THE WORKS OF RICHARD SIBBES

THE WORKS OF
RICHARD SIBBES

VOLUME 1

Edited with Memoir by
Alexander B. Grosart

THE BANNER OF TRUTH TRUST

THE BANNER OF TRUTH TRUST

Head Office
3 Murrayfield Road
Edinburgh, EH12 6EL
UK

North America Office
610 Alexander Spring Road
Carlisle, PA 17015
USA

banneroftruth.org

The Complete Works of Richard Sibbes
first published in 7 volumes 1862-64
This reprint of volume 1 first published by
the Banner of Truth Trust 1973
Reprinted 1979, 2001, 2023

*

ISBN
Print: 978 0 85151 169 6

*

Printed in the USA by
Versa Press Inc.,
East Peoria, IL.

CONTENTS.

*** The 'Notes' prefixed to the several Treatises and Sermons will shew, that in the present volume are included the whole of the works *published by Sibbes himself:* 'The Description of Christ,' and 'The Sword of the Wicked,' being restored to their proper places, as introductory to 'The Bruised Reed,' and 'The Soul's Conflict,' respectively.'—G.

EDITOR'S ADVERTISEMENT.

Having now in my library the whole of the works of Sibbes, *with the exception of two small volumes,* I beg to note them here, in the hope that thereby I may secure them.

(1.) The Saint's Comforts, being the substance of divers sermons preached on Ps. cxxx., the beginning; The Saint's Happiness, on Ps. lxxiii. 28; The Rich Pearl, on Mat. xiii. 45, 46; The Success of the Gospel, on Luke vii. 34, 35; Mary's Choice on Luke x. 38–40. By a Reverend Divine now with God. Printed at London by Thos. Cotes, and are to be sold by Peter Cole, at the sign of the Glove, in Cornhill, near the Exchange. 1638. 12mo.

(2.) Antidotum contra Naufragium Fidei et Bonæ Conscientiæ, Concio Latinè. . . 2 Tim. i. 14. Pp. 78. 18mo.

In view of the bibliographical list (see *a* of this Preface), it is also exceedingly desirable to have the following editions:—

(3.) Bruised Reed. *4th edition.* 1632. 18mo.

(4.) Two Sermons on First Words of Christ's Last Sermon. 4to. 1636. *1st edition.*

(5.) Spiritual Man's Aim. *2d edition.*

(6.) Fountain Sealed. *2d edition.*

(7.) Divine Meditations. *2d edition.*

PREFACE.

In presenting the public with the first volume of what, it is hoped, will prove a standard edition of the hitherto uncollected and inedited works of Dr Richard Sibbes, I may be permitted to make the following remarks :—

(*a*) Sibbes has had no preceding editor. The edition (so-called), of his 'Works,' noted below,* contains a mere fraction, and those which are included have been mutilated and most carelessly printed. It were invidious to point out the abounding blunders of these volumes. 'This edition,' says the late William Pickering, our English Aldus, 'which purports to be the entire works of Sibbes, contains only a small portion; besides being incorrectly printed, and omitting the prefaces, dedications, and tables.' †

There have been many editions, more or less accurate, and more or less attractive in their typography, of separate treatises,—especially of the Bruised Reed and Soul's Conflict. These, so far as known to us, will be recorded in a bibliographical list of editions in the concluding volume.

(*b*) It may therefore be pleaded, that any shortcomings, whether of omission or commission, claim indulgence, in that the editor has had wholly to prepare his text from the original and early editions ;‡

* The Works of the Reverend Richard Sibbes, D.D., late Master of Catherine Hall, in the University of Oxford (*sic*), and Preacher of Gray's Inn, London, &c. Aberdeen, 1812. 3 Vols. 8vo.

† 'Bruised Reed,' reprint of 1838, p. xxi.

‡ To explain ;—Adams's 'Sermons' were collected by himself from the early 4tos into a folio, and so *it* is an editor's text. Had Sibbes's numerous writings been brought together into a folio or otherwise, by himself, or under his authority, it is plain that the labour of editing would have been much simplified.

and that these, excepting the three small volumes published by or under the sanction of the author, swarm with misprints and mispunctuations. The posthumous publication of the larger proportion explains this. It can hardly be hoped that in every case perfect accuracy has been attained, as many points must always remain to some extent matter of opinion ; but I have given a good deal of thought and pains to the production of an accurate text. It need scarcely be said, that in nothing save the modernisation of the orthography and punctuation, are Sibbes's words touched.

(*c*) By the kind help of friends interested in the work, every quotation and reference, coming within the general rule laid down for this series,* has been verified or filled in, as the case may be. Occasional casual references and allusions have been traced. It is believed that no quotation of any moment has been overlooked. This does not apply to the mere pointing of a sentence or barbing of an appeal with a saying introduced after the fashion of the age, as 'one saith,' or 'the heathen saith.' But when traced, even those have been given.

(*d*) To the treatises embraced in this volume, which were published originally and superintended subsequently by the author in different editions, the 'various readings' are appended as foot-notes. The letters *a*, *b*, *c*, &c., refer to the few 'notes' of the editor, added at the close of each treatise. These might have been multiplied; but his design is simply to explain names, dates, facts. The old significant words that occur will be given as a 'glossary' in the last volume, with references to the places where they occur. This may prove a not unacceptable addition to the stores of the 'Philological Society,' in their laudable endeavour to furnish that great desideratum, a national dictionary of our English tongue.

(*e*) Foı the 'Memoir' I have done my humble best. None can regret its deficiencies more than myself. Yet has it, as the whole undertaking, been done lovingly and *as an honest piece of work.* Those who have engaged in kindred investigations will best appreciate the difficulties involved. As compared with preceding memoirs of Sibbes (or notices rather, for no one exceeds at the most five of our pages), ıt will be found more ample. I have been enabled to enrich it with new matter, to recover old which was lost or neglected; and to bring together what is scattered through many volumes. I felicitate myself upon the possession of Zachary Catlin's MS.† Writing of one who came under the persecution

* See 'Editorial Note,' Adams' Works, vol. i. pp. ix, x.

† See Appendix A. to Memoir.

of Laud, and who was a 'Puritan' of the true stamp, the policy of Laud must come under review. On that policy I have decided opinions, which I have not concealed. But I trust I have not spoken uncourteously, much less untruthfully. There are some minds that cannot speak well of their own favourites except at the expense of others. They cannot laud the Churchman without, to use a word of Sibbes's, 'depraving' the Puritan, or the Puritan without impaling the Churchman. Such men would quench Orion that Saturn's rings may gleam the brighter. Whereas our dark world needs both, needs all its stars. *Let them all shine.* Our great names are not so numerous, either in Church or State, that we can afford to obscure any of our historic lights. Let all irradiate the firmament of fame.

(*f*) It would have unduly extended the 'Memoir' to have included an analysis and estimate of the works of Sibbes, or a view of his 'opinions' and 'character' as reflected therein. This I hope to overtake in a short essay, to be given in the course of the issue of the works, in which I trust to be able to throw some little light on his relations to other writers and theirs to him, and perchance to guide the casual reader to the treasures of rare thought, ripe wisdom, spiritual insight, beauty of illustration, sweetness of consolation, of this incomparable old worthy.

(*g*) The pleasant duty remains of returning my warm thanks to very many friends and correspondents. It were to savour of ostentation to name all who have rendered assistance, or endeavoured to do so. But I must mention a few. To the Rev. John Eyton Bickersteth Mayor, M.A., Fellow of St John's College; the Rev. Charles Kirkby Robinson, M.A., Master of St Catherine's College; Charles Henry Cooper, Esq., F.S.A., and Thompson Cooper, Esq., F.S.A.; Mr Wallis,—all of Cambridge, I owe special acknowledgments for various favours, and for local inquiries most obligingly made and communicated. My thanks are similarly due to Dr Hessey, preacher of Gray's Inn, London; and to the Rev. Paul M. Stedman, vicar of Thurston; the Rev. W. G. Tuck, rector of Tostock; the Rev. A. H. Wratislaw, Bury St Edmunds, from each of whom I have received many tokens of their interest in my labours, as well by letter, as personally on occasion of a visit to Suffolk. From his Grace the Duke of Manchester; Richard Almack, Esq., Mel ford, Sudbury; James Spedding, Esq., editor of Bacon; Joshua Wilson, Esq., Nevill Park, Tunbridge Wells; Edward Foss, Esq., Churchill House, Dover; William Durrant Cooper, Esq., F.S.A.; Albert Way, Esq., F.S.A.; R. Siegfried, Esq., Trinity College, Dublin; Jonathan B. Bright, Esq., Waltham, Massachusetts,

United States; the Rev. W. G. Lewis, Westbourne Grove; the Rev. George Thomson, Hackney; the Rev. E. Pattison, Gedding; the Rev. Robert Redpath, M.A., London; W. E. Whitehouse, Esq., Birmingham, I have received various *memorabilia*, communicated with such ungrudging alacrity and kindness as much to deepen the obligation.

I beg to thank the Rev. J. C. Robertson, Canterbury; the Rev. Hastings Robinson, D.D., Great Warley; the Rev. William West, Hawarden; the Rev. William Webster, M.A., Richmond; Charles Bird, Esq., London; the Rev. Dr Cairns, Berwick; the Rev. Dr Bonar, Kelso; the Rev. Dr Bryce, Belfast; and the Rev. Thomas Smith, M.A., Edinburgh, and numerous anonymous correspondents, for service in verification of references in this volume and those that are to follow. I am sure the edition will owe much to the willing hand and vigilant eye of the last-named gentleman, as General Editor of the series, in revision of the proofs with myself.

It would be ungrateful not to acknowledge the unvarying courtesy with which I have been permitted access to the stores of the great libraries, *e. g.*, British Museum, where Mr Watt, as he is to all, was ever eager to assist; Red Cross Street; University and Advocates', Edinburgh. Nor can I withhold a grateful word from the Editors and Correspondents of 'Notes and Queries,' and other literary journals, whose columns I have had occasion to use. I have endeavoured to leave no source of information unconsulted, and have given the authority for my statements, whether in Memoir or Notes. 'For in all faculties, their writings have been of longest continuance, who have made fairest use of other authors.' 'For mine owne, either judgment or opinion' also, with the foregoing, in the words of Sir John Hayward, 'as I do nothing the more value the spider's for that she draweth it out of her own bowels; so doe I not esteeme the lesse of the honeycombe, because it is gathered out of many flowers.'—(Sanctuary of a Troubled Soul, Part ii. To the Reader, 1631. 18mo). Wherever I have been indebted to a predecessor, it is duly recorded.

And now, with unfeigned diffidence in myself and my part, but with the conviction that no common service is being rendered to Christian literature by this edition of Sibbes, I would say, in the words of Isaak Walton, 'If I have prevented an abler person, I beg pardon of him and my reader.'—(*Intr. to Life of Herbert.*)

A. B. G.

1st Manse,
Kinross, 2d *May* 1862.

MEMOIR OF
RICHARD SIBBES

MEMOIR OF RICHARD SIBBES, D.D.

CHAPTER I.

'MEMORIALS' THAT MIGHT HAVE BEEN.

Izaak Walton—Dr William Gouge—Richard Baxter—John Davenport, B.D.—Leading. 'Puritans'—Sibbes's own indifference.

THERE are more than common reasons to cause regret that hitherto there has not been, and in this later time can scarcely be, a worthy life of the '*heavenly*' RICHARD SIBBES (the adjective, like the 'venerable' Bede, the 'judicious' Hooker, the 'holy' Baxter, being the almost invariable epithet associated with every mention of his name, through many generations after his departure).* I look upon my own gatherings, after no small expenditure of time and endeavour, all the more sorrowfully because of these reasons. I would fain have placed upon the honoured forehead of the author of the 'Bruised Reed' and 'Soul's Conflict' a wreath of 'amaranthine flowers;' but alas! have instead with difficulty gleaned a few crushed and withered leaves, some poor spires of faded grass and braids of grave-stone moss, with perchance a sprig of not altogether scentless thyme; whereas in the course of my researches, I have come upon various notices and scintillations of revelation, which shew how different it might have been had contemporaries discharged their duty. These tantalizing indications

* 'Heavenly.' The famous Dr Manton thus speaks of him: 'This is mentioned .... because of that excellent and peculiar gift which the worthy and reverend author had in unfolding and applying the great mysteries of the gospel in a sweet and mellifluous way; and, therefore, was by his hearers usually termed the "sweet dropper"—sweet and heavenly distillations usually dropping from him with such a native elegancy, as is not easily to be imitated.'—(To the Reader .... Commentary .... on 2 Cor. i.). 'That "heavenly" man,' says Zachary Catlin; and Neal, 'His works discover him to have been of a "heavenly," evangelical spirit.'—(Hist. of the Puritans, vol. i. 582, edition, 3 vols. 8vo, 1837.)

of personal knowledge, and of reserved and now lost information, may perhaps most fitly introduce our narrative.

First of all, in that 'Last Will and Testament,' over which so many eyes have brimmed with unsorrowing tears—drawn out 'in a full age,' very shortly before the venerable writer went up to lay his silver crown of gray hairs at His feet—good, gentle, blithely garrulous Izaak Walton bequeaths, among numerous other tokens and legacies, his copies of the 'Bruised Reed' and 'Soul's Conflict,' and there gleams upon the antique deed, like a ray of sunlight, these noteworthy words about them :—'To my son Izaak, I give Doctor Sibbes his Soul's Conflict, and to my daughter his Bruised Reed, DESIRING THEM TO READ THEM SO AS TO BE WELL ACQUAINTED WITH THEM.'* Nor was this the only expression of esteem for Sibbes by the 'old man eloquent.' In a copy of 'The Returning Backslider,' now preserved in Salisbury Cathedral library, he has written this inscription :—

> 'Of this blest man, let this just praise be given,
> Heaven was in him, before he was in heaven.—IZAAK WALTON.'

Pity that either Wotton was not assigned to another, or that Richard Sibbes made not a sixth to the golden five 'Lives' of this most quaintly-wise and wisely-quaint of all our early English biographers. How lovingly, how tenderly, with salt of wit and warbling of poetic prose, would he have made 'sacrifice to the memory' (his own phrase) of Master Richard Sibbes, the more than equal of Donne or Herbert, Sanderson or Wotton, and only in degree, not in kind, beneath Hooker himself.

Again, in Sibbes's own will, the usual sum was left to Dr William Gouge of 'Blackfryer's, London,' to preach a funeral sermon. The wording runs, 'To my reverend frende Dr Gouge, I doe give as a testimony of my love, twenty shillings, desiring him to take the paynes to preach my funeral sermon.' Pity once more that this noble preacher, whose great 'Exposition of Hebrews' is worthy of a place beside the kindredly-massive folios of John Owen, having preached it, as he doubtless did, gave not his 'sermon' to the press. Spoken by one who was his fellow-student at the university, and who knew and greatly loved him, while men's eyes were yet wet for him, while the tones of his 'sweet-dropping' voice (Manton's word) still lingered in the groined roof of the chapel of Gray's Inn, it must have contained not a little that we of the nineteenth century would have prized. It is vexatious that importunity should have got printed this large-thoughted man s

* 'Will of Walton.' Introductory Essay to 'The Angler' by Major, 4th edition, 1844, pp. xlii.–vi.

funeral sermons, for a 'Mrs Margaret Ducke!' and numerous others equally unknown, and secured not this.

Further, Richard Baxter, his survivor for upwards of half a century, might have been the biographer of Sibbes. In the story of his earlier days, in that marvellous 'Reliquiæ Baxterianæ,' which won the heart of Coleridge, he speaks gratefully of him:—'About that time [his fifteenth year] it pleased God that a poor pedlar came to the door that had ballads and some good books, and my father bought of him Dr Sibbes's Bruised Reed. This also I read, and found it suited my state and seasonably sent me, which opened more the love of God to me, and gave me a livelier apprehension of the mystery of redemption, and how much I was beholden to Jesus Christ.'* This circumstance alone, observes Granger, in his meagre and chary fashion missing the right word 'immortal,' would have rendered his (Sibbes's) name memorable.'† How priceless would have been a life of Sibbes from this like-minded man, as a companion to his Alleine! How thankfully should we have spared half a dozen of his 'painful' controversial books for half a dozen pages of such a memoir!

Nor is my roll of casualties—shall I say?—done. In the address 'to the Christian Reader,' prefixed to 'The knowledge of Christ indispensably required of all men who would be saved' (4to, 1653), of JOHN DAVENPORT, who, like Gouge, was Sibbes's contemporary, coadjutor, and bosom friend, he informs us of a grievous loss to himself and to us:—'My far distance from the press,' he says, dating from his sequestered 'study in Newhaven,' New England, 'and the hazards of so long a voyage by sea, had almost discouraged me from transmitting this copy; foreseeing that whatsoever σφαλματα‡ are committed by the printer, men disaffected will impute it to the author; and being sensible of my great loss of some manuscripts by a wreck at sea, together WITH THE LIVES OF SUNDRY PRECIOUS ONES, about six years since.' From the peculiarly close and endeared friendship between the two, there can be little doubt that among those precious ones would be Richard Sibbes.

Then again, we have Thomas Goodwin, Thomas Manton, and Philip Nye, Simeon Ash, and Jeremiah Burroughs, John Sedgwick, Arthur Jackson, James Nalton, and John Dod, John Hill, John Goodwin, Robert Towne, Joseph Church, Lazarus Seaman, William Taylor, Ezekiel Culverwell, in truth, all the foremost puritan names of the period, as the writers of 'Prefaces,' 'Epistles,' 'Dedications.'

* 'Baxter,' R. B., pp. 3, 4, lib. i., pt. 1, 1696, folio.

† 'Granger,' Biog. Hist. of England, 2d edition, 1776.

‡ That is, 'slips, blunders.'

addresses 'To the Reader,' in the original quartos and duodecimos as they were issued in quick succession. In these there are provoking hints, so to speak, of withheld information. Thus say Ash, Nalton, and Church: 'The scope and business of this epistle is not so much to commend the workman (whose name is a sweet savour to the church), as to give a short and summary view of the generals handled in this treatise. THOUGH MUCH MIGHT BE SAID of this eminent saint, if either detraction had fastened her venomous nails in his precious name, or the testimony of the subscribers of this epistle might give the book a freer admission into thy hands.'* Again, John Goodwin thus pleads: 'Good reader, to discourse the worth or commendations of the author, especially the pens of others having done sacrifice unto him in that kind, *I judge it but an unpertinency*, and make no question but that if I should exchange thoughts or judgments with thee herein, *I should have but mine own again*.'† A sketch of our saintly Calvinist by the great Arminian would have been worth having.

Once more, Arthur Jackson, William Taylor, and James Nalton, deem any enlargement supererogatory: 'WE NEED SAY NOTHING OF THE AUTHOR, his former labours sufficiently 'speak for him in the gates,' his memory is HIGHLY HONOURED AMONGST THE GODLY LEARNED. He that enjoys the glory of heaven needs not the praises of men upon earth.'‡

Further, how many pleasant memories lay behind, when Jeremiah Burroughs thus poured out his reverence and love: 'Bless God for . . . . . this work, AND THE MAN THAT INDITED IT, a man, for matter always full, for notions sublime, for expression clear, for style concise—a man spiritually rational and rationally spiritual—one that seemed to see the insides of nature and grace and the world and heaven, by those perfect anatomies he hath made of them all.'§

Finally (for it were endless to cite all), in the 'Marrow of Ecclesiastical History' (folio, 1675), in the address 'to the Christian Reader,' signed 'Simeon Ash, John Wall,' we read: 'Here, *we might have given in a true though short character* of some precious servants and ministers of Christ, whose graces were admired whilst they lived, and whose memory their surviving friends do much honour, viz., Dr Preston, SIBBES, Taylor, Stoughton,' &c.

There are again and again such things, in every variety of loving

* 'To the Reader.' Heavenly Conference betwixt Christ and Mary, 12mo, 1654. 4to, 1656.

† 'To the Reader,' Exposition of 3d chapter of Philippians, &c., 4to, 1639.

‡ 'To the Reader,' Glorious Feast of the Gospel, 4to, 1650.

§ 'To the Reader,' The Christian's Portion, 12mo. 1638.

epithet, but we look in vain for any adequate memorial of the tender and tenderly treasured friendships; for even the welcome gossip that abounds, of far inferior men.

The 'evil days and evil tongues,' the crowding and trampling of events, England's 'Ιλιὰς κακῶν, that made men hold their breath and ask, 'What next?' explains, if it does not mitigate, the neglect of Sibbes's friends to place on record their knowledge and wealth of regard for him. He departed when the shadows of great calamities were falling, huge and dark, over the nation—calamities that were to recall, as with a clarion-blast, John Milton from Italy; and it is easily to be understood, how, under such circumstances, there was delay issuing in forgetfulness. To all this must be added Sibbes's own splendid indifference to any blazoning of his name or fame, other than what might come spontaneously. His three small volumes—all that were published during his own life, under his own sanction—were literally compelled from him. Of the first, the 'Bruised Reed,' he tells us, with a touch of complaint, almost of anger, '*To prevent further inconvenience,* I was drawn to let these notes pass with some review, considering there was an *intendment of publishing them by some who had not perfectly taken them.* And these first as being next at hand.' Of the 'Soul's Conflict,' he says also, 'I began to preach on the text about twelve years since in the city, and afterwards finished the same in Gray's Inn. After which, *some having gotten imperfect notes, endeavoured to publish them without my privity.* Therefore, to do *myself right, I thought fit to reduce them to this form.*'

All this was the expression, not of passing irritation, much less of petulancy wearing the vizard of modesty, but of principle. For, in his 'Description of Christ,' the introductory sermons to the 'Bruised Reed' (which are now restored to their proper place), he had deprecated all eagerness after human applause. 'Let us commit the fame and credit,' says he, 'of what we are or do to God. *He will take care of that,* let us take care to be and to do as we should, and then *for noise and report,* let it be good or ill as God will send it. . . . . *If we seek to be in the mouths of men, to dwell in the talk and speech of men,* God will abhor us. . . . . Therefore let us labour to be good *in secret.* Christians should be as minerals, rich in the depth of the earth. That which is least seen is his (the Christian's) riches. We should have our treasure deep; for the discovery of it, we should be ready when we are called to it; and for all other accidental things, let it fall out as God in his wisdom sees good. . . . . God will be careful enough to get us applause. . . . . As much reputation as is fit for a man will follow him in being and doing what he should. *God will look to that.* Therefore we should not set up sails to our own meditations, that unless we be carried with the wind of applause, to be becalmed, and not go a whit forward, but we should be carried with the Spirit of God, and with a holy desire to serve God and our brethren, and to do all the good we can, and never care for the speeches of the world, ... We should, from the example of Christ, labour to subdue this infirmity, which we are sick of naturally. . . .' Then, in words that have the ring of Bacon in them, 'We shall have glory enough, and be known enough to devils, to angels, and men, *ere long*. Therefore, as Christ lived a hidden life—that is, he was not known what he was, that so he might work our salvation, so let us be content to be hidden ones.' More grandly, and even more like a stray sentence from 'The Essayes,' he elsewhere gives the secret of his unconcern as to what men might say or leave unsaid of him. 'THERE WILL BE A RESURRECTION OF CREDITS, as well as of bodies. We'll have glory enough BY AND BY.' The very ease, nay, negligence of that 'by and by' (recalling Henry Vaughan's 'other night,' in his superb vision of the great ring of eternity), sets before us one who 'looked not at the things that are *seen and temporal*, but at the things unseen and eternal,' one who would shine not in the lower firmament of human fame, but up higher, in the 'new heavens,' as a star for ever and ever.

With all explanations, and all the modesty of Sibbes himself, we cannot help lamenting that his contemporaries so readily acquiesced in his choice of being a 'hidden one.'

But I must now try to put together such particulars as have been found, and in proceeding to do so it can only be needful to remind those who have attempted similar service, of the Greek proverb—Τοῖς σιτου 'αποροῦσι σπουδάζονται οἱ ὄροβοι—which may be freely rendered, 'Chick-peas are eagerly sought after when we lack corn.'

CHAPTER II.

PARENTAGE AND BIRTH—BIRTH-PLACE AND SCHOOLS.

Suffolk—Martyrs and 'Puritans'—Name, its various orthography—Bishop Mountagu—'*Blue blood*'—Tennyson—Birth-place, Tostock, not Sudbury—Zachary Catlin—The old English Village—Removal to Thurston—The 'Wheel-wright'—School at Pakenham—Richard Brigs—The 'boy father of the man'—John Milton—Contemporary 'boys'—Grammar-school at Bury St Edmunds—Father begrudges 'expense'—Master Sibbes put in the 'wheel-wright's' shop—Friends step in.

RICHARD SIBBES was a native of Suffolk, one of the great martyr and puritan counties of England, that furnished many of the early fugitives to Holland, a very unusual proportion of the emigrants to New England (whose lustrous names are still talismans over the Atlantic), and nearly a hundred of the 'ejected' two-thousand of 1662. The name 'Sibbes' is variously spelled. The spelling now given, and adopted in our title-page, is his own signature to his own dedications and 'epistles to the reader.' But he is frequently called Sibbs, and such is the orthography of his Will, as well as of his heirs and their descendants. There is a third variation, Sybbes or Sybesius. But it is the Latinized form, as it occurs in Richterus Redivivus.* A fourth, Sibs, is common to many of the original editions, and furnishes a side-thrust in a play upon the word to Bishop Mountagu, in his 'Appello ad Cæsarem' (1625), that over-clever 'Defence.' Even thus early Sibbes was speaking bravely out in his post at 'Gray's Inn' against the semi-popish practices of the prelates; and the venal bishop, afraid to strike openly, must needs hint dislike in this taunt, 'So . . . . with our Puritans, very *Sibs* unto those fathers of the society, every moderate man is bedaubed with these goodly habiliments of Arminianism, popery, and what not, unless he will be frantic with them for their holy cause.'† This may, perchance, be a mere jesting use of the word 'sib,' but the capital S and plural, and the man, seem to indicate an intended hit at our author, ever outspoken against such as the unquestionably astute but also unquestionably unscrupulous Richard Mountagu. The earliest occurrence of the name that I have met with is in a Robert Sibbes or Sybbs of Cony-Weston, Norfolk, who, in 1524, purchased Ladie's Manor, Rockland-Tofts, which again was sold by his son and heir, also a Robert, in 1594.‡ Perhaps, by further inquiries, it might be possible to connect the neighbouring Norfolk with the Suffolk Sibbeses; and, though I have searched in vain in Burke's 'Armoury,' and all through the Davy 'Suffolk MSS.,'§ for genealogical record, it is possible that further research might even shew 'blue blood' in the descent of the author of the 'Bruised Reed.' But it would serve

* 'Richterus Redivivus.' In a curious letter of Christopher Arnold, containing new and apparently unused information about Milton. Writing to Geo. Richter (from Lond., A.D. 7 Aug. (*sic*) 1651, printed in Richterus Redivivus, p. 485), he says, 'In Academia Cantabrigiensi vir peramans mei, Abrah. Whelocus, Arab. atque Anglo-saxonicæ Linguarum Professor et Bibliothecarius publicus codices manuscriptos cum primis Græcos, &c. . . . . Obstupui in Johannitica (bibliotheca), cum mihi magnum sacrorum librorum Græcobarbarorum copiam ostenderent, a benefactore quodam anonymo, suasione Richardi Sybbes, S. Th. Prof. et hujus Coll. quondam socii senioris, A.D. 1628, dono oblatorum.'

† 'Appello ad Cæsarem, a Just Appeale from Two Unjust Informers.' By Richard Mountagu. 4to, 1625, p. 139.

‡ Blomefield's Norfolk, vol. i., pp. 481–82. § In British Museum. Addl. MSS.

little purpose to do so, or to prove him '*sib*' to this, that, or the other great family. The far-fountained 'red' ichor that has come down from

'The grand old gardener and his wife'*

suffices, the more especially as, at the time of his birth at least, our author's family was assuredly lowly, and of the people :

'Kind hearts are more than coronets,
And simple faith than Norman blood.'†

In all preceding notices, Sudbury, the old town, so far back as Edward III.'s times inhabited by the Flemings, is given as Sibbes's birth-place. 'At Sudbury,' says Neal ('History of the Puritans'), and Brook ('Lives of the Puritans'), and so all the 'Biographical Dictionaries.' '*Nigh* Sudbury,' says Fuller; '*At the edges* of Suffolk, *near* Sudbury,' says Clarke. This is a mistake. The town, 'as great as most, and ancient as any,' according to Thomas Fuller, that can boast of Thomas Gainsborough and Thomas Constable later, as natives, and of Faithful Teate, William Jenkyn, and Samuel Peyto earlier, as ministers, can afford to give up an honour to which it has no claim. Tostock, not Sudbury, was his birth-place. The 'registers' of the period, of Sudbury and Tostock alike, have perished; but a contemporary manuscript 'Memoir' of Sibbes, from the pen of Zachary Catlin (of whom more anon), which the stream of time, while engulphing so much else of what was precious and what was worthless, has floated down and placed by lucky accident in my possession, states the fact. As this contemporary manuscript must be frequently laid under contribution in the sequel, it may be as well to give here its proem, which is sufficient, apart from what will subsequently appear, to attest its authority and trustworthiness. 'At the request of a noble friend, Sir William Spring, I have here willingly contributed to the happy memory of that worthy man of God, Dr Sibbes, a few such flowers as I could collect, either from the *certain relation of those that knew his first education, or from mine own observation of him* at that distance whereat we lived. And if anything here recorded may seem convenient for his purpose, who is (as I am informed)

* and † Tennyson. 'Lady Clara Vere de Vere.' Even were it possible to trace the name of Sibbes up to 'Norman blood,' we must remember our Scottish proverbs :—

A' Stuarts are no *sib* to the king, } = Though of the same name,
A' Campbells are no *sib* to the duke, } not of the same family.

Moreover, as he says himself of another (Sherland), 'What should I speak of these things, when he has personal worth enough? I need not go abroad to commend this man, for there were those graces and gifts in him that made him so esteemed, that verily I think no man of his place and years lived more desired, and died more lamented.' ('Christ is Best,' page 347 of this volume of the works.)

about to publish the lives of some worthies deceased, I shall think my labour well bestowed. For I am not of that philosopher's mind, who lighting upon a book newly put forth, entitled, "The Encomium of Hercules," cast it away, saying, *Et quis Lacedæmoniorum eum vituperavit?* accounting it a needless work to praise him whom no man did or could find fault withal. I rather judge it a commendable thing to perpetuate and keep fresh the memory of such worthy men whose examples may be of use for imitation in this declining and degenerate age.'* I give his *ipsissima verba* of the birth-place, as above, and embrace in the quotation the birth-date as well. 'But I come to the matter. This Richard, the eldest son of Paul Sibs and Johan [= Joanna ?] was born at Tostock, in Suffolk, four miles from Bury, anno domini 1577.'† The source of the blunder of making Sudbury the birth-place is evidently confounding '*Bury*' St Edmunds with Sud*bury*. Tostock is 'nigh' the former, but not 'nigh' the latter, and cannot at all be described as 'on the edges' of Suffolk, being fifteen or twenty miles in the interior. Tostock, to which I thus restore, if not in the popular sense a great, at least a revered, name, and one of which any place might be proud, remains to-day very much as we may suppose it to have been two hundred years ago, except perhaps that 'its tide of work has ebbed away,' and it is now wholly rural. It is a small sequestered village in Thedwestry hundred, about, as we have seen, four miles from Bury St Edmunds, and about thirteen miles from Sudbury.

> 'A quaint, old, gabled place
> With Church stamped on its face.

Exactly such a 'village' as 'Our Village' has made dear to us all. Its few picturesquely scattered houses cluster around an unenclosed 'common' (once abundant in 'merry England,' but now sparse), and present fine specimens of what every year is seeing disappear —the peaked-roofed, mossy-thatched, or saffron-tiled 'homes' of our forefathers of the 16th and 17th centuries, with every 'coign of vantage' of the over-hanging upper storeys and lozenge-paned windows,

> 'Held by old swallows on a lease of love
> Unbroken, immemorial;'

and little gardens a-front flinging out into the air the breath of

* Above and throughout I modernise the orthography; but in Appendix A to this Memoir I reprint from my MS. the whole very interesting document. Thither I refer for further information concerning its author.

† Neal gives 1579, and is followed by others; but the misprint is corrected by the statement that his death took place in 1635, in his 57th year, which, however, ought to be 58th. The 'Registers' of Tostock that remain commence long subsequent to 1577, and hence the date of his birth-*day* is lost.

old-fashioned flowers. It is pleasant in our day to come upon such a virgin spot.

'For it is well, amid the whirr
Of restless wheels and busy stir,
To find a quiet spot where live
Fond, pious thoughts conservative,
That ring to an old chime,
And bear the moss of time.

. . . .

'And sweeter far and grander too
The ancient civilisation grew,
With holy war and busy work
Beneath the spire and round the kirk
Than miles of brick and stone
In godless monotone.'

The 'church,' lichened and lady-ferned, but in excellent preservation, is approached by a fragrant lane that strikes off from 'the rectory,'

' . . . . where the budding purple rose,
Prolific of its gifts, the long year through
Breaks into beauty.

It is dedicated to St Andrew.

'Nor gargoyle lacks, grotesque and quaint,
Nor saintly niche without its saint,
Nor buttress lightsome, nor the tower,
Where the bell marks the passing hour,
And peals out with our mirth,
And tolls our earth to earth.'

The 'font'—from which no doubt little Richard Sibbes was baptized—is noticeable. The 'benches' are of dark oak, grotesquely carved. The graves around are ozier-woven, and on some of the stones, the once great Suffolk name of Bacon, is still to be read; also in the wrecks of the 'Registers' that remain, the mighty name of Wolsey occurs, as elsewhere in the neighbourhood (by a strange link with Germany and the Reformation), is to be found that of Luther. We visited the primitive hamlet on one of the finest of English September days, and our Scottish eye and heart were touched with the quiet English scenery, long familiar by the 'landscapes' of Suffolk's Gainsborough and Constable, and her poets, Bloomfield and Crabbe. There were the 'Cart on a Road,' 'Cows crossing a Ford,' 'Boys a-straddle on a Gate,' the 'Stile,' ringed with honey-suckle, and now the glowing, and now the bleak originals of 'The Farmer's Boy' and of 'The Borough.' Tostock was a cheery, sunny, many-memoried birth-place; to this hour, with its sister-villages, possessing traditions of martyrs and reformers, Rowland Taylor and Yeoman, and, farther off.

Hooper and Coverdale and John Rogers, and legends of the Tudors and the Commonwealth. For a 'Puritan' none could have been more fitting, for all around were the family seats of grand old Puritan worthies, Barton-Mere, Talmach Hall, Pakenham, Nether Hall, where 'godly ministers' were ever welcome to the Barnardistons and Brights, Veres and Brooks, Winthrops and Riches, Springs and Cavendishes, and the Bacon stock.

But Sibbes was very soon removed thence to Thurston, a similar hamlet only about three miles distant. Here, our old worthy the Vicar of Thurston informs us, Mr and Mrs Sibbes 'lived in honest repute, brought up and married divers children, purchased some houses and lands, and there both deceased.'

There will be something to say afterward of these 'divers children' who were 'married;' but it is to be regretted that, the 'registers having perished, no positive light can be cast on the dates of the decease of the elder folks, except that the father was dead before 1608. Concerning him this is Catlin's testimony: 'His father was by his trade a wheel-wright, a skilful and painful workman, and a good, sound-hearted Christian.' 'Skilful and painful'* were very weighty words then, particularly 'painful,' which was the highest praise that could be given to a laborious, faithful, evangelical minister of the gospel. It is found in many an olden title-page, and underneath many a grave, worn face. A 'mill-wright,' or 'wheel-wright,' for they are interchangeable, was by no means an unimportant 'craftsman' in those days. In country places, such as Thurston and Tostock, where division of labour could not be carried so far as in the large towns, the 'wheel-wright' was compelled to draw largely upon his own resources, and to devise expedients to meet pressing emergencies as they arose. Necessarily this made him dexterous, expert, and 'skilful' in mechanical arrangements. If thus early, the whole of Smiles's description, on whose authority I am writing this,† does not hold (for he speaks of him devising steam-engines, pumps, cranes, and the like); yet in those primitive days, perhaps more than some generations later, such tradesmen were, in all cases of difficulty, resorted to, and looked upon as a very important class of workmen; while the nature of their business tended to make them thoughtful, decided, self-reliant. The cradle of little Richard, therefore, would seem to have been rocked at a fireside not altogether unprosperous. And yet there must have been in the outset somewhat of poverty and struggle, or, the elder Sibbes will need the full benefit of Catlin's character of him. For our guileless

* Painful = full of pains, *i.e.*, painstaking, laborious.

† Smiles's Life of Brindley, in Lives of the Engineers, vol. i. p. 312.

chronicler, carrying us swiftly onward, adds immediately thereafter, 'This Richard he brought up in learning at the grammar school, *though very unwillingly in regard of the charge.*' We will in charity give Master Paul Sibs, wheel-wright, the benefit of the vicar's testimony, and ascribe the 'unwillingness' to the *res angustæ domi.* Whether or not, the 'charge,' I fear, had prematurely removed the little fellow from the school to the wheel-wright's bench, but for his own bookish tastes, and the watchful interest of friends. This is explicitly affirmed in what follows. The sentence above, that tells us of the unwilling school-learning, through the 'charge,' thus continues—'had not the youth's strong inclination to his books, and well profiting therein, with some importunities of friends, prevailed so far as to continue him at school till he was fit for Cambridge.' Most truly the 'boy was father of the man.' I turn again to the Izaak Walton-like words of the Vicar of Thurston. He says—'Concerning his love to his book, and his industry in study, I cannot omit the testimony of Mr Thomas Clark, high constable, who was much of the same age, and went to school together with him at the same time, with one Mr Richard Brigs (afterward head master of the Free School at Norwich), then teaching at Pakenham church. He hath often told me that, when the boys were dismissed from school at the usual hours of eleven and five or six, and the rest would fall to their pastime, and sometimes to playing the wags with him, as being harmless and meanly apparelled (for the most part in leather), it was this youth's constant course, as soon as he could rid himself of their unpleasing company, to take out of his pocket or satchel one book or other, and so to go reading and meditating till he came to his father's house, which was near a mile off, and so he went to school again. This was his order, also, when his father sent him to the Free School at Bury, three or four miles off, every day. Whereby the said Mr Clark did then conceive, that he would in time prove an excellent and able man, who of a child was of such a manly staidness, and indefatigable industry in his study.'* Milton's immortal portraiture of '*The* Child' may be taken to describe Master Richard:—

> 'When I was yet a child, no childish play
> To me was pleasing; all my mind was set,
> Serious to learn and know, and thence to do,
> What might be public good.'—*Paradise Regained.* [B. i. 201-204.]

The 'school near Pakenham church' has long since disappeared,

* '*Staidness*' is the very word Lord Brooke uses to describe the youthhood of Sir Philip Sidney: and indeed his whole description is reflected in the above. Cf. the Life of the renowned Sir Philip Sidney (ed. 1652), pp. 6, 7.

and no memorial whatever has been transmitted of it. The mansion of Pakenham was the seat of the Gages, whence the mother of Sir Nicholas Bacon, father of *the* Bacon, came; and later was the residence of Sir William Spring, at whose request Catlin drew up his notice of Sibbes. Probably, we err not in tracing back the after-friendship with Sibbes to those school-boy days. One likes to picture little Master Richard in his leathern suit (not at all uncommon at the period), studiously walking day by day from Pakenham to Thurston, and home again. Nor can we avoid thinking of other 'boys,' who were then likewise 'at school,' and destined to cross one another's paths. Not a few of them will be found united in intimate friendship with the little leathern-suited pupil of Master Brigs. With others he came into conflict. They are relegated to a footnote.*

Having obtained all that he could, apparently, at the school of Master Brigs (of whom nothing has come down), little Richard, as our last citation from the vicar's manuscript has anticipated us in stating, was sent to Bury St Edmunds, to the 'Free School' there, by which must be intended the still famous 'School' founded by Edward VI.; and we can very well understand the zest with which one so thoughtful and eager would avail himself of the advantages of such an institution. Dr Donaldson has failed to enrol Sibbes among the celebrities of the school, an omission which, it is to be hoped, will

* Contemporary 'boys.' The greatest of all, Master Willie Shakespeare, rising into his teens, has only very lately been tossing his auburn curls at Stratford 'school;' and, still a 'boy,' is now wooing his fair Anne Hathaway. Master Joseph Hall is playing about Bristow Park, Ashby-de la-Zouch, under the eye of Mistress Winifred, of whom he was to write so tenderly as his more than Monica. Away in the downs of Berks, diminutive Willie Laud is playing at marbles under the acacia-walk of Reading. Master George Herbert is ruffling the humour of his stately brother, afterwards Lord Herbert of Cherbury, the '*doubter*,' by overturning a glass of malmsey on his slashed hose and 'roses of his shoon.' In not distant Tarring, Master John Selden is already storing up in the wizard cave of memory those treasures of learning the world is one day to marvel at. Masters Phineas and Giles Fletcher are truanting in the linden glades of their father's vicarage. Masters George Wither and Francis Quarles are agog (in strange contrast with their grim scorn of such 'gaudery,' by-and-bye) over their new lace-frill. Master William Browne is chasing the butterflies in Tavistock. Masters Ussher and Hobbes are perchance busy over their A B C. Francis Beaumont and John Fletcher are still asunder. Master Massinger, tossing ha'pence under the minster of Salisbury, no vision yet of the 'Virgin Martyr,' and no shadow of the '*stranger's* grave' he is to fill. Moreover, as Master Sibbes was thus footing it between Thurston and Bury, men were alive who had seen martyr faces, 'pale i' the fire.' In the words of Bourne, of a few years earlier, 'The English air was thick with sighs and curses. Great men [were] heavy-hearted at the misery which had fallen upon the land . . . . and he [may] have listened to their earnest, mournful talk. (Memoirs of Philip Sidney, by H. R. Fox Bourne, 8vo, 1862, pp. 9, 10.)

henceforward be supplied, for any school may boast of a name so venerable as the author of the 'Bruised Reed.' In the 'registers of the school the name of Sibbes has not been recorded. One would have been glad to know some of his schoolmates. I am not aware that history or biography has named any of them, none at any rate more distinguished than himself. The statutes and other documentary manuscripts of the school have been lost, and nothing is known of its celebrated scholars till 1610—long subsequent to Sibbes—when the list is headed by that twin-brother to Pepys, Sir Symonds D'Ewes. Only one Master is given before 1583, a Philip Mandevill. In 1583, the office was filled by a John Wright, M.A., and in 1596, by Edmund Coote, M.A., who seems to have published his 'English Schoolmaster' (hardly to be placed beside 'The Schoolmaster' of Roger Ascham, though not without merit), during his short term of office.

The earliest extant list of 'boys' is dated 1656. It is a fine glimpse of the student-boy old Catlin gives, leisurely footing from Pakenham to Thurston, and it is to be remembered he did the same to the more distant Bury. We can avouch that, in this good year Eighteen hundred and sixty-two, twenty-fourth of Queen Victoria I., few more pleasant rural roads can be found than that which now winds from Thurston to Bury. On either side are picturesque hurdle-fences tangled with purple cornel, or hedge-rows odorous with hawthorn spray. But it must have been very different in Master Richard's time. Macadam was still unborn; and even a century and half later, Arthur Young* has anything but praise for this turnpike. 'I was forced,' he tells us in reference to it, 'to move as slow in it as in any unmended lane in Wales. For ponds of liquid dirt, and a scattering of loose flints, just sufficient to lame every horse that moves near them, with the addition of cutting vile grips across the road, under the pretence of letting the water off, but without effect, altogether render at least twelve out of these sixteen miles (between Bury and Sudbury) as infamous a turnpike as ever was beheld.' Alas! for bookish, studious Master Richard, if he found his school-walk such a Slough-of-Despond.

Sent to Bury 'Free School' (visiting which I looked up at the time-stained bust of its youthful royal founder with interest for Sibbes's sake, who, perchance, practised his first Latin in spelling out the not over-elegant or accurate inscription beneath), there would, no doubt, be rapid advancement. But the 'child' had become a 'lad,' and again there was threatened interruption to his school-learning. I

* 'Six Weeks' Tour through the Southern Counties of England and Wales.' 2d ed. 1769. Pp. 88, 89.

find an objurgation rising to my lips against this so 'unwilling' father; but it is silenced by the recollection of the vicar's testimony: 'He was a skilful and painful workman, and a good, sound-hearted Christian.' Master Catlin, I suspect thy sweet-nurtured charity was blind to Master Paul Sibs's penuriousness! It may have been, again let us say, pressure of circumstances, many mouths to be fed, multiplied 'work' demanding another pair of hands. Still it is not altogether what we should like, to find Master Richard again hindered. 'His father,' continues our vicar, 'at length *grew weary of his expenses for books and learning*, took him from school, bought him an axe and some other tools, and set him to his own trade, to the great discontent of the youth, whose genius wholly carried him another way.' So Master Paul Sibs proposed, but Another disposed. The lad was destined to work for his generation—and many generations—with other tools than these.

CHAPTER III.

STUDENT AND PREACHER AT CAMBRIDGE.

Leaves Bury St Edmunds for 'St John's College,' Cambridge—Greaves—Knewstub—Rushbrook—Enters as 'sub-sizar'—Jeremy Taylor '*pauper scholaris*'—Progress—Degrees—B.A.—'Fellow'—M.A.—'Taxer'—B.D.—Paul Bayne—'*Conversion*'—A 'Preacher'—Lectureship of 'Trinity,' Cambridge—Memorial—'Hobson'—Accepts—Results—Samuel Clarke—Thomas Cawton—John Cotton—'Word in season' to Thomas Goodwin—Prevalent 'preaching.'

Once more vigilant friends stepped in. They saw the 'youth' set utterly against the grain, at the wheel-wright's bench. 'Whereupon,' approvingly, with the faintest touch of rebuke, chronicles good Zachary Catlin: 'Mr Greaves, then minister of Thurston, and Mr Rushbrook, an attorney there, knowing the disposition and fitness of the lad, sent him, *without his father's consent*, to some of the Fellows of St John's College of their acquaintance, with their letters of recommendation; where, upon examination, he was so well approved of, that he was presently entertained as a sub-sizar, shortly after chosen scholar of the house, and at length came to be Fellow of the College, and one of the taskers of the university; his father being hardly brought to allow him twenty nobles a year towards his maintenance in Cambridge, to which some good friends in the country, Mr Greaves, Mr Knewstub, and some others, made some addition, for a time, as need required.' I am sure all my readers will wish that we knew more of those 'good friends.' All honour to the memory of 'Mr Greaves and Mr Rushbrook.' Of 'Mr Knewstub,' the scholarly, the pious, the brave-hearted, no admirer of the Puritans needs to be informed. His is truly a historic *clarum et venerabile nomen.* His letter of recommendation to St John's College would have the greater weight, in that he was one of its greatest lights, and, subsequently, its benefactor. One is pleased, nevertheless, to learn that it was 'upon examination,' not mere 'recommendation,' the youth was received. He was then in his eighteenth year. Entered as a sub-sizar, which is even beneath a sizar, young Sibbes must have been placed at a disadvantage. Jeremy Taylor, however, was entered as '*pauper scholaris,*' lower still. That has transfigured, if not ennobled, the lowly 'sizar.' Certainly the more honour is due to those who, starting with the meanest, have won for themselves the highest places. How many who entered among the highest are forgotten, while the lapse of time only brightens the lustre of our 'sub-sizar' and the '*pauper scholaris.*'

The career of Sibbes at the university was singularly successful, and indicates in the son of the wheel-wright of Tostock and Thurston, no common energy and devotion to study. It is probable that his 'school-learning' at Pakenham and Bury St Edmunds, alike, was frequently interrupted and hindered. Nevertheless, he seems to have at once placed himself abreast of the most favoured students. The records and registers of St John's College, shew that he passed B.A. in 1598-9; was admitted 'Fellow' 3d April 1601, commenced M.A. in 1602, taxer (the 'tasker' of Catlin) in 1608, was elected 'College Preacher' feast of 1st March 1609, and graduated B.D. in 1610.

We must return upon these dates. When Sibbes, in 1595, proceeded to Cambridge, '*without the consent of his father,*' but with kind words of cheer and something more from Mr Greaves, Mr Knewstub, and Mr Rushbrook, it does not appear that he had any specific intentions in regard to the future. An academic life was evidently his ambition; but to what profession, whether divinity, law, or medicine, he was ultimately to devote himself, was probably left undetermined. An event, or more accurately, *the* one great event and 'change' in every man—his *conversion* (I like and therefore use the good old puritan, because Biblical, word), in all likelihood led him to decide to serve God in the ministry of the gospel of his Son. Paul Bayne, sometimes Baine and Baines, one of the most remarkable of the earlier '*Doctrinal* Puritans' (that name of stigma imposed by Laud), whose 'Letters,' second only to those of Samuel Rutherford, and other minor books, were long the chosen fireside reading of every puritan household, and whose 'Exposition of Ephesians' is worthy to take its place beside Rogers and Byfield on Peter, Jenkyn on Jude, Petter on Mark, Elton on Colossians and Romans, Newton on John, and their kindred folios, that lie now-a-days like so many unworked mines of gold—had succeeded Perkins as preacher at St Andrew's, Cambridge, 'and it pleased God,' says Clarke, 'to make him an instrument of the conversion of that holy and eminent servant of Christ, Dr Sibbes.' Sibbes himself is reverently reticent on the momentous matter, even in his preface to Bayne's 'Exposition of the first chapter of Ephesians' (published separately in 1618), making no allusion to it; but it probably took place somewhere about 1602–3.* In 1602, having passed M.A., he shortly thereafter became a 'preacher.' By 1608 'he was a preacher of good note.' Where he did preach we are not informed. In his address to the reader prefixed to the 'Soul's Conflict,' he states that the 'Sermons' which compose it had been preached first of all 'about twelve years' before 'in the city,' *i.e.*, London, and afterwards at 'Gray's Inn.' I have utterly failed to come upon any memorial of this 'city' ministry; but it is probable that it was commenced between 1602 and 1607. Elected 'College Preacher' in 1609, he must have been then well known and distinguished.

In 1610, when he had graduated B.D., another very important event happened. In that year a 'Memorial' was addressed to him, which, in so far as I can learn, appears to have been the origin of the subsequently celebrated 'Trinity Lectureship,' held since by some of the greatest names of the church. The memorial gives us

* 'Conversion . . . . reticent.' This is quite in accord with Sibbes's declared sentiments. I would refer the reader to 'The Description of Christ,' pp. 30, 31. There he will find not more sound than admirably expressed counsels and warnings as to the 'vainglory' of publishing abroad things too solemn to be so dealt with. I assume the responsibility of affirming, that at no period have those warnings been more demanded than the present. Every one who 'loves the Lord,' who prays and longs for the coming of 'the kingdom,' who mourns the wordliness and coldness of all sections of Christ's divided church, must rejoice in the past two years' awakening and 'revival.' I would gladly recognise the work of the Spirit of God in much that has taken place. I verily believe very many have been 'born again,' and more who were half asleep have been stirred and quickened. At the same time, it were to be unfaithful and untruthful to blink the 'evil' that has mingled with the 'good.' It becomes every reverent soul to protest against those premature declarations of 'conversions,' and publication of 'experiences' that have got so common. It is perilous to forget the Master's words, Luke xvii. 20. Paul was fourteen years a 'servant' of Christ before he made known his ineffable rapture and vision. Modern 'converts,' do not allow as many hours to expire ere their whole story is blazoned in the public prints. Surely a thing so awful and so sacred, unless in very exceptional instances, is for the ear of God alone. The Tract Societies would act wisely if they circulated by thousands as a 'Tract for the Times,' Sibbes's priceless words of 'Vainglory.'

insight into the popularity of Sibbes as a preacher.* The orthography and wording of the original are retained :—

'A Coppye of the general request of the inhabitants of o^{r} p'ishe deliv'ed to Mr Sibs, publique p'acher of the house of Cambridge.

'We whose names ar heerunderwritten, the Churchewardens and P'ishioners of Trinity p'ishe in Cambridge, with the ful and fre consent of Mr Jhon Wildbore o^{r} minister, duely considering the extream straytnes & div'se other discomodities concerning the accustomed place of y^{r} exercise & desireing as much as in vs lyeth y^{e} more publique benefit of yor ministery, doe earnestlye entreat you wold be pleesed to accept of o^{r} p'ishe Churche, which al of vs doe willinglye offer you for & concerning the exercising of yo$_{r}$ ministery & awditorye at the awntient and usual daye & houre. In witnes hereof wee have heervnto set to o^{r} hands this 22th (*sic*) of Noveber 1610.

'JOHN WILBORE, Minister.
'EDWARD ALMOND, } Churchewardens.
'THOMAS BANKES, }
(Signed also by 29 Parishioners.)

The churchwardens of the parish having kindly permitted access to their 'Records,' I find amongst them a list of the names of the subscribers to the lectureship in the several parishes of the town, with the amount of each person's subscription, which runs generally 13s. 4d., 10s., and 6s. 8d. per annum. Three gave £1 per annum each, of whom one was Mr Hobson, the carrier, immortalised by Milton, and later by Steele in the 'Spectator,' and to this day a 'household word' in Cambridge, in kindly eccentric association with the proverb, 'Hobson's choice, that or none,' which no one book-read will need explained. One thing is noticeable, that a goodly number of the signatures to the memorial are with marks +. This is of the last interest and not a little touching. The 'common people' heard Sibbes, like his Master, 'gladly,' and the 'straytnes of the place' hindered others. This is a sign of change for the better in Cambridge very worthy of observation. The old longing after that full preaching of the gospel which had characterised the period of Perkins's seraphic yet pungent ministry, was revived. Sibbes responded to the memorial, and immediately it was felt that 'Trinity' had a man of mark as its 'Lecturer,' the coequal of Bayne of St Andrew's. How those saintly servants of the same Lord would rejoice to be fellow-helpers of each other, the younger 'serving' with the elder, as a son with a father. The lectureship of 'Trinity' was a complete success. Besides the townsmen, many scholars resorted to him, whereby he became, in the words of Clarke, a 'worthy instrument of begetting many sons

* 'Trinity Lectureship.' The 'Memorial' is given by Mr Cooper in his Annals of Cambridge, iii. 168.

and daughters unto God, besides the edifying and building up of others.'*

We have incidental confirmations of the weighty testimony of the 'Pastor of St Bennet Fink, London.' More generally, in that curious little rarity of Puritan biography, 'The Life and Death of that Holy and Reverend man of God, Mr Thomas Cawton'† (1662), we read 'He conscientiously and constantly laboured to counter-work those factors of hell, and drove a trade for God in bestirring himself to insinuate into any lad that was ingenious, and was very successful therein, to the astonishment and confusion of his opposers. Many had great cause to bless God for him, and their first acquaintance with him, for his bringing them to Dr Preston's and *Dr Sibbes, his Lectures* in those times.' More specially, Cotton Mather, the Thomas Fuller of New England, tells us of one memorable conversion through his instrumentality—John Cotton, who was in turn the 'leader to Christ' of a greater than himself, Dr Preston, and whom Oliver Cromwell himself addressed as 'my esteemed friend.'‡

It were like to rubbing off with coarse fingers the powder from a moth's wing, in any wise to change the loving and grave narrative. It is as follows:—'Hitherto we have seen the life of Mr Cotton while he was not yet alive! Though the restraining and preventing grace of God had kept him from such outbreakings of sin as defile the lives of most in the world, yet like the old man who for such a cause ordered this epitaph to be written on his grave, "Here lies an old man who lived but seven years," he reckoned himself to have been but a dead man as being "alienated from the life of God," until he had experienced that regeneration in his own soul, which was thus accomplished. The Holy Spirit of God had been at work upon his young heart, by the ministering of that reverend and renowned preacher of righteousness, Mr Perkins; but he resisted and smothered those convictions through a vain persuasion, that if he became a godly man 'twould spoil him for being a learned one. Yea, such was the secret enmity and prejudice of an unregenerate soul against real holiness, and such the torment which our Lord's witnesses give

* Clarke, Lives of Thirty-two English Divines, 3d edition, 1677, folio, p. 143.

† 'Cawton,' p. 11.

‡ Cotton and Cromwell. The letter of the great Protector, alluded to, a very striking one, will be found in Brook's Lives of the Puritans, iii. 158–9. It is also given with characteristic annotation in Carlyle's 'Cromwell,' iii. 221–225 (3d ed. 1850). When, may I ask in a foot-note, will America give us worthy editions of the still inedited and uncollected 'Works' of John Cotton, Thomas Hooker, Davenport, and others of their kindred? Surely this were better than much that has been reprinted over the Atlantic.

to the consciences of the earthly-minded, that when he heard the bell toll for the funeral of Mr Perkins, his mind secretly rejoiced in his deliverance from that powerful ministry by which his conscience had been so oft beleaguered; the remembrance of which things afterwards did break his heart exceedingly! *But he was at length more effectually awakened by a sermon of Dr Sibs*, wherein was discoursed the misery of those who had only a negative righteousness, or a civil, sober, honest blamelessness before men. Mr Cotton became now very sensible of his own miserable condition before God; and the errors of those convictions did stick so fast upon him, that after no less than three years disconsolate apprehensions under them, the grace of God made him a thoroughly renewed Christian, and filled him with a sacred joy which accompanied him into the fulness of joy for ever. For this cause, as persons truly converted unto God have a mighty and lasting affection for the instruments of their conversion, *thus Mr Cotton's veneration for Dr Sibs* was after this very particular and perpetual, and it caused him to have the picture of that great man in that part of his house where he might oftenest look upon it.'*

Various similar *memorabilia* might be here adduced from the Puritan 'Biographies' and 'Histories.' One additional 'word in season,' spoken to Dr Thomas Goodwin, may suffice. In his earlier days this celebrated divine leant to Arminianism rather than to Calvinism, and it was through Sibbes that his views were cleared, to his life-long satisfaction, on the point of Jesus Christ being the Head and Representative of his people. It is also recorded that, in familiar discourse with Goodwin, Sibbes said, 'Young man, if you ever would do good, you must preach the gospel, and the free grace of God in Christ Jesus.'† The counsel was as a 'nail in a sure place,' and no reader of Goodwin needs to be told how fully and magnificently he sets forth the 'grace' of God in Christ.

Well was it that such men as Paul Bayne and Richard Sibbes were preachers in such a place and at such a time. From contemporary accounts it is apparent, that notwithstanding the profound impression 'on the town' by Perkins, and notwithstanding that there were a few who, Mary-like, 'kept all the things' they had heard from him, 'and pondered them in their hearts,' Cambridge was sunken down, as a whole, to all its former indifferentism and formality. The preaching that was fashionable among the 'wits' of

* Cotton. Magnalia Christi Americana: or the Ecclesiastical History of New England, book iii., c. i., § 5, p, 15. Folio, 1702.

† Robert Trail, A.M., Justification by Faith, Works, vol. i. p. 261 (edition 4 vols. 8vo, 1810).

the university was a very different thing from the stern reproofs, bold invectives, burning remonstrances, prophet-like appeals of William Perkins. What was now cultivated and extolled was a frivolous, florid eloquence, that boasted itself on its deftly-turned tropes, its high-flown paraphrases of the classics, especially Seneca and Cicero, and the Fathers, the multiplied quotations of the 'sermons' published shewing like purple patches on a thread-bare robe. There was trick of manner, mellifluous cadence, simpering refinement, nothing more. The Senhouses *et hoc genus omne* sprinkled *eau-de-cologne* over their hearers (if they durst it had been '*holy* water'), while parched lips were athirst for the '*living* water'—tickled the ear when the heavily-laden soul sought pardon, the weary rest, the bruised balm. The cross lifted up on Calvary beneath the pallid heavens—the cross as proclaimed by Paul—was 'vulgar,' and to be kept out of sight. The awful blood must first be wiped off—the coarse nails withdrawn. Whoso gainsays, let him turn to their extant 'Sermons.' But amid the faithless some faithful were found. There were some not ashamed of *the* gospel,' some who could stand and withstand 'the loud laugh.' The 'towns-people' would have that which the 'collegians' (so they called them) rejected. In such circumstances we may conceive that the ministry of Sibbes could scarcely fail to be a ministry of power. 'The Day' alone will fully reveal its fruits.

CHAPTER IV.

'PREACHER' AT GRAY'S INN, LONDON.

'Deprived' of Lectureship and 'Outed' from Fellowship—Sir Henry Yelverton—'Preacher' at Gray's Inn—Correction of date—The 'Chapel'—The 'Inn'—Segar MS.—The Auditory—Lord Bacon.

From 1610 to 1615, Sibbes held his lectureship and other honours without molestation. But in the latter year he was deprived ('outed,' says Clarke) both of his fellowship and lecture. Even thus early Laud was at work against all Puritanism and 'preaching ;' and this was the manner of his working. However, as in many other instances, while there was unquestionable hardship and hurt done by the double deprivation, it 'fell out for the furtherance of the gospel.' Sir Henry Yelverton, that 'constant patron to godly ministers,' stepped in and secured the 'preachership' of 'Gray's Inn,' London, for him. All preceding authorities give 1618—the 'Synod of Dort' year—or 'about 1618,' as the date of this well-timed appointment. This is incorrect. I found the following entry in the 'Order-Books:' *

'Quinto die, Feb. A.D. 1616.

'At this penton [pension] Mr Richd. Sibbs is chosen preacher of Graies Inne; and it is ordered that he shal be continually resident, and shall not take any other benefice or livinge.' †

This appointment introduced him at a bound to the first society of the metropolis.

Among the treasures of the British Museum is a noble folio, drawn up from the books of 'Gray's Inn,' by Segar, one of the society's former 'butlers.' ‡ In it, with superb blazonry of shield and scutcheon, and all the 'pomp of heraldry,' are registered the names of those who were resident 'readers, benchers, ancients, barristers, students,' from the earliest date. If one had the Greek of Homer, or the 'large utterance' of Milton, or even the rhetoric of Macaulay, it were possible to revivify the auditory of the 'chapel.' A more illustrious can scarcely be imagined. The flower of the old nobility, the greatest names of the state and of history, men who mark epochs, were embraced in it. I have looked through the roll from 1616 to 1635—the period of Sibbes's office—and almost at random I note Abbots and Ashleys, Audleys and Amhersts, Bacons and Barnardistons, Boyles and Brookes, Bradshaws and Barrows, Cromwells and Cholmleys, Cornwallises

* 'Order Books.' These are deposited at 'Gray's Inn,' where I had the privilege of an unrestricted examination of them. The volume from which I make all my excerpts, is a huge folio, marked 'Gray's Inn. Book of Orders. II. of Eliz. to XVIII. of Chs. II.'

† 'Chapel' of 'Gray's Inn.' I cull from the above authority a record of the foundation of the 'preachership' to which Sibbes was elected:—

CHAPELL.

'It appeareth as well by a deed of the Cort of Augmentacons, bearinge date the 10th of November, in ye 33th (*sic*) yeare of ye reigne of King Henry 8. As also by an Exemplificacon thereof, made ye 12th November in ye said yeare. As also by another Exemplificacon thereof, granted by ye late Queen Elizab., dated at Westminster the 12th of ffebruary, in the fourth yeare of her reigne. That ye treasurer of ye Cort of Augmentacons, of ye said revenue of ye crowne, for the time beinge, should yearely pay out of ye said treasurres to ye treasurer of ye house of Graye's Inn, Nigh Holborne, in ye county of Midd. for ye time being, ye sume of vi xiij iiij[d] (£6, 13s. 4d), in recompense of a yearly stipend of vij xiij iiij (£7, 13s. 4d), wch. was duely proved before ye said Cort of Augmentacons to be issuinge out of ye possessions of ye late monasterie of St Bartholomew in Smithfield, besides London; and of right payable, time out of mind, by ye prior and convent of the said monastrie and their p'decessors, for ye findinge of a chaplaine to celebrate divine service in ye chapell of Graye's Inn aforesaid, for ye students, gent., and fellowes of ye said house,' &c. &c. &c.

‡ 'Segar.' Harleian MSS., 1912. 94, c. 25. Plut. xlvii. E folio.

and Chetwinds, Drakes and Egertons, Fairfaxes and Fitzgeralds, Nevills and Pelhams, Riches and Sidneys, Staffords and Stanleys, Standishes and Talbots, Wallers, and Vaughans, and Veres.* Truly the wheel-wright's son has a worthy audience; ay, and what is better, he is worthy of the audience.

At the date of Sibbes's appointment, the greatest of all the names enumerated, Francis Bacon, had 'chambers' in Gray's Inn; and, after his fall, was a permanent resident.† When it was dark with him, he had Sibbes for his 'preacher.' Am I wrong in thinking that the touching appeal of the stricken Lord Chancellor to his peers, recorded by every biographer, 'I am a *bruised reed*,' may have been a reminiscence of the golden-syllabled words which he had heard from the 'preacher' at Gray's Inn?

I know not that the author of the Bruised Reed is once named

* 'Gray's Inn.' I may give in a foot-note, from Segar's folio, the earlier history of the Society with which the name of Sibbes is so indissolubly associated. Having recited certain ancient mediæval-Latin records, which are also supplemented by prior relations to the Dean and Chapter of St Paul's, the chronicler proceeds:—

'By all wch severall offices, it appeares that the said manor of Portepole, now Gray's Inne, or within ye which a part of Graye's Inne is now situate, was anciently the Inheritance of the Grayes. But I do not find in any of ye said former, &c. . . . that any Gray, lord or owner of ye said manor or messuage, did at any time reside there. Reginald de Gray, in ye 44th year of ye reign of Kinge Edw. 3, for ye yearly rent of Q (?), as is mentioned in ye office, then found after his decease. And in ye w[ch] office (the same beinge in form[r] inquisitions named mesuagium), is thereby found to be hospitium and in lease whereby it's manifested yt. ye house then and yet knowne by the name of Gray's Inn, was demised to some p'sons of speciall regard and rank, *and not to meane ones, or p'sons of meane or privat behav[r]*, but to such as were united into a Society p'fessinge ye lawes, that in those dayes begunn to congregat and setle themselves within ye Court (?) as an associated company entertayning hospitalitie together. And then this house grew to be off an higher title in denominacon and became to be totally termed by ye Intitulacon of Hospitium in Portopole. And it also appeareth that ye said Reginald de Gray devised ye said messuage as aforesaid in ye reigne of King Edw. 3, in his life-time, and at his death was held for hospitium and by the jury before whom ye said inquisition was taken in ye said 44th yeare of Edw. 3d (a[o] 1370), was found to bee hospitium, and not mesuaginm. Imediatly whereupon ye said hospitium is called Grey's Inne, or Hospitium Graiorum, for that that estate had been soe long and by soe many severall descents in yt name,' &c. &c. &c.

This quaint and curious narrative, which I believe is now for the first time published, explains the origin of the name 'Gray's Inn.' Those interested will find much additional information in Segar,—all the more valuable that many of the originals were destroyed by a fire at Gray's Inn. These missing portions have been transcribed, but not very accurately, for the Hon. Society.

† 'Bacon and Gray's Inn.' See an interesting chapter of an unusually interesting, but not very accurate, book, Meteyard's 'Hallowed Spots of Ancient London' (4to, 1862), entitled 'York House, Strand, and Gray's Inn,' pp. 80–99. An engraving of 'Gray's Inn' is given on page 90. I need hardly say that all the old buildings, and the 'faire gardenne,' with its Bacon-planted elms, have long disappeared.

in all Bacon's writings, but then neither is Shakespeare. Still, I cannot help rejoicing that, in his closing years of humiliation and penitence, while he was building up the Cyclopean masonry of his 'Novum Organum,' he had Richard Sibbes to lift his thoughts higher. I delight to picture to myself the mighty thinker and the heavenly preacher walking in the 'faire gardenne' of the Inn, holding high and sanctified discourse.* I fancy I can trace the influence of Sibbes on Bacon, and of Bacon on Sibbes. There are in Sibbes many aphoristic sayings, pregnant seeds of thought, felicitous 'similies' (so marked on the early margins), that bear the very mintage of the 'Essays;' and again there is in them an insight into Scripture, a working in of its cloth-of-gold with his own meditations, an apposite quotation of its facts and words, that surely came of the sermons and private talk under the elms with Sibbes. It is something to know that two such men knew each other.

The 'Bruised Reed' and 'Soul's Conflict,' and indeed nearly all his works, present specimens of the kind of preaching to which the auditory of 'Gray's Inn' listened from Sunday to Sunday. One is gladdened to think that such men heard such preaching, so wise, so grave, so fervid, so Christful. There grew out of it life-long friendships.

CHAPTER V.

PROVOSTSHIP OF TRINITY COLLEGE, DUBLIN.

Archbishop Ussher—Dr John Preston—Letter of Sibbes—Sir William Temple—Letters of Ussher to Archbishop Abbot and the Hon. Society of Gray's Inn—Sibbes to Ussher—Archbishop Abbot to Ussher—Declines the Provostship.

Installed as 'preacher' at Gray's Inn, Sibbes seems to have acted up to the letter of his appointment; which, it will be remembered, required that he was 'to be continually resident,' and 'to take no other benefice or living.' This he continued apparently to do, with the exception of occasional 'sermons' in the 'city' or in Cambridge, until 1626. In that year new honours came to him. Archbishop Ussher sought to have him made provost of Trinity College, Dublin; and he was elected, on the death of Dr John Hills, 'Master' of St Katherine Hall (now College), Cambridge. A very interesting correspondence remains in relation to

* One asks wistfully if they took any note of one William Shakespeare, who, within three months of the appointment to the 'preachership' at 'Gray's Inn,' was laid beside his little Hamnet by the Avon! (Died, 23d April 1616.)

the former, which I would now introduce. He had long been in intimate friendship with the illustrious primate of Ireland, who, on his visits to London, was wont to invite himself to his 'study.'* One early notice of their mutual regard is contained in a portion of a letter from Dr John Preston to Ussher. It is as follows: 'March 16. 1619.—Your papers you shall surely have with you; and if there be no remedy that I cannot see you myself, I shall entreat you *to make plain to Mr Sibbes* (or whom else you will) the last point especially, when the LXX weeks began, though I should speak to you about many other things.'† The following brief letter of Sibbes himself a few years onward, 1622, gives us a further glimpse of their relations, as well as of various memorable names and occurrences. Ussher was then Bishop of Meath.

Mr R. Sibbs to the Bishop of Meath.‡

I could not, Right Reverend Sir, omit so fit an opportunity of writing unto you as the coming of two of my worthy friends, Sir Nathaniel Rich and Mr Crew; though it were but to signify unto you that I retain a thankful and respectful remembrance of your lordship's former love and kindness. Mr Crew is already known unto you; Sir Nathaniel, I think, a stranger yet unto you; you shall find him for sincerity, wisdom, and right judgment worthy your inward acquaintance. How matters stand here you shall have better information from those worthy gentlemen than from me. For Cambridge matters, I suppose your lordship hath already heard that Dr Ward is chosen professor in Dr Davenant's place; there is hope of Mr Preston's coming to be lecturer at Lincoln's Inn, which place is now void. Mrs More, Mr Drake and his wife, Mr Dod, with others that love you heartily in the Lord, are in good health, the Lord be praised. Sir Henry Savil hath ended his days, secretary Murray succeeding him in Eton, but report will prevent my letter in this and other matters. Sir, I long to see your begun historical discourse of the perpetual continuity of a visible church, lengthened and brought to these latter times. No one point will stop the clamour of our adversaries more, nor furnish the weaker with a better plea. Others not very well affected to the Waldenses, &c., for some tenets . . . have gone about to prove what you do some other ways. But perhaps the present exigence of your Church is such as taketh up your daily endeavours and thoughts. And I know the zeal of your heart for the public good will put you forward for whatsoever is for the best advantage of the common cause. I fear lest the encountering with that daring chal-

* 'Ussher and Sibbes.' Brook's 'Lives of the Puritans,' vol. ii. p. 416. From Brook's own copy, interleaved and containing additional MS. notes. In the library of Joshua Wilson, Esq, Tunbridge Wells.

† 'Preston and Ussher.' This and the succeeding correspondence I take from 'The whole Works of the Most Rev. James Ussher, D.D., Lord Archbishop of Armagh and Primate of all Ireland. With a Life of the Author, and an Account of his Writings. By Charles Richard Elrington, D.D., Regius Professor of Divinity in the University of Dublin. Dublin: Hodges & Smith. 16 vols. 8vo, 1847, *seq.*' See vol. xvi. p. 373. Elrington supersedes Parr (who also gives the most of the letters), and I therefore take the whole from him.

‡ 'Sibbes to Usher.' Letter cclxiii. Vol. xvi. p. 395, 396.

lenger breed you a succession of troubles. How far you have proceeded in this matter we know not. The Lord lead you through all conflicts and businesses, with comfortable evidence of his wisdom in guiding you, and goodness in a blessed issue.

Your Lordship's in all Christian affection and service,

R. SIBBS.

Gray's Inn, March 21. 1622.

Advancing to 1626–27, Ussher was now archbishop and primate, and involved in an imbroglio of political and ecclesiastical difficulties. His was only a splendid exile. He writes, half-mournfully, half in dread, under date 'Feby. 9th, 1626:'—'As for the general state of things here, they are so desperate that I am afraid to write anything thereof.'* He was specially 'troubled' in the matter of 'Trinity College,' of which he was the patron. Sir William Temple was provost, and from his great age, utterly inefficient, and even in dotage. There were perpetual disputes between him and the 'fellows,' so much so that the removal of the provost, in some quiet manner, was felt to be the only method of preserving the discipline and good order of the college. To this Ussher addressed himself, and ultimately persuaded the old man—a not unhistoric name—to resign, on condition that Sibbes took his place. This we learn from a letter of the primate to Archbishop Abbot, to whom, on 10th January 1626–27, he writes:—'The time is now come wherein we have at last wrought upon Sir William Temple to give up his place, *if the other may be drawn over*.' That 'other' was Sibbes. But all difficulty about the resignation, with or without conditions, was unexpectedly removed by the death of Sir William, who expired on the 15th of January 1626–27, five days only after the date of Ussher's letter,—upon which he again wrote Abbot in favour of Sibbes. The whole correspondence is of the last interest, and is self-explanatory. It may now be given in order, the more so, that, excepting one of the letters, it has been overlooked or left unused:—

The Archbishop of Armagh to the most Reverend GEORGE ABBOT, *Archbishop of Canterbury.*†

MY MOST GRACIOUS LORD,—When I took my last leave of you at Lambeth, I made bold to move your grace for the settlement of the provostship of our college here upon some worthy man, whensoever the place should become void. I then recommended unto you Mr Sibbes, the preacher of Gray's Inn, with whose learning, soundness of judgment, and uprightness of life I was very well acquainted; and it pleased your grace to listen unto my motion, and give way to the coming over of the person named, when time required. The time, my lord, is now come, wherein we have at last wrought Sir William Temple to give up his place, if the other may be

* Ussher, xv. 365–6. † Ussher, letter cxxi. xv. 361–2.

drawn over. And therefore I most humbly entreat your grace to give unto Mr Sibbes that encouragement he deserveth; in whose behalf I dare undertake that he shall be as observant of you, and as careful to put in execution all your directions, as any man whosoever. The matter is of so great importance for the good of this poor church, and your fatherly care, as well of the church in general, as our college in particular, so well known, that I shall not need to press you herein with many words. And therefore, leaving it wholly to your grace's grave consideration, and beseeching Almighty God to bless you in the managing of your weighty employments, I humbly take my leave, and rest,

Your grace's in all duty, ready to be commanded,

J. A.

Drogheda, January 10. 1626.

At the same time, the primate addressed a similar letter to the 'Honourable Society of Gray's Inn,' to deprecate their putting any obstacles in the way of Sibbes's acceptance. By a slip of the pen, he inserts—'*Lincoln's*,' instead of 'Gray's' Inn. As himself formerly 'preacher' in 'Lincoln's,' the mistake was natural:—

*The Archbishop of Armagh to the Honourable Society of Gray's-Inn.**

My most worthy Friends,—I cannot sufficiently express my thankfulness unto you for the honour which you have done unto me, in vouchsafing to admit me into your society, and to make me a member of your own body. Yet so is it fallen out for the present, that I am enforced to discharge one piece of debt with entering into another. For thus doth the case stand with us. Sir William Temple, who hath governed our college at Dublin these seventeen years, finding age and weakness now to increase upon him, hath resolved to ease himself of that burthen, and resign the same to some other. Now of all others whom we could think of, your worthy preacher Mr Sibbes is the man upon whom all our voices have here settled, as one that hath been well acquainted with an academical life, and singularly well qualified for the undertaking of such a place of government. I am not ignorant what damage you are to sustain by the loss of such an able man, with whose ministry you have been so long acquainted; but I consider withal, that you are at the well-head, where the defect may quickly be supplied; and that it somewhat also tendeth to the honour of your Society, that out of all the king's dominions your house should be singled out for the place unto which the seminary of the whole Church in this kingdom should have recourse for help and succour in this case. And therefore my most earnest suit unto you is, that you would give leave unto Mr Sibbes to repair hither, at leastwise for a time, that he may see how the place will like him. For which great favour our whole Church shall be obliged unto you: and I, for my part, shall evermore profess myself to rest

Your own in all Christian service, Ready to be commanded,

J. A.

Drogheda, January 10. 1626.

Further:—

The Archbishop of Armagh to the most Reverend George Abbot, *Archbishop of Canterbury.*†

My very good Lord,—I wrote unto your grace heretofore concerning

* Ussher, letter cxx., xv. 363–4. † Ussher, letter cxxi., xv. 365.

the substitution of Mr Sibbes into the place of Sir William Temple. But having since considered with myself how some occasions may fall out that may hinder him from coming hither, and how many most unfit persons are now putting in for that place, I have further emboldened myself to signify thus much more of my mind unto you, that in case Mr Sibbes do not come unto us, I cannot think of a more worthy man, and more fitted for the government of that college, than Mr Bedel, who hath heretofore remained with Sir Henry Wotton at Venice, and is now beneficed about Berry. If either he, or Dr Featly, or any other worthy man whom you shall think fit, can be induced to accept of the place; and your grace will be pleased to advise the fellows of the college to elect him thereunto; that poor house shall ever have cause to bless your memory for the settlement of it at such a time as this, where so many labour to make a prey of it.

Of the 'occurrences' that might 'fall out' to hinder Sibbes from coming, the primate had been informed in our next letter:—

Mr R. Sibbs *to the Archbishop of Armagh.**

Right Rev. and my very good Lord,—I answered your letters presently upon the receipt of them, but out of a mind diversely affected as divers things presented themselves to me; it much moved me when I perceived your great care of the place, the cost, the trouble, the more than ordinary inclination towards me, far beyond any deserts of mine. Yet as I signified to your grace, when I consider God's providence in raising me so little before, to another place, and that compatible with my present employment here in London, it moveth me to think it were rash to adventure upon another place. And I have entered into a course of procuring some good to the college, which is like to be frustrate, if I now leave them, and they exposed to some who intend to serve their own turn of them. The scandal whereof would lie upon me. The judgment of my friends here is for my stay, considering I am fixed already, and there must be a call for a place; as to a place, they allege the good which may be done, and doubtfulness of good succession here; and that it were better that some other man had that place that were not so fixed here. These and such like considerations move them to think, that when your lordship shall know how it is with me at this time, that you will think of some other successor. Nothing of a great time so much troubled me. I humbly desire you, my lord, to take in good part this my not accepting, considering now there be other difficulties than were when you were in England with us. It is not yet openly known that I refuse it, that so you may have time of pitching upon another. I write now this second time, fearing lest my former letter might miscarry. I could set the comfort by you against many objections, were not that late chief in Cambridge. I count it one part of my happiness in especial manner, that ever I knew your lordship; the remembrance of you will be fresh in my heart whilst I live, which will move me to desire the multiplying of all happiness upon you and yours.

I have not delivered the letter to my lord of Canterbury, because it hath reference to the business as it concerneth me. The Lord continue to honour you in his service for the good of many, and to keep you in these dangerous times.—Your Grace's to command in the Lord,

R. Sibbs.

Gray's Inn, Feb. 7. A.D. 1626.

I humbly desire you to remember my service and respects to Mrs Ussher.

* Ussher, letter cclxxxvi., xvi 440–1.

Upon receipt of this the primate wrote :*—'But now very lately, even by the last packet, I have received a letter from Mr Sibbs, signifying his doubtfulness of accepting the place of provost here (he having beine *at the same time* chosen head of another college in Cambridge), which hath much altered our intentions.' A few days later, Ussher was informed more definitely by Dr Samuel Ward of Sibbes's election to the Mastership of 'Catherine Hall.' I give an extract, with context, as it introduces to us an eminent ornament of Sibbes's circle :—

Dr Samuel Ward *to* Ussher—London, 'Feb. 13. 1626.'†

The 25th of January deceased your good friend and mine, Mr Henry Alvey, at Cambridge. I was with him twice when he was sick: the first time I found him sick, but very patient and comfortable. He earnestly prayed that God would give him patience and perseverance. The later time I came he was in a slumber, and did speak nothing: I prayed for him, and then departed. Shortly after he departed this life. He desired to be buried privately, and in the churchyard, and in a sheet only, without a coffin, for so, said he, was our Saviour. But it was thought fitting he should be put in a coffin, and so he was: I was at his interring the next day at night. Thus God is daily collecting his saints to himself. The Lord prepare us all for the *dies ascensionis*, as St Cyprian styleth it. Since the death of Dr Walsall, Dr Goslin, our vice-chancellor, and Dr Hill, master of St Katherine Hall, are both dead. In their places succeed, in Bennet College, Dr Butts; in Caius College, Mr Bachcroft, one of the fellows; *in Katherine Hall, Mr Sibbes of Gray's Inn.*

Notwithstanding Sibbes's intimation, that he had not delivered the primate's letter to Abbot, he must have subsequently changed his mind, and done so. To Ussher's recommendation, Archbishop Abbot lent a cordially willing ear. This appears by his letter in reply, which would also seem to indicate that Sibbes had been persuaded to go over to Ireland, probably to consult personally with his friend:—

The most Reverend George Abbot, *Archbishop of Canterbury, to the Archbishop of Armagh.*‡

My very good Lord,—I send unto you Mr Sibbes, who can best report what I have said unto him. I hope that college shall in him have a very good master, which hitherto it hath not had. You shall make my excuse to the fellows that I write not unto them. You shall do well to pray to God that he will bless his church; but be not too solicitous in that matter, which will fall of itself, God Almighty being able and ready to support his own cause. But of all things take heed that you project no new ways; for if they fail you shall bear a grievous burden; if they prosper, there shall be no thanks to you. Be patient, and tarry the Lord's leisure. And so commending me unto you, and to the rest of your brethren, I leave you to the Almighty, and remain,

Your lordship's loving brother, G. Cant.

Lambeth, March 19. 1626.

Sibbes no doubt found, on his arrival in Dublin, that the 'place

* Ussher, letter cccxci., xvi. 453. † Ussher, xv. 369. ‡ Ussher, xv. 375

was likely to prove harassing, and to lead him into controversy. A sentence from a letter of Joseph Mede, in like circumstances, explains his declinature :—'I would not,' he writes to Ussher, 'be willing to adventure into a strange country upon a litigious title, having seen the bad experience at home of perpetual jars and discontents from such beginnings.' * Similar reasons, combined with the attractions of Gray's Inn and Cambridge, led Sibbes to return, leaving the provostship of Trinity College, Dublin, to be filled by the afterwards revered Bishop Bedell.

CHAPTER VI.

MASTER OF CATHARINE HALL, CAMBRIDGE.

Accepts Mastership—Relaxation of 'order' at Gray's Inn—Founder of Catharine Hall and its celebrities—Its condition—'Troublous times'—Dr John Preston—Trinity Lectureship—Bishopric declined—Friendship between Sibbes and Preston—Fellow-labourers—Conversion of Preston—The effect of the preaching of the two Puritan Masters—Auditory of St Mary's—Memorials of Trinity Lecture—Success of Sibbes as Master—Clarke and Fuller—Fellows.

Having declined the Provostship of Trinity College, Dublin, Sibbes at once accepted the Mastership of Catharine Hall, Cambridge, to which, as has been narrated, he was almost simultaneously elected. No record remains of the influence used to secure this coveted and often contested honour for the 'outed' Fellow and 'deprived' Lecturer. It is not improbable that it was to Dr John Preston, the Puritan Master of the 'nest of Puritans' (so his enemies designated it), Emmanuel, that he was indebted. Preston was then in the height of his favour with the Duke of Buckingham,—the acceptance of whose patronage is one of the stains upon the memory of the Puritans. He had long been in close friendship with the preacher of Gray's Inn.

There must have been some relaxation of the 'order' under which Sibbes accepted the appointment of preacher to Gray's Inn,—to admit of his accepting the mastership of Catharine Hall, without resignation of the other. The statute is very explicit, as will be seen :—'15 Nov. 40 Eliz. (1598–9).—The divinity-reader to be chosen shall be nominated, having *no ecclesiastical preferment* other than a prebend without cure of souls, nor readership in any other place ; and shall keep the same place as long as he continues thus qualified, and no longer ; and to be charged with reading but twice a week, except when there is a communion.'†

* Ussher, as *ante*, p. 455–56, vol. xvi.

† This 'order' was made in the term previous to the election of the successor of

There were then, as now, the two distinct offices of reader, sometimes called chaplain, and of preacher, sometimes called lecturer, and as in above order, 'divinity-reader.'* So that it was the more easy to arrange for Sibbes's absence during the week. From an entry, under date 19th Jan. 1612, we learn that 'The preacher, ye chaplain, ye steward . . . . . . were to be allowed such commons as *gentlemen.*'† Not as 'gentleman' merely, but as associate and friend, was Sibbes regarded. The anxiety of the 'ancients, barristers, students,' to retain his services, would also smoothe the way to place in practical desuetude the 'order' as to '*no other ecclesiastical preferment.*' Be all this as it may, Sibbes entered on the mastership of Catharine Hall forthwith.‡

Catharine or Katharine Hall, on whose Mastership Sibbes thus entered, was then, as it continues, one of the minor Colleges of the University. Yet is it not without its own celebrities, even the foremost names of English theology, Church and Puritan, before and since. It proudly tells of John Bradford the martyr, John Maplet, John Overall, William Strong, Ralph Robinson, Ralph Brownrig, John Arrowsmith, William Spurstowe, James Shirley (the dramatist), John Lightfoot, Thomas Goodwin, John Ray, William Wotton, John Strype, Thomas Sherlock, Joseph Milner, and has recently lost Charles Hardwick. It was founded by a Robert Woodlark, D.D.,§ (whose name has passed away like his namesake's song of a previous summer), in 1475; and took its name in honour of the 'virgin and martyr St Katherine.' Its original endowment, beyond 'the tenements and garden,' was small for even those days.

a certain Dr Crooke, who was preacher from 1583 to 1599. His successor was a Mr Fenton, elected 7th Feb., 41st Eliz., 1598–99. In respect to the preacher being unmarried, the 'order' was rigid, and probably explains why Sibbes remained so to the end. I cull a couple of entries that don't say very much for the chivalry of the Gray's Inn authorities :—1612. 'A ffine paid upon change of life.' 1630, 'Noe women to come into any pt. of ye Chapell.' 1647, 'No familie to bee in the house.'—Segar MS.

* 'Chaplain.'—I note certain little memoranda in relation to the 'Chaplain,' as distingushed from the 'preacher:' the later from Segar, being one of the items included in the destroyed originals—the warrrant itself having perished; and the earlier from the 'order-book' at Gray's Inn:—1625, Warrant (granted) to pay to the treasurer of Gray's Inn £6 : 13 : 4, June 25. yearly, during pleasure, for a chaplain to read service daily in the chapel there. An earlier entry runs thus:—'5th Feb. 1620. Mr Finch allowed 4/ a week for reading in the Chappell.'

† 'Order-Book' Gray's Inn, p. 16, Segar MS.

‡ In Carter's History of the University of Cambridge (pp. 202–6), and Graduati Cantabrigienses, Dr Brownrig is erroneously stated to have been elected Master of Catharine Hall in 1631. Even so accurate a writer as Mr Russell ('Memorials of Fuller', p. 114) repeats the blunder.

§ 'Dr Woodelark.' The Cambridge Antiquarian Society have published a Catalogue of Books presented by the founder to 'Catharine Hall.'

It had some subsequent 'benefactors,' among whom appear, earlier and later, Barnardistons and Claypoles. At the period of Sibbes's election, the buildings were dilapidated, the revenues limited, the students few in number. But he threw his whole soul into his office, and speedily not only attracted a fair share of young men, but also persuaded his many noble and wealthy friends to become 'benefactors.' So early as 1630, there were no fewer than twenty-eight new entries of students; and, by that time, the hall was renovated and adorned.

Sibbes entered on his mastership in 'troublous times.' When deprived of his 'lectureship' at Trinity—which in all probability, as we said, originated with the memorial addressed to him by the parishioners—he was succeeded by a John Jeffrey, of Pembroke Hall, who resigned in 1624. Upon his resignation a remarkable contest for the situation ensued. The 'townsmen'—who were now leavened with Puritanism through his preaching, and that of his associates—were desirous of electing Dr Preston; and to make it better worth his acceptance, raised the stipend from £40 or £50, to £80 a year. He was opposed by Paul Micklethwaite, fellow of Sidney College, who was supported by the Bishop of Ely, Francis White, a creature of Laud's, and the heads of colleges. It is difficult to understand on what plea there was interference with the 'townsmen.' They had themselves originated the lectureship; had themselves appointed Sibbes, had themselves supported it. But the matter came before the king at Royston, and so intense was the royal wish to root out Puritanism, his primate inciting him to the dastardly work, that Dr Preston was actually offered a bishopric, the see of Gloucester being then void. He refused to withdraw. He accepted and entered upon the lectureship. All honour to the man who spurned a mitre, its honours and revenues alike, when offered at the price of proving false to the earnest desires of 'the people' to have the gospel, the very gospel, preached to them,—wherein, in the high but truthful encomium of Goodwin, he did 'bow his more sublime and raised parts to lowest apprehension.'* When Sibbes returned to Cambridge therefore, he found in Preston one like-minded, while equally did Preston find in him one worthy to stand by his side, and 'display a banner because of the truth.'

Preston and Sibbes, from the date of the mastership of the latter, were the two great centres of influence in Cambridge, in so far as the *preaching* of the gospel was concerned. They loved one another with a love that was something wonderful. They were as

* To the Reader. . . . Sermons before His Majesty, 1630. 4to.

David and Jonathan in earlier, and as Luther and Melanchthon in later, days. They were never found apart when anything was to be done for THEIR MASTER. To the last it was so; and when the prematurely old Master of 'Emmanuel' died, he left all his papers to his beloved friend the Master of Catharine Hall, along with John Davenport, sending words of kindly greeting by Lord Say and Seale to Gray's Inn. As Sibbes's return to Cambridge, and association with Preston, formed a marked era in his life and life-work, it is needful to dwell for a little on the history of his friend.

Dr Preston was a man of extraordinary force of character and splendour of eloquence, and burned with the zeal of a seraph. Very remarkable were his antecedents. For years, like John Cotton, he had been the glory of the 'wits' for his learning and faculty of utterance. But by John Cotton's first sermon after his 'change,' he had been smitten as between joints and marrow, soul and spirit, and thenceforward had known nothing but Christ Jesus crucified. Cotton Mather tells the story of his conversion finely, and we may pause over it for a moment. 'Some time after this change upon the soul of Mr Cotton,' he says, 'it came to his turn again to preach at St Mary's; and because he was to preach, an high expectation was raised through the whole university that they should hear a sermon flourishing indeed with all the learning of the whole university. Many difficulties had Mr Cotton in his own mind, and what course to steer.' And then he proceeds to tell how he decided 'to preach a plain sermon, even such a sermon as in his own conscience he thought would be most pleasing unto the Lord Jesus Christ; and he discoursed practically and powerfully, but very solidly, upon the plain doctrine of repentance.' What then? 'The vain wits of the university, disappointed thus with a more excellent sermon, that shot some troublesome admonitions into their consciences, discovered their vexation at this disappointment by their not humming, as according to their sinful and absurd custom they had formerly done; and the vice-chancellor, for the very same reason also, graced him not as he did others that pleased him. Nevertheless,' adds Mather, 'the satisfaction which he enjoyed in his own faithful soul abundantly compensated unto him the loss of any human favour or honour; nor did he go without many encouragements from some doctors, then having a better sense of religion upon them, who prayed him to persevere in the good way of preaching which he had now taken.' And then he continues, with exultation, 'But perhaps the greatest consolation of all, was a notable effect of the sermon then preached. The famous Dr

Preston, then a fellow of Queen's College in Cambridge, and of great note in the university, came to hear Mr Cotton, with the same "itching ears" as others were then led withal. For some good while after the beginning of the sermon, his frustrated expectation caused him to manifest his uneasiness all the ways that were then possible; but before the sermon was ended, like one of Peter's hearers, he found himself "pierced at the heart." His heart within him was now struck with such resentment of his own interior state before the God of heaven, that he could have no peace in his soul, till, with a "wounded soul," he had repaired unto Mr Cotton, from whom he received those further assistances wherein he became a "spiritual father" unto one of the greatest men in his age.'*

These were men who believed in a 'living,' presiding God, and who were not ashamed to recognise, nor afraid to avouch, 'the finger of God,' the very interference of God, as real as when the Lord met Saul of Tarsus, in the turning of a human soul to Himself. They saw in Sibbes reaching the conscience of John Cotton, and in John Cotton touching the heart of Dr Preston, so many links of the mighty chain of predestination, whose last link is fast to the throne of the Eternal. They are weaker and not wiser men who scorn such faith. It is not to be wondered at, then, that in the correspondence of the Puritans in Cambridge of this period, it was felt to be 'of God,' that quick as one preacher of the word, in its blessed height and depth, breadth and length, was removed thence, another succeeded. William Perkins was taken away, but Paul Bayne was 'sent' in his room. Paul Bayne was removed, and Sibbes was sent; Sibbes was 'outed,' and John Preston took his place; and now while the Master of Emmanuel was longing for one who might be a fellow-helper with him, again came Richard Sibbes. The hearts of the praying few were cheered, and under the awakening, rich, full, grand, proclamations of the 'grace of God that bringeth salvation,' all Cambridge was moved. Preston was from day to day at Emmanuel and Trinity, and Sibbes from day to day at Catharine Hall, preaching as 'dying men to dying men;' knowing nothing among them save Jesus Christ and him crucified, yea, regarding the demand of the 'wits' for 'polite' preaching as but an awful echo of the olden cry, 'Let him come down from the cross and we will believe him.'

From the title-pages of the early editions of their Sermons, we find that they were, again and again, appointed to preach at St Mary's, the church of the whole University. On these occasions

* Magnalia, as *ante* page 16.

there was such a galaxy of men assembled as could not have been seen elsewhere in all the world. The effect was electric, among gentle as among simple. It rejoices one to scan the roll of the names of those who were then Masters, Fellows, and Students, and all of whom were found in attendance on the preaching of Sibbes and Preston. With relation to Sibbes, we read 'The Saint's Safety' and 'Christ is Best,' 'Christ's Sufferings for Man's Sin' and 'The Church's Visitation,' and 'The Saints' Hiding-place,' with deepened interest, as, turning to the original title-pages, we find they were addressed to auditories that included the foremost names of the age. The dates inform us that these sermons, which are almost unrivalled for largeness, I might even say grandeur, of thought, richness of gospel statement, impressiveness and pungency of application, and music of diction, were delivered when the several colleges sent to St Mary's names such as these. Foremost stands John Milton, then at Christ's, and himself writing sonnets on the very themes of Sibbes's discourses. Next comes Jeremy Taylor, just entered '*pauper scholaris,*' as Sibbes assumed the Mastership. Behind him, already renowned as a 'public orator,' mark George Herbert. Side by side with him rises the girlish face, with its strange shadow of sorrow, of Matthew Wren, destined to belie God's handwriting in that face, by becoming a 'persecutor.' Very different is the next that meets our eye, William Gouge, of King's. And beside him is one who will be the preacher's successor at Catharine Hall, Ralph Brownrig, looking wistfully upward with his large, beaming eyes. Snug in some sequestered pew, taking keen note of all in that marvellous memory of his, see Thomas Fuller. Worn and weary, yet moved to listen, picture Edmund Castell and Abraham Whelock. Sitting at the foot of the pulpit stairs are Charles Chauncy and Richard Holdsworth, and dreamy Peter Sterry from Emmanuel. Taking notes, and wishing the hour-glass were turned again, is Joseph Mede. Fronting the preacher, and intent as any, lo! the young Lord Wriothesly, son of Shakespeare's Earl of Southampton, and young Sir Dudley North, son of Lord North of Kirkling, both of Sibbes's own college, St John's. Linking himself arm-in-arm with the preacher as he descends, mark stormy John Williams, afterwards Bishop and 'Lord Keeper.' And thus might be recounted, almost by the hundred, names that still shine like a winter's night of stars. St Mary's pews and lobbies, crowded, above and below, with such hearers, to such preachers, is a noticeable mark of progress.*

Perhaps I cannot better illustrate the advance of Puritanism

* I have gathered these names, after Masson (Life of Milton, i. 92–99), from numerous sources, but mainly from Cooper's 'Annals of Cambridge,' Wood's 'Athenæ'

in Cambridge than by here submitting a hitherto unpublished document of this period, 1626–27, recovered from the 'Churchwardens' books of the parish.* It very strikingly reveals the interest pervading the community in the Trinity lectureship.

The document explains itself. I adhere to its orthography—

'Whereas, such p'sons as are interessed in the seates of the gallerie of this church ("Trinity") to sit there dureinge the time of the lecture, haveinge paid for the same to the p'ish, and yet, notwithstanding, are displaced by others haveinge not interest there, to their greivance and wronge; and, unles redresse herein be speedely had, such p'sons soe greived will withdraw their cotribucons from the said lecture. For remedie whereof, it is ordered and agreed unto, by a joynt consent of all the p'shioners, that from henceforth noe p'son nor p'sons of what condyc'on soever, except such who have interest in the seats, shal be permytted to goe up into the galleries untyl the bell have done tollinge; and then, yf any place be voyd, or may be spared to p'mytt, in the first place, grave divines, and after them such others as shall be lyked of by such as shall keep the dore: and yf any who have interest in the seates shall bringe any stranger to be placed there, and will have him to have his place in the gallerie, then such p'son bringing such stranger, to keepe belowe, and take his place els where for such tyme; and yf any person interessed in the seats doe not repair to the church before the bell have done tollinge, then he to lose his place for that tyme.

'It is likewise ordered, by ye like consent, that such p'sons as have interest in any of ye seates in ye church, shall not have it particularly to themselves to place and displace whom they will, but only to have ye use of the seats, duringe the tyme of the lecture, for theire owne p'sons, and to receave into them such other of the parish, yf any such come, as shall belonge to such seate, and such others likewise as are people of qualitye who doe contribute to ye lecture; and not to receave any children into their seats.

'It is further ordered that noe seats eyther in ye galleries or in ye church shall hereafter be disposed of to any w[th]out the consent of the parishiners at a publiq meetinge in the church.†

Thus moving the 'whole city,' Sibbes and Preston went hand-in-hand; and long after they were gone, when a very different spirit

(by Bliss), Fuller's 'Worthies' (by Nichols), and the 'Lives of Nicholas Ferrar, and of Matthew Robinson,' two of, I trust, a series of like 'Biographies,' under the scholarly editorial care of Mr Mayor of St John's. Consult also the 'Memoirs' of each name given. All, however, wishing to get real insight into Cambridge-life of the period, I must again and again refer to Mr Masson's 'Milton.' Sibbes's popularity and success is testified by all who write about him, and I can trace none who was so frequently called to preach in St Mary's.

* From 'Between the Churchwarden's Accounts for 1626 and 1627, Trinity Parish, Cambridge.' Kindly pointed out to me by Mr Wallis, and obligingly transcribed, with his usual exactness, by Mr Cooper.

† It may be as well to round off, in a foot-note, such additional memoranda as are in my possession about the lectureship. On 11th May 1630, there was again interference and controversy, Dr Thomas Goodwin being the lecturer. A letter respecting it was addressed to the vice-chancellor by Dudley Carleton, Viscount Dorchester, one of the principal secretaries of state. This 'letter' may be here given from

reigned in Cambridge, born of the wild licence of the Restoration, white-headed men would recall their honoured names with a sigh.

But, while thus faithful as a 'servant of Jesus Christ' in preaching, Richard Sibbes had the faculty of government. Catharine Hall soon found itself on an equality with its sister colleges. He returned from Sunday to Sunday, while the 'Courts' sat, to Gray's Inn, and was ever forward to plead the claims of his 'little house,' with his noble friends there.

We have many testimonies to his influence and usefulness in both. Of the former, Samuel Clarke observes: 'About the year 1618 (1616), he was chosen Preacher to Gray's Inn, one of the learnedest societies in England, where his ministry found such general approbation and acceptance that, besides the learned lawyers of the house, many noble personages, and many of the gentry and citizens, resorted to hear him, and many, till this day

the Baker MSS. (xxvii. 137), as inserted in Cooper's Annals of Cambridge (iii. 229–30).

To my Reverend Friend Mr Dr BUTS, *Vice-chan, &c.*

SIR,—By reason of his Majesties late directions concerning lecturers, that they should read divine service according to the Liturgy, before their lectures, and the afternoone sermons to be turned into catechising, some doubt hath beene made of the continuance of the lecture at Trinity Church, in Cambr. which for many yeares past hath beene held at one of the clocke in the afternoone, without divine service read before yt, and cannot be continued at that hower, if the whole service should be reade before the sermon begin. Whereupon his Majestie hath been informed that the same is a publick lecture, serving for all the parishes in that town (being fourteen in number), and that the university sermon is held at the same tyme, which would be troubled with a greater resort than can be well permitted, yf the towne sermon should be discontinued: and that the same being held at the accustomed hower, there will be tyme enough left after that sermon ended, and the auditory departed thence to their own parish churches, as well for divine service as for catechising in that and all other churches in the towne, which could not well be, yf divine service should be read in that church before the lecture; besides the catechising in that church, would hereby be lost. Upon these motives his Majesty, being graciously pleased that the said lecture may be continued at the accustomed hower, and in manner as yt hath been heretofore used, hath given me in charge to make knowne to you his royall pleasure accordingly, but under this caution, that not only divine service, but catechising be duely read and used after that sermon ended, both in that and the rest of the churches of the towne; and that the sermon doe end in convenient tyme for that purpose, soe as no pretext be made, either for the present or in future tyme, by color of the foresaid sermon, to hinder either divine service or catechising, which his Majestie is resolved to have maintained. And so I bidd you heartily farewell, and rest, Yours to doe you service, DORCHESTER.

From Whitehall, the 11th of May 1630.

Mr Cooper annotates: 'Randolph in a poem "On Importunate Dunnes," after a curious malediction on the Cambridge tradesmen, adds—

"And if this vex 'um not, I'le grive the town,
With this curse, State, put *Trinity-lecture* down."'

Randolph's Poems, ed. 1643, p. 119.

(1674–77), bless God for the benefit which they received of him.'* Besides this, various regulations and 'orders' as to seats and right of entrance in the order-books, inform us of over-crowded attendance. Thus, under 1623, 'All strangers to be kept out of the Chapell at Sermon, but such as are brought in by some of y[e] society.' Perhaps even more significant of a crowd is what follows: 'And all y[e] gentlemen to goe out of y[e] Chappell bare-headed in decent manner.'

Of the latter, again, Clarke says, 'About the year 1625, or '26, he was chosen Master of Katharine Hall in Cambridge, the government whereof he continued till his dying day; and, indeed, like a faithful governor, he was always very solicitous and careful to procure and advance the good of that little house. For he procured good means and maintenance, by his interest in many worthy persons, for the enlargement of the College, and was a means and instrument to establish learned and religious Fellows there; inasmuch as, in his time, it proved a very famous society for piety and learning, both in Fellows and Scholars.'† To the same effect, though with characteristic quaintness, Fuller testifies, 'He found the House in a mean condition, the wheel of St. Katharine having stood still (not to say gone backwards) for some years together; he left it replenished with scholars, beautified with buildings, better endowed with revenues.'‡ Somewhat boastfully, perhaps, Daniel Milles, in his list of Masters, thus describes Sibbes:—

'Ricardus Sibbs, Sacræ Theologiæ Professor,§ omnium quos præsens ætas viderit vir pientissimus, concionator mellitissimus, qui haud paucorum corda suavitate dicendi emolliit, et vivendi sanctitate ad bonam frugem plane rapuit. Hic erat qui collegium istud partim temporum injuria, partim Præfectorum socordia et avaritia bonis suis spoliatum, et omni honore exutum, ad pristinam famam et dignitatem restituit, quiaque erat apud omnes pios autoritate maximâ, largam benefactorum messem, in hoc vacuum gymnasium feliciter diduxit. Adeo ut non nudo Præfecti nomine dignus videatur, sed alter fundator censeri debeat.'

Other testimonies, as of Eachard,‖ might be given, were it needful; and, indeed, the tribute of Sir Philip Sidney to Hubert Languet must have been his, from many,

"......... hating what is naught,
For faithful heart, clean hands, and mouth as true.
With his sweet skill my skill-less youth he drew
To have a feeling taste of Him that sits
Beyond the heaven, *far more beyond our wits.*'

(*Arcadia*, Book iii. pp. 397–8, ed. 1755.)

Of the Fellows, during Sibbes's Mastership, may be named Anthony

* 'Clarke,' as *ante*, p. 144.

† 'Clarke,' as *ante*, p. 144.

‡ Fuller, 'Worthies.' edited by Nichols. 2 vols. 4to. 1811. Vol. ii. p. 348.

§ *i.e.*, D.D.

‖ 'Eachard,' History of England, p. 451.

Pym (1628), probably a relative of *the* John Pym, who was a personal friend, and mentioned in his will; William Spurstowe (1630);* John Sibbes (1631), his nephew; Charles Pym (1631), brother of Anthony; Roger Fleetwood (1632); Joseph Spurstowe (1634).

CHAPTER VII.

SIBBES AND LAUD—'THE PALATINATE.'

The Puritans watched—The Elector Palatine—Disasters—Shame of England—Battle of Prague—Frederick and Elizabeth fugitives—Persecution—Circular Letter by Sibbes, Gouge, Taylor, and Davenport—Citation before the Star-Chamber—Pronounced 'Notorious Delinquents.'

All the emotion and interest to hear such preaching as was that of Sibbes and Preston, while it gives a measure of the progress of Puritanism (using the word in its recognised historic and lustrous sense), is also to the student of the period a measure of the hate with which the king (in so far as he had stamina enough to hate) and Bishop Laud, now rising into notice, regarded it. So early as 1611, the latter was a '*whisperer*,' a '*busy-body*,' ever going about with sly, stealthy-paced, panther-like foot-fall, and keen, cold eye, if by any means, he might possess himself of *secrets*. Between Gray's Inn, and Catharine Hall, and St Mary's, with not unfrequent 'sermons' elsewhere, Sibbes had noble vantage-ground for noble service, and he was occupying it to the full; and Laud was ready to pounce upon him. I have now to narrate the occasion. Sibbes was not a man to narrow his activities to his own immediate sphere, or to his own country. He watched with profoundest interest the progress of the great Protestant sister-countries, rejoicing in their joy and mourning with their mourning. In 1620, he had spoken burning words 'of the Palatinate;' words that reveal the common shame of England for her king's pusillanimous desertion of the Elector Frederick, a man true and good in himself, and knit by the tenderest ties to the king of England. From shore to shore the nation had rung with acclaim over revolting Bohemia—the land of John Huss and many martyr-names. They had said 'Amen' to the rejection of Ferdinand II., and their hearts beat high for the Elector Palatine chosen in his stead, when he fearlessly said 'Yes' to the call. History tells the tragic sequel.

* Spurstowe. The date, 1630, of Spurstowe's 'fellowship' (he was afterwards Master), shews that Mr Masson has made a slip in enumerating his name among the distinguished 'fellows' under Dr Hill's Mastership. Life of Milton, i. 97. I cannot make even this small reference to Mr Masson without, in common with every literary man since the issue of his book, acknowledging my indebtedness to his industry, and almost prodigal elucidation and illustration of contemporary events and names.

Then opened what proved the 'Thirty Years' War,' in which the emperor, and pope, and the king of Spain were leagued against Frederick, and against the Protestant Union in him. All Europe looked on. Our own England was humiliated, all but treasonous, as James talked his foolish talk and lived his unclean life, and forgot daughter, son-in-law, Protestantism—all. Driven to do something, he did his little when too late. In November 1620, the Protestants were smitten in one decisive battle—Prague; and Frederick and his queen, losing Bohemia, losing the Palatinate, losing all, fled as refugees to Holland. What followed, only the great sealed 'book' above will declare. The triumphant enemy 'played havoc;' and, through many dark and terrible years, the sufferings of the Protestants of Bohemia and the 'palatinate,' were something unimaginable. The cry reached England, and public help was sought and denied. But it went not everywhere unheard, unheeded. The Puritans, Sibbes among the first, recognised their brotherhood, and out of their own private resources sought to do a little, if it were only to shew their sympathy. I have been fortunate enough to recover a touching memorial of their efforts. Preserved among very different papers in Her Majesty's Record Office is a 'circular' letter, which, in the pathos of its simple words, goes right to the heart. Here it is:—

Whereas, a late information is given to his Matie of the lamentable distresses of two hundred and forty godly preachers, with their wifes and families, and sundrie thousands of godly private persons with them, cast out of their house and homes, out of their callings and countreys, by the furie of the mercilesse papists in the Upper Palatinate, whose heavie condicion is such as they are forced to steale their servises of religion in woods and solitarie places, not without continual feare and damage of their lives; and whose present want is such as they would be very thankfull for coarse bread (and) drinke if they could gett it. As tenderinge the miserie and want of deare brethren and sisters, desire all godly persons to whom these presents may come, as fellowe feelinge members of the same body of Jesus Christ, to comiserate their present want and enlarge their hearts and hands for some present and private supply for them till some publique means (which hereafter may be hoped) may be raised for their reliefe, assuring themselves that whatsoever is cast into heaven, and falleth into the lappe of Christ in his members, shall return with abundant increase in the harvest; neither lett any be discouraged least their bounty should miscarrie, for we knowe a sure and safe way whereby whatsoever is given shall undoubtedly come to their hands to (whom) it is intended.

2 Martii 1627. (Signed) Tho. Taylor.
Richard Sibbs.
John Davenport.
William Gouge.*

* 'Circular.' Described in 'Calendar of State Papers, Domestic Series of the Reign of Charles I., 1627–28.' By John Bruce, 1858 (Longman).

One of two copies of this affecting 'circular' is endorsed by Laud, and the names noted so carefully, that the Sibbs within is corrected to Sibbes without. One marvels what ground even a Laud could find for opposition, much less persecution, in so piteous an appeal. But when there is a will to hurt or hinder, an occasion is not ill to devise. Perchance the vehement words, '*merciless papists*,' stung. At any rate, the four honoured men, Richard Sibbes, William Gouge, Thomas Taylor, John Davenport, were summoned before the Star Chamber, and reprimanded. It is not at all wonderful that William Prynne, in his 'Canterburie's Doom,' should ask, '*By what law of the land*'—a question, by the way, that rings all through the charges of this extraordinary book, like a Gerizzim curse—'did they convert Doctor Gouge, Doctor Sibbes, Doctor Taylor, and Master Davenport, as notorious delinquents, only for setting their hands to a certificate upon entreaty, testifying the distressed condition of some poor ministers of the Palatinate, and furthering a private contribution among charitable Christians for their relief, when public collections failed?'

It does not appear what further steps, if any, were taken; but one thing is certain, the miserable persecution did not 'silence' Sibbes. For he not only preached, but published passionately rebuking words against the national lukewarmness. 'What,' asks he, 'shall the members of Christ suffer in other countries, and we profess ourselves to be living members, and *yet not sympathize with them?* We must be conformable to our Head, before we can come to heaven.' * What a pass things had reached, when those in authority would have shut even the hand of private charity against such sufferers! It is impossible to restrain indignation when reading of James's more than poltroonly, more than mean, desertion of his own 'flesh and blood,' not to speak of Protestantism; but doubly base was Laud's interference to stamp out as a pestilent thing, this little effort to relieve 'godly preachers and private persons.' It only added to that thunder-cloud, which in a few years was to launch its lightnings on his own head, and whose preluding shadows were even now darkening the sky: such retribution as comes

> 'When the quick darting lightning's flash
> Is the clear glitter of His golden spear.'†

---

* 'Soul's Conflict.' † Cecil and Mary, by Jackson, p. 19 (1858.)

CHAPTER VIII.

SIBBES AND LAUD AGAIN—'THE IMPROPRIATION FEOFEES.'

The Preacher of Gray's Inn under surveillance—Controversy not sought by Sibbes—Loyal to Church and State—The Puritans no 'Schismatics'—Witness-bearing—Wonder and yet no Wonder—Laud's 'Beauty of Holiness'—'Solemnity'—Persecution—'Silencing'—William Prynne—Puritan Literature—Laudian-Bishop's Literature—Sibbes against Popery—Lord Keeper Finch—The 'Impropriation' Scheme—Sibbes a 'Feoffee'—Checks upon Laud—'Overthrow' of 'Feoffees'—Confiscation—Banishment—Verdict upon Laud.

The Star Chamber citation, because of The Palatinate, with its result—a severe reprimand, and treatment as of 'notorious delinquents,'—was only a slighter issue of that unsleeping and vengeful resolution to suppress all Puritanism, which through upwards of a quarter of a century, Laud had planned. Accordingly, though defeated in the matter of the Palatinate, in so far as '*silencing*' Sibbes and his compeers was concerned, they, in common with all the 'good men and true' of the period—for really it appears that every man of note in his day, who was not his creature, was the object of his annoyance—were *watched*.* Nor is it at all difficult to understand, that such preaching as was being heard from Sunday to Sunday at 'Gray's Inn,' and down in Cambridge, and by crowds in St Mary's, when reported to him, as everything was reported—must have been superlatively offensive. We do not find Sibbes mixed up with the controversies of the day. There is in his works a noteworthy absence of those fires of intolerant passion that burn so fiercely in many of the writings and actings of his contemporaries. Never once do we meet with him in the ante-chamber of 'the Court,' or mingling with the venal crowds that in unholy rivalry bade high and higher, or more properly low and lower, for place, seeking to cover their 'multitude of sins,' not with charity, but lawn sleeves. He lived serenely apart from the miserable squabbling and personal resentments, and exacerbations of the semi-political, semi-theological polemics that agitated state and church. He was loyal, even tenderly charitable to those in authority; and true to the church, if only the church would be true to him, by being true to its Head. Let us hear what he was saying about both in those days. Of the State he thus speaks:—'Sometimes it falleth out that those that are under the government of others are most

* 'Watched.' Scattered up and down Sibbes's writings are various indications of his knowledge of this espionage, *e. g.*, 'So in coming to hear the word of God, some come to observe the elegancy of words and phrases, *some to catch advantage, perhaps, against the speaker, men of a devilish temper.*'—('Bowels Opened,' pp. 130–31.)

injurious, by waywardness and harsh censures, herein disparaging and discouraging the endeavours of superiors for public good. In so great weakness of man's nature, and especially in this crazy age of the world, *we ought to take in good part any moderate happiness we enjoy by government;* and not be altogether as a nail in the wound, exasperating things by misconstruction. *Here love should have a mantle to cast upon the lesser errors of those above us. Oftentimes the poor man is the oppressor by unjust clamours. We should labour to give the best interpretation to the actions of governors that the nature of the actions will possibly bear.'* * Similar sentiments abound. Of the Church we have many wise and considerate words. He had no wish for separation: none of the Puritans had, until they were driven to it. So far from seeking to divide 'the church' and injure it—the refrain of many an accusation—Sibbes has sarcasms that perhaps might have been spared, against those who even then felt they could not remain within her pale. 'Fractions,' he says, with an approach to unkindness very unusual with him, 'always breed factions.' He could not mean it; but this was capable of being turned by Laud to his own account. He was quick as a sleuth-hound to discern taint of treason. But we have more full and explicit statements. Thus with more than ordinary vehemence he expostulates, accuses:—'What a joyful spectacle is this to Satan and his faction, to see those that are separated from the world fall in pieces among themselves! Our discord is our enemy's melody. *The more to blame those that for private aims affect differences from others, and will not suffer the wounds of the church to close and meet together.'*†

Was this man, so truly a man of peace, one to track and keep under surveillance, as though he had been at once traitor and fanatic? Whence came it? The answer is too easy. Though 'slow to speak,' and sweet-natured to a fault, he was fearless when the occasion demanded it.‡ Even immediately on saying the above,

* Bruised Reed, c. xvii. † Bruised Reed, c. xvii.

‡ 'Sweet-natured to a fault.' Brook ('Lives of the Puritans,' ii. 419) remarks: 'This reverend divine was eminently distinguished for a meek and quiet spirit, being *always unwilling to offend those in power.*' This is too general, for however gentle, Sibbes, when roused, spoke out with no thought of who might be, or might not be, offended. For, says he, 'It argues a base disposition, either for frown or favour, to desert a good cause in evil times' ('Bowels Opened,' 1st edition, 1639, 4to, p. 45). Brook continues, from Calamy (Calamy's Account, vol. ii. pp. 605, 606): 'This trait in his character will appear from the following anecdote:—A fellowship being vacant in Magdalen College, for which Archbishop Laud recommended his bell-ringer at Lambeth, with an ardent design of quarrelling with

he takes care to guard himself from misconstruction, by adding:—'Which must not be understood, as if men should dissemble their judgment in any truth where there is just cause of expressing themselves; for the least truth is Christ's, and not ours: and therefore we are not to take liberty to affirm or deny at our pleasure. There is a due in a penny, as well as in a pound; *therefore we must be faithful in the least truth, when season calleth for it.*' But again, so gentle and unpolemic was he, he continues finely:—'But in some cases peace, by keeping our faith to ourselves, Rom. xiv. 22, is of more consequence than the open discovery of some things we take to be true: *considering the weakness of man's nature is such, that there can hardly be a discovery of any difference in opinion, without some estrangement of affection.* So far as men are not of one mind, they will hardly be of one heart, except where grace and the peace of God, Col. iii. 15, bear great rule in the heart. *Therefore, open show of difference is never good but when it is necessary;* however some, from a desire to be somebody, turn into by-ways, and yield to a spirit of contradiction in themselves.'* And then, Leighton-like, he turns away from the distractions around him, and thinks of the 'rest that remains.' 'Our blessed Saviour, when he was to leave the world, what doth he press upon his disciples more than peace and love? And in his last prayer, with what earnestness did he beg of his Father that they might be one, as he and the Father were one! John xvii. 21. But what he prayed for on earth, we shall only enjoy perfectly in heaven. *Let this make the meditation of that time the more sweet to us.*'† Even so—

'Search well another world; who studies this,
Travels in clouds; seeks manna where none is.'‡

One wonders, and yet does not wonder, how such a peaceable and loveable man came to be thus harassed. But what has the dove done to make the serpent strike its fang into it? Simply

them if they refused, or of putting a spy upon them if they accepted, Dr Sibbes, who was ever unwilling to provoke his superiors, told the fellows that Lambeth-house would be obeyed; and that the person was young, and might in time prove hopeful. The fellows therefore consented, and the man was admitted.' This 'anecdote' carries improbability in the face of it, and neither Calamy nor Brook adduce any authority. Sibbes could have no voice in 'Magdalen,' in the election or rejection of a 'fellow.' Nor is there the slightest memorial of such an appointment as is stated. Surely if it had been made, name and date would have been notorious. Amid the many charges against Laud, this has no place either in Prynne or elsewhere. Calamy is not guilty, ordinarily, of introducing mere idle gossip, but it would seem that in the present instance he has.

* and † Bruised Reed, c. xvii.

‡ Henry Vaughan, Silex Scintillans. Edition by Lyte, 1847, page 17.

crossed its path. What the lamb, to cause the wolf to take it by the throat? Again, simply *crossed its path.* Sibbes had done that with Laud. While the king, under his mitred councillor's tuition, was straining every nerve to un-Sabbath Sunday, Sibbes and his co-Puritans held fast its inviolable authority. While proclamations, unsanctioned by Parliament, were issued to substitute the May-pole for the Cross, the Book of Sports for the Book of God, and the village green for the sanctuary, Sibbes held up the cross and summoned the people to the sanctuary. While all doctrinal preaching, all declarations of the *grace* of God in Jesus Christ, was sought to be put down (precursor of the infamous 'Directions'), Sibbes avouched his Calvinism, and spoke with no bated breath of Arminianism. While *churchmen* of the school of Laud would have men regard transubstantiation as a '*school nicety*,' bowing to the table of the Lord, as '*becoming reverence*,' images in churches worthy 'commemoration,' sacerdotal absolution and confession to a priest as '*proper things*,' the Lord's Supper not as a sacrament, but as a sacrifice,—Sibbes protested, and gave them their proper designation, with no periphrasis or courtly phrase, of papistical innovation and delusions of the devil. I am not sure that I would make all his and the Puritans' side-thrusts against 'the papist' my own. I fear I cannot acquit either them or him of 'upbraiding,' and even blameable uncharity for the men, in the honesty of his indignation against their doctrines and measures. But we must not forget the circumstances of 'the time.' He was old enough to remember the Armada, sent to his own Suffolk shore under a pope's blessing, and a 'bull' being nailed to the palace-door with a pope's ban. He was cognizant of innumerable plots, not merely against our religious, but also our civil, liberties. He heard claims asserted, not for equality, but supremacy. And then there were those high in authority, coquetting with that popery that had incarnadined England with her best blood, and had been got rid of at a cost inestimable. He could not but speak, and, speaking as a patriot and Protestant, it was not easy to '*prophesy smooth things*.' Perhaps Laud would have endured Sibbes's bold and passionate rebuke of the prevailing sins of the age, and even, however galled, have winked at his full and fervid assertions of the principles of the reformation from popery, and clear and articulate condemnation of Arminianism, had he gone no further. But words were not only to be answered with words, be it granted unadvised words, with occasional kindredly unadvised words. Action was to be met with action, if 'the church' were not to be only a masked re-establishment of popery, and if the Calvinism of its fathers were not to degenerate into *ultra*-Arminianism; and it was done, as we shall see. Peter Heylin was now at the ear of Laud; and Hacket observes, that 'they that watched the increase of Arminianism, said, confidently, that it was from the year 1628 that the tide of it began to come in;' and this because it was from that year that 'all the preferments were cast on one side.'* Similar is the testimony concerning the favour shewn to popery. Thus opposing Laud in his two darling objects, it is easy to foresee that one like Sibbes, resident in London,' could not fail to come into conflict with the vigilant and suspicious head of the church. Nor are we to suppose that, if *he* was watched by Lambeth's police, Lambeth went unwatched. How far the primate was going in his 'papistical tendencies,' may be gathered from one notorious exhibition. Besides its bearing on the persecution springing out of the impropriation scheme, it gives point to a suggestive hit by Sibbes, which was probably the thing that stung Laud to further action against him and his coadjutors in another blessed work. I therefore give the record of it from the admittedly authoritative pages of Rushworth and Wharton, *in extenso*:—On Sunday the 16th of January 1630–1, a new church—St Catherine Creed—in Leadenhall Street, was consecrated. It had been re-built, and had been suspended by the primate from all divine service, sermons or sacraments, until it should be re-consecrated. Laud and a number of his clergy came in the morning to perform the ceremony. Then as strange and sad a 'performance' as ever men beheld was enacted, regard being had to the fact that the performer was the Protestant Primate of England:—

'At the bishop's approach to the west door,' says Rushworth, 'some that were prepared for it cried, with a loud voice, "Open, open, ye everlasting doors, that the king of glory may enter in!" and presently the doors were opened, and the bishop, with some doctors, and many other principal men, went in, and immediately, falling down upon his knees, with his eyes lifted up, and his arms spread abroad, uttered these words: "This place is holy; the ground is holy: in the name of the Father, Son, and Holy Ghost, I pronounce it holy." Then he took up some of the dust, and threw it up into the air, several times, in his going up towards the chancel.† When they approached near to the rail and communion-table, the bishop bowed towards it several times; and, returning, they went round the church in procession, saying the 100th Psalm, and after that the 19th Psalm, and then said a form of prayer, commencing, "Lord Jesus

* Hacket . . . Life of Williams, Lord Keeper. Pt. ii. p. 42 and p. 82.

† Masson, 'Life of Milton,' i. 350, adds here this foot-note:—This was sworn to on Laud's trial by two witnesses; but Laud denies it, and moreover, says that, if it had been true, it would not have been a popish ceremony, as the Romish pontifical prescribes, not 'dust,' but 'ashes' to be thrown up on such occasions.

Christ," &c., and concluding, "We consecrate this church, and separate it unto thee, as holy ground, not to be profaned any more to common use." After this, the bishop being near the communion-table, and taking a written book in his hand (a copy, as was afterwards alleged, of a form in the Romish pontifical, but according to Laud, furnished him by the deceased Bishop Andrewes), pronounced curses upon those that should afterwards profane that holy place by musters of soldiers, or keeping profane law-courts, or carrying burdens through it; and at the end of every curse, bowed towards the east, and said, "Let all the people say, Amen." When the curses were ended, he pronounced a number of blessings upon all those that had any hand in framing and building of that sacred and beautiful church, and those that had given, or should hereafter give, any chalices, plate, ornaments, or utensils; and at the end of every blessing, he bowed towards the east, and said, "Let all the people say, Amen." After this followed the sermon, which being ended, the bishop consecrated and administered the sacrament in manner following:—As he approached the communion-table, he made several lowly bowings; and coming up to the side of the table, where the bread and wine were covered, he bowed seven times; and then, after the reading of many prayers, he came near the bread, and gently lifted up a corner of the napkin wherein the bread was laid; and when he beheld the bread, he laid it down again, flew back a step or two, bowed three several times towards it, then he drew near again, and opened the napkin, and bowed as before. Then he laid his hand on the cup, which was full of wine, with a cover upon it, which he let go again, went back, and bowed thrice towards it; then he came near again, and lifting up the cover of the cup, looked into it, and seeing the wine, let fall the cover again, retired back, and bowed as before. Then he received the sacrament, and gave it to some principal men; after which, many prayers being said, the solemnity of the consecration ended.'

That was the sort of thing that the primate and his like-minded bishops, sought to impose on men as 'SOLEMNITY!' That '*mountebank* holiness' (it is Sir Philip Sidney's word of scorn) was to be its translation of the grand old 'Beauty of Holiness,' (1 Chron. xvi. 29; Ps. xxix. 2, and xcvi. 9).* It is no light occasion that

* 'Beauty of holiness.' The vehement words of John Milton, stern as Jeremiah, a few year later, are memorable, and may not be passed by:—'Now for their demeanour within the church, how have they disfigur'd and defac't that more than angelick brightnes, the unclouded serenity of Christian religion, *with the dark overcasting of superstitious coaps and flaminical vestures*. . . . Tell me, ye priests, wherefore this gold, wherefore these roabs and surplices, over the gospel? Is our religion guilty of the first trespasse, and hath need of cloathing to cover her nakednesse? What does this else but cast an ignominey upon the perfection of Christ's ministery by seeking to adorn it with that which was the poor remedy of our shame? Believe it, wondrous doctors, *all corporeal resemblances of inward holinesse and beauty are now past*.' (The Reason of Church Government, B. II. ch. ii. p. 154. Mitford's Milton. Prose Works, vol. i. Pickering.) Elsewhere, denouncing the 'chaff of over-dated ceremonies,' he thus describes the Laudian 'prelaty:'—'They began to draw down all the divine intercourse betwixt God and the soul, yea, the very shape of God himself, into an exterior and bodily form, urgently pretending a necessity and obligement of joining the body in a formal reverence and worship circumscribed: they hallowed it, they fumed it, they sprinkled it, they bedecked it, not in robes of

calls for one's judgment of another in so awful and sacred a thing as his religion, however it may be darkened by superstition, or lightened by the fires of the wildest fanaticism. Deplorable, therefore, as this mummery may be to us, we may not pronounce that it was an unreal, much less that it was a farcical thing to its chief actor. Such a soul as his, so small, so narrow, may have found channel deep enough for its reverence in such return upon an effete ritualism. We may agree with Macaulay's epithet of 'imbecile,' but not with the Puritan's angry charge of 'hypocrite.' But when one realises that prison, fine, the knife, the shears, persecution to the death, were the award of every honest soul that refused to regard as the 'Beauty of Holiness' such exaggerations of even popery, it is hard to withhold an anathema, ringing as Paul's, on the memory of him who devised, and of the craven bishops who cravenly enforced them. There the spider-soul sat, in its craft, spreading out its net-work over broad England, and by its Harsnets and Curles, Mountagus and Buckridges, Bancrofts and Wrens, and Mainwarings, united in a brotherhood of evil, sought to entrap all who held to the divine simplicity of the New Testament. The secret threads, revealed by the tears of the persecuted, as by the morning dew is revealed the drop-spangled and else concealed web of the open-air spider, thrilled news up to the hand that grasped all, and forth the fiat went. 'Within a single year, at this period,' says Neal, 'many lecturers were put down, and such as preached against Arminianism or the new ceremonies were suspended and silenced, among whom were the Rev. Mr John Rogers of Dedham, Mr Daniel Rogers of Wethersfield, Mr Hooker of Chelmsford, Mr White of Knightsbridge, Mr Archer, Mr William Martin, Mr Edwards, Mr Jones, Mr Dod, Mr Hildersam, Mr Ward, Mr Saunders, Mr James Gardiner, Mr Foxley, and many others.' *

We have the burning words of Prynne, that at a 'later day,' in the day of his humiliation, the primate had to meet. Thus forcibly is the charge put—nor was it ever touched :—

'As he thus preferred Popish and Arminian clergymen to the chief eccle-

pure innocency, but of pure linen, with other deformed and fantastic dresses, in palls and mitres, gold and gewgaws, fetched from Aaron's old wardrobe or the flamen's vestry; then was the priest sent to con his motions and his postures, his liturgies and lurries, till the soul, by this means of overbodying herself, given up to fleshly delights, bated her wing apace downwards.' In our own day, one has characterised the same phenomenon, as presented by Tractarianism, which, indeed, was the harvest of the baleful seed sown by Laud, as 'a thing of flexions and genuflexions, postures and impostures, with a dash of man-millinery.'

* Hist. of Puritans, Vol. i. p. 589, &c. (ed., 3 vols. 8vo, 1837.)

siastical preferments in our church, so, on the contrary, (following the counsel of Cautzen, the Mogonutive Jesuit, in his politics, see 'Look about you'), he discountenanced, suspended, silenced, suppressed, censured, imprisoned, persecuted most of the prime, orthodox, diligent preaching ministers of the realm, and forced many of them to fly into America, Holland, and other foreign places, to avoid his fury, only for opposing his popish innovations, and expressing their fears of the change of our religion. Not to trouble you with any forementioned instances of Mr Peter Smart, Mr Henry Burton, Mr Snelling, and others, we shall instance in some fresh examples. . . . .' Mr Samuel Ward's case, and Mr Chauncy's case, are then narrated. 'To these we could add,' he proceeds, 'Mr Cotton, Mr Hooker, Mr Davenport, Mr Wells, Mr Peters, Mr Glover, and sundry other ministers, driven into New England and other plantations.' And then 'Dr Stoughton, *Dr Sibbes*, Dr Taylor, Dr Gouge, Mr White of Dorchester, Mr Rogers of Dedham, with sundry more of our most eminent preaching, orthodox divines, were brought into the High Commission, and troubled or silenced for a time by his procurement upon frivolous pretences, but in truth because they were principal props of our Protestant religion against his Popish and Arminian innovations.'*

Now, we have the actual books containing the actual preaching of these men, and the numerous others who shared their persecution. They are in our libraries; and he must be either a bold or a very foolish man, not only rash, but reckless, who gainsays that, *remove these books from the Christian literature of the period and you remove the very life-blood of that literature.*

The most recent, truthful, and catholic of 'the church' historians, Mr Perry,† admits that all the practical writers of the age were of the puritans and sufferers for nonconformity; and he names a few, Willet and Dyke, Preston and Byfield, Bolton and Hildersam, and Sibbes. 'This fact,' he candidly observes, 'must needs have told with extreme force against the interests of the church. It was doubtless alleged that the church divines could only speak when their position or their order was menaced, but in the face of the great and crying sins and scandals of the age they were dumb and tongue-tied;' and he might have added, in view also of the gross ignorance and darkness in which whole districts of the country were shrouded.

I should make larger reservation or exceptions in favour of 'church' writers than Mr Perry does; for I find in Thomas Adams and Anthony Farindon, and others, whom I love equally with the foremost of the puritans, the same preaching with theirs. Still it remains that the men whom Laud delighted to honour were the men who were vehement enough to bring men to 'the church,' but not at all concerned about bringing them to Christ; ready to dispense

* 'Canterburie's Doom,' pp. 362, *seq.* 1646, folio.

† The History of the Church of England from the death of Elizabeth to the present time. By the Rev. G. G. Perry, M.A., Rector of Waddington. Vol. I. 1861. (Saunders, Otley, & Co.) See C. ix. p. 326.

the sacraments, but oblivious of their antitype; swift to jangle in hot controversies on 'super-elementation,' but cold about the one transcendent change; reverers of the altar, but despisers of the cross. We have defences of the church, its tithes and dignities, its upholstery and repairs, *ad nauseam*. We have the primate himself fervid about his genu-flexions and reverence to the *name* of Christ, and the name only; and a Mountagu, ribald as Billingsgate against holy Samuel Ward. They were, as was jested of a modern Lord Chancellor, buttresses rather than pillars of 'the church.' We look in vain all through the extant writings of the bishops named, from Laud downward, for anything approaching one earnest, heartfelt utterance as from a servant of Jesus Christ to perishing sinners, one living word to men as 'under wrath,' nay, for one flash of genius, one gush of human feeling. They had no answer for the 'Anxious Inquirer' as he cried—

'I am a sinner, full of doubts and fears,
Make me a humble thing of love and tears.'*

There exists not a more meagre, inane, contemptible literature, taken as a whole, than that composed of the Laudian books *proper;* for it were a historic blunder, as well as a slander, to include Hall or Ussher or Bedell or Davenant among them, from the mere accident of their first appointment, more or less, coming from Laud. Yet we must believe that what they printed and gave to the world was their best, and at least was the preaching their auditories heard. On the other hand, it equally remains unchallengeable that the men whom Laud delighted to persecute were the only men then in England who were really discharging, in the fear of God, their office of preachers of the gospel, men, at the same time, of generous loyalty, and lovers, with the deepest affection, of that reformed church from which they were driven in 1662.

Such having been the state of things, it is only what we should expect, to find even the unpolemic and gentle Sibbes speaking out against the doings and tendencies of the men in authority. There is a time to be silent, *and* a time to speak. Fealty to truth demanded plain words, and translating of words into acts. Nor was either awanting. For words take these, over which we can conceive even the rheumy eyes of the primate flashing fire. They are taken from sermons preached during this period, and afterwards fearlessly published. I venture to italicise some few lines:—

'What shall we think them to be of that take advantages of the bruisedness and infirmities of men's spirits to relieve them with false peace for

* Hartley Coleridge. Poems, ii. p. 387 (edition 1851).

their own worldly ends? A wounded spirit will part with anything. Most of the gainful points of popery, as confession, satisfaction, merit, purgatory, &c., spring from hence, but they are physicians of no value, or rather tormentors than physicians at all. *It is a greater blessing to be delivered from "the sting of these scorpions" than we are thankful for. Spiritual tyranny is the greatest tyranny*, and then especially when it is where most mercy should be shewed; yet even there some, like cruel surgeons, delight in making long cures, to serve themselves upon the misery of others. It bringeth men under a terrible curse, "when they will not remember to shew mercy, but persecute the poor and needy man, that they might even slay the broken in heart," Ps. cix. 16.

'Likewise, to such as raise temporal advantage to themselves out of the spiritual misery of others, join such as raise estates by betraying the church, *and are unfaithful in the trust committed unto them*, when the CHILDREN SHALL CRY FOR THE BREAD OF LIFE, AND THERE IS NONE TO GIVE THEM, *bringing thus upon the people of God that heavy judgment* of a spiritual famine, starving Christ in his members. Shall we so requite so good a Saviour, who counteth the love and mercy shewed in "feeding his lambs," John xxi. 15, as shewed to himself?

'Last of all, they carry themselves very unkindly towards Christ, who stumble at this his low stooping unto us in his GOVERNMENT and ORDINANCES, that are *ashamed of the simplicity of the gospel*, that count preaching foolishness.

'They, out of the pride of their heart, think they may do well enough without the help of the WORD and SACRAMENTS, and think CHRIST TOOK NOT STATE ENOUGH UPON HIM, AND THEREFORE THEY WILL MEND THE MATTER WITH THEIR OWN DEVICES, whereby they may give the better content to flesh and blood, *as in popery*.'*

Elsewhere, in his most eloquent sermon entitled 'The Saint's Safety in Evil Times,' he thus fearlessly speaks:—

'I beseech you consider, what hurt have we ever had by the "Reformation" of religion? Hath it come naked unto us? Hath it not been attended with peace and prosperity? Hath God been "a barren wilderness to us?" Jer. ii. 31. Hath not God been a wall of fire about us? which if he had not been, it is not the water that compasseth our island could have kept us.†

Once more, in the 'Ungodly's Misery,' also 'preached' at this period, we have these plain-spoken words:—

'What is the gospel but salvation and redemption by Christ *alone?* Therefore, Rome's church is an apostate church, and may well be styled an adulteress and a whore, because she is fallen from her husband Christ Jesus. And what may we think of those that would bring light and darkness, Christ and Antichrist, the ark and Dagon, together, that would reconcile us, as if it were no great matter?'‡

Still again, in his exceeding precious sermons on Canticles, he strikes high, even right at the prelates, on their neglect of abounding error:—

'Thus,' says he, 'popery grew up *by degrees*, till it overspread the

* 'Bruised Reed,' page 78.

† 'Saint's Safety,' page 312.

‡ 'Ungodly's Misery,' p. 388.

church, *whilst the watchmen that should have kept others awake* FELL ASLEEP THEMSELVES. And thus we answer the papists when they quarrel with us about the beginning of their errors. They ask of us when such and such an heresy began; we answer, THAT THOSE THAT SHOULD HAVE OBSERVED THEM WERE ASLEEP. Popery is a "mystery," that *crept into the church by degrees* UNDER GLORIOUS PRETENCES. *Their errors had modest beginnings.*' *

These two words, 'glorious pretences,' must have been treasured up by Laud. They reappear in his 'Answers' to the 'Charges' against him, as I shall notice anon.

These were fiery words, and given to the world in print, the former in 'The Bruised Reed,' in 1629–30, the latter in 'The Saint's Safety,' in 1632–3, they could not fail to rouse the primate. Almost immediately upon his appointment to the preachership of Gray's Inn, Laud had sought to have him deprived and silenced; for tidings had reached him of the Trinity lectureship and the evangelical, 'soul-fatting' (good old Bolton's word) preaching there. But Lord Keeper Finch had interfered to defeat his machinations, a right good service by not the best of men I fear, which he did not forget to plead when he stood at the bar of the House. Thus did he bring it up, the little quarto containing the full 'speech' being now before me:—'I hope for my affection in religion no man doubteth me. What my education was, and under whom I lived for many yeares, is well knowne. I lived neere thirty years in the society of Gray's Inne; and if one (that was a reverend preacher there in my time, Doctor Sibs) were now living, he were able to give testimony to this House that when a party ill-affected in religion sought to tyre and weary him out, he had his chiefest encouragement and help from me.' Let the erring Lord Keeper have the benefit of this redeeming trait.

Defeated in this earlier effort, Laud postponed, but did not abandon, his purpose. He soon found a pretext. As was observed before, Sibbes was a man of beneficent action as well as of beneficent words; and holding as he did that the church was for the nation, and not the nation for the church,—that the ministry was for the preaching of the gospel,—he joined hand and heart in counterworking those schemes, that, by quenching every 'golden candlestick' within which burned the oil of the sanctuary, sought to bring back the darkness and superstitions of the worst of popish times. Things had come to the crisis of endurance. If Laud and his myrmidons would 'deprive,' 'out,' 'silence,' 'persecute' the humble, faithful, godly preachers of salvation by grace, who were bearing the 'heat and burden' of work, and would intrude men, from the bishop to his humblest curate, who enforced a thinly-veiled popery in

* 'Bowels Opened,' pp. 84–5.

practice, and *un*scriptural, *anti*scriptural teaching in doctrine, something was demanded that should neutralise such doings. What was devised is matter of history. 'Feoffees' were appointed—the sacred 'twelve' in number—to raise funds, and buy in from time to time such 'impropriations' as were in the hands of laymen, when they could be purchased, and then to appoint therein as lecturers those who would really do the work of preaching. Superadded was the appointment of similar lecturers in the more neglected regions where lay-impropriations were not purchasable. Years before Sibbes had expressed his earnest wish that a 'lecturer' were in every dark corner of England.* It was a noble enterprise, and was nobly responded to. The best and wisest, the purest and holiest men of the age, took their part in the undertaking. I hesitate not to avouch, that there was scarcely a man whose name is now remembered for good, but was found subscribing amply and co-operating zealously for its accomplishment. The national heart was stirred, and it was found to beat in the right place. Sibbes, along with his old friends and coadjutors, Davenport and Gouge, was appointed one of the 'Feoffees.' It needs not to be told how this drew down the vengeance of Laud. The scheme had been more or less hindered from its inauguration in 1626, but not till 1632–3 (coincident with Sibbes's defences of 'The Reformation from Popery') was open action taken. The delay was caused by no relenting, much less forgetfulness. But events in the interval had transpired to 'give pause.' James had died, and his son reigned in his stead. The plague had passed over the metropolis in 1625, and there was 'lamentation and woe' in tens of thousands of households, again returning dolefully in 1630. There were political movements, also, that whitened to pallor the proudest cheek. One 'Mr Cromwell' had come up to Parliament in 1627–8. Besides 'the Petition of Right,' and the extorted and memorable *Soit fait comme il est desiré*, and the 'Declaration,' most uncourtly words fell from Masters Pym and Hampden and Eliot, and many others. But very especially was there plain-speaking, in his own stammering but forcible and resolute fashion, by 'Mr Cromwell' about increase of 'popery.' The House of Commons resolved itself into a Committee of Religion. Let Thomas Carlyle, tell the issue. 'It was,' says he, 'on the 11th day of February 1628–9, that Mr Cromwell, member for

* His words are memorable: 'If it were possible, it were to be wished that there were set up some lights in all the dark corners of this kingdom, that might shine to those people that sit in darkness and in the shadow of death.'—(Saint's Safety, p. 331 of the present volume.)

Huntingdon (then in his thirtieth year), stood up and made his first speech, a fragment of which has found its way into history, and is now known to all mankind. He said: "He had heard by relation from one Dr Beard (his old schoolmaster at Huntingdon) that Dr Alabaster (prebendary of St Paul's and rector of a parish in Herts) had preached flat popery at Paul's Cross; and that the Bishop of Winchester (Dr Neile) had commanded him, as his diocesan, he should preach nothing to the contrary. Mainwaring, so justly censured in this House for his sermons, was, by the same bishop's means, preferred to a rich living. If these are the steps to church-preferment, what are we to expect?"'* We shall probably not greatly err if we conclude that even the 'red face' of Laud blanched under that question of 'Mr Cromwell,' knowing as he well did that the facts named were only two out of many, and knowing also the 'stuff' of which the men were made who were upon the inquisition. Then came 'remonstrances' and 'declarations' stronger still, and they who drew them up meant to have what they demanded. True, the chief speakers were 'indicted' in the Star-Chamber, and ultimately sent to the Tower, 'Mr Cromwell,' and 'Mr Pym,' and 'Mr Hampden' alone excepted (marvellous and suggestive exceptions). There lay Denzil Holles and Sir John Eliot, John Selden, Benjamin Valentine, and William Couton, Sir Miles Hobart and William Longe, William Strode and Sir Peter Hayman. For eleven years it was decreed to be penal so much as to speak of assembling another Parliament. There were 'wars and rumours of wars,' too. Every one who at all knows the time can see that a constraint which could not be disregarded was put upon Laud in the matter of his persecuting for religion. He durst not go in the teeth of the unmistakeable menaces of the last memorable Parliament. He noted down everything, and certainly would not fail to note down what Rous and Pym, Eliot and Selden, had said. Let us hear a little of what was said. Francis Rous, trembling like an old Hebrew prophet with his 'burden,' had denounced that 'error of Arminianism which makes the grace of God lackey it after the will of man,' and called on the House to postpone questions of goods and liberties to this question, which concerned 'eternal life, men's souls, yea, God himself.' Sir John Eliot repudiated the claim that 'the bishops and clergy alone should interpret church doctrine; and, professing his respect for some bishops, declared that there were others, *and two especially*, from whom nothing orthodox could come, and to empower whom to interpret *would be the ruin of national religion.*' John Selden, grave and calm, referred to individual cases in which

* Cromwell's Letters and Speeches, 3d edition, i. 29.

Popish and Arminian books were allowed, while Calvinistic books were restrained, notwithstanding that there was no law in England to prevent the printing of any books, but only a decree in Star-Chamber.' And then on one occasion the whole House stood up together, and vowed a vow against '*innovations in the faith.*' The issue of that, passed with closed doors, and with clenching of teeth and gripping of sword-hilts, none will soon forget. We have to do with only one of the three 'Resolutions:—'Whoever shall bring in innovation of religion, or by favour or countenance seem to extend Popery or Arminianism, or other opinion disagreeing from the true and orthodox church, shall be reputed a capital enemy to this kingdom and commonwealth.' *

After these things it is remarkable that the king, a man without mind, and Laud, a man without either mind or heart, should at all have adventured to go against the mind and heart of England. But so it was. There was of necessity greater secrecy, very much of covert plotting against the liberties, civil and religious, of England. The 'feoffees' at last, borne with involuntarily from 1626, were summoned before the Star Chamber and High Commission both. And that was but the execution of Laud's cherished purpose from the beginning. For in that strangest of strange 'Diaries,' the oddest combination, that ever has been written, of piety and grovelling superstition, of faith and the most babyish credulity, (for Pepys' is wisdom itself in comparison †), we light upon this entry:—

'Things which I have projected to do, if God bless me in them—

'III. To overthrow the feoffment, dangerous both to Church and State, going under the specious pretence of buying in impropriations.'

Opposite these words, a few out of many equally deplorable, that a little onward came to be to their writer terrible as the mystic 'handwriting' of Babylon's palace-wall, is inscribed 'DONE.' And it was *done*—for the moment; but it was a tremendous success to its doer. If only Nemesis had been touched with ruth to blot out the handwriting! But no! There the entry stood, when perhaps not altogether lawfully or honourably, at least not courteously, the diary was seized:—

* Consult for the facts introduced Masson's Life of Milton, i. 181, 329, *seq.*; Carlyle's 'Cromwell;' John Forster's 'Statesmen of the Commonwealth,' and others of his historical works about this period.

† Pepys. I do not know if his prescient entry in favour of the Puritans has been remarked. Having witnessed Ben Jonson's 'Bartholomew Fair,' he jots down, 'And is an excellent play; the more I see it the more I love the wit of it; *only the business of abusing the Puritans* begins to grow stale, and of no use, *they being the people that at last will be found the wisest.*' See Index of any edition of 'Diary' under 'Bartholomew Fair.'

'Feb. 13. 1632.

'*Wednesday.*—The feoffes that pretended to buy in impropriations were dissolved in the Chequer Chamber. *They were the main instruments for the Puritan faction to undo the Church.* THE CRIMINAL PART RESERVED.'*

Reserved! Ay, and transferred!

Those who had engaged in the impropriation scheme, including Sibbes, having been thus summoned before the Star-Chamber, were dealt with, not as honourable and good men, but as 'criminals and traitors.' The verdict was—CONFISCATION of the funds and BANISHMENT of the men!

Some fled to Holland, some to New England.† Had the nation's

* Laud's 'Works,' vol. iii. p. 216, 217.

† Of the 'fugitives' associated with Sibbes in the 'feoffees' scheme, the most eminent was John Davenport. In Anderson's Life of Lady Mary Vere, in 'Memorable Women of Puritan Times,' some very touching letters of his are given from the Brit. Museum MSS. (Birch 4275, No. 69). Two extracts will shew the anxiety in which these godly men were kept, and at the same time shew how far they were from wishing to be 'schismatics,' or in any way to injure the church. First of all, while he and Sibbes and others were under the ban of the 'High Commission' as mentioned above, he writes, 'I have had divers purposes of writing to your honour, only I delayed in hope to write somewhat concerning the event and success of our High Commission troubles; but I have hoped in vain, for to this day we are in the same condition as before, delayed till the finishing of the session in Paliament, which now is unhappily concluded without any satisfying contentment to the king or commonwealth. *Threatenings were speedily revived against us by the new Bishop of London, Dr Laud, even the next day after the conclusion of the session.* We now expect a fierce storm from the enraged spirits of the two bishops; ours, as I am informed, hath a particular aim at me upon a former quarrel, so that I expect ere long to be deprived of my pastoral charge in Coleman Street. But I am in God's hand, not in theirs, to whose good pleasure I do contentedly and cheerfully submit myself.'

A more beautiful charity, or more modest assertion of conscience, than in our next extract, can scarcely be imagined.

'Be not troubled, much less discouraged, good madam, at any rumours you meet with concerning my present way. The persecution of the tongue is more fierce and terrible than that of the hand. At this time I have some of both. . . . . . The truth is, I have not forsaken my ministry, nor resigned up my place, *much less separated from the church,* but am only absent a while to wait upon God, upon the settling and quieting of things, for light to discover my way, being willing to lie and die in prison, if the cause may be advantaged by it, but choosing rather to preserve the liberty of my person and ministry for the service of the church elsewhere, *if all doors are shut against me here.* . . . . . . The only cause of all my present sufferings is the alteration of my judgment in matters of conformity to the ceremonies established, whereby I cannot practise them as formerly I have done; *wherein I do not censure those that do conform* (*nay, I account many of them faithful and worthy instruments of God's glory;* and I know that I did conform with as much inward peace as now I do forbear; in both my uprightness was the same, but my light different). In this action I walk by that light which shineth into me. . . . . . . With much advice of many ministers of eminent note and worth, I have done all that I have done hitherto, and with desire of pitching upon that way wherein God might be most glorified. In his due time he will manifest it.'

tongue not been cut out—no Parliament sat for years!—there had been stormy debates on that!

So far as Sibbes was concerned, it does not appear that any part of the sentence was ever put into execution. He continued preacher at Gray's Inn, and Master of Catharine Hall. This assures us that powerful friends, the Brooks and Veres, Manchesters and Warwicks, must have stood by him. But there was no compromise on his part. I find that almost like a menace, and most surely a defiance, Sibbes introduced into a sermon, preached immediately after the decision, an explicit eulogy of Sherland, the recorder of Northampton, for what he had done toward the impropriation scheme; and published the sermon.*

Still it was crushed, the 'monies' confiscated, the 'purchases' reversed, the whole holy enterprise branded, and its agents disgraced. One thing is to be recalled. Among the 'things projected,' Laud enumerates, with imbecile forgetfulness, precisely such a scheme of purchase of 'impropriations'—by HIMSELF.† So that it stands confessed that not the thing itself was dangerous and illegal, but the doers of it. Let only him and his appoint to the places, and all was well and right. But let men such as Sibbes, Gouge, Taylor, Davenport in the Church, and the foremost men for worth in the State, their enemies themselves being witnesses, be the appointers, and instantly it smells of 'treason, stratagem, wiles.' These or those dangerous to Church and State? What is the award of posterity? And yet defenders have been found for the transparently mendacious and infamous act. Such jeer at the paltry minority of Puritanism, oblivious of what a living poet has finely expressed—

'. . . . . You trust in numbers, I
Trust in One only.' ‡

Let us see how Laud himself met it when it came in awful resurrection back upon him. Every one is aware that the suppression of the 'feoffment-impropriation' scheme formed one of the counts in the great roll of accusation, whose issue was the block on Tower Hill. A careful record was kept of charges and answers, and the whole have been republished in the Works of Laud. It is but fitting that what he had to say should appear. Here, then, are 'charge' and 'defence.' The whole case, so vital as between Laud and the Puritan worthies, among whom Richard Sibbes was prominent, can then be judged of:—

* See 'Christ is Best,' in the present volume, p. 349.

† See the whole list in his works, as after-referenced.

‡ Cecil and Mary, as *ante*, p. 10.

That whereas divers gifts and dispositions of divers sums of money were heretofore made by divers charitable and well-disposed persons, for the buying in of divers impropriations, for the maintenance of preaching the word of God in several churches; the said archbp., about eight years last past, wilfully and maliciously caused the said gifts, feoffments, and conveyances, made to the uses aforesaid, to be overthrown in his majesty's Court of Exchequer, contrary to law, as things dangerous to the Church and State, under the specious pretence of buying in appropriations; whereby that pious work was suppressed and trodden down, to the great dishonour of God and scandal of religion.

This article is only about the feoffments. That which I did was this: I was (as then advised upon such information as was given me) clearly of opinion, that this was a cunning way, under a glorious pretence, to overthrow the church government, by getting into their power more dependency of the clergy than the king, and all the peers, and all the bishops in all the kingdom had. And I did conceive the plot the more dangerous for the fairness of the pretence; and that to the State as well as the Church. Hereupon, not "maliciously" (as 'tis charged in the article), but conscientiously, I resolved to suppress it, if by law it might be done. Upon this, I acquainted his majesty with the thing, and the danger which I conceived would in few years spring out of it. The king referred me to his attorney, and the law. Mr Attorney Noye, after some pause upon it, proceeded in the exchequer, and there it was, by judicial proceeding and sentence, overthrown. If this sentence were according to law and justice, then there's no fault at all committed. If it were against law, the fault, whate'er it be, was the judges', not mine; for I solicited none of them. And here I humbly desired, that the Lords would at their leisure read over the sentence given in the exchequer,* which I then delivered in; but by reason of the length, it was not then read. Whether after it were, I cannot tell. I desired likewise that my counsel might be heard in this and all other points of law.

1. The first witness was Mr Kendall.† He says, that speaking with me about Presteen, 'I thanked God that I had overthrown this foeffment.'

2. The second witness, Mr Miller,‡ says he heard me say, 'They would have undone the church, but I have overthrown their feoffment.' These two witnesses prove no more than I confess. For in the manner aforesaid, I deny not but I did my best in a legal way to overthrow it. And if I did thank God for it, it was my duty to do so, the thing being in my judgment so pernicious as it was.

3. The third witness was Mr White, one of the feoffees.§ He says, 'that coming as counsel in a cause before me, when that business was done, I fell bitterly on him as an underminer of the church.' I remember well his coming to me as counsel about a benefice. And 'tis very likely I spake my conscience to him, as freely as he did his to me; but the particulars I remember not; nor do I remember his coming afterwards to me to

* Sir Leolin Jenkins hath a copy of it out of the records of the exchequer. W. S. A. C. (See Rushworth's Collections, vol. ii. pp. 151, 152.)

† 'William Kendall.'—Prynne's Cant. Doom, p. 388.

‡ 'Tempest Miller.'—Ibid.

§ John White. He was, in 1640, M.P. for Southwark, and chairman of the Committee for Religion. He was commonly called 'Century' White from the title of his celebrated tractate, 'The First Century of Malignant Priests,' (Wood. Ath. Ox. iii. 144, 145).

Fulham; nor his offer 'to change the men or the course, so the thing might stand.' For to this I should have been as willing as he was; and if I remember right, there was order taken for this in the decree of the Exchequer. And his majesty's pleasure declared, that no penny so given should be turned to other use. And I have been, and shall ever be, as ready to get in impropriations, by any good and legal way, as any man (as may appear by my labours about the impropriations in Ireland). But this way did not stand either with my judgment or conscience.

1. First, because little or nothing was given by them to the present incumbent, to whom the tithes were due, if to any; that the parishioners which payed them, might have the more cheerful instruction, the better hospitality, and more full relief for their poor.

'2. Secondly, because most of the men they put in, were persons disaffected to the discipline, if not the doctrine, too, of the Church of England.

'3. Thirdly, because no small part was given to schoolmasters, to season youth *above*, for their party; and to young students in the universities, to purchase them and their judgments to their side, against their coming abroad into the church.

'4. Fourthly, because all this power to breed and maintain a faction, was in the hands of twelve men, who were they never so honest, and free from thoughts of abusing this power, to fill the church with schism, yet who should be successors, and what use should be made of the power, was out of human reach to know.'

5. Because this power was assumed by, and not to themselves, without any legal authority, as Mr Attorney assured me.

He further said, 'that the impropriations of Presteen, in Radnorshire, was specially given to St Antolin's, in London.* I say the more the pity, considering the poorness of that country, and the little preaching that was among that poor people, and the plenty which is in London. Yet because it was so given, there was care taken after the decree, that they of St Antolin's had consideration, and I think to the full. He says, 'that indeed they did not give anything to the present incumbents, till good men came to be in their places.' Scarce one incumbent was bettered by them. And what then? In so many places not one 'good man' found? 'Not one factious enough against the church, for Mr White to account him good?' Yet he thinks 'I disposed these things afterwards to unworthy men.' 'Truly, had they been at my disposal, I should not wittingly have given them to Mr White's worthies.' But his majesty laid his command upon his attorney, and nothing was done or to be done in these things, but by his direction. For Dr Heylin, if he spake anything amiss concerning this feoffment, in any sermon of his† he is living to answer it; me it concerns not. 'Mr Brown in the sum of the charge omitted not this. And I answered as before. And in his reply he

* This impropriation was, after the forfeiture, granted by King Charles I. to the rector of Presteign for ever. This grant was revoked during the Rebellion, but confirmed by King Charles II. at the beginning of his reign.

† The Sermon to which reference is here made, was preached by Heylin, at St Mary's, Oxford, July 11. 1630, at the Act. The passage relating to the feoffees will be found in Prynne (Cant. Doom, p. 386), who transcribed it from a MS. copy of the Sermon in Abp. Laud's study; and in Heylin (Cypr. Ang. p. 199, Lond. 1671). who appears in his turn to have transcribed it from Prynne.

turned again upon it, that it must be a crime in me, because I projected to overthrow it. But, under favour, this follows not. For to project (though the word 'projector' sounds ill in England), is no more than to forecast and forelay any business. Now as 'tis lawful for me, by all good and fit means, to project the settlement of anything that is good; so is it as lawful, by good and legal means, to project the overthrow of anything that is cunningly or apparently evil. And such did this feoffment appear to my understanding, and doth still.' As for reducing of impropriations to their proper use, they may see (if they please) in my Diary (whence they had this) another project to buy them into the church's use. For given they will not be. But Mr Pryn would shew nothing, nor Mr Nicolas see anything, but what they thought would make against me.

Of this Defence, it must be said in the apophthegm of Helps, 'It would often be as well to condemn a man unheard, as to condemn him upon the reasons which he openly avows for any course of action.'* Still, in common with the whole of the 'Answers,' as tragically told in the 'History of the Troubles,'† it exhibits no little astuteness and dexterity, and more than all his resoluteness in assertion of conscience. There is also characteristic strategy shewn in his retreats behind others who acted with him, now Attorney-General Noye, and now the king himself, with an almost humorous contrast in the surrender of Heylin to his fate. While then we cannot altogether deny that an answer (not reply merely, but answer) is returned, nor that his infamy was shared; yet there lies behind all the indisputable fact, that here was an association of the very salt of Church and State, seeking from their own resources to purchase in a legal way,—in the very way their accuser himself had done, and still proposed to do,—'impropriations' in the hands of laymen who were not only willing, but wishful, to part with them, and to place therein, through the recognised authorities, men of kindred character with themselves, in order that the gospel might be fully preached, and the people cared for—and Laud prevents. It is not more strange than sad, that in this nineteenth century, men should be found maintaining that Laud did right—that in entering among 'the things to be done,' the overthrow of the 'Feoffees,' or the frustration of an earnest effort whereby men of God, in the truest sense, would have '*fed* the flock of God, which he hath redeemed with his own blood,' he came to a resolution, and in the execution of it performed a service, to be remembered and praised, not deplored. But, indeed, such defences only mask a deeper hatred. For often, as Lovell Beddoes puts it—

* Thoughts in the Cloister and the Crowd. 1835, 12mo, page 9.

† The History of the Troubles and Trial of Archbishop Laud. Works (edited by Scott and Bliss in 'Anglo-Cathclic Library'), vol. iv. pp. 302–306.

'These are the words that grow, like grass and nettles
Out of dead men; and speckled hatreds hide,
Like toads, among them.'*

There is always a certain nimbus of glory around a decollated head, and I am disposed to concede that a truer man, great among the small, fell on Tower Hill than he whose face paled on the awful block of Whitehall window, though it was a king's and has been canonized as a martyr's. There was a stout-heartedness in the face of fearful odds in the stricken and forsaken primate throughout his trial that commands a measure of respect; and, perhaps, such is the inscrutable mystery of poor human nature, he deceived himself into a conscientious suppression of all consciences that differed from his own. Neither would I forget that one or two, or even three or four—Hall and Prideaux, Ussher, Davenant, and William Chillingworth—may be named, who, self-contradictorily, were advanced in the church more or less by him.† I will not conceal this, though historic candour compels me to affirm that, in so far as they fell in with his wishes (taking Bishop Hall as an example), they stained the white of their souls, and that Ussher and the apostolic Bedell and Chillingworth protested against the ultimate development of his views and actings.

I gladly give him all praise for his honest and courageous word to the king, when his irreverent Majesty came in too late and interrupted 'prayers.' It was a brave and worthy request that he made that the king should be present 'at prayers as well as sermon every Sunday.'‡

I found no common joy also in coming, in the arid pages of the 'Diary,' upon these pitying words about a very venerable Puritan, gleaming like a drop of dew, or even a human tear:—'In Leicester the dean of the Arches suspended one Mr Angell, who had continued a lecturer in that great town for these divers years, without any license at all to preach, yet took liberty enough. I doubt his violence hath cracked his brain, and do therefore use him more tenderly, *because I see the hand of God hath overtaken him.*'§

Brook ('Lives of the Puritans'‖) testily criticises the entry. The conclusion was false, for the 'violence' of the good Angell was the 'fine frenzy' of a man in awful earnest, in a fashion which Laud could not so much as apprehend. Still he is entitled to the full advantage of it, and to have it placed beside the kindred touch-

* Poems: Posthumous and Collected, vol. i. p. 109.

† 'Advanced.' The most has been made of this in the following acute and, in certain respects, valuable pamphlet:—'A Letter to the Rev. J. C. Ryle, A.B., in Reply to his Lecture on "Baxter and his Times." By a Clergyman of the Diocese of Exeter. Exeter, 1858. 8vo.'

‡ Diary, Nov. 14. 1626. § Ap. for 1634, pp, 325–6. ‖ Brook, iii. 236.

ing notices of his dying servants, his love for whom is remarkable.* But with every abatement, unless we are to blur the noblest names of the Christianity of England; to write 'false' against its truest, and refuse honour to men who, rather than fail in fealty to what they believed was written in the word of God, hazarded all that was dear to them; unless we are to overtop the loftiest intellects by one of the lowest, and sanctified genius and learning by one who was no scholar, and even could not write tolerable English, we must denounce every attempt to exalt and extol the morbid craving for an impossible 'uniformity' of this hard, cruel, unlovingly zealous, and unlovable man, around whom there hangs but a single gentle memory of tenderness to frailty or mercy to penitence; from whose pen there never once flowed one true word for Christ or the salvation of souls; from whom, in his darkened end, there came not so much as that remorseful touch that wins our sympathy for a Stephen Gardiner, '*Erravi cum Petro at non flevi cum Petro.*'† Claverhouse, the 'bloody,' and the first Charles, the 'false,' have been idealised. We look upon their pensive faces, and feel how traitorous they must have been to their better nature. But Laud it is not possible to idealise. The more, successive biographers have elucidated his history; they have only the more made him a definite object of contempt. He was elevated above men who, by head and shoulders (and we know what the head includes), were taller than himself.‡ The stilts fell from beneath him, and he found his level, as 'imbecile' (it is Lord Macaulay's word), as contemptible, as worthless a man as ever rose to power—a mitred Robespierre. A certain party are voluble in pronouncing their judgments upon the victims of Laud. It were to play false to truth to let them go unanswered; and the present is undoubtedly an occasion demanding such answer and out-speaking. But—

'I say not that the man I praise
By that poor tribute stands more high,
I say not that the man I blame
Be not of purer worth than I;

* Laud's servants. I give one entry in Diary:—'Sept. 23. 1621.—Thy. Mr Adam Torless, my ancient, loving, and faithful servant, then my steward, after he had served me full forty-two years, died, to my great loss and grief.'

† Gardiner. Foss's Judges of England, v. 370.

‡ A few wise words from 'Thoughts in the Cloister and the Crowds' may enforce our remarks —'Perhaps it is the secret thought of many that an ardent love of power and wealth, however culpable in itself, is nevertheless a proof of superior sagacity. But in answer to this it has been well remarked, that even a child can clench its little hand the moment it is born; and if they imagine that the successful, at any rate, must be sagacious, let them remember the saying of a philosopher, that the meanest reptiles are found at the summit of the loftiest pillars.' (Pp. 20–1.)

But when I move reluctant lips
For holy justice, human right,
The sacred cause I strive to plead
Lends me its favour and its might.'*

CHAPTER IX.

SIBBES'S 'INTRODUCTIONS' TO WORKS OF CONTEMPORARIES.

Whitaker—Duke of York—Paul Bayne—Henry Scudder—Ezekiel Culverwell—Dr John Preston—John Smith—John Ball—Richard Capel.

But I turn the leaf, and pass on in our 'Memoir.' And it is a pleasant change to turn from a Laud, chaffering over the breadth of a phylactery; from a Mountagu, overwhelming holy men, such as Samuel Ward, with the ribaldry of a 'Gagg for the new gospel!—no, a new gagg for an old goose!' from a Wren, tracking every 'two or three' who sought to meet together in the name of the Lord, to Richard Sibbes at his post, discharging his duties as a minister of Christ through 'good and evil report,' and sustaining the kindliest relationship with all the 'good men and true' of his contemporaries. There are pleasant memorials of the latter in various occasional productions, such as 'prefaces' and 'epistles dedicatory,' which Sibbes from time to time prefixed to good books of good men. These I would now bring together. They give us some very precious glimpses of his society, from a pretty early date to near the close. They are, indeed, so many little 'essays' on religious subjects, written in his very best style, and breathing all the sweetness, and informed with all the spirituality, of his larger writings. Where can we turn to more felicitous words about 'faith,' and 'prayer,' and 'holiness,' and the 'Christian life'? while there is a modesty of praise of the author introduced, whether living or dead, in striking contrast with the adulation then prevalent. First of all, I find among the 'Epicedia in Obitum Gul: Whitakeri,'† a copy of Greek verses to the memory of that truly great man, whose mother was Elizabeth Nowell, sister of Dr Alexander Nowell, and who, if he had found such a biographer as Nowell has in Archdeacon Churton, would be better known to the present generation. As a Master of Sibbes's own College of St John's, and as having married a sister first of Samuel and Ezekiel Culverwell, and next the widow of Dudley Fenner, and in every-day association with the Culverwells

* 'Passion-Flowers,' by Mrs Howe. Boston, 1854, p. 118.

† Works, Geneva, fol. 1610, vol. i. p. 706; previously published in 1596. 4to.

and Fenners, Cartwright, Fuller, Chadderton, and Dod, Whitaker could not but be known and esteemed by him. He was venerated by all parties. He was, says even the atrabilious Anthony Wood, 'one of the greatest men his college ever produced, the desire and love of the present times and the envy of posterity, that cannot bring forth a parallel.'* 'The learned Whitaker,' observes Leigh, 'the honour of our schools and the angel of our church, than whom our age saw nothing more memorable.'† 'Who,' exclaims Bishop Hall, 'ever saw him without reverence, or heard him without wonder?'‡ Whitaker died in 1596, the second year of Sibbes's studentship. It is significant that the verses of such a mere youth received a place beside the tributes of the greatest men of the age :—

Τὴν ὀρθὴν πάροδον πολλοις, 'ῥαιστῆρα Παπιστῶν
    Σαυτὸν γνωρίζεις, Ουϊτάχηρε, σοφοις
Ἕξοχος ἁπάντων, ὅ δ' ἀνεδραμεν ἔρνεϊ ἴσος,
    Καὶ Μουσῶν ὀρθῶς τὰς ἀνέῳγε θύρας.
Ἔυθετα τ' ἐκδίδου, 'ρ' ἔμφρων καὶ πλοια κυβερνῶν
    Τὴν λύμην κακὴν ζῶν τε θανών τ' ἔφυγε.
Νῦν γε ἀείμνηστον φήμην, κῦδος τε μέγιστον,
    Λιπὼν, πηγάζει δόγματα θεσπέσια.

R[ICHARD] S[IBBES].§

It is hardly worth while turning these verses into English, but one remark is suggested by them. Spite of the ''ῥαιστῆρα Παπιστῶν' (= hammer of the papists), won by his controversies with Campian and Bellarmine and others, Bellarmine thought so highly of Whitaker that he sent for his portrait, and gave it a prominent place in his study ; and when his friends were introduced to him he used to point to it and say, 'he was the most learned heretic he ever read.'||

Though it anticipates the order in date, it may be as well to introduce here the only other verses of Sibbes that are known (this time Latin)—on the birth of the Duke of York :—¶

* Fasti Oxon. (ed. by Bliss, vol. i. p. 210, &c.)

† Edward Leigh's Treatise of Religion and Learning, folio, 1656, p. 363.

‡ Quoted in Leigh, *supra*, p. 364. Hall wrote an English 'Elegy' and Latin verses on Whitaker. The former will be found in Caroli Horni Carmen Funebre in Obitum Ornatissimi viri Gul., Whitakeri, &c. Lond. 4to, 1596. The latter prefixed to Whitaker's Prælectiones, 1599, 4to. Both, in Hall's Works by Peter Hall, xii. 323–25 and 330.

§ Given *verbatim et literatim* from the volume of Whitaker.

|| Wood's Athenæ, *ante*. For full notice of Whitaker, with, as usual, ample authorities, consult Cooper's Athenæ Cantab., vol. ii., p. 196, *seq*.

¶ From 'Ducis Eboracensis Fasciæ a Musis Cantabrigiensibus,' 1633, p. 6. For pointing out both the Greek and Latin verses I am indebted to Charles H. Cooper, Esq., Cambridge, not more erudite than willing to place his multitudinous collections at the disposal of a fellow-labourer.

IN NATALEM DUCIS EBORACENSIS AUSPICATISSIMUM.

Anglia ter felix, ternâ jam prole beata:
  Pax regno namque est pignore firma novo.
Major si ex populi numero sit gloria regis;
  Natorum ex numero an non magè surgit honos?
Candidiora nitent tria Lilia, tresque Leones
  Exultant, sceptra ut nobilitata vident,
Fratribus et binis stipatur utrinque Maria:
  Delicias junctas cum Patre Mater habet.
Regia stirps crescit; crescunt hinc gaudia regni:
  Crescat et hinc summo gloria summa Deo!

At Tu, Magne puer, Regum de stemmate germen,
  Cura Dei, Patriæ spes nova, vive, vige.
Gloria Te niveis semper circumvolet alis,
  Teque ipso major crescito, parve puer!
Gratia te et virtus semper comitentur euntem!
  In vultu et labris sessitet ipsa *Charis!*
Angelicusque chorus tua stet cunabula circum,
  Sitque *Duci* semper *Dux* DEUS atque *Comes!*
Et nati natorum, et qui nascentur ab illis
  Perpetuent seriem, *Carole* magne, tuam!
Germinet usquè, ferax jam faustè, regia vitis
  Germinet, O fructus edat et usquè novos!

R[ICHARD] S[IBBES], *Aulæ Sanctæ Catharinæ Præfectus.**

It were a waste of pains to translate these lines. Neither their subject nor their merit claims this.†

It is clear that Sibbes wanted the *afflatus* of the poet, of whom the old axiom, one of the world's *memorabilia*, must ever hold, *nascitur non fit.* And alas! for the '*gratia*,' and other prayers! for this Duke of York became the Second Charles of England.

Returning upon our chronology, Paul Bayne, whose 'ministry' along with Sibbes has been described in an earlier part of this Memoir,‡ having died in 1617, there was issued immediately a quarto volume containing an Exposition of the 1st chapter of the Epistle to the Ephesians.§ Its main theme is 'Predestination,' one of the '*doctrinal*' points forbidden by royal proclamation to be discussed. Soberly, wisely, suggestively, and with much beauty of wording does Sibbes introduce his 'father in the gospel.'

'Notwithstanding the world's complaint of the surfeit of books (hasty wits being over forward to vent their unripe and misshapen conceits), yet

* This also is given *verbatim* from the volume.

† Perhaps the classical scholar will agree with me, that in the couplet,

Gratia te et virtus semper comitentur euntem,
In vultu et labris sessitet ipsa Charis!

= 'May grace itself sit on thy countenance and lips,' we have a reminiscence of a fragment from Diodorus πειθώ τις ἐπικάθισεν ἐπι τοις χείλεσιν = 'Persuasion sat upon his lips.' Quoted in Keightley's History of Greece, p. 160.

‡ See pages xxxvi, xxxviii.

§ Commentary on 1st Chapter of Ephesians, handling the controversy of Predestination, 4to, 1618.

in all ages there hath been, and will be necessary uses of holy treatises, appliable to the variety of occasions of the time; because men of weaker conceits cannot so easily of themselves discern how one truth is inferred from another, and proved by another, especially when truth is controverted by men of more subtile and stronger wits. Whereupon, as God's truth hath in all ages been opposed in some branches of it; so the divine providence that watcheth over the church, raised up some to fence the truth, and make up the breach. Men gifted proportionably to the time, and as well furnished to fight God's battles, as Satan's champions have been to stand for him: neither have any points of Scripture been more exactly discussed, than those that have been most sharply oppugned, opposition whetting both men's wits and industry, and in several ages men have been severally exercised. The ancientest of the fathers had to deal with them without (the Pagans), and especially with proud heretics, that made their own conceits the measure of holy truth, believing no more than they could comprehend in the articles of the Trinity, and natures of Christ, whence they bent their forces that way, and for their matter wrote more securely. Not long after, the enemies of grace, and flatterers of nature, stirred up St Augustine to challenge the doctrine of God's predestination and grace out of their hands, which he did with great success, as fitted with grace, learning, and wit for such a conflict, and no Scriptures are more faithfully handled by him, than those that were wrested by his opposites, and such as made for the strengthening of of his own cause. In other writings he took more liberty, his scholars Prosper, Fulgentius and others interest themselves in the quarrel.

In process of time, men desirous of quiet, and tired with controversies, began to lay aside the study of Scriptures, and hearken after an easier way of ending strife, by the determination of one man (the Bishop of Rome), whom virtually they made the whole church; so the people were shut up under ignorance and implicit faith, which pleased them well, as easing them of labour of search, as upon the same irksomeness of trouble in the eastern parts, they yielded to the confusion and abomination of Mahometism.

And lest scholars should have nothing to do, they were set to tie and untie school knots, and spin questions out of their own brain, in which brabbles they were so taken up, that they slightly looked to other matters; as for questions of weight they were schooled to resolve all into the decisive sentence of the see apostolic, the authority of which they bent their wits to advance; yet then wisdom found children to justify her: for Scriptures that made for authority of princes and against usurpation of popes, were well cleared by Occam, Marsilius, Patavinus, and others, as those of predestination and grace by Ariminensis, Bradwardine, and their followers, against Pelagianism, then much prevailing. At length the apostasy of popery spread so far, that God in pity to his poor church, raised up men of invincible courage, unwearied pains, and great skill in tongues and arts to free religion, so deeply enthralled; from whence it is that we have so many judicious tractates and commentaries in this latter age. And yet will there be necessary use of farther search into the Scriptures as new heresies arise, or old are revived, and further strengthened. The conviction of which, is then best when their crookedness is brought to the straight rule of Scriptures to be discovered. Besides, new expositions of Scriptures will be useful, in respect of new temptations, corruptions in life and cases of conscience, in which the mind will not receive any satisfying resolution, but from explication and application of Scriptures. Moreover, it is not unprofitable that there should be divers treatises of the same portion of Scriptures, because the same truth may be better conveyed to the conceits of some men, by some men's handling than others', one man relishing one man's gifts more than another. And it is not meet that the glory of God's goodness and wisdom should be obscured, which shineth in the variety of men's gifts, especially seeing the depth of Scripture is such, that though men had large hearts, as the sand of the sea shore, yet could they not empty out all things contained; for though the main principles be not many, yet deductions and conclusions are infinite, and until Christ's second coming to judgment, there will never want new occasion of further search and wading into these deeps.

In all which respects this exposition of this holy man, deserves acceptance of the church, as fitted to the times (as the wise reader will well discern). Some few places are not so full as could be wished, for clearing some few obscurities; yet those that took the care of setting them out, thought it better to let them pass as they are, than be over-bold with another man's work, in making him speak what he did not, and take them as they be. The greatest shall find matter to exercise themselves in; the meaner, matter of sweet comfort and holy instruction, and all confess, that he hath brought some light to this excellent portion of Scripture.

He was a man fit for this task, a man of much communion with God, and acquaintance with his own heart, observing the daily passages of his life, and exercised much with spiritual conflicts. As St Paul in this epistle never seemeth to satisfy himself in advancing the glory of grace, and the vileness of man in himself, so this our Paul had large conceits of these things, a deep insight into the mystery of God's grace, and man's corruption: he could therefore enter further into Paul's meaning, having received a large measure of Paul's spirit. He was one that sought no great matters in the world, being taken up with comforts and griefs, unto which the world is a stranger; one that had not all his learning out of books; of a sharp wit, and clear judgment: though his meditations were of a higher strain than ordinary, yet he had a good dexterity, furthered by his love to do good, in explaining dark points with lightsome similitudes. His manner of handling questions in this epistle is press, and school-like, by arguments on both sides, conclusions, and answers, a course more suitable to this purpose than loose discourses.

In setting down the object of God's predestination, he succeeds him in opinion, whom he succeeded in place;* in which point divines accord not who in all other points do jointly agree against the troubles of the church's peace, in our neighbour countries; for some would have man lie before God in predestinating him, as in lapsed and miserable estate; others would have God in that first decree to consider man abstracted from such respects, and to be considered of, as a creature alterable, and capable either of happiness or misery, and fit to be disposed of by God, who is Lord of his own to any supernatural end; yet both agree in this: First, that there was an eternal separation of men in God's purpose. Secondly, that this first decree of severing man to his ends, is an act of sovereignty over his creature, and altogether independent of anything in the creature, as a cause of it, especially in comparative reprobation, as why he rejected Judas, and not Peter; sin foreseen cannot be the cause, because that was common to both, and therefore could be no cause of severing. Thirdly, all agree in this, that damnation is an act of divine justice, which supposeth demerit; and therefore the execution of God's decree is founded on sin, either of nature, or life, or both. My meaning is not to make the cause

* Perkins.

mine, by unnecessary intermeddling. The worthiness of the men on both side is such, that it should move men to moderation in their censures either way. Neither is this question of like consequence with others in this business, but there is a wide difference between this difference and other differences. And one cause of it, is the difficulty of understanding, how God conceives things, which differs in the whole kind from ours, he conceiving of things altogether and at once without discourse, we one thing after another, and by another. Our comfort is, that what we cannot see in the light of nature and grace, we shall see in the light of glory, in the university of heaven; before which time, that men should in all matters have the same conceit of things of this nature, is rather to be wished for, than to be hoped. That learned bishop (now with God) that undertook the defence of Mr Perkins, hath left to the church, together with the benefit of his labours, the sorrow for his death, the fame of his worth, an example likewise of moderation, who, though he differed from Mr Perkins in this point, yet shewed that he could both assent in lesser things, and with due respect maintain in greater matters.* If we should discern of differences, the church would be troubled with fewer distempers; I speak not as if way were to be given to Vorstian, lawless, licentious liberty of prophecy; that every one, so soon as he is big of some new conceit, should bring forth his abortive monster: for thus the pillars of Christian faith would soon be shaken, and the church of God, which is a house of order, would become a Babel, a house of confusion. The doleful issues of which pretended liberty, we see in Polonia, Transylvania, and in countries nearer hand. We are much to bless God for the king's majesty's firmness this way, unto whose open appearing in these matters, and to the vigilancy of some in place, we owe our freedom from that schism, that troubleth our neighbours.

But for diversity of apprehensions of matters far remote from the foundation; these may stand with public and personal peace. I will keep the reader no longer from the treatise; the blessing of heaven go with it, that through the good done by it, much thanksgiving may be to God in the Church! Amen. R. SIBBS.

Gray's Inn.

Our next name is Henry Scudder, whom Richard Baxter and John Owen united to praise while he was alive. In 1620, he published his inestimable little treatise, worthy companion to his 'Christian's Daily Walk in Holy Security and Peace,' entitled 'Key of Heaven, the Lord's Prayer Opened.'† To it Sibbes prefixed a 'Recom-

* The 'learned bishop' is Robert Abbot, Bishop of Salisbury, and the reference is to his 'Defence of the Reformed Catholick of W. Perkins against Dr W. Bishop.' 4to, 1611.

† A Key of Heaven: the Lord's Prayer opened, and so applied, that a Christian may learn how to pray, and to procure all things which may make for the glory of God, and the good of himself, and of his neighbour. Containing likewise such doctrines of faith and goodness, as may be very useful to all that desire to live godly in Christ Jesus. The second edition, enlarged by the author. Mat. vii. 7, Ask, and it shall be given you; seek, and ye shall find; knock, and it shall be opened unto you. *Oratio justi clavis cœli.* London: Printed by Thomas Harper, for Benjamin Fisher, and are to be sold at the sign of the Talbot in Aldersgate Street. 1688. This 'Key' has been erroneously included among Sibbes's own writings, *e.g.*, Brook ('Lives of Puritans, ii. 420), and even in Dr Bliss's Sale-Catalogue.

mendation,' which is in itself an Essay on Prayer, of rare value. Scudder was a contemporary of Sibbes in Cambridge, of Christ's Church. Afterwards he became successively minister at Drayton, in Oxfordshire, and at Collingborn-Dukes, in Wiltshire. In the year 1643, he was chosen one of the 'Assembly of Divines,' and was exemplary in his attendance. His books are pre-eminently scriptural and practical, and there are occasional similes and scraps of out-of-the-way incidents of a quaint beauty and appositeness. It is easy to understand that such a man would be dear to Richard Sibbes.* Thus he writes :—

To be much in persuading those that be favourites of some great person, to use that interest for their best advantage, were an endeavour somewhat needless, considering natural self-love inclineth men in such cases to be sensible enough of their own good. Yet so dull is our apprehension of matters that are of an higher nature, that though we have the ear of God always open unto us, and free access to the throne of grace through Christ who appeareth in heaven for us, carrying our names in his breast, yet we need stirring up to improve this blessed liberty, though the whole world be not worth this one prerogative, that we can boldly call God Father. This disproportion of our carriage ariseth in part from Satan's malice, who laboureth to keep us in darkness, that we believe not, or mind not our best privileges, which if we did, how glorious would our lives appear! how comfortably and fruitfully should we walk! what honour should God have by us! what sweet sacrifice from us! how should we overlook all opposite power! But now by reason we are prone to believe Satan, and the lies of our own heart; and ready to call truth itself into question, as if these things were too good to be true, no marvel if we pass our days so deadly. For what use of an hidden and locked up treasure, if we use not this key of prayer to fetch from thence for all our need? What benefit of all the precious promises made in Christ unto us, unless we allege them unto God, and with a reverend boldness bind him with his own word, which he can no more deny, than cease to be God? If we took these things to heart, God should hear oftener from us, we would be more in heaven than we are, seeing we should bring as much grace and comfort from God as we could bring faith to grasp and carry away.

Besides this fore-mentioned mindlessness of our privileges, since the fall the soul naturally loveth to spend and scatter itself about these present sensible things, and cannot without some strife gather itself together, and fix upon heavenly things. Now this talking with God requireth an actual bent of the mind, and carrieth up the whole soul into heaven, and exerciseth, as all the parts, so all the graces of the soul, faith especially, prayer being nothing else but the flame of faith. And Satan knowing that when we send up our desires to God, it is to fetch supply against him, troubleth the soul, weak of itself, with a world of distractions. Where he cannot corrupt the doctrine of prayer (as in popery) with heresies and superstitious follies, there he laboureth to hinder the exercise of it. Wherein we should be so far from being discouraged, that we should reason rather that must needs be an excellent duty which is so irksome to the flesh, and which the devil so eagerly sets against. This should encourage us to this exercise, wherein

* Scudder. Consult Brook's 'Lives of the Puritans,' ii. 504, *seq.*

lieth all our strength, that if in spite of Satan's annoyance and our own indisposition, we will set upon this duty, we shall find ourselves by little and little more raised up to heaven, and our hearts more and more enlarged, God rewarding the use of that little grace we find at the first, with increase of strength and comfort. To him that hath (in the exercise of that he hath) shall be given more. We should labour not to be ignorant of Satan's enterprises, who besides his diverting our minds from prayer, and disturbing us in it, laboureth by all means to draw us to some sin, the conscience whereof will stop our mouths, and stifle our prayers, and shake our confidence, and eclipse our comfort; which he oft aimeth more at than the sin itself unto which he tempteth us. We should labour therefore to preserve ourselves in such a state of soul, wherein we might have boldness with God, and wherein this gainful trading with him might not be hindered.

To pass over many other causes of the neglect of this intercourse, and dealing with God by prayer, we may well judge, as one of the chief, a self-sufficiency whereby men dwell too much in themselves. He that hath nothing at home will seek abroad. The poor man (saith Solomon) speaketh supplications. If we were poor in spirit, and saw our own emptiness, it would force us out of ourselves. Alas! what temptation can we resist, much less overcome, without fresh succour? What cross can we endure without impatience, if we have not new support? What success can we look for, yea, in common affairs, without his blessing? What good can we do, nay, think of, without new strength? When we do any good by his power, do we not need pardon for the blemishes of our best performances? What good blessing can we enjoy, so as we defile not ourselves in it, without a further blessing, giving us with the thing the holy use of it? Yet we see most men content to receive blessings as they come from God's general providence, without regarding any sanctified use by prayer, whereas holy men, knowing that God will be sought unto even for those things of which he hath given a promise, Ezek. xxxvi. 37, in obedience to this his divine order, desire to receive all from him as a fruit of their prayers. And God's manner is to keep many blessings from his children until they have begged them, as delighting to hear his children speak. The consideration whereof moveth those that have nearest communion with God to acknowledge him in all their ways, depending on him for direction, strength, success, whereupon he delighteth in shewing himself more familiarly unto them in the sweetest experiences of his love, guiding them by his counsel whilst they abide here, and after, bringing them to glory, Ps. xxxvii. 24. As other graces grow in those that are in the state of grace, so this spirit of prayer receiveth continual increase upon more inward acquaintance with God, and their own estates. Whence they can never be miserable, having God to pour forth their spirits and ease their hearts unto, who cannot but regard the voice of his own Spirit in them. But of ourselves, such is our case, that God who knoweth us better than we know ourselves, saith, we know not what or how to pray, Rom. viii. 26. This language of Canaan is strange unto us. Which our blessed Saviour in mercy considering, stirred up a desire in his disciples to be taught of him the Son, how to speak to the Father. Where thereupon he teacheth them a form, which for heavenly fulness of matter, and exactness of order, sheweth that it could come from no other Author.

This holy pattern comprising so much in so little, all things to be desired in six short petitions, it is needful for the guides of God's people to lay open the riches of it to the view of those that are less exercised. An endeavour which his excellent majesty thought not unbeseeming the greatness of a king. For the use of a set form of prayer, and this in special, I will make no question; yet in the use of this prayer, we may dwell more in the meditation and enforcing such petitions as shall concern our present occasions. For instance, if ever there were time of praying, 'Let thy kingdom come,' let Christ arise and his enemies be scattered, then certainly now is the time for us to ascend up into heaven by our prayers, and awake Christ, that he would rebuke the winds and waves, and cause a calm; that he would be strong for his church, in maintaining his own cause. It is God's manner, before any great work for his church, to stir up the spirits of his beloved ones to give him no rest. How earnest was Daniel with the Lord immediately before the delivery out of Babylon, Dan. xi. And undoubtedly, if we join the forces of our prayers together, and set upon God with an holy violence, he would set his power, his wisdom, his goodness on work for the exalting of his church, and ruin of the enemies of it. Now is the time for Moses his hands to be upheld, whilst Amalek goeth down.

The prevailing power of prayer with God in times of danger, appeareth not only in the sacred history of the Bible, but hath been recorded in all ages of the church. In the primitive church, A.D. 175, the army of Christians was called the thundering legion, because, upon their prayers, God scattered their enemies with thunder, and refreshed themselves with showers in a great drought.

After, in the good Emperor Theodosius his time, A.D. 394, upon an earnest prayer to Christ, the winds fought from heaven for him against his enemies, as they did for us in 1588. And continually since, God never left the force of faithful prayer without witness. If we would observe how God answereth prayers, we should see a blessed issue of all the holy desires he kindles in our hearts; for he cannot but make good that title whereby he is styled, 'a God hearing prayer,' Ps. lxv. 2, which should move us to sow more prayers into his bosom, the fruit whereof we should reap in our greatest need. It would be a strong evidence in these troublesome times of the future good success of the church, if we were earnest in soliciting Christ with these words which himself hath taught us, 'Let thy kingdom come.' For put him to it, and 'he will never fail those that seek him,' Ps. ix. 10. He loveth importunity.

But to speak something of this treatise of this godly and painful minister of Christ, which is written by him without affectation, as desirous to clothe spiritual things with a spiritual manner of writing, the diligent and godly reader shall observe a sound, clear, substantial handling of the greatest points that naturally fall within the discourse, and a more large and useful unfolding of many things, than in former treatises. It appeareth he sought the good of all; so that, besides the labours of other holy men, there will be just cause of blessing God for his assistance in this work. To whose blessing I commend both it and the whole Israel of God.

Gray's Inn. R. SIBBES.

Passing on to 1623–4, we have a delightful 'epistle' prefixed to Ezekiel Culverwell's 'Treatise of Faith . . . . . applied especially unto the use of the weakest Christians.'* This little volume had

* A Treatise of Faith. Wherein is declared how a man may live by faith, and find relief in all his necessities. Applied especially unto the use of the weakest Christians. By Ezekiel Culverwell. The just shall live by faith. The seventh

passed through seven editions by 1633; and it were well if its popularity could be revived; for it overflows with profound thought, sagacious counsel, pungent appeal, and true eloquence. But let Dr Gouge characterise it and its author. 'God,' he says, 'sent Ezekiel Culverwell, as of old he sent Ezekiel Buzi, to set forth the promises of God mòre plentifully and pertinently than ever before; and that to breed faith where it is not, to strengthen it where it is weak, to settle it where it wavereth, to repair it where it decayeth, to apply it aright to every need, to extend it to sanctification as well as to justification, and to point out the singular use of it in matters temporal, spiritual, and eternal.' And he adds—'What I say of him, I know of him; for from mine infancy have I known him, and under his ministry was I trained up in my younger years, he being at least two-and-twenty years older than myself.'*

Let us now read Sibbes's 'Epistle to the Christian Reader:'—

The leading of a happy life (the attainment whereof this treatise directeth unto) is that which all desire, but God's truth only discovereth, and faith only enjoyeth. In the first Adam, our happiness was in our own keeping; but he, by turning from God to the creature, made proof what and whence he was; a creature raised out of nothing, and without the supporting power of him in whom all things consist, subject to fall into a state worse than nothing again. Hence God, out of his infinite power, and depth of goodness intending the glory of his mercy, in restoring man, would not trust man with his own happiness; but would have it procured and established in the person of a second Adam, in whom we recover a surer estate than we lost in the first. For though Adam's soul was joined to God, yet that knitting was within the contingent and changeable liberty of his own will; but now we are brought to God in an everlasting covenant of mercy, by faith in Christ; who, by taking the nature of man into unity of his person, and not the person of any, became a public person, to be the author of eternal salvation to all that receive him; and so gathering us that were scattered from God, into one head, bringeth us back again to God, by a contrary way to that whereby we fell, that is, by cleaving to God by faith, from whom we fell by distrust. A fit grace for the state of grace, giving the whole glory to God, and emptying the soul of all self-sufficiency, and enlarging it to receive what is freely wrought and offered by another. Thus we come to have the comfort, and God the glory of mercy; which sweet attribute moved him to set all other attributes on work to make us happy. Out of the bowels of which mercy, as he chose us to eternal salvation in Christ, so vouchsafeth he all things necessary to life and godliness. And as the same love in God giveth us heaven, and furnisheth us with all things needful in the way, until we come thither; so the same faith which saveth us, layeth hold likewise on the promises of necessary assistance, comfort, provision, and protection: and

edition, corrected and amended. Ephes. vi. 16, 'Above all, taking the shield of faith.' Rom. xv. 4, 'Whatsoever things were written aforetime, were written for our learning, that we through patience and comfort of the Scriptures might have hope.' London: Printed by J. D. for Hen. Overton, and are to be sold at his shop at the entering in of Pope's-head Alley, out of Lumbard Street, 1633.

* 'To the Christian Reader,' prefixed to Treatise of Faith, *supra.*

this office it performeth in all the several stations of this life, until it hath brought us unto the enjoying of him 'in whose presence is fulness of joy for evermore,' Ps. xvi. 11.

We see that same love in parents, which moveth them to give an inheritance to their sons, moveth them likewise to provide for them, and to train them up in experience of their fatherly care. So it pleaseth our first and best Father, besides the main promise of salvation, to give us many other rich and precious promises, that in taste of his goodness and truth in these, we may at length yield up our souls to him, as to our faithful Creator, 1 Pet. iv. 19, with the more assured comfort; and the longer we live here, be more rooted in faith. 'I know whom I have trusted,' 2 Tim. i. 12, saith aged St Paul. But alas! how little is that we know of his ways, Job xxvi. 14, because we observe him not, making good his word unto us! 'All his ways are mercy and truth,' Ps. xxv. 10, and every 'word is a tried word,' Ps. xii. 6. For the better help of God's people, to know their portion in those good things, which their father not only layeth up for them, Ps. xxxi. 19, for times to come, but layeth out for them here as his wisdom seeth fit; this reverend and holy man of God hath compiled this treatise, wherein he layeth open the veins of promises hidden in the Scriptures, to the view of every Christian, and digesteth them in their orders; and withal, sheweth their several value and use, for the beautifying of a holy life; which wits less exercised, of themselves, would not so well have discerned.

Now that we may the rather benefit ourselves by this treatise, it will not be inconvenient to know these four things.

First, that it supposeth a reader grounded in the knowledge of the nature and properties of God, of Christ and his offices, of the covenant of grace, and such like: because as in an arch, one stone settleth another, so there is such a linking together of points in divinity, that one strengtheneth another. For from whence hath faith that efficacy, but because it is that which is required in the covenant, to lay hold on the free promises? And whence have the promises their strength, but from the constant nature of Jehovah; who giveth a being to his word, and is at peace with us, by the all-sufficient sacrifice of the Mediator of the new covenant? Words have their validity from the authority of the speaker. Were not faith founded on the word of an infinite God, so thoroughly appeased, the soul would sink in great temptations, whereas now even mountains vanish before a believing soul. For what can stand against Christ, who is able to subdue all to himself? Hence it is, that now we are by faith, Phil. iii. 21, safer than Adam in Paradise, because we have a promise, which he wanted. Safer it is to be as low as hell with a promise, than in paradise without it, because faith wrought by the power of God, hath what strength God hath, on whom it resteth, and therefore worketh such wonders: God honouring that grace, which honours him so much.

But howsoever the knowledge of these things serveth the argument in hand; yet it must not be expected, that he should be long in these things, which are but coincident, and should be foreknown: which I speak, because some of weaker judgment, not considering the just bounds of treatises, may expect larger handling of some things. Whereas he hath laboured especially to furnish the argument in hand, and not to load the discourse.

In the second place, it must be known, that the fruit of these things belong to such as are in Christ, in whom all promises are yea and amen, made and performed. He that by the immortal seed of the word and Spirit is born again, may claim a title to that he is born unto. These promises be as well his inheritance, as heaven itself is. For clearing of this, there be three degrees of promises; one of salvation to absolute and personal obedience; but this, by reason of weakness of the flesh, driveth us to a despair of ourselves, and so to the second promise of life by Christ. This requireth nothing but receiving by faith, which is wrought in those that are given to Christ, whilst grace is offered, the Spirit clothing the words with a hidden and strong power, and making them operative; when they are commanded to believe, their hearts are opened to believe. To persons in this estate, are made a third kind of promises, of all that is needful in this world, until all promises end in performance. Of both these promises, and the last especially, this book speaketh.

Thirdly, it must be pressed upon those that mean to profit, that they resolve to come under Christ's government, and be willing to be led by the Spirit into all revealed truth. Wisdom is easy to such as are willing; and the victory is as good as gotten, when the will is brought from thraldom to base affections, to resolve to be guided. For such a heart lieth open to God's gracious working, and the Spirit readily closeth with such a spirit, as putteth not bars of obstinacy.

Notwithstanding, we must know in the fourth place, that when we are at the best, we shall yet be in such a conflicting state, as that we shall long after that glorious liberty of the sons of God, after we have done the work God hath given us to do. For God will have a difference betwixt heaven and earth; and sharpen our desire of the coming of his kingdom, which nothing doth so much, especially in times of outward prosperity, as those tedious combats of the inner man. And yet let this raise up our spirits, that it is so far that this remainder should prejudice our interest in happiness, that thereby we are driven every day to renew our claim to the promise of pardon, and so to live by faith until this unclean issue be dried up. These sour herbs help us to relish Christ the better. Moreover, though in this life our endeavours come short of our desires, and we always allow a greater measure than we can attain unto; yet we may, by stirring up the graces begun in us, and by suing God upon those promises of his Spirit and grace, whereby he hath made himself a debtor unto us, come to that measure, whereby we shall make the profession of religion glorious, and lovely in the eyes of others, and comfortable to ourselves; and so shine far brighter than others do. Why then do we not, in the use of all sanctified means, beg of God, to make good the promises wherein he hath caused us to trust? Do we not, beside life of our bodies, desire health and strength to discharge all the offices of civil life? And why should we not much more (if the life of God be in us) labour after health and vigour of Spirit, and for that anointing of the Holy Ghost, whereby we may do and suffer all things, so as we may draw others to a liking of our ways? The truth is, Satan laboureth to keep us under belief of particular promises, and from renewing our covenant, in confidence, that God will perfect the work that he hath begun, and not repent him of his earnest. So far as thus we cherish distrust, we lie open to Satan. Strengthen faith, and strengthen all. Let us therefore at once set upon all duties required, and be in love with an holy life, above all other lives, and put ourselves upon God's mercy and truth; and we shall be able from experience, so far to justify all God's ways as that we would not be in another state for all the world. What greater encouragement can we wish, than that our corruptions shall fall more and more before the Spirit, and we shall be able to do all things through Christ that strengtheneth us?

To make these ways of God more plain unto us, this pains is taken by this man of GOD. Not to disparage the labours of other holy men (as far as I can judge), there is nothing in this kind more fully, judiciously, or savourily written, with greater evidence of a spirit persuaded of the goodness and truth of what it sets down. And though (distinct from respect to the author) the treatise deserveth much respect, yet it should gain the more acceptance, especially of those that are babes and young men in Christ, that it is written by a father of long and reverend esteem in the church; who hath begun in all these rules to others. As for our bodies, so for our souls, we may more securely rely on an old experienced physician. He commendeth it unto thee, having felt the kindly working of it upon himself. The Lord by his Spirit convey these truths into thy heart, and upon good felt hereby in thy soul, remember to desire God that he may still bring forth more fruit in his age, until he hath finished his course with credit to the gospel, and an assured hope of a blessed change.

Gray's Inn. RICHARD SIBBES.

We place along with this another 'epistle' by Sibbes, prefixed to another small book by Culverwell. The copy of this in my library, was formerly in the possession of Charles I., and has his royal arms enstamped in gold on each side. Judging from its appearance, it must have been well read. The book is entitled, 'Time Well Spent in Sacred Meditations, Divine Observations, Heavenly Exhortations;' and the 'Epistle Dedicatory' is addressed to an 'excellent Christian woman,' who seems to have been greatly beloved by Sibbes, Mrs More.* It runs as follows:—

To the right worshipful and truly religious MRS MORE.

RIGHT WORSHIPFUL AND WORTHY MRS MORE.—The church of God hath not only benefit by exact and just treatises knit together in a methodical dependency of one part from another, but likewise of sententious independent speeches, that have a general lustre of themselves, as so many flowers in a garden, or jewels in a casket, whereof every one hath a distinct worth of themselves; and this maketh them the more acceptable, that being short they are fitter for the heart to carry, as having much in a little.

This moved this reverend man of God, to spend what spare hours his sickness would afford him about thoughts in this kind. He was many years God's prisoner under the gout and stone, such diseases as will allow but little liberty to those that are arrested and tortured by them. So fruitful an expense of time in so weak and worn a body is seldom seen, scarce any came to him but went away better than they came; God gave much strength of spirit to uphold his spirit from sinking under the strength of such diseases. It were a happy thing if we that are ministers of Christ, would on all conditions and times think of our calling, that our office is not tied to one day in a week, and one hour or two in that day, but that upon all fit occasions we are to quicken ourselves and others in the way homeward, as guides to heaven. We read not of the opening of heaven but to some great purpose. So it should be with the man of God, he should not open his mouth and let any thing fall (so far as frailty and the necessary occurrences of human life will permit) but what might minister some grace to the hearers.

The reason why I made choice of you to dedicate them unto, is not that

* Mrs More. She is named in his Will.

I might discharge mine own debt unto you with another man's coin, but that I could not think of any fitter than yourself, whom this ancient minister of Christ esteemed always very much for eminency of parts and grace, and you him as a man faithful, and one that maintained his ministerial authority with good success in his place; God allotting your habitation in your younger years in that part of the country where he lived, and where you first learned to know God and yourself. In those times those parts were in regard of the air unhealthful, yet that air was so sweetened with the savoury breath of the gospel, that they were termed the holy land. Hereupon I thought meet to commend these sententious speeches by your name to others. Which though (divers of them) may seem plain, yet what they want in show they have in weight, as coming from a man very well experienced in all the ways of God. The Lord follow you with his best blessings, that you may continue still to adorn the gospel of Christ in your place!

Yours in all Christian service, R. SIBBES.

Before passing on to other 'Epistles' of a public kind, I would here introduce a letter to Ussher, of probably 1628–29, which happens to have been preserved. It reveals to us the keen zest and interest with which Sibbes observed what was transpiring, 'Petition of Right,' and the like. It falls in here fittingly as an introduction to the next 'Epistle,' as there is in it a passing notice of the last illness of the 'Master' of 'Emmanuel.'

MR R. SIBBS *to the Archbishop of Armagh.*

RIGHT REVEREND,—My duty and service premised. I am forced of the sudden in midst of straits and distractions to write unto you, your servant being presently to depart here: but I choose rather thus to express my remembrance of your grace, than to let slip so fit an opportunity. I hope I shall always carry you in my heart, and preserve that deserved respect I owe to you, who are oft presented to me as one that God hath shewed himself unto in more than ordinary measure, and set up high in the affections of the best. I know not the man living more beholden to God, in those respects, than yourself. It went for current here a while that you were dead, which caused the hearts of many to be more refreshed upon hearing the contrary. It is very ill losing of men of much meaner service in the church in these almost desperate times. Yesterday there was an agreement between the two houses about a petition of right, whereby the liberty of the subject is like to be established. Here is much joy for it, if it prove not a lightning before death. Our fears are more than our hopes yet. Doctor Preston is inclining to a consumption, and his state is thought doubtful to the physicians. The neighbour schism getteth still more strength with us. *Boni deficiunt, mali perficiunt.* I cannot now enlarge myself, your servant hastening hence. The Lord still delight to shew himself strong with you, and to shield you in the midst of all dangers, and glorify himself by you, to the great comfort of his church, and the disheartening of his enemies! I desire your grace to remember my respect to your wife, humbly thanking you both for your undeserved love.—Your Grace's in all Christian service, to be commanded, R. SIBBS.*

May 27.

* Ussher, *ante* xvi. letter ccccxxii.

We have a series of prefaces, in union with John Davenport, to various posthumous works of Dr John Preston, of whom I have had occasion to speak repeatedly in this memoir. I trust that the time is not distant when we shall have a worthy edition of his writings to place beside those of Sibbes. No books had such a wide, nay, universal audience through many generations. Edition followed upon edition, and now it is not easy to collect them all. It is mournful to think how Cambridge neglects her most illustrious sons!

The Preston epistles call for no comment beyond an explanatory word. I give them in order:—

I. The 'New Covenant or Saint's Portion.'*

Dedication.

Illustrissimis, et Honoratissimis Viris, Theophilo Comiti Lincolniensi, et Gulielmo Vice-Comiti Say et Sele, Dominis suis submississimè colendis has Johannis Prestoni, S.S. Theol. Doct., et Collegii Immanuelis Magistri Primitias Devotissimi, Tam Authoris, Dum Viveret, Quam Ipsorum, Qui Supersunt, Obsequii Testimonium, L.M.D.D.D.

RICHARDUS SIBS.
JOHANNES DAVENPORT.

To the Reader.

It had been much to have been desired (if it had so pleased the Father of spirits), that this worthy man had survived the publishing of these and other his lectures; for then, no doubt, they would have come forth more refined and digested; for, though there was very little or no mistake in taking them from his mouth, yet preaching and writing have their several graces. Things livened by the expression of the speaker, sometimes take well, which after, upon a mature review, seem either superfluous or flat. And we oft see men very able to render their conceits in writing, yet not the happiest speakers.

Yet we, considering (not so much what might have been, as) what now may be for the service of the church, thought good rather to communicate them thus, than that they should die with the author. He was a man of an exact judgment and quick apprehension, an acute reasoner, active in good, choice in his notions; one who made it his chief aim to promote the cause of Christ and the good of the church, which moved him to single out arguments answerable, on which he spent his best thoughts. He was honoured of God to be an instrument of much good, whereunto he had advantage by those eminent places he was called unto. As he had a short

* The New Covenant, or the Saint's Portion: a Treatise unfolding the All-Sufficiency of God, Man's Uprightness, and the Covenant of Grace. Delivered in fourteen sermons upon Gen. xvii. 1, 2; whereunto are adjoined four sermons upon Eccles. ix. 1, 2, 11, 12. By the late faithful and worthy minister of Jesus Christ, John Preston, Dr in Divinity, Chaplain in Ordinary to his Majesty, Master of Emmanuel College in Cambridge, and sometimes preacher of Lincoln's Inn. The fourth edition, corrected. 'He hath given a portion to them that fear him: he will ever be mindful of his covenant,' Ps. cxi. 5. London: Printed by I. D. for Nicholas Bourne, and are to be sold at the south entrance of the Royal Exchange. 1630, 4to.

race to run, so he made speed, and did much in a little time. Though he was of an higher elevation and strain of spirit than ordinary, yet, out of love to do good, he could frame his conceits so as might suit with ordinary understandings. A little before his death (as we were informed by the Right Honourable the Lord Viscount Say and Sele, in whose piety, wisdom, and fidelity he put great repose), he was desirous that we should peruse what of his was fit for public use.

We are not ignorant that it is a thing subject to censure to seem bold and witty in another man's work, and, therefore, as little is altered as may be. And we desire the reader rather to take in good part that which is intended for public good, than to catch at imperfections, considering they were but taken as they fell from him speaking. And we entreat those that have anything of his in their hands, that they would not be hasty, for private respects, to publish them, till we, whom the author put in trust, have perused them. We purpose (by God's help) that what shall be judged fit shall come forth. We send forth these sermons of God's All-Sufficiency, and Man's Uprightness, and the Covenant of Grace first, as being first prepared by him that had the copies, and because the right understanding of these points hath a chief influence into a Christian life. The Lord give a blessing answerable, and continue still to send forth such faithful labourers into his harvest!

RICHARD SIBS.
JOHN DAVENPORT.

II. The 'Breastplate of Faith and Love.'*

Dedication.

Illustrissimo, Nobilissimoque Viro, Roberto Comiti Warwicensi, Johannis Prestoni, S.T.D., et Collegii Immanuelis Q.† Magistri (cujus tutelæ, dum in vivis esset, Primogenitum suum in Disciplinam et Literis expoliendum tradidit), posthumorum tractatuum partem de natura fidei, ejusque efficacia, deque amore et operibus bonis, Devotissimi, tam authoris, dum viveret, quam ipsorum qui supersunt, obsequii testimonium. M.D.D.D.

RICHARDUS SIBS.
JOHANNES DAVENPORT.

To the Christian Reader.

CHRISTIAN READER—Innumerable are the sleights of Satan, to hinder a Christian in his course towards heaven, by exciting the corruption of his own heart to disturb him, when he is about to do any good; or by discouraging him with inward terrors, when he would solace himself with heavenly comforts; or by disheartening him under the fears of sufferings,

* The Breastplate of Faith and Love. A treatise, wherein the ground and exercise of faith and love, as they are set upon Christ their object, and as they are expressed in good works, is explained. Delivered in 18 sermons upon three several texts, by the late faithful and worthy minister of Jesus Christ, John Preston, Dr in Divinity, chaplain in ordinary to his Majesty, Master of Emmanuel College in Cambridge, and sometimes Preacher of Lincoln's Inn. The fourth edition. 'But let us who are of the day be sober, putting on the breastplate of faith and love,' 1 Thess. v. 8. 'What will it profit, my brethren, if a man say he have faith, and hath not works? Can faith save him?' James ii. 14. Imprinted at London by R. Y. for Nicholas Bourne and are to be sold at the south entrance of the Royal Exchange. 1634.

† Qu. 'quondam?'—ED.

when he should be resolute in a good cause. A type whereof were the Israelites, whose servitude was redoubled when they turned themselves to forsake Egypt. Wherefore we have much need of Christian fortitude, according to that direction, 'Watch ye, stand fast, quit yourselves like men,' 1 Cor. xvi. 13; especially since Satan, like a serpentine crocodile pursued, is by resistance put to flight.

But as in wars (which the Philistines knew well in putting their hope in Goliath) the chief strength of the soldiers lieth in their captain, so in spiritual conflicts all a Christian's strength is in Christ, and from him. For before our conversion we were of no strength; since our conversion we are not sufficient of ourselves to think a good thought. And to work out from the saints all self-confidence, God, by their falls, teacheth them 'to rejoice in the Lord Jesus, and to have no confidence in the flesh.'

Whatsoever Christ hath for us, is made ours by faith, which is the hand of the soul enriching it by receiving Christ, who is the treasure hid in the field, and with him, those unsearchable riches of grace, which are revealed and offered in the gospel; yea, it is part of our spiritual armour. That which was fabulously spoken of the race of giants is truly said of a Christian, he is born with his armour upon him; as soon as he is regenerate he is armed. It is called a breastplate, Θώραξ, 1 Thess. v. 8, because it preserves the heart; a long, large shield, Θυρεὸς of θύρα, Eph. vi. 16 (as the word signifieth), which is useful to defend the whole man from all sorts of assaults. Which part of spiritual armour, and how it is to be managed, is declared in the former part of the ensuing treatise, in ten sermons.

Now, as all rivers return into the sea whence they came, so the believing soul, having received all from Christ, returneth all to Christ. For thus the believer reasoneth, Was God's undeserved, unexpected love such to me that he spared not his only-begotten Son, but gave him to die for me? It is but equal that I should live to him, die for him, bring in my strength, time, gifts, liberty, all that I have, all that I am, in his service, to his glory. That affection, whence these resolutions arise, is called love, which so inclineth the soul that it moveth in a direct line towards that object wherein it expecteth contentment. The soul is miserably deluded in pursuing the wind, and is taking aim at a flying fowl, whilst it seeks happiness in any creature; which appears in the restlessness of those irregular agitations and endless motions of minds of ambitious, voluptuous, and covetous persons, whose frame of spirit is like the lower part of the elementary region, the seat of winds, tempests, and earthquakes, full of unquietness; whilst the believer's soul, like that part towards heaven which is always peaceable and still, enjoyeth true rest and joy. And indeed the perfection of our spirits cannot be but in union with the chief of spirits, which communicateth his goodness to the creature according to its capacity. This affection of love, as it reflecteth upon Christ, being a fruit and effect of his love to us apprehended by faith, is the subject of the second part of the following treatise, in seven sermons.

The judicious author, out of a piercing insight into the methods of the tempter, knowing upon what rocks the faith of many suffers shipwreck; that neither the weak Christian might lose the comfort of his faith through want of evidences, nor the presumptuous rest upon a fancy instead of faith, nor the adversaries be emboldened to cast upon us, by reason of this doctrine of justification by faith only, their wonted nicknames of Solifidians and Nullifidians; throughout the whole treatise, and more especially in the last sermon, he discourseth of good works as they arise from faith and love. This is the sum of the faithful and fruitful labours of this reverend, learned, and godly minister of the gospel, who, whilst he lived, was an example of the life of faith and love, and of good works, to so many as were acquainted with his equal and even walking in the ways of God, in the several turnings and occasions of his life. But it will be too much injury to the godly reader to be detained longer in the porch, We now dismiss thee to the reading of this profitable work, beseeching God to increase faith, and to perfect love in thy heart, that thou mayest be fruitful in good works.

Thine in our Lord Jesus Christ, RICHARD SIBBS.
JOHN DAVENPORT.

III. The Saint's Daily Exercise. *

To the Reader.

COURTEOUS READER,—To discourse largely of the necessity and use of this piece of spiritual armour, after so many learned and useful treatises upon this subject, may seem superfluous, especially considering that there is much spoken to this purpose, for thy satisfaction, in the ensuing treatise, wherein, besides the unfolding of the nature of this duty (which is the saint's daily exercise), and strong enforcement to it, there is an endeavour to give satisfaction in the most incident cases, want of clearing whereof is usually an hindrance to the cheerful and ready performance thereof. In all which, what hath been done by this reverend and worthy man we had rather should appear in the treatise itself, to thy indifferent judgment, than to be much in setting down our own opinion. This we doubt not of, that, by reason of the spiritual and convincing manner of handling this argument, it will win acceptance with many, especially considering that it is of that nature wherein, though much have been spoken, yet much more may be said with good relish to those that have any spiritual sense; for it is the most spiritual action, wherein we have nearer communion with God, than in any other holy performance, and whereby it pleaseth God to convey all good to us, to the performance whereof Christians find most backwardness and indisposedness, and from thence most dejection of spirit, which also in these times is most necessary, wherein, unless we fetch help from heaven this way, we see the church and cause of God like to be trampled under feet. Only remember, that we let these sermons pass forth as they were delivered by himself in public, without taking that liberty of adding or detracting, which perhaps some would have thought meet; for we thought it best that his own meaning should be expressed in his own words and manner, especially considering there is little which perhaps may seem superfluous to some, but may, by God's blessing, be useful to others. It would be a good prevention of many inconveniences in this kind, if able men would be persuaded to publish their own works in their lifetime; yet we think it a good service to the church when that defect is supplied by giving

* The Saint's Daily Exercise; a Treatise unfolding the whole Duty of Prayer. Delivered in five sermons upon 1 Thes. v. 17. By the late faithful and worthy minister of Jesus Christ, John Preston, Dr in Divinity, Chaplain in Ordinary to his Majesty, Master of Emmanuel College in Cambridge, and sometime Preacher of Lincoln's Inn. The fourth edition, corrected. 'The effectual fervent prayer of a righteous man availeth much,' James v. 16. 'If I regard iniquity in my heart, the Lord will not hear my prayer,' Ps. lxvi. 18. London: Printed by W. I. for Nicholas Bourne, and are to be sold at the south entrance of the Royal Exchange. 1630. 4to.

some life to those things, which otherwise would have died of themselves. The blessing of these labours of his we commend unto God, and the benefit of them unto thee, resting thine in our Lord Jesus Christ,

RICHARD SIBS.
JOHN DAVENPORT.

IV. The Saints' Qualification. *

Dedication.

Illustrissimo, Nobilissimo Viro, Philippo, Pembrochiæ, et Montis Gomerici Comiti, Baroni Herbert de Cardiffe et Sherland, Ordinis Garterii Equiti, Regiæ Domus Camerario, Regiæ Majestati a Secretioribus Consiliis, &c., triplicem hunc Johannis Prestoni, S.S., Theologiæ Doct. Colleg. Immanuelis Nuper Magist. et Regiæ Majest. a Sacris, Tractatum, de Humiliatione, Nova Creatura, Præparatione ad Sacram Synaxin, in Devotissimæ, Tam authoris, quam Ipsorum, Observantiæ Testimonium, L.M.D.D.D.

RICHARDUS SIBS.
JOANNES DAVENPORT.

To the Christian Reader.

The good acceptance the sermons of this worthy man have found amongst well-disposed Christians, hath made us the willinger to give way to the publishing of these, as coming from the same author. The good they may thus do prevails more for the sending of them forth than some imperfections (that usually accompany the taking of other men's speeches) may do to suppress them. Something may well be yielded to public good in things not altogether so as we wish. They are enforced upon none that shall except against them, they may either read or refuse them at their pleasure. The argument of them is such as may draw the more regard, being of matters of necessary and perpetual use.

For 'Humiliation' we never so deeply see into the grounds of it (sinfulness of nature and life); or, so far as we see, look upon it with that eye of detestation we should; and therefore a holy heart desireth still further light to be brought in, to discover whatsoever may hinder communion with God, and is glad when sin is made loathsome unto it, as being its greatest enemy, that doth more hurt than all the world besides, and the only thing that divides between our chief good and us. As this humiliation increaseth, so in the like proportion all other graces increase; for the more we are emptied of ourselves, the more we are filled with the fulness of God. The defects of this appear in the whole frame of a Christian life,

* The Saints' Qualification: or, a treatise—1, of humiliation, in ten sermons; 2, of sanctification, in nine sermons; whereunto is added a treatise of communion with Christ in the sacrament, in three sermons. Preached by the late faithful and worthy minister of Jesus Christ, John Preston, Doctor in Divinity, chaplain in ordinary to his majesty, master of Emmanuel College in Cambridge, and sometime preacher of Lincoln's Inn. The third edition, corrected. 'When men are cast down, then thou shalt say, There is lifting up: and he shall save the humble person,' Job xxii. 29. 'Cast away from you all your transgressions, whereby ye have transgressed, and make you a new heart, and a new spirit,' &c., Ezek. xviii. 31. 'He that eats my flesh and drinks my blood, dwelleth in me and I in him,' John vi. 56. London; Printed by R. B. for N. Bourne, and are to be sold by T. Nicholes at the Bible in Pope's-head Alley. 1637. 4to.

which is so far unsound as we retain anything of corrupted self, unhumbled for.

The foundation of Christianity is laid very low; and therefore the treatise of 'Humiliation' is well premised before that of the 'New Creature.' God will build upon nothing in us. We must be nothing in ourselves before we be raised up for a fit temple for God to dwell in, whose course is to pull down before he build. Old things must be out of request before all become new; and without this newness of the whole man from union with Christ, no interest in the new heavens can be hoped for, whereinto no defiled thing shall enter, as altogether unsuitable to that condition and place. Nothing is in request with God but this new creature, all things else are adjudged to the fire; and without this it had been better be no creature at all. By this we may judge of the usefulness of discourses tending this way. One thing more thou art to be advertised of (courteous reader), and that is, of the injurious dealing of such as for private gain have published what they can get, howsoever taken, without any acquainting either of those friends of the author's that resided in Cambridge (to whose care he left the publishing of those things that were delivered there) or of us, to whom he committed the publishing of what should be thought fit for public view of that which was preached in London. Hereby not only wrong is done to others, but to the deceased likewise, by mangling and misshaping the birth of his brain; and therefore once again we desire men to forbear publishing of anything until those that were entrusted have the review. And so we commit the treatise and thee to God's blessing.

RICHARD SIBS.
JOHN DAVENPORT.

In 1632, Sibbes introduced to the world the excellent folio of John Smith on 'The Creed,'* and the well-known and still vital treatise of John Ball on 'Faith.'† John Smith was 'preacher of the word at Clavering in Essex.' He succeeded Bishop Andrewes as lecturer in St Paul's Cathedral. Anthony Wood speaks of him as being skilled in the original languages, and well acquainted with the writings of the ablest divines. He died in November 1616.‡

* An Exposition of the Creed; or, an Explanation of the Articles of our Christian Faith. Delivered in many afternoon sermons, by that reverend and worthy divine, Master John Smith, late preacher of the Word at Clavering in Essex, and sometime Fellow of St John's College, in Oxford. Now published for the benefit and behoof of all good Christians, together with an exact table of all the chiefest doctrines and uses throughout the whole book. 'Uprightness hath boldness.' Heb. xi. 6, 'But without faith it is impossible to please him: for he that cometh unto God must believe that he is, and that he is a rewarder of them that diligently seek him.' At London: Imprinted by Felix Kyngston, for Robert Allot, and are to be sold at his shop, at the sign of the Black Bear, in Paul's Churchyard. 1632.

† A Treatise of Faith. Divided into Two Parts, the first shewing the Nature, the second the Life of Faith, both tending to direct the weak Christian how he may possess the whole word of God as his own, overcome temptations, better his obedience, and live comfortably in all estates. By John Ball. Hab. ii. 4, 'The just shall live by his faith.' The third edition, corrected and enlarged. London: Printed by Robert Young, for Edward Brewster, and are to be sold at his shop, at the sign of the Bible, upon Fleet Bridge. 1637. 4to.

‡ Wood's Athenæ (ed. by Bliss), ii. 188. And see Chalmers's Biog. Dict., *sub. voce*

So far as I have been able to read his folio, I must regard Sibbes's Introduction as its most valuable feature. Pearson, indeed, overshadows all such works. John Ball has been very lovingly written of by very many. Wood and Clarke, Thomas Fuller, and Richard Baxter, and Simeon Ash join in speaking 'well' of him. His books, larger and smaller, are worthy of a place beside those of Sibbes. His 'Power of Godliness' (1657), a thin folio, is marked by extraordinary acquaintance with the workings of the human heart. There are touches of weird subtlety, and one in reading can easily understand the stillness of his auditory. His treatise on 'Faith' is rich and practical.* With these few words, let us turn to the two 'epistles:'—

I. Smith on the Creed.

To the Christian Reader.

It is available, for the better entertainment of this work, to know something concerning the author, concerning the work itself, and concerning the argument; for the author, my acquaintance with him was especially towards the declining part of his years, at what time (as they speak of the sun towards setting) the light and influence which comes from worthy men is most mild and comfortable. The gifts of men then, perhaps, are not so flourishing as in their younger time, but yet more mature, and what cometh from them is better digested. In the prime of his years he was trained up in St John's College, in Oxford, being there Fellow of the House, and for piety and parts esteemed highly in the University of those that excelled in both. Afterwards he grew to that note that he was chosen to read the lecture in Paul's, succeeding therein that great, learned man, Doctor Andrewes, late Lord Bishop of Winchester, which he discharged not only to the satisfaction, but to the applause of the most judicious and learned hearers, witnessed by their frequency and attention. Not long after he was removed to a pastoral charge in Clavering, in Essex, where being fixed till his death, he shined as a star in his proper sphere.

This good man's aim was to convey himself by all manner of ways into the heart, which made him willingly heard of all sorts; for witty things only, as they are spoken to the brain, so they rest in the brain, and sink no deeper; but the heart (which vain and obnoxious men love not to be touched), that is the mark a faithful teacher aims to hit. But because the way to come to the heart is often to pass through the fancy, therefore this godly man studied by lively representations to help men's faith by the fancy. It was our Saviour Christ's manner of teaching to express heavenly things in an earthly manner; and it was the study of the wise man, Solomon, becoming a preacher, to find out pleasant words, or words of delight, Eccles. xii. 10. But when all pains are taken by the man of God, people will relish what is spoken according as their taste is. It falleth out here as it doth in a garden, wherein some walk for present delight, some carry flowers away with them to refresh them for a time; some, as bees, gather honey, which they feed on long afterwards; some, spider-like, come to suck that which may feed that malignant and venomous disposition that they bring with them. There cannot be a better character of a man than

* Consult Brook, 'Lives of the Puritans,' ii. 440, *seq.*

to observe what he relisheth most in hearing; for as men are, so they taste, so they judge, so they speak. Ezekiel, besides prophetical gifts fit for so high a calling, had no doubt a delightful manner of expression of himself, whereupon the wickeder sort of Jews, engaged in sinful courses, came to hear him but as a musician to please their ears, neglecting the authority of his person and the weight of his message, Ezek. xxxiii. 32. It is no wonder, therefore, if in these days people stick in the bark and neglect the pith; though sometimes it falleth out with some, as with Augustine hearing Ambrose, whilst they bite at the bait of some pleasing notions, they are, at the same time, catched with the Spirit's hook.

He was skilful in the original languages, and thereupon an excellent textman, well read in writers that were of note in the several ages of the church, which made him a well furnished and able divine. His judgment was clear and his conscience tender, and, which helped him most, he brought to the great work of the ministry an holy and gracious heart, which raised and carried him to aims above himself and the world. In his conversing he was modest, fruitful, wise, and winning; in his expressions witty and graceful, insomuch that he hath left a fresh and sweet remembrance of them to this day. Towards his end he grew more spiritual, setting light by all things here below, and only waited (as his expression was) for the coming of the Comforter; at length, his work being finished, breathing out his life with that wish of the spouse, 'Yea, come, Lord Jesus,' Rev. xxii. 20. Thus much I thought not unfit to be made known of the man.

Now, for the work itself, it must be considered by the learned reader that these things were spoken, though to a people high-raised in knowledge, and more refined than ordinary by his teaching, yet to the people, not with a purpose that they should come to the view and censure of the learned. But though they were delivered to the people, yet are they not so popular, but (if my love to the man and the work deceive me not) they will leave the best reader either more learned or more holy, or both. It must, therefore, be remembered, for the more favourable acceptation of this work, that these sermons were taken by one of his parish, a man, though pious and of good parts, yet not skilful in the learned languages; and therefore it must needs be that many apt and acute sentences of the fathers, by which this learned man did use to beautify and strengthen the points he delivered, are fallen to the ground and lost, for lack of skill to take up. But howsoever much of the spirits be lost, yet here you have the corpse and bulk of the discourse, and not without some life and vigour, wherein this is peculiar in his manner of handling, that he hath chosen fit texts of Scripture to ground his exposition of every article upon.

Now, for the argument itself, the Creed, I think it fit to premise something, because it hath been omitted by the author, or at least not gathered with the rest. The Creed is of middle authority, between divine and human, and called the Apostles' Creed, not only for consanguinity with the apostles' doctrine, but because it is taken out of the apostles' writings, and therefore of greatest authority next to the Scriptures. It is nothing else but a summary comprehension of the counsel and work of God concerning our supernatural condition here and hereafter. The doctrine of salvation is spread through the Scriptures as spirits in the arteries and blood in the veins, as the soul in the body. And here, for easier carriage, the most necessary points are gathered together, as so many pearls or precious stones, that we might have a ready use of them upon all occasions, being, as it were, a little Bible or Testament that Christians of all ranks, as suited for all conditions, may bear about with them everywhere without any trouble. In every article there is both a shallow and a depth, milk for babes and meat for strong men. Though there be no growth in regard of fundamental principles (which have been alike in all ages of the church), yet there hath and will be a proficiency in regard of conclusions drawn out of those principles. The necessities of every Christian, and the springing up of unsound opinions in the church, will continually enforce diligence and care in the further explication and application of these fundamental truths.

It will not, therefore, be amiss to set down a few directions for the more clear understanding of the Creed, and for the better making use of it. And first, for the understanding of it, it hath the name of Creed or Belief, from the act exercised about it, to shew that it doth not only contain doctrine to be believed, but that that doctrine will do us no good unless, by mingling it with our faith, we make it our belief. Therefore, both the act and the object are implied in one word, Belief. Secondly: From the execution in creation and incarnation we must arise to God's decree; nothing done in time which was not decreed before all times, 'Known unto the Lord are all his works from the beginning of the world,' Acts xv. 18. Thirdly: We must arise from one principal benefit to all that follow and accompany it, as in forgiveness of sins, follow righteousness, peace, and joy, the spirit of sanctification, Christian liberty, &c. Though the articles be nakedly pro pounded, yet are we to believe all the fruits and privileges. So to God's creating of heaven and earth we must join his providence in upholding and ruling all things in both. Fourthly: In the consequent we are to understand all that went before by way of cause or preparation, as in the crucifying of Christ, his preceding agony and the cause of it, our sins, and the love of God and Christ in those sufferings, &c. Fifthly: Though we are to believe circumstances as well as the thing itself, yet not with the same necessity of faith, as it is more necessary to believe that Christ was crucified than that it was under Pontius Pilate; though when any circumstance is revealed we ought to believe it, and to have a preparation of mind to believe whatsoever shall be revealed. Yet in the main points this preparation of mind is not sufficient, but there must be a present and an expressed faith. We must know that, as in the law, he that breaketh one commandment breaketh all, because all come from the same authority; so, in the grounds of faith, he that denies one in the true sense of it denies all, for both law and faith are copulatives. The singling out of anything is contrary to the obedience of faith. *Fides non eligit objectum.*

For particular and daily use, we must know, first, that every article requires a particular faith, not only in regard of the person believing, but likewise in regard of the application of the article believed; or else the devil might say the creed, for he believes there is a Creator, and that there is a remission of sins, &c.; but because he hath no share in it, it enrageth him the more. Our adversaries are great enemies to particular faith, and think we coin a thirteenth article when we enforce particular assurance, because, say they, particular men are not named in the Scripture, and what is not in Scripture cannot be a matter of faith. But there is a double faith, a faith which is the doctrine we do believe, and faith which is the grace whereby we believe; and this faith is a matter of experience wrought in our hearts by the Spirit of God. It is sufficient that that faith which we do believe is contained in the Scriptures. Now whereas they object that we make it a thirteenth article, their fourteenth apostle adds to these twelve many more articles of faith, which he enforceth to be believed, with the same necessity of faith as these twelve; neither hath he only entered upon Christ's prerogative in minting new articles of faith, but likewise they have usurped over all Christian churches by adding Roman to the catholic church in the creed. A bold imposture!

But for special faith, the main office of the Holy Spirit is in opening general truths, to reveal our particular interest in those truths, and to breed special faith whereby we make them our own, because the Spirit of God reveals the mind of God to every particular Christian, 1 Cor. ii. 11, 12; for as the things believed are truths above nature, so the grace of faith whereby we believe is a grace above nature, created as a supernatural eye in the soul, to see supernatural truths.

Secondly, Where sacred truths are truly apprehended, there the Spirit works an impression in the soul suitable to the things believed; every article hath a power in it which the Spirit doth imprint upon the soul. The belief of God to be the Father Almighty breeds an impression of dependence, reverence, and comfort. The belief and knowledge of Christ crucified is a crucifying knowledge. The true knowledge and faith in Christ rising, is a raising knowledge. The knowledge of the abasement of Christ is an abasing knowledge; because faith sees itself one with Christ in both states. We cannot truly believe what Christ hath wrought for us, but at the same time the Spirit of Christ worketh something in us.

Thirdly, It is convenient for the giving of due honour to every person to consider of the work appropriated to every one: all come from the Father; all are exactly performed by the Son in our nature for the redemption of those that the Father hath given him. The gathering out of the world of that blessed society (which we call the church) into an holy communion, and the sanctifying of it, and sealing unto it all the privileges believed, as forgiveness of sins, resurrection of the body, and life everlasting, &c., proceed from the Holy Ghost.

Fourthly, It has pleased the great God to enter into a treaty and covenant of agreement with us his poor creatures, the articles of which agreement are here comprised. God, for his part, undertakes to convey all that concerns our happiness, upon our receiving of them, by believing on him. Every one in particular that recites these articles from a spirit of faith makes good this condition, and this is that answer of a good conscience, which Peter speaks of, 1 Pet. iii, whereby being demanded what our faith is, every one in particular answers to every article, I believe; I not only understand and conceive it, but assent unto it in my judgment as true, and consent to it in my will as good, and build my comfort upon it as good to me: this act of belief carries the whole soul with it.

Fifthly, Though it is we that answer, yet the power by which we answer is no less than that whereby God created the world and raised Christ from the dead. The answer is ours, but the power and strength is God's, whereby we answer, who performs both his part and ours too in the covenant. It is a higher matter to believe than the common sort think it. For this answer of faith to these truths, as it is caused by the power of God's Spirit, so is it powerful to answer all temptations of Satan, all seducements of the world, all terrors of conscience from the wrath of God and the curse of the law; it setteth the soul as upon a rock above all.

Sixthly, These articles are a touchstone at hand to try all opinions by, for crooked things are discerned by bringing them to the rule. What directly, or by immediate and mere consequence, opposeth these, is to be rejected as contrary to the platform of wholesome doctrine. That one monster of opinions, of the bread into the body of Christ by transubstantiation, overthrows at once four articles of the Creed—the incarnation of Christ, ascension, sitting at the right hand of God, and coming to judgment; for if Christ's body be so often made of a piece of bread, being in so many places at once here upon earth, how can all these articles be true?

Again, seventhly, These grounds of faith have likewise a special influence in direction and encouragement unto all Christian duties. A holy life is but the infusion of holy truths. Augustine saith well, *Non bene vivitur, ubi bene de Deo non creditur:* men of an ill belief, cannot be of a good life; whereupon the apostles' method is, to build their exhortations to Christian duties upon the grounds of Christian faith. But we must remember, that as faith yields a good life and conscience, so a conscience is the vessel to preserve the doctrine of faith, else a shipwreck of faith will follow. If there be a delighting in unrighteousness, there will not be a love of the truth; and if we love not the truth, then there will be a preparedness to believe any lie, and that by God's just judgment, 2 Thes. ii. 12.

Eighthly. As these fundamental truths yield strength to the whole frame of a Christian life, so they are so many springs and wells of consolation for God's people to draw from; whereupon that good Prince George Anhalt (who in Luther's time became a preacher of the gospel), intending to comfort his brother Prince John, raiseth his comfort from the last three articles —remission of sins, resurrection of the body, and life everlasting; which, as they have their strength from the former articles, are able to raise any drooping spirit, and therefore in the greatest agonies it is the readiest way to suck comfort from these benefits. But I omit other things, intending only to say something by way of preface. And thus, good reader, I commend this work unto thee, and both it and thee to God's blessing.

Thine in the Lord, R. SIBBES.

II. Ball on 'Faith.'

The Preface to the Reader.

Glorious things are spoken of the grace of graces (faith) in the Scriptures, God setting himself to honour that grace that yields up all the honour unto him in Christ: who indeed is the life of our life, and the soul of our soul. Faith only as the bond of union bringeth Christ and the soul together, and is as an artery that conveys the spirit from him as the heart, and as the sinews which convey the spirit to move all duty from him as head, whence St Paul maketh Christ's living in us, and our living by faith all one, Gal. ii. 20. Now that which giveth boldness and liberty to faith, is not only God's assignment of this office to it in the covenant of grace to come unto Christ, and unto him in Christ, to receive grace, but likewise the gracious promises whereby the great God hath engaged himself as a debtor to his poor creature, for all things needful to life and godliness, until that blessed time when we shall be put into a full possession of all things we have now only in promise, when faith shall end in fruition, and promises in performances.

Faith first looks to this word of promise, and in the promise to Christ, in whom and for whom they are yea and amen, both made and performed. And in Christ it eyeth God in whom it last resteth, as its proper centre and foundation; otherwise how should we weak sinful creatures dare to have any intercourse with God that dwelleth in that light that none can attain unto, if he had not come forth and discovered his good pleasure in Christ the substantial Word, and in the word inspired by the Holy Ghost for the good of those whom God meant for to make heirs of salvation? Now these promises whereon all our present comfort and future hope dependeth lie hid in the Scriptures, as veins of gold and silver in the bowels of the earth, and had need be laid open, that God's people may know what upon good grounds to lay claim unto. Those, therefore, that search these mines to bring to light these treasures, deserve well of God's church. We commend (and not without cause) the witty industry of those that from springs remote bring rivers to cities, and by pipes from these rivers derive water to every man's house for all domestical services; much more should we esteem of the religious pains of men that brings these waters of life home for every man's particular use, in all the passages and turnings of this life.

In which regard, I do not doubt, but the pains of this godly, painful, and learned man will find good entertainment of all children of the promises that hope to inherit them, who hath with great pains, and with good evidence of spiritual understanding, endeavoured to clear most matters concerning faith, and likewise discovered the variety and use of the promises, with teaching Christians how to improve their riches in Christ here spread before them, how to use the shield of faith and the sword of the Spirit upon all occasions, that so they might not only be believing but skilful Christians, knowing how to manage and make the best advantage of their faith and the word of faith. Which if they could do, there would another manner of power and beauty shine in their lives than doth. He is a man that hath formerly deserved well of the church, but in more special manner fitted for a treatise of this nature, as having been put to it to know by experience what it is to live by faith, having in sight for matters of this life very little whereupon to depend. Those that are driven to exercise their faith cannot but find God faithful, as never failing those that trust in him, they see more of God than others do.

If it be objected that others of late time have digged in the same mine and laboured in the same field, and to good purpose and success, I answer, it is true, the more this age is bound to God that directs the spirits of men to so useful, so necessary, an argument, seeing without faith we have no communion with the fountain of life, nothing in this world that can yield settled comfort to ground the soul upon, seeing without it the fairest carriage is but empty and dead morality, neither finding acceptance with God nor yielding comfort to us in our greatest extremities, and by it God himself and Christ, with all that he hath done, suffered, conquered, becometh ours and for our use. Besides, none that I know have written in our language so largely of this argument; and such is the extent and spiritualness of this heavenly point, that many men and of the greatest graces and parts, may with great benefit to the church dive and dig still into this mystery. Neither let any except against the multitude of quotations of Scriptures; they are brought under their proper head, and set in their proper place, and the matter itself is cut out into variety of parts. Store (as we used to speak) is no sore, we count it a delight to take out of a full heap; the more light the conviction is the stronger; what suits not at one time will suit our spirits and occasions at another, and what taketh not with one may take with another. But the full and well handling of matters in this treatise carries such satisfaction with it, that it frees me from necessity of further discourse, and mine own present weakness of body taketh me off. Only I was willing to yield that testimony to the fruitful pains of a faithful labourer in God's vineyard, and I judge it deserved. Receive it, therefore, Christian reader, with thanks to God that stirreth up such helpers of that faith by which we live, stand, conquer, and in which we must die, if we look to receive the end of our faith, the salvation of our souls.

RICHARD SIBBES.

The last epistle known to me is prefixed to a very striking and suggestive book, to wit, Richard Capel's 'Treatise of Temptations.'* Nearly related to the noble family of Capel, he was yet a staunch Puritan and 'Nonconformist:' his son Daniel having also been one of the 'ejected' of 1662. He was very much esteemed by Sibbes, who left to him a memorial 'ring' in his will.† The book itself is well fitted to comfort the despondent, and may be placed beside Brook's 'Precious Remedies for Satan's Devices,' which it somewhat resembles, though wanting in the wonderful learning and ingenuity of illustration of that most learned and vivid of the later Puritans. The 'epistle' follows:—

To the Christian Reader.

After the angels left their own standing, they envied ours, and out of envy became both by office and practice tempters, that they might draw man from that happy communion with God, unto that cursed condition with themselves. And success in this trade hath made them both skilful and diligent, especially now, their time being but short. And if neither the first or second Adam could be free from their impudent assaults, who then may look for exemption? The best must most of all look to be set upon as having most of Christ in them, whom Satan hates most, and as hoping and disheartening of them, to foil others, as great trees fall not alone; no age or rank of Christians can be free. Beginners he labours to discourage; those that have made some progress, he raiseth storms against; those that more perfect he labours to undermine by spiritual pride; and above all other times, he is most busy when we are weakest, then he doubles and multiplies his forces, when he looks either to have all, or lose all. His course is either to tempt to sin or for sin. To sin, by presenting some seeming good to draw us from the true good, to seek some excellency besides God in the creature, and to this end he labours in the first place to shake our faith in the word; thus he dealt with Adam, and thus he dealeth with all his posterity. And besides immediate suggestions, he cometh unto us, by our dearest friends, as unto Christ by Peter; so many tempters, so many devils in that ill office, though neither they or we are oft aware of it; the

* Tentations: their nature, danger, cure. By Richard Capel, sometime Fellow of Magdalen College in Oxford. The sixth edition. The fourth part left enlarged by the author, and now there is added his remains to the work of Tentations. To which thou hast prefixed an abridgment of the author's life, by Valentine Marshall, of Elmore, in Gloucestershire. 1 Cor. x. 13, There hath no tentation taken you, but such as is common to man: but God is faithful, who will not suffer you to be tempted above that you are able; but will with the tentation also make a way to escape, that ye may be able to bear it. London: Printed by Tho. Ratcliffe, for John Bartlet, long since living in the Goldsmith's Row in Cheapside, at the Gilt Cup; since at St Austine's Gate; now in the New buildings on the south side of Paul's near St Austine's Gate, at the sign of the Gilt Cup, and at the Gilt Cup in Westminster Hall, over against the Upper Bench. 1659.

† Consult Brook, *supra*, iii. 289 *seq*.

nearest friend of all our own flesh, is the most dangerous traitor, and therefore most dangerous because most near, more near to us than the devil himself, with which, if he had no intelligence, all his plots would come to nothing; this holding correspondence with him, layeth us open to all danger; it is this inward bosom enemy that doth us most mischief. When Phocas (like another Zimry) had killed his master, Mauricius the emperor, he laboured like Cain, to secure himself with building high walls, after which he heard a voice telling him, that though he built his walls never so high, yet sin within the walls would undermine all. It is true of every particular man, that if there were no tempter without, he would be a tempter to himself; it is this lust within us that hath brought us an ill report upon the creature. This is that which makes blessings to be snares unto us; all the corruption which is in the world is by lust, which lieth in our bosom, 2 Pet. i. 4, and as Ahithophel, or Judas, by familiarity betrayeth us, yea, oftentimes in our best affections, and actions, nature will mingle without * zeal, and privy pride will creep in, and taint our best performances with some corrupt aim. Hence it is, that our life is a continual combat. A Christian, so soon as new born, is born a soldier, and so continueth until his crown be put upon him; in the mean time our comfort is, that ere long, we shall be out of the reach of all tentation; 'the God of peace will tread down Satan under our feet,' Rom. xvi. 20. A carnal man's life is nothing but a strengthening and feeding of his enemy, a fighting for that which fighteth against his soul. Since Satan hath cast this seed of the serpent into our souls, there is no sin so prodigious, but some seed of it lurketh in our nature; it should humble us to hear what sins are forbidden by Moses, which if the Holy Ghost had not mentioned, we might have been ashamed to hear of, they are so dishonourable to our nature; the very hearing of the monstrous outrages committed by men, given up of God, as it yields matter of thanks to God for preservation of us, so of humility, to see our common nature so abused, and so abased by sin and Satan. Nay, so catching is our nature of sin, that the mention of it, instead of stirring hatred of it, often kindles fancy to a liking of it; the discovery of devilish policies and stratagems of wit, though in some respects to good purpose, yet hath no better effect in some, than to fashion their wits to the like false practices; and the innocency of many ariseth not from the love of that which is good, but from not knowing of that which is evil.

And in nothing the sinfulness of sin appears more than in this, that it hindereth all it can, the knowledge of itself, and if it once be known, it studieth extenuation, and translation upon others; sin and shifting came into the world together; in St James his time, it seems that there were some that were not afraid to father their temptations to sin, upon him that hateth it most (God himself), whereas God is only said to try, not to tempt. Our adversaries are not far from imputing this to God, who maintain concupiscence, the mother of all abominations, to be a condition of nature as first created, only kept in by the bridle of original righteousness, that from hence, they might the better maintain those proud opinions of perfect fulfilling the law, and meriting thereby. This moved St James to set down the true descent and pedigree of sin; we ourselves are both the tempters and the tempted; as tempted we might deserve some pity, if as tempters we deserve not blame. In us there is both fire and matter for fire to take hold on. Satan needs but to blow, and oftentimes not that neither; for many, if concupiscence stir not up them, they will stir up concupiscence. So long

* Qu. 'with our?'—Ed.

as the soul keeps close to God and his truth, it is safe; so long as our way lieth above, we are free from the snares below. All the danger first riseth from letting our hearts loose from God by infidelity, for then presently our heart is drawn away by some seeming good, whereby we seek a severed excellency and contentment out of God, in whom it is only to be had. After we have once forsaken God, God forsakes us, leaving us in some degree to ourselves, the worst guides that can be; and thereupon, Satan joins forces with us, setting upon us as a friend, under our own colours; he cannot but miscarry that hath a pirate for his guide. This God suffereth to make us better known to ourselves; for by this means, corruption that lay hid before, is drawn out, and the deceitfulness of sin the better known, and so we are put upon the daily practice of repentance and mortification, and driven to fly under the wings of Jesus Christ. Were it not for temptations, we should be concealed from ourselves; our graces as unexercised, would not be so bright, the power of God should not appear; so in our weakness, we would not be so pitiful and tender towards others, nor so jealous over our own hearts, nor so skilful of Satan's method and enterprises, we should not see such a necessity of standing always upon our guard; but though, by the overruling power of God, they have this good issue, yet that which is ill of itself, is not to be ventured on, for the good that cometh by accident. The chief thing wherein one Christian differs from another is watchfulness, which though it require most labour, yet it bringeth most safety; and the best is no farther safe, than watchful, and not only against sins, but tentations, which are the seeds of sin, and occasions which let in tentations. The best, by rash adventures upon occasion, have been led into temptations, and by temptation into the sin itself; whence sin and temptation come both under the same name, to shew us that we can be no further secure from sin, than we be careful to shun temptations. And in this every one should labour so well to understand themselves, as to know what they find a temptation to them. That may be a temptation to one which is not to another; Abraham might look upon the smoke of Sodom, though Lot might not; because that sight would work more upon Lot's heart than Abraham's. In these cases a wise Christian better knows what to do with himself than any can prescribe him. And because God hath our hearts in his hand, and can either suspend or give way to temptations, it should move us especially to take heed of those sins, whereby, grieving the good Spirit of God, we give him cause to leave us to our own spirits; but that he may rather stir up contrary gracious lustings in us, as a contrary principle. There is nothing of greater force to make us out of godly jealousy 'to fear always.' Thus daily 'working out our salvation,' that God may delight to go along with us, and be our shield, and not to leave us naked in the hands of Satan, but second his first grace with a further degree, as temptations shall increase. It is he that either removeth occasions, or shutteth our hearts against them, and giveth strength to prevail over them; which gracious promise you cannot be too thankful for. It is a great mercy when temptations are not above the supply of strength against them. This care only taketh up the heart of those who, having the life of Christ begun in them, and his nature stamped upon them, have felt how sweet communion and acquaintance with God in Christ, and how comfortable the daily walking with God, is; these are weary of anything that may draw away their hearts from God, and hinder their peace. And therefore they hate temptations to sin as sin itself, and sin as hell itself, and hell most of all, as being a state of eternal separation from all comfortable fellowship with God. A man that is a stranger from the life of God, cannot resist temptation to sin, as it is a sin, because he never knew the beauty of holiness; but from the beauty of a civil life, he may resist temptations to such times * as may weaken respect, and from love of his own quiet, may abstain from those sins that will affright conscience. And the cause why civil men fear the less disturbance from temptations is, because they are wholly under the power of temptation, till God awaken their heart. What danger they see not, they feel not, the strong man holds his possession in them, and is too wise, by rousing them out of their sleep to give them occasion of thoughts of escape. None more under the danger of temptation, than they that discern it not; they are Satan's stales, 'taken by him at his pleasure,' whom Satan useth to draw others into the same snare. Therefore Satan troubleth not them, nor himself about them; but the true Christian fears a temptation in everything. His chief care is, that in what condition soever he be, it prove not a temptation to him. Afflictions, indeed, are more ordinarily called temptations, than prosperity, because Satan by them breedeth an impression of sorrow and fear, which affections have an especial working upon us in the course of our lives, making us often to forsake God, and desert his cause. Yet snares are laid in everything we deal with, which none can avoid but those that see them. None see, but those whose eyes God opens; and God useth the ministry of his servants for this end, to open the eyes of men, to discover the net, and then, as the wise man saith, 'In vain is the net spread before the sight of any bird.' *Domine, quis evadet laqueos istos multos nisi videat istos? Et quis videbit istos, nisi quem illuminaveris lumine tuo? ipse enim pater tenebrarum laqueos suos abscondit. Soliloq. cap.* 16. Which goeth under Augustine's name. Tom. 9.

This moved this godly minister, my Christian friend, to take pains in this useful argument, as appeareth in this treatise, which is written by him in a clear, quick, and familiar style; and for the matter and manner of handling, solid, judicious, and scholar-like; and which may commend it the more, it is written by one that, besides faithfulness and fruitfulness in his ministry, hath been a good proficient in the school of temptation himself, and therefore the fitter, as a skilful watchman, to give warning and aim to others; for there be spiritual exercises of ministers more for others than for themselves. If by this he shall attain, in some measure, what he intended, God shall have the glory, thou the benefit, and he the encouragement to make public some other labours.—Farewell in the Lord,

RICHARD SIBBES.

These 'epistles' and 'prefaces' shew the cordial relations sustained by Sibbes towards his fellow-divines and contemporaries; and down to a late period, the booksellers found it a profitable advertisement to say of a book, 'Recommended by Dr Sibbes.' †

* Qu. 'sins?'—ED.

† 'Recommended by Dr Sibbes.' The various books of Preston are usually thus advertised; and those of Burroughs, Hooker, and Cotton as 'approved by Dr Sibbes.' Eglesfield and Cole in their book-lists supply various examples.

CHAPTER X.

SIBBES VICAR OF TRINITY, CAMBRIDGE—PEACE-MAKER.

Presentation to Vicarage of Trinity by the King—Another relaxation of 'order' of Gray's Inn—Lord Keeper Williams—'Tender Conscience'—'Consolatory Letter' —Thomas Goodwin—'Summer visits'—Earls of Manchester and Warwick—Truro and Say and Seal—Brooks and Veres—Thurston—'Mother and brethren.'

From the manner in which Sibbes escaped the practical effects of the 'High Commission' and 'Star-Chamber' decisions, in striking contrast with Davenport and Hooker, and others of the fugitives to Holland and New England, and from the fearless way in which he continued to preach the same sentiments, it is evident that he must have personally commanded the weightiest regard, and secured influence that could not be disregarded. In 1627, he passed D.D. In 1633 (shortly after the overthrow of the 'Feoffees' scheme, which makes it the more memorable), he was presented by the king, Charles I., on its resignation by Thomas Goodwin, who scarcely held it a year,* to 'the vicarage of the holy and undivided Trinity, in the town of Cambridge.' We have the fact in the 'Fœdera:—

'Ricardus Sibbes, clericus, in Sacra Theologia Professor, habet consimiles Literas Patentes de presentatione ad Vicariam sanctæ et individuæ Trinitatis in Villa Cantabrigiæ, Diocesis Eliensis, per resignationem ultimi Incumbentis ibidem jam vacantem, et ad nostram presentationem pleno jure spectantem; et deriguntur hæ Literæ Reverendo in Christo Patri Domino Francisco Eliensi Episcopo. Teste Rege apud Westmonasterium, vicesimo primo die Novembris 1633.' †

This 'presentation' speaks much for Sibbes; for at this date Laud was filling every place with men of his own kind. We have not the means of determining by what influence this appointment was obtained. One tells us Goodwin resigned 'in favour of Sibbes,' but that could scarcely be, inasmuch as he at the same time resigned all his offices and honours in the University. Besides, the difficulty is only removed back a stage; how did it come about that a Puritan resigned and another stepped into his place? It may be that it was a tacit recompence for the former injustice of 'outing' him from his lectureship of Trinity and his fellowship; but it is more probable that on the 'Feoffees'' decision, the powerful friends of the preacher at Gray's Inn interfered in such a way as to let the primate understand that they, at any rate, were not to be trifled with; and that then he secured, or at least did not hinder, this 'presentation.'

But there is the further difficulty of the 'order' of Gray's Inn, that their preacher was not only to be continually resident, but

* Rymer's Fœdera, xix., 440, No. 81, ed. 1732.

† *Ibid.*, xix., 536.

likewise to have no other ecclesiastical preferment. As Sibbes actually accepted and acted as vicar, the 'order' must once more have been relaxed in his favour. Indeed, I suspect that 'order' was originally passed for a personal object and from a personal reason. The immediate predecessor of Sibbes was a Mr Fenton,—in all likelihood, though no Christian name appears in the 'Order-Books' of Gray's Inn, the same with Roger Fenton, D.D., who was a great pluralist, and who died 16th January 1615–16. He held the prebend, rectory, and vicarage of St Pancras, and the rectory of St Stephen's, Walbrook, and also the vicarage of Chigwell, Essex, till his death. Probably he neglected his duties as preacher at Gray's Inn. Hence the check put upon his successor.* For one so faithful in the discharge of his office, and who was regarded by all as a personal friend, there would be no great difficulty in making arrangements, in order to his accepting the 'presentation,' and still continuing the honoured preacher of Gray's Inn.

It is greatly to be lamented that the most diligent and persistent research has failed to add any memorials to the fact of his entrance on the vicarage of Trinity. Though he must have been non-resident, he would have many opportunities to officiate during 'vacation' time at the Inn.

This is the last public honour recorded as having been conferred upon Sibbes. What remains to be told partakes of the privacy of his daily life.

One little fact, half-casually recorded in that extraordinary folio, 'Scrinia Reserata: a Memorial offer'd to the great deservings of John Williams, D.D., who some time held the place of Lord Keeper of the Great Seal of England, &c., &c., &c., by John Hacket, late Lord Bishop of Litchfield and Coventry,' 1693—a book *sui generis*, and than which none gives profounder insight into the 'form and pressure of the age,'—brings out a very beautiful side of Sibbes's character, and dates to us, if I err not, one of the most interesting, biographically, of his minor writings. Vindicating Williams—a vindication which, the more successful it is, the more it damages the strangely contradictory character of the Lord Keeper—from the rumour of favouring Puritans, Hacket thus introduces Sibbes :—

'Another rank for whose sake the Lord Keeper suffer'd, were scarce an handful, not above three or four in all the wide Bishoprick of Lincoln, who did not oppose, but by an ill education seldom used the appointed ceremonies. Of whom when he was certified by his commissaries and officials.

* 'Check put upon his successor.' For these facts and the inference from them I owe thanks to Dr Hessey

he sent for them, and confer'd with them with much meekness, sometimes remitted them to argue with his chaplain. If all this stirred them not, *he commended them to his old collegiate Dr Sibbes*, or Dr Gouch (Gouge), *who knew the scruples of these men's hearts*, and how to bring them about, the best of any about the city of London.'*

There is such a fascination, spite of all his errors, or it may be crimes, about the hot-blooded Welshman, so stormy and impulsive, so wise and yet so foolish, that one is glad to find, that even when he was 'Lord Keeper,' and surrounded by very different men, he forgot neither him who was once his humble fellow-student of St John's, nor the staunch puritan of 'Blackfryers,' William Gouge, also a contemporary at Cambridge, but—

'They had been friends, when friendship is
A passion and a blessedness;
And in a tender sacrament
Unto the house of God they went,
And plighted love,—caressing
The same dear cup of blessing.

'They had been friends in youth, most dear;
In studious night, and mirthful cheer,
And high discourse, and large debate,
Unmixed by bitterness or hate—
Their fellowship, I ween,
A pleasant thing had been.'

It is specially pleasing to know what was the occasion of again associating the students of earlier years—to wit, tender dealing with tender consciences. I like to place that over against his after humiliating repudiation of all Puritans, extorted from him while under the shadow of a charge of treason, and in a letter to LAUD.† He was truthful in his favour; untruthful in his disfavour. The fact also dates, as I have intimated, one of the minor writings of Sibbes, which illustrates how he would discharge the office assigned to him. It is entitled:—

A CONSOLATORY LETTER To an afflicted Conscience: full of pious admonitions and Divine Instructions. Written by that famous Divine, Doctor SIBBS: and now published for the common good and edification of the Church. Ecclesiastes vi. 18, *Be not thou just overmuch, neither make thy selfe overwise; wherefore shouldest thou be desolate.*

[Woodcut portrait. Ætat: Suæ 58.] London, Printed for *Francis Coules*. 1641.‡

* i. 95. 'Scrinia' seems to have been a favourite title. The historical student will recall also 'Scrinia Ceciliana.'

† Works of Laud. vi. pp. 312–314. Sept. 9. 1633.

‡ For a copy of this excessively rare 'Letter,' published in a thin 4to, pp. 6, I am indebted to the kindness of Joshua Wilson, Esq., Nevill Park, Tunbridge Wells, who has devoted much time to good purpose in investigating the history, and biography, and bibliography of Puritanism. His 'Historical Inquiry concerning the Principles, &c., of English Presbyterians' (1835) has not gathered all its renown yet.

I introduce this 'Letter' here, retaining its ortnography:—

Deare Sir,

I understand by your Letter, that you have many and great tryals; some externall and bodily, some internall and spirituall: as the deprivall of inward comfort, the buffetings (and that in more then ordinary manner), of your soule, with Satans temptations: and (which makes all those inward and outward, the more heavy and insupportable) that you have wanted Christian society with the Saints of God, to whom you might make knowne your griefes, and by whom you might receive comfort from the Lord, and incouragement in your Christian course.

Now that which I earnestly desire in your behalfe, and hope likewise you doe in your owne, is that you may draw nearer to God, and be more conformable to his command by these afflictions; for if our afflictions be not sanctified, that is, if we make not an holy use of them by purging out the old leaven of our ingenerate corruptions, they are but judgments to us, and makes way for greater plagues: Ioh v. 14. And therefore the chiefe end and ayme of God in all the afflictions which he sends to his children in love, is, that they may be partakers of his holinesse, and so their afflictions may conduce to their spirituall advantage and profit, Heb. xii. 10. The Lord aymes not at himselfe in any calamities he layes on us, (for God is so infinitely all-sufficient, that we can adde nothing to him by all our doings or sufferings) but his maine ayme is at our Melioration and Sanctification in and by them. And therefore our duty in every affliction and pressure, is thus to thinke with our selves: How shall we carry and behave our selves under this crosse, that our soules may reap profit by it? This (in one word) is done by our returning and drawing nearer to the Lord, as his holy Apostle exhorts us, Iames iv. 8. This in all calamities the Lord hath a speciall eye unto, and is exceeding wroth if he finde it not.

The Prophet declares *That his anger was not turned from Israel, because they turned not to him that smote them*, Isa. i. 4, 5. Now it is impossible that a man should draw nigh to God, and turne to him, if he turne not from his evill wayes: for in every conversion there is *Terminus à quo*, something to be turned from, as well as *Terminus ad quod*, something to be turned to.

Now, that we must turn to, is God; and that we must turne from, is sinne; as being diametrally opposite to God, and that which separates betweene God and us.

To this purpose we must search and try our hearts and wayes, and see what sinnes there be that keepe us from God, and separate us from his gracious favour: and chiefly we must weed out our speciall bosom-sins. This the ancient Church of God counsels each other to doe in the time of their anguish and affliction, Lam. iii. 39, 40, *Let us search and try our wayes, and turne againe to the Lord:* for though sinne make not a finall divorce betwixt God and his chosen people, yet it may make a dangerous rupture by taking away sense of comfort, and suspending the sweet influence of his favour, and the effectuall operation of his grace.

And therefore (deare Sir) my earnest suit and desire is, that you would diligently peruse the booke of your conscience, enter into a thorow search and examination of your heart and life; and every day before you goe to bed, take a time of recollection and meditation, (as holy *Isaac* did in his private walkes, Gen. xxiv. 63), holding a privy Session in your soule, and indicting your selfe for all the sins, in thought, word, or act committed, & all the good duties you have omitted. This self-examination, if it be so strict and rigid as it ought to be, will soone shew you the sins whereto you are most inclinable (the chiefe cause of all your sorrowes), and consequently, it will (by God's assistance) effectually instruct you to fly from those venomous and fiery serpents, which have so stung you.

And though you have (as you say) committed many grievous sinnes, as abusing God's gracious ordinances, and neglecting the golden opportunities of grace: the originall, as you conceive of all your troubles; yet I must tell you, there is another *Coloquintida* in the pot, another grand enormity (though you perceive it not) and that is your separation from Gods Saints and Servants in the Acts of his publike Service and worship. This you may clearly discern by the affliction it selfe, for God is methodicall in his corrections, and doth (many times) so suite the crosse to the sinne, that you may reade the sin in the crosse. You confesse that your maine affliction, and that which made the other more bitter, is, that God tooke away those to whom you might make your complaint; and from whom you might receive comfort in your distresse. And is not this just with God, that when you wilfully separate your selfe from others, he should separate others from you? Certainly, when we undervalue mercy, especially so great a one as the communion of Saints is, commonly the Lord takes it away from us, till we learne to prize it to the full value. Consider well therefore the haynousnesse of this sin, which that you may the better conceive, First, consider it is against Gods expresse Precept, charging us not to forsake the assemblies of the Saints, Heb. x. 20, 25. Again, it is against our own greatest good and spirituall solace, for by discommunicating & excommunicating our selves from that blessed society, we deprive our selves of the benefit of their holy conference, their godly instructions, their divine consolations, brotherly admonitions, and charitable reprehensions; and what an inestimable losse is this? Neither can we partake such profit by their prayers as otherwise we might: for as the soule in the naturall body conveyes life and strength to every member, as they are compacted and joyned together, and not as dis-severed; so Christ conveyes spirituall life and vigour to Christians, not as they are disjoyned from, but as they are united to the mysticall body, the Church.

But you will say *England* is not a true Church, and therefore you separate; adhere to the true Church.

I answer, our Church is easily proved to be a true Church of Christ: First, because it hath all the essentialls, necessary to the constitution of a true Church; as sound preaching of the Gospell, right dispensation of the Sacraments, Prayer religiously performed, and evill persons justly punisht (though not in that measure as some criminals and malefactors deserve:) and therefore a true Church.

2. Because it hath begot many spirituall children to the Lord, which for soundnesse of judgement, and holinesse of life, are not inferiour to any in other Reformed Churches. Yea, many of the Separation, if ever they were converted, it was here with us: (which a false and adulterous Church communicated.)

But I heare you reply, our Church is corrupted with Ceremonies, and pestered with prophane persons. What then? must we therefore separate for Ceremonies, which many think may be lawfully used. But admit they be evils, must we make a rent in the Church for Ceremonious Rites, for circumstantiall evils? That were a remedy worse than the disease. Besides, had not all the true Churches of Christ their blemishes and deformities, as you may see in seaven *Asian* Churches? Rev. ii. and iii. And though you may finde some Churches beyond Sea free from Ceremonies, yet notwithstanding they are more corrupt in Preachers, (which is the maine) as in prophanation of the Lord's day, &c.

As for wicked and prophane Persons amongst us, though we are to labour by all good meanes to purge them out, yet are we not to separate because of this residence with us: for, there will bee a miscellany and mixture in the visible Church, as long as the world endures, as our Saviour shewes by many parables: Matth. xiii. If therefore we should be so overjust as to abandon all Churches for the intermixture of wicked Persons, we must saile to the Antipodes, or rather goe out of the world, as the Apostle speaks: it is agreed by all that *Noahs* Arke was a type and embleme of the Church. Now as it had been no lesse then selfe-murder for *Noah*, *Sem*, or *Iaphet*, to have leapt out of the Arke, because of that ungracious *Cains* * company; so it is no better then soule-murder for a man to cast himself out of the Church, either for reall or imaginall corruptions. To conclude, as the Angell injoyned *Hagar* to returne, and submit to her Mistris *Sarah*, so let me admonish you to returne your selfe from these extravagant courses, and submissively to render your self to the sacred communion of this truly Evangelicall Church of *England*.

I beseech you therefore, as you respect Gods glory and your owne eternall salvation, as *There is but one body and one spirit, one Lord, one Baptisme, one God and Father of all, who is above all, and through all, and in us all; so endeavour to keep the unity of the spirit in the bond of peace*, Eph. iv., as the Apostle sweetly invites you. So shall the peace of God ever establish you, and the God of peace ever preserve you; which is the prayer of

Your remembrancer at the Throne of Grace R. SIBS.

The preceding 'Letter,' the more valuable because of the paucity of such memorials of Sibbes, was in all likelihood addressed to Thomas Goodwin, D.D., who has been designated the Atlas and patriarch of Independency. Francis White, Bishop of Ely, within whose jurisdiction the Church of Trinity, Cambridge, lay, being one of the ultra-zealous adherents of Laud, had put every obstacle possible in the way of Goodwin's acceptance, and subsequently of his installation; but he was ultimately installed as vicar, having passed from the curacy of St Andrew's, Cambridge, thereto. On the succession of Laud to the primacy, his special charge to his bishops was to watch over the lecturers, and 'watch over' had a terrible significance. White harassed all within his diocese who sought to preach evangelically. He renewed his attacks upon Goodwin. The result was, that, dissatisfied with the restrictions imposed upon preaching that truth which, from the time of Sibbes's barbed words to him, he had found to be the very life of his own soul, he resigned at once his vicarage, lectureship of Trinity, and fellowship of Catharine Hall, and removed, as it would appear, to London, where he began to propagate his new views and conclusions in regard to church government. He shrank not from the name, then of evil omen, of 'Separatist.' † The

* Qu. 'Cham's ?'—ED.

† Consult Dr Halley's Memoir of Goodwin in this series, II, xxiii–iv.

whole circumstances of the case, their previous friendship, their mutual sentiments, warrant, I apprehend, the supposition that this grave, loving, skilful, and admirable letter was addressed to Thomas Goodwin. If so, it was unsuccessful in winning him back to 'the church.' Methinks Sibbes would have acted more faithfully as well as more consistently, had he followed the example of his friends, Goodwin, John Cotton, John Davenport, Thomas Hooker, Samuel Stone, and their compeers. The spirit that pervades his letter is worthier than his arguments. It seems difficult to see how Goodwin could have remained within the pale of the church, gagged and hindered as he was in what was to him momentous beyond all earthly estimate; and it was equally impossible to give 'assent and consent' to what those in authority pronounced to be the 'beauty of holiness,' and teaching of the Book of Common Prayer. Sibbes allowed of neither. By the powerful influence of his many friends, while certainly, as we have seen, summoned before Star Chamber and High Commission, he held on in his way of preaching the same gospel everywhere. That explains his remaining within the church. Who doubts for a moment, that, if his mouth had been shut, as was Goodwin's, on the 'one thing,' Sibbes would have placed himself beside his friend? Perhaps there would have been more of lingering effort to get above the difficulties, more pain in sundering of the ties that bound him to the church, more sway given to heart than head. Still the final decision, beyond all debate, would have been that of the 'two thousand' of 1662. The more shame to those who compelled such loyal lovers of 'the church' to leave her. This letter gives us insight into Sibbes's method of procedure in dealing with the scruples of the conscientious. It is to be regretted that we have no more of such letters, and none of his conversations with them. But we have the fact, upon various authority, that he was at all times ready to speak a word in season, and on principle, contrived to *sanctify* all his intercourse with his fellow-men, as well more privately as publicly. He had many opportunities of influencing for good some of the finest minds of the age; and he availed himself of such opportunities. He was wont, Samuel Clarke informs us, 'in the summer time, to go abroad to the houses of some worthy personages, *where he was an instrument of much good,* not only by his private labours, but by his prudent counsel and advice, that upon every occasion he was ready to minister unto them.' * Charles Stanford has well limned to us such visits in Alleine's day. If you wish, he says, 'to see what Puritan life was like in "the high places," go with Mr Alleine and

* Clarke, *ante*, p. 145.

his brother Norman, to spend an evening with Admiral Blake at his country house at Knowle.' * Instead of Alleine let us go with Sibbes, and instead of Admiral Blake at Knowle, let the visit be to John Pym, or to Lady Mary Vere, or to Sir Robert and Lady Brooke, or any of those great and true families, whose heads

'. . . . . bore, without abuse,
The grand old name of gentleman,'

and 'feared God,' and were 'lovers of all good men.' Suppose Colonel Hutchinson and the Puritan Admiral to be also guests. There would be the simple meal,—the Bible would be brought in, —there would be prayer,—there would be conversation such as Christians love, and which they can only have when in 'their own company,'—there would probably be discourse, in logical forms, on some of the mysteries of Christian truth,—of course, there would be reasonings over some 'case of conscience.' Dr Gouge would be apt to get prosy, in discussing the opinions of Fragosa, Talet, Sayrus, and Roderiques, or of Doctors Ursinus or Lobetius; Master Davenport would interpose a 'why' or 'how;' and Richard Sibbes would close with some sweet words from John or the Lord himself, modestly confirming his own elucidations of them from Bernard, or with a quaint saying from Luther, or a wise apophthegm from Augustine. Then there would be a flow of graceful and varied talk, not only on politics ('Petition of Right,' and so on), but on books, pictures, gardening, or the last scientific experiments of the 'Oxford Society;' and the tall-browed statesman, and the great sailor, 'would affect a droll concern to prove before the ministers, by the aptness and abundance of their Latin quotations, that in becoming 'leader in the House' and admiral, they had not forfeited their claim to be considered good classics.' You could not find better types of the winning, yet stately Christian gentleman, than among such Puritan circles; and where will you match their 'fair ladyes?' We have confirmation of the 'visits' and of their results in the several 'epistles' and 'dedications' of his posthumous writings. Each of these records personal intercourse and kindnesses, and the tenderest cherishing of his memory. He was a frequent guest with the Earls of Manchester and Warwick, and Ladies Anne and Susanna, their Countesses, Lord Say and Seal, Lord Roberts, Baron Truro, and Lady Lucie his consort, but most of all with the Brooks and Veres, with whom he lived on the most familiar terms. The 'dedications' and 'epistles' will be found in their respective

* Joseph Alleine: his Companions and Times, pp. 131–2; and Hepworth Dixon's Life of Blake, p. 267. I accommodate, rather than quote from Stanford's picturesque and masterly work.

places; but, as it reflects interesting light and mutual honour on both, I must introduce in full the 'epistle dedicatory' of the 'Fountain Sealed,' to 'the truly noble and much honoured lady, the Lady Elizabeth Brooke, wife to Sir Robert Brooke,' and also glean a few biographic sentences from others. The 'epistle' to Lady Brooke, one of the most remarkable women of England, at a period when there were many such, is as follows:—

To the truly noble and much honoured lady, the LADY ELIZABETH BROOKE, *wife to Sir Robert Brooke.*

'Madam,—Besides that deserved interest your Ladyship held in the affections and esteem of this worthy man more than any friend alive, which might entitle you to all that may call him author, this small piece of his acknowledgeth a more special propriety unto your Ladyship. For though his tongue was as the pen of a ready writer in the hand of Christ, who guided him, yet your Ladyship's hand and pen was in this his scribe and amanuensis, whilst he dictated a first draught of it in private, with intention for the public. In which labour, both of humility and love, your Ladyship did that honour unto him which Baruch, though great and noble, did but receive in the like transcribing the words of Jeremiah from his mouth, wherein yet your Ladyship did indeed but write the story of your own life, which hath been long exactly framed to the rules herein prescribed. We, therefore, that are intrusted in the publishing of it, deem it but an act of justice in us to return it thus to your Ladyship, unto whom it owes even its first birth, that so, wherever this little treatise shall come, there also this that you have done may be told and recorded for a memorial of you. And we could not but esteem it also an addition of honour to the work, that no less than a lady's hand, so pious and so much honoured, brought it forth into the world, although in itself it deserveth as much as any other this blessed womb did bear. The Lord, in way of recompense, write all the holy contents of it yet more fully and abundantly in your ladyship's heart, and all the lineaments of the image of Jesus Christ, and seal up all unto you by his blessed Spirit, with joy and peace, to the day of redemption.—Madam, we are your Ladyship's devoted, THOS. GOODWIN.
PHILIP NYE.

It was no uncommon thing for ladies moving in the highest circles thus to 'take down' the sermons of their ministers, or discharge the office of amanuenses. Contemporaneously with Lady Brooke we find Lady Elizabeth Rich, another of Sibbes's friends, transcribing and preparing for the press WILLIAM STRONG'S great folio 'Of the Covenants.'* Of Lady Brooke, her biographer Parkhurst states, among many other things of note, that—

'She used a mighty industry to preserve what either instructed her mind or affected her heart in the sermons she had heard. To these she gave great attention in the Assembly, and heard them repeated in her family. And thus she would discourse of them in the evening; and in the following week she had them again repeated, and discoursed the matter of them to some of her family in her chamber. And besides all this, *she wrote the substance of them*, and then digested many of them into questions and

* 1678. Dedication by Theophilus Gale to Lady Elizabeth Rich.

answers, or under heads of common-places, and then they became to her matter for repeated meditation. And by these methods she was always increasing her knowledge, or confirming the things that were known.' *

Addressing Lord Roberts, Baron Truro, and Lady Lucie, John Sedgwick thus commences his 'dedication' of the 'Beams of Divine Light:'—

'RIGHT HONOURABLE AND TRULY NOBLE,—It was not so much the nobility of your blood, as that of grace given unto you from the divine hand, *which did so much interest you in the love and esteem of that worthy servant of Christ*, the author of this work, in whom Urim and Thummim met, whose whole course being a real and vital sermon, sweetly consonant to the tenor of his teaching, made him amiable living and honourable dead, in the opinion of as many as well knew him. This was the thing, I suppose, which wrought unto him from you, *as well as from many others of your noble stock and rank*, more than an ordinary esteem.' †

Again, in like manner he addresses Robert, Earl of Warwick, and Lady Susanna, in 'Light from Heaven:'—

'For me to commend the author, were to make the world to judge him either *a stranger unto you, or a man that had not ingratiated himself with you whilst he lived near unto you.* I well knew that he had an honourable opinion of you both, and of yours. . . . . You that knew and loved him so well shall, in vouchsafing to read over these ensuing sermons, find his spirit in them.' ‡

These 'testimonies' might be greatly multiplied, and it is very pleasing to know that one who so carried about with him the 'sweet savour' of Christ was thus welcomed at the Kimboltons, and Cockfields, and Hevinghams, and other of the family seats and castles of the nobility and gentry. It is especially honourable to Sibbes that he received such cordial welcome from the nobles and gentry of his own native county of Suffolk. The Tostock 'wheelwright's' son reversed the too often true saying of a prophet not being without honour 'save in his own country and among his own kin.' The Day will declare the good effected by these summer visits and 'conferences in private, done aptly, pithily, and profitably . . . . much in few words.' §

While thus a visitor among the 'great ones,' he did not forget his birth-place or school-boy haunts, his 'mother, and brethren.' I turn here to the manuscript of the Vicar of Thurston:—

'Anno Domini 1608. I came to be minister of Thurston, and he was then a Fellow of the College, and a preacher of good note in Cambridge, and we soon grew well acquainted. For whensoever he came down into the

* Quoted in Wilford's 'Memorials and Characters,' folio, 1741, page 210. Consult pp. 209–213, and Appendix xvii.

† Ep. Ded., 4to, 1639. ‡ Ep. Ded., 4to, 1638.

§ 'Epistle Dedicatory' to 'Evangelical Sacrifices,' 4to, 1640.

country to visit his mother and brethren (his father being deceased) he would never fail to preach with us on the Lord's day, and for the most part twice, telling me that it was a work of charity to help a constant and a painful preacher, for so he was pleased to conceive of me. And if there were a communion appointed at any time he would be sure not to withdraw himself after sermon, but receiving the bread and wine at my hands, he would always assist me in the distribution of the cup to the congregation.'

The church of Thurston, in which Sibbes thus ministered, has only within these two years disappeared. Its great tower fell, and it was found necessary to rebuild the whole. This has been done nearly in fac-simile of the original.* The parsonage of the excellent vicar remains. It has degenerated into a kind of farmer's house, but on a recent visit I found many traces of former elegance and comfort. It is two-storied, with lozenge-paned windows, and heavy sculptured doorway. In front is an avenue of noble chesnuts and beeches, and pollard limes. The 'garden' must have been of considerable extent. Imagination was busy calling up Sibbes and Catlin walking arm-in-arm along the mossed avenue. I stepped across the threshold of the ancient house, sat down by the carved mantel-pieced fireside with reverence. It was something to know that there our worthies had many and many a time exchanged loving words, perhaps smoked a pipe.

Finely does the vicar continue his personal reminiscences of the visits to Thurston, and of his friend's kindnesses. We must again listen to him :—

'As for his kindness to his kindred, and neglect of the world, it was very remarkable. For this I can testify of my own knowledge, that, purchasing of Mr Tho. Clark and others in our town a messuage and lands at several times to the value of fifty pounds per annum, he paid the fines to the lords but never took one penny of the rents or profits of them, *but left the benefit wholly to his mother and his two brethren* as long as he lived. So much did this heavenly-minded man of God' ('heavenly' seems instinctively to drop from every one who writes of him) 'slight this present world (which the most men are so loth to part withal when they die) that he freely and undesired parted with it whilst he lived, requiring nothing of them but only to be liberal to the poor. Nay, over and besides, if any faithful, honest man came down from Cambridge or London, where he lived, by whom he might conveniently send, he seldom or never failed to *send his mother* a

* An engraving of the church as it was before its fall is given in one of those privately printed family histories, for which we are indebted to the love of the Americans towards their mother country. 'The Brights of Suffolk, England; represented in America by the descendants of Henry Bright jun., who came to New England in 1630, and settled in Watertown, Massachusetts. By J. B. Bright. For private circulation. Boston. 1 vol. royal 8vo. 1858.' See opposite page 109. This book is of the deepest interest, well arranged, and illustrated lavishly with portraits and other illustrations.' Mr Bright in the most obliging manner sent me a copy.

piece of gold, for the most part a ten shilling piece, but five shillings was the least,* and this he continued as long as his mother lived. And would she have been persuaded to exchange her country life for the city, he often told me that he would willingly have maintained her there in good view and fashion, *like his mother*, but she had no mind to alter her accustomed course of life in her old days, contenting herself with her own means, and that addition which her son made thereunto.'

And still farther the good old man continues, with a love and reverence most affecting, and that only a *true* man could have secured :—

'For his special kindness to myself, in particular, I cannot omit that, being trusted by personages of quality with divers sums of money for pious and charitable uses, he was pleased, among many others, not to forget me. At one time he sent me down three twenty-shilling pieces of gold enclosed in a letter, and at two other times he delivered to me with his own hand two twenty-shilling pieces more; and so far was this humble saint from pharisaical ostentation and vainglory, and from taking the honour of these good works to himself, that he plainly told me that these gratuities were not of his own cost, but being put in trust, and left to his own discretion in the distribution, he looked upon me as one that took great pains in my ministry and in teaching scholars, and at that time labouring under the burden of a great charge of children, and so thought me a fit object of their intended charity. And from myself his love descended down to my son for my sake, for whom (before he had ever seen him, being then at the grammar-school at Bury, he then, chosen Master of Katherine Hall, promised me a scholarship there of five pounds a year, and to provide for him a tutor and a chamber. And such was his constancy of spirit and his reality, that whatsoever promise he made me he would be sure both to remember it and to make it good as freely as he first made it, that was unasked and undesired. And for these manifold kindnesses all that he desired at my hands was no more but this, *that I would be careful of the souls of my people, and, in special, of his mother, his brethren, and his sisters,* and would give them good counsel in their disposing themselves in marriage, or upon any other occasion, as I saw they stood in need. And this one thing I may not pass over concerning myself, that in his last will and testament he gave me a legacy of forty shillings, with the title of "his loving friend," which I the rather mention, because I had not the least thought to have been in that sort remembered by him at his death, living at no less distance from him than of threescore miles. In a word, such was the lowliness of this sweet servant of God, such his learning, parts, piety, prudence, humility, sincerity, love, and meekness of spirit (whereof every one was a loadstone to attract, unite, and fasten my spirit close to his), that I profess ingenuously no man that ever I was acquainted withal got so far into my heart or lay closer there, so that many times I could not part from him with dry eyes. But who am I? or what is it to be beloved of me, *especially for him that had so many and great friends as he had?* Yet even to me the great God is pleased to say, "My son, give me thy heart," and this poor and contrite heart I know he will not despise; and this heart of mine, as small as it is, yet is too great to close with a proud, profane, worldly, malicious heart, though it be in a prince. But true virtue and

* This may fairly be considered equal to a pound of our present money.

grace are the image of God himself, and where they are discerned by wisdom's children they command the heart and are truly lovely and venerable, whereas carnal notions and unmortified affections (whereof this man of God was as free as any man I know living), they do render a man, whatever he be, if not hateful and contemptible, yet at least less lovely and honourable. But my love to this good man hath transported me beyond my purpose, which was to speak of some things less visible to others, especially concerning his first education. For when he came to the university and the city, there his life and actions were upon a public theatre, and his own words, without a trumpet, would praise him in the gates. As for his kindness to his kindred and to myself, I know none that took more notice of them than I, and therefore I could not hide them from the world upon this occasion without some kind of sacrilege.'

Thanks, chatty Zachary, for thy golden words! Thou wert a meet companion of Richard Sibbes! Would that we might recover thy '*Hidden Treasure*,'* for, of a truth, it must breathe thy very spirit! All the notices of the author of The Bruised Reed and Soul's Conflict harmonise with the tribute of the vicar of Thurston. Whether it be Clark or Thomas Fuller, Prynne or Eachard, or his numerous 'prefacers,' he is invariably spoken of with the most touching kindliness.

CHAPTER XI.

'THE BEGINNING OF THE END.'

Retrospect—Character—Humility—the English Leighton—his 'Cygnea-Cantio' vel Concio.

We have now reached 'the beginning of the end.' A few months later, and Richard Sibbes lay dying. But at this point, I would observe, that up to the latest he continued faithfully to execute his office as a '*preacher of the word*.' Left alone (for Preston was gone: and Cotton, and Davenport, and Hooker, and many others of his circle, were fugitives in New England), he had ever-increasing demands made upon him, and no 'door of entrance' was opened into which he did not enter, still

'Hoping through the darkest day.'†

He continued to preach at Gray's Inn, in the good old way, the simple gospel that Paul preached, and that of all men JOHN CALVIN, following Augustine, in his estimate, had best interpreted.

* The following is the title, from Crowe's Catalogue of our English writers on Old and New Testament, &c., 1668:—'Hidden-Treasure, two sermons on Mat. xiii. 44. 4to. 1633.' Can any reader help to this?

† Poems by Currer, Ellis, and Acton Bell, p. 34, 12mo. 1846.

He resided with enlarged acceptability as Master of Catharine Hall, adding to its Fellows, and Students, and Revenues, and from 1632–3, he was, as already recorded, Vicar of Trinity, Cambridge. One incidental sentence informs us, that he was very fully, if not over, occupied, even before his presentation to the Vicarage of Trinity. It occurs at the close of the address 'To the Christian Reader' prefixed to 'The Bruised Reed :' 'What I shall be drawn to do in this kind,' he says, '*must be by degrees, as leisure in the midst of many interruptions will permit.*'

His was a self-sacrificing, self-consuming life. Quaintly does Mather put it of another. 'There,' he says, ''twas that, like a silk-worm, he spent his own bowels or spirits to procure the "garments of righteousness" for his hearers; there 'twas . . . he might challenge the device and motto of the famous Dr Sibs, a wasting lamp, with this inscription, "*Prælucendo pereo*," or, "My light is my death."'*

Another casual reference indicates earlier personal sickness. He closes one of his 'Epistles' prefixed to Ball† by saying, 'Mine own weakness of body taketh me off.'

His published writings afford the best evidence of what stamp his preaching was. The most cursory reader is struck with the Paul-like kindling of emotion, the Paul-like burning of utterance, as often as the name of Christ occurs; and it is most interesting to mark the majestic procession of his words as he walks along some great avenue of thought, leading up to the cross, and from the cross, in farther vista, to the house of many mansions, and to the throne of sculptured light. Very beautifully does Clarke put this:—

His learning was mixed with humility, whereby he always esteemed lowly of himself, and was ready to undervalue his own labours, though others judged them to breathe spirit and life, to be strong of heaven, speaking with authority and power to men's consciences. His care in the course of his ministry was to lay a good foundation in the heads and hearts of his hearers. And though he were a wise master-builder, and that in one of the eminentest auditories for learning and piety that was in the land, as was said before, yet according to the grace which was given to him (which was indeed like that of Elisha in regard of the other prophets, 2 Kings i. 9, the elder brother's privilege, a double portion), *he was still taking all occasions to preach of the* FUNDAMENTALS *to them;* and amongst the rest, of the incarnation of the Son of God, one of the chief fundamentals of our faith, one of the chief of those wonders in the mercy-seat which the cherubim gaze at, which the angels desire to pry into, 1 Pet. i. 12. And preaching at several times, and by occasion of so many several texts of Scripture concerning this subject, there is scarce any one of those incomparable benefits which accrue to us thereby, nor any of those holy impressions which the meditation hereof ought to make on our hearts, which was not by him

* Life of Urian Oakes. Magnalia Am. as *ante*, b. iv. pp. 186, 187. † *Ante* p. cvi.

sweetly unfolded, as may appear by those sermons now in print. 'And therefore,' saith a reverend divine, 'the *noted humility of the author* I less wonder at, finding how often his thoughts dwelt upon the humiliation of Christ.'*

The 'reverend divine' referred to was Thomas Fuller, who plays with the conceit in his own wisely-witty way. We cannot pass it by :—

He was most eminent for that grace which is most worth, yet costs the least to keep it, viz., *Christian humility*. Of all points of divinity, he most frequently pressed that of Christ's incarnation; and if the angels desired to pry into that mystery, no wonder if this angelical man had a longing to look therein. A learned divine imputed this good doctor's great humility to his much meditating on that point of Christ's humiliation when he took our flesh upon him. If it be true what some hold in physic, that *omne par nutrit suum par*, that the vitals of our body are most strengthened by feeding on such meats as are likest unto them, I see no absurdity to maintain that men's souls improve most in those graces whereon they have most constant meditation, whereof this worthy doctor was an eminent instance.†

Aye, quaint and loveable Fuller, and there is a higher authority than 'physic' for it, even 2 Cor. iii. 18, 'We all, with open face beholding as in a glass the glory of the Lord, *are changed into the same image* from glory to glory, even of the Lord, the Spirit.'

Thus growing in holiness and humility, Richard Sibbes passed along his 'pilgrimage.' We have found that he lived in troublous times, and that he did not escape his own share of its trials and persecution. It had argued time-serving or a cold neutrality had it been otherwise. We find him also taking a fitting stand for 'the truth,' and speaking brave and noble words, and flinching not from giving them to the world. At the same time, it must be apparent to all who have followed our memoir thus far, that naturally Sibbes was of a 'meek and quiet spirit,' willing to bear and forbear much. I picture him as an English 'Leighton,' as *he* has been pourtrayed in a little volume of 'poems,' entitled 'The Bishop's Walk.'‡ We have to change very little in the scenery, have but to translate 'Dunblane' to the 'fair garden' lined with elms, of Gray's Inn, or to the acacia-bordered 'Walk' of St Catherine Hall, Cambridge, or, perhaps, to the bosky glades of the Veres, or Brooks, or Manchesters, or Warwicks. I invite my readers to judge :—

* Clarke, *ante* p. 144.

† Fuller's 'Worthies,' *ante* p. 343 of vol. ii.

‡ The Bishop's Walk and the Bishop's Times, By Orwell. Cambridge: Macmillan and Co. 1861. The measure will reveal the source of earlier quotations in this memoir; and certainly the gifted author promises to take a high place among the poets of Scotland. It may be noted here, that among the few Puritan books in the library of Leighton (preserved at Dunblane) are Sibbes's Bruised Reed (6th edition, 1638) and Soul's Conflict (4th edition, 1638).

Two hundred years have come and gone,
Since that fine spirit mused alone
On the dim walk, with faint green shade
By the light-quivering ash-leaves made,
And saw the sun go down
Beyond the mountains brown.

Slow pacing with a lowly-look,
Or gazing on the lettered book
Of Tauler, or A Kempis, or
Meek Herbert with his dulcimer,
In quaintly pious vein
Rehearsing a deep strain:

Or in the Gold-mouthed Greek he read
High rhetoric, or what was said
Of Augustine's experience,
Or of the Gospel's grand defence
Before assembled lords,
In Luther's battle-words.

Slow-pacing, with a downcast eye,
Which yet, in rapt devotion high,
Sometimes its great dark orb would lift,
And pierced the veil, and caught the swift
Glance of an angel's wing,
That of the Lamb did sing;

And with the fine pale shadow, wrought
Upon his cheek by years of thought,
And lines of weariness and pain,
And looks that long for home again;
So went he to and fro
With step infirm and slow.

A frail, slight form—no temple he,
Grand, for abode of Deity;
Rather a bush, inflamed with grace,
And trembling in a desert place,
And unconsumed with fire,
Though burning high and higher.

A frail, slight form, and pale with care,
And paler from the raven hair
That folded from a forehead free
Godlike of breadth and majesty—
A brow of thought supreme
And mystic, glorious dream.

And over all that noble face
Lay somewhat of soft pensiveness
In a fine golden haze of thought,
That seemed to waver light, and float
This way and that way still,
With no firm bent of will.

God made him beautiful, to be
Drawn to all beauty tenderly,
And conscious of all beauty, whether
In things of earth or heaven or neither;
So to rude men he seemed
Often as one that dreamed.

But true it was that, in his soul,
The needle pointed to the pole,
Yet trembled as it pointed, still
Conscious alike of good and ill;
In his infirmity
Looking, O Lord, to thee.

Beautiful spirit! fallen, alas,
On times when little beauty was;
Still seeking peace amid the strife,
Still working, weary of thy life,
Toiling in holy love,
Panting for heaven above:

I mark thee, in an evil day,
Alone upon a lonely way;
More sad-companionless thy fate,
Thy heart more truly desolate,
Than even the misty glen
Of persecuted men.

For none so lone on earth as he
Whose way of thought is high and free
Beyond the mist, beyond the cloud,
Beyond the clamour of the crowd,
Moving, where Jesus trod,
In the lone walk with God.

We have here the very man before us, and the very books he loved, and the very age he 'fell on,' and from which he was 'taken away.' Looking at the portrait, over and over engraved for the early quartos and duodecimos, and his one folio, Richard Sibbes must have been a man of larger mould, of more massive head, ampler brain-chamber, keener vision than Robert Leighton.* As

* Russell, in his 'Memorials of Fuller' (1844), and Mr Mayor, in his prefatory remarks to Catlin's MS., from the Baker MSS., have anticipated the comparison of Sibbes with Leighton. The former says—'Dr Richard Sibbes . . . a writer surpassed by none in that purity and depth of true spirituality, which also characterised

one studies the ruff-girted 'Master'-capped face, a more robust soul looks out from the benignant eyes. The seamed and lined forehead tells of deeper thinking, not without storms of doubt and wrestling (that always *so* leave their mark, like the waves on the sea-shore sands, as though the soul's mystic sea beat there). But the 'inner men,' in their spiritual-mindedness, unworldliness, meekness, humility, peacefulness, surely very closely resemble one another.

But now the stage darkens for 'the end,'

'Like a cave's shadow enter'd at mid-day.' *

He has to preach but other two 'sermons,' and then go forth on the last great journey. With strange fitness he chooses for his texts, John xiv. 1, 2, 'Let not your heart be troubled; ye believe in God, believe also in me. In my Father's house are many mansions; if it were not so, I would have told you.' These two sermons will appear in an early volume.

CHAPTER XII.

'THE VALLEY OF THE SHADOW OF DEATH.'

Last Illness—Finishes 'The Soul's Conflict'—Draws up his 'Will'—'Falls on Sleep.'

Having preached the last of these two 'sermons,' he 'fell sick that very night, June 28,' with some un-named illness. Feeling that he was indeed dying, he, on 'July 1,' put the finishing touches to his 'Address to the Christian Reader,' for the 'Soul's Conflict,' which had been passing through the press during his absence at Cambridge. Glancing over the proof-sheets, he detected certain passages which he found misunderstood, and noticed them; but apparently was too weak to do more. On the 4th, he 'set his house in order,' by revising and altering his 'last will and testament.' He had many friends, gentle and simple, and it is with no common satisfaction that it is in our power to present this closing memorial:—†

Leighton in a succeeding age,' p. 81. The latter—'When we consider the beauty of Sibbes' language, and the gentleness of his temper, in both which respects he almost deserves the name of the Puritan Leighton, we cannot but wonder at the general neglect which has obscured his memory,' p. 253.

* 'Adon:' Poems. By Mrs Clive. 1856. P. 39.

† Extracted from the Principal Registry of Her Majesty's Court of Probate, in the Prerogative Court of Canterbury.

'In the name of God, amen, I, Richard Sibbs, Doctor of Divinity, weake in body, but of p'fect memory, doe make and ordaine this my last will and testament, in manner and forme followeing: First, I comend and bequeath my soule into the hands of my gratious Saviour, whoe hath redeemed it wth his most pretious blood, and appeares now in heaven to receave it, with humble thankes that he hath vouchsafed I should be borne and live in the best tymes of the gospell, and have my interest in the comforte of it; as alsoe, that he hath vouchsafed me the honour of being a publisher thereof wth some measure of faythfullnes. My body I would have to be buried at the discretion of my executors. And as for that outward estate that God, in his rich goodnes, hath blessed me w^th^all, my minde and will is as followeth: First, I give and bequeath unto my brother Thomas Sibbs of Thurston, in the countie of Suffolk,* all my messuages, lands, and tenements, with the appurtenances, lyeing and being in Thurston aforesaid, or elsewhere, for and dureing the terme of his naturall life; and after my said brother's decease, to John Sibbs, sonne of my late brother John Sibbs, and now a student at Katherine Hall, in Cambridge,† and to his heires for ever: Item, I give unto my sister, Margaret Mason, fourtie pounds; and unto the children of my late sister, Susann Lopham, deceased, the some of thirty pounds, to be equally devided amongst them; as likewise, I give unto the children of my late sister, Elizabeth King, deceased, the some of fourtie pounds, to be equally devided amongst them; the said threescore and ten pounds, soe given to the children of my said sisters, I would have payed to the said children, severally and proporconably, at the dayes of their marriage, or when they shall accomplish their severall ages of one-and-twenty yeares, or otherwise sooner, at the discretion of my executors: Item, I give unto my uncle Sibbs, yf he be liveing, fourtie shillings; and unto the children of my late aunte . . . . . who dwelt in or neer Walding-feild, in Essex,‡ the some of three pounds: Item, I give unto my cosen, Jeremy Huske, unto my cosins, Anne Beckett and Elizabeth Beckett, to every of them fourtie shillings: Item, I give unto the poore of the said towne of Thurston twentie shillings: Item, I give unto such of my poore kindred as are now dwelling at Stowlangton, § in Suffolke, or elsewhere, whoe are now knowne to my executors, fourtie shillings, to be disposed according to the discretion of my executors: Item, I give unto James Joyner of London, whoe hath beene very faithfull in his service unto me tenn pounds; and to my loveing frends, Mr Dermer, haberdasher, dwelling on Ludgate Hill, twenty shillings, and to his wife twentie shillings, and to Widdow Dermer twentie shillings; and to my good friends Goodman Pinkaur and Goodman Rocke, dwelling in Perpoole Lane, to each of them twenty shillings: Item, I give unto Mr Nicholas Parry, steward of Grayes Inne, three pounds; and to Mr Guy, cheife cooke there, a ring of tenn shillings; and to his under servants, to be disposed at his discretion, the some of twenty shillings in the whole: Item, I give unto the three cheife butlers of Grayes Inne, to every of them, twenty shillings; alsoe, I give unto the inferiour servants of that house twenty shillings, to be disposed of according to the discretion of the steward; and as for that Hono^ble^ Society of Grayes Inne, I have nothing to bequeath unto it but the prayers of a sicke and dyeing man, that it may continue to be still a semenary of worthy men,

* See B in Appendix to this Memoir. † *Ibid.*

‡ This is a slip. It is in Suffolk, near Sudbury, on borders of Essex.

§ Stowlangtoft, three miles from Thurston.

whoe may be alwayes ready to maintaine religion and justice, wth humble thankes for all their kindnesse and loveing respects towardes mee: Item, I give unto my auncient and deare frend, ould Mr Mew, in remembrance of my love, one of Mr Downham's books, called a Direccon to a Christian Life;* and to my deare and very worthy frend, Mr John Pym,† a ring of fourtie shillings: Item, I give unto my very good frend, Mr William Mew, one silver spoone, now in the custody of James Joyner aforenamed: Item, I give unto the poore of the parrish where I shal be buried twenty shillings: Item, I give unto my very worthy, religious, and bountifull frend, Mrs Mary Moore,‡ as a poore remembrance of my harty love unto her, one ryng of fourtie shillings; and to my very worthy frends S[r] Robert Brooke of Langly, to his lady,§ and to his brother, Mr John Brooke, to each of them a ring of fourtie shillings; and to my kind frend, Mr Stevens of Gloucestershire, a ring‖ of twentie shillings; and to my worthy friend, Mr Capell, ¶ late preacher in Gloucestershire, twenty shillings: Item, I give five pounds to the poore of the p'ishes of Trinity and St Andrews, in Cambridge: Item, Whereas there is due unto me, from the Colledge of St Katherine, in Cambridge, one hundred pounds, for w[ch] Mr Goodwyn and Mr Arrow Smith ** stand bound to mee, haveing the seale of the said colledge for their securetie, I doe hereby give and bequeath unto the said colledge, for ever, the said some of one hundred pounds, for the setling of a scholarship of fower pounds p. ann.; to w[ch] said schollership my will and desire is, that my kinsman, John Sibbs, aforemenconed, shal be first elected and admitted; and that in all future eleccons, when the same shal be void in tyme to come, yf any of my kindred shal be then students in the said colledge, the p'son soe of kynne to me shal be p[r]ferred before another: Item, I give unto my loveing frend, Mr Catline, preacher of Thurston, fourtie shillings: Item, I give unto my good frend, Mr Almond of Cambridge, fyve pounds, praying him to imploy the same for the benefit of his sonne and my godsonne: Item, I give unto my godsonne, Richard Clerk, fortie shillings; and whereas, by the will of Mrs Gardiner, late of London, widdow, deceased, I was desired to dispose a certain some of money, in such manner as in her said will is specified, all w[ch] money hath beene accordingly disposed, excepting only fyve pounds, payable unto Mr Symons of Katherine Hall, my will therefore is that payment be made of the said fyve pounds unto Mr Symonds aforesaid; and to my reverend frende, Dr Gouge, I doe give, as a testimony of my love, twenty shillings, desiring him to take the paynes to preach my funerall sermon: †† Item, My will is, that my reverend frend, Mr Downeham, shall have two of those bookes of his owne making backe againe w[ch] were by him delivered unto me, and are remayning in my studie at Grayes Inne; all the rest of my goods and chattles, my funerall, debts, and legacies being payed and discharged, I give unto my brother and kinsman before named—that is to saie, to my brother Thomas Sibbs, and my nephew John Sibbs, formerly menconed, whome, together wth John Godbold of Grayes Inne,

* Published 1622, and entitled 'A Guide to Godliness; or, a Treatise of a Christian Life.' The author was John Downame or Downham, B.D., brother of George, Bishop of Derry. He died 1644.

† See references *in loc.* at p. cxxxvii, Appendix A

‡ Sibbes dedicates Culverwell's 'Time Well-spent' to her, *ante* p. xciii, *seq.*

§ See reference *in loc.* p. cxxxvii, Appendix A.

‖ *Ibid.* ¶ *Ibid.* ** Drs Goodwin and Arrowsmith.

†† See Mr Mayor's note *in loc.* Appendix A.

Esquire, I doe hereby ordayne, constitute, and appoynt to be the executors of this my last will and testament, giving unto the said Mr Godbould a peece of my owne plate, such as himself shall choose out of that plate of myne, which is now in the custody of the said James Joyner; and I doe entreate my worthy and very loveing frends, S[r] Nathaniel Rich, Sir Nathaniell Barnardiston,* and S[r] William Spring, Knighte,† to be overseers of this my will, desireing my executors, in all things of difficulty, to be advised by them in the execution of the same; and as a remembrance of my love to every of the said overseers of my will, I give unto each of them a ring of twentie shillings.—In wittnes whereof I have hereunto set my hand and seale, this fourth daye of July, in the eleaventh yeare of the raigne of our sov'aigne Lord Charles, by the grace of God, kinge of England, Scotland, France, and Ireland, defender of the faith, &c., and in the yeare of our Lord God 1635. Signed, sealed, and published to be the last will and testament of the said Richard Sibbs in the presence of us.

PROBATUM fuit testamentum sup[r]scriptum apud London coram ven[ll] viro magistro Willimo Merricke legum doctore: Surrogato ven[lis] viri Domini Henrici Marten militis, legum etiam doctoris, curiæ prerogativæ Cantuar. magistri, custodis sive com[rll] legitime constituti; undecimo die mensis Julii anno Domini millesimo sexcentesimo tricesimo quinto, Juramentis Thomæ Sibbs et Johannis Sibbs duorum executorum in senior ‡ testamento nominatorum: Quibus commissa fuit administracio omnium et singulorum bonorum piriu (?) et creditorum dicti defuncti de bene et fideliter administrando eadem ad sancta dei evangelia juratis: Reservata potestate similem commissionem faciendi Johanni Godbould Ar: alteri executori etiam in senior ‡ testamento nominato cum ven'it eand[m] petitum.'

His will was drawn up on Saturday the 4th, and then he quietly waited his 'change.' '*Paulisper O senex, oculos claude, nam statim lumen Dei videbis*' ('Shut thine eyes a little, old man, and immediately thou shalt see the light of God'§).

Thus remembering his kinsmen and friends left behind, even the humblest, and looking UPWARD, he 'WALKED THROUGH the valley of the shadow of death,' and went, from the Sabbath below (*it was a Sabbath morning*) to the Sabbath above, to 'be with the Lord.' 'Blessed are the dead who die in the LORD. . . . Yea, saith THE SPIRIT, for they rest from their labours, *and their works do follow them*,' Rev. xiv. 13. He died 5th July 1635, in the 58th year of his age. An entry in the 'Register' of St Andrew's Church, Holborn (within which parish Gray's Inn is situate), tells us he was buried there on the next day:—

* Sir Nathaniel Barnardiston. The 'Rich' and 'Barnardiston' families are historic in their warm support of the Puritans. It were superfluous to annotate names that are found in every Puritan 'History.'

† Sir William Spring, Knt. He was of Pakenham, near Bury St Edmunds, of the ancient family of Lavenham. See Burke's 'Extinct' Baronetcies; also *ante* page xxvi.

‡ Qu. 'superscripts?'—ED.

§ Sozomen, lib. ii. cap. ii. Stanford's Alleine, p. 21.

'1635. July 6. Richard Sibbes, D.D., sometime preacher in Gray's Inn, died in his chambers at Gray's Inn, 5th.' *

1.

'Servant of God! well done;
Rest from thy loved employ;
The battle fought, the victory won,
Enter thy Master's joy.'
—The voice at midnight came;
He started up to hear:
A mortal arrow pierced his frame.
He fell,—but felt no fear.

2.

Tranquil amid alarms,
It found him in the field,
A veteran slumbering on his arms,
Beneath his red-cross shield:
His sword was in his hand,
Still warm with recent fight,
Ready that moment at command,
Through rock and steel to smite.

3.

The pains of death are past,
Labour and sorrow cease,
And life's long warfare closed at last,
His soul is found in peace.
Soldier of Christ! well done;
Praise be thy new employ;
And while eternal ages run
Rest in thy Saviour's joy. †

I would have my readers turn to the perhaps over-garrulous, yet interesting 'reflections' upon the death of Sibbes,‡ and add only a few words by Ashe, Church, and Nalton:—

'This bright star, who sometimes with his light refreshed the souls of many of God's people while he shone on the horizon of our church, set, as we say, *between the evening of many shadows and the morning of a bright hoped-for reformation*, which, though for the present (1654) overcast, yet being so agreeable to the mind of Jesus Christ, and ushered in with the groans and prayers of so many of his saints, we doubt not but will in God's own time break forth gloriously, to the dissipating of those clouds and fogs which at the present do eclipse and darken it.' § Even so:—

'God's saints are shining lights; . . . .
They are indeed as pillar-fires,
Seen as we go;
They are that city's shining spires
We travel to.' ‖

A. B. G.

* It has been found impossible to identify his grave; no stone, the simplest, marks it. Is there to be no memorial raised?

† James Montgomery, 'The Christian Soldier.' Poetical Works, p. 305, ed. 1 vol. 8vo. 1851.

‡ Appendix A, p. cxxxviii, *seq.* See also B, pp. cxl–xli, in Appendix, for notices of Sibbes's family and name; and C, p. cxli, for references concerning his successors at Gray's Inn and Catharine Hall

§ 'To the Reader,' Heav. Conf. between Christ and Mary, 12mo. 1654.

‖ Vaughan, as *ante* p. 39.

APPENDIX TO MEMOIR.

A, page xxvi, *et alibi*.—ZACHARY CATLIN.

It has been deemed proper to give in full, in this appendix, the 'Memoir' of Sibbes, drawn up by Zachary Catlin (the manuscript of which; as has been stated, is in my possession). Accordingly it is subjoined, *verbatim et literatim* from the original holograph with signature. Two copies of this 'Memoir' are preserved at Cambridge; one among the Baker MSS. (xxxviii. 441–446); the other, recently presented, in University Library.* That by Baker has been edited with scrupulous fidelity by Rev. J. E. B. Mayor, M.A.; and forms one of the 'Communications' of the Cambridge Antiquarian Society (read December 1. 1856, No. vii. pp. 252–264). It is to be regretted that it abounds with the most singular misreadings; for which Baker, not Mr Mayor, must be held responsible. Mr Mayor's notes, characteristically full of out-of-the-way reading, are appended. They are marked M. That in University Library, Mr Cooper informs me, 'is a transcript written about 1750, and contains some slight verbal variations from the Baker MS.,' but he adds, 'these variations can be of little value, because the scribe read the olden hand so imperfectly, that he throughout calls the subject of the memoir "Gibbs."'

Of Catlin very little is known beyond the incidental notices of himself and father, in his memoir of Sibbes. The 'Diary of John Rous, incumbent of Santon Downham, Suffolk, from 1625 to 1642, edited by Mary A. E. Green, (Camden Society, 4to, 1856,)' introduces him thus:—

Thirston.—Mr Catlin's sermon.

'Upon Shrovemoonday, February 13. [A.D. 1632], Mr Catlin preaching at Bury, gave out before his sermon that it was good the ministers of the combination wold meete to consulte of the making of the combination, that those ministers that wold doe good might be put in seasonably for it. I learned since, that a newe-come minister was put in first in the combination, to beginne on Plough Moonday, but as it seemed would not goe before the graver preachers, and, therefore, lefte the day unprovided; but Mr Catlin by entreaty, preached at that time, *ex improviso*, and after wold have beene freed of this his owne time, but could not (thus he said before the sermon), and in his sermon said thus much obiter, which I heard. We are blamed for our churches, but it is certaine, that these courtes extracte more from us than will repayer our churches, adorne them, and keepe them so.' Pp. 68, 69.

* A third is in Harl. MSS., 6037, fol. 17.

Mr Mayor has overlooked the marginal-note, 'Thirston,' when he asks if our Zachary Catlin were 'the Mr Catlin mentioned by John Rous.' 'Thirston,' *i.e.*, Thurston, gives the answer in the affirmative.

Mr Cooper has favoured me with a note of various Catlins of the several colleges, Cambridge. There is a Zachary Catlin of Christ's, B.A. 1598, M.A. 1602. This was probably our Zachary. There is a Jonathan Catlin of Catharine-Hall, B.A. 1631, M.A. 1635, who was most likely the son mentioned as cared for by Sibbes.

The name, spelled 'Catling' and 'Catlyn,' occurs in Mr Bright's volume (*ante* page cxxi), as an 'overseer' in the will of one of the Nether-hall Brights, and elsewhere as a 'witness' (see pp. 108, 128). I have been unable to trace to any library the two sermons published by him (*ante* page cxxiii). Considerable 'Notes' on the family and name of Catelyne or Catlin (unpublished), will be found in 'Davy's Suffolk Collections,' vol. xlvi. (pp. 312–24). . . . Pedigrees C, Caa—Cha; Mus. Brit. Jure Emptionis, 19, 122. Plut. clxxvi. E. With these slight memoranda, I beg now to submit, 'Dr Sibbs, his Life, by Zachary Catlin.'

At the Request of a Noble Friend, S[ir] W. Spring,* I haue here willingly contributed to the happy memory of that worthy man of God Doctour Sibs a few such Flowers, as I could collect, eyther from the certain Relation of those yt knew his first Education, or from mine own observation of him, at that distance, whereat we lived. And if any thing here recorded, may seem convenient for His purpose, who is (as I am informed) about to publish the Lives ‡ of some Worthyes lately deceased, I shall think my labour well bestow'd. For I am not of that Philosopher's mind, who lighting upon a Book newly put forth, entitled, The encomium of Hercules, cast it away, saying, Et quis Lacedæmoniorum eum vituperavit? accounting it a needles § work to prayse him, whom noe man did, or could find fault withal. I rather iudge it a commendable thing, to perpetuate and keep Fresh the Memory of such worthy men, whose examples may be of use, for Imitation, in this declining, and degenerate Age. But I come to the matter.

Mr Clark of London.†

He was born 577.

This Richard, the eldest Son of Paul Sibs and Johan, was born at Tostock|| in Suffolk, 4 miles from Bury, anno domini 1577, from whence his Parents soon removed, to a Town adioining, called, Thurston, where they lived in honest Repute, brought up, and maried divers children, purchased some Houses and Lands, and there they both Deceased. His Father was by his Trade, a Wheelewright, a skilful and painful workman, and a good sound harted Christian. This Richard he brought up to Learning, at the Grammar Schole, though very ¶ unwillingly, in regard of the charge, had not the youth's strong Inclination to his Book, and wel profiting therein, with some Importunity of Freinds prevailed so far, as to continue him at Schole, til he was fit for Cambridge. Concerning his loue to his Book, and his Industry in study, I cannot omit the Testimony of Mr. Thomas Clark, High Constable, who was

His industry in his study.

* See Prynne's 'Canterb. Doome,' p. 376.—M.

† Mr Clark of London. Probably 'Samuel Clarke,' who included a Memoir of Sibbes in his 'Thirty-two lives' (*ante* p. xxxvii), without however using Catlin's MS. Perhaps as the volume was published in 1652, and the MS. is dated November 1st of that year, it may not have reached him in time. But neither does any trace of it appear in subsequent editions.—G. ‡ 'Plan' in Baker, by Mr Mayor.—G.

§ 'Useless' in Baker, by Mr Mayor. I designate the remaining mis-readings by M. B.—G. || 'Tastock' in M. B.—G. ¶ 'Yet' in M. B.—G.

much of the same Age, and went to schole, together with him, at the same Time, wth one M$^{r.}$ Rich. Brigs (afterward, Head Master of the Free Schole at Norwich) then teaching at Pakenham church. He hath often told me, that when the Boies were dismist from Schole, at the usuall Houres of eleuen, and 5, or 6, and the rest would fal to their pastime, and sometimes to plaiing the Waggs with him, being haimlet* and meanly apparel'd, for ye most part in Leather, it was this Youth's constant course, as soon as he could rid himself of their unpleasing company, to take out of his Pocket or Sachel, one Book or other, and so to goe reading† and meditating, til he came to his Father's house, wch was neere a mile of, and so as he went to Schole agen. This was his order also, when his Father sent him to the Free Schole at Bury, 3, or 4 Miles off, every day. Whereby ye said M$^{r.}$ Clark, did then conceive y^{t} he would in Time prove an excellent and Able man, who of a child was of such a manly staydnes § and indefatigable industry in his study. His Father at length grew weary of his expenses for books and learning, took him from Schole, bought him an Axe and some other tooles, and set him to his own Trade, to the great discontent of the youth, whose Genius wholy caried him another way. Whereupon, M$^{r.}$ *Greaves* ‖ then Minister of Thurston, and M$^{r.}$ Rushbrook an Attorney there, knowing the disposition and fitnes of the lad, sent him, without his Father's consent, to some of the Fellowes of S$^{t.}$ John's colledge, of their acquaintance, with their Letters of Recommendation, where, upon examination, he was so wel approved off, that he was presently entertained as a Subsizar, shortly after chosen Scholer of the House, and at length came to be Fellow of ye Colledge,¶ and one of the Taskers of ye University, His Father being hardly brought to allow him 20 Nobles a yeare toward his maintenance in Cambr., to which some good friends in the country, M^{r}. *Greaves*,** M^{r}. Knewstub,†† and some others, made some addition, for a Time as need required.

ἐαν ῆ φιλομαθης, ἐση πολυμαθης. Tis one signe of a scholar to be φιλόπονος. —Ascham.‡

His profiting in Cambr.

Anno domini 1608, I came to be Minister of Thurston, and he was then a Fellow of the Colledge, and a Preacher of good Note in Cambr., and wee‡‡ soon grew§§ wel acquainted, for whensoeuer he came down into ye Country, to visit his Mother and brethren (his Father being deceased) he would never faile to preach with us, ‖‖ on the Lords day, and for the most part, twice, telling me, that it was a work of charity, to help a constant and painful preacher, for so he was pleased to conceiue of me. And If there were a Communion appointed at any Time, he would be sure not to withdraw himselfe after sermon, but receiving the Bread and wine at my hands, he would always assist me in the distribution of ye cup to the congregation.

As for his kindnes to his kindred,¶¶ and neglect of the world, it was very remarkable, for this I can testify of my own knowledge, that purchasing of M$^{r.}$ Tho. Clark, and others in our Town, a Mesuage and Lands, at seueral times, to the value of fifty pounds per annum, he paid the Fines to the Lords, but never took one peny of the Rents or profits of them, but left the Benefit wholly to his

His kindnes to his kindred and his singular neglect of ye world.

* 'Humble' in M. B.—G. † 'Studying' in M. B.—G.

‡ Not given in M. B.—G. § 'Stryde' in M. B.—G. ‖ 'Gwinn' in M. B.—G.

¶ 'That house' in M. B.—G. ** 'Graves' in M. B.—G.

†† See Brook's 'Puritans,' vol. ii. p. 308, *seq.;* Clarke's 'Lives of Thirty-two English Divines,' ed. 1677, p. 133; Geffrey Whitney's 'Emblems,' p. 223; Bancroft's 'Daungerous Positions,' pp. 5, 57 (Bk. 2, c. 10), 44 (Bk. 3, c. 2), 120, 122, 143; Sutcliffe's 'Answere to Throckmorton,' p. 47; Prynne's 'Canterb. Doome,' p. 376.—M. ‡‡ 'Was' in M. B.—G. §§ 'Grown' in M. B.—G.

‖‖ 'Me' in M. B.—G. ¶¶ 'Friends' in M. B.—G.

Mother, and his 2 Brethren,* as long as he liued. So much did this Heavenly-minded Man of God slight this present world (which the most men are so loth to part withal, when they Dye) that he freely and undesired, parted with it, whilst he liued, requiring nothing of them, but only to be liberal to the poore. Nay ouer and besides, if any faithful honest man came down from Cambridge or London, where he liued, by whom he might conveniently send, he seldome or never fayled to send his Mother a Peice of Gold, for the most part, a ten shillings Piece, but 5 shillings was the least, and this he continued as long, as his Mother liued. And would she haue been persuaded to exchange her Country Life for the citty, he often told me, yt he would willingly have maintain'd her there, in good view and fashion, like his Mother, but she had no mind to alter her accustomed course of Life, in her old daies, contenting her self with her own Meanes, and that Addition, w[ch] her Son made thereunto.

His special kindness to me.

And for his special kindnes to my self, in particular, I cannot omit, that being Trusted by Personages of Quality, with diuers sumes of mony, for pious and charitable uses, he was pleased, among many others, not to forget Me. At one Time he sent me down three Twenty shillings peices of gold inclosed in a Letter: and at 2 other Times, deliver[ed] me, with his own hand, two Twenty shilling pieces more: and so far was this Humble Saint from Pharisaical ostentation, and vain glory, and from taking the honour of these good works to himself, that he plainly told me, that these Gratuities were not of his own cost, but being put in Trust, and † left to his own Discretion, in the distribution, he lookt upon Mee as One, that took great Paines in my ministry, and in teaching Scholers, and at that Time Labouring under the Burden of a great charge of children, and so thought me a fit object of their intended charity. And from myselfe His love descended down to my Son, for my sake, for whom ‡ (before he had euer seen him, being then at the Grammar Schole at Bury) he, then chosen M[r] of Katherin Hal, promis'd me a Schollership there, of 5 pound a yeare, and to provide for him a Tutour and a chamber. And such was his constancy of spirit, and his Reality, that whatsoeuer promise he made me, he would be sure, both to Remember it, and to make it good, as freely as he first made it, that was, unaskt and undesired: and for these manyfold kindnesses, all that he desired at my hands, was no more but this, that I would be careful of the soules of my people, and in special of his Mother, his Brethren, and his sisters, and would give them good counsel, in their disposing themselves in Marriage, or upon any other occasion, as I saw, they stood in need. And this one thing, I may not passe over, concerning myself, that in his last wil and Testament, he gave me a Legacy of 40 sh. with the Title of his Loving Freind, w[ch] I the rather mention, because I had not the least thought, to haue been in yt sort remembred by him, at his Death, liuing || at no lesse distance from him, then of three score miles. In a word, such was the Loueliness of this sweet ¶ seruant of God, such his learning, parts, piety, prudence, humility, sincerity, Loue and meeknes of Spirit (whereof euery one was a Lodeston to attract unto, and fasten my spirit, close to his) that (I professe ingenuously) no man yt euer I was acquainted withal, got so far into my hart, or lay **

His singular humility.

His reality in his promises. Pollicitis dives quilibetis esse potest.§

* 'Brothers' in M. B., and so elsewhere.
† 'As' in M. B.—G.
‡ 'For whom' dropped in M. B.—G.
§ Not in M. B.
|| 'Being' in M. B.—G.
¶ 'Same' in M. B.—G.
** 'Was' in M. B.—G.

so close therein: So that many Times I could not part from him, with dry eyes. But who am I? or what is it to be belov'd of me, especially for Him, that had so many and so great Friends, as he had? yet even to Me, the great God is pleased to say, My son give me thy Heart, and this poor and contrite hart, I know, he wil not despise, And this Hart of mine, as small as it is, yet is too great, to close with a Proud, Profane, worldly, malicious hart, though it be in a Prince. But true* Vertue and Grace, are the Image of God himself, and where they are discerned† by Wisdom's children, they command the Hart, and are truly louely and venerable, whereas Carnal, vitious, and unmortified Affections (whereof this Man of God, was as Free, as any man, I know liuing) they do render a man (whateuer he bee), if not hateful and contemptible, yet at least less louely and honourable. But my Love to this good Man hath transported me beyond my purpose, wch was to speake of some things, lesse visible to others, especially concerning his first Education: for when he came to the University and the Citty, there his Life, and Actions were upon a publick Theatre, and his own works, without a Trumpet, would prayse him in the Gates. As for his kindnes to his kindred, and to my selfe, I know none, yt took more notice of them, then I, and therefore I could not hide them from the world (upon this occasion) without some kind of Sacriledge.

Prov. 23 26.
Psal. 51. 17.
Prov. 31. 31 and 23.
His death July 5th 1635 ætat 58.

But from his Life, I passe to his Death, and the disposing of his worldly estate, wherein are some things very Remarkable, and coming to my certain knowledge and observation, I neyther wil, nor dare‡ conceal them. His Death was some what soden; for having preach't at Graye's Inne, upon the Lords Day, on that sweet Text, Joh. xiv. 1, 2, 'Let not your Harts be troubled, ye belieue in God, Believe also in me. In my Father's House are many Mansions,' as if he had presag'd his own Death, he fel sick that very night, and died on ye Tuesday‖ following, being the 5th of July A.D. 1635. Ætatis suæ 58, his Physitian, that knew his Body best¶ being then out of ye Citty; yet having his senses, and some respite of Time, as he set his Soule, so he set his House in order, revising his former will, and altering, what he thought fitt to be altered. And first, he Bequeathed and commended** his Soule, into the hands of his gracious Saviour, who Redeemed it, with his most precious Blood, and appeared then in heaven, to receive it. He gave him humble thanks, that he had vouchsafed him, to be born, and to live, in the Best Times of the Gospel, *(mark this)* and to have his Interest in the comfort of it. As also that he had vouchsafed him the Honour of being a Publisher of it, with some measure of Faithfulnes (mark this, you that contemne ye office of the ministry). His Body he ordered to be buried, at the pleasure of his Executors. And for his worldly estate, wherewith God had blessed him, he thus disposed of it. His House and Lands at Thurston, to the value of 50 lib. a year, or more, he gave to his youngest and only Brother then liuing, Thomas Sibs, for ye terme of his natural Life, and the Remainder to John Sibs, the son of John, his second Brother deceased: and between these two, he diuided all his

His Cygnea Cantio vel concio §
His last will.
Note.
How he disposed his lands and personal estate.

* 'This' in M. B.—G. † 'Discovered' in M. B.—G. ‡ 'Doe' in M. B.—G.

§ This is the title given to Whitaker's last 'sermon,' published 1599, 4to.—G.

‖ This is a slip for Sunday. See Memoir, page cxxx., and title-page of 'last sermons,' in this volume.—G.

¶ 'Best' in M. B.—G. ** 'Committed' in M. B.—G.

personal estate, which clearly amounted to 650 lib. (his large Legacies, and funeral charges being discharged and satisfied) making them, ye exequestors of his Wil and Test[t]. To the children of his 3 sisters deceased he gave 110 lib. To other poore kindred 13 lib. To his faithful Servant, James Joynar, 10 lib. To other 5 in London, 5 lib. To the poore of the parishes of Trinity and S[t.] Andrew's in Cambridge, 5 lib. To the poore of the Parish of Thurston, and of the parish, where he should be buried, 2 lib. To the Steward of Grayes Inne, 3 lib. To the 3 cheife Butlars, 3 lib. To their Servants, 1 lib. To the chiefe Cook, a Ring of 10 sh. To his under Servants, 1 lib. To his deare and worthy Friend M[r]. Jo. Pym,* a Ring of 2 lib. To S[r]. Rob[t.] Brook† of Langley, his Lady, and Brother, 3 Rings of 6 lib. To Mr. Stephens‡ a Ring of 2 lib. To M[r.] Capell,§ Preacher, 1 lib. To his loving friend Mr. Catlin, Preacher of Thurston, 2 lib. To Mr. Almond of Cambr. for his Son (ye Doctours Godson), 5 lib. To his Godson Rich[d.] Clark, 2 lib. To Mr. Gouge ‖ of London, whom he requested to preach at his Funeral, 1 lib.¶ To S[r.] Nath. Rich ;** to S[r.] Nath. Barnardiston ;†† and to S[r.] W[m.] Spring, Supervisors of his will, 3 Rings of 3 lib. To M[rs.] Mary Moore, a Ring of 2 lib. To Mr. Jo. Godbold of Gray's Inn Esq., one of ye exequatours of his Will, the best peice of plate he had, valued at 10 lib. To Katherin-Hal in Cambr, for the setling of a Scholarship of 4 lib. per annum for ever, 100 lib. All wich Legacies amount to the total summe of 288 lib. 10 sh.

Legacies given out 288 lib. 10 sh.

His enlarging Katherin Hal.

During the Time yt he was M[r]. of Kath-Hal, he was the Meane by his great friends, of buying in the Inne, adioininge ye Colledge, called The Bull, and so of enlarging the Buildings of the Colledge, to the value of 500 lib. as I am informed: But I leave this to ‡‡ a *melius Inquirendum*. O what a Pious and charitable disposition do these things discouer, in this precious Saint, to be had in everlasting Remembrance.

* Besides the common sources for Pym's life, consult the 'Charisteria and Epist Eucharist.' of Degory Whear, his tutor and acquaintance of many years' standing. 'Charist.' Dedn. and pp 101, 102; 'Epist. Eucharist.' Nos. 21—28. Pym was a friend and connection of Brownrigg's. B's 'Life,' pp. 190, 191.—M.

† Sir Robert Brook of Langley, his Lady . . . . See 'Dedication' of 'Fountain Sealed' (*ante* page cxix)—G.

‡ Dr Stephens, editor of 'Statius,' Master of Bury? 'Life of Isaac Milles,' 1721, pp. 8–12, 74.—M.

§ Richard Capel, Wood's 'Athenæ,' ed. Bliss, iii. 421, Clark's 'Lives' (as above), p. 303 *seq.*—M.

‖ Dr Wm. Gouge. See his life in Clark (as above), p. 234 *seq.*, Harwood's 'Alumni Etonenses,' p. 202, Wm. Lilly's 'Life,' ed. 1774, p. 29, Prynne's 'Canterb. Doome,' p. 362, Life of Row' in Clark's 'Lives of Eminent Persons,' (1683), pt. ii. p. 106, Brook's 'Lives of the Puritans,' iii. 165, *seq.*—M. Also 'Memoir' prefixed to his Exposition of 'Hebrewes,' folio, 1655, vol. i.—G.

¶ From a tract bound in the volume marked R. 10. 16 in the University Library of Cambridge (p. 525) it appears that 10s. was commonly charged to the poor, and 20s. to the rich, for a funeral sermon. The tract contains the answer of George Finch (a Cambridge man, brother to Lord Finch) to the articles against him A.D. 1641.—M.

** See Birch's James I., vol. ii., p. 55, and Whear's 'Charisteria,' p. 127.—M.

†† See his life in Clarke's 'Lives of Eminent Persons,' (1683), pt. ii., p. 105, *seq.* Cf. *ibid.* pp. 161, 163, 169, 172, 175; Calamy's 'Account,' pp. 636, 637; 'Contin.' p. 786.—M.

‡‡ The Black Bull was given by will to Cath. Hall by Dr Gostlin, for the founding of six scholars, &c.—M.

I shal conclude with an Observation, w[ch] I made of the Time, when this holy man, and some other Godly and precious Divines, were taken out of this world, by the wise Providence of God. Tis that of ye Prophet Is: 57, I. That Righteous and merciful men are taken away, from the Evill to come. They enter into Peace, and rest in their Graues, as in Beds of Sleep. Thus ye Lord said, concerning good Josia, I wil gather thee to the Fathers, and thou shalt go to thy Grave in Peace, And thine eyes shall not see all ye Evil, w[ch] I wil bring upon this place. In like manner, the Lord took away, about the same Time, with this Reverend man diuers, that their eyes might not see that great Evils, then ready to break out, upon these 3 kingdoms. To instance in some few, D[r.] Sibs died July 5, 1635; M[r.] Sam. Ward,* that Worthy Preacher of Ipswich, was censured in the High commission, and silencet in October follow[g] ye same yeare 1635, and died, as I remember 1638. The Irish Rebellion, the slaughter of 100,000 Protestants in a yeare, the long, fatal war, between the King and Parl[t].

The time of his death. Isa. 57, 1.

2 K. 22. 19, 20.

Dr Sibs, Mr Sam. Ward.

M[r.] Rogers† also, that Zealous and powerful Preacher of Dedham in Essex, died Octob: 15: 1636. And I may not forget my own father also, M[r.] Robert Catlin,‡ an aged and a faithfull Minister in Rutlandshire, about four score yeares old died July 24: 1637: who Being unable any longer to serue his great Pastoral cure, he came over to Barham, neere Ipswich, to dy amongst his children (here) in Suffolk: who lying on his sick Bed, heard M[r.] Fenton, a Minister relating the Heavy censure, that was then newly passed upon the Bishop of Lincoln, and Deane of Westminster, Doctour Williams, reputed at that Time a very good Man, whom my Father knew to be a great Freind to the Good ministers in his Diocese, and a great enimy to the setting the Tables Altarwise, and to the Altar worship, w[ch] then began to be much advocated, and one that had done many munificent works of charity, and had given yearely a great summe to the Releife of the Lady Elizabeth. The Bishop, by the malice of Archbishop Laud and others his enemies, was suspended in the High Commission ab officio or beneficio, censured in the Star-Chamber, fined 10,000 lib. and cast into the Towre of London about July 15, 1637: from whence he was fetchet out the beginning of this Parl[t.] Nov. 3d, 1640, with great applause. My Father, I say, hearing of this Bishop's censure (wherein my Brother Wm. Catlin, a minister was deeply concerned, as being a witness for ye Bishop), He brake out into these words, before the 2 Ministers, and others then present in the chamber. Alas poore England, thou hast now seen thy best daies; I that am 4 score yeares old, and I have in al my time seene no alteration in Religion, nor any foreign Enemy setting

Mr Rogers of Dedham.

Mr Robert Catlin.

Dr. Williams cast into ye Tower.

* See Brook's 'Lives of the Puritans,' vol. ii. p. 452, *seq.*, with the authors there cited; also Heylin's 'Cyprianus Angl.' p. 120, *seq.;* Prynne's 'Canterb. Doome,' pp. 157, 159, 361, 375; Birch's 'James I.,' vol. ii. pp. 226, 228, 232; Clark's 'Lives of Eminent Persons' (1683), pt. ii. pp. 154, 159; D'Ewes' 'Autobiography,' vol i. p. 249; Calamy's 'Account,' p. 636 —M. Also Mr Ryle's Memoir, prefixed to his 'Sermons' in present series (see Adams's, iii.).—G.

† See his life in Brook's 'Lives of the Puritans,' vol. ii. p. 421: and Bastwick's 'Utter Routing,' p. 474, Prynne's 'Canterb. Doome,' pp. 363, 373, Calamy's 'Account,' p. 606, Clark's 'Lives of Eminent Persons' (1683), p. 64 (Life of Blackerby), Mather's 'Life of T. Hooker,' p. 8, Mather's 'Life of John Cotton,' pp. 24, 25.—M. Also Chester's 'John Rogers' . . . pages 245, *seq.* (1 vol. 8vo, 1861).—G.

‡ This account has been printed in Brook's 'Lives of the Puritans,' vol. ii. pp. 428, 429.—M.

foot in England, nor any Ciuil wars, amongst ourselves, do now forsee euil daies a comming. But I shal go to the grave in Peace. Blessed be that God, whom I have served, who hath accepted my weake service, and wil be mine exceeding great reward. And within a few houres, he departed this Life, and lies Buried in the Chauncell of the Parish Church at Barham, Doctour Young of Stow Market,* preaching at his Funeral: and as he Blessed God (with Dr. Sibs) yt he had lived in the best Times of the Gospel, so there was no great difference in the Time of their death. And shortly after the death of these men were those sparkles of discontent kindled between the Scots and us, wch were the sad Præludia, or beginnings of this late Universal Conflagration. The King went against the Scots, as far as York, in March 1638: and the Scots were proclaimed Traitours in the Churches of England, in April following, and though this Proclamation were revoked, yet who knows not, what Tragical events have follow'd in al the 3 Kingdoms, to this very day,† to the astonishment of Heaven and Earth. This is ye very observation of Reverend Beza in his 70th Epistle: That as often as God kindleth and setteth vp these Lights (men of singular graces and special use in ye church) so often he testifies his good wil to yose Times and Places in a certen special and peculiar manner. But when he extinguishes these Lights and puts them out, it must be accounted as an evident testimony of his sore Displeasure. For (saith he) it is apparant in al Histories that when greivous Tempests are comming upon a People, The Lord is wont to withdraw his especial servants into the Haven beforehand, wch agrees with yt of ye Prophet Isay 2. 2, 3, 5. Behold ye Lord wil take away out of Judah and Jerusalem ye Judges and ye Prophets; the Wise man and ye Councellour and ye Honourable: and the People shal bee oppressed one of another etc. And no marvel, for such men are the το κατεχος . . . meanes as a shield to keep off the wrath of God from the Places where they live. The Lord with held the Flood of waters from ye old world, til Noah was safely shut up in the Ark, and the very selfe same day (saith the Text) were the Fountaines of the Deep broken up and the windowes of Heaven opened. The Angel told Lot he could do nothing against wicked Sodom, till he was got out of that place. The Lord held off the king of Babilon from beseiging Jerusalem til good Josia was at rest. And ere the Roman Army sate down before it, the Lord by a Miracle warned the Christian Jewes to remove from thence to Pella. Again, no sooner was that worthy Bishop of Hippo St Augustin deceased, but the City was taken and sacked by the Goths and Vandals. No sooner was Martin Luther translated to a better Life, but the Smalcaldick warre brake out wch wasted almost al the Protestants in Germany. No sooner was that worthy man, aged Pareus taken from Heydelberg, but presently Marques Spinola with his Army entered the Town. And no sooner had the Lord taken away these worthy Divines, but presently the Fire of war and confusion (a iust punishment for our great and crying sins) brake out upon these 3 nations. For if the Foundations (of Religion and Government) be cast down and destroy'd, what can the Righteous do. The voice of wise men is not heard in the cry of Fooles: The counsel of moderate and unbiased men is not regarded in such a

King went against ye Scots. March 1638.

Bezæ Ep. 70.

Gen. 7. 16. 11. 13.

Gen. 13. 22.

2 Chron. 34. 28, and 36. 6.

Josephus.

Augustine.

M. Luther.

D. Pareus.

Psal. 11. 3.

* The celebrated Scottish tutor and friend of John Milton.

† From 'very day,' on to 'The Lord in Mercy,' not in M.-B.—G.

Tempest of clamour, violence, and confusion. Such men would have been slighted and lay'd aside in such Times as these. The Lord therefore hath put them into their safe harbour and Haven of Rest, while wee that survive are tossed to and fro upon the turbulent Eurypus of Anabaptistical, Anarchical, Fanatical, and Atheistical barretings and Vittlitigations.*

The Lord in Mercy vouchsafe to stil the Raging of the waters, Ps. 65. 7.
and the madnes of (that many headded monster) the People, Isay. 39. 8.
that once more his faithful Servants in these 3 Nations, may Matt: 8. 25.
enjoy a blessed calm. That there may yet once again, be Peace and Truth in our Daies. Lord save us, or we perish.

Compiled and attested, by Zachary Catlin, Minister of Thurston, Nov. 1. 1652: Anno ætatis 69: currente.

(I have presented Catlin's MS. to 'University Library,' Cambridge).

B, pages xxix and cxxxi.—SIBBES'S FAMILY AND NAME.

The Will of Sibbes (*ante* p. cxxviii, *seq.*), enumerates various relatives deceased and alive. His father had died before 1608, and his mother, Catlin informs us, also predeceased him. Dr Sibbes himself never married, perhaps through the 'order' of Gray's Inn, that forbad its 'preacher' to marry. The name seems to have utterly died out, not in Suffolk merely, but everywhere. While all the other Puritans of this Series are living names, I have failed to trace any Sibbes beyond 1737. No doubt the blood has been transmitted in the issue of the several sisters named in the 'Will.'

The following *memorabilia* from the sources enumerated above each, contain all that I have been able to collect about the family and name.

I. Catharine-Hall 'Registers.'

(1.) John Sibbes, B.A. 1635 (mentioned in 'Will').

(2.) Richard . . . B.A. 1664, M.A. 1668. (See entry in Thurston 'Register,' Mo. 2.)

(3.) Robert . . . B.A. 1675.

(4.) Richard . . . B.A. 1716.

II. Tostock 'Registers.'

The merest fragment of the 'Registers' of Tostock has been preserved; and the first occurrence of the name of Sibbes therein, it will be observed, is long posterior to his death.

1. Hannah Sibbs, the daughter of Thomas Sibbs (probably a grand-nephew), and Elizabeth his wife, was baptized the 6th day of January 1679.

2. Francis, ye daughter of Thomas Sibbes and Elizabeth his wife, was baptized ye 5th of June 1683.

*** See an entry from Thurston 'Register,' of her marriage.

3. Richard, the son of Thomas Sibbs and Elizabeth his wife, was baptized May ye 1st 1688.

From the 'deaths' we find 'Thomas Sibbes was buried January ye 18th 1690,' and 'Elizabeth Sibbes, widow, was buried, August 9th 1706.'

4. John Nunn and Sarah Sibbes (probably a grand-neice), both of this parish, were married, April 12. 1697.

Of this marriage were born :—

(1.) Mary, 'baptized December ye 30th 1702.'

(2.) John, 'baptized January ye 9th 1706.' (Died in a few days.)

(3.) Esther, 'baptized May ye 26th 1708.'

* Qu. 'Vile litigations?'—Ed.

Of 'Sarah Sibbes' = Mrs Nunn, we read, 'Sarah, the wife of John Nunn of Thurston, was buried here, April 28th 1719.' A 'Frances Nunn of Rattlesden, was buried, Feb. 18. 1725.'

A third branch is as follows :—

5. 'John Limner of Chevington, and Elizabeth Sibbes (probably another grand-niece), of this town, were married, August ye 23d 1700.'

There was issue :—

'Esther, daughter of John Limner and Elizabeth his wife, . . baptized Octob. ye 15th 1701.'

III. Thurston 'Registers,' as Tostock.

Only two occurrences of the name of Sibbes are found :—

1. Titulus Matrimonii, 1707.

'Robert Steggles of Tostock, and Frances Sibbes of Thurston, married, Ap. 23.' (See under Tostock, No. 2.)

2. 'Mr Richard Sibbes, clerk, rector of Gedding 65 years, aged 93, Feb. 2. 1737.'

This was doubtless the 'Richard' of the Cambridge list (*supra* No. 2). He was probably non-resident. In the 'registers' of Gedding, only one entry during the whole period of his incumbency, bears his signature as 'rector.'

IV. Bright's 'Brights of Suffolk' (*ante* pp. lxxxv–vi).

In the family papers of 'the Netherhall Family,' John Sibbes, no doubt the Doctor's nephew, appears as a 'witness' in a dispute about a 'meadow' (page 127). On the back of a letter (January ye 6th 1703), is a memorandum by Thomas Bright, relating to accounts and rents, under the heads of Thurston, Pakenham, Barton, and Tostock, in which, among others, occur the names of 'John, Robert, and Thomas Sibbes,' perhaps 'tenants' on the estate. Finally, in a letter, 'June 10. 1729,' a Mr Howard writes to the famous beauty, 'Mary Bright,' that 'yesterday he view[d] Mr Sibbs' copyhold lands, held of her manor.'

C, page cxxvi.—SUCCESSORS OF SIBBES IN HIS OFFICES.

1. 'Preacher,' Gray's Inn.

13th November 1635. Hannibal Potter, Dr of Divinity, chose preacher.

9th February 1641. Mr Jackson is chose lecturer, to preach twice of a Sunday.

28th May 1647. Mr Horton chose preacher.

13th January 1662. Mr Caley, preacher and lect[r] of this Society, if he please to accept thereof.

12th November 1662. Mr Cradock chose lect[r], wth same allowance as Mr Wilkins.

2. 'Master,' Catherine Hall, Cambridge.

There was a keen contest for the 'Mastership.' The subsequently celebrated Bishop Brownrig was appointed. For interesting notice, with references, of Brownrig, and for the papers relating to the disputes, consult Mr Mayor's 'Autobiography of Matthew Robinson' (pp. 130–146); also 'Garrard's Letter to Strafford (September 1. 1635, Strafford's Letters, vol. i. p. 462).

A DESCRIPTION OF CHRIST.

A DESCRIPTION OF CHRIST.

NOTE.

THE title-page, which is given below,* of the original and only early edition of the 'Description of Christ' bears, it will be observed, that it consists of the 'leading—*i. e.*, introductory—sermons to that treatise called the Bruised Reed.' Hence its position in our reprint. It seemed proper to place the two together.

The 'Description,' as having been published posthumously, will not compare in finish with the more famous 'Bruised Reed,' and, indeed, occasionally (as at p 6, line 10 from bottom, p. 13, line 8 from bottom), partakes very much of the nature of those 'notes . . . by some who had not perfectly taken them,' to which Sibbes deprecatingly refers in his address to the 'Christian reader,' prefixed to the latter. Still, in substance, if not in composition, the 'Description' is valuable; and having been published in the 'Beams of Divine Light' according 'to the doctor, his own appointment,' it carries his authority. It is to be hoped that in no after-reprints will the 'Description' and 'Bruised Reed' be disjoined. G. †

* Original Title page—

A
DESCRIPTION
OF CHRIST,
In { His neerenesse to God,
His calling,
His qualification,
His execution of his calling.
In three Sermons.
Being the leading Sermons to that Treatise called the Bruised Reed, preached
upon the precedent words.
By the late Reverend and learned Divine, Richard Sibs,
Doctor in Divinitie, Master of Katherine Hall in
Cambridge, and sometimes Preacher at
Grayes Inne.
Isa. 61. 1.
The Spirit of the Lord God is upon me, because the Lord hath annoynted
me to preach good tidings unto the meeke.
London.
Printed by G. M. for N. Bourne and R. Harford, and are to be sold at the south
entrance of the Royall Exchange, and at the guilt Bible in Queenes-head-
Alley in Pater-noster-row. MDCXXXIX.

† Throughout the present edition of Sibbes, those foot-notes without any signature or initial belong to the author or his original editors. For all others prefixed or subjoined to the several treatises, &c., having G. attached, the Editor is responsible.

A DESCRIPTION OF CHRIST.

Behold my servant, whom I have chosen; my beloved, in whom my soul is well pleased: I will put my Spirit upon him, and he shall shew judgment to the Gentiles. He shall not strive, nor cry; neither shall any man hear his voice in the streets, &c.—MATT. XII. 18.

THE words are the accomplishment of a prophecy, taken out of Isaiah xlii. 1, 2, as we may see by the former verse, 'that it might be fulfilled.' Now the occasion of bringing them in here in this verse, it is a charge that Christ gives, verse 16, that they should not discover and make him known for the miracles he did. He withdraws himself; he was desirous to be concealed, he would not live to the view over much, for he knew the rebellious disposition of the Jews, that were willing to change their government, and to make him king; therefore, he laboured to conceal himself all kind of ways. Now, upon this charge, that they should tell nobody, he brings in the prophet Isaiah prophesying of him, 'Behold my servant, &c.; he shall not strive nor cry, neither shall any man hear his voice in the streets.' Other kings labour that their pomp and magnificence may be seen; but he shall not mind ostentation, he shall not be contentious nor clamorous. For these three things are meant when he saith, 'he shall not strive, nor cry, neither shall his voice be heard in the streets;' he shall not yield to any ostentation, for he came in an abased state to work our salvation; he shall not be contentious, nor yet clamorous in matter of wrong; there shall be no boasting any kind of way, as we shall see when we come to the words. You see, then, the inference here.

The inference in the prophet Isaiah is to comfort the people, and to direct them how to come to worship the true God, after he had declaimed against their idolatry, as we see in the former chapter, 'Behold my servant,' &c. Great princes have their ambassadors, and the great God of heaven hath his Son, his servant in whom he delights, through whom, and by whom, all intercourse between God and man is.

It is usual in the prophecies, especially of Isaiah, that evangelical prophet, when he foretells anything comfortable to the people, in the promise of temporal things, he riseth to stablish their faith in better things, by adding thereto a prophecy, and promise of Christ the Messiah, to insinuate thus much, I will send you the Messiah, that is a greater gift than this that I have promised you; therefore you may be sure of the less, as the apostle reasons excellently, 'If he spared not his own son, but delivered him to death for us all, how shall he not with him give us all things?' Rom. viii. 32. So here, I have promised you deliverance out of Babylon, and this and that; do you doubt of the performance? Alas! what is that in comparison of a greater favour I intend you in Christ, that shall deliver you out of another manner of Babylon? 'Behold my servant whom I have chosen;' and in Isaiah vii. 14, 'Behold a virgin shall conceive, and bear a son,' &c. I will send you the Messiah; God shall become man; therefore, I will not stand for any outward favour or deliverance whatsoever. So he goes to the grand promise, that they might reason from the greater to the less.

There is another end, why in other promises there is mention of the promise of the Messiah, to uphold their faith. Alas! we are unworthy of these promises, we are laden with sin and iniquity. It is no matter, I will send you the Messiah. 'Behold my servant in whom my soul delighteth,' and for his sake I will delight in you. I am well pleased with you, because I am well pleased in him; therefore, be not discouraged. 'All the promises are yea and amen in Jesus Christ,' 2 Cor. i. 19; for all the promises that be, though they be for the things of this life, they are made for Christ, they are yea in him, and they are performed for his sake, they are amen in him. So much for the occasion of the inference in the evangelist St Matthew, and likewise in the prophet Isaiah.

To come more directly to the words, 'Behold my servant whom I have chosen, my beloved in whom my soul is well pleased,' &c.

In the words you have *a description of Christ, his nearness to God:* 'Behold my servant whom I have chosen, my beloved in whom my soul is well pleased.' And then his *calling and qualification:* 'I will put my Spirit upon him.' And the *execution of that calling:* 'He shall shew judgment to the Gentiles.' Then the *quiet and peaceable manner* of the execution of his calling: 'He shall not strive nor cry, neither shall any man hear his voice in the streets,' &c.

Behold!—This word is as it were a beacon lighted up to all the rest. In all the evangelists you have this word often repeated, and the prophets likewise when they speak of Christ; there is no prophecy almost but there is this word, 'Behold.'

Why? Not to spend time in the variety of acceptions (= acceptations), but to speak of it as may serve for the present purpose. The use of it in the prophet, especially out of which these words are taken, was to present Christ to the hearts of the people of God then; therefore, he saith, 'Behold,' for Christ was present to the believers then; he did profit before he was, he did good before he was exhibited, because he was 'the Lamb of God slain from the beginning of the world,' Rev. xiii. 8; he was yesterday as well as to-day, and to-morrow as well as to-day, 'yesterday, to-day, and the same for ever,' Heb. xiii. 8; he was present to their faith, and present to them in types and sacrifices, and present in God's acceptation of him for them; therefore, the prophets mount up with the wing of prophecy, and in regard of the certainty of the things to come, they speak as if they were present, as if they had looked on Christ present, 'Behold my servant,' and 'Behold a virgin,' &c.

But that is not all. Another use of this word 'behold,' was to call the people's minds from their miseries, and from other abasing objects that dejected them, and might force despair. Why do you dwell upon your unworthiness and sin? raise up your mind, 'Behold my servant whom I have chosen,' &c. This is an object worth beholding and admiration, especially of a distressed soul that may see in Christ whatsoever may comfort it.

A third end of it is to raise the mind from any vulgar, common, base contents.* You look on these things, and are carried away with common trivial objects, as the poor disciples when they came to the temple; they stood wondering at the stones. What wondrous stones! what goodly building is here! Mark xiii. 1. So shallow-minded men, they see any earthly excellency, they stand gazing. Alas, saith Christ, do you wonder at these things? So the prophet here raiseth up the minds of men to look on an object fit to be looked on, 'Behold my servant,' &c. So that the Holy Ghost would have them from this saving object, Christ, to raise satisfaction to their souls every way. Are you dejected? here is comfort; are you sinful? here is righteousness; are you led away with present contentments? here you have honours, and pleasures, and all in Christ Jesus. You have a right to common pleasures that others have, and besides them you have interest to others that are everlasting pleasures that shall never fail, so that there is nothing that is dejecting and abasing in man, but there is comfort for it in Christ Jesus; he is a salve for every sore, a remedy for every malady; therefore, 'Behold my servant.'

This word 'behold,' it is a word of wonderment, and, indeed, in Christ there are a world of wonders, everything is wonderful in him. Things new and wonderful, and things rare, and things that are great, that transcend our capacity, are wonderful, that stop our understanding that it cannot go through them. Vulgar things, we see through them quickly, but when we see things that stay our understandings, that raise our understandings higher, and that are more capacious than our understandings, here is matter of admiration and wonder. Now whatsoever may make wonderment is in Jesus Christ, whose name is Wonderful, as it is in Isa. ix. 7; therefore the prophet saith, 'Behold.'

My servant.—Christ is called a servant, first, in respect of his creation, because being a man, as a creature he was a servant. But that is not all.

He was a servant in respect of his condition. Servant implies a base and low condition, Philip. ii. 7. Christ took upon him the form of a servant; he emptied himself; he was the lowest of all servants in condition: for none was ever so abased as our glorious Saviour.

And then, it is a name of office, as well as of base condition. There are ordinary servants and extraordinary, as great kings have their servants of state. Christ besides his abasement, he was a servant of state, he was an ambassador sent from the great God; a prophet, a priest, and a king, as we shall see afterwards; an extraordinary servant, to do a piece of service that all the angels in heaven, and all the men on the earth joined together, could not perform. This great master-piece of service was to bring God and man together again, that were at variance, as it is, 1 Peter iii. 18, 'to bring us to God.' We were severed and scattered from God. His office was to gather us together again, to bring us all to one head again, to bring us to himself, and so to God, to reconcile us, as the Scripture phrase is, Col. i. 20. Now, it being the greatest work and service that ever was, it required the greatest servant; for no creature in the world could perform it. All the angels of heaven would have sunk under this service, to have undergone satisfaction to divine justice; for the angels themselves, when they sinned, they could not recover themselves, but sunk under their own

* That is, 'contentments.'—Ed.

sin eternally. Thus we see how he is God's servant, who set him apart, and chose him to this service.

And then he was a servant to us; for the Son of man came to minister, not to be ministered unto, Matt. xx. 28. He washed his disciples' feet. He was a servant to us, because he did our work and suffered our punishment; we made him serve by our sins, as the prophet saith, Isa. xliii. 24. He is a servant that bears another man's burden. There was a double burden—of obedience active, and obedience passive. He bore them both. He came under the law for us, both doing what we should have done, and indeed far more acceptably, and suffering that we should have suffered, and far more acceptably. He being our surety, being a more excellent person, he did bear our burden, and did our work, therefore he was God's servant, and our servant; and God's servant, because he was our servant, because he came to do a work behoveful to us.

Herein appears the admirable love and care of God to us wretched creatures, here is matter of wonderment.

If we look to him that was a servant;

If we look to that in God and him, that made him stoop to be a servant;

If we look to the manner of the performance of this service;

If we look to the fruit of that service; they are all matter of wonderment.

If we look to the person that was this servant; the apostle, in Philip. ii. 6, will tell you, he thought it not robbery to be equal with God, yet he took upon him the shape of a servant. Was not this wonderful, for God to become man, the glorious God to abase himself, to be a servant? God-man, glorious God, and base servant; for the living God to die, for the incomprehensible God to be enclosed in the womb of a virgin, for glory itself to be abased, for riches to become poor, what matter of wonderment is here! The very angels stand at a gaze and wonder, they pry into these things, 1 Peter i. 12; his name may well be wonderful.

There are four notable conjunctions that are especially wonderful, two in us, and two above us.

One in us, is the conjunction of so excellent a thing as the soul breathed in by God. The soul of man is an admirable thing. The world is not worth it in the judgment of him that gave himself for it. That this should be joined to a piece of earth (indeed, I am wonderfully made, saith David, Ps. cxxxix. 14) in regard of his body, but the conjunction of the soul and body together, so excellent a substance to so base a thing as earth, to a piece of red, well-coloured earth (*a*),* to a lump of flesh, it is a wondrous conjunction.

But there is a more supernatural conjunction of man when all of us, sinners as we are, are knit to Christ our head, and head and members make one Christ. Here is a wondrous conjunction. St Paul calls it a mystery, Eph. v. 32. These conjunctions in us are wonderful.

But now, to go higher, in Christ there are more wonderful conjunctions; for the greatest and the meanest to join together, for God and man to come together, the Lord of all and a servant, and such a servant as should be under a curse, for the Highest of all to come to the deepest abasement. For there was no abasement ever so deep as Christ's was, in a double regard.

First, None ever went so low as he, for he suffered the wrath of God, and bore upon him the sins of us all; none ever was so low.

And then in another respect his abasement was greatest, because he

* The letters *a*, *b*, *c*, &c., in the text, refer to notes appended to the respective treatise, &c.—G.

descended from the highest top of glory; and for him to be man, to be a servant, to be a curse, to suffer the wrath of God, to be the lowest of all—Lord, whither dost thou descend? Here is a wonder in these conjunctions.

Next to Christ's abasement was Adam's; because he was the most excellent, being in the state of innocency, and carrying the image of God, and being familiar with God. For him presently to come into that fearful condition, it was the greatest abasement; because it was from the greatest dignity that made the abasement of Christ so great. For lordship to submit to service, for God to be man, the blessed God to become a curse, here is matter of wonder indeed.

In Christ, again, there was a conjunction of perfect body, perfect soul, and perfect God, and all make one Christ. In the Trinity there is a conjunction of three persons in one nature. That is a wondrous conjunction, but it belongs not to our present purpose. Here you see there is matter of wonder in the person, that Christ should be a servant.

There is matter of wonder likewise in that from whence he is a servant. Whence comes it that Christ is a servant? It is from the wondrous love of God, and the wondrous love of Christ. To be so abased, it was wondrous love in God to give him to us to be so abased, and the wondrous misery we were in, that we could not otherwise be freed from; for such was the pride of man, that he, being man, would exalt himself to be like God. God became man, he became a servant to expiate our pride in Adam, so that it is wondrous in the spring of it. There was no such love as Christ's to become a servant, there was no such misery as we were in, out of which we were delivered by this abasement of Christ becoming a servant; so it is wondrous in that regard, springing from the infinite love and mercy of God, which is greater in the work of redemption and reconciliation than in the creation of the world, for the distance between nothing and something was less than the distance between sin and happiness. For nothing adds no opposition; but to be in a sinful state there is opposition. Therefore it was greater love and mercy for God, when we were sinful, and so obnoxious to eternal destruction, to make us of sinners, not only men, but to make us happy, to make us heirs of heaven out of a sinful and cursed estate, than to make us of nothing something, to make us men in Adam, for there God prevailed over nothing, but here his mercy triumphed over that which is opposite to God, over sinfulness and cursedness. To shew that the creature cannot be so low but there is somewhat in God above the misery of the creature, his mercy shall triumph over the basest estate where he will shew mercy. Therefore there is mercy above all mercy and love above all love, in that Christ was a servant.

Thirdly, It is wondrous in regard of the fruit we have by this service of Christ, the work of our redemption, to be translated from the kingdom of Satan to the glorious liberty of the sons of God, Rom. viii. 21, to be brought out of darkness into marvellous light. It is a marvellous matter of wonder, the good we have by this abasement of Christ, 'Behold what love the Father hath shewed us, that we should be called the sons of God!' 1 John iii. 1. Now, all this comes from Christ's being a servant. Our liberty comes from his service and slavery, our life from his death, our adoption and sonship and all comes from his abasement. Therefore it is a matter of wonderment for the great things we have by it, O the depth, O the depth, saith St Paul, Rom. xi. 33. Here are all dimensions in this excellent work that Christ hath wrought by his abasement, by his incarnation, and taking upon him the form of a servant, and dying for us; here is the height and breadth, and length and depth of the love of God in Christ. O the riches of God's mercy! The apostles they stand in a wonder and admiration of this, and indeed, if anything be to be admired, it is Christ, that wondrous conjunction, the wondrous love that wrought it, and the wondrous fruit we have by it.

It is the baseness of our nature we can wonder at shallow things. There cannot be foolery, but there will be many about it presently, and stand admiring every empty idle thing that the nature of man is carried away with; whereas indeed there is nothing worthy of admiration but the wonderful love of God. O how wonderful are thy works, saith David, of the works of creation, Ps. viii. 1. The work of creation and of providence whereby God guides the world are wonderful, and the psalmist cries out of the folly of men, that do not regard the work of the Lord, 'Fools regard not this' Ps. xiv 1; 'The works of the Lord are worthy to be considered, they are known of all that delight in them,' Ps. cxi. 2. But if these things be so wonderful, and to be regarded and delighted in, alas! what is all the work of redemption! Great is the mystery of godliness, God manifested in the flesh, &c., 1 Tim. iii. 16. There are mysteries, matters of admiration, but carnal men think these trival matters, they can hear matters of more rarity; and when they speak of these things, alas! they are too wise to wonder, tush, they know the gospel well enough, whereas indeed, as we see here, they are things that deserve the admiration of angels; and as they deserve it, so the angels pry into these excellent secrets in Jesus Christ, 1 Pet. i. 12.

Christ was a servant by office and by condition. We must not rest in this base condition; for he took upon him the form of a servant that he might be an excellent servant. There is both baseness and excellency in the word servant; for his humiliation was a degree of his exaltation, and a part of his advancement. If we regard his human nature, it was an advancement for man's nature to be grafted into God by conception and incarnation; but if we regard his Godhead, for him to conceal himself, and lay aside the beams and rays of majesty, and clothe himself with man's flesh, this was the first degree of humiliation. It was an advancement to his flesh, but it was a concealing and hiding to his Godhead. For God to become a servant this was an abasement: but then consider the excellency of the service, how God delighted in it, and how useful it was to us, and we shall see that he was a servant by way of excellency. There was first in Christ human flesh, abased flesh, and then glorious flesh. Abasement was first necessary for Christ; for he could not have performed the office of a servant, unless he had undertaken the condition of a servant. He must first be abased and then glorious, our ill must be his before his good could be ours; and how could he undergo our ill, our sin and misery, and the curse due to us, but he must be abased? Our sins must be imputed to him, and then his righteousness and whatsoever is good is ours; so here is both the abasement of his condition, and the excellency of his office to be a king, priest, and prophet to his church, as we shall see afterwards.

Is the Lord Christ a servant? This should teach us not to stand upon any terms. If Christ had stood upon terms, if he had refused to take upon him the shape of a servant, alas! where had we and our salvation been? And yet wretched creatures, we think ourselves too good to do God and our brethren any service. Christ stood not upon his greatness, but, being equal with God, he became a servant. Oh! we should dismount from the tower of our conceited excellency. The heart of man is a proud creature, a proud piece of flesh. Men stand upon their distance. What! shall I stoop to him? I am thus and thus. We should descend from the heaven of our conceit, and take upon us the form of servants, and abase ourselves to do good to others, even to any, and account it an honour to do any good to others in the places we are in. Christ did not think himself too good to leave heaven, to conceal and veil his majesty under the veil of our flesh, to work our redemption, to bring us out of the cursed estate we were in. Shall we think ourselves too good for any service? Who for shame can be proud when he thinks of this, that God was abased? Shall God be abased, and man proud? Shall God become a servant, and shall we that are servants think much to serve our fellow-servants? Let us learn this lesson, to abase ourselves; we cannot have a better pattern to look unto than our blessed Saviour. A Christian is the greatest freeman in the world; he is free from the wrath of God, free from hell and damnation, from the curse of the law; but then, though he be free in these respects, yet, in regard of love, he is the greatest servant. Love abaseth him to do all the good he can; and the more the Spirit of Christ is in us, the more it will abase us to anything wherein we can be serviceable.

Then, again, here is comfort for us, that Christ, in whatsoever he did in our redemption, is God's servant. He is appointed by God to the work; so, both God and Christ meet together in the work. Christ is a voluntary in it, for he emptied himself, he took upon him the form of a servant, Phil. ii. 6, he came from heaven voluntarily. And then withal the Father joins with him, the Father appointed him and sent him, the Father laid him as the corner-stone, the Father sealed him, as it is, John vi. 27, the Father set him out, as it is, Rom. iii. 25. 'He hath set him out as the propitiatory.' Therefore, when we think of reconciliation and redemption, and salvation wrought by Christ, let us comfort ourselves in the solidity of the work, that it is a service perfectly done. It was done by Christ, God-man. It is a service accepted of God, therefore God cannot refuse the service of our salvation wrought by Christ. Christ was his servant in the working of it. We may present it to God, it is the obedience of thy servant, it is the satisfaction of thy servant. Here is that will give full content and satisfaction to conscience, in this, that whatsoever Christ did, he was God's servant in it. But we shall better understand the intent of the Holy Ghost when we have gone over the rest of the words, 'Behold my servant whom I have chosen.'

Christ was chosen before all worlds to be the head of the elect. He was predestinate and ordained by God. As we are ordained to salvation, so Christ is ordained to be the head of all that shall be saved. He was chosen eternally, and chosen in time. He was singled out to the work by God; and all others that are chosen are chosen in him. There had been no choosing of men but in him; for God saw us so defiled, lying in our filth, that he could not look upon us but in his Son. He chose him, and us in him.

Here is meant, not only choosing by eternal election to happiness, but a choosing to office. There is a choosing to grace and glory, and a choosing to office. Here, it is as well meant, a choosing to office, as to grace and glory. God, as he chose Christ to grace and glory, so he chose him to the office of Mediatorship. Christ did not choose himself; he was no usurper. No man calls himself to the office, as it is in Heb. v. 4; but Christ was called and appointed of God. He was willing, indeed, to the work, he took it voluntary upon him; but as Mediator, God chose him, God the Father and he joining together.

If we respect eternal salvation, or grace, or office, Christ was chosen in respect of his manhood; for, as it is well observed by divines, Christ is the head of all that are predestinate; and the human nature of Christ could not merit its choice, it could not merit its incarnation, it could not merit union with the Godhead, it was merely from grace. How could Christ's manhood deserve anything of God before it was? Things must have a subsistence before they can work: our blessed Saviour is the pattern of all election, and his manhood could not merit to be knit to the second person; as how could it, being a creature? Therefore the knitting of the human nature of Christ to his divine, it is called the grace of union. The choosing of the human nature of Christ to be so gracious and glorious, it was of grace.

Christ he was both a chosen servant and a choice servant. In calling him a chosen servant, it implies his excellency, as a chosen vessel, Acts ix. 15, a chosen arrow in God's quiver, Lament. iii. 13, so a chosen servant, every way excellent.

This adds to our comfort, that whatsoever Christ did for us, he did it as chosen; he is a chosen stone, as St Peter saith, 1 Peter ii. 6, 'a precious corner-stone;' though refused of the builders, yet precious in God's sight!

Was Christ a chosen servant of God, and shall not we take God's choice? Is not God's choice the best and the wisest? Hath God chosen Christ to work our salvation, and shall we choose any other? Shall we run to saints' mediation, to the virgin Mary, and others, for intercession, which is a part of Christ's office? Who chose Mary, and Peter, and Paul to this work? There is no mention in Scripture of them for this purpose, but behold *my servant*, whom I have chosen.

God in paradise did choose a wife for Adam, so God hath chosen a husband for his church; he hath chosen Christ for us: therefore it is intolerable sacrilegious rebellion and impudency to refuse a Saviour and Mediator of God's choosing, and to set up others of our own, as if we were wiser to choose for ourselves than God is. We may content ourselves well enough with God's choice, because he is the party offended.

Besides, it is folly to go out from Christ, where there is all fulness and content, to leave God's chosen servant, and to go to any other servant, to any broken vessel. God rests in this servant as Pharaoh did in Joseph, the second person in the kingdom, Gen. xli. 40, 43. Therefore let God's choice and ours agree.

And this directs us also, in our devotions to God, how to carry ourselves in our prayers and services, to offer Christ to God. Behold, Lord, thy chosen servant, that thou hast chosen to be my Mediator, my Saviour, my all in all to me, he is a mediator and a Saviour of thine own choosing, thou canst not refuse thy own choice; if thou look upon me, there is nothing but matter of unworthiness, but look upon him whom thou hast chosen, my head and my Saviour!

Again, if Christ be a chosen servant, O let us take heed how we neglect Christ. When God hath chosen him for us, shall not we think him worthy to be embraced and regarded; shall we not kiss the Son with the kiss of love, and faith, and subjection? He is a Saviour of God's own choosing, refuse him not. What is the reason that men refuse this chosen stone? They will not be laid low enough to build upon this corner stone, this hidden stone. The excellency of Christ is hidden, it appears not to men, men will not be squared to be built upon him. Stones for a building must be framed, and made even, and flat. Men stick out with this and that lust, they will not be pared and cut and fitted for Christ. If they may have their lusts and wicked lives, they will admit of Christ. But we must make choice of him as a stone to build upon him; and to be built on him, we must be made like him. We like not this laying low and abasing, therefore we refuse this corner stone, though God hath made him the corner of building to all those that have the life of grace here, or shall have glory hereafter.

The papists admit him to be a stone, but not the only stone to build on, but they build upon him and saints, upon him and works, upon him and traditions. But he is the only corner stone. God hath chosen him only, and we must choose him only, that we may be framed and laid upon him to make up one building. So much for that, 'Behold my servant whom I have chosen.'

My Beloved, in whom my soul is well pleased.—How do we know that these words in the prophet Isaiah are fitly appliable to Christ? By the greatest authority that ever was from the beginning of the world, by the immediate voice of God the Father from heaven, who applies these words in Isaiah to Christ, Matt. iii. 17, in his inauguration when he was baptized, 'This is my beloved Son, in whom I am well pleased,' this is that my Son, that beloved, *ὁ ἀγάπητὸς*, the beloved Son, so beloved that my soul delights in him, he is capable of my whole love, I may pour out my whole love upon him. 'In whom I am well pleased,' it is the same with that here, 'in whom my soul delighteth,' the one expresseth the other.

How, and in what respect is Christ thus beloved of God?

First as he is God, the Son of God, the engraven image of his Father, so he is *primum amabile*, the first lovely thing that ever was. When the Father loves him, he loves himself in him, so he loves him as God, as the second person, as his own image and character.

And as man he loves him, for as man he was the most excellent creature in the world, he was conceived, fashioned, and framed in his mother's womb by the Holy Ghost. It is said, Heb. x. 5, God gave him a body. God the Father by the Holy Ghost fashioned and framed and fitted him with a body, therefore God must needs love his own workmanship.

Again, there was nothing in him displeasing to God, there was no sin found in his life any way, therefore as man he was well pleasing to God. He took the manhood and ingrafted it into the second person, and enriched it there; therefore he must needs love the manhood of Christ, being taken into so near a union with the Godhead.

As God and man mediator especially, he loves and delights in him. In regard of his office, he must needs delight in his own ordinance and decree. Now he decreed and sealed him to that office, therefore he loves and delights in him as a mediator of his own appointing and ordaining, to be our king, and priest, and prophet.

Again, he loved and delighted in him, in regard of the execution of his office both in doing and suffering. In doing, the evangelist saith, 'He did all things well,' Mark vii. 37. When he healed the sick, and raised the dead, and cured all diseases, whatsoever he did was well done. And for his suffering, God delighted in him for that, as it is in John x. 17, 'My Father loves me, because I lay down my life;' and so in Isa. liii. 12, 'He shall divide him a portion with the great, because he poured out his soul unto death;' and in Phil. ii. 9, 'Because he abased himself to the death of the cross, 'God gave him a name above all names:' therefore God loves and delights in him for his suffering and abasement.

It is said of Noah, Gen. viii. 21, that he offered a sacrifice after the flood, and 'the Lord smelled a sweet savour of his sacrifice,' and thereupon he saith, 'I will not curse the earth again.' So God loves and delights in Christ as he offered himself a sacrifice of a sweet smelling savour wherein God rests; he felt such a sweet savour in the sacrifice of Christ, he is so delighted in it, that he will never destroy mankind, he will never destroy any that believe in Christ. The sacrifice of Noah was a type of Christ's sacrifice.

Now, that Christ's sacrifice was so acceptable to God, there is a direct place for it in Eph. v. 2, 'Walk in love, as Christ hath loved us, and hath given himself an offering and a sacrifice to God of a sweet smell.' And indeed how many sweet savours were there in the sacrifice of Christ offered on the cross! Was there not the sweet savour of obedience? he was 'obedient to the death of the cross,' Phil. ii. 8. There was the sweet savour of patience, and of love to mankind. Therefore God delighted in him, as God, as man, as mediator God-man, in his doings, in his sufferings, every way.

Doth God delight thus in Christ, in his person, or considered mystically? I answer; both. God loves and delights in Christ mystical, that is, in Christ and his members, in whole Christ. 'This is my beloved Son, in whom I am well pleased,' not only with whom alone by himself, but 'in whom,' in him as God, in him in body and soul, in him as head of the church, in him mystically, in all that are under him any kind of way. God delights in him, and all his.

Is it possible that he should delight in the head, and refuse the members? that he should love the husband, and mislike the spouse? O no; with the same love that God loves Christ, he loves all his. He delights in Christ and all his, with the same delight. There is some difference in the degree, 'that Christ in all things may have the pre-eminence,' Col. i. 18, but it is the same love; therefore our Saviour sets it down excellently in his own prayer, he desires 'that the same love wherewith his Father loved him may be in them that are his,' John xvii. 20, that they may feel the love wherewith his Father loves him, for he loved him and his members, him and his spouse, with all one love.

This is our comfort and our confidence, that God accepts us, because he accepts his beloved; and when he shall cease to love Christ, he shall cease to love the members of Christ. They and Christ make one mystical Christ. This is our comfort in dejection for sin. We are so and so indeed, but Christ is the chosen servant of God, 'in whom he delighteth,' and delights in us in him. It is no matter what we are in ourselves, but what we are in Christ when we are once in him and continue in him. God loves us with that inseparable love wherewith he loves his own Son. Therefore St Paul triumphs, Rom. viii. 35, 'What shall separate us from the love of God in Christ Jesus?' This love, it is founded in Christ, 'therefore neither things present, nor things to come (as he goes on there gloriously), shall be able to separate us.' You see what a wondrous confidence and comfort we have hence, if we labour to be in Christ, that then God loves and delights in us, because he loves and delights in Christ Jesus.

And here is a wondrous comfort, that God must needs love our salvation and redemption when he loves Christ, because 'he poured out his soul to death to save us.' Doth not God delight that we should be saved, and our sins should be forgiven, when he loves Christ because he abased himself for that purpose? What a prop and foundation of comfort is this, when the devil shall present God to us in a terrible hideous manner, as an avenging God, 'and consuming fire,' &c., Heb. xii. 29; indeed out of Christ he is so. Let us present to ourselves thoughts of God as the Scripture sets forth God to us; and as God sets forth himself, not only in that sweet relation as a Father to Christ, but our father, 'I go to my Father and your Father, to my God and your God,' John xx. 17, having both one God, and love and care. There is none of us all but the devil will have a saying to us, either in the time of our life, in some terrible temptation, especially when any outward abasement comes, or at the hour of death; and all the cordials we have gathered out of the word will then be little enough to support the drooping soul, especially in the hour of temptation. O beloved, what a wondrous stay and satisfaction to a distressed conscience doth this yield, that Christ in all that he hath wrought for us is God's chosen servant, 'whom he loves and delights in,' and delights in him for this very work, that he abased himself and gave himself for us, that he wrought God's work, because he wrought reconciliation for us! If we can believe in Christ, we see here what ground of comfort we have, that God loves and delights in us, as he doth in his own Son.

And what a comfort is it now, in our daily approach to God, to minister boldness to us in all our suits, that we go to God in the name of one that he loves, 'in whom his soul delights,' that we have a friend in court, a friend in heaven for us, that is at the right hand of God, and interposeth himself there for us in all our suits, that makes us acceptable, that perfumes our prayers and makes them acceptable. His intercession is still by virtue of his service, dying for us. He intercedes by virtue of his redemption. If God love him for the work of redemption, he loves him for his intercession, therefore God must needs regard the prayers made by him, by virtue of his dying for us, when he loves him for dying for us. Be sure therefore, in all our suits to God, to take along our elder brother, to take our beloved brother, take Benjamin with us, offer all to God in him, our persons to be accepted in him, our prayers, our hearing, our works, and all that we do, and we shall be sure to speed; for he is one in whom the soul of God delights. There must be this passage and repassage, as God looks upon us lovely in him, and delights in us as we are members of him. All God's love and the fruits of it come to us as we are in Christ, and are one with him. Then in our passage to God again we must return all, and do all, to God in Christ. Be sure not to go to a naked God; for so he is 'a consuming fire,' but go to him in the mediation of him whom he loves, 'and in whom his soul delighteth.'

And shall God love him and delight in him, and shall not our soul delight in Christ? This therefore should stir up our affections to Christ, to be faithful in our conjugal affection as the spouse of Christ, to say, 'My beloved is mine and I am my beloved's,' Cant. ii. 16. Christ calls his church, 'My love and my dove,' Cant. vi. 9. Doth Christ delight in us, and God delight in Christ, and shall not we delight in Christ that delights in us, and in whom God delights? In the 1 Cor. xvi. 22, the apostle is bold to pronounce a bitter curse, 'Anathema Maran-atha,' upon him that loves not the Lord Christ Jesus, a most bitter curse. When Christ shall become a servant to do our work for us, to suffer for us, to bear the burden of our sins upon the tree, to become our husband, to bestow his riches upon us, to raise us to the same condition with himself, and withal to be such a one as God hath chosen out to love and delight in as the best object of his love, and most capable of it, and for us not to solace and delight ourselves in him that God delights in, when God delights in him for our sake. God loves and delights in him for the work of salvation and redemption by his blood, and shall not we love and embrace him for his love which is for our good? What good hath God by it but only the glory of his mercy, in saving our souls through Christ? Therefore if God love him for the good he doth to us, much more should we love him for the fruit of it that we receive ourselves.

It should shame us therefore when we find dulness and coldness upon us, that we can hear of anything better than of Christ; and arguments concerning Christ are cold to us. Alas! where is our love, and joy, and delight; and when we can make no better but a carnal use of the incarnation and other benefits by Christ! We should therefore desire God to shed the love of Christ into our hearts more and more, that we may feel in our souls the love that he bears to us, and may love God and Christ again, for that that he hath done for us.

Hence we have also a ground of estimation of Christians to be excellent persons. Doth God value poor sinful souls so much as to give Christ for them to become a Saviour? doth he delight in Christ for giving himself for them? and shall not we love one another whom God and Christ so loves?

But if God love and delight in those that are in Christ, with the same love and delight that he hath in him, how shall I know that I am in Christ, and that God thus delights in me?

Briefly, a man may know that he is in Christ, if he find the Spirit of Christ in him; for the same Spirit when Christ took our nature, that sanctified that blessed mass whereof he was made, when there was a union between him and the second person, the same Spirit sanctifies our souls and bodies. There is one Spirit in the head and in the members. Therefore if we find the Spirit of Christ in us, we are in Christ and he in us. Now this Spirit is renewing, 'Whosoever is in Christ is a new creature,' 2 Cor. v. 17; all is new, 'old things are done away,' the old manner of language, the old disposition, old affections, old company, all old things are past, all is new; and if a man be a new creature, he hath right and title to 'the new heaven and new earth,' 2 Pet. iii. 13. Let us examine the work of grace in us. If there be no change in us we have no present interest in Christ. We have to do with him because he is still wooing us to be in him, but as yet we have no title to him.

The very beholding of Christ is a transforming sight. The Spirit that makes us new creatures, and stirs us up to behold this servant, it is a transforming beholding. If we look upon him with the eye of faith, it will make us like Christ; for the gospel is a mirror, and such a mirror, that when we look into it, and see ourselves interested in it, we are changed from glory to glory, 2 Cor. iii. 18. A man cannot look upon the love of God and of Christ in the gospel, but it will change him to be like God and Christ. For how can we see Christ, and God in Christ, but we shall see how God hates sin, and this will transform us to hate it as God doth, who hated it so that it could not be expiated but with the blood of Christ, God-man. So, seeing the holiness of God in it, it will transform us to be holy. When we see the love of God in the gospel, and the love of Christ giving himself for us, this will transform us to love God. When we see the humility and obedience of Christ, when we look on Christ as God's chosen servant in all this, and as our surety and head, it transforms us to the like humility and obedience. Those that find not their dispositions in some comfortable measure wrought to this blessed transformation, they have not yet those eyes that the Holy Ghost requireth here. 'Behold my servant whom I have chosen, my beloved in whom my soul delighteth.'

I will put my Spirit upon him.—Now we come to the qualification of Christ for his calling, in these words, I will put my Spirit upon him—that is, I will clothe him with my Spirit, I will put it, as it were, upon him as a garment.

Now there were divers degrees of Christ's receiving the Spirit at several times. For he was conceived by the Holy Ghost. The Holy Ghost did sanctify that blessed mass whereof his body was framed in the womb of the virgin, he was quickened in the womb in his conception by the Holy Ghost, and he was graced by the Holy Ghost, and led by the Spirit in all things before his baptism. But afterward, when he came to set upon his office, to be the prophet and priest and king of his church, that great office of saving mankind, which he did not solemnly set upon till he was thirty years old, then God poured upon him a special portion of the Spirit, answerable to that great calling, then the Spirit lighted upon him, Matt. iii. 16. Christ was ordained to his office by the greatest authority that ever any was ordained from the beginning of the world. For at his baptism, when he was ordained and set apart to his office, there was the Father from heaven uttered an audible voice, 'This is my beloved Son, in whom I am well pleased,' Mat. iii. 17; and there was Christ, the party baptized and installed into that great office; then there was the Holy Ghost, in the form and shape of a dove. It being a matter of the greatest consequence that ever was in the world, greater than the creation, it was fit it should be done with the greatest authority; and so it was, the Father, Son, and Holy Ghost being present at the admission of Christ into his office. This is especially here intended, though the other be included, I will put my Spirit upon him—that is, I will anoint him, as it is in Isa. lxi. 1, 'The Spirit of the Lord is upon me,' saith Christ, 'because the Lord hath anointed me to preach good tidings to the meek, to bind up the broken-hearted, to proclaim liberty to the captives, to open the prison for them that are bound, to proclaim the acceptable year of the Lord'—that is, the year of jubilee, for that was a type of Christ, to preach the gospel deliverance to all that are in captivity, servitude, and thraldom under Satan and sin. This was accomplished when Christ, at his baptism, entered upon his office. God put his Spirit upon him, to set him apart, to ordain him, and to qualify him with abundance of grace for the work; for there are these three things especially meant by putting the Spirit upon him, separation or setting apart, and ordaining, and enriching with the gifts of the Spirit.

When any one is called to great place, there is a setting apart from others, and an ordaining to that particular, and a qualifying. If it be a calling of God, he qualifies where he ordains always.

But Christ had the Spirit before. What doth he mean, then, when he saith he will put the Spirit upon him now?

I answer, he had the Spirit before, answerable to that condition he was in. Now he received the Spirit answerable to that condition he was to undertake. He was perfect then for that condition. Now he was to be made perfect for that office he was to set upon. He was always perfect. He had abundance of Spirit for that estate he was in, but now he was to enter upon another condition, to preach the gospel, to be a prophet, and after to be a priest. Therefore he saith now especially, I will put my Spirit upon him.

Now, this putting of the Spirit, it is expressed in Isa. lxi. 1, and other places, by anointing. There were three sorts of persons that were anointed before Christ, prophets, priests, and kings. Now Christ was to be a prophet, a priest, and a king. Therefore he was to be anointed with the Spirit, to enable him to these three offices.

I might here take occasion to enlarge myself in the offices of Christ, but I will only speak of them as the text ministereth just occasion.

There are three main defects in man since the fall.

There is ignorance and blindness.

There is rebellion in the will and affections.

And in regard of his condition, by reason of the sins of nature and life, a subjection to a cursed estate, to the wrath of God and eternal damnation.

Now, answerable to these three grand ills, whosoever shall be ordained a saviour must provide proportionable remedies for these. Hereupon comes a threefold office in Christ, that is ordained to save man, to cure this threefold mischief and malady.

As we are ignorant and blind, he is a prophet to instruct us, to convince us of the ill state we are in, and then to convince us of the good he intends us, and hath wrought for us, to instruct us in all things concerning our everlasting comfort. He is such a prophet as teacheth not only the outward, but the inward man. He openeth the heart, he teacheth to do the things he teacheth. Men teach what we should do, but they teach not the doing of them. He is such a prophet as teacheth us the very things; he teacheth us to love and to obey, &c.

And answerable to the rebellion and sinfulness of our dispositions, he is a king to subdue whatsoever is ill in us, and likewise to subdue all opposite power without us. By little and little he will trample all enemies under his feet, and under our feet, too, ere long.

Now, as we are cursed by reason of our sinful condition, so he is a priest to satisfy the wrath of God for us. He was made a curse for us, Gal. iii. 13. He became a servant, that, being so, he might die, and undergo the cursed death of the cross; not only death, but a cursed death, and so his blood might be an atonement as a priest. So, answerable to the threefold ill in us, you see here is a threefold office in Christ.

Now Christ performs these three offices in this order.

First of all he is a prophet. When he was baptized the Spirit was put upon him, as in Isa. lxi. 1, to preach deliverance to the captives. First, he preached wherefore he came into the world, why God sent him, and discovered to the world the state they were in; and when he had preached as a prophet, then as a priest, he died, and offered himself a sacrifice.

After death his kingly office was most apparent. For then he rose again as a triumphant king over death and all our enemies, and ascended in his triumphant chariot to heaven, and there he sits gloriously as a king in his throne at the right hand of God. So that however at his baptism, and before, when he was sanctified in his mother's womb, he was both king, priest, and prophet, yet in regard of the order of manifestation, he manifested himself first to be a prophet, secondly a priest, and thirdly to be a king. For his kingly office brake forth but seldom in the time of his abasement. Sometimes it did, to shew that he was ruler and commander of earth and sea, and devils, and all. He wrought miracles, but the glorious manifestation of his kingly office, it was after his resurrection.

Now, the fundamental, the chief office to which he was anointed by the Spirit, upon which the rest depends, it was his priestly office; for wherefore was his teaching, but to instruct us what he must do and suffer for us, and what benefit we have by his sacrifice—reconciliation with God, and freedom from the wrath of God, and right unto life everlasting, by his obedience to the cursed death of the cross? And how comes he to be a king to rule over us by his Holy Spirit, and to have a right unto us, but because as a priest he died for us first? He washed us with his blood, he purged us with his blood, and then he made us kings and priests, Rev. i. 5. All other benefits came from this—he washed our souls in his blood first. Whatsoever we have from God, is especially from the great work of Christ as a priest abasing himself, and dying for us; and thereupon he comes to be a prophet and a king. Thus we see the order of Christ's offices, how they come to be fruitful to us, the rest especially, by virtue of his priestly office.

Note this by the way: Christ's priestly office, his sacrificing himself for us, includes two branches. A priest was to offer sacrifice and to pray for the people. Our Saviour Christ did both in the days of his humiliation, in his prayer in John xvii. There, as a priest, he commends his sacrifice to God before he died; and now he is in heaven making intercession for us, to the end of the world. He appears for us there. We see, then, to what purpose God put the Spirit upon Christ, to enable him to be a prophet, a priest, and a king, and thereupon to take away those mischiefs and evils that we were subject and enthralled to; so that we have a supply for all that may any way abase us and cast us down, in the all-sufficiency that is in Christ Jesus, who was anointed with the Spirit for this end.

It may be objected, Christ was God himself; he had the Spirit, and gives the Spirit; therefore, how could the Spirit be put upon him?

I answer, Christ is both God and man. Christ, as God, gives the Spirit to his human nature; so he communicates his Spirit. The Spirit is his Spirit as well as the Father's. The Spirit proceeds from them both. Christ, as man, receives the Spirit. God the Father and the Son put the Spirit upon the manhood of Christ; so Christ both gives and receives the Spirit in diverse respects. As God, he gives and sends the Spirit. The spiration and breathing of the Spirit is from him as well as from the Father, but as man he received the Spirit.

And this is the reason of it: next under the Father, Son, and Holy Ghost, Christ the Mediator, was to be the spring and original of all comfort and good. Therefore, Christ's nature must not only be sanctified and ordained by the Spirit; but he must receive the Spirit to enrich it, for whatsoever is wrought in the creature is by the Spirit. Whatsoever Christ did as man, he did by the Spirit. Christ's human nature, therefore, must be sanctified, and have the Spirit put upon it. God the Father, the first person in Trinity, and God the Son, the second, they work not immediately, but by the Holy Ghost, the third person. Therefore, whatsoever is wrought upon the creature, it comes from the Holy Ghost immediately. So Christ received the Holy Ghost as sent from the Father and the Son. Now as the Holy Spirit is from the Father and the Son, so he works from the Father and the Son. He sanctifieth and purifieth, and doth all from the Father and the Son, and knits us to the Father and the Son; to the Son first, and then to the Father. Therefore it is said, 'The grace of our Lord Jesus Christ, the love of God the Father, and the communion of the Holy Ghost,' 2 Cor. xiii. 14; because all the communion we have with God is by the Holy Ghost. All the communion that Christ as man had with God was by the Holy Ghost; and all the communion that God hath with us, and we with God, is by the Holy Ghost: for the Spirit is the bond of union between Christ and us, and between God and us. God communicates himself to us by his Spirit, and we communicate with God by his Spirit. God doth all in us by his Spirit, and we do all back again to God by the Spirit. Because Christ, as a head, as the second Adam, was to be the root of all that are saved, as the first Adam was the root of all that are damned, he was therefore to receive the Spirit, and to have it put upon him in a more excellent and rich manner: for we must know that all things are first in Christ, and then in us.

God chose him first, and then he chose us. God singled him out to be the Saviour, the second Adam, and he calls us in Christ.

God justified Christ from our sins, being our surety, taking our sins upon him. We are justified, because he by his resurrection quit himself from the guilt of our sins, as having paid the debt.

Christ is the first fruits of them that rise again, 1 Cor. xv. 20. We rise again because he is risen. Christ first ascended; we ascend in Christ. Christ is first loved; we are loved in the Beloved. Christ is first blessed; we are blessed with all spiritual blessings in Jesus Christ, Eph. i. 3. So, whatsoever is in us, we have it at the second hand. We have the Spirit in us, but he is first in Christ; God hath put the Spirit in Christ, as the spring, as the second Adam, as a public person, that should receive the Spirit for us all. He is first in all things; Christ must have the pre-eminence. He hath the pre-eminence in all, both before time, in time, and after time, in election, in whatsoever is done here in this world, and in glorification. All is first in Christ, and then in us. He is the elder brother.

We must understand this, to give Christ his due honour and respect, and to know whence we have all we have. Therefore the Spirit is said here, first, to be 'put upon Christ.' We have not the Holy Ghost immediately from God, but we have him as sanctifying Christ first, and then us; and whatsoever the Holy Ghost doth in us, he doth the same in Christ first, and he doth it in us because in Christ. Therefore, in John xvi. 14, 15, Christ saith, He shall take of mine. Whatsoever the Holy Ghost works in us, he takes of Christ first. How is that?

Thus: the Holy Ghost comforts us with reasons from Christ. He died, and hath reconciled us to God; therefore, now God is at peace with thee. Here the Holy Ghost takes a ground of comfort from the death of Christ. When the Holy Ghost would raise a man up to holiness of life, he tells him, Christ thy Saviour and head is quickened, and is now in heaven, therefore we ought to rise to holiness of life. If the Holy Ghost be to work either comfort or grace, or anything, he not only doth the same thing that he did first in Christ, but he doth it in us by reasons from Christ, by grounds fetched from Christ. The Holy Ghost tells our souls that God loves Christ first, and he loves us in Christ, and that we are those that God gave Christ for, that we are those that Christ makes intercession for in heaven. The Holy Ghost witnesseth to us the love of the Father and the Son, and so he fetcheth from Christ whatsoever he works.

And hence the work of the Holy Ghost is distinguished from illusions and delusions, that are nothing but frantic conceits of comfort that are groundless. The Holy Ghost fetcheth all from Christ in his working and comfort, and he makes Christ the pattern of all; for whatsoever is in Christ, the Holy Ghost, which is the Spirit of Christ, works in us as it is in Christ. Therefore, in John i. 13, it is said, 'of his fulness we receive grace for grace'—that is, grace answerable to his grace. There are three things that we receive answerable to Christ by the Spirit.

We receive grace—that is, the favour of God answerable to the favour

God shews his Son. He loves his Son, he is graciously disposed to him, and he loves us.

So grace habitual. We have grace in us answerable to the grace in Christ. We have love answerable to his love, patience answerable to his patience, obedience and humility answerable to that in Christ. The Spirit works a conformity to Christ in all things.

Likewise, in the third place, the Spirit assures us of the same privileges that issue from grace. Christ is a Son; the Spirit tells us we are sons. Christ is an heir; the Spirit tells us we are heirs with Christ. Christ is the king of heaven and earth; the Spirit tells us that we are kings, that his riches are ours. Thus we have 'grace for grace,' both favour and grace in us, and privileges issuing from grace, we have all as they are in Christ. Even as in the first Adam we receive of his emptiness, curse for curse, ill for ill; for his blindness and rebellion we are answerable; we are born as he was after his fall: so in the second Adam, by his Spirit, we receive grace for grace.

Hence issues this, that our state now in Christ is far more excellent than our state in Adam was.

How doth it spring hence?

Thus, Christ is God-man. His nature was sanctified by the Spirit; he was a more excellent person, he gives and sends the Spirit. Adam was only a mere man, and therefore his goodness could not be so derived to his posterity; for, however the Holy Ghost was in Adam, yet the Holy Ghost did not so fill him, he was not so in him as in Christ. The Holy Ghost is in Christ in a more excellent manner; for Christ being equal with God, he gave the Holy Ghost; the Holy Ghost comes from Christ as God. Now the second Adam being a more excellent person, we being in Christ the second Adam, we are in a more excellent, and in a more safe estate; we have a better keeper of our happiness than Adam. He being a mere man, he could not keep his own happiness, but lost himself and all his posterity. Though he were created after the image of God, yet being but a mere man, he shewed himself to be a man—that is, a changeable creature; but Christ being God and man, having his nature sanctified by the Spirit, now our happiness is in a better keeping, for our grace hath a better spring. The grace and sanctification we have, it is not in our own keeping, it distils into us answerable to our necessities; but the spring is indeficient, it never fails, the spring is in Christ. So the favour that God bears us, it is not first in us, but it is first in Christ; God loves him, and then he loves us; he gives him the Spirit, and us in him. Now, Christ is the keeper both of the love of God towards us and the grace of God; and whatsoever is good he keeps all for us, he receives all for himself and for us; he receives not only the Spirit for himself, but he receives it as Mediator, as head: for 'we all of his fulness receive grace for grace.' He receives it as a fountain to diffuse it, I say. This shews us our happy and blessed condition in Jesus Christ, that now the grace and love of God and our happiness, and the grace whereby we are sanctified and fitted for it, it is not in our own keeping originally, but in our head Christ Jesus.

These be comfortable considerations, and, indeed, the life and soul of a Christian's life and comfort. If we conceive them aright, they will quicken us to obedience, and we shall know what the gospel is. To come to make some use of it.

I might observe this, that none should take that office upon them to which they are not called of God, nor qualified by his Spirit, especially ministers, because Christ did not set upon his office, till the Spirit was put upon him. The Spirit must enable us and fit us for everything. But I leave that, and come to that which concerns us all.

First, then, hath God put the Spirit upon Christ, as the evangelist saith in John iii. 34, 'He whom God hath sent'—that is Christ—'he speaketh the word of God: for God gives him not the Spirit by measure.' God doth not stand measuring grace out to Christ, but he pours it out upon him, full measure, running over, because he receives it not for himself alone, but for us. We receive the Spirit by measure, Eph. iv. 7, 'according to the measure of the gift of Christ.' Christ gives us all a measure of sanctifying knowledge and of every grace, till we 'grow to be a perfect man in Christ,' Eph. iv. 13. Therefore it is called the 'first fruits of the Spirit,' Rom. viii. 23, as much as shall fit us for heaven, and grace sufficient, though it be not that measure we shall have hereafter, or that we would have here. Christ had a full measure, the fulness of a fountain, diffusive, not only abundance for himself, but redundance, and overflowing for the good of others; he being the head of the church, not only a head of eminence, but of influence to bestow and convey all grace in him to all his members, proportionable to the service of every member. Therefore he received not the Spirit according to measure—that is, sparingly—but it was showered upon him; he was filled and clothed with the Holy Ghost. Is it so?

Let us labour, then, to see where to have supply in all our wants. We have a full treasury to go to. All treasure is hid in Christ for us. What a comfort is this in anything we want! If we want the favour of God, go to his beloved Christ, desire God to love us in his beloved, and to accept us in his gracious Son, in him whom he hath made his servant, and anointed with his Spirit for that purpose.

If we want particular graces, go to the well-head Christ, consider of Christ now filled for us, as it was in Aaron. The oil that was poured on Aaron's head ran down to his beard, and to the skirts of his clothing, Ps. cxxxiii. 2, the meanest parts of his garment were bedewed with that oil: so the graces of God's Spirit poured upon our head Christ, our Aaron, our High Priest, run down upon us, upon all ranks of Christians, even upon the skirts, the weakest and lowest Christians. Every one hath grace for grace; we all partake of the oil and anointing of our spiritual Aaron, our High Priest. If we want anything, therefore, let us go to him. I can do all, saith St Paul, in Christ that strengtheneth me, Philip. iv. 13. Go to him for patience, for comfort, for everything, because God hath put his Spirit upon him, to supply all our wants; he hath the oil of gladness above his fellows, Ps. xlv. 7; but for his fellows he hath the oil of grace more than any, but it is not only for him, but for us all. Therefore, let us have comfortable meditations of the fulness of Christ, and make use of it, all this is for me. In Col. ii. 9, St Paul sets it out, 'in him the fulness of the Godhead dwells personally;' for that is meant by σωματικῶς, and it follows after, 'in him we are complete.' Wherefore is all the fulness that is in him? to shew that in him we are complete. So, in 1 John v. 20, 21, to shew how the spirits of the apostles agree, in this saith he, 'we know that the Son of God is come in the flesh, and hath given us an understanding to know him that is true, and we are in him that is true, even in his Son Jesus Christ. This is true God and eternal life.' Christ is true God and eternal life for us all; for our comfort, 'we know that the Son of God is come, and hath given us an understanding, &c. Little children, keep yourselves from idols.' How doth this depend upon the other? Thus;

will you go to idols, stocks and stones, devices of men's brain, for supply of grace and comfort? Christ, whom God hath sent, he is come into the world; he is God and eternal life. 'God hath given eternal life, and this life is in his Son,' 1 John v. 11; therefore, why should you go to idols?

What is the ground of popish idolatries and abominations? They conceive not aright of the fulness of Christ, wherefore he was ordained, and sent of God; for if they did, they would not go to idols and saints, and leave Christ. Therefore let us make this use of it, go out of Christ for nothing. If we want favour, go not to saints, if we want instruction, go not to traditions of men. He is a prophet wise enough, and a priest full enough to make us accepted of God. If we want any grace, he is a king able enough, rich enough, and strong enough to subdue all our rebellions in us, and he will in time by his Spirit overcome all, 'Stronger is he that is in us than he that is in the world,' 1 John iv. 4. The spirit in the world, the devil and devilish-minded men, they are not so strong as the Spirit of Christ; for by little and little the Spirit of Christ will subdue all. Christ is a king, go not out of him therefore for anything. 'Babes, keep yourselves from idols,' 1 John v. 21. You may well enough, you know whom to go to.

Therefore let us shame ourselves. Is there such a store-house of comfort and grace every way in Christ? Why are we so weak and comfortless? Why are we so dejected as if we had not such a rich husband? All our husband's riches are ours for our good, we receive of it in our measure, why do we not go to the fountain and make use of it? Why, in the midst of abundance, are we poor and beggarly? Here we may see the misery of the world. Christ is a prophet to teach us the way to heaven, but how few be there that will be directed by him! Christ is a king to subdue all our spiritual and worst enemies, to subdue those enemies that kings tremble at, to subdue death, to subdue the fear of judgment and the wrath of God, and yet how few will come under his government! 'Christ is the light of the world,' John ix. 5, yet how few follow him! Christ is the way, yet how few tread in his steps! Christ is our wisdom and our riches, yet how few go to him to fetch any riches, but content themselves with the transitory things of this life! Men live as if Christ were nothing, or did nothing concern them, as if he were a person abstracted from them, as if he were not a head or husband, as if he had received the Spirit only for himself and not for them, whereas all that is in Christ is for us. I beseech you therefore let us learn to know Christ better, and to make use of him.

Again, if Christ hath 'the Spirit put upon him for us all,' then in our daily slips and errors make this use, to offer Christ to God with this argument. Take an argument from God himself to bind him. God will be bound with his own arguments. We cannot bind him with ours, but let us go to him and say, Lord, though I be thus and thus sinful, yet for Christ Jesus' sake thy servant, whom thou lovest and hast put thy Spirit upon him to be a priest, and to make intercession for me, for his sake pardon, for his sake accept. Make use of God's consecration of Christ by the Spirit to God himself, and bind him with his own mediator, and with his own priest of his own ordaining. Thou canst not, Lord, refuse a Saviour and mediator of thine own, sanctified by thine own Spirit, whom thou hast set apart, and ordained and qualified every way for this purpose. Let us go to God in the name of this mediator Jesus Christ every day, and this is to make a good use of this, that God hath 'put his Spirit upon him.'

But to make a use of trial, how shall we know that this comfort belongs to us, that Christ hath the Spirit put upon him for us or no, whether he be ordained a king, priest, and prophet for us? That which I said before will give light to this. We must partake of the same Spirit that Christ hath, or else we are none of his members. As we partake of his name, so we must also of his anointing. Thereupon we are called Christians, because we partake of the anointing and Spirit of Christ, and if we have the Spirit of Christ, it will work the same in us as it did in Christ, it will convince us of our own ill, of our rebellions, and cursed estate, and it will convince us likewise of the good we have in him. And then, he is a Spirit of union, to knit us to Christ, and make us one with him, and thereupon to quicken us, to lead us, and guide us, and to dwell in us continually, to stir up prayers and supplications in us, to make us cry familiarly to God as to a Father, to comfort and support us in all our wants and miseries, as he did Christ, 'to help our infirmities,' as the apostle at large, in Rom. viii. 20, sets down the excellent office of the Holy Ghost, what he doth in those that are Christ's. Let us therefore examine ourselves, what the Spirit doth in us, if Christ be set apart to redeem us as a priest. Surely all his offices go together. He doth by the same Spirit rule us, Rev. i. 5, 'He hath washed us in his blood, and made us kings and priests.' Whosoever he washeth in his blood he maketh him a king and a priest, he makes him by the power of his Spirit able to rule over his base corruptions. We may know then, whether we have benefit by Christ by his Spirit, not only by the Spirit witnessing that we are the sons of God, but by some arguments whereby the Spirit may witness without delusion. For though the Spirit of Christ tells us that we are Christ's, yet the proof must be from guiding and leading, and comforting and conforming us to Jesus Christ, in making us kings and prophets, enlightening our understandings to know his will, and conforming us to be like him. The Spirit of Christ is a Spirit of power and strength. It will enable us to perform duties above nature, to overcome ourselves and injuries, it will make us to want and to abound, it will make us able to live and to die, as it enabled Christ to do things that another man could not do. So a Christian can do that, and suffer that that another man cannot do and suffer, because he hath the Spirit of Christ.

At the least, whosoever hath the Spirit of Christ, he shall find that Spirit in him striving against that which is contrary, and by little and little getting ground. Where there is no conflict, there is no Spirit of Christ at all. I will not be large in the point, only I speak this by way of trial, to know whether we have the Spirit of Christ in us or no. If not, we have nothing to do with Christ; for Christ saves us not as he is out of us only. Christ was to do something of himself that we have no share in, only the good of it is ours. He was to redeem us by his blood, to be a sacrifice. The title to heaven and salvation was wrought by Christ out of us. But there is somewhat that he doth not only for us, but he works in us by his Spirit, that is, the fitting of us for that he hath given us title to, and the applying of that that he hath done for us. Whosoever therefore hath any benefit by Christ, he hath the Spirit to apply that to himself and to fit and qualify him to be a member of such a head, and an heir of such a kingdom. Whosoever Christ works anything for, he doth also work in them. There is a Spirit of application, and that Spirit of application, if it be true, it is a Spirit of sanctification and renovation fitting us every way for our condition.

Let us not abuse ourselves, as the world commonly doth, concerning Christ. They think God is merciful, and Christ is a Saviour. It is true, but what hath he wrought in thee by his Spirit? hast thou the Spirit of Christ?

or 'else thou art none of his,' Rom. viii. 9. Wherever Christ is, he goes with his Spirit to teach us to apply what Christ hath done for us, and to fit us to be like him. Therefore, let those that live in any sins against conscience, think it a diabolical illusion to think God and Christ is merciful. Aye, but where is the work of the Spirit? All the hope thou hast is only that thou art not in hell as yet, [only] for the time to come; but for the present I dare not say thou hast anything to do with Christ, when there is nothing of the Spirit in thee. The Spirit of Christ conforms the spouse to be like the husband, and the members to be like the head. Therefore, beg of Christ that he would anoint himself king in our hearts, and prophet and priest in our hearts, to do that that he did, to know his will as a prophet, to rule in us as a king, and to stir up prayers in us as a priest, to do in some proportion that that he doth, though it be in never so little a measure, for we receive it in measure, but Christ beyond measure. We must labour for so much as may manifest to us the truth of our estate in Christ, that we are not dead but living branches.

Now Christ gives and conveys his Spirit especially, and most of all since his ascension and sitting at the right hand of God, for after his resurrection he declared his victory over all his enemies, and therefore was able to give the Spirit without opposition, and upon his resurrection, death and hell and the anger of God were overcome, and our sins were satisfied for. Now Christ was head indeed, having trod all his enemies under his feet; now he was enabled to give the Spirit. But upon his ascension into heaven, and his sitting there, he was more enabled. For even as the sun being so high above the earth, doth convey his light and heat and influence upon the inferior bodies, so Christ being so highly advanced, is fitter to infuse his Spirit and grace here below since his exaltation. Therefore, the church is fuller of grace, and grace hath been more spread and diffused since the ascension of Christ than before, and the evangelist gives it as a reason, 'The Spirit was not yet given, because Christ was not ascended,' John vii. 39; intimating that, after his ascension, there was a more full portion of the Spirit given, God being fully appeased by the death of Christ, and Christ staying the advantage that was fittest to give the Spirit. Now God the Father gives the Spirit with the Son, so in both regards there was a greater fulness of the Spirit. Therefore, the prophets speaking of the times of Christ, especially of his exaltation, shew that then they should be filled with the Spirit, that the Spirit should be poured upon all flesh more abundantly than before. And that is the reason that the apostles so differed from themselves, before and after Christ's ascension. What a wondrous alteration was there! Peter before, he flies even at the voice of a maid, and they were full of contention and vainglory: but after we see, when the Spirit, the Holy Ghost, came down after Christ's ascension into heaven, how courageous and valorous they were, that they accounted it a matter of glory to suffer anything; and, indeed, we have more or less valour and courage, the more or less Spirit we have. Now they having received more abundance of Spirit, hereupon they were more courageous and undaunted at one time than another. And this abundance of the Spirit comes especially since Christ's advancement.

But how or by what means doth Christ give his Spirit to us? This Spirit that is so necessary for us, it is given by the ministry of the gospel, which is the ministry of the Spirit. 'Received ye the Holy Ghost by the works of the law, or by the hearing of faith preached?' Gal. iii. 2. When the love of God in Christ, and the benefits by Christ, are laid open in the preaching of the gospel to us, God gives his holy Spirit, the Spirit of Christ. Now God in Christ would save us by a triumphant and abundant love and mercy, and the Spirit of God never goes but where there is a magnifying of the love and mercy of God in Christ; therefore the ministry of the gospel, which only discovers the amity and love of God to mankind, being now reconciled in Christ, it is accompanied with the Spirit, to assure us of our part and portion in those benefits, for the Spirit is the fruit of God's love as well as Christ. Christ is the first gift, and the Spirit is the second, therefore that part of the word that discovers God's exceeding love to mankind, leaving angels when they were fallen, in their cursed estate, and yet giving his Son to become man, and 'a curse for us:' the discovery of this love and mercy of God, and of his Son Christ to us, is joined with the Spirit. For by the Spirit we see our cursed estate without the love and mercy of God in Christ, and likewise we are convinced of the love of God in Christ, and thereupon we love God again, and trust to his mercy, and out of love to him perform all cheerful obedience. Whatsoever we do else, if it be not stirred by the Spirit, apprehending the love of God in Christ, it is but morality. A man shall never go to heaven but by such a disposition and frame and temper of soul as is wrought by the Holy Ghost, persuading the soul first of the love and favour of God in Christ. What are all our performances if they be not out of love to God? and how shall we love God except we be persuaded that he loves us first? Therefore the gospel breeds love in us to God, and hath the Spirit together with it, working a blessed frame of sanctification, whereby we are disposed to every good duty. Therefore if we would have the Spirit of God, let us attend upon the sweet promises of salvation, upon the doctrine of Christ; for together with the knowledge of these things, the Holy Ghost slides and insinuates and infuseth himself into our souls.

Therefore the ministers of the gospel should be much in laying open the riches of God in Christ. In unfolding Christ, all other things will follow, as St Paul in Titus ii. 11, 12, 'The grace of God hath shined, hath appeared gloriously, teaching us to deny all ungodliness and worldly lusts, and to live holily and soberly in this present world.' Where the grace and love of God is persuaded and shed into the soul, all will follow.

What is the reason that former times were called dark times (and so they were), the times of popery a dark age? Christ was veiled, the gospel was veiled, there was no preaching of salvation by Christ alone, people were sent to stocks and stones, and to saints, and instead of the word, they were sent to legends and such things. Christ was obscured, thereupon they were dark ages. Those ages wherein the Spirit of God is most, is where Christ is most preached, and people are best always where there is most Spirit; and they are most joyful and comfortable and holy, where Christ is truly laid open to the hearts of people. The preaching of mere morality, if men be not careful to open Christ, to know how salvation is wrought by Christ, and how all good comes by Christ, it will never make a man perfectly good and fit him for heaven. It may make a man reform many abuses, like a philosopher, which hath its reward and respect amongst men, but nothing to give comfort at the hour of death and the day of judgment. Only that whereby the Spirit is conveyed, is the knowledge and preaching of Christ in his state and offices.

Again, the Spirit of Christ is given in obedience to this gospel, Acts v. 32. He gives the Holy Ghost to them that obey him. Now, there is the obedience of faith, and the obedience of life. When the soul is wrought to obedience, to believe, and to be directed by God, then the Holy Spirit is given in a further measure still. The Holy Ghost is given to them that obey, to them that do not resist the Spirit of God. For in the ministry of the gospel the Spirit is given in some degree to reprobates. It is offered, it knocks at the hearts of the vilest persons, that live in filthy and false courses of life, whose tongues and bodies are all instruments of an unsanctified soul to offend God. They have gracious motions offered them, but then they do not obey them. Therefore the Spirit seizeth not upon them, to rule in them. They have the Spirit knocking upon them; he doth not dwell in them, and take up his lodging in them. The Spirit is given to them that obey the sweet motions of it. Now, who is it that hears the blessed word of God, the blessed tidings of salvation, but he hath sweet motions of the Spirit to be in love with God, and the mercy of God, and to hate sin a little for a time, then presently upon it corruption joins and swells against those motions, and they only rest in the bare motion, and never come to any perfection. This is the state of reprobates in the church. They have many motions by the Holy Ghost, but their hearts are not subdued to obedience, not to constant obedience. Therefore, if we would have the Spirit of Christ, let us labour to subject ourselves unto it. When we have any good motion by the ministry of the word, or by conference, or by reading of good things (as holy things have a savour in them, the Spirit breathes in holy exercises), Oh give way to the motions of God's Spirit. We shall not have them again perhaps, turn not back those blessed messengers, let us entertain them, let the Spirit dwell and rule in us. It is the most blessed lodger that ever we entertained in all our lives. If we let the Spirit guide and rule us, it will lead us and govern and support us in life and death, and never leave us till it have raised our bodies (the Spirit of Christ in us at length will quicken our dead bodies), Rom. viii. 11, it will never leave us till it have brought us to heaven. This is the state of those that belong to God, that give way to the motions of God's Spirit to rule and guide them. Therefore, if we would have the Spirit of Christ, let us take heed of rebelling against it.

This is the state of many of us,—the Lord be merciful to us, and cure us,—that we do not only not receive the motions of the Spirit deeply into us, but if they be such as cross us in our pleasures and profits, though the word and Spirit join together, there is a rising of the proud spirit of man against so much of the Spirit and the motions of it, and against such parts of the word as crosseth us. This will be laid heavy to our charge one day, that we would bring the Spirit of God to our corruptions, and not bring our hearts to God's Spirit; and hereupon be those phrases in the Scripture of tempting the Spirit. Ananias and Sapphira tempted the Spirit, Acts v. 9—that is, when men will do that which is naught, and try whether God will forgive them, and put it off or no. How many are there that tempt the Spirit, that put it off, 'Perhaps I shall have the like motions another time,' 'I shall have better occasion when I can gain no more, when I can have my pleasure no more.' Thus men resist the Spirit, as St Stephen saith, Acts vii. 51—that is, when the Spirit discovers to them what they should believe, and what they should do, and they see it crosseth their resolution to be naught. Hereupon they resist the work of the Spirit, that else would close with their souls, and sanctify them, and fit them for heaven, if they would give way to it. And there is a quenching of the Spirit—that is, when men have sweet motions of the Spirit, and presently by some ill language or course of life they defile their vessels, and quench the sweet motions of the Spirit. Let us take heed of all these, of tempting, of resisting, and quenching the Spirit. For undoubtedly, living in the bosom of the church, we have many heavenly motions, especially those that have so much goodness in them as to attend upon God's ordinances. They have those motions at those times that they never have after perhaps, but they either resist them or quench them, and wrong and grieve the Spirit, as St Paul saith, 'Grieve not the Spirit of God, whereby you are sealed to the day of redemption,' Eph. iv. 30. Men speak or do somewhat that grieves the Spirit of God in them, their conscience being enlightened by the Spirit, tells them that they have done that which is naught; yet notwithstanding, for this or that advantage, to please this or that company, they will speak or do that which is ill, and then the Spirit that was given in some measure before is grieved at this carnal and sinful liberty. Therefore, if ye would be guided by the Spirit of Christ, take heed of all these, and of such like courses.

Another means whereby we may come to obtain the Spirit is prayer. To be guided by the Spirit of Christ, next to Christ himself, our Saviour, is the most excellent thing in the world, therefore it is worth the begging and getting. 'How much more shall your heavenly Father give his Holy Spirit to them that ask him?' Luke xi. 13, insinuating that we can ask nothing greater than the Spirit. A man that hath a sanctified judgment, next the forgiveness of his sins through Christ, he begs nothing more than the Spirit to witness the favour of God in Christ, and to fit him for other favours, especially to fit us for the world to come. God can give nothing greater, nor can we beg nothing greater, if we have sanctified judgments, than the Spirit of God. Therefore let us have an high esteem of the Holy Spirit, of the motions of it, and out of an high esteem in our hearts beg of God the guidance of the Spirit, that he would lead us by his Spirit, and subdue our corruptions, that we may not be led by our own lusts, and so consequently by Satan, that leads us by our own lusts in the way that leads to perdition. So much for that, 'I will put my Spirit,' &c.

And he shall shew judgment to the Gentiles.—After Christ was fully furnished, as he was furnished with the Spirit of God, and with a commission from heaven, from Father, Son, and Holy Ghost, having this high commission, and gifts for it by the Spirit, he falls upon his office presently. We are never fit for anything till we have the Spirit, and when we have the Spirit it is active and vigorous and working. 'He shall shew judgment to the Gentiles.'

What is meant by judgment here?

By judgment is meant laws. He shall declare his laws, his truth, and, together with declaring the truth of the gospel, which is his evangelical law, he shall declare it in the soul, and bow the neck of the inward man to the obedience of this his judgment. Christ then, by himself and his apostles and ministers, shall declare his truth, which is the sceptre of his government, to the Gentiles; and not only declare it as princes do their laws, by proclamations and statutes, &c., but he shall declare it to the heart by his Spirit.

Now, in the Hebrew language, ordinarily, wise government is called judgment (*b*). He shall declare judgment, that is, his manner of government, he shall declare it by his Spirit, and cause our spirits to submit to it.

And, indeed, grace is called judgment, in the phrase of Scripture, the grace of sanctification, because it is agreeable to judgment, to God's law. It is agreeable to it, and wrought by it in the soul, and it is the best judgment. For grace whereby the soul is subject to the judgment and law and rule of God, it must needs be the best judgment, because it is agreeable to God's judgment. Grace judgeth aright of things, and subdues all things, the affections and inward man to itself.

But why is the word of God called judgment?

It is called so frequently in the Psalms, and in other places of Scripture, because the truth of God shews what God doth judge. Judgment is originally in God, who is the first truth and the first good. The first truth judgeth best of truths; what is light and what is darkness, what is truth and what is error, what is good and what is ill, what is safe and what is dangerous. All will grant that God is the first light and the first truth; therefore, he doth originally judge of the difference of things; for even as in the creation he put an eternal difference between light and darkness, and severed things that were in the confused chaos, and established an orderly world, that heaven should be above, and earth below, that one thing should be above another, and all in judgment; so in the governing of mankind, he shews his judgment by his word, and that word shews how God judgeth of things. Laws shew judgment, what is to be done, and what is not to be done. The gospel shews God's judgment, what he will have us believe and hope for, and how we must carry ourselves in way of thankfulness. If we do this, then the gospel, the word of God, judgeth what shall become of us; 'we shall be saved,' Mark xvi. 16. If we do the contrary, the word again judgeth what our state shall be, 'we shall be damned,' *ibid.* So it is called judgment, because it judgeth what is good and what is ill, and because it determineth what shall become of us if we obey or disobey.

Hereupon it is that the word of God is a glass wherein we may see our own condition infallibly, what will become of us. The word of God judgeth thus: he that lives in such and such sins shall come to this end, God will inflict these and these judgments upon him. Judgment, in the first place, is, You shall do this and this, because it is good. Judgment, in the second place, is, Because you have not done this, this shall befall you. So the evangelical judgment of the gospel is this, 'He that repents and believes shall not perish, but have everlasting life,' John iii. 15; but he that arms and furnisheth his heart to rebellion, he shall perish in his sins, 'He that believeth not is condemned already, the wrath of God hangs over his head,' John iii. 18. So from this, that God's truth is called judgment, we may know how to judge of ourselves, even as God judgeth in his word. We may see our own faces and conditions there. He that is a man of death may see it in the word, and he that is appointed for happiness may there see his condition.

Again, not only the word of God, the gospel, which is out of us in the book of God, is called judgment, but the work of God in the soul, sanctification, is called judgment. Hence, we may observe what is the most judicious course in the world, the most judicious frame of soul, when it is framed to the judgment and truth of God, being the first truth. When a man is sanctified and set in a holy frame, it is from a sanctified judgment. The flesh is subject to the Spirit. Here is all in a gracious order. The baser part doth not rule the higher, but the higher part of the soul, a sanctified judgment, rules all, because the whole is in right judgment. Therefore, sanctification is called judgment, and other courses, though they be never so fashionable, are but madness and folly and disorder in the censure in the Scripture. Nothing is judgment and true wisdom, but sanctification and obedience flowing from sanctification. Therefore, saith Moses, in Deut. iv. 6, 'Then shall you be known to be a wise people when you obey the laws that I have given you.' Only that, shews a wise, judicious man to be obedient to God's truth by the Spirit sanctifying him. Without the truth of God and the Spirit in us, framing our souls answerable to the truth, we are out of all good order; for then the affections that should be ruled, rule us; then the body and the lusts of the body rule the soul; and the devil rules by both. What a shameful disorder is this, when a man shall be ruled by the devil and his own lusts, that he should tread under feet and trample upon! And this is the state of all that have not this judgment in them, that have not the word of God written in their hearts, bowing and bending them by the Spirit of God to spiritual obedience. To prove this, I will name but one place among many, Tit. iii. 3; he shews the state of all men that are not brought into subjection by this judgment, by the word and Spirit of truth. We, ourselves, saith he, 'were sometimes foolish and disobedient;' till this judgment is set up in us, we are foolish in our understandings, and disobedient in our wills and affections, deceived and misled by the devil and our own lusts: for that follows upon folly. Those that are foolish and disobedient are deceived and led away to eternal destruction. 'There is a way that seems good in a man's own eyes, but the issues of it are death,' saith Solomon, Prov. xiv. 12. This is the state of all men that are not led with the judgment of God's truth and Spirit, sanctifying and framing their souls to obedience, they are foolish and disobedient and deceived, and so it will prove with them in the end, 'serving diverse lusts, and pleasures, living in malice and envy, hating one another,' Titus iii. 3. Now when God by his blessed truth and Spirit sets up his rule in the heart, it brings all into captivity; as St Paul saith, it brings all the inner man into subjection: 'The word of God is the weapon of God; these judgments are mighty in operation, together with the Spirit, to beat down all strongholds and to set up another judgment there; it brings all into captivity to the truth and command of God, and to the motions of the Spirit, 2 Cor. x. 4, 5 (*c*). The word and Spirit beat down all the strongholds that are raised up in the heart by Satan, and our corruptions. So we see here what is meant by this phrase, 'he shall declare judgment to the Gentiles.' It is a militant word, therefore I have stood somewhat the longer in unfolding of it.

Now this is wrought by the preaching of the gospel, 'he shall declare judgment to the Gentiles.' All grace comes by declaring; 'The gospel is the power of God to salvation,' Rom. i. 16. Let but the gospel (which is God's judgment how men shall be saved, and how they shall walk in obedience by way of thankfulness to God) be declared, and all that belong to God shall come in, and yield homage to it, and be brought in subjection. The devil in the antichristian state knows this well enough. Therefore he labours to hinder the declaration of judgment by all means; he will not have God's judgments but men's traditions declared. He knows the declaring of God's judgments will breed an alteration quickly in men's dispositions: For when he saith, he shall declare judgment to the Gentiles, he means the consequent as well as the thing, he shall so declare judgment that they shall yield spiritual obedience and come in and be saved.

Let the devil do his worst, let all seducers of souls do their worst, if they would but give way to the preaching of the gospel, let but judgment be declared, let God's arm be stretched forth in delivering the truth, he would soon gain souls out of the captivity and bondage of Satan. They know it well enough; therefore by all the ways they can, they stop the preaching of the gospel, and disgrace and hinder it, and set up men's traditions instead of the gospel. But I will not enlarge myself farther upon these words, but go on to the next.

He shall not strive nor cry, neither shall any man hear his voice in the streets.—These words set down the mild and sweet and amiable manner of Christ's carriage upon earth. Here, in his first coming to work the great work of our redemption, he did not carry the matter in an outward glorious manner, in pomp; but he would have his miracles concealed ofttimes and himself hidden. His Godhead was hid under the veil of his manhood. He could not have wrought our salvation else. If the devil and the world had known Christ to be as he was, they would never have made those attempts against him. Therefore, considering he had such a dispensation to work our salvation as a king, priest, and prophet, he would not cry and contend and strive, he would not come with any great noise.

Now, here is an opposition to the giving of the law, and likewise to the coming and carriage of civil princes. You know when the law was given all the mount was on fire, and the earth thereabout quaked and trembled, and the people fled. They could not endure to hear the voice of God speaking in the mount; there was such a terrible smoke and fire, they were all afraid. Thus came Moses. Now, did Christ come as Moses? Was the gospel delivered by Christ as the law was, in terrors and fears? Oh, no. Christ came not in such a terrible manner, in thunder and lightning; but the gospel, it came sweetly. A dove, a mild creature, lit upon the head of Christ when he was baptized, to shew his mild manner of carriage; and he came with blessing in his mouth in his first sermon of all: 'Blessed are the poor in spirit, blessed are they that mourn, blessed are they that hunger and thirst after righteousness,' Matt. v. 3, 4, 6. The law came with curses: 'Cursed is every one that continueth not in all things written in the law to do them,' Gal. iii. 10. Christ came in another manner; the gospel was delivered in a mild, sweet manner. Christ, as an ambassador, came sweetly to entreat and beseech. There is a crying, indeed, but it is a crying out of love and entreaty, not a shouting in a terrible manner as was at the giving of the law, no, nor as at the coming of other civil princes into a city, with shouting and noise of trumpets, with pomp, and state, and great attendants. Christ came not into the world to execute his kingdom and office in such pomp and noise as it is said of Agrippa, Acts xxv. 23, 'He came with great pomp.' So worldly princes carry things thus, and it is needful in some sort. People must have shows and pomp; the outward man must have outward things to astonish it withal. It is a policy in state so to do. But Christ came in another manner. He came not to make men quake and tremble that came to speak and deal with him. He came not with clamour and fierceness; for who would have come to Christ then? But he came in a mild, and sweet, and amiable manner. We see a little before the text (ver. 16), upon occasion of the inference of these words, he commands and chargeth them that they should not discover him and make him known. When he had done a good work he would not have it known.

Now, there are three things especially insinuated in this description, 'He shall not strive nor cry, neither shall any man hear his voice in the street.' That Christ should not be outwardly glorious to publish his own excellency, nor contentious; he should not cry nor quarrel, nor he should not be clamorous, if he had any wrong, to be all on fire presently, but he should be as a meek lamb, he should make no noise, he should not come in vainglory or clamour, &c.

But here we must know that Christ was a wise discerner of the fitness of times; for sometimes he would have things published, sometimes he would not; sometimes he would be known, sometimes he would not. Christ, in his second coming, shall come all in majesty and glory with his angels, and all the earth shall appear before him; but now his wisdom told him, now he came to save the world as a prophet, priest, and king, to work man's salvation, that he must hide and conceal himself; and so he ordered all his courses by discretion. Every sacrifice must be salted with salt, everything should be seasoned with the salt of discretion. This is the steward of all our actions, to know what is fit. Christ knew it was fittest to conceal himself now at this time.

Now, by Christ's example we should learn this, not to be vainglorious, not to make a great noise. You have some, if they do anything that is good, presently all the world must know it. This was not Christ's disposition. It is a disposition that is hardly wrought out of man's heart without an exceeding great measure of the Spirit of God; for we see good men have been given this way. David would number the people, that it might be known what a great monarch he was, what a great number of people he had, 2 Sam. xxiv. He was a good man, yet vainglorious. He smarted for it. So good Hezekiah. Ambassadors were sent to him from the king of Babylon, and that they should know that Hezekiah was no beggarly prince, out must come the vessels of the temple and all his treasures, to shew what a rich king the king of Judah was, 2 Kings xx. 13, *et seq.* His vainglory cost him all his riches, as the prophet told him. So the disciples. Before they received a great measure of the Spirit, how vainglorious were they! They contended for the higher place; therefore they advise Christ to go up to Jerusalem, that he might be known. As Jehu said to Jonadab, 'Come up and see my zeal for the Lord of hosts,' 2 Kings x. 16, he accounts it nothing unless it be seen. So flesh and blood. If there be anything done that is good, all the world must know it presently. Christ chargeth them that no noise should be made, but that they should conceal him.

What should we learn hence?

To be of Christ's disposition, that is, to have no more care of the knowledge of things than the light of the things themselves will discover, to do works of light, and if the things themselves will break forth to men's eyes and they must see our light shine, then let them, and imitate our good works; but for us to blazon them abroad ourselves, it is not the spirit of Christ.

Let us labour to have humility of spirit, that that may grow up with us in all our performances, that all things that we speak and do may savour of a spirit of humility, that we may seek the glory of God in all things more than our own.

And let us commit the fame and credit of what we are or do to God. He will take care of that. Let us take care to be and to do as we should, and then for noise and report, let it be good or ill as God will send it. We know ofttimes it falls out that that which is precious in man's eye is abominable in God's. If we seek to be in the mouths of men, to dwell in the talk and speech of men, God will abhor us, and at the hour of death it will not comfort us what men speak or know of us, but sound comfort must be from our own conscience and the judgment of God. Therefore, let us labour to be good in secret. Christians should be as minerals, rich in the depth of the earth. That which is least seen is his riches. We should have our treasure deep. For the discovery of it we should be ready when we are called to it, and for all other accidental things, let them fall out as God in his wisdom sees good. So let us look through good report and bad report to heaven; let us do the duties that are pleasing to God and our own conscience, and God will be careful enough to get us applause. Was it not sufficient for Abel, that though there was no great notice taken what faith he had, and how good a man he was, yet that God knew it and discovered it? God sees our sincerity and the truth of our hearts, and the graces of our inward man, he sees all these, and he values us by these, as he did Abel. As for outward things there may be a great deal of deceit in them, and the more a man grows in grace, the less he cares for them. As much reputation as is fit for a man will follow him in being and doing what he should. God will look to that. Therefore we should not set up sails to our own meditations, that unless we be carried with the wind of applause, to be becalmed and not go a whit forward; but we should be carried with the Spirit of God and with a holy desire to serve God, and our brethren, and to do all the good we can, and never care for the speeches of the world, as St Paul saith of himself: 'I care not what ye judge of me, I care not what the world judgeth, I care not for man's judgment,' 1 Cor. iv. 3. This is man's day. We should, from the example of Christ, labour to subdue this infirmity which we are sick of naturally. Christ concealed himself till he saw a fitter time. We shall have glory enough, and be known enough to devils, to angels, and men ere long. Therefore, as Christ lived a hidden life, that is, he was not known what he was, that so he might work our salvation, so let us be content to be hidden men. A true Christian is hidden to the world till the time of manifestation comes. When the time came, Christ then gloriously discovered what he was; so we shall be discovered what we are. In the mean time, let us be careful to do our duty that may please the Spirit of God, and satisfy our own conscience, and leave all the rest to God. Let us meditate, in the fear of God, upon these directions for the guidance of our lives in this particular.

NOTES.

(a) P. 6.—'Red, well-coloured earth.' The allusion is to the name of Adam, or man—אָדָם, red, ruddy—and to his derivation, as recorded in Gen. ii. 7.

(b) P. 26.—'In the Hebrew language ordinarily wise government is called judgment.' This holds of various Hebrew terms. In the passage explained (Isa. xlii. 1), the term rendered judgment, is מִשְׁפָּט, which is equivalent to תּוֹרָה, *law*.

(c) P. 28.—2 Cor. x. 4, 5. Sibbes's translation of this somewhat difficult passage may be profitably compared with Alford, Stanley, Hodge, and others, *in loc.* It is surprising how many of these unpretending and almost incidental renderings anticipate the results of the highest scholarship of our time. He may not be—who is?—invariably accurate critically, but he rarely fails in his insight into the 'mind of the Spirit.' G.

THE BRUISED REED AND SMOKING FLAX.

NOTE.

The editions of the 'Bruised Reed and Smoking Flax' known to the editor are, with the letters used to designate those collated for the present publication, as follows:—

(*a*) The Brvised Reede, and Smoaking Flax. Some Sermons contracted out of the 12. of Matth. 20. At the desire, and for the good of weaker Christians. By R. Sibbes, D.D. Zach. 4. 10, Who hath despised the day of small things?

London, Printed for R. Dawlman, dwelling at the signe of the Brazen Serpent in Paul's Church-yard. 1630. 18mo. A.

This is the *first* edition.

(*b*) 'The second Edition, enlarged.' 1631. 18mo. B.

(*c*) 3d edition 1631. 18mo.

(*d*) 4th „ 1632. 18mo.

(*e*) 5th „ 'corrected,' 1635. 18mo. E

(*f*) 6th „ 1638. 18mo.

(*g*) 6th „ [so designated] 'corrected, and divided into chapters.' 1658. 18mo. G.

The text of our reprint is E, as having been the last issued during the lifetime of Sibbes. The 'corrections' and 'enlargements' of B, and the original readings of A, are noted. These will shew the watchful pains which Sibbes took in the matter even of style. It also deepens the regret that so many of his writings labour under the disadvantage of posthumous publication.

The division 'into chapters,' which we probably owe to the celebrated John Goodwin, who also prefixed an admirable 'Epistle' to another of Sibbes's volumes (Exposition of Philippians, c. iii., &c., &c., 4to, 1639), it has been deemed advisable to retain. It is the form in which all subsequent editions have appeared.

The 'various readings,' are given as foot-notes.

G

TO THE RIGHT HONOURABLE

SIR HORATIO VERE, KNIGHT,

LORD VERE OF TILBURY, AND GENERAL OF THE ENGLISH FORCES

UNDER THE HIGH AND MIGHTY LORDS

THE STATES GENERAL OF THE UNITED PROVINCES IN THE NETHERLANDS :*

AND TO HIS PIOUS CONSORT,

THE LADY MARY VERE,†

INCREASE OF GRACE, ETC.

RIGHT HONOURABLE,

Soldiers that carry their lives in their hands had need, above all others, to carry grace in their hearts, that so having made peace with God, they may be fit to encounter with men; and having by faith in Christ disarmed death before they die, they may sacrifice their life with the more

* Sir Horatio Vere was the youngest son of Geffrey de Vere, Esq., who again was son of John Vere, 15th Earl of Oxford. He was born at Kirkby Hall, Essex, in 1565. As the titles of the present 'Epistle Dedicatory' shew, he was a military commander of note, only second to his illustrious brother Sir Francis. Returning from a campaign in Bohemia, in 1622–3, the king (James I.), according to Camden, 'received him so graciously and thankfully, that forgetting himself, he stood bare to him.' On the accession of Charles I., in 1625, he was, in consideration of his eminent services, raised to the peerage, by the title of Lord Vere, Baron Tilbury. He was the first peer created by Charles. He died, May 2. 1635, only three months before Sibbes himself. Besides the tribute of the author of the 'Bruised Reed,' to the worth of Sir Horatio, Fuller has burnished his name as of one renowned for piety, meekness, and valour. A volume of poems, now rarely to be met with, was published on his death. It is entitled, 'Elegies, celebrating the happy memory of Horatio Vere.' (London, 1642, 8vo.) For full 'Memoirs' of him, consult the *Extinct Peerage* books. G.

† Lady Mary Vere.—Anderson in his 'Memorable omen of the Puritan Times,' (2 vols., 1862, *just issued*,) has given a singularly interesting, and on the whole, accurate account of this remarkable Lady. (See vol. i. pp. 31–85.) It was to her the Parliament entrusted the care of the children of Charles I. She died on the 25th of December 1671, in the ninety-first year of her age. Gurnall preached her funeral sermon. G.

courage and comfort, which to neglect, being a matter of eternity, is not valour, but desperate madness, because in this business, as in oversights of war, there is no place for a second repentance, the first error being unrecoverable. In evils above the strength of man to prevail against* and his patience to endure, there God hath planted the affection of fear, which might stir us up to avoid the danger by flying to him in Christ, who being our friend, it is no matter who is our enemy: we may be killed, but cannot be hurt; so safe it is to be under his command that hath command over death, hell, judgment, and all that we most fear. Yet such is our nature, that by familiarity with danger, we grow by degrees insensibly to be hardened against it, and to look no further than death, as if to die were only to give up the ghost, and then an end of all. And hereupon it is, that they that follow the wars are generally taken to be men not most religious; the more respect those of that profession deserve, that have learned upon what terms to live and die, that are sure of a better life before they leave this, that have laid up their life in Christ; amongst whom, Right Honourable, the world hath a long time taken notice of you, in whom both religion and military employment, meekness of spirit with height of courage, humility with honour, by a rare and happy combination have met together. Whereby you have much vindicated your profession from common imputation, and shewed that piety can enter into tents, and follow after camps, and that God hath his Joshuas and his Corneliuses in all ages. But I will not use many words of yourself to yourself, because though you have done much that may and will be spoken, yet you love not to hear or speak of what you have done.

It may seem to some unbefitting to offer a discourse of a 'bruised reed' to such a strong and flourishing cedar. But experience sheweth that the strongest plants in God's house are exposed sometimes to strong winds of temptation, and thereupon meet with bruisings, that they may the better know by whose strength they stand, and that the greatest may learn to go out of themselves to the same common rock and fountain of strength with the meanest. David was a valiant man; yet upon experience of his oft failings and recoveries, he became towards God as a weaned child. Lowliness of mind to Godward and greatness of spirit against His enemies may well stand together; for the way to be above all other things is to submit to God first. Besides, this text speaketh of the prevailing government of Christ in his church and in his children, which may be an encouragement to your Lordship still, not only to own the cause of Christ in these times, wherein men are ashamed of what they should glory in, and glory in their shame; but likewise to fight the Lord's battles, when called to it, and help him against the mighty, for victory attendeth Christ's side in the end. Though God, to revenge the quarrel of his covenant, suffer his enemies to prevail yet for a time, to harden them the more, yet they have undertaken a damned cause; and howsoever the church hath justly provoked God, yet the cause shall stand impregnable against all created

* 'Against,' added first in B.

power of devils and men. We naturally desire victory, and many desire it more than truth or goodness, which only are victorious; and so out of a depraved judgment they cross their own desires, seeking to overcome in that wherein it were safer for them to be overcome. These* are sure to meet with shame in the conclusion instead of victory; or else we must deny Christ to be King of his church and Judge of the world. Proceed on still, Honourable Lord, to stand for Christ both in peace and war, and this shall be found to your honour when Christ shall come 'to be glorious in his saints,' 2 Thess. i. 10, that he thought you worthy to honour himself by, when others, that oppose or betray the cause of Christ for base ends, shall not dare to hold up their heads.

I would not divide you from your Honourable Lady, being obliged to both, and both being one, as in other bands, so in that above nature, in love to the best things; both exemplary in all religious courses; both in your places, likewise, having been employed in great services for the common good, so that not only this but foreign States are bound to bless God for you both. Going on in these ways, you will find God making his promise good of honouring them that honour him.

I do not so far overvalue this poor work as to think it worthy of your Honours, but thus I thought meet to witness my deserved respect to you both. If I be to blame for suffering these sermons, long since preached, thus to come forth, others must divide the fault with me, who had brought it to that pass that it was almost necessary for me to take this course. The Lord continue to bless your Honours, with all your branches, and to maintain his grace in you, 'until he hath brought forth judgment unto victory,' Mat. xii. 20.

Your Honours' to command in the Lord,

RICHARD SIBBES.

* 'They,' in A.

TO THE GENERAL READER.

To prevent a further inconvenience, I was drawn to let these notes pass with some review, considering there was an intendment of publishing them, by some who had not perfectly taken them; and these first, as being next at hand: and having had occasion lately of some fresh thoughts concerning this argument, by dealing with some, the chief ground of whose trouble was the want of considering of the gracious nature and office of Christ; the right conceit of which is the spring of all service to Christ, and comfort from him. God hath laid up all grace and comfort in Christ for us, and planted a wonderful sweetness of pity and love in his heart towards us. As God his father hath *fitted him with a body*, Heb. x. 7, so with a heart to be a merciful Redeemer. What do* the Scriptures speak but Christ's love and tender care over those that are humbled? and besides the mercy that resteth in his own breast, he works the like impression in his ministers and others, *to comfort the feeble-minded, and to bear with the weak*, 1 Thess. v. 14. Ministers by their calling are friends of the Bride, and to bring Christ and his Spouse together, and therefore ought, upon all good occasions, to lay open all the excellencies of Christ, and amongst others, as that he is highly born, mighty, One 'in whom all the treasures of wisdom are hid,' Col. ii. 3, &c., so likewise gentle, and of a good nature, and of a gracious disposition. It cannot but cheer the heart of the spouse, to consider, in all her infirmities and miseries she is subject to,† that she hath a husband of a kind disposition, that knows how to give the honour of mild usage to the weaker vessel, that will be so far from rejecting her, because she is weak, that he will pity her the more. And as he is kind at all times, so especially when it is most seasonable; he will speak to her heart, 'especially in the wilderness,' Hos. ii. 24. The more glory to God, and the more comfort to a Christian soul, ariseth from the belief and application of these things, the more the enemy of God's glory and man's comfort labours to breed mispersuasions of them, that if he cannot keep men from heaven, and bring them into that cursed condition he is in himself, yet he may trouble them in their passage; some and none of the worst, Satan prevails withal so far as to neglect the means, upon fear they should, being so sinful, dishonour God and increase their sins; and so they lie smothering under this temptation, as it were bound hand and foot by Satan, not daring to make out to Christ, and yet are secretly upheld by a spirit of faith, shewing itself in hidden sighs and groans unto God. These are abused by false representations of Christ; all whose ways to such being ways of mercy, and all his thoughts, thoughts of love. The more Satan is malicious

* 'Doth,' in A and B.

† 'Unto,' in A and B.

in keeping the soul in darkness, the more care is to be had of establishing the soul upon that which will stay it. Amongst other grounds to build our faith on, as the free offer of grace to all that will receive it, Rev. xxii.17; the gracious invitation of all that are weary and heavy laden, Matt. xi. 28; those that have nothing to buy withal, Isa. lv. 1; the command binding to believe, 1 John. iii. 23; the danger of not believing, being shut up prisoners thereby under the guilt of all other sins, John xvi. 9; the sweet entreaty to believe, and ordaining ambassadors to desire peace, 2 Cor. v. 20; putting tender affections into them, answerable to their calling, ordaining sacraments for the sealing of the covenant. Besides these, I say, and such moving inducements, this is one infusing vigour and strength into all the rest, that they proceed from Christ, a person authorised, and from those bowels that moved him not only to become a man, but a curse for us; hence it is, that he '*will not quench the smoking wick or flax.*' It adds strength to faith to consider, that all expressions of love issue from nature in Christ, which is constant. God knows that, as we are prone to sin, so, when conscience is thoroughly awaked, we are as prone to despair for sin; and therefore he would have us know, that he setteth himself in the covenant of grace to triumph in Christ over the greatest evils and enemies we fear, and that his thoughts are not as our thoughts are, Isa. v. 8; that he is God, and not man, Hos. xi. 9; that there are heights, and depths, and breadths of mercy in him above all the depths of our sin and misery, Eph. iii. 18; that we should never be in such a forlorn condition, wherein there should be ground of despair, considering our sins be the sins of men, his mercy the mercy of an infinite God. But though it be a truth clearer than the sunbeams, that a broken-hearted sinner ought to embrace mercy so strongly enforced; yet there is no truth that the heart shutteth itself more against than this, especially in sense of misery, when the soul is fittest for mercy, until the Holy Spirit sprinkleth the conscience with the blood of Christ, and sheddeth his love into the heart, that so the blood of Christ in the conscience may cry louder than the guilt of sin; for only God's Spirit can raise the conscience with comfort above guilt, because he only is greater than the conscience. Men may speak comfort, but it is Christ's Spirit that can only comfort. Peace is the *fruit of the lips*, but yet *created* to be so, Isa. lvii. 19. No creature can take off wrath from the conscience, but he that set it on, though all the prevailing arguments be used that can be brought forth, till the Holy Ghost effectually persuadeth, by a divine kind of rhetoric, which ought to raise up our hearts to him who is the comforter of his people, that he would seal them to our souls. Now God dealing with men as understanding creatures, the manner which he useth in this powerful work upon their consciences, is by way of friendly intercourse, as entreaty and persuasion, and discovery of his love in Christ, and Christ's gracious inclination thus even to the weakest and lowest of men. *Loquitur Deus ad modum nostrum, agit ad modum suum.* And, therefore, because he is pleased by such like motives to enter into the heart and settle a peace there, we ought with reverence to regard all such sanctified helps, and among the rest this of making use of this comfortable description of Christ by God the Father, in going boldly in all necessities to the throne of grace. But we must know this comfort is only the portion of those that give up themselves to Christ's government, that are willing in all things to be disposed of by him. For here we see in this Scripture both joined together, mercy to bruised reeds, and yet government prevailing by degrees over corruptions. Christ so favoureth weak ones, as that he frameth their souls to a better condition than they are in. Neither can it be otherwise, but that a soul looking for mercy should submit itself at the same time to be guided. Those relations of husband, head, shepherd, &c., imply not only meekness and mercy, but government likewise. When we become Christians to purpose, we live not exempt from all service, but only we change our Lord. Therefore, if any in an ill course of life snatch comforts before they are reached out unto them, let them know they do it at their own perils. It is as if some ignorant man should come into an apothecary's shop, stored with variety of medicines of all sorts, and should take what comes next to hand, poison perhaps, instead of physic. There is no word of comfort in the whole book of God intended for such *as regard iniquity in their hearts*, Ps. lxvi. 18; though they do not act it in their lives. Their only comfort is, that the sentence of damnation is not executed, and thereupon there is yet opportunity of safer thoughts and resolutions, otherwise they stand not only convicted but condemned by the word; and Christ *that rideth on the white horse*, Rev. vi. 2, will spend all his arrows upon them, and wound them to death. If any shall bless himself in an ill way, God's wrath shall burn to hell against such. There is no more comfort to be expected from Christ, than there is care to please him. Otherwise to make him an abettor of a lawless and loose life, is to transform him into a fancy, nay, into the likeness of him whose works he came to destroy, 1 John iii. 8, which is the most detestable idolatry of all. One way whereby the Spirit of Christ prevaileth in his, is to preserve them from such thoughts; yet we see people will frame a divinity to themselves, pleasing to the flesh, suitable to their own ends, which, being vain in the substance, will prove likewise vain in the fruit, and as a building upon the sand.

The main scope of all, is, to allure us to the entertainment of Christ's mild, safe, wise, victorious government, and to leave men naked of all pretences, why they will not have Christ to rule over them, when we see salvation not only strongly wrought, but sweetly dispensed by him. His government is not for his own pleasure, but for our good. We are saved by a way of love, that love might be kindled by this way in us to God again; because this affection melteth the soul, and mouldeth it to all duty and acceptable manner of performance of duty. It is love in duties that God regards, more than duties themselves. This is the true and evangelical disposition arising from Christ's love to us, and our love to him again; and not to fear to come to him, as if we were to take an elephant by the tooth. It is almost a fundamental mistake, to think that God delights in slavish fears, whenas the fruits of Christ's kingdom are peace and joy in the Holy Ghost: for from this mistake come weak, slavish, superstitious conceits.

Two things trouble the peace of Christians very much (1), their weaknesses hanging upon them, and (2) fear of holding out for time to come. A remedy against both is in this text, for Christ is set out here as a mild Saviour to weak ones; and, for time to come, his powerful care and love is never interrupted, until he bring forth judgment to victory. And thereupon it is that both the means of salvation and grace wrought by means, and glory the perfection of grace, come all under one name of the KINGDOM OF GOD so oft; because whom by means he brings to grace, he will by grace bring to glory.

This makes * the thoughts of the latter judgment comfortable unto us, that he who is then to be our judge, cannot but judge for them who have been ruled by him here; for whom he guides by his counsel, those he

* 'Maketh,' in A and B.

brings to glory, Ps. lxxiii. 24. If our faith were but as firm as our state in Christ is secure and glorious, what manner of men should we be?

If I had gone about to affect writing in a high strain, I should have missed of mine end, and crossed the argument in hand. For shall we that are servants quench those weak sparks which our Lord himself is pleased to cherish? I had rather hazard the censure of some, than hinder the good of others; which, if it be any ways furthered by these few observations, I have what I aimed at. I intended not a treatise, but opening of a text; what I shall be drawn to do in this kind must be by degrees, as leisure in the midst of many interruptions will permit: the Lord guide our hearts, tongues, and pens for his glory and the good of his people.

RICHARD SIBBES.

THE BRUISED REED AND SMOKING FLAX.

A bruised reed shall he not break, and smoking flax shall he not quench, till he send forth judgment unto victory.—MATT. xii. 20.

[CHAPTER I.—*The Text opened and divided. What the Reed is, and what the Bruising.*]

THE prophet Isaiah being lifted up, and carried with the wing of prophetical spirit, passeth over all the time between him and the appearing of Jesus Christ in the flesh, and seeth with the eye of prophecy, and with the eye of faith, Christ as present, and presenteth him, in the name of God, to the spiritual eye of others, in these words: 'Behold my servant whom I have chosen,' &c., Isa. xliii. 10. Which place is alleged by Saint Matthew as fulfilled now in Christ, Matt. xii. 18. Wherein is propounded—

First, the calling of Christ to his office.

Secondly, the execution of it.

I. For his calling: God styleth him here his righteous servant, &c. Christ was God's servant in the greatest piece of service that ever was; a chosen, and a choice servant: he did and suffered all by commission from the Father: wherein we may see the sweet love of God to us, that counts the work of our salvation by Christ his greatest service; and that he will put his only beloved Son to that service. He might well prefix *Behold,* to raise up our thoughts to the highest pitch of attention and admiration. In time of temptation, misgiving consciences look so much to the present trouble they are in, that they need be roused up to behold him in whom they may find rest for their distressed souls. In temptations it is safest to behold nothing but Christ the true brazen serpent, the true *Lamb of God that taketh away the sins of the world,* John i. 29. This saving object hath a special influence of comfort into the soul, especially if we look not only on Christ, but upon the Father's authority and love in him. For in all that Christ did and suffered as Mediator, we must see *God in him reconciling the world unto himself,* 2 Cor. v. 19.

What a support to our faith is this, that God the Father, the party offended by our sins, is so well pleased with the work of redemption! And what a comfort is this, that seeing God's love resteth on Christ, as well pleased in him, we may gather that he is as well pleased with us, if we be in Christ! For his love resteth in whole Christ, in Christ mystical, as well as Christ natural, because he loveth him and us with one love. Let us, therefore, embrace Christ, and in him God's love, and build our faith safely on such a Saviour, that is furnished with so high a commission.

See here, for our comfort, a sweet agreement of all three persons: the Father giveth a commission to Christ; the Spirit furnisheth and sanctifieth to it; Christ himself executeth the office of a Mediator. Our redemption is founded upon the joint agreement of all three persons of the Trinity.

II. For the execution of this his calling, it is set down here to be modest, without making a noise, or raising dust by any pompous coming, as princes use to do. '*His voice shall not be heard.*' His voice indeed was heard, but what voice? '*Come unto me, all ye that are weary and heavy laden,*' Mat. xi. 28. He cried, but how? '*Ho, every one that thirsteth, come,*' &c., Isa. lv. 1. And as his coming was modest, so it was mild, which is set down in these words: The bruised reed shall he not break, &c. Wherein we may observe these three things:—

First, The condition of those that Christ had to deal withal. (1.) They were *bruised reeds;* (2.) *smoking flax.*

Secondly, Christ's carriage toward* them. He *brake not* the bruised reed, nor *quenched* the smoking flax: where more is meant than spoken; for he will not only not break the bruised reed, nor quench, &c., but he will cherish them.

Thirdly, The constancy and progress of this his tender care, '*until judgment come to victory*'—that is, until the sanctified frame of grace begun in their hearts be brought to that perfection, that it prevaileth over all opposite corruption.

1. For the *first,* the condition of men whom he was to deal withal is, that they were bruised reeds, and smoking flax; not trees, but reeds; and not whole, but bruised reeds. The church is compared to weak things; to a dove amongst the fowls; to a vine amongst the plants; to sheep amongst the beasts; to a woman, which is the weaker vessel: and here God's children are compared to bruised reeds and smoking flax. First,† we will speak of them as they are bruised reeds, and then as smoking flax.

They are bruised reeds before their conversion, and oftentimes after: before conversion all (except such as being bred up in the church, God hath delighted to shew himself gracious unto from their childhood), yet in different degrees, as God seeth meet; and as difference is in regard of temper, parts, manner of life, &c., so in God's intendment of employment for the time to come; for usually he empties such of themselves, and makes them nothing, before he will use them in any great services.

(1.) This bruised reed is a man that for the most part is in some misery, as those were that came to Christ for help, and (2) by misery is brought to see sin the cause of it; for whatsoever pretences sin maketh, yet bruising or breaking is the end of it; (3) he is sensible of sin and misery, even unto bruising; and (4), seeing no help in himself, is carried with restless desire to have supply from another, with some hope, which a little raiseth him out of himself to Christ, though he dareth not claim any present interest of mercy. This spark of hope being opposed by doubtings, and fears rising from corruption, maketh him as smoking flax; so that both these together, a *bruised* reed and *smoking* flax, make up the state of a poor dis-

* 'Towards,' in A and B. † 'And first,' in A and B.

tressed man. Such an one as our Saviour Christ termeth poor in spirit, Mat. v. 3, who seeth a want, and withal seeth himself indebted to divine justice, and no means of supply from himself or the creature, and thereupon mourns, and upon some hope of mercy from the promise and examples of those that have obtained mercy, is stirred up to hunger and thirst after it.

[Chapter II.—*Those that Christ hath to do withal are Bruised.*]

This bruising is required [1] before conversion (1), that so the Spirit may make way for itself into the heart by levelling all proud, high thoughts, and that we may understand ourselves to be what indeed we are by nature. We love to wander from ourselves and to be strangers at home, till God bruiseth us by one cross or other, and then we *bethink ourselves*, and come home to ourselves with the prodigal (Luke xv. 17.)

A marvellous hard thing it is to bring a dull and a shifting heart to cry with feeling for mercy. Our hearts, like malefactors, until they be beaten from all shifts, never cry for the mercy of the Judge. Again (2), this bruising maketh us set a high price upon Christ. The gospel is the gospel indeed then; then the fig-leaves of morality will do us no good. And (3) it maketh us more thankful, and (4) from thankfulness more fruitful in our lives; for what maketh many so cold and barren, but that bruising for sin never endeared God's grace unto them? Likewise (5), this dealing of God doth establish us the more in his ways, having had knocks and bruisings in our own ways. This is the cause oft of relapses and apostasies, because men never smarted for sin at the first; they were not long enough under the lash of the law. Hence this inferior work of the Spirit in *bringing down high thoughts*, 2 Cor. x. 5, is necessary before conversion. And, for the most part, the Holy Spirit, to further the work of conviction, joineth some affliction, which, sanctified, hath a healing and purging power.

Nay, [2] after conversion we need bruising, that (1) reeds may know themselves to be reeds, and not oaks; even reeds need bruising, by reason of the remainder of pride in our nature, and to let us see that we live by mercy. And (2) that weaker Christians may not be too much discouraged when they see stronger shaken and bruised. Thus Peter was bruised when he wept bitterly, Matt. xxvi. 75. This reed, till he met with this bruise, had more wind in him than pith. 'Though all forsake thee, I will not,' &c., Matt. xxvi. 35. The people of God cannot be without these examples. The heroical deeds of those great worthies do not comfort the church so much as their falls and bruises do. Thus David was bruised, Ps. xxxii. 3–5, until he came to a free confession, without guile of spirit; nay, his sorrows did rise in his own feeling unto the exquisite pain of breaking of bones, Ps. li. 8. Thus Hezekiah complains that God had 'broken his bones' as a lion, Isa. xxxviii. 13. Thus the chosen vessel St Paul needed the messenger of Satan to buffet him, lest he should be lifted up above measure, 2 Cor. xii. 7.

Hence we learn that we must not pass too harsh judgment upon ourselves or others when God doth exercise us with bruising upon bruising; there must be a conformity to our head, Christ, who 'was bruised for us,' Isa. liii. 5, that we may know how much we are bound unto him. Profane spirits, ignorant of God's ways in bringing his children to heaven, censure broken-hearted Christians for desperate persons, whenas God is about a gracious good work with them. It is no easy matter to bring a man from nature to grace, and from grace to glory, so unyielding and untractable are our hearts.

[Chapter III.—*Christ will not Break the Bruised Reed.*]

2. The second point is, that Christ will not '*break the bruised reed.*' Physicians, though they put their patients to much pain, yet they will not destroy nature, but raise it up by degrees. Chirurgeons* will lance and cut, but not dismember. A mother that hath a sick and froward child will not therefore cast it away. And shall there be more mercy in the stream than in the spring? Shall we think there is more mercy in ourselves than in God, who planteth the affection of mercy in us? But for further declaration of Christ's mercy to all bruised reeds, consider the comfortable relations he hath taken upon him of husband, shepherd, brother, &c., which he will discharge to the utmost; for shall others by his grace fulfil what he calleth them unto, and not he that, out of his love, hath taken upon him these relations, so thoroughly founded upon his Father's assignment, and his own voluntary undertaking? Consider his borrowed names from the mildest creatures, as lamb, hen, &c., to shew his tender care; consider his very name Jesus, a Saviour, given him by God himself; consider his office answerable to his name, which is that he should 'heal the broken-hearted,' Isa. lxi. 1. At his baptism the Holy Ghost sate on him in the shape of a dove, to shew that he should be a dove-like, gentle Mediator. See the gracious manner of executing his offices. As a prophet, he came with blessing in his mouth, 'Blessed be the poor in spirit,' &c., Matt. v. 3, and invited those to come to him whose hearts suggested most exceptions against themselves, 'Come unto me, all ye that are weary and heavy laden,' Matt. xi. 28. How did his bowels yearn when 'he saw the people as sheep without a shepherd!' Matt. ix. 36. He never turned any back again that came unto him, though some went away of themselves. He came to die as a priest for his enemies. In the days of his flesh he dictated a form of prayer unto his disciples, and put petitions unto God into their mouths, and his Spirit to intercede in their hearts; and now makes intercession in heaven for weak Christians, standing between God's anger and them; and shed tears for those that shed his blood. So he is a meek King; he will admit mourners into his presence, a king of poor and afflicted persons: as he hath beams of majesty, so he hath bowels of mercies and compassion; 'a prince of peace,' Isa. ix. 6. Why was he 'tempted, but that he might succour those that are tempted,' Heb. ii. 18. What mercy may we not expect from so gracious a mediator, 1 Tim. ii. 5, that took our nature upon him that he might be gracious. He is a physician good at all diseases, especially at the binding up of a broken heart; he died that he might heal our souls with a plaster of his own blood, and by that death save us, which we were the procurers of ourselves, by our own sins; and hath he not the same bowels in heaven? 'Saul, Saul, why persecutest thou me?' Acts ix. 4, cried the head in heaven, when the foot was trodden on, on earth. His advancement hath not made him forget his own flesh; though it has freed him from passion, yet not from compassion towards us. The lion of the tribe of Judah will only tear in pieces those that 'will not have him rule over them,' Luke xix. 17. He will not shew his strength against those that prostrate themselves before him.

* 'Surgeons,' in A and B.

Use 1. What should we learn from hence, but 'to come boldly to the throne of grace,' Heb. iv. 16, in all our grievances? Shall our sins discourage us, when he appears there only for sinners? Art thou bruised? Be of good comfort, he calleth thee; conceal not thy wounds, open all before him, keep not Satan's counsel. Go to Christ though trembling; as the poor woman, if we can but 'touch the hem of his garment,' Matt. ix. 20, we shall be healed and have a gracious answer. Go boldly to God in our flesh; for this end that we might go boldly to him, he is flesh of our flesh, and bone of our bone. Never fear to go to God, since we have such a Mediator with him, that is not only our friend, but our brother and husband. Well might the angels proclaim from heaven, 'Behold, we bring you tidings of joy,' Luke ii. 10. Well might the apostle stir us up to 'rejoice in the Lord again and again,' Phil. iv. 4: he was well advised upon what grounds he did it. Peace and joy are two main fruits of his kingdom. Let the world be as it will, if we cannot rejoice in the world, yet we may rejoice in the Lord. His presence maketh any condition comfortable. 'Be not afraid,' saith he to his disciples, when they were afraid as if they had seen a ghost, 'it is I,' Matt. xiv. 27, as if there were no cause of fear where he is present.

Use 2. Let this stay us when we feel ourselves bruised. Christ his course is first to wound, then to heal. No sound, whole soul shall ever enter into heaven. Think in temptation, Christ was tempted for me; according to my trials will be my graces and comforts. If Christ be so merciful as not to break me, I will not break myself by despair, nor yield myself over to the roaring lion Satan, to break me in pieces.

Use 3. Thirdly, See the contrary disposition of Christ, and Satan and his instruments. Satan setteth upon us when we are weakest, as Simeon and Levi upon the 'Shechemites, when they were sore,' Gen. xxxiv. 25; but Christ will make up in us all the breaches sin and Satan have made; he 'binds up the broken-hearted,' Isa. lxi. 1. And as a mother tendereth most the most diseased and weakest child, so doth Christ most mercifully incline to the weakest, and likewise putteth an instinct into the weakest things to rely upon something stronger than themselves for support. The vine stayeth itself upon the elm, and the weakest creatures have oft the strongest shelters. The consciousness of the church's weakness makes her willing to lean on her beloved, and to hide herself under his wing.

[Chapter IV.—*Signs of one truly bruised.—Means and measure of bruising, and comfort to such.*]

Objection. But how shall we know whether we are such as those that may expect mercy?

Answer 1. By bruising here is not meant those that are brought low only by crosses, but such as by them are brought to see their sin, which bruiseth most of all. When conscience is under the guilt of sin, then every judgment brings a report of God's anger to the soul, and all less* troubles run into this great trouble of conscience for sin. As all corrupt humours run to the diseased and bruised part of the body, and as every creditor falls upon the debtor when he is once arrested, so when conscience is once awaked, all former sins and present crosses join together to make the bruise the more painful. Now, he that is thus bruised will be content with nothing

* 'Lesser,' in A and B.

but with mercy from him that hath bruised him. 'He hath wounded, and he must heal,' Isa. lxi. 1. Lord, thou hast bruised me deservedly for my sins, bind up my heart again,* &c. 2. Again, a man truly bruised judgeth sin the greatest evil, and the favour of God the greatest good. 3. He had rather hear of mercy than of a kingdom. 4. He hath mean conceits of himself, and thinketh he is not worth the earth he treads on. 5. Towards others he is not censorious, as being taken up at home, but is full of sympathy and compassion to those that are under God's hand. 6. He thinketh those that walk in the comforts of God's Spirit the happiest men of the world. 7. 'He trembleth at the word of God,' Isa. lxvi. 2, and honoureth the very feet of those blessed instruments that bring peace unto him, Rom. x. 15. 8. He is more taken up with the inward exercises of a broken heart than with formality, and yet careful to use all sanctified means to convey comfort.

Question. But how shall we come to have this temper?

Answer. First, we must conceive of bruising either as a state into which God bringeth us, or as a duty to be performed by us. Both are here meant. We must join with God in bruising of ourselves. When he humbles us, let us humble ourselves, and not stand out against him, for then he will redouble his strokes; and let us justify Christ in all his chastisements, knowing that all his dealing towards us is to cause us to return into our own hearts. His work in bruising tendeth to our work in bruising ourselves. Let us lament our own untowardness, and say, Lord, what an heart have I that needs all this, that none of this could be spared! We must lay siege to the hardness of our own hearts, and aggravate sin all we can. We must look on Christ, who was bruised for us, look on him whom we have pierced with our sins. But all directions will not prevail, unless God by his Spirit convinceth us deeply, setting our sins before us, and driving us to a stand. Then we will make out for mercy. Conviction will breed contrition, and this humiliation. Therefore desire God that he would bring a clear and a strong light into all the corners of our souls, and accompany it with a spirit of power to lay our hearts low.

A set measure of bruising ourselves cannot be prescribed; yet it must be so far, as 1, we may prize Christ above all, and see that a Saviour must be had; and 2, until we reform that which is amiss, though it be to the cutting off our right hand, or pulling out our right eye. There is a dangerous slighting of the work of humiliation, some alleging this for a pretence for their overly dealing with their own hearts, that Christ will not break the bruised reed; but such must know that every sudden terror and short grief is not that which makes us bruised reeds; not a *little hanging down our heads like a bulrush*, Isa. lviii. 5, but a working our hearts to such a grief as will make sin more odious unto us than punishment, until we offer an holy violence against it; else, favouring ourselves, we make work for God to bruise us, and for sharp repentance afterwards. It is dangerous, I confess, in some cases with some spirits, to press too much and too long this bruising, because they may die under the wound and burden before they be raised up again. Therefore it is good in mixed assemblies to mingle comfort, that every soul may have its due portion. But if we lay this for a ground, that there is more mercy in Christ than sin in us, there can be no danger in thorough dealing. It is better to go bruised to heaven than sound to hell. Therefore let us not take off ourselves too soon, nor pull off the plaster before the cure be wrought, but keep ourselves under

* 'Lord . . . . again,' not in A and B, but in E.

this work till sin be the sourest, and Christ the sweetest, of all things. And when God's hand is upon us in any kind, it is good to divert our sorrow for other things to the root of all, which is sin. Let our grief run most in that channel, that as sin bred grief, so grief may consume sin.

Quest. But are we not bruised unless we grieve more for sin than we do for punishment?

Ans. Sometimes our grief from outward grievances may lie heavier upon the soul than grief for God's displeasure; because in such cases the grief works upon the whole man, both outward and inward, and hath nothing to stay it, but a little spark of faith: which, by reason of the violent impression of the grievance, is suspended in the exercises of it: and this is most felt in sudden distresses which come upon the soul as a torrent or land-flood, and especially in bodily distempers, which by reason of the sympathy between the soul and the body, work upon the soul so far as they hinder not only the spiritual, but often the natural acts. Hereupon St James wisheth in affliction to pray ourselves, but in case of sickness to *send for the elders*, James v. 14; that may, as those in the gospel, offer up the sick person to God in their prayers, being unable to present their own case. Hereupon God admitteth of such a plea from the sharpness and bitterness of the grievance, as in David, Ps. vi., &c. 'The Lord knoweth whereof we are made, he remembereth we are but dust,' Ps. ciii. 14; that our strength is not the strength of steel. It is a branch of his faithfulness unto us as his creatures, whence he is called 'a faithful Creator,' 1 Pet. iv. 19; 'God is faithful, who will not suffer us to be tempted above that we are able,' 1 Cor. x. 13. There were certain commandments which the Jews called the hedges of the law: as to fence men off from cruelty, he commanded they should 'not take the dam with the young, nor seethe the kid in the mother's milk,' Exod. xxiii. 19; 'nor muzzle the mouth of the ox,' 1 Cor. ix. 9. Hath God care of beasts, and not of his more noble creature? And therefore we ought to judge charitably of the complaints of God's people which are wrung from them in such cases. Job had the esteem with God of a patient man, notwithstanding those passionate complaints. Faith overborne for the present will get ground again; and grief for sin, although it come short of grief for misery in violence, yet it goeth beyond it in constancy; as a running stream fed with a spring holdeth out, when a sudden swelling brook faileth.

For the concluding of this point, and our encouragement to a thorough work of bruising, and patience under God's bruising of us, let all know that none are fitter for comfort than those that think themselves furthest off. Men, for the most part, are not lost enough in their own feeling for a Saviour. A holy despair in ourselves is the ground of true hope, Hos. xiv. 3. In God the fatherless find mercy: if men were more fatherless, they should feel more God's fatherly affection from heaven; for God that dwelleth in highest heavens, Isa. lxvi. 2, dwelleth likewise in the lowest soul. Christ's sheep are weak sheep, and wanting in something or other; he therefore applieth himself to the necessities of every sheep. 'He seeks that which was lost, and brings again that which was driven out of the way, and binds up that which was broken, and strengthens the weak,' Ezek. xxxiv. 16; his tenderest care is over the weakest. The lambs he carrieth in his bosom, Isa. xl. 11; 'Peter, feed my lambs,' John xxi. 15. He was most familiar and open to the troubled souls. How careful was he that Peter and the rest of the apostles should not be too much dejected after his resurrection! 'Go, tell the disciples, and tell Peter,' Mark xvi. 7.

Christ knew that guilt of their unkindness in leaving of him had dejected their spirits. How gently did he endure Thomas his unbelief! and stooped so far unto his weakness, as to suffer him to thrust his hand into his side (*a*).

[CHAPTER V.—*Grace is little at first.*]

For the second branch, God will not quench the smoking flax, or wick, but will blow it up till it flameth. In smoking flax there is but a little light, and that weak, as being not able to flame, and this little mixed with smoke.

The observations hence are, first, *That in God's children, especially in their first conversion, there is but a little measure of grace, and that little mixed with much corruption, which, as smoke, is offensive.* Secondly, *That Christ will not quench this smoking flax.*

Obs. 1. For the first, *Grace is little at the first.* There are several ages in Christians, some babes, some young men: grace is as 'a grain of mustard seed,' Matt. xvii. 20. Nothing so little as grace at first, and nothing more glorious afterward: things of greatest perfection are longest in coming to their growth. Man, the perfectest creature, comes to perfection by little and little; worthless things, as mushrooms and the like, like Jonah's gourd, soon spring up, and soon vanish. A new creature is the most excellent frame in all the world, therefore it groweth up by degrees; we see in nature that a mighty oak riseth of an acorn. It is with a Christian as it was with Christ, who sprang out of the dead stock of Jesse, out of David's family, Isa. liii. 2, when it was at the lowest, but he grew up higher than the heavens. It is not with the trees of righteousness as it was with the trees of paradise, which were created all perfect at the first. The seeds of all the creatures in this goodly frame of the world were hid in the chaos, in that confused mass at the first, out of which God did command all creatures to arise; in the small seeds of plants lie hid both bulk and branches, bud and fruit. In a few principles lie hid all comfortable conclusions of holy truth. All these glorious fireworks of zeal and holiness in the saints had their beginning from a few sparks.

Let us not therefore be discouraged at the small beginnings of grace, but look on ourselves, as 'elected to be blameless and without spot,' Eph. i. 4. Let us only look on our imperfect beginning to enforce further strife to perfection, and to keep us in a low conceit. Otherwise, in case of discouragement, we must consider ourselves, as Christ doth, who looks on us as such as he intendeth to fit for himself. Christ valueth us by what we shall be, and by that we are elected unto. We call a little plant a tree, because it is growing up to be so. 'Who is he that despiseth the day of little things?' Zech. iv. 10. Christ would not have us despise little things.

The glorious angels disdain not attendance on little ones; little in their own eyes, and little in the eyes of the world.

Grace, though little in quantity, yet is much in vigour and worth.

It is Christ that raiseth the worth of little and mean places and persons. Bethlehem the least, Micah v. 2, Mat. ii. 6, and yet not the least; the least in itself, not the least in respect Christ was born there. The second temple, Hag. ii. 9, came short of the outward magnificence of the former; yet more glorious than the first, because Christ came into it. The Lord of the temple came into his own temple. The pupil of the eye is very little, yet seeth a great part of the heaven at once. A pearl, though little, yet is of much esteem: nothing in the world of so good use, as the least dram of grace.*

[Chapter VI.—*Grace is mingled with Corruption.*]

Obs. 2. But grace is not only little, but mingled with corruption; whereof it is, that a Christian is said to be smoking flax. Whence we see, that *grace doth not waste corruption all at once, but some is left to conflict withal.* The purest actions of the purest men need Christ to perfume† them, and so is his office. When we pray, we need to pray again for Christ to pardon the defects of them. See some instances of this smoking flax. Moses at the Red Sea, being in a great perplexity, and knowing not what to say, or which way to turn him, groaned to God: no doubt this was a great conflict in him. In great distresses we know not what to pray, but the Spirit makes request with sighs that cannot be expressed, Rom. viii. 26. Broken hearts can yield but broken prayers.

When David was before the king of Gath, 1 Sam. xxi. 13, and disfigured himself in an uncomely manner, in that smoke there was some fire also; you may see what an excellent psalm he makes upon that occasion, Ps. xxxiv.; wherein, upon experience, ver. 18, he saith, 'The Lord is near unto them that are of a contrite spirit.' Ps. xxxi. 22, 'I said in my haste, I am cast out of thy sight; there is smoke: yet thou heardest the voice of my prayer; there is fire.' 'Master, carest thou not that we perish?' Mat. viii. 25, cry the disciples; here is smoke of infidelity, yet so much light of faith as stirred them up to pray to Christ. 'Lord, I believe:' there is light; 'but help my unbelief,' Mark ix. 24: there is smoke.

Jonah cries, ii. 4, 'I am cast out of thy sight:' there is smoke; 'yet will I look again to thy holy temple:' there is light.

'O miserable man that I am,' Rom. vii. 24, saith St Paul upon sense of his corruption; but yet breaks out into thanks to God through Jesus Christ our Lord.

'I sleep,' saith the Church in the Canticles, 'but my heart wakes,' Cant. v. 2. In the seven Churches, which for their light are called 'seven golden candlesticks,' Rev. ii. iii., most of them had much smoke with their light.

The ground of this mixture is, that we carry about us a double principle, grace and nature. The end of it is especially to preserve us from those two dangerous rocks which our natures are prone to dash upon, security and pride; and to force us to pitch our rest on justification, not sanctification, which, besides imperfection, hath some soil.

Our spiritual fire is like our ordinary fire here below, that is, mixed; but fire is most pure in its own element above; so shall all our graces be when we are where we would be, in heaven, which is our proper element.

Use. From this mixture it is, that the people of God have so different judgments of themselves, looking sometimes at the work of grace, sometimes at the remainder of corruption, and when they look upon that, then they think they have no grace; though they love Christ in his ordinances and children, yet dare not challenge so near acquaintance as to be his. Even as a candle in the socket sometimes sheweth its light, and sometimes the show of light is lost; so sometimes well persuaded they are of themselves, sometimes at a loss.

* 'As the least dram of grace *is*,' in A and B.

† 'Perform,' in A and B.

[CHAPTER VII.—*Christ will not quench small and weak beginnings.*]

Doct. Now for the second observation, *Christ will not quench the smoking flax.* First, because this spark is from heaven, it is his own, it* is kindled by his own spirit. And secondly, it tendeth to the glory of his powerful grace in his children, that he preserveth light in the midst of darkness,—a spark in the midst of the swelling waters of corruption.

There is an especial blessing in that little spark; 'when wine is found in a cluster, one saith, Destroy it not; for there is a blessing in it,' Isa. lxv. 8. We see how our Saviour Christ bore with Thomas in his doubting, John xx. 27; with the two disciples that went to Emmaus, who staggered 'whether he came to redeem Israel or no,' Luke xxiv. 21: he quenched not that little light in Peter, which was smothered: Peter denied him, but he denied not Peter, Mat. xxvi. 'If thou wilt, thou canst,' said one poor man in the gospel, Mat. viii. 2; 'Lord, if thou canst' said another, Mark ix. 22; both were this smoking flax, neither of both were quenched. If Christ had stood upon his own greatness, he would have rejected him that came with his *if*, but Christ answers his *if* with a gracious and absolute grant, 'I will, be thou clean.' The woman that was diseased with an issue did but touch, and with a trembling hand, and but the hem of his garment, and yet went away both healed and comforted. In the seven churches, Rev. ii. and iii., we see he acknowledgeth and cherisheth anything that was good in them. Because the disciples slept of infirmity, being oppressed with grief, our Saviour Christ frameth a comfortable excuse for them, 'The spirit is willing, but the flesh is weak,' Mat. xxvi. 41.

If Christ should not be merciful, he would miss of his own ends; 'there is mercy with thee that thou mayest be feared,' Ps. cxxx. 4. Now all are willing to come under that banner of love which he spreadeth over his: 'therefore to thee shall all flesh come,' Ps. lxv. 2. He useth moderation and care, 'lest the spirit should fail before him, and the souls which he hath made,' Isa. lvii. 16. Christ's heart yearned, the text saith, 'when he saw them without meat, lest they should faint,' Mat. xv. 32; much more will he have regard for the preventing of our spiritual faintings.

Here see the opposite disposition between the holy nature of Christ, and the impure nature of man. Man for a little smoke will quench the light; Christ ever we see cherisheth even the least beginnings. How bare he with the many imperfections of his poor disciples. If he did sharply check them, it was in love, and that they might shine the brighter. Can we have a better pattern to follow than this of him by whom we hope to be saved? 'We that are strong ought to bear with the infirmities of them that are weak,' Rom. xv. 1. 'I become all things to all men, that I may win some,' 1 Cor. ix. 22. O that this gaining and winning disposition were more in many! Many, so far as in us lieth, are lost for want of encouragement. See how that faithful fisher of men, St Paul, labours to catch his judge, 'I know thou believest the prophets,' Acts xxvi. 27; and then wisheth all saving good, but not bonds; he might have added them too, but he would not discourage one that made but an offer, he would therefore wish Agrippa only that which was good in religion. How careful was our blessed Saviour of little ones that they might not be offended, Mat. xii. xiii. How doth he defend his disciples from malicious imputations of the Pharisees! How careful not to put new wine into old vessels, Mat. ix. 17, not to alienate new beginners

* 'That,' in A.

with the austerities of religion (as some indiscreetly). O, saith he, they shall have time to fast when I am gone, and strength to fast when the Holy Ghost is come upon them.

It is not the best way to fall foul presently with young beginners for some lesser vanities, but shew them a more excellent way, and breed them up in positive grounds, and other things will be quickly out of credit with them. It is not amiss to conceal their wants, to excuse some failings, to commend their performances, to cherish their towardness, to remove all rubs out of their way, to help them every way to bear the yoke of religion with greater ease, to bring them in love with God and his service, lest they distaste it before they know it. For the most part we see Christ planteth in young beginners a love which we call 'the first love,' Rev. ii. 4, to carry them through their profession with more delight, and doth not expose them to crosses before they have gathered strength; as we breed up young plants, and fence them from the weather, until they be rooted.* Mercy to others should move us to deny ourselves in our lawful liberties oftentimes, in case of offence of weak ones; it is the 'little ones that are offended,' Matt. xviii. 6. The weakest are aptest to think themselves despised, therefore we should be most careful to give them content.

It were a good strife amongst Christians, one to labour to give no offence, and the other to labour to take none. The best men are severe to themselves, tender over others.

Yet people should not tire and wear out the patience of others: nor should the weaker so far exact moderation from others, as to bear out themselves upon their indulgence, and so to rest in their own infirmities, with danger to their own souls, and scandal to the church.

Neither† hereupon must they set light by the gifts of God in others, which grace teacheth to honour wheresoever they are found, but know their parts and place, and not enterprise anything above their measure, which may make their persons and their case obnoxious to scorn. When blindness and boldness, ignorance and arrogance, weakness and wilfulness, meet together in one, it renders men odious to God, it maketh men burdensome in society, dangerous in their counsels, troublers of better designs, untractable and uncapable of better direction, miserable in the issue: where Christ sheweth his gracious power in weakness, he doth it by letting men understand themselves so far as to breed humility, and magnifying of God's love to such as they are: he doth it as a preservative against discouragements from weakness, seeing it bringeth men into a less distance from grace, as being an advantage to poverty of spirit, than greatness of condition and parts, which yield to corrupt nature fuel for pride. Christ refuseth none for weakness of parts, that none should be discouraged; accepteth of none for greatness, that none should be lifted up with that which is of so little reckoning with God. It is no great matter how dull the scholar be, when Christ taketh upon him to be the teacher: who as he prescribeth what to understand, so he giveth understanding itself even to the simplest.

The church suffereth much from weak ones, therefore we may challenge liberty to deal with them, as mildly, so oftentimes directly. The scope of true love is to make the party better, which by concealment oftentimes is hindered; with some a spirit of meekness prevaileth most, but with some a rod. Some must be 'pulled out of the fire,' Jude 23, with violence, and they will bless God for us in the day of their visitation. We see our Saviour multiplies woe upon woe when he was to deal with hard-hearted

* 'Well-rooted,' in A. † 'Neither . . . simplest.' This paragraph first added in B

hypocrites ,Mat. xxiii. 13, for hypocrites need* stronger conviction than gross sinners, because their will is nought, and thereupon usually their conversion is violent. An hard knot must have an answerable wedge, else in a cruel pity we betray their souls. A sharp reproof sometimes is a precious pearl, and a sweet balm. The wounds of secure sinners will not be healed with sweet words. The Holy Ghost came as well in fiery tongues, as in the likeness of a dove, and the same Holy Spirit will vouchsafe a spirit of prudence and discretion, which is the salt to season all our words and actions. And such wisdom will teach us 'to speak a word in season,' Isa. l. 4, both to the weary, and likewise to the secure soul. And, indeed, he had need have 'the tongue of the learned,' Isa. l. 4, that shall either raise up or cast down; but in this place I speak of mildness towards those that are weak and are sensible of it. These we must bring on gently, and drive softly, as Jacob did his cattle, Gen. xxxiii. 14, according to their pace, and as his children were able to endure.

Weak Christians are like glasses which are hurt with the least violent usage, otherwise if gently handled will continue a long time. This honour of gentle use we are to give to 'the weaker vessels,' 1 Pet. iii. 7, by which we shall both preserve them, and likewise make them useful to the church and ourselves.

In unclean bodies if all ill humours be purged out, you shall purge life and all away. Therefore though God saith, that 'he will fine them as silver is fined,' Zech. xiii. 9; yet, Isa. xlviii. 10, he said, 'he hath fined them, but not as silver,' that is, so exactly as that no dross remaineth, for he hath respect to our weakness. Perfect refining is for another world, for the world of the souls of perfect men.

[Chapter VIII.—*Tenderness required in ministers toward young beginners.*]

1. Divines had need to take heed therefore how they deal with these in divers particulars: as first let them be careful they strain not things too high (*b*), making those general and necessary evidences of grace, which agree not to the experience of many a good Christian, and lay salvation and damnation upon those things that are not fit to bear so great a weight, whereupon men are groundlessly cast down lower by them, than they can hastily be raised up again by themselves or others. The ambassadors of so gentle a Saviour should not be over-masterly, setting up themselves in the hearts of people where Christ alone should sit as in his own temple. Too much† respect to man was one of the inlets of popery. 'Let a man account of us as of the ministers of Christ,' 1 Cor. iv. 1, neither more nor less, just so much. How careful was St Paul in cases of conscience not to lay a snare upon any weak conscience.

They should take heed likewise that they hide not their meaning in dark speeches, speaking in the clouds. Truth feareth nothing so much as concealment, and desireth nothing so much as clearly to be laid open to the view of all: when it is most naked, it is most lovely and powerful.

Our blessed Saviour, as he took our nature upon him, so he took upon him our familiar manner of speech, which was part of his voluntary abasement. St Paul was a profound man, yet became as a nurse to the weaker sort, 1 Thess. ii. 7.

That spirit of mercy that was in Christ should move his servants to be

* 'Do need,' in A and B. † 'Too much .... just so much,' added first in B

content to abase themselves for the good of the meanest. What made the 'kingdom of heaven suffer violence,' Matt. xi. 22, after John the Baptist's time, but that comfortable truths were with that plainness and evidence laid open, that the people were so affected with them, as they offered a holy violence to them?

Christ chose those to preach mercy, which had felt most mercy, as St Peter and St Paul; that they might be examples of what they taught. St Paul 'became all things to all men,' 1 Cor. ix. 2, stooping unto them for their good. Christ came down from heaven, and emptied himself of majesty in tender love to souls; shall we not come down from our high conceits to do any poor soul good? shall man be proud after God hath been humble? We see the ministers of Satan turn themselves into all shapes to 'make proselytes,' Matt. xxiii. 15. A Jesuit will be every man. We see ambitious men study accommodation of themselves to the humours of those by whom they hope to be raised;* and shall not we study application of ourselves to Christ, by whom we hope to be advanced, nay, are already sitting with him in heavenly places? After we are gained to Christ ourselves, we should labour to gain others to Christ. Holy ambition and covetousness will move us to put upon ourselves the disposition of Christ: but we must put off ourselves first.

We should not, thirdly, rack their wits with curious or 'doubtful disputes,' Rom. xiv 1; for so we shall distract and tire them, and give occasion to make them cast off the care of all. That age of the church which was most fertile in nice questions, was most barren in religion: for it makes people think religion to be only a matter of wit, in tying and untying of knots; the brains of men given that way are hotter usually than their hearts.

Yet notwithstanding, when we are cast into times and places wherein doubts are raised about main points, here people ought to labour to be established. God suffereth questions oftentimes to arise for trial of our love and exercise of our parts. Nothing is so certain as that which is certain after doubts. *Nil tam certum quâm quod ex dubio certum.* Shaking settles and roots. In a contentious age, it is a witty thing to be a Christian, and to know what to pitch their souls upon; it is an office of love here to take away the stones, and to smooth the way to heaven. Therefore, we must take heed that, under pretence of avoidance of disputes, we do not suffer an adverse party to get ground upon the truth; for thus may we easily betray both the truth of God and souls of men.

And likewise those are failing that, by overmuch austerity, drive back troubled souls from having comfort by them; for by this carriage many smother their temptations, and burn inwardly, because they have none into whose bosom they may vent their grief and ease their souls.

We must neither bind where God looseth, nor loose where God bindeth, nor open where God shutteth, nor shut where God openeth; the right use of the keys is always successful. In personal application there must be great heed taken; for a man may be a false prophet, and yet speak the truth. If it be not a truth to the person to whom he speaketh; if he 'grieve those whom God hath not grieved,' Lam. iii. 33, by unseasonable truths, or by comforts in an ill way, the hearts of the wicked may be strengthened. One man's meat may be another's bane.

If we look to the general temper of these times, rousing and waking Scriptures are fittest; yet there be many broken spirits need soft and oily words. Even in the worst time the prophets mingled sweet comfort for

* 'To raise themselves,' in A and B.

the hidden remnant of faithful people. God hath comfort; 'Comfort ye my people,' Isa. xl. 1, as well as 'lift up thy voice as a trumpet,' Isa. lviii. 1.

And here likewise there needs a caveat. Mercy doth not rob us of our right judgment, as that we should take stinking* fire-brands for smoking flax. None will claim mercy more of others, than those whose portion is due severity. This example doth not countenance lukewarmness, nor too much indulgence to those that need quickening. Cold diseases must have hot remedies. It made for the just commendations of the church of Ephesus, 'that it could not bear with them which are evil,' Rev. ii. 2. We should so bear with others, as we discover withal a dislike of evil. Our Saviour Christ would not forbear sharp reproof, where he saw dangerous infirmities in his most beloved disciples. It bringeth under a curse 'to do the work of the Lord negligently,' Jer. xlviii. 10; even where it is a work of just severity, as when it is sheathing the sword in the bowels of the enemy. And those whom we suffer to be betrayed by their worst enemies, their sins, will have just cause to curse us another day.

It is hard to preserve just bounds of mercy and severity, without a spirit above our own; which we ought to desire to be led withal in all things. That 'wisdom which dwelleth with prudence,' Prov. viii. 12, will guide us in these particulars, without which virtue is not virtue, truth not truth. The rule and the case must be laid together; for if there be not a narrow insight, seeming likeness in conditions will be the breeder of errors in our opinions of them. Those fiery, tempestuous, and destructive spirits in popery, that seek to promote their religion by cruelty, shew that they are strangers to that wisdom which is from above, which maketh men gentle, peaceable, and ready to shew that mercy they have felt before themselves. It is a way of prevailing, as agreeable to Christ, so likewise to man's nature, to prevail by some forbearance and moderation.

And yet oft we see a false spirit in those that call for moderation. It is but to carry their own projects with the greater strength; and if they prove of the prevailing hand, they will hardly shew that moderation to others they now call for from others. And there is a proud kind of moderation likewise, when men will take upon them to censure both† parties, as if they were wiser than both, although,‡ if the spirit be right, a looker on may see more than those that are in conflict.

[CHAPTER IX.—*Governors should be tender of weak ones, and also private Christians.*]

2. So in the censures of the church, it is more suitable to the spirit of Christ to incline to the milder part, and not to kill a fly on the forehead with a beetle (*c*), nor shut men out of heaven for a trifle. The very snuffers of the tabernacle were made of pure gold, to shew the purity of those censures, whereby the light of the church is kept bright. That power that is given to the church is given for edification, not destruction. How careful was St Paul, that the incestuous Corinthian, 2 Cor. ii. 7, repenting, should not be swallowed up with too much grief.

As for civil magistrates, they, for civil exigences and reasons of state, must let the law have its course; yet thus far they should imitate this mild king, as not to mingle bitterness and passion with authority derived from God. Authority is a beam of God's majesty, and prevaileth most where

* 'Smoking,' in A and B. † 'Either party,' in A. ‡ 'Though,' in A and B.

there is least mixture of that which is man's. It requireth more than ordinary wisdom to manage it aright. This string must not be too much strained up, nor too much let loose. Justice is an harmonical thing. Herbs hot or cold beyond a certain degree, kill. We see even contrary elements preserved in one body by a wise contemperation. Justice in rigour is oft extreme injustice, where some considerable circumstances should incline to moderation; and the reckoning will be easier for bending rather to moderation than rigour.

Insolent carriage toward miserable persons, if humbled, is unseemly in any who look for mercy themselves. Misery should be a loadstone of mercy, not a footstool for pride to trample on.

Sometimes it falleth out that those that are under the government of others, are most injurious by waywardness and harsh censures, herein disparaging and discouraging the endeavours of superiors for public good. In so great weakness of man's nature, and especially in this crazy age of the world, we ought to take in good part any moderate happiness we enjoy by government; and not be altogether as a nail in the wound, exasperating things by misconstruction. Here love should have a mantle to cast upon lesser errors of those above us. Oftentimes the poor man is the oppressor by unjust clamours. We should labour to give the best interpretation to the actions of governors that the nature of the actions will possibly bear.

In the last place, there is something for private Christians, even for all of us in our common relations, to take notice of: we are debtors to the weak in many things.

1. Let us be watchful in the use of our liberty, and labour to be inoffensive in our carriage, that our example compel them not. There is a commanding force in an example, as Peter, Gal. ii. Looseness* of life is cruelty to ourselves, and to the souls of others. Though we cannot keep them from perishing which will perish, in regard of the event; yet if we do that which is apt of itself to destroy the souls of others, their ruin is imputable to us.

2. Let men take heed of taking up Satan's office, in depraving the good actions of others, as he did Job's, 'doth he serve God for nought?' Job i. 9, or slandering their persons, judging of them according to the wickedness that is in their own hearts. The devil getteth more by such discouragements, and these reproaches that are cast upon religion, than by fire and fagot. These, as unseasonable frosts, nip all gracious offers in the bud; and as much as in them lieth, with Herod, labour to kill Christ in young professors. A Christian is a hallowed and a sacred thing, Christ's temple; 'and he that destroyeth his temple, him will Christ destroy,' 1 Cor. iii. 17.

3. Amongst the things that are to be taken heed of, there is amongst private Christians a bold usurpation of censure towards others, not considering their temptations. Some will unchurch and unbrother in a passion. But distempers do not alter true relations; though the child in a fit should disclaim the mother, yet the mother will not disclaim the child.

There is therefore in these judging times good ground of St James's caveat, that there should not 'be too many masters,' James iii. 1; that we should not smite one another by hasty censures, especially in things of an indifferent nature; some things are as the mind of him is that doth them, or doth them not; for both may be unto the Lord.

A holy aim in things of a middle nature makes the judgments of men,

* 'A looseness,' in A.

although seemingly contrary, yet not so much blameable. Christ, for the good aims he seeth in us, overlooketh any ill in them, so far as not to lay it to our charge.

Men must not be too curious in prying into the weaknesses of others. We should labour rather to see what they have that is for eternity, to incline our heart to love them, than into that weakness which the Spirit of God will in time consume, to estrange us. Some think it strength of grace to endure nothing in the weaker, whereas the strongest are readiest to bear with the infirmities of the weak.

Where most holiness is, there is most moderation, where it may be without prejudice of piety to God and the good of others. We see in Christ a marvellous temper of absolute holiness, with great moderation, in this text. What had become of our salvation, if he had stood upon terms, and not stooped thus low unto us? We need not affect to be more holy than Christ; it is no flattery to do as he doth, so it be to edification.

The Holy Ghost is content to dwell in smoky, offensive souls. O that that Spirit would breathe into our spirits the like merciful disposition! We endure the bitterness of wormwood, and other distasteful plants and herbs, only because we have some experience of some wholesome quality in them; and why should we reject men of useful parts and graces, only for some harshness of disposition, which, as it is offensive to us, so grieveth themselves?

Grace whilst we live here is in souls, which as they are unperfectly renewed, so they dwell in bodies subject to several humours, which will incline the soul sometimes to excess in one passion, sometimes to excess in another.

Bucer was a deep and a moderate divine; upon long experience he resolved to refuse none in whom he saw, *aliquid Christi*, something of Christ.

The best Christians in this state of imperfection are like gold that is a little too light, which needs some grains of allowance to make it pass. You must grant the best their allowance. We must supply out of our love and mercy, that which we see wanting in them.

The church of Christ is a common hospital, wherein all are in some measure sick of some spiritual disease or other; that we should all have ground of exercising mutually the spirit of wisdom and meekness.

1. This that we may the better do, let us put upon ourselves the spirit of Christ. The spirit of God carrieth a majesty with it. Corruption will hardly yield to corruption in another. Pride is intolerable to pride. The weapons of this warfare must not be carnal, 2 Cor. x. 4. The great apostles would not set upon the work of the ministry, until they were 'clothed as it were with power from on high,' Luke xxiv. 49. The Spirit will only work with his own tools. And we should think what affection Christ would carry to the party in this case. That great physician, as he had a quick eye and a healing tongue, so had he a gentle hand, and a tender heart.*

2. And secondly, put upon us the condition of him whom we deal withal: we are, or have been, or may be such: make the case our own, and withal consider in what near relation a Christian standeth unto us, even as a brother, a fellow-member, heir of the same salvation. And therefore let us take upon ourselves a tender care of them every way; and especially in cherishing the peace of their consciences. Conscience is a tender and

* Nil sic spiritualem virum indicat quam alieni peccati tractatio.—*Aug*[*ustine*] in Gal. vi.

delicate thing, and so must be used, It is like a lock, if the wards be troubled, it will be troublesome to open.*

[Chapter X.—*Rules to try whether we be such as Christ will not quench.*]

For trial, to let us see whether we be this smoking flax which Christ will not quench. In this trial remember these:—1. *Rules.* 2. *Signs.*

1. We must have two eyes, one to see imperfections in ourselves and others; the other to see what is good. 'I am black,' saith the church, 'but yet comely,' Cant. i. 5. Those ever want comfort that are much in quarrelling with themselves, and through their infirmities are prone to feed upon such bitter things, as will most nourish that distemper they are sick of. These delight to be looking on the dark side of the cloud only.

2. We must not judge of ourselves always according to present feeling; for in temptations we shall see nothing but smoke of distrustful thoughts. Fire may be raked up in the ashes, though not seen; life in the winter is hid in the root.

3. Take heed of false reasoning; as because our fire doth not blaze out as others, therefore we have no fire at all; and by false conclusions come to sin against the commandment in bearing false witness against ourselves. The prodigal would not say he was no son, but that he was not worthy to be called a son, Luke xv. 19. We must neither trust to false evidence, nor deny true; for so we should dishonour the work of God's Spirit in us, and lose the help of that evidence which would cherish our love to Christ, and arm us against Satan's discouragements. Some are so faulty this way, as if they had been hired by Satan, the 'accuser of the brethren,' Rev. xii. 10, to plead for him, in accusing themselves.

4. Know, for a ground of this, that in the covenant of grace, God requires the truth of grace, not any certain measure; and a spark of fire is fire as well as the whole element. Therefore we must look to grace in the spark as well as in the flame. All have not the like strong, yet the like precious faith, 2 Pet. i. 1, whereby they lay hold, and put on, the perfect righteousness of Christ. A weak hand may receive a rich jewel; a few grapes will shew that the plant is a vine, and not a thorn. It is one thing to be wanting in grace, and another thing to want grace altogether. God knoweth we have nothing of ourselves, therefore in the covenant of grace he requireth no more than he giveth, and giveth what he requireth, and accepteth what he giveth: 'He that hath not a lamb may bring a pair of turtle doves,' Lev. xii. 6. What is the gospel itself but a merciful moderation, in which Christ's obedience is esteemed ours, and our sins laid upon him, and wherein God of a judge becometh the father, pardoning our sins and accepting our obedience, though feeble and blemished! We are now brought to heaven under the covenant of grace by a way of love and mercy.

It will prove a special help to know distinctly the difference between the covenant of works and the covenant of grace, between Moses and Christ; Moses without all mercy breaketh all bruised reeds, and quencheth all smoking flax. For the law requireth, 1, personal; 2, perpetual; 3, perfect obedience; 4, and from a perfect heart; and that under a most terrible curse, and giveth no strength, a severe task-master, like Pharaoh's requiring the whole tale, and yet giving no straw. Christ cometh with blessing

* Nil magis ad misericordiam inclinat quam proprii periculi cogitatio.—*August*[*ine*].

after blessing even upon those whom Moses had cursed, and with healing balm for those wounds which Moses had made.

The same duties are required in both covenants; as, 'to love the Lord with all our hearts, with all our souls,' &c., Deut. vi. 5. In the* covenant of works, this must be taken in the rigour; but under the covenant of grace, as it is a sincere endeavour proportionable to grace received (and so it must be understood of Josias, and others, when it is said, 'they loved God with all their hearts,' &c.), it must have an evangelical mitigation.

The law is sweetened by the gospel, and becometh delightful to the inner man, Rom. vii. 22. Under this gracious covenant sincerity is perfection. This is the death in the pot in the Roman religion,† that they confound two covenants; and it deads the comfort of drooping ones, that they cannot distinguish them. And thus they suffer themselves to be held under bondage,' Isa. lxi. 1, 2, when Christ hath set them free; and stay themselves in the prison, when Christ hath set open the doors before them.

5. Grace sometimes is so little as is undiscernible to us; the Spirit sometimes hath secret operations in us, which we know not for the present; but Christ knoweth. Sometimes in bitterness of temptation, when the Spirit struggles with sense of God's anger, we are apt to think God an enemy; and a troubled soul is like troubled water,‡ we can see nothing in it; and so far as it is not cleansed, it will cast up mire and dirt. It is full of objections against itself, yet for the most part we may discern something of the hidden life, and of these smothered sparks.

In a gloomy day there is so much light whereby we may know it to be day, and not night; so there is something in a Christian under a cloud, whereby he may be discerned to be a true believer, and not a hypocrite. There is no mere darkness in the state of grace, but some beam of light, whereby the kingdom of darkness wholly prevaileth not.

[CHAPTER XI.—*Signs of smoking flax which Christ will not quench.*]

These things premised, let us know for a trial, 1. First, *if there be any holy fire in us, it is kindled from heaven* by the 'Father of lights, who commandeth light to shine out of darkness,' 2 Cor. iv. 6. As it is kindled in the use of means, so it is fed. The light in us, and the light in the word, spring one from the other, and both from one Holy Spirit; and, therefore, those that regard not the word, it is because there 'is no light in them,' Isa. viii. 20. Heavenly truths must have a heavenly light to discern them. Natural men see heavenly things, but not in their own proper light, but by an inferior light. God in every converted man putteth a light into the eye of his soul, proportionable to the light of truths revealed unto him. A carnal eye will never see spiritual things.

2. Secondly, *the least divine light hath heat with it in some measure;* light in the understanding breedeth heat of love in the affections. *Claritas in intellectu parit ardorem in affectu.* In what measure the sanctified understanding seeth a thing to be true, or good, in that measure the will embraces it. Weak light breeds weak inclinations; a strong light, strong inclinations. A little spiritual light is of strength enough to answer strong objections of flesh and blood, and to look through all earthly allurements and opposing§ hindrances, presenting them as far inferior to those heavenly objects it eyeth.

* 'This,' in A and B.

† Roman religion = Popery.—G.

‡ 'Waters,' in A and B.

§ 'And all,' in A and B.

All light that is not spiritual, because it wanteth the strength of sanctifying grace, yieldeth* to every little temptation, especially when it is fitted and suited to personal inclinations. This is the reason why Christians that have light little for quantity, but yet heavenly for quality, hold out, when men of larger apprehensions sink.

This prevailing of light in the soul is because, together with the spirit of illumination, there goeth, in the godly, a spirit of power, 2 Tim. i. 7, to subdue the heart to truth revealed, and to put a taste and relish into the will, suitable to the sweetness of the truths; else a mere natural will will rise against supernatural truths, as having an antipathy and enmity against them. In the godly, holy truths are conveyed by way of a taste; gracious men have a spiritual palate as well as a spiritual eye. Grace altereth the relish.

3. Thirdly, where this heavenly light is kindled, *it directeth in the right way*. For it is given for that use, to shew us the best way, and to guide in the particular passages of life; if otherwise, it is but common light, given only for the good of others. Some have light of knowledge, yet follow not that light, but are guided by carnal reason and policy; such as the prophet speaks of, 'All you that kindle a fire, walk in the light of your own fire, and in the sparks that you have kindled; but this you shall have of mine hand, ye shall lie down in sorrow,' Isa. l. 11. God delights to confound carnal wisdom, as enmity to him, and robbing him of his prerogative, who is God only wise. We must, therefore, walk by his light, and not the blaze of our own fire. God must light our candle, Ps. xviii. 28, or else we are like to abide in darkness. Those sparks that are not kindled from heaven, are not strong enough to keep us from lying down in sorrow, though they make a greater blaze and show than the light from above, as madmen do greater things than sober, but by a false strength: so the excess of these men's joy ariseth from a false light, 'the candle of the wicked shall be put out,' Job xviii. 6.

The light that some men have, it is like lightning, which after a sudden flash leaveth them more in darkness. They can love the light as it shines, but hate it as it discovers and directs. A little holy light will enable to keep the word, and not betray religion, and deny Christ's name, as Christ speaketh of the church of Philadelphia, Rev. iii. 8.

4. Fourthly, where this fire is, *it will sever things of diverse natures, and shew a difference between things, as gold and dross.* It will sever between flesh and spirit, and shew that this is of nature, this of grace. All is not ill in a bad action, or good in a good action. There is gold in ore, which God and his Spirit in us can distinguish. A carnal man's heart is like a dungeon, wherein is nothing to be seen but horror and confusion; this light maketh us judicious and humble, upon clearer sight of God's purity, and our own uncleanness; and maketh us able to discern of the work of the Spirit in another.

5. Fifthly, so far as a man is spiritual, *so far is light delightful unto him*, as willing to see anything amiss, that he may reform, and any further service discovered that he may perform, because he truly hateth ill and loveth good; if he goeth against light discovered, he will soon be reclaimed, because light hath a friendly party within him. Whereupon, at a little sight of his error he is soon counselable, as David in his intendment to kill Nabal, and blessed God afterwards, when he is stopped in an ill way, 1 Sam. xxv. 32.

* 'It yieldeth,' in A and B.

In a carnal man, the light breaks in upon him, but he labours to shut the passages, he hath no delight to come to the light. It is impossible before the Spirit of grace hath subdued the heart, but that it should sin against the light, either by resisting of it, or keeping it prisoner under base lusts, and burying it, as it were, in the earth; or perverting of it, and so making it an agent and factor for the flesh, in searching out arguments to plead for it, or abusing that little measure of light they have, to keep out a greater, higher, and more heavenly light; and so, at length, make that light they have a misleading guide to utter darkness. And the reason is, because it hath no friend within, the soul is in a contrary frame; and light always hindereth that sinful peace that men are willing to speak to themselves: whence we see it oft enrages men the more, as the sun in the spring breedeth aguish distempers, because it stirreth humours, and doth not waste them. There is nothing in the world more unquiet than the heart of a wicked man, that sitteth under means of knowledge, until, like a thief, he hath put out the candle, that he may sin with the less check. Spiritual light is distinct, it seeth spiritual good, with application to ourselves; but common light is confused, and lets sin lie quiet. Where fire is in any degree, it will fight against the contrary matter. God hath put irreconcilable hatred between light and darkness at first, so between good and ill, flesh and spirit, Gal. v. 17; grace will never join with sin, no more than fire with water. Fire will mingle with no contrary, but preserveth its own purity, and is never corrupted as other elements are. Therefore, those that plead and plot for liberties of the flesh, shew themselves strangers from the life of God. Upon this strife, gracious men oft complain that they have no grace, but they contradict themselves in their complaints; as if a man that seeth should complain he cannot see, or complain that he is asleep, when the very complaint, springing from a displeasure against sin, sheweth that there is something in him opposite to sin. Can a dead man complain? Some things, though bad in themselves, yet discover good; as smoke discovers some fire. Breaking out in the body shews strength of nature. Some infirmities discover more good than some seeming beautiful actions. Excess of passion in opposing evil, though not to be justified, yet sheweth a better spirit than a calm temper, where there is just cause of being moved. Better it is that the water should run something muddily, than not at all. Job had more grace in his distempers, than his friends in their seeming wise carriage. Actions soiled with some weaknesses, are more accepted than complemental performances.

6. Sixthly, fire, where it is in the least measure, *is in some degree active*; so the least measure of grace is *working*, as springing from the Spirit of God, which, from the working nature of it, is compared to fire. Nay, in sins, when there seemeth nothing active, but corruption, yet there is a contrary principle, which breaks the force of sin, so that it is not out of measure sinful, as in those that are carnal, Rom. vii. 13.

7. Seventhly, fire maketh metals *pliable and malleable, so doth grace, where it is begun;* it worketh the heart to be pliable and ready for all good impressions. Untractable spirits shew that they are not so much as smoking flax.

8. Eighthly, fire turneth all, as much as it can, to fire; so grace *laboureth to breed the like impression in others, and make as many good as it can.* Grace likewise maketh a gracious use even of natural and civil things, and doth spiritualise them. What another man doth only civilly, a gracious man will do holily. Whether he eateth or drinketh, or whatsoever

he doth, he doth all to the glory of God, 1 Cor. x. 31, making everything serviceable to the last end.

9. Ninthly, *sparks by nature fly upwards; so the Spirit of grace carrieth the soul heaven-ward, and setteth before us holy and heavenly aims.* As it was kindled from heaven, so it carries us back to heaven. The part followeth the whole: fire mounteth upward, so every spark to its own element. Where the aim and bent of the soul is God-wards, there is grace, though opposed. The least measure of it is holy desires springing from faith and love, for we cannot desire anything which we do not believe first to be, and the desire of it issues from love. Hence desires are counted a part of the thing desired, in some measure; but then they must be, *first, constant*, for constancy shews that they are supernaturally natural, and not enforced; *secondly*, they must be *carried to spiritual things*, as to believe, to love God, &c.: not out of a special exigent, because, if now they had grace, they think they might escape some danger, but as a loving heart is carried to the thing loved for some excellency in itself; and *thirdly*, with desire there is grief when it is hindered, which stirs up to prayer: 'Oh that my ways were so directed, that I might keep thy statutes!' Ps. cxix. 5; O miserable man that I am, who shall deliver? &c., Rom. vii. 24; *fourthly*, desires put us onward still: O that I might serve God with more liberty; O that I were more free from these offensive, unsavoury, noisome lusts!

10. Tenthly, fire worketh itself, if it hath any matter to feed on, *into a larger compass, and mounteth higher and higher, and the higher it riseth, the purer is the flame;* so where true grace is, it groweth in measure and purity. Smoking flax will grow to a flame; and as it increaseth, so it worketh out the contrary, and refineth itself more and more. *Ignis, quo magis lucet, eo minus fumat.* Therefore, it argueth a false heart to set ourselves a measure in grace, and to rest in beginnings, alleging that Christ will not quench the smoking flax. But this merciful disposition in Christ is joined with perfect holiness, shewed in perfect hatred to sin; for rather than sin should not have its deserved punishment, himself became a sacrifice for sin, wherein his Father's holiness and his own most of all shined. And besides this, in the work of sanctification, though he favours his work in us, yet favours he not sin in us; for he will never take his hand from his work, until he hath taken away sin, even in its very being, from our natures. The same Spirit that purified that blessed mass whereof he was made, cleanseth us by degrees to be suitable to so holy a head, and frameth the judgment and affection of all to whom he sheweth mercy, to concur with his own, in labouring to further his ends, in abolishing of sin out of our nature.

[Chapter XII.—*Scruples hindering comfort removed.*]

Use. From the meditation of these rules and signs, much comfort may be brought into the souls of the weakest; which, that it may be in the more abundance, let me add something for the helping them over some few ordinary objections and secret thoughts against themselves, which getting within the heart, oftentimes keep them under.

1. Some think they have no faith at all, because they have no full assurance; whenas the fairest fire that can be will have some smoke. The best actions will smell of the smoke. The mortar wherein garlic hath been stamped, will always smell of it; so all our actions will savour something of the old man.

2. In weakness of body some think grace dieth, because their performances are feeble, their spirits, being the instruments of their souls' actions, being wasted; not considering that God regards those hidden sighs of those that want abilities to express them outwardly. He that pronounceth them blessed that consider the poor, will have a merciful consideration of such himself.

3. Some again are haunted with hideous representations to their fantasies, and with vile and unworthy thoughts of God, of Christ, of the word, &c., which, as busy flies, disquiet and molest their peace; these are cast in like wildfire by Satan, as may be discerned by the, 1, strangeness; 2, strength and violence; 3, horribleness of them even unto nature corrupt. *Vellem servari Domine, sed cogitationes non patiuntur.* A pious soul is no more guilty of them, than Benjamin of Joseph's cup put into his sack. Amongst other helps prescribed by godly writers, as abomination of them, and diversion from them to other things, &c., let this be one, to complain unto Christ against them, and to fly under the wings of his protection, and to desire him to take our part against his and our enemy. Shall every sin and blasphemy of man be forgiven, and not these blasphemous thoughts, which have the devil for their father, when Christ himself was therefore molested in this kind, that he might succour all poor souls in the like case?

But* there is a difference betwixt Christ and us in this case, by reason that Satan had nothing of his own in Christ, his suggestions left no impression at all in his holy nature; but, as sparks falling into the sea, were presently quenched. Satan's temptations of Christ were only suggestions on Satan's part, and apprehensions of the vileness of them on Christ's part. To apprehend ill suggested by another, is not ill. It was Christ's grievance, but Satan's sin. But thus he yielded himself to be tempted, that he might both pity us in our conflicts, and train us up to manage our spiritual weapons as he did. Christ could have overcome him by power, but he did it by argument. But when Satan cometh to us, he findeth something of his own in us, which holdeth correspondency and hath intelligence with him; there is the same enmity in our nature to God and goodness in some degree, that is in Satan himself; whereupon his temptations fasten for the most part some taint upon us. And if there wanted a devil to suggest, yet sinful thoughts would arise from within us; though none were cast in from without, we have a mint of them within: these thoughts, *morosa cogitatio*, if the soul dwell on them so long as to suck or draw from and by them any sinful delight, then they leave a more heavy guilt upon the soul, and hinder our sweet communion with God, and interrupt our peace, and put a contrary relish into the soul, disposing of it to greater sins. All scandalous breakings out are but thoughts at the first. Ill thoughts are as little thieves, which, creeping in at the window, open the door to greater; thoughts are seeds of actions. These, especially when they are helped forward by Satan, make the life of many good Christians almost a martyrdom. In this case it is an unsound comfort that some minister, that ill thoughts arise from nature, and what is natural is excusable; but we must know, that nature, as it came out of God's hands at the first, had no such risings out of it: the soul, as inspired of God, had no such unsavoury breathings; but since that by sin it betrayed itself, it is in some sort natural to it to forge sinful imaginations, and to be a furnace of such sparks; and this is an aggravation

* 'But' . . . . to 'subjection in himself.' This long paragraph first introduced in B.

of the sinfulness of natural corruption, that it is so deeply rooted, and so generally spread in our nature.

It furthereth humiliation to know the whole breadth and depth of sin; only this, that our nature now, so far as it is unrenewed, is so unhappily fruitful in ill thoughts, ministers this comfort, that it is not our case alone, as if our condition herein were severed from others, as some have been tempted to think, even almost to despair; none, say they, have such a loathsome nature as I have. This springs from ignorance of the spreading of original sin, for what can come from an unclean thing, but that which is unclean? 'As in the water face answers face, so the polluted heart of one man answereth to the heart of another,' Prov. xxvii 19, where grace hath not made some difference. As in annoyances from Satan, so here, the best way is to lay open our complaints to Christ, and cry with St Paul, *Domine sim patior*, 'O miserable man that I am, who shall deliver me from this body of death?' Rom. vii. 24, 25: upon this venting of his distressed soul, he presently found comfort; for he breaketh into thanksgiving, 'Thanks be to God,' &c. And it is good to take advantage from hence to hate this noisome body of death the more, and to draw nearer unto God, as that holy man after his 'foolish and beastly thoughts,' Ps. lxxiii. 22 and 28, did, and to keep our hearts closer to God, seasoning them with heavenly meditations in the morning, storing up good matter that our heart may be a good treasury, and begging of Christ his Holy Spirit to stop that cursed issue, and to be a living spring of better thoughts in us. Nothing more abaseth the spirits of holy men that desire to delight in God after they have escaped the common defilements of the world, than these unclean issues of spirit, as being most contrary to God, who is a pure Spirit: but the very irksomeness of them yields matter of comfort against them; they force the soul to all spiritual exercises, to watchfulness, and a more near walking with God, and to raise itself to thoughts of a higher nature, which the truth of God, works of God, communion of saints, the mystery of godliness, the consideration of the terror of the Lord, of the excellency of the state of a Christian, and conversation suitable, do abundantly minister. They discover to us a necessity of daily purging and pardoning grace, and of seeking to be found in Christ, and so bring the best often upon their knees.

But our chief comfort is, that our blessed Saviour, as he bade Satan avaunt from himself after he had given way awhile to his impudency, Mat. iv. 10; so he will command him to be gone from us, when it shall be good for us; he must be gone at a word. And he can and will likewise in his due time rebuke the rebellious and extravagant stirrings of our hearts, and bring all the thoughts of the inner man in subjection to himself.

4. Some think, when they begin once to be troubled with the smoke of corruption more than they were before, therefore they are worse than they were. It is true, that corruptions appear now more than before, but they are less.

For, first, sin, the more it is seen the more it is hated, and thereupon is the less. Motes are in a room before the sun shines, but they then only appear.

Secondly, contraries, the nearer they are one to another, the sharper is the conflict betwixt them: now of all enemies the spirit and the flesh are nearest one to another, being both in the soul of a regenerate man, and in faculties of the soul, and in every action that springeth from those faculties, and therefore it is no marvel the soul, the seat of this battle, thus divided in itself, be as smoking flax.

Thirdly, the more grace, the more spiritual life, and the more spiritual life, the more antipathy to the contrary; whence none are so sensible of corruption, as those that have the most living souls.

And fourthly, when men give themselves to carnal liberties, their corruptions trouble them not, as not being bound* and tied up; but when once grace suppresseth their extravagant and licentious excesses, then the flesh boileth, as disdaining to be confined; yet they are better now than they were before. That matter which yields smoke was in the torch before it was lighted; but it is not offensive till the torch begins to burn. Let such know, that if the smoke be once offensive to them, it is a sign that there is light. It is better to enjoy the benefit of light, though with smoke, than to be altogether in the dark.

Neither is smoke so offensive, as light is comfortable to us, it yielding an evidence of truth of grace in the heart; therefore, though it be cumbersome in the conflict, yet it is comfortable in the evidence. It is better corruption should offend us now, than by giving way to it to redeem a little peace with loss of comfort afterwards. Let such therefore as are at variance and odds with their corruptions, look upon this text as their portion of comfort.

[CHAPTER XIII.—*Set upon Duties notwithstanding Weaknesses.*]

Here is an use of encouragement to duty, that Christ will not quench the smoking flax, but blow it up. Some are loath to perform good duties, because they feel their hearts rebelling, and duties come off untowardly. We should not avoid good actions for the infirmities cleaving unto them. Christ looketh more at the good in them that he meaneth to cherish, than the ill in them that he meaneth to abolish. A sick man, though in eating he something increaseth the disease, yet he will eat, that nature may get strength against the disease; so though sin cleaveth to what we do, yet let us do it, since we have to deal with so good a Lord, and the more strife we meet withal, the more acceptance. Christ loveth to taste of the good fruits that come from us, although they will always relish of the old stock. A Christian complaineth he cannot pray. O I am troubled with so many distracting thoughts, and never more than now. But hath he put into thine heart a desire to pray? He will hear the desires of his own Spirit in thee. 'We know not what to pray for as we ought' (nor do anything else as we ought), 'but the Spirit helpeth our infirmities, with inexpressible sighs and groans,' Rom. viii. 26, which are not hid from God. 'My groanings are not hid from thee,' Ps. xxxviii. 9. God can pick sense out of a confused prayer. These desires cry louder in his ears than thy sins. Sometimes a Christian hath such confused thoughts, he can say nothing, but as a child crieth, O Father, not able to shew what it needs, as Moses at the Red Sea.

These stirrings of spirit touch the bowels of God, and melt him into compassion towards us, when they come from the spirit of adoption, and from a striving to be better.

Object. Oh, but is it possible, thinketh the misgiving heart, that so holy a God should accept such a prayer?

Ans. Yes, he will accept that which is his own, and pardon that which is ours. 'Jonah prayed in the whale's belly,' Jonah ii. 1, being burdened with the guilt of sin, yet God heareth him. Let not, therefore, infirmities discourage us. St James takes away this objection, v. 17. Some might object, If I were as holy as Elias, then my prayers might be regarded;

* 'Bounded,' in G.

but, saith he, 'Elias was a man of like passions to us,' he had his passions as well as we; for do we think that God heard him because he was without fault? No, surely. But look we to the promises: 'Call upon me in the day of trouble, and I will hear thee,' Ps. l. 15; 'Ask and ye shall receive,' Matt. vii. 7; and such like. God accepteth our prayers, though weak. 1. Because we are his own children, they come from his own Spirit. 2. Because they are according to his own will. 3. Because they are offered in Christ's mediation, and he takes them, and mingleth them with his own odours, Rev. viii. 3. There is never a holy sigh, never a tear we shed, lost. And as every grace increaseth by exercise of itself, so doth the grace of prayer. By prayer we learn to pray. So, likewise, we should take heed of a spirit of discouragement in all other holy duties, since we have so gracious a Saviour. Pray as we are able, hear as we are able, strive as we are able, do as we are able, according to the measure of grace received. God in Christ will cast a gracious eye upon that which is his own. Would St Paul do nothing, because 'he could not do the good he would?' Phil. iii. 14. Yes, he 'pressed to the mark.' Let us not be cruel to ourselves when Christ is thus gracious.

There is a certain meekness of spirit whereby we yield thanks to God for any ability at all, and rest quiet with the measure of grace received, seeing it is God's good pleasure it should be so, who giveth the will and the deed, yet so as we rest not from further endeavours. But when, upon faithful endeavour, we come short of that we would be, and short of that others are, then know for our comfort, Christ will not quench the smoking flax, and that sincerity and truth, as before was said, with endeavour of growth, is our perfection. It is comfortable what God saith, 'He only shall go to his grave in peace, because there is some goodness,' 1 Kings xiv. 13, though but some goodness. 'Lord, I believe,' Mark ix. 24, with a weak faith, yet with faith; love thee with a faint love, yet with love; endeavour in a feeble manner, yet endeavour. A little fire is fire, though it smoketh. Since thou hast taken me into thy covenant to be thine of an enemy, wilt thou cast me off for these infirmities, which, as they displease thee, so are they the grief of my own heart?

[Chapter XIV.—*The Case of Indisposition Resolved, and Discouragements.*]

1. From what hath been spoken, with some little addition, it will not be difficult to resolve that case which some require help in, namely, whether we ought to perform duties, our hearts being altogether indisposed. For satisfaction we must know, 1, Our hearts of themselves do linger after liberty, and are hardly brought under the yoke of duty; and the more spiritual the duty is, the more is their untowardness. Corruption getteth ground, for the most part, in every neglect. It is as in rowing against the tide, one stroke neglected will not be gained in three; and therefore it is good to keep our hearts close to duty, and not to hearken unto the excuses they are ready to frame.

2. In the setting upon duty, God strengtheneth his own party that he hath in us. We find a warmness of heart, and increase of strength, the Spirit going along with us, and raising us up by degrees, until it leaveth us as it were in heaven. God often delighteth to take the advantage of our indisposition, that he may manifest his work the more clearly, and that all the glory of the work may be his, whose all the strength is.

3. Obedience is most direct when there is nothing else to sweeten the action. Although the sacrifice be imperfect, yet the obedience with which it is offered hath acceptance.

4. That which is won as a spoil from our corruptions will have such a degree of comfort afterwards, as for the present it hath of cumber. Feeling and freeness of spirit is oft reserved until duty be discharged; reward followeth work. In and after duty we find that experience of God's presence which, without obedience, we may long wait for, and yet go without. This hindereth not the Spirit's freedom in blowing upon our souls when it listeth, John iii. 8. For we speak only of such a state of soul as is becalmed, and must row, as it were, against the stream. As in sailing, the hand must be to the stern, and the eye to the star; so here, put forth that little strength we have to duty, and look up for assistance, which* the Spirit, as freely, so seasonably will afford.

Caution. (1.) Yet in these duties, that require as well the body as the soul, there may be a cessation till strength be repaired. Whetting doth not let (*d*), but fit. (2.) In sudden passions there should be a time to compose and calm the soul, and to put the strings in tune. The prophet would have a minstrel to bring his soul into frame, 1 Sam. xvi. 16, 17.

So likewise we are subject to discouragements in suffering, by reason of impatience in us. Alas! I shall never get through such a cross. But if God bring us into the cross, he will be with us in the cross, and at length bring us out more refined; we shall lose nothing but dross, Zech. xiii. 9. Of our own strength we cannot bear the least trouble, and by the Spirit's assistance we can bear the greatest. The Spirit will join his shoulders to help us to bear our infirmities. 'The Lord will put his hand to heave us up,' Ps. xxxvii. 24. 'You have heard of the patience of Job,' saith James, chap. v. 11. We have heard likewise of his impatiency too; but it pleased God mercifully to overlook that. It yields us comfort also in desolate conditions, as contagious sicknesses, and the like, wherein we are more immediately under God's hand. Then Christ hath a throne of mercy at our bed's side, and numbers our tears and our groans. And, to come to the matter we are now about, the Sacrament,† it was ordained not for angels, but for men; and not for perfect men, but for weak men; and not for Christ, who is truth itself, to bind him, but because we are ready, by reason of our guilty and unbelieving hearts, to call truth itself into question. Therefore it was not enough for his goodness to leave us many precious promises, but he giveth us seals to strengthen us; and, what though we are not so prepared as we should, yet let us pray as Hezekiah did: 'The Lord pardon every one that prepareth his heart to seek the Lord God of his fathers, though he be not cleansed according to the purification of the sanctuary,' 2 Chron. xxx. 19. Then we come comfortably to this holy sacrament, and with much fruit. This should carry us through all duties with much cheerfulness, that, if we hate our corruptions, and strive against them, they shall not be counted ours. It is not I, saith St Paul, but 'sin that dwelleth in me,' Rom. vii. 17; for what displeaseth us shall never hurt us, *quod non placet, non nocet,* and we shall be esteemed of God to be that we love, and desire, and labour to be. What we desire to be we shall be, and what we desire truly to conquer we shall conquer; for God will fulfil the desire of them that fear him, Ps. cxlv. 19. The desire is an earnest of the thing desired. How little encouragement will carry us to the affairs of

* 'Which . . . . afford,' not in A, B, but in E.

† Marginal note—This was preached at the Sacrament.

this life! And yet all the helps God offers will hardly prevail with our backward natures. Whence are, then, discouragements? 1. Not from the Father, for he hath bound himself in covenant 'to pity us as a father pitieth his children,' Ps. ciii. 13, and to accept as a father our weak endeavours; and what is wanting in the strength of duty, he giveth us leave to take up in his gracious indulgence, whereby we shall honour that grace wherein he delights, as much as in more perfect performances. *Possibilitas tua mensura tua.*

2. Not from Christ, for he by office will not quench the smoking flax. We see* how Christ bestoweth the best fruits of his love upon persons, for condition mean, for parts weak, for infirmities, nay, for grosser falls, offensive: *first,* thus it pleaseth him to confound the pride of flesh, which usually taketh measure of God's love by some outward excellency. *Secondly,* thus he is delighted to shew the freedom of his grace and his prerogative royal, that 'whosoever glorieth, may glory in the Lord,' 1 Cor. i. 31.

In the eleventh to the Hebrews, among that cloud of witnesses, we see Rahab, Gideon, and Samson, ranked with Abraham the father of the faithful, Heb. xi. 31, 32. Our blessed Saviour, as he was the image of his Father, so in this he was of the same mind, glorifying his Father for revealing the mystery of the gospel to simple men, neglecting those that carried the chief reputation of wisdom in the world, Heb. xi. 31, 32.

It is† not unworthy of the remembering that which Saint Augustine speaketh‡ of a silly man in his time, destitute almost altogether of the use of reason, who when he was most patient of all injuries done to himself, yet from a reverence of religion he would not endure any injury done to the name of Christ; insomuch that he would cast stones at those that blasphemed, and would not in that case spare his own governors; which sheweth that the parts of none are so low, as that they are beneath the gracious regard of Christ; where it pleaseth him to make his choice, and to exalt his mercy, he passeth by no degree of wit, though never so plain.

3. Neither do discouragements come from the Spirit;§ he helps our infirmities, and by office is a comforter, Rom. viii. 26. If he convinceth of sin, and so humbleth us, it is that he may make way to shew his office of comforting us. Discouragements, then, must come from ourselves and Satan, who laboureth to fasten on us a loathing of duty.

[CHAPTER XV.—*Of infirmities. No cause of discouragement. In whom they are. And how to recover peace lost.*]

And among other causes of discouragement, some are much vexed with scruples, even against the best duties; partly by distemper of body, helped by Satan's malice, casting dust in their eyes, in their way to heaven; and partly from some remainder of ignorance, which like darkness breedeth fears; and as ignorance of other things, so especially of this merciful disposition in Christ, the persuasion of which would easily banish false fears, they conceive of him as one sitting at a catch for all advantages against them; wherein they may see how they wrong not only themselves but his goodness. This scrupulosity, for the most part, is a sign of a godly soul,

* 'We see' . . . . to 'wisdom in the world.' This paragraph added first in B.
† 'It is' . . . to 'never so plain.' This paragraph not in A, B, but in E.
‡ Aug. de peccatorum meritis et remiss., lib. i. cap. 14.
§ 'Not from the Spirit,' in A.

as some weeds are of a good soil: therefore are they the more to be pitied, for it is a heavy affliction, and the ground of it in most is not so much from trouble of conscience, as from sickness of fantasy. The end of Christ's coming was to free us from all such groundless fears.

There is still in some, such ignorance of that comfortable condition we are in under the covenant of grace, as by it they are much discouraged. Therefore we must know, 1, That weaknesses do not break covenant with God. They do not between husband and wife; and shall we make ourselves more pitiful than Christ, who maketh himself a pattern of love to all other husbands? 2. Weaknesses do not debar us from mercy, nay, they incline God the more, Ps. lxxviii. 39. Mercy is a part of the church's jointure, 'Christ marries her in mercy,' Hos. ii. 19. The husband is bound to bear with the wife, as 'being the weaker vessel,' 1 Pet. iii. 7; and shall we think he will exempt himself from his own rule, and not bear with his weak spouse?

3. If Christ should not be merciful to our infirmities, he should not have a people to serve him.

Put case therefore we be very weak, yet so long as we are not found amongst malicious opposers and underminers of God's truth, let us not give way to despairing thoughts; we have a merciful Saviour. But lest we flatter ourselves without ground, we must know that weaknesses are accounted either, 1, Imperfections cleaving to our best actions; or, 2, Such actions as proceed from want of age in Christ, whilst we are babes; or, 3, From want of strength, where there hath been little means; or, 4, They are sudden indeliberate breakings out, contrary to our general bent and purpose, whilst our judgment is overcast with the cloud of a sudden temptation. After which, 1, we are sensible of our infirmity; 2, We grieve for it; 3, And from grief, complain; and 4, With complaining strive and labour to reform; and 5, In labouring get some ground of our corruption.

Weaknesses* so considered, howsoever they be matter of humiliation, and the object of our daily mortification, yet may stand with boldness with God, neither is a good work either extinguished by them, or tainted so far as to lose all acceptance with God. But to plead for an infirmity is more than an infirmity; to allow ourselves in weaknesses is more than a weakness. The justification of evil sealeth up the lips, so that the soul cannot call God Father with that child-like liberty, or enjoy sweet communion with him, until peace be made by shaming ourselves, and renewing our faith. Those that have ever been bruised for sin, if they fall they are soon recovered. Peter was recovered with a gracious look of Christ; David by Abigail's words. Tell a thief or a vagrant that he is out of the way, he regards it not, because his aim is not to walk in any certain way, but as it serveth his own turn.

For the further clearing of this, we must conceive, 1, That wheresoever sins of infirmity are, there in that person must be the life of grace begun. There can be no weakness, where there is no life. 2. There must be a sincere and general bent to the best things; though for a sudden a godly man be drawn or driven aside in some particulars, yet by reason of that interest the Spirit of Christ hath in him, and because his aims are right for the main, he will either recover of himself, or yield to the counsel of others. 3. There must be a right judgment allowing of the best ways, or else the heart is rotten, and infuseth corruption into the whole conversation, so that all their actions become infected at the spring-head; they justify looseness, and condemn God's ways, as too much strictness; their principles whereby they work are not good. 4. There must be a conjugal love to Christ, so

* 'Weaknesses' . . to 'perfecteth his strength.' This paragraph first added in B.

as upon no terms they will change their Lord and husband, and yield themselves absolutely over to be ruled by their own lusts, or the lusts of others.

A Christian's carriage towards Christ may in many things be very offensive, and cause some strangeness; yet he will own Christ, and Christ him; he will not resolve upon any way wherein he knows he must break with Christ.

Where the heart is thus in these respects qualified, there we must know this, that Christ counteth it his honour to pass by many infirmities, nay, in infirmities he perfecteth his strength. There be some almost invincible infirmities,* as forgetfulness, heaviness of spirit, sudden passions, fears, &c., which though natural, yet are for the most part tainted with sin; of these,† if the life of Christ be in us, we are weary, and would fain shake them off, as a sick man his ague; otherwise it is not to be esteemed weakness so much as wilfulness, and the more will, the more sin; and little sins, when God shall awake the conscience, and 'set them in order before us,' Ps. l. 21, will prove great burdens, and not only bruise a reed, but shake a cedar. Yet God's children never sin with full will, because there is a contrary law of the mind, whereby the dominion of sin is broken, which always hath some secret working against the law of sin. Notwithstanding‡ there may be so much will in a sinful action, as may wonderfully waste our comfort afterward, and keep us long upon the rack of a disquieted conscience, God in his fatherly dispensation suspending the sense of his love. So much as we give way to our will in sinning, in such a measure of distance we set ourselves from comfort. Sin against conscience is as a thief in the candle, which wasteth our joy, and thereby weakeneth our strength. We must know, therefore, that wilful breeches in sanctification will much hinder the sense of our justification.

Quest. What course shall such take to recover their peace?

Ans. Such must give a sharp sentence against themselves, and yet cast themselves upon God's mercy in Christ, as at their first conversion. And now they had need to clasp about Christ the faster, as they see more need in themselves, and let them remember the mildness of Christ here, that will not quench the smoking flax. Ofttimes we see that, after a deep humiliation, Christ speaks more peace than before, to witness the truth of this reconciliation, because he knows Satan's enterprises in casting down such, lower, and because such are most abased in themselves, and are ashamed to look Christ in the face, by reason of their unkindness. We see God did not only pardon David, but after much bruising gave him wise Solomon to succeed him in the kingdom. We see in the Canticles, chap. vi. 44, that the church, after she had been humbled for her slighting of Christ, Christ sweetly entertains her again, and falleth into commendation of her beauty. We must know for our comfort that Christ was not anointed to this great work of the mediator for lesser sins only, but for the greatest, if we have but a spark of true faith to lay hold on him. Therefore, if there be any bruised reed, let him not except himself, when Christ doth not except him; 'Come unto me, all ye that are weary and heavy laden,' &c., Matt. xi. 28. Why should we not make use of so gracious a disposition? we are only therefore poor, because we know not our riches in Christ. In time of temptation, rather believe Christ than the devil, believe truth from truth itself, hearken not to a liar, an enemy, and a murderer.

* A necessitatibus meis libera me Domine.—*Aug* [*ustine*].

† 'If . . . . in us,' added in B. ‡ 'Yet,' in A.

[CHAPTER XVI.—*Satan not to be believed, as he representeth Christ unto us.*]

Since Christ is thus comfortably set out unto us, let us not believe Satan's representations of him. When we are troubled in conscience for our sins, his manner is then to present him to the afflicted soul as a most severe judge armed with justice against us. But then let us present him to our souls, as thus offered to our view by God himself, as holding out a sceptre of mercy, and spreading his arms to receive us. When we think of Joseph, Daniel, John the Evangelist, &c., we frame conceits of them with delight, as of mild and sweet persons; much more when we think of Christ, we should conceive of him as a mirror of all meekness. If the sweetness of all flowers were in one, how sweet must that flower needs be? In Christ all perfections of mercy and love meet; how great then must that mercy be that lodgeth in so gracious a heart? whatsoever tenderness is scattered in husband, father, brother, head, all is but a beam from him, it is in him in the most eminent manner. We are weak, but we are his; we are deformed, but yet carry his image upon us. A father looks not so much at the blemishes of his child, as at his own nature in him; so Christ finds matter of love from that which is his own in us. He sees his own nature in us: we are diseased, but yet his members. Who ever neglected his own members because they were sick or weak? none ever hated his own flesh. Can the head forget the members? can Christ forget himself? we are his fulness, as he is ours. He was love itself clothed with man's nature, which he united so near to himself, that he might communicate his goodness the more freely unto us; and took not our nature when it was at the best, but when it was abased, with all natural and common infirmities it was subject unto. Let us therefore abhor all suspicious thoughts, as either cast in or cherished by that damned spirit, who as he laboured to divide between the Father and the Son by jealousies, 'If thou be the Son of God,' &c., Matt. iv. 6, so his daily study is, to divide betwixt the Son and us, by breeding mispersuasions in us of Christ, as if there were not such tender love in him to such as we are. It was his art from the beginning to discredit God with man, by calling God's love into question, with our first father Adam; his success then makes him ready at that weapon still.

Object. But for all this, I feel not Christ so to me, saith the smoking flax, but rather the clean contrary; he seemeth to be an enemy unto me, I see and feel evidences of his just displeasure,

Ans. Christ may act the part of an enemy a little while, as Joseph did, but it is to make way for acting his own part of mercy in a more seasonable time; he cannot hold in his bowels long. He seemeth to wrestle with us, as with Jacob, but he supplies us with hidden strength, at length to get the better. Faith pulls off the vizard from his face, and sees a loving heart under contrary appearances. *Fides Christo larvam detrahit.* At first he answers the woman of Canaan crying after him not a word; 2, Then gives her a denial; 3, Gives an answer tending to her reproach, calling her dog, as being without the covenant; yet she would not be so beaten off, for she considered the end of his coming. As his Father was never nearer him in strength to support him, than when he was furthest off in sense of favour to comfort him; so Christ is never nearer us in power to uphold us, than when he seemeth most to hide his presence from us. The influence of the Sun of righteousness pierceth deeper than his light. In such cases, whatsoever Christ's present carriage is towards us, let us oppose his nature and office against it; he cannot deny himself, he cannot but discharge the office his Father hath laid upon him. We see here the Father hath undertaken that he shall not 'quench the smoking flax;' and Christ again undertaking for us to the Father, appearing before him for us, until he presents us blameless before him, John xvii. 6, 11. The Father hath given us to Christ, and Christ giveth us back again to the Father.

Object. This were good comfort, if I were but as smoking flax.

Ans. It is well that thy objection pincheth upon thyself, and not upon Christ; it is well thou givest him the honour of his mercy towards others, though not to thyself: but yet do not wrong the work of his Spirit in thy heart. Satan, as he slandereth Christ to us, so he slandereth us to ourselves. If thou beest not so much as smoking flax, then why dost thou not renounce thy interest in Christ, and disclaim the covenant of grace? This thou darest not do. Why dost thou not give up thyself wholly to other contents? This thy spirit will not suffer thee. Whence come these restless groanings and complaints? lay this thy present estate, together with this office of Christ to such, and do not despise the consolation of the Almighty, nor refuse thy own mercy. Cast thyself into the arms of Christ, and if thou perishest, perish there; if thou dost not, thou art sure to perish. If mercy be to be found anywhere, it is there.

Herein appears Christ's care to thee, that he hath given thee a heart in some degree sensible: he might have given thee up to hardness, security and profaneness of heart, of all spiritual judgments the greatest. He that died for his enemies, will he refuse those, the desire of whose soul is towards him? He that by his messengers desires us to be reconciled, will he put us off when we earnestly seek it at his hand? No, doubtless, when he prevents us by kindling holy desires in us, he is ready to meet us in his own ways. When the prodigal set himself to return to his father, his father stays not for him, but meets him in the way. 'When he prepares the heart to seek, he will cause his ear to hear,' Ps. x. 17. He cannot find in his heart to hide himself long from us. If God should bring us into such a dark condition, as that we should see no light from himself, or the creature, then let us remember what he saith by the prophet Isaiah, 'He that is in darkness, and seeth no light,' Isa. l. 10, no light of comfort, no light of God's countenance, 'yet let him trust in the name of the Lord.' We can never be in such a condition, wherein there will be just cause of utter despair; therefore let us do as mariners do, cast anchor in the dark. Christ knows how to pity us in this case; look what comfort he felt from his Father in his breakings, Isa. liii. 5, the like we shall feel from himself in our bruising.

The sighs of a bruised heart carry in them some report, as of our affection to Christ, so of his care to us. The eyes of our souls cannot be towards him, but that he hath cast a gracious look upon us first. The least love we have to him is but a reflection of his love first shining upon us. As Christ did in his example whatsoever he gives us in charge to do, so he suffered in his own person whatsoever he calleth us to suffer, that he might the better learn to relieve and pity us in our sufferings. In his desertion in the garden, and upon the cross, he was content to want that unspeakable solace in the presence of his Father, both to bear the wrath of the Lord for a time for us, and likewise to know the better how to comfort us in our greatest extremities. God seeth it fit we should taste of that cup of which his Son drank so deep, that we might feel a little what sin is, and what his Son's love was; but our comfort is, that Christ drank the dregs of the cup for us, and will succour us, that our spirits utterly fail not under that little taste of his displeasure which we may feel. He became not only a man, but a curse, a man of sorrows for us. He was broken, that we should not be broken; he was troubled, that we should not be desperately troubled; he became a curse, that we should not be accursed. Whatsoever may be wished for in an all-sufficient comforter, is all to be found in Christ, 1. Authority from the Father, all power was given him,' Matt. xxviii. 18. 2. Strength in himself, as having his name the mighty God, Isa. ix. 6. 3. Wisdom, and that from his own experience, how and when to help. 4. Willingness, as being flesh of our flesh, and bone of our bone, Isa. ix. 6.

[CHAPTER XVII.—*Reproof of such as sin against this merciful disposition in Christ. Of quenching the Spirit.*]

We are now to take notice of divers sorts of men that offend deeply against this merciful disposition of Christ: as, 1, Such as go on in all ill courses of life upon this conceit, as if it were in vain to go to Christ, their lives have been so ill; whenas so soon as we look to heaven, all encouragements are ready to meet us and draw us forward. Amongst others this is one allurement, that Christ is ready to welcome us, and lead us further. None are damned in the church but those that will. Such as either enforce upon themselves hard conceits of Christ, that they may have some show of reason to fetch contentment from other things: as that unprofitable servant, Matt. xxv. 30, that would needs take up a conceit, that his master was a hard man; hereby to flatter himself in his unfruitful courses, in not improving that talent which he had.

2. Such as take up a hope of their own, that Christ will suffer them to walk in the ways to hell, and yet bring them to heaven: whereas all comfort should draw us nearer to Christ, else it is a lying comfort, either in itself or in our application of it.

And 3. Those that will cast water themselves upon those sparks which Christ labours to kindle in them, because they will not be troubled with the light of them.

Such must know that the Lamb can be angry, and they that will not come under his sceptre of mercy, shall be crushed in pieces by his sceptre of power, Ps. ii. 9. Though he will graciously tender and maintain the least spark of true grace, yet where he findeth not the spark of grace, but opposition to his Spirit striving with them, his wrath once kindled shall burn to hell. There is no juster provocation than when kindness is churlishly refused.

When God would have cured Babylon, and she would not be cured, then she was given up to destruction, Jer. li. 9.

When Jerusalem would not be gathered under the wing of Christ, then their habitation is left desolate, Matt. xxiii. 37, 38.

When wisdom stretcheth out her hand and men refuse, then wisdom will laugh at men's destruction, Prov. i. 26. Salvation itself will not save those that spill the potion, and cast away the plaster. A pitiful case, when this merciful Saviour shall delight in destruction: when he that made men shall have no mercy on them, Isa. xxvii. 11.

O, say the rebels of the time, God hath not made us to damn us. Yes, if you will not meet Christ in the ways of his mercy, it is fit you should 'eat the fruit of your own ways, and be filled with your own devices,' Prov. i. 31.

This will be the hell of hell, when men shall think, that they have loved their sins more than their souls; when they shall think, what love and mercy hath been almost enforced upon them, and yet they would perish. The more accessary we are in pulling a judgment upon ourselves, the more the conscience will be confounded in itself, when they shall acknowledge Christ to be without all blame, themselves without excuse.

If men appeal to their own consciences, they will tell them, the Holy Spirit hath often knocked at their hearts, as willing to have kindled some holy desires in them. How else can they be said to resist the Holy Ghost, but that the Spirit was readier to draw them to a further degree of goodness than stood with their own wills? whereupon those in the church that are damned are self-condemned before. So that here we need not rise to higher causes, when men carry sufficient cause* in their own bosoms.

4. And the best of us all may offend against this merciful disposition, if we be not watchful against that liberty our carnal disposition will be ready to take from it. Thus we reason, if Christ will not quench the smoking flax, what need we fear that any neglect on our part can bring us under a comfortless condition? If Christ will not do it, what can?

Ans. You know the apostle's prohibition notwithstanding, 1 Thess. v. 19, 'Quench not the Spirit.' These cautions of not quenching are sanctified by the Spirit as means of not quenching. Christ performeth his office in not quenching, by stirring up suitable endeavours in us; and none more solicitous in the use of the means than those that are most certain of the good success. The ground is this: the means that God hath set apart for the effecting of any thing, fall under the same purpose that he hath to bring that thing to pass; and this is a principle taken for granted, even in civil matters; as who, if he knew before it would be a fruitful year, would therefore hang up his plough and neglect tillage?

Hence the apostle stirs up from the certain expectation of a blessing, 1 Cor. xv. 57, 58, and this encouragement here from the good issue of final victory is intended to stir us up, and not to take us off. If we be negligent in the exercise of grace received, and use of means prescribed, suffering our spirits to be oppressed with multitudes and variety of cares of this life, and take not heed of the damps of the times, for such miscarriage God in his wise care suffereth us oft to fall into a worse condition for feeling, than those that were never so much enlightened. Yet in mercy he will not suffer us to be so far enemies to ourselves, as wholly to neglect these sparks once kindled. Were it possible that we should be given up to give over all endeavour wholly, then we could look for no other issue but quenching; but Christ will tend this spark, and cherish this small seed, so as he will preserve in the soul always some degree of care. If we would make a comfortable use of this, we must consider all those means whereby Christ doth preserve grace begun; as *first*, holy communion, whereby one Christian heateth another; 'two are better than one,' &c., Eccles. iv. 9. 'Did not our hearts burn?' Luke xxiv. 32, said the disciples. *Secondly*, much more communion with God in holy duties, as meditation and prayer, which doth not only kindle, but addeth a lustre to the soul. *Thirdly*, we feel by experience the breath of the Spirit to go along with the ministerial breath, whereupon the apostle knits these two together: 'Quench not the Spirit;' 'despise not prophecies,' 1 Thess. v. 19, 20. Nathan by a few words blew up the decaying sparks in David. Rather than God will suffer his fire in us to die, he will send some Nathan or other, and something always is left

* 'Of their own damnation,' in A and B.

in us to join with the word as connatural to it; as a coal that hath fire in it will quickly catch more to it: smoking flax will easily take fire. *Fourthly*, grace is strengthened by the exercise of it; 'Up and be doing, and the Lord be with thee,' 1 Chron. xxii. 16, said David to his son Solomon: stir up the grace that is in thee, for so holy motions turn to resolutions, resolutions to practice, and practice to a prepared readiness to every good work.

Caution. Yet let us know that grace is increased in the exercise of it, not by virtue of the exercise itself, but as Christ by his Spirit floweth into the soul, and bringeth us nearer unto himself the fountain, and instilleth such comfort in the act, whereby the heart is further enlarged. The heart of a Christian is Christ's garden, and his graces are as so many sweet spices and flowers, which his Spirit blowing upon makes* them to send forth a sweet savour: therefore keep the soul open for entertainment of the Holy Ghost, for he will bring in continually fresh forces to subdue corruption, and this most of all on the Lord's day. John was in the Spirit on the Lord's day, even in Patmos, the place of his banishment, Rev. i. 10; then the gales of the Spirit blow more strongly and sweetly. As we look, therefore, for the comfort of this doctrine, let us not favour our natural sloth, 'but exercise ourselves to godliness,' 1 Tim. iv. 7, and labour to keep this fire always burning upon the altar of our hearts, and dress our lamps daily, and put in fresh oil, and wind up our souls higher and higher still: resting in a good condition is contrary to grace, which cannot but promote itself to a further measure; let none turn this 'grace into wantonness,' Jude 4. Infirmities are a ground of humility, not a plea for negligence, not an encouragement to presumption. We should be so far from being ill, because Christ is good, as that those coals of love should melt us; therefore those may well suspect themselves in whom the consideration of this mildness of Christ doth not work that way: surely where grace is, corruption is as 'smoke to their eyes, and vinegar to their teeth,' Prov. x. 29. And therefore they will labour in regard of their own comfort, as likewise for the credit of religion and the glory of God, that their light may break forth. If a spark of faith and love be so precious, what an honour will it be to be rich in faith! Who would not rather walk in the light, and in the comforts of the Holy Ghost, than to live in a dark, perplexed estate? and not rather to be carried with full sail to heaven, than to be tossed always with fears and doubts? The present trouble in conflict against a sin is not so much as that disquiet which any corruption favoured will bring upon us afterward; true peace is in conquering, not in yielding. The comfort in this text intended is for those that would fain do better, but find their corruptions clog them; that are in such a mist, that ofttimes they cannot tell what to think of themselves; that fain would believe, and yet oft fear they do not believe, and think that it cannot be that God should be so good to such sinful wretches as they are; and yet they allow not themselves in these fears and doubts.

5. And among others, how do they wrong themselves and him, that will have other mediators to God for them than he? Are any more pitiful than he, who became man to that end, that he might be pitiful to his own flesh? Let all at all times repair to this meek Saviour, and put up all our suits in his prevailing name. What need we knock at any other door? can any be more tender over us than Christ? What encouragement have we to commend the state of the church in general, or of any broken-hearted Christian, unto him by our prayers? Of whom we may speak unto Christ, as they of Lazarus, Lord, the church which thou lovest, and gavest thyself

* 'Maketh,' in A and B.

for, is in distress: Lord, this poor Christian, for whom thou wert bruised, Isa. liii. 5, is bruised and brought very low. It cannot but touch his bowels when the misery of his own dear bowels is spread before him.

6. Again, considering this gracious nature in Christ, let us think with ourselves thus: when he is so kind unto us, shall we be cruel against him in his name, in his truth, in his children? how shall those that delight to be so terrible 'to the meek of the earth,' Zech. ii. 3, hope to look so gracious a Saviour in the face? they that are so boisterous towards his spouse, shall know one day they had to deal with himself in his church. So it cannot but cut the heart of those that have felt this love of Christ, to hear him wounded who is the life of their lives, and the soul of their souls: this maketh those that have felt mercy weep over Christ, whom they have pierced with their sins. There cannot but be a mutual and quick sympathy between the head and the members. When we are tempted to any sin, if we will not pity ourselves, yet we should spare Christ, in not putting him to new torments. The apostle could not find out a more heart-breaking argument to enforce a sacrificing ourselves to God, than to conjure us by the mercies of God in Christ, Rom. xii. 1.

7. This mercy of Christ likewise should move us to commiserate the state* of the poor church, torn by enemies without, and rending itself by divisions at home. It cannot but work upon any soul that ever felt comfort from Christ, to consider what an affectionate entreaty the apostle useth to mutual agreement in judgment and affection. 'If any consolation in Christ, if any comfort of love, if any fellowship of the Spirit, if any bowels and mercies, fulfil my joy, be like-minded,' Phil. ii. 1; as if he should say, Unless you will disclaim all consolation in Christ, &c., labour to maintain the unity of the Spirit in the bond of peace. What a joyful spectacle is this to Satan and his faction, to see those that are separated from the world fall in pieces among themselves! Our discord is our enemy's melody.

The more to blame those that for private aims affect differences from others, and will not suffer the wounds of the church to close and meet together. Which must not be understood, as if men should dissemble their judgment in any truth where there is just cause of expressing themselves; for the least truth is Christ's and not ours, and therefore we are not to take liberty to affirm or deny at our pleasures. There is a due in a penny as well as in a pound, therefore we must be faithful in the least truth, when season calleth for it. Then our 'words are like apples of gold with pictures of silver,' Prov. xxv. 11. One word spoken in season, will do more good than a thousand out of season. But in some cases peace, by 'keeping our faith to ourselves,' Rom. xiv. 22, is of more consequence than the open discovery of some things we take to be true; considering the weakness of man's nature is such that there can hardly be a discovery of any difference in opinion, without some estrangement of affection. So far as men are not of one mind, they will hardly be of one heart, except where grace and the peace of God, Col. iii. 15, bear great rule in the heart: therefore open show of difference is never good but when it is necessary; howsoever some, from a desire to be somebody, turn into by-ways, and yield to a spirit of contradiction in themselves; yet, if St Paul may be judge, 'are they not carnal?' 1 Cor. iii. 3; if it be wisdom, it is wisdom from beneath: for the wisdom from above, as it is pure, so it is *peaceable*, James iii. 17. Our blessed Saviour, when he was to leave the world, what doth he press upon his disciples more than peace and love? And in his

* 'Estate,' in A and B.

last prayer, with what earnestness did he beg of his Father that 'they might be one, as he and the Father were one!' John xvii. 21. But what he prayed for on earth, we shall only enjoy perfectly in heaven. Let this make the meditation of that time the more sweet unto us.

8. And further, to lay open offenders in this kind, what spirit shall we think them to be of, that take advantages of the bruisedness and infirmities of men's spirits to relieve them with false peace for their own worldly ends? A wounded spirit will part with anything. Most of the gainful points of popery, as confession, satisfaction, merit, purgatory, &c., spring from hence, but they are physicians of no value, or rather tormentors than physicians at all. It is a greater blessing to be delivered from the 'sting of these scorpions,' Rev. ix. 5, than we are thankful for. Spiritual tyranny is the greatest tyranny, and then especially when it is where most mercy should be shewed; yet even there some, like cruel surgeons, delight in making long cures, to serve themselves upon the misery of others. It bringeth men under a terrible curse, 'when they will not remember to shew mercy, but persecute the poor and needy man, that they might even slay the broken in heart,' Ps. cix. 16.

Likewise, to such as raise temporal advantage to themselves out of the spiritual misery of others, join such as raise estates by betraying the church, and are unfaithful in the trust committed unto them: when the children shall cry for the bread of life, and there is none to give them, bringing thus upon the people of God that heavy judgment of a spiritual famine, starving Christ in his members; shall we so requite so good a Saviour, who counteth the love and mercy shewed 'in feeding his lambs,' John xxi. 15, as shewed to himself?

Last of all, they carry themselves very unkindly towards Christ, who stumble at this his low stooping unto us in his government and ordinances, that are ashamed of the simplicity of the gospel, that count preaching foolishness.

They, out of the pride of their heart, think they may do well enough without the help of the word and sacraments, and think Christ took not state enough upon him; and therefore they will mend the matter with their own devices, whereby they may give the better content to flesh and blood, as in popery. What greater unthankfulness can there be than to despise any help that Christ in mercy hath provided for us? In the days of his flesh, the proud Pharisees took offence at his familiar conversing with sinful men, who only did so as a physician to heal their souls. What defences was St Paul driven to make for himself, for his plainness in unfolding the gospel? The more Christ, in himself and in his servants, shall descend to exalt us, the more we should, with all humility and readiness, entertain that love, and magnify the goodness of God, that hath put the great work of our salvation, and laid the government upon so gentle a Saviour, that will carry himself so mildly in all things wherein he is to deal betwixt God and us, and us and God. The lower Christ comes down to us, the higher let us lift him up in our hearts: so will all those do that have ever found the experience of Christ's work in their heart.

[CHAPTER XVIII.—*Of Christ's judgment in us, and his victory, what it is.*]

We come to the third part, the constant progress of Christ's gracious power, until he hath set up such an absolute government in us, which shall prevail over all corruptions. It is said here, he will cherish his beginnings of grace in us, until he bring forth judgment unto victory. By judgment here, is meant the kingdom of grace in us, that government whereby Christ sets up a throne in our hearts. Governors among the Jews were first called judges, then kings: whence this inward rule is called judgment; as likewise, because it agrees unto the judgment of the word, which the psalmist oft calleth judgment, Ps. lxxii. 1, 2, because it agreeth to God's judgment. Men may read their doom in God's word, what it judgeth of them God judgeth of them. By this judgment set up in us, good is discerned, allowed, and performed; sin is judged, condemned, and executed. Our spirit being under the Spirit of Christ, is governed by him, and so far as it is governed by Christ, it governs us graciously.

Christ and we are of one judgment, and of one will. He hath his will in us; and his judgments are so invested into us, as that they are turned into our judgment, we carrying 'his law in our hearts, written by his Spirit,' Jer. xxxi. 33. The law in the inner man and the law written, answer as counterpanes each other.

The meaning then is, that the gracious frame of holiness set up in our hearts by the Spirit of Christ, shall go forward until all contrary power be brought under. The spirit of judgment will be a spirit of burning, Isa. iv. 4, to consume whatsoever opposed corruption like rust eats into the soul. If God's builders fall into errors, and build stubble upon a good foundation, God's Spirit, as a spiritual 'fire, will reveal this in time, 1 Cor. iii. 13,' and waste it. They shall, by a spirit of judgment, condemn their own errors and courses. The whole work of grace in us is set out under the name of judgment, and sometimes wisdom, because judgment is the chief and leading part in grace; whereupon that gracious work of repentance is called a change of the mind,* and an after-wisdom. As on the other side, in the learned languages, the words that do express wisdom imply likewise the general relish and savour of the whole soul,† and rather more the judgment of taste than of sight, or any other sense, because taste is the most necessary sense, and requireth the nearest application of the object of all other senses. So in spiritual life, it is most necessary that the Spirit should alter the taste of the soul, so as that it might savour the things of the Spirit so deeply, that all other things should be out of relish.

And as it is true of every particular Christian, that Christ's judgment in him shall be victorious, so likewise of the whole body of Christians—the church. The government of Christ, and his truth, whereby he ruleth as by a sceptre, shall at length be victorious in spite of Satan, antichrist, and all enemies. Christ 'riding on his white horse,' Rev. vi. 2, hath a bow, and goeth forth conquering, Rev. xix. 11, in the ministry, that he may overcome either to conversion or to confusion. But yet I take judgment for Christ's kingdom and government within us principally. 1. Because God especially requireth the subjection of the soul and conscience as his proper throne. 2. Because if judgment should prevail in all other‡ about us and not in our own hearts, it would not yield comfort to us; hereupon it is the first thing that we desire when we pray, 'Thy kingdom come,' that Christ would come and rule in our hearts. The kingdom of Christ in his ordinances serves but to bring Christ home into his own place, our hearts.

The words being thus explained, that judgment here includeth the government of both mind, will, and affections, there are divers conclusions that naturally do spring from them.

* μετάνοια. † φρονεῖν, sapere. ‡ 'Others,' in A and B.

[CHAPTER XIX.—*Christ is so mild that yet he will govern those that enjoy the comfort of his mildness.*]

The first conclusion from the connection of this part of the verse with the former is, that Christ is upon those terms mild, so that he will set up his government in those whom he is so gentle and tender over. He so pardons as he will be obeyed as a king; he so taketh us to be his spouse, as he will be obeyed as a husband. The same Spirit that convinceth us of the necessity of his righteousness to cover us, convinceth us also of the necessity of his government to rule us. His love to us moveth him to frame us to be like himself, and our love to him stirreth us up to be such as he may take delight in, neither have we any more faith or hope than care to be purged as he is pure; he maketh us subordinate governors, yea, kings under himself, giving us grace not only to set against, but to subdue in some measure our base affections. It is one main fruit of Christ's exaltation that he may turn every one of us from our wickedness, Acts iii. 26. 'For this end Christ died and rose again and liveth, that he should be Lord of the dead and living,' Rom. xiv. 9. God hath bound himself by an oath that he would grant us, that 'without fear we might serve him in holiness and righteousness in his sight,' Luke i. 75, not only in the sight of the world.

1. This may serve for a trial to discern who may lay just claim to Christ's mercy; only those that will take his yoke, and count it a greater happiness to be under his government, than to enjoy any liberty of the flesh; that will take whole Christ, and not single out of him what may stand with their present contentment; that will not divide Lord from Jesus, and so make a Christ of their own: none ever did truly desire mercy pardoning, but desired mercy healing. David prayeth for a new spirit, as well as for sense of pardoning mercy, Ps. li. 10.

2. This sheweth that those are misled, that make Christ to be only righteousness to us, and not sanctification, except by imputation: whereas it is a great part of our happiness to be under such a Lord, who was not only born for us, and given unto us, but 'hath the government likewise upon his shoulders,' Isa. ix. 6, 7, that is our Sanctifier as well as our Saviour, our Saviour as well by the effectual power of his Spirit from the power of sin, as by the merit of his death from the guilt thereof; so that this, 1, Be remembered, that the first and chief ground of our comfort is, that Christ as a priest offered himself as a sacrifice to his Father for us. The guilty soul flieth first to Christ crucified, made a curse for us. Thence it is that Christ hath right to govern us, thence it is that he giveth us his Spirit as our guide to lead us home.

2. In the course of our life, after that we are in state of grace, and be overtaken with any sin, we must remember to have recourse first unto Christ's mercy to pardon us, and then to the promise of his Spirit to govern us.

3. And when we feel ourselves cold in affection and duty, it is the best way to warm ourselves at this fire of his love and mercy in giving himself for us.

4. Again, remember this, that Christ, as he ruleth us, so it is by a spirit of love from a sense of his love, whereby his commandments are easy to us. He leadeth us by his free Spirit, a Spirit of liberty: his subjects are voluntaries. The constraint that he layeth upon his subjects is that of love: he

draweth us with the cords of love sweetly. Yet remember withal, that he draweth us strongly by a Spirit of power, for it is not sufficient that we have motives and encouragements to love and obey Christ from that love of his, whereby he gave himself for us to justify us; but Christ's Spirit must likewise subdue our hearts, and sanctify them to love him, without which all motives would be ineffectual. Our disposition must be changed, we must be new creatures; they seek for heaven in hell that seek for spiritual love in an unchanged heart. When a child obeys his father, it is so from reasons persuading him, as likewise from a child-like nature which giveth strength to these reasons: it is natural for a child of God to love Christ so far as he is renewed, not only from inducement of reason so to do, but likewise from an inward principle and work of grace, whence those reasons have their chief forces; first, we are made partakers of the divine nature, and then we are easily induced and led by Christ's Spirit to spiritual duties.

[Chapter XX.—*The spiritual government of Christ is joined with judgment and wisdom.*]

The second conclusion is, that Christ's government in his church and in his children is a wise and well-ordered government, because it is called judgment, and judgment is the life and soul of wisdom. Of this conclusion there are two branches: 1. That the spiritual government of Christ in us is joined with judgment and wisdom. 2. Wheresoever true spiritual wisdom and judgment is, there likewise the Spirit of Christ bringeth in his gracious government. For the first, a well-guided life by the rules of Christ standeth with the strongest and highest reason of all; and therefore holy men are called the 'children of wisdom,' Luke vii. 31, and are able to justify, both by reason and experience, all the ways of wisdom. Opposite courses are folly and madness. Hereupon St Paul saith, that a 'spiritual man judgeth all things,' 1 Cor. ii. 15, that appertain to him, and is judged of none that are of an inferior rank, because they want spiritual light and sight to judge; yet this sort of men will be judging, 'and speaking ill of what they know not,' 2 Pet. ii. 12; they step from ignorance to prejudice and rash censure, without taking right judgment in their way, and therefore their judgment comes to nothing. But the judgment of a spiritual man, so far forth as he is spiritual, shall stand, because it is agreeable to the nature of things: as things are in themselves, so they are in his judgment. As God is in himself infinite in goodness and majesty, &c., so he is to him; he ascribes to God in his heart his divinity and all his excellencies. As Christ is in himself the only mediator, and all in all in the church, Col. iii. 11, so he is to him, by making Christ so in his heart. 'As all things are dung in comparison of Christ,' Phil. iii. 8, so they are to Paul, a sanctified man. As the very worst thing in religion, 'the reproach of Christ is better than the pleasure of sin for a season,' Heb. xi. 26; so it is to Moses, a man of a right esteem. 'As one day in the courts of God is better than a thousand elsewhere,' Ps. lxxxiv. 10, so it is to David, a man of a reformed judgment. There is a conformity of a good man's judgment to things as they are in themselves, and according to the difference or agreement put by God in things, so doth his judgment differ or agree.

Truth is truth, and error, error, and that which is unlawful is unlawful, whether men think so or no. God hath put an eternal difference betwixt light and darkness, good and ill, which no creature's conceit can alter; and therefore no man's judgment is the measure of things further than it agrees to truth stamped upon things themselves by God. Hereupon, because a wise man's judgment agrees to the truth of things, a wise man may in some sense be said to be the measure of things; and the judgment of one holy wise man to be preferred before a thousand others. Such men usually are immoveable as the sun in its course, because they think, and speak, and live by rule. 'A Joshua and his house will serve God,' Josh. xxiv. 15, whatsoever others do, and will run a course contrary to the world, because their judgments lead them a contrary way. Hence it is that Satan hath a spite at the eye of the soul, the judgment, to put out that by ignorance and false reason, for he cannot rule in any until either he hath taken away or perverted judgment: he is a prince of darkness, and ruleth in darkness of the understanding, Therefore he must first be cast out of the understanding by the prevailing of truth, and planting it in the soul. Those therefore that are enemies of knowledge help Satan and antichrist, whose kingdom, like Satan's, is a kingdom of darkness, to erect their throne. Hence it is promised by Christ, that 'the Holy Ghost shall convince the world of judgment,' John xvi. 8; that is, that he is resolved to set up a throne of government, because the great lord of misrule, 'Satan, the prince of the world,' is judged by the gospel, and the Spirit accompanying it, his impostures are discovered, his enterprises laid open; therefore when the gospel was spread, the oracles ceased, 'Satan fell from heaven like lightning,' Luke x. 18; men were 'translated out of his kingdom into Christ's,' Col. i. 13. Where prevailing is by lies, there discovery is victory; 'they shall proceed no further, for their folly shall be manifest to all,' 2 Tim. iii. 9. So that manifestation of error giveth a stop to it, for none will willingly be deceived. Let truth have full scope without check or restraint, and let Satan and his instruments do their worst, they shall not prevail; as Jerome saith of the Pelagians in his time.* The discovery of your opinions is the vanquishing of them, your blasphemies appear at the first blush.

Use. Hence we learn the necessity, that the understanding be principled with supernatural knowledge, for the well managing of a Christian conversation.

There must be light to discover a further end than nature, for which we are Christians, and a rule suitable directing to that end, which is the will of God in Christ, discovering his good pleasure toward us, and our duty towards him; and in virtue of this discovery we do all that we do, that any way may further our reckoning: 'The eye must first be single, and then the whole body and frame of our conversation will be light,' Matt. vi. 22; otherwise both we and our course of life are nothing but darkness. The whole conversation of a Christian is nothing else but knowledge digested into will, affection, and practice. If the first concoction in the stomach be not good, that in the liver cannot be good; so if there be error in the judgment, it mars the whole practice, as an error in the foundation doth the building: God will have 'no blind sacrifices, no unreasonable services,' Mal. i. 13, but will have us to 'love him with all our mind,' Rom. xii. 1, that is, wih our understanding part, as well as 'with all our hearts,' Luke x. 27, that is, the affecting part of the soul.

This order of Christ's government by judgment is agreeable unto the soul, and God delighteth to preserve the manner of working peculiar unto man, that is, to do what he doth out of judgment: as grace supposeth

* Sententias vestras prodidisse, superasse est.—Hieron. in Epist. ad Ctesiphon: rima fronte apparent blasphemiæ.

nature as founded upon it, so the frame of grace preserveth the frame of nature in man. And, therefore Christ bringeth all that is good in the soul through judgment, and that so sweetly, that many out of a dangerous error think, that that good which is in them and issueth from them is from themselves, and not from the powerful work of grace. As in evil, the devil so subtilly leadeth us according to the stream of our own nature, that men think that Satan had no hand in their sin; but here a mistake is with little peril, because we are ill of ourselves, and the devil doth but promote what ill he findeth in us. But there are no seeds of supernatural goodness at all in us. God findeth nothing in us but enmity; only he hath engraven this in our nature to incline in general to that which we judge to be good. Now when he shall clearly discover what is good in particular, we are carried to it; and when convincingly he shall discover that which is ill, we abhor it as freely as we embraced it before.

From whence we may know, when we work as we should do or no, that is, when we do what we do out of inward principles, when we fall not upon that which is good, only because we are so bred, or because such or such whom we respect do so, or because we will maintain a side, so making religion a faction; but out of judgment, when what we do that is good, we first judge it in ourselves so to be; and what we abstain from that is ill, we first judge it to be ill from an inward judgment. A sound Christian, as he enjoyeth the better part, so hath first made choice of it with Mary, Luke x. 42; he established all his thoughts by counsel, Prov. xx. 18. God indeed useth carnal men to very good service, but without a thorough altering and conviction of their judgment.* He worketh by them, but not in them, therefore they do neither approve the good they do, nor hate the evil thev abstain from.

[CHAPTER XXI.—*Where true wisdom and judgment is, there Christ sets up his government.*]

The second branch is, that wheresoever true wisdom and judgment is, there Christ hath set up his government; because where wisdom is, it directs us not only to understand, but to order our ways aright. Where Christ by his Spirit as a prophet teaches, he likewise as a king by his Spirit subdueth the heart to obedience of what is taught. This is that teaching which is promised of God, when not only the brain, but the heart itself, is taught: when men do not only know what they should do, but are taught the very doing of it; they are not only taught that they should love, fear, and obey, but they are taught love itself, and fear and obedience itself. Christ sets up his chair in the very heart, and alters the frame of that, and makes his subjects good, together with teaching of them to be good. Other princes can make good laws, but they 'cannot write them in their people's hearts,' Jer. xxxii. 40. This is Christ's prerogative, he infuseth into his subjects his own Spirit, 'Upon him there doth not only rest the spirit of wisdom and understanding, but likewise the spirit of the fear of the Lord,' Isa. xi. 2. The knowledge which we have of him from himself, is a transforming knowledge, 2 Cor. iii. 18. The same Spirit that enlighteneth the mind, inspireth gracious inclinations into the will and affections, and infuseth strength into the whole man. As a gracious man judgeth as he should, so he affecteth and doth as he judgeth, his life is a commentary of his inward

* 'Judgments,' in A and B.

man; there is a sweet harmony betwixt God's truth, his judgment, and his whole conversation. The heart of a Christian is like Jerusalem when it was at the best, a city compact within itself, Psa. cxii. 3; where are set up the thrones of judgment, Ps. cxxii. 5. Judgment should have a throne in the heart of every Christian. Not that judgment alone will work a change, there must be grace to alter the bent and sway of the will, before it will yield to be wrought upon by the understanding. But God hath so joined these together, as that whensoever he doth savingly shine upon the understanding, he giveth a soft and pliable heart; for without a work upon the heart by the Spirit of God, it will follow its own inclination to that which it affecteth, whatsoever the judgment shall say to the contrary: there is no connatural proportion betwixt an unsanctified heart and a sanctified judgment. For the heart unaltered will not give leave to the judgment coldly and soberly to conclude what is best: as the sick man whilst his aguish distemper corrupteth his taste, is rather desirous to please that, than to hearken what the physician shall speak. Judgment hath not power over itself where the will is unsubdued, for the will and affections bribe it to give sentence for them, when any profit or pleasure shall come in competition with that which the judgment in general only shall think to be good; and, therefore, it is for the most part in the power of the heart, what the understanding shall judge and determine in particular things. Where grace hath brought the heart under, there unruly passions do not cast such a mist before the understanding, but that in particular it seeth that which is best; and base respects, springing from self-love, do not alter the case, and bias the judgment into a contrary way; but that which is good in itself shall be good unto us, although it cross our particular worldly interests.

Use. The right conceiving of this hath an influence into practice, which hath drawn me to a more full explanation: this will teach us the right method of godliness, to begin with judgment, and then to beg of God, together with illumination, holy inclinations of our will and affections, that so a perfect government may be set up in our hearts, and that our 'knowledge may be with all judgment,' Phil. i. 9, that is, with experience and feeling. When the judgment of Christ is set up in our judgments, and thence, by the Spirit of Christ, brought into our hearts, then it is in its proper place and throne; and until then, truth doth us no good, but helpeth to condemn us. The life of a Christian is a regular life, and he that walketh by the rule, Gal. vi. 16, of the new creature, peace shall be upon him: 'he that despiseth his way and loveth to live at large, seeking all liberty to the flesh, shall die,' Prov. xix. 16. And it is made good by St Paul, 'If we live after the flesh, we shall die,' Rom. viii. 13.

We learn likewise, that men of an ill governed life have no true judgment: no wicked man can be a wise man. And that without Christ's Spirit the soul is in confusion, without beauty and form, as all things were in the chaos before the creation. The whole soul is out of joint till it be set in again by him whose office is to 'restore all things.' The baser part of the soul which should be subject, ruleth all, and keepeth under that little truth that is in the understanding, holding it captive to base affections; and Satan by corruption getteth all the holds of the soul, till Christ, stronger than he, cometh, and driveth him out, and taketh possession of all the powers and parts of soul and body, to be weapons of righteousness, to serve him, and then new lords new laws. Christ as a new conqueror changeth the fundamental laws of old Adam, and establisheth a government of his own.

[Chapter XXII.—*Christ's government is victorious.*]

The third conclusion is, that this government is victorious. The reasons are:—

1. Because Christ hath conquered all in his own person first, and he is God over all, blessed for evermore; and therefore over 'sin, death, hell, Satan, the world,' &c., Rom. ix. 5. And as he hath overcome them in himself, so he overcomes them in our hearts and consciences. We use to say, conscience maketh a man a king or a caitiff, because it is planted in us to judge for God, either with us or against us. Now if natural conscience be so forcible, what will it be when besides its own light it hath the light of divine truth put into it? It will undoubtedly prevail, either to make us hold up our heads with boldness, or abase us beneath ourselves. If it subject itself by grace to Christ's truth, then it boldly overlooks death, hell, judgment, and all spiritual enemies, because then Christ sets up his kingdom in the conscience, and makes it a kind of paradise.

The sharpest conflict which the soul hath is between the conscience and God's justice: now if the conscience, sprinkled with the blood of Christ, hath prevailed over assaults fetched from the justice of God as now satisfied by Christ, it will prevail over all other opposition whatsoever.

2. We are to encounter with accursed and damned enemies; therefore, if they begin to fall before the Spirit in us, they shall fall: if they rise up again, it is to have the greater fall.

3. The Spirit of truth, to whose tuition Christ hath committed his church, and the truth of the Spirit, which is the sceptre of Christ, abide for ever; therefore the soul begotten by the immortal seed of the Spirit, 1 Pet. i. 23, and this truth, must not only live for ever, but likewise prevail over all that oppose it, for both the word and Spirit are mighty in operation, Heb. iv. 12; and if the ill spirit be never idle in those whom God delivereth up to him, we cannot think that the Holy Spirit will be idle in those whose leading and government is committed to him. No; as he dwelleth in them, so he will drive out all that rise up against him, until he be all in all.

What is spiritual is eternal. Truth is a beam of Christ's Spirit, both in itself and as it is ingrafted into the soul, therefore it, and the grace, though little, wrought by it, will prevail. A little thing in the hand of a giant will do great matters. A little faith strengthened by Christ will work wonders.

4. 'To him that hath shall be given,' Matt. xxv. 29; the victory over any corruption or temptation is a pledge of final victory. As Joshua said when he set his foot upon the five kings which he conquered, 'Thus God shall do with all our enemies,' Josh. x. 25; heaven is ours already, only we strive till we have full possession.

5. Christ as king brings in a commanding light into the soul, and bows the neck, and softens the iron sinew of the inner man; and where he begins to rule, he rules for ever, 'his kingdom hath no end,' Luke i. 33.

6. The end of Christ's coming was to destroy the works of the devil, both for us and in us; and the end of the resurrection was, as to seal unto us the assurance of his victory; so, 1, To quicken our souls from death in sin; 2, To free our souls from such snares and sorrows of spiritual death as accompany the guilt of sin; 3, To raise them up more comfortable, as the sun breaks forth more gloriously out of a thick cloud; 4, To raise us out of particular slips and failings, stronger; 5, To raise us out of all troublesome and dark conditions of this life; and, 6, At length to raise our

bodies out of the dust. For the same power that the Spirit shewed in raising Christ, our head, from the sorrows of death, and the lowest degree of his abasement; the same power obtained by the death of Christ from God, now appeased by that sacrifice, will the Spirit shew in the church, which is his body, and in every particular member thereof.

And this power is conveyed by faith, whereby, after union with Christ in both his estates of humiliation and exaltation, we see ourselves not only 'dead with Christ, but risen and sitting together with him in heavenly places,' Eph. ii. 6. Now we, apprehending ourselves to be dead and risen, and thereupon victorious over all our enemies in our head, and apprehending that his scope in all this is to conform us to himself, we are by this faith changed into his likeness, 2 Cor. iii. 18, and so become conquerors over all our spiritual enemies, as he is, by that power which we derive from him who is the storehouse of all spiritual strength for all his. Christ at length will have his end in us, and faith resteth assured of it, and this assurance is very operative, stirring us up to join with Christ in his ends.

And so for the church in general, by Christ it will have its victory: Christ is 'that little stone cut out of the mountain without hands, that breaketh in pieces that goodly image,' Dan. ii. 35, that is, all opposite government, until it become 'a great mountain, and filleth the whole earth.' So that the stone that was cut out of the mountain, becomes a mountain itself at length. Who art thou, then, O mountain, that thinkest to stand up against this mountain? All shall lie flat and level before it: he will bring down all mountainous, high, exalted thoughts, and lay the pride of all flesh low. When chaff strives against the wind, stubble against the fire, when the heel kicks against the pricks, when the potsherd strives with the potter, when man strives against God, it is easy to know on which side the victory will go. The winds may toss the ship wherein Christ is, but not overturn it. The waves may dash against the rock, but they do but break themselves against it.

Object. If this be so, why is it thus with the church of God, and with many a gracious Christian? the victory seemeth to go with the enemy.

Ans. For answer, remember, 1, God's children usually in their troubles overcome by suffering; here lambs overcome lions, and doves eagles, by suffering, that herein they may be conformable to Christ, who conquered most when he suffered most; together with Christ's kingdom of patience there was a kingdom of power.

2. This victory is by degrees, and therefore they are too hasty-spirited that would conquer so soon as they strike the first stroke, and be at the end of their race at the first setting forth; the Israelites were sure of their victory in their voyage *(f)* to Canaan, yet they must fight it out. God would not have us presently forget what cruel enemies Christ hath overcome for us; 'Destroy them not, lest the people forget it, saith the Psalmist, Ps. lix. 11. That so by the experience of that annoyance we have by them, we might be kept in fear to come under the power of them.

3. That God often worketh by contraries: when he means to give victory, he will suffer us to be foiled at first; when he means to comfort, he will terrify first; when he means to justify, he will condemn us first; whom he means to make glorious, he will abase first. A Christian conquers, even when he is conquered; when he is conquered by some sins, he gets victory over others more dangerous, as spiritual pride, security, &c.

4. That Christ's work, both in the church and in the hearts of Christians, often goeth backward, that it may go the better forward. As seed rots in

the ground in the winter time, but after comes better up, and the harder the winter the more flourishing the spring, so we learn to stand by falls, and get strength by weakness discovered—*virtutis custos infirmitas*—we take deeper root by shaking; and, as torches flame brighter by moving, thus it pleaseth Christ, out of his freedom, in this manner to maintain his government in us. Let us herein labour to exercise our faith, that it may answer Christ's manner of carriage towards us; when we are foiled, let us believe we shall overcome; when we are fallen, let us believe we shall rise again. Jacob, after he had a 'blow upon which he halted, yet would not give over wrestling,' Gen. xxxii. 24, till he had gotten the blessing; so let us never give over, but in our thoughts knit the beginning, progress, and end together, and then we shall see ourselves in heaven out of the reach of all enemies. Let us assure ourselves that God's grace, even in this imperfect estate, is stronger than man's free will in the state of first perfection, being* founded now in Christ, who, as he is the author, so will be 'the finisher, of our faith,' Heb. xii. 2; we are under a more gracious covenant.

That † which some say of faith rooted, *fides radicata*, that it continueth, but weak faith may come to nothing, seemeth to be crossed by this Scripture; for, as the strongest faith may be shaken, so the weakest where truth is, is so far rooted, that it will prevail. Weakness with watchfulness will stand out, when strength with too much confidence faileth. Weakness, with acknowledging of it, is the fittest seat and subject for God to perfect his strength in; for consciousness of our infirmities driveth us out of ourselves to him in whom our strength lieth.

Hereupon it followeth that weakness may stand with the assurance of salvation; the disciples, notwithstanding all their weaknesses, are bidden to rejoice, Luke x. 20, that their names are written in heaven. Failings, with conflict, in sanctification should not weaken the peace of our justification, and assurance of salvation. It mattereth not so much what ill is in us, as what good; not what corruptions, but how we stand affected to them; not what our particular failings be, so much as what is the thread and tenor of our lives; for Christ's mislike of that which is amiss in us, redounds not to the hatred of our persons,‡ but to the victorious subduing of all our infirmities.

Some have, after conflict, wondered at the goodness of God, that so little and shaking faith should have upheld them in so great combats, when Satan had almost catched them. And, indeed, it is to be wondered how much a little grace will prevail with God for acceptance, and over our enemies for victory, if the heart be upright. Such is the goodness of our sweet Saviour, that he delighteth still to shew his strength in our weakness.

Use 1. First, therefore, for the great consolation of poor and weak Christians, let them know, that a spark from heaven, though kindled under greenwood that sobs (*g*) and smokes, yet it will consume all at last. Love once kindled is strong as death, much water cannot quench it, and therefore it is called a vehement flame, or flame of God, Cant. viii. 6, kindled in the heart by the Holy Ghost; that little that is in us is fed with an everlasting spring. As the fire that came down from heaven in Elias his time, 1 Kings xviii. 38, licked up all the water, to shew that it came from God, so will this fire spend all our corruption; no affliction without, or corruption within, shall quench it. In the morning we see oft clouds gather about the sun, as if they would hide it, but the sun wasteth them by little and little, till it come to its full strength. At the first, fears and doubts hinder

* 'And it is,' in A. † 'That . . . lieth,' added first in B. ‡ 'Person,' in A and B.

the breaking out of this fire, until at length it gets above them all, and Christ prevails; and then he backs his own graces in us. Grace conquers us first, and we by it conquer all things else; whether it be corruptions within us, or temptations without us.

The church of Christ, begotten by the word of truth, hath the doctrine of the apostles for her crown, and tramples the moon, that is, the world, and all worldly things, 'under her feet,' Rev. xii. 1; 'every one that is born of God overcometh the world,' 1 John v. 4. Faith, whereby especially Christ rules, sets the soul so high, that it overlooks all other things as far below, as having represented to it, by the Spirit of Christ, riches, honour, beauty, pleasures of a higher nature.

Now that we may not come short of the comfort intended, there are two things especially to be taken notice of by us: 1. Whether there be such a judgment or government set up in us, to which this promise of victory is made. 2. Some rules or directions how we are to carry ourselves, that the judgment of Christ in us may indeed be victorious.

The evidences whereby we may come to know that Christ's judgment in us is such as will be victorious, are, 1, If we be able from experience to justify all Christ's ways, let flesh and blood say what it can to the contrary, and can willingly subscribe to that course which God hath taken in Christ, to bring us to heaven, and still approve a further measure of grace than we have attained unto, and project and forecast for it. No other men can justify their courses, when their conscience is awaked. 2. When reasons of religion be the strongest reasons with us, and prevail more than reasons fetched from worldly policy. 3. When we are so true to our ends and fast to our rule, as no hopes or fears can sway us another way, but still we are looking what agrees or differs from our rule. 4. When we 'can do nothing against the truth, but for the truth,' 2 Cor. xiii. 8, as being dearer to us than our lives; truth hath not this sovereignty in the heart of any carnal man. 5. When if we had liberty to choose under whose government we would live, yet out of a delight in the inner man to Christ's government we would make choice of him only to rule us before any other, for this argues, that we are like-minded to Christ, a free and a voluntary people, and not compelled unto Christ's service, otherwise than by the sweet constraint of love. When we are so far in liking with the government of Christ's Spirit, that we are willing to resign up ourselves to him in all things, for then his kingdom is come unto us, when our wills are brought to his will. It is the bent of our wills that maketh us good or ill.

6. A well ordered uniform life, not by fits or starts, shews a well ordered heart a ɪn a cloc;k when the hammer strikes well, and the hand of the dial points well, it is a sign that the wheels are right set. 7. When Christ's will cometh in competition with any earthly loss or gain, yet if then, in that particular case, the heart will stoop to Christ, it is a true sign; for the truest trial of the power of grace is in such particular cases which touch us nearest, for there our corruption maketh the greatest head. When Christ came near home to the young man, Matt. x. 22, in the gospel, he lost a disciple of him. 8. When we can practise duties pleasing to Christ, though contrary to flesh, and the course of the world, and when we can overcome ourselves in that evil to which our nature is prone, and standeth so much inclined unto, and which agreeth to the sway of the times, and which others lie enthralled under, as desire of revenge, hatred of enemies, private ends, &c., then it appears that grace is in us above nature, heaven above earth, and will have the victory.

For the further clearing of this and helping of us in our trial, we must know there be three degrees of victory. 1. When we resist though we be foiled. 2. When grace gets the better though with conflict. 3. When all corruption is perfectly subdued. Now we have strength but only to resist, yet we may know Christ's government in us will be victorious, because what is said of the devil is said of all our spiritual enemies, 'If we resist, they shall in time fly from us,' James iv. 7; because 'stronger is he that is in us,' that taketh part with his own grace, 'than he that is in the world,' 1 John iv. 4. And if we may hope for victory upon bare resistance, what may we not hope for when the Spirit hath gotten the upper hand?

[Chapter XXIII.—*Means to make Grace victorious.*]

For the second, that is, directions.

We must know, though Christ hath undertaken this victory, yet he accomplisheth it by training us up to fight his battles; he overcometh in us, by making us 'wise to salvation,' 2 Tim. iii. 15; and in what degree we believe Christ will conquer, in that degree we will endeavour by his grace that we may conquer; for faith is an obedient and a wise grace. Christ maketh us wise to ponder and weigh things, and thereupon to rank and order them so as we may make the fitter choice of what is best. Some rules to help us in judging are these:

(1.) To judge of things as they help or hinder the main; (2.) as they further or hinder our reckoning; (3.) as they make us more or less spiritual, and so bring us nearer to the fountain of goodness, God himself; (4.) as they bring us peace or sorrow at the last; (5.) as they commend us more or less to God, and wherein we shall approve ourselves to him most; (6.) likewise to judge of things now, as we shall do hereafter when the soul shall be best able to judge, as when we are under any public calamity, or at the hour of death, when the soul gathereth itself from all other things to itself. (7.) Look back to former experience, see what is most agreeable unto it, what was best in our worst times. If grace is or was best then, it is best now. And (8.) labour to judge of things as he doth who must judge us, and as holy men judge, who are led by the* Spirit; more particularly, (9.) what those judge, that have no interest in any benefit that may come by the thing which is in question: for outward things blind the eyes even of the wise; we see papists are most corrupt in those things where their honour, ease, or profit is engaged; but in the doctrine of the Trinity, which doth not touch upon these things, they are sound. But it is not sufficient that judgment be right, but likewise ready and strong.

1. Where Christ establisheth his government, he inspireth care to keep the judgment clear and fresh, for whilst the judgment standeth straight and firm, the whole frame of the soul continueth strong and impregnable. True judgment in us advanceth Christ, and Christ will advance it. All sin is either from false principles, or ignorance, or mindlessness, or unbelief of true. By inconsideration and weakness of assent, Eve lost her hold at first, Gen. iii. 6. It is good, therefore, to store up true principles in our hearts, and to refresh them often, that in virtue of them our affections and actions may be more vigorous. When judgment is fortified, evil finds no entrance, but good things have a side within us, to entertain them. Whilst true convincing light continueth, we will not do the least ill of sin for the greatest

* 'His.' in A and B.

ill of punishment. 'In vain is the net spread in the eyes of that which hath wings,' Prov. i. 17. Whilst the soul is kept aloft, there is little danger of snares below; we lose our high estimation of things before we can be drawn to any sin.

And because knowledge and affection mutually help one another, it is good to keep up our affections of love and delight, by all sweet inducements and divine encouragements; for what the heart liketh best, the mind studieth most. Those that can bring their hearts to delight in Christ know most of his ways. Wisdom loveth him* that loves her. Love is the best entertainer of truth; and when it is not 'entertained in the love of it,' 2 Thess. ii. 10, being so lovely as it is, it leaveth the heart, and will stay no longer. It hath been a prevailing way to begin by withdrawing the love to corrupt the judgment; because as we love, so we use to judge; and therefore it is hard to be affectionate and wise in earthly things; but in heavenly things, where there hath been a right information of the judgment before, the more our affections grow, the better and clearer our judgments will be, because our affections, though strong, can never rise high enough to the excellency of the things. We see in the martyrs, when the sweet doctrine of Christ had once gotten their hearts, it could not be gotten out again by all the torments the wit of cruelty could devise. If Christ hath once possessed the affections, there is no dispossessing of him again. A fire in the heart overcometh all fires without.

3. Wisdom likewise teacheth us wherein our weakness lieth, and our enemy's strength, whereby a jealous fear is stirred up in us, whereby we are preserved; for out of this godly jealousy we keep those provocations which are active and working, from that which is passive and catching in us, as we keep fire from powder. They that will hinder the generation of noisome creatures will hinder the conception first, by keeping male and female asunder. This jealousy will be much furthered by observing strictly what hath helped or hindered a gracious temper in us; and it will make us take heed that we consult not with flesh and blood in ourselves or others. How else can we think that Christ will lead us out to victory, when we take counsel of his and our enemies?

4. Christ maketh us likewise careful to attend all means whereby fresh thoughts and affections may be stirred up and preserved in us. Christ so honoureth the use of means, and the care he putteth into us, that he ascribeth both preservation and victory unto our care of keeping ourselves. 'He that is begotten of God keepeth himself,' 1 John v. 18, but not by himself, but by the Lord, in dependence on him on the use of means. We are no longer safe than wise to present ourselves to all good advantages of acquaintance, &c. By going out of God's walks we go out of his government, and so lose our frame, and find ourselves overspread quickly with a contrary disposition. When we draw near to Christ, James iv. 8, in his ordinances, he draws near unto us.

5. Keep grace in exercise. It is not sleepy habits, but grace in exercise, that preserveth us. Whilst the soul is in some civil or sacred employment, corruptions within us are much suppressed, and Satan's passages stopped, and the Spirit hath a way open to enlarge itself in us, and likewise the guard of angels then most nearly attends us; which course often prevails more against our spiritual enemies than direct opposition. It stands upon Christ's honour to maintain those that are in his work.

6. Sixthly, in all directions we must look up to Christ the quickening

* 'Them,' in A and B.

Spirit, and resolve in his strength. Though we are exhorted to 'cleave to the Lord with full purpose of heart,' Acts xi. 23, yet we must pray with David, 'Lord, for ever keep it in the thoughts of our hearts, and prepare our hearts unto thee,' 1 Chron. xxix. 18. Our hearts are of themselves very loose and unsettled, 'Lord, unite our hearts unto thee to fear thy name,' Ps. lxxxvi. 11, or else, without him, our best purposes will fall to the ground. It is a pleasing request, out of love to God, to beg such a frame of soul from him, wherein he may take delight; and therefore in the use of all the means we must send up our desires and complaints to heaven to him for strength and help, and then we may be sure that 'he will bring forth judgment unto victory.'

7. Lastly, it furthers the state of the soul, to know what frame it should be in, that so we may order our souls accordingly. We should always be fit for communion with God, and be heavenly-minded in earthly business, and be willing to be taken off from them, to redeem time for better things. We should be ready at all times to depart hence, and to live in such a condition as we would be content to die in. We should have hearts prepared for every good duty, open to all good occasions, and shut to all temptations, keeping our watch, and being always ready armed. So far as we come short of these things, so far we have just cause to be humbled, and yet press forward, that we may gain more upon ourselves, and make these things more familiar and lovely unto us; and when we find our souls any ways falling downwards, it is best to raise them up presently by some waking meditations, as of the presence of God, of the strict reckoning we are to make, of the infinite love of God in Christ, and the fruits of it, of the excellency of a Christian's calling, of the short and uncertain time of this life; how little good all those things that steal away our hearts will do us ere long, and how it shall be for ever with us thereafter, as we spend this little time well or ill, &c. The more we give way for such considerations to sink into our hearts, the more we shall rise nearer to that state of soul which we shall enjoy in heaven. When we grow regardless of keeping our souls, then God recovers our taste of good things again by sharp crosses. Thus David, Solomon, Samson, &c., were recovered. It is much easier kept than recovered.

Object. But, notwithstanding my striving, I seem to stand at a stay.

Ans. 1. Grace, as the seed in the parable, grows, we know not how, yet at length, when God seeth fittest, we shall see that all our endeavour hath not been in vain. The tree falleth upon the last stroke, yet all the former strokes help it forward.

Ans. 2. Sometimes victory is suspended because some Achan is not found out, Judges xx. 26, or because we are not humble enough, as Israel had the worst against the Benjamites till they fasted and prayed; or because we betray our helps, and stand not upon our guard, and yield not presently to the motions of the Spirit, which mindeth us always of the best things, if we would regard it. Our own consciences will tell us, if we give them leave to speak, that some sinful favouring of ourselves is the cause. The way in this case to prevail is, 1, To get the victory over the pride of our own nature, by taking shame to ourselves, in humble confession to God; and then, 2, To overcome the unbelief of our hearts, by yielding to the promise of pardon; and then, 3, In confidence of Christ's assistance, to set ourselves against those sins which have prevailed over us; and then prevailing over ourselves, we shall easily prevail over all our enemies, and conquer all conditions we shall be brought into.

[Chapter XXIV.—*All should side with Christ.*]

Use 2. If Christ will have the victory, then it is the best way for nations and states to 'kiss the Son,' Ps. ii. 12, and to embrace Christ and his religion, to side with Christ, and to own his cause in the world. His side will prove the stronger side at last. Happy are we if Christ honour us so much as to use our help 'to fight his battle against the mighty,' Judges v. 23. True religion in a state is as the main pillar of a house, and staff of a tent that upholds all. 2. So for families, let Christ be the chief governor of the family; and 3, Let every one be as a house of Christ, to dwell familiarly in, and to rule. Where Christ is, all happiness must follow. If Christ goeth, all will go. Where Christ's government in his ordinances and his Spirit is, there all subordinate government will prosper. Religion inspireth life and grace into all other things; all other virtues, without it they are but as a fair picture without a head. Where Christ's laws are written in the heart, there all other good laws are best obeyed. None despise man's law but those that despise Christ's first. *Nemo humanam authoritatem contemnit, nisi qui divinam prius contempsit.* Of all persons, a man guided by Christ is the best; and of all creatures in the world, a man guided by will and affection, next the devil, is the worst. The happiness of weaker things stands in being ruled by stronger. It is best for a blind man to be guided by him that hath sight, it is best for sheep, and such like shiftless creatures, to be guided by man, and it is happiest for man to be guided by Christ, because his government is so victorious that it frees us from the fear and danger of our greatest enemies, and tends to bring us to the greatest happiness that our nature is capable of. This should make us to joy when Christ reigneth in us. When 'Solomon was crowned, the people shouted,' so that the earth rang,' 1 Kings i. 39, 40. Much more should we rejoice in Christ our king.

And likewise for those whose souls are dear unto us, our endeavour should be that Christ may reign in them also, that they may be baptized by Christ with this fire, Matt. iii. 11, that these sparks may be kindled in them. Men labour to cherish the spirit and mettle, as they term it, of those they train up, because they think they will have use of it in the manifold affairs and troubles of this life. Oh, but let us cherish the sparks of grace in them; for a natural spirit in great troubles will fail, but these sparks will make them conquerors over the greatest evils.

Use 3. If Christ's judgment shall be victorious, then popery, being an opposite frame, set up by the wit of man to maintain stately idleness, must fall. And it is fallen already in the hearts of those upon whom Christ hath shined. It is a lie, and founded upon a lie, upon the infallible judgment of a man subject to sin and error. When that which is taken for a principle of truth becomes a principle of error, the more relying upon it, the more danger.

[Chapter XXV.—*Christ's government shall be openly victorious.*]

It is not only said, *judgment shall be victorious, but that Christ will bring it openly forth to victory.* Whence we observe that grace shall be glory, and run into the eyes of all. Now Christ doth conquer, and hath his own ends, but it is in some sort invisibly. His enemies within and without us seem to have the better. But he will bring forth judgment unto victory, to the view of all. The wicked that now shut their eyes shall see it to their torment. It shall not be in the power of subtle men to see or not see what they would. Christ will have power over their hearts; and as his wrath shall immediately seize upon their souls against their wills, so will he have power over the eyes of their souls, to see and know what will increase their misery. Grief shall be fastened to all their senses, and their senses to grief.

Then all the false glosses which they put upon things shall be wiped off. Men are desirous to have the reputation of good, and yet the sweetness of ill; nothing so cordially opposed by them as that truth which layeth them open to themselves, and to the eyes of others, their chief care being how to daub with the world and their own consciences. But the time will come when they shall be driven out of this fools' paradise, and the more subtle their conveyance of things hath been, the more shall be their shame. Christ, whom God hath chosen to set forth the chief glory of his excellencies, is now veiled in regard of his body the church, but will come ere long to be glorious in his saints, 2 Thess. i. 10, and not lose the clear manifestation of any of his attributes; and will declare to all the world what he is, when there shall be no glory but that of Christ and his spouse. Those that are as smoking flax now shall then 'shine as the sun in the firmament,' Matt. xiii. 43, and their 'righteousness break forth as the noon-day,' Ps. xxxvii. 6.

The image of God in Adam had a commanding majesty in it, so that all creatures reverenced him; much more shall the image of God in the perfection of it command respect in all. Even now there is a secret awe put into the hearts of the greatest, towards those in whom they see any grace to shine, from whence it was that Herod feared John Baptist; but what will this be in their day of bringing forth, which is called 'the day of the revelation of the sons of God?' Rom. viii. 19.

There will be more glorious times when 'the kingdoms of the earth shall be the Lord Jesus Christ's,' Rev. xi. 10, and he shall reign for ever; then shall judgment and truth have its victory; then Christ will plead his own cause; truth shall no longer be called heresy and schism, nor heresy catholic doctrine; wickedness shall no longer go masked and disguised; goodness shall appear in its own lustre, and shine in its own beams; things shall be what they are, 'nothing is hidden but shall be laid open,' Matt. x. 26; iniquity shall not be carried in a mystery any longer; deep dissemblers that think to hide their counsels from the Lord shall walk no longer invisible as in the clouds. As * Christ will not quench the least spark kindled by himself, so will he damp the fairest blaze of goodly appearances which are not from above.

Use. If this were believed, men would make more account of sincerity, which will only give us boldness, and not seek for covershames; the confidence whereof, as it maketh men now more presumptuous, so it will expose them hereafter to the greater shame.

If judgment shall be brought forth to victory, then those that have been ruled by their own deceitful hearts and a spirit of error, shall be brought forth to disgrace; that God that hath joined grace and truth with honour, hath joined sin and shame together at last; all the wit and power of man can never be able to sever what God hath coupled. Truth and piety may be trampled upon for a time, but as the two witnesses, Rev. xi. 11, after

* 'As Christ . . . . above,' not in A, B, but in E.

they were slain rose again, and stood upon their feet, so whatsoever is of God shall at length stand upon its own bottom. There shall be a resurrection not only of bodies but of credits. Can we think that he that threw the angels out of heaven will suffer dust and worms' meat to run a contrary course, and to carry it away always so? No; as verily as Christ is 'King of kings and Lord of lords,' Rev. xix. 16, so will he dash all those pieces of earth 'which rise up against him, as a potter's vessel,' Ps. ii. 9. Was there ever any fierce against God and prospered? Job ix. 4. No; doubtless the rage of man shall turn to Christ's praise, Ps. lxxvi. 10. What was said of Pharaoh shall be said of all heady enemies, who had rather lose their souls than their wills, that they are but raised up for Christ to get himself glory in their confusion.

Let us, then, take heed that we follow not the ways of those men, whose ends we shall tremble at; there is not a more fearful judgment can befal the nature of man, than to be given up to a reprobate judgment of persons and things, because it cometh under a woe 'to call ill good, and good ill,' Isa. v. 20.

How will they be laden with curses another day, that abuse the judgment of others by sophistry and flattery, deceivers and being deceived? 2 Tim. iii. 13. Then the complaint of our first mother Eve will be taken up but fruitlessly, Gen. xiii. 3; the serpent hath deceived me; Satan in such and such hath deceived me; sin hath deceived me; a foolish heart hath deceived me. It is one of the highest points of wisdom to consider upon what grounds we venture our souls. Happy men will they be, who have by Christ's light a right judgment of things, and suffer that judgment to prevail over their hearts.

The soul of most men is drowned in their senses and carried away with weak opinions, raised from vulgar mistakes and shadows of things. And Satan is ready to enlarge the imagination of outward good and outward ill, and make it greater than it is, and spiritual things less, presenting them through false glasses. And so men, trusting in vanity, vanquish themselves in their own apprehensions. A woful condition, when both we and that which we highly esteem shall vanish together, which will be as truly as Christ's judgment shall come to victory; and in what measure the vain heart of man hath been enlarged, to conceive a greater good in things of this world than there is, by so much the soul shall be enlarged to be more sensible of misery when it sees its error. This is the difference betwixt a godly wise man and a deluded worldling; that which the one doth now judge to be vain, the other shall hereafter feel to be so when it is too late. But this is the vanity of our natures, that though we shun above all things to be deceived and mistaken in present things, yet in the greatest matters of all we are willingly ignorant and misled.

[Chapter XXVI.—*Christ alone advanceth this government.*]

The fifth conclusion is, that this government is set up and advanced by Christ alone; he bringeth judgment to victory. We both fight and prevail 'in the power of his might,' Eph. vi. 10; we overcome by the Spirit, obtained by 'the blood of the Lamb,' Rev. xii. 11.

It is he alone that 'teacheth our hands to war and fingers to fight,' Ps. cxliv. 1. Nature, as corrupted, favours its own being, and will maintain itself against Christ's government. Nature, simply considered, cannot raise itself above itself to actions spiritual of a higher order and nature; therefore the divine power of Christ is necessary to carry us above all our own strength, especially in duties wherein we meet with greater opposition; for there not only nature will fail us, but ordinary grace, unless there be a stronger and a new supply. In taking up a burden that is weightier than ordinary, if there be not a greater proportion of strength than weight, the undertaker will lie under it; so to every strong encounter there must be a new supply of strength, as in Peter, Matt. xxvi. 69, when he was assaulted with a stronger temptation, being not upheld and shored up with a mightier hand, notwithstanding former strength, foully fell. And being fallen, in our raisings up again it is Christ that must do the work, 1, By removing; or 2, Weakening; or 3, Suspending opposite hinderances; 4, And by advancing the power of his grace in us, to a further degree than we had before we fell; therefore when we are fallen, and by falls have gotten a bruise, let us go to Christ presently to bind us up again.

Use. Let us know, therefore, that it is dangerous to look for that from ourselves which we must have from Christ. Since the fall, all our strength lies in him, as Samson's in his hair, Judges xvi. 17; we are but subordinate agents, moving as we are moved, and working as we are first wrought upon, free so far forth as we are freed, no wiser nor stronger than he makes us to be for the present in anything we undertake.* It is his Spirit that actuates and enliveneth, and applieth that knowledge and strength we have, or else it faileth and lieth as useless in us; we work when we work upon a present strength; therefore dependent spirits are the wisest and the ablest. Nothing is stronger than humility, that goeth out of itself; or weaker than pride, that resteth upon its own bottom, *Frustra nititur qui non innititur;* and this should the rather be observed, because naturally we affect a kind of divinity, *affectatio divinitatis*, in setting upon actions in the strength of our own parts; whereas Christ saith, 'Without me you,' apostles that are in a state of grace, 'can do nothing,' John xv. 5, he doth not say you can do a little, but nothing. Of ourselves,† how easily are we overcome! how weak to resist! we are as reeds shaken with every wind; we shake at the very noise and thought of poverty, disgrace, losses, &c., we give in presently, we have no power over our eyes, tongues, thoughts, affections, but let sin pass in and out. How soon are we overcome of evil! whereas we should overcome evil with good. How many good purposes stick in the birth, and have no strength to come forth! all which shews how nothing we are without the Spirit of Christ. We see how weak the apostles themselves were, till they were endued with strength from above, Matt. xxvi. 69. Peter was blasted with the speech of a damsel, but after the Spirit of Christ fell upon them, the more they suffered, the more they were encouraged to suffer; their comforts grew with their troubles; therefore in all, especially difficult encounters, let us lift up our hearts to Christ, who hath Spirit enough for us all, in all our exigencies, and say with good Jehoshaphat, 'Lord, we know not what to do, but our eyes are towards thee,' 2 Chron. xx. 12; the battle we fight is thine, and the strength whereby we fight must be thine. If thou goest not out with us, we are sure to be foiled. Satan knows nothing can prevail against Christ, or those that rely upon his power; therefore his study is, how to keep us in ourselves, and in the creature: but we must carry this always in our minds, that that which is begun in self-confidence will end in shame.

* Sic se habent mortalium corda: quæ scimus, cum necesse non est, in necessitate nescimus.—*Ber*[*nard*] *de consid.*

† 'Of ourselves . . . . troubles,' added first in B.

The manner of Christ's *bringing forth judgment to victory*, is by letting us see a necessity of dependence upon him; hence proceed those spiritual desertions wherein he often leaveth us to ourselves, both in regard of grace and comfort, that we may know the spring head of these to be out of ourselves. Hence it is that in the mount, that is, in extremities, God is most seen, Gen. xxii. 13. Hence it is that we are saved by the grace of faith, that carrieth us out of ourselves to rely upon another; and that faith worketh best alone, when it hath least outward support. Hence it is, that we often fail in lesser conflicts, and stand out in greater, because in lesser we rest more in ourselves, in greater we fly to the rock of our salvation, which is higher than we, Ps. lxi. 2. Hence likewise it is, that we are stronger after foils, because hidden corruption, undiscerned before, is now discovered, and thence we are brought to make use of mercy pardoning, and power supporting. One main ground of this dispensation is, that we should know it is Christ that giveth both the will and the deed, and that as a voluntary work* according to his own good pleasure. And therefore we should 'work out our salvation in a jealous fear and trembling,' Phil. ii. 12, lest by unreverent and presumptuous walking, we give him cause to suspend his gracious influence, and to leave us to the darkness of our own heart.

Those that are under Christ's government have the spirit of revelation, whereby they see and feel a divine power sweetly and strongly enabling them for to preserve faith, when they feel the contrary, and hope in a state hopeless, and love to God under signs of his displeasure, and heavenly-mindedness in the midst of worldly affairs and allurements, drawing a contrary way. They feel a power preserving patience, nay, joy in the midst of causes of mourning, inward peace in the midst of assaults. Whence† is it that, when we are assaulted with temptation, and when compassed with troubles, we have stood out, but from a secret strength upholding us? To make so little grace so victorious over so great a mass of corruption, this requireth a spirit more than human; this is as to preserve fire in the sea, and a part of heaven even as it were in hell. Here we know where to have this power, and to whom to return the praise of it. And it is our happiness, that it is so safely hid in Christ for us, in one so near unto God and us. Since the fall, God will not trust us with our own salvation, but it is both purchased and kept by Christ for us, and we for it through faith, wrought by the power of God, and laying hold of the same: which power is gloriously set forth by St Paul, 1, To be a great power; 2, An exceeding power; 3, A working and a mighty power; 4, Such a power as was wrought in raising Christ from the dead, Eph. i. 19. That grace which is but a persuasive offer, and in our pleasure to receive or refuse, is not that grace which brings us to heaven; but God's people feel a powerful work of the Spirit, not only revealing unto us our misery, and deliverance through Christ, but emptying us of ourselves as being redeemed from ourselves, and infusing new life into us, and after strengthening us, and quickening of us when we droop and hang the wing, and never leaving us till perfect conquest.

[Chapter XXVII.—*Victory not to be had without fighting.*]

The sixth conclusion is, that this prevailing government shall not be without fighting. There can be no victory where there is no combat. In

* 'Worker,' in A and B. † 'Whence . . . us,' added in B.

Isaiah it is said, 'He shall bring judgment in truth,' Is. xlii. 3; here it is said, he shall send forth judgment unto victory. The word 'send forth' hath a stronger sense in the original (*h*), to send forth with force; to shew, that where his government is in truth, it will be opposed, until he getteth the upper hand. Nothing is so opposed as Christ and his government, both within us and without us. And within us most in our conversion, though corruption prevails not so far as to make void the powerful work of grace, yet there is not only a possibility of opposing, but a proneness to oppose, and not only a proneness, but an actual withstanding the working of Christ's Spirit, and that in every action, but yet no prevailing resistance so far as to make void the work of grace, but corruption in the issue yields to grace.

There is much ado to bring Christ into the heart, and to set a tribunal for him to judge there; there is an army of lusts [in] mutiny against him. The utmost strength of most men's endeavours and parts is to keep Christ from ruling in the soul; the flesh still laboureth to maintain its own regency, and therefore it cries down the credit of whatsoever crosseth it, as God's blessed ordinances, &c., and highly prizeth anything, though never so dead and empty, if it give way to the liberty of the flesh.

And no marvel if the spiritual government of Christ be so opposed: 1. Because it is government, and that limits the course of the will, and casteth a bridle upon its wanderings; everything natural resists what opposeth it; so corrupt will labours to bear down all laws, and counteth it a generous thing not to be awed, and an argument of a low spirit to fear any, even God himself, until unavoidable danger seizeth on men, and then those that feared least out of danger fear most in danger, as we see in Belshazzar, Dan. v. 6.

2. It is spiritual government, and therefore the less will flesh endure it. Christ's government bringeth the very thoughts and desires, which are the most immediate and free issue of the soul, into obedience. Though a man were of so composed a carriage, that his whole life were free from outward offensive breaches, yet with Christ to be 'carnally or worldly-minded is death,' Rom. viii. 6: he looketh on a worldly mind with a greater detestation than any one particular offence.*

But Christ's Spirit is in those who are in some degree earthly-minded.

Truth it is, but not as an allower and maintainer, but as an opposer, subduer, and in the end as a conqueror. Carnal men would fain bring Christ and the flesh together, and could be content with some reservation to submit to Christ; but Christ will be no underling to any base affection; and therefore, where there is allowance of ourselves in any sinful lust, it is a sign the keys were never given up to Christ to rule us.

3. Again,† this judgment is opposed, because it is judgment, and men love not to be judged and censured. Now Christ, in his truth, arraigneth them, giveth sentence against them, and bindeth them over to the latter judgment of the great day. And therefore they take upon them to judge that truth that must judge them; but truth will be too good for them. Man hath a day now, which St Paul calls 'man's day,' 1 Cor. iv. 33, wherein he getteth upon his bench, and usurpeth a judgment over Christ and his ways; but God hath a day wherein he will set all straight, and his judgment shall stand. And the saints shall have their time, when they shall

* Gravius est peccatum diligere quam perpetrare, &c.—*Greg*[*ory*]. *Moral.*, lib. xxv. cap. 11.

† 'Again . . . . opposed,' added in B.

sit in judgment upon them that judge them now, 1 Cor. vi. 2. In the mean time, Christ will rule in the midst of his enemies, Ps. cx. 3, even in the midst of our hearts.

Use. It is therefore no sign of a good condition to find all quiet, and nothing at odds; for can we think that corruption, which is the elder in us, and Satan, the strong man that keepeth many holds in us, will yield possession quietly? No; there is not so much as a thought of goodness discovered by him, but he joineth with corruption to kill it in the birth. And as Pharaoh's cruelty was especially against the male children, so Satan's malice is especially against the most religious and manly resolutions.

This, then, we are always to expect, that wheresoever Christ cometh, there will be opposition. When Christ was born, all Jerusalem was troubled; so when Christ is born in any man, the soul is in an uproar, and all because the heart is unwilling to yield up itself to Christ to rule it.

Wheresoever Christ cometh he breedeth division, not only, 1, between man and himself; but, 2, between man and man; and 3, between church and church: of which disturbance Christ is no more the cause than physic is of trouble in a distempered body, of which noisome humours are the proper cause; for the end of physic is the peace of humours. But Christ thinketh it fit that the thoughts of men's hearts should be discovered, and he is as well for the falling as the rising of many in Israel, Luke ii. 34.

Thus the desperate madness of men is laid open, that they had rather be under the guidance of their own lusts, and by consequence of Satan himself, to their endless destruction, than put their feet into Christ's fetters, and their necks under his yoke; whereas, indeed, Christ's service is the only true liberty. His yoke is an easy yoke, his burden but as the burden of wings to a bird, that maketh her fly the higher. Satan's government is rather a bondage than a government, unto which Christ giveth up those that shake off his own, for then he giveth Satan and his factors power over them, since they will not 'receive the truth in love,' 2 Thess. ii. 20: take him, Jesuit, take him, Satan, blind him and bind him and lead him to perdition. Those that take the most liberty to sin are the most perfect slaves, because most voluntary slaves. The will in everything is either the best or the worst; the further men go on in a wilful course, the deeper they sink in rebellion; and the more they cross Christ, doing what they will, the more they shall one day suffer what they would not. In the mean time, they are prisoners in their own souls, bound over in their consciences to the judgment of him after death, whose judgment they would none of in their lives. And is it not equal that they should feel him a severe judge to condemn them, whom they would not have a mild judge to rule them?

[CHAPTER XXVIII.—*Be encouraged to go on cheerfully, with confidence of prevailing.*]

For conclusion and general application of all that hath been spoken, unto ourselves. We see the conflicting, but yet sure and hopeful state of God's people. The victory lieth not upon us, but upon Christ, who hath taken upon him, as to conquer for us, so to conquer in us. The victory lieth neither in our own strength to get, nor in our enemies to defeat it. If it lay upon us, we might justly fear. But Christ will maintain his own government in us, and take our part against our corruptions; they are his enemies as well as ours. 'Let us therefore be strong in the Lord, and in the power of his might,' Eph. vi. 10. Let us not look so much who are our enemies, as who is our judge and captain, nor what they threaten, but what he promiseth. We have more for us than against us. What coward would not fight when he is sure of victory? None are here overcome, but he that will not fight. Therefore, when any base fainting seizeth upon us, let us lay the blame where it is to be laid.

Discouragement* rising from unbelief and ill report, brought upon the good land by the spies, moved God to swear in his wrath, that they should not enter into his rest. Let us take heed a spirit of faint-heartedness, rising from seeming difficulty and disgrace, cast upon God's good ways, provoke not God to keep us out of heaven. We see here what we may look for from heaven. O beloved, it is a comfortable thing to conceive of Christ aright, to know what love, mercy, strength we have laid up for us in the breast of Christ. A good conceit of the physician, we say, is half the cure; let† us make use of this his mercy and power every day, in our daily combats. Lord Jesus, thou hast promised not to quench the smoking flax, not to break the bruised reed; cherish thine own grace in me, leave me not to myself, the glory shall be thine. Let us not suffer Satan to transform Christ unto us, to be otherwise than he is to those that are his. Christ will not leave us, till he hath made us like himself, 'all glorious within and without, and presented us blameless before his Father,' Jude 24. What a comfort is this in our conflicts with our unruly hearts, that it shall not always be thus! Let us strive a little while, and we shall be happy for ever. Let us think when we are troubled with our sins, that Christ hath this in charge of his Father, 'that he shall not quench the smoking flax,' until he hath subdued all. This putteth a shield into our hands to beat back all 'the fiery darts of Satan,' Eph. vi. 16. He will object, (1.) thou art a great sinner; we may answer, Christ is a strong Saviour; but he will object, (2.) thou hast no faith, no love; yes, a spark of faith and love; but (3.) Christ will not regard that; yes, 'he will not quench the smoking flax;' but (4.) this is so little and weak, that it will vanish and come to nought: nay, but Christ will cherish it, until he hath brought judgment to victory. And thus much for our comfort we have already, that even when we first believed, we overcame God himself, as it were, by believing the pardon of all our sins; notwithstanding the guilt of our own consciences, and his absolute justice. Now having been prevailers with God, what shall stand against us if we can learn to make use of our faith?

O what a confusion is this to Satan, that he should labour to blow out a poor spark, and yet should not be able to quench it; that a grain of mustard seed should be stronger than the gates of hell; that it should be able to remove mountains of oppositions and temptations cast up by Satan and our rebellious hearts between God and us. Abimelech could not endure that it should be said, 'a woman had slain him,' Jud. ix. 54; and it must needs be a torment to Satan, that a weak child, a woman, and decrepit old man should, by a spirit of faith, put him to flight.

Since there is such comfort where there is a little truth of grace, that it will be so victorious, let us oft try what God hath wrought in us, search our good as well as our ill, and be thankful to God for the least measure of grace, more than for any outward thing; it will be of more use and comfort than all this world, which passeth away and cometh to nothing. Yea, let us be thankful for that promised and assured victory, which we may rely on without presumption, as St Paul doth; 'thanks be to God, that hath given us

* 'Discouragement . . . . heaven,' added in B.

† 'Let . . . thine,' a transposition of A and B here.

victory in Jesus Christ,' 1 Cor. xv. 57. See a flame in a spark, a tree in a seed; see great things in little beginnings; look not so much to the beginning, as to the perfection, and so we shall be in some degree joyful in ourselves, and thankful unto Christ.

Neither* must we reason from a denial of a great measure of grace, to a denial of any at all in us; for faith and grace stand not in an indivisible point, so as he that hath not such and such a measure hath none at all; but as there is a great breadth between a spark and a flame, so there is a great wideness between the least measure of grace and the greatest; and he that hath the least measure, is within the compass of God's eternal favour; though he be not a shining light, yet he is a smoking wick, which Christ's tender care will not suffer him to quench.

And let all this that hath been spoken allure those that are not yet in state of grace, to come under Christ's sweet and victorious government, for though we shall have much opposition, yet if we strive, he will help us; if we fail, he will cherish us; if we be guided by him, we shall overcome; if we overcome, we are sure to be crowned. And for the present state of the church, we see now how forlorn it is, yet let us comfort ourselves, that Christ's cause shall prevail; 'Christ will rule, till he hath made his enemies his footstool,' Ps. cx. 1, not only to trample upon, but to help him up to mount higher in glory. 'Babylon shall fall, for strong is the Lord who hath condemned her,' Rev. xviii. 8. Christ's judgment not only in his children, but also against his enemies, shall be victorious, for he is 'King of kings and Lord of lords,' Rev. xix. 1. God will not always† suffer antichrist and his supports to revel and ruffle in the church as they do.

If we look to the present state of the church of Christ, it is as Daniel in the midst of lions, as a lily amongst thorns, as a ship not only tossed, but almost covered with waves. It is so low, that the enemies think they have buried Christ, in regard of his gospel, in the grave, and there they think to keep him from rising; but Christ as he rose in his person, so he will roll away all stones, and rise again in his church. How little support hath the church and cause of Christ at this day! how strong a conspiracy is against it! the spirit of antichrist is now lifted up, and marcheth furiously; things seem to hang on a small and invisible thread. But our comfort is, that Christ liveth and reigneth and standeth on Mount Sion in defence of them that stand for him, Rev. xiv. 1; and when States and kingdoms shall dash one against another, Christ will have care of his own children and cause, seeing there is nothing else in the world that he much esteemeth. At this very time the delivery of his church, and the ruin of his enemies, is in working; we see no things in motion till Christ hath done his work, and then we shall see that the Lord reigneth.

Christ and his church, when they are at the lowest, are nearest rising: his enemies at the highest are nearest a downfall.

The Jews are not yet come in under Christ's banner; but God, that hath persuaded Japhet to come into the tents of Shem, will persuade Shem to come into the tents of Japhet, Gen. ix. 27. The 'fulness of the Gentiles is not yet come in,' Rom. xi. 25, but Christ, that hath the 'utmost parts of the earth given him for his possession,' Ps. ii. 8, will gather all the sheep his Father hath given him into one fold, that there may be one sheepfold and one shepherd, John x. 16.

The faithful Jews rejoiced to think of the calling of the Gentiles; and why should not we joy to think of the calling of the Jews?

* 'Neither . . . quench,' not in A, B, but in E. † 'God will not,' &c., added in B.

The gospel's course hath hitherto been as that of the sun, from east to west, and so in God's time may proceed yet further west (*i*). No creature can hinder the course of the sun, nor stop the influence of heaven, nor hinder the blowing of the wind, much less hinder the prevailing power of divine truth, until Christ hath brought all under one head, and then he will present all to his Father; these are they thou hast given unto me; these are they that have taken me for their Lord and King, that have suffered with me; my will is that they be where I am, and reign with me. And then he will deliver up the kingdom even to his Father, and put down all other rule, and authority, and power, 1 Cor. xv. 24.

Let us then bring our hearts to holy resolutions, and set ourselves upon that which is good, and against that which is ill, in ourselves or others, according to our callings, upon this encouragement, that Christ's grace and power shall go along with us. What had become of that great work of reformation of religion in the latter-spring of the gospel, if men had not been armed with invincible courage to outstride all lets, upon this faith, that the cause was Christ's, and that he would not be wanting to his own cause. Luther ingenuously confessed, that he carried matters often inconsiderately, and with mixture of passion; but upon acknowledgment, God took not advantage of his errors, but the cause being God's, and his aims being holy, to promote the truth, and being a mighty man in prayer, and strong in faith, God by him kindled that fire which all the world shall never be able to quench. According to our faith, so is our encouragement to all duties, therefore let us strengthen faith, that it may strengthen all other graces. This very belief, that faith shall be victorious, is a means to make it so indeed. Believe it, therefore, that though it be often as smoking flax, yet it shall prevail. If it prevail with God himself in trials, shall it not prevail over all other opposition? 'Let us wait a while, and we shall see the salvation of the Lord,' Exod. iv. 13.

The Lord reveal himself more and more unto us in the face of his Son Jesus Christ, and magnify the power of his grace in cherishing those beginnings of grace in the midst of our corruptions, and sanctify the consideration of our own infirmities to humble us, and of his tender mercy to encourage us; and persuade us, that since he hath taken us into the covenant of grace, he will not cast us off for those corruptions; which as they grieve his Spirit, so they make us vile in our own eyes. And because Satan labours to obscure the glory of his mercy, and hinder our comfort by discouragements, the Lord add this to the rest of his mercies, that, since he is so gracious to those that yield to his government, we may make the right use of this grace, and not lose any portion of comfort that is laid up for us in Christ. And [may] he vouchsafe to let the prevailing power of his Spirit in us be an evidence of the truth of grace begun, and a pledge of final victory, at that time when he will be all in all, in all his, for all eternity. Amen. Finis.*

* Added here to G is the following couplet:—

Quassatâ (Lector) quid arundine vilius, aut te?
At non frangeris, si pius, Unctus ait— G. J.

It may be thus rendered:

Than shaken reed what can more worthless be?
Reader, just such thou art:
But hast thou faith?
Then take good heart;
The Anointed saith,
Nor it nor thou by him shall broken be.

The initials are probably those of John Goodwin reversed. G.

NOTES.

(a) P. 49.—'Stooped so far . . . . as to suffer him to thrust his hand into his side.' It is questionable if Thomas really did this. His early faith recovered itself in presence of the Lord, and the narrative seems rather to indicate that he did not avail himself of the tenderly-forgiving offer of his Master. See Archbishop Whately's lecture on the apostle Thomas in his Lectures on the Apostles, (2d ed. 1853).

(b) P. 53.—'Strain not things too high, making those general and necessary evidences of grace which agree not,' &c. This characteristically gentle warning reminds us of an anecdote of the excellent Ebenezer Erskine, one of the founders of what is now the United Presbyterian Church. He had been delivering a course of sermons on '*Marks* of Grace,' and had spent much time in shewing how many things men might possess and nevertheless be 'hypocrites.' Chancing some time after to be on a visit to a very saintly but lowly 'aged' believer, who was apparently dying, the good man was startled by an exclamation, 'Oh! Mr Erskine, if I were just as good as one of your —— hypocrites, I would be happy.' The words struck home, and Erskine was wont to tell it, and to add that the remark opened his eyes to the danger by over-high 'marks' of causing God's own dearest children to 'write bitter things against themselves' without cause. This anecdote, related by one whose grandfather attended Mr Erskine at Stirling, strikingly enforces Sibbes's counsel.

(c) P. 55.—'Kill a fly on the forehead with a beetle.' 'Beetle' = mallet. In the margin opposite the passage in A, B, and E, is 'As Parisien.' Query, Peter Lombard?

(d) P. 67.—'Let' [= hinder]. Few words present such a curious example of utter reversal of meaning as this. Formerly to let was to 'hinder,' now it means to 'permit.' It occurs in the former sense both in O. T. and N. T., *e. g.*, Isa. xliii. 13, and Rom. i. 13; 2 Thess. ii. 7. It is here referred to once for all.

(e) P. 68.—'Catch' = on the watch. This supplies Richardson's lack (in his great Dictionary), of an example of 'catch' in the meaning here.

(f) P. 85.—'Voyage' = a travel, a journey; but now limited to *travel* by sea. Milton uses it repeatedly in the earlier sense. See *P. L.*, ii., 426, 919; vii. 431. *P. R.* i., 103.

(g) P. 86.—'Sobs.' To 'sob' means to 'sop' or 'soak,' and 'sobs,' as applied to kindled 'greenwood,' is vividly descriptive.

(h) P. 96.—'Send forth hath a stronger sense in the original.' Consult and compare Dr J. A. Alexander on the passage in his commentary on Isaiah (ed. by Eadie, 1848).

(i) P. 100.—'The gospel's course hath hitherto been as that of the sun, from east to west, and so in God's time may proceed further west.' This remarkable anticipation may be placed side by side with the better known but much later, and admittedly grander, vaticination of Berkeley :—

> '*Westward* the course of empire takes its way;
> The four first acts already past,
> A fifth shall close the drama with the day;
> Time's noblest offspring is the last.

The 'Priest' of Bemerton, George Herbert, may have had his equally memorable couplet suggested by Sibbes's words, the 'Bruised Reed' having preceded 'The Temple' by three years :—

> 'Religion stands a-tiptoe in our land,
> Ready to pass to the American strand.'
>
> *Church Millitant.*

Sibbes and his Puritan contemporaries turned with wistful eye to '*New* England,' and read in the light of the present position of America among the nations of the earth, it is curious to note the mingled hope and dread with which the mighty unknown continent was regarded. John Cotton, John Davenport, Thomas Hooker, and many other of Sibbes's personal friends, became fugitives thither. For various curious *memorabilia* on the subject of this note (Sibbes's being an addition thereto), consult Mayor's Nicholas Ferrar, pp. 52–3. G.

THE SWORD OF THE WICKED.

THE SWORD OF THE WICKED.

NOTE.

The title-page, a copy of which is given below [*], will, as in the case of 'The Description of Christ,' in its relation to 'The Bruised Reed,' explain the position of 'The Sword of the Wicked' in the present publication. It will be observed that it consists of the *leading*, *i.e.*, introductory sermons to that treatise, called 'The Soule's Conflict.' As such, it falls to be associated therewith. The 'Sword of the Wicked' forms a small portion of one of the posthumously-published quartos of Sibbes, entitled 'Evangelicall Sacrifices' [1640]. It labours under the same disadvantage with the 'Description,' as compared with its companion treatise, the 'Soul's Conflict,' being even more unfinished; but abounds with pungent and vigorous writing.

G.

[*] Title-page—

The
SWORD
of
THE WICKED.
In two Sermons.
Being the leading Sermons to that Treatise
called
The Soules Conflict.
By
The late Learned and Reverend Divine,
Rich. Sibbs:
Doctor in Divinity, Mr of Katherine Hall
in Cambridge, and sometimes Preacher
to the Honourable Society of
Grayes-Inne.
Psal. 57. 4.
Their Tongue is a sharpe Sword.
London,
Printed by E. P. for N. B. and R. H. 1639. 4to.

THE SWORD OF THE WICKED.

As with a sword in my bones, mine enemies reproach me; while they say unto me daily, Where is thy God?—Psalm XLII. 10.

The Psalms are, as it were, the anatomy of a holy man; they lay the inside of a true devout man outward, even to the view of others.

If the Scriptures be compared to a body, the Psalms may well be the heart, they are so full of sweet and holy affections and passions. In other portions of Scripture, God speaks to us; in the Psalms, holy men (especially David, who was the penman of most of them), speak to God, wherein we have the passages of a broken, humble soul to God. Among the rest, in this Psalm David lays open variety of passions. His condition at this time was such, as that he was an exiled man, from his own house and his own friends, and which grieved him worst of all, from the tabernacle, the house of God. It was upon the occasion of Saul's persecution, or of Absalom's, his son; but I take it rather of Saul's, that hunted him as a partridge in the wilderness. Hereupon you have a discovery, how this holy man of God stood affected with this case and condition of his. First he lays open his grief. His grief ariseth from his desire. He that loves most and desireth most, he always grieves most; and all other affections have their scantling (*a*) from love, which is the firstborn affection of the soul. Therefore, before he lays out his grief, he sets out his desire to the house of God, the want whereof grieved him most of all. 'As the hart panteth after the water brooks, so panteth my soul after thee, O God,' ver. 1. As the chased hart panteth after water, so the soul thirsteth for God, for the living God, 'O when shall I come and appear before God?' ver. 2.*

Then after his desire, he lays forth his grief, 'My tears have been my meat day and night, while they continually say unto me, Where is thy God?' ver. 3. Grievances never come alone, but as Job's messengers, they come one after another, even to God's children. When he is disposed to correct them, they are multiplied. Therefore, here is not only a grief of want, that he was debarred of those sweet comforts which he had before in the tabernacle, but here is likewise a grief from the reproach of his enemies, that took occasion from his disconsolate estate to upbraid him, 'Where is thy

* This opening paragraph is very nearly identical with the commencement of the 'Soul's Conflict.'—G.

God?' 'My tears have been my meat day and night, while they continually say unto me, Where is thy God?' He dissolves the cloud of his grief into the shower of tears, 'My tears have been my meat.' They were so plentiful that they did feed his soul as it were.

Then he sets down another ground of his grief, from the remembrance of his former happiness; as usually, that doth make the grief raw and more sensible, for *felix miser*, *maxime miser*, he that hath been happy in former time and now is miserable, is most miserable of all, because his former happiness makes him most sensible. Therefore, of all men in hell, the torment of great men is most, because they had most sense of comfort in this world; mighty men shall be mightily tormented, that is all the privilege they shall have in hell. Therefore, to aggravate his grief, O, saith he, when I remember what comfort I had formerly in the house of God, I pour out my soul. It was not enough that he poured out his tears, or words, but I pour out my soul, for in former times, 'I went with the multitude to the house of God,' ver. 4, and led a goodly train to the house of God, the picture of a good magistrate, and a good master of a family; he goes not alone to the house of God, but he leads his train, he is attended on by his servants. David went not alone into the house of God, but with the multitude, 'with the voice of them that kept holiday,' ver. 4. Well, he had grief enough, his heart was full of grief. Now in the next verse he takes up his soul, and expostulates with himself, 'Why art thou so sad, O my soul? and why art thou disquieted in me? hope thou in God, for I shall yet praise him for the help of his countenance,' ver. 5. So you see here, he is not so flat in his grief that he gives over-long way to it, but he even falls a chiding of his soul, 'Why art thou cast down, O my soul? why art thou disquieted within me?' O! but yet grief will not be so stilled! affliction is not quelled at the first, nor grief stilled and stayed at the first. Therefore it gathers upon him again in the next verse, 'O my God, my soul is cast down within me, when I remember thee from the land of Jordan, and of the Hermonites, from the hill Mizar.' When I remember thee from these places, my soul is cast down again, and my afflictions are multiplied; though he had fallen out with his soul before, for his impatience. 'One deep calls to another,' deep calls upon deep, 'as the noise of the water-spouts,' ver. 7. He compares affliction to water-spouts, as it is in Scripture. 'All thy waves and billows have gone over me,' ver. 7. Even as one deep calls to another, so one affliction calls to another. Then when he had given a little way again to his grief, and complained to God, he takes up his soul another time; yet, saith he, 'The Lord will command his lovingkindness in the day time, and in the night his song shall be with me, and I will pray to the God of my life,' ver. 8. He presents to himself the goodness of God, to comfort his soul. And he presents to him in the next verse his own resolution, 'I will say to God (for the time to come) my rock, why hast thou forgotten me? and why go I mourning, for the oppression of the enemy,' ver. 9. So here he stays his soul once again; he presents to his soul the lovingkindness of God, with renewing his resolution to seek God: an effectual way to stay the soul, by considering God's love and mercy, and by renewing our resolutions and purposes to cleave to God, 'I will say to God my rock, why hast thou forgotten me?'

Aye, but here is a third assault of grief again, for there is a spring of corruption in us, and such a principle in us as will yield murmurings and discontent again and again; therefore in the verse I have read to you, he comes again to complain, 'As with a sword in my bones, mine enemies reproach me; while they say unto me daily, Where is thy God?' ver. 10. He had complained once of this before, but it had a fresh working with his thoughts again, 'As with a sword in my bones,' &c. Hereupon, he is forced the third time to expostulate, and to fall out with his soul, 'Why art thou cast down, O my soul? and why art thou disquieted? hope thou in God, for I shall yet praise him, who is the health of my countenance, and my God,' ver. 11. He comes to his former remedy, he had stilled his grief once before with the same meditation and upbraiding of his own soul, and chiding himself; but he comes to it here as a *probatum est*, as a tried remedy, he takes up his soul very short, 'Why art thou so cast down, O my soul? why art thou disquieted within me?' You see how David's passions here are interlaced with comforts, and his comforts with passions, till at last he gets the victory of his own heart. Beloved, neither sin, nor grief for sin, are stilled and quieted at the first. You have some short-spirited Christians, if all be not quiet at the first, all is lost with them; but it is not so with a true Christian soul, with the best soul living. It was not so with David: when he was in distemper, he checks himself; the distemper was not yet stilled, he checks himself again; then the distemper breaks out again, then he checks himself again; and all little enough to bring his soul to a holy, blessed, quiet temper, to that blessed tranquillity and rest that the soul should be in, before it can enjoy its own happiness, and enjoy sweet communion with God. As you see in physic, perhaps one purge will not carry away the peccant humour, then a second must be added; perhaps that will not do it, then there must be a third; so when the soul hath been once checked, perhaps it will not do, we must fall to it again, go to God again. And then it may be there will be breaking out of the grief and malady again; we must to it again, and never give over; that is the right temper of a Christian.

Before I come to the words, observe in general this, *that a living soul, the soul that is alive in grace, that hath the life of grace quickening it, is most sensible of all, in the want of spiritual means.* As here, the grief of griefs was (which he begins with), that he was banished from the tabernacle.

What shall we think therefore of those that excommunicate themselves from God's assembly, where there is the Father, Son, and Holy Ghost, all the Trinity dispensing their bounty, and where the prayers of God's people meet together in one as it were, and bind God? What shall we think of them that prefer their private devotions, as they say, before God's assemblies? Surely they are not of David's mind; and it is a shrewd argument, that they never had the life of grace in them yet: for where life is, there will be hunger and thirst. *Acrius urgent quæ ad naturam.* It is a true aphorism, those things press upon nature hardest that touch upon the necessities of nature, rather than those that touch upon delight. We can want delights, but necessities of nature we cannot; therefore hunger and thirst, they are such passions as will not be quiet. Delicacies and novelties the soul of a hungry man can be content to want, but not spiritual food for the soul. We see how famine wrought upon the patriarchs, it made them go down into Egypt for food. I note it only by the way, that men may know how to judge of themselves, when they can very well be content, without a blessed supply of holy means. Holy David, when the means was but dark and obscure, when the canon was not enlarged, when all was in types and clouds, yet he felt that comfort in the tabernacle and in the ordinances of God, that he could not endure the want of them; but as the hart brayeth after the water-brooks, so his soul panted after God. But to come to the words themselves,

'As with a sword in my bones, mine enemies reproach me, when they say unto me daily, where is thy God?'

Here are two things considerable in the words.

The carriage and disposition and expression of others to David.

And *David's affection towards it, how he was disposed towards it, how he did bear it.*

For their disposition, they were enemies, *mine enemies, &c.*

The expression of it, *they reproach me.*

The specialty of that expression, how they reproached him, they said unto him, '*Where is thy God?*' They do reproach him in his religion.

The aggravation of that specialty is, they say, openly to his face, they go not behind my back, they esteem so slightly of me, they say it to my face. And continually too, they are never weary, they say daily, Where is thy God? They are enemies, they reproach, they reproach in this, 'Where is thy God?' and they do it impudently, and daily.

How doth David entertain this usage? how doth he carry himself all this while? He must needs be sensible of it, and therefore he expresseth it in most significant words. Oh, saith he, these things were as *a sword in my bones.* There be diverse readings of the words; but we will take them as they are laid down, being very well, *as with a sword in my bones* (or as it is in the margin, (*b*) *as killing in my bones*), mine enemies reproach me. It was as killing to him, it did go to his heart, it cut him to the quick. As a sword is to the body and bones, so are their words to my soul, I cannot endure it, it is death to me. It is a most emphatical manner of expressing the enemies' disposition and carriage. Thus you have the words unfolded. I will but touch some particulars; those that I think most needful for us to take notice of, I will dwell more upon. *Mine enemies*, saith he, *reproach me.*

Mine enemies. There hath been contrary seeds from the beginning of the world, and will be while Satan is in the world. Till he be cast into the 'burning lake,' and be there in perpetual chains adjudged to torment, he will raise up men alway that shall be of his side. And as long as that grand enemy is, and as long as men are that will be subject to his government, as alway there will be, he will have a great faction in the world. And by reason that he hath a party in us, the flesh, he will have the greatest party in the world. The most go the broad way, so that *God's children*, even David himself, *shall not want enemies.*

Mine enemies. It is strange that he should have enemies, that was so harmless a man, that when they were sick and distressed, he prayed for them, and put on sackcloth for them, as it is Ps. xli. This compassionate, sweet-natured man, yet notwithstanding you see he had enemies, and enemies that would discover themselves to reproach him, and that bitterly; in the bitterest manner, they reproach him in his religion. It is a large point, if I should give myself liberty in it. I do but touch it, that we may be armed by this observation, against the scandal of opposition, that if we meet with enemies in the world, we should not be much offended at it; grieve we may, but wonder we need not. Was there ever any that did more good than our Saviour Christ? 'He went about doing good,' Acts x. 38. He did never a miracle that was harmful (but only of the swine that were drowned in the sea, and that was their own fault), but he went about doing all the good he could; yet, notwithstanding, we see what malicious opposites he had. That that is true of the head must be true in the members. Therefore, we should rejoice in our conformity to Christ, if it be in a good cause, that we find enemies and opposition. *O imperator,*

&c., saith he, O the emperor is become a Christian. It was a blessed time. Oh! but the devil is not made a Christian yet, and he will never be made good: for he is *in termino*, as we say, he is in his bounds, his nature is immoveable; he is in hell in regard of his estate, though he be loose to do mischief. Now, until the devil be good, God's children shall never want enemies; and he will never be good. Therefore, though there were good kings and good governors over all the world, yet good men shall never want enemies as long as the devil is alive, as long as he hath any thing to do in the world. Enemies therefore we must look for, and such enemies as will not conceal their malice neither: for that were something if they would suffer their malice to boil and concoct in their own hearts, but that will not be, but 'out of the abundance of the heart the mouth will speak.' Where there is a bad treasury, there will be a bad vent;* therefore we see here, they reproach him, '*mine enemies*.'

Reproach me. It is the proper expression of malice, reproach; and it is that that the nature of man can least endure of all. The nature of man can endure an outward wrong, a loss or a cross, but a reproach, especially if it be a scornful reproach, the nature of man is most impatient of. For there is no man, but he thinks himself worthy of some respect. Now a reproachful scorn shews a disrespect, and when the nature of man sees itself disrespected, it grows to terms of impatience. There is not the meanest man living but he thinks himself worthy of some regard. Therefore I cannot blame David, even out of the principle of nature, to be affected here when they reproached him, and gave him vile terms, 'mine enemies *reproach me*.' Their tongues were tipt from hell, and they did but utter that that was in their hearts. If the tongues of wicked men, as St James saith, be a world of mischief, what is the whole man? what is the heart, and tongue, and life, and all of wicked men?

Now this reproach of wicked men, it is a grievous persecution, as Ishmael persecuted Isaac in that manner, as it is, Gal. iv., taken out of the story in Genesis. I will not enter into the commonplace of reproach; it is taken by the by here.

Only by the way, let it be a support to us. If we be reproachfully used in the world, let us not be much cast down. It is no credit for a man to do that that the devil and his instruments do; nor it is no discredit for us to suffer that that David suffered. Let this satisfy thee, there is not the vilest man living but hath this weapon to serve the devil with, a reproachful tongue. He that sits upon the ale bench, that rakes in the channel,† the basest wretch in the world, hath a tongue to serve the devil with in reproaches. It is no credit for them to do that that the vilest person in the world can do; and it is no shame for thee to suffer that that the best man that ever lived did suffer. So much for that, *mine enemies reproach me.*

But what is the specialty of this reproach? To come to that more particularly. *They say unto me, Where is thy God?*

They touch him in his religion. They saw him persecuted by Saul, scorned by Saul's courtiers; they see him driven up and down, as a partridge in the wilderness; they saw him banished from the sanctuary, destitute of friends; they saw him in this disconsolate estate, and they judge by sense and appearance, that they thought he was a man that God regarded not at all; therefore say they, *Where is thy God?*

God's children are impatient, as far as they are men, of reproaches; but so far as they are Christian men, they are impatient of reproaches in reli-

* That is, 'out-goiug.'—ED. † That is, 'the kennel' or sewer.—ED.

gion: *Where is now thy God?* They were not such desperate atheists as to think there was no God, to call in question whether there were a God or no, though indeed they were little better; but they rather reproach and upbraid him with his singularity, *Where* is *thy* God? You are one of God's darlings; you are one that thought nobody served God but you; you are one that will go alone—*your* God.

So this is an ordinary reproach, an ordinary part for wicked men, to cast at the best people, especially when they are in misery. What is become of your profession now? What is become of your forwardness and strictness now? What is become of your much reading and hearing now; and your doing such things now? What is become of your God that you bragged so of, and thought yourselves so happy in, as if he had been nobody's God but yours? We may learn hence the disposition of wicked men. It is a character of a poisonful, cursed disposition to upbraid a man with his religion.

But what is the scope? The scope is worse than the words, *Where is thy God?* The scope is to shake his faith, and his confidence in God; and this is that that touched him so nearly while they upbraided him, *Where is thy God?* Indeed, they had some probability and show of truth; for now God seemed opposite to him, when he was banished from his house, from that blessed communion with him that he had. Their purpose was therefore to shake his faith and affiance in God; and herein they shewed themselves right, the children of the devil, whose scope is to shake the faith and affiance of God's people, in all his temptations, and by his instruments. For the devil knows well enough, that as long as God and the soul join together, it is in vain to trouble any man; therefore he labours to put jealousies, to accuse God to man, and man to God. He knows there is nothing in the world can stand against God. As long as we make God our confidence, all his enterprises are in vain. His scope is therefore to shake our affiance in God: *Where is thy God?* So he dealt with the Head of the church, our blessed Saviour himself, when he came to tempt him. 'If thou be the Son of God, command these stones to be made bread,' Matt. iv. 3. He comes with an *if;* he laboured to shake him in his sonship. The devil, since he was divided from God himself eternally, is become a spirit of division; he labours to divide the Son from the Father; he labours to divide even God the Father from his own Son: *If thou be the Son of God.* So he labours to sever Christians from their head, Christ; subjects from their princes, and princes from their subjects; friends from friends, and one from another;—he is a spirit of division: *Where is thy God?* There was his scope, to breed division, if he could, between his heart and God, that he might call God into jealousy, as if he had not regarded him: thou hast taken a great deal of pains in serving thy God; thou seest how he regards thee now: *Where is thy God?*

We should labour to make this use of it, to counter-work Satan; to strengthen that most of all, that the devil labours to shake most of all. Shall the devil labour to shake our faith and affiance in God above all other things, and shall we not labour to strengthen that? Above all things, let us look to our head, as the serpent winds about and keeps his head. Keep faith, and keep all. If faith be safe, all is safe; let us strengthen that, and strengthen all; weaken that, and we weaken all. What cares Satan for other sins that we fall into? He aims at our assurance, that we may doubt of God's love, whom we have been so bold as to sin against. That is it he aims at, to make weak faith in the particular acts of sin we commit. He knows that sin naturally breeds doubts, as flesh breeds worms.

Where sin is, if it be in never such a little degree, he knows it will breed doubts and perplexities, and where they are, he hath that he would have. He labours to hinder that sweet communion that should be between the soul and God: *Where is now thy God?* You see wicked men are the children of the devil right in this.

Again, they instance here in matter of religion against him. You see how ready wicked and devilish-minded men are, to tread over the hedge where it is lowest, as the proverb is, to add affliction to affliction, especially in that that may touch a man nearest. They could not touch him nearer than in this, *Where is thy God?* They knew it well enough, where is now your religion? This, they thought, would anger him to the heart. Here is a devilish disposition. You have a terrible psalm for it, Ps. cix., of those that add affliction to the afflicted; *they are cursed persons.* This is the disposition of wicked men, they have no mercy. Malice, we say, is unsatiable. One would think that our Saviour Christ, when he was upon the cross, racked there in all his parts, a man exposed to so much misery and scorn as he was, that they should have had pity upon him; but upon the cross they reproached him, Aha, he saved others, himself he cannot save; let him come from the cross, and we will believe in him. What a bitter sarcasm was this, that came from hell itself! Nay, when he was dead, one would have thought their malice should have been buried with his body. Malice is ordinarily among men living, not the dead; but when he was dead, *This impostor said, &c.*, Matt. xxvi. 61. They laboured to bury his good name, that nothing tending to his honour might remain of him. Indeed, it is the nature of malice to wish the not being of the thing it maliceth, no, not the name. *Let his name perish from the earth*, Ps. xli. 5. It was extremity of malice to work upon this disadvantage, when they see him thus afflicted, to vex him with that he was most affected with, *Where is thy God?*

Therefore, let those that feel and feed that devilish disposition in themselves to insult over God's people, especially in matters of religion to vex them, and when there is a wound already, to make the affliction greater, to add affliction to affliction, let them judge of what disposition they are.

They say unto me. You see here another circumstance, *they say unto me.* They are so impudent that they are not afraid to reproach him to his face; *they say unto him*, as if they would stand to their reproach. This is one circumstance of aggravation. Indeed malice is very impudent, when it is come to the extremity. I only observe it, that if we meet with such insolency of malice, not to be discouraged; it hath been thus before, and thus it will be to the end of the world.

And, then, they are not wearied, their malice is unwearied; they say to me, *Daily.* Day by day their malice is fed with a spring, with a malicious heart. A malicious heart and a slanderous tongue alway go well together. The devil, that was the first grand slanderer, hath communion with a malicious heart, and he foments malice, and cherisheth that malicious, poisonful disposition; and a malicious disposition never wants malicious words. As one saith of anger and fury, it ministereth weapons (*c*), so we may say of malice and hatred, it ministereth words alway. A malicious heart will never want words: they say to me, *daily.* These are but circumstances, but yet they are somewhat considerable, for they tend to the aggravation of the disconsolate estate of this holy man, that he should meet with such wretched men, that had no pity at all on him, but say to him daily,

Where is now thy God? You see, then from hence that God is a God, as the prophet saith, ofttimes hiding himself, Isa. xlv. 15, that God vails himself ofttimes to his children. Not only from the eyes of wicked men, that they think godly men deserted of God, but sometimes from the very sense and feeling of God's children themselves. They are in such desertions that they are fain to complain that God hath hid himself, and is as a stranger to them. This is the state of God's children in this world. Though God love them dearly, 'as the apple of his eye, and as the signet on his hand,' Zech. ii. 8, and Jer. xxii. 24, yet notwithstanding his carriage to them is ofttimes so strange, that those that look upon their estate in this world think they are men, as it were, forlorn and destitute of God. And this estate must needs be, because of necessity there must be a conformity between us and our Saviour. It was so with our Saviour, 'My God, my God, why hast thou forsaken me?' Matt. xxvii. 46. God was never nearer him in all his life than then, and yet he cries out, 'My God, my God, why hast thou forsaken me?' And as he spake, so the rest thought of him, as if he had been a man forsaken; and so here they say to this holy man, *Where is thy God?*

Therefore let us lay up this likewise for the strengthening of our faith in the like case, that we be not overmuch discouraged. If God hide himself, if others think our estates miserable, and ourselves think ourselves so, it is no strange matter. It was thus with David. He was so neglected of God that they thought God had clean forsaken him. *Where is thy God?*

Our life is now hid with Christ, as the apostle saith, Col. iii. 3. We have a blessed and glorious life, but it is hid in our Head. Even as in winter time the trees have a life, but it is hid in the root, so a Christian hath a blessed condition at all times, but his glory and happiness is hid in his Head, and there is a cloud between him and his happiness.

Therefore let us support ourselves with this in all times, was God gone from David indeed when they said, 'Where is thy God?' Oh no; God was as near David now as ever he was, nay, rather nearer. God was never nearer Moses than when he was sprawling upon the water in that ark they had made for him, Ex. ii. 3. He was never nearer Daniel than when he was in the lion's den, Dan. vi. 19. God came between the lion's teeth and Daniel. And, as I said, he was never nearer our Saviour than when he was on the cross. And he was never nearer to David than when they said, 'Where is thy God?' When trouble is near, God is never far off. That is an argument to make God near, *Lord, be not far off, for trouble is near.* And extremity and danger and trouble, it is God's best opportunity to be with his children, however he do not help for the present ofttimes. '*Where is thy God?*'

David might rather have said to them, Where are your eyes? where is your sight? for God is not only in heaven, but in me. Though David was shut from the sanctuary, yet David's soul was a sanctuary for God; for God is not tied to a sanctuary made with hands. God hath two sanctuaries, he hath two heavens: the heaven of heavens and a broken spirit. God dwelt in David as in his temple. God was with David and in him; and he was never more with him, nor never more in him, than in his greatest afflictions. They wanted eyes, he wanted not God. Though sometimes God hide himself, not only from the world, but from his own children, yet he is there; howsoever their sorrow is such that it dims their sight (as we see in Hagar), so that they cannot see him for the present, Gen. xxi. 19. He sometimes looks in their face, as we see Mary. She could not see Christ distinctly, but thought him to be the gardener. There is a kind of concealment a while in heavenly wisdom, yet, notwithstanding, God is with his children always, and they know it by faith, though not by feeling always. As we know what Jacob said, 'God was in this place, and I was not aware,' Gen. xxviii. 16, when he slept upon the stone, and had that heavenly vision; so it is with God's people in their trouble. God is with his church and children, and wicked men are not aware of it. Christ is in them, and they are not aware of it. Christ was in the saints when Saul persecuted them, and Paul was not aware of it, 'Saul, Saul, why persecutest thou me? Who art *thou*, Lord?' saith he. Alas! he dreamed not of Christ. However wicked men of the world think, yet God is near his own children, in the most disconsolate condition that can be. It is, when they say, '*Where is thy God?*' as if a man should ask what is become of the moon between the old and the new, when the dark side is towards us, when we see no moon at all for a time, till the new come? The moon is near, and more enlightened with the sun then than at other times, and is nearer to him. So in afflictions. However the dark side of God's children be toward the world, that they cannot see them, yet their light side is towards God. God shines upon them, and enlightens them more then at that time with solid comfort, that keeps them from sinking, than at other times. Therefore it was an ignorant question of them to ask, *Where is thy God?* It shewed they were ignorant of the passages of God's dealing with his children, as indeed none are greater atheists than your scoffers. *Where is thy God?* as if God had been only a God of observation, to be observed outwardly in all his passages towards his children, whereas, as I said, he is a God hiding himself ofttimes; and he shews himself in contrary conditions most of all, most comfortably. His work is by contraries. But these carnal men were ignorant of the mysteries of religion, and the mysteries of divine providence towards God's children. Therefore their question savours of their disposition, *Where is now thy God?* Thus briefly I have gone over their disposition and carriage towards the holy man David, that they were enemies of hostile nature and disposition, and they reproached him, and daily, and that in his religion, *Where is thy God?*

I beseech you let us look to it in time, that it may not be truly said to us, by way of upbraiding, *Where is now thy God?* God may be strange to us indeed; let us so carry ourselves as that God may own us in the worst times. If they had said this truly, how grievous had it been to David! but it was more malice than truth. For David found experience of God. He might rather have upbraided them, *Where is your God?* and there is no wicked man, but a man may in his greatest extremity upbraid him, and that in truth, Where is your God? your riches, honour, and estate? where is all this that you supported yourself with, and bore yourself so big on, that you despised all others? what has become of all now? A man cannot stand in a thing that stands not itself. A man cannot build on that that hath no good foundation. Now all men that are not truly religious, they have some idol or other that will deceive them. Therefore a man may truly say to them, that which they falsely and maliciously say to God's people, *Where is your God?*

So much for their disposition and carriage. Now how stands David affected with this? that is the second part.

As with a sword in my bones. It was as a sword to his bones. Now that that toucheth the bones is the most exquisite grief. That that we call the grief of the teeth, you see what an exquisite grief it is in that little member. When the bones are cut or touched, it is a most exquisite grief. *As with a sword in my bones, my enemies reproach me.* What was the matter that this reproach, *Where is thy God?* touched him so to the quick? What was the cause? The causes were diverse.

First of all concerning God: for when they said to him, 'Where is thy God?'

First, It tended to the reproach of God, as if God were so fickle a friend as to desert his best friends in the time of misery. This touched upon God by way of disparagement, therefore it must needs touch David, who was God's friend.

Then, again, it touched God in another thing, in his manner of providence, as if he had been a God of the hills and not of the valleys; as if he had been a God for one time and not for another. Where is now thy God? What is become of him?

Again, in the third place, it touched upon him in this, as if he had favoured them, being cursed, formal hypocrites, more than David; as if he had favoured their formal, hypocritical, base, dead courses, that were most abominable to God. For these persecutors were Saul's courtiers, and other enemies. Wicked men, they thought to justify their own ways by this reproach, You see we are as good as you. God respects us; we fall not into such miseries; we have recourse to Saul, though he have cast out you and others, &c. So it tended to God's reproach in that, as if God had justified their course, as if they had been dearer to him that were most abominable.

And this is to make an idol of God, to make God justify those courses that he most abhors, as it is in Ps. l., 'Thou thoughtest I was like unto thee.' Because God lets a wicked man alone, thou thoughtest that I was a companion for thee, and would take thee by the hand; whereas God will not do so.

In these three respects, especially, God was wronged when they said, 'Where is thy God?' as if he had not been a true and faithful friend to his children; and, besides, as if he had not a providence over his children in the worst condition; as if he had allowed and liked of the base carriage, and condition, and profession of these wretched men as well as of David's. '*Where is now thy God?*' You see God respects us as well as you. But there was no such matter; he respected David more than a thousand of them.

Again, this touched upon religion itself, this reproach, 'Where is now thy God?' where is your goodly profession? as if it were in vain to serve God, a horrible reproach to religion. It is not in vain altogether to serve the devil; he bestows somewhat upon his servants. This was a base thought, to think that God would do no good to them that serve him. That is the fountain of all good, that doeth good to his enemies, that suffers his sun to shine upon his enemies, Mat. v. 45. For him to desert his friends, for a man to be truly religious and get nothing by it, this tended to the reproach of religion; and through David's sides they strike at God and religion, as if it were in vain to serve God, as they said in Malachi's time, Mal. iii. 14. And, indeed, this is in the hearts of men now-a-days. If they see a man that makes care and conscience of his ways, under a cloud, or that he doth not so prosper in the world as others do, they begin to have weak conceits of the profession of religion, as if that were the cause, as if there was nothing gotten by serving of God. But we may be loose professors, and go in a libertine course, and please God as well as others. This is a great grief to God's children. They know well enough it is not in vain to serve God. God is not a barren wilderness, Jer. ii. 31, to those that serve him; they are not barren ground that are careful in his service. So you see upon what ground he was thus affected, because God and religion were touched in it.

Take away a godly man's religion, and his God whom he serves in religion, you take away his life; touch him in that, you touch him in his best freehold. Therefore, when these malicious enemies say, *Where is thy God?* they could not more touch David than so. Profane men of the world come and tell them of religion and such things. Alas! they turn it off with scorn, for they would have the world know that they are not very religious; they never speak of God and of religion but in scorn, or by way of discourse. But a man that is religious to purpose, and makes it his trade, makes it that whereby he hopes to be saved, he takes to heart any thing that is spoken against religion, their words are *as a sword in his bones*, while they say unto him, *Where is thy God?* It is better to be distempered than not to be moved, when God and religion are touched. The Holy Ghost that appeared in the shape of a dove, Matt. iii. 16, appeared at another time in fiery tongues, Acts ii. 3, to shew that the meek spirit of God is zealous other whiles in his children. This was another reason he was thus affected.

And, *thirdly*, in this reproach of theirs, thus violent, 'Where is now thy God?' here was a damping of the spirits of all good men in those times, that should hear of this reproach. Words affect strangely; they have a strange force with men, especially in weak fancies, that are not grounded in their judgment and faith. The spies made a shrewd oration, and brought an ill report on the land: Oh! it is a land that devours the inhabitants, Num. xiii. 32. It was a speech discomfortable, and it wrought so, that it made them all murmur and be discouraged. It is not to be thought what mischief comes from speech cunningly handled. This malicious speech, 'Where is thy God?' and what is become of all thy devotion at the tabernacle, that thou didst frequent so, and drewest others, a great train with thee, what is become of all now? When weak men, that had the beginnings of goodness in them, should see a man reproached for this, questionless it would damp the beginnings of goodness. O would not this go to the heart of David, to see insolent men to quench good things in good men with reproaches! Well, we see what reason the holy man David had to be so sensible of this reproach, for they said unto him daily, 'Where is thy God?'

Now, therefore, to make some use of it to ourselves, let us enter into our own souls, and examine with what spirits and feeling we hear God reproached, and religion reproached, and hindered, and disgraced any kind of way. If we be not sensible of this, and sensible to the quick, we may suspect we are not of David's spirit, that was a man after God's own heart, 1 Samuel xiii. 14; Acts xiii. 22. It was a cutting of his bones, when they came to disparage his religion, and profession, and to touch him in that. Shall a man see men forsake religion, and go backward, and desert the cause of God, and see it oppressed, and not be affected with all this? Certainly he hath a dead soul. That which hath no grief, when there is cause of grief, certainly it is to be accounted but as dead flesh. That heart is but dead flesh that is not touched with the sense of religion.

And to come a little nearer to our times, when we can hear of the estate of the church abroad, the poor church in the Palatinate, in Bohemia, (*d*) and those places, you see how like a canker, superstition is grown up amongst them; when we hear of these things and are not affected, and do not send up a sigh to God, it is a sign we have hollow and dead hearts. No question but if we were there among those malignant spirits that are there, their speeches are daily such, as these wicked men's were to David, What is become of your reformation? What is become of your new religion? Where is that now, I pray? You that do upbraid us with idolatry, what is become of your religion? No question but they have these sarcasms and bitter speeches daily; and those that have the Spirit of God, they are grieved to the heart. If we have the Spirit of God and of Christ in our breasts, and anything of the spirit of David and of holy men, we will grieve at this.

The apostle St Paul, when Elymas laboured to stop, when one was to be converted, he breaks out, 'Thou child of the devil, and enemy of all good, why dost thou not cease to pervert the right ways of God?' Acts xiii. 10. A man that is not fired in this case, hath nothing at all in him. When we see wicked men go about to pervert religion, and overturn all, and we are not stirred at it, it is an ill sign.

Let us, therefore, take a trial of ourselves, how we stand affected in case of religion. He that hath no zeal in him hath no love. By an antiperistasis, an opposition of the contrary increaseth the contrary; if a man have any goodness, if it be environed with opposition, it will intend (*e*) the goodness and increase it. Lot shewed his goodness in Sodom the more, because of the wickedness of the Sodomites. When a man is in vile company, and hears religion disgraced, and good persons scoffed at, and will not have a word to justify good causes and good persons, he hath no life at all of religion; for if he had, he would then have more religion than ordinary, the contrary would then intend, and increase the contrary. There was a blessed mixture of many affections in this grief of the holy man David, when he said, 'their words were as a sword in his bones.' There was great grief, not only for himself, as a man being sensible of reproaches, for men are men; and not out of corrupt nature, but out of the principles of nature, they are sensible of reproaches. Here was grief in respect of God, and in respect of himself; and here was the love of God and the love of religion in this grief. Here was zeal in this, and a sweet mixture of blessed affections; a sweet temper in this, when he saith, 'their words were as a sword in my bones.'

Let us make a use of trial, bring ourselves to this pattern, and think, if we do come short of this, then we come short of that that should be in us. But especially let us consider with what hearts we entertain those doleful and sad reports of foreign churches, and with what consideration and view we look upon the present estate of the church, whether we be glad or no. There are many false spirits that either are not affected at all, or else they are inwardly glad of it; they are of the same disposition that those cursed Edomites were of, 'Down with it, down with it, even unto the ground,' Ps. cxxxvii. 7. I hope that there are but few such amongst us here, therefore I will not press that. But if we be dead-hearted, and are not affected with the cause of the church, let us suspect ourselves, and think all is not well. The fire from heaven is not kindled in our hearts. Our hearts are not yet the altar where God hath kindled that heavenly fire, if we can hear religion disgraced, and good causes go backward, and not be affected. 'Curse ye Meroz.' Why? Because 'they went not out to help the Lord,' Jud. v. 23. If those be cursed that do not help, as they can, by their prayers, then surely they are cursed that are dead-hearted, that are not affected at all, that join with the persecutors, that cry, 'Down with it even to the ground,' and say, 'Aha, so we would have it.' If those be cursed that help not forward the cause of the church, at least by their prayers, and strive and contend for 'the faith once given,' Jude 3, what shall we think of those that are not affected at all? nay, which is worst of all, that hinder good causes, that are scorners of religion and good causes, what shall we think of those wretched spirits? How opposite are they to the spirit of David!

To add one thing more, we may learn hence the extent of the commandments, how to enlarge the commandments. Our Saviour, Christ, when he came to preach the gospel, he began with the enlargement of the commandments, shewing the spiritual meaning and extent of the law, 'He that calleth his brother Raca, or fool, is in danger of hell fire,' and 'He that looks on a woman to lust after her, hath committed adultery with her in his heart,' Mat. v. 22, 28. You see here the prophet David, when he speaks of their reproach, he speaks of it as if they had a murderous intention; and in the event and issue it is a kind of murder. *As with a sword in my bones, my enemies reproach me*, &c. This sword were but words. He is a murderer in God's esteem, and so it will prove if he repent not, that wounds another man with his tongue. For what doth the Holy Ghost here in David? Doth he not set out words by swords? Is it not oft in the Psalms, 'Their words are as swords, the poison of asps is under their lips?' Rom. iii. 13. There is an excellent place you have for this in Prov. xii. 18, 'There is that speaks like the piercing of a sword, but the tongue of the wise is health.' A good man hath a healing tongue, he hath a medicinal, salving tongue; but a wicked man, his words are as swords, and, as he saith here, their speaking is as the piercing of a sword. Therefore, hence let us learn not to think ourselves free from murder when we have killed nobody, or free from adultery when we are free from the gross act. This is but a pharisaical gloss upon the commandments; but if we will understand the commandments of God as they are to be understood, we must enlarge them as the Scripture enlargeth them. He that prejudiceth the life and comfort of any man, he is a murderer of him in God's esteem; and he that labours to cut another man to the heart with sharp, piercing words, in God's esteem he is a murderer. Those that, though among men, they cannot say black is their eye, and pride themselves, as if they were very religious men; yet, notwithstanding, they are men that are not wanting of their tongues, men that care not to speak bitterly and sharply of others. If they did consider of this, it would take them down, and make them think a little meaner of themselves, when, indeed, in God's construction, they are little better than murderers. 'As with a sword in my bones, mine enemies reproach me, while they say to me daily, Where is thy God?' So much for these words.

NOTES.

(*a*) P. 105.—'Scantling' = a proportion, or simply, portion. This is a somewhat peculiar use of a not very common word. It occurs in Shakspeare once in the same sense with that here:

'. . . . . Trust to me, Ulysses,
Our imputation shall be oddly pois'd
In this wild action: for the success,
Although particular, shall give a *scantling*
Of good or bad unto the general.'—*Troilus and Cressida*, i. 3.

See also Locke, Human Understanding, b. ii., c. 21.

(*b*) P. 108.—'As killing in my bones.' The strong impression 'killing,' or even as it might be rendered, murder, is a literal equivalent of the original (רֶצַח), which is intended to express excruciating pain. Compare Ezekiel xxi. 22, rendered 'slayeth' in auth. version.

(*c*) P. 111.—'As one saith of anger.' The reference is to Virgil, Æn., lib. i., v. 150:

> '. . . . . . . *Furor arma ministrat ;*
> Tum pietate gravem ac meritis, si forte virum quem
> Conspexere,' &c.

(*d*) P. 115—'The poor church in the Palatinate.' Our memoir shews the deep interest Sibbes, in common with the 'Puritans,' took in the persecuted Protestants of Bohemia.

(*e*) P. 116.—'Intend' = stretch, and so augment. Richardson illustrates the word from Barrow.

G.

THE SOUL'S CONFLICT WITH ITSELF,

AND VICTORY OVER ITSELF BY FAITH.

A TREATISE OF THE INWARD DISQUIETMENTS OF DISTRESSED SPIRITS, WITH COMFORTABLE REMEDIES TO ESTABLISH THEM.

THE SOUL'S CONFLICT, AND VICTORY OVER ITSELF BY FAITH.

NOTE.

The several editions of the 'Soul's Conflict,' known to the Editor, and collated for the present publication, are, with the letters used to designate them, as follows:—

(*a*) The Sovles Conflict with it selfe, and Victorie over it selfe by Faith. A Treatise of the inward disquietments of distressed spirits, with comfortable remedies to establish them. '*Returne unto thy rest, O my soule, for the Lord hath dealt bountifully with thee.*'

By R. Sibbs, D.D., Master of Katherine Hall, in Cambridge, and Preacher at Grayes Inne, London.

Printed at London, by M. Flesher, for R. Dawlman, at the Brazen Serpent, in Paul's Churchyard. 1635. 12mo. A.

*** This is the *first* edition.

(*b*) There was a re-issue in same year—1635—of A. It is distinguishable from it by having 'Victory' for 'Victorie' in title-page, and by certain corrections, and one alteration. The chief interest attaching to it rests on the latter, upon which Bishop Patrick makes his charge against the Puritans of 'falsification.' See note at end of treatise.

(*c*) 2d edition, 1635. 12mo. C.

(*d*) Another called '2d edition,' 1636. 12mo. D.

(*e*) 3d edition, 1636. 12mo. E.

(*f*) 4th edition, 1638. 12mo. F.

(*g*) Another called '4th edition,' 1651. 12mo. G.

(*h*) 5th edition, 1658. 12mo, H.

The text of our reprint is A (see title-page *supra*), with collations from B; C to H consist simply of reproductions of C, and which, except in the addition of the 'Verses' by Benlowes and Quarles, follows B. I have preferred A as our text, from its having been published by Sibbes himself, but have carefully noted the 'corrections' and alteration *supra* as unquestionably made by his authority. The division into chapters of C has been retained, as facilitating perusal.

G.

TO THE RIGHT WORSHIPFUL

SIR JOHN BANKES, KNIGHT,

THE KING'S MAJESTY'S ATTORNEY-GENERAL,*

SIR EDWARD MOSELY, KNIGHT,

HIS MAJESTY'S ATTORNEY OF THE DUCHY [OF LANCASTER],†

SIR WILLIAM DENNY, KNIGHT,

ONE OF THE KING'S LEARNED COUNCIL,‡

SIR DUDLEY DIGGES, KNIGHT,

ONE OF THE MASTERS OF THE CHANCERY;||

AND THE REST OF THE WORSHIPFUL,

READERS AND BENCHERS, WITH THE ANCIENTS, BARRISTERS, STUDENTS,

AND ALL OTHERS BELONGING TO THE HONOURABLE SOCIETY OF GRAY'S INN,

R[ICHARD] SIBBES

DEDICATETH THESE SERMONS, PREACHED AMONGST THEM, IN TESTIMONY OF HIS DUE OBSERVANCE, AND DESIRE OF THEIR SPIRITUAL AND ETERNAL GOOD.

* Sir John Bankes was a man of mark in his generation. He was constituted Lord Chief Justice of the Common Pleas, from being attorney, as above described, in 1640–41. He adhered to Charles I; and was employed against Hampden the patriot, in the case of ship-money. His wife's noble defence of Corfe Castle, and its fall by treachery in the next year, has been well told by a descendant in a volume dedicated to the story of Corfe Castle. He died in 1644, at Oxford.—Consult Foss's admirable Judges of England, vol. vi.; also Lloyd's 'Memoires,' pp. 586–7, 1668.

† Sir Edward Mosely or Mosley was of the family of Ancoats, near Manchester. now represented by Sir Oswald Mosley, Bart.

‡ Sir William Denny was of Cambridgeshire and Ireland.—See *Burke*.

|| Sir Dudley Digges, like Bankes, is a historical character. After fulfilling various senatorial and diplomatic appointments, and suffering imprisonment more than once, he was admitted Master in Chancery in 1631, and received a grant of the reversion of the office of Master of the Rolls after the death of Sir Julius Cæsar He obtained possession of it at Sir Julius's death, in April 1636, and held it till his own, in March 18. 1639. He is one of Fuller's 'Worthies.'—See Foss, as *supra*.

G.

TO THE CHRISTIAN READER.

There be two sorts of people always in the visible church, one that Satan keeps under with false peace, whose life is nothing but a diversion to present contentments, and a running away from God and their own hearts, which they know can speak no good unto them; these speak peace to themselves, but God speaks none. Such have nothing to do with this Scripture, Ps. xlii. 11; the way for these men to enjoy comfort, is to be soundly troubled. True peace arises from knowing the worst first, and then our freedom from it. It is a miserable peace that riseth from ignorance of evil. The angel 'troubled the waters,' John v. 4, and then it* cured those that stepped in. It is Christ's manner to trouble our souls first, and then to come with healing in his wings.

But there is another sort of people, who being drawn out of Satan's kingdom and within the covenant of grace, whom Satan labours to unsettle and disquiet: being the 'god of the world,' 2 Cor. iv. 4, he is vexed to see men in the world, walk above the world. Since he cannot hinder their estate, he will trouble their peace, and damp their spirits, and cut asunder the sinews of all their endeavours. These should take themselves to task as David doth here, and labour to maintain their portion and the glory of a Christian profession. For whatsoever is in God or comes from God, is for their comfort. Himself is the *God of comfort*, Rom. xv. 5; his Spirit most known by that office, John xiv. 26. Our blessed Saviour was so careful that his disciples should not be too much dejected, that he forgat his own bitter passion to comfort them, whom yet he knew would all forsake him: 'Let not your hearts be troubled,' saith he, John xiv. 1, 27. And his own soul was troubled to death, that we should not be troubled: 'whatsoever is written is written for this end,' 2 Cor. ii. 9; every article of faith hath a special influence in comforting a believing soul. They are not only food, but cordials; yea, he put himself to his oath, that we might not only have consolation, but *strong consolation*, Heb. vi. 18. The sacraments seal unto us all the comforts we have by the death of Christ. The exercise of religion, as prayer, hearing, reading, &c., is, that 'our joy may be full,' 2 John 12. The communion of saints is chiefly ordained to comfort the feeble-minded and to strengthen the weak, 1 Thess. v. 14. God's government of his church tends to this. Why doth he sweeten our pilgrimage, and let us see so many comfortable days in the world, but that we should serve him with cheerful and good hearts? As for crosses, he doth but cast us down, to raise us up, and empty us that he may fill us, and

* 'It,' removed in C.

melt us that we may be 'vessels of glory,' Rom. ix. 23, loving us as well in the furnace, as when we are out, and standing by us all the while. 'We are troubled, but not distressed; perplexed, but not in despair; persecuted but not forsaken,' 2 Cor. iv. 8. If we consider from what fatherly love afflictions come, how they are not only moderated but sweetened and sanctified in the issue to us, how can it but minister matter of comfort in the greatest seeming discomforts? How then can we let the reins of our affections loose to sorrow without being injurious to God and his providence? as if we would teach him how to govern his church.

What unthankfulness is it to forget our consolation, and to look only upon matter of grievance! to think so much upon two or three crosses, as to forget a hundred blessings! to suck poison out of that from which we should suck honey! What folly is it to straiten and darken our own spirits! and indispose ourselves from doing or taking good! A limb out of joint can do nothing without deformity and pain; dejection takes off the wheels of the soul.

Of all other, Satan hath most advantage of discontented persons, as most agreeable to his disposition, being the most discontented creature under heaven; he hammers all his dark plots in their brains. The discontentment of the Israelites in the wilderness provoked God to 'swear that they should never enter into his rest,' Ps. xcv. 11. There is 'another spirit in my servant Caleb,' saith God, Num. xiv. 24. The spirit of God's people is an encouraging spirit. Wisdom teaches them, if they feel any grievances, to conceal them from others that are weaker, lest they be disheartened. God threatens it as a curse to give a trembling heart, and sorrow of mind, Deut. xxviii. 65; whereas on the contrary, joy is as oil to the soul, it makes duties come off cheerfully and sweetly from ourselves, graciously to others, and acceptably to God. A prince cannot endure it in his subjects, nor a father in his children, to be lowering at their presence. Such usually have stolen waters, Prov. ix 17, to delight themselves in.

How many are there, that upon the disgrace that follows religion, are frighted from it? But what are discouragements, to the encouragements religion brings with it? which are such as the very angels themselves admire at. Religion indeed brings crosses with it, but then it brings comforts above those crosses. What a dishonour is it to religion to conceive that God will not maintain and honour his followers; as if his service were not the best service! what a shame is it for an heir of heaven to be cast down for every petty loss and cross! to be afraid of a man whose breath is in his nostrils, Isa. ii. 22, in not standing to a good cause, when we are sure God will stand by us, assisting and comforting us, whose presence is able to make the greatest torments sweet! *Tua presentia, Domine, Laurentio ipsam craticulam dulcem fecit.*

My discourse tends not to take men off from all grief and mourning; 'Light for the righteous is sown in sorrow,' Ps. xcvii. 11. Our state of absence from the Lord, and living here in a vale of tears, our daily infirmities, and our sympathy with others, requires it; and where most grace is there is most sensibleness, as in Christ. But we must distinguish between grief and that sullenness and dejection of spirit, which is with a repining and taking off from duty. When Joshua was overmuch cast down at Israel's turning their backs before their enemies, God reproves him, 'Get thee up, Joshua, why liest thou upon thy face?' Josh. vii. 10.

Some would have men, after the committing of gross sins, to be presently comfortable, and believe, without humbling themselves at all. Indeed, when we are once in Christ, we ought not to question our state in him, and if we do, it comes not from the Spirit; but yet a guilty conscience will be clamorous and full of objections, and God will not speak peace unto it till it be humbled. God will let his best children know what it is to be too bold with sin, as we see in David and Peter, who felt no peace till they had renewed their repentance. The way to rejoice 'with joy unspeakable and glorious,' 1 Pet. i. 8, is to stir up sighs 'that cannot be uttered,' Rom. viii. 26. And it is so far, that the knowledge of our state in grace should not humble us, that very ingenuity considering God's love to us, out of the nature of the thing itself, worketh sorrow and shame in us, to offend his Majesty.

One main stop that hinders Christians from rejoicing is, that they give themselves too much liberty to question their grounds of comfort and interest in the promises. This is wonderful, comfortable say they, but what is it to me, the promise belongs not to me? This ariseth from want of giving all 'diligence to make their calling sure,' 2 Pet. i. 10, to themselves. In watchfulness and diligence we sooner meet with comfort than in idle complaining. Our care, therefore, should be to get sound evidence of a good estate, and then likewise to keep our evidence clear; wherein we are not to hearken to our own fears and doubts, or the suggestion of our enemy, who studies to falsify our evidence, but to the word, and our own consciences enlightened by the Spirit; and then it is pride and pettishness to stand out against comfort to themselves. Christians should study to corroborate their title. We are never more in heaven, before we come thither, than when we can read our evidences. It makes us converse much with God, it sweetens all conditions, and makes us willing to do and suffer anything. It makes us have comfortable and honourable thoughts of ourselves, as too good for the service of any base lust, and brings confidence in God both in life and death.

But what if our condition be so dark that we cannot read our evidence at all?

Here look up to God's infinite mercy in Christ, as we did at the first, when we found no goodness in ourselves, and that is the way to recover whatsoever we think we have lost. By honouring God's mercy in Christ, we come to have the Spirit of Christ; therefore, when the waters of sanctification are troubled and muddy, let us run to the witness of blood. God seems to walk sometimes contrary to himself; he seems to discourage, when secretly he doth encourage, as the 'woman of Canaan,' Matt. xv. 21–23; but faith can find out these ways of God, and untie these knots, by looking to the free promise and merciful nature of God. Let our sottish and rebellious flesh murmur as much as it will, Who art thou? and what is thy worth? yet a Christian 'knows whom he believes,' 2 Tim. i. 12. Faith hath learned to set God against all.

Again, we must go on to add grace to grace. A growing and fruitful Christian is always a comfortable Christian; the oil of grace brings forth the oil of gladness. Christ is first a king of righteousness, and then a king of peace, Heb. vii. 2; the righteousness that he works by his Spirit brings a peace of sanctification, whereby though we are not freed from sin, yet we are enabled to combat with it, and to get the victory over it. Some degree of comfort follows every good action, as heat accompanies fire, and as beams and influences issue from the sun; which is so true, that very heathens, upon the discharge of a good conscience, have found comfort and peace answerable; this is a reward before our reward, *præmium ante præmium*.

Another thing that hinders the comfort of Christians is, that they forget what a gracious and merciful covenant they live under, wherein the perfection that is required is to be found in Christ. Perfection in us is sincerity; what is the end of faith but to bring us to Christ? Now imperfect faith, if sincere, knits us* to Christ, in whom our perfection lies.

God's design in the covenant of grace is to exalt the riches of his mercy above all sin and unworthiness of man; and we yield him more glory of his mercy by believing, than it would be to his justice to destroy us. If we were perfect in ourselves, we should not honour him so much, as when we labour to be found in Christ, having his righteousness upon us, Philip. iii. 9.

There is no one portion of Scripture oftener used to fetch up drooping spirits than this: '*Why art thou cast down, O my soul?*' It is figurative, and full of rhetoric, and all little enough to persuade the perplexed soul quietly *to trust in God;* which, without this retiring into ourselves and checking our hearts, will never be brought to pass. Chrysostom brings in a man loaden with troubles, coming into the church, where, when he heard this passage read, he presently recovered himself, and becomes another man, (Homil. in Genes. xxix.). As David, therefore, did acquaint himself with this form of dealing with his soul, so let us, demanding a reason of ourselves, Why we are cast down; which will at least check and put a stop to the distress, and make us fit to consider more solid grounds of true comfort.

Of necessity the soul must be something calmed and stayed before it can be comforted. Whilst the humours of the body rage in a great distemper, there is no giving of physic; so when the soul gives way to passion, it is unfit to entertain any counsel, therefore it must be stilled by degrees, that it may hear reason; and sometimes it is fitter to be moved with ordinary reason (as being more familiar unto it), than with higher reasons fetched from our supernatural condition in Christ, as from the condition of man's nature subject to changes, from the uncomeliness of yielding to passion for that which it is not in our power to mend, &c.; these and such like reasons have some use to stay the fit for a while, but they leave the core untouched, which is sin, the trouble of all troubles. Yet when such considerations are made spiritual by faith on higher grounds, they have some operation upon the soul, as the influence of the moon having the stronger influence of the sun mingled with it becomes more effectual upon these inferior bodies. A candle light being ready at hand is sometimes as useful as the sun itself.

But our main care should be to have evangelical grounds of comfort near to us, as reconciliation with God, whereby all things else are reconciled to us, adoption and communion with Christ, &c., which is never sweeter than under the cross. Philip Lansgrave of Hesse, being a long time prisoner under Charles the Fifth, was demanded what upheld him all that time? who answered that 'he felt the divine comfort of the martyrs.' *Respondit divinas consolationes martyrum se sensisse.* There be divine comforts which are felt under the cross, and not at other times.

Besides personal troubles, there are many much dejected with the present state of the church, seeing the blood of so many saints to be shed, and the enemies oft to prevail; but God hath stratagems, as Joshua at Ai, Josh. vii. He seems sometimes to retire, that he may come upon his enemies with the greater advantage. The end of all these troubles will no doubt be the ruin of the antichristian faction; and we shall see the church in her more perfect beauty when the enemies shall be in that place which is fittest

* 'Us,' omitted in C.

for them, the lowest, that is, the footstool of Christ, Ps. cx. 1. The church, as it is highest in the favour of God, so it shall be the highest in itself. 'The mountain of the Lord shall be exalted above all mountains,' Isa. ii. 2. In the worst condition, the church hath two faces, one towards heaven and Christ, which is always constant and glorious; another towards the world, which is in appearance contemptible and changeable. But God will in the end give her beauty for ashes, and glory double to her shame, Isa. lxi. 3, and she shall in the end prevail; in the mean time, the power of the enemies is in God's hand, *robur hostium apud Deum.* The church of God conquers when it is conquered, even as our head Christ did, who overcame by patience as well as by power. Christ's victory was upon the cross. The spirit of a Christian conquers when his person is conquered.

The way is, instead of discouragement, to search all the promises made to the church in these latter times, and to turn them into prayers, and press God earnestly for the performance of them. Then we shall soon find God both cursing his enemies and blessing his people out of Zion, by the faithful prayers that ascend up from thence.

In all the promises we should have special recourse to God in them. In all storms there is sea room enough in the infinite goodness of God for faith to be carried with full sail.

And it must be remembered that in all places where God is mentioned, we are to understand God in the promised Messiah, typified out so many ways unto us. And to put the more vigour into such places in the reading of them, we in this latter age of the church must think of God shining upon us in the face of Christ, and our Father in him. If they had so much confidence in so little light, it is a shame for us not to be confident in good things, when so strong a light shines round about us, when we profess we believe 'a crown of righteousness is laid up for all those that love his appearing,' 2 Tim. iv. 8. Presenting these things to the soul by faith, setteth the soul in such a pitch of resolution, that no discouragements are able to seize upon it. 'We faint not,' saith St Paul. Wherefore doth he not faint? Because 'these light and short afflictions procure an exceeding weight of glory,' 2 Cor. iv. 17.

Luther, when he saw Melancthon, a godly and learned man, too much dejected for the state of the church in those times, falls a chiding of him, as David doth here his own soul: 'I strongly hate those miserable cares,' saith he, 'whereby thou writest thou art even spent. It is not the greatness of the cause, but the greatness of our incredulity. If the cause be false, let us revoke it. If true, why do we make God in his rich promises a liar? Strive against thyself, the greatest enemy. Why do we fear the conquered world, that have the conqueror himself on our side?' '*Ego miserrimas curas, quibus te consumi scribis, vehementer odi. Quod sic regnant in corde tuo, non est magnitudo causæ, sed magnitudo incredulitatis nostræ. Si causa falsa est revocemus. Si vera, cur facimus illum tantis promissis mendacem; luctare contra teipsum maximum hostem.*'*

Now, to speak something concerning the publishing of this treatise. I began to preach on the text about twelve years since in the city, and afterwards finished the same at Gray's Inn. After which, some having gotten imperfect notes, endeavoured to publish them without my privity. Therefore, to do myself right, I thought fit to reduce them to this form. There

* These remarkable words of a remarkable man are found in letters addressed to Melancthon during the Diet of Augsburg, A.D. 1530. They are effectively quoted by D'Aubigné, Hist. of Reformation, b. xiv., § x., c. 6.—G.

is a pious and studious gentleman of Gray's Inn, that hath of late published observations upon the whole psalm,* and another upon this very verse† very well; and many others, by treatises of faith,‡ and such like, have furthered the spiritual peace of Christians much. It were to be wished that we would all join to do that which the apostles gloried in, 'to be helpers of the joy of God's people,' 2 Cor. i. 24. By reason of my absence while the work was in printing, some sentences were mistaken. Some will be ready to deprave the labours of other men; but, so good may be done, let such ill-disposed persons be what they are, and what they will be, unless God turn their hearts. And so I commend thee and this poor treatise to God's blessing.

R. SIBBES.

GRAY'S INN, *July* 1. 1635.

* 'Whole psalm.' This probably refers to William Bloy's 'Meditations on the 42d Psalm.' 1632.

† 'Very verse.' Query, Dr John Reading's 'David's Soliloquy; being the Substance of Several Sermons on Psalm xlii. 11. 1630?'

‡ 'Faith.' Sibbes had himself prefaced Ball, and Preston, and Culverwell on 'Faith.'

*** Sir Egerton Brydges, in his Restituta, iii. p. 500, has this note:—'One of these (on 'Faith'), was written by the Rev. John Rogers, minister of Dedham in Essex; but I cannot point out the two writers previously alluded to.' G.

IN OPUS POSTHUMUM ADMODUM REVERENDI,

MIHIQUE MULTIS NOMINIBUS COLENDI, RICHARDI SIBBES, S. T. PROFESSORIS, AULÆ SANCTÆ. CATH. PRÆFECTI DIGNISSIMI.

VADE, liber, pie dux animæ, pie mentis Achates;
  Te relegens, fructu ne pereunte legat;
Quam fœlix prodis! Præ sacro codice sordent,
  Bartole, sive tui; sive, Galene, tui.

Fidu præco Dei, cœlestis cultor agelli,
  Assidui pretium grande laboris habet:
Quo mihi nec vitâ melior, nec promptior ore,
  Gratior aut vultu, nec fuit arte prior.

Nil opus ut nardum caro combibat uncta Sabæum,
  Altáve marmoreus sydera tangat apex:
Non eget hic urnâ, non marmore; nempe volumen
  Stat sacrum, vivax marmor, et urna, pio.

Qui Christo vivens incessit tramite cœli,
  Æthereúmque obiit munus, obire nequit:
Ducit hic angelicis æqualia sæcula lustris,
  Qui verbo studium contulit omne suum.

Perlegat hunc legum cultrix veneranda senectus,
  Et quos plena Deo mens super astra vehit:
Venduntur (quanti!) circum palatia fumi!
  Hic sacer altaris carbo minoris erit?

Heu! pietas ubi prisca? profana ô tempora! mundi
  Fæx! vesper! prope nox! ô mora! Christe veni.
Si valuere preces unquam, et custodia Christi,
  Nunc opus est precibus, nunc ope, Christe, tuâ.

Certat in humanis vitiorum infamia rebus,
  Hei mihi! nulla novis sufficit herba malis?
Probra referre pudet; nec enim decet: exprobret illa
  Qui volet; est nostrum flere, silendo queri.

Flere? Tonabo tuas, pietas neglecta, querelas:
  Quid non schisma, tepor, fastus, et astus agunt?
Addo—Sed historicus Tacitus fuit optimus. Immo
  Addam—sphærarum at musica muta placet.

EDV. BENLOSIO.*

CRESSINGÆ TEMPLARIORUM,
Prid. Cal. Febr. MDCXXXV.†

* Edward Benlowes, Esq. He was of Brenthall. Essex. Consult Brydges's Restituta, iii. 41, 42; and Wood's Fasti Oxon. (ed. by Bliss), ii. 358. His principal book is his 'Theophila.' Samuel Butler, Pope, and Bishop Warburton. have satirized his poetry. It is to be feared his tribute to Sibbes will not neutralize the general condemnation. He was a good man, and the friend of good men, to his own impoverishment.

† Sibbes died *July* 5. 1635, and yet this poem, dated '*February* 1635,' is *in memoriam.* The explanation is that prior to 1752, the year in England was reckoned not from 1st January, but from 25th March. All those days, therefore, intervening between the 31st of December and the 25th of March, which we should now date as belonging to a particular year, were then dated as belonging to the year preceding that. Hence while Benlowes wrote according to our reckoning in 1636, he still dates 1635. G.

ON THE WORK OF MY LEARNED FRIEND DOCTOR SIBBES.

FOOL that I was! to think my easy pen
Had strength enough to glorify the fame
Of this known author, this rare man of men,
Or give the least advantage to his name.
  Who think by praise to make his name more bright,
  Shew the sun's glory by dull candle-light.*

Blest saint! thy hallow'd pages do require
No slight preferment from our slender lays;
We stand amazed at what we most admire:
Ah, what are saints the better for our praise!
  He that commends this volume does no more
  Than warm the fire or gild the massy ore.*

Let me stand silent, then. O may that Spirit
Which led thine hand direct mine eye, my breast,
That I may read and do, and so inherit
(What thou enjoy'st and taught'st) eternal rest!
  Fool that I was! to think my lines could give
  Life to that work, by which they hope to live.

FRA[NCIS] QUA[RLES].†

* Sir Egerton Brydges, in his Restituta, annotates here.—'This is much in unison with Shakespeare's thought:—

" To gild refined gold, to paint the lily,
To seek the beauteous eye of heaven to garnish,
Is wasteful and ridiculous excess." '

Aristotle might haply here have been introduced by the Commentators. *e.g.*, 'They who demonstrate plain things, light a candle to see the sun,' iii. p. 499.

† Francis Quarles. There is no doubt that this was the quaint poet of the 'Emblems,' and many other volumes not so well known as they deserve to be. It was common to contract names thus, formerly. The 'Garden of Spiritual Flowers,' (1622) is worded on title-page, 'A Garden of Spirituall Flowers, planted by Ri. Ro., Will. Per., Ri. Gree., M. M., and Geo. Web.,' designating severally, Richard Rogers, William Perkins, Richard Greene, &c., &c., and so in many other instances. G.

THE SOUL'S CONFLICT WITH ITSELF.

Why art thou cast down, O my soul? and why art thou disquieted within me? hope thou in God; for I shall yet praise him, who is the health of my countenance, and my God.—PSALM XLII. 11.

THE Psalms are, as it were, the anatomy of a holy man, which lay the inside of a truly devout man outward to the view of others. If the Scriptures be compared to a body, the Psalms may well be the heart, they are so full of sweet affections and passions. For in other portions of Scripture God speaks to us; but in the Psalms holy men speak to God and their own hearts, as

In this Psalm we have *the passionate passages of a broken and troubled spirit.*

At this time David was a banished man, banished from his own house, from his friends, and, which troubled him most, from the house of God, upon occasion of Saul's persecution, who hunted him as a partridge upon the mountains. See how this works upon him.

1. *He lays open his desire springing from his love;* love being the prime and leading affection of the soul, from whence grief springs, from being crossed in that we love. For the setting out of which his affection to the full, he borroweth an expression from the hart. No hart, being chased by the hunters, panteth more after the waters than my heart doth after thee, O God, ver. 1. Though he found God present with him in exile, yet there is a sweeter presence of him in his ordinances, which now he wanted and took to heart. Places and conditions are happy or miserable as God vouchsafeth his gracious presence more or less; and, therefore, 'When, O when shall it be that I appear before God?' ver. 2.

2. Then, after his strong desire, *he lays out his grief,* which he could not contain, but must needs give a vent to it in tears; and he had such a spring of grief in him as fed his tears day and night, ver. 3. All the ease he found was to dissolve this cloud of grief into the shower of tears.

Quest. But why gives he this way to his grief?

Ans. Because, together with his exiling from God's house, he was upbraided by his enemies with his religion, 'Where is now thy God?' ver. 3. Grievances come not alone, but, as Job's messengers, Job i., follow one another. These bitter taunts, together with the remembrance of his former happiness in communion with God in his house, made deep impressions in his soul, when he 'remembered how he went with the multitude into the house of God,' ver. 4, and led a goodly train with him, being willing, as a good magistrate and master of a family, not to go to the house of God alone, nor to heaven alone, but to carry as many as he could with him. Oh! the remembrance of this made him pour forth, not his words or his tears only, but his very soul. Former favours and happiness make the soul more sensible of all impressions to the contrary. Hereupon, finding his soul over sensible, he expostulates with himself, 'Why art thou cast down, O my soul? and why art thou disquieted within me?' &c.

But though the remembrance of the former sweetness of God's presence did somewhat stay him, yet his grief would not so be stilled, and therefore it gathers upon him again. One grief called upon another, ver. 7, as one deep wave follows another, without intermission, until his soul was almost overwhelmed under these waters; yet he recovers himself a little with looking up to God, who he expected would with speed and authority send forth his lovingkindness, with command to raise him up and comfort him, and give him matter of 'songs in the night,' ver. 8. For all this, his unruly grief will not be calmed, but renews assaults upon the return of the reproach of his enemies. Their words were as swords, ver. 10, unto him, and his heart being made very tender and sensible of grief, these sharp words enter too deep; and thereupon he hath recourse to his former remedy, as being the most tried, to chide his soul, and charge it to trust in God.

Chapter I.—*General Observations upon the Text.*

Obs. 1. Hence in general we may observe that *grief gathered to a head will not be quieted at the first.* We see here passions intermingled with comforts, and comforts with passions; and what bustling there is before David can get the victory over his own heart. You have some short-spirited Christians that, if they be not comforted at the first, they think all labour with their hearts is in vain, and thereupon give way to their grief. But we see in David, as distemper ariseth upon distemper, so he gives check upon check and charge upon charge to his soul, until at length he brought it to a quiet temper. In physic, if one purge will not carry away the vicious humour, then we add a second; if that will not do it, we take a third. So should we deal with our souls. Perhaps one check, one charge will not do it, then fall upon the soul again; send it to God again, and never give over until our souls be possessed of our souls again.

Again, in general observe in David's spirit that *a gracious and living soul is most sensible of the want of spiritual means.*

Reason. The reason is because spiritual life hath answerable taste, and hunger and thirst after spiritual helps.

We see in nature that those things press hardest upon it that touch upon the necessities of nature, rather than those that touch upon delights; for these further only our comfortable being, but necessities uphold our being itself, *acrius urgent quæ necessitatis sunt, quam quæ spectant ad voluptatem.* We see how famine wrought upon the patriarchs to go into Egypt: where we may see what to judge of those who willingly excommunicate themselves from the assemblies of God's people, where the Father, Son, and Holy Ghost are present, where the prayers of holy men meet together in one, and, as it were, bind God, and pull down God's blessing. No private devotion hath that report of acceptance from heaven.

Obs. 3. A third general point is, that *a godly soul, by reason of the life of grace, knows when it is well with it and when it is ill, when it is a good day with it and when a bad.* When God shines in the use of means, then the soul is, as it were, in heaven; when God withdraws himself, then it is in darkness for a time. Where there is but only a principle of nature, without sanctifying grace, there men go plodding on and keep their rounds, and are at the end, where they were at the beginning; not troubled with changes, because there is nothing within to be troubled; and, therefore, dead means, quick means, or no means, all is one with them, an argument of a dead soul. And so we come particularly and directly to the words, '*Why art thou cast down, O my soul? and why art thou disquieted within me?*' &c.

The words imply, 1, *David's state wherein he was;* and 2, express his *carriage in that state.*

His estate was such that in regard of outward condition, he was in variety of troubles; and that in regard of inward disposition of spirit, he was first *cast down*, and then *disquieted.*

Now for his carriage of himself in this condition, and disposition, he dealeth roundly with himself. David reasoneth the case with David, and first checketh himself for being too much *cast down*, and then for being too much *disquieted.*

And then layeth a charge upon himself *to trust in God;* wherein we have the duty he chargeth upon himself, which is to *trust in God*, and the grounds of the duty:

First, from confidence of better times to come, which would yield him matter of *praising God.*

And then by a representation of God unto him, as a saving God in all troubles, nay, as salvation itself, an open glorious Saviour in the view of all, *The salvation of my countenance.* And all this enforced from David's interest in God, *He is my God.*

Obs. 1. Whence observe first, from the state he was now in, that *since guilt and corruption hath been derived by the fall, into the nature of man, it hath been subjected to misery and sorrow, and that in all conditions, from the king that sitteth on the throne to him that grindeth on the mill.* None ever have* been so good or so great, as could raise themselves so high as to be above the reach of troubles.

1. And that choice part of mankind, the first-fruits and excellency of the rest, which we call the church, more than others; which appears by consideration both of the head, the body, and members of the church. For the *head* Christ, he took our flesh as it was subject to misery after the fall, and was, in regard of that which he endured, both in life and death, a man of sorrows.

2. For the *body*, the church, it may say from the first to the last, as it is, Ps. cxxix. 1, 'From my youth up they have afflicted me.' The church began in blood, hath grown up by blood, and shall end in blood, as it was redeemed by blood.

3. For the *members*, they are all predestinated to a conformity to Christ their head, as in grace and glory, so in abasement, Rom. viii. 29. Neither is it a wonder for those that are born soldiers to meet with conflicts, for travellers to meet with hard usage, for seamen to meet with storms, for strangers in a strange country, especially amongst their enemies, to meet with strange entertainment.

A Christian is a man of another world, and here from home, which he

* 'Hath,' in C.

would forget, if he were not exercised here, and would take his passage for his country. But though all Christians agree and meet in this, that 'through many afflictions we must enter into heaven,' Acts xiv. 22, yet according to the diversity of place, parts, and grace, there is a different cup measured to every one.

Use. And therefore it is but a plea of the flesh, to except against the cross, 'never was poor creature distressed as I am.' This is but self-love, for was it not the case both of head, body, and members, as we see here in David a principal member? when he was brought to this case, thus to reason the matter with himself, 'Why art thou cast down, O my soul? and why art thou disquieted within me?'

Obs. 2. From the frame of David's spirit under these troubles, we may observe, that as the case is thus with all God's people, to be exercised with troubles, *they are sensible of them oftentimes, even to casting down and discouraging*. And the reason is (1), they are flesh and blood, subject to the same passions, and made of the same mould, subject to the same impressions from without as other men. And (2) their nature is upheld with the same supports and refreshings as others, the withdrawing and want of which affecteth them. And (3) besides those troubles they suffer in common with other men, by reason* of their new advancement and their new disposition they have in and from Christ their head, they are more sensible in a peculiar manner of those troubles that any way touch upon that blessed condition, from a new life they have in and from Christ; which will better appear if we come more particularly to a discovery of the more special causes of this distemper, some of which are, 1. Without us. 2. Some within us.

Chapter II.—*Of Discouragements from without.*

I. *Outward causes of discouragement.*

1. *God himself:* who sometimes withdraws the beams of his countenance from his children, whereupon the soul even of the strongest Christian is disquieted; when together with the cross, God himself seems to be an enemy unto them. The child of God, when he seeth that his troubles are mixed with God's displeasure, and perhaps his conscience tells him that God hath a just quarrel against him, because he hath not renewed his peace with his God, then this anger of God puts a sting into all other troubles, and adds to the disquiet. There were some ingredients of this divine temptation, as we call it, in holy David at this time; though most properly a divine temptation be, when God appears unto us as an enemy, without any special guilt of any particular sin, as in Job's case.

And no marvel if Christians be from hence disquieted, whenas the Son of God himself, having always enjoyed the sweet communion with his Father, and now feeling an estrangement, that he might be a curse for us, complained in all his torments of nothing else, but 'My God, my God, why hast *thou* forsaken me? Matt. xxvii. 46. It is with the godly in this case as with vapours drawn up by the sun, which, when the extracting force of the sun leaves them, fall down again to the earth from whence they are drawn. So when the soul, raised up and upheld by the beams of his countenance, is left of God, it presently begins to sink. We see when the body of the sun is partly hid from us, for totally it cannot, in an eclipse by the body of the moon, that there is a drooping in the whole frame of nature;

* 'By reason,' added in B.

so it is in the soul, when there is anything that comes between God's gracious countenance and it.

2. Besides, if we look down to inferior causes, the soul is oft cast down by Satan, who is all for casting down, and for disquieting. For being a cursed spirit, cast and tumbled down himself from heaven, where he is never to come again, [he] is hereupon full of disquiet, carrying a hell about himself; whereupon all that he labours for is to cast down and disquiet others, that they may be, as much as he can procure, in the same cursed condition with himself. He was not ashamed to set upon Christ himself with this temptation of casting down, and thinks Christ's members never low enough, till he can bring them as low as himself.

By his envy and subtilty we were driven out of paradise at the first, and now he envies us the paradise of a good conscience; for that is our paradise until we come to heaven, into which no serpent shall ever creep to tempt us. When Satan seeth a man strongly and comfortably walk with God, he cannot endure that a creature of meaner rank by creation than himself should enjoy such happiness. Herein, like some peevish men which are his instruments, men too contentious and bred up therein, as the salamander in the fire, who when they know the cause to be naught, and their adversaries to have the better title, yet, out of malice, they will follow them with suits and vexations, though they be not able to disable their opposites' title. If their malice have not a vent in hurting some way, they will burst for anger.

It is just so with the devil; when he seeth men will to heaven, and that they have good title to it, then he follows them with all dejecting and uncomfortable temptations that he can. It is his continual trade and course to seek his rest in our disquiet, he is by beaten practice and profession a tempter in this kind.

3. Again, what Satan cannot do himself by immediate suggestions, that he labours to work by his instruments, who are all for casting down of those who stand in their light, as those in the psalm, who cry, 'Down with him, down with him, even to the ground,' Ps. cxxxvii. 7; a character and stamp of which men's dispositions we have in the verse before this text; 'Mine enemies,' saith David, 'reproach me.' As sweet and as compassionate a man as he was, to pray and put on sackcloth for them, Ps. xxxv. 13, yet he had enemies, and such enemies, as did not suffer their malice only to boil and concoct in their own breasts, but out of the abundance of their hearts, they reproached him in words. There is nothing the nature of man is more impatient of than of reproaches; for there is no man so mean but thinks himself worthy of some regard, and a reproachful scorn shews an utter disrespect, which issues from the very superfluity of malice.

Neither went they behind his back, but were so impudent to say it to his face. A malicious heart and a slandering tongue go together, and though shame might have suppressed the uttering of such words, yet their insolent carriage spake as much in David's heart, Ps. xxxix. 1. We may see by the language of men's carriage what their heart saith, and what their tongue would vent if they dared.

And this their malice was unwearied, for they said daily unto him, as if it had been fed with a continual spring. Malice is an unsatiable monster, it will minister words, as rage ministers weapons. But what was that they said so reproachfully, and said daily? 'Where is now thy God? ver. 3. They upbraid him with his singularity, they say not now, Where is God, but Where is thy God, that thou dost boast so much on, as if thou hadst some special interest in him? where we see that the scope of the devil and wicked men is to shake the godly's faith and confidence in their God. As Satan laboured to divide betwixt Christ and his Father, 'If thou beest the Son of God, command that these stones be made bread,' Matt. iv. 3, so he labours to divide betwixt Father and Son and us. They labour to bring God in jealousy with David, as if God had neglected him bearing himself so much upon God. They had some colour of this, for God at this time had vailed himself from David, as he does oft from his best children, for the better discovery of the malice of wicked men; and doth not Satan tip the tongues of the enemies of religion now, to insult over the church now lying a bleeding!* What's become† of their reformation, of their gospel? Nay, rather what's become of your eyes, we may say unto them? For God is nearest to his children when he seems farthest off. 'In the mount of the Lord it shall be seen,' Gen. xxii. 14; God is with them, and in them, though the wicked be not aware of it; it is all one, as if one should say betwixt the space of the new and old moon, Where is now the moon? whenas it is never nearer the sun than at that time.

Quest. Where is now thy God?

Ans. In heaven, in earth, in me, everywhere but in the heart of such as ask such questions, and yet there they shall find him too in his time, filling their consciences with his wrath; and then, where is their God? where are their great friends, their riches, their honours, which they set up as a god? what can they avail them now?

But how was David affected with these reproaches? Their words were as swords, 'as with a sword in my bones,' &c., ver. 10, they spake daggers to him, they cut him to the quick when they touched him in his God, as if he had neglected his servants, whenas the devil himself regards those who serve his turn. Touch a true godly man in his religion, and you touch his life and his best freehold; he lives more in his God than in himself; so that we may see here, there is a murder of the tongue, a wounding tongue as well as a healing tongue. Men think themselves freed from murder if they kill none, or if they shed no blood, whereas they cut others to the heart with bitter words. It is good to extend the commandment to awake the conscience the more, and breed humility, when men see there is a murdering of the tongue. We see David, therefore, upon this reproach, to be presently so moved, as to fall out with himself for it, 'Why art thou so cast down and disquieted, O my soul?' This bitter taunt ran so much in his mind, that he expresseth it twice in this psalm; he was sensible that they struck at God through his sides; what they spake in scorn and lightly, he took heavily. And indeed, when religion suffers, if there be any heavenly fire in the heart, it will rather break out, than not discover itself at all. We see by daily experience, that there is a special force in words uttered from a subtle head, a false heart and a smooth tongue, to weaken the hearts of professors, by bringing an evil report upon the strict profession of religion; as the cunning and false spies did upon the good land, Num. xiii. 27, as if it were not only in vain, but dangerous to appear for Christ in evil times. If the example of such as have faint spirits will discourage in an army, as we see in Gideon's history, Judges vii., then what will speech enforced both by example and with some show of reason do?

4. To let others pass, we need not go further than ourselves, for to find causes of discouragement; there is a seminary of them within us. Our flesh, an enemy so much the worse, by how much the nearer, will be ready

* This was preached in the beginning of the troubles of the church. [1623. G.]
‡ 'What becomes,' in C.

to upbraid us within us, 'Where is now thy God?' why shouldst thou stand out in a profession that finds no better entertainment?

CHAPTER III.—*Of Discouragements from within.*

But to come to some particular causes *within* us. There is cause oft in the body of those in whom a melancholy temper prevaileth. Darkness makes men fearful. Melancholy persons are in a perpetual darkness, all things seem black and dark unto them, their spirits, as it were, dyed black. Now to him that is in darkness, all things seem black and dark; the sweetest comforts are not lightsome enough unto those that are deep in melancholy. It is, without great watchfulness, Satan's bath; which he abuseth as his own weapon to hurt the soul, which, by reason of its sympathy with the body, is subject to be misled. As we see where there is a suffusion of the eye by reason of distemper of humours, or where things are presented through a glass to the eye, things seem to be of the same colour; so whatsoever is presented to a melancholy person, comes in a dark way to the soul. From whence it is that their fancy being corrupted, they judge amiss, even of outward things, as that they are sick of such and such a disease, or subject to such and such a danger, when it is nothing so; how fit are they then to judge of things removed from sense, as of their spiritual estate in Christ?

II. *Causes privative, of discouragement in ourselves.*

1. To come to causes more near the soul itself, as when there is want of that which should be in it, as of *knowledge in the understanding*, &c. Ignorance, being darkness, is full of false fears. In the night time men think every bush a thief. Our forefathers in time of ignorance were frighted with everything; therefore it is the policy of popish tyrants, taught them from the prince of darkness, to keep the people in darkness, that so they might make them fearful, and then abuse that fearfulness to superstition; that they might the better rule in their consciences for their own ends; and that so having entangled them with false fears, they might heal them again with false* cures.

2. Again, though the soul be not ignorant, yet if it be *forgetful and mindless*, if, as the apostle saith, 'you have forgot the consolation that speaks unto you,' &c., Heb. xii. 5. We have no more present actual comfort than we have remembrance; help a godly man's memory, and help his comfort; like unto charcoal, which, having once been kindled, is the more easy to take fire. He that hath formerly known things, takes ready acquaintance of them again, as old friends; things are not strange to him.

3. And further, *want of setting due price upon comforts;* as the Israelites were taxed for setting nothing by the pleasant land. It is a great fault when, as they said to Job, 'the consolation of the Almighty seem light and small unto us,' Job xv. 11, unless we have some outward comfort which we linger after.

4. Add unto this, *a childish kind of peevishness;* when they have not what they would have, like children, they throw away all; which, though it be very offensive to God's Spirit, yet it seizeth often upon men otherwise gracious. Abraham himself, wanting children, Gen. xv. 2, undervalued all other blessings. Jonah, because he was crossed of his gourd, was weary of his life. The like may be said of Elias, flying from Jezebel. This peevishness is increased by a too much flattering of their grief, so far as to justify

* 'False' is misprinted 'safe' in A and B. 'False,' the correction, is from C.

it; like Jonas, 'I do well to be angry even unto death,' Jonah iv. 9; he would stand to it. Some, with Rachel, are so peremptory, that they 'will not be comforted,' Jer. xxxi. 15, as if they were in love with their grievances. Wilful men are most vexed in their crosses. It is not for those to be wilful that have not a great measure of wisdom to guide their wills; for God delights to have his will of those that are wedded to their own wills, as in Pharaoh. No men more subject to discontentments than those who would have all things after their own way.

5. Again, one main ground is, *false reasoning, and error in our discourse*, as that we have no grace when we feel none. Feeling is not always a fit rule to judge our states by, that God hath rejected us, because we are crossed in outward things, whenas this issues from God's wisdom and love. How many imagine their failings to be fallings, and their fallings to be fallings away; infirmities to be presumptions; every sin against conscience, to be the sin against the Holy Ghost; unto which misapprehensions, weak and dark spirits are subject. And Satan, as a cunning rhetorician, here enlargeth the fancy, to apprehend things bigger than they are. Satan abuseth confident spirits another contrary way; to apprehend great sins as little, and little as none. Some also think that they have no grace, because they have not so much as grown Christians; whereas there be several ages in Christ. Some, again, are so desirous and enlarged after what they have not, that they mind not what they have. Men may be rich, though they have no millions, and be not emperors.

6. Likewise, some are much troubled, because they proceed by *a false method and order* in judging of their estates. They will begin with election, which is the highest step of the ladder; whereas they should begin from a work of grace wrought within their hearts, from God's calling them by his Spirit, and their answer to his call, and so raise themselves upwards to know their election by their answer to God's calling. 'Give all diligence,' saith Peter, 'to make your calling and election sure,' 2 Pet. i. 10, your election by your calling. God descends down unto us from election to calling, and so to sanctification; we must ascend to him, beginning where he ends. Otherwise it is as great folly as in removing of a pile of wood, to begin at the lowest first, and so, besides the needless trouble, to be in danger to have the rest to fall upon our heads. Which, besides ignorance, argues pride, appearing in this, that they would bring God to their conceits, and be at an end of their work before they begin.

This great secret of God's eternal love to us in Christ is hidden in his breast, and doth not appear to us, until in the use of means God by his Spirit discovereth the same unto us; the Spirit letteth into the soul so much life and sense of God's love in particular to us, as draweth the soul to Christ, from whom it draweth so much virtue as changeth the frame of it, and quickeneth it to duty, which duties are not grounds of our state in grace, but issues, springing from a good state before; and thus far they help us in judging of our condition, that though they be not to be rested in, yet as streams they lead us to the spring-head of grace from whence they arise.

And of signs, some be more apt to deceive us, as being not so certain, as 'delight and joy in hearing the word,' Mat. xiii. 20, as appeareth in the third ground; some are more constant and certain, as love to those that are truly good, and to all such, and because they are such, &c. These as they are wrought by the Spirit, so the same Spirit giveth evidence to the soul of the truth of them, and leadeth us to faith from whence they come, and faith leads us to the discovery of God's love made known to us in hearing the word opened. The same Spirit openeth the truth to us, and our understandings to conceive of it, and our hearts to close with it by faith, not only as a truth, but as a truth belonging to us.

Now this faith is manifested, either by itself reflecting upon itself the light of faith, discovering both itself and other things, or by the cause of it, or by the effect, or by all. Faith is oft more known to us in the fruit of it, than in itself, as in plants, the fruits are more apparent than the sap and root. But the most settled knowledge is from the cause, as when I know I believe, because in hearing God's gracious promises opened and offered unto me, the Spirit of God carrieth my soul to cleave to them as mine own portion, Eph. i. 13. Yet the most familiar way of knowledge of our estates is from the effects to gather the cause, the cause being oftentimes more remote and spiritual, the effects more obvious and visible. All the vigour and beauty in nature which we see, comes from a secret influence from the heavens which we see not; in a clear morning we may see the beams of the sun shining upon the top of hills and houses before we can see the sun itself.

Things in the working of them, do issue from the cause, by whose force they had their being; but our knowing of things ariseth from the effect, where the cause endeth. We know God must love us before we can love him, and yet we oft first know that we love him, 1 John iv. 19; the love of God is the cause why we love our brother, and yet we know we love our brother whom we see more clearly, than God whom we do not see, ver. 20.

It is a spiritual peevishness that keeps men in a perplexed condition, that they neglect these helps to judge of their estates by, whereas God takes liberty to help us sometime to a discovery of our estate by the effects, sometimes by the cause, &c. And it is a sin to set light by any work of the Spirit, and the comfort we might have by it, and therefore we may well add this as one cause of disquietness in many, that they grieve the Spirit, by quarrelling against themselves and the work of the Spirit in them.

7. Another cause of disquiet is, that men by a natural kind of popery *seek for their comfort too much sanctification*, neglecting justification, relying too much upon their own performances. St Paul was of another mind, accounting all but dung and dross, compared to the righteousness of Christ, Philip. iii. 8, 9. This is that garment, wherewith being decked, we please our husband, and wherein we get the blessing. This giveth satisfaction to the conscience, as satisfying God himself, being performed by God the Son, and approved therefore by God the Father. Hereupon the soul is quieted, and faith holdeth out this as a shield against the displeasure of God and temptations of Satan. Why did the apostles in their prefaces join grace and peace together,* but that we should seek for our peace in the free grace and favour of God in Christ?

No wonder why papists maintain doubting, who hold salvation by works, because Satan joining together with our consciences will always find some flaw even in our best performances; hereupon the doubting and misgiving soul comes to make this absurd demand, as, Who shall ascend to heaven? Ps. xxiv. 3, which is all one as to fetch Christ from heaven, and so bring him down to suffer on the cross again. Whereas if we believe in Christ we are as sure to come to heaven as Christ is there. Christ ascending and

* Grace and peace. See 1 Cor. i. 3; 2 Cor. i. 2; Gal. i. 3; Eph. i. 2; 1 Peter . 2; Rev. i. 4, &c., &c.—G.

descending, with all that he hath done, is ours. So that neither height nor depth can separate us from God's love in Christ, Rom. viii. 39.

But we must remember, though the main pillar of our comfort be in the free forgiveness of our sins, yet if there be a neglect in growing in holiness, the soul will never be soundly quiet, because it will be prone to question the truth of justification, and it is as proper for sin to raise doubts and fears in the conscience, as for rotten flesh and wood to breed worms.

8. And therefore we may well join this as a cause of disquietness, *the neglect of keeping a clear conscience.* Sin, like Achan, or Jonah in the ship, is that which causeth storms within and without. Where there is not a pure conscience, there is not a pacified conscience; and therefore though some, thinking to save themselves whole in justification, neglect the cleansing of their natures and ordering of their lives, yet in time of temptation they will find it more troublesome than they think. For a conscience guilty of many neglects, and of allowing itself in any sin, to lay claim to God's mercy, is to do as we see mountebanks sometimes do, who wound their flesh to try conclusions upon their own bodies, how sovereign the salve is; yet oftentimes they come to feel the smart of their presumption, by long and desperate wounds. So God will let us see what it is to make wounds to try the preciousness of his balm; such may go mourning to their graves. And though, perhaps, with much wrestling with God they may get assurance of the pardon of their sins, yet their conscience will be still trembling, like-as David's, though Nathan had pronounced unto him the forgiveness of his sin, Ps. li., till God at length speaks further peace, even as the water of the sea after a storm is not presently still, but moves and trembles a good while after the storm is over. A Christian is a new creature and walketh by rule, and so far as he walketh according to his rule, peace is upon him, Gal. vi. 16. Loose walkers that regard not their way, must think to meet with sorrows instead of peace. Watchfulness is the preserver of peace. It is a deep spiritual judgment to find peace in an ill way.

9. Some again reap the fruit of their *ignorance of Christian liberty,* by unnecessary scruples and doubts. It is both unthankfulness to God and wrong to ourselves, to be ignorant of the extent of Christian liberty. It makes melody to Satan to see Christians troubled with that they neither should or need. Yet there is danger in stretching Christian liberty beyond the bounds. For a man may condemn himself in that he approves, as in not walking circumspectly in regard of circumstances, and so breed his own disquiet, and give scandal to others.

10. Sometimes also, God suffers men to be disquieted for *want of employment,* who, in shunning labour, procure trouble to themselves; and by not doing that which is needful, they are troubled with that which is unnecessary. An unemployed life is a burden to itself. God is a pure act, always working, always doing; and the nearer our soul comes to God, the more it is in action and the freer from disquiet. Men experimentally feel that comfort, in doing that which belongs unto them, which before they longed for and went without; a heart not exercised in some honest labour works trouble out of itself.

11. Again, *omission of duties and offices of love* often troubles the peace of good people; for even in time of death, when they look for peace and desire it most, then looking back upon their former failings, and seeing opportunity of doing good wanting to their desire (the parties perhaps being deceased to whom they owed more respect), are hereupon much disquieted, and so much the more because they see now hope of the like advantages cut off.

A Christian life is full of duties, and the peace of it is not maintained without much fruitfulness and looking about us. Debt is a disquieting thing to an honest mind, and duty is debt. Hereupon the apostle layeth the charge, 'that we should owe nothing to any man but love,' Rom. xiii. 8.

12. Again, one special cause of too much disquiet is, *want of firm resolution in good things*. The soul cannot but be disquieted when it knows not what to cleave unto, like a ship tossed with contrary winds. Halting is a deformed and troublesome gesture; so halting in religion is not only troublesome to others and odious, but also disquiets ourselves. 'If God be God, cleave to him,' 1 Kings xviii. 21. If the duties of religion be such as will bring peace of conscience at the length, be religious to purpose, practise them in the particular passages of life. We should labour to have a clear judgment, and from thence a resolved purpose; a wavering-minded man is inconsistent in all his ways, James i. 6. God will not speak peace to a staggering spirit that hath always its religion and its way to choose. Uncertain men are always unquiet men: and giving too much way to passion maketh men in particular consultations unsettled. This is the reason why, in particular cases, when the matter concerns ourselves, we cannot judge so clearly as in general truths, because Satan raiseth a mist between us and the matter in question.

III. *Positive causes.*

May be, 1. *When men lay up their comfort too much on outward things*, which, being subject to much inconstancy and change, breed disquiet. Vexation always follows vanity, when vanity is not apprehended to be where it is. In that measure we are cast down in the disappointing of our hopes, as we were too much lifted up in expectation of good from them. Whence proceed these complaints: Such a friend hath failed me; I never thought to have fallen into this condition; I had settled my joy in this child, in this friend, &c. But this is to build our comfort upon things that have no firm foundation, to build castles in the air, as we use to say. Therefore it is a good desire of the wise man Agur to desire God 'to remove from us vanity and lies,' Prov. xxx. 8; that is, a vain and false apprehension pitching upon things that are vain and lying, promising that* contentment to ourselves from the creature which it cannot yield. Confidence in vain things makes a vain heart, the heart becoming of the nature of the thing it relies on. We may say of all earthly things as the prophet speaketh, 'here is not our rest,' Mic. ii. 10.

It is no wonder, therefore, that worldly men are oft cast down and disquieted, when they walk in a vain shadow, Ps. xxxix. 6, as likewise that men given much to recreations should be subject to passionate distempers, because here, things fall out otherwise than they looked for; recreations being about matters that are variable, which especially falls out in games of hazard, wherein they oft spare not divine providence itself, but break out into blasphemy.

Likewise men that grasp more businesses than they can discharge, must needs bear both the blame and the grief of losing or marring many businesses, it being almost impossible to do many things so well as to give content to conscience; hence it is that covetous and busy men trouble both their hearts and their houses. Though some men, from a largeness of parts and a special dexterity in affairs, may turn over much, yet the most capacious heart hath its measure, and when the cup is full, a little drop may

* 'a,' in C.

cause the rest to spill. There is a spiritual surfeit, when the soul is overcharged with business; it is fit the soul should have its meet burden and no more.

2. As likewise, those that *depend too much upon the opinions of other men.* A very little matter will refresh, and then again discourage, a mind that rests too much upon the liking of others—*Sic leve sic parvum est animum quod laudis avarum subruit aut reficit.* Men that seek themselves too much abroad, find themselves disquieted at home. Even good men many times are too much troubled with the unjust censures of other men, specially in the day of their trouble. It was Job's case; and it is a heavy thing to have affliction added to affliction. It was Hannah's case, who, being troubled in spirit, was censured by Eli for distemper in brain, 1 Sam. i. 14; but for vain men who live more to reputation than to conscience, it cannot be that they should long enjoy settled quiet, because those in whose good opinion they desire to dwell, are ready often to take up contrary conceits upon slender grounds.

3. It is also a ground of overmuch trouble, when *we look too much and too long upon the ill in ourselves and abroad.* We may fix our eyes too long even upon sin itself, considering that we have not only a remedy against the hurt by sin, but a commandment to rejoice always in the Lord, Philip. iv. 4. Much more may we err in poring too much upon our afflictions; wherein we may find always in ourselves upon search, a cause to justify God, and always something left to comfort us; though we naturally mind more one cross than a hundred favours, dwelling over long upon the sore.

So likewise, our minds may be too much taken up in consideration of the miseries of the times at home and abroad, as if Christ did not rule in the midst of his enemies, and would not help all in due time; or as if the condition of the church in this world were not for the most part in an afflicted and conflicted condition. Indeed there is a perfect rest both for the souls and bodies of God's people, but that is not in this world, but is kept for hereafter; here we are in a sea, where what can we look for but storms?

To insist upon no more, one cause is, that we do usurp upon God, and take his office upon us, by troubling ourselves in forecasting the event of things, whereas our work is only to do our work and be quiet, as children when they please their parents take no further thought; our trouble is the fruit of our folly in this kind.

Use 1. That which we should observe from all that hath been said is, that we be not over hasty in censuring others, when we see their spirits out of temper, for we see how many things there are that work strongly upon the weak nature of man. We may sin more by harsh censure than they by overmuch distemper; as, in Job's case, it was a matter rather of just grief and pity, than great wonder or heavy censure.

Use 2. And, for ourselves, if our estate be calm for the present, yet we should labour to prepare our hearts, not only for an alteration of estate, but of spirit, unless we be marvellous careful beforehand, that our spirits fall not down with our condition. And if it befalls us to find it otherwise with our souls than at other times, we should so far labour to bear it, as that we do not judge it our own case alone, when we see here David thus to complain of himself, 'Why art thou cast down, O my soul?' &c.

Chapter IV.—*Of casting down ourselves, and specially by sorrow—evils thereof.*

To return again to the words, 'Why art thou cast down, O my soul?' &c., or, Why dost thou cast down thyself? or, Art cast down by thyself?

Obs. 1. Whence we may further observe, *that we are prone to cast down ourselves*, we are accessory to our own trouble, and weave the web of our own sorrow, and hamper ourselves in the cords of our own twining. God neither loves nor wills that we should be too much cast down. We see our Saviour Christ, how careful he was that his disciples should not be troubled, and therefore he labours to prevent that trouble which might arise by his suffering and departure from them, by a heavenly sermon; 'Let not your hearts be troubled,' &c., John xiv. 1. He was troubled himself that we should not be troubled. The ground, therefore, of our disquiet is chiefly from ourselves, though Satan will have a hand in it. We see many, like sullen birds in a cage, beat themselves to death. This casting down of ourselves is not from humility, but from pride; we must have our will, or God shall not have a good look from us, but as pettish and peevish children, we hang our heads in our bosom, because our wills are crossed.

Use. Therefore, in all our troubles we should look first *home to our own hearts*, and stop the storm there; for we may thank our own selves, not only for our troubles, but likewise for overmuch troubling ourselves in trouble. It was not the troubled condition that so disquieted David's soul, for if he had had a quiet mind, it would not have troubled him. But David yielded to the discouragements of the flesh, and the flesh, so far as it is unsubdued, is like the sea that is always casting mire and dirt of doubts, discouragements, and murmurings in the soul; let us, therefore, lay the blame where it is to be laid.

Obs. 2. Again, we see, *it is the nature of sorrow to cast down, as of joy to lift up.* Grief is like lead to the soul, heavy and cold; it sinks downwards, and carries the soul with it. The poor publican, to shew that his soul was cast down under the sight of his sins, hung down his head, Luke xviii. 13; the position of his body was suitable to the disposition of his mind, his heart and head were cast down alike. And it is Satan's practice to go over the hedge where it is lowest; he adds more weights to the soul by his temptations and vexations. His sin cast him out of heaven, and by his temptations he cast us out of our paradise, and ever since, he labours to cast us deeper into sin, wherein his scope is, to cast us either into too much trouble for sin, or presumption in sin, which is but a lifting up, to cast us down into deep despair at length, and so at last, if God's mercy stop not his malice, he will cast us as low as himself, even into hell itself.

Reason. The ground hereof is because, *as the joy of the Lord doth strengthen, so doth sorrow weaken the soul.* How doth it weaken?

1. By weakening the execution of the functions thereof, because it drinketh up the spirits, which are the instruments of the soul.

2. Because it contracteth, and draweth the soul into itself from communion of that comfort it might have with God or man. And then the soul being left alone, if it falleth, hath none to raise it up, Eccl. iv. 10.

Use. Therefore, if we will prevent casting down, let us prevent grief the cause *of it*, and sin the cause of that. Experience proves that true which the wise man says, 'Heaviness in the heart of a man makes it stoop, but a good word makes it better,' Prov. xii. 25. It bows down the soul, and therefore our blessed Saviour inviteth such unto him, 'Come unto me, ye who are heavy laden with the burden of your sins,' Matt. xi. 28. The body bends under a heavy burden, so likewise the soul hath its burden, 'Why art thou cast down, O my soul? why so disquieted?' &c.

Obs. 3. Whence we see, 1, that casting down breeds disquieting: because it springs from pride, which is a turbulent passion, whenas men cannot stoop to that condition which God would have them in; this proceeds from discontentment, and that from pride. As we see a vapour enclosed in a cloud causeth a terrible noise of thunder, whilst it is pent up there, and seeketh a vent; so all the noise within proceeds from a discontented swelling vapour. It is air enclosed in the bowels of the earth which shakes it, which all the four winds cannot do.

No creature under heaven so low cast down as Satan, none more lifted up in pride, none so full of discord. The impurest spirits are the most disquiet and stormy spirits, troublesome to themselves and others; for when the soul leaves God once, and looks downwards, what is there to stay it from disquiet? Remove the needle from the pole-star, and it is always stirring and trembling, never quiet till it be right again. So, displace the soul by taking it from God, and it will never be quiet. The devil cast out of heaven and out of the church, keeps ado; so do unruly spirits led by him.

Now I come to the remedies.

1. *By expostulation with himself*, Why art, &c.
2. *By laying a charge upon himself*, Trust in God.

Trust in God. It is supposed here, that there is no reason, which the wisdom from above allows to be a reason, why men should be discouraged; although the wisdom from beneath, which takes part with our corruption, will seldom want a plea. Nay, there is not only no reason for it, but there are strong reasons against it, there being a world of evil in it.

For, 1. *It indisposes a man to all good duties*, it makes him like an instrument out of tune, and like a body out of joint, that moveth both uncomely and painfully. It unfits to duties to God, who loves a cheerful giver, and especially a thanksgiver. Whereupon the apostle joins them both together, 'In all things be thankful, and rejoice evermore,' 1 Thess. v. 17, 18. In our communion with God in the sacraments, joy is a chief ingredient. So in duties to men, if the spirit be dejected, they are unwelcome, and lose the greatest part of their life and grace; a cheerful and a free spirit in duty is that which is most accepted in duty. We observe not so much what, as from what affection a thing is done.

2. *It is a great wrong to God himself*, and it makes us conceive black thoughts of him, as if he were an enemy. What an injury is it to a gracious father that such whom he hath followed with many gracious evidences of his favour and love should be in so ill a frame as once to call it into question!

3. So *it makes a man forgetful of all former blessings*, and stops the influence of God's grace for the time present and for that to come.

4. So, again, *for receiving of good*, it makes us unfit to receive mercies. A quiet soul is the seat of wisdom; therefore, meekness is required for the receiving of that 'engrafted word which is able to save our souls,' James i. 21. Till the Spirit of God meekens the soul, say what you will, it minds nothing; the soul is not empty and quiet enough to receive the seed of the word. It is ill sowing in a storm; so a stormy spirit will not suffer the word to take place. Men are deceived when they think a dejected spirit to be an humble spirit. Indeed, it is so when we are cast down in the

sense of our own unworthiness, and then as much raised up in the confidence of God's mercy. But when we cast ourselves down sullenly, and neglect our comforts, or undervalue them, it proceeds from pride; for it controls, as much as in us lies, the wisdom and justice of God, when we think with ourselves, Why should it be so with us? as if we were wiser to dispose of ourselves than God is. It disposeth us for entertaining any temptation. Satan hath never more advantage than upon discontent.

5. Besides, *it keeps off beginners from coming in*, and entering into the ways of God, bringing an ill report upon religion, causing men to charge it falsely for an uncomfortable way, whenas men never feel what true comfort meaneth till they give up themselves to God. And it damps, likewise, the spirits of those that walk the same way with us, whenas we should, as good travellers, cheer up one another both by word and example. In such a case the wheels of the soul are taken off, or else, as it were, want oil, whereby the soul passeth on very heavily, and no good action comes off from it as it should, which breeds not only uncomfortableness, but unsettledness in good courses. For a man will never go on comfortably and constantly in that which he heavily undertakes. That is the reason why uncheerful spirits seldom hold out as they should. St Peter knew this well, and therefore he willeth that there should be 'quietness and peace betwixt husband and wife, that their prayers be not hindered,' 1 Pet. iii. 7, insinuating that their prayers are hindered by family breaches; for by that means those two that should be one flesh and spirit are divided, and so made two, and when they should mind duty their mind is taken up with wrongs done by the one to the other.

There is nothing more required for the performing of holy duties than uniting of spirits, and therefore God would not have the sacrifice brought to the altar before reconciliation with our brother, Matt. v. 24. He esteems peace so highly, that he will have his own service stay for it. We see when Moses came to deliver the Israelites out of bondage, Exod. ix., their mind was so taken up with their grief that there was nobody within to give Moses an answer; their souls went altogether after their ill usage.

Use. Therefore, we should all endeavour and labour for a calmed spirit, that we may the better serve God in praying to him and praising of him; and serve one another in love, that we may be fitted to do and receive good, that we may make our passage to heaven more easy and cheerful, without drooping and hanging the wing. So much as we are quiet and cheerful upon good grounds, so much we live, and are, as it were, in heaven. So much as we yield to discouragement, we lose so much of our life and happiness, cheerfulness being, as it were, that life of our lives and the spirit of our spirits by which they are more enlarged to receive happiness and to express it.

CHAPTER V.—*Remedies of casting down · to cite the soul, and press it to give an account.*

Obs. 1. But to come to some helps:

First, in that he expostulates with himself, we may observe that one way to raise a dejected soul is *to cite it before itself, and, as it were, to reason the case.* God hath set up a court in man's heart, wherein the conscience hath the office both of informer, accuser, witness, and judge; and if matters were well carried within ourselves, this prejudging would be a prevention of future judging. It is a great mercy of God that the credit and comfort of man are so provided for that he may take up matters in himself, and so prevent public disgrace. But if there be not a fair dispatch and transaction in this inferior court within us, there will be a review in a higher court. Therefore, by slubbering over our matters we put God and ourselves to more trouble than needs. For a judgment must pass, first or last, either within us or without us, upon all unwarrantable distempers. We must not only be ready to give an account of our faith, upon what grounds we believe; but of all our actions, upon what grounds we do what we do; and of our passions, upon what grounds we are passionate; as in a well-governed state, uproar and sedition is never stirred, but account must be given. Now in a mutiny, the presence and speech of a venerable man composeth the minds of the disordered multitude; so likewise in a mutiny of the spirit, the authority that God hath put into reason, as a beam of himself, commands silence, and puts all in order again.

Reason. And there is good reason for it, for man is an understanding creature, and hath a rule given him to live by, and therefore is to be countable of every thought, word, action, passion. Therefore the first way to quiet the soul, is, to ask a reason of the tumult raised, and then many of our distempers for shame will not appear, because though they rage in silent darkness, yet they can say nothing for themselves, being summoned before strength of judgment and reason. Which is the reason why passionate men are loth that any court should be kept within them; but labour to stop judgment all they can. If men would but give themselves leave to consider better of it, they would never yield to such unreasonable motions of the soul; if they could but gain so much of their unruly passions, as to reason the matter within themselves, to hear what their consciences can tell them in secret, there would not be such offensive breakings out. And therefore, if we be ashamed to hear others upbraiding us, let us for shame hear ourselves; and if no reason can be given, what an unreasonable thing is it for a man endowed with reason to contrary his own principles! and to be carried as a beast without reason; or if there be any reason to be given, then this is the way to scan it, see whether it will hold water or not. We shall find some reasons, if they may be so called, to be so corrupt and foul, that if the judgment be not corrupted by them, they dare not be brought to light, but always appear under some colour and pretext; for sin, like the devil, is afraid to appear in its own likeness, and men seek out fair glosses for foul intentions. The hidden, secret reason is one, the open is another; the heart being corrupt sets the wit awork, to satisfy corrupt will; such kind of men are afraid of their own consciences, as Ahab of Micaiah, 1 Kings xxii. 16, because they fear it would deal truly with them; and therefore they take either present order for their consciences, or else, as Felix put off Paul, Acts xxiv. 25, they adjourn the court for another time. Such men are strangers at home, afraid of nothing more than themselves, and therefore in a fearful condition, because they are reserved for the judgment of the great day, if God doth not before that set upon them in this world. If men, carried away with their own lusts, would give but a little check, and stop themselves in their posting to hell, and ask, What have I done? What am I now about? Whither will this course tend? How will it end? &c., undoubtedly men would begin to be wise. Would the blasphemer give away his soul for nothing (for there is no engagement of profit or pleasure in this as in other sins, but it issues merely out of irreverence, and a superfluity of profaneness), would he, I say, draw so heavy a guilt upon himself for nothing, if he would but make use of his reason? Would an old man, when he is very near his journey's end, make longer provision for a short way, if he would ask himself a reason? But, indeed, covetousness is an unreasonable vice.

If those also of the younger sort would ask of themselves, why God should not have the flower and marrow of their age? and why they should give their strength to the devil? it might a little take them off from the devil's service. But sin is a work of darkness, and therefore shuns not only the light of grace, but even the light of reason. Yet sin seldom wants a seeming reason. Men will not go to hell without a show of reason. But such be sophistical fallacies, not reasons; and, therefore, sinners are said to play the sophisters with themselves. Satan could not deceive us, unless we deceived ourselves first, and are willingly deceived. Wilful sinners are blind, because they put out the light of reason, and so think God, like themselves, blind too, Ps. l. 21, and, therefore, they are deservedly termed madmen and fools; for, did they but make use of that spark of reason, it would teach them to reason thus: I cannot give an account of my ways to myself; what account shall I, or can I, give then to the Judge of all flesh ere it be long.

And as it is a ground of repentance in stopping our course to ask, What have I done? so likewise of faith and new obedience, to ask, What shall I do for the time to come? and then upon settling, the soul in way of thanks will be ready to ask of itself, 'What shall I return to the Lord?' &c. So that the soul, by this dealing with itself, promoteth itself to all holy duties till it come to heaven.

1. The reason why we are thus backward to the keeping of this court in ourselves is *self-love*. We love to flatter our own affections, but this self-love is but self-hatred in the end. As the wise man says, he that regards not this part of wisdom, 'hates his own soul, and shall eat the fruits of his own ways,' Prov. i. 31.

2. As likewise it issues from an *irksomeness of labour*, which makes us rather willing to seem base and vile to ourselves and others, than to take pains with our own hearts to be better, as those that are weary of holding the reins give them up unto the horse neck, and so are driven whither the rage of the horse carrieth them. Sparing a little trouble at first, doubles it in the end; as he who will not take the pains to cast up his books, his books will cast up him in the end. It is a blessed trouble that brings sound and long peace. This labour saves God a labour, for therefore he judgeth us, because we would not take pains with ourselves before, 1 Cor. xi. 31.

3. And *pride* also, with a desire of liberty, makes men think it to be a diminishing of greatness and freedom either to be curbed, or to curb ourselves. We love to be absolute and independent; but this, as it brought ruin upon our nature in Adam, so it will upon our persons. Men, as Luther was wont to say, are born with a pope in their belly, they are loath to give an account, although it be to themselves, their wills are, instead of a kingdom to them, *mens mihi pro regno*.

Let us, therefore, when any lawless passions begin to stir, deal with our souls as God did with Jonah, 'Doest thou well to be angry?' Jonah iv. 4, to fret thus. This will be a means to make us quiet; for, alas! what weak reasons have we often of strong motions. Such a man gave me no respect, such another looked more kindly upon another man than upon me, &c. You have some of Haman's spirit, Esth. v. 13, that for a little neglect would ruin a whole nation. Passion presents men that are innocent as guilty to us, *facit ira nocentes;* and because we will not seem to be mad without reason, pride commands the wit to justify anger, and so one passion maintains and feeds another.

Obs. 2. Neither is it sufficient to *cite the soul before itself; but it must be pressed to give an account,* as we see here David doubles and trebles the expostulation; as oft as any distemper did arise, so oft did he labour to keep it down. If passions grow too insolent, Eli's mildness will do no good, 1 Sam. ii. 24. It would prevent much trouble in this kind to subdue betimes, in ourselves and others, the first beginnings of any unruly passions and affections; which, if they be not well tutored and disciplined at the first, prove as headstrong, unruly, and ill nurtured children, who, being not chastened in time, take such a head, that it is oft above the power of parents to bring them in order. A child set at liberty, saith Solomon, 'breeds shame, at length, to his parents,' Prov. xxix. 15. Adonijah's example shews this. The like may be said of the affections set at liberty; it is dangerous to redeem a little quiet by yielding to our affections, which is never safely gotten but by mortification of them.

Those that are in great place are most in danger, by yielding to themselves, to lose themselves; for they are so taken up with the person for a time put upon them, that they, both in look and speech and carriage, often shew that they forget both their natural condition as men, and much more their supernatural as Christians; and therefore are scarce counselable by others or themselves in those things that concern their severed condition, that concerneth another world. Whereas it were most wisdom so to think of their place they bear, whereby they are called gods, Ps. lxxxii. 6, 7, as not to forget they must lay their person aside, and 'die like men,' 2 Sam. xxiv. 4. David himself that in his afflicted condition could advise with himself, and check himself, yet in his free and flourishing estate neglected the counsel of his friends. Agur was in jealousy of a full condition, and lest instead of saying, what have I done? why am I thus cast down, &c., he should say, 'Who is the Lord?' Prov. xxx. 9.

Meaner men in their lesser sphere often shew what their spirits would be, if their compass were enlarged.

It is a great fault in breeding youth, for fear of taking down of their spirits, not to take down their pride, and get victory of their affections: whereas a proud unbroken heart raiseth us more trouble often than all the world beside. Of all troubles, the trouble of a proud heart is the greatest. It was a great trouble to Haman to lead Mordecai's horse, Esth. vi. 1, which another man would not have thought so; the moving of a straw is troublesome to proud flesh. And therefore it is good to 'bear the yoke from our youth,' Lam. iii. 27; it is better to be taken down in youth, than to be broken in pieces by great crosses in age. First or last, self-denial and victory over ourselves is absolutely necessary; otherwise faith, which is a grace that requireth self-denial, will never be brought into the soul, and bear rule there.

Quest. But, what if pressing upon our souls will not help?

Ans. Then speak to God, to Jesus Christ by prayer, that as he rebuked the winds and the waves, and went upon the sea, so he would walk upon our souls, and command a calm there. It is no less power to settle a peace in the soul, than to command the seas to be quiet. It is God's prerogative to rule in the heart, as likewise to give it up to itself, which, next to hell is the greatest judgment; which should draw us to the greater reverence and fear of displeasing God. It was no ill wish of him,* that desired God to free him from an ill man, himself. *Domine, libera me a malo homine, meipso.*

CHAPTER VI.—*Other observations of the same nature.*

Obs. 3. Moreover we see that *a godly man can cast a restraint upon himself*, as David here stays himself in falling. There is a principle of grace, that stops the heart, and pulls in the reins again when the affections are loose. A carnal man, when he begins to be cast down, sinks lower and lower, until he sinks into despair, as lead sinks into the bottom of the sea. 'They sunk, they sunk, like lead in the mighty waters,' Exod. xv. 5. A carnal man sinks as a heavy body to the centre of the earth, and stays not if it be not stopped: there is nothing in him to stay him in falling, as we see in Ahithophel and Saul, 2 Sam. xvii. 23, who, wanting a support, found no other stay but the sword's point. And the greater their parts and places are, the more they entangle themselves; and no wonder, for they are to encounter with God and his deputy, conscience, who is King of kings, and Lord of lords. When Cain was cast out of his father's house, his heart and countenance was always cast down, for he had nothing in him to lift it upwards. But a godly man, though he may give a little way to passion, yet, as David, he recovers himself. Therefore as we would have any good evidence that we have a better spirit in us than our own, greater than the flesh or the world, let us, in all troubles we meet with, gather up ourselves, that the stream of our own affections carry us not away too far.

There is an art or skill of bearing troubles, if we could learn it, without overmuch troubling of ourselves, as in bearing of a burden there is a way so to poise it that it weigheth not over heavy: if it hangs all on one side, it poises the body down. The greater part of our troubles we pull upon ourselves, by not parting our care so, as to take upon us only the care of duty, and leave the rest to God; and by mingling our passions with our crosses, and like a foolish patient, chewing the pills which we should swallow down. We dwell too much upon the grief, when we should remove the soul higher. We are nearest neighbours unto ourselves. When we suffer grief, like a canker, to eat into the soul, and like a fire in the bones, to consume the marrow and drink up the spirits, we are accessory to the wrong done both to our bodies and souls: we waste our own candle, and put out our light.

Obs. 4. We see here again, that *a godly man can make a good use of privacy*. When he is forced to be alone he can talk with his God and himself; one reason whereof is, that his heart is a treasury and storehouse of divine truths, whence he can speak to himself, by way of check, or encouragement of himself: he hath a Spirit over his own spirit, to teach him to make use of that store he hath laid up in his heart. The Spirit is never nearer him than when by way of witness to his spirit he is thus comforted; wherein the child of God differs from another man, who cannot endure solitariness, because his heart is empty; he was a stranger to God before, and God is a stranger to him now, so that he cannot go to God as a friend. And for his conscience, that is ready to speak to him that which he is loth to hear: and therefore he counts himself a torment to himself, especially in privacy.

We read of great princes, who after some bloody designs were as terrible

* Augustine.—ED.

to themselves,* as they were formerly to others, and therefore could never endure to be awaked in the night, without music or some like diversion. It may be, we may be cast into such a condition, where we have none in the world to comfort us; as in contagious sickness, when none may come near us, we may be in such an estate wherein no friend will own us. And therefore let us labour now to be acquainted with God and our own hearts, and acquaint our hearts with the comforts of the Holy Ghost; then, though we have not so much as a book to look on, or a friend to talk with, yet we may look with comfort into the book of our own heart, and read what God hath written there by the finger of his Spirit. All books are written to amend this one book of our heart and conscience. *Ideo scribuntur omnes libri, ut emendetur unus*. By this means we shall never want a divine to comfort us, a physician to cure us, a counsellor to direct us, a musician to cheer us, a controller to check us, because, by help of the word and Spirit, we can be all these to ourselves.

Obs. 5. Another thing we see here, that God hath made *every man a governor over himself*. The poor man, that hath none to govern, yet may he be a king in himself. It is the natural ambition of man's heart to desire government, as we see in the bramble, Judges ix. Well then, let us make use of this disposition to rule ourselves. Absalom had high thoughts. O, if I were a king, I would do so and so! so our hearts are ready to promise, if I were as such and such a man in such and such a place, I would do this and that.

But how dost thou manage thine own affections? How dost thou rule in thine house, in thyself? Do not passions get the upper hand, and keep reason under foot? When we have learned to rule over our own spirits well, then we may be fit to rule over others. 'He that is faithful in a little, shall be set over more,' Matt. xxv. 21. 'He that can govern himself,' in the wise man's judgment, 'is better than he that can govern a city,' Prov. xvi. 32. He that cannot, is like a city without a wall, where those that are in may go out, and the enemies without may come in at their pleasure. So where there is not a government set up, there sin breaks out, and Satan breaks in without control.

Obs. 6. See again, the *excellency of the soul, that can reflect upon itself, and judge of whatsoever comes from it*. A godly man's care and trouble is especially about his soul, as David here looks principally to that, because all outward troubles are for to help that. When God touches our bodies, our estates, or our friends, he aims at the soul in all. God will never remove his hand, till something be wrought upon the soul, as 'David's moisture was as the drought in summer,' Ps. xxxii. 4, so that he roared, and carried himself unseemly for so great and holy a man, till his heart was subdued to deal without all guile with God in confessing his sin; and then God forgave him the iniquity thereof, and healed his body too. In sickness, or in any other trouble, it is best the divine should be before the physician, and that men begin where God begins. In great fires, men look first to their jewels, and then to their lumber; so our soul is our best jewel. A carnal, worldly man is called, and well called, a fleshly man, because his very soul is flesh, and there is nothing but the world in him. And therefore, when all is not well within, he cries out, My body is troubled, my state is broken, my friends fail me, &c.; but all this while, there is no care for the poor soul, to settle a peace in that.

* As Charles IX. after the massacre in France. Thuanus, lib. 57. Somnum post casum Sanbartholomæum nocturni horrores plerumque interrumpebant et rursus adhibiti symphoniaci expergefacto conciliabant.

The possession of the soul is the richest possession, no jewel so precious. The account for our own souls, and the souls of others, is the greatest account, and therefore the care of souls should be the greatest care. What an indignity is it, that we should forget such souls to satisfy our lusts! to have our wills! to be vexed with any, who by their judgment, example, or authority, stop, as we suppose, our courses! Is it not the greatest plot in the world, first, to have their lusts satisfied; secondly, to remove, either by fraud or violence, whatsoever standeth in their way; and, thirdly, to put colours and pretences upon this to delude the world and themselves, employing all their carnal wit and worldly strength for their carnal aims, and fighting for that which fights against their own souls? For, what will be the issue of this but certain destruction?

Of this mind are not only the dregs of people, but many of the more refined sort, who desire to be eminent in the world; and to have their own desires herein, give up the liberty of their own judgments and consciences to the desires and lusts of others. To be above others, they will be beneath themselves, having those men's persons in admiration for hope of advantage, whom otherwise they despise; and so, substituting in their spirits man in the place of God, lose heaven for earth, and bury that divine spark, their souls, capable of the divine nature, and fitter to be a sanctuary and temple for God to dwell in, than by closing with baser things to become base itself. We need not wonder that others seem base to carnal men, who are base both in and to themselves. It is no wonder they should be cruel to the souls of others, who are cruel to their own souls; that they should neglect and starve others, that give away their own souls in a manner for nothing. Alas! upon what poor terms do they hazard that, the nature and worth whereof is beyond man's reach to comprehend! Many are so careless in this kind, that if they were thoroughly persuaded that they had souls that should live for ever, either in bliss or torment, we might the more easily work upon them. But as they live by sense, as beasts, so they have no more thoughts of future times than beasts, except at such times as conscience is awaked by some sudden judgment, whereby God's wrath is revealed from heaven against them. But happy were it for them, if they might die like beasts, whose misery dies with them.

To such an estate hath sin brought the soul, that it willingly drowneth itself in the senses, and becomes, in some sort, incarnate with the flesh.

We should therefore set ourselves to have most care of that, which God cares most for, which he breathed into us at first, set his own image upon, gave so great a price for, and values above all the world besides. Shall all our study be to satisfy the desires of the flesh, and neglect this?

Is it not a vanity to prefer the casket before the jewel, the shell before the pearl, the gilded potsherd before the treasure? and is it not much more vanity to prefer the outward condition before the inward? The soul is that which Satan and his hath most spite at, for in troubling our bodies or estates, he aims at the vexation of our souls. As in Job (ch. i.) his aim was to abuse that power God had given him over his children, body, and goods, to make him, out of a disquieted spirit, blaspheme God. It is an ill method to begin our care in other things, and neglect the soul, as Ahithophel, who set his house in order, when he should have set his soul in order first, 2 Sam. xvii. 23. Wisdom begins at the right end. If all be well at home, it comforts a man, though he meets with troubles abroad. Oh, saith he, I shall have rest at home; I have a loving wife and dutiful children: so whatsoever we meet withal abroad, if the soul be quiet, thither we can retire with comfort. See that all be well within, and then all troubles from without cannot much annoy us.

Grace will teach us to reason thus—God hath given mine enemies power over my liberty and condition, but shall they have power and liberty over my spirit? It is that which Satan and they most seek for; but never yield, O my soul! and thus a godly man will become more than a conqueror; when in appearance he is conquered, the cause prevails, his spirit prevails, and is undaunted. A Christian is not subdued till his spirit is subdued. Thus Job prevailed over Satan and all his troubles, at length. This tormenteth proud persons, to see godly men enjoy a calm and resolute frame of mind in the midst of troubles; when their enemies are more troubled in troubling them, than they are in being troubled by them.

Obs. 7. We see likewise here, *how to frame our complaints.* David complains not of God, nor of his troubles, nor of others, but of his own soul; he complains of himself to himself, as if he should say, Though all things else be out of order, yet, O my soul, thou shouldst not trouble me too, thou shouldst not betray thyself unto troubles, but rule over them. A godly man complains to God, yet not of God, but of himself. A carnal man is ready to justify himself and complain of God, he complains not to God, but of God, at the least, in secret murmuring, he complains of others that are but God's vials; he complains of the grievance that lies upon him, but never regards what is amiss in himself within; openly he cries out upon fortune, yet secretly he striketh at God, under that idol of fortune, by whose guidance all things come to pass; whilst he quarrels with that which is nothing, he wounds him that is the cause of all things; like a gouty man that complains of his shoe, and of his bed, or an aguish man of his drink, when the cause is from within. So men are disquieted with others, when they should rather be disquieted and angry with their own hearts.

We condemn Jonah for contending with God, and justifying his unjust anger, but yet the same risings are in men naturally, if shame would suffer them to give vent to their secret discontent; their heart speaks what Jonah his tongue spake. Oh! but here we should lay our hand upon our mouth, and adore God, and command silence to our souls.

No man is hurt but by himself first. We are drawn to evil, and allured from a true good to a false by our own lusts, 'God tempts no man,' James i. 13. Satan hath no power over us further than we willingly lie open to him. Satan works upon our affections, and then our affections work upon our will. He doth not work immediately upon the will. We may thank ourselves in willingly yielding to our own passions, for all that ill Satan or his instruments draws us unto. Saul was not vexed with an evil spirit, 1 Sam. xvi., till he gave way to his own evil spirit of envy first. The devil entered not into Judas, Mat. xxvii. 3, until his covetous heart made way for him. The apostle strengtheneth his conceit against rash and lasting anger from hence, that by this we give way to the devil, Eph. iv. 27. It is a dangerous thing to pass from God's government, and come under Satan's.

Satan mingleth himself with our own passions, therefore we should blame ourselves first, be ashamed of ourselves most, and judge ourselves most severely. But self-love teacheth us a contrary method, to translate all upon others; it robs us of a right judgment of ourselves. Though we desire to know all diseases of the body by their proper names, yet we will conceive of sinful passions of the soul under milder terms; as lust under love, rage under just anger, murmuring under just displeasure, &c. Thus whilst we flatter our grief, what hope of cure! Thus sin hath not only made all the creatures enemies to us, but ourselves the greatest enemies to ourselves; and therefore we should begin our complaints against ourselves, and discuss ourselves thoroughly. How else shall we judge truly of other things without us, above us, or beneath us? The sun when it rises, enlightens first the nearest places, and then the more remote; so where true light is set up, it discovers what is amiss within first.

Obs. 8. Hence also we see, that *as in all discouragements a godly man hath most trouble with his own heart, so he knows how to carry himself therein*, as David doth here.

For the better clearing of this, we must know there be divers kinds and degrees of conflicts in the soul of man whilst it is united to the body.

1. First, between one corrupt passion and another, as between covetousness and pride; pride calls for expense, covetousness for restraint. Oft passions fight not only against God and reason, to which they owe a homage, but one against another; sin fights against sin, and a lesser sin is oftentimes overcome by a greater. The soul in this case is like the sea tossed with contrary winds: and like a kingdom divided, wherein the subjects fight both against their prince, and one against another.

2. Secondly, there is a natural conflict in the affections, whereby nature seeks to preserve itself, as betwixt anger and fear; anger calls for revenge, fear of the law binds the soul to be quiet. We see in the creatures, fear makes them abstain from that which their appetites carry them unto. A wolf comes to the* flock with an eagerness to prey upon it, but seeing the shepherd standing in defence of his sheep, returns and doth no harm; and yet for all this, as he came a wolf, so he returns a wolf.

A natural man may oppose some sin from an obstinate resolution against it,† not from any love of God, or hatred of sin, as sin, but because he conceives it a brave thing to have his will; as one hard weapon may strike at another, as a stone wall may beat back an arrow. But this opposition is not from a contrariety of nature, as is betwixt fire and water.

3. Thirdly, there is a conflict of a higher nature, as between some sins and the light of reason helped by a natural conscience. The heathen could reason from the dignity of the soul, to count it a base thing to prostitute themselves to beastly lusts, so as it were degrading and unmanning themselves. *Major sum et ad majora natus quam ut corporis mei sim mancipium.* (Seneca, Ep. 65). Natural men, desirous to maintain a great opinion of themselves, and to awe the inferior sort by gravity of deportment in carriage, will abstain from that which otherwise their hearts carry them unto, lest yielding should render them despised, by laying themselves too much open; as because passion discovers a fool as he is, and makes a wise man thought meaner than he is; therefore a prudent man will conceal his passion. Reason refined and raised by education, example, and custom, doth break in some degree the force of natural corruption, and brings into the soul, as it were, another nature, and yet no true change; as we see in such as have been inured to good courses, they feel conscience checking them upon the first discontinuance and alteration of their former good ways, but this is usually from a former impression of their breeding, as the boat moves some little time upon the water by virtue of the former stroke; yet at length we see corruption prevailing over education, as in Jehoash, who was awed by the

* 'A,' in C.

† 'A natural . . . . love.' In A reads, 'a natural man may oppose an obstinate resolution to commit some sin not from love.' Corrected in B as above.—G.

reverent respect he bare to his uncle Jehoiada, he was good 'all his uncle's days,' 2 Kings xii. 2. And in Nero, in whom the goodness of his education prevailed over the fierceness of his nature, for the first five years (*a*).

4. Fourthly, but in the church, where there shineth a light above nature, as there is a discovery of more sins, and some strength, with the light to perform more duty; so there is a further conflict than in a man that hath no better than nature in him. By a discovery of the excellent things of the gospel, there may be some kind of joy stirred up, and some degree of obedience: whence there may be some degree of resistance against the sins of the gospel, as obstinate unbelief, desperation, profaneness, &c. A man in the church may do more than another out of the church, by reason of the enlargement of his knowledge; whereupon such cannot sin at so easy a rate as others that know less, and, therefore, meet with less opposition from conscience.

5. Fifthly, There is yet a further degree of conflict betwixt the sanctified powers of the soul and the flesh, not only as it is seated in the baser parts, but even in the best faculties of the soul, and as it mingles itself with every gracious performance: as in David, there is not only a conflict between sin and conscience, enlightened by a common work of the Spirit; but between the commanding powers of the soul sanctified, and itself unsanctified, between reasons of the flesh and reasons of the Spirit, between faith and distrust, between the true light of knowledge and false light. For it is no question but the flesh would play its part in David, and muster up all the strength of reason it had. And usually flesh, as it is more ancient than the spirit, we being first natural, then spiritual, so it will put itself first forward in devising shifts, as Esau comes out of the womb first before Jacob, Gen. xxv. 25; yet hereby the spirit is stirred up to a present examination and resistance, and in resisting, as we see here, at length the godly gets the victory. As in the conflict between the higher parts of the soul with the lower, it clearly appears that the soul doth not rise out of the temper of the body, but is a more noble substance, commanding the body by reasons fetched from its own worth; so in this spiritual conflict, it appears there is something better than the soul itself, that hath superiority over it.

Chapter VII.—*Difference between good men and others in conflicts with sin.*

Quest. But how doth it appear that this combat in David was a *spiritual combat?*

Ans. 1. First, *A natural conscience is troubled for sins against the light of nature only*, but David for inward and secret corruptions, as discouragement and disquietness arising from faint-trusting in God.

David's conflict was not only with the sensual, lower part of his soul, which is carried to ease and quiet and love of present things, but he was troubled with a mutiny in his understanding between faith and distrust; and therefore he was forced to rouse up his soul so oft to trust in God; which shews that carnal reason did solicit him to discontent, and had many colourable reasons for it.

2. Secondly, *A man endued with common grace is rather a patient than an agent in conflicts;* the light troubles him against his will, as discovering and reproving him, and hindering his sinful contentments; his heart is more biassed another way if the light would let him; but a godly man labours to help the light, and to work his heart to an opposition against

sin; he is an agent as well as a patient. As David here doth not suffer disquieting, but is disquieted with himself for being so. A godly man is an agent in opposing his corruption, and a patient in enduring of it, whereas a natural man is a secret agent in and for his corruptions, and a patient in regard of any help against them; a good man suffers evil and doth good, a natural man suffers good and doth evil.

3. Thirdly, *A conscience guided by common light withstands distempers most by outward means;* but David here fetcheth help from the Spirit of God in him, and from trust in God. Nature works from within, so doth the new nature. David is not only something disquieted, and something troubled for being disquieted, but sets himself thoroughly against his distempers; he complains and expostulates, he censures and chargeth his soul. The other, if he doth anything at all, yet it is faintly; he seeks out his corruption as a coward doth his enemy, loath to find him, and more loath to encounter him.

4. Fourthly, *David withstands sin constantly, and gets ground.* We see here he gives not over at the first, but presseth again and again. Nature works constantly, so doth the new nature. The conflict in the other is something forced, as taking part with the worser side in himself; good things have a weak, or rather no party in him, bad things a strong; and therefore he soon gives over in this holy quarrel.

5. Fifthly, *David is not discouraged by his foils,* but sets himself afresh against his corruptions, with confidence to bring them under.* Whereas he that hath but a common work of the Spirit, after some foils, lets his enemy prevail more and more, and so despairs of victory, and thinks it better to sit still than to rise and take a new fall; by which means his latter end is worse than his beginning; for beginning in the spirit, he ends in the flesh. A godly man, although upon some foil, he may for a time be discouraged, yet by holy indignation against sin he renews his force, and sets afresh upon his corruptions, and gathers more strength by his falls, and groweth into more acquaintance with his own heart and Satan's malice, and God's strange ways in bringing light out of darkness.

6. Sixthly, An ordinary Christian may be disquieted for being disquieted, as David was, but then it is only as disquiet hath vexation in it; but David here striveth against the unquietness of his spirit, not only as it brought vexation with it, but *as it hindered communion with his God.*

In sin there is not only a guilt binding over the soul to God's judgment, and thereupon filling the soul with inward fears and terrors; but in sin likewise there is—1, A contrariety to God's holy nature; and, 2, A contrariety to the divine nature and image stamped upon ourselves; 3, A weakening and disabling of the soul from good; and, 4, A hindering of our former communion with God, sin being in its nature a leaving of God, the fountain of all strength and comfort, and cleaving to the creature. Hereupon the soul, having tasted the sweetness of God before, is now grieved, and this grief is not only for the guilt and trouble that sin draws after it, but from an inward antipathy and contrariety betwixt the sanctified soul and sin. It hates sin as sin, as the only bane and poison of renewed nature, and the only thing that breeds strangeness betwixt God and the soul. And this hatred is not so much from discourse and strength of reason, as from nature itself rising presently against its enemy; the lamb presently shuns the wolf from a contrariety: antipathies wait not for any strong reason, but are exercised upon the first presence of a contrary object.

* That is, 'defeats.'—Ed.

7. Seventhly, Hereupon ariseth the last difference, that because the soul hateth sin as sin, therefore it *opposeth it universally and eternally, in all the powers of the soul; and in all actions, inward and outward, issuing from those powers*. David regarded no iniquity in his heart, but hated every evil way, Ps. lxvi. 18; the desires of his soul were, that it might be so directed that he might keep God's law, Ps. cxix. 5. And if there had been no binding law, yet there was such a sweet sympathy and agreement betwixt his soul and God's truth, that he delighted in it above all natural sweetness; hence it is that St John saith, 'He that is born of God cannot sin,' 1 John iii. 9; that is, so far forth as he is born of God, his new nature will not suffer him; he cannot lie, he cannot deceive, he cannot be earthly-minded, he cannot but love and delight in the persons and things that are good. There is not only a light in the understanding, but a new life in the will, and all other faculties of a godly man; what good his knowledge discovereth, that his will makes choice of, and his heart loveth; what ill his understanding discovers, that his will hateth and abstains from. But in a man not thoroughly converted, the will and affections are bent otherwise; he loves not the good he doth, nor hates the evil he doth not.

Use. Therefore let us make a narrow search into our souls upon what grounds we oppose sin, and fight God's battles. A common Christian is not cast down because he is disquieted in God's service, or for his inward failings that he cannot serve God with that liberty and freedom he desires, &c. But a godly man is troubled for his distempers, because they hinder the comfortable intercourse betwixt God and his soul, and that spiritual composedness and sabbath of spirit, which he enjoyed before, and desires to enjoy again. He is troubled that the waters of his soul are troubled so that the image of Christ shines not in him as it did before. It grieves him to find an abatement in affection, in love to God, a distraction or coldness in performing duties, any doubting of God's favour, any discouragement from duty, &c. A godly man's comforts and grievances are hid from the world; natural men are strangers to them. Let this be a rule of discerning our estates, how we stand affected to the distempers of our hearts; if we find them troublesome, it is a ground of comfort unto us that our spirits are ruled by a higher Spirit; and that there is a principle of that life in us, which cannot brook the most secret corruption, but rather casts it out by a holy complaint, as strength of nature doth poison, which seeks its destruction. And let us be in love with that work of grace in us, which makes us out of love with the least stirrings that hinder our best condition.

Obs. 9. See again, *We may be sinfully disquieted for that which is not a sin to be disquieted for*. David had sinned if he had not been somewhat troubled for the banishment from God's house, and the blasphemy of the enemies of the church; but yet, we see, he stops himself, and sharply takes up his soul for being disquieted. He did well in being disquieted, and in checking himself for the same; there were good grounds for both. He had wanted spiritual life if he had not been disquieted, [but] he abated the vigour and liveliness of his life by being overmuch disquieted.

CHAPTER VIII.—*Of unfitting dejection, and when it is excessive. And what is the right temper of the soul herein.*

Quest. § I. *Then, how shall we know when a man is cast down and disquieted, otherwise than is befitting?*

Ans. There is a threefold miscarriage of inward trouble.

1. *When the soul is troubled for that it should not be vexed for*, as Ahab, when he was crossed in his will for Naboth's vineyard, 1 Kings xxi. 1, 2, *seq.*

2. *In the ground*, as when we grieve for that which is good, and for that which we should grieve for; but it is with too much reflecting upon our own particular.

As in the troubles of the state or church, we ought to be affected; but not because these troubles hinder any liberties of the flesh, and restrain pride of life, but from higher respects; as that, by these troubles God is dishonoured, the public exercises of religion hindered, and the gathering of souls thereby stopped, as the states and commonwealths, which should be harbours of the church, are disturbed, as lawless courses and persons prevail, as religion and justice are triumphed over and trodden under. Men usually are grieved for public miseries from a spirit of self-love only, because their own private is embarked in the public. There is a depth of deceit of the heart in this matter.

3. So for the *measure*, when we trouble ourselves, though not without cause, yet without bounds.

The spirit of man is like unto moist elements, as air and water, which have no bounds of their own to contain them in, but those of the vessel that keeps them. Water is spilt and lost without something to hold it, so it is with the spirit of man, unless it be bounded with the Spirit of God. Put the case, a man be disquieted for sin, for which not to be disquieted is a sin, yet we may look too much, and too long upon it; for the soul hath a double eye, one to look to sin, another to look up to God's mercy in Christ. Having two objects to look on, we may sin in looking too much on the one, with neglect of the other.

Quest. § II. *Seeing then, disquieting and dejection for sin is necessary, how shall we know when it exceeds measure?*

Ans. 1. First, *when it hinders us from holy duties, or in the performance of them*, by distraction or otherwise; whereas they are given to carry us to that which is pleasing to God, and good to ourselves.

Grief is ill when it taketh off the soul from minding that it should, and so indisposeth us to the duties of our callings. Christ upon the cross was grieved to the utmost, yet it did not take away his care for his mother, John xix. 26, 27: so the good thief, Luke xxiii. 42, in the midst of his pangs laboured to gain his fellow, and to save his own soul, and to glorify Christ. If this be so in grief of body, which taketh away the free use of reason and exercise of grace more than any other grief, then much more in grief from more remote causes; for in extremity of body the sickness may be such as all that we can perform to God is a quiet submission and a desire to be carried unto Christ by the prayers of others; we should so mind our grief as not to forget God's mercy, or our own duty.

2. Secondly, *when we forget the grounds of comfort*, and suffer our mind to run only upon the present grievance. It is a sin to dwell on sin and turmoil our thoughts about it, when we are called to thankfulness. A physician in good discretion forbids a dish at some times to prevent the nourishment of some disease, which another time he gives way unto. So we may and ought to abstain from too much feeding our thoughts upon our corruptions in case of discouragement, which at other times is very necessary. It should be our wisdom in such cases to change the object, and

labour to take off our minds, and give them to that which calls more for them. Grief oft passeth unseasonably upon us, when there is cause of joy, and when we are called to joy; as Joab justly found fault with David for grieving too much, when God had given him the victory, and rid him and the state of a traitorous son, 2 Sam. xix. 5, *seq*. God hath made some days for joy, and joy is the proper work of those days. 'This is the day which the Lord hath made,' Ps. cxviii. 24. Some in a sick distemper desire that which increaseth their sickness; so some that are deeply cast down, desire a weakening* ministry, and whatever may cast them down more, whereas they should meditate upon comforts, and get some sweet assurance of God's love. Joy is the constant temper which the soul should be in. 'Rejoice evermore,' 1 Thes. v. 16, saith the apostle. If a sink be stirred, we stir it not more, but go into a sweeter room. So we should think of that which is comfortable, and of such truths as may raise up the soul, and sweeten the spirit.

3. Thirdly, Grief is too much, *when it inclines the soul to any inconvenient courses:* for if it be not looked to, it is an ill counsellor, when either it hurts the health of our bodies, or draws the soul, for to ease itself, to some unlawful liberty. When grief keeps such a noise in the soul, that it will not hear what the messengers of God, or the still voice of the Spirit saith. As in combustions, loud cries are scarce heard, so in such cases the soul will neither hear itself nor others. The fruit of this overmuch trouble of spirit is increase of trouble.

Quest. § III. Another question may be, *What that sweet and holy temper is the soul should be in, that it may neither be faulty in the defect, nor too much abound in grief and sorrow?*

Ans. 1. The soul must be raised *to a right grief*.

2. The grief that is raised, though it be right, yet it must be *bounded*. Before we speak of raising grief in the godly, we must know there are some who are altogether strangers to any kind of spiritual grief or trouble at all; such must consider, that the way to prevent everlasting trouble, is to desire to be troubled with a preventing trouble. Let those that are not in the way of grace think with themselves what cause they have not to take a minute's rest while they are in that estate. For a man to be in debt both body and soul, subject every minute to be arrested and carried prisoner to hell, and not to be moved; for a man to have the wrath of God ready to be poured out upon him, and hell gape for him, nay, to carry a hell about him in conscience, if it were awake, and to have all his comfort here hanging upon a weak thread of this life, ready to be cut and broken off every moment, and to be cursed in all those blessings that he enjoys; and yet not to be disquieted, but continually treasuring up wrath against the day of wrath, by running deeper into God's books: for a man to be thus, and not to be disquieted, is but the devil's peace, whilst the strong man holds possession. A burning ague is more hopeful than a lethargy. The best service that can be done to such men, is to startle and rouse them, and so with violence to pull them out of the fire, as Jude speaks, ver. 23, or else they will another day curse that cruel mercy that lets them alone now. In all their jollity in this world, they are but as a book fairly bound, which when it is opened is full of nothing but tragedies. So when the book of their consciences shall be once opened, there is nothing to be read but lamentations and woes. Such men were in a way of hope, if they had but so much

* 'Weakening.' In A and B 'wakening,' but corrected in C as above.

apprehension of their estates, as to ask themselves, 'What have I done?' If this be true that there are such fearful things prepared for sinners, why am I not cast down? why am I no more troubled and discouraged for my wicked courses? Despair to such is the beginning of comfort; and trouble the beginning of peace. A storm is the way to a calm, and hell the way to heaven.

(1.) But for raising of a right grief in the soul of a holy man, *look what is the state of the soul in itself, in what terms it is with God:* whether there be any sin hanging on the file (*b*) unrepented of. If all be not well within us, then here is place for inward trouble, whereby the soul may afflict itself.

God saw this grief so needful for his people, that he appointed certain days for afflicting them, Lev. xvi. 29; because it is fit that sin contracted by joy should be dissolved by grief; and sin is so deeply invested into the soul, that a separation betwixt the soul and it cannot be wrought without much grief. When the soul hath smarted for sin, it sets then the right price upon reconciliation with God in Christ, and it feeleth what a bitter thing sin is, and therefore it will be afraid to be too bold with it afterward; it likewise aweth the heart so, that it will not be so loose towards God as it was before; and certainly that soul that hath felt the sweetness of keeping peace with God, cannot but take deeply to heart, that there should be any thing in us that should divide betwixt us and the fountain of our comfort, that should stop the passage of our prayers and the current of God's favours both towards ourselves and others; it is such an ill as is the cause of all other ill, and damps all our comforts.

(2.) *We should look out of ourselves also*, considering whether for troubles at home and abroad, God calls not to mourning or troubling of ourselves; grief of compassion is as well required as grief of contrition.

It is a dead member that is not sensible of the state of the body. Jeremiah, for fear he should not weep enough for the distressed state of the church, desired of God, 'that his eyes might be made a fountain of tears,' Jer. ix. 1. A Christian, as he must not be proud flesh, so neither must he be dead flesh; none more truly sensible either of sin or of misery, so far as misery carries with it any sign of God's displeasure, than a true Christian; which issues from the life of grace, which, where it is in any measure, is lively. and therefore sensible; for God gives motion and senses for the preservation of life. As God's bowels are tender towards us, so God's people have tender bowels towards him, his cause, his people, and his church. The fruit of this sensibleness, is earnest prayer to God. As Melancthon said well, If I cared for nothing, I would pray for nothing, *Si nil curarem nil orarem.**

Grief being thus raised, must, as we said before, be *bounded and guided.*

(1.) God hath framed the soul, and planted such affections in it, as may answer all his dealing towards his children; that when he enlargeth himself towards them, then the soul should enlarge itself to him again; when he opens his hand, we ought to open our hearts; when he shews any token of displeasure, we should grieve; when he troubles us, we should trouble and grieve ourselves. As God any way discovereth himself, so the soul should be in a suitable pliableness. Then the soul is as it should be, when it is ready to meet God at every turn, to joy when he calls for it, to mourn when he calls for that, to labour to know God's meaning in every thing.

* Melancthon. . . . The following is the exact saying:—'Ad alium, qui à curis eum dehortabatur: Si *nihil*, inquit, *curarem, nihil orarem.*'—Dicta Melancthonis, in his Life in Melchior Adam's Vitæ Germ. Theolog. ed. Frankfort, 1653, p. 358.—G.

(2.) Again, God hath made the soul for a communion with himself, which communion is especially placed in the affections, which are the springs of all spiritual worship. Then the affections are well ordered, when we are fit to have communion with God, to love, joy, trust, to delight in him above all things. The affections are the inward movings of the soul, which then move best when they move us to God, not from him. They are the feet of the soul, whereby we walk with, and before God. When we have our affections at such command, that we can take them off from any thing in the world, at such times as we are to have more near communion with God in hearing or prayer, &c., as Abraham when he was to sacrifice left whatsoever might hinder him at the 'bottom of the mount,' Gen. xxii. 5. When we let our affections so far into the things of the world, as we cannot taken them off when we are to deal with God, it is a sign of spiritual intemperancy. It is said of the Israelites that they brought Egypt with them into the wilderness; so many bring the world into their hearts with them when they come before God.

(3.) But because our affections are never well-ordered without judgment, as being to follow, not to lead, it is an evidence that the soul is in a fit temper, when there is such a harmony in it, as that we judge of things as they are, and affect as we judge, and execute as we affect. This harmony within breeds uniformity and constancy in our resolutions, so that there is, as it were, an even thread drawn through the whole course and tenor of our lives, when we are not off and on, up and down. It argues an ill state of body when it is very hot, or very cold, or hot in one part, and cold in another; so unevenness of spirit argues a distemper. A wise man's life is of one colour, like itself. The soul bred from heaven, so far as it is heavenly-minded, desires to be, like heaven, above all storms, uniform, constant; not as things under the sun, which are always in changes, constant only in inconstancy. Affections are as it were the wind of the soul, and then the soul is carried as it should be, when it is neither so becalmed that it moves not when it should, nor yet tossed with tempests to move disorderly; when it is so well balanced that it is neither lift up nor cast down too much, but keepeth a steady course. Our affections must not rise to become unruly passions, for then as a river that overfloweth the banks, they carry much slime and soil with them. Though affections be the wind of the soul, yet unruly passions are the storms of the soul, and will overturn all, if they be not suppressed. The best, as we see in David here, if they do not steer their hearts aright, are in danger of sudden gusts. A Christian must neither be a dead sea, nor a raging sea.

(4.) Our affections are then in best temper, when they become so many graces of the Spirit, as when love is turned to a love of God, joy, to a delight in the best things, fear, to a fear of offending him more than any creature, sorrow, to a sorrow for sin, &c.

(5.) They are likewise in good temper, when they move us to all duties of love and mercy towards others; when they are not shut where they should be open, nor open where they should be shut.

Yet there is one case where exceeding affection is not over-exceeding, as in an ecstasy of zeal upon a sudden apprehension of God's dishonour, and his cause trodden under foot. It is better in this case, rather scarce to be our own men, than to be calm or quiet. It is said of Christ and David, that their hearts were eaten up with a holy zeal for God's house, Ps. lxix. 9, cxix. 139, Isa. lix. 19. In such a case, Moses, unparalleled for meekness, was turned into a holy rage, Exod. xxxii. 19. The greatness of the provocation, the excellency of the object, and the weight of the occasion, bears out the soul, not only without blame, but with great praise, in such seeming distempers. It is the glory of a Christian to be carried with full sail, and as it were with a spring-tide of affection. So long as the stream of affection runneth in the due channel, and if there be great occasions for great motions, then it is fit the affections should rise higher, as to burn with zeal, to be 'sick of love,' Cant. ii. 5., to be more vile for the Lord, as David, 2 Sam. vi. 22, to be counted out of our wits, 2 Car. v. 13, with St Paul, to further the cause of Christ and the good of souls.

Thus we may see the life of a poor Christian in this world. 1. He is in great danger, if he be not troubled at all. 2. When he is troubled, he is in danger to be over-troubled. 3. When he hath brought his soul in tune again, he is subject to new troubles. Betwixt this ebbing and flowing there is very little quiet. Now because this cannot be done without a great measure of God's Spirit, our help is to make use of that promise of giving 'the Holy Ghost to them that ask it,' John. xi. 13. To teach us when, how long, and how much to grieve; and when, and how long, and how much to rejoice, the Spirit must teach the heart this, who as he moved upon the waters before the creation, so he must move upon the waters of our souls, for we have not the command of our own hearts. Every natural man is carried away with his flesh and humours, upon which the devil rides, and carries him whither he list; he hath no better counsellors than flesh and blood, and Satan counselling with them. But a godly man is not a slave to his carnal affections, but as David here, labours to bring into captivity the first motions of sin in his heart.

Chapter IX.—*Of the soul's disquiets, God's dealings, and power to contain ourselves in order.*

Obs. 1. Moreover we see, that *the soul hath disquiets proper to itself, besides those griefs of sympathy that arise from the body*; for here the soul complains of the soul itself, as when it is out of the body it hath torments and joys of its own. And if those troubles of the soul be not well cured, then by way of fellowship and redundance they will affect the outward man, and so the whole man shall be enwrapt in misery.

Obs. 2. From whence we further see, that *God, when he will humble a man, need not fetch forces from without.* If he let but our own hearts loose, we shall have trouble and work enough, though we were as holy as David; God did not only exercise him with a rebellious son out of his own loins, but with rebellious risings out of his own heart. If there were no enemy in the world, nor devil in hell, we carry that within us, that, if it be let loose, will trouble us more than all the world besides. Oh that the proud creature should exalt himself against God, and run into a voluntary course of provoking him, who can not only raise the humours of our bodies against us, but the passions of our minds also to torment us! Therefore it is the best wisdom not to provoke the great God, for 'are we stronger than he,' 1 Cor. x. 22, that can raise ourselves against ourselves? and work wonders not only in the great world, but also in the little world, our souls and bodies, when he pleases?

Obs. 3. We see likewise hence a *necessity of having something in the soul above itself.* It must be partaker of a diviner nature than itself; otherwise, when the most refined part of our souls, the very spirit of our minds, is out of frame, what shall bring it in again? Therefore we must conceive in a godly man, a double self, one which must be denied, the other which must deny; one that breeds all the disquiet, and another that stilleth what the other hath raised. The way to still the soul, as it is under our corrupt self, is not to parley with it, and divide government for peace sake, as if we should gratify the flesh in something, to redeem liberty to the spirit in other things; for we shall find the flesh will be too encroaching. We must strive against it, not with subtlety and discourse, so much as with peremptory violence silence it and vex it. An enemy that parleys will yield at length. Grace is nothing else but that blessed power, whereby as spiritual we gain upon ourselves as carnal. Holy love is that which we gain of self-love; and so joy, and delight, &c. Grace labours to win ground of the old man, until at length it be all in all; indeed we are never ourselves perfectly, till we have wholly put off ourselves; nothing should be at a greater distance to us than ourselves. This is the reason why carnal men, that have nothing above themselves but their corrupt self, sink in great troubles, having nothing within to uphold them, whereas a good man is wiser than himself, holier than himself, stronger than himself; there is something in him more than a man. There be evils that the spirit of man alone, out of the goodness of nature, cannot bear; but the spirit of man, assisted with an higher Spirit, will support and carry him through. It is a good trial of a man's condition to know what he esteems to be himself. A godly man counts the inner man, the sanctified part, to be himself, whereby he stands in relation to Christ and a better life. Another man esteems his contentment in the world, the satisfaction of his carnal desires, the respect he finds from men by reason of his parts, or something without him, that he is master of; this he counts himself, and by this he values himself, and to this he makes his best thoughts and endeavours serviceable: and of crosses in these things he is most sensible, and so sensible, that he thinks himself undone if he seeth not a present issue out of them.

That which most troubles a good man in all troubles is himself, so far as he is unsubdued; he is more disquieted with himself than with all troubles out of himself; when he hath gotten the better once of himself, whatsoever falls from without is light. Where the spirit is enlarged, it cares not much for outward bondage; where the spirit is lightsome, it cares not much for outward darkness; where the spirit is settled, it cares not much for outward changes; where the spirit is one with itself, it cannot* bear outward breaches; where the spirit is sound, it can bear outward sickness. Nothing can be very ill with us, when all is well within. This is the comfort of a holy man, that though he be troubled with himself, yet by reason of the spirit in him, which is his better self, he works out by degrees whatever is contrary, as spring-water, being clear of itself, works itself clean, though it be troubled by something cast in, as the sea will endure no poisonful thing, but casts it upon the shore. But a carnal man is like a spring corrupted, that cannot work itself clear, because it is wholly tainted; his eye and light is darkness, and therefore no wonder if he seeth nothing. Sin lieth upon his understanding, and hinders the knowledge of itself; it lies close upon the will, and hinders the striving against itself.

True self that is worth the owning, is when a man is taken into a higher condition, and made one with Christ, and esteems neither of himself nor others, as happy for anything according to the flesh. 1. He is under the law and government of the Spirit, and so far as he is himself, works accord-

* Qu. 'can?'—ED.

ing to that principle. 2. He labours more and more to be transformed into the likeness of Christ, in whom he esteemeth that he hath his best being. 3. He esteems of all things that befall him, to be good or ill, as they further or hinder his best condition. If all be well for that, he counts himself well, whatsoever else befalls him.

Another man, when he doth anything that is good, acts not his own part; but a godly man, when he doth good, is in his proper element; what another man doth for by-ends and reasons, that he doth from a new nature, which, if there were no law to compel, yet would move him to that which is pleasing to Christ. If he be drawn aside by passion or temptation, that he judgeth not to be himself, but taketh a holy revenge on himself for it, as being redeemed and taken out from himself; he thinks himself no debtor, nor to owe any service to his corrupt self. That which he plots and projects and works for is, that Christ may rule everywhere, and especially in himself, for he is not his own but Christ's, and therefore desires to be more and more emptied of himself, that Christ might be all in all in him.

Thus we see what great use there is of dealing with ourselves, for the better composing and settling of our souls. Which, though it be a course without glory and ostentation in the world, as causing a man to retire inwardly into his own breast, having no other witness but God and himself; and though it be likewise irksome to the flesh, as calling the soul home to itself, being desirous naturally to wander abroad and be a stranger at home; yet it is a course both good in itself, and makes the soul good.

For by this means the judgment is exercised and rectified, the will and affections ordered, the whole man put into an holy frame fit for every good action. By this the tree is made good, and the fruit cannot but be answerable; by this the soul itself is set in tune, whence there is a pleasant harmony in our whole conversation. Without this, we may do that which is outwardly good to others, but we can never be good ourselves. The first justice begins within, when there is a due subjectiou of all the powers of the soul to the spirit, as sanctified and guided by God's Spirit; when justice and order is first established in the soul, it will appear from thence in all our dealings. He that is at peace in himself, will be peaceable to others, peaceable in his family, peaceable in the church, peaceable in the state. The soul of a wicked man is in perpetual sedition; being always troubled in itself, it is no wonder if it be troublesome to others. Unity in ourselves is before union with others.

To conclude this first part, concerning intercourse with ourselves. As we desire to enjoy ourselves, and to live the life of men and of Christians, which is, to understand our ways; as we desire to live comfortably, and not to be accessory of yielding to that sorrow which causeth death; as we desire to answer God and ourselves, when we are to give an account of the inward tumults of our souls; as we desire to be vessels prepared for every good work, and to have strength to undergo any cross; as we desire to have healthy souls, and to keep a sabbath within ourselves; as we desire not only to do good, but to be good in ourselves: so let us labour to quiet our souls, and often ask a reason of ourselves, why we should not be quiet?

Chapter X.—*Means not to be overcharged with sorrow.*

To help us further herein, besides that which hath been formerly spoken, 1. *We must take heed of building an ungrounded confidence of happiness for time to come*, which makes us when changes come, 1, Unacquainted with them; 2, Takes away expectation of them; 3, And preparation for them. When any thing is strange and sudden, and lights upon us unfurnished and unfenced, it must needs put our spirits out of frame. It is good therefore to make all kind of troubles familiar to us, in our thoughts at least, and this will break the force of them. It is good to fence our souls beforehand against all assaults, as men use to keep out the sea, by raising banks; and if a breach be made, to repair it presently.

We had need to maintain a strong garrison of holy reasons against the assaults of strong passions; we may hope for the best, but fear the worst, and prepare to bear whatsoever. We say that a set diet is dangerous, because variety of occasions will force us upon breaking of it; so in this world of changes we cannot resolve upon any certain condition of life, for upon alteration the mind is out of frame. We cannot say this or that trouble shall not befall; yet we may, by help of the Spirit, say, nothing that doth befall shall make me do that which is unworthy of a Christian.

That which others make easy by suffering, that a wise man maketh easy by thinking of beforehand. *Quæ alii diu patiendo levia faciunt, sapiens levia facit diu cogitando.* If we expect the worst, when it comes, it is no more than we thought of; if better befalls us, then it is the sweeter to us, the less we expected it. Our Saviour foretells the worst, 'In the world you shall have tribulation,' John xvi. 33; therefore look for it; but then He will not leave us. Satan deludes with fair promises; but when the contrary falls out, he leaves his followers in their distresses. We desire peace and rest, but we seek it not in its own place; 'there is a rest for God's people,' Heb. iv. 9, but that is not here, nor yet; but it remains for them; 'they rest from their labours,' Rev. xiv. 13, but that is after they 'are dead in the Lord.' There is no sound rest till then. Yet this caution must be remembered, that we shape not in our fancies such troubles as are never likely to fall out. It comes either from weakness or guiltiness, to fear shadows. We shall not need to make crosses; they will, as we say of foul weather, come before they be sent for. How many evils do people fear, from which they have no further hurt than what is bred only by their causeless fears! Nor yet, if they be probable, must we think of them so as to be altogether so affected, as if undoubtedly they would come, for so we give certain strength to an uncertain cross, and usurp upon God, by anticipating that which may never come to pass. It was rashness in David to say, 'I shall one day perish by the hand of Saul,' 1 Sam. xxvii. 1.

If they be such troubles as will certainly come to pass, as parting with friends and contentments, at least, by death; then, 1. Think of them so as not to be much dismayed, but furnish thy heart with strength beforehand, that they may fall the lighter. 2. Think of them so as not to give up the bucklers to passion, and lie open as a fair mark for any uncomfortable accident to strike to the heart; nor yet so think of them as to despise them, but to consider of God's meaning in them, and how to take good by them. 3. Think of the things we enjoy, so as to moderate our enjoying of them, by considering there must be a parting, and therefore how we shall be able to bear it when it comes.

2. If we desire not to be overcharged with sorrow when that which we fear is fallen upon us, we must then beforehand look *that our love to any thing in this world shoot not so far as that, when the time of severing cometh, we part with so much of our hearts by that rent.* Those that love too much will always grieve too much. It is the greatness of our affections which causeth

the sharpness of our afflictions. He that cannot abound without pride and high-mindedness, will not want without too much dejectedness. Love is planted for such things as can return love, and make us better by loving them; wherein we shall satisfy our love to the full. It is pity so sweet an affection should be lost. So sorrow is for sin, and for other things, as they make sin the more bitter to us. The life of a Christian should be a meditation how to unloose his affections from inferior things. He will easily die that is dead before in affection. But this will never be, unless the soul seeth something better than all things in the world, upon which it may bestow itself. In that measure our affections die in their excessive motion to things below, as they are taken up with the love and admiration of the best things. He that is much in heaven in his thoughts is free from being tossed with tempests here below. The top of those mountains that are above the middle region are so quiet as that the lightest things, as ashes, lie still, and are not moved. The way to mortify earthly members, that bestir themselves in us, is to mind things above, Col. iii. 1, 5. The more the ways of wisdom lead us on high, the more we avoid the snares below.

In the uncertainty of all events here, labour to frame that contentment in and from our own selves which the things themselves will not yield; frame peace by freeing our hearts from too much fear, and riches by freeing our hearts from covetous desires. Frame a sufficiency out of contentedness. If the soul itself be out of tune, outward things will do no more good than a fair shoe to a gouty foot.

And seek not ourselves abroad out of ourselves in the conceits of other men. A man shall never live quietly that hath not learned to be set light-by of others. He that is little in his own eyes will not be troubled to be little in the eyes of others. Men that set too high a price upon themselves, when others will not come to their price, are discontent. Those whose condition is above their worth, and their pride above their condition, shall never want sorrow; yet we must maintain our authority, and the image of God in our places, for that is God's and not ours; and we ought so to carry ourselves as we approve ourselves to their consciences, though we have not their good words. 'Let none despise thy youth,' saith St Paul to Timothy, 1 Tim. iv. 12—that is, walk so before them as they shall have no cause. It is not in our own power what other men think or speak, but it is in our power, by God's grace, to live so that none can think ill of us, but by slandering, and none believe ill but by too much credulity.

3. When anything seizeth upon us, we must take heed we *mingle not our own passions with it;* we must neither bring sin to, nor mingle sin with, the suffering; for that will trouble the spirit more than the trouble itself. We are more to deal with our own hearts than with the trouble itself. We are not hurt till our souls be hurt. God will not have it in the power of any creature to hurt our souls, but by our own treason against ourselves.

Therefore we should have our hearts in continual jealousy, for they are ready to deceive the best. In sudden encounters some sin doth many times discover itself, the seed whereof lieth hid in our natures, which we think ourselves very free from. Who would have thought the seeds of murmuring had lurked in the meek nature of Moses? that the seeds of murder had lurked in the pitiful heart of David? 2 Sam. xii. 9, that the seeds of denial of Christ, Matt. xxvi. 72, had lien hid in the zealous affection of Peter towards Christ? If passions break out from us, which we are not naturally inclined unto, and over which by grace we have got a great conquest, how watchful need we be over ourselves in those things, which, by temper, custom, and company we are carried unto! and what cause have we to fear continually that we are worse than we take ourselves to be!

There are many unruly passions lie hid in us, until they be drawn out by something that meeteth with them; either—

(1.) *By way of opposition*, as when the truth of God spiritually unfolded meets with some beloved corruption, it swelleth bigger. The force of gunpowder is not known until some spark light on it; and oftentimes the stillest natures, if crossed, discover the deepest corruptions. Sometimes it is drawn out by dealing with the opposite spirits of other men. Oftentimes retired men know not what lies hid in themselves.

(2.) *Sometimes by crosses*, as many people, whilst the freshness and vigour of their spirits lasteth, and while the flower of age, and a full supply of all things continueth, seem to be of a pleasing and calm disposition; but afterwards, when changes come, like Job's wife, they are discovered, Job ii. 9. Then that which in nature is unsubdued, openly appears.

(3.) *Temptations likewise have a searching power to bring that to light in us which was hidden before.* Satan hath been a winnower and a sifter of old, Luke xxii. 3. He thought if Job had been but touched in his body, he would have cursed God to his face, Job i.

Some men, out of policy, conceal their passion until they see some advantage to let it out, as Esau smothered his hatred until his father's death. *Aperta perdunt odia vindictæ locum.* When the restraint is taken away, men, as we say, shew themselves in their pure naturals. Unloose a tiger or a lion, and you know what he is. *Solve leonem et senties.*

(4.) Further, *let us see more every day into the state of our own souls.* What a shame is it that so nimble and swift a spirit as the soul is, that can mount up to heaven, and from thence come down into the earth in an instant, should, whilst it looks over all other things, overlook itself! that it should be skilful in the story almost of all times and places, and yet ignorant of the story of itself! that we should know what is done in the court and country, and beyond the seas, and be ignorant of what is done at home in our own hearts! that we should live known to others, and yet die unknown to ourselves! that we should be able to give account of anything better than of ourselves to ourselves! This is the cause why we stand in our own light, why we think better of ourselves than others, and better than is cause; this is that which hindereth all reformation, for how can we reform that which we are not willing to see, and so we lose one of the surest evidences of our sincerity, which is, a willingness to search into our hearts, and to be searched by others. A sincere heart will offer itself to trial.

And therefore let us sift our actions, and our passions, and see what is flesh in them, and what is spirit, and so separate the precious from the vile. It is good likewise to consider what sin we were guilty of before, which moved God to give us up to excess in any passion, and wherein we have grieved his Spirit. Passion will be more moderate when thus it knows it must come to the trial and censure. This course will either make us weary of passion, or else passion will make us weary of this strict course. We shall find it the safest way to give our hearts no rest till we have wrought on them to purpose, and gotten the mastery over them.

When the soul is inured to this dealing with itself, it will learn the skill to command, and passions will be soon commanded, as being inured to be examined and checked; as we see dogs, and such like domestical creatures, that will not regard a stranger, yet will be quieted in brawls presently by the voice of their master, to which they are accustomed. This fits us for service. Unbroken spirits are like unbroken horses, unfit for any use until they be thoroughly subdued.

(5.) And it were best to prevent, as much as in us lieth, *the very first risings*, before the soul be overcast. Passions are but little motions at the first, but grow as rivers do, greater and greater, the farther they are carried from their spring. The first risings are the more to be looked unto, because there is most danger in them, and we have least care over them. Sin, like rust, or a canker, will by little and little eat out all the graces of the soul. There is no staying when we are once down the hill, till we come to the bottom. No sin but is easier kept out than driven out. If we cannot prevent wicked thoughts, yet we may deny them lodging in our hearts. It is our giving willing entertainment to sinful motions that increaseth guilt, and hindereth our peace. It is that which moveth God to give us up to a further degree of evil affections. Therefore what we are afraid to do before men, we should be afraid to think before God. It would much further our peace to keep our judgments clear, as being the eye of the soul, whereby we may discern in every action and passion what is good and what is evil; as likewise to preserve tenderness of heart, that may check us at the first, and not brook the least evil being discovered. When the heart begins once to be kindled, it is easy to smother the smoke of passion, which otherwise will fume up into the head, and gather into so thick a cloud as we shall lose the sight of ourselves, and what is best to be done. And therefore David here labours to take up his heart at the first; his care was to crush the very first insurrections of his soul, before they came to break forth into open rebellion. Storms we know rise out of little gusts. Little risings neglected cover the soul before we are aware. If we would check these risings, and stifle them in their birth, they would not break out afterwards to the reproach of religion, to the scandal of the weak, to the offence of the strong, to the grief of God's Spirit in us, to the disturbance of our own spirits in doing good, and to the disheartening of us in troubling of our inward peace, and thereby weakening our assurance. Therefore let us stop beginnings as much as may be; and so soon as they begin to rise, let us begin to examine what raised them, and whither they are about to carry us, Ps. iv. 4. The way to be still is to examine ourselves first, and then censure what stands not with reason. As David doth, when he had given way to unbefitting thoughts of God's providence, 'So foolish,' saith he, 'was I, and as a beast before thee,' Ps. lxxiii. 22.

Especially then, look to these sinful stirrings when thou art to deal with God. I am to have communion with a God of peace, what then do turbulent thoughts and affections in my heart? I am to deal with a patient God, why should I cherish revengeful thoughts? Abraham drove away the birds from the sacrifice, Gen. xv. 11. Troublesome thoughts, like birds, will come before they be sent for, but they should find entertainment accordingly.

(6.) In all our grievance let us look to something that may *comfort us, as well as discourage*; look to that we enjoy, as well as that we want. As in prosperity God mingles some crosses to diet us, so in all crosses there is something to comfort us. As there is a vanity lies hid in the best worldly good, so there is a blessing lies hid in the worst worldly evil. God usually maketh up that with some advantage in another kind, wherein we are inferior to others. Others are in greater place, so they are in greater danger. Others be richer, so their cares and snares be greater: the poor in the world may be richer in faith than they, James ii. 5. The soul can better digest and master a low estate than a prosperous, and under some abasement, it is in a less distance from God. Others are not so afflicted as we, then they have less experience of God's gracious power than we. Others may have more healthy bodies, but souls less weaned from the world. We would not change conditions with them, so as to have their spirits with their condition. For one half of our lives, the meanest are as happy and free from cares, as the greatest monarch, that is, while both sleep; and usually the sleep of the one is sweeter than the sleep of the other. What is all that the earth can afford us, if God deny health? and this a man in the meanest condition may enjoy. That wherein one man differs from another, is but title, and but for a little time; death levelleth all.

There is scarce any man, but the good he receives from God is more than the ill he feels, if our unthankful hearts would suffer us to think so. Is not our health more than our sickness? do we not enjoy more than we want, I mean, of the things that are necessary? are not our good days more than our evil? but we would go to heaven upon roses, and usually one cross is more taken to heart, than a hundred blessings. So unkindly we deal with God. Is God indebted to us? doth he owe us any thing? those that deserve nothing, should be content with any thing.

We should look to others as good as ourselves, as well as to ourselves, and then we shall see it is not our own case only. Who are we that we should look for an exempted condition from those troubles which God's dearest children are addicted unto?

Thus when we are surprised contrary to our looking for and liking, we should study rather how to exercise some grace, than give way to any passion. Think, now is a time to exercise our patience, our wisdom, and other graces. By this means we shall turn that to our greatest advantage, which Satan intendeth greatest hurt to us by. Thus we shall not only master every condition, but make it serviceable to our good. If nature teach bees, not only to gather honey out of sweet flowers, but out of bitter, shall not grace teach us to draw even out of the bitterest condition something to better our souls? we learn to tame all creatures, even the wildest, that we may bring them to our use: and why should we give way to our own unruly passions?

(7.) It were good to have in our eye *the beauty of a well-ordered soul*, and we should think that nothing in this world is of sufficient worth to put us out of frame. The sanctified soul should be like the sun in this, which though it worketh upon all these inferior bodies, and cherisheth them by light and influence, yet is not moved nor wrought upon by them again, but keepeth its own lustre and distance; so our spirits, being of a heavenly breed, should rule other things beneath them, and not be ruled by them. It is a holy state of soul to be under the power of nothing beneath itself. Are we stirred? then consider, is this matter worth the loss of my quiet? What we esteem, that we love; what we love, we labour for; and therefore let us esteem highly of a clear, calm temper, whereby we both enjoy our God and ourselves, and know how to rank all things else. It is against nature for inferior things to rule that which the wise Disposer of all things hath set above them. We owe the flesh neither suit nor service; we are no debtors to it.

The more we set before the soul that quiet estate in heaven which the souls of perfect men now enjoy, and itself ere long shall enjoy there, the more it will be in love with it, and endeavour to attain unto it. And because the soul never worketh better, than when it is raised up by some strong and sweet affection—*anima nunquam melius agit, quam ex imperio alicujus insignis affectus*—let us look upon our nature, as it is in Christ, in whom it is pure, sweet, calm, meek, every way lovely. This sight is a changing sight; love is an affection of imitation; we affect a likeness to him we love. Let us 'learn of Christ to be humble and meek,' and then we 'shall find rest to our souls,' Mat. xi. 29. The setting of an excellent idea and platform before us, will raise and draw up our souls higher, and make us sensible of the least moving of spirit, that shall be contrary to that, the attainment whereof we have in our desires. He will hardly attain to mean things, that sets not before him higher perfection. Naturally we love to see symmetry and proportion, even in a dead picture, and are much taken with some curious piece. But why should we not rather labour to keep the affections of the soul in due proportion? seeing a meek and well ordered soul is not only lovely in the sight of men and angels, but is much set by, by the great God himself. But now the greatest care of those that set highest price upon themselves is, how to compose their outward carriage in some graceful manner, never studying how to compose their spirits; and rather how to cover the deformity of their passions than to cure them. Whence it is that the foulest inward vices are covered with the fairest vizards, and to make this the worse, all this is counted the best breeding.

The Hebrews placed all their happiness in peace, and when they would comprise much in one word, they would wish peace. This was that the angels brought news of from heaven, at the birth of Christ, Luke ii. 14. Now peace riseth out of quietness and order, and God that is 'the God of peace, is the God of order' first, 1 Cor. xiv. 33. What is health, but when all the members are in their due positure,* and all the humours in a settled quiet? Whence ariseth the beauty of the world, but from that comely order wherein every creature is placed; the more glorious and excellent creatures above, and the less below? So it is in the soul; the best constitution of it is when by the Spirit of God it is so ordered, as that all be in subjection to the law of the mind. What a sight were it for the feet to be where the head is, and the earth to be where the heaven is, to see all turned upside down? And to a spiritual eye it seems as great a deformity, to see the soul to be under the rule of sinful passions.

Comeliness riseth out of the fit proportion of divers members to make up one body, when every member hath a beauty in itself, and is likewise well suited to other parts. A fair face and a crooked body, comely upper parts, and the lower parts uncomely, suit not well; because comeliness stands in oneness, in a fit agreement of many parts to one. When there is the head of a man, and the body of a beast, it is a monster in nature; and is it not as monstrous for to have an understanding head, and a fierce untamed heart? It cannot but raise up a holy indignation in us against these risings, when we consider how unbeseeming they are. What do these base passions in a heart dedicated to God, and given up to the government of his Spirit? what an indignity is it for princes to go afoot, and servants on horseback? for those to rule, whose place is to be ruled? as being good attendants, but bad guides. It was Ham's curse to be a 'servant of servants,' Gen. ix. 25.

(8.) This must be strengthened with a strong *self-denial*, without which there can be no good done in religion.

There be two things that most trouble us in the way to heaven, corruption within us, and the cross without us: that which is within us must be denied, that that which is without us may be endured. Otherwise we

* That is, 'position.'—ED.

cannot follow him by whom we look to be saved. The gate, the entrance of religion, is narrow; we must strip ourselves of ourselves before we can enter; if we bring any ruling lust to religion, it will prove a bitter root of some gross sin, or of apostasy and final desperation.

Those that sought the praise of men more than the praise of God, John xii. 43, could not believe, because that lust of ambition would, when it should be crossed, draw them away. The young man thought it better for Christ to lose a disciple than that he should lose his possession, and therefore went away as he came, Mat. xix. 22. The 'third ground,' Mat. xiii. 25, came to nothing; because the plough had not gone deep enough to break up the roots, whereby their hearts were fastened to earthly contentments. This self-denial we must carry with us through all the parts of religion, both in our active and passive obedience; for in obedience there must be a subjection to a superior; but corrupt self neither is subject, nor can be, Rom. viii. 7. It will have an oar in everything, and maketh everything, yea, religion, serviceable to itself. It is the idol of the world, or rather the god that is set highest of all in the soul; and so God himself is made but an idol. It is hard to deny a friend who is another self, harder to deny a wife that lieth in the bosom, but most hard to deny ourselves. Nothing so near us as ourselves to ourselves, and yet nothing so far off. Nothing so dear, and yet nothing so malicious and troublesome. Hypocrites would part with the fruit of their body, Mic. vi. 7, sooner than the sin of their souls.

Chapter XI.—*Signs of victory over ourselves, and of a subdued spirit.*

Quest. But how shall we know whether we have by grace got the victory over ourselves or not?

Ans. I answer, 1. *If in good actions we stand not so much upon the credit of the action as upon the good that is done.* What we do as unto God, we look for acceptance from God. It was Jonah his fault to stand more upon his own reputation than the glory of God's mercy. It is a prevailing sign when, though there be no outward encouragements, nay, though there be discouragements, yet we can rest in the comfort of a good intention. For usually inward comfort is a note of inward sincerity. Jehu must be seen, or else all is lost, 2 Kings x. 16.

2. It is a good evidence of some prevailing when, *upon religious grounds, we can cross ourselves in those things unto which our hearts stand most affected.* This sheweth we reserve God his own place in our hearts.

3. When, being privy to our own inclination and temper, we have gotten such *a supply of Spirit as that the grace which is contrary to our temper appears in us.* As oft we see none more patient than those that are naturally inclined to intemperancy of passion, because natural proneness makes them jealous over themselves. Some, out of fear of being overmuch moved, are not moved so much as they should be. This jealousy stirreth us up to a careful use of all helps. Where grace is helped by nature, there a little grace will go far; but where there is much untowardness of nature, there much grace is not so well discerned. Sour wines need much sweetening. And that is most spiritual which hath least help from nature, and is won by prayer and pains.

4. When we are not *partial when the things concern ourselves.* David could allow himself another man's wife, and yet judgeth another man

worthy of death for taking away a poor man's lamb, 2 Sam. xii. 4. Men usually favour themselves too much when they are chancellors in their own cause, and measure all things by their private interest. He hath taken a good degree in Christ's school that hath learned to forget himself here.

5. It is a good sign when, upon discovery of self-seeking, *we can gain upon our corruption;* and are willing to search and to be searched, what our inclination is, and where it faileth. That which we favour we are tender of, it must not be touched. A good heart, when any corruption is discovered by a searching ministry, is affected as if it had found out a deadly enemy. Touchiness and passion argues guilt.

6. This is a sign of a man's victory over himself, when he loves health and peace of body and mind, with a supply of all needful things, chiefly for this end, *that he may with more freedom of spirit serve God in doing good to others.* So soon as grace entereth into the heart, it frameth the heart to be in some measure public; and thinks it hath not its end in the bare enjoying of anything, until it can improve what it hath for a further end. Thus to seek ourselves is to deny ourselves, and thus to deny ourselves is truly to seek ourselves. It is no self-seeking when we care for no more than that, without which we cannot comfortably serve God. When the soul can say unto God, Lord, as thou wouldst have me serve thee in my place, so grant me such a measure of health and strength, wherein I may serve thee.

Object. But what if God thinks it good that I shall serve him in weakness, and in want and suffering?

Ans. Then it is a comfortable sign of gaining over our own wills, when we can yield ourselves to be disposed of by God, as knowing best what is good for us. There is no condition but therein we may exercise some grace, and honour God in some measure. Yet because some enlargement of condition is ordinarily that estate wherein we are best able to do good in, we may in the use of means desire it, and upon that resign up ourselves wholly unto God, and make his will our will, without exception or reservation, and care for nothing more than we can have with his leave and love. This Job had exercised his heart unto; whereupon in that great change of condition he sinned not, Job ii. 10; that is, fell not into the sins incident to that dejected and miserable state; into sins of rebellion and discontent. He carried his crosses comely, with that staidness and resignedness which became a holy man.

7. It is further a clear evidence of a spirit subdued, when *we will discover the truth of our affection towards God and his people, though with censure of others.* David was content to endure the censure of neglecting the state and majesty of a king, out of joy for settling the ark, 2 Sam. vi. 22. Nehemiah could not dissemble his grief for the ruins of the church, though in the king's presence, Neh. ii. 3. It is a comfortable sign of the wasting of self-love, when we can be at a point what becomes of ourselves, so it go well with the cause of God and the church.

Now the way to prevail still more over ourselves, as when we are to do or suffer anything, or withstand any person in a good cause, &c., is, not to think that we are to deal with men, yea, or with devils, so much as with ourselves. The saints resisted their enemies to death, by resisting their own corruptions first. If we once get the victory over ourselves, all other things are conquered to our ease. All the hurt Satan and the world do us, is by correspondency with ourselves. All things are so far under us, as we are above ourselves. *Te vince, et mundus tibi victus est,* &c.

For the further subduing of ourselves, it is good to follow sin to the first hold and castle, which is corrupt nature; the streams will lead us to the spring head. Indeed, the most apparent discovery of sin is in the outward carriage; we see it in the fruit before in the root, as we see grace in the expression before in the affection. But yet we shall never hate sin thoroughly until we consider it in the poisoned root from whence it ariseth.

That which least troubles a natural man doth most of all trouble a true Christian. A natural man is sometimes troubled with the fruit of his corruption, and the consequents of guilt and punishment that attend it; but a true-hearted Christian with corruption itself. This drives him to complain, with St Paul, 'O wretched man that I am, who shall deliver me,' not from the members only, but 'from this body of death?' Rom. vii. 24, which is as noisome to my soul as a dead carrion is to my senses, which, together with the members, is marvellously nimble and active, and hath no days, or hours, or minutes of rest; always laying about it to enlarge itself, and like spring water, which, the more it issueth out, the more it may.

It is a good way, upon any particular breach of our inward peace, presently to have recourse to that which breeds and foments all our disquiet. Lord! what do I complain of this my unruly passion? I carry a nature about me subject to break out continually upon any occasion. Lord! strike at the root, and dry up the fountain in me. Thus David doth arise from the guilt of those two foul sins of murder and adultery, Ps. li. 5, to the sin of his nature, the root itself; as if he should say, Lord, it is not these actual sins that defile me only, but if I look back to my first conception, I was tainted in the spring of my nature.

This is that which put David's soul so much out of frame; for from whence was this contradiction? and whence was this contradiction so unwearied in making head again and again against the checks of the Spirit in him? Whence was it that corruption would not be said nay? Whence were these sudden and unlooked for objections of the flesh? but from the remainder of old Adam in him, which, like a Michal within us, is either scoffing at the ways of God, or, as a Job's wife, fretting and thwarting the motions of God's Spirit in us; which prevails the more because it is home-bred in us, whereas holy motions are strangers to most of our souls. Corruption is loath that a new comer-in should take so much upon him as to control, as the Sodomites thought much that Lot, being a stranger, should intermeddle amongst them, Gen. xix. 9. If God once leave us, as he did Hezekiah, to try what is in us, what should we find but darkness, rebellion, unruliness, doubtings, &c., in the best of us. This flesh of ours hath principles against all God's principles, and laws against all God's laws, and reasons against all God's reasons. Oh, if we could but one whole hour seriously think of the impure issue of our hearts, it would bring us down upon our knees in humiliation before God! But we can never whilst we live, so thoroughly as we should, see into the depth of our deceitful hearts, nor yet be humbled enough for what we see; for though we speak of it and confess it, yet we are not so sharpened against this corrupt flesh of ours as we should. How should it humble us that the seeds of the vilest sin, even of the sin against the Holy Ghost, is in us? And no thank to us that they break not out. It should humble us to hear of any great enormous sin in another man, considering what our own nature would proceed unto if it were not restrained (*c*). We may see our own nature in them as face answering face, Prov. xxvii. 19. If God should take his Spirit from us, there is enough in us to defile a whole world; and although we be ingrafted into Christ, yet we carry about us a relish of the old stock still. David was a man of a good natural constitution, and, for grace, a man after God's own heart, and had got the better of himself in a great measure, and had learned to overcome himself in matter of revenge, as in Saul's case, 1 Sam. xxiv. 6; yet now we see the vessel is shaken a little, and the dregs appear that were in the bottom before. Alas! we know not our own hearts till we plough with God's heifer, till his Spirit bringeth a light into our souls. It is good to consider how this impure spring breaks out diversely in the diverse conditions we are in. There is no estate of life, nor no action we undertake, wherein it will not put forth itself to defile us; it is so full of poison that it taints whatsoever we do, both our natures, conditions, and actions. In a prosperous condition, like David, we think we shall never be moved, Ps. xxx. 6. Under the cross the soul is troubled, and drawn to murmur, and to be sullen, and sink down in discouragement, to be in a heat almost to blasphemy, to be weary of our callings, and to quarrel with everything in our way. See the folly and fury of most men in this, for us silly worms to contradict the great God. And to whose peril is it? Is it not our own? Let us gather ourselves with all our wit and strength together; alas! what can we do but provoke him, and get more stripes? We may be sure he will deal with us as we deal with our children. If they be froward and unquiet for lesser matters, we will make them cry and be sullen for something. Refractory, stubborn horses are the more spurred, and yet shake not off the rider.

CHAPTER XII.—*Of original righteousness, natural corruption, Satan's joining with it, and our duty thereupon.*

Object. § I. But here mark a plot of spiritual treason. Satan, joining with our corruption, setteth the wit on work to persuade the soul that this inward rebellion is not so bad, because it is natural to us, as a condition of nature rising out of the first principles in our creation, and was curbed in by the bridle of original righteousness, which they would have accessary and supernatural, and therefore allege that concupiscence is less odious and more excusable in us, and so no great danger in yielding and betraying our souls unto it, and by that means persuading us that that which is our deadliest enemy hath no harm in it, nor meaneth any to us.*

Ans. This rebellion of lusts against the understanding is not natural, as our nature came out of God's hands at the first, Gen. i. 27; for this, being evil and the cause of evil, could not come from God, who is good and the cause of all good, and nothing but good, who, upon the creation of all things, pronounced them good, and, after the creation of man, pronounced of all things that they were very good, ver. 31. Now, that which is ill and very ill cannot be seated at the same time in that which is good and very good. God created man at the first right; he of himself 'sought out many inventions,' Eccles. vii. 29. As God beautified the heaven with stars, and decked the earth with variety of plants, and herbs, and flowers, so he adorned man, his prime creature here below, with all those endowments that were fit for a happy condition; and original righteousness was fit and due

* Most of the most dangerous opinions of popery, as justification by works, state of perfection, merit, satisfaction, supererogation, &c., spring from hence, that they have slight conceits of concupiscence as a condition of nature. Yet some of them, as Michael Bayns, professor at Louvain, &c., are sound in the point.

to an original and happy condition. Therefore, as the angels were created with all angelical perfections, and as our bodies were created in an absolute temper of all the humours, so the soul was created in that sweet harmony wherein there was no discord, as an instrument in tune, fit to be moved to any duty; as a clean, neat glass, the soul represented God's image and holiness.

§ II. Therefore it is so far, that concupiscence should be natural, that the contrary to it, namely, righteousness, wherein Adam was created, was natural to him; though it were planted in man's nature by God, and so in regard of the cause of it, was supernatural; yet because it was agreeable to that happy condition, without which he could not subsist, in that respect it was natural, and should have been derived, if he had stood, together with his nature, to his posterity. As heat in the air, though it hath its first impression from the heat of the sun, yet is natural, because it agreeth to the nature of that element; and though man be compounded of a spiritual and earthly substance, yet it is natural that the baser earthly part should be subject to the superior, because where there is different degrees of worthiness, it is fit there should be a subordination of the meaner to that which is in order higher. The body naturally desires food and bodily contentments, yet in a man endued with reason, this desire is governed so as it becomes not inordinate. A beast sins not in its appetite, because it hath no power above to order it. A man that lives in a solitary place, far remote from company, may take his liberty to live as it pleaseth him; but if he comes to live under the government of some well-ordered city, then he is bound to submit to the laws and customs of that city, under penalty upon any breach of order; so the risings of the soul, howsoever in other creatures they are not blameable, having no commander in themselves, above them, yet in man they are to be ordered by reason and judgment.

Therefore it cannot be, that concupiscence should be natural, in regard of the state of creation. It was Adam's sin; which had many sins in the womb of it, that brought this disorder upon the soul. Adam's person first corrupted our nature, and nature being corrupted, corrupts our persons, and our persons being corrupted, increase the corruption of our nature, by custom of sinning, which is another nature in us. As a stream, the farther it runs from the spring head, the more it enlargeth its channel, by the running of lesser rivers into it, until it empties itself into the sea; so corruption, till it be overpowered by grace, swelleth bigger and bigger, so that though this disorder was not natural, in regard of the first creation, yet since the fall it has become natural, even as we call that which is common to the whole kind, and propagated from parents to their children, to be natural; so that it is both natural and against nature, natural now, but against nature in its first perfection.

And because corruption is natural to us, therefore, 1, We delight in it; whence it comes to pass, that our souls are carried along in an easy current, to the committing of any sin without opposition. 2. Because it is natural, therefore it is unwearied and restless, as light bodies are not wearied in their motion upwards, nor heavy bodies in their motion downwards, nor a stream in its running to the sea, because it is natural: hence it is that the 'old man,' Eph. iv. 22, is never tired in the 'works of the flesh,' Gal. v. 19, nor never drawn dry. When men cannot act sin, yet they will love sin, and act it over again by pleasing thoughts of it, and by sinful speculations suck out the delight of sin; and are grieved, not for their sin, but because they want strength and opportunity to commit it; if sin would not leave them, they would never leave sin. This corruption of our nature is not wrought in us by reason and persuasions, for then it might be satisfied with reasons, but it is in us by way of a natural inclination, as iron is carried to the loadstone; and till our natures be altered, no reason will long prevail, but our sinful disposition, as a stream stopped for a little while, will break out with greater violence. 3. Being natural, it needs no help, as the earth needs no tillage to bring forth weeds. When our corrupt nature is carried contrary to that which is good, it is carried of itself, as when Satan lies or murders, it comes from his own cursed nature; and though Satan joineth with our corrupt nature, yet the proneness to sin, and the consent unto it, is of ourselves.

Quest. § III. But how shall we know that Satan joins with our nature, in those actions unto which nature itself is prone?

Ans. Then Satan adds his help, when our nature is carried more eagerly than ordinary to sin; as when a stream runs violently, we may know that there is not only the tide, but the wind that carrieth it.

So in sudden and violent rebellions, it is Satan that pusheth on nature left to itself of God. A stone falls downwards by its own weight, but if it falls very swiftly, we know it is thrown down by an outward mover. Though there were no devil, yet our corrupt nature would act Satan's part against itself; it would have a supply of wickedness, as a serpent doth poison, from itself, it hath a spring to feed it. *Nemo se palpet de suo, Satan est, &c.* (Augustine).

But that man, whilst he lives here, is not altogether excluded from hope of happiness, and hath a nature not so large and capable of sin as Satan's; whereupon he is not so obstinate in hating God and working mischief as he, &c. Otherwise there is, for kind, the same cursed disposition, and malice of nature against true goodness in man, which is in the devils and damned spirits themselves.

It is no mitigation of sin, to plead it is natural; for natural diseases, as leprosies, that are derived from parents, are most dangerous, and least curable. Neither is this any excuse, for because as it is natural, so it is voluntary, not only in Adam, in whose loins we were, and therefore sinned, but likewise in regard of ourselves, who are so far from stopping the course of sin either in ourselves or others, that we feed and strengthen it, or at least give more way to it, and provide less against it than we should, until we come under the government of grace; and by that means we justify Adam's sin, and that corrupt estate that followeth upon it, and shew, that if we had been in Adam's condition ourselves, we would have made that ill choice which he made. And though this corruption of our nature be necessary to us, yet it is no violent necessity from an outward cause, but a necessity that we willingly pull upon ourselves, and therefore ought the more to humble us; for the more necessarily we sin, the more voluntarily, and the more voluntarily, the more necessarily, the will putting itself voluntarily into these fetters of sin.* Necessity is no plea, when the will is the immediate cause of any action. *Quicquid sibi imperavit animus, obtinuit* (Seneca). Men's hearts tell them they might rule their desires if they would; for tell a man of any dish which he liketh, that there is poison in it, and he will not meddle with it: so tell him that death is in that sin which he is about to commit, and he will abstain, if

* 'Fetters of sin.' Margin-note in C—Suspirabam ligatus, non ferro aliquo, sed mea ferrea voluntate, vellem meum tenebat inimicus, et inde mihi catenam fecerit. Augustine, Conf. G

he believe it to be so ; if he believe it not, it is his voluntary unbelief and atheism.

If the will would use that sovereignty it should, and could, at the first, we should be altogether freed from this necessity. Men are not damned because they cannot do better, but because they will do no better ; if there were no will, there would be no hell, *Cesset voluntas propria et non erit infernus.* For men willingly submit to the rule and law of sin, they plead for it, and like it so well, as they hate nothing so much as that which any way withstandeth those lawless laws.

Those that think it their happiness to do what they will, that they might be free, cross their own desires, for this is the way to make them most perfect slaves. When our will is the next immediate cause of sin, and our consciences bear witness to us that it is so, then conscience is ready to take God's part in accusing ourselves ; our consciences tell us to our faces that we might do more than we do to hinder sin, and that when we sin, it is not through weakness, but out of the wickedness of our nature.

Our consciences tell us that we sin not only willingly, but often with delight, so far forth as we are not subdued by grace, or awed by something above us, and that we esteem any restraint to be our misery. And where by grace the will is strengthened, so that it yields not a full consent, yet a gracious soul is humbled even for the sudden risings of corruption that prevent deliberation. As here David, though he withstood the risings of his heart, yet he was troubled, that he had so vile a heart that would rise up against God, and therefore takes it down. Who is there that hath not cause to be humbled, not only for his corruption, but that he doth not resist with that strength, nor labour to prevent it with that diligence which his heart tells him he might?

We cannot have too deep apprehensions of this breeding sin, the mother and nurse of all abominations ; for the more we consider the height, the depth, the breadth, and length of it, the more shall we be humbled in ourselves, and magnify the height, the depth, the breadth, and the length of God's mercy in Christ, Eph. iii. 18. The favourers of nature are always the enemies of grace. This, which some think and speak so weakly and faintly of, is a worse enemy to us than the devil himself ; a more near, a more restless, a more traitorous enemy, for by intelligence with it the devil doth us all the hurt he doth, and by it maintains forts in us against goodness. This is that which, either by discouragement or contrariety, hinders us from good ; or else, by deadness, tediousness, distractions, or corrupt aims, hinders us in doing good. This putteth us on to evil, and abuseth what is good in us, or from us, to cover or colour sin, and furnishes us with reasons either to maintain what is evil, or shifts to translate it upon false causes, or fences to arm us against whatsoever shall oppose us in our wicked ways ; though it neither can nor will be good, yet it would be thought to be so by others, and enforces a conceit upon itself that it is good. It imprisons and keeps down all light that may discover it, both within itself and without itself, if it lie in its power ; it flatters itself, and would have all the world flatter it too, which, if it doth not, it frets, especially if it be once discovered and crossed. Hence comes all the plotting against goodness, that sin may reign without control. Is it not a lamentable case that man, who, out of the very principles of nature, cannot but desire happiness and abhor misery, yet should be in love with eternal misery in the causes of it, and abhor happiness in the ways that lead unto it? This sheweth us what a wonderful deordination and disorder is brought upon man's nature; for every other creature is naturally carried to that which is helpful unto it, and shunneth that which is any way hurtful and offensive. Only man is in love with his own bane, and fights for those lusts that fight against his soul.

§ IV. Our duty is, 1. To labour to see this sinful disposition of ours, not only as it is discovered in the Scriptures, but as it discovers itself in our own hearts. This must be done by the light and teaching of God's Spirit, who knows us and all the turnings and windings and byways of our souls, better than we know ourselves. We must see it as the most odious and loathsome thing in the world, making our natures contrary to God's pure nature, and of all other duties making us most indisposed to spiritual duties, wherein we should have nearest communion with God, because it seizeth on the very spirits of our minds.

2. We should look upon it as worse than any of those filthy streams that come from it; nay, than all the impure issues of our lives together. There is more fire in the furnace than in the sparkles; there is more poison in the root than in all the branches. For if the stream were stopped, and the branches cut off, and the sparkles quenched, yet there would be a perpetual supply. As in good things, the cause is better than the effect, so in ill things the cause is worse. Every fruit should make this poisonful root more hateful to us, and the root should make us hate the fruit more, as coming from so bad a root, as being worse in the cause than in itself; the affection is worse than the action, which may be forced or counterfeited. We cry out upon particular sins, but are not humbled as we should be for our impure dispositions, without the sight of which there can be (1.) no sound repentance arising from the deep and thorough consideration of sin; (2.) no desire to be new moulded, without which we can never enter into so holy a place as heaven; (3.) no self-denial, till we see the best things in us are enmity against God; (4.) no high prizing of Christ, without whom our natures, our persons, and our actions are abominable in God's sight; (5.) nor any solid peace settled in the soul, which peace ariseth not from the ignorance of our corruption, or compounding with it, but from sight and hatred of it, and strength against it.

3. Consider the spiritualness and large extent of the law of God, together with the curse annexed, which forbids not only particular sins, but all the kinds, degrees, occasions, and furtherances of sin in the whole breadth and depth of it, and our very nature itself, so far as it is corrupted; for want of which we see many 'alive without the law,' Rom. vii. 9, jovial and merry from ignorance of their misery, who, if they did but once see their natures and lives in that glass, it would take away that liveliness and courage from them, and make them vile in their own eyes. Men usually look themselves in the laws of the state wherein they live, and think themselves good enough, if they are free from the danger of penal statutes; this glass discovers only foul spots, gross scandals, and breakings out; or else they judge of themselves by parts of nature, or common grace, or by outward conformity to religion, or else by that light they have to guide themselves in the affairs of this life, by their fair and civil carriage, &c.; and thereupon live and die without any sense of the power of godliness, which begins in the right knowledge of ourselves, and ends in the right knowledge of God. The spiritualness and purity of the law should teach us to consider the purity and holiness of God; the bringing of our souls into whose presence will make us to abhor ourselves, with Job, 'in dust

and ashes,' Job xlii. 6. Contraries are best seen by setting one near the other; whilst we look only on ourselves, and upon others amongst whom we live, we think ourselves to be somebody. It is an evidence of some sincerity wrought in the soul, not to shun that light which may let us see the foul corners of our hearts and lives.

4. The consideration of this likewise should enforce us to carry a double guard over our souls. David was very watchful, yet we see here he was surprised unawares by the sudden rebellion of his heart. We should observe our hearts as governors do rebels and mutinous persons. Observation awes the heart. We see to what an excess sin groweth in those that deny themselves nothing, nor will be denied in anything; who, if they may do what they will, will do what they may; who turn liberty into licence, and make all their abilities and advantages to do good, contributary to the commands of overruling and unruly lusts.

Were it not that God partly by his power suppresseth, and partly by his grace subdueth the disorders of man's nature for the good of society, and the gathering of a church upon earth, corruption would swell to that excess, that it would overturn and confound all things together with itself. Although there be a common corruption that cleaves to the nature of all men in general, as men (as distrust in God, self-love, a carnal and worldly disposition, &c.), yet God so ordereth it, that in some there is an ebb and decrease, in others, God justly leaving them to themselves, a flow and increase of sinfulness, even beyond the bounds of ordinary corruption, whereby they become worse than themselves, either like beasts in sensuality, or like devils in spiritual wickedness. Though all be blind in spiritual things, yet some are more blinded; though all be hard-hearted, yet some are more hardened; though all be corrupt in evil courses, yet some are more corrupted; and sink deeper into rebellion than others.

Sometimes God suffers this corruption to break out in civil men, yea even in his own children, that they may know themselves the better, and because sometimes corruption is weakened not only by smothering, but by having a vent, whereupon grace stirs up in the soul a fresh hatred and revenge against it; and lets us see a necessity of having whole Christ, not only to pardon sin, but to purge and cleanse our sinful natures.

Caution. But yet that which is ill in itself, must not be done for the good that comes by it by accident; this must be a comfort after our surprisals, not an encouragement before.

5. And because the divine nature, wrought in us by divine truth, together with the Spirit of God, is the only counter-poison against all sin, and whatsoever is contrary to God in us, therefore we should labour that the truth of God may be grafted in our hearts, that so all the powers of our souls may relish of it, that there may be a sweet agreement betwixt the soul and all things that are spiritual, that truth being engrafted in our hearts, we may be engrafted into Christ, and grow up in him, and put him on more and more, and be changed into his likeness. Nothing in heaven or earth will work out corruption, and change our dispositions, but the Spirit of Christ, clothing divine truths with a divine power to this purpose.

6. When corruption rises, pray it down, as St Paul did, 2 Cor. xii. 8, and to strengthen thy prayer, claim the promise of the new covenant, that God would 'circumcise our hearts,' and 'wash us with clean water,' that he would 'write his law in our hearts, and give us his Holy Spirit when we beg it,' Ezek. xxxvi. 25–27; and look upon Christ as a public 'fountain open for Judah and Jerusalem to wash in,' Zech. xiii. 1. Herein consists our com-

fort, 1, that Christ hath all fulness for us, and that our nature is perfect in him; 2, That Christ in our nature hath satisfied divine justice, not only for the sin of our lives, but for the sin of our nature. And, 3, That he will never give over until by his Spirit he hath made our nature holy and pure as his own, till he hath taken away not only the reign, but the very life and being of sin out of our hearts. 4, That to this end he leaves his Spirit and truth in the church to the end of the world, that the seed of the Spirit may subdue the seed of the serpent in us, and that the Spirit may be a never-failing spring of all holy thoughts, desires, and endeavours in us, and dry up the contrary issue and spring of corrupt nature.

And Christians must remember, when they are much annoyed with their corruptions, that it is not their particular case alone, but the condition of all God's people, lest they be discouraged by looking on the ugly deformed visage of old Adam, which affrighteth some so far that it makes them think, no man's nature is so vile as theirs; which were well if it tended to humiliation only; but Satan often abuseth it towards discouragement and desperation. Many out of a misconceit think that corruption is greatest when they feel it most, whereas indeed, the less we see it and lament it, the more it is. Sighs and groans of the soul are like the pores of the body, out of which in diseased persons sick humours break forth and so become less. The more we see and grieve for pride, which is an immediate issue of our corrupted nature, the less it is, because we see it by a contrary grace; the more sight the more hatred, the more hatred of sin, the more love of grace, and the more love the more life, which the more lively it is, the more it is sensible of the contrary. Upon every discovery and conflict corruption loses some ground, and grace gains upon it.

CHAPTER XIII.—*Of imagination, sin of it, and remedies for it.*

§ I. And amongst all the faculties of the soul, most of the disquiet and unnecessary trouble of our lives arises from the vanity and ill government of that power of the soul which we call *imagination* and *opinion*, bordering between the senses and our understanding; which is nothing else but a shallow apprehension of good or evil taken from the senses. Now because outward good or evil things agree or disagree to the senses, and the life of sense is in us before the use of reason, and the delights of sense are present, and pleasing and suitable to our natures, thereupon the imagination setteth a great price upon sensible good things; and the judgment itself since the fall, until it hath a higher light and strength, yieldeth to our imagination. Hence it comes to pass that the best things, if they be attended with sensible inconveniences, as want, disgrace in the world, and such like, are misjudged for evil things; and the very worst things, if they be attended with respect in the world, and sensible contentments, are imagined to be the greatest good; which appears not so much in men's words (because they are ashamed to discover their hidden folly and atheism), but the lives of people speak as much, in that particular choice which they make. Many there are who think it not only a vain but a dangerous thing to serve God, and a base thing to be awed with religious respect; they count the ways that God's people take no better than madness, and that course which God takes in bringing men to heaven by a plain publishing of heavenly truths, to be nothing but foolishness; and those people that regard it, are esteemed, as the Pharisees esteemed them that heard Christ, ignorant, base, and despicable persons. Hence arise all those false prejudices against the ways of holiness, as they in the Acts were shy in entertaining the truth, because it was 'a way everywhere spoken against,' Acts xxviii. 22. The doctrine of the cross hath the cross always following it, which imagination counteth the most odious and bitter thing in the world.

This imagination of ours is become the seat of vanity, and thereupon of vexation to us, because it apprehends a greater happiness in outward good things than there is, and a greater misery in outward evil things than indeed there is; and when experience shews us that there is not that good in those things which we imagine to be, but, contrarily, we find much evil in them which we never expected, hereupon the soul cannot but be troubled. The life of many men, and those not the meanest, is almost nothing else but a fancy; that which chiefly sets their wits awork and takes up most of their time is how to please their own imagination, which setteth up an excellency, within itself, in comparison of which it despiseth all true excellency and those things that are of most necessary consequence indeed. Hence springs ambition and the vein of being great in the world; hence comes an unmeasurable desire of abounding in those things which the world esteems highly of. There is in us naturally a competition and desire of being equal or above others in that which is generally thought to make us happy and esteemed amongst men. If we be not the only men, yet we will be somebody in the world; something we will have to be highly esteemed for, wherein if we be crossed, we count it the greatest misery that can befall us.

And, which is worse, a corrupt desire of being great in the opinion of others creeps into the profession of religion, if we live in those places wherein it brings credit or gain. Men will sacrifice their very lives for vainglory. It is an evidence a man lives more to opinion and reputation of others than to conscience, when his grief is more for being disappointed of that approbation which he expects from men, than for his miscarriage towards God. It mars all in religion when we go about heavenly things with earthly affections, and seek not Christ in Christ, but the world. What is popery but an artificial frame of man's brain to please men's imaginations by outward state and pomp of ceremonies, like that golden image of Nebuchadnezzar, wherein he pleased himself so, that, to have uniformity in worshipping the same, he compelled all, under pain of death, to fall down before it, Dan. iii. 6. This makes superstitious persons always cruel, because superstitious devices are the brats of our own imagination, which we strive for more than for the purity of God's worship. Hence it is, likewise, that superstitious persons are restless (as the woman of Samaria) in their own spirits, as having no bottom, but fancy instead of faith.

§ II. Now, the reason why imagination works so upon the soul is, because it stirs up the affections answerable to the good or ill which it apprehends, and our affections stir the humours of the body, so that oftentimes both our souls and bodies are troubled hereby.

Things work upon the soul in this order: 1. Some object is presented. 2. Then it is apprehended by imagination as good and pleasing, or as evil and hurtful. 3. If good, the desire is carried to it with delight; if evil, it is rejected with distaste, and so our affections are stirred up suitably to our apprehension of the object. 4. Affections stir up the spirits. 5. The spirits raise the humours, and so the whole man becomes moved, and oftentimes distempered; this falleth out by reason of the sympathy between the soul and body, whereby what offendeth one redoundeth to the hurt of the other.

And we see conceived* troubles have the same effect upon us as true. Jacob was as much troubled with the imagination of his son's death as if he had been dead indeed. Imagination, though it be an empty, windy thing, yet it hath real effects. Superstitious persons are as much troubled for neglecting any voluntary service of man's invention, as if they had offended against the direct commandment of God. Thus superstition breeds false fears, and false fear brings true vexation. It transforms God to an idol, imagining him to be pleased with whatsoever pleases ourselves, whenas we take it ill that those who are under us should take direction from themselves and not from us in that which may content us. Superstition is very busy, but all in vain. 'In vain they worship me,' Mat. xv. 9, saith God. And how can it choose but vex and disquiet men, when they shall take a great deal of pains in vain, and, which is worse, to displease most in that wherein they think to please most. God blasteth all devised service with one demand, 'Who required these things at your hands?' Isa. i. 12. It were better for us to ask ourselves this question beforehand, Who required this? Why do we trouble ourselves about that which we shall have no thank for? We should not bring God down to our own imaginations, but raise our imaginations up to God.

Now, imagination hurteth us, 1. By false representations. 2. By preventing reason, and so usurping a censure of things before our judgments try them, whereas the office of imagination is to minister matter to our understanding to work upon, and not to lead it, much less mislead it, in anything. 3. By forging matter out of itself without ground; the imaginary grievances of our lives are more than the real. 4. As it is an ill instrument of the understanding to devise vanity and mischief.

§ III. The way to cure this malady in us is, 1. *To labour to bring these risings of our souls into the obedience of God's truth and Spirit*, 2 Cor. x. 5. For imagination, of itself, if ungoverned, is a wild and a ranging thing; it wrongs not only the frame of God's work in us, setting the baser part of a man above the higher, but it wrongs likewise the work of God in the creatures and everything else, for it shapes things as itself pleaseth; it maketh evil good if it pleaseth the senses, and good evil if it be dangerous and distasteful to the outward man, which cannot but breed an unquiet and an unsettled soul. As if it were a god, it can tell good and evil at its pleasure; it sets up and pulls down the price of what it listeth. By reason of the distemper of imagination, the life of many is little else but a dream. Many good men are in a long dream of misery, and many bad men in as long a dream of happiness, till the time of awaking come, and all because they are too much led by appearances. And as in a dream men are deluded with false joys and false fears, so here; which cannot but breed an unquiet and an unsettled soul. Therefore, it is necessary that God, by his word and Spirit, should erect a government in our hearts to captivate and order this licentious faculty.

2. Likewise, it is good *to present real things to the soul*, as the true riches and true misery of a Christian, the true honour and dishonour, true beauty and deformity, the true nobleness and debasement, of the soul. Whatever is in the world are but shadows of things in comparison of those true realities which religion affords. And why should we vex ourselves about a vain shadow? Ps. xxxix. 6.

* That is, 'apprehended.'—Ed.

The Holy Ghost, to prevent further mischief by these outward things, gives a dangerous report of them, calling them vanity, unrighteous mammon, Luke xvi. 9, uncertain riches, thorns, yea, nothing, Prov. xxiii. 5; because, though they be not so in themselves, yet, our imagination overvaluing them, they prove so to us upon trial. Now, knowledge that is bought by trial is often dear bought; and therefore God would have us prevent this by a right conceit of things beforehand, lest trusting to vanity we vanish ourselves, and trusting to nothing we become nothing ourselves, and, which is worse, worse than nothing.

3. Oppose *serious consideration against vain imagination;* and because our imagination is prone to raise false objects, and thereby false conceits and discourses in us, our best way herein is to propound true objects of the mind to work upon, as, 1. To consider the greatness and goodness of Almighty God and his love to us in Christ. 2. The joys of heaven and the torments of hell. 3. The last and strict day of account. 4. The vanity of all earthly things. 5. The uncertainty of our lives, &c. From the meditation of these truths the soul will be prepared to have right conceits of things, and discourse upon true grounds of them, and think with itself that if these things be so indeed, then I must frame my life suitable to these principles. Hence arise true affections in the soul, true fear of God, true love and desire after the best things, &c. The way to expel wind out of our bodies is to take some wholesome nourishment, and the way to expel windy fancies from the soul is to feed upon serious truths.

4. Moreover, to the well ordering of this unruly faculty, it is necessary that *our nature itself should be changed;* for as men are, so they imagine; as the 'treasure of the heart is,' Mat. xii. 35, such is that which comes from it. *Mala mens, malus animus*, an evil heart cannot think well. Before the heart be changed, our judgment is depraved in regard of our last end; we seek our happiness where it is not to be found. 'Wickedness comes from the wicked,' 1 Sam. xxiv. 13, as the proverb is. If we had as large and as quick apprehensions as Satan himself, yet if the relish of our will and affections be not changed, they will set the imaginations awork, to devise satisfaction to themselves. For there is a mutual working and reflux betwixt the will and the imagination; the imagination stirs up the will, and as the will is affected, so imagination worketh.

When the law of God by the Spirit is so written in our hearts, that the law and our hearts become agreeable one to the other, then the soul is inclined and made pliable to every good thought. When the heart is once taught of God to love, it is the nature of this sweet affection, as the apostle saith, to 'think no evil,' 1 Cor. xiii. 5, either of God or man; and not only so, but it carries the bent of the whole soul with it to good, so that we love God not only with all our heart, but with all our mind, Mat. xxii. 37, that is, both with our understanding and imagination. Love is an affection full of inventions, and sets the wit awork to devise good things; therefore our chief care should be, that our hearts may be circumcised and purified, so as they may be filled with the love of God, and then we shall find this duty not only easy, but delightful unto us. The prophet healed the waters by casting salt into the spring, 2 Kings ii. 20, so the seasoning of the spring of our actions seasons all. And indeed, what can be expected from man, whilst he is vanity, but vain imaginations? What can we look for from a viper but poison? A man naturally is either weaving spiders' webs, or hatching cockatrices' eggs, Isa. lix. 5, that is, his heart is exercised either in vanity or mischief; for not only the frame of the heart, but what the heart frameth, is evil continually, Gen. vi. 5. A wicked man that is besotted with false conceits, will admit of no good thoughts to enter.

5. Even when we are good, and devise good things, yet there is still some sickness of fancy remaining in the best of us, whereby we work trouble to ourselves; and therefore it is necessary we should labour *to restrain and limit our fancy*, and stop these waters at the beginning, Prov. vii. 14, giving no not the least way thereunto. If it begins to grow wanton, tame the wildness of it by fastening it to the cross of Christ (whom we have pierced with our sins, Zech. xii. 10; and amongst other, with these sins of our spirits), who hath redeemed us from our vain thoughts and conversations, 1 Peter i. 18; set before it the consideration of the wrath of God, of death, and judgment, and the woful estate of the damned, &c., and take it not off till thy heart be taken off from straying from God. When it begins once to run out to impertinences, confine it to some certain thing, and then upon examination we shall find it bring home some honey with it; otherwise it will bring us nothing but a sting from the bitter remembrance of our former misspent thoughts and time, which we should redeem and fill up with things that most belong to our peace, Luke xix. 47. Idleness is the hour of temptation, wherein Satan joins with our imagination, and sets it about his own work, to grind his grease;* for the soul as a mill, either grinds that which is put into it, or else works upon itself. Imagination is the first wheel of the soul, and if that move amiss, it stirs all the inferior wheels amiss with it. It stirs itself, and other powers of the soul are stirred by its motion; and therefore the well ordering of this is of the greater consequence. For as the imagination conceiveth, so usually the judgment concludeth, the will chooseth, the affections are carried, and the members execute.

If it break loose, as it will soon run riot, yet give no consent of the will to it. Though it hath defiled the memory, yet let it not defile the will. Though it be the first-born of the soul, yet let it not, as Reuben, ascend unto the father's bed—that is, our will,—and defile that which should be kept pure for the Spirit of Christ.† Resolve to act nothing upon it, but cross it before it moves to the execution and practice of anything. As in sickness, many times we imagine, by reason of the corruption of our taste, physic to be ill for us, and those meats which nourish the disease to be good, yet care of health makes us cross our own conceits, and take that which fancy abhors; so if we would preserve sound spirits, we must conclude against groundless imagination, and resolve that whatsoever it suggests cannot be so, because it crosses the grounds both of religion and reason. And when we find imagination to deceive us in sensible things, as melancholy persons are subject to mistake, we may well gather that it will much more deceive us in our spiritual condition; and indeed, such is the incoherence, impertinency, and unreasonableness of imagination, that men are oft ashamed and angry with themselves afterwards, for giving the least way to such thoughts; and it is good to chastise the soul for the same, that it may be more wary for time to come. Whilst men are led

* Qu. 'grist?'—Ed.

† Bernard. The following is the reference of Sibbes *supra*:—'Plane exclamandum nobis est cum Sancto Jacobo atque dicendum Reuben primogenitus, &c. Rubea enim et carnalis atque sanguinea hujusmodi concupiscentia est, quæ tunc cubile nostrum ascendit, cum non solum memoriam tangit cogitatione, sed et ipsum voluntatis stratum ingreditur, et polluit prava dilectione. Bene autem primogenitus noster dicitur appetitus ille carnalis,' &c. &c.—Sermo de triplici genere cogitationum nostrarum. Edn. Antwerp, 1616, p. 411. G.

with imagination, they work not according to right rules prescribed to men, but as other baser creatures, in whom phantasy is the chief ruling power; and therefore, those whose will is guided by their fancies, live more like beasts than men.

We allow a horse to prance and skip in a pasture, which if he doth when he is once backed by the rider, we count him an unruly and unbroken jade; so howsoever in other creatures we allow liberty of fancy, yet we allow it not in man to frisk and rove at its pleasure, because in him it is to be bridled with reason.

6. Especially take heed of those *cursed imaginations out of which, as of mother roots, others spring forth;* as questioning God's providence, and care of his children, his justice, his disregarding of what is done here below, &c., thoughts of putting off our amendment for time to come, and so blessing ourselves in any evil way, thoughts against the necessity of exact and circumspect walking with God, &c., Eph. v. 15. When these and such like principles of Satan's and the flesh's divinity take place in our hearts, they block up the soul against the entrance of soul-saving truths, and taint our whole conversation, which is either good or evil, as the principles are by which we are guided, and as our imagination is, which lets in all to the soul.

The Jews in Jeremiah's time were forestalled with vain imaginations against sound repentance, and therefore his counsel is, 'Wash thine heart, O Jerusalem! how long shall vain thoughts lodge within thee?' Jer. iv. 14.

7. Fancy will the better be kept within its due bounds, *if we consider the principal use thereof.* Sense and imagination is properly to judge what is comfortable or uncomfortable, what is pleasing or displeasing to the outward man, not what is morally or spiritually good or ill; and thus far by the laws of nature and civility we are bound to give fancy contentment both in ourselves and others, as not to speak or do anything uncomely, which may occasion a loathing or distaste in our converse with men; and it is a matter of conscience to make our lives as comfortable as may be. As we are bound to love, so we are bound to use all helps that may make us lovely, and endear us into the good affections of others. As we are bound to give no offence to the conscience of another, so to no power or faculty either of the outward or inward man of another. Some are taken off in their affection by a fancy, whereof they can give but little reason; and some are more careless in giving offence in this kind, than stands with that Christian circumspection and mutual respect which we owe one to another. The apostle's rule is of large extent, 'Whatsoever things are not only true, and honest, and just, but whatsoever things are lovely and of good report, &c., think of these things,' Phil. iv. 8. Yet our main care should be to manifest ourselves rather to men's *consciences* than to their *imaginations.*

8. It should be our wisdom, likewise, *to place ourselves in the best conveniency of all outward helps, which may have a kind working upon our fancy; and to take heed to the contrary, as time, place, and objects,* &c. There be good hours and good messengers of God's sending, golden opportunities wherein God uses to give a meeting to his children, and breathes good thoughts into them. Even the wisest and holiest men, as David and Solomon, &c., had no further safety than they were careful of well-using all good advantages, and sequestering themselves from such objects as had a working power upon them. By suffering their souls to be led by their fancies, and their hearts to run after their eyes, they betrayed and robbed themselves of much grace and comfort, thereupon Solomon cries out with

grief and shame from his own experience, 'Vanity of vanities,' &c. Eccles. i. 2. Fancy will take fire before we be aware. Little things are seeds of great matters. Job knew this, and therefore made a 'covenant with his eyes,' Job xxxi. 1; but a 'fool's eyes are in the corners of the earth,' saith Solomon, Prov. xvii. 24.

Sometimes the ministering of some excellent thought—*præclara cogitatio*—from what we hear or see, proves a great advantage of spiritual good to the soul. Whilst St Augustine out of curiosity delighted to hear the eloquence of St Ambrose, he was taken with the matter itself, sweetly sliding together with the words into his heart.* Of later times, whilst Galeaceus Caracciolus, an Italian marquis, and nephew to Pope Paul V., was hearing Peter Martyr reading upon 1 Corinthians, and shewing the deceivableness of man's judgment in spiritual things, and the efficacy of divine truth in those that belong unto God, and further using a similitude to this purpose: 'If a man be walking afar off, and see people dancing together, and hear no noise of the music, he judges them fools and out of their wits; but when he comes nearer and hears the music, and sees that every motion is exactly done by art, now he changes his mind, and is so taken up with the sweet agreement of the gesture and the music, that he is not only delighted therewith, but desirous to join himself in the number. So it falls out, saith he, with men: whilst they look upon the outward carriage and conversation of God's people, and see it differing from others, they think them fools; but when they look more narrowly into their courses, and see a gracious harmony betwixt their lives and the word of God, then they begin to be in love with the "beauty of holiness," and join in conformity of holy obedience with those they scorned before.' This similitude wrought so with this nobleman, that he began, from that time forward, to set his mind to the study of heavenly things.†

One seasonable truth falling upon a prepared heart, hath oftentimes a sweet and strong operation. Luther confesseth that having heard a grave divine, Staupicius, say 'that that is kind repentance which begins from the love of God,' ever after that time the practice of repentance was sweeter to him. This speech of his likewise took well with Luther, that in doubts of predestination we should begin from the wounds of Christ, *doctrina prædestinationis incipit a vulneribus Christi*,—that is, from the sense of God's love to us in Christ, we should arise to the grace given us in election before the world was, 2 Tim. i. 9.

The putting of lively colours upon common truths hath oft a strong working both upon the fancy and our will and affections. The spirit is refreshed with fresh things, or old truths refreshed. This made the preacher seek to find out pleasing and acceptable words, Eccl. xii. 10: and our Saviour Christ's manner of teaching was by a lively representation to men's fancies, to teach them heavenly truths in an earthly, sensible man-

* See the memorable 'confession' in 'The Confessions' of Augustine, Book V., xiii. 23; xiv. 24. A few words may interest:—'Though I took no pains to learn *what* he spake, but only to hear *how* he spake. . . . . . yet together with the words which I would choose, came also into my mind the things which I would refuse; for I could not separate them. And while I opened my heart to admit "how eloquently he spake," there also entered, "how truly he spake;" but this by degrees.'

† The authority given in the margin is 'Beza in his life.' This is a translation from the Italian, and was published in 1596. No less than two translations into English are extant: one, 4to, 1608, and another, 4to, 1612. Sibbes's quotations are from c. iii. The whole passage is given from the quaint translation of 1608, in Note *d*.

G

ner; and indeed, what do we see or hear but will yield matter to a holy heart to raise itself higher?

We should make our fancy serviceable to us in spiritual things, and take advantage by any pleasure, or profit, or honour which it presents our thoughts withal, to think thus with ourselves, 'what is this to the true honour, and to those enduring pleasures,' &c.? And seeing God hath condescended to represent heavenly things to us under earthly terms, we should follow God's dealing herein. God represents heaven to us under the term of a banquet, and of a kingdom, &c., Luke x. 32; our union with Christ under the term of a marriage, yea, Christ himself, under the name of whatsoever is lovely or comfortable in heaven or earth. So the Lord sets out hell to us by whatsoever is terrible or tormenting. Here is a large field for our imagination to walk in, not only without hurt, but with a great deal of spiritual gain. If the wrath of a king be as the roaring of a lion, Prov. xix. 12, what is the wrath of the King of kings? If fire be so terrible, what is hell fire? If a dark dungeon be so loathsome, what is that eternal dungeon of darkness? If a feast be so pleasing, what is the 'continual feast of a good conscience?' Prov. xv. 15. If the meeting of friends be so comfortable, what will our meeting together in heaven be? The Scripture, by such like terms, would help our faith and fancy both at once. A sanctified fancy will make every creature a ladder to heaven. And because childhood and youth are ages of fancy, therefore it is a good way to instil into the hearts of children betimes, the loving of good and the shunning of evil, by such like representations as agree with their fancies, as to hate hell under the representation of fire and darkness, &c. Whilst the soul is joined with the body, it hath not only a necessary but a holy use of imagination, and of sensible things whereupon our imagination worketh. What is the use of the sacraments but to help our souls by our senses, and our faith by imagination? As the soul receives much hurt from imagination, so it may have much good thereby.

But yet it ought not to invent or devise what is good and true in religion. Here fancy must yield to faith, and faith to divine revelation. The things we believe are such as neither 'eye hath seen, nor ear heard, neither came into the heart of man,' 1 Cor. ii. 9, by imagination stirred up from anything which we have seen or heard. They are above, not only imagination, but reason itself, in men and angels. But after God hath revealed spiritual truths, and faith hath apprehended them, then imagination hath use while the soul is joined with the body, to colour divine truths, and make lightsome what faith believes; for instance, it doth not devise either heaven or hell; but when God hath revealed them to us, our fancy hath a fitness of enlarging our conceits of them, even by resemblance from things in nature, and that without danger; because the joys of heaven and the torments of hell are so great that all the representations which nature affords us fall short of them.

Imagination hath likewise some use in religion, by putting cases to the soul, as when we are tempted to any unruly action we should think with ourselves, what would I do if some holy, grave person whom I much reverence should behold me? Whereupon the soul may easily ascend higher, God sees me, and my own conscience is ready to witness against me, &c.

It helps us also in taking benefit by the example of other men. Good things are best learned by others expressing of them to our view. The very sight often, nay, the very thought of a good man doth good, as representing to our souls some good thing which we affect—*est aliquid quod ex magno viro vel tacente proficias*—which makes histories and the lively characters and expressions of virtues and vices useful to us. The sight, yea, the very reading of the suffering of the martyrs hath wrought such a hatred of that persecuting church as hath done marvellous good. The sight of justice executed upon malefactors works a greater hatred of sin in men than naked precepts can do. So outward pomp and state in the world doth further that awful respect due to authority, &c.

9. Lastly, it would much avail for the well ordering of our thoughts *to set our souls in order every morning, and to strengthen and perfume our spirits with some gracious meditations*,* especially of the chief end and scope wherefore we live here, and how every thing we do or befalls us may be reduced and ordered to further the main. The end of a Christian is glorious, and the oft thoughts of it will raise and enlarge the soul, and set it on work to study how to make all things serviceable thereunto. It is a thing to be lamented that a Christian born for heaven, having the 'prize of his high calling,' Phil. iii. 14, set before him, and matters of that weight and excellency to exercise his heart upon, should be taken up with trifles, and fill both his head and heart with vanity and nothing, as all earthly things will prove ere long; and yet if many men's thoughts and discourses were distilled, they are so frothy that they would hardly yield one drop of true comfort.

§ IV. *Obj.* Oh, but, say some, thoughts and imaginations are free, and we shall not be accountable for them.

Ans. This is a false plea, for God hath a sovereignty over the whole soul, and his law binds the whole inward and outward man. As we desire our whole man should be saved by Christ, so we must yield up the whole man to be governed by him; and it is the effect of the dispensation of the gospel, accompanied with the Spirit, to captivate whatsoever is in man unto Christ, and to bring down all 'high towering imaginations,' 2 Cor. x. 5, that exalt themselves against God's Spirit. There is a divinity in the word of God, powerfully unfolded, which will convince our souls of the sinfulness of natural imaginations, as we see in the idiot, (*e*) 1 Cor. xiv. 24, 25, who, seeing himself laid open before himself, cried out, that 'God was in the speaker,' 1 Cor. xiv. 25.

There ought to be in man a conformity to the truth and goodness of things, or else, 1, we shall wrong our own souls with false apprehensions; and 2, the creature, by putting a fashion upon it otherwise than God hath made; and 3, we shall wrong God himself, the author of goodness, who cannot have his true glory but from a right apprehension of things as they are. What a wrong is it to men when we shall take up false prejudices against them without ground! and so suffer our conceits to be envenomed against them by unjust suspicions, and by this means deprive ourselves of all that good which we might receive by them; for our nature is apt to judge and accept of things as the persons are, and not of persons according to the things themselves. This faculty exercises a tyranny in the soul, setting up and pulling down whom it will. Job judged his friends altogether vain, Job xxvii. 12, because they went upon a vain imagination and discourse, judging him to be an hypocrite, which could not but add much to his affliction. When men take a toy† in their head against a person or place, they are ready to reason as he did, 'Can any good come out of Nazareth?' John vi. 46.

* 'Meditations.' Sibbes himself practised this excellent counsel, as witness his golden little volume of 'Meditations,' first published in 1638, 18mo.

† That is, 'fancy.'—G.

It is an indignity for men to be led with surmises and probabilities, and so to pass a rash judgment upon persons and things. Oftentimes falsehood hath a fairer gloss of probability than truth; and vices go masked under the appearance of virtue, whereupon seeming likeness—*similitudo mater errorum*—breeds a mistake of one thing for another; and Satan oftentimes casts a mist before our imagination, that so we might have a misshapen conceit of things. By a spirit of illusion he makes worldly things appear bigger to us, and spiritual things lesser than indeed they are; and so by sophisticating of things our affections come to be misled. Imagination is the womb, and Satan the father of all monstrous conceptions and disordered lusts, which are well called deceitful lusts, Eph. iv. 22, and lusts of ignorance, 1 Tim. vi. 9, foolish and noisome lusts, because they both spring from error and folly, and lead unto it.

We see, even in religion itself, how the world, together with the help of 'the god of the world,' 2 Cor. iv. 4, is led away, if not to worship images, yet to worship the image of their own fancy. And where the truth is most professed, yet people are prone to fancy to themselves such a breadth of religion as will altogether leave them comfortless when things shall appear in their true colours. They will conceit to embrace truth without hatred of the world, and Christ without his cross, and a godly life without persecutions. They would pull a rose without pricks. Which, though it may stand with their own base ends for a while, yet will not hold out in times of change, when sickness of body and trouble of mind shall come. Empty conceits are too weak to encounter with real griefs.

Some think orthodox and right opinions to be a plea for a loose life, whereas there is no ill course of life but springs from some false opinion. God will not only call us to account how we have believed, disputed, and reasoned, &c., but how we have lived. Our care, therefore, should be to build our profession, not on seeming appearances, but upon sound grounds, that the gates of hell cannot prevail against. The hearts of many are so vain that they delight to be blown up with flattery, because they would have their imaginations pleased, yea, even when they cannot but know themselves abused, and are grieved to have their windy bladder pricked, and so to be put out of their conceited happiness. Others, out of a tediousness in serious and settled thoughts, entertain everything as it is offered to them at the first blush, and suffer their imaginations to carry them presently thereunto without further judging of it. The will naturally loves variety and change, and our imagination doth it service herein, as not delighting to fix long upon anything. Hereupon men are contented, both in religion and in common life, to be misled with prejudices upon shallow grounds; whence it is that the best things and persons suffer much in the world. The power and practice of religion is hated under odious names, and so condemned before it is understood; whence we see a necessity of getting spiritual eye-salve, for without true knowledge the heart cannot be good, Prov. xix. 2.

It is just with God that those who take liberty in their thoughts should be given up to their own imaginations, Rom. i. 28, to delight in them, and to be out of conceit with the best things, and so to reap the fruit of their own ways. Nay, even the best of God's people, if they take liberty herein, God will let loose their imagination upon themselves, and suffer them to be entangled and vexed with their own hearts. Those that give way to their imaginations, shew what their actions should be, if they dared; for if they forbear doing evil out of conscience, they should as well forbear imagining evil, for both are alike open to God and hateful to him; and, therefore, oft where there is no conscience of the thought, God gives men up to the deed. The greatest and hardest work of a Christian is least in sight, which is the well ordering of his heart. Some buildings have most workmanship under ground. It is our spirits 'that God, who is a Spirit,' John iv. 24, hath most communion withal; and the less freedom we take to sin here, the more argument of our sincerity, because there is no law to bind the inner man but the law of the Spirit of grace, whereby we are 'a law to ourselves,' Rom. ii. 14. A good Christian begins his repentance where his sin begins, in his thoughts, which are the next issue of his heart. God counts it an honour when we regard his all-seeing eye so much, as that we will not take liberty to ourselves in that which is offensive to him, no, not in our hearts, wherein no creature can hinder us. It is an argument that the Spirit hath set up a kingdom and order in our hearts, when our spirits rise within us against any thing that lifts itself up against goodness.

§ V. *Obj.* Many flatter themselves, from an impossibility of ruling their imaginations, and are ready to lay all upon infirmity and natural weakness, &c.

Ans. But such must know that if we be sound Christians, the Spirit of God will enable us to do all things, evangelically, that we are called unto, if we give way without check to the motions thereof. Where the Spirit is, it is such a light as discovers not only dunghills, but motes themselves, even light and flying imaginations, and abaseth the soul for them, and by degrees purgeth them out; and if they press, as they are as busy as flies in summer, yet a good heart will not own them, nor allow himself in them, but casts them off, as hot water doth the scum, or as the stomach doth that which is noisome unto it. They find not that entertainment here which they have in carnal hearts, where the scum soaks in, which are stews of unclean thoughts, shambles of cruel and bloody thoughts, exchanges and shops of vain thoughts, a very forge and mint of false, politic, and undermining thoughts, yea often a little hell of confused and black imaginations. There is nothing that more moveth a godly man to renew his interest every day in the perfect righteousness and obedience of his Saviour, than these sinful stirrings of his soul, when he finds something in himself always enticing and drawing away his heart from God, and intermingling itself with his best performances. Even good thoughts are troublesome if they come unseasonably, and weaken our exact performance of duty.

§ VI. But here some misconceits must be taken heed of.

1. As we must take heed that we account not our imaginations to be religion, so we must not account true religion, and the power of godliness, to be a matter of imagination only; as if holy men troubled themselves more than needs, when they stand upon religion and conscience, seeking to approve themselves 'to God in all things,' 1 Thess. v. 12, and endeavouring, so far as frailty will permit, to 'avoid all appearances of evil,' 1 Thess. v. 22. Many men are so serious in vanities and real in trifles, that they count all which dote not upon such outward excellencies as they do, because the Spirit of God hath revealed to them things of a higher nature, to be fantastics and humorous * people, and so impute the work of the Spirit to the flesh, God's work to Satan, which comes near unto blasphemy. They imagine good men to be led with vain conceits, but good

* That is, 'whimsical.'—G.

men know them to be so led. Not only St Paul, Acts xxvi. 24, but Christ himself, John x. 20, were counted beside themselves, when they were earnest for God and the souls of his people. But there is enough in religion to bear up the soul against all imputations laid upon it: the true children of wisdom are always able to justify their mother, Mat. xi. 19, and the conscionable practice of holy duties, if founded upon such solid grounds as shall hold out when heaven and earth shall vanish.

2. We must know that—as there is great danger in false conceits of the way to heaven, when we make it broader than it is, for by this means we are like men going over a bridge, who think it broader than it is, but being deceived by some shadow, sink down, and are suddenly drowned; so men mistaking the straight way to life, and trusting to the shadow of their own imagination, fall into the bottomless pit of hell before they are aware;—in like manner the danger is great in making the way to heaven narrower than indeed it is, by weak and superstitious imaginations, making more sins than God hath made. The wise man's counsel is, that we should not make ourselves over-wicked, nor be foolisher than we are, Eccl. vii. 17, by devising more sins in our imagination than we are guilty of.

It is good in this respect, to know our Christian liberty, which being one of the fruits of Christ's death, we cannot neglect the same, without much wrong not only to ourselves, but to the rich bounty and goodness of God. So that the due rules of limitation be observed, from authority, piety, sobriety, needless offence of others, &c., we may with better leave, use all those comforts which God hath given to refresh us in the way to heaven, than refuse them. The care of the outward man binds conscience so far, as that we should neglect nothing which may help us in a cheerful serving of God, in our places, and tend to the due honour of our bodies, which are the 'temples of the Holy Ghost,' 1 Cor. iii. 16, 17, and companions with our souls in all performances, so that under this prete ıce we take not too much liberty to satisfy the lusts of the body. Intemperate use of the creatures is the nurse of all passions; because our spirits, which are the soul's instruments, are hereby inflamed and disturbed. It is no wonder to see an intemperate man transported into any passion.

3. Some out of their high and airy imaginations, and out of their iron and flinty philosophy, will needs think outward good and ill, together with the affections of grief and delight stirred up thereby, to be but opinions and conceits of good and evil only, not true, and really so founded in nature, but taken up of ourselves. But though our fancy be ready to conceit a greater hurt in outward evils than indeed there is, as in poverty, pain of body, death of friends, &c., yet we must not deny them to be evils. That wormwood is bitter, it is not a conceit only, but the nature of the thing itself, yet to abstain from it altogether, for the bitterness thereof, is a hurtful conceit. That honey is sweet, it is not a conceit only, but the natural quality of it is so; yet out of a taste of the sweetness, to think we cannot take too much of it, is a misconceit paid home with loathsome bitterness. Outward good and outward evil, and the affections of delight and sorrow rising thence, are naturally so, and depend not upon our opinion. This were to offer violence to nature, and to take man out of man, as if he were not flesh but steel. Universal experience, from the sensibleness of our nature in any outward grievance, is sufficient to damn this conceit.

The way to comfort a man in grief, is not to tell him that it is only a conceit of evil, and no evil indeed that he suffers. This kind of learning will not down with him, as being contrary to his present feeling. But the way is, to yield unto him that there is cause of grieving, though not of over-grieving, and to shew him grounds of comforts stronger than the grief he suffers. We should weigh the degrees of evil in a right balance, and not suffer fancy to make them greater than they are; so as that for obtaining the greatest outward good, or avoiding the greatest outward ill of suffering, we should give way to the least evil of sin. This is but a policy of the flesh to take away the sensibleness of evil, that so those checks of conscience and repentance for sin, which is oft occasioned thereby, might be taken away; that so men may go on enjoying a stupid happiness, never laying anything to heart, nor afflicting their souls, until their consciences awaken in the place of the damned, and then they feel that grief return upon them for ever, which they laboured to put away when it might have been seasonable to them.

§ VII. I have stood the longer upon this, because Satan and his instruments, by bewitching the imagination with false appearances, misleadeth not only the world, but troubleth the peace of men 'taken out of the world,' James i. 27, 1 John iv. 5, 6, whose estate is laid up safe in Christ, who, notwithstanding, pass their few days here in an uncomfortable, wearisome, and unnecessary sadness of spirit, being kept in ignorance of their happy condition by Satan's juggling and their own mistakes, and so come to heaven before they are aware. Some again pass their days in a golden dream, and drop into hell before they think of it. But it is far better to dream of ill, and when we awake to find it but a dream, than to dream of some great good, and when we awake to find the contrary.

As the distemper of the fancy—*læsa phantasia*—disturbing the act of reason, oftentimes breeds madness in regard of civil conversation; so it breeds, likewise, spiritual madness, carrying men to those things, which, if they were in their right wits, they would utterly abhor. Therefore we cannot have too much care upon what we fix our thoughts. And what a glorious discovery is there of the excellencies of religion that would even ravish an angel, which may raise up, exercise, and fill our hearts! We see our fancy hath so great a force in natural conceptions, that it oft sets a mark and impression upon that which is conceived in the womb. So, likewise, strong and holy conceits of things, having a divine virtue accompanying of them, transform the soul, and breed spiritual impressions answerable to our spiritual apprehensions. It would prevent many crosses, if we would conceive of things as they are. When trouble of mind, or sickness of body, and death itself cometh, what will remain of all that greatness which filled our fancies before? Then we can judge soberly, and speak gravely of things. The best way of happiness, is not to multiply honours or riches, &c., but to cure our conceits of things, and then we cannot be very much cast down with anything that befalls us here.

Therefore, when anything is presented to our souls, which we see is ready to work upon us, we should ask of ourselves upon what ground we entertain such a conceit, whether we shall have the same judgment after we have yielded to it as now we have? and whether we will have the same judgment of it in sickness and death and at the day of reckoning as we have for the present? That which is of itself evil, is always so at one time as well as another. If the time will come when we shall think those things to be vain, which now we are so eagerly set upon, as if there were some great good in them, why should we not think so of them now, whenas the reforming of our judgment may do us good, rather than to be led on with a pleasing error until that time, wherein the sight of our error will fill our hearts with horror and shame, without hope of ever changing our condition?

Here, therefore, is a special use of these soliloquies, to awake the soul and to stir up reason cast asleep by Satan's charms, that so scattering the clouds through which things seem otherwise than they are, we may discern and judge of things according to their true and constant nature. Demand of thy soul, Shall I always be of this mind? Will not the time come when this will prove bitterness in the end? Shall I redeem a short contentment with lasting sorrow? Is my Judge of my mind? Will not a time come when all things shall appear as they are? Is this according to the rule? &c.

To conclude, therefore, whereas there be divers principles of men's actions, as, 1, Natural inclination, inclining us to some courses more than others; 2, Custom, which is another nature in us; 3, Imagination, apprehending things upon shallow grounds, from whence springs affectation, whereby we desire glory in things above our own strength and measure, and make show of that, the truth whereof is wanting in us; 4, True judgment, discerning the true reasons of things; 5, Faith, which is a spiritual principle planted in the soul, apprehending things above reason, and raising us up to conceive of all things as God hath discovered them. Now a sound Christian should not be lightly led with those first common grounds of natural inclination, custom, opinion, &c., but by judgment enlightened, advanced, and guided by faith. And we must take heed we suffer not things to pass suddenly from imagination to affection, without asking advice of our judgment, and faith in the way, whose office is to weigh things in God's balance, and, thereupon, to accept or refuse them.

CHAPTER XIV.—*Of help by others. Of true comforters and their graces. Method. Ill success.*

§ I. But because we are subject to favour, and flatter ourselves, it is wisdom to take the benefit of a second self, that is, a well chosen friend, living or dead, books I mean, which will speak truly, without flattery, of our estates. 'A friend is made for the time of adversity,' Prov. xvii. 17; and two are better than one, Eccl. iv. 9, for, by this means, our troubles are divided, and so more easily borne. The very presence of a true-hearted friend yields often ease to our grief. Of all friends, those that by office are to speak a word to a weary soul are most to be regarded, as speaking to us in Christ's stead. Oftentimes, especially in our own case, we are blinded and benighted with passion, and then the judgment of a friend is clearer. Loving friends have a threefold privilege: 1, Their advice is suitable, and fit to our present occasion, they can meet with our grievance, so cannot books so well; 2, What comes from a living friend, comes lively, as helped by his Spirit; 3, In regard of ourselves, what they say is apprehended with more ease, and less plodding and bent of mind. There is scarce anything wherein we see God more in favour towards us, than in our friends, and their seasonable speeches, our hearts being naturally very false and willingly deceived. God often gives us up to be misled by men, not according to his, but our own naughty hearts. As men are, so are their counsellors, for such they will have, and such God lets them have. Men, whose wills are stronger than their wits, who are wedded to their own ways, are more pleased to hear that which complies with their inclinations, than a harsh truth which crosses them. This presages ruin, because they are not counselable. Wherefore God suffers them to be led through a fool's paradise to a true prison, as men that will neither hear themselves nor others who would do them good against their wills. It was a sign God would destroy Eli's sons, when they would hear no counsel, 1 Sam. ii. 25. God fills such men with their own ways, Prov. xiv. 14. Men in great place, often in the abundance of all things else, want the benefit of a true friend, *Ideo amicus deest quia nihil deest*, because, under pretence of service of them, men carry their own ends. As great men* flatter themselves, so they are flattered by others, and so robbed of the true judgment of themselves. Of all spiritual judgments this is the heaviest, for men to be given up to such a measure of self-willness, and to refuse spiritual balm to heal them. Usually such 'perish without remedy,' Prov. xxix. 1, because to be wilfully miserable is to be doubly miserable, for it adds to our misery, that we brought it willingly upon ourselves.

It is a course that will have a blessing attending it, for friends to join in league, one to watch over another, and observe each other's ways. It is a usual course for Christians to join together in other holy duties, as hearing, receiving of the sacrament, prayer, &c.; but this fruit of holy communion which ariseth from a mutual observing one another is much wanting. Whence it is that so many droop, so many are so uncheerful in the ways of God, and lie groaning under the burden of many cares, and are battered with so many temptations, &c., because they are left only to their own spirits. What an unworthy thing is it that we should pity a beast overloaden, and yet take no pity of a brother! *(f)* whereas there is no living member of Christ but hath spiritual love infused into him and some ability to comfort others. Dead stones in an arch uphold one another, and shall not living? It is the work of an angel to comfort; nay, it is the office of the Holy Ghost to be a Comforter, not only immediately, but by breathing comfort into our hearts, together with the comfortable words of others. Thus one friend becomes an angel, nay, a god, to another. And there is a sweet sight of God in the face of a friend; for though the comfort given by God's messengers be ordinarily most effectual, as the blessing of parents, who are in God's room, is more effectual than the blessing of others upon their children, yet God hath promised a blessing to the offices of communion of saints performed by one private man towards another. Can we have a greater encouragement than, under God, to be gainer of a soul, which is as much in God's esteem as if we should gain a world? Spiritual alms are the best alms. Mercy shewed to the souls of men is the greatest mercy, and wisdom in winning of souls is the greatest wisdom in the world, because the soul is especially the man, upon the goodness of which the happiness of the whole man depends. What shining and flourishing Christians should we have if these duties were performed! As we have a portion in the communion of saints, so we should labour to have humility to take good, and wisdom and love to do good. A Christian should have feeding lips and a healing tongue. The leaves, the very words, of the tree of righteousness have a curing virtue in them.

Some will shew a great deal of humanity in comforting others, but little Christianity; for as kind men they will utter some cheerful words, but as Christians they want wisdom from above to speak a gracious word in season, Isa. l. 4, 2 Tim. iv. 2. Nay, some there are who hinder the saving working of any affliction upon the hearts of others by unseasonable and unsavoury discourses, either by suggesting false remedies, or else diverting

* 'Great men' in C, is simply 'as they.'

men to false contentments, and so become spiritual traitors rather than friends, taking part with their worst enemies, their lusts and wills. Happy is he that in his way to heaven meeteth with a cheerful and skilful guide and fellow-traveller, that carrieth cordials with him against all faintings of spirit. It is a part of our wisdom to salvation to make choice of such a one as may further us in our way. An indifferency for any company shews a dead heart. Where the life of grace is, it is sensible of all advantages and disadvantages. How many have been refreshed by one short, apt, savoury speech, which hath begotten, as it were, new spirits in them.

In ancient times, as we see in the story of Job, chap. ii. 12, it was the custom of friends to meet together to comfort those that were in misery, and Job takes it for granted, that 'to him that is afflicted pity should be shewed from his friends,' chap. vi. 14. For besides the presence of a friend, which hath some influence of comfort in it, 1. The discovery of his loving affection hath a cherishing sweetness in it. 2. The expression of love in real comforts and services, by supplying any outward want of the party troubled, prevails much. Thus Christ made way for his comforts to the souls of men by shewing outward kindness to their bodies. Love, with the sensible fruits of it, prepareth for any wholesome counsel. 3. After this, wholesome words carry a special cordial virtue with them, especially when the Spirit of God in the affectionate speaker joins with the word of comfort, and thereby closeth with the heart of a troubled patient. When all these concentre and meet together in one, then is comfort sealed up to the soul. The child in Elizabeth's womb sprang at the presence and salutation of Mary, Luke i. 41. The speech of one hearty friend cannot but revive the spirits of another. Sympathy hath a strange force, as we see in the strings of an instrument, which being played upon, as they say, the strings of another instrument are also moved with it. After love hath once kindled love, then the heart, being melted, is fit to receive any impression. Unless both pieces of the iron be red hot, they will not join together. Two spirits warmed with the same heat will easily solder together.

§ II. In him that shall stay the mind of another there had need to be an excellent temper of many graces, as, 1. Knowledge of the grievance, together with wisdom to speak a word in season, and to conceal that which may set the cure backwards. 2. Faithfulness with liberty, not to conceal anything which may be for his good, though against present liking. The very life and soul of friendship stands in freedom, tempered with wisdom and faithfulness. 3. Love with compassion and patience to bear all, and hope all, and not to be easily provoked by the waywardness of him we deal with. Short-spirited men are not the best comforters. God himself is said to 'bear with the manners of his people in the wilderness,' Acts xiii. 18. It is one thing to bear with a wise sweet moderation that which may be borne, and another thing to allow or approve that which is not to be approved at all, *Non est idem ferre, si quid ferendum non est, et probare si quid probandum non est.* Where these graces are in the speaker, and apprehended so to be by the person distempered, his heart will soon embrace whatsoever shall be spoken to rectify his judgment or affection. A good conceit of the spirit of the speaker is of as much force to prevail as his words. Words especially prevail, when they are uttered more from the bowels than the brain, and from our own experience, which made even Christ himself a more compassionate High Priest. When men come to themselves again they will be the deepest censurers of their own miscarriage.

§ III. Moreover to the right comforting of an afflicted person, special care must be had of discerning the true ground of his grievance; the core must be searched out. If the grief ariseth from outward causes, then it must be carried into the right channel, the course of it must turn another way, as in staying of blood. We should grieve for sin in the first place, as being the evil of all evils. If the ground be sin, then it must be drawn to a head, from a confused grief to some more particular sin, that so we may strike the right vein; but if we find the spirit much cast down for particular sins, then comfort is presently to be applied. But if the grief be not fully ripe, then, as we use to help nature in its offers to purge, by physic, till the sick matter be carried away; so when conscience, moved by the spirit, begins to ease itself by confession, it is good to help forward the work of it, till we find the heart low enough for comfort to be laid upon. When Paul found the jailor cast down almost as low as hell, he stands not now upon further hammering, and preparing of him for mercy, that work was done already, but presently stirs him up to 'believe in the Lord Jesus Christ,' Acts xvi. 31. Here being a fit place for an interpreter to declare unto man his righteousness, and his mercy that belongs unto him, after he hath acknowledged his personal and particular sins, which the natural guilt of the heart is extremely backward to do, and yet cannot receive any sound peace till it be done. If signs of grace be discerned, here likewise is a fit place to declare unto man the saving work of grace in his heart, which Satan labours to hide from him. Men oft are not able to read their own evidences without help.

In case of stiffness and standing out, it is fit the man of God, 1 Tim. vi. 11 and 2 Tim. iii. 17, should take some authority upon him, and lay a charge upon the souls of men in the name of Christ, to give way to the truth of Christ, and to forbear putting off that mercy which is so kindly offered, when we judge it to be their portion; which course will be successful in hearts awed with a reverend fear of grieving God's Spirit. Sometimes men must be dealt roundly withal, as David here deals with his own soul, that so whilst we ask a reason of their dejection, they may plainly see they have no reason to be so cast down. For oftentimes grievances are irrational, rising from mistakes; and counsel, bringing into the soul a fresh light, dissolves those gross fogs, and setteth the soul at liberty. What grief is contracted by false reason, is by true reason removed.* Thus it pleaseth God to humble men, by letting them see in what need they stand one of another, that so the communion of saints may be endeared. Every relation wherein we stand towards others, are so many bonds and sinews whereby one member is fitted to derive comfort to another, 'through love the bond of perfection,' Col. iii. 14; all must be done in this sweet affection. A member out of joint must be tenderly set in again, and bound up, which only men guided by the spirit of love seasoned with discretion are fit to do. They are taught of God to do what they should. The more of Christ is in any man, the more willingness and fitness to this duty; to which this should encourage us, that in strengthening others we strengthen ourselves, and derive upon ourselves the blessing pronounced on those that 'consider the needy,' Ps. xli. 1, which will be our comfort here and crown hereafter, that God hath honoured us, to be instruments of spiritual good to others. It is an injunction to 'comfort the feeble-minded,' 1 Thes. v. 14, and there is an heavy imputation on those that 'comforted not the weak,' Ezek. xxxiv. 4; when men will not own men in trouble, but estrange themselves as the

* 'Removed,' is in B and C 'altered.'

herd of deer forsakes and pushes away* the wounded deer from them. And those that are any ways cast down, must stoop to those ways which God hath sanctified to convey comfort; for though sometimes the Spirit of God immediately comforts the soul, which is the sweetest, yet for the most part the 'Sun of righteousness that hath healing in his wings,' Mal. iv. 2, conveyeth the beams of his comfort by the help of others, in whom he will have much of our comfort to lie hid; and for this very end it pleaseth God to exercise his children, and ministers especially, with trials and afflictions, that so they, having felt what a troubled spirit is in themselves, might be able to comfort others in their distresses with the same comfort wherewith they have been comforted, 2 Cor. vii. 7. God often suspends comfort from us to drive us to make use of our Christian friends, by whom he purposeth to do us good, *Si illatas molestias lingua dicat, a conscientia dolor emanat, vulnera enim clausa plus cruciant.*—Greg. Oftentimes the very opening of men's grievances bringeth ease, without any further working upon them. The very opening of a vein cools the blood. If God in the state of innocency thought it fit man should have a helper, if God thought it fit to send an angel to comfort Christ in his agonies, shall any man think the comfort of another more than needs? Satan makes every affliction, by reason of our corruption, a temptation to us, whereupon we are to encounter not only with our own corruptions, but with our spiritual wickednesses, Eph. vi. 12; and need we not then that others should join forces with us to discover the temptation, and to confirm and comfort us against it? For so reason joining with reason, and affection with affection, we come by uniting of strength to be impregnable. Satan hath most advantage in solitariness, and thereupon sets upon Christ in the wilderness, Mat. iv., and upon Eve single, Gen. iii., and it added to the glory of Christ's victory, that he overcame him in a single combat, and in a place of such disadvantage. Those that will be alone, at such times, do as much as in them lieth to tempt the tempter himself, to tempt them. The preacher gives three reasons why 'two are better than one,' Eccles. iv. 9. 1. Because if one fall, the other may lift him up. As that which is stronger shoreth up that which is weaker, so feeble minds are raised and kept up by the stronger; nay, oftentimes he that is weaker in one grace is stronger in another. One may help by his experience and meekness of love, that needs the help of another for knowledge. 2. If two lie together, one may warm another by kindling one another's spirits. Where two meet together upon such holy grounds and aims, there Christ by his Spirit makes up another, and this threefold cable who shall break? Mat. xviii. 20. While Joash lived, Jehoiada stood upright; while Latimer and Ridley lived, they kept up Cranmer by intercourse of letters and otherwise, from entertaining counsels of revolt. The disciples presently upon Christ's apprehension fainted, notwithstanding he laboured by his heavenly doctrine to put courage and comfort into them. 3. If any give an onset upon them, there is two to withstand it, spirit joining with spirit; and because there is an acquaintance of spirits as well as of persons, those are fittest to lay open our minds unto, in whom upon experience of their fidelity our hearts may most safely rely, *Solatium vitæ, habere cui pectus aperias.*† We lose much of our strength in the loss of a

* 'Forsakes and pushes away,' in B and C 'Forsake and push away,' and 'estrange themselves' dropped.

† Ambrose. The reference is to Ambrose de Off. Min. lib. iii. cap. 22, and is more exactly as follows:—'Solatium quippe vitæ hujus est, ut habeas cui pectus aperias tuum.'—G.

true friend; which made David bemoan the loss of his friend Jonathan, 'Woe is me for thee, my brother Jonathan!' 2 Sam. i. 20. He lost a piece of himself, by losing him whom his heart so clave unto. St Paul accounted that God had shewed especial mercy to him, in the recovery of Epaphroditus, Phil. ii. 27.

§ IV. But there are divers miscarriages in those that are troubled, which make the comfort of others of none effect.

1. When the troubled party deals not directly, but doubleth with him that is to help him. Some are ashamed to acknowledge the true ground of their grievance, pretending sorrow for one thing, when their hearts tell them it ariseth from another: like the lapwings, which make greatest noise farthest from their nest, because they would not have it discovered. This deceit moved our blessed Saviour, who knew what was in the hearts of men, to fit his answers many times, rather to the man than to the matter.

2. Some rely too much upon particular men, Oh if they had such a one they should do well, and mislike others, fitter perhaps to deal with them, as having more thorough knowledge of their estates, because they would have their disease rather covered than cured, or if cured, yet with soft words, whereas no plaster worketh better than that which causes smart. Some out of mere humorous fondness must have that which can hardly be got, or else nothing pleases them. David must needs have the 'waters of Bethlehem,' 2 Sam. xxiii. 15, when others were nearer hand. And oftentimes when men have not only whom they desire, but such also who are fit and dexterous in dealing with a troubled spirit, yet their souls feel no comfort, because they make idols of men; whereas men at the best are but conduits of comfort, and such as God freely conveyeth comfort by, taking liberty oft to deny comfort by them, that so he may be acknowledged the 'God of all comfort,' 2 Cor. i. 3.

3. Some delude themselves, by thinking it sufficient to have a few good words spoken to them, as if that could cure them; not regarding to apprehend the same, and mingle it with faith, without which, good words lose their working, even as wholesome physic in a dead stomach.

Besides miscarriages in comforting, times will often fall out in our lives, that we shall have none either to comfort us, or to be comforted by us, and then what will become of us unless we can comfort ourselves? Men must not think always to live upon alms, but lay up something in store for themselves, and provide oil for their own lamps, and be able to draw out something from the treasury of their own hearts. We must not go to the surgeon for every scratch. No wise traveller but will have some refreshing waters about him. Again, we are often driven to retire home to our own hearts, by uncharitable imputations of other men. Even friends sometimes become miserable comforters. It was Job's case, chap. ii.; his friends had honest intentions to comfort him, but erred in their manner of dealing. If he had found no more comfort by reflecting upon his own sincerity, than he received from them, who laboured to take it from him, he had been doubly miserable. We are most privy to our own intentions and aims, whence comfort must be fetched; let others speak what they can to us, if our own hearts speak not with them, we shall receive no satisfaction. Sometimes it may fall out, that those which should unloose our spirits when they are bound up, mistake; the key misses the right wards, and so we lie bound still. Opening of our estate to another is not good but when it is necessary; and it is not necessary, when we can fetch supply from our own store. God would have us tender of our reputations, except in some special cases, wherein we are to give glory to God, Josh. vii. 19, by a free and full confession. Needless discovery of ourselves to others, makes us fear the conscience of another man, as privy to that which we are ashamed he should be privy unto; and it is neither wisdom nor mercy to put men upon the rack of confession, further than they can have no ease any other way. For by this means we raise in them a jealousy towards us, and oft without cause, which weakeneth and tainteth that love which should unite hearts in one.

CHAPTER XV.—*Of flying to God in disquiets of souls; eight observations out of the text.*

Quest. What if neither the speech of others to us, nor the rebuke of our own hearts, will quiet the soul? Is there no other remedy left?

Ans. Yes; then look up to God, the father and fountain of comfort, as David doth here; for the more special means whereby he sought to recover himself was by laying a charge upon his soul to trust in God. For having let his soul run out too much, he begins to recollect himself again, and resign up all to God.

§ I. *Quest.* But how came David to have the command of his own soul, so as to take it off from grief, and to place it upon God? Could he dispose of his own heart himself?

Ans. The child of God hath something in him above a man; he hath the Spirit of God to guide his spirit. This command of David to his soul was under the command of the great commander. God commands David to trust in him, and at the same time infuseth strength into his soul by thinking of God's command, and trusting to God's power, to command itself to trust in God; so that this command is not only by authority, but by virtue likewise of God's command. As the inferior orbs move as they are moved by a higher, so David's spirit here moves as it is moved by God's Spirit, which inwardly spake to him to speak to himself.

David, in speaking thus to his own soul, was, as every true Christian is, a prophet and an instructor to himself; it is but as if inferior officers should charge in the name and power of the king. God's children have a principle of life in them from the Spirit of God, by which they command themselves. To give charge belongs to a superior. David had a double superior above him, his own spirit as sanctified, and God's Spirit guiding that. Our spirits are the Spirit's agents, and the Holy Spirit is God's agent, maintaining his right in us. As God hath made man a free agent, so he guides him, and preserves that free manner of working which is agreeable to man's nature.

By this it appears that David's moving of himself did not hinder the Spirit's moving of him, neither did the Spirit's moving of him hinder him from moving himself in a free manner; for the Spirit of God moveth according to our principles, it openeth our understandings to see that it is best to trust in God; it moveth so sweetly, as if it were an inbred principle, and all one with our own spirits. If we should hold our will to move itself, and not to be moved by the Spirit, we should make a god of it, whose property is to move other things, and not to be moved by any.*

We are in some sort lords over our own speeches and actions, but yet under a higher lord. David was willing to trust in God, but God wrought

* Ergone ita liberi esse volunt, ut nec Deum volunt habere Dominum?—Aug. de Spir. et Lit.

that will in him. He first makes our will good, and then works by it. It is a sacrilegious liberty that will acknowledge no dependence upon God. We are wise in his wisdom, and strong in his strength, who saith, 'Without me ye can do nothing,' John xv. 5. Both the bud of a good desire, and the blossom of a good resolution, and the fruit of a good action, all comes from God. Indeed, the understanding is ours whereby we know what to do, and the will is ours whereby we make choice of what is best to be done; but the light whereby we know, and the guidance whereby we choose, that is from a higher agent, which is ready to flow into us with present fresh supply, when by virtue of former strength we put ourselves forward in obedience to God.* Let but David say to his soul being charged of God to trust, I charge thee, my soul, to trust in him, and he finds a present strength enabling to it. Therefore, we must both depend upon God as the first mover, and withal set all the inferior wheels of our souls agoing, according as the Spirit of God ministers motion unto us. So shall we be free from self-confidence, and likewise from neglecting that order of working which God hath established. David hearkened what the Lord said, before he said anything to himself,—so should we. God's commands tend to this, that we should command ourselves. God, and the minister under God, bid us trust in him, but all is to no purpose till grace be wrought in the soul, whereby it bids itself. Our speaking to others doth no good, till they, by entertaining what we say, speak the same to their own souls.

In this charge of David upon his own soul, we may see divers passages and privileges of a gracious heart in trouble.

§ II. *Obs.* 1. As 1. *That a Christian, when he is beaten out of all other comforts, yet hath a God to run unto.* A wicked man beaten out of earthly comforts, is as a naked man in a storm, and an unarmed man in the field, or as a ship tossed in the sea without an anchor, which presently dashes upon rocks, or falleth upon quicksands; but a Christian, when he is driven out of all comforts below, nay, when God seems to be angry with him, he can appeal from God angry to God appeased, he can wrestle and strive with God by God's own strength, fight with him with his own weapons, and plead with God by his own arguments. What a happy estate is this! Who would not be a Christian, if it were but for this, to have something to rely on when all things else fail? The confusion and unquietness which troubles raise in the soul may drive it from resting in itself, but there can never be any true peace settled, until it sees and resolves what to stay upon.

§ III. 2. We see here that *there is a sanctified use of all troubles to God's children.* First, they drive them *out of themselves*, and then draw them nearer to God. Crosses, indeed, of themselves estrange us more from God, but by an overruling work of the Spirit they bring us nearer to him. The soul of itself is ready to misgive, as if God had too many controversies with it, to shew any favour towards it; and Satan helpeth. Because he knows nothing can stand and prevail against God, or a soul that relieth on him, therefore he labours to breed and increase an everlasting division betwixt God and the soul. But let not Christians muse so much upon their trouble, but see whither it carries them, whether it brings them nearer unto God or not. It is a never-failing rule of discerning a man to be in the state of grace, *when he finds every condition draw him nearer to God;* for thus it

* Certum est, nos velle cum volumus, sed ille facit ut velimus.—Aug. For the thought, not the words, see Conf., Book VII., iii. 5, and elsewhere repeatedly.—G.

appears that such love God, and are called of him, unto whom 'all things work together for the best,' Rom. viii. 28.

§ IV. 3. Again, hence we see that the Spirit of God by these *inward speeches* doth awake the soul, and keep it in a holy exercise, by stirring up the grace of faith to its proper function. It is not so much the having of grace, as grace in *exercise*, that preserves the soul. Therefore, we should by this and the like means 'stir up the grace of God in us,' 2 Tim. i. 6, that so it may be kept a-working, and in vigour and strength. It was David's manner to awake himself, by bidding both 'heart and harp to awake,' Ps. lvii. 8. It is the waking Christian, that hath his wit and his grace ready about him, who is the safe Christian. Grace dormant, without the exercise, doth not secure us. It is almost all one, in regard of present exigence, for grace not to be and not to work. The soul without action is like an instrument not played upon, or like a ship always in the haven. Motion is a preservative of the purity of things. Even life itself is made more lively by action. The Spirit of God, whereby his children are led, is compared to things of the quickest and strongest actions, as fire and wind, &c. God himself is a pure act, always in acting; and everything, the nearer it comes to God, the more it hath its perfection in working. The happiness of man consists chiefly in a gracious frame of spirit, and actions suitable sweetly issuing therefrom. The very rest of heavenly bodies is in motion in their proper places. By this stirring up the grace of God in us, sparkles come to be flames, and all graces are kept bright. Troubles stir up David;* David being stirred, stirs up himself.

§ V. 4. We see likewise here a further use *of soliloquies or speeches to our own hearts*. When the soul by entering into itself sees itself put out of order, then it enjoins this duty of trusting in God upon it. If we look only on ourselves, and not turn to God, the work of the soul is imperfect. Then the soul worketh as it should, whenas by reflecting on itself, it gathers some profitable conclusion, and leaveth itself with God. David, upon reflecting on himself, found nothing but discouragement; but when he looks upward to God, there he finds rest. This is one end why God suffers the soul to tire and beat itself, that, finding no rest in itself, it might seek to him. David yields not so much to his passion as that it should keep him from God. Therefore, let no man truly religious pretend, for an excuse, his temper or provoking occasions, &c., for grace doth raise the soul above nature. Grace doth not only stop the soul in an evil way, but carries it to a contrary good, and raiseth it up to God. Though holy men be subject to 'like passions with others,' James v. 17, as it is said of Elias, yet they are not so enthralled to them, as that they carry them wholly away from their God; but they hear a voice of the Spirit within them, calling them back again to their former communion with God; and so grace takes occasion, even from sin, to exercise itself.

§ VI. 5. Observe further, that *distrust is the cause of all disquiet*. The soul suffers itself by something here below to be drawn away from God, but can find no rest till it return to him again. As Noah's dove had no place to set her foot upon, Gen. viii. 11, till it was received into the ark from whence it came. And it is God's mercy to us, that when we have let go our hold of God, we should find nothing but trouble and unquietness in any-

* A connective 'and' in C.

thing else, that so we might remember from whence we are fallen, and return home again. That is a good trouble which frees us from the greatest trouble, and brings with it the most comfortable rest. It is but an unquiet quiet, and a restless rest which is out of God. It is a deep spiritual judgment for a man to find too much rest in the creature. The soul that hath had a saving work upon it, will be always impatient until it recovers its former sweetness in God. After God's Spirit hath once touched the soul, it will never be quiet until it stands pointed God-ward.

Obj. But conscience may object, upon any offence is God offended, and therefore not to be trusted?

Ans. It is true, where faith is not above natural conscience; but a conscience 'sprinkled with the blood of Christ,' Heb. x. 22, is not scared from God by its infirmities and failings, but as David here is rather stirred up to run unto God by his distemper; and it had been a greater sin than his distemper not to have gone unto God. Those that have the spirit of sons in their hearts, run not further from God after they have a little strayed from him; but, though it be the nature of sinful passions to breed grief and shame, yet they will repair to God again, and their confidence overcomes their guilt, so well are they acquainted with God's gracious disposition.

Yet we see here, David thinks not of trusting in God, till first he had done justice upon his own soul, in rebuking the unruly motions thereof. Censure for sin goeth before favour in pardoning sin or boldness to ask pardon of God. Those that love God must hate ill, Ps. xcvii. 10. If our consciences condemn us of allowing any sin, we cannot have boldness with God, who is light and can abide no darkness, and 'greater than our consciences,' 1 John iii. 20.

§ VII. 6. Moreover, hence we see *it is no easy thing to bring God and the heart together*. David here as he often checks his heart, so he doth often charge his heart. Doubts and troubles are still gathering upon him, and his faith still gathering upon them. As one striving to get the haven, is driven back by the waves, but recovering himself again, gets forward still, and after often beating back, at length obtains the wished haven, and then is at rest, so much ado there is to bring the soul unto God, the harbour of true comfort. It were an easy thing to be a Christian, if religion stood only in a few outward works and duties, but to take the soul to task, and to deal roundly with our own hearts, and to let conscience have its full work, and to bring the soul into spiritual subjection unto God, this is not so easy a matter, because the soul out of self-love is loath to enter into itself, lest it should have other thoughts of itself than it would have. David must bid his soul trust, and trust, and trust again before it will yield. One main ground of this difficulty is, that contrary which is in the soul by reason of contrary principles. The soul so far as it is gracious commands, so far as it is rebellious resists, which drew holy Austin to a kind of astonishment: 'The soul commands the body and it yields,' saith he, 'it commands itself, and is resisted by itself. It commands the hand to move, and it moveth with such an unperceivable quickness that you can discern no distance betwixt the command and the motion. Whence comes this? but because the soul perfectly wills not, and perfectly enjoins not that which is good, and so far forth that it fully wills not, so far it holds back.'* There should

* Unde hoc monstrum et quare istud? . . . . . Non ex toto vult, non ex toto imperat, in tantum non fit quod imperat, in quantum non vult.—Augustine, Confess., Book VIII., ix. 21.

be no need of commanding the soul if it were perfect, for then it would be of itself, what it now commandeth. If David had gotten his soul at perfect freedom at the first, he needed not have repeated his charge so often upon it. But the soul naturally sinks downward, and therefore had need often to be wound up.

§ VIII. 7. We should therefore labour to bring our souls, as David doth here, to a firm and peremptory resolution, and not stand wavering, and as it were equally balanced betwixt God and other things; but enforce our souls. We shall get little ground of infidelity else. Drive your souls, therefore, to this issue, either to rely upon God, or else to yield up itself to the present grievance. If by yielding, it resolves to be miserable, there's an end, but if it desires rest, then let it resolve upon this only way, to trust in God. And well may the soul so resolve, because in God there arè grounds of quieting the soul, above all that may unsettle it; in him there is both worth to satisfy, and strength to support the soul. The best way to maintain inward peace, is to settle and fix our thoughts upon that which will make us better, till we found our hearts warmed and wrought upon thereby, and then, as the prophet speaks, 'God will keep us in peace, peace,' that is, 'in perfect and abundant peace,' Isa. xxvi. 3. This resolution stayed Job, that though God should kill him, yet he resolved 'to trust in him,' Job xiii. 15. Answerable to our resolution is our peace, the more resolution the more peace. Irresolution of itself, without any grievance, is full of disquiet. It is an unsafe thing always to begin to live, to be always cheapening and paltering with God; come to this point once, trust God I ought, therefore, trust God I will, come what may or will.

And it is good to renew our resolutions again and again: for every new resolution brings the soul closer to God, and gets further in him, and brings fresh strength from him; which, if we neglect, our corruption joining with outward hindrances will carry us further and further backward, and this will double, yea multiply our trouble and grief to recover ourselves again. We have both wind and tide against us, we are going up the hill, and, therefore, had need to arm ourselves with resolution. Since the fall, the motion of the soul upward, as of heavy bodies, is violent, in regard of corruption which weighs it downward, and, therefore, all enforcement is little enough. Oppose, therefore, with David, an invincible resolution, and then doubt not of prevailing. If we resolve in God's power and not our own, and be 'strong in the Lord,' Eph. vi. 10, and not in ourselves, then it matters not what our troubles or temptations be either from within, or without, for trust in God at length will triumph.

Here is a great mercy, that when David had a little let go his hold of God, yet God would not let go his hold of him, but by a spirit of faith draws him back again to himself. God turns us unto him, and then we return. 'Turn us again,' saith the psalmist, 'cause thy face to shine upon us, and we shall be saved,' Ps. lxxx. 19. When the soul leaves God once, it loses its way and itself; and never returns till God recalls it again. *Animus æger semper errat.* If moral principles, cherished and strengthened by good education, will enable the soul against vicious inclinations, so that, though some influence of the heavens work upon the air, and the air upon the spirits, and the spirits upon the humours, and these incline the temper, and that inclines the soul of a man such and such ways, yet breeding in the refineder sort of civil persons will much prevail to draw them another way. What, then, may we think of this powerful grace of faith which is altogether supernatural? Will not this carry the soul above all natural inclinations whatsoever, though strengthened by outward occasions, if we resolve to put it to it? David was a king of other men, but here he shews that he was a king of himself. What benefit is it for a man to be ruler over all the world, and yet remain a slave to himself?

§ IX. 8. Again, David here doth not only resolve, but *presently takes up his soul, before it strayed too far from God.* The further and the longer the soul wanders from God, the more it entangles itself, and the thicker darkness will cover the soul, yea, the loather it is to come to God again, being ashamed to look God in the face after discontinuing of acquaintance with him; nay, the stronger the league grows betwixt sin and the soul, and the more there groweth a kind of suitableness betwixt the soul and sin. Too long giving way to base thoughts and affections, discovers too much complacency and liking of sin. If we once give way, a little grief will turn into bitter sorrow, and that into a settled pensiveness and heaviness of spirit; fear will grow into astonishment, and discouragement into despair. If ever we mean to trust God, why not now? How many are taken away in their offers and essays, before they have prepared their hearts to cleave unto God! The sooner we give up ourselves to the Lord, the sooner we know upon what terms we stand, and the sooner we provide for our best security, and have not our grounds of comfort to seek when we shall stand most in need of them. Time will salve up grief in the meanest of men; reason, in those that will suffer themselves to be ruled thereby, will cure, or at least stay the fits of it, sooner; but faith, if we stir it up, will give our souls no rest, until it hath brought us to our true rest, that is, to God. Therefore we should press the heart forward to God presently, that Satan make not the rent greater.

§ X. 9. Lastly, here we see, that *though the soul be overborne by passion for a time, yet if grace hath once truly seasoned it, it will work itself into freedom again.* Grace, as oil, will be above. The eye when any dust falls into it, is not more tender and unquiet, till it be wrought out again, than a gracious soul is, being once troubled. The spirit, as a spring, will be cleansing of itself more and more. Whereas the heart of a carnal man is like a standing pool, whatsoever is cast into it, there it rests. Trouble and disquietness in him are in their proper place. It is proper for the sea to rage and cast up dirt. God hath set it down for an eternal rule, that vexation and sin shall be inseparable. Happiness and rest were severed from sin in heaven when the angels fell, and in paradise when Adam fell, Gen. iii., and will remain for ever separated, until the breach be made up by faith in Christ. *Jussisti Domine, et sic est, ut omnis inordinatus affectus sibi sit pœna.* —Aug.

CHAPTER XVI.—*Of trust in God: grounds of it; especially his providence.*

But to come nearer to the unfolding of this trust in God, which David useth here as a remedy against all distempers. Howsoever confidence and trust be an affection of nature, yet by the Spirit's sanctifying and carrying it to the right object, it becomes a grace of wonderful use. In the things of this life, usually he that hopes most is the most unwise man, he being most deceived that hopes most, because he trusts in that which is uncertain;

and therefore deceitful hope is counted but the dream of a waking man. But in religion it is far otherwise; here hope is the main supporting grace of the soul, springing from faith in the promises of God.

Trust and hope are often taken in the same sense, though a distinction betwixt them hath sometimes its use. Faith looks to the word promising, hope to the thing promised in the word; faith looks to the authority of the promiser, hope especially to the goodness of the promise; faith looks upon things as present, hope as to come hereafter. God as the first truth, is that which faith relies on; but God as the chief good is that which hope rests on. Trust or confidence is nothing else but the strength of hope. If the thing hoped for be deferred, then of necessity it enforces waiting, and waiting is nothing else but hope and trust lengthened.

Howsoever there may be use of these and such like distinctions, yet usually they are taken promiscuously, especially in the Old Testament. The nature and use of faith is set out by terms of staying, resting, leaning, rolling ourselves upon God, &c., which come all to one, and therefore we forbear any further curious distinction.

Now, seeing trusting in God is a remedy against all distempers, it is necessary that we should bring the object and the act, God and the soul, together; for effecting of which it is good to know something concerning God and something concerning trust. God only is the fit object of trust. He hath all the properties of that which should be trusted on. A man can be in no condition wherein God is at a loss and cannot help him. If comforts be wanting, he can create comforts, not only out of nothing, but out of discomforts. He made the whale that swallowed up Jonah a means to bring him to the shore, Jonah i. 17. The sea was a wall to the Israelites on both sides, Exod. xiv. 22. The devouring flames were a great refreshing to the three children in the fiery furnace, Dan. iii. That trouble which we think will swallow us up, may be a means to bring us to our haven; 'so mighty is God in power, and so excellent in working,' Isa. xxviii. 29. God then, and God only, is a fit foundation for the soul to build itself upon, for the firmer the foundation is, the stronger will the building be; therefore those that will build high must dig deep. The higher the tree riseth, the deeper the root spreadeth and fasteneth itself below. So it is in faith: if the foundation thereof be not firm, the soul cannot build itself strongly upon it. Faith hath a double principle to build on, either a principle of being, or a principle of knowing. The principle of being is God himself, the principle of knowing is God's word, whereby God cometh forth 'out of that hidden light which none can attain unto,' 1 Tim. vi. 16, and discovereth his meaning towards us for our good.

This then must, 1, be supposed for a ground, *that there is a God*, and that God *is*, that is, hath a full and eternal being, and giveth a being, and an order of being, to all things else. Some things have only a being, some things life and being, some things sense, &c., and some things have a more excellent being, including all the former, as the being of creatures endued with reason. If God had not a being, nothing else could be. In things subordinate one to another, take away the first, and you take away all the rest. Therefore this proposition, God is, is the first truth of all; and if this were not, nothing else should be, as we see if the heavenly bodies do not move, there is no motion here below.

2. In the divine nature or being, there is a subsisting of three persons, every one so set out unto us, as fitted for us to trust in; the Father as a Creator, the Son as a Redeemer, the Holy Ghost as a Comforter, and all

this is in reference to us. God in the first person hath decreed the great work of our salvation, and all things tending to the accomplishment of it. God in the second person hath exactly and fully answered that decree and plot, in the work of our redemption. God in the third person discovers and applies all unto us, and fits us for communion with the Father and the Son, from whom he proceeds.

3. God cannot be comfortably thought upon out of Christ our Mediator, in whom he was 'reconciling the world to himself,' 1 Cor. v. 19, as being a friend both to God and us, and therefore fit to bring God and the soul together, being a middle person in the Trinity. In Christ, God's nature becomes lovely to us, and ours to God; otherwise there is an utter enmity betwixt his pure and our impure nature. Christ hath made up the vast gulf between God and us. There is nothing more terrible to think on, than an absolute God out of Christ.

4. Therefore, for the better drawing of us to trust in God, we must conceive of him under the sweet relation of a Father. God's nature is fatherly now unto us, and therefore lovely.

5. And for further strengthening our faith it is needful to consider what excellencies the Scripture giveth unto God, answerable to all our necessities. What sweet names God is pleased to be known unto us by for our comfort, 'as a merciful, gracious, long-suffering God,' &c. Exod. xxxiv. 6.

When Moses desired to see the glory of God, God thus manifested himself, in the way of goodness: 'I will make all my goodness pass before thee,' Exod. xxxiii. 16.

Whatsoever is good in the creature is first in God as a fountain; and it is in God in a more eminent manner and fuller measure. All grace and holiness, all sweetness of affection, all power and wisdom, &c. as it is in him, so it is from him: and we come to conceive these properties to be in God, 1, by feeling the comfort and power of them in ourselves; 2, by observing these things in their measure to be in the best of the creatures, whence we arise to take notice of what grace and what love, what strength and wisdom, &c., is in God, by the beams of these which we see in his creature, with adding in our thoughts fulness peculiar to God, and abstracting imperfections incident to the creature. For that is in God in the highest degree, the sparkles whereof is but in us.

6. Therefore it is fit that unto all other eminencies in God, we should strengthen our faith by considering those glorious singularities, which are altogether incommunicable to the creature, and which gives strength to his other properties, as that God is not only gracious and loving, powerful, wise, &c., but that he is infinitely, eternally, and unchangeably so. All which are comprised in and drawn from that one name Jehovah, as being of himself, and giving a being to all things else, of nothing; and able, when it pleaseth him, to turn all things to nothing again.

7. As God is thus, so he makes it good by answerable actions and dealing towards us, by his continual providence, the consideration whereof is a great stay to our faith; for by this providence God makes use of all his former excellencies for his people's good, for the more comfortable apprehension of which, it is good to know that God's providence is extended as far as his creation. Every creature, in every element and place whatsoever, receiveth a powerful influence from God, who doth what pleaseth him, both in heaven and earth, in the sea, and all places. But we must know God doth not put things into a frame, and then leave them to their own motion, as we do clocks, after we have once set them right, and ships, after

we have once built them, commit them to wind and waves; but as he made all things, and knows all things, so, by a continued kind of creation, he preserves all things in their being and working, and governs them in their ends. He is the first mover that sets all the wheels of the creature aworking. One wheel may move another, but all are moved by the first. If God moves not, the clock of the creature stands. If God should not uphold things, they would presently fall to nothing, from whence they came. If God should not guide things, Satan's malice, and man's weakness, would soon bring all to a confusion. If God did not rule the great family of the world, all would break and fall to pieces, whereas the wise providence of God keepeth everything on its right hinges. All things stand in obedience to this providence of God, and nothing can withdraw itself from under it. If the creature withdraw itself from one order of providence, it falls into another. If man, the most unruly and disordered creature of all, withdraw himself from God's gracious government of him to happiness, he will soon fall under God's just government of him to deserved misery. If he shakes off God's sweet yoke, he puts himself under Satan's heavy yoke, who, as God's executioner, hardens him to destruction. And so, whilst he rushes against God's will, he fulfils it; and whilst he will not willingly do God's will, God's will is done upon him against his will.

The most casual things fall under providence, yea, the most disordered thing in the world, sin, and, of sins the most horrible that ever the sun beheld, the 'crucifying of the Lord of life,' Acts iii. 15, was guided by a hand of providence to the greatest good. For that which is casual in regard of a second cause, is not so in regard of the first, whose providence is most clearly seen in casual events that fall out by accident, for in these the effect cannot be ascribed to the next cause. God is said to kill him who was unwarily slain by the falling of an axe or some instrument of death, Deut. xix. 5.

And though man hath a freedom in working, and of all men the hearts of kings are most free, yet even these are 'guided by an overruling power,' Prov. xxi. 1, as the rivers of water are carried in their channels whither skilful men list to derive them.

For settling of our faith the more, God taketh liberty in using weak means to great purposes, and setting aside more likely and able means; yea, sometimes he altogether disableth the greatest means, and worketh often by no means at all. It is not for want of power in God, but from abundance and multiplying of his goodness that he useth any means at all. There is nothing that he doth by means but he is able to do without means.

Nay, God often bringeth his will to pass by crossing the course and stream of means, to shew his own sovereignty and to exercise our dependence, and maketh his very enemies the accomplishers of his own will, and so to bring about that which they oppose most. Hence it is that we believe under hope against hope, Ps. cxxxv. 6.

But we must know, God's manner of guiding things is without prejudice to the proper working of the things themselves. He guideth them sweetly according to the instincts he hath put into them; for,

1. He furnishes creatures with a virtue and power to work, and likewise with a manner of working suitable to their own nature; as it is proper for a man, when he works, to work with freedom, and other creatures by natural instinct, &c.

2. God maintaineth both the power and manner of working, and perfecteth and accomplisheth the same by acting of it, being nearer to us in

all we do than we are to ourselves. *Intimior intimo nostro.* 3. He applies and stirs up our abilities and actions to this or that particular as he seeth best. 4. He suspends or removes the hindrances of all actions, and so powerfully, wisely, and sweetly orders them to his own ends. When any evil is intended, God either puts bars and lets to the execution of it, or else limiteth and boundeth the same, both in regard of time and measure, so that our enemies either shall not do the evil at all, or else not so long a time or not in such a height of mischief as their malice would carry them to. The rod of the wicked may light upon the back of the righteous, Ps. cxxv. 3, but it shall not rest there. God knows how to take our enemies off, sometimes by changing or stopping their wills, by offering considerations of some good or ill, danger or profit, to them; sometimes by taking away and weakening all their strength, or else by opposing an equal or greater strength against it. All the strength our enemies have rests in God, who, if he denies concourse and influence, the arm of their power, as Jeroboam's, when he stretched it out against the prophet, shrinks up presently.

God is not only the cause of things and actions, but the cause, likewise, of the cessation of them, why they fall not out at all. God is the cause why things are not, as well as why they are. *Deus est prima causa cujuscunque non esse.* The cause why men favour us not, or, when they do favour us, want present wisdom and ability to help us, is from God's withdrawing the concurrence of his light and strength from them. If a skilful physician doth us no good, it is because it pleaseth God to hide the right way of curing at that time from him. Which should move us to see God in all that befalls us, who hath sufficient reason, as to do what he doth, so not to do what he doth not, to hinder as well as to give way.

The God of spirits hath an influence into the spirits of men, into the principles and springs of all actions; otherwise he could not so certainly foretell things to come. God had a work in Absalom's heart in that he refused the best counsel. There is nothing independent of him who is the mover of all things, and himself unmoveable.

Nothing so high, that is above his providence; nothing so low, that is beneath it; nothing so large, but is bounded by it; nothing so confused, but God can order it; nothing so bad, but he can draw good out of it; nothing so wisely plotted, but God can disappoint it, as Ahithophel's counsel; nothing so simply and unpoliticly carried, but he can give a prevailing issue unto it; nothing so freely carried, in regard of the next cause, but God can make it necessary in regard of the event; nothing so natural, but he can suspend it in regard of operation, as heavy bodies from sinking, fire from burning, &c.

It cannot but bring strong security to the soul, to know that in all variety of changes and intercourse of good and bad events, God, and our God, hath such a disposing hand. Whatsoever befalls us, all serves to bring God's electing love, and our glorification together, God's providence serveth his purpose to save us. All sufferings, all blessings, all ordinances, all graces, all common gifts, nay, our very falls, yea, Satan himself with all his instruments, as over-mastered, and ruled by God, have this injunction upon them, to further God's good intendment to us, and a prohibition to do us no harm. Augustus taxed the world for civil ends, but God's providence used this as a means for Christ to be born at Bethlehem. Ahasuerus could not sleep, and thereupon calls for the chronicles, the reading of which occasioned the Jews' delivery, Esth. vi. 1. God oft disposeth little occasions to great purposes. And by those very ways whereby proud men have gone about to withstand God's counsels, they have fulfilled them, as we see in the story of Joseph and Moses, 'in the thing wherein they dealt proudly, he was above them,' Exod. x. 11. *Divinum consilium, dum devitatur, impletur; humana sapientia, dum reluctatur, comprehenditur.*—Greg.

CHAPTER XVII.—*Of graces to be exercised in respect of Divine Providence.*

We are under a providence that is above our own; which should be a ground unto us, of exercising those graces that tend to settle the soul, in all events. As,

1. Hence to lay our hand upon our mouths, and command the soul an holy silence, not daring to yield to the least rising of our hearts against God. 'I was dumb, and opened not my mouth, because thou didst it,' Ps. xxxix. 9, saith David. Thus Aaron, when he had lost his two sons, both at once, and that by fire, Lev. x. 1, 2, and by fire from heaven, which carried an evidence of God's great displeasure with it, yet held his peace. In this silence and hope is our strength. Flesh and blood is prone to expostulate with God, and to question his dealing, as we see in Gideon, Jeremiah, Asaph, Habakkuk, and others, 'If the Lord be with us, why then is all this befallen us?' Jud. vi. 13; but, after some struggling between the flesh and the spirit, the conclusion will be, yet howsoever matters go, 'God is good to Israel,' Ps. lxxiii. 1. Where a fearful spirit, and a melancholy temper, a weak judgment, and a scrupulous and raw conscience meet in one, there Satan and his, together with men's own hearts, which, like sophisters, are continually cavilling against themselves, breed much disquiet, and makes the life uncomfortable. Such, therefore, should have a special care, as to grow in knowledge, so to stick close to sure and certain grounds, and bring their consciences to the rule. Darkness causeth fears. The more light, the more confidence. When we yield up ourselves to God, we should resolve upon quietness, and if the heart stirs, presently use this check of David, 'Why art thou disquieted?'

God's ways seem oft to us full of contradictions, because his course is to bring things to pass by contrary means. There is a mystery not only in God's decree concerning man's eternal estate, but likewise in his providence, as why he should deal unequally with men otherwise equal. His judgments are a great depth, which we cannot fathom, but they will swallow up our thoughts and understandings. God oft wraps himself in a cloud, and will not be seen till afterward. Where we cannot trace him, we ought with St Paul to admire and adore him. When we are in heaven, it will be one part of our happiness to see the harmony of those things that seem now confused unto us. All God's dealings will appear beautiful in their due seasons, though we for the present see not the contiguity and linking together of one with another.

2. Hence likewise proceeds a holy resigning of ourselves to God, 'who doth all things according to the counsel of his own will,' Dan. xi. 16; Eph. i. 11. *Voluntas Dei, necessitas rei.* His will is a wise will; it is guided by counsel, a sovereign prevailing will. The only way to have our will is to bring it to God's will. If we could delight in him, we should have our heart's desire. Thus David yields up himself to God: 'Here I am; let the Lord deal with me as seemeth good unto him, 2 Sam. xv. 26. And thus Eli, when God foretold by Samuel the ruin of his house, quiets him-

self: 'It is the Lord; let him do what seemeth him good,' 1 Sam. iii. 18. Thus our blessed Saviour stays himself: 'Not my will, but thy will be done.' And thus the people of God, when Paul was resolved to go to Jerusalem, submitted, saying, 'The will of the Lord be done,' Acts xxi. 14, —a speech fit to proceed out of the heart and mouth of a Christian. *Vox vere Christianorum.*

We may desire and long after a change of our condition, when we look upon the grievance itself, but yet remember still that it be with reservation, when we look upon the will of God, as, 'How long, Lord, holy and true,' &c. Rev. vi. 10. Out of inferior reasons we may with our Saviour desire a removal of the cup; but when we look to the supreme reason of reasons, the will of God, here we must stoop and kiss the rod. 'Thus humbling ourselves under his mighty hand,' 1 Peter v. 6, which by murmuring and fretting we may make more heavy, but not take off, still adding new guilt and pulling on new judgments.

3. The way patiently to suffer God's will, is to inure ourselves first to do it. Passive obedience springs from active. He that endures anything will endure it quietly, when he knows it is the will of God, and considers that whatever befalls him comes from his good pleasure. Those that have not inured themselves to the yoke of obedience, will never endure the yoke of suffering; they fume and rage 'as a wild boar in a net,' Isa. li. 20, as the prophet speaks. It is worth the considering, to see two men of equal parts under the same cross, how quietly and calmly the one that establisheth his soul on Christ will bear his afflictions, whereas the other rageth as a fool, and is more beaten.

Nothing should displease us that pleaseth God: neither should anything be pleasing to us that displeaseth him. This conformity is the ground of comfort. Our own will takes away God, as much as in it lies. *Propria voluntas Deum quantum in ipsa eximit.* 'If we acknowledge God in all our ways, he will direct our paths, and lead us the way that we should go,' Prov. iii. 6. The quarrel betwixt God and us is taken up, when his will and our will are one; when we have sacrificed ourselves and our wills unto God; when, as he is highest in himself, so his will hath the highest place in our hearts. We find by experience that, when our wills are so subdued, that we delight to do what God would have us do, and to be what God would have us be, that then sweet peace presently riseth to the soul.

When we can say, Lord, if thou wilt have me poor and disgraced, I am content to be so; if thou wilt have me serve thee in this condition I am in, I will gladly do so. It is enough to me that thou wouldst have it so. I desire to yield readily, humbly, and cheerfully to thy disposing providence. Thus a godly man says amen to God's amen, and puts his *fiat* and *placet* to God's. As the sea turns all rivers into its own relish, so he turns all to his own spirit, and makes whatsoever befalls him an exercise of some virtue. A heathen could say that calamities did rule over men, but a wise man hath a spirit overruling all calamities; much more a Christian. For a man to be in this estate, is to enjoy heaven in the world under heaven. God's kingdom comes where his will is thus done and suffered.

None feel more sweet experience of God's providence than those that are most resolute in their obedience. After we have given glory to God in relying upon his wisdom, power, and truth, we shall find him employing these for our direction, assistance, and bringing about of things to our desired issue, yea, above whatever we looked for, or thought of.

In all cases that fall out, or that we can put to ourselves, as in case of extremity, opposition, strange accidents, desertion, and damps of spirit, &c., here we may take sanctuary, that we are in covenant with him who sits at the stern and rules all, and hath committed the government of all things to his Son, our brother, our Joseph, the second person in heaven. We may be sure that no hurt shall befall us that he can hinder; and what cannot he hinder 'that hath the keys of hell and of death?' Rev. i. 18, unto whom we are so near that he carries 'our names in his breast, and on his shoulders,' Heb. iv. 15, as the high priest did those of the twelve tribes. Though his church seems a widow neglected, ye he will make the world know that she hath a husband will right her in good time.

Quest. But it may be demanded, What course is to be taken for guidance of our lives in particular actions, wherein doubts may arise what is most agreeable to the will of God?

Ans. 1. We must not put all carelessly upon a providence, but first consider what is our part; and, so far as God prevents us with light, and affords us helps and means, we must not be failing in our duty. We should neither outrun nor be wanting to providence. But in perplexed cases, where the reasons on both sides seem to be equally balanced, see whether part make more for the main end, the glory of God, the service of others, and advancement of our own spiritual good. *Summa ratio quæ pro religione facit*. Some things are so clear and even, that there is not a best between them, but one may be done as well as the other, as when two ways equally tend to one and the same place.

2. We are not our own, and therefore must not set up ourselves. We must not consult with flesh and blood either in ourselves or others, for self-love will deprave all our actions, by setting before us corrupt ends. It considers not what is best, but what is safest. By-respects sway the balance the wrong way.

3. When things are clear, and God's will is manifest, further deliberation is dangerous, and for the most part argues a false heart; as we see in Balaam, who, though he knew God's mind, yet would be still consulting, till God in judgment gave him up to what his covetous heart led him unto, 2 Pet. ii. 15. A man is not fit to deliberate till his heart be purged of false aims; for else God will give him to the darkness of his own spirit, and he will be always warping, unfit for any bias. Where the aims are good, there God delighteth to reveal his good pleasure. Such a soul is level and suitable to any good counsel that shall be given, and prepared to entertain it. In what measure any lust is favoured, in that measure the soul is darkened. Even wise Solomon, whilst he gave way to his lust, had like to have lost his wisdom.

We must look to our place wherein God hath set us. If we be in subjection to others, their authority in doubtful things ought to sway with us. It is certain we ought to obey; and if the thing wherein we are to obey be uncertain unto us, we ought to leave that which is uncertain and stick to that which is certain; in this case we must obey those that are gods under God. Neither is it the calling of those that are subjects, to inquire over curiously into the mysteries of government; for that, both in peace and war, breeds much disturbance, and would trouble all designs (*g*).*

The laws under which we live are particular determinations of the law of God [in some duties of the second table. For example, the law of God

* See note '*g*' for the charge based on the subsequent alteration of this passage and context.

says, 'Exact no more than what is thy due,' Luke iii. 13. But what in particular is thy due, and what another man's, the laws of men determine],* and therefore ought to be a rule unto us so far as they reach; though it be too narrow a rule to be good only so far as man's law guides unto.† Yet law being the joint reason and consent of many men for public good, hath a use for guidance of all actions that fall under the same. Where it dashes not against God's law, what is agreeable to law is agreeable to conscience.

The law of God in the due enlargement of it, to the least beginning and occasions, is exceeding broad, and allows of whatsoever stands with the light of reason or the bonds of humanity, civility, &c., and whatsoever is against these is so far against God's law. So that higher rules be looked to in the first place, there is nothing lovely or praiseworthy among men but ought to be seriously thought on.

Nature of itself is wild and untamed, and impatient of the yoke; but as beasts that cannot endure the yoke at first, after they are inured awhile unto it bear it willingly, and carry their work more easily by it, so the yoke of obedience makes the life regular and quiet. The meeting of authority and obedience together, maintains the peace and order of the world.

So of that question.‡

5. Though blind enfolded§ obedience, such as our adversaries would have, be such as will never stand with sound peace of conscience, which always looks to have light to direct it; for else a blind conscience would breed blind fears; yet in such doubtful cases wherein we cannot wind out ourselves, we ought to light our candles at others whom we have cause to think, by their place and parts, should see further than we. In matters of outward estate, we will have men skilful of our counsel; and Christians would find more sound peace, if they would advise with their godly and learned pastors and friends. Where there is not a direct word, there is place for the counsel of a prudent man, *sententia boni viri*. And it is a happiness for them whose business is much, and parts not large, to have the benefit of those that can give aim, and see further than themselves. The meanest Christian understands his own way, and knows how to do things with better advantage to his soul than a graceless though learned man; yet is still glad of further discovery. In counsel there is peace, the thoughts being thus established, Prov. xx. 18.

When we have advised and served God's providence in the use of means, then if it fall out otherwise than we look for, we may confidently conclude that God would not have it so, otherwise to our grief we may say it was the fruit of our own rashness.

Where we have cause to think that we have used better means in the search of grounds, and are more free from partial affections than others, there we may use our own advice more safely. Otherwise what we do by consent from others, is more secure and less offensive, as being more countenanced.

In advice with others, it is not sufficient to be generally wise, but experienced and knowing in that we ask, which is an honour to God's gifts where we find them in any kind. When we set about things in passion,

* The words in brackets inserted first in B. See note *g*.—G.

† The following margin-note first added in B: 'Nimis angusta innocentia est ad legem bonum esse.'—G.

‡ Inserted first in C.

§ 'Blinde enfolded' in A, and therefore given in text; but 'blindfold' in B and C.—G.

we work not as men or Christians, but in a bestial manner. The more passion, the less discretion; because passion hinders the sight of what is to be done. It clouds the soul, and puts it on to action without advisement. Where passions are subdued, and the soul purged and cleared, there is nothing to hinder the impression of God's Spirit; the soul is fitted as a clean glass to receive light from above. And that is the reason why mortified men are fittest to advise with in the particular cases incident to a Christian life.

After all advice, extract what is fittest, and what our spirits do most bend unto; for in things that concern ourselves God affords a light to discern, out of what is spoken, what best suiteth us. And every man is to follow most what his own conscience, after information, dictates unto him; because conscience is God's deputy in us, and under God most to be regarded, and whosoever sins against it, in his own construction sins against God. God vouchsafeth every Christian in some degree the grace of spiritual prudence, whereby they are enabled to discern what is fittest to be done in things that fall within their compass.

It is good to observe the particular becks* of providence, how things join and meet together. Fit occasions and suiting of things are intimations of God's will. Providence hath a language which is well understood by those that have a familiar acquaintance with God's dealing; they see a train of providence leading one way more than to another.

Take especial heed of not grieving the Spirit when he offers to be our guide, by studying evasions, and wishing the case were otherwise. This is to be lawgivers to ourselves, thinking that we are wiser than God. The use of discretion is not to direct us about the end, whether we should do well or ill (for a single heart always aims at good), but when we resolve upon doing well, and yet doubt of the manner how to perform it. Discretion looks not so much to what is lawful, for that is taken for granted, but what is most expedient. A discreet man looks not to what is best, so much as what is fittest in such and such respects, by eyeing circumstances, which, if they sort not, do vary the nature of the thing itself.

And because it is not in man to know his own ways, we should look up unto Christ, the great Counsellor of his church, to vouchsafe the spirit of counsel and direction to us; that 'make our way plain before us,' by suggesting unto us, 'this is the way, walk in it,' Isa. xxx. 21. We owe God this respect, to depend upon him for direction in the particular passages of our lives, in regard that he is our Sovereign, and his will is the rule, and we are to be accountable to him as our judge. It is God only that can see through businesses, and all helps and lets that stand about.

After we have rolled ourselves upon God, we should immediately take that course he inclines our hearts unto, without further distracting fear. Otherwise it is a sign we 'commit not our way to him,' 1 Pet. iv. 19, when we do not quietly trust him, but remain still as thoughtful as if we did not trust him. After prayer and trust follows 'the peace of God,' Phil. ii. 4, and a heart void of further dividing care. We should therefore presently question our hearts, for questioning his care, and not regard what fear will be ready to suggest, for that is apt to raise conclusions against ourselves, out of self-conceited grounds, whereby we usurp upon God and wrong ourselves.

It was a good resolution of the three young men in Daniel, 'We are not careful to answer thee, O king,' Dan. iii. 16. We know our duty, let God do with us as he pleaseth. If Abraham had hearkened to the voice of nature,

* That is, signals, indications.—G.

he would never have resolved to sacrifice Isaac, but because he cast himself upon God's providing, God in the mount provided a ram instead of his son.

CHAPTER XVIII.—*Other grounds of trusting in God, namely, the Promises, and twelve directions about the same.*

§ I. But for the better settling of our trust in God, a further discovery is necessary than of the nature and providence of God; for though the nature of God be written in the book of the creatures in so great letters, as he that runs may read, and though the providence of God appears in the order and use of things, yet there is another book whereby to know the will of God towards us, and our duty towards him. We must therefore have a knowledge of the promises of God, as well as of his providence, for though God hath discovered himself most graciously in Christ unto us, yet had we not a word of promise, we could not have the boldness to build upon Christ himself. Therefore, from the same grounds, that there is a God, there must be a revealing of the will of God, for else we can never have any firm trust in him further than he offers himself to be trusted. Therefore hath God opened his heart to us in his word, and reached out so many sweet promises for us to lay hold on, and stooped so low, by gracious condescending mixed with authority, as to enter into a covenant with us to perform all things for our good; for promises are, as it were, the stay of the soul in an imperfect condition, and so is faith in them until all promises shall end in performance, and faith in sight, and hope in possession.

Now these promises are, 1, for their spring from whence they proceed, free engagements of God, for if he had not bound himself, who could? and 2, they are for their value precious; and 3, for their extent large, even of all things that conduce to happiness; and 4, for their virtue quickening and strengthening the soul, as coming from the love of God, and conveying that love unto us by his Spirit in the best fruits thereof; and 5, for their certainty, they are as sure as the love of God in Christ is, upon which they are founded, and from which 'nothing can separate us,' Rom. viii. 39. For all promises are either Christ himself, the promised seed, or else they are of good things made to us in him and for him, and accomplished for his sake. They are all made first to him as heir of the promise, as Angel of the Covenant, as head of his body, and as our elder brother, &c. For promises being the fruits of God's love, and God's love being founded first on Christ, it must needs follow that all the promises are both made, and made good to us in and through him, who is 'yesterday, and to-day, and for ever the same,' Heb. xiii. 8.

That we should not call God's love into question, he not only gives us, (1) his word, but a binding word, his promise; and not only (2) a naked promise, but hath (3) entered into a covenant with us, founded upon full satisfaction by the blood of Christ, and unto this covenant sealed by the blood of the Lord Jesus, he hath (4) added the seals of sacraments, and unto this he hath added (5) his oath, that there might be no place left of doubting to the distrustful heart of man. There is no way of securing promises amongst men, but God hath taken the same to himself, and all to this end that we might not only know his mind towards us, but be fully persuaded of it, that as verily as he lives, he will make good whatever he hath promised for the comfort of his children. What greater assurance can there be than for being itself to lay his being in pawn? and for life itself to lay life to pawn, and all to comfort a poor soul?

The boundless and restless desire of man's spirit will never be stayed without some discovery of the chief good, and the way to attain the same. Men would have been in darkness about their final condition and the way to please God, and to pacify and purge their consciences, had not the word of God set down the spring and cause of all evil, together with the cure of it, and directed us how to have communion with God, and to raise ourselves above all the evil which we meet withal betwixt us and happiness, and to make us every way 'wise to salvation,' 2 Tim. iii. 15. Hence it is that the Psalmist prefers the manifestation of God by his word before the manifestation of him in his most glorious works, Ps. xix. 7.

And thus we see the necessity of a double principle for faith to rely on: 1, God; and 2, the Word of God revealing his will unto us, and directing us to make use of all his attributes, relations, and providence for our good; and this word hath its strength from him who gives a being and an accomplishment unto it; for words are as the authority of him that uttereth them is. When we look upon a grant in the word of a king, it stays our minds, because we know he is able to make it good; and why should it not satisfy our souls to look upon promises in the word of God? whose words, as they come from his truth and express his goodness, so they are all made good by his power and wisdom.

By the bare word of God it is that the heavens continue, and the earth, without any other foundation, hangs in the midst of the world; therefore well may the soul stay itself on that, even when it hath nothing else in sight to rely upon. By his word it is that the covenant of day and night, and the preservation of the world from any further overflowing of waters, 2 Peter iii. 7, continueth, which, if it should fail, yet his covenant with his people shall abide firm for ever, though the whole frame of nature were dissolved.

When we have thus gotten a fit foundation for the soul to lay itself upon, our next care must be, by trusting, to build on the same. All our misery is either in having a false foundation, or else in loose building upon a true. Therefore, having so strong a ground as God's nature, his providence, his promise, &c., to build upon, the only way for establishing our souls is, by trust, to rely firmly on him.

Now the reason why trust is so much required, is because, 1, it emptieth the soul; and 2, by emptying enlargeth it; and 3, seasoneth and fitteth the soul to join with so gracious an object; and 4, filleth it by carrying it out of itself unto God, who presently, so soon as he is trusted in, conveys himself and his goodness to the soul; and thus we come to have the comfort, and God the glory of all his excellencies. Thus salvation comes to be sure unto us, whilst faith, looking to the promises, and to God freely offering grace therein, resigns up itself to God, making no further question from any unworthiness of its own.

And thus we return to God by cleaving to him, from whom we fell by distrust, living under a new covenant merely of grace, Jer. xxxi. 3, and no grace fitter than that which gives all to Christ. Considering the fountain of all our good is, out of ourselves, in him, it being safest for us, who were so ill husbands at the first, that it should be so, therefore it is fit we should have use of such a grace that will carry us out of ourselves to the spring head.

The way, then, whereby faith quieteth the soul, is by raising it above all discontentments and storms here below, and pitching it upon God, thereby uniting it to him, whence it draws virtue to oppose and bring under whatsoever troubles its peace. For the soul is made for God, and never finds rest till it returns to him again (*h*). When God and the soul meet, there will follow contentment. God simply considered, is not all our happiness, but God as trusted in; and Christ as we are made one with him. The soul cannot so much as 'touch the hem of Christ's garment,' but it shall find 'virtue coming from him,' Mat. ix. 20, to sanctify and settle it. God in Christ is full of all that is good. When the soul is emptied, enlarged, and opened by faith to receive goodness offered, there must needs follow sweet satisfaction.

§ II. 1. For the better strengthening of our trust, it is not sufficient that we trust in God and his truth revealed, *but we must do it by light and strength from him.* Many believe in the truth by human arguments, but no arguments will convince the soul but such as are fetched from the inward nature, and powerful work of truth itself. No man can know God, but by God; none can know the sun, but by its own light; none can know the truth of God, so as to build upon it, but by the truth itself and the Spirit revealing it by its own light to the soul. That soul which hath felt the power of truth in casting it down, and raising it up again, will easily be brought to rest upon it. It is neither education, nor the authority of others that profess the same truth, or that we have been so taught by men of great parts, &c., will settle the heart, until we find an inward power and authority in the truth itself shining in our hearts by its own beams. Hence comes unsettledness in time of troubles, because we have not a spiritual discerning of spiritual things. Supernatural truths must have a supernatural power to apprehend them, therefore God createth a spiritual eye and hand of the soul, which is faith. In those that are truly converted, all saving truths are transcribed out of the Scripture into their hearts, 'they are taught of God,' Isa. liv. 13, so as they find all truths, both concerning the sinful estate and the gracious and happy estate of man in themselves. They carry a divinity in them and about them, so as from a saving feeling they can speak of conversion, of sin, of grace, and the comforts of the Spirit, &c., and from this acquaintance are ready to yield and give up themselves to truth revealed, and to God speaking by it.

2. Trust is never sound but upon a spiritual conviction of the truth and goodness we rely upon, for the effecting of which the Spirit of God must likewise *subdue the rebellion and malice of our will,* that so it may be suitable and level to divine things, and relish them as they are. We must apprehend the love of God, and the fruits of it, as better than life itself, and then choosing and cleaving to the same will soon follow; for as there is a fitness in divine truths to all the necessities of the soul, so the soul must be fitted by them to savour and apply them to itself; and then from an harmony between the soul and that which it applies itself unto there will follow, not only peace in the soul, but joy and delight surpassing any contentment in the world besides.

3. As there is in God to satisfy the whole soul, so trust *carries the whole soul to God.* This makes trust not so easy a matter, because there must be an exercise of every faculty of the soul, or else our trust is imperfect and lame. There must be a knowledge of him whom we trust, and why we trust, an affiance and love, &c. Only they that know God will trust in him; not that knowledge alone is sufficient, but because the sweetness of

God's love is let into the soul thereby, which draweth the whole soul to him. We are bidden to trust perfectly in God; therefore, seeing we have a God so full of perfection to trust in, we should labour to trust perfectly in him.

4. And it is good for the exercise of trust to *put cases to ourselves of things that probably may fall out*, and then return to our souls to search what strength we have if such things should come to pass. Thus David puts cases. Perfect faith dares put the hardest cases to its soul, and then set God against all that may befall it, Ps. iii. 6; xlvi. 3; xxvii. 3.

5. Again, *labour to fit the promise to every condition thou art in*. There is no condition but hath a promise suitable, therefore no condition but wherein God may be trusted, because his truth and goodness are always the same. And in the promise, look both to the good promised and to the faithfulness and love of the promiser. It is not good to look upon the difficulty of the thing we have a promise against, but who promiseth it, and for whose sake, and so see all good things in Christ made over to us.

6. We should labour likewise *for a single heart to trust in God only*. There is no readier way to fall than to trust equally to two stays, whereof one is rotten, and the other sound; therefore as in point of doctrine we are to rely upon Christ only, and to make the Scriptures our rule only; so in life and conversation, whatever we make use of, yet we should enjoy and rely upon God only; for either God is trusted alone or not at all. Those that trust to others things with God, trust not him but upon pretence to carry their double minds with less check.

7. Again, labour that thy soul may *answer all the relations wherein it stands to God*, by cleaving to him, (1) as a Father, by trusting on his care; (2) as a Teacher, by following his direction; (3) as a Creator, by dependence on him; (4) as a Husband, by inseparable affection of love to him; (5) as a Lord, by obedience, &c. And then we may with comfort expect whatsoever good these relations can yield; all which, God, regarding more our wants and weaknesses than his own greatness, hath taken upon him.

8. Shall these relations *yield comfort from the creature, and not from God himself*, in whom they are in their highest perfection? shall God make other fathers and husbands faithful, and not be faithful himself? All our comfort depends upon labouring to make these relations good to our souls.

And as we must wholly and only trust in God, so likewise we must trust him in all conditions and times, for all things that we stand in need of, until that time comes, wherein we shall stand in need of nothing: for as the same care of God moved him to save us, and to preserve us in the world till we be put in possession of salvation; so the same faith relies upon God for heaven and all necessary provision till we come thither. It is the office of faith to quiet our souls in all the necessities of this life, and we have continual use of trusting while we are here; for even when we have things, yet God still keeps the blessing of them in his own hands, to hold us in a continual dependence upon him. God trains us up this way, by exercising our trust in lesser matters, to fit us for greater. Thus it pleaseth God to keep us in a depending condition until he see his own time; but so good is God that as he intends to give us what we wait for, so will he give us the grace and spirit of faith, to sustain our souls in waiting till we enjoy the same. The unruliness of a natural spirit is never discovered more, than when God defers; therefore we should labour the more not to withdraw our attendance from God.

9. Further, we must know that the condition of a Christian in this life,

is not to see what he trusts God for; 'he lives by faith, and not by sight,' 2 Cor. v. 7; and yet there is such a virtue in faith, which makes evident and present, things to come and unseen; because God, where he gives an eye of faith, gives also a glass of the word to see things in, and by seeing of them in the truth and power of him that promiseth, they become present, not only to the nnderstanding to apprehend them, but to the will to rest upon them, and to the affections to joy in them. It is the nature of faith to work, when it seeth nothing, and oftentimes best of all then, because God shews himself more clearly in his power, wisdom, and goodness, at such times; and so his glory shines most, and faith hath nothing else to look upon then, whereupon it gathers all the forces of the soul together, to fasten upon God.

It should therefore be the chief care of a Christian to strengthen his faith, that so it may answer God's manner of dealing with him in the worst times; for God usually (1, that he might perfectly mortify our confidence in the creature; and 2, that he might the more endear his favours and make them fresh and new unto us; and 3, that the glory of deliverance may be entirely his, without the creatures sharing with him; and 4, that our faith and obedience may be tried to the uttermost, and discovered) suffers his children to fall into great extremities before he will reach forth his hand to help them, as in Job's case, &c. Therefore Christians should much labour their hearts to trust in God in the deepest extremities that may befall them, even when no light of comfort appears either from within or without, yea then especially, when all other comforts fail, Isa. iv. 10. Despair is oft the ground of hope. When the darkness of the night is thickest, then the morning begins to dawn. That which, to a man unacquainted with God's dealings, is a ground of utter despair, the same, to a man acquainted with the ways of God, is a rise of exceeding comfort; for infinite power and goodness can never be at a loss, neither can faith which looks to that, ever be at a stand; whence it is that both God and faith work best alone. In a hopeless estate a Christian will see some door of hope opened, 1, because God shews himself nearest to us, when we stand most in need of him; 'Help, Lord, for vain is the help of man,' Ps. lx. 11. God is never more seen than in the mount. He knows our souls best, and our souls know him best, in adversity. Ps. xxxi. 7; then he is most wonderful in his saints. 2. Because our prayers then are strong cries, fervent and frequent. God is sure to hear of us at such a time, which pleaseth him well, as delighting to hear the voice of his beloved.

10. For our better encouragement in these sad times, and to help our trust in God the more, *we should often call to mind the former experiences, which either ourselves or others have had of God's goodness, and make use of the same for our spiritual good.* 'Our fathers trusted in thee,' saith the head of the church, 'and were not confounded,' Ps. xxii. 14. God's truth and goodness is unchangeable, 'he never leaves those that trust in him,' Ps. ix. 10. So likewise in our own experiences, we should take notice of God's dealings with us in sundry kinds; how many ways he hath refreshed us, and how good we have found him in our worst times. After we have once tried him and his truth, we may safely trust him. God will stand upon his credit, he never failed any yet, and he will not begin to break with us. If his nature and his word and his former dealing hath been sure and square, why should our hearts be wavering? 'Thy word,' saith the Psalmist, 'is very pure (or tried), therefore thy servant loveth it,' Ps. cxix. 140; the word of God is 'as silver tried in the furnace, purified seven times,'

Ps. xii. 6. It is good therefore to observe and lay up God's dealings. Experience is nothing else but a multiplied remembrance of former blessings, which will help to multiply our faith. Tried truth and tried faith unto it, sweetly agree and answer one another. It were a course much tending to the quickening of the faith of Christians, if they would communicate one to another their mutual experiences. This hath formerly been the custom of God's people, 'Come and hear, all ye that fear God, and I will declare what he hath done for my soul,' Ps. lxvi. 16; and David urgeth this as a reason to God for deliverance, that then 'the righteous would compass him about,' Ps. cxlii. 7, as rejoicing in the experience of God's goodness to him. The want of this makes us upon any new trial, to call God's care and love into question, as if he had never formerly been good unto us; whereas every experiment of God's love should refresh our faith upon any fresh onset. God is so good to his children even in this world, that he trains them up by daily renewed experiences of his fatherly care; for besides those many promises of good things to come, he gives us some evidence and taste of what we believe here; that by that which we feel we might be strengthened in that we look for, that so in both (1, sense of what we feel; and 2, certainty of what we look for) we might have full support.

11. But yet we must trust God, *as he will be trusted*, namely, *in doing good*, or else we do not trust him but tempt him. Our commanding of our souls to trust in God, is but an echo of what God commands us first; and therefore in the same manner he commands us, we should command ourselves. As God commands us to trust him in doing good, so should we 'commit our souls to him in well doing,' 1 Pet. iv. 19, and trust him when we are about his own works, and not in the works of darkness. We may safely expect God in his ways of mercy, when we are in his ways of obedience; for religion, as it is a doctrine of what is to be believed, so it is a doctrine according to godliness; and the mysteries of faith are mysteries of godliness, because they cannot be believed but they will enforce a godly conversation. Where any true impression of them is, there is holiness always bred in that soul; therefore a study of holiness must go jointly together with a study of trusting in God. Faith looks not only to promises, but to directions to duty, and breeds in the soul a liking of whatsoever pleaseth God. There is a mutual strengthening in things that are good; trusting stirs to duty, and duty strengthens trusting by increasing our liberty and boldness with God.

12. Again, we must maintain in our souls, *a high esteem of the grace of faith*, the very trial whereof is 'more precious than gold,' 1 Pet. i. 7. What then is the grace of faith itself, and the promises which it layeth hold on? Certainly they transcend in worth whatever may draw us from God; whence it is that the soul sets a high price upon them, and on faith that believes them. It is impossible that anything in the world should come betwixt the heart and those things, if once we truly lay hold on them, to undermine faith or the comfort we have by it. The heart is never drawn to any sinful vanity, or frighted with any terror of trouble, till faith first loseth the sight and estimation of divine things, and forgets the necessity and excellency of them. Our Saviour Christ, when he would stir up a desire of faith in his disciples, Luke xvii. 6, shewed them the power and excellency of the same. Great things stir up faith, and keep it above, and faith keeps the soul that nothing else can take place of abode in it. When the 'great things of God,' Hos. viii. 12, are brought into the heart by faith, what is there in the whole world that can out-bid them? assurance of these

things, upon spiritual grounds, overrules both sense and reason, or what ever else prevails with carnal hearts.

Chapter XIX.—*Faith to be prized, and other things undervalued, at least not to be trusted to as the chief.*

That faith may take the better place in the soul, and the soul in God, the heart must continually be taught of what little worth all things else are, as reputation, riches, and pleasures, &c.; and to see their nothingness in the word of God, and in experience of ourselves and others, that so our heart being weaned from these things, may open itself to God, and embrace things of a higher nature. Otherwise baser things will be nearer the soul than faith, and keep possession against it, so that faith will not be suffered to set up a throne in the heart. There must be an unloosing of the heart, as well as a fastening of it, and God helps us in both; for, besides the word discovering the vanity of all things else out of God, the main scope of God's dealing with his children in any danger or affliction whatsoever, is to embitter all other things but himself unto them. Indeed it is the power of God properly which makes the heart to trust, but yet the Spirit of God useth this way to bring all things else out of request with us in comparison of those inestimable good things, which the soul is created, redeemed, and sanctified for. God is very jealous of our trust, and can endure no idol of jealousy to be set up in our hearts. Therefore it behoves us to take notice, not only of the deceitfulness of things, but of the deceitfulness of our hearts in the use of them. Our hearts naturally hang loose from God, and are soon ready to join with the creature. Now the more we observe our hearts in this, the more we take them off, and labour to set them where they should be placed; for the more we know these things, the less we shall trust them.

Obj. But may we not trust in riches, and friends, and other outward helps at all?

Ans. Yes, so far as they are subordinate to God, our chief stay, with reservation and submission to the Lord; only so far, and so long as it shall please him to use them for our good. Because God ordinarily conveys his help and goodness to us by some creature, we must trust in God to bless every mercy we enjoy, and to make all helps serviceable to his love towards us. In a word, we must trust and use them in and under God, and so as if all were taken away, yet to think God, being all-sufficient, can do without them, whatsoever he doth by them, for our good. Faith preserves the chastity of the soul, and cleaving to God is a spiritual debt which it oweth to him, whereas cleaving to the creature is spiritual adultery.

It is an error in the foundation to substitute false objects in religion, or in Christian conversation; for, 1, in religion; trusting in false objects, as saints, and works, &c., breeds false worship, and false worship breeds idolatry, and so God's jealousy and hatred. 2. In Christian conversation; false objects of trust breed false comforts and true fears; for in what measure we trust in anything that is uncertain, in the same measure will our grief be when it fails us. The more men rely upon deceitful crutches, the greater is their fall. God can neither endure false objects, nor a double object, as hath been shewed, for a man to rely upon anything equally in the same rank with himself. For the propounding of a double object, argues a double heart, and a double heart is always unsettled, James i. 8;

for it will regard God no longer than it can enjoy that which it joins together with him. Therefore it is said, 'You cannot serve two masters,' Luke xvi. 13, not subordinate one to another; whence it was that our Saviour told those worldly men which followed him, 'that they could not believe in him, because they sought honour one of another,' John v. 44; and in case of competition, if their honour and reputation should come into question, they would be sure to be false to Christ, and rather part with him than their own credit and esteem in the world.

David here, by charging his soul to trust in God, saw there was nothing else that could bring true rest and quiet unto him; for whatsoever is besides God is but a creature; and whatever is in the creature is but borrowed and at God's disposing, and changeable, or else it were not a creature. David saw his error soon, for the ground of his disquiet was trusting something else besides God; therefore when he began to say, 'My hill is strong, I shall not be moved,' &c., Ps. xxx. 6, then presently his soul was troubled. Out of God there is nothing fit for the soul to stay itself upon; for,

1. Outward things are not fitted to the spiritual nature of the soul. They are dead things and cannot touch it, being a lively spirit, unless by way of taint.

2. They are beneath the worth of the soul, and therefore debase the soul, and draw it lower than itself; as a noble woman, by matching with a mean person, much injures herself, especially when higher matches are offered. Earthly things are not given for stays wholly to rest on, but for comforts in our way to heaven. They are no more fit for the soul, than that which hath many angles is fit to fill up that which is round, which it cannot do, because of the unevenness and void places that will remain. Outward things are never so well fitted for the soul, but that the soul will presently see some voidness and emptiness in them, and in itself in cleaving to them; for that which shall be a fit object for the soul, must be, 1, for the nature of it spiritual, as the soul itself is; 2, constant; 3, full and satisfying; 4, of equal continuance with it; and 5, always yielding fresh contents. We cast away flowers, after once we have had the sweetness of them, because there is not still a fresh supply of sweetness. Whatever comfort is in the creature, the soul will spend quickly, and look still for more; whereas the comfort we have in God is 'undefiled and fadeth not away,' 1 Peter i. 4. How can we trust to that for comfort, which by very trusting proves uncomfortable to us? Outward things are only so far forth good, as we do not trust in them. Thorns may be touched, but not rested on, for then they will pierce. We must not set our hearts upon things which are never evil to us, but when we 'set our hearts upon them,' Ps. lxii. 10.

By trusting anything but God, we make it, 1, an idol; 2, a curse, and not a blessing, Jer. xvii. 5; 3; it will prove a lying vanity, not yielding that good which we look for; and 4, a vexation, bringing that evil upon us we look not for.

Of all men Solomon was the fittest to judge of this, because, 1, he had a large heart, able to comprehend the variety of things; and 2, being a mighty king, had advantages of procuring all outward things that might give him satisfaction; and 3, he had a desire answerable, to search out and extract whatever good the creature could yield. And yet, upon the trial of all, he passeth this verdict upon all, that they are but 'vanity,' Eccles. i. 2. Whilst he laboured to find that which he sought for in them, he had like to have lost himself; and seeking too much to strengthen himself by foreign combination, he weakened himself the more thereby, until he came to know where the 'whole of man consists,' Eccles. xii. 13. So that now we need not try further conclusions after the peremptory sentence of so wise a man.

But our nature is still apt to think there is some secret good in the forbidden fruit, and to buy wisdom dearly when we might have it at a cheaper rate, even from former universal experience.

It is a matter both to be wondered at and pitied, that the soul having God in Christ set before it, alluring it unto him, that he might raise it, enlarge it, and fill it, and so make it above all other things, should yet debase and make itself narrower and weaker by leaning to things meaner than itself.

The kingdom, sovereignty, and large command of man continueth while he rests upon God, in whom he reigns, in some sort, over all things under him; but so soon as he removes from God to anything else, he becomes weak, and narrow, and slavish presently; for,

The soul is as that which it relies upon. If on vanity, itself becomes vain; for that which contents the soul must satisfy all the wants and desires of it, which no particular thing can do, and the soul is more sensible of a little thing that it wants than of all other things which it enjoys.

But see the insufficiency of all other things, out of God, to support the soul in their several degrees. 1. First, all outward things can make a man no happier than outward things can do; they cannot reach beyond their proper sphere; but our greatest grievances are spiritual. 2. And as for inward things, whether gifts or graces, they cannot be a sufficient stay for the mind; for (1), Gifts, as policy and wisdom, &c., they are, at the best, very defective, especially when we trust in them, for wisdom makes men often to rebel, and thereupon God delighteth to blast their projects, Isa. xlvii. 10. None miscarry oftener than men of the greatest parts, as none are oftener drowned than those that are most skilful in swimming, because it makes them confident.

And for grace, though it be the beginning of a new creature in us, yet it is but a creature, and therefore not to be trusted in; nay, by trusting in it we imbase it, and make it more imperfect. So far as there is truth of grace, it breeds distrust of ourselves, and carries the soul out of itself to the fountain of strength.

3. And for any works that proceed from grace, by trusting thereunto they prove like the reed of Egypt, which not only deceives us, but hurts us with the splinters. Good works are good, but confidence in them is hurtful; and there is more of our own in them, for the most part, to humble us, than of God's Spirit to embolden us so far as to trust in them. Alas! they have nothing from us but weakness and defilement, and therefore since the fall God would have the object of our trust to be out of ourselves in him, and to that purpose he useth all means to take us out of ourselves and from the creature, that he only might be our trust.

4. Yea, we must not trust itself, but God whom it relies on, who is therefore called our trust. All the glorious things that are spoken of trust are only made good by God in Christ, who, as trusted, doth all for us.

God hath prescribed trust as the way to carry our souls to himself, in whom we should only rely, and not in our imperfect trust, which hath its ebbing and flowing. Neither will trust in God himself for the present suffice us for future strength and grace, as if trusting in God to-day would suffice to strengthen us for to-morrow; but we must renew our trust for fresh supply upon every fresh occasion. So that we see God alone must be the object of our trust.

There is still left in man's nature a desire of pleasure, profit, and of whatever the creature presents as good, but the desire of gracious good is altogether lost, the soul being wholly infected with a contrary taste. Man hath a nature capable of excellency and desirous of it, and the Spirit of God in and by the word reveals where true excellency is to be had; but corrupt nature leaving God seeketh it elsewhere, and so crosseth its own desires, till the Spirit of God discovers where these things are to be had, and so nature is brought to its right frame again by turning the stream into the right current. Grace and sinful nature have the same general object of comfort, only sinful nature seeks it in broken cisterns, and grace in the fountain, Jer. ii. 13. The beginning of our true happiness is from the discovery of true and false objects, so as the soul may clearly see what is best and safest, and then stedfastly rely upon it.

It were an happy way to make the soul better acquainted with trusting in God, to labour to subdue at the first all unruly inclinations of the soul to earthly things, and to take advantage of the first tenderness of the soul to weed out that which is ill, and to plant knowledge and love of the best things in it; otherwise, where affections to anything below get much strength in the soul, it will by little and little be so overgrown that there will be no place left in it either for object or act, God or trust. God cannot come to take his place in the heart by trust, but where the powers of the soul are brought under, to regard him and those great things he brings with him above all things else in the world besides.

In these glorious times wherein so great a light shineth, whereby so great things are discovered, what a shame is it to be so narrow-hearted as to fix upon present things. Our aims and affections should be suitable to the things themselves set before us. Our hearts should be more and more enlarged, as things are more and more revealed to us. We see in the things of this life, as wisdom and experience increaseth, so our aims and desires increase likewise. A young beginner thinks it a great matter if he have a little to begin withal, but as he grows in trading, and seeth further ways of getting, his thoughts and desires are raised higher. Children think as children, but riper age puts away childishness, 1 Cor. xiii. 11, when their understandings are enlarged to see what they did not see before. We should never rest till our hearts, according to the measure of revelation of those excellent things which God hath for us, have answerable apprehension of the same. Oh, if we had but faith to answer those glorious truths which God hath revealed, what manner of lives should we lead!

Chapter XX.—*Of the method of trusting in God; and the trial of that trust.*

13. Lastly, to add no more, our trusting in God *should follow God's order in promising*. The first promise is of forgiveness of sin to repentant believers; next, 2, of healing and sanctifying grace; then, 3, the inheritance of the kingdom of heaven to them that are sanctified; 4, and then the promises of all things needful in our way to the kingdom, &c. Now answerably, the soul being enlightened to see its danger, should look first to God's mercy in Christ pardoning sin, because sin only divides betwixt God and the soul; next to the promises of grace for the leading of a Christian life, for true

faith desires healing mercy as well as pardoning mercy, and then to heaven and all things that may bring us thither.

By all this we see that it is not so easy a matter as the world takes it, to bring God and the soul together by trusting on him. It must be effected by the mighty power of God, raising up the soul to himself, to lay hold upon the glorious power, goodness, and other excellencies that are in him, Eph. i. 20. God is not only the object, but the working cause of our trust; for such is our proneness to live by sense and natural reason, and such is the strangeness and height of divine things, such our inclination to a self-sufficiency and contentment in the creature, and so hard a matter is it to take off the soul from false bottoms, by reason of our unacquaintance with God and his ways; besides, such guilt still remains upon our souls for our rebellion and unkindness towards God, that it makes us afraid to entertain serious thoughts of him; and so great is the distance betwixt his infinite majesty, before whom the very angels do cover their faces, and us, by reason of the unspiritualness of our nature, being opposite to his most absolute purity, that we cannot be brought to any familiarity with the Lord, so as to come into his holy presence with confidence to rely upon him, or any comfort to have communion with him, till our hearts be sanctified and lifted up by divine vigour infused into them.

Though there be some inclination, by reason of the remainder of the image of God in us, to an outward moral obedience of the law, yet, alas, we have not only no seeds of evangelical truths and of faith to believe them, but an utter contrariety in our natures, as corrupted, either to this, or any other good. When our conscience is once awaked, we meditate nothing but fears and terrors, and dare not so much as think of an angry God, but rather how we may escape and fly from him. Therefore, together with a deep consideration of the grounds we have of trusting God, it is necessary we should think of the indisposition of our hearts unto it, especially when there is greatest need thereof, that so our hearts may be forced to put up that petition of the disciples to God, 'Lord, increase our faith,' Luke xvii. 5; Lord, help us against our unbelieving hearts, &c. By prayer and holy thoughts stirred up in the use of the means, we shall feel divine strength infused and conveyed into our souls to trust.

The more care we ought to have to maintain our trust in God, because, besides the hardness of it, it is a radical and fundamental grace; it is, as it were, the mother-root and great vein whence the exercise of all graces have their beginning and strength. The decay of a plant, though it appears first from the withering of the twigs and branches, yet it arises chiefly from a decay in the root; so the decay of grace may appear to the view, first in our company, carriage, and speeches, &c.; but the primitive and original ground of the same is weakness of faith in the heart; therefore, it should be our wisdom, especially, to look to the feeding of the root. We must, 1, Look that our principles and foundation be good; and, 2, Build strongly upon them; and, 3, Repair our building every day as continual breaches shall be made upon us, either by corruptions and temptations from within or without; and we shall find that the main breaches of our lives arise either from false principles or doubts, or mindlessness of those that are true. All sin is a turning of the soul from God to some other seeming good, but this proceeds from a former turning of the soul from God by distrust. As faith is the first return of the soul to God, so the first degree of departing from God is by infidelity, and from thence comes a departure by other sins, by which, as sin is of a winding nature, our unbelief more increaseth, and so the rent and breach betwixt our souls and God is made greater still, which is that Satan would have, till at length, by departing further and further from him, we come to have that peremptory sentence of everlasting departure pronounced against us; so that our departure from God now is a degree to separation for ever from him. Therefore, it is Satan's main care to come between God and the soul, that so unloosing us from God, we might more easily be drawn to other things; and if he draws us to other things, it is but only to unloose our hearts from God the more; for he well knows, whilst our souls cleave close to God, there is no prevailing against us by any created policy or power.

It was the cursed policy of Balaam to advise Balak to draw the people from God, by fornication, that so God might be drawn from them. The sin of their base affections crept into the very spirits of their mind, and drew them from God to idolatry. Bodily adultery makes way for spiritual. An unbelieving heart is an ill heart, and a treacherous heart, because it makes us to 'depart from God, the living God,' &c., Heb. iii. 12. Therefore we should especially take heed of it as we love our lives, yea, our best life, which ariseth from the union of our souls with God.

None so opposed as a Christian, and in a Christian nothing so opposed as his faith, because it opposeth whatsoever opposes God, both within and without us. It captivates and brings under whatsoever rises up against God in the heart, and sets itself against whatsoever makes head against the soul.

And because mistake is very dangerous, and we are prone to conceive that to trust in God is an easy matter, therefore it is needful that we should have a right conceit of this trust, what it is, and how it may be discerned, lest we trust to an untrusty trust, and to an unsteady stay.

We may by what hath been said before, partly discern the nature of it, to be nothing else but an exercise of faith, whereby looking to God in Christ through the promises, we take off our souls from all other supports, and lay them upon God for deliverance and upholding in all ill, present or future, felt or feared, and the obtaining of all good, which God sees expedient for us.

1. Now that we may discern the truth of our trust in God the better, we must know, that true trust is willing to be tried and searched, and can say to God as David, 'Now, Lord, what wait I for, my hope is in thee,' Ps. xxxix. 7; and as it is willing to come to trial, so it is able to endure trial, and to hold out in opposition, as appears in David. If faith hath a promise, it will rely and rest upon it, say flesh and blood what it can to the contrary. True faith is as large as the promise, and will take God's part against whatsoever opposes it.

2. And as faith singles not out one part of divine truth to believe and rejects another, so it relies upon God for every good thing, one as well as another; the ground whereof is this, the same love of God that intends us heaven, intends us a supply of all necessaries that may bring us thither.

A child that believes his father will make him heir, doubts not but he will provide him food and nourishment, and give him breeding suitable to his future condition. *Fides non eligit objectum.* It is a vain pretence to believe that God will give us heaven, and yet leave us to shift for ourselves in the way.

3. Where trust is rightly planted, it gives boldness to the soul in going to God; for (1) it is grounded upon the discovery of God's love first to us, and seeth a warrant from him for whatsoever it trusts him for. Though the things themselves be never so great, yet they are no greater than God is willing to bestow. Again, (2) trust is bold because it is grounded upon

the worthiness of a mediator, who hath made way to God's favour for us, and appears now in heaven to maintain it towards us.

4. Yet this boldness is with humility, which carries the soul out of itself; and that boldness which the soul by trust hath with God, is from God himself. It hath nothing to allege from itself but its own emptiness and God's fulness, its own sinfulness and God's mercy, its own humble obedience and God's command; hence it is that the true believer's heart is not lifted up, nor swells with self-confidence; as trust comes in, that goes out. Trust is never planted, and grows but in an humble and low soul. Trust is a holy motion of the soul to God, and motion arises from want. Those, and those only, seek out abroad that want succour at home. *Motus ex indigentia.* Plants move not from place to place, because they find nourishment where they stand; but living creatures seek abroad for their food, and for that end have a power of moving from place to place. And this is the reason why trust is expressed by *going to God.*

5. Hereupon trust is a dependent grace, answerable to our dependent condition. It looks upon all things it hath or desires to have as coming from God and his free grace and power. It desireth not only wisdom, but to be wise in his wisdom, to see in his light, to be strong in his strength. The thing itself contents not this grace of trust, but God's blessing and love in the thing. It cares not for anything further than it can have it with God's favour and good liking.

6. Hence it is that trust is an obsequious * and an observing grace, stirring up the soul to a desire of pleasing God in all things, and to a fear of displeasing him. He that pretends to trust the Lord in a course of offending may trust to this, that God will meet him in another way than he looks for. He that is a tenant at courtesy will not offend his lord. Hence it is that the apostle enforceth that exhortation to work out our salvation with fear and trembling, Phil. ii. 12, 13, because it is God that worketh the will and the deed, and according to his good pleasure, not ours. Therefore faith is an effectual working grace; it works in heaven with God, it works within us, commanding all the powers of the soul; it works without us, conquering whatsoever is in the world on the right hand to draw us from God, or on the left hand to discourage us; it works against hell and the powers of darkness; and all by virtue of trusting, as it draweth strength from God. It stirs up all other graces, and keeps them in exercise, and thereupon the acts of other graces are attributed to faith, as Heb. xi. It breeds a holy jealousy over ourselves, lest we give God just cause to stop the influence of his grace towards us, so to let us see that we stand not by our own strength. Those that take liberty in things they either know or doubt will displease God, shew they want the fear of God; and this want of fear shews their want of dependency, and therefore want of trust. Dependency is always very respective; † it studieth contentment and care to comply. This was it made 'Enoch walk with God, and study how to please him,' Heb. xi. 5. When we know nothing can do us good or hurt but God, it draws our chief care to approve ourselves to him. Obedience of faith and obedience of life will go together; and therefore he that commits his soul to God to save, will commit his soul to God to sanctify and guide in a way of well pleasing, 1 Peter iv. 19. Not only the tame, but most savage creatures, will be at the beck of those that feed them, though they are ready to fall violently upon others. Disobedience, therefore, is against the principles of nature.

* That is, complying, yielding.—G.

† That is, 'respectful.'—Ed.

7. This dependency is either in the use of means, or else when means fail us. True dependency is exactly careful of all means. When God hath set down a course of means, we must not expect that God should alter his ordinary course of providence for us; deserved disappointment is the fruit of this presumptuous confidence. The more we depend on a wise physician, the more we shall observe his directions, and be careful to use what he prescribes; yet we must use the means as means, and not set them in God's room, for that is the way to blast our hopes. The way to have anything taken away and not blest, is to set our heart too much upon it. Too much grief in parting with anything, shews too much trust in the enjoying of it; and therefore he that uses the means in faith, will always join prayer unto God, from whom, as every good thing comes, so likewise doth the blessing and success thereof. Where much endeavour is and little seeking to God, it shews there is little trust. The widow that trusted in God, continued likewise 'in prayers day and night,' 1 Tim. v. 5.

The best discovery of our not relying too much on means is, when all means fail, if we can still rely upon God, as being still where he was, and hath ways of his own for helping of us, either immediately from himself, or by setting awork other means, and those perhaps very unlikely, such as we think not of. God hath ways of his own. Abraham never honoured God more than when he trusted in God for a son against the course of nature; and when he had a son, was ready to sacrifice him, upon confidence that God would raise him from the dead again, Gen. ii. 2. This was the ground upon which Daniel, with such great authority, reproved Belshazzar, that he had not a care to glorify God, in whose hands 'his breath was, and all his ways,' Dan. v. 23. The greatest honour we can do unto God, is when we see nothing, but rather all contrary to that we look for, then to shut our eyes to inferior things below, and look altogether upon his all-sufficiency. God can convey himself more comfortably to us when he pleaseth, without means than by means. True trust, as it sets God highest in the soul, so in danger and wants it hath present recourse to him, as the conies to the rocks, Prov. xxx. 26.

8. And because God's times and seasons are the best, it is an evidence of true trust when we can wait God's leisure and not make haste, and so run before God; for else the more haste the worse speed. God seldom makes any promise to his children but he exerciseth their trust in waiting long before, as David for a kingdom, Abraham for a son, the whole world for Christ's coming, &c.

9. One main evidence of true trust in God is here in the text; we see here it hath a quieting and stilling virtue, for it stays the soul upon the fulness of God's love, joined with his ability to supply our wants and relieve our necessities, though faith doth not, at the first especially, so stay the soul as to take away all suspicious fears of the contrary. There be so many things in trouble that press upon the soul, as hinder the joining of God and it together, yet the prevailing of our unbelief is taken away, the reign of it is broken. If the touch of Christ in his abasement on earth drew virtue from him, Mark v. 30, certain it is that faith cannot touch Christ in heaven but it will draw a quieting and sanctified virtue from him, which will in some measure stop the issues of an unquiet spirit. The needle in the compass will stand north, though with some trembling.

A ship that lies at anchor may be something tossed, but yet it still remains so fastened, that it cannot be carried away by wind or weather. The soul, after it hath cast anchor upon God, may, as we see here in David, be disquieted awhile, but this unsettling tends to a deeper settling. The more we believe, the more we are established. Faith is an establishing grace, by faith we stand, and stand fast, and are able to withstand whatsoever opposeth us. For what can stand against God, upon whose truth and power faith relies? The devil fears not us, but him whom we fly unto for succour; it is the ground we stand on secures us, not ourselves.

As it is our happiness, so it must be our endeavour, to bring the soul close to God, that nothing get between, for then the soul hath no sure footing. When we step from God, Satan steps in by some temptation or other presently. It requires a great deal of self-denial to bring a soul either swelling with carnal confidence, or sinking by fear and distrust, to lie level upon God and cleave fast to him. Square will lie fast upon square, but our hearts are so full of unevenness, that God hath much ado to square our hearts fit for him, notwithstanding the soul hath no rest without this.

The use of trust is best known in the worst times, for naturally in sickness we trust to the physician, in want to our wit and shifts, in danger to policy and the arm of flesh, in plenty to our present supply, &c.; but, when we have nothing in view, then indeed should God be God unto us. In times of distress, when he shews himself in the ways of his mercy and goodness, then we should especially magnify his name, which will move him to discover his excellencies the more, the more we take notice of them. And, therefore, David strengthens himself in these words, that he hoped for better times, wherein God would shew himself more gracious to him, because he resolved *to praise him*.

This trusting joints the soul again, and sets it in its own true resting-place, and sets God in his own place in the soul, that is, the highest; and the creature in its place, which is to be under God, as in its own nature, so in our hearts. This is to ascribe 'honour due unto God,' Ps. xxix. 2; the only way to bring peace into the soul. Thus, if we can bring our hope and trust to the God of hope and trust, we shall stand impregnable in all assaults, as will best appear in these particulars.

CHAPTER XXI.—*Of quieting the spirit in troubles for sin; and objections answered.*

To begin with troubles of the spirit, which indeed are the spirit of troubles, as disabling that which should uphold a man in all his troubles. A spirit set in tune and assisted by a higher spirit, will stand out against ordinary assaults, but when God, the God of the spirits of all flesh, shall seem contrary to our spirits, whence then shall we find relief?

Here all is spiritual, God a Spirit, the soul a spirit, the terrors spiritual, the devil, who joins with these, a spirit, yea that which the soul fears for the time to come, is spiritual, and not only spiritual, but eternal, unless it pleaseth God at length to break out of the thick cloud wherewith he covers himself, and shine upon the soul, as in his own time he will.

In this state,* comforts themselves are uncomfortable to the soul. It quarrels with everything. The better things it hears of, the more it is vexed. Oh! what is this to me, what have I to do with these comforts? the more happiness may be had, the more is my grief. As for comforts from God's inferior blessings, as friends, children, estate, &c., the soul is ready to misconstrue God's end in all, as not intending any good to him thereby.

In this condition God doth not appear in his own shape to the soul, but

* 'Estate,' in C.

in the shape of an enemy; and, when God seems against us, who shall stand for us? Our blessed Saviour in his agony had the angels to comfort him; but had he been a mere man, and not assisted by the Godhead, it was not the comfort, no not of angels that could have upheld him, in the sense of his Father's withdrawing his countenance from him. Alas! then, what will become of us in such a case, if we be not supported by a spirit of power and the power of an almighty Spirit?

If all the temptations of the whole world and hell itself were mustered together, they were nothing to this, whereby the great God sets himself contrary to his poor creature.* None can conceive so, but those that have felt it. If the hiding of his face will so trouble the soul, what will his frown and angry look do? Needs must the soul be in a woeful plight, whenas God seems not only to be absent from it, but an enemy to it. When a man sees no comfort from above, and looks inward and sees less; when he looks about him, and sees nothing but evidences of God's displeasure; beneath him, and sees nothing but desperation; clouds without, and clouds within, nothing but clouds in his condition here, he had need of faith to break through all, and see sun through the thickest cloud.

Upon this, the distressed soul is in danger to be set upon by a temptation, called the temptation of blasphemy, *tentatio blasphemiarum*, that is, to entertain bitter thoughts against God, and especially against the grace and goodness of God, wherein he desires to make himself most known to his creature. In those that have wilfully resisted divine truths made known unto them, and, after taste, despised them, a persuasion that God hath forsaken them, set on strongly by Satan, hath a worse effect. It stirs up a hellish hatred against God, carrying them to a revengeful desire of opposing whatsoever is God's, though not always openly, for then they should lose the advantage of doing hurt, yet secretly and subtilly, and under pretence of the contrary. To this degree of blasphemy God's children never fall, yet they may feel the venom of corruption stirring in their hearts, against God and his ways which he takes with them; and this adds greatly to the depth of their affliction, when afterward they think with themselves what hellish stuff they carry in their souls. This is not so much discerned in the temptation, but after the fit is somewhat remitted.

In this kind of desertion, seconded with this kind of temptation, the way is to call home the soul, and to check it, and charge it to trust in God, even though he shews himself an enemy; for it is but a show, he doth but put on a mask, with a purpose to reveal himself the more graciously afterward. His manner is to work by contraries. In this condition God lets in some few beams of light, whereby the soul casts a longing look upon God, even when he seems to forsake it. It will, with Jonah in the belly of hell, look back to the holy temple of God, Jonah ii. 4, it will steal a look unto Christ. Nothing more comfortable in this condition, than to fly to him, that by experience knew what this kind of forsaking meant, for this very end that he might be the fitter to succour us in the like distress, Heb. iv. 15, 16.

Learn, therefore, to appeal from God to God, oppose his gracious nature, his sweet promises to such as 'are in darkness, and see no light,' Isa. l. 10, inviting them to trust in him, though there appear to the eye of sense and reason nothing but darkness. Here make use of that sweet relation of God in Christ becoming a Father to us. 'Doubtless thou art our Father,' Isa.

* Nihil est tentatio vel universi mundi et totius inferni in unum constata, ad eam qua Deus contrarius homini ponitur.—*Luther.*

lxiii. 16. Flesh would make a doubt of it, and thou seemest to hide thy face from us, yet *doubtless* thou art our Father, and hast in former time shewed thyself to be so; we will not leave thee till we have a blessing from thee, till we have a kinder look from thee. This wrestling will prevail at length, and we shall have such a sight of him, as shall be an encouragement for the time to come, when 'we shall be able to comfort others, with those comforts whereby we have been refreshed ourselves,' 2 Cor. i. 4. With the saint's case remember the saint's course, which is to trust in God. So Christ the Head of the church commits himself to that God, whose favour for the present he felt not; so Job resolves upon trust, though God should kill him, Job xiii. 15.

Obj. But these holy persons were not troubled with the guilt of any particular sin, but I feel the just displeasure of God kindled against me for many and great offences.

Ans. True it is, that sin is not so sweet in the committing, as it is heavy and bitter in the reckoning. When Adam had once offended God, paradise itself was not paradise to him. The presence of God, which was most comfortable before, was now his greatest terror, had not God, out of his free, infinite, and preventing mercy, come betwixt him and hell, by the promise of the blessed seed. This seed was made sin to satisfy for sin; sin passive in himself to satisfy for sin active in us, 1 Cor. v. 21.

When God once charges sin upon the soul, alas! who shall take it off? when the great God shall frown, the smiles of the creature cannot refresh us. Sin makes us afraid of that which should be our greatest comfort; it puts a sting into every other evil. Upon the seizing of any evil, either of body, soul, or condition, the guilty soul is embittered and enraged; for from that which it feels, it fore-speaks to itself worse to come, it interprets all that befalls as the messengers of an angry God, sent in displeasure to take revenge upon it. This weakeneth the courage, wasteth the spirits, and blasteth the beauty even of God's dearest ones, Ps. xxxix. 11. There is not the stoutest man breathing, but if God sets his conscience against him it will pull him down, and lay him flat, and fill him with such inward terrors, as he shall be more afraid of himself, than of all the world beside. This were a doleful case, if God had not provided in Christ a remedy for this great evil of evils, and if the Holy Spirit were not above the conscience, able as well to pacify it by the sense of God's love in Christ, as to convince it of sin, and the just desert thereby.

Obj. But my sins are not the sins of an ordinary man, my spots are not as the spots of the rest of God's children.

Conceive of God's mercy as no ordinary mercy, and Christ's obedience as no ordinary obedience. There is something in the very greatness of sin, that may encourage us to go to God, for the greater our sins are, the greater the glory of his powerful mercy pardoning, and his powerful grace in healing will appear. The great God delights to shew his greatness in the greatest things. Even men glory, when they are put upon that, which may set forth their worth in any kind. God 'delighteth in mercy,' Mic. vii. 18. It pleaseth him, nothing so well, as being his chief name, which then we take in vain, when we are not moved by it to come unto him.

That which Satan would use as an argument to drive us from God, we should use as a strong plea with him. Lord, the greater my sins are, the greater will be the glory of thy pardoning mercy. David, after his heinous sins, cries not for mercy, but for 'abundance of mercy;' 'according to the multitude of thy mercies, do away mine offences,' Ps. li. 1. His mercy is not only above his own works, but above ours too. If we could sin more than he could pardon, then we might have some reason to despair. Despair is a high point of atheism, it takes away God and Christ both at once. Judas, in betraying our Saviour, was an occasion of his death as man, but in despairing he did what lay in him to take away his life as God.

When, therefore, conscience, joining with Satan, sets out the sin in its colours, labour thou by faith to set out God in his colours, infinite in mercy and lovingkindess. Here lies the art of a Christian; it is divine rhetoric thus to persuade and set down the soul. Thy sins are great, but Adam's was greater, who being so newly advanced above all the creatures, and taken into so near an acquaintance with God, and having ability to persist in that condition if he would, yet willingly overthrew himself and all his whole posterity, by yielding to a temptation, which though high, as being promised to be like unto God, yet such as he should and might have resisted. No sin we can commit, can be a sin of so tainting and spreading a nature; yet, as he fell by distrust, so he was recovered by trusting, and so must we by relying on a second Adam, whose obedience and righteousness from thence reigns, Rom. v. 17, to the taking away not only of that one sin of Adam, and ours in him, but of all, and not only to the pardon of all sin, but to a right of everlasting life. The Lord thinks himself disparaged, when we have no higher thoughts of his mercy than of our sins, when we bring God down to our model, whenas 'the heavens are not so much higher than the earth, than his thoughts of love and goodness are above the thoughts of our unworthiness,' Isa. lv. 9. It is a kind of taking away the Almighty to limit his boundless mercy in Christ, within the narrow scantling* of our apprehension; yet infidelity doth this, which should stir up in us a loathing of it above all other sins. But this is Satan's fetch,† when once he hath brought us into sins against the law, then to bring us into sins of a higher nature, and deeper danger, even against the blessed gospel, that so there may be no remedy, but that mercy itself might condemn us.

Al lthe aggravations that conscience, and Satan helping it, are able to raise sin unto, cannot rise to that degree of infiniteness, that God's mercy in Christ is of. If there be a spring of sin in us, there is a spring of mercy in him, and a fountain open daily to wash ourselves in, Zech. xiii. 1. If we sin oft, let us do as St Paul, who prayed oft 'against the prick of the flesh,' 2 Cor. xii. 7, 8. If it be a devil of long continuance, yet fasting and prayer will drive him out at length, Mat. xvii. 21.

Nothing keeps the soul more down than sins of long continuance, because corruption of nature hath gotten such strength in them, as nature is added to nature, and custom doth so determine and sway the soul one way, that men think it impossible to recover themselves. They see one link of sin draw on another, all making a chain to fasten them to destruction. They think of necessity they must be damned, because custom hath bred a necessity of sinning in them, and conceive of the promise of mercy, as only made to such as turn from their sinful courses, in which they see themselves so hardened that they cannot repent.

Certain it is, the condition is most lamentable, that yielding unto sin brings men unto. Men are careful to prevent dangerous sicknesses of body, and the danger of law concerning their estates; but seldom consider into what a miserable plight their sins, which they so willingly give themselves up unto, will bring them. If they do not perish in their sins, yet their yielding will bring them into such a doleful condition, that they would give

* That is, 'small portion.'—G. † That is, 'artifice.'—G.

the whole world, if they were possessors of it, to have their spirits at freedom from this bondage and fear.

To such as bless themselves in an ill way upon hope of mercy, we dare not speak a word of comfort, because God doth not, but threatens his wrath shall burn to hell against them. Yet because while life continues there may be, as a space, so a place and grace for repentance, these must be dealt withal in such a manner, as they may be stayed and stopped in their dangerous courses; there must be a stop before a turn.

And when their consciences are thoroughly awaked with sense of their danger, let them seriously consider whither sin, and Satan by sin, is carrying of them, and lay to heart the justice of God, standing before them as an angel with a drawn sword, ready to fall upon them if they post on still.

Yet to keep them from utter sinking, let them consider withal, the unlimited mercy of God, as not limited to any person, or any sin, so not to any time. There is no prescription of time can bind God. His mercy hath no certain date that will expire, so as those that fly unto it shall have no benefit. Invincible mercy will never be conquered, and endless goodness never admits of bounds or end.*

What kind of people were those that followed Christ? Were they not such as had lived long in their sinful courses? He did not only raise them that were newly dead, but Lazarus, that had lien 'four days in the grave,' John xi. 39. They thought Christ's power in raising the dead had reached to a short time only, but he would let them know that he could as well raise those that had been long as lately dead. If Christ be the physician, it is no matter of how long continuance the disease be. He is good at all kind of diseases, and will not endure the reproach of disability to cure any. Some diseases are the reproaches of other physicians, as being above their skill to help, but no conceit more dangerous when we are to deal with Christ.

'The blessed martyr Bilney was much offended when he heard an eloquent preacher inveighing against sin, saying thus, Behold, thou hast lien rotten in thy own lusts, by the space of sixty years, even as a beast in his own dung, and wilt thou presume in one year to go forward towards heaven, and that in thine old age, as much as thou wentest backward from heaven to hell in sixty years?' 'Is not this a goodly argument?' saith Bilney. 'Is this preaching of repentance in the name of Jesus? It is as if Christ had died in vain for such a man, and that he must make satisfaction for himself. If I had heard, saith he, such preaching of repentance in times past, I had utterly despaired of mercy.' We must never think the door of hope to be shut against us, if we have a purpose to turn unto God. As there is nothing more injurious to Christ, so nothing more foolish and groundless than to distrust, it being the chief scope of God in his word to draw our trust to him in Christ, in whom is always open a breast of mercy for humbled sinners to fly unto.

But thus far the consideration of our long time spent in the devil's service should prevail with us, as to take more shame to ourselves, so to resolve more strongly for God and his ways, and to account it more than sufficient that we have spent already so much precious time to so ill purposes; and the less time we have, to make the more haste to work for God, and bring all the honour we can to religion in so little a space. Oh, how doth it grieve those that have felt the gracious power of Christ in converting their souls, that ever they should spend the strength of their parts in the work of his and their enemy! and might they live longer, it is their

* Bonitas invicti non vincitur, et infinita misericordia non finitur.—*Fulgent*[*ius*].

full purpose for ever to renounce their former ways. There is bred in them an eternal desire of pleasing God, as in the wicked there is an eternal desire of offending him, which eternity of desires God looks to in both of them, and rewards them accordingly, though he cuts off the thread of their lives.

But God in wisdom will have the conversions of such as have gone on in a course of sinning, especially after light revealed, to be rare and difficult. Births in those that are ancienter, are with greater danger than in the younger sort. *Cavendum est vulnus quod dolore curatur.* God will take a course, that his grace shall not be turned into wantonness. He oft holds such upon the rack of a troubled conscience, that they and others may fear to buy the pleasure of sin at such a rate. Indeed, where sin abounds, there grace superabounds; but then it is where sin, that abounded in the life, abounds in the conscience in grief and detestation of it, as the greatest evil. Christ groaned at the raising of Lazarus, which he did not at others, because that although to an almighty power all things are alike easy, yet he will shew that there be degrees of difficulties in the things themselves, and make it appear to us that it is so. Therefore, those that have enjoyed long the sweet of sin, may expect the bitterest sorrow and repentance for sin.

Yet never give place to thoughts of despair, as coming from him that would overturn the end of the gospel, which lays open the riches of God's mercy in Christ; which riches none set out more than those that have been 'the greatest of sinners,' 1 Tim. i. 15, as we see in Paul. We cannot exalt God more than by taking notice, and making use of that great design of infinite wisdom in reconciling justice and mercy together, so as now he is not only merciful, but 'just in pardoning sins,' Rom. iii. 26. Our Saviour, as he came towards the latter age of the world, when all things seemed desperate; so he comes to some men in the latter part of their days. The mercy shewed to Zaccheus and the good thief was personal, but the comfort intended by Christ was public, therefore still trust in God.

In this case, we must go to God, with whom all things are possible, to put forth his almighty power, not only in the pardoning, but in subduing our iniquities. He that can make a camel go through a needle's eye, can make a high conceited man lowly, a rich man humble. Therefore, never question his power, much less his willingness, when he is not only ready to receive us when we return, but persuades and entreats us to come in unto him, yea, after backsliding and false dealing with him, wherein he allows no mercy to be shewed by man, yet he will take liberty to shew mercy himself, Jer. iii. 2.

Obj. But I have often relapsed and fallen into the same sin again and again.

Ans. If Christ will have us pardon our brother seventy-seven times,* can we think that he will enjoin us more than he will be ready to do himself, when in case of shewing mercy he would have us think his thoughts to be far above ours? Adam lost all by once sinning, but we are under a better covenant, a covenant of mercy, and are encouraged by the Son to go to the Father every day for the sins of that day.

Where the work of grace is begun, sin loses strength by every new fall; for hence issues deeper humility, stronger hatred, fresh indignation against ourselves, more experience of the deceitfulness of our hearts, renewed resolutions until sin be brought under. That should not drive us from God, which God would have us make use of to fly the rather to him. Since there is a throne of grace set up in Jesus Christ, we may boldly make use of it, and let us be ashamed to sin, and not be ashamed to glorify God's mercy in

* Qu. 'seventy times seven times?'—Ed.

begging pardon for sin. Nothing will make us more ashamed to sin than thoughts of so free and large mercy. It will grieve an ingenuous spirit to offend so good a God. Ah, that there should be such a heart in me as to tire the patience of God, and dam up his goodness as much as in me lies! But this is our comfort, that the plea of mercy from a broken spirit to a gracious Father will ever hold good. When we are at the lowest in this world, yet there are these three grounds of comfort still remaining:—1. That we are not yet in the place of the damned, whose estate is unalterable. 2. That whilst we live, there is time and space for recovering of ourselves. 3. That there is grace offered, if we will not shut our hearts against it.

Obj. Oh, but every one hath his time; my good hour may be past.

Ans. That is counsel to thee; it is not past if thou canst raise up thy heart to God, and embrace his goodness. Shew by thy yielding unto mercy, that thy time of mercy is not yet out, rather than by concluding uncomfortably, willingly betray thyself to thy greatest enemy, enforcing that upon thyself, which God labours to draw thee from. As in the sin against the Holy Ghost, fear shews that we have not committed it; so in this, a tender heart fearing lest our time be past, shews plainly that it is not past.

Look upon examples; when the prodigal in his forlorn condition was going to his father, his father stayed not for him, but 'meets him' in the way, Luke xv. 20; he did not only go, but ran to meet him. God is more willing to entertain us than we are to cast ourselves upon him; as there is 'a fountain opened for sin, and for uncleanness,' Zech. xiii. 1, so it is a living fountain of living water, that runs for ever, and can never be drawn dry.

Caution. Here remember, that I build not a shelter for the presumptuous, but only open a harbour for the truly humbled soul to put himself into.

CHAPTER XXII.—*Of sorrow for sin, and hatred for sin, when right and sufficient. Helps thereto.*

Obj. Ah! there's my misery; If I could be humbled for sin, I might hope for mercy, but I never yet knew what a broken heart meant; this soul of mine was never as yet sensible of the grief and smart of sin. How then can I expect any comfort?

Ans. 1. *It is one of Satan's policies to hold us in a dead and barren condition, by following us with conceits, that we have not sorrowed in proportion to our offences.* True it is, we should labour that our sorrow might in some measure answer to the heinousness of our sins; but we must know sorrow is not required for itself in that degree as faith is. If we could trust in God without much sorrow for our sins, then it would not be required, for God delights not in our sorrow as sorrow. God in mercy both requires it and works it, as thereby making us capable vessels of mercy, fit to acknowledge, value, and walk worthy of Christ. He requires it as it is a means to embitter sin, and the delightful pleasures thereof unto us, and by that means bring us to a right judgment of ourselves, and the creature, with which sin commits spiritual adultery, that so we may recover our taste before lost. And then when with the prodigal we return unto ourselves, having lost ourselves before, we are fit to judge of the baseness of sin, and of the worth of mercy; and so upon grounds of right reason, be willing to alter our condition, and embrace mercy upon any terms it shall please Christ to enjoin.

Ans. 2. Secondly, if we could grieve and cast down ourselves beneath the earth, as low as the nethermost pit, *yet this would be no satisfaction to God for sin;* of itself, it is rather an entrance, and beginning of hell.

Ans. 3. Thirdly, we must search what is *the cause of this want of grief which we complain of*, whether it be not a secret cleaving to the creature, and too much contentment in it, which oft stealeth away the heart from God, and brings in such contentment as is subject to fail and deceive us; whereupon from discontentment we grieve, which grief, being carnal, hinders grief of a better kind.

Usually the causes of our want of grief for sin are these:—*First,* a want of serious consideration, and dwelling long enough upon the cause of grief, which springs either from an unsettledness of nature, or distractions from things without. Moveable dispositions are not long affected with anything. One main use of crosses is to take the soul from that it is dangerously set upon, and to fix our running spirits. For though grief for crosses hinders spiritual grief, yet worldly delights hinder more. That grief is less distant from true grief, and therefore nearer to be turned into it.

And *secondly*, put case we could call off our minds from other things, and set them on grief for our sins, yet it is only God's Spirit that can work our hearts to this grief; and for this end, perhaps, God holds us off from it, to teach us that he is the teacher of the heart to grieve. And thereupon it is our duty to wait till he reveal ourselves so far to ourselves, as to stir up this affection in us.

Thirdly, Another cause may be a kind of *doubleness of heart*, whereby we would bring two things together that cannot suit. We would grieve for sin so far as we think it an evidence of a good condition; but then because it is an irksome task, and because it cannot be wrought without severing our heart from those sweet delights it is set upon; hence we are loath God should take that course to work grief, which crosseth our disposition. The soul must therefore, by self-denial, be brought to such a degree of sincerity and simplicity as to be willing to give God leave to work this 'sorrow, not to be sorrowed for,' 2 Cor. vii. 10, by what way he himself pleaseth. But here we must remember again that this self-denial is not of ourselves, but of God, who only can take us out of ourselves, and if our hearts were brought to a stooping herein to his work, it would stop many a cross, and continue many a blessing which God is forced to take from us, that he may work that grief in us which he seeth would not otherwise be kindly wrought.

Ans. 4. God giveth some *larger spirits*, and so their sorrows become larger. Some upon quickness of apprehension, and the ready passages betwixt the brain and the heart, are quickly moved. Where the apprehension is deeper, and the passages slower, there sorrow is long in working, and long in removing. The deepest waters have the stillest motion. Iron takes fire more slowly than stubble, but then it holds it longer.

Ans. 5. Again, *God that searcheth and knows our hearts* better than ourselves, *knows when and in what measure it is fit for to grieve.* He sees it is fitter for some dispositions to go on in a constant grief. We must give that honour to the wisdom of the great physician of souls to know best how to mingle and minister his potions. And we must not be so unkind to take it ill at God's hands when he, out of gentleness and forbearance, ministers not to us that churlish physic he doth to others, but cheerfully embrace any potion that he thinks fit to give us.

Some holy men have desired to see their sin in the most ugly colours, and God hath heard them in their requests. But yet his hand was so heavy upon them that they went always mourning to their very graves, and thought it fitter to leave it to God's wisdom to mingle the potion of sorrow than to be their own choosers.* For a conclusion, then, of this point, if we grieve that we cannot grieve, and so far as it is sin, make it our grief; then put it amongst the rest of our sins, which we beg pardon of, and help against, and let it not hinder us from going to Christ, but drive us to him. For herein lies the danger of this temptation, that those who complain in this kind think it should be presumption to go to Christ, whenas he especially calleth the 'weary and heavy laden sinner to come unto him,' Mat. xi. 28, and therefore such as are sensible that they are not sensible enough of their sin must know, though want of feeling be quite opposite to the life of grace, yet sensibleness of the want of feeling shews some degree of the life of grace. The safest way in this case is from that life and light that God hath wrought in our souls, to see and feel this want of feeling, to cast ourselves and this our indisposition upon the pardoning and healing mercy of God in Christ.

Caution. We speak only of those that are so far displeased with themselves for their ill temper, as they do not favour themselves in it, but are willing to yield to God's way in redressing it, and do not cross the Spirit, moving them thus with David to check themselves, and to trust in God. Otherwise, an unfeeling and careless state of spirit will breed a secret shame of going to God, for removing of that we are not hearty in labouring against, so far as our conscience tells us we are enabled.

The most constant state the soul can be in, in regard of sin, is, upon judgment, to condemn it upon right grounds, and to resolve against it. Whereupon repentance is called an after wisdom and change of the mind.† And this disposition is in God's children at all times. And for affections, love of that which is good, and hatred of that which is evil, these likewise have a settled continuance in the soul. But grief and sorrow rise and fall as fresh occasions are offered, and are more lively stirred up upon some lively representation to the soul of some hurt we receive by sin, and wrong we do to God in it. The reason hereof is, because till the soul be separated from the body, these affections have more communion with the body, and therefore they carry more outward expressions than dislike or abomination in the mind doth. We are to judge of ourselves more by that which is constant than by that which is ebbing and flowing.

Quest. But what is the reason that the affections do not always follow the judgment, and the choice or refusal of the will?

Ans. 1. Our soul being a finite substance, is carried with strength but one way at one time.

2. Sometimes God calls us to joy as well as to grieve, and then no wonder if grief be somewhat to seek.

3. Sometimes when God calleth to grief, and the judgment and will goeth along with God, yet the heart is not always ready, because, it may be, it hath run out so far that it cannot presently be called in again.

4. Or the spirits, which are the instruments of the soul, may be so wasted

* Here in margin is placed a name, thus, 'Mr Leaver.' Probably the reference is to the excellent but despondent Thomas Leaver, chaplain to Edward VI., and subsepuently one of the refugees at Frankfort. See Fuller's 'Worthies' (i. 547, ed. 1811. 2 vols. 4to); and Bale, de Scrip. Brit. (Cent. ix. 86). There were various eminent Nonconformists of the same name, descendents of Thomas Leaver, contemporary with Sibbes. See Nonconf. Memorial by Palmer (ii. 358; iii. 58, 78, ed. 3 vols. 8vo, 1802).—G.

† 'Change of the mind= μετάνοια.—G.

that they cannot hold out to feed a strong grief; in which case the conscience must rest in settled judgment and hatred of ill, which is the surest and never failing character of a good soul.

5. Ofttimes God in mercy takes us off from grief and sorrow, by refreshing occasions, because sorrow and grief are affections very much afflicting both of body and soul.

Quest. When is godly sorrow in that degree wherein the soul may stay itself from uncomfortable thoughts about its condition?

Ans. 1. When we find strength against that sin which formerly we fell into, and ability to walk in a contrary way; for this answers God's end in grief, one of which is a prevention from falling for the time to come. For God hath that affection in him which he puts into parents, which is by smart to prevent their children's boldness of offending for the time to come.

Ans. 2. When that which is wanting in grief is made up in fear. Here there is no great cause of complaint of the want of grief, for this holy affection is the awe-band of the soul, whereby it is kept from starting from God and his ways.

Ans. 3. When after grief we find inward peace; for true grief being God's work in us, he knows best how to measure it. Therefore, whatsoever frame God brings my soul into, I am to rest in his goodness, and not except against his dealing. That peace and joy which riseth from grief in the use of means, and makes the soul more humble and thankful to God, and less censorious and more pitiful to others, is no illusion nor false light.

Ans. 4. The main end of grief and sorrow is to make us value the grace and mercy of God in Christ, above all the contentments which sin feeds on. Which, where it is found, we may know that grief for sin hath enough possessed the soul before. The sufficiency of things is to be judged by an answerableness to their use and ends. God makes sin bitter, that Christ may be sweet. That measure of grief and sorrow is sufficient which brings us and holds us to Christ.

Ans. 5. Hatred, being the strongest, deepest, and steadiest affection of the soul against that which is evil, grief for sin is then right, when it springs from hatred, and increaseth further hatred against it.

1. Now the soul may be known to hate sin when it seeks the utter abolishing of it; for hatred is an implacable and irreconcileable affection.

2. True hatred is carried against the whole kind of sin, without respect of any wrong done to us, but only out of a mere antipathy and contrariety of disposition to it, as the lamb hateth the whole kind of wolves, and man hateth the whole kind of serpents. A toad does us no harm, but yet we hate it.

3. That which is hateful to us, the nearer it is the more we shun and abhor it, as venomous serpents and hurtful creatures, because the nearness of the object affects us more deeply. Therefore, if our grief spring from true hatred of sin, it will make no new league with it, but grieve for all sin, especially for our own particular sins, as being contrary to the work of God's grace in us, then is grief an affection of the new creature, and every way of the right breed.

4. But for fuller satisfaction in this case, we must know there is sometimes grief for sin in us, when we think there is none. It wants but stirring up by some quickening word. The remembrance of God's favours and our unkindness, or the awaking of our consciences by some cross, will raise up this affection feelingly in us. As in the affection of love many think that they have no love to God at all; yet let God be dishonoured in

his name, truth, or children, and their love will soon stir, and appear in just anger.

In want of grief for sin, we must remember, first, that we must have this affection from God, before we can bring it unto God.

And, therefore, in the second place, our chief care should be not to harden our hearts against the motions of the Spirit stirring us to seasonable grief, for that may cause a judicial hardness from God. God oft inflicteth some spiritual judgment as a correction upon men, for not yielding to his Spirit at the first; they feel a hardness of heart growing upon them. This made the church complain, 'Why hast thou hardened our hearts from thy fear?' Isa. lxiii. 17. Which if Christians did well consider, they would more carefully entertain such impressions of sorrow, as the Spirit in the use of the means, and observation of God's dealing towards themselves or others, shall work in them, than they do. It is a saying of Austin, 'Let a man grieve for his sin, and joy for his grief.' Though we can neither love, nor grieve, nor joy of ourselves, as we should, yet our hearts tell us, we are often guilty of giving a check to the Spirit's stirring these affections in us, which is a main cause of the many sharp afflictions we endure in this life, though God's love in the main matter of salvation be most firm unto us.

Third, We must not think to have all this grief at first, and at once, for oftentimes it is deeper after a sight and feeling of God's love than it was before. God is a free agent, and knows every man's several mould, and the several services he is to use them in, and oft takes liberty afterwards to humble men more, when he hath enabled them better to bear it, than in their first entrance into religion. Grief before springs commonly from self-love and fear of danger. Let no man suspect his estate, because God spares him in the beginning. For Christians many times meet with greater trial after their conversion than ever they thought on. When men take little fines, they mean to take the greater rent. God will have his children, first or last, to feel what sin is; and how much they are beholden to him for Christ.

This grief doth not always arise from poring on sin, but by oft considering of the infinite goodness of God in Christ, and thereby reflecting on our own unworthiness, not only in regard of sin past, but likewise of the sin that hangeth upon us, and issues daily from us. The more holy a man is, the more he sees the holiness of God's nature, with whom he desires to have communion, the more he is grieved that there should be anything found in him displeasing to so pure a Majesty.

And as all our grief comes not at first, so God will not have it come all at once, but to be a stream always running, fed with a spring, yet within the banks, though sometimes deeper, sometimes shallower. Grief for sin is like a constant stream; grief for other things is like a torrent, or swelling waters, which are soon up, soon down; what it wants in greatness is made up in continuance.

Fourth, Again, if we watch not our nature, there will be a spice of popery, which is a natural religion, in this great desire of more grief; as, if we had that, then we had something to satisfy God withal, and so our minds will run too much upon works. This grief must not only be wrought by God revealing our sin, and his mercy unto us in Christ; but when it is wrought, we must altogether rest, in a sense of our own emptiness, upon the full satisfaction and worthiness of Christ our Saviour.

All this that hath been said tends not to the abating of our desire to have a tender and bleeding heart for sin; but that in the pursuit of this desire, we be not cast down so as to question our estates, if we feel not that measure of grief which we desire and endeavour after, or to refuse our portion of joy which God offers us in Christ, considering grief is no further good than it makes way for joy; which caused our Saviour to join them together: blessed are the mourners, for they shall be comforted.' Being thus disposed, we may commit our souls to God in peace, notwithstanding Satan's troubling of us in the hour of temptation.

Chapter XXIII.—*Other spiritual causes of the soul's trouble discovered and removed; and objections answered.*

Another thing that disquiets and casts down the soul very much is, that inward conflict betwixt grace and corruption. This makes us most work, and puts us to most disquietment. *Proximorum odia sunt acerbissima.* It is the trouble of troubles to have two inhabitants so near in one soul, and these to strive one against another, in every action, and at all times in every part and power in us: the one carrying us upward, higher and higher still, till we come to God; the other pulling us lower and lower, further from him. This cannot but breed a great disquiet, when a Christian shall be put on to that which he would not, and hindered from that which he would do, or troubled in the performance of it, Rom. vii. 21–23. The more light there is to discern, and life of grace to be sensible hereof, and the more love of Christ, and desire from love to be like to him, the more irksome will this be. No wonder then that the apostle cried out, 'O wretched man that I am,' &c., Rom. vii. 24.

Here is a special use of trust in the free mercy of God in justification, considering all is stained that comes from us. It is one main end of God's leaving us in this conflicting condition, that we may live and die by faith in the perfect righteousness of Christ, whereby we glorify God more than if we had perfect righteousness of our own. Hereby likewise we are driven to make use of all the promises of grace, and to trust in God for the performance of them, in strengthening his own party in us, and not only to trust in God for particular graces, but for his Spirit, which is the spring of all graces, which we have through and from Christ, who will help us in this fight until he hath made us like himself. We are under the government of grace; sin is deposed from the rule it had, and shall never recover the right it had again. It is left in us for matter of exercise, and ground of triumph.

Obj. Oh, say some, I shall never hold out, as good give over at first as at last; I find such strong inclination to sin in me, and such weakness to resist temptation, that I fear I shall but shame the cause; I shall one day perish, by the hand of Satan strengthening my corruption.

Ans. Why art thou thus troubled? 'Trust in God,' grace will be above nature; God above the devil, the spirit above the flesh. Be strong in the Lord, the battle is his, and the victory ours beforehand. If we fought in our own cause and strength, and with our weapons, it were something; but as we fight in the power of God, so are 'we kept by that mighty power through faith unto salvation,' 1 Pet. i. 5. It lies upon the faithfulness of Christ, to put us into that possession of glory which he hath purchased for us; therefore charge the soul to make use of the promises, and rely upon God for perfecting the good work that he hath begun in thee.

Corruptions be strong, but stronger is he that is in us than that corruption that is in us. When we are weak in our own sense, then are we strong in him who perfecteth strength in our weakness, felt and acknowledged. Our corruptions are God's enemies as well as ours, and, therefore, in trusting to him and fighting against them, we may be sure he will take our part against them.

Obj. But I have great impediments and many discouragements in my Christian course.

Ans. What if our impediments be mountains, faith is able to remove them. 'Who art thou, O mountain?' Zech. iv. 7, saith the prophet. What a world of impediments were there betwixt Egypt and the land of Canaan, betwixt the return out of Babylon and Jerusalem; yet faith removed all by looking to God's power and truth in his promise. The looking too much to the Anakims and giants, and too little to God's omnipotency, shut the Israelites out of Canaan, and put God to his oath that they should 'never enter into his rest,' Ps. xcv. 11; and it will exclude our souls from happiness at length, if, looking too much upon these Anakims within us and without us, we basely despair and give over the field, considering all our enemies are not only conquered for us by our Head, but shall be conquered in us, so that in strength of assistance we fight against them. God gave the Israelites' enemies into their hands, but yet they must fight it out; and what coward will not fight when he is sure of help and victory?

Obj. But I carry continually about me a corrupt heart; if that were once changed, I could have some comfort.

A new heart is God's creature, and he hath promised to create it in us, Ps. li. 10, Eph. ii. 10. A creating power can, not only bring something out of nothing, but contrary out of contrary. Where we are sure of God's truth, let us never question that power to which all things are possible. If our hearts were as ill as God is powerful and good, there were some ground of discouragement. In what measure we give up our hearts to God, in that measure we are sure to receive them better. That grace which enlargeth the heart to desire good is therefore given that God may increase it, being both a part and a pledge of further grace, Ezek. xxxvi. 25. There is a promise of pouring clean water upon us which faith must sue out. Christ hath taken upon him to purge his spouse, and make her fit for himself, Eph. v. 26, 27.

Obj. But I have many wants and defects to be supplied.

Ans. It pleaseth him that in Christ 'all fulness shall dwell,' Col. i. 19, from whose fulness grace sufficient is dispensed to us answerable to the measure of our faith, whereby we fetch it from the fountain. The more we trust, the more we have. When we look, therefore, to our own want, we should look withal to Christ's fulness and his nearness to us, and take advantage from our misery to rest upon his all-sufficiency whose fulness is ours, as himself is. Our fulness, with our life, is hid in Christ, and distilled into us in such measure as his wisdom thinketh fit and as sheweth him to be a free agent, and yet so as the blame for want of grace lieth upon us, seeing he is beforehand with us in his offers of grace; and our own consciences will tell us that our failings are more from cherishing of some lust than from unwillingness in him to supply us with grace.

Obj. But God is of pure eyes, and cannot endure such services as I perform.

Ans. Though God be of pure eyes, yet he looks upon us in 'Him who is blameless and without spot,' Heb. ix. 14, who, by virtue of his sweet-smelling sacrifice, appears for us in heaven, and mingles his odours with our services;

and in him will God be known to us by the name of a kind Father, not only in pardoning our defects, but accepting our endeavours. We offer our services to God, not in our own name, but in the name of our High Priest, who takes them from us, and presents them to his Father as stirred up by his Spirit and perfumed by his obedience. Jonah's prayer was mingled with a great deal of passion and imperfection, yet God could discern something of his own in it, and pity and pardon the rest.

CHAPTER XXIV.—*Of outward troubles disquieting the spirit, and comforts in them.*

As for the outward evils that we meet withal in this life, they are either such, 1, As deprive us of the comforts our nature is supported withal; or else, 2, They bring such misery upon our nature or condition that hinders our well-being in this world.

1. For the first, trust in God, and take out of his all-sufficiency whatsoever we want. Sure we are by his promise that we shall want nothing that is good. What he takes away one way, he can give another; what he takes away in one hand, he can give another; what he withholds one way, he can supply in a better.* Whatsoever comfort we have in goods, friends, health, or any other blessings, it is all conveyed by him, who still remains, though these be taken from us. And we have him bound in many promises for all that is needful for us. We may sue him upon his own bond. Can we think that he who will give us a kingdom, will fail us in necessary provision to bring us thither, who himself is our portion?

2. As for those miseries which our weak nature is subject to, they are all under Christ. They come and go at his command; they are his messengers, sent for our good, and called back again when they have done what they came for. Therefore, look not so much upon them as to Him for strength and comfort in them, mitigation of them, and grace to profit by them.

To strengthen our faith the more in God, he calleth himself a buckler for defence from ill, and an 'exceeding great reward,' Gen. xv. 1, for a supply of all good; a sun for the one, and a shield for the other. Trust him, then, with health, wealth, good name, all that thou hast. It is not in man to take away that from us which God will give us and keep for us. It is not in man's power to make others conceive what they please of us.

Among crosses this is that which disquieteth not the mind least, to be deceived in matter of trust, whenas if we had not trusted we had not been deceived. The very fear of being disappointed made David in his haste think 'all men were liars,' Ps. cxvi. 11. But as it is a sharp cross, so nothing will drive us nearer unto God, who never faileth his.

Friends often prove as the 'reed of Egypt, as a broken staff,' Ezek. xxix. 6, 'and as a deceitful brook,' Job vi. 15, that fails the weary passenger in summer time, when there is most need of refreshing; and it is the unhappiness of men, otherwise happy in the world, that during their prosperous condition, they know not who be their friends; for when their condition declines, it plainly appears, that many were friends of their estates, and not of their persons. But when men will know us least, God will know us most. He knows our souls in adversity, and knows them so as to support and comfort them, and that from the spring-head of comfort, whereby the sweetest comforts are fetched. What God conveyed before by friends, that he doth now instil immediately from himself. The immediate comforts are

* In Margin, 'Amaziah.'

the strongest comforts. Our Saviour Christ told his disciples, that they would 'leave him alone; yet, saith he, I am not alone, but the Father is with me,' John xvi. 32. At St Paul's first appealing 'all forsook him, but the Lord stood by him,' 2 Tim. iv. 16. He wants no company that hath Christ for his companion, *Solus non est cui Christus comes est.*—Cypr[ian.] 'I looked for some to take pity,' saith David, 'but there was none, Ps. lxix. 20. This unfaithfulness of man is a foil to set out God's truth, who is never nearer than when trouble is nearest. There is not so much as a shadow of change in him or his love.

It is just with God when we lay too much weight of confidence upon any creature, to let us have the greater fall. Man may fail us .and yet be a good man, but God cannot fail us and be God, because he is truth itself. Shall God be so true to us, and shall not we be true to him and his truth?

The like may be said in the departure of our friends. Our life is oft too much in the life of others, which God takes unkindly. How many friends have we in him alone! who rather than we shall want friends, can make our enemies our friends. A true believer is to Christ as his mother, brother, and sister, because he carries that affection to them, as if they were mother, brother, and sister, to him indeed, Mat. xii. 50. As Christ makes us all to him, so should we make him all in all to ourselves. If all comforts in the world were dead, we have them still in the living Lord.

Sicknesses are harbingers of death, and in the apprehension of many they be the greatest troubles, and tame great spirits, that nothing else could tame. Herein we are more to deal with God than with men, which is one comfort sickness yieldeth above other troubles. It is better to be troubled with the distempers of our own bodies, than with the distempers of other men's souls; in which we have not only to deal with men, but with the devil himself, that ruleth in the humours of men.

The example of Asa, 2 Chron. xvi. 12, teaches us in this case not to lay too much trust upon the physician, but with Hezekiah first look up to God, and then use the means, 2 Kings xix. 14, 15. If God will give us a *quietus est*, and take us off from business by sickness, then we have a time of serving God by patient subjection to his will. If he means to use our service any further, he will restore our health and strength to do that work he sets us about. Health is at his command, and sickness stays at his rebuke. In the mean, the time of sickness is a time of purging from that defilement we gathered in our health, till we come purer out; which should move us the rather willingly to abide God's time. Blessed is that sickness that proves the health of the soul. We are best, for the most part, when we are weakest, *Optimi sumus dum infirmi sumus.* Then it appears what good proficients we have been in time of health.

Carnal men are oft led along by false hopes suggested by others, and cherished by themselves, that they shall live still and do well till death comes and cuts off their vain confidence and their life both at once, before ever they are acquainted what it is to trust in God aright, in the use of means. We should labour to learn of St Paul in desperate cases, to receive the sentence of death, and not to trust in ourselves, but in God 'that raiseth the dead,' 2 Cor. i. 9. He that raiseth our dead bodies out of the grave, can raise our diseased bodies out of the bed of sickness, if he hath a pleasure to serve himself by us.

In all kind of troubles, it is not the ingredients that God puts into the cup so much afflicts us, as the ingredients of our distempered passions mingled with them. The sting and core of them all is sin. When that is not only pardoned, but in some measure healed, and the proud flesn eaten out, then a healthy soul will bear anything. After repentance, that trouble that before was a correction, becomes now a trial and exercise of grace. 'Strike, Lord,' saith Luther, 'I bear anything willingly, because my sins are forgiven.' We should not be cast down so much about outward troubles, as about sin, that both procures them and envenoms them. We see by experience, when conscience is once set at liberty, how cheerfully men will go under any burden; therefore labour to keep out sin, and then let come what will come.

It is the foolish wisdom of the world to prevent trouble by sin, which is the way indeed to pull the greatest trouble upon us. For sin dividing betwixt God and us, moveth him to leave the soul to entangle itself in its own ways. When the conscience is clear, then there is nothing between God and us to hinder our trust. Outward troubles rather drive us nearer unto God, and stand with his love. But sin defileth the soul, and sets it further from God. It is well-doing that enables us to commit our souls cheerfully unto him, 1 Pet. iii. 21. Whatsoever our outward condition be, 'if our hearts condemn us not, we may have boldness with God,' 1 John. iii. 21. In any trouble our care should be, not to avoid the trouble, but sinful miscarriage in and about the trouble, and so trust God. It is a heavy condition to be under the burden of trouble, and under the burden of a guilty conscience both at once. When men will 'walk in the light of their own fire, and the sparks which they have kindled themselves, it is just with God that they should lie down in sorrow,' Isa. l. 11.

Whatsoever injuries we suffer from those that are ill affected to us, let us commit our cause to the 'God of vengeance,' Isa. lix. 17, and not meddle with his prerogative. He will revenge our cause better than we can, and more perhaps than we desire. The wronged side is the safer side.* If, instead of meditating revenge, we can so overcome ourselves as to pray for our enemies, and deserve well of them, we shall both sweeten our own spirits, and prevent a sharp temptation which we are prone unto; and have an undoubted argument that we are sons of that Father that doth good to his enemies, and members of that Saviour that prayed for his persecutors, Luke xxiii. 34. And withal by 'heaping coals,' Rom. xii. 20, upon our enemies, shall melt them either to conversion or to confusion.

But the greatest trial of trust is in our last encounter with death, wherein we shall find not only a deprivation of all comforts in this life, but a confluence of all ill at once; but we must know, God will be the God of his unto death, and not only unto death, but in death. We may trust God the Father with our bodies and souls which he hath created; and God the Son with the bodies and souls which he hath redeemed; and the Holy Spirit with those bodies and souls that he hath sanctified. We are not disquieted when we put off our clothes and go to bed, because we trust God's ordinary providence to raise us up again. And why should we be disquieted when we put off our bodies and sleep our last sleep, considering we are more sure to rise out of our graves than out of our beds? Nay, we are raised up already in Christ our Head, 'who is the resurrection and the life,' John xi. 25, in whom we may triumph over death, that triumpheth over the greatest monarchs, as a disarmed and conquered enemy. Death is the death of itself, and not of us. If we would have faith ready to die by, we must exercise it well in living by it, and then it will no more fail

* Melior est tristitia iniqua patientis, quam lœtitia iniqua facientis.—*Aug.*

us than the good things we lay hold on by it, until it hath brought us into heaven, where that office of it is laid aside. Here is the prerogative of a true Christian above an hypocrite and a worldling, whenas their trust, and the thing they trust in, fails them, then a true believer's trust stands him in greatest stead.

In regard of our state after death, a Christian need not be disquieted, for the angels are ready to do their office in carrying his soul to paradise, those 'mansions prepared for him,' John xiv. 2. His Saviour will be his judge, and the Head will not condemn the members; then he is to receive the fruit and end of his faith, the reward of his hope; which is so great and so sure, that our trusting in God for that, strengtheneth the heart to trust him for all other things in our passage; so that the refreshing of our faith in these great things, refreshes its dependence upon God for all things here below. And how strong helps have we to uphold our faith in those great things which we are not able to conceive of, till we come to possess them! Is not our husband there? and hath he not taken possession for us? Doth he not keep our place for us? Is not our flesh there in him? and his Spirit below with us? Have we not some first-fruits and earnest of it before hand? Is not Christ now fitting and preparing of us daily, for what he hath prepared and keeps for us? Whither tends all we meet with in this world, that comes betwixt us and heaven, as desertions, inward conflicts, outward troubles, and death at last, but to fit us for a better condition hereafter, and by faith therein to stir up a strong desire after it? 'Comfort one another with these things,' saith the apostle, 1 Thes. iv. 18; these be the things will comfort the soul.

CHAPTER XXV.—*Of the defects of gifts, disquieting the soul; as also the afflictions of the church.*

Among other things, there is nothing more disquiets a Christian, that is called to the fellowship of Christ and his church here, and to glory hereafter, than that he sees himself unfurnished with those gifts that are fit for the calling of a saint; as likewise for that particular standing and place wherein God hath set him in this world, by being a member of a body politic.

For our Christian calling, we must know that Christianity is a matter rather of grace than of gifts, of obedience than of parts. Gifts may come from a more common work of the Spirit; they are common to castaways, and are more for others than for ourselves. Grace comes from a peculiar favour of God, and especially for our own good. In the same duty, where there is required gifts and grace, as in prayer, one may perform it with evidence of greater grace than another of greater parts. Moses, a man not of the best speech, was chosen before Aaron to speak to God, Exod. vii. 11; and to strive with him by prayer, whilst Israel fought with Amalek with the sword, Exod. xvii 11. It is a business more of the heart than of the tongue, more of groans than of words, which groans and sighs the spirit will always stir up even in the worst condition. Yet for parts there is no member, but it is fitted with some abilities to do service in the body, and by faith may grow up to a greater measure. For God calls none to that high condition, but whom in some measure he fits to be an useful member, and endows with a public spirit.

But that is the measure which Christ thinks fit; who will make up that in the body which is wanting in any particular member. God will increase the measure of our gifts as occasion shall be offered to draw them forth;

for there is not the greatest but may have use both of the parts and graces of the meanest in the church. And here the soul may by a spirit of faith go to God in this manner: Lord, the state* of Christianity unto which thy love in Christ hath called and advanced me, is a high condition; and there is need of a great measure of grace to uphold the credit and comfort of it. Whom thou callest unto it, thou dost in some measure furnish to walk worthy of it. Let this be an evidence to my soul of the truth of thy call, that I am enabled by the Spirit for those duties that are required; in confidence of which assistance I will set upon the work: 'Thou hast promised to give wisdom to them that ask it, and to upbraid none with their unworthiness. Nay, 'thou hast promised the Spirit of all grace to those that beg it,' James i. 5. It is that which I need, and it is no more than thou hast promised.

Caution. Only it must be remembered, that we do not walk above our parts and graces, the issue whereof will be discouragement in ourselves and disgrace from others.

The like may be said for our particular calling, wherein we are to express the graces of our Christian calling, and 'serve one another in love,' Gal. v. 13, as members of the state as well as of the church. Therefore every one must have, 1, a calling; 2, a lawful; 3, a useful calling; 4, a calling fitted for his parts, that he may be even for his business, *pares negotio;* 5, a lawful entrance and calling thereunto; 6, and a lawful demeanour in the same. Though the orb and sphere we walk in be little, yet we must keep within the bounds of it, because for our carriage in that, we must give a strict account; and there is no calling so mean but a man shall find enough to give a good account for (*i*). Our care must be to know our work, and then to do it; and so to do it as if it were unto God, with conscience of moderate diligence; for over-doing and over-working anything comes either from ostentation or distrust in God; and negligence is so far from getting any blessing, that it brings us under a 'curse for doing God's work negligently,' Jer. xlviii. 10. For we must think our callings to be services of God, who hath appointed us our standing therein.

That which belongs to us in our calling is care of discharging our duty; that which God takes upon him is assistance, and good success in it. Let us do our work, and leave God to do his own. Diligence and trust in him is only ours, the rest of the burden is his. In a family the father's and the master's care is the greatest; the child's care is only to obey, and the servant's to do his work; care of provision and protection doth not trouble them. Most of our disquietness in our calling is, that we trouble ourselves about God's work. Trust God and be doing, and let him alone with the rest. He stands upon his credit so much, that it shall appear we have not trusted him in vain, even when we see no appearance of doing any good. Peter fished all night and catched nothing, yet upon Christ's word he casts in his net again, and caught so many fish as break his net, Luke v. 6. Covetousness, when men will be richer than God would have them, troubles all; it troubles the house, the whole family, and the house within us, our precious soul, which should be a quiet house for God's spirit to dwell in, whose seat is a quiet spirit. If men would follow Christ's method, and 'seek first the kingdom of heaven,' Mat. vi. 33, all other things would be cast upon them. If thoughts of insufficiency in our places discourage us, remember what God saith to Moses, when he pretended disability to speak, 'Who hath made man's mouth, have not I the Lord?' Exod. iv. 11. All our sufficiency for every calling is from God.

* 'Estate,' in C.

Obj. But you will say, though by God's blessing my particular condition be comfortable, yet the state of God's people abroad, and the miseries of the times, disquiet me.

Ans. We complain of the times, but let us take heed we be not a part of the misery of the times: that they be not the worse for us. Indeed he is a dead member that takes not to heart the ill of the times, yet here is place for that complaint, 'Help, Lord,' Ps. xii. 1. In these tempests do as the disciples did, cry to Christ to rebuke the tempests and storms, Mat. viii. 25. This is the day of Jacob's trouble, let it also be the day of Jacob's trust; let the body do as the head did in the like case, and in time it shall be with the body as it is with the head.

In this case it is good to lay before God all the promises made to his church, with the examples of his presence in it, and deliverance of the same in former times. God is never nearer his church than when trouble is near. When in earth they conclude an utter overthrow, God is in heaven concluding a glorious deliverance. Usually after the lowest ebb, follows the highest spring-tide. Christ stands upon Mount Zion. There is a counsel in heaven, that will dash the mould of all contrary counsels on earth; and which is more, God will work the raising of the church, by that very means by which his enemies seek to ruin it. 'Let us stand still and behold the salvation of the Lord,' Exod. xiv. 13. God gave too dear a price for his church, to suffer it long in the hands of merciless enemies.

As for the seeming flourishing of the enemies of God's church, it is but for a time, and that a short time, and a measured time. 'The wicked plot against the just,' Ps. xxxvii. 12; they 'are plotters and ploughers of mischief,' Job iv. 8; they are skilful and industrious in it, but they reap their own ruin. 'Their day is a coming,' Ps. xxxvii. 12, and 'their pit is in digging,' Ps. xciv. 13; take heed therefore of fretting, Ps. xxxvii. 7; because of the man 'that bringeth wicked devices to pass, for the arms of the wicked shall be broken,' Ps. xxxvii. 17.* We should help our faith by observing God's executing of judgment in this kind. It cannot but vex the enemies of the church, to see at length a disappointing of their projects; but then to see the mould of all their devices turned upon their own heads, will more torment them.

In this case, it will much comfort to go into the sanctuary, for there we shall be able to say, 'Yet God is good to Israel,' Ps. lxxiii. 17. God hath an ark for his. There is no condition so ill, but there is balm in Gilead, comfort in Israel. The depths of misery are never beyond the depths of mercy. God oft for this very end, strips his church of all helps below, that it may only rely upon him: and that it may appear that the church is ruled by a higher power than it is opposed by. And then is the time when we may expect great deliverances of the church, when there is a great faith in the great God.

From all that hath been said, we see that the only way to quiet the soul is, to lay a charge upon it to trust God, and that unquietness and impatiency are symptoms and discoveries of an unbelieving heart.

CHAPTER XXVI.—*Of divine reasons in a believer. Of his minding to praise God, more than to be delivered.*

To go on. '*I shall yet praise him.*'

In these words David expresseth the reasons and grounds of his trust,

* Read Psalms x., xxxvii., xciv., cxxix., &c.

namely, from the interest he had in God by experience and special covenant: wherein in general we may observe, *that those who truly trust in God, labour to back their faith with sound arguments.* Faith is an understanding grace; it knows whom it trusts, and for what, and upon what grounds it trusts. Reason of itself cannot find what we should believe, yet when God hath discovered the same, faith tells us there is great reason to believe it. Faith useth reason, though not as a ground, yet as a sanctified instrument to find out God's grounds, that it may rely upon them. He believes best, that knows best why he should believe. Confidence, and love, and other affections of the soul, though they have no reason grafted in them, yet thus far they are reasonable, as that they are in a wise man raised up, guided, and laid down with reason; or else men were neither to be blamed nor praised for ordering their affections aright; whereas not only civil virtue, but grace itself is especially conversant in ruling the affections by sanctified reason.

The soul guides the will and affections otherwise than it doth the outward members of the body. It sways the affections of confidence, love, joy, &c., as a prince doth his wiser subjects, and as counsellors do a well ordered state, by ministering reasons to them; but the soul governs the outward members by command, as a master doth a slave,—his will is enough. The hand and foot move upon command, without regarding any reason; but we will not trust and rejoice in God without reason, or a show of reason at the least.

Sin itself never wanted a reason, such as it is, but we call it unreasonable, because it hath no good reason for it; for reason being a beam of God, cannot strengthen any work of darkness. God having made man an understanding creature, guides him by a way suitable to such a condition, and that is the reason why God in mercy yields so far to us in his word, as to give us so many reasons of our affiance in him. What is encouragement and comfort but a demonstration to us of greater reasons to raise us up, than there are to cast us down?

David's reasons here, are drawn partly from some promise of deliverance, and partly from God's nature and dealing with him, whom, as he had formerly found a healing and a saving God, so he expects to find him still; and partly from the covenant of grace, *He is my God.*

The chief of his reasons are fetched from God, what he is in himself, and what he is and will be to his children, and what to him in particular. Though godly men have reasons for their trust, yet those reasons be divine and spiritual, as faith itself is; for as naturally as beams come from the sun, and branches from the root, even so by divine discourse one truth issueth from another. And as the beams and the sun, as the root and branches are all of one nature, so the grounds of comfortable truths, and reasons taken from those grounds, are both of the same divinity and authority, though in time of temptation discourse is oft so troubled, that it cannot see how one truth riseth from another. This is one privilege of heaven, that our knowledge there shall not be so much discoursive, proving one thing by another, as definitive, seeing things in their grounds with a more present view; the soul being then raised and enlarged to a present conceiving of things, and there being no flesh and blood in us to raise objections that must be satisfied with reasoning.

Sometimes in a clearer state of the soul, faith hath not so much use of reasons, but upon near and sweet communion with God, and by reason of some likeness between the soul that hath a divine nature stamped upon it, and God, it presently, without any long discourse, runneth to God, as it were, by a supernatural instinct, as by a natural instinct a child runneth to his father in any distress. Yea, and from that common light of nature, which discovereth there is a God, even natural men in extremities will run to God, and God as the author of nature will sometimes hear them, as he doth the young ravens that cry unto him; but comfortably, and with assurance, only those have a familiar recourse unto him, that have a sanctified suitable disposition unto God, as being well acquainted with him.

Sometimes again faith is put to it to use reasons to strengthen itself, and therefore the soul studieth arguments to help itself by, either from inward store laid up in the soul, or else it hearkeneth and yields to reasons suggested by others; and there is no gracious heart but hath a frame suitable and agreeable to any holy and comfortable truth that shall be brought and enforced upon it. There is something in his spirit that answers whatever comes from the Spirit of God. Though perhaps it never heard of it before, yet it presently claims kindred of it, as coming from the same blessed spring, the Holy Spirit; and, therefore, a gracious heart sooner takes comfort than another, as being prepared to close with it.

The reasons here brought by David, are not so much arguments to convince his judgment, as motives and inducements to incline his will to trust in God; for trusting being a holy relying upon God, carrieth especially the will to him. Now the will is led with the goodness of things, as the understanding is led with truth. The heart must be sweetened with consideration of love and mercy in him whom we trust, as well as convinced of his ability to do us good. The cords that draw the heart to trust are the cords of love, and the cords of love are especially the love of him to us whom we love; and, therefore the most prevailing reasons that carry the whole heart, are such as are drawn from the sweetness of God, whereby the heart is opened and enlarged to expect all good, and nothing but good from him.

But we must remember that neither reasons from the truth and power of God, nor inducements or allurements from the goodness of God, will further prevail with the soul, than it hath a fresh light and relish brought into it by the Spirit of God, to discern of those reasons, and answer the contrary.

I shall yet praise him,* or I will yet praise him, I shall because I will, and I will praise him because I shall have occasion to praise him. When God by grace enlarges the will, he intends to give the deed. God's children, wherein their wills are conformable to God's will, shall have their wills fulfilled. God intends his own glory in every mercy, and he that praises him glorifies him, Ps. l. 23. When our wills, therefore, carry us to that which God wills above all, we may well expect he will grant us what we will.

'I shall praise him,' because I have prayed unto him. It is God's direction, to call upon him in trouble, Ps. l. 15, and it is his promise to deliver, and then both his direction and promise that we shall glorify him. When troubles stir up prayer, God's answer to them will stir up praises. David, when he says I shall praise God, pre-supposes that God will deliver him, that he may have ground of praising his name; and he knew God would deliver him, because as from faith he had prayed for deliverance, so he knew that it was God's order in his dealing, to revive after drooping, and to

* 'I shall yet,' to 'fail before him.' This very sweet paragraph, by a strange oversight, was omitted in B, and has slipped out from every subsequent edition. Probably it was displaced in B to allow of the additions referred to in Note *g*. The paragraph, 'David minds,' &c., that immediately follows, is twice printed in B, and the closing sentence of the one omitted *above*, occurs at page 531, without any connection with what precedes.—G.

refresh after fainting. God knows otherwise that our spirits would fail before him.

I will praise him. David* minds praising of God more than his own delivery, because he knew his own delivery was intended on God's part, that he might be glorified. It is an argument of an excellent spirit, when all self-respects are drowned in the glory of God: and there is nothing lost therein, for our best being is in God. A Christian begins with loving God for himself; but he ends in loving himself in and for God: and so his end, and God's end, and the end of all things else, concentre and agree in one. We may aim at our own good, so we bring our hearts to refer it to the chief good, as a less circle may well be contained in a greater, so that the lines drawn from both circles, meet in one middle point. It is an excellent ground of sincerity to desire the favour of God, not so much out of self-aims, as that God may have the more free and full praise from us, considering the soul is never more fit for that blessed duty, than when it is in a cheerful plight.

It rejoiced David more that he should have a large heart to serve God, than that he should have enlargement of condition. Holy dispositions think not so much of the time to come, that it will be sweet to them, as that it will further God's praise. True grace raiseth the soul above self-respects, and resteth not till it comes to the chief end wherein its happiness consists.

God is glorified in making us happy, and we enjoying happiness, must glorify God. Although God condescend so low unto us, as not only to allow us, but to enjoin us to look to our own freedom from misery, and enjoyment of happiness, yet a soul thoroughly seasoned with grace, mounteth higher, and is carried with pure respects to advance God's glory; yea, sometimes so far as to forget its own happiness. It respects itself for God, rather than God for itself. A heavenly soul is never satisfied, until it be as near God as is attainable. And the nearer a creature comes to God, the more it is emptied of itself, and all self-aims. Our happiness is more in him, than in ourselves. We seek ourselves most when we deny ourselves most. And the more we labour to advance God, the more we advance our own condition in him.

I will praise. David thinks of his own duty in praising God more than of God's work in delivering him. Let us think of what is our duty, and God will think of what shall be for our comfort. We shall feel God answering what we look for from him, in doing what he expects from us. Can we have so mean thoughts of him as that we should intend his glory, and he not much more intend our good?

This should be a strong plea unto us in our prayers to prevail with God, when we engage ourselves, upon the revelation of his mercy to us, to yield him all the praises. Lord, as the benefit and comfort shall be mine, so the praises shall be thine!

It is little less than blasphemy to praise God for that which by unlawful shifts we have procured; for besides the hypocrisy of it, in seeming to sacrifice to him, when we sacrifice, indeed, to our own wits and carnal helps, we make him a patron of those ways which he most abhors; and it is idolatry in the highest degree to transform God so in our thoughts, as to think he is pleased with that which comes from his greatest enemy. And there is a gross mistake to take God's curse for a blessing. To thrive in an ill way is a spiritual judgment, extremely hardening in the heart.

* 'Here,' inserted in B.

It is an argument of David's sincerity here that he meant not to take any indirect course for delivering himself, because he intended to praise God, which as no guilty conscience can offer, being afraid to look God in the face, so God would abhor such a sacrifice were it offered to him. St Paul was stirred up to praise God, but withal he was assured 'God would preserve him from every evil work,' 2 Tim. iv. 18.

Sometimes, indeed, where there is no malicious intention, God pardons some breakings out of flesh and blood, endeavouring to help ourselves in danger, so far as not to take advantage of them to desert us in trouble; as in David, who escaped from Achish by counterfeiting, 1 Sam. xxvii. 10; and this yields a double ground of thankfulness, partly for God's overlooking our miscarriage, and partly for the deliverance itself. Yet this indulgence of God will make the soul more ashamed afterward for these sinful shifts; therefore, it must be no precedent to us. There can neither be grace nor wisdom in setting upon a course wherein we can neither pray to God for success in, nor bless God when he gives it. In this case God most blesseth where he most crosseth, and most curseth where the deluded heart thinks he blesseth most.

CHAPTER XXVII.—*In our worst condition we have cause to praise God; still ample cause in these days.*

'*I shall yet praise him*, or *yet I will praise God*;' that is, however it goeth with me, yet, as I have cause, so I have a spirit to praise God. When we are at the lowest, yet it is a mercy that we are not consumed. We are never so ill but it might be worse with us. Whatsoever is less than hell is undeserved. It is a matter of praise that yet we have time and opportunity to get into a blessed condition. 'The Lord hath afflicted me sore, but he hath not delivered me to death,' saith David, Ps. xviii. 18.

In the worst times there is a presence of God with his children.

1. In moderating the measure of the cross, that it be not above their strength.

2. In moderating the time of it, 'The rod of the wicked shall not rest long upon the lot of the righteous,' Ps. cxxv. 3. God limits both measure and time.

3. He is present in mixing some comfort, and so allaying the bitterness of a cross.

4. Yea, and he supports the soul by inward strength, so as though it faint, yet it shall not utterly fail.

5. God is present in sanctifying a cross for good, and at length, when he hath perfected his own work in his, he is present for a final deliverance of them. A sound-hearted Christian hath always a God to go to, a promise to go to, former experience to go to, besides some present experiences of God's goodness which he enjoys. For the present he is a child of God, a member of Christ, an heir of heaven. He dwells in the love of God in the cross as well as out of it. He may be cast out of his happy condition in the world, but never out of God's favour.

Obj. If God's children have cause to praise God in their worst condition, what difference is there betwixt their best estate and their worst?

Ans. Howsoever God's children have continual occasion to praise God, yet there be some more especial seasons of praising God than others; there be days of God's own making of purpose to rejoice in, wherein we may say,

'This is the day which the Lord hath made, let us rejoice therein,' Ps. cxviii. 24. And this I think is chiefly intended here. David comforts himself with this, that however it was now with him, yet God would deal so graciously with him hereafter that he should have cause to bless his name.

Though in evil times we have cause to praise God, yet so we are, and such are our spirits, for the most part, that affliction straitens our hearts. Therefore, the apostle thought it the fittest duty in affliction to pray. 'Is any afflicted? let him pray,' saith James; 'is any joyful? let him sing psalms,' James v. 13; shewing that the day of rejoicing is the fittest day of praising God. Every work of a Christian is beautiful in its own time. The graces of Christianity have their several offices at several seasons. In trouble, prayer is in its season. 'In the evil day call upon me,' saith God, Ps. xci. 15. In better times praises should appear and shew themselves. When God manifests his goodness to his, he gives them grace with it to manifest their thankfulness to him. Praising of God is then most comely, though never out of season, when God seems to call for it by renewing the sense of his mercies in some fresh favour towards us. If a bird will sing in winter, much more in the spring. If the heart be prepared in the winter-time of adversity to praise God, how ready will it be when it is warmed with the glorious sunshine of his favour!

Our life is nothing but as it were a web woven with interminglings of wants and favours, crosses and blessings, standings and fallings, combat and victory, therefore there should be a perpetual intercourse of praying and praising in our hearts. There is always a ground of communion with God in one of these kinds, till we come to that condition wherein all wants shall be supplied, where indeed is only matter of praise. Yet praising God in this life hath this prerogative, that here we praise him 'in the midst of his enemies,' Ps. cx. 2. In heaven all will be in concert with us. God esteems it an honour in the midst of devils, and wicked men, whose life is nothing but a dishonour of him, to have those that will make his name, as it is in itself, so great in the world.

David comforts himself in this, that he should praise God, which shews he had inured himself well before to this holy exercise, in which he found such comfort, that he could not but joy in the forethoughts of that time, wherein he should have fresh occasion of his former acquaintance with God. Thoughts of this nature enter not into a heart that is strange to God.

It is a special art, in time of misery to think of matter of joy, if not for the present, yet for the time to come; for joy disposeth to praise, and praise again stirs up joy; these mutually breed one another, even as the seed brings forth the tree, and the tree brings forth the seed. It is wisdom, therefore, to set faith on work, to take as much comfort as we can from future promises, that we may have comfort and strength for the present, before we have the full possession of them. It is the nature of faith to antedate blessings, by making them that are to be performed hereafter, as present now, because we have them in the promise. If God had not allowed us to take many things in trust for the time to come, both for his glory and our good, he would never have left such rich promises to us. For faith doth not only give glory to God, for the present, in a present believing of his truth, and relying upon him, but as it looks forward, it sees an everlasting ground of praising God, and is stirred up to praise him now, for that future matter of praise, which it is sure to have hereafter. The very hopes of future good made David praise God for the present. If the happy condition we look for were present, we would embrace it with present praises. Now, 'faith is the evidence of things not seen,' Heb. xi. 1, and gives a being to that which is not; whereupon a true believing soul cannot but be a praising soul. For this end God reveals beforehand what we shall have, that beforehand we should praise him, as if we possessed it. For that is a great honour to his truth, when we esteem of what he speaks as done, and what he promiseth as already performed. Had we not a perpetual confidence in the perpetuity of his love to us, how is it possible we should praise him?

Obj. But we want those grounds for the time to come which David had; he had particular promises, which we want.

Ans. 1. Though we want Urim and Thummim and the prophets, to foretell us what the times to come shall be, yet we have the canon of Scripture enlarged; we live under a more glorious manifestation of Christ, and under a more plentiful shedding of the Spirit, whereby that want is abundantly supplied. We have general promises for the time to come, that 'God will never fail nor forsake us,' Deut. xxxi. 6; 'that he will be with us in fire and in water, that he will give an issue to the temptation, and that the issue of all things shall be for our good, that we shall reap the quiet fruit of righteousness,' Heb. xii. 11; 'and no good thing will he withhold from them that lead a godly life,' &c., Ps. lxxxiv. 11. If we had a spirit of faith to apply these generals, we should see much of God's goodness in particular.

2. Besides general promises, we have some particular ones for the time to come; of the confusion of antichrist, of the conversion of the Jews, and fulness of the Gentiles, &c., which, though we perhaps shall never live to see, yet we are members of that body, which hereafter shall see the same; which should stir up our hearts to praise God, as if we did enjoy the present fulfilling of them ourselves, for faith can present them to the soul as if they were now present.

3. Some that have a more near communion with God, may have a particular faith of some particular deliverances, whereupon they may ground particular prayer. Luther praying for a sick friend [Frederick Myco] who was very comfortable and useful to him, had a particular answer for his recovery, whereupon he was so confident, that he sent word to his friend, that he should certainly recover. Latimer prayed with great zeal for three things. 1. That Queen Elizabeth might come to the crown. 2. That he might seal the truth with his heart's blood. 3. And that the gospel might be restored 'once again, once again,' which he expressed with great vehemency of spirit; all which three, God heard him in. But the privileges of a few must not be made a general rule for all. Privileges go not out of the persons, but rest there. Yet if men would maintain a nearer communion with God, there is no doubt but he would reveal himself in more familiar manner to them, in many particulars, than usually he doth. Those particular promises in the 91st Psalm and other places, are made good to such as have a particular faith, and to all others, with those limitations annexed to promises of that nature, so far forth as God seeth it will conduce* to their good and his own glory, and so far forth as they depend upon him in the use of means; and is not this sufficient to stay a gracious heart?

But not to insist upon particular promises and revelations, the performance whereof we enjoy here in this present life, we have rich and precious promises of final and full deliverance from all evil, and perfect enjoying of

* 'Induce, in C.

all good in that life which is to come; yet not so to come, but that we have the earnest and first fruits of it here; all is not kept for heaven. We may say with David, 'Oh how great is thy goodness, which thou hast laid up for them that fear thee,' Ps. xxxi. 19; and not only so, but how great is that goodness which thou hast wrought in them that trust in thee, even before the sons of men! God treasures not up all his goodness for the time to come, but lays much of it out daily before such as have eyes to behold it.

Now God's main end in revealing such glorious promises of the life to come is, that they might be a ground of comfort to us, and of praise to him even in this life; and indeed what can be grievous in this world to him that hath heaven in his eye? What made our blessed Saviour 'endure the cross, and despise the shame, but the joy of glory to come, set before him?' Heb. xii. 2.

The duty that David brought his heart to, before he had a full enjoyment of what he looked for, was patient waiting, it being God's use to put a long date oftentimes to the performances of his promises. David after he had the promise of a kingdom, was put off a long time ere he was invested to it; Abraham was an old man before he enjoyed his son of the promise; Joseph stayed a long time before he was exalted; our blessed Saviour himself was thirty-four years old before he was exalted up into glory.

God defers, but his deferring is no empty space, wherein no good is done, but there is in that space a fitting for promises. Whilst the seed lieth hid in the earth, time is not lost, for winter fits for spring, yea, the harder the winter, the more hopeful the spring; yet were it a mere empty space, we should hold out, because of the great things to come; but being only a preparing time, we should pass it with the less discouragement. Let this support us in all the thwartings of our desire. It is a folly to think, that we should have physic and health both at once. We must endure the working of God's physic. When the sick humour is carried away and purged, then we shall enjoy desired health. God promiseth forgiveness of sin, but thou findest the burden of it daily on thee. Cheer up thyself: when the morning is darkest, then comes day; after a weary week comes a sabbath, and after a fight victory will appear. God's time is best, therefore resolve upon waiting his leisure. For the better demeaning of ourselves herein, we must know we must so wait, that we provoke not in the mean time his patience on whom we depend, by putting forth our hand to any evil, which indeed is a crossing of our hopes. Therefore, *waiting upon God* is always joined with *doing good*. There is an influence in the thing hoped for, in the spirit of him that truly hopes, stirring him up to a suitable conformity, by purging himself of whatsoever will not stand with the holiness of that condition. Waiting implies all graces, as patience, perseverance, long-suffering in holding out, notwithstanding the tediousness of time deferred, courage, and breaking through all difficulties that stand between. For what is waiting, indeed, but a continuing in a gracious inoffensive course, till the accomplishment of our desires?

Whence we may discern a main difference betwixt a Christian and a carnal man, who is short-spirited, and all for the present. He will have his good here, whereas a saint of God continues still waiting, though all things seem contrary to what he expects. The presence of things to come is such to faith, as it makes it 'despise the pleasure of sin for a season,' Heb. xi. 25. What evidence of goodness is it for a man to be good only upon the apprehension of something that contents him? Here is the glory of faith, that it can upon God's bare promise, cross itself in things pleasing to nature, and raise up the soul to a disposition some ways answerable to that blessed estate which, though yet it enjoys not, yet it is undoubtedly persuaded of, and looks for. What can encourage us more to wait than this, that the good we wait for is greater than we are able to conceive, yea, greater than we can desire or hope for?

This was no presumptuous resolution of David's own strength, but it issued from his present truth of heart, so far as he knew the same; together with an humble dependence upon God, both for deliverance, and a heart to praise him for it; because God's benefits are usually entire, and are sweetened with such a sense of his love, as causeth a thankful heart, which to a true Christian, is a greater blessing than the deliverance itself, as making the soul better. David doth acknowledge with humble admiration, that a heart enlarged comes from God, 'Who am I,' saith he, 'and who are my people?' 1 Chron. xxix. 14.

He mentioneth here praising God, instead of deliverance, because a heart enlarged to praise God is indeed the greatest part of the deliverance; for by it the soul is delivered out of its own straits and discontent.

CHAPTER XXVIII.—*Divers qualities of the praise due to God, with helps therein; and notes of God's hearing our prayers.*

Though this be God's due and our duty, and itself a delightful thing, yet it is not so easy a matter to praise God, as many imagine. Music is sweet, but the setting of the strings in tune is unpleasing. Our souls will not be long in tune, and it is harsh to us to go about the setting them in order. Like curious clocks, a little thing will hinder the motion; especially passion, which disturbs not only the frame of grace in us, but the very frame of nature, putting man out of the power and possession of himself; and therefore David here, when he had thoughts of praising God, was fain to take up the quarrel betwixt him and his soul first. Praising sets all the parts and graces of the soul awork; and therefore the soul had need gather itself and its strength together to this duty.

It requires especially self-denial, from a conscience* of our own wants, weaknesses, and unworthiness; it requires a giving up of ourselves, and all ours to be at God's dispose.† The very ground and the fruit which it yields are both God's; and they never gave themselves truly up to God, that are not ready to give all they have to him whensoever he calls for it. Thankfulness is a sacrifice, and in sacrifices there must be killing before offering, otherwise the sacrifice will be as the offering up some unclean creature. Thanksgiving is an incense, and there must be fire to burn that incense. Thanksgiving requires not only affections, but the heat of affections. There must be some assurance of the benefit we praise God for; and it is no easy matter to maintain assurance of our interest in the best things.

Yet in this case, if we feel not sense of assurance, it is good we should praise God for what we have. We cannot deny but God offers himself in mercy to us, and that he intends our good thereby, for so we ought to construe his merciful dealing towards us, and not have him in jealousy without ground. If we bring our hearts to be willing to praise God, for that we cannot but acknowledge comes from him, he will be ready in his time to shew himself more clearly to us. We taste of his goodness many ways, Rom. ii. 4, and it is accompanied with much patience; and these in

* That is, 'consciousness.'—ED.

† That is, 'disposal.'—G.

their natures lead us not only to repentance, but likewise to thankful acknowledgment; and we ought to follow that which God leads us unto, though he hath not yet acquainted us with his secrets.

It is good in this case to help the soul with a firm resolution, and to back resolution with a vow, not only in general that we will praise, but particularly of something within our own power, provided it prove no snare to us. For by this means the heart is perfectly gained, and the thing is as good as done in regard of God's acceptance and our comfort; because strong resolutions discover sincerity without any hypocritical reservation and hollowness. Always so much sincerity as a man hath, so much will his inward peace be. Resolution as a strong stream bears down all before it. Little good is done in religion without this, and with it, all is as good as done.

So soon as we set upon this work we shall feel our spirits to rise higher and higher, as the waters in the sanctuary, Ezek. xlvii., as the soul grows more and more heated. See how David riseth by degrees. Be glad in the Lord, Ps. xxxii. 11, and then, rejoice, ye righteous, and then, shout for joy all ye that are upright in heart. The Spirit of God will delight to carry us along in this duty, until it leaves our spirits in heaven, praising God with the saints and glorious angels there. To him that hath and useth it shall be given, Mat. xxv. 29. He that knoweth God aright will honour him by trusting of him; he that honours him by trusting him, will honour him by praying; and he that honours him by prayer, shall honour him by praises; he that honours him by praises here, shall perfect his praises in heaven; and this will quit the labour of setting and keeping the soul in tune. This trading with God is the richest trade in the world. When we return praises to him, he returns new favours to us, and so an everlasting, ever increasing intercourse betwixt God and the soul is maintained. David here resolved to praise God, because he had assurance of such a deliverance as would yield him a ground of praising him.

Praising of God may well be called incense, because, as it is sweet in itself, and sweet to God, so it sweetens all that comes from us. Love and joy are sweet in themselves, though those whom we love and joy in should not know of our affection, nor return the like; but we cannot love and joy in God but he will delight in us. When we neglect the praising of God, we lose both the comfort of God's love and our own too. It is a spiritual judgment to want or lose the sight or sense of God's favours, for it is a sign of want of spiritual life, or at least liveliness; it shews we are not yet in the state of those whom God hath chosen to set forth the riches of his glory upon.

When we consider that, if we answer not kindness and favour shewed unto us by men, we are esteemed unworthy of respect, as having sinned against the bond of human society and love, we cannot but much more take shame to ourselves, when we consider the disproportion of our carriage, and unkind behaviour towards God, when, instead of being temples of his praise, we become graves of his benefits. What a vanity is this in our nature, to stand upon exactness of justice, in answering petty courtesies of men, and yet to pass by the substantial favours of God, without scarce taking notice of them! The best breeding is to acknowledge greatest respects where they are most due, and to think, that if unkindness and rudeness be a sin in civility, it is much more in religion. The greatest danger of unthankfulness is in the greatest matter of all. If we arrogate any spiritual strength to ourselves in spiritual actions, we commit either sacrilege, in robbing God of his due, or mockery, by praising him for that which we hold to be of ourselves. If injustice be to be condemned in man, much more in denying God his due, religion being the first due. It takes much from thankfulness, when we have common conceits of peculiar favours. Praise is not comely in the mouth of fools; God loves no 'blind sacrifice,' Mal. i. 8.

We should, therefore, have wisdom and judgment, not only to know upon what grounds to be thankful, but in what order, by discerning what be the best and first favours whence the rest proceed, and which add a worthiness to all the rest. It is good to see blessings, as they issue from grace and mercy. It much commends any blessing, to see the love and favour of God in it, which is more to be valued than the blessing itself, as it much commends anything that comes from us, when we put a respect of thankfulness, and love to God upon it; and if we observe, we shall find the unkindness of others to us, is but a correction of our unkindness to God.

In praising God it is not good to delay, but take advantage of the freshness of the blessing. What we add to delay, we take from thankfulness; and withal lose the prime and first-fruits of our affections. It is a wise redeeming of time to observe the best seasons of thankfulness. A cheerful heart will best close with a cheerful duty, and therefore it is not good to waste so fit a temper in frivolous things; but after some contentment given to nature, let God have the fruit of his own planting, otherwise it is even no better than the refreshing of him that standeth by a good fire and crieth, 'Ah, ah, I am warm,' Isa. xliv. 16.

David doth not say, 'I will thank God,' but 'I shall praise him,' though he intends that. Thanks is then best when it tends to praising, and there ends; for thanks alone shew respect to our own good only, praises to God's glory; and in particular to the glory of such excellencies whence the benefit comes; and from thence the soul is enlarged to think highly of all God's excellencies.

Hannah, upon particular thanks for her hearing about a child, 1 Sam. ii. 1, takes occasion to set out God's other excellencies, and riseth higher and higher, from one to many, from the present time to that which was to come; from particular favours to herself, she stirs up others to praise God for his mercy to them. So David: 'Deliver me, O God, and my tongue shall sing of thy praises,' Ps. li. 14. He propounds this as an engagement of the Lord to help him, because it should tend to the enlargement of his glory; he was resolved to improve God's favour this way.

The Spirit of God works like new wine, enlarging the spirit from one degree of praising God to another; and because it foresees the eternity of God's love, as far as it can, it endeavours an eternity of God's praise. A gracious heart upon taste of favour shewed to itself, is presently warmed to spread the praise of God to others; and the more it sees the fruit of trusting God, and his truth in performing promise, the more it still honours that trusting, as knowing that it lies upon God's honour to honour those that honour him, 1 Sam. ii. Blessing will procure blessing. The soul hath never such freedom from sin as when it is in a thankful frame; for thankfulness issues from a heart truly humbled and emptied of itself, truly loving and rejoicing in God; and upon any sin the spirit is grieved and straitened, and the lips sealed up in such a heart; for the conscience upon any sin looks upon it not only as disobedience against God's will and authority, but as unthankfulness to his goodness; and this melteth a godly heart most of all. When Nathan told David God had done this and this for him, and was ready to do more, he could not hold in the confession of his sin, but relented and gave in presently, 2 Sam. xii. 8.

We ought not only to give thanks, but to be thankful, to meditate and study the praises of God. Our whole life should be nothing else but a continual blessing of his holy name, endeavouring to bring in all we have, and to lay it out for God and his people, to see where he hath any receivers. Our goodness is nothing to God. We need bring no water to the fountain nor light to the sun. Thankfulness is full of invention, it deviseth liberal things. Though it be our duty to be good stewards of our talents, yet thankfulness adds a lustre, and a more gracious acceptance, as having more of that which God calls for.

Our praising God should not be as sparks out of a flint, but as water out of a spring, natural, ready, free, as God's love to us is. Mercy pleases him, so should praise please us. It is our happiness when the best part in us is exercised about the best and highest work. It was a good speech of him that said, If God had made me a nightingale, I would have sung as a nightingale, but now God hath made me a man, I will sing forth the praises of God, which is the work of a saint only. 'All thy works bless thee, and thy saints praise thee,' Ps. cxlv. 10. All things are either blessings in their nature, or so blessed, as they are made blessings to us by the overruling command of him, who maketh all things serviceable to his. Even the worst things in this sense are made spiritual to God's people against their own nature. How great is that goodness which makes even the worst things good!

Little favours come from no small love, but even from the same love that God intends the greatest things to us; and are pledges of it. The godly are more thankful for the least favours than worldly men for the greatest. The affection of the giver enhances the gift.

O then let us labour to improve both what we have, and what we are, to his glory. It discovers that we love God, not only with all our understanding, heart, and affection, but, when with all our might and power, so far as we have advantage by any part, relation, or calling whatsoever, we endeavour to do him service. We cannot have a greater honour in the world, than to be honoured of God, to be abundant in this kind.

Our time here is short, and we shall all ere long be called to a reckoning; therefore let us study real praises. God's blessing of us is in deed, and so should ours be of him. Thanks in words is good, but in deeds is better; leaves are good, but fruit is better; and of fruit, that which costs us most. True praise requires our whole man, the judgment to esteem, the memory to treasure up, the will to resolve, the affections to delight, the tongue to speak of, and the life to express the rich favours of God. What can we think of! what can we call to mind! What can we resolve upon! what can we speak! What can we express in our whole course better than the praises of him, 'of whom, and through whom, and to whom we and all things are!' Rom. xi. 36.

Our whole life should speak nothing but thankfulness; every condition and place we are in should be a witness of our thankfulness. This will make the times and places we live in the better for us. When we ourselves are monuments of God's mercy, it is fit we should be patterns of his praises, and leave monuments to others. We should think life is given us, to do something better than live in. We live not to live. Our life is not the end of itself, but the praise of the giver. God hath joined his glory and our happiness together. It is fit that we should refer all that is good to his glory, that hath joined his glory to our best good, in being glorified in our salvation.

David concludes, that he should certainly praise God, because he had prayed unto him. Prayers be the seeds of praises. I have sown, therefore I will reap. What we receive as a fruit of our prayers, is more sweet than what we have by a general providence.

Obj. But how do we know that God hears our prayers?

Ans. 1. If we regard them ourselves, and expect an issue. Prayer is a sure adventure. We may well look for a return.

2. It is a sign that God hath heard our prayers, when he stirs up thankfulness aforehand upon assurance. Thankfulness cannot be without either the grace of God, by which we are thankful, or some taste of the things we are thankful for. God often accepts the prayer, when he doth not grant the thing, and will give us thereby occasion of thanksgiving for his wise care in changing one blessing for another fitter for us. God regards my prayers, when by prayer my heart is wrought to that frame which he requires, that is, an humble subjection to him, from an acknowledgment of my wants, and his fulness. There is nothing stirred up in our hearts by the Spirit, no, not so much as a gracious desire, but God will answer it, if we have a spirit to wait.

3. We may know God hath accepted our prayer, when he makes the way easy and plain after prayer, by a gracious providence; when the course of things begin to change, and we meet with comforts instead of former crosses, and find our hearts quieted and encouraged against what we most feared.

4. Likewise earnestness in prayer is a sign God hears our prayers, as fire kindled from heaven sheweth God accepts the sacrifice. The ground of prevailing by our prayer, is, that they are put up in a gracious name, and for persons in favour, and dictated by God's own Spirit. They work in the strength of the blessed Trinity, not their own, giving God the glory of all his excellencies.

It is God's direction 'to call upon him in trouble,' Ps. l. 15, and it is his promise to deliver; and then both his direction and promise that we shall glorify him. When troubles stir up prayer, God's answer to them will stir up praises. David when he saith, I shall praise God, presupposes God would deliver him, that he might have ground of praising his name. And he knew God would deliver him, because as from faith he had prayed for deliverance, so he knew it was the order of God's dealing, to revive after drooping, and refresh after fainting. God knows otherwise that our spirits would fail before him.

A thankful disposition is a special help in an afflicted condition, for thankfulness springs from love, and 'love rejoiceth in suffering,' Acts xv. 21. Thankfulness raises the soul higher than itself. It is trading with God, whereby, as we by him, so he gains by us. Therefore the saints used this as a motive to God, that he would grant their desires, because the living praise him, and not the dead, Isa. xxxviii. 19. If God expect praise from us, sure he will put us into a condition of praise.

Unthankfulness is a sin detestable both to God and men, and the less punishment it receives from human laws, the more it is punished inwardly by secret shame, and outwardly by public hatred, if once it prove notorious. When God's arrests come forth for denying him his tribute, he chiefly eyes an unthankful heart, and hates all sin the worse, as there is more unthankfulness in it. The neglect of kindness is taken most unkindly. Why should we load God with injuries, that loadeth us with his blessings? Who would requite good with evil? Such men's mercies will prove at last so many indictments against them.

Use. I beseech you therefore labour to be men of praises. If in any duty we may expect assistance, we may in this, that altogether concerns God's glory. The more we praise God, the more we shall praise him. When God by grace enlarges the will, he intends to give the deed. God's children, wherein their wills are conformable to God's will, are sure to have them fulfilled. In a fruitful ground, a man will sow his best seed. God intends his own glory in every mercy, and he that 'praises him, glorifies him,' Ps. l. 23. When our wills therefore carry us to that which God wills above all, we may well expect he will satisfy our desires. The living God is a living fountain, never drawn dry. He hath never done so much for us, but he can and will do more. If there be no end of our praises, there shall be no end of his goodness; no way of thriving like to this. By this means we are sure never to be very miserable. How can he be dejected, that by a sweet communion with God sets himself in heaven? nay, maketh his heart a kind of heaven, 'a temple, a holy of holies,' 2 Cor. vi. 16, wherein incense is offered unto God. It is the sweetest branch of our priestly office, to offer up these daily sacrifices. It is not only the beginning, but a further entrance of our heaven upon earth, and shall be one day our whole employment for ever.

Praise is a just and due tribute for all God's blessings; for what else especially do the best favours of God call for at our hands? How do all creatures praise God, but by our mouths? It is a debt always owing, and always paying; and the more we pay, the more we shall owe. Upon the due discharge of this debt, the soul will find much peace. A thankful heart to God for his blessings, is the greatest blessing of all. Were it not for a few gracious souls, what honour should God have of the rest of the unthankful world? Which should stir us up the more to be trumpets of God's praises in the midst of his enemies, because this, in some sort, hath a prerogative above our praising God in heaven; for there God hath no enemies to dishonour him.

This is a duty that none can except against, because it is especially a work of the heart. All cannot shew their thankfulness in giving, or doing, great matters, but all may express the willingness of their hearts. All *within us* may praise his holy name, Ps. ciii. 1, though we have little or nothing *without* us; and that within us is the thing God chiefly requires. Our heart is the altar on which we offer this incense. God looks not to quantity, but to proportion. He accepts a mite where there is no more to be had.

Quest. But how shall we be enabled to this great duty?

Ans. 1. *Enter into a deep consideration of God's favours, past, present, and to come;* think of the greatness and suitableness of them to our condition, the seasonableness and necessity of them every way unto us. Consider how miserable our life were without them, even without common favours; but as for spiritual favours, that make both our natural and civil condition comfortable, our very life were death, our light were darkness without these. In all favours think not of them so much, as God's mercy and love in Christ, which sweetens them. Think of the freeness of this love, and the smallness of thy own deserts. How many blessings doth God bestow upon us, above our deserts, yea, above our desires, nay, above our very thoughts! He had thoughts of love to us when we had no thoughts ourselves. What had we been if God had not been good unto us! How many blessings hath God bestowed upon us, that we never prayed for! and yet we are not so ready to praise God, as to pray unto him. This more desire of what we want than esteeming of what we have, shews too much prevailing of self-love. But,

2. Secondly, *comparing also ourselves with others*, will add a great lustre to God's favour, considering we are all hewed out of one rock, and differ nothing from the meanest, but in God's free love. Who are we, that God should single us out for the glory of his rich mercy?

3. Considering, likewise, *that the blessings of God to us are such as if none but we had them, and God cares for us as if he had none else to care for in the world besides.* These things well pondered should set the greater price upon God's blessings. What are we in nature and grace but God's blessings?—what is in us, about us, above us? What see we, taste we, enjoy we, but blessings? All we have, or hope to have, are but dead favours to us, unless we put life into them by a spirit of thankfulness. And shall we be as dead as the earth, as the stones we tread on? Shall we live as if we were resolved God should have no praise by us? Shall we make ourselves gods, ascribing all to ourselves? Nay, shall we, as many do, fight against God with his own favours, and turn God's blessings against himself? Shall we abuse peace to security? plenty to ease, promises to presumption, gifts to pride? How can we please the devil better than thus doing? Oh, the wonderful patience of God, to continue life to those whose life is nothing else but a warring against him, the giver of life!

As God hath thoughts of love to us, so should our thoughts be of praïses to him, and of doing good in our places to others for his sake. Think with thyself, Is there any I may honour God by relieving, comforting, counselling? Is there any of Jonathan's race? 2 Sam. ix. 1. Is there any of Christ's dear ones? I will do good to them, that they together with me, and for me, may praise God, Psalm cxviii. 1. As David here checks himself for the failing and disquietness of his spirit, and, as a cure thereof, thinks of praising God, so let us, in the like case, stir up our souls as he did, and say, 'Praise the Lord, O my soul, and all that is within me, set forth his holy name,' Psalm ciii. 1. We never use our spirits to better purpose, than when by that light we have from God, we stir them up to look back again to him.

By this it will appear to what good purposes we had a being here in the world, and were brought into communion with Christ by the gospel. The carriage of all things to the right end shews whose we are, and whither we tend. It abundantly appears by God's revealing of himself many ways to us, as by promises, sacraments, sabbaths, &c., that he intended to raise up our hearts to this heavenly duty. The whole gracious dispensation of God in Christ tends to this, that our carriage should be nothing else but an expression of thankfulness to him; that by a free, cheerful, and gracious disposition, we might shew we are the people of God's free grace, set at liberty from the spirit of bondage, to serve him without fear, Luke i. 74, with a voluntary, child-like service, all the days of our lives.

CHAPTER XXIX.—*Of God's manifold salvation for his people, and why open, or expressed in the countenance.*

I proceed.

He is the salvation of my countenance.

As David strengthens his trust in God, by reason fetched from the future goodness of God, apprehended by faith, so he strengthens that reason with another reason fetched from God, whom he apprehends here as the salvation of his countenance. We need reason against reason, and reason upon reason, to steel and strengthen the soul against the onset of contrary reasons.

He is the salvation of my countenance; that is, he will so save as I shall see, and my enemies shall see it; and upon seeing, my countenance shall be cheered and lifted up; God's saving kindness shall be read in my countenance, so that all who look on me shall say, God hath spoken peace to my soul, as well as brought peace to my condition.

He saith not salvation, but salvations (*j*); because as our life is subject to many miseries, in soul, body, and state, public and private, &c., so God hath many salvations. If we have a thousand troubles, he hath a thousand ways of help, *Mille mali species, mille salutis erunt.* As he hath more blessings than one, so he hath more salvations than one. He saves our souls from sin, our bodies from danger, and our estates from trouble. He is the Redeemer of his people; and not only so, but 'with him is plenteous redemption,' Ps. cxxx. 7, of all persons, of all parts both of body and soul, from all ill, both of sin and misery, for all times, both now and hereafter. He is an everlasting salvation.

David doth not say, God will save me; but God is salvation itself, and nothing but salvation. Our sins only stop the current of his mercy, but it being above all our sins, will soon scatter that cloud, remove that stop, and then we shall see and feel nothing but salvation from the Lord. 'All his ways are mercy and peace,' Ps. xxv. 10, to a repentant soul that casts itself upon him.

Christ himself is nothing else but salvation clothed in our flesh. So old Simeon conceived of him, when he had him in his arms, Luke ii. 29, and was willing thereupon to yield up his spirit to God, having seen Christ, the salvation of God. When we embrace Christ in the arms of our faith, we embrace nothing but salvation. He makes up that sweet name given him by his Father, and brought from heaven by an angel to the full, Luke ii. 14; a name in the faith of which it is impossible for any believing soul to sink.

The devil, in trouble, presents God to us as a revenging destroyer, and unbelief presents him under a false vizard; but the skill of faith is, to present him as a Saviour clothed with salvation. We should not so much look what destruction the devil and his threaten, as what salvation God promiseth. To God belong 'the issues of death,' Ps. lxviii. 20; and of all other troubles, which are lesser deaths. Cannot he that hath vouchsafed an issue in Christ from eternal death, vouchsafe an issue from all temporal evils? If he will raise our bodies, cannot he raise our conditions? He that brought us into trouble can easily make a way out of it when he pleaseth. This should be a ground of resolute and absolute obedience, even in our greatest extremities, considering God will either deliver us from death, or by death, and at length out of death.

So then, when we are in any danger, we see whither to go for salvation, even to him that is nothing else but salvation; but then we must trust in him, as David doth, and conceive of him as salvation, that we may trust in him. If we will not trust in salvation, what will we trust in? and if salvation itself cannot save us, what can? Out of salvation there is nothing but destruction, which those that seek it anywhere out of God, are sure to meet with.

How pitiful then is their case, who go to a destroyer for salvation! that seek for help from hell!

Here also we see to whom to return praise in all our deliverances, even to the God of our salvation. The Virgin Mary was stirred up to magnify the Lord; but why? 'Her spirit rejoiced in God her Saviour,' Luke i. 47. Whosoever is the instrument of any good, yet salvation is of the Lord; whatsoever brings it, he sends it. Hence in their holy feasts for any deliverance, the cup they drank was called the cup of salvation; and therefore David when he summons his thoughts, what to render unto God, he resolves upon this, to take 'the cup of salvation,' Ps. cxvi. 13. But always remember this, that when we think of God as salvation, we must think of him as he is in Christ to his. For so everything in God is saving, even his most terrible attributes of justice and power. Out of Christ, the sweetest things in God are terrible. Salvation itself will not save out of Christ, who is the only way of salvation, called the way, the truth, and the life, John xiv. 6.

David addeth, 'He is the salvation of my countenance,' that is, he will first speak salvation to my soul, and say, I am thy salvation; and when the heart is cheered, which is as it were the sun of this little world, the beams of that joy will shine in the countenance. True joy begins at the centre, and so passeth to the circumference, the outward man. The countenance is as the glass of the soul, wherein you may see the naked face of the soul, according as the several affections thereof stand. In the countenance of an understanding creature, you may see more than a bare countenance. The spirit of one man may see the countenance of another's inner man in his outward countenance; which hath a speech of its own, and declares what the heart saith, and how it is affected.

Quest. But how comes God to be the salvation of our countenance?

Ans. I answer, *God only graciously shines in the face of Jesus Christ, which we with the eye of faith beholding, receive those beams of his grace, and reflect them back again.* God shineth upon us first, and we shine in that light of his countenance upon us. 'The joy of salvation,' Ps. li. 12, especially of spiritual and eternal salvation, is the only true joy: all other salvations end at last in destruction, and are no further comfortable than they issue from God's saving love.

God will have the body partake with the soul. As in matter of grief, so in matter of joy, the lantern shines in the light of the candle within.

2. Again, *God brings forth the joy of the heart into the countenance, for the further spreading and multiplying of joy to others.*

Next unto the sight of the sweet countenance of God, is the beholding of the cheerful countenance of a Christian friend, rejoicing from true grounds. Whence it is that the joy of one becomes the joy of many, and the joys of many meet in one; by which means, as many lights together make the greater light, so many lightsome spirits make the greater light of spirit: and God receiveth the more praise, which makes him so much to delight in the prosperity of his children. Hence it is, that in any deliverance of God's people, 'the righteous do compass them about,' Ps. cxlii. 7, to know 'what God hath done for their souls;' and keep a spiritual feast with them in partaking of their joy. And the godly have cause to joy in the deliverance of other Christians, because they suffered in their afflictions, and it may be in their sins the cause of them, which made them somewhat ashamed. Whence it is, that David's great desire was, that 'those who feared God might not be ashamed because of him,' Ps. lxix. 6: insinuating that those who fear God's name are ashamed of the falls of God's people. Now when God delivers them, this reproach is removed, and those that had part in their sorrow have part in their joy.

3. Again, God will have salvation so open, that it shall appear in the countenance of his people, *the more to daunt and vex the enemies.* Cainish hypocrites hang down their heads, when God lifts up the countenance of their brethren. When the countenance of God's children clears up, then their enemies' hearts and looks are cloudy. Jerusalem's joy is Babylon's sorrow. It is with the church and her enemies as it is with a balance, the scales whereof, when one is up, the other is down. Whilst God's people are under a cloud, carnal people insult over them, as if they were men deserted of God. Whereupon they hang down their heads, and the rather, because they think that by reason of their sin, Christ and his religion will suffer with them. Hence David's care was, that the miseries of God's people 'should not be told in Gath,' 2 Sam. i. 20. The chief reason why the enemies of the church gnash their teeth at the sight of God's gracious dealing, is, that they take the rising of the church to be a presage of their ruin: a lesson which Haman's wife had learned, Esther vi. 13.

This is a comfort to us in these times of Jacob's trouble and Zion's sorrow. The captivity of the church shall return, 'as rivers in the south,' Ps. cxxvi. 1. Therefore the church may say, 'Rejoice not over me, O my enemy; though I am fallen, I shall rise again,' Mic. vii. 8. Though Christ's spouse be now as black as the pots, yet she shall be as white as the dove, Ps. lxviii. 13. If there were not great dangers, where were the glory of God's great deliverance? The church at length will be as 'a cup of trembling,' and as 'a burdensome stone,' Zech. xii. 2. The blood of the saints cry, their enemies' violence cries, the prayers of the church cry, for deliverance and vengeance upon the enemies of the church; and as that 'importunate widow,' Luke xi. 5, will at length prevail. Shall the importunity of one poor woman prevail with an unrighteous judge, and shall not the prayers of many that cry unto the righteous God take effect? If there were armies of prayers, as there are armies of men, we should see the stream of things turned another way. A few Moseses in the mount would do more good than many soldiers in the valley. If we would lift up our hearts and hands to God, he would lift up our countenance. But alas! we either pray not, or cross our own prayers, for want of love to the truth of God and his people.

It is we that keep antichrist and his faction alive, to plague the unthankful world. The strength he hath is not from his own cause, but from our want of zeal. We hinder those hallelujahs by private brabbles,* coldness and indifferency in religion. The church begins at this time a little to lift up her head again. Now is the time to follow God with prayers, that he would perfect his work, and plead his own cause; that he would be revenged not only of ours, but his enemies; that he would wholly free his church from that miserable bondage. These beginnings give our faith some hold to be encouraged to go to God, for the fulfilling of his gracious promise, that the church may rejoice in the salvation of the Lord. God doth but look for some to seek unto him; Christ doth but stay until he is awaked by our prayers. But it is to be feared that God hath not yet perfected his work in Zion. The church is not yet fully prepared for a full and glorious deliverance. If God had once his ends in the humiliation of the church for sins past, with resolution of reformation for the time to come, then this age, perhaps, might 'see the salvation of the Lord,' which the

* That is, 'squabbles.'—G.

generations to come shall be witness of, 'we should see Zion in her perfect beauty,' Ps. l. 2. The generations of those that came out of Egypt saw and enjoyed the pleasant land which their progenitors were shut out of; who by reason of their murmuring and looking back to Egypt, and forgetfulness of the wonders which God had done for and before them, perished in the wilderness.

Use. There is little cause, therefore, of envying the present flourishing of the enemies of the church, and of joining and colluding * with them; for it will prove the wisest resolution to resolve to fall and rise with the church of Christ, considering the enemies themselves shall say, God hath done great things for them; kings shall lay their crowns at 'Christ's feet,' and 'bring all their glory to the church,' Rev. xxi. 24.

And for every Christian this may be a comfort, that though their light for a time may be eclipsed, yet it shall break forth. David at this time was accounted an enemy of the state, and had a world of false imputations laid upon him, which he was very sensible of; yet we see here, he knew at length God would be 'the salvation of his countenance.'

Obj. But some, as Gideon, may object, 'If God intend to be so gracious, why is it thus with us?' Judges vi. 13.

Ans. The answer is, salvation is God's own work, humbling and casting down is his strange work, whereby he comes to his own work. For, when he intends to save, he will seem to destroy first; and when he will justify, he will condemn first; whom he will revive, he will kill first. Grace and goodness countenanced by God, have a native inbred majesty in them, which maketh the face to shine, and borroweth not its lustre from without, which God at length will have to appear in its own likeness, howsoever malice may cast a veil thereon, and disguise it for a time. And though wickedness, as it is base born, and a child of darkness, may shelter itself under authority a while, yet it shall hide itself and run into corners. The comfort of comforts is, that at that great day, the day of all days, that day 'of the revelation of the righteous judgment of God,' the righteous shall then shine as the sun in the firmament, Dan. xii. 3; then Christ will come to be glorious in his saints, and will be the salvation of the countenance of all his. Then all the works of darkness shall be driven out of countenance, and adjudged to the place from whence they came. In the mean time, let us, with David, support ourselves with the hopes of these times.

CHAPTER XXX.—*Of God, our God, and of particular application.*

My God.

These words imply a special interest that the holy man had in God, as his God, being the ground of all which was said before; both of the duty of trusting, and of praising, and of the salvation that he expected from God. He is my God, therefore be not disquieted, but trust him. He is my God, therefore he will give me matter to praise him, and will be the salvation of my countenance. God hath some special ones in the world, to whom he doth as it were pass over himself, and whose God he is by virtue of a more special covenant; whence we have these excellent expressions, 'I will be your God, and you shall be my people,' Jer. xxxi. 33; 'I will be your Father, and you shall be my sons and daughters,' 2 Cor.

* That is, 'falling in with.'—G.

vi. 18. Since the fall, we having lost our communion with God the chief good, our happiness stands in recovering again fellowship with him. For this end we were created, and for this redeemed, and for effecting of this the word and sacraments are sanctified to us; yea, and for this end God himself, out of the bowels of his compassion, vouchsafed to enter into a gracious covenant with us, founded upon Jesus Christ, and his satisfaction to divine justice; so that by faith we become one with him, and receive him as offered of his Father to 'be all in all to us,' Col. iii. 11.

Hence it is that Christ hath his name Immanuel, God with us. Not only because he is God and man too, both natures meeting in one person, but because being God in our nature, he hath undertook this office to bring God and us together. The main end of Christ's coming and suffering was to reconcile, and to gather together in one; and, as Peter expresseth it, 'to bring man again to God,' 1 Pet. iii. 18. Immanuel is the bond of this happy agreement, and appears for ever in heaven to make it good. As the comfort hereof is great, so the foundation of it is sure and everlasting. God will be our God so long as he is Christ's God, and because he is Christ's God, John xx. 10. Thus the father of the faithful, and all other holy men before Christ, apprehended God to be their God in the Messiah to come. Christ was the ground of their interest. He was yesterday to them as well as to-day to us, Heb. xiii. Hence it is that God is called the portion, Psalm lxxiii. 26, of his people, and they his jewels, Mal. iii. 25; he is their only rock and strong tower, Psalm lxxi. 3, and they his peculiar ones.

Use. Well may we wonder that the great God should stoop so low, to enter into such a covenant of grace and peace, founded upon such a mediator, with such utter enemies, base creatures, sinful dust and ashes as we are. This is the wonderment of angels, a torment of devils, and glory of our nature and persons; and will be matter of admiration and praising God unto us for all eternity.

As God offereth himself to be ours in Christ, else durst we lay no claim to him, so there must be in us an appropriating grace of faith, to lay hold of this offer. David saith here, *My God.* But by what spirit? By a spirit of faith which, looking to God's offer, maketh it his own whatsoever it lays hold of. God offereth himself in covenant, and faith catcheth hold thereon presently. With a gracious offer of God there goeth a gracious touch of his Spirit to the soul, giving it sight and strength, whereby, being aided by the same Spirit, it layeth hold on God shewing himself in love. God saith to the soul, I am thy salvation; and the soul saith again, Thou art my God. Faith is nothing else but a spiritual echo, returning that voice back again, which God first speaks to the soul. For what acquaintance could the soul claim with so glorious a Majesty, if he should not first condescend so low as to speak peace and whisper secretly to the soul, that he is our loving God and Father, and we his peculiar ones in Christ; that our sins are all pardoned, his justice fully satisfied, and our persons freely accepted in his dear Son?

But to come more particularly to the words, *My God.* The words are pregnant. In the womb of them, all that is graciously and comfortably good is contained. They are the spring-head of all particular blessings. All particular relations and titles that it pleaseth God to take upon him, have their strength from hence, that God is our God. More cannot be said, and less will not serve the turn. Whatsoever else we have, if we have not God, it will prove but an empty cistern at last. He is our proper element. Everything desires to live in its own element: fishes in the sea, birds in the air; in this they are best preserved.

There is a greater strength in this 'My God,' than in any other title. It is more than if he had said, My King, or My Lord. These are words of sovereignty and wisdom; but this implies not only infinite power, sovereignty, and wisdom, but likewise infinite bounty and provident care; so that when we are said to be God's people, the meaning is, that we are not only such over whom God hath a power and command, but such as toward whom he shews a loving and peculiar respect.

In the words is implied: 1. A propriety and interest in God. 2. An improvement of the same for the quieting of the soul.

David here lays a particular claim, by a particular faith, unto God. The reason is: 1. The virtue of faith is, as to lay hold, so to appropriate to itself, and make its own, whatever it lays hold on; and it doth no more in this than God gives it leave by his gracious promises to do.

2. As God offers, so faith receives; but God offers himself in particular to the believing soul by his Spirit, therefore our faith must be particular. That which the sacraments seal, is a peculiar interest in Christ. This is that which hath always upheld the saints of God, and that which is ever joined with the life of Christ in us. 'The life that I live,' saith Paul, 'is by the faith of the Son of God, who loved me, and gave himself for me,' Gal. ii. 20. The spirit of faith is a spirit of application.

This is implied in all the articles of our faith. We believe God to be our Father, and Christ to be born for us; that he died for us, and rose again for our good, and now sits at the right hand of God, making requests for us in particular.

3. This is that which distinguisheth the faith of a true Christian from all hypocrites and castaways whatsoever. Were it not for this word of possession, *mine*, the devil might say the Creed to as good purpose as we. He believes there is a God and a Christ; but that which torments him is this, he can say *my* to never an article of faith.

4. A general apprehension of God's goodness and mercy may stand with desperation. Take away *my* from *God*, and take away God himself in regard of comfort. *Tolle meum, tolle Deum.* What comfort was it for Adam, when he was shut out of Paradise, to look upon it after he had lost it? The more excellencies are in God, the more our grief if we have not our part in them. The very life-blood of the gospel lies in a special application of particular mercy to ourselves. All relations that God and Christ have taken upon them imply a necessity of application. What if God be a rock of salvation, if we do not rest upon him? What if he be a foundation, and we do not build on him? What if he offers himself as a husband, if we will not accept of him, what avails it us? How can we rejoice in the salvation of our souls, unless we can in particular say, '*I* rejoice in God *my* Saviour.'

5. Without particular application, we can neither entertain the love of God, nor return love again, by which means we lose all the comfort God intends us in his word, which of purpose was written for our solace and refreshment. Take away particular faith, and we let out all the spirits of cheerful and thankful obedience.

This possessive particle, *my*, hath place in all the golden chain of our salvation. The first spring of all God's claim to us as his, is in his election of us. We were by grace his, before we were. Those that are his from that eternal love, he gives to Christ. This is hid in the breast of God, till he calls us out of the rest of the world into communion with Christ.

In answering of which call, by faith, we become one with Christ, and so one with him. Afterwards, *in justification*, we feel God experimentally to be reconciled unto us, whence arises joy and inward peace. And then, upon further *sanctification*, God delights in us as his, bearing his own image, and we from a likeness to God delight in him as ours in his Christ, and so this mutual interest betwixt God and us continues, until at last God becomes all in all unto us.

Obj. But how can a man that is not yet in the state of grace say with any comfort, My God?

Ans. Whilst a man 'regards iniquity in his heart,' Ps. lxvi. 18, without any remorse or dislike of the same, if he saith, My God, his heart will give his tongue the lie, however in an outward profession and opinion of others he may bear himself as if God were his, upon false grounds. For there can be no more in a conclusion, than it hath from the principle and premises out of which it is drawn. The principle here is, that God is the God of all that trust in him. Now if we can make it good, that we truly trust in God, we may safely conclude of comfort from him; for the more certain clearing of which, try yourselves by the signs of trust delivered.*

It is no easy matter to say in truth of heart, *My God;* the flesh will still labour for supremacy. God should be all in all unto us; but this will not be till these bodies of flesh, together with the body of sin, be laid aside. He that says, God is my God, and doth not yield up himself unto God, raiseth a building without a foundation, layeth a claim without a title, and claimeth a title without an evidence, reckoning upon a bargain, without consent of the party with whom he would contract.

But if a man shall, out of the sight and sense of sin, thirst after mercy in Christ, and call unto God for pardon, then God, who is a God 'hearing prayer,' Ps. lxv. 2, and delighteth to be known by the name of merciful, will be ready to close and meet with the desire of such a soul, so far as to give it leave to rely upon him for mercy, and that without presumption, until he further discovers himself graciously unto it; upon sense of which grace the soul may be encouraged to lay a further claim unto God, having further acquaintance with him. Hence are those exhortations so oft in the prophets, to 'turn unto the Lord our God,' Zech. i. 3, because upon our first resolution to turn unto God, we shall find him always ready to answer those desires that he stirs up by his own Spirit in us.

We are not therefore to stay our turning unto God, till we feel him saying to our hearts, '*I am thy God*,' Isa. xli. 10; but when he prevents us by his grace, enabling us to desire grace, let us follow the work begun in the strength of what grace we have, and then God will further manifest himself in mercy to us.

Yet God, before we can make anything towards him, lets into our hearts some few beams of mercy, thereby drawing us unto him, and reaching us out a hint to lay hold upon.

And as sin causeth a distance betwixt God and us, so the guilt of sin in the conscience, causeth further strangeness, insomuch that we dare not look up to heaven, till God open a little crevice to let in a little light of comfort at least into our souls, whereby we are by little and little drawn nearer to him. But this light at the first is so little, that in regard of the greater sense of sin, and a larger desire of grace, the soul reckons the same as no light at all, in comparison of what it desires and seeks after. Yet the comfort is, that this dawning light will at length clear up to a perfect day.

* See chap. xviii. pp. 212–218.

Thus we see how this claim of God to be our God, is still in growth until full assurance, and that there is a great distance betwixt the first act of faith in cleaving to God, offering himself in Christ to be ours, and between the last fruit, of faith the clear and comfortable feeling, that God is our God indeed. We first by faith apply ourselves to God, and then apply God to us, to be ours; the first is the conflicting exercise of faith, the last is the triumph of faith; therefore faith properly is not assurance. And to comfort us the more, the promises are specially made to the act of faith; fuller assurance is the reward of faith.

Obj. If God hath not chosen me in Christ to be his, what ground have I to trust in him? I may cast away myself upon a vain confidence.

Ans. We have no ground at first to trouble ourselves about God's election. Secret things belong to God, Deut. xxix. 29. God's revealed will is, 'that all that believe in Christ shall not perish,' John iii. 15. It is my duty therefore, knowing this, to believe, by doing whereof, I put that question, whether God be mine or no? out of all question; for all that believe in Christ are Christ's, and all that are Christ's are God's. It is not my duty to look to God's secret counsel, but to his open offer, invitation, and command, and thereupon to adventure my soul. And this adventure of faith will bring at length a rich return unto us. In war men will adventure their lives, because they think some will escape, and why not they? In traffic beyond the seas many adventure great estates, because some grow rich by a good return, though many miscarry. The husbandman adventures his seed, though sometime the year proves so bad, that he never sees it more.* And shall not we make a spiritual adventure in casting ourselves upon God, when we have so good a warrant as his command, and so good an encouragement as his promise, that he will not fail those that rely on him? God bids us 'draw near to him, and he will draw near to us,' Deut. xxix. 29. Whilst we in God's own ways draw near to him, and labour to entertain good thoughts of him, he will delight to shew himself favourable unto us. Whilst we are striving against an unbelieving heart, he will come in and help us, and so fresh light will come in.

Pretend not thy unworthiness and inability, to keep thee off from God, for this is the way to keep thee so still. If anything help us, it must be God, and if ever he help us, it must be by casting ourselves upon him; for then he will reach out himself unto us in the promise of mercy to pardon our sin, and in the promise of grace to sanctify our natures. It was a good resolution of the lepers, 'If we enter into the city, the famine is there, and we shall die, say they; if we sit still, we shall die also: let us therefore fall into the host of Assyrians, if they save us, we shall live; if they kill us, we shall but die,' 2 Kings vii. 4. *Omnia in rebus humanis spes futurorum agunt.* So we should reason: if we sit still under the load of our sin, we shall die; if we put ourselves into the hands of Christ, if he save us, we shall live; if he save us not, we shall but die. Nay, surely he will not suffer us to die. Did ever Christ thrust any back from him, that put themselves upon him? unless it were by that means to draw them the nearer unto him, as we see in the 'woman of Canaan,' Mat. xv. 27. His denial was but to increase her importunity. We should therefore do as she did, gather all arguments to help our faith. Suppose I am a dog, saith she, yet I am one of the family, and therefore have right to the crumbs that fall. So, Lord,

* Quis pollicetur serenti, proventum; naviganti portum; militanti victoriam? Ideo navigantes vitam ventis credunt, etc. Ideo terris frumenta credimus ut cum usuris credita recipiamus.—*Salvian*[*us*].

I have been a sinner, yet I am thy creature; and not only so, but such a creature as thou has set over the rest of the works of thy hands; and not only so, but one whom thou hast admitted into thy church by baptism, whereby thou wouldst bind me to give myself unto thee beforehand; and more than this, thou hast brought me under the means, and therein hast shewed thy will concerning my turning towards thee. Thou hast not only offered me conditions of peace, but wooed me by thy ministers to give up myself unto thee, as thine in thy Christ. Therefore I dare not suspect thy good meaning towards me, or question thy intendment,* but resolve to take thy counsel, and put myself upon thy mercy. I cannot think, if thou hadst meant to cast me away, and not to own me for thine, thou wouldst ever have kindled these desires in me. But it is not this state I rest in, my purpose is to wait upon thee, until thou dost manifest thyself farther unto me. It is not common favours that will content me, though I be unworthy of these; because I hear of choice blessings towards thy chosen people, that thou enterest into a peculiar covenant withal, sure mercies, Isa. lv. 3; and such as accompany salvation. These be the favours I wait for at thy hand. 'O visit me with the salvation of thy chosen,' Ps. cvi. 4, 5. O remember me with the favour of thy people, that I may see 'the good of thy chosen.' Whilst the soul is thus exercised, more sweetness falls upon the will and affections, whereby they are drawn still nearer unto God; the soul is in a getting and thriving condition. For God delights to shew himself gracious to those that strive to be well persuaded of him, concerning his readiness to shew mercy to all that look towards him in Christ. In worldly things, how do we cherish hopes upon little grounds! if there shineth never so little hope of gain or preferment, we make after it: why then should we forsake our own mercy, which God offers to be our own, if we will embrace it, having such certain grounds for our hope to rest on?

It was the policy of the servants of Benhadad to watch if any word of comfort fell from the king of Israel, and when he named Benhadad his *brother*, they catched presently at that, and cheered themselves, 1 Kings xx. 33. Faith hath a catching quality at whatsoever is near to lay hold on. Like the branches of the vine, it windeth about that which is next, and stays itself upon it, spreading further and further still. If nature taught Benhadad's servants to lay hold upon any word of comfort that fell from the mouth of a cruel king, shall not grace teach God's children to lie in wait for a token that he will shew for good to them? How should we stretch forth the arms of our faith to him, that 'stretcheth out his arms all the day long to a rebellious people!' Isa. lxv. 2. God will never shut his bosom against those, that in an humble obedience fly unto him. We cannot conceive too graciously of God. Can we have a fairer offer, than for God in Christ to make over himself unto us? which is more than if he should make over a thousand worlds. Therefore our chief care should be first by faith to make this good, and then to make it useful unto us, by living upon it as our chiefest portion, which we shall do: 1, By proving God to be our God in particular; 2, By improving of it in all the passages of our lives.

CHAPTER XXXI.—*Means of proving and evidencing to our souls that God is our God.*

1. Now we prove it to our souls, that God is ours, when we take him at his offer, when we bring nothing but a sense of our own emptiness with us,

* That is, 'design, intention.'—G.

and a good conceit of his faithfulness and ability to do us good, when we answer God in the particular passages of salvation, which we cannot do, till he begins unto us. Therefore if we be God's, it is a certain sign that God is ours. If we choose him, we may conclude he hath chosen us first: 'if we love him, we may know that he hath loved us first,' 1 John iv. 19. If we apprehend him, it is because he hath apprehended us first. Whatsoever affection we shew to God, it is a reflection of his first to us. If cold and dark bodies have light and heat in them, it is because the sun hath shined upon them first. Mary answers not *Rabboni* till Christ said *Mary* to her, John xx. 16. If we say to God, I am thine, it is because he hath first said unto us, Thou art mine; after which, the voice of the faithful soul is, 'I am my beloved's, and my beloved is mine,' Cant. vi. 3.* We may know God's mind to us in heaven, by the return of our hearts upwards again to him; only as the reflected beams are weaker than the direct, so our affections, in their return to God, are far weaker than his love falling upon us. God will be to us whatsoever we make him by our faith to be. When by grace we answer his condition of trusting, then he becomes ours to use for our good.

2. We may know God to be *our God* when we pitch and plant all our happiness in him, when the desires of our souls are towards him, and we place all our contentment in him. As this word *my* is a term of appropriation springing from a special faith, so it is a word of love and peculiar affection, shewing that the soul doth repose and rest itself quietly and securely upon God. Thus David proves God to be his God, by early seeking of him, by thirsting, and longing after his presence, and that upon good reason, 'because God's lovingkindness was better to him than life,' Ps. lxiii. 1, 2, 3, &c. This he knew would 'satisfy his soul as with marrow and fatness.' So St Paul proved Christ to be his Lord, by 'accounting all else as dung and dross in comparison of him,' Phil. iii. 8.

Then we make God our God, and set a crown of majesty upon his head, when we set up a throne for him in our hearts, where self-love before had set up the creature above him; when the heart is so unloosed from the world, that it is ready to part with anything for God's sake, giving him now the supremacy in our hearts, and bringing down every high thought, in captivity to him; making him our trust, our love, our joy, our delight, our fear, our all; and whatsoever we esteem or affect else, to esteem and affect it under him, in him, and for him; when we cleave to him above all, depending upon him as our chief good, and contenting ourselves in him, as all-sufficient to give our souls fit and full satisfaction; when we resign up ourselves to his gracious government, to do and suffer what he will, offering ourselves and all our spiritual services as sacrifices to him; when faith brings God into the soul as ours, we not only love him, but love him dearly, making it appear that we are at good terms with God, we are at a point for other things. How many are there that will adventure the loss of the love of God for a thing of nothing, and redeem the favour of men with the loss of God's! Certain it is, whatsoever we esteem, or affect most, that, whatsoever it be in itself, yet we make it our god—*Amor tuus, Deus tuus.* The best of us all may take shame to ourselves herein in that we do not give God his due place in us, but set up some idol or other in our hearts above him.

When the soul can without hypocrisy say, *My God*, it engageth us to universal and unlimited obedience. We shall be ambitious of doing that

* Dicat anima, secura dicat, Deus meus es tu, qui dicit animæ nostræ: Salus tua ego sum.—*Aug*[*ustine*] in Ps. cxxxii.

which may be acceptable and well pleasing to him; and, therefore, this is prefixed as a ground before the commandments, enforcing obedience. 'I am the Lord thy God,' therefore 'thou shalt have no other gods before me,' Exod. xx. 3, whomsoever else we obey, it must be in the Lord, because we see a beam of God's authority in them; and it is no prejudice to any inferior authority, to prefer God's authority before it, in case of difference one from the other. *Nemini fit injuria cui præponitur Deus.*

When we know we are a *peculiar people*, we cannot but be '*zealous of good works*,' Tit. ii. 14. 'If I be a Father, where is mine honour?' Mal. i. 6. Special relations are special enforcements to duty.

4. The Spirit of God, which knows the deep things of God and the depths of our hearts, doth reveal this mutual interest betwixt God and those that are his, it being a principal work of the Spirit to seal this unto the soul, by discovering such a clear and particular light in the use of means, as swayeth the soul to yield up itself wholly to God. When we truly trust, we may say with St Paul, 'I know whom I have trusted,' 2 Tim. i. 12; he knew both that he trusted, and whom he trusted. The Spirit of God, that reveals God to be ours, and stirs up faith in him, both reveals this trust to our souls, and the interest we have in God thereby. 'The Lord is my portion, saith my soul,' Lam. iii. 24; but God said so to it first. If instinct of nature teaches dams to know their young ones, and their young ones them, in the midst of those that are alike, shall not the Spirit of God much more teach the soul to know its own father? As none knows what is in man, but the spirit of man, so none knows what love God bears to those that are his, but the Spirit of God in his. All the light in the world cannot discover the sun unto us, only it discovers itself by its own beams. So all the angels and saints in heaven cannot discover to our souls the love that is in the breast of God towards us, but only the Spirit of God, which 'sheds it into our hearts,' Rom. v. 5. The Spirit only teaches this language, My God. It is infused only into sanctified hearts; and, therefore, ofttimes mean men enjoy it, when great, wise, and learned persons are strangers to it, Mat. xi. 25.

5. The Spirit when it witnesseth this to us is called 'the Spirit of adoption,' Rom. viii. 15, and hath always accompanying of it a spirit of supplication, whereby with a familiar, yet reverend * boldness, we lay open our hearts to God as a dear father. All others are strangers to this heavenly intercourse. In straits they run to their friends and carnal shifts, whereas an heir of heaven runs to his Father, and tells him of all.

6. Those that are God's, are known to be his by special love-tokens that he bestows upon them, as,

(1.) The special graces of his Spirit. Princes' children are known by their costly jewels, and rich ornaments. It is not common gifts, and glorious parts that set a character upon us to be God's, but grace to use those gifts, in humility and love, to the glory of the giver.

(2.) There is in them a suitableness and connaturalness of heart to all that is spiritual, to whatsoever hath God's stamp upon it, as his truth and his children, and that because they are his. By this likeness of disposition, we are fashioned to a communion with him. Can two walk together and not be agreed? It is a certain evidence that we are God's in Christ, if the Spirit of God hath wrought in us any impression like unto Christ, who is the image of his Father. Both Christ looking upon us, and our looking upon Christ by faith, as ours, hath a transforming and conforming power.

(3.) Spiritual comforts in distress, such as the world can neither give,

* That is, 'reverent.'—Ed.

nor take away, shew that God looks upon the souls of his with another eye, than he beholdeth others. He sends a secret messenger that reports his peculiar love to their hearts. He knows their souls, and feeds them with his '*hidden manna*,' Rev. ii. 17. The inward peace they feel is not in freedom from trouble, but in freeness with God in the midst of trouble.

(4.) Seasonable and sanctified corrections, whereby we are kept from being led away by the error of the wicked, shew God's fatherly care over us as his. Who will trouble himself in correcting another man's child? yet we oftener complain of the smart we feel, than think of the tender heart and hand that smites us, until our spirits be subdued; and then we reap the quiet fruit of righteousness. Where crosses work together for the best, we may know that we love God, Rom. viii. 28, and are loved of him. Thriving in a sinful course is a black mark of one that is not God's.

7. Then we make it appear that God is our God, when we side with him, and are for him and his cause in ill times. When God seems to cry out unto us, 'Who is on my side, who?' 2 Kings ix. 32; then if we can say as those in Isaiah, whereof one says, 'I am the Lord's, and another calls himself by the name of Jacob, and another subscribes with his hand unto the Lord,' Isa. xliv. 6, it is a blessed sign. Thus the patriarchs and prophets, apostles and martyrs, were not ashamed of God, and God was not ashamed to own them. Provided that this boldness from God proceed not only from a conviction of the judgment, but from spiritual experience of the goodness of the cause, whereby we can justify in heart what we justify in words. Otherwise men may contend for that with others, which they have no interest in themselves. The life must witness for God as well as the tongue. It is oft easier for corrupt nature to part with life rather than with lust.

This siding with God, is with a separation from whatsoever is contrary. God useth this as an argument to come out of Babylon, because we are his people: 'Come out of her, my people,' Rev. xviii. 4. Religion is nothing else but a gathering and a binding of the soul close to God. That fire which gathers together the gold, separates the dross. Nature draws out that which is wholesome in meats, and severs the contrary. The good that is to be had by God, is by cleaving to him, and him only. God loves an ingenuous and full protestation, if called to it. It shews the coldness of the times when there is not heat enough of zeal to separate from a contrary faith. God is a jealous God, and so we shall find him at last. When the day of severing comes, then they that have stood for him, shall not only be his, but his treasure, and his jewels, Mal. iii. 17.

There is none of us all but may some time or other fall into such a great extremity, that when we look about us, we shall find none to help us: at which time we shall throughly know, what it is to have comfort from heaven, and a God to go unto. If there be anything in the world worth labouring for, it is the getting sound evidence to our souls that God is ours. What madness is it to spend all our labour to possess ourselves of the cistern, when the fountain is offered to us? O beloved, the whole world cannot weigh against this one comfort, that God is ours. All things laid in the other balance, would be too light. A moth may corrupt, a thief may take away that we have here, but who can take our God away? Though God doth convey some comfort to us by these things, yet when they are gone, he reserves the comfort in himself still, and can convey that, and more, in a purer and sweeter way, where he plants the grace of faith to fetch it from him. Why then should we weaken our interest in God, for any thing this earth affords? What unworthy wretches are those, that to please a sinful man, or to feed a base lust, or to yield to a wicked custom will, as much as in them lieth, lose their interest in God? Such, little consider what an excellent privilege it is to have a sure refuge to fly unto in time of trouble. God wants not ways to maintain his, without being beholden to the devil. He hath all help hid in himself, and will then most shew it, when it shall make most for his own glory. If God be ours, it is a shame to be beholden to the devil, that ever it should be said, Satan by base courses hath made us rich. God thinks any outward thing too mean for his children, severed from himself, therefore he gives his Son, the express image of himself, 2 Cor. iv. 4, unto them. For which cause David, when he had even studied to reckon up the number of God's choice blessings, concludes with advancing of this above all, 'yea rather happy are they whose God is the Lord,' Ps. xliv. 15. If this will not satisfy the soul, what can? Labour therefore to bring thy soul to this point with God, 'Lord, if thou seest it fit, take away all from me, so thou leavest me thyself: whom have I in heaven but thee, and there is none on earth that I desire in comparison of thee?' Ps. lxxiii. 25.

CHAPTER XXXII.—*Of improving our evidences for comfort in several passages of our lives.*

That we lose not any measure of comfort in this so sweet a privilege, we must labour for skill to improve and implead the same in the several passages and occasions of our lives, and let it appear in the retail, that whatsoever is in God is mine. If I am in a perplexed condition, his wisdom is mine; if in great danger, his power is mine; if I lie sighing under the burden of sin, his grace is mine; if in any want, his all-sufficiency is mine. 'My God,' saith St Paul, 'will supply all your wants,' Philip. iv. 19. If in any danger, I am thine. Lord, save me, I am thine, the price of thy Son's blood; let me not be lost, thou hast given me the earnest of thy Spirit, and set thy seal upon me for thy own, let me neither lose my bargain nor thou thine. What is religion itself but a spiritual bond? whereby the soul is tied to God as its own, and then singles out of God whatsoever is needful for any occasion: and so binds God with his own covenant and promise. Lord, thou hast made thyself to be mine, therefore now shew thyself so, and be exalted in thy wisdom, goodness, and power, for my defence. To walk comfortably in my Christian course, I need much grace, supply me out of thy rich store. I need wisdom to go in and out inoffensively before others, furnish me with thy Spirit. I need patience and comfort, thou that art the God of all consolation, bestow it on me.

In time of desertion put Christ betwixt God and thy soul, and learn to appeal, from God out of Christ, to God in Christ. Lord, look upon my Saviour, that is near unto thee as thy son, near to me as my brother, and now intercedes at thy right hand for me. Though I have sinned, yet he hath suffered, and shed his precious blood to make my peace. When we are in any trouble, let us still wait on him, and lie at his feet, and never let him go till he casts a gracious look upon us.

So if we be to deal with God, for the church abroad, we may allege unto him that whatsoever provocations are therein, and deformity in regard of abuses and scandals; yet it is his church, his people, his inheritance, his name is called upon, in it, and the enemies of it are his enemies. God hath engaged himself to the friends of the church, that 'they shall prosper that love it,' Ps. cxxii. 6; and therefore we may with a holy boldness press him for a blessing upon the same.

So for our children and posterity, we may incline God to respect them, because they are under his covenant, who hath promised to be our God, and the God of our seed. 'Thine they were, thou gavest them me: all that I have is thine; these are those children which thou of thy rich grace hast given me. They are thine more than mine; I am but a means under thee to bring them into the world, and to be a nurse unto thy children; take care therefore of thine own children, I beseech thee, especially, when I can take no care of them myself; thou slumberest not, thou diest not, I must,' John xvii.

Flesh and blood think nothing is cared for, but what it seeth cared for by itself. It hath no eyes to see a guard of providence, a guard of angels. It takes no knowledge that that is best cared for, that God cares for. Those that have God for their God, have enlarged hearts as they have enlarged comforts. They have an everlasting spring that supplies them in all wants, refreshes them in all troubles, and then runs most clearly and freshly, when all other streams in the world are dried and stopped up. Were we skilful in the art of faith, to improve so great an interest, what in the world could much dismay us? Faith will set God against all.

It should fill our hearts with an holy indignation against ourselves, if either we rest in a condition wherein we cannot truly say, God is our God, or if, when we can in some sincerity of heart say this, that we make no better advantage thereby, and maintain not ourselves answerable to such a condition. What a shame is it for a nobleman's son to live like a beggar! for a great rich man to live like a poor peasant; to famish at a banquet; to fall when we have so many stays to lay hold on! Whereas if we could make this clear to our souls, that God is ours, and then take up our thoughts with the great riches we have in him, laid open in Christ, and in the promises, we need trouble ourselves about nothing, but only get a large vessel of faith, to receive what is offered, nay, enforced upon us.

When we can say, God is our God, it is more than if we could say, heaven is mine; or whatever good the creature affords is mine. Alas! what is all this, to be able to say, God is mine, who hath in him the sweetness of all these things, and infinitely more? If God be ours, goodness itself is ours. If he be not ours, though we had all things else, yet ere long nothing would be ours. What a wondrous comfort is this, that God hath put himself over to be ours! that a believing soul may say with as great confidence, and greater too, that God is his, than he can say his house is his, his treasure is his, his friends are his! Nothing is so much ours as God is ours, because by his being ours in covenant, all other things become ours; and if God be once ours, well may we trust in him. God and ours joined together make up the full comfort of a Christian. God! there is all to be had; but what is that to me unless he be *my* God? All-sufficiency with propriety * fully stayeth the soul.

David was now banished from the sanctuary, from his friends, habitation, and former comforts; but was he banished from his God? No; God was his God still. When riches, and friends, and life itself cease to be ours, yet God never looseth his right in us, nor we our interest in him. This comfort that God is ours, reacheth unto the resurrection of our bodies and to life everlasting. God is the God of Abraham, and so of every true believer, even when his body is turned into dust. Hence it is that 'the lovingkindness of the Lord is better than life,' Ps. lxiii. 3, because when life departs,

* That is, 'property, possession.'—G.

yet we live for ever in him. When Moses saw the people drop away so fast in the wilderness, and wither like grass, 'Thou art our foundation,' saith he, 'from one generation to another; thou art God from everlasting to everlasting,' Ps. xc. 2. When we leave the world, and are no more seen here, yet we have a dwelling-place in God for ever. God is ours from everlasting in election, and to everlasting in glory, protecting us here and glorifying us hereafter. David, that claimed God to be his God, is gone, but David's God is alive. And David himself, 'though his flesh see corruption,' Acts ii. 27, yet is alive in his God still.

That which is said of wily persons that are full of fetches * and windings, and turnings in the world, that such will never break, may much more truly be said of a right godly man, that hath but one grand policy to secure him in all dangers, which is to run to his God as to his tower of offence and defence; such a one will never be at a desperate loss so long as God hath any credit, because he never faileth those that fly unto him; and that because his mercy and truth never fails. The very lame and the blind, the most shiftless † creatures, when they had gotten the strong hold of Zion, thought then they might securely 'scorn David and his host,' 2 Sam. v. 6, 7, because though they were weak in themselves, yet their hold was strong; but we see their hold failed them at length, which a Christian's will never do.

Obj. But God seems to have small care of those that are his in the world; those who believe themselves to be his jewels, are counted the offscouring of the world, and most despised.

Ans. We must know that such have a glorious life in God, but it is 'hidden with Christ in God,' Col. iii. 3, from the eyes of the world, and sometimes from their own. Here they are hidden under infirmities, afflictions, and disgraces, but yet never so hidden but that God sometimes lets down a beam of comfort and strength, which they would not lose, to be freed from their present condition, though never so grievous. God comes more immediately to them now than formerly he was used; nay, even when God seems to forsake them and to be their enemy, yet they are supported with such inward strength that they are able to make good their claim with Christ their head, and cry 'My God' still. God never so departs but he always leaves somewhat behind him which draws and keeps the heart to him. We are like poor Hagar, who, when the bottle of water was spent, fell a crying, Gen. xxi. 17, when there was a fountain close by, but her tears hindered her from seeing it. When things go ill with us in our trades and callings, and all is spent, then our spirits droop, and we are at our wits' end, as if God were not where he was. Oh, consider, if we had all and had not God, we had nothing. If we have nothing, and have God, we have enough, for we have him that hath all, and more than all, at his command. If we had all other comforts that our hearts can desire, yet if God withdraw himself, what remains but a curse and emptiness? What makes heaven but the presence of God? and what makes hell but the absence of God? Let God be in any condition, though never so ill, yet it is comfortable; and usually we find more of God in trouble than when we are out of trouble. The comforts of religion never come till others fail. Cordials are kept for faintings. When a curtain and a veil is drawn betwixt us and the creature, then our eyes are only upward to God, and he is more clearly seen of us.

In the division of things, God bequeaths himself to those that are his for their portion as the best portion he can give them. There are many goodly

* That is, 'artifices.'—G

† That is, 'without expedients.'—G.

things in the world, but none of these are a Christian's portion. There is in him to supply all good and remove all ill, until the time come that we stand in need of no other good. It is our chief wisdom to know him, our holiness to love him, our happiness to enjoy him. There is in him to be had whatsoever can truly make us happy. We go to our treasure and our portion in all our wants; we live by it and value ourselves by it. God is such a portion, that the more we spend on him the more we may. 'Our strength may fail, and our heart may fail, but God is our portion for ever,' Ps. lxxiii. 26. Everything else teaches us, by the vanity and vexation we find in them, that our happiness is not in them. They send us to God; they may make us worse, but better they cannot. Our nature is above them, and ordained for a greater good; they can go but along with us for a while, and their end swallows up all the comfort of their beginning, as Pharaoh's lean kine swallowed up the fat, Gen. xli. 20. If we have no better portion here than these things, we are like to have hell for our portion hereafter. What a shame will it be hereafter, when we are stript of all, that it should be said, Lo, this is the man that took not God for his portion. If God be once ours, he goes for ever along with us, and when earth will hold us no longer, heaven shall. Who that hath his senses about him would perish for want of water when there is a fountain by him? or for hunger, that is at a feast? God alone is a rich portion. O, then, let us labour for a large faith, as we have a large object. If we had a thousand times more faith, we should have a thousand times more increase of God's blessings. When the prophet came to the widow's house, as many vessels as she had were filled with oil, 1 Kings xvii. 14. We are straitened in our own faith, but not straitened in our God. It falls out oft in this world that God's people are like Israel at the Red Sea, environed with dangers on all sides. What course have we, then, to take, but only to look up and wait for the salvation of our God? This is a breast full of consolation; let us teach our hearts to suck and draw comfort from hence.

Is God *our* God, and will he suffer anything to befall us for our hurt? Will he lay any more upon us than he gives us strength to bear? Will he suffer any wind to blow upon us but for good? Doth he not set us before his face? Will a father or mother suffer a child to be wronged in their presence if they can help it? Will a friend suffer his friend to be injured if he may redress him? And will God, that hath put these affections into parents and friends, neglect the care of those he hath taken so near unto himself? No, surely. His eyes are open to look upon their condition; his ears are open to their prayers; a 'book of remembrance,' Mal. iii. 16, is written of all their good desires, speeches, and actions; he hath bottles for all their tears, Ps. lvi. 8; their very sighs are not hid from him, Ps. lxxix. 11; he hath written them upon the 'palms of his hands,' Isa. xlvi. 16, and cannot but continually look upon them. Oh, let us prize the favour of so good a God, who, though he dwells on high, yet will regard things so low, and not neglect the mean estate of any; nay, especially delights to be called the 'comforter of his elect,' John xiv. 16, and the God of those that are in misery, and have none to fly unto but himself.

But we must know that God only thus graciously visits his own children; he visits with his choicest favours those only that *fear his name*, Ps. xxv. 14. As for those that either secretly undermine or openly oppose the cause and church of God and join with his enemies, such as savour not the things of God, but commit spiritual idolatry and adultery with God's enemies, the world and the devil, God will answer these as once he did the

Israelites, when in their necessity they would have forced acquaintance upon him, 'Go to the gods whom ye have served,' Judges x. 14, to the great men whose persons you have obeyed for advantage, to your riches, to your pleasures, which you have loved more than God or goodness. You would not lose a base custom, an oath, a superfluity, a thing of nothing, for me; therefore, I will not own you now. Such men are more impudent than the devil himself, that will claim acquaintance with God at last when they have carried themselves as his enemies all their days. Satan could tell Paul and Silas they were 'the servants of the living God,' Acts xvi. 17, but he would not make that plea for himself, knowing that he was a cursed creature.

Miserable, then, is their condition who live in the world, nay, in the church, without God, Eph. ii. 12. Such are in a worse estate than pagans and Jews; for, living in the house of God, they are strangers from God and from the covenant of grace; usurping the name of Christians, having, indeed, nothing to do with Christ.

Some of these, like spiritual vagabonds, as Cain, excommunicate themselves from God's presence in the use of the means, or rather like devils, that will have nothing to do with God, because they are loath to be tormented before their time. They think every good sermon an arraigning of them, and therefore keep out of reach.

Others will present themselves under the means, and carry some savour away with them of what they hear, but it is only till they meet with the next temptation, unto which they yield themselves presently slaves. These shewed themselves under a general profession, as they did, who called themselves Jews and were nothing less. But, alas! an empty title will bring an empty comfort at last. It was cold comfort to the rich man in flames, Luke xvi. 25, that Abraham called him son; or to Judas, that Christ called him friend, Mat. xxvi. 50; or to the rebellious Jews, that God styles them his people, Isa. l. 2. Such as our profession is, such will our comfort be. True profession of religion is another thing than most men take it to be. It is made up of the outward duty, and the inward man too, which is, indeed, the life and soul of all. What the heart doth not in religion is not done. *Quod cor non facit non fit.*

God cares for no retainers that will only wear his livery, but serve themselves. 'What hast thou to do to take his name into thy mouth, and hatest to be reformed? Ps. l. 16. Saul lived in the bosom of the church, yet, being a cruel tyrant, when he was in a desperate plunge, his outward profession did him no good; and, therefore, when he was environed with his enemies he uttered this doleful complaint, 'God hath forsaken me, and the Philistines are upon me,' 1 Sam. xxviii. 15. A pitiful case! Yet so will it be with all those that rest in an outward profession, thinking it enough to compliment * with God when their hearts are not right within them. Such will at length be forced to cry, sickness is upon me, death is upon me, hell is before me, and God hath forsaken me. I would have none of God heretofore, now God will have none of me. When David himself had offended God by numbering the people, then God counted him but plain David, 'Go and say to David,' &c., 2 Sam. xxiv. 12; whereas before, when he purposed to build a temple, then, 'Go, tell my servant David,' 2 Sam. vii. 5. When the Israelites had set up an idol, then God fathers them on Moses, '*Thy* people which *thou* hast brought out of Egypt.' He would not own them as at other times then. They are my people still whilst they keep covenant. No care, no present comfort, in this near relation.

* That is, 'to pretend compliance.'—G.

The price of the pearl is not known till all else be sold, and we see the necessary use of it. So the worth of God in Christ is never discerned till we see our lost and undone condition without him, till conscience flies in our faces, and drags us to the brink of hell; then, if ever we taste how good the Lord is, we will say, 'Blessed is the people whose God is the Lord.' Heretofore I have heard of his lovingkindness, but that is not a thousandth part of what I see and feel. The joy I now apprehend is unutterable, unconceivable.

Oh then, when we have gotten our souls possessed of God, let our study be to preserve ourselves in his love, to walk close with him, that he may delight to abide with us and never forsake us! How basely doth the Scripture speak of whatsoever stands in our way! It makes nothing of them. What is man but vanity, and less than vanity! All nations but as 'a drop of the bucket,' as the 'dust of the balance,' Isa. xl. 15, things not at all considerable. Flesh looks upon them as through a multiplying glass, making them greater than they are; but faith, as God doth, sees them as nothing.

This is such a blessed condition, as may well challenge all our diligence in labouring to be assured of it; neither is it to be attained or maintained without the strength and prime of our care. I speak especially of, and in regard of, the sense and comfort of it. For the sense of God's favour will not be kept without keeping him in our best affections above all things in the world, without keeping of our hearts always close and near to him, which cannot be, without keeping a most narrow watch over our loose and unsettled hearts, that are ready to stray from God and fall to the creature. It cannot be kept without exact and circumspect walking, without constant self-denial, without a continual preparation of spirit, to want and forsake anything that God seeth fit to take from us.

But what of all this? Can we cross ourselves, or spend our labours to better purpose? One sweet beam of God's countenance will requite all this. We beat not the air, we plough not in the sand, neither sow in a barren soil; God is no barren wilderness. Nay, he never shews so much of himself as in suffering, and parting with anything for him, and denying ourselves of that which we think stands not with his will. Great persons require great observance. We can deny ourselves, and have men's persons in great admiration, for hope of some advantage; and is any more willing and more able to advance us than the great all-sufficient God? A Christian, indeed, undergoes more troubles, takes more pains, especially with his own heart, than others do. But what are these to his gains? What return so rich as trading with God? What comfort so great as these that are fetched from the fountain? One day spent in enjoying the light of God's countenance is sweeter than a thousand without it. We see here, when David was not only shut out from all comforts, but lay under many grievances, what a fruitful use he makes of this, that God was his God. It upholdeth his dejected, it stilleth his unquiet, soul; it leadeth him to the rock that was higher than he, and there stayeth him. It filleth him with comfortable hopes of better times to come. It sets him above himself, and all troubles and fears whatsoever.

Therefore wait still in the use of means till God shine upon thee; yea, though we know our sins in Christ are pardoned, yet there is something more that a gracious heart waits for us;* that is, a good look from God, a further enlargement of heart, and an establishing in grace. It was not

* Qu. 'waits for?'—Ed.

enough for David to have his sins pardoned, but to 'recover the joy of salvation,' and 'freedom of spirit,' Ps. li. 12. Therefore the soul should always be in a waiting condition, even until it be filled with the fulness of God, as much as it is capable of. Neither is it quiet alone, or comfort alone, that the soul longs after, no, nor the favour of God alone, but a gracious heart to walk worthy of God. It rests not whilst anything remains that may breed the least strangeness betwixt God and us.

CHAPTER XXXIII.—*Of experience and faith, and how to wait on God comfortably. Helps thereto.*

My God. These words further imply a special experience, that David's soul had felt of the goodness of God. He had found God distilling the comfort of his goodness and truth through the promises, and he knew he should find God again the same as he was, if he put him in mind of his former gracious dealing. His soul knew right well, how good God was, and he could seal to those truths he had found comfort by, therefore he thus speaks to his soul: *My soul,* what, *my soul,* that hast found God so good, so oft, so many ways, thou *my* soul to be discouraged, having God, and my God, with whom I have taken so much sweet counsel, and felt so much comfort from, and found always heretofore to stick so close unto me! Why shouldst thou now be in such a case, as if God and thou had been strangers one to another? If we could treasure up experiments,* the former part of our life would come in to help the latter; and the longer we live the richer in faith we should be; even as in victories, every former overthrow of an enemy helps to obtain a succeeding victory. The use of a sanctified memory is to lose nothing that may help in time of need. He had need be a well-tried and a known friend upon whom we lay all our salvation and comfort.

We ought to trust God upon other grounds, though we had never tried him; but when he helps our faith by former experience, this should strengthen our confidence, and shore up † our spirits, and put us on to go more cheerfully to God, as to a tried friend. If we were well read in the story of our own lives, we might have a divinity of our own, drawn out of the observation of God's particular dealing towards us; we might say, this and this truth I dare venture upon, I have found it true, I dare build all my happiness upon it. As Paul, 'I know whom I have trusted,' 2 Tim. i. 12, I have tried him, he never yet failed me, I am not now to learn how faithful he is to those that are his. Every new experience is a new knowledge of God, and should fit us for new encounters. If we have been good in former times, God remembers the 'kindness of our youth,' Jer. ii. 2; we should therefore remember the kindness of God even from our youth. Evidence of what we have felt, helps our faith in that which for the present we feel not.

Though it be one thing to live by faith, and another thing to live by sight, yet the more we see, and feel, and taste of God, the more we shall be led to rely on him, for that which as yet we neither see nor feel. 'Because thou hast been my helper,' saith David, 'therefore in the shadow of thy wings will I rejoice,' Ps. lxiii. 7. The time was, Lord, when thou shewedst thyself a gracious Father to me, and thou art unchangeable in thy nature, in thy love, and in thy gifts.

Yea, when there is no present evidence, but God shews himself as con-

* That is, 'experiences.'—G.

† That is, 'support.'—G.

trary to us, yet a former taste of God's goodness will enable to lay claim unto him still. God's concealing of himself is but a wise discipline for a time, until we be enabled to bear the full revealing of himself unto us for ever. In the mean time, though we have some sight and feeling in God, yet our constant living is not by it; the evidence of that we see not, is that which more constantly upholds the soul, than the evidence of anything we see or feel.

Yea, though our experience, by reason of our not minding of it in trouble, seems many times to stand us in no stead, but we fare as if God had never looked in mercy upon us; yet even here, some virtue remains of former sense, which with the present spirit of faith, helps us to look upon God as ours, as we have a present strength from food received and digested before. Vessels are something the better for that liquor they keep not, but runs through them.

But if experience should wholly fail, there is such a divine power in faith, as a very little beam of it, having no other help than a naked promise, will uphold the soul. Howsoever, we must neglect no help, for God oft suspends his comfort till we have searched all our helps. Though we see no light, yet we ought to search all crevices for light, and rejoice in the least beam of light, that we may see day by. It is the nature of true faith to search and pry into every corner, and if after all nothing appears, then it casts itself upon God as in the first conversion, when it had nothing to look upon but the offer of free mercy.* If at that time without former experience we did trust God, why not now, when we have forgotten our experience? The chief grounds of trusting God are always the same, whether we feel or feel not; nay, though for the present we feel the contrary, faith will never leave wrestling till it hath gotten a blessing. When faith is driven to work alone, having nothing but God, and his bare promise to rely upon, then God thinks it lies upon his credit to shew himself as a God unto us. God's power in creating light out of darkness is never more exalted, than when a guilty soul is lifted up by God to look for mercy, even when he seems armed with justice, to execute vengeance upon him; then the soul is brought to a near conformity unto Christ, who, 1, when he had the guilt of the sins of the whole world upon him; 2, when he was forsaken, and that after he had enjoyed the sweetest communion with his Father that ever creature could do; and not only so, but, 3, felt the weight of God's just displeasure against sin; and, 4, was abased lower than ever any creature was; yet still he held fast God as *his God*.

In earthly matters, if we have a title to anything by gift, contract, inheritance, or howsoever, we will not be wrangled out of our right. And shall we not maintain our right in God, against all the tricks and cavils of Satan and our own hearts? We must labour to have something, that we may shew that we are within the covenant. If we be never so little entered into the covenant, we are safe. And herein lies the special comfort of sincerity, that though our grace be little, yet it is of the right stamp, and shews us, that we are servants, and sons, though unworthy to be so. Here a little truth will go far. Hence it is that the saints in all their extremities still allege something, that shews that they are within the covenant; we are thy children, thy people, and thy servants, &c. God is mindful of his covenant, but is well pleased, that we should mind him of it too; and mind it ourselves to make use of it, as David doth here. He knew if he could bring his soul to his God, all would be quiet.

* Cum omnium incertus sit eventus, ad ea accedimus de quibus bene sperandum esse credimus.—*Sen*[*eca*].

God is so ready to mercy, that he delighteth in it, and delighteth in Christ, through whom he may shew mercy, notwithstanding his justice, as being fully satisfied in Christ. Mercy is his name that he will be known by. It is his glory which we behold in the face of Christ, who is nothing but grace and mercy itself. Nay, he pleads reasons for mercy, even from the sinfulness and misery of his creature, and maintains his own mercy against all the wrangling cavils of flesh and blood, that would put mercy from them; and hearken more willingly to Satan's objections, than God's arguments, till at length God subdues their spirits so far, as they become ashamed for standing out so long against him. How ready will God be to shew mercy to us when we seek it, that thus presseth upon us, when we seem to refuse it! If God should take advantage of our waywardness, what would become of us? Satan's course is to discourage those that God would have encouraged, and to encourage those whom God never speaks peace unto; and he thinks to gain both ways. Our care therefore should be, when we resolve upon God's ways, to labour that no discouragement fasten upon us, seeing God and his word speak all comfort to us.

And because the best of a Christian is to come, we should raise up our spirits to wait upon God, for that mercy which is yet to come. All inferior waitings for good things here, do but train us up in the comfortable expectation of the main.

This waiting on God requires a great strength of grace, by reason not only, 1, of the excellency of the things waited for, which are far beyond anything we can hope for in the world; but, 2, in regard of the long day which God takes before he performeth his promise; and, 3, from thence the tediousness of delay; 4, the many troubles of life in our way; 5, the great opposition we meet with in the world; 6, and scandals * ofttimes even from them that are in great esteem for religion; 7, together with the untowardness of our nature in being ready to be put off by the least discouragement. In these respects there must be more than a human spirit to hold up the soul, and carry it along to the end of that which we wait for.

But if God be our God, that love which engaged him to bind himself to us in precious promises, will furnish us likewise with grace needful, till we be possessed of them. He will give us leave to depend upon him both for happiness, and all sanctifying and quieting graces, which may support the soul, till it come to its perfect rest in God. For God so quiets the hearts of his children, as withal he makes them better and fitter for that which he provides for them. Grace and peace together. Our God is the God of grace and peace, of such graces as breed peace.

1. As he is a God of *love*, nay, love itself to us, so a taste of his love, raising up our love, is better than wine, full of nothing but encouragement. It will fetch up a soul from the deepest discouragement. This grace quickeneth all other graces. It hath so much spirits in it as will sweeten all conditions. Love enables to wait, as Jacob for Leah, seven years, Gen. xxxix. Nothing is hard to love; it carries all the powers of the soul with it.

2. As he is a God of *hope*, so by this grace, as an anchor fastened in heaven within the vail, he stayeth the soul; that though as a ship at anchor it may be tossed and moved, yet not removed from its station. This hope, as cork, will keep the soul, though in some heaviness, from sinking, and, as a helmet, bear off the blows, that they endanger not our life, Eph. vi. 17.

3. As God is a God of hope, so by hope, of *patience*, which is a grace whereby the soul resigneth up itself to God in humble submission to his

* That is, 'stumbling-blocks.'—G.

will, because he is our God, as David in extremity comforted himself 'in the Lord his God,' Ps. lxxxvi. 17. Patience breeds comfort, because it brings experience with it of God's owning of us to be his, Rom. v. 4. The soul, shod and fenced with this, is prepared against all rubs and thorns in our way, so as we are kept from taking offence. All troubles we suffer, do but help patience to its perfect work, Rom. v. 3; by subduing the unbroken sturdiness of our spirits, when we feel by experience, we get but more blows, by standing out against God.

4. The Spirit of God, likewise, is a spirit of *meekness*, whereby, though the soul be sensible of evil, yet it moderates such distempers, as would otherwise rob a man of himself; and together with patience, keepeth the soul in possession of itself. It stays murmurings and frettings against God or man. It sets and keeps the soul in tune. It is that which God, as he works, so he much delights in, and sets a price upon it, as the chief ornament of the soul. The 'meek of the earth seek God, and are hid in the day of his wrath,' Zeph. ii. 3; whereas, high spirits that compass themselves with pride as with a chain, Ps. lxxiii. 6, thinking to set out themselves by that which is their shame, are looked upon by God afar off. Meek persons will bow when others break; they are raised when others are plucked down, and stand when others that mount upon the wings of vanity, fall, Mat. v. 5; these prevail by yielding, and are lords of themselves, and other things else, more than other unquiet-spirited men: the blessings of heaven and earth attend on these.

5. So, likewise, *contentedness with our estate* is needful for a waiting condition, and this we have in our God, being able to give the soul full satisfaction. For outward things God knows how to diet us. If our condition be not to our mind, he will bring our mind to our condition. If the spirit be too big for the condition, it is never quieted, therefore God will level both. Those wants be well supplied, that are made up with contentedness, and with riches of a higher kind. If the Lord be our Shepherd, we can want nothing, Ps. xxiii. 1. This lifteth the 'weary hands and feeble knees,' even under 'chastisement,' Heb. xii. 12, wherein though the soul mourneth in the sense of God's displeasure, yet it rejoiceth in his fatherly care.

6. But patience and contentment are too low a condition for the soul to rest in, therefore the Spirit of God raiseth it up to a spiritual enlargement of *joy*. So much joy, so much light; and so much light, so much scattering of darkness of spirit. We see in nature how a little light will prevail over the thickest clouds of darkness; a little fire wastes a great deal of dross. The knowledge of God to be our God, brings such a light of joy into the soul, as driveth out dark uncomfortable conceits; this light makes lightsome. If the light of knowledge alone makes bold, much more the light of joy arising from our communion and interest in God. How can we enjoy God, and not joy in him? a soul truly cheerful rejoiceth that God whom it loveth, should think it worthy to endure anything for him. This joy often ariseth to a spirit of glory, even in matter of outward abasement. If the trouble accompanied with disgrace continue, the Spirit of glory rests upon us, and it will rest so long until it make us more than conquerors, even then when we seem conquered; for not only the cause, but the spirit riseth higher, the more the enemies labour to keep it under, as we see in Stephen, Acts vii.

With this joy goeth a spirit of courage and confidence. What can daunt that soul, which in the greatest troubles hath made the great God to be its own? Such a spirit dares bid defiance to all opposite power, setting the soul above the world, having a spirit larger and higher than the world, and seeing all but God beneath it, as being in heaven already in its head. After Moses and Micah had seen God in his favour to them, how little did they regard the angry countenances of those mighty princes, that were in their times the terrors of the world! The courage of a Christian is not only against sensible danger, and of flesh and blood, but against principalities and powers of darkness, against the whole kingdom of Satan, the god of the world, whom he knows shortly shall be trodden under his feet, Rom. xvi. 20. Satan and his may for a time exercise us, but they cannot hurt us. True believers are so many kings and queens, so many conquerors over that which others are slaves to. They can overcome themselves in revenge, they can despise those things that the world admires, and see an excellency in that which the world sets light by; they can set upon spiritual duties, which the world cannot tell how to go about, and endure that which others tremble to think of, and that upon wise reasons, and a sound foundation; they can put off themselves, and be content to be nothing, so their God may appear the greater, and dare undertake and undergo anything for the glory of their God. This courage of Christians among the heathens was counted obstinacy, but they knew not the power of the Spirit of Christ in his, which is ever strongest when they are weakest in themselves; they knew not the privy armour of proof that Christians had about their hearts, and thereupon counted their courage to be obstinacy.*

Some think the martyrs were too prodigal of their blood, and that they might have been better advised; but such are unacquainted with the force of the love of God kindled in the heart of his child, which makes him set such a price upon Christ and his truth, that he counts not 'his life dear unto him,' Acts xx. 24; he knows he is not his own, but hath given up himself to Christ, and therefore all that is his, yea, if he had more lives to give for Christ, he should have them. He knows he shall be no loser by it. He knows it is not a loss of his life, but an exchange for a better.

We see the creatures that are under us will be courageous in the eye of their masters, that are of a superior nature above them; and shall not a Christian be courageous in the presence of his great Lord and Master, who is present with him, about him, and in him? Undoubtedly, he that hath seen God once in the face of Christ, dares look the grimmest creature in the face, yea, death itself under any shape. The fear of all things flies before such a soul. Only a Christian is not ashamed of his confidence. Why should not a Christian be as bold for his God, as others are for the base gods they make to themselves?

7. Besides a spirit of *courage*, for establishing the soul, is required a spirit of *constancy*, whereby the soul is steeled and preserved immoveable in all conditions, whether present or to come, and is not changed in changes. And why? but because the spirit knows that God, on whom it rests, is unchangeable. We ourselves are as quicksilver, unsettled and moveable, till the spirit of constancy fix us. We see David sets out God in glorious terms, borrowed from all that is strong in the creature, to shew that he had great reason to be constant, and cleaving to him. 'He is my rock, my buckler, the horn of my salvation, my strong tower,' &c., Ps. xviii. God is a rock so deep, that no floods can undermine; so high, that no waves can reach, though they rise never so high, and rage never so much. When we stand upon this rock that is higher than we, we may overlook

* Tertul[lian] in Apol.—Also Pliny in his famous letter to the Emperor Trajan. His 'inflexibilis obstinatio' has passed into a world's proverb.—G.

all waves, swelling, and foaming, and breaking themselves, but not hurting us. And thereupon may triumphantly conclude with the apostle, that 'neither height, nor depth, shall ever separate us from the love of God,' Rom. viii. 39. Whatsoever is in the creature he found in his God, and more abundant. The soul cannot with an eye of faith look upon God in Christ, but it will be in its degree, as God is, quiet and constant. The spirit aimeth at such a condition as it beholdeth in God towards itself.

This constancy is upheld by endeavouring to keep a constant sight of God, for want of which it oft fares with us, like men, that having a city or tower in their eye, passing through uneven grounds, hills, and dales, sometimes get the sight thereof, sometimes lose it, and sometimes recover it again, though the tower be still where it was, and they nearer to it than they were at first. So it is oft with our uneven spirits: when once we have a sight of God, upon any present discouragement, we let fall our spirits, and lose the sight of him, until by an eye of faith we recover it again, and see him still to be where he was at first. The cherishing of passions take away the sight of God, as clouds take away the sight of the sun; though the sun be still where it was, and shineth as much as ever it did. We use to say, when the body of the moon is betwixt the sun and us, that the sun is eclipsed, when indeed not the sun but the earth is darkened: the sun loseth not one of its glorious beams. God is oft near us, as he was unto Jacob, and we are 'not aware of it,' Gen. xxviii. 17. God was near the holy man Asaph, when he thought him afar off. 'I am continually with thee,' saith he; 'thou holdest me by my right hand,' Ps. lxxiii. 27. Mary in her weeping passion could not see Christ before her; he seemed a stranger unto her. So long as we can keep our eye upon God, we are above the reach of sin or any spiritual danger.

Chapter XXXIV.—*Of confirming this trust in God: seek it of God himself. Sins hinder not: nor Satan. Conclusion and Soliloquy.*

§ I. But to return to the drawing out of our trust by *waiting*. Our estate in this world is still to wait, and happy it is that we have so great things to wait for; but our comfort is, that we have not only a 'furniture of graces,' 2 Pet. i. 5, one strengthening another as stones in an arch, but likewise God vouchsafeth some drops of the sweetness of the things we wait for, both to increase our desire of those good things, as likewise to enable us more comfortably to wait for them. And though we should die waiting, only cleaving to the promise, with little or no taste of the good promised; yet this might comfort us, that there is a life to come, that is, a life of sight and sense, and not only of taste but of fulness, and that for 'evermore,' Ps. xvi. 11. Our condition here is to live by faith and not by sight; only to make our living by faith more lively, it pleaseth God when he sees fit, to increase our earnest of that we look for. Even here God waits 'to be gracious to those that wait for him,' Isa. xxx. 18. And in heaven Christ waits for us, we are part of his 'fulness,' Eph. i. 23; it is part of his joy that 'we shall be where he is,' John xvii. 24; he will not therefore be long without us. The blessed angels and saints in heaven wait for us. Therefore let us be content as strangers to wait a while till we come home, and then we 'shall be for ever with the Lord,' Rev. xxii. 5; there is our eternal rest, where we shall enjoy both our God and ourselves in perfect happiness, being, as without need, so without desire, of the least change. When the time of our departure thither comes, then we may say as David, 'Enter now, my soul, into thy rest,' Ps. cxvi. 7. This is the 'rest which remaineth for God's people,' Heb. iv. 9, that is worth the waiting for, when we shall rest from all labour of sin and sorrow, and lay our heads in the bosom of Christ for ever.

It stands us therefore upon to get this great charter more and more confirmed to us, that God is *our God*, for it is of everlasting use unto us. It first begins at our entering into covenant with God, and continues not only unto death, but entereth into heaven with us. As it is our heaven upon earth to enjoy God as ours, so it is the very heaven of heaven, that there we shall for ever behold him, and have communion with him.

The degrees of manifesting this propriety * in God are divers, rising one upon another, as 'the light clears up by little and little till it comes to a perfect day,' Prov. iv. 18. 1. As the ground of all the rest, we apprehend God to be a God of some peculiar persons, as favourites above others. 2. From hence is stirred up in the soul a restless desire, that God would discover himself so to it, as he doth to those that are his, that he would 'visit our souls with the salvation of his chosen,' Ps. cvi. 4. 3. Hence follows a putting of the soul upon God, an adventuring itself on his mercy. 4. Upon this, God, when he seeth fit, discovers by his Spirit that he is ours. 5. Whence followeth a dependence on him as ours, for all things that may carry us on in the way to heaven. 6. Courage and boldness in setting ourselves against whatsoever may oppose us in the way, as the three young men in Daniel, 'Our God can deliver us if he will,' Dan. iii. 17. 'Our God is in heaven,' &c., Ps. cxv. 3. 7. After which springs a sweet spiritual security, whereby the soul is freed from slavish fears, and glorieth in God as ours in all conditions. And this is termed by the apostle, not only assurance, but the 'riches of assurance,' Col. ii. 2. Yet this is not so clear and full as it shall be in heaven, because some clouds may after arise out of the remainder of corruption, which may something overcast this assurance, until the light of God's countenance in heaven for ever scatters all.

There being so great happiness in this nearness betwixt God and us, no wonder if Satan labour to hinder the same, by interposing the guilt and heinousness of our sins, which he knows of themselves will work a separation; but these, upon our first serious thought of returning, will be removed. As they could not hinder our meeting with God, so they may cause a strangeness for a time, but not a parting, a hiding of God's countenance, but not a banishing of us from it. Peter had denied Christ, and the rest of the apostles had left him all alone; yet our Saviour, after his resurrection, forgets all former unkindnesses; he did not so much as object it to them, but sends Mary, who herself had been a great sinner, as an apostle to the apostles, and that presently, to tell them that he was risen, Mat. xxviii. 7; his care would have no delay. He knew they were in great heaviness for their unkindness. Though he was now entered into the first degree of his glory, yet we see his glory made him not forget his poor disciples. Above all, he was most careful of Peter, as deeper in sin than the rest, and therefore deeper in sorrow. 'Go tell Peter,' he needs most comfort. But what is the message? that 'I ascend not to my Father alone, but to your Father; not to my God only, but to your God,' John xx. 17.

And shall not we be bold to say so after Christ hath taught us, and put this claim into our mouths? If once we let this hold go, then Satan hath us where he would; every little cross then dejects us. Satan may darken

* That is, 'property, interest in.'—G.

the joy of our salvation, but not take away the God of our salvation. David, after his crying sin of murder, prays, 'Restore unto me the joy of thy salvation,' Ps. li. 12; this he had lost; but yet in the same psalm he prays, 'Deliver me from blood, O God, thou God of my salvation,' Ps. li. 14; therefore, whatsoever sense, reason, temptation, the law, or guilt upon conscience shall say, nay, however God himself, by his strange carriage to us may seem to be, yet let us cast ourselves upon him, and not suffer this plea to be wrung from us, but shut our eyes to all, and look upon God 'all-gracious and all-sufficient, who is the Father, the begetter of comfort,' 2 Cor. i. 3; the God, the creator of consolation, not only of things that may comfort, but of the comfort itself conveyed through these unto us. 'Who is a God like unto our God, that passeth by the sins of the remnant of his people?' Micah vii. 18. This should not be thought on without admiration; and indeed there is nothing so much deserves our wonderment as such mercy, of such a God, to such as we.

Since God hath 'avouched us to be his peculiar people,' Deut. xxvi. 18, let us avouch him, and since he hath passed his word for us, let us pass our words for him that we will be his, and stand for him, and to our power advance his cause. Thus David out of an enlarged spirit saith, 'Thou art my God, and I will praise thee; thou art my God, and I will exalt thee,' Ps. cxix. 28. Whatsoever we engage for God, we are sure to be gainers by. The true Christian is the wisest merchant, and makes the best adventure. He may stay long, but is sure of a safe and a rich return. A godly man is most wise for himself. We enter on religion, upon these terms, to part with ourselves, and all, when God shall call for it.

§ II. God much rejoiceth in sinners converted, as monuments of his mercy, and because the remembrance of their former sins whets them on to be more earnest in his service, especially after they have felt the sense of God's love. They even burn with a holy desire of honouring him, whom before they dishonoured, and stand not upon doing or suffering anything for him, but cheerfully embrace all occasions of expressing obedience.* God hath more work from them than from others; why then should any be discouraged?

Neither is it sins after our conversion, that nullify this claim of God to be *ours*. For this is the grand difference betwixt the two covenants, that now God will be merciful to our sins, 'if our hearts by faith be sprinkled with the blood of Christ,' Heb. x. 22. Though one sin was enough to bring condemnation, yet the free gift of grace in Christ is of many offences unto justification. And we have a sure ground for this, for the righteousness of Christ is God's righteousness, and God will thus glorify it, that it shall stand good to those that by faith apply it against their daily sins, even till at once we cease both to live and sin. For this very end was the Son of God willingly 'made sin,' Gal. iii. 13, that we might be freed from the same. And if all our sins laid upon Christ could not take away God's love from him, shall they take away God's love from us, when by Christ's blood our souls are purged from them?

O mercy of all mercies, that when we were once his, and gave away ourselves for nothing, and so became neither his nor our own, that then he would vouchsafe to become ours, and make us his by such a way, as all the angels in heaven stand wondering at; even his Son, not only taking our nature and miserable condition, but our sin upon him, that that being done

* Ex ipso dolore suo compuncti, inardescunt amore Dei. Damna præcedentia lucris sequentibus compensant.—*Greg*[*ory*].

away, we might through Christ have boldness with God as ours, who is now in heaven appearing there for us, until he bring us home to himself, and presents us to his Father for his for ever!

Think not then only that we are God's and he ours, but from what love and by what glorious means this was brought to pass. What can possibly disable this claim, when God for this end hath founded a covenant of peace so strongly in Christ, that sin itself cannot disannul it? Christ was therefore manifest, 'that he might destroy this greatest work of the devil,' 1 John iii. 5, 8. Forgiveness of sins now is one chief part of our portion in God. It is good therefore not to pore and plod so much upon sin and vileness by it, as to forget that mercy that rejoiceth over judgment. If we once be God's, though we 'drink this deadly poison, it shall not hurt us,' Mark xvi. 18. God will make a medicine, an antidote of it; and for all other evils, the fruit of them is by God's sanctifying the same, the taking away sin out of our natures; so that lesser evils are sent to take away the greater. If God could not over-rule evils to his own ends, he would never suffer them.

§ III. I have stood the longer upon this, because it is the *one thing needful*, Luke x. 42; the one thing we should desire, that this one God, in whom and from whom is all good, should be ours. All promises of all good in the new covenant, spring first from this, that God 'will be ours, and we shall be his,' Jer. xxxii. 38. What can we have more? and what is in the world less that will content us long, or stand us in any stead, especially at that time when all must be taken from us? Let us put up all our desires for all things we stand in need of, in this right we have to God in Christ, who hath brought God and us together. He can deny us nothing, that hath not denied us himself. If he be moved from hence to do us good, that we are his, let us be moved to fetch all good from him, on the same right that he is ours.

The persuasion of this will free us from all pusillanimity, lowliness, and narrowness of spirit, when we shall think that nothing can hurt us, but it must break through God first. If God give quietness, who shall 'make trouble?' Job xxxiv. 29. If God be with us, who can be against us? This is that which puts comfort into all other comforts, that maketh any burden light; this is always ready for all purposes. Our God is a present and a seasonable help. All evils are at his command to be gone, and all comforts at his command to come. It is but, go comfort, go peace, to such a man's heart: cheer him, raise him; go salvation, rescue such and such a soul in distress. So said and so done presently. Nay, with reverence be it spoken, so far doth God pass over himself unto us, that he is content himself to be commanded by us. 'Concerning the work of my hands command you me,' Isa. xlv. 11; lay the care and charge of that upon me. He is content to be out-wrestled and overpowered by a spirit of faith, as in Jacob, and the woman of Canaan, to be as it were at our service. He would not have us want anything wherein he is able to help us. And what is there wherein God cannot help us? If Christians knew the power they have in heaven and earth, what were able to stand against them? What wonder is it if faith overcome the world, if it overcomes him that made the world? that faith should be almighty, that hath the Almighty himself ready to use all his power for the good of them to whom he hath given the power of himself unto? Having therefore such a living fountain to draw from, such a centre to rest in, having all in one, and that one ours, why should we knock at any other door? We may go boldly to God now, as made 'ours, being bone of our bone, and flesh of our flesh.' We may go more comfortably to God, than to any angel or saint. God in the second person hath vouchsafed to take our nature upon him, but not that of angels. Our God and our man, our God-man is ascended unto the high court of heaven, to his and our God, clothed with our nature. Is there any more able and willing to plead our cause, or to whom we may trust business with, than he, who is in 'heaven for all things for us, appertaining to God?' Heb. v. 1.*

It should therefore be the chief care of a Christian, upon knowledge of what he stands in need of, to know where to supply all. It should raise up a holy shame and indignation in us, that there should be so much in God, who is so near unto us in Christ, and we make so little use of him. What good can any thing do us if we use it not? God is ours to use, and yet men will rather use shifts and unhallowed policies, than be beholden to God, who thinks himself never more honoured by us than when we make use of him. If we believe anything will do us good, we naturally make out for the obtaining of it. If we believe anything will hurt us, we study to decline it. And certain it is, if we believed that so much good were in God, we would then apply ourselves to him, and him to ourselves. Whatsoever virtue is in anything, it is conveyed by application and touching of it; that whereby we touch God, is our faith, which never toucheth him, but it draws virtue from him. Upon the first touch of faith, spiritual life is begun. It is a bastard in nature, to believe anything can work upon another without spiritual or bodily touch. And it is a monster in religion to believe that any saving good will issue from God, if we turn from him, and shut him out, and our hearts be unwilling. Where unbelief is, it binds up his power. Where faith is, there it is between the soul and God, as betwixt the iron and the loadstone, a present closing and drawing of one to the other. This is the beginning of eternal life, so to 'know God the Father and his Son Christ,' John xvii. 4, as thereby to embrace him with the arms of faith and love as ours, by the best title he can make us, who is truth itself.

Since then our happiness lies, out of ourselves, in God, we should go out of ourselves for it, and first get into Christ, and so unto God in him; and then labour, by the Spirit of the Father and the Son, to maintain acquaintance with both, that so God may be ours, not only in covenant, but in communion, hearkening what he will say to us, and opening our spirits, disclosing our wants, consulting and advising in all our distresses with him. By keeping this acquaintance with God, 'peace and all good is conveyed to us,' Job xxii. 21.

Thereafter as we maintain this communion further with him, we out of love study to please him, by exact walking according to his commands; then we shall feel increase of peace as our care increaseth; then he will 'come and sup with us,' Rev. iii. 20, and be free in his refreshing of us; then he will shew himself more and more to us, and manifest still a further degree of presence in joy and strength, until communion in grace ends in communion in glory.

But we must remember, as David doth here, to desire and delight in God himself more than in anything that is God's. It was a sign of St Paul's pure love to the Corinthians when he said, 'I seek not yours, but

* Tutius et jucundius loquor ad meum Jesum quam ad aliquem sanctorum Dei &c. Quod ego sum, fieri dignatus est Deus, non factus est quod angeli. Ad curiam Dei sui, Dei tui, præcessit Deus tuus, homo tuus; tunica tua indutus illic assidue pro nobis interpellat.—*Aug*[*ustine*].

you,' 2 Cor. xii. 14. We should seek for no blessing of God so much as for himself.

What is there in the world of equal goodness to draw us away from our God? If to preserve the dearest thing we have in the world, we break with God, God will take away the comfort we look to have by it, and it will prove but a dead contentment, if not a torment to us. Whereas, if we care to preserve communion with God, we shall be sure to find in him whatsoever we deny for him, honour, riches, pleasures, friends, all; so much the sweeter, by how much we have the more immediately from the spring-head. We shall never find God to be our God more than when, for making of him to be so, we suffer anything for his sake. We enjoy never more of him than then.

At the first we may seek to him, as rich to supply our wants, as a physician to cure our souls and bodies; but here we must not rest till we come to rejoice in him as our friend, and from thence rise to an admiration of him for his own excellencies, that being so high in himself, out of his goodness would stoop low to us. And we should delight in the meditation of him, not only as good to us, but as good in himself; because goodness of bounty springs from goodness of disposition. He doth good, because he is good.

A natural man delights more in God's gifts than in his grace. If he desires grace, it is to grace himself, not as grace, making him like unto God, and issuing from the first grace, the free favour of God; by which means men come to have the gifts of God without God himself; *dona Dei, sine Deo*. But, alas! what are all other goods, without the chief good? They are but as flowers, which are long in planting, in cherishing, and growing, but short in enjoying the sweetness of them. David here joys in God himself; he cares for nothing in the world but what he may have with his favour; and whatever else he desires, he desires only that he may have the better ground from thence to praise his God.

§ IV. The sum of all is this, *the state of God's dear children in this world is to be cast into variety of conditions*, wherein, they, consisting of nature, flesh, and spirit, every principle hath its own and proper working. They are sensible as flesh and blood; they are sensible to discouragements as sinful flesh and blood; but they recover themselves, as having a higher principle, God's Spirit, above flesh and blood in them.

In this conflicting state, every principle labouring to maintain itself, at length by help of the Spirit, backing and strengthening his own work, grace gets the better, keeping nature within bounds, and suppressing corruption. And this the soul, so far as it is spiritual, doth by gathering itself to itself, and by reasoning the case so far, till it concludes, and joins upon this issue, that the only way to attain sound peace is, when all other means fail, to trust in God. And thereupon he lays a charge upon his soul so to do, as being a course grounded upon the highest reason, even the unchangeable goodness of God; who, out of the riches of his mercy, having chosen a people in this world, which should be to the glory of his mercy, will give them matter of setting forth his praise, in shewing some token of good upon them, as being those on whom he hath fixed his love, and to whom he will appear not only a Saviour, but salvation itself; nothing but salvation. As the sun is nothing but light, so whatsoever proceeds from him to them tends to further salvation. All his ways towards them lead to that; which ways of his, though for a time they are secret, and not easily found out, yet at length God will be wonderful in them, to the admiration of his enemies themselves, who shall be forced to say, God hath done great things for them; and all from this ground, that God is our God in covenant; which words are a stern * that rule and guide the whole text.

For why should we not be disquieted when we are disquieted? Why should we not be cast down when we are cast down? Why should we trust in God as a Saviour, but that he is *our God*, making himself so to us in his choicest favours? doing that for us which none else can do, and which he doth to none else that are not his in a gracious manner. This blessed interest and intercourse betwixt God's Spirit and our spirits, is the hinge upon which all turns; without this no comfort is comfortable; with this, no trouble can be very troublesome.

Without this assurance there is little comfort in soliloquies; unless, when we speak to ourselves, we can speak to God as ours. For in desperate cases our soul can say nothing to itself to still itself, unless it be suggested by God. Discouragements will appear greater to the soul than any comfort, unless God comes in as ours.

See therefore David's art; he demands of himself why he was so cast down? The cause was apparent, because there were troubles without and terrors within, and none to comfort. Well, grant this, saith the Spirit of God in him, as the worst must be granted; yet, saith the Spirit, Trust in God. *So I have.*

Why, then, wait in trusting; 'light is sown for the righteous,' Ps. xcvii. 11; it comes not up on the sudden. We must not think to sow and reap both at once. If trouble be lengthened, lengthen thy patience.

What good will come of this?

God will wait to do thee that good, for which thou shalt praise him; he will deal so graciously with thee, as he will deserve thy praise; he will shew thee his salvation. And new favours will stir thee up to sing new songs. Every new recovery of ourselves or friends is as it were a new life, and ministers new matter of praise. And upon offering this sacrifice of praise, the heart is further enlarged to pray for fresh blessings. We are never fitter to pray than after praise.

But in the mean time I hang down my head, whilst mine enemies carry themselves highly, and my friends stand aloof.

God in his own time, which is best for thee, will be the salvation of thy countenance; he will compass thee about with songs of deliverance, and make it appear at last that he hath care of thee.

But why then doth God appear as a stranger to me?

That thou shouldst follow after him with the stronger faith and prayer; he withdraws himself, that thou shouldst be the more earnest in seeking after him. God speaks the sweetest comfort to the heart in *the wilderness.* Happily thou art not yet low enough, nor purged enough. Thy affections are not thoroughly crucified to the world, and therefore it will not yet appear that it is God's good will to deliver thee. Wert thou a fit subject of mercy, God would bestow it on thee.

But what ground hast thou to build thyself so strongly upon God?

He hath offered and made himself to be *my God*, and so hath shewed himself in former times; and I have made him *my God*, by yielding him his sovereignty in my heart; besides the present evidence of his blessed Spirit, clearing the same, and many peculiar tokens of his love which I daily do enjoy; though sometimes the beams of his favour are eclipsed.

* That is, 'rudder' or 'helm,' using the place for the thing.—G.

Those that are God's, besides their interest and right in him, have oft a sense of the same, even in this life, as a foretaste of that which is to come. To the seal of grace stamped upon their hearts, God superadds a fresh seal of joy and comfort, by the presence and witness of his Spirit; and shews likewise some outward token for good upon them, whereby he makes it appear that 'he hath set apart him that is godly for himself, as his own,' Ps. iv. 3.

Thus we see that discussing of objections in the consistory of the soul settles the soul at last, faith at length silencing all risings to the contrary. All motion tends to rest, and ends in it. God is the centre and resting-place of the soul, and here David takes up his rest, and so let us. Then whatsoever times come, we are sure of a hiding-place and sanctuary.

FINIS.

'Although the fig-tree shall not blossom, neither shall fruit be in the vines, the labour of the olive shall fail, and the fields shall yield no meat, &c., yet I will rejoice in the Lord, I will joy in the God of my salvation,' Hab. iii. 17.

'He that dwelleth in the secret place of the Most High, shall lodge under the shadow of the Almighty. I will say of the Lord, He is my refuge, and my fortress; My God, in him will I trust,' Ps. xci. 1, 2.

'My strength and my heart faileth, but God is the strength of my heart, and my portion for ever,' Ps. lxxiii. 26.

NOTES.

(a) P. 153.—Nero. Consult Long's excellent memoir of this worst of all the Cæsars, in Dr Smith's Dictionary of Greek and Roman Biography and Mythology.

(b) P. 158.—'File.' 'In good sadness, I do not know; either it is there, or it is upon a *file*, with the duke's other letters, in my tent.'—*All's Well that Ends Well*, iv. 3.

(c) P. 171.—'Restrained.' The touching saying told of many, from John Bradford to John Newton, and certainly used by the latter, on seeing a criminal ascending the gallows, 'There goes John Newton, but for the grace of God,' illustrates this.

(d) Caracciolus. The following are the title-pages of the translations referred to in foot-note, page 184:—

1. 'Newes from Italy of a second Moses, or the Life of Galeacius Caracciolus the noble Marquesse of Vico.' 4to. London. 1608.

2. 'A President to the Nobilitie of Court and Countrey, in the Life of Galeacius Caracciolus, the noble Marquesse of Vico in the Kingdome of Naples.' 4to. 1612.

The incident noted by Sibbes is thus narrated:—

'At that time *Peter Marytr Vermilius*, a *Florentine*, was a publik preacher and reader at *Naples*. This man was a canon regular (as they call them), a man since then of great name for his singular knowledge in Christian religion, his godly manners and behaviours, and for his sweet and copious teaching; for he afterwards, casting away his monkes coule, and renouncing the superstitions of Poperie, he shone so brightly in God's church, that he dispersed and strangely drove away the darknesse and mists of popery. *Galeacius* was once content at *Cæserta* his motion to be drawen to heare *Peter Marytr's* sermon, yet not so much for any desire he had to learne, as moved and tickled with a curious humour to heare so famous a man as then *Martyr* was accounted at that time. *Peter Marytr* was in hand with *Paul's* first

Epistle to the *Corinthians*; and as he was shewing the weakness and deceitfulnes of the iudgement of man's reason in spirituall things, as likewise the power and efficasy of the word of God in those men in whom the Lord worketh by his Spirit, amongst other things, he vsed this similie or comparison—If a man walking in a large place see a farre off men and women dancing together, and heare no sound of instrument, he will iudge them mad, or at least foolish; but if he come neerer them, and perseive their order, and heare their musicke, and marke their measures and their courses, he will then be of another minde, and not onely take delight in seeing them, but feele a desire in himself to beare them company, and dance with them. Even the same (said *Martyr*) betides many men, who, when they behold in others a suddain and great change of their looks, apparell, behaviour, and whole course of life, at the first sight they impute it to melancholy, or some other foolish humour; but if they looke more narrowly into the matter, and begin to heare and perceive the harmony and sweet concent of God's Spirit and his word in them (by the ioint power of which two this change was made and wrought, which afore they counted folly), then they change their opinion of them, and, first of all, begin to like them, and that change in them, and afterwards feele in themselves a motion and desire to imitate them, and to be of the number of such men, who, forsaking the world and his vanities, doe thinke that they ought to reforme their lives by the rule of the gospell, that so they may come to true and sound holinesse. This comparison, by the grace of God's Spirit, wrought so wonderfully with *Galeacius* (as himselfe hath often tolde his friends), that from that houre he resolved with himselfe more carefully to restraine his affections from following the world and his pleasures, as before they did, and to set his mind about seeking out the truth of religion, and the way to true happinesse. To this purpose he began to reade the Scriptures every day, being perswaded that truth of religion and soundnesse of wisdom was to be drawen out of that fountaine, and that the highway to heaven was thence to be sought. And further, all his acquaintance and familiarity did he turne into such company as out of whose life and conferences he was perswaded he might reape the fruit of godlinesse and pure religion; and thus farre in this short time had the Lord wrought with him by that sermon, as, first, to consider with himselfe seriously whether he was right or no; secondly, to take up an exercise continuall of reading Scripture; thirdly, to change his former company, and make choice of better. And this was done in the year one thousand five hundred fortie and one, and in the foure and twentieth yeare of his age.'

There is a marginal note, having relation to the chapter, and not to any particular sentence in it—'See how the first step of a man's conversion from popery is true and sound mortification of carnal lusts, and a change of life. See, also, how the first means to bring a man out of error to the truth is study of holy Scriptures.'

(e) P. 186.—'Idiot.' The original word here (1 Cor. xiv. 24), 'ἰδιώτης, which Sibbes renders literally, and which Wickliffe had so done long before, meant, at the period, simply a private person, as opposed to officials, and not at all, as now, a fatuous person.

(f) P. 192.—'Pity a beast over-loaden, and yet take no pity of a brother.' Sterne, weeping and moralising over a 'dead ass,' and at the very time neglecting his nearest relatives, has long 'pointed this moral.'

(g) P. 209.—Bishop Patrick and the 'Soul's Conflict.' The paragraph commencing 'The laws under which we live,' as stated in the foot-note (page 209), forms the basis of an extraordinary charge against the Puritans by Bishop Patrick, only less extraordinary than his mode of putting it. It occurs in his, it must be allowed us to say, miscalled '*Friendly* Debate betwixt two Neighbours, the one a Conformist, the other a Nonconformist,' described below.*

Perhaps the better way to deal with the charge will be to give it in full, and then see what can be said about it. Be it observed, that *C.* stands for Conformist, and *N. C.* for Nonconformist. The passage is as follows (part ii., 1669, pp. 219–222; in Taylor's scholarly edition of Patrick's Works, vol. v., pp. 655–57) :—

C. I must add, that you are all guilty of too much confidence, and talk as if you were infallible in your conclusions. When you see, therefore, the folly of it in another, mend it in yourselves; and do not talk hereafter as if all godly men had

* The 'Friendly Debate.' Part 1st, 1668; part 2d, 1669; part 3d, 1669-70; appendix to part 3d, 1669-70, with a postscript. Curiously enough, the 6th edition, 'enlarged and corrected,' does not include part 3d, or any of the additions, though published long subsequently, viz., in 1683-4.

ever been of your mind; no man of a tender conscience but held it unlawful to prescribe anything in God's worship. Everybody knows Cartwright, Reynolds, Greenham were of this opinion, as the prefacer boldly told you; and it is a wonder he did not add Dr Sibbes. For so some of your party took care the world should believe, and *chose rather to corrupt his writings, than have it thought he was of another persuasion*

N. C. I shall never believe it.

C. You may choose; but I shall prove that this good man's writings were *abused presently after his death* in this very point. For in his book called the Soul's Conflict he gave this direction, among others, to guide a soul in doubtful cases—'The laws under which we live are particular determinations of the law of God, and therefore ought to be a rule to us, *so far as they reach.* Though it be too narrow a rule to be good only so far as man's law guides unto, yet law, being the joint reason and consent of many men for public good, *hath an use* for the guiding of our actions *that are under the same. Where it dashes not against God's law,* what is agreeable to law is agreeable to conscience.' Thus the rule stood when the book first came out.* But in a very short time after, when he was newly laid in his grave, the first words were changed into these—'The laws under which we live are particular determinations of the law of God in some duties *of the second table.*'† *In which they made two restrictions of that which he had said in general words; first, they restrained the rule to the second table, and not to all things neither, but only some duties; and then they add a whole sentence, by way of example, which* was not in the first edition, *which I make no doubt was done on purpose, lest any man who read the book should think it was the Doctor's opinion, that we should conform to the orders of our governors about the worship of God, where the law of God hath determined nothing in particular, and their laws do not cross his. But what is there done by the Jesuits worse than this? What greater injury to the dead than thus to play tricks with their books, and change their words at your pleasure.*

N. C. It is very strange.

C. I have something more to tell you. As they have added here, so they have taken away in another place just before it. He is answering, I told you, this question, What course must we take for guidance of our lives in particular actions wherein doubts may arise, what is most agreeable to God's will? And one advice is this—'We must look to our place wherein God hath set us. If we be in subjection to others, their authority in doubtful things ought to sway with us.' A dangerous rule, some men thought; and therefore in the next edition *they left out those words,* 'in doubtful things;' and also blotted out this whole sentence which follows—'It is certain we ought to obey *(viz., in doubtful things of which he is speaking)*, and if the things wherein we are to obey be certain to us, we ought to leave that which is uncertain, and stick to that which is certain. In this case, we must obey those that are under God.'

N. C. Are you sure of this?

C. As sure as that I see you; though I must tell you there was a neat device to hide this fraud: for they *reprinted the book speedily with the very same title-page that was before, without giving notice that it was a second edition; and by leaving out those lines, and adding an example, as I told you, to illustrate the rule as they had restrained it, they made the pages exactly even as they were at the first.*‡ *Afterward the book was divided into chapters; and in all editions since, you will find these rules* (chap. 17) *with these alterations.*

N. C. By his own appointment, it is like.

C. Why did they not tell us so?

N. C. I know not.

C. I will tell you then. They were loth to tell a plain lie; for the Doctor died within three days after he had writ his preface to the first impression, *and therefore, it is most likely, made no alterations.* That preface was dated July the first 1635,§ and he died July the fourth. So I gather from those who put out his two last sermons, preached June 21st and 28th; and he died, say they, the Lord's day following.

* First Edition, 1635, page 364.

† From page 364 of B. I note this, as Taylor in his edition of the 'Friendly Debate' mistakenly gives a reference to C.—G.

‡ There are two editions of 1635, one of his own, another of somebody's else, but so ordered, that they seem the same. At least, they reprinted that sheet (wherein these things are contained) with these alterations, which I add lest I should not be rightly understood by all.

§ Mr Taylor adds a foot-note here—'The day of the month is not appended in the first unaltered edition, a copy of which is in the Bodleian Library.' This is an overlook. The 'unaltered edition' A is now before me, and it bears the date 'July 1. 1635.' Mr Taylor apparently turned to the 'Epistle Dedicatory,' which is undated, instead of to the address 'To the Reader.'—G.

Immediately after which came out a new impression of the same year 1635, *but not called a second edition, which they would have us believe was not till* 1636; a mere cheat, as I confidently affirm, *having seen and compared all.*

Not satisfied with the preceding, the charge is renewed, and, if possible, intensified in a 'general preface' to the '6th edition' [1684, § ix.; in Taylor's edition *supra*, vol. v., pp. 262–3]. That the whole may be before our readers, this fresh assault may also be given:—

'And let me beseech all those who shall cast their eyes on this preface, by no means to hearken to one sort of people among them, but to look upon them as men of an evil mind, that are perniciously bent to their own and all our destruction; such, I mean, as persuade them to read nothing that is said for their information, and take as great care to continue their scruples as we do to remove them. An instance of which we had long ago in the corrupting of Dr Sibbes's book, called the Soul's Conflict, which hath been in many hands since, and might have done much to the settling men's minds in dutiful obedience to authority, if they of the then discontented party had not falsified his words, and quite altered the sense of his discourse. For it was intended to satisfy weak and doubtful people in those very things, as well as others, which still trouble this church; but lest they should receive such satisfaction as to conform to public orders, when they were in any uncertainty of mind about them (as Dr Sibbes honestly advised them to do, nay, told them they ought to do, notwithstanding their doubts and scruples), there was care taken to have that passage quite blotted out of his book immediately upon his death, which happened as soon as the book had seen the light. Read the second part of this treatise, pp. 225, 226, &c., and then consider what kind of conscience this is, and how impudently it pretends to tenderness, which is so strait-laced about a ceremony, and takes such a liberty as this to *deprave* other men's writings, and make them speak contrary to their meaning. If they could be persuaded to reflect whose practice this is, and how odious it hath made those who have been guilty of it, it is possible they might be ashamed to find this foul and (as they would call it in others) anti-Christian dealing among themselves.'

Such is the charge and case of the bishop against the Puritans in all its length and breadth, and I would now make a few remarks upon it. It only requires, I apprehend, a statement of matters-of-fact to set the whole aside. But it were to dishonour the memory of the Puritans to emulate the spirit of the bishop in vindicating them.

[*a*] The text of the *sentences* (let the word be marked) in question *is* found in 'Soul's Conflict' A, the original edition, as given in the 'Friendly Debate;' and the changes alleged are accurately represented from 'Soul's Conflict' B. But—

[*b*] The following specific notice, which the bishop, as will be shewn, knew of, but apparently found it convenient to ignore, warrants us in affirming that the omissions and additions of B, were made, if not from the dictation, at least with the sanction of Sibbes himself. It is taken from the close of the address 'To the Christian Reader:'—'By reason,' he says, 'of my absence while the work was in printing, SOME SENTENCES were MISTAKEN.'* Now, that the '*sentences*' in debate were those herein referred to, is self-evident, from this fact, that they are THE ONLY SENTENCES IN THE WHOLE BOOK changed in B. Nor is this all. For—

[*c*] As if to guard against the abuse of the 'general rule' laid down in the mistaken sentences, in absence of the after-limitations inserted in B, he adds—'Some men will be ready to *deprave* the labours of other men's, but, so good may be done, let all such ill-disposed persons be what they are, and what they will be, unless God turn their hearts.'† I remark by the way—

[*d*] That it is the more necessary to attend to the intimation by Sibbes of 'mistaken *sentences*,' inasmuch as Pickering's beautiful, but, unfortunately, inaccurate, reprint of the 'Soul's Conflict,' by a strange oversight, omits it.‡

[*e*] It may be very safely left with every unprejudiced reader to decide whether it be not plain, from the above words of Sibbes, that some of his friends, Goodwin, or Nye, or Ash (to whom he confided his MSS.), had called his attention to the '*sentences*,' and received from him the modifications and corrections inserted in B, and from B to H, and in all subsequent editions. The specific noting of certain 'mistaken sentences' has no meaning otherwise. It must be kept in mind also,

* See page 127, line 11 from bottom, of our reprint in this volume.

† Ibid., line 10 from bottom.

‡ 'The Bruised Reed' and other pieces in the companion volume to the 'Soul's Conflict,' by Pickering, has the same beauty of typography, but even more inaccuracies.

that the 'Soul's Conflict' was posthumously published, having only been printed off while the author was on his death-bed. Again, I remark—

[*f*] That the mistake would be the more readily made, from the circumstance, that, in common with all the writings of Sibbes, he seems to have taken as the groundwork of the 'Soul's Conflict,' the brachy-graphic notes of others written down from his lips on delivery. These he simply revised.* Having in my library a volume of such 'notes,' I speak with the less hesitation.

[*g*] In the matter of editions, and the related 'charge' of 'trick,' and 'falsification,' and 'corruption,' it is UNTRUE that they [*i.e.*, the Puritans] reprinted the book speedily, with the very same title-page that was before, WITHOUT giving notice that it was a SECOND EDITION. B, was NOT a 'reprint,' was not a 'new edition,' but simply A, with leaf 364–5 inserted, and 'victory' in title-page, instead of 'victorie,' and C, *the* 'second edition,' DOES bear on its title-page these words, 'The Second Edition,' and the date, not of 1636, as the bishop would have us believe, but of 1635. I have a copy in my library, and another will be found in, respectively, University Library, Cambridge, and the Library of Trinity College, Dublin. I place below the *verbatim et literatim et punctatim* title-page.†

[*h*] It would be very idle to enter into a controversy as to the relative teaching of the sentences, as in A and B. Every dispassionate reader of both must admit that there is no change in the sentiment, but simply an expansion by way of explanation. In the original form, it was said, 'The laws under which we live . . . . . . ought to be a rule unto us, *so far as they reach*;' and it was only illustrating the extent of the obligation of the rule to add in B, 'in some duties of the second table,' &c. Would Bishop Patrick really have us regard Sibbes as teaching that the 'rule' did extend beyond the 'second table,' while we read so unmistakably, in A and B alike, the qualification, '*Where it dashes not against God's law?*' Every one who knows the works of Sibbes, knows that in a venal and time-serving semi-popish period he held with all his might, that in matters of *conscience*, the law of God contained in the word of God was the supreme and only arbiter. It is worse than slander to maintain that he would have had men 'conform to the orders of our governors about the worship of God' apart therefrom. The utmost he says, and he says even that with the preliminary caution, 'though it be TOO NARROW A RULE to be good ONLY [carefully italicised in A and B], so far as man's law guides unto,' is this . . . 'yet law . . . hath AN USE for the guiding of our actions THAT ARE UNDER THE SAME.'

This is sufficiently explicit, and conclusively meets that unquestioning submission to 'the powers that be,' which offered its inodorous incense at the shrine of James I., and his son Charles I.—that worshipping of 'the right divine of kings to *govern wrong*,' by which, in the indignant couplet of old Benjamin Bennet—

'The SOV'REIGN'S WILL becomes our—LAW,
The CHURCH'S WILL our—CREED.'

[*i*] As to the 'blotting out' of the second sentence (first in order), animadverted upon by the bishop, it may be sufficient to observe, that the omission of the words, 'in doubtful cases,' is explained and accounted for by the fuller statement, with example, thereafter given; and equally is the deletion of the remainder accounted for, partly by its being a mere tautology in view of the after fuller statement, and partly that there was necessarily abridgment here to admit of corresponding enlargement there, within the compass of the one leaf in B, as in A.

* 'Revised.' See address to 'Christian Reader' prefixed to 'Bruised Reed' and 'Soul's Conflict,' and the various prefaces to the posthumously published volumes. The B. R. and S. C. seem to have been more fully written out by Sibbes himself; but as Mr Ryle observes of Ward, even they, and much more the others, have all the characteristics of compositions intended for ears rather than for eyes, for hearers rather than for readers. In the haste of revision, it is easily to be understood how Sibbes passed by the 'mistaken sentences.'

† 'The SOVLES CONFLICT with it selfe, AND VICTORY over it self by *Faith*: A Treatise of the inward disquietments of distressed spirits, with comfortable remedies to establish them. Returne unto thy rest O my soule, for the Lord hath dealt bountifully with thee. By *R. Sibbs* D.D. Master of *Katherine Hall* in Cambridge, and Preacher of *Grayes Inne* London. The Second Edition. LONDON Printed by M. F. for *R. Dawlman* at the Brazen Serpent in Pauls Churchyard. 1635. 12°.' By the way, it may be noticed as an incidental confirmation of above, as to B being identical with A, that Benlowes' and Quarles's 'Verses' did *not* appear in it, but first in C. There was a '*second* edition' also of 1636, which perhaps explains, but does not in the slightest extenuate, the bishop's rash and reckless assertion, seeing he boasts of having seen and compared ALL. But indeed D, as in the case of A and B, is palpably from the same types, a mere further issue of C. Hence, probably, the designating C and D 'the second edition,' the only change being in the date 1635 into 1636. It will be noticed from our prefatory note to 'Soul's Conflict,' that there were two 'fourth' editions likewise. Nichols, in his Introduction to Pearson on the Creed, has shewn how publishers were wont to continue issuing edition upon edition, with the same date. I believe this to have been done with Sibbes's 'Soul's Conflict,' and that the long apparent interval between edition of 1651 and that of 1658 is thus explained.

That this is the true explanation, will be readily granted.

[j] When it is remembered who were the literary executors and editors of all Sibbes's writings. If the honoured and venerable names of Thomas Goodwin, Philip Nye, Jeremiah Burroughs, Simeon Ashe, James Nalton, be not sufficient to put to flight all charges of *unauthorised* changes or omissions, much more of 'trick,' 'falsification,' 'corruption,' then none may hope to do so. But apart altogether from Sibbes's own explicit declaration, that 'some sentences' had been 'mistaken,' and his deprecation of any 'depraving' of his writings on the strength (or rather weakness) of such mistake, the *character* of the men is more than sufficient to meet the accusations and insinuations of the 'Friendly Debate.' Finally,

[k] The use of the peculiar word 'deprave,'* in the second statement of his case, reveals the bishop's knowledge of Sibbes's special intimation concerning the mistaken sentences, a circumstance which aggravates his disingenuousness.

I would only add, that a similar examination of the numerous other kindred charges of the 'Friendly Debate' will satisfy any one that scarcely a page is without its over or under statement, that its citations are wrested from their context, that dogma is substituted for proof, and loud assertion for argument, while the entire spirit and temper evidence a contest for victory rather than truth.

(h) P. 214.—'The soul is made for God, and never finds rest till it returns to him again.' This seems to be a reminiscence of the well-known saying of Augustine, 'Thou madest us for thyself, and our heart is restless, until it rests in thee,' (Confess. Book i. 1).

(i) P. 243.—'No calling so mean . . . . enough to give account for.' I have marked this searching observation, in order to confirm it with the great and worthy John Brown of Haddington's 'Hint to Ministers,' than which few things are more striking. It was originally addressed to Dr Waugh, when a young man, and subsequently published in the 'Evangelical Magazine.' The Rev. John Brown of Haddington, *clarum et venerabile nomen*, in a letter of paternal counsels and cautions to one of his pupils newly ordained over a *small* congregation, wrote thus—'I know the vanity of your heart, and that you will feel mortified that your congregation is very small, in comparison with those of your brethren around you; but assure yourself on the word of an old man, that when you *come to give an account of them to the Lord Christ, at his judgment-seat, you will think you have had enough.*'—Memoir of Dr Waugh, by Drs Hay and Belfrage. 1839. 8vo. Pages 64–5.

(j) P. 259.—'Salvations.' Sibbes here notes the bold and unusual expression which would seem to indicate such abundant help as meets abounding need. It is interesting to find one thus early turning from time to time to the original Hebrew as well as Greek. G.

* 'Deprave.' See *ante* page 127, line 10 from bottom.

THE SAINT'S SAFETY IN EVIL TIMES.

THE SAINT'S SAFETY IN EVIL TIMES.

NOTE.

The 'Saint's Safety' forms a moiety of the only remaining volume published by Sibbes himself. The full title-page is given below.* These two masterly discourses form Nos. 8 and 9 of the folio, entitled 'The Saint's Cordials.' (2d edition, 1637; 3d edition, 1658). Our text follows the edition of 1633. That of 1634 is the same book with a new title.—G

* Title-page—

THE
SAINTS
SAFETIE IN
EVILL TIMES.
Delivered at St Maries in *Cambridge* the fift of *November* upon occasion of the POWDER-PLOT.
Whereunto is annexed a *Passion-Sermon*, Preached at MERCER'S CHAPPEL *London* upon Good-Friday.
As also the Happinesse of enjoying Christ laid open at the Funerall of Mr *Sherland* late Recorder of *Northampton*.
Together with the most vertuous life and Heavenly end of that Religious GENTLEMAN.
BY
R. Sibbes, D.D., Master of *Katherine-Hall* in *Cambridge*, and Preacher at *Grayes-Inne* LONDON.
John 3. 30.
Let him increase, let me decrease.
LONDON,
Printed by M. Flesher for *R. Dawlman* at the Brazen Serpent in Pauls Church-yard. 1633.

THE SAINT'S SAFETY IN EVIL TIMES.

Behold, he travaileth with iniquity, and hath conceived mischief, and brought forth a lie.—Ps. VII. 14.

THESE be the words of David. The title shews the occasion, which was the malicious slander and cruel practices of Ahithophel or Shimei, in the time of Absalom's rebellion. The words express the *conception, birth, carriage*, and *miscarriage*, of a *plot* against David. In which you may consider, 1. What his *enemies* did. 2. What *God* did. 3. What *we all* should do: his enemies' *intention*, God's *prevention*, and our *duty;* his enemies' intention, *he travaileth with iniquity, and conceiveth mischief;* God's prevention, *he brought forth a lie;* our duty, *Behold.*

His enemy's *intention* or *action* is set out by proportion to a bodily conception. The Holy Ghost delights to present unto us the plots of wicked men under the resemblance of a bodily conception and birth, by reason of the analogy between both. The mind hath its conceptions as well as the body. The seed of this conception was some wicked thought either raised up by the heart itself, or cast in by Satan, that envious man. Not only wicked men, but their devices, are the seed of the serpent. The understanding was the womb to conceive, the will to consent. The conception was the hatching of a mischievous plot; the quickening of it was the resolution and taking it in hand; the impregnation, growing big, and travailing of it, was the carriage of it the due time; the birth itself was the execution expected, but yet miscarried and stillborn. They intended the destruction of David, but brought forth their own ruin.

1. *Quo minor necessitas peccandi, eo majus peccatum.* For the conception, observe the aggravation of the sin, he conceiveth. (1.) He was not put upon it, or forced unto it; it was voluntary. The more liberty we have not to sin, makes our sin the greater. He did not this in passion, but in cold blood. The less will, less sin. *Involuntarium minuit de ratione peccati.* Here could be no plea, because nothing is more voluntary than plotting. Where the will sets the wit a work to devise, and the body to execute mischief, it shews the spreading and largeness of sin in any man; for the will being the desire of the whole man, carries the whole man with it.

Voluntas appetitus totius suppositi. Besides, when a man sins voluntarily, there is less hope of amendment, because his will is not counselable; if the defect were in the understanding of a man, then sound direction might set it right; but where the will is set upon a thing, and is the only reason of itself (as when a man will, because he wills) there counsel will not be heard; for, tell a roving person that he is out of the way, he knows it well enough already, and means not to take your direction; but tell an honest traveller that ignorantly mistakes his way, and he will thank you. So tell a popish atheist that he is in an error, he heeds it not, because he is a papist for bye-ends, not in judgment, and resolves to be so, bring what reasons you can, his hope being to rise that way. Though the will follow some kind of understanding, yet it is in the power of the will what the understanding shall consult and determine of; and, therefore, unless the malice of the will be first taken away by grace, it will always bias our judgments the wrong way.

2. Neither was this plot only voluntary, but with delight, because it was a conception; births are with more pain. Delight carries the whole strength and marrow of the soul with it; much of the soul is where delight is.

3. Again, it was a spiritual sin. The spirit of a man is the chief seat of God's good Spirit, wherein he frames all holy devices and good desires. The spirit is either the best or the worst part in a man. Here Satan builds his nest and forges all his designs, his masterpieces, his powder-plots. The chief curse or blessing of God is upon the spirits of men. If men be raised never so high in the world, yet if they are given to a malicious and devilish spirit, they are under a most heavy judgment, carrying Satan's stamp upon them. Diseases that seize upon the spirits of men, as pestilential diseases, &c., are more deadly than those that seize upon the humours. Spiritual wickednesses are the most desperate wickednesses. Sins are more judged by the mind than by the fact.

4. And as it was a spiritual sin, so it was artificial. There was a great deal of art and cunning in it; and in evil things, the more art, the worse. Art commends other things, but it makes sin the more *sinful*. *Doli non sunt doli, ni astu colas*. When men are witty to work mischief, and wise to do evil, then they are evil in grain. It is best to be a bungler at this occupation. Ingenuous men carry their hatred open; but this plot was spun with so fine a thread as could not easily be discerned.

5. Again, they were very diligent in it, for it was a curious web. And as in weaving, head and hand, eye and foot, all go together, so here they mustered up all their wits. Judas is awake when Peter sleeps.

6. And which is worst of all, they were so well pleased with the brat of their own brain that they travailed of it. It increases guilt when men upon view and sight of their plot grow so far in love with it that they long to be delivered of it. The more the soul dwells upon any sinful plot, the more estrangement there is from God; because the happiness of the soul consists in cleaving to God the fountain of all good. The more deliberation any man takes in sinning, the more his soul is pleased with wickedness. A heart long exercised in sin will admit of no impression of grace; for the spirits are so absorbed with other designs that they are dry and dead to better things. Many thousands are in hell at this day for suffering their spirits to shove them too far into sin. Many suck out the delight of sin before they act it, as Esau pleased himself by thinking 'the day of mourning for his father would come, wherein he might be revenged of his brother,' Gen. xxvii. 41.

7. Yet this sin was not only spiritual and imminent, but transient likewise. It reached against the second table, and, therefore, against the principles of nature, and against society, out of which God gathers a church. There was false witness and murder in this sin. In this respect it is that

the sins of the second table are greater than the sins of the first, because they are against more clear light. A natural conscience hath a clearer eye in these things. Here is light upon light; for both grace and nature condemn these sins. Yet for order in sinning, the rise of all sin against man, is our sinning against God first, for none sin against men, but they sin against God in the first place, whereupon the breach of the first commandment is the ground of the breach of all the rest; for if God were set up in the heart in the first place, there parents would be honoured, and all kind of injury suppressed for conscience sake. The Scripture gives this as a cause of the notorious courses of wicked men, 'that God is not in all their thoughts,' Ps. x. 4. They forget there is a God of vengeance and a day of reckoning. The fool would needs enforce upon his heart, 'that there is no God,' Ps. xiv. 1, and what follows: 'Corrupt they are, there is none doth good, they eat up my people as bread,' &c. They make no more bones of devouring men and their estates, than they make conscience of eating a piece of bread. What a wretched condition hath sin brought man unto, that the great God who 'filleth heaven and earth,' Jer. xxiii. 24, should yet have no place in the heart which he hath especially made for himself! The sun is not so clear as this truth, that God is, for all things in the world are because God is. If he were not, nothing could be. It is from him that wicked men have that strength they have to commit sin, therefore sin proceeds from atheism, especially these plotting sins; for if God were more thought on, he would take off the soul from sinful contrivings, and fix it upon himself.

But by whom and against whom was this plotting? by children of the church, not uncircumcised Philistines. Opposition is bitterest betwixt those that are nearest, as betwixt the flesh and the spirit in the same soul, between hypocrites and true-hearted Christians in the same womb of the church. Brethren they were, but false brethren; children, but strange children. Children by the mother's side, all bred in the same church, but had not the same father. Children by the mother's side only, are commonly persecutors. Popish spirits count it presumption to know who is their father, which shews them to be bastard children. The greatest sins of all are committed within the church, because they are committed against the greatest light; whereupon that great sin against the Holy Ghost (which, like Jonah his whale, devours all at once) is not committed out of the church at all. Oh! beloved, how should we reverence the blessed truth of God and gracious motions of his Spirit! If it be sin to kill infants in the womb, what is it to kill the breed of the blessed Spirit in our hearts!

But against whom was this plot directed? Even against David, a prophet and a king, a kingly prophet, a man after God's own heart, 1 Sam. xiii. 14; Acts xiii. 22, though not according to theirs; a sacred person, and therefore inviolable. 'Touch not mine anointed, and do my prophets no harm,' Ps. cv. 15, was a prohibition from heaven. David was a man eminent in goodness, and goodness invested in greatness is a fair mark for envy to shoot at. What men for sloth care not to do, for weakness cannot, or for pride will not, imitate, that they malign, sitting cursing and fretting at the bottom of the hill, at those which they see go above them, whose life giveth witness against them. When goodness shines forth, it presently meets with envy, until it come to the height to be above envy, as the sun at the highest hath no shadow. Envy hath an ill eye. It cannot look on goodness without grief. The spirit that is in us lusteth after envy. Pursuing of goodness in men, and men for goodness, is a sin of a deep dye, because whosoever hates a man for goodness, hates goodness itself; and he that hates goodness itself hates it most in the fountain, and so becomes a hater of God himself; and if Christ were in such a man's power he should escape no better than his members do. For Christ is joined either in love or hatred with his cause and children. He and his have common friends and common enemies. Men think they have to deal with silly men, but they shall one day find that they have to deal with the great Lord of heaven and earth.

But what was the manner of carrying their design? This cruel plot was cunningly carried, for they kill him in his good name first, and accuse him as an enemy to the state, that so their slanders may make way for violence. Satan is a liar first, and then a murderer, yea therefore a liar that he may be a murderer the better. He is first a serpent, then a liar; and first a lion couchant, then a lion rampant. He teaches his scholars the same method. Cruelty marcheth furiously, and under warrant with privilege, when it hath slander to countenance it. Taint men once in the opinion of the world, and then they lie open to any usage. It is not only safe but glorious to oppose such, and thus virtue comes to have the reward due to wickedness, and passes under public hatred. The open cause and pretence is one, and the inward moving cause another, which perhaps lies hid till the day of 'revelation of the secrets of all flesh,' Rom. ii. 5, as in a clock the wheels and the hand appear openly, but the weights that move all are out of sight.

But what course took David herein? Innocency was his best apology, and when that would not do, then patience. He saw God in the wrongs he suffered, 'God bade Shimei,' &c., 2 Sam. xvi. 10. But this invites more injuries, therefore by prayer he lays open his soul to God. David's prayer prevailed more in heaven than Ahithophel's policy could do on earth. Carnal men are pregnant and full of wiles and fetches* to secure themselves, but godly men have one only refuge and hiding-place, yet that is a great one, namely, to run to God by prayer, as to their rock and tower of defence in their distresses. From all this that hath been said there ariseth these conclusions:—

First, that *even the best of God's saints are liable to be the subjects of the plots of wicked men.* (1.) From an antipathy between the two contrary seeds in them. (2.) Because God will not have his children love the world, therefore he suffers the world to hate them. (3.) They are strangers here, and therefore no wonder if they find strange entertainment from them that think themselves at home. There hath ever been from the beginning of the world a continual conspiracy of Satan and his instruments against God and goodness. Emperors and kings became Christians, but Satan never yet became a Christian, but hath always bestirred himself to maintain the first division, and never yet wanted a strong faction in the world.

Secondly, observe that *it is the character of a man wicked in an high degree, to contrive wickedness.* The reason is: (1.) Because it is a disposition of such as are given up by God to a reprobate sense, and it is reckoned among other vile sins, that they are full of maliciousness, and inventors of ill, &c. A son of Belial carries a froward heart and devises mischief, Prov. vi. 14. (2.) It shews that malice is so connatural to such, that they cannot sleep unless they cause some to fall; 'wickedness comes from the wicked' (as *naturally* and *speedily*), Prov. iv. 16, as poison from a spider. (3.) It argues such kind of men work out of a vicious habit, which is a stamping of a second ill nature upon the former, whenas their hearts are exercised

* That is, 'artifices.'—G.

to do mischief. (4.) It shews they are of the devil's trade, whose only work is to hurt and mischief all he can, those that are broken loose from him. Certainly such people as these are the children of the devil in an higher degree than ordinary. It is said, when Judas began to betray Christ, 'the devil entered into him,' Luke xxii. 3. He was the child of the devil in some degree before, but now the devil took stronger possession of him; his unnatural treason did in some sort change him into the very form of the devil. When Simon Magus sought to turn away the deputy from the faith, St Paul had no fitter terms for him than to style him, 'Thou full of all subtlety and mischief, and child of the devil,' Acts xiii. 10. And indeed there is no disposition so contrary to the sweet Spirit of God, which is a Spirit of love and goodness, as this is.

Use 1. Learn hence therefore, as you love God, to abhor this hateful disposition. The serpent indeed was 'wiser than all the beasts of the field,' Gen. iii. 1, yet when he became an instrument of mischief, he was cursed above all the rest, Gen. iii. 14. Satan labours to serve his turn of the best wits; but what greater curse can befal a man than to serve the basest creature in the basest service, and that with our best abilities? Men of a devilish spirit carry God's curse under zeal,* yea, they carry the devil in their brain, in all their works of darkness; for, alas, what should the subtlety of foxes, and fierceness of lions, and malice of devils do, in an heart dedicated to Christ? Such men work from a double principle, the illness of their own disposition within, and Satan going with the tide of that, whose chief labour is to make a prey of men of the best parts, that by them he may either snare others, or else vex them that have so much wit or grace as not to be catched by his baits. This is a course contrary to humanity as we are men, contrary to ingenuity† as we are civil men, and contrary to religion as we are Christian men, and plainly argueth that such persons are led with another spirit than their own, even by the prince that ruleth in the air.

Our care and duty, therefore, should be to submit our spirits to the sweet guidance and government of God's good Spirit, to be contented that every device and imagination of our hearts should be captivated to higher and better reasons than our own.

We are not wise enough of ourselves that our own wills and wit should be our first movers. Everything is perfected by subjection to a superior; where there should be a subordination to higher wisdom, there to withdraw our understanding and wills, is mere rebellion. That which the prophet speaks is too true of many in these days, 'Thy wisdom hath made thee to rebel,' Is. xlvii. 10. Such are too wise to be saved.

Use 2. We need not be ashamed to learn some things of our very enemies. If they be so pragmatical for evil, why should not we be as active for good? I am sure we serve a better Master. True love is full of inventions; it will be devising of good things. So soon as ever our nature is changed, the stream of the soul is turned another way, the bent of it is for God. Alas, it is a small commendation to be only passively good, and it is a poor excuse to be only passively ill. A good Christian thinks it not enough to see good done by others, but labours to have a hand in it himself; and he that suffers evil to be done, which he might have opposed and hindered, brings the guilt thereof upon his own head. 'Curse you Meroz,' saith God, 'for not helping the Lord against the mighty,' &c., Jud. v. 23. What shall we think then of those that help the mighty against the Lord, that cast oil to kindle where they should cast water to quench, that inflame the rage of

* Qu. 'seal?'—Ed. † That is, 'ingenuousness.'—Ed.

great persons, when they should labour to reduce all to a moderation? Of this spirit was that apostate which stirred up the emperor to kill man, woman, and child of the Protestants, with all their kindred and alliance, fearing lest any living should revenge the other's quarrel.*

We see God hath stooped so low as to commend his cause unto us, as if he stood in need of our help, and usually what good he doth to us is conveyed by men like ourselves; therefore, we should labour to appear on his side, and own his cause and children. In the house of God there be vessels of all kinds. Some are of more honourable use than others. Some make the very times and places good where they live, by an influence of good. Others, as malignant planets, threaten misery and desolation where-ever they come. These are the calamities of the times. Men may know whether they be vessels of mercy or no, by the use they are put to; the basest of people are fit enough to be executioners; the worst of men are good enough to be rods of God's wrath. How much better is it to be full of goodness, as the Scripture speaks of Josiah and Hezekiah, &c.! Indeed, what is a man, but his goodness? Such men live desired, and die lamented. Yea, their very 'name is as the ointment of the apothecary poured out,' Cant. i. 3. They leave a sweet savour in the church behind them.

Now I come to their miscarriage. They brought forth a lie; a lie in regard of their expectation, their hopes deceiving them, but a just defeating in regard of God. It was contrary to their desire, but agreeable to God's justice. Neither were they disappointed only so as to miss of what they intended, but they met with that misery they intended not; yea, even with that very misery which they thought to bring upon David.

This defeating ariseth by five steps: 1, they were *disappointed;* 2, they fell into *danger;* 3, they were *contrivers* of this danger *themselves;* 4, there was a penal *proportion*, they *fell* into the *same* danger which they plotted for *another;* 5, they were a means of doing *good* to him whom they devised *evil* against; and *raised* him, whom they thought to pull *down*. *David* sped the better for Shimei's malice, and Ahithophel's policy. See all these five likewise in the example of Haman and Mordecai. 1, Haman missed of his plot; 2, he fell into danger; 3, he fell into the same danger which he contrived himself; 4, he fell into the same danger which he contrived for Mordecai; and 5, was the means of Mordecai's advancement. It had been enough to have woven a spider's web, which is done with a great deal of art, and yet comes to nothing; but to hatch a cockatrice's egg, that brings forth a viper which stings to death, this is a double vexation. Yet thus God delighteth to catch the 'wise in the imagination of their own hearts,' Luke i. 51, and to pay them in their own coin. The wicked carry a lie in their right hand; for they trust in man, which is but a *lie;* and, being liars themselves too, no marvel if their hopes prove deceitful, so that, while they sow the wind, they reap the whirlwind, Hosea viii. 7.

Reason. (1.) The reason of God's dealing in this kind is, *first*, in regard of *himself*. God will not lose the glory of any of his attributes; he will be known to be God only wise, and this he will let appear, then especially, when wicked men think to overreach him.

(2.) Secondly, in regard of his tender care over his children, they are as the apple of his eye; and as they are very near, so they are very dear to him. They cost him dear; they are his jewels, and he gave a *Jewel* of infinite price for them. He is interested in their quarrels, and they in his.

* Qu. 'Massacre of St Bartholomew, 1572?'—G.

If they be in any misery, God's bowels yearn for them. He is always awake, and never slumbereth, as we see in the parable, the master of the house waked while the servants slept, Mat. xxv. 1, *et seq*. God's eye is upon them for good. He hath them written in the 'palms of his hands, Isa. xlix. 16. Christ carries them always in his breast. Christ, who is the husband of his church, is Lord of heaven and earth, and hath all power committed to him, Mat. xxviii. 18, John xvii. 2, and will rule in the midst of his enemies. He is the only Monarch of the world, and makes both all things and persons serviceable to his own end and his church's good. He is higher than the highest. Satan, the god of the world, 2 Cor. iv. 4, is but his and his church's slave. All things are the church's, to further its best good.

(3.) Another reason is, *the insolence of the enemies*, whose *fierceness turns* at length *to God's praise*, Ps. ix. 16; for as he is a just Lord, so he will be known to be so by executing of judgment. It shall appear that there is 'a God that judgeth the earth,' Ps. lviii. 11.

(4.) Again, God's children will give him *no rest*. When he seems to sleep, they will awake him with their prayers. 'They will not let him go without a blessing from him,' Gen. xxxii. 26. They will prevail by importunity, as the widow in the gospel, Luke xviii. 5. Having to deal with a just God, in a just cause, against common enemies, his as well as theirs, they bind him with his own promises; and he is content to be bound, because he hath bound himself first. He will not lose that part of his title whereby he is known to be a 'God hearing prayers,' Ps. lxv. 2.

Obj. But it will be objected that wicked men do not only set themselves against the people of God, but prevail over them, even to the scorn of the beholders. Tully could say '*The gods shew how much they esteem of the Jewish nation, by suffering them so often to be conquered.*'* Hath not antichrist a long time prevailed, and was it not foretold that the beast should prevail? Rev. xiii. Where is, then, the *bringing forth of a lie?*

Ans. I answer, (1.) the enemies have power, but no more than is given them of God, as Christ answered Pilate, John xix. 11. They prevail indeed, but it is for a time, a limited time, and that a short one too, ten days, &c., Rev. ii. 10: and what is this to that vast time of their torment? The time will come, when there shall be no more time for them to persecute in.

(2.) Besides, even when they do prevail, it is but over part only, not over the whole. They prevail over persons, it may be, not over the cause: that stands impregnable. They prevail over men's lives, perhaps, but not over their spirits, which is that they chiefly aim at. A true Christian conquers when he is conquered. Stephen prevailed over his enemies when they seemed to prevail over him. God put glory upon him, and a spirit of glory into him, Acts vii.

(3.) The church's enemies may prevail in some place, but then, as the sea, they lose in another. The more they cut down God's people, as Pharaoh did the Israelites, the more they multiply; and the more they are kept straight,† the more they spread and are enlarged. God suffers the enemies of his truth to prevail, in some passages, to harden their hearts the more for destruction, as Pharaoh prevailed in oppressing the Israelites,

* This is one of only two notices of the Jews, that are found in the voluminous works of Cicero. It occurs in Orat. Pro L. Flacco, c. 28. As Sibbes rather paraphrases than translates, the true and vivid original may be given:—'. . . . Nunc vero hoc magis, quod illa gens, quid de imperio, nostro sentiret ostendit armis; quam cara Diis immortalibus esset, docuit, quod est victa, quod elocata, quod servata.'—G.

† Qu. 'strait?'—ED.

and Herod in killing John, &c. But yet, lay the beginning and the end together, and then we shall see they prevailed not, and so far as they did prevail, it tended only to hasten their own ruin, because the present success lifts up the heart. We see antichrist prevailed, but spiritually, only over those 'whose names were not written in the Lamb's book of life,' Rev. xiii. 7, and outwardly over the saints; for so it was prefixed, Rev. xviii. 24, that he should *make war* with the saints, *and overcome them:* and this was objected as a fiery dart against the Christians in those times, that therefore they might think their cause naught, because they were so prevailed over;* but they, by help of the Spirit of God, understood so much of the Revelation as concerned themselves, and used this as a weapon, confessing that they were the conquered people of God, but yet the people of God still. But the chief stay and satisfaction of the soul herein, is to look to the day of the righteous judgment of God, when we shall see all promises performed, all threatenings executed, and all enemies trodden for ever under Christ and his church's feet.

Use 1. This is a point of marvellous comfort, when Israel can say, 'They have afflicted me from my youth, but yet they have not prevailed over me,' Ps. cxxix. 1. The gates of hell may set themselves against the church, but shall not prevail. The church is not ruled by man's counsel. We neither live nor die at man's appointment. Our lives are not in our own hands, or Satan's, or our enemies', but in God's. They can do no more, they shall do no less, than God will, who is our life, and the length of our days. God may give way a while, that the 'thoughts of many may be revealed,' Luke ii. 35, and that his glory may shine the more in raising his children, and confounding his enemies; but he will put a period in his due time, and that is the best time. There is a day of Jacob's trouble, when his enemies say, 'This is Sion, whom none regards,' Jer. xxx. 7; but God sets bounds both to the time of his children's trouble, and to the malice of the wicked. 'Their rod shall not rest over-long upon the back of the righteous,' Ps. cxxv. 3. God will put a *hook into the nostrils* of these leviathans, and draw them which way he pleaseth.

Use 2. Again, we see here that mischievous attempts are successless in the end; for did ever any harden themselves against God and prosper long? Let Cain speak, let Pharaoh, Haman, Ahithophel, Herod; let the persecutors of the church for the first two hundred years; let all that ever bore ill-will towards Sion, speak, and they will confess they did but kick against the pricks, and dash against the rocks. The greatest torment of the damned spirit is, that God turns all his plots for the good of those he hates most. He tempted man to desire *to become like God*, Gen iii. 5, that so he might ruin him; but God *became man*, and so restored him. God serveth himself of this archpolitician and all his instruments; they are but executioners of God's will while they rush against it. Joseph's brethren sold him that they might not worship him, and that was the very means whereby they came at length to worship him. God delights to take the oppressed party's part. Wicked men cannot do God's children a greater pleasure than to oppose them, for by this means they help to advance them.

Why wicked plots miscarry. The ground of the miscarriage of wicked plots is, that Satan and his, maintain a damned cause, and their plots are under a curse. Every one that prays, 'Thy kingdom come,' prays by consequence against them as opposers of it; and how can the men and plots of so many curses but miscarry, and prove but as the untimely fruit of a

* Cicero, *ante.*—G.

woman? They are like the grass on the house-top, which perks above the corn in the field, but yet no man prays for a blessing upon it. When men come by a goodly corn-field, every one is ready to say, God bless this field, &c. Beloved, it is a heavier thing than atheistical spirits think of, to be under the curse of the church; for as God blesseth out of Sion, so usually the heaviest curses come out of Sion. Woe be to the Herods and Julians of the world, when the church, either directly or indirectly, prays against them.

Use 3. This is a ground of staying the souls of God's people in seeming confusion of things. There is an harmony in all this discord. God is fitting his people for a better condition even when they are at the worst, and is hardening and preparing the wicked for confusion, even when they are at the best. 'The wicked practise against the righteous, but God laugheth them to scorn,' Ps. ii. 4; for he seeth all their plottings, and his day is a-coming. Whilst they are digging pits for others, there is a pit a-digging and a grave a-making for themselves. They have a measure to make up, and a treasure to fill, which at length will be broken open, which, methinks, should take off them which are set upon mischief from pleasing themselves in their plots. Alas! they are but plotting their own ruin, and building a Babel which will fall upon their own heads. If there were any commendation in plotting, then that great plotter of plotters, that great engineer, Satan, would go beyond us all, and take all the credit from us. But let us not envy Satan and his in their glory. They had need of something to comfort them. Let them please themselves with their trade. The day is coming wherein the daughter of Sion shall laugh them to scorn. There will be a time wherein it shall be said, 'Arise, Sion, and thrash,' Micah iv. 13. And usually the delivery of God's children is joined with the destruction of his enemies; Saul's death, and David's deliverance; the Israelites' deliverance, and Egyptians' drowning. The church and her opposites are like the scales of a balance; when one goes up, the other goes down.

Haman's wife had learned this, that if her husband began once to fall before the Jews, he should surely fall. Wicked men have an hour, and they will be sure to take it; and God hath his hour too, and will be as sure to take that. The judgments of the wicked are mercies to the church. So saith David, 'He slew mighty kings, Og king of Bashan, for his mercy endureth for ever,' &c., Ps. cxxxvi. 20.

God hath but two things in the world that he much regardeth; his truth, and his church, begotten by his truth;* and shall we think that he will suffer long, wretched men who turn that wit and power which they have from him against his truth and church? No, assuredly; but he will give them up by that very wit of theirs, to work their own destruction; they shall serve their turn most whom they hate most. God sits in heaven, and laughs them to scorn. Shall God laugh, and we cry? They take counsel together on earth, but God hath a counsel in heaven that will overthrow all their counsels here. Mark the bitter expressions in Scripture, 'Why do the heathen rage,' Ps. ii. 1, without fear or wit? 'Go to now, saith God, gather a council,' &c., Isa. viii. 9. Beloved, it goes to the heart of proud persons to be scorned, especially in the miscarriage of that which they count their masterpiece; they had rather be counted devils than fools. Let us *work wisely*, saith Pharaoh, when he was never more fool, Exod. ii. 10. They usurp upon God, and promise themselves great

* 'God hath but two things,' &c. This sentiment, which is repeated in the 'Fountain Sealed,' is quoted by Bishop Patrick in his 'Friendly Debate,' against Bridge. See Taylor's edition of Patrick, vol. v. pp. 509–10.—G.

matters for the time to come, whereas that is only God's prerogative, and they neither know what the womb of their counsels, nor what the womb of to-morrow, may bring forth. That which they are big of may prove an abortive, or a viper to consume the womb that bred it. 'Go to now,' saith the prophet, 'all ye that kindle a fire: walk in the light of your fire, but take this of me, you shall lie down in sorrow,' &c., Isa. li. 11. The Scripture is full of such expostulations and upbraidings. 'Man is become like one of us, saith God,' Gen. iii. 22. When men will have a way of their own, and think themselves wiser than God, then it stands upon God's honour to outwit them. 'Yet God is wise,' saith the prophet, Isa. xxxi. 2. You think to go beyond God. Deceive not yourselves. *God is wise*, and you shall find him to be so. He hath a way to go beyond you. Do not many men spin a fine thread, and weave a fair web, when by their turnings and devices they turn themselves into hell? 'Woe be to them that dig deep,' saith the prophet, 'and think to hide their counsels from the Lord,' Hosea ix. 2, 3. God hath an eye to see into the most secret and dark conveyances of business. God hath a key to open the closet of their hearts, let them be never so close locked up. Oh, that men would more fear this all-seeing eye of God, and be wise for themselves, and not against themselves. It is a miserable wisdom when men are wise to work their own ruin. Beloved, when men have had all their plots, God hath a plot still beyond them. He takes them failing in something or other. Their devices are like a curious clock; if the least thing be out of frame, all is marred. God suffers them to spin a fine thread a great while, and at length cuts the web, and there is an end. And they may thank themselves for all this, for they carry a justification of God in their own breasts. They perish because they will perish; and this will be the torment of all torments to graceless persons, that they pulled destruction upon themselves. Malice blinds the understanding in Satan and his instruments; for, if their malice were not above their wit, would they, to gratify their ill affections, knowingly rush into the displeasure of God, and into such courses as will unavoidably bring their ruin? Malice drinks up the greatest part of its own poison. 'His own iniquity shall take the wicked himself,' saith Solomon, 'and he shall be holden with the cords of his own sin,' Prov. v. 22.

This may be enlarged to all sinful courses. Every sinner worketh a deceitful work, and *bringeth forth a lie.* Augustine saith well, *every sin is a lie* (*a*). Men would be happy, yet they will not live so as they may be happy; what more deceitful than this? It will be the complaint of every sinner at length, that was Eve's, the 'serpent hath deceived me,' Gen. iii. 13. It was St Paul's complaint, Rom. viii. 8, and it will be the complaint of all sinful wretches at the last day. What hath pride profited us? what can the favour of men, upon whom we bear ourselves, do us good now? Sin promiseth us contentment, continuance, secresy, full satisfaction, &c., but doth it make good this? Were ever any, when the beginning and ending was laid together, established by wickedness? Take it from God himself (we have a commission to speak it),' Say, it shall not go well with the wicked, though they escape an hundred times,' Eccl. viii. 12, 13, yet it is but a reprieval for some further service which God hath to do by them. 'Be not deceived, God is not mocked,' Gal. vi. 7. When we can be more subtle than the devil, or more strong than God, we may think to thrive by sin. Can we think God will alter the course of divine justice for us? had we not better believe this than find it so hereafter? Beloved, hell is for those to feel that will not believe. Certain it is, that those who will sin, notwithstanding God's justice, shall be severely punished, notwithstanding his mercy. God is not more peremptory in any one thing than in this, 'If any man bless himself in an ill way, my wrath shall smoke against him,' Deut. xxix. 19, 20; therefore it is a good prayer, *Lord, give me not over to lying*, that is, not to trust in that which will lie and deceive me.

This is the unhappiness of us ministers, all other professions are believed when they discover danger, but 'who believeth our report?' Isa. liii. 1. We are men's 'enemies, because we tell them the truth,' Gal. iv. 16; we labour to take away the sweet morsels from men, their Herodiases (*b*), and to divide betwixt men and their sins, which they love better than their souls. No creature but man, loves that which will be its own bane. Only wretched man seeks happiness in the way to misery, and heaven in the way to hell. I beseech you therefore, as you would not be deceived, (as indeed who would?) take heed of the deceitful works of darkness. Satan that tempts us is but a lying spirit (which he is not ashamed to confess), 1 Kings xxii. 22, and sin is like unto him. What got Ahab by his vineyard? Judas by his thirty pieces of silver? what got Haman, and so of the rest, by their sins at the last? Men are usually ashamed of an ill bargain, because the very thought thereof upbraids them with weakness and folly. Whatever we get by sin for the present, it will prove the worst bargain that ever we made. Oh, therefore, let us use our wits and parts to better purpose; if we will needs be plotting, let us plot for eternity; that is worth the plotting for. Let us plot how to avoid Satan's plot. Our time is short, opportunity, the flower of time, shorter. Our talents are many, our accounts strict, our judge unpartial. Let us be 'sowing to the Spirit,' Gal. vi. 8; let us labour to be like our Judge, who went about doing his Father's work, John xvii. 4, and came to destroy the works of the devil, 1 John iii. 8. Oh, beloved, shall we build up that which Christ came to destroy? All his miracles tended to good; he wrought the salvation of those that wrought his destruction; he shed his blood for those that shed his blood. Satan is all for mischief, and rather than he will not do hurt, he is content to be set about drowning of swine, Mark v. 14. And such are all those that are led with his spirit, men witty to destroy and acute to malice others, who take a great deal of pains to go to hell and carry others with them. Those that are skilful in the story of nature, write of the scorpion, that he whets his tail often upon stones, that so it may be sharp and ready for a mischief. Some crooked wits there are which make it their exercise to vex the quiet of the land; it is as natural to them as poison to a scorpion.

But our happiness is, how to be like the idea, the pattern of all grace, and the glory of our nature, by whom we hope to be saved. Our happiness is to bring forth fruit, and our own fruit 'in due season,' Ps. i. 3; to have opportunity, ability, and a heart to do good. How comfortable is death when it takes men so doing? The time will be ere long, when it will comfort us above all things in the world besides, that we have been honoured to be instruments of doing good, and stood in the gap to hinder evil. Beloved, we serve a good master. We shall not lose a good word for a good cause. There is a 'book of remembrance, Mal, iii. 16, for every good word and work we do. When wicked men have beaten their brains, spent their spirits, and wasted their strength, what becomes of them at length? A conscience often wounded will receive no comfort, but take God's part against itself. When the other powers are wearied, then conscience comes and doth its office; then the eyes of the soul are open to see what it would not see before, then sin that 'lay at the door,' Gen. iv. 7 (*c*), at the going out of this life, flieth in our faces. Pleasure and profit, for which wicked men project and contrive so much, comes all to nothing; but sin itself, and the punishment of it, abides for ever. Men, like popes, will dispense with themselves, and conceit a latitude and breadth in their courses, that they may do so and so, and yet do well at last, but who tells them this? Is it not a spirit of illusion? Indeed, punishment is often deferred; it comes not like thunder and lightning all at once, yet as sure as God is true, sin will be bitterness in the end. When the honey is gone, the sting will remain.

To conclude this point; when we are tempted to any hurtful design, let us look upon Christ, and that great project for our redemption undertaken by him, and reason thus with ourselves: hath he plotted and wrought my salvation, and shall I plot against him in his members?

I beseech you, stir up your hearts to conceive and bring forth good purposes. Satan is an enemy to all strong resolutions and masculine conceptions, endeavouring to kill them in the very birth. Alas, how many good thoughts are conceived whilst the word is hearing, which yet prove abortive and stick in the birth! How few actions come to their due ripeness and perfection! I am sure our encouragements to good are far more than our encouragements to evil. We serve a better master, and for better wages. They may prosper for a time, but nothing is more wretched than the happiness of wicked men; it first hardens them, and then destroys them, Prov. i. 32.

Our only way is, 1, to get into Christ 'the true vine,' John xv. 1, then we shall take and bear fruit presently, and draw and suck out of him the same disposition.

2. And then lay up good principles, and look with a single eye to the main end of our life, and see that all the particular passages of our life tend to that. It is an argument of a narrow heart to be wise in some particular business, for some particular end, and yet to be careless in the main. Other creatures are carried by a particular instinct to some particular thing. A spider is witty to catch flies, a bird to build nests, &c. As man hath larger parts, so he should have larger aims.

That which we should especially labour for is, 1, to be good in ourselves; and 2, to do all the good we can to others, even as God our Father is good, and doth good; and the further our good extends, the more we resemble our Father. Such as we are, such are our thoughts, such are our devices. A good man will devise of liberal things, &c. Every vermin can do mischief. We see some are never in their element but when they are plotting or working mischief, as if they were born for no other end but to exercise the graces of men better than themselves. It is a poor commendation to be counted a cunning person for self ends. Alas! the heart of man, which is 'deceitful above measure,' Jer. xvii. 9, hath abundance of turnings and windings in it, and can suggest tricks enough to circumvent the best of us.

I come, in the third place, to our duty, which is to 'behold,'—the ordinary beacon kindled to discover some extraordinary thing.

Quest. But what is here to be beheld?

Ans. Behold the subtlety, malice, and restless endeavour of the enemies of goodness. Is it not a matter with grief to be beheld, that one member should tear another? that one, professing the same religion, should study to supplant and devour another? Behold, likewise, their bootless enterprise, *they bring forth a lie.*

But especially behold the mercy of God to his children; his wisdom in discovering, his justice in confounding, the mischievous practices of their enemies, making them the workers of their own ruin.

The things which especially deserve our beholding are either, 1, things excellent, and so are all God's works in their season, yea, justice itself; or, 2, things rare, as comets and eclipses; or else, 3, great things, as stars of the first magnitude, &c.

Even such, and much more, is God's mercy to his children, and justice against his enemies. Behold what great things he hath done for them, Ps. cxxvi. 2. Shall the heathen say so, and shall not Israel much more? Beloved, we ought to seek out God's works, and shall we not take notice of them when they are offered to our view? This is especially the duty of the saints of God. 'All thy works praise thee, and thy saints bless thee,' saith David, Ps. cxlv. 10. The works of God praise him by our mouths and by our tongues. Were it not for some few that by a more divine light and spiritual eye see more of God than others do, what glory should God have in the world? God hath not brought us on the stage of this world to be mere gazers, but to extract something out for our own use, and to give him the glory of his excellencies. But we are too wise to admire anything. It is a matter too mean for our parts to take notice of God and his works. You have some that can see nothing in the works of God worth the admiring; and yet they will have men's persons in admiration, in hope of some advantage by them. We are apt to admire any outward excellency, like the disciples, before the Holy Ghost came upon them, who stood admiring of the goodly stones of the temple. When our minds are thus taken up, it were good if we heard Christ speaking to us as he did to them, 'Are these the things you wonder at?' Mark xiii. 1.

Beloved, it is our duty to observe special occurrences, not out of any Athenian curiosity, but to begin our employment in heaven now, whilst we are upon earth; to take occasion from thence to bless God. We should compare the rule and the event together, and observe what truth or attribute God makes good by that which is so fallen out; see how God commenteth upon himself by his own actions; and from observation of particulars it is good to rise to generals, as Deborah from the destruction of one enemy to the destruction of all. 'So let all thy enemies perish, O Lord,' Judges v. 31. This was Moses's song, and Hannah's, and the Virgin Mary's, &c. They mounted from a consideration of their own particular, and had their thoughts enlarged with the mercy and justice of God, to others in succeeding generations.

And among all God's works we should more take notice of his mercy to the church than of his justice towards his enemies, because his justice is, as it were, a foil to give lustre to his mercy. God delighteth more in mercy, as being his proper work, issuing from his own bowels, than in works of justice that are occasioned by the malice of men. God is wonderful in his saints, and more in saving them than in destroying his enemies. Considering, therefore, that mercy bears the chief office in the great works of God, we ought to dwell most in consideration thereof, and feed our thoughts more with the meditation of his saving works to his church than of the ruin of his enemies.

We pray *hallowed be thy name.* Unless we practise what we pray for, we mock God, and deceive our own souls. Let not God lose any glory by us; let not us lose such a pledge of future happiness as glorifying God is. 'Oh that men would praise the Lord,' saith David, who, fearing lest God should lose any glory from his creatures, stirs up angels and all creatures to 'bless the Lord,' Ps. cxlviii. 2, 3. God takes it very unkindly when we do not observe especially, the excellent pieces of his workmanship. 'A fool considereth not this,' &c., Ps. xcii. 6.

The Lord hath done marvellous things for his church of late, whereof we should rejoice. We should do as Moses did when he came out of the sea, and as the church, in resemblance of that deliverance from Egypt, did, who sang the song of Moses, being delivered from their spiritual Pharaoh, Rev. xv. 3.

We see now the vial poured upon the sun, we see the prophecies against antichrist's kingdom in fulfilling. God hath vouchsafed to strengthen our faith by experience. We have something to lay hold on, which may encourage us to expect more from God, and to look for those hallelujahs to be sung from all creatures in heaven and earth, upon the utter confusion of antichrist; which, whosoever labours to hinder any kind of way, hinders the glory of God, and the joy of his people.

It is good to observe how the Scripture sets out the enemies of God's church, in a double representation, 1, as terrible, terming them lions, bulls, &c.; 2, as base, comparing them to chaff and dust before the wind, dung, &c., Ps. x. 4, that when we see them in their present ruff and jollity, we should stay ourselves with consideration of their future baseness. Faith looks on things as present, because it looks upon them in the word of Jehovah, who will give a being to all his promises and threatenings; and therefore faith is called the subsistence of 'things not seen,' Heb. xi. 1, (*d*) because it gives a kind of being of things to the mind and affections of man, as if they were present. Therefore the believing of the final deliverance of God's people, and the ruin of his enemies, cannot but raise up the souls of good men to a marvellous degree of joy and thankfulness to God. Who would not fear to cleave to antichrist, if they did but present to themselves by faith, the certain ruin of that state, which the Scripture sets down, in a prophetical manner, as a thing already present? 'Babylon is fallen,' &c., Rev. xviii. 2.

But to come to a more particular application, suitable to the present time. The occasion and the text are as parallel as may be. Our gunpowder-plotters (*e*) were as pregnant in mischief as ever these. For conception, it could not but come from beneath the vault. There was the very quintessence of devilishness in it. Satan emptied all his bowels, as it were, in this project. If all the devils in hell were set awork to devise the like, they could hardly do it. There was scarce from the beginning of the world, a design more prodigious and unmerciful, of greater depth and extent of villany. Were [it] not [for] this anniversary commemoration of it, posterity would hardly believe that a plot so hellish could be hatched in the hearts of men, of English men, of Catholic men, as they would be termed, of men so borne withal, notwithstanding their dangerous correspondency with foreign enemies, and but half subjects, their better parts, their spirits, being subject to another visible head, who can untie the bond of allegiance at his pleasure.

Neither did they only conceive this hellish wickedness, but were big of it, and kept it close many months, and pleased themselves in the same, as monstrous and misshapen as it was. There wanted neither wit, nor counsel, nor combination, nor secret encouragement to effect it.

Nay, it was an holy villany, sealed with oaths, sacrament, and all the bonds of secrecy that could be invented. Oh horrible profanation, to set God's seal to Satan's plot. But God, who delighteth to confound all presumptuous attempts, discovered it when it should have come to the birth, and so it proved but the untimely fruit of a woman.

They *brought forth a lie*, for whereas they intended to have blown up king and kingdom, churchmen and church, statesmen, yea, the whole state itself, all at once, without any warning to prepare themselves for another world, they not only missed of this, but brought that ruin upon themselves which they intended to others; whereas they thought for ever to have established their (religion, shall I call it, or idolatry, or) superstition, they have by this means made it more odious than ever before; as the northern gentleman could say, that though he was not able to dispute, yet he had two arguments against popery, equivocation and the gunpowder-treason. But they turn it off easily, as they think. Alas! it was but the plot of a company of unfortunate gentlemen. It was our happiness that they were unfortunate; whereas if it had succeeded well, they would have had other terms for it. Successful villany goeth for virtue.

Well, the net is broken, and we are delivered. God thought of us when we thought not of him, and awaked for us when we were asleep (here is a place for *behold*), for what a miserable face of things would there have been if their plot had succeeded!

Now what return shall we make for all this? They conceived mischief, let us conceive praise, and travail of holy resolutions to give up ourselves to God, who hath given us our king, our state, yea, ourselves to ourselves. He hath given us our lives more than once, every one of us in particular, especially in the last heavy visitation.* But had it not been better for many in regard of their own particular, to have been swept away in that deluge, than to live longer to treasure up further wrath to themselves? Many are not content to go to hell alone, but they will draw as many others as they can into their fellowship here, and torment hereafter. Oh beloved, the preservation of such, is but a reservation to further judgment! What good got the king of Sodom by being delivered once, and then after to be consumed with 'fire and brimstone from heaven? Gen. xix. What got Pharaoh by being delivered from ten plagues, and then to perish in the sea? Exod. xiv. What are all our temporal deliverances, if we live still in sin, go on in sin, die in our sins, and so perish eternally? Blessings, without return of due thanks, increase the guilt of sin, and the increase of guilt causeth the increase of judgments.

The most proper homogeneal way of thanks, is to stir up ourselves to a greater hatred of that religion. They would fain free it, as if it were the fault of some persons only; but alas! what can be else distilled from those dangerous points they hold (as that, *the pope hath temporal jurisdiction over princes, that he may excommunicate them; that he may, out of fulness of power, dispense with the oath of allegiance: that he cannot err; that subjection to him is a point of absolute necessity to salvation, &c.*) What, I say, can be distilled from these opinions, but treason in a people that live under a prince of a contrary religion? The dispositions of many of them are better than their positions.

However perhaps the present pope† may be more moderate and neutral, yet this is the infusion of their religion wherever it prevails, and these tenets shall be acted and in full force when they please, and it will please them when it shall be for the advantage of the Catholic cause. This was Bellarmine's tenet, *If the pope should err in commanding vice or forbidding virtue, the church is bound to believe vice to be good, and virtue to be ill, or*

* The plague.—G.

† Urban VIII *(f)*.—G.

*else it should sin against conscience; for it is bound to believe what he commands.** Thus they make the judgment of man the rule of truth and falsehood, good and evil; whereas truth is truth, and that which is false is false, whether men think so or no. There is an intrinsical evil in evil, which the judgment of any man cannot take away; and the truth and goodness of things stands upon eternal grounds, not flexible or alterable by the will of any creature; otherwise it were all one as to think the course of the sun should be guided by a dial. Is there any hope of their coming to us when they had rather have the rules of nature and religion, which are as unmoveable as a mountain of brass, to vary, than be thought to confess that the pope may err! which indeed is the grand and leading error of all. But how should we expect our words should prevail, whenas the great works of God prevail not at all with them? The efficacy of error is so strong in many, that though they should see the vial poured out 'upon the throne of the beast,' Rev. xvi. 10, yet will they not repent.

For ourselves, we cannot better shew our thankfulness for this deliverance, by means whereof we enjoy our lives and our religion, than to preserve that truth, that is grounded upon the foundation of truth, which hath been derived unto us from those that went before, who held out the same truth; that hath been sealed by the blood of so many martyrs; that hath been established by the authority of gracious princes; that God hath given witness to by so many deliverances; that concurs with the confessions of all reformed churches; that God hath blessed with a constant tenor of peace, even to the rejoicing of all neighbour churches, to the envy of our enemies, and to the admiration of all.

We see all countries round about us in a confusion, and we, as it were the 'three young men in the fiery furnace,' safe, Dan. iii., without so much as smoke or smell of fire; as if we were the only people of God's delight. Now, what is that which God careth most for amongst us, but his truth? which, if we suffer, as much as in us lieth, to take any detriment, God may justly make us the spectacles of his wrath to others, as others have been to us. Beloved, God hath a cause and a people in the world, which he esteemeth more than all the world besides. Let us therefore own God's cause and people; his side one day will prove the better side.

I beseech you consider, what hurt have we ever had by the Reformation of religion? hath it come naked unto us? hath it not been attended with peace and prosperity? hath God 'been a barren wilderness to us?' Jer. ii. 31. Hath not God been a wall of fire about us? which, if he had not been, it is not the water that compasseth our island could have kept us. So long as we keep Christ's truth, Christ will keep us. Otherwise, trust to it, Christ and his truth will leave us. No nation under heaven hath so much cause to say 'Behold' as we have. Men are ready upon all occasions to be sensible of civil grievances (as in Solomon's time gold was as stones in the street, 2 Chron. i. 15, ix. 27), but we should be sensible of the spiritual favours we enjoy. If we look upon other kingdoms abroad, what nation under heaven hath the like cause to bless God for religion, for prince, for peace, &c., as we have? Beloved, we cannot better deserve of our king, church, and state, than to give up our lives to God who hath thus blessed us. The greatest enemies of a church and state, are those that provoke the highest Majesty of heaven, by obstinate courses against the light that shineth in their own hearts. It is seriously to be considered what Samuel saith to the people; and therefore, if not for love of our-

* See original in note *g*.—G.

selves, yet for the love of our king, religion, and state, let us take heed of provoking courses, and take heed of tiring the patience of God over-long. To conclude all, it is prayer that gets, but thankfulness witnessed by obedience that keeps, blessings. And what can our thoughts devise, our tongues utter, or our lives express, better, than the praise of our good God, that ever loadeth us with his benefits? that so God may delight still to shew himself unto us in the ways of his mercy, and think thoughts of love towards us, and dwell amongst us to the world's end.

NOTES.

(*a*) P. 306.—Augustine saith well, every sin is a lie. From De Civitate Dei, xlv. iv. 1, 'Unde non frustra dici potest, omne peccatum esse mendacium.'

(*b*) P. 307.—'Sweet morsels . . . . their Herodians.' This is probably a misprint for Herodiases, and the reference to Mat. xiv. 3, 6, Mark vi. 17, 22.

(*c*) P. 307.—'Sin . . . lay at the door,' Gen. iv. 7. For very interesting remarks on this passage, in the sense of Sibbes's quotation, consult Kalisch *in loc*, specially page 139 (Hist. and Critical Commentary on Old Testament . . . Genesis. 1858).

(*d*) P. 310.—'The *subsistence* of things not seen,' Heb xi. 1. ὑπόστασις is rendered 'substance' in our authorised version. Professor Sampson of America *in loc* accepts Sibbes's translation, and observes, 'It is not only true of faith, that it is a "firm persuasion" of the existence of such things, but that it gives them, so to speak, "*present subsistence.*" It gives them the force of present realities. This sense, therefore, includes the other, and is for this reason preferable, that, while it expresses all that is expressed by the other, it gives more fulness and strength to the apostle's words' (Critical Commentary on Hebrews. New York, 1856).

(*e*) P. 310.—'Our gunpowder plotters.' Sibbes preached numerous sermons on the anniversary of the memorable conspiracy known by the name of 'the gunpowder plot.' It was so designated from its design having been, by springing a mine under the Houses of Parliament, to destroy the three estates of the realm. It was discovered on Nov. 5th. 1605. An excellent summary of the facts will be found in a small volume dedicated to 'the plot,' by the Rev. Thomas Lathbury of Bristol, and a full 'history' in the standard work of David Jardine, Esq.

(*f*) P. 311.—'The present pope . . . . Urban VIII.' Consult Ranké (History of the Popes, ii. 104, *seq.*) for the extraordinary career of this very remarkable pope. His bearing toward England at the time of Sibbes's sermon explains the half-favourable opinion expressed. He was raised to the tiara in 1623, and died in 1644.

(*g*) P. 311.—This extraordinary quotation will be found in Bellarmine, De Pontifice, book iv. c. 5—'Si autem Papa erraret præcipiendo vitia vel prohibendo virtutes, teneretur Ecclesia credere vitia esse bona et virtutes malas, nisi vellet contra conscientiam peccare.' G.

THE SAINT'S SAFETY IN EVIL TIMES:*

MANIFESTED BY ST PAUL, FROM HIS EXPERIENCE OF GOD'S GOODNESS IN GREATEST DISTRESSES.

Notwithstanding the Lord stood with me, and strengthened me, that by me the preaching might be fully known, and that all the Gentiles might hear: and I was delivered out of the mouth of the lion. And the Lord shall deliver me from every evil work, and will preserve me unto his heavenly kingdom; to whom be glory for ever and ever. Amen.—2 TIM. IV. 17, 18.

BLESSED St Paul, being now an old man, and ready to sacrifice his dearest blood for the sealing of that truth which he had carefully taught, sets down in this chapter what diverse entertainment he found, both from God and man, in the preaching of it. As for men, he found they dealt most unfaithfully with him, when he stood most in need of comfort from them. Demas, a man of great note, in the end forsook him; Alexander the coppersmith (thus it pleases God to try his dearest ones with base oppositions of worthless persons) did him most mischief; weaker Christians forsook him, &c. But mark the wisdom of God's Spirit in the blessed apostle, in regard of his different carriage towards these persons. Demas, because his fault was greater, by reason of the eminency of his profession, him he brands to all posterity, for looking back to Sodom and to the world, after he had put his hand to the plough. Alexander's opposing, because it sprung from extremity of malice towards the profession of godliness, him he curseth. 'The Lord reward him,' &c. Weaker Christians, who failed him from want of some measure of spirit and courage, retaining still a hidden love to the cause of Christ, their names he conceals, with prayer that God would not lay their sin to their charge. But whilst Paul lived in this cold comfort on earth, see what large encouragement had he from heaven! 'Though all forsook me, yet,' says he, 'God did not forsake me, but stood by me, and I was delivered out of the mouth of the lion. And the Lord will deliver me,' &c.

In the words, we have, in Paul's example, an expressing of that general truth set down by himself: 'And not only so, but we glory in tribulations

* In the 'Saint's Cordial's' editions of this sermon, it is said to have been 'preached at Paul's Crosse, upon a speciall solemne occasion, Aug. 5.'—G.

also, knowing that tribulation worketh patience; and patience, experience; and experience, hope,' &c., Rom. v. 3. So here affliction breeds experience of God's mercy in our deliverance, and experience breeds hope of deliverance for the time to come; and both his experience and hope stirs him up to glorify God, who was his deliverer; so that here offer unto us to be unfolded—

1. Paul's *experience of God's loving care of him in his deliverance past.*

2. *His assured hope, built upon his experience, for the time to come;* set down in two branches:

(1.) *The Lord will deliver me from every evil work.*

(2.) *He will preserve me to his heavenly kingdom.*

3. *The issue he maketh of both; as they flow from God's grace, so he ascribes him the glory of both.* 'To whom be glory for ever and ever. Amen.'

For the first, I find that most, both ancient and modern writers, by *lion* understand Nero, that cruel tyrant, thirsty of blood, especially of Christians (*h*). Some also understand it to be a proverbial speech, to express extremity of danger, both which are true. But if we take the words in the just breadth of the apostle's intent, we may by lion understand *the whole united company of his cruel enemies,* as David in many places hath the like; and, by the mouth of the *lion,* the present danger he was in by reason of their cruel malice. Whence observe:

1. *That enemies of the truth are (oft for power, always for malice) lions.*

2. *That God suffers his dearest children to fall into the mouths of these lions.*

3. *That in this extremity of danger God delivers them.*

For the second, his hope built upon his experience; both* branches thereof hath its limitation and extent. The Lord shall deliver me, not from evil suffering, but from evil works. This he could boldly build on. He could not conjecture what he should suffer, because that was in the power of others; but he could build upon this, what God would give him grace to do. And so he limits his confidence, 'He will deliver me from evil works, and he will preserve me.' From what? From danger? from death? No; here is the limitation: 'He will preserve me to his heavenly kingdom.' He will not preserve me from death (and yet he will do that whilst I can do his service by my life), but sure I am he will preserve me beyond death to a state of security and happiness. 'He will preserve me to his heavenly kingdom.'

And then for the third. After his experience, confidence, and hope well built, as his fashion is, when his heart was once warmed, he breaks out into *thanksgiving,* in the consideration of God's favours past, and to come. His tongue is large thereupon, and God hath the fruit of it. 'To whom be glory for ever;' and lastly, he seals up all with the word, 'Amen.'

'I was delivered out of the mouth of the lion,' &c. Beloved, by nature we are all lions, and nothing will alter us, save the effectual knowledge of Christ. Education may civilise, but not subdue. A sound knowledge of God's truth hath a changing power; for when the spirit becomes tender, and when the heart, which lies in a cursed estate, under and in danger of, the wrath of a just God, whose eye cannot spare iniquity unrepented of, is cited and affrighted effectually by the spirit of bondage, it will cast down, and pull sorrow from the strongest spirit, making it melting and tender. Again, in this estate, when the soul hath felt favour shining upon it; when

* That is, 'each of the' branches.—G.

the eye is opened to see the high prerogatives and exceeding riches of Christ; when we find ourselves that we are delivered from the lion's mouth, we cannot but shew that pity to others, which we felt from God ourselves. Paul thirsts as eagerly after the conversion of others now, as ever he did for their blood before, Acts ix. 22. The jailor also, a man by nature, custom, and calling, hardened in the practice of cruelty, Acts xvi. 33; yet after he had felt the power of God's blessed truth, shewed forth those bowels of pity he felt from Christ, which were shut before (*i*).

Let us then be thankful, that God hath changed us from being lions, and with meekness submit ourselves unto God's ordinances, desiring him to write his law, not only in our understandings, but in our very hearts and bowels, that we may not only know that we should walk harmless and full of good, Jer. xxxi. 33, but be so indeed, resembling him by whom we hope to be saved, in a right serviceable pliableness to all duties of love.

And because our imperfect measure of mortification in this life, hinders us from a full content in one another's communion, let this make us the more willing to be translated to God's holy mount, where, being purged from all such lusts as hinder our peace and love, we shall fully enjoy one another, without the least falseness or distrust. Then shall we see total accomplishment of these promises, which are but in part fulfilled in this life.

Obs. 1. That God suffereth his children to fall into the *mouth of lions*, or into some danger proportionable, wherein they shall see no help from him, is a truth clear as the sun. The history of the church in all ages shews as much. Was not Christ in the mouth of the lion, so soon as born, when Herod sought to kill him? Mat. ii. 13. Did not Satan and all the spiritual powers of hell daily come about him, like ramping and roaring lions? And hath it not been thus with God's church from Abel to this present, as appears by the children of Israel in Egypt, at the Red Sea, and in their journey to Canaan, being environed round about with cruel enemies, and dangers on every side, like Daniel in the midst of lions? So far God gave them up to the power of their enemies, that the wisest of the heathen judged them a forlorn people, hateful to God and men.* For particular instances, see Job and David, so near as there was but a step between them and death.

Besides, God often awakens the consciences of his children, and exerciseth them with spiritual conflicts; their sins, as so many lions, stand up against them, ready to tear their souls. Nay, rather than those that belong to God shall want that, which will drive them unto him, God himself will be a lion unto them, as unto Ephraim, Hos. v. 14,† which made David pray, 'Oh Lord, rebuke me not in thine anger, neither chasten me in thy hot displeasure,' Ps. vi. 1. Of all the troubles which a child of God undergoeth in his way to heaven, these bring him lowest. When the body is vexed and spirit troubled, it is much; but when God frowns, when neither heaven nor earth yields comfort to a distressed soul, no evil in the world is like to this. Imagine the horror and straits of such a soul, when all things seem against it, and itself against itself, as near to the pains of the very damned in hell.

The reasons of this dispensation of God are: 1, because we are so desperately addicted to present things, and so prone to put confidence in the

* Cicero. See *ante*, p. 303.—G.

† 'For I will be unto Ephraim as a lion, and as a young lion to the house of Judah: I, even I, will tear and go away; I will take away, and none shall rescue him.'

arm of flesh, that unless God driveth us from these holds, by casting us into a perplexed estate, we shall never know what it is to live by faith in God alone, when all other props are pulled away, and when the stream of things seems cross unto us. That God therefore may train us up to live the spiritual life of the just, which is by faith in him, when all else fail, he suffereth us to fall into the lion's mouth, that so our prayers, which are the flame of faith, may be more ardent and piercing, rather cries than words. 'Why criest thou unto me,' saith God to Moses, Exod. xiv. 15. When was this? Even when he knew not what way to turn him. It was out of the depths that David cried most earnestly unto God, Ps. cxxx. 1; and Christ, in the days of his flesh, cried unto God with strong cries and tears, in a deep distress, and was also heard in that which he feared, Heb. v. 7. Strong troubles force from the afflicted strong cries. Even experience shews, in prosperity, and a full estate, how faint and cold the prayers and desires of men are.

2. Besides, it is meet that the secrets of men's hearts should be discovered; for when all is quiet, we know not the falsehood of our own hearts. Some over-value their strength, as Peter, Mat. xxvi. 33; others underprize themselves, and the gifts and graces of God's Spirit in them, thinking that they want faith, patience, love, &c., who yet, when God calleth them out to the cross, shine forth in the eyes of others, in the example of a meek and faithful subjection. The wisdom of God therefore judgeth it meet, that there should be times of sifting, that both the church and ourselves may know what good or ill is in us, what soundness or looseness remains in our hearts. When, therefore, we are wanting in fanning ourselves, God in love takes the fan into his hand.

It is likewise behoveful that false brethren may be discovered. Afflictions are well called trials, because then it is known what metal men are made of, whether pure or reprobate silver. Think it not strange then, when our estate seems desperate. It is but with us after the manner of God's dearest ones; why should we have a severed condition from them? Remember this, that God, as he suffers his children to fall into the lion's mouth, so he delivers them out; and that he never leaves his, especially in extremity, but in fit case of soul to receive the greatest comfort, and to render him the greatest glory. For then it is known to be God's work: our extremity is his opportunity. God will especially shew himself at such a time, and make it appear that the church stands not by man's strength. When Christians are at a loss, and know not which way to turn themselves, then is God nearest hand and careth most for them.

And this the Lord doth, both for the greater shame of those that contrive mischief (when they make themselves surest to bring their wicked plots and purposes to pass, then their designs are most frustrated); as also to draw on others not yet called; that they, seeing God's immediate care over his church and children, may come in and obtain like protection and deliverance.

The manner how God delivereth his children out of the lion's mouth is diverse.

Divers ways how God delivers from the lion's mouth:—1. *By suspending their malice for the time.* As in Noah's ark the fierceness of the wild creatures was stopped by divine power from preying upon the tamer, so the lions' mouths were stopped from preying upon Daniel in the lions' den, Dan. vi. 22.

2. *By stirring up one lion against another;* as the Persians against the

Babylonians, Grecians against Persians, Romans against the Grecians, and the other barbarous nations, as the Goths and Vandals, against them; so whilst lions spit their fury one upon another, the sheep are quiet. Thus the Turks and other enemies have kept popish princes from raging and tyrannising over the church to the height of their malice.

3. *By casting something unto these lions, to divert them another way from their intended prey;* as when a man is in danger, a dog is cast unto the lion (*j*). Thus, when Saul was ready to devour David, the Philistines made a breach upon him, invaded the land, and turned his fury another way, 2 Sam. xxiii. 27.

4. *By altering and changing lions to be lambs;* as when Paul was set upon havoc and mischief, God, by changing his heart, gave the churches cause to glorify God for him, of whom before they were most afraid.

5. *God shews himself a lion to these lions;* by breaking their teeth and jaw-bones, striking them with sudden and fearful judgment; as Herod, Acts xii. 23, and the persecuting emperors; and as in '88, when God with his four winds fought for us against the enemies of his truth.*

6. *By making them lions to themselves:* witness Ahithophel, Saul, and other such-like enemies of God's children.

7. Again, *God maketh them friends without changing their disposition,* by putting into their hearts some conceit for the time, which inclineth them to favour: as in Nehemiah, God put it into the king's heart to favour his people, Neh. ii. 8. Esau, Gen. xxxiii. 4, was not changed, only God for the time changed his affections to favour Jacob. So God puts it into the hearts of many, groundedly-naught, to favour the best persons.

8. Lastly, *God maketh his own children sometimes lions to their adversaries;* for the image of God shining in his children, hath a secret majesty in it, and striketh an awe upon wicked men. So Pharaoh at length could not endure to see Moses and Aaron any more, Exod. x. 28; and Felix trembled whilst Paul disputed of temperance and judgment, Acts xxiv. 25.

Use; of instruction and consolation. Thus we see the Lord knows how to deliver his, and can if he will; and will do it in their extremities, when is most for his glory, his people's comfort, and confusion of his own and their enemies. Never despair therefore of thyself or the church of God: it shall, rather than fail, breed in the lion's den. Paul salutes the Philippians, from the church in Cæsar's house, Phil. iv. 22, a place in appearance little fitter for a church than hell itself. What though things seem past recovery abroad? When they are at the worst, then are they nearest mending. When the task of brick was doubled by Pharaoh upon Israel, Exod. v. 11, then came Moses to work out their deliverance. When the Jews heard news of their liberty to return from captivity, they were as those that dreamed, Ps. cxxvi. 1; they could not suddenly believe it, it seemed so strange a thing, in that their hopeless estate. Learn we then, from this dealing of God with his people, in the midst of all extremities, to allege unto God the extremity we are in: 'Help, Lord, for vain is the help of man,' Ps. lx. 11, is a prevailing argument. Allege the pride of enemies, the presumption of those that fear not God, &c., and that he only, can give issue from death, when he will. And as God brings us to heaven by contraries, so let us in one contrary believe another: hope against hope, in misery look for mercy, in death for life, in guiltiness for forgiveness.

* The reference is to the Armada, proudly called 'the Invincible.' It arrived in the Channel July 19th 1588, and was utterly defeated next day by Drake and Howard.—G.

Learn to wrestle with God when he seemeth thy enemy; oppose unto God his former dealings, his nature, his promise, &c. Job had learned this, 'Though he kill me, yet will I trust in him,' Job xiii. 15. Be of Jacob's resolution, 'I will not leave hold of thee, until I get a blessing,' Gen. xxxii. 26. Whatsoever we are stript of, let us never forsake our own mercy, Jonah ii. 8. This one word, 'I despair,' takes away God and Christ all at once. We must remember our sins are the sins of men, but mercy is the mercy of God. God will never leave us, but be with us, whilst we are with him. The world and all comforts in it, leave a man when they can have no more use of him nor he of them. Satan leaves his sworn vassals at their wits' end when he hath brought them into danger. But blessed be for ever our gracious God, then of all other times he is nearest to help us, when we stand most in need of him. He was never nearer Moses than when Moses seemed furthest from comfort, Exod. iii. 2; never nearer Jacob than when heaven was his canopy and a stone his pillow, Gen. xxviii. 12; never nearer Joseph than when in prison; Jonah, than in the belly of the whale, for God went down with him; never nearer Paul than when in the dungeon, Acts xvi. 25. A Christian is not alone when left alone, not forsaken when forsaken, 2 Cor. iv. 9. God and his angels supply them the want of other comforts. Is it not a greater comfort that a prince should come in person to a subject and cheer him up, than send a meaner man? 'And whence is this to me,' said Elizabeth, 'that the mother of my Lord should come unto me? Luke i. 43. Is it not the greatest comfort to a Christian soul when God, in want of means, comes immediately himself unto us, and comforts us by his Spirit? For in defect of second causes, comforts are ever sweetest. Therefore, in all extremities let us wait and hope still for mercy. 'If the vision stay,' saith Habakkuk, 'wait, for it will come,' Hab. ii. 3.

Differences of godly and wicked. This is a main difference betwixt the child of God and a person destitute of sound grace; for the child of God in extremity, recovers himself, as David, after a great conflict, gets still the upper hand, 'Yet, my soul, keep thou silence unto God, for God is yet good to Israel,' Ps. lxxiii. 1, as if he should say, Though, when I look upon my present outward condition, I stagger, yet, when I consider more deeply of his dealing, I am resolved God is good to Israel. Thus, after much tossing, they get up upon that rock which is higher than they. But those who are not upright-hearted, in any great extremity, sink down with despair, as heavy bodies, to the centre of the earth, without stop. The reason is, in their best estate they never were acquainted with relying upon God, but bore themselves up with fleshly helps, which, being taken away, they must needs fall downright. But a sincere Christian, in midst of his flourishing estate, acquainteth himself with God, and sets not his heart upon present things. Job says, that which he feared in his best case, that befel unto him, Job iii. 25. Therefore they can rest upon God's mercy when other props are taken away.

Of our support in spiritual losses. Yet there be divers degrees of upholding us when we are at a spiritual loss. For usually, in what measure we, in the times of our peace and liberty, inordinately let loose our affections, in that measure are we cast down, or more deeply in discomfort. When our adulterous hearts cleave to outward things more than becomes chaste hearts, it makes the cross more sharp and extreme. For that which is not enjoyed with over much pleasure, is parted withal without over much grief. But for spiritual extremities, oftentimes the strongest, feel them with quickest sense; for God herein respects not always sins past, or more or less measure of grace, as in Job's case, who could, without much distemper of soul, endure extremities of body and estate, but when God wrote bitter things against him, presently he begins to sink, and but begins only; for when he was at worst, he stays himself upon his Redeemer, to the glory of God's grace, and shame of the devil. Thus sometimes God makes his children triumph, whom he sets as champions in defiance of Satan. They, in weakness, think they shall utterly fail and perish, but their standing out in greatest conflicts shews the contrary.

But to come to that which I intend chiefly to insist on, 'the Lord shall deliver me from every evil work,' &c., wherein we may see—

1. *The author of his safety.*
2. *The deliverance itself.*

The author is the Lord. No less than an almighty power is necessary to deliver from any evil work. For such is our inclinableness to join with temptation, such the malice and strength of our enemy, so many be the snares, and so cunningly spread in everything we deal withal, that whatsoever delivereth us must be above Satan and our own evil hearts; more wise, more powerful, more gracious to preserve us than any adverse power can be to draw us unto evil works. In which case, well said Moses when God, in his wonted glorious presence, refused to go along with them. O, saith Moses, if thou go not with us, carry us not hence, Exod. xxxiii. 15.

'Deliver' supposeth danger, possible or present. Beloved, our lives are such as stand in need of perpetual deliverance. Our estate here is wavering. The church lives always in tents, and hath never any hope of rest until the day of triumph. Therefore, after forgiveness of sins, follows 'lead us not into temptation;' because, though sins past be forgiven, yet we are in danger to be led into temptation. Let none promise a truce to himself, which God promiseth not. If Satan and our corruptions join, we cannot be quiet. After sins of youth we are in danger of sins of riper age; for though by grace, in some sort, sin be subdued, yet, until it be wholly mortified, there will be some stirring up, until that which is imperfect in us be abolished.

But I hasten to that which follows. 'The Lord will deliver me from every evil work.'

Whence, from the form of the argument, observe that we ought to reason with God from former experience to future, 1 Sam. xvii. 37; 2 Cor. i. 10. Yea, it is a binding argument with God. He loves to be sued and pressed from former mercies, and suffers them to be bonds unto him. Men will not do so, because their fountain is soon drawn dry; but God is a spring that can never be emptied. As he was able to help in former time, so he is also for the time to come. He is always, I AM JEHOVAH; always where he was; his arm is not shortened. What he hath done heretofore he can do now.

Use. We should therefore register God's favours, which is the best use we can put our memories to, and make them so many arguments to build upon him for time to come, as David, 'The Lord that delivered me,' saith he, 'out of the paw of the lion, and out of the paw of the bear, will deliver me out of the hand of this Philistine,' 1 Sam. xvii. 37. Oh, were we but acquainted with this kind of reasoning with God, how undaunted would we be in all troubles! We should be as secure for the time to come as for the time past, for all is one with God. We do exceedingly wrong our own souls, and weaken our faith, by not minding of God's favours. How strong in faith might old men be, that have had many experiences of God's love, if they would take this course! Every former mercy should strengthen our faith for a new, as conquerors, whom every former victory encourageth to a new conquest. So old favours should help us to set upon God afresh.

But what is the limitation here? 'From every evil work.' Which words we will first touch a little severally, and then consider more particularly of them.

Sometimes God speaks of duties as they issue from man, because, indeed, the will is man's, from whence the duty comes, and therefore the Scripture speaks, as though the duty came from us, because the powers are ours from whence they spring. Sometimes the Scripture speaks of holy duties as they issue from a higher power, from God. So here, the Lord will deliver me from every evil work, he means that God would stir up his heart to a care to avoid evil works. We are agents and patients in all we do. We are agents, because the powers are ours; we are patients, because the Lord doth all. Now it is the language of the Holy Ghost for the most part, when he speaks of good duties, to go to the fountain, especially when faith is to be strengthened.

Quest. But how doth God deliver?

Ans. By keeping us from occasions, or by ministering strength if occasions be offered. By giving occasions of good, and by giving a heart to entertain those occasions. He preserves us from evil works, (1) *by planting the graces of faith and of fear in us*, whereby we are preserved; and by peace, which guards our souls from despair and tumultuous thoughts. Yea, he preserves us from evil works, through faith, unto his heavenly kingdom, Phil. iv. 7.

In a word, (2) *God preserves his children by making them better*, by weakening corruptions, by his Spirit stirring up a clear sight and hatred of the same in them, and by withdrawing occasions which might prevail over us, and by keeping us from betraying ourselves unto them; by chaining up Satan until our strength be such as may encounter him. A great mercy it is, though little thought on, that God letteth not loose Satan upon us every moment. How should this stir us up, with David, to thankfulness and dependence upon God.

He delivers also wicked men from dangers, not out of any love to their persons, but because he hath some base service for them to undertake, to exercise the patience of his children, and vex others better than themselves, which is not fit for godly men to do. They are only God's rod, and their deliverance is no preservation, but a reservation to worse mischief. It is not a bettering deliverance.

But God delivers his, graciously, not only from danger, but from those evil works they are subject to fall into in their danger. It is not ill to suffer ill, but to do ill. For doing ill makes God our enemy; suffering ill doth not. Doing ill, stains and defiles the soul, and blemisheth the image of God in us; suffering ill doth none of this. Doing ill, hinders communion and acquaintance with God; suffering ill doth not. God is more immediately acquainted with the soul in suffering ill. Doing ill is the cause of all ills; suffering ill comes from doing ill. The ill of sin, is the ill of ills, because it is evil itself, and the cause of all other whatsoever. We may thank our ill in doing, for our ill in suffering; and therefore the apostle is well assured what he says, 'The Lord will deliver me from every evil work,' not from every inward infirmity and weakness, but from every evil work that is scandalous and offensive to him.

It is an aggravation of ill when it is manifested; for then it either taints or grieves others. Indeed so soon as the resolution of the soul hath passed it, when the will resolves on such a thing, it is done, both in good and evil, before God. But in regard of the world, and of the church we live in; the bringing of the work upon the stage, as it were, is an aggravation of evil; because, besides the hurt which is done to evil men, good men are either hurt or vexed at it. Therefore the apostle saith, 'the Lord will deliver me from every evil work.' This, a Christian should especially labour for, that God in all things would keep him free from sin. Yea, this differenceth a Christian from another man. Take a carnal man when he is like to fall into danger, he studies how to get out of suffering evil, not how to prevent doing evil; he plots, devises, and entangles himself in his own wit, and makes the matter worse by equivocation, and such like sinful courses, as we might learn from the papists, if we had not enough from our own breast. But Paul's care was to be delivered from *evil works*. For a man indeed is never overcome, let him be never so vexed in the world by any, till his conscience be cracked. If his conscience and his cause stand upright, he prevails still; 'in all these things we are more than conquerors,' Rom. viii. 37, saith the apostle. The meaning is, sufferings cannot quell our courage, they cannot stain our conscience, they do not hurt the cause, but it gets victory in despite of them; so that our courage is undaunted and our conscience abides unstained. Let it be our care therefore to take heed of evil works. Look into the world and see what is the care of most men we converse with, Oh, if they can get such a place, if they can get such an estate! Aye, but it cannot be had without sinful abasement, without cracking of conscience, and unlawful engagement. Oh, say they, it is no matter, God will pardon all, I care not so I may have my wish. This is the heart of many graceless persons that are not led with heavenly respects. But take a Christian, and he had rather beg, do anything in the world, than do a thing unworthy his profession, unbeseeming the gospel, or that high calling whereunto he is called. 'Shall such a man as I do this?' Neh. vi. 11; he will not, and therefore his care is to take heed of ill works; for then he is sure to have God his friend, who hath riches and honour enough for him, because 'the earth is the Lord's and the fulness thereof,' Ps. xxiv. 1. This is the care of a judicious well-instructed Christian.

But mark the *extent* from *every* evil work. St Paul' scare is not for one or two, but that God would keep him from *every* evil work. Why so?

Why St Paul says from every evil work. Because he that truly hates one sin, will hate all the kinds of it. Both come from the same love of God. He that loves God as he should, will hate whatsoever God hates; 'and have respect to all God's commandments,' as the psalmist speaks, Ps. cxix. 128. Partial obedience is indeed no obedience at all; for he that obeys one, and not another, obeys not simply because of the commander, to yield obedience unto him; but only to satisfy his own corrupt nature, picking and choosing what pleases himself, which belongs not to an inferior, but to a superior to do. And therefore, such make themselves gods, in that they single out easy things that do not oppose their lusts, which are not against their reputation, &c., and therein perhaps they will supererogate, and do more than they need, only because they will have a compensation with God, that he should quit with them for other things. I have done that, and therefore he must bear with me in this. Oh! but there is no compensation here. A man is never so straitened but he may escape without sin. There is no pretence will serve; but we must abstain from *every* evil work. Satan keeps many men in his snare by this, and so he hath them safe in one sin, he cares not; therefore he will suffer them to hear, read, and pray, &c., holding them fast in one reigning sin, wherein he will let them alone till the time of some great affliction, or death; and then he will roar upon them. Oh beloved! we cannot provide worse for our own souls, than to cherish a purpose of living in any one sin, for that is enough for the devil to hold his possession in us by, and at the hour of death to claim us for his own. 'If we regard any iniquity in our heart, the Lord will not hear our prayers,' Ps. lxvi. 18. I beseech you therefore, let us labour to have clear consciences, freeing ourselves from a purpose to live in any sin; that in all our slips and failings we may say with an honest heart, my purpose was not to do this, but to refrain from wickedness.

Again, he speaks of this for the time to come; the Lord *will* deliver me from evil. A true Christian is as careful to avoid sin for the time to come, as to be freed from the guilt of sins past. Judas may desire to have his conscience freed from former sins, but Judas cannot desire to be a good man for the time to come. Nothing argues a good conscience more than this. The most wicked wretch that breathes, may desire to have his conscience stilled, and yet never have any purpose or power to abstain from sin; but like a dog, after he hath disgorged himself, return to his vomit again. True repentance is a turning from former evils to a contrary good. Our grief no further yields comfort of sound repentance, than it hath care attending, for prevention of sin; according to that which Christ said to the woman taken in adultery, 'Go, and sin no more,' John v. 14, and as David prays, 'Purge me, O Lord, and cleanse me, but withal, establish me with thy free Spirit for the time to come,' Ps. li. 2, 12. As if he should say, Lord, I know it is not in man to order his own ways, I desire not the forgiveness of my sins that thereby I might with more liberty offend thy majesty, but with pardoning grace, I beg preventing grace. No false heart can move such a desire as this to God. A gracious heart that prays aright, prays as well that God would preserve him from future sin, as forgive him his former sins. It is a ridiculous thing of the papists to make confession of a sin which they mean to commit: as some late traitors confessed such and such things which they were to act, and were straight absolved for it. So your cursed duellists, that will pray and repent, when they mean presently to fall one upon another. Is this repentance, when a man is inveigled with the sin he means to commit; and cannot overcome himself in the case of revenge? Do these men think they repent? No, certainly; repentance is of sins past, and the carriage of every true Christian is to avoid evil for the time to come.

Again, it is here a perpetuated act: The Lord will deliver me still from every evil work. Whence you see that in every evil work we are tempted to, we need delivering grace; as to every good work, assisting grace. Indeed, our whole life, if we look upwards, is nothing but a deliverance, but if we look to ourselves, it is nothing but danger and a warfare, and therefore we have need of a deliverance. How little a temptation turns over a great man! as sometimes a little wind turns over your mighty galleys. We see this in David and Solomon; and, if God leave us to ourselves, even the strongest man in the world, how soon is he overturned! In the midst of sinful occasions, how ready are we to join with them, and betray our own souls!

But from the whole, take it as it comes from God altogether, the truth is thus much, *that a Christian, who is privy to his own soul of good intentions to abstain from all ill for the present, may presume that God will assist him against all ill works for the time to come.* I say a Christian, that hath his conscience telling him that he means to be better, and is not in league with any sin, may believe this for the time to come, that God will keep him from evil works. I speak this, because many who are yet sinners think it in vain to strive, for they shall never be better. What dost thou talk, man? Hast thou a mind to be better? God will meet thee one time or other. Is thy will at liberty? He that gives thee the will, will also give thee the deed. Is not this the promise, that God will deliver thee from every evil work? And, therefore, away with all discouragements.

Obj. O but there are sons of Anak, mighty giants, that molest me; my sins are as so many giants to stop my proceeding; I shall never be better!

Solution. Say not so; nay, rather thou *wilt* not be better. Thou art in league with some secret sin, thy heart riseth against those that reprove thee of it, thine own conscience tells thee that thy heart is naught; for if thou wouldst set thyself to obey God in truth, assuredly he would deliver thy soul. And therefore the apostle, to prevent such doubts, speaks of deliverance from evil works as coming from God.

Obj. But some may object, We sin every day; and 'if we say we have no sin, we deceive ourselves, and the truth is not in us,' 1 John i. 8.

Ans. You must not understand this phrase legally, in the rigour of it, as that God will deliver us from every ill thought, or rising in the heart, or from every outward slip and failing, &c.; but by every evil work, the apostle means every reproachful sin that breaks the peace of our conscience, that swallows up a man's salvation. From such kind of sins that bring a stain and discredit unto a man's profession, that wound his soul, and may discourage others, the Lord will deliver his; he will keep them from greater sins altogether, and from being in league with lesser. You know in falls there are several degrees; there is a slip, a falling, and a falling on all four; as we say, a flat falling. Now God will deliver his children from falling so foully.

2. *How God delivers from ill works by not delivering.* Nay, sometimes he will deliver them from evil works, by not delivering them from evil works. He will deliver from great ill works, by letting them alone in lesser ill works. God delivers from evil divers ways; he delivers from falling into ill, and he delivers out of ill when we are fallen; he delivers from ill likewise by supporting us; nay, which is more, he delivers from ill works by ill works.

Quest. How is that?

Solution. How do physicians deliver from an apoplexy? from a lethargy? Is it not by casting the sick person into an ague, to awaken that dull sickness? So God, to cure the conscience of a man, when he sees him in danger of security by those soul-killing sins, pride, covetousness, looseness, hypocrisy, and the like, suffers him sometimes to fall into less offences, to awake his conscience, that being roused up he may fly to God's mercy in Christ. So infinite is God's care this way, that he will deliver either from ill works, or from the evil of ill works; or, if he deliver not from ill works, yet he will deliver us from worse works by those ill works. Austin saith, I dare presume to say, it is profitable for some men to fall.* If a man be of a proud, peremptory disposition, or of a blockish, dull, and

* 'It is profitable for some men to fall.' Consult 'Confessio Book I., xi. 18; and Book VII. xx. 26.—G.

secure nature, it is good he should be acquainted what sin he carries in his breast, where his corruptions are, &c., that so he may know himself and his danger the better.

Use. I beseech you make use of this, to help your faith and thankfulness. When we are delivered from evil works, it is God that doth it. The consideration whereof, methinks, should strengthen our faith against Satan and all his fiery darts, and encourage us to set confidently upon any corruption that we are moved to by others, or our own natural inclination. It is God's enemy, and it is my enemy; it is opposite to God's will, and it is an enemy to my comfort. God will take my part against that which is opposite to him. He hath promised me to assist me against every evil work by his Holy Spirit. A Christian is a king, Rev. i. 6; and he hath the triumphing Spirit of Christ in him, which will prevail over all sin in time.

Obj. But some poor soul may object, Alas! I have been assaulted by such a corruption, a long time, in a grievous manner, and am not yet delivered from it.

Ans. God doth by little and little purge out corruption. As every stroke helps the fall of the oak, the first stroke helps forward; so every opposing of corruption, never so little, helps to root it out, and it is weakened by little and little, till death accomplish more mortification.

But to proceed. God doth not only deliver from evil works, but preserves us to his heavenly kingdom. We must take *preserve* here in its full breadth. He preserves us whilst he hath any work for us to do in this life; and when he will have us live no longer, he will preserve us to heaven; howsoever, by death he takes us away, yet even then the Lord still preserves us.

Under-preservers of the saints. He will preserve us in our outward estate, by himself, and by under-preservers, for there be many such under God; as angels that are his ministering spirits, and magistrates, who are the shields of the earth; they may preserve under God; and likewise ministers, that are the chariots and horsemen of Israel, and good laws, &c. But God is the first turner of the wheel; we must see him in all other preservers whatsoever. And therefore the apostle, in the language of the Holy Ghost, and of Canaan, saith here, 'The Lord will preserve me,' Ps. xlvii. 9; 2 Kings ii. 12. And rather than a man shall miscarry when God hath anything for him to do, God will work a miracle.

The three men could not be burned in the fire, Dan. iii. 25 and vi. 12; God so suspended the force thereof. Daniel could not be devoured of the greedy lions, &c. Rather than God's purpose shall fail, that a man should perish before the time that God hath allotted him, the lions shall not devour, and the fire shall not burn. God hath measured our glass and time, even to a moment; and as our Saviour Christ, out of knowledge of this heavenly truth, saith, 'My time is not yet come,' John vii. 6, so let us know that, till our hour comes, all the devils in hell cannot hurt one hair of our head. And this is a wondrous ground of confidence, that we should carry ourselves above all threatenings, and above all fears whatsoever. 'Thou canst do nothing except it were given thee,' John xix. 10, saith Christ to bragging Pilate, who boasted of his power. Alas! what can all the enemies of God's people do except God permit them?

If a king or a great man should say to an inferior, Go on; I will stand by thee, and preserve thee; thou shalt take no harm: what an encouragement were this! Oh, but when God shall say to a Christian, Walk humbly before me, keep close to my word, be stedfast in the ways of holiness, fear not man, you are under my protection and safeguard: what an encouragement is this to a believing soul!

But put case we cannot be preserved from death; for so it was here with the apostle, he died a bloody death. Why, let us observe his blessed carriage in all this, and do likewise. I regard not that, saith he; do your worst, God will preserve me still. So it should be the bent of a Christian's soul to come to God with this limitation, in his faith and in his prayer: Lord, if thou wilt not deliver me from suffering ill, preserve me from doing ill; if thou wilt not preserve me from death, preserve me from sinful works. This we may build on, that either God will preserve us in life, or if we die, he will preserve us in death to his heavenly kingdom. And *sometimes God preserves by not preserving from death;* for indeed death keeps a man from all danger whatsoever. He is out of all gun-shot, when he is once dead. Death is a deliverance and a preservation of itself: it sends a man to heaven straight; and therefore the apostle knew what he said, 'The Lord will preserve me to his heavenly kingdom.'

That is, he will preserve me till I be possessed of heaven; he will go along with me in all the passages of my life; he will carry me through all, and bring me thither at last. As the angel that struck off Peter's bolts, 'shined in the prison,' Acts xii. 7, and carried him out into the city, so God by his Spirit shines into our souls, and carries us through all the passages of this life, never leaving us, till he have brought us to his heavenly kingdom.

And not to open unto you things that are beyond my conceit, much more my expression, what a state this heavenly kingdom is, unto which St Paul hoped to be preserved! Observe, briefly, thus much :—1, It is a kingdom of all conditions the freest; 2, the most glorious; 3, the most abundant in all supplies; 4, it is a heavenly kingdom; 5, it is an everlasting kingdom.

The excellency of the heavenly kingdom. Things, the nearer the heavens they are, the purer they are. 1, heaven is a most holy kingdom: no uncleanness can enter there; 2, it is a large kingdom; and 3, an everlasting kingdom. Other men's kingdoms determine with their persons; perhaps they may live to out-live their glory in the world, as Nero did (the king that Paul was under now, when he wrote this epistle), who came to a base end. But this kingdom can never be shaken. God's preservation shall end in eternal glory.

Use 1. *Here is a special ground to God's children of perseverance in well-doing.* What! doth God undertake even from himself, to deliver us from evil works, which might endanger our salvation, and to preserve us until he have put us into heaven! Where is the popish doctrine of falling away, then? *Obj.* Oh, but I may sin, and so fall away. *Sol.* Aye, but God will deliver us from evil works; he takes away that objection. He that keeps heaven for us, keeps us for heaven, till he have put us into possession of it. 'We are kept (we are guarded (*k*), as the word is) by the power of God to salvation,' 1 Pet. i. 5. Salvation is kept for us, and we for that. If we endanger heaven any way, it is by ill works, and God keeps us from them. What a most comfortable doctrine is this!

Use 2. But, to add a second against that foolish, vain, and proud point of *popish merit.* We see what a strain they are in. 1. Before conversion they will have merit of congruity, that it befits the goodness of God, when we do what we can, that we should have grace. 2. When we are in the state of grace, they will have merit of condignity; but how can that be, whenas free grace runs along in all? God preserves us from evil works, and preserves us to his heavenly kingdom, of his mere love and mercy. Where then is the merit of man? Indeed, we do good when we do good, but God enables us; we speak to the praise of God, but he opens our mouth; we believe, but God draws our heart to it: as Austin says, we move, but God moves us.*

Use 3. I beseech you, observe further here: *How complete God's favours are to his. He deals like a God, that is, fully and eternally, with his children.* If he deliver, it is from the greatest evil; if he preserve, it is to the greatest good. Who would not serve such a master? Oh, the baseness of the vile heart of man, that is a slave to inferior things, and afraid to displease men, never considering what a blessed condition it is, to be under the government of a gracious God, that will keep us from ill, if it be for our good, for ever, outwardly from evil works, inwardly from the terrors of an ill conscience, that will preserve us here in this world, and give us heaven when we have done. I beseech you, let this complete and full dealing of God quicken us to a holy courage and constancy in his service.

Use 4. And see here a *point of heavenly wisdom; to look, when we are in any danger, with the apostle, to the heavenly kingdom.* When we are sick, look not at death. Paul cared not for that, but says he, 'The Lord will preserve me to his kingdom.' He looked to the bank of the shore. As a man that goes through a river hath his eye still on the shore, so the apostle had his eye fixed upon heaven still. I beseech you therefore, in all dangers and distresses whatsoever, if you would keep your souls without discouragements, as you should, be much in heaven in your thoughts, minding the things above, and conversing with God in your spirits. Look to the crown that is held out to us; let our minds be in heaven before our souls. It is a wondrous help to our weakness in the time of trouble, not to think, I am full of pain, I must be turned into the grave, and rot, and what shall become of me then? &c. Away with this carnal reasoning. It much weakens faith, and damps the hearts of Christians.

Use 5. Again, *How doth this arm the soul with invincible courage in any trouble.* God may call me to trouble, but he will preserve me in it that I shall not stain my conscience. What a ground of patience is this! Patience is too mean a word; what a ground of joy and triumphing is it! 'We rejoice under the hope of glory,' Rom. v. 2. A Christian should triumph in soul over all evils whatsoever, and be, as the apostle saith, 'more than a conqueror,' Rom. viii. 37; considering that God will be present with him all his life long, and after that, bring him to an everlasting kingdom. What an encouragement is this! Heaven is holy, and shall we not fit ourselves for that blessed estate? There is much holiness required for heaven; the sinful, wicked, malicious, poisonful world, lays reproaches upon holiness; but 'without it no man shall see God,' Heb. xii. 24. Doth that man believe he shall obtain a heavenly kingdom, who never fits himself with holiness for it? Oh no; 'Faith and hope have this efficacy in the breast, wheresoever they are, to frame the heart to the thing believed.' If I believe a kingdom to be where righteousness and holiness dwelleth, this belief forceth me to carry myself answerable to the state there, 2 Pet. iii. 13. And therefore, saith the apostle, 'our conversation (*l*) is in heaven, from whence we look for the Saviour,' &c., Philip. iii. 20. Because he was assured of heaven, therefore he conversed as a citizen of heaven before he came there. He praised God,

* 'We move, but God moves us.' A frequent saying in his 'Confessions.' Consult Book VII., iii. 4.—G.

kept himself undefiled of the world, and conversed with the best people; every way he carried himself, as much as earth would suffer him, as they do in heaven. Certainly, 'he that hath the hope of a heavenly kingdom, is pure as Christ is pure,' 1 John iii. 3. He endeavours and aims to be holy as God is holy, who hath called him. Faith is of efficacy to conform a Christian's carriage to the likeness of him whom he believes to be so excellent. And therefore they are infidels, and have no saving faith; profane persons, who live in sins that stain their consciences, and blemish their conversation, not believing that there is a heaven. 'Deceive not yourselves; neither whoremongers, nor adulterers, nor extortioners,' &c., 1 Cor. vi. 9, shall inherit the kingdom of God. Do men who live in these sins, without remorse, think to come to heaven? as though they should come out of the puddle to heaven? No, no; 'away, you workers of iniquity, I know you not,' Mat. xxv. 41, saith Christ. Let no man cherish presumptions of a heavenly kingdom, except he abstain from all sins against conscience. The apostle, when he would urge to holiness of life, uses this argument: 'If you be risen with Christ, seek those things that are above, where Christ is, at the right hand of the Father,' Col. iii. 1.

Well, let us oft, I beseech you, present unto our souls the blessed condition to come, which will be effectual to quicken and stir us up to every good duty, and comfort us in all conditions whatsoever. What will a man care for crosses and losses and disgraces in the world, that thinks of a heavenly kingdom? What will a man care for ill usage in his pilgrimage, when he knows he is a king at home? We are all strangers upon earth, now in the time of our absence from God; what if we suffer indignities, considering that we have a better estate to come, when we shall be somebody! What if we pass unknown in the world! It is safe that we should do so; God will preserve us to his heavenly kingdom, and all that we suffer and endure here, it is but a fitting for that place. David was a king anointed many years ere he was actually possessed of his kingdom; but all that time between his anointing and his investing into the kingdom, it was a preparation of him by humility, that he might know himself, and learn fitness to govern aright. So we are anointed kings as soon as we believe; for when we believe in Christ, who is a king, priest, and prophet, we communicate with his offices; we have the same blessed anointing poured on our head, and runs down about us, Ps. cxxxiii. 2. But we must be humbled by crosses, and fitted for it; we must be drawn more out of the world, and be heavenly-minded first.

Rules to discern what our interest in heaven is. Would you know some rules of discerning whether heaven belongs to you or not? In brief, do but remember the *qualification of them that must reign;* those that labour daily to purge themselves of all pride and self-confidence; that see no excellency in the creature, in comparison of heaven; that see a vanity in all outward things which makes them humble in the midst of all their bravery; those that see themselves empty of all, without God's favour, 'the poor in spirit, &c., theirs,' saith Christ, 'is the kingdom of heaven,' Mat. v. 3.

2. *Faith makes us kings*, because thereby we marry the King of heaven; the church is the queen of heaven, and Christ is the king of heaven. Where this grace is in truth, happiness belongs to that soul.

3. *Those that are kings have a royal spirit.* The hopes of a young prince puts into him a great deal of spirit, otherwise, perhaps, above his disposition. So all that are kings have a royal spirit in some measure, which raiseth them above all earthly things, and maketh them see all other things to be nothing

in comparison of Christ, to be but 'dross and dung,' as holy St Paul saith, Philip. iii. 8. Those therefore that are slaves to their base lusts, to riches, honour, pleasure, &c., know not what belongs to this heavenly kingdom. What, do men think to reign in heaven, when they cannot reign over their own base corruptions! We see David prays to God for an 'enlarged spirit,' Ps. li. 12, that he might be capable of the best things; and certainly those that have this knowledge are of a spirit above the world, '*more excellent than their neighbours*,' as the wise man saith, Prov. xii. 26. You cannot shake them with offers of preferment, or with fears; they will not venture their hope of eternity for this or that base earthly thing; they are of a more royal spirit than so.

I beseech you therefore, let us discern of our spirits what they are; whether God hath established us with a free spirit or not. The kingdom of heaven is begun upon earth; the door whereby we must enter in is here. Those graces must be begun here which must fit us for happiness hereafter. As the 'stones of the temple,' 1 Kings vi. 7, were first hewn and then laid upon the temple, so we must be hewn and fashioned here, ere we can come thither. Those that are not fitted and squared now, must never think to be used of God as living stones of his temple then. A word now of Paul's use of all, and so I conclude:

'*To whom be glory for ever and ever.*'

When he had mentioned the heavenly kingdom, and set himself by faith, as it were, in possession of it, he presently begins the employment of heaven, 'to praise and glorify God,' even whilst he was on earth. For faith stirs us up to do that which we shall do, when we obtain the thing believed. It is called 'the evidence of things not seen,' Heb. xi. 1; and makes them, as it were, present to the soul. Because when we are in heaven indeed, we shall do nothing else but praise God. Faith apprehends it, as if he were now there, for all is sure to faith, God having said it, who will do it; and sets the soul upon that employment here, which it shall have eternally with God hereafter.

It is therefore Christian wisdom, to fix our souls on good meditations, to have them wedded to good thoughts, to have those *præclaras cogitationes*, befitting Christians, that may lead us comfortably in our way to heaven. Let a man think of God's deliverances past, and that will strengthen his faith for the future deliverances. Let him think of future deliverances, and that will lead him to a kingdom, to praise God; and this praising of God will stretch his soul, for ever and for ever; as if there were no time sufficient to glorify God, that is so excellent and glorious. What a blessed condition is this, to have God's Spirit warming our souls and perfuming our spirits with holy ejaculations, continually putting us upon the employment of heaven, till at length it hath safely brought us thither.

Here then is the use of all uses. What is the former use which Paul makes of the experience of God's deliverance? The Lord hath delivered me, and therefore he will deliver me. But what use doth he make of this, that God will deliver him? To glorify God. Here is the end of all ends, to praise God. Happy we when God's end and our end meet together. He hath made all for his own glory; and when we, with a single eye, can aim at that too, what a sweet harmony is there!

1. To direct us in this duty in praising God, let us with Paul, for I go no further than the text leads me, *seriously meditate on God's mercies, both past and to come*. Nothing moves thankfulness more than this. A Christian when he looks backward hath comfort, and when he looks forward he sees

comfort still: for preservation, and kingdoms, and crowns abide for him. If a man would praise God, therefore, let him consider how graciously God hath dealt with him. He hath delivered me already by Jesus Christ, from sin and eternal wrath; and he will deliver me from every evil work to come, that may endanger my salvation. Think of these things, and see whether your hearts can be cold and dead or no; see if your spirits can be straitened. Certainly both heart and mouth will be full. Thou canst not but say, in the apprehension of God's mercies, 'To him be glory for ever.'

2. *Consider the kinds of favours thou receivest.* They are either positive or privative, spiritual or temporal. Positive—the Lord will preserve me; privative—the Lord will deliver me from every evil work. Temporal—the Lord in this life will keep me; spiritual—he will deliver me from the power of sin. Eternal—he will preserve me to his heavenly kingdom. Think forward or backward, outward or inward, spiritual or temporal: wherever you look, tell me if you can do otherwise than break out with the holy apostle in the praises of so good a God.

And 3. *Think of the greatness of all these:* the greatness of the deliverance from sin and damnation. The apostle, to make himself the more thankful, saith he was delivered out of the mouth of the lion. He had large apprehensions of God's goodness. So should we, beloved, consider the greatness of the misery we are in by nature, being slaves of Satan, in danger to slip into hell every moment; and when God hath secured us from this, think of the greatness of the benefit, a 'heavenly kingdom.' When we think, not only of the benefits, but of the greatness of them, it is a wondrous encouragement to be thankful. Labour then to have a due and high esteem of every mercy. God hath brought us out of *darkness into marvellous light*, saith the apostle, 1 Pet. ii. 9; *great is the mystery of godliness*, 1 Tim. iii. 16; and *the unsearchable riches of his grace*, Eph. iii. 8. He had not words big enough to express God's goodness. 'Oh, the height, and breadth, and depth, and length of his love,' Eph. ii. 18. When we consider these dimensions, our thankfulness must be answerable.

4. Again, if you would be thankful, *labour to have humble spirits, to see God in all things;* and then you will sacrifice to him alone; not to thy parts and graces, friends, abilities, &c. The meek are fit to pray to God. 'Seek the Lord, ye meek of the earth,' Zeph. ii. 3; and an humbled, meek, soul, is the fittest to praise God of any other. He that knows he is worthy of nothing, will bless God for anything. He that knows he hath nothing in himself, will be thankful for the least measure of grace. An humble soul is a thankful soul. We see it was Paul's disposition here. He gives all to God, which makes him so break out in praising his name.

5. Again, if we would be thankful, as Paul here, and begin heaven upon earth, *labour to be assured of salvation*, and perseverance in thy Christian course. The papists, that speak against assurance and perseverance, kill prayer and praising of God. Shall a man praise God for that which he doubts of? I cannot tell whether God will damn me or not; perhaps I am but fitted as a sheep to the slaughter, &c. How shall a man praise God for any blessing he enjoys, when these thoughts are still with him? How shall a man praise God for salvation, when perhaps he shall not come to it? How shall a man praise God for that which perhaps he may fall from before he die? when perhaps he is God's to-day, and may be the devil's to-morrow? How can there be a hearty thanks, but when a man can say, 'The Lord will deliver me from every evil work,' that by mine own weakness, and Satan's malice, I may occasionally fall into, betwixt this and

heaven? Therefore, if we would praise God as we should, let us work our hearts to labour after assurance of God's favour; let us redeem our precious time, and every day set some time apart to strengthen our evidences for heaven, which will set us in a continual frame to every good work.

Thus we see, out of Paul's example, how we should be disposed here, to be in heaven before our time. For *undoubtedly he who praiseth God is so much in heaven, as he is given to thankfulness;* for he is in that employment now, which shall be there altogether. But how long doth he desire that God should have glory? For ever and ever.

Obs. A Christian should have the extent of his desires of God's glory carried to eternity. Upon what ground? Because God intends him glory for ever and ever. A Christian that is assured of his salvation, is assured that God will eternally glorify him. He knows that Christ is king for ever; he knows that Christ is a priest for ever; he knows that the state and condition that he is kept for, is everlasting: 'it is an inheritance immortal and undefiled, that fadeth not away,' 1 Pet. i. 4; and therefore he saith, Hath God eternal thoughts of my good? and is Christ an eternal head, an eternal king to rule me, both in life and in death? Surely I will extend my desires of his glory as far as he extends his purpose to do me good. Now, his purpose to do me good is for eternity, and my desire that he may have glory shall be for eternity, *world without end*, Eph. iii. 21. This is the disposition of a gracious soul, not that God may be honoured by him alone, but of all. To whom be praise, not by me, but by all. I am not sufficient enough to praise him. To him be praises in the churches, throughout all ages, for ever. David had not largeness enough in himself to bless God; and therefore he stirs up his spirits and all within him to praise his holy name, Ps. ciii. 1, as if all were too little to set out the glory of God's infinite goodness, mercy, wisdom, and power: those gracious attributes that shew themselves glorious in bringing man to salvation, and in governing the church.

Use. Learn this duty therefore: *if we will make good to our own souls, that we are in the state of grace, we must plot for eternity, and endeavour to lay a ground and foundation, that the church may flourish for eternity.* No man can warrant himself to be a good Christian, but he that labours to have the church and commonwealth flourish; to have a happy kingdom, happy government, and happy laws. Not only to have the church in his own family, but that the church may flourish in those that stand up when we are gone the way of all flesh; and therefore to declare the mind of God, and his favours to us, and our children, that they may strengthen their experience, with their fathers' experience, and say to God, Thou art the God of my fathers, therefore be my God. Those that are called to places of dignity, should consider that it is required at their hands to labour that there should be means to continue religion, even to the world's end, if it may be, and to stop all the breaches in this kind. And if it were possible, it were to be wished that there were set up some lights in all the dark corners of this kingdom, that might shine to those people that sit in darkness, and in the shadow of death.

2. One way is, *to have a care that there be no breaches made upon the sound doctrine that is left unto us, and hath been sealed up by the blood of so many martyrs.* We had it dearly. It hath been taught by our forefathers, and sealed with their blood; and shall we betray it? No; let us labour to deliver it to our posterity, from hand to hand, to the coming of Christ; and then we shall in effect, and not in word only, do that which Paul saith

here—labour to glorify God for ever and ever, both in the church and in heaven. Surely those that will glorify God in heaven, he will have them so disposed to glorify him on earth.

It is a dangerous thing when persons are naught. We see what comes of it, especially if they be great. It is said of Manasseh, when God had forgiven him his sin, yet afterwards God plagued the kingdom for the sins that Manasseh committed, 2 Kings xxiv. 3. How can this be? Because he by his sin, though he repented himself, yet set the kingdom in an evil frame. And no question but he had naughty principles; and among people that are given to licentiousness, if there be anything in great men, it will go to posterity after them. So that when governors are naught, they are not only a poison to the church and state while they live, but the mischief of it is after and after still. And so it is in the best things. If the governor be good, he lays a foundation of good for the kingdom in time to come, as well as for his own time.

How will it shame a man when he shall think, I do these things now, but what will posterity think of me? what will be the remembrance of it when I am gone? Then my name will stink. The wicked emperor Nero was of this resolution when he should die: 'Let heaven and earth mingle together,' saith he, 'when I am gone.'* He knew himself to be so naught, and that he should be so evil spoken of, that he wished there were no posterity, but that the world might end with him. So it is the wishes of those that are wretches themselves, and that lay a foundation of wretched times after. They wish that heaven and earth may mingle, that no man might censure them when they are gone. What a shameful condition is it for men to gratify a number of unruly lusts, and give such sway to them as to do ill while they live, and to lay a foundation of misery for after times.

On the contrary, what a good thing is it, like Josiah and Nehemiah, to be full of goodness while we live, and to lay a foundation of happiness and prosperity to the church and state when we are gone! What a happy thing is it, when a man is gone, to say such a man did such a thing! He stood stoutly for the church, for religion; he was a public man; he forgot his own private good for the public; he deserved well of the times wherein he lived. What a blessed commendation is this, next to heaven, to have a blessed report on earth, and to carry such a conscience as will comfort a man that he hath carried himself well, and abounded in well-doing.

I beseech you let us think of this 'for ever and ever.' It is not enough that we be good in our times that are circumscribed to us. But as God hath given us immortal souls, and preserves us to immortal glory, and a crown of immortality, so let our thoughts and desires be immortal, that God may be glorified in the church, world without end. Oh, what a sweet comfort will it be when we are on our deathbed, to think what we have done in our lifetimes! Then all our good actions will come and meet together, to comfort and refresh our souls.

Encouragements to glorify God. The better to encourage us to glorify God while we are here, and to lay a foundation to eternise his glory for the time to come, consider, 1. *God's gracious promise:* 'Those that honour me I will honour,' 1 Sam. ii. 30. If we had enlarged hearts to honour God, God would honour us. He hath passed his word for it. If a king should say so, O how would we be set on fire! how much more when the King of kings saith it!

* The dying saying of Nero has been recorded, 'Dedecorosè vixi, turpiùs peream.' —See Tacitus, lib. xv.—G.

2. Consider that *we honour ourselves when we honour God.* Nay, the more we honour God, the more we are bound to God; for it is from him that we honour him. The sacrifice comes from him, as well as the matter for which we sacrifice. He found a ram for Abraham to sacrifice, Gen. xxii. 13. He gives the heart to be thankful. The more we are thankful, the more we shall be thankful, and the more we ought to be thankful for our thankfulness.

3. *The more we praise God, the more we should praise him,* for it is the gift of God. When God sees we honour him, and frame ourselves that we may be such as may honour him, by emptying and disabling ourselves to be sufficient to do him any service, he will bestow more upon us. As men cast seed upon seed where there is fruitful ground, but they will sow nothing upon a barren heath. So the more we set ourselves to do good in our places, the more we shall have advantage thereunto; and the more we do good, the more we shall do good. When God sees we improve our talents so well that he trusts us withal, he will trust us with more.

4. Again, consider *our glorifying and praising God causeth others to do so,* which is the main end wherefore we live in this world. It is the employment of heaven, and we are so much in heaven as we are about this work. And when God gives us hearts to glorify him here, it is a good pledge that he will afterward glorify us in heaven. Who would lose the comfort of all this, to be barren, and yield to his base, unbelieving, dead heart? to save a little here? to sleep in a whole skin? and adventure upon no good action? Who would not rather take a course that hath such large encouragements attending it both in life and death? I beseech you think of these things. Christ, ere long, will come to be glorified in all those that believe, 2 Thes. i. 10. He will come to be glorified in his saints. Our glory tends to his glory. Shall we not glorify him all we can here, by setting forth his truth, by countenancing his children and servants, by doing good, and deserving well of ungrateful times we live in? Let men be as unthankful as they will, we look not to them, but to the honour of God, the credit of religion, the maintenance of the truth, &c. Let men be as they will be, base and wicked, enemies to grace and goodness, we do it not to them, but to God. Consider this. Will Christ come from heaven ere long to be glorified in us, and shall not we labour to glorify him while we are here? He will never come to be glorified in any hereafter, but those that glorify him now. As we look, therefore, that he should be glorified in us, and by us, let us glorify him now; for so he condescends to vouchsafe to be glorified in us and by us, that he may also glorify us.

Quest. St Paul saith, the wife is the glory of the husband, 1 Cor. xi. 7. What means he by this? *Solution.* That is, she reflects the graces of a good husband. If he be good, she is good; she reflects his excellencies. So let every Christian soul that is married to Christ, be the glory of Christ, reflect his excellencies, be holy as he is holy, 1 Pet. i. 15, fruitful as he was in doing good, meek and humble as he was; every way be his glory; and then, undoubtedly, when he comes to judge us, he will come to be glorified in us, having been before glorified by us.

Beloved, these and such considerations should set us on work how to do Christ all the honour we can. As David saith, 'Is there any of Jonathan's posterity alive, that I may do good unto them for his sake?' 2 Sam. ix. 1, so, considering we shall be so glorified by Christ, and that he will do so much for us in another world, we should inquire, Is there any of Christ's posterity here, any of his children in this world, that I may do good unto them? Is there any way wherein I may shew my thankfulness, and I will do it? Let us consider that we shall be for ever and ever glorified. The expression of it is beyond conceit. We shall never know it till we have it. Let this, I beseech you, stir us up to study how we may be thankful to God, set forth his glory, and deserve well of the church and times wherein we live. God hath children and a cause in the world which he dearly loves, let us own the same, and stand for it to the uttermost of our power, maugre all the spite and opposition of Satan and his wicked instruments.

The Lord in mercy settle these truths upon our hearts, and encourage us in his most holy way.

NOTES.

(*h*) P. 315.—'I find that most ancient and modern writers by lion understand Nero. . . . . This is the common view of 'the Fathers;' and, of contemporaries of Sibbes, of Thomas Hall of King's Norton. All wishing to obtain much learning and quaint application will not be disappointed if they consult the latter's 'Exposition' of 2 Timothy, c. iii.–iv. (folio, 1658). See pp. 449–50. 'When we consider the position of the apostle,' observe Webster and Wilkinson, 'the good confession he maintained in spite of desertion and discouragement, we may reasonably conceive he refers to ὁ ἀντίδικος ἡμῶν διαβολος ὡς λεων ὠρυόμενος, 1 Peter v. 8.' (Greek Testament, with Notes Grammatical and Exegetical, vol. ii. 1861.) It will be noticed that Sibbes adopts the impersonal reference. Psalm xxii. 21, Proverbs xxvi. 13, illustrate his interpretation.

(*i*) P. 316.—'Jailor . . . . . bowels of pity.' See this subject treated with no common power and pathos from the text, Acts xvi. 33, 'He washed their stripes,' by Bishop Brownrig, who succeeded Sibbes as Master of Katherine Hall. ('Sermons,' folio, vol. i. pp. 273–291.)

(*j*) P. 318.—'Casting something unto these lions, to divert them another way.' A singularly beautiful expansion of this thought may here be given from a volume of 'Sermons,' by the late Rev. Dr Henderson of Galashiels, with whom Sibbes was an especial favourite:—

'Death is the last enemy,—the last with whom the believer shall be called to contend during his period of conflict and trial. When the struggle is over, which issues in the dissolution of his earthly tabernacle, it may be said that his "warfare is accomplished." He may appear to the eye of sense to sink and perish in the mortal strife; but to the eye of faith, in the view of the angel bands who look on, and in his sight to whom belong the issues from death, he escapes and triumphs. He has passed from the land of the enemy—from the field of war and danger. He has left his body, indeed, behind, a prey to corruption. Death may wreak on *it* his fury. *But it is as one who has thrown down his garment to be torn and trampled by the wild beasts in its rage; while he himself hastens away to the refuge which opens before him.* So does the soul enter into rest. . . . ' (Sermons on Doctrinal and Practical Subjects. 1 vol. 8vo, 1843, pp. 244–5.)

(*k*) P. 326.—'We are kept (we are *guarded*, as the word is).' Sibbes very frequently quotes this text; and invariably returns upon his rendering of 'guarded' instead of 'kept.' Demarest, who adopts it, may profitably be consulted. (Translation and Exp. of 1 Peter. New York, 1851.)

(*l*) P. 327.—'Our *conversation* is in heaven. . . . . He conversed as a *citizen* of heaven before he came there, Philip iii. 20. The original is τὸ πολίτευμα = commonwealth, or perhaps citizenship. Cf. Ellicott *in loc*, who gives the literature of the text and word. G.

CHRIST IS BEST; OR, ST PAUL'S STRAIT.

CHRIST IS BEST; or, ST PAUL'S STRAIT.

NOTE.

'Christ is Best' follows the 'Saint's Safety in Evil Times' in the volume described, (See note at page 296). Its separate title-page is given below.* It forms No. 11 of 'Saints' Cordials,' (2d ed. 1637, and 3d ed. 1658); and is therein entitled, 'Christ is Best; or, A Sweet Passage to Glory.'—G.

* Title-page—

CHRIST IS BEST:

OR,

ST PAUL'S STRAIT,

A

SERMON PREA-
ched at the Funerall of
Mr Sherland, late Recorder of Northampton.

By R. SIBBS, D.D. [as before].

Psal. 42. 2.

London, Printed by M. F. for R. Dawlman, at the
Brazen Serpent in Paul's Church-
yard. 1634. 8°.

CHRIST IS BEST;

OR,

ST PAUL'S STRAIT.

For I am in a strait between two, having a desire to depart, and to be with Christ, which is best of all; nevertheless, to abide in the flesh is most needful for you.—PHIL. I. 23, 24.

THE apostle Paul here, had a double desire, one in regard of himself, to be with Christ; another, out of his love of God's church and people, to abide still in the flesh; and between these two he is in a great strait, not knowing which to choose. But the love of the church of Christ triumphed in him, above the love of his own salvation, so as he was content, out of self-denial, to want the joys of heaven for a time, that he might yet further comfort the people of God.

In the words you have, 1, *St Paul's straits;* 2, his *desires* that caused them, as in regard of himself, which was *to be with Christ;* so, in respect of the church of God, which was *to abide still here;* 3, the reasons of both, (1) *to be with Christ* is far better for me, (2) *to abide in the flesh* more needful for you; and 4, his resolution upon all, being willing for the church's good *still to abide here,* rather than go to heaven and enjoy his own happiness.

St Paul's soul was as a ship, between two winds, tossed up and down, and as iron between two loadstones, drawn first one way, then another; the one loadstone was his own good, to be in heaven; the other was the good of God's people, to abide still in the flesh.

Obs. Observe hence *that the servants of God are oftentimes in great straits.* Some things are so exceeding bad that, without any deliberation or delay at all, we ought presently to abominate them, as Satan's temptations to sin, to distrust, despair, &c. Some things also are so good that we should immediately cleave unto them, as matters of religion and piety. There should be no delay in these holy businesses. Deliberation here, argues weakness. Some things, again, are of an ambiguous and doubtful nature, requiring our best consideration. Such was Paul's strait in this place. He had reasons swaying him on both sides; and such is the happy estate of a Christian, that whatsoever he had chosen had been well for him; only, God who rules our judgments, will have us to make choice. God might have determined whether Paul should live or die, but he would not without Paul's choice. That which is good, is not good to us, but upon choice and advice. When God hath given us abilities to discourse and examine things, he will have us make use of them, and therefore the apostle useth reasons on both sides, it is better to die for me, it is better to live for you, &c.

Wicked men have their deliberations, and their straits too; but it is with the rich man in the gospel, what they shall do, how they may pull down their barns, and build bigger, &c., Luke xii. 18. Their main strait is at the hour of death; live they cannot, die they dare not. There is so much guilt of sin upon their consciences, they know not which way to turn themselves. Oh, what fearful straits will sin bring men into! But the apostle was straitened in an higher nature than this, whether it were better for the glory of God (which he aimed at above all) for him to go to heaven and enjoy happiness in his own person, or to abide still, for the comfort of God's saints, on earth.

The ground of this difficulty and strait was his present desire.

I have a desire. Desires are the immediate issue of the soul, the motion and stirring of the same to something that likes it. When there is anything set before the soul having a magnetical force, as the loadstone, to draw out the motions thereof, we call that desire, though for the present it enjoys it not.

1. St Paul's desire was, *spiritual;* not after happiness, so much as holiness. 'O miserable man that I am,' saith he, 'who shall deliver me from this body of death?' Rom. vii. 24. His desire of death was to be freed from the *body of sin*, more than to be taken out of the flesh; and his desire of holiness, to have Christ's image stamped on his soul, was more than of eternal happiness. Nature cannot do this. It is a work above the flesh, for that will not hear of departing, but rather bids God and Christ depart from it.

2. This desire came from a *taste of sweetness in communion with Christ;* and those desires that most ravish the soul in apprehension of heavenly things are ever the most holy. St Paul knew what a sweet communion Christ was.

3. It was a *constant* desire. He doth not say I desire, but I have a desire, I carry the same about me, and that carries me to a love of Christ and his members.

4. It was *efficacious*, not a naked velleity, not a wish of the sluggard, I would, and I would, but a strong desire, carrying him even through death itself to Christ. Desires thus qualified are blessed desires. As where we see vapours arise, there are springs usually below them, so where these desires are, there is always a spring of grace in that soul. Nothing characteriseth a Christian so much as holy and blessed desires, for there is no hypocrisy in them.

I desire to depart. There must be a *parting* and a departing; there must be a parting in this world with all outward excellencies, from the sweet enjoyment of the creatures; there must be a parting between soul and body, between friend and friend, and whatever is near and dear unto us. All shall determine in death.

And there must be a *departing* also. Here we cannot stay long; away we must; we are for another place. Oh that we could make use of these common truths! How far are we from making a right use of the mysteries of salvation, when we cannot make use of common truths which we have daily experience of! Holy Moses, considering the suddenness of his departure hence, begged of God to teach him to number his days, that he might apply his heart unto wisdom, Ps. xc. 12.

Death is but a departing (*a*), which word is taken from loosing from the shore, or removing of a ship to another coast. We must all be unloosened from our houses of clay, and be carried to another place, to heaven. Paul labours to sweeten so harsh a thing as death, by comfortable expressions of it. It is but a sleep, a going home, a laying aside our earthly tabernacle, to teach us this point of heavenly wisdom, that we should look on death as it is now in the gospel, not as it was in the law and by nature; for so it is a passage to hell, and lets us in to all miseries whatsoever.

Some things are desirable for themselves, as happiness and holiness; some things are desirable not for themselves, but as they make way to better things, being sour, and bitter to nature themselves; as physic is desired not for itself, but for health. We desire health for itself, and physic for health, so *to be with Christ* is a thing desirable of itself; but because we cannot come to Christ but by the dark passage of death, saith Paul, *I desire to depart*, that so my death may be a passage to Christ; so that death was the object of St Paul's desire so far as it made way for better things.

I desire to depart, and to be with Christ.

To be with Christ that came from heaven to be here on earth with us, and descended that we should ascend; to be with him, that hath done and suffered so much for us; to be with Christ that delighted to be with us; to be with Christ that emptied himself, and became of no reputation, that became poor to make us rich; to be with Christ our husband, now contracted here, that all may be made up in heaven, this was the thing Paul desired.

Quest. Why doth he not say, I desire to be in heaven?

Ans. Because heaven is not heaven without Christ. It is better to be in any place with Christ than to be in heaven itself without him. All delicacies without Christ are but as a funeral banquet. Where the master of the feast is away, there is nothing but solemnness. What is all without Christ? I say the joys of heaven are not the joys of heaven without Christ; he is the very heaven of heaven.

True love is carried to the person. It is adulterous love, to love the thing, or the gift, more than the person. St Paul loved the person of Christ, because he felt sweet experience that Christ loved him; his love was but a reflection of Christ's love first. He loved to see Christ, to embrace him, and enjoy him that had done so much and suffered so much for his soul, that had forgiven him so many sins, &c.

The reason is, because it is best of all. To be with Christ is to be at the spring-head of all happiness. It is to be in our proper element. Every creature thinks itself best in its own element, that is the place it thrives in, and enjoys its happiness in; now Christ is the element of a Christian. Again, it is far better, because to be with Christ is to have the marriage consummate. Is not marriage better than the contract? is not home better than absence? To be with Christ is to be at home. Is not triumph better than to be in conflict? but to be with Christ is to triumph over all enemies, to be out of Satan's reach. Is not perfection better than imperfection? Here all is but imperfect, in heaven there is perfection; therefore that is much better than any good below, for all are but shadows here, there is reality. What is riches? what are the worm-eaten pleasures of the world? What are the honours of the earth, but mere shadows of good? 'At the right hand of Christ are pleasures indeed,' Ps. xvi. 11, honours indeed, riches indeed; there is reality.

If we speak of grace, and good things, it is better to be with Christ than enjoy the graces and comforts of the Holy Ghost here. Why? because they are all stained and mixed. Here our peace is interrupted with desertion and trouble. Here the joys of the Holy Ghost are mingled with sorrow. Here the grace in a man is with combat of flesh and spirit, but in heaven there is pure peace, pure joy, pure grace: for what is glory but the perfection of grace. Grace indeed is glory here, but it is glory with conflict. The Scripture calls grace glory sometimes, but it is glory with imperfection. Beloved, perfection is better than imperfection, therefore to be with Christ is far better.

And is it much 'far better' to die, that we may be with Christ, than to live here a conflicting life? Why should we then fear death, that is but a passage to Christ? It is but a grim sergeant that lets us into a glorious palace, that strikes off our bolts, that takes off our rags, that we may be clothed with better robes, that ends all our misery, and is the beginning of all our happiness. Why should we therefore be afraid of death? it is but a departure to a better condition? It is but as Jordan to the children of Israel, by which they passed to Canaan. It is but as the Red Sea by which they were going that way. Therefore we have no reason to fear death. Of itself it is an enemy indeed, but now it is harmless, nay, now it is become a friend, amicable to us, a sweet friend. It is one part of the church's jointure, death. 'All things are yours,' saith the apostle, Paul and Apollos, 'life and death,' 1 Cor. iii. 22. Death is ours and for our good. It doth us more good than all the friends we have in the world. It determines and ends all our misery and sin; and it is the suburbs of heaven. It lets us into those joys above. It is a shame for Christians therefore, to be afraid of that that Paul here makes the object of his desire.

But may not a good Christian fear death?

I answer, Not, so far as a Christian is led with the Spirit of God, and is truly spiritual; for the Spirit carries us upward. But as far as we are earthly and carnal, and biassed downward to things below, we are loath to depart hence. In some cases God's children are afraid to die, because their accounts are not ready. Though they love Christ, and are in a good way, yet notwithstanding, because they have not prepared themselves by care, as a woman that hath her husband abroad and desires his coming, but all is not prepared in the house, therefore she desires that he may stay awhile; so the soul that is not exact, that is not in that frame that it should be in, saith, 'Oh stay a while that I may recover my strength, before I go hence and be no more seen,' Ps. xxxix. 13; but as far as we are guided by the Spirit of God sanctifying us, and are in such a condition as we should be in, so far the thoughts of death ought not to be terrible to us; nor indeed are they.

Beloved, there is none but a Christian that can desire death; because it is the end of all comfort here, it is the end of all callings and employments, of all sweetness whatsoever in this world. If another man that is not a Christian, desire heaven, he desires it not as heaven, or to be with Christ as Christ; he desires it under some notion suitable to his corruption; for our desires are as ourselves are, as our aims are. No carnal worldly man, but hath carnal worldly aims. A worldly man cannot go beyond the world. It is his sphere. A carnal man cannot go beyond the flesh. Therefore a carnal man cannot desire heaven. A man that is under the power of any lust, can desire nothing but the satisfying of that lust. Heaven is no place for such. None but a child of God can desire that; for if we consider heaven, and *to be with Christ*, to be *perfect holiness*, can he desire it that hates holiness here? can he desire the image of God upon him that hates it in others and in himself too? can he desire the communion of saints, that of all societies hates it the most? can he desire to be free from sin, that engulfs himself continually in sin? He cannot, and therefore as long as he is under the thraldom and dominion of any lust he may desire heaven indeed, but it is only so far as he may have his lusts there, his pleasures, honours, and riches there too. If he may have heaven with that, he is contented; but alas! brethren, heaven must not be so desired. St Paul did otherwise; he desired *to be dissolved, to be with Christ.* He desired it as the perfection of the image of God, under the notion of holiness and freedom from sin, as I said before.

Which is far better.

Obs. Again, we see that *God reserves the best for the last* (*b*). God's last works are his best works. The new heaven and the new earth are the best; the second wine that Christ created himself was the best; spiritual things are better than natural. A Christian's last is his best.

God will have it so, for the comfort of Christians, that every day they live, they may think, my best is behind, my best is to come, that every day they rise, they may think, I am nearer heaven one day than I was before, I am nearer death, and therefore nearer to Christ. What a solace is this to a gracious heart! A Christian is a happy man in his life, but happier in his death, because then he goes to Christ; but happiest of all in heaven, for then he is *with Christ.* How contrary to a carnal man, that lives according to the sway of his own base lusts! He is miserable in his life, more miserable in his death, but most miserable of all after death. I beseech you, lay this to heart. Methinks, considering that death is but a way for us to be with Christ, *which is far better,* this should sweeten the thinking of death to us, and we should comfort ourselves daily that we are nearer happiness.

Quest. But how shall we attain this sanctified sweet desire that Paul had, to die, and be with Christ?

Ans. 1. *Let us carry ourselves as Paul did,* and then we shall have the same desires. St Paul, before death, in his lifetime, 'had his conversation in heaven,' Phil. iii. 1. His mind was there, and his soul followed after. There is no man's soul comes into heaven, but his mind is there first. It was an easy matter for him to desire to be with Christ, having his conversation in heaven already. Paul in meditation was, where he was not, and he was not where he was. He was in heaven when his body was on earth.

2. Again, *St Paul had loosed his affections from all earthly things;* therefore it was an easy matter for him to desire to be with Christ. 'I am crucified to the world, and the world is crucified to me,' &c., Gal. vi. 14. If once a Christian comes to this pass, death will be welcome to him. Those whose hearts are fastened to the world, cannot easily desire Christ.

3. Again, holy St Paul *laboured to keep a good conscience in all things.* 'Herein I exercise myself, to have a good conscience towards God and men,' &c., Acts xxiv. 16. It is easy for him to desire to be dissolved, that hath his conscience *sprinkled with the blood of Christ,* Heb. x. 22, free from a purpose of living in any sin. But where there is a stained, defiled, polluted conscience, there cannot be this desire; for the heart of man, naturally, as the prophet saith, 'casts up mire and dirt,' Isa. lvii. 20. It casts up fears, and objections, and murmurings, and repinings. Oh, beloved, we think not what mischief sin will do us, when we suffer it to seize upon our consciences; when it is once written there *with the claw of a diamond,*

and *with a pen of iron*, Jer. xvii. 1, who shall get it out? Nothing but great repentance and faith, applying the blood of Christ. It is no easy matter to get it off there, and to get the conscience at peace again; and when conscience is not appeased, there will be all clamours within. It will fear to appear before the judgment-seat. A guilty conscience trembles at the mention of death. Therefore I wonder how men that live in swearing, in looseness, in filthiness, in deboisedness* of life, that labour to satisfy their lusts and corruptions, I wonder how they can think of death without trembling, considering that they are under the guilt of so many sins. Oh, beloved, the exercising of the heart to keep a clear conscience, can only breed this desire in us to depart, and to be with Christ. You have a company of wretched persons, proud enough in their own conceits, and censorious. Nothing can please them, whose whole life is acted by Satan joining with the lusts of their flesh, and they do nothing but put stings into death every day, and arm death against themselves, which when once it appears, their conscience, which is a hell within them, is wakened, and where are they? They can stay here no longer; they must appear before the dreadful Judge; and then where are all their pleasures and contentments, for which they neglected heaven and happiness, peace of conscience, and all? Oh, therefore let us walk holily with our God, and maintain inward peace all we can, if we desire to depart hence with comfort.

4. Again, Paul had got *assurance that he was in Christ, by his union with him.* 'I live not,' saith he, 'but Christ lives in me,' Gal. ii. 19. Therefore labour for assurance of salvation, that you may feel the Spirit of Christ in you, sanctifying and altering your carnal dispositions to be like his. 'I know whom I have trusted,' 2 Tim. i. 12, saith he. He was as sure of his salvation, as if he had had it already. How few live as if they intended any such matter as this, assurance of salvation, without which how can we ever desire to be dissolved, and to be with Christ? Will a man leave his house, though it be never so mean, when he knows not whither to go? Will a man leave the prison, when he knows he shall be carried to execution? Oh, no; he had rather be in the dungeon still. So when there is guilt on the soul, that it is not assured of salvation, but rather hath cause to fear the contrary, can it say, 'I desire to depart, and be with Christ,' &c.? No; they had rather abide in the flesh still, if they could, for ever, for all eternity. Therefore, if we would come to Paul's desire, labour to come to the frame of the holy apostle's spirit. He knew whom he had believed; he was assured that nothing could separate him from the love of God, neither life, nor death, nor anything whatsoever that could befall him, Rom. viii. 38, 39.

5. *Paul had an art of sweetening the thoughts of death.* He considered it only as a departure from earth to heaven. When death was presented unto him as a passage to Christ, it was an easy matter to desire the same; therefore it should be the art of Christians to present death as a passage to a better life, to labour to bring our souls into such a condition, as to think death not to be a death to us, but the death of itself. Death dies when I die, and I begin to live when I die. It is a sweet passage to life. We never live till we die. This was Paul's art. He had a care to look beyond death, to heaven; and when he looked upon death, he looked on it but as a passage to Christ: so let it be our art and skill. Would we cherish a desire to die, let us look on death as a passage to Christ, and look beyond it to heaven. All of us must go through this dark passage to Christ (*c*), which when we consider as Paul did, it will be an easy matter to die.

* That is, 'debauchery.'—G.

I come now to the next words—*Nevertheless, to abide in the flesh is more needful for you.*

This is the other desire of Paul, that brought him into this strait. He was troubled whether he should die, which was far better for himself, or live, which was more needful for them; but the love of God's people did prevail in holy St Paul, above the desire of heaven, and the present enjoying his own happiness. Oh, the power of grace in the hearts of God's children, that makes them content to be without the joys of heaven for a time, that they may do God's service, in serving his church here upon earth.

Obs. 1. Observe hence, *that the lives of worthy men, especially magistrates and ministers, are very needful for the church of God.*

The reason is, because God's manner of dispensation is, to convey all good to men, by the means of men like ourselves for the most part; and this he doth to knit us into a holy communion one with another. Therefore it is needful that holy men should abide. In regard of the church of God, their lives are very useful.

If we consider good, the great benefit that comes by them, we shall easily yield to this; for what a deal of sin doth a good magistrate stop and hinder! When there were good judges and good kings in Israel, see what a reformation there was. Antichrist could not come in when the Roman empire flourished, 2 Thes. ii. 7, though now the Roman empire hinder the fall of antichrist, because antichrist hath given her the cup of fornication, and they are drunk with the whore's cup; but at the first it was not so. Beloved, whilst good magistrates and good ministers continue in a place, there is a hindrance of heresies and sin, &c. If they be once removed, there is a floodgate opened for all manner of sin and corruption to break in at. Yea, there is abundance of good comes in by gracious persons.

1. By their *counsel and direction:* 'The lips of the righteous feed many,' Prov. vii. 21.

2. By their *reformation of abuses, by planting God's ordinances and good orders,* whereby God's wrath is appeased. They stand in the gap, and stop evil. They reform it, and labour to establish that which is pleasing to God.

3. Gracious persons, in what condition soever they are, *carry the blessing of God with them.* Wheresoever they are, God and his blessing goes along with them.

4. They do a great deal of good *by their pattern and example.* 'They are the lights of the world,' Philip. ii. 15, that give aim to others in the darkness of this life.

5. They can by their *prayers bind God,* as it were, *that he shall not inflict his judgments.* They do a world of good by this way. A praying force and army is as good as a fighting army. Moses did as much good by prayer, as the soldiers in the valley when they fought with Amalek. They are favourites with God in heaven, therefore St Paul saith, *It is needful for you that I abide in the flesh.* Gracious men are public treasures, and storehouses, wherein every man hath a share, a portion; they are public springs in the wilderness of this world, to refresh the souls of people; they are trees of righteousness, that stretch out their boughs for others to shelter under, and to gather fruit from. You have an excellent picture of this in Daniel, in the dream of Nebuchadnezzar, Dan. iv. 21. The magistrates there, are compared to a great tree, wherein the birds build their nests, and the beasts shelter themselves; so a good magistrate, especially

if he be in great place, is as a great tree for comfort and shelter. Oh, beloved, the lives of good men are very useful. A good man, saith the philosopher, is a common good; because as soon as ever a man becomes gracious, he hath a public mind, as he hath a public place, nay, whether he hath a public place or no, he hath a public mind. It is needful, therefore, that there be such men alive.

If this be so, then we may lament the death of worthy men, because we lose part of our strength in the loss of such, God's custom being to convey much good by them; and when there is scarcity of good men, we should say with Micah, Woe is me, the good is perished from the earth, Micah vii. 2. They keep judgments from a place, and derive a blessing upon it. Howsoever the world judgeth them, and accounts them not worthy to live, yet God accounts the world unworthy of them. They are God's jewels, they are his treasure and his portion, therefore we ought to lament their death, and to desire their lives; and we ought to desire our own lives, as long as we may be useful to the church; and be content to want heaven for a time. Beloved, it is not for the good of God's children that they live; as soon as ever they are in the state of grace they have a title to heaven, but it is for others. When once we are in Christ, we live for others, not for ourselves. That a father is kept alive, it is for his children's sake; that good magistrates are kept alive, it is for their subjects' sake; that a good minister is kept alive, out of the present enjoying of heaven, it is for the people's sake that God hath committed to him to instruct; for, as Paul saith here, in regard of my own particular, *it is better for me to be with Christ.*

Use. If God convey so much good by worthy men to us, then what wretches are they that malign them, persecute them, &c., speak ill of those that speak to God for them? Doth the world continue for a company of wretches, a company of profane, blasphemous, loose, disorderly livers? Oh no; for if God had not a church in the world, a company of good people, heaven and earth would fall in pieces. There would be an end presently. It is for good people only that the world continues. They are the pillars of the tottering world, they are the stakes in the fence, they are the foundation of the building, and if they were once taken out, all would come down; there would be a confusion of all. Therefore those that oppose and disquiet gracious and good men are enemies to their own good; they cut the bough which they stand on; they labour to pull down the house that covers themselves, being blinded with malice and a diabolical spirit. Take heed of such a disposition. It comes near to the sin against the Holy Ghost to hate any man for goodness; because, perhaps, his good life reproacheth us. Such a one would hate Christ himself if he were here. How can a man desire to be with Christ when he hates his image in another? Therefore if God convey so much good by other men that are good, let us make much of them, as public persons, as instruments of our good. Take away malice, and pride, and a poisonful spirit, and all their good is ours. What hinders that we have no good by them? Pride and an envious spirit, &c.

Obs. A second thing that I observe hence is this, *holy and gracious men, that are led by the Spirit of God, can deny themselves and their own best good for the church's benefit.* They know that God hath appointed them as instruments to convey good to others; and knowing this, they labour to come to Paul's spirit here, to desire to live, to have life in patience, and death in desire in regard of themselves; for it were much better for a good man to be in heaven, out of misery, out of this conflicting condition with the devil and devilish-minded men.

Reason 1. The reason is, because a good man, as soon as he is a good man, *hath the spirit of love in him*, and 'love seeketh not its own,' 1 Cor. xiii. 5, but the good of another; and as the love of Christ and the love of God possesseth and seizeth upon the soul, so self-love decays. What is gracious love but a decay of self-love? The more self-love decays, the more we deny ourselves.

2. Again, God's people have the *Spirit of Christ in them*, who minded not his own things, 1 Cor. x. 24. If Christ had minded his own things, where had our salvation been? Christ was content to leave heaven, and to take our nature upon him, to be Emmanuel, God with us, that we might be with God for ever in heaven. He was content, not only to leave heaven, but to be born in the womb of a virgin. He was content to stoop to the grave. He stooped as low as hell in love to us. Now, where Christ's Spirit is, it will bring men from their altitudes and excellencies, and make them to stoop to serve the church, and account it an honour to be an instrument to do good. Christ was content to be accounted, not only a servant of God, but of the church. 'My righteous servant,' &c., Isa. liii. 11. Those that have the Spirit of Christ have a spirit of self-denial of their own. We see the blessed angels are content to be ministering spirits for us, and it is thought to be the sin of the devil, pride, when he scorned to stoop to the keeping of man, an inferior creature to himself. The blessed angels do not scorn to attend upon a poor child, 'little ones.' A christian is a consecrated person, and he is none of his own. He is a sacrifice as soon as he is a Christian. He is Christ's. He gives himself to Christ; and as he gives himself, so he gives his life and all to Christ, as Paul saith of the Corinthians, they gave themselves and their goods to him, 2 Cor. viii. 5. When a Christian gives himself to Christ, he gives all to Christ; all his labour and pains, and whatsoever he knows that Christ can serve himself of him for his church's good and his glory. He knows that Christ is wiser than he; therefore he resigns himself to his disposal, resolving, if he live, *he lives to the Lord;* and if he die, *he dies to the Lord*, Rom. xiv. 8; that so, whether he live or die, *he may be the Lord's*.

Use 1. Oh, beloved, that we had the spirit of St Paul, and the Spirit of Christ, *to set us a work to do good while we are here*, 'to deny ourselves,' Titus ii. 12. Oh, it would be meat and drink, as it was to our blessed Saviour Christ, to do good all kinds of ways. Consider all the capacities and abilities we have to do good, this way and that way, in this relation and that relation, that we may be trees of righteousness, that the more we bear the more we may bear. God will mend his own trees. He will purge them and prune them to 'bring forth more fruit,' John xv. 2. God cherisheth fruitful trees. In the law of Moses, when they besieged any place, he commanded them to spare fruitful trees. God spares a fruitful person till he have done his work. We know not how much good one man may do, though he be a mean person. Sometimes one poor wise man delivereth the city, Eccles. ix. 15; and the righteous delivereth the land. We see for one servant, Joseph, Potiphar's house was blessed, Gen. xxxix. 3. Naaman had a poor maidservant that was the occasion of his conversion, 2 Kings v. Grace will set anybody a-work. It puts a dexterity into any, though never so mean. They carry God's blessing wheresoever they go, and they bethink themselves when they are in any condition to do good, as he saith in Esther iv. 14, 'God hath called me to this place, perhaps for this end.' We should often put this *quære* to ourselves, Why hath God called me to this place? for such and such a purpose?

Now, that we may be fruitful as Paul was, let us labour to have humble spirits. God delights in an humble spirit, and not in a proud spirit, for that takes all the glory to itself. God delights to use humble spirits, that are content to stoop to any service for others, that think no office too mean.

2. Get *loving* hearts. Love is full of invention, how shall I glorify God? how shall I do good to others? how shall I bring to heaven as many as I can? Love is a sweet and boundless affection, full of holy devices.

3. Labour to have *sufficiency in our places,* that you may have ability to do good. Oh, when these meet together, ability and sufficiency; and a willing, a large, and gracious heart and a fit object to do good to, what a deal of good is done then!

4. And when we find *opportunity of doing any good, let us resolve upon it,* resolve to honour God, and serve him in spite of flesh and blood; for we must get every good work that we do out of the fire, as it were; we must get it out with travail, and pains. We carry that about us that will hinder us. Let us therefore labour to have sincere aims in that we do to please God, and then resolve to do all the good we can.

To stir us up to be more and more fruitful in our places, let us consider we live for others, and not for ourselves, when we are good Christians once. It was a good speech of that godly Palsgrave, great grandfather to him that is (Frederick the godly they called him), when he was to die, *Satis vobis,* saith he, *I have lived hitherto for you, now let me live for myself.* We live here all our life for others, therefore let us think while we live, how we may do most good in the church of God.

For encouragement hereunto consider, God will undertake to recompense all the good we do, to a 'cup of cold water,' Mark ix. 41. We shall not lose a sigh, a groan, for the church. God would account himself dishonoured if it should not be rewarded. He hath pawned his faithfulness upon it; 'he is not unfaithful to be unmindful of your good works,' Heb. vi. 10.

Nay, we have a present reward and contentment of conscience: as light accompanies fire, so peace and joy accompany every good action. All is not reserved for heaven. A Christian hath some beginnings of happiness here. When he doth that that is contrary to flesh and blood, how full of sweet joy is a fruitful soul! Those that are fruitful in their places never want arguments of good assurance of salvation. It is your lazy, lukewarm Christian that wants assurance. Therefore I beseech you be stirred up, to live desired in the world, and die lamented; labour to be useful in your places all you can; to be as the olive and fig-tree, delighting God and man, and not to cumber the ground of the church with barrenness. Sins of omission,—because men were not fruitful in their places,—was a ground of damnation; 'cast the unprofitable servant into outer darkness,' Mat. xxv. 30; put case he did no harm; aye, but he was *unprofitable.* Such was the cursed disposition of Ephraim; he brought forth fruit to himself. Oh this looking to ourselves. When we make ourselves the beginning and the end of all the good we do, it is an argument of a barren person. None ever came to heaven but those that denied themselves.

I see I cannot proceed in this point. You may by the Spirit of God enlarge it in your thoughts and bring home what hath been said, to your own souls. Labour that you may be such as others may make use of you, and not be the burdens and calamities of the time, as many are, that live for nothing but to do good men good by vexing of them. That is all the good they do; by vexing their patience they exercise their grace a contrary way.

Let us not be briars and unfruitful plants, labouring to be great by the public miseries. As they say, great fishes grow big by devouring many little ones; as a dragon comes to be great by devouring many little serpents, so many grow great by the ruin of others. Oh beloved, it had been better for such that they had never been born. Therefore as we desire to have comfort when we die, let us labour to be fruitful while we live. St Paul, when the time came that he should die, when he had done his work, you see he that was thus full of self-denial, how gloriously he ended his days. The second Epistle to Timothy was the last epistle that ever he wrote, and when he had done his work, saith he, 'I have fought a good fight, I have kept the faith, I have finished my course: from henceforth there is a crown of righteousness reserved for me,' 2 Tim. iv. 7. What a glorious end is here! and indeed those that are thus careful, and fruitful in their lives and conversations, end their days full of comfort, and resign their souls to God with full assurance of a blessed change, and only those. For you have many, when they come to die, what hinders them? Oh I have been unfruitful, I have not done that good that I might, I have not 'wrought out my salvation with fear and trembling,' Philip. ii. 12. In such a thing I have done ill, such a thing I have omitted. So they are enemies to their own comfort. Enlarge this in your own meditations, and consider what will comfort you hereafter, when you shall need most comfort. So I leave the text, and come to the occasion.

This holy and blessed man whose funeral now we solemnize, was of St Paul's spirit. He did *desire to die, and be with Christ;* he had a desire while he lived to take all opportunities to do good. I speak of that time when he lived, that is, when he was good, for we live no longer than we are good. Let us not reckon that life, wherein we do no good. After God had wrought upon his heart, he had a public heart to do good. If I wanted matter to speak of, I could tell you of his alliance and birth, having two worthy judges of reverend esteem, the one his grandfather, the other his uncle. The one bred him, the other cherished and promoted his study and endeavours; but what should I speak of these things when he hath personal worth enough? I need not go abroad to commend this man, for there were those graces and gifts in him that made him so esteemed, that verily, I think, no man of his place and years lived more desired, and died more lamented.

1. For his parts of nature, they were pregnant and solid; but as one said to Melancthon, his disposition and loving mind did gain as much love from men as his parts, though they were great.

2. His learning was good; for beside his own profession, he was a general scholar, and had good skill in that we call elegant learning, and controverted points of divinity. He was a good divine. Indeed, in the turning of his life, when he should have adventured upon a profession, he had some thoughts of being a divine, had not his friends, especially his uncle, Judge Yelverton, (*d*) disposed him otherwise, by promoting his study in the law; and when he took upon him that profession, he grew so in it, that he was a credit to the profession for integrity, sincerity, and ability.

3. For his disposition he was every way a man of an excellent sweet temper; mild, and yet resolute; meek, and yet bold where cause was; discreet, yet not over-discreet, so as not to stand out in a good cause in the defence of it; he was humble, yet thought himself too good to be instrumental to any services other than stood with the peace of his conscience; he was tractable and gentle, yet immovably fixed to his principles of piety

and honesty; he was exact in his life, yet not censorious; very conscionable and religious, but without any vain curiosity; indeed, he was everyway of a sweet temper. If he stood out in dislike of any, in any matter, he carried it usually with evidence of such sincerity, and denial of self-seeking, that he usually prevailed where he put in.

4. To come to his private personal carriage, it was very pious. He was wont to sequester himself from his employment and labour, to bring his heart under to God, to the guidance of God's Spirit: his study was to study to die; for he gathered choice things out of the sermons he heard about death, many years before he died, to lay up store of provision against that time; and two or three terms before he died he had a special care to inquire of nearer communion with God. He inquired of those he conversed with of the way to attain the same, and was willing to hear any discourses that tended that way.

5. For his care of the Sabbath, it was his delight. His custom was, after sermon, to retire and ruminate upon what he had heard, to turn it into his spirit. Alas, for want of this, how many sermons are lost in this great city! how much seed is spilt in vain! What nourishment can there be without digestion? it is the second digestion that breeds nourishment; when we chew things, and call them to mind again, and make them our own. This was his custom every Sabbath.

6. For his carriage to others, he was a constant friend, and his study was, to labour to make those good he conversed withal. He conversed with few, but they were the better for him, he was so fruitful; and he would have intimate society with none, but he would do good or take good from them. You have many in the society where he lived, that may bless God all the days of their life that ever they knew him.

7. For his carriage in his government of the place where he lived, I think there are none that are able to judge, but will give him the testimony of a faithful, prudent governor. He was so careful of the town where he was recorder, that he provided for them after his death, and gave them a large legacy, two hundred merks, to set the poor on work.

8. For the honourable society wherein he was a governor, he carried himself with that resolution, for good order and good exercises, and was such a strict opposer of any abuse, which he judged to be so, that the house will have a special want of him.* I fear, rather, I desire from my soul, that that honourable society may so flourish as they may have no want of good Master Sherland.

9. For his more public carriage, by virtue of his place at Northampton, where he was recorder, he was called to be a member of the body-representative in Parliament, wherein both his ability and spirit appeared to all that knew him. You may see by this what manner of man we have lost.

He died before he was come to the middle of his years, a young man to speak of; and he did a great deal of work in a little time. God had ripened him for his business extraordinarily, and gave him a spirit to bestir himself to do all the good he could. These be wondrous ill times, beloved, to lose such men as he was; therefore we have cause to lay it to heart the more. The commonwealth wants him, the town and country where he lived will want him, the society where he was a governor will want him, the family where he was a governor will find a miss in him. He went wisely in and out; he was able for family duties; he had more than ordinary sufficiency;

* Qu. 'want of him, I fear: rather, I desire?' &c.—Ed.

he was of Joshua's mind, 'Choose who you will serve, but I and my house will serve the Lord,' Josh. xxiv. 15; and to help him the more, he had the happiness to marry into a religious family; he had a good helper.

Now for the church. Though his profession was the law, yet that will have a great want of him. He was a hearty and true promoter of the cause of religion, and shewed his love to the church, by his care of it now he is departed. He gave four hundred pounds to buy in impropriations; he gave an hundred pounds for the breeding up of poor scholars, and there is never a good minister round about where he lived, but had encouragement from him. Indeed, he was a man of special use and service; and as he honoured God in his life, so God hath honoured him in his death, as you may see by this honourable assembly of worthy people, met in love to him.

His death was, as the death of strong men useth to be, with conflicts between nature and his disease, but with a great deal of patience; and in his sickness time he would utter Paul's disposition, Oh, saith he, you keep me from heaven, you keep me from glory, being displeased with those that kept him alive, with conference out of love.

He had a large heart to do good, for though he were fruitful, and studied to be fruitful, yet oft in his sickness in a complaining manner he would say, Oh, I have not been so wise for my own soul as I ought to be; I have not been provident enough in taking opportunities of doing and receiving good.

Beloved, shall such a man as he was, so careful, so fruitful, so good, shall he complain thus? what shall a company of us do? Beloved, those that have warmed their hearts at the fire of God's love, they think zeal itself to be coldness, and fruitfulness to be barrenness. Love is a boundless affection. He spake not this from want of care; but love knows no bounds. Therefore he took the more opportunities of doing good.

Well, I beseech you, beloved, let not this example pass without making good use of it. God will call us to a reckoning, not only for what we hear, but for what we see: he will call us to a reckoning for the examples of his people. Therefore, as we see here what a holy disposition was in St Paul, and in this blessed man now with God, so let us labour to find the same disposition in ourselves. Paul hath now his desire; he is dissolved, and he is with Christ, that is best of all. This holy man hath his desire; he desired not to be kept from his glory and happiness, on which his mind was set before. Let us therefore labour with God in the use of good means, to have the same disposition; and in this moment let us provide for eternity; out of eternity before, and eternity after, issueth this little spot of time to do good in. Let us sow to the Spirit, account all time lost that either we do not or take not, good in. Opportunity is God's angel. Time is short, but opportunity is shorter. Let us catch at all opportunities. This is the time of worship. Oh, let us sow now. Shall we go to sowing then, when the time comes that we should reap? Some begin to sow when they die, that is the reaping time. While we have time let us do all good, especially where God loves most, to those that are good.

Consider the standings and places that God hath set us in; consider the advantages in our hands, the price that we have; consider that opportunity will not stay long. Let us therefore do all the good we can, and so if we do, beloved, we shall come at length to reap that, that this blessed saint of God, St Paul here in the text, and this blessed man, for whose cause we are now met, do enjoy. Therefore, if we desire to end our days in joy and comfort, let us lay the foundation of a comfortable death now betimes. To die well is not a thing of that light moment as some imagine: it is no easy matter. But to die well is a matter of every day. Let us daily do some good that may help us at the time of our death. Every day by repentance pull out the sting of some sin, that so when death comes, we may have nothing to do but to die. To die well is the action of the whole life. He never dies well for the most part that dies not daily, as Paul saith of himself, 'I die daily,' 1 Cor. xv. 31; he laboured to loose his heart from the world, and worldly things. If we loose our hearts from the world and die daily, how easy will it be to die at last! He that thinks of the vanity of the world, and of death, and of being with Christ for ever, and is dying daily, it will be easy for him to end his days with comfort. But the time being past, I will here make an end. Let us desire God to make that which hath been spoken effectual, both concerning Paul, and likewise concerning this blessed man, for whose cause we are met together.*

* Sherland. In addition to the splendid eulogy of Sibbes, it may be noted here, that Sherland was one of the lay 'feofees' to buy in livings. (Fuller's Church History, ed. Brewer, vi. 67; and see Prynne's Canterburie's Doom, p. 385.) He impeached Buckingham. (Heylin's Laud, p. 143.)—G.

NOTES.

(a) P. 339.—'Death is but a *departing* . . . which word is taken from loosing from the shore, or removing of a ship to another coast.' See Luke viii. 38, and 2 Tim. iv. 6, and Phil. 1. 23 (all in the Greek).

(b) P. 341.—'God reserves the best for the last.' This more than once repeated saying of Sibbes, probably suggested to Thomas Brooks the titles of two of his minor writings, *(a)* 'A String of Pearls; or the Best Things Reserved till Last,' (1657); *(b)* 'A Believer's Last Day is his Best Day,' (1651).

(c) P. 342.—'All of us must go *through this dark passage to Christ.*' Sir William Davenant has finely used this saying—

'O harmless Death! whom still the valiant brave,
The wise expect, the sorrowful invite,
And all the good embrace, *who know the grave*
A short dark passage to eternal light.'

Longfellow has the same thought:

'The grave is but a cover'd bridge, leading from light
To light, *through a brief darkness.*'

(d) P. 347.—'Judge Yelverton.' Consult Foss's 'Judges of England.'

G.

CHRIST'S SUFFERINGS FOR MAN'S SIN.

CHRIST'S SUFFERINGS FOR MAN'S SIN.

NOTE.

'Christ's Sufferings' follows 'Christ is Best,' and closes the 'first part' of the volume. It was reprinted in the 'Saint's Cordial's' (2d edition, 1637; 3d edition, 1658), forming No. 7. The separate title-page is subjoined.*—G.

* Title-page—

CHRISTS
SUFFERINGS,
FOR
MANS SINNE.

Laid open in a Passion Sermon at *Mercers Chappell* London, vpon Good Friday.

By R. SIBBS, D.D.

ISAY. 53. 5.
He was wounded for our *transgressions, and bruised for* our *iniquities; the chastisement of our peace was upon* him, *and with* his *stripes are* wee *healed.*

LONDON,
Printed by *M. F.* for *R. Dawlman*, at the Brazen Serpent in *Pauls* Church-yard. 1634.

CHRIST'S SUFFERINGS FOR MAN'S SIN.

About the ninth hour Jesus cried with a loud voice, Eli, Eli, lama sabachthani? that is to say, My God, my God, why hast thou forsaken me?—MAT. XXVII. 46.

THE dying speeches of men of worth, are most remarkable. At that time they stir up all their spirits and abilities which remain, that they may speak with greatest advantage to the hearts of others, and leave the deeper impression behind them.

These be some of the last words of our blessed Saviour's, uttered from the greatest affection, with the greatest faith, and to the greatest purpose, that ever any words were spoken, and therefore deserve your best attention.

In this portion of Scripture you have Christ's compellation, *My God;* and his complaint, *Why hast thou forsaken me?* 1. A compellation with an ingemination or reduplication of the words, *My God, my God,* to shew the strength of his affection and desire of help at this time.

2. A complaint by way of expostulation, *Why hast thou forsaken me?* I will draw all that I have to say into these four propositions:

1. That Christ was *forsaken.*

2. That he was very *sensible of it,* even unto complaint, *Why hast thou forsaken me?*

3. His *disposition and carriage in this extremity. His faith failed not; My God, my God.* His present grief tied him the closer and faster to his God.

4. Neither was it only faith, but a faith *flaming in prayer,* whereby he expressed that God was his God. He not only prayed but cried to him, 'My God, my God,' &c. This is the sum of what I intend.

1. Christ being in extremity was *forsaken.*

2. Being forsaken, he was very *sensible of it;* and from sensibleness complains, pouring out his soul into the bosom of his Father.

3. And not only complains, but *believes certainly that his Father will help him.*

4. And to strengthen his *faith* the more, he puts it forth in *prayer.* The fire of faith in his heart kindled into a flame of prayer (and that not in an ordinary manner, but in strong supplications), he cried out, 'My God, my God, why hast thou forsaken me?' To come to the particulars.

Obs. 1. *Christ was forsaken.*

I will briefly touch upon some circumstances, and then fall upon the point itself, as,

1. The *time* wherein he was *forsaken*—a time of darkness (*the sixth hour*), in which there was a darkness over the whole earth, and in the land of Judea especially. Neither had he darkness without only, but within likewise. His soul was troubled from a sense of his Father's displeasure, Mat. xxvi. 38. Two eclipses seized upon him together,—the one of the glorious light of the sun, the other of the light of his Father's countenance. He must needs be in a disconsolate estate, and doubly miserable, that is encompassed with such darkness. Whatsoever was done to Christ our surety, shall be done to all that are out of him. Blackness of darkness is reserved for them. As Christ wanted the comfort of light from heaven, so those that are out of Christ shall have no comfort from any creature at the last: the sun shall not shine upon them, the earth shall not bear them, they shall not have a drop of water to cool their tongues. They were formerly rebels against God, and now every creature is ready to serve the Lord against them. When the king is displeased with a man, which of his servants dare to countenance him?

This darkness being in Judea, did likewise portend the miserable condition of the Jews here, and that eternal darkness in the world to come, which should be their portion if they repented not.

2. Another circumstance may be this, *God was a great while ere he removed his heavy displeasure from Christ.* He was three hours in torment; and though God delayed him long, yet he said nothing till now by way of complaint. We should beware of darkness of spirit in trouble. God may delay help to his dearest children, as here he did to his only Son, to perfect the work of sanctification in them. Therefore, submit to his will, rest contented with whatever he sends, look to thy Head and Saviour, &c. But of this more anon.

3. *His greatest grief and conflicts were towards his latter end*, towards the shutting up and close of his life. Though a little after he saith, 'All is finished,' yet now he cries out, 'My God, my God, why hast thou forsaken me?' Afflictions are sharpest toward our ends. I speak this for prevention of discomfort in those that find extremities upon them. When miseries are extreme, help is nearest. They will either mend or end then. The darkness is thickest a little before the morning appears; and Satan raged most a little before his casting down.

As also to prevent security from seizing upon people. Take heed of deferring repentance till thy last hours; there may be a confluence of many extremities then upon thee, pains of body, terrors of conscience, Satan's temptations, God's wrath, &c. When all these meet together, and the poor soul, in its best strength, finds enough to do to conflict with any one of them, what an unhappy condition will that be! Oh, put not off your repentance to this time. But I pass these circumstances, and come to the point of forsaking itself.

In the unfolding whereof I will shew,

1. In what *sense* Christ was *forsaken*.
2. In what *parts* he was forsaken.
3. Upon what *ground*. And, .
4. To what *end* all this forsaking of Christ was.

For the first, forsaking is nothing else but when God leaves the creature to itself, either in regard of comfort or of grace and assistance. I will shew you how Christ was left of his Father, and how he was not left.

(1.) *How Christ was not forsaken.* He was not forsaken in regard of *God's love*, for '*My Father loveth me*,' saith he, John iii. 35, 'because I give my life for my sheep,' John x. 11. God never loved Christ more than now, because he was never more obedient than at this present.

(2.) Nor in regard of *union*, for there was no separation of his divine nature from the human. There was a suspension of vision, indeed; he saw no comfort for the present from God, but there was no dissolution of union; for the divine nature did many things in this seeming forsaking. That was it which supported his human nature to sustain the burden of our sin and the wrath of God, as also that gave merit and worth of satisfaction to his sufferings.

(3.) Neither was this forsaking in regard of *grace*, as if faith, or love, or any other grace, were taken from Christ. Oh, no; for he believed, before he said, '*My* God, *my* God.' Would he have committed his dearest jewel into the hands of God if he had not believed in him?

Quest. How, then, was Christ forsaken?

Ans. 1. *In regard of his present comfort and joy.* He could not else have been a sacrifice; for as we cannot suffer by way of conformity to Christ, unless there be some desertion, that we may know the bitterness of sin, no more could Christ have suffered for our iniquities had there not been a suspension of light and comfort from his gracious soul.

2. He was not only privatively deprived of all joy and happiness, but *positively he felt the wrath and fury of the Almighty*, whose just displeasure seized upon his soul for sin, as *our surety*. All outward comforts likewise forsook him. The sun withdrew his light from above, and everything below was irksome to him. He suffered in all the good things he had, body, soul, good name, in his eyes, ears, hands, &c. He was reproached, and forsaken of all comforts about him. He had not the common comfort of a man in misery, pity; none took compassion upon him; he was the very object of scorn.

Quest. But in what part was Christ forsaken?

Ans. In all, both in body and soul too, as may plainly appear.

(1.) First, because he was our surety, and we had stained our souls, and bodies too, offending God in both (but in soul especially, because that is the contriver of all sin, the body being but the instrument). Some sins we call spiritual sins, as pride, malice, infidelity, and the like; these touch not the body, yet are the greatest sins of all other.

(2.) Secondly, if he had not suffered in his soul the sense of God's displeasure why should he thus cry out, whenas the poor thieves that suffered by him made no such exclamation? If he had suffered in body only, the sufferings of Paul and Moses had been more, for they wished to be separated from the joys of heaven out of a desire to promote God's glory on earth. Therefore it was, he saith in the garden, 'My soul is heavy unto death,' Mat. xxvi. 38.

Obj. Some will grant that Christ suffered in soul, but, say they, it was by way of sympathy, for there are sufferings of soul immediately from God, and sufferings by way of sympathy and agreement with the body, whenas the soul hath a fellow-feeling of the torments thereof; and so Christ suffered in soul indeed.

Ans. That is not all, beloved, but there were immediate sufferings, even of his soul also, which he groaned under. God the Father laid a heavy stroke upon that. He was smitten of the Lord, Isa. liii. 4; and when God deals immediately with the soul himself, and fills it with his wrath, no creature in the world is able to undergo the same. None can inflict punishment upon the soul but God only. Satan may urge and press arguments of discouragement, and affright us with God's displeasure; but the inflicting of anger upon the soul issues immediately from the hand of the Almighty. We must here, therefore, consider God as a righteous Judge, sitting in heaven in his judgment-seat, taking the punishment of the sins of all his people upon Christ. There was a meeting together of all the sins of the faithful, from Adam to the last man that shall be in the world, as it were, in one point upon him, and the punishment of all these was laid on his blessed shoulders, who suffered for them in both body and soul.

3. *Conclusion.* But how could Christ be forsaken of God, especially so forsaken as to suffer the anger of his father, being an innocent person?

Ans. 1. I answer, first, the Paschal lamb was an innocent creature, yet if the Paschal lamb be once made a sacrifice, it must be killed. Though Christ were never so unblameable, yet, if he will stoop to the office of a surety, he must pay our debt, and do that which we should have done. If a prince's son become a surety, though his father love him and pity him never so much, yet he will say, Now you have taken this upon you, you must discharge it.

2. Secondly, as in natural things the head is punished for the fault of the body, so Christ, by communicating his blessed nature with ours, made up one mystical body, and suffered for us.

Quest. But upon what ground should Christ become our surety?

Ans. 1. Because he was able to discharge our debt to the uttermost. He was more eminent than all mankind, having two natures in one, the manhood knit to the Godhead.

2. Christ most willingly gave himself a sacrifice for us.

3. He was designed and predestinated to this office, yea, he was anointed, set out, and sealed for this business by God himself; and is not this sufficient ground why he should become our surety? especially if we consider,

4. That Christ took the communion of our nature upon him for this very end, that he might be a full surety, that his righteousness being derived to us, and our guilt to him, God's wrath might be satisfied in the self-same nature that offended. You see in societies and cities, if some people offend, the whole city is oftentimes punished. Though perhaps many are guiltless in it, yet by reason of the communion, all are punished. So likewise a traitor's son, that never had any hand in his father's sin, but behaved himself as an honest subject should do, yet, having communion with the person of his father, being indeed a piece of him, is thereupon justly disinherited by all law.

Obj. But how could Christ take our sins upon him and not be defiled therewith?

Quest. He took not the *stain* of our sins, but the *guilt* of them. Now in guilt there is two things.

1. A worthiness and desert of punishment.

2. An obligation and binding over thereunto.

Christ took not the desert of punishment upon him, from any fault in himself; he took whatsoever was penal upon him, but not culpable. As he was our surety, so he everyway discharged our debt, being bound over to all judgments and punishments for us.

Now we owe unto God a double debt.

1. A debt of obedience; and if that fail,

2. A debt of punishment.

And both these hath Christ freed us from: first, by obeying the will ot his Father in everything; and, secondly, by suffering whatsoever was due to us for our transgressions.

Some heretics that would shake the foundation of our faith, will grant Christ to be a *Mediator* to intercede for us, and a *Redeemer* to set us at liberty from slavery, &c., but *not* to be a *surety* to pay our debt, by way of satisfaction to God for us.

Let such remember, that God's pleasure to redeem lost mankind, is not so much by way of power and strength, as by way of justice, and therefore it is said, Heb. vii. 22, 'Christ is become our surety;' and Paul, when he became a mediator to Philemon for Onesimus, a fugitive servant, did it by way of surety, 'If he owe thee anything I will discharge it,' Philem. 18; and Christ Jesus our Mediator blessed for ever, so intercedeth unto God for us, as that he fully satisfies his justice for our offences.

Quest. But why was Christ thus forsaken of his Father?

Ans. 1. To satisfy God for *our forsaking of him.* Christ's forsaking was satisfactory for all our forsakings of God. Beloved, we all forsook God in Adam, and indeed what do we else in every sin we commit, but forsake the Lord, and turn to the creature? what are all our sins of pleasure, profit, ambition, and the like, but a leaving of *the fountain of living waters*, to fetch contentment from 'broken cisterns,' Jer. ii. 13.

2. But Christ was chiefly forsaken, *that he might bring us home again to God*, that there might be no more a separation betwixt his blessed Majesty and us.

Some shallow heretics there are, that would have Christ to be an *example* of *patience* and *holiness* in his life and death, and do us good that way only.

Oh no, beloved, the main comfort we receive from Christ is by way of satisfaction. There must be first grace, and then peace in our agreement with God. Sweetly, saith Bernard, I desire indeed to follow Christ as an example of humility, patience, self-denial, &c., and to love him with the same affection that he hath loved me; but I must eat of the Passover-Lamb, that is, I must chiefly feed on Christ dying for my sins. So every true Christian soul desires to follow Christ's obedience, humility, patience, &c., and to be transformed into the likeness of his blessed Saviour. Whom should I desire to be like more than him, that hath done so much for me? But yet the main comfort I receive from Christ, is by eating his body and drinking his blood; my soul feeds and feasts itself most of all upon the death of Christ, as satisfying for my sins. And what a comfort is it that Christ being our surety, hath made full satisfaction for all our sins. Surely * we shall never be finally and wholly forsaken, because Christ was forsaken for us. Now we may think of God without discomfort, and of sin without despair. Now we may think of the law of death, the curse and all, and never be terrified—why? Christ our surety hath given full content of divine justice for wrath and law, sin and curse, &c. They are all links of one chain, and Christ hath dissolved them all. Now sin ceaseth, wrath ceaseth, the law hath nothing to lay to our charge; death's sting is pulled out. How comfortably, therefore, may we appear before God's tribunal! Oh, beloved, when the soul is brought as low as hell almost, then this consideration will be sweet, that Christ was forsaken as a surety for me; Christ overcame sin, death, God's wrath, and all for me; in him I triumph over all these. What welcome news is this to a distressed sinner! Whenever thy soul is truly humbled in the sense of sin, look not

* That is, 'assuredly.'—G.

at sin in thy conscience (thy conscience is a bed for another to lodge in), but at Christ. If thou be a broken-hearted sinner, see thy sins in Christ thy Saviour taken away; see what he hath endured and suffered for them; see not the law in thy conscience, but see it discharged by Christ; see death disarmed through him, and made an entrance into a better life for thee. Whatsoever is ill, see it in Christ before thou seest it in thyself; and when thou beholdest it there, see not only the hurt thereof taken away, but all good made over to thee; for 'all things work together for the best to them that love God,' Rom. viii. 28. The devil himself, death, sin, and wrath, all help the main; the poison and mischief of all is taken away by Christ, and all good conveyed to us in him. We have grace answerable to his grace. He is the first seat of God's love, and it sweetens whatever mercy we enjoy, that it comes from the fountain, *God the father*, through Christ unto us. I beseech you embrace the comfort that the Holy Ghost affords us from these sweet considerations.

Again, in that Christ was forsaken; and not only so, but endured the displeasure and immediate wrath of God, seizing upon his soul, and filling his heart with anguish at this time, we may learn hence.

How to discern the ugliness of sin. 1. *In what glass to look upon the ugly thing, sin, to make it more ugly unto us.* Beloved, if we would conceive aright of sin, let us see it in the angels tumbled out of heaven, and reserved in chains of darkness for offending God, Jude 6; see it in the casting of Adam out of paradise, Gen. iii. 23, 24, and all us in him; see it in the destruction of the old world, and the Jews carried to captivity, in the general destruction of Jerusalem, &c. But if you would indeed see the most ugly colours of sin, then see it in Christ upon the cross, see how many sighs and groans it cost him, how bitter a thing it was to his righteous soul, forcing him to weep tears of blood, and send forth strong cries to his Father, 'My God, my God, why hast thou forsaken me?' If sin but imputed to Christ our surety, so affected him that was God-man, and lay so heavy upon his soul, what will it do to those that are not in Christ? Certainly, the wrath of God must needs burn to hell; he will be a 'consuming fire,' Heb. xii. 29, to all such. See sin therefore chiefly in the death of Christ. How odious it is to God, that it could be no otherwise purged away than by the death of his beloved Son. All the angels in heaven, and all the creatures in the world could not satisfy divine justice for the least sin. If all the agonies of all creatures were put into one, it were nothing to Christ's agony; if all their sufferings were put into one, they could not make satisfaction to divine justice for the least sin. Sin is another manner of matter than we take it to be. See the attributes of God, his anger against it, his justice and holiness, &c. Beloved, men forget this. They think God is angry against sin indeed, but yet his justice is soon satisfied in Christ. Oh, we must think of the Almighty as a holy God, separated from all stain and pollution of sin whatsoever, and so holy that he enforced a separation of his favour from Christ, for becoming our surety, and Christ underwent a separation from his Father, because he undertook for us. So odious is sin to the holy nature of God, that he left his Son while he struggled with his wrath for it; and so odious was sin to the holy nature of Christ, that he became thus a sacrifice for the same. And so odious are the remainders of sin in the hearts of the saints, that all that belong to God have the Spirit of Christ, which is as fire to consume and waste the old Adam by little and little out of them. 'No unclean thing must enter into heaven,' Rev. xxi. 27. Those that are not in Christ by faith, that have not a shelter in him, must suffer for their transgressions eternally, 'Depart, ye cursed, into everlasting fire,' Mat. xxv. 41; so holy is God that he can have no society and fellowship with sinners.

Do you wonder why God so much hates sin, that men so little regard, not only the lewd sort of the world, but common dead-hearted persons, that set so little by it, that they regard not spiritual sins at all, especially hatred, malice, pride, &c., clothing themselves with these things as a comely garment? Certainly you would not wonder that God hates sin, if you did but consider how sin hates God? What is sin but a setting of itself in God's room, a setting the devil in God's place? for when we sin we leave God, and set up the creature, and by consequence Satan, that brings the temptation tc us; setting him in our hearts before God. Beloved, God is very jealous, and cannot endure that filthy thing sin, to be in his room. Sin is such a thing as desires to take away God himself. Ask a sinner when he is about to sin, Could you not wish that there were no God at all, that there were no eye of heaven to take vengeance on you? Oh aye, with all my heart. And can you then wonder that God hates sin so, when it hates him so, as to wish the not being of God? Oh marvel not at it, but have such conceits of sin as God had when he gave his Son to die for it, and such as Christ had, when in the sense of his Father's anger he cried thus, 'My God, my God,' &c.

The deeper our thoughts are of the odiousness of sin, the deeper our comfort and joy in Christ will be after; therefore I beseech you work your hearts to a serious consideration what that sin is that we cherish so much, and will not be reproved for, and which we leave God and heaven, and all to embrace; conceive of it as God doth, that must be a Judge, and will one day call us to a strict account for the same.

If Christ cried out thus, 'My God, my God, why hast thou forsaken me?' as being our surety for our sins, we may see what to conceive of sin, and of God the better.

But above all things I desire you to see often in this glass, in this book of Christ crucified (it is an excellent book to study), the mercy of God and the love of Christ, the height, and depth, and breadth of God's love in Jesus Christ, which hath no dimensions. What set God on work to plot this excellent work of our salvation and redemption by such a surety,—was it not mercy? Did not that awaken wisdom to reconcile justice and mercy to* Christ? But what stirred up this wisdom of God? Oh, bowels of compassion to man! He would not have man perish, when the angels did, without remedy.

Therefore let us desire to be inflamed with the love of God, that hath loved us so much. All the favours of God in Christ tend, next after satisfaction to justice, to inflame our hearts to love him again. Wherefore else are the favours of creation and providence? How sweet is God in providing for our bodies, giving us not only for necessity, but abundance, withholding no comfort that is good for us, &c.

But chiefly in his masterpiece, God would have us apprehend the greatest love of all other, because there he hath set himself to glorify his mercy more than anything else! Therefore we may well cry with the apostle, 'Oh the height of his love,' &c., Ephes. iii. 18. I beseech you fix your thoughts on this, think not now and then slightly of it, but dwell on the meditation of the infinite love of God in Christ, till your hearts be enlarged and warmed and inflamed with the consideration thereof; and then love will set you forward

* Qu. 'by?'—Ed.

to all good works. What need we bid you be liberal to the poor, to be good subjects, just in your dealings, &c.? All this may be spared when there is a loving heart. And when shall we have loving hearts? When they are kindled and fired at God's fire; when they are persuaded of God's love, then the apprehension of his love will breed love in our hearts again; and that is the reason why the apostles are not so punctual as heathen authors in particularities of duties. They force upon men especially the love of God, and the ground-points of religion, as knowing when the heart is seasoned with that once, it is ready prepared to every good duty. Think seriously of this, 'The love of Christ constraineth me,' 2 Cor. v. 14. There is a holy violence in love; there is a spiritual kind of tyranny and prevailing in this grace.

One thing further we may learn from this forsaking of Christ, viz., that,

It is no strange thing for God's dear children to be forsaken.

To have the apprehension of their sins, and the wrath of God, to be forsaken, in regard of sense of all comfort, do we not see it done in the natural Son? and shall we wonder that it is done in the adopted sons? We see this forsaking was in the natural branch, and shall we wonder that it is done in the grafted branches? It was done to the green tree, and shall we wonder if it be done in the dry? No, certainly.

The whole church complains, Ps. lxix. 21; of drinking gall and wormwood, Ezek. xxxvi. 3; that God was hid in a cloud, Lam. iii. 15, &c. Both the head complains, and the body too, as we see in David, Job, and other saints; so that there is a kind of desertion and forsaking that the child of God must undergo.

Quest. What is the ground and end of it?

Ans. 1. First, God's prerogative is such, that sometimes when there is no great sin to provoke him to withdraw comfort, yet will he leave holy men to themselves, to shew that he will do as pleaseth him.

2. Another ground is, our own estate and condition. We are here absent from the Lord, strangers on earth. Now we would take our pilgrimage for our country, if we had always comfort and new supplies of joy.

3. Again, our disposition is to live by sense more than by faith. We are as children in this. We would have God ever smile upon us, that we might walk in abundance of comfort; and I cannot blame Christians for desiring it, if they desire the work of grace in the first place; if they desire the work of God in them, rather than the shining of comfort by the Spirit, for that is the best work. Now because Christians desire rather to live by sight than by faith, wherein they might honour God more, he leaves them ofttimes. Sight is reserved for another world, for the church triumphant. There we shall have sight enough; we shall see God face to face.

4. Sometimes God's children are negligent, and keep not a holy watch over their souls; they cleave to the creature too much, and then no wonder though God forsake them, since they will have stolen waters of their own, and fetch comfort elsewhere.

5. But one main ground is, conformity to Christ. He suffered for our sins, and God will conform the members in some measure to their head. Though Christ drank the cup of God's wrath to the bottom, yet we must sip and taste a little, that we may know how much we are beholden to Christ; and there are few that come to heaven, few that truly belong to God, but they know what sin is, and what the wrath of God is, first or last. The wrath of God is the best corrosive in the world to eat out sin. A little anger of God felt in the conscience will make a man hate pride and malice, and all sin whatsoever.

Quest. But for what end doth God leave his children, as he did here our blessed Saviour?

Ans. 1. In regard of himself.

2. In regard of his children.

1. In regard of himself, he leaves them that he may comfort them more afterwards; that he may bring more love with him; and that they may love him more than before. There will, after a little forsaking, be a mutual reflection of love between God and a Christian. God delights to shew himself more abundantly after a little forsaking, and the soul enlargeth itself after it hath wanted the love of God; for want enlargeth the capacity of the soul, and want makes it stretch itself to receive more comfort when it comes. God doth this for the increase of his love to us, and of our love to him again. He both draws nigh to us, and goes away, in regard of feeling for our good.

2. That we may be more watchful over our hearts for the time to come; that there may be a more perfect divorce and separation wrought in us to the creatures. Our adulterous hearts have 'stolen delights' that God likes not; and, therefore, when we have smarted for it in the anger and displeasure of God, a divorce will be wrought. It is hard to work a separation from sin, sin and the soul being so nearly invested together; yet God therefore uses this way of spiritual desertion to effect the same.

3. Likewise to make a Christian soul ransack and search the ground of all the comforts that are left him by God. It will make him rifle and search all the Scriptures. Is there any comfort for me, poor wretch, that am troubled with sin? It will make him search the experience of other Christians. Have you any word of comfort for me? It will make him regard a gracious man as 'one of a thousand.' It will make him stretch his heart in all the degrees of grace. Have I any evidence that I am the child of God, and not a cast-away? It will make him search his heart in regard of corruption. Is there any sin that I am not willing to part with? &c. Beloved, God many times leaves us; and not only leaves us, but makes our naked conscience smart for sin. Oh! this is a quickening thing! A child of God that is of the right stamp will not endure to be under God's wrath long. Oh, it is bitter! He knows what it is to enjoy communion with God. He will not endure it. Therefore, it stirs him up to all manner of diligence whatsoever.

Quest. But is there no difference between Christ's sufferings and smart, for sin and ours?

Ans. Yes (1), the sufferings of Christ came from the vindictive * and revenging † hand of God, as a just Judge; but ours proceed from him as a loving Father; for God, when we are in Christ, is changed. He layeth aside the person of a Judge. Having received full satisfaction in Christ, he is now in the relation of a sweet Father to us.

(2.) Again, there is difference in the measure. We take but a taste of the cup, sweetened with some comfort and moderated; but Christ drank deep of the same.

(3.) In the end and use. The sufferings and forsaking of Christ were satisfactory to divine justice; but ours are not so, but only medicinal. The nature of them is quite changed. They are not for satisfaction; for then we should die eternally; disable the satisfaction of Christ. They are crosses indeed, but not curses. Whatsoever we suffer in soul or body is a cross, but not a curse unto us; because the sting is pulled out. They are all medicinal cures to fit us for heaven. Whatsoever we suffer in our in-

* That is, 'vindicative, vindicatory.'—G

† That is, 'avenging.'—G.

ward or outward man, prepares us for glory, by mortifying the remainders of corruptions, and fitting us for that blessed estate.

(4.) All other men's deaths are for themselves. As Leo saith, *Singula in singulis (a)*; they are single deaths for single men. But it is otherwise here; for all the children of God were forsaken in their head, crucified in their head, and died in Christ their head. Christ's death was a public satisfaction. No man dieth for another, let the papists say what they will; only Christ died for all, and suffered for his whole body. And thus much of the first general, that *Christ was forsaken.*

2. The second is this, *Christ was very sensible of it*, even to complaint and expostulation, *My God, My God*, &c. Why should it be thus between the Father and the Son? between such a Father and such a Son, a kind, loving Father to his natural, obedient, and only Son? The word is strong, beloved, he was not only forsaken, but exposed to danger, and left in it, being very sensible of the same. Every word here expresseth some bowels. He doth not say, the Jews have forsaken me; or my beloved disciples and apostles that I made much of have forsaken me, or Pilate would not do the duty of a true judge; my feet are pierced, my head is wounded, my body is racked, hanging on the cross, &c.; he complains of none of these, though they were things to be complained of, and would have sunk any creature to have felt that in his body that he did, but that which went nearest to him, was this, 'Oh, my God, why hast *thou* forsaken me?' I stand not upon others forsaking, but why hast *thou* forsaken me? I stand more upon *thy* forsaking than the forsaking of all others. Christ was very sensible of this; it went to his very heart.

But what special reason was there that Christ should take this so deeply?

1. First of all, because *the lovingkindness of the Lord is better than life itself*, as David the type of Christ well said, Ps. xiii. 3; the forsaking of God being indeed worse than death. The lovingkindness of the Lord is that that sweeteneth all discomforts in the world; the want of that embitters all comforts to us. If we be condemned traitors, what will all comforts do to a condemned man? The want of God's love embitters all good, and the presence thereof sweeteneth all ill; death, imprisonment, and all crosses whatsoever. Therefore Christ having a sanctified judgment, in the highest degree, judgeth the loss of this to be the worst thing.

2. *The sweeter the communion is with God the fountain of good, the more intolerable and unsufferable is the separation from him;* but none had ever so near and sweet a communion with God as Christ our Mediator had, for he was both God and man in one person, the beloved Son of his Father. Now the communion before being so near and so sweet unto him, a little want of the same must needs be unsufferable. Things the nearer they are, the more difficult the separation will be; as when the skin is severed from the flesh, and the flesh from the bones, oh, it is irksome to nature; much more was Christ's separation from the sense of his Father's love. Those that love, live more in the party loved, than in themselves. Christ was in love with the person of his Father, and lived in him. Now to want the sense of his love, considering that love desires nothing but the return of love again, it must needs be death unto him.

3. Another ground that Christ was thus sensible, was, *because he was best able to apprehend the worth of communion with God, and best able to apprehend what the anger of God was.* He had a large judgment, and a more capacious soul than any other; therefore being filled with the wrath of God,

he was able to hold more wrath than any man else. He could deepest apprehend wrath, that had so deep a taste of love before.

4. Again, in regard of his body: the grief of Christ, both in *body* and *soul*, was the greatest that ever was, for he was in the strength of his years; he had not dulled his spirits with intemperancy; he was quick and able to apprehend pain, being of an excellent temperature.

Use. Was Christ so exceeding sensible of the want of his Father's love, though it were but a while? I beseech you then, let us have merciful considerations of those that suffer in conscience, and are troubled in mind. Oh, it is another manner of matter than the world takes it for! It is no easy thing to conflict with God's anger, though but a little. It was the fault of Job's friends; they should have judged charitably of him, but they did not. Take heed, therefore, of making desperate conclusions against ourselves or other, when the arrows of the Almighty stick in us, when we smart and shew our distemper in the apprehension of the terrors of the Lord seizing upon our souls. God is about a gracious work all this while; the more sensible men are of the anger of God, the more sensible they will be of the return of his favour again.

There are some insensible, stupid creatures, that are neither sensible of the afflictions they suffer in body, nor of the manifestation of God's anger on their soul. Notwithstanding, he follows them with his corrections, yet they are as dead flesh, unmoveable; therefore, 'Why should I smite them any longer,' &c., Isa. i. 5, saith God.

This comes from three grounds:

(1.) From *pride*, when men think it a shame for such Roman spirits as they are to stoop.

(2.) Or from *hypocrisy*, when they will not discover their grief, though their conscience be out of tune.

(3.) Or else out of *stupid blockishness*, which is worst of all, when they are not affected with the signs of God's wrath. It is a good thing to be affected with the least token of God's displeasure, when we can gather by good evidence that God hath a quarrel against us. You see how sensible Christ was, and so will it be with us if we get not into him betimes; we shall be sensible of sin one day whether we will or no; conscience is not put in us for nought. You may stupify and stifle the mouth of conscience with this or that trick now, but it will not be so for ever; it will discharge its office, and lay bitter things to our charge, and stare in our faces, and drive us to despair one day. Sin is another matter when it is revealed to conscience than we take it, howsoever we go blockishly and stupidly on now. It is sweet in the temptation and allurement, but it hath an ill farewell and sting. If we could judge of sin as we shall do when it is past, especially when we come to our reckoning at the hour of death, and at the day of judgment, then we would be of another mind; then we would say that all sinners, as the Scripture terms them, 'are fools,' Ps. xciv. 8. But to go on.

Christ we see expresseth his sensibleness by complaint; 'My God, my God, why hast thou forsaken me?'

Caution. Here some cautions must be rendered that we do not mistake. Christ complains not *of* God but *to* God.

Obj. Was Christ ignorant of the cause of God's forsaking him?

Ans. No, he knew the cause, for his sufferings were intolerable; but taking our nature upon him, he takes our speech also, and expresseth himself like to a miserable man; having the greatest affliction that ever was upon a creature. The divine nature of Christ stopped the excess of any passion; he was turbated but not perturbated; he was moved with the sins of men, but not removed; he was as water in a clear glass. There is nothing but water though you stir it never so much: if there were mud in it, it would soon be unclean. We cannot stir our affections and complain but with a tincture of sin. It was not so with Christ. He knew when to raise and when to allay his affections; and though there were much nature in these affections, a natural shunning of grief, and a natural desire of God's presence; yet here was grace to direct and sanctify the same; for nature sometimes carries grace with a stronger wind, more fully when they go both in one current, as here. It was grace to have the love of God, yea, it was death to be without it, and it was sinless nature to desire ease; for without sin nature may desire ease, so it be with submission of itself to God. For the soul may have divers desires as there are divers objects presented to it. When the soul apprehends release and ease, it rejoices and is glad; but when upon higher considerations and better ends there is pain presented to the soul to do it good, the soul may desire that, and upon deliberation choose that it refused before. A man may have his hand cut off, and cast his wares into the sea, that he would not willingly do, yet when upon deliberation he considers, I shall save my life by it, he will do it. So Christ by a natural desire, without sin, might desire release of pain, but when it was presented to him, what shall become of the salvation of men and obedience to God then? Upon these considerations, that respected higher ends, there might be another choice; so in things subordinate one to another, one thing may cross another, and yet all be good too.

But you must know this likewise, that forsaking and to be sensible of forsaking, is no sin, especially when it is not contracted by any sin of ours. It is a suffering, but not a sin; and to be sensible of it is no sin. It is rather a sin to be otherwise affected. God allows those affections that he hath planted in us: he hath planted fear and sorrow in presenting dolorous objects. If a man do not sorrow in objects of sorrow, he is not a man after God's making. God allows grief and fear in afflictions and trouble, always remembering it be with submission to him, 'Not as I will, but as thou wilt,' Matt. xxvi. 30.

Again, consider Christ was now in a conflicting condition between doubting and despair, the powers of hell being round about him. Satan as he was busy about him at the entrance into his office, Mat. iv. 1–11, so he was now vexing his righteous soul with temptations, 'God hath forsaken thee,' and this and that. We know not the malice of Satan at such a time; but certainly the powers of hell were all let loose then upon him. The truth is, God had a purpose to finish his sufferings presently upon his complaint, and because he will have us all receive what we receive, even Christ himself, by prayer and opening our desires to him, God suffers Christ to complain, and pour out his supplication into his bosom, that presently after, he might be released of all, seeing he had now fully satisfied for the sins of man.

Use. The use of it in a word is this, *That God having stooped so low to poor creatures, to be a father and a friend to them,* will suffer them familiarly (as there is a great deal of familiarity in the spirit of adoption), yet reverently, to lay open their griefs into his bosom, and reason the case with his Majesty, without sin, Why, Lord, am I thus forsaken? what is the matter? where are the sounding of thy bowels? where are thy former mercies? &c. There is another kind of familiarity between God and his children than the world takes notice of; yet withal remember, they are not murmuring complaints, but seasoned with faith and love, as here, *my* God, *my* God still. Whence you see that,

Christ in his greatest extremities had a spirit of faith.

3. There is a question between the papists and us about Christ's faith; they will have him to be a comprehender and a traveller, &c. Indeed, he needed no justifying faith to apply anything from without him, because he had righteousness enough of his own; but yet to depend upon God as his Father, so he had faith; neither was he alway in the state of happiness, for that distinction is a confusion of the abasement of Christ and his exaltation. Howsoever, there was the happiness of union (the human nature being alway united to the Godhead), yet there was not alway the happiness of vision; he did not see the face of God, for then why did he cry out, 'My God, my God,' &c.? Sight was due to him from his incarnation in himself considered, not as our surety. Now that which made a stop of the influence of comfort to his soul was, that he might fully suffer for our sins, that he might be humbled and tempted, and suffer even death itself. Therefore, in regard of the state of humiliation, there was faith in him, faith of dependence; there was hope in him, and he made great use thereof to support himself.

Quest. But what supported the faith of Christ in this woeful, rueful estate he was in, being forsaken of God as our surety?

Ans. Christ presented to his faith these things.

1. The unchangeable nature of God, *my God,* &c. 'Whom he once loves, he loves to the end,' John xiii. 1; therefore he lays claim to him; thou hast been my God heretofore, and so thou art still.

2. Again, faith presented to the soul of Christ, God's manner of dealing. He knew well enough that God by contraries brings contraries to pass. He brings to heaven by the gates of hell, he brings to glory by shame, to life by death, and therefore resolves, notwithstanding this desertion, I will depend upon *my* God.

3. Again, Christ knew well enough that God is nearest in support when he is furthest off in feeling. So it is oft, where he is nearest the inward man, to strengthen it with his love, he is furthest off in comfort to outward sense. To whom was God nearer than Christ in support and sanctifying grace? and yet to whom was he further off in present feeling? Christ knew that there was a secret sense of God's love, and a sensible sense of God's love; he had a secret sense of God that he was his Father, because he knew himself to be his Son, but he had it not sensibly. Faith must be suitable to the thing believed. Now Christ, in saying My God, suits his faith to the truth that was offered to him; he knew God in the greatest extremity to be nearest at hand. 'Be not far off, for trouble is near,' &c., Ps. xxii. 11.

This should teach us in any extremity or trouble, to set faith on work, and feed faith with the consideration of God's unchangeable nature, and the unchangeableness of his promises, which endure for ever. We change, but the promise changeth not, and God changeth not; *my God* still: 'The word of the Lord endureth for ever,' 1 Pet. i. 25. God deals with his people in a hidden manner; he supports with secret, though not with sensible comfort, and will be nearest when he seems to be furthest off his children. I beseech you, acquaint yourselves with these things, and think it not strange that God comes near you in desertions, considering that it was so with Christ. Present to thy soul the nature of God, his custom and manner of dealing, so shalt thou apprehend favour in the midst of wrath, and glory in the midst of shame. We shall see life in death; we shall see through the thickest clouds that are between God and us. For as God shines in the heart in his love secretly through all temptations and troubles, so there is a spirit of faith goes back to him again: my God, my God. For faith hath a quick eye, and seeth through contraries. There is no cloud of grief but faith will pierce through it, and see a father's heart under the carriage of an enemy. Christ had a great burden upon him, the sins of the whole world; yet he breaks through all. I am now sin, I bear the guilt of the whole world, yet under this person that I sustain, I am a son, and God is my God still, notwithstanding all this weight of sin upon me. And shall not we, beloved, say, My God, in any affliction or trouble that befalls us? Oh yes. In the sense of sin, which is the bitterest of all, and in the sense of God's anger, in losses and crosses, in our families &c., let us break through those clouds, and say, My God, still.

Obj. But you will say, I may apprehend a lie; perhaps God is not my God, and then it is presumption to say so.

Ans. Whosoever casts himself upon God, out of the sense of sin, to be ruled by God for the time to come, shall obtain mercy. Now, dost thou so? doth thy conscience tell thee, I cast myself upon God for better direction; I would be ruled as God and the ministry of the Word would have me hereafter. If so, thou hast put this question out of question: thou doubtest whether God be thy God; I tell thee God is the God of all that seek him, and obey him in truth. But thy conscience tells thee thou dost this, certainly then, whatsoever thou wert before, God is now beforehand with thee. He offers himself to be thy God, if thou trust in him, and wilt be ruled by him; and not only so, but he entreats us (we should beseech him, but he entreats us, such is his love), nay, he commands us to believe in his Son Jesus Christ. Now, when I join with God's entreaty, Oh Lord, thou offerest thyself, thou invitest me, thou commandest me, I yield obedience and submit to thy good word; then the match is stricken and made up in doing so. God is thy God, and Christ is thy Christ, and thou must improve this claim and interest here, in all the passages of thy life long. Lord, thou art my God, therefore teach me; thou art my God, I have given myself to thee, I have set up thee in my heart above all things, thou art in my soul above all sin, above all profits and pleasures whatsoever, therefore save me, and deliver me, have pity upon me, &c. The claim is good when we have truly given ourselves up to him, else God may say, 'Go to the gods you have served,' Jud. x. 14; men were your gods, for whom you cracked your consciences, riches and pleasure were your gods, go to them for succour.

Oh, beloved, it is a harder matter to say, *My God*, in the midst of trouble, than the world takes it. There was a great conflict in Christ when he said, My God, when he brake through all molestations and temptations of Satan, together with the sense of wrath, and could say notwithstanding, My God. There was a mighty strong spirit in him. But no wonder; faith is an almighty grace, wrought by the power of God, and laying hold upon that power, it lays hold upon omnipotency, and therefore it can do wonders, it overcomes the invincible God. He hath made a promise, and cannot deny his promise; he cannot deny himself and his truth. Put case his dealing be as an enemy. His promise is to be as a friend to those that trust in him: he is merciful, forgiving sins; his nature now is such. Satisfaction to his justice makes him shew mercy.

I speak this that you might beg of God the gift of faith, which will carry you through all temptations and afflictions, yea, even through the shadow of death; as David saith, 'Though I walk in the valley of the shadow of death, yet will I fear no ill,' Ps. xxiii. 4. Why? Because thou art with me, my God and my shepherd. Though we be in the valley of the shadow of death, yet notwithstanding, if God be with us, if we be in covenant with him, and can lay just claim to his promise, by giving up ourselves to him, we shall not fear. One beam of God's countenance, when we are in covenant with him, will scatter all clouds whatsoever. I beseech you, therefore, labour more and more for this precious grace of faith, and increase it by all sanctified means, hearing the word, reading the Scriptures, and treasuring up promises, considering what special use we have of this above all other graces. But to proceed.

Christ here doth not only believe, but

4. *He vents his faith by prayer.*

Good works are but faith incarnate, faith working. They differ not much from it. So prayer is but faith flaming, the breath of faith, as it were. For when troubles possess the soul, it sends out its ambassador presently, it speeds prayer forth, and prayer stays not till it come to heaven, and there takes hold upon God, and gets a message and answer from him back, to comfort the soul. Faith and prayer are all one in a manner. When the soul hath any great desire of grace, or is in grief, apprehending the displeasure of God, faith would, if it could, work to heaven; but we are on earth, and cannot till we die. Therefore when it cannot go to heaven, it sends prayer, and that mounts the soul aloft, and wrestles with God, and will give him no rest till the petition be granted, and it can say, My God.

Therefore, if you have any faith at all, exercise it, and make it bright by often prayer: 'The prayer of faith prevails much,' James v. 15. How shall they call on him in whom they have not believed? Indeed it is no prayer at all without faith; great faith, great prayer; weak faith, weak prayer; no faith, no prayer: they both go on in an even strength. Christ here prays to God under this complaint, *Why hast thou forsaken me?* There is a hidden prayer in it, Oh do not forsake me, deliver me out, &c.

I beseech you, even as you would have comfort from the fountain of comfort, that usually conveys all grace and comfort to us by a spirit of prayer, labour to be much in communion with God in this blessed exercise, especially in troubles: 'Call upon me in the day of trouble,' Ps. l. 15. The evil day is a day of prayer; of all days, in the day of trouble especially, 'make your request known to God,' Phil. iv. 6.

Obj. But perhaps God will not hear me.

Ans. Yes, this fruit follows: 'The peace of God which passeth all understanding shall keep your hearts and minds,' Philip. iv. 7. When you have eased your souls into the bosom of God by prayer, you may go securely, and know that he will let you reap the fruit of your prayers in the best time.

Obj. Yea, but I have prayed long, and have had no answer.

Ans. Wait in prayer; God's time is the best time. The physician keeps his own time; he turns the glass,* and though the patient cry out that he torments him, it is no matter, he knows his time. The goldsmith will not take the metal out of the fire till it be refined. So God knows what to do; wait his good leisure. In the mean time, because we must have all from God by prayer, I beseech you, derive all from him this way; pray for evreything, and then we shall have it as a blessing indeed.

* The allusion is to the 'hour-glass,' the then common measure of time, as the watch is now.—G.

Obj. But put the case I cannot pray, as sometimes we are in such a case that we cannot make a large prayer to God.

Ans. Then do as Christ did, cry; if thou canst not pray, groan and sigh, for they are the groans and the sighs of God's Spirit in thee. There is a great deal of oratory in these words. What is the use of eloquence but to persuade? and what could persuade God more than when Christ shewed how he esteemed his love, and how he was now, in the absence of it, environed with grief before him? Here was rhetoric. If Christ had not spoken, his wounds had said enough, and his pitiful case spake sufficiently. Everything hath a voice to cry for mercy. But he adds his voice to all, and cries vocally aloud, 'My God, my God, why hast thou forsaken me?'

Beloved, if you acquaint yourselves with God in prayer, then you may go readily to him in any extremity. Therefore, in time of health and prosperity, cherish communion with his blessed Majesty, make him your friend; and upon every good occasion improve this plea, O my God. If we have riches, if we have a friend in the court, we will improve them; if we have anything, we will make use of it. Have we a God, and will we not improve him? Have we a God that is our God, and do we want grace? Do we want comfort, and strength, and assistance, and have we a God, the fountain of all, to go to? Shall we have such a prerogative as this, to have Jesus Christ to be our great peacemaker, that we may go boldly to the throne of grace through him, and shall we not improve the same? We may go boldly to God, and welcome, because God is infinite, and the more we go and beg, the more he gives. We cannot exhaust that fountain. O let us improve this blessed prerogative; then we shall live the life of heaven upon earth. Especially when the conscience is troubled with sin, as Christ was now with the displeasure of his Father, then let us go to God, and plead with his Majesty, and we may plead lawfully with him—Lord, thy justice is better satisfied in Christ, than if thou shouldst send me to hell; if thou wilt, thou mayest destroy me (for conscience must come to a great resignation; it cannot desire mercy, but it must see its own misery); Lord, thou mayest justly call me to hell, but it would not be so much for thy glory; thou art more glorious in satisfying thy justice in Christ, than if thou shouldst damn me to hell. Why? Because God's justice is better satisfied in Christ. Man sinned, but God-man satisfied for sin; man would be like God in pride, God becomes man in humility. The expiation of God is greater than the sin of man. He prayed for his persecutors, and gave his life for them. Doth not this proportion more the justice of God than the sin of man? The law doth but require a nocent person, a guilty person to suffer. Christ was innocent. The law requires that man should suffer. Christ was God. Therefore Christ hath done more than satisfied the law. The satisfaction of Christ is more than if we had suffered. We are poor men,—creatures. That was the satisfaction of God-man. Our sins are the sins of finite persons, but he is infinite. Therefore, the soul may plead, Lord, I am a wretched sinner, but I should take away thee, and take away Christ, if I should despair; I should make thee no God, and make Christ no Christ, if I should not accept of mercy; for Christ is given to me, and I labour to make him mine own, by laying hold of him. Faith hath a power to make everything its own that it toucheth; particular faith (which is the only true comfortable faith) makes general things mine. When the soul can lay a particular claim to God as his God, by giving himself to him only, then we may plead in Christ better satisfaction to God's justice, than if he should cast us into hell. What a stay is this for a distressed soul to make use of!

Beloved, the church of God, the mystical body of Christ, is thus forsaken in other countries, besides many particular humble, broken-hearted Christians at home, who find no beams of God's love and mercy. What shall we do? Let the body imitate the head, even go to God in their behalf, and pour out your complaints before him: Lord, where are thy mercies of old? where are thy ancient bowels to thy church? why should the enemy triumph, &c. God delights when we lay open the miseries of his people, and our own particular grievances before him. If there be a spirit of faith in it, oh! it works upon his bowels. If a child can but say, O father, O mother! though he can say not a word more, the bowels are touched, there is eloquence enough; so when we can lay open the pitiful state of God's poor church, what a blessing may we obtain for them? It is thy church, Lord, thine own people, thy name is called upon them, and they call upon thy name; though they have sinned, yet thou deservest to be like thyself, and Christ hath deserved mercy for them. Thus, if we contend with God, and keep not silence, and give God no rest, faith would work wonders. The state of the church would not be long as it is, if we would all improve our interest in heaven in their behalf. Beloved, Christ struggled with the powers of darkness and the wrath of his Father a while, but presently after, all was finished; so let us contend boldly, 'Fight the good fight of faith,' 2 Tim. iv. 7, and not yield to desperate suggestions. Let faith stir up prayer, and prayer go to God; and ere long it shall be said of the church, and of all particular troubles, All is finished. Then we shall enjoy the sweet presence of God, 'where is fulness of joy,' Ps. xvi. 11, and that *for evermore*. The presence of God is that the child of God desires above all things in the world; it quickens and strengthens him; it puts zeal and fire into him; it doth all. What will not the presence of God do when a man enjoys his face? Therefore, let us be content to conflict here, to be exercised a while in faith and prayer. We shall surely say ere long, 'I have finished my course, I have kept the faith; henceforth is laid up for me a crown of righteousness,' 2 Tim. iv. 8.

I beseech you learn these lessons and instructions from our blessed Saviour. We cannot have a better pattern than to be like him, by whom we all hope to be saved another day. So much for this time.

NOTE.

Page 362, line 3d from top, 'As Leo saith,' &c. The reference (rather than quotation) is to Leo, Serm. 64, De Passione Domini, 13, wherein occurs the following:—'Singulares quippe in singulis mortes fuerunt, nec alterius quisquam debitum suo fine persolvit, cum inter filios hominum unus solus Dominus Noster Jesus extiterit in quo omnes crucifixi, omnes mortui, omnes sepulti, omnes etiam sint suscitati.' G.

THE CHURCH'S VISITATION.

THE CHURCH'S VISITATION.

NOTE.

'The Church's Visitation' forms a treatise expository of 1 Pet. iv. 17–19, in four separate but related discourses. The original title-page is given below.* It makes the 'second part' of the volume described at page 296. These four sermons were reprinted in the 'Saints Cordials' (2d ed. 1637, 3d ed. 1658), where they are numbered as 12th to 15th.—G.

* Title-page—

THE
CHVRCHES
VISITATION:
DISCOVERING
The many difficulties and tryalls of
Gods Saints on earth:
Shewing wherein the fountaine of
their happinesse consists:
Arming Christians how to doe, and
suffer for CHRIST;
And directing them how to commit
themselves, and all their wayes to
God in holinesse here, and
happinesse hereafter.

Preached in sundry Sermons at Grayes-
Inne, LONDON,

BY R. S. D.D.

LONDON,
Printed by *M. F.* for *R. Dawlman*, at the
Brazen Serpent in *Pauls* Church-
yard. 1634.

THE CHURCH'S VISITATION.

SERMON I.

For the time is come that judgment must begin at the house of God, and if it begin at us, what shall the end be of them that obey not the gospel? &c.—1 PET. IV. 17, 18, 19.

OUR nature, as it is very backward to do good, so likewise to suffer evil; therefore the blessed apostle exhorts us at the latter end of this chapter, 'not to think it strange concerning the fiery trial, but to rejoice, inasmuch as we are made partakers of Christ's sufferings; wherein are many grounds of patience and comfort to the children of God.

(1.) That the thought of troubles should not be *strange* but *familiar* to them. Acquainting our thoughts with them, taketh away offence at them; though it be a *fiery trial*, yet it shall consume nothing but dross.

(2.) *Then* Christ joineth with us *in suffering*. Better to be in trouble with Christ, than in peace *without* him.

(3.) *The issue will be glorious;* for the Spirit of glory will not only support us with his presence, but rest still upon us.

To other grounds of comfort, he addeth some in the words of my text, as,

1. First, *that the church is God's house*, and therefore he will have a care of it.

2. That he will do it in the fittest *season*. Such is the exigence of the church and people of God, that they require a sharp visitation; and, therefore, such is God's love, that he appoints out a certain time for them.

3. From the different conditions of the *godly* and *ungodly* in *suffering;* both suffer, but differ much; (1) in order, *God begins with his own house;* (2) in measure, *where shall the ungodly appear?* Their judgment shall be most terrible and certain. It is set down by way of interrogation and admiration; what shall their end be? And as Pharaoh's dreams were doubled for more certainty, so here is a double question to make the matter more out of question, [1] what shall their end be that obey not the gospel? [2] where shall the ungodly and sinners appear?

Here is no unnecessary waste of words and arguments, for the Spirit of God knows that all is little enough to fortify the soul against the evil day. Unless the soul be well balanced, it will soon be overturned when storms arise. Therefore, the apostle in these three verses sets down, 1, some *foundations* of comfort; and, 2, an *encouragement* to build upon them, 'wherefore let them that suffer,' &c.

The points considerable in the 17th verse are these:—

1. *That God's church is his house.*

2. *That this house of his will need purging; it will gather soil.*

3. *When God sees the exigent of it, that it must be so, he will be sure to visit and judge his own house.*

4. *That there is a certain time when he will do it, which those that are wise may easily gather.* For God comes not upon his church on the sudden, as a storm, or tempest, &c., but he gives them fair warning. There is a season when God begins judgment with his own house.

5. Lastly, *Why God begins with his own church and people.*

Of these in order.

Obs. 1. *That the Church of God is his own house.* First, *The Church of God is God's house.* God hath two houses, the *heavens*, which are called his house, because he manifests his glory there, and the *church* here below, wherein he manifests his *grace*. Yea, the whole world, in a sort, is his house, because he manifests his power and wisdom in it; but heaven and his church, in a more peculiar manner; and that in these respects:

(1.) Because God by his grace hath *residence* in his church.

(2.) Because by the means of salvation,—the *word*, and *sacraments* there administered,—he doth *feed* his church, as in a house.

(3.) A man *rests* and takes *contentment* in his *house;* so God takes his best contentment in his church and *people;* they are the most beloved of all mankind.

(4.) As in a house we use to lay up our jewels and precious things; so God lays up in his church whatsoever is precious,—his praises, his graces, yea, whatsoever is good and of high esteem, that he bestows upon his church and people.

For the further clearing of this, we must know that the church and children of God are said to be his house, either,

[1.] As a *family* is said to be a house; or,

[2.] As the *fabric* or *building* is said to be the house.

God provides for his church as his own house. First, a man provides for his family, and he that neglects it, is worse than an infidel, 1 Tim. v. 8; so doth God provide for his church. The very dragons and ostriches, the worst of the creatures, all have some respect to their young ones; much more will God provide for his own. And as a man protects his house from all enemies, so will God protect his church and people, and be *a wall of fire*, and a defence round about them.

Now there is a mixture in the church, as in a house, of good and bad vessels; but the godly are especially God's house. As for hypocrites and false professors, they are no more in the house, than the excrements are in the body; they are in the body, but not of the body; and therefore, as Ishmael, Gen. xxi. 10, they must be cast out at length.

The heart of true Christians is God's private closet. And as in every house or building, there are some open places, and some private closets, &c., so is it here. God hath his private chamber, and his retiring-place, which is the heart of every true Christian. He counts it not sufficient to dwell in his house at large, but he will dwell in the best part of it, the heart and the affections. Therefore 'he knocks at the doors of our hearts for entrance,' Rev. iii. 20, and his best children are glad he will reside in them. They set him up in the highest place of their souls, and set a crown upon him;

their desire is, that God may govern and rule their whole conversation; they have no idol above God in their hearts.

Use 1. What a wonderful mercy is this, that we are God's house; that he will vouchsafe to dwell and take up his lodging in such defiled houses as our souls are. It is no mean favour, that God should single out us poor wretches, to have his residence and abiding place in our souls, considering there is so much wickedness in the hearts of the best of us.

Oh what comfort ariseth to a Christian soul from the due meditation of this point. If we are God's house, then God will be our house; 'Thou art our habitation,' saith Moses, 'from generation to generation,' Ps. xc. 1. Howsoever we shuffle in the world, now here and now there, having no certain place of abode, but are here to day, and gone to-morrow, yet in God we have an house, 'Thou art our habitation;' he is ours, and we are his. And what a comfort is this that we are God's house. Certainly God will provide for his own house. He that lays this charge upon others, and hath put that affection and care of provision into others for their families, will he neglect his own? he that makes us love, and puts that natural affection into us of those that belong unto us, hath he not infinitely more in himself? whenas that which we have, is but a beam or ray from his infinite brightness.

Use 2. This should then, instruct us to labour that God may dwell largely and comfortably in us, to deliver up all to this keeper of our house, and suffer him to rule and reign in us. The Romish Church is become the habitation of devils; that which was Bethel, is now become Bethaven (*a*). Why? because they would not suffer God to rule in his own house, but would have coadjutors with Christ, as if he were not a sufficient head of the church to govern it, but he must have a vicar, the pope; who, as if Christ were took * weak, will not suffer him to exercise his kingly office, unless he may support and help him. Thus they set up the abomination of desolation in the temple of God.

O beloved, it much concerns us to cleanse and purify our hearts, that so we may entertain Christ, and he may delight to abide and dwell with us. You know how heinously he took it, when his house was made a den of thieves, Luke xix. 46, and will he not take it much worse that our hearts should be made the very sinks and cages of all manner of uncleanness?

How should we beg and cry to God that he would whip out these noisome lusts and corruptions out of the temple of our hearts by any sharp correction or terror of conscience whatsoever, rather than suffer them to reside there, still to grieve his good Spirit. We should take a holy state upon us, as being *temples of the Holy Ghost*, and therefore too good to be defiled with sin. Our hearts should be as the holy of holies; and therefore the apostle exhorts us 'to abstain from all filthiness both of flesh and spirit,' for this cause, 'that God may dwell amongst us,' 2 Cor. vii. 1; for, 'what communion hath light with darkness?' 2 Cor. vi. 14.

Use 3. Are God's people his house? Then let the enemies of the church take heed how they deal with them, for God will have a special care of his own house. Howsoever he may seem for a time to neglect his children, yet remember this, they are his house still; and no ordinary house, but a temple, wherein sacrifice is offered to him continually; and 'he that destroyeth the temple of God, him will God destroy,' 1 Cor. iii. 17.

Quest. Here a question would be answered, which some uncharitable spirits make, and that is this, Whether England be the house of God, or no?

* Qu. 'too?'—Ed.

Ans. That the Church of England is God's house. I answer: the whole catholic militant church is but one house of God, though there be divers branches of the same. As there is but one main ocean of the sea, yet as it washeth upon the British coast it is called the British sea; and as it washeth on the Germans, the German sea, &c. It hath divers names of the divers countries which it passeth through, nevertheless there is still but one main sea; so it is with the house of God. God hath but one true church in the whole world, which spreads itself into divers nations and countries upon the face of the earth; one branch whereof is among us at this day.

Quest. How prove you that?

Ans. Doth not Christ dwell amongst us by his ordinances, and by his Spirit working effectually in the same? If a house be not in perfect repair, is it not still a house? I beseech you, let us rather give God cause to delight to dwell within us, than call in question whether he dwelleth amongst us or no.

Obs. 2. *That the house of God needs visiting and purging, and the reasons of it.* But to proceed. Hence further we see that the house of God after some time will need visiting and purging, seeing it will soon gather soil. There will abuses and disorders creep into it, so that it will need reformation. And this the apostle seems to insinuate when he saith, 'The time is come that judgment must begin at the house of God.' The Lord saw cause for what he did. For,

1. First,—Such is the weakness of man's nature, that evil things soon discourage us; and good things, except we wrestle with our spirits, prove a snare to the best. Even the church of God, after a long time of peace, is apt to gather corruption, as water doth by standing, and as the air itself will do if it have not the wind to purge it. And as it is in the bodies of men, if they be not curiously looked unto; after a certain time, they will gather such a burden of humours as will rise to a distemper, so that they must be let blood or purged, &c., so it is with the church of God. Such is the infirmity of man's nature and the malice of Satan, that enemy to mankind, that the best of God's people will quickly gather some distemper or other, and stand in need of purging. You know a house will gather dust of itself, though clean at the first.

2. Most certain it is that the church of God cannot be long without some affliction, considering that it is now in a state of pilgrimage, absent from God, in another world as it were. We live in a gross, corrupt air, and draw in the corruption of the times, one defiling another. 'I am a man of polluted lips,' saith Isaiah, 'and dwell with men of polluted lips,' Isaiah vi. 5; ill neighbours made him the worse.

Use. This should stir us up to lament the miserable estate of man's nature, that even the best of men, the church and people of God, whilst they remain in this world, stand in need of continual purging and winnowing. Crosses are as necessary to us as our daily bread, because we carry that about us which wants them. We are as much beholden to God's corrections as to his comforts, in this world. The church needs keeping under, for the most part. God will not have us settle upon our dregs, Ps. lv. 19; Jer. xlviii. 11. This should teach us to bewail our condition, and to desire to be at home, where we shall need no purging, where we shall be as free from sorrow as from sin, the cause of it.

Obs. 3. *That God will come to visit and purge his house when need is.* Observe we further, *that as the church will stand in need of chastisements, so*

God will come and visit his temple when need is, and but when need requires neither ;* for God is no tyrant, yet he will shew that he hates sin wheresoever he finds it, even in his own dear children and servants, Amos iii. 2.

If God should bear with the abuses and sins of his own church and people, it would seem that sin was not so contrary to his holy disposition as it is. Therefore, in whomsoever he finds sin, he will punish it. Our blessed Saviour found this true, when he took upon him the imputation of our sins, and became but only a surety for us. You see how it made him cry out, 'My God, my God, why hast thou forsaken me?' Mat. xxvii. 46. Those glorious creatures, the very angels themselves, when they kept not their own standing, God would endure them no longer, but thrust them out of heaven.

Obj. But why doth God chiefly afflict his own people more than others?

Ans. 1. *Why God afflicts his own people before others. Because they are of his own family, and are called by his name,* Num. vi. 27. Now the disorders of the family tend to the disgrace of the governor of it. The sins of the church touch God more nearly than others, and therefore 'judgments must begin at the sanctuary first,' Ezek. iv. 6. 'I will be sanctified in all that come near me,' saith God when he smote Aaron's sons, Lev. x. 3. The nearer we come to God, if we maintain not the dignity of our profession, undoubtedly the more near will God come to us in judgment. We see the angels, who came nearest to God of all others, when once they sinned against him, they were tumbled out of heaven, and cast into the bottomless pit. Heaven could then brook them no longer.

2. Beloved, *the gospel suffers much through the sides of professors.* What saith the wicked worldling? These be your professors! See what manner of lives they lead! what little conscience they make of their ways! &c. Little do men know how much religion is vilified, and the ways of God evil spoken of, through the loose carriage of professors of the gospel, as if there were no force in the grace and favour of God to make us love and obey him in all things; as if religion consisted in word only, and not in power. What a scandal is this to the cause of Christ! It is no marvel God begins with them first. 'You have I known above all the families of the earth, and therefore will I punish you,' Amos iii. 2. A man may see and pass by dirt in his grounds, but he will not suffer it in his dining chamber; he will not endure dust to be in his parlour.

3. *The sins of the godly more heinous than others.* The sins of God's house admit of a greater aggravation than the sins of others; for, (1) they are committed against more *light;* (2) against more *benefits and favours;* (3) their sins in a manner are *sacrilege.* What! to make 'the temple of God a den of thieves,' to defile their *bodies* and *souls,* that are bought with the precious blood of Jesus Christ, is this a small matter? Again, (4) their sins are *idolatry;* for they are not only the *house* of God, but the *spouse* of God.

Now, for a spouse to be false and adulterous, this is greater than fornication, because the bond is nearer; so the nearer any come to God in profession, the higher is the aggravation of their sin, and as their sin grows, so must their punishment grow answerable and proportionable. They, therefore that know God's will most of all others, must look for most stripes if they do it not, Luke xii. 47, 48.

Use 1. *No privilege can exempt us from God's judgment.* Hence, therefore, learn that no privilege can exempt us from God's judgments, nay, rather the contrary. Where God doth magnify his rich goodness and mercy to a people, and is, notwithstanding, dishonoured by them, he will at last,

* That is, 'He will neither visit nor purge it, except when need requires.'—ED.

magnify his righteous justice in correcting such disobedient wretches. Some of the fathers (Augustine, Salvianus) were forced to justify God in visiting his church more sharply than other people, because Christians are so much worse than others, by how much they should be better. Their sins open the mouths of others to blaspheme. We should not bear out ourselves on this, that we are God's house, but fear so much the more to offend him, else all our privileges will but increase our guilt, not our comfort.

Use 2. Secondly, if God begins with his own house, let the church be severe in punishing sin there most of all; because God's wrath will break out first there. What a shame is it that the heathen should make such sharp laws against adultery and other sins, and we let them pass with a slight or no punishment at all! No doubt but God blesseth a State most, when sin is discountenanced and condemned most; for then it is the State's sin no longer, but lieth upon particular offenders. But I hasten.

Obs. 4. *God appoints a particular time for his visitation.* As God will visit his church, *so there is a certain time for it.* God, as he hath appointed a general day to *judge the world in*, so he appoints particular times of judgment in this life; he is the wise dispenser of times. God doth not always whip his church, but his ordinary course is to give them some respite, as, Acts ix. 31, after Paul's conversion, the church had joy, and grew in the comforts of the Holy Ghost. God hath rejoicing days for his people as well as mourning days; fair weather as well as foul; and all to help them forward in the way to heaven. Beloved, God gives many happy and blessed times to encourage weak ones at their first coming on, that they may the better grow up in goodness, and not be nipped in the bud; but after a certain time, when through peace and encouragement they grow secure and careless, and scandalous in their lives, then he takes them in hand and corrects them. God hath scouring days for his vessels.

Quest. What be those times wherein God will visit his church?

Ans. 1. *What be the times of God's visitation?* I answer, in general, the time of visiting the church of God is from Abel to the last man that shall be in the earth. The church began with blood, continues with blood, and shall end with blood. The whole days of the church are a time of persecution. 'From my youth upward,' saith the psalmist, 'I have suffered,' Ps. lxxxviii. 15. So may the church of God say, 'Even from my cradle, from my infancy,' I have been afflicted; yea, 'for thy sake we are killed all the day long, and counted as sheep for the slaughter,' Ps. xliv. 22. But this is not here meant.

2. *The church is afflicted when the light of the gospel hath most clearly shined.* The time for the church of God to suffer is when the glorious manifestation of the gospel is more than in former times. We see the ten first persecutions were after that general promulgation of the gospel, whereby the world was more enlightened than formerly (*b*). We read in the Revelation of a *white horse* that Christ rides on, and a *pale horse* of famine, and a *red horse* of persecution that followed after him, Rev. vi. 2, 4, 8. So presently after the preaching of the gospel, comes the fan and the axe, or though not very presently, yet after a certain time, when our need requires it; for God will wait a while to see how we entertain his glorious gospel, and whether we walk worthy of it or not.

3. *That now is the time of the church's affliction.* More particularly, even now is the time of Jacob's trouble; even now God hath put a cup into the church's hand, and it must go round. The sword hath a commission to devour, which is not yet called in.

Quest. But what be the more especial times wherein a man may know some judgment is like to fall upon the church of God?

Ans. 1. *How we may know when some judgment approacheth.* The Scripture is wondrous full in the point. God usually, before any heavy judgment, visits a people with lesser judgments. His footsteps first appear in some small token of his displeasure; but if that prevails not, then *he brings a greater.*

Sign 1. 'This, and this have I done,' saith the Lord, 'and yet ye have not returned unto me,' Amos iv. 6, 7. There be droppings before the ruin of a house. Lesser judgments make way for greater, as a little wedge makes way for a greater; and, therefore, where less afflictions prevail not, there cannot but be an expectation of greater. 'Why should I smite you any more?' saith God; 'you fall away more and more,' Isa. i. 5; that is, I must have a sweeping judgment to carry you clean away.

Sign 2. Again, usually before some great calamity *God takes away worthy men,* 'the councillor, and the captain, and the man of war,' Isa. iii. 2, 3. This is is a fearful presage that God threateneth some destruction, for they are the pillars of the church and the strength of the world; they are those that make the times and places good wherein they live; for they keep away evil and do good by their example and by their prayers many ways. A good man is a common good. The city thrives the better, as Solomon saith, for a righteous man, Prov. xi. 10, 11, Eccles. ix. 15. Therefore, we have cause to rejoice in them, and it is an evil sign when such are removed.*

Sign 3. God usually visits a people when some *horrible crying sins reign amongst them,* as (1) atheism. Beloved, God stands upon his prerogative then, when he is scarce known in the world; when they say, Where is God? God sees us not, &c. So, likewise (2), when idolatry prevails. This is spiritual adultery and a breach of covenant with God. Again (3), when divisions grow amongst a people. Union is a preserver. Where there is dissension of judgment, there will soon be dissension of affections; and dissipation will be the end if we take not heed. For the most part, ecclesiastical dissensions end in civil; and therefore we see, before the destruction of Jerusalem, what a world of schisms and divisions were amongst the Jews. There were Pharisees and Sadducees, &c. It was the ruin of the ten tribes at length, the rent that Jeroboam caused in religion. It is a fearful sign of some great judgment to fall upon a church, when there is not a stopping of dissensions. They may be easily stopped at first, as waters in the beginning; but when they are once gotten into the very vital parts of the church and commonwealth, we may see the mischief, but it is hardly † remedied.

Sign 4. Again, *when sin goes with some evil circumstances and odious qualities, which aggravate the same in the sight of God,* as when sin grows ripe, and abounds in a land or nation. At such a time as this a man may know there is some fearful judgment approaching.

Quest. But when is sin ripe?

Ans. 1. When it is impudent; when men grow bold in sin, making it their whole course and trade of life. When men's wicked courses are their 'conversation,'‡ they cannot tell how to do otherwise.

2. When sin grows common and spreads far. It is an ill plea to say, Others do so as well as I. Alas! the more sin, the more danger.

3. When there is a security in sinning, without fear or dread of the Almighty, as if men would dare the God of heaven to do his worst. Oh,

* Compare reflections on Sibbes's own death, by Catlin. Appendix to Memoir, pp. cxxxiii–v.—G.

† That is, 'with difficulty.'—G.

‡ That is, 'habitual.' Compare 2 Peter ii. 7; 1 Peter i. 15, *et alibi.*—G.

beloved, such persons as go on still in their sins to provoke the Lord, do put a sword, as it were, into God's hands to destroy themselves.

The old world, you know, was very secure. No doubt, they mocked at holy Noah when he made the ark, as if he had been a doting old man. Notwithstanding, he foretold them of the wrath to come. And our Saviour, Christ, saith, 'Before the end of the world it shall be as in the days of Noah,' Mat. xxiv. 38. Beloved, God hath his 'old worlds' still. If we have the same course and security of sinning, we must look for the same judgments. And, therefore, compare times with times. If the times now answer former times, when God judged them, we may well expect the same fearful judgments to fall upon us.

Sign 5. *Unfruitfulness threateneth a judgment upon a people.* When God hath bestowed a great deal of cost and time, he looks we should answer his expectation in some measure. The fig-tree in the gospel had some respite given it, by reason of the prayers of the vine-dresser; but afterward, when it brought forth no fruit, it was cut down and cast into the fire. Beloved, who amongst us would endure a barren tree in his garden? That which is not fit for fruit is most fit for fire. We can endure a barren tree in the wilderness, but not in our orchards. When God, the great husbandman in his church, sees that upon so great and continual cost bestowed upon us, we remain yet unfruitful, he will not suffer us long to cumber the ground of his church.

Sign 6. Again, *decay in our first love* is a sign of judgment approaching. God threatened the church of Ephesus to remove his candlestick from among them, for their 'decay in their first love,' Rev. ii. 4; that having surfeited of plenty and peace, he might recover her taste by dieting of her. Decay in love proceeds from disesteem in judgment; and God cannot endure his glorious gospel should be slighted, as not deserving the richest strain of our love. The Lord takes it better where there is but little strength and a striving to be better, than when there is great means of grace and knowledge, and no growth answerable, but rather a declining in goodness. I beseech you lay these things to heart. The Lord is much displeased when Christians are not so zealous as they should be; when there is not that sweet communion of saints among them, to strengthen and encourage one another in the ways of holiness as there might be; when there is not a beauty in their profession to allure and draw on others to a love and liking of the best things; when there is not a care to avoid all scandals that may weaken respect to good things, and bring an evil report on the ways of God; when they labour not with their whole hearts to serve the Lord in a cheerful manner, &c. The very not serving God answerable to encouragements, is a certain sign of ensuing danger, Deut. xxviii. 47.

Use. Therefore, I beseech you, let us look about us whether these be not the times wherein we live, that judgment must begin at the house of God. The Lord complains in Jeremiah, Jer. viii. 7, that the turtle and other silly creatures knew the time of their standing and removing, but his people did not know his judgments. Do the creatures know their times and seasons, and shall Christ complain that we know not the day of our visitation? What a shame is this! I beseech you, let us know and consider our times. If we have a time of sinning, God will have a time of punishing.

And have we not just cause to fear that judgment is not far from us, when we see a great part of God's house on fire already in our neighbouring countries? We have had lesser judgments, and they have not wrought kindly with us; we need a stronger purge. If we look to the carriage of men, what sin is less committed now than formerly? How few renew their covenant with God, in sincerity of resolution, to walk closely with him!

And what the judgment will be, we may probably foresee, for usually the last judgment is the worst. We have had all but war, the worst of all; for in other judgments we have to deal with God, but in this we are to deal with men, whose very mercies are cruelties, Prov. xii. 10. The sword hath a long time been shaken over our heads, a cloud of war hath hung over us to affright us, but we rest still secure in our sinful courses, and think 'to-morrow shall be as to-day,' Isa. lvi. 12, and that 'no evil shall come nigh us,' &c., Micah iii. 11. O the frozen hearts of Christians, that thrust the evil day far from them! do we not see the whole world in a manner in a combustion round about us, and we, as 'the three young men in the fiery furnace,' Dan. iii., untouched? Beloved, we have outstripped them in abominable wickedness; and however the Lord is pleased that we should only hear a noise and rumour of war, yet we in this land have deserved to drink as deep of the cup of the Lord's wrath as any people under heaven.

Quest. What course should we take to prevent the judgment of God, and keep it from us?

Ans. Of the means to prevent and escape God's judgments. 1. *Labour to meet God by speedy repentance, before any decree be peremptorily come forth against us.* As yet there is hope to prevail; for, blessed be God, as we have many things to fear, so we have many things to encourage us to go unto God with comfort. We have enjoyed a succession of gracious princes that have maintained the truth of God amongst us; we have many godly magistrates and ministers, together with the ordinances, and many other experiences of God's love vouchsafed unto us. We have yet time to seek the Lord. Let us not defer till the very time of judgment come upon us; for that is but self-love.

Note. Assure thyself thus much, thou canst have no more comfort in troubles and afflictions when they do come, than thou hast care to prevent them before they come; answerable to our care in preventing now, will be our comfort then.

Therefore if we would be hid in the day of God's wrath; if we would have God to set his mark upon us, and write us in his book of remembrance, and to gather us when he 'makes up his jewels,' Mal. iii. 16; if we would have him to own us then, look to it now, get now into Christ, be provided now of a sound profession of religion, and that will be as an ark to shelter us in the evil day. What we know let us do, and then we shall be built on a rock, that if waves or anything come, we shall not be stirred.

Usually God in dangerous times leaveth some ground of hope, which worketh differently with men. Such as are carnal, grow presumptuous hereupon; but the godly are drawn nearer to God upon any appearance of encouragement; the good things they enjoy from God, work in them a more earnest desire to please him.

It is the custom of the Spirit of God to make doubtful, imperfect, and as it were half promises, to keep his people still under some hope; whence we read of these and such like phrases in Scripture, 'It may be God will shew mercy,' Amos v. 15; and 'who knoweth whether he will hear us?' &c., Joel ii. 14.

2. Again, *examine and try, upon what ground thou professest religion*, whether it will hold water or no, and stand thee in stead when evil times shall come. Beloved, it nearly concerns us all, seriously to consider and narrowly to search,

upon what grounds we venture our lives and souls; try our graces, our knowledge, repentance, faith, love, &c., of what metal they are. Those that have coin, bring it to the touchstone, and if it prove counterfeit they presently reject it and will have none of it. O that we had this wisdom for matters of eternity! If men would search and plough up their own hearts, they would not need the ploughing of God's enemies. We should not need God's judgments, if we would judge ourselves. The church complained that the enemies had made long furrows on her back, but if she had ploughed herself, she had saved the enemies that labour, Ps. cxxix. 3.

3. Before any judgment comes, *let us store up the fruits of a holy life;* every day be doing something; do that now, which may comfort thee then; store up comforts against the evil day. When the 'night is come, we cannot work,' John ix. 4. Let us therefore 'walk while we have the light,' John xii. 35; let us look about us and do what good we can 'whilst we have time,' as the apostle saith, 1 Cor. vii. 29. The time will come ere long that thou wilt wish, O that I had that opportunity and advantage of doing good as I have had! O that I had such means of doing good as I have had! but then it will be too late; then that whereby thou shouldst do good, will be in thy enemies' hands; and therefore, while we have time, let us be doing and receiving all the good we can.

4. Again, if we would have God to shield us, and be an hiding-place in the worst times, *let us mourn for our own sins and the sins of the times wherein we live.* Let us keep ourselves unspotted of the sins of the world; let us not bring sticks to the common fire; let us not make the times worse for us, but better, that the times and places we live in may bless God for us.

And let us not only mourn for the sins of the times, but labour also to repress them all we can, and stand in the gap, endeavouring by our prayers and tears to stop God's judgments.

5. *And we should set a high price upon that religion and the blessings of God which we do enjoy*, lest we force God to take them from us; and so we come to know that, by the want of it, which we did not value when we possessed it. Oh, let us esteem the treasure of the gospel at a higher rate than ever we have done. We see how it is slighted by most of the world; how they shake the blessed truths of God, and call them into question, being indifferent for any religion. Is this our proficiency, beloved? It behoves us to store up all the sanctified knowledge we can, and to take heed we yield not to any, that would either weaken our judgment in religion, or our affections to the best things. We should, every one in his place, labour to stop dissensions in this kind, and knit our hearts together as one man in unity and concord. Factions have always fractions going with them. Unity makes strong, but division weakeneth any people. Even Satan's kingdom, Mat. xii. 25, 26, divided against itself, cannot stand.

What is the glory of England? Take away the gospel, and what have we that other nations have not better than ourselves? Alas, if we labour not to maintain truth, we may say with Eli's daughter, 'The glory of God is departed from us,' 1 Sam. iv. 21.

Sarah had her handmaid; and so hath religion been attended with prosperity and peace, preservation and protection amongst us, even to the admiration * of other countries. Shall we not, therefore, make much of that religion, which, if we had it alone, joined with many crosses and sufferings, yet were an inestimable and unvaluable blessing? And shall we not now much more, considering it hath been attended by so many mer-

* That is, 'wonder.'—G.

cies, cherish and maintain the same all we can? Do we think it will go alone when it goes, whensoever God removes it from us? No, no. Therefore, I beseech you, let us highly esteem of the gospel, whilst we do enjoy it. If we suffer that to be shaken any way, our peace and prosperity will then leave us, and judgment upon judgment will come upon us. If we will not regard the truth of God, which he esteemeth most, he will take away outward prosperity, which we esteem most.

But I come to the fifth point, *that judgment must begin at the house of God.*

Quest. Why doth God begin with his own church and people?

Ans. Reason 1. Usually because he useth *wicked* men and the *enemies* of his church for that base service, *to correct and punish them.*

Reason 2. *To take away all excuse from wicked men.* That they, seeing how severely God deals with his own dear children, might be stirred up to look about them, and consider what will become of themselves at the last, if they go on in their sinful courses. So many crosses as befall God's children, so many evidences against secure carnal persons; for if God deal thus with the green tree, what will he do with the dry? If he scourge his children thus with rods, certainly the slaves shall be whipped with scorpions.

Reason 3. God begins with his own servants, *that his children might be best at last.* If he should not begin with them, they would grow deeper in rebellion against him, and attract more soil and filth to themselves, and be more and more engaged to error and corruption. God's love to his people is such, that he regards their correction before the confusion of his enemies.

Reason 4. Again, God doth this, *that when he sends them good days afterwards, they might have the more taste and relish of his goodness.* After an afflicted life, we are more sensible of happy times. God deals favourably, therefore, with a man when he crosseth him in the beginning of his days, and gives him peace in his latter end.

This is a point of marvellous comfort and encouragement to the faithful servants of God; for,

Use 1. *Though God correct them sharply, yet he shews thereby they are of his household.* When a man corrects another, we may know it is his child or servant, &c. God shews that we are of his house and family by the care he takes to correct us. The vine is not hated because it is pruned, but that it may bring forth more fruit; the ground is not hated because it is ploughed, nor the house because it is cleansed.

Quest. But what is meant by judgment here?

Ans. Judgment is correction moderated to God's children. Judgment is twofold in Scripture. The statutes of God are called judgments, and the corrections of God are called judgments. The statutes are called judgments, because they judge what we should do, and what we should not do. Now, when we do not that we should, he is forced to judge us actually with real judgments.

The real judgments of God are either (1), upon the *wicked*, and so they are judgments *in fury*, for there is not the least taste of his love in them to wicked men. They can make no sanctified use of them, because they are not directed to them for their good; or (2), to *God's children*, and so they are *moderate corrections;* and therefore the prophet so often urgeth, 'Correct us, Lord, in judgment,' &c., Jer. x. 24. God always moderates afflictions to his own children, but as for the wicked, he sweeps them away as dung, as dross, and as chaff, &c.

Use 2. Again, *it is a comfort to God's children that he begins with them first.* Rather than God will suffer them to perish and be condemned with the world, he begins with them here. They have their worst first, and the better is to come.

Use 3. This likewise is some comfort, that the *time* when God corrects his children is most *seasonable* and fit for them. God pruneth his trees in the fittest time. A plant cut unseasonably, dieth, but being cut in due time it flourishes the better. All the works of God are beautiful in their season. Every Christian may truly say, God loves me better than I do myself. He knows the best time of purging and visiting his people. 'This is the time of Jacob's trouble,' &c., Micah ii. 3. Therefore we should lay our hands upon our mouths, kiss the rod, and stoop under judgments, as considering God's time to be the best time, and that he knows better what is good for us than we do ourselves.

Thus you see, though we have cause of fearing God's judgments, yet there is something to comfort us in the midst of all. God mingles our comforts and crosses together whilst we are here, both to keep us in awe of offending his Majesty, and to encourage us in well-doing. *Securitatis custos timor*. Therefore let us always look what matter of fear and what matter of hope we have, for both these are operative affections. *Spes exercitat ad opus*. Oh that I could stir up this blessed fear in you. It is that which preserves the soul; and God hath promised that 'he will put his fear into our hearts, that we shall not depart from him,' Jer. xxxii. 40. I beseech you, ply the throne of grace, and desire the Lord that it may be to every one of your souls according to his good word.

Labour likewise for encouragement in the ways of holiness. Blessed be God, yet we have a time of respite. God forbears us with much patience and goodness. Answerable to our good courses that we take now, will be our comfort in the evil day. If we carelessly go on in sin, and think it time enough to renew our covenant with God then, when his judgments are abroad and ready to cease* upon us, we do but delude our own souls, and expose ourselves to inevitable dangers. Mark what the Lord saith, Because I called, and you would not hear, &c., therefore will I laugh at your destruction, Prov. i. 24, 26. Is it not strange that the merciful God should laugh at the calamity of his poor creatures? Yet thus it is with every wilful sinner that dallies with God, and puts off his repentance from time to time. God will take pleasure in the ruin of such a man, and laugh when his fear cometh, because those that seek him then, do it not out of any love or liking of God and the ways of goodness, but merely out of self-love and respect to their own welfare.

* Qu. 'rest?' or 'fall?'—Ed.

NOTES.

(*a*) Page 375.—'That which was Bethel, is now become Bethaven.' That is, what was 'Bethel,' which means 'house of God,' was become 'Bethaven,' which means 'house of idols;' a sort of *jeu de mot* applied to Bethel, after it became the seat of the worship of the golden calves.

(*b*) Page 378..—'First ten persecutions.' The first was under Nero, A.D. 64; the second under Domitian, 95; the third under Trajan, 100; the fourth under Adrian, 118; the fifth under Severus, 197; the sixth under Maximinus, 235: the seventh under Decius, more bloody than any preceding; the eighth under Valerian, 257; the ninth under Aurelian, 272; and the tenth under Dioclesian, which lasted ten years, 302. G.

THE UNGODLY'S MISERY.

SERMON II.

And if it first begin at us, what shall the end of those be that obey not the gospel!—1 Pet. IV. 17.

These words are propounded by way of admiration,* as if the apostle had been at his wits' end, and could not certainly set down how great the judgment should be, of those that obey not the gospel, it was so terrible and unavoidable. The points considerable are these :—

Three points considerable. 1. *That the seeming prosperity of the wicked shall have an end.*

2. *That it is wisdom to consider the end of graceless persons.*

3. *The description of them;* in these words, *they are such as obey not the gospel.*

Obs. 1. *The seeming prosperity of the wicked shall have an end.* It is naturally in the hearts of carnal persons, to think it shall be always well with them, whereas the prophet saith, the happiness of a wicked man is but 'as a candle, that ends in a snuff,' Prov. xxiv. 20, or like a rose, the beauty whereof suddenly fades, and nothing remains but the prickles. The favours of men, for which they so much offend God, shall have an end; their strength shall end, their pleasure shall end, (alas, they are but pleasures of sin for a season!) their life itself, the foundation of all their comforts, that shall have an end; but their sins, by which they have offended God, shall never have an end. See what a fearful judgment follows every wicked wretch; that which he sins for, his honour, riches, delights, all shall vanish and come to nothing; they shall not be able to afford him one drop or dram of comfort at his dying day; but the sin itself, the guilt of that, and the punishment due to the same, shall endure for ever, to torment his soul, without serious repentance and turning to God in time.

Obs. 2. *The happiness of the wicked is momentary; their misery endless.* But secondly, if the happiness of wicked men shall have an end, and their misery shall have no end, *let us not be dazzled with their present happiness, so as to imitate their evil ways;* let us tremble at their courses, whose end we tremble at. If we walk in the same path, shall we not come to the

* That is, 'amazement.'—G.

same end? All wicked men that delight in the company one of another here, are brethren in evil, and shall be like a company of tares, all cast into hell-fire together hereafter. It is pity they should be severed then that will not be severed now. Those men's courses, therefore, which we follow here, of their judgment we shall participate eternally afterwards.

Use. Let this admonish us to have nothing to do with sinful persons, nor to be troubled with their seeming prosperity. 'They stand in slippery places,' Ps. lxxiii. 18. God lets them alone for a while, but their pleasure will end in bitterness at last; all their riches shall end in poverty and beggary. 'They shall not have a drop of water to cool their tongues,' Luke xvi. 24, 25. All their honour and greatness shall end in confusion and shame, and lie in the dust ere long. Indeed, we should rather pity them, if we consider their latter ends. Alas, what shall become of them ere long! The fall of these wretches shall be so terrible, that Peter could not set it down, but leaves it to the admiration of the reader, What shall the end of such be! &c.

One difference betwixt a wise man and a fool is, that a wise man considers his end, and frames his life suitable thereunto. Therefore if we would be truly wise, let us consider the end of those things in this world, which wicked men offend God for, and set so light by heaven and everlasting happiness for the procurement of. Alas, whatsoever is here, shall have an end! A Christian should frame his course answerable to eternity, that when his happiness shall end in this world, it may begin in the world to come, else we may outlive our happiness.

Present happiness aggravates future and eternal misery. This is the misery of wicked men, that their souls are eternal, but their happiness is determined in this life. Here that ends; but their misery is infinite, and hath no end at all. Look what degree of excellency any creature hath, if it be good; the same degree of misery it hath if it be evil. What made the angels worse than other creatures when they sinned, but only this? they were most excellent creatures, and therefore when they became evil, their excellency did but help them to subsist and be more capable of punishment. A wise man understandeth his misery. *Sapiens miser plus miser.* Now the angels when they fell became more miserable, because they were more capacious, and sensible of it, being spirits.

So man being sinful and evil, his end will be more miserable than any inferior creature, because he was more happy. His happiness helps him to more misery. How should this stir up every one to look about him, and not to prize himself by any outward excellency whatsoever! The more excellent thou art, the more miserable if thou sin against God. It is of all unhappiness the most unhappy thing, for a man to live happily here a while, and be eternally miserable afterwards; for our former happiness tends to nothing else but to make us more sensible of future miseries. What is all the felicity of great persons, when they die and leave this world? Alas, it soon comes to nothing, and serves but to make them apprehensive of more misery than meaner persons are capable of: what shall the end of such be? &c.

Obs. 3. *The endless miseries of the wicked should warn us from the love of their present pleasures and profits.* From this, that the apostle leaves the punishment of all sinful wretches to admiration and wonderment, rather than to expression, for indeed it is above expression, we may learn—*when we are tempted to any sin or unlawful course, to consider thus with ourselves: Shall I, for a pleasure that will end, have a judgment that shall never end?*

for the favour of men that will fail, shall I lose the perpetual favour of God, whose wrath is a consuming fire, and burns to hell? shall I for a little profit, lose my soul eternally? Beloved, as the good things of a Christian, even in this life, are admirable beyond expression, 'peace that passeth all understanding,' Philip. iv. 7, and 'joy unspeakable and glorious,' 1 Pet. i. 8, &c., so when God awakens our consciences, those gripes and pangs and terrors of soul, which follow after sin committed, are unutterable and inconceivable. I beseech you therefore, whenever you are solicited to sin, for profit or pleasure, &c., set before your eyes the fading and perishing condition of these things, and the everlastingness of that judgment which attends upon them. Oh that we were wise this way!

Obs. 3. I come now to the third particular; *Those that obey not the gospel*, wherein we have—

1. A description of the *thing*.
2. And then of the *persons*.

The thing is the *gospel of God;* the persons are *wicked men*. God is the author of the gospel. It comes out of his breast, sealed with authority. Whence learn this, by the way, *that in refusing the blessed gospel, we have to deal with God himself*. It is God's word and gospel. Therefore when you reject it, you reject God; in receiving it, you receive God. You deal with God himself, when you deal with the ministers of his word. Therefore whenever you partake of the ordinances, say, with good Cornelius, 'We are now in the presence of God, to hear what he will say,' Acts x. 33.

Quest. But, what is it to obey the gospel?

Ans. To obey the gospel is to *entertain the offers of it;* for indeed though the gospel command us to believe in the Son of God, yet withal it offers the very command unto us; to believe in Christ, being in effect a command to receive him, which supposeth an act of giving and tendering something to us. Now when we do not receive and entertain with our whole heart Christ and his benefits, freely offered, we disobey the gospel, and so procure danger to ourselves.

But more particularly, he obeys the gospel *that is sensible of his own miserable and sinful condition, and from a sense thereof hungereth after the grace and favour offered in Jesus Christ to pardon sin*, which when he hath once obtained, [he] walks answerable to that great mercy received. He that receives whole Christ to justify him, and sanctify him too; that receives Christ as a king to rule him as well as a priest to save him, such a one receives the gospel. But those that are not sensible of their misery, or if they be, will not go to Christ, but, as desperate persons, fling away the potion that should cure them, these are far from obeying the gospel of God. Such likewise as pretend, Oh, Christ is welcome with the pardon of sin, but yet live in gross wickedness, against knowledge and conscience, and suffer him not to bear sway in their hearts, as if Christ came by blood alone, and not by water; whereas indeed he came as well by water to sanctify us, as by blood to die for us.

Many there are that think they obey the gospel, who are indeed very rebels and enemies unto it. They welcome the gospel, and they hate popery, &c., but notwithstanding they will be their own rulers, and live as they list; they will not deny themselves in their beloved sins; they are full of revenge, notwithstanding the gospel saith, 'This is my commandment, that you love one another,' John xv. 12. That 'bids them deny ungodliness and worldly lusts, and live soberly,' Titus ii. 12; yet they will riot, and follow their base courses still. The gospel teacheth a man to acknowledge God in all his ways, to deal with God in all things he goes about. Now, when a man lives without God in the world, saying, *God is merciful*, and *Christ is a Saviour*, and yet persists in those ways which seem good in his own eyes, never looking to God to guide him, or his law to rule him, how can such a one be said to obey the gospel?

That works have no place in the act of justification. But some others there are amongst us, that regard not Christ and his satisfaction alone, but join faith and works together in justification; they will have other priests, and other intercessors than Christ. Alas! beloved, how are these men fallen from Christ to another gospel, as if Christ were not an all-sufficient Saviour, and able to deliver to the uttermost! What is the gospel but salvation and redemption by Christ alone? Gal. ii. 16.

Therefore Rome's church is an apostate church, and may well be styled an adulteress and a whore, because she is fallen from her husband Christ Jesus.

And what may we think of those that would bring light and darkness, Christ and antichrist, the ark and Dagon together; that would reconcile us, as if it were no such great matter! Beloved, they that join works with Christ in matter of justification, err in the foundation. The very life and soul of religion consists in this. What was the reason the Jews stumbled at this stumblingblock, and were never benefited by Christ? Why? They set up a righteousness of their own, which could not stand, but soon failed them. So when a man sets up a righteousness of his own, neglecting the righteousness of Christ, it is impossible he should ever be saved, living and dying in that error, Philip. iii. 10.

Why disobedience against the gospel is so great a sin. Therefore, I beseech you, take heed of disobeying the gospel of Jesus Christ in any kind whatsoever, for of all sins this is the greatest, as shall appear by these reasons.

Reason 1. First, *because sins against the gospel are sins against those attributes, wherein God will glorify himself most*, as his grace, mercy, loving-kindness, &c. Therefore the gospel is called grace, because it publisheth, offers, and applies grace. Now sins against mercy are greater than sins against justice; for God hath made all things for the glory of his mercy. Even among men, are not sins against favours the greatest sins? To wrong a man whether he deserves well or ill is an offence. But what man will have his courtesies rejected, though never so mean? Love deserves love; favour deserves respect again. But now when we obey not the gospel, we neglect and despise the goodness and mercy of God. Oh what excellent blessings doth the gospel reveal, if we had hearts to value them! Doth not the gospel bring salvation! Is it not the word of *grace*, the word of *life*, the word of the *kingdom?* Beloved, I beseech you, lay these things to heart, for whensoever you refuse the gospel of Christ, you refuse with it the word of grace, of the kingdom of heaven, and eternal life, and all. Therefore the sins of the gospel must needs be the greatest sins.

Reason 2. Again, *sins against the greatest light are most sinful.* What makes sin out of measure sinful, but this, when it is committed against a great measure of light? What makes a man fall foul? It is not when he falls in a mist, or in a dark night, every one will pity him then; alas, he wanted light; but when he falls at noon-day. Beloved, had we lived in former times, when the light was not poured forth so abundantly as now it is, our sin had been the less; but now in this clear sunshine of the gospel, for us to live in sins condemned by so great a light, either in our judgment or practice, it must needs make our sin the greater. 'If I had not come and spoken to them,' saith our Saviour, 'they had had some pretence for their sins,' John xv. 22; but when Christ had once poken, all excuse was taken away; they could not then say they knew not the will of God; and this is the reason of that speech of the apostle, 'Now you are in the light, walk as children of light,' Eph. v. 8. 'And this is the condemnation, that men hate light (not that men for want of light stumble, but), that men love darkness more than light,' John iii. 19. It is not the sin itself, but the love and liking of sin which aggravates men's wickedness, whenas the malice and poison of their hearts rebel against the discovery of God's good pleasure in Christ.

Negative infidelity is a lesser sin than disobedience to the gospel. No people out of the church are capable of this sin; for how can they sin by infidelity and unthankfulness for the gospel that never had it? And therefore negative infidelity is, as it were, no sin in comparison, 'If I had not come among them, they had had no sin,' saith Christ, John xv. 22. Negative I call that, whenas men believe not, having no means, as infidels and heathens, &c. And therefore as they sin without the gospel, so they shall be damned without the gospel. The rule of their damnation shall be the law of nature written in their hearts; for this is an undoubted truth, *no man ever lived answerable to his rule;* and therefore God hath just ground of damnation to any man, even from this, that he hath not lived answerable to the rule of his own conscience. So that we need not fly to reprobation, &c.

Reason 3. Again, another aggravation of sins against the gospel is, *that they sin against the better covenant.* The first covenant was, *Do this and live*, against which we all sinned, and *were under the curse.* But now we are under a more gracious covenant, *a covenant of mercy*, 'Believe in the Lord Jesus Christ and we shall be saved.' Therefore sin now must needs be more heinous; for if we sin against the gospel, either by presumption or despair, or else by profaneness, professing the gospel but denying the power of it, &c., 2 Tim. iii. 5, there is no remedy left for us. If a man sin against the law, against moral honesty and civil righteousness, there is a remedy in the gospel for him; but when a man sins against the sweet love and goodness of God, in rejecting the gospel of his dear Son, mercy itself shall not save such an one. That must needs be a strange sin that makes a man worse than a Sodomite, yet we read it 'shall be easier for Sodom and Gomorrah in that day,' Mat. x. 15, than for those that hear the gospel, the blessed allurements and invitations to believe, and to lead an holy life answerable to our faith and calling, and yet live in sins against conscience, despising the precious blood of Christ.

Herod was a wretched man, yet notwithstanding it was said, he added this to all, 'he put John in prison, a preacher of the gospel,' Luke ii. 20. Sins against the gospel in a loose malignant professor, are many times worse than all the rest. Oh therefore take heed of sinning against the favour and goodness of God; for this will confound us at the day of judgment, when we shall think, What! was so great mercy offered me, and did I slight it in this manner? Have I lost the favour of God, eternal life, and the glorious company of the saints in heaven, for a base pleasure of sin for a season? to gratify a brutish lust? Have I lost Christ and all the good by him for ever, only to satisfy my sinful disposition? to please a carnal friend? &c. Oh, how will this lie heavy upon the soul another day! We shall not need accusers. Our own hearts shall justify the sentence of God against us, be it never so sharp, that we have refused mercy, so often tendered to us in the blood of Christ. Mark what St Paul saith, 'The Lord Jesus shall be revealed from heaven in flaming fire, taking vengeance upon those that know not God, and obey not his glorious gospel,' 2 Thess. i. 7, 8. He saith not only on those that are swearers and profane persons, but ignorant sots that care not to know God, though they be not open sinners. He saith not, those that persecute the gospel or oppose it, shall be punished with eternal destruction from the presence of God, which is true; but those that sin in a less degree, 'such as obey not the gospel, 2 Thess. i. 8; that value not this inestimable jewel; that sell not all to buy this pearl, Mat. xiii. 46; unto whom all the world is not dross and dung, Philip. iii. 8, in respect of the glorious gospel of Christ Jesus. How shall they escape 'which neglect so great salvation?' Heb. ii. 3.

Oh, say some, this concerns not me, I thank God there is mercy in Christ, and I hope for pardon, &c. Beloved, here is the bane of men's souls, they will be their own carvers, and take of the gospel what they list. Oh, so much of Christ as concerns their own good they will have; so much as concerns their pleasure and profit; so much as they may have, and be proud too, and be devilish and evil in their life and conversation too. This they allow of. And it is pity he should live *that regards not Christ* in justification. But so much as concerns mortification and self-denial, as crosses them in their sinful courses, this they are strangers to. But, we must know, the gospel doth not only bring salvation, but it teacheth a man 'to deny ungodliness and worldly lusts,' Titus ii. 12; to put off himself, his whole self, that he might have no judgment, nor no affection contrary to God.

To make this more plainly appear, take these few instances.

Instance 1. The very first lesson which the gospel enjoineth, is to 'cut off our right hand, and pull out our right eye,' that is, to deny ourselves in those sins which are most useful and gainful to us. Now when this is pressed in particular, to some that live in their secret beloved sins, presently they begin to hate this blessed truth, and the ministry thereof. They know so much as will damn them, but so much, as without the which they cannot be saved, that they oppose. Contenting themselves with a bare form and outside of religion, they come to church, and take their books, and read, and hear, and receive the sacrament, &c., and in these outward performances they rest. Alas, beloved, what are these? I tell you, all the privileges of the gospel do but aggravate thy damnation, if thou are not better by them; for as they are in themselves invaluable privileges, and even ravish the heart of a true child of God; so when they are not entertained to purpose, they make our sin the more heinous. Every man is willing to accept of Christ, but it must be upon their own terms; and what are those? So they may enjoy their worldly delights; so they may increase their estates by such unlawful means, and not be crossed. So long they are content that Christ and the gospel shall be theirs; but otherwise, if they cannot enjoy Christ upon their own terms, that is, if they cannot go to heaven and to hell too, they will rather regard their own profits and pleasures, than regard Christ. Oh, how do these poor wretches delude their own souls! Beloved, the embracing and obeying the gospel is a spiritual marriage betwixt Christ and the believer. Now, you know in marriage the will is given up to the husband; the wife is no more her own, but at his disposing. So when once we are truly united unto Christ, we take him for better for worse. We must suffer with him, yea, live and die with him, and esteem him above all; we must take Christ upon his own terms, or else he will not be had. If we love not 'him above father and mother (yea and life itself), we are not worthy of him,' Mat. x. 37; and therefore all that do not thus obey the gospel are rebels, and shall have the reward of rebels if they repent not in time. Were it not a comely thing, think you, for a company of traitors that had this condition propounded to them, if you will come in and live as good subjects you shall have a pardon, for them to go on presumptuously in their rebellion still, and think to have favour when they please? Would not a sharp execution be the just desert of such persons?

Instance 2. Again, Christ propounds pardon and forgiveness of sins upon this condition, that we will come in and live as wives* and as obedient subjects to his blessed Spirit, and not in swearing, filthiness, and other abominable courses, of which the Scripture saith, 'such shall never inherit the kingdom of heaven,' 1 Cor. vi. 9; and yet notwithstanding, Satan hath so bewitched many poor wretches, that they think their case is good, and it shall go well with them, be their lives never so loose and opposite to the ways of God. They bless themselves when God doth not bless them, but rather curse them to their faces. The devil himself is likely to be saved as soon as such graceless persons as these, without repentance. No, no; if ever they expect a pardon, they must live as subjects; if they frame not themselves to be guided by Christ, and come under his government, to be ruled according to his will, they have nothing to do with mercy and salvation: 'those mine enemies, that will not have me rule over them, bring them hither, and slay them before me,' &c., Luke xix. 27. We mock Christ if we will not suffer him to rule us.

Obj. But I cannot obey the gospel of myself.

Ans. It is true we cannot, no more than we can obey the law; nay, it is harder to obey the gospel than to obey the law in a man's own strength; for there are the seeds of the law in our nature, but there are none of the gospel. That is merely† supernatural. The promises are above nature to apprehend them; therefore a supernatural strength is required to plant the excellent grace of faith in our hearts. But though we be as unable to believe and obey the gospel as the law, yet here is the difference; together with the unfolding of our miseries by the gospel, the Spirit of God goes along to sustain us. The law finds us dead, and gives us no strength, but leaves a man cursed still; the gospel likewise finds us dead, but it leaves us not so, and therefore it is called 'the ministry of the Spirit,' Gal. iii. 5. 'Received you the Spirit by the law, or by the gospel?' Gal. iii. 2. God's blessed Spirit goes together with the sweet message of salvation and eternal life, and this Spirit doth not only open our understandings, but incline and bend our wills and affections to embrace the truth that is offered. Seeing, therefore, the Spirit which accompanieth the gospel is mighty and powerful in operation, let none pretend impossibility. For though they find not the sweet blaze of the Spirit at the first or second hearing, yet let them still attend upon grace, 'waiting at wisdom's gate,' Prov. viii. 34, and the angel will come at length and stir the waters. God will make the means effectual first or last, to those that in truth of heart seek unto him; for the gospel is the chariot of the Spirit, and the golden conduit through which the Spirit runs, and is conveyed to us. Therefore if thou wouldst not disobey the gospel, withstand not the Spirit of God working by the same.

How the Spirit works with the gospel. Now the Spirit works with the gospel by degrees. 1. It bringeth some to be willing to hear the gospel, who yet presently neglect and disregard the same. 2. Others are more obedient for a time, 'as the stony ground,' Mat. xiii. 5, but because they

* That is, as 'submissive.' See page 390, line 7 from bottom.—G.

† That is, 'wholly.'—G.

opened not their hearts to the working of the Spirit only, but will be ruled partly by carnal wisdom, and partly by the Spirit, it leaves them at last altogether. 3. But some there are who give up themselves wholly to the government of Christ, to be ruled in all things by his blessed Spirit, highly esteeming the treasures of heaven, and comforts of a better life, above all the fading outward felicities which this world can afford; who would not gain any earthly thing, hurt their consciences, or once defile themselves with unfruitful works of darkness; fearing lest they should in anything dishonour Christ, or grieve his good Spirit; and to such only hath the gospel come in power.

Therefore, I beseech you, seriously consider of this truth. *If you would not disobey the gospel, disobey not the Spirit accompanying the same;* deal faithfully with your own souls. Which of you all hath not some time or other had his heart warmed with the sweet motions of God's Spirit? Oh, do not resist these holy stirrings within you; give way to the motions of the blessed Spirit of God; second them with holy resolutions to practise the same; let them sink deep into your hearts, root them there, and never give over the holy meditation of them, till you make them your own, till you come to see grace and the state of Christianity, to be the most amiable and excellent thing in the world, and sin and carnal courses to be the most accursed thing in the world, worse than any misery, than any beggary, torment, or disgrace whatsoever. Beloved, till we have our spirits wrought upon to this high esteem of good things, and to a base undervaluing of all things else, we shall rebel against Christ first or last; for until such time as the heart of man is overpowered with grace, he cannot but disobey the gospel, either by shutting it out altogether, or by making an evil use of what he knoweth, thereby turning the 'grace of God into wantonness,' Jude 4, or else by revolting from the truth received altogether. When times of temptation come, unsound Christians will do one of these three, either despise, refuse, or revolt from the truth. Therefore I beseech you, let your hearts be cast into the mould and fashion of the gospel of Christ, let it be soundly bottomed and engrafted in you, that so you may grow more and more obedient to the truth revealed, and so your end shall not be theirs here, *which obey not the gospel of Jesus Christ.*

Quest. But how may I come to obey the gospel?

Ans. Beg earnestly of God, in the use of the means (else prayer is but a tempting of God), *that thy soul may be convinced what evil is in thee, and what evil is towards thee, unless thou repent.* Labour for sound conviction; for you shall not need to stir up a man that is condemned to seek out for a pardon, or a man that feels the smart of his wound to get balm to cure it. Oh, no; when our hearts are once truly humbled and pierced with a sight of our sins, then Christ will be Christ indeed unto us. Now mercy is sweet at such a time; anything for a Saviour then, and not before. Therefore labour every day to see more and more into the venomous and filthy nature of sin; make it as odious to thy soul as possibly thou canst; hearken to the voice of conscience; give it full scope to speak what it can, that so thou mayest fly to Christ. Consider how God plagueth us in this world for sin; how it fills us with fears and horrors, causing our consciences to torment us, and fly in our faces; consider what threatenings are denounced against sin and sinners, for the time to come; consider the fearful judgments of God upon others for sin, how it cast Adam out of paradise, the angels out of heaven, being so offensive to God, that it could no otherwise be expiated than by the death and bloodshedding of the Lord Jesus. I beseech you, let your hearts dwell upon these things, and consider with yourselves how bitter you have found it to offend God, though now it be a time of mercy.

2. Secondly, consider how the gospel lays open Christ unto us; 'This is his commandment, that we believe in the Lord Jesus,' 1 John iii. 23. He that commands us to do no murder, not to steal, &c., commands us likewise to believe in Christ. He commands us to love our own souls so much, as to take the remedy which may cure them; so that now it is our duty to be good to our poor souls; and we offend God if we be not merciful to our own souls. Oh! what a favour is this, that God should lay a charge upon me not to reject my own mercy, as it is in Jonah, 'They who follow lying vanities forsake their own mercies,' Jonah ii. 8. If I do not love my own soul, and accept of mercy offered, 'I make God a liar,' 1 John v. 10, and offend his majesty.

3. Again, consider how God allures those that might except against mercy. Alas, I am laden with sin, will some poor soul say! Why! 'Come unto me, all you that are heavy laden, and I will ease you,' Mat. xi. 28. But I have offended God, I have broken my peace, &c., yet 'I beseech you, be reconciled to God,' 2 Cor. v. 20; though you have offended, yet there is hope. Do but consider how ready God is to help you, how continual his mercies are, and how he stretcheth out his hands to receive us.

4. Consider further, what a sweet regiment* it is to be under Christ, as a king, and as an husband. Will he not provide for his own family, for his own subjects? Beloved, it is not mere dominion that Christ stands upon; he aims at a fatherly and husband-like sovereignty, for the good of his children and spouse. It is their welfare he looks after. Therefore, I beseech you, be in love with the government of Jesus Christ, his blessed Spirit. Oh! it is a sweet regiment!* For the Spirit of God leads us quietly, enlightening our understandings upon judicious grounds what to do, by strength of reason; altering our natures, and bettering us every way, both in our inward and outward man. It never leaves teaching and guiding of us till it hath brought us to heaven and happiness.

To conclude, mark what the apostle saith here, 'What shall be the end of those that obey not the gospel?' He cares not what they know. Many say, we have heard the word, and we have received the sacrament, &c. It is no matter for that, how stands the bent of your souls? what hath your obedience been? This is that God looks after. Every man can talk of religion, but where is the practice? A little obedience is worth all the discourse and contemplation in the world; for that serves but to justify God's damning of us, if we live not answerably. Value not yourselves, therefore, by your outward profession, neither judge of your estate in grace, by the knowledge of good things. Nothing but the power of godliness, expressed in our lives, will yield real comfort in the day of trial.

Our obedience must be free. And we should labour that our obedience be 'free and cheerful,' Ps. cx. 3; always upon the wing, as we say, for that is evangelical obedience. God's people under the gospel are a voluntary, ready people, 'zealous of good works,' Tit. ii. 14. Oh! beloved, did we but consider what God hath done for us here, and what he means to do for us in another world, how would our hearts be enlarged in duty to his majesty! Did we but consider of his inestimable love in the Lord Christ, pardoning such wretches as we are, and not only so, but accepting our service and us to life everlasting; taking us from the lowest misery to the highest happiness; from the lowest hell to the highest heaven; of traitors

* That is, 'government.'—C.

to be sons; of slaves to be heirs of the kingdom, &c. Oh! did we but seriously consider and believe these things, how would they warm our hearts, and make us pliable and constant to every good work and way!

The apostle having tasted the sweet favour of God in Christ, might well use it as a motive to quicken others. 'I beseech you by the tender mercies of Christ,' &c., Rom. xii. 1. He knew this was a powerful argument, and if that wrought not upon men's hearts, nothing would.

Let our obedience, therefore, be cheerful; for now we are not in the oldness of the letter. We have not a legal covenant since Christ's coming, but we serve God 'in the newness of the Spirit,' Rom. vii. 6; that is, considering that the Spirit is given in more plenty since his ascension, we should be more spiritual and heavenly in our service of God. Considering that our Head is already entered into that high and holy place, and we, ere long, shall be present with him, having but a spot of time to pass here below, how ready and zealous should we be in obedience to God's will! and not suffer a heavy lumpishness and deadness of spirit to seize upon us in holy performances. But I hasten to the second amplification.

THE DIFFICULTY OF SALVATION.

SERMON III.

If the righteous scarcely be saved, where shall the wicked and ungodly appear? —1 Pet. IV. 18.

What is meant here by righteousness, to wit, a man endued with evangelical righteousness. By 'righteous' here, is meant that evangelical righteousness which we have in the state of the gospel, namely, the righteousness of Christ imputed to us; for Christ himself being ours, his obedience and all that he hath becomes ours also; and whosoever partaketh of this righteousness which is by faith, hath also a righteousness of sanctification accompanying the same, wrought in his soul by the Spirit of God, whereby his sinful nature is changed and made holy; for 'if any man be in Christ, he is a new creature,' 2 Cor. v. 17. The same Spirit that assures us of our interest in Christ, purifies and cleanseth our hearts, and worketh a new life in us, opposite to our life in the first Adam; from whence flows new works of holiness and obedience throughout our whole conversation. There must be an inward inherent righteousness, before there can be any works of righteousness. An instrument must be set in tune before it will make music; so the Spirit of God must first work a holy frame and disposition of heart in us, before we can bring forth any fruits of holiness in our lives. For we commend not the works of grace as we do the works of art, but refer them to the worker. All that flows from the Spirit of righteousness are works of righteousness. When the soul submits itself to the spirit, and the body to the soul, then things come off kindly. Take a man that is righteous by the Spirit of God: he is righteous in all relations; he gives every one his due; he gives God his due; spiritual worship is set up in his heart above all; he gives Christ his due by affiance in him; he gives the holy angels their due, by considering he is always in their presence, that their eye is upon him in every action he doth, and every duty he performs; the poor have their due from him; those that are in authority have their due. If he be under any, he gives them reverence and obedience, &c.; 'he will owe nothing to any man but love,' Rom. xiii. 8; he is righteous in all his conversation; he is a vessel prepared for every good work. I deny not but he may err in some particular; that is nothing to the purpose. I speak of a man as he is in the disposition and bent of his heart to God and goodness, and so there is a thread of a righteous course, that runs along through his whole conversation. The constant tenure of his life is righteous. He hungers and thirsts after righteousness, and labours to be more and more righteous still, every way, both in justification, that he may have a clearer evidence of that, as also in sanctification, that he may have more of the 'new creature' formed in him, that so he may serve God better and better all his days. Now, if this man shall *scarcely be saved*, where shall the sinner and ungodly appear? Where you have two branches.

1. *The righteous shall scarcely be saved.*

2. *The terrible end of sinners and ungodly*, where shall they appear? &c.

Now in that the righteous man thus described by me *shall scarcely be saved*, consider two things.

1. *That the righteous shall be saved.*

2. *That they shall scarcely be saved.*

The righteous are saved. What do I say? the righteous *shall be saved?* He is saved already. 'This day is salvation come to thine house,' saith Christ to Zaccheus, Luke xix. 9. 'We are saved by faith, and are now set in heavenly places together with him,' Eph. ii. 6. We have a title and interest to happiness already. There remains only a passage to the crown by good works. We do not, as the papists do, work to merit that we have not, but we do that we do in thankfulness for what we have. Because we know we are in the state of salvation; therefore we will shew our thankfulness to God in the course of our lives.

How can we miss of salvation when we are saved already? Christ our head being in heaven, will draw his body after him. What should hinder us? The world? Alas! * we have that *faith* in us, 'which overcometh the world,' 1 John v. 4. As for the flesh, you know what the apostle saith, 'We are not under the law, but under grace,' Rom. vi. 14. The spirit in us always lusteth against the flesh, and subdues it by little and little; neither can Satan nor the gates of hell prevail against us; for the grace we have is stronger than all enemies against us.

God the Father is our Father in Christ, and his love and gifts are without repentance, Rom. xi. 29. When once we are in the state of salvation, 'he will preserve us by faith to salvation,' 1 Pet. i. 5; and we are knit to God the Son, who will lose none of his members. The marriage with Christ is an everlasting union; whom he loves, 'he loves to the end,' John xiii. 1. As for God the Holy Ghost, saith Christ, 'I will send the Comforter, and he shall be with you to the end,' John vi. 14, 16. The blessed Spirit of God never departs where he once takes up his lodging. There is no question, therefore, of the salvation of the righteous; they are, as it were, saved already.

Use. Let this teach us thus much, that in all the changes and alterations which the faith of man is subject unto, he is sure of one thing: all the troubles, and all the enemies of the world shall not hinder his salvation. 'If it be possible the elect should be deceived,' Mat. xxiv. 24; but it is not possible. O what a comfort is this, that in the midst of all the oppositions and plottings of men and devils, yet notwithstanding, somewhat we have, that is not in the power of any enemy to take from us, nor in our own power to lose, namely, *our salvation.* Set this against any evil whatsoever, and it swallows up all. Put case a man were subject to an hundred deaths, one after another, what are all these to salvation? Put case a man were in such grief, that he wept tears of blood; alas! in the day of salvation all tears shall

* This is one of many instances, in Sibbes, of a peculiar use of the interjection 'Alas!' See also last line of this page.—G.

be wiped from his eyes. Set this, *I shall be saved*, against any misery you can imagine, and it will unspeakably comfort and revive the soul beyond all.

Obj. But it is here said, he *shall scarcely be saved*.

Ans. This is not a word of doubt, but of difficulty. It is not a word of doubt of the event, whether he shall be saved or no—there is no doubt at all of that—but it is a word of difficulty in regard of the way and passage thither. So it is here taken, which leads me to a second point, that *the way to come to salvation is full of difficulties*.

1. Because there is much ado to get Lot out of Sodom, to get Israel out of Egypt. It is no easy matter to get a man out of the state of corruption. O the sweetness of sin to an unregenerate man! O how it cuts his very heart to think what pleasures and what profits, and what friends, and what esteem amongst men he must part withal! What ado is there to pull him out of the kingdom of Satan, wherein the *strong man*, Luke xi. 21, held him before!

2. Again, it is hard in regard of the sin that continually cleaves to them in this world, which doth, as it were, shackle them, and compass them about in all their performances. 'They would do well, but sin is at hand,' Rom. vii. 21, ready to hinder and stop them in good courses; so that they cannot serve God with such cheerfulness and readiness as they desire to do. Every good work they do, it is, as it were, pulled out of the fire; they cannot pray, but the flesh resists; they cannot suffer, but the flesh draws back. In all their doing and suffering they carry an enemy in their own bosoms that hinders them. Beloved, this [is] no small affliction to God's people. How did this humble Paul, when no other affliction lay upon him! 'O wretched man that I am, who shall deliver me from this body of death?' Rom. vii. 24. It was more troublesome to him than all his irons and pressures whatsoever.

3. Besides, it is a hard matter in regard of Satan; for he is a great enemy to the peace of God's children. When they are once pulled out of his kingdom, he sends floods of reproaches and persecutions after them, and presently sends hue and cry, as Pharaoh after the Israelites. Oh, how it spites him! What! shall a piece of dust and clay be so near God, when I am tumbled out of heaven myself! Though I cannot hinder him from salvation, I will hinder his peace and joy; he shall not have heaven upon earth.* I will make him walk as uncomfortably as I can. Thus the devil, as he is a malignant creature, full of envy against God's poor saints, so he is a bitter enemy of the peace and comfort which they enjoy; and therefore troubles them with many temptations from himself and his instruments, to interrupt their peace, and make the hearts of God's people sad all he can.

4. Then, by reason of great discouragements and ill-usage which they find in the world from wicked men, who are the devil's pipes, led with his spirit to vex and trouble the meek of the earth; for, though they think not of it, Satan is in their devilish natures; he joins and goes along with their spirits in hating and opposing the saints of God; for, indeed, what hurt could they do but by his instigation? How are good men despised in the world! How are they made the only butt† to shoot at! Alas! beloved, we should rather encourage men in the ways of holiness. We see the number of such as truly fear God is but small, soon reckoned up. They are but as grapes after the vintage, or a few berries after the shaking; one of a city, two of a tribe, Micah vii. 1, Jer. iii. 14. They have little encouragements from any, but discouragements on all sides.

* 'Heaven upon earth' is the title of one of Thomas Brooks's most Sibbes-like works.—G

† That is, 'a mark.'—G.

5. Besides this, scandal makes it a hard matter to be saved; to see evil courses and evil persons flourish and countenanced in the world. Oh, it goes to the heart of God's people, and makes them stagger at God's providence. It is a bitter temptation, and shakes the faith of holy men, as we see, Ps. lxxiii., Jer. xii. 1, 2. Again, it makes the heart of a good Christian bleed within him, to see scandals arise from professors of the gospel, when they are not so watchful as they should be, but bring a reproach upon religion by their licentious lives.

Yea, God's children suffer much for their friends, whose wicked courses are laid to their charge, and sometimes even by their friends; for whilst they live here, the best of all are subject to some weakness or other, which causeth even those that are our encouragers, through jealousy or corruption, one way or another, to dishearten and trouble us in the way to heaven.

6. This, likewise, makes the way difficult; we are too apt to offend God daily, giving him just cause to withdraw his Spirit of comfort from us, which makes us go mourning all the day long; wanting those sweet refreshments of spiritual joy and peace we had before. The more comfort God's child hath in communion with God, the more he is grieved when he wants it. When Christ wanted the sweet solace of his Father upon the cross, how did it trouble him! 'My God, my God, why hast thou forsaken me?' Mat. xxvii. 46. How did he sweat water and blood in the garden, Luke xxii. 44, when he felt but a little while his Father's displeasure for sin! Thus is it with all God's children; they are of Christ's mind in their spiritual desertions.

And when they have gotten a little grace, how difficult is it to keep it! to keep ourselves in the sense of God's love! to manage our Christian state aright! to walk worthy of the gospel, that God may still do us good, and delight to be present with us! What a great difficulty is it to be always striving against the stream, and when we are cast back to get forward still, and not be discouraged till we come to the haven! None comes to heaven but they know how they come there.

Why God will have the righteous with such difficulty saved. Now, God will have it thus to sweeten heaven unto us. After a conflicting life peace is welcome; heaven is heaven indeed after trouble. We can relish it then. Because God will discard hypocrites in this life, who take up so much of religion as stands with their ease and credit in the world, avoiding every difficulty which accompanies godliness, but, so they may swim two ways at once, go on in their lusts still and be religious withal. This they approve of. Therefore, God will have it a hard matter to be saved, to frustrate the vain hopes of such wretches. Alas! it is an easy matter to be an hypocrite, but not to live godly.

Use. If the righteous be saved with much ado, then never enter upon the profession of religion with vain hopes of ease and pleasure, that it shall be thus and thus with thee, &c. Herein thou dost but delude thy own soul, for it will prove otherwise. Forecast, therefore, what will fall, and get provision of grace beforehand to sustain thee. As, if a man were to go a dangerous journey, he provides himself of weapons and cordials, and all the encouragements he can, lest he should faint in the way; whereas he that walks for his pleasure provides nothing. He cares not for his weapon or his cloak, because if a storm comes he can run under shelter or into a house, &c. He that makes religion a recreation can walk a turn or two for his pleasure, and when any difficulty arises can retire and draw in his horns again. An hypocrite hath his reservations and politic ends, and therefore what needs he any great provision to support him, when he knows how to wind out of trouble well enough, rather than to stand courageously to anything. But a true Christian, that makes it the main work of his life to please God, arms himself for the worst that can befall him, and will be saved through thick or thin, smooth or rough, whatsoever comes on it. So God will save his soul, he cares not, but rejoiceth, with Paul, if by any means he can attain the resurrection of the dead, Phil. iii. 11, by any means, it is no matter what. Let fire and fagot meet with him, yet he is resolved not to retire for any trouble or persecution whatsoever that stands between him and happiness. He is purposely armed to break through every opposition to the best things, and whatever may separate his soul from the favour of God. I beseech you, beloved, think of these things, and let it be your wisdom to make the way to heaven as easy as you can. To this end,

1. *Beg the Spirit of Christ.* You know the Holy Spirit is full of life and strength; it is a Spirit of light and comfort and whatsover is good. The Spirit of God is like the wind; as it is subtle in operation and invisible, so it is strong and mighty, it bears all before it. Oh! therefore, get this blessed Spirit to enlighten thee, to quicken thee, to support thee, &c., and it will carry thy soul courageously along, above all oppositions and discouragements whatsoever in the way to happiness.

2. *Get likewise the particular graces of the Spirit*, which will much cheer thee in thy Christian course. Above all, labour for a spirit of humility. An humble man is fit to do or suffer anything. A proud man is like a gouty hand, or a swelled arm, unfit for any Christian performance; he is not in a state to do good; but an humble man is thankful that God will honour him so far as to let him suffer for the cause of Christ. He is wondrous empty and vile in his own eyes, and admires* why God should reserve such infinite matters for so base a worm as he is.

When Christ would have us take his yoke upon us, he advises us 'to learn of him to be meek and lowly,' &c., Mat. xi. 29. Some might say, This yoke is heavy, it will pinch me and gall me. No, saith our Saviour, it shall be very light and easy. But how shall I get it to be so? Why! get but an humble and meek spirit, and that will bring rest to your souls.

3. Again, *labour for a spirit of love.* 'Love is strong as death,' Cant. viii. 6; it will carry us through all. The love of Christ in the martyrs, when the fire was kindled about them, made them despise all torments whatsoever. This will warm our hearts and make us go cheerfully to work. Let but a spirit of love be kindled in God's child, and it is no matter what he suffers; cast him into the fire, cast him into the dungeon, into prison, whatsoever it be, he hath that kindled in his heart, which will make him digest anything. We see the disciples, when they had the Spirit of Christ within them to warm their hearts, what cared they for whipping, or stocks, &c.? You see even base, carnal love will make a man endure poverty, disgrace, what not! and shall not this fire that comes from heaven, when it is once kindled in our hearts, prevail much more? What will make our passage to heaven sweet if this will not? Nothing is grievous to a person that loves.

4. *Exercise your hope likewise.*. Set before your eyes the crown and kingdom of heaven; those admirable things contained in the word of God, which no tongue can express. Let hope feed upon these delicates; cast anchor in heaven, and see if it will not make thee go on cheerfully in a Christian course.

Faith will *overcome the world;* all the snares of prosperity that would hinder us on the right hand. Faith, it presents things of a higher nature to the soul; better than they. Faith likewise overcomes temptations on the

* That is, 'wonders.'—G.

left hand; all terrors and discomforts whatsoever. It considers these are nothing to 'the terror of the Lord,' 2 Cor. v. 11. Therefore 'faith is called the evidence of things not seen,' Heb. xi. 1, because it presents things that are absent as present to the soul. If life and happiness be once truly presented to our hearts, what can all the world do to hinder our passage thither?

5. Lastly, we should much endeavour *the mortification of our lusts;* for what is it that makes the way to heaven irksome unto us? Is it not this corrupt and proud flesh of ours, which will endure nothing, no, not the weight of a straw, but is all for ease and quiet, &c.? It is not duty which makes our way difficult, 'for it was meat and drink to Christ, to do the will of his Father,' John iv. 34.

Quest. Why is it not so with us?

Ans. Because he was born without sin. When Satan came he found nothing of his own in him; but when he solicits us, he finds a correspondency betwixt our corrupt hearts and himself, whereby having intelligence what we haunt, and what we love, he will be sure to molest us. The less we have of the works of Satan in us, the less will be our trouble; and the more we do the will of God, and strive against our corruptions, the more will be our comfort. This will make holy duties delightful to us; but if we favour and cherish corruption, it will make religion harsh. For the ways of wisdom are ways of pleasure in themselves, and to the regenerate, &c. I come now to the second clause.

'*Where shall the sinner and ungodly appear?*'

What he means by sinner. By sinner he means him that makes a trade of sin. As we say, a man is of such a trade, because he is daily at work of it, and lives by it, so a man is a trader in sin, that lives in corrupt courses. For it is not one act that denominates a sinner, but the constant practice of his life.

Now this question, Where shall the ungodly appear? implies a strong denial, He shall be able to appear nowhere; especially in these three times.

1. *In the day of public calamity*, when God's judgments are abroad in the world. The wicked are as chaff before the wind, as wax before the sun, as stubble before the fire. When God comes to deal with a company of graceless wretches, how will he consume and scatter them, and sweep them away as dung from the face of the earth! he will universally make a riddance of them at once. Where shall a Nabal stand when judgment comes upon him? 1 Sam. xxv. 37. Alas! his heart is become a stone. Where shall Belshazzar appear when he sees the handwriting upon the wall? Dan. v. Oh how the wicked tremble and quake when God comes to judge them in this world, though they were a terror to others before!

2. But where shall they stand *in the hour of death?* when the world can hold them no longer; when friends shall forsake them; when God will not receive them; when hell is ready to devour them, &c.

3. And lastly, where shall the sinner appear *at the day of judgment*, that great and terrible day of account, when they shall see all the world in a combustion round about them, and the Lord Jesus coming in flaming fire, 'with his mighty angels, to take vengeance on such as obey not the gospel?' 2 Thess. i. 8. How will they then call for 'the mountains to cover them, and the hills to fall upon them, to hide them from the face of him that sitteth on the throne, and from the wrath of the Lamb,' &c., Rev. vi. 16. Beloved, I beseech you, let the meditation of these things sink deep into your hearts, dwell upon them, remember that they are matters which nearly concern your soul, and no vain words, touching you and your welfare.

THE SAINT'S HIDING-PLACE IN THE EVIL DAY.*

SERMON IV.

Wherefore let them that suffer according to the will of God commit their souls to him in well-doing, as to a faithful Creator.—1 Pet. IV. 19.

Though divinity be clear in other differences from carnal or natural reasons, yet it hath homogeneal reasons and grounds of its own, whence come inferences as natural as for the tree to bear fruit, or the sun to shine; so upon the former divine grounds (for it is a matter of suffering wherein we must have pure divinity to support our souls), the apostle comes to bring a spiritual inference suitable to the same in the words read unto you. *Wherefore*, concluding all to be true that was said before, *let them that suffer*, &c. Wherein consider, 1. That the state and condition of God's children is to *suffer*. 2. The dispensation of that *suffering*, they suffer not at all adventures, but *according to the will of God*. 3. Their duty in this estate, namely, *to commit the keeping of their souls to God*.

In the *duty* we have these particulars comprehended:—1. An action, *to commit*. 2. An object, what we must commit, *the soul*. 3. The person to whom, *to God*. 4. The manner, *in well-doing*. Lastly. The reason which should move us hereunto, implied in these words, *as unto a faithful Creator*. Whatsoever may support the doubting of a godly man in any trouble, and enforce upon him this duty of committing his soul to God, is briefly comprised in this, that God stands in that near relation of a Creator, yea, of a faithful Creator, to us. This is the scope of the words.

Obs. 1. *That the state of God's children is to suffer*, yea, to suffer *of God;* for sometimes he seems to be an enemy to his dearest servants, as unto Job. But chiefly they are in a militant estate and condition here.

1. *Why God's children must suffer here.* Because they live among those that they cannot but suffer from, wheresoever they live. Suppose they live among Christians, yet there are many Christians in name that are not so in deed. There hath been secret underminers in all ages; and what else may they look for but suffering from these? All that ever truly feared God and

* This title of the present sermon, which is taken from the reprint in the 'Saint's Cordials,' is preferred, to that placed over it in the original volume, viz., 'The Saints Safety in Evil Times,' inasmuch as at page 297, *seq.*, other two bear this heading.—G.

made conscience of their ways have found afflictions among false brethren. It was never heard of that a sheep should pursue a wolf.

2. They must suffer also in regard of themselves; for the truth is, the best of us all have many lusts to be subdued, and a great deal of corruption to be purged out, before we can come to heaven, that pure and holy place into which no unclean thing can enter, Rev. xxi. 27. Though a garden be never so fruitful, yet after a shower it will need weeding. So, after long peace, the church of God gathers soil, and needs cleansing.

Obj. But some carnal wretch will say, I thank God I never suffered in my life, but have enjoyed peace and prosperity, and my heart's content in everything.

Ans. In the best estate there will be suffering one way or other. Then, suspect thyself to be in a bad estate, for every true Christian suffers in one kind or other, either from without or within. Sometimes God's children are troubled more with corruption than with affliction; at other times their peace is troubled both with corruption within and with affliction without; at the best, they have sufferings of sympathy. Shall the members of Christ suffer in other countries, and we profess ourselves to be living members, and yet not sympathise with them? We must be conformable to our Head before we can come to heaven. But the dispensation of our suffering is according to the will of God, where note two things.

1. *That it is God's will we should suffer.*

2. *When we suffer we suffer according to his will.*

To pass briefly over these, as not being the thing I aim at,

God's will concerning our suffering is permissive in respect of those that do us harm; but in regard of our patient enduring injuries, it is his approving and commanding will. We are enjoined to suffer, and they are permitted to wrong us.

Obj. It seems, then, there is some excuse for those that persecute the saints. They do but *according to God's will;* and if it be so, who dares speak against them?

Ans. It is not God's commanding will, but his suffering will. He useth their malice for his own ends. God lets the rein loose upon their necks. As a man is said to set a dog upon another when he unlooseth his chain, so God is said to command them when he lets them loose to do mischief. They are full of malice themselves, which God useth as physicians do their poison to cure poison. God and they go two contrary ways, as a man in a ship walks one way, but is carried another. In the death of Christ the will of Judas and the rest went one way, and God's will another. So, in all our sufferings, when God useth wicked men, their will is destructive and hostile, but God's will is clean otherwise, aiming at the good of his people in all this. Nebuchadnezzar did the will of God in *carrying the people captive.* However, he thought not so, Isa. x. 7. Every sinful wretch that offers violence to the poor saints, imagine they do God good service in it, whenas, indeed, they do but execute the malice and venom of their own hearts. In the highest heavens, as they say in philosophy, the first thing moved is by a violent motion. The sun is carried about the heavens violently against its own proper motion, which inclines to a clean contrary course. So God dealeth with wicked men; he carries them they know not whither. They are set to do mischief, and God useth their sinful dispositions for his own ends, which plainly shews that God is without all fault, and they without all excuse.

Obs. But observe further, *that we never suffer but when God will.* And, beloved, his will is not that we should always suffer, though generally our estate be so in one kind or other. God is *not always chiding*, Ps. ciii. 9, but hath times of breathing and intermission, which he vouchsafes his children for their good. He knows if we had not some respite, some refreshment, we should soon be consumed and brought to nothing. 'The Lord knows whereof we are made, and considers we are but dust,' Ps. ciii. 14. Therefore he saith, 'Though for a season you are in heaviness, yet rejoice,' &c., 1 Pet. i. 6.

And this the Lord doth out of mercy to his poor creatures, that they might not sink before him, but gather strength of grace, and be the better fitted to bear further crosses afterwards. You know, Acts ix. 31, after Saul's conversion, when he was become a Paul, then the church had rest, and increased in the comforts of the Holy Ghost. God gives his people pausing times, some *lucida intervalla* (*a*). Our time of going into trouble is in God's hands; our time of abiding trouble is in God's hands; our time of coming out is in God's hands. As in our callings he preserves our going out and our coming in, so in every trouble that befalls us we come in and tarry there, and go out of the same when he pleaseth. He brings us to the fire as the goldsmith puts his metals and holds them there, till he hath refined them and purged out the dross, and then brings them out again. 'Our times,' as David saith excellently, 'are in thy hands, O Lord,' Ps. xxxi. 15. Beloved, if our times were in our enemies' hands we should never come out. If they were in our own hands we should never stay in trouble, but come out as soon as we come in; nay, we would not come into trouble at all if we could choose. Beloved, everything of a Christian is dear unto God; his health is precious, his blood is precious; especially precious to the Lord is the death of his saints, Ps. cxvi. 15. Do you think, therefore, he will let them suffer without his will? No; he will have a valuable consideration of all those that are malignant persecutors of his people at last. And it is for matters better than life that God lets his children suffer here; for, alas! this life is but a shadow, as it were, nothing. God regards us not as we are in this present world, but as strangers; therefore, he suffers us to sacrifice this life upon better terms than life, or else he would never let us suffer for his truth, and seal it with our dearest blood, as many of the saints have done.

Use. I beseech you, therefore, considering all our sufferings are by the appointment and will of God, let us bring our souls to an holy resignation unto his Majesty, not looking so much to the grievance we are under as to the hand that sent it. We should with one eye consider the thing, with another eye the will of God in the same. When a man considers, I suffer now, but it is by the will of God; he puts me upon it, how cheerfully will such an one commit his soul to the Lord! It is as hard a matter to suffer God's will as to do his will. Passive obedience is as hard as active. In the active we labour that what we do may please God; in the passive we must endeavour that what he doth may please us. Our hearts are as untoward to the one as to the other. Therefore, let us beg of God to bring our wills to the obedience of his blessed will in everything. Would you have a pattern of this? Look upon our blessed Saviour, to whom we must be conformable in obedience if ever we will be conformable in glory. 'Lo, I come,' saith he; 'I am ready to do thy will, O Lord,' Heb. x. 9. What was the whole life of Christ but a doing and a suffering of God's will? 'Behold, it is written in the volume of thy book that I should do thy will,' ver. 7, and here I am ready pressed for it. It should be, therefore, the disposition of all those that are led by the Spirit of Christ, as all must be that hope to reign with him, to be willing to suffer with Christ here, and say with him, Lord, I am here ready to do and suffer whatsoever thou requirest! When once we are brought to this, all the quarrel is ended between God and us.

I come now to that which I chiefly intend, which is the Christian's duty. *Let him commit his soul to God in well-doing.* Wherein observe,

1. The manner *how* he must commit, *in well-doing.*
2. What, *his soul.*
3. To whom, *to God.*
4. The reasons moving, implied in these words, *as unto a faithful Creator.*

Now this *well-doing* must be distinguished into two times.

1. *Before our suffering.* When a son of Belial shall offer violence to a poor saint of God, what a comfort is this, that he suffers in well-doing! Oh, beloved, we should so carry ourselves that none might speak evil justly against us, that none, unless it were wrongfully, might do us hurt. We should be in an estate of well-doing continually in our general and particular callings. We must not go out of our sphere, but serve God in our standings, that if trouble comes it may find us in a way of well-pleasing, either doing works of charity or else the works of our particular calling wherein God hath set us. In all that befalls thee look to this, that thou suffer not as an evil doer, 1 Pet. iv. 15.

2. So likewise *in suffering,* we must commit our souls to God in well-doing in a double regard.

1. *We must carry ourselves* generally *well in all our sufferings.*
2. In particular, *we must do well to them that do us wrong.*

First, I say, *in* affliction our carriage must be generally good in respect of God, by a meek behaviour under his hand, without murmuring against him.

2. In regard of the cause of God, that we betray it not through fear or cowardice, through base aims and intentions, &c., but endeavour to carry it with a good conscience in all things. When we make it clear by managing anything, that we are led with the cause and conscience of our duty, it works mightily upon them that wrong us. (1.) It wins those that are indifferent; and (2.) confounds the obstinate, and stops their mouths. Therefore, let us carry ourselves well, not only before, but in suffering. We may not fight against them with their own weapons, that is, be malicious as they are malicious, and rail as they rail. Beloved, this is as if a man should see another drink poison, and he will drink, too, for company; he is poisoned with malice, and thou, to revenge thyself, wilt be poisoned too. What a preposterous course is this! Ought we not rather to behave ourselves as befits the cause of Christ, as becomes our Christian profession, and as befits him whose children we are?

We should have an eye to God, and an eye to ourselves, and an eye to others, and an eye to the cause in hand; so we shall do well. We must not commit our souls to God in idleness, doing nothing at all, nor yet in evil doing, but in well doing. We must have a care, if we would suffer with comfort, not to study how to avoid suffering by tricks, so to hurt the cause of Christ. This is to avoid suffering, by sin, to leap out of one danger into another. Is not the least evil of sin worse than the greatest evil of punishment? What doth a man get by pleasing men, to displease God? Perhaps a little ease for the present. Alas! what is this to that inexpressible horror and despair which will one day seize upon thy soul eternally for betraying the blessed cause and truth of Christ? How can we expect God should own us another day, when we will not own him in his cause, and his members, to stand for them now? Think on that speech of our Saviour, 'Whosoever shall be ashamed of me, or of my words in this adulterous and sinful generation, of him shall the Son of man be ashamed when he cometh in the glory of his Father,' Mark viii. 38.

Therefore, avoid not any suffering *by sin.* See how blessed St Paul carried himself in this case. 'The Lord,' saith he, 'hath delivered me, and will deliver me,' 2 Tim. iv. 18. From what? from death? No; *from every evil work.* What! will God keep him from evil sufferings? No; for immediately after he was put to death. What then? Why! he will preserve me from every evil work, that is, from every sinful act, which may hurt the cause of Christ, or blemish my profession. This was it Paul chiefly regarded; not whether he will preserve me from death or trouble, I leave that to him; but this I hope and trust to, that he will preserve me from every evil work to his heavenly kingdom. Thus should it be with every Christian in the cause of religion, or in a cause of justice, &c.; for there is not any good cause but it is worth our lives to stand in, if we be called to it. It is necessary we should be just; it is not so necessary we should live (*b*). A Christian's main care is how to do well; and if he can go on in that course, he is a happy man.

Obj. But I cannot do well, but I shall suffer ill.

Ans. Labour, therefore, to carry thyself well in suffering evil, not only in the general, but even in particular, towards those persons that do thee wrong; endeavour to requite their evil with good. There is a great measure of self-denial required to be a Christian, especially in matter of revenge, 'to pray for them that curse us, to do good to them that persecute us,' &c., and so 'heap coals of fire upon our enemies' heads,' Prov. xxv. 22, Rom. xii. 20. How is that? There are—

1. Coals of conversion.
2. Coals of confusion.

How in suffering we heap coals of fire. You know coals do either melt or consume. If they belong to God, we shall heap coals of fire to convert them, and make them better by our holy carriage in suffering. If they be wicked, graceless wretches, we shall heap coals of fire to consume them; for it will aggravate their just damnation when they do ill to those that deserve well of them.

Obj. Some will say, Christianity is a strange condition, that enforceth such things upon men, that are so contrary to nature.

Ans. It is so, indeed, for we must be new-moulded before ever we can come to heaven. We must put off our whole self; and he is gone a great way in religion, that hath brought his heart to this pass. None ever overcame himself in these matters out of religious respects, but he found a good issue at last. It is a sweet evidence of the state of grace, none better, when a man can love his very enemies, and those that have done him most wrong; it is an argument that such a man hath something above nature in him. What is above nature, if this be not, for a man to overcome himself in this sweet appetite of revenge? Revenge is most natural to a man; it is as sugar, as the heathen saith; and for a man to overcome himself in that, it argues the power of grace and godliness in such a one.

As Christianity is an excellent estate, an admirable advancing of a man to a higher condition, so it must not seem strange for those that are Christians to be raised to a higher pitch of soul than other men. See how our

Saviour dealt in this particular, 'Father, forgive them, they know not what they do,' Luke xxiii. 34; and so likewise Stephen, being led by the same Spirit of Christ, desired God 'not to lay this sin to their charge,' Acts vii. 60; and so all the martyrs in the first state of the church, when the blood of Christ was warm, and the remembrance of Christ was fresh, were wont to pray for their enemies, committing their souls to God in well doing.

The excellent victory of suffering. I beseech you let us labour by all means possible to bring our hearts hereunto. If anything overcome, this will do it, *to suffer well.* The church of God is a company of men that gain and overcome by suffering in doing good. Thus the dove overcomes the eagle, the sheep overcomes the wolf, the lamb overcomes the lion, &c. It hath been so from the beginning of the world. Meek Christians, by suffering quietly, have at length overcome those that are malicious, and have gained even their very enemies to the love of the truth. What shall we think, then, of the greatest part of the world, who never think of suffering, which is the first lesson in Christianity, but study their ease and contentment, accounting the blessed martyrs too prodigal of their blood, &c.?

Others there are, who, if once they come to suffer, presently fall to shifting and plotting, how to get forth again by unlawful means; oftentimes making shipwreck of a good conscience, and dishonouring the gospel of God. I beseech you consider these things. Every man would have Christ, and be religious, so long as they may enjoy peace and quietness; but if once trouble or persecution arises, then farewell religion; they cast off their profession then. I wish this were not the case of many seeming Christians in these our days.

But suppose a man carry himself *ill* in *suffering?*

There is not the least promise of comfort in Scripture to such a man, unless he *return*, and seek the Lord by timely repentance; for all encouragement is to *well-doing*. Oh, what a pitiful thing is it for the soul to be in such a state, as that it dares not commit itself to God! A man in evil doing cannot go home to his own conscience for comfort, nor have any inward peace in the least action he performs, so long as he doth it with false aims, and carnal affections, &c. Who would deprive himself of the comfort of suffering in a good cause for want of integrity? I beseech you, therefore, carry yourselves well in anything you either do or suffer, otherwise no blessing can be expected; for we tempt the Lord, and make him accessory to us, when we commit our souls to him in ill-doing: even as your pirates and other miscreants in the world, that will rob and steal, and do wickedly, and yet pray to God to bless them in their base courses (*c*); what is this but to make God like themselves, as if he approved their theft and horrible blasphemy?

But *what* must we commit to God *in well-doing?* The keeping of our *souls.* The soul is the more excellent part, witness he that purchased the same with his dearest blood. 'What will it profit a man,' saith our Saviour, 'to gain the whole world and lose his own soul?' Mark viii. 36. Who could know the price of a soul better than he that gave his life for redemption of it? Yea, if the whole world were laid in one balance and the soul in another, the soul were better than all. Therefore, whatsoever estate thou art in, let thy first care be for thy soul, that it may go well with that. You know in any danger or combustion, suppose the firing of an house, that which a man chiefly looks after is his jewels and precious things, 'I have some wealth in such a place, if I could but have that I care for no more, let the rest go;' so it is with a Christian, whatsoever becomes of him in this world, he looks to his precious soul, that that may be laid up safely in the hands of God. Suppose a man were robbed by the highway, and had some special jewel about him, though every thing else were taken away from him, yet so long as that is left he thinks himself a happy man, and saith, they have taken away some luggage, but they have left me that which I prize more than all: so it is with a Christian, let him be stripped of all he hath, so his soul be not hurt, but all safe and well there, he cares not much.

Quest. But what should we desire our souls to be *kept from* in this world?

Ans. From sin and the evil consequences thereof. Beloved, we have great need our souls should be kept by God; for alas! what sin is there but we shall fall into it, unless God preserve us in peace and comfort, and assurance of a better estate. What would become of our poor souls if we had them in our own keeping? Ahithophel had the keeping of his own soul, and what became of him? First, he did run into the sins of treason, and afterwards, being a wicked politician, and an atheist, having no delight in God, was the executioner of himself (*d*). We shall be ready, as Job saith, to tear our own souls if God hath not the keeping of them; we shall tear them with desperate thoughts, as Judas, who never committed his soul to God, but kept it himself, and we see what became of him. The apostle bids us go to God in prayer, and committing our souls to him, to keep from sin, despair, distrust, and all spiritual evil whatsoever, 'and then the peace of God which passeth all understanding,' as the word in the original is, 'shall guard* our souls in Christ,' Phil. iv. 7. Our souls have need of guarding, and we of ourselves are not sufficient to do it; therefore we should commit them unto God, for except he preserve us we shall soon perish.

Wicked men think that they have no souls. I am ashamed to speak of it, and yet notwithstanding the courses of men are such, that they enforce a man to speak that which he is ashamed of. What do I speak of committing your souls to God, when many thousands in the world live as if they had no souls at all? I am persuaded that your common swearers, and profane wretches, who wrong their souls to pleasure their bodies, and prostitute both body and soul, and all to their base lusts, think for the time that they have no souls; they think not that there is such an excellent immortal substance breathed into them by God, which must live for ever in eternal happiness or endless misery. Did they believe this they would not wound and stain their precious souls as they do; they would not obey every base lust out of the abundance of profaneness in their hearts, even for nothing, as many notorious loose persons do. Oh could we but get this principle into people, that they have immortal souls, which must live for ever, they would soon be better than they are; but the devil hath most men in such bondage that their lives speak that they believe they have no souls, by their ill usage of them.

Obj. But must we not commit our *bodies* and our *estates* to God, as well as our souls?

Ans. Yes, all we have; for that is only well kept which God keeps; but yet in time of suffering we must be at a point† with these things. If God will have our liberty, if he will have our life and all, we must hate all for Christ's sake; but we must not be at such a point with our souls, we must keep them close to God, and desire him to keep them *in well-doing*.

Obj. Suppose it come to an exigent, that we must either sin and hurt our souls, or else lose all our outward good things?

* See note *k*, page 334.—G.

† That is, 'make light of.'—Ed.

Ans. Our chief care must be over our souls. We must desire God to preserve our souls, whatsoever becomes of these; our principal care must be that that be not blemished in the least kind; for, alas! other things must be parted with first or last. This body of ours, or whatsoever is dear in the world, must be stripped from us, and laid in the dust ere long. But here is our comfort, though our body be dead, yet our souls are themselves still; dead St Paul is Paul still. Our body is but the case or tabernacle wherein our soul dwells; especially a man's self is his soul; keep that and keep all. I beseech you, therefore, as things are in worth and excellency in God's account, let our esteem be answerable. You have many compliments in the world, how doth your body, &c., mere compliments indeed, but how few will inquire how our souls do? alas! that is in poor case. The body perhaps is well looked unto, that is clothed, and care taken that nothing be wanting to it, but the poor soul is ragged and wounded, and naked. Oh that men were sensible of that miserable condition their poor souls are in.

Beloved, the soul is the better part of a man, and if that miscarries, all miscarries. If the soul be not well, the body will not continue long in a good estate. Bernard saith sweetly, 'Oh, body, thou hast a noble guest dwelling in thee, a soul of such inestimable worth that it makes thee truly noble.' Whatsoever goodness and excellency is in the body, is communicated from the soul; when that once departs, the body is an unlovely thing, without life or sense. The very sight of it cannot be endured of the dearest friends. What an incredible baseness is it therefore, that so precious a thing as the soul is, should serve these vile bodies of ours! Let the body stay its leisure; the time of the resurrection is the time of the body. In this life it should be serviceable to our souls in suffering and doing whatsoever God calls us unto. Let our bodies serve our souls now, and then body and soul shall for ever after be happy; whereas, if we, to gratify our bodies, do betray our souls, both are undone.

Beloved, the devil and devilish-minded men, acted with his spirit, have a special spite to the soul. Alas! what do they aim at in all their wrongs and injuries to God's children? Do they care to hurt the body? indeed, they will do this rather than nothing at all; they will rather play at small game than sit out. The devil will enter into the swine rather than stand out altogether. Some mischief he will do, however; but his main spite is at the soul, to vex and disquiet that, and taint it with sin all he can. Considering therefore that it is Satan's aim to unloose our hold from God, by defiling our souls with sin, so to put a divorce betwixt his blessed majesty and us, oh! let it be our chief care to see to that which Satan strikes at most! He did not so much care, in Job's trouble, for his goods, or for his house, or children, &c. Alas! he aimed at a further mischief than this! his plot was how to make him blaspheme and wound his soul, that so there might be a difference betwixt God and him. He first tempts us to commit sin, and afterwards to despair for sin.

Quest. But to whom must the soul be *committed?*

Ans. Our souls must be committed to God. Commit the keeping of your souls to God. Indeed, he only can keep our souls. We cannot keep them ourselves; neither can anything else in the world do it. Some when they are sick will commit themselves to the physician, and put all their trust in him. When they are in trouble they will commit themselves to some great friend; when they have any bad, naughty cause to manage, they will commit themselves to their purse, and think that shall bear them out in anything. One thinks his wit and policy shall secure him, another that his shifts may shelter him, &c.; and indeed the heart of man is so full of atheism, that it can never light upon the right object, *to trust God alone*, until it sees everything else fail, as being insufficient to support the soul, or to yield any solid comfort in times of extremity and distress.

Quest. But why must we commit our souls to God?

Ans. Because he is a *faithful Creator*. Whence observe,

Obs. That the soul of man being an understanding essence, will not be satisfied and settled without sound reasons. Comfort is nothing else but reasons stronger than the evil which doth afflict us; when the reasons are more forcible to ease the mind than the grievance is to trouble it. It is no difficult matter to commit our souls to God when we are once persuaded that he is a *faithful Creator*. A man commits himself to another man, and hath no other reason for it, but only he is persuaded of his ability and credit in the world; that he is a man of estate and power to do him good. So it is in this business of religion. Our souls are carried to anything strongly when they are carried by strong reasons, as in this particular of trusting God with our souls. When we see sufficient reasons inducing thereto, we easily resign them into his hands. This shews that popery is an uncomfortable religion, which brings men to despair. They have no reason for what they maintain. What reason can they give for their doctrine of doubting, transubstantiation, perfect obedience to the law, &c.? These are unreasonable things. The soul cannot yield to such absurdities. It must have strong reasons to stablish it, as here, to consider God as a *faithful Creator*, &c. There is something in God to answer all the doubts and fears of the soul, and to satisfy it in any condition whatsoever. This is the very foundation of religion; not that any worth can accrue to the Creator from the creature, but that there is an all-sufficiency in the Creator to relieve the poor creature. If a man consider in what order God created him, it will make him trust God. Paradise and all in it were ready for him, so soon as he came into the world. God created us after his own image, that as he was Lord of all things, so we should be lord of the creatures. They were all at his service, that he might serve God. Therefore after everything else was created, he was made, that so God might bring him as it were to a table ready furnished.

And not only in nature, but in holiness, having an immortal and invisible soul resembling God. We must take God here as a Creator of our whole man, body and soul, and of *the new creature* in us. God made man at the first, but that was not so much as for God to be made man, to make us new creatures. God created our bodies out of the dust, but our souls come immediately from himself. He breathes them into us, and in this respect he is a higher Creator than in the other; for when we had marred our first making, and became more like beasts than men, for indeed every one that is not like God sympathiseth with beasts or devils one way or other, God in Christ made us new again. Yea, God became man to enrich us with all grace and goodness, to free us from the hands of Satan, and bring us to an eternal state of communion with himself in heaven. For all the old heaven and the old earth shall pass away, and the old condition of creatures, and a new life shall be given them. God that made the new heaven and the new earth, hath made us for them. Considering therefore that God gave us our first being, and when we were worse than naught, gave us a second being in regard to our new creation, how should it stir us up to commit our souls unto him! especially if we consider that in him we 'live and move and have our being,' Acts xvii. 28; that there is not the least thought and affection to goodness in us but it comes from God; we are what we are by his grace.

Quest. What is the reason that love descends so much?

Ans. Because a man looks upon that which is his own and loves it. Now God looks upon us as upon those into whom he hath infused mercy and goodness, and he loves his own work upon us; and therefore having begun a good work, will perfect the same. Do not men delight to polish their own work? As in the first creation God never took off his hand till he had finished his work, so in the second creation of our souls he will never remove his hand from the blessed work of grace till he hath perfected the same; therefore we may well commit our souls to him.

Obj. But suppose a man be in a desperate estate, and hath no way of escaping?

Ans. Remember that God is the same still; he hath not forgot his old art of creating, but is as able to help now as ever, and can create comforts for thee in thy greatest troubles. As in the first creation he made light out of darkness, order out of confusion, so still he is able out of thy confused and perplexed estate to create peace and comfort. Thou knowest not what to do perhaps, thy mind is so troubled and disquieted; why, commit thy soul to God; he can raise an excellent frame out of the chaos of thy thoughts. Therefore be not dismayed; consider thou hast God in covenant with thee, and hast to deal with an almighty Creator, who can send present help in time of need. Dost thou want any grace? dost thou want spiritual life? Go to this Creator, he will put a new life into thee; he that made all things of nothing can raise light out of thy dark mind, and can make fleshy thy stony heart, though it be as hard as a rock. Therefore never despair, but frequent the means of grace, and still think of God under this relation of a Creator; and when he hath begun any good work of grace in thee, go confidently to His Majesty, and desire him to promote and increase the same in thy heart and life. Lord, I am thy poor creature, thou hast in mercy begun a blessed work in me, and where thou hast begun thou hast said thou wilt make an end. When thou createdst the world, thou didst not leave it till all was done; and when thou createdst man thou madest an end. Now, I beseech thee, perfect the *new creature* in my soul. As thou hast begun to enlighten mine understanding and to direct my affections to the best things, so I commit my soul unto thee for further guidance and direction to full happiness.

NOTES.

(a) P. 403.—'Lucida Intervalla.' This is the title of a very singular volume by Carkesse. 4to. 1679.

(b) P. 405.—'It is necessary we should be just; *it is not so necessary we should live*.' The memorable reprimand of the man who, engaged in a disreputable business, and defending himself against the sarcasms of Dr Samuel Johnson, pleaded he 'must live.' 'Not at all, Sir; there is no necessity for *your* living,' enforces the apophthegm of Sibbes. It is one of the gems preserved by Boswell.

(c) P. 406.—'Miscreants . . . . that will rob and steal and do wickedly, and yet pray to God to bless them in their base courses.' The 'Thugs' and the appalling system of 'Thuggism' furnish apt examples of this. Consult Arnold's 'Marquis Dalhousie's Administration of the Punjaub,' just issued, for narrative of their suppression in India. It contains many startling illustrations of Sibbes's words.

(d) P. 407.—'Ahithophel . . . *a wicked politician*.' 'Ahithophel,' or the 'Wicked Politician,' is the title of one of Nathaniel Carpenter's curious tractates. 4to. 1629.

G.

THE SAINT'S HIDING-PLACE IN THE EVIL DAY.*

SERMON V.

Wherefore let them that suffer according to the will of God, commit their souls to him in well-doing, as to a faithful Creator.—1 PET. IV. 19.

I AM now to treat of that other attribute of God, which should move us to trust in him, namely, as he is a *faithful* Creator. Now God is faithful, 1. In his *nature*. He is I AM, always like himself, immutable and unchangeable. 2. In his *word*. He expresseth himself as he is. The word that comes from God is an expression of the faithfulness of his nature. 3. In his *works*. 'Thou art good, and dost good,' as the psalmist saith, Ps. cxix. 68. God being faithful in himself, all must needs be so that proceeds from him. Whatsoever relation God takes upon him, he is faithful therein. As he is a Creator, so he preserves and maintains his own work. As he is a Father, he is faithful in discharging that duty to the full, for his children's good. As he is our Friend, he likewise performs all the duties of that relation, &c. And why doth God stoop so low to take these relations upon him, but only to shew that he will certainly accomplish the same to the utmost? Whence is it that men are faithful in their relations one towards another, that the father is faithful to his child? Is it not from God, the chief Father? That a friend should be faithful to his friend, is it not from God, the great Friend?

All his ways are mercy and truth, Ps. xxxv. 10. They are not only merciful and good and gracious, but mercy and truth itself. If he shew himself to be a Father, he is a true father, a true friend, a true creator and protector. As one saith, 'Shall I cause others to fear, and be a tyrant myself?'† All other faithfulness is but a beam of that which is in God. Shall not he be most faithful that makes other things faithful?

Now, this faithfulness of God is here a ground of this duty of committing ourselves to him; and we may well trust him whose word hath been seven times tried in the fire, Ps. xii. 6. There is no dross in it. Every word of God is a sure word; his truth is a shield and buckler; we may well trust in it. Therefore, when you read of any singular promise in the New

* Title.—See Note p. 401.

† Qu.—'Be a tyrant to myself?'—G. Rather, 'Shall I cause others to fear tyrants, and be a tyrant myself?'—ED.

Testament, it is said, 'This is a faithful saying,' &c., 1 Tim. i. 15; that is, this is such a speech as we may trust to; it is the speech of a *faithful* Creator.

Considering, therefore, that God is so faithful every way in his promises and in his deeds, let us make especial use of it. Treasure up all the promises we can of the forgiveness of sins, of protection and preservation; that he will never leave us, but be *our God to death*, &c., and then consider withal that he is faithful in performing the same. When we are affrighted by his majesty and his justice, and other attributes, then think of his mercy and truth. He hath clothed himself with faithfulness, as the psalmist saith. In all the unfaithfulness of men whom thou trustest, depend upon this, that God is still the same, and will not deceive thee.

When we have man's word, we have his sufficiency in mind, for men's words are as themselves are. What will not the word of a king do? If a man be mighty and great, his word is answerable. This is the reason why we should make so much of the word of God, because it is the word of Jehovah, a mighty Creator, who gives a being to all things, and can only be Lord and Master of his word. We know God's meaning no otherwise than by his word. Till we come to the knowledge of vision in heaven, we must be content with the knowledge of revelation in the word.

And in every promise, single out that which best suiteth with thy present condition. If thou art in any great distress, think upon the almighty power of God. Lord, thou hast made me of nothing, and canst deliver me out of this estate. Behold, I fly unto thee for succour, &c. If thou art in perplexity for want of direction, and knowest not what to do, single out the attribute of God's wisdom, and desire him to teach thee the way that thou shouldst go. If thou art wronged, fly to his justice, and say, O God, to whom vengeance belongeth, hear and help thy servant. If thou be surprised with distrust and staggering, then go to his truth and faithfulness. Thou shalt always find in God something to support thy soul in the greatest extremity that can befall thee; for if there were not in God a fulness to supply every exigent* that we are in, he were not to be worshipped, he were not to be trusted.

Man is lighter than vanity in the balance. Every man is a liar, that is, he is false. We may be so, and yet be men too, but God is essentially true. He cannot deceive and be God too. Therefore ever, when thou art disappointed with men, retire to God and to his promises, and build upon this, that the Lord will not be wanting in anything may do thee good. With men there is breach of covenant, nation with nation, and man with man. There is little trust to be had in any; but in all confusions here is comfort. A religious person may cast himself boldly into the arms of the Almighty, and go to him in any distress, as to a faithful Creator that will not forsake him.

Use. Oh, let us be ashamed that we should dishonour him who is ready to pawn his faithfulness and truth for us. If we confess our sins, 'God is faithful to forgive them,' 1 John i. 9. He will not suffer us to be tempted 'above that which we are able,' 1 Cor. x. 13. When we perplex ourselves with doubts and fears whether he will make good his promise or not, we disable His Majesty. Do we not think God stands upon his truth and faithfulness? Undoubtedly he doth, and we cannot dishonour him more

* That is, exigency. Brooks uses 'exigents' in the title of one of his raciest books, viz., 'The Mute Christian under the Smarting Rod, with Sovereign Antidotes against the most miserable *Exigents*.' 12mo, 1669.—G.

than to distrust him, especially in his evangelical promises. We make him a liar, and rob him of that which he most glories in, his mercy and faithfulness, if we rest not securely upon him.

See the baseness of man's nature. God hath made all other things faithful that are so, and we can trust them; but are ever and anon questioning the truth of his promise. We may justly take up Salvian's complaint in his time, 'Who hath made the earth faithful to bring forth fruit,' saith he, 'but God? Yet we can trust the ground with sowing our seed. Who makes man faithful, who is by nature the most slippery and unconstant creature of all other, but God only? Yet we can trust a vain man, whose breath is in his nostrils, and look for great matters at his hands, before an all-sufficient God, that changeth not. Who makes the seas and the winds faithful, that they do not hurt us, but God? And yet we are apt to trust the wind and weather sooner than God, as we see many seamen that will thrust forth their goods into the wide ocean in a small bark, to shift any way, rather than trust God with them.'

Yea, let Satan, by his wicked instruments, draw a man to some cursed politic reasons, for the devil doth not immediately converse with the world, but in his instruments, and he will sooner trust him than God himself. So prone are our hearts to distrust the Almighty, to call his truth in question, and to trust the lies of our own hearts and other men's, before him. Let us, therefore, lament our infidelity, that having such an omnipotent and faithful creator to rely upon, yet we cannot bring our hearts to trust in him. There are two main pillars of a Christian's faith :—

1. The power of God.
2. The goodness of God.

These two, like Aaron and Hur, hold up the arms of our prayers. Let our estate be never so desperate, yet God is a Creator still. Let our sins and infirmities be never so great, yet he hath power to heal them. Oh, how should this cheer up our souls, and support our drooping spirits in all our strivings and conflicts with sin and Satan, that we yield not to the least temptation, having such an almighty God to fly unto for succour.

We must not trust the creature. 'Cursed is that man which makes flesh his arm,' Jer. xvii. 5. He that we trust in, must be no less than a Creator. 'Cease from man, whose breath is in his nostrils,' saith God, he is a poor creature as thyself is; raised of nothing, and shall come to dust again. If we would be trusting, as we needs must, for we are dependent persons, and want many things whilst we are here, let us go to the fountain, and not to broken cisterns for comfort.

It is no small privilege for a Christian to have this free access to God in times of extremity. Be we what we can be, take us at our worst in regard of sin or misery, yet we are his creatures still. I am the clay, thou art the potter; I am a sinful wretch, yet I am the workmanship of thy hands. O Lord, thou hast framed me and fashioned me, &c. No wicked person in the world can, upon good ground, plead in this manner, though they may say to God, *I am thy creature*, yet they have not the grace in their troubles to plead this unto him. Why, Lord, though I be a rebellious son, and am not worthy to be called thy servant, yet I am thy creature, though a sinful one. Surely, had we faith, we would take hold by a little. The soul of man is like the vine, it winds about and fastens upon every little help. Faith will see day at a little hole; and where it sees anything it will catch at it, as the woman of Canaan. Christ calls her dog. Why, be it so, Lord, *I am a dog*, yet I am one of the family though I be a dog; therefore *have mercy on me.*

Oh, it is a sweet reasoning thus to cling about God, and gather upon him; it is a special art of faith. Though a carnal man may reason thus, as having a ground from the truth of the thing, yet he hath not grace to reason out of an affection thereunto. Though he should say, Lord, I am thy creature; yet his heart tells him thus, if he would hearken to it, I am thy creature, Lord, but I have made all my members that I have received from thee, instruments to sin against thee, and I purpose not to reform; my tongue is an instrument of swearing, lying, and profane speeches; my hands are instruments of bribery and violence, continually working mischief in thy sight; my feet carry me to such and such filthy places, and abominable courses; mine own heart tells me that I fight against thee, my Creator, with those very limbs and weapons which thou hast given me. Beloved, the conscience of this so stifles the voice of a wilful sinner, that notwithstanding he acknowledgeth himself to be God's creature, yet he cannot with any comfort plead for mercy at his hand in times of distress.

But to a right godly man this is an argument of special use and consequence; in the midst of troubles he may allege this, and it binds God to help him. We see great ones when they raise any, though perhaps there is little merit in them, yet they call them their creatures; and this is a moving argument with such to polish their own work still, and not to desert them. Will it not be a prevailing argument with God then, for a Christian to plead with him? Lord, thou hast raised me out of nothing, yea, out of a state worse than nothing; I am thy poor creature, forsake not the work of thine own hands. We may see what a fearful thing sin is in God's eye, that the works of *our* hands should make God depart from the work of *his* hands, as he will certainly do at the day of judgment: 'Depart, you cursed,' &c., Mat. xxv. 41. Though we be his creatures, yet because we have not used those gifts and abilities which he hath given us to serve His Majesty, he will not endure the sight of us in that day.

But that you may the better practise this duty of committing your souls to God, take these directions.

1. *Directions how to commit our souls to God.* First, *see that thou be thy own man.* It is an act of persons free to covenant. Our souls must be ours before we can commit them to God. Naturally we are all slaves to Satan; the *strong man* hath possession of us, and therefore our first care must be to get out of his bondage, to which purpose we should much eye the sweet promises and invitations of the gospel, alluring us to accept of mercy and deliverance from sin and death, as—'Come unto me, all you that are weary and heavy laden,' &c., Mat. xi. 28, and so cast the guilt of our souls upon God to pardon first, and then to sanctify and cleanse, that we may no more return to folly, but lead an unspotted life before him for the time to come.

It is therefore a silly course and dangerous, which poor worldly wretches take, who think *Lord, have mercy upon them,* will serve their turn, and that God will certainly save their souls; whenas they were never yet in the state of grace or reconciliation with him, nor never had any divorce made between them and their sins, and consequently never any league between God and their souls to this day.

Beloved, when once a man hath alienated his soul from God by sin, he hath then no more command of it; for the present it is quite out of his power. Now, when we would commit our souls to God aright, we must first commit them to him to pardon the guilt of sin in them. When this is done, God will give us our souls again, and then they may truly be said to be our own, and not before. It is the happiness of a Christian that he is not his own, but that whether he live or die, he is the Lord's.

Direction 2. In the second place, *we must labour to find ourselves in covenant with God;* that is, *to find him making good his promises to us, and ourselves making good our promises to him.* For a man cannot commit himself to God, unless he find a disposition in his heart to be faithful to him.

There is a passive fidelity, and an active. 1. Passive faithfulness is in the things that we give trust unto, as, such a one is a sure, trusty man, therefore I will rely upon him. 2. Active faithfulness in the soul is, when we cast ourselves upon a man that is trusty, and depend upon him. The more a man knows another to be faithful, the more faithful he will be in trusting of him; and thus we must trust God, if ever we expect any good at his hands; and our dependence on him binds him to be the more faithful to us. He is counted a wicked man indeed, that will deceive the trust committed to him. Trust begets fidelity; it makes a good man the more faithful, when he knows he is trusted.

Learn therefore to know thyself to be in covenant with God, and to trust him with all thou hast; train up thyself in a continual dependence upon him. He that trusts God with his soul, will trust him every day in everything he hath or doth. He knows well, that whatsoever he enjoys is not his own, but God's; and this stirs him to commit all his ways and doings to his protection, esteeming nothing safe but what the Lord keeps. He sees 'it is not in sinful man to direct his own steps,' Jer. x. 23; and therefore resigns up his estate, his calling, his family, whatsoever is near and dear unto him, to the blessed guidance and direction of the Almighty. Oh, thinks he, that I were in covenant with God, that he would own me for his, and take the care of me, how happy should my condition then be!

He will likewise commit the church and state wherein he lives to God; and strengthens his faith daily by observing God's faithful dealing with his people in every kind.

How behoveful it is for Christians thus to inure themselves to be acquainted with God by little and little, first trusting him with smaller matters, and then with greater. How can a man trust God with his soul, that distrusts him for the petty things of this life? 'They that give to the poor are said to lend unto the Lord,' Prov. xix. 17; and 'if we cast our bread upon the waters, we shall find it again,' Eccles. xi. 1. Beloved, he that parts with anything to relieve a poor saint, and will not trust God with his promise to recompense it again, but thinks all is gone, and he shall never see it more, &c., exceedingly derogates from the truth and goodness of the Almighty, who hath promised to return with advantage whatsoever we give that way. He hath secret ways of his own to do us good, that we know not of. A man is never the poorer for that which he discreetly gives. It is hard to believe this; but it is much harder for a man to commit his soul to God when he dies, with assurance that he shall partake of mercy, and be saved at the last day.

Direction 3. Again, *take heed of these evil and cursed dispositions that hinder us from the performance of this duty;* as namely, carnal wit and policy, and carnal will and affection, &c. There is a great deal of self-denial to be learned, before we can go out of ourselves and commit all to God; ere we can cast ourselves into his arms, and lay ourselves at his feet. Therefore take heed that we be not ruled, either by our own carnal policy or others', to knit ourselves to that; for I beseech you, do but think, what is true in all stories, not only in the Scripture, but elsewhere, the most unfortunate men that ever were, otherwise wise enough, were always too confident of themselves. The greatest swimmers, you know, are often drowned, because relying overmuch on their own skill, they cast themselves into danger, and are swallowed up of the deep. Even confidence in wit is usually unfortunate, though it be great. Let Solomon be an example. You see how he strengthened himself by carnal supports; but what became of all? Alas, it soon vanished and came to nothing. The Jews would run to the reed of Egypt, and that ran into their hands; instead of helping, it hurt them. God takes delight to overthrow the ripeness of all the carnal policy of man, that advanceth itself against his word and gospel. Take heed of confidence in prosperity, in wit, in strength; take heed of whatsoever hinders the committing of our souls to God; and alway remember, that honesty is the best policy; and that God reconciled in Christ is the best sanctuary to flee unto. 'The name of God is a strong tower,' saith Solomon; 'the righteous flee thereto, and are safe,' Prov. xviii. 10.

That carnal policy hinders our safety. Let Christians therefore have nothing to do with carnal shifts, and politic ends; for they have a strong rock, and a sure hold to go to; the Almighty is their shield. Beloved, God will be honoured by our trusting of him, and those that will be wiser than God, and have other courses distinct and contrary to him, must look for confusion in all their plots. A Christian should thus think with himself, let God be wise for me; his wisdom shall be my direction; his will shall be the rule of my life; he shall guide me and support me; I will adventure upon no course that I dare not commit my soul with comfort to God in.

Oh beloved, if we tender our own welfare, let us shun all unwarrantable courses, and adventure upon no action whatsoever, wherein we cannot upon good grounds desire the Lord's protection. It is a fearful estate for a man to undertake such courses, as that he cannot if he were surprised by judgment, suddenly commit himself to God in. The throne of iniquity shall not abide with God; he will not take a wicked man by the hand, nor own him in a distressful time.

Study therefore, I beseech you, to be always in such a blessed condition, as that you may, without tempting of God, in a holy boldness of faith, resign up your souls to him. A guilty conscience cannot seek the Lord; naturally it runs away from him. Peace is not easily gotten, nor the gap soon made up; therefore preserve conscience clear and unspotted, if thou wouldst have God thy refuge in time of need. Adam when he had sinned ran from God; Peter, when our Saviour discovered more than an ordinary majesty in his miracles, said, 'Lord, depart from me, I am a sinful man,' Luke v. 8. It is the work of flesh and blood to depart from God, but when a man goes to God, it is a sign he hath more than flesh and blood in him; for this cannot be done without a supernatural work of faith; which alone will make a sinful conscience fly to God, and look to him as a father in Christ, and desire him by his almighty power, whereby he created heaven and earth, to create faith in the soul. And when thou hast cast thy soul into the arms of the Almighty, labour to settle it there, and to quiet thyself in the discharge of thy duty; say thus, now I have done that which belongs to me, let God do that which belongs to him; I will not trouble myself about God's work, but in well-doing commit my soul to him, and let him alone with the rest.

Christians should not outrun God's providence, and say, what shall become of me? this trouble will overwhelm me! &c. but serve his providence in the use of the means, and then leave all to his disposal. Especially this duty is needful in the hour of death, or when some imminent danger approacheth; but then it will be an hard work, except it be practised aforehand.

Direction 4. Labour therefore for *assurance of God's love betimes*, get infallible evidences of thy estate in grace, that thou art a renewed person, and that there is a thorough change wrought in thy heart; that God hath set a stamp upon thee for his own, and that thou hast something above nature in thee; then mayest thou cheerfully say, 'Father, into thy hands I commend my spirit; I am thine, Lord, save me, &c.,' Luke xxiii. 46, otherwise having no interest in God, how canst thou expect any favour from him? Oh the sweet tranquillity and heaven upon earth which those enjoy who have God to be their friend!

This lays a heavy prejudice upon antichristian religion, which maintains a doctrine of doubting, affirming that we ought not to labour for assurance of God's favour. Oh beloved, what deprives a poor Christian soul of comfort more than this? Alas! how can a man at the hour of death commit his soul into the hands of Almighty God, that staggers whether he be his child or no? and knows not whether he shall go to heaven or hell? Therefore it should be our daily endeavour, as we would have comfort in the time of resigning and giving up our souls to God, to gather evidences of a good estate; that we are in covenant with him; that he is our Father; and that we are his children in Christ Jesus.

For will a man trust his jewels with an enemy, or with a doubtful friend? How can the swearer commit his soul to God? How can loose livers and your filthy, unclean wretches, that live in continual enmity against the Lord, commit themselves with any comfort unto him? They pray, 'Lead us not into temptation,' Mat. vi. 13, and yet run daily into temptations, into vile houses and places of wickedness, wherein they feed their corruptions, and nothing else. They say, 'Give us this day our daily bread,' and yet use unwarrantable courses, seeking to thrive by unlawful means.

Beloved, a man can commit his soul with no more comfort to God than he hath care to please him. If a man knows such a one hath his evidences and leases, and may hurt him when he list, how careful will he be of provoking or giving offence to such a man? Suppose we knew a man that had the keeping of a lion, or some cruel beast, and could let it loose upon us at his pleasure, would we not speak such a one fair, and give him as little cause of discontent as may be? Beloved, God hath devils and wicked men in a chain, and can, if we offend him, set loose all the powers of darkness upon us; he can make conscience fly in our faces, and cause us to despair and sink. All our evidences and assurances of salvation are in God's hands; he can bring us into a state full of discomfort and misery, and make us in a manner to feel the very flashes and scorchings of hell itself. Oh who would offend this God, much less live in the practice of any sin, and yet think of committing their souls to him!

Direction 5. To encourage you the more to trust in God, *observe the constant course of his dealing towards you.* 'Lord, thou hast been my God from my youth,' saith David; 'upon thee have I hung ever since I was took out of my mother's womb; forsake me not in my gray hairs, when my strength faileth me,' &c., Ps. lxxi. 6, 9, xvii. 18. We should gather upon God, as it were, from former experience of his goodness, and trust him for the time to come, having formerly found him true. Beloved, it is good to lay up all the experiments of God's love we can, that we may trust him at the hour of death; for all our strength then will be little enough to uphold our faith. When many troubles shall meet in one, as it were in a centre, then a world of fears and distractions will seize upon our souls, the guilt of sin past, thoughts of judgment to come, forsaking of our former lusts and delights, trouble of mind, pain of body, &c. We have need of much acquaintance with God, and assurance of his love at such a time. Therefore let us learn daily to observe the experience of his goodness towards us, how when we have committed ourselves to him in youth, he hath been a God from time to time in such and such dangers to us. Ancient Christians should be the best Christians, because they are enriched with most experiences. It is a shame for ancient Christians to stagger, when they yield up their souls to God, as if they had not been acquainted with him heretofore. You see how David pleads to God, 'Thou hast redeemed me,' Ps. xxxi. 5; he goes to former experience of his mercy; therefore now into thy hands I commend my spirit in this extremity. This psalm is a practice of this precept; here is the precept, 'Commit your souls to God, as a faithful Creator;' here is the practice of David, 'Into thy hands I commend my spirit, for thou hast redeemed me, O Lord God of truth,' &c. Therefore, I beseech you, let us treasure up experience of God's goodness, that so when extremities shall come, we may go boldly to him, upon former acquaintance with his majesty; and being strengthened with former experience. I beseech you, let us labour to practise these and the like rules prescribed, to encourage us in the performance of so necessary a duty.

Obj. But will not God keep us without we commit ourselves unto him?

Ans. We must commit our souls to God if we would be preserved. I answer, God having endued us with understanding and grace, will do us good in the exercise of those powers and graces that he hath given us; he will preserve us, but we must pray for it. Christ himself must ask before he can have: 'Ask of me, and I will give thee the heathen for thine inheritance,' Ps. ii. 8, &c. We should therefore make it a continued act, every day of our lives, to commit all we have to the Lord's disposal; and to that end observe how he dischargeth the trust committed to him upon all occasions; how faithful he is in delivering his poor church in greatest extremities, and ourselves also even in our worst times. 'Thou never failest those that trust in thee,' saith David, and 'How excellent is thy lovingkindness, O God, therefore the children of men shall trust under the shadow of thy wings,' Ps. xxxvi. 7. Daily experience of God's lovingkindness will make us daily to trust under the shadow of his wings. It should therefore be our continual course to observe the goodness, kindness, faithfulness, and other attributes of God, and often to support our souls with them.

Think, I beseech you, how he numbers the very bones of men; they are all written in his book of providence; he knows every joint, every part which he hath made; he knows his own workmanship; therefore we may well commit our souls to him. Doth God number our superfluities, and not our natural and essential parts? Even our very hairs are numbered; our tears are taken notice of, and put into his bottle; our steps are told; our desires are known; our groans are not hid. We shall not lose a sigh for sin, so particular is God's providence. He watcheth continually over us. There is not any of our members but they are all written in his book, so that he will not suffer 'a bone to be broken,' Ps. xxxiv. 20. We should therefore daily resign up our souls to his merciful tuition,* and bind ourselves to lead unblameable lives before him, resolving against every sinful course, wherein we would be afraid to look his Majesty in the face. What a comfortable life were the life of Christians, if they would exercise them-

* That is, 'protection.'—ED.

selves to walk as in the presence of the Almighty! This is that which the Scripture speaks of Enoch, Gen. v. 24, and the rest, who are said to have walked with God; that is, to have committed themselves and their souls to him, as *to a faithful Creator.*

Obj. Of wicked men's preserving, who do not commit their souls to God. It may be objected, here is a great deal of labour and striving against corruptions indeed; may not a man walk with God without all this ado? We see wicked men, that never commit their souls to God, grow fat and lusty, and have as good success in the world as the strictest men that are.

Ans. 1. I answer, God many times preserves such wretches; but, alas! that preservation is rather a reservation for a worse evil to come upon them. 'There is a pit a-digging for the wicked,' Ps. xxxvii. 13, 38. He flourisheth and bears out all impudently, under hope of success; but his grave is a-making, and his present prosperity will but aggravate his future misery.

2. Sometimes God preserves wicked men for other ends. It may be he hath some to come of their loins, who of wicked shall be made good.

3. Again, God will be in no man's debt. Those that are civilly good shall have civil prosperity, as the Romans had. They had a commonwealth well governed, and they prospered many years together. As Chaucer observes, God preserves wicked men from many calamities; he gives them civil wisdom, good carriage, &c.; and answerable to those common gifts, he gives them preservation and protection, &c.; but then there is vengeance on their souls the while. Those that commit not themselves carefully and watchfully to God, have dead, secure souls, without any life of grace or power of godliness in them. I speak this to waking Christians, that would know in what case they should live; walking in the sense and assurance of God's love; they, I say, ought to practise this duty of committing the keeping of their souls to God in well-doing, as to a faithful Creator.

What it is to commit our souls to God. Neither is it so easy a matter to commit our souls to God as many fondly imagine. It is not the mumbling over a few prayers, saying, Lord, receive my soul, &c., will serve the turn. These are good words indeed, and soon learned; but, alas! who cannot do this? Our study, therefore, should be to know the depth and meaning of the same; how that we are not only to commit the essence of our souls to God, that he would take them into heaven when we die; but also to commit the affections of our souls to him, that he might own us and govern us whilst we live; for how are our souls known, but by those active expressions in our affections, which immediately issue from them, when we commit all our thoughts, desires, and affections to him, setting him highest in our souls, and making him our hope, our trust, our joy, our fear, &c.?

Thus I have spoken of the duty, and of the *thing* to be committed, *our souls;* and *to whom, to God;* and the *manner, in well-doing;* and *why? because he is a faithful Creator.*

Now, I beseech you, consider how nearly it concerns us all to be thoroughly acquainted with the practice of this duty. God knows what extremities we may fall into. Certainly in what condition soever we be, either public or private, whether in contagion and infection, or war and desolation, happy are we if we have a God to go to. If we have him to retire to in heaven, and a good conscience to retire to in ourselves, we may rest secure. 'Though the earth be removed, and the mountains be carried into the midst of the sea,' Ps. xlvi. 2, 4, yet we shall be safe; that is, though the order of nature were confounded, yet there is a river shall refresh the house of God. There are chambers of divine protection, that the

Christian enters into, as the prophet saith, 'Enter into thy chambers,' Isa. xxvi. 20; and God is his habitation still. If a Christian had no shelter in the world, yet he hath an abiding place in God continually; as God dwells in him, so he dwells in God. Satan and all other the enemies of man must break through God before they can come to us, when once we commit ourselves to him, as to a tower and habitation, and enter into him as into an hiding place. The enemies must wrong him before they can hurt us, so blessed an estate it is to be in God, having commended our souls to him, as unto a *faithful Creator.*

Obj. But we see many of God's dear children, that commit themselves to his care and protection, miscarry, and go by the worst in the world.

Ans. 1. Beloved, it is not so, for when they commit themselves to God, they are under safety; and if he keep them not *out* of trouble, yet he will preserve them *in* trouble. 'I will be with thee in the fire, and in the water,' saith God, Isa. xl. He saith not, I will keep you out of the fire, and out of the water, for he brought many holy martyrs into it; some were drowned, some burned, &c. Though God will not keep us out of trouble, yet he will preserve our spirits in trouble; nay, God many times by a small trouble preserves us from a greater. Even the sufferings of the godly are oft preservations to them. Was not Jonah preserved by the whale? What had become of him if that had not swallowed him up? A whale that one would have thought should be a means to destroy him, was a means to carry him to the coast, and bring him safely to land.

Again, God seems for a time indeed to neglect his children when they commit themselves unto him, but mark the issue; 'all the works of God are beautiful in their season,' Eccl. iii. 11. He suffers them it may be, a long time to be in danger and trouble, till he hath perfected the work of mortification in their hearts, and crucified their confidence in earthly things, till he hath made them more sensible of the evil of sin, and watchful against it; but wait a while, and you shall see 'that the end of the righteous man is peace,' Ps. xxxvii. 37.

God's presence and assistance to support his children in trouble is invincible; they have gladness and comfort that we wot not of; they commit the safety of their souls to God, and he seems to neglect them, if we look to their outward man, but they have a paradise in their conscience. God preserves their souls from sin, and their consciences from despair. They have an invisible protection. There was a fence about Job that the devils saw, and a guard of angels that Elias saw, and that his servant saw afterwards, 2 Kings vi. 14, 15. Wicked men see not the guard of spirits that is about the children of God; as Christ saith, 'they have meat the world knows not of,' John iv. 32; they feed on hidden comforts.

As for carnal men, they do not commit themselves to God; they have no preservation, but rather a reservation to further evil. Pharaoh was kept from the ten plagues, but was drowned in the sea at last; and Sodom was kept by Abraham; he fought for them, but yet it was destroyed with fire and brimstone afterwards.

Let us then try our trust in God. Those that intend to embark themselves and their estates in a ship, will be sure to try it first. This committing of our souls to God, must be our ship to carry us through the waves of this troublesome wor d to the heavenly Canaan of rest and peace. We should therefore search and prove the same, whether it be indeed safe and sound, able to support our souls in the evil day, and not leak and prove insufficient for us.

How to know when we trust God aright. *Trial* 1. Those that commit themselves to God aright, *are far from tempting his majesty*. God will be trusted, but not tempted. What though things fall not out according to thy expectation; yet wait thou, and think God hath further ends than thou knowest of. God will do things in the order of his providence, therefore if we neglect that, it is our own fault if he do not help us. If Christ had committed his health to God, and had cast himself down from the pinnacle, what an act had this been! but he would not so tempt the Almighty. Neither should we unadvisedly run into dangers, but serve his providence upon all occasions. God useth our endeavour to this very end. He saves us not always immediately, but by putting wisdom into our hearts to use lawful means, and using those means he will save us in them. A Christian therefore should be in a continual dependence upon God, and say, I will use these means, God may bless them; if not, I will trust him; he is not tied to the use of means, though I be.

Trial 2. Again, those that commit their souls, or anything to God, *find themselves quieted therein*. Is it not so amongst men? If a man commit a jewel to a trusty friend, is he not secure presently? Have we not God's word and faithfulness engaged, that he will not leave us nor forsake us, but continue our all-sufficient God and portion to our lives' end? Why then are we disquieted? Those that are full of cares and fears may talk their pleasure, but they never yet had any true confidence in God: for faith is a quieting grace, it stills the soul; 'being justified by faith, we have peace with God,' Rom. v. 1. Those that are hurried in their life with false doubts and perplexities, 'What shall become of me? What shall I eat, and what shall I drink?' &c., though they use lawful means, yet commit not themselves to God as they should; for where there is a dependence upon God in the use of means, there is an holy silence in the party. All stubborn and tumultuous thoughts are hushed in him. 'My soul, keep silence to the Lord,' saith David, 'and trust in God; why art thou so vexed within me?' Ps xlii. 11. Still there is a quieting of the soul where there is trust. Can that man put confidence in God that prowls for himself, and thinks he hath no Father in heaven to provide for him? Doth that child trust his father, that, besides going to school, thinks what he shall put on? how he shall be provided for, and what inheritance he shall have hereafter? Alas: this is the father's care, and belongs not to him. Wheresoever these distractions are, there can be no yielding up of the soul to God in truth.

There be two affections which mightily disturb the peace of Christians. 1. Sinful cares; and 2. sinful fears. To both which we have remedies prescribed in the Scripture. 1. 'Fear not, little flock,' saith Christ, 'for it is your Father's will to give you a kingdom,' Luke xii. 32; as if he had said, Will not he that gives you heaven, give you other things? In nothing be careful, saith the apostle, that is, in a distracting manner, but do your duty, and then 'let your requests be made known to God, and the peace of God shall keep you,' Phil. iv. 7; and therefore were we redeemed from the hands of our enemies, that we might 'serve him without fear all our days,' Luke i. 74.

A Christian should keep an inward sabbath in his soul, and go quietly on in doing all the good he can. What a fearful thing is it to see men lie grovelling in the earth, and live without God in the world, troubling and turmoiling themselves how to compass this thing and that thing, as if they had no God to seek unto, nor no promise to rely upon.

Trial 3. Again, where this committing of a man's self and his soul to God is, *there will be a looking to God only, in all a man doth,* not fearing any danger or opposition that may befall him from without. As the three young men said to Nebuchadnezzar, 'Our God can keep us if he will,' Dan. iii. But what if he will not? 'Yet know, O king, that we will not worship nor fall down before thy image.' So it is with a Christian; foreseeing some danger, disgrace, or displeasure of this or that man which may befall him, he resolveth notwithstanding, in despite of all, to commit himself to God in doing his duty, come what will. Whether God will save him or no, he will not break the peace of his conscience, or do the least evil. He is no fool, but foresees what may befall him for well-doing. This inconvenience may come, and that trouble, yet he sets light by these. He hath an eye to heaven, and sees more good to himself in the Creator that gave him his being of nothing, and more good for the time to come, that will make him a blessed saint in heaven, than there can be ill in the creature. Therefore, come what can come, his heart is fixed to trust the Lord, and rather than he will displease him, desert his honour and his cause, or do any unworthy action, he will commit himself to God in the greatest dangers.

Reason of trusting in God. The ground hereof is this: a Christian is the wisest man in the world, and he understands well enough that God is all-sufficient. He sees there is a greater good in God than he can have in the creature, and counts it madness to offend God to please the creature; because there is a greater evil to be expected from God than from the creature, though it were the greatest monarch in the world. Considering, therefore, that he hath his best good in his union with God, and in keeping his peace with him, he will not break with him for any creature. And thus he doth wisely, for he knows if he lose his life he shall have a better life of God than he hath in his body; for God is his life, God is his soul and his comfort, and he hath his being from God. He is his Creator, and he hath a better being in God when he dies than he had when he lived; for our being in God makes us happy, and therefore Christ saith, *He that loves his life,* before God and a good cause, *hates it,* and *he that hates his life* when Christ calls for it, *loves it,* John xii. 25, for he hath a better life in him. We give nothing to God, but he returns it a thousand times better than we gave it. Let us yield our lives to him. We shall have them in heaven if they be taken away on earth. He will give us our goods a thousandfold. We shall have more favour in God than in any creature, and therefore a Christian, out of this ground, commits himself to God, though he foresee never so much danger like to fall upon him.

Trial 4. Again, if we do *in deed and not in pretence* commit ourselves to God, as to a faithful Creator, *we will not limit his majesty,* as many carnal hearts do. Oh, if God will do so and so for them, then they would trust him. If they had but so much to live on a year, and such comings in, &c., then they would depend upon God. But they must have a pawn and so much in hand first. What a shame is it that we should trust the vilest man in the world as far as we see him, and yet, unless we have somewhat to lean on, we will not trust God! Beloved, when a man limits God in anything, such a one may talk, but he trusts him not at all. Indeed, we should indent with God, and tie him to look to the salvation of our souls; but for other things leave them to his own wisdom, both for the time, for the manner and measure, do what he will with us. Suppose it come to the cross, hath he not done greater matters for us? Why then should we distrust him in lesser? If times come that religion flourish or goes downward, yet rely on him still: Hath he not given his Son to us, and will he not give heaven also? Why do we limit the Holy One of Israel, and not cast ourselves upon him, except he will covenant to deal thus and thus with us?

A true Christian hath his eye always heavenward, and thinks nothing too good for God. O Lord, saith he, of thee I have received this life, this estate, this credit and reputation in the world. I have what I have, and am what I am of thee, and therefore I yield all to thee back again. If thou wilt serve thyself of my wealth, of myself, of my strength, thou shalt have it. If thou wilt serve thyself of my credit and reputation, I will adventure it for thee. If thou wilt have my life, of thee I had it, to thee I will restore it, I will not limit thy majesty; come of it what will, I leave it to thy wisdom; use me and mine as thou wilt; only be gracious to my soul, that it may go well with that, and I care not. Thus we should wholly resign ourselves to the Lord's disposal, and thereby we shall exceedingly honour his majesty, and cause him to honour us, and to shew his presence to us for our good, which he will assuredly do if we absolutely yield up ourselves to him. But if a man will have two strings to his bow, and trust him so far but not so far, so he may be kept from this danger or that trouble, &c., this is not to deal with God as an omnipotent Creator; for he that doth a thing truly in obedience to God, will do it generally to all his commands. So far as the reason of his obedience reaches, his trust extends. He that commits anything to God will commit all to him. He chooseth not his objects. But upon the same ground that he commits his soul to God when he dies, he commits his estate, liberty, and all he hath while he lives. He can never rely on God for greater matters, that distrusts him in lesser.

Trial 5. Again, a man that truly trusts God *will commit all his ways unto him;* he will take no course but what he is guided in by the Lord. He looks for wisdom from above, and saith, Lord, though it is not in me to guide my own way; as thy word shall lead me, and the good counsel of thy Spirit in others direct me, so I will follow thee. He that commits not his ways to God, will not commit his comforts to him. God must be our counsellor as well as our comforter. Therefore the wise man bids us 'acknowledge God in all our ways, and lean not to our own wisdom,' Prov. iii. 5. Most men look how safe their counsels are, not how holy and agreeable to God. Is this to trust in him? Will God save us at last, and yet suffer us to live as we list now? Deceive not yourselves; he that will have his soul saved must commit it to God beforehand to be sanctified.

Trial 6. Again, those that commit themselves aright to God *will commit their posterity to him*, their wives and children, &c.

Obj. Why! do not men make their wills and commit their goods to them?

Solution. Oh! but how do they resign them? How covetous and full of distrust are they! I must leave such a child so much and so much; and why, I pray you? Because God cannot bless him else? O fearful! is God tied to means? cannot he bless with a little as well as with a great deal? Is not 'the earth the Lord's, and the fulness thereof?' Ps. xxiv. 1. Why must God have so much in hand, or else he cannot enrich and raise up thy children? Oh! consider, he hath declared himself to be the father of the fatherless, and looks to the widow in a special manner; he doubles his providence there; he provides for all, but takes special notice of them; therefore quiet thyself, they are in covenant with God, and God is thy God, and the God of thy seed also; therefore if thou wilt commit thy soul, why not thy wife, children, goods? &c.

Look into the course of God's people in all times. Those that have left but little with honest dealing, God hath blessed the same exceedingly; whereas those that have left great matters ill gotten, instead of a blessing have often left a curse and a snare behind them. Why then should men take indirect courses, and wound their consciences for worldly pelf?

Consid. 1. Consider, 1, thy children are God's and not thine; he gave them to thee at first, and he can provide hereafter when thou art gone. Thou art the father of their body, but he is the father of their soul.

2. He provided for them before they were born. Doth not he provide care and affection in the mother's heart? Doth he not provide suck in the mother's breasts? and will he not care for them now they are born as well as he did before they came into the world? It is atheism to think such a thought. Those that commit themselves to God in one thing will do so in all things, otherwise they deceive their own souls; for it is a universal act that runs through their whole life. Committing is an action of trust, and there is a kind of intercourse of trust between God and a Christian continually.

Trial 7. Lastly, those that commit themselves to God *will be faithful stewards in whatsoever he hath trusted them withal.* Thou committest thyself and thy health and estate to God, and at length thou wilt commit thy soul when thou diest unto him. Very well; but what doth God trust thee withal? Hath he not trusted thee with a body and a soul, with a portion of goods, with place, time, strength, and abilities to do good? Hast thou not all thou hast from God as a steward, to improve for thy Master's advantage? If ever thou expectest the performance of what thou hast put in him, be faithful in that trust which he hath committed to thee. Those that have misused their bodies and wounded their souls in their lives, how can they commit them to God at their deaths? How dares the soul look up to him, when the life hath been nothing else but a perpetual offending of his majesty?

I beseech you, let us learn this wholesome lesson! Great is our benefit thereby. 'He that trusts in the Lord shall be as Mount Sion, that cannot be moved.' We may be shaken, but shall never be removed. The earth is shaken with earthquakes, but the earth keeps its own centre still. Our best peace is in God, and our chiefest safety in his protection. 'I laid me down to rest, because thou, Lord, watchest over me,' Ps. iii. 5, saith the prophet; and, 'Return, O my soul, to thy rest, for the Lord hath been very beneficial to thee,' Ps. cxvi. 7. Is it not a good thing to have a sweet security of soul that whether I sleep or wake, whether I be at home or abroad, live or die, I have a providence watching over me better than mine own? When I yield myself up to God, his wisdom is mine, his strength is mine; whatsoever he hath it is for me, because I am his. What a heaven upon earth is this, that a Christian, out of a holy familiarity with God, can resign up his soul to him upon all occasions! Set heaven and salvation aside, what greater happiness can be desired? How sweet is a man's rest at night after he hath yielded himself to God by faithful prayer?

Use. Exhortation. I beseech you, let us be acquainted with the practice of this duty, and labour to be in such a state as God may own us, and receive our poor souls to himself. Let us keep them pure and undefiled, and labour to improve our talents, that when we give anything to God, we may say, Lord, according to the grace I have received I have kept it, and therefore now return it to thee again.

Beloved, when trouble of conscience comes, when sickness and death comes, what will become of a man that hath not this sweet acquaintance with

God? He was a stranger to God in the time of prosperity, and God is now a stranger to him in adversity. Saul was a profane-spirited man; he did not acquaint himself with God in the time of his happiness, and therefore in time of distress he goes first to the witch, and then to the sword-point. So fareth it with all wicked wretches in their great extremities. No sooner doth any evil betide them, or the least danger approach them, let conscience never so little fly in their faces, &c., but presently they go to cursed means, and run upon desperate conclusions.

Therefore, as we desire to die even in God's arms, and yield up ourselves into the very hands of the Almighty with comfort, let us daily inure ourselves to this blessed course of committing ourselves and all our ways to him in doing good.

'Come and see,' saith the Scripture, John i. 46. Beloved, if you will not believe me, make trial of this course a while. Did you once taste the sweetness of it, how would your drooping spirits be cheered up!

Let a man continually keep a good conscience, and he shall be satisfied with peace at last. Suppose he meets with danger and opposition in the world, this may seem harsh at the first. Oh, but he shall know afterwards what it is to part with anything for Christ's sake, to commit his cause, or whatsoever he hath, unto God, as to a faithful Creator! Then we taste of God to the purpose when we put him to it, for God will not be indebted to us. We never find such sweet immediate comfort from him as when we deny ourselves comfort of the creature for his sake.

Little do we know what times may befall us. There is much danger abroad, and we have cause to fear, not far from us. It may be the clouds even now hang over our heads. Oh, if we would be hid in the day of the Lord's wrath, and have no evil come nigh our dwellings, let us, above all things in the world, make sure our interest in Christ, and title to the promise. We should seek to know God more, and then we would trust him more. 'They that know thy name will trust in thee,' saith David, Ps. ix. 10. Oh, the blessed estate of a Christian, that now he may be acquainted with God; that through Christ there is a throne of grace to fly unto! I beseech you, improve this happy privilege; and then, come what will, come famine, come danger of war or pestilence, &c., God will be a sanctuary and an abiding place to you. A Christian carries his rock and sure defence about him. 'I will be unto them a little sanctuary in all places,' saith God. What a comfort is it to have a 'wall of fire' still compassing us about, a shield that our enemies must break through before they can come at us! He that trusts in God shall be recompensed with mercy on every side. It is no matter what dangers compass him. Though he be in the midst of death and hell, or any trouble whatsoever, if he commits himself to God in obedience, out of good grounds of faith in his word, hes hall be safe in the evil day.*

* As explained in prefatory note, 'The Church's Visitation' forms the 'second part' of a volume. I annex the quaint notice for the guidance of readers, as wishing to preserve everything traceable to the pen of Sibbes:—

To THE READER.—Reader, in this Booke there are two parts. The one begins at the *Church's Visitation*, and goes on orderly to page 240, and there it ends. This I call the *second part*. All the rest, from the beginning and so forward, I count the first part. Therefore, when thou art directed to the fourth or fifth page, because thou shouldest not looke in both nor mistake, I have set it thus: 1, 4, which is, 1 part, 4 page; or 2, 5, the second part and fifth page.'

END OF VOL. I.

INDEX

NOTE. The principle acted upon in the construction of this General Index was to select *thoughts* rather than mere *words*. An effort has been made to include all the former. The 'Tables' given in the original and early editions are *substantially* incorporated, but frequently under more definite and concise headings. Where, as in '*Christ*,' the references would have been so numerous as to confuse, as many as possible have been distributed under other topics. G.

THE WORKS OF
RICHARD SIBBES

THE WORKS OF
RICHARD SIBBES

VOLUME 2

Edited by
Alexander B. Grosart

THE BANNER OF TRUTH TRUST

THE BANNER OF TRUTH TRUST

Head Office
3 Murrayfield Road
Edinburgh, EH12 6EL
UK

North America Office
610 Alexander Spring Road
Carlisle, PA 17015
USA

banneroftruth.org

The Complete Works of Richard Sibbes
first published in 7 volumes 1862-64
This reprint of volume 2 first published by
the Banner of Truth Trust 1983
Reprinted 2001, 2023

*

ISBN
Print: 978 0 85151 370 6

*

Printed in the USA by
Versa Press Inc.,
East Peoria, IL.

CONTENTS.

BOWELS OPENED;

OR, EXPOSITORY SERMONS ON CANTICLES IV. 16, V. VI.

THE SPOUSE, HER EARNEST DESIRE AFTER CHRIST.

A BREATHING AFTER GOD.

THE RETURNING BACKSLIDER;

Or, A Commentary upon Hosea XIV.

THE GLORIOUS FEAST OF THE GOSPEL.

PREFATORY NOTE.

HAVING embraced in Volume I. the whole of the works of Sibbes published by himself, together with related portions restored to their proper places (*e. g.*, 'The Description of Christ,' and 'The Sword of the Wicked'), the present volume contains his larger Treatises from the Old Testament, together with lesser kindred 'Sermons,' which will be followed by his Commentaries on portions of the New Testament.

A. B. G.

BOWELS OPENED,

BEING EXPOSITORY SERMONS ON CANT. IV. 16, V., VI.

NOTE.

The expository sermons which compose the treatise, entitled, in the quaint phraseology of the age, 'Bowels Opened,' (no doubt derived from the Hebraic idea of the seat of the affections being in the 'bowels,' Cant. v. 4; and compare 1 John iii. 17) passed through three editions, as follows:—

(*a*) 1st edition, 4to, 1639.

(*b*) 2d edition, 4to, 1641. There is no intimation of its being a '2d edition;' but it really was so. The pagination is wholly different from *a*.

(*c*) 3d edition, 4to, 1648. This *is* designated '3d edition,' and the pagination differs from *a* and *b*. Prefixed to it is a portrait of Sibbes, *ætat* 58. Underneath it are these lines, without signature or initial:

'Thy learning, meekness, wisedome, heavenly minde,
Soe full of love, soe zealous, soe discreete,
Thy works, ye Church, yea Heaven, where they doe finde
A crowne—declare, for earth they were not meete.
Whoe, slighting thee, himselfe preferrs before,
Let him gett to thee,—he shall then know more.'

Our text follows *a*, with comparison of *b* and *c* for correction of misprints. Its title-page is given below.* G.

* Original title page:—

BOWELS
OPENED,
OR
A DISCOVERY OF THE
Neere and deere Love, Union and
Communion betwixt Christ and the
Church, and consequently betwixt
Him and every beleeving soul.
Delivered in divers Sermons on the Fourth Fifth
and Sixt Chapters of the CANTICLES
By that Reverend and Faithfull Minister of the
Word, DOCTOR SIBS, late Preacher unto
the Honourable Societie of *Grayes Inne*, and Master
of Katharine Hall in Cambridge.
Being in part finished by his owne pen in his life
time, and the rest of them perused and corrected
by those whom he intrusted with the
publishing of his works.
CANT.4.10.
Thou hast ravished my heart, my Sister, my Spouse: thou hast ravished my heart with one of thine eyes, and with one chaine of thy necke.
LONDON.
Printed by *G. M.* for *George Edwards* in the Old Baily in
Greene-Arbour at the signe of the Angell, MDCXXXIX.†

† It may be noted that Obadiah Sedgwick's famous folio on 'The Covenants,' (1661) is entitled, 'The Bowels of Tender Mercy Sealed in the Everlasting Covenant.' Thomas Willocks and Faithful Teat have similarly quaintly-titled treatises on 'Canticles.' This book seems to have had a special attraction for the Puritan Divines.
G.

HONORATISSIMO DOMINO,

DOMINO EDWARDO VICE-COMITI MANDEVILLE,*

QUEM, UT VERÆ NOBILITATIS DELICIAS, CANDORIS NIVEM,
IN RES CHRISTI, ET ALIORUM COMMODA EFFUSISSIMUM, SUSPICIMUS, COLIMUS;
UNAQUE CONCIONES HAS IN CANTICA POSTHUMAS
IN AMORIS GRATIAM QUO AUTHOREM IPSE COMPLEXUS EST NOSTRÆQUE IN DNEM
ILLIUS MERITISSIMÆ OBSERVANTIÆ TESTIMONIUM

D.D.

THOMAS GOODWIN.†
PHILIPPUS NYE.‡

* For full and interesting notices of this great historic name, consult Burke, and any of the 'Peerages;' also the recently issued family papers at Kimbolton, by the present Duke of Manchester. He was the patron and beloved friend of John Howe.—G.

† The celebrated Dr Thomas Goodwin, who discharged the office of 'prefacer' or editor for many of his Puritan contemporaries, *e.g.*, besides Sibbes, Burroughes, and Hooker. Cf. Memoir by Dr Halley.—G.

‡ Philip Nye was one of the foremost men in the great Puritan struggle. He died in 1672. Cf. 'Nonconf. Memorial,' i. 95, 96; and Hanburg's 'Historical Memorials relating to the Independents,' throughout the work.—G.

TO THE CHRISTIAN READER.

The perusal of this book being committed unto me by an ancient and a faithful friend of mine, I found it, I confess, so full of heavenly treasure, and such lively expressions of the invaluable riches of the love of Christ towards all his poor servants that sue and seek unto him, that I sent unto the godly and learned author, earnestly entreating him to publish the same, judging it altogether unmeet that so precious matter should be concealed from public use: when he excused himself, by undervaluing his own meditations; but withal signified his desire of the church's good, if by anything in his works it might never so little be promoted. I could not but declare myself in recommending this treatise as a very profitable and excellent help both to the understanding of that dark and most divine Scripture, and also to kindle in the heart all heavenly affections unto Jesus Christ.

It is well known how backward I am and ever have been to cumber the press, but yet I would not be guilty in depriving the dear children of God of the spiritual and sweet consolations which are here very plentifully offered unto them.

And the whole frame of all these sermons is carried with such wisdom, gravity, piety, judgment, and experience, that it commends itself unto all that are godly wise; and I doubt not but that they shall find their temptations answered, their fainting spirits revived, their understandings enlightened, and their graces confirmed, so as they shall have cause to praise God for the worthy author's godly and painful labours. And thus desiring the Father of all mercies and the God of all comfort to bless this work to the consolation and edification of those that seek his favour and desire to fear his holy name, I rest

Thine in Jesus Christ,

J[OHN] DOD.*

* John Dod is one of the most venerable of Puritan 'worthies.' He lived to a 'great age.' Born in 1549, he died in 1645. Consult Brook ('Lives of the Puritans,' vol. iii. pp. 1–6); also Clark ('Lives of Thirty-two English Divines,' folio, 1677, pp. 168–178).—G.

BOWELS OPENED.

SERMON I.

I am come into my garden, my sister, my spouse: I have eaten my honey-comb with my honey; I have drunk my wine with my milk: eat, O friends; drink, yea, drink abundantly, O beloved.—Cant. V. 1.

Other books of Solomon lie more obvious and open to common understanding; but, as none entered into the holy of holies but the high priest, Lev. xvi. 2, *seq.*, and Heb. ix. 7, so none can enter into the mystery of this Song of songs, but such as have more near communion with Christ. Songs, and specially marriage songs, serve to express men's own joys, and others' praises. So this book contains *the mutual joys and mutual praises betwixt Christ and his church.*

And as Christ and his church are the greatest persons that partake of human nature, so whatsoever is excellent in the whole world is borrowed to set out the excellencies of these two great lovers.

It is called 'Solomon's Song,' who, next unto Christ, was the greatest son of wisdom that ever the church bred, whose understanding, as it was 'large as the sand of the sea,' 1 Kings iv. 29, so his affections, especially that of love, were as large, as we may see by his many wives, and by the delight he sought to take in whatsoever nature could afford. Which affection of love, in him misplaced, had been his undoing, but that he was one beloved of God, who by his Spirit raised his soul to lovely objects of a higher nature. Here in this argument there is no danger for the deepest wit, or the largest affection, yea, of a Solomon, to overreach. For the knowledge of the love of Christ to his church is above all knowledge, Eph. iii. 19. The angels themselves may admire it, though they cannot comprehend it. It may well, therefore, be called the 'Song of Solomon;' the most excellent song of a man of the highest conceit* and deepest apprehension, and of the highest matters, *the intercourse betwixt Christ, the highest Lord of lords, and his best beloved contracted spouse.*

There are divers things in this song that a corrupt heart, unto which all things are defiled, may take offence; but 'to the pure all things are pure,' Titus i. 15. Such a sinful abuse of this heavenly book is far from the intention of the Holy Ghost in it, which is by stooping low to us, to take

* That is, 'imagination.'—G.

advantage to raise us higher unto him, that by taking advantage of the sweetest passage of our life, *marriage*, and the most delightful affection, *love*, in the sweetest manner of expression, *by a song*, he might carry up the soul to things of a heavenly nature. We see in summer that one heat weakens another; and a great light being near a little one, draws away and obscures the flame of the other. So it is when the affections are taken up higher to their fit object; they die unto all earthly things, whilst that heavenly flame consumes and wastes all base affections and earthly desires. Amongst other ways of mortification, there be two remarkable—

1. *By embittering all earthly things unto us, whereby the affections are deaded* to them.*

2. *By shewing more noble, excellent, and fit objects*, that the soul, issuing more largely and strongly into them, may be diverted, and so by degrees die unto other things. The Holy Spirit hath chosen this way in this song, by elevating and raising our affections and love, to take it off from other things, that so it might run in its right channel. It is pity that a sweet stream should not rather run into a garden than into a puddle. What a shame is it that man, having in him such excellent affections as love, joy, delight, should cleave to dirty, base things, that are worse than himself, so becoming debased like them! Therefore the Spirit of God, out of mercy and pity to man, would raise up his affections, by taking comparison from earthly things, leading to higher matters, that only deserve love, joy, delight, and admiration. Let God's stooping to us occasion our rising up unto him. For here the greatest things, the 'mystery of mysteries,' the communion betwixt Christ and his church, is set out in the familiar comparison of a marriage, that so we might the better see it in the glass of comparison, which we cannot so directly conceive of; as we may see the sun in water, whose beams we cannot so directly look upon. Only our care must be not to look so much on the colours as the picture, and not so much on the picture as on the person itself represented; that we look not so much to the resemblance as to the person resembled.†

Some would have Solomon, by a spirit of prophecy, to take a view here of all the time, from his age to the second coming of Christ, and in this song, as in an abridgment, to set down the several passages and periods of the church in several ages, as containing divers things which are more correspondent to one age of the church than another (*a*). But howsoever this song may contain, we deny not, a story of the church in several ages, yet this hinders not, but that most passages of it agree to the spiritual estate of the church in every age, as most interpreters have thought. In this song there is,

1. A strong desire of the church of nearer communion with Christ; and then,
2. Some declining again in affection.
3. After this we have her recovery and regaining again of love; after which,
4. The church falls again into a declining of affection; whereupon follows a further strangeness of Christ to her than before, which continues until,
5. That the church, perceiving of Christ's constant affection unto her, notwithstanding her unkind dealing, recovers, and cleaves faster to Christ than ever , chap. iii.

These passages agree to the experience of the best Christians in the state of their own lives. This observation must carry strength through this whole song, that *there is the same regard of the whole church, and of every particular member, in regard of the chiefest privileges and graces that accompany salvation.* There is the same reason of every drop of water as of the

* That is, 'deadened.'—G. † That is, 'represented.'—G.

whole ocean, all is water; and of every spark of fire as of the whole element of fire, all is fire. Of those homogeneal bodies, as we call them, there is the same respect of the part and of the whole. And therefore, as the whole church is the spouse of Christ, so is every particular Christian; and as the whole church desires still nearer communion with Christ, so doth every particular member. But to come to the words, 'I am come into my garden,' &c.

This chapter is not so well broken and divided from the former as it might have been, for it were better and more consequent* that the last verse of the former chapter were added to the beginning of this.

'*Awake, O north wind; and come, thou south; blow upon my garden, that the spices thereof may flow out. Let my beloved come into his garden, and eat his pleasant fruits*,' Cant. iv. 16.

And therefore, by reason of connection of this chapter with the former verse, we will first speak somewhat of it briefly, only to make way for that which follows. The words contain—

1. *A turning of Christ's speech to the winds to blow upon his garden, with the end why*, 'that the spices thereof may flow out.'

2. *We have an invitation of Christ, by the church, to come into his garden*, with the end, 'to eat his pleasant fruits.'

Quest. It may be a question whether this command be the words of Christ or the desire of his spouse?

Ans. The words are spoken by Christ, because he calls it '*my* garden,' and the church after invites him to eat of '*his* pleasant fruits,' not of hers. Yet the words may be likewise an answer to a former secret desire of the church, whereof the order is this: The church being sensible of some deadness of spirit, secretly desires some further quickening. Christ then answers those desires by commanding the winds to blow upon her. For ordinarily Christ first stirs up desires, and then answers the desires of his own Spirit by further increase, as here, 'Awake, thou north wind; and come, thou south; and blow upon my garden,' &c.

1. For the first point named, we see here that Christ *sends forth his Spirit, with command to all means*, under the name of 'north and south wind,' to further the fruitfulness of his church. The wind is nature's fan. What winds are to the garden, that the Spirit of Christ, in the use of means, is to the soul. From comparison fetched from Christ's commanding the winds, we may in general observe, that *all creatures stand in obedience to Christ, as ready at a word, whensoever he speaks to them.* They are all, as it were, asleep until he awakes them. He can call for the wind out of his treasures when he pleases: he holds them in his fist, Prov. xxx. 4.

Use. Which may comfort all those that are Christ's, that they are under one that hath all creatures at his beck under him to do them service, and at his check to do them no harm. This drew the disciples in admiration to say, 'What manner of man is this, that even the winds and the seas obey him?' Mat. viii. 27. And cannot the same power still the winds and waves of the churches and states, and cause a sudden calm, if, as the disciples, we awake him with our prayers.

2. Secondly, we see here that Christ speaks to *winds contrary one to another*, both in regard of the coasts from whence they blow, and in their quality; but both agree in this, that both are necessary for the garden: where we see that *the courses that Christ takes, and the means that he uses with his church, may seem contrary; but by a wise ordering, all agree in the wholesome issue.* A prosperous and an afflicted condition are contrary: a

* That is, 'in sequence.'—G.

mild and a sharp course may seem to cross one another; yet sweetly they agree in this, that as the church needeth both, so Christ useth both for the church's good. The north is a nipping wind, and the south a cherishing wind; therefore the south wind is the welcomer and sweeter after the north wind hath blown. But howsoever, all things are ours: 'Paul, Apollos, Cephas, things present and to come, life, death,' &c., 1 Cor. iii. 21, 22; 'all things work together for good to us, being in Christ,' Rom. viii. 28.

Use 1. Hence it is that the manifold wisdom of Christ *maketh use of such variety of conditions;* and hence it is that the Spirit of Christ is mild in some men's ministries, and sharp in others: nay, in the very same minister, as the state of the soul they have to deal withal requires.

Use 2. Sometimes, again, *the people of God need purging, and sometimes refreshing.* Whereupon the Spirit of God carries itself suitably to both conditions; and the Spirit in the godly themselves draws good out of every condition, sure [as] they are that all winds blow them good, and [that] were it not for their good, no winds should blow upon them. But in regard that these times of ours, by long peace and plenty, grow cold, heavy, and secure, we need therefore all kinds of winds to blow upon us, and all little enough. Time was when we were more quick and lively, but now the heat of our spirits is* abated. We must therefore take heed of it, and 'quicken those things that are ready to die,' Rev. iii. 2; or else, instead of the north and south wind, God will send an east wind that shall dry up all, as it is, Hos. xiii. 15.

Use 3. Again, if Christ can raise or lay, bind up or let loose, all kind of winds at his pleasure, then if means be wanting or fruitless, it is he that says to the clouds, Drop not, and to the winds, Blow not. Therefore, *we must acknowledge him in want or plenty of means.* The Spirit of Christ in the use of means is a free agent, sometimes blows strongly, sometimes more mildly, sometimes not at all. No creature hath these winds in a bag at command, and therefore it is wisdom to yield to the gales of the Spirit. Though in some other things, as Solomon observes, it may hinder to observe the winds, Eccles. xi. 4, yet here it is necessary and profitable to observe the winds of the Spirit.

Now, for the clear understanding of what we are to speak of, let us first observe—

1. Why the Spirit of God, in the use of the means, is compared to wind. And then,

2. Why the church is compared to a garden; which shall be handled in the proper place.

But first for the wind.

1. 'The wind bloweth where it listeth,' as it is John iii. 8. So the Spirit of God blows freely, and openeth the heart of some, and poureth grace plentifully in them.

2. The wind, especially the north wind, *hath a cleansing force.* So the Spirit of God purgeth our hearts 'from dead works to serve the living God, making us partakers of the divine nature,' 2 Pet. i. 4.

3. The wind *disperseth and scattereth clouds, and makes a serenity in the air.* So doth the Spirit disperse such clouds as corruption and Satan raise up in the soul, that we may clearly see the face of God in Jesus Christ.

* It is printed 'are.' But such inaccuracy is not uncommon in Sibbes and his contemporaries. If the nearer noun be plural, it, and not the nominative proper, regulates the use of the verb. This remark is made once for all, that apparent misprints may not be placed to oversight.—G.

4. The wind hath *a cooling and a tempering quality, and tempers the distemper of nature.* As in some hot countries there be yearly anniversary winds, which blow at certain times in summer, tempering the heat; so the Spirit of God allayeth the unnatural heats of the soul in fiery temptations, and bringeth it into a good temper.

5. The wind being subtle, *searcheth into every corner and cranny.* So the Spirit likewise is of a searching nature, and discerneth betwixt the joints and the marrow, betwixt the flesh and the Spirit, &c., searching those hidden corruptions, that nature could never have found out.

6. The wind hath *a cherishing and a fructifying force.* So the Spirit is a quickening and a cherishing Spirit, and maketh the heart, which is as a barren wilderness, to be fruitful.

7. The wind hath *a power of conveying sweet smells in the air, to carry them from one to another.* So the Spirit in the word conveyeth the seeds of grace and comfort from one to another. It draws out what sweetness is in the spirits of men, and makes them fragrant and delightful to others.

8. The wind, again, *bears down all before it, beats down houses, and trees, like the cedars in Lebanon,* turns them up by the roots, and lays all flat. So the Spirit is mighty in operation. There is no standing before it. It brings down mountains, and every high thing that exalts itself, and lays them level; nay, the Roman and those other mighty empires could not stand before it.

For these respects and the like, the 'blowing of the Spirit' is compared to wind. For which end Christ here commands the wind to 'blow upon his garden.'

1. *To blow,* &c. See here the order, linking, and concatenation of things one under another. To the prospering of a poor flower or plant in a garden, not only soil is needful, but air and wind also, and the influence of heaven; and God commanding all, as here the winds to blow upon his garden. To this end, as a wonderful mercy to his people, it is said, 'And it shall come to pass in that day, I will hear, saith the Lord: I will hear the heavens, and they shall hear the earth; and the earth shall hear the corn, the wine, and the oil; and they shall hear Jezreel,' Hos. ii. 21, 22. As the creatures are from God, so the order and dependence of creatures one from another, to teach us not only what to pray for, but also what to pray fitly for; not only to pray for the dew of heaven, but also for seasonable and cherishing winds. It is not the soil, but the season, that makes fruitful, *Non ager sed annus facit fructus,* and that from seasonable winds and influences. So in spiritual things there is a chain of causes and effects: prayer comes from faith, Rom. x. 14; faith from the hearing of the word; hearing from a preacher, by whom God by his Spirit blows upon the heart; and a preacher from God's sending. If the God of nature should but hinder and take away one link of nature's chain, the whole frame would be disturbed. Well, that which Christ commands here, is for the winds to 'blow upon his garden.'

And we need blowing: our spirits will be becalmed else, and stand at a stay; and Satan will be sure by himself, and such as are his bellows, to blow up the seeds of sinful lusts in us. For there are two spirits in the church, the one always blowing against the other. Therefore, the best had need to be stirred up; otherwise, with Moses, Exod. xvii. 12, their hands will be ready to fall down, and abate in their affection. Therefore we need blowing—

1. In regard of our natural inability.

2. In regard of our dulness and heaviness, cleaving to nature occasionally.

3. In regard of contrary winds from without.

Satan hath his bellows filled with his spirit, that hinders the work of grace all they can; so that we need not only Christ's blowing, but also his stopping other contrary winds, that they blow not, Rev. vii. 1.

4. In regard of the estate and condition of the new Covenant, wherein all beginning, growth, and ending, is from grace, and nothing but grace.

5. Because old grace, without a fresh supply, will not hold against new crosses and temptations.

Use. Therefore when Christ draws, let us run after him; when he blows, let us open unto him. It may be the last blast that ever we shall have from him. And let us set upon duties with this encouragement, that Christ will blow upon us, not only to prevent us, but also to maintain his own graces in us. But O! where is this stirring up of ourselves, and one another, upon these grounds!

Quest. But, *why is the church compared to a garden?*

Ans. Christ herein takes all manner of terms to express himself and the state of the church, as it is to him, to shew us that wheresoever we are, we may have occasion of heavenly thoughts, to raise up our thoughts to higher matters. His church is his 'temple,' when we are in the temple; it is a 'field' when we are there; a 'garden,' if we walk in a garden. It is also a 'spouse' and a 'sister,' &c. But more particularly the church is resembled to a garden.

1. *Because a garden is taken out of the common waste ground, to be appropriated to a more particular use*. So the church of Christ is taken out of the wilderness of this waste world, to a particular use. It is in respect of the rest, as Goshen to Egypt, Exod. ix. 26, wherein light was, when all else was in darkness. And indeed wherein doth the church differ from other grounds, but that Christ hath taken it in? It is the same soil as other grounds are; but, he dresseth and fits it to bear spices and herbs.

2. *In a garden nothing comes up naturally of itself*, but as it is planted and set. So nothing is good in the heart, but as it is planted and set by the heavenly husbandman, John xv. 4; and Mat. xv. 3. We need not sow the wilderness, for the seeds of weeds prosper naturally. The earth is a mother to weeds, but a stepmother to herbs. So weeds and passions grow too rank naturally, but nothing grows in the church of itself, but as it is set by the hand of Christ, who is the author, dresser, and pruner of his garden.

3. Again, *in a garden nothing uses to be planted but what is useful and delightful*. So there is no grace in the heart of a Christian, but it is useful, as occasion serves, both to God and man.

4. Further, *in a garden there are variety of flowers and spices*, especially in those hot countries. So in a Christian, there is somewhat of every grace. As some cannot hear of a curious flower, but they will have it in their garden, so a Christian cannot hear of any grace but he labours to obtain it. They labour for graces for all seasons, and occasions. They have for prosperity, temperance and sobriety; for adversity, patience and hope to sustain them. For those that are above them, they have respect and obedience; and for those under them, suitable usage in all conditions of Christianity. For the Spirit of God in them is a seminary of spiritual good things. As in the corruption of nature, before the Spirit of God came to us, there was the seminary of all ill weeds in us, so when there is a new quality and new principles put in us, therewith comes the seeds of all graces.

5. Again, *of all other places, we most delight in our gardens to walk there and take our pleasure*, and take care thereof, for fencing, weeding, watering, and planting. So Christ's chief care and delight is for his church. He walks in the midst of the 'seven golden candlesticks,' Rev. ii. 1; and if he defend and protect States, it is that they may be a harbour to his church.

6. And then again, as in gardens there had wont to have *fountains and streams which run through their gardens*, (as paradise had four streams which ran through it); so the church is Christ's paradise; and his Spirit is a spring in the midst of it, to refresh the souls of his upon all their faintings, and so the soul of a Christian becomes as a watered garden.

7. So also, 'their fountains were sealed up,' Cant. iv. 12; so the joys of the church and particular Christians are, as it were, sealed up. A stranger, it is said, 'shall not meddle with this joy of the church,' Prov. xiv. 10.

8. Lastly, *a garden stands always in need of weeding and dressing*. Continual labour and cost must be bestowed upon it; sometimes planting, pruning, and weeding, &c. So in the church and hearts of Christians, Christ hath always somewhat to do. We would else soon be overgrown and turn wild. In all which, and the like respects, Christ calleth upon the winds 'to blow upon his garden.'

Use 1. If then the church be a severed portion, then *we should walk as men of a severed condition from the world*, not as men of the world, but as Christians; to make good that we are so, by feeling the graces of God's Spirit in some comfortable measure, that so Christ may have something in us, that he may delight to dwell with us, so to be subject to his pruning and dressing. For, it is so far from being an ill sign, that Christ is at cost* with us, in following us with afflictions, that it is rather a sure sign of his love. For, the care of this blessed husbandman is to prune us, so as to make us fruitful. Men care not for heath and wilderness, whereupon they bestow no cost. So when God prunes us by crosses and afflictions, and sows good seed in us, it is a sign he means to dwell with us, and delight in us.

2. And then also, we should not strive so much for *common liberties* of the world that common people delight in, but for *peculiar graces*, that God may delight in us as his garden.

3. And then, let us learn hence, *not to despise any nation or person*, seeing God can take out of the waste wilderness whom he will, and make the desert an Eden.

4. Again, *let us bless God for ourselves*, that our lot hath fallen into such a pleasant place, to be planted in the church, the place of God's delight.

5. And this also should move us *to be fruitful*. For men will endure a fruitless tree in the waste wilderness, but in their garden who will endure it? Dignity should mind us of duty. It is strange to be fruitless and barren in this place that we live in, being watered with the dew of heaven, under the sweet influence of the means. This fruitless estate being often watered from heaven, how fearfully is it threatened by the Holy Ghost, that 'it is near unto cursing and burning,' Heb. vi. 8. For in this case, visible churches, if they prosper not, God will remove the hedge, and lay them waste, having a garden elsewhere. Sometimes God's plants prosper better in Babylon, than in Judea. It is to be feared God may complain of us, as he doth of his people, 'I have planted thee a noble vine; how art thou then come to be degenerated?' Jer. ii. 21. If in this case we regard iniquity in our heart, the Lord will not regard the best thing that comes from us, as our prayers, Heb. xii. 17.

* That is, 'expense.'—G.

We must then learn of himself, how and wherein to please him. Obedience from a broken heart is the best sacrifice. Mark in [the] Scriptures what he abhors, what he delights in. We use to say of our friends, Would God I knew how to please them. Christ teacheth us, that 'without faith it is impossible to please him,' Heb. xi. 6. Let us then strive and labour to be fruitful in our places and callings. For it is the greatest honour in this world, for God to dignify us with such a condition, as to make us fruitful. 'We must not bring forth fruit to ourselves,' as God complains of Ephraim, [Israel], Hos. x. 1. Honour, riches, and the like, are but secondary things, arbitrary at God's pleasure to cast in; but, to have an active heart fruitful from this ground, that God hath planted us for this purpose, that we may do good to mankind, this is an excellent consideration not to profane our calling. The blessed man is said to be, 'a tree planted by the water side, that brings forth fruit in due season,' Ps. i. 3. But it is not every fruit; not that fruit which Moses complains of, Deut. xxxii. 32, the wine of dragons, and the gall of asps: but good fruit, as John speaks; 'Every tree that bringeth not forth good fruit, is hewn down, and cast into the fire,' Mat. iii. 10.

6. Lastly, in that the church is called Christ's garden, this may *strengthen our faith in God's care and protection.* The church may seem to lie open to all incursions, but it hath an invisible hedge about it, a wall without it, and a well within it, Zech. ii. 5. God himself is a wall of fire about it, and his Spirit a well of living waters running through it to refresh and comfort it. As it was said of Canaan, so it may be said of the church, 'The eye of the Lord is upon it all the year long,' Deut. xi. 12, and he waters it continually. From which especial care of God over it, this is a good plea for us to God, 'I am thine, save me;' I am a plant of thine own setting; nothing is in me but what is thine, therefore cherish what is thine. So, for the whole church the plea is good: 'The church is thine; fence it, water it, defend it, keep the wild boar out of it.' Therefore the enemies thereof shall one day know what it is to make a breach upon God's vineyard. In the mean time, let us labour to keep our hearts as a garden, that nothing that defileth may enter. In which respects the church is compared to a garden, upon which Christ commands the north and south wind, all the means of grace, to blow.

But to what end must these winds blow upon the garden?

'That the spices thereof may flow out.'

The end of this blowing is, you see, 'that the spices thereof may flow out.' Good things in us lie dead and bound up, unless the Spirit let them out. We ebb and flow, open and shut, as the Spirit blows upon us; without blowing, no flowing. There were gracious good things in the church, but they wanted blowing up and further spreading, whence we may observe, that,

Obs. 1. *We need not only grace to put life into us at the first, but likewise grace to quicken and draw forth that grace that we have.* This is the difference betwixt man's blowing and the Spirit's. Man, when he blows, if grace be not there before, spends all his labour upon a dead coal, which he cannot make take fire. But the Spirit first kindles a holy fire, and then increases the flame. Christ had in the use of means wrought on the church before, and now further promoteth his own work. We must first take in, and then send out; first be cisterns to contain, and then conduits to convey. The wind first blows, and then the spices of the church flow out. We are first sweet in ourselves, and then sweet to others.

Obs. 2. Whence we see further, that *it is not enough to be good in our-*

selves, but our goodness must flow out; that is, grow more strong, useful to continue and stream forth for the good of others. We must labour to be, as was said of John, burning and shining Christians, John v. 35. For Christ is not like a box of ointment shut up and not opened, but like that box of ointment that Mary poured out, which perfumes all the whole house with the sweetness thereof. For the Spirit is herein like wind; it carries the sweet savour of grace to others. A Christian, so soon as he finds any rooting in God, is of a spreading disposition, and makes the places he lives in the better for him. The whole body is the better for every good member, as we see in Onesimus, Phil. 11. The meanest persons, when they become good, are useful and profitable; of briars, become flowers. The very naming of a good man casts a sweet savour, as presenting some grace to the heart of the hearer. For then we have what we have to purpose, when others have occasion to bless God for us, for conveying comfort to them by us. And for our furtherance herein, therefore, the winds are called upon to awake and blow upon Christ's garden, 'that the spices thereof may flow out.'

Obs. 3. Hence we see, also, that *where once God begins, he goes on, and delights to add encouragement to encouragement, to maintain new setters up in religion,* and doth not only give them a stock of grace at the beginning, but also helps them to trade. He is not only Alpha, but Omega, unto them, the beginning and the ending, Rev. i. 8. He doth not only plant graces, but also watereth and cherisheth them. Where the Spirit of Christ is, it is an encouraging Spirit; for not only it infuseth grace, but also stirs it up, that we may be ready prepared for every good work, otherwise we cannot do that which we are able to do. The Spirit must bring all into exercise, else the habits of grace will lie asleep. We need a present Spirit to do every good; not only the power to will, but the will itself; and not only the will, but the deed, is from the Spirit, which should stir us up to go to Christ, that he may stir up his own graces in us, that they may flow out.

Use. Let us labour, then, in ourselves to be full of goodness, that so we may be fitted to do good to all. As God is good, and does good to all, so must we strive to be as like him as may be; in which case, for others' sakes, we must pray that God would make the winds to blow out fully upon us, 'that our spices may flow out' for their good. For a Christian in his right temper thinks that he hath nothing good to purpose, but that which does good to others.

Thus far of Christ's command to the north and south wind to awake and blow upon his garden, that the spices thereof may flow out. In the next place we have—

II. Christ's invitation by the church to come into his garden, with the end thereof, 'to eat his pleasant fruits.'

Which words shew *the church's further desire of Christ's presence to delight in the graces of his own Spirit in her.* She invites him to come and take delight in the graces of his own Spirit; and she calls him 'Beloved,' because all her love is, or should be, imparted and spent on Christ, who gave himself to a cursed death for her. Our love should run in strength no other way, therefore the church calls Christ her 'Beloved.' Christ was there before, but she desires a further presence of him, whence we may observe, that

Wheresoever grace is truly begun and stirred up, there is still a further desire of Christ's presence; and approaching daily more and more near to the soul, the church thinks him never near enough to her until she be in heaven with him. The true spouse and the bride always, unless in desertion and temptation, crieth, 'Come, Lord Jesus, come quickly,' Rev. xxii. 20. Now, these degrees of Christ's approaches to the soul, until his second coming, are, that he may manifest himself more and more in defending, comforting, and enabling his church with grace. Every further manifestation of his presence is a further coming.

Quest. But why is the church thus earnest?

Reason 1. First, because *grace helps to see our need of Christ,* and so helps us to prize him the more; which high esteem breeds a hungering, earnest desire after him, and a desire of further likeness and suitableness to him.

Secondly, because the church well knows that when Christ comes to the soul *he comes not alone, but with his Spirit, and his Spirit with abundance of peace and comfort.* This she knows, what need she hath of his presence, that without him there is no comfortable living; for wheresoever he is, he makes the soul a kind of heaven, and all conditions of life comfortable.

Use. Hence we may see that those that do not desire the presence of Christ in his ordinances are, it is to be feared, such as the wind of the Holy Ghost never blew upon. There are some of such a disposition as they cannot endure the presence of Christ, such as antichrist and his limbs,* whom the presence of Christ in his ordinances blasts and consumes. Such are not only profane and worldly persons, but proud hypocrites, who glory in something of their own; and therefore their hearts rise against Christ and his ordinances, as laying open and shaming their emptiness and carnalness. The Spirit in the spouse is always saying to Christ, 'Come.' It hath never enough of him. He was now in a sort present; but the church, after it is once blown upon, is not satisfied without a further presence. It is from the Spirit that we desire more of the Spirit, and from the presence of Christ that we desire a further presence and communion with him. Now,

The end and reason why Christ is desired by the Church to come into his garden is 'to eat his pleasant fruits;' that is, to give him contentment. And is it not fit that Christ should eat the fruit of his own vine? have comfort of his own garden? to taste of his own fruits? The only delight Christ hath in the world is in his garden, and that he might take the more delight in it, he makes it fruitful; and those fruits are precious fruits, as growing from plants set by his own hand, relishing of his own Spirit, and so fitted for his taste. Now, the church, knowing what fitted Christ's taste best, and knowing the fruits of grace in her heart, desireth that Christ would delight in his own graces in her, and kindly accept of what she presented him with. Whence we see that

A gracious heart is privy to its own grace and sincerity when it is in a right temper, and so far as it is privy is bold with Christ in a sweet and reverend† *manner.* So much sincerity, so much confidence. If our heart condemn us not of unsincerity, we may in a reverend† manner speak boldly to Christ. It is not fit there should be strangeness betwixt Christ and his spouse; neither, indeed, will there be, when Christ hath blown upon her, and when she is on the growing hand. But mark the order.

First, Christ blows, and then the church says, 'Come.' Christ begins in love, then love draws love. Christ draws the church, and she runs after him, Cant. i. 4. The fire of love melts more than the fire of affliction.

Again, we may see here in the church a carefulness to please Christ. As it is the duty, so it is the disposition, of the church of Christ, to please her husband.

* That is, 'members,' = adherents.—G. † That is, 'reverent.'—ED.

1. The reason is, first, our happiness stands in his contentment, and all cannot but be well in that house where the husband and the wife delight in, and make much of, each other.

2. And again, after that the church hath denied herself and the vanities of the world, entering into a way and course of mortification, whom else hath she to give herself to, or receive contentment from? Our manner is to study to please men whom we hope to rise by, being careful that all we do may be well taken of them. As for Christ, we put him off with anything. If he likes it, so it is; if not, it is the best that he is like to have.

Uses. 1. Oh! let us take the apostle's counsel, 'To labour to walk worthy of the Lord, &c., unto all well-pleasing, increasing in knowledge, and fruitfulness in every good work,' Col. i. 9, 10. And this knowledge must not only be a general wisdom in knowing truths, but a special understanding of his good-will to us, and our special duties again to him.

2. Again, that we may please Christ the better, labour to be cleansed from that which is offensive to him: let the spring be clean. Therefore the psalmist, desiring that the words of his mouth and the meditations of his heart might be acceptable before God, first begs 'cleansing from his secret sins,' Ps. xix. 12.

3. And still we must remember that he himself must work in us whatsoever is well-pleasing in his sight, that so we may be perfect in every good thing to do his will, having grace whereby we may serve him acceptably. And one prevailing argument with him is, that we desire to be such as he may take delight in: 'the upright are his delight.' It cannot but please him when we desire grace for this end that we may please him. If we study to please men in whom there is but little good, should we not much more study to please Christ, the fountain of goodness? Labour therefore to be spiritual; for 'to be carnally minded is death,' Rom. viii. 6, and 'those that are in the flesh cannot please God.'

The church desires Christ to come into his garden, 'to eat his pleasant fruits,' where we see, *the church gives all to Christ.* The garden is his, the fruit his, the pleasantness and preciousness of the fruit is his. And as the fruits please him, so the humble acknowledgment that they come from him doth exceedingly please him. It is enough for us to have the comfort, let him have the glory. It came from a good spirit in David when he said, 'Of thine own, Lord, I give thee,' &c., 1 Chron. xxix. 14. God accounts the works and fruits that come from us to be ours, because the judgment and resolution of will, whereby we do them, is ours. This he doth to encourage us; but because the grace whereby we judge and will aright, comes from God, it is our duty to ascribe whatsoever is good in us, or comes from us, unto him; so God shall lose no praise, and we lose no encouragement. The imperfections in well-doing are only ours, and those Christ will pardon, as knowing how to bear with the infirmities of his spouse, being 'the weaker vessel,' 1 Pet. iii. 7.

Use. This therefore should cheer up our spirits in the wants and blemishes of our performances. They are notwithstanding precious fruits in Christ's acceptance, so that we desire to please him above all things, and to have nearer communion with him. *Fruitfulness unto pleasingness may stand with imperfections,* so that we be sensible of them, and ashamed for them. Although the fruit be little, yet it is precious, there is a blessing in it. Imperfections help us against temptations to pride, not to be matter of discouragement, which Satan aims at. And as Christ commands the north and south wind to blow for cherishing, so Satan labours to stir up an east pinching wind, to take either from endeavour, or to make us heartless in endeavour. Why should we think basely of that which Christ thinks precious? Why should we think that offensive which he counts as incense? We must not give false witness of the work of grace in our hearts, but bless God that he will work anything in such polluted hearts as ours. What though, as they come from us, they have a relish of the old man, seeing he takes them from us, 'perfumes them with his own sweet odours,' Rev. viii. 3, and so presents them unto God. He is our High Priest which makes all acceptable, both persons, prayers, and performances, sprinkling them all with his blood, Heb. ix. 14.

To conclude this point, let it be our study to be in such a condition wherein we may please Christ; and whereas we are daily prone to offend him, let us daily renew our covenant with him, and in him: and fetch encouragements of well-doing from this, that what we do is not only well-pleasing unto him, but rewarded of him. And to this end desire him, that he would give command to north and south, to all sort of means, to be effectual for making us more fruitful, that he may delight in us as his pleasant gardens. And then what is in the world that we need much care for or fear?

Now, upon the church's invitation for Christ to come into his garden, follows his gracious answer unto the church's desire, in the first verse of this fifth chapter:

'I am come into my garden, my sister, my spouse: I have gathered my myrrh with my spice; I have eaten my honeycomb with my honey; I have drunk my wine with my milk: eat, O friends; drink, yea, drink abundantly, O beloved,' Cant. v. 1.

Which words contain in them *an answer to the desire of the church in the latter part of the verse formerly handled:* 'Awake, thou north wind; and come, thou south,' &c.

Then, ver. 2, is set forth *the secure estate of the church at this time,* 'I sleep, but my heart waketh;' in setting down whereof the Holy Ghost here by Solomon shews likewise,

The loving intercourse betwixt Christ and the church one with another.

Now Christ, upon the secure estate and condition of the church, desires her 'to open unto him,' ver 2; which desire and waiting of Christ is put off and slighted with poor and slender excuses: ver. 3, 'I have put off my coat; how shall I put it on?' &c.

The success* of which excuses is, that Christ seems to go away from her (and indeed to her sight and sense departs): ver. 6, 'I opened to my beloved; but my beloved had withdrawn himself,' &c.; whereupon she lays about her, is restless, and inquires after Christ from the watchmen, who misuse, 'wound her, and take away her veil from her,' ver. 7.

Another intercourse in this chapter here is, that *the church for all this gives not over searching after Christ,* but asks the daughters of Jerusalem what was become of her beloved, ver. 8; and withal, in a few words, but full of large expression, she relates her case unto them, that 'she was sick of love,' and so 'chargeth them to tell her beloved,' 'if they find him.' Whereupon a question moved by them, touching her beloved, ver. 9, 'What is thy beloved more than another beloved?' she takes occasion, being full of love, which is glad of all occasion to speak of the beloved, to

* That is, 'the result.'—G.

burst forth into his praises, by many elegant expressions, verses 10, 11, 12, &c.

1. In general, setting him at a large distance, beyond comparison from all others, to be 'the chiefest of ten thousand,' ver. 10.

2. In particulars, ver. 11, &c.: 'his head is as most fine gold,' &c.

The issue whereof was, that the 'daughters of Jerusalem' become likewise enamoured with him, chap. vi. 1; and thereupon inquire also after him, 'Whither is thy beloved gone, O thou fairest among women?' &c. Unto which demand the church makes answer, chap. vi. 2; and so, ver. 3 of that chapter makes a confident, triumphant close unto all these grand passages forenamed, 'I am my beloved's, and my beloved is mine,' &c.; all of which will better appear in the particulars themselves.

The first thing then which offereth itself to our consideration is *Christ's answer to the church's invitation*, chap. iv. 16:

'I am come into my garden, my sister, my spouse: I have gathered my myrrh with my spice; I have eaten my honeycomb with my honey; I have drunk my wine with my milk: eat, O friends; drink, yea, drink abundantly, O beloved.' In which verse we have,

I. Christ's answer to the church's petition, 'I am come into my garden.'

II. A compellation, or description of the church, 'My sister, my spouse.'

III. Christ's acceptation of what he had gotten there, 'I have gathered my myrrh with my spice; I have eaten my honeycomb with my honey.' There is,

IV. An invitation of all Christ's friends to a magnifique* abundant feast, 'Eat, O friends; drink, yea drink abundantly, O beloved.'

I. For the first, then, in that Christ makes such a real answer unto the church's invitation, 'I am come into my garden,' &c., we see, *that Christ comes into his garden.* 'Tis much that he that hath heaven to delight in, will delight to dwell among the sons of sinful men; but this he doth for us, and so takes notice of the church's petition.

'Let my beloved come into his garden, and eat his pleasant fruit.' The right speech of the church that gives all to Christ, who, when she hath made such a petition, hears it. The order is this—

First of all, God *makes his church lovely*, planteth good things therein, and then stirs up in her good desires: both fitness to pray from an inward gracious disposition, and holy desires; after which, Christ hearing the voice of his own Spirit in her, and regarding his own preparations, he answers them graciously. Whence, in the first place, we may observe, that,

God makes us good, stirs up holy desires in us, and then answers the desires of his holy Spirit in us.

A notable place for this we have, Ps. x. 17, which shews how God first prepares the heart to pray, and then hears these desires of the soul stirred up by his own Spirit, 'Lord, thou hast heard the desires of the humble.' None are fit to pray but the humble, such as discern their own wants: 'Thou wilt prepare their hearts, thou wilt make thine ear to hear.' So Rom. viii. 26, it is said, 'Likewise the Spirit also helpeth our infirmities; for we know not what we should pray for as we ought: but the Spirit itself maketh intercession for us, with groanings which cannot be uttered.' Thus the Spirit not only stirs up our heart to pray, but also prepares our hearts unto it. Especially this is necessary for us, when our thoughts are confused with trouble, grief, and passions, not knowing what to pray. In

* That is, 'magnificent.'—G.

this case the Spirit dictates the words of prayer, or else, in a confusion of thoughts, sums up all in a volley of sighs and unexpressible groans. Thus it is true, that our hearts can neither be lifted up to prayer, nor rightly prepared for it, in any frame fitting, but by God's own Spirit. Nothing is accepted of God toward heaven and happiness, but that which is spiritual: all saving and sanctifying good comes from above. Therefore God must prepare the heart, stir up holy desires, dictate prayer; must do all in all, being our 'Alpha and Omega,' Rev. i. 8.

1. Now God hears our prayers, First, *Because the materials of these holy desires are good in themselves, and from the person from whence they come, his beloved spouse*, as it is in Cant. ii. 14, where Christ, desiring to hear the voice of his church, saith, 'Let me see thy countenance, and let me hear thy voice; for sweet is thy voice, and thy countenance is comely.' Thus the voice of the Spouse is sweet, because it is stirred up by his own Spirit, which burns the incense, and whence all comes which is savingly good. This offering up of our prayers in the name of Christ, is that which with his sweet odours perfumes all our sacrifices and prayers; because, being in the covenant of grace, God respects whatsoever comes from us, as we do the desires of our near friends, Rev. viii. 3.

2. And then, again, God hears our prayers, *because he looks upon us as we are in election, and choice of God the Father, who hath given us to him*. Not only as in the near bond of marriage, husband and wife, but also as he hath given us to Christ; which is his plea unto the Father, John xvii. 6, 'Thine they were, thou gavest them me,' &c. The desires of the church please him, because they are stirred up by his Spirit, and proceed from her that is his; whose voice he delights to hear, and the prayers of others for his church are accepted, because they are for her that is his beloved.

To confirm this further, see Isa. lviii. 9. 'Thou then shalt cry, and the Lord shall answer; thou shalt call, and presently he shall say, Here I am,' &c. So as soon as Daniel had ended that excellent prayer, the angel telleth him, 'At the beginning of thy supplications the decree came forth,' &c., Dan. ix. 23. So because he knows what to put into our hearts, he knows our desires and thoughts, and therefore accepts of our prayers and hears us, because he loves the voice of his own Spirit in us. So it is said, 'He fulfils the desires of them that fear him; and he is near to all that call upon him, to all that call upon him in truth,' Ps. cxlv. 18. And our Saviour, he saith, 'Ask and ye shall receive,' &c., Mat. vii. 7. So we have it, 1 John v. 14, 'And we know if we ask anything according to his will, he heareth us.'

Use 1. Let it therefore be a singular comfort to us, that in all wants, so in that of friends, when we have none to go to, yet we have God, to whom we may freely pour out our hearts. There being no place in the world that can restrain us from his presence, or his Spirit from us, he can hear us and help us in all places. What a blessed estate is this! None can hinder us from driving this trade with Christ in heaven.

Use 2. And let us make another use of it likewise, to be a means to stir up our hearts to make use of our privileges. What a prerogative is it for a favourite to have the fare * of his prince! him we account happy. Surely he is much more happy that hath God's care, him to be his father in the covenant of grace; him reconciled, upon all occasions, to pour out his heart before him, who is merciful and faithful, wise and most able to help us. 'Why are we discouraged, therefore; and why are we cast down,' Ps.

* Qu. 'care?' or 'fare?'—ED.

xlii. 11, when we have such a powerful and such a gracious God to go to in all our extremities? He that can pray can never be much uncomfortable.

Use 3. So likewise, it should stir us up to keep our peace with God, that so we may always have access unto him, and communion with him. What a pitiful case is it to lose other comforts, and therewith also to be in such a state, that we cannot go to God with any boldness! It is the greatest loss of all when we have lost the spirit of prayer; for, if we lose other things, we may recover them by prayer. But when we have lost this boldness to go to God, and are afraid to look him in the face, as malefactors the judge, this is a woful state.

Now there are diverse cases wherein the soul is not in a state fit for prayer. As that first, Ps. lxvi. 18, 'If I regard iniquity in my heart, the Lord will not regard my prayer.' If a man hath a naughty heart, that purposeth to live in any sin against God, he takes him for an enemy, and therefore will not regard his prayer. Therefore we must come with a resolute purpose to break off all sinful courses, and to give up ourselves to the guidance of God's Spirit. And this will be a forcible reason to move us thereunto, because so long as we live in any known sin unrepented of, God neither regards us nor our prayers. What a fearful estate is this, that when we have such need of God's favour in all estates; in sickness, the hour of death, and in spiritual temptation, to be in such a condition as that we dare not go to God! Though our lives be civil,* yet if we have false hearts that feed themselves with evil imaginations, and with a purpose of sinning, though we act it not, the Lord will not regard the prayers of such a one; they are abominable. The very 'sacrifice of the wicked is abominable,' Prov. xv. 8.

2. Another case is, when we will not forgive others. We know it is directly set down in the Lord's prayer, 'Forgive us our trespasses, as we forgive them that trespass against us,' Mat. vi. 14; and there is further added, ver. 15, 'If you forgive not men their trespasses, neither will your heavenly Father forgive you.' If our hearts tell us we have no disposition to pardon, be at peace and agreement, then we do but take God's name in vain when we ask him to forgive our sins, and we continue in envy and malice. In this case God will not regard our prayers, as it is said, 'I care not for your prayers, or for any service you perform to me,' Isa. i. 15. Why? 'For your hands are full of blood,' Isa. lxvi. 1. You are unmerciful, of a cruel, fierce disposition, which cannot appear before God rightly, nor humble itself in prayer. If it doth, its own bloody and cruel disposition will be objected against the prayers, which are not mingled with faith and love, but with wrath and bitterness. Shall I look for mercy, that have no merciful heart myself? Can I hope to find that of God, that others cannot find from me? An unbroken disposition, which counts 'pride an ornament,' Ps. lxxiii. 6, that is cruel and fierce, it cannot go to God in prayer. For, whosoever would prevail with God in prayer must be humble; for our supplications must come from a loving, peaceable disposition, where there is a resolution against all sin, Ps. lxxiii. 1. Neither is it sufficient to avoid grudging and malice against these, but we must look that others have not cause to grudge against us, as it is commanded: 'If thou bring thy gifts to the altar, and there rememberest that thy brother hath ought against thee; leave there thy gift before the altar, and go thy way; first be reconciled to thy brother, and then come and offer thy gift,' Mat. v. 23. So that if

* That is, 'moral.'—G

we do not seek reconciliation with men unto whom we have done wrong, God will not be reconciled to us, nor accept any service from us.

If then we would have our prayers and our persons accepted or respected, let us make conscience of that which hath been said, and not lose such a blessed privilege as this is, that God may regard our prayers. But here may be asked—

Quest. How shall I know whether God regard my prayers or not?

Ans. 1. First, *When he grants the thing prayed for, or enlargeth our hearts to pray still.* It is a greater gift than the thing itself we beg, to have a spirit of prayer with a heart enlarged; for, as long as the heart is enlarged to prayer, it is a sign that God hath a special regard of us, and will grant our petition in the best and fittest time.

2. When *he answers us in a better and higher kind,* as Paul when he prayed for the taking away of the prick of the flesh, had promises of sufficient grace, 2 Cor. xii. 7–9.

3. When, again, *he gives us inward peace, though he gives not the thing,* as Phil. iv. 6, 'In nothing be careful, but in all things let your requests be made to God with prayer and thanksgiving.'

Obj. But sometimes he doth not answer our requests.

Ans. It is true he doth not, but 'the peace of God which passeth all understanding guards our hearts and minds in the knowledge and love of God,' Philip. iv. 7. So though he answers not our prayers in particular, yet he vouchsafes inward peace unto us, assuring us that it shall go well with us, though not in that particular we beg. And thus in not hearing their prayers, yet they have their hearts' desire when God's will is made known. Is not this sufficient for a Christian, either to have the thing, or to have inward peace, with assurance that it shall go better with them than if they had it; with a spirit enlarged to pray, till they have the thing prayed for. If any of these be, God respects our prayers.

Again, in that Christ is thus ready to come into his garden upon the church's invitation, we may further observe, that

Christ vouchsafes his gracious presence to his children upon their desire of it.

The point is clear. From the beginning of the world, the church hath had the presence of Christ alway; for either he hath been present in sacrifices, or in some other things, signs of his presence, as in the 'bush,' Exod. iii. 2, or some more glorious manifestation of his presence, the ark, Exod. xxv. 22, and in the cloud and pillar of fire, Exod. xiii. 21, and after that more gloriously in the temple. He hath ever been present with his church in some sign or evidence of his presence; he delighted to be with the children of men. Sometimes before that he assumed a body, and afterward laid it down again, until he came, indeed, to take our nature upon him, never to leave it again. But here is meant a spiritual presence most of all, which the church in some sort ever had, now desires, and he offers, as being a God 'hearing prayer,' Ps. lxv. 2. And to instance in one place for all, to see how ready Christ hath always been to shew his presence to the church upon their desire. What else is the burden of the 107th Psalm but a repetition of God's readiness to shew his presence in the church, upon their seeking unto him, and unfeigned desire of it, notwithstanding all their manifold provocations of him to anger? which is well summed up, Ps. cvi. 43, 'Many times did he deliver them, but they provoked him with their counsel, and were brought low for their iniquity. Nevertheless, he regarded their affliction when he heard their cry.'

It doth not content the church to have a kind of spiritual presence of

Christ, but it is carried from desire to desire, till the whole desire be accomplished; for as there are gradual presences of Christ, so there are suitable desires in the church which rise by degrees. Christ was present, 1, by his gracious spirit; and then, 2, more graciously present in his incarnation, the sweetest time that ever the church had from the beginning of the world until then. It being 'the desire of nations,' Hag. ii. 7, for the description of those who lived before his coming is from 'the waiting for the consolation of Israel,' that is, for the first coming of Christ. And then there is a 3d and more glorious presence of Christ, that all of us wait for, whereby we are described to be such 'as wait for the coming of Christ,' Mark xv. 43. For the soul of a Christian is never satisfied until it enjoy the highest desire of Christ's presence, which the church knew well enough must follow in time. Therefore, she especially desires this spiritual presence in a larger and fuller measure, which she in some measure already had. So, then, Christ is graciously present in his church by his Holy Spirit. 'I will be with you,' saith he, 'unto the end of the world,' Mat. xxviii. 20. It is his promise. When I am gone myself, 'I will not leave you comfortless,' John xiv. 18, but leave with you my vicar-general, the Holy Spirit, the Comforter, who shall be alway with you. But—

Quest. How shall we know that Christ is present in us?

Ans. To know this, we shall not need to pull him from heaven. We may know it in the word and sacraments, and in the communion of saints; for these are the conveyances whereby he manifests himself, together with the work of his own gracious Spirit in us; for, as we need not take the sun from heaven to know whether or not it be up, or be day, which may be known by the light, heat, and fruitfulness of the creature; and as in the spring we need not look to the heaven to see whether the sun be come near us or not, for looking on the earth we may see all green, fresh, lively, strong, and vigorous; so it is with the presence of Christ. We may know he is present by that light which is in the soul, convincing us of better courses to be taken, of a spiritual life, to know heavenly things, and the difference of them from earthly, and to set a price upon them. When there is, together with light, a heat above nature, the affections are kindled to love the best things, and to joy in them; and when, together with heat, there is strength and vigour to carry us to spiritual duties, framing us to a holy communion with God, and one with another; and likewise when there is every way cheerfulness and enlargement of spirit, as it is with the creature when the sun approacheth. For these causes the church desires Christ, that she may have more light, life, heat, vigour, strength, and that she may be more cheerful and fruitful in duties. The soul, when it is once made spiritual, doth still desire a further and further presence of Christ, to be made better and better.

What a comfort is this to Christians, that they have the presence of Christ so far forth as shall make them happy, and as the earth will afford. Nothing but heaven, or rather Christ in heaven itself, will content the child of God. In the mean time, his presence in the congregation makes their souls, as it were, heaven. If the king's presence, who carries the court with him, makes all places where he is a court, so Christ he carries a kind of heaven with him. Wheresoever he is, his presence hath with it life, light, comfort, strength, and all; for one beam of his countenance will scatter all the clouds of grief whatsoever. It is no matter where we be, so Christ be with us. If with the three children in a fiery furnace, it is no matter, if 'a fourth be there also,' Dan. iii. 25. So if Christ be with us, the flames nor nothing shall hurt us. If in a dungeon, as Paul and Silas were, Acts xvi. 24, if Christ's presence be there, by his Spirit to enlarge our souls, all is comfortable whatsoever. It changeth the nature of all things, sweeteneth everything, besides that sweetness which it brings unto the soul, by the presence of the Spirit; as we see in the Acts, when they had received the Holy Ghost more abundantly, they cared not what they suffered, regarded not whipping; nay, were glad 'that they were accounted worthy to suffer anything for Christ,' Acts v. 41. Whence came this fortitude? From the presence of Christ, and the Comforter which he had formerly promised.

So let us have the Spirit of Christ that comes from him; then it is no matter what our condition be in the world. Upon this ground let us fear nothing that shall befall us in God's cause, whatsoever it is. We shall have a spirit of prayer at the worst. God never takes away the spirit of supplication from his children, but leaves them that, until at length he possess them fully of their desires. In all Christ's delays, let us look unto the cause, and to our carriage therein; renew our repentance, that we may be in a fit state to go to God, and God to come to us. Desire him to fit us for prayer and holy communion with him, that we may never doubt of his presence.

THE SECOND SERMON.

I am come into my garden, my sister, my spouse: I have gathered my myrrh with my spice; I have gathered my honeycomb with my honey; I have drunk my wine with my milk: eat, O friends; drink, yea, drink abundantly, O beloved.'—CANT. V. 1.

THIS song is a mirror of Christ's love, a discovery of which we have in part in this verse; wherein Christ accepts of the invitation of the church, and comes into his garden; and he entertains her with the terms of sister and spouse. Herein observe *the description of the church, and the sweet compellation*, 'my sister, my spouse;' where there is both affinity and consanguinity, all the bonds that may tie us to Christ, and Christ to us.

1. His sister, by blood.

2. His spouse, by marriage.

Christ is our brother, *and the church, and every particular true member thereof, is his sister*. 'I go,' saith Christ, 'to my Father and to your Father, to my God and to your God,' John xx. 17. 'Go,' saith he, 'and tell my brethren.' This was after his resurrection. His advancement did not change his disposition. Go, tell my brethren that left me so unkindly; go, tell Peter that was most unkind of all, and most cast down with the sense of it. He became our brother by incarnation, for all our union is from the first union of two natures in one person. Christ became bone of our bone and flesh of our flesh, to make us spiritually bone of his bone and flesh of his flesh.

Therefore let us labour to be like to him, who for that purpose became like to us, Immanuel, God with us, Isa. vii. 14; that we might be like him, and 'partake of the divine nature,' 2 Pet. i. 4. Whom should we rather desire to be like than one so great, so gracious, so loving?

Again, 'Christ was not ashamed to call us brethren,' Heb. ii. 11, nor 'abhorred the virgin's womb,' to be shut up in those dark cells and straits; but took our base nature, when it was at the worst, and not only our nature, but our miserable condition and curse due unto us. Was he not ashamed of us? and shall we be ashamed to own him and his cause? Against this cowardice it is a thunderbolt which our Saviour Christ pronounceth, 'He that is ashamed of me before men, him will I be ashamed of before my Father, and all the holy angels,' Mark viii. 38. It argues a base disposition, either for frown or favour to desert a good cause in evil times.

Again, *It is a point of comfort to know that we have a brother who is a favourite in heaven;* who, though he abased himself for us, is yet Lord over all. Unless he had been our brother, he could not have been our husband; for husband and wife should be of one nature. That he might marry us, therefore, he came and took our nature, so to be fitted to fulfil the work of our redemption. But now he is in heaven, set down at the right hand of God: the true Joseph, the high steward of heaven; he hath all power committed unto him; he rules all. What a comfort is this to a poor soul that hath no friends in the world, that yet he hath a friend in heaven that will own him for his brother, in and through whom he may go to the throne of grace boldly and pour out his soul, Heb. iv. 15, 16. What a comfort was it to Joseph's brethren that their brother was the second person in the kingdom.

Again, *It should be a motive to have good Christians in high estimation, and to take heed how we wrong them*, for their brother will take their part. 'Saul, Saul, why persecutest thou me?' Acts ix. 4, saith the Head in heaven, when his members were trodden on upon earth. It is more to wrong a Christian than the world takes it for, for Christ takes it as done to himself. Absalom was a man wicked and unnatural, yet he could not endure the wrong that was done to his sister Tamar, 2 Sam. xiii. 1. Jacob's sons took it as a high indignity that their sister should be so abused, Gen. xxxiv. Hath Christ no affections, now he is in heaven, to her that is so near him as the church is? Howsoever he suffer men to tyrannise over her for a while, yet it will appear ere long that he will take the church's part, for he is her brother.

'My sister, my spouse.'

The church is the daughter of a King, begotten of God; the sister and spouse of a King, because she is the sister and spouse of Christ, and the mother of all that are spiritual kings. The church of Christ is every way royal. Therefore we are kings because we are Christians. Hence the Holy Ghost doth add here to sister, spouse. Indeed, taking the advantage of such relations as are most comfortable, to set out the excellent and transcendant relation that is between Christ and his church; all other are not what they are termed, so much as glasses to see better things. Riches, beauty, marriage, nobility, &c., are scarce worthy of their names. These are but titles and empty things. Though our base nature make great matters of them, yet the reality and substance of all these are in heavenly things. True riches are the heavenly graces; true nobility is to be born of God, to be the sister and spouse of Christ; true pleasures are those of the Spirit, which endure for ever, and will stand by us when all outward comforts will vanish. That mystical union and sweet communion is set down with such variety of expressions, to shew *that whatsoever is scattered in the creature severally is in him entirely*. He is both a friend and a brother, a head and a husband, to us; therefore he takes the names of all. Whence we may observe further,

That *the church is the spouse of Christ.* It springs out of him; even as

Eve taken out of Adam's rib, so the spouse of Christ was taken out of his side. When it was pierced, the church rose out of his blood and death; for he redeemed it, by satisfying divine justice; we being in such a condition that Christ must redeem us before he would wed us. First, he must be *incarnate in our nature* before he could be a fit husband; and then, because we were in bondage and captivity, we must be redeemed before he could marry us: 'he purchased his church with his own blood,' Acts xx. 28. Christ hath right to us, he bought us dearly.

Again, another foundation of this marriage between Christ and us, is *consent*. He works us by his Spirit to yield to him. There must be consent on our part, which is not in us by nature, but wrought by his Spirit, &c. We yield to take him upon his own terms; that is, that we shall leave our father's house, all our former carnal acquaintance, when he hath wrought our consent. Then the marriage between him and us is struck up.

Some few resemblances will make the consideration of this the more comfortable.

1. The husband takes his wife under his own name. She, losing her own name, is called by his. So we are called Christians, of Christ.

2. The wife is taken with all her debt, and made partaker of the honours and riches of her husband. Whatsoever he hath is hers, and he stands answerable for all her debts. So it is here: we have not only the name of Christ upon us, but we partake his honours, and are kings, priests, and heirs with him, Rev. i. 5, 6. Whatsoever he hath, he hath taken us into the fellowship of it; so that his riches are ours, and likewise, whatsoever is ours that is ill, he hath taken it upon him, even the wrath due to us. For he came between that and us, when he was made sin and a curse for us, 2 Cor. v. 21; so there is a blessed change between Christ and us. His honours and riches are ours. We have nothing to bestow on him, but our beggary, sins and miseries, which he took upon him.

3. Those that bring together these two different parties, are the friends of the bride; that is, the ministers, as it is, John iii. 23. They are the *paranymphi*, the friends of the bride, that learn of Christ what to report to his spouse, and so they woo for Christ, and open the riches, beauty, honour, and all that is lovely in him, which is indeed the especial duty of ministers—to lay open his unsearchable riches, that the church may know what a husband she is like to have, if she cleave to him; and what an one she leaves, if she forsake him. It was well said in the council of Basil, out of Bernard, '*Nemo committit sponsam suam Vicario; nemo enim Ecclesiæ sponsus est,*'—None commits his wife to a vicar, for none is the husband of the church. To be husband of the church is one of the incommunicable titles of Christ, yet usurped by the pope. Innocent the Third was the first that wronged Christ's bed by challenging the title of Sponsus, husband of the church. Bernard forbids his scholar Eugenius this title (Epist. ccxxxvii. ad Eugenium). It is enough for ministers to be friends of the Bride. Let us yield him to be husband of the church, that hath given himself to sanctify it with washing of water and blood, Eph. v. 26. We are a wife of blood to him.

In this sweet conjunction we must know, that by nature we are clean otherways than spouses; for what was Solomon's wife, Pharaoh's daughter? A heathen, till she came to be Solomon's spouse. And as we read in Moses, the strange woman must have her hair cut off, and her nails pared, Deut. xxi. 12. Before she should be taken into the church, there must be an alteration; so before the church, which is not heathenish, but indeed hellish by nature, and led by the spirit of the world, be fit to be the spouse of Christ, there must be an alteration and a change of nature, Is. xi. 6–8; John iii. 3. Christ must alter, renew, purge, and fit us for himself. The apostle saith, Eph. v. 24, it was the end of his death, not only to take us to heaven, but to sanctify us on earth, and prepare us that we might be fit spouses for himself.

Use 1. *Let us oft think of this nearness between Christ and us*, if we have once given our names to him, and not be discouraged for any sin or unworthiness in us. Who sues a wife for debt, when she is married? *Uxori lis non intenditur*. Therefore answer all accusations thus:—'Go to Christ.' If you have anything to say to me, go to my husband. God is just, but he will not have his justice twice satisfied, seeing whatsoever is due thereunto is satisfied by Christ our husband. What a comfort is this to a distressed conscience! If sin cannot dismay us, which is the ill of ills and cause of all evil, what other ill can dismay us? He that exhorts us to bear with the infirmities one of another, and hath enjoined the husband to bear with the wife, as the weaker vessel, 1 Pet. iii. 7, will not he bear with his church as the weaker vessel, performing the duty of an husband in all our infirmities?

Use 2. Again, his desire is to make her better, and not to cast her away for that which is amiss. And for outward ills, they are but to refine, and make us more conformable to Christ our husband, to fit us for heaven, the same way that he went. They have a blessing in them all, for he takes away all that is hurtful, he pities and keeps us 'as the apple of his eye,' Zech. ii. 8. Therefore, let us often think of this, since he hath vouchsafed to take us so near to himself. Let us not lose the comfort that this meditation will yield us. We love for goodness, beauty, riches; but Christ loves us to make us so, and then loves us because we are so, in all estates whatsoever.

Use 3. And if Christ be so near us, *let us labour for chaste judgments*, that we do not defile them with errors, seeing the whole soul is espoused to Christ. Truth is the spouse of our understandings. *Veritas est sponsa intellectus*. It is left* to us to be wanton in opinions, to take up what conceit we will of things. So we ought to have chaste affections, not cleaving to base things. It hath been ofttimes seen, that one husband hath many wives, but never from the beginning of the world, that one wife hath had many husbands. God promiseth to betroth his church to him in righteousness and faithfulness, that is, as he will be faithful to her, so she shall by his grace be faithful to him; faithfulness shall be mutual; the church shall not be false to Christ. So there is no Christian soul must think to have many husbands; for Christ in this case is a jealous husband. Take heed therefore of spiritual harlotry of heart, for our affections are for Christ, and cannot be better bestowed. In other things we lose our love, and the things loved; but here we lose not our love, but this is a perfecting love, which draws us to love that which is better than ourselves. We are, as we affect;† our affections are, as their objects be. If they be set upon better things than ourselves, they are bettered by it. They are never rightly bestowed, but when they are set upon Christ; and upon other things as they answer and stand with the love of Christ. For the prime love, when it is rightly bestowed, it orders and regulates all other loves whatsoever. No man knows how to use earthly things, but a Christian, that hath first pitched his love on Christ. Then seeing all things in him, and in all them, a beam

* Qu. 'not left?'—ED. † That is, 'choose.'—G.

of that love of his, intending happiness to him, so he knows how to use everything in order. Therefore let us keep our communion with Christ, and esteem nothing more than his love, because he esteems nothing more than ours.

Quest. But how shall we know, whether we be espoused to Christ or not?

Ans. 1. Our hearts can tell us, *whether we yield consent to him or not.* In particular, whether we have received him, as he will be received, as a right husband, that is, *whether we receive him to be ruled by him,* to make him our head. For the wife, when she yields to be married, therewith also surrenders up her own will, to be ruled by her husband. So far she hath denied her own will; she hath no will of her own. Christ hath wisdom enough for us, and himself too, whose wisdom and will must be ours. To be led by divine truths so far as they are discovered unto us, and to submit ourselves thereunto, is a sign of a gracious heart, that is married to Christ.

Ans. 2. Again, *a willingness to follow Christ in all conditions as he is discovered in the word.* To suffer Christ to have the sovereignty in our affections, above all other things and persons in the world; this is the right disposition of a true spouse. For as it was at the first institution, there must be a leaving of father, and mother, and all, to cleave to our husband*: so here, when anything and Christ cannot stand together, or else we shall never have the comfort of his sweet name. Many men will be glad to own Christ to be great by him, but as St Austin complains in his time, Christ Jesus is not loved for Jesus his own sake. *Vix diligitur Jesus propter Jesum,* but for other things, that he brings with him, peace, plenty, &c.—as far as it stands with these contentments. If Christ and the world part once, it will be known which we followed. In times of peace this is hardly† discerned. If he will pay men's debts, so as they may have the credit and glory of the name to be called Christians, if he will redeem them from the danger of sin, all is well; but only such have the comfort of this communion, as love him for himself. Let us not so much trouble ourselves about signs as be careful to do our duty to Christ, and then will Christ discover his love clearly unto us.

Use 4. Now, they that are not brought so near to this happy condition by Christ, may yet have this encouragement, there is yet place of grace for them. Let them therefore consider but these three things.

1. The excellency of Christ, and of the state of the church, when it is so near him.

2. The necessity of this, to be so near him.

3. That there is hope of it.

There is in Christ whatsoever may commend a husband; birth, comeliness, riches, friends, wisdom, authority, &c.

1. The excellency of this condition to be one with Christ, is, *that all things are ours.* For he is the King, and the church the Queen of all. All things are serviceable to us. It is a wondrous nearness, to be nearer to Christ than the angels, who are not his body, but servants that attend upon the church. The bride is nearer to him than the angels, for, 'he is the head and husband thereof, and not of the angels,' Heb. ii. 16. What an excellent condition is this for poor flesh and blood, that creeps up and down the earth here despised!

2. But especially, if we consider *the necessity of it.* We are all indebted for more than we are worth. To divine justice we owe a debt of obedience,

* See Gen. ii. 24 and Mat. xix. 5; Mark x. 7, but it is 'wife,' not 'husband.'—G.

† That is with 'difficulty.'—G.

and in want of that we owe a debt of punishment, and we cannot answer one for a thousand. What will become of us if we have not a husband to discharge all our debts, but to be imprisoned for ever?

A person that is a stranger to Christ, though he were an Ahithophel for his brain, a Judas for his profession, a Saul for his place, yet if his sins be set before him, he will be swallowed up of despair, fearing to be shut up eternally under God's wrath. Therefore, if nothing else move, yet let necessity compel us to take Christ.

3. Consider not only how suitable and how necessary he is unto us, but what *hope there is to have him*, whenas he sueth to us by his messengers, and wooeth us, whenas we should rather seek to him; and with other messengers sendeth a privy messenger, his Holy Spirit, to incline our hearts. Let us therefore, as we love our souls, suffer ourselves to be won. But more of this in another place. The next branch is,

III. *Christ's acceptation.* 'I have gathered my myrrh with my spice,' &c. So that, together with Christ's presence, here is a gracious acceptance of the provision of the church, with a delight in it, and withal, a bringing of more with him. The church had a double desire, 1, That Christ would come to accept of what she had for him of his own grace, which he had wrought in her soul; and 2, She was also verily persuaded that he would not come empty handed, only to accept of what was there, but also would bring abundance of grace and comfort with him. Therefore she desires acceptation and increase; both which desires he answers. He comes to his garden, shews his acceptation, and withal he brings more. 'I have gathered my myrrh with my spice. I have eaten my honeycomb with my honey; I have drunk my wine with my milk,' &c. Whence we observe,

That God accepts of the graces of his children, and delights in them.

First, Because *they are the fruits that come from his children, his spouse, his friend.* Love of the person wins acceptance of that which is presented from the person. What comes from love is lovingly taken.

Second, They are the graces of his Spirit. If we have anything that is good, all comes from the Spirit, which is first in Christ our husband, and then in us. As the ointment was first poured on Aaron's head, Ps. cxxxiii. 2, and then ran down upon his rich garments, so all comes from Christ to us. St Paul calls the wife 'the glory of her husband,' 1 Cor. xi. 7, because, as in a glass, she resembleth the graces of her husband, who may see his own graces in her. So it is with Christ and the church. Face answereth to face, as Solomon saith in another case, Prov. xxvii. 19. Christ sees his own face, beauty, glory, in his church; she reflects his beams; he looks in love upon her, and always with his looks conveys grace and comfort; and the church doth reflect back again his grace. Therefore Christ loves but the reflection of his own graces in his children, and therefore accepts them.

Third, His kindness is such *as he takes all in good part.* Christ is love and kindness itself. Why doth he give unto her the name of spouse and sister, but that he would be kind and loving, and that we should conceive so of him? We see, then, the graces of Christ accepting of us and what we do in his strength. Both we ourselves are sacrifices, and what we offer is a sacrifice acceptable to God, through him that offered himself as a sacrifice of sweet smelling savour, from which God smells a savour of rest. God accepts of Christ first, and then of us, and what comes from us in him. We may boldly pray, as Ps. xx. 3, 'Lord, remember all our offerings, and accept all our sacrifices.' The blessed apostle St Paul doth will us 'to offer up ourselves,' Rom. xii. 1, a holy and acceptable sacrifice to God, when we are once in Christ. In the Old Testament we have divers manifestations of this acceptation. He accepted the sacrifice of Abel, as it is thought, by fire from heaven, and so Elijah's sacrifice, and Solomon's, by fire, 1 Kings xviii. 38; 1 Chron, xxi. 26. So in the New Testament he shewed his acceptation of the disciples meeting together, by a mighty wind, and then filling them with the Holy Ghost, Acts ii. 3. But now the declaration of the acceptation of our persons, graces, and sacrifice that we offer to him, is most in peace of conscience and joy in the Holy Ghost, and from a holy fire of love kindled by the Spirit, whereby our sacrifices are burned. In the incense of prayer, how many sweet spices are burned together by this fire of faith working by love; as humility and patience in submitting to God's will, hope of a gracious answer, holiness, love to others, &c.

Use 1. If so be that God accepts the performances and graces, especially the prayers of his children, let it be an argument to encourage us *to be much in all holy duties*. It would dead the heart of any man to perform service where it should not be accepted, and the eye turned aside, not vouchsafing a gracious look upon it. This would be a killing of all comfortable endeavours. But when all that is good is accepted, and what is amiss is pardoned, when a broken desire, a cup of cold water shall not go unrespected, nay, unrewarded, Mat. x. 42, what can we desire more? It is infidelity which is dishonourable to God and uncomfortable to ourselves, that makes us so barren and cold in duties.

Use 2. Only let our care be to *approve our hearts unto Christ*. When our hearts are right, we cannot but think comfortably of Christ. Those that have offended some great persons are afraid, when they hear from them, because they think they are in a state displeasing to them. So a soul that is under the guilt of any sin is so far from thinking that God accepts of it, that it looks to hear nothing from him but some message of anger and displeasure. But one that preserves acquaintance, due distance, and respect to a great person, hears from him with comfort. Before he breaks open a letter, or sees anything, he supposes it comes from a friend, one that loves him. So, as we would desire to hear nothing but good news from heaven, and acceptation of all that we do, let us be careful to preserve ourselves in a good estate, or else our souls will tremble upon any discovery of God's wrath. The guilty conscience argues, what can God shew to me, being such a wretch? The heart of such an one cannot but misgive, as, where peace is made, it will speak comfort. It is said of Daniel that he was a man of God's desires, Dan. ix. 23; x. 11, 19; and of St John, that Christ so loved him that he leaned on his breast, John xxi. 20. Every one cannot be a Daniel, nor one that leans on Christ's bosom. There are degrees of favour and love; but there is no child of God but he is beloved and accepted of him in some degree. But something of this before in the former chapter.

'I have gathered my myrrh with my spice; I have eaten my honeycomb with my honey,' &c.

That is, I have taken contentment in thy graces, together with acceptation. There is a delight, and God not only accepts, but he delights in the graces of his children. 'All my delight,' saith David, 'is in those that are excellent,' Ps. xvi. 3. But this is not all, Christ comes with an enlargement of what he finds.

Christ comes, and comes not empty whensoever he comes, but with abundance of grace. If St Paul, who was but Christ's instrument, could tell the Romans, 'I hope to come to you in abundance of grace and comfort,' Rom. xv. 29, because he was a blessed instrument to convey good from Christ to the people of God, as a conduit-pipe, how much more shall Christ himself, where he is present, come with graces and comfort! Those that have communion with Christ, therefore, have a comfortable communion, being sure to have it enlarged, for 'to him that hath shall be given,' Mat. xxv. 29. It is not only true of his last coming, when he shall come to judge the quick and the dead, 'I come, and my reward is with me,' Rev. xxii. 12, but also of all his intermediate comings that are between. When he comes to the soul, he comes not only to accept what is there, but still with his reward with him, the increase of grace, to recompense all that is good with the increase thereof. This made his presence so desired in the gospel with those that had gracious hearts. They knew all was the better for Christ, the company the better, for he never left any house or table where he was, but there was an increase of comfort, and of grace. And as it was in his personal, so it is in his spiritual presence. He never comes, but he increases grace and comfort.

Therefore, let us be stirred up to have communion with Christ, by this motive, that thus we shall have an increase of a further measure of grace. Let us labour to be such as Christ may delight in, for our graces are honey and spices to him, and where he tastes sweetness he will bring more with him. To him that overcometh he promiseth 'the hidden manna,' Rev. ii. 17. They had manna before, but he means they shall have more abundant communion with me, who am 'the hidden manna.' There is abundance in him to be had, as the soul is capable of abundance. Therefore we may most fruitfully and comfortably be conversant in holy exercises and communion with Christ, because our souls are fit to be enlarged more and more, till they have their fulness in heaven; and still there is more grace and comfort to be had in Christ, the more we have to deal with him.

But to come to shew what is meant by honey and wine, &c. Not to take uncertain grounds from these words, but that which may be a foundation for us to build comfort and instruction on, we will not shew in particular what is meant by wine and honey (for that is not intended by the Holy Ghost), but shew in general how acceptable the graces of the Spirit of Christ are to him, that they feed him and delight him, as wine and honey do us, because in the covenant of grace he filleth us by his Spirit of grace, to have comfort in us as we have in him. For, except there be a mutual joy in one another, there is not communion. Therefore Christ furnisheth his church with so much grace as is necessary for a state of absence here, that may fit her for communion with him for ever in heaven. As Isaac sent Rebecca, before the marriage, jewels and ornaments to wear, Gen. xxiv. 22, that she might be more lovely when they met, so our blessed Saviour, he sends to his spouse from heaven jewels and ornaments, that is, graces, wherewith adorned, he may delight in her more and more till the marriage be fulfilled. Therefore in this book the church is brought in, delighting in Christ, and he in the church. 'Thy love,' saith the church to him, 'is sweeter than wine,' Cant. i. 2. Christ saith to the church again, 'Thy love is sweeter than wine.' Whatsoever Christ saith to the church, the church saith back again to Christ, and he back again to the church. So there is a mutual contentment and joy one in another. 'Eat, O friends, drink,' &c.

Here is an invitation. When he comes stored with more grace and comfort, he stirs them up; both the church, others, and all that bear goodwill to his people, that they would delight in the graces and comforts of his church. Whence observe, that

Obs. We ought to rejoice in the comforts and graces of others, and of ourselves.

He stirreth up the church here, as well as others; for he speaks to all, both to the church and the friends of it. He had need to stir her up to enjoy the comfort of her own grace; for they are two distinct benefits, to have grace, and to know that we have it, though one Spirit work both, 1 Cor. ii. 12. The Spirit works grace, and shews us the things that God hath given us, yet sometimes it doth the one, and not the other. In the time of desertion and of temptation, we have grace, but we know it not; right to comfort, but we feel it not. There is no comfort of a secret, unknown treasure; but so it is with the church, she doth not always take notice of her own graces, and the right she hath to comfort.

We have need to have Christ's Spirit to help us to know what good is in us. And indeed a Christian should not only examine his heart for the evil that is in him, to be humbled; but what good there is, that he may joy and be thankful. And since Christ accepts the very first fruits, the earnest, and delights in them, we should know what he delights in, that we may go boldly to him; considering that it is not of ourselves, but of Christ, whatsoever is graciously good. Therefore we ought to know our own graces; for Christ, when he will have us comfortable indeed, will discover to us what cause we have to rejoice, and shew us what is the work of his own Spirit, and our right to all comfort.

And so, for others, we should not only joy in ourselves, and in our own condition and lot; but also in the happy condition of every good Christian. There is joy in heaven at the conversion of one sinner, Luke xv. 10. God the Father joys to have a new son; God the Son to see the fruit of his own redemption, that one is pulled out of the state of damnation; and God the Holy Ghost, that he hath a new temple to dwell in; the angels, that they have a new charge to look to, that they had not before, to join with them to praise God. So there is joy in heaven; the Father, Son, and Holy Ghost, with the angels, joy at it; and all true-hearted Christians joy in the graces one of another.

Reasons. For, 1. God, Christ, and the Holy Ghost have glory by it; and 2, the church hath comfort by the increase of a saint. 3. The prayer of a Christian adds new strength to the church. What a happy condition is it when God's glory, the church's comfort and strength, and our own joy, meet together. So that we should all take notice of the grace of God in others.

We ought to take notice of the works of God in creation and providence, when we see plants, stars, and such like, or else we dishonour God. What then should we do for his gifts and graces in his children, that are above these in dignity? should we not take notice of what is graciously good, and praise God for it? Thus they did for Paul's conversion, 'they glorified God.' For when they saw that Paul of a wolf was become not only a sheep, but a shepherd and leader of God's flock, they glorified God, Gal. i. 24.

So the believing Jews, when the Gentiles were converted, 'they glorified God, that he had taken the Gentiles to be his garden and people,' Acts xi. 18. When Paul and others had planted the gospel, and God gave the increase, the godly Jews rejoiced at that good. So, we that are Gentiles, should rejoice to hear of the conversion of the Jews, and pray for it; for then there will be a general joy when that is. Want of joy shews want of grace.

There is not a surer character of a Satanical and Cainish disposition, than to look on the graces of God's children with a malignant eye: as Cain, who hated his brother, because his works were better than his, 1 John iii. 12. Those that deprave * the graces of God in others, and cloud them with disgraces, that they may not shine, and will not have the sweet ointment of their good names to spread, but cast dead flies into it, shew that they are of his disposition that is the accuser of the brethren. It is a sign of the child of the devil. All that have grace in them, are of Christ's and of the angels' disposition. They joy at the conversion and growth of any Christians. Here, such as they, are styled friends and beloved; and indeed none but friends and beloved can love as Christ loves, and delight as Christ delights.

THE THIRD SERMON.

I am come into my garden, my sister, my spouse: I have gathered my myrrh with my spice; I have eaten my honeycomb with my honey; I have drunk my wine with my milk; eat O friends; drink, yea, drink abundantly, O beloved! I sleep, but my heart waketh, &c.—CANT. v. 1, 2.

It hath been shewed how Christ and the church were feasting together. She entreated his company 'to come into his garden and eat his pleasant fruits.' He, according to her desire, was come; and not only feasted on the church's provision, but also brought more with him. Christ taking walks in his garden, that is, his church, and every particular soul, which is as a sweet paradise for him to delight in, is much refreshed; and in witness of acceptance brings increase. What greater encouragement can we wish, than that we, being by nature as the earth, since the fall, accursed, should be the soil of Christ's delight, planted and watered by him; and that what we yield should be so well taken of him. We are under so gracious a covenant that all our services are accepted; not only our honey, but honeycomb; not only our wine, but our milk; our weak services as well as our strong; because the Spirit which we have from him sweeteneth all. As in nature there is one common influence from heaven, but yet variety of flowers, violets, roses, gilliflowers, spices, all sweet in their several kind, with a different kind of sweetness: so all graces have their beginning from the common influence of Christ's Spirit, though they differ one from another; and are all accepted of the 'Father of lights,' from whence they come, James i. 17. Christ wonders at his own grace, 'O woman, great is thy faith,' Matt. xv. 28; and Cant. iii. 6, 'Who is this that cometh out of the wilderness like pillars of smoke, perfumed with myrrh and frankincense, with all powders of the merchant?'

Let not the weakest of all others be discouraged. Christ looks not to what he brings, so much as out of what store; that which is least in quantity may be most in proportion, as the widow's mite was more in acceptance than richer offerings, Luke xxi. 3, 'A pair of turtle doves,' Levit. v. 7, was accepted in the law, and those that brought but goats' hair to the building of the tabernacle, Exod. xxxv. 6.

The particulars here specified that Christ took delight in, and inviteth others to a further degree of delight in, are

Myrrh and spice, honey and honeycomb, milk.

* That is, 'speak evil of.'—G.

Which shew, 1. The sweetness of grace and spiritual comfort. 2. The variety. 3. The use.

Myrrh and spices, 1, refresh the spirits, and 2, preserve from putrefaction; which are therefore used in embalming. If the soul be not embalmed with grace, it is a noisome, carrion soul; and as it is in itself, so whatsoever cometh from it is abominable.

Milk and honey nourish and strengthen; and *wine* increaseth spirits; and thereupon encourageth and allayeth sorrow and cares. 'Give wine to him that is ready to die,' Prov. xxxi. 6. The sense of the love of Christ is sweeter than wine; it banisheth fears, and sorrow, and care.

From this mutual delight between Christ and his spouse we observe next, that

There is a mutual feasting betwixt Christ and his church. The church bringeth what she hath of his Spirit; and Christ comes with more plenty.

For there being so near a covenant between him and us, we are by his grace to perform all offices on our part. We invite him, and he inviteth us. There is not the meanest Christian in whom there is not somewhat to welcome Christ withal; but Christ sends his provision before, and comes, as we say, to his own cost. He sends a spirit of faith, a spirit of love, a spirit of obedience. 1. Some are content to invite others, but are loth to go to others, as if it were against state. They would have wherewith to entertain Christ, but are unwilling to be beholden to Christ. 2. Some are content to have benefit by Christ, as his righteousness to cover them, &c., but they desire not grace to entertain Christ; but a heart truly gracious desireth both to delight in Christ, and that Christ may delight in it. It desireth grace together with mercy, holiness with happiness. Christ could not delight in his love to us, if we by his grace had not a love planted in our hearts to him. But to come to speak of this feast.

We see it pleaseth Christ to veil heavenly matters with comparisons fetched from earthly things, that so he may enter into our souls the better by our senses.

1. Christ maketh us a *feast, a marriage feast, a marriage feast with the King's Son*, of all feasts the most magnificent. A feast, first, in regard of the choice rarities we have in Christ. We have the best, and the best of the best. 'Fat things, and the marrow of fatness; wine, and wine on the lees,' Isa. xxv. 6, refined, that preserveth the strength. The comforts we have from Christ, are the best comforts; the peace, the best peace; the privileges, the highest privileges. 'His flesh,' crucified for us, to satisfy divine justice, 'is meat indeed; his blood, shed for us, is drink indeed,' John vi. 55; that is, the only meat and drink to refresh our souls; because these feed our souls, and that to eternal life. The love of God the Father in giving Christ to death; and Christ's love in giving himself, together with full contentment to divine justice; this gift it is that the soul especially feeds on. What could Christ give, better than himself to feed on? He thought nothing else worthy for the soul to feed on; and this it daily feeds on, as daily guilt riseth from the breakings out of the remainder of corruption. Other dainties are from this; from hence we have the Spirit, and graces of the Spirit. If he giveth himself, will he not give all things with himself?

2. As Christ maketh a feast of choice things for his elect and choice spouse, *so there is variety*, as in a feast. 'Christ is made to us of God, wisdom, righteousness, sanctification, and redemption,' 1 Cor. i. 30, that we should not be too much cast down with thought of our own folly, guilt, unholiness, and misery. There is that in Christ which answereth to all our wants, and

an all-sufficiency for all degrees of happiness. Therefore, he hath terms from whatsoever is glorious and comfortable in heaven and earth. Christ is all marrow, all sweetness. All the several graces and comforts we have, and the several promises whereby they are made over and conveyed unto us, are but Christ dished out in several manner, as the need of every Christian shall require. Christ himself is the ocean, issuing into several streams, to refresh the city of God. We can be in no condition, but we have a promise to feed on, and 'all promises are yea and amen,' 2 Cor. i. 20,' made to us 'in Christ,' and performed to us 'for Christ.'

3. Therefore, as we have in Christ a feast for variety, so for *sufficiency of all good*. No man goeth hungry from a feast. It was never heard for any to famish at a feast. In Christ there is not only abundance, but redundance, a diffusive and a spreading goodness; as in breasts to give milk, in clouds to drop down showers, in the sun to send forth beams. As Christ is full of grace and truth, so he fully dischargeth all his offices. There is an overflowing of all that is good for our good. He that could multiply bread for the body, he can multiply grace for our soul. If he giveth life, he giveth it in abundance, John x. 10. If he giveth water of life, he giveth rivers, not small streams, John vii. 38. If he giveth peace and joy, he giveth it in abundance; his scope is to fill up our joy to the full. As he is able, so 'is he willing to do for us far more abundantly than we are able to think or speak,' Eph. iii. 20. Where Christ is present, he bringeth plenty with him. If wine be wanting at the first, he will rather turn water into wine, than there should be a fail.

4. In a feast there is variety of *friendly company;* so here friends are stirred up to refresh themselves with us. We have the blessed Trinity, the angels, and all our fellow-members in Christ to come with us.

There is no envy in spiritual things, wherein whatsoever the one hath, the other hath not the less.

5. In a feast, because it is intended for rejoicing, *there is music;* and what music like to the sweet harmony between God, reconciled in Christ, and the soul, and between the soul and itself, in inward peace and joy of the Holy Ghost, shedding the love of Christ in the soul. We do not only joy, but glory, under hope of glory, and in afflictions, and in God now as ours, in whom now by Christ we have an interest, Rom. vi. 2–10. When we come sorrowful to this feast, we depart cheerful. This, as David's harp, stills all passions and distempers of spirit.

The founder and master of the feast is Christ himself; and withal is both guest, and banquet, and all. All graces and comforts are the fruits of his Spirit; and he alone that infused the soul, can satisfy the soul. He that is above the conscience can only quiet the conscience. He is that wisdom that 'sends forth maids,' Prov. ix. 3, his ministers, to invite to his feast. It is he that cheereth up his guests, as here. Those that invited others, brought ointment, and poured it out upon them, to shew their welcome, and to cheer them up, as may appear by our Saviour's speech to the Pharisee that invited him, Luke vii. 44. So we have from Christ both the oil of grace and oil of gladness. 'He creates the fruits of the lips to be peace,' Isa. lvii. 19, speaking that peace and joy to the heart that others do to the ear. 'He raiseth pastors according to his own heart, to feed his sheep,' Jer. iii. 15.

The vessels wherein Christ conveyeth his dainties are the ministry of the word and sacraments. By the word and sacraments we come to enjoy Christ and his comforts and graces; and by this feast of grace we come at length to the feast of feasts, that feast of glory, when we shall be satisfied with the image of God, and enjoy fulness of pleasures for evermore; and, which adds to the fulness, we shall fully know that it shall be a never-interrupted joy.

We see, then, that we cannot please Christ better than in shewing ourselves welcome, by cheerful taking part of his rich provision. It is an honour to his bounty to fall to; and it is the temper of spirit that a Christian aims at, to 'rejoice always in the Lord,' Phil. iv. 4, and that from enjoying our privileges in him. We are not bidden to mourn always, but to 'rejoice always,' and that upon good advisement; 'Rejoice,' and 'I say again,' saith St Paul, 'rejoice.' Indeed, we have causes of mourning, but it is that the seed of joy should be sown in mourning; and we can never be in so forlorn a condition, wherein, if we understand Christ and ourselves, we have not cause of joy. 'In me,' saith Christ, 'ye shall have peace,' John xvi. 33. The world will feed us with 'bread of affliction,' Hos. ix. 4. If the world can help it, we shall have sorrow enough; and Christ knows that well enough, and stirs us up to a cheerful feeding on that he hath procured for us. He hath both will, and skill, and power, and authority to feed us to everlasting life, for the Father sent him forth, and sealed him to that purpose. All the springs of our joy are from him, Ps. lxxxvii. 7.

Our duty is to accept of Christ's inviting of us. What will we do for him, if we will not feast with him? We will not suffer with him, if we will not feast with him; we will not suffer with him, if we will not joy with him, and in him. Happy are they that come, though compelled by crosses and other sharp ways. If we rudely and churlishly refuse his feast here, we are like never to taste of his feast hereafter. Nothing provokes so deeply as kindness despised. It was the cause of the Jews' rejection. 'How shall we escape,' not if we persecute, but 'if we do but neglect so great salvation?' Heb. ii. 3.

That which we should labour to bring with us is a taste of these dainties, and an appetite to them. The soul hath a taste of its own, and as all creatures that have life have a taste to relish and distinguish of that which is good for them, from that which is offensive, so wheresoever spiritual life is, there is likewise a taste suitable to the sweet relish that is in spiritual things. God should lose the glory of many excellent creatures if there were not several senses to discern of several goodness in them. So if there were not a taste in the soul, we could never delight in God, and his rich goodness in Christ.

Taste is the most necessary sense for the preservation of the creature, because there is nearest application in taste; and that we should not be deceived in taste, we hear, see, and smell before, and if these senses give a good report of the object, then we taste of it and digest it, and turn it into fit nourishment. *Omnis vita gustu ducitur.* So the spirit of man, after judgment of the fitness of what is presented, tastes of it, delights in it, and is nourished by it. There is an attractive, drawing power in the soul, whereby every member sucks that out of the food that is convenient for it. So the soul draws out what is well digested by judgment, and makes it its own for several uses.

The chief thing that Christ requireth is a good stomach to these dainties.

1. The means to procure an appetite. We are first *to be sensible of spiritual wants and misery.* The passover lamb was eaten with sour herbs; so Christ crucified, relisheth best to a soul affected with bitterness of sin. Whilst men are rich in their conceit, they go empty away. The duties and

performances they trust to, are but husks, windy, empty chaff. Swelling is not kind nourishment.

2. *That which hinders the sharpness of the stomach are, cold defluxions, that dull and flat the edge of it.* So upon plodding upon the world, cold distillations drop upon the soul, and take away the savour and desire of heavenly things. These things fill not. There is both a vanity of emptiness, and a vanity of short continuance in them. 'Why should we lay out our money,' Isa. lv. 2, spend our time, our wits, our endeavour so much about them? This makes so many starvelings in religion.

Besides, there be other noisome affections to be purged, as 1 Pet. ii. 1, ['Wherefore laying aside all malice, and all guile, and hypocrisies, and envies, and all evil speakings,' which breed a distaste and disaffection to spiritual things;] as malice and guile, &c. How can Christ be sweet to that soul unto which revenge is sweet!

3. *Exercise quickens appetite.* Those that exercise themselves unto godliness, see a need of spiritual strength to maintain duty. A dull formalist keeps his round, and is many years after where he was before; sees no need of further growth or strength. A Christian life, managed as it should be indeed, as it hath much going out, so it must have much coming in. It will not else be kept up. Those that have a journey to go, will refresh themselves for afterward, lest they faint by the way.

4. *Company likewise* of such as 'labour for that blessed food that endureth to life eternal,' John vi. 27, provoketh to fall too as the rest do, especially if they be equal or go beyond us in parts. For we will reason with ourselves, Have not I as much need as they? If these things be good for them, then they are good for me.

Thus St Paul foretelleth, that the example of the Gentiles should provoke the Jews to come in, and taste of the banquet Christ hath provided for both, Rom. xi. 25, 26. Especially this should stir us up earnestly to take our part in that Christ hath provided, because we know not how soon the table may be taken away. When men see the dishes in removing, though before they have discoursed away much time of their supper, yet then they will fall fresh to it. We know not how long wisdom will be inviting of us. It will be our wisdom to take our time, lest we put off so long, as wisdom herself laughs at our destruction; and a famine be sent, of all famines the most miserable, a famine of the word, and then we may pine away eternally without comfort. Christ will not always stand inviting of us. If we will none of his cheer, others will, and shall, when we shall starve.

Let this draw us on, that we see here Christ's hearty and free welcome, the gracious look that we are like to have from him. He counts it an honour, since he hath made such rich provision, for us to take part, and for our part, shew our unwillingness, that such free kindness should be refused. We cannot honour his bounty more than to feed liberally of that he liberally sets before us. We are glad to perceive our friends upon invitation to think themselves welcome. Let us open our mouth wide, since Christ is so ready to fill it. We are not straitened in his love, but in our own hearts. The widow's oil failed not till her vessels failed, 2 Kings iv. 6. We are bidden to delight in the Lord, and in whom should we delight, but where all fulness is to be had to delight in? Our spirits are not so large as those blessed comforts are which we are called to the enjoyment of. If the capacity of our souls were a thousand times larger, yet there is so large a sea of comfort in Christ, as they are not able to comprehend it. A taste of these good things breeds 'joy unspeakable,' and 'peace that passeth all understanding,' Philip. iv. 7. What will the fulness do? This taste we feel in the ordinances will bring us to that fulness hereafter. Oh, let us keep our appetites for these things which are so delightful, so suitable to the soul. How great is that goodness which he both lays up for hereafter, and lays out for his, even here in this life!

In some ages of the church, the feasts that Christ hath made have been more solemn and sumptuous than in other thereafter, as Christ hath been more or less clearly and generally manifested. At Christ's first coming there was a greater feast than before; because the riches of God's love in Christ were then laid open, and the pale of the church was enlarged by the coming in of the Gentiles. So will there be a royal feast, when the Jews shall be converted. 'Blessed then shall those be that shall be called to the supper of the Lamb,' Rev. xix. 9. Suppers are in the end of the day, and this supper shall be furnished towards the end of the world.

But then will be the true magnificent supper, when all that belong to God's election shall meet together, and feed upon that heavenly manna for ever. Then there will be nothing but marrow itself, and wine without all dregs. In all our contentments here, there is some mixture of the contrary; then nothing but pure quintessence. In the mean time, he lets fall some manna in this our wilderness, he lets us relish that now. It will not putrefy as the other manna did, but endure, and make us endure for ever. It's the true 'bread of life.'

Mark how Christ draws his spouse on to drink, and drink abundantly. There is no danger of taking too much. Where the spring is infinite, we can never draw these wells dry, never suck these breasts of consolation too much; and the more strong and cheerful we are, the better service we shall perform, and the more accepted. Delight is as sugar, sweet in itself, and it sweetens all things else. The joy of the Lord is our strength. Duties come off more gracefully, and religion is made more lovely in the eyes of all, when it comes forth in strength and cheerfulness. Christ's housekeeping is credited hereby. In our Father's house is plenty enough, Luke xv. 17. When the martyrs had drunk largely of this wine, it made them forget friends, riches, honours, life itself. The joy stirred up by it, carried them through all torments.

If any be hindered by conceit of unworthiness, if affected deeply with it, let them consider what kind of men were compelled to the banquet, the blind, the lame, Luke xiv. 21. See a lively picture of God's mercy in the example of the prodigal. He fears sharp chiding, and the father provides a rich banquet. He *goeth* to his father, but the father *runs* to meet him, Luke xv. 20. Did Christ ever turn back any that came unto him, if they came out of a true sense of their wants?

'Eat, O friends.' Christ, out of the largeness of his affections, multiplieth new titles and compellations—'beloved' and 'friends.' Christ provides a banquet, and invites his friends, not his enemies. Those good things that neither 'eye hath seen, nor ear hath heard, that are above our conceit to apprehend,' 1 Cor. ii. 9; these are provided for 'those that love him,' not that hate him. He mingles another cup for them, 'a cup of wrath,' and they are to 'drink up the very dregs of it,' Ps. lxxv. 8. Friendship is the sweetness, intimateness, and strength of love. In our friends our love dwells and rests itself. Conjugal friendship is the sweetest friendship. All the kinds and degrees of friendship meet in Christ towards his spouse. It is the friendship of a husband, of a brother; and if there be any relation in the world wherein friendship is, all is too little to express the love of Christ.

In friendship there is mutual consent, an union of judgment and affections. There is a mutual sympathy in the good and ill one of another, as if there were one soul in two bodies (*b*). There be mutual friends and mutual enemies. 'Do I not hate them,' saith David, 'that hate thee?' Ps. cxxxix. 21. There is mutual love of one another for their own sakes. In flattery, men love themselves most; in semblance, love others, but all is in reflection to themselves.

There is liberty which is the life of friendship; there is a free intercourse between friends, a free opening of secrets. So here Christ openeth his secrets to us, and we to him. We acquaint him with the most hidden thoughts of our hearts, and we lay open all our cares and desires before him. Thus Abraham was called God's friend, 2 Chron. xx. 7, and the disciples Christ's friends, John xv. 15. It is the office of the Spirit to reveal the secrets of Christ's heart to us, concerning our own salvation. He doth not reveal himself to the world.

In friendship, there is mutual solace and comfort one in another. Christ delighteth himself in his love to his church, and his church delighteth herself in her love to Christ. Christ's delight was to be with the sons of men, and ours is to be with him.

In friendship there is a mutual honour and respect one of another; but here is some difference in this friendship. For though Christ calls us friends, and therein in some sort brings himself down to us, yet we must remember that this is a friendship of unequals. Christ's honouring of us is his putting honour upon us. Our honouring of him is the giving him the 'honour due to his name,' 1 Chron. xvi. 29. This friendship must be maintained by due respect on our parts. As he is our friend, so he is our king, and knows how to correct us if we forget our distance. If he here seem to use us hardly, it is that he may use us the more kindly after. He suffers much for us, therefore we may well allow him the liberty of seasonable correcting of us.

He that inspireth friendship into others will undoubtedly keep the laws of friendship himself, will count our enemies his enemies. The enemies of the church shall one day know that the church is not friendless.

And as his friendship is sweet, so constant in all conditions. He useth not his friends as we do flowers, regard them only when they are fresh; but he breeds that in us that may make us such as he may still delight in us. If other friends fail, as friends may fail, yet this friend will never fail us. If we be not ashamed of him, he will never be ashamed of us. How comfortable would our life be if we could draw out the comfort that this title of *friend* affordeth! It is a comfortable, a fruitful, an eternal friendship.

'I sleep, but my heart waketh.' Here the church expresseth a changeable passage of her spiritual condition, after she had recovered herself out of a former desertion, expressed in the beginning of the third chapter; and enjoyed a comfortable intercourse with Christ. Now she falleth into a deeper desertion and temptation, from the remainder of corruption getting strength. The church now falleth asleep, then was awake in the night, and sought her beloved. Here is no present awaking, no seeking; there no misusage by the watchmen, as here. There she findeth him more speedily; here she falls sick with love before Christ discovereth himself.

Before we come to the words, observe in general,

Obs. 1. *That the state of the Church and every Christian is subject to spiritual alterations.* The church is always 'beloved,' a 'spouse,' a 'friend;' but in this one state there falleth out variety of changes. No creature subject to so many changes as man. From a state of innocency he fell into a state of corruption. From that he, by grace, is restored to a state of grace, and from grace to glory, where his condition shall be as Christ's now is, and as heaven the place is, altogether unchangeable. And in that state of grace, how many intercourses be there! the foundation of God's love to us, and grace in us always remaining the same. Once beloved, for ever beloved.

We see here, after a feast, the church falleth asleep. See it in Abraham, sometimes 'strong in faith,' sometimes fearful. David sometimes standing, sometimes falling, sometimes recovering himself and standing faster, sometimes triumphing, 'The Lord is the light of my countenance, whom shall I fear?' Ps. xxvii. 1; sometimes, again, 'I shall one day fall by the hands of Saul,' 1 Sam. xxvii. 1. In the very same psalm he begins with 'Rebuke me not in thy wrath,' and ends with 'Away, ye wicked,' Ps. vi. 1, 10. Elias, though zealous, yet after flies for his life, 1 Kings xix. So Job, Peter, sometimes resolute and valiant, other while sinks for fear, Job vi.; Mat. xiv. 30.

The reason. The ground is, by reason of variety of outward occurrences working upon the diversity of principles in us, nature and grace. Both nature and grace are always active in us in some degree. When corruption gets strength, then we find a sick state creeping upon us, and lose our former frame. It is with the soul as with the body. In a certain period of time it gathereth ill humours, which break out into aguish distempers at length; so the relics of a spiritual disease not carried away, will ripen and gather to a head. This should teach us, when we are well, to study to keep an even course, and to watch over the first stirrings, and likewise, if we see some unevenness in our ways, not to censure ourselves or others over harshly. Exact evenness is to be striven after here, but to be enjoyed in another world.

Obs. 2. We see, by comparing the state of the church here with the state of it in the third chapter, that *where corruption is not thoroughly purged, and a careful watch kept over the soul, thereafter* a recovery, will follow a more dangerous distemper.* Corruption will not only strive for life, but for rule. If there had been a thorough reformation in the church after her former trouble, and a thorough closing with Christ, she would not thus have fallen into a more dangerous condition. We see David, in his later times, falls to 'numbering of the people,' 2 Sam. xxiv. 1, *seq.*; and Samson, after he had done great services for the church, at length shamefully betrays his strength; and he that had ruled others submits to be ruled by a base strumpet, Jud. xvi. Jonah, for not thorough repenting for his running from his calling, falls after to quarrel with God himself, Jonah iv. 9. It is the best, therefore, to deal thoroughly with our hearts, else flesh unsubdued will owe us a greater shame, and we shall dishonour our own beginnings. Yet this is the comfort, that this will occasion deeper humility and hatred of sin in those that are God's, and a faster cleaving to God than ever before, as we see in the church here. Afterwards grace will have the better at last.

Obs. 3. We may observe the *ingenuity† of the church in laying open her own state.* It is the disposition of God's people to be ingenuous in opening their state to God, as in David, Nehemiah, Ezra, &c.

The reason is thus:—

(1.) By a free and full confession we give *God the honour of his wisdom in knowing of our own condition, secret and open.* We give him the honour of mercy that will not take advantage against us, the honour of power and

* Qu. 'there, after?'—ED. † That is, 'ingenuousness.'—G.

authority over us, if he should shew his strength against us. We yield unto him the glory of all his chief prerogatives; whereupon Joshua moveth Achan to a free confession, 'My son, give glory to God,' Joshua vii. 19.

(2.) *We shame Satan*, who first takes away shame of sinning, and then takes away shame for sin. He tempts us not to be ashamed to do that we are ashamed to confess, so we, by silence, keep Satan's counsel against our own souls. If we accuse ourselves, we put him out of office who is the 'accuser of the brethren,' Rev. xii. 10.

(3.) We *prevent, likewise, malicious imputations from the world.* Austin answered roundly and well when he was upbraided with the sins of his former age: 'What thou,' saith he, 'findest fault with, I have condemned in myself before.' *Quæ tu reprehendis, ego damnavi.*

(4.) This ingenuous dealing *easeth the soul*, giving vent to the grief of it. Whiles the arrow's head sticks in the wound, it will not heal. Sin unconfessed is like a broken piece of rusty iron in the body, *ferrum in vulnere.* It must be gotten out, else it will, by rankling and festering, cause more danger. It is like poison in the stomach, if it be not presently cast up it will infect the whole body. Is it not better to take shame to ourselves now, than to be shamed hereafter before angels, devils, and men? How careful is God of us, by this private way to prevent future shame!

(5.) This faithful dealing with ourselves is oft a means of *present delivery out of any trouble.* David, in Ps. xxxii. 4, was in a great distemper both of body and spirit; his moisture was turned into the drought of summer. It is thought he made this psalm between the time of his sin and his pardon. What course taketh he? 'I said,' saith he, that is, 'I resolved to confess my sin, and thou forgavest the iniquity of my sin,' ver. 5. Upon a free and full, a faithful and ingenuous confession, without all guile of spirit, he found ease presently, both in soul and body. The cause of God's severe dealing with us is, that we should deal severely with ourselves. The best trial of religion in us is by those actions whereby we reflect on ourselves by judging and condemning of ourselves, for this argueth a spirit without guile. Sin and shifting* came into the world together. The subtilty of proud nature, especially in eminency, is such that sins may pass for virtues, because sin and Satan are alike in this, they cannot endure to appear in their own colour and habit, and so those that oppose it shall be accounted opposers of good. This guile of spirit hath no blessedness belonging to it. Take heed of it.

Obs. 4. Mark, further, one sign of a gracious soul, *to be abased for lesser defects, sleepiness, and indisposition to good.* One would think drowsiness were no such great matter. Oh, but the church had such sweet acquaintance with Christ, that every little indisposition that hindered any degree of communion was grievous to her! You shall have a Judas, a Saul, an enormous offender confess great falls that gripe his conscience. All shall be cast up, that the conscience, being disburdened, may feel a little ease; but how few have you humbled for dulness of spirit, want of love, of zeal, and cheerfulness in duty? This, accompanied with strife against it, argues a good spirit indeed.

A carnal man is not more humbled for gross sins than a gracious Christian for wants in good actions, when it is not with him as it hath been, and as he would. The reason is, where there is a clear and heavenly light, there lesser motes are discernible; and spiritual life is sensible of any obstruction and hindrance. This goeth in the world for unnecessary nicety (*c*).

* That is, 'evasions, expedients.'—G.

The world straineth not at these gnats. But those upon whose hearts the sun of righteousness hath shined have both a clear sight and a tender heart.

To come to the words, 'I sleep.' The church fetcheth a comparison from the body to express the state of the soul. It is one use of our body to help us in spiritual expressions. Whilst the soul dwelleth in the body, it dependeth much in the conceiving of things upon the phantasy,* and the phantasy upon the senses. We come to conceive of spiritual sleep by sleep of the body, which we are all well enough acquainted with.

The church, as she consists of a double principle, flesh and spirit mingled together in all parts, as darkness and light in the twilight and dawning of the day ; so here she expresseth her condition in regard of either part. So far as she was carnal, she slept; so far as she was spiritual, she was awake.

In this mixed condition the flesh for the present prevailed, yet so as the spirit had its working; 'she slept, but her heart waked.'

The words contain a confession, 'I sleep;' and a correction, 'but my heart waketh.' She hath a double aspect, one to the ill, 'her sleeping;' the other to the good, 'the heart in some degree awaked.' The Spirit of God is a discerning Spirit, it discovereth what is flesh and what is spirit.

So that we must not conceive this sleep to be that dead sleep all men are in by nature, nor to be that judicial sleep, that spirit of slumber, which is a further degree of that natural sleep to which God giveth up some, as a seal of their desperate condition; but here is meant that sleep that ariseth out of the remainder of corruption unsubdued, and now, is here in the church, prevailing over the better part. Flesh and spirit have both their intercourse in us, as Moses and Amalek had. Unless we stand upon our guard, the flesh will get the upper ground, as we see here. The best are no further safe than they are watchful.

For the clear understanding of this, observe some correspondency in the resemblance; wherein too much curiosity is loathsome,† and postill-like (*d*); and calleth the mind too much from the kernel to the shell.

Bodily and spiritual sleep resemble each other in the causes, in the effects, and in the dangerous issue.

1. The sleep of the body cometh from the *obstruction and binding up of the senses by vapours which arise out of the stomach.* So there be spiritual fumes of worldly cares and desires that obstruct the senses of the soul. Therefore our blessed Saviour counts it a spiritual surfeiting, when the soul is oppressed with care about the world, Luke xxi. 34. Lusts bring the soul a-bed. Prosperity is a strong vapour. If it overcome not the brain, yet it weakeneth it, as strong waters do. See it in Solomon himself.

2. The disciples fell asleep in the garden when they were *oppressed with heaviness and sorrow,* Luke xxii. 45, which passions will have the like effect upon the soul.

3. Sleep ariseth oft from *weariness and want of spirits.* So there is a spiritual weariness arising from discouragements and too much expense‡ of the strength of the soul upon other matters; upon impertinencies that concern not the best state of the soul.

4. Some are brought asleep by *music.* So many, by flattering enticements and insinuations of others, joining with their own flattering, deceitful heart, are cast into a spiritual sleep.

5. Sleep ariseth from *want of exercise.* When there is a cessation from spiritual exercise, about the proper object of it, there followeth a spiritual sleep. Exercise keeps waking.

* That is, 'fancy.'—G. † That is, 'offensive.'—G. ‡ That is, 'expenditure.'—G.

6. Sleep ariseth oft from *cold diseases, as lethargies*; from cold, gross humours. Cold, earthly, gross affections about the things here below, benumb the soul, and bring it into a heavy, drowsy, sleepy temper.

7. Sometimes sleep is caused by *some kind of poison*, especially the poison of asps, which kills in sleeping. And do not sinful delights do the like to the soul? Insensible evils are the most dangerous evils.

8. Otherwhile *slothful, yawning company* dispose to sleep. There is no more ordinary cause of spiritual sleep, than conversing with spiritual sluggards, that count it a high point of wisdom not to be forward in religion. These formal, proud persons, as they are cold themselves, so they labour to cast water upon the heat of others. Nay, those that are otherwise good, if declining in their first love, will incline others to a fellowship in the same secure temper, lest they should be upbraided by the vigilancy of others. They are like in the effects.

1. Men disposed to be asleep *desire to be alone*. Those likewise that are disposed to take a spiritual nap, will avoid company, especially of such as would awake them. They will hardly endure rousing means.

2. Men will *draw the curtains and shut out light*, when they mean to compose themselves to rest. So when men favour themselves in some ways not allowable, they are afraid to be disquieted by the light. Light both discovereth, awaketh, and stirs up to working. And men when they are loth to do what they know, are loth to know what they should do. 'They that sleep, sleep in the night,' 1 Thess. v. 7. Asa, otherwise a good king, shut up the prophet in prison for doing his duty, 2 Chron. xvi. 10. Much of the anger that men bear against the word laid open to them, is because it will not suffer them to sleep quietly in their sins. Such as will suffer them to live quietly in their sins,—they are quiet and honest men. There cannot be a worse sign than when men will not endure wholesome words. It is a sign they are in an ill league with that they should above all wage war against.

3. In sleep, *phantasy ruleth, and dreams in phantasy*. Men in sleep dream of false good, and forget true danger.

Many cherish golden dreams; dream of meat, and when they awake, their soul is empty, Isa. xxix. 8. Vain hopes are the dreams of waking men, as vain dreams are all the waking of sleeping and carnal men, whose life is but a dream.

In sleep, there is no exercise of senses or motion. As then, men are not sensible of good or ill, they move neither to good or ill. Motion followeth sensibleness. What good we are not sensible of, we move not unto. Hence sleep is of kin to death, for the time, depriving us of the use of all senses; and a secure professor in appearance differs little from a dead professor. Both of them are unactive in good; and what they do, they do it without delight, in an uncomely and unacceptable manner, unbeseeming the state of a Christian. It is all one to have no senses, and not to use them. We may say of men in this sleepy temper, as the Scripture speaks of idols, 'they have eyes and see not, ears and hear not,' &c., Ps. cxv. 5.

So likewise they are alike in danger. In sleep, the preciousest thing men carry about them is taken away without resistance; and they are ready to let loose what they held fast before, were it never so rich a jewel. And it is so in spiritual sleepiness. Men suffer the profession of the truth to be wrung from them, without much withstanding; and with letting fall their watch, let fall likewise, if not their grace, yet the exercise of their graces, and are in danger to be robbed of all.

There is no danger but a man in sleep is fair for, and exposed unto. Sisera was slain asleep, Jud. v. 26, and Ishbosheth at noonday, 2 Sam. iv. 7; and there is no temptation, no sin, no judgment, but a secure, drowsy Christian is open for; which is the ground of so oft enforcing watchfulness by the Spirit of God in the Scriptures. As spiritual deadness of spirit is a cause of other sin, so likewise it is a punishment of them. God poureth a spirit of 'dead sleep upon men, and closeth up their eyes,' Isa. xxix. 10, till some heavy judgment falleth upon them; and how many carnal men never awake in this world, till they awake in hell! No wonder therefore that Satan labours to cast men into a dead sleep all that he can; and deludes them, with dreams of a false good, that their estate is good, and like so to continue; that to-morrow shall be as to-day; that no danger is near, though God's wrath hangeth over their head, ready to be revealed from heaven.

Thus we see how the resemblance holds. Some apply this to Constantine's time, about three hundred years after Christ, when the church upon peace and plenty grew secure, and suffered ecclesiastical abuses to creep in. Religion begat plenty, and the daughter devoured the mother. This made the writers of the ecclesiastical stories, to question whether the church hath more hurt by open persecution or peace, when one Christian undermineth and rageth against another.* Human inventions were so multiplied, that not long after, in Augustine's time, he complained that the condition of the Jews was more tolerable than theirs; † for though the Jews were under burdens, yet they were such as were imposed by God himself, and not human presumptions. But Gerson many hundred years after increaseth his complaint.‡ If, O Augustine, thou saidst thus in thy time, what wouldst thou have said if thou hadst lived now, when men, as a toy§ taketh them in the head, will multiply burdens? And he was not afraid to say, that the number of human Constitutions was such, that if they were observed in rigour, the greatest part of the church would be damned. Thus, whilst the husbandmen slept, the envious man Satan slept not, but sew|| his tares. Thus popery grew up by degrees, till it overspread the church, whilst the watchmen that should have kept others awake, fell asleep themselves. And thus we answer the papists, when they quarrel with us about the beginning of their errors. They ask of us, when such and such an heresy began? We answer, that those that should have observed them, were asleep. Popery is a mystery that crept into the church by degrees, under glorious pretences.¶ Their errors had modest beginnings. Worshipping of images arose from reserving the pictures of friends, and after that were brought into the church. Invocation of saints arose from some of the fathers' figurative turning of their speech to some that were dead. Transubstantiation had rise from some transcendent, unwary phrases of the fathers. The papacy itself, from some titles of the Romish Church and bishop. Nothing in popery so gross, but had some small beginnings, which being neglected by those that should have watched over the church, grew at length unsufferable. No wonder if the papists be cast into a dead sleep; they have drunk too deep of the whore's cup. They that worship images are, as the Scrip-

* Theodoret, lib 5.

† Augustine, Epist. ad Januar. cxix. Tolerabilior Judæorum conditio quam nostra.

‡ Si tuo tempore hæc dicebas (O sapiens Augustine) quid nostra tempestate dixisses? Si tenerentur in suo rigore, maxima pars Ecclesiæ damnaretur. Gerson de vit. spiritual.

§ That is, 'trifle.'—G.

|| That is, 'sowed.'—G.

¶ See Memoir of Sibbes, vol. i. p. lxv.

ture saith, 'like unto them, they have eyes and see not,' &c., Ps. cxv. 5. They cannot discern of their errors, though they be never so ridiculous and senseless, as prayer in an unknown tongue, and such like.

And upon this state of the church let us add this caution.

A Caution. If the best men be so prone to sleep, then we cannot safely at all times build upon their judgment. The fathers of the church were not always awake. There be few of them, but in some things we may appeal from themselves sleeping, to themselves waking. The best, having some darkness left in their understandings, and some lusts unsubdued in their affections, may write and speak sometimes out of the worst part and principle that is in them, as well as out of the best, when they keep not close to the rule.

When our adversaries press us with the authority of fathers, we appeal to them, where they speak advisedly and of purpose.* When they were not awaked by heretics, they speak sometimes unworthily, and give advantages to heretics that followed. It is the manner of our adversaries to make the unwarrantable practice of the ancienter time a rule of their practice, and the doubtful opinions of the ancients their own grand tenets; wherein in both they deal unsafely for themselves, and injuriously towards us, when we upon grounds in some things dissent; which liberty (oft when they should not) they will take to themselves.

But howsoever this sleepy condition agreeth to the former times of the church, yet I wish there were not cause to apply it to ourselves, in this latter age of the church, wherein many of the ancient heresies are revived; and besides, the evils that accompany long peace take hold of us, and will prevail too far, if we do not rouse up ourselves. The church is in the commonwealth, and usually they flourish and fall together. When there is a sleep of the church, for the most part there is a sleep of the state. A civil sleep is, when in grounds of danger there is no apprehension of danger; and this sleep is a punishment of spiritual sleep, when with Ephraim a state hath 'grey hairs, and knoweth it not,' Hos. vii. 9; when judgments abroad will not awake men. When noise and pinching will not awake, the sleep must needs be deep. The whole world almost is in combustion round about us; and many countries thought themselves as safe, a little before their troubles, as we now think ourselves. If fear of outward dangers will not awake, then spiritual dangers will not, as being more secret, and not obvious to sense. No wonder, then, if few will believe our report of the fearful condition of wicked men in the world to come. A man may be startled and awaked with outward dangers that is spiritually sottish, but he that is careless of outward danger, will be regardless of what we say in spiritual dangers. The fear of danger may be the greater, when, as it was amongst the Jews, those that should be watchful themselves, and awake others, instead of awaking, rock the cradle, and cry 'Peace, peace, the temple of the Lord, the temple of the Lord,' Jer. vii. 4. Yet we must never forget to be mindful, with thankfulness, for peace and the gospel of peace, which yet by God's blessing we enjoy, always suspecting the readiness of nature to grow secure under the abundance of favours, and so to bless ourselves in that condition.

Signs of a sleepy state. 1. Now we know that sleep is creeping upon us, by *comparing our present condition with our former*, when we were in a more wakeful frame, when the graces of God's Spirit were in exercise in us. If we differ from that we were, then all is not well.

* Patres in maximis sunt nostri, in multis varii, in minimis vestri.—*Wh*[*itaker*].

2. Compare ourselves again with that *state and frame that a Christian should be in;* for sometimes a Christian goes under an uncomfortable condition all the days of his life, so that he is not fit to make himself his pattern. The true rule is, that description that is in the word, of a waking and living Christian. What should a man be, take him at the best, the varying from that is a sleepy estate. As, for instance, a Christian should walk 'in the comfort of the Holy Ghost,' Acts ix. 31, live and walk by faith; he should depend upon God, and resist temptations. Faith should work by love, and love to ourselves should move us to honour ourselves as members of Christ, to disdain to defile ourselves by sin. Our hope, if it be waking, will purge us, and make us suitable to the condition we hope for in heaven, and the company we hope to have fellowship with there.

3. Again, *look to the examples of others that are more gracious.* I have as many encouragements to be thankful to God, and fruitful. They enjoy no more means than I; and yet they abound in assurance, are comfortable in all conditions. I am down in a little trouble, subject to passion, to barrenness, and distrust, as if there were no promises of God made to sowing in righteousness. Thus a man may discern he is asleep, by comparing himself with others that are better than himself.

4. Again, it is evident that we are growing on to a sleepy condition by this, when we find *a backwardness to spiritual duties,* as to prayer, thanksgiving, and spiritual conference. It should be the joy of a Christian, as it is his prerogative, to come into the presence of Christ, and to be enabled to do that, that is above himself. When what is spiritual in a duty will not down with us, it is a sign our souls are in a sleepy temper. There is not a proportion between the soul and the business in heavenly duties. Whom do we speak to but God? whom do we hear speak in the word but God? what should be the temper of those that speak to God, and hear him speak to them? It should be regardful, reverent, observant. Those that are watchful to the eye of a prince, what observance they shew, when they are to receive anything from him or to put up any request to him. 'Offer this to thy king,' saith the Lord by Malachi, Mal i. 8. When a man comes drowsily to God, to sacrifice, to hear, to pray, &c., offer this carriage to man; will he take it at thy hands? Oh the mercy of our patient God, that will endure such services as we most frequently perform! By this indisposedness to duty more or less, may we discover our sleepiness.

5. When the soul begins to *admire outward excellencies;* when it awakes much to profits, pleasures, and honours; when men admire great men, rich men, great places. The strength and fat of the soul are consumed by feeding on these things; so that when it comes to spiritual things it must needs be faint and drowsy. By these and the like signs, let us labour to search the state of our souls.

Motives against sleepiness. 1. And to stir us up the more, *consider the danger of a secure, sleepy estate.* There is no sin but a man is exposed unto in a secure estate. Therefore the devil labours all he can to cast men into this temper; which he must do before he can make him fall into any gross sin. When he is asleep, he is in a fit frame for any ill action; he is in a temper fit for the devil to work upon; to bring into any dream or error; to inflame the fancies and conceits with outward excellencies. The devil hath a faculty this way, to make outward things great that are nothing worth, and to make such sins little as, if we were awake, would affright us. He works strongest upon the fancy, when the soul is sleepy or a little drowsy.

There is no man that comes to gross sin suddenly. But he falls by little and little; first to slumber, and from slumber to sleep, and from sleep to security; and so from one degree to another. It is the inlet to all sins, and the beginning of all danger. Therefore the Lord takes a contrary course with his. When he would preserve a state or person, he plants in them first a spirit of faith, to believe that there is such a danger, or such a good to be apprehended, upon watching and going on in a course befitting that condition; and then faith, if it be a matter of threatening, stirs up fear, which waketh up care and diligence. This is God's method, when he intends the preservation of any.

2. A man in his sleep *is fit to lose all.* A sleepy hand lets anything go with ease. A man hath grace and comfort; he lets it go in his spiritual sleepiness,—grace in a great measure, and the sense and comfort of it altogether. A Christian hath always the divine nature in him, that works in some degree; yet notwithstanding in regard of his present temper and feeling, he may be in such a case, that he shall differ nothing from a reprobate, nay, he may come to feel more than any ordinary wicked man feels whiles he lives in the world, as divers good Christians do. And all this, through their carelessness,—that they suffer themselves to be robbed of first beginnings, by yielding to delights, company, and contentments. Feeding their conceits with carnal excellencies, so favouring corruptions, and flattering that that is naught in them, they lose the comfort of all that is good. Who would do this for the gaining of a little broken sleep; I say broken sleep, for the better a man is, the more unquietly shall he sleep in such a state. He shall feel startlings and frights in the midst of his carnal delights if he belong to God.

3, Besides, *God meets them with some crosses in this world*, that they shall gain nothing by it. There is none of God's children that ever gained by yielding to any corruption, or drowsiness, though God saved their souls. It is always true, a secure state is a sure forerunner of some great cross, or of some great sin. God cannot endure such a temper of soul; lifeless and unfeeling performances and sacrifices, to him that hath given us such encouragements. It must needs be distasteful to God, when we go drowsily and heavily about his work. 'Cursed is he that doth the work of the Lord negligently,' Jer. xlviii. 10. If it were to sheath his sword in the bowels of his enemy, to which man is exceedingly prone, yet if it be not done with diligence and an eye to God, a man is cursed in it.

4. And it is an *odious temper to God.* For doth not he deserve cheerful service at our hands? hath he been a 'wilderness' to us? doth he not deserve the marrow of our souls? doth not his greatness require it at our hands, that our senses be all waking? and doth not his mercy deserve, that our love should take all care, to serve him that is so gracious and good to us? Is it not the fruit of our redemption to serve him without fear, in holiness and righteousness all the days of our lives? Luke i. 14.

5. It is a state not only odious to God, but *irksome to our own spirits.* The conscience is never fully at peace in a drowsy state or in drowsy performances.

Likewise it is not graceful to others. It breeds not love in them to good things, but dislike. Carnal men, let them see a Christian not carry himself waking, as he should, though they be a thousand times worse themselves, yet notwithstanding they think it should not be so. Such a course doth not suit with so much knowledge and so much grace.

Let a man consider, wherefore God hath given the powers of the soul and the graces of the Spirit. Are they not given for exercise, and to be employed about their proper objects? A man is not a man, a Christian is not a Christian, when he is not waking. He so far degenerates from himself, as he yields unto any unbeseeming carriage. Wherefore hath God given us understanding, but to conceive the best things? Wherefore have we judgment, but to judge aright between the things of heaven and earth? Wherefore have we love planted in us, but to set it on lovely objects? Wherefore faith, but to trust God over all? Wherefore hatred, but to fly ill? Wherefore have we affections, but for spiritual things? When therefore our affections are dull, and lose their edge to these things, being quick only to earthly things, what a temper is this! How doth a man answer his creation, the state of a new creature! Wherefore are all graces planted in the soul, as faith and love, and hope and patience, but to be in exercise, and waking? To have these, and to let them sleep and lie unexercised, so far a Christian forgets himself, and is not himself. A Christian as a Christian, that is, in his right temper, should be in the act and exercise of what is good in him, upon all occasions; as we say of God, he is a pure act, because he is always in working. The Spirit of God is a pure act, in whom is no suffering but all action, about that that is fit for so glorious a nature. So it is with the spirit of a man, that hath the Spirit of God. He is in act, in exercise, in operation, as the Spirit is more or less in him. So he is more or less in operation, more or less fruitful. What a world of good might Christians do, if they were in a right temper! What a deal of ill might they escape and avoid that they lie in, if they would rouse up their souls to be as Christians should be, and as their soul and conscience tells them they ought and might be, did they rightly improve the means they have!

THE FOURTH SERMON.

I sleep, but my heart wakes, &c.—CANT. V. 2.

THE words, as it hath been shewed, contain a confession, 'I sleep,' and a correction, 'my heart waketh.' The confession hath been handled, now something of the correction or exception.

'My heart waketh.' The word heart, you know, includes the whole soul, for the understanding is the heart, 'an understanding heart,' Job xxxviii. 36. To 'lay things up in our hearts,' Luke ii. 51, there it is memory; and to cleave in heart is to cleave in will, Acts xi. 23. To 'rejoice in heart,' Isa. xxx. 29, that is in the affection. So that all the powers of the soul, the inward man, as Paul calleth it, 2 Cor. iv. 16, is the heart.

'I sleep, but my heart waketh.' Indeed the church might have said, My heart sleepeth, but my heart waketh. For it is the same faculty, the same power of the soul, both in the state of corruption, and of grace, in which the soul is; as in the twilight we cannot say, this is light and that is darkness, because there is such a mixture. In all the powers of the soul there is something good and something ill, something flesh and something spirit. The heart was asleep, and likewise was awake. 'I sleep, but my heart waketh.'

Obs. 1. You see here, then, first of all, in this correction, *that a Christian hath two principles in him*, that which is good, and that which is evil, whence issueth the weakness of his actions and affections. They are all mixed, as are the principles from which they come forth.

Obs. 2. We may observe, further, *that a Christian man may know how it is with himself.* Though he be mixed of flesh and spirit, he hath a distinguishing knowledge and judgment whereby he knows both the good and evil in himself. In a dungeon where is nothing but darkness, both on the eye that should see and on that which should be seen, he can see nothing; but where there is a supernatural principle, where there is this mixture, there the light of the Spirit searcheth the dark corners of the heart. A man that hath the Spirit knoweth both; he knoweth himself and his own heart. The Spirit hath a light of its own, even as reason hath. How doth reason know what it doth? By a reflect act inbred in the soul. Shall a man that is natural reflect upon his state, and know what he knows, what he thinks, what he doth, and may not the soul that is raised to an higher estate know as much? Undoubtedly it may. Besides, we have the Spirit of God, which is light, and self-evidencing. It shews unto us where it is, and what it is. The work of the Spirit may sometimes be hindered, as in times of temptation. Then I confess a man may look wholly upon corruption, and so mistake himself in judging by that which he sees present in himself, and not by the other principle which is concealed for a time from him. But a Christian, when he is not in such a temptation, he knows his own estate, and can distinguish between the principles in him of the flesh and spirit, grace and nature.

Again, we see here in that the church saith, 'but my heart waketh,' that she doth acknowledge there is good as well as evil. As the church is ingenious* to confess that which is amiss, 'I sleep,' so she is as true in confessing that which is good in herself, 'but my heart waketh,' which yields us another observation.

Obs. 3. We should *as well acknowledge that which is good as that which is evil in our hearts.*

Because we must not bear false witness, as not against others, much less against ourselves. Many help Satan, the accuser, and plead his cause against the Spirit, their comforter, in refusing to see what God seeth in them. We must make conscience of this, to know the good as well as the evil, though it be never so little.

To come in particular, what is that good the church here confesseth, when she saith that 'her heart waketh?'

(1.) She in her sleepy estate, *first*, hath her *judgment sound in that which is truth, of persons, things, and courses.* Christians are not so benighted when they sleep, or given up to such a reprobate judgment, as that they discern not differences. They can discern that such are in a good way, and such are not; that such means are good, and such are not. A Christian ofttimes is forced to do work out of judgment, in case his affections are asleep or distracted; and such works are approved of God, as they come from a right judgment and conviction, though the evil of them be chastised.

(2.) But all is not in the judgment. The child of God asleep hath a *working in the will.* Choosing the better part, which he will cleave to, he hath a general purpose 'to please God in all things,' and no settled purpose in particular for to sleep. Thus answerable to his judgment, therefore, he chooseth the better part and side; he owns God and his cause, even in evil times, cleaving in resolution of heart to the best ways, though with weakness.

Take David in his sleepy time between his repentance and his foul sin. If one should have asked him what he thought of the ways of God and of

* That is, 'ingenuous.'—G.

the contrary, he would have given you an answer out of sound judgment thus and thus. If you should have asked him what course he would have followed in his choice, resolution, and purpose, he would have answered savourly.

(3.) Again, there remaineth *affection answerable to their judgment*, which, though they find, and feel it not for a time, it being perhaps scattered, yet there is a secret love to Christ, and to his cause and side, joined with joy in the welfare of the church and people of God; rejoicing in the prosperity of the righteous, with a secret grief for the contrary. The pulses will beat this way, and good affections will discover themselves. Take him in his sleepy estate, the judgment is sound in the main, the will, the affections, the joy, the delight, the sorrow. This is an evidence his heart is awake.

(4.) *The conscience likewise is awake.* The heart is taken ofttimes for the conscience in Scripture. A good conscience, called a merry heart, is 'a continual feast,' Prov. xv. 15. Now, the conscience of God's children is never so sleepy but it awaketh in some comfortable measure. Though perhaps it may be deaded* in a particular act, yet notwithstanding there is so much life in it, as upon speech or conference, &c., there will be an opening of it, and a yielding at the length to the strength of spiritual reason. His conscience is not seared. David was but a little roused by Nathan, yet you see how he presently confessed ingeniously† that he had sinned, 2 Sam. xii. 13. So, when he had numbered the people, his conscience presently smote him, 2 Sam. xxiv. 10; and when he resolved to kill Nabal and all his family, which was a wicked and carnal passion, in which there was nothing but flesh; yet when he was stopped by the advice and discreet counsel of Abigail, we see how presently he yielded, 1 Sam. xxv. 32, *seq.* There is a kind of perpetual tenderness of conscience in God's people. All the difference is of more or less.

(5.) And answerable to these inward powers is the *outward obedience of God's children.* In their sleepy estate they go on in a course of obedience. Though deadly and coldly, and not with that glory that may give others good example or yield themselves comfort, yet there is a course of good duties. His ordinary way is good, howsoever he may step aside. His fits may be sleepy when his estate is waking. We must distinguish between a state and a fit. A man may have an aguish fit in a sound body. The state of a Christian is a waking state in the inward man. The bye-courses he falleth into are but fits, out of which he recovers himself.

Use 1. Whence, for use, let us magnify the goodness of God, that will remain by his Spirit, and let it stay to preserve life in such hearts as ours are, so prone to security and sleepiness. Let it put us in mind of other like merciful and gracious doings of our God for us, that he gave his Spirit to us when we had nothing good in us, when it met with nothing but enmity, rebellion, and indisposedness. Nay, consider how he debased himself and became man, in being united to our frail flesh, after an admirable‡ nearness, and all out of mercy to save us.

Use 2. If so be that Satan shall tempt us in such occasions, let us enter into our own souls, and search the truth of grace, our judgment, our wills, our constant course of obedience, and the inward principle whence it comes, that we may be able to stand in the time of temptation. What upheld the church but this reflect act, by the help of the Spirit, that she was able to judge of the good as well as of the ill? Thus David, 'The desires of our souls are towards thee,' Ps. xxxviii. 9; and though all this have befallen us,

* That is, 'deadened.'—G. † That is, 'ingenuously.'—G. ‡ That is, 'wonderful.'—G.

yet have we not forgotten thy name, Ps. xliv. 20. This will enable us to appeal to God, as Peter, 'Lord, thou knowest I love thee,' John xxi. 15. It is an evidence of a good estate.

Obs. 1. 'My heart waketh.' *God's children never totally fall from grace.* Though they sleep, yet their heart is awake. The prophet Isaiah, speaking of the church and children of God, Isa. vi. 13, saith, 'It shall be as a tree, as an oak whose substance is in them, when they cast their leaves.' Though you see neither fruit nor leaves, yet there is life in the root, 'the seed remains in them.' There is alway a seed remaining. It is an immortal seed that we are begotten by. Peter, when he denied his Master, was like an oak that was weather-beaten; yet there was life still in the root, 1 Pet. i. 3, Mat. xxvi. 32, *seq.* For, questionless, Peter loved Christ from his heart. Sometimes a Christian may be in such a poor case, as the spiritual life runneth all to the heart, and the outward man is left destitute; as in wars, when the enemy hath conquered the field, the people run into the city, and if they be beaten out of the city, they run into the castle. The grace of God sometimes fails in the outward action, in the field, when yet it retireth to the heart, in which fort it is impregnable. 'My heart waketh.'

When the outward man sleeps, and there are weak, dull performances, and perhaps actions amiss, too, yet notwithstanding 'the heart waketh.' As we see in a swoon or great scars, the blood, spirits, and life, though they leave the face and hands, &c., yet they are in the heart. It is said in the Scripture of Eutychus, 'His life is in him still,' though he seemed to be dead, Acts xx. 9. As Christ said of Lazarus, John xi. 4, so a man may say of a Christian in his worst state, His life is in him still; he is not dead, but sleeps; 'his heart waketh.'

Obs. 2. *This is a sound doctrine and comfortable, agreeable to Scripture and the experience of God's people.* We must not lose it, therefore, but make use of it against the time of temptation. There are some pulses that discover life in the sickest man, so are there some breathings and spiritual motions of heart that will comfort in such times. These two never fail on God's part, his love, which is unchangeable, and his grace, a fruit of his love; and two on our part, the impression of that love, and the gracious work of the new creature. 'Christ never dies,' saith the apostle, Heb. vii. 25. As he never dies in himself, after his resurrection, so he never dies in his children. There is always spiritual life.

Use for comfort. 'The heart waketh.' This is a secret of God's sanctuary, only belonging to God's people. Others have nothing to do with it. They shall ever love God, and God will ever love them. The apostle, 1 Cor. xiii. 8, saith, 'Love never fails.' Gifts, you know, shall be abolished, because the manner of knowing we now use shall cease. 'We see through a glass,' &c., 'but love abideth,' 1 Cor. xiii. 12. Doth our love to God abide for ever, and doth not his love to us, whence it cometh? Ours is but a reflection of God's love. Let us comfort ourselves, therefore, in this for the time to come, that in all the uncertainty of things in this life we have to-day and lose to-morrow, as we see in Job, there is somewhat a saint may build on that is constant and unmoveable. 'I am the Lord, I change not; therefore you sons of Jacob are not consumed,' Mal. iii. 6. God should deny himself, as it were, which he cannot do, and his own constant nature, if he should vary this way.

Obs. 3. *A Christian is what his heart and inward man is.* It is a true speech of divines, God and nature begin there. Art begins with the face and outward lineaments, as hypocrisy, outward painting and expressions;

but grace at the centre, and from thence goes to the circumference. And therefore the church values herself here by the disposition and temper of her heart. Thus I am for my outward carriage, &c. 'I sleep, but my heart, that waketh.'

Therefore, let us enter into our consciences and souls, for the trial of our estates, how it is with our judgments. Do we allow of the ways of God and of the law of the inward man? How is it with our affections and bent to good things? how with our hatred, our zeal? Is it not more for outward things than for inward? We know what Jehu said to Jonadab, when he would have him into his chariot, 'Is thine heart as mine? Then come to me,' 2 Kings x. 15. So saith Christ, Is thine heart as mine? then give me thy hand. But first God must have our hearts, and then our hands. A man otherwise is but a ghost in religion, which goes up and down, without a spirit of its own; but a picture that hath an outside, and is nothing within. Therefore, especially, let us look to our hearts. 'Oh, that there were such an heart in this people,' saith God to Moses, 'to fear me always, for their good,' Deut. v. 29. This is it that God's children desire, that their hearts may be aright set. 'Wash thy heart, O Jerusalem,' saith the prophet, 'from thy wickedness,' &c., Jer. iv. 14. Indeed, all the outward man depends upon this. Therefore, Satan, if he can get this fort, he is safe, and so Satan's vicar, Prov. iv. 23. It was a watchword that was in Gregory XIII. his time, in Queen Elizabeth's days, 'My son, give me thy heart. Dissemble, go to church, and do what you will; but, *da mihi cor*, be in heart a papist, and go where you will' (*e*). God is not content with the heart alone. The devil knows if he have the heart he hath all; but God, as he made all, both soul and body, he will have all. But yet in times of temptation the chief trial is in the heart.

And from hence we may have a main difference between one Christian and another. A sound Christian doth what he doth from the heart; he begins the work there. What good he doth he loves in his heart first, judgeth it to be good, and then he doeth it.

An hypocrite doth what he doth outwardly, and allows not inwardly of that good he doth. He would do ill, and not good, if it were in his choice. The good that he doth is for by-ends, for correspondence, or dependence upon others, or conformity with the times, to cover his designs under formality of religion, that he may not be known outwardly, as he is inwardly, an atheist and an hypocrite. So he hath false aims; his heart is not directed to a right mark. But it is otherwise with God's child. Whatsoever good he doth, it is in his heart first; whatsoever ill he abstains from, he doth it from his heart, judging it to be naught; therefore he hates it, and will not do it. Here is a main difference of the church from all others. It wakes in the heart, though the outward man sleeps. But other men's hearts sleep when they wake, as you know some men will walk and do many things in their sleep. An hypocrite is such a kind of man. He walks and goes up and down, but his heart is asleep. He knows not what he doth, nor doth he the thing out of judgment or love, but as one asleep, as it were. He hath no inward affection unto the things he doth. A Christian is the contrary; his heart is awake when he is asleep.

Another difference from the words you may have thus. A Christian, by the power of God's Spirit in him, is sensible of the contrarieties in him, complains, and is ashamed for the same. But an hypocrite is not so; he is not sensible of his sleepiness. 'I sleep,' saith the church. So much as the church saith she slept, so much she did not sleep; for a man that is asleep cannot say he is asleep, nor a dead man that he is dead. So far as he saith he is asleep, he is awake. Now, the church confesseth that she was asleep by that part that was awake in her. Other men do not complain, are not sensible of their sleepiness and slumbering, but compose themselves to slumber, and seek darkness, which is a friend of sleep. They would willingly be ignorant, to keep their conscience dull and dumb as much as they can, that it may not upbraid them. This is the disposition of a carnal man; he is not sensible of his estate as here the church is.

Obs. 4. *A waking state is a blessed state.* The church you see supports and comforts herself that she was waking in her inward man, that she was happy in that respect.

Quest. How shall we do to keep and preserve our souls in this waking condition, especially in these drowsy times?

Ans. 1. *Propound unto them waking considerations.* What causeth our sleeps but want of matters of more serious observation? None will sleep when a thing is presented of excellency more than ordinary. To see, and know, and think of what a state we are now advanced unto in Christ; what we shall be ere long, yet the fearful estate we should be in, if God leave us to ourselves! a state of astonishment, miserable and wretched, beyond speech, nay, beyond conceit!* Thus did the blessed souls in former times exercise their thoughts, raise, and stir them up by meditation, that so they might hold their souls in a high esteem of the best things, and not suffer them to sleep. We never fall to sleep in earthly and carnal delights, till the soul let its hold go of the best things, and ceaseth to think of, and to wonder at them. What made Moses to fall from the delights of Egypt? He saw the basest things in religion were greater than the greatest things in the court, yea, in the world. 'He esteemed the reproach of Christ better than the greatest treasures of Egypt,' Heb. xi. 26.

2. Make the *heart think of the shortness and vanity of this life*, with the uncertainty of the time of our death; and of what wondrous consequent† it is to be in the state of grace before we die. The uncertainty of the gales of grace, that there may be a good hour which, if we pass, we may never have the like again, Luke xix. 42, Mat. xxiii. 37; as the angel descended at a certain hour into the pool of Bethesda, John v. 4, when those that entered not immediately after, went away sick as they came. So there are certain good hours which let us not neglect. This will help to keep us waking.

3. *The necessity of grace*, and then the free dispensing of it in God's good time, and withal the terror of the Lord's-day, 'Remembering,' saith St Paul, 'the terror of the Lord, I labour to stir up all men,' &c., 2 Cor. v. 11. Indeed it should make us stir up our hearts when we consider the terror of the Lord; to think that ere long we shall be all drawn to an exact account, before a strict, precise judge. And shall our eyes then be sleeping and careless? These and such like considerations out of spiritual wisdom we should propound to ourselves, that so we might have waking souls, and preserve them in a right temper.

Ans. 2. *To keep faith waking.* The soul is as the object is that is presented to it, and as the certainty of the apprehension is of that object. It conduceth much therefore to the awakening of the soul to keep faith awake. It is not the greatness alone, but the presence of great things that stirs us. Now it is the nature of faith to make things powerfully present to the soul; for it sets things before us in the word of Jehovah, that made all things of

* That is 'conception.'—G. † That is, 'consequence.'—G.

nothing, and is Lord of his word, to give a being to whatsoever he hath spoken, Heb. xi. 1. Faith is an awakening grace. Keep that awake, and it will keep all other graces waking.

When a man believes, that all these things shall be on fire ere long; that heaven and earth shall fall in pieces; that we shall be called to give an account, [and that] before that time we may be taken away—is it not a wonder we stand so long, when cities, stone walls fall, and kingdoms come to sudden periods? When faith apprehends, and sets this to the eye of the soul, it affects the same marvellously. Therefore let faith set before the soul some present thoughts according to its temper. Sometimes terrible things to awaken it out of its dulness; sometimes glorious things, promises and mercies, to waken it out of its sadness, &c. When we are in a prosperous estate let faith make present all the sins and temptations that usually accompany such an estate, as pride, security, self-applause, and the like. If in adversity, think also of what sins may beset us there. This will awaken up such graces in us, as are suitable to such an estate, for the preventing of such sins and temptations, and so keep our hearts in 'exercise to godliness,' 1 Tim. iv. 7; than which, nothing will more prevent sleeping.

Ans. 3. And withal, *labour for abundance of the Spirit of God.* For what makes men sleepy, and drowsy? The want of spirits. We are dull, and overloaden with gross humours, whereby the strength sinks and fails. Christians should know, that there is a necessity, if they will keep themselves waking, to keep themselves spiritual. Pray for the Spirit above all things. It is the life of our life, the soul of our soul. What is the body without the soul, or the soul without the Spirit of God? Even a dead lump. And let us keep ourselves in such good ways, as we may expect the presence of the Spirit to be about us, which will keep us awake.

Ans. 4. *We must keep ourselves in as much light as may be.* For all sleepiness comes with darkness. Let us keep our souls in a perpetual light. When any doubt or dark thought ariseth, upon yielding thereunto comes a sleepy temper. Sleepiness in the affections ariseth from darkness of judgment. The more we labour to increase our knowledge, and the more the spiritual light and beams of it shine in at our windows, the better it will be for us, and the more shall we be able to keep awake. What makes men in their corruptions to avoid the ministry of the word, or anything that may awake their consciences? It is the desire they have to sleep. They know, the more they know, the more they must practise, or else they must have a galled conscience. They see religion will not stand with their ends. Rich they must be, and great they will be; but if they suffer the light to grow upon them, that will tell them they must not rise, and be great, by these and such courses. A gracious heart will be desirous of spiritual knowledge especially, and not care how near the word comes; because they ingeniously* and freely desire to be spiritually better. They make all things in the world yield to the inward man. They desire to know their own corruptions and evils more and more. And therefore love the light 'as children of the light, and of the day,' 1 Thess. v. 5. Sleep is a work of darkness. Men therefore of dark and drowsy hearts desire darkness, for that very end that their consciences may sleep.

Ans. 5. *Labour to preserve the soul in the fear of God:* because fear is a waking affection, yea, one of the wakefullest. For, naturally we are more moved with dangers, than stirred with hopes. Therefore, that affection, that is most conversant about danger, is the most rousing and waking

* That is, 'ingenuously.'—G.

affection. Preserve therefore the fear of God by all means. It is one character of a Christian, who, when he hath lost almost all grace, to his feeling, yet the fear of God is always left with him. He fears sin, and the reward of it, and therefore God makes that awe the bond of the new covenant. 'I will put my fear into their hearts, that they shall never depart from me,' Jer. xxxii. 39. One Christian is better than another, by how much more he wakes, and fears more than another. Of all Christians, mark those are most gracious, spiritual, and heavenly, that are the most awful and careful of their speeches, courses, and demeanours; tender even of offending God in little things. You shall not have light and common oaths come from them, nor unsavoury speeches. Sometimes a good Christian may in a state of sleepiness be faulty some way. But he grows in the knowledge of the greatness of God, and the experience of his own infirmities, as he grows in the sense of the love of God. He is afraid to lose that sweet communion any way, or to grieve the Spirit of God. Therefore, always as a man grows in grace, he grows in awfulness, and in jealousy of his own corruptions. Therefore let us preserve by all means this awful affection, the fear of God. Let us then often search the state of our own souls; our going backward or forward; how it is between God and our souls; how fit we are to die, and to suffer; how fit for the times that may befall us. Let us examine the state of our own souls, which will preserve us in a waking estate; especially examine ourselves in regard of the sins of the place, and the times where we live; of the sins of our own inclination, how we stand affected and biassed in all those respects, and see how jealous we are of dangers in this kind. Those that will keep waking souls, must consider the danger of the place where they live, and the times; what sins reign, what sins such a company as they converse with, are subject unto, and their own weakness to be led away with such temptations. This jealousy is a branch of that fear that we spake of before, arising from the searching of our own hearts, and dispositions. It is a notable means to keep us awake, when we keep our hearts in fear of such sins as either by calling, custom, company, or the time we live in, or by our own disposition, we are most prone to.

There is no Christian, but he hath some special sin, to which he is more prone than to another, one way or other, either by course of life, or complexion. Here now is the care and watchfulness of a Christian spirit, that knowing by examination, and trial of his own heart, his weakness, he doth especially fence against that, which he is most inclined to; and is able to speak most against that sin of all others, and to bring the strongest arguments to dishearten others from practice of it.

Ans. 6. In the last place it is a thing of no small consequence, *that we keep company with waking and faithful Christians*, such as neither sleep themselves or do willingly suffer any to sleep that are near them.

It is a report, and a true one, of the sweating sickness, that they that were kept awake by those that were with them, escaped; but the sickness was deadly if they were suffered to sleep. It is one of the best fruits of the communion of saints, and of our spiritual good acquaintance, to keep one another awake. It is an unpleasing work on both sides. But we shall one day cry out against all them that have pleased themselves and us, in rocking us asleep, and thank those that have pulled us 'with fear,' Jude 23, out of the fire, though against our wills.

Let us labour upon our own hearts in the conscionable* use of all these means, in their several times and seasons, that we may keep our hearts

* That is, 'conscientious.'—G.

waking; and the more earnest ought we to be, from consideration of the present age and season in which we live.

Certainly a drowsy temper is the most ordinary temper in the world. For would men suffer idle words, yea, filthy and rotten talk to come from their mouths if they were awake? Would a waking man run into a pit? or upon a sword's point? A man that is asleep may do anything. What do men mean when they fear not to lie, dissemble, and rush upon the pikes of God's displeasure? When they say one thing and do another, are they not dead? or take them at the best, are they not asleep? Were they awake, would they ever do thus? Will not a fowl that hath wings, avoid the snare? or will a beast run into a pit when it sees it? There is a snare laid in your playhouses, gaming houses, common houses, that gentlemen frequent that generally profess religion, and take the communion. If the eye of their souls were awake, would they run into these snares, that their own conscience tells them are so? If there be any goodness in their souls, it is wondrous sleepy. There is no man, even the best, but may complain something, that they are overtaken in the contagion of these infectious times. They catch drowsy tempers, as our Saviour saith, of those latter times. 'For the abundance of iniquity, the love of many shall wax cold,' Mat. xxiv. 12. A chill temper grows ever from the coldness of the times that we live in, wherein the best may complain of coldness; but there is a great difference. The life of many, we see, is a continual sleep.

Let us especially watch over ourselves, in the use of liberty and such things as are in themselves lawful. It is a blessed state, when a Christian carries himself so in his liberty, that his heart condemns him not for the abuse of that which it alloweth, and justly in a moderate use. Recreations are lawful; who denies it? To refresh a man's self, is not only lawful, but necessary. God knew it well enough, therefore hath allotted time for sleep, and the like. But we must not turn recreation into a calling, to spend too much time in it.

Where there is least fear, there is most danger always. Now because in lawful things there is least fear, we are there in most danger. It is true for the most part, *licitis perimus omnes*, more men perish in the church of God by the abuse of lawful things, than by unlawful; more by meat, than by poison. Because every man takes heed of poison, being* he knows the venom of it, but how many men surfeit, and die by meat! So, many men die by lawful things. They eternally perish in the abuse of their liberties, more than in gross sins. Therefore let us keep awake, that we may carry ourselves so in our liberties, that we condemn not ourselves in the use of them. We will conclude this point with the meditation of the excellency of a waking Christian. When he is in his right temper, he is an excellent person, fit for all essays.† He is then impregnable. Satan hath nothing to do with him, for he, as it is said, is then a wise man, and 'hath his eyes in his head,' Eccles. iii. 4. He knows himself, his state, his enemies, and adversaries, the snares of prosperity and adversity, and of all conditions, &c. Therefore, he being awake, is not overcome of the evil of any condition, and is ready for the good of any estate. He that hath a waking soul, he sees all the advantages of good, and all the snares that might draw him to ill, Mark xiii. 37. What a blessed estate is this! In all things therefore watch; in all estates, in all times, and in all actions. There is a danger in everything without watchfulness. There is a scorpion under every stone,

* That is, 'seeing it is.'—G.

† That is, 'attempts.' Sibbes's spelling is 'assaies,'—Qu.' assaults?'—G.

as the proverb is, a snare under every blessing of God, and in every condition, which Satan useth as a weapon to hurt us; adversity to discourage us, prosperity to puff us up: when, if a Christian hath not a waking soul, Satan hath him in his snare, in prosperity to be proud and secure; in adversity to murmur, repine, be dejected, and call God's providence into question. When a Christian hath a heart and grace to awake, then his love, his patience, his faith is awake, as it should be. He is fit for all conditions, to do good in them, and to take good by them.

Let us therefore labour to preserve watchful and waking hearts continually, that so we may be fit to live, to die, and to appear before the judgment seat of God; to do what we should do, and suffer what we should suffer, being squared for all estates whatsoever.

THE FIFTH SERMON.

It is the voice of my Beloved that knocketh, saying, Open to me, my sister, my love, my dove, my undefiled; for my head is filled with dew, and my locks with the drops of the night.—CANT. V. 2.

HITHERTO, by God's assistance, we have heard largely both of the church's sleeping and heart-waking; what this sleeping and heart-waking is; how it comes; the trials of these opposite dispositions; of the danger of sleeping, and excellency of heart-waking; and of the helps and means, both to shun the one and preserve the other. Now, the church, having so freely and ingeniously* confessed what she could against herself, proceeds yet further to acquaint us with the particulars in her heart-waking disposition, which were twofold. She heard and discerned 'the voice of her Beloved,' who, for all her sleep, was her Beloved still; and more than that, she remembers all his sweet words and allurements, whereby he pressed her to open unto him, saying, 'Open to me, my love, my dove, my undefiled;' which is set out and amplified with a further moving argument of those inconveniences Christ had suffered in his waiting for entertainment in her heart, 'For my head is filled with dew, and my locks with the drops of the night,' all which aggravates her offence; and his rare goodness and patience towards miserable sinners, so to wait from time to time for admission into our wretched souls, that he may rule and govern them by his Holy Spirit. Therefore, we had great reason to shun this sleepy distemper of soul, which for the present so locks up 'the everlasting gates of our soul, that the King of glory cannot enter in,' Ps. xxiv. 7, and to strive for this blessed heart-waking disposition, which may help us at all times to see our dangers, and, by God's blessing, recover us out of them, as here the church doth at length, though first smarting and well beaten by the watchmen, in a world of perplexities ere she can recover the sense of her former union and communion with Christ.

And surely we find by experience what a woful thing it is for the soul which hath once tasted how gracious the Lord is, to be long without a sense of God's love; for when it looks upon sin as the cause of this separation, this is for the time as so many deaths unto it. Therefore, the church's experience must be our warning-piece to take heed how we grieve the Spirit, and so fall into this spiritual sleep. Wherein yet this is a good sign, that yet we are not in a desperate dead sleep when we can with her say,

'It is the voice of my Beloved that knocks, saying, Open unto me,' &c.

* That is, 'ingenuously.'—G.

In which words you have,

1. The church's acknowledgment of Christ's voice.

2. Of his carriage towards her.

1. Her acknowledgment is set down here, 'It is the voice of my Beloved.'

2. His carriage, 'He knocks,' &c. Wherein,

(1.) His patience in suffering things unworthy and utterly unbeseeming for him. He doth not only 'knock,' but he continues knocking, till 'his head was filled with dew, and his locks with the drops of the night.'

(2.) His friendly compellation, 'Open to me, my love, my dove, my undefiled.' Lo, here are sweet actions, sweet words, and all to melt the heart of the spouse!

First, *the church's acknowledgment* is to be considered, confessing, 'It is the voice of her beloved.' The first thing to be observed in this acknowledgment is, that the church, however sleepy and drowsy she was, yet notwithstanding, her heart was so far awake as to know the voice of her husband. The point is this,

Obs. That a Christian soul doth know and may discern the voice of Christ, yea, and that even in a lazy, sleepy estate, but much more when in a good and lively frame. God's believers are Christ's sheep, John x. 3. Now, 'My sheep,' saith Christ, 'hear my voice,' verse 4. It is the ear-mark, as it were, of a Christian, one of the characters of the new man, 'to taste words by the ear,' as Job saith, Job xii. 11. He hath a spiritual taste, a discerning relish in his ear, because he hath the Spirit of God, and therefore relisheth what is connatural, and suitable to the Spirit. Now, the voice of Christ without in the ministry, and the Spirit of Christ within in the heart, are connatural, and suitable each to other.

And surely so it is, *that this is one way to discern a true Christian from another, even by a taste in hearing.* For those that have a spiritual relish, they can hear with some delight things that are most spiritual. As the heathen man said of a meadow, that some creatures come to eat one sort of herbs, others another, all that which is fit for them; men to walk therein for delight; all for ends suitable to their nature; so, in coming to hear the word of God, some come to observe the elegancy of words and phrases, some to catch advantage perhaps against the speaker, men of a devilish temper; and some to conform themselves to the customs of the places they live in, or to satisfy the clamours of a troubled conscience, that will have some divine duty performed, else it goes on with much vexation. But every true Christian comes and relisheth what is spiritual; and when outward things can convey in similitudes spiritual things aptly to the mind, he relisheth this, not as elegant and pleasing his fancy so much, as for conveying the voice of Christ unto his soul, so that a man may much be helped to know his state in grace and what he is, by his ear. 'Itching ears,' 2 Tim. iv. 3, usually are such as are 'led with lust,' as the apostle saith, and they must be clawed. They are sick, and nothing will down with them. They quarrel with everything that is wholesome, as they did with manna. No sermons will please them, no bread is fine and white enough; whereas, indeed, it is their own distemper is in fault. As those that go in a ship upon the sea, it is not the tossing but the stomach that causeth a sickness, the choler within, and not the waves without, so the disquiet of these men, that nothing will down with them, is from their own distemper. If Christ himself were here a-preaching, they would be sure to cavil at something, as then men did when he preached in his own person, because they labour of lusts, which they resolve to feed and cherish.

And again, observe it against our adversaries. What say they? How shall we know that the word is the word of God? For this heretic saith thus, and this interprets it thus. This is the common objection of the great rabbis amongst them in their writings, how we can know the word to be God's, considering there are such heresies in the churches, and such contrariety of opinions concerning the Scriptures read in the churches.

Even thus to object and ask is an argument and testimony that these men have not the Spirit of Christ, for 'his sheep know his voice,' John x. 3, who, howsoever they cannot interpret all places of Scripture, yet they can discern in the Scripture what is suitable food for them, or in the unfolding of the Scriptures in preaching they can discern agreeable food for them, having a faculty to reject that which is not fit for nourishment, to let it go. As there is in nature passages fit for concoction and digestion and for rejection, so there is in the soul to work out of the word, even out of that which is hard, yet wholesome, what is fit for the soul and spirit. If it be cast down, it feeds upon the promises for direction and consolation; and what is not fit for nourishment, that it rejects, that is, if it be of a contrary nature, heterogeneal. Therefore, we answer them thus, that 'God's sheep hear his voice,' John x. 4; that his word left in the church, when it is unfolded, his Spirit goes together with it, breeding a relish of the word in the hearts of people, whereby they are able to taste and relish it, and it hath a supernatural power and majesty in it which carries its own evidence with it. How shall we know light to be light? It carries evidence in itself that it is light. How know we that the fire is hot? Because it carries evidence in itself that it is so. So if you ask how we know the word of God to be the word of God; it carries in itself inbred arguments and characters, that the soul can say none but this word can be the word of God; it hath such a majesty and power to cast down, and raise up, and to comfort, and to direct with such power and majesty, that it carries with it its own evidence, and it is argument enough for it, 1 Cor. xiv. 24, 25; 2 Cor. x. 4, 5. And thus we answer them, which they can answer no way but by cavils. 'God's sheep hear the voice of Christ.' He speaks, and the church understands him, 'and a stranger's voice they will not hear,' John x. 5.

And indeed, this is the only sure way of understanding the word to be of God, from an inbred principle of the majesty in the word, and a powerful work thereof on the soul itself; and an assent so grounded is that which makes a sound Christian. If we should ask, what is the reason there be so many that apostatize, fall away, grow profane, and are so unfruitful under the gospel, notwithstanding they hear so much as they do? The answer is, their souls were never founded and bottomed upon this, that it is the word of God, and divine truth, so as to be able to say, I have felt it by experience, that it is the voice of Christ. Therefore they so soon apostatize, let Jesuits, or seducers set upon them. They were never persuaded from inbred arguments, that the voice of Christ is the word of God. Others from strictness grow profane, because they were never convinced by the power and majesty of the truth in itself; and then in the end they despair, notwithstanding all the promises, because they were never convinced of the truth of them. They cannot say Amen to all the promises. But the church can say confidently, upon sound experience, 'It is the voice of my beloved,' &c.

Again, whereas the church saith here, It is the voice of my beloved, &c., and knows this voice of her beloved, we may note—

Obs. That the church of God, and every Christian, takes notice of the means that God useth for their salvation.

A Christian is sensible of all the blessed helps he hath to salvation. To a dead heart, it is all one whether they have means or no means; but a Christian soul takes notice of all the means. 'It is the voice of my beloved that knocketh.' It seeth Christ in all.

And mark what the church saith, moreover, 'It is the voice of my beloved.' She acknowledgeth Christ to be beloved of her, though she were asleep. So then here is a distinction between the sleep of a Christian and the dead sleep of another natural man. The one when he sleeps, his heart doth not only wake, but it is awake to discern the voice of Christ. It can relish in reading what is spiritual and good, what is savoury, and what not. And likewise take a Christian at the worst: when he is asleep, he loves Christ, he will do nothing against him. 'I can do nothing,' saith Paul, 'against the truth, but for the truth,' 2 Cor. xiii. 8. He will do nothing against the cause of religion. There is a new nature in him, that he cannot do otherwise. He cannot but love; he cannot sin with a full purpose, nor speak against a good cause, because he hath a new nature, that leads him another way. Christ is her beloved still though she sleep.

Obs. Take a Christian at the lowest, his heart yearns after Christ.

Acknowledging him to be his beloved, there is a conjugal chastity in the soul of a Christian. Holding firm to the covenant and marriage between Christ and it, he keeps that unviolable. Though he may be untoward, sleepy, and drowsy, yet there is always a conjugal, spouse-like affection. 'It is the voice of my beloved,' &c.

Now, leaving the church's notice of the voice of Christ, we come to Christ's carriage towards her.

1. 'He knocketh;' and then we have—

2. His patience in that carriage. 'My head is filled with dew, and my locks with the drops of the night,' &c. Here is patience and mercy, to endure this indignity at the church's hand, to stand at her courtesy to come in; besides, 3, the compellation, afterwards to be spoken of. The general observation from Christ's carriage is this—

Obs. That Christ still desires a further and further communion with his church.

Even as the true soul that is touched with the Spirit, desires nearer and nearer communion with Christ; so he seeks nearer and nearer communion with his spouse, by all sanctified means. Christ hath never enough of the soul. He would have them more and more open to him. Our hearts are for Christ, who hath the heaven of heavens, and the soul of a believing Christian for himself to dwell in. He contents not himself to be in heaven alone, but he will have our hearts. He knocks here, waits, speaks friendly and lovingly, with such sweet words, 'My love, my dove,' &c. We had a blessed communion in the state of innocency, and shall have a glorious communion in heaven, when the marriage shall be consummated; but now the time of this life is but as the time of the contract, during which there are yet many mutual passages of love between him and his spouse, a desire of mutual communion of either side. Christ desires further entertainment in his church's heart and affection, that he might lodge and dwell there. And likewise there is the like desire in the church, when she is in a right temper; so that if any strangeness be between Christ and any man's soul, that hath tasted how good the Lord is, let him not blame Christ for it, for he delights not in strangeness. He that knocks and stands knocking, while his locks are bedewed with the drops of the night, doth he delight in strangeness, that makes all this love to a Christian's soul? Certainly no.

Therefore look for the cause of his strangeness at any time in thine own self. As, *whether we cast ourselves imprudently into company, that are not fit to be consulted withal*, in whom the Spirit is not, and who cannot do us any good, or they cast themselves to us. Evil company is a great damping, whereby a Christian loseth his comfort much, especially that intimate communion with God ; whence we may fall into security.

Again, *discontinuing of religious exercises doth wonderfully cause Christ to withdraw himself*. He makes no more love to our souls, when we neglect the means, and discontinue holy exercises, and religious company, when we stir not up the graces of God's Spirit. Being this way negligent, it is no wonder that Christ makes no more love to our souls, when we prize and value not the communion that should be between the soul and Christ, as we should. 'Whom have I in heaven but thee?' Ps. lxxiii. 25. 'Thy lovingkindness is better than life,' saith the psalmist, Ps. lxiii. 3. When we prize not this, it is just with Christ to make himself strange. Where love is not valued and esteemed, it is estranged, and for a while hides itself. So that these, with other courses and failings, we may find to be the ground and reason of the strangeness between Christ and the soul, for certainly the cause is not in him. For we see here, he useth all means to be entertained by a Christian soul: 'he knocks.'

You know what he says to the church of Laodicea—'Behold, I stand at the door, and knock,' Rev. iii. 20 ; so here—'It is the voice of my beloved that knocketh.' Therefore, in such a case, search your own hearts, where, if there be deadness and desertion of spirit, lay the blame upon yourselves, and enter into a search of your own ways, and see what may be the cause.

Now, to come more particularly to Christ's carriage here, knocking at the heart of the sleepy church, we see that *Christ takes not the advantage and forfeiture of the sins of his church, to leave them altogether, but makes further and further love to them*. Though the church be sleepy, Christ continues knocking. The church of Laodicea was a lukewarm, proud, hypocritical church ; yet 'Behold,' saith Christ, 'I stand at the door, and knock,' Rev. iii. 20 ; and it was such a church as was vainglorious and conceited. 'I am rich, and want nothing, when she was poor, blind, and naked,' Rev. iii. 17. And here he doth not only stand knocking, but he withal suffereth indignities—'the dew' to fall upon him, which we shall speak more of hereafter. Christ, therefore, refuseth not weak sinners. He that commands, 'that we should receive him that is weak in the faith,' Rom. xiv. 1, and not cast him off from our fellowship and company, will he reject him that is weak and sleepy? No. What father will pass by or neglect his child, for some failings and weaknesses? Nature will move him to respect him as his child.

Now, Christ is merciful both by his office and by his nature. Our nature he took upon him, that he might be a merciful Redeemer, Heb. ii. 17. And then as God also, he is love, 'God is love,' 1 John iv. 16 : that is, whatsoever God shews himself to his church, he doth it in love. If he be angry in correcting, it is out of love ; if merciful, it is out of love ; if he be powerful in defending his church, and revenging himself on her enemies, all is love. 'God is love,' saith John, John iv. 8 : that is, he shews himself only in ways, expressions, and characters of love to his church. So Christ, as God, is all love to the church. And we see the Scriptures also to set out God as love, both in his essence and in his relations. 1. In relations of love to his church, he is a father: 'As a father pitieth his child, so the Lord pities them that fear him,' Ps. ciii. 13. And, 2. Also in those sweet attributes of love, which are his essence, as we see, Exod.

xxxiv. 6. When God describes himself to Moses, after his desire to know him, in the former chapter, 'Thou canst not see me and live;' yet he would make him know him, as was fit for him to be known—'Jehovah, Jehovah, strong, merciful, gracious, long-suffering,' &c., Exod. xxxiv. 6. Thus God will be known in these attributes of consolation. So Christ, as God, is all love and mercy. Likewise Christ, as man, he was man for this end, to be all love and mercy. Take him in his office as Jesus, to be a Saviour; he carrieth salvation in his wings, as it is in Mal. iv. 2, both by office and by nature.

And here how excellently is the expression of Christ's mercy, love, and patience set out! He knocks, 'my beloved knocks,' &c., saying, 'Open.' He knocks for further entrance, as was shewed before. Some he had already, but he would have further. As you know we have divers rooms and places in our houses. There is the court, the hall, the parlour, and closet: the hall for common persons, the parlour for those of better fashion, the closet for a man's self, and those that are intimate friends. So a Christian hath room in his heart for worldly thoughts, but his closet, his inmost affections, are kept for his inmost friend Christ, who is not content with the hall, but will come into the very closet. He knocks, that we should open, and let him come into our hearts, into our more intimate affections and love. Nothing will content him but intimateness, for he deserves it. As we shall see, he knocks for this end. But how doth he knock?

Every kind of way. 1. It is taken from the fashion of men in this kind, God condescending to speak to us in our own language. Sometimes, you know, there is a knocking or calling for entrance by voice, when a voice may serve, and then there needs no further knocking.

Sometimes both by voice and knocking. If voice will not serve, knocking comes after. So it is here. Christ doth knock and speak, useth a voice of his word, and knocks by his works, and both together sometimes, whether by works of mercy or of judgment. He labours to enter into the soul, to raise the sleepy soul that way. He begins with mercy usually.

(1.) By *mercies*. All the creatures and blessings of God carry in them, as it were, a voice of God to the soul, that it would entertain his love. There goes a voice of love with every blessing. And the love, the mercy, and the goodness of God in the creature, is better than the creature itself. As we say of gifts, the love of the giver is better than the gift itself. So the love of God in all his sweet benefits is better than the thing itself. And so in that we have. There is a voice, as it were, entreating us to entertain God and Christ in all his mercies, yea, every creature, as one saith, and benefit, speaks, as it were, thus to us: We serve thee, that thou mayest serve him that made thee and us. There is a speech, as it were, in every favour. Which mercies, if they cannot prevail, then,

(2.) Come *corrections*, which are the voice of God also. 'Hear the rod, and him that smiteth,' Micah vi. 9.

2. But hath the rod a voice? Yes, for what do corrections speak, but amendment of the fault we are corrected for? So we must hear the rod. All corrections tend to this purpose. They are as knockings, that we should open to God and Christ. And because corrections of themselves will not amend us, God to this kind of knocking adds a voice. He teacheth and corrects together, 'Happy is that man that thou correctest, and teachest out of thy law,' saith the psalmist, Ps. xciv. 12. Correction without teaching is to little purpose. Therefore God adds instruction to correction. He opens the conscience,

so that it tells us it is for this that you are corrected; and together with conscience, gives his Spirit to tell us it is for this or that you are corrected; you are to blame in this, this you have done that you should not have done. So that corrections are knockings, but then especially when they have instruction thus with them. They are messengers from God, both blessings and corrections, Lev. xxvi. 24, *seq.* They will not away, especially corrections, till they have an answer, for they are sent of God, who will add seven times more; and if the first be not answered, then he sends after them. He will be sure to have an answer, either in our conversion or confusion, when he begins once.

3. Many other ways he useth to knock at our hearts. *The examples of those we live among that are good, they call upon us,* Luke xiii. 2, 3; 1 Cor. x. 33. The patterns of their holy life, the examples of God's justice upon others, are speeches to us. God knocks at our door then. He intends our correction when he visits another, when, if we amend by that, he needs not take us in hand.

4. But besides all this, there is a more near knocking that Christ useth to the church, *his ministerial knocking.* When he was here in the days of his flesh, he was a preacher and prophet himself, and now he is ascended into heaven, he hath given gifts to men, and men to the church, Eph. iv. 11, *seq.*, whom he speaks by, to the end of the world. They are Christ's mouth, as we said of the penmen of holy Scripture. They were but the hand to write; Christ was the head to indite. So in preaching and unfolding the word they are but Christ's mouth and his voice, as it is said of John, Mat. iii. 3. Now he is in heaven, he speaks by them, 'He that heareth you heareth me, he that despiseth you despiseth me,' Luke x. 16. Christ is either received or rejected in his ministers, as it is said of Noah's time, 'The Spirit of Christ preached in the days of Noah to the souls now in prison,' &c., 1 Pet. iii. 19. Christ as God did preach, before he was incarnate, by Noah to the old world, which is now in prison, in hell, because they refused to hear Christ speak to them by Noah. Much more now, after the days of his flesh, that he is in heaven, he speaks and preacheth to us, which, if we regard not, we are like to be in prison, as those souls are now in prison for neglecting the preaching of Noah, 1 Pet iii. 19. So the ministers are Christ's mouth. When they speak, he speaks by them, and they are as ambassadors of Christ, whom they should imitate in mildness. 'We therefore, as ambassadors, beseech and entreat you, as if Christ by us should speak to you; so we entreat you to be reconciled unto God,' 2 Cor. v. 20. And you know what heart-breaking words the apostle useth in all his epistles, especially when he writes to Christians in a good state, as to the Philippians, 'If there be any bowels of mercy, if there be any consolation in Christ,' then regard what I say, 'be of one mind.' Phil. ii. 1. And among the Thessalonians he was as a nurse to them, 1 Thess. ii. 7. So Christ speaks by them, and puts his own affections into them, that as he is tender and full of bowels himself, so he hath put the same bowels into those that are his true ministers.

He speaks by them, and they use all kind of means that Christ may be entertained into their hearts. They move all stones, as it were, sometimes threatenings, sometimes entreaties, sometimes they come as 'sons of thunder,' Mark iii. 17; sometimes with the still voice of sweet promises. And because one man is not so fit as another for all varieties of conditions and spirits, therefore God gives variety of gifts to his ministers, that they may knock at the heart of every man by their several gifts. For some have more rousing, some more insinuating gifts; some more legal, some more evangelical spirits, yet all for the church's good. John Baptist, by a more thundering way of preaching, to make way for Christ to come, threateneth judgment. But Christ, then he comes with a 'Blessed are the poor in spirit,' 'blessed are they that hunger and thirst for righteousness,' &c., Mat v. 3. All kind of means have been used in the ministry from the beginning of the world.

5. And because of itself this ministry it is a dead letter; therefore he joins that with the word, which knocks at the heart together with the word, not severed from it, but is the life of it. *Oh! the Spirit is the life, and soul of the word;* and when the inward word, or voice of the Spirit, and the outward word or ministry go together, then Christ doth more effectually knock and stir up the heart.

Now this Spirit with sweet inspirations knocks, moves the heart, lightens the understanding, quickens the dull affections, and stirs them up to duty, as it is, Isa. xxx. 21, 'And thine ears shall hear a voice behind thee saying, This is the way, walk in it.' The Spirit moves us sweetly, agreeable to our own nature. It offers not violence to us; but so as in Hosea xi. 4, 'I drew them by the cords of a man.' That is, by reasons and motives befitting the nature of man, motives of love. So the Spirit, together with the word, works upon us, as we are men by rational motives, setting good before us, if we will let Christ in to govern and rule us; and by the danger on the contrary, so moving and stirring up our affections. These be 'the cords of a man.'

6. And besides his Spirit, God hath planted in us a *conscience* to call upon us, to be his vicar; a little god in us to do his office, to call upon us, direct us, check and condemn us, which in great mercy he hath placed in us.

Thus we see what means Christ useth here—his voice, works, and word; works of mercy and of correction; his word, together with his Spirit, and the conscience, that he hath planted, to be, as it were, a god in us; which together with his Spirit may move us to duty. This Austin speaks of when he says, *Deus in me*, &c. 'God spake in me oft, and I knew it not' (*f*). He means it of conscience, together with the Spirit, stirring up motives to leave his sinful courses. God knocked in me, and I considered it not. I cried, *modò* and *modò*, *sine modo*. I put off God, now I will, and now I will, but I had no moderation, I knew no limits. And whilst Christ thus knocketh, all the three persons may be said to do it. For as it is said elsewhere, that 'God was and is in Christ reconciling the world,' &c., 2 Cor. v. 19. For whatsoever Christ did, he did it as anointed, and by office. And therefore God doth it in Christ, and by Christ, and so in some sort God died in his human nature, when Christ died. So here the father beseecheth when Christ beseecheth, because he beseecheth, that is sent from him, and anointed of the Father. And God the Father stoops to us when Christ stoops, because he is sent of the Father, and doth all by his Father's command and commission, John v. 27. So besides his own bowels, there is the Father and the Spirit with Christ, who doth all by his Spirit, and from his Father, from whom he hath commission. Therefore God the Father, Son, and Holy Ghost knock at the heart. 'Open to me, my love, my dove, my undefiled;' but Christ especially by his Spirit, because it is his office.

Obj. But some may object, Christ can open to himself, why doth he not take the key and open, and make way for himself? Who will knock, when he hath the key himself? and who will knock, when there is none within to open? Christ can open to himself, and we have no free will, nor power to open.

Bellarmine makes this objection, and speaks very rudely, that he is an unwise man to knock, where there is no man within to open; and that if Christ knock, and we cannot open, it is a delusion to exhort to open, and that therefore there must needs be free will in us to open *(f*)*.

The answer is, *first*, Christ speaks to the spouse here, and so, many such exhortations are given to them that have the Spirit of God already, who could by the help thereof open. For good and gracious men are moved first by the Spirit, and then they move; they are *moti moventes*, and *acti agentes*. They are acted first by the Spirit, and then they do act by it, not of themselves; as the inferior orbs move not, but as they are moved by the superior. The question is not of them in the state of grace, but at their first conversion, when especially we say that Christ speaks to them that he means to convert. He knocks at their hearts, and opens together with his speech. Then there goes a power that they shall open; for his words are operative words. As it was in the creation, 'Let there be light,' it was an operative word, 'and there was light,' Gen. i. 3. Let there be such a creature, it was an operative working word, and there was such a creature presently. So he opens together with that word. With that invitation and command there goes an almighty power to enable the soul to open. Were it not a wise reason to say, when Christ called to Lazarus to 'come forth,' John xi. 43, that we should reason he had life to yield to Christ, when he bade him come forth? No, he was rotten, in his grave, almost; but with Christ's speaking to Lazarus, there went an almighty power, that gave life to him, by which life he heard what Christ said, 'Arise, Lazarus.' So Christ by his Spirit clothes his word in the ministry, when he speaks to people with a mighty power. As the minister speaks to the ear, Christ speaks, opens, and unlocks the heart at the same time; and gives it power to open, not from itself, but from Christ. Paul speaks to Lydia's ear, Christ to her heart, and opened it, as the text says, Acts xvi. 13, whereby she believes;* so Christ opens the heart.

Quest. But why doth he thus work?

Ans. Because he will preserve nature, and the principles thereof; and so he deals with us, working accordingly. The manner of working of the reasonable creature, is to work freely by a sweet inclination, not by violence. Therefore when he works the work of conversion, he doth it in a sweet manner, though it be mighty for the efficaciousness of it. He admonisheth us with entreaty and persuasion, as if we did it ourselves. But though the manner be thus sweet, yet with this manner there goeth an almighty power. Therefore he doth it strongly as coming from himself, and sweetly, as the speaking is to us, preserving our nature. So the action is from him, which hath an almighty power with it. As holy Bernard saith, 'Thou dealest sweetly with my soul in regard of myself;' that is, thou workest upon me, as a man with the words of love, yet strongly in regard of thyself. For except he add strength with sweetness, the work will not follow; but when there are both, an almighty work is wrought in the soul of a Christian; and so wrought, as the manner of man's working is preserved in a sweet and free manner, whilst he is changed from contrary to contrary. And it is also with the greatest reason that can be, in that now he sees more reason to be good, than in the days of darkness he did to be naught, God works

* 'Lydia's Heart Opened,' is the title of one of Sibbes's most delightful minor books.—G

so sweetly. God speaks to us after the manner of men, but he works in us as the great God. He speaks to us as a man in our own language, sweetly; but he works in us almightily, after a powerful manner, as God. So we must understand such phrases as these, 'I knock; open to me, my love, my dove,' &c. We may take further notice,

Obs. That the heart of a Christian is the house and temple of Christ.

He hath but two houses to dwell in; the heavens, and the heart of an humble broken-hearted sinner, Isa. lvii. 15.

Quest. How can Christ come into the soul?

Ans. He comes into the heart by his Spirit. It is a special entertainment that he looks for. Open thine ears that thou mayest hear my word; thy love, that thou mayest love me more; thy joy, that thou mayest delight in me more; open thy whole soul that I may dwell in it. A Christian should be God's house, and a true Christian is the true temple of God. He left the other two temples therefore; but his own body, and his church he never leaves. For a house is for a man to solace himself in, and to rest in, and to lay up whatsoever is precious to him. So with Christ. A man will repair his house, so Christ will repair our souls, and make them better, and make them more holy, and spiritual, and every way fit for such a guest as he is.

Quest. How shall we know whether Christ dwells in our hearts or not?

Ans. We may know *by the servants what master dwells in an house.* If Christ be in the soul, there comes out of the house good speeches. And we watch the senses, so as there comes nothing in to defile the soul, and disturb Christ, and nothing goes out to offend God. When we hear men full of gracious sweet speeches, it is a sign Christ dwells there. If we hear the contrary, it shews Christ dwells not there. For Christ would move the whole man to do that which might edify and comfort.

Again, where Christ comes, *assistance comes there.* When Christ was born, all Jerusalem was in an uproar; so, when Christ is born in the soul, there is an uproar. Corruption arms itself against grace. There is a combat betwixt flesh and spirit. But Christ subdues the flesh by little and little. God's image is stamped upon the soul where Christ is; and if we have opened unto the Lord of glory, he will make us glorious.

Christ hath never enough of us, nor we have never enough of him till we be in heaven; and, therefore, we pray, 'Thy kingdom come.' And till Christ comes in his kingdom, he desires his kingdom should come to us. Open, saith he, *stupenda dignatio*, &c., as he cries out. It is a stupendous condescendence, when he that hath heaven to hold him, angels to attend him, those glorious creatures; he that hath the command of every creature, that do yield presently homage when he commands, the frogs, and lice, and all the host of heaven are ready to do his will! for him to condescend and to entreat us to be good to our own souls, and to beseech us to be reconciled to him, as if he had offended us, who have done the wrong and not he, or as if that we had power and riches to do him good; here greatness beseecheth meanness, riches poverty, all-sufficiency want, and life itself comes to dead, drowsy souls. What a wondrous condescending is this! Yet, notwithstanding, Christ vouchsafes to make the heart of a sinful, sleepy man to be his house, his temple. He knocks, and knocks here, saying, 'Open to me,' &c.

Use 1. This is useful many ways, as *first, cherish all the good conceits* we can of Christ.* Time will come that the devil will set upon us with sharp temptations, fiery darts, temptations to despair, and present Christ amiss,

* That is, 'conceptions.'—G.

as if Christ were not willing to receive us. Whenas you see he knocks at our hearts to open to him, useth mercies and judgments, the ministry of his Spirit and conscience, and all. Will not he then entertain us, when we come to him, that seeks this entertainment at our hands? Certainly he will. Therefore, let us labour to cherish good conceits of Christ. This is the finisher and beginning of the conversion of a poor sinful soul, even to consider the infinite love and condescendence of Christ Jesus for the good of our souls. We need not wonder at this his willingness to receive us, when we first know that God became man, happiness became misery, and life itself came to die, and to be 'a curse for us,' Gal. iii. 13. He hath done the greater, and will he not do the less? Therefore, think not strange that he useth all these means, considering how low he descended into the womb of the virgin for us, Ephes. iv. 9.

Now such considerations as these, being mixed with the Spirit and set on by him, are effectual for the conversion of poor souls. Is there such love in God to become man, and to be a suitor to woo me for my love? Surely, thinks the soul then, he desires my salvation and conversion. And to what kind of persons doth he come? None can object unworthiness. I am poor: 'He comes to the poor,' Isa. xiv. 32 and xxix. 19. I am laden and wretched: 'Come unto me, all ye that are weary and laden,' Mat. xi. 28. I have nothing: 'Come and buy honey, milk, and wine, though you have nothing,' Isa. lv. 1. He takes away all objections. But I am stung with the sense of my sins: 'Blessed are they that hunger and thirst,' &c., Mat. v. 6. But I am empty of all: 'Blessed are the poor in spirit,' Mat. v. 3. You can object nothing, but it is taken away by the Holy Ghost, wisely preventing* all the objections of a sinful soul. This is the beginning of conversion, these very conceits. And when we are converted, these thoughts, entertained with admiration of Christ's condescending, are effectual to give Christ further entrance into the soul, whereby a more happy communion is wrought still more and more between Christ and the soul of a Christian.

Use 2. *Oh, but take heed that these make not any secure.* For, if we give not entrance to Christ, all this will be a further aggravation of our damnation. How will this justify the sentence upon us hereafter, when Christ shall set us on the left hand, and say, 'Depart from me,' Mat. xxv. 41, for I invited you to come to me, I knocked at the door of your hearts, and you would give me no entrance. Depart from us, said you; therefore, now, Depart you from me. What do profane persons in the church but bid Christ depart from them, especially in the motions of his Spirit? They entertain him in the outward room, the brain; they know a little of Christ, but, in the heart, the secret room, he must not come there to rule. Is it not equal that he should bid us, 'Depart, ye cursed, I know you not'? Mat. xxv. 41; you would not give entrance to me, I will not now to you, as to the foolish virgins he speaks, Mat. xxv. 12, and Prov. i. 28. Wisdom knocks, and hath no entrance; therefore, in times of danger, they call upon her, but she rejoiceth at their destruction. Where God magnifies his mercy in this kind, in sweet allurements, and inviting by judgments, mercies, ministry, and Spirit, he will magnify his judgment after. Those that have neglected heaven with the prerogatives and advantages in this kind, they shall be cast into hell. 'Woe to thee, Chorazin,' &c., Mat. xi. 21, as you know in the gospel. This is one thing that may humble us of this place and nation, that Christ hath no further entrance, nor better entertainment

* That is, 'anticipating.'—G.

after so long knocking! for the entertaining of his word is the welcoming of himself, as it is, Col. iii. 16. 'Let the word of God dwell plentifully in you.' And, 'Let Christ dwell in your hearts by faith,' Eph. iii. 17. Compare those places; let the word dwell plenteously in you by wisdom, and let Christ dwell in your hearts by faith. For then doth Christ dwell in the heart, when the truth dwells in us. Therefore, what entertainment we give to his truth, we give to himself. Now what means of knocking hath he not used among us a long time? For works of all sorts, he hath drawn us by the cords of a man, by all kind of favours. For mercies, how many deliverances have we had (no nation the like; we are a miracle of the Christian world) from foreign invasion, and domestical conspiracies at home? How many mercies do we enjoy! Abundance, together with long peace and plenty. Besides, if this would not do, God hath added corrections with all these, in every element, in every manner. Infection in the air, judgments in inundations. We have had rumours of wars, &c. Threatenings, shakings of the rod only, but such as might have awaked us. And then he hath knocked at our hearts by the example of other nations. By what he hath done to them, he hath shewed us what he might justly have done to us. We are no better than they.

As for his ministerial knocking: above threescore years we have lived under the ministry of the gospel. This land hath been Goshen, a land of light, when many other places are in darkness. Especially we that live in this Goshen, this place, and such like, where the light shines in a more abundant measure. Ministers have been sent, and variety of gifts. There hath been piping and mourning, as Christ complains in his time, that they were like froward children, that neither sweet piping nor doleful mourning would move to be tractable to their fellows. 'They had John, who came mourning,' Mat. xi. 17, and Christ comforting with blessing in his mouth. All kind of means have been used.

And for the motions of his Spirit, who are there at this time, who thus live in the church under the ministry, who cannot say that God thereby hath smote their hearts, those hard rocks, again and again, and awaked their consciences, partly with corrections public and personal, and partly with benefits? Yet notwithstanding, what little way is given to Christ! Many are indifferent, and lukewarm either way, but rather incline to the worst.

Let us then consider of it. The greater means, the greater judgments afterwards, if we be not won by them. Therefore let us labour to hold Christ, to entertain him. Let him have the best room in our souls, to dwell in our hearts. Let us give up the keys to him, and desire him to rule our understandings, to know nothing but him, and what may stand with his truth, not to yield to any error or corruption. Let us desire that he would rule in our wills and affections; sway all, give all to him. For that is his meaning, when he says, 'Open to me,' so that I may rule, as in mine own house, as the husband rules in his family, and a king in his kingdom. He will have all yielded up to him. And he comes to beat down all, whatsoever is exalted against him; and that is the reason men are so loth to open unto him. They know if they open to the Spirit of God, he will turn them out of their fool's paradise, and make them resolve upon other courses of life, which, because they will not turn unto, they repel the sweet motions of the Spirit of Christ, and pull away his graces, building bulwarks against Christ, as lusts, strange imaginations, and resolutions, 2 Cor. x. 3–5. Let the ministers say what they will, and the Spirit move as he will, thus they live, and thus they will live. Let us take notice, therefore, of all the means that God useth to the State, and to us in particular, and every one labour to amend one. Every soul is the temple, the house, Christ should dwell in. Let every soul, therefore, among us, consider what means Christ useth to come into his soul to dwell with him, and to rule there.

And what shall we lose by it? Do we entertain Christ to our loss? Doth he come empty? No; he comes with all grace. His goodness is a communicative, diffusive goodness. He comes to spread his treasures, to enrich the heart with all grace and strength, to bear all afflictions, to encounter all dangers, to bring peace of conscience, and joy in the Holy Ghost. He comes, indeed, to make our hearts, as it were, a heaven. Do but consider this. He comes not for his own ends; but to empty his goodness into our hearts. As a breast that desires to empty itself when it is full; so this fountain hath the fulness of a fountain, which strives to empty his goodness into our souls. He comes out of love to us. Let these considerations melt our hearts for our unkindness, that we suffer him to stand so long at the door knocking, as it is said here.

If we find not our suits answered so soon as we would, remember, we have made him also wait for us. Perhaps to humble us, and after that to encourage us, he will make us wait; for we have made him wait. Let us not give over, for certainly he that desires us to open, that he may pour out his grace upon us, he will not reject us when we come to him, Mat. vii. 7; Hab. ii. 3. If he answers us not at first, yet he will at last. Let us go on and wait, seeing there is no one duty pressed more in Scripture than this. And we see it is equity, 'He waits for us,' Isa. xxx. 18. It is good reason we should wait for him. If we have not comfort presently when we desire it, let us attend upon Christ, as he hath attended upon us, for when he comes, he comes with advantage, Isa. lx. 16. So that when we wait, we lose nothing thereby, but are gainers by it, increasing our patience, Isa. lxiv. 4; James i. 4. The longer we wait, he comes with the more abundant grace and comfort in the end, and shews himself rich, and bountiful to them that wait upon him, Isa. xl. 1, *et seq.*

THE SIXTH SERMON.

It is the voice of my beloved that knocketh, saying, Open unto me, my love, my dove, my undefiled, &c.—CANT. V. 2.

IN the first part of this verse hath been handled the church's own condition, which she was in, after some blessed feelings that she had of the love of Christ.

Now, in the next words, the church sets down an acknowledgment of the carriage of Christ to her in this her sleepy condition. 'It is the voice of my beloved that knocks, saying, Open to me, my sister, my love, my dove,' &c. She acknowledgeth Christ's voice in her sleepy estate, and sets down his carriage thus, 'how he knocks', and then also speaks, 'Open to me,' and then sets down what he suffered for her, 'My head is filled with dew, and my locks with the drops of the night.' And that nothing might be wanting that might move her heart to respect this his carriage towards her, he useth sweet titles, a loving compellation, 'Open to me,' saith he, 'my sister, my love, my dove, my undefiled,' as so many cords of love to draw her. So here wants neither loving carriage, sweet words, nor patience. 'It is the voice of my beloved that knocketh.'

The church, as she takes notice of the voice of Christ, so she doth also of the means he useth, and seeth his love in them all. 'It is the voice of my beloved that knocketh, saying, Open to me,' &c. Here is also another distinguishing note of a sound Christian from an unsound. A sanctified spirit sees Christ in the means. This is, says the heart, the word of Christ, and this the mercy of Christ, to take such pains with my soul, to send his ministers, to provide his ordinances, to give gifts to men, and men to the church, Eph. iv. 11, 12. 'It is the voice of my beloved that knocketh.'

But we must especially understand it of the ministerial voice, whereby Christ doth chiefly make way for himself into the heart, and that by all kind of ways dispensed therein: as gifts of all sorts, some rougher, some milder, all kind of methods and ways in the ministry to make way for himself. First of all by the threatenings of the law, and by terrors. As John was sent before Christ, and as the storm went before the still and calm voice, wherein God came to Elias, 1 Kings xix. 12, so he useth all kinds of courses in the ministry. And ministers, by the direction of the Spirit, turn themselves, as it were, into all shapes and fashions, both of speech and spirit, to win people to God, in so much, that God appeals to them, 'What could I have done more for my church, that I have not done?' Isa. v. 4.

Use. Therefore let us take notice of this voice of Christ in the word, and not think as good Samuel thought, that Eli spake, when God spake, 1 Sam. iii. 5. Let us think that God speaks to us in the ministry, that Christ comes to woo us, and win us thereby.

And we ministers are the friends of the Bridegroom, who are to hear what Christ saith and would have said to the church; and we must pray to him, that he would teach us what to teach others. We are to procure the contract, and to perfect it till the marriage be in heaven. That is our work.

And you that are hearers, if you do not regard Christ's sweet voice in the ministry, which God hath appointed for the government of the world, know that there is a voice that you cannot shake off. That peremptory voice at the day of judgment, when he will say, 'Go, ye cursed, into hell fire,' &c., Mat. xxv. 30. And that God who delights to be styled 'a God hearing prayer,' Ps. lxv. 2, will not hear thee, but saith, 'Such a one as turns his ear away from hearing the law, his prayer is abominable,' Prov. xxviii. 9. It is a doleful thing, that he that made us, and allureth us in the ministry, that follows us with all evidences of his love, and adds, together with the ministry, many sweet motions of his Spirit, that he should delight in the destruction of his creatures, and not endure the sight of them, 'Depart away from me, ye cursed, into hell fire,' &c. There are scarce any in the church, but Christ hath allured at one time or other to come in, and in many he opens their understandings in a great measure, and knocks upon their hearts, that they, as it were, half open unto Christ, like Agrippa, that said to Paul, 'Thou almost persuadest me to be a Christian,' Acts xxvi. 28. So Herod 'did many things, and he heard gladly,' Mark vi. 20. They are half open, seem to open, but are not effectually converted. But at last they see, that further yielding will not stand with that which they resolve not to part with, their lusts, their present condition, that they make their God, and their heaven. Whereupon they shut the door again. When they have opened it a little to the motions of God's Spirit, they dare give no further way, because they cannot learn the first lesson in Christ's school, to deny themselves and take up their cross.

This is an undoubted conclusion. Our blessed Saviour giveth such means and motions of his Spirit to the vilest persons in the church, that their own hearts tell them, they have more means and sweeter motions than they yield to, and that the sentence of condemnation is not pronounced upon them for merely not knowing of Christ, but upon some grounds of rebellion, in that they go not so far as they are provoked,* and put on † by the Spirit of God. They resist the Holy Spirit. There can be no resistance where there is not a going beyond the desire and will of him whom he resisteth, Acts vii. 51. A man doth not resist, when he gives way as far as he is moved. There is no wicked man in the church, that gives so much way as he is moved and stirred to by the Spirit and word of God.

Away then with these impudent, ungracious objections about God's decree for matter of election. Let us make it sure. And for any ill conceits that may rise in our hearts about that other of reprobation, let this damp them all, that in the church of God, he offers unto the vilest wretch so much means, with the motions of his Spirit, as he resisting, proves inexcusable; his own rebellion therefore being the cause of his rejection. Let men cease from cavilling; God hath that in their own breast, in the heart of every carnal man, which will speak for God against him, and stop his mouth that he shall be silent and speechless at the day of judgment, Mat. xxii. 12.

Thus we see that Christ doth condescend so low as to account it almost a part of his happiness to have our souls for a temple to dwell in, to rule there. Therefore he makes all this earnest suit, with strong expressions what he suffereth.

And since Christ bears this great and large affection to his poor church, it may encourage us to pray heartily for the same, and to spread before God the state thereof. Why, Lord? it is that part of the world that is thy sister, thy love, thy dove, thy undefiled; the communion with whom thou lovest above all the world besides. It is a strong argument to prevail with God. Therefore let us commend the state of the church at this time, or at any time, with this confidence. Lord, it is the church that thou lovest. They thought they prevailed much with Christ when they laboured to bring him to Lazarus, saying, 'Lord, he whom thou lovest is sick,' John xi. 3. So say we, the church whom thou lovest, that is, thy only love, in whom thy love is concenterate,‡ as it were, and gathered to a head, as though thou hadst no other love in the world but thy church, this thy love is in this state and condition. It is good to think of prevailing arguments; not to move God so much as our own hearts; to strengthen our faith to prevail with God, which is much fortified with the consideration of Christ's wondrous loving expression to his poor church. Then come to Christ, offer thyself, and he will meet thee. Are not two loving well-wishers well met? When thou offerest thyself to him, and he seeks thy love, will he reject thee when thou comest to him that seeks thy love, and seeketh it in this passionate, affectionate manner, as he doth? Therefore, be of good comfort. He is more willing to entertain us than we are to come to him.

And for those that have relapsed any kind of way, let them not be discouraged to return again to Christ. The church here was in a drowsy, sleepy estate, and used him unkindly; yet he is so patient, that he waits her leisure, as it were, and saith, 'Open to me, my sister, my love,' &c. Thomas was so untoward, that he would not believe, 'unless he did see the

* That is, 'stirred up.'—G. † That is, 'incited.'—G. ‡ That is 'concentrated.'—G.

print of the nails,' &c., in Christ's body. Yet Christ was so gracious as he condescendeth to poor Thomas, John xx. 27. So to Peter after he was fallen, Mark xvi. 7, and to the church after backsliding.

'Open to me, my sister,' &c. Hence observe further,

That Christ hath never enough of his church till he hath it in heaven, where are indeed the kisses of the spouse, and of Christ. In the mean while 'Open, open,' still. Christ had the heart of the spouse in some measure already; but yet there were some corners of the heart that were not so filled with Christ as they should be. He was not so much in her understanding, will, joy, delight, and love, as he would be. Therefore, open thy understanding more and more to embrace me, and divine truths that are offered thee. Open thy love to solace me more and more. For God in Christ, having condescended to the terms of friendship, nay, to intimate terms of friendship in marriage with us; therefore* the church in her right temper, hath never enough of Christ, but desires further union, and communion still. It being the description of the people of God, that 'they love the appearance of Christ,' 2 Tim. iv. 8; Rev. xxii. 20, as they loved his first appearance, and waited for 'the consolation of Israel,' Luke ii. 25; so they love his second appearing, and are never quiet, till he comes again in the flesh, to consummate the marriage begun here. So Christ also he is as desirous of them, yea, they are his desires that breed their desires. 'Open to me, my sister, my love, my dove,' &c. Again his love and pity moves him to desire further to come into us. Christ knows what is in our hearts. If he be not there, there is that that should not be there. What is in the brain where Christ is not? A deal of worldly projects, nothing worth. What is in our joy if Christ be not there? Worldly joy, which cleaves to things worse than itself. If a man were anatomised, and seen into, he would be ashamed of himself, if he did see himself. Christ therefore, out of pity to our souls, would not have the devil there. Christ knows it is good for our souls to give way to him, therefore he useth all sweet allurements, 'Open to me, my sister, my love,' &c. Christ hath never his fill, till he close with the soul perfectly; so that nothing be in the soul above him, nothing equal to him. Therefore 'Open, open,' still.

Again, he sets down, to move the church the more to open to him, the inconveniences that he endured, 'My head is filled with dew,' &c. Wherein he shews what he suffered, which sufferings are of two sorts: in himself; in his ministers. In himself, and in his own blessed person, what did he endure! What patience had he in enduring the refractory spirits of men, when he was here! How many indignities did he digest† in his disciples after their conversion! Towards his latter end, his head was not only filled with the drops, but his body filled with drops of blood. Drops of blood came from him, because of the anguish of his spirit, and the sense of God's wrath for our sins. Upon the cross, what did he endure there! That sense of God's anger there, was only for our sins. 'My God, my God, why hast thou forsaken me?' Mat. xxvii. 46. What should we speak of his going up and down doing good, preaching in his own person, setting whole nights apart for prayer! And then for what he suffers in his ministers. There he knocks, and saith, 'Open,' in them. And how was he used in the apostles that were after him, and in the ministers of the church ever since! What have they endured! for he put a spirit of patience upon them. And what indignities endured they in the primitive church, that were the publishers of the gospel! Those sweet publishers

* 'As,' deleted here.—G.

† That is, 'bear.'—G.

thereof, drawing men to open to Christ, were killed for preaching. So cruel is the heart, that it offereth violence to them that love them most, that love their souls. And what greater love than the love of the soul! Yet this is the Satanical temper and disposition of men's hearts. They hate those men most, that deal this way most truly and lovingly with them. It is not that the gospel is such an hard message. It is the word of reconciliation, and the word of life; but the heart hates it, because it would draw men from their present condition; and 'therefore condemnation is come into the world, in that men hate the light, because their works are evil,' John iii. 19. Is there anything truly and cordially hated but grace? and are any persons heartily and cordially hated in the world so much as the promulgers and publishers of grace, and the professors of it? because it upbraids most of all, and meddles with the corruptions of men, that are dearer to them than their own souls.

Now, what patience is there in Christ to suffer himself in his messengers, and his children to be thus used! Nor it is not strange to say that Christ stands thus in his ministers; for it is said, 'That Christ by his Spirit preached in the days of Noah, to the souls now in prison,' 1 Pet. iii. 19. Christ preached in Noah's time, before he was incarnate, much more doth he preach now. And as he was patient then to endure the old world, unto whom Noah preached a hundred and twenty years; so he is patient now in his ministers to preach still by the same Spirit, even to us still, and yet the entertainment in many places is, as Paul complains, 'Though the more I love you, yet the less I am beloved of you,' 2 Cor. xii. 15.

Use 1. *Let these things move us to be patient towards God and Christ, if we be corrected in any kind*, considering that Christ is so patient towards us, and to wait upon him with patience. How long hath he waited for our conversion! How long doth he still wait for the thorough giving up of our souls to him! Shall we think much, then, to wait a little while for him?

Use 2. *And let this Spirit of Christ strengthen us likewise in our dealing with others*, as to bear with evil men, and as it is, 'to wait, if God will at any time give them repentance,' 2 Tim. ii. 25, 26. Neither may we be so short-spirited, that if we have not an answer, presently to give over. We should imitate Christ here. Never give over as long as God continues life with any advantage and opportunity to do good to any soul. Wait, if God at any time will give them grace. 'Open to me, my sister, my love,' &c.

Use 3. *Let this again work upon us, that our Saviour Christ here would thus set forth his love, and his patience in his love*, in bearing with us thus, under the resemblance of a silly suitor that comes afar off, and stands at the door, and knocks. That Christ should stoop thus in seeking the good of our souls, let this win and quicken our hearts with all readiness and thankfulness to receive him when he comes to work in our souls. Considering that Christ hath such a care of us by himself, his ministers, and the motions of his Spirit, who joins with his ministry, let not us therefore be careless of our own souls, but let it move our hearts to melt to him. The motives may be seen more in the particular compellations. 'Open to me, my sister, my love,' &c.

'My sister.' This was spoken of before in the former verse. The church of God is Christ's sister and spouse. We are knit to him both by consanguinity and by affinity. The nearest affinity is marriage, and the nearest consanguinity is sister. So that there are all bonds to knit us to Christ. Whatsoever is strong in any bond, he knits us to him by it. Is there any love in an husband, a brother, a mother, a friend, in an head to the members? in anything in the world? Is there any love scattered in any relation, gather it all into one, and all that love, and a thousand times more than that, is in Christ in a more eminent manner. Therefore he styles himself in all these sweet relations, to shew that he hath the love of all. Will a sister shut out a brother, when the brother comes to visit her, and do her all good? Is this unkindness even in nature, to look strangely upon a man that is near akin, that comes and saith, 'Open to me, my sister?' If the sister should shut out the brother, were it not most unnatural? And is it not monstrous in grace, when our brother comes for our good, and in pity to our souls, to let him stand without doors? Remember that Christ hath the same affections, to account us brothers and sisters, now in heaven, as he had when he was upon the earth. For after his resurrection, saith he to his disciples, 'I go to my God, and to your God, to my Father, and to your Father,' John xx. 17. He calls himself our brother, having one common Father in heaven, and one Spirit, and one inheritance, &c. This is a sweet relation. Christ being our brother, his heart cannot but melt towards us in any affliction. Joseph dissembled a while, out of politic wisdom, Gen. xlii. 7, *seq.*, but because he had a brother's heart to Benjamin, therefore at last he could not hold, but melted into tears, though he made his countenance as though he had not regarded. So our Joseph, now in heaven, may seem to withdraw all tokens and signs of brotherly love from us, and not to own us; but it is only in show, he is our brother still. His heart, first or last, will melt towards his brethren, to their wonderful comfort. 'My sister,' &c.

'My love.' That word we had not yet. It is worthy also a little standing on, for all these four words be, as it were, the attractive cords to draw the spouse, not only by shewing what he had suffered, but by sweet titles, 'My love, My dove.'

What, had Christ no love but his spouse? Did his love go out of his own heart to her, as it were? It is strange, yet true. Christ's love is so great to his church and children, and so continual* to it, that his church and people and every Christian soul is the seat of his love. That love in his own breast being in them, they are his love, because he himself is there, and one with them, John xvii. 26.

He loves all his creatures. They have all some beams of his goodness, which he must needs love. Therefore he loves them as creatures, and as they be more or less capable of a higher degree of goodness; but for his church and children, they are his love indeed.

Quest. But what is the ground of such love?

Ans. 1. He *loves them as he beholds them in his father's choice*, as they are elected of God, and given unto himself in election. 'Thine they are, thou gavest them me,' John xvii. 6. Christ, looking on us in God's election and choice, loves us.

Ans. 2. Again, *he loves us because he sees his own graces in us*. He loves what is his in us. Before we be actually his, he loves us with a love of good will, to wish all good to us. But when we have anything of his Spirit, that our natures are altered and changed, he loves us with a love of the intimatest friendship, with the love of an head, husband, friend, and what we can imagine. He loves his own image. Paul saith 'that the wife is the glory of her husband,' 1 Cor. xi. 7, because whatsoever is in a good husband, the wife expresseth it by reflection. So the church is the glory of Christ; she reflects his excellencies, though in a weak measure. They

* That is, 'abiding.'—G.

shew forth his virtues or praises, as Peter speaks, 1 Pet. ii. 9. Thus he sees his own image in her, and the Holy Ghost in his church. He loves her, and these in her, so as whether we regard the Father or himself or his Spirit, the church is his love.

Ans. 3. *If we consider also what he hath done and suffered for her*, we may well say the church is his love. Besides the former favours, not to speak of election, he choosed us before we were. In time he did choose us by actual election, by which he called us. We had an existence, but we resisted. He called us when we resisted. And then also he justified us, and clothed us with his own righteousness, and after feeds us with his own body. As the soul is the most excellent thing in the world, so he hath provided for it the most excellent ornaments. It hath food and ornaments proportionable. What love is this, that he should feed our souls with his own body, and clothe us with his own righteousness! 'He loved me,' saith Paul, Gal. ii. 20. What was the effect of his love? 'He gave himself for me.' He gave himself, both that we might have a righteousness to clothe us with in the sight of God, and he gave himself that he might be the bread of life, 'My flesh is meat indeed, and my blood is drink indeed,' John vi. 55. The guilty, the self-accusing soul feeds upon Christ dying for its sins. Again, Rev. i. 6, you have his love set forth, 'He loved us;' and how doth he witness it? 'He hath washed us with his own blood, and hath made us kings, and priests, &c. The like you have, 'He loved us, and gave himself a sweet sacrifice to God for us,' Eph. v. 2. When this world is at an end, we shall see what his love is. He is not satisfied till we be all in one place. What doth he pray for to his Father? 'Father, I will that those whom thou hast given me be with me where I am,' &c., John xvii. 24. Run through all the whole course of salvation, election, vocation, justification, glorification, you shall see his love in all of them. But it were an infinite argument to follow to shew the love of Christ, which is beyond all knowledge, Eph. iii. 19; and it is too large for us to know all the dimensions of it, to see the height, breadth, depth, and length of it, which we should ever think, speak, and meditate of, because the soul is then in the most fit temper to serve, love, and glorify God, when it is most apprehensive of his great love.

1. This phrase imports divers things. 1. *That there is no saving love to any out of the church*, which is his *love.* It is, as it were, confined in the church, as if all the beams of his love met in that centre, as we see when the beams of the sun meet in a glass, they burn, because many are there united. So in the church all his love doth meet.

2. Then the church is his love also, *because whatsoever she hath or hopes for is from his love, and is nothing but his love.* The church, as it is a church, is nothing but the love of Christ. That there is a church so endowed, so graced, so full of the hope of glory, it is out of his love.

And for the properties of it. (1.) It is a *free love, a preventing love.* He loved us before ever we could love him. He loved us when we resisted him, and were his enemies.

(2.) It is a most *tender love*, as you have it in Isa. xlix. 15, 'Can a mother forget her sucking child? If she should, yet will not I forget thee. Thou art written on the palms of my hands,' &c. He hath us in his heart, in his eye, in his hand, in a mother's heart, and beyond it. He hath a tender eye and a powerful hand to maintain his church, Deut. xxxiii. 3.

(3.) It is a *most transcendent and careful love.* All comparisons are under it.

(4.) And it is *a most intimate invincible love*, that nothing could quench it.

As we see here the church droopeth, and had many infirmities, yet she is Christ's love. So that the love of Christ is a kind of love that is unconquerable; no water will ever quench it; no sin of ours; no infirmity. So as it is very comfortable that the church considered under infirmities is yet the love of Christ. 'I sleep, but my heart waketh,' yet Christ comes with 'My love, my dove,' &c.

Quest. But what, cannot Christ see matter of weakness, sinfulness, hatred, and dislike in the church?

Ans. Oh yes, to pity, help, and heal it, but not at all to diminish his love, but to manifest it so much the more. His love is a tender love, sensible of all things wherewith we displease him, yet it is so invincible and unconquerable, that it overcomes all. Again, he sees ill indeed in us, but he sees in us some good of his own also, which moves him more to love, than that that is ill in us, moves him to hate. For what he sees of ours, he sees with a purpose to vanquish, mortify, and eat it out. The Spirit is as fire to consume it. He is as water to wash it. But what he sees of his own, he sees with a purpose to increase it more and more, and to perfect it. Therefore he says, 'my love,' notwithstanding that the church was asleep.

Use. This therefore serves greatly for our comfort, to search what good Christ by his Spirit hath wrought in our hearts; what faith, what love, what sanctified judgment, what fire of holy affections to him, and to the best things. O let us value ourselves by that that is good, that Christ hath in us. We are Christ's love notwithstanding we are sleepy. If we be displeased with this our state; that as Christ dislikes it, so if we by the Spirit dislike it, the matter is not what sin we have in us, but how we are affected to it. Have we that ill in us, which is truly the grief of our hearts and souls, which as Christ dislikes, so we abhor it, and would be purged, and rid of it; and it is the grief of our hearts and souls, that we cannot be better, and more lovely in Christ's eye! then let us not be discouraged. For Christ esteems of his church highly, even as his very love, even at that time when she was sleepy; and may teach us in time of temptation not to hearken to Satan, who then moves us to look altogether upon that which is naught in us, thereby to abate our love to Christ, and our apprehension of his to us. For he knows if we be sensible of the love of Christ to us, we shall love him again. For love is a kind of fire, an active quality, which will set us about glorifying God, and pulling down Satan's kingdom. As we say in nature, fire doth all; (what work almost can a man work without fire, by which all instruments are made and heated? &c.). So grace doth all with love. God first doth manifest to our souls his love to us in Christ, and quicken us by his Spirit, witnessing his love to us, wherewith he warms our hearts, kindles and inflames them so with love, that we love him again; which love hath a constraining, sweet violence to put us upon all duties, to suffer, to do, to resist anything. If a man be in love with Christ, what will be harsh to him in the world? The devil knows this well enough; therefore one of his main engines and temptations is to weaken our hearts in the sense of God's love and of Christ's. Therefore let us be as wise for our souls as he is subtle, and politic against them; as watchful for our own comfort, as he is to discomfort us, and make us despair. Let us be wise to gather all the arguments of Christ's love that we can.

Quest. But how shall we know that Christ loves us in this peculiar manner?

Ans. 1. *First*, search what course he takes and hath taken to *draw thee nearer unto him*. 'He chastiseth every one that he loveth,' Heb. xii. 6. Seasonable corections sanctified, is a sign of Christ's love; when he will not suffer us to thrive in sin; when we cannot speak nor do amiss; but either he lasheth us in our conscience for it, and by his Spirit checks us, or else stirs up others, one thing or other to make us out of love with sin.

2. Again, we may gather Christ's love by this, *if we have any love to divine things, and can set a great price upon the best things;* upon the word, because it is Christ's word; upon grace, prizing the image of Christ, and the new creature. When we can set an high value upon communion with Christ, the sense of his love in our hearts, and all spiritual prerogatives and excellencies above all things, this is an excellent argument of Christ's love to us. Our love is but a reflection of his; and therefore if we have love to anything that is good, we have it from him first. If a wall that is cold become hot, we say, the sun of necessity must shine on it first, because it is nothing but cold stone of itself. So if our hearts, that are naturally cold, be heated with the love of divine things, certainly we may say, Christ hath shined here first; for naturally our hearts are of a cold temper. There is no such thing as spiritual love growing in our natures and hearts.

You have many poor souls helped with this, who cannot tell whether Christ love them or no; but this helps them a little, they can find undoubted arguments of their love to Christ, his image, and servants, and of relishing the word, though they find much corruption: and this their love to divine things tells them by demonstrations from the effects, *that Christ loves them*, because there is no love to divine and supernatural things without the love of Christ first. And the graces in our hearts, they are love tokens given to the spouse. Common favours he gives, as Abraham gifts to his servants and others, but special gifts to his spouse. If therefore there be any grace, a tender and soft heart, a prizing of heavenly things, love to God's people and truth, then we may comfortably conclude Christ loves us; not only because they are reflections of God's love, but because they are jewels and ornaments that Christ only bestows upon his spouse; and not upon reprobates, such precious jewels as these, John xv. 15.

3. *By discovering his secrets to us*, Ps. xxv. 14, for that is an argument of love. Doth Christ by his Spirit discover the secret love he hath borne to us before all worlds? Doth he discover the breast of his Father, and his own heart to us? This discovery of secret affections, of entire love, sheweth our happy state. For that is one prerogative of friendship, and the chiefest discovery of secrets, when he gives us a particular right to truths, as our own, that we can go challenge them, these are mine, these belong to me, these promises are mine. This discovery of the secret love of God, and of the interests we have in the promises, is a sign that Christ loves us, and that in a peculiar manner we are his love.

Use 1. Let us be like our blessed Saviour, that where we see any saving goodness in any, let us love them; for should not our love meet with our Saviour's love? Shall the church of God be the love of Christ, and shall it be our hatred? Shall a good Christian be Christ's love, and shall he be the object of my hatred and scorn? Can we imitate a better pattern? O let us never think our estate to be good, except every child of God be our love as he is Christ's love. Can I love Christ, and cannot I love * him in whom I see Christ? It is a sign that I hate himself, when I hate his image. It is to be wondered at that the devil hath prevailed with any so much, as to think they should be in a good estate, when they have hearts rising against the best people, and who, as they grow in grace, so they grow in their dislike of them. Is here the Spirit of Christ?

* That is, 'can I not love.'—ED.

Use 2. And let them likewise be here reproved that are glad to see any Christian halt, slip, and go awry. The best Christians in the world have that in part, which is wholly in another man; he hath flesh in him. Shall we utterly distaste a Christian for that? The church was now in a sleepy condition, and yet, notwithstanding, Christ takes not the advantage of the weakness of the church to cashier,* and to hate her, but he pities her the more, and takes a course to bring her again into a good state and condition. Let us not therefore be glad at the infirmities and failings of any, that discover any true goodness in them. It may be our own case ere long. It casts them not out of Christ's love, but they dwell in his love still; why should we then cast them out of our love and affections? Let them be our loves till, as they are the love of Christ, notwithstanding their infirmities.

THE SEVENTH SERMON.

My love, my dove, my undefiled: for my head is filled with dew, and my locks with the drops of the night. I have put off my coat; how shall I put it on? I have washed my feet; and how shall I defile them?—CANT. V. 2, 3.

THAT the life of a Christian is a perpetual conflicting, appears evidently in this book, the passages whereof, joined with our own experiences, sufficiently declare what combats, trials, and temptations the saints are subject unto, after their new birth and change of life; now up, now down, now full of good resolutions, now again sluggish and slow, not to be waked, nor brought forward by the voice of Christ, as it was with the church here. She will not out of her sleep to open unto Christ, though he call, and knock, and stand waiting for entrance. She is now desirous to pity herself, and needs no Peter to stir her up unto it (*g*). The flesh of itself is prone enough to draw back, and make excuses, to hinder the power of grace from its due operation in us. She is laid along, as it were, to rest her; yet is not she so asleep, but she discerns the voice of Christ. But up and rise she will not.

Thus we may see the truth of that speech of our Saviour verified, 'That which is born of the flesh is flesh, and that which is born of the Spirit is spirit,' John iii. 6. The flesh pulls her back: the Spirit would raise her up to open to Christ. He in the meanwhile makes her inexcusable, and prepares her by his knocking, waiting, and departing; as for a state of further humiliation, so for an estate of further exaltation. But how lovingly doth he speak to her!

1. 'Open unto me, my love.' He calls her my love, especially for two respects; partly because *his love was settled upon her*. It was in his own breast, but it rested not there, but seated itself upon, and in the heart of his spouse, so that she became Christ's love. We know the heart of a lover is more where it loves than where it lives, as we use to speak; and indeed, there is a kind of a going out, as it were, to the thing beloved, with a heedlessness of all other things. Where the affection is in any excess, it carries the whole soul with it.

2. But, besides this, when Christ saith my love, he shews, that as his love goes, and plants, and seats itself in the church, *so it is united to that, and is not scattered to other objects*. There are beams of God's general love scattered in the whole world; but this love, this exceeding love, is only fas-

* That is, 'dismiss.'—G.

tened upon the church. And, indeed, there is no love comparable to this love of Christ, which is above the love of women, of father, or mother, if we consider what course he takes to shew it. For there could be nothing in the world so great to discover his love, as this gift, and gift of himself. And therefore he gave himself, the best thing in heaven or in earth withal, to shew his love. The Father gave him, when he was God equal with his Father. He loved his church, and gave himself for it. How could he discover his love better, than to take our nature to shew how he loved us? How could he come nearer to us, than by being incarnate, so to be bone of our bone, and flesh of our flesh; and took our nature to shew how he loved it, Eph. v. 30. Love draws things nearer wheresoever it is. It drew him out of heaven to the womb of the virgin, there to be incarnate; and, after that, when he was born not only to be a man, but a miserable man, because we could not be his spouse unless he purchased us by his death. We must be his spouse by a satisfaction made to divine justice. God would not give us to him, but with salving* his justice. What sweet love is it to heal us not by searing, or lancing, but by making a plaster of his own blood, which he shed for those that shed his, in malice and hatred. What a wondrous love is it, that he should pour forth tears for those that shed his blood! 'O Jerusalem, Jerusalem,' &c., Mat. xxiii. 37; that he prayed for those that persecuted him, Luke xxiii. 34; and what wondrous love is it now that he sympathiseth with us in heaven, accounting the harm that is done to the least member he hath, as done to himself! 'Saul, Saul, why persecutest thou me?' Acts ix. 4, and that he should take us into one body with himself, to make one Christ, 1 Cor. xii. 27. And he doth not content himself with anything he can do for us here, but his desire is, that we may be one with him more and more, and be for ever with him in the heavens, as you have it in that excellent prayer, John xvii. 24.

Use 1. Now this should stir us up *to be fully persuaded of his love, that loves us so much.* Christ's love in us, is as the loadstone to the iron. Our hearts are heavy and downwards of themselves. We may especially know his love by this, that it draws us upwards, and makes us heavenly minded. It makes us desire further and further communion with him. Still there is a magnetical attractive force in Christ's love. Wheresoever it is, it draws the heart and affections after it.

Use 2. And we may know from hence one argument to prove *the stability of the saints, and the immortality of the soul,* because Christ calls the church his love. The want of love again, where it is entire, and in any great measure, is a misery. Christ therefore should suffer, if those he hath planted his love upon, whom he loves truly, either should fall away for ever, or should not be immortal for ever. Christ will not lose his love. And as it is an argument of persevering in grace, so is it of an everlasting being, that this soul of ours hath; because it is capable of the love of Christ, seeing there is a sweet union and communion between Christ and the soul. It should make Christ miserable, as it were, in heaven, the place of happiness, if there should not be a meeting of him and his spouse. There must therefore be a meeting; which marriage is for ever, that both may be for ever happy one in another, Hos. ii. 20.

Use 3. Let us often *warm our hearts with the consideration hereof, because all our love is from this love of his.* Oh the wonderful love of God, that both such transcendent majesty, and such an infinite love should dwell together. We say majesty and love never dwell together, because love is an abasing of the

* That is, 'preserving.'—G.

soul to all services. But herein it is false, for here majesty and love dwell together in the heart of one Christ, which majesty hath stooped as low as his almighty power could give leave. Nay, it was an almighty power that he could stoop so low and yet be God, keeping his majesty still. For God to become man, to hide his majesty for a while, not to be known to be God, and to hide so far in this nature as to die for us: what an almighty power was this, that could go so low and yet preserve himself God still! Yet this we see in this our blessed Saviour, the greatest majesty met with the greatest abasement that ever was, and all out of love to our poor souls. There was no stooping, no abasement that was ever so low as Christ was abased unto us, to want for a time even the comfort of the presence of his Father. There was an union of grace; but the union of solace and comfort that he had from him was suspended for a time, out of love to us. For he had a right in his own person to be in heaven presently. Now for him to live so long out of heaven, and ofttimes, especially towards his suffering, to be without that solace (that he might be a sacrifice for our sins), to have it suspended for a time, what a condescending was this? It is said, Ps. cxiii. 6, that God stoops 'to behold the things done here below.' It is indeed a wondrous condescending, that God will look upon things below; but that he would become man, and out of love to save us, suffer as he did here, this is wondrous humility to astonishment! We think humility is not a proper grace becoming the majesty of God. So it is not indeed, but there is some resemblance of that grace in God, especially in Christ, that he should, to reveal himself, veil himself with flesh, and all out of love to us. The consideration of these things are wondrous effectual, as to strengthen faith, so to kindle love. Let these be for a taste to direct our meditations herein. It follows,

'My dove.' We know when Christ was baptized, the Holy Ghost appeared in the shape of a dove, Mat. iii. 16, as a symbol of his presence, to discover thus much: (1.) *That Christ should have the property and disposition of a dove.* 'And be meek and gentle.' For indeed he became man for that end, to be 'a merciful Saviour.' 'Learn of me, for I am meek and lowly,' Mat. xi. 28, 29. 'And I will not quench the smoking flax, nor break the bruised reed,' &c., Mat. xii. 20, said he; and therefore the Spirit appeared upon him in the shape of a dove. As likewise, (2.) *To shew what his office should be.* For even as the dove in Noah's ark was sent out, and came home again to the ark with an olive branch, to shew that the waters were abated; so Christ was to preach deliverance from the deluge of God's anger, and to come with an olive leaf of peace in his mouth, and reconciliation, to shew that God's wrath was appeased. When he was born, the angels sung, 'Glory to God on high, on earth peace, and goodwill towards men,' Luke ii. 14. Now, as Christ had the Spirit in the likeness of a dove; so all that are Christ's, the spouse of Christ, have the disposition of Christ. That Spirit that framed him to be like a dove, frames the church to be a dove; as the ointment that was poured on Aaron's head: it ran down upon the lowest skirts of his garments, Ps. cxxxiii. 3.

Now, the church is compared to a dove, partly *for the disposition that is and should be in the church resembling that creature;* and partly, also, *for that the church is in a mournful suffering condition.*

I. *For the like disposition as is found in a dove.* There is some good in all creatures. There is no creature but it hath a beam of God's majesty, of some attribute; but some more than others. There is an image of virtue even in the inferior creatures. Wherefore the Scripture sends us to them for many virtues, as the sluggard to the ant, Prov. vi. 6. And indeed we may see the true perfection of the first creation, the state of it, more in the creatures than in ourselves ; for there is no such degeneration in any creature as there is in man.

Now, that which in a dove the Scripture aims at, 1, we should resemble a dove in is, his *meekness* especially. The church is meek both to God and man, not given to murmurings and revengement. Meek: that is, 'I held my tongue without murmuring,' as it is in the psalm; 'I was dumb,' &c., Ps. xxxix. 2: which is a grace that God's Spirit frames in the heart of the church, and every particular Christian, even to be meek towards God by an holy silence ; and likewise towards men, to put on the 'bowels of meekness,' as we are exhorted, 'As the elect of God, put on the bowels of meekness and compassion,' &c., Col. iii. 12. Hereby we shall shew ourselves to be Christ's, and to have the Spirit of Christ. And this grace disposeth us to a nearer communion with God than other graces. It is a grace that God most delights in, and would have his spouse to be adorned with, as is shewed, 1 Pet. iii. 4, where the apostle tells women, it is the best jewel and ornament that they can wear, and is with God of great price. Moses, we read, was a mighty man in prayer, and a special means to help and fit him thereunto, was because he was the meekest man on earth, Num. xii. 3; and therefore, 'seek the Lord, seek meekness,' Zeph. ii. 3; and it fits a man for communion with God, 'for God resisteth the proud, and giveth grace to the meek and humble,' 1 Pet. v. 5. It is a grace that empties the soul of self-conceit, to think a man's self unworthy of anything, and so makes it capacious, low, and fit for God to fill with a larger measure of his Spirit. It takes away the roughness and swelling of the soul, that keeps out God and grace. Therefore in that grace we must especially be like this meek creature, which is no vindictive creature, that hath no way to revenge itself.

Again, 2, *it is a simple creature, without guile*. It hath no way to defend itself, but only by flight. There is a simplicity that is sinful, when there is no mixture of wisdom in it. There is a simplicity, that is, a pure simplicity; and so God is simple, which simplicity of God is the ground of many other attributes. For thereupon he is eternal, because there is nothing contrary in him; there is no mixture in him of anything opposite. So that is a good simplicity in us, when there is no mixture of fraud, no duplicity in the soul. 'A double-hearted man is inconstant and unstable in all his ways,' James i. 8. Now simplicity, as it is a virtue, so we must imitate the dove in it; for there is a sinful, dove-like silliness. For, Hos. vii. 11, Ephraim is said there to be 'like a silly dove without heart; they call to Egypt, they go to Assyria.' There is a fatal simplicity, usually going before destruction, when we hate those that defend us, and account them enemies, and rely more upon them that are enemies indeed than upon friends. So it was with Ephraim before his destruction: 'He was a silly dove without heart; he called to Egypt, and went to Assyria,' false friends, that were enemies to the church of God ; yet they trusted them more than God or the prophets. Men have a world of tricks to undermine their friends, to ruin them, and to deserve ill of those that would with all their hearts deserve well of them, when yet in the mean time they can gratify the enemy, please them, and hold correspondence with them, as here Ephraim did. 'Ephraim is a silly dove,' &c. This, therefore, is not that which we must aim at, but to be simple and children concerning evil, but not in ignorance and simplicity that way.

3. Again, *this creature is a faithful creature*. That is mainly here aimed

at. It is faithful to the mate. So the Christian soul, by the Spirit of God, it is made faithful to Christ, it keeps the judgment chaste, is not tainted with errors and sins. He keeps his affections chaste likewise, sets nothing in his heart above Christ. 'Whom hath he in heaven but him, and what is there in earth he desires beside him?' Ps. lxxiii. 25. You know in the Revelation, the spouse of Christ is brought in like a virgin contracted, but the Romish Church like a whore. Therefore the church of God must take heed of the Roman Church, for that is not a dove. We must be virgins, who must keep chaste souls to Christ, as you have it—'Those that follow the Lamb wheresoever he goeth, they have not defiled themselves with women,' Rev. xiv. 4. The meaning is spiritual, namely, that they have not defiled themselves with idolatry and spiritual fornication; they have chaste hearts to Christ. So in this respect they resemble the dove. These, therefore, that draw away from the love of religion to mixture, to be meretrices* and harlots in religion, they are not Christ's doves. As far as they yield to this, it is an argument that they have false hearts. Christ's church is a dove. She keeps close and inviolate to him.

4. Again, *this creature is of a neat† disposition*. It will not lodge where it shall be troubled with stench, and annoyed that way; and likewise feeds neatly on pure grain; not upon carrion, as you see in the ark, when the raven was sent out it lights upon carrion, of which there was then plenty, and therefore never came into the ark again, Gen. viii. 7. But the dove, when she went out, would not light upon carrion or dead things; and so finding no fit food, came back again to the ark. So the Christian soul in this respect is like a dove, that will not feed upon worldly carrion, or sinful pleasures, but upon Christ and spiritual things. The soul of a carnal and a natural man useth to feed upon dust, earth and earthly things. When the soul of a true Christian, that hath the taste of grace, feeds neatly, it will not feed on that which is base and earthly, but upon heavenly and spiritual things.

5. It is *gregaria avis*, a bird that loves communion and fellowship, as the prophet speaks, 'Who are those that flock to the windows as doves,' Isa. lx. 8; for so they use to flock to their houses by companies. So the children of God love the communion and fellowship one of another, and keep severed from the world as soon as ever they are separated from it, delighting in all those of the same nature. Doves will consort with doves, Christians with Christians, and none else. They can relish no other company. These and such like properties may profitably be considered of the dove. The much standing upon these were to wrong the intendment‡ of the Spirit of God; to neglect them altogether were as much. Therefore we have touched upon some properties only.

II. Now, *for the sufferings of the church* it is like a dove in this. *The dove is molested by all the birds of prey*, it being the common prey of all other ravenous birds. So the poor church of God is persecuted and molested. 'Oh that I had wings like a dove,' &c., saith holy David, Ps. lv. 6. It is an old speech, and is for ever true, that crows and such, escape better than doves. The punishment that should light on ravens, ofttimes it lights on doves. Thus God's dove, God's church, is used.

But what defence hath God's poor church? Why, no defence. But,

First, *flight*, even as the dove hath nothing but flight. It hath no talons to wound, but it hath flight. So we are to fly to God as to our mountain; fly to the ark, that God may take us in. The church of God

* That is, 'courtezans.'—G. † That is, 'cleanly.'—G. ‡ That is, 'design.'—G.

hath no other refuge but to be housed in God and Christ, Prov. xviii. 10. He is our ark.

Secondly, and to *mourn;* as Hezekiah saith of himself, 'He mourned as a dove, and chattered like a crane,' Isa. xxxviii. 14. The state of the church of God is like the turtle's, to mourn in all afflictions, desertions, and molestations of wicked men; to mourn to God, who hears the bemoanings of his own Spirit in them. And woe to all other birds, the birds of prey, when the turtles do mourn because of their cruelty. It is a presage of ruin to them, when they force the turtle to sorrow and mourning.

Thirdly, And then, thirdly, they have another refuge besides flight and mourning, which is *to build high from vermin* that would otherwise molest them. Instinct teacheth them thus to escape their enemies by building high, and so to secure themselves. So there is in God's children a gracious instinct put, an antipathy to the enemies of it; which tends to their safety, in that they mingle not themselves with them. And likewise God breeds in them a familiarity with himself, and stirs them to build in him as on a rock, to be safe in him.

Objec. But you will object, If the church of God be his dove, why is it so with it as it is, that God should suffer his love, and his dove, and his turtle thus as it were to be preyed upon? 'Give not the soul of the turtle to the beasts,' saith the psalmist, Ps. lxxiv. 19. If the church were God's dove, he would esteem more of it than he doth, and not suffer it to be persecuted thus?

Ans. God never forsakes his dove, but is an ark for it to fly to, a rock for it to build on. The dove hath always a refuge in God and in Christ in the worst times. You have a notable place for this, 'Though you have lien among the pots,' that is, smeared and sullied, 'yet they shall be as the wings of a dove covered with silver, and her feathers with yellow gold. When the Almighty scattered kings in it, it was white as the snow in Salmon,' Ps. lxviii. 13, 14. So though the church of God lies among the pots awhile, all smeared, and soiled, and sullied with the ill-usage of the world, yet as long as it keeps itself a dove, unspotted of the filth of the world and sin (though it be smeared with the ill-usage thereof), we see what God promiseth here, 'yet shall they be as the wings of a dove covered with silver, and her feathers with yellow gold.' So God will bring forth his dove with glory out of all these abasements at length. So much for the title of dove. It follows,

'My undefiled.' Undefiled is a high word to be applied to the church of God here; for the church, groaning under infirmities, to be counted perfect and undefiled. But Christ, who judgeth aright of his church, and knows best what she is, he yet thus judgeth of her. But, how is that? The church is undefiled, especially *in that it is the spouse of Christ, and clothed with the robes of his righteousness.* For there is an exchange so soon as ever we are united to Christ. Our sins are upon him, and his righteousness is made ours; and therefore in Christ the church is undefiled. Christ himself the second person is the first lovely thing next the Father; and in Christ all things as they have relation to him are loved, as they are in him. Christ's human nature is next loved to the second person. It is united, and is first pure, holy, and beloved. Then, because the church is Christ mystical, it is near to him; and, in a manner, as near as that sacred body of his, both making up one Christ mystical. And so is amiable and beloved even of God himself, who hath pure eyes; yet in this respect looks upon the church as undefiled.

Christ and his church are not to be considered as two when we speak of this undefiledness, but as one. And the church having Christ, with all that is Christ's, they have the field, and the pearl * in the field together. And Christ giving himself to the church, he gives his righteousness, his perfection, and holiness; all is the church's.

Quest. But how can it be the church's, when it is not in the church, but in Christ?

Ans. It is safe for the church that it is in Christ, who is perfect and undefiled for us; to make us appear so. And so it is in Christ, the second Adam, for our good. It is not in him as another person, but it is in him as the church's Head, that make both one Christ. The hand and the foot see not; but both hand and foot have benefit by the eye, that sees for them. There is no member of the body understands, but the head does all for them. Put the case we have not absolute righteousness and undefiledness in our own natures and persons inhering in us. Yet we have it in Christ, that is one with us, who hath it for our good. It is ours, for all the comfort and good that we may have by it; and thereupon the church in Christ is undefiled; yea, even then when it feels its own defilements. And here ariseth that wondrous contradiction that is found in a believer's apprehension. The nature of faith is to apprehend righteousness in the sense of sin, happiness in the sense of misery, and favour in the sense of displeasure.

And the ground of it is, because that at the same time the soul may be in some measure defiled in itself, and yet notwithstanding be undefiled in her head and husband Christ. Hence the guilty soul, when it feels corruption and sin, yet notwithstanding doth see itself holy and clean in Christ the head. And so at once there is a conscience of sin, and no more conscience of sin, as the apostle saith, Heb. x. 2, when we believe in Christ, and are purged with his blood, that is, there is no more guilt of sin binding over to eternal damnation, yet notwithstanding always there is a conscience of sin, for we are guilty of infirmities, 'And if we say we have no sin, we lie, and deceive ourselves, 1 John i. 8.

Obj. But, how can this be, that there should be conscience of sin, and no conscience of sin, a sinner, and yet a perfect saint and undefiled?

Ans. 1. *The conscience knows its own imperfection, so it is defiled*, and accuseth of sin. *And as it looks to Christ, so it sees itself pure, and purged from all sin.* Here is the conquest, fight, and the victory of faith in the deepest sense of sin, pollution, and defilement in ourselves, at the same time to see an absolute and perfect righteousness in Jesus Christ. Herein is even the triumph of faith, whereby it answers God. And Christ, who sees our imperfections, but it is to purge and cleanse them away, not to damn us for them, at the same time he sees us in his own love clothed with his righteousness, as one with himself, endowed with whatsoever he hath; his satisfaction and obedience being ours as verily as anything in the world is. Thus he looks on us, and thus faith looks upon him too, and together with the sight and sense of sin, at the same time it apprehends righteousness, perfect righteousness, and so is undefiled. This is the main point in religion, and the comfort of Christians, to see their perfection in Christ Jesus, and to be lost in themselves, as it were, and to be only 'found in him, not having their own righteousness, but the righteousness of God in him,' Phil. iii. 9. This is a mystery which none knows but a believing soul. None see corruption more, none see themselves freed more. They have an inward sight to see corruption, and an inward faith to see God takes not advantage at it. And

* That is, 'treasure.' See Mat. xiii. 44.—G.

surely there can be no greater honour to Christ than this. In the sense of sin, of wants, imperfections, stains, and blemishes, yet to wrap ourselves in the righteousness of Christ, God-man; and by faith, being thus covered with that absolute righteousness of Christ, with boldness to go, clothed in the garments of this our elder brother, to the throne of grace. This is an honour to Christ, to attribute so much to his righteousness, that being clothed therewith, we can boldly break through the fire of God's justice, and all those terrible attributes, when we see them all, as it were, satisfied fully in Christ. For Christ, with his righteousness, could go through the justice of God, having satisfied it to the full for us. And we being clothed with this his righteousness and satisfaction, may go through too.

Ans. 2. But besides that, there is another undefiledness in the church, in respect to which she is called undefiled, that is, *in purity of disposition, tending to perfection.* And God respects her according to her better part, and according to what he will bring her in due time. For we are chosen unto perfection, and to be holy in his sight; and perfectly holy, undefiled, and pure. We are not chosen to weak beginnings.

In choosing us, what did God aim at? Did he aim at these imperfect beginnings, to rest there? No; we were elected and chosen to perfection. For, as it is in this natural life, God purposed that we should not only have all the limbs of men, but grow from infancy to activeness and perfection. As God at first intended so much for our bodies, no question he intends as much also for the soul, that we should not only have the lineaments of Christianity, a sanctified judgment, with affections in part renewed, but he hath chosen us to perfection by degrees. As the seed first lies rotting in the ground, then grows to a stalk, and then to an ear, so God's wisdom shines here, by bringing things by degrees to perfection and undefiledness. His wisdom will have it thus (or else his power might have it otherwise), because he will have us to live by faith, to trust his mercy in Christ, and not to the undefiledness that is begun in us, but to admire that which we have in Christ himself.

And, indeed, it is the character of a judicious believing Christian soul, that he can set a price and value the righteousness of Christ, out of himself, labouring, living, and dying to appear in that; and yet to comfort and sustain himself during this conflict and fight between the flesh and the Spirit, that in time this inherent grace shall be brought to perfection.

And Christ, he looks upon us as he means to perfect the work of grace in us by little and little, as he means to purge and cleanse us, as Eph. v. 26, 27. The end of redemption is, that he might purge his church, and so never leave it till he have made it 'a glorious spouse in heaven.' He looks upon us as we shall be ere long, and therefore we are said 'to be dead to sin,' while we are but dying to it. And, saith he, 'you have crucified the flesh with the affections, and lusts thereof,' Gal. v. 24, when we are but crucifying it. But it is said so because it is as sure to be done as if it were done already. As a man, when he is condemned, and going to his execution, he is a dead man, so there is a sentence passed upon sin and corruption. It shall be abolished and die. Therefore it is dead in sentence, and is dying in execution. It is done; 'They that are in Christ have crucified the flesh, with the lusts thereof,' Gal. v. 24. It is as sure to faith as if it were done already. So we are said 'to sit in heavenly places with Christ,' Eph. ii. 6. We are with him already. For Christ having taken us so near in affection to himself, he will never leave us till he have made us such as he may have full contentment in, which is in heaven, when the contract between him and us shall be fulfilled in consummation of the marriage. Thus faith looks, and Christ looks thus upon us. Which should comfort us in weakness, that God regards us not in our present imperfections, but as he means to make us ere long. In the mean time, that he may look upon us in love, he looks upon us in the obedience of his son, in whom whatsoever is good shall be perfected at the last.

Use 1. What should we do then, if Christ doth make his church thus, 'his love,' 'his dove,' 'his undefiled,' by making his love to meet in it as the centre thereof, whereunto he doth confine all his love, as it were? *We should confine our love to him again; and have no love out of Christ,* since he hath no love out of us. There should be an everlasting mutual shining and reflection between him and the soul. We should lay open our souls to his love, as indeed he desires especially the communion of our affections. We should reflect love to him again. This perpetual everlasting intercourse between Christ and his spouse, is her main happiness here, and her eternal happiness in heaven. In looking on him who hath done so much for us, he shines on us, and we look back again upon him. Doth Christ love us so intimately, and so invincibly, that no indignities nor sin could overcome his love, which made, that he endured that which he hates most, 'to become sin for us,' 2 Cor. v. 21, nay, the want of that, which was more to him than all the world, the want of the sense of the favour of God for a time. 'My God, my God, why hast thou forsaken me?' Hath Christ thus infinitely loved us, and shall not we back again make him our love? In their degree the saints of God have all done so. It was a good speech of Ignatius the martyr, 'My love Christ was crucified!' (*h*) So a Christian should say, 'My love was crucified,' 'My love died,' 'My love is in heaven.' And for the things on earth, I love them as they have a beam of him in them; as they lead me to him. But he is my love, there my love is pitched, even upon him. This is the ground of these Scripture phrases, 'But our conversation is in heaven, from whence we look for the Saviour, the Lord Jesus Christ,' &c., Phil. iii. 20; and 'set your affections on the things that are above,' Col. iii. 1. Why? Christ our love is there. The soul is more where it loves, than where its residence is. It dies, as it were, to other things, and lives in the thing it loves. Therefore our thoughts and affections, our joy and delight should be drawn up to Christ; for indeed his love hath such a magnetical attractive force, that where it is, it will draw up the heavy iron, the gross soul; and make it heavenly. For there is a binding, a drawing force in this excellent affection of love.

Use 2. 'My love, my dove,' &c. *There are all words of sweetness.* He labours to express all the affection he can. For the conscience is subject to upbraid, and to clamour much. So that there must be a great deal of persuasion to still the accusing conscience of a sinner, to set it down, make it quiet, and persuade it of God's love. Therefore he useth all heavenly rhetoric to persuade and move the affections.

Use 3. In this that the church is undefiled in Christ, let us learn when afflicted in conscience, not so much *to judge of ourselves by what we feel in ourselves, as by what faith suggests.* In Christ therefore let us judge of ourselves by what we are as in him. We are poor in ourselves, but have riches in him. We die in ourselves in regard of this life, but we have a life in him, an eternal life; and we are sinners in ourselves, but we have a righteousness in him whereby we are righteous in his sight, 1 Cor. v. 21. We are foolish, unskilful, and ignorant in ourselves, but he is our wisdom in all whatsoever is amiss in us. Let us labour to see a full supply of our wants made up in Christ. This is to glorify God as much as if we could fulfil the law perfectly. If we were as undefiled as Adam was, we could not glorify God more, than when we find ourselves and our conscience guilty of sins, yet thus by the Spirit of God to go out of ourselves, and to see ourselves in Christ, and thus to cast ourselves on him, embrace him, and take that gift of God given us, Christ offered to us, because God so commands, John iv. 10. We honour God more than if we had the obedience that Adam had at first before his fall. For now in the covenant of grace, he will be glorified in his mercy, in his forgiving, forbearing, rich, transcendent mercy, and in going beyond all our unworthiness and sins, by shewing that there is a righteousness provided for us, the righteousness of God-man; whose obedience and satisfaction is more than our disobedience, because it is the disobedience of man only, but his obedience and righteousness is the obedience and righteousness of God-man. So it satisfieth divine justice, and therefore ought to satisfy conscience to the full. Our faith must answer Christ's carriage to us. We must therefore account ourselves in him 'undefiled,' because he accounts us so. Not in ourselves, but as we have a being in him, we are undefiled.

Use 4. Again, see here, Christ accounts us, even in regard of habitual grace, *undefiled, though we have for the present many corruptions.* Let us therefore learn a lesson of moderation of so excellent a teacher; let us not be ashamed to learn of our Saviour. What spirit shall we think they have, that will unchurch churches, because they have some defilement and unbrotherly brethren, accounting them no churches, no brethren, because they have some imperfections? Why hath not Christ a quarrel to the church then? is he blind? doth his love make him blind? No; he seeth corruption, but he seeth better things; somewhat of his own, that makes him overlook those imperfections, because they are such as he means to mortify, subdue, wear away, and to fire out by the power of his Spirit, which as fire shall waste all those corruptions in time. So it is with the church. Put the case, she hath some corruptions; that it be not with her, as it should be, yet she is a church notwithstanding. The church of Corinth, we see, Paul styles them saints and brethren, with all those sweet names, 1 Cor. i. 2, notwithstanding they had many corruptions among them.

Use 5. We have a company of malignant spirits, worse than these a great deal, atheistical persons, that have no religion at all, who, out of malice and envy, *watch for the halting of good Christians;* who can see nothing but defilement in those that have any good in them, nothing but hypocrisy, moppishness, all that is naught; who, if they can devise any blemish, put it upon them. Whereas Christ sees a great deal of ill in the church, but he sees it to pardon, subdue, and to pity the church for it, extolling and magnifying its goodness. What spirits are those of that watch to see imperfections in others, that their hearts tell them are better than they, that they may only disgrace them by it; for goodness they will see none.

Use 6. And likewise, it should teach us *not to wrong ourselves with false judgment.* We should have a double eye: one eye to see that which is amiss in us, our own imperfections, thereby to carry ourselves in a perpetual humility; but another eye of faith, to see what we have in Christ, our perfection in him, so to account of ourselves, and glory in this our best being, that in him we have a glorious being,—such an one whereby God esteems us perfect, and undefiled in him only. The one of which sights should enforce us to the other, which is one end, why God in this world leaves corruption in his children. Oh, since I am thus undefiled, shall

I rest in myself? Is there any harbour for me to rest in mine own righteousness? Oh, no; it drives a man out of all harbour. Nay, I will rest in that righteousness which God hath wrought by Christ, who is God-man. That will endure the sight of God, being clothed with which, I can endure the presence of God. So, this sight of our own unworthiness and wants should not be a ground of discouragement, but a ground to drive us perfectly out of ourselves, that by faith we might renew our title to that righteousness, wherein is our especial glory. Why should we not judge of ourselves as Christ doth? Can we see more in ourselves than he doth? Yet, notwithstanding all he sees, he accounts us as undefiled.

Use 7. Again, since he accounts us undefiled, because he means to make us so, and now looks on us as we shall be, in all our foils* and infirmities, let us comfort ourselves, *it shall not thus be always with us*. Oh, this flesh of mine shall fall and fall still, and shall decay as Saul's house, and the Spirit at the last shall conquer in all this! I am not chosen to this beginning, to this conflicting course of life. I am chosen to triumph, to perfection of grace: this is my comfort. Thus we should comfort ourselves, and set upon our enemies and conflict in this hope of victory: 'I shall get the better of myself at the last.' Imperfection should not discourage, but comfort us in this world. We are chosen to perfection. Let us still rejoice, in that 'we are chosen to sanctification,' which is a little begun, being an earnest of other blessings. Let us not rest in the pledge or in the earnest, but labour for a further pledge of more strength and grace. For those that have the Spirit of Christ, will strive to be as much unspotted and as heavenly as they can, to fit themselves for that heavenly condition as much as may be. When, because they cannot be in heaven, yet they will converse there as much as they can; and because they cannot be with such company altogether, they will be as much as they may be; labouring as they are able to be that which they shall be hereafter. Imperfection contents them not, and therefore they pray still in the Lord's prayer, 'Thy kingdom come,' Mat. vi. 10. While there is any imperfection, their hearts are enlarged more and more; nothing contents them but perfection. And indeed God accounts us thus unspotted for this end, because he would encourage us. Where he sees the will and endeavour, he gives the title of the thing desired.

I have put off my coat; how shall I put it on? I have washed my feet; how shall I defile them? Verse 3.

Here is an ingenious† confession made by the church of her own untowardness. Notwithstanding all Christ's heavenly rhetoric and persuasion that he did use, yet she draws back, and seems to have reason so to do. 'I have put off my coat; how shall I put it on again' to let thee in? 'I have washed my feet, &c. It is a phrase taken from the custom of those hot countries, wherein they used to wash their feet. 'I have washed my feet; how shall I defile them' to rise and open the door to thee? There is a spiritual meaning herein, as if she had said, I have some ease by this sleepy profession, some freedom from evil tongues, and some exemption and immunity from some troubles I was in before. I was then, perhaps, too indiscreet. Now wilt thou call me again to those troubles, that I have wisely avoided? No; 'I have put off my coat; how shall I put it on? I have washed my feet, how shall I defile them?' I affect‡ this estate very well; I am content to be as I am, without troubling of myself. Thus the church puts off Christ. This I take to be the meaning of the words. That which is observable is this: *that it is not an easy*

* That is, 'falls.'—G. † That is, 'ingenuous.'—G. ‡ That is, 'like.'—G.

matter to bring the soul and Christ together into near fellowship. We see here how the church draws back; for the flesh moves either not to yield at all to duty, or to be cold, uncertain, and unsettled therein. The flesh knows that a near communion with Christ cannot stand with favouring any corruption, and therefore the flesh will do something, but not enough. It will yield to something, but not to that that it should do, to that communion and fellowship that we ought to have with Christ. To instance in some particulars, as a rule and measure to somewhat of which we should be.

Obs. 1. *A Christian life should be nothing but a communion and intercourse with Christ,* a walking in the Spirit; and to be spiritual, and to favour the things of the Spirit altogether, he should study to adorn his profession by a lively and cheerful performance of duty, Mat. v. 16, and be exemplary to others; and should be in such a frame as he should 'walk continually in the comforts of the Holy Ghost' undismayed and undaunted, 'and abound in the fruits of the Spirit,' Acts ix. 20,' and do all the good he can wheresoever he comes. He should 'keep himself unspotted of the world,' James i. 27, go against the stream, and be continually in such a temper, as it should be the joy of his heart to be dissolved, and to be with Christ, 2 Tim. iv. 6. One might go on thus in a world of particulars, which would be too long. If we could attain to this excellency, it were an happy life, a heaven upon earth. This we should aim at. Will the flesh endure this, think you? No, it will not; which you shall see more particularly in this next observation, which is,

Obs. 2. That *one way, whereby the unregenerate part in us hinders this communion with Christ,* and the shining of a believer in a Christian course, *is by false pretences, reasons, and excuses.* 'I have washed my feet; I have put off my coat,' &c.

The flesh never wants excuses and pretences (there was never any yet came to hell, but they had some seeming pretence for their coming thither) to shift and shuffle off duties. There was never yet any careless, sinful course but it had the flesh to justify it with one reason or other; and therefore it is good to understand the sophistical shifts* of the flesh, and pretences and shows which it hath. And as it is good to know the truth of God, and of Christ revealed in his word, so is it to know the falseness and deceitfulness of our own hearts. They are both mysteries almost alike, hard to be known. Labour we then more and more to know the falsehood of our own disposition, and to know the truth of God. To give instance in a few particulars. You see in the church the difficulty of her communion with Christ comes from the idle pretences and excuses she hath. Every one hath his several pretexts, as his state and condition is. We think we should be losers if we give ourselves to that degree of goodness which others do; whereas God doth curse those blessings which men get with neglect of duty to him. If we seek 'first the kingdom of heaven, all other things that are good for us shall be cast upon us,' Mat. vi. 33.

Obj. Thou shalt lose the favour of such a one?

Ans. Never care for that favour thou canst not keep with God's favour. The favour of man is a snare. Take heed of that favour that snares thee. Thou losest their favour and company, but thou gainest the favour of Christ, and company of angels.

Obj. But they will rail on thee, and reproach thee with thy old sins?

Ans. Care not, 'God will do thee good for that,' as David said when Shimei cursed him, 2 Sam. xvi. 12.

* That is, 'expedients.'—G.

Obj. But I shall lose my pleasure?

Ans. O! but such pleasures end in death. They are but pleasures of sin for a season, and thou shalt not lose by the change. 'The ways of wisdom are pleasant ways,' Prov. iii. 17. One day religiously spent in keeping of a good conscience, what a sweet farewell hath it! Joy is in the habitation of the righteous. It becomes the righteous to be joyful. However outwardly it seems, yet there is a paradise within. Many such objections the flesh makes. Some take scandal at the prosperity of the wicked, and affliction of the saints, and from hence take occasion to rot in their dregs of sin. But what saith Christ? 'Happy is the man who is not offended in me,' Mat. xi. 6. As for the prosperity of the wicked, envy them not. They stand in slippery places, and flourish like a green bay tree, but presently they vanish. Take no offence at them, nor at the cross. Look not at this, but at the ensuing comfort. 'Blessed are they that suffer for righteousness sake,' 1 Pet. iii. 14. Bind such words to your head as your crown. God reserves the best comforts to the worst times; his people never find it otherwise.

Obj. Ay, but if I be thus precise, the times are so bad, I shall be alone.

Ans. Complain not of the times, when thou makest them worse. Thou shouldst make the times better. The worse the times are, the better be thou; for this is thy glory, to be good in an evil generation. This was Lot's glory, 2 Pet. ii. 7. Paul tells what ill times they were; but, saith he, 'our conversation is in heaven, from whence we look for a Saviour,' Phil. iii. 20. What brings destruction on God's people, but their joining with the wicked? When they joined with the children of men, then came the flood. These and the like pretences keep men altogether from goodness, or else from such a measure as may bring honour to God and comfort to themselves.

Or if men be great, why, this is not honourable to do thus, as you know what Michal said to David, 'How glorious was the king of Israel this day! like a fool,' &c., 2 Sam. vi. 20. To attend upon the word of God with reverence, to make conscience of religion, Oh! it stands not with greatness, &c. But the Spirit of God answereth this in him, 'I will yet be more vile for God,' verse 22. It is a man's honour here to stand for God and for good things; and it is our honour that God will honour us so much.

Those likewise that are worldly have excuses also. 'Alas! I must tend my calling.' And they have Scripture for it too. 'He that provides not for his family is worse than an infidel,' 1 Tim. v. 8, as if God had set up any callings to hinder the calling of Christianity; as if that were not the greatest calling, and the best part that will abide with us for ever; as if it were not the part of a Christian to redeem time from his calling to the duties of Christianity. I have no time, saith the worldling; what will you have me to do? Why, what time had David, when he meditated on the law of God day and night? Ps. i. 2. He was a king. The king is bound to study the Scriptures. And yet whose employment is greater than the employment of the chief magistrate? Deut. xvii. 18, 19.

And thus every one, as their state and condition is, they have several pretences and excuses. Those that are young, their excuse is, we have time enough for these things hereafter. Others, as those that were negligent to build the second temple, 'the time is not yet, say they,' Hag. i. 2; whenas the uncertainty of this life of ours, the weightiness of the business, the danger of the custom of sin, the engaging of our hearts deeper and deeper into the world, makes it a more difficult thing to be a Christian. It more and more darkens our understanding, the more we sin; and the more it estrangeth our affections from good things, the more we have run out in an evil course. Time is a special mercy; but then thou hast not time only, but the means, good company, and good motions. Thou mayest never have such a gale again; thy heart may be hardened through the deceitfulness of sin. Again, who would want the comforts of religion for the present? As Austin saith, 'I have wanted thy sweetness too long.'* What folly is it to want the sweetness and comfort of religion, so long as we may have it.

Some others pretend, the uncomfortableness of religion, I shall want my comforts; whenas indeed there is no sound comfort without having our hearts in a perfect communion with Christ, walking with God, and breaking off from our evil courses. What is the reason of discomforts, unresolvedness, and unsettledness? when we know not where we are, whither we go, or what our condition is. Unsettledness breeds discomfort; and indeed there is no pleasure so much as the pleasure that the serving of God hath with it. As the fire hath light and heat always in it, so there is no holy action that we perform throughly, but as it hath an increase of strength, so there is an increase of comfort and joy annexed to it. There is a present reward annexed to all things that are spiritually good. They carry with them present peace and joy. The conscience hath that present comfort which consumes all discouragements whatsoever, as is always found in the experience of that soul that hath won so much of itself, as to break through discouragements to the practice of holy duties. Believers have a joy and comfort 'that others know not of,' Rev. ii. 7; an hidden kind of manna and contentment.

These and a thousand such like discouragements men frame to themselves: 'My health will not serve,' 'I shall endanger my life.' 'There is a lion in the way,' saith the sluggard, Prov. xxvi. 13, who, with his excuses, 'thinks himself wiser than the wisest in the city,' verse 16. There is none so wise as the sluggard, for belly-policy teacheth him a great many excuses, which he thinks will go for wisdom, because by them he thinks to sleep in a whole skin. He is but a sluggard for all that; and though he plead 'yet a little while,' poverty, not only outward, but spiritual poverty and barrenness of soul, 'will come upon him as an armed man,' Prov. vi. 11, and leave him destitute of grace and comfort, when he shall see at last what an evil course of life he hath led, that he hath yielded so much to his lazy flesh to be drawn away by discouragements from duties that he was convinced were agreeable to the word. Now, what may be the grounds and causes of these false pretences and excuses which hinder us from holy duties? There be many causes.

1. First of all, one cause of this in us is this: Naturally, so far as we are not guided by a better spirit than our own, *we are inclined too much to the earthly present things of this life*, because they are present and pleasant, and we are nuzled up† in them, and whatsoever pulls us from them is unwelcome to us. This is one ground.

2. Again, join with this, that naturally, since the fall, the soul of man having lost wisdom to guide it to that which is truly good, hath wit enough left *to devise untoward shifts,‡ to excuse that which is evil.* In this fallen estate the former abilities to devise things throughly good is turned to a matter of untoward wit, joined with shifting.§ 'God made man right, but

* 'Confessions,' Book X. [xxvii.], 38. 'Too late loved I thee, O thou beauty of ancient days, yet ever new! too late I loved thee.'—G. † That is, 'nestled.'—G

‡ That is, 'expedients.'—G. § That is, 'expediency.'—G..

he hath sought out many inventions,' Eccles. vii. 29. Carnal wit serves carnal will very well; and carnal lusts never want an advocate to plead for them, namely, carnal reason. From the bent, therefore, of the soul to ill things, pleasure, ease, and honour, such a condition as pleaseth the outward man since the fall, the bent and weight of the soul goeth this way, together with wit. Having lost the image of God in holy wisdom, there is shifting. This is a ground also why delays are joined with shifts.

3. Again, there is another ground, that *corrupt nature*, in this like the devil and sin, which never appear in their own colours, *sets a man on this way*. Who would not hate the devil if he should appear in his own likeness? or sin, if it should appear in his own colours? And therefore wit stretcheth itself to find out shifts. For, says the heart, unless there be some shifts and pretences to cover my shame, I shall be known to be what I am indeed, which I would be loth were done. I would have the sweet but not the shame of sin, the credit of religion, but not put myself to the cost which cometh with true religion, to deny myself. Corrupt courses never appear in their own colours. They are like the devil for this.

4. And then, again, naturally there is a great deal of *hypocrisy in us*. We may do duties to satisfy conscience, for somewhat must be done, to hear now and then, read and come to prayer betwixt sleeping and waking, yawning prayers, when we can do nothing else. Somewhat must be done. Conscience else will cry out of us that we are atheists, and shall be damned. Some slubbering service must be done therefore. Yet notwithstanding, herein is our hypocrisy, that we cannot bring our hearts to do it, as it should be done, to purpose; for though it be true that there is much imperfection in the best actions, the best performances, yet this is hypocrisy when men do not do it as God may accept it, and as it may yield themselves comfort. The heart draws back. Duties it will and must do, but yet will not do them as it shall have comfort by them. This is inbred in the heart naturally. Conscience forceth to do something, though the flesh and corruption pulls back. This is the disposition of all men, till they have got the victory of their own atheistical hearts.

5. And then, again, another ground may be this, *a false conceit of God and of Christ*, that they will take anything at our hands. Because we love ourselves, and think that we do very well, we think that God is such a one as we are, as it is, 'Thou thoughtest that I was like unto thee,' &c., Ps. l. 21, that God will be put off with anything, and any excuse will serve the turn. You have not a swearer, a filthy, careless person, but he thinks God is merciful, and Christ died for sinners; and I was provoked to it, &c. Still he thinks to have some excuse for it, and that they will stand good with God. This atheism is in us naturally, and when we are palpably to blame in the judgment of others and ourselves in our sober wits, yet we put more ignorance and carelessness on God than on ourselves. 'Tush, God regards it not.' It is the times. I would be better. It is company whom I must yield unto, &c. They think God will accept these things from them.

6. But one main ground thereof is, *the scandals that we meet withal in the world*, which, indeed, is a ground, because our own false hearts are willing to catch at anything. You see, say they, these men that make profession of religion, what they are; and then the devil will thrust some hypocrisy* into the profession of religion, and they judge all by one or two, and will be sure to do it. Therein stands their ingenuity; and if they can see any infirmity in them that are incomparably better than themselves, Oh, they are safe.

* Qu. 'hypocrite?'—G.

Here is warrant enough to dislike religion and all good courses, because some do and so,* as if the course of religion were the worse for that. Thus they wrap themselves in those excuses, as men do their hands to defend them from pricks. This is the vile poison of our hearts, that will be naught, and yet, notwithstanding, will have reason to be so. The speech is, wickedness never wanted pretexts, which, as it is true of great wickedness, much more is it of that which goes in the world for drowsy lukewarm profession, under which many sink to hell before they are aware. They never want reason and pretexts to cover their sin. There is a mint and forge of them in the soul. It can coin them suddenly. Thus we see our wits do serve us excellently well to lay blocks in our own way to hinder us from heaven. We are dunces, and dull to do anything that is spiritually good, whereof we are incapable. But if it be to lay blocks in our own way to heaven, to quarrel with God and his ordinances, with the doctrine of salvation, with the instruments, teachers, and those that lead us a better way, that our wit will serve for. But to take a course to do us good another day, to lay up comforts in which we might end and close up our days, there we are backward, and have shift upon shift. This is added for the further explication of it, because of the necessity of the point; for except our hearts be discovered to us, we shall never know what religion means, save to know so much as may, through the winding, turning, shifting, and falsehood of our own nature, bring us to hell. Wherein we are worse enemies to ourselves than the devil is, who could not hurt us unless we did betray ourselves. But he hath factors in us to deal for him. Our own carnal wit and affection, they hold correspondency with him; whence all the mischief that he doth us is by that intercourse that our nature hath with Satan. That is the Delilah which betrayeth all the Sampsons, sound worthy Christians in the world, to their spiritual enemies. Therefore, we can never be sufficiently instructed what a vile nature we have, so opposite to religion, as far as it is saving. Corrupt nature doth not oppose it so far as it is slubbered over, but so far as may bring us to that state we should be in. We have no worse enemies than our own hearts. Therefore, let us watch ourselves continually, and use all blessed means appointed of God whereby we may escape out of this dangerous, sleepy disposition of soul, which cost the church so dear, as we shall hear, God willing, hereafter.

THE EIGHTH SERMON.

I have put off my coat; how shall I put it on? I have washed my feet; how shall I defile them?—CANT. V. 3.

WE are now, by God's assistance, to speak of *the remedies against the lazy distempers we are prone unto in spiritual things;* where we left off the last day.

Quest. What course should we take, then, to come forth from this distempered laziness? That we may attain a spiritual taste and relish of heavenly things, so as not to loathe religious exercises; or delay and put them off with excuses?

Ans. 1. First of all, *resolve not to consult with flesh and blood in anything.* For it always counsels us for ease, as Peter counselled Christ, 'Master, pity thyself,' Mat. xvi. 22. So we have a nature in us like unto Peter,

* Qu. 'so and so?'—ED.

Spare, favour, pity thyself. Like Eve, and Job's wife, we have a corrupt nature that is always soliciting from* God, and drawing us unto vanity, Gen. iii. 6 and Job ii. 10. Take heed of counselling with flesh and blood; for if men were in a city environed round about with enemies, would they consult with them what they should do for defence of the city? Were it not a mad part? And is it not a greater madness when Christians will consult with flesh and blood what they should do in duties of obedience, which will always put us upon terms of ease, the favour of men, content, and the like, which, if a man yield to, he shall never enter into heaven? Take heed therefore of consulting with our enemy, seeing Satan hath all the correspondency he hath by that enemy which we harbour in our bosom. In which case the hurt he doth us by his sophistry comes by ourselves. We betray ourselves by our carnal reason, whereby Satan mingleth himself with our imaginations and conceits. Let us therefore beware we listen not to the counsel of flesh and blood, especially when the matter comes to suffering once, for there of all other things flesh and blood doth draw back. Every one hath a Peter in himself that saith, 'Spare thyself.' Thou art indiscreet to venture thyself upon this and that hazard. But where the judgment is convinced of the goodness of the cause, whether it be religion or justice (for the first or for the second table, that matters not), if the judgment be convinced of the thing, then consult not with flesh and blood, whatsoever the suffering be. It is not necessary that we should live in riches, honours, pleasures, and estimation with the world. But it is necessary we should live honest men and good Christians. Therefore, when flesh and blood objecteth in this kind, consult not with it. First, because it is an enemy, and therefore is to be suspected and neglected; secondly, because it is said, 'flesh and blood shall not inherit the kingdom of heaven,' 1 Cor. xv. 50.

2. And therefore we should practise that first lesson in religion, *heavenly wisdom*. To aid us wherein, Christ, knowing what an enemy we are to ourselves in the ways of God, saith, 'Let a man deny himself, and take up his cross, and follow me,' Mat. xvi. 24. There is no following of Christ, considering that our flesh is so full of cavils and excuses, unless we practise that heavenly lesson of Christ, 'to deny ourselves,' our whole self, our wit and reason, in the matters of God: our will and affections. Say nay to all the sluggishness of the flesh; silence all presently, as soon as ever they discourage thee from holy ways. Consider whence they come, which is enough; from God's and our enemy, and the worst enemy we have, that lieth in our own bosom. And to enable us the better, mark what Paul saith, 'We are no more debtors to the flesh,' &c., Rom. viii. 12. We owe nothing to it. I owe not such obedience, such subjection, to the flesh and carnal reason; I have renounced it long since. What! am I obnoxious to a man unto whom I owe no service? We owe the flesh no service or obedience. What! shall we yield to that which we have long since renounced?

3. And withal, *in spiritual courses, let us arm ourselves with resolution*. First, conclude is it so or not so. Let our judgments be convinced. For resolution is a disposition arising from the will immediately; but it is of the will, by sound judgment, convinced of the goodness of the thing, after which the will resolves. Get resolution from soundness of conviction that such things are good, and that they are best for us, and best for us at this time, the sooner the better; that there is an absolute necessity to have

* That is, '*away* from.'—G.

them, and that they are everlastingly good. Oh! these considerations will put us on amain to obtain the same. It is our duty, and we shall sin against God, against our conscience, against the Spirit of God, and against others that take like liberty by our examples, if we yield to our base lusts and suggestions in this kind.

And to help resolution the more, let us have before our eyes the examples of God's worthies, who (like unto David's worthies, who brake through the host of the Philistines for water, 2 Sam. xxiii. 16) have in all ages broken through all discouragements, and made a conscience more to please God, to hold communion and fellowship with Christ, than to hold any correspondency with the world. Look to blessed Paul, 'What do ye vexing of me and breaking my heart? I am ready not only to go to Jerusalem, but to die for Christ's sake,' Acts xxi. 13. And look to Christ how he shakes off Peter, 'Get thee behind me, Satan,' &c., Mat. xvi. 23. Look to Moses, how he shook off all the solicitations of a court, 'Because he had an eye to the recompence of the reward,' Heb. xi. 16. Look to Joshua, 'I and mine house will serve the Lord,' Josh. xxiv. 15. Let others of the world do what they will; if others will go to the devil, let them; for myself, I and my house, those that I have charge of, will serve the Lord. This was a noble resolution which was in good Nehemiah, 'Shall such a man as I flee?' Neh. vi. 11. What! shall I flee? shall I do this, yield to this base discouragement? shall I discourage others, like those spies of Canaan, by mine example? Hence it is that Hebrews 11th, in that notable chapter, that little 'book of martyrs,' after the catalogue of those worthies set down there, that which we are exhorted and pointed to in the beginning of the next chapter, is unto the practice of the like virtues, in imitation, having before us 'such a cloud of witnesses,' wherewith being compassed, the exhortation is, 'Let us therefore shake off everything that presseth down, and the sin that hangeth so fast on,' &c., Heb. xii. 1 (*i*). As the cloud was a guide to them to Canaan out of Egypt, so the cloud of good examples is as it were a light to go before us to the heavenly Canaan.

In this case above all, let us look to Christ, 'who is the author and finisher of our faith,' Heb. xii. 2. This will make us break through discouragements and resolve indeed. What could hinder him? His love is so fiery, that nothing could hinder him to come from heaven to the womb of the virgin; from thence to the cross, and so to the grave, to be abased lower than ever any creature was. His love to us so carried him through all discouragements and disgraces. 'Consider him, who endured such speaking against of sinners,' Heb. xii. 3. The consideration of Christ's love and example will carry us through all discouragements whatsoever.

4. And further, *let us be able by sound reasons to justify the ways of God, and to answer cavils; to give account of what we do to ourselves and others*, with reasons why we sanctify the Sabbath, have such communion with God in prayer, neglect the fashions of the world, &c. To have reasons ready from Scripture is an excellent thing; when we are able to justify whatsoever we do by the word, against all the quarrels of our own hearts and others. When we are led to do things only by the example of others, or by respects, then we are ofttimes put to it on the sudden by temptations, being not able to justify what we do. Let us labour therefore to do things upon good grounds, and be able to justify all the ways of religion, as they are easily justified. For nothing in this world stands with so much reason, as exactness in the ways of God. There is so much reason for nothing in the world, as to be not only Christians, but exact Christians as Paul saith

to Agrippa, 'Would to God you were not almost, but altogether as I am, saving these bonds,' Acts xxvi. 29, to make conscience of all ways and courses. It stands with the most reason of the world, so to justify religion by reasons unanswerable, that may set down corrupt nature, and stop the mouth of the devil himself. And herein let us propound sound and strong questions to ourselves often. Are those things that I am moved to do good, or are they not? If they be good, why do I not do them? If they be bad, why do I do them at all? If they be good, why do I stick at them? How do I prove them to be good? Have alway ready some Scripture, or reason from thence, which is as good. The reasons of the word are most divinely strong, let them be ready against all objections whatsoever, as against slight oaths, think of that of Christ, that we must give an account for all idle words, Mat. xii. 36. How much more for atheistical oaths! So against grosser sins learn reason, a civil man, an heathen, would not do thus.

So also when the flesh moveth us to any backwardness in religious courses, let us have some Scripture ready, or reasons deducted from it. As, 1. *From the dignity of our profession, from the great hopes we have to be glorious another day.* And reason the matter, How doth this that I am moved to, suit with my hopes and expectation to come? How furthers it my journey homewards? And consider this likewise. 2. *That no excuse will serve the turn at the day of judgment, but such an one as ariseth from an invincible infirmity, or an unremovable impediment.* Such an excuse, taken from an invincible infirmity, may then serve the turn. As, when we cannot possibly do a thing, from impediments that all the means in the world cannot remove, as, a poor man cannot be liberal, &c. Excuses also, fetched from impossible impediments, as from invincible weakness, may avail. If a man have an infirm body, that he cannot do that which another man can. These excuses, with a gracious God, will serve the turn: which are not so much excuses, as a just plea. But otherwise, our untoward excuses will not serve the turn. What hindered them in the gospel who were invited to the supper? Luke xiv. Excuses from oxen, wives, &c. Was it not lawful to buy oxen? and was it not lawful for the married to take content in a wife? 'Another had married a wife.' Were not all these things lawful? Very lawful. The farm hurts not, if it hinder not, nor the wife, oxen, nor anything. But in this case, when we regard these things more than the invitation to come to the feast of holy things, here is the malice of the devil, which brings that doleful message, 'They shall never taste of my feast,' Luke xiv. 24. There is such an infinite disproportion between the good of religion, peace of conscience, joy in the Holy Ghost here, and heaven and happiness hereafter, and between anything in this world, that to allege any hindrance whereby we cannot keep a good conscience, and preserve assurance of salvation, is most extreme folly and atheism. I believe not a better life, the disproportion being so great between the state of this life and a better, if I fetch excuses from the things of this life, to keep me from religion, the fear of God, and working out my salvation with fear and trembling. These excuses will not serve the turn. Not only with God at the day of judgment, but also our own consciences will tell us, that we are hypocrites to make such or such a plea. Therefore, when men become false, thereby to provide for wife or children, and take corrupt courses to keep them from religion, with pretext of their callings, lest they should lose one day in seven, this employment cannot prosper, which slights over duties under false pretences. Oh, they can toil for the pelf of the world! But for matters of their souls, they turn off all shamefully, as if there were not a God to judge them, a heaven to reward them, or a hell to punish them. Will such excuses serve the turn? Oh, no; they cannot with conscience, much less with God the Judge, who is greater than our conscience. This is another way to cut off these idle cavils, to consider that these excuses cannot serve the turn, neither to comfort conscience in this world, nor to uphold us in our plea at the day of judgment. Remember that.

5. And then again, *Let us inure ourselves to bear the yoke of religion from our youth*, which will make it easy afterwards. It were an excellent thing if those who are young, in the prime of their years, would inure themselves to the exercise of religion. This would make it easy unto them, to read the word of God, to open their spirits unto him in prayer. It may please God hereby (though they be negligent herein), yet they may be called to religion. But for an old man there is much work to do to read, to get anything into his brain, when his memory is pestered with other things, and corrupt nature in him is armed with a world of excuses, that might have been prevented by a timely and seasonable training up in a course of religion. Profane young persons know not what they do when they put off religion. Have they excuses now? They will have many more hereafter, when Satan and corruption will be much stronger. O! let them bear the yoke of religion, that is, inure themselves to duties that become Christians, which may facilitate and make it easy and pliable, that it may not be harsh to our nature. If a man do not hear, pray, and read, he can never have faith, grace, knowledge, mortification of corruption, wherein religion stands. But because these lead to duties that are hard to nature, and harsh, it is wisdom to inure young ones thereto betimes, that, having used themselves to these preparing duties, they may be the more fitted for the essential ones; that, having things in the brain by reading and hearing, grace may be wrought in the heart, it being a more easy passage from the brain to the heart. When a man is converted, it is an easy matter to bring it from the brain unto the heart; whereas a man that hath been negligent in his youth must then be instructed in the principles of religion. Therefore, it is a miserable case (though men be never so politic in the world) to have been negligent herein till age. It breeds a great deal of difficulty to them, ere they can come to be in such a state as a Christian should be in. Remember this, therefore, to do as Paul adviseth Timothy, a young man, 'to exercise himself in godliness,' 1 Tim. iv. 7. It is a good thing for all that are young to exercise themselves to all duties of religion, or else pretences will grow up with age, whereby they will be indisposed every day more than other. Experience shews it generally. We may believe it. If we will not, we shall find it hereafter too true by woful experience.

6. And then again, by little and little, not only to be inured to the yoke of religion, but likewise *to endure difficulties, opposition, and hardship;* as the apostle stands upon it to Timothy, 'to endure hardship and afflictions from the beginning,' 2 Tim. ii. 3. If the thing be good and warrantable, neglect the speeches of the world. What are the speeches of a company of men in the state of nature, in their miserable condition, to regard them, so as not to endure hardship in such things, of the goodness whereof we are convinced? But in these days men take up a delicate profession of religion. Men will be religious, but they will suffer nothing, not a taunt or a scoff. They will part with nothing; be at no loss; suffer no cross; be at no pains with religion further than may stand with all earthly content of this world. This delicate profession, if anything among us, threateneth

the removing of the gospel and blessed truths we enjoy, because we will not part with any pleasure now. How will they suffer afflictions for the gospel, if such times come, that will not part with a vain oath, a corrupt fashion of life, a superfluity, that will not part with a rotten unsavoury discourse, which discovereth a rotten spirit, and infecteth others? Here is a profession of religion, indeed, that cannot have so much mastery of the corrupt heart as to deny and overcome itself in things that are grossly ill! How will a man part with his blood and life, that will not part with things that he should part withal? not only with something to the poor and to good uses, but to part with some sinful course of life, and wicked and ungodly lusts that fight against the soul; who will not endure not so much as a check; who, rather than they will go under that censure wherewith the world is pleased to disgrace religion, they will live and die like atheists. This extreme tenderness in the matters of God and of salvation is the cause why many eternally perish.

7. Again, to cut off all vain excuses, *let us oft have in thought of our heart what we should be, and what we should all aim at, and how far we come all short of it.* A Christian that hopes of good of his religion should live by faith, and depend upon God in the use of lawful means. If he be as he should be, he ought to walk with God, keep his watch with him, and do nothing unbeseeming the eye of God. When his corruption draws him to be careless, then he is not as he should be; for in a right temper, he ought to be fitted to every good work, ready for all opportunities of doing anything that is good, because the time of this life is the seedtime, the time of doing good. The time of reaping is in the world to come. When, therefore, the heart is shut, when any opportunity is offered of doing good, he may conclude certainly, I am cold and dull; pretend what I will, I am not as I should be. A Christian ought to 'abound in the work of the Lord,' 1 Cor. xv. 58, especially having such abundance of encouragements as we have. What a world of encouragements hath a Christian! There are none to* those of religion, from the inward content that it brings here, at the hour of death, and in glory hereafter. When we are drawn to be scanty, niggardly, and base to things that are good, surely this is not as it should be. Pretend what we will to the contrary, this is a fault. A Christian should at all times be fit to yield and to render up his soul unto God, because our life is uncertain. When, therefore, we are moved by corruption to live in a state that we cannot abide to die in, because we are under the guilt of some sin, then certainly, pretend what we will, our state is so far naught, as far as there is unfitness and unwillingness to die. Let us have in the eye of our soul, therefore, what a Christian should be, aim at it, and think that when we stop at a lower measure and pitch, that, pretend what we will, all is but from carnal wit and policy, the greatest enemy that religion hath.

We pray in the Lord's Prayer, 'Thy kingdom come; thy will be done in earth, as it is done in heaven:' great desires, and which should be the desires of all our hearts. But herein we play the hypocrites. Whilst we pray thus, that the kingdom of God may come, that Christ may rule in our hearts over lusts and desires; yet notwithstanding, we pretend this and that excuse, whereby we may be led with this and that lust. We cross our own prayers. Yet it sheweth what pitch we should aspire to, 'To sanctify the Lord in our hearts,' to delight in him, and trust in him above all. When we do not this, we fall short of our own prayers. And when

* That is, 'there are no encouragements compared with.'—ED.

we cannot bring our hearts to suffer, and to do what God would have us to do, but are led away with our own wills, we are not as we should be. Our wills should be conformable to Christ's in all things. It is our prayer, and therefore we should aim at it. Now, when flesh and blood sets up a pitch of religion, I am well enough; and yet prays, 'Hallowed be thy name; thy kingdom come; thy will be done,' &c.,—such a man is an hypocrite. For his prayer leads him further and further still, till he come to heaven, where is all perfection; until when, our life is a life of endeavour and progress. Though we be never so perfect, yet Christ may more rule and set up his kingdom yet more in the heart, and further bring our will to his in all things. When flesh and blood sets up cavils against this, we play the hypocrites with God, and cross ourselves. Therefore, let us justify a measure of religion beyond our present pitch, whatsoever it is; justify it more and more still. Think, we are never as we should be till we be in heaven; and never bless ourselves, but think that we should always be on the growing hand; and whatsoever excuse comes to hinder us from zealousness and earnestness, though it carry a show of reason in the profession of religion, account it to come from our corrupt hearts.

8. Again, *remember to do all things to God and not to man, in our callings both of religion and in our particular callings;* and then whatsoever discouragement there is from men, we should not be discouraged. We shall hear men continually complain of others, that they are unthankful persons; and why should we do anything for them? Why! do it to God. If it fall within our callings, let us do justice and shew mercy. God will accept, though men do not. It cuts off many discouragements in duties. It is best to have God's reward. In this world it is good to meet with naughty unthankful persons, because else we should meet with all our reward here. It is good to do somewhat for God's sake, and for religion, let people be as unthankful as they will; to say, I did it not to you, but to God. If a man regard the discouragement of the world, he shall never do that which is good, people in the world are so unthankful and regardless to those that wish them best, and that do best to them. But if a man do a thing to God, and do it out of duty and conscience, he may hold on; have he never so many discouragements in the world, he shall lose nothing. All shall be rewarded, and is regarded.

9. Likewise, be sure to carry this in mind, *that sin is the greatest evil, and grace and goodness the best thing in the world.* Therefore, there is no excuse for sin, from anything in the world, for it is the worst thing in the world, which stains the soul, and hinders it from comfort. And for grace and goodness in the inward man, it is the best thing in the world. Therefore, purchase this, though with disadvantage. It is best to avoid sin, though with enduring evil; yea, to avoid the least sin, by enduring the greatest evil. It is wisdom to do good with disadvantage, when the disadvantage is bounded only in this life, the thing that I do being a thing which furthers my reckoning at the day of account. Therefore, have this alway in consideration, whatsoever I suffer in this world, I will not sin. This will cut off a world of excuses.

Therefore, let us labour to cut off all cavils, and to 'arm ourselves.' It is the apostle Peter's exhortation, 1 Pet. iv. 1. As David's worthies brake through the pikes to fetch him water from the well of Bethlehem, 2 Sam. xxiii. 16, so all Christian worthies that look to be crowned, let them be armed inwardly with resolution for good things, take up resolutions that they will do it. As Paul tells his scholar Timothy of his purpose, 'Thou knowest my purpose, and manner of living,' 2 Tim. iii. 10. This is the manner of a Christian life: that this, I will not break for all the world. So, there is a purpose of living honestly a manner of life, not by starts, now and then to speak a word, and to do a good deed; but there is a a purpose and a manner of life for it. He resolves always for the best things.

And to this end beg of God his Spirit, which is above all impediments. The more Spirit, the more strength and courage against impediments. The more we attend upon holy means, the more spiritual and heavenly light and life is set up in the soul. The more spiritual we are, the more we shall tread under foot all those things that stand between us and heaven. Let us therefore labour more and more for the Spirit, and then we shall offer an holy violence unto good things; as it was said of John Baptist's time, 'The kingdom of God suffered violence,' Mat. xi. 12. Men were so eager of it, as that they surprised it as a castle, by violence. There is no way to take heaven but by offering violence to discouragement, corruption, and whatsoever stands in the way. The violent only takes heaven by force.* Now when we are spiritual, we shall not pretend, that 'there is a lion in the way,' that there are difficulties, as the sluggard doth, that thinks himself wiser than many men who can render a reason. But we shall go boldly and courageously on; and know that there are more encouragements for good, and stronger, than the world hath allurements to be naught, which are but for the present life; but we have inward ones, which will hold out in the hour of death and after. Therefore, go on boldly and resolutely in good things, always remembering to beg the Spirit of God, that may arm our spirits with invincible courage.

Now the Spirit of God brings faith with it, which is a conquering, victorious grace over the world, and 'sees him that is invisible,' Heb. xi. 27; which brings love also, 'which is strong as death,' Cant. viii. 6: wherewith the soul being warmed, it constraineth us to do duties in spite of all impediments. The Spirit of God will strengthen our hope also of heaven, which strengthens us against all discouragements which stand in our way. For this hope is on greater and better grounds than discouragements are; and he that giveth us this hope, will enable us to possess it.

Therefore labour first, *to have a clear understanding of the things of God, and of the excellency of them;* for light will cause heat Why did the kingdom of heaven in John Baptist's time, 'suffer violence?' Why were men then so violent to cleave unto Christ? Because from that time the gospel was more clearly manifested. And heavenly truths, the more they are discovered and laid open (there is such an excellency in them), the more they work upon the heart and affections. Therefore, 'the kingdom of heaven suffered violence.' And where are people more earnest after good things, than in these places where the evangelical truths of God are laid open most? There they break through all discouragements whatsoever.

And so, *labour for faith to believe those truths:* which is the most victorious and conquering grace, that will carry us through all discouragements whatsoever; because it will set greater things before us, than the discouragements are. Are we afraid of men? Faith, it sets hell before us. Are we allured by the world? It sets heaven before us. It conquers the world, with all the discouraging temptations thereof. Are the discouragements

* This recalls the little book of Thomas Watson's, called 'Heaven taken by Storm,' memorable as having been the occasion of the conversion of the celebrated Colonel Gardiner, whose life by Doddridge is one of our Christian classics.—G

from impossibilities? O, it is hard, I cannot do it. Aye, but, saith Paul, 'I am able to do all things through Christ that strengthens me,' Phil. iv. 13. There is a kind of omnipotency in faith, 'O woman, be it unto thee as thou wilt,' Mark xv. 28. We have abundance of strength in Christ. Faith is but an empty hand, that goes to Christ to draw from him what it hath need of; 'In Christ I can do all things.'

So, *to have our hearts warmed with love to him*. This grace of the Spirit will make us pass through all discouragements, for it hath a constraining power. 'The love of Christ constrains us,' saith the apostle, 2 Cor. v. 14. If our hearts once be warmed with the love of Christ, this will make us to think nothing too dear for Christ, and will cut off all excuses and pretences whatsoever, which come from coldness of affection. 'Love is strong as death,' as we have it in this book, 'much water cannot quench it,' Cant. viii. 6. All oppositions and discouragements whatsoever, all the water which the devil and the world hath or useth, cannot quench the heavenly fire of love, when it is kindled in any measure. What carried the blessed saints and martyrs of God in all times through the pikes of all discouragements? The Spirit of God, by the spirit of love, from a spirit of faith, and heavenly conviction of the excellency and truth of the things. They saw such a light, which wrought upon their affections, and carried them amain against the stream (contrary to the stream of the times wherein they lived), that the worse the times were, the better they were.

10. And let us consider again, *that Christ will not be always thus alluring us*; that we shall not always have these encouragements, such truths and motions of God's Spirit, as perhaps we feel now. Therefore, when we feel any good motion stirred up toward Christ, entertain it presently. Happily we shall never hear of it again. The longer we defer and put it off, the worse. As a man that is rowing in a boat, let him neglect his stroke, the neglecting of one may make him tug at it five or six times after to overtake those that are before him. So nothing is gotten by sloth and negligence. We do but cast ourselves back the more.

11. And let us help ourselves *with setting the glory to come before our eyes*, with Moses to have a patriarch's eye to him 'that is invisible,' to see 'a country afar off,' Heb. xi. 27. Now, 'we are nearer salvation than when we believed.' Let us help our backward souls this way: that so, having still glory in our eyes, it may help us to go through all discouragements, whatsoever they be. We know Zaccheus, when he was afraid that he should not see Christ, went before the multitude; and getting up upon the top of a tree, thus helps himself. So doth grace help itself by glory. And so far is grace from objecting and pretending lets,* as it makes supplies in God's service; as David, who in this case was pleased to be accounted vile, 2 Sam. vi. 22. Let us look unto the recompence of the reward; not to the present discouragements, but to the prize at the end of the race. What makes a soldier to fight hard for the victory in the end? The sweetness of the triumph. What makes a husbandman go through all discouragements? He hopes to receive a crop in the end. Consider the issue which followeth after a conscionable, careful, and Christian life, after a more near and perfect walking with God, maintaining communion with him. Let there be what discouragements there will be in the world, 'the end thereof is peace.' 'The end of that man is peace,' Ps. xxxvii. 37. Upon this ground, the apostle exhorts us, 'to be fruitful and abundant in the work of the Lord; knowing that your labour is not in vain in the Lord,' 1 Cor. xv. 58.

* That is, 'hindrances.'—G.

THE NINTH SERMON.

I rose to open to my beloved; but my beloved had withdrawn himself.—
CANT. V. 6.

NATURALLY we are prone to delays in heavenly things, and then to cover all with excuses. A man is a sophister to himself, whom he first deceives, before the devil or the world deceive him; which is the reason why so oft in Scripture you have this mentioned: 'Be not deceived, God is not mocked,' Gal. vi. 7. 'Be not deceived, neither adulterer, nor covetous person, nor such and such, shall ever enter into the kingdom of heaven,' 1 Cor. vi. 9. 'Be not deceived,' which is an intimation that naturally we are very prone to be deceived in points of the greatest consequence in the world, to flatter ourselves, as the church doth here, with false excuses. 'I have put off my coat,' &c. But we shall now see in this next verse what becomes of all those excuses and backwardness of the church whereby she puts oft Christ.

'My beloved put in his hand by the hole of the door, and my bowels were moved for him.

'I rose to open to my beloved; and my hands dropped with myrrh, and my fingers with sweet-smelling myrrh, upon the handles of the lock.

'I rose to open to my beloved; but my beloved had withdrawn himself,' &c., ver. 4–6.

This comes of her sluggishness and drowsiness, that Christ absented and withdrew himself. There are three things here set down in these verses now read.

1. *Christ's withdrawing of himself.*

2. *His gracious dealing, having withdrawn himself.*

He doth not altogether leave his church, but 'puts his finger into the hole of the door,' and then leaves some sweetness behind him before he goes. After which is set down,

3. *The success of Christ's departure and withdrawing of himself from her.*

(1.) *Her bowels were moved in her*, which were *hard* before.

(2.) *She rose up out of her bed*, wherein formerly she had framed and composed herself to rest.

(3.) *She seeks and calls after him.*

But the doctrinal points which are to be observed out of these verses are these,

Obs. 1. *That Christ doth sometimes use to leave his children, as he did the church here.*

Obs. 2. *That the cause is from the church herself*, as we see how unkindly she had used Christ, to let him attend her leisure so long. Therefore he, taking a holy state upon him, leaves the church. The cause of his forsaking us is in ourselves. We may thank ourselves for it.

Obs. 3. That though Christ deal thus with us, yet notwithstanding *he never leaves us wholly, without some footsteps of his saving grace and everlasting love; some remainders and prints he leaves upon the soul*, so as it lingers after him, and never rests till it find him. He always leaves something. There is never a total desertion; as we see here in Christ's dealing, 'he puts his finger into the hole of the door.' He stands at the door, and leaves myrrh behind him, something in the heart that causeth a lingering and restless affection in her towards Christ.

Obs. 4. *That the church, by reason of this gracious dealing of Christ, (leaving somewhat behind him) is sensible of her former unkindness, is restless, and stirs up herself to endeavour more and more, till she have recovered her former communion and sweet fellowship with Christ which she had before.* She never gives over till Christ and she meet again in peace, as we shall see in the prosecution. These be the chief points considerable.

Obs. 1. First, *Christ doth use sometimes to leave his church*, as here he doth, 'My beloved had withdrawn himself,' &c.

But what kind of leaving is it?

We must distinguish of Christ's leavings and withdrawings of himself. They are either in regard of outward or inward comforts and helps.

1. *Outward*, as Christ leaves his church sometimes *by taking away the means of salvation*, the ministry, or *by taking away outward comforts*, which is a withdrawing of his; especially if he accompany the taking of them away with some signs of his displeasure or sense of his anger, as usually it falls out. This doth embitter all crosses and losses, namely, when they come from Christ as a testimony of his anger for our former unkindness.

2. Sometimes his forsaking is *more inward*, and that is double, either in regard of *peace and joy*, sweet inward comfort that the soul had wont to feel in the holy ordinances by the Spirit of Christ; or in regard of *strength and assistance*. There is a desertion in regard of comfort and in regard of strength. Sometimes he leaves them to themselves, in regard of strength and supportation, to fall into some sin, to cure some greater sin perhaps.

Now that Christ thus leaves his church, it is true of all, both of the body and of each particular member of the church.

(1.) It is true of the *whole body of the church*, for you have the church complaining, Isa. xlix. 14, 'God hath forgotten me,' 'Can a mother forget her child?' saith God again. So Ps. xliv. 9; and in other places the church complains of forsakings. The Scripture is full of complaints in this kind.

(2.) It is true of the *several members*, and especially of the most eminent members, as we see holy Job complains, as if God had 'set him,' as it were, 'a butt to shoot at,' Job vi. 4, and had opposed himself against him. So David complains, Ps. lxxxviii. 11, Ps. lxxvii. 9, and Ps. lx. 1, and in other Psalms, of God's anger. 'Correct me not in thine anger,' Ps. vi. 1. The Psalms are full of this, so as it would be time unprofitably spent to be large in a point so clear, that every one knoweth well enough who reads and understands the Psalms. So Jonah likewise felt a kind of forsaking when he was in the midst of the sea, when the waves were without and terrors within, when he was in the midst of hell, as it were, Jonah ii. 2. Thus, you see, the instances clear the point.

The ends that God hath in it are many. (1.) *To endear his presence the more to us*, which we slighted too much before. It is our corruption, the not valuing of things till they be gone. We set not the true price upon them when we enjoy them. When we enjoy good things, we look at the grievances which are mingled with the good, and forget the good; which, when it is gone, then we remember the good. The Israelites could remember their onions and garlic, and forget their slavery, Num. xi. 5. So, because manna was present, they despised manna, and that upon one inconvenience it had, 'it was ordinary with them,' Num. xxi. 5. Thus the corrupt heart of man is prone in the enjoying of favours. If it have any grievance, it murmurs at that; and it troubles and makes them forget all the goodness and sweetness of what they enjoy. But, on the contrary, when God withdraws those good things from us, then we forget those former inconveniences, and begin to think what good we had by them. This is the poison and corruption of our nature.

(2.) Again, Christ seems to forsake us, *to try the truth of the graces and affections in us*, whether they be true or not; and to cause us to make after him, when he seems to forsake us, as undoubtedly we shall, where there is truth of grace planted in the heart in any measure.

(3.) And in regard of others, he doth it *to teach us heavenly wisdom, how to deal with those in affliction*, 2 Cor. i. 4. It makes us wise, tender, and successful in dealing with others, when we have felt the like particular grievance ourselves, as Gal. vi. 1, 'Brethren, if a man be overtaken in a fault, you that are spiritual restore such a one in the spirit of meekness, considering thyself, lest thou also be tempted.' Experience of spiritual grief in this kind, will make us fit, able, and wise every way to deal with others.

(4.) This serves likewise *to wean us from the world, in the plenty and abundance of all earthly things.* For take a Christian that hath no cross in the world, let him find some estrangement of Christ from his spirit, that he finds not the comforts of the Holy Ghost, and that enlargement which in former times he enjoyed, and all the wealth he hath, the earthly contentments he enjoys, please him not, nor can content that soul, which hath ever felt sweet communion with Christ. Again, how should we pray with earnestness of affection, 'Thy kingdom come,' in the time of prosperity, except there were somewhat in this kind to raise up the soul to desire to be gone? Now, it is our subjection to these alterations and changes, ebbings and flowings, sometimes to have the sense of God's love in Christ, and sometimes to want it; sometimes to feel his love, and sometimes again the fruits of his anger and displeasure, which serves exceedingly to stir up men's desires of heaven.

(5.) In this place here, the especial end was *To correct the security, and ill carriage of the church.*

And, likewise (6.) *to prepare the church, by this desertion and seeming forsaking, for nearer communion.* For, indeed, Christ did not forsake her, but to her feeling, to bring her, in the sequel, to have nearer communion and union with himself than ever she had before. God forsakes, that he may not forsake. He seems strange, that he may be the more friendly. This is Christ's usage. He personates an adversary, when he intends to shew the greatest effects of his love, as we may see afterwards in the passages following.

And also, (7.) *to make us to know thoroughly the bitterness of sin*, that we may grow up to a further hatred of that which deprives us of so sweet a communion. We think sin a trifle, and never know it enough till the time of temptation; that conscience be awakened and opened; that it appears in its right colours.

And then, again, (8.) *that we may know what Christ suffered and underwent for us, in the sense of God's wrath, in the absence of his favour for a time.* This the human nature could never have suffered, if his divinity had withdrawn itself. Now, all of us must sip of that cup, whereof Christ drank the dregs, having a taste what it is to have God to forsake us. For the most part, those believers who live any time (especially those of great parts), God deals thus with. Weaker Christians he is more indulgent unto. At such times we know of what use a Mediator is, and how miserable our condition were without such an one, both to have borne and overcome the wrath of God for us, which burden he could never have undergone, but had sunk under it, but for the hypostatical union.

Use 1. Let us not, therefore, *censure any Christian, when we find that their course hath been good and gracious, yet notwithstanding they seem to want comfort.* Let us not wonder at them, as if God had utterly forsaken them. Indeed, sometimes they think themselves forsaken, and the world thinks them so too, 'that God regards them not,' Ps. lxvi. 18. They are people of no respect either to God or to others, as you have the church in the Psalms complaining, as if God had forsaken them,' Ps. xliv. 9 ; so they think themselves forsaken, and the world thinks them so too, and neglects them. Therefore, in so doing, we shall censure the generation of the righteous. It was thus with the Head of the church, with the whole church, and with every particular member. Neither is it fit we should always enjoy the sense of God's love. Christ by heavenly wisdom dispenseth of his sweetness, comforts, and peace, as may stand with our souls' best good, and we should as much take heed of censuring ourselves in that condition, as if we were rejected and cast away of God. We must judge ourselves at such times by faith, and not by feeling; looking to the promises and word of God, and not to our present sense and apprehension.

Use 2. Again, if this be so, learn *to prepare and look for it beforehand, and to get some grounds of comfort, some promises out of the word, and to keep a good conscience.* O it is a heavy thing, when God shall seem to be angry with us, and our conscience at the same time shall accuse us; when the devil shall lay sins hard to our charge, and some affliction at the same time lie heavy upon the sore and guilty soul. If we have not somewhat laid up beforehand, what will become of the poor soul, when heaven, and earth, and hell, and all shall seem to be against it. There are few that come to heaven, but they know what these things mean. It is good, therefore, to look for them, and to prepare some comforts beforehand.

But what here should be the inward moving cause? It is in the church herself; for mark the coherence. She had turned off Christ with excuses, pretences, and dilatory answers; and now presently upon it Christ forsakes her in regard of her feeling, and of the sweet comfort she formerly enjoyed. The point is,

Obs. 2. *That the cause rests in ourselves why Christ withdraws comfort from our souls.*

If we search our own hearts we shall find it so, and usually the causes in ourselves are these, as it was in the church here: 1. *When we are unkind to Christ,* and repel the sweet motions of the Spirit. 2. *When we improve not the precious means of salvation that we enjoy.* 3. *When we are careless of our conversation and company.* 4. *When we linger after carnal liberties and ease.* 5. *When we yield to carnal policy* and shifts to keep us off from the power of religion, to go on in a lukewarm course. 6. *When we linger after earthly things and comforts,* and wrap ourselves up in fleshly policy for ease. 7. *When we tremble not at God's judgments and threatenings, and at the signs of them;* with many such things. Where these dispositions are, we need not wonder if we find not the comforts of Christ and of the Holy Ghost in us, with the gracious presence of his Spirit. The cause is in ourselves. But security hath been at large spoken of before, where the church's sleep was handled.* Therefore, the point shall not be here enlarged, but only some use made of it, as may serve for the present purpose.

Use 1. If Christ should take away the comforts that we enjoy, and

* See pp. 35–44, *et seq.*—G.

remove himself and his dwelling from us, for he is now yet among us and knocks at our doors, *do we not give him just cause to depart?* What a spirit of slumber possesseth us, which will be awaked with nothing to seek after Christ! How few lay hold upon God, press upon him, wrestle with him by prayer, to hide themselves before the evil day come, as they should do! Therefore, if Christ have absented himself a long time from the church in general, and withdrawn the comfort and presence of his ordinances; and, in particular, withheld the sweet comforts of our spirits and our peace, so that we see him in the contrary signs of his displeasure and anger, as if he did not regard and respect us, we have given him just cause so to do. We see here how the church used Christ; and so do we, with the like security, and a spirit of slumber, with unkindness. Notwithstanding all the provocations that Christ useth to win us, he leaves us not, until he be left first, for he desires to have nearer acquaintance, communion, and fellowship with the soul, as we have seen in the former verse, 'My love, my dove, my undefiled, open to me,' &c. Therefore, if we do not enjoy more acquaintance with Christ than we do, and walk more in the comforts of the Holy Ghost, it is merely from our own indisposition and security, Acts ix. 31. Therefore, let us censure ourselves in this kind, and not call Christ an enemy, as if he had forgotten, and God had forsaken. Take heed of such a spirit of murmuring. If such a state befall us, let us labour to lay our hand upon our mouth and to justify Christ. It is just with thee thus to leave me, to give me over to this terror, to deal thus with me, that have dealt so unkindly with thee. So to justify God, and accuse ourselves, is the best way to recover spiritual comfort.

Obs. 3. Well, for the third point. *That howsoever Christ be provoked by the church's ingratitude, drowsiness, and careless carriage, to leave her in regard of her feeling, and of inward comfort; yet notwithstanding he is so gracious, as to leave something behind him, that shews indeed, that he had not left the church altogether, but only in some regard.* For howsoever Christ, in regard of some order of his providence, leave it, yet in regard of another order of his providence, care and mercy, he doth not leave it, so as one way which he takes must sometimes give place to another way of his working in ordering things. Sometimes he is present in a way of comfort, that is one order of his dispensation; and when he sees that that is neglected, then he withdraws his comforts and hides his gracious countenance. Yet he is then present still in another order and way, though we discern it not, that is, in a way of humbling the soul, letting it see its sin. So here, howsoever Christ had withdrawn himself in regard of this manner of his dealing, in respect of comfort, that the church did not now see his grace, favour; yet he left behind him a spirit of grace, to affect her heart with grief, sorrow, and shame, and to stir up her endeavours to seek after him, as it is said here: 'I rose to open to my beloved; and my hands dropped myrrh, and my fingers sweet smelling myrrh, upon the handles of the locks.'

Here observe these three things, which shall be briefly named, because they shall be touched elsewhere.

Obs. 1. *Christ's grace is the cause of our grace.* He first leaves myrrh, and then her fingers drop myrrh. Our oil is from his oil. The head being anointed, 'the oil ran down to the skirts of Aaron's garments,' Ps. cxxxiii. 2, xxxvi. 9; 'Out of his fulness we receive grace for grace,' John i. 16, that is, our grace is answerable to the grace of Christ. We have all from him, favour for his favour. Because he is beloved, we are beloved. We have the grace of sanctification from him. He was sanctified with the Spirit, therefore we are sanctified. We have grace of privilege for his grace. He is the Son of God, therefore we are sons. He is the heir of heaven, therefore we are heirs. So that of his grace it is we receive all. Whether we take grace for favour, or for the grace of sanctification, or the grace of privilege and prerogative, all our graces are from his, 'our myrrh from his myrrh.'

Use. This should teach us, *the necessity of dependence upon Christ*, for whatsoever we have or would have; which dependence upon Christ is the life of our life, the soul of our souls.

Again, observe from hence, that the church's fingers dropped myrrh when she opened the door, and stirred up herself to endeavour. When first her bowels were moved, then she makes to the door, and then her hands dropped myrrh, so that,

Obs. 2. *We find experience of the grace of Christ, especially when we stir up ourselves to endeavour*. 'Arise and be doing, and the Lord shall be with thee,' 1 Chron. xxviii. 20, saith David to Solomon. So let us rouse up ourselves to endeavour, and we shall find a gracious presence of Christ, and a blessed assistance of the Spirit of Christ, who will shew himself in the midst of endeavours. 'To him that hath shall be given:' what is that? To him that hath, if he exercise and stir up the grace of God in him, shall be given, Mat. xxv. 29. Therefore, let us stir up the graces of God in us; let us fall upon actions of obedience, second them with prayer. Whatsoever we pray for and desire, set upon the practice thereof. We mock God else, except we endeavour for that we desire. There was myrrh left on the door, but she feels it not till she arose, opened the door, and laid her hand upon the lock.

I speak to any Christian's experience, if in the midst of obedience they do not find that comfort they looked for, and that it is meat and drink to do God's will. Therefore keep not off and say, I am dead and drowsy, therefore I shall be still so. You are deceived; fall upon obedience and practising of holy duties, and in the midst thereof thou shalt find the presence and assistance of God's Spirit. That will comfort thee.

Obs. 3. The third thing observable from hence is this, *that God's graces are sweet*. Pleasant and sweet, compared here to myrrh, which was an ingredient in the holy oil. Grace makes us sweet. Prayers are sweet, as it is in Rev. viii. 4. Christ mingleth them with his own sweet odours, and so takes and offers them to God. Holy obedience is sweet and delightful to God and to the conscience. It brings peace and delight to others. Therefore they are called fruits. Fruit doth not only imply and shew the issuing of good things from the root, but there is also a pleasantness in it. So there is a delightfulness in good works, as there is in fruit to the taste. Therefore if we would be sweet and delightful to God, let us labour to have grace. If we would think of ourselves with contentment, and have inward sweetness, let us labour for the graces of God's Spirit. These are like myrrh. 'The wicked are an abomination unto the Lord,' Prov. xv. 8, who abhors them, and whatsoever is in them. But 'the righteous and sincere man is his delight,' Prov. xv. 8. Therefore, if we would approve ourselves to God, and feel that he hath delight in us, labour to be such as he may delight in.

Use. Wherefore let the discouraged soul make this use of it, *not to be afraid to do that which is good, upon fear we should sin*. Indeed, sin will cleave to that we do, but Christ will pardon the sin, and accept that which is sweet of his own Spirit. Let us not esteem basely of that which Christ esteems highly of, nor let that be vile in our eyes that is precious in his. Let us labour to bring our hearts to comfortable obedience, for it is a sweet sacrifice to God.

Now, whence came all this? From this that is mentioned, 'My beloved put in his hand by the hole of the door, and my bowels were moved for him,' ver. 4. First, for that expression, he put his finger in by the hole of the door. It implies here that Christ, before he departed, left by his Spirit an impression on the church's heart, which deeply affected her to seek after him.

The fingers spoken of are nothing but 'the power of his Spirit.' As the usual Scripture phrase is, 'This is God's finger,' 'God's mighty hand,' Exod. viii. 19, without which all ordinances are ineffectual. 'Paul may plant, and Apollos may water,' 1 Cor. iii. 6, 7, but all is nothing without the working of the Spirit, the motions whereof are most strong, being God's finger, whereby he wrought all that affection in the church which is here expressed. Christ, before he leaveth the church, 'puts his finger into the hole of the door,' that is, he works somewhat in the soul by his Spirit, which stirred up a constant endeavour to seek after him. For why else follows it, 'her bowels were moved after him'? which implies a work of the Spirit upon her bowels, expressed in her grief for his absence, and shame for her refusing his entrance, and whereby her heart was moved and turned in her to seek after him. From whence, thus explained, observe,

Obs. 1. *That outward means will do no good, unless the finger of Christ come to do all that is good.*

The finger of Christ is the Spirit of Christ—that is, a kind of divine power goes from him in hearing and speaking the word of God, and in prayer. There is more than a man's power in all this. If these work any effect, Christ 'must put his finger in.' When duties are unfolded to us in the ministry of the word, all is to no purpose, but the sounding of a voice, unless the finger of Christ open the heart, and work in the soul.

Use 1. Let us make this use of it, therefore, *not to rest in any means whatsoever*, but desire the presence of Christ's finger to move and to work upon our hearts and souls. Many careless Christians go about the ordinances of God, and never regard this power of Christ, this mighty power, 'the finger of Christ.' Thereupon they find nothing at all that is divine and spiritual wrought in them. For, as it required a God to redeem us, to take our nature, wherein he might restore us, so likewise it requires the power of God to alter our natures. We could not be brought into the state of grace without divine satisfaction, and we cannot be altered to a frame of grace without a divine finger, the finger of God working upon our hearts and souls. This should move us, in all the ordinances of God that we attend upon, to lift up our hearts in the midst of them, 'Lord, let me feel the finger of thy Spirit writing thy word upon my heart.' 'Turn us, O Lord, and we shall be turned,' Jer. xxxi. 18. Pray for this quickening and enlivening, for this strengthening Spirit. All comes by it.

From this that it is said here, 'that Christ puts his finger into the hole of the door before he removed it,' and withdrew himself, observe,

Obs. 2. How graciously Christ doth deal with us, *that he doth always leave some grace before he doth offer to depart.* Let us therefore, for the time to come, lay and store this up as a ground of comfort, that howsoever Christ may leave us, yet, notwithstanding, he will never leave us wholly; but as he gave us his Holy Spirit at first, so he will continue Him in us by some gracious work or other, either by way of comfort, or of strength to uphold us. Perhaps we may need more sorrow, more humility, than of any other grace. For winter is as good for the growing of things as the spring, because were it not for this, where would be the killing of weeds and worms, and preparing of the ground and land for the spring? So it is as needful for Christians to find the presence of Christ in the way of humiliation and abasement, causing us to afflict our own souls, as to feel his presence in peace, joy, and comfort. In this life we cannot be without this gracious dispensation. We may therefore comfort ourselves, that howsoever Christ leaves us, yet he will always leave somewhat behind him, as here he left some myrrh after him upon the handle of the door. Some myrrh is left always behind him upon the soul, which keeps it in a state and frame of grace, and sweetens it. Myrrh was one of the ingredients in the holy oil, as it is Exod. xxx. 30; and so this leaving of myrrh behind him signifies the oil of grace left upon the soul, that enabled the church to do all these things, which are after spoken of.

Obj. But you will say, How doth this appear, when in some desertion a Christian finds no grace, strength, or comfort at all, that nothing is left?

Ans. It is answered, *they always do*. Take those who at any time have had experience of the love of God, and of Christ formerly, take them at the worst, you shall find from them some sparkles of grace, broken speeches of tried secret comfort, some inward strength and struggling against corruptions; their spirits endeavouring to recover themselves from sinking too low, and with something withstanding both despair and corruption. Take a Christian at the worst, there will be a discovery of the Spirit of Christ left in him, notwithstanding all desertion. This is universally in all in some measure, though perhaps it is not discerned to a Christian himself, but to those that are able to judge. Sometimes others can read our evidences better than ourselves. A Christian that is in temptation cannot judge of his own estate, but others can. And so, at the very worst, he hath always somewhat left in him, whereby he may be comforted. Christ never leaves his church and children that are his wholly. Those that are wholly left, they never had saving grace, as Ahithophel, Cain, Saul, and Judas were left to themselves. But for the children of God, if ever they found the power of sanctifying grace, 'Christ whom he loves, he loves to the end,' John xiii. 1, from whom he departs not, unless he leaves somewhat behind him, that sets an edge upon the desires to seek after him.

Use 2. Make this second use of it, *to magnify the gracious love and mercy of Christ*, that when we deserve the contrary, to be left altogether, yet notwithstanding so graciously he deals with us. Behold, in this his dealing, the mercy of Christ. He will not suffer the church to be in a state of security, but will rather, to cure her, bring her to another opposite state of grief and sorrow, as we shall see in the next point, how that which Christ left in the heart of the church so afflicted her 'that her bowels were turned in her.' Whereupon she riseth, seeks, and inquires after Christ by the watchmen and others. So she saith of herself,

'My bowels were moved in me,' &c. What was that? My heart was affected full of sorrow and grief for my unkind dealing with Christ. Hereby those affections were stirred up, that were afore sleepy and secure, to godly grief, sorrow, and shame. For God hath planted affections in us, and joined them with conscience, as the executioners with the judge. So that, whenas conscience accuseth of any sin, either of omission or commission, affections are ready to be the executioners within us. Thus to prevent eternal damnation, God hath set up a throne in our own hearts, to take revenge and correction by our own affections, godly sorrow and mourning, as here the church saith, 'My bowels were turned in me.' It was a shame and grief, springing out of love to Christ, that had been so kind, patient, and full of forbearance to her. 'My bowels were turned in me;' that is, sorrow and grief were upon me for my unkind dealing.

The observation from hence is,

That security and a cold, dull state produceth a contrary temper. That is, those that are cold, dull, secure, and put off Christ, he suffers them to fall into sharp sorrows and griefs.

We usually say, Cold diseases must have hot and sharp remedies. It is most true spiritually. Security, which is a kind of lethargy, a cold disease, forgetting of God and our duty to him, must have a hot and sharp cure. And the lethargy is best cured by a burning ague. So Christ deals here. He puts his finger in at the hole of the door, and leaves grace behind to work upon the bowels of the church, to make her grieve and be ashamed for her unkind dealing. Thus he cures security by sorrow. This is the best conclusion of sin.

And we may observe withal, *that even sins of omission, they bring grief, shame, and sorrow.* And in the issue, through Christ's sanctifying them, these which they breed consume the parent. That is, sin brings forth sorrow, shame, and grief, which are a means to cure sin. Security breeds this moving of the bowels, which moving helps security. Would we therefore prevent sorrow, shame, and grief? Take heed then of security, the cause that leads to them; yea, of sins of omission, wherein there is more danger than in sins of commission. The sins of carnal, wicked men are usually sins of commission; most which break out outrageously, and thereby taint themselves with open sins. But the sins of God's people, who are nearer to him, are for the most part sins of omission; that is, negligence, coldness, carelessness in duty, want of zeal, and of care they should have in stirring up the graces of God in them; as the church here, which did not give way to Christ, nor shook off security.

Use. Let us esteem as slightly as we will of sins of omission and carelessness, *they are enough to bring men to hell if God be not the more merciful.* It is not required only that we do no harm, and keep ourselves from outward evils; but we must do good in a good manner, and have a care to be fruitful and watchful, which if we do not, this temper will bring grief, shame, and sorrow afterwards. As here, even for sins of omission, deadness, and dulness, we see the church is left by Christ, 'and her bowels are turned in her.' For careless neglect and omission of duty to God is a presage and forerunner of some downfal and dejection. And commonly it is true, when a man is in a secure and careless state, a man may read his destiny (though he have been never so good); nay, the rather if he be good. Such a one is in danger to fall into some sharp punishment, or into some sin; for of all states and tempers, God will not suffer a Christian to be in a secure, lazy, dead state, when he cannot perform things comfortably to God, or himself, or to others. A dead, secure estate is so hateful to him (decay in our first love, this lukewarm temper) that he will not endure it. It either goes before some great sin, cross, affliction, or judgment.

'My bowels were moved in me.' And good reason. It was a suitable correction to the sin wherein she offended. For Christ, his bowels were turned towards her in love and pity, 'My love, my dove, my undefiled,' in which case, she neglecting him, it was fit she should find 'moving of bowels' in another sense, out of love too, but in shame and mourning. Christ here leaves her to seek after him, that had waited and attended her leisure before, as we shall see after.

The next thing we may hence observe in that, 'that her bowels were turned in her,' from something left in the hole of the door by the Spirit of Christ, is,

That Christ hath our affections in his government.

He hath our bowels in his rule and government, more than we ourselves have. We cannot of ourselves rule our grief, shame, sorrow, or such affections as these. The wisest man in the world cannot award* grief and sorrow when God will turn it upon his bowels, and make a man ashamed and confounded in himself. All the wit and policy in the world cannot suppress those affections. For Christ rules our hearts, 'The hearts of kings are in his hand, as the rivers of water,' Prov. xxi. 1, as well as the hearts of ordinary persons.

If he set anything upon the soul to afflict it and cast it down, it shall afflict it, if it be but a conceit. If he will take away the reins from the soul, and leave it to its own passion, removing away its guard; for he by his Spirit guards our souls with peace, by commanding of tranquillity; so as let him but leave it to itself, and it will tear itself in sunder, as Ahithophel, who being left to himself, did tear himself in pieces, 2 Sam. xvii. 23. Cain also being thus left, was disquieted, tormented, and wracked† himself, Gen. iv. 13. So Judas in this case, being divided in himself, you see what became of him, Mat. xxvii. 5. Let Christ but leave us to our own passion of sorrow, what will become of us but misery? He hath more rule therefore of our passions than we ourselves have, because we cannot rule them graciously, nor can we stay them when we would.

Use. Therefore this should *strike an awe in us of God, with a care to please him.* For there is not the wisest man in the world, but if he remove his guard from his soul, and leave him to himself; if there were no devil in hell, yet he would make him his own tormentor and executioner. Therefore the apostle makes this sweet promise. He bids them pray to God; 'and the peace of God which passeth all understanding should guard their souls,' &c., Philip. iv. 7. So the word is in the original.‡ It is a great matter for the keeping of God's people, to have their souls guarded.

'Her bowels were turned in her.'

Here again, as the conclusion of all this, we seeing this estate of the church, *may wonder at Christ's carriage towards her in this world.* Christ is wonderful in his saints, and in his goodness towards them, 2 Thess. i. 10; sometimes alluring them, as we see Christ the church here; wondrous in patience, notwithstanding their provocation of him; wondrous in his desertions; wondrous in leaving something behind him in desertions. Those that are his he will not leave them without grace, whereby they shall seek him again. Nay, the falling out of lovers shall be the renewing of fresh and new love, more constant than ever the former was. Thus our blessed Saviour goes beyond us in our deserts, taking advantage even of our security; for our greater good, making all work to good in the issue, Rom. viii. 28; which shall end in a more near and close communion between Christ and his church than ever before. Carnal men feel not these changes, ebbings and flowings. They are not acquainted with God's forsakings. Indeed their whole life is nothing but a forsaking of God, and God's forsaking of them, who gives

* That is, 'ward off.'—ED.

† Qu. 'racked?'—G.

‡ See note *k*, vol I. page 334.—G.

them outward comforts, peace and friends in the world, wherein they solace themselves. But for inward communion with him, any strength to holy duties, or against sin, for to be instruments for God's honour, and service, to do any good, they are careless. For they live here to serve their own turns, leaving their state and inheritance behind them. The Scripture saith, 'They have no changes, therefore they fear not God,' Ps. lv. 19; and so they go down to hell quietly and securely. Oh! but it is otherwise with God's children. They are tossed up and down. God will not suffer them to prosper, or live long in a secure, drowsy, sinful state, the continuance wherein is a fearful evidence that such an one as yet hath no saving grace, nor that he yet belongs to God, seeing Christ hates such an estate, and will not suffer his to be long therein, but will shift and remove them from vessel to vessel, from condition to condition, till he have wrought in them that disposition of soul that they shall regard and love him more and more, and have nearer and nearer communion with him.

THE TENTH SERMON.

I opened to my beloved; but my beloved had withdrawn himself and was gone: my soul failed when he spake; I sought him, but could not find him; I called him, but he gave no answer.—CANT. V. 6.

THUS we see that the life of a Christian is trouble upon trouble, as wave upon wave. God will not suffer us to rest in security, but one way or other he will fire us out of our starting-holes, and make us to run after him. How much better were it for us, then, to do our works cheerfully and joyfully, 'so to run as we may obtain,' 1 Cor. ix. 24, than to be thus hurried up and down, and through our own default, coming into desertions, and there receiving rebukes and blows and delays ere we have peace again, as it fell out with the church in the sequel; for this text is but the beginning of her seeming misery. The watchmen, after this, 'found her, and wounded her,' &c., verse 7. But heaven is more worth than all, now that her affections are set on fire. From thence she bestirs herself, is resolute to find out her beloved, whom she highly values above all this world. How her affections were stirred by Christ's putting in his finger at the hole of the door, we have heard. Now follows her action thereupon; for here is rising, opening, seeking, calling, and inquiring after Christ.

Action follows affection. After her bowels are moved, she ariseth and openeth; from whence we may further observe—

Obs. 1. *That where truth of affection is, it will discover itself in the outward man, one way or other.* If there be any affection of love and piety to God, there will be eyes lift up, knees bended down, and hands stretched forth to heaven. If there be any grief for sin, there will be the face dejected, the eyes looking down, some expression or other. If there be a desire, there will be a making forth to the thing desired; for the outward man is commanded by the inward, which hath a kind of sovereign commanding power over it, and says, Do this, and it doth it; Speak this, and it speaks it. Therefore, those whose courses of life are not gracious, their affections and their hearts are not good; for where the affections are good, the actions will be suitable. 'Her bowels were moved in her,' and presently she shews the truth of her affection, in that she maketh after him.

1. *Her soul failed when he spake.*
2. *She makes after him.*

'My soul failed when he spake: I sought him, but I could not find him.'—Of Christ's withdrawing himself, we spake in general before, wherefore we will leave that and proceed.

'My soul failed when he spake.' That is, her soul failed when she remembered what he had spoke when he stood at the door and said, 'Open to me, my sister, my love, my dove, my undefiled: for my head is wet with the dew,' &c. Now, when God's Spirit had wrought upon her, then she remembered what Christ had said. All those sweet allurements were effectual now unto her, especially when she saw that after those sweet allurements Christ had withdrawn himself; for that is the meaning or these words, 'My soul failed when he spake unto me.' He did not speak now; but her soul failed after he spake; for so it should be read, that is, after she remembered his speech to her; for now, when she opened, he was not there. Therefore, he could not speak to her.

Obs. 2. *The word of Christ, howsoever for the present it be not effectual, yet afterwards it will be in the remembrance of it.* To those that are gracious, it will be effectual when the Holy Ghost comes to seal it further upon their hearts. Christ spake many things to his disciples which they forgot; but when afterwards the Holy Ghost the Comforter was come, his office was, 'to bring all things to their remembrance that they had forgotten before,' John xiv. 26. The Holy Ghost taught them not new things, but brought former things to their remembrance; for God will make the word effectual at one time or other. Perhaps the word we hear is not effectual for the present; it may afterwards, many years after, when God awakes our consciences.

And as this is true of God's children, the seed now sown in them will not grow up till many years after, so it is true also of those that are not God's children. They think they shall never hear again of those things they hear. Perhaps they will take order by sensuality, hardening of their hearts, and through God's judgments withal concurring, that conscience shall not awake in this world. But it shall awake one day; for it is put into the heart to take God's part, and to witness against us for our sins. It shall have and perform its office hereafter, use it as you will now; and it will preach over those things again that you now hear. You shall hear again of them, but it shall be a barren hearing. Now we may hear fruitfully to do us good, but afterwards we shall call to mind what we have heard, and it shall cut us to the heart. Dives, we know, had Moses and the prophets to instruct him, but he never heeded them in his life, until afterwards to his torment, Luke xvi. 29. So men never heed what they hear and read; they put off all, and lay their consciences asleep; but God will bring them afterwards to remembrance. But because it is a point especially of comfort to the church;

Labour we all of us to make this use of it, to be diligent and careful to hear and attend upon the ordinances of God; for howsoever that we hear is not effectual for the present, but seems as dead seed cast into the heart, yet God will give it a body after, as the apostle speaks, at one time or other, 1 Cor. xv. 38. And that which we hear now, the Holy Ghost will bring it to our remembrance when we stand in most need of it.

'My soul failed when he spake.' She was in a spiritual swoon and deliquium* upon his withdrawing, whence the point considerable is,

* That is, 'fainting, sinking.'—G.

That Christ doth leave his church sometimes, and bring it very low in their own apprehensions, that their hearts fail them for want of his presence. So it was with David, Ps. xxxviii. 2, 3; so with Jonah, Jonah ii. 2; so with the church, Lam. iii. 1, *seq.* We see it at large.

Reason. The necessity of our souls and of our estates require this. As sometimes a body may be so corrupt, that it must be brought as low as possible may be, before there will be a spring of new and good blood and spirits, so we may fall into such a state of security, that nothing will bring us to a right temper but extreme purging. And usually God deals thus with strong wits and parts, if they be holy. David and Solomon were men excellently qualified; yet when they tasted of the pleasures and contentments of the world too deep, answerably they had; and so usually others shall have such desertions as will make them smart for their sweetness, as was shewed before.

But upon what occasions doth a Christian think especially that God doth leave, forsake, and fail him?

First. This failing and fainting of the soul is sometimes upon an apprehension, *as if God and Christ were become enemies*, as Job saith, vii. 20, and as having set us as a butt to shoot at. But this is not all that a gracious and pure heart sinks for.

But also *secondly*. *For the absence of Christ's love, though it feel no anger.* Even as to a loving wife, her husband not looking lovingly upon her as he used to do, is enough to cast her down, and cause her spirits to fail; so for God to look upon the soul, put the case, not with an angry, yet with a countenance withdrawn, it is sufficient to cast it down. For any one that hath dependence upon another, to see their countenance withdrawn, and not to shew their face as before, if there be but a sweet disposition in them, it is enough to daunt and dismay them.

Nay, *thirdly*. Moreover, *when they find not that former assistance in holy duties;* when they find that their hearts are shut up and they cannot pray as formerly when they had the Spirit of God more fully; and when they find that they cannot bear afflictions with wonted patience—certainly Christ hath withdrawn himself, say they. This is first done when we hear the word of God, not with that delight and profit as we were wont. When they find how they come near to God in holy communion, and yet feel not that sweet taste and relish in the ordinances of God as they were wont to do, they conclude, certainly God hath hid his face. Whereupon they are cast down, their spirits fail. And do not wonder that it should be so, for it is so in nature. When the sun hides itself many days from the world, it is an uncomfortable time; the spirits of the creatures lower and wither. We see it so in the body, that the animal spirits in the brain, which are the cause of motion and sense, if they be obstructed, there follows an apoplexy and deadness. So it is between Christ and the soul. He is the 'Sun of righteousness,' Mal. iv. 2, by whose beams we are all comforted and cheered, which when they are withheld, then our spirits decay and are discouraged. Summer and winter arise from the presence and absence of the sun. What causeth the spring to be so clothed with all those rich ornaments? The presence of the sun which comes nearer then. So what makes the summer and winter in the soul, but the absence or presence of Christ! What makes some so vigorous beyond others, but the presence of the Spirit! As it is in nature, so it is here. The presence of Christ is the cause of all spiritual life and vigour; who when he withdraws his presence a little the soul fails.

'My soul failed when he spake to me: I sought him, but I could not find him; I called, but he gave me no answer.'

Obs. 1. The church redoubleth her complaint to shew her passion. *A large heart hath large expressions.* She took it to heart that Christ did not shew himself in mercy. Therefore she never hath done. I sought him but I could not find him, I called but he gave me no answer. Affection makes eloquent and large expressions.

Obs. 2. But mainly observe from this failing of the church, *the difference between the true children of God and others.* The child of God is cast down when he finds not the presence of God as he was wont; his spirits fail. A carnal man, that never knew what this presence meant, regards it not, can abide the want of it. He finds, indeed, a presence of God in the creature which he thinks not of. There is a sweetness in meat, drink, rest, and a contentment in honour, preferment, and riches; and thus God is present always with him, but other presence he cares not for. Nay, he shuns all other presence of God, labouring to avoid his spiritual presence. For what is the reason that a carnal man shuns the applying of the word and the thinking of it, but because it brings God near to his heart, and makes him present? What is the reason he shuns his own conscience; that he is loath to hear the just and unanswerable accusations that it would charge upon him, but because he cannot abide the presence of God in his conscience? What is the reason he shuns the sight of holier and better men than himself? 1 Kings xvii. 18. They present God to him, being his image, and call his sins to memory, and upbraid his wicked life. Hence comes that Satanical hatred more than human in carnal, vile men, to those that are better than themselves; because they hate all presence of God, both in the word, ministry, and all God's holy servants. All such presence of God they hate; whereof one main reason is, because they are malefactors, wicked rebels, and intend to be so. And as a malefactor cannot endure so much as the thought of the judge, so they cannot think of God otherwise, in that course they are in, than of a judge; whereupon they tremble and quake at the very thought of him, and avoid his presence.

You know that great man, Felix, Paul spake to in the Acts, Acts xxiv. 25, when he spake of the judgment to come, and those virtues, as temperance and righteousness, which he was void of, and guilty of the contrary vices; he quaked, and could not endure to hear him speak any longer. Wicked men love not to be arraigned, tormented, accused, and condemned before their time, Mark v. 7. Therefore, whatsoever presents to them their future terrible estate, they cannot abide it. It is an evidence of a man in a cursed condition, thus not to endure the presence of God. But what shall God and Christ say to them at the day of judgment? It was the desire of such men not to have to do with the presence of God here, and it is just with Christ to answer them there as they answer him now; 'Depart, depart, we will have none of thy ways,' say they, Job xxii. 17. 'Depart, ye cursed,' saith he. He doth but answer in their own language, 'Depart, ye cursed, with the devil and his angels,' Mat. xxv. 41.

But you see the child of God is clean of another temper. He cannot be content to be without the presence of God and of his Spirit, enlightening, quickening, strengthening, and blessing of him in spiritual respects. When he finds not his presence helping him, when he finds Christ his life is absent from him, he is presently discouraged. For 'Christ is our life,' Col. iii. 4. Now, when a man's life fails all fails. When, therefore, a man finds his spiritual taste and comfort not as it was before, then Oh, 'the life of my life' hath withdrawn himself, and so is never quiet till he have recovered his life again, for 'Christ is his life,' Col. iii. 4.

And because there is a presence of God and of Christ in the word and sacraments—a sweet presence, the godly soul, he droops and fails if he be kept from these. He will not excommunicate himself, as many do, that perhaps are asleep when they should be at the ordinances of God. But if he be excommunicated and banished, O how takes he it to heart! 'As the hart panteth after the water brooks, so longeth my soul after thee, O God,' Ps. xlii. 1. The whole 84th Psalm is to that purpose, 'O how amiable are thy tabernacles, O Lord of hosts.' He finds a presence of God in his word and sacraments, and when he doth not taste a sweet presence of God therein, he droops and sinks.

A carnal man never heeds these things, because he finds no sweetness in them; but the godly, finding Christ in them, they droop in the want of them, and cannot live without them. 'Whither shall we go?' saith Peter to Christ, 'thou hast the words of eternal life,' John vi. 68. I find my soul quickened with thy speaking. So a soul that feels the quickening power of the ordinances, he will never be kept from the means of salvation, but he droops and is never well till he have recovered himself again.

Again, another difference may be observed. Carnal men, when they find the sense of God's anger, they seek not God's favour, but think of worse and worse still, and so run from God till they be in hell. But those that are God's children, when they fail and find the sense of God's displeasure, they are sensible of it, and give not over seeking to God. They run not further and further from him.

The church here, though she found not Christ present with her, yet she seeks him still and never gives over. Whence again we may observe,

3. *That although the church be said to fail and not to find Christ, yet he is present then with her.* For who enabled her to seek him? To explain this, there is a double presence of Christ.

1. Felt.

2. Not felt.

1. *The presence felt,* is, when Christ is graciously present and is withal pleased to let us know so much, which is a heaven upon earth. The soul is in paradise then, when she feels 'the love of God shed abroad in the heart,' and the favourable countenance of God shining upon her. Then she despiseth the world, the devil, and all, and walks as if she were half in heaven already. For she finds a presence and a manifestation of it, a more glorious state than the world can afford.

2. But, there is a presence of Christ *that is secret;* when he seems to draw us one way, and to drive us another, that we are both driven and drawn at once: when he seems to put us away, and yet, notwithstanding, draws us. When we find our souls go to Christ, there is a drawing power and presence; but when we find him absent, here is a driving away. As we see here in the church and in the 'woman of Canaan,' Mat. xv. 21, *seq.* We see what an answer she had from Christ, at first none, and then an uncomfortable, and lastly a most unkind answer. 'We must not give the children's bread to dogs,' Mat. xv. 27. Christ seemed to drive her away, but, at the same time, he by his Spirit draws her to him, and was thereby secretly present in her heart to increase her faith. When Christ wrestled with Jacob, though he contended with him, yet the same time he gave Jacob power to overcome him, to be Israel, a prevailer over him, Gen. xxxii. 28. So, at the same time, the church seems to fail and faint, yet,

notwithstanding, there is a secret, drawing power pulling her to Christ, whereby she never gives over, but seeks and calls still after him.

It is good to observe this kind of Christ's dealing, because it will keep us that we be not discouraged when we find him absent. If still there be any grace left moving us to that which is good, if we find the Spirit of God moving us to love the word and ordinances, to call upon him by prayer, and to be more instant, certainly we may gather there is a hidden, secret presence here that draws us to these things. Nay more, that the end of this seeming forsaking and strangeness is to draw us nearer and nearer, and at length to draw us into heaven to himself. God's people are gainers by all their losses, stronger by all their weaknesses, and the better for all their crosses, whatsoever they are. And you shall find that the Spirit of God is more forceible in them after a strangeness, to stir them up more eagerly after Christ than before, as here the church doth: for her eagerness, constancy, and instantness, it groweth as Christ's withdrawing of himself groweth.

Use 1. Let us therefore learn hence *how to judge of ourselves*, if we be in a dead, lifeless state, both in regard of comfort and of holy performances, whether we be content to be so. If we be not contented, but make towards Christ more and more, it is a good sign that he hath not forsaken us, that he will come again more gloriously than ever before, as here we shall see after, it was with the church. He seems strange, but it is to draw the church to discover her affection, and to make her ashamed of her former unkindness, and to sit surer and hold faster than she did before. All ends in a most sweet communion.

Use 2. We should labour, therefore, *to answer Christ's dealings in suitable apprehensions of soul*, when he is thus present secretly, though he seem, in regard of some comforts and former experience of his love, to withdraw himself. It should teach us to depend upon him, and to believe, though we feel not comfort, yea, against comfort, when we feel signs of displeasure. If he can love and support me, and strengthen my soul, and shew it a presence of that which is fit for me, certainly I should answer thus with my faith, I will depend upon him, though he kill me, as Job did, Job xiii. 15. Our souls should never give over seeking of Christ, praying and endeavouring, for there is true love where he seems to forsake and leave. Therefore I ought in these desertions to cleave to him in life and in death.

THE ELEVENTH SERMON.

I opened to my beloved; but my beloved had withdrawn himself, and was gone: my soul failed when he spake: I sought him, but I could not find him; I called him, but he gave me no answer.—CANT. V. 6, 7.

THE pride and security of the spouse provokes the Lord, her husband, oft to bring her very low, they being incompatible with Christ's residence.

Pride is an affection contrary to his prerogative; for it sets up somewhat in the soul higher than God, the highest.

Security is a dull temper, or rather distemper, that makes the soul neglect her watch, and rely upon some outward privilege. Where this ill couple is entertained, there Christ useth to withdraw himself, even to the failing and fainting of the soul.

The spouse is here in her fainting fit, yet she seeks after Christ. Still she gives not over. So Jonah, 'I am cast out of thy presence,' says he, 'yet notwithstanding I will look toward thy holy temple,' Jonah ii. 4. And David, 'I said in my haste, I am cast out of thy sight; yet notwithstanding thou heardest the voice of my prayer,' Ps. xxxi. 22. He said it, but he said it in his haste. God's children are surprised on the sudden to think they are cast away; but it is in haste, and so soon as may be, they recover themselves. 'I said it is my infirmity,' said David, Ps. lxxvii. 10. It is but in a passion. Here then is the difference between the children of God and others in desertions; they arise, these lie still and despair. There is 'life in the substance of the oak,' Isa. vi. 13, that makes it lift up its head above ground, though it be cut down to the stumps. Nay, we see further here, the church is not taken off for any discouragements, but her faith grows stronger, as the woman's of Canaan did, Mat. xv. 21, *seq.*

The reason whereof is—1, faith looks to the promise, and to the nature of God, not to his present dealing.

And then, 2. God, by a secret work of his Spirit, though he seem to be an enemy, yet notwithstanding draws his children nearer and nearer to him by such his dealing. All this strangeness is but to mortify some former lust, or consume some former dregs of security.

'I sought him, but I could not find him.' Here one of the greatest discouragements of all other is, when prayer, which is left to the church as a salve for all sores, hath no answer. This is the complaint, but indeed an error, of the church; for Christ did hear the church, though he seemed to turn his back.

But how shall we know that God hears our prayers?

First. Amongst many other things this is one. When he gives us inward peace, then he hears our prayers, for so is the connection, Phil. iv. 6, 7.

Or *secondly.* If we find a spirit to pray still, a spirit to wait and to hold out, it is an argument that God either hath or will hear those prayers.

And as it is an argument that God hears our prayers, so is it of the presence of Christ. For how could we pray but from his inward presence? Christ was now present, and more present with the church when he seemed not to be found of her, than he was when she was secure; for whence else comes this eagerness of desire, this spirit of prayer, this earnestness of seeking? 'I called, but he gave no answer,' &c.

Directions how to carry ourselves in such an estate. How shall we carry ourselves when it falls out that our hearts fail of that we seek for, when we pray without success, and find not a present answer, or are in any such-like state of desertion.

1. *We must believe against belief,* as it were, 'hope against hope, and trust in God,' Rom. iv. 18, howsoever he shews himself to us as an opposite.* It is no matter what his present dealing with his church and children here is; the nature of faith is to break through all opposition, to see the sun behind a cloud, nay, to see one contrary in another, life in death, a calm in a storm, &c., 1 Cor. vi. 8, 9, *seq.*

2. *Labour for an absolute dependence upon Christ, with a poverty of spirit in ourselves.* This is the end of Christ's withdrawing himself, to purge us of self-confidence and pride.

* That is, 'opponent.—G.

3. *Stir up your graces.* For as nature joining with physic helps it to work and carry away the malignant humours, so by the remainder of the Spirit that is in us, let us set all our graces on work until we have carried away that that offends and clogs the soul, and not sink under the burden. For this is a special time for the exercising of faith, hope, love, diligence, care, watchfulness, and such-like graces.

And let us know for our comfort, that even this conflicting condition is a good estate. In a sick body it is a sign of life and health approaching when the humours are stirred, so as that a man complains that the physic works. So when we take to heart our present condition, though we fail and find not what we would, yet this will work to the subduing of corruption at length. It is a sign of future victory when we are discontent with our present ill estate. Grace will get the upper hand, as nature doth when the humours are disturbed.

4. Again, when we are in such a seeming forlorn estate, *let us have recourse to former experience.* What is the reason that God vouchsafes his children for the most part in the beginning of their conversion, in their first love, experience of his love to ravishment? It is, that afterwards they may have recourse to that love of God then felt, to support themselves, and withal to stir up endeavours, and hope; that finding it not so well with them now as formerly it hath been, by comparing state with state, desires may be stirred up to be as they were, or rather better, Hosea ii. 7.

And as the remembrance of former experiences serve to excite endeavour, so to stir up hope, I hope it shall be as it was, because God is immutable; I change, but Christ alters not. The inferior elementary world changes. Here is fair weather and foul, but the sun keeps his perpetual course. And as in the gloomiest day that ever was, there was light enough to make it day and to distinguish it from night, though the sun did not shine, so in the most disconsolate state of a Christian soul, there is light enough in the soul to shew that the Sun of righteousness is there, and that Christ hath shined upon the soul, that it is day with the soul, and not night, Ps. cxii. 4.

5. And learn when we are in this condition *to wait God's leisure*, for he hath waited ours. It is for our good, to prepare us for further blessings, to mortify and subdue our corruptions, to enlarge the capacity of the soul, that the Lord absents himself. Therefore Bernard saith well, '*Tibi accidit*,' &c., 'Christ comes and goes away for our good.' When he withdraws the sense of his love, the soul thereupon is stretched with desire, that it may be as it was in former time, in the days of old. Thus much for that. 'I sought, but could not find him: I called, but he gave me no answer.'

Obj. Here we must answer one objection before we leave the words. This seems to contradict other Scriptures, which promise that those that seek shall find, Matt. vii. 7.

Ans. It is true they that seek shall find, but not presently. God's times are the best and fittest. They that seek shall find, if they seek constantly with their whole heart in all the means. Some do not find, because they seek in one means and not in another. They seek Christ in reading and not in the ordinance of hearing, in private meditation, but not in the communion of saints. We must go through all means to seek Christ, not one must be left. Thus if we will seek him, undoubtedly he will make good his promise. Nay, in some sort, 'he is found before he is sought,' for he is in our souls to stir up desire of seeking him. He prevents us with desires, and answers us in some sort before we pray, Isa. lxv. 24. When he gives us a spirit of prayer, it is a pledge to us, that he means to answer us.

Therefore it is a spiritual deceit when we think Christ is not in us, and we are neglected of him, because we have not all that we would have. Among many other deceits that Christians deceive themselves with in this kind, these be two.

1. That they judge grace *by the quantity and not by the value and price of it;* whereas the least measure of grace and comfort is to be esteemed, because it is an immortal seed cast into the soul by an immortal God, the Father of eternity,* Isa. ix. 6.

2. Another deceit is, that we judge of ourselves *by sense and feeling, and not by faith.*

'The watchman that went about the city found me, and smote me, and took away my veil from me.' Here the poor church, after the setting down of her own exercise in her desertion, now sets out some outward ill dealing she met with, and that from those that should have been her greatest comforters. 'The watchmen that went about the city found me, they wounded me: the keepers of the walls took away my veil from me.'

Thus we see how trouble follows trouble. 'One depth calls upon another.' Inward desertion and outward affliction go many times together. The troubles of the church many times are like Job's messengers. They come fast one upon another, because God means to perfect the work of grace in their hearts. All this is for their good. The sharper the winter the better the spring. Learn hence first of all therefore in general,

That it is no easy thing to be a sound Christian. We see here, when the church had betrothed herself to Christ and entertained him into her garden, thereafter she falls into a state of security and sleep, whence Christ labours to rouse her up. Then she useth him unkindly. After which he withdraws himself, even so far that her heart fails her. Then, as if this were not enough, the watchmen that should have looked to her, 'they smite her, wound her, and take away her veil.' See here the variety of the usage of the church and changes of a Christian; not long in one state, he is ebbing and flowing.

Therefore let none distaste the way of godliness for this, that it is such a state as is subject to change and variety, whereas carnal men are upon their lees and find no changes.

Obj. But you will say, All Christians are not thus tossed up and down, so deserted of God and persecuted of others.

Ans. I answer, indeed there is difference. Whence comes this difference? From God's liberty. It is a mystery of the sanctuary, which no man in the world can give a reason of, why of Christians both equally beloved of God, some should have a fairer passage to heaven, others rougher and more rugged. It is a mystery hid in God's breast. It is sufficient for us, if God will bring us any way to heaven, as the blessed apostle saith, 'if by any means I might attain to the resurrection of the dead,' Phil. iii. 11; either through thick or thin, if God will bring me to heaven it is no matter. 'If I by any means.'

'The watchmen that went about the city smote me,' &c. By the watchmen here are meant especially governors of state and church.

Why are they called watchmen?

It is a borrowed speech, taken from the custom of cities that are beleaguered. For policy's sake they have watchmen to descry the danger they are liable unto. So magistrates be watchmen of the state. Ministers are the watchmen for souls, 'watching over our souls for good,' Heb. xiii. 17.

Quest. Why doth God use watchmen?

* That is, the 'Everlasting Father' of authorised translation.—G.

Ans. 1. Not for any defect of power in him, but for demonstration of his goodness. For he is the great watchman, who watcheth over our commonwealths, churches, and persons. He hath an eye that never sleeps. 'He that watcheth Israel neither slumbers nor sleeps,' Ps. cxxi. 4. Yet notwithstanding he hath subordinate watchmen, not for defect of power, but for demonstration of goodness. He manifests his goodness in that he will use variety of subordinate watchers.

And likewise to shew his power in using many instruments, and his care for us when he keeps us together with his own subordinate means.

And in this that God hath set over us watchers, ministers especially, it implies that *our souls are in danger*. And indeed there is nothing in the world so beset as the soul of a poor Christian. Who hath so many and so bad enemies as a Christian? and amongst them all, the worst and greatest enemy he hath is nearest to him, and converseth daily with him, even himself. Therefore there must needs be watchmen to discover the deceits of Satan and his instruments, and of our own hearts; to discover the dangers of Jerusalem, and the errors and sins of the times wherein we live. The church is in danger, for God hath set watchmen. Now God and nature doth nothing in vain or needlessly.

Again, in that God takes such care for the soul, it shews the *wondrous worth of it*. Many arguments there be to shew that the soul is a precious thing. It was breathed by God at first. Christ gave his life to redeem it. But this is an especial one, that God hath ordained and established a ministry and watchmen over it. And as God hath set some watchmen over others, so hath he appointed every man to be a watchman to himself. He hath given every man a city to watch over, that is, his own estate and soul. Therefore let us not depend altogether on the watching of others. God hath planted a conscience in every [one] of us, and useth as others to our good, so our own care, wisdom, and foresight, these he elevateth and sanctifieth.

'The watchmen that went about the city found me, they smote me, they wounded me,' &c.

Come we now to the carriage of these watchmen. Those that should have been defensive prove most offensive.

They smote the church and wounded her many ways, though it be not discovered here in particular. As (1.) with their ill and scandalous life; and (2.) sometimes with corrupt doctrine, and otherwhiles with bitter words; and (3.) their unjust censures, as we see in the story of the church, especially the Romish Church. They have excommunicated churches and princes. But not to speak of those synagogues of Satan, come we nearer home and we may see amongst ourselves sometimes those that are watchmen, and should be for encouragement, they smite and wound the church, and take away her veil, 3 John 10.

What is it to take away the veil?

You know, in the times of the Old Testament, a veil was that which covered women for modesty, to shew their subjection; and it was likewise an honourable ornament. 'They took away the veil,' that is, that wherewith the church was covered. They took away that that made the church comely, and laid her open, and as it were naked.

Now both these ways the church's veil is taken away by false and naughty watchmen.

1. As the veil is a token of subjection, when by their false doctrines they labour *to draw people from Christ, and their subjection to him.*

The church is Christ's spouse. The veil was a token of subjection. Now they that draw the people to themselves, as in popish churches, that desire to sit high in the consciences of people, and so make the church undutiful, 'they take away the veil of subjection,' and so force Christ to punish the church, as we see in former ages.

2. As the veil is for honour and comeliness, so 'they take away the veil' of the church, when they *take away the credit and esteem of the church;* when they lay open the infirmities and weaknesses of the church. This is strange that the watchmen should do this; yet notwithstanding oftentimes it falls out so that those that by place are watchmen, are the bitterest enemies of the church. Who were bitterer enemies of the poor church in Christ's time than the scribes, pharisees, and priests?

And so in the time of the prophets. Who were the greatest enemies the church had, but false priests and prophets?

Quest. What is the ground of this, that those men that by their standing should be encouragers, are rather dampers of the church's zeal in pursuit of it?

Ans. There are many grounds of it.

Sometimes it falls out from a spirit of envy in them at the graces of God's people, which are wanting in themselves. They would not have others better than themselves.

Sometimes from idleness, which makes them hate all such as provoke them to pains. They raise up the dignity of outward things too much, as we see in popery. They make everything to confer grace, as if they had a special virtue in them. But they neglect that wherewith God hath joined an efficacy, his own ordinances.

Use 1. This should teach us, *to be in love with Christ's government*, and to see the vanity of all things here below, though they be never so excellent in their ordinance. Such is the poison of man's heart, and the malice of Satan, that they turn the edge of the best things against the good of the church.

What is more excellent than magistracy? yet many times the point of sword is directed the wrong way. 'I have said ye are gods,' Ps. lxxxii. 6. They should govern, as God himself would govern, and ask with themselves, Would God now, if he were a watchman of the state, do thus and thus? But I wish woeful experience did not witness the contrary.

So ministers are Christ's ambassadors, 2 Cor. v. 20, and should carry themselves even as Christ would do. They should strengthen the feeble knees and bind up the broken hearted, nor* discourage; and not sew pillows under the armholes of wicked and carnal men, Ezek. xiii. 18. But, alas! we see the edge of the ordinance is oftentimes turned another way by the corrupt, proud, unbroken hearts of men and the malice of Satan.

Use 2. Again, it should teach us *not to think the worse of any for the disgraces of the times.* The watchmen here take away the veil of the church, and her forwardness is disgraced by them. Take heed, therefore, we entertain not rash conceits of others upon the entertainment they find abroad in the world, or among those that have a standing in the church, for so we shall condemn Christ himself. How was he judged of the priests, scribes, and pharisees in his times? And this hath been the lot of the church in all ages. The true members thereof were called heretics and schismatics. The veil was taken off. It is the poisonful pride of man's heart that, when it cannot raise itself by its own worth, it will endeavour to raise itself

* Qu. 'not?'—G.

by the ruin of others' credit through lying slanders. The devil was first a slanderer and liar, and then a murderer, John viii. 44. He cannot murder without he slander first. The credit of the church must first be taken away, and then she is wounded. Otherwise, as it is a usual proverb, Those that kill a dog make the world believe that he was mad first; so they always first traduced the church to the world, and then persecuted her. Truth hath always a scratched face. Falsehood many times goes under better habits than its own, which God suffers, to exercise our skill and wisdom, that we might not depend upon the rash judgment of others, but might consider what grounds they have; not what men do, or whom they oppose, but from what cause, whether from a spirit of envy, idleness, jealousy, and pride, or from good grounds. Else, if Christ himself were on earth again, we should condemn him, as now men do the generation of the just, whom they smite and wound, and take away their veil from them.

THE TWELFTH SERMON.

The watchmen that went about the city found me, they smote me, they wounded me: the keepers of the walls took away my veil from me.—CANT. V. 7.

THE watchmen, those that by their place and standing should be so, they smote the church. As Bernard complains, almost five hundred years ago, 'Alas, alas!' saith he, 'those that do seek privileges in the church are the first in persecuting it;' and as his fashion is to speak in a kind of rhetoric, 'they were not pastors, but impostors.' There be two ordinances without which the world cannot stand.

1. Magistracy.
2. Ministry.

Magistrates are nursing fathers and nursing mothers to the church.

Ministers are watchmen by their place and standing.

Now, for shepherds to become wolves, for watchmen to become smiters, what a pitiful thing is it! But thus it is. The church hath been always persecuted with these men under pretence of religion, which is the sharpest persecution of all in the church. It is a grievous thing to suffer of an enemy, but worse of a countryman, worse then that of a friend, and worst of all, of the church. Notwithstanding, by the way, we must know that the persecuted cause is not always the best, as Austin was forced to speak in his time against the Donatists *(j)*. Sarah was a type of the true, and Hagar of the false, church. Now, Sarah, she corrected Hagar. Therefore, it follows not that the suffering cause is alway the better. Therefore, we must judge of things in these kind of passages by the cause, and not by the outward carriage of things.

'They took away my veil.'

Quest. What shall we do in such cases, if we suffer any indignity, if the veil be taken off? That is, if our shame, infirmities, and weaknesses be laid open by false imputations.

Ans. In this case it is the 'innocency of the dove' that is to be laboured for, and withal the wisdom of the serpent, Mat. x. 16. If innocency will not serve, labour for wisdom, as indeed it will not alone. The wicked would then labour for subtilty to disgrace righteous persons.

Obj. But what if that will not serve neither? Christ was wisdom itself, yet he suffered most.

Ans. When innocency and wisdom will not do it (because we must be conformable to our head), then we must labour for patience, knowing that one hair of our heads shall not fall to the ground without the providence of the Almighty.

Commend our case, as Christ did, by faith and prayer to God that judgeth.

'I charge you, O daughters of Jerusalem, if you see my beloved, that you tell him that I am sick of love,' &c.

Here the church, after her ill usage of the watchmen, is forced to the society of other Christians not so well acquainted with Christ as herself. 'I charge you, O daughters of Jerusalem, if you find my beloved,' &c., 'tell him,' &c. What shall they tell him?

'Tell him I am sick of love.'

The church is restless in her desire and pursuit after Christ till she find him. No opposition, you see, can take off her endeavour.

1. Christ seems to leave her inwardly.
2. Then she goeth to the watchmen. They 'smite and wound' her.
3. Then she hath recourse to the daughters of Jerusalem for help.

Generally, before we come to the particulars, from the connection we may observe this,

That love is a fire kindled from heaven.

Nothing in the world will quench this grace, Cant. viii. 7. 8; no opposition; nay, opposition rather whets and kindles endeavour.

The church was nothing discouraged by the ill usage of the watchmen, only she complains; she is not insensible. A Christian may without sin be sensible of indignities; only it must be the 'mourning of doves,' Isa. xxxviii. 14, and not the roaring of bears. It must not be murmuring and impatiency, but a humble complaining to God that he may take our case to heart, as the church doth here. But as sensible as she was, she was not a whit discouraged, but seeks after Christ still in other means. If she find him not in one, she will try in another. We see here the nature of love. If it be in any measure perfect, it casteth out all fear of discouragements.

And, indeed, *it is the nature of true grace to grow up with difficulties.* As the ark rose higher with the waters, so likewise the soul grows higher and higher, it mounts up as discouragements and oppositions grow. Nay, the soul takes vigour and strength from discouragements, as the wind increaseth the flame. So the grace of God, the more the winds and waves of affliction oppose it, with so much the more violence it breaks through all oppositions, until it attain the desired hope.

To apply it: those therefore that are soon discouraged, that pull in their horns presently, it is a sign they are very cold, and have but little grace. For where there is any strength of holy affection, they will not be discouraged, nor their zeal be quenched and damped. Therefore they subordinate religion to their own ends, as your temporary believers. Where is any love to Christ, the love of Christ is of a violent nature. It sways in the heart, as the apostle speaks, 'The love of Christ constraineth us,' 2 Cor. v. 14.

If we find this unconquerable resolution in ourselves, notwithstanding all discouragements to go on in a good cause, let us acknowledge that fire to be from heaven; let us not lose such an argument of the state of grace, as suffering of afflictions with joy. The more we suffer, the more we should rejoice, if the cause be good, as the apostles rejoiced 'that they were accounted worthy to suffer any thing,' Acts v. 41.

'I charge you, O daughters of Jerusalem, if you find my beloved, that ye tell him I am sick of love.'

She goes to the 'daughters of Jerusalem' for help. Whence we may learn,

That, *if we find not comfort in one means, we must have recourse to another.*

If we find not Christ present in one, seek him in another; and perhaps we shall find him where we least thought of him. Sometimes there is more comfort in the society of poor Christians, than of the watchmen themselves.

'I charge you, O daughters of Jerusalem,' &c.

Where we have, 1. A charge given. 'I charge,' &c.

2. The parties charged, 'the daughters of Jerusalem.'

3. The particular thing they are charged with, that is, if they find Christ, 'to tell him she is sick of love.'

The parties charged, are 'the daughters of Jerusalem,' the daughters of the church, which is called Jerusalem, from some resemblances between Jerusalem and the church. Some few shall be touched, to give light to the point.

1. Jerusalem was a city compact in itself, as the Psalmist saith, Ps. cxxii. 3, so is the church, the body of Christ.

2. Jerusalem was chosen from all places of the world, to be the seat of God; so the church is the seat of Christ. He dwells there in the hearts of his children.

3. It is said of Jerusalem, they went up to Jerusalem, and down to Egypt, and other places: so the church is from above, Gal. iv. 26. 'The way of wisdom is on high,' Prov. xv. 24. Religion is upward. Grace, glory, and comfort come from above; and draw our minds up to have our conversation and our desires above.

4. Jerusalem was 'the joy of the whole earth;' so the church of God, what were the world without it, but a company of incarnate devils?

5. In Jerusalem, records were kept of the names of all the citizens there; so all the true citizens of the church, their names are written in the book of life in heaven, Heb. xii. 23.

The daughters of Jerusalem therefore are the true members of the church that are both bred and fed in the church, 1 Peter i. 20; 1 Peter ii. 2. Let us take a trial of ourselves, whether we be daughters of Jerusalem or no. That we may make this trial of ourselves.

1. *If we find freedom in our conscience from terrors and fears.* If we find spiritual liberty and freedom to serve God, it is a sign that we are daughters of Jerusalem, because Jerusalem was free, Gal. iv. 26.

2. Or if we *mind things above, and things of the church.* If we take to heart the cause of the truth, it is a sign we are true 'daughters of Jerusalem.' We know what the Psalmist saith, 'Let my right hand forget her cunning if I forget thee, O Jerusalem, if I do not prefer Jerusalem before my chief joy,' Ps. cxxxviii. 5, 6. If the cause of the church go to our hearts; if we can joy in the church's joy, and mourn in the church's abasement and suffering, it is a sign we are true daughters of Jerusalem, and lively* members of the body of Christ. Otherwise, when we hear that the church goes down, and that the adverse part prevails, and we joy, it is a sign we are daughters of Babylon and not of Jerusalem.

Therefore let us ask our affections what we are, as Austin writes excellently in his book *De Civitate Dei.* 'Ask thy heart of what city thou art.'

But what saith the church to the daughters of Jerusalem? In the first place, 'I charge you.'

* That is, 'living.'—G.

It is a kind of admiration supplied thus: 'I charge you, as you love me your sister, as you love Christ, as you tender my case that am thus used, as you will make it good that you are daughters of Jerusalem and not of Babylon, 'tell my beloved, that I am sick of love.' It is a strong charge, a defective speech, which yields us this observation,

That true affections are serious in the things of God and of religion.

She lays a weight upon them, 'I charge you, O daughters of Jerusalem.' True impressions have stong expressions. Therefore are we cold in matters of religion in our discourses; it is because we want these inward impressions. The church here was full, she could not contain herself, in regard of the largeness of her affections. 'I charge you, O daughters of Jerusalem,' &c.

We may find the truth of grace in the heart, by the discoveries and expressions in the conversation in general.

'I charge you, O daughters of Jerusalem, if you find my beloved, that ye tell him I am sick of love.'

The church here speaks to others meaner than herself. She would have the church tell Christ, by prayer, the surest intelligencer, how she was used, how she languished, and was sick for him, and cannot be without him.

Quest. Why did not the church tell Christ herself?

Ans. So she did as well as she could, but she desired the help of the church this way also. Sometimes it is so with the children of God that they cannot pray so well as they should, and as they would do; because the waters of the soul are so troubled, that they can do nothing but utter groans and sighs, especially in a state of desertion, as Hezekiah could but chatter, Isa. xxxviii. 14; and Moses could not utter a word at the Red Sea, though he did strive in his spirit, Ex. xiv. 15. In such cases they must be beholden to the help of others.

Sometimes a man is in body sick, as James saith, 'If any man be sick, let him send for the elders, and let them pray,' James v. 14. There may be such distemper of body and soul, that we are unfit to lay open our estate to our own content. It is oft so with the best of God's children; not that God doth not respect those broken sighs and desires, but they give not content to the soul. The poor palsy man in the gospel, not able to go himself, was carried on the shoulders of others, and let through the house to Christ, Mark ii. 2, 3. Ofttimes we may be in such a palsy estate, that we cannot bring ourselves to Christ, but we must be content to be borne to him by others.

'I charge you, O daughters of Jerusalem, that ye tell my beloved I am sick of love.'

Whence the point that I desire you would observe is,

That at such times as we find not our spirits enlarged from any cause outward and inward, to comfort and joy, then is a time to desire the prayers and help of others.

It is good to have a stock going everywhere; and those thrive the best that have most prayers made for them; have a stock going in every country. This is the happiness of the saints. To enforce this instruction, to desire the prayers of others, we must discover, that there is a wondrous force in the prayers of Christians one for another. It is more than a compliment. Would it were so!

The great apostle Paul, see how he desires the Romans, that they would strive and contend with God after a holy violence, by their joint prayers for him, Rom. xv. 30; so he desires the Thessalonians that they would pray for him, 'that he might be delivered from unreasonable men,' 2 Thes. iii. 2. It is usual with him to say, 'Pray, pray,' and for us too; for such are gracious in the court of heaven. Despise none in this case. A true, downright, experienced Christian's prayers are of much esteem with God. Our blessed Saviour himself, when he was to go into the garden, though his poor disciples were sleepy, and very untoward, yet he would have their society and prayers, Mat. xxvi. 38 (*k*).

'I charge you, O daughters of Jerusalem, if you find my beloved, that ye tell him I am sick of love.'

To speak a little of the matter of the charge, 'I am sick of love.' I love him, because I have found former comfort, strength, and sweetness from him, that I cannot be without him. To be love-sick, then, in the presence of the church, is to have strong affections to Christ; from which comes wondrous disquietness of spirit in his absence. Here is somewhat good, and somewhat ill. This is first her virtue, that she did fervently love. This was her infirmity, that she was so much distempered with her present want. These two breed this sickness of love. Whence we observe,

Where the thing loved is not present, answerable to the desires of the soul that loves, there follows disquiet and distemper of affections. That is here termined sickness of love.*

The reason hereof is, *natural contentment is in union with the thing loved.* The more excellent the thing is that is loved, the more contentment there is in communion with it; and where it is in any degree or measure hindered, there is disquiet. Answerable to the contentment in enjoying, is the grief, sorrow, and sickness in parting. The happiness of the church consisting in society with Christ, therefore it is her misery and sickness to be deprived of him, not to enjoy him whom her soul so dearly loveth. There are few in the world sick of this disease. I would there were more sick of the love of Christ. There are many that surfeit rather of fulness, who think we have too much of this manna, of this preaching, of this gospel. There is too much of this knowledge of the ordinances. These are not sick of love.

Use. Make a use, therefore, of trial, whether we be in the state of the church or no, *by valuing and prizing the presence of Christ in his ordinances, the word and sacraments.*

There are many fond† sicknesses in the world. There is Amnon's sickness, that was sick of love for his sister Tamar, 2 Sam. xiii. 2; his countenance discovered it. And Ahab, he is sick in desiring his neighbour's vineyard, 1 Kings xxi. 1, *seq.* You have many strange sicknesses. Many sick with fires kindled from the flesh, from hell, but few sick of this sickness here spoken of.

1. If we find ourselves carried to Christ, to run in that stream as strong as the affections of those that are distempered with sickness of the love of other things, *it will discover to us whether we be truly love-sick or not.*

2. Take a man that is sick for any earthly thing, whether of Ahab's or Amnon's sickness, or of anything, take it as you will, *that which the soul is sick of in love, it thinks of daily.* It dreams of it in the night. What do our souls therefore think of? What do our meditations run after? When we are in our advised and best thoughts, what do we most think of? If of Christ, of the state of the church here, of grace and glory, all is well. What makes us, in the midst of all worldly discontentments, to think all dung and dross in comparison of Christ, but this sickness of love to Christ.

* That is, 'termed.'—G. † That is, 'foolish.'—G.

If our love be in such a degree as it makes us sick of it, it makes us not to hear what we hear, not to see what we see, not to regard what is present. The soul is in a kind of ecstasy; it is carried so strongly, and taken up with things of heaven. It is deaded to other things, when our eyes are no more led with vanity than if we had none, and the flesh is so mortified as if we were dead men, by reason of the strength of our affections that run another way, to better things which are above.

3. *Thus we see it is in love.* Talk with a man that is in any heat of affections, you talk with one that is not at home, you talk with one absent. The soul is more where it loves than where it dwells. Surely where love is in any strength it draws up the soul, so that a man ofttimes, in his calling and ordinary employments, doth not heed them, but passeth through the world as a man at random. He regards not the things of the world; for Christ is gotten into his heart, and draws all the affections to himself. Where the affection of love is strong, it cares not what it suffers for the party loved, nay, it glories in it. As it is said of the disciples, when they were whipped and scourged for preaching the gospel, it was a matter of glory to them, Acts v. 41. It is not labour, but favour. It is not labour and vexation, but favour that is taken, where love is to the party loved. Where the love of Christ is, which was here in the church, labour is no labour, suffering is no suffering, trouble is no trouble.

4. Again, *it is the property of the party that is sick of this disease, to take little contentment in other things.* Tell a covetous worldling that is in love with the world a discourse of learning, what cares he for learning? Tell him of a good bargain, of a matter of gain, and he will hearken to that. So it is with the soul that hath felt the love of Christ shed abroad in his heart. Tell him of the world, especially if he want* that which he desires, the peace and strength that he found from Christ in former times, he relisheth not your discourse.

Labour we, therefore, every day more and more to have larger and larger affections to Christ. The soul that loves Christ, the nearer to Christ the more joyful it is; when he thinks of those mutual embracings, when Christ and his soul shall meet together there. This happiness is there, where the soul enjoys the thing loved; but that is not here, but in heaven. Therefore, in the mean time, with joy he thankfully frequents the places where Christ is present in the word and sacrament. And, that we may come to have this affection, let us see what our souls are without him; mere dungeons of darkness and confusion, nothing coming from us that is good. This will breed love to the ordinances; and then we shall relish Christ both in the word and sacrament. For he is food for the hungry soul, and requires nothing of us but good appetites; and this will make us desire his love and presence.

THE THIRTEENTH SERMON.

I charge you, O daughters of Jerusalem, if ye find my beloved, that ye tell him I am sick of love. What is thy beloved more than another beloved, O thou fairest among women? &c.—CANT. V. 8, 9.

THE soul, as it is of an immortal substance, so in the right and true temper thereof, [it] aspireth towards immortality, unless when it is clouded and overpressed with that 'which presseth downwards, and the sin which hangeth so fast on,' as the apostle speaks, Heb. xii. 1,* which is the reason of those many and diverse tossings and turmoilings of the enlightened soul, now up, now down, now running amain homewards, and now again sluggish, idle, and lazy; until roused up by extraordinary means, it puts on again. As the fire mounteth upwards unto its proper place, and as the needle still trembleth till it stand at the north; so the soul, once inflamed with an heavenly fire, and acquainted with her first original, cannot be at rest until it find itself in that comfortable way which certainly leads homewards. An instance whereof we have in the church here, who, having lost her sweet communion with Christ, and so paid dearly for her former neglect and slighting his kind invitations, as being troubled, restless in mind, 'beaten and wounded by the watchmen,' bereft of her veil, &c. Yet this heavenly fire of the blessed Spirit, this 'water of life,' John iv. 10, so restlessly springing in her, makes her sickness of love and ardent desire after Christ to be such, that she cannot contain herself, but breaks forth in this passionate charge and request—

'I charge you, O daughters of Jerusalem, if ye find my beloved, that ye tell him I am sick of love.'

Thus we may see that the way to heaven is full of changes. The strength of corruption overclouds many times, and damps our joys. How many several tempers hath the church been in! Sometimes she is all compounded of joy, vehemently desiring kisses of her best beloved. She holds her beloved fast, and will not let him go; and sometimes, again, she is gone, hath lost her beloved, is in a sea of troubles, seeks and cannot find him, becomes sluggish, negligent, overtaken with self-love, after which when she hath smarted for her omissions, as here again, she is all a-fire after Christ, as we say, no ground will hold her, away she flies after him, and is restless until she find him. Where by the way we see, *that permanency and stability is for the life to come; here our portion is to expect changes, storms, and tempests.* Therefore they must not be strange to particular persons, since it is the portion of the whole church, which thus by sufferings and conformity to the head, 2 Cor. iv. 17, 18, must enter into glory, while God makes his power perfect in our weakness, 2 Cor. xii. 9, overcomes Satan by unlikely means, and so gets himself the glory, even out of our greatest infirmities, temptations, and abasements.

But God, though he make all things work for good unto his children, Rom. viii. 28, even the devil, sin, and death, desertions, afflictions and all; yet we must be warned hereby not to tempt God, by neglecting the means appointed for our comfortable passage, but open to Christ when he knocks, embrace him joyfully in his ordinances, and let our hearts fly open unto him. For though, through his mercy, our wounds be cured, yet who would be wounded to try such dangerous experiments, as here befell the church in her desertions, for her sluggish negligence, deadness, and self-love?

So that we see there is nothing gotten by favouring ourselves in carnal liberty, security, or by yielding to the flesh. The church stood upon terms with Christ when he would have come in to her; but what ensued hereupon? She fell into a grievous desertion, and not only so, but finds very hard usage abroad, all which she might have prevented by watchfulness, carefulness, and opening to Christ knocking. It is a spiritual error, to which we are all prone, to think that much is gained by favouring ourselves,

* See Note *i*.—G.

but we shall find it otherwise. See here, again, that God will bear with nothing, though in his own, but he will sharply punish them even for omissions, and that not only with desertion, but sometimes they shall meet with oppositions in the world.

David cannot scape with a proud thought in numbering of the people, but he must smart for it, and his people also, 2 Sam. xxiv. 1. God is wondrous careful of his children to correct them, when he lets strangers alone, Amos iii. 2. It is a sign of love, when he is at this cost with us. And it should tie us to be careful of our behaviour, not to presume upon God's indulgence; for the nearer we are to him, the more careful he is over us: 'He will be sanctified in all that come near him,' Lev. x. 3. We see the Corinthians, because they come unreverently to the Lord's table, though otherwise they were holy men, 'some of them are sick, some weak, others sleep, that they might not be condemned with the world,' 1 Cor. xi. 30.

Let none, therefore, think the profession of religion to imply an immunity, but rather a straighter* bond; for 'judgment begins at the house of God,' 1 Pet. iv. 17. Whatsoever he suffers abroad, he will not suffer disorders in his own house, as the prophet says, 'You only have I known of all the families of the earth, therefore you shall not go unpunished,' Amos iii. 2. The church is near him, his spouse whom he loveth, and therefore he will correct her, not enduring any abatement, or decay of the first love in her. And for this very cause he threateneth the church of Ephesus, 'to remove her candlestick,' Rev. ii. 5.

To proceed. The poor church here is not discouraged, but discovers and empties herself to the daughters of Jerusalem. As it is the nature of culinary fire, not only to mount upwards, but also to bewray itself by light and heat, so of this heavenly fire, when it is once kindled from above, not only to aspire in its motion, but to discover itself, in affecting others with its qualities. It could not contain itself here in the church, but that she must go to the daughters of Jerusalem. 'I charge you, O daughters of Jerusalem, if ye find my beloved, that ye tell him that I am sick of love.' Therefore they may doubt that they have not this heavenly fire kindled in them, that express it not seriously; for of all affections, it will not be concealed. David wonders at his own love: 'Oh, how I love thy law! Oh, how amiable are thy tabernacles!' Ps. cxix. 97.

Again, we see here, *that where the soul is sick of love, it stands not upon any terms, but it humbleth and abaseth itself*. We say that affection stands not with majesty. Therefore Christ's love to us moved him to abase himself in taking our nature, that he might be one with us. Love stood not upon terms of greatness. We see the church goes to those that were meaner proficients in religion than herself, to pour out her spirit to them, 'to the daughters of Jerusalem.' She abaseth herself to any service, 1 Thess. ii. 8. Love endureth all things, 1 Cor. xiii. 7, anything to attain to the thing loved; as we see Hamor the son of Shechem,† he would endure painful circumcision for the love he bore to Dinah, Gen. xxxiv. 24. So, Acts v. 41, it is said they went away rejoicing, after they were whipped, because they loved Christ. The spirit of love made them rejoice, when they were most disgracefully used.

Sometimes where this affection of heavenly love is prevalent, so that a man is sick of it, the distempers thereof redounds to the body, and reflects upon that, as we see in David: 'That his moisture became as the drought of summer,' Ps. xxxii. 4; because there is a marriage and a sympathy

* Qu. 'straiter?'—ED. † 'Shechem the son of Hamor.'—ED.

between the soul and the body, wherein the excessive affections of the one redound and reflect upon the other.

'Tell him that I am sick of love.' Here is a sickness, but not unto death, but unto life; a sickness that never ends but in comfort and satisfaction. Blessed are those that hunger and thirst after Christ, they shall be satisfied, Mat. v. 6, as we shall see afterwards more at large.

Knowledge gives not the denomination, *for we may know ill and be good, and we may know good and be evil;* but it is the affection of the soul which cleaves to the things known. The truth of our love is that gives the denomination of a state to be good or ill. Love is the weight and wing of the soul, which carries it where it goes; which, if it carry us to earth, we are base and earthly; if to heaven, heavenly. We should have especial care how we fix this affection; for thereafter as it is, even so is our condition. 'Ask thy love of what city thou art, whether of Jerusalem or Babylon,' as Austin saith. Now the daughters of Jerusalem reply unto the church, wondering at her earnestness,

'What is thy beloved more than another beloved, O thou fairest among women? what is thy beloved more than another beloved, that thou dost so charge us?'

Instead of giving satisfaction to her, they reply with asking new questions, 'What is thy beloved more than another beloved, O thou fairest among women? what is thy beloved,' &c. Wherein ye have a doubling of the question, to shew the seriousness of it. Of this their answer there are two parts.

1. A loving and sweet compellation, 'O thou fairest among women.'

2. The question doubled, 'What is thy beloved more than another beloved?' And again, 'What is thy beloved,' &c., 'that thou dost so charge us?' As if they should say, 'Thou layest a serious charge upon us; therefore there is some great matter surely in thy beloved that thou makest such inquiry after him.' Thus the weaker Christians being stirred up by the example of the stronger, they make this question, and are thus inquisitive. But to speak of them in their order.

'O thou fairest among women.' Here is the compellation. The church is the fairest among women in the judgment of Christ. So he calls her, 'O thou fairest among women,' Cant. i. 8; and here the fellow-members of the church term her so too; fair, and the fairest, incomparably fair.

Quest. But how cometh she to be thus fair?

Ans. 1. *It is in regard that she is clothed with Christ's robes.* There is a woman mentioned clothed with the sun, Rev. xii. 1. We were all ennobled with the image of God at the first, but after we had sinned we were bereft of that image. Therefore now all our beauty must be clothing, which is not natural to man, but artificial; fetched from other things. Our beauty now is borrowed. It is not connatural with us. The beauty of the church now comes from the Head of the church, Christ. She shines in the beams of her husband, not only in justification, but in sanctification also.

2. The church is lovely and fair again, *as from Christ's imputative righteousness, so from his righteousness inherent in her, the graces she hath from him.* For of him we receive grace for grace. There is never a grace but it is beautiful and fair; for what is grace but the beams of Christ, the Sun of righteousness? So that all must be fair that comes from the first fair, all beautiful that comes from the first beauty.

This beauty of grace, whereby it makes the church so fair, springs from these grounds.

First. *In that it is from a divine principle and original. It is not basely bred, but from heaven.* And therefore it raiseth the soul above nature, and makes the subjects wherein it is as far surpass all other men, as men do beasts.

Secondly. In regard of the continuance, *it is everlasting, and makes us continue for ever.* 'All flesh is grass, and as the flower of grass,' saith the prophet, Isa. xl. 6; and it is repeated in the New Testament in divers places. All worldly excellency is as the flower of grass. 'The grass withereth and the flower fadeth, but the word of the Lord (that is, the grace that is imprinted in the soul by the Spirit with the word), that abideth for ever,' 1 Pet. i. 24, and makes us abide likewise.

Use 1. From this fairness of the church, let us take occasion to contemplate of the excellency of Christ that puts this lustre of beauty upon the church. Moses married a woman that was not beautiful, but could not alter the complexion and condition of his spouse. But Christ doth. He takes us wallowing in our blood, deformed and defiled. He is such a husband as can put into his church his own disposition, and transform her into his own proportion. He is such a head as can quicken his members; such a root as instils life into all his branches; such a foundation as makes us living stones. There is a virtue and power in this husband above all.

Obj. But she is black.

Ans. She is so, indeed, and she confesseth herself to be so. 'I am black, but comely,' Cant. i. 5. (1.) Black in regard of the afflictions and persecutions of others she meets with in this world.

(2.) Black, again, in regard of scandals; for the devil hates the church more than all societies in the world. Therefore, in the society of the church there are often more scandals than in other people; as the apostle tells the Corinthians there was incest amongst them, the like was not among the heathen, 1 Cor. v. 1.

(3.) She is black through the envy of the world, that looks more at the church's faults than virtues.

(4.) The church is black and unlovely, nothing differing from others, in regard of God's outward dealing. 'All falls alike to all,' Eccles. ix. 2. They are sick and deformed. They have all things outwardly whatsoever in common with others.

(5.) Lastly and principally, she is black, in respect of her infirmities and weaknesses; subject to weakness and passions, as other men. The beauty of the church is inward, and undiscerned to the carnal eye altogether. The Scribes and Pharisees see no virtue in Christ himself. It is said, 'that he came among his own, and his own could not discern of him: the darkness could not comprehend that light,' John i. 5, 11. Now, as it was with Christ, so it is much more with the church. Let this, then, be the use of it.

Use 2. *Oppose this state of the church to the false judgment of the world.* They see all black, and nothing else that is good. Christ sees that which is black, too; but then his Spirit in them (together with the sight of their blackness) seeth their beauty, too. 'I am black, but comely,' &c. Be not discouraged, therefore, at the censure of the world. Blind men cannot judge of colours. It is said of Christ, 'he had no form or beauty in him, when we shall see him,' Isa. liii. 2. (1.) Not in outward glory, nor (2.) in the view of the world. If we be, therefore, thought to be black, we are no otherwise thought of than the church and Christ hath been before us.

Use 3. Again, let us make this use of it *against Satan in the time of temptation.* Doth Christ think us fair for the good we have? Doth he not altogether value us by our ill? and shall we believe Satan, who joins with the distempers of melancholy or weakness we are in (which he useth as a weapon against the soul), to make us think otherwise? 'Satan is not only a murderer, but a liar from the beginning,' John viii. 44. We must not believe an enemy and a liar withal. But consider how Christ and the church judgeth, that have better discerning. And let us beware we be not Satans* to ourselves; for if there were no devil, yet in the time of temptation and desertion we are subject to discouragement, to give false witness against ourselves. We are apt to look on the dark side of the cloud. The cloud that went before the Israelites had a double aspect, one dark, the other light, Exod. xiv. 20. In temptation we look on the dark side of the soul, and are witty in pleading against ourselves. Oh, but consider what Christ judgeth of us, 'O! thou fairest among women;' and what those about us that are learned, who can read our evidences better than we ourselves, do judge of us. Let us trust the judgment of others in time of temptation more than our own.

Use 4. Learn again here, *what to judge of the spirits of such kind of men as are all in disgracing and defacing the poor church.* Their table talk is of the infirmities of Christians. They light upon them as flies do upon sore places, and will see nothing that is good in them. Oh! where is the Spirit of Christ, or of the church of Christ, in them that thus bescratch the face of the church? when yet ofttimes their hearts tell them these poor despised ones will be better than themselves one day, for grace shall have the upper hand of all excellences.

The church is fair and fairest. Grace is a transcendent good. All the excellency of civility and morality is nothing to this. This denominates the church the fairest. She is not gilt, but pure gold; not painted, but hath a true natural complexion. All other excellencies are but gilt, painted excellencies. 'The whore of Babylon,' she is wondrous fair! But wherein doth her beauty consist? In ornaments and ceremonies to abuse silly people that go no further than fancy. It is an excellency that comes not to the judgment, but the excellency of the church is otherwise. She is 'the fairest among women.' She hath a natural fairness. As gold is pure gold, so the church is of a pure composition, glorious within. It is for the false, whorish church to be glorious without only, but the true church is glorious within. But that which we should especially observe is, *that we should labour to answer this commendation; not only to be fair, but the fairest; to be transcendently, singularly good; to do somewhat more than others can; to have somewhat more in us than others have.*

For it is answerable to the state of a Christian. Is a Christian in an excellent rank above other men? Let him shew it by a carriage more gracious, more fruitful and plentiful in good works. There is a kind of excellency affected in other things, much more should we desire to be excellent in that that is good, that we may not be fair only, but the fairest. This the apostle St Paul excellently presseth to Titus, his scholar, Tit. ii. 14,† and to all of us in other places, that we should be 'a peculiar people, zealous of good works,' not only to do them, but to be zealous of them, and to go before others in them, standing as standard-bearers. Therefore those that think they may go too far in religion, that they may be too fruitful, are not worthy the name of the spouse of Christ; for she is fair, yea, the fairest among women, 'The righteous is more excellent than his neighbour,' Prov. xii. 26. Therefore we should excel in good works, as the apostle

* That is, 'accusers' or 'adversaries.'—G.

† 'Jesus Christ, who gave himself for us that he might redeem us from all iniquity, and purify unto himself a *peculiar* people.'

exhorts us, 'to labour after things that are excellent,' 1 Cor. xii. 31; 2 Pet. i. 8, as if he should say, Is there anything better than other, labour for that. You have some so far from this disposition that they cry down the excellencies of others, lest the fairness of others might discover their blackness. Thus we leave the compellation, and come to the question.

Quest. 'What is thy beloved more than another beloved?' And they double it, 'What is thy beloved more than another beloved, that thou so chargest us?'

Questions are of divers natures. We shall not stand upon them. This is not a question merely of ignorance, for they had some knowledge of Christ, though weak. Nor was it a curious nor a catching question, like those of the scribes and pharisees unto Christ, to instance in that of Pilate, 'What is truth?' John xviii. 38, when Christ had told him the truth. 'What is truth?' saith he, in a scornful, profane manner (*l*), as indeed profane spirits cannot hear savoury words, but they turn them off with scorn, 'What is truth?' This here in the text is not such, but a question tending to further resolution and satisfaction, 'What is thy beloved more than another beloved?'

First of all, observe that these of the church here were stirred up by the examples of other members of the church to be inquisitive after Christ, so to be satisfied. Hence observe *that there is a wondrous force in the examples of Christians to stir up one another.* We see here, when the church was sick of love, the other part of the members began to think, what is the reason the church is so earnest to seek after Christ? There is some excellency sure in him. For wise men do not use great motions in little matters. Great things are carried with great movings. We use not to stir up tragedies for trifles, to make mountains of mole-hills. The endeavours and carriages of great persons that be wise, judicious, and holy are answerable to the nature of things. And indeed the church judgeth aright in this. Then see the force of good example. Any man that hath his wits about him, when he sees others serious, earnest, and careful about a thing, whereof for the present he can see no reason, especially if they have parts equal or superior to himself, will reason thus presently:—

What is the matter that such a one is so earnest, so careful, watchful, laborious, inquisitive? It is not for want of wit; surely he hath parts enough, he understands himself well. And then he begins to think, sure I am too cold. Hereupon come competition and co-rivality,* surely I will be as good as he.

Use. Let us labour, therefore, to be exemplary to others, and to express the graces of God; for thus we shall do more than we are aware. There is a secret influence in good example. Though a man say nothing, saith one, there is a way to profit from a good man though he hold his peace. His course of life speaks loud enough. We owe this to all, even to them that are without, to do them so much good as to give them a good example, and we wrong them when we do not, and hinder their coming on by an evil or a dead example.

Let this be one motive to stir us up to it, *that answerable to the good we shall do in this kind shall be our comfort in life and death, and our reward after death.* For the more spreading our good is either in word, life, or conversation, the more our consciences shall be settled in the consideration of a good life well spent, our reward shall be answerable to our communication and diffusion of good; and whereas otherwise it will lie heavy on the

* That is, 'mutual emulation.'—G.

conscience, not only in this life, but at the day of judgment and after; when we shall think not only of the personal ill that we stand guilty of, but exemplary ill also.

It should move those therefore of inferior sort to look to all good examples, as the church here to the love of the other part of the church. Wherefore are examples among us but that we should follow them? We shall not only be answerable for abuse of knowledge, but also of good examples we have had and neglected. Doth God kindle lights for us, and shall not we walk by their light? It is a sin not to consider the sun, the moon, the stars, the heavens, and works of nature and providence, much more not to consider the works of grace. But one place of Scripture shall close up all, which is, Rom. xi. 11, that the example of us Gentiles at length shall stir up and provoke the Jews to believe. To those stiff-necked Jews example shall be so forcible that it shall prevail with them to believe and to be converted. If example be of such force as to convert the Jews that are so far off, how much more is it or should it be to convert Christians! Wondrous is the force of good example! So we come to the question itself,

'What is thy beloved more than another beloved?' &c.

We see there is excellent use of holy conference. The church coming to the daughters of Jerusalem, speaking of Christ her beloved, that she is 'sick of love,' &c., the daughters of Jerusalem are inquisitive to know Christ more and more. Here is the benefit of holy conference and good speeches. One thing draws on another, and that draws on another, till at length the soul be warmed and kindled with the consideration and meditation of heavenly things. That that is little in the beginning may bring forth great matters. This question to the church and talking with her, 'I charge you, if you find my beloved, to tell him that I am sick of love,' breeds questions in others, 'What is thy beloved?' &c. Whence, upon the description of her beloved, her heart is kindled, she findeth her beloved; so that talking of holy and heavenly things is good for others and ourselves also.

It is good for others, as it was good for the daughters of Jerusalem here; for thereupon they are stirred up to be inquisitive after Christ. And it was good for the church herself, for hereupon she took occasion to make a large commendation of Christ, wherein she found much comfort.

2. Good conference, then, is *good for ourselves;* for we see a little seed brings forth at length a great tree, a little fire kindleth much fuel, and great things many times rise out of small beginnings. It was a little occasion which Naaman the Assyrian* had to effect his conversion, 2 Kings v. 2. There was a poor banished woman, a stranger, who was a Jewish maidservant. She told her lord's servants that there was a prophet in Jewry that could heal him, whereupon he came thither, and was converted and healed. And Paul sheweth that the very report of his bonds did a great deal of good in Cæsar's house, Philip. i. 13. Report and fame is a little matter, but little matters make way for the greater.

This may put us in mind *to spend our time fruitfully in good conference, when in discretion it is seasonable.* We know not, when we begin, where we may make an end. Our souls may be carried up to heaven before we are aware, for the Spirit will enlarge itself from one thing to another. 'To him that hath shall be given more and more still,' Mat. xiii. 12. God graciously seconds good beginnings. We see the poor disciples, when they were in a damp for the loss of Christ, after he comes, meets them, and talks of holy things. In that very conference their hearts were warmed and

* 'Syrian.'—ED.

kindled, Luke xxiv. 32. For, next to heaven itself, our meeting together here, it is a kind of paradise. The greatest pleasure in the world is to meet with those here whom we shall ever live with in heaven. Those who are good should not spend such opportunities fruitlessly.

And to this end, labour for the graces of the communion of saints; for there is such a state. We believe it as an article of our creed. How shall we approve ourselves to be such as have interest unto the communion of saints, unless we have spirits able to communicate good to others? pitiful and loving spirits, that we may speak a word in due season.

What a world of precious time is spent in idle conversing, as if the time were a burden, and no improvement to be made of the good parts of others. Sometimes, though we know that which we ask of others as well as they do, yet notwithstanding good speeches will draw us to know it better, by giving occasion to speak more of it, wherewith the Spirit works more effectually and imprints it deeper, so that it shall be a more rooted knowledge than before; for that doth good that is graciously known, and that is graciously known that the Spirit seals upon our souls. Perhaps the knowledge I have is not yet sealed sufficiently; it is not rooted by conference. Though I hear the same things again, yet I may hear them in a fresh manner, and so I may have it sealed deeper than before. Experience finds these things to be true.

Again, *we should labour here to have our hearts inquisitive.* The heathen man accounted it a grace in his scholar, and a sign that he would prove hopeful, because he was full of questions. Christians should be inquisitive of the ways of righteousness; inquisitive of the right path which leads to heaven; how to carry themselves in private, in their families; how in all estates; inquisitive of the excellency of Christ. 'What is thy beloved more than another beloved?' Questions end usually in resolutions; for the soul will not rest but in satisfaction. Rest is the happiness of the soul, as it were. When a question is moved, it will not be quiet till it have satisfaction. Therefore doubting at the first, breeds resolution at the last. It is good therefore to raise questions of the practice of all necessary points; and to improve the good parts and gifts of others that we converse with, to give satisfaction. What an excellent improvement is this of communion and company, when nothing troubles our spirit, but we may have satisfaction from others upon our proposing it. Perhaps God hath laid up in the parts of others, satisfaction to our souls; and hath so determined that we shall be perplexed and vexed with scruples, till we have recourse to some whom he hath appointed to be helpful to us in this kind. Many go mourning a great part of their days in a kind of sullenness this way, because that they do not open their estate to others. You see here the contrary practice of the church. She doubles the question: 'What is thy beloved more than another beloved, O thou fairest among women? what is thy beloved more than another beloved, that thou dost so charge us?

THE FOURTEENTH SERMON.

What is thy beloved more than another beloved, O thou fairest among women? what is thy beloved more than another beloved, that thou dost so charge us? My beloved is white and ruddy, the chiefest among ten thousand.—CANT. V. 9, 10.

THE last time we met we left the church sick of love; which strange affection in her, together with her passionate charge to the daughters of Jerusalem, moved them to make this question unto her, 'What is thy beloved more than another beloved,' &c. To be in love is much; to conceal it is grievous; to vent it with such fervency and passion breeds astonishment in these younger Christians, who wonder what that is which can so draw away the church's love, and run away with her affections. They knew no such excellencies of the person the church so admired, and therefore they double the question unto her, 'What is thy beloved?' &c. 'what is thy beloved?' &c. Whereby we see the excellency of the soul which aspires still towards perfection; not resting in any state inferior to the most excellent. Therefore also is the church's sickness of love here, who desires a nearer union and communion with Christ than she at this time had.

For there are degrees of spiritual languishing. *Till we be in heaven we are always under some degree of this sickness of love;* though the soul have more communion at one time than at another. Yea, the angels are under this wish to see Christ, together with his church, in full perfection. So that until we be in heaven, where shall be a perfect reunion of soul and body, and of all the members of the church together, there is a kind of sickness attending upon the church and a languishing.

The question asked is,

'What is thy beloved more than another's beloved, O thou fairest among women?'

What! now fair when her veil was taken away? now fair when the watchmen abased* her? now fair when she was disgraced? Yes; now fair, and now fair in the sight of the daughters of Jerusalem, and in the sight of Christ that calls her the fairest among women. So that under all disgraces, infirmities, and scandals; under all the shame that riseth in the soul upon sin; under all these clouds there is an excellency of the church. She is, 'the fairest among women,' notwithstanding all these. 'O thou fairest among women.'

Quest. Whence comes this fairness, under such seeming foulness and disgrace?

Ans. It comes from without. It is borrowed beauty, as you have it, Ezek. xvi. 1, 2. By nature we lie in our blood. There must be a beauty put upon us. We are fair with the beauty that we have out of Christ's wardrobe. The church shines in the beams of Christ's righteousness; she is not born thus fair, but new-born fairer. The church of Christ is all glorious, but it is within, not seen of the world, Ps. xlv. 13. She hath a life, but it is a hidden life, 'our glory and our life is hidden in Christ,' Col. iii. 3. It is hid sometimes from the church itself, who sees only her deformity and not her beauty, her death but not her life, because her 'life is hid.' Here is a mystery of religion, *The church is never more fair than when she judgeth herself to be most deformed; never more happy than when she judgeth herself to be miserable: never more strong than when she feels herself to be weak; never more righteous than when she feels herself to be most burdened with the guilt of her own sins,* because the sense of one contrary forceth to another. The sense of ill forceth us to the fountain of good, to have supply thence. 'When I am weak, then am I strong,' saith Paul, 2 Cor. xii. 10. Grace and strength is perfect in weakness.

Use. This should teach us what to judge of the church and people of God; even under their seeming disgraces, yet to judge of them as the excellentest people in the world, 'All my delight is in those that are ex-

* Qu. 'abused?'—G.

cellent,' Ps. xvi. 3; to join ourselves to them. Especially this is here to be understood of the church, as it is the mystical body of Christ; not as a mixed body, as a visible church, 'but as it is the temple of the Holy Ghost,' 1 Cor. iii. 17.

The visible church hath terms of excellency put upon it sometimes, but it is in regard of the better part. As gold unrefined is called gold, because gold is the better part; and a heap of wheat unwinnowed is called wheat, though there be much chaff in it. The body of Christ itself hath always excellent terms given it, 'O thou fairest among women.'

Those that look upon the church with the spectacles of malice can see no such beauty in her, though to espy out faults (as the devil could in Job, Job i. 9, *seq.*), to quarrel, to slander, they are quick-sighted enough. But we see here the church in the judgment of the 'daughters of Jerusalem,' that she is the 'fairest among women.'

The papists have a painted beauty for their catholic church, but here is no such beauty. It becomes a whore to be painted to be as fair as her hands can make her, with feigned beauty. But the church of Christ hath a beauty from her husband, a real, spiritual beauty, not discerned of the world.

Use. This should be of use to God's children themselves, *to help them in the upbraidings of conscience* (as if they had no goodness in them), *because they have a great deal of ill.* Christians should have a double eye, one to set and fix upon that which is ill in them, to humble them; and another upon that which is supernaturally gracious in them, to encourage themselves. They should look upon themselves as Christ looks upon them, and judge of themselves as he judgeth of them, by the better part. He looks not so much what ill we have, for that shall be wrought out by little and little, and be abolished. It is condemned already, and it shall be executed by little and little, till it be wholly abolished. But he looks upon us in regard of the better part. So should we look upon ourselves, though otherwhiles upon our black feet (our infirmities) when we are tempted to pride and haughtiness. But always let the mean thoughts we conceive of ourselves make us to fly to Christ.

'What is thy beloved more than another beloved?'

Here is a question, and a question answered with a question. Questions they breed knowledge; as the Greek proverb is, doubtings breed resolution. Whereupon the inquisitive soul usually proves the most learned, judicious, and wise soul. Therefore that great philosopher* counted it as a virtue amongst his scholars that they would be inquisitive. So the scholars of righteousness are inquisitive, 'They inquire the way to Canaan, and the way to Zion with their faces thitherwards,' Jer. l. 5.

It is a special part of Christians' wisdom to improve the excellency of others by questions; to have a bucket to draw out of the deep wells of others. As Solomon saith, 'The heart of a wise man is as deep waters, but a man of understanding can tell how to fetch those waters out.' There be many men of deep and excellent parts which are lost in the world, because men know not how to improve them. Therefore it is good, while we have men excellent in any kind, to make use of them. It is an honour to God as well as a commodity to ourselves. Doth God suffer lights to shine in the world that we should take no notice of them? It is a wrong to ourselves and a dishonour to God.

'What is thy beloved more than another beloved?' &c.

A further point from hence is, *that if we would give encouragement to others*

* That is, Socrates in Plato's 'Dialogues.'—G.

to repair to us for any good, we should learn to be so excellent as to adorn religion.

'O thou fairest among women, what is thy beloved?' &c. They inquire of her, because they have a good conceit of her. A world of good might be done if there were bred a good conceit of men in others. We say in sickness, A good conceit of the physician is half the cure. So in teaching, a good conceit of the teacher is half the learning. 'The daughters of Jerusalem' had a good conceit here in their questioning of the church. 'O thou fairest among women, what is thy beloved more than another beloved?'

Let us labour, therefore, to be such as may bring honour and credit to religion, and make it lovely; that what we do may make others think we do what we do to great purpose; which is ofttimes a special means and occasion of their conversion. Though properly the cause of conversion be the Spirit of God in the ordinances, yet the inducement, many times, and occasion, is the observation of the course and carriage of those that excel and are known to be eminent in parts and in graces. Emulation adds spurs to the soul. Do they take such courses that are wiser than I, and shall not I take the like course too? Paul saith, the emulation of the Gentiles shall be a means of the conversion of the Jews, Rom. xi. 11. When they shall see them embrace Christ, they will be encouraged to do so also. What shall we think, therefore, of them that live so as that they bring an evil report, scandal, and reproach upon religion? Great and fearful is their wickedness, that by their ill conversation, like Hophni and Phinehas, discredit the ordinances of the Lord, 1 Sam. ii. 17.

Now the church thus answers the former question touching Christ, 'My beloved is white and ruddy, the chiefest of ten thousand.' She is not afraid to set out her beloved's beauty; for there is no envy in spiritual things. It is want of wisdom amongst men to commend a thing that is very lovely to others, and so to set an edge upon their affections when they cannot both share; and the more one hath, the less another hath of all things here below. But in spiritual things there is no envy at the sharing of others in that we love ourselves, because all may be loved alike. Christ hath grace and affection enough for all his. He hath not, as Esau speaks, but 'one blessing.' No, he can make all his happy. Therefore the church stands not upon terms. When the 'daughters of Jerusalem' inquire about her beloved, I tell you freely, says she, what my beloved is. First, in general, the answer is, 'My beloved is white and ruddy, the chiefest among ten thousand.' Then afterwards there is a specification of the particulars. She will not stand upon the gross, but admires* at every parcel in the thing beloved. Every thing is lovely, as we shall see in particulars afterwards.

'My beloved is white and ruddy, the chiefest among ten thousand.'

We will take that which is safe, because we will have sure footing, as near as we can, in this mystical portion of Scripture.

Quest. What is that white and ruddy? Why doth the church set forth the spiritual excellencies of Christ by that which is most outwardly excellent and most beautiful?

Ans. Because of all complexions, the mixed complexion of these two colours, white and ruddy, is the purest and the best. Therefore she sets out the beauty and the spiritual excellency of Christ by this 'white and ruddy.' Beauty ariseth of the mixture of these two. First, she sets out the beauty of Christ positively; and then, by way of comparison, 'the chiefest among ten thousand.

* That is, 'wonders.'—G.

But what is this white and ruddy? what is beauty?

1. To the making of beauty there is required a sound, healthy constitution, so as *the particulars have a due proportion*. There must be a harmony of the parts, one suiting with one another; for comeliness stands in oneness, when many things, as it were, are one. Uncomeliness is in diversity, when diverse things are jumbled together that belong to many heads; as we say it is uncomely to have an old man's head on a young man's shoulders. But when all things are so suited that they make one, agreeing exactly, there is beauty and comeliness.

2. Besides soundness of constitution and comeliness of proportion, *there is a grace of colour* that maketh beauty, which ariseth out of the other. So that soundness and goodness of constitution, together with the exact proportion of the variety of parts, having with it this gracefulness of colour and complexion, makes up that which we call beauty. In a word, then, this carnation colour, white and ruddy, may be understood of that excellent and sweet mixture that makes such a gracefulness in Christ. In him there is wonderful purity and holiness, and yet a wonderful weakness. There is God the 'great God' and a piece of earth, of flesh in one person; a bloody, pierced, and a glorious shining body; humility and glory: justice, wonderful justice, and yet exceeding love and mercy: justice to his enemies, mercy to his children.

Obs. Christ is a most beautiful person, not as God only, but as man, the Mediator, God and man. The person of the Mediator is a beautiful person, as Ps. xlv. 2, there is a notable description of Christ and of his church, 'Thou art fairer than the children of men, grace is poured into thy lips,' &c.

But the loveliness and beauty of Christ *is especially spiritual*, in regard of the graces of his Spirit. A deformed person, man or woman, of a homely complexion and constitution, yet, notwithstanding, when we discern them by their conversation to be very wise and of a lovely and sweet spirit, very able and withal wondrous willing to impart their abilities, being wondrous useful; what a world of love doth it breed, though we see in their outward man nothing lovely? The consideration of what sufficiency is in Christ, wisdom, power, goodness, and love, that made him come from heaven to earth, to take our nature upon him, to marry us, and join our nature to his (that he might join us to him in spiritual bonds): the consideration of his meekness and gentleness, how he never turned any back again that came to him, should make us highly prize him. Indeed some went back of themselves (as the young man in discontent, Mat. xix. 32), Christ turned them not back; nay, he loved the appearance of goodness in the young man, and embraced him. He is of so sweet a nature that he never upbraided those that followed him with their former sins, as Peter with denial, and the like. He is of so gracious a nature that he took not notice of petty infirmities in his disciples, but tells them of the danger of those sins that might hurt them: being of so sweet a nature that 'he will not quench the smoking flax, nor break the bruised reed,' Isa. xlii. 3; his whole life being nothing but a doing of good, 'he did all things well' (as the gospel speaks), excellent well, Mark vii. 37.

Now, the consideration of what a gracious Spirit is in Christ, must needs be a loadstone of love, and make him beautiful. Therefore Bernard saith well, When I think of Christ, I think at once of God, full of majesty and glory; and, at the same time, of man, full of meekness, gentleness, and sweetness. So, let us consider of Christ as of the 'mighty God,' powerful; and withal consider of him as a gentle and mild man, that came riding meekly on an ass, as the Scripture sets him out,' Mat. xxi. 5. He was for comers, and gave entertainment to all: 'Come unto me, all ye that are weary and heavy laden,' &c., Mat. xi. 28. For the most weak and miserable person of all had the sweetest entertainment of him, 'He came to seek and to save that which was lost,' Luke xix. 10. Let us, I say, think of him both as of the great God, and withal as of meek man: the one to establish our souls, that he is able to do great matters; the other to draw us to him because he loves us. We are afraid to go to God, 'a consuming fire,' Heb. xii. 29; but now let us think we go to bone of our bone and flesh of our flesh, to our brother, to one that out of his goodness abased himself of purpose that we might be one with him: who loved us more than his own life, and was contented to carry the curse for us, that we might be blessed of God for ever, and to suffer a most painful and shameful death, that so he might make us heirs of everlasting life.

Christ is spiritually lovely, 'the chiefest of ten thousand.' The church sets him out by comparison, 'a standard-bearer,' a carrier of the 'banner of ten thousand.' For, as the goodliest men use to carry the ensign, the banner; so he, the goodliest of all other, is the standard-bearer.

Obs. Whence we gather, *that Christ, as he is beautiful and good, so he is incomparably, beyond all comparison good;* 'He is a standard bearer, one among ten thousand; anointed with the oil of gladness above his fellows,' Ps. xlv. 7.

First, *for that he is so near to God by the personal union.*

And in regard likewise, *that all others have all from him.* Of his fulness we receive grace for grace, John i. 16. Ours is but a derivative fulness. His glory and shining is as the shining of the body of the sun; ours as the light of the air, which is derived from the glory of the sun. Ours is but the fulness of the stream, and of the vessel, but the fulness of the fountain and of the spring is his. Thereupon he is called 'the head of the church,' Col. i. 18; the head is the tower of the body which hath all the five senses in it, and wisdom for the whole body. It seeth, heareth, understandeth, and doth all for the body; having influence into the other parts of it. So Christ is above all, and hath influence into all his church, not only eminence, but influence.

What is excellent in the heavens? The sun. So Christ is the 'Sun of righteousness,' Mal. iv. 2. The stars. He is the 'bright morning star,' Rev. xxii. 16. The light. He is the 'light of the world,' John ix. 5. Come to all creatures; you have not any excellent amongst them but Christ is styled from it. He is 'the lion of the tribe of Judah,' Rev. v. 5, the 'lily,' Cant. ii. 1, and the 'rose,' Cant. ii. 1, and 'the Lamb of God that taketh away the sins of the world,' John i. 29, 'the tree of Life,' &c., Rev. xxii. 2. There is not a thing necessary to nature, but you have a style from it given to Christ, to shew that he is as necessary as bread and water, and the food of life, John vi. 35; John iv. 14. When we see light, therefore, think of the 'true light,' John ix. 5. When the sun, think of the 'Sun of righteousness,' Mal. iv. 2. So remember 'the bread and water of life,' in our common food. Therefore the sacraments were ordained, that as we go to the sea by the conduct of rivers, so we might go to the sea of all excellency and goodness by the conduct of these rivers of goodness, to be led by every excellency in the creature, to that of our mediator Christ, who is 'the chiefest among ten thousand.'

To come more particularly to speak of his excellencies, omitting his two natures in one person, God and man; that we may consider his offices, a king, priest and prophet. He being the chief in all these, so all good kings before him were types of him, as also the prophets and priests. He was all in one. Never any before him was king, priest, and prophet, as he was king, priest, and prophet in one. So in every respect he was incomparable above all.

1. *Such a king, as is king of kings;* and subdueth things unconquerable to all other kings, even the greatest enemies of all; such a king as conquered the world, death, hell, and sin, all things that are terrible. Death you know is called 'the king of fears,* because it terrifieth even kings themselves. Christ is such a king as takes away these terrible greatest ills of all; such a king as rules over the soul and conscience, the best part of man, where he settles and stablisheth peace; such a king as sets up his kingdom in our very souls and hearts, guides our thoughts, desires, actions, and affections, setting up a peaceable government there. So he is an incomparable king even in regard of that office. 'He is the chiefest of ten thousand;' such a king as carries the government upon his own shoulders, as it is Isa. ix. 6. He devolves not the care to another, to make it as he list and so be a cypher himself, but he carries all upon his own shoulder. He needs not a pope for his vicar.

2. Again, as a *priest, such a high priest as offered himself a sacrifice by his* eternal Spirit. He as God offered up his manhood. Such a priest as hath satisfied the wrath of God, and reconciled God to man. All other priests were but types of this priest, who is such a priest as never dies, 'but lives for ever to make intercession for us in heaven,' by virtue of that sacrifice which he offered in the days of his flesh. He was both priest and sacrifice. Such a 'priest as is touched with our infirmities;' so mild and gentle, full of pity and mercy. No priest to this priest. God only smelt a sweet smell from this sacrifice.

3. And for his *prophetical office, he is a prophet beyond all others.* Such a one as can instruct the soul. Other men can propound doctrines, but he can open the understanding, and hath the key of the heart, the 'key of David which can open the soul,' Luke xxiv. 45. By his Holy Spirit he can make the very simple full of knowledge, Prov. i. 4. Such a prophet as hath his chair in the very heart of man; this great 'Bishop of our souls,' 1 Pet. ii. 25, 'the Angel of the covenant,' that Λογὸς, 'the messenger of the Father.' So he is 'the chief of ten thousand,' consider him as king, as priest, or as prophet.

Use. The use of this is exceeding pregnant, comfortable, and large, that we have such a Saviour, such an eminent person, so near, so peculiar to us. Our beloved, my beloved. If he were *a* 'beloved, the chief of ten thousand,' it were no great matter, but he is mine. He is thus excellent; excellent considered with propriety in it, and a peculiar propriety.† Peculiarity and propriety, together with transcendent excellency, makes happy if there be any enjoying of it. Therefore repent not yourselves of your repentings, but think I have not cast away my love, but have set it upon such an object as deserves it, 'for my beloved is the chiefest of ten thousand.'

* Cf. Job. xviii. 14.—G

† That is, 'property' = right.—G.

THE FIFTEENTH SERMON.

My beloved is white and ruddy, the chiefest among ten thousand.—CANT. V. 10.

LOVE is such a boundless affection, that where it once breaks forth in praises upon a good foundation, it knows no measure; as we see here in the church, who being provoked and, as it were, exasperated by the 'daughters of Jerusalem' to explain the excellency of him she had with so much affection incessantly sought after, that she might justify her choice (ere she descend into particulars), she breaks forth into this general description of her beloved; whereby she cuts off from all hopes of equalling him, 'My beloved is white and ruddy' (exceeding fair), nay, 'the chief among ten thousand' (none like him). She would not have us think she had bestowed her love but on the most excellent of all, 'the chief of ten thousand.' Well were it for us that we could do so in our love, that we might be able to justify our choice; not to spend it on sinful, vain, and unprofitable things, which cause repentance and mourning in the conclusion, whereof the church here worthily cleareth herself; in that she had chosen 'the chief among ten thousand.'

And most justly did she place her affections upon so excellent an object, who was so full of 'all the treasures of wisdom and knowledge, the life of our life, in whom dwelt all the fulness of the Godhead bodily,' Col. i. 11, 19; in whom was a gracious mixture and compound of all heavenly graces; where greatness and goodness, justice and mercy, God and man, meet in one person. Such an one who breaks no 'bruised reed, nor quenches the smoking flax,' Mat. xii. 20, who refuses not sinners, but invites them unto him, offering to heal all and cure all who come unto him. He is a king indeed, John xviii. 37. But this also approves her choice; he rules all, commands all, judges all. What then can she want who hath such a friend, such a husband? whose government is so winning, mild, and merciful?

He is not such a monarch as loves to get authority by sternness, like Rehoboam, 1 Kings xii. 12, but by those amiable graces of gentleness and love. All the excellencies of holiness, purity, and righteousness, are sweetly tempered with love and meekness in him. You may see, for instance, how he takes his disciples' part against the Pharisees, and the poor woman's that came to wash his feet and kissed them, against the Pharisee that had invited him to dinner, Luke vii. 44. The church is a company of despised people, that are scorned of Pharisaical proud spirits; who perhaps have morality and strength of parts to praise them with. Now Christ takes part with the broken spirits, against all proud spirits. Howsoever he be gone to heaven (where he is full of majesty), yet he hath not forgotten his meekness nor changed his nature, with change of honour. He is now more honoured than he was, for 'he hath a name above all names, in heaven or in earth,' Acts iv. 12; yet he is pitiful still. 'Saul, Saul, why persecutest thou me?' Acts ix. 4. He makes the church's case his own still. Together with beams of glory, there are bowels of pity in him, the same that he had here upon earth; which makes him so lovely to the truly broken-hearted, believing soul, 'My beloved is white and ruddy.'

He is set out likewise by comparing him with all others whatsoever, 'He is the chief of ten thousand;' a certain number for an uncertain, that is, the chief among all. In all things Christ hath the pre-eminence. 'He is the first-born from the dead,' Rom. viii. 29; 'he is the first-born of every creature,' Col.

i. 15; he is the eldest brother; he is the chief among all. For all kings, priests, and prophets before were but types and shadows of him. He, the body, the truth, and the substance. And (as was shewed before) he is all three in one, king, priest, and prophet; the great doctor* and prophet of his church, that spake by all the former prophets, and speaks by his ministers to the end of the world. 'The angel of the covenant,' that Λογὸς, the Word, that expresseth his Father's breast; that as he came from the bosom of his Father, so lays open his counsel to mankind. It was he that spake by Noah, and preached by his Spirit to the souls that are now in prison, as Peter speaks, 1 Pet. iii. 19. So, 'he is the chief among all.' But especially in regard of his righteousness; for which Paul 'accounted all dung and dross, to be found in Christ, not having his own righteousness, but the righteousness that is in Christ,' Phil. iii. 8; which is more than the righteousness of an angel, being the righteousness of God-man, and above all the righteousness of the law.

Quest. But what is this to us or to the church?

Ans. Yes; for his beauty and excellency is the church's, because he is the church's. 'My beloved is white and ruddy, and my beloved is the chief among ten thousand.' It is the peculiar interest that the church hath in Christ that doth relish her spirit; excellency with propriety in him; 'I am my beloved's, and my beloved is mine.' The more excellent the husband is, the more excellent is the wife. She only shines in his beams. Therefore it is the interest that we have in Christ that endears Christ to us. But to come to more particular application of it. Is Christ thus excellent, super-excellent, thus transcendently excellent, 'white and ruddy,' the chief of ten thousand?' This serves,

1. *To draw those that are not yet in Christ unto him.*
2. *To comfort those that are in Christ.*

Use 1. First, those that are not yet in Christ, not contracted to him, to draw them; *what can prevail more than that which is in Christ?* Beauty and excellencies, greatness and goodness. And indeed one main end of our calling, the ministry, is, to lay open and unfold the unsearchable riches of Christ; to dig up the mine, thereby to draw the affections of those that belong to God to Christ.

Use 2. But it is not enough to know that there are excellencies in Christ to draw us to him, but, *there must be a sight of our misery; what beggars we are, and how indebted.* Before we are in Christ we are not our own. The devil lays claim to us that we are his; death lays claim to us. We are under sin; we cannot satisfy one of a thousand; therefore this enforceth to make out to join with him that can discharge all our debts, answer all our suits, and non-suit Satan in the court of heaven. When once we are married to the Lord of heaven and earth, all is ours. We have a large charter, 'All things are yours, and you are Christ's, and Christ is God's,' 1 Cor iii. 22, 23.

Quest. Why are all things ours?

Ans. Because we are married to Christ, who is Lord of all. It is the end of our calling to sue for a marriage between Christ and every soul. We are the friends of the bride, to bring the church to him; and the friends of the church, to bring Christ to them. It is the end of our ministry to bring the soul and Christ together; and let no debts, no sins hinder. For especially he invites such as are sensible of their sins. 'Where sin abounds, grace abounds much more,' Rom. v. 20. 'Come unto me, all ye that are

* That is, 'teacher.'—G.

weary and heavy laden,' Mat. xi. 28. And, 'he came to seek and to save that which was lost,' Luke xix. 10. He requires no more, but that we be sensible of our debts and miseries, which sense he works likewise by his Holy Spirit.

Use 3. Again, for those that have entertained Christ, *let them see what an excellent gracious person they have entertained*, who is 'the chief of ten thousand.' The world thinks them a company of silly, mean people, that make choice of Christ, religion, the word, and such things; but there is a justification of their choice. They choose him that is 'the chief of ten thousand.' 'Let him kiss me with the kisses of his mouth,' saith the spouse, 'for thy love is better than wine, nay, than life itself,' Cant. i. 2. A Christian must justify the choice that he hath made with Mary 'of the good part,' Luke x. 42; against all those that shall disparage his choice. Let the world account Christians what they will; that they are a company of deluded, besotted persons, fools and madmen; the Christian is the only wise man. Wisdom is seen in choice especially; and here is the choice of that which is excellent and most excellent of all, 'the chief of ten thousand.'

Use 4. So also, *we may see here the desperate and base folly of all whatsoever*, save true Christians. What do they make choice of to join to? that which is base, the condemned world, vain, transitory things; and refuse Christ. Are they in their right wits who refuse a husband that is noble for birth, rich for estate, mighty for power, abundant in kindness and love itself, every way excellent, and take a base, ignoble, beggarly person? This is the choice of the world. God complains, 'Israel would none of me,' &c., Ps. lxxxi. 11. What shall we judge therefore of those that will none of Christ when he woos and sues them; but prefer with Esau a 'mess of pottage,' before their eternal birthright, Heb. xii. 16; with Adam, an apple before paradise; and with Judas, thirty pieces of silver before Christ himself. This is the state of many men. To be married to Christ is to take him for an husband; to be ruled by him in all things. Now when we prefer base commodities and contentments before peace of conscience and the enjoying of his love—what is it, but for pelf and commodity, thirty pieces of silver (perhaps for sixpence, a thing of nothing), to refuse Christ. Yet this is the condition of base worldlings that live by sense and not by faith. So then as it serves to comfort those that have made a true choice; so it serves to shew the madness and folly of all others, which one day will feel their hearts full of horror and confusion, and their faces of shame, when they shall think, What? hath Christ made such suit to my heart to win my love? hath he ordained a ministry for to bring me in? made such large promises? is he so excellent? and was this discovered to me, and yet would I none of him? what did I choose, and what did I leave? I left Christ with all his riches, and made choice of the 'pleasures and profits of sin, which are but for a season,' Heb. xi. 25. When the conscience is once thoroughly awaked, this will torment it,—the punishment of loss, not of loss simply, as the loss of Christ and the loss of heaven, but the loss of Christ and of heaven so discovered and opened. Therefore there is no condition in the world so terrible as of those that live in the church, and hear those things of Christ crucified unfolded to them before their eyes. As Paul speaks of the ministry, it makes Christ's cross so open to them as if he had been crucified before their eyes, Gal. iii. 1. Yet notwithstanding [they] yield to their base heart's desires and affections before these excellencies; which if they had a spirit of faith would draw their hearts to him.

Therefore let us consider how we hear those things. It concerns us nearly. On the one side we see what we get if we join with Christ; we have him and his. On the contrary, we lose him; and not only so, but we gain eternal misery, and perish eternally. O what baseness of mind possesseth us! Christ left all things in love to us, and we leave Christ for any paltry thing in the world; almost to please and content the humours of sinful men, to attain a few empty titles, to get a little wealth, enjoy a little pleasure. You see then the equity of that terrible commination* that you have, 'If any man love not the Lord Jesus Christ, let him be Anathema Maran-atha,' 1 Cor. xvi. 22. Let him be accursed for ever that loves not the Lord Jesus Christ. If any man sin there is a remedy to discharge his sin in Jesus Christ, if he will marry him and take him; but when Christ is offered and we will have none of him, we sin against the gospel; and then there is no remedy; there is nothing but 'Anathema and Maran-atha.' Therefore the most dangerous sins of all, are those against the light of the gospel; when yet we choose rather to live as we list, than to join ourselves to Christ. To this purpose, Heb. ii., St Paul makes an use of the first chapter, wherein he sets out the excellency of Christ, whom the angels adore. He is so beautiful, so lovely that God the Father is in love with him, and pronounceth, 'This is my beloved Son,' Mat. iii. 17. In the beginning of the second chapter, 'Wherefore,' saith he, 'how shall we escape if we neglect so great salvation; for if they escaped not that despised Moses' law, &c., how shall we escape if we neglect so great salvation?' Heb. ii. 3. He says not, if we oppose Christ, but if we neglect him, if we do not love so great salvation; as 2 Thess. i. 8, it is said, 'Christ will come in flaming fire to take vengeance of all those that do not know God, and obey not the gospel of Christ,' though they do not persecute it.

Use 1. Therefore this *reproves all civil, moral persons that think they have riches enough.* Not only debauched persons, but self-sufficient persons, that think they have any righteousness of their own. Let them know that 'Christ shall come in flaming fire, to take vengeance of such.' This is the scope of the second psalm, which ye know sets out the excellency of Christ, 'I have set my king upon Zion,' Ps. ii. 6. God the Father there anoints Christ king of the church. To what end? 'That we should kiss the Son,' kiss him with the kiss of subjection, as subjects do their prince; with the kiss of love, as the spouse doth her husband; and with the kiss of faith. But what if we do not kiss him, and subject ourselves to him, love him, and believe in him? 'If his wrath be once kindled, happy are all those that trust in him.' He is a lamb, but such a one as can be angry. It is said, 'The kings and great persons of the world fly from the wrath of the Lamb,' Rev. vi. 16. He that is so sweet, mild, and gentle, if we join with him, on the contrary, if we come not unto him, we shall find the wrath of the Lamb a terrible wrath, which the greatest potentates in the world shall desire to be hid from. 'If his wrath be once kindled, blessed are all those that trust in him,' and woe be to them that do not receive him.

Use 2. For us that profess ourselves to be in Christ, and to be joined to him that is thus excellent, let us make this use, *to make him the rule of our choice in other things.* In the choice of friends, choose such as are friends to Christ. Take heed of society with idolaters, or with profane, wretched persons. If you will be joined to Christ, and profess yourselves to be so, then let us join to none but those that we can enjoy and Christ too. So in marriage, let the rule of choice be the love of Christ. And likewise, let the measure of our respect to all things be the respect to Christ. Let us

* That is, 'denunciation, threatening.'—G.

measure our love to wife and children, to kindred, friends, and to all creatures whatsoever, as it may stand with love to Christ. Obey in the Lord, marry in the Lord, do all things in the Lord, so as may stand with the love and allowance of the Lord, 1 Cor. vii. 39, 40.

Use 3. Make also a use of direction, *how to come to value Christ thus*, as to keep an high esteem of him. For this follows infallibly and undeniably, if Christ be 'the chief of ten thousand,' he must have the chief of our affections 'above ten thousand.' For, as he is in excellency, he must have place in our hearts answerable thereunto; for then our souls are as they should be, when they judge of, and affect things as they are in themselves.

1. First, let us enter into a serious consideration *of the need we have of Christ, of our misery without him, of our happiness if we be joined with him.* The soul being thus convinced, the affections must needs follow the sanctified judgment.

What will come of it if Christ be set in the highest place in our heart? If we crown him there, and make him 'King of kings and Lord of lords,' in a hearty submitting of all the affections of the soul to him? While the soul continues in that frame it cannot be drawn to sin, discomfort, and despair. The honours, pleasures, and profits that are got by base engagements to the humours of men, what are these to Christ? When the soul is rightly possessed of Christ and of his excellency, it disdains that anything should come in competition with him.

2. Again, *it stands firm against all discouragements whatsoever:* for it sets Christ against all, who is the 'chief of ten thousand.' The soul in this case will set Christ against the anger and wrath of God, against Satan, and all our spiritual enemies. Christ is the angel of the covenant. Satan is a lion, a roaring lion; Christ the lion of the tribe of Judah. Satan a serpent, a dragon; but Christ, the true brazen serpent, the very looking upon whom will take away all the stings and fiery darts of Satan whatsoever. Wherefore it is said, 1 John v. 4, that faith is that that 'overcometh the world.' How doth faith overcome the world? Because it overcomes all things in the world, as, on the right hand, pleasures and profits and honours, and on the left hand, threatenings, pains, losses, and disgraces, by setting Christ against all.

3. Again, if we would have a right judgment and esteem of Christ, *let us labour to wean our affections as much as may be from other things.* Fleshly hearts that have run so deeply into the world, and vanities of this present life, it is in a sort an extraordinary task for them to be drawn away and pulled from the world, as a child from a full breast, which they have sucked so long. Now, for sweet affections that are tender, it is an excellent advantage they have to consider betimes that there is that in religion and in the gospel which is worth their best and prime affections, the flower and marrow of them. Let them begin, with young Timothy, 2 Tim. iii. 15, Daniel, and Joseph, to love Christ from their childhood. It is a desperate folly, on the other hand, to put off the regard of good things till after, when we shall be less fit, when the understanding will be darkened, and the affections blunted, when we shall not have that edge, nature being decayed, and the world having taken such possession of the soul that we shall not value this excellency. Therefore let us begin betimes to make up the marriage between Christ and the soul. No time, indeed, is too late, but it were to be wished that those that are young would be thus wise for their souls betimes.

4. Besides, if we would highly value Christ, *beg of God a spirit that we*

may judge aright of our corruptions, for in what measure we can discern the height, and breadth, and depth of our corrupt nature, in that measure shall we judge of the height, and breadth, and depth of the excellency of Christ. The sweetest souls are the most humble souls. Those that love Christ most are those that have been stung most with the sense of their sins. Where sin most abounds in the sense and feeling of it, grace much more abounds in the sense and feeling of that, Rom. v. 20. Did ever soul love Christ more than that woman that had so many devils cast out of her? Luke viii. 2. And Paul, that had such great sins forgiven? Doth any man so love his creditor as he that hath much debt forgiven him? It is our Saviour Christ's own reason. Therefore these two go always with the true church. 1. The true knowledge of the corruption of nature, and misery by reason of it; and 2. The true sense and feeling of it, with true and hearty sorrow for it, &c. In popery they slight original sin, that mother, breeding sin. Actual sins be venial, and many sins no sins. And therefore they esteem so slightly of Christ that they join saints, the pope, works and satisfaction with him. Because they know not the depth of the malady, how black sin is, what a cursed estate we are in by nature, they have slight, shallow, and weak conceits of sin. Therefore they have answerable weak and shallow conceits of Christ and of his righteousness and excellency. Therefore the conviction of our sins goeth before the conviction of righteousness in Christ, as it is said, 'The Holy Ghost shall convince the world of sin and then of righteousness,' John xvi. 8. For except the soul be convinced of sin, and of ill in itself, it will never be truly convinced of good and of righteousness in Christ.

The Passover was always eaten with sour herbs, because it should add a relish to the feast. So Christ, the true Passover, we never relish truly without sour herbs, the consideration of sin, with the desert of it. Christ savours otherwise to a man humbled for his sins than he doth to another man not touched therewith; otherwise to a poor man than he doth to a rich; otherwise to a man that the world goes not well on his side than to a prosperous man. One savoury discourse of Christ relisheth more to an afflicted soul than seven discourses with such as are drunk with prosperity, not having a brain strong enough to conceive, nor an appetite to relish heavenly things.

Therefore why do we murmur at the cross, when all is to recover our spiritual taste and relish? Solomon had lost his taste and relish of Christ. He never made his song of songs when he was in his idolatrous way, nor was so in love with Christ and his excellencies when he doted so much upon his wives. No; but when he had recovered his spirit's taste and relish of heavenly things once, then made he the book of the preacher. When he had run through variety of things, and saw all to be nothing but vexation of spirit, and besides that vanity, then he passeth his verdict upon all things, that they were vanity. So it is with us, we can hardly prize Christ without some afflictions, some cross or other. Therefore here the church is fain to endure a spiritual desertion, to set an edge upon her affections. Now, when she is thus in her desertions, 'Christ is white and ruddy, the chief of ten thousand.'

We value more, and set a higher price on things in the want of them—such is our corruption—than in the enjoying of them. And if God remember us not with affliction, then let us afflict, humble, and judge ourselves; enter into our own souls, to view how we stand affected to Christ, to heaven, and to heavenly things. How do I relish and esteem them? If I have lost my esteem and valuing, where have I lost it? Consider in what sin, in what pleasure, in what company I lost it; and converse no more with such as dull our affections to heavenly things.

4. And *let us make use likewise of our infirmities and sins to this purpose, to set an high price on the excellencies of Christ.* We carry about us always infirmities and corruptions. What use shall we make of them? Not to trust to our own righteousness, which is 'as a defiled cloth,' Isa. lxiv. 6, but fly to Christ's righteousness, which is the righteousness of God-man, all being as dung and dross in regard of that. Often think with thyself, What am I? a poor sinful creature; but I have a righteousness in Christ that answers all. I am weak in myself, but Christ is strong, and I am strong in him. I am foolish in myself, but I am wise in him. What I want in myself I have in him. He is mine, and his righteousness is mine, which is the righteousness of God-man. Being clothed with this, I stand safe against conscience, hell, wrath, and whatsoever. Though I have daily experience of my sins, yet there is more righteousness in Christ, who is mine, and who is the chief of ten thousand, than there is sin in me. When thus we shall know Christ, then we shall know him to purpose.

THE SIXTEENTH SERMON.

My beloved is white and ruddy, the chiefest among ten thousand. His head is as fine gold; his locks are bushy and black as a raven; his eyes are as the eyes of doves, by the rivers of waters, washed with milk, and fitly set, &c.—CANT. V. 10, 11, 12, 13.

Obj. Hence likewise we may answer some doubts that may arise; as why the death of one man, Christ, should be of value for satisfaction for the sins of the whole world. How can this be?

Ans. O but what kind of man was he? 'The chief among ten thousand,' especially considering that his excellency ariseth from the grace of his personal union of God and man. The first Adam tainted thousands, and would have tainted a world of men more if there had been more; but he was mere man that did this. And shall not Christ, God and man, the second Adam, advance the world, and ten thousand worlds if there had been more? He is chief among ten thousand.

'His head is as most fine gold; his locks are bushy and black as a raven,' &c.

1. Positively, 'He is white and ruddy.' 2. Comparatively, 'He is the chiefest of ten thousand.'

The church doth not think it sufficient, in general, to set out Christ thus; but she descends into a particular description of him by all the parts of a body that are conspicuous. First, in general observe hence, *that it is the nature of love upon all occasions to reflect upon the thing loved.* As the church here, from things that are excellent in the world, borrows phrases and comparisons to set out the excellency of Christ, exalting him above any other thing. Whatsoever the soul of a Christian sees in heaven or earth, it takes occasion thence to think of Christ.

Again, in general, observe from hence, seeing the church fetcheth comparison from doves' eyes, from the body of a man and other things, *that there are some beams of excellency in every creature.* There is somewhat of

God in every creature. This makes the meditation of the creature to be useful. There is none, even the meanest, but it hath a being, and thereby in a sort sets out the being of God. Why doth God style himself a shield, a rock, a buckler, a shadow, and the like? but to shew that there is something of him in these. And therefore to teach us to rise from them to him, in whom all those excellencies that are scattered in them are united.

In innocency we knew God, and in him we had knowledge of the creature; but now we are fain to help ourselves from the knowledge of the creature to rise to the knowledge of God.

'His head is as fine gold.' A little in general. See the boldness and largeness of the church's affections, who, though she had been ill entreated by the watchmen and others, yet is she not disheartened for all this. No; she goes on and sets out particular commendations of her beloved. Where love hath any strength, no water can quench it. You see the church here found but cold entertainment from the watchmen and others that should have been better.

Nay, she was in desertion, yet she was not discouraged. Nay, not from the desertion that Christ left her in; but she seeks after him whom her soul loved. Oh! this is the sign of a true, sanctified soul, touched from heaven, never to give over seeking of Christ; nor setting out his praises. No, though it thinks itself not beloved of Christ. Ask such ones, Do you love God, his children, and his word? Oh! you shall have them eloquent. No words are enough to set out their affections.

And this is one reason, which we may note by the way, why God plants in his children, at their first conversion, a sweet love, which we call, 'the first love,' that when desertions come they may call to mind what they felt from Christ, and what they bore to him; and thereupon the church concludes, 'I will return to my first love, for then was I better than now,' Hos. ii. 7. The church here, from what doth she commend her beloved, but from somewhat that was left in her soul, some inward taste of the love of Christ in her? She called to mind how it was with her before in the former part of this, and in the latter end of the former chapter; what an excellent estate she had been in. This helped her to recover herself.

Now you may say, Why is she so exact in reckoning up so many particulars of her beloved, his head, locks, eyes, lips, and such like?

Why? 1. It is from largeness of affection. A large heart hath alway large expressions. When we are barren in expressions towards Christ, and of good things, whence comes this but from narrow, poor affections? The church had large affections; therefore she had suitable expressions.

And then, 2. She is thus particular, because Christ hath not one but many excellencies. Everything in him is excellent, inward and outward, as his head, &c. For indeed beauty consists not in sweetness of colour only, but in affinity and proportion of all parts. Now there is all sweet proportion in Christ. So it should be with Christians. They should not have one excellency, but many. Those that receive grace for grace from Christ, John i. 16, have not only head, eyes, hands, and feet good; but all lovely, 'grace for grace,' answerable to the variety of graces in Jesus Christ, in whom all things jointly, and everything severally, are lovely.

Then, 3. She sheweth her particular care and study, to be exact in this knowledge of Christ. To rip him up and anatomise him thus, from head to foot, it argueth she had studied Christ well, ere she could attain this excellency. So it should be the study and care of every Christian, to study the excellencies of Christ, not only in the gross, to say as much as you have in the Creed; he was born for us of the Virgin Mary, was crucified, dead, and buried, &c., which every child can say; but to be able to particularize the high perfections and excellencies of Christ, as the church here; to study his nature, offices, the state he was in, and how he carried himself in his humiliation and exaltation; what good we have by both states, redemption by his abasement; application of it by his advancement; what he did for us on earth; what he doth in heaven; what in justification, adoption, sanctification, and in the glory to come. Study everything, and warm the heart with the meditation of them.

This particular spreading and laying open the excellencies of Christ is a thing worthy of a Christian. We make slight work of religion. We can be particular and eloquent enough in other things, but in that wherein all eloquence is too little, how barren are we! how shamefaced to speak of Christ and his excellencies in base company, as if it were a dishonour! Let us therefore learn this from the church here, to be much in thoughts and meditations of the excellencies of Christ, and so our expressions will be answerable to our meditations. So the holy fathers that were godly (till another kind of divinity came into the world, of querks* and subtilties) there was none of them but was excellent this way. Paul admirable, accounting 'all dung and dross in comparison of Christ.' In speaking of him, when he begins, he goes on from one thing to another, as if he were ravished, and knew not how nor where to end.

The soul hath sights of Christ that God shews to it, and which the soul presents to itself by the help of the Spirit. The sights that God in this kind shews, are to those in affliction especially; as Daniel and Isaiah saw Christ in his glory in a vision. So Ezekiel had a vision, and John, Rev. i., where Christ was presented to him gloriously. So there is a glorious description of Christ present to the church, Rev. iv. 5.

And as there are sights let down from God into the soul, so there are sights that the soul frames of Christ, such as the church here conceives of him by faith. Thus Moses saw him before he was incarnate, and Abraham saw his day and rejoiced, John viii. 56: so should we now have spiritual sights, ideas of Christ framed to our souls. This is to bestow our souls as we should do (*m*). So much for general, now we come to some particulars. 'His head is as fine gold; his locks are bushy and black as a raven.'

'His head is as fine gold.' He begins to set out the excellency of the chief part, the head. The head of Christ is God, as it is 1 Cor. xi. 3. He is above all, and God only is above him. All is yours, and you are Christ's, and Christ is God's, 1 Cor. iii. 22, 23. But that is not so much intended here, as to shew Christ's headship over the church, as God and man. His head is as fine gold, that is, his government and headship is a most sweet and golden government.

Daniel ii. You have an image of the monarchies; the first whereof had a golden head, which was the Chaldean. The best monarchy is set out by the best metal,—gold; so Christ, the head of the church, is a precious head, a head of gold.

A head hath an eminency above all others; an influence and motion above all other parts. It is the seat of the senses. So this golden head is more eminent than all, governs the whole church and hath influence into all. In him we live, and move, and have our being, Acts xvii. 28.

Quest. Why is Christ as king thus resembled to an head of gold?

Ans. Because gold is the chief, the most precious, durable metal of all

* That is, 'quirks,' = tricks.—G.

others. Christ is a king for ever, and hath an everlasting government. Gold is also the most pliable metal. You may beat it out to leaves more than any other metal whatsoever. Christ is all gold indeed. His love hath beat himself out as low as may be, all for our good. What abasement like to Christ's? That which is most precious is most communicating, as the sun, a glorious creature. What doth so much good as it? So Christ, as he is the most excellent of all, 'the chief of ten thousand,' so is he also the most communicative. What good to the good that Christ did? He was beaten, out of love to mankind, to lowest abasement for us. Though this be not mainly aimed at here, yet, by the way, speaking of gold, we may present to ourselves such comfortable meditations.

Use 1. Well then, is Christ such an excellent head, a golden head, 'in whom are hid all the treasures of wisdom, Col. ii. 3, to govern his church? *What need we then go to that triple crown, having such a golden head?* The apostasy of the church hath found out another golden head. Is not Christ precious enough? Let us take heed of leaving the head Christ, as it is Col. ii. 19. It is a damnable thing to forsake him. Let the apostatical * church alone with her antichrist.

2. Again, if Christ be a golden head, let us his members *labour every one to be suitable.* Though there be difference between the head and the members in many respects, especially in those three formerly named, eminency, government, and influence, yet for nature they are one. Head and members make but one. So that as the head of the body is gold, so should every member be. Therefore the seven churches are styled seven golden candlesticks. Everything in the tabernacle was gold, even to the snuffers, to shew that in the church everything is excellent. The tabernacle was gold, most of it, though it was covered with badgers' skins. The church indeed hath a poor covering as of badgers' skins, not gilded as hypocrites; but it is precious within. Again, Christ, as he is gold, so he is fine gold, whole gold. He hath not only the crown on him, but his head is gold itself. Other kings, their crowns are of gold, but their heads are not so. But there is such a precious treasure of wisdom in him that his head is gold. So let the church and every Christian labour, not to be gilt, but gold; to be thoroughly good; to have the inside as good as the outside, the heart as good as the conversation. The church is glorious within, Ps. xlv. 13. Beloved, is Christ an excellent golden head, and shall we have a base body? Is he fit to be united to a golden head that is a common drunkard, a swearer, that is a beast in his life and conversation? Is this suitable?

3. Again, is our head so golden, and whatsoever excellency we have, is it from our head? Therefore as the church in the Revelation, '*let us cast all our crowns at his feet,*' Rev. iv. 10. Have we crowns of gold? anything that is excellent within, any grace, any comfort? Let us lay it down at his feet, for all is from him. Natural men have golden images of their own. Israel would have golden calves. Nebuchadnezzar sets up a golden image, and all must worship it. So in the declining times of the church: they framed golden images, that is, a golden whorish religion, gilded, and painted, framed by their own brain, whereunto all must stoop. But the true gold is that we must respect and submit ourselves unto and admire. Others are but golden dreams and images, as Nebuchadnezzar's was. Christ's head is of fine gold.

All must be fine gold that comes from this head. His word is gold, sometimes† purged in the fire. His ordinances gold, in the Scripture

* That is, 'apostate.'—ED. † Qu. 'seven times?'—ED.

phrase, Ps. xix. 10. The city, the new Jerusalem, which signifies the state of the church in this world, when it shall be refined to the utmost, all is of gold; the walls of precious stones; the gates of pearl; and the pavement of the streets of pure gold, Rev. xxi. 21, to shew the excellency of reformation; which golden times are yet to come. In the mean time let us go on and wait for them.

'His locks are bushy, and black as a raven.' I think this is but complemental, to fill up the other. It is nothing but a commendation of his freshness, a foil to beauty. Therefore not particularly to be stood upon.

'His eyes are as doves' eyes by the rivers of waters,' &c. His eyes are as doves' eyes, and such eyes as are by the rivers of waters; where they are cleansed and washed with milk that they may be the clearer, and fitly set; neither goggle eyes, nor sunk into the head, but fitly set, as a jewel in a ring; neither too much in, nor too much out, to set out the comeliness of this part, the eye, which is the glory of the face.

Quest. Why is Christ said to have the eyes of doves?

Ans. The dove hath many enemies, especially the white dove is a fair mark for the birds of prey. Therefore God hath given that creature a quick sight, that she might discern her enemies. Thus the Scripture helps us to conceive of the quickness of Christ's eye, Rev. v. 6. There are seven horns and seven eyes, which are the seven Spirits of God. Here Christ the lamb, hath seven eyes and seven horns. What be these? Christ hath not only horns of power, as the enemies have horns of violence.—He hath horn against horn; but seven eyes, that is, a quick sight to see all the danger the church is in, and seven eyes. Seven is a word of perfection, that is, he hath many eyes, an accurate sight. He hath not only an eye of providence over the whole world, but an eye of grace and favour, lively, and lovely in regard of his church. All things are naked and open before his eyes, as it is, Heb. iv. 13. He can see through us, he knows our very hearts and reins, which he must do *ex officio*, because he must be our judge. He that is judge of all had need to have eyes that will pierce through all. It had need be a quick eye that must judge of the heart and affections. But what may we learn hence? That we have a Saviour that hath doves' eyes, that is, clear eyes, able to discern.

Use 1. Take it as a point first, *of all comfort to the church*, that when we have any imputation [that] lies upon us, that we are thus and thus, Christ hath quick eyes, he knows our hearts. Thou knowest, saith Peter, Lord, that I love thee, John xxi. 15. In all false imputations, rest in the eyesight of Christ. He knows it is otherwise with us.

Use 2. Then again, *in all abasement, know that there is an eye that sees all.* He sees with his eye and pities with his heart. As he hath a quick eye, so he hath a tender heart. Though he seems to sleep and to wink, it is but that we may wake him with our prayers; which when we have done, we shall see that Christ hath seen all this while, and that the violence the enemies of God have offered to his church, the spouse, hath been in his sight, and that they shall know at length to their cost.

Likewise it is a point of terror to all hypocrites and others, that think to blindfold Christ again. Can they blindfold him in heaven that hath this sharp eye? No; he sees all their courses and projects, what they are and what they tend to; and as he sees them, so he will spread them all open ere long.

Use 3. And as it is a point of comfort and terror, so it is a point of *instruction to us all, that we having to deal with a judge that sees all, to wor-*

ship Christ in spirit. If we had knowledge that such an eye of God is fixed upon us in all places, in all our affections and actions, would we give liberty to base and filthy thoughts, to cruel designs, and to treacherous aims and intents? to hatch a hell, as it were, in our hearts, and to carry a fair show outwardly. It could not be. Men are not afraid of their thoughts, affections, desires, and inward delights of their soul, because there is no eye of justice upon them. But if they did consider that the all-seeing God did observe these inward evils, and would call them to account one day for them, then they would be as well afraid to think ill as to do ill.

'His cheeks are as beds of spices, and as sweet flowers.'

Cheeks are the grace of the face. They are used here to denote the presence of Christ, which is sweet as spices and flowers. Not only his presence is glorious in heaven, when we shall see that goodly person of Christ that became man for us, that transforming sight that shall make us like himself, but the spiritual presence of Christ in his ordinances which we are capable of here, this is as spices and flowers.

Obj. But you will say, cheeks, face, and presence present colours to the eye, and not smells, as spices and flowers, which are the peculiar object of another sense.

Ans. Oh, but Christ is the object of all the senses. Beloved, he is not only beauty to the eye, but sweetness to the smell, and to the taste. Therefore faith hath the name of all the senses, to see, hear, taste, and smell, and doth all, because it carries us to Christ, that is instead of all to us. But the point is,

That the manifestation of Christ to his church and children by his Spirit in any of his ordinances, is a sweet manifestation, and delectable as spices and flowers; as it is, Cant. i. 3; 'Because of the savour of thy good ointments, thy name is as an ointment poured out, therefore the virgins love thee.' The very name of Christ, when he is known and laid open by the ministry, is a precious ointment, and the virgins, that is, all chaste souls, follow him by the smell of his ointments. All his ordinances convey a sweetness to the soul. His sacraments are sweet, his word sweet, the communion of saints sweet. The presence of the sun, you know, is known in the spring time by the freshness of all things, which put forth the life and little liveliness they have in them, some in blossoming, and some in flowers. That which lay, as it were, dead in winter, it comes out when the sun draws near; so when Christ comes and shews his presence and face to the soul, he refresheth and delights it.

Hence we see they are enemies to Christ and to the souls of God's people that hinder the manifestation of Christ, whereby his face might be seen, and his lovely cheeks discerned. Those that hate and undermine the ordinances of God, they hinder the comforts of their own souls.

And they are enemies to Christ. For when hath Christ glory but when the virgins follow him in the scent of his sweet ointments? When the soul, in the sense of his sweetness, follows him, and cleaves to him with joy, love, and delight, this makes Christ Christ, and sets him up in the heart above all others. This is the proper work of the ordinances. Those, therefore that are enemies to the ordinances of Christ, are enemies to the souls of God's people, and to the glory and honour of Christ himself. Thus far we may go safely, upon comparison of this with the other Scriptures.

THE SEVENTEENTH SERMON.

His lips are like lilies, dropping sweet-smelling myrrh; his hands are as gold rings set with beryl; his belly is as bright ivory overlaid with sapphire: his legs, &c.—CANT. V. 13.

IN speaking of these particulars we are to be very wary, for we have not that foundation as we have in other generals. For no doubt but the Spirit of God here did more intend to set out the large affection that the church had to Christ, than to insinuate any great particularity in every one of these. Therefore let us only cull out, and take those things that are of more easy explication.

'His lips are as lilies, dropping down sweet myrrh.'

That is, his doctrine is as sweet as the lilies, and sound as the myrrh, keeping from putrefaction, it being the nature of myrrh, as it is sound itself, so to make other things sound. In like manner, the speech of Christ makes the soul sound that embraceth it. What was ever more sweet than the truth of Christ? When he spake himself, they all hung upon his lips, Luke iv. 20, as the phrase is in the gospel (*n*), as a man hangs upon the lips of another whom he desires and delights to hear speak, and they marvelled at the gracious words that came out of his lips. Grace was in his lips, Ps. xlv. 2. All was sweet that came from him, for it came from the excellency of his Spirit. His words were dyed in these affections of his heart. In the learned language, the same word signifieth speech and reason (*o*), to intimate that speech is but the current of reason from the heart, the seat of reason. Therefore Christ's speeches were sweet, because his heart was sweet, full of all love, grace, mercy, and goodness, Mat. xii. 34, 35. His heart was a treasure. His lips must needs then be sweet. Beloved, therefore let us hence take a trial of ourselves, what our condition is, whether the words that come from Christ when he speaks in his ministry to us be sweet or not.

The word, to some kind of men, is like the northern air, which parcheth and cutteth. Ahab could not endure the breath of Elias, 1 Kings xxi. 18, *seq.*, nor Herodias the breath of John Baptist, Mark vi. 16, nor the Pharisees the breath of Stephen and Paul, Luke vii. 54, Acts xxii. 22. So too many now-a-days cannot endure the breath of divine truth, when it cuts and pierceth. These words are arrows that stick. If they stick not savingly, they stick to killing. If we cannot endure Christ's breath, we are not his spouse, nor have any communion with him.

'His lips are like lilies, dropping sweet myrrh,' &c.

This is one excellency of Christ and of his truth, that it preserves the soul in a pure estate. It is pure itself, and so it preserves the soul. Myrrh is a liquor that keeps from putrefaction. There is nothing that keeps the soul, but the word that endures for ever. Whereas, on the other side, error is of a putrefying nature, corrupting and defiling the soul.

'His hands are as gold rings set with beryl,' &c.

Hands are the instruments of actions. Christ's actions are precious. Whatsoever he doth to the church, nay, even when he doth use evil men to afflict and exercise the church, he hath a hand there, a golden, a precious hand, in the evil hand of wicked men. God doth all things by Christ. He is, as it were, God's hand, which all things pass through. Joseph was the second man of Egypt, through whose hands all things came to the rest,

Heb. i. 2, John v. 22; so all things come through Christ's hands to us; and whatsoever is his handiwork is good. Even as it is said in the days of his flesh, 'he did all things well,' Mat. vii. 37, so still, in the church all his workmanship is exceeding well. Though we cannot see the excellency of it, it is all well both in the government of the church and his workmanship in our hearts, 'the new creature.'

'His belly is as bright ivory overlaid,' &c.

His belly, that is, his inward parts. In the Hebrew (*p*), it is used for the inward affections. They are as bright ivory overlaid with sapphires, that is, they are pure. All the inside of Christ, all his affections that he bears, are wondrous good. His love, his desires, his joys, his hatred, all pure, like pure water in a crystal glass. It may be stirred sometimes, but still it is clear. There are no dregs at the bottom, because there was no taint of sin in him.

'His legs are as pillars of marble set on sockets of fine gold,' &c.

That is, all his passages and ways are constant and firm, even as pillars of marble. His children are so likewise, as far as they are endued with his Spirit. Christ is yesterday, to-day, and the same for ever, Heb. xiii. 8. In regard of his enemies, he is set out in another manner of similitude, 'as having legs of brass to trample them all in pieces,' Rev. i. 15. But in respect of his constant truth and ways of goodness to his church, his legs are as pillars of marble.

'His countenance is as Lebanon, excellent as the cedars.'

Lebanon was a goodly forest lying on the north side of Judea, wherein were excellent plants of all kinds, especially cedars. Christ his countenance is as Lebanon, excellent as the cedars, that is, his presnece is goodly, stately, and majestical. So it is and will be when he shews himself, indeed, for the vindicating of his church. Then the enemies thereof shall know that his presence is as Lebanon, and excellent as the cedars.

The children of God are like to cedars, too, for they are Christ mystical. Other men are as shrubs to them, men of no value; but they are cedars, and grow as cedars in Lebanon, from perfection to perfection, bearing most fruit in their age. Wicked men sometimes are cedars, too, and are said to grow and flourish as the cedars in Lebanon. But look a while, and you shall see their place no more. They have no good root, no good foundation, Ps. xxxvii. 10. A Christian is a cedar set in Christ the chief cedar. He is a plant that grows in him. He hath an eternal root, and, therefore, he flourisheth eternally.

'His mouth is most sweet, he is altogether lovely.'

His mouth is most sweet. She doubles this commendation. She had said before, his lips are as lilies dropping sweet myrrh. Here she saith again of his mouth, it is most sweet, to shew that this is the chief lovely thing in Christ. The repetition argueth the seriousness of the church's affection to Christ, and of the excellency of that part. The main lovely thing is that which comes from his heart by his words and his lips; as, indeed, the most excellent thing that we can think of is the expression of the heart of God in Christ, and of Christ's love to us. 'His mouth is most sweet.' And, indeed, the best discovery of a true affection to Christ, and of a true estate in grace, is from our affection to the word of Christ. Wheresoever there is interest into Christ, there is a high respect to the word. 'My sheep hear my voice,' John x. 4; and you know what Peter saith, John vi. Many of Christ's hearers and followers forsook him, upon some hard speeches, as they thought, that came from him. Saith Christ to Peter,

'Will ye also leave me?' Peter answered again, 'Whither, Lord, shall we go? Thou hast the words of eternal life,' John vi. 68. The apostles, that had the Spirit of God, perceived an incredible graciousness to sit on his lips, and therefore they hung upon his lips. 'Whither shall we go? Thou hast the words of eternal life.' If we leave his speech, we leave our comfort, we leave our life.

As a comment hereupon, see Ps. xix., where we have a high commendation of God's excellency; first, from the book of nature, the works of God: 'the heavens declare the glory of God;' then from the word of God; and herein the psalmist is wondrous large. 'The law of the Lord is perfect, converting the soul; the testimonies of the Lord are sure, making wise the simple; the statutes of the Lord are right, and rejoice the heart; the commandments of the Lord are sure, and enlighten the eyes; more to be desired than gold, yea, than fine gold; sweeter also than the honey or the honeycomb.'

But mark the order. When is the word of God precious as gold, sweeter than the honey or the honeycomb, but when the former commendation takes place? Where the word is perfect, converting the soul, and where it is sure, making wise the simple, and where the fear of the Lord is clean, &c., there it is more to be desired than fine gold, and sweeter than the honeycomb. So the church here finding, first of all, the word to be a converting word, and giving understanding to the simple, she cannot but speak of the sweetness of the word of Christ. His lips are as lilies dropping sweet-smelling myrrh. His mouth is most sweet. Thus a man may know his estate in grace by his relish of the word.

There is a divine and a heavenly relish in the word of God; as, for instance, take the doctrine of his providence, 'that all things shall work together for the best to them that love God,' Rom. viii. 28. What a sweet word is this! A whole kingdom is not worth this promise, that whatsoever befalls a Christian in this world, there is an overruling providence to sway all to good, to help forward his eternal good.

That Christ will be present with us in all conditions, what a sweet word and promise is this! Mat. xxviii. 20; 'that he will give his Holy Spirit, if we beg it,' Luke xi. 13; 'that he will not fail us nor forsake us,' Heb. xiii. 5; that 'if we confess our sins, and lay them open, he is merciful to forgive them,' 1 John i. 9; that 'if our sins were as red as scarlet, they shall all be white as wool,' Isa. i. 18. What kind of incredible sweetness is in these to a heart that is prepared for these comforts! The doctrine of reconciliation, of adoption, of glory to come, of the offices of Christ and such like, how sweet are they! They relish wondrously to a sanctified soul.

Let us therefore discern of our estate in grace by this, how do we relish divine truths? Are they connatural and suitable to us? Do we love them more than our appointed food? Are they dearer unto us than thousands of gold and silver? Do we like them above all other truths whatsoever? Ps. cxix. 72, 127. Every truth in its rank is lovely, and is a beam of God. For truth is of God wheresoever we find it. But what are other truths to this heavenly, soul-saving truth? this gospel-truth that is from Christ? 'His mouth is most sweet.'

In our nature there is a contrary disposition and antipathy to divine truth. We love the law better than the gospel, and any truth better than the law. We love a story, any trifling, baubling thing concerning our ordinary callings, better than divine truth. In divine truth, as things are more spiritual, so the more remote they are naturally from our love and liking. Evangelical truths will not down with a natural heart; such an one had rather hear a quaint point of some vice or virtue finely stood upon than anything in Christ, because he was never truly convinced of his corrupt and miserable estate by nature. But when the grace of God hath altered him, and his eyes are open to see his misery, then of all truths the truth of Christ favours* best. Those truths that come out of the mouth of Christ, and out of the ministry concerning Christ, they are the most sweet of all. Oh! how sweet are those words in the gospel to the poor man, 'Thy sins are forgiven thee,' Mat. ix. 2. Do you think they went not to his heart? So to the woman, Luke vii. 47. Her many sins are forgiven her, for she loved much. Oh! they were words that went to her soul! And to the thief on the cross, 'This day thou shalt be with me in paradise,' Luke xxiii. 43. How do you think those words affected him? So it is with us if ever we have been abased in the sense of our sins. Oh! how sweet is a promise of mercy then! 'He that brings it is as one of ten thousand, that comes to declare to man his righteousness, Job. xxxiii. 23; to lay open the mercy that belongs to a distressed soul. Oh! the very feet of those that bring these glad tidings are beautiful! Rom. x. 15. When our blessed Saviour, after his resurrection, spake to Mary, and called her by her name, after that she had sought him and could not find him, 'O Rabboni,' saith she. The words of Christ they melted her presently. Let Christ once call us by our names, for he knows us by name, as he knew Moses, Exod. xxxiv. 27, Isa. xliii. 1; let him by his Spirit speak to us by name, and own us, then we call him Rabboni. We own him again, for what is our love but the reflection of his back again? Therefore saith the psalmist, 'Let me hear the voice of joy and gladness, that the bones that thou hast broken may rejoice,' Ps. li. 8. 'Let me hear;' that is, I long for thy word to hear it; not the bare ministerial word, but the word of the Spirit. But the church resteth not here, but saith further,

'He is altogether lovely.' Altogether desirable; as if she should say, What should I stand upon particulars? he is altogether, from top to toe, amiable, lovely, and delectable.

'He is altogether lovely.' Lovely to God, to us, to the soul; lovely to him that can best judge of loveliness. The judgment of God I hope will go current with us; and what doth God the Father judge of Christ? 'This is my beloved Son,' Mat. iii. 17. He is the Son of God's love, Col. i. 13, as God cannot but love his own image. He is lovely also as man, for he was pure and holy; lovely as mediator by office, for he was anointed by God to convey the Father's love to us. He must needs be lovely in whom all others are loved. This is my beloved Son, in whom I am well pleased; out of him I am well pleased with nobody. And indeed he was filled with all graces that might make him lovely. All the treasures of wisdom are in him, and of his fulness we all receive grace for grace. He is made a storehouse of all that is good for us.

He is lovely to God in whatsoever he did. He carried himself lovely, and pleased his Father in all his doings and sufferings. God loved him especially, 'because he was obedient, even unto the death of the cross. Therefore God gave him a name above all names; that at the name of Jesus every knee should bow, both in heaven and in earth,' Phil. ii. 8–10. As for the angels, they look upon him with admiration. They attended

* Qu. 'savours?'—ED.

him, and accounted it an honour to wait upon him. He is lovely to all above us, and shall he not be lovely to us?

Obj. But you will say, Was he lovely when he was nailed on the cross, hung between two thieves, when he wore a crown of thorns, was whipped, laid grovelling on the ground, when he sweat water and blood? What loveliness was in him when he was laid in his grave?

Ans. Oh! yes; then he was most lovely of all to us, by how much the more he was abased for us. This makes him more lovely that out of love he would abase himself so low. When greatness and goodness meet together, how goodly is it! That Christ, so great a majesty, should have such bowels of compassion! Majesty alone is not lovely, but awful and fearful; but joined with such condescending grace, is wondrous amiable. How lovely a sight is it to see so great a person to be so meek and gentle! It was so beyond comparison lovely in the eyes of the disciples, that they stood and wondered to see him, who was the eternal Word of the Father, condescend to talk with a poor Samaritan woman, John iv. 6, *seq*. And what loveliness of carriage was in him to Peter, undeserving, after he had denied and forsworn him, yet to restore him to his former place that he had in his heart, loving him as much as ever he did before! In a word, what sweetness, gentleness, bowels of meekness, pity, and compassion did he discover to those that were in misery! We cannot insist upon particulars.

There is a remarkable passage in the story of Alphonsus the king, not very well liked of some. When he saw a poor man pulling of his beast out of a ditch, he put to his hand to help him; after which, as it is recorded, his subjects ever loved him the better. It was a wonderful condescending. And is it not as wonderful that the King of heaven and earth should stoop so low as to help us poor worms out of the ditch of hell and damnation? and that, when he hath set us in a state of deliverance, he should not leave us there, but advance us to such a state and condition as is above our admiration, which neither heart can conceive nor tongue express? Is not this wonderful condescending?

Use 1. That we may further improve this point, Is Christ altogether lovely; so lovely to us, and so beloved of God the Father? *Let us then rest upon his obedience and righteousness;* build upon it, that God cannot refuse that righteousness whose whole subject is altogether lovely. Let us come clothed in the garments of our Elder Brother, and then doubt not of acceptance; for it is in Christ that he loves us. In this well-beloved Son it is that God is well pleased with us. If we put on Christ's righteousness, we put on God's righteousness; and then how can God hate us? No more than he hates his own Son. Nay, he loves us, and that with the same love wherewith he loves him; for he loves whole Christ mystical, Head and members, John xvii. 23. Let this strengthen our faith, that if Christ be so altogether lovely in himself and to the Father, then we may comfortably come before the Father, clothed with the garments of him our Elder Brother, and so rest ourselves on the acceptation of his mediation, that is so beloved a mediator.

Use 2. Again, if Christ be so lovely, 'altogether lovely,' then *let us labour to be in him*, that so we may be lovely to God; because he is the first amiable thing in the world, in whom we are all lovely. All our loveliness is in beloved Christ.

Use 3. Again, if Christ be so lovely, *here only we have whereupon to spend the marrow of our best affections*. Is it not pity we should lose so much of our affections as we do upon other things? Christ is altogether lovely; why should we doat upon other things so much, and set up idols in our hearts above Christ? Is he altogether lovely, and shall not he have altogether our lovely affections, especially when we are commanded, under pain of a curse, to love the Lord Jesus? *Anathema Maran-atha* to those that love not Christ, 1 Cor. xvi. 22. Let us therefore labour to place all our sweet affections that are to be exercised upon good, as love, joy, and delight, upon this object, this lovely deserving object, Christ, who is 'altogether lovely.' When we suffer a pure stream, as it were, to run through a dirty channel, our affections to run after the things of the world, which are worse than ourselves, we lose our affections and ourselves.

Let, therefore, the whole stream of our affections be carried unto Christ. Love him, and whatsoever is his; for he being altogether lovely, all that comes from him is lovely. His promises, his directions, his counsels, his children, his sacraments, are all lovely. Whatsoever hath the stamp of Christ upon it, let us love it. We cannot bestow our hearts better, to lose ourselves in the love of Christ, and to forget ourselves and the love of all. Yea, to hate all in comparison of him, and to account all 'dung and dross' compared with Christ, is the only way to find ourselves. And indeed we have a better condition in him, than in the world or in ourselves. Severed from him, our condition is vain, and will come to nothing; but that we have in him is admirable and everlasting. We cannot conceive the happiness which we poor wretches are advanced to in Christ; and what excellent things abide for us, which come from the love of God to us in Christ, who is so altogether lovely. Therefore let us labour to kindle in our hearts an affection towards Christ, all that we can, considering that he is thus lovely.

Use 4. And let us make an use of trial, *whether he be thus lovely to us, or no*. We may see hence whether we love Christ or no. We may judge of our love by our esteem.

1. *How do we value Christ?* what price doth the church set on him? 'He is the chief of ten thousand.' What place, then, should he have in our hearts? If he be the chief of ten thousand, let us rather offend ten thousand than offend him. Let us say, with David, 'Whom have I in heaven but thee?' &c., Ps. lxxiii. 25. And when the soul can say to Christ, or any that is Christ's (for I speak of him in the latitude of his truths, promises, sacraments, and communion with his children), 'What have I in heaven but thee?' &c., then it is in a happy condition. If these things have the same place in our esteem, as they have in respect of their own worth, then we may say truly, without hypocrisy, 'He is altogether lovely to us,' that we truly love him.

2. In the next place, *are we ready to suffer for Christ?* We see the church here endures anything for Christ. She was misused of the watchmen. They scorned her, and her 'veil is taken away,' yet notwithstanding, she loves Christ still. Do we stand ready disposed to suffer for Christ? of the world to be disgraced and censured? and yet are we resolved not to give over? Nay, do we love Christ the more, and stick to his truth the faster? Certainly where the love of Christ is, there is a spirit of fortitude, as we may see in the church here, who is not discouraged from Christ by any means. He is still the chief of ten thousand. When she was wronged for seeking after him, yet he was altogether lovely. Whereas, on the other hand, you have some that, for frowns of greatness, fear of loss, or for hope of rising, will warp their conscience, and do anything. Where now is love to Christ and to religion? He that loves Christ, loves him the more for his cross, as the Holy Ghost hath recorded of some, that they

'rejoiced that they were thought worthy to suffer for Christ,' Acts v. 41. So the more we suffer for him, the more dear he will be to us. For indeed he doth present himself in love and comfort most, to those that suffer for his sake; therefore their love is increased.

3. Again, where love is, *there it enlargeth the heart*, which being enlarged, enlargeth the tongue also. The church hath never enough of commending Christ, and of setting out his praise. The tongue is loosed, because the heart is loosed. Love will alter a man's disposition. As we see in experience, a man base of nature, love will make him liberal; he that is tongue-tied, it will make him eloquent. Let a man love Christ, and though before he could not speak a word in the commendation of Christ, and for a good cause, yet, I say, if the love of Christ be in him, you shall have him speak and labour earnestly in the praises of God. This hot affection, this heavenly fire, will so mould and alter him, that he shall be clean another man. As we see in the church here, after that there was kindled a spirit of love in her, she cannot have done with Christ. When she had spoke what she could, she adds, 'He is altogether lovely.' Those that cannot speak of Christ, or for Christ, with large hearts in defence of good causes, but are tongue-tied and cold in their affections, where is their love? Put any worldly man to a worldly theme that he is exercised in, and speaks of daily, he hath wit and words at will; but put him to a theme of piety, you lose him: he is out of his theme, and out of his element. But 'tis not so with those that have ever felt the love of God in Christ. They have large affections. How full is Saint Paul! He cannot speak of Christ, but he is in the height, breadth, length, and depth of the love of God in Christ, and the knowledge of God above all knowledge. Thus we may discern the truth of our love by the expressions of it here as in the church.

4. Again, *the church here is never content till she find Christ*; whatsoever she had, nothing contents her. She wanted her beloved. As we see here, she goes up and down inquisitive after him till she find him. So it is with a Christian. If he have lost, by his own fault, his former communion with Christ, he will not rest nor be satisfied; but searcheth here and there in the use of this and that means. He runs through all God's ordinances and means till he find Christ. Nothing in the world will content him, neither honour, riches, place, or friends, till he find that which he once enjoyed, but hath now for a season lost, the comfort and assurance of God's love in Christ.

Now, if we can sit down with other things, and can want Christ and the assurance of salvation, that sweet report of the Spirit that we are his, and yet be contented well enough, here is an ill sign that a man is in an ill condition. The church was not so disposed here. She was never quiet, nor gives over her inquisition and speaking of Christ (that by speaking of the object she might warm her affections), until at the last she meets with Christ. These and the like signs there are of the truth of the love of Christ. But where there is a flaming love of Christ there is this degree further, a desire of the appearance of Christ, a desire of his presence. For if Christ be so lovely in his ordinances, if we find such sweetness in the word and sacraments, in the communion of saints, in the motions of the Spirit, what is the sweetness, think you, which the souls in heaven enjoy, where they see Christ face to face, see him as he is? Hereupon the spouse saith, 'Let him kiss me with the kisses of his mouth.' Oh, that I might live in his presence. This is the desire of a Christian soul when the flame of love is kindled in any strength, 'Oh, that I might see him.' And therefore it longs even for death; for as far as a man is spiritual, he desires to be dissolved and to be with Christ; as Simeon, when he saw him, though in his abasement, 'Now I have enough; let thy servant depart in peace, for mine eyes have seen thy salvation,' Luke ii. 30. The presence of Christ, though it were but in the womb, when Mary, the mother of Christ, came to Elizabeth, it caused the babe that was in her womb to spring. Such comfort there is in the presence of Christ, though he be but in the womb, as it made John to spring. What, then, shall be his presence in heaven? How would it make the heart spring there, think you? For that which is most lovely in Christ is to come. Therefore the saints that have any degree of grace in the New Testament, they are set out by this description. They were such as loved the appearing of our Lord Jesus Christ. How can it be otherwise? If they love Christ, they love the appearing of Christ, wherein we shall be made lovely, as he is lovely.

Here we are not 'altogether lovely;' for we have many dregs of sin, many infirmities and stains. Shall we not, then, desire that time wherein, as he is 'altogether lovely,' so shall we be made a fit spouse for so glorious a husband?

To conclude this point, let us try our affections by the church's affections in this place, whether Christ be so lovely to us or not. It is said, 'There is no beauty in him when we shall see him, and he was despised of men,' Isa. liii. 2. He was so, in regard of his cross and sufferings, to the eye of the world and of carnal men. Herod scorned him; when Pilate sent him to him, made nobody of him, as the word in the original is (*q*). They looked upon the outside of Christ in the flesh when he was abased. 'There was no form nor beauty in him,' saith the Holy Ghost, that is, to the sight of carnal men; but those that had the sight of their sins with spiritual eyes, they could otherwise judge of Christ. The poor centurion saw an excellency in him when he said, 'He was not worthy that he should come under his roof,' Mat. viii. 8. The poor thief saw the excellency of Christ upon the cross in those torments. 'Lord, remember me when thou comest into thy kingdom,' Luke xxiii. 42.

So those souls that were enlightened, that had the sight of their misery and the sight of God's love in Christ, had a high esteem of Christ in his greatest abasement. Therefore, if we have a mean esteem of the children of God as contemptible persons, and of the ordinances of God as mean things, and of the government of Christ (such as he hath left in his word) as base, it is an argument of a sinful, unworthy disposition. In such a soul Christ hath never been effectually by his Spirit; for everything in him is lovely, even the bitterest thing of all. There is a majesty and excellency in all things of Christ. The censures of the church are excellent when they proceed and issue forth with judgment, as they should do, 'to deliver such a man over to Satan, that he may be saved in the day of the Lord,' 1 Cor. v. 5.

Now, if the ordinances of Christ, the word and sacraments, and the shutting sinners out of the church, if these things be vilified as powerless things, it shews a degenerate, wicked heart, not acquainted with the ways of God. If we have a mean esteem of men that suffer for Christ and stand out for him, if we account them so and so, shall we think ourselves Christians in the mean time? When Christ is altogether lovely, shall they be unlovely that carry the image of Christ? Can we love him that begets, and hate them that are begotten of him? Can we love Christ, and hate Christians? It cannot be.

Now, that we may get this affection and esteem of Christ that is so lovely,

Let us labour to make our sins bitter and loathsome, that Christ may be sweet.

Quest. What is the reason we set no higher a price of Christ?

Ans. Because we judge not of ourselves as we are indeed, and want spiritual eye-salve to see into ourselves rightly.

2. *And let us attend upon the means of salvation, to hear the unsearchable riches of Christ.* What makes any man lovely to us, but when we hear of their riches, beauty, and good intent to us? In the word we are made acquainted with the good intent of Christ towards us, the riches of mercy in forgiving our sins, and riches of glory prepared for us. The more we hear of him, of his riches and love to us, the more it will inflame our love to Christ. Those that live where the ordinances of Christ are held forth with life and power, they have more heavenly and enlarged affections than others have, as the experience of Christians will testify.

3. Again, if we would esteem highly of Christ that he may be lovely to us, *let us join with company that highly esteem of Christ, and such as are better than ourselves.* What deads the affections so much as carnal, worldly company, who have nothing in them but civility? By converse with them who have discourse of nothing but the world, if a man have heavenly affections, he shall quickly dull them, and be in danger to lose them. They may be conversed with in civil things, but when we would set to be heavenly and holy minded, let us converse with those that are of an heavenly bent. As we see here, 'the daughters of Jerusalem' are won to love Christ. By what? By conversing with the church. Upon the discourse that the church makes of his excellencies, in particular, they begin to ask, Where is Christ, as in the next chapter; and so are all brought to the love of Christ.

THE EIGHTEENTH SERMON.

His mouth is most sweet; yea, he is altogether lovely. This is my beloved, and this is my friend, O daughters of Jerusalem.—CANT. V. 16.

Whither is thy beloved gone, O thou fairest among women? whither is thy beloved turned aside? that we may seek him with thee? My beloved is gone down, &c.—CANT. VI. 1, 2.

BY this time the church hath well quit herself in that safe subject, commending her beloved; first in general, and then in particular. She affirms in effect, there was none like him in general; which she after makes good, in all the particulars of her description. Now she sums up all with a kind of superabundant expression. What shall I say more of him? if that which is said be not enough, then know farther, he is altogether lovely. There were no end to go through all his perfections; but look on him wholly, 'he is altogether lovely,' and therefore deserves my love. So that there is no cause why you should wonder at the strength of my affections, and care to find out this my beloved and this my friend, O ye daughters of Jerusalem. Thus we see how the pitch of an enlightened soul is bent. It aspires to things suitable to itself; to God-wards; to union and communion with Christ; to supernatural objects. Nothing here below is worthy the name of its beloved. It fastens not on earthly, base things. But this is my beloved, and this is my friend, this so excellent a person, this Jedidiah,* this beloved Son, this judge of all, Lord of all, this chief of ten thousand. Here the church pitches her affections, which she conceals, not as ashamed thereof, but in a kind of triumphing, boasting of her choice. She concludes all with a kind of resolute assurance, that the object of this her choice is far beyond all comparison.

'This is my beloved, and this is my friend, O daughters of Jerusalem.'

Which is the closing up of her commendations of Christ. 'This is my beloved, and this my friend,' &c. Which shall only be touched, because we had occasion to speak thereof before. She calls Christ her beloved. Howsoever he had withdrawn himself in regard of the comfort and communion she had with him before, yet he is her beloved still.

That which is specially to be stood upon is, that the church here doth set out not only in parcels, but in general, her beloved Christ. This is my beloved. She doth, as it were, boast in her beloved. Whence observe:

A Christian soul seems to glory as it were in Christ.

'This is my beloved, and this is my friend, O ye daughters of Jerusalem.' But to unfold more fully this point, there be three or four ends why the church thus stands upon the expression of the excellencies of Christ, in particular and in general.

1. The one, *to shew that it is most just that she should love and respect him in whom there is all this to deserve love.* Both in himself, in regard of his own excellencies, so, and in relation to us, in regard of his merits and deserts.

2. Secondly, *to justify her large affections before the world and all opposites.*† For the world thinks, what mean these who are called Christians to haunt the exercises of religion, to spend so much time in good things? They wonder at it for want of better information. Now the church here, to justify her large expressions, says, 'This is my beloved, this is my friend, O ye daughters of Jerusalem.'

3. *And not only to justify, but likewise to glory therein*, as you have it, Ps. xliv. 8. The church there boasts of God, 'I will make my boast of thee all the day long.' So that Christians may not only justify their course of life against enemies, but in some sort boast of Christ, as Paul oft doth. And he shews the reason of it, that God hath made Christ to us all in all, wisdom, righteousness, sanctification, and redemption, 1 Cor. i. 30, that whosoever glorieth might glory in the Lord, ver. 31. For it is not a matter of glorying in the church when she hath such a head and such a husband. 'This is my beloved.' The wife shines in the beams of her husband. Therefore this yields matter not only of justification but of glory.

4. And next, in the fourth place, the church is thus large and shuts up all with a repetition, 'This is my beloved,' *to enlarge her own affections and to feed our‡ own love.* For love feeds upon this fuel, as it were; upon expressions and meditations of the person or thing loved. Love is, as it were, wages of itself. The pains it takes is gain to itself. To the church here, it is an argument pleasing. She dilates upon a copious theme. I may truly say there is no greater comfort to a Christian, nor a readier way to enlarge the affections after Christ, than to speak oft of the excellencies of Christ; to have his tongue as the pen of a ready writer furnished this way, 'This is my beloved,' &c.

* That is, 'beloved of Jehovah.'—G. † That is, 'opponents.'—ED.

‡ Qu. 'her?'—ED.

5. In the fifth place, another end of this may be, *to aggravate her own shame*, as indeed God's children are much in this argument; that upon their second thoughts of Christ's worthiness, and therewithal reflecting upon their own unworthiness and unkindness, they may relish Christ the better. Therefore the church here, that it might appear to herself, for her humiliation, how unkind she had been to shut the door against Christ when he knocked (whereupon he deservedly did withdraw himself, and made her seek him so long sorrowing), I tell you, says she, what a kind of beloved he is, thus and thus excellent. How did the consideration of God's kindness and love melt David's heart after that horrible sin in the matter of Uriah, 2 Sam. xii. 13; and the sweet looks of Christ upon Peter, Mat. xxvi. 75, that had been so unkind, melted him. So here the church, when she considered how unkind she had been to Christ her beloved, so incomparably excellent above other beloveds, to let him stand at the door, till his locks were wet with the dew of the night, the consideration hereof made her ashamed of herself. What! so excellent, so deserving a person as my beloved is to me, to be used of me so! what indignity is this! Thus to raise up the aggravation of her unkindness, no question but the church takes this course. For God's children are not as untoward worldlings and hypocrites, afraid to search and to understand themselves. The child of God loves to be well read in his own heart and unworthy ways. Therefore he lays all the blame he can upon himself every way. He knows he loseth nothing by this; for there is more mercy in Christ than there is sin in him. And the more sin abounds in his own feeling, the more grace shall abound. He knows the mystery of God's carriage in this kind. Therefore for this end, amongst the rest, she says, 'This is my beloved, and this is my friend,' whom I have so unkindly used.

6. And the last reason why the church is thus large was, *to draw and wind up the affections of those well-meaning Christians that were comers on, who were inquisitive of the way to Zion*. O ye daughters of Jerusalem, that you may know that there is some cause to seek after Christ more than you have done before, I tell you what an excellent person my beloved is; to whet their affections more and more. And we see the success of this excellent discourse in the beginning of the next chapter. 'Whither is thy beloved gone?' &c.

These and the like reasons there are of the large expressions of the church, of the excellencies of Christ. 'This is my beloved, and this is my friend, O ye daughters of Jerusalem.' But we will single out of these reasons for use, that which I think fittest for us to make use of.

Let us then oft think of the excellencies of Christ for this end, *to justify our endeavours and pains we take in the exercises of religion, and to justify God's people from the false imputations of the world, that they lay upon them*; as if they were negligent in other matters, and were too much busied in spiritual things. You see how large the church is in setting out the excellencies of her beloved, and then she shuts up all (being able to say no more) justifying our cause, 'This is my beloved, and this is my friend.' Do you wonder that I seek so much after him then? or wonder you at Christians, when they take such pains to keep their communion with Christ in a holy walking with, and depending upon God? These are no wonders, if you consider how excellent Christ is, what he hath done for us, and what he keeps for us in another world? that he will preserve us to his heavenly kingdom, till he put us into possession of that glorious condition that he hath purchased? Let the hearts of men dwell upon the consideration of these things, and then you shall see that God's children are rather to be blamed that they are no more careful, watchful, and industrious, than to be taxed that they are so much. Our Saviour Christ said, 'Wisdom is justified of all her children,' Mat. xi. 19. If you will make good that you are children of wisdom, you must be able to justify the wisdom of God every way, to justify your reading, hearing, your communion of saints; to justify all the exercises of religion from an experimental taste and sweetness of them, as the church doth here, 'This is my beloved.' What says Joshua? 'This choice I have made; do you what you will, it matters me not, but I and my house will serve the Lord,' Josh. xxiv. 15. So Paul makes a voluntary profession of his affection, Rom. i. 2, 'I am not ashamed of the gospel of Jesus Christ.' Let the gospel be entertained in the world as it will, and let others think of me as they will, that I am forward in the preaching of it; I am not ashamed of it. And good reason he had not to be ashamed; for it is the power of God to salvation, to all that believe; yea the saving power to us. And have not I cause to stand in the defence of it? And so he saith, 'I know whom I have believed,' &c., 2 Tim. i. 12. I am not ashamed to suffer bonds for his sake. Though the world thought him a mean person, 'I will not be scorned out of my faith and religion by shallow, empty persons, that know not what Christ and religion meaneth.' No; 'I know whom I have believed; he is able to keep that that I have committed to him against that day.' Let us therefore be able to justify from a judicious apprehension, sweet divine truths. You see what justifications there are of the church of God, 'Wherefore should the heathen say, Where is now their God?' Micah vii. 10, and Ps. xlii. 10. Oh, it went to David's heart, when they said, 'Where is now their God,' 'What was become of his God,' when he was left in trouble, as the church here. And what doth he answer? Doth he let it go with a question? No, says he; our God is in heaven, Ps. cxiii. 4, and hath done whatsoever he pleased.

And this justification of religion, you may know by this sign. It is with the desertion of all discourses opposite to religion whatsoever. He that justifies the truth, he esteems meanly of other courses and discourses. Therefore in the next verse the church vilifies the idols. Our God is in heaven, and doth whatsoever he pleaseth; the idols are silver and gold, the work of men's hands: they have eyes and see not, ears and hear not, Ps. cxv. 6. And the more we justify Christ, the more we will be against antichrist and his religion. We may know the owning of the one truth by the vilifying the other. Let us labour therefore to grow to such a convincing knowledge of Christ; the good things in him; and the ways of God, as we may be able to stand out against all opposition of the gates of hell whatsoever.

And to this end proceed in the study of Christ, and to a deeper search of him, and of the excellencies and good things in him, that we may say as Micah vii. 18, 'Who is a God like to thee, that pardons sins and iniquities?' and as David, Ps. cxiii., 'Who is a God like our God, that humbleth himself to behold the things done here below?'

And desire also to this purpose, the spirit of revelation, that which Paul prays for, Eph. iii. 18, 'that we may know that knowledge that is above all knowledge, the height, depth, and breadth of God's love in Christ.' So sweet is God in the greatest abasements of his children, that he leaves such a taste in the soul of a Christian, that from thence he may be able to say, 'This is my beloved,' when his beloved seems not to care for him. When the church seemed to be disrespected and neglected of Christ, yet she says, 'This is my beloved, and this is my friend, O ye daughters of Jerusalem.'

Shall rich men boast of their riches? Shall men that are in favour, boast of the favour of great persons? Shall a man that hath large possessions boast and think himself as good and as great as his estate is? Shall a base-minded worldling be able to boast? 'Why boastest thou thyself, O mighty man?' Ps. lii. 1. Nay, you shall have malignant-spirited men boast of their malignant destructive power. I can do this and that mischief. Shall a man boast of mischief, that he is able to do mischief? and hath not a Christian more cause to boast in God and in salvation? Lord, shine on me, says David, Ps. iv. 6, let me enjoy the light of thy countenance; and that shall bring me more joy than they have, when their corn and wine increaseth. Know this, as he goes on in the same psalm, that God accepts the righteous man.

Therefore let us think we have much more cause to boast of God and of Christ in a spiritual manner, than the worldling hath of the world. Is not God and Christ our portion? and having Christ, have we not all things with Christ? Put case all things be took from us. If a man have Christ, he is rich though he have nothing else. If he have all without him, his plenty is (as a father saith, and as it is in truth) beggary. But whosoever hath Christ may thus rejoice with David, 'The lot is fallen to me in pleasant places; yea, I have a goodly heritage,' Ps. xvi. 6. Would we have more than God in Christ, a ring with a diamond very precious in it? Now the daughters of Jerusalem, hearing this large expression of affection, ask,

'Whither is thy beloved gone, O thou fairest among women? whither is thy beloved turned aside? that we may seek him with thee,' chap. vi. 1.

Here is another question. The first which the daughters of Jerusalem ask is, 'What is thy beloved?' whereupon the church took occasion to express what her beloved was: upon her expression closing up all with this general, 'This is my beloved, and this is my friend.'

Then the second question is, 'Whither is thy beloved gone?' One question begets another; and indeed if this question be well satisfied, what is Christ above others? this will follow again. Where is he? How shall I get him? How shall I seek him? What is the reason this second question is seldom made? Whither is he gone? how shall I get Christ? Because the former question, namely, 'What is Christ? is so seldom made. For if we did once know what Christ is, we would be sure with the daughters of Jerusalem to ask whither is he gone, that we may seek him with thee.

We see here is a growth in the desires of the daughters of Jerusalem, whence we learn,

That grace, though it be in never so little proportion at the first, it is growing still.

From the first question, 'What is thy beloved?' here is a second, upon better information, 'Whither is thy beloved gone, that we may seek him with thee?' Nothing is less than grace at the first, nothing in the world so little in proportion. The kingdom of heaven is compared to a grain of mustard seed, Mat. xiii. 31, *seq.* That is, the work of grace in the heart, as well as in the preaching of the gospel, in the beginning is little. It is true of the work of grace, as well as of the word of grace, that it is like a grain of mustard seed at first. 'What is thy beloved?' inquires the church at first; but when she hears of the excellency of Christ, then, 'Whither is thy beloved gone?' Grace begets grace. There is a connection and knitting together in religion. Good things beget good things. It is a strange thing in religion how great a matter ariseth of a little beginning. The woman of Samaria had but a small beginning of grace, and yet she presently drew many of her neighbours to believe in Christ. So Andrew, John i. 41. As soon as he was converted, he finds his brother Simon, and tells him that he had found the Messiah, and so brings him to Christ. And Philip, as soon as he had got a spark of faith himself, he draws also Nathanael to come to Christ. Paul speaks of his bonds, how the noise of them was in Cæsar's court, Philip. i. 13, and many believed the very report, which, howsoever it is not a working cause, yet it may be a preparing, inducing, leading cause to such things, from one thing to another, till there follow this change and full conversion. You see here the daughters of Jerusalem growing. Therefore, let us labour to be under good means. Some of the Romists and others, which are ill affected and grounded in that point, they think that the efficacy of grace is, as we call it, from the congruity, fitness, and proportion of the means to the heart and will of man. And thereupon God converts one and not another, because there is a congruous and fit offering of means to him when he is fitly disposed, and another is not fitly disposed. Therefore, there follows not upon it effectual calling. So that the virtue of the means offered depends upon suitableness and fitness in the party to whom the means are offered, and not upon the power and blessing of God. Verily, this is plausible, and goes down very roundly with many weak persons; but this is a false and a gross error, for unless God by his Holy Spirit do work by the means, no planting and watering will bring any increase, and change the heart and mind. Though there were greater means in Christ's time when he wrought these miracles, than any time before, yet all those could not convert that froward generation; and it was Moses's complaint in the wilderness, where they had abundance of means, 'God hath not given you a heart to perceive, and eyes to see, and ears to hear until this day,' Deut. xxix. 4. When a man is planted under good means and frequents them, then ordinarily it pleaseth God, by the inward workings of his own powerful Spirit, to work greater matters; and those that keep out of God's reach, that will not come into places where they may hear good things, there is no hope of them. Though there be many ill fish in the net, yet there is no hope to catch them that are without the net. So those that are kept out of all opportunities and occasions whereby God's Spirit may work upon them, there is no hope of them.

Let us learn this heavenly wisdom, to advantage ourselves this way, by improving all good opportunities whatsoever whereby we may learn; for God works by outward means. Good company and good discourse, these breed excellent thoughts. As, therefore, we love our souls, take all advantages wherein the Spirit of God works. We shall find incredible fruit thereof, more than we would believe. But to come to the question.

1. See here, first of all, in this question *the blessed success of the church's inquiry after Christ* in the daughters of Jerusalem after they heard the large explications of the excellencies of Christ, especially by the church, whom they had a good conceit of, for they call her 'the fairest among women.'

And seeing, likewise, the confidence of the church, she stands to it, 'This is my beloved;' yea, also, eagerness in the church to seek after him, they would seek him with her. So that where these meet, a large unfolding of the truth of God, and that by persons that are known to be good, well accepted, and conceited of, and where there is a large demonstration of real affection, and the things are spoken of with confidence, as knowing what they say; the word, I say, so managed, it is never without wondrous success.

(1.) For in the course of reason, what can I have to say, considering the party who speaks is an excellent person? He is wiser and holier than I; he takes to heart these things; and shall not I affect that which those that have better parts and graces do?

(2.) Then, withal, I see not only excellent persons do it, but I see how earnest they are. Surely there is some matter in it; for persons so holy, so wise, and gracious to be so earnest, surely either they are to blame, or I am too dull and too dead; but I have most cause to suspect myself.

(3.) And to see them carried with a spirit of confidence, as if they were well enough advised when they deliver this, 'This is my beloved,' in particular, and then to shut up all in general, 'This is my beloved, and this is my friend;' I say, when there is grace and life in the heart, and earnestness with confidence, this, together with the explication of the heavenly excellencies of Christ and of religion, it hath admirable success. As here in the church, 'the fairest among women,' the 'daughters of Jerusalem,' seeing the church was so earnest, confident, and so large in the explication of the excellencies of Christ, see how it works. It draws out this question with resolution. They join with the church in seeking Christ, 'Whither is thy beloved gone, O thou fairest among women? whither is thy beloved turned aside? that we may seek him with thee.' Where by the way observe, as the church before doubles it, 'This is my beloved, and this is my friend,' so they answer with a double question, 'Whither is thy beloved gone? whither is he turned aside? O thou fairest among women,' &c. From this appellation note,

2. If we would be happy instruments to convert others, being converted ourselves, *labour to be such as the world may think to be good and gracious*. 'O thou fairest among women,' fair in the robes of Christ took* out of his wardrobe. All the beauty and ornaments that the church hath she hath from Christ. Let us labour to be such as the world may conceit are good persons. We say of physicians, when the patient hath a good conceit of them, the cure is half wrought. So the doctrine is half persuaded when there is a good conceit of the speaker.

3. Again, *labour to be earnest*. If we would kindle others, we must be warmed ourselves; if we would make others weep, we must weep ourselves. Naturalists could observe this. The church spake this with large expressions, indeed, more than can be expressed. Let us labour to be deeply affected with what we speak, and speak with confidence as if we knew what we spoke, as the apostle John doth, in the beginning of his epistle, to bring others to be better persuaded of his doctrine. He affirmeth 'that which was from the beginning, which we have heard, which we have seen with these our eyes, which we have looked upon, and these hands of ours have handled of the word of life' he delivered to them, 1 John i. 1.

For when we are confident from spiritual experience, it is wonderful how we shall be instruments of God to gain upon others. So Peter. 'We followed not,' says he, 'deceivable fables, when we opened unto you the power and coming of our Lord Jesus Christ, but with our eyes we saw his majesty,' 2 Pet. i. 16.

Do not think it belongs only to the ministry. There is an art of conversion that belongs to every one that is a grown Christian, to win others.

'Whither is thy beloved gone, O thou fairest among women?'

The next observation out of the words, because it is the especial, which works upon the daughters of Jerusalem, is from the large explication of Christ.

* That is, 'taken.'—G

That which most of all stirs up holy affections to search after Christ is the large explications of his excellencies.

Then be in love with the ministry of the gospel and the communion of saints, who have their tongues and their hearts taught of God to speak excellently. Their tongues are as refined silver; their hearts are enriched to increase the communion of saints, Prov. x. 20. Mark this one excellency of that excellent ordinance of God in Christ, whereof Paul saith, Eph. iii. 7, 8, 'To me is committed this excellent office, to lay open the unsearchable riches of Christ;' such riches as may draw you to wonder, such 'as eye hath never seen, nor ear heard, nor hath entered into the heart of man to conceive,' 1 Cor. ii. 9; and so to draw the affections of people after them.

And because it is the special office of the ministry to lay Him open, to hold up the tapestry, to unfold the hidden mysteries of Christ, labour we, therefore, to be alway speaking somewhat about Christ, or tending that way. When we speak of the law, let it drive us to Christ; when of moral duties, to teach us to walk worthy of Christ. Christ, or somewhat tending to Christ, should be our theme and mark to aim at.

Therefore what shall we judge of those that are hinderers of this glorious ordinance of Christ in the gospel? They are enemies of conversion and of the calling of God's people; enemies of their comfort. And what shall we think of those wretched and miserable creatures that, like Cain, are vagabonds? who wander, and will not submit themselves to any ordinance meekly, but keep themselves out of this blessed opportunity of hearing the excellencies of Christ, which might draw their hearts to him? We are made for ever, if Christ and we be one. If we have all the world without him, it is nothing; if we have nothing in the world but Christ, we are happy. Oh! happy then when this match is made between Christ and the soul! The friends of the bride and of Christ, they, laying open the unsearchable riches of Christ to the spouse, draw the affections, work faith, and so bring the bride and the bridegroom together.

Thus far of the question. Now we have the church's answer to the daughters of Jerusalem.

'My beloved is gone into his garden, to the beds of spices, to feed in the gardens, and to gather lilies.'

The question was not for a bare satisfaction, but from a desire the church had to seek Christ. 'Whither is thy beloved gone, that we may seek him?' It was not a curious question, but a question of inquisition tending to practice. Many are inquisitive; but when they know another man's meaning, it is all they desire. Now I know your meaning, will they say, but I mean not to follow your counsel. The daughters of Jerusalem had a more sincere intention, 'O thou fairest among women, whither is thy beloved turned aside? *that we may seek him with thee*.' Whereunto the church answered,

'My beloved is gone into his garden, to the beds of spices, to feed in the gardens.' Where we see,

The church is not squeamish, but directly answers to the question. For there is no envy in spiritual things, because they may be divided *in solidum*. One may have as much as another, and all alike. Envy is not in those things that are not divisible; in other things, the more one hath, another hath the less. But there is no envy in grace and glory, because all may share alike. Therefore here is no envy in the answer, as if she denied the daughters of Jerusalem the enjoying of her beloved. No. If you will know, says she, I will tell you directly whither my beloved is gone.

'My beloved is gone into his garden, to the bed of spices,' &c.

God hath two gardens. The church catholic is his garden, and every particular church are gardens and beds of spices, in regard that many Christians are sown there that Christ's soul delights in, as in sweet spices. This was spoken of before at large in chapter v. 1, why the church is called a garden, being a severed place from the waste.* The church is severed from the wilderness of the world in God's care and love; likewise he tends and weeds his church and garden. As for the waste of the world, he is content the wilderness should have barren plants, but he will not endure such in his garden. Therefore those that give themselves liberty to be naught in the church of God, he will have a time to root them out. Trees that are not for fruit shall be for the fire; and above all other trees their doom shall be the heaviest that grow in God's garden without fruit. That fig-tree shall be cursed, Luke xiii. 6–9.

Men are pleased with answering the bill of accusation against them thus: Are we not baptized? and do we not come to church? &c. What do you make of us? Yet they are abominable swearers, and filthy in their lives. To such I say, the more God hath lift you up and honoured you in the use of the means, the more just shall your damnation be, that you bring forth nothing but briers and brambles, Heb. vi. 4, *seq.*, the grapes of Sodom and the vine of Gomorrah, Deut. xxxii. 32. Heavy will the doom be of many that live in the church's bosom, to whom it had been better to have been born in America (*r*), in Turkey, or in the most barbarous parts in the world. They have a heavy account to make that have been such ill proficients under abundance of means. Therefore it ought to be taken to heart.

'My beloved is gone into his garden, to the beds of spices, to feed in the gardens, and to gather lilies.'

That is, having first planted them lilies here, to gather them, and to transport them out of the garden here to the garden in heaven, where there shall be nothing but lilies. For the church of God hath two gardens or paradises since the first paradise (whereof that was a resemblance), the paradise of the church and the paradise of heaven. As Christ saith to the good thief, 'This day thou shalt be with me in paradise,' Luke xxiii. 43; so those that are good plants in the paradise of the church, they shall be glorious plants also in the paradise of heaven. We must not alway be here; we shall change our soil, and be taken into heaven. 'He is gone into his garden to gather lilies.'

1. Christians are compared to lilies for their *purity and whiteness*, unspotted in justification; and for their endeavours in sanctity and holiness, wherein also at length they shall be wholly unspotted. It is the end they are chosen to, 'to be holy without blame before him in love,' Eph. i. 4. God and Christ looks upon them without blame, not as they are here defiled and spotted, but as they intend, by little and little, to purge and purify themselves by the Spirit that is in them, that they may be altogether without blame. They are lilies, being clothed with the white garment of Christ's righteousness, not having a natural whiteness and purity (*s*). The whiteness and purity of God's children is borrowed. All their beauty and garments are taken out of another's wardrobe. The church is all glorious within; but she borrows her glory, as the moon borrows all her light from the sun. The church's excellency is borrowed. It is her own, but by gift; but being once her own, it is her own for ever.

The church before was likened to a garden culled out, an Eden, a para-

* See pp. 8–10.—G.

dise. Now there, you know, were four streams, sweet and goodly rivers, which watered paradise; the heads of which rivers were without it. So the church of God, her graces are her own; that is, the Spirit of God comes through her nature, purgeth and purifieth it; but the spring of those graces, as in paradise, is out of herself.

2. And then the lily is *a tall, goodly plant*. Therefore the church is compared to them. Other men are compared to thorns, not only for a noxious, hurtful quality in them, but for their baseness likewise. What are thorns good for, but to cumber the ground, to eat out the heart of it, to hide snakes, and for the fire? Wicked men are not lilies, but thorns. They are base, mean persons. Antiochus, Dan. xi. 21, is said to be a vile person, though he were a king, because he was a naughty* man. Wicked men, though they be never so great, being void of the grace of God, are vile persons. Though we must respect them in regard of their places, yet as they are in their qualification, they are vile and base thorns. But the church is not so, but as a lily among thorns, that is, among vile and abominable persons.

Use 1. The use is *to comfort God's children*. They have an excellency and glory in them, which, howsoever it is not from them, yet it is theirs by gift, and eternally theirs. Therefore let them comfort themselves against all the censures of sinful persons that labour to trample them under foot, and think basely and meanly of them, as of the offscouring of the world. Let the unworthy world think of them as they will, they are lilies in God's esteem, and are so indeed; glorious persons that have the Spirit of glory resting upon them, 1 Pet. iv. 14, and whom the world is not worthy of, Heb. xi. 38, though their glory be within. Therefore let us glory in it, that God vouchsafeth saving grace to us above any other privilege.

Use 2. Again, it comforts us in all our wants whatsoever, that *God will take care for us*. Christ useth this argument. God saith, he clotheth the lilies of the field with an excellent beauty; he cares even for the meanest plants, and will he not take care for you, O ye of little faith? Mat. vi. 29. Doth he care for lilies, that are to-day, and to-morrow are cast into the oven? and shall he not care for the lilies of paradise, the living lilies, those holy reasonable lilies? Undoubtedly he will. Our Saviour Christ's reason is undeniable. He that puts such a beauty upon the poor plants, that flourish to-day in the morning, and wither before night; he that puts such a beauty upon the grass of the field; will he not put more excellency upon his children? will he not provide for them, feed them? Undoubtedly he will. Thus we have shewed why God's children in the church of God are compared to lilies.

'To gather lilies.' Christ is said to gather these lilies, that is, he will gather them together. Christ will not have his lilies alone, scattered. Though he leaves them oft alone for a while, yet he will gather them to congregations and churches. The name of a church in the original is *Ecclesia* (*t*). It is nothing but a company gathered out of the world. Do we think that we are lilies by nature? No; we are thorns and briers. God makes us lilies, and then gathers us to other lilies, that one may strengthen another. The Spirit of God in his children is not a spirit of separation of Christians from Christians, but a spirit of separation from the waste, wild wilderness of the world, as we say of fire, *Congregat homogenea et disgregat heterogenea*. It congregates all homogeneal things, as gold, which it gathers, but disgregates heterogeneal things, consumeth dross. So the

* That is, 'wicked.'—G.

Spirit of God severs thorns, and gathers lilies; gathers Christians together in the church, and will gather them for ever in heaven.

Thus we see the answer of the church to the daughters of Jerusalem, what it was, with the occasion thereof; the question of the daughters of Jerusalem, 'Whither is thy beloved gone?' So that the church was beholden to the daughters of Jerusalem for ministering such a question, to give her occasion to know better what her beloved was. Indeed, we many times gain by weaker Christians. Good questions, though from weak ones, minister suitable answers. It is a Greek proverb, that 'doubting begets plenty and abundance,' for doubting at the first begets resolution at last. O! that we could take occasion hence to think of this. What excellent virtue is in the communion of saints, when they meet about heavenly exercises! What a blessing follows when, though at the entry their affections may be flat and dull, yet they part not so! Christ heats and inflames their hearts to do much good to one another. O! those that shall for ever live together in heaven, should they not delight to live more together on earth?

THE NINETEENTH SERMON.

I am my beloved's, and my beloved is mine; he feedeth among the lilies.—CANT. VI. 3.

THESE words are a kind of triumphant acclamation upon all the former passages; as it were, the foot of the song. For when the church had spoken formerly of her ill-dealing with Christ, and how he thereupon absented himself from her, with many other passages, she shuts up all at last with this, 'I am my beloved's, and my beloved is mine.'

Now she begins to feel some comfort from Christ, who had estranged himself from her. O! saith she, notwithstanding all my sufferings, desertions, crosses, and the like, 'I am my beloved's, and my beloved is mine,' words expressing the wondrous comfort, joy, and contentment the church now had in Christ; having her heart inflamed with love unto him, upon his manifesting of himself to her soul. 'I am my beloved's, and my beloved is mine: he feedeth among the lilies.'

There is a mutual intercourse and vicissitude of claiming interest betwixt Christ and his church. I am Christ's, and Christ is mine. 'I am my beloved's, and my beloved is mine.'

From the dependence and order of the words coming in after a desertion for a while, observe,

That Christ will not be long from his church.

The spiritual desertions (forsakings, as we use to call them), howsoever they be very irksome to the church (that loves communion with Christ), and to a loving soul to be deprived of the sense of her beloved, yet notwithstanding they are but short. Christ will not be long from his church. His love and her desire will not let him. They offer violence. Why art thou absent? say they. Why art thou so far off, and hidest thyself? Joseph may conceal himself for a space, but he will have much ado so to hold long, to be straitened to his brethren. Passion will break out. So Christ may seem hard to be entreated, and to cross his own sweet disposition, as to the woman of Canaan, but he will not long keep at this distance. He is soon overcome. 'O! woman, great is thy faith; have what thou wilt,' Mat. xv. 28. When she strove with him a little (as faith is a striving grace), see how she did win upon him! So the angel and Jacob may strive for a while, but Jacob at the length proves Israel; he prevails with God, Gen. xxxii. 24, *seq*. So it is with the Christian soul and Christ. Howsoever there be desertion, for causes before mentioned, because the church was negligent, as we hear, and partly for the time to come, that Christ, by his estrangement, might sweeten his coming again howsoever there may be strangeness for a time, yet Christ will return again to his spouse.

Use 1. The use should be not only *for comfort to stay us in such times, but to teach us likewise to wait, and never give over*. If the church had given over here, she had not had such gracious manifestations of Christ to her. Learn hence, therefore, this use, to wait God's leisure. God will wait to do good to them that wait on him, Isa. xxx. 18. If we wait his leisure, he will wait an opportunity of doing good to us. When God seems not to answer our prayers, let us yet wait. We shall not lose by our tarrying. He will wait to do us good.

Use 2. In the next place, observe, after this temporary desertion, *Christ visits his church with more abundant comfort than ever before*.

Now, the church cannot hold, 'My beloved is mine, and I am his;' and Christ cannot hold, but falls into a large commendation of his spouse back again. As she was large in his commendations, so he is large in hers, and more large. He will have the last word. Therefore, learn by this experience, 'that all things work together for the best to them that love God,' Rom. viii. 28. All things. What? evil? Ay, evil. Why, even sin turns to their humiliation; yea, and desertion (those spiritual ills), turns to their good; for Christ seems to forsake for a while, that he may come after with more abundance of comfort. When once he hath enlarged the soul before with a spacious desire of his coming, to say, O! that he would come; when the soul is thus stretched with desire in the sense of want, then he fills it again till it burst forth, 'My beloved is mine, and I am his.' It was a good experiment of Bernard, an holy man in ill times, *tibi accidit*, &c., speaking of Christ's dealing with his church. He comes and he goeth away for thy good. He comes for thy good to comfort thee; after which, if thou be not careful to maintain communion with him, then he goeth away for thy good, to correct thy error, and to enlarge thy desire of him again, to teach thee to lay sure and faster hold upon him when thou hast him, not to let him go again.

If you would see a parallel place to this, look in Cant. iii., where there is the like case of the spouse and Christ, 'By night on my bed I sought him.' The church sought Christ not only by day, but by night, 'I sought him whom my soul loved.' Though she wanted him, yet her soul loved him constantly. Though a Christian's soul have not present communion with Christ, yet he may truly say, My soul loves him, because he seeks him diligently and constantly in the use of all the means. So we see the church, before my text, calls him my beloved still, though she wanted communion with him. Well, she goes on, 'I sought him, but I found him not.' Would the church give over there? No; then she riseth and goeth about the city, and about the streets, and 'seeks him whom her soul loved,' seeks him, and will not give over. So I sought him, but I wanted the issue of my seeking, I found him not. What comes upon that? 'The watchmen go about the city, and find her.' Of whom, when by her own seeking she could not find Christ, she inquires, 'Saw you him whom my soul loveth?' She inquires of the watchmen, the guides of God's people, who could not satisfy her fully. She could not find her beloved, yet what doth she, she shews, verse 4. It was but a little that she stayed, after she had used all means, private and public—in her bed, out of her bed—by the watchmen and others, yet, saith she, it was but a little that I was past from them. She had not an answer presently, though the watchmen gave her some good counsel. It was not presently, yet not long after. Christ will exercise us a while with waiting: 'It was but a little that I passed from them, but I found him whom my soul loved.' After all our seeking, there must be waiting, and then we shall find him whom our soul loveth. Perhaps we have used all means, private and public, and yet find not that comfort we look for. Oh, but wait a while! God hath a long time waited for thee. Be thou content to wait a while for him. We shall not lose by it, for it follows in the next verse; after she had found him whom her soul loved, 'I held him, I would not let him go.' So this is the issue of desertions. They stir up diligence and searching, in the use of means, private and public; and exercise patience to wait God's leisure, who will not suffer a gracious soul to fail of its expectation. At length he will fulfil the desires of them that fear him, Ps. cxlv. 19; and this comes of their patience. Grace grows greater and stronger. 'I held him, and would not let him go, until I had brought him unto my mother's house.' Thus you see how the Spirit expresseth the same truth in another state of the church. Compare place with place. To go on.

'I am my beloved's, and my beloved is mine.' The words themselves are a passionate expression of long-looked-for consolation. Affections have eloquence of their own beyond words. Fear hath a proper expression. Love vents itself in broken words and sighs, delighting in a peculiar eloquence suitable to the height and pitch of the affection, that no words can reach unto. So that here is more in the words breathed from such an inflamed heart, than in ordinary construction can be picked out, 'I am my beloved's,' &c., coming from a full and large heart, expressing the union and communion between Christ and the church, especially after a desertion. 'I am my beloved's, and my beloved is mine.'

First, I say, the union, viz., the union of persons, which is before all comfort and communion of graces, 'I am my beloved's, and my beloved is mine.' Christ's person is ours, and our persons are his. For, as it is in marriage, if the person of the husband be not the wife's, his goods are not hers, nor his titles of honour; for these come all to her, because his person is hers: he having passed over the right of his own body and of his person to his wife, as she hath passed over all the right of herself to her husband. So it is in this mystical marriage. That that entitles us to communion of graces is union of persons between Christ and his church. 'I am my beloved's, and my beloved himself is mine.' And indeed nothing else will content a Christian's heart. He would not care so much for heaven itself, if he had not Christ there. The sacrament, word, and comforts, why doth he esteem them? As they come from Christ, and as they lead to Christ. It is but an adulterous and base affection to love anything severed from Christ.

Now, from this union of persons comes a communion of all other things whatsoever. 'I am my beloved's, and my beloved is mine.' If Christ himself be mine, then all is mine (*u*). What he hath done, what he hath suffered, is mine; the benefit of all is mine. What he hath is mine. His prerogatives and privileges to be the Son of God, and heir of heaven, and the like, all is mine. Why? Himself is mine. Union is the foundation of communion. So it is here with the church, 'I am my beloved's.' My person is his, my life is his, to glorify him, and to lay it down when he will. My goods are his, my reputation his. I am content to sacrifice all for him. I am his, all mine is his. So you see there is union and communion mutually, between Christ and his church. The original and spring hereof is Christ's uniting and communicating himself to his church first. The spring begins to* the stream. What hath the stream or cistern in it, but what is had from the spring? First we love him, because he loved us first, 1 John iv. 19. It was a true speech of Augustine, *Quicquid bonum*, &c.: whatsoever is good in the world or lovely, it is either God or from God; it is either Christ or from Christ. He begins it. It is said in nature, love descends. The father and the mother love the child before the child can love them. Love, indeed, is of a fiery nature. Only here is the dissimilitude, fire ascends, love descends. It is stronger, descending from the greater to the less, than ascending up from the meaner to the greater, and that for this amongst other reasons,

Because the greater person looks upon the lesser as a piece of himself—sees himself in it. The father and mother see themselves in their child. So God loves us more than we can love him, because he sees his image in us. Neither is there only a priority of order. He loves us first, and then we love him. But also of causality. He is the cause of our love, not by way of motive only. He loves us, and therefore from an ingenuous spirit we must love him again. But he gives us his Spirit, circumciseth our hearts to love him, Deut. xxx. 6; for all the motives or moral persuasions in the world, without the Spirit, cannot make us love, 1 Thess. iv. 9. We are taught of God to love one another, our brethren whom we see daily, saith Paul, much more need we to be taught to love him whom we never saw, so that his love kindles ours by way of reflection.

In the new covenant God works both parts, his own and our parts too. Our love to him, our fear of him, our faith in him, he works all, even as he shews his own love to us.

If God love us thus, what must we do? Meditate upon his love. Let our hearts be warmed with the consideration of it. Let us bring them to that fire of his love, and then they will wax hot within us, and beg the Spirit, 'Lord, thou hast promised to give thy Spirit to them that ask it,' Luke xi. 10, and to circumcise our hearts to love thee, and to love one another, 'give thy Holy Spirit, as thou hast promised.'

In a word, these words, 'I am my beloved's, and my beloved is mine,' to join them both together.

1. They imply a *mutual propriety*,† Christ hath a propriety in me, and I in Christ. Peculiar propriety. Christ is mine, so as I have none in the world. So mine, 'whom have I in heaven but Christ?' and what is there in earth in comparison of him? He is mine, and mine in a peculiar manner, and I am his in a peculiar manner. There is propriety with peculiarity.

2. Then, again, these words, 'I am his,' implies *mutual love*. All is mutual in them, mutual propriety, mutual peculiarity, and mutual love. I love Christ so as I love nothing else. There is nothing above him in my heart, as Christ loves me more than anything else, saith the church, and every Christian. He loves all, and gives outward benefits to all, but to me

* That is, 'originates, or gives its beginning to.'—ED.

† That is, 'property.'—G.

he hath given himself, so love I him. As the husband loves all in the family, his cattle and his servants, but he gives himself to his spouse. So Christ is mine, himself is mine, and myself am Christ's. He hath my soul, my affections, my body, and all. He hath a propriety in me, and a peculiarity in me. He hath my affection and love to the uttermost, as I have his, for there is an intercourse in these words.

3. Then, again, they imply *mutual familiarity*. Christ is familiar to my soul, and I to Christ. He discovers himself to me in the secret of his love, and I discover myself to him in prayer and meditation, opening my soul to him upon all occasions. God's children have a spirit of prayer, which is a spirit of fellowship, and talks, as it were, to God in Christ. It is the language of a new-born Christian. He cries to his Father. There is a kind of familiarity between him and his God in Christ, who gives the entrance and access to God. So that where there is not a kind of familiarity in prayer and opening of the soul to Christ upon all occasions, there is not this holy communion. Those that are not given to prayer, they cannot in truth speak these words, as the church doth here, 'I am my beloved's, and my beloved is mine,' for they imply sweet familiarity.

4. Then, again, they imply *mutual likeness* one to another. He is mine, and I am his. The one is a glass to the other. Christ sees himself in me, I see myself in him. For this is the issue of spiritual love, especially, that it breeds likeness and resemblance of the party loved in the soul that loveth; for love frameth the soul to the likeness of the party loved. I am his, I resemble him. I am his, I have given myself to him. I carry his picture and resemblance in my soul, for they are words of mutual conformity. Christ, out of love, became like me in all things, wherein I am not like the devil, that is, sin excepted. If he became like me, taking my nature that I might be near him in the fellowship of grace, 'My beloved is mine,' I will be as like him as possibly I can, I am his. Every Christian carries a character of Christ's disposition as far as weakness will suffer. You may know Christ in every Christian; for as the king's coin carries the stamp of the king (Cæsar's coin bears Cæsar's superscription), so every Christian soul is God's coin, and he sets his own stamp upon it. If we be Christ's, there is a mutual conformity betwixt him and us.

Now, where you see a malicious, unclean, worldly spirit, know that is a stamp of the devil, none of Christ's. He that hath not the Spirit of God is none of his. Now, where the Spirit of Christ is, it stamps Christ's likeness upon the soul. Therefore we are exhorted, Phil. ii. 5, to be like-minded to Christ.

5. Again, these words, 'I am my beloved's, and my beloved is mine,' imply a *mutual care* that Christ and the soul have of the good of one another, of each other's honour and reputation. As Christ hath a care of our good, so a Christian soul, if it can say with truth and sincerity I am Christ's, it must needs have care of Christ's good, of his children, religion, and truth. What! will such a soul say, Shall Christ care for my body, soul, and salvation, and stoop to come from heaven to save me, and shall I have no care for him and his glory? He hath left his truth and his church behind him, and shall not I defend his truth, and stand for the poor church to the utmost of my power against all contrary power? Shall not I stand for religion? Shall it be all one to me what opinions are held? Shall I pretend he cares for me, and shall I not care for that I should care for? Is it not an honour to me that he hath trusted me to care for anything? that he will be honoured by my care? Beloved, it is an honour for us that we may speak

a good word for religion, for Christ's cause, for his church, against maligners and opposers; and we shall know one day that Christ will be a rewarder of every good word. Where this is said in sincerity, that Christ is mine, and I am Christ's, there will be this mutual care.

6. Likewise there is implied a *mutual complacency* in these words. By a complacency I mean a resting, contenting love. Christ hath a complacency and resting in the church; and the church hath a sweet resting contentment in Christ. Christ in us and we in him. A true Christian soul that hath yielded up its consent to Christ, when it is beaten in the world, vexed and turmoiled, it can rely on this, 'I have yet a loving husband;' yet I have Christ.

Let this put us upon a search into ourselves, what we retire to, when we meet with afflictions. Those that have brutish and beastly souls retire to carnal contentments, to good fellowship; forget, besot, and fly away from themselves; their own consciences and thought of their own trouble. Whereas a soul that hath any acquaintance with God in Christ, or any interest into Christ, so that it may say, that Christ is mine, and I am Christ's, there will be contentment and rest in such a soul, whatsoever it meets with in the world.

7. The last thing implied is *courage*, a branch of the former. Say all against it what they can, saith the resolved soul, I will be Christ's. Here is courage with resolution. Agreeable hereto is that, 'One shall say I am the Lord's, and another shall call himself by the name of Jacob; another shall subscribe and surname himself by the name of Israel,' Isa. xliv. 5. Where there is not this resolution in good causes, there is not the Spirit of Christ; there is no interest into Christ. It is but a delusion and self-flattery to say I am Christ's, when there is not resolution to stand to Christ. These words are the expression of a resolved heart, I am, and I will be Christ's; I am not ashamed of my bargain; of the consent I have given him; I am and I will be his. You have the like in Micah iv. 5, 'All people will walk every one in the name of his god, they will resolve on that, and we will walk in the name of the Lord our God for ever and for ever.' So that where these words are spoken in truth, that 'I am Christ's,' there is necessarily implied, I will own him and his cause for ever and ever.

He hath married me for ever and ever; therefore, if I hope to have interest in him for comfort for ever and ever, I must be sure to yield myself to him for ever and ever; and stand for his cause, in all oppositions, against all enemies whatsoever. These and such like places in Scripture run parallel with this in the text, 'I am my beloved's, and my beloved is mine,' not only holding in the person, but in the cause of Christ. Every man hopes his god will stand for him against the devil, who accuseth us daily. If we will have Christ to stand for us, and to be an advocate to plead our cause as he doth in heaven, we must resolve to stand for him against all enemies, heretics, schismatics, persecutors whatsoever; that we will walk in the name of our God for ever and ever.

Quest. But when the case is not thus with us, and that neither we can feel comfort from Christ, nor have this assurance of his love to us, what should we judge of such?

Solution. We should not wonder to see poor souls distempered when they are in spiritual desertions, considering how the spouse cannot endure the absence of Christ. It is out of love therefore in the deepest plunge she hath this in her mouth, '*my* beloved.' Therefore let us not judge amiss of ourselves or others, when we are impatient in this kind.

But for a more full answer, in want of feeling of the love of Christ in regard of that measure we would (for there is never altogether a want of feeling, there is so much as keeps from despair alway, yet), if we carry a constant love towards him, mourn to him and seek after him as the church here; if the desire of our souls be after him, that we make after him in the use of means, and are willing to speak of him as the church here, feel or feel not, we are his, and he will at length discover himself to us.

Let such drooping spirits consider, that as he will not be long from us, nor wholly, so it shall not be for our disadvantage that he retires at all. His absence at length will end in a sweet discovery of himself more abundantly than before. He absents himself for our good, to make us more humble and watchful for the time to come; more pitiful to others; more to prize our former condition; to justify the ways of God more strictly; to walk with him; to regain that sweet communion which by our negligence and security we lost. When we are thus prepared by his absence, there ensues a more satisfying discovery of himself than ever before.

But when is the time that he comes? Compare this with the former chapter. He comes after long waiting for him. The church waited for him, and waited in the use of all means. She runs to the watchmen, and then inquires after him of the daughters of Jerusalem. After this she finds him. After we have waited and expected Christ in the use of means, Christ at length will discover himself to us; and yet more immediately, it was after the church had so deservedly exalted him in such lofty praises, 'This is my beloved, the chief of ten thousand; he is altogether lovely.' When we set our hearts to the high exaltation of Christ above all things in the world, proclaiming him 'the chief of ten thousand,' this at the last breeds a gracious discovery, 'I am my beloved's, and my beloved is mine,' for Christ when he sees us faithful, and so loving that we will not endure his absence, and so constantly loving, that we love him notwithstanding some discouragements, it melts him at the last, as Joseph was melted by his brethren.

'I am my beloved's, and my beloved is mine.'

In the words, you see a mutual interest and owning between Christ and the church. Howsoever in the order of words, the church saith, 'I am my beloved's' first, yet in order of nature Christ is ours first, though not in order of discovery. There is one order of knowing, and another order of causing. Many things are known by the effect, but they issue from a cause. I know he is mine, because I am his. I have given myself to him. I know it is day, because the sun is up. There is a proof from the effect. So I know a man is alive, because he walks. There is a proof of the cause by the effect. 'I am his;' I have grace to give myself up to him. Therefore I know he loves me. He is mine. Thus I say in order of discovery; but in order of nature, he is first mine, and then I am his. 'My beloved is mine, and I am my beloved's.'

The union and communion betwixt us and Christ hath been already spoken of.

Now to speak of the branches, 'I am my beloved's, and my beloved is mine.' That Christ is first ours; and then we are his, because he is ours; and the wondrous comfort that issues hence—that Christ himself is ours.

How comes Christ to be ours? (1.) Christ is ours by his Father's gift. God hath given him for us. (2.) Christ is ours by his own gift. He hath given himself for us. (3.) And Christ is ours by his Spirit that witnesseth so much to our spirits. For the Spirit is given for this purpose, to shew us all things that are given us of God, whereof Christ is the chief. Therefore the Spirit of Christ tells us that Christ is ours; and Christ being ours, all that he hath is ours.

If he be ours, if we have the field, we have all the treasures in the field. If we have him, we have all his. He was born for us; his birth was for us; he became man for us; he was given to death for us. And so likewise, he is ours in his other estate of exaltation. His rising is for our good. He will cause us to rise also, and ascend with him, and sit in heavenly places, judging the world and the angels. We recover in this second, what we lost in the first, Adam.

Use 1. This is a point of wondrous comfort *to shew the riches of a Christian*, his high estate, that Christ is his.

And Christ being ours, God the Father and the Holy Spirit and all things else in the world, the rich promises, are ours; for in Christ they are all made, and for him they shall be performed. For, indeed, he is the chief promise of all himself, and all are 'yea and amen in him,' 2 Cor. i. 20. Can we want righteousness, while we have Christ's righteousness? Is not his garment large enough for himself and us, too? Is not his obedience enough for us? Shall we need to patch it up with our own righteousness? He is ours, therefore his obedience is ours.

Use 2. And this should be a ground likewise of *contentation* in our condition and state whatsoever*,—Christ himself is ours. In the dividing of all things, some men have wealth, honours, friends, and greatness, but not Christ, nor the love of God in Christ, and therefore they have nothing in mercy. But a Christian, he hath Christ himself. Christ is his by faith and by the Spirit's witness. Therefore, what if he want those appendencies,† the lesser things? He hath the main; what if he want a riveret, a stream? He hath the spring, the ocean; him, in whom all things are, and shall he not be content? Put case a man be very covetous, yet God might satisfy him. What! should anxious thoughts disquiet us, when we have such bills, such obligations from him who is faithfulness itself? When a Christian cannot say, honour, favour, or great persons are his, yet he can say, he hath that that is worth all, more than all; Christ is his.

Obj. Oh! may some say, this is but a speculation,—Christ is yours. A man may want and be in misery for all that.

Ans. No; it is a reality. Christ is ours, and all things else are ours. He that can command all things is mine. Why then, do I want other things? Because he sees they are not for my good. If they were, he would not withhold them from me. If there were none to be had without a miracle, no comfort, no friends, he could and would make new out of nothing, nay, out of contraries, were it not better for me to be without them.

Use 3. That you may the more fully feed on this comfort, *study the excellencies of Christ* in the Scripture, the riches and honour that he hath, the favour he is in with his Father, with the intercession that he makes in heaven, John xvii. Study his mercy, goodness, offices, power, &c., and then come home to yourselves, 'All this is mine, for he is mine; the love of God is mine.' God loves him, and therefore he loves me, because we are both one. He loves me with the same love that he loves his Son. Thus we should make use of this, that Christ is ours. I come to the second.

'I am my beloved's.'

This is a speech of reflection, second in nature, though first in place and

* That is, 'contentment.'—G. † That is, 'additions.'—G.

in discovery to us. Sometimes we can know our own love, when we feel not so much the love of Christ, but Christ's love must be there first. 'I am my beloved's,' 1 John iv. 19.

How are we Christ's beloved ?

1. We are his, first of all, *by his Father's gift;* for God in his eternal purpose gave him for us, and gives us to him, as it is in the excellent prayer, 'Father, thine they were, and thou gavest them me,' John xvii. 6. I had not them of myself first, but thine they were before all worlds were. Thou gavest them me to redeem them, and my commission doth not extend beyond thy gift. I die for all those that thou gavest me. I sanctify myself for them, that they may be sanctified. So we are Christ's in his Father's gift. But that is not all, though it be the chief, fundamental, principal ground of all.

For, 2. We are his likewise by *redemption.* Christ took our nature, that he might die for us, to purchase us. We cost him dear. We are a bloody spouse to Christ. As that froward woman wrongfully said to Moses, 'Thou art a bloody husband unto me,' Exod. iv. 25, so Christ may without wrong say to the church, 'Thou art a spouse of blood to me.' We were, indeed, to be his spouse, but first he must win us by conquest in regard of Satan, and then satisfy justice. We were in such debt by sin, lying under God's wrath, so as, till all debts were paid, we could not in the way of justice be given as a spouse to Christ.

3. Nor is this all ; but we are Christ's *by marriage* also. For when he purchased us, and paid so dear for us, when he died and satisfied divine justice, he did it with a purpose to marry us to himself. We have nothing to bring him but debt and misery ; yet he took upon him our nature to discharge all, that he might marry us, and take us to himself. So we are his by marriage.

4. Then again, we are his *by consent.* We have passed ourselves over unto him. He hath given himself to us, and we have given ourselves to him back again. To come to some use of it, if we be Christ's, as Christ is ours.

Use 1. First, it is a point of *wondrous comfort.* God will not suffer his own to want. He is worse than an infidel that will suffer his family to perish. When we are once of Christ's family, and not only of his family, but of his body, his spouse, can we think he will suffer us to want that which is needful ?

2. Then again, as it comforts us against want, so it likewise *fenceth us against all the accusations of Satan.* I am Christ's ; I am Christ's. If he have anything to say, lo ! we may bid him go to Christ. If the creditor comes to the wife, she is not liable to pay her own debts, but saith, Go to my husband. So in all temptations, learn hence to send Satan whither he should be sent. When we cannot answer him, send him to Christ.

3. And for the time to come, what a ground of comfort is this, that we are Christ's, as well as he is ours. What a plea doth this put into our mouths for all things that are beneficial to us. 'Lord, I am thine ; save me,' saith the psalmist. Why ? 'Save me, because I am thine, I am thine ; Lord, teach me and direct me,' Ps. xxvii. 11. The husband is to direct the spouse. The head should direct all the senses. All the treasures of wisdom are in Christ, as all the senses are in the head for the good of the body. All fulness dwells in him. Therefore, plead with him, I want wisdom ; teach me and instruct me how to behave myself in troubles, in dangers, in fears. If it be an argument strong enough amongst men,

weak men, I am thine, I am thy child, I am thy spouse, &c, shall we attribute more pity and mercy to ourselves than to the God of mercy and comfort, who planted these affections in the creature? Shall he make men tender and careful over others, and shall not he himself be careful of his own flock? Do we think that he will neglect his jewels, his spouse, his diadem, and crown? Isa. lxii. 3. He will not.

But you will urge experience. We see how the church is used, even as a forlorn widow, as if she had no husband in the world, as an orphan that had no father. Therefore, how doth this stand good?

Ans. 1. The answer is, all that the church or any particular Christian suffers in this world, it is but that there may be *a conformity between the spouse and the husband.* The Head wore a crown of thorns, and went to heaven and happiness through a great deal of misery and abasement in the world, the lowest that ever was. And it is not meet that the church should go to heaven another way.

Ans. 2. Then again, all this is but *to fashion the spouse to be like to Christ,* but to bring the church and Christ nearer together. That is all the hurt they do, to drive the church nearer to Christ than before. Christ is as near to his church as ever in the greatest afflictions, by his Spirit. Christ cries out on the cross, 'My God, my God, why hast thou forsaken me?' It is a strange voice, that God should be his God, and yet, notwithstanding, seem to forsake him. But God was never more his God than at that present. Indeed, he was not his God in regard of some feelings that he had enjoyed in former times. He seemed to be forsaken in regard of some sense, as Christ seems to forsake the church in regard of some sense and feeling, but yet his God still. So the church may say, I am thine still. Though she seem to be forsaken in regard of some feelings, yet she is not deserted in regard of God's care for support of the inward man and fashioning to Christ. The church hath never sweeter communion with Christ than under the greatest crosses; and, therefore, they many times have proved the ground of the greatest comforts. For Christ leads the church into the wilderness, and then speaks to her heart, Hos. ii. 14. Christ speaks to the heart of his spouse in the wilderness, that is, in a place of no comfort. There are no orchards or pleasures, but all discomforts there. A man must have it from heaven, if he have any good in the wilderness. In that wilderness, that is, in a desolate, disconsolate estate, Christ speaks to the heart of his children. There is in the wilderness oftentimes a sweet intercourse of love, incomparably beyond the time of prosperity.

Ans. 3 Again, to stay your hearts, *know this will not be long;* as we see here, the church seemed to be forsaken and neglected, fell into the hands of cruel watchmen, and was fain to go through this and that means, but it was not long ere she met with him whom she sought after. It may be midnight at this time, but the night continues not long; it will be morning ere long. Therefore the church may well say, 'Rejoice not against me, O mine enemy; for though I be fallen, I shall rise again; though I sit in darkness, the Lord will be a light unto me,' as it is Mic. vii. 8. It shall not be always ill with the church. Those that survive us shall see other manner of days than we see yet, whatsoever we shall ourselves.

4. Hence we have also an use of trial. Whosoever are Christ's, they have hearts to give themselves to him. As he gives himself, not his goods or his honours, but himself for his church, so the church gives herself to Christ. My delight is in him; he hath myself, my heart, my love and affection, my joy and delight, and all with myself. If I have any honour,

he shall have it. I will use it for his glory. My riches I will give them to him and his church and ministry and children, as occasion shall serve. I am his, therefore all that I have is his, if he ask it at my hands. It is said of the Macedonians, they gave themselves to Christ, and then their riches and goods, 2 Cor. viii. 5. It is an easy matter to give our riches to Christ when we have given ourselves first. A Christian, as soon as ever he becomes a Christian, and ever after, to death, and in death too, he gives up himself to Christ. They that stand with Christ, and will give this or that particular, will part only with idle things that they may spare, are they Christ's? No. A Christian gives himself and all his to Christ. So we see here what we should do if Christ be ours. Let us give up ourselves to him, as it is Rom. xii. 1. The issue of all that learned profound discourse in the former part of the epistle, that Christ justifieth us by his righteousness and merit, and sanctifies us by his Spirit, and hath predestinated and elected us, and refused others, is this, 'I beseech you, give up your bodies and souls, and all as a living sacrifice, holy and acceptable unto God.

In brief, these words imply renunciation and resignation. 'I am his,' that is, I have given up myself to him, therefore I renounce all others that stand not with his love and liking. I am not only his by way of service, which I owe him above all that call for it, but I am his by way of resignation. If he will have me die, I will die. If he will have me live here, I will. I have not myself to dispose of any longer. I have altogether alienated myself from myself. I am his to serve him, his to be disposed of by him. I have renounced all other.

Therefore here we have another answer to Satan, if he come to us and solicit us to sin. Let the Christian's heart make this answer, *I am not mine own*. What hath Satan and his instruments to do with me? Is my body his to defile? Is my tongue his to swear at his pleasure? Shall I make the temple of God the member of an harlot? As the apostle reasons, 'Shall I defile my vessel with sin?' 1 Cor. vi. 15. What saith converted Ephraim? 'What have I any more to do with idols? for I have seen and observed him?' Hos. xiv. 8. We ought to have such resolutions ready in our hearts. Indeed, when a Christian is resolute, the world counts such to be lost. He is gone. We have lost him, say your dissolute, profane persons. It is true they have lost him indeed, for he is not his own, much less theirs, any longer. But he is found to God and himself and the church. Thus we see what springs from this, that Christ is ours, and that we are Christ's back again. Let us carry this with us even to death; and if times should come that God should honour us by serving himself of us in our lives, if Christ will have us spend our blood, consider this, I am not mine own in life nor death, and it is my happiness that I am not my own. For if I were mine own, what should I do with myself? I should lose myself, as Adam did. It is therefore my happiness that I am not mine own, that I am not the world's, that I am not the devil's, that none else hath to do with me, to claim any interest in me, but I am Christ's. If I do anything for others, it is for Christ's sake. Remember this for the time to come. If there be anything that we will not part with for Christ's sake, it will be our bane. We shall lose Christ and it too. If we will not say with a perfect spirit, I am his, my life, my credit, my person is his, anything his; look what we will not give for him, at length we shall lose and part with it and him too.

THE TWENTIETH SERMON.

I am my beloved's, and my beloved is mine; he feedeth among the lilies.—CANT. VI. 3.

THE church, you see here, though she stood out a while against all Christ's invitation and knocking, yet at length she is brought to yield herself up wholly unto Christ, and to renounce herself, which course God takes with most, yea, in a manner with all his people, ere they go out of this world, to lay all high things low, beat down every high thought and imagination which exalteth itself against him, 2 Cor. x. 5, that they may give themselves and all they have to Christ, Luke xiv. 26, if he call for it. For he that doth not so is not worthy of Christ. If we do not this, at least in preparation of mind, let us not own the name of Christians, lest we own that which shall further increase and aggravate our condemnation, professing religion one way, and yet alienating our minds to our lusts and pleasures of the world another way. To have peculiar love-fits of our own, distinct from Christ, how stands this with 'I am my beloved's, and my beloved is mine'? How stands it with the self-resignation that was spoken of before?

Now this follows upon apprehension of Christ being ours. 'I am my beloved's, because my beloved is mine first.' There are four reasons why Christ must be given to us before we can give ourselves to him by this self-resignation.

1. *Because he is the chief spring of all good affections*, which he must place in us; loving us, ere we can love him, 1 John iv. 10, 19.

2. *Because love descends.* Though it be of a fiery nature, yet in this it is contrary, for love descends, whereas fire ascends. The superior, first loves the inferior. Christ must descend in his love to us, ere we can ascend to him in our affections.

3. *Because our nature is such that we cannot love but where we know ourselves to be loved first.* Therefore God is indulgent to us herein; and that we may love him, he manifests his love first to us.

4. *Because naturally ourselves, being conscious of guilt, are full of fears from thence.* So that if the soul be not persuaded first of Christ's love, it runs away from him, as Adam did from God, and as Peter from Christ, 'Depart from me, for I am but a sinful man,' Luke v. 8. So the soul of every man would say, if first it were not persuaded of God's love in Christ, 'Who amongst us shall dwell with the everlasting burnings?' Isa. xxxiii. 14. Therefore to prevent that disposition of soul which would rise out of the sense of guilt and unworthiness, God first speaks to us in Christ; at length saying unto our souls, 'I am thy salvation,' whereupon the soul first finding his love, loves him back again, of whom it finds itself so much beloved; so that our love is but a reflection of his, 'I am my beloved's, because my beloved is mine.'

It is with the Spirit of God as with the spirits in the soul and body of a man, there is a marriage betwixt the body and soul. The spirits join both together, being of a middle nature; for they have somewhat spiritual near the soul, and somewhat bodily near the body. Therefore they come between the body and the soul, and are the instruments thereof, whereby it works. So it is with the Spirit of God. The same Spirit that tells the soul that Christ is ours, the same Spirit makes up the match on our part, and gives us up to Christ again.

Let this then be the trial that we are Christ's, by the spiritual echo that our souls make to that report which Christ makes to our souls, whether in promises or in instructions.

Use 1. See hence likewise the nature of faith, for these are the words of faith as well as of love. Faith hath two branches, it doth give as well as take. Faith receives Christ, and says, Christ is mine; and the same faith saith, I am Christ's again. Indeed, our souls are empty; so that the main work of faith is to be an empty hand, *mendica manus* (as Luther calls it); a beggar's hand to receive. But when it hath received it gives back again, both ourselves and all that we can do. The churches of Macedonia 'gave themselves,' and then 'they gave their goods,' 2 Cor. viii. 5. Where faith is, there will be a giving of ourselves and our goods; and, by a proportion, our strength, wits, and all back again. This discovers a great deal of empty false faith in the world; for undoubtedly if it were true faith there would be a yielding back again.

Use 2. And again, these words discover the mutual coherence of justification and sanctification, and the dependence one upon another. 'I am my beloved's, and my beloved is mine.' Christ is mine; his righteousness is mine for my justification; I am clothed with Christ as it is, 'The spouse there is clothed with the sun,' Rev. xii. 1, with the beams of Christ. But is that all? No. 'I am my beloved's;' I am Christ's. There is a return of faith in sanctification. The same Spirit that witnesseth Christ is ours, it sanctifies and alters our disposition, that we can say, I am Christ's. It serves to instruct us therefore in the necessary connection of these two, justification and sanctification, against the idle slander of papists, that sinfully traduce that doctrine, as if we were Solifideans (*v*), as if we severed justification from sanctification. No. We hold here that whensoever Christ is ours, there is a spirit of sanctification in us, to yield all to Christ, though this resignation be not presently perfect.

Use 3. This likewise helps us, by way of direction, to understand the covenant of grace, and the seals of the covenant, what they enforce and comprise; not only what God will do to us, but the duty we are to do to him again, though we do it in his strength. A covenant holds not on one side, but on both. Christ is mine, and I am Christ's again. 'I will be their God,' but they must have grace 'to be my people,' Lev. xxvi. 12; and then the covenant is made up. The covenant of grace is so called, because God is so gracious as to enable us to perform our own part.

And so in the seals of the covenant in baptism. God doth not only bind himself to do thus and thus to us, but binds us also to do back again to him. So in the communion, we promise to lead a new life, renewing our covenant; and therefore we must not think that all is well (when we have received our Maker), though we continue in a scandalous, fruitless course of life. No. There is a promise in the sacrament (the seal of the covenant of grace), to yield up ourselves to God, to return to Christ again with our duty. Then we come as we should do when we come thus disposed. This for direction, 'My beloved is mine, and I am my beloved's.'

Use 4. To proceed to make an use of comfort *to poor, doubting Christians*. 'I am my beloved's,' is the voice of the whole church, that all ranks of Christians, if they be true, may without presumption take up. I have not so much faith, so much love, so much grace, so much patience as another, saith a poor Christian; therefore I am none of Christ's. But we must know that Christ hath in his church of all ranks, and they are all his spouse, one as well as another, there is no exception. There is a little spirit of emulation, and a spice of envy, in Christians that are weaker. If they have not all that great measure of grace which they see in others, they fear they have none at all; as if there were no babes in Christ's school as well as men and grown persons.

Then again, we see here the nature of faith in the whole church. It is the same that is in every particular, and the same in every particular as it is in the whole church. The whole church saith, 'I am my beloved's, and my beloved is mine.' I appropriate him. There is a spirit of appropriation in the whole, and there is so in each particular. Every Christian may say with Paul, 'I live by faith in the Son of God, that hath loved me, and gave himself for me,' Gal. ii. 20; and with Thomas, 'My God, and my Lord,' John xx. 28.

The ground hereof is, because they are all one in Christ, and there is one and the same Spirit in the whole church and every particular Christian, as in pipes, though of different sounds, yet there is the same breath in them. So Christians may have different sounds, from the greater or lesser strength of grace that is in the one and in the other, but all comes from the same breath, the same Spirit. The Spirit in the bride saith Come, Rev. xxii. 17, the whole church saith it, and every particular Christian must say it; because, as the body is acted by one spirit, and makes but one natural body, though consisting of many parts weaker and stronger, so should there be a harmony in this mystical body acted by that one Spirit of Christ, who so regards all, as if there were but one, and regards every one so, as he doth not forget the whole. *Sic omnibus attentus ut non detentus, &c.* Christ so attends to all, that he is not detained from any particular, and he so attends every particular, that he is not restrained from all. There is the same love to all as to one, and to every one, as if there were no other. He so loves each one, that every Christian may say as well as the whole church, Christ is mine, and I am Christ's.

In those things that we call homogeneal, there is the same nature in each quantity as in the whole, as there is the same nature in one drop of water as in the whole ocean, all is water; and the same respect of a spark, and of all the element of fire. So Christ bears the same respect to the church as to every particular, and to every particular as to the church.

Use 5. To come to make an use of direction, *how to come to be able to say this,* 'I am my beloved's, and my beloved is mine.' For answer hereto, take notice in the first place, from the dependence. Christ must be first ours, before we can give ourselves to him.

(1.) Therefore, we must dwell on the consideration of Christ's love. This must direct and lead our method in this thing. Would we have our hearts to love Christ, to trust in him, and to embrace him, why then think what he is to us. Begin there; nay, and what we are: weak, and in our apprehension, lost. Then go to consider his love, his constant love to his church and children. 'Whom he loves, he loves to the end,' John xiii. 1. We must warm our souls with the consideration of the love of God in him to us, and this will stir up our faith to him back again. For we are more safe in that he is ours, Gal. iv. 9, Philip. iii. 12, than that we give ourselves to him. We are more safe in his comprehending of us, than in our clasping and holding of him. As we say of the mother and the child, both hold, but the safety of the child is that the mother holds him. If Christ once give himself to us, he will make good his own part alway. Our safety is more on his side than on ours. If ever we have felt the love of Christ, we may comfort ourselves with the constancy and perpetuity thereof. Though, perhaps, we find not our affections warmed to him at all times, nor alike, yet the strength of a Christian's comfort lies in this, that first, 'Christ is mine,' and then, in the second place, that 'I am his.' Now, I say, that we may be able to maintain this blessed tradition of giving ourselves to Christ,

(2.) Let us dwell on the consideration of his love to us, and of the necessity that we have of him; how miserable we are without him, poor, beggarly, in bondage to the devil. Therefore we must have him to recover us out of debt, and to enrich us. For Christ's love carries him forth, not only to pay all our debts for us, but to enrich us; and it is a protecting, preserving love, till he brings us to heaven, his own place, where we shall ever be with him. The consideration of these things will warm our hearts, and for this purpose serves the ministry.

(3.) We should therefore, in the next place, attend upon the word, for this very end. Wherefore serves the ministry? Among many others, this is one main end—'to lay open the unsearchable riches of Christ.' Therein you have something of Christ unfolded, of his natures, offices, and benefits we have by him,—redemption, and freedom, and a right to all things in him, the excellencies of another world. Therefore attend upon the means of salvation, that we may know what riches we have in him. This will keep our affections close to Christ, so as to say, 'I am his.'

(4.) And labour we also every day more and more to bring all our love to him. We see in burning-glasses, where the beams of the sun meet in one, how forcible they are, because there is an union of the beams in a little point. Let it be our labour that all the beams of our love may meet in Christ, that he may be as the church saith, our beloved. 'My beloved is mine, and I am my beloved's,' saith she, as if the church had no love out of Christ. And is it love lost? No; but as Christ is the church's beloved, so the church is Christ's love again, as we see in this book oft, 'My love, my dove.' As all streams meet in the great ocean, so let all our loves meet in Christ. We may love other things, and we should do so, but no otherwise than as they convey love to us from Christ, and may be means of drawing up our affections unto Christ. We may love our friends, and we ought to do so, and other blessings of God; but how? No otherwise than as tokens of his love to us. We love a thing that our friends send to us. O, but it is as it doth convey his affection to us. So must we love all things, as they come from God's love to us in Christ.

And, indeed, whatsoever we have is a love-token, even our very afflictions themselves. 'Whom I love, I rebuke and chastise,' Heb. xii. 6.

(5.) Again, that we may inflame our hearts with the love of Christ, as we are exhorted by Jude, 21, let us consider the vanity of all things that entice us from Christ, and labour every day more and more to draw our affections from them, as we are exhorted—'Hearken, O daughter, and consider, and incline thine ear; forget also thine own people, and thy father's house: so shall the king greatly desire thy beauty,' Ps. xlv. 10. So, if we will have Christ to delight in us, that we may say we are his, let us labour to sequester our affections more and more from all earthly things, that we may not have such hearts, as St James speaketh of, adulterous hearts. 'O ye adulterers and adulteresses! know ye not that the love of the world is enmity with God?' James iv. 4.

Indeed there is reason for this exhortation; for all earthly things, they are all vain and empty things. There is an emptiness in whatsoever is in the world, save Christ. Therefore we should not set our affections too much upon them. A man cannot be wise in loving anything but Christ, and what he loves for Christ. Therefore let us follow that counsel, to draw ourselves from our former company, acquaintance, pleasures, delights, and vanities. We cannot bestow our love and our affections better than upon Christ. It is a happiness that we have such affections, as joy, delight, and love, planted in us by God; and what a happiness is it, that we should have such an excellent object to fill those affections, yea, to transcend and more than satisfy them! Therefore the apostle wisheth that they might know all the dimensions of God's love in Christ. There is a 'height, breadth, length, and depth of the love of God,' Eph. iii. 18.

And let us think of the dimensions, the height, breadth, and depth of our misery out of Christ. The more excellent our natures are, the more miserable they are if not changed; for look what degree of excellency we have, if it be not advanced in Christ, we have so much misery being out of him. Therefore let us labour to see this, as to value our being in him, so to be able, upon good grounds, to say, 'I am my beloved's, and my beloved is mine.'

(6.) Again, let us labour to walk in the light of a sanctified knowledge to be attained by the gospel, for as it is, 'the end of all our preaching is to assure Christ to the soul,' 1 John v. 13, that we may be able to say without deceiving our own souls, 'I am my beloved's, and my beloved is mine.' All preaching, I say, is for this end. The terror of the law and the discovery of corruption is to drive us out of ourselves to him; and then to provoke us to grow up into him more and more. Therefore saith John, 'All our preaching is that we may have fellowship with the Father and the Son, and they with us,' 1 John i. 7. And what doth he make an evidence of that fellowship? 'walking in the light, as he is light,' or else we are liars. He is bold in plain terms to give us the lie, to say we are Christ's, and have communion with the Father and the Son, when yet we walk in darkness. In sins against conscience, in wilful ignorance, the darkness of an evil life, we have no communion with Christ. Therefore if we will have communion with him, let us walk in the light, and labour to be lightsome in our understandings, to have a great deal of knowledge, and then to walk answerable to that light and revelation that we have. Those that live in sins against conscience, and are friends to the darkness of ignorance, of an evil life, Oh they never think of the fellowship with Christ and with God! These things are mere riddles to them; they have no hope of them, or if any, their hope is in vain. They bar themselves of ever having comfortable communion with Christ here; much less shall they enjoy him hereafter in heaven.

Therefore labour every day more and more to grow rich in knowledge, to get light, and to walk in that light; to which end pray with the holy apostle, 'That you may have the Spirit of revelation,' Eph. i. 17, that excellent Spirit of God, to reveal the things of God, that we may have the light discovered to us.

What a world of comfort hath a Christian that hath light in him and walks in that light, above another man. Whether he live or die, the light brings him into fellowship with the Father of lights. He that hath this light knows his condition and his way, and whither he goeth. When he dieth he knows in what condition he dieth, and upon what grounds. The very light of nature is comfortable, much more that of grace. Therefore labour to grow daily more and more in the knowledge and obedience of the light.

All professors of the gospel are either such as are not Christ's, or such as are his. For such as are not yet, that you may be provoked to draw to fellowship with Christ, do but consider you are as branches cut off, that will wither and die, and be cast into the fire, unless you be grafted into the living stock, Christ. You are as naked persons in a storm, not clothed with anything to stand against the storm of God's wrath. Let this force you to get into Christ.

Use 6. And next for encouragement consider, *Christ offereth himself to all in the gospel;* and that is the end of the ministry, to bring Christ and our souls together, to make a spiritual marriage, to lay open his riches and to draw you to him, 1 John i. 9. If you confess your sins, he will forgive them, and you shall have mercy, 'He relieves those that are wearied and heavy laden,' Mat. xi. 28, and bids those come to him that are thirsty, Isa. lv. 1. Christ came to seek and to save that which was lost. Christ offers himself in mercy to the worst soul.

Therefore if there be any that have lived in evil courses, in former times, consider that upon repentance all shall be forgotten, and as a mist scattered away and cast into the bottom of the sea. Christ offers himself to you. These are the times, this is the hour of grace. Now the water is stirring for you to enter; do but entertain Christ, and desire that he may be yours to rule you and guide you, and all will be well for the time to come.

Obj. Do not object, *I am a loathsome creature, full of rebellions.*

Ans. Christ doth not match with you, because you are good, but to make you good. Christ takes you not with any dowry. All that he requires is to confess your beggary and to come with emptiness. He takes us not because we are clean, but because he will purge us. He takes us in our blood when he first takes us, Ezek. xvi. 9. Let none despair either for want of worth or of strength, Eph. v. 27. Christ seeth that for strength we are dead, and for worth we are enemies; but he gives us both spiritual strength and worth, takes us near to himself and enricheth us. Let none therefore be discouraged. It is our office, thus to lay open and offer the riches of Christ. If you will not come in, but love your sinful courses more than Christ, then you perish in your blood, and we free our hands, and may free our souls from the guilt thereof. Therefore as you love your own souls, come in at length and stand out no longer.

And for those that have in some measure given themselves up to Christ, and can say, 'He is mine and I am his,' let them go on with comfort, and never be discouraged for the infirmities that hang about them. For one part of Christ's office is to purge his church by his Spirit more and more; not to cast her away for her infirmities, 'but to wash and cleanse it more and more till it be a glorious spouse like himself,' Eph. v. 27. For if the husband will, by the bond of nature, bear with the infirmities of the wife, as the weaker vessel, doth not Christ bind himself by that which he accounts us bound? Is there more love and mercy, and pity in us to those that we take near us, than there is in Christ to us? What a most blasphemous thought were this to conceive so! Only let us take heed of being in league with sin; for we cannot give our souls to Christ, and to sinful courses too. Christ will allow of no bigamy or double marriage. Where he hath anything to do, we must have single hearts, resolving, though I fall, yet I purpose to please Christ, and to go on in a good conversation; and if our hearts tell us so, daily infirmities ought not to discourage us.

We have helps enough for these. First, Christ bids us ask forgiveness; and then we have the mercy of Christ to bear with weaker vessels. Then his advocation.* He is now in heaven to plead for us. If we were perfect, we needed not that office, 1 John ii. 2. Let none be discouraged therefore; but let us labour more and more that we may be able to comprehend in some measure the love of Christ, so will all duties come off sweetly and easily; and then we shall be enabled to suffer all things, not only willingly, but cheerfully, and rejoice in them. Love is of the nature of fire, which as it severeth and consumeth all that is opposite, all dross and dregs, and dissolves coldness, so it quickens and makes active and lively. It hath a kind of constraining force, a sweet violence. As the apostle saith, 'the love of Christ constraineth,' 2 Cor. v. 24.

Let a man that loves the Lord Jesus Christ in sincerity, be called to part with his life, he will yield it as a sacrifice with comfort. Come what will, all is welcome, when we are inflamed with the love of Christ; and the more we suffer, the more we find his love. For he reserves the manifestation of his love most for times of suffering; and the more we find the manifestation of his love, the more we love him back again, and rejoice in suffering for him that we love so. Whether they be duties of obedience, active or passive, doing or suffering, all comes off with abundance of cheerfulness and ease, where the love of Christ is, that the soul can say, 'I am my beloved's, and my beloved is mine.' Nothing in the world is able to make such a soul miserable. It follows.

'He feedeth among the lilies. The church here shews where Christ feeds.

Quest. But the question is, Whether it be the feeding of the church and people that is meant, or whether he feeds himself?

Ans. For answer, he both feeds his church among the lilies, and delights himself to be there. The one follows the other. Especially it is meant of the church. Those that are his, he feeds them among the lilies. How?

Lilies are such kind of flowers as require a great deal of nourishment, and grow best in valleys and fat ground. Therefore when she saith, 'He feeds among the lilies,' the meaning is, he feeds his church and people in fat pastures, as sheep in such grounds as are sweet and fruitful. Such are his holy word and the communion of saints. These are especially the pastures wherein he feeds his church. The holy truths of God are the food of the soul, whereby it is cherished and nourished up to life everlasting. This whole book is a kind of pastoral (to understand the word a little better), a 'song of a beloved' concerning a beloved. Therefore Christ in many places of this book, he takes upon him the term and carriage, as it were, of a loving shepherd, who labours to find out for his sheep the fattest, fruitfulest, best, and sweetest pastures, that they may grow up as calves of the stall, as it is Malachi iv. 2, that they may grow and be well liking.

You have, to give light to this place, a phrase somewhat like this, where he follows the point more at large, Cant. i. 7. The church there prays to Christ, 'Tell me, O thou whom my soul loveth, where thou feedest, where thou makest thy flocks to rest at noon.' Those that are coming up in the church desire to know with whom they may join, and what truths they may embrace. 'Tell me where thou feedest, and where thou makest thy flock to rest at noon:' that is, in the greatest heat and storm of persecution, as at noon-day the sun is hottest. 'For why should I be as one that turns aside by the flocks of thy companions?' that is, by those that are not true

* That is, 'advocacy.'—ED.

friends, that are false shepherds; why should I be drawn away by them? I desire to feed where thou feedest among thy sheep. Why should I be as one that turns aside by the flocks of those that are emulators to thee? as antichrist is to Christ. Thus the church puts forth to Christ, whereunto Christ replies, verse 8. 'If thou know not, O thou fairest among women, go thy way forth by the footsteps of the flocks, and feed thy kids beside the shepherds' tents:' that is, if thou know not, go thy way forth, get thee out of thyself, out of the world, out of thy former course, put thyself forward, stay not complaining, go on, put thyself to endeavour, go thy way forth. Whither? 'In the footsteps of the flocks.' See the steps of Christians in the best times of the church in former times. Tread in the steps of those that lived in the best ages of the church. 'Feed thy kids,' thy Christians, 'beside the shepherds' tents,' the best shepherds. Mark where the apostles and prophets fed their sheep; there feed thou. And mark the footsteps of the flock that have lived in the best times; for of all times since the apostles and prophets, we must follow those virgin best times. All churches are so far true churches, as they have consanguinity with the primitive apostolical and prophetical churches.

Therefore, 'we are now to go out by the footsteps of the flock.' Mark the footsteps of former Christians, Abraham, Moses, and David; and in Christ's time, of John, Peter, and the rest. Blessed saints! walk as they walked, go their way, and 'feed yourselves by the shepherds' tents.' Mark the shepherds where they have their tents! So these words have reference to the prophetical, especially to the evangelical times, whereunto we must conform ourselves; for the latter times are apostate times. After a certain season the church kept not her purity; which the Scriptures foretold directly, that we should not take scandal at it. The church did fall to a kind of admiration of antichrist, and embraced doctrines of devils, 1 Tim. iv. 1. Therefore now we must not follow these companies that lead into by-paths, contrary to the apostolical ways, but see wherein our church agrees with the apostolical churches and truth, and embrace no truth for the food of our souls, but that we find in the gospel. For antichrist feeds his flocks with wind, and with poison, and with empty things. For what hath been the food in popery? Sweet and goodly titles; as if they, poor souls, had the best pastors in the world, whenas they administer to them nothing but that which will be the bane of their souls, full of poison and fraud. This is spoken to unfold that place which gives light to this, spoken of the pastoral care of Christ, 'he feeds his flock among the lilies,' plentifully and sweetly. From hence may be briefly observed, first,

That Christ feeds as well as breeds. And we have need of feeding as well as breeding. Where dost thou feed? that is, build up thy children, and go on with the work begun in them. We have need to be fed after we are bred; and Christ (answerable to our exigence and necessity) he feeds as well as breeds; and that word which is the seed to beget us, is that which feeds too, 1 Peter i. 23. What is the seed of the new birth? The word of God, the holy promises, they are the seed, the Spirit mingling with them, whereby a Christian is born, and being born, is cherished and bred. Therefore, 'as new-born babes,' saith the apostle, 'desire the sincere milk of the word, that you may grow thereby,' 1 Peter ii. 1. So that the same thing is both the seed of a Christian, and that which breeds him; the blessed truth and promises of God.

Quest. If you ask, why we must grow up and be fed still?

Ans. 1. Do but ask your own souls, whether there be not a perpetual renewing of corruption, which still breaks out into new guilt every day. Therefore we have need to feed every day anew upon the promises, upon old promises with new affections. Somewhat breaks out ever and anon which abaseth the soul of a Christian, that makes him go with a sharp appetite to the blessed truths that feed his soul.

Ans. 2. And then again, we need a great deal of strength, which is maintained by feeding. Besides the guilt of the soul, there needs strength for duty, which must be fetched from the blessed word of God; and the comforts thence, whereby we are able to withstand and resist, to stand and do all that we do.

Ans. 3. And then we are set upon by variety of temptations within and without, which require variety of wisdom and strength, all which must be gotten by feeding; and therefore you see a Christian for his subsistence and being, hath need of a feeding, cherishing, and maintaining still, by the sweet and blessed directions and promises out of the word of God.

Therefore you may see what kind of atheistical creatures those are, and how much they are to be regarded, that turn off all with a *compendium* in religion, Tush, if we know that we must love God above all, and our neighbours as ourselves, and that Christ died for all, we know enough, more than we can practise. They think these *compendiums* will serve the turn, as if there were not a necessity of growing still further and further in distinct knowledge. Alas! the soul needs to be fed continually. It will stagger else, and be insufficient to stand against temptation, or to perform duties.

A second general point out of the text is this, *that as Christ feedeth still his flock and people, so he feeds them fully, plentifully, and sweetly among the lilies.* There are saving truths enough. There is an all-sufficiency in the book of God. What need we go out to man's inventions, seeing there is a fulness and all-sufficiency of truth there? Whatsoever is not in that is wind, or poison. In the word is a full kind of feeding. In former times when they had not the Scriptures, and the comforts of them to feed on, what did the poor souls then? and what do those remaining in popery feed on? Upon stones as it were. There was a dream of an holy man in those times, divers hundred years agone, that he saw one having a deal of manchet* to feed on, and yet all the while the poor wretch he fed on stones. What folly and misery is this, when there are delicate things to feed on, to gnaw upon stones! And what is all the school learning almost, (except one or two that had better spirits than the rest) but a gnawing upon stones, barren distinctions, empty things, that had no substance in them? They had the Scriptures, though they were locked up in Latin, an unknown tongue. They had the sweet pastures of Christ to feed in; and yet all this while they fed, as it were, on stones.

This should shew us, likewise, our own blessedness that live in these times, wherein the streams of the gospel run abundantly, sweetly, and pleasantly. There is a fulness among us, even in the spirits of the worst sort. There is a fulness almost to loathing of that heavenly manna: but those souls, who ever were acquainted with the necessity of it, rather find a want than a fulness; and still desire to grow up to a further desire, that as they have plentiful means, so they may have plentiful affections after, and strength by those means. Let us know our own happiness in these times. Is it not a comfort to know where to feed and to have pastures to go to, without suspicion of poison? that we may feed ourselves with comforts fully without fear of bane, or noisome mingling of *coloquintida* in the pot, which would

* That is, 'white-bread.' See Holinshed, Description of England, B. ii. c. 6.—G.

disrelish all the rest? to know that there are truths that we may feed on safely? This the church in the former place, Cant. i. 6, 7, accounted a great privilege, 'Oh, shew me where thou feedest at noon.' In the greatest heat of persecution, that I may feed among them. So then it is a great privilege to know where to feed, and so to be esteemed, that thereby we may be stirred up to be thankful for our own good, and to improve these privileges to our souls' comfort.

But the second branch that must be touched a little is, *that there is fulness nowhere but in God's house; and that there, and there only, is that which satisfieth the soul with fatness and sweetness.*

Nay, not only the promises, but the very rebukes, of Scripture, are sweet. The rebukes of a friend, they feed the soul. For we have many corruptions which hinder our communion with God, so that a Christian delights to have his corruptions rebuked; for he knows, if he leave them, he shall grow into further communion with Christ, wherein stands his happiness in this world, and the fulness of his happiness in the world to come.

If this be so, let us know then that when we come to religion we lose not the sweetness of our lives, but only translate them to a far more excellent and better condition. Perhaps we fed before upon vain authors, upon (as it were) gravel, vain company; but now we have our delight (and perhaps find more pleasure) in better things. Instead of that which fed our idle fancy (vain treatises and the like), now we have holy truths to delight our souls. Believe it, a Christian never knows what comfort is to purpose till he be downright and sincere in religion. Therefore Austin saith of himself, 'Lord, I have wanted thy sweetness over long. I see all my former life (that I thought had such sweetness in it) was nothing at all but husks, empty things. Now I know where sweetness is, it is in the word and truth.'* Therefore let us not misconceive of religion as of a mopish and dull thing, wherein we must lose all comfort. If we give ourselves over to the study thereof, must we so? Must we lose our comfort? Nay, we have no comfort till we be religious indeed. Christ feeds not his among thorns and briers and stinking weeds, but among lilies. Dost thou think he feeds thee among unsavoury, harsh, fretting, galling things? No; 'he feeds among lilies.' Therefore when thou comest to religion, think that thou comest to comfort, to refresh thy soul. Let us make use of this for our soul's comfort, to make us in love more with the ways of Christ.

Now, to seal this further, see what the Scripture saith in some parallel places. 'The Lord is my shepherd;' and what is the use that David presently makes hereof? Why, 'I shall want nothing,' Ps. xxiii. 1. He will feed me plentifully and abundantly. The whole psalm is nothing but a commenting upon that word, 'the Lord is my shepherd.' How doth he perform the duty of a shepherd? 'He makes me to lie down in green pastures, and leads me by the still waters.' It is not only meant of the body, but of the soul chiefly, 'he restoreth my soul;' that is, when my soul languisheth and is ready to faint, he restores it, and gives me as it were a new soul; he refresheth it. We see say,† re-creation is the creating of a thing anew. So he restores my soul; he gives me my soul anew, with fresh comforts. Thus the blessed Shepherd doth, and how? Because 'he feeds among the lilies,' the promises of the gospel. Then he doth not only do good to the body and soul, but he guides all our ways, all our goings out, 'he leads us in the paths of righteousness.' And why?

* Confessions, b. x. p. [xxviii.] 38.—G.

† That is, 'we see that people, etymologists, say.'—ED.

Because I deserve so much at his hands? No; 'for his own name's sake,' because he hath a love to me; because he hath purchased me with his blood, and given his life for his sheep; hath bought me so dear, though there be no worth in me. He goes on, 'Though I walk through all temptations and troubles,' which are as 'the valley of the shadow of death,' that is, where there is nothing but disconsolation and misery; 'yet I will fear none ill; thou, with thy rod and staff, dost comfort me.' If I, as a wandering sheep, venture to go out of the way, thou, out of thy care, being a sweet and loving shepherd, wilt pull me in with thy hook and staff again. He hath not care only to feed us, but to govern us also. What a sweet Shepherd and Saviour have we in covenant, that deals thus with us! And so he proceeds, 'Thou wilt prepare my table in the presence of mine enemies.' And for the time to come he promiseth himself as much, that God, as he hath been a Shepherd for the present, to provide all things necessary for body and soul and guidance, so surely the goodness of the Lord shall follow me all the days of my life; for he is a perpetual Shepherd. He will not leave us till he hath brought us to heaven. Thus we see in this place the sweet care of Christ.

The like place you have—'He shall feed his flock like a shepherd; he shall gather the lambs with his arms, and carry them in his bosom, and shall gently lead those that are with young,' Isa. xl. 11. So he leads them into the pastures, and feeds them plentifully and sweetly, not only with sweet things, but with a tender care, which is sweeter. As a shepherd, he takes into his bosom the poor lambs that cannot walk themselves, and the sheep that are heavy with young. He cares for them; 'he gently leads them' that are poor, weak Christians, that struggle and conflict with many temptations and corruptions. Christ hath a tender care of them. He carries them, as it were, in his bosom and in his arms, and leads them gently; for indeed all Christ's sheep are weak. Every one hath somewhat to complain of. Therefore he hath a tender care; he feeds them tenderly and sweetly, or else they might perish.

Another place notable for this purpose, see Ezek. xxxiv. 14, *seq.*, wherein you have the same metaphor from a loving shepherd; and it is but a comment upon the text. Therefore, being parallel places, they may help our memories: 'I will feed them in good pastures upon the high mountains of Israel; there shall their fold be; there shall they lie in a good fold, and in a fat pasture. I will feed my flock, and cause them to lie down, saith the Lord God. I will seek that which is lost, and bring back that which was driven away; I will bind up that which was broken, and strengthen that which is sick, and destroy the fat and the strong, and feed them with judgment.' Those that are Christ's true sheep have somewhat to complain of. Either they are sick, or broken, or driven away. Somewhat is amiss or other. But Christ's care preventeth all the necessities of his sheep. He hath a fit salve for all their sores.* And, to apply this to the business in hand,† doth not Christ feed us 'among the lilies?' Doth he not now feed us with his own body and blood in the sacrament? Would you have better food? 'My body is meat indeed, and my blood is drink indeed,'—that is, it is the only meat, with an emphasis; the only meat and drink that our souls could feed upon. God gave his Son to death, to shed his blood for my sins. What would become of the hunger-bitten, thirsty soul, that is

* This is the title of one of Thomas Powell's excellent practical treatises, viz.:—'Salve for Soul-Sores.'—G.

† That is, celebration of the sacrament.—G.

stung with Satan and his temptations, were it not for the blood of Christ to quench our thirst, and the body of Christ given by the Father to death for sin? Were it not that the soul could think upon this, where were the comfort of the soul? All this is represented to us here in the sacrament. We feed on the body and blood of Christ spiritually, and are refreshed thereby, as verily as our bodies are refreshed with the bread and wine. For God doth not feed us with empty symbols and representations, but with things themselves, that the soul which comes prepared by faith is partaker of Christ crucified, and is knit to him, though now in heaven. There is as sure an union and communion between Christ and the Christian soul, as there is between the food and the body, when it is once digested.

Therefore let us come to this blessed, to this sweet food of our souls with hungry appetites and thankful hearts, that God hath given us the best comforts of his word, and fed us with the sweet comforts of the sacraments, as a seal of the word. We should even spend our lives much in thankfulness for this, that he will feed us so sweetly, that thinks nothing is good enough for our food, but his own self, with his own gracious word and truth. Thus we should be very thankful unto God, and now at this time labour to get hungry appetites fit for this blessed food to receive it.

How shall we do that?

1. Think seriously of the former part of thy life, and this week past. For Christ, the food of the soul, relisheth well with the sour herbs of repentance. Let us stir up in our hearts repentance for our sins, and sorrow in the consideration of our own corrupt nature and life; and when we have felt our corruptions and have the sense of our want, then Christ will be sweet to us. The paschal lamb was to be eaten with sour herbs; so Christ our passover must be eaten with repentance.

2. Then withal there must be purging. There are many things which clog the stomach. Come not with worldly, wicked, malicious affections, which puff up the soul, James i. 21; 'but lay aside,' as the apostle wisheth, 'all guile, malice, and superfluity,' 1 Pet. ii. 1. Empty the soul of all sin and prepossessing* thoughts or affections.

3. And then consider the necessity of spiritual strength, that we have need to grow up more and more in Christianity, to be feeding still. We have need of strong faith and strong assurance that Christ is ours, and that we are his. Let us often frequent this ordinance, and come prepared as we should, and we shall find Christ making good his own ordinance, in his own best time; so as we shall be able to say, in truth of heart, experimentally and feelingly with the church, 'My beloved is mine, and I am his. He feedeth among the lilies.'

FINIS.

NOTES.

(a) P. 4.—'Some would have Solomon, by a spirit of prophecy, to take a view here of all the time,' &c. For a very full and valuable, though, in respect of the early English expositors (of whom there are many in whole or part), defective and meagre, '*Historical Sketch of the Exegesis of the Book*,' consult Ginsburg's 'Song of Songs, ... with a Commentary, Historical and Critical,' (London, Longman, 1857, 8vo) pp. 20–101. The opinions referred to by Sibbes will be found duly recorded.

* That is, 'pre-occupying.'—G.

(*b*) P. 35.—'One soul in two bodies.' This definition of friendship, which is again and again introduced by Sibbes and his contemporaries, is ascribed to Aristotle by Diogenes Laertius (v. § 20), as follows: ἐρωτηθεὶς τί ἐστι φίλος, ἔφη, μία ψυχὴ δύο σώμασιν ἐνοικοῦσα. Cf. Aristotle, Eth. Nic., ix. 8, § 2, Ovid. Trist., iv. 4, 72. Probably Sibbes derived it from Augustine (a favourite with him), who applies it to his friend Nebridius. Materials for an interesting paper on this saying, in its multiform variations, have accumulated in my hands.

(*c*) P. 37.—'This goeth in the world for unnecessary *nicety*.' This reminds us of an anecdote of the saintly Richard Rogers, who was remarkable for seriousness and gravity in all kinds of company. Being once engaged in conversation with one of the 'wits,' who said to him, 'Mr Rogers, I like you and your company very well, only you are *too precise*;' he replied, 'Oh, sir, I serve a *precise God*.'—Firmin's Real Christian, p. 67, ed. 1670.

(*d*) P. 38.—'Postill-like.' The allusion, no doubt, is to the over-subtle distinctions and uselessly curious speculations of the *scholastic* expositions of Scripture, which are called 'Postilla.' Various had been translated in the time of Sibbes, under the title of 'Postils.'

(*e*) P. 48.—'*Da mihi cor*.' Jesuitism, even in its present working, proceeds on this maxim, of which there have been many startling evidences.

(*f*) P. 60.—'God spake in me oft, and I knew it not.' This is the touching burden of the early chapters of Augustine's *Confessions*.

(*f**) P. 61.—'Ballarmine makes this objection,' &c. An ignorat eos aperire non posse? An stultus non esset, qui ostium vicini pulsaret, si certo sciret neminem intus esse qui aperire posset. Bell. de gratia et lib.: arbit. lib. i., cap. xi.

(*g*) P. 74.—'She is now desirous to pity herself, and needs no Peter to stir her up to it.' The allusion is to Mat. xvi. 22. In our translation it is rendered, 'Be it far from thee, Lord,' which obscures the pathos of the devoted apostle's mistaken, but most loving appeal. It should be '*Pity thyself*.' Hence Sibbes's reference.

(*h*) P. 84.—'It was a good speech of Ignatius the martyr,' &c. There are various sayings resembling this in the epistles of Ignatius, *e.g.*, to the Ephesians, c. xviii., to the Trallians, c. ix–xi., to the Romans, c. ii.–iv., and vi. Probably Sibbes refers to the ancient narrative of the 'martyrdom of Ignatius.' Cf. § 2. Patrum Apostolicorum Opera, ed. Hefele. 8vo. 1847.

(*i*) P. 93.—Hebrews xii. 1. Cf. Sibbes's translation, with Alford, Webster and Wilkinson, and Dr Sampson, *in loc.* He repeats this and other renderings in his various books.

(*j*) P. 121.—'Austin was forced to speak in his time against the *Donatists*.' For a very masterly account of this and other of the great fathers' controversies, consult Wigger's 'Historical Presentation of Augustinism and Pelagianism from the Original Sources,' (ed. by Emerson. Andover, 1840. 8vo).

(*k*) P. 125.—'He [the Lord] . . . would have their [disciples'] society and *prayers*.' This is the popular view, but, like the popular understanding of Thomas, thrusting his fingers into the side and nail-prints of the risen Saviour, (See note *a*, vol. i., p. 101), is probably a popular mistake. Our Lord sought the society of his disciples certainly; but nowhere do we read of his asking any one to pray *for* him. It is an awful peculiarity of the divine man 'Emanuel,' that he never did that,—one of a multitude of subsidiary assertions of his divinity.

(*l*) P. 132.—'"What is truth?" saith he, in a scornful, profane manner.' This, almost verbatim the opening words of Bacon's Essay on 'Truth,' reminds one, with others, of Sibbes's intercourse with him, noticed in our memoir.

(*m*) P. 149.—'So should we now . . . . have ideas of Christ framed to our souls,' &c. For a very valuable, and, in many respects, remarkably acute and suggestive discussion of the question of framing 'ideas of Christ,' a subject keenly debated in the last century in Scotland, consult the following little-known book, by Ralph Erskine—'Faith no Fancy; or a Treatise of Mental Images . . . . . shewing that our imaginary idea of Christ as Man (when supposed to belong to saving faith, whether in its act or object), imports nothing but ignorance, atheism, idolatry, great falsehood, and gross delusion.' . . . . . Edinburgh, 1745, 12mo. This little work may be pronounced the pioneer of the philosophy known as Scottish. Apart from its bearing on the passage of Sibbes, it will be found to contain much uncommon thought on 'ideas,' equal, to say the least, to the subsequent writings of Reid.

(*n*) P. 153.—'All hung upon his lips, as the phrase is in the gospel.' The reference is to Luke iv. 20, which is here given in the original, to confirm Sibbes's remark,—Καὶ πτύξας τὸ βιβλίον ἀποδοὺς τῷ ὑπηρέτῃ, ἐκάθισε καὶ πάντων ἐν τῇ συναγωγῇ οἱ ὀφθαλμοὶ ἦσαν ἀτενίζοντες αὐτῷ. ἀτενής = 'intent,' 'earnestly fixed,' from τείνω, cf. xxii. 56. Acts iii. 12, x. 4, xiv. 9.

(*o*) P. 153.—'In the learned language, the same word signifieth speech and reason.' Query—Is the allusion to λογος?

(*p*) P. 154.—'His belly . . . . In the Hebrew it is used for the inward affections.' See prefatory note to the present treatise of 'Bowels Opened.'

(*q*) P. 160.—'When Pilate sent him to him, [Herod] made *nobody* of him, as the word in the original is.' Sibbes's reference is to Luke xxiii. 11, rendered in authorised version, 'set him at nought,' but literally runs, 'having set him at nought,' *i.e.*, etymologically, treated him as if he were nobody, or of no consideration. The verb is ἐξουθενέω.

(*r*) P. 169.—'Heavy will the doom be of many that live in the church's bosom, to whom it had been better to have been born in America, in Turkey' . . . . . The juxtaposition of America *and* Turkey is in curious contrast with the present position of America among the *Christian* nations of the world. Yet with all this idea of the 'barbarousness' of America (which was common to Sibbes with his contemporaries), the Puritans shrank not from exiling themselves thither when the question of their religious liberties came up. Hooker, Davenport, Cotton, Stone, and numerous others of Sibbes's friends thus expatriated themselves.

(*s*) P. 169.—'They are lilies, being clothed with the white garment,' &c. It is pity to destroy the 'fine fancies' of Sibbes on the supposed 'whiteness' of the lily; but he was thinking of the home, not of the eastern 'lily,' which is purple coloured, not 'white.' The 'purple' gives greater vividness to the Lord's allusion to the imperial robes of Solomon, Mat. vi. 28, 29.

(*t*) P. 170.—'The name of a church in the original is Ecclesia,' *i.e.*, ἐκκλησία. Cf. 1 Cor. xi. 18, and Robinson and Liddell and Scott, *sub voce*.

(*u*) P. 173.—'If Christ himself be mine, then all is mine.' The well-known hymn, 'If God be mine' *(anonymous)*, is little more than a paraphrase of these sweet words of Sibbes.

(*v*) P. 183.—'As if we were Solifideans.' This sect derived its name from *solus*, alone, and *fides*, faith. The following quotations will illustrate Sibbes:—

'Such is first the persuasion of the *solifidians*, that all religion consists in *believing* aright, that the being of orthodox (as that is opposed to erroneous) opinions is all that is on our part required to render our condition safe, and our persons acceptable in the sight of God.'—Hammond. Works, i., p. 480.

'That we may be able to answer the Papists, who charge us with *solifidianism*, as if we were of this opinion, that if a man do but trust in Christ, that is, be but confidently persuaded that he will save him, and pardon him, this is sufficient, and, consequently, he that is thus persuaded need not take any farther care of his salvation, but may live as he list.'—Tillotson, iii., ser. 174. G.

THE SPOUSE,

HER EARNEST DESIRE AFTER CHRIST.

NOTE.

'The Spouse' is one of two sermons published together, but independent, in 1638. The general title-page of both is given below [*]; also the separate title of 'The Spouse' [†]. Prefixed is an 'Epistle Dedicatory,' which will be found on the opposite page. 'The Spouse,' though from an earlier chapter of Canticles, as being subordinate, follows 'Bowels Opened.' **G.**

* and † Title-pages—

TWO
SERMONS:
PREACHED
By that Faithfull
and Reverend Divine,
RICHARD SIBBES,
D.D. and sometimes Prea-
cher to the Honourable So-
ciety of *Grayes-Inne;*
And Master of *Katherine*
Hall in CAMBRIDGE.
Printed at *London* by *T. Cotes*,* and
are to sold by *Andr. Kembe*, at his Shop
at S *Margarets* Hill in *Southwarke*, 1638.

On the back of this title we read, 'Imprimator [sic] Tho. Wykes. Aprill 12. 1638.'

THE
S P O V S E,
HER
Earnest desire after
Christ her Husband.
OR,
A Sermon preached on
CANT. I. Vers. 5.
By that Faithfull and Reve-
rend Divine, *Richard Sibbes*,
D. D. and sometimes preacher
to the Honorable Societie
of *Grayes-Inne;*
And Master of *Katherine* Hall in
Cambridge.

PSAL. 73. 25.
Whom have I in Heaven but thee?
and there is none upon earth that I
desire besides thee.

* It may be noted here that Coates was the publisher of the famous second folio of the works of Shakespeare, 1632.—G.

TO THE RIGHT WORSHIPFUL

SIR JOHN HOWLAND, KNIGHT.

SIR,—These two sermons were brought unto me for that learned and religious divine, whose name they bear; and so far as I am able to judge, the style and spiritualness of the matter argue no less. Being earnestly requested to peruse them, I thought fit to commend them to the world under your name, because I know that you so well affected the author. My request unto you is, that you would be pleased to accept the dedication of them as a testimony of his sincere affection, who labours, and prays for your good in the best things.

Your Worship's to be commanded in all Christian service,

R. T.*

* These initials R. T., probably represent Robert Town or Towne. In the 'Nonconformist's Memorial,' (iii. 438) he is stated to have been one of the 'Ejected' of 1662, being at the time in Howorth, Yorkshire, the same it is presumable with Haworth, since rendered so renowned by the Brontës, and a little earlier by Grimshawe. He had at a former period been Vicar of Ealand, Halifax. He died in 1663, aged about 70. Palmer adds, 'It was said that he had imbibed some unsound principles, but he was a man of good character.' Neither Calamy, nor Palmer, nor any of the Puritan historians, enumerate writings by him. But at the end of Burrough's 'Saint's Happiness,' (4to 1660), Nathanael Brook announces the following: 'Reassertion of grace? *Vindiciæ Evangelii*, or the Vindication of the Gospel; a reply to Mr Anthony Bridges [*sic* but Burgess is meant] *Vindiciæ Legis*, and to Mr Rutherford, by Robert Town.'—G.

THE SPOUSE, HER EARNEST DESIRE AFTER CHRIST.

Let him kiss me with the kisses of his mouth: for thy love is better than wine.
—Cant. I. 2.

The Holy Ghost is pleased here to condescend to our infirmities; and, that we might help ourselves in our spiritual estate by our bodies, he speaketh here of heavenly things after an earthly manner, and with a comfortable mystery. As in other places the Holy Ghost sets out the joys of heaven by a sweet banquet, so here he sets out the union that we have with Christ by the union of the husband with the wife; and that we might the better understand what this union is, he condescends to our weakness, that we might see that in a glass which we through our corruptions cannot otherwise discern. This book is nothing else but a plain demonstration and setting forth of the love of Christ to his church, and of the love of the church to Christ; so familiarly and plainly, that the Jews take great scandal at it, and would not have any to read this book till they are come to the age of thirty years, lest they thereby should be tempted to incontinency; wherein they would seem wiser than God himself. But the Holy Ghost is pleased thus by corporeal to set out these spiritual things, which are of a higher nature, that by thinking and tasting of the one they might be stirred up to translate their affections (which in youthful age are most strong) from the heat of natural love to spiritual things, to the things of God; and all those who are spiritually minded (for whom chiefly the Scriptures were written) will take special comfort and instruction thereby, though others take offence and scandal at it. So here, the union between Christ and his spouse is so familiarly and livelily set forth by that union which is between the husband and the wife, that, though ungodly men might take offence at it, yet the godly may be bettered by it.

'Let him kiss,' &c. These words are the words of the spouse to Christ, containing in them two particulars.

First, *an earnest desire*, in these words, 'Let him kiss me with the kisses of his mouth.'

In which note three parts.

First, the person desiring, the church.

Secondly, the person desired, Christ.

Thirdly, the things desired, a familiar kiss of his mouth.

Secondly, *the ground of the desire*, fetched from the excellency of the thing desired, in these words, 'For thy love is sweeter than wine.'

From the whole in general observe *a spiritual contract between Christ and his church.* There is a civil contract between man and wife, answerable to which the spiritual contract between Christ and his church holds firm resemblance.

1. That this civil contract may hold, *both parties must consent.* So it is between Christ and his spouse. He was so in love with mankind, that he hath taken our nature upon him; and this his incarnation is the ground of all our union with Christ. First, his incarnation is the cause or ground of our union with him in grace here; and, secondly, our union in grace is the ground of our union in glory. Now, that we may be a spouse to him, he gives us his Spirit to testify his love to us, that we might give our consent to him again, as also that we might be made a fit spouse for him.

2. Likewise in marriage there is *a communicating of all good things.* So it is here. Christ here in this spiritual contract gives himself, and with himself all good things. The Spirit is the church's. His happiness is the church's. His graces are the church's. His righteousness is the church's. In a word, all his privileges and prerogatives are the church's; as saith the apostle, 'All things are Christ's, and Christ is yours,' 1 Cor. iii. 21; for all are Christ's, and all that are Christ's are yours by this spiritual contract. This excellency is set down by the prophet Hosea in his second chapter and latter end, where he, speaking of this spiritual contract between Christ and his church, saith, Hos. ii. 19, &c. 'In that day when he shall marry her unto himself in faithfulness, he will make a covenant for her with all creatures, with the beasts of the field, the fowls of heaven, and all that creepeth upon the earth.' So that upon this contract cometh in a league between the church and all the creatures. All that he hath done, all that he hath suffered by this contract is made ours. We have the benefit of all.

Obj. But what have we to bestow upon him again?

Solution. Nothing at all; neither portion nor proportion, beauty nor riches, but our miserable and base condition that he took upon him.

Use. This is *a well-spring of much comfort*, and *a ground of much duty.*

1. Christ condescended so far unto us, to such a near league, as to take us to be his spouse, who hath all things. What then can we want when we are at the fountain of all things? We can want no protection, for that is the covering of this well. We can want no good thing but he will supply it. We have free access unto him, as the wife hath to her husband. Who hath free access to the husband if the wife hath not? So who hath free access to Christ but the spouse?

Obj. Yea, but we have infirmities.

Solution. True, indeed; but shall man bear with his wife because she is the 'weaker vessel,' 1 Pet. iii. 7, and shall not Christ much more with his spouse? Herein then is our chiefest comfort, that this union, this contract, is not for a time, but for ever: 'I have married thee unto myself for ever,' Hos. ii. 19. And therefore we shall never want protection nor direction, nor anything that is good for us.

2. Now, the duty on our part is to love him again with a mutual love, and obedient love; to honour him as Sarah did Abraham, by calling him Lord, 1 Pet. iii. 6; and manifest it by doing what he would have thee to do, and by suffering what he would have thee to suffer.

To come to particulars.

First, *of the person desiring*, 'Let him kiss me.'

'Me' is here the speech of the whole church, and so of every particular member which is the spouse of Christ.

Doct. All Christian favours belong to all Christians alike. We have one faith, one baptism, one Spirit. As every Christian may say 'me,' so may the whole church, and every Christian as well as the church. All Christian privileges belong to all alike.

Use 1. Herein have comfort then, that whatsoever belongs to the church in general, belongs to every member in particular.

Use 2. This teacheth us to reason from one spiritual thing to another, as thus Abraham believed, 'and it was counted to him for righteousness,' Rom. iv. 22; and therefore if I believe I shall be counted righteous. David sinned, and David repented and found mercy; and therefore if I, &c. So all privileges belong alike to all Christians. Every Christian soul is the spouse of Christ as the whole church is. Therefore St Paul propounds himself an example to all that would believe in Christ. 'God had mercy on him,' 1 Tim. i. 16, and therefore he encourageth all to come unto Christ, by this, that he will have mercy on thee, as he had on him. Whatsoever is promised to the whole church, that apply to thy own soul in particular; and whatsoever is required of the whole church, that is required of thee in particular by Christ, if thou be a member. But though in spiritual favours all have a like portion, yet it is not so in outward things; but some are rich, some are poor, some honourable, some base. But in the best privileges and best gifts there is an equal extending to all alike, to the poor Christian as well as to the rich, to him that is base in the eye of the world, as well as to him that is honourable.

Secondly, *of the person desired*, 'Let him.'

Many make love to the spouse; as the devil, the world, and the flesh. The devil and carnal persons make love to the soul, to draw her away from Christ, but she looks to Christ still. 'Let *him* kiss me.' She goes not as the papists do, to Peter and Paul, but to Christ and to Christ alone. He 'is my well-beloved, and I am his,' Cant. ii. 16; he is my peculiar, and I am his peculiar; none have 'I in heaven but him, and there is none that I desire in comparison of him,' Ps. lxxiii. 25. He hath singled out me, and I have singled out him, 'Let him kiss me.'

Thirdly, *of the thing desired*, 'Let him kiss me,' &c.

The thing desired, it is a kiss. There are divers sorts of kisses spoken of in Scripture. There is a kiss of superiors to inferiors, and of inferiors to superiors. There is an holy kiss, Rom. xvi. 16, 1 Cor. xvi. 20, and an hypocritical kiss, as Joab to Amasa, 2 Sam. xx. 9, and as Judas to Christ, Mat. xxvi. 49. There are kisses of love; so Jonathan kissed David, 1 Sam. xx. 41. There are kisses also of subjection, as, Kiss ye the Son, &c., Ps. ii. 12. But here is the kiss of a superior to an inferior. 'Let him kiss me with the kisses of his mouth,' that is, let him shew me further testimony of his love by his presence; let me enjoy further communion with him still; let him further assure me of his love. Consider what the church meant; howsoever she had interest in this spiritual contract and covenant at the first, yet the church, according to the different degrees of time, had different degrees of desires to be further and further assured of his love. As in Solomon's time, so before from the beginning, there was a desire in the church of the kisses of Christ, that is, that he would come in our nature, and that he would manifest by little and little, clearer and clearer, his coming in the flesh; and accordingly he did by degrees reveal himself, as first in paradise, 'The seed of the woman shall break the serpent's head, Gen. iii. 15; then to Abraham, 'In thy seed shall all the families of the earth be blessed,' Gen. xii. 3. After that to one tribe, Gen. xlix. 10, the tribe of Judah, Heb. vii. 14; then to one family of that tribe, the house of David, Luke i. 27; then a virgin shall conceive, Isa. vii. 14; and after that pointed out by the finger of John the Baptist, 'Behold the Lamb of God that takes away the sins of the world,' John i. 29. So you see how Christ did reveal himself more and more by degrees unto his church. Answerable to these degrees were the desires of the church for the coming of Christ, as the prophet Isaiah saith, 'Come down and break the heavens,' Isa. lxiv. 1.; and then prophesied of by those that waited for the consummation of Israel. So that before Christ came in the flesh the church had a longing desire after his incarnation, as here, 'Let him kiss me with the kisses of his mouth.' But that is not all. For she knew this should not be till the last days, and therefore desireth some further means of acquaintance and knowledge of him, desiring that he would manifest himself more and more by his word, by his grace, and by his Spirit; and therefore as then the desire of the church was for the coming of Christ, so now that which Christians desire and long after is, to go to him that they may remain with him in glory. They love his appearance, but because this shall not be yet, though the church be still in expectation of it, therefore she desireth to hear his words, and to have him kiss her with his mouth in his word. But this is not all; but let me find his Spirit now walking with me here, and further, 'kiss me with his mouth,' by increasing his graces in me, manifesting his love unto me more and more. This is the desire of the church, and of every Christian soul, that Christ would thus kiss her; that he would reveal himself every day more and more unto her, in his word, in his sacraments, by his Spirit, by his graces, by increasing of them. This is the desire of the church and of every Christian soul, that Christ would thus 'kiss her with the kisses of his mouth.'

Now we are come to the ground of this desire, taken from the excellency of the love of Christ, which is here said by experience of the whole church, and of every Christian soul, to be 'sweeter than wine.'

From hence we note two things.

Doct. 1. *First, that every Christian soul and the spouse in general hath a sweet taste of the love of Christ even in this life.*

Doct. 2. *That after this contract and taste of this love, she hath ever springing up in her a further desire of the increase and manifestation of it.*

Doct. 1. For the first, as after the contract there is a more manifestation of love than was before, yet not a full manifestation of love till after the marriage, so Christ, though he do give his spouse a taste of his love here, and sends love-tokens unto her, some graces whereby his love is made more manifest than before (as Isaac sent to Rebekah some jewels and bracelets to manifest his love to her, Gen. xxiv. 53); yet his love is not fully manifested in this life, but is kept until the great solemnity. Christ cannot delight in the spouse unless she be decked with his graces, and therefore he gives her of them; and these are not only a taste of his favours, but the fruit of his favours.

The reasons are diverse.

Reason 1. The first reason is *to solace their long absence*, that they may not faint, but having a sweet taste of his love here, may stay their hearts thereupon until the day wherein he will fully manifest his love unto them. The Lord seeth his children are subject to be oppressed with heaviness here; therefore he gives them a taste of his love here, that thereby they might be comforted, when nothing else can.

Reason 2. The Lord gives his children a sweet taste of his love here, *that when they by weakness and frailty fall away and lose their first love, when by their former taste they might return and recover themselves again*, considering how sweet, and how strong that love was, that once they had enjoyed from Christ, and hereby they might say with the church, 'I will return,' &c., Hos. ii. 7.

Reason 3. The third reason is, *because the manifestation of this his love doth wonderfully strengthen a Christian to go lightly through the heaviest affliction;* for when Christ assures a Christian of his love, then affliction will seem grievous, but he will through all, he will suffer whatsoever shall befall him for Christ's sake with joy.

Reason 4. Lastly, Christ gives his church, and so every Christian, a taste of his love in this life, *because he knows we have many temptations in this world which are ready to steal away our affections*, as carnal pleasures, riches, honours, and the like. Now that these might not draw away our affections, he gives us a taste of his love, which is better than all other things, 'which is sweeter than wine,' that by this our affections might be preserved chaste to him. So then Christ gives us, his spouse, a sweet taste of his love in this life, that afflictions on our left hand might not too much press us down and discomfort us; nor the pleasures and delights on our right hand steal away our hearts from him.

Use. The use is to teach us to *admire* at the goodness of God* in this, that he is pleased so to provide for us, as to keep us from being too much overcome with heaviness through the multitude of temptations and afflictions which in this life we are subject unto; expelling the bitterness thereof with the sweetness of his love, thereby preserving our affections chaste unto himself.

Now we come to the second doctrine.

Doct. 2. *That the church (and so every Christian) after this contract and taste of Christ's love, hath evermore springing up in them an insatiable desire for a further taste and assurance of his love.*

The reasons of this doctrine are two.

Reason 1. The first reason is taken from the nature of true love, *which is never satisfied.* And hence it is, that though Christ give his spouse a taste of his love in his word, by sending his ambassadors, his ministers with his love-letters, the gospel of peace, giving therein a taste of his love, as also by his Spirit, by his sacraments, by his graces; yet all this will not satisfy her soul, but Christ having once manifested his love unto her, there is a continual desire to have a further taste and assurance of it.

Reason 2. The second reason is drawn *from Christ's infinite riches*, infinite in his glory, in his power, in his beauty, in his pleasures, and joys, and the like. He hath all things, 'All power is given him in heaven and in earth,' Mat. xxviii. 18; every way infinite in himself; and hence it is, that the spouse hath an infinite desire to have a further taste of his love, and a nearer communion with him. So you see whether we regard the nature of love, which is never satisfied, or whether we consider his infinite riches, both manifest this truth, that there is an insatiable desire in a Christian, to be further filled with, and more fully assured of, the love of Christ.

* That is, 'wonder.'—G.

Where grace is, there is a further desire of growth in grace. It is an higher degree of love to desire the enjoying of the presence of Christ, than to enjoy heaven itself; but this will not be yet.

Use 1. Therefore let us try our love *by our labouring for that sight of Christ which we may have;* as in his ordinances where he manifests himself in a special manner. Is it the great grief of thy soul that thou art shut from the presence of Christ in his ordinances, from the congregation of the saints, where he by familiar kisses useth to manifest his love to thee more and more? I can but wonder that some persons dare to take upon them the name of Christianity, and yet think that men be too holy. These want this character of a Christian, viz., a further desire of the manifestation of Christ's love. Many of them neglect the ordinances of God, or if they do come there, they desire not further inward kisses of his love, but content themselves with the outward.

When the Spirit should witness and seal up the love, the love of Christ to their souls, by an inward kiss, they only content themselves with the outward, the bare hearing of the word. But where this further desire of familiarity with Christ is not, there is but a barren soul, there is no taste of Christ's love. If there were a taste, there would be a further desire of growth in that love. There are some that make a profession of religion, as many that marry to cloak their adultery; so these profess Christ, to cover their strong covetousness and strong faults, that they may have the more strength to commit sin. We must not content ourselves without these outward kisses, but give, as the outward man, so sacrifice the inward man, Rom. vii. 22, the soul unto God. Let those that find, after this trial, these desires springing up in them, comfort themselves in this, that they are Christ's, and Christ shall manifest his love more and more unto them. For God hath promised to grant the desires of the righteous, Ps. xxxvii. 4. Hast thou then a longing desire to have a further taste of the love of Christ? Use the means, and then be sure that Christ will manifest his love more and more unto thy soul.

Use 2. The second use is for exhortation and spiritual direction *how we shall come to a further assurance, sign, and fruit of Christ's love.* If we desire this, we must labour to have, first, *chaste judgments*, and secondly, *chaste affections. A chaste judgment* from error, heresy, and schism; and our affections chaste from the world, from pleasures and the like. For Christ is wonderful jealous of our judgments, and of our love. Therefore Paul desires to present the Corinths* a 'pure virgin unto Christ,' 2 Cor. xi. 2. So then, as we must affect† goodness, so we must profess truth. We must have chaste judgments as well as chaste affections. The spouse of Christ, as she is pure in affections, so she is pure in judgment; she hears his voice and follows him. Whatsoever comes not from the word, receive it not, but reject it. Thus much for the judgment.

So likewise labour for *chaste affections*. Christ will not have us to divide our affections; partly for him, and partly for the world, or partly to pleasures, and partly to him. He will not have it so. He will have the whole heart and whole affections, or he will have neither heart nor affections. If we give our hearts to the world or to the pleasures of the world, the love of which is enmity with God, James iv. 4, then have we an adulterous heart; which to do is a double sin. As for a wife to commit whoredom is a double sin, there is adultery and breach of marriage covenant; so to embrace the world after we are contracted unto Christ, is spiritual whoredom and a

* That is, 'Corinthians.'—G.

† That is, 'love.'—G.

breach of our covenant in spiritual contract. Take heed of worldly-minded ness, which will glue thy affections to the earth, and will not suffer them to be lifted up to Christ. Take heed of the pleasures of the world, lest they drown thy soul, as they do the souls of many that profess themselves to be Christians.

Use 3. Thirdly, if we will grow in the assurance of the love of Christ, and have more familiar kisses of his mouth, then labour *to get an humble heart*, by searching out our own unworthiness in respect of what we are, or were by nature. Indeed, we may disparage our credits by abasing ourselves in respect of men, but never can we be too much humbled to our Saviour in acknowledging ourselves unworthy of all that we have. There is no danger in thus debasing ourselves to our Saviour, nay, it is for our honour with God. For those that thus honour him he will honour with his graces; for he giveth grace to the humble, and with such a spirit he delights to dwell, Isa. lxvi. 2. Let us with humility, then, acknowledge all to be from his free grace, and with Jacob, acknowledge ourselves to be less than the least of his mercies, Gen. xxxii. 10.

Use 4. Fourthly, if we will grow in the assurance of the love of Christ, *we must give Christ no peace.* Take no nay of him, till he hath given thee the kisses of his love. Many times he delays the manifesting of his love—what though? Yet wait his pleasure, for he hath waited long upon thee. We see Mary Magdalen, what ado she made when she could not find Christ. He having manifested himself unto her at the beginning, at length he calleth her by her name, demanding for what she wept, and whom she sought, Luke vii. 47. Give him no rest, take no denial, till he answer thee, for he will do it. What did the woman of Canaan? She gave him no rest till he did apply himself unto her, Mat. xv. 22, *seq.* Jacob wrestled with God, and would not let him go, till he had assured him of his love and favour, Gen. xxxii. 24, *seq.* He hath promised to grant the desires of the righteous, Ps. xxxvii. 4. Hath he given us such strong desires after him? Then continue constant importuning him by prayer, and he cannot stand out with us long; he cannot deny us some further assurance of his love.

Use 5. Again, *take everything to thine advantage*, as his former love and favour, his power, fidelity, and stability. Take advantage from these, and plead for thy desires, as the woman of Canaan. Christ accounts her a dog, Mat. xv. 26. I am indeed so, saith she. She taketh advantage of his words, and thereby pleads for her desire. As the servants of Benhadad catch at words of comfort from Ahab, 1 Kings xx. 33; so continually take advantage from your own experience. He hath been thus and thus good unto thee, these and these means thou hast enjoyed, and thus and thus hath it wrought for my good; I will therefore follow him now until he assure me of his love in a further degree.

Use 6. Again, consider thou must be *modest in thy desires of this kind.* Desire no great matter at the first. I mean, not full assurance of the love of Christ at the first; but observe the degrees of his kisses, and manifestation of his love. The thief on the cross desired but to be remembered of Christ when he came into his kingdom, Luke xxiii. 42,—no great matter; so do thou desire any taste of his love, though never so little. Indeed, so the children of God do. First they desire the pardon of their sins, and having obtained this, they grow more and more in desiring the graces of the Spirit, as seals to assure them of the pardon of them, and of his love unto them, and nearer communion with him.

Obj. But this communion is not alway felt.

Sol. 1. I answer, if Christ be strange to us, *it is from ourselves, not from Christ;* for he is all love. It is either because our loose hearts run after some carnal contents; and then no marvel though Christ shew himself strange unto us, and we go mourning all the day long, without a sense of his love.

Or else, 2, It is when *we will not seek for his kisses*, a further taste of his love, as we should, in his ordinances, nor exercise those graces that we have as we should, in attending upon the ordinance, resting by faith upon God's promise for a blessing.

Or else, 3, *We are so negligent, that we do not stir up those graces of God in us by private duties.*

Or else, 4, *We join ourselves to evil company*, or to persons led with an evil spirit. These are the causes why Christ is strange to us.

Or else, 5, It is to exercise and try our faith, and to let us see ourselves and our own weakness. Thus he left Peter. Otherwise, it is Christ, his nature, to manifest himself and his love by familiar kisses of his mouth. Search into your hearts, and you shall find that these and such like are the causes why Christ is strange unto you, and why you are senseless* of your communion with him.

Use 7. Consider, again, when it is, *at what time is it that we have the sweetest kisses, and are most refreshed with Christ's love.* Is it not when we put our strength to good means, as when we strive with God in prayer, and labour in humility rightly, and profitably to use all his ordinances? Mark these two well as a means to preserve and increase the assurance of Christ's love in you.

First, *how you fall into deadness*, and the causes of it.

Secondly, *how you come to have most communion with Christ*, and at what time, and after what performances. Canst thou say, I was thus and thus dead and senseless of Christ's love, but now I am thus and thus comforted and refreshed? either when thou deniedst anything to thyself, which thy heart stood strongly for, or when thou hadst been most careful in holy duties. If we deny ourselves in anything, that our hearts stand strongly for, because it hinders us in holy courses, God will be sure to recompense us in spiritual things abundantly, yea, and in temporal things many times.

Use 8. Consider, again, *when I was afflicted and had none else to comfort me, then the Lord was most sweet unto me, then he refreshed my soul with a sense of his love.*

These may help us much in getting a further assurance of Christ's love. Be stirred up, then, to desire to be where Christ is, and to have the kisses of his love in his ordinances, as further testimonies of his favour, and never rest from having a desire to increase in grace and communion with Christ. So shall you never want assurance of a good estate, nor comfort in any good estate. Cast such a man into a dungeon, he hath paradise there. Why? Because Christ comes to him. And if we have this communion with Christ, then though we are compassed about with death, yet it cannot affright us, because the great God is with us, Ps. xxiii. 4. Do with such a one what you will; cast him into hell, if it were possible; he having a sweet communion with Christ, will be joyful still; and the more sense we have of the love of Christ, the less we shall regard the pleasures or riches of the world. For what joy can be compared with this, that

* That is, 'unconscious of,' 'without assurance of.'—G.

the soul hath communion with Christ? All the world is nothing in comparison.

Now, then, seeing you cannot requite this love of Christ again, yet shew your love to Christ in manifesting love to his members, to the poor, to such poor especially as have the church of God in their families. As the woman poured oil on the head of Christ, so shall we do well to pour some oil upon the feet of Christ. That which we would do to him, if he were here, let us do to his members, that thereby we may further our communion with Christ.

FINIS.

A BREATHING AFTER GOD.

A BREATHING AFTER GOD.

NOTE.

The 'Breathing after God' is placed immediately after the sermons from Canticles, as being not only on the same subject, though from a different portion of Holy Scripture, but also as partaking very much of their spirit. The original title-page is given below.* Prefixed is the miniature portrait, by Marshall, found in several of Sibbes's smaller volumes. **G.**

* Title-page :—

A
BREATHING
AFTER GOD,
OR
A CHRISTIANS
DESIRE OF GODS
PRESENCE,
BY
The late Reverent [*sic*] and worthy
Divine RICHARD SIBS,
Doctor in Divinity, Master of
Katherine Hall in *Cambridge*, and
sometime Preacher of
Graies-Inne.
Psal. 42. 1.
As the Hart panteth after the water brooks;
so panteth my soul after thee, O God.
Lam. 3. 56.
Hide not thine eare at my breathing.
LONDON
Printed by *John Dawson* for *R. M.*
and are to be sold by *Thomas Slater*,
at the Swan in *Duck-lane.* 1639.

TO THE CHRISTIAN READER.

MAN in this world, especially since his defection from God, standing at a distance from his happiness in respect of full possession, it is not the least part of his bliss to be happy in expectation. Happiness being by all men desirable, the desire of it is naturally engrafted in every man; and is the centre of all the searchings of his heart and turnings of his life. But the most of men, like the men of Sodom, grope and find not the right door, Gen. xix. 11. Only to a true Christian, by a supernatural light, is discovered both the right object, and the right way to felicity. Upon this discovery, finding himself, while he is here, a stranger to his happiness, he desires to take leave of this sublunary condition, that he may enjoy him who is 'the desire of all nations,' Hag. ii. 7.

Now although God cast common blessings promiscuously upon good and bad; yet he holds his best favours at a distance, as parents do cherries or apples from their children, to whet their appetites the more after them. And indeed the best perfection of a Christian in his military* condition, is, in desire and expectation; and it is enough to him that; for that he hath God's acceptation, who knowing whereof we are made, and how unable to hold weight in the 'balance of the sanctuary,' Dan. v. 27, takes his best gold with grains of allowance.

The soul of man is like a cipher, which is valued by that which is set before it. If it weary itself in the desire of earthly things, like the silk-worm, it finisheth its work with its own destruction. But if on things above, when this earthly tabernacle is turned to ashes, there shall result a glorious phœnix for immortality.

There are no characters better distinguishing a Christian, than those that are inward (hypocrisy like sale-work, may make a fair show outward; an hypocrite may perform external works, but cannot dissemble inward affections), and amongst them, none better discovers his temper, than the beating of the pulse of his desires, which this worthy author (who departed not without being much desired† and no less lamented) hath most livelily set forth in the ensuing treatise; which a Christian, holding as a glass before him, may discern whether he have life or no by these breathings.

* That is 'militant.'—G.

† That is, 'longed after.'—G

For the object here propounded, what more desirable than the chief good? For the place, where can it be more desired, than in his house, where his presence is manifested? What better end to be in that house, than to behold God in the 'beauty of holiness?' Ps. xxix. 2. What term of happiness better than 'for ever'? This was the desire of the holy prophet David, and that it may be thy desire, is the desire of

Thy Christian friend,

H. I.*

* These initials are in all probability those of John Hill, reversed, intentionally or by a misprint. See note on p. 251.—G.

A BREATHING AFTER GOD.

One thing have I desired of the Lord, that I will seek after; that I may dwell in the house of the Lord all the days of my life; to behold th   uty of the Lord, and to inquire in his temple.—Ps. XXVII. 4.

THIS psalm is partly a prophecy. It was made after some great deliverance out of some great trouble. The blessed prophet David, having experience of God's goodness suitable to the trouble he was in, in the first part of this excellent psalm he shews—

I. His *comfort;* and, II. His *courage;* and, III. His *care.*

I. His *comfort.* It was altogether *in the Lord,* whom he sets out in all the beauties and excellency of speech he can. He propounds the Lord to him in borrowed terms. 'The Lord is my light and my salvation, the strength of my life,' Ps. xxvii. 1. So he fetcheth comfort from God, the spring of comfort, 'the Father of all comfort,' 2 Cor. i. 4. He labours to present God to him in the sweetest manner that may be. He opposeth him to every difficulty and distress. In darkness, he is 'my light;' in danger, he is 'my salvation;' in weakness, he is 'my strength;' in all my afflictions and straits, he is the 'strength of my life.' Here is the art of faith in all perplexities whatsoever, to be able to set somewhat in God against every malady in ourselves. And this is not simply set out, but likewise with a holy insultation.* 'The Lord is my light and salvation; whom shall I fear?' Ps. xxvii. 1. It is a question proceeding from a holy insultation, and daring of all other things. 'The Lord is the strength of my life; of whom shall I be afraid?' That is one branch of his comfort.

The second branch and ground of his comfort is, 2. *The goodness of God in the ruin and destruction of his enemies.* 'When the wicked, even mine enemies and foes, came upon me to eat up my flesh, they stumbled and fell,' Ps. xxvii. 2. He describes his enemies by their malice, and by their ruin.

[1.] His enemies were *cruel enemies,* blood-suckers, eaters of flesh. We call them cannibals. As indeed men that have not grace, if they have greatness, and be opposed, their greatness is inaccessible; one man is a devil to another. The Scripture calls them 'wolves, that leave nothing

* That is, 'defiance.'—G.

till morning,' Zeph. iii. 3. As the great fishes eat up the little ones, so great men they make no more conscience of eating up other men, than of eating bread; they make no more bones of overthrowing men and undoing them, than of eating bread. 'They eat up my people as they eat bread,' Ps. xxvii. 2.

[2.] But notwithstanding their cruelty, *they were overthrown*. Saith David, 'when my foes came upon me to eat up my flesh, they stumbled and fell.' For, indeed, God's children, when they are delivered, it is usually with the confusion of their enemies. God doth two things at once, because the special grievance of God's children it is from inward and outward enemies. He seldom or never delivers them but with the confusion of their enemies. So he sets down his own comfort in the Lord, by the confusion of his enemies. This will be most apparent at the day of judgment, when Satan, and all that are led by his spirit, all the malignant church, shall be sent to their own place, and the church shall be for ever free from all kind of enemies. When the church is most free, then the enemies of the church are nearest to destruction; like a pair of balances, when they are up at the one end, they are down at the other. So when it is up with the church, down go the enemies. So here are the two branches of his comfort.

II. Now his *courage* for the time to come, that is, in the third verse. 'Though an host encamp against me, my heart shall not fear.' He puts the case of the greatest danger that can be. Though an host of men should encompass me, 'my heart shall not fear; though war rise against me, in this I will be confident.' Here is great courage for the time to come. *Experience breeds hope and confidence*. David was not so courageous a man of himself; but upon experience of God's former comfort and assistance, his faith brake as fire out of the smoke, or as the sun out of a cloud. Though I was in such and such perplexities, yet for the time to come I have such confidence and experience of God's goodness, that I will not fear. He that seeth God by a spirit of faith in his greatness and power, he sees all other things below as nothing. Therefore he saith here, he cares not for the time to come for any opposition; no, not of an army. 'If God be with us, who can be against us?' Rom. viii. 31. He saw God in his power; and then, looking from God to the creature, alas! who was he? As Micah, when he had seen God sitting upon his throne; what was Ahab to him, when he had seen God once? So when the prophet David had seen God once, then 'though an host encamp against me, I will not fear,' &c. Thus you have his comfort in the double branch of it; his courage, also, and his confidence for the time to come.

III. What is his *care?* That is the next. I will not analyse the psalm farther than the text. After his comfort in the Lord, and in the confusion of his enemies, and his courage for the time to come, he sets down his care, 'One thing have I desired of the Lord, and that will I seek after, that I may dwell in the house of the Lord all the days of my life,' &c. This was his care. He had so sweet experience of the goodness and power of God, being light, and salvation and strength to him in confounding his enemies, that he studied with himself how to be thankful to God; and this he thought fittest in the open great congregation, in the church of God, among many others. Therefore he saith, 'One thing have I desired of the Lord, and that will I seek after still, that I may dwell in the house of the Lord all the days of my life.'

Now, in the words of the text that I have read, there is contained the holy prophet's care and desire, set down first in general, 'One thing have I desired of the Lord, and that I will seek after.'

And then a specification of that desire he specifies. What is that one thing he desired? That 'I may dwell in the house of the Lord,' with the circumstance of time, 'all the days of my life.'

Now, after the desire in general, set out here by the object in general, the transcendent object, 'One thing have I desired of the Lord,' and likewise by the frequency and fervency of the desire, 'I will seek after it still.' I have desired it, and I will not cease. So my desire, it shall not be a flash soon kindled, and soon put out. No; but 'one thing have I desired of the Lord, and that I will seek still.' I will not be quiet till my desire be accomplished. There is the general desire, and the degrees of it.

The particular is, 'that I may dwell in the house of the Lord.'

Then the grounds and ends of the particular desire of dwelling in the 'house of the Lord,' because it is 'the house of God.' There is a strong argument to move him to dwell in the house of God. It is good dwelling where God dwells, where his angels dwell, and where his Spirit dwells, 'in the house of the Lord.' There is one argument that moved him, 'I desire to dwell there,' because it is the house of God, which is set out by the extent of time, that 'I may dwell in the house of God all the days of my life,' till I be housed in heaven, where I shall need none of these ordinances that I stand in need of in this world. 'I desire to dwell in the house of the Lord all the days of my life.'

Then the second end is, 'To behold the beauty of God.' That was one end of his desire, to dwell in the house of God; not to feed his eyes with speculations and goodly sights (as indeed there were in the tabernacle goodly things to be seen). No; he had a more spiritual sight than that. He saw the inward spiritual beauty of those spiritual things. The other were but outward things, as the apostle calls them. I desire to dwell in the house of the Lord, 'to behold the beauty of the Lord,' the inward beauty of the Lord especially.

And then the third end of his desire is, 'that I may inquire in his temple.' He desired to dwell in the house of God, because it was the house of God, and to see the beauty of God, the sweet, alluring beauty of God, that appeared in his ordinances; and then his desire was to dwell in the house of God, that he might inquire more and more of the meaning of God still, because there is an unfathomed bottom, and an endless depth of excellency in divine things, that the more we know, the more we may, and the more we seek, the more we may seek. They are beyond our capacity; they do not only satisfy, but transcend it. Therefore, he desires still further and further to wade deeper into these things, 'to inquire in God's temple.' Thus ye see the state of the verse. There is a general desire propounded. 'One thing have I desired of the Lord, and that will I seek after.'

And then the desire specified, 'to dwell in the house of the Lord, and to see the beauty of the Lord, and to inquire in his temple.' These be the three ends.

'One thing have I desired of the Lord,' &c.

To speak first of this desire generally propounded, 'One thing have I desired,' &c.

And then of the increase of it, in that he saith, 'I will seek after it still.' He desired it, and he would seek more and more after it.

In the desire, consider—

First, the *object*, 'one thing.'

And then the *desire* or *seeking itself*.

First, the *object*, 'one thing.'

Quest. Was there but one thing for holy David to make the object of his desire? Was there but one thing needful? Alas! this poor life of ours, it is a life of necessities. How many things are needful for our bodies? How many things are needful for the decency of our condition? How many things need we for our souls? It is a life of necessities. How, then, doth he say, 'One thing have I desired?'

Ans. Yes. His meaning is, comparatively, I seek for other things in their order and rank, and as they may stand with the main; but, indeed, one thing principally. All the rest will follow. 'Seek ye first the kingdom of God, and all the rest will be cast on you,' Mat. vi. 33. The best way to have all other things, is to seek one thing in the first place. Therefore, in heavenly wisdom he saith, I desire *unum unicè*; one thing after an entire manner. That I desire more than all things else.

Hence we may see that,

There is a difference of degrees of things. God hath established in the world degrees of things. There are some good and some ill by his permission; and of good, there are some that are greater goods, and some less. There are spiritual goods, and outward goods; and of spiritual good, there are some that are means leading to that which is spiritually good, and some that are spiritual good things in their own essence and nature. The leading preparing things are the means of salvation, the word, and sacraments, and being in the visible church. The true spiritual good, the good that we get by these things, faith and love, and spiritual inward strength. Now that there is degrees of things, the prophet here insinuates when he saith, 'One thing have I desired;' that is, of all these variety of things, he desired the best, that includes all in it. God, to exercise the wisdom that he hath given to man, hath planted a difference in the creatures, and hath given a faculty to man to make a right choice in those differences; and then man makes a right choice when he chooseth as God chooseth. Now, God makes choice of spiritual things to be the best things, and them he gives to his best friends. He knows they will make us good, and supply all outward wants whatsoever, and sanctify all estates and conditions to us, and they are eternal, suitable to the spiritual nature of our souls. God knows this very well. Therefore, God hath set spiritual things, as the one only thing; and so the soul, when it is made spiritual, and hath the image of God upon it, it chooseth as God chooseth.

'One thing have I desired.'

Quest. But here it may be asked, why doth he say, 'one thing?' He desired not only to live near the tabernacle, but to hear and see, to have the word read, and he desired thereupon grace, and then nearer communion with God by grace, to have more communion here, and fuller communion in heaven. Here is more than one thing.

Ans. I answer, it is all one. As a chain that hath many links, yet it is but one chain; so all these are but one. 'I desire one thing.' What is that? To live in the church of God, to enjoy the ordinances of God, and they will draw on faith and fear, &c. The Spirit accompanying the ordinances, it will be a spirit of faith, and repentance, and grace; and by those graces of faith, and the rest that accompany the ordinances, I shall have nearer communion with God here, and eternal and everlasting communion with God in heaven; and all these are but one, because they are all links of one chain. Therefore, when he saith, 'One thing have I desired,' he means that one thing that will draw on all other.

That is the scope of a gracious heart, when it attends upon the means of salvation, and lives in the church; not to hear that it may hear, and there an end, and to read that it may read, to perform it as a task, and all is done; but to have the work of the Spirit together with it, to have the ministry of the Spirit in the gospel, and the Spirit to increase faith, and faith to increase all other graces, and so by grace to grow into nearer communion with God in Christ. That is the scope of every good hearer. Therefore, he speaks to purpose when he saith, 'One thing have I desired.'

But to speak a little more of the object, why doth he say, 'One thing?'

First, *it is from the nature of God.* We must have the whole bent and sway of our souls to him. He will have no halting. The devil is content with half, if we will sin, because then he is sure of all; but God will have the whole heart. 'My son, give me thy whole heart,' Prov. xxiii. 26; and 'Thou shalt love the Lord with all thy heart, and with all thy soul,' Luke x. 27. The bent and sway of the soul must be that way; for it is the nature of excellent things, except we desire them in the chief place, they take state upon them.* God takes state upon him in this case. He will not have us serve him and Mammon, Mat. vi. 24. He will not have the heart divided.

Second. Then again, *it is from the nature of the soul.* Therefore, he saith, 'One thing.' It is the nature of the soul, when it is upon many things, it can do nothing well. Therefore, that I may be religious to purpose, 'One thing have I desired.' A stream cut into many channels runs weakly, and is unfit to carry anything. Babylon was so taken. They cut the river into many channels, and then he that took it easily passed over them. (*a*) When the soul is divided into many channels, to many things, that it looks after this thing and that thing, and that with expense and intention of care and endeavour, alas! where is the desire of one thing necessary all the while? For the soul cannot go with that strength as it should, except it mind one thing. The soul of man is a finite thing. Therefore, except it gather its strength, as a stream, that riseth of many particular lesser rivers, which makes it run stronger; so the soul it cannot desire one thing as it should, except it bring all other petty streams to it, and make that the main desire, to be saved in another world, and to have communion and fellowship with God in Christ Jesus, by the Spirit of grace in this world, in the use of the means. Unless this be the main care, the soul takes no good when it is so much set on other things.

Then, *thirdly*, he sets down this 'one thing,' to 'dwell in the house of God,' to grow in grace there 'as a cedar,' to be a 'tree planted there,' *from the very nature of grace*, which is to unite things to the main. The Spirit of grace sets before the eye of the soul heavenly spiritual things in their greatness and excellency; and the Spirit of grace, seeing there are many useful things in this world, it hath an uniting, knitting, subordinating power, to rank all things so as they may agree to and help the main. Grace confines the soul to one thing. Man, after his fall, 'sought out many inventions,' Eccles. vii. 29, saith the wise man. He was not content with his condition when he stood, but 'he sought out many inventions. When man falls to the creature, he knows not where to stay. No creature can afford a stay and rest for the soul long. The soul is never quiet till it come

* That is, 'are offended.'—G.

to God again,* and that is the one thing the soul desireth. The soul being sanctified by the Spirit of God, it subordinates all things to this one thing. David desired many things besides this one thing, but not in that degree, but as they might stand with the desire of this one thing necessary. Grace subordinates and ranks all things so as that the best things have the pre-eminence. Therefore, he might well say, 'one thing,' from the disposition that grace hath to rank all things to one. It is a promise in the covenant of grace. Saith God, 'I will give you one heart,' Jer. xxxii. 39. As soon as a man becomes a Christian, he hath one heart.' His heart before was divided. There was variety of objects it was set upon; God had the least piece. The flesh had a piece, and this delight and that delight had a piece; but saith God, 'I will give you one heart,' that is, a heart uniting itself in desire to the best things, and regulating all things, so as all shall be but one, that a man shall 'use the world as though he used it not,' so as it shall help to the main. As I said, little streams they help the main stream running into it, so grace hath a subordinating power over all things in the world, as they may help the main. 'One thing have I desired,' and I desire other things, as they may help the main. Grace will teach us that art. It hath a special art that way. So we see both in regard of God, and in regard of the soul being finite, and in respect of the wise disposing of grace that aims at the main, and ranks all things as they may help the main, he doth well say, 'One thing have I desired.'

Use. This shews *the vanity and baseness of every worldly man, that makes the main work and labour his by-work, and the by-work his main work.* That that is the 'one thing necessary,' Luke x. 42, is set after all. Indeed, without grace, this is so. The first work of grace is to set the soul in order, to subdue base affections, to sanctify the judgment; and when it hath set the soul in tune and order, then it is fitted to set a right price on things, to rank and order them as it should. So much shall be sufficient to unfold the object itself in general, 'One thing have I desired.'

Now I come to the affection itself, set forth here by the degrees.

'One thing have I desired, *and that I will seek after.*

I have desired it, and I will desire it still. Desires are the issues of the heart. Thoughts and desires are the two primitive issues of the heart, the births of the heart. Thoughts breed desires. Thoughts in the mind or brain, the brain strikes the heart presently. It goes from the understanding to the will and affections. What we think of, that we desire, if it be good. So thoughts and desires, they immediately spring from the soul; and where they are in any efficacy and strength, they stir up motion in the outward man. The desires of the soul, being the inward motion, they stir up outward motion, till there be an attaining of the thing desired, and then there is rest. Desire to the thing desired is like *motus ad quietem*, as motion is to rest. When motion comes once to rest, it is quiet. So desire, which is the inward motion, it stirs up outward motion, till the thing desired be accomplished, and then the soul rests in a loving content, and enjoying of the thing desired.

Now this desire, it was a spiritual desire. 'One thing have I desired of the Lord.' Holy desires, they issue from choice. A holy, wise desire, when it is not a mere notion, it ariseth from a choice of a thing that is good; for desire is nothing but the embracing and closing with a thing that is good. The understanding must choose the good first, before the soul embrace it. The will is but the carriage of the soul, the furthering and

* Augustine.—See note *h*, vol. I., page 214.—G.

promotion of the soul to the good things discovered; so it supposeth a choice of good things.

And choice supposeth an esteem of the things before we choose them; and that supposeth a deliberate judging that works an esteem. So that it was no hasty, sudden thing this desire; but it rose from the sanctified judgment of David, that bred a holy esteem of these excellent things; the means of salvation, having the Spirit of God accompanying of them, containing such excellent comforts as they do. I say this desire supposes a right judgment, and thence an esteem; thence a choice upon all, choosing these things above all other contentments and things in the world besides. For at this time he wanted in his family the comfort of his wife and house, &c. Tush, what do I regard these things? If I could enjoy the sweet, and strong, and comfortable presence of God in his ordinances, other things I could bear well enough, the want of house, and wife and children, the pleasures and contentments of my country. Therefore, 'One thing have I desired.' It was a desire out of a high esteem and choice of that one thing he speaks of.

The point of doctrine that I will observe in brief, because I hasten to the main thing, is this,

That the Spirit of God in the hearts of his children is effectual in stirring up holy desires.

There is nothing that characteriseth and sets a stamp upon a Christian so much as desires. All other things may be counterfeit. Words and actions may be counterfeit, but the desires and affections cannot, because they are the immediate issues and productions of the soul; they are that that comes immediately from the soul, as fire cannot be counterfeit. A man may ask his desires what he is? According to the pulse of the desires, so is the temper of the man. Desires are better than actions a great deal; for a man may do a good action, that he doth not love, and he may abstain from an ill action, that he hates not. But God is a Spirit, and looks to the spirit especially. It is a good character of a Christian, that his desire, for the most part, is to good; the tenor and sway and bent of his desire is to good. 'One thing have I desired.' The Spirit of God is effectual in stirring up these desires.

Quest. But how shall we know that these desires are the chief things to distinguish an hypocrite from a true Christian, and whether they be true or no?

Ans. To go no farther than the text: desires are holy and spiritual,

If they be about holy and spiritual things. 'One thing have I desired,' saith David. What was that? To be rich and great in the world, and to be revenged on my enemies? No, no; that is not the matter. I have many enemies; God will take a course that they shall fall. That that I desire, is to have nearer communion with God; I desire to enjoy the ordinances of God. So his desire it was set on spiritual objects, and that argued it was a holy desire.

2. And then again, his desire. It was a *fervent desire,* as he saith, 'One thing have I desired, and that will I seek after.' It was not a blaze or flash, that was soon in and soon out. It was not a mere velleity, a kind of inefficacious desire. Fervency shewed that his desire was sound. He would not be quieted without the thing accomplished.

3. And then *constancy,* when a man will not be taken off. There is not the wickedest man in the world, but he hath good flashes, good offers, and desires sometimes. 'Lord, have mercy upon me,' &c. He hath good

ejaculations sometimes. Ay, but what is the bent and sway of his desires? This was David's constant desire. As it was about spiritual, and was a fervent and eager desire, that he would not be quieted, so it was constant. That that is natural is constant, and that that is supernaturally natural. That that is natural in spiritual things, it is constant; nature is constant. For how doth nature differ from art? Artificial things are for a time. Teach a creature beyond his nature, he will shew his naturals. So let an hypocrite act a part, if it be not his nature, he will soon turn to his naturals, and shew that he is an hypocrite again. Constancy and perpetuity in good things, a tenor of good desires, shew that the heart is good, because it is constant.

4. And then again, this desire here, of David, it was kindled *from the love of God, and not out of base ends.* Holy desires are kindled in the soul from the love of God; for what saith he here? 'One thing have I desired.' What was that? 'To dwell in the house of the Lord.' What to do? 'To behold the beauty of God;' to see God in his excellency and beauty and worthiness. All his desire was from this, that his soul was enamoured with the beauty of God's house. The love of God stirred up this blessed desire in the prophet. Therefore, it was a holy and spiritual desire.

5. Again, as they spring from the love of God, *so they tend to the honour of God;* for what comes from heaven, goes to heaven back again. As waters that come from a spring, they go as high as the place they come from; so holy desires, being kindled from heaven from a spirit of love, they go to heaven again. The love of God stirs them up, and he seeks God's glory, and honour, and inward communion with God in this. For a man out of a natural desire may desire holy things sometimes, to be free from such or such a sin, and to have such and such a grace, not out of a desire to honour God; but if he had grace, he sees he might escape troubles, he might be free from temporal judgments, and he might ingratiate himself, and commend himself to this or that person, whom he desires to benefit by. Therefore, he desires as much grace as may help forward his intentions in the world. He joins the world and God together. Oh! no, these are not the desires that distinguish a Christian from another man; but those that spring from the love of God, that proceed inwardly from the truth of the heart, and that the things themselves please God, and that there is a loveliness in them, and that they tend to the honour of God especially, and our own good in a secondary place. This is a character of good desires. Thus we see, though I should go no further than the text, how we may distinguish holy and heavenly desires from other desires. 'One thing have I desired, and that will I seek,' &c.

Therefore, let us examine what our desires are, what our bent is. Desires issue from the will and affections, and they shew the frame of the soul more than anything in the world. As the springs in low places are discovered by the steams and vapours that come out of the place, men gather that there is a spring below, because of the ascent of vapours; so the vapouring out of these desires shew that there is a spring of grace in the heart; they discover that there is a spring within.

And let those that mourn in Sion, that have some evidence (though they are not so good as they would be), let them look to their hearts. What is thy desire? What is the bent of thy soul? When a man is once converted and turned, wherein is his turning? Especially, his mind and judgment and esteem of things are altered. There is a change of mind, and withal the desire and bent of the soul is altered; that if a man ask him, and examine what the bent is of all the course of his life, oh! that God might be glorified, that his church and cause might prosper, that others might be converted; this is the bent of his soul; not that he might be great in the world, and ruin those that stand in his way (this shews that a man is a rotten hypocrite). The bent and sway of the soul shews what a man is.

Because I would not have any deceived in the point, take one evidence and sign more with you, and that shall be instead of all, and it is out of the text too, 'One thing have I desired, and that will I seek after,' not by prayer only, but in the use of all means; as, indeed, he was never quiet till he was settled again in Sion, nor then neither till he had gotten materials for the temple, and a place for God's honour 'to dwell in,' Deut. xii. 11. If desires be not the desires of the sluggard, there will be endeavour; as we see in the desire of David here, 'One thing have I desired, and that will I seek.' He used all means to enjoy communion with God sweetly.

The sluggard lusts and hath nothing. So there are many spiritual sluggards that lust and have nothing, because they shew not their desire in their endeavours. There will be endeavour where the desire is true. For desire springs from the will, the will being the appetite of the whole man, *Voluntas appetitus*, &c. The understanding carries not, but the will. When the will will have a thing, it carries all the parts. Hereupon, when the desire is true, it stirs up all the powers and faculties to do their duty, to seek to attain the accomplishment and possession of that that is desired.

Those, therefore, that pretend they have good desires to God, and yet live scandalously and negligently, and will take no pains with their souls, alas! it is the sluggard's desire, if they take not pains to remove all lets and hindrances. For a man may know the desire of a thing is good when he labours to set the hindrances out of the way, if he can. If the lets and hindrances be not impossible, he will remove it, if he can. Therefore, those that pretend this and that, 'There is a lion in the way,' Prov. xxvi. 13, when they might remove it, if they would, there is no true desire; for desire is with the removing of all possible hindrances of the thing desired.

Quest. But to resolve one question. How shall I know whether my desire be strong enough and ripe enough or no to give me comfort?

Ans. I answer, if the desire of grace *be above the desire of any earthly thing*, that a man may say with David, 'One thing have I desired,' I desire to be free from sin, as a greater blessing to my soul, than to be free from any calamity, Oh! it is a good sign. And surely a man can never have comfort of his desire till his desires be raised to that pitch. For none ever shall come to heaven that do not desire the things that tend to heaven, above all earthly things; nor none shall ever escape hell that do not think it worse and more terrible than all earthly miseries. God brings no fools to heaven that cannot discern the difference of things. Therefore, let us know, that our desires are to little purpose if we have some desire to be good, &c.; but we have a greater desire to be rich and great in the world, to have such and such place. If the desire of that be greater than to be gracious with God, if we hate poverty, and disgrace, and want, and this and that more than sin and hell, to which sin leads, it is a sign that our judgments are rotten and corrupt, and that our desire is no pure spiritual desire. For it is not answerable to the thing desired; there is no proportion. David saith here, 'One thing have I desired.' His desire carried him amain to 'one thing necessary,' above all other things whatsoever. Thus you see out of the text, what are the distinguishing notes of true desires from those that are false. I need name no more, if we consider what hath been spoken.

Now for our comfort, if we find these holy desires: Oh! let us take comfort in ourselves: for 'God will fulfil the desires of them that fear him,' Ps. xxxvii. 4. Holy desires, they are the birth of God's Spirit, and there is not one of them that shall be lost; for God regards those desires, 'My groanings are not hid from thee,' Ps. xxxviii. 9; my groanings in trouble, and desires of grace. There is not the least thing stirred up in the soul by the Spirit of God, but it prevails with God in some degree, answerable to the degree of worth in it. Therefore, if we have holy desires stirred up by God, God promotes those desires. God will regard his own work, and to 'him that hath shall be given,' Mat. xiii. 12. 'Lord, be merciful to thy servants, that desire to fear thy name,' saith Nehemiah, i. 11.* It is a plea that we may bring to God, 'Lord, I desire to please thee,' as it is, 'The desire of our souls is to thy name, O Lord,' Isa. xxvi. 8. We fail sometimes, that we cannot perform actions with that zeal and earnestness as we should; but the desire and bent of our soul is to thy name. A Christian may make it his plea to God,—truly our desires are towards thy name, and we have some suitable endeavours; and our desires are more that way than to anything in the world. It is a good plea, though we be much hindered and pulled back by our corruptions. So much for that, the act upon this object, 'One thing have I desired.'

Of whom doth he desire it? Of the Lord.

'One thing have I desired of the Lord.'

It was not a blind desire of the thing, *but a desire directed to the right object, to God*, to fulfil it. Holy desires are such as we are not ashamed of, but dare open them to God himself in prayer, and desires to God. A Christian, what he desires as a Christian, he prays for, and what he prays for he desires; he is a hypocrite else. If a man pray, as St Austin, in his confessions,† that God would free him from temptations, and yet is unwilling to have those loving baits from him, he prays, but he doth not desire. There are many that pray; they say in their prayers, 'Lead us not into temptation,' Mat. vi. 13, and yet they run into temptation; they feed their eyes, and ears, and senses with vain things. You know what they are well enough, their lives are nothing but a satisfying of their lusts, and yet they pray, 'Lead us not in temptation.' And there are many persons that desire that, that they dare not pray for, they desire to be so bad. But a Christian what he desires, he prays for. I desire in earnest to be in the house of the Lord, I desire it of the Lord, I put up my request to him; and what I pray to him for, I earnestly desire indeed. Learn this in a word, hence, that,

When we have holy desires stirred up by God, turn them to prayers.

A prayer is more than a desire. It is a desire put up to God. Let us turn our desires into prayers. That is the way to have them speed.

'One thing have I desired of the Lord.'

The reason why we should, in all our desires, make our desires known to God, is to keep our acquaintance continually with God. We have continual use of desires of grace, and desires of mortification of corruptions, and of freedom from this and that evil that is upon us. As many desires as we have, let them be so many prayers; turn our desires into prayers to God, and so maintain our acquaintance with God. And we shall never come from God

* Misprinted 'Ezechias' = Hezekiah.—G.

† Conf. A reminiscence rather than translation, of a recurring sentiment in the 'Confessions.'—G.

without a blessing and comfort. He never sends any out of his presence empty, that come with a gracious heart, that know what they desire. And it brings peace with it, when we make our desires known to God by our prayer. It brings 'peace that passeth understanding,' Philip. iv. Put case God doth not hear our request, that he doth not grant what we ask. 'The peace of God which passeth understanding, shall keep your hearts and minds.' So that when we put up our requests to God with thankfulness for what we have received, the soul will find peace. Therefore I say, let us turn all our desires into prayers, to maintain perpetual communion and acquaintance with God. Oh! it is a gainful and comfortable acquaintance.

It is an argument, and sign of a good conscience, for a man to go oft to God with his desires. It is a sign that he is not in a wicked course; for then he dares not appeal to the presence of God. Sore eyes cannot endure the light; and a galled conscience cannot endure God's presence. Therefore it is good to come oft into the presence of God. It shews that the heart doth not regard iniquity. 'If I regard iniquity in my heart, God will not hear my prayers.' Ps. lxvi. 18. It is an argument of a good conscience to come oft into the presence of God. But I will not enter into the common place of prayer.

We see next his earnestness, 'I have desired it of the Lord, *and I will seek after it*.'

I will follow God still. Here is his importunity in prayer, his fervency, his uncessancy and perseverance, as the apostle exhorts, he persevered in prayer, Eph. vi. 18. 'I will seek after it.' In prayer, and in the use of all good means, I will do what I can. So you see one qualification of prayer, *it must be with perseverance and importunity*. God loves importunate suitors. Though we cannot endure to be troubled with such persons, yet God loves importunate suitors, as we see in Luke xviii. 1–8, in the parable of the widow. God there vouchsafes to compare himself to an unrighteous judge, that 'cared neither for God nor man,' yet the importunity of the widow moved him to regard her. So the poor church of God, she is like a widow, with her hair hanging about her. 'This is Zion, whom none regardeth;' yet this widow, the poor church of God, and every particular member of it, they are importunate with the Judge of heaven and earth, with God; and will not he more regard the importunity of his children whom he loves, and delights in, that 'call upon him day and night'? Ps. cii. 2, will not he regard their petitions, when an unrighteous judge shall care for the importunity of a poor widow? Thus you see the excellent fruit of importunity in our blessed Saviour himself, and here in David, 'I will seek after it,' I will have no nay. Therefore we are exhorted in the Scriptures, not to keep silence, to give God no rest. 'You that are the Lord's remembrancers, keep not silence, give him no rest.' As Jacob with the angel, wrestle with him, leave him not till we have a blessing. As the woman of Canaan, let us follow him still, and take no nay. Oh this is a blessed violence, beloved, when we can set upon God, and will have no nay, but renew suit upon suit, and desire on desire, and never leave till our petitions be answered. Can the hypocrite pray alway? Would you know a comfortable note to distinguish an hypocrite from a true Christian? take it hence, will the hypocrite pray alway? Sometimes he will pray; but if God answer him not presently he gives over; but God's children pray always, if the ground be good, if they see the excellency of the thing, and the necessity, and withal join at the amiableness of it, that it may be gotten. When they see the excellency, and the necessity and usefulness of the thing, and the attainableness of it, and that it is attainable in the use of means, they need no more, they will never give over. That is the reason of that in the petitions, 'Thy kingdom come, thy will be done in earth as it is in heaven,' Mat. vi. 10. But can we do the will of God on earth as it is done in heaven? and doth God's glorious kingdom of heaven come while we are here on earth? No; it doth not, but the soul that is guided with the spirit of prayer, it rests not in this or that degree, but prays till it be in heaven, 'Thy kingdom come.' I have grace now, but I desire glory. 'Thy will be done.' I desire to do it as thy saints in heaven, though I cannot do it; but I desire, and I will not give God rest, but pray, till all my prayers be answered in heaven; and then I shall do the will of God as it is done in heaven indeed. Thus we ought eagerly, and constantly to persevere in our desires, till they be fully satisfied, or else we are but hypocrites.

Let us make conscience, I beseech you, of this duty more than we have done, and never give God over for grace; for strength against our corruptions; for his church; for the prosperity of the means of salvation; for those things that we have ground for; let us never give him over till we see he hath answered our desires. And when he hath answered our desires, let us go on still to desire more; for this life is a life of desires. The life of accomplishment is heaven. Then all our desires shall be accomplished, and all promises performed, and not before then. This is a life of desires, and we must be in a state of desires and prayers still till we be in heaven.

Quest. What is the reason that God doth not presently accomplish our desires?

Ans. There be diverse reasons. *First* of all *he loves to hear the desires of his servants*, he loves to be sued unto; because he knows it is for our good. It is music that best pleaseth God's ears to hear a soul come to him to request, especially spiritual things of him, which he delights most to give, which he knows is most useful and best for us. This pleaseth him so marvellously, that he will not presently grant it, but leads us along and along, that still he may hear more and more from us.

2. And then *to keep us in a perpetual humble subjection and dependence on him*, he grants not all at once, but leads us along, by yielding a little and a little, that so he may keep us in a humble dependence.

3. And then *to exercise all our graces;* for a spirit of prayer is a spirit of exercise of all grace. We cannot pray, but we must exercise faith, and love to God and his church; and a sanctified judgment to esteem what are the best things to be prayed for; and to exercise mortification. 'If I regard sin, God will not regard my prayers,' Ps. lxvi. 18. A spirit of prayer is a spirit that puts all into exercise; therefore God, to keep us in the exercise of all grace, answers not at the first.

4. And then he would have us *to set a high price upon what we desire and seek after.* If we had it at the first, we should not set so high an esteem and price of it.

5. And then, that *we might better use it when we have it.* Then we use things as we should do when we have gotten them with much ado; when we have won them from God with great importunity, then we keep and preserve them as we should. These and the like reasons may be given, and you may easily conceive them yourselves. Therefore let us not be offended with God's gracious dispensation if he answer not our desires presently, but pray still; and if we have the spirit of prayer continued to us, that

spirit of prayer is better than the thing we beg a great deal. Ofttimes God answers us in a better kind, when he gives us a spirit of prayer; for increasing a spirit of prayer in us, he increaseth all graces in us. What is it we would have? this or that particular grace. But when God gives us a spirit of prayer, he answers us better than in the thing we ask, for there is all grace. He will answer in one kind or other. But I will not be large in these points. You see then what was the affection of the holy prophet, to that one thing. 'One thing have I desired.' And he did not only desire it, but turned his desire into a prayer. He prayed to God; and he not only prayed once or twice, but he seeks it still, till God vouchsafed to grant it.

Obj. Well, but that that he prayed for, he was assured of, and therefore what need he pray for it? He had a promise, 'He shall prepare a table before mine enemies, my cup doth overflow,' Ps. xxiii. 5, 6. But what is that to this? These be things of this life. Oh! but, saith he, God will be good to me in the things of another life, and all the days of my life too. 'Doubtless the lovingkindness of the Lord shall follow me all the days of my life, and I shall dwell in the house of the Lord.' He takes in trust his dwelling in the house of God; and that the lovingkindness of God should follow him all the days of his life, he was assured of it, and yet here he seeks it and prays for it.

Ans. I note it, to shew that the assurance of the thing takes not away the earnestness of prayer. Daniel was assured (Dan. ix. 4, *seq.*) that God would deliver the Jews out of Babylon. He had read Jeremiah's prophecies, he knew the time was accomplished; yet we see what an earnest prayer he makes there. Christ knew that God heard him in all his desires, that he should have all good from God, being his only Son, yet he prayed whole nights sometimes, and a whole chapter, John xvii., is an excellent prayer of his. So that the assurance of the thing takes not away prayer to God; nay, it stablisheth it, for God so makes good his promises for the time to come, as that he makes them good this way, he will be sought to by prayer. And I may know hence that he will make good his promises for the time to come to me, if I have a spirit of prayer for them; if I pray for perseverance to the end, that God would vouchsafe me grace to live in the church, and to grow up as a cedar. God surely means to grant this, because he hath given me holy and gracious desires, which he would not have given me, but that he means to give the thing. For this is an encouragement to pray, when I know I shall not lose my labour. I pray, because I have a promise to have it, and I know the promise runs upon this. 'But I will be sought unto of the house of Judah for this,' Ezek. xxxvi. 37. For if we have it, and have not sought it by prayer, for the most part we cannot have a comfortable use of it, unless we have things as the fruit of our prayers. Though there be not a particular prayer for every particular thing we have of God, yet unless it be the fruit of the general prayer, that we put up daily, we cannot have comfort in it; if God give it by a general providence, as he fills 'the bellies of the wicked with good things,' Ps. xvii. 14. But if we will have things for our good in particular, we must receive them as the fruit of our prayers from God. You see here he seeks, and desires that that he had a promise to have, 'One thing have I desired of the Lord, and that will I seek.'

'That I may dwell in the house of the Lord.'

It was generally propounded before. 'One thing have I desired, and that will I seek after,' with all my might. And what is that? The specification of it is this:

'That I may dwell in the house of the Lord for ever.'

His desire is, not only to be in God's house, but to dwell in it, to abide; and not for a little while, but to dwell, and to dwell 'all the days of my life.'

The house of God then was the tabernacle, the sanctuary. The temple was not yet built. He desired to be near the tabernacle, to dwell in the sanctuary, the place of God's worship. In the tabernacle, which in those times was the house of God, there was the ark and the mercy-seat, types of many glorious things in the New Testament; the holy of holies, &c. And he desired to dwell in the tabernacle, to be near the ark, the house of God. Why? Because God manifested his presence there, more than in other places. The ark hath God's name in diverse places of Scripture; because God gave his answers in the ark, in the propitiatory, or mercy-seat. They came there to know his meaning, what he would have; he gave his answer there. He is said to dwell between the cherubins. There were two cherubins upon the mercy-seat, and God is said to dwell between the cherubins, Exod. xxxv. 22; that is, there he was present to give answers to the high priest, when he came to ask. David knew this well enough, that God had vouchsafed a more special presence in the tabernacle, than in all the places of the world, and therefore, saith he, 'I desire to dwell in the house of the Lord all the days of my life.'

'House,' we take for the persons that are in it, and persons that are ordered, or else it is a confusion, and not a house. It is a company of those that are voluntary. They come not by chance into our house, those that are members of our society; but there is an order. There is a governor in a house, and some that are under government, and there is a voluntary conjunction and combination. So the church is a voluntary company of people that is orderly, some to teach, and some to be instructed; and thereupon it is called a house.

And it is called the house of God, because he is present there, as a man delights to be present in his house. It is the place where God will be met withal. As a man will be found in his house, and there he will have suitors come to him, where he reveals his secrets. A man rests, he lies, and lodgeth in his house. Where is a man so familiar as in his house? And what other place hath he such care to protect and provide for as his house? And he lays up his treasures, and his jewels in his house. So God lays up all the treasures of grace and comfort in the visible church. In the church he is to be spoken with as a man is in his house. There he gives us sweet meetings; there are mutual spiritual kisses. 'Let him kiss me with the kisses of his mouth,' Cant. i. 2. A man's house is his castle, as we say, that he will protect and provide for. God will be sure to protect and provide for his church. Therefore he calls the church of God, that is, the tabernacle (that was the church at that time), the house of God. If we apply it to our times, that that answers the tabernacle now, is particular visible churches under particular pastors, where the means of salvation are set up. Particular visible churches now are God's tabernacle (*b*). The church of the Jews was a national church. There was but one church, but one place, and one tabernacle; but now God hath erected particular tabernacles. Every particular church and congregation under one pastor, their meeting is the church of God, a several church independent. Our national church, that is, the Church of England, because it is under a government civil, which is not dependent upon any other foreign prince, it is a particular church from other nations.

In that God calls the church his house, it shews the special respect that he hath to his church. God, though he be present everywhere, yet he is present in another manner in his church. As for instance, the soul is present in all the parts of the body; but the soul, as far as it understands, is only in the brain; as far as it is the fountain of life, it is in the heart. It hath offices and functions in all the parts; but in the special function, the rational function of it, as it discourseth and reasoneth, it is in the brain. So for our apprehension's sake, God is everywhere; but as he sanctifies and pours out his blessings, and opens, and manifests his secrets, so he is in his church especially. God is everywhere, but he is in another way in heaven than in other places. He is there gloriously. So in earth he is everywhere, but he is in another manner in the church (the heaven upon earth), than in other places. He is there as in his house to protect them, and provide for them as his family; and there he abides by his ordinances, and takes solace, and delight. God delights himself in his church and children that attend upon his ordinances. 'Where two or three are met together, I will be in the midst of them,' Mat. xviii. 20. When God's people meet together in the church, God is present among them. So you see in what respect the tabernacle then, and particular churches now, which answer it, are called the house of God.

Let us learn this for our duty, as well as consider our comfort, in that the church is the house of God, *let us carry ourselves as we should, decently, in the house of God.* Those that are to look to the house of God, they should purge out all unclean corners, that God may delight to dwell in his house still, that we give him no cause to depart out of his house. 'That I may *dwell in the house of the Lord,*' *&c.*

The act here is, that I 'may dwell in house of the Lord.' He did not desire to be in it for a day or a little time, to salute it, and so leave to it; but to 'dwell in the house of the Lord,' and to dwell there for ever. You see here that Christians have a constant love to the best things, a constant desire to dwell in the house of God. You may think it a strange desire of this holy man to dwell in the house of God; but think then of the continuedness of his desire, it was even to heaven itself; he desired 'to dwell in the house of God for ever.'

For what end?

1. I desire to dwell in the house of God, that I may dwell *in the love of God, and in the care of God to me in Christ for ever.* I do not desire to dwell in the house of God, as it is a meeting, and there an end; but I desire to dwell in the house of God, that I may dwell in the love and care of God, and not only dwell in his care and love to me, and his care and esteem of me; but,

2. That I may dwell *in my love to him,* that I may 'abide in his love,' and faith in him; that I may abide in Christ. It is not only for a man to abide in the house of God, and go no further than so, but to abide in the love of God; and in our love, and care, and faith, and dependence upon him, to make God our house, to live, and walk, and abide in, 'to dwell in God,' as St John saith, 1 John iv. 13; not only in the house of God, but God himself. And the upshot of all his desire, was to abide in heaven for ever. The desires of God's people never rest till they come to their proper centre, and there they are quiet. There is a rest of all desires in heaven; as fire, it never rests till it come to its element above, and heavy bodies rest not till they come to the centre below. So holy desires, that are the motion of the soul, they rest not till they come to the centre, the place of rest. So we must conceive of David's desire to dwell in the

house of the Lord, to dwell in the care, and love, and protection of God for ever, to dwell in love, and faith, and dependence, and in the whole stream of my soul for ever while I live; and then abide in heaven, where there are 'pleasures for evermore,' as he saith in another place, Ps. xvi. 11.

Therefore when we have any thoughts and desires, while we are here below, of grace and comfort, &c., let us extend, and stretch our desires to the last, to heaven itself, where all desires shall be accomplished, where all promises shall have their full performance. It is a poor thing only to desire to live in the church militant, and there is an end. No; here is the comfort of God's people, that in their prayers and desires, and their endeavours suitable to their prayers and desires, they all lead them to heaven; and there they have their full accomplishment. They have a constant desire to dwell in the house of God.

1. The reason is, because the soul in this world *is never fully satisfied with the good things of God's house till it be in heaven.* This life is a life of desires and longing; the church is but contracted to Christ in this world; the marriage shall be consummate in another world. Therefore the church desires still further and further communion with Christ in his ordinances here, and for ever in heaven.

2. And then *there are remainders of corruptions still, that dead and dull our performances, and put us on to actions that grieve our spirits and the Spirit of God;* to this end, that we may have a perpetual supply of the Spirit. We desire to dwell in the house of the Lord, because there is corruption in us still, till grace hath wrought it out fully.

3. *There is more and more to be had still in the house of God.* We never come to be full. The soul it is wondrous capable, being a spiritual essence. It is capable of more grace and comfort than we can have in this world. Therefore we pray, 'Thy will be done on earth as it is in heaven.' A Christian desires to dwell in the house of the Lord here, till he come to dwell in heaven, till he be translated from the temple here, to the temple in heaven. In Ephes. iv. 11, *seq.*, God hath ordained a ministry to the edification of the church, not only to constitute the church, as some think and say, that preaching must constitute a church, and after praying must edify it. Oh! let both go together. 'God gave gifts to men,' to preach, to edify the church more and more. So long as there is use of building more and more, so long there is need of the ministry. Therefore he desired to 'dwell in the house of the Lord.'

4. But the especial reason why he desired it, was *because he knew God was also present in his own house, and there is no good thing can be wanting where God is present.* It is the presence of God that makes all things sweet and comfortable. What makes heaven to be heaven, but because God is there? If the soul of a Christian were among angels, angelical comforts would not be desired, if God were not there. If there were all the delights in the world, it would not care for them, except God were present. Heaven were not heaven without the presence of God. The presence of God in a dungeon, in a lion's den, makes it a paradise, a place of pleasure; the presence of God makes all conditions comfortable. If there be not the presence of God, the greatest comfort in the world is nothing. What makes the church esteemed of by holy men? God is present there; and wheresoever God is present, in the communion of saints, especially in his ordinances, we should esteem them by this, that God is present. What makes hell to be hell? There is no presence of God there; no testi-

mony of his presence in hell; nothing but 'utter darkness.' What makes the life of man comfortable? There is some presence of God in everything. There is a presence of God in meat, in drink, in friends, that a man may say, Oh, here is a good God, here is some presence of God. There is not the vilest reprobate in the world, but he hath some testimony of God's presence. He tastes of God in somewhat or other; though he see not God in it (but like a beast is drowned in the use of the creature), yet God shews himself to him in some comfort. But when God shall remove all his presence from a man, that is hell itself. What is hell but where there is no presence of God? When there is no communion with the chief good, that the fountain of good is removed, a man is in darkness, and horror, that is hell, as we see in Dives, Luke xvi. 4, *seq.* It is the presence of God that makes things comfortable. That is heaven, to enjoy nearer and nearer communion with God.

Therefore let us labour to enjoy the presence of God in his ordinances, that we may have a heaven upon earth, that we may desire still more and more to delight in them, till we come to heaven, where all desires shall be accomplished, and there shall be no more desire. David knowing that God was present in his church, he saith, 'Oh that I might dwell in the house of God all the days of my life.'

See the constant disposition of God's children hence. It is a torment to carnal men to watch one hour with Christ. 'Could you not watch with me one hour?' Mat. xxvi. 40, saith he to his disciples. It is a torment to give God the hearing; to sanctify the Lord's day. Alas! it cannot stand with their carnal dispositions. But God's people long, and have a longing desire. 'One thing have I desired, that I may dwell in the house of the Lord.' Men that have not depth of grace, they are like comets. They blaze for a time; but when they are not fed with vapours from below, there is a dispartition not long after. But fixed stars are always in the firmament; they never vary. So a true Christian is as a fixed star, he is fixed in the firmament, in his desire. 'One thing have I desired, that I may dwell in the house of the Lord all the days of my life;' and God seconds his desire, and saith amen to it; as I shall have occasion to press after, in the use in the latter part of the verse. 'That I may dwell in the house of the Lord.'

'*To behold the beauty of the Lord.*'

This was another ground of the eager, constant, unsatisfied desire, 'To dwell in the house of the Lord,' that he might 'see the beauty of the Lord,' or the delight, the sweetness of God. Beauty is too particular a word to express the fulness of the Holy Ghost, the pleasantness or the delight of God. Take the word in a general sense, in your apprehensions. It may be the object of all senses, inward and outward. Delight is most transcendent for pleasantness; for indeed God in his ordinances, is not only beauty to the eye of the soul, but is ointment to the smell, and sweetness to the taste, and all in all to all the powers of the soul. God in Christ, therefore, he is delightful and sweet. 'That I may see the beauty of the Lord.'

In this clause here are discovered these two things, the object and the act.

There are these two points. *That God is beautiful.* And this is seen in his ordinances, and in his church, especially, 'to see the beauty' of God's house. And *it is the happiness of a Christian*, and he esteems it so by the Spirit of God, to see, and to be partaker of this beauty of God. Sight is put for the more full enjoying, one sense put for another, as indeed sight is taken for all the senses, inward and outward. It is no benefit to us, though there be beauty, if we have not eyes to see it, all is lost; therefore he desired to dwell in the house of the Lord, that he might 'see the beauty of the Lord.'

Now, concerning the beauty of God, I will not speak of it at large, or singly of the excellencies of God. The text aims especially at the beauty of God, *as discovered in his ordinances, in his church.* A man may speak gloriously, and largely of the beauty of God, of his excellency. That his wisdom is wondrous excellent, and beautiful, that is seen in the ordering of things, and his power is wonderful beautiful, and his mercy, &c. All this is true; but what is all to us, though God be never so beautiful in himself, if he be not beautiful to us in Christ, and in his church? Therefore we will come to that that the holy prophet here aims at, 'The beauty of the Lord;' that is, God is especially beautiful in his church, in his ordinances, and that was the ground of his desire. *Omne pulchrum est amabile*, every beautiful thing is an attractive of love. It is no wonder he desired to dwell in the house of the Lord, because there was the beauty of the Lord, and the most excellent beauty of all.

The beauty of the Lord is especially the amiable things of God, which is his mercy and love, that makes all other things beautiful that is in the church.

What makes his power sweet to his children? and his justice, in confounding their enemies, and giving rewards? and his wisdom sweet, in reconciling justice and mercy together wisely in Christ? All that makes this so lovely, is his grace and love, that set his wisdom on work, to devise a way to reconcile justice and mercy by Christ Emmanuel, God and man. So that that is most beautiful in God is grace; as you have it, Exod. xxxiv. 6. When Moses desired to see the glory of God, how doth God describe himself to Moses? 'Jehovah, Jehovah strong, gracious, merciful, longsuffering, full of kindness.' So that if we would see the glory of God, it appears most in grace, and mercy, and lovingkindness, and such sweet attributes. This makes all things in God amiable; for now we can think of his justice, and not fear. It is fully satisfied in Christ. We can think of his power with comfort. It serves for our good to subdue all our enemies. There is no atttibute, though it be terrible in itself, but it is sweet and amiable, because God looks graciously on us in his beloved.

Now this grace and love and mercy of God shines to us in the face of Christ as beloved, as I have shewed out of that text, 2 Cor. iii. 18, 'We all behold the glory of God as in a glass (*c*), that is, we behold the love of God in Jesus Christ, in the mirror of the gospel. We must take God, not as considered abstractively* and simply, but God in Christ; for other notions of God are terrible. God will not otherwise be seen by the eye of the soul, nor otherwise known, than in Christ. Now God in the Messiah is very delightful in his house. This beauteous grace of God shines in the face of Jesus Christ, 2 Cor. iv. 6. For God is so gracious and merciful, as that his justice must be fully satisfied, that is, only in Christ; that being satisfied, God in Christ looks on us with a gracious look. So that God is beautiful now in regard of his mercy and grace, as it is revealed in Jesus Christ, as he looks upon us in the face of his beloved Son. There are two objects of religious worship. God the Father, Son, and Holy Ghost, and Christ Mediator. The beauty of both is wondrous in the church,

* That is, 'abstractly.'—G.

wondrous towards the church of God, and it is most apparent in the ordinances of God in the church. Christ is 'altogether lovely,' Cant. v. 16. Christ in whom God is a Father, and reconciled to us; and now we can sweetly think of, 'He is altogether lovely, the chief of ten thousand.' The church sets him out there particularly, his head, his arms, his breasts, his eyes. 'His lips drop myrrh,' Cant. v. 13. She singles out every excellency of Christ, and dwells upon it in her meditation, and sums up all together, 'Christ is lovely.' What makes beauty but a mixture of diverse colours? as we say, white and red mix together sweetly. Now to see justice and mercy in Christ so sweetly mixed, what an excellent beauty it makes! To see the justice of God fully satisfied, that his mercy might run amain to us now. Here is a sea indeed if we should enter into it, to see the love of God, which is the most beautiful and amiable grace of all; the love of God in Christ, and the love of Christ towards us.

Christ was never more lovely to his church than when he was most deformed for his church; 'there was no form nor beauty in him,' Isa. liii. 2, when he hung upon the cross. Oh! there was a beauty to a guilty soul, to see his surety enduring the wrath of God, overcoming all his enemies, and nailing the law to his cross. And that should endear Christ to us above all things. He should be the dearer to us, the more vile and base he was made for us, and he should be most lovely in our eyes, when he was least lovely in his own, and when he was deformed, when our sins were upon him. We should consider those times especially. The world is most offended at that, that a Christian most joys in. 'God forbid that I should joy in anything but in the cross of Christ,' Gal. vi. 14, saith St Paul; so we should joy in and love that especially in Christ.

Now this love of God in Christ, and this love of Christ, is expressed to us in the Scriptures at large; it is published by the ministry, sealed by the sacrament. It is too large an argument for me to wade into. I need but only give you a touch and taste of it.

Now, that that makes the house of God so beautiful, then, *is the love of God, and the love of Christ shewed and manifested, and the presence of God, of Christ, and of the Holy Ghost in the church.* Take it for the persons; God the Father, as he hath revealed himself a Father in Christ, he is among the people of God in the church, and there is God the Son, and the Holy Ghost, dispensing graces and comfort there. It is the presence of the king that makes the court, and it is the presence of God in the church that makes it so glorious and so excellent as it is. 'Glorious things are spoken of thee, thou city of God,' Ps. lxxxvii. 3.

The church likewise is beautiful *in regard of the angels, that are alway attending in our assemblies*, and see how we carry ourselves. Here is not only the Father, Son, and Holy Ghost distributing grace and mercy, but likewise the blessed angels, as pure instruments are in our assemblies. Therefore in the curtains, in the hangings of the ark, there were pictures of cherubins, to shew that the angels attend about the church, especially the church gathered together; for God more respects the church gathered together than any several member. We are all temples severally, but especially the church is the temple when it is met together. Now by the cherubins in the curtains of the tabernacle, was set forth the angels' attendance upon the church. They are servants to do good to the church; and they are fellow-students with us. They study the mysteries of salvation, the beauty of God, the wonderful transcendent love, and grace, and mercy of God to his church, as it is in 1 Pet. i. 10, 11. 'The angels pry into the mysteries of salvation;' they are students with us of those blessed mysteries. Something is revealed to them, some grace and mercy to the church, that they knew not before experimentally.

And it is beautiful likewise in regard *of the church itself.* The people of God themselves are beautiful; for order is beautiful. Now it is an orderly thing to see many together to submit themselves to the ordinance of God. 'The glory of a king is in the multitude of subjects,' Prov. xiv. 28; and it is a glorious thing for God to have many subjects meekly meeting together to attend his pleasure. An army is a beautiful thing, because of the order, and of the well disposed ranks that are within it. In this regard the church is beautiful.

That which makes the house of God beautiful more especially, *is the means of salvation:* not only God's presence, but the means, solemn and public prayer, the word and sacraments, and likewise the government, that should be in purging the church,—all make the church of God beautiful and lovely. All the ordinances of God in the church of God have a delight in them to spiritual senses.

1. *As for the ordinance of the word,* it is wondrous delightful, 'sweeter than the honeycomb,' Ps. xix. 10, especially the ordinance unfolding the word, the word as it is preached, which is the 'opening of the box.' A box of sweet ointment, if it be not opened, it casts not a sweet savour all the house over; but when the box is opened, the savour comes over all the house. So the publishing of the word in the ordinance, is the opening of the box, the lifting up of the brazen serpent. If the serpent were [not] lift up for the wounded person, he could not behold it. Now [that] Christ is lift up in the ordinance, every wounded soul may look to Christ. The preaching of the word, is the lifting up of the banner of Christ's love. As it is in the Canticles, Christ's love as a banner draws all after him. When the beauty of Christ is unfolded, it draws the wounded, hungry soul unto him. The preaching of the word doth that that shews the sweet love of God in Jesus Christ. This makes the ordinance of the ministry so sweet. The ordinance of the ministry is that that distributes the portion to every child of God. The ministers of God are stewards, as it were, to distribute comfort and reproof to whom it belongs. Now where there is a convenient distributing of the portion to every one, that makes the ordinance of God so beautiful, when the waters of life are derived from the spring of the Scripture to every particular man's use. The word, in the application of it, is a sweet thing. For good things, the nearer they are brought home, the more delightful they are. This ordinance of preaching, it lays open the 'riches of Christ.' There may be a great deal of riches wrapped up in a treasury, but this opens the treasury, as St Paul saith, 'to lay open the unsearchable riches of Christ,' Eph. iii. 8. The ministry of the word is ordained to lay open the treasure to God's people, that they may know what riches they have by Christ; and the end of the ministry is to win the people's love to Christ. Therefore they come between the bride and bridegroom to procure the marriage; therefore they lay open that that procures the contract here, and the consummation in heaven; so to woo for Christ, and 'beseech them to be reconciled to God,' 2 Cor. v. 20. This is the end of the ministry. This makes the church of God so beautiful, that it hath this ordinance in it, to bring God, and Christ, and his people together: to contract them together. There be rich mines in the Scripture, but they must be digged up. The ministry serves to dig up those mines. God hath therefore set apart this calling of the ministry, to shew what belongs

to God's people. Thus you see in this respect, of the ordinance of the ministry, God is beautiful in his house.

2. Then likewise for the other ordinance, *the sacrament, it is a sweet and delightful thing.* There is a wondrous beauty in the sacrament; for therein we taste the love of God, and the love of Christ. That they would condescend so low, as to seal our faith with the sacrament, to help our souls by our bodies, by outward things; to help our souls by that that feeds our bodies, to teach us what feeds our souls, namely, the death of Christ, as satisfying divine justice,—the thinking and digesting of this is wondrous comfortable, as any food is to the body, and incomparably more sweet, considering our continual necessity to relish that spiritual food, and our daily sins and breaches, that enforce a daily necessity to relish Christ. That God should appoint such means, that he should in the sacrament feed us with his own body and blood. He thought he could not manifest his love enough, unless he had told us that he would give himself to us, and make over himself wholly to us: You shall have me, my body and blood; as in the sacrament we are as verily partakers of the body and blood of Christ, as we are of the bread and wine. Our souls have as much spiritual growth by Christ, and his benefits, as our bodies have by the outward elements. He feeds us with himself; he esteems and prizeth our souls that are bought with his blood, so that he thinks no food good enough but his own body and blood. What a gracious sweet love is this! He is both the inviter and the banquet, and all. He invites us to himself.

3. There is a loveliness likewise *in all other ordinances that belong to the church; as in the good order and government of the church, in purging the church of offenders;* the discipline that is in the church, which is as the snuffers in the sanctuary to purge the lights; so that there should be a casting out of persons that are openly scandalous. The lights should be purged, the temple should be cleansed, scandals should be removed, that God's house might be the more beautiful. They are blemishes of God's house, open swearers and blasphemers. Those that live in scandalous sins, they are spots in the assembly, they are leaven, and this leaven should be purged out; and where there is the vigour of this, there is a great beauty of the church. Where these things are looked to as they should be, they are the bonds, and nerves, and sinews that knit and tie a church together. It makes a church wondrous lovely, the neglect of which makes the church as a garden overgrown. So you see how, in respect of the ordinances of the word, and of the sacrament, and this government that should be, that the house of God is a beautiful place.

4. Then again, it is a comfortable, a sweet and delightful thing, *the praises of God.* It is a marvellous sweet thing, when all as one man hear together, pray together, sing together hymns, and spiritual songs, and praise God together, and receive the sacrament together, all as one man,—what a comely thing is this to a spiritual eye! Every Christian hath a beauty severed in himself; but when all meet together, this is more excellent. As we say of the *via lactea,* or milky way in the heavens (we call it so), it is nothing but a deal of light from a company of little stars, that makes a glorious lustre. So if there be a beauty in every poor Christian, what a beauty is there when all meet together! A beauty, nay, strength too; for the prayer and the praise of such, they offer a holy violence to God, they can obtain anything at his hands. We see burning glasses, when there is a confluence, and meeting of divers beams in one point, it strengthens the heat, and inflames a thing; so when there are many sweet desires meet

together, many strong desires of spiritual things, they bind God. There is not only beauty but strength in the prayers of the church. They are in Christ's own esteem comeliness. He loves to see his church, especially when they are together. 'Let me see thy face, and hear thy voice, thou that hidest thyself in the clefts of the rock,' Cant. ii. 14. He marvellously desires to see his children, and to hear them speak, especially when they present themselves before him. Harmony is a sweet and pleasant thing. The comparing of the state of the church in former times with the present, is a harmonious thing. David, he lived under the Old Testament, and yet he saw under that the New, so we should see the Old in the New, compare them together, to see shadows in substances, types in truths. So that there is nothing in the church, but it gives special delight.

5. God's beauty likewise appears, his gracious, amiable, sweet beauty, in his house, his church in regard *of the evidences of his love that he bears to his church, in protecting it, and providing for it.* 'They shall not need a wall,' saith he in Zechariah, 'I will be a wall of fire,' Zech. ii. 5. God hath a special care of his congregation. 'God dwells in the congregation of the righteous,' Ps. lxxxii. 1. He hath his dwelling, his special residence there, where his name is called on. This will appear more if we see all the sweet privileges and comforts that are in the house of God. God is not only beautiful in himself, but in regard of the privileges that the church hath from him. For all our beauty and excellency is borrowed. The church shines in the beams and beauty of Christ. Now these privileges that the church hath by Christ, to name a few. (1.) *We see in the golden chain of salvation,* what sweet, amiable love is in all those links; as what a wondrous sweet love of God is it. (2.) *To call men out of the wilderness of the world,* out of the kingdom of Satan, to be his children! A marvellous love to single us out of the rest of mankind to be Christians, and being Christians, to be professors of the truth, and being so, to be true professors of the truth. What a wondrous love of God was it to call us, and thereby to have the eternal purpose of God opened to us. As when we are drawn to God by his Spirit and by the ministry, then the good pleasure of God, that was hid from eternity, is discovered to the soul. Here is the amiable love of God.

(3.) And then in *the pardon, and forgiveness of sins, and justification after*—what a wondrous grace is that forgiveness of sins, and adoption to be the sons and heirs of God, 'fellow-heirs with Jesus Christ,' Rom. viii. 17, and thereupon to have angels our attendants. What beauty have we in justification, to be clothed with the righteousness of Christ; that perfect righteousness, that can answer the justice of God much more Satan's cavils and the troubles of our own consciences. That that satisfieth the justice of God, being the righteousness of God-man, it will satisfy conscience, and Satan's temptations. It is a garment without spot. Satan can pick no hole in that glorious garment, the righteousness of Christ. If we have the wardrobe of Christ, we shall be beautiful in that we have from Christ, we shall shine in his beams.

(4.) So go to *sanctification.* How amiable is God in the privilege of sanctification, to set his image upon us, to make us new creatures, to be like his Son, that before were like the devils, full of malice and base affections. Now for God by his Spirit to frame a new temple for his Spirit to dwell in, to set his stamp upon us, what a wondrous beauty is this! The church of God is the house where God frameth new creatures. There he sets a stamp upon his creatures.

The graces that belong to the church of God are wondrous delight. 'Wisdom makes a man's face to shine,' Eccles. viii. 1; and there is no wisdom out of the church. All is but darkness and folly. So of all other graces whatsoever. Graces are the anointing of the Spirit, the oil of the Spirit. They make sweet and delightful, delightful to God, and to the church, and to one another. They are anointed with the oil of gladness and of grace. It ran first upon Christ's head, upon Aaron's head, but then upon the skirts, the meanest Christian.

And so the beginning of glory here; for all is not kept for the life to come. For God distils some drops of glory beforehand. We see the beauty of God here, marvellously even in this world, in regard of the beginning of glory. For upon justification, and the beginning of holiness wrought in our nature by the Spirit, we have inward peace of conscience, and joy and comfort in all discomforts whatsoever. We have not only the oil of grace, but the oil of comfort. Oh! the comfort of the children of God, that are members of the church, that are so in the church, that they are of the church too, that are of the church visible, so as they are of the church invisible. Oh! the comfort that belongs to them, all the comfort in God's book. So you see the wondrous sweet prerogatives and privileges we have in all the passages of salvation in the house of God, and in God reconciled in Jesus Christ.

Nay, God is so lovely to those that are his, his church and people, he is so good to Israel, that he makes everything good to them in the issue. 'All things work for the best to them that love God,' Rom. viii. 28, in the issue. He makes a covenant between everything. So that all the endeavours of Satan and his instruments, all their plottings, shall turn for the good of the church. When they think to do most hurt, they do most good; so sweet, and good, and gracious is God.

Indeed, 'glorious things are spoken,' Ps. lxxxvii. 3, of the people of God. Take the church for a visible congregation, a mixed congregation; glorious things are spoken of that. It is the house of God. Take it as visible, 'the vessels of honour and dishonour,' 2 Tim. ii. 20, and the field, the 'tares and the wheat,' Mat. xiii. 1, *seq.*, it is God's field. Though we take the church as visible, it hath a glorious name for the good that is in it, specially for the wheat. But take the church of God for the company of his children that are gathered by the means dwelling in the visible church, enjoying the visible means: so they are the house and temple of Christ, the 'temple of the Holy Ghost, the body of Christ, the spouse of Christ.' They are God's delight, they are spiritual kings and priests, &c. The most glorious things that can be, all other excellencies in the world, are but titular things, mere shadows of things. There is some little reality, but it is nothing in comparison, it is scarce worth the name of reality, but Solomon calls them 'vanity of vanities.' In comparison of the excellencies of the church all is nothing. I might be large in these particulars. It is enough to give you the generals of the delights and excellencies of God's house, 'the beauty of the Lord.' We see amiableness of God in Christ, in his ordinances, the privileges that we have in the ordinances, graces, and comforts. Indeed the church of God, beloved, is a paradise. Since we were cast out of the first paradise, this second paradise is the church of God, and the third is heaven itself. This paradise, this church, it is the seminary* of young plants, that must be transplanted hence to heaven in due time. In paradise there was the tree of life, Gen. iii. 22; in the church, there is the tree of life,

* That is, 'seed-plot.'—G.

Christ. In paradise there was waters, streams, the rivers of paradise, Gen. ii. 10; so there 'is a river that makes glad the city of God,' Ps. xlvi. 4, streams of grace and comfort that run through the church of God.

In the church we are as plants by the rivers of waters, that bring forth fruit in due season, as it is in Ps. i. 3, *seq*. Speaking of blessed men that live in the church, 'Blessed is the man that meditates in the word day and night,' that attends upon the ordinances. He is 'planted as a tree by the waters' side,' his leaf is alway green. What food to that food that is ministered to us in the word, and sacraments—Christ himself to feed us to life eternal! And what raiment to the raiment of justification; for Christ to clothe these poor souls of ours, poor, naked, beggarly souls! What riches to the riches of God's graces and comforts! What strength to that that is in the church, to overcome our own corruptions and lusts! What beauty to the image of God shining and stamped on his children! What company so sweet, as those that we meet with in the earth, in good exercises, and that we shall live ever with in heaven! What company to God the Father, Son, and Holy Ghost, and the angels, that we enjoy in the church! What discourse so sweet, as that of God, hearing him speak in his word, and us speaking to him by prayer, so that it is a resemblance of heaven upon earth, the church of God!

Therefore we should be in love with the beauty of God's temple and sanctuary. And the rather because all things now in this age of the church wherein we live are in a more glorious manner than in David's time. David when he saw the beauty of God's sanctuary, it was but in a shadow; and when he looked upon the mercy-seat, then he did think of Christ, the true propitiatory, the true mercy-seat. When he looked on the high priest, he thought on Christ the true high priest. When he thought of Canaan, it put him in mind of heaven, whereof Canaan was a type. When he saw the sacrifices, he thought of the true sacrifice for our sins, Christ. When he thought of the oblations and incense, he thought of the sacrifice of thankfulness. When he thought of the passover, he thought of Christ the true passover, whose blood is sprinkled on our souls, that the destroying angel hath nothing to do with us. He saw all in shadows; we see them naked. So our condition is more glorious in this latter age of the church, than it was in David's time. Therefore our desires should be more stirred up; for instead of the shadow we have the substance. Then the Spirit was but dropped, but the Father hath poured out the Spirit since Christ's time. Then the pale of the church was straitened, now it is enlarged. Then there was but one church, the national church of the Jews. Then the service of God was wondrous burdensome, and chargeable, but it is not so now. So that there be many differences. All things are more lightsome and clear now than they were then. Therefore having many things to commend the frequenting of the congregation more than David had in his time, we should much more make this one thing our desire 'to dwell in the house of the Lord, all the days of our life, to *behold the beauty of the Lord*.'

Quest. If this be so, that there is such a beauty in the house of God, then what shall we think of those that see no such beauty at all, that see no such delight and contentment in the house of God?

Ans. I answer, it is a discovery to them, if they would think of it, *that they have no spiritual senses at all;* as St Austin saith of men that complain, that they do not taste and relish these things. Surely, saith he, thou wantest a spiritual palate to taste these things. What do swine care for sweet marjoram or roses? They care more for a dunghill or a puddle. What do your base filthy swine in men's shape care for these things? They care more for pleasures and such things, that they may spend their lives as beasts. Now when we speak of the delights, and dainties, and excellencies of God's house, we speak to those that we wish, and we hope have spiritual senses answerable to these things. Every creature delights in its proper element. These things are the element of a Christian. Beetles delight in dirt, and swine in mire, the fish in the sea, man hath his element here, and spiritual things are the element of a Christian, so far as he is a Christian, and that is his *ubi*, the place that he delights in. I speak to such. They can make it good in some measure, that 'one day in the house of God is better than a thousand elsewhere,' Ps. lxxxiv. 10, that one hour in the unfolding the sweet mysteries of salvation, it is worth twenty-four hours in other employment; and they are so taken with the sweetness, that they are content that God should take them out of the world, in the unfolding of these sweet things. When they hear the promises of salvation opened, though by a poor weak man, yet when it is in the ministry, it so ravisheth their hearts, that they are content to go to heaven at the same time; it so convinceth them of the excellency of religion. I speak to such of the beauty of God.

Now David here, he desires to behold God's beauty, to see or consider this excellency of God in his church, for to true delight these things must concur. There must be something sweet in the thing itself. There must be a power in the soul to apprehend it. There must be an affection in the soul to that good thing. If the affection be flat, though there be never so beautiful and sweet things, and a power to apprehend them, if there be not affection, they are nothing; and then, upon the affection, there must be complacency and contentment in the thing when we have it. All these things are in delight from that that is beautiful and pleasant, David desired to see. He knew there was a beauty in the presence of God in his ordinances and gifts and graces; but he desired to see and to contemplate these things, that the faculties and powers of his soul might be answerable to the things, that as they were excellent, so he might have a power in his soul answerable. And then he had affections to carry that power of his soul to the things, 'One thing have I desired.' And then there was a complacency and delight in the things, upon enjoining,* answerable, as we see how he expressed his delight when he danced before the ark. We see what a psalm he made when he did but purpose 'to build the temple,' Ps. cxxxii. He had a wondrous joy. So answerable to our delights is our joy and complacency in the thing when we have it.

Now that he might have the sweeter complacency, he desired to see the beauty and the things in God's house. Of all senses, sight hath this property above the rest (as it is more spiritual, more refined, and more capable; a man may see many things at once, it is a quick sense; so), it hath this privilege, it stirs affections more than any sense, more than hearing, that is a more dull sense. Things stir affections more that are seen, than by that we hear. He desired therefore to see the beauty of God's house, that he might be enamoured. Of sight comes love.

David had spiritual eyes, and he desired to feed his spiritual eye-sight with the best object that could be, for therein is the happiness of man. Wherein stands a man's happiness? When there is a concurrence of the most excellent object, with the most excellent power and faculty of the

* Qu. 'enjoying?'—Ed.

soul, with delight and content in it. Now he desired to see the beauty of God in his house, that his soul might be ravished in the excellency of the object, and that the highest powers of his soul, his understanding, will, and affections might be fully satisfied, that he might have full contentment. Since the fall, all our happiness is out of ourselves, it is derived from God in Christ; and it is taken out of the promises of God in the word. For God will be seen in Christ, and God and Christ will be seen in the glass of the ordinances till we come to heaven, and there we shall see 'face to face,' 1 Cor. xiii. 12. So that now all our happiness is fetched by looking on the love of God, out of ourselves, fetched out of the ordinances. David desired to see the beauty of God. God's love is diffusive. It spreads and communicates itself to his church in the ordinances. Thus he, knowing, desired more and more to communicate of this diffusive, abundant, transcendent love of God.

Quest. But how shall we come to have these desires that David had, to see the beauty of God?

Ans. In a word—we must have *spiritual senses.* The spiritual life of a Christian is furnished with spiritual senses. He hath a spiritual eye and a spiritual taste to relish spiritual things, and a spiritual ear to judge of holy things, and a spiritual feeling. As every life, so this excellent life hath senses and motion suitable to it. Now we should labour to have this spiritual life quickened in us, that we may have a quick sight of heavenly things; and a taste of heavenly things, that we may smell the ointment of Christ. 'For the sweetness of thy ointments the virgins run after thee,' Cant. i. 3. The soul hath senses answerable to the body, let us desire God *to cleanse all our senses, and to reveal himself in Christ more and more in the ordinances.*

This St Paul calleth the 'Spirit of revelation,' Eph. i. 17. Let us pray to God that in his ordinances he would discover that amiable love of his in Christ, to shine on us in the face of his Son, in his ordinances; for the Spirit must help us to see the beauty of God. When we have spiritual senses, except the Spirit give us a spiritual light to see, we cannot see. Therefore let us desire that God would give us spiritual senses, to the spiritual light.

When God made the world, light was the first creature. Why? That all the excellency of the creature might be discerned by light. If God had made never so many excellent creatures, if the light had not discovered them, where had been his glory? So there are many excellent, beautiful things in Christ, wonderful grace and comfort; if these be discovered in the word and we have no senses, and no light, if there be not light in the understanding, God shall want his glory, and we the comfort.

It is light that makes things that are beautiful to be beautiful to us. A blind man cannot judge of colours, nor a deaf man of sounds and harmony. A man that hath lost his taste cannot judge of sweetness, so that there must be senses, and the Spirit of God must reveal these things unto us.

And likewise let us labour more and more to *see our own deformity, and then we shall see Christ's beauty, the more we desire to know our own vileness.* Indeed the Spirit of God carries these parallel one with another. He discovers by the same light our own deformity and necessity, and the beauty and excellency of God in Jesus Christ. The one will set an edge on the other, and he that will come to see the height and breadth, and depth of God's love in Christ, must see the height, and breadth, and depth of his own corruption, and our misery by it out of Christ. And they are good thoughts for us, every day to think of these two objects, the misery of the condition of man out of Christ, and the excellency now that we have in Jesus Christ; the amiableness of Christ towards us, and our amiable condition in him. He delights in us, as we delight in him. The consideration of this, and of the loathsome, terrible, fearful condition out of him, will keep us closer to Christ, and make us value the ordinances more, that we may grow up in faith and knowledge of Christ more and more, till we come to a fulness in Christ.

And present to the eye of our souls, God in Christ *in the relations he hath taken upon him*, to be a Father in Christ. Let us make that benefit of this beauty that is presented to us in the gospel, especially when it is unfolded in the ministry, because Satan hath a special policy to present God and Christ otherwise to us. Especially in the time of temptation, he presents God as a judge, sitting upon his throne, and God as a 'consuming fire,' Heb. xii. 29. It is true he is so out of Christ, but in him he hath taken the relation of a father, and looketh on us sweetly in the relation of sons. Christ must be considered in the sweet relation of a Saviour, and the Holy Ghost in the sweet relation of a comforter; and the word is all written for our comfort, if we believe, and the sacraments feed us to eternal life. Let us represent these things beautifully to the soul, and this will strengthen faith, and cherish affection, that Satan shall not rob us of our comfort, nor say to us, what do you, ye unclean persons, loathsome creatures, what do you come to the sacrament, and come to the holy things of God? It is true, if we mean to be so still, but as soon as ever the desire of our souls is to come to God, and that there is a divorce between us and our sins, and we desire to leave them, let us have all the sweet conceits of God that may be. We see in Revelations, Laodicea was lukewarm, and that is a hateful temper. 'Behold,' saith he, 'I stand and knock, if any man open to me, I will come, and sup with them,' Rev. iii. 20. A strange love, to come to them that were in such a lukewarm estate. He was ready to cast them out. His stomach was loaden with them. 'I stand at the door and knock,' yet if any of you lukewarm professors will open, I will come and sup with him, and refresh him with the refreshings of God. So in Cant. v., when the church slighted Christ and offended him, yet he woos his church. 'My locks are wet with the dew of the night,' Cant. v. 2. Oh! marvellous patience, that notwithstanding her lukewarmness and neglect, yet Christ gives not over! Let us not entertain hard conceits of God in Christ, but labour to present them sweetly to our meditations.

This is the wisdom of a Christian, to have sights of faith, that is, to present several things that faith may work on to strengthen itself, as for faith to have a sight of God in Christ, a gracious Father; and to have a spiritual sight of Christ sending ambassadors wooing and beseeching us to be reconciled; and a sight of the joys of heaven, that we shall have full possession of after. Let us think of them, and present them to our souls; and present to our souls by meditation, the excellency, and royalty, and prerogative of God's children, that they are the most excellent people in the world. These sights that faith helps itself by, are an excellent means to make us in love with the beauty of God's house. But to answer two or three objections briefly before I proceed to more particulars.

Obj. Some will object, what need we now in these glorious times of the church stand upon the ordinances so much? Indeed in darker times there was more need, &c.

Ans. I will not be large, but to answer in a word. *The more God dis-*

covers himself, and his excellent things here, the more we should express our thankfulness in labouring to grow in knowledge; for there is such a breadth in them, that we can never have enough of them, and there is such a daily exigence of spiritual things, of comforts and graces, that are all conveyed in the use of means, that a Christian cannot be without them; he can no more be without the use of the ordinances than he can without his daily food.

Obj. Oh! but what need we be so eager and earnest after these things as some are? Is not now and then enough?

Ans. Are we better than David? See how earnest he was, Ps. lxxxiv. and Ps. xlii. 'As the hart panteth after the rivers of water, so my soul thirsteth after thee, O God,' Ps. xlii. 1, lxxiv. 2. For there is a presence of God in his ordinances that other men are not sensible of. There is a presence to their spirits that they feel that they marvellously love, and are affected with. And if they want the presence of God, as David here, they are wondrously discouraged. As good Nehemiah, when he heard it went not well with the church, he grew sad; and David, we see how he takes it here when he was banished, as it were, from the house and ordinances of God. But I will not stand long upon these objections.

Obj. Some think they may as well read at home good books and sermons, and not come to the ordinances.

Ans. But David *loved the ordinances; he loved the place.* Might not he think of what he heard before? might not he have help of the prophets? Oh! but there is a blessing in the very meeting, 'Where two or three are met together, I will be in the midst of them,' Mat. xviii. 20. And Christ walks in the midst 'of the golden candlesticks,' Rev. i. 12. There is a more powerful, gracious presence in the very assemblies of God's people. Put case thou mayest do much good in private, with contempt of the public ordinance; it is a cursed study. Like manna that did stink when it was gathered out of season. When it was gathered when it should not, it putrefied. There is a curse upon that study, and upon that knowledge that we get when we should attend upon the public means. For it is not knowledge that will bring to heaven, for the devil hath that, but it is knowledge sanctified, seizing upon the affections. Now, what is it that maketh us good? The Spirit working with the ordinance; and will the Spirit work when we neglect the ordinance? It is but a pretence. They spend their time otherwise, it is to be feared not so well. But put the case they should, there never comes good of it. It may enrich them in knowledge to grow more devilish; but more holy they cannot be, for holiness comes from the Spirit, and the Spirit will work by his own ordinances. So much for that, and of all other objections in regard of the beauty of God.

I will not raise any objections, but only answer those that commonly popish spirits trouble some withal. I will answer, I say, some of them briefly.

Obj. They trouble us about our churches. Indeed, if your particular churches were churches of God, if you could make that good, then you might delight in them, but you are heretics and schismatics; your churches are not good churches. Thus they trouble good Christians that are of the simpler sort; especially with this, where was your church a hundred years ago? before Luther's time? (*d*) Your church is an upstart, and your congregations are nothing but a meeting of a company of heretics together.*

* The commonplaces of the popish controversy. Consult Faber's 'Difficulties of Romanism.'—G.

Ans. Beloved, that *that makes a church to be a catholic church, to be a branch of the catholic church,* which we believe in the creed, *it is the catholic faith.* The faith and truth that is the seed of the church, it is begotten of the word of God. Wheresoever the word, the catholic truth of God, is, there is the church, a branch of the catholic church. Now our faith that we believe hath consanguinity with the first churches; for what do we believe, but it is fetched out of the Testament, and from the primitive church? And indeed in their own confession, if they would be modest, that might be extorted from them, that we are more catholic, and our doctrine is more catholic than theirs. Why? For that that agrees with the ancient truth, 'and faith once given,' as St Jude saith, ver. 3, it runs through all ages; and that wherein we agree with them is more agreeable and catholic than that they hold severed from us. It is more catholic in regard of all times, before Christ, and in Christ's time, and in the apostles' times; and that that the papists themselves hold with us, is more catholic than that they hold severed. Now wherein they differ from us, and we account them heretics, they differ from the Scriptures, and from the church six hundred years after Christ; and many of them are of late standing. Therefore in those tenets of ours we agree with the papists, and with the primitive church. What do we hold but they hold? But they add traditions that are pernicious. We hold the Scriptures. They hold that, and traditions too. We hold two sacraments. They add five more. We hold Christ to be the Mediator. They make saints mediators too. Whatsoever we hold they hold, but they add their own patcheries* to them. Therefore our doctrine is more catholic, because we have the evidence of Scripture for all ours, and we have them to justify ours; and wherein they differ from us, they have neither Scripture nor antiquity; but they are only a company, a mass of things of their own. But I will not be much in this point. And then, say they, where was your church before Luther's time, and two hundred years ago? Where was it? Where their church was. Our church was amongst them, in the midst of them. Witness their fire and inquisition, and persecution! They found out our church well enough.

But to make it a little clearer. The church of God, take it in general for good and bad in it, and for the means of salvation that they had in some measure, it may be called a kind of visible church, though very corruptly; and so considered, our church, those that possessed our religion, was the best of that church in the declining times of it. As in a lump of gold that is not yet refined to bullion there is gold, and a great deal of earth: take it in the whole, we say it is gold; but when it is refined to bullion, we say it is gold severed. Now our church in the midst of popery was as gold in the midst of earth unrefined; that is, there were† many Romish Churches, and ours was in the midst of them, the temple in the midst of the court; that is, the true church in the visible church. There were a great company that held the tenets of the gospel, especially at the hours of death, that denied popery. But then there were some that were refined as bullion after, as the Waldenses,‡ that were a severed company of people, besides other holy men and women that grew up by hearing somewhat of Christ in their sermons, and somewhat in the sacrament. They left out that that was bad, and took that that was good. Besides the lump of gold, there was some refined gold, when popery was in its perfection; and those they termed Waldenses, and the like. There was alway a company that held the

* That is, 'patchwork,' = additions.—G. † Misprinted 'was.'—G.

‡ Consult Stanley Faber's 'Waldenses and Albigenses'—able and trustworthy.—G.

truth against them. I am sorry to mention these things, in a point tending more to edification. Our churches therefore are refined churches, that is, gold singled out of the dross of popery. They are a corrupt, and our church a refined, a visible congregation.

Now to cut off these objections, to come nearer to ourselves, to make good our particular congregations, and to shew that of necessity we ought to frequent them, and to take heed of all objections that the devil and the flesh may make to bring us out of love with our particular congregations, know therefore these three or four rules in a word.

First, that there hath been *a church from the beginning af the world, where God hath been worshipped.* Christ is a King, and he must have a kingdom. To believe a catholic church is an article of our faith, and there cannot be an act without an object. I have faith, I believe a visible church, therefore there must be a church. So that there hath been a church from the beginning of the world. It is an article of our faith.*

Secondly, the mark whereby this church is known *is especially the truth of God.* That is the seed of the church, the truth of God discovered by his word and ordinance. To which is annexed the sacraments and ecclesiastical government; but the former most necessary. And these three were typified in the ark; for there was the law signifying the word, and the pot of manna signifying the sacrament, and the rod to shew the discipline. Those three were, as it were, types of the three marks of the church. But especially the word. For that is the seed of the new birth. Wheresoever the word hath been published, and there hath been an order of teachers, and people submitting themselves, there is a church, though perhaps there might be some weakness in other regards. A man is a man though he want the ornaments of a man; and a city without walls is a city. Put case there might be some weakness in some things, yet as long as the vitals of the church remain it is a church.

The third thing that I observe, to clear this point, to hasten to things of more edification, is this, *abuse takes not away the use.* A neglectful use or abuse takes not away the true use of things. Put case the Scripture be abused many ways, that the sacraments have many additions, that these things are not so pure; yet it takes not away the just use; for then we take away the cause of things. Then the conclusion of all is this, that of necessity, notwithstanding somewhat may be found fault with in all visible churches, some errors there may be; yet we ought to cleave to a visible church, because it hath been alway, and we ought to know it by these marks. If the word of God be taught there, then of necessity we must cleave to it. 'God added to the church such as should be saved,' Acts ii. 47, to the visible church. Those that are saved must be saved in submission to the visible church. But these things I list not† to be large in. This may give satisfaction.

Use 1. If this be so, that we ought to submit to the ordinance of God in the visible church, to come into the ark as it were (the visible church is called the ark), or else we must be drowned and perish, *what shall we think then of those that are cast out of the church by excommunication* (but that is for their good)? But their case is very ill, because they are cut off from the house and beauty of God. Their case is miserable. But it is worse with those that depart out of themselves, as apostates, &c. Some are cast out, some are apostates and go out. They fall away from the church of God to the Romish strumpet,

* Consult Pearson, and also John Smith, *in loc.*—G.

† That is, 'choose not.'—G.

to Babylon; being dazzled with the pomp of that church, not seeing the spiritual beauty of the ordinances of God with us. What think we of those that ought to join with visible congregations, that excommunicate themselves willingly, such as schismatics, and such profane separatists, that when they may, will not; partly because they will not have their consciences awaked, and partly because they will give liberty to the flesh to other things at that time. Some are cast out, and some go out, some excommunicate themselves. They are of the disposition of the devils, that will not be 'tormented before their time,' Mat. viii. 29. They think they shall hear somewhat that will awake their conscience, and they are very unwilling to have conscience awaked, but they will have all their torment at once. All these are in a woeful condition. If the gracious presence of God be in the church above all other places in the world (as we see David desired 'to dwell in the house of God, that he might see the beauty of God') if there be a beauty in the divine ordinances, how miserable are those that are cast out, or that go out! that rent themselves from the church, or willingly excommunicate themselves like wild creatures? They are worse than Cain. He grieved when he was to depart the presence of God. He fell into a desperate temper. They are worse than he, that when they have the liberty of the ordinances of God, they go on in a wild licentious course, and neglect all means that God hath sanctified to bring them to heaven.

Use 2. But to come nearer, to make an use of trial, *how shall we know whether we have benefit by, and whether we be truly in love with, the beauty of God's house or no, because many come hither?* As in Noah's ark there were beasts that were clean and unclean, so there are many that come to the visible congregations; they are in the church (as excrements are in the body), but they are not of it.

To know therefore whether we come to purpose, and heartily love the beauty of God in his ordinances, and comforts and graces, as David did here or no, we may know it easily, *for sight*, as I said before, *it works affection.* We may know by our affection whether we see the excellency of God or no in his ordinances. There is no sense that stirs up affection answerable to sight; the affection of love especially.

How shall we know that we love the ordinances of God?

That is an affection that of all others is least to be concealed. What we love we will boldly profess; we will joy and delight in it if we have it. You see how David joyed in the ordinance of God, how he danced before the ark. There was no joy that he had comparable. He preferred it before all other joy that he had whatsoever. It was a transcendent joy. And what we love and delight in we meditate much on. 'Oh how I love thy law! my meditation is on it continually,' Ps. cxix. 97. Our minds will run on it. Therefore we are exhorted to think of the word of God, to have it before our eyes, to have it written before us in our courses, that we may meditate upon it at home and abroad. Moses he gave those helps. Where there is love there is meditation. Those that love the good things of God, their minds will be often on them.

Again, there will be *zeal for the holy things of God.* A man will not endure them to be disgraced, but he will have a good word to speak in the defence of God's ordinances, of holy things and religion. Those that suffer religion to be betrayed in the company of base carnal people, they have never seen the beauty of God's house; [they] that have not a word to say. Those that have seen God's beauty, and felt the comfort of the delights of

God's house, they are able to justify it against all opposers whatsoever, that there is good to be taken and done there, by their own experience, by the comfort they have felt. They will be able to tell others what 'the Lord hath done for their souls,' Ps. lxvi. 16, and in their souls, what graces they have been strengthened in, what comfort they have felt. They can discover this, and can justify all the ordinances of God from their own experience. Do not we see daily under the ordinance of God by weak men, the blind see, the spiritually deaf hear, the spiritually dumb be able to speak, to pray to God; the dead, those that are dead in sin, they receive life. Do not all these justify the excellency of God's ordinance, which gives spiritual life, and spiritual senses? Those therefore that have been dead in former time in sinful courses, and have found the power of God's Spirit with his ordinances, they are able to justify it. Those that are not able to justify these things by some experience, they never felt any good by them. By these and the like evidences, we may try the truth of our affection, whether we have seen this beauty or no to purpose.

Quest. If we find that we have little comfort and strength by the word of God, that we have not seen the beauty of it, what shall we do, what course shall we take?

Ans. 1. *Wait still.* Wait still at the pool for the angel's stirring, John v. 4; for God at length will discover his power by his Spirit; he will discover his goodness, if not at the first, yet at length. Therefore let us use all sanctified means. And know this for a rule, that God's Spirit is an excellent worker. He will only work by his own instruments.

2. And *come to the ordinances with a spirit of faith*, because they are God's ordinances. God will discover himself in some excellency or other; he will discover some comfort and grace, somewhat that is useful to our souls to build us up to eternal life. Let us come with a particular faith that he will do so. Faith must answer God's promise. God hath promised, 'where two or three are met together in his name, he will be in the midst of them.' He hath made a promise to bless all his ordinances. Therefore let our particular faith answer God's ordinances. Lord, I go to thy house to hear thy word, to receive thy sacrament in thy fear, in reverence of thy majesty, and in a spirit of faith, I expect thee to make good thy own ordinance. This brings a marvellous efficacy with it. If we go with a particular faith, know that God will be as good as his word. This course we must take to see the beauty of the Lord.

3. And then, as I said before, *often let our thoughts be upon these spiritual excellencies.* Let us balance and weigh things in our thoughts. Love comes from judgment, love comes from an esteem of things, of the goodness of things, and that comes from a right judgment. Let us therefore labour to have a right judgment of things to be as they are. Solomon was the wisest man, next to him that was God-man, that ever was, and he knew what spiritual things were, and what all other things in the world were, and what verdict doth he give? This is the whole man, 'to fear God and keep his commandments, Eccl. xii. 13. And how doth he commend wisdom in Prov. viii. 1, *seq.* All precious things are nothing in comparison of the wisdom of God's word. But what saith he of other things? He that had run through all things by experience, and thought to extract the quintessence of all that the creature could give, he saith they were but 'vanity and vexation of spirit,' Eccles. i. 2; trust my experience. Therefore let us be able to lay in the balance the good that we get or may get by the blessed ordinances of God, with other things whatsoever. Oh the beauty and excel-

lency of spiritual things, it is above all other beauty whatsoever! Alas! what is outward beauty? it is but a lump of well-coloured earth.* What is gold, and all the lustre of it? It is but earth refined. And what are all honours and goodly delights that way? It is but a puff of smoke, it is nothing; in one word, it is vanity, and experience proves this every day. Oh! but the 'word of the Lord endureth for ever,' 1 Pet. i. 25, that is, the comforts, and the privileges that we have by the word of God, they endure for ever; and then more especially the comfort of them when outward comforts fail most, even upon our deathbed. When conscience is awakened then, and hath presented to it the former life, and the guilt of many sins, what will comfort a man then? his goodly apparel, or his goodly feature, or his great place and honour? (Perhaps these will increase his grief as they have been instruments of sin.) Oh no; this will do him good. Such a comfort I heard in such a sermon; such good things I heard read, and such good things come to my mind; such experience I have of God's Spirit working at such and such a time; these will testify that God's Spirit went with his ordinance to fasten somewhat on my soul, and they will comfort when nothing else will.

Let us oft compare all other things with the beauty of God, and his ordinances, as if all were nothing to them. Thus holy Moses, he saw a beauty and a glory in the despised people of God that made brick; he saw they were the people that God set his delight on, and that the church of God was there. When he saw that, he despised all the glory of Pharaoh's court, and accounted the worst thing in religion, 'the reproach and shame,' better than all the pleasures of sin, Heb. xi. 23. Beloved, the bitterest things in the ordinance of God are better than any worldly thing. What is the bitterest thing in the ordinance of God? Reproofs! They are as precious balm. If the ordinance of God meet with our particular sins, and tell us, and discover to us what an enemy it is, that it will be the bane of our souls if we live in it, and it send us away to look to ourselves, this will be as a precious balm; our souls will come to be saved by it. And if for religion we suffer reproach and shame, it will be as a crown, as holy Moses accounted the reproach of Christ better than the treasures of Egypt, Heb. xi. 26. If the worst and bitterest things in God's ordinance be so sweet, what are the best things of all? The comforts of religion. What is the peace of conscience and joy in the Holy Ghost, and eternal glory in heaven? What are the excellencies of religion, when the shame and disgrace are to be preferred before all other things whatsoever?

So blessed St Paul, he weighed things after this fashion. He was an excellent man, and had excellent privileges to glory in. Oh but, saith he, I account all 'dung and dross' in comparison of the excellent knowledge of Christ that he had, Phil. iii. 8. Our blessed Saviour, that was the most able of all to judge, he would have all 'sold for the pearl,' that is, for the field where the pearl is (*e*), to buy that, to get the ordinances of God. He accounts him a wise man that will sell all for that. And when Martha and Mary entertained him, Mary sat at his feet to hear him expound the truth of God; 'she chose the better part,' Luke x. 42, saith Christ. If we will believe him 'in whom all the treasures of wisdom are,' in his judgment, 'Mary chose the better part;' 'One thing is necessary,' saith he. He justified David's choice, 'One thing have I desired;' and saith Christ, 'One thing is necessary.' All things in comparison of that are not necessary; they may well enough be spared. Thus we see how we may come to love God

* See note *a*, vol. I., p. 31.—G.

in his ordinances, and to see the 'beauty of holiness,' the beauty of God in his sanctuary.

4. And because there are two things needful to see a beauty, *an object revealed, and a sight,* let us desire God *to reveal himself in his ordinances to us more and more, and desire him to give us spiritual eyes more and more to see him.* Sometimes he hides himself in his ordinances, that we cannot see the beauty of things. Let us therefore desire him to reveal himself, to take away that veil that is between us and holy things, and between us and grace, and comfort, that he would take away that spiritual veil, and reveal himself to us, and shine on us in Christ, that he would manifest his love to us, and give us spiritual eyes to see him.

Prayer is an excellent means before we come; and when we are there, and oft in attending on the ordinances, let us lift up our hearts to God to reveal his truths to us.

There are many veils between us and holy things. Let us desire God to take them all away—of error, and ignorance, and unbelief—and to shine so clearly to us by his Spirit, that we may see him more clearly. And objects have a special influence when they are clearly discerned. Now a man may more clearly see and feel God at peace with him by the Spirit, and clearly see and feel the comfort of forgiveness of sins, and of any promise that is unfolded; and it hath a marvellous influence upon the affections, to comfort and to breed peace and joy. And that is one sign that we profit by the ordinance of God, when it is so with us; when we find an influence from the things, upon our daily prayers, to work peace and comfort, and spiritual strength against temptations and corruptions. All in the ordinance is by the power of the Spirit. Therefore we are to pray to God that he would join his Holy Spirit, that he would reveal his secrets to us, and with revelation work an influence into our souls, that there may be a distilling of grace and comfort through the ordinances to our souls. Prayer must accompany the ordinances; because the ordinance of itself is an empty thing unless the Spirit accompany it.

To stir us up a little to this, more and more to see the beauty of God in his ordinances, to see the glory of God, as the Scripture speaks—indeed God is not only delightful and beautiful, but glorious in his ordinances; and the ark is called the 'glory of God,' Exod. xl. 34; and the knowledge of God in Christ it is a glorious knowledge, and the gospel is called a 'glorious gospel,' 1 Tim. i. 11—*this will only* make us truly glorious.* These things, they put a glory upon our souls. St Paul calls it 'the glorious grace,' Eph. i. 6. What a glorious thing is it when, by the ordinance of God, a weak man shall have power against the strong devil, against all the 'gates of hell,' Mat. xvi. 18; when a poor creature, 'flesh and blood,' by some virtue distilled through the ordinance by the Spirit of God, shall have such a strong faith in the promise of forgiveness of sins; such a faith in the promise that all such† turn to his good; that God is reconciled to him in Christ; that all the gates of hell shall not prevail over a weak soul. And what a glorious grace is it when, by the use and attendance upon the ordinance of God, a poor soul shall have strength over these corruptions and sins that others are slaves to, and cannot get the victory over, that when they see the spiritual beauty in God's ordinances, they grow out of taste with all other things that others are besotted with, that are of more excellent natural parts than they, what a glory of grace is this! Therefore let us with all fear and reverence attend upon the ordinances of

* That is, 'this only.'—G. † Qu. 'shall?'—Ed.

God, that God may be glorious in us by his Spirit, and strengthen us against Satan and our beloved corruptions.

2. *And let us know what our souls were made for.* What are our souls more for than to dwell in the meditation of the beauty of God? What are our souls made for, but for excellent things? and what is excellent but in God's ordinances? Is the soul made to study debates and jars between man and man in our particular callings? Is the soul made to get a little wealth, that we shall leave perhaps to an unthrifty generation after? Are our souls, that are the most excellent things under heaven (the world is not worth a soul; they are the price of the blood of the Son of God; in his judgment the world is not worth a soul), are they for these things? No. They are for union and communion with God in his ordinances, to grow in nearer communion with God by his Spirit, to have more knowledge and affection, more love and joy and delight in the best things daily. Our souls are for these things that will make us gracious here, and glorious for ever after in heaven.

It is a great deordination,* when we study and care only for earthly things, and have slight conceits of those things that are incomparably the best things, in the judgment of God and of Christ himself, and of Solomon, and of all good men.

3. And the rather let us be stirred up to affect these things, *lest God depart from us.* The glory of God departed out [of] the temple before the destruction of Jerusalem, Ezek. xi. 23; so the glory of God, that is, a visible sign of his glory, it departs from a church; the beauty and excellency of God departs when we esteem them not. And if anything in the world make God to leave a church, as he left the Jews, and as he may leave any particular church (he will alway have a catholic church in the world; but he is not tied to England or France, or any country), if anything move him to this, it is because there is not a prizing of the heavenly things we have; of the blessed liberty we have to meet God in his ordinances; that we have not a care to improve these ordinances, to get grace and comfort against the evil day. For however we esteem these things, God sets a high price on them; and if we do not, God will deprive us of them, or of the power and beauty of them. Therefore as we desire God to continue his ordinances, and his blessing, and power in his ordinances, let us improve them the best way to get grace and comfort. He hath made a great progress in religion, that hath gotten a high esteem and a sanctified judgment of the best things. Though perhaps he find himself dull and dead, and complain of it, yet when God shines so far that he is able to approve, and to justify the best things, that they touch his affections so much, that the bent of his soul is that way, and he cannot be long without them, and he finds much comfort by them, though it be joined with much corruption, these things argue a good temper and frame of soul.

And of all other dispositions of soul, let us preserve that spiritual disposition of soul, whereby our soul is fitted to the things themselves. The things of God's Spirit are holy and excellent, when there is such a taste and relish wrought in the soul suitable to the things. There is a happy combination then. We may know there is a powerful work of the things upon the soul, for all grace wrought by the things of God, we may know it when the soul hath a suitable relish of them, and longs after them, and delights in them, and improves them to the best; and such a soul never wants evidence of a good Christian. Ask a Christian what is the best evidence of

* That is, 'disordering,' = placing out of order.—G.

salvation, and that you belong to God? 'My sheep hear my voice,' John x. 4, saith Christ, 'and as children new born, desire the sincere milk of the word, that ye may grow thereby,' 1 Pet. ii. 2. A man may know he is a true child of the church if he desire the sincere milk of the word, to grow better and more holy and comfortable. If he delight in the voice of God in the ministry, and so be affected to the truth and ordinances of God, it is a comfortable character of a good Christian. There are more hidden evidences sometimes, but this for an ordinary evidence is a good one and comfortable. David marvellously comforted himself with this. 'Oh! how do I love thy law,' Ps. cxix. 97. Oh! that we could say as he did, 'Oh how do I love thy law, and love thy truth,' that we could wonder at our own affections, that we could delight in this beauty of God, as David saith here, 'One thing have I desired of the Lord, and that will I seek after, that I may dwell in the house of the Lord all the days of my life, to behold the beauty of the Lord,' &c.

FINIS.

NOTES.

(*a*) P. 217.—'Babylon was so taken,' &c. Consult Herodotus, I. 177, *seq.*, with the annotations and illustrations of Rawlinson, *in loc.;* also Xenophon, *Cyrop.* vii. 5. For very interesting explorations confirmatory of the fact cf. Rich, 'Babylon and Persepolis;' Ainsworth, 'Researches in Assyria;' and Chesney, 'Exped. for Survey of Euphrates.' It need hardly be stated that it was Cyrus who took Babylon in the manner referred to by Sibbes.

(*b*) P. 226.—'Particular visible churches are now God's tabernacle.' In a tract by Philip Nye, entitled 'The Lawfulness of the Oath of Supremacy, and Power of the King in Ecclesiastical Affairs' (4to, 1683, p. 41), the above and other context is quoted. On the margin is placed 'Gospel Anointings,' which misled us into inquiring after such a book (of which none had ever heard) by Sibbes. Another tractate, by Bartlet, his 'Model of the Primitive Congregational Way' (4to, 1647), explains the mistake of Nye. The following was evidently his authority:—'I shall produce only one more that was famous for his *Gospell-anointings* [in italics, the usual mode of expressing quotations], and little thought by most men to have been of this judgment [in the margin here, "see Dr Sibbs"]. And yet you shall find in a little treatise of his (printed before these troubles brake forth in England), called *A Breathing after God*, that he speaks fully to this purpose, his subject leading him to discover himself herein, being, as I suppose, a little before his death.' Bartlet then quotes the passages to which the present note refers. The manner in which Nye was led into his mistake is quite apparent on an examination of Bartlet's tractate. Sibbes's name in the margin is exactly opposite the words 'his *Gospell Anointings*,' while the title of the book actually quoted does not apppear till several lines lower on the page.

(*c*) P. 230.—'As I have shewed out of that text, 2 Cor. iii. 18,' &c. The sermons here referred to comprise the second half of Sibbes's 'Excellency of the Gospel above the Law.' 18mo, 1639.

(*d*) P. 240.—'Where was your church before Luther?' &c. There have been many polemical answers to this taunting question. For *thoroughness* none perhaps excels the old Scottish tractate by Andrew Logie, 'Answer to the question, Where was your religion before Luther?' Aberdeen, 1634, 4to.

(*e*) P. 245.—'The field where the pearl is.' Either Sibbes uses pearl as = treasure, or here, and elsewhere, he makes a slip. It is 'treasure,' not a 'pearl,' that is hidden in the 'field.'—Mat. xiii. 44. G.

THE RETURNING BACKSLIDER.

THE RETURNING BACKSLIDER.

NOTE.

'The Returning Backslider' passed through three editions, viz. :—

(*a*) 1st, 1639, 4to, } Portrait *ætat* 58 prefixed, without the verses. (See prefatory
(*b*) 2d, 1641, 4to, } note to 'Bowels Opened.')

(*c*) 3d, 1650, 4to.

It will be remembered that it is on a copy of this work that Isaak Walton's memorable couplet is found (Memoir of Sibbes, vol. i., page xx). Our text follows *c*. Its title-page is given below.* The 'Saint's Privilege' therein mentioned is an admirable little treatise on John xvi. 8–10, which will be included, with other of Sibbes's minor writings, in a subsequent volume. It will be remembered that Bishop Reynolds also has a series of expository sermons on 14th chapter of Hosea, entitled 'Israel's Prayer in Time of Trouble, with God's gracious Answer,' 4to, 1638.

G.

* Title-page :—

THE
RETVRNING
BACKSLIDER:
OR,
A COMMENTARIE
upon the whole XIV. Chapter
of the Prophecy of the Prophet HOSEA.
Wherein is shewed the large extent of GODS free Mercy,
even unto the most miserable forlorne and wretched sinners
that may be, upon their Humiliation and Repentance.
Also the Saints Priviledge, *&c.*
Preached by that Learned and Iudicious Divine, Dr. SIBS, late Preacher to the Honourable Society of *Grayes Inne*, and Master of
Katherine-Hall in CAMBRIDGE.
Published by his own Permission before his Death.
The third Edition.
JEREM. 3. 12, 13.
Goe and Proclaime these words towards the North, and say, Return thou Backsliding Israel, saith the LORD ; *and I will not cause mine Anger to fall upon you : for I am merciful, saith the* LORD, *and I will not keep anger for ever. Onely acknowledge thine iniqnity*, &c.
LONDON.
Printed by *T. Mab* and *A. Coles* for JOHN SAYWELL dwelling in *Little Brittain* without *Aldersgate* at the signe
of the *Grey-hound.* M D C L.

TO THE READER.

GOOD READER! this treatise begs the favour of those concerning whom especially it is said Christ came for, poor trembling sinners, 'the blind,' 'the prisoners of hope,'* and such who by the assiduity, iteration, and multitude of Satan's discouragements and temptations, sit, as it were, in darkness, and in the valley of death, to whom every sour thing is sweet. Because these, most of all, relish and stand in need of mercy; for when the least flame of that unsupportable wrath breaks forth in show, which is poured out like fire, and 'kindled by the breath of the Lord of Hosts, like a river of brimstone,'† which can make 'the mountains quake, the hills melt,'‡ 'burn up the earth, and all that is therein,'§ the poor soul for the time thinking on nothing but 'blackness and darkness of tempest,'‖ whilst bypast sins, without sight of the Mediator, stares them in the face, with millions of unconceivable horrors and astonishments: then to see light in darkness, mercy in wrath, the sunshine of righteousness, a gracious God appeased by a Mediator, with some sight and sense of its interest therein, this must needs overjoy the troubled soul, which is the main subject of this book. How gracious God is to encourage miserable sinners to return! What encouragements and helps he gives them, what effects his gracious working hath in them, and how sweetly they close with him again! Wherefore, though this mess comes not unto thee set forth in a 'lordly dish,'¶ not having passed, since the preaching thereof, under the exquisite hand of the most worthy author, yet despise it not. For many times, though things of greater judgment affect the understanding most, yet things of lesser conciseness work more upon the affections in a plain flowing way, which happiness, with all other felicities, he wisheth thee, who is ever

Thine in the best bonds,

J. H.**

* Isa. lxi. 1. † Isa. xxx. 33. ‡ Amos ix. 5, 13. § 2 Peter iii. 12. ‖ Heb. xii. 18. ¶ Judges v. 25.

** This J. H. was probably the John Hill who writes an 'Epistle Dedicatory' to Elton's work on the 'Ten Commandments,' entitled, 'God's Holy Mind Tovching Matters Morall,' &c. (4to, 1625). He therein addresses the parishioners of 'St Marie Magdalen's in Barmondsey,' (*i.e.*, Bermondsey), who were formerly under the charge of Elton, as his; but there appears to be little known of him beyond this. He is not the 'John Hill' noticed in the Nonconformist's Memorial, ii. 54.—G.

THE RETURNING BACKSLIDER.

SERMON I.

O Israel, return unto the Lord thy God; for thou hast fallen by thine iniquity. Take with you words, and turn to the Lord; say unto him, Take away all iniquity, &c.—Hos. XIV. 1, 2.

The whole frame of godliness is a mystery, Col. i. 26. The apostle called it 'a great mystery,' comprehending all under these particulars: 'God was manifested in the flesh, justified in the Spirit, seen of angels, preached unto the Gentiles, believed on in the world, received up into glory,' 1 Tim. iii. 16. Amongst which mysteries, this may well be the 'mystery of mysteries.' 'God was manifest in the flesh,' which includeth also another mystery, the graciousness and abundant tender mercy of God towards miserable, wretched, and sinful creatures; even in the height of their rebellion, appointing such a remedy to heal them. Which is the subject of this chapter, and last part of this prophecy: which, as it thunders out terrible judgments against hard-hearted impenitent sinners (such as were the most part of Israel), so is it mingled full of many and sweet consolations to the faithful, in those times, scattered amongst the wicked troop of idolaters then living.

The time when Hosea prophesied was under the reign of Uzziah, Jotham, Ahaz, and Hezekiah, kings of Judah; and in the days of Jeroboam, the son of Joash, king of Israel, in whose days idolatry was first universally set up, and countenanced by regal power. This Jeroboam, 'who caused Israel to sin,' 1 Kings xv. 34, that he might strengthen himself, made use of religion, and profanely mixed it with his civil affairs in carnal policy, and so leavened the whole lump of Israel with idolatry, that shortly after, the whole ten tribes, for their sin, and their injustice, cruelty, lust, security, and such other sins as accompanied and sprang from this brutish idolatry, were led away captive by the king of Assyria, and the Lord's righteous judgment made manifest upon them.

There being, notwithstanding, amongst these some faithful ones, though thinly scattered, who mourned for, and by their good examples, reproved these abominable courses: there being also a seed of the elect unconverted; and of the converted, some that were carried down too far in the strength of this stream of wickedness: in this chapter, therefore, being the conclusion of this prophecy, there are many excellent and heavenly encouragements; also many earnest incitements to repentance and returning to the Lord, with free and gracious promises, not only of pardon and acceptance, but of great rewards in things spiritual and temporal to such as should thus return.

'O Israel, return unto the Lord thy God, for thou hast fallen by thine iniquity.'

'Take with you words, and turn to the Lord; say unto him, Take away all iniquity,' &c.

In this chapter we have,

1. *An exhortation to repentance, with the motives enforcing the same:* 'O Israel, return unto the Lord thy God,' ver. 1.

2. *The form:* 'Take with you words, and say unto the Lord,' &c., ver. 2.

3. *A restipulation, what they should do: and return back again, having their prayers granted.* 1. *Thanksgiving:* 'So will we render the calves of our lips.' 2. *Sound reformation of their beloved sin:* 'Ashur shall not save us,' &c.; *with the reason thereof:* 'For in thee the fatherless findeth mercy,' ver. 3.

4. *God's answer to their petitions.* 1. *In what he will do for them:* 'Heal their backsliding, love them freely, and be as the dew unto Israel;' *with the reason thereof:* 'For mine anger is turned away from him,' ver. 4. 2. *What he will work in them, a proportionable speedy growth in height, breadth, and depth:* 'He shall grow as the lily, and cast forth his roots as Lebanon,' &c.; which mercy is further amplified *by a blessing poured out also upon their families:* 'They that dwell under his shadow shall return,' ver. 5–7.

5. There is set down a further effect of this repentance and gracious work in them, *a sound and strong well-rooted indignation against their former darling sins;* 'Ephraim shall say, What have I any more to do with idols?' backed with a *strong consolation:* 'I have heard him and observed him,' &c., ver. 8.

6. *The diverse event and issue* of this God's so gracious dealing, is shewed both in the godly and wicked. 1. The wise and prudent understand and know that the ways of the Lord are right, and shall walk in them; but, 2. 'The transgressors shall fall therein,' ver. 9.

'O Israel, return unto the Lord thy God, for thou hast fallen by thine iniquity.'

Every word hath his weight, and, in a manner, is an argument to enforce this returning.

'O Israel!' Israel, we know, 1, is a word *of covenant.* Jacob was Israel, a prince and wrestler with God, as they also ought to be. Therefore he enforceth, You also ought to return, because you are Israel. And, 2, It was also an *encouragement* for them to return, because God so acknowledgeth them to be Israel, and will be gracious unto them, though they were such hideous sinners.

'Return,' saith he, 'unto the Lord Jehovah,' who is the chief good. For when a man returneth to the creature, which is a particular, changeable good, unsatisfying [to] the soul, he is restless still until he come unto Jehovah, who is the all-sufficient, universal good, who fills and fills the soul abundantly. Therefore, 'return' to him who is the fountain of all good, and giveth a being unto all things, and not to 'broken cisterns,' Jer. ii. 13. He is Jehovah, like himself, and 'changeth not.' And then he is *thy* God. Therefore, return to him who is thy God in covenant, who will make good his gracious covenant unto thee, and did choose thee to be 'his people before all the nations of the world.' This, therefore, is also an encouragement to return. And then,

'Thou hast fallen by thine iniquity.' Therefore, because thou art fallen by thy iniquities, and thine own inventions have brought these miseries upon thee, and none but God can help thee out of these miseries, seeing he only can, and is willing to forgive thy sins and revive thee, therefore,

'O Israel, return unto the Lord thy God, for thou hast fallen by thine iniquity.'

Now, in that he forewarneth them of the fearful judgments to come, which were to fall upon them unless they were prevented by true repentance, hence in general it is to be observed,

That *God comes not as a sudden storm upon his people, but gives them warning before he smites them.*

This is verified in Scripture. When the cry of Sodom and Gomorrah was great, the Lord said, 'Because the cry of Sodom and Gomorrah is great, and because their sin is very grievous, I will go down now and see whether they have done altogether according to the cry of it which is come unto me; and if not, I will know,' Gen. xviii. 20, 21. And wherefore was the ark of Noah so long in building, but to give warning to that sinful age, which were nothing bettered by it. The like we have of Pharaoh and all the Egyptians, who had so many warnings and miracles shewed before their destruction came, Exod. xi. 1, *seq.* Thus God dealt in Amos: 'Therefore, thus will I do unto thee; and because I will do this unto thee, prepare to meet thy God, O Israel,' Amos iv. 12. 'O Jerusalem, Jerusalem,' saith Christ, 'thou that killest the prophets, and stonest them which are sent unto thee, how often would I have gathered thy children together, even as a hen gathereth the chickens under her wings, and ye would not,' Mat. xxiii. 37. What need we stand upon proofs? Are not all the threatenings of Scripture as so many warning-pieces of approaching judgments?

1. The reason hereof is, *his own nature.* 'He is a God of long-suffering,' Exod. xxxiv. 6. He made the world in six days, yet hath continued it six thousand years, notwithstanding the many sins and provocations thereof, 'his mercies being over all his works,' Ps. cxlv. 9.

2. And partly *from a special regard to his own dear children*, these terrible threatenings not being killing and wounding, but, like Jonathan's warning arrows, who, though he shot, yet meant no other harm to David save to forewarn him of harm, 1 Sam. xx. 20.

Use. Let us, therefore, observe God's gracious and mild dealing in so much mercy, who giveth us so many warnings by his servants, and lesser judgments which we have had amongst us; let us take notice and believe, so as belief may stir up fear, and fear may provoke care, and care stir up endeavours to provide us an ark, even a hiding-place betimes, before winter and worse times come upon us.

Hence issueth another general point, that

The best provision for preventing of destruction is spiritual means.

God himself is a spirit, and spiritual means reach unto him who is the first mover of the great wheel of all the affairs of this world. It is preposterous to begin at the second cause. We trouble ourselves in vain there, when we neglect the first. We should therefore begin the work in heaven, and first of all take up that quarrel which is between God and our souls. If this be done first, we need not fear the carriage of second things, all which God, out of his good providence and gracious care, will frame to work for good to his, Rom. viii. 28, for whose sakes, rather than help should fail, he will create new helps, Isa. iv. 5. Wherefore, in all things it is best to begin with God.

The third general point is this, that

Of all spiritual means, the best is to return to the Lord.

In this returning, 1. *There must be a stop.* Those who have run on in evil ways must first stop their lewd courses. For naturally from our birth and childhood we are posting on to hell; and yet such is our madness (unless the Spirit of God shew us ourselves) to be angry with those who stand in our way.

To make this stop, then (which is always before returning).

(1.) There must be *examination and consideration whither our ways tend.* There be stopping considerations, which both waken a man and likewise put rubs in his way; if a man, upon examination, find his ways displeasing unto God, disagreeing from the rule, and consider what will be the end and issue of them (nothing but death and damnation), and withal consider of the day of judgment, the hour of death, the all-seeing eye of God, and the like. So the consideration of a man's own ways, and of God's ways towards him, partly when God meets him with goodness;—I have hitherto been a vile wretch, and God hath been good to me, and spared me;—and partly when God stops a wicked man's ways with thorns, meets him with crosses and afflictions. These will work upon an ingenious* spirit, to make him have better thoughts and deeper considerations of true happiness, and the way unto it. God puts into the heart of a man, whom he intends to save, serious and sad considerations, what estate he is in, whither his course leads; and withal he lets them feel some displeasure of his, towards them, in those ways, by his ways towards them; whereupon they make a stop.

(2.) There must be *humiliation, with displeasure against ourselves,* judging and taking revenge of ourselves, working and reflecting on our hearts, taking shame to ourselves for our ways and courses; and withal, there must concur some hope of mercy. For so long as there is hue and cry, as we say, after a traitor, he returns not, but flies still and hastes away; but offer a pardon, and he returneth. So, unless there be hope of pardon, to draw a man again to God, as the prodigal was moved to return by hope of mercy and favour from his father, Luke xv. 18, we will not, we dare not else return.

(3.) There must be a *resolution to overcome impediments.* For when a man thinks or resolves to turn to God, Satan will stir up all his instruments, and labour to kill Christ in his infancy, and to quench good while it is in the purpose only. The dragon stood watching for the birth of the child, Rev. xii. 4; so doth Satan observe the birth of every good resolution and purpose, so far as he can know them, to destroy them.

Use. Let it be thought of by us in all our distresses, and in whatsoever other evidences of God's anger, whether this means have been taken up by us. It will be thus known.

[1.] Turning is a change of the posture of the body; so is this *of the frame of the mind.* By this we know a man is in a state of turning. The look of his intentions, purposes, the whole bent of his soul is set another way, even upon God; and his word is the star of direction towards which he bends all his thoughts.

[2.] *His present actions, also, be contrary to his former.* There is not only a change of the disposition of his soul, 'Behold all things are become new;' not some things, but all; not only 'new,' but with a 'behold' new, 2 Cor.

* That is, 'ingenuous.'—G.

v. 17. This change undoubtedly sheweth that there is a true conversion and unfeigned.

[3.] *By our association.* He that turns to God, turns presently to the company of God's people. Together with the change of his nature and course of life, there is a change of company; that is, of such as we make choice of for amity and friendship, Isa. xi. 10, *seq.* Other company, by reason of our callings, and occasionally, may be frequented.

[4.] It is a sign that one is not only turned, but hath gone backwards from sin a great way, *when the things of heaven only are great things in his eyes.* For, as the further a man goeth from a place, the lesser the things behind him seem, so the greater the things before, he being nearer to them. The more sublime and high thoughts a man hath of the ways of God, and the meaner thoughts of the world and worldly matters he esteemed so highly of in the days of his vanity, the more he is turned unto God.

This returning is further enforced, saying, 'Return unto the Lord thy God.'

It is very emphatical and significant in the original (*a*). Return, *usque ad Jehovam*, even to Jehovah, as though he should say, Do not only begin to return towards Jehovah, but so return as you never cease coming till you come to Jehovah.

'Even unto the Lord thy God.'

It is not enough to make a stop, and forbear the practising of our former sins; but we must come home, even unto the Lord our God, to be pardoned and healed of him.

The prodigal son had been never a whit the better to see his sin and misery, and to be grieved for his wicked life past, unless he had come unto his father for pardon and comfort, Luke xv. 20. And when those were pricked in their hearts at Peter's sermon, asking Peter 'what they should do?' he exhorted them, 'To repent, every one to be baptized in the name of Jesus Christ, for the remission of sins, and so they should receive the Holy Ghost,' Acts ii. 38. And when Christ invites all those who 'are weary and heavy laden to come unto him,' Mat. xi. 28, he bids them not now be further humbled and grieved for their sins, but by faith to come unto him to be healed, and so they should find rest and peace to their souls. It is not sufficient for a wounded man to be sorry for his brawling and fighting, and to say, he will fight no more; but he must come to the surgeon to have his wounds stopped, dressed, and healed, or else it may cost him his life. So it is not enough to be humbled and grieved for sin, and to resolve against it. We shall relapse again, do what we can, unless we come under the wing of Christ, to be healed by his blood.

Use. Many think they have repented, and are deceived upon this false ground. They are and have been grieved for their sins and offences; are determined to leave and forsake them, and that is all they do. They never lay hold on Christ, and come home to God.

'For thou hast fallen by thine iniquity.'

Here divers points might be insisted on.

1. *That where there is a falling into sin, there will be a falling into misery and judgment.*

This is made good in the experience of all times, ages, persons, and states. Still the more sinful any were, the more fearful judgments fell upon them; and as soon as any man came into a sinful state, he entered into a declining state; as Jacob said of his son Reuben, who had defiled his bed, 'Unstable as water, thou shalt not excel; because thou wentest up to thy father's bed,' Gen. xlix. 4. So sin still debaseth a man. So much sin, so much loss of excellency.

The use hereof is, *first*, against those that complain of their troubles and miseries, as though God and men had dealt hardly with them; whereas their own ways, indeed, have brought all these evils upon them, Lam. iii. 39. God is a sufficient, wise, and holy disposer and orderer of all the ways of men, and rewarder of good and evil doings. God being wise and just in his disposing of all things, it must needs follow, that it shall go well with those that are good; as the prophet speaks, 'Say unto the just, that it shall be well with them, for the reward of their works shall be given them,' Isa. iii. 10. And if it fall out otherwise than well with men, the blame must be laid on their own sin. As the church confesseth, and therefore resolveth, 'I will bear the indignation of the Lord, because I have sinned against him, until he plead my cause, and execute judgment for me; he will bring me forth in the light, and I shall see his righteousness,' Micah vii. 9. If Adam sin, he shall find a hell in a paradise. If Paul return, and return to God, he shall find a heaven in a dungeon.

Secondly, It should move us therefore to seek unto God by unfeigned repentance, to have our sins taken away and pardoned; or else, however we may change our plagues, yet they shall not be taken away; nay, we shall still, like Pharoah, change for the worst; who, though he had his judgments changed, yet sin, the cause, remaining, he was never a whit the better, but the worse, for changing, until his final ruin came.

'The wages of sin is death,' Rom. vi. 23. Sin will cry till it hath its wages. Where iniquity is, there cannot but be falling into judgment. Therefore they are cruel to their own souls that walk in evil ways; for undoubtedly God will turn their own ways upon their own heads. We should not therefore envy any man, be he what he will, who goeth on in ill courses, seeing some judgment is owing him first or last, unless he stop the current of God's wrath by repentance. God, in much mercy, hath set up a court in our hearts to this end, that, if we judge ourselves in this inferior court, we may escape, and not be brought up into the higher. If first they be judged rightly in the inferior court, then there needs no review. But otherwise, if we by repentance take not up the matter, sin must be judged somewhere, either in the tribunal of the heart and conscience, or else afterwards there must be a reckoning for it.

Thirdly, Hence we learn, since the cause of every man's misery is his own sin, *that therefore all the power of the world, and of hell, cannot keep a man in misery, nor hinder him from comfort and happiness, if he will part with his sins by true and unfeigned repentance.* As we know, Manasseh, as soon as he put away sin, the Lord had mercy upon him, and turned his captivity, 2 Chron. xxxiii. 12, 13. So the people of Israel, in the Judges. Look how often they were humbled and returned to God, still he forgave them all their sins. As soon as they put away sin, God and they met again. So that, if we come to Christ by true repentance, neither sin nor punishment can cleave to us, Ps. cvi. 43, 44; cvii. 1, 9.

'Thou hast fallen,' &c. Fallen blindly, as it were. Thou couldst not see which way thou wentest, or to what end thy courses did tend. Therefore thou art come into misery before thou knowest where thou art. A sinner is blind, 'The god of this world hath put out his eyes,' 2 Cor. iv. 4. They see not their way, nor foresee their success. The devil is ever for our falling. That we fall into sin, and then fall into misery, and so fall into despair, and into hell, this pleaseth him. 'Cast thyself down,' saith he to Christ, Mat. iv. 6. 'Down with it, down with it,' saith Edom, Ps. cxxxvii. 7. Hell is beneath. The devil drives all that way.

Use. Take heed of sin! take heed of blindness! Ponder the path of your feet! keep your thoughts heavenward! stop the beginnings, the first stumblings! pray to God to make our way plain before us, and not to lead us into temptation!

'Take with you words, and turn to the Lord: say unto him,' &c., ver. 2.

These Israelites were but a rude people, and had not so good means to thrive in grace as Judah had. Therefore he prompts them here with such words as they might use to God in their returning. 'Take with you words,' whereby we see how gracious God is unto us in using such helps for our recovery, and pitying us more than we pity ourselves. Is not this a sufficient warrant and invitation to return, when the party offended, who is the superior, desires, entreats, and sues unto the offending, guilty inferior, to be reconciled?' 2 Cor. v. 5.

But this is not all. He further sheweth his willingness in teaching us, who are ignorant of the way, in what manner and with what expressions we should return to the Lord. He giveth us not only words, and tells us what we shall say, but also giveth his Spirit so effectually therewith, as that they shall not be lifeless and dead words, but 'with unexpressible sighs and groans unto God,' Rom. viii. 26, who heareth the requests of his own Spirit. Christ likewise teacheth us how to pray. We have words dictated, and a spirit of prayer poured upon us; as if a great person should dictate and frame a petition for one who were afraid to speak unto him. Such is God's graciousness; and so ready is he in Jesus Christ to receive sinners unto mercy.

'Take unto you words.' None were to appear empty before the Lord at Jerusalem, but were to bring something. So it is with us. We must not appear empty before our God. If we can bring nothing else, let us bring words; yea, though broken words, yet if out of a broken and contrite heart, it will be a sacrifice acceptable.

This same taking of words or petitions, in all our troubles and afflictions, must needs be a special remedy, it being of God's own prescription, who is so infinite in knowledge and skill. Whence we observe, that

They who would have help and comfort against all sins and sorrows, must come to God with words of prayer.

As we see in Jonah's case, in a matchless distress, words were inforcive,* and did him more good than all the world besides could. For after that he had been humbled, and prayed out of the whale's belly, the whale was forced to cast him out again, Jonah ii. 10. So the prodigal son being undone, having neither credit nor coin, but all in a manner against him, yet he had words left him: 'Father, I have sinned against heaven and before thee, and am no more worthy to be called thy son: make me as one of thy hired servants,' Luke xv. 18, *seq.* After which, his father had compassion on him. And good Hezekiah, being desperately sick of a desperate disease, yet when he set his faith a-work, and took with him words, which comfort only now was left unto him, we know how after he had turned his face towards the wall, and prayed with words, God not only healed him of that dangerous disease, but also wrought a great miracle for his sake, causing the sun to come back ten degrees, Isa. xxxviii. 2, 8. Thus, when life seemed impossible, yet words, prayers, and tears prevailed with God. Jehoshaphat, also, going to war with Ahab, against God's commandment,

* That is, 'prevailing, or invested with a power of enforcing.'—ED.

and in the battle, being encompassed with enemies, yet had words with him ready, and after prayer found deliverance, 1 Kings xxii. 32. Elijah, likewise, after a great drowth and famine, when rain had been three years wanting, and all in a manner out of frame for a long time, 'took with him words,' James v. 18; and God sent rain abundantly upon the earth again.

The reason is, because prayer sets God on work; and God, who is able and willing to go through with his works, sets all the creatures on work, Hos. ii. 21, 22. As we heard of Elijah, when he prayed for rain, the creatures were set a-work to effect it, 1 Kings xviii. 45, *seq.*

Obj. Where it may be objected, Oh, but rain might come too late in that hot country, where all the roots and herbs might be withered and dried up in three years' space.

Ans. Yet all was well again. The land brought forth her increase as formerly. For faithful prayer never comes too late, because God can never come too late. If our prayers come to him, we shall find him come to us. Jehoshaphat, we read, was in great distress when three kings came against him; yet when he went to God by unfeigned and hearty fasting and prayer, God heard him, fought for him, and destroyed all his enemies, 2 Chron. xx. 3. *seq.* The Scripture sheweth, also, how after Hezekiah's prayer against Sennacherib's blasphemies and threatenings, the Lord sent forth his angel, and destroyed in one night a hundred fourscore and five thousand of the Assyrians, 2 Chron. xxxii. 21, *seq.*

Use 1. This is, first, *for reproof* of those who, in their distresses, set their wit, wealth, friends, and all a-work, but never set God a-work, as Hezekiah did in Sennacherib's case. The first time he turned him off to his cost, with enduring a heavy taxation, and yet was never a whit the better for it, 2 Kings xviii. 15, *seq.;* for Sennacherib came shortly after and besieged Jerusalem, until Hezekiah had humbled himself and prayed; and then God chased all away and destroyed them. He had better have done so at first, and so saved his money and pains, too. The like weakness we have a proof of in Asa, who, when a greater army came against him of ten hundred thousand men, laid about him, prayed and trusted in God, and so was delivered, with the destruction of his enemies, 2 Chron. xiv. 11, yet in a lesser danger, 2 Chron. xvi. 2, against Baasha, king of Israel, distrusted God, and sent out the treasures of the house of God and of his own house unto Benhadad, king of Syria, to have help of him, by a diverting* war against Baasha, king of Israel, which his plot, though it prospered, yet was he reproved by the prophet Hanani, and wars thenceforth denounced against him, 2 Chron. xvi. 7. This Asa, notwithstanding this experiment, afterwards sought unto the physician, before he sought unto God, 2 Chron. xvi. 12.

Use 2. Secondly. *This blameth that barrenness and want of words to go unto God*, which, for want of hearts, we often find in ourselves. It were a strange thing to see a wife have words enough for her maids and servants, and yet not to be able to speak to her husband. We all profess to be the spouse of Christ. What a strange thing, then, is it to be full when we speak to men, yet be so empty and want words to speak to him! A beggar, we know, wants no words, nay, he aboundeth with variety of expressions; and what makes him thus fruitful in words? His necessity, and, in part, his hope of obtaining.

These two make beggars so earnest. So would it be with us. If we found sufficiently our great need of Christ, and therewith had hope, it

* That is, 'diverging or dividing.—G.

would embolden us so to go to God in Christ, that we should not want words. But we want this hope, and the feeling of our necessities, which makes us so barren in prayer.

Prepare thyself, therefore, to prayer, by getting unto thee a true sense of thy need, acquaintance with God, and hope to obtain, and it will make thee fervent in prayer, and copious in thy requests.

Use 3. Thirdly, this is for *consolation*. Though one should want all other means, yet whatsoever their misery be, if they can take words, and can pray well, they shall speed well, Isa. xxxviii. 3. If the misery be for sin, confess it, and ask pardon for it, and they shall have it, 'and be cleansed from all unrighteousness,' 1 John i. 9. Words fetch the comfort to us, though it be the 'blood of Christ only that hath paid the debt,' Isa. liii. 5.

THE SECOND SERMON.

Take with you words, and turn to the Lord; say unto him, Take away all iniquity, and receive us graciously: so will we render the calves of our lips. —Hos. XIV. 2.

As we lost ourselves in the first Adam, so the mercy of God, in the covenant of grace, found out a way to restore us again by the 'second Adam,' 1 Cor. xv. 47, Jesus Christ, in whom all the promises are 'yea and amen; yesterday and to-day, and the same for ever,' Heb. xiii. 8. And as the wisdom of God did freely find out this way at first, comforting our first parents with it in paradise; so this bowels of incomprehensible love of his hath so gone on from time,* in all ages of the church, comforting and raising up the dejected spirits of his church, from time to time, and awakening them out of their drowsiness and sleepy condition. And many times, the greater sinners he dealt with, the greater mercies and tender bowels of compassion were opened unto them, in many sweet and gracious promises tendering forgiveness, and inviting to repentance; as here in this chapter, and whole prophecy, is shewed. What tribe so wicked, so full of idolatry and rebellion, as Ephraim? and yet here Ephraim and Israel are taught a lesson of repentance. As the tender nurse feeds her child, and puts meat in its mouth, so here the Lord puts words in the mouth of this rebellious people.

'Take with you words, and turn unto the Lord.'

Obj. What need God words, he knows our hearts before we speak unto him?

Ans. It is true: God needs no words, but we do, to stir up our hearts and affections; and because he will have us take shame unto ourselves, having given us our tongues as an instrument of glorifying him, he will have our 'glory,' Ps. xvi. 9; lvii. 8, used in our petitions and thanksgivings. And therefore, in regard of ourselves, he will, as was said, have us take words unto ourselves, for exciting of the graces of God in us by words, blowing up of the affections, and for manifestation of the hidden man of the heart. God will be glorified by the outward, as well as by the inward man.

'And turn to the Lord.' He repeats the exhortation of returning, to

* That is, 'from time to time,' or 'through all time.'—ED.

shew that *words must not be empty, but such as are joined with a purpose of turning to God.* For otherwise, to turn to him with a purpose to live in any sin, is the extremity of profane impudence. To come to ask a pardon of the king, with a resolution to live still in rebellion against him, what is this but mockery, as if one should come with a dagg* to shoot him? Such is our case, when we come to ask forgiveness, with a purpose to offend. It is the extremity of profaneness, to come to ask a pardon, to the intent that we may sin still. Therefore he repeats it again, 'Take unto you words, and turn to the Lord.' The form is—

'Take away all iniquity, and receive us graciously,' or 'do good to us:' 'so will we render the calves of our lips;' wherein we have,

1. A *petition:* (1.) *To take away all iniquity;* (2.) *To receive them graciously.*

2. A *re-stipulation,* or promise of thankfulness back again to the Lord, 'So will we render the calves of our lips.' So that we may observe, hence—

What God will grant us. He will have us ask of him. 'Yet for all these things I will be sought unto of the house of Israel,' Ezek. xx. 31, saith God; because he will have us acknowledge our homage and dependence upon him. Therefore we must ask what he hath purposed to give. 'Take away all iniquity,' &c., where there is an implication of a confession of their sins and great iniquities. 'Take away iniquity,' and 'Take away all iniquity,' that is, our manifold guilt. So, before petition, there must be a free and full confession, as was shewed before.

Now, this confession here is made to God, and to God only, saith Austin in this case. Because it is a point in controversy, it is good to hear what the ancients say. There are a curious sort of men, who are busy to search into other men's lives, and are careless in amending their own. Saith he, 'What have I to do with men to hear me confess, when I have offended God? We must confess to God, and to God only.'† But in some cases there may be public and private confession to men. Public, in public offences, for the satisfaction of the church, and the glory of God; for preventing of scandal. Private, to ministers, for the quieting of conscience. But this is only in some cases. Men go not to the chirurgeon, as the papists would have it, for every little prick of their finger. No; but yet in some cases it is good to open the matter to a minister, 'who hath the tongue of the learned,' Isa. l. 4. But the sin is toward God, against him, he only being able to forgive sins, as the Pharisees confessed: 'None can forgive sins but God,' Mark ii. 7. The papists, therefore, herein are worse than the Pharisees.

The petition is, 'Take away iniquity,' and 'all iniquity.' Why all?

First. Because where there is any true goodness in the heart, that hatred which carries the bent of the soul against one sin, is alike against all, as I shewed; and the devil carries thousands to hell by this partial obedience, because he knows at any time where to have such. God and a purpose to sin will not stand together, nor dwell in a heart that allows itself in any sin, be it never so small. He saith, Take away all, because the Spirit of God works in a man renewed, such a disposition of sincerity to hate all alike.

Secondly, he saith, 'Take away all iniquity,' because the heart, which desires to be at peace with God, desires also to be like God, who hates all sin. Therefore, saith the sanctified soul, forgive all sin. Take all away, that I may have nothing in me displeasing unto thee. I desire to join

* That is, 'small pistol.'—G. † Augustine, Conf. Introd., *et alibi.*—G.

with the Lord; to hate what he hateth, and as he hateth; to carry a perfect hatred to the whole kind. 'Take away all iniquity.' Hatred is not satisfied, but with the utter abolishing of the thing hated. Therefore it hath this extent here. 'Take away all sin,' both the guilt and the reign of every sin, that none may rule in me; nay, by little and little, purge out all. 'Take away iniquity,' and the train of all which it draws after it—judgments. 'Take away iniquity,' that is, forgive the sin, and overcome the power of it by sanctifying grace, and remit the judgments attending it.

'Take it away.' That is, take away the guilt of it utterly by pardon, and the remainders thereof by sanctifying grace, so as the Spirit may rule, and be all in all in us. They see sin is an offensive thing, and therefore they say, 'Take it away,' as an offensive, odious thing, and as a burden. For howsoever it be sweet as honey in the committing it, afterwards, when the conscience is thoroughly awaked, it is most offensive and bitter. So as in this case, a sinner would gladly run from his own conscience, and from himself; run anywhere from the tormenting and racking thoughts of conscience awaked, and withal hates the place where it was committed, and the company with whom, yea, the thoughts of them. As Absalom hated Tamar after he had lien with her, so a sinner awaked from sin hates what he formerly loved. As good men love the circumstances of anything which puts them in mind of any good they have done, loving both place and person. So it is with a sinner. When his conscience is awaked, he hates all things which puts him in mind of his sins. Therefore, 'Take it away,' forgive it, cast it into the bottom of the sea, blot it out of thy remembrance, cover it, impute it not; all which phrases shew a taking away.

Therefore, I beseech you, let us examine ourselves hereby, whether our desire of forgiveness be sound or not. If we desire sin should be taken away, we cannot think of it with comfort. For in that many think with delight of their old sins, what do they else, but repeat them over again and again? But where the heart is soundly touched with a saving sense of sin, O then he cries, 'Take it away;' take it out of my conscience, that it cause not despair there; and out of thy remembrance, that no advantage be taken against me for it. 'Take it away.' But it is no otherwise taken away than by satisfying of divine justice. How much are we beholden to Christ, therefore, who hath borne and taken away our sins, and as the scape-goat, gone away with the burden of all into the wilderness of oblivion. Blessed be God, and the Lamb of God, that taketh away the sins of the world! We can never bless God too much, nor sufficiently, for Christ. 'Blessed be God, the Father of our Lord Jesus Christ,' Eph. i. 3. Now we may think of sin without shame and despair. O blessed state, when a man can think of his former odious, and filthy, loathsome sins, and yet not despair! Because, when he believes in Christ, the blood of Christ purgeth all away, takes away all sin. He hath taken them away.

You see here, in the first place, they pray for the taking away of their iniquity. For, take away this, and all other mercies follow after, because this only is it which stops the current of God's favours, which removed, the current of his mercies run amain. As when the clouds are gone, the sun shines out; so let our sins be removed, and God's favour immediately shines upon us. Therefore, first 'Take away all iniquity,' and then we shall see nothing but thy fatherly face in Christ. You see what the care of God's children is, to seek mercy and favour in the first place; as David, 'Have mercy on me, O Lord!' Ps. li. 1. This he begs first of all. Whereas God had threatened other terrible judgments, as that the sword should never depart from his house, &c., yet he neglects all, as it were, and begs only for mercy, 'to take away iniquity.' For a sinner is never in such a blessed condition as he should be in, until he prize and desire mercy above all; because, though we be in misery, until then, with sinful Ephraim, Hos. vii. 14, we howl upon our beds for corn and wine, preferring earthly, sensual things before all. But that soul and conscience which is acquainted with God, and the odiousness of sin, that soul God intends to speak peace unto in the end, desires pardon of sin and mercy above all. For it knows that God is goodness itself, and that, when the interposing clouds are vanished, God cannot shew himself otherwise than in goodness, grace, and mercy. 'Take away all iniquity.'

Quest. Before I go further, let me answer one question. Ought we not to think of our former sins? Shall God take them away altogether out of the soul?

Ans. Oh no! Take them away out of the conscience, O Lord, that it do not accuse for them; but not out of the memory. It is good that sin be remembered, to humble us, to make us more thankful, pitiful, and tender-hearted unto others, to abase us and keep us low all the days of our life, and to make us deal gently and mercifully with others, being sensible of our own frailties. As they are naught in the conscience, so they are good to the memory. Therefore, let us think often of this, what the chief desire of our souls to God should be for—mercy, to have sin taken away. In all the articles of our creed, that of chiefest comfort is, that of 'remission of sins.'* Wherefore are all the other articles of Christ, his birth, death, and crucifying, but that he might get the church? and that the privileges thereof might be, 'forgiveness of sins, resurrection of the body, and life everlasting;' but forgiveness of sins is in the first place.

Quest. But may some say, How shall I know whether or no my sins be forgiven?

1. By something that goes before.
2. By something which follows after.

Ans. There is somewhat which goes before, viz.:—

First, an humble and hearty confession, as, 'If we confess our sins, he is faithful and just to forgive us our sins, and to cleanse us from all unrighteousness,' 1 John i. 9. Therefore, whether I feel it or not, if I have heartily, fully, and freely confessed, my sins are forgiven. God in wisdom and mercy may suspend the feeling thereof, for our humiliation, and for being over-bold with Satan's baits; yet I ought to believe it. For I make God a liar else, if I confess heartily, and acknowledge my debt, to think that he hath not cancelled the bond.

Secondly, sin is certainly pardoned, *when a man finds strength against it;* for where God forgives, he gives strength withal: as to the man whom he healed of the palsy, 'Thy sins are forgiven thee; take up thy bed and walk,' Mat. ix. 2, 6. When a man hath strength to return to God, to run the way of his commandments, and to go on in a Christian course, his sins are forgiven, because he hath a spirit of faith to go on and lead him forward still. Those who find no strength of grace, may question forgiveness of sins. For God, where he takes away sin, and pardons it, as we see here in this text, after prayer made to take away iniquity, he 'doth good to us.'

The *third* evidence is, *some peace of conscience;* though not much, perhaps, yet so much as supports us from despair, as, 'Therefore, being justified by faith, we have peace with God through our Lord Jesus Christ,' Rom. v. 1;

* Creed, Article X.—G.

that is, being acquitted from our sins by faith, we have peace with God; so much peace, as makes us go boldly to him. So that one may know his bonds are cancelled, and his sins forgiven, when with some boldness he dare look God in the face in Jesus Christ. A Judas, an Ahithophel, a Saul, because they are in the guilt of their sins, cannot confess comfortably, and go to God, which, when with some boldness we can do, it is a sign that peace is made for us.

Fourth. Again, where sin is pardoned, *our hearts will be much enlarged with love to God;* as Christ said to the woman, 'Her sins, which are many, are forgiven her, because she loved much,' Luke vii. 47. Therefore, when we find our hearts inflamed with love to God, we may know that God hath shined upon our souls in the pardon of sin; and proportionably to our measure of love is our assurance of pardon. Therefore we should labour for a greater measure thereof, that our hearts may be the more inflamed in the love of God. It is impossible that the soul should at all love God angry, offended, and unappeased; nay, such a soul wisheth that there were no God at all, for the very thoughts thereof terrify him.

Fifthly. Again, where sin is forgiven, *it frames the soul suitably*, to be gentle, merciful, and to pardon others. For, usually, those who have peaceable consciences themselves are peaceable unto others; and those who have forgiveness of sins, can also forgive others. Those who have found mercy have merciful hearts, shewing that they have found mercy with God. And, on the contrary, he that is a cruel, merciless man, it is a sign that his heart was never warmed nor melted with the sense of God's mercy in Christ. Therefore, 'as the elect of God,' saith the apostle, 'put on bowels of compassion,' 1 Peter iii. 8, as you will make it good that you are the elect of God, members of Christ, and God's children.

Therefore, let us labour for the forgiveness of our sins, that God would remove and subdue the power of them, take them away, and the judgments due to them, or else we are but miserable men, though we enjoyed all the pleasures of the world, which to a worldly man are but like the liberty of the tower* to a condemned traitor, who though he have all wants supplied with all possible attendance, yet when he thinks of his estate, it makes his heart cold, damps his courage, and makes him think the poorest car-man or tankard-bearer, at liberty, happier than he, who would not change estates with him. So it is with a man that hath not sued out his pardon, nor is at peace with God. He hath no comfort, so long as he knows his sins are on the file,† that God in heaven is not at peace with him, who can arm all the creatures against him to be revenged of him. In which case, who shall be umpire betwixt God and us, if we take not up the controversy betwixt him and our souls? Therefore, it being so miserable a case to want assurance of the forgiveness of sins, it should make us be never an hour quiet till we have gotten it, seeing the uncertainty of this life, wherein there is but a step betwixt hell, damnation, and us. Therefore sue unto God, ply him with broken and humble hearts, that he would pardon all the sins of our youth and after-age, known and unknown, that he would pardon all whatsoever. 'Take away all iniquity.'

'And do good to us.' For so it is in the original,‡ but it is all one, 'Receive us graciously, and do good to us.' All the goodness we have from God, it is out of his grace, from his free grace and goodness. All grace, every little thing from God is grace. As we say of favours received of

* That is, the state-prison.—G. † See note *b*, vol. I. p. 289.—G.
‡ See note *a*.—G.

great persons, this is his grace, his favour; so this is a respect which is put upon all things which we receive from God, when we are in covenant, all is gracious. Take we the words as they are, the more plain, in the original. 'Take good, and do good to us:' take good out of thy treasure of goodness, and do good to us, bestow upon us thy own good. First, 'take away our iniquities,' and then take good out of thy bounty, 'and do good to us.' Whence we see—

Doct. That God's mercy to his children is complete and full.

For he takes away ill, and doth good. Men may pardon, but withal they think that they have done wondrous bountifully when they have pardoned. But God goes further. He takes away ill, and doth good; takes good out of his fountain, and doth good to us.

Use. Therefore, let us make this use of it, to be encouraged, when we have the first blessing of all, forgiveness of sins, to go to him for more and more, and gather upon God further and further still. For because he is a fountain of goodness that can never be drawn dry, he is wondrously pleased with this. We cannot honour him more than by making use of his mercy in the forgiveness of sins; and of his goodness, in going to him for it; and having interested ourselves in his goodness, go to him for more. Lord, thou hast begun: make an end; thou hast forgiven my sins; I want this and that good; together with the pardon of my sins, do me good. 'Receive us graciously,' or, 'do us good.' Now, good is the loadstone of the soul, the attractive that draws it. Therefore, after forgiveness of sins, he saith, 'do good.' The petition is easy, God will soon grant it. For nothing else interposeth betwixt God and us, and makes two, but sin, which being removed, he is all goodness and mercy. 'All his ways are mercy and truth,' Ps. xxv. 10. Yea, even his sharpest ways are mercy, all mercy. When sin is forgiven, there is goodness in all, in the greatest cross and affliction. 'Do good to us.'

The soul, we see, desires good, and needs good. It is a transcendent word here, and must be understood according to the taste of God's people, of a sanctified soul. 'Do good.' Especially do spiritual good to us. Together with the forgiveness of sins, give us the righteousness of Jesus Christ, sanctifying grace, such good as may make us good first. For the desire must be such as the person is, who makes it. Wicked men, as it is said of Balaam, have good gifts, without the good God; but we must not be so pleased with gifts, unless we be good ourselves, and see God making us good. 'Can an evil tree bring forth good fruit?' Mat. vii. 18. Therefore, the apostle calls the regenerate person 'God's workmanship,' &c., Eph. ii. 10. We are God's good work, and then we do good works; being made good, good comes from us. 'Do good to us.'

It is an acknowledgment of their own emptiness, 'Do good to us.' We are blind in our own understandings, enlighten us. We are perplexed, set us right. We are dull, quicken us. We are empty, fill us. We are dark, shine upon us. We are ready to go out of the way, establish us. Every way do good to us suitable to our wants. The best that we can bring to thee is emptiness. Therefore do thou good to us; fill us with thy fulness. Do good to us every way, whereby thou usest to convey spiritual things to thy servants' souls. Give us first thy grace, thy Spirit, which is the spring of all good things; for the Spirit of God is a Spirit of direction, of strength, of comfort, and all. Therefore he who hath the Spirit of God hath the spring of all. That is begged in the first place. And then give us good magistrates, to rule us well, and good ministers, who are the dispensers of grace, instruments of our salvation, the conduit pipes whereby thou derivest and conveyest good to us. When thou hast made us good, continue the means of salvation for our good every way. The church, when she saith, 'Do good to us,' hath a large desire. Here be seeds of wondrous large things in these two short petitions, 'Take away all iniquity,' and 'do good to us.' *A bono Deo*, &c. From the good God nothing can come but what is good. Therefore do good to us in all spiritual things. The prophet David aims at this excellent good, saying that other men are for corn, wine, and oil, and say, 'Who will shew us any good? But, Lord, lift thou up the light of thy countenance upon us,' Ps. iv. 6, 7. Thy lovingkindness is better than life, therefore do good to us. When thou hast forgiven our sins, shine graciously upon us in Jesus Christ.

And it extends its limits likewise to outward prosperity, this desire of doing good. Let us have happy days! Sweeten our pilgrimage here! Let our profession of religion be comfortable! Do not lay more crosses upon us than thou wilt give us strength to bear! Do good to us every way! But mark the wisdom of the Holy Ghost in dictating of this prayer to them. He speaks in general, 'Do good to us;' not to do this or that good, but he leaves it to the wisdom of God, as they here frame their hearts unto the will of God. 'Do good to us,' spiritual. That needs no limitation, because we cannot more honour God than to depend upon him for all spiritual good things. Thou art wiser, and knowest what is good for us better than we ourselves. Beggars ought to be no choosers. Therefore 'do good to us,' for the particulars we leave them to thy wisdom. Oh, beloved, it is a happy and blessed privilege to be under the conduct of so wise and all-sufficient a God, who is good, and as he is good, knows best what is good for us. We would have riches, liberty, and health; aye, but it may be it is not good for us. 'Do good to us.' Thou, Lord, knowest what is best. Do in thine own wisdom what is best.

Use. Which should teach us not to limit the Holy One of Israel in our desires of any outward thing whatsoever. Especially desire forgiveness and spiritual good things, leaving the rest to his wise disposing. Yet notwithstanding, out of the sense of pain and grief, we may pray either for the mitigation or removing of a cross, if God be so pleased. Because he hath put in us self-love, not sinful, but love of preserving our nature, therefore he permits us, if it may stand with his good pleasure, to desire the good of our outward man, as, Lord, give us bodily health, for we cannot else be instruments of serving thee. With reservation of God's good pleasure, we may desire such and such things, conditionally, that when we see God will have it otherwise, we rest contented, sit down quietly, knowing that whatsoever health, sickness, or crosses he sends, it comes from his goodness and love, and shall turn to our good at length. If we love God, all shall work for good.

'Take away our iniquity, and do us good.' We should make this petition for the church and ourselves. Pardon our sins, and do good to us, to our persons, to the state, to the times wherein we live, to the church at home and abroad, do good to all.

And we may observe this from the order, and know what good we have. It comes from God in love, when it comes after forgiveness of sins. How then, may we take comfort of all the good things we have enjoyed, having seen many good days, enjoyed many good blessings, in health, wealth, good magistracy, ministry, peace, plenty, and the like! If all this goodness of God lead us to God, and draw us nearer to him, 'after forgiveness of sins,' grounded on the former evidences I spake of, then they come in love. But never let us think to have true comfort with a blessing, or any good thing we enjoy, till we have assurance of God's love and mercy in the forgiveness of sins, lest God strip us naked of all the good things we have, and make us as naked as Dives in hell, who had not anything that was good to refresh his body or soul. So that all good things we enjoy here without this, will only aggravate our condemnation. Let us observe, therefore, how all our good things are joined with spiritual good (whether we ourselves are made better by them or not), having our sins pardoned. I beseech you, let us renew our requests for forgiveness of sins every day, making our accounts even with God, desiring grace to set our souls in a holy and sanctified frame with God, that ourselves may be good, our conversation good, and that then he would 'do good to us' all other ways, and sanctify all other things. This is the method of God's Spirit in setting us right onwards in our heavenly journey, first to have forgiveness of sins, then sanctification, to be better ourselves, and then to look for peaceable and comfortable days in this world, if God see it good. What can be more? 'Take away all iniquity, and do us good,' all manner of good.

Therefore, since all good comes from God, the first and chief good, let us labour to have communion with him by all sanctified means, that so he may take away our ill, and do us every way good to our souls, bodies, conditions. Oh, what a blessed thing is it for a Christian to keep a strict and near communion with the fountain of goodness, who can do more for us than all the world besides! When we are sick on our deathbeds, or when conscience is thoroughly awaked, then to speak peace comfortably to us in this great extremity, is more worth than all this world. Therefore let us labour to keep communion with God, that he may speak peace to our souls when nothing else can.

I beseech you, therefore, let us take heed how we break or walk loosely with God, seeing we can have no further comfort of any good thing we enjoy, than we are careful to keep and maintain our peace and communion with him at all times. And when we run into arrearages with God, then be sure we lie not in sin, but say, 'Take away all iniquity, and do good to us,' labouring to be in such an estate as God may give us his Holy Spirit, both to make us good and to sanctify unto us all other good. There be good things which are good of themselves, and which make all other things good. Thus, by communion with God, we ourselves are made good, and all other things likewise are made good to us, all his ways being mercy and truth unto those who fear him. Therefore resign we ourselves and all that we have unto his wisdom and disposing, because ofttimes there is good where we imagine the worst of evils to be, as it is sometimes good to have a vein opened to be purged. The physician thinks so, when yet the patient, impatient of reason's issue, thinks not so. But as the physician is wiser than the patient, to know what is best for him, so God is wiser than man, to know what is good for him, who intends us no hurt when he purgeth us by affliction.

All our care, therefore, should be to annihilate ourselves, to come with empty, poor souls to God, 'Do good to us.' In which case it is no matter what our ill be, if he do us good, who hath both pardon and rich grace to remove the evil of sin, and convey all grace unto us out of his rich treasury.

'So will we render the calves of our lips.'

Here is the re-stipulation or promise. They return back again to God, for there is no friendship maintained without rendering. When God hath entered into covenant with us, then there is a kind of friendship knit up betwixt him and us, he becoming our friend. We must not, therefore, be like graves, to swallow up all, and return nothing, for then the intercourse betwixt God and us is cut off. Therefore the same Spirit which teacheth them to pray, and to 'take to them words,' teacheth them likewise to take unto them words of praise, that there may be a rendering according to receiving, without which we are worse than the poorest creature that is, which rendereth according to its receipt. The earth, when it is ploughed and sowed, it yields us fruit. Trees being set, yield increase. Beasts being fed, render in their kind. Yea, the fiercest, untamed beasts, as we read of the lion, have been thankful in their kind. The heavens, saith the psalmist, declare the glory of God, and the firmament shews forth his praise, Ps. xix. 1. So there must be a return, if we be not worse than beasts. Therefore the church here promiseth a return by the same Spirit which stirred her up to pray. 'So will we render the calves of our lips.'

Now, this promise which the church makes here of praise, is a kind of vow, 'So will we render,' &c. To bind one's-self is a kind of vow. The church therefore binds herself, that she may bind God; for binding herself by vow to thankfulness, she thereby binds God; who is moved with nothing we can do so much as with setting forth of his praise, which was his end in all the creation, the setting forth of his glory. The end of the new creature is the end of all things both in nature and grace; the end whereof is God's glory, from whence all things come and wherein all things end: as we say of a circle, all things begin and end in it. All other things are for man, and man for God's glory. When the soul can say, 'Lord, this shall be for thy honour, to set forth thy praise,' it binds God. Hence, that they might move God to yield to their prayers, they bind themselves by a kind of vow. Do thus, O Lord, and thou shalt not lose by it, thou shalt have praise; 'so will we render thee the calves of our lips.'

So promises and vows of praise are alleged as an argument to prevail with God, for the obtaining of that the church begs for: 'So will we render,' &c. Not to enter into the commonplace of vows, only thus much I say, that there is a good use of them, to vow and promise thankfulness when we would obtain blessings from God. That which a promise is to men, that a vow is to God; and usually they go together in Scripture, as it is said of David, that 'he vowed unto God, and sware unto the mighty God of Jacob,' Ps. cxxxii. 2. So we have all in baptism vowed a vow. So that it is good to renew our vows often, especially that of new obedience; and in this particular to vow unto him that we will praise him, and strive that his glory be no loser by us.

1. It is good thus to vow, if it were but *to excite and quicken our dulness and forgetfulness of our general vow;* to put us in mind of our duty, the more to oblige us to God and refresh our memories. This bond, that having promised, now I must do it, provokes the soul to it. As it helps the memory, so it quickens the affections.

2. Besides, as by nature we are forgetful, *so we are inconstant;* in which respect it is a tie to our inconstant and unsteady natures. For there are none who have the Spirit of God at all, with any tenderness of heart, but will thus think: I have vowed to God. If it be a heinous thing to break with men, what is it wittingly and willingly to break with the great God? A vow is a kind of oath. This is the sacrifice of fools, to come to God, and yet neither to make good our vows, nor endeavour to do it.

Let us consider therefore what we have done in this case. By permission of authority, there was a fast lately, when we all renewed our vows (we mocked God else), [and] received the communion. Will God be mocked, think you? No; but howsoever man may forget, God will not, but will come upon us for non-payment of our vows and covenants. Lay we it to heart therefore what covenants we have made with God of late. And then, for the time to come, be not discouraged if you have been faulty in it. There is a general vow, wherein, though we have failed (if we be his children, and break not with God in the main, cleaving to him in purpose of heart, occasionally renewing our purposes and covenants), yet let not Satan discourage us for our unfaithfulness therein. But be ashamed of it, watch more, look better to it for the time to come, and make use of the gracious covenant; and, upon recovery, say with the church, 'So will we render the calves of our lips.'

It was the custom under the Jewish policy, you know, to offer sacrifices of all sorts. But the Spirit of God speaks here of the church of the Jews under the New Testament; especially what they should be after their conversion, having reference to the Jews in Christ's time, and to the believing Jews in all times, implying thus much; howsoever, not legal sacrifices of calves, bullocks, sheep, and lambs, yet the 'calves of the lips,' which God likes better, are acceptable to him. And it likewise implies some humiliation of the church. Lord, whatsoever else we could offer unto thee, it is thine own, though it were the beasts upon a thousand mountains; but this, by thy grace, we can do, to 'praise thee,' Ps. l. 23. For God must open and circumcise our lips and hearts before we can offer him the 'calves of our lips.' Thus much the poorest creature in the world may say to God, Lord, 'I will render thee the calves of my lips.' Other things I have not. This I have by thy gracious Spirit, a heart somewhat touched by the sense of thy favour. Therefore 'I will render thee the calves of my lips;' that is, praise, as the apostle hath it, 'By him therefore let us offer the sacrifice of praise to God continually; that is, the fruit of our lips, giving thanks to his name,' Heb. xiii. 15. 'So will we render thee the calves of our lips.' Whence the point is,

Doct. That God's children at all times have their sacrifices.

There is indeed one kind of sacrificing determined* and finished by the coming of Christ, who was the last sacrifice of propitiation for our sins. The more to blame those who yet maintain a daily sacrifice, not of laud and praise, but of cozening and deluding the world, in saying mass for the sins of the quick and the dead; all such sacrifices being finished and closed up in him, our blessed Saviour; who, 'by one sacrifice,' as the apostle speaks, 'hath perfected them that are sanctified,' Heb. x. 14, vii. 27; and that, 'by one sacrifice, when he offered up himself,' Heb. x. 12; when all the Jewish sacrifices ended. Since which, all ours are but a commemoration of Christ's last sacrifice, as the fathers say: the Lord's supper, with the rest, which remain still; and the sacrifice of praise, with a few others, I desire to name.

1. First, The sacrifice of a broken heart, whereof David speaks, Ps. li. 17; which sacrifice of a wounded, broken heart, by the knife of repentance, pleaseth God wondrously well.

2. And then, a broken heart that offers Christ to God every day; who, though he were offered once for all, yet our believing in him, and daily presenting his atonement made for us, is a new offering of him. Christ is

* That is, 'abolished' = fulfilled.—G.

crucified and sacrificed for thee as oft as thou believest in Christ crucified. Now, upon all occasions we manifest our belief in Christ, to wash and bathe ourselves in his blood, who justifieth the ungodly. So that, upon a fresh sight of sin, with contrition for it, he continually justifieth us. Thus, when we believe, we offer him to God daily; a broken heart first, and then Christ with a broken heart.

3. And then when we believe in Christ, we offer and sacrifice ourselves to God; in which respect we must, as it were, be killed ere we be offered. For we may not offer ourselves as we are in our lusts, but as mortified and killed by repentance. Then we offer ourselves to God as a reasonable and living sacrifice, when we offer ourselves wholly unto him, wit, understanding, judgment, affections, and endeavour; as Paul saith of the Macedonians, 'they gave themselves to God first, and then their goods,' 2 Cor. viii. 5. In sum, it is that sacrifice Paul speaks of, 'to present our bodies a living sacrifice, holy, acceptable unto God,' &c., Rom. xii. 1. For a Christian who believeth in the Lord Jesus is not his own, but sacrificeth himself to him that was sacrificed for him. As Christ is given to us, so he that believes in Christ gives himself back again to Christ. Hereby a man may know if he be a true Christian, and that Christ is his, if he yields up himself to God. For 'Christ died and rose again,' saith the apostle, 'that he might be Lord both of quick and dead,' Rom. xiv. 9. 'Therefore,' saith he, 'whether we live or die, we are not our own,' Rom. xiv. 8. What we do or suffer in the world, in all we are sacrificed. So saith a sanctified soul, My wit, my will, my life, my good, my affections are thine; of thee I received them, and I resign all to thee as a sacrifice. Thus the martyrs, to seal the truth, as a sacrifice, yielded up their blood. He that hath not obtained of himself so much as to yield himself to God, he knows not what the gospel means. For Christian religion is not only to believe in Christ for forgiveness of sin; but the same faith which takes this great benefit, renders back ourselves in lieu of thankfulness.

So that, whatsoever we have, after we believe, we give all back again. Lord, I have my life, my will, my wit, and all from thee; and to thee I return all back again. For when I gave myself to believe in thy dear Son, I yielded myself and all I have to thee; and now, having nothing but by thy gift, if thou wilt have all I will return all unto thee again; if thou wilt have my life, my goods, my liberty, thou shalt have them. This is the state of a Christian who hath denied himself. For we cannot believe as we should unless we deny ourselves. Christianity is not altogether in believing this and that; but the faith which moves me to believe forgiveness of sins, carries us also unto God to yield all back again to him.

4. More especially, among the sacrifices of the New Testament are alms, as, 'To do good and to communicate forget not, for with such sacrifices God is well pleased,' Heb. xiii. 16.

5. And among the rest, the sacrifice of praise, which is in the same chapter, verse 15. First, he saith, By him, that is, by Christ, let us offer the sacrifice of praise to God continually, that is, the fruit of our lips: which is but an exposition of this place, which, because it is especially here intended, I will a little enlarge myself in.

The 'calves of our lips' implies two things:

Not only thankfulness to God, but glorifying of God, in setting out his praise. Otherwise to thank God for his goodness to us, or for what we hope to receive, without glorifying of him, is nothing at all worth. For in glorifying there are two things.

1. *A supposition of excellency.* For that cannot be glorified, which hath no excellency in it. Glory in sublimity hath alway excellency attending it. And

2. *The manifestation of this glory.*

Now, when all the excellencies of God, as they are, are discovered and set out, his wisdom, mercy, power, goodness, all-sufficiency, &c., then we glorify him. To praise God for his favours to us, and accordingly to glorify him, is 'the calves of our lips;' but especially to praise him. Whence the point is—

That the yielding of praise to God is a wondrous acceptable sacrifice.

Which is instead of all the sacrifices of the Old Testament, than which the greatest can do no more, nor the least less; for it is the sacrifice and fruit of the lips. But to open it. It is not merely the sacrifice of our lips; for the praise we yield to God, it must be begotten in the heart. Hereupon the word, λογὸς, speech, signifieth both reason and speech, there being one word in the learned language for both.* Because speech is nothing but that stream which issues from the spring of reason and understanding: therefore, in thanksgiving there must not be a lip-labour only, but a thanksgiving from the lips, first begotten in the heart, coming from the inward man, as the prophet saith, 'Bless the Lord, O my soul; and all that is within me, bless his holy name,' Ps. ciii. 1. Praise must come from a sound judgment of the worth of the thing we praise for. It must come from an affection which desires that God may have the glory, by the powers of the whole inward man, which is a hard matter, to rouse up ourselves to praise God with all the powers of our soul, 'all that is within me, praise his holy name,' Ps. ciii. 1. There goeth judgment, resolution of the will, strength of affections, and all with it.

And then again, besides this, 'the calves of our lips' carries us to work. The oral thanksgiving must be justified by our works and deeds; or else our actions will give our tongue the lie, that we praise him with the one, but deny him in the other. This is a solecism, as if one should look to the earth, and cry, O ye heavens! So when we say, God be praised, when yet our life speaks the contrary, it is a dishonouring of God. So the praise of our lips must be made good and justified by our life, actions, and conversation. This we must suppose for the full understanding of the words, 'We will render,' from our hearts, 'the calves of our lips;' which we must make good in our lives and conversations, ever to set forth thy praise in our whole life.

Quest. But why doth the prophet especially mention lips, 'the calves of our lips,' which are our words?

Ans. 1. Partly, because Christ, who is the Word, delights in our words.

2. Because our tongue is our glory, and that whereby we glorify God.

3. And especially because our tongue is that which excites others, being a trumpet of praise, ordained of God for this purpose. Therefore, 'the calves of our lips;' partly, because it stirs up ourselves and others, and partly, because God delights in words, especially of his own dictating. To come then to speak more fully of praise and thanksgiving, let us consider what a sweet, excellent, and prevailing duty this is, which the church, to bind God, promiseth unto him, 'the calves of our lips.' I will not be long in the point, but only come to some helps how we may come to do it.

First, this praising of God must be *from an humble, broken heart.* The

* Cf. p. 153 and note *o*, p. 195.—G.

humble soul that sees itself not worthy of any favour, and confesseth sin before God, is alway a thankful soul. 'Take away our iniquity, and then do good to us.' We are empty ourselves. Then will 'we render thee the calves of our lips.' What made David so thankful a man? He was an humble man; and so Jacob, what abased him so in his own eyes? His humility: 'Lord, I am less than the least of thy mercies,' Gen. xxxii. 10. He that thinks himself unworthy of anything, will be thankful for everything; and he who thinks himself unworthy of any blessing, will be contented with the least. Therefore, let us work our hearts to humility, in consideration of our sinfulness, vileness, and unworthiness, which will make us thankful: especially of the best blessings, when we consider their greatness, and our unworthiness of them. A proud man can never be thankful. Therefore, that religion which teacheth pride, cannot be a thankful religion. Popery is compounded of spiritual pride: merit of congruity, before conversion; merit of condignity, and desert of heaven, after; free will, and the like, to puff up nature. What a religion is this! Must we light a candle before the devil? Is not nature proud enough, but we must light a candle to it? To be spiritually proud is worst of all.

2. And with our own unworthiness, add this: *a consideration of the greatness of the thing we bless God for;* setting as high a price upon it as we can, by considering what and how miserable we were without it. He will bless God joyfully for pardon of sin, who sees how miserable he were without it, in misery next to devils, ready to drop into hell every moment. And the more excellent we are, so much the more accursed, without the forgiveness of sins. For the soul, by reason of the largeness thereof, is so much the more capable and comprehensible of misery; as the devils are more capable than we, therefore are most accursed. Oh, this will make us bless God for the pardon of sin! And likewise, let us set a price upon all God's blessings, considering what we were without our senses, speech, meat, drink, rest, &c. O beloved! we forget to praise God sufficiently for our senses. This little spark of reason in us is an excellent thing; grace is founded upon it. If we were without reason, what were we? If we wanted sight, hearing, speech, rest, and other daily blessings, how uncomfortable were our lives! This consideration will add and set a price to their worth, and make us thankful, to consider our misery without them. But, such is our corruption, that favours are more known by the want, than by the enjoying of them. When too late, we many times find how dark and uncomfortable we are without them; then smarting the more soundly, because in time we did not sufficiently prize, and were thankful for them.

3. And then, *labour to get further and further assurance that we are God's children, beloved of him.* This will make us thankful both for what we have and hope for. It lets out the life-blood of thankfulness, to teach doubting or falling from grace. What is the end, I beseech you, why the glory to come is revealed before the time? That we shall be sons and daughters, kings and queens, heirs and co-heirs with Christ, and [that] 'all that he hath is ours?' Rom. viii. 17. Is not this knowledge revealed beforehand, that our praise and thanksgiving should beforehand be suitable to this revelation, being set with Christ in heavenly places already. Whence comes those strong phrases? 'We are raised with Christ; sit with him in heavenly places,' Eph. ii. 6; 'are translated from death to life,' Col. i. 13; 'transformed into his image;' 'partakers of the divine nature,' &c., 2 Pet. i. 4. If anything that can come betwixt our believing,

and our sitting there, could disappoint us thereof, or unsettle us, it may as well put Christ out of heaven, for we sit with him. If we yield to the uncomfortable popish doctrine of doubting, we cannot be heartily thankful for blessings; for still there will rise in the soul surmises, I know not whether God favour me or not: it may be, I am only fatted for the day of slaughter; God gives me outward things to damn me, and make me the more inexcusable. What a cooler of praise is this, to be ever doubting, and to have no assurance of God's favour! But when upon good evidence, which cannot deceive, we have somewhat wrought in us, distinct from the greater number of worldlings, God's stamp set upon us; having evidences of the state of grace, by conformity to Christ, and walking humbly by the rule of the word in all God's ways: then we may heartily be thankful, yea, and we shall break forth in thanksgiving; this being an estate of peace, and 'joy unspeakable and glorious,' 1 Pet. i. 8, wherein we take everything as an evidence of God's love.

Thus the assurance of our being in the state of grace makes us thankful for everything. So by the contrary, being not in some measure assured of God's love in Christ, we cannot be thankful for everything. For it will always come in our mind, I know not how I have these things, and what account I shall give for them. Therefore, even for the honour of God, and that we may praise him the more cheerfully, let us labour to have further and further evidences of the state of grace, to make us thankful both for things present and to come, seeing faith takes to trust things to come, as if it had them in possession. Whereby we are assured of this, that we shall come to heaven, as sure as if we were there already. This makes us praise God beforehand for all favours; as blessed Peter begins his epistle, 'Blessed be the God and Father of our Lord Jesus Christ, which, according to his abundant mercy, hath begotten us again unto a lively hope, by the resurrection of Jesus Christ from the dead, to an inheritance incorruptible and undefiled, and that fadeth not away, reserved in heaven for you,' &c., 1 Pet. i. 3, 4. As soon as we are newborn, we are begotten to a kingdom and an inheritance. Therefore, assurance that we are God's children will make us thankful for grace present, and that to come, as if we were in heaven already. We begin then the employment of heaven in thanksgiving here, to praise God beforehand with cherubims and angels. Let us, then, be stirred up to give God his due beforehand, to begin heaven upon earth; for we are so much in heaven already, as we abound and are conversant in thanksgiving upon earth.

THE THIRD SERMON.

So will we render the calves of our lips. Asshur shall not save us; we will not ride upon horses: neither will we say any more to the works of our hands, Ye are our gods: for in thee the fatherless findeth mercy.—Hos. XIV. 2, 3.

THE words, as we heard heretofore, contain a most sweet and excellent form of returning unto God, for miserable, lost, and forlorn sinners; wherein so far God discovers his willingness to have his people return unto him, that he dictates unto them a form of prayer, 'Take with you words, and turn to the Lord; say unto him, Take away iniquity.' Wherein we see how detestation of sin must be as general as the desire of pardon, and that none heartily pray to God to 'take away all iniquity' who have not grace truly to hate all iniquity. 'And do good to us,' or do graciously to us; for there is no good to us till sin be removed. Though God be goodness itself, there is no provoking or meriting cause of mercy in us. But he finds cause from his own gracious nature and bowels of mercy to pity his poor people and servants. It is his nature to shew mercy, as the fire to burn, a spring to run, the sun to shine. Therefore, it is easily done. As the prophet speaks, 'Who is a God like unto thee?' Micah vii. 18.

Where we come to speak of the re-stipulation, 'So will we render the calves of our lips.' Where God's favour shines, there will be a reflection. Love is not idle, but a working thing. It must render or die. And what doth it render? Divers sacrifices of the New Testament, which I spake of; that of a broken heart; of Christ offered to the Father, to stand betwixt God's wrath and us; ourselves as a living sacrifice; alms-deeds and praise, which must be with the whole inward powers of the soul.

'Praise is not comely in the mouth of a fool,' saith the wise man, nor of a wicked man. Saith God to such, 'What hast thou to do to take my words in thy mouth, since thou hatest to be reformed, and hast cast my words behind thee?' Ps. l. 16, 17. There are a company who are ordinary swearers and filthy speakers. For them to praise God, James tells them that these contrary streams cannot flow out of a good heart, James iii. 10, 11. Oh, no; God requires not the praise of such fools.

I gave you also some directions how to praise God, and to stir up yourselves to this most excellent duty, which I will not insist on now, but add a little unto that I then delivered, which is, *that we must watch all advantages of praising God from our dispositions.* 'Is any merry? let him sing,' saith James, v. 13. Oh! it is a great point of wisdom to take advantages with the stream of our temper to praise God. When he doth encourage us by his favours and blessings, and enlarge our spirits, then we are in a right temper to bless him. Let us not lose the occasion. This is one branch of redeeming of time, to observe what state and temper of soul we are in, and to take advantage from thence. Is any man in heaviness? he is fit to mourn for sin. Let him take the opportunity of that temper. Is any disposed to cheerfulness? Let him sacrifice that marrow, oil, and sweetness of spirit to God. We see the poor birds in the spring-time, when those little spirits they have are cherished with the sunbeams, how they express it in singing. So when God warms us with his favours, let him have the praise of all.

And here I cannot but take up a lamentation of the horrible ingratitude of men, who are so far from taking advantage by God's blessings to praise him, that they fight like rebels against him with his own favours. Those tongues which he hath given them for his glory, they abuse to pierce him with blasphemy; and those other benefits of his, lent them to honour him with, they turn to his dishonour; like children who importunately ask for divers things, which, when they have, they throw them to the dog. So favours they will have, which, when they have obtained, they give them to the devil; unto whom they sacrifice their strength and cheerfulness, and cannot be merry, unless they be mad and sinful. Are these things to be tolerated in these days of light? How few shall we find, who, in a temper of mirth, turn it the right way?

1. But to add some encouragements to incite us to praise God unto the former, I beseech you let this be one, that *we honour God by it.* It is a

well-pleasing sacrifice to him. If we would study to please him, we cannot do it better than by praising him.

2. And *it is a gainful trading with God*. For in bestowing his seed, where he finds there is improvement in a good soil, with such a sanctified disposition as to bless him upon all occasions, that there comes not a good thought, a good motion in the mind, but we bless God who hath injected such a good thought in our heart; there, I say, God delights to shower down more and more blessings, making us fruitful in every good work to the praise of his name. Sometimes we shall have holy and gracious persons make a law that no good or holy motion shall come into their hearts, which they will not be thankful for. Oh! when God seeth a heart so excellently disposed, how doth it enrich the soul! It is a gainful trade. As we delight to bestow our seed in soils of great increase, which yield sixty and an hundredfold, if possible, so God delights in a disposition inclined to bless him upon all occasions, on whom he multiplies his favours.

3. And then, in itself, *it is a most noble act of religion*, it being a more base thing to be always begging of God; but it argueth a more noble, raised, and elevated spirit, to be disposed to praise God. And it is an argument of less self-love and respect, being therefore more gainful to us. Yea, it is a more noble and royal disposition, fit for spiritual kings and priests thus to sacrifice.

4. Again, indeed, *we have more cause to praise God than to pray;* having many things to praise him for, which we never prayed for. Who ever prayed for his election, care of parents in our infancy, their affection to us, care to breed and train us to years of discretion, besides those many favours daily heaped upon us, above all that we are able to think or speak? Therefore, praise being a more large sacrifice than prayer, we ought to be abundant in it. For those that begin not heaven upon earth, of which this praise is a main function, they shall never come to heaven, after they are taken from the earth; for there is no heavenly action, but it is begun upon earth, especially this main one, of joining with angels, seraphim, and cherubim, in lauding God. Shall they praise him on our behalf, and shall not we for our own? We see the choir of angels, when Christ was born, sang, 'Glory be to God on high, on earth peace, and goodwill towards men,' Luke ii. 14. What was this for? Because Christ the Saviour of the world was born; whereby they shew that we have more benefit by it than they. Therefore, if we would ever join with them in heaven, let us join with them upon earth. For this is one of the great privileges mentioned by the author to the Hebrews, unto which we be come to, 'communion with the spirits of just men made perfect, and to the company of innumerable angels,' Heb. xii. 22, 23. We cannot better shew that we are come to that blessed estate and society spoken of, than by praising God.

5. And lastly, if we be much in praising God, *we shall be much in joy*, which easeth misery. For a man can never be miserable that can be joyful; and a man is always joyful when he is thankful. When one is joyful and cheerful, what misery can lie upon him? Therefore, it is a wondrous help in misery to stir up the heart to this spiritual sacrifice of thanksgiving by all arguments, means, and occasions. Our hearts are temples, and we are priests. We should alway, therefore, have this light and incense burning in our hearts, as the fire did alway burn on the altar in Moses's time, that we may have these spiritual sacrifices to offer continually. Where this is not, the heart of that man or woman is like 'the abomination of desolation,'

Dan. xii. 11, which, when the daily sacrifice was taken away, was set up in the temple. And certainly where there is not praising of God, the heart is 'an abomination of desolation,' having nothing in it save monsters of base lusts and earthly affections.

Ques. But how shall we know that God accepts these sacrifices of praise?

Ans. How did he witness the acceptation of those sacrifices under the old law? 'By fire from heaven,' Judges vi. 21; 1 Kings xviii. 24, *et seq.* This was ordinary with them. So, if we find our hearts warm, cheered and encouraged with joy, peace, and comfort in praising God; this is as it were a witness by fire from heaven that our sacrifices are accepted. Let this now said be effectual to stir you up to this excellent and useful duty of thanksgiving, without multiplying of more arguments, save to put you in mind of this, that as we are exhorted to 'delight ourselves in the Lord,' Ps. xxxvii. 4, one way, among the rest, to do it, is to 'serve him with cheerfulness.' It is an excellent thing to make us delight in God, who loves a cheerful giver and thanksgiver. 'So will we render the calves of our lips.' But to proceed.

After this their solemn covenant and promise of yielding praise to God, that if he would forgive all their sins, and do good to them, then he should have the best they could do to him again: praise here is a promise of new obedience, which hath two branches,

1. *A renunciation of the ill courses they took before.*

'Asshur shall not save us; we will not ride upon horses; neither will we say any more to the works of our hands, Ye are our gods.'

2. Then there is *a positive duty implied* in these words, 'For in thee the fatherless findeth mercy.'

Whereof, the one springs from the other; 'Asshur shall not save us, we will not ride upon horses; neither will we say any more to the works of our hands, Ye are our gods.' Whence comes all these? 'For in thee the fatherless findeth mercy.' Thou shalt be our rock, our trust, our confidence for ever. What will follow upon this? 'Asshur shall not save us any longer; we will not ride upon horses,' &c. For we have pitched and placed our confidence better; on him in whom 'the fatherless findeth mercy.'

'Asshur shall not save us.' The confidence which this people had placed partly in Asshur, their friends and associates, and partly in their own strength at home, now promising repentance, they renounce all such confidence in Asshur, horses and idols. 'Asshur shall not save us,' &c.

First, for this, 'Asshur shall not save us,' that is, the Assyrians, whom they had on the one side, and the Egyptians on the other: it being, as we see in the prophecies of Isaiah and Jeremiah, ordinary with God's people, in any distress, to have recourse to the Assyrians, or Egyptians, as if God had not been sufficient to be their rock and their shield. We see how often the Lord complains of this manner of dealing. 'Woe unto them that go down into Egypt for help, and stay on horses, and trust in chariots, because they are many,' &c., Isa. xxx. 2, and xxxi. 1. The prophets, and so this prophet, are very full of such complaints: it being one of the chief arguments he presseth, their falseness in this, that in any fear or peril, they ran to the shelter of other nations, especially these two, Egypt and Assyria, as you have it, 'Ephraim feedeth on wind, and followeth after the east wind; he daily increaseth lies and desolation, and they do make a covenant with the Assyrians, and oil is carried into Egypt,' Hosea xii. 1, that is, balm, who had this privilege above all other nations, to abound in precious balms; which balm and oil they carried into Egypt, to win their favour against the Assyrians. Sometimes they relied on the one, and sometimes on the other, the story and causes whereof were too tedious to relate. Wherefore I come to the useful points arising hence. 'Asshur shall not save us.'

1. That man, naturally, is prone to put confidence in the creature.

2. That the creature is insufficient and unable to yield us this prop to uphold our confidence.

3. That God's people, when they are endowed with light supernatural to discern and be convinced hereof, are of that mind to say, 'Asshur shall not save us.'

But, to make way to these things, we must first observe two things for a preparative.

Doct. First, That reformation of life must be joined with prayer and praise. There was prayer before, and a promise of praise; but, as here, there must be joined reformation of their sin. That it must be so, it appears, first, for *prayer*. It is said, 'If I regard iniquity in my heart, the Lord will not hear my prayer,' Ps. lxvi. 18. And for *praise*, 'The very sacrifice of the wicked (who reforms not his ways) is abominable,' Prov. xv. 8. So that, without reformation, prayer and praise is to no purpose. Therefore it is brought here after a promise of praise. Lord, as we mean to praise thee, so we intend a thorough reformation of former sins, whereof we were guilty. We will renounce Asshur, and confidence in horses, idols, and the like. Therefore let us, when we come to God with prayer and praise, think also of reforming what is amiss. Out with Achan, Josh. vii. 19. If there be any dead fly, Eccles. x. 1, or Achan uncast out, prayer and praise is in vain. 'Will you steal, lie, commit adultery, swear falsely, and come and stand before me,' saith the Lord, by the prophet Jeremiah, Jer. vii. 9. Will you offer to pray to me, and praise me, living in these and these sins? No; God will abhor both that prayer and praise, where there is no reformation. 'What hast thou to do to take my name in thy mouth, since thou hatest to be reformed, and hast cast my words behind thee, saith God,' Ps. l. 16, where he pleads with the hypocrite for this audacious boldness in severing things conjoined by God. Therefore, as we would not have our prayers turned back from heaven, which should bring a blessing upon all other things else: as we would not have our sacrifices abominable to God, labour to reform what is amiss, amend all, or else never think our lip-labour will prove anything but a lost labour without this reformation.

A *second* thing, which I observe in general, before I come to the particulars, is,

Doct. That true repentance is, of the particular sin which we are most addicted to, and most guilty of.

The particular sin of this people, whom God so instructs here, was their confidence in Assyria, horses, and idols. Now therefore repenting, they repent of the particular, main sins they were most guilty of; which being stricken down, all the lesser will be easy to conquer. As when Goliath himself was stricken down, all the host of the Philistines ran away, 1 Sam. xvii. 51. So when Goliath shall be slain in us, the reigning, ruling, domineering sin, the rest will easily be conquered.

Use. Therefore let us make an use of *examination* and trial of our repentance. If it be sound, it draws with it a reformation; as in general, so especially of our particular sins. As those confess and say, 'Above all other things we have sinned in this, in asking a king,' 1 Sam. xii. 8. We were naught, and had offended God many ways before; but herein we have been exceeding sinful, in seeking another governor, being weary of God's gracious government over us. So a gracious heart will say, I have been a wretch in all other things, but in this and that sin above all other. Thus it was with the woman of Samaria, when she was put in mind by Christ of her particular grand sin, that she had been a light woman, and had had many husbands, he whom she lived with now not being her husband, John iv. 18. This discovery, when Christ touched the galled part, did so work upon her conscience that it occasioned a general repentance of all her other sins whatsoever. And, indeed, sound repentance of one main sin will draw with it all the rest. And, for the most part, when God brings any man home to him, he so carries our repentance, that, discovering unto us our sinfulness, he especially shews us our Delilah, Isaac, Herodias, our particular sin; which being cast out, we prevail easily against the rest. As the charge was given by the king of Aram against Ahab, 'Fight neither against great nor small, but only against the king of Israel,' 2 Chron. xviii. 30; kill him, and then there will be an end of the battle. So let us not stand striking at this and that sin (which we are not so much tempted to), if we will indeed prove our repentance to be sound; but at that main sin which by nature, calling, or custom we are most prone unto. Repentance for this causes repentance for all the rest; as here the church saith, 'Asshur shall not save us; we will not ride upon horses,' &c.

It is a grand imposture, which carries many to hell; they will cherish themselves in some gross main sin, which pleases corrupt nature, and is advantageous to them; and by way of compensation with God, they will do many other things well, but leave a dead fly to mar all; whereas they should begin here especially. Thus much in general, which things premised, I come to the forenamed particulars. First,

Doct. That naturally we are apt and prone to confidence in outward helps and present things.

This came to our nature from the first fall. What was our fall at first? A turning from the all-sufficient, unchangeable God, to the creature. If I should describe sin, it is nothing but a turning from God to one creature or other. When we find not contentment and sufficiency in one creature, we run to another. As the bird flies from one tree and bough to another, so we seek variety of contentments from one thing to another. Such is the pravity of our nature since the fall. This is a fundamental conclusion. Man naturally will, and must, have somewhat to rely on. The soul must have a bottom, a foundation to rest on, either such as the world affords, or a better. Weak things must have their supports. As we see, the vine being a weak thing, is commonly supported by the elm, or the like supply. So is it with the soul since the fall. Because it is weak, and cannot uphold nor satisfy itself with itself, therefore it looks out of itself. Look to God it cannot, till it be in the state of grace; for being his enemy, it loves not to look to him or his ways, or have dealing with him. Therefore it looks unto the creature, that next hand unto itself. This being naturally since the fall, that what we had in God before when we stood, we now labour to have in the creature.

Reason 1. Because, as was said, having lost communion with God, somewhat we must have to stay the soul.

2. *Secondly*, Because Satan joins with our sense and fancy, by which we are naturally prone to live, esteeming of things not by faith and by deeper

grounds, but by fancy. Now, fancy having communion with sense, what it discovers and presents for good and great, fancy makes it greater. And the devil, above all, having communion with that faculty of fancy, and so a spirit of error being mixed therewith, to make our fancy think the riches of the world to be the only riches; the greatness and goodness of the creature to be the only greatness and goodness; and the strength thereof the only strength. This spirit of error joining with our own spirits, and with the deceit of our natures, makes us set a higher value on the creature, enlargeth and enrageth the fancy, making it spiritually drunk, so as to conceive amiss of things.

Use. Briefly for use hereof, it being but a directing point to others. Let us take notice of our corruption herein, and be humbled for it; taking in good part those afflictions and crosses which God sends us, to convince and let us see that there is no such thing in the creature as we imagined; because naturally, we are desperately given to think that there is somewhat more therein than there is. Now affliction helps this sickness of fancy, embittering unto us all confidence in the creature. Therefore it is a happy and a blessed thing to be crossed in that which we over-value, as these Israelites here did the Assyrians and the Egyptians: for being enemies, they trusted in a 'broken reed,' 2 Kings xviii. 21, as we shall see further in the second point.

Doct. How these outward things cannot help us.

How prone soever we are to rely upon them, they are in effect nothing. They cannot help us, and so are not to be relied upon. 'Asshur shall not save us.' Indeed it will not, it cannot. These things cannot aid us at our most need. So that that which we most pitch upon, fails us when we should especially have help. Some present vanishing supply they yield, but little to purpose. They have not that in them which should support the soul at a strait, or great pinch, as we say.

Reason. The reason is largely given by Solomon in the whole book of Ecclesiastes, 'All is vanity and vexation of spirit,' Eccles. i. 14. There is a vanity in all the creatures, being empty and not able to support the soul. They are vain in their continuance, and empty in regard of their strength. They are gone when we have need of them. Riches, as the wise man saith, are gone, and have wings to fly away, in our most need, Prov. xxiii. 5. So friends are fugitive good things, being like to the brooks mentioned in Job, vi. 15: which when in summer there is need of, then they are dried up, and yet run amain in winter, when there is no need of them. So, earthly supports, when there is no need of them, then they are at hand; but when we have most need of them, are gone. 'They are broken cisterns,' as the prophet calls them, Jer. ii. 13. Cisterns, that is, they have a limited capacity. A cistern is not a spring. So all their support, at the best, is but a bounded and a mixed sufficiency; and that also which will quickly fail: like water in a cistern, which if it be not fed with a continual spring, fails or putrefies presently. Likewise these outward things are not sufficient for the grievance; for being limited and bounded, the grievance will be above the strength of the creature; which though sometime it be present and do not fail, yet the trouble is such, that it is above the strength of the creature to help. So that for these and the like respects, there is no sufficiency, nor help to be expected from the creature. 'Asshur shall not save us.' He is not a sufficient ground of trust. Why?

1. He is but a creature.
2. He is an enemy.

3. He is an idolater.

So that, take him in all these three relations, he is not to be trusted.

1. *He is a creature.* What is a creature? Nothing, as it were. Saith the prophet, 'All creatures before him are as nothing, and as a very little thing.' And what it is, when he pleaseth, he can dissolve it into nothing, turn it into dust. Man's breath is in his nostrils, Isa. ii. 22. 'All flesh is grass, and all his glory as the flower of grass,' Ps. ciii. 15. If a man trust the creature, he may outlive his trust. His prop may be taken from him, and down he falls. Asshur must not be trusted, therefore, as a creature, nor as a man, for that brings us within the curse. Thus saith the Lord, 'Cursed be the man that trusteth in man, and maketh flesh his arm,' &c., Jer. xvii. 5. So trusting in the creature not only deceives us, but brings us within the curse. In that respect, Asshur must not be trusted.

2. But Asshur likewise was an *enemy*, and a secret enemy. For howsoever the ten tribes unto whom Hosea prophesied were great idolaters, yet they were somewhat better than Asshur, who was without the pale of the church, and a wholly corrupted church. Therefore, they were enemies to the ten tribes, and, amongst other reasons, because they were not so bad as they, nor deeply enough dyed with idolatry.

Many think they may comply with popery in some few things, to gain their love, and that there may be joining with them in this and that; but do we think that they will ever trust us for all this? No; they will alway hate us, till we be as bad as they, and then they will despise us, and secure themselves of us. Therefore, there is no trusting of papists, as papists; not only creatures, but as false, and as enemies. For this is the nature of wicked men. They will never trust better than themselves, till they become as bad as they are, after which they despise them. Say they, Now we may trust such and such a one; he is as bad as we, becom'd* one of us. Which is the reason why some of a naughty dispositson take away the chastity and virginity of men's consciences, making them take this and that evil course, and then they think they have such safe, being as bad as themselves. Wherein they deal as Ahithophel's politic, devilish counsel was, that Absalom should do that which was naught, and then he should be sure that David and he should never agree after that, 2 Sam. xvi. 21; and that then by this discovery the wicked Jews, set on mischief, might secure themselves of Absalom. So they, now that they join with us, God will forsake them; we shall have them our instruments for anything. First, they would have the ten tribes as bad as they, and then give them the slip whensoever they trusted them.

3. Again, neither were they to be trusted *as idolaters*, to have league and society with them. There may be some commerce and traffic with them, but amity and trust, none. Asshur and Egypt were horrible idolaters, and therefore not to be trusted in that respect. As we see the prophet in this case reproved good Jehoshaphat, when he had joined with wicked Ahab, king of the ten tribes, 'Shouldst thou help the ungodly, and love them that hate the Lord? therefore wrath is upon thee from before the Lord,' 2 Chron. xix. 2. So we see it is a dangerous thing to be in league with idolaters, even such as the ten tribes were, who had some religion amongst them. This good king was chidden for it.

'We will not ride upon horses.'

What kind of creature a horse is, it is worth the seeing. What a description God gives of him, that we may see what reason the Spirit of God hath

* That is, 'become.'—G.

to instance in the horse. Saith God to Job, 'Hast thou given the horse strength? hast thou clothed his neck with thunder? canst thou make him afraid as a grasshopper? the glory of his nostrils is terrible. He paweth in the valley, and rejoiceth in his strength: he goeth on to meet the armed men. He mocketh at fear, and is not affrighted; neither turneth he back from the sword. The quiver rattleth against him, the glittering spear and the shield. He swalloweth the ground with fierceness and rage: neither believeth he that it is the sound of the trumpet. He saith among the trumpets, Ha, ha; and he smelleth the battle afar off, the thunder of the captains, and the shouting,' Job xxxix. 19–21. A notable and excellent description of this warlike creature. And yet for all this excellency, so described by the Spirit of God, in another place the psalmist saith, 'A horse is a vain thing for safety, neither shall he deliver any by his great strength,' Ps. xxxiii. 17. 'Some trust in chariots, and some in horses; but we will remember the name of the Lord our God,' Ps. xx. 7. So in another place, 'The horse is prepared against the day of battle, but victory is of the Lord,' Prov. xxi. 31.

How oft have you in the Psalms that proud warlike creature disparaged, because naturally men are more bewitched with that than with any other creature. If they have store of horses, then they think they are strong. Therefore God forbids the king 'to multiply horses to himself, nor cause the people to return to Egypt, to the end he should multiply horses,' &c., Deut. xvii. 16, because God is the strength of his church, when there is no multitude of horses. You see it is a bewitching creature, and yet a vain help. A place like this we have, Isa. ii. 7, complaining there of the naughty people which were among the Jews, at that time as bad as the Israelites. Saith he, 'Their land also is full of silver and gold; neither is there any end of their treasures; their land is also full of horses, neither is there any end of their chariots.' What, is there a fault in that? No. Luther saith, 'Good works are good, but the confidence in them is damnable.' So gold and silver, horses and chariots, are good creatures of God. But this was their sin, confidence in these things. 'There is no end of their treasures.' If they had treasure enough, they should do well enough. 'Their land also was full of horses.' Was this a fault? No; but their confidence in them. They thought they were a wise people to have such furniture and provision of munition for war. But God was their king, and the chief governor of his people; and for them to heap up these things, to trust over-much in them, it was a matter of complaint. 'Their land also is full of idols.'

Thus you see there is no confidence to be put neither in the one nor the other, neither in the association of foreign friends, who will prove deceitful, 'reeds of Egypt,' that not only deceive, but the splinters thereof fly about, and may run up into the hand. Such are idolaters and false friends, deceitful and hurtful. Nor in home. There is no trust in horses, munition, or such like. What doth this imply? That to war and have provision in that kind is unlawful and unnecessary, because he finds fault here with horses and the like? No; take heed of that; for John Baptist, if the soldier's profession had been unlawful, he would have bid them cast away their weapons; but he bids them 'do violence to no man, neither accuse any falsely,' &c., Luke iii. 14. And God would never style himself 'the Lord of hosts, and a man of war,' Isa. xlii. 13, and 'he that teacheth our hands to war, and our fingers to fight,' Ps. xviii. 34, unless it were good in the season. Therefore war is lawful, seeing in the way to heaven we live in the midst of enemies.

Therefore it is but an anabaptistical fancy to judge war to be unlawful. No, no; it is clean another thing which the Holy Ghost aims at: to beat back carnal confidence. For it is an equal fault to multiply help and to neglect them. Either of both are fatal many times: to multiply horses, trusting in them, or to spoil horses and other helps vainly, so to weaken a kingdom. Therefore there is a middle way for all outward things, a fit care to serve God's providence, and when we have done, trust in God without tempting of him; for to neglect these helps is to tempt him, and to trust in them, when we have them, is to commit idolatry with them. Beware of both these extremes, for God will have his providence served in the use of lawful means. When there is this great care in a Christian commonwealth, there is a promise of good success, because God is with us. Otherwise, what is all, if he be our enemy? So we see the second point made good, *that these outward things of themselves cannot help*. Therefore comes this in the third place:—

Obs. That when God alters and changes and mouldeth anew the heart of a man to repentance, he altereth his confidence in the creature.

A Christian State will not trust in Asshur, nor in horses. It is true both of State and persons. The reason will follow after in the end of the verse, 'For in thee the fatherless findeth mercy.' Because, when a man hath once repented, there is a closing between God and him, and he seeth an all-sufficiency in God to satisfy all his desires. Therefore he will use all other things as helps, and as far as it may stand with his favour. For he hath Moses's eye put in him, a new eye to see him that is invisible, Heb. xi. 27, to see God in his greatness, and other things in their right estimate as vain things. What is repentance but a change of the mind, when a man comes to be wise and judicious, as indeed repentant men are the only wise men? Then a man hath an esteem of God to be *El-shadai*, all-sufficient, and all other things to be as they are, uncertain; that is, they are so today, as that they may be otherwise to-morrow, for that is the nature of the creatures. They are *in potentia*, in a possibility to be other things than they are. God is alway 'I AM,' alway the same. There is not so much as a shadow of changing in him. Wherefore, when the soul hath attained unto this spiritual eyesight and wisdom, if it be a sinful association with Egypt or Asshur, with this idolater or that, he will not meddle; and as for other helps, he will not use them further than as subordinate means. When a man is converted, he hath not a double, not a divided heart, to trust partly to God and partly to the creature. If God fail him,* he hath Asshur and horses enough, and association with all round about. But a Christian he will use all helps, as they may stand with the favour of God, and are subordinate under him. Now for trial.

Quest. How shall we know whether we exceed in this confidence in the creature or not?

Sol. 1. We may know it by *adventuring on ill courses and causes*, thinking to bear them out with Asshur and with horses. But all the mercenary soldiers in the world, and all the horses at home and abroad, what can they do when God is angry? Now, when there is such confidence in these things as for to out-dare God, then there is too much trust in them. That trust will end in confusion, if it be not repented of, for that lifts up the heart in the creature. And as the heathen man observes, 'God delights

* That is, the 'double-minded' man.—G.

to make great little, and little great.' It is his daily work to 'cast down mountains, and exalt the valleys,' Isa. xl. 4. Those that are great, and boast in their greatness, as if they would command heaven and earth, God delights to make their greatness little, and at length nothing, and to raise up the day of small things. Therefore the apostle saith, 'If I rejoice, it shall be in my infirmities,' 2 Cor. xii. 9, in nothing else; for God delights to shew strength in weakness.

2. *By security and resting of the soul in meaner things*, never seeking to divine and religious helps when we are supplied with those that are outward. For these people, when they trusted to Assyria and Egypt, those false supports and sandy foundations, they were careless of God, and therefore must trust in somewhat else. Wherefore, if we see a man secure and careless, certainly he trusts too much to uncertain riches, to Asshur, to Egypt, to friends, or to outward helps. His security bewrays that. If a man trust God in the use of the means, his care will be to keep God his friend by repentance and daily exercises of religion, by making conscience of his duty. But if he trust the means and not God, he will be careless and weak in good duties, dull and slow, and, out of the atheism of his heart, cry, Tush! if God do not help me, I shall have help from friends abroad, and be supported with this and that at home, horses and the like, and shall be well.

Use 1. Let us therefore enter into our own souls, and examine ourselves, how far forth we are guilty of this sin, and think we come so far short of repentance. For the ten tribes here, the people of God, when they repented, say, 'Asshur shall not save us; we will not ride upon horses.' He speaks comparatively, as trusted in. Therefore, let us take heed of that boasting, vain-glorious disposition, arising from the supply of the creature. Saith God, 'Let not the wise man glory in his wisdom; neither let the mighty man glory in his might: let not the rich man glory in his riches; but let him that glorieth glory in this, that he understandeth and knoweth this, that I am the Lord, which exercise lovingkindness, judgment, and righteousness in the earth,' &c., Jer. ix. 23, 24. Let a man glory that he knows God in Christ to be his God in the covenant of grace; that he hath the God of all strength, the King of kings and Lord of lords to be his: who hath all other things at his command, who is independent and all-sufficient. If a man will boast, let him go out of himself to God, and plant himself there; and for other things, take heed the heart be not lift up with them.

1. Consider what kind of thing boasting is. It is idolatry, for it sets the creature in the place and room of God.

2. And it is also spiritual adultery, whereby we fix our affections upon the creature, which should be placed on God; as it is in James, 'Ye adulterers and adulteresses, know ye not that the friendship of the world is enmity with God?' &c., James iv. 4.

3. Habakkuk calls it drunkennness, Hab. ii. 4, 5, for it makes the soul drunk with sottishness and conceitedness, so as a man in this case is never sober, until God strip him of all.

4. And then again, it puts forth the eye of the soul. It is a kind of white, that mars the sight. When a man looks to Asshur, horses, and to outward strength, where is God all this while? These are so many clouds, that they cannot see God, but altogether pore upon the creature. He sees so much greatness there, that God seems nothing. But when a man sees God in his greatness and almightiness, then the creature is

nothing, Job xlii. 6. But until this be, there is a mist and blindness in the eye of the soul.

And when we have seen our guiltiness this way (as who of us in this case may not be confounded and ashamed of relying too much on outward helps ?), then let us labour to take off our souls from these outward things, whether it be strength abroad or at home. Which that we may do, we must labour for that obedience which our Saviour Christ exhorts us unto in self-denial, Mat. xvi. 24, not to trust to our own devices, policy, or strength, wit, will, or conceits, that this or that may help us, nor anything. Make it general ; for when conversion is wrought, and the heart is turned to God, it turns from the creature, only using it as subordinate to God. We see, usually, men that exalt themselves in confidence, either of strength, of wit, or whatsoever, they are successless in their issue. For God delights to confound them, and go beyond their wit, as we have it, Isa. xxx. 3. They thought to go beyond God with their policy, they would have help out of Egypt, this and that way. Oh, saith the prophet, but for all this, God is wise to see through all your devices ; secretly hereby touching them to the quick, as sottish persons, who thought by their shallow brains to go beyond God. You think religious courses, and the obedience God prescribeth to you, to be idle, needless courses ; but, notwithstanding, God is wise. He will go beyond you, and catch you in your own craft. 'Therefore, the strength of Pharaoh shall be your shame, and the trust in the shadow of Egypt your confusion,' Isa. xxx. 3. Thus God loves to scatter Babels fabrics, Gen. xi. 8, and holds that are erected in confidence of human strength against him. He delights to catch the wise in their own craft, to beat all down, lay all high imaginations and things flat before him, that no flesh may glory in his sight. There is to this purpose a notable place in Isaiah : 'Behold, all ye that kindle a fire, that compass yourselves about with sparks,' Isa. l. 11. For they kindled a fire, and had a light of their own, and would not borrow light from God : 'Walk in the light of your fire, and in the sparks that ye have kindled.' But what is the conclusion of all ? 'This shall ye have of mine hand.' I dare assure you of this, saith the prophet. 'You shall lie down in sorrow.' Those that walk by the light and spark of their own fire, this they shall have at God's hands : 'they shall lie down in sorrow.'

Let us therefore take heed of carnal confidence. You have a number who love to sleep in a whole skin, and will be sure to take the safest courses, as they think, not consulting with God, but with 'flesh and blood.' It might be instanced in stories of former times, how God hath crossed emperors, and great men in this kind, were it not too tedious. But for present instance, you have many who will be of no settled religion. Oh, they cannot tell, there may be a change. Therefore they will be sure to offend neither part. This is their policy, and if they be in place, they will reform nothing. Oh, I shall lay myself open to advantages, and stir up enemies against me. And so they will not trust God, but have carnal devices to turn off all duty whatsoever. It is an ordinary speech, but very true, policy overthrows policy. It is true of carnal policy. When a man goes by carnal rules to be governed by God's enemy and his own, with his own wit and understanding, which leads him to outward things, this kind of policy overthrows all policy, and outward government at length. Those that walk religiously and by rule, they walk most confidently and securely, as the issue will shew. Therefore, consider that, set God aside, all is but vanity. And that,

First, In regard they do not yield that which we expect they should yield. There is a falsehood in the things. They promise this and that in shows, but when we possess them, they yield it not. As they have no strength indeed, so they deceive.

2. Then, also, there is a mutability in them; for there is nothing in the world but changes. There is a vanity of corruption in them. All things at last come to an end, save God, who is unchangeable.

3. Then again, besides the intrinsical vanity in all outward things, and whatsoever carnal reason leads unto, they are snares and baits unto us, to draw us away from God, by reason of the vanity of our nature, vainer than the things themselves. Therefore take heed of confidence in anything, or else this will be the issue: we shall be worse than the things we trust. 'Vanity of vanities, all things are vanity,' Eccles. i. 1; and man himself is lighter than vanity, saith the psalmist, Ps. lxii. 9. He that trusts to vanity, is worse than vanity. A man cannot stand on a thing that cannot stand itself,—*stare non stante*. A man cannot stand on a thing that is mutable and changeable. If he doth, he is vain with the thing. Even as a picture drawn upon ice, as the ice dissolves, so the picture vanisheth away. So it is with all confidence in the creature whatsoever. It is like a picture upon ice, which vanisheth with the things themselves. He that stands upon a slippery thing, slips with the thing he stands on. If there were no word of God against it, yet thus much may be sufficient out of the principles of reason, to shew the folly of trusting to Asshur, and horses, and the like.

Let this be the end of all, then, touching this carnal confidence: to beware that we do not fasten our affections too much upon any earthly thing, at home or abroad, within or without ourselves. For 'God will destroy the wisdom of the wise,' 1 Cor. i. 19. Let us take heed, therefore, of all false confidence whatsoever. Let us use all outward helps, yet so as to rely upon God for his blessing in the use of all. And when they all fail, be of Jehoshaphat's mind: 'Lord, we know not what to do,' 2 Chron. xx. 12. The creature fails us, our helps fail us; 'but our eyes are upon thee.' So when all outward Asshurs, and horses, and helps fail, despair not; for the less help there is in the creature, the more there is in God. As Gideon with his army, when he thought to carry it away with multitudes, God told him there were too many of them to get the victory by, lest Israel should vaunt themselves of their number, and so lessened the army to three hundred, Jud. vii. 2; so it is not the means, but the blessing on the means which helps us. If we be never so low, despair not. Let us make God ours, who is all-sufficient and almighty, and then if we were brought a hundred times lower than we are, God will help and raise us. Those who labour not to have God, the Lord of hosts, to go out with their armies, if they had all the Asshurs and horses in the world, all were in vain. It was therefore a good resolution of Moses. Saith he to God, 'If thy presence go not with us, carry us not hence,' Exod. xxxiii. 15. He would not go one step forward without God. So, if we cannot make God our friend to go out before us, in vain it is to go one step forward. Let us therefore double our care in holy duties, renewing our covenant with God, before the decree come out against us. The more religious, the more secure we shall be. If we had all the creatures in the world to help us, what are they but vanity and nothing, if God be our enemy! These things we know well enough for notion; but let us labour to bring them home for use, in these dangerous times abroad. Let us begin where we should, that our work may be especially in heaven. Let us reform our lives, being moderately careful, as Christians should, without tempting God's providence, using rightly all civil supports and helps seasonably, and to the best advantage; for, as was said, the carelessness herein for defence may prove as dangerous and fatal to a State, as the too much confidence and trust in them.

THE FOURTH SERMON.

Asshur shall not save us; we will not ride upon horses; neither will we say any more to the works of our hands, Ye are our gods: for in thee the fatherless findeth mercy.—Hos. xiv. 3.

We shewed you heretofore at large, how the Spirit of God, by the prophet, doth here dictate a form of turning unto these Israelites, 'Take unto you words;' and then teacheth them what they should return back again, thanks. 'So will we render the calves of our lips.' Wherein they shew two things. 1. They that have no great matters to render, oxen or sheep, &c. 2. They shew what is most pleasing unto God, the calves of our lips; that is, thanksgiving from a broken heart, which, as the Psalmist speaks, pleaseth God better than 'a bullock that hath horns and hoofs,' Ps. lxix. 31. But this is not enough. The Holy Ghost therefore doth prescribe them, together with prayer and thanksgiving, reformation. 'Asshur shall not save us; we will not ride upon horses; neither will we say any more to the works of our hands, Ye are our gods: for in thee the fatherless findeth mercy.' So that here you have reformation joined with prayer and praise. Whence we observed divers things: that without reformation our prayers are abominable; that in repentance there must be reformation of our special sin; which here they do. Take this one thing more in the third place, which shall be added to the former.

Obs. In reformation, we must go not only to the outward delinquencies, but to the spring of them, which is some breach of the first table.

The root of all sin, is the deficiency of obedience to some command of the first table. When confidence is not pitched aright in God, or when it is misapplied, and misfastened to the creature: when the soul sets up somewhat for a stay and prop unto it, which it should not do, this is a spiritual and subtle sin, and must be repented of, as here, 'Asshur shall not save us,' &c. It were good therefore for all those who seriously intend the work of repentance, to take this course. If the gross fault be of the second table, take occasion of sorrow and mourning thence. But when you have begun there, resolve and bring all to the breeding sin of all, which is the fastening of the soul falsely, when it is not well fastened and bottomed in the root. And therefore it was well done by Luther, who, in a Catechism of his, brings in the first commandment into all the commandments of the first and second table, 'Thou shalt have no other gods but me.' Therefore thou shalt sanctify the Sabbath, honour thy father and mother, shalt not take my name in vain, shalt not commit adultery, shalt not steal, &c., (*b*). Because he that hath no God but that God in his heart, will be sure to sanctify the Sabbath, honour his father and mother, not commit adultery, nor steal. And whence come all the breaches of the second table? Hence, that there is not the true fear and love of God in our hearts; and it is just with God, for their spiritual sins, to give them up to carnal and gross sins. Therefore, though the Israelites here had many gross sins to repent of, yet they go to the spring-head, the breeding sin of all, false confidence. This is to deal thoroughly, to go to the core. 'Asshur shall not save us; we will not ride upon horses.' From whence, in the third place, may descend to the next branch of their sin, idolatry.

'Neither will we say any more to the works of our hands, Ye are our gods.'

All false confidence hath two objects: for it is always either,

1. Out of religion; or,
2. In religion.

For the first, all ill confidence and trust, if it be out of religion, it is in the creature; either,

1. Out of us; or,
2. In ourselves.

Secondly, if it be in religion, it is in a false god, as here, 'Neither will we say any more to the works of our hands, Ye are our gods.' Observe hence in the first place.

Obs. Man naturally is prone to idolatry.

The story of the Bible, and of all ages, sheweth how prone men are to idolatry and will-worship, and what miseries ensued thereupon. Amongst other instances, we see how presently after that breach in the kingdom of David and Solomon, by Jeroboam's setting up of two calves, how suddenly they fell to idolatry, 1 Kings xiii. 33, *seq.;* 2 Chron. xiii. 8. So that after that, there was not one good king amongst them all, until the nation was destroyed. And so in the story of their antiquities, see how prone they were to idolatry in the wilderness. Moses doth but go up to the mount, and they fall to idolatry, cause Aaron to make a calf, and dance round about it, Exod. xxxii. 4, *seq.*; Ps. cvi. 19. The thing is so palpable, that it need not be stood upon, that man's nature is prone to idolatry which will not raise itself up to God, but fetch God to itself, and conceive of him according to its false imaginations.

Now idolatry is two ways committed, in the false, hollow, and deceitful heart of man: either,

1. By attributing to the creature that which is proper to God only, investing it with God's properties; or,
2. By worshipping the true God in a false manner.

1. So that, in the *first* place, idolatry *is to invest the creature with God's properties.* Go to the highest creature, Christ's human nature. We have some bitter spirits (Lutherans they call them) Protestants, who attribute to the human nature of Christ, that which only is proper to God, to be every where, and therefore to be in the sacrament, (*c*). You have some come near them, both in their opinion and in their bitterness. They will have a *nescio quomodo.* Christ is there though they know not how. But this is to make Christ's human nature a god, to make an idol of it. So prayers to saints and angels, this makes idols of them, because it invests them with properties to know our hearts, which he must know unto whom we pray. And then, it gives unto them that which is proper to God, worship and prayer. But, we must call upon none but whom we must believe in, and we must believe in none but God. Therefore, worshipping of saints or angels is idolatry.

Secondly, idolatry *is to worship the true God in a false manner;* to fix his presence to that we should not fix it to; to annex it to statues, images, crucifixes, the picture of the Virgin Mary and the like. Not to run into the common place of idolatry, but to come home unto ourselves.

Quest. Whether are the papists idolaters or not, like unto these Israelites, who say (being converted), 'Neither will we say unto the works of our hands, Ye are our gods ?'

Ans. I answer, Yes ; as gross as ever the heathens were, and worse. The very Egyptians, they worshipped none for gods but those who were alive ; as a papist himself saith (though he were an honest papist), the Egyptians worshipped living creatures, but we are worse than they ; for we worship stocks and stones, and a piece of bread in the sacrament. And to this purpose, one of their Jesuits confesseth this, and yielded the question for granted, that if there be not a transubstantiation of the bread turned into the body and blood of Christ, we are worse idolaters than these and these nations ; because we worship a piece of bread, which is a dead thing. But we assume (according to the Scriptures, the judgment of the church, and of the truth itself), the bread is not transubstantiated, at least it is a doubtful matter, for if it be not the intention of the priest, it is not. See here upon what hazard they put the souls of people !

Obj. But they have many shifts for themselves ; as, among the rest, this is one, that *they do not worship the image, but God or Christ before the image.*

Ans. To which the answer is, that the fathers who wrote against the heathens meet with this pretence. The Pagans had this excuse. We worship not this statue of Jupiter, but Jupiter himself. Thus they have no allegation for themselves, but the heathen had the same, which the ancient Fathers confuted. They are guilty of idolatry in both the forenamed kinds. For, first, they worship things that they should not, as appears by their invocation of saints, vows to them ; their temples, altars, and the like, full of their images, giving them honour due unto God. And then, they worship the true God in a false manner before their images. There is no kind of idolatry but they are grossly guilty of it. Whereof let this be the use.

Use 1. *First* of all, of *thankfulness*, that God hath brought us into Goshen, into a kingdom of light ; that we are born in a time and place of knowledge of the true God, wherein is the true worship of the true God. It is a matter that we cannot be too thankful to God for.

Quest. How shall we shew ourselves thankful ?

Ans. In keeping fast the true worship of God we have, and keeping out idolatry ; in reviving laws in that kind, if not making new. What if there were liberty given for men to go about the country to poison people ! Would we endure such persons, and not lay hold of them ? So in that we are freed from Jesuits who go about to poison the souls of God's people, let us shew our thankfulness for this, and shun idolatry of all sorts whatsoever.

Use 2. *Secondly*, See from hence that there can be *no toleration of that religion*, no more, as was said, than to suffer and tolerate poisoners. As they said of coloquintida in their pottage, 2 Kings iv. 40, so 'there is death in the pot' of Romish religion. Therefore it were good to compel them to come in and serve the Lord their God. As it is said, good Josiah compelled those in his time to serve the Lord, 2 Chron, xxxiv. 33, so it were good such courses were taken to reform and reclaim them. As Saint Augustine said of himself in his time, being a Donatist, he altered his judgment by force. In which case it would be with them as with children, who, when they are young, must be forced to school, but afterwards they thank them who forced them. So it is in religion, though it cannot be forced, yet such might afterwards bless God for them who brought them to the means; who, instead of their blindness, trained them up in more knowledge, by forcing them to use the means for which, when God should open their eyes, they might bless God another day. But this point of gross idolatry, so largely handled in books, is only touched by the way, that we may hate idolatry the more; which could not be left out, the words leading to say somewhat of it, seeing how these converts here hate it, and out of that hatred make this profession, 'Neither will we say any more to the works of our hands, Ye are our gods,' &c.

But this is not all; we must know that there be other idols than the idols which we make with our hands. Besides these religious idols, there be secular idols in the world, such as men set up to themselves in their own hearts. Whatsoever takes up the heart most, which they attribute more to than to God, that is their idol, their god. A man's love, a man's fear, is his god. If a man fear greatness rather than God, that he had rather displease God than any great person, they are his idols for the time. 'The fear of a man brings a snare,' Prov. xxix. 25, saith the wise man. And those who get the favour of any in place, sacrifice therefore their credit, profession, religion, and souls, it is gross idolatry; dangerous to the party, and dangerous to themselves. It was the ruin of Herod to have that applause given to him, and taken by him, 'The voice of God, and not of man,' Acts xii. 22. So for any to be blown up with flatterers, that lift them up above their due measure, it is an exceeding wrong to them, prejudiceth their comfort, and will prove ill in the conclusion; indeed, treason against their souls.

So there is a baser sort of idolaters, who sacrifice their credit and state, whatsoever is good within them, their whole powers, to their base and filthy pleasures. Thus man is degenerate since his fall, that he makes that his god which is meaner than himself. Man, that was ordained for everlasting happiness and communion with God, is now brought to place his happiness and contentment in base pleasures. Whereas it is with the soul of man for good or ill, as it applies itself to that which is greater or meaner than itself. If it apply itself to confidence and affiance in God, then it is better. For it is the happiness of the soul to have communion with the Spring of goodness, as David speaks, 'It is good for me to draw near to God,' &c., Ps. lxxiii. 28. When we suffer the soul to cleave in affiance to earthly things, it grows in some measure to the nature of the things adhered to. When we love the world and earthly things, we are earthly. Till the Spirit of God touch the soul, as the loadstone doth the heavy iron, drawing it up, as it were, it will cleave to the creature, to baser things than itself, and so makes the creature an idol, which is the common idolatry of these times. Some make favour, as the ambitious person; some their pleasures, as baser persons of meaner condition; and some riches. Every man as their temper and as their temptations are.

Now, it is not enough to be sound in religion one way in the main; but we must be sound every way, without any touch of idolatry. In a special manner the apostle calls the 'covetous man an idolater,' Eph. v. 5, because he makes riches his castle, thinking to carry anything with his wealth. But his riches oftentimes prove his ruin; for whatsoever a man loves more than God, God will make it his bane and ruin; at least, be sure to take it away, if God mean to save the party. Therefore, here they say, 'Asshur shall not save us; we will not ride upon horses; neither will we say any more to the works of our hands, Ye are our gods.'

'For in thee the fatherless findeth mercy.'

Here he shews the reason of their rejecting of all false confidence in

Asshur, in horses, in idols; because they had planted their confidence in the true God. They said so when they had smarted by Asshur, and by idolatry. Then 'Asshur shall not save us,' &c. They knew it by rule before; but till God plagued them, as he did oft by Asshur and by Egypt, when he broke the reed that it did not only not uphold them, but run into their hands, they made no such acknowledgment. Hence observe,

Obs. Usually it is thus with man, he never repents till sin be embittered to him. He never alters his confidence till his trusts be taken away. When God overthrows the mould of his devices, or brings them upon his own head, setting him to reap the fruit of his own ways, embittering sinful courses to him, then he returns. Instruction without correction doth for the most part little good. When Asshur had dealt falsely with them, and idolatry would do them no good, then they begin to alter their judgment. What makes men, after too much confidence in their wit, when they have, by their plots and devices, gone beyond what they should do, and wrapped and entangled themselves in a net of their own weaving, as we say, alter their judgment? They are then become sick of their own devices. This makes the change. For till then the brain hath a kind of net to wrap our devices in. So, many have nets in their brains, wherewith they entangle themselves and others with their idle devices; which, when they have done, and so woven the web of their own misery, then they begin to say, as the heathen saith when he was deceived, 'O fool am I, I was never a wise man!' Then they begin to say, I was a fool to trust such and such. I have tried such and such policies, and they have deceived me. I will now alter my course. And surely men of great parts are seldom converted till God confound their plots, and lays flat all their false confidence. When Asshur disappoints them, then 'Asshur shall not save us,' &c.

Use. Therefore make this use of it, *not to be discouraged when God doth confound any carnal plot or policy of ours*, as to think that God hates either a nation or a person when they have ill success in plots and projects which are not good. Nay, it is a sign rather that God intends good, if they make a right use it. God intends conversion, to translate false confidence from the creature to himself, and to learn us to make God wise for us. It is a happy thing when in this world God will disappoint a man's courses and counsels, and bring him to shame, rather than he should go on and thrive in an evil and carnal course, and so end his days. There is no evidence at all which can be given of a reprobate, because there may be final repentance, repentance at the last. But this is one and as fearful a sign as may be, to thrive and go on in an evil course to the end. When God shall disappoint and bring a man to shame in that he prided in and built upon, it is a good sign. If thereupon we take advantage to turn to God, and lay a better bottom and foundation, as we see here, 'Asshur shall not save us; we will not ride upon horses,' &c.

'For in thee the fatherless findeth mercy.'

As if he should say, We have that supply of strength and comfort from thee that Asshur, horses, and idols cannot give. Therefore we will alter our confidence, to fix and pitch it upon thee, and trust thee; because 'in thee the fatherless findeth mercy.' We shall not need to say, In thee will we trust; for, if God be apprehended thus, as one in whom 'the fatherless findeth mercy,' affiance will follow. For the object is the attractive and loadstone of the soul; so that if a fit object be presented unto it, affiance, confidence, and trust will of itself follow. Therefore the Spirit of God forbears multiplication of words, and sets down this, 'For in thee the fatherless findeth mercy;' and doth not say, In thee will I trust, for that is implied. Whatsoever conceives that God is so gracious and merciful to despicable, miserable persons, such as are set down in this one particular, 'fatherless,' they cannot but trust in God. Therefore the one is put for the other, 'for in thee the fatherless findeth mercy.' Whence, from the dependence of the words, observe,

Obs. That it is not sufficient to disclaim affiance in the creature, but we must pitch that affiance aright upon God.

We must not only take it off where it should not be placed, but set it where it should be. 'Cease from evil, and learn to do well,' Isa. i. 16, 17. Trust not in the creature. 'Cease from man,' as the prophet saith, 'whose breath is in his nostrils,' Isa. ii. 22; 'Commit thy ways to God, trust in him,' Ps. xxxvii. 5. The heathen, by the light of nature, knew this, that for the *negative* there is no trusting in the creature, which is a vain thing. They could speak wonderful wittily* and to purpose of these things, especially the Stoics. They could see the vanity of the creature. But for the *positive* part, where to place their confidence, that they were ignorant in. And so for the other part here, 'Neither will we say any more to the works of our hands, Ye are our gods.' Idolaters can see the vanity of false gods well enough. In Italy you have thousands of the wittier and learneder sort, who see the folly and madness of their religion. And among ourselves, how many witty men can disclaim† against popery, who yet in their lives and conversations are not the better for it; because they think it enough to see the error that misleads them, though they never pitch their confidence as they should do. It is not enough therefore to rest in the negative part. A negative Christian is no Christian; not to be an idolater, not to be a papist; no, there must be somewhat else. We must bring forth good fruit, Mat. iii. 10, or else we are for the fire, and are near to cursing and burning, Heb. vi. 8. This is spoken, the rather because many think themselves well when they can disclaim against the errors of popery; and that they are good Christians, because they can argue well. Oh! such make religion nothing but a matter of opinion, of canvassing an argument, &c. But it is another manner of matter, a divine power exercised upon the soul, whereby it is transformed into the obedience of divine truth, and moulded into it. So that there must be a positive as well as a negative religion; a cleaving to God as well as a forsaking of idols.

Again, in the severing of these idols from God, we must know and observe hence,

Obs. That there is no communion between God and idols.

'Neither will we say any more to the works of our hands, Ye are our gods: for in thee the fatherless findeth mercy.' There must be a renouncing of false worship, religion, and confidence, before we can trust in God. 'Ye cannot serve God and Mammon,' saith Christ, Mat. vi. 24. We cannot serve Christ and Antichrist together. We may as well bring north and south, east and west together, and mingle light and darkness, as mix two opposite religions. You see here, one of them is disclaimed ere affiance be placed in the other. Therefore the halters betwixt two religions are here condemned. It was excellent well said by Joshua. They had there some mixture of false worship, and thought therewith to serve also Jevovah. 'No,' saith he, 'you cannot serve Jehovah,' Josh. xxiv. 19. What is Joshua's meaning when he saith they could not? Not only that they had no power of themselves; but, you are a naughty, false

* That is, 'with wit' = wisdom.—G.

† That is, 'declaim.'—G.

people, you think to jumble God's worship and that of heathens together; 'you cannot serve God' thus. So a man may say to those who look Romewards, for worldly ends, and yet will be Protestants, You cannot serve God; you cannot be sound Christians, halting thus betwixt both. These are not compatible, they cannot stand together; you must disclaim the one if you will cleave to the other. We see the ground here, 'Neither will we say any more to the works of our hands, Ye are our gods: for in thee the fatherless findeth mercy.'

Again, whereas upon disclaiming of false confidence in the creatures and idols, they name this as a ground, 'For in thee the fatherless findeth mercy,' observe,

In what measure and degree we apprehend God aright to be the all-sufficient true God, in that measure we cast away all false confidence whatsoever.

The more or less we conceive of God as we should do, so the more or less we disclaim confidence in the creature. Those who in their affections of joy, love, affiance, and delight, are taken up too much with the creature, say what they will, profess to all the world by their practice that they know not God. By the contrary, those who know and apprehend him in his greatness and goodness as he should be apprehended, in that proportion they withdraw their affections from the creature and all things else. It is with the soul in this case as with a balance. If the one scale be drawn down by a weight put in it, the other is lifted up. So where God weighs down in the soul, all other things are light; and where other things prevail, there God is set light. 'Asshur shall not save us,' for he can do us no good; nor 'horses,' because they are vain helps. How attained they to this light esteem of Asshur and horses? 'For in thee the fatherless findeth mercy.' That which is taken from the creature, they find in God. And this is the reason why the world so malign good and sound Christians. They think, when God gets, that they lose a feather, as we say, some of their strength. Surely so it is; for when a Christian turns to God and becomes sound, he comes to have a mean esteem of that which formerly was great in his sight. His judgment is otherwise, as we see here, Asshur, horses, idols, and all, they esteem nothing of them. Horses and the like are good, useful, and necessary to serve God's providence in the use of means; not to trust in, or make co-ordinate with God. In the world especially, great persons would be gods in the hearts of people; therefore, when they see any make conscience of their ways, they think they lose them; because now they will do nothing but what may stand with the favour of God. Thus far from the connection. Now to the words themselves.

'For in thee the fatherless findeth mercy.'

Wherein we have set forth unto us for our consideration of God's rich goodness towards poor miserable sinners—

1. The attribute of God, *mercy*.

2. The fit object thereof, *the fatherless*.

Mercy is God's sweetest attribute, which sweeteneth all his other attributes; for, but for mercy, whatsoever else is in God were matter of terror to us. His justice would affright us. His holiness likewise (considering our impurity) would drive us from him. 'Depart from me,' saith Peter to our Saviour, 'for I am a sinful man,' Luke v. 8. And when the prophet Isaiah saw God in his excellency a little, then he said, 'Woe is me, for I am undone, because I am a man of unclean lips,' &c., Isa. vi. 5. His power is terrible; it would confound us; his majesty astonish us. Oh!

but mercy mitigates all. He that is great in majesty, is abounding in mercy; he that hath beams of majesty, hath bowels of mercy. Oh! this draweth especially miserable persons. 'In thee the fatherless findeth mercy.' And now, in the covenant of grace, this mercy sets all awork. For it is the mercy of God by which we triumph now in the covenant of grace; in that mercy which stirred up his wisdom to find out a way for mercy by satisfying his justice. So that the first moving attribute of God that set him awork about that great work of our salvation by Jesus Christ, in the covenant of grace, was mercy, his tender mercy, his bowels of mercy. Therefore, of all others, that attribute is here named. 'For in thee the fatherless findeth mercy.'

Mercy in God, supposeth misery in the creature, either present or possible; for there is, 1. A preventing; 2. A rescuing mercy.

A *preventing mercy*, whereby the creature is freed from possible misery that it might fall into; as it is his mercy that we are not such sinners in that degree as others are. And every man that hath understanding is beholden to God for their preventing, as well as for their rescuing mercy. We think God is merciful only to those unto whom he forgives great sins. Oh! he is merciful to thee that standeth. Thou mightst have fallen foully else. Mercy supposeth misery, either that we are in, or may fall into. So that mercy in God may admit of a threefold consideration.

1. It supposeth *sin*. So there is a *pardoning mercy* for that. Or,
2. *Misery*; that is, a *delivering mercy*. Or,
3. *Defect or want in the creature*, which is, *supplying mercy*.

Wheresoever mercy is conversant, it is usually about one of these three, either sin, or misery, or defects and wants; that is, to persons in misery. For, indeed, the word is more general than fatherless. Deserted persons, that are forsaken of others, and have no strength of their own, they are here meant by the fatherless, who have no means, wisdom, power, or ability of their own, but are deserted and forsaken of others. Whence the chief truth that offers itself to be considered of us is this,

That God is especially merciful to those persons who stand most in need of mercy.

First, Because *these do relish mercy most*, and give him the glory of it, applying themselves most to his mercy, being beaten out of the creature; and the more we have communion with God, being driven out of the creature and other comforts, the more he discovers himself to us. As the nearer we are to the fire, the hotter it is; so the nearer we are to God, the more good and gracious he every way shews himself unto us. Now, what makes us near him, but extremity of misery, whereby we are beaten from all other holds whatsoever? It is acknowledged to be his work, when he doth it for those that are deserted of all others, Hosea v. 15. Then he hath the chief glory of it. This is one end why God suffers his children to fall into extremity of great sorrows and perplexities, to fall very low in depths of miseries (as the Scripture speaks), Ps. cxxx. 1, that he might discover a depth of his mercy beyond the depth of their misery, to shew that there is a depth deeper than that depth, for their misery is finite. Oh! but the bowels of his compassions are infinite, both in measure and time. 'His mercy endureth for ever,' Ps. cxxxvi. 1, *seq.*

Again, *God is jealous of their affiance and confidence*, knowing that naturally, unless we fall into some straits and weaning extremities, we shall place our affiance upon the creature. Therefore, he deals thus with us. He knows our sickness well enough, that we are desperately addicted to present things. Therefore, to cure this sickness in us, he draws us by extremities from the creature to himself, which, when it fails, we go to him. 'Help, Lord!' Why? 'For vain is the help of man,' Ps. lx. 11. It is time then to help. 'Help, Lord, for the godly are perished from the earth,' Ps. xii. 1. It is time to help, Lord, for if thou do not, none will; whereby they come to have their confidence upon the rock, which is worth all. Other men, they run from creature to creature, from help to help, as sick bodies do to this and to that drug, and to this and that potion. They seek to many things to beg comfort from; but a Christian hath a sure foundation that he may stay upon. 'In thee the fatherless findeth mercy.'

To come now to speak of the words as they lie in the whole. They carry another instruction,

That God is very gracious and merciful to fatherless and distressed persons.

As we have it, Ps. x. 18, 'that God will judge the fatherless and oppressed; that the man of the earth may no more oppress;' so Ps. cxlvi. 9, it is said, 'The Lord preserveth the strangers, he relieveth the fatherless and widow,' &c. And for the general we have it, 'The Lord relieveth all that fall, and raiseth up all that be bowed down,' Ps. cxlv. 14. God he opens his ear to hear their cry, to judge the fatherless and the oppressed. The like we have in Exodus, 'Also thou shalt not oppress a stranger,' for ye know the heart of a stranger, seeing ye were strangers in the land of Egypt,' Exod. xxiii. 9. And saith he, 'Thou shalt not afflict any widow or fatherless child. If thou afflict them in any wise, and they cry at all unto me, I will surely hear their cry,' Exod. xxii. 21. These, among many, are direct places to shew the truth of this, that God is merciful, not only in general, but to those persons set down by a *synecdoche*, a figure where one is set down for all of the same kind. God is merciful to all persons, in any kind of misery or distress whatsoever. As the apostle speaks, God is he 'who comforteth the abject person,' 2 Cor. vii. 6, the forlorn, the castaway persons of the world; and he is 'a very present help in trouble,' Ps. xlvi. 1. So as when there are none to help, then he awaketh and rouseth up himself to lay hold for us. 'His own arm brings salvation for his own sake.'* So when there is misery, and none to help, God will find cause and ground from his own bowels to shew mercy, to take pity and compassion upon his poor church and children. Which should teach us,

Use 1. First of all, *to take notice of this most excellent attribute of God*, and to make use of it upon all occasions at our most need, then to present to our souls God thus described and set out by his own Spirit, to be 'he that comforteth the abject,' and sheweth mercy to the fatherless and oppressed. This we should make use of for the church in general, and for every one of ourselves in particular. The church hath been a long time like a forlorn widow, as it were. God hath promised that he will have a care of the 'widow and the fatherless,' and so he will of his poor church.

We see in the parable, the widow, with her importunity, prevailed with an unrighteous judge, Luke xviii. 5. The church now being like a widow, what is wanting but a spirit of supplication and prayer? Which spirit, if the church had to wrestle with God, and lay hold upon him as Jacob did, Hos. xii. 4, and not suffer God to rest till he had mercy on his poor church, certainly it would be better with it than it is, for God comforteth the widow, Isa. lxii. 7. If one, what will he do for the whole spouse, which hath so long been a despicable and forlorn widow? And for the time to come it ought to minister matter of comfort for the church. Certainly, God that

* Isa. xli. 17, lix. 16, lxiii. 5, xlviii. 9.

is merciful to the fatherless, he will be merciful to the poor church. We see in the Revelation, though the woman was persecuted by the dragon, yet there were given two wings of a great eagle to her, that she might fly unto the wilderness, where she had a place provided of God, Rev. xii. 14. It alludes to the story of the Israelites when they came out of Egypt. God provided for them in the wilderness. They had manna from heaven, and water out of the rock; and till they came to Canaan, God provided every way for them in a marvellous manner. So God will be sure to provide for his in the wilderness of this world. He will have a harbour still for the church, and a hiding-place from the stormy tempests of her adversaries, Isa. iv. 5, 6. Therefore let us not despair, but stir up a spirit of prayer for the church, that he who shews mercy to the fatherless, and commands mercy to be shewed to the widow, that he would shew that himself which he requires of us. And why may not we hope and trust for it. The church in this world is, as it were, a fatherless person, a pupil, an orphan, a sheep in the midst of wolves, as Daniel in the lions' den, as a ship tossed in the waves, as a lily among thorns. It is environed with enemies, and of itself, like the poor sheep, is shiftless.* What is the church but a company of weak persons? Not so witty† for the world as worldly-wise men are, not so strong in the arm of flesh, nor so defenced, but a company of persons who have a hidden dependence upon God we know not how, and hang, as it were, by a thread, as the church in this land, and abroad in other places. The true church is maintained, we know not how. God keeps up religion, the church, and all, because he is merciful to the fatherless, who have no shifting wits, as the worldly Ahithophels have. God is wise for them that are not wise for themselves, and powerful for them that have little strength of their own. Therefore let us not be discouraged though we be weak creatures, a little flock, like a company of sheep, yet notwithstanding we have a strong shepherd, Ps. xxiii 1. The church is like a vine, a poor, despicable, withered, crooked, weak plant, which winds about, and must be supported, or else it sinks to the ground; yet it is a fruitful plant, Isa. v. 1, 7. So the church of God, a number of weak Christians professing religion, they want many helps, yet God supports them, and hath ordained this and that haven for them, as this magistrate and that person. God hath one support or other for them. While they are fruitful and true vines, God will have a care of them, though they be never so weak and despised in the eye of the world, Isa. liv. 11.

Use 2. Again, this should teach us *to make God our all-sufficiency in all estates whatsoever*, and not to go one hair's breadth from a good conscience, for fear of after-claps.‡ I may be cast into prison, I may lose my goods. What of all this? Is not God all-sufficient? And is not he especially seen in comforting of those who stand in most need of comfort, who want other helps? And will he be indebted to any man who stands out in a good quarrel for his cause? Isa. xli. 17. Will he not give needful supply, if not in this world, yet in a better, of all comforts whatsoever? It is a good supply when the loss is in outward things, and the supply in inward peace, grace, and strength. It is a happy loss that is lost to the advantage, Isa. lx. 17; lxiv. 5. There was never any man yet, from the beginning of the world, who lost by cleaving to religion and good causes. God ever made it up one way or other. Therefore this is a ground of courage to cast ourselves upon doing good when God offers the occasion, relying upon

* That is, 'without expedients.'—G.

† That is, 'wise.'—G.

‡ That is, 'judgments, trials.'—G.

God, as Esther did, 'If I perish, I perish,' Esther iv. 16. She meant, 'If I perish, I shall not perish.' Such have a better condition in the love and favour of God than they had before, or should have had, if they had not perished. It is the way not to perish, so to perish. It is as clear and true as the sunshine, but we want faith to believe it.

Use 3. And then, again, let us make use of it in another kind, to resist another temptation. What will become of my poor children, if I do thus and thus, stand thus and thus, and go on in my innocency? What will become of thy children? It was well spoken by Lactantius, 'Because God would have men stand out and die in a good cause willingly, therefore he hath promised in a special manner to be a father to the fatherless, and a husband to the widow' (*d*). Are we the chief fathers of our children? No; we are but under God, to bring those who are his children into the world. We are but instruments. God is the chief father, best and last father, 'The everlasting father,' Isa. ix. 6, who takes upon him to be a father to the fatherless, whom he chargeth all not to hurt. Experience shews how he blesseth the posterity of the righteous, who have stood in defence of the truth. Therefore let us make no pretences either for baseness, dejection of spirit, or covetousness, to keep us from well doing, for God will reward all.

Quest. Oh, say some, I could be content not to be so worldly, but it is for my children.

Ans. What saith the apostle? 'Let those who are married be as if they were not married,' 1 Cor. vii. 29, meaning in regard of this scraping of wealth together by unlawful means of covetousness, or in regard of readiness to do works of mercy. What, doth God appoint one ordinance of marriage, to take a man off of all duties? No; notwithstanding this we must do fitting works of mercy. God will be the father of the fatherless. Many use oppression, and go to hell themselves to make their children rich. Who commands us to make our children, in show, a while happy here, to make our souls and bodies miserable for ever? There is a moderate care, as the apostle speaks, so that 'he who cares not for his own, is worse than an infidel,' 1 Tim. v. 8; but we must not make this pretence to excuse injurious and extortive courses. But let God alone. He will do all things well; trust him. Or, if anything should befall us otherwise than well, what if it do? God is the God of the fatherless. Whatsoever he takes away, he supplies it better another way. For whence have the creatures that infusion to help? Is it not from God? And when the creature is taken away, is not God where he was?

Use 4. And let us also learn hence that we answer God's dealing, in shewing mercy to the fatherless and such as stand in need, as the apostle exhorts, 'Put on, therefore, as the elect of God, holy and beloved, bowels of mercy,' &c., Col. iii. 12, as if he should say, as you would prove yourselves to be elect members of Christ and children of God, so shew your likeness in this particular, 'The bowels of mercy and compassion.' This hath ever been, and yet is at all times, a character of God's children, and shall be to the end of the world. It is a sign such a one hath found bowels of mercy, that is ready upon all occasions to pour forth those bowels of compassion upon others, as hard-heartedness this way shews a disposition which yet hath not rightly tasted of mercy. As we say in another case, those that are appeased in their consciences, in the sense of the forgiveness of sins, they are peaceable to others, because they feel peace. So here, those that feel mercy will be merciful, those that have felt love will be loving to others.

'A good man is merciful to his beast, but the mercies of the wicked are cruel,' Prov. xii. 10. Those, therefore, that are hard-hearted and unmerciful, hardening themselves against the complaints of the miserable, there is, for the present, no comfort for them, that the Spirit of God hath wrought any change in their hearts; for then it would stamp the image of God upon them, they would be merciful to the fatherless, widow, and distressed persons. What shall we think, then, of a generation of men who, by gripping usury and the like courses, have made many widows miserable? Let such profess what they will, whilst they are thus hard-hearted they have not the bowels of Christ. God is so merciful that you see, as the Jews call them (*e*), he hath hedges of the commandments, that is, he hath some remote commands which are not of the main, and all to hedge from cruelty, as, 'Thou shalt not kill the dam upon the nest,' Deut. xxii. 6; 'Thou shalt not seethe a kid in his mother's milk,' Exod. xxiii. 19. What tends this to? Nothing but to shew the mercy and bowels of God, and that he would have us to abstain from cruelty. He that would not have us murder, would have us keep aloof off, and not be merciless to the very dumb creatures, birds and beasts. Therefore let us labour to express the image of our heavenly father in this.

Use 5. Again, we should use this *as a plea against dejectedness at the hour of death*, in regard of those we leave behind us, not to be troubled what shall become of them, when we are to yield up our souls to God; but know that he hath undertaken to be 'the Father of the fatherless, and of the widow.' Therefore, for shame, for shame! learn, as to live, so to die by faith; and as to die by faith in other things, so to die in this faith; that God, as he will receive thy soul, so he will receive the care of thy posterity. Canst thou with affiance yield up thy soul unto God, and wilt thou not with the same confidence yield thy posterity? Thou art an hypocrite, if this distract and vex thee, when yet thou pretendest to die in the faith of Christ. Canst thou yield thy soul, and yet art grieved for thy posterity? No; leave it to God. He is all-sufficient. 'The earth is the Lord's, and the fulness thereof,' Ps. xxiv. 1. We need not fear to put our portion in his hands. He is rich enough. 'The earth and all is his.' Therefore, when we are in any extremity whatsoever, rely on this mercy of so rich and powerful a God; improve it, for it is our portion, especially in a distressed condition. Were it not for faith, wrought by the blessed Spirit of God, he would lose the glory of this attribute of mercy. Now, faith is a wise power of the soul, that sees in God what is fit for it, singling out in God what is fit for the present occasion of distress. Is a man in any extremity of misery? let him look to mercy. Is a man oppressed? let him look to mercy, to be revenged of his enemies. Is a man in any perplexity? let him look to mercy, joined with wisdom, which is able to deliver him. Religion is nothing else but an application of the soul to God, and a fetching out of him somewhat (as he hath discovered himself in the covenant) fit for all our exigents; as there is somewhat in God, and in the promises, for all estates of the soul. Faith, therefore, is witty to look to that in God which is fit for its turn. Let us therefore take heed of Satan's policy herein, who in our extremity, useth this as a weapon to shake our faith. 'Tush,' as it is in the psalm, 'God hath forsaken and forgotten him,' Ps. x. 11. Hath he so? Nay; because I am in extremity, and deserted above others, rather God now regards me more than before; because, 'he scourgeth every son whom he receiveth,' Heb. xii. 6. So retort Satan's fiery darts back again. For indeed, that is the time wherein God exalts and shews himself most glorious and triumphant in mercy, where misery is greatest. 'Where sin abounds, there grace abounds much more,' Rom. v. 20. So where misery abounds, mercy superabounds much more. Therefore let us be as wise for our souls, as Satan can be malicious against them. What he useth for a weapon to wound the soul, use the same as a weapon against him.

To end all, *let faith in God's mercy answer this his description;* and let it be a description ingrafted into us at such a time. Doth God care for the fatherless, and mean persons, who are cast down and afflicted? Why, then, I will trust that God who doth so, being in this case myself. If he will help in extremity, trust him in extremity; if he will help in distress, trust him in distress; if he will help when all forsake, trust him when we are forsaken of all, Hab. iii. 17. What if a stream be taken away? yet none can take away God from thee. What if a beam be taken away? thou hast the sun itself. What if a particular comfort be taken away? So long as God, 'who comforteth the abject,' and is merciful to the distressed, fatherless, and widows, continues with thee, thou needst not fear. A man cannot want comfort and mercy, so long as the Father of mercies is in covenant with him. If he sin, he hath pardoning mercy for him; if weak, he hath strengthening mercy; if in darkness, he hath quickening mercy; if we be dull, dead, and in danger, there is rescuing mercy; and if subject to dangers we may fall in, there is for that preventing mercy, Ps. xxxii. 10. Therefore there is mercy ready to compass God's children about in all conditions. When they are environed with dangers, yet God is nearer to guard their souls, than the danger is to hurt them.

Therefore let us take the counsel of the blessed apostle. 'Be careful for nothing; but in everything, by prayer and supplication, with thanksgiving, let your requests be known to God.' And what then? Will God grant that I pray for? Perhaps he will not; but yet, 'the peace of God, which passeth all understanding, shall guard your hearts and minds through Christ Jesus,' Philip. iv. 6, 7. As if he should say, in nothing be overcareful. Let your care be, when ye have used the means, to depend upon God for support in the event and issue of all. If God deny you what you pray for, he will grant you that which is better. He will set up an excellent inward peace there, whereby he will stablish the soul in assurance of his love, pardon of sins, and reconciliation: whereby their souls shall be guarded, and their hearts and minds preserved in Christ. So they become impregnable in all miseries whatsoever, when they have 'the peace of God, which passeth all understanding,' to guard them within. Therefore let us not betray and lose our comforts for want of making use of them, or for fear some should call us hypocrites. And, on the other side, let us not flatter ourselves in an evil course; but make the conscience good, which will bear us out in all miseries, dangers, and difficulties whatsoever. Nothing makes losses, crosses, banishment, imprisonment, and death so terrible and out of measure dreadful unto us, but the inward guilt and sting in the inside, the tumults of conscience, Gen. xlii. 21. Clear this well once, make all whole within, let conscience be right and straight, let it have its just use and measure of truth and uprightness, and go thy way in peace; I warrant thee, thou shalt hold up thy head, and wind thyself out of all dangers well enough: nothing shall daunt or appal thy courage. For, saith Solomon, 'The righteous is bold as a lion,' Prov. xxviii. 1. What can, what should he fear, who is heir of all things,' Rev. xxi. 7, whose all things are, and who is reconciled to God in Christ, having all the angels and creatures for his servants, Heb. i. 14, for whose sake 'all things must needs work together for good?' Rom. viii. 28.

THE FIFTH SERMON.

I will heal their backsliding, I will love them freely: for mine anger is turned away from them.—Hos. XIV. 4.

THE superabounding mercies and marvellous lovingkindnesses of a gracious and loving God to wretched and miserable sinners, as we have heard, is the substance and sum of this short, sweet chapter, wherein their ignorance is taught, their bashfulness is encouraged, their deadness is quickened, their untowardness is pardoned, their wounds are cured, all their objections and petitions answered; so as a large and open passage is made unto them, and all other miserable penitent sinners, for access unto the throne of grace. If they want words, they are taught what to say; if discouraged for sins past, they are encouraged that sin may be taken away; yea, all iniquity may be taken away. 'Take away all iniquity.' If their unworthiness hinder them, they are taught for this, that God is gracious. 'Receive us graciously.' If their by-past unthankfulness be any bar of hindrance unto them, they are taught to promise thankfulness. 'So will we render the calves of our lips.' And that their repentance may appear to be sound and unfeigned, they are brought in, making profession of their detestation of their bosom sins, of false confidence and idolatry. 'Asshur shall not save us; we will not ride upon horses; neither will we say any more to the works of our hands, Ye are our gods.' And not only do they reject their false confidence, to cease from evil, but they do good, and pitch their affiance where it should be. For 'in thee the fatherless findeth mercy.'

None must therefore be discouraged, or run away from God, for what they have been, for there may be a returning. God may have a time for them, who, in his wise dispensation, doth bring his children to distress, that their delivery may be so much the more admired by themselves and others, to his glory and their good. He knows us better than we ourselves. How prone we are to lean upon the creature. Therefore he is fain to take from us all our props and supports, whereupon we are forced to rely upon him. If we could do this of ourselves, it were an excellent work, and an undoubted evidence of the child of God, that hath a weaned soul in the midst of outward supports, to enjoy them, as if he possessed them not; not to be puffed up with present greatness, not to swell with riches, nor be high-minded; to consider of things to be as they are, weak things, subordinate to God, which can help no further than as he blesseth them. But to come to the words now read.

'I will heal their backsliding, and love them freely,' &c.

After that the church had shewed her repentance and truth of returning to God: now in these words, and the other verses, unto the end of the chapter (saving the last verse, which is a kind of acclamation issuing from all the rest of the foregoing verses, 'Who is wise, and he shall understand these things?' &c.), is set down an answer unto that prayer, repentance, and reformation which the church made; all the branches of which their former suit the Lord doth punctually* answer. For they had formerly

* That is, 'point by point.'—ED.

prayed, 'Take away all iniquity, and receive us graciously; do good unto us.' Unto which he answers here, 'I will heal their backsliding,' &c.

Which is thus much: I will pardon their iniquities, I will accept graciously of them, I will love them freely, and so of the rest, as will appear afterwards; and, in sum, God answers all those desires which formerly he had stirred up in his people. Whence, ere we come to the particulars, observe in general,

Obs. Where God doth give a spirit of prayer, he will answer.

It needs no proof, the point is so clear and experimental. All the saints can say thus much from their experience of God's gracious dealing with them; and the Scriptures are full of such instances and promises, which we all know. To name a place or two for all the rest, 'Call upon me in the day of trouble, I will deliver thee, and thou shalt glorify me,' Ps. l. 15. So in another place, 'And it shall come to pass that before they call, I will answer; and whilst they speak, I will hear,' Isa. lxv. 24. It hath been made good to persons, as Daniel, Elijah, Solomon, Jacob, and others; and it hath been, and is, made good unto all ages of the church, from time to time, and shall be unto the end of the world. And therefore the prophet sets down this as a conclusion undeniable from the premises, 'O thou that hearest prayer, unto thee shall all flesh come,' Ps. lxv. 2. Whence he draws this excellent consolation, 'Iniquities prevail against me; as for our transgressions, thou shalt purge them away.'

Reason. The reason is strong, because they are the motions of his own Spirit, which he stirs up in us. For he dictates this prayer unto them, 'Take with you words,' &c., 'and say unto the Lord, Take away all iniquity, and receive us graciously.' So that, where God stirs up holy desires by his Spirit, he will answer exactly; there shall not a sigh be lost. 'Likewise,' saith the apostle, 'the Spirit also helps our infirmities: for we know not what we should pray for as we ought: but the Spirit itself makes intercession for us, with groanings which cannot be uttered,' Rom. viii. 26. Therefore there cannot a groan be lost, nor a darting of a sigh. Whatsoever is spiritual must be effectual, though it cannot be vented in words. For God hath an ear, not only near a man's tongue, to know what he saith; but also in a man's heart, to know what he desires, or would have. As the observing, careful, tender mother many times knows what the child would have though it cannot speak; so God, he knows the desires, sighs, and groans of the heart when we cannot speak. For sometimes there may be such a confusion upon the soul, by reason of divers disturbances, that it cannot express nor vent itself in words. Therefore the Spirit vents itself then in sighs and groans, which are heard and accepted, because they are the desires of his own Spirit. Thus much the prophet David excellently sheweth, 'Lord, thou hast heard the desire of the humble: thou wilt prepare their heart, thou wilt cause thine ear to hear,' Ps. x. 17. God, he first prepares the heart to pray, then his ear to hear their prayers and desires. If this will not encourage us to be much in suit to God, and put up our petitions to him, to labour for a spirit of prayer, I know not what will prevail; when we know that no petition shall be turned back again unanswered. When we are to deal with princes upon earth, they oftentimes regard neither the persons nor their petitions, but turn their backs upon both. Oh! but a Christian hath the ear of God and heaven open upon him; such credit in heaven, that his desires and groans are respected and heard. And undoubtedly a man may know that he shall be heard when he hath a spirit of prayer; in one kind or other, though not in the particulars or kinds we ask, hear he will for our good.

God will not lose the incense of his own Spirit, of a spirit of prayer which he stirs up, it is so precious. Therefore let us labour to have a spirit of prayer, which God regards so much; seeing for a certain, wheresoever he gives a spirit of prayer, he means to give that we pray for; but according to his heavenly wisdom, as here his answer is,

'I will heal their backsliding, I will love them freely,' &c.

God answers them exactly unto all they prayed for, beginning first with the ground of all our comfort, 'forgiveness of sins.' According to their petition, 'Take away all iniquity,' he answers, 'I will heal their backsliding,' or their rebellion. Backsliding is an aggravation of sin. Every sin is not a rebellion, apostasy, or backsliding · for there be also sins of infirmities. We usually rank sins thus, in

1. Sins of ignorance.
2. Sins of infirmity.
3. Sins against knowledge, with a higher hand; and
4. The sins against the Holy Ghost.

Now, this is more than to cure sins of ignorance and of infirmity when he saith, 'I will heal their backsliding.'

Quest. But why doth he answer the higher pitch of an aggravation, when their petition was in a lower strain only, 'Take away all mine iniquity'?

Ans. To shew that he would answer them fully; that is, that he would heal all sins whatsoever, not only of ignorance and of infirmity, but also sins willingly committed, their rebellions and backslidings. For, indeed, they were backsliding. From the time of Jeroboam, that made the rent, the ten tribes grew worse and worse continually, so that they had been utterly extinguished, but that God was wondrous gracious to send them prophets to preserve many that they should not bow the knee to Baal, being merciful to them to bear with their backsliding so long. For besides their calves, they had false gods. They did not only worship the true God in a false manner by the calves, but they had Baals also. So that we see, God, when he will comfort, will comfort to purpose, and take away all objections that the soul can make, a guilty soul being full of objections. Oh! my sins are many, great, rebellions and apostasies. But, be they what they will, God's mercy in Christ is greater and more. 'I will heal their backsliding,' or their rebellion. God is above conscience. Let Satan terrify the conscience as he will, and let conscience speak the worst it can against itself, yet God is greater. Therefore, let the sin be what it will, God will pardon all manner of sins. As they pray to pardon all, so he will 'take away all iniquity, heal their backsliding.' But to come nearer the words.

'I will heal,' &c. The healing meant here is especially in the pardon of their sins, answerable to their desires in justification. And there is a healing also in sanctification by the Spirit. When God takes away the venom from the wound, then God cures in sanctification. Both are meant, but especially the first. In a wound we know there is,

1. The malignity and venom of it; and then,
2. The wound itself, so festered and rankled.

Now, pardoning grace in justification takes away the anguish and malice of the wound, so that it ceaseth to be so malignant and deadly as to kill or infect. And then sanctification purgeth and cleanseth the wound and heals it up. Now, God through Christ doth both. The blood of Christ doth heal the guilt of sin, which is the anger and malignity of it; and by the Spirit of Christ he heals the wound itself, and purgeth out the sick and peccant humour by little and little through sanctification. God is a perfect healer. 'I will heal their backsliding.' See here the state of the church and children of God. They are prone to backsliding and turning away. We are naturally prone to decline further and further from God. So the church of God, planted in a family in the beginning of the world, how soon was it prone to backsliding. This is one weakness since the fall. It is incident to our nature to be unsettled and unsteady in our holy resolutions. And whilst we live in the midst of temptations, the world, together with the fickleness of our own nature, evil examples, and Satan's perpetual malice against God and the poor church, are ill pilots to lead us out of the way. This is spoken to make us careful how to shun backsliding. For we see how many opinions are foisted in amongst us, and have got some head, that durst not before once be named amongst us. Popery spreads itself amain. Even churches are prone to backsliding. Therefore, St Paul's advice is, 'Be not high-minded, but fear; for if God spared not the natural branches, take heed lest he also spare not thee,' Rom. xi. 20, 21. What is become of Rome? So the same will become of us if we stop not our backslidings.

Now, in that God's promise is, 'I will heal their backslidings,' observe, in the first place,

That sin is a wound and a disease.

Now, as in sickness there is, 1, grief troubling and vexing the party who feels it; and, 2, deformity of the place affected, which comes by wounds and weaknesses; so in all sin, when we are sensible of it, there is first grief, vexation, and torment of conscience, and then, again, deformity. For it takes away the beauty and vigour of the soul, and dejects the countenance. It debaseth a man, and takes away his excellency. As Jacob saith of Reuben, 'Unstable as water, thou shalt not excel, because thou wentest up to thy father's bed,' Gen. xlix. 4. Saith God to Cain, 'Why art thou wroth, and why is thy countenance fallen?' Gen. iv. 6. And the prophet David, he confesseth, 'When I kept silence, my bones waxed old through my roaring all the day long,' Ps. xxxii. 3, 4. So again, 'There is no soundness in my flesh, because of thine anger; neither is there any rest in my bones, because of my sin,' Ps. xxxviii. 3. So that sin is a wound and a disease, whether we consider the miseries it brings on soul and body, or both. Therefore, howsoever a sinful person think himself a goodly person, and wear his sins as ornaments about him, pride, lust, and the like, yet he is a deformed, loathsome person in the eyes and presence of God; and when conscience is awakened, sin will be loathsome, irksome, and odious unto himself, fill him full of grief and shame, so that he cannot endure the sight of his own soul.

Now, all sins whatsoever are diseases. The first sin of all sins, which we call hereditary, original sin, what was* it but an hereditary disease? A leprosy, which we drew from our first parents, spread over all the soul, having the seeds and spawn of all sin in it. The church of Rome makes it less than other sins, as indeed popery is ignorant both of the height of grace and of the depth of corruption, for if they knew the one, they would be more capable of the other. Why do they not conceive aright of grace and of the height of it? Because they know not the depth of original sin. And, indeed, the true knowledge of this disease is proper only to the child of God in the true church. None but he knows what original sin is. Others can dispute and talk of it, but none feels it but the child of God. Now, all other particular, actual sins be diseases flowing from hence. So that all diseases in this kind arise either, 1, from ourselves, as we have a

* Qu. 'is it?'—G.

seminary of them in our own hearts; or else, 2, from the infection and contagion of others; or, 3, from Satan, who hath society with our spirits, as men have with the outward man, coming in by his suggestions, and our entertaining of them. So that in that respect sin is like unto a wound and a disease, in regard of the cause of them.

And, in regard of the effects, sin is like a disease. Diseases, if they be neglected, breed death itself, and become incurable. So it is with the diseases and sins of the soul. Neglect them, and the best end of them will be despair in this world. Whereupon we may have advantage to fly unto the mercy of God in Christ. This is the end of sin, either to end in a good despair or in a fruitless barren despair, at the hour of death leading to hell, when they have no grace to repent. 'The wages of sin is death,' &c., Rom. vi. 23. Sin itself is a wound, and that which riseth from sin is a wound too, doubting and despair; for this disease and wound of sin breeds that other disease, a despair of mercy, which is the beginning of hell, the second death. These things might be further enlarged. But for the present only in general know that sin is *a disease and a wound of the soul;* so much worse than the diseases of the body, by how much the soul is more precious than it, and the death of the soul more terrible than the death of the body. Sin is a disease and a wound; for what is pride but a swelling? What is anger but an intemperate heat of the soul, like an ague, as it were? What is revenge but a wildfire in the soul? What is lust but a spreading canker in the soul, tending to a consumption? What is covetousness but a sword, a perpetual wounder of the soul, piercing it through with many sorrows? What is security but, as it were, the lethargy and apoplexy of the soul? And so we might go on in other resemblances (*f*).

Quest. But, it may be demanded, how shall we know that we are sick of this sickness and disease you speak of?

Ans. How do we know that we are sick in body? If the body be extreme cold we know there is a distemper, or if it be extreme hot. So if the soul be so extreme cold that no heavenly motives or sweet promises can work upon it, stir it up, then certainly there is a disease upon the soul.

If the soul be inflamed with revenge and anger, that soul is certainly diseased. The temper of the soul is according to the passions thereof. A man may know by his passions when he hath a sick soul.

If a man cannot relish good diet, then we count him a sick man; so when a man cannot relish holy discourse nor the ordinances of God. You have some men that can relish nothing but profits and pleasures, and such vanities, but no divine thing. Such have sick souls undoubtedly.

So, again, a man may know there is a deadly sickness and soreness upon the soul, 1, when it is senseless of its wounds; and, 2, is senseless of that which passeth from it. As men, we say, are ready to die when excremental things pass from them without any sense, so a man may know that he is desperately soul-sick when oaths, lies, and deceitful speeches pass from him, and yet he is senseless of them. They think not of them. They mean no harm. Doth that argue a sound state of body, when a man is so desperately ill that he feels not his bodily hurts? And is this a good state of soul, when these filthy things come out from it insensibly? It is an argument of extreme deadness of spirit and irreverence, and of a desperate sin-sick soul, when there is no dread or awe of the majesty of God. Let such look about them. It is an aggravation of the danger of the soul this kind of temper. We usually say, when the stomach is so weak that it can hold no nourishment without casting it up again as fast as it receives it, certainly such an one is sick, and in a dangerous state of body. So when a man hears and hears, and reads and reads, and digests nothing into nourishment, but all is left where he heard it, it is a sign they have sick souls when their retentive power is so weak. And there is certainly some sickness, some dangerous obstruction in that soul that cannot digest the wholesome word of God, to make use of it; some noisome lust then certainly obstructs the soul, which must be purged out.

It is a pitiful thing to see the desperate condition of many now, who, though they live under the tyranny of sin, yet flatter their own disease, and account them their greatest enemies who any way oppose their sick humour. What do they most cordially hate? The sound preaching of the word. The very sight of such an one whose calling hath been to put us in mind of our sins, evil courses, and vanities of the world, is loathsome and offensive to carnal men, in whom corruption is grown up to such a tyranny that it sways the whole soul to devise how to satisfy it. Man is so diseased that those lusts in him, which he should labour to subdue and mortify by the power of the Spirit, do so oversway him that all his life is nothing else but a disease and backsliding into sin. And as if we were not corrupt enough ourselves, how many are there who feed their corruptions when they frequent ill places and company, whom they cannot do without, and are as fish in the water, feeding the old man in them. So that such are not only sick, but defend, maintain, and feed their sickness, their whole life being spent this way, which they laugh at, and make 'pride their chain and ornament,' Ps. lxxiii. 6, as the prophet speaks. This is spoken that we may take up a lamentation for the vileness of man's nature, and to teach us how to judge aright of men when they devise how to have their liberty strengthened to go to hell, as it were, with an high hand, having their will so fortified that no man is able to deal with them, thwart them, or teach them anything. If it were offered to most men to have what estate they would in this world, what are their wishes and desires? O that I might live as I list, that I might have what would content my pleasures without control, that I might have no crosses, but go smoothly on! Yet this, which is the desire of most men, is the most cursed estate of all, and most to be lamented. Thus it appeareth sin is a wound and a disease. What use may we make of it?

Use 1. If this be so, then, in the first place, let us know and consider, *that no man who lives in sins unrepented of and uncured, is to be envied, be they never so great.* Who will envy a man that hath a rotten body, covered over with glorious attire? when every man knows that he carries a rotten disease about him; either some disease in the vital parts, or from the rottenness of sin, which puts a kind of shame and scorn. Can we pity a man thus in glorious attire, having a filthy body under it? thus covering their nakedness, in whose case we would not for anything be. And are they not much more to be pitied, who have ulcerous souls, galled and pierced through with many sins? When we see men that are blasphemers, swearers, men guilty of much blood and filthiness, and of many sins hanging upon them, to envy such a man's greatness is extreme folly. Oh, he carries his death's wound about him, as we say. He is stricken already in his side with a deadly dart. Without the healing mercy of God, there is but a step betwixt him and eternal death; wherefore no man is to be envied for his sinful greatness.

Use 2. Again, if this be so, that sin is a disease and wound of the soul, *let us therefore labour to cure it presently.* It is desperate folly in men to neglect their bodies, when they know that they are prone to such and such diseases, which are growing upon them every day. How careful are men, perceiving thus much, to prevent diseases by timely physic! All sins are diseases, and growing like diseases, run from ill to worse, worse and worse. 'Wicked men,' saith the apostle, 'grow worse and worse,' 2 Tim. iii. 13. Therefore, if sin be a disease, prevent it presently. For as we see, heretics and other the like are hardly sound but at the first, and then are hardly cured. So, if we neglect the diseases of our souls, they will breed a consumption of grace, or such an ill temper of soul, as that it cannot well desire to repent. Nay, when a man lives in wicked, rebellious courses long, God will give him up to such terrors of conscience, that it will not be pacified, but upbraid itself. I have been a sinful, wretched creature; mercy hath been offered me again and again, but now it is too late, having outstood all the means of grace, and rejected them. When they have considered that their lives have for a long time been a mere rebellion, and that they have put off the checks of conscience, the admonitions of the word and Spirit, with the motions thereof. It is long in this case before a man can have peace. For answerable to the continuance in sin, is the hardness of the cure, if it be cured at all.

Therefore there is no dallying with sin. I shall repent at length, but not now. Yet a while I will continue these and these courses, I shall do well enough, &c.; as if a man who were sick, or desperately wounded, should say, I shall do well, and yet neglect to send for the physician. None are so desperately foolish in case of the body, why should we for our souls? Is not that in much more hazard than the body, if we had spiritual eyes to consider of it? The truth is, people are not convinced of this, that sin is such a sickness, which is the reason they are so careless of it. But when the conscience is awaked, as it will be one day, here or in hell, then they will be of another mind. Nay, in this world, when friends, nor riches, nor anything can comfort, then they cry out, O that they had not been so foolish! They would give a world, if they had it, for peace of conscience! This will be the best of it, for men that go on in sin. Therefore, before hardness of heart grow upon us, that disease following the disease of sin, let us take heed, and labour to have our souls healed in time. Thus we have found that sin is a sickness; for so much is implied, when he saith, 'I will heal their backsliding.' Whence the direct observation is,

That God is the great physician of the soul.

For he saith here, 'I will heal their backsliding;' so that healing implies the taking away of—

1. The guilt of sin, which is the venom of it, by justification.
2. The rage of sin, which is the spreading of it, by sanctification.
3. The removing the judgment upon our estate.

For, unless God be the more merciful, these things follow. Where there is sin, and breaking of his law, there is a state binding over to damnation and guilt. When there is a sinful disposition raging, and bringing us from one degree of sin to another, then there is God's judgment and wrath revealed from heaven against this. Now, when God heals, he heals perfectly, but in some regards slowly, as we shall see hereafter. In regard of forgiveness of sins, he healeth perfectly. But by little and little in regard of the other, of sanctification. He stops up the issues of our corruption by little and little. For other things, and judgments in this world, he removes the malice, and takes away the sting of them, which is the venom; as he saith afterward, 'For mine anger is turned away,' which being removed and turned from things, then they are no more judgments. What cared Paul for imprisonment, when he knew God's wrath accompanied not the stocks? Acts xvi. 19, *seq.* Let wrath be taken from the suffering, that the soul be sound, then it is no matter what condition a man be in, he carries heaven and paradise with him. Therefore, so far God removes those diseases and sicknesses of condition, as they carry venom in them; so changing the condition, that whatsoever we suffer, it hath the nature of an exercise, medicine, or correction only. But that which envenoms all, and makes the least cross a curse, and sinks deep, is the anger of God joined with things, Ps. lxxxix. 46. The least cross, when it carrieth with it the anger and vengeance of God, and reports that to the soul, I have offended God, and it is just with him thus to inflict wrath upon me: this is terrible, and it puts a sting to the cross. Now, God here promiseth to remove that, 'I will heal their backsliding.' This principally, in the first place, is meant of healing in regard of justification; taking away that guilt from the soul which enthrals it, and binds it over to condemnation and judgment. God will set the soul at a spiritual liberty, and so heal it. Thus you see the point clear, that God is the great physician of the soul.

Reason 1. For God who made the soul, *knows all the diseases, windings, and turnings of it.* He is an excellent anatomist: 'all things are naked and open before his eyes,' Heb. iv. 13. He knows the inward part of the soul, the seat of all sin. We know not ourselves as he knows us. There is a mystery of self-deceit in the heart, which he knows who can search all the hidden corners of the heart, which is the reason why he is so good a physician, and so excellent. Because he is a discerner and searcher of the heart, who can see all, and so can cure all, being above the sting of conscience, he hath a remedy above the malady. He is greater than our conscience. Therefore he can cure our conscience.

Reason 2. And in the next place, *as he can heal our souls, so he is willing to do it,* which his willingness we may know by the medicine he doth it by, his own dear Son. He hath provided a plaster of his Son's blood to heal us. And besides his own inward willingness, being now a gracious father to us in Christ Jesus, he sends his ambassadors to heal and cure us in his name, 2 Cor. v. 20, to apply his medicines, and to beseech and entreat us to be reconciled. God, by them, entreats us to entreat him for pardon and mercy, and is so willing to be entreated, that ere we shall set out he teacheth us words, as we heard, 'Take unto you words,' &c. As he is an able, so he is a willing physician. Christ, the great physician, together with his Father, expects not that we should first come to him, but he comes first, and sends to us. The physician came to the sick, though for the most part the sick, if able, go to the physician, 1 John iv. 9, 10. But here is the contrary. He came from heaven, took our nature upon him, and therein died, by which his blood-shedding, he satisfied the wrath of God, justly offended with us, Isa. liii. 10. So he heals our souls that way, having undergone the anger and wrath of God, that his blood might quench and appease that anger by a plaster thereof made, and applied to our souls, Isa. liii. 11, 12.

Do we doubt of his willingness, when he comes to us and calls us, 'Come unto me, all ye that labour and are heavy laden, and I will give you rest'? Mat. xi. 28. It is his office which he hath assumed to heal our soul. The many cures he hath done sheweth the ability and willingness of the physician; cures whereof we are incapable, by reason of our mean condition. A king, as his place is greater, so sometimes his sins are greater than others are; yet he cured Manasseh, that sinful king, 2 Chron. xxxiii. 23, together with Mary Magdalen, Paul, Peter, and the rest, who were a company healed by this physician. Therefore all this is for the glory of our physician. We may see what he can do by what he hath done; as amongst us physicians are sought after according to their skill and cures done. Consider in the sacrament how ready God is to cure and to heal us, how gracious he is in the sacrament of baptism, wherein he engageth us to believe, admitting us into the covenant, and preventing us with mercy, before we knew what a covenant or seal was, Ezek. xvi. 6, *seq.* And so to persuade us of his willingness to forgive our sins and heal our rebellions, he hath ordained the sacrament, not for his sake, but to strengthen our weak faith, and help us. The point is easy for matter of our understanding, but hard in regard of use and application, especially when it should be made use of, in time of temptation. Then let us lay it up as a comfortable point, this gracious promise of God, 'I will heal their backsliding, I will love them freely,' &c. Lay this up against the hour of temptation, make use of it then, alleging unto God his own promise and nature, as David did, 'Lord, remember the promise wherein thou hast caused me to trust,' Ps. cxix. 49. Thou hast promised pardoning and healing [of] all our trangressions, &c. Remember thy free promises made in Jesus Christ. God cannot deny himself nor his word, but loves to have his bonds sued. Remember this. And when conscience is surprised with any sin, though it be never so great, look not on the disease so much as who is the physician, and what his plaster and medicine is. God is the physician, and the blood of Christ is the plaster. What if our sins be mountains! There is an ocean and a sea of mercy to swell above and cover these mountains of our sins, Mic. vii. 18, 19. Our sins in this case are like fire, which, falling into the sea, is by and by quenched. What if our sins be of never so long standing (as these their backslidings here had continued hundreds of years, wherein they were a backsliding generation), yet it is no matter of what standing or continuance the disease is, so long as God hath promised to be the physician, and the blood of Christ is the plaster that healeth us, Isa. i. 18, 19. The question is not, What? How many? How great? and of what continuance our sins? but how we stand affected towards them, hate them, and resolve against them? That sin cannot hurt us which we fight against, mourn for, complain of, resolve to leave, and truly hate. Let us never stand, then, in comparisons with our sins, which bear no proportion to the infinite skill and power of our great physician, and to the infinite work of Christ's all-sufficient satisfaction. What canst thou object, O man? 'It is Christ that justifieth the ungodly, who art thou that condemneth? It is he that died, yea, rather, who is risen again, who is also at the right hand of God, and also maketh intercession for us,' Rom. viii. 33, 34. Thou canst not satisfy for the least sin. God hath laid upon him the iniquities of us all, Lev. xvi. 21. 'The chastisements of our peace was upon him, and with his stripes we are healed,' Isa. liii. 5.

Let us, therefore, be wise for afterwards, hear, read, lay up, and meditate for the time to come. For times will come, if we belong to God, that nothing will content or pacify the soul but the infinite worth and merit of an infinite and free mercy apprehended in the face of Jesus Christ. When our sins are set in order before us, the sins of our youth, middle, and old age, our sins against conscience, against the law and gospel, against examples, vows, promises, resolutions, and admonitions of the Spirit and servants of God; when there shall be such a terrible accuser, and God shall perhaps let the wounds of conscience fly open and join against us; when wrath shall appear, be in some sort felt, and God presented to the soul as 'a consuming fire,' Heb. xii. 29, no comfort in heaven or earth appearing, hell beneath seeming ready to revenge against us the quarrel of God's covenant, Oh then for faith to look through all these clouds! to see mercy in wrath! love in correction! Heb. xii. 6, life in death! the sweetness of the promises! the virtue and merit of Christ's sufferings, death, resurrection, and intercession at the right hand! the sting of death removed, 1 Cor. xv. 55, sin pardoned and done away, and glory at hand! In sum, this promise made good, which leads unto all this happiness, as we shall by and by hear, 'I will heal their backsliding, I will love them freely, for mine anger is turned away.' Oh, this is a marvellous matter, then, to be persuaded of! Therefore let us make a right use of these words in due season, for they are 'like apples of gold, with pictures of silver,' Prov. xxv. 11, like balm to a green wound, like delivery in a shipwreck. But, indeed, all comparisons come far short of this illustration, as the terror of incensed wrath in the fearful apprehension of eternal, unspeakable misery, is beyond any other fear, apprehension, or joy.

But lest this grace be abused by others (for we must not withhold the children's bread, for fear others partake with them unto whom it belongs not), let them know thus much: that those who turn this grace into wantonness, and will be evil, because God is thus gracious—that there is no word of comfort in the whole Scripture for them, who stand resolved to go on in their sins, presuming of mercy. See what God saith in this case, 'Lest there should be among you a root that beareth gall and wormwood; and it come to pass when he heareth the words of this curse, that he bless himself in his heart, saying, I shall have peace, though I walk in the imagination of mine heart, to add drunkenness to thirst: the Lord will not spare him, but then the anger of the Lord and his jealousy shall smoke against that man, and all the curses that are written in this book shall lie upon him, and the Lord shall blot out his name from under heaven,' Deut. xxix. 18–20. 'God will wound the hairy scalp of such an one,' Ps. lxviii. 21, who goes on in his wickedness, and means to be so. And in the New Testament those who thus make a progress in sin, what do they? They are said 'to treasure up unto themselves wrath against the day of wrath, and revelation of the righteous judgment of God,' Rom. ii. 5. Therefore God's word speaks no comfort to those who purpose to live in any sin. All the comfort that can be spoken to such is, that yet they are not in hell; that yet they have time to return to this great Physician of the soul. But take such an one in his present condition, he can have no comfort in this estate, wherein there is but a step between him and hell. So as when the rotten thread of this uncertain life shall fail, or is cut asunder, down they fall. We have no comfort here for them, till they return. This precious balm belongs to the wounded conscience. Briefly for use then.

Use. Seeing that our God is a healing God, as we can admire the wisdom, skill, and excellency of our physician, so let us much more make use of him upon all occasions. Trust and cleave to him, not like good Asa (but not good in this), who forgot himself, and sent first to the physicians, 2 Chron. xvi. 12. But let us especially rely upon God, and look to him, who can 'create help,' Isa. iv. 5, and must bless all means whatsoever. He is a healing God, who will heal all rebellions, and the most grievous sicknesses. He is a physician that is good for all turns. There are some diseases which are called the scorn of physicians, as the gout, the ague, and the like; wherein, in some cases, they are put to a stand, and know not what to do. But God is never at a loss. His skill cannot be set down. He is good at all diseases, to pardon all manner of sins. Therefore let us go to him for cure, seeing there is neither sin, nor grief, nor terror of conscience arising thereupon, which can be so great but God can cure both the sin and the terror, if we take a right course, and speak peace to the soul. God is a healing God, arising when he comes 'with healing in his wings,' Mal. iv. 2. As he saith, 'I will heal their rebellion,' &c. And as he is a healing physician, so he puts his patients to no charge. For as he saith, 'I will heal their backslidings;' so he saith, 'I will love them freely.'

Therefore let us the more build upon this truth, which is indeed the sum of all godliness. For what is the gospel but the triumph of mercy? Do but consider the scope of God in the new covenant, whereof the sacrament is a seal, which is only to shew forth the exaltation of the grace and mercy of God in Jesus Christ, above all unworthiness whatsoever. For all there is for the glory of his mercy. For in the covenant of grace, mercy doth triumph against judgment and justice; which mercy of God in Christ is said by the apostle 'to reign unto life everlasting, by Jesus Christ our Lord,' Rom. v. 21. It reigns, and hath a regiment* above, and over all. For mercy in God stirred up his wisdom to devise a way, by shedding of the blood of Christ Jesus, God-man, to satisfy divine justice, and rejoice against it. But whence comes this, that justice should be so satisfied? Because a way is found out, how none of God's attributes are losers by mercy. Wherefore in any temptation, when we are prone to doubt of God's love, say, What! shall we wrong God more, by calling in question his mercy, and the excellency of his lovingkindness, which is more than any other sin we have committed? This is a sin superadded against his mercy, power, goodness, graciousness, and love in healing of sin; which takes away the glory of God in that attribute, wherein he labours to triumph, reign, and glorify himself most, and 'which is over all his works,' Ps. cxlv. 9. Therefore he that offends herein, in denying God the glory of his great, tender, unspeakable mercy, whereby he would glorify himself most in the covenant of grace, he offends God most.

Therefore let us, at such times as God awakens conscience, be so far from thinking that God is unwilling to cure and help us, as to think that hereby we shall honour God more by believing than we dishonoured him by our sin. For the faith of an humble, contrite sinner, it glorifies God more than our better obedience in other things doth; because it gives him the glory of that wherein he delights, and will be most glorified, the glory of his mercy and truth, of his rich, abundant mercy that hath no bounds. There is no comparison between the mercy of God in the covenant of grace, and that to Adam in the state of nature. For in the first he did good to a good man; first he made him good, and then did him good. But when man did degenerate, and was fallen into such a cursed estate as we are, for God then to be good to a sinner, and freely to do good, here is goodness indeed, triumphant goodness. Cain was a cursed person, who said, 'My punishment is greater than can be borne,' Gen. iv. 13. We know who spake it. No; God is a physician for all diseases. If they be 'crimson sins,' he can make them 'white as wool,' Isa. i. 18.

* That is, 'government.'—G.

Who would not be careful therefore to search his wounds, his sins to the bottom? Let the search be as deep as we can, considering that there is more mercy in God, than there can be sin in us. Who would favour his soul? especially considering, if he neglect searching of it, sins will grow deadly and incurable upon that neglect. Let this therefore encourage us not to spare ourselves, in opening the wounds of our souls to God, that he may spare all. Thus we saw formerly, the church here is brought in dealing plainly with God, and confessing all (for she had an excellent teacher), and God answers all; beginning with this, 'I will heal their backsliding.' They were idolaters, and guilty of the sins of the second table in a high measure (no petty sins), yet God saith, 'I will heal their backsliding,' &c. Which being healed, then an open highway is made for all other mercies whatsoever, which is the next point we observe hence:

Obs. That the chief mercy of all, which leads unto all the rest, is the pardon and forgiveness of sins.

Healing of the guilt of sin, we see, is set in the front of these petitions formerly shewed; which as it is the first thing in the church's desire, 'Take away all iniquity,' &c, so it is the first thing yielded to in God's promise, 'I will heal their backsliding,' &c. Pardon of sin, and cure of sin, whereby the conscience ceaseth to be bound over to condemnation, is the first and chiefest blessing of God, and is that for which the church falls out in a triumph. 'Who is a God like unto thee, that pardoneth iniquity, and passeth by the transgression of the remnant of his heritage, because he delighteth in mercy,' &c., Micah vii. 18, 19, 20. And this is that excellent and sweet conclusion of the new covenant also, whereupon all the rest of those former foregoing mercies there are grounded. For, 'I will forgive their iniquity, and I will remember their sin no more,' Jer. xxxi. 34. Yea, this is the effect of that grand promise made to his church after the return of their captivity. 'In those days, and at that time, saith the Lord, the iniquity of Israel shall be sought for, and there shall be none; and the sins of Judah, and they shall not be found; for I will pardon them whom I reserve,' Jer. l. 20. The point is plain and clear enough; it needs no following. The reason is,

Because it takes away the interposing cloud. God is gracious in himself. Pardon of sin removes the cloud betwixt God's gracious face and the soul. Naturally, God is a spring of mercy; but our sins stop the spring. But when sin is pardoned, the stop is taken away, and the spring runs amain. God is not merciful as a flint yields fire, by force; but as a spring, whence water naturally issues.

Quest. Seeing forgiveness of sins unstops this spring, why do we not feel this mercy?

Ans. Surely, because some sin or other is upon the file uncancelled,* perhaps unconfessed; or because we are stuffed with pride, that we believe not; or are so troubled, or trouble ourselves, that we apprehend not, or believe not the pardon of sins confessed and hated. But sure it is, forgiveness of sins unstops the spring of mercy, and unveils God's gracious face in Jesus Christ unto us. Sin being not pardoned, this stops, as the prophet speaks. Our iniquity is that which keeps good things from us. Therefore the chief mercy is that which removes, that which unstops the current of all mercy. 'I will heal their backsliding,' &c. Look at a condemned prisoner in the tower! Let him have all contentment; as long as he is in the displeasure of the prince, stands condemned, and the sentence

* See note *b*, vol. I., p. 289.—G.

unreversed, what true contentment can he have? None at all. So it is with a sinner, that hath not his pardon and *quietus est* from heaven. Yield him all contentment which the world can afford; all the satisfaction that can issue from the creature; yet what is this to him, as long as he hath not mercy, and that his conscience is not pacified, because it is not cleansed and washed with the blood of Christ?

Sin is like Jonah: whilst he was in the ship, there was nothing but tempest, Jonah i. 4; like Achan in the army, Joshua vii. 11, 12: whilst he was not found out, God's judgment followed the camp. Sin is that which troubleth all. Therefore it must be taken away first; and therewith all evil is taken away. Therefore, the first mercy is a forgiving, pardoning, and quieting mercy. When the blood of Jesus Christ, by the hand of faith, is sprinkled upon the soul, God creating a hand of faith to sprinkle and shed it upon the soul, 'Christ loved me, and gave himself for me,' then the soul saith, Though my sins be great, yet the satisfaction of Christ is greater. God hath loved me, and gave his own Son for me; and I apply this to myself, as it is offered to me, and take the offer. This pacifieth the soul, as it is written, 'The blood of Christ, who through the eternal Spirit offered himself without spot to God, is that which purgeth our conscience from dead works to serve the living God,' Heb. ix. 14. To a repentant sinner, this 'blood of sprinkling speaks better things than the blood of Abel,' Heb. xii. 24: not as his blood cried for vengeance, but mercy, mercy. When the soul is thus pacified, there is the foundation of all other mercy whatsoever. The order is this: when God is reconciled, all is reconciled; when God is at peace with us in the forgiveness of sins, then all is peaceable at home and abroad. Conscience is in peace within, and all the creatures at peace without; all which, with all that befalls us, have a command to do us no hurt; as David gave charge to the people, of Absalom. When God is reconciled and at peace, all things are at peace with us. For is not he Lord of hosts, who hath the command of all the creatures? Therefore this grace of forgiveness is the chief grace.

To shew it in one instance more. David was a king and a prophet, a comely and a valorous person. But what esteemed he most? Did he say, Blessed is the man who is a king, or a prophet, or a valiant warrior, or hath dominion, obedience, or great possessions, as I have? Oh, no. 'Blessed is the man whose sins are forgiven, and whose iniquities are covered,' Ps. xxxii. 1. You see wherein this holy man David sets and pitcheth happiness, in the forgiveness of sins. Blessed is such a man. Though he were a king, he knew well enough that if his sins were not pardoned and covered he had been a wretched man.

Use 1. Therefore, this should teach us to desire of God continually *the pardon of our sins;* and we should make it the chief desire of our souls that God would shine upon them in Jesus Christ, pardon and accept us in his beloved. They go together.

Use 2. And *bless him for this above all other blessings*, as it is Ps. ciii. 1, 3, 'Bless the Lord, O my soul; and all that is within me, bless his holy name,' &c. Why? 'Who forgiveth all thy iniquities, and healeth all thy diseases.' We should bless God most of all for this, that he hath devised a way by Christ to receive satisfaction for sin, to pardon it, and say unto our souls, 'I am thy salvation,' Ps. xxxv. 3. This is the greatest favour of all.

Quest. But you ask, How shall I know that God hath healed my soul in regard of the forgiveness of sins?

Ans. The answer is, *If, together with pardon of sin, he heal sin.* For God, when he takes away the venom of a wound that endangers death, the deadly disease, he takes away also the swelling of the wound and glowing of it. When he ceaseth to make it deadly, he heals the soul withal, and *subdues our iniquities*, as his promise is, Micah vii. 19. So there is, together with pardoning mercy, curing mercy in regard of sanctification. Where God is a Father to make us sons, he is a Father to beget us anew. So where Christ comes by blood to wash away our sins, he comes by water also and the Holy Ghost; where he is a Comforter in the forgiveness of sins, he is a sanctifier. And the soul of a distressed sinner looks to the one as well as the other. Ask the soul of any man who is truly humbled, What do you chiefly desire? Oh, that God would pardon my sins! But is that all? No; that he would also heal my sins and subdue my rebellions, that I may not any longer be under the government and tyranny of my lusts, but under God's gracious government, who will guide me better than before, Hos. ii. 7. This we see to be the order in the Lord's prayer. After we are taught to say, 'Forgive us our trespasses,' it follows, 'And lead us not into temptation, but deliver us from evil,' which is for the time to come, Mat. vi. 12, 13. So David, 'Cleanse me from my secret sins, and keep me, that presumptuous sins have not dominion over me,' &c., Ps. xix. 12, 13. So that this is the desire of an afflicted conscience truly humbled, curing as well as covering of sin. This is a sure evidence that our sins are pardoned.

2. Then again, *when there is peace:* when the soul feels this, it is a sign that God hath healed the soul. 'For,' saith the apostle, 'being justified by faith, we have peace with God through our Lord Jesus Christ,' Rom. v. 1. The blood of Christ hath a pacifying power in forgiveness of sins. When Jonah was cast out, there was a calm, Jonah i. 12; so when sin is cast out and pardoned, there is a calm in the soul, which comes from the forgiveness of sins.

3. Again, healing is known by this, *if we have hearts willing to be searched*, for then our will is cured, which in the state of grace is more than our obedience. When we would be better than we are, then certainly our will is not in league with corruptions. Now, where the will is so much sanctified, I resolve to be better, I would be better, and I use all means, being glad when any joins with me against my corruptions, I am glad of all such advantages, here is a good sign. As now, when a man goes to church, and desires, 'O that my corruptions might be met withal! O that I might be laid open to myself, and know myself better than I have formerly done!' this is the desire of an ingenuous soul. Where there is no guile of soul, a man is glad to have himself and his corruptions discovered, whereas another frets and kicks, and rageth against the word of God, which is a sign that there is some league betwixt him and his sin. You have some that, above all things in the world, they would not have such and such downright ministers. O take heed; this is a sign of a hollow heart, and that a man is in love with his disease. Can there be a cure where there is a love of the disease?

4. Not to name many, the last, which is a high pitch, shall be, *by our estimation of things here and above.* What hath this healing wrought in thee? What estimation of things? How is thy heart weaned from the world? How are thy affections set on things which are above? Col. iii. 1. When a sick man is soundly recovered, though his distempered palate could not relish the best meats in his sickness, yet now he relishes and

loves the best most of all. Look, then, to ourselves. How forget we, with blessed St Paul, 'the things which are behind, pressing hard to the mark which is before, for the high prize of that calling'? Philip. iii. 13. How stand we affected, to long for our country? this world being only the place of our pilgrimage. Surely a soul that is soundly healed is an undervaluing soul, to use this world and all things therein as though we used them not; and it is also a valuing soul, to covet spiritual things above all, 1 Cor. vii. 29, 31. 'O,' saith David, 'how I love thy law, it is my meditation all the day; I love thy commandments above gold, yea, above fine gold,' Ps. cxix. 97, 127. The joy of this estate 'is a joy unspeakable and glorious,' 1 Pet. i. 8, of which it is said 'the stranger shall not meddle with,' Pro. xiv. 10. Thus much concerning the disease. Before we come to the cure a question ariseth.

Quest. Whence, then, comes a calm in a carnal person?

Ans. From ignorance and deadness of conscience, or from diversion. As a sick man, when he talks with another man that is his friend, his mind is diverted that he feeleth not his sickness all the while, so wicked men, either their consciences are seared, and they go on in sin, or else they have diversions. Great persons are loath to hear, and are usually full of diversions from the time they rise till they sleep again. All diversions busy conscience about other things; so they keep themselves, that it may not trouble them. But the peace of a true Christian comes from another ground, from sound knowledge of his disease, and from sound satisfaction, by faith knowing Christ, the Spirit of God sealing this knowledge to the soul. If peace be thus settled, it is a sign of a sound cure.

Quest. But you will say, How shall I know that my sins are pardoned when I am subject to those sins still?

Ans. Not to speak of transient actual sins, that are past and pardoned, when we have repented of them; but of the root of all sin, which is weakness and corruption in us, fortified, and, as it were, intrenched by nature, occasions and custom. Of this the question is, How to discern of pardon, the root of sin remaining, and now and then foiling us? The answer is affirmative. We may have that sin pardoned, which yet occasionally may foil us still. For a man is in the state of health, though he have the dregs of a disease hanging upon him, whereby a man ofttimes hath some little fit of the disease. When nature and physic hath prevailed over the disease, yet after that, there may be grudgings. So when God hath cured the soul by pardon, and hath begun to cure in sanctification, the cure is wrought, though some dregs remain, because those dregs are carried away with daily physic, and daily flying to God, 'Lord, forgive our debts; Lord, heal us.' Every prayer and renewing of repentance carries some debt away, till death comes, that excellent physician, which once for all perfectly cures both soul and body, bringing both there where both shall have perfection.

Quest. But you will say, Is God's grace weak, that it cannot carry away all dregs of corruption as well as pardon? Why is pardon in the forgiveness of sins absolute, when yet God suffers the dregs to remain, so as we still are subject to the disease of sin?

Ans. God is wise. Let us not quarrel with our physician, for he is wiser than we ourselves. For he makes these relics medicinal to us, as thus: naturally we are prone to security and spiritual pride, therefore he makes a medicine of our infirmities, to cure spiritual pride and security, and to set us a-work. Therefore the Jebusites, and the residue of that kind, were left uncast out from among Israel, that thereby he might prove Israel, and lest they should be a prey unto wild beasts to devour them, Judges iii. 1. So some remainders of the flesh are left still in the best, that these wild beasts might not prey upon their souls. Spiritual pride, which is a detestable sin, robbing and denying God of his prerogative, and security, the grave of the soul, to cure these two especially, God makes the relics and remainders of sin a medicine unto us.

Quest. Why doth God suffer these infirmities and diseases to remain in us?

Ans. Diseases are suffered, to put us in mind of infirmities in the root, which we knew not before. For if these should not sometimes break forth into a disease, we would think our nature were pure. Therefore God suffers them to break forth into diseases. Who would have thought that Moses had been passionate? Certainly, himself did not know himself, at the waters of strife, that the seeds of anger should be in the meekest man in the world! Num. xx. 2. Who would have thought that David, whose heart smote him for cutting off the lap of Saul's garment, 1 Sam. xxiv. 4, that so mild a man should have cruelty in him, and yet after that he committed murder? Who would have thought that Peter, who made such protestations of love to Christ, that though all men forsook him, yet he would not; yet after that should deny his Master, and forswear him? Matt. xxiii. 33, 69, &c. All which was to shew us, that it is useful for us sometimes to have our corruptions break out, to put us in mind what inward weaknesses we have unknown and unsearched in us, and that we may know the depth of our corruption. God's children are gainers by all their infirmities and weaknesses, whereby they learn to stand stronger. Here is a main difference betwixt the slips of God's children, and the ordinary evil courses of others. They grow worse and worse. The oftener they fall into sin, the more they are settled upon their dregs. But God's child hath the remainders of corruption in him, from whence he hath infirmities, and whence he breaks into diseases. But notwithstanding, corruption is a loser hereby. For the oftener he falls into sin, it is the weaker and weaker. For the more he sees the root of it, the more he hates it, resolves and strives against it, till it be consummated by repentance and sanctifying grace. Let no man therefore be too much cast down for infirmities, though ofttimes they break out, if thereupon we find a renewed hatred, repentance, and strength against them. For God looks not so much, how much corruption there is in us, as how we stand affected to it, and what good there is, whether we be in league with it, and resist it. It is not sin that damns men, but sin with the ill qualities, sin unconfessed, not grieved for, and unresisted, else God hath holy ends in leaving corruption in us, to exercise, try us, and keep us from other sins. Therefore sin is left uncured.

Now the way to have it cured, both in the pardon and likewise in sanctification, we have it in the context. What doth God say? 'I will heal their backsliding,' &c. After they had searched their hearts, and thereupon found iniquity, and then prayed, 'Take away all iniquity;' after they had desired a divorce from their sins, 'Asshur shall not save us;' and when they had some faith that God would cure them, and accordingly put confidence in God, 'the Father of the fatherless;' then saith God, 'I will heal their backsliding.' So that sense of pardon in the forgiveness of sins, and sense of grace, comes after sight, sense, weariness, and confession of sin. God doth not pardon sin, when it is not seen, sorrowed for, nor confessed, and where there is not some degree of faith, to come to God, 'the

Father of the fatherless,' and the great Physician of souls. When we do this, as it is said in the context, then we find the forgiveness of sins, with the gracious power of God's Spirit healing of our diseases, 'I will heal their backsliding.'

Let us therefore remember this, lest we deceive our souls, for it is not so easy a thing to attain unto forgiveness of sins as we think.

And then again, though forgiveness of sins be free, yet notwithstanding there is a way whereby we come to forgiveness of sins that costs us somewhat. God humbles the soul first, brings a man to himself, to think of his course, to lay open his sins and spread them before God in confession, and working upon the soul hearty repentance; so to come to God, and wait for forgiveness of sins, perhaps a good while before there be a report of it. There are none who have sins forgiven, but they know how they come by it. For there is a predisposition wrought in man's soul by the Spirit, which teacheth him what estate he is in, and what his danger is, whereupon follows confession; and upon that, peace. God keeps his children many times a long while upon the rack before he speaks peace unto them in the forgiveness of sins, because he would not have them think slightly of the riches of his mercy. It is no easy matter to attain unto the sense of the forgiveness of sins, though indeed we should strive to attain it, that so we may walk in the comforts of the Holy Ghost. The difficulty of obtaining or recovering the sense of forgiveness, may be seen in David after his fall. Did he easily obtain sense of pardon? Oh no! God held him on the rack a long time, 'He roared all the day long, his moisture was turned into the drought of summer,' Ps. xxxii. 3, 4. But when he had resolved a thorough, and no slight, confession; when he had resolved to shame himself and glorify God; then saith he, 'And thou forgavest my sin.' But till he dealt thoroughly with his soul without all guile, he felt no comfort. So it is with the children of God. When in the state of grace they fall into sin, it is no slight 'Lord, have mercy upon me' that will serve the turn; but a thorough shaming of themselves before God, and a thorough confession, resolving and determining to be under another government; to have Christ to govern them as well as to pardon them. God will no otherwise do it. Because he would glorify his rich mercy herein; for who would give mercy its due glory, if forgiveness were easily attained, without shaming of ourselves? If it came easily, without protestation and waiting upon God, as the church here, we should never be thoroughly humbled for our sins, and God would never have the glory of his mercy, nor known to be so just in hating of sin in his dear children, who long ago upon such terms have attained sense of forgiveness of sins. It is worth our trouble to search our souls and to wait at Christ's feet, never to give over until we have attained the sense of forgiveness of sin. It is heaven upon earth to have our consciences enlarged with God's favour in the pardon of sin.

What is the reason that many profess that God is merciful, and Christ hath pardoned their sins, &c.? If the ground be right, it is a high conceit of mercy; and such have been soundly humbled for their sins. But dost thou profess so, who livest carelessly in thy sins, and licentiously still? Surely* thy ground is naught, for hadst thou been upon the rack, in God's scalding-house, and smarted soundly for sin, wouldst thou take pleasure still to live in sin? Oh no! Those that go on carelessly in their actions and speeches, not caring what they are, did they ever smart for sin,

* That is, 'assuredly.'—G.

who carry themselves thus? Surely these were never soundly humbled for sin, nor confessed them with loathing and detestation. Therefore let us mark the context here inferred. After they had confessed, prayed, and waited, resolving reformation in their false confidence, then God promiseth, 'I will heal their backsliding.' It is a fundamental error in a Christian course, the slighting of true humiliation, which goes along in all the fabric and frame of a Christian course. Let a man not be soundly humbled with the sight of his sins, his faith is weaker, and his sanctification and comfort the slighter. Whereas, if a man would deal truly with his own heart, set up a court there, and arraign, judge, and condemn himself (which is God's end in all his dealings, afflictions, and judgments inflicted upon us), the deeper we went in this course, the more would our comfort be, and the report of God's mercy, in the sense of that which follows, 'I will love them freely: for mine anger is turned away.'

THE SIXTH SERMON.

I will love them freely: for mine anger is turned away. I will be as the dew unto Israel; he shall grow as the lily, and cast forth his root as Lebanon. —HOS. XIV. 4, 5.

IT was a good speech of St Austin, 'Those that are to petition great persons, they will obtain some who are skilful, to frame their petitions; lest by their unskilfulness they provoke anger, instead of carrying away the benefit desired.' So it is here with God's people, being to deal with the great God, and not being able to frame their own petitions, God, as we heard before, doth it for them, and answers them graciously with the same mercies which he had suggested them to ask; his answer being exact to their petitions, 'I will heal their backsliding, I will love them freely,' &c., wherein God exceeds all physicians in the world whatsoever. For they have nature to help them. Physic is the midwife of nature, helping it to do that which it cannot do itself. Physic can do nothing to a dead man. But God is so great a physician, that he first gives life, and after that spiritual life is in some degrees begun; by little and little he heals more and more. 'I will heal their backslidings.'

We have an error crept in amongst some of the meaner, ignorant sort of people, who think that God sees no sin when he hath once pardoned men in justification; who falsely smooth themselves in this wicked, sensual conceit, think they can commit no sin offensive to God; as though God should frame such a justification for men, to blindfold him, and cast dust, as it were, in his eyes; or justify men, to make them loose and idle. No; it is false, as appeareth by this place; for how can God heal that he sees not? He sees it not to be revenged on them for it; but he sees sin, to correct it and to heal it. He sees it not after a revengeful, wrathful justice, to cast us into hell and damn us for it; but he sees it after a sort, to make us smart and lament for it, and to have many times a bitter sense of his wrath and forsaking, as men undone without a new supply of comfort and peace from heaven. Let a man neglect sanctification, daily sorrow and confession of sin, and now and then even craving new pardon for sins past, casting all upon a fantastic conceit of faith in their justification: what follows but pride, hardness of heart, contempt of others, and neglect of better than themselves, and proneness out of God's judgment, to fall from ill to worse, from one error to another? In this case the heart is false and deceitful. For whilst it pretends a glorious faith to look back to Christ, to live by faith, and lay all on him by justification, it winds itself out of all tasks of religion, sets the heart at liberty, neglects sanctification and mortification of lusts, and beautifying the image of God in them, giving too much way to the flesh. Therefore, away with this false and self-conceited opinion, which draws poison out of that which God speaks to confirm and stablish us, 'That he sees no iniquity in Jacob,' &c., Num. xxiii. 21. Whence from these hyperbolical speeches, they think that God seeth not that which we ourselves see. But, 'He heals our backslidings,' therefore he sees them. For how can he heal a wound, if he see it not? He sees it, but not to their destruction who are freely justified by his grace. But we will leave this point, it being too much honour to them to spend time in confutation of it, and will rather say unto it, as Isaiah speaks of a menstruous cloth, 'Get thee hence,' Isa. xxx. 22.

Now as God is a most gracious God, never weary of well-doing and comforting his people, because it is his nature to be merciful, so he hath suitable expressions of it; he goes on with mercy upon mercy, lovingkindness upon lovingkindness. He had promised before, 'I will heal their backslidings,' take in sum all their apostasy, all shall be healed. But this is not all. He answers all the accusations and doubts of Satan, who is still objecting against us our unworthiness, misery, wretchedness to have such favours conferred on such filthy creatures. Therefore, he takes off all with this which followeth. As they had prayed, 'Receive us graciously;' so the answer is full, and suitable to their request, 'I will love them freely.'

Put case, they out of conscience of their own guilt should see no worth in themselves, or cause why they should be respected, yet I see reason in mine own love. 'I will love them freely.'

Quest. But may some say, How can God love freely?

Ans. Ask thyself. Doth not a father and mother love their child freely? What doth the child deserve of the father and mother a great while? Nothing. But the mother hath many a weary night and foul hand with it. Hath God planted an affection in us to love our children freely; and shall not God much more, who gives this love and plants it in us, be admitted to love freely? But indeed there is absurdity and infidelity in distrust. For it is against reason, to deny the mighty God that which we have in ourselves. If he did not love freely, how could he love us at all? What could he foresee in us to love for beforehand? The very manhood of Christ deserved not the grace of union, it was freely given.

'I will love them freely.' That which, first of all, we observe hence is thus much, *that God loves his people freely.* So saith the apostle, 'God commendeth his love towards us, in that while we were yet sinners, Christ died for us; much more being justified by his blood, we shall be saved from wrath through him,' Rom. v. 8, 9. The like we have in Ezekiel. Saith God, 'Therefore, say unto the house of Israel, Thus saith the Lord God, I do not this for your sakes, O house of Israel, but for mine holy name's sake, which ye have profaned among the heathen whither ye went,' Ezek. xxxvi. 22. Adam when he had sinned that main, great sin, what did he? Fly from God, run away; and when God called to him, and debated the matter with him, he accused God, and excused himself, Gen.

iii. 12, 13. Yet for all this God pitied him, and clothed him, and made him that promise of the blessed seed. What desert was there here in Adam! nay, rather the quite contrary; yet God loved him freely. The same may be said of St Paul, for the time past a persecutor, what deserving was there in him? None at all; yet he found God's free love in his conversion; for, saith God to Ananias, 'He is a chosen vessel unto me, to bear my name before the Gentiles,' Acts ix. 15. Here was no deserving in St Paul, but God's free election, which in time took place, Acts ix. 5. And so we may say of the prodigal, having spent all, his father pardoned all, and loved him freely, Luke xv. 20.

Reason 1. The reason hereof is, *because it is his name and nature to be gracious*, and to love freely; and whatsoever is God's nature, that hath a freedom in the working.

Reason 2. *Because no creature can deserve anything at God's hands.* (1.) Because by nature we are all God's enemies; and therefore what can enemies deserve? Nothing but wrath and vengeance. (2.) If we have any graces, they are the gift of God; and therefore we deserve nothing by them, they being of his own gift. So St James speaks, 'Every good gift, and every perfect gift, is from above, and cometh down from the Father of lights, with whom is no variableness, nor shadow of turning,' James i. 17. And St Paul saith, 'That of him, and through him, and to him, are all things,' Rom. xi. 36. What should follow hereupon? 'To him be glory for ever.'

Use 1. This, in the *first place*, serves for *reproof of our adversaries of the Romish Church*, who say that God loves us for something foreseen in us, which is good, or for somewhat which in time we would do to deserve favour at his hands. But both are false. The cause of love is free from himself; for, 'when we have done our best,' yet, saith the Holy Ghost, 'we are unprofitable servants.' Luke xvii. 10.

Use 2. *Secondly*, It is for reproof of *God's own dear children*, who, because they find no deserving in themselves, are therefore discouraged at the sight of their own unworthiness; whereas, quite contrary, the sight of our own unworthiness should make us the more fit subjects for Christ's free love, which hath nothing to do with them that stand upon deserving. Many of God's dear children are troubled with temptations, doubts, and fears of God's love and favour towards them, because they expect to find it in the fruits of grace, and not in free grace itself. If we would have any sound peace, let us look for it in free grace. Therefore the blessed apostle, in the entrance of his salutations in his epistles, still joineth grace, and then peace, to shew us that if we look for sound peace, we can nowhere find it but in grace. We would find peace in the grace that is in us, but it is labour in vain, for we shall never find it but in free grace.

Use 3. Hence we may also be *comforted in the certainty of our salvation;* for that grace, and love, and favour, whereby we are saved, is in God, not in us. Now, whatsoever is in him is immutable and sure. So saith the apostle, 'Nevertheless, the foundation of God standeth sure, having this seal, the Lord knoweth them that are his; and let every one that nameth the name of Christ depart from iniquity,' 2 Tim. ii. 19. Where speaking of election, which comes from the free love of God, he makes that a sure foundation to build on. If there be a reformation 'to depart from iniquity,' we may be comfortably assured of our salvation. And as it is with election, so is it with all the other fruits of God's love: vocation, adoption, justification, and perseverance. The foundation of God, fastly sealed in the way of holiness, stands good and sure in all, Rom. iii. 24; John xiii. 1.

Use 4. This further teacheth us *thankfulness unto God*, who hath so freely loved us; for if there were deserving on our part, what place were left for thankfulness? We know, one who deserves nothing, and hath small matters bestowed upon him, at least will be thankful for such favours. But when one is so far from deserving anything, that by the contrary he deserveth all plagues and punishments, hath yet many and abundant mercies bestowed freely upon him, this doth exceedingly provoke (especially a generous spirit) to a suitable thankfulness, as much as may be.

Use 5. And let it likewise breed *confidence in us to God, in all our miseries*, both for pardon of sin, help in distress, and comfort in sorrows, because he 'loves us freely,' and did love us whilst we were enemies. Make, therefore, upon all occasions, the apostle's use of it. 'For if, when we were enemies, we were reconciled to God by the death of his Son, much more, being reconciled, we shall be saved by his life,' Rom. v. 10.

'I will love them freely.'

In the next place, from hence we observe another point, which necessarily followeth upon the former,—*that God did not then begin to love them, when he said, 'I will love them freely;' but to discover that love unto them, which he carried unto them from all eternity.* For instance hereof, St Paul was beloved of God, ere God manifested his love unto him; as he testifieth to himself, that the discovery of this free love was, 'when it pleased God, who separated me from my mother's womb, and called me by his grace, to reveal his son in me,' &c., Gal. i. 15, 16. So the apostle blesseth God, in his salutation unto them, 'who had blessed them with all spiritual blessings in heavenly places in Christ,' Eph. i. 3. But whence fetcheth he the ground hereof? 'According as he hath chosen us in him, before the foundatiom of the world, that we should be holy and unblameable before him in love,' verse 4. We need not multiply places more to prove it. Our adversaries would fain seem to clear God only in all,* and so shroud their arguments under such needless pretences, shift off all places, name we never so many, with their strong heads, distinctions, and sophisms. But God will one day give them no thanks for their labour: the will of God (how unequal soever in our eyes, who cannot with our shallow conceits sound the depth of such mysteries) being ground enough to justify all his actions whatsoever. We will therefore come to some reasons of the point.

Reason 1. Because *whatsoever is in God*, manifested in time, *is eternal and everlasting in him, without beginning and ending;* for whatsoever is in God is God. God is not loving, but love, 1 John iv. 8; and he is not only true, but truth itself, John xiv. 6. He is not wise only, but wisdom itself, 1 Cor. i. 24. And therefore his love, discovered in time, must needs be from all eternity.

Secondly, If God did then first begin to love us, when he manifested his love unto us, *then there should be a change in God*, because he should love them now that he did not formerly love. As we see, those who loved Paul after his conversion loved him not before. There was then a change in the church. In which case, if God should so love, he should be changeable, and so be like unto man.

Thirdly, And then, again, *Christ's prayer*, John xvii., *makes it clear* that the love of God beginneth not with the manifestation thereof; for Christ there, knowing all the Father's secrets, as coming out of the bosom of the

* That is, 'would fain seem only to clear God in all.'—G.

Father, intimates the contrary, where he makes one end of his prayer for them to be, 'That the world may know that thou hast loved them, as thou hast loved me,' John xvii. 23. Now, how he loved Christ is also shewed a little after, 'For thou lovedst me before the foundation of the world,' verse 24. Therefore the saints and children of God are loved with an everlasting former love, not beginning at that instant discovery thereof.

Use 1. The use hereof is, first of all, against those *who measure God's love and favour by their own feeling*, because, as God loved them before, so he loves them as well and as dearly still; when he hideth his face from them, as when he suffered his lovingkindness to shine most comfortably upon them. He loved Christ as dearly when he hanged on the tree, in torment of soul and body, as he did when he said, 'This is my beloved son, in whom I am well pleased,' Mat. iii. 17; yea, and when he received him up into glory. The sun shineth as clearly in the darkest day as it doth in the brightest. The difference is not in the sun, but in some clouds which hinder the manifestation of the light thereof. So God loveth us as well when he shineth not in the brightness of his countenance upon us as when he doth. Job was as much beloved of God in the midst of his miseries as he was afterwards when he came to enjoy the abundance of his mercies, Job xlii. 7.

'I will love them freely,' &c.

The last point which we gather from hence, as a special ground of comfort, is this,

That this free love and favour of God is the cause of all other mercies and free favours, whereby he discovereth his love unto us.

(1.) It is the cause *of election*, 'Even so, then, at this present time also there is a remnant, according to the election of grace,' Rom. xi. 5. So (2.), For *vocation*. When the apostle had shewed that the Ephesians were saved by grace, he adds, 'That in the ages to come he might shew the exceeding riches of his grace, in his kindness towards us through Christ Jesus,' Eph. ii. 7. He afterwards sheweth, when this grace began first to have being, 'For we are his workmanship, created unto good works, which God hath before ordained that we should walk therein,' Eph. ii. 10. (3.) *Forgiveness of sins*. 'In whom we have a redemption through his blood, even the forgiveness of sins, according to the riches of his grace.' Eph. i. 7. So (4.), For the *grace of love*. 'We love him because he loved us first,' 1 John iv. 19. (5.) For *justification and sanctification*. It is said 'that Christ hath loved us.' Why? 'For he hath washed us from our sins in his own blood,' Rev. i. 5; and St John saith, 'He hath made us kings and priests unto God and his Father.' [1.] Kings to fight against the world, the flesh, and the devil. [2.] Priests to teach, instruct, reprove, and comfort ourselves and others by the word of God, and then to offer up the sacrifice of a broken heart, in prayers and praises. All comes from freedom of love. (6.) So *every good inclination* comes hence, 'for it is God which worketh in us, both to will and to do of his good pleasure,' Phil. ii. 13. So (7.) *Every good work*. 'For we are his workmanship, created in Christ Jesus unto good works, which he had before ordained that we should walk therein,' 'for by grace ye are saved,' saith he, 'through faith,' Eph. ii. 8, 10. So (8.) For *eternal life*. The apostle sheweth, 'It is the gift of God, through Jesus Christ our Lord,' Rom. vi. 23.

Use 1. This should teach us, in the first place, *to be humbled*, in that we are so miserable, naughty servants, doing so little work, nay, nothing as we should, yet should have so good wages. But 'God loves us freely,' &c. It should rather humble us the more than puff us up in pride, in regard that there was nothing in us which might deserve anything at God's hand, 1 Cor. iv. 7; Eph. ii. 9.

Use 2. And hence also it followeth that if he loved us from everlasting with a free love, John xvii. 23, 24, in a sort as he loved Christ, that therefore the *effects of his love towards us shall never fail*, as the apostle sheweth, 'The gifts and calling of God are without repentance,' Rom. xi. 29. Faith and repentance, being fruits of his love wrought in us, shall hold out. Therefore the weakness of these graces, as they shall not hinder our salvation, no more should they discourage us, or hinder the comfort of our profession; because that faith and repentance which we have is not any work of ours, but the work of God's free love in us. Therefore they shall be continued and accepted. For our perseverance doth not stand in this, that we have strength in ourselves to continue faithful to God, but because he, out of his free love, continueth faithful to us, and will never fail nor forsake them whom he hath once taken into his everlasting favour, on whom he hath set his everlasting free love, as the apostle speaks of Christ, 'Who also shall confirm you unto the end, that ye may be blameless in the day of our Lord Jesus Christ.' But upon what ground? 'God is faithful, by whom we were called unto the fellowship of his Son, Jesus Christ our Lord,' 1 Cor. i. 8, 9. So that if any of the elect should fall away, God should be unfaithful. The case in perseverance is not how faithful we are, but how faithful God is, who 'guides us here with his counsel in all things, and afterwards receiveth us into glory,' Ps. lxxiii. 24. So in another place, after the apostle had prayed, 'Now the very God of peace sanctify you wholly; and I pray God your whole spirit and soul and body be preserved blameless unto the coming of the Lord Jesus Christ.' What maketh the ground of this his prayer? 'Faithful is he that calleth you, who also will do it,' 1 Thess. v. 23, 24.

Use 3. If, then, we would have God to manifest his free love to us, let us strive to be *obedient to his commandments*, and stir up our hearts by all means to love him who hath so freely loved us.

Quest. Now, how should we manifest our love toward God?

Ans. First, in *loving his word*, as Ps. xix. and Ps. cxix. Secondly, in *loving his people*, 1 John v. 1, 2. Thirdly, in *longing for* and loving his *second coming*, Rev. xxii. 20.

Now followeth the reason of the discovery of this free love shewed now in time to them.

'For mine anger is turned away from him.'

Here is the third branch of God's answer to their petition, 'Mine anger is turned away from him,' which is included and implied in the former, 'I will heal their backsliding.' How could he do this if he were angry? No; he saith, 'I will love them freely,' which argues that his anger was appeased. God knoweth that variety of words and expressions are all little enough to raise up and comfort a doubting, wounded, galled soul, which, when it is touched with a sense of sin and of his displeasure, cannot hear words enough of comfort. This God knows well enough, and therefore he adds expression upon expression, 'I will heal their backsliding, I will love them freely, for mine anger is turned away from him.' The soul which is touched with the sense of wrath, and defiled with the stains of sin's dreadful impressions, receives all this cheerfully, and more too. Therefore, in such cases we must take in good part the largeness of God's expressions,

'For mine anger is turned away from him.' To unfold the words, therefore,

Anger is the inward displeasure which God hath against sin, and his purpose to punish it, accompanied with threatenings upon his purpose, and execution upon his threatenings. The point to be observed in the first place is,

That there is anger in God against sin.

We need not stand to prove the point, it is so manifest to every man. The Scripture is copious in it. If we consider either judgments executed upon sinners, threatenings against sin, or the saint's complaining of it, as Ps. lxxiv. 1, Job xlii. 7, Ps. vi. 1, Ps. xc. 11, Ps. xxxviii. 1, 3, Isa. lxiii. 6, with many the like places, prove that there is anger in God against sin. We will rather see the reason of it.

Because there is an antipathy betwixt him and sin, which is contrary to his pure nature. Sin, as it opposeth God, so it is contrary unto him; and, indeed, sin would turn him out of his sovereignty. For what doth a man, when he sins wittingly and willingly, but turn God out of his government, and causes the devil to take up God's room in the heart? When a man gives way to sin, then the devil rules, and he thinks his own lusts better than God's will, and his own carnal reason in contriving of sin above God's wisdom in his word; therefore, he is a proud rebel. Sin is such a kind of thing, that it labours to take away God; for it not only puts him out of that part of his throne, man's heart, but for the time a man sins, he could wish there were no God to take vengeance of him. Can you wonder, therefore, that God is so opposite to that which is so opposite to his prerogative royal as sin is?

The truth is, God is angry with nothing else but with sin, which is the only object of his anger. That which foolish persons make a trifle and sport of, swearing, filthy speaking, and lying, is the object of God's anger, Ps. xiv. 1. For this offence of sin he did not spare the angels of heaven, 2 Pet. ii. 4, but tumbled them thence, never to return again. Sin also thrust Adam out of paradise, Gen. iii. 23, and made God angry with him and the whole world, so as to destroy it with a flood of water, Gen. vi. 13, and will at last make him burn and consume all with a deluge of fire, 2 Pet. iii. 12. Yea, it made him in a sort angry with his own dear Son, when he underwent the punishment of sin as our surety, so that he cried out, 'My God, my God, why hast thou forsaken me?' Mat. xxvii. 46. If God thus shewed his anger against sin, in punishing it in Christ our surety, who was made sin for us, and yet had no sin in himself, how will he punish it much more in those who are not in Christ? Those who stand in their own sin and guilt, what will become of them? So that God is angry with sin, and with nothing else.

The second thing we gather from this, where he saith, 'My anger is turned away from him,' God's anger being taken especially for judgments, is,

That God's anger is the special thing in afflictions.

They come from his anger, as hath been shewed. Therefore he saith, 'I will take mine anger from you,' whereby he means judgments, the effect of his anger. For in the Scriptures anger is ordinarily taken for the fruits and effects of God's anger, which are terrible judgments, as we may see, Deut. xxix. 20, and so in many other places.

Quest. [Why are] judgments, then, called God's anger?

Ans, 1. Because they issue from his anger and displeasure; for it is not the judgments, but the anger in them, which lies heavy upon the soul,

When they come from God's anger, they are intolerable to the conscience: else, when we suffer ill, knowing that it is not from God's anger, but for trial of our graces, or for exercise, we bear it patiently. Therefore God saith, 'Mine anger is turned away from him:' for this, unremoved, embittereth every cross, though it be never so small. Let God's anger be upon a man, and he will make a conceit, a very light thing, to be as a heavy cross upon him, and vex him both in body and state more than mightier crosses at some other time shall. Will you see this in one instance, where God threatened his own dear people thus: 'And the Lord will smite thee with the botch of Egypt, and with the emrods, and with the scab, and with the itch, whereof thou canst not be healed,' Deut. xxviii. 27. What! is a scab, and an itch, and the like, such a terrible judgment, which in these days is set so light by? O yes! When it comes with God's displeasure; when the least scratch is set on fire by God's anger, it shall consume us, it proves uncurable, as there it is threatened: 'whereof thou canst not be healed.' When the vermin came in God's anger upon that hard-hearted king, all Pharaoh's skill, and his magicians' skill, could not beat them out, because, as they confessed, 'this was the finger of God,' Exod. viii. 19. Let any thing come as a messenger of God's anger, it comes with vengeance, and sticks to the soul, like a 'fretting leprosy,' Lev. xiv. 45, 46, which, when it entered into a house, many times could not be gotten out again with pulling out stones, or scraping them, till the house were demolished. So, when God's anger is raised and kindled against a person, you may remove this and that, change place and company, and use of helps; yet it will never leave fretting till it have consumed him, unless it be removed by repentance. If it be never so small a scratch or itch, all the physic in the world shall not cure it. For as the love of God makes all other things in God comfortable unto us, so it is his anger which makes all his attributes terrible. As, for his power, the more he loves me, the more he is able to do me good. But otherwise, the more he is angry and displeased, the more his other attributes are terrible. If he be wise, the more he will find out my sins: if he be powerful and angry, the more he can revenge himself on me. Is he angry and just? the more woe to me. So there is nothing in God when he is angry, but it is so much the more terrible. For this puts a sting in everything: which, when it is removed out of malignant creatures armed with a sting, then they are no more hurtful. The sting of every evil and cross, is God's anger and wrath. This being removed, nothing hurts. All crosses then are gentle, mild, tractable, and medicinal, when God hath once said, 'For mine anger is turned away from him.' After that's gone, whatsoever remaineth is good for us, when we feel no anger in it. What is that which blows the coals of hell, and makes hell hell, but the anger of God, seizing upon the conscience? This kindles Tophet, and sets it a-fire like a river of brimstone, Isa. xxx. 33. Therefore this is a wondrous sweet comfort and encouragement when he saith, 'For mine anger is turned away from him.' Whence, in the next place, we may observe,

That God will turn away his anger upon repentance.

When there is this course taken, formerly mentioned, to turn unto the Lord and to sue for pardon, to vow reformation, 'Asshur shall not save us,' and a thorough reformation of the particular sin; and when there is wrought in the heart faith to rely on God's mercy, as the 'Father of the fatherless,' in whom they 'find mercy,' then God's anger is turned away. God, upon repentance, will turn away his anger. The point is clear. We see, when the Lord hath threatened many grievous judgments and plagues for sin, one upon the neck of another, denounced with all variety of expressions in the most terrible manner; yet, after all that thundering, Deut. xxviii. and xxix., it follows, 'And it shall come to pass, when all these things are come upon thee, the blessings and the curses, which I have set before thee, and thou shalt call them to mind among all the nations whither the Lord thy God hath driven thee, and shalt return unto the Lord thy God, &c.; that then the Lord thy God will turn thy captivity, and have compassion upon thee,' &c., Deut. xxx. 1, 2, 3. After repentance, you see the promise comes presently after; not that the one is the meritorious cause of the other; but there is an order of things. God will have the one come with the other. Where there is not sense of sin and humiliation, and thence prayer to God for pardon, with reformation and trusting in his mercy, there the anger of God abides still. But where these are, 'his anger is turned away.' God hath established his order, that the one of these must still follow the other.

Another excellent place to the forenamed, we have in the Chronicles, 'If my people that are called by my name shall humble themselves and pray,' (as they did here in this chapter, 'take words unto yourselves') 'and seek my face and turn from their wicked ways,' 2 Chron. vii. 14; as they did here, 'Asshur shall not save us, we will not ride upon horses,' &c. We will no more rely on the barren false helps of foreign strength. What then? 'I will hear from heaven, and will forgive their sin, and will heal their land,' 2 Chron. vii. 14. Here is the promise, whereof this text is a proof. So in all the prophets there is a multiplication of the like instances and promises; which we will not stand upon now, as not being controversial. It is God's name so to do, as we may see in that well known place of Exodus. 'Jehovah, Jehovah, God, merciful and gracious, longsuffering, and abundant in goodness and truth; keeping mercy for thousands, forgiving iniquity, and transgression, and sin,' &c., Exod. xxxiv. 6, 7. And so it is said, 'At what time soever a sinner repents himself of his sins from the bottom of his heart, I will put all his sins out of my remembrance, saith the Lord God,' Hebrews viii. 12. The Scripture is plentiful in nothing more; especially it is the burden of Ezek. xviii. and xxxiii., forgiveness of sins, and removal of wrath upon repentance.

And for example. See one for all the rest. Let the greater include the lesser. Manasseh was a greater sinner than any of us all can be; because he was enabled* with a greater authority to do mischief, (all which no private man, nor ordinary great man, is capable of, not having the like power); which he exercised to the full in all manner of cruelty, joined with other gross and deadly sins; and yet the Scripture shews that, upon his humiliation and praying, he found mercy. God turned away his anger, 2 Chron. xxxiii. 12, 13.

That of the prodigal is a parable also fitted for this purpose, who had no sooner a resolution to return to his father, Luke xv. 23. *Filius timet convitium, &c.* The son fears chiding; the father provides a banquet. So God doth transcend our thoughts in that kind. We can no sooner humble ourselves to pray to him heartily, resolving to amend our ways and come to him, but he lays his anger aside to entertain terms of love and friendship with us. As we see in David, who was a good man, though he slubbered over the matter of repentance, all which while God's hand was so heavy upon him, that his moisture was turned into the drought of summer, he

* That is, 'endued.'—G.

roaring all the day long, Ps. xxxii. 3, 4. But when once he dealt throughly in the business, and resolved, 'I will confess my transgression unto the Lord; and thou forgavest the iniquity of my sin.' Let our humiliation be real and thorough, with prayer for pardon, and purpose to reform, and presently God will shew mercy.

The reason is clear, because it is his nature so to do. His nature is more inclined to mercy than anger. For him to be angry, it is still upon supposition of our sins. But to be merciful and gracious, it always proceeds from his own bowels, whether we be sinners or not. Without all supposition, God is still merciful unto whom he will shew mercy. 'Who is a God like unto thee,' saith the prophet, 'that pardoneth iniquity? he passeth by the transgression of the remnant of his heritage, and retaineth not his anger for ever; because he delighteth in mercy.' Things naturally come easily, without pain; as beams from the sun, water from the spring, and as heat from fire; all which come easily, because they are natural. So mercy and love from God come easily and willingly. It is his nature to be gracious and merciful. Though we be sinners, if we take this course here, as the church doth, to pray and be humbled, then it will follow, 'Mine anger is turned away from him.' The use is,

First, to observe *God's truth in the performance of his gracious promises*, who, as he makes gracious promises to us, so he makes them good. His promise is, 'If we confess our sins, he will forgive them and be merciful,' Prov. xxviii. 13. So here he says, 'Mine anger is turned away.' As they confess, so he is merciful to forgive them. It is good to observe the experiments* of God's truth. Every word of God is a shield, that is, we may take it as a shield. It is an experimental truth, whereby we may arm our souls. This is an experimental truth, that when we are humbled for our sins, God, he will be merciful unto our sins, and allay his anger, as it is in this text. Therefore it is said, 'Those that know thy name will trust in thee, for thou never failest those who put their trust in thee,' Ps. ix. 10. Let us then open our hearts unto God, and confess our sins unto him; and if we resolve amendment, we shall find the truth of his gracious promises. He will turn aside his anger, and will never fail us, if we put trust in him. 'The name of the Lord is a strong tower, and the righteous fly to it and are safe,' Prov. xviii. 10. This name of mercy, grace, and favour, is a strong tower to distressed consciences. Let us therefore remember to fly unto it, when our consciences are awaked and distressed with sin, and sense of God's displeasure. Seeing these kinds of promises are as a city of refuge, let us run unto them, and we shall not be pulled from the horns of this altar, as Joab once was from his, 1 Kings ii. 28; but shall at all times find grace and mercy to help us at the time of need. It is a comfortable point, 'Mine anger is turned away from him.'

Quest. But it may be said, How is God's anger turned away from his children, when they feel it ofttimes after in the course of their lives?

Ans. The answer is, that there is a double anger of God, whereby we must judge of things, for either it is,

1. Vindicative; or, 2. Fatherly anger.

God, ofter our first conversion, he removeth his vindicative anger, after which, though sometimes he threaten and frown upon us, yet it is with a fatherly anger, which God also removes, with the shame and correction attending it, when we reform and amend our wicked ways.

There is, 1. A child of anger; 2. A child under anger.

God's children are never 'children of wrath,' Eph. ii. 3, and anger, after

* That is, 'experiences' = trials of.—G.

their first conversion. But sometimes children under wrath, if they make bold with sin, so as they cannot use their right of sonship, to go boldly to the throne of grace. Because then, though they have the right of fear,* they conceive of God as angry with them, and cannot use it, so long as they live in any sin against conscience, and so continue, until they reform and humble themselves, as the church doth here ; after which they can and do rejoice again, claim their right, and are not either children of wrath, or under wrath. David, after he had sinned that foul sin, Ps. li. was a child under wrath, not a child of wrath. So, if we make bold to sin, we are children under wrath, for ofttimes God begins correction at his own house, if there be any disorder there, 1 Pet. iv. 17. You know God was so angry with Moses, that he was not suffered to enter into the land of Canaan, Num. xx. 12. And David, when he had numbered the people, God was angry with him, 2 Sam. xxiv. 1 ; and with the Corinthians also, for unreverent receiving of the Lord's Supper, 1 Cor. xi. 30. But here is a course prescribed to remove his fatherly anger, and to enjoy the beams of his countenance, and sunshine of his favour in Christ. If we humble ourselves, confess our sins, and fly unto him, as the church here doth, then we shall find this made good, 'For mine anger is turned away from him.' But it may be asked,

Quest. In times of affliction, how may we know God's anger to be removed, when yet we endure the affliction ?

Ans. The answer is, that God is infinitely wise, and in one affliction hath many ends ; as,

1. When he afflicts them, it is to correct them for their sins ; after which, when they have pulled out the sting of sin by confession and humiliation, if afflictions continue, his anger doth not continue.

2. Affliction sometimes is for an exercise of patience and faith, and trial of their graces, and for the exemplary manifestation to others of God's goodness to them.

But even then they may know that things come not in anger unto them by this ; that after repentance God speaks peace unto their conscience ; so that, though the grievance continue, it is with much joy in the Holy Ghost, and peace of conscience, in which case, the soul knows that it is for other ends that God continues it. Therefore the first thing in any affliction is, to remove away the core and sting thereof by humbling ourselves, as the church here doth, after which our consciences will be at peace for other things. God hath many ends in correcting us. He will humble us, improve our afflictions to the good of others, and will gain himself honour by our afflictions, sufferings, and crosses. When God hath shed abroad his love in our hearts by his Spirit, then we can rejoice in tribulation, and rejoice under hope, Rom. v. 5. Though the afflictions continue, because the sting is gone, anger is removed.

'For mine anger is turned away from him.'

The last point we observe from hence, and gather from all these general truths, is this,

Where there is not humiliation for sin, and hearty prayer to God, with reformation of our ways, flying unto God for mercy, who is merciful to the fatherless, there God's wrath continues.

For as where they are performed his anger is turned away, so must it needs follow, that where they are not performed, his anger continueth. Therefore, let us examine ourselves. The Spirit of God here speaks of

* Qu. 'the right, of fear they conceive?' &c.—ED.

'healing backslidings,' and of 'turning away iniquity.' Let us look well to ourselves, and to the present state of things, that our diseases be soundly cured, our personal diseases; and then let us be sensible of the diseases of the land, and pray for them. For there are universal diseases and sins of a kingdom, as well as personal. And we are guilty of the sins of the times, as far as we are not humbled for them. Paul tells those who did not punish the incestuous person, 'Why are you not humbled rather for this deed?' 1 Cor. v. 2. Where there is a public disease, there is a public anger hanging over upon that disease; the cure whereof is here prescribed, to be humbled, as for ourselves, so for others. Therefore let us beware of sin (if we would shun wrath), especially of idolatry, or else we shall be sure to smart for it, as Ephraim did, of whom the Spirit of God saith, 'When Ephraim spake trembling, he exalted himself in Israel; but when he offended in Baal, he died,' Hosea xiii. 1. Ephraim had got such authority, what with his former victories, and by the signs of God's favour among them, that when he spake 'there was trembling,' and he 'exalted himself in Israel;' but when he 'offended once in Baal,' that is, when he became an idolater, 'he died.' It is meant of the civil death especially, that he lost his former credit and reputation. We see then the dangerous effects of sin, especially of idolatry. Wherefore let us fortify ourselves against it, and bless God that we live under such a gracious, just, and mild king, and good government, where there are such laws against this great sin especially, and beseech God long to continue his life and prosperity for our good amongst us. For use then.

Remember, when we are to deal with God, *that he is the great Mover of all things;* who, if he be angry, can overturn all things, and cross us in all things; and can also heal us of all our diseases. But what must we do if we would be healed? We must take the course prescribed here, 'Take unto us words;' humble ourselves, and have no confidence in Asshur, munition, people, or in 'the works of our hands;' but trust in God, so shall we be happy and blessed. Whatsoever our enemies be, yet if we can make God our rock, fortress, and shield, then it is no matter who be our enemies. 'If he be on our side, who can be against us?' Rom. viii. 31. Let us all, ministers and all, reform ourselves, and stand in the gap, after the course here prescribed, and go to God in a right manner; so we may dissipate all the clouds of anger which may seem to hang over our heads, and find God experimentally making this promise good to us, which he made then to his people, 'I will heal their backsliding, I will love them freely: for mine anger is turned away from him.'

Therefore let us do as Jacob did with Esau, when he came incensed with mighty displeasure against his brother. Jacob comes before him humbly, prostrates himself before him, and so turns away his anger, Gen. xxxiii. 3. So when God is angry with us, and comes against us, let us humble ourselves before him to appease him. As Abigail quieted David, by humbling herself before him, when he had a purpose to destroy her family, 1 Sam. xxv. 23, *seq.*, so let us come before God in humility of soul, and God will turn away his anger. As when there was a great plague begun in the army, Aaron stood with his censer betwixt the living and the dead, offering incense and making atonement for them, whereby the plague was stayed, Num. xvi. 48; so in any wrath felt or feared, for ourselves or the State we live in, let every one hold his censer and offer the incense of prayer, 'Take with you words,' Rev. viii. 4. God is wondrously moved to pity by the incense of these sweet odours offered up by

Christ unto the Father. Believe it, it is the only safe course to begin in heaven. Such a beginning will have a blessed ending. Other courses, politic and subordinate helps must also be taken, but all is to no purpose, unless we begin in heaven; because all things under God are ruled and moved by him; who, when he is favourable, makes all the creatures pliable unto us, but especially makes this good, 'I will heal their backsliding, I will love them freely; for mine anger is turned away from him.'

THE SEVENTH SERMON.

I will be as the dew unto Israel: he shall grow as the lily, and cast forth his root as Lebanon. His branches shall spread, and his beauty shall be as the olive tree, and his smell as Lebanon.—HOSEA XIV. 5, 6.

THE church, as we heard, had been humbled, and therefore is comforted. It is usual in the Scriptures, especially in the prophetical parts thereof, after terrible threatenings to come with sweet promises; because God in all ages hath a church.* Therefore God in this chapter takes this course. He makes gracious promises to this people, grounded upon the former part of the chapter, wherein God had dictated unto them a form of prayer, repentance, and reformation. 'Take with you words, and turn to the Lord: say unto him, Take away all iniquity, and receive us graciously,' &c. Whereupon a reformation is promised, 'Asshur shall not save us, we will not ride upon horses,' &c. Which was a reformation of that national sin which they were guilty of, false confidence. Now, as we have heard, God answers them to every particular. He makes a gracious promise, 'that he will heal their backsliding,' according to their prayer, 'Take away all iniquity.' And to that, 'receive us graciously,' he answers, 'I will love them freely, for mine anger is turned away from him.'

Now, it cannot be but that God should regard the desires of his own Spirit, when both the words and Spirit proceed from him. Therefore he goes on more fully to answer their desire of 'doing good to them,' saying, 'I will be as the dew to Israel,' &c.

In which words the holy prophet doth first, by a metaphor and borrowed speech, set down the ground of all happiness. So that there is here given a more full satisfaction to the desires of the church.

1. The cause of all—'I will be as the dew,' &c.

2. The particular persons to whom—'to Israel.'

3. The fruit of this follows—'he shall grow as the lily, and cast forth his root as Lebanon.'

Now the words read are a fuller satisfaction to the desires of God's people, which were stirred up by his own Spirit. 'I will be as dew unto Israel.' Where,

1. You have set down the cause of all, which follows. God by his gracious Spirit will be 'as the dew unto Israel.'

2. And then upon that, the prosperous success this dew of God's Spirit hath in them, 'They shall grow as the lily.'

Obj. 1. Aye, but the lily grows, but hath no stability. Everything that grows is not well rooted. Therefore he adds, in the second place, 'They

* Joel ii. 27, 28; Hos. ii. 14, 15; Isa. i. 18, 19; Deut. iii. 1, *seq;* Jer. iii. 12; Jer. xxx. 1, *seq*.

shall cast out their roots as Lebanon;' that is, with growth they shall have stability; not only grow in height speedily, but also grow fast in the root with firmness.

Obj. 2. And likewise, as everything that grows in root and firmness, doth not spread itself, he says, he shall not only grow upward, and take root downwards, 'but his branches shall spread;' whereby he shall be more fruitful and comfortable to others.

Obj. 3. Oh! but everything that grows, is rooted and spread, is not for all that fruitful; therefore, he saith, they shall be as the olive tree, 'His beauty shall be as the olive tree for fruitfulness.'

Obj. 4. Yet, though the olive be fruitful, it hath no pleasant smell nor good taste. Therefore he adds another blessing to that. They shall, in regard of their pleasantness to God and man, that shall delight in them, be 'as the smell of Lebanon;' which was a wondrous pleasant, delightful place, which yielded a pleasant savour round about. So we see what a complete kind of growth this is, wherein blessing upon blessing is promised. The Holy Ghost cannot enough satisfy himself in variety of comfortable expressions. Nothing is left unsatisfied that the heart can propound. He will make them grow, be stedfast, fruitful, delightful, and pleasant. So that we have here to consider:

1. The favour and blessing that he promiseth, to be 'as the dew to Israel.'
2. The excellency of it in divers particulars.
3. The order wherein it is promised.

Before we come to the words themselves, if we remember and read over the former part of the prophecy, we shall find it full of terrible curses, all opposite unto that here promised: to shew,

We can never be in so disconsolate a state, but God can alter all.

He hath a right hand as well as a left; blessings as well as curses; mercy as well as justice; which is more proper to his nature than that. Therefore let Christian souls never be discouraged with their condition and state whatsoever it is.

Reason. For, as there are many maladies, so there are many remedies opposite to them. As Solomon saith, 'This is set over against that,' &c., Eccles. vii. 14. If there be a thousand kinds of ills, there are many thousand kinds of remedies. For God is larger in his helps than we can be in our diseases and distresses, whatsoever they are, Zech. i. 19, 20, 21. Therefore it is good to make this use of it, to be so conceited of God, as may draw us nearer unto him upon all occasions.

Again, we see here how large the Spirit of God is in expressions of the particulars. 'I will be as the dew unto Israel: and he shall grow as the lily, and cast forth his roots as Lebanon. His branches shall spread, and his beauty be large,' &c. Whereunto tends all this largeness of expression? God doth it in mercy unto us, who especially need it, being in a distressed, disconsolate estate. Therefore they are not words wastefully spent. We may marvel sometimes, in Isaiah, and so in some other prophets, to see the same things in substance so often repeated, though with variety of lively expressions, as it is, for the most part, the manner of every prophet. Surely, because it is useful and profitable, the people of God need it. There is, nor never was any man in a drooping, sinking condition, but he desires line upon line, word upon word, promise upon promise, expression upon expression.

Obj. One would think, is not a word of God sufficient?

Ans. Yes, for him, but not for us. We have doubting and drooping hearts, and therefore God adds sacraments and seals; not only one sacrament, but two; and in the sacrament not only bread, but wine also; to shew that Christ is all in all. What large expressions are here, thinks a profane heart, what needs this? As if God knew us not better than we know ourselves. Whensoever thou art touched in conscience with the sense of thy sins, and knowest how great, how powerful, how holy a God thou hast to deal with, who can endure no impure thing, thou wilt never find fault with his large expressions in his word and sacraments; and with the variety of his promises, when he translates out of the book of nature into his own book, all expressions of excellent things to spread forth his mercy and love. Is this needless? No; we need all. He that made us, redeemed us, preserves us, knows us better than we know ourselves. He who is infinite in wisdom and love takes this course.

And mark again, in the next place, how the Holy Ghost fetcheth here this comfort from things that are most excellent in their kind. 'They shall grow as the lily,' that grows fairly and speedily; 'and they shall take root as Lebanon.' To shew that a Christian should be the excellent in his kind, he compares him in his right temper and state, to the most excellent things in nature; to the sun, to lions, trees of Lebanon, cedars, and olive trees for fruitfulness; and all to shew that a Christian should not be an ordinary man. All the excellencies of nature are little enough to set out the excellency of a Christian. He must be an extraordinary singular man. Saith Christ, 'What singular thing do ye?' Mat. v. 47. He must not be a common man. Therefore, when God would raise his people, he tells them, they should not be common men, but grow as lilies, be rooted as trees, fruitful as olives, and pleasant, beautiful, as the goodly, sweet-smelling trees of Libanus. How graciously doth God condescend unto us, to teach us by outward things, how to help our souls by our senses, that when we see the growth, fruitfulness, and sweetness of other things, we should call to mind what we should be, and what God hath promised we shall be, if we take this course and order formerly prescribed. Indeed, a wise Christian, endowed with the Spirit of God, extracts a quintessence out of everything, especially from those that God singles out to teach him his duty by. When he looks upon any plant, fruit, or tree that is pleasant, delightful, and fruitful, it should put him in mind of his duty.

'I will be as the dew to Israel,' &c.

These sweet promises in their order follow immediately upon this, that God would freely love them, and cease to be angry with them. Then he adds the fruits of his love to their souls, and the effects of those fruits in many particulars; whence first of all we observe,

God's love is a fruitful love.

Wheresoever he loves, he makes the things lovely. We see things lovely, and then we love them; but God so loves us that in loving us he makes us lovely. So saith God by the prophet, 'I have seen his ways, and will heal him; I will lead him also, and restore comforts unto him and to his mourners,' Isa. lvii. 18. And from this experience of the fruitfulness of God's love, the church is brought in rejoicing, 'I will greatly rejoice in the Lord; my soul shall be joyful in my God: for he hath clothed me with the garments of salvation, he hath covered me with the robe of righteousness, as a bridegroom decketh himself with ornaments, and as a bride adorneth herself with her jewels,' Isa. lxi. 10. Thus he makes us such as may be amiable objects of his love that he may delight in.

Reason. For his love is the love, as of a gracious, so of a powerful, God, that can alter all things to us, and us to all things. He can bring us good out of everything, and do us good at all times, according to the church's prayer, 'Do good unto us.'

Use. Wherefore, seeing God can do us good, and since his love is not only a pardoning love, to take away his anger, but also so complete and fruitful a love, so full of spiritual favours, 'I will be as the dew unto Israel, and he shall grow up as the lily,' &c., let us stand more upon God's love than we have formerly done, and strive to have our hearts inflamed with love towards God again, as the prophet David doth, 'I love the Lord, because he hath heard my voice and my supplications,' Ps. cxvi. 1. It may be for outward condition that even where God loves they may go backwards so and so; but for their best part, their souls, God will be as the 'dew to them,' and 'they shall grow as Lebanon.' God will be good to them in the best things; and a Christian, when he begins to know what the best things are, concerning a better life, he then learneth to value spiritual blessings and favours above all other whatsoever. Therefore God suits his promises to the desires of his children, that he would water their dry souls, that he would be as the dew unto them. God's love is a fruitful love, and fruitful in the best things. As we know what David saith, 'There be many who say, Who will shew us any good? Lord, lift thou up the light of thy countenance upon us. Thou hast put gladness in my heart, more than in the time that their corn and their wine increased,' Ps. iv. 6, 7. So God fits his gracious promise, answerable to the desires of a gracious heart,

'I will be as the dew to Israel.'

2. To come to the words, in particular, for this is the ground of all that follows, 'I will be as the dew unto Israel.'

Quest. How will God be as the dew to Israel?

Ans. This is especially meant of, and performed to, the church under the New Testament, especially next unto Christ's time, when the dew of grace fell in greatest abundance upon the church. The comfortable, sanctifying, fruitful grace of God is compared to dew in many respects.

First, *the dew doth come from above.* God sends it, it drops from above, and cannot be commanded by the creature. So all other gifts, and especially this perfect gift, the grace of God, comes from above, from the Father of lights. There is no principle of grace naturally within a man. It is as childish to think that grace comes from any principle within us, as to think that the dew which falls upon a stone is the sweat of the stone, as children think that the stone sweats, when it is the dew that has fallen upon it. Certainly our hearts, in regard of themselves, are barren and dry. Wherefore, God's grace, in regard of the original, is compared to dew, which should teach us to go to God, as the church doth here, and pray him to deal graciously with us, to do good to us, for this cause laying open our souls unto him, to shed his grace into them.

Secondly, *the dew doth fall insensibly and invisibly.* So the grace of God. We feel the comfort, sweetness, and operation of it, but it falls insensibly without observation. Inferior things here feel the sweet and comfortable influence of the heavens, but who sees the active influence upon them? which, how it is derived from superior bodies to the inferior, is not observable. As our Saviour speaks of the beginnings of grace and workings of it, 'The wind bloweth where it listeth, and thou hearest the sound thereof, but canst not tell whence it cometh or whither it goeth: so is every one that is born of the Spirit,' John iii. 8. It works we know not how. We feel the work, but the manner of working is unknown to us. Grace, therefore, is wrought undiscernibly. No man can see the conversion of another; nay, no man almost can discern his own conversion at first. Therefore, this question should not much trouble you, Shew us the first hour, the first time of your conversion and entrance into the state of grace. Grace, to many, falls like the dew, by little and little, drop and drop, line upon line. It falls sweetly and undiscernibly upon them at the first. Therefore, it is hard to set down the first time, seeing, as our blessed Saviour speaks, grace at the first is wondrous little, likened to a grain of mustard-seed; but though it be small at first, yet nothing is more glorious and beautiful afterwards, for from a small seed it grows to overspread and be great, shooting out branches, Mark iv. 31, 32. And as the root of Jesse was a despised stock, and in show a dead root, yet thence Christ rose, a branch as high as heaven; so the beginning of a Christian is despised and little, like a dead stock, as it were; but they grow upward and upward still, till they come to heaven itself, Prov. iv. 18. Thus we see there is nothing in the world more undiscernible in the beginning than the work of grace, which must make us not over-curious to examine exactly the first beginnings thereof, because it is as the falling of the dew, or 'the blowing of the wind.'

Thirdly, Again, as it falls undiscernibly and invisibly, so *very sweetly and mildly*, not violating the nature or course of anything, but rather helping and cherishing the same; or if it make any change in anything, it doth it mildly and gently. So usually, unless it be in some extraordinary case, God works upon the soul by his grace mildly and sweetly. Grace works sweetly upon the soul, preserving its freedom; so as man, when he begins to be good, shall be freely good, from inward principles wrought in him. His judgment shall like the course he takes, and be clean opposite to others that are contrary, from an inward principle; as free now in altering his course, as formerly he was in following the other. There is no violence, but in regard of corruption. God works strongly and mildly: strongly, for he changeth a stone into a fleshly heart; and yet sweetly: he breaks not any power of nature, but advanceth it. For grace doth not take away or imprison nature, but lifts it up, and sets it at liberty. For it makes the will stronger and freer, the judgment sounder, the understanding clearer, the affections more orderly. It makes all things better, so that no violence is offered to nature.

Fourthly, Again, grace is compared to dew, *in regard of the operations of dew*. For, what effects hath dew upon the earth?

(1.) *It cools the air when it falls*, and then with coolness it hath a fructifying virtue; for falling especially on tender herbs and plants, it soaks into the root of them, and makes them fruitful. So it is with the grace of God's Spirit. It cools the soul, scorched with the sense of God's anger; as indeed all our souls will be, when we have to deal with God, who is 'a consuming fire,' Heb. xii. 29, till we take that course to look upon him in Christ for the pardon of sin; after which his grace and the sense of it cooleth, assuageth, and speaks peace to an uncomfortable, disconsolate heart. This voice, 'Son, be of good comfort, thy sins are forgiven thee.' Oh, this hath a cooling in it! and this also, 'This day shalt thou be with me in paradise.' Oh, how it cooled and cheered the good thief, and comforted him! And so when God says unto the soul, 'I am thy salvation;' Oh, when the soul feels this, how is it cooled and refreshed!

(2.) And the soul is not only cooled and refreshed, but *it is also sweetened and made fruitful with comfort to the soul.* If we were to see a man in the pangs of conscience, stung with fiery temptations, as with so many fiery serpents and poisoned darts, which drink up the spirits, and presents God a consuming fire ; and hell beneath, full of insupportable torments, set on by the insupportable wrath of God : then we should know what it were to have grace in this efficacious manner, cooling and refreshing the soul, that hath these fiery darts stuck into it of violent strong temptations, which to the present sense are the flashes and beginnings of hell. Oh, it is an excellent thing to have the grace of God in such a case to assuage and cool the maladies of a distressed soul, which for the present seems to burn in a flame of wrath ! As it cools, so also it makes the heart fruitful, our hearts of themselves being as the barren wilderness and wild desert. Now God by his grace turns 'the wilderness into water-springs,' as it appeareth in many places of the prophets. Saith God, 'For I will pour water upon him that is thirsty, and floods upon the dry ground ; I will pour my Spirit upon thy seed,' &c., Isa. xliv. 3 ; xlv. 8. So grace, it turns the barren wilderness, the heart, dry of itself, and makes it fruitful. We know what Paul said of Onesimus, a fruitless servant, nay, a fugitive thief. He is unfruitful no longer, saith he, now that he is become a convert, another, a new man, now he will do good service, Phil. xvi. A man is no sooner altered by the dew of grace, but howsoever formerly he were a naughty, hurtful person, of whom every man was afraid because of his wickedness, yet now he is a fruitful person, and strives to bring forth fruits worthy of amendment of life, Mat. iii. 8.

Fifthly, And we may add one more, in the next place, *in regard of the unresistibleness thereof;* for as nothing can hinder the dew from falling from the sweet influence of heaven unto us, or hinder the working of those superior bodies upon the inferior, or hinder the wind from blowing ; so who can hinder God's grace ? Job xxxviii. 37. They may, out of malice, hinder the means of it, and hinder the gracious working of the Spirit, by discouragements in others ; which is a sign of a devilish spirit, when yet God hath a hand in that too after a sort. For it raineth in one city, and not in another, by God's appointment ; but nothing can hinder, where God will have the dew and water, and shine of the influence of grace, work. Nothing in the world can stop it. So it is said in that excellent prophecy of Christ and his kingdom, 'He shall come down like rain upon the mown grass, as showers that water the earth,' which as they cool and fructify, so come they unresistibly, Ps. lxxii. 6.

Use. Let none, therefore, be discouraged with the deadness, dryness, and barrenness of their own hearts; but let them know that God doth graciously promise, if they will take the course formerly set down, to be 'as the dew unto them.' Therefore let them come unto the ordinances of God, with wondrous hope, confidence, and faith, that he will be as dew unto them ; that, seeing he hath appointed variety of ordinances, the word and sacraments, he will bless those means of his own ordaining and appointing, for his own ends. He that hath graciously appointed such means of grace, will he not bless them ? especially having promised, 'I will be as the dew unto Israel.' Therefore let us attend upon the ordinances, and not keep away, though our hearts be barren, dry, and unfruitful. God is above the heart, and able to turn the wilderness into a fruitful place. He can make the heart a fit habitation for himself to dwell in. Let us by faith attend upon the ordinances. If we find not comfort in one ordinance, let us go unto another, and another. Comfort and help shall come, especially if, with the church, we 'go a little further,' Cant. iii. 4; for the promise is, 'I will be as the dew unto Israel.'

But mark the order wherein he makes this promise.

First, He gives grace to pray to him. 'Take away all iniquity, and receive us graciously;' 'Do good to us.'

Then, *second, he gives a spirit of reformation*, promising amendment; whereupon this followeth, 'that he will forgive their sins, love them freely,' &c., and be 'as the dew unto Israel.' He will be as the dew unto Israel; but he will give them grace first to be humbled, confess sin, and pray to God for grace and forgiveness. There is an order of working in the soul. God giveth justification before sanctification; and before he freeth from the guilt of sin, he gives grace to confess sin. 'If we confess our sins, he is faithful and just to forgive us our sins, and to cleanse us from them,' saith St John, 1 John i. 9. Where these go before, grace will follow; and where they do not, there will be no sanctification. Therefore let us consider the order; for wheresoever God 'takes away iniquity,' and heals their souls, in regard of the guilt of their sins, unto those he will be as dew. Therefore, if we have still barren souls, without desires or strength to goodness, certainly our sins are still upon the file;* for justification is never without holiness of life. 'Whosoever is in Christ, he is a new creature,' 2 Cor. v. 17. When this is done, God will be 'as the dew;' because he doth pardon our sins for this cause, that he may thereby fit us to be entertained in the covenant; and are we fit to be in covenant with him, until our natures be altered? Therefore, whensoever he enters into covenant with any, he changeth their natures, that they may be friends, and have communion with him. Then the same soul which crieth, 'Take away all iniquity,' desireth also the dew of grace to make it better. This order is not only necessary on God's part, but in regard of the soul also. For was there ever any soul, from the beginning of the world, that truly desired forgiveness of sins, which did not also therewith desire grace? Such a soul were but a hypocritical soul. For if it be rightly touched with sorrow, it desires as well ability to subdue sin, as forgiveness of sin; holiness and righteousness, with forgiveness, Luke i. 75.

Use 1. Therefore, lest we deceive ourselves, let this be an use of trial from the order, *that if we find not grace wrought in our natures to restrain sin, and alter our former lewd courses, our sins are not yet forgiven.* For, wheresoever God takes away sin, and 'loves freely,' there also he gives the best fruits of his love, bestows the dew of his grace, to work upon and alter our natures. Christ came not by blood alone, to die for us; but by water also, to sanctify us, 1 John v. 6. He will not only 'love freely,' but he will be 'as the dew,' where he loves freely. Therefore, if we have not sanctifying grace, we have not as yet pardoning grace. For we know the prophet joins them both together. 'Blessed is the man unto whom the Lord imputeth not iniquity, and in whose spirit there is no guile,' Ps. xxxii. 1, 2. If we retain a guileful, false spirit, our sins are not forgiven. We see both these are put together.

Use 2. And seeing all these good things come from God, it is necessary to take notice of what hath been said of God's goodness, *that we do not rob God of his due glory, nor ourselves of the due comfort that we may draw thence.* The Egyptians had the river Nylus, that overflowed the land every year, caused by anniversary winds, which so blew into the mouth of the river, that it could not discharge itself into the sea; whereupon it over-

* See Note *b*, vol. I. p. 289.—G.

flowed the banks, and left a fruitful slime upon the ground, so that they needed not rain as other countries, because it was watered with Nylus. Hereupon they did not depend upon God's blessing, nor were so holy as they should; but were proud of their river, as is intimated by Moses unto the people. 'But the land whither thou goest in to possess it, is not as the land of Egypt, from whence ye came out, where thou sowest thy seed, and wateredst it with thy foot, as a garden of herbs: but the land whither ye go to possess it is a land of hills and valleys, and drinketh water of the rain of heaven: a land which the Lord thy God careth for,' &c., Deut. xi. 10, 11. They having more immediately rain from heaven, saw God's hand in watering it, whereas the Egyptians did not. And what makes a papist to be so unthankful? He thinks he can with his own industry water his own ground with somewhat in himself. What makes another man thankful, on the other side? Because he knoweth he hath all things by dependence from the first Cause: for as in nature, 'In God we live, move, and have our being,' Acts xvii. 28, much more in grace. We have all our nourishment, spiritual being, moving, and life from the dew of heaven. All our heat is from the Sun of righteousness,' Mal. iv. 2, which makes a Christian life to be nothing else but a gracious dependence. 'I can do all things,' saith St Paul,' Philip. iv. 13. Big and great words! Oh, but it is 'through Christ that strengthens me.' These things must not be forgotten. For a child of the church is a child of grace. By grace he is what he is; he hath all from heaven. Suitable to the former place is that in Ezekiel. 'And the land of Egypt shall be desolate and waste; and they shall know that I am the Lord; because he hath said, The river is mine, and I have made it,' Ezek. xxix. 9. He shall be desolate, because he boasts and brags of his river, and depends not upon God for the sweet showers of the former and the latter rain. They boasted because it was a fat, fruitful country, which the Romans called their granary. But we must look for all from heaven. God by his Spirit will be as the dew.

You know in paradise there were four rivers that watered the garden of God, that sweet place, and made it fruitful; but the heads of all these rivers were out of paradise, Gen. ii. 10. So it is with the church of God, 'There is a river, the streams whereof makes glad the city of God,' as the Psalmist speaks, Ps. xlvi. 4: many precious comfortable graces, the particulars whereof follow. But where is the head-spring of the river? It is in heaven. We have all from God, through Christ the Mediator. So, though we have of the water and dew, yet notwithstanding the head and spring of all is from without the church; in heaven, in Christ, in the Mediator. And, therefore, in all the excellent things we enjoy in the church, let us look to the original first cause, Christ by his Spirit. He is 'as the dew' to his church.

Use 3. This affords likewise an *use of direction*, how to come to have grace to sanctify and alter our natures.

Ans. Do as the church doth here; desire it of God. Lord, teach me to see and know my sins: Lord, 'Take away all iniquity, and receive me graciously;' Heal my soul, for I have sinned against thee. O love me freely. Turn away thy angry face from my sins, and be as the dew unto my barren soul; my dead soul, O quicken it; make good thy promise, come swiftly, come speedily, come unresistibly, 'like rain upon the mown grass,' Ps. lxxii. 6; as showers, to water with the dew of grace, and fructify my dry, parched soul. Thus we should be earnest with God for grace for ourselves, and for the churches abroad, for our church and state at home. Therefore, let such an use be made of it generally, as God, and not other foreign helps, may especially be trusted in: for it is the only way to destruction, to let God alone, and to trust to this body and that body. For in this case, many times, God makes those we trust in our destruction, as the Assyrians and Babylonians were the ruin of the ten tribes. But begin always first in heaven: set that great wheel a-working, and he will make all things comfortable, especially for our souls. Then we shall not only find him to make good this promise, 'I will be as the dew unto Israel;' but the residue which follow after.

'He shall grow as the lily,' &c.

Those unto whom God is dew, [he gives] a double blessing. He will make them grow, and so grow as they shall grow up as the lily. Thistles, and nettles, and ill weeds grow apace also, but not as lilies. But God's children are lilies, and then they grow as lilies.

Quest. How do Christians grow like lilies?

Ans. First, *for beauty and glory.* There is such a kind of glory and beauty in that plant, that it is said by our Saviour, that Solomon 'in all his royalty was not arrayed like one of these,' Mat. vi. 29. Because his was a borrowed glory from the creature, but the lily hath a native beauty of its own.

2. Again, the lily hath *a sweet and fragrant smell.* So have Christians a sweetness and shining expressed in their conversation; as we have it a little after, 'His smell shall be as Lebanon,' &c.

3. And then again, in regard *of purity and whiteness.* So, Christians are pure and unspotted in their conversation, and their aim is purity and unspottedness. Whiteness betokens an unstained conversation. So the people and children of God, they are lilies, beautiful and glorious in the eyes of God, and of all those who have spiritual eyes, to discern what spiritual excellency is; howsoever in regard of the world, their life be hidden. Their excellency is veiled with infirmities, afflictions, and disgraces by the malignant church; yet in God's esteem, and in the esteem of his children, they are lilies. All the dirt in the world cast upon a pearl cannot alter the nature of it. So, though the world go about to besmear these lilies with false imputations, yet they are lilies still, and have a glory upon them. For they have a better spirit and nature than the world hath. And they are sweeter in their conversation than the world; for when they have begun to be Christians, they sweeten their speeches and discourses. There is no Christian who is not of a sweet conversation. So far as grace hath altered him, he is beautiful, lovely, and sweet, and hath the whiteness of sincerity.

4. Now as God's children are lilies, and then grow as lilies for sweetness, glory, and beauty; so they are like lilies, especially in regard of *sudden growth.* When God gives a blessing, there is a strange growth on a sudden, as it is observed of this plant, that it grows very much in a night. So God's children, when his blessing is upon them, they thrive marvellously in a short space. To make this clear. When the dew of grace fell in our Saviour's time upon the Christian world, what a world of lilies grew suddenly! Three thousand in one day, at one sermon, converted by Peter, Acts ii. 41. The kingdom of heaven suffered violence in John Baptist's time, that is, the people thronged after the means of grace, and offered a holy violence to the things of God, Mat. xi. 12. So when this dew of grace fell, it was prophesied of it, 'The youth of thy womb,' saith he, 'shall be as the morning dew,' Ps. cx. 3. The dew comes out of the womb

of the morning, for the morning begets it: 'Thy youth shall be as the dew of the morning,' that is, they shall come in great abundance, as we see it fell out in the first spring of the gospel. In the space of forty years, by the preaching of the apostles, what a deal of good was done through a great part of the world! How did the gospel then break out like lightning, by means of that blessed apostle Paul, who himself carried it through a great part of the world!

And now, in the second spring of the gospel, when Luther began to preach, in the period of a few years, how many countries were converted and turned to the gospel! England, Scotland, Swethland,* Denmark, the Palatinate, a great part of France, Bohemia, and of the Netherlands. How many lilies grew up here on a sudden! Sudden growths are suspected, and well they may be. But when God will bless, in a short space a great deal of work shall be done. For God is not tied to length of time. He makes water to be wine every year in tract of time; for he turns the water of heaven into the juice of the grape. So there is water turned into wine; that done in tract of time, which he can do in a shorter time, as he did in the gospel, John ii. 1, &c. Where is the difference? That he did that miraculously in a short time, which he usually effects in continuance of time. So now many times he doth great matters in a short time, that his power may be known and seen the more, as we see now in these wars of Germany (*g*) how quickly God hath turned his hand to help his church, and hiss for a despised, forgotten nation to trample down the insulting, afflicting, menacing power of the proud enemy. And he can do so still, if our sins hinder him not. Surely if we stand still and behold the salvation of the Lord, we shall see great matters effected in a little time. 'They shall grow as the lily.' The accomplishment of this promise is not wholly yet come, for there be blessed times approaching, wherein, when the Jews are converted, 'they shall grow as the lily' in those glorious times there spoken of, at the conversion of the Jews and 'fulness of the Gentiles' coming in, Rom. xi. 12, the accomplishment whereof we expect, to the rejoicing of our hearts, that they should at length prove indeed with us the true children of Abraham.

Use 1. Therefore, we should make this use of all. Labour that the dew of God may prove the dew of grace, that God would make us lilies. If we would be beautiful and glorious, have a lustre upon us, and be as much beyond others as pearls are beyond common stones, and as lilies are better than thorns and briers, let us labour to have the grace of God, so to be accounted lilies, whatsoever the world accounts of us.

Use 2. Again, if the work be wrought upon us, though the imputations of the world be otherwise, let us comfort ourselves, God accounts me a lily. Set this against the base esteem of the world, considering how God judgeth, and those who are led by his Spirit, who judge better of us. And in all association, combination, and linking in acquaintance, labour to join with those that are lilies, who cast a good and a sweet savour. For we shall gain by their acquaintance whom Solomon affirmeth to be better and more excellent than their brethren, Prov. xii. 26. What are other people then? They are but thorns. Therefore, let not those which are lilies have too much or near acquaintance with thorns, lest they prick us, and, as our blessed Savour saith, turning again all to be-rent† us, Mat. vii. 6. It is said of our blessed Saviour in the Canticles, 'He feedeth among the lilies,' ii. 16. And, indeed, where is there any true delight to be had under

* That is, 'Sweden.'—G.

† That is, 'rend.'—G.

heaven but in their company who are gracious? What can a man receive from profane spirits in regard of comfort of soul? Nothing. They are as the barren wilderness that can yield nothing. Their hearts are empty. Therefore, their tongues are worth nothing. But let our delight be with David, toward the most excellent of the land, Ps. ci. 6, and then we shall not only 'grow as the lily,' but, as it followeth, 'we shall cast forth our roots as Lebanon.'

'And cast forth his roots as Lebanon.'

Because we have spoken of growth, and shall have occasion to touch it hereafter, we will not be large in the point. God here promiseth a growth not only to the church, but to every particular Christian; and it is very necessary it should be so. For without growth neither can we give God his due honour, nor he receive the smell of a sweet sacrifice from us, as is fit. Nor can we without it withstand our enemies, or bear our crosses that God may call us to. Again, without growth and strength we cannot perform those great duties that God requires at our hands, of thankfulness; nor do things so cheerfully and sweetly as may be comfortable to us. In some* without growth we can do nothing acceptably either to God or his people. The more grace, the more acceptance, which is spoken that we may value the promises, this especially, that we shall grow up in grace and knowledge 'as the lily, and cast forth our roots as Lebanon.'

Quest. But how shall we come to grow?

Ans. 1. Go to God, *that we may continually have from him the sanctifying dew of his grace.* Go first for pardon of sin, then for a heart to reform our ways, to enter in a new covenant for the time to come, that we will not 'trust in Asshur,' but will renounce our particular personal sins; after which we shall find sanctifying grace, so as the dew of God's Spirit will make us grow. Therefore take this order to improve the promises. Go to God for his love in Christ, for the pardoning of sin, and accepting of us in him, that we may find a sense of his love in accepting of our persons, in the pardoning of our sin, which is the ground of love; for then this sense of his love will kindle our love towards him again, feeling that we are in the state of grace. Then go to God for his promise in this order: Lord, thou hast promised that thou wilt be as the dew, and that we shall grow as lilies. Make good thy promise then, that I may find the effectual power of it transforming my soul into the blessed image of thy dear Son!

2. And know *that we must use all the means of growth, together with the promise;* for, in the things of this life, if a man were assured that the next year would be a very plentiful year, would men therefore, because they were thus forewarned, hang up their ploughs, and not prepare their ground? No; but they would the rather be encouraged to take pains, because they know that howsoever God be pleased to vouchsafe plenty, yet he will do it in the use of means, observing and depending on his providence. So when he hath made gracious promises of the dew of his grace, and of growth as lilies, &c., this implieth a subordinate serving of his gracious providence. Therefore it is a way to stir us up unto the use of all means rather, and not to take us off from them. Even as God, when he told the Israelites, 'I will give you the land of Canaan,' Gen. xvii. 8, did only promise it, leaving the remainder to their conquest in the use of means. Should this have made them cast away their swords? No; but it was that they might fight, and fight the more courageously. So when God hath promised growth in grace, should this make us careless? Oh no; it should make us

* Qu. 'in sum?'—ED.

more diligent and careful, and comfort us in the use of means, knowing that our labour shall not be in vain in the Lord, 1 Cor. xv. 58. Now, Lord, I know I shall not lose my labour in hearing, in receiving of the sacrament, in the communion of saints, and use of sanctified means, for thou hast made a gracious promise that 'I shall grow as the lily,' and that thou wilt be 'as the dew unto me.' Therefore make thy good work begun, effectual unto my poor soul, that it may flourish and be refreshed as a watered garden. But there are several sorts of growth formerly touched, either

1. A growing upward; or
2. A growing in the root; or
3. A spreading and growing in the fruit, and sweetness.

Therefore Christians must not always look to have their growth in one and the same place, but must wisely consider of God's prudent dealing with his children in this kind, as will be further seen hereafter in the particulars.

'He shall cast forth his roots as Lebanon.'

That is, he shall cast and spread, and so put forth his roots as Lebanon. He shall grow upward and downward. In regard of firmness, he shall be more rooted. In what proportion? Trees grow upwards, in that proportion they take root downwards, because otherwise they may be top-heavy and overturn, a blast of wind taking advantage of their tallness and weakness, to root them out the sooner. Therefore, proportionable to their spreading above, there must be a rooting in the ground. As the prophet speaks to Hezekiah of God's people, 'And the remnant that is escaped of the house of Judah shall yet again take root downward, and bear fruit upward,' 2 Kings xix. 30. There must be firmness in the root, as well as growth in the branches, for which cause God here promiseth to the church and every Christian stability and fixedness, that as he groweth upward like the lily, so he should grow downward, firm and strong.

Quest. Now, whence comes this rootedness and firm stability of God's children?

Ans. Especially from this, that they are now in the covenant of grace, rooted in Christ, who is God-man, in whom they are firmly rooted. In Adam we had a root of our own, but now our root is in Christ. All grace is first poured into Christ's blessed nature, John i. 16, and then at a second hand, 'out of his fulness we all receive grace for grace.' Being rooted in Christ we become firm, for there is in him an everlasting marriage and union. 'The root beareth us, we bear not the root,' Rom. xi. 18. Christ beareth us, we bear not him. So now, in the covenant of grace, all the firmness is out of us. Even as salvation itself was wrought out of us by a mediator, so it is kept by a mediator out of us. All goodness, grace, and favour of God to us is not in us, but in Christ; but it is so out of us, as Christ and we are one. But now we only speak of the cause of our firmness and stability, that because we are in the state of grace we have an everlasting firmness, as we are in Christ Jesus. God now making a second covenant, he will not have it disannulled as the first was, for his second works are better than his first. His first covenant was, 'Do this and live,' Lev. xviii. 5; but his second is, 'Believe this and live,' Rom. x. 9. So as howsoever our state in grace be but little, yet it is of a blessed, growing, spreading, firm nature, so sure as what is begun in grace will end in glory. Where God gives the first fruits he will give tenths, yea, the full harvest and all, because by the covenant of grace we are one with Christ, who is an everlasting head that never dies. Subservient to this now we have promised in the covenant of grace that we shall never depart from him, and that he will never depart from us to do us good. He puts an awe-band into our hearts, that we shall never depart from him. But this point being often touched, leaving it, we will come to answer some objections.

Obj. 1. It may seem that these things are not so. God's children do not always grow and spread themselves, but they are often overturned and fall.

Ans 1. This is nothing. They are moved, but not removed. They are as Mount Zion, which cannot be removed, but abideth for ever, Ps. cxxv. 1, which, though it may be shaken with earthquakes, yet is not removed thereby. The gates of hell and sorrows of death may set sore upon them, but not prevail against them, Mat. xvi. 18. They may fall, but not fall away. They may be as a weather-beaten tree, but not as a tree pulled up by the roots. Therefore they are compared here to a tree whose root stands fast still. Thus much the church, after a sore trial and endurance of much affliction, confesseth, 'All this is come upon us, yet have we not forgotten thee, neither have we dealt falsely in thy covenant; our heart is not turned back, neither have our steps declined from thy way, though thou hast broken us in the place of dragons, and covered us with the shadow of death,' &c., Ps. xliv. 17, 18, 19.

And again, though they fall, yet they learn to stand fast by their falls, are gainers by their losses, and become stronger by their weaknesses. As tall cedars, the more they are shaken by the winds, the more deeply they take rooting; so Christians, the more storms and blasts they have, the more they are fastly rooted. That which we think to be the overthrow of God's children, doth but root them deeper. As Peter after his fall took deeper rooting, and David, &c., so after all outward storms and declinings, here is the fruit of all. They take deeper rooting, whilst their sins are purged away by their fiery afflictions, Isa. xxx. 15.

Qbject. 2. But why then are they not more comfortable in their lives, in feeling and seeing of God's wise ordering of things?

Ans. 1. *First,* Because though God work strongly and surely in them, *yet he doth it for the most part slowly,* as the wise man speaks, 'all his works being beautiful in time,' Eccl. iii. 11. Therefore they apprehend not their comforts as they ought, and so go mourning the longer: the time of knitting divine experiences together not being yet come.

Secondly, Because the anguish of the cross, if it be quick and sharp, many times *takes away the apprehensions of God's excellent ends in the same;* as the children of Israel could not hearken unto Moses, for anguish and vexation of spirit, Exod. vi. 9. 'No affliction,' saith the apostle, 'for the present is joyous,' though afterwards it brings forth the quiet fruit of righteousness, Heb. xii. 11.

Thirdly, Then again, *Satan's malice,* who casts in floods of temptations, *is great.* So that the soul cannot enjoy that sweet tranquillity and peace it otherwise might, casting in doubts and numbers of what-ifs into the soul. So that for a time, he causes a strong diversion in them, whence after that, there followeth peace again, when those temptations are seen and overcome.

Fourthly, It is long also of ourselves, who are not armed for crosses and afflictions, until we are suddenly surprised by them. And then leaving our watchfulness, and forgetting our consolation, we are struck down for the present by them, and cannot support ourselves against them.

Fifthly, and lastly, It comes also *from God's wise ordering and disposing providence,* who will not do all at once. Our comforts must come by degrees, now a little and then a little. Our experience, and so our comforts, come together, after we have honoured God in dependence upon his will and pleasure. And yet this hinders not, but a Christian grows still, though he be for the present insensible of it, as a man is alive and grows whilst he sleeps, though he be not sensible of it. Other objections have been formerly touched.

'He shall cast forth his roots as Lebanon.'

We see then that the state of God's children is a firm and a stable condition, whence we may observe the difference betwixt God's people and others. God's people are rooted, and spread their root; but the other have rottenness in their root, being cursed, without any foundation. For take a man who is not a good Christian, where is his foundation? Only in the things of this world. Now all here is vanity, and we ourselves by trusting vanity become vain, 'Every man in his best estate is altogether vanity,' Ps. lxii. 9, vanity in himself, and trusts in vanity. What stableness can there be in vanity? Can a man, *stare non stante*, stand in a thing that stands not in itself? Will a picture continue that is drawn upon the ice? Will it not fail and melt away, when the ice upon which it is drawn thaws? So all these who have not the dew of God's grace, they are as a picture upon the water, have no foundation, and stand upon that which cannot stand itself. Therefore the Scripture compareth them to the worst of grass, which hath no good root; grass upon the housetop, which hath no blessing of those that come by, but there stands perking up above others, Ps. cxxix. 6. So it is with men that have no grace, they can perk up above others; but as they have no stable root, nor the blessing of God's people, stability with the Spirit of God inwardly, and the prayers of God's people to water and bless them, so they perish and wither quickly. Nay, whole nations, if wicked, have no foundation. What is become of the great monarchies of the world, the Assyrian, Persian, Grecian and Roman monarchies? And for cities themselves, they have died like men, and had their periods. Only a Christian hath a kingdom, a stable condition which cannot be shaken, Heb. xii. 28. He takes his root strongly, and grows stronger and stronger till he grows to heaven, nay, indeed, while he lives, he is rooted in heaven before his time; for though we be in earth, we are rooted in heaven. Christ our root is in heaven, and his faith which is wrought from heaven, carrieth us to Christ in heaven; and love, that grace of union, following the union of faith, carrieth us to Christ also. Even before our time, we are there in faith, love, and joy. Therefore a poor Christian is firm and stable even in this life, having union with Christ. Though he creep upon the earth, and seem a despised person, yet his root is heaven, where he hath union with Christ. 'His life is hid with God in Christ,' who 'when he shall appear,' he shall appear with him likewise in glory, Col. iii. 3, 4. Therefore, if Christ be firm, the estate of a Christian must needs be firm, for he is a cedar. Another man is as grass or corn upon the house-top. 'All flesh is grass,' saith the prophet, Isa. xl. 6.

Obj. Aye, but they have wit, and memory, and parts, &c. Yet they are but as the flower of the grass, perhaps better than ordinary grass, 'but the grass withereth, and the flower fadeth.' What continueth then? Oh, the word of the Lord, and comfort and grace by that word, 'endures for ever,' 1 Pet. i. 25, and makes us endure for ever. This is excellently set down by the prophet David. We see there, the righteous man is compared to a tree planted by the water side, his leaf fails not, Ps. i. 3. So a Christian is planted in Christ, he is still on the growing hand, and his leaf shall not wither: 'Those who are planted in the house of the Lord, shall flourish in the courts of our God, they shall still bring fruit in their old age, they shall be fat and flourishing, they shall grow like a cedar in Lebanon,' Ps. xcii. 13.

Use 1. This clear difference should stir us up to *be comforted in our condition, which is firm and stable.* Why do we value crystal above glass? Because it is brighter, and of more continuance. Why do we value continuing things? inheritance above annuities? Because they continue. If by the strength of our discourse, we value things answerable to their lasting, why should we not value the best things? Our estate in grace, this is a lasting condition: for a Christian is like a cedar that is rooted, and takes deeper and deeper root, and never leaves growing till he grow to heaven. 'He shall cast forth his roots as Lebanon.'

Use 2. Again, let all them make use of it, *that find not the work of grace upon their hearts.* Oh! let them consider what a fading condition they are in. They think they can do great matters. Perhaps they have a destructive power. They labour to do mischief, to crush whom they will in this world. But what is all this? We see what the psalmist saith of a Doeg, a cursed man, who had a destroying power. 'Why boastest thou thyself in mischief, O mighty man? the goodness of God endureth continually,' Ps. lii. 1. Why boastest thou thyself, that thou canst do mischief and overturn God's people? &c. Know this, that the good will of God continues. Boast not thyself; thy tongue deviseth mischief, as a sharp razor; God shall destroy thee for ever. He shall cast thee away and pull thee out of thy dwelling, and root thee out of the land of the living. Those men that rejoice in a destructive power, in their ability to do mischief, and exercising of that ability all they can, they shall be plucked out of their place, and rooted out of the land of the living. And as it is in Job, they shall be hurled away as a man hurls a stone out of a sling, Job. xxvii. 21. Then what shall the righteous say? They shall see and fear, and say, 'Lo, this is the man that made not God his strength, but trusted in the abundance of his riches, and strengthened himself in wickedness,' Ps. lii. 7. He thought to root himself so fast, that he should never be removed; but at the last it shall come to pass, that all that see him shall say, 'Lo, see what is become of him! this is the man that trusted in his riches, and made not God his strength.' What is become of him? Saith David of himself, 'I am like a green olive tree in the house of God; I trust in the mercy of God for ever and ever,' Ps. lii. 8. Let them trust, if they will, in riches, power, strength, and favour with Saul and great men; yet notwithstanding, be Doeg what he will, 'I shall be a green olive planted in the house of God,' &c.

So here is a double use the Scripture makes of these things. 1. The godly man rejoiceth in his condition; and 2, Other men fear and grow wise, not to trust to their fading condition. They are, as the prophet speaks, 'as a bay tree,' Ps. xxxvii. 35, that flourishes for a time, and then after come to nothing, 'their place is nowhere found.' They keep a great deal of do in the world for a time, but afterwards, where is such an one? Their place is nowhere found, nowhere comfortably. They have a place in hell, but comfortably a place nowhere. This is the estate of all those who have not a good root. For, saith Christ, 'Every plant that my heavenly Father hath not planted, shall be rooted up,' Mat. xv. 13. It is true of every condition, and of every man, if God have not planted him in that excellent state, or do not in time, he shall be rooted up. For the time will come that the earth will hold him no longer. He roots himself now in the earth, which then shall cast him out. He cannot stay here long. Heaven will not receive him, then hell must. What a miserable thing is this, when we place and bottom ourselves upon things that will not last! when ourselves shall outlast our foundation! when a man shall live for ever, and that which he builds on is fading! What extremity of folly is this, to build on riches, favour, greatness, power, inheritance, which either must be taken from him, or he from them, he knoweth not how soon!

What makes a man miserable, but the disappointing of his hopes and crossing of his affections? Now when a man pitcheth his soul too much upon his worldly things, from which there must be a parting, this is, as it were, the rending of the skin from the flesh, and the flesh from the bones. When a man's soul is rent from that he pitcheth his happiness on, this maketh a man miserable; for misery is in disappointing the hopes, and crossing the affections. Now only a Christian plants his heart and affections on that which is everlasting, of equal continuance with his soul. As he shall live for ever, so he is rooted for ever in that which must make him everlastingly happy. These things we hear, and they are undeniably true. But how few make use of them, to desist from going on in a plodding, swelling desire of an earthly condition, to overtop other men. Such labour to grow in tallness and height, but strive not to be rooted. Now that which grows perking up in height, overtopping other things, yet without root, what will become of it? It will be turned up by the roots.

Now, how shall we grow to be rooted? For to attain hereunto, it is not only necessary to apply the promises, and challenge God with them, but to consider also what ways he will make them good.

First, Labour to know God and his free grace in Jesus Christ. 'Grow in grace, and in the knowledge of our Lord Jesus Christ,' 2 Pet. iii. 18. They go both together. The more we grow in the knowledge of our Lord Jesus Christ, and of the grace of God in him, the more grace and rootedness we shall have. For that which the soul doth clearly apprehend, it fastens upon in that measure it apprehendeth it. Clearness in the understanding breeds earnestness in the affections, and fastness too. So the more we grow in knowledge, the more we root ourselves in that we know. And therefore the apostle prays for the Ephesians, that they might have the Spirit of revelation, &c., that they might know the height, breadth, depth, and length of God's love that passeth knowledge. 'For this cause I bow my knees unto the Father of our Lord Jesus Christ, of whom the whole family of heaven and earth is named, that he would grant you, according to the riches of his glory, to be strengthened by his Spirit in the inner man; that Christ may dwell in your hearts by faith; that ye, being rooted and grounded in love,' in the sense of God's love to us, and so of our love to him again (for we are not rooted in love to God, till we be rooted in the sense of God's love to us), 'that you may be able to comprehend with all saints the height and breadth,' &c., Ephes. iii. 14.

Second, And withal, *labour to know the gracious promises of Christ.* For we are knit to him by virtue of his word and promises, which like himself are 'yea and amen.' 'Jehovah, yesterday, to-day, and the same for ever,' 2 Cor. i. 20. So all his promises made in him, they are 'yea and amen,' in themselves firm, and firm to us in him. They are 'yea and amen;' that is, they are made and performed in Christ, in whom they are sure to be performed; and thereupon they are firm too. God made them, who is Jehovah, and they are made in Christ that is Jehovah. So God the Father Jehovah, he promiseth, and he makes them good in Christ Jehovah, who is unchangeable.

Thirdly, But this is not enough. We must *labour to have our hearts stablished*, that they may rely firmly on that which is firm. For if a thing be never so firm, except we rely firmly on it, there is no stability or strength from it. Now, when there is strength in the thing, and strength in the soul, that strength is impregnable and unconquerable strength. In Christ they are 'yea and amen;' in whom he stablisheth us, anoints us, seals us, and gives us the earnest of the Spirit in our hearts.

How doth God stablish us upon the promises? The rest which followeth is an explication of this. When he gives us the 'earnest of the Spirit,' 2 Cor. i. 22, and seals us to be his, in token he means to make good the bargain, then we are established. But we are never firmly established till we get the assurance of salvation. Then, as the promises are yea and amen in themselves, so we are stablished upon them when we are sealed and have earnest of the Spirit. Let us labour therefore to grow in the knowledge of God's love in Christ, to know the height, breadth, depth, and length of it, and to grow in all the gracious promises which are made in Christ, who is Amen himself, as his promises are; and then, when we are sealed and anointed by the Spirit, we shall be so stablished that nothing shall move us. Therefore let us use all means for the establishing of growth in us, the word and sacraments especially. For as baptism admits us into the house of God, so by the sacrament of the Lord's supper, the blessed food of the soul, we are strengthened. In the use of these means, let us make suit unto God to make good his gracious promise unto us, that we shall 'grow as lilies, and take root as the cedars in Lebanon.'

Let us know, that we ought every day to labour to be more and more rooted. Do we know what times may befall us? We have need to grow every day, to grow upward, and in breadth and in depth. If we considered what times we may live to, it should force us to grow every way, especially in humility, that root and mother of graces, to grow downward in that; to grow in knowledge and faith, until we be filled with the fulness of God.

Obj. A poor Christian ofttimes makes this objection, Oh! I do not grow! Therefore I fear my state; I am oft shaken! Therefore this promise is not fulfilled to me!

Ans. To this I answer, Christians may be deceived; for they do grow ofttimes in firmness, strength, and stability, though they do not spread out. They may grow in refinedness, that that which comes from them may be more pure, and less mixed with natural corruption, pride, self-love, and the like. This is a temptation that old men are subject to especially, in whom the heat of nature decays, who think withal that grace decays. But it is not so; for ofttimes when grace is carried with the heat of nature, it makes a greater show, being helped by nature. The demonstration, but not the truth, of grace is thus helped. Therefore this clause of the promise is made good in old Christians. They are every day more and more rooted, firm, stable, and judicious, and more able in those graces which belong to their place and condition. Therefore they should not be discouraged though they be not carried with the stream and tide of nature, helped with that vigour that sometime was in them. They grow in judiciousness, mortifiedness, in heavenly-mindedness, and in ability to give good counsel to others. This is well, for we grow not in grace one way, but divers ways; not only when we grow in outward demonstration, and in many fruits and actions, but when we grow in refinedness and judiciousness, as was said, then we are said to grow likewise.

Yet notwithstanding it should be the endeavour of all to grow what they can in grace. When, if they grow not so fast as others, let them know that there are several ages in Christ. A young Christian cannot be so planted and so deeply rooted as another that is of a greater standing. This should not discourage any, seeing there are 'babes in Christ,' 1 Cor. iii. 1, as well as 'strong men,' Rom. xv. 1. Therefore where there is truth of heart, with endeavour to grow better and better, and to use all means, let no man be discouraged. Remember alway this for a truth, that we may grow, and we ought to grow, and the children of God ordinarily have grown more and more, both in fruitfulness and stedfastness every way, but not with a like growth in measure or time. Therefore labour to make use of these promises, and not to favour ourselves in an ungrowing estate, for grace is of a growing nature. If it grow not in fruitfulness, yet it grows in the root; as a plant sometimes grows in fruitfulness, sometimes in the root. There is more virtue in winter time in the root than in the fruit which is gone. So a Christian groweth one way if not another; though not in outward demonstration, yet in humiliation. God sometimes sees it necessary that our branches should not spread for a while, but that we should grow in humility; by some faults and sins we fall and slip into, that we may see our own weakness and look up.

Let us labour therefore, who have so long enjoyed such store of blessed means, under the dew of God's grace and the influence of his Spirit, in the paradise of God, his house and church. Having so long lived in this Eden, let us labour now to spread and grow in fruitfulness, that so we may be filled with the fulness of God. It is the chief thing of all, to be rooted and grow in grace. You see, God when he would single out a blessing, he tells them not that they shall grow rich, that they shall spread out and grow rich in the world. No! But, you whom I love freely, take this as a fruit of it, 'you shall grow as the lily,' you shall grow fruitful 'as the olive,' &c. This is the comfort of a Christian. Though he grows downward oft in the world, and things of this natural life, yet he grows upward in another condition: as lilies and cedars, they grow downwards one way, but they grow upwards another. Perhaps they may decay in their state and favour, and in their practice and cunning in this life; but a Christian, if he be in the use of right means, and put in suit the gracious promises, he is sure still to grow in grace, in faith, in love, and in the inner man.

Is not this a comfort, that a Christian hath a comfortable meditation of the time to come in all his crosses? that it is for better and better still; that as in time he is nearer heaven, so he shall be fitter and fitter, and nearer and nearer still, with a disposition suitable to the place; that the time to come is the best time; and that he shall grow every way, in height, in breadth, in depth and length, and apprehension of God's love, and that the more he grows in knowledge of these things, the more he shall grow in all dimensions, being as sure of things to come as of things past, and that neither things present nor to come shall ever separate him from the love of God in Christ? Rom. viii. 35. What a comfortable state is a Christian in, who is always on the mending hand, that is such a child of hope, when the hope of the wicked shall perish! Let us labour, therefore, that we may be in such a case and state of soul as that thoughts of the time to come may be comfortable, that when we think we must be transplanted hence out of the paradise and Eden of God's church into a heavenly paradise, that all our changes shall be for the better. What a fearful thing is it to be in the state of nature! What foundation hath a man in that estate, who hath no root here, and that root he hath will fail him ere long? How fearful is it for such a man to think of a change, when it is not a change for the better?

Here is wisdom. If we will be wise to purpose, let us be wise this way. Labour, in the first place, to prize God's favours, and to know how to come by them in the use of all means. Look to God for the performance of these gracious promises. For they are not of what we shall do in ourselves, but what God will do in the covenant of grace. And if a Christian should not be rooted and grow stronger and stronger, we should not fail, but God and Christ should fail, who is our root and bears us up. Therefore, God hath taken upon him the performance of all these things. What remaineth for us but a careful using of all means? and in the use of all, a going out of ourselves to God, that he would be 'as the dew to us,' and cause us, by the dew of his Spirit, to grow more and more rooted in grace as long as we live in this world? And then our rooting and stability lies upon God, not upon us. He fails if we fail, who hath undertaken that 'we shall grow as the lily, and cast forth our roots as Lebanon.'

THE EIGHTH SERMON.

His branches shall spread, his beauty shall be as the olive-tree, and his smell as Lebanon. They that dwell under his shadow shall return; they shall revive as the corn, and grow as the vine: the scent thereof shall be as the vine of Lebanon.—HOS. XIV. 6, 7.

WE have heard at large heretofore what petitions God put into the heart and mouth of his church, as also what gracious answer God gives his own petitions. He cannot deny the prayers made by his own Spirit; and as he is goodness in itself, so he shews it in this, that he goes beyond all that we can desire, think, or speak. His answer is more transcendent, as the apostle speaks. He does 'exceeding abundantly above all that we ask or think,' &c., Ephes. iii. 19, 20. For whereas they in particular and in brief say, 'Do good to us, and receive us graciously,' he tells them, 'He will be as the dew unto them.' And from thence, being dew to them, is their spreading and growing as a lily, and casting of their roots as Lebanon. 'And their branches shall spread,' &c. And all this to encourage us to come to so powerful and large-hearted a God, who, as he is able to do more than we desire of him, so he will also do it. 'He will be as the dew unto us.' This is the general of all, for all other fruitfulness comes from this: 1. God will be as the dew; and then, 2. They shall grow as the lily, and cast their roots as the cedars in Lebanon. They shall not only grow upward, but downward, for the lily quickly spreads itself forth; but they shall be like the trees of Lebanon for stedfastness, and then spread in breadth, grow in all dimensions, which is fulfilled of the church in general, and of every particular Christian, when once he is in Christ, using sanctified means. They grow, then, in the root, and upright, and in every dimension. 'His branches shall spread.' And then,

'His beauty shall be as the olive-tree.'

Which, though fruitful and excellent, yet because it hath no sweet smell, it is added,

'His smell shall be as Lebanon.'

These excellencies promised to the church of God are not all in one tree, but yet they are in some sort in every Christian. What agrees not all to one plant agrees to the 'plants of righteousness.' They grow upwards and downwards, spread, and are savoury and fruitful. All agrees to a tree of righteousness. We say of man, He is a little world, a compendium of this great world, as indeed there is a comprising of all the excellencies of the world in man, for he hath a being with those creatures who have only that, and therewith he hath growing sense and reason, whereby he hath communion with God, and those understanding spirits, the angels. So that he is, as it were, a sum of all the excellencies of the creatures, a little world indeed (*h*). The great world hath nothing, but the little world hath the same in some proportion. So it is in grace. A Christian hath all excellencies in him, that are in the world. There is not an excellency in any thing, but it is an higher kind in a Christian. He hath the beauty of the lily, and he grows up in spreading, smell, and fruitfulness. His wisdom exceeds that of all the creatures. There is not an excellency in nature, but we have some proportionable excellency in grace which is above it. God useth these outward things to help us, that we should do both body and soul good by the creatures. Whatsoever doth our bodies good, either by necessity or delight, they help our souls; as plants and trees not only refresh the outward man, and the senses, but also they teach our souls, as here the Holy Ghost teacheth them by outward things. First it is said,

'His branches shall spread.'

When God enriches the soul with saving grace, one shall grow every way and flourish abundantly, extending forth their goodness on every side largely to the knowledge and open view of others; and then further,

'His beauty shall be as the olive-tree.'

What is the beauty of the olive-tree? To be useful, fruitful, and to bring forth good fruit. Indeed, the glory of a tree is to be loaden with fruit, and useful fruit; which is the best property of fruit, to be useful and delightful. So the glory of a Christian, who is a plant of righteousness, of God's own planting, is to abound in fruits of righteousness. Indeed, the olive is a very fruitful tree, and the oil which comes and distils from it hath many excellent properties agreeing to graces.

1. Amongst the rest, it is a royal kind of liquor, that will be above the rest. So grace it commands all other things; it gives a sanctified use of the creature, and subdues all corruption.

2. And then it is unmixed. It will mingle with nothing. Light and darkness will not mingle, no more will grace and corruption; for the one is hostile to the other, as Solomon speaks, 'The just is abomination to the wicked,' Prov. xxix. 27.

3. Further, it is sweet, strengthening, and feeding the life, as in Zechariah there is mention made of two olives before the Lord, which feed the two candlesticks, Zech. iv. 3. And olives of grace have always fatness distilling from Christ to feed his lamp with oil. God's church hath always oil; and those that are olives, they keep the church by their particular calling.

1. He shall be fruitful as the olive; and,

2. Abundant in fruit, as the olive.

3. Constant in fruit, like the olive.

For it bears fruit much, and never fails, no not in winter, and hath a perpetual greenness. Indeed, the child of God hath a perpetual verdure; as it is, Ps. i. 3, 'His leaf never fails,' because that which is the cause of flourishing never fails him. Which causes are two,

1. Moisture.
2. Heat.

For we know, moisture and heat, these two are the causes of all kindly growth. If a tree have more moisture than heat, then it is waterish; if it have more heat than moisture, then there is no bigness in the fruit. So true it is, that moisture and heat are the causes of fruitfulness in a good proportion. So God's children, having the Sun of righteousness always shining upon them, and being always under the dew of grace (the promise being, 'to be as the dew to Israel'), having all dew to fall upon them for moisture, and having the Sun of righteousness to shine upon them to make them fruitful, their leaf never fails, they never give over bringing forth fruit; because they have in them causes perpetuating fruitfulness, though not alike; because Christ by his Spirit is a voluntary, and not a natural, cause of their fruitfulness, that is, he is such a cause, as works sometimes more and sometimes less, to shew that grace springs not from ourselves, and to acquaint us with our own weakness and insufficiency. Heaven is the perfection of all, both graces and comforts. Wherefore Peter calls the state of heaven, 'an inheritance, immortal and undefiled, that fades not away,' 1 Peter i. 4. Why is that an estate of grace and comfort, more than this of this world? Because it is a never-fading estate. There they are alway in one tenure; and because Christ shews himself alway there. There is abundance of water to moisten them, and heat to cherish them. There is no intermingling or stopping in growth, as is here. Therefore it is an inheritance that fadeth not away, having the supply of a perpetual cause of flourishing.

This in some degree is true of the church on earth. It is the inheritance of God that fades not, and Christians therein are olives that bring forth fruit constantly, having a perpetual freshness and greenness. So the righteous man is compared to the cedars of Lebanon, Ps. xcii. 12, which bring forth much fruit in their age. He shall be fruitful as the olive. From all which this point, formerly touched, followeth:

That it is the excellency and glory of a Christian, to be fruitful in his place.

Both to be fruitful in his place as a Christian, and in his particular calling; to be fruitful as a magistrate, as a minister, as a governor of a family, as a neighbour, as a friend; to be fruitful in all. Because in religion, every near relation is as it were a joining together of the body in Christ, one to another, by which some good is derived from one to another. God uses these relations as conduits to convey graces. A good Christian, the meanest of them is a good neighbour, and doth a great deal of good, being fruitful as a neighbour, fruitful as a friend; much more as a husband, as a magistrate, as a minister. These relations are a knitting to Christ, by which fatness and sap are derived from the head for the good of the whole body. Therefore a Christian in all relations is fruitful. When he comes to be a Christian, he considers, like good Mordecai, what good he may do; as he told Esther, 'What if thou be called to the kingdom for this purpose,' Esther iv. 14? So a Christian will reason with himself, What if I be called to be a magistrate, or a minister, for this purpose? What if I be called to be a friend, for such or such a purpose, to do this or this good? Indeed such are gracious *quære's** made to a man's soul, to inquire for what purpose hath God raised me? To do this or that? To be idle, or barren, or noisome? O no; to be a plant of God's planting. My glory shall be my fruitfulness in my place.

* That is, 'queries.'—G.

Therefore let us every one consider with ourselves, wherefore God hath set us in the church in our particular standings. Wherein let us remember this, that howsoever God may endure barrenness out of the church, in want of means, yet he will never endure it under means. It is better for a bramble to be in the wilderness, than in an orchard; for a weed to be abroad, than in a garden, where it is sure to be weeded out, as the other to be cut down. If a man will be unprofitable, let him be unprofitable out of the church. But to be so where he hath the dew of grace falling on him, in the means of salvation, where are all God's sweet favours, to be a bramble in the orchard, to be a weed in the garden, to be noisome in a place where we should be fruitful, will God the great husbandman endure this? He will not long put it up. But that he exerciseth his children with such noisome trees to try them, as he hath some service for these thorns to do, to scratch them. So, were it not for such-like services for a time, he would weed them out and burn them. For whatsoever is not for fruit, is for the fire. 'Yea, every tree that bringeth forth not good fruit, shall be hewn down and cast into the fire,' Mat. iii. 10.

And the more to stir us up hereunto, let us know that wheresoever the dew of grace falls, and where there is the means of salvation, that at that very time there is an axe, an instrument of vengeance, laid to the root of the tree, which is not struck down presently, but 'it is laid to the root,' Mat. iii. 10; that is, vengeance is threatened to the tree, to that plant which hath the means, and brings not forth good fruit in time and season. What is the end thereof? To be hewn down and cast into the fire. As we see the church of the Jews, when Christ came, the Messiah, the great prophet of the church, never was there more means of salvation; yet even then, what saith John Baptist? 'Now,' even now, 'is the axe laid unto the root of the tree,' Mat. iii. 10; and indeed, in a few years after, the whole tree, the church of the Jews, was cut down. And, Rev. vi. 2, 4, we see, after the rider on the 'white horse,' which is the preaching of the gospel, there comes a 'red, bloody horse,' and 'a pale horse,' war and famine. After the 'white horse,' his triumphant chariot, the preaching of the gospel. If this take not place, that it win and gain not, what follows after? 'The red and the pale horse,' war, famine, and destruction. It will not be always with us as it is; for the gospel having been so long preached, we having been so long planted in God's paradise, the church, if we bear not fruit, 'the axe is laid to the root of the tree.' God will strike at the root, and root up all. Therefore let every one in their place be fruitful.

Every one that is fruitful, God hath a special care of. If any tree were fruitful, the Israelites in their conquest were to spare that, because it was useful, and they might have use of it, Deut. xx. 19, 20. So God will always spare fruitful trees, and have a special care of such in common calamities. Let us therefore be exhorted not only to bring forth fruit, but to bring forth fruit in abundance, to study to excel in good works. The word in the original is, 'a standard-bearer' (*i*), to stand before others in good works. As it is in Titus, 'labour to be as standard-bearers,' Titus iii. 8, to go before others in good works. Strive to out-go others in fruitfulness; for therein is the excellency. For those both in the sight of God and men are in most esteem who are most fruitful in their callings and places. The more we excel in fruitfulness, the more we excel in comfort; and the more we excel this way, the more we may excel. For God will tend and prune good trees, that they may bring forth more and better fruit, John xv. 2. And the more majesty we walk with, the more we damp the enemies, seeing them all under our feet. A growing Christian never wants abundance of encouragements, for he sees such grounds of comfort, as that he walks impregnable and invincible in all the discouragements of this world, breaking through all. As Solomon saith, it is a comely thing to see a lion walk, Prov. xxx. 29, 30. So much more it is to see a valiant, strong, well-grown Christian, who is bold as a lion, abound in good works.

It is said, 'His beauty shall be as the olive, and his smell as Lebanon.' The olive of itself hath no sweet smell. Therefore it is made up by another resemblance,

'His smell shall be as Lebanon.'

Lebanon stood on the north side of Judea, and was a place abounding with goodly trees, and all sweet plants whatsoever, which cast a wondrous sweet scent and smell afar off; as some countries abound so in sweet fruits and simples, as oranges, lemons and the like, that the fragrancy of the smell is smelt of passengers as they sail along the coast (*j*). So was this Lebanon a place full of rare fruits and fragrant flowers, which cast a scent afar off. Now, hence the Holy Ghost fetcheth the comparison. 'They shall smell as Lebanon,' that is, as those plants in Lebanon which cast a sweet and delightful smell afar off. Whence we will only observe this;

That a Christian by his fruitfulness doth delight others.

He is sweet to God and man, as the olive and the vine speak of their fruitfulness. 'They delight God and man,' Judges ix. 9, 13. So a Christian, both alive and dead, he is pleasing and delightful to the spirits of others, to God, and all that have the Spirit of God. As for God himself, we know that works of mercy are, as it were, a sweet odour. He is delighted with good works, as with sacrifice, Philip. iv. 18, smelling a sweet savour from them; and their prayers ascend as sweet incense before him, Ps. cxli. 2. Every good work is pleasing and delightful to God, who dwells in an humble heart, and broken spirit. 'The upright are his delight,' Prov. xi. 20. We see likewise how Christ commends the graces of his church, which whole book is full of praises in this kind one of another. The church sets out the praises of Christ, and Christ the praises of the church. The church is sweet: 'Oh, let me hear thy voice, for it is sweet and lovely,' Cant. ii. 14. The church's voice is sweet, praying to God, or praising him. So whatsoever comes from the Spirit of God in the hearts of his children, is sweet. God lays to heart the voice of his children.

And as it is true of God, so is it of God's people. They are delighted with the favour of those things that come from other of God's people. For they have graces in them, and therewith the Spirit of God, which is as fire to set a-work all those graces in them. For it is the nature of fire, where it encounters with sweet things, to kindle them, and make them smell more fragrant and sweet. So a spirit of love makes all sweet and pleasing whatsoever, in the children of God. It puts a gracefulness upon their words, making their reproofs, admonitions, comforts, and whatsoever comes from them, to have a delightfulness in them; because all is done in love, and comes from the Spirit of God, which carrieth a sweetness in it, to all those endowed with the same Spirit.

Use 1. Let this be an encouragement to be in love with the state of God's children, that so our works, and whatsoever comes from us, as far as it is spiritual, may be acceptable unto God and to the church, while we are living, nay, when we are dead. The very works of holy men, when they are dead, are as a box of ointment, as the ointment of the apothecary; as the wise man says of Josiah, whose very name was like the ointment of the apothecary.* So the name of those who have stood out for good, and have been good in their times, it carries a sweetness with it when they are gone. The church of God riseth out of the ashes of the martyrs, which hitherto smells sweet, and puts life in those who come after, so precious are they both dead and alive (*k*).

Use 2. And then, let it be an encouragement to be led by God's Spirit, and planted in God's house, and to be fruitful in our places, that so we may delight God and man, and when we are gone, leave a good scent behind us. Good men, as it were, with their good scent they leave behind them, perfume the times, which are the better for them dead and alive. What a sweet savour hath Paul left behind him, by his writings to the church, even to the end of the world! What fragrancy of delightful smells have the holy ancient fathers and martyrs left behind them! A good man should be like the box of ointment spoken of in the gospel, which when it was opened, the whole house was filled with the sweetness thereof, Mat. xxvi. 7, *seq*. So a good man should labour to be full of sweetness, willingness and abilities to do good, all kindled by a spirit of love in him; that when he is opened, all should be pleasing and delightful that cometh from him. Christ never opened his mouth, but good came from him; and the heavens never opened in vain. Therefore, in opening of our mouths, we should labour to fill the places where we are with a good savour. Oh, how contrary is this to the condition of many! What comes from them? Filthy speeches and oaths; nay, that which should be their shame they glory in. We see it is the glory of a tree to be fruitful, and to cast forth a good savour, like the trees of Lebanon. What vile spirits, then, are such men led withal, who delight to offend God and man with their impious speeches! who yet are so bold as to shew their faces, to outdare others that are better than themselves. Such are contrary to all God's senses. The Scripture condescends so far to our capacity, as to attribute senses unto God, of feeling, smelling, and touching, &c. So God is said to look upon his children with delight, and to hear their prayers. 'Let me hear thy voice,' &c., Cant. ii. 14. And he tastes the fruit that comes from them. So, on the contrary, all his senses are annoyed with wicked men and vile persons, who are abominable to God, as the Scripture speaks. As a man that goes by a stinking dunghill, stops his nose, and cannot endure the scent, so the blasphemous breath of graceless persons, it is abominable to God, as it were; God cannot endure such an odious smell; and for his eyes, he cannot endure iniquity, to look upon the wicked; and for his ears, their prayers are abominable. How abominable, then, are their persons whence those prayers proceed! They have proud hearts, hating God and man. Wherefore, praying out of necessity, not love to him, they are abominable. And so for feeling. Your sacrifices are a burden unto me, I cannot bear them, Isa. i. 11; and the prophet complaineth that God was burdened and loaded under their sins, 'as a cart pressed till it be ready to break under the sheaves,' Amos ii. 13. All his senses are offended with wicked men. This, hardened wretches think not of, that, whilst God fills their bellies with good things, go on in sin-security. But the time will come when they shall know the truth of these things, what it is to lead an odious, abominable life, contrary to God and all good men. Hence we see what we should be, that we may give a sweet scent: 'His smell shall be as Lebanon.'

* The passage is in Ecclesiasticus xlix. 1. This is the first reference that we have found in Sibbes to the Apocrypha.—ED.

Wicked men know this very well, that the lives, speeches, and courses of good men, for the most part, are fruitful beyond theirs. Therefore, what they can, they labour to cast aspersions upon them, that they may not smell so sweet. So, crying down those who are better than themselves, that they may be the less ill thought of, and setting a price upon all things in themselves, and their companions. Take me a knot of cursed companions, and they are the only stout, the only wise and learned men: all learning it must live and die with them; and all other men, though incomparable beyond them in abilities, in grace, in fruitfulness to do good, they are nobody. And this policy the devil teacheth them. But this will not serve the turn; for God, both in life and after death, will raise up the esteem of such who have been fruitful, when 'the memory of the wicked shall rot,' Prov. x. 7, and not be mentioned without a kind of loathing. Therefore let no man trust to this foolish policy, to cry down all others that are better than themselves, thinking thereby themselves shall be better esteemed. This will not do; for as all other things, so our good name is at God's disposing. It is not in the world to take away the good name or acceptance of good people; for they shall have, in spite of the world, a place in the hearts of God's people, who are best able to judge. The next thing promised is,

'They that dwell under his shadow shall return.'

The Holy Ghost, it seems, cannot express in words and comparisons enough, the excellent condition of the church, and of the children of God, when they are once brought into the state of grace. The former words concern the excellency of the children of God in themselves, and these the fruitfulness and goodness of them that are under them, who shall be brought into the families and places where they live. 'They that dwell under his shadow,' under the shadow of Israel, 'shall return and revive as the corn, and grow as the vine,' &c. For so it is most fitly meant of Israel. For formerly it is said, 'I will be as the dew unto Israel.' Originally it is meant of Christ's shadow; but because whosoever dwells under the church's shadow dwells under Christ's, therefore it is most fitly applied to Israel. They that dwell under Israel's shadow shall return.' What returning? Return to God by repentance. This is supposed; for those that dwell in the church of God, if they belong to God, by the help of good means they shall attain to reformation and repentance. But it is especially meant of that which follows upon it, 'They shall return;' that is, they shall revive, as a man's spirits after a swoon are said to return, and things after a seeming decay and deadness are said to be quickened and return again. So all that dwell under the shadow of Israel, they shall return to God by repentance. 'They shall return,' having a greater vigour and liveliness, recovering that which they seemed to have lost before.

'They that dwell under his shadow shall return.'

When God will bless any people, he will bless all that belong to them and are under them, because they are blessed in blessing them, even as we are touched when our children are stricken. God strikes the father in the child, the husband in the wife, the master in the servant, because there is some relation and dependence betwixt them. As it is in ill so it is in good. God blesseth the father in the child, the king in the subject, and the subject in the king. God blesseth one in another. And in blessing, because God loves the church, all the friends of the church are the better for it. They prosper that love the church, Ps. cxxii. 6, though they be not members of it. All that bless Abraham shall be blessed. Though they be not actually good, yet if they wish him well, a blessing is promised. So when

God blesseth a man to purpose, he blesseth all that belong to him. All that be under his shadow fare the better. The point to be handled is this,

That the church itself yields a shadow, being shadowed itself by Christ, who spreads his wing over it. Now, what is the use of a shadow?

1. It is for a retiring place to rest in.
2. It is for defence against the extremity of heat.
3. It is for delight, if the shades be good and wholesome.

For, as philosophers express the nature of trees, there be some trees which yield noisome shadows, some trees have a heavy, noxious, dangerous shadow, because there comes a scent from the tree, as naturalists observe, which annoys the brains. But he speaks here of good trees. Israel is a tree that yields a shadow unto all; that is, all that are under Israel shall rest quietly, and not be annoyed with the heat of God's wrath, and the like. They shall be delighted, having a sweet refreshing under the church.

God, in Scripture, is often said to be a shadow, and his people to be under 'the shadow of his wings,' Ps. xxxvi. 7. But God and the church are all one in this, for they that are under the church's shadow are under God's shadow; for the church is Christ's, and Christ God's. Therefore to be under the church is to be under God, and to be in the church is to be under God's protection. They both agree, as we see, Mic. v. 7. The church is said to be dew, because God bedews the church, and the church bedews others; and here the promise is, 'I will be as the dew unto Israel,' where the same name is attributed unto God. Christ is a vine, and the church is a vine, John xv. 1. Christ is a dew and a shadow. So is the church, because Christ communicates his excellencies to her, and she hers unto others. Therefore there can be no offence in applying this to the church, which is the proper meaning of the place; for the church is a shadow for rest and freedom from annoyance unto all that come under her.

Quest. To clear this a little. What solace and rest do men find under the shadow of the church?

Ans. There is a rest and a peace in the church, for all things are at peace with the church, even the very stones in the field, Job v. 23; nothing can hurt the children of the church, 'God will be and is a sun and shield unto them,' Ps. xxxiv. 11: a shield to keep off all ill, and a sun to confer all good unto them. So his promise is to Abraham, 'I will be thy buckler, and thine exceeding great reward,' Gen. xv. 1. A buckler to keep ill from him, and 'an exceeding great reward' for good. Therefore it is a sweet shadow to be under the church, where God is all in all to them, who makes all things work for good unto them, even the greatest evil. Now, what a delightful thing is it to have a resting-place with them which either suffer no ill, or God turns all ill to their great good! where God is a 'sun and a shield,' a 'buckler,' and an 'exceeding great reward,' as he is to his church and children!

And then, again, God is about his church as a 'wall of fire,' Zech. ii. 5, to protect it, not only as a shadow to keep off storms, but as a wall of fire to keep off and consume enemies. God, in regard of protection of his church, is a compassing unto them, as it is in Job. Saith Satan, 'Hast thou not made a hedge about him, and all that he hath?' Job i. 10. There was a hedge about Job, his wife, children, and goods, which the devil durst not enter, nor make a gap in, until God gave him leave. Therefore those that are under the shadow of the church, they are safe, and may rest quietly.

But this is especially understood spiritually. The church is a shadow, and herself under a shadow spiritually, that is, in regard of spiritual evils, from the worst enemies. For out of the church, where is any fence for the greatest ill of all, the wrath of God? In the church of God there is set down a way of pacification, how the wrath of God is taken off and appeased in reconciliation by the death and sufferings of Jesus Christ, whereby the believing soul attaineth peace and joy unspeakable and glorious. Out of the church there is no means at all to pacify the greatest ill. Therefore there is no true rest out of the church, nothing but stings and torments of conscience. And as there is a shelter against the wrath of God, which burns to the bottom of hell, so here is a remedy against death and damnation. For now death is made a friend to the church, and the children of the church, for the sting of it is taken away, so that it doth them more good than anything in the world, ending all their misery and sinning, and opening a passage unto eternal happiness. All other petty ills that attend upon death are nothing. There is a rest from all these whatsoever, for all afflictions have a sanctified use to God's people for their good. There is therefore a rest and refreshing in the church for all that come under it.

And as this is true of the church in general, so it is true of particular families, that are little churches. There is rest and happiness in them. God blesseth all under the roof of a godly man. Whosoever comes under that shadow comes for a blessing, or for further hardening. We see in the current of Scripture ordinarily that when God converted any one man, he converted his whole family. 'Salvation is this day come to thy house,' saith Christ to Zaccheus, Luke xix. 9. When salvation came to his heart, it came to his house; all was the better for it. So the jailor, when he believed, he and his whole house were baptized, Acts xvi. 33. When God blesseth the governor once, then it is supposed all the house comes under the covenant of grace. Abraham and his house were blessed, Gen. xxii. 17. But this holds not always, for there was a Ham in good Noah's family. Still there will be the ravens and wild beasts among the tame beasts. There will be an Ishmael in Abraham's family, a Doeg in the church of Judah, a Judas in Christ's family, and a Demas among God's people. That is, let the family be never so good, you shall have some by God's judgment naught in the same. As it is said of Jeremiah's figs, the good figs were exceeding good, and the bad exceeding bad, Jer. xxiv. 3. There is none so good as those that are in a gracious family, and none so naught as such who are naught there. Because they are cursed and under a curse, being bad under such gracious means, being like the ground which receives the rain and showers from heaven, and yet is not the better for it, and so is accursed, Heb. vi. 7, 8. If a man who is untoward were in a gracious family, it is supposed he would be better, but those who are naught, where they should be good, under abundance of means, such are in danger to be sealed to eternal destruction. Such being bad, are very bad, who though they break not out to dangerous enormities, because of the place, yet to have a barren, untractable heart under abundance of means, is to be hardened to destruction, without a special mercy to make it work afterwards. For some who have lived in gracious families, though for the present the seed fructified not, yet have afterwards found that seed fructify after a long time, and have blessed God that ever they came under such a shadow. Therefore, though such barrenness be a dangerous sign, yet must we not suddenly either condemn ourselves or others in this case. Because in the things of God in the church it is as in nature. The seed springs not as soon as it is sown. So that grace at length which hath seemed to lie dead, after many years may sprout out. Monica, St Austin's mother, was a gracious woman whilst he was an untoward young man, as appeareth by his own Confessions, yet his mother having prayed much for him, he was converted after her death, and became a glorious father and instrument of the church's good (*l*). It is ordinary amongst us. Many, when they have gone astray, reflect home upon themselves, consider under what means they have been, calling to mind the gracious instructions they have had, and so, by God's assistance, are new men. Therefore let none despair in regard of time or place, because God may have further aims than we can reach to. But unless God give a special blessing after such watering, it is for the increase of condemnation not to profit under such abounding means, but still to be like Pharaoh's lean kine, full fed and lean still, Gen. xli. 17, *seq*. For the promise is, 'Those that are under his shadow shall return.'

There is here a fit occasion offered to spend much time in pressing care upon those that are governors, that even out of love unto those that are under them, they would labour to be gracious; because if they be gracious, God will give them those that are in their family. The whole family was baptized when the master was baptized; and when any man was called, the whole family came within the covenant. When Shechem and Hamor were circumcised, all the city was circumcised also, Gen. xxxiv. 24. It is true especially of governors. There is no man hath grace for himself alone. God gives special graces to special persons, to be a means to draw on many others. Wheresoever grace is, it is of a spreading nature. It is said here of such, 'their branches shall spread.' It is communicative, and of a piercing nature, a little whereof will work strangely. As we know, a little short speech of a poor maid to Naaman the Assyrian,* how it wrought, and was the occasion of his conversion, 2 Kings v. 3. So a little savoury speech will often minister occasion of many heavenly thoughts. God so assists it with his Spirit, that it often doth a great deal of good.

Quest. But why are all in the family the better for the governor that is good?

Ans. Because God gives them grace and wisdom to walk holy before them, and to shine as lights, expressing and shewing forth the virtues of God which they have felt; as we see David professeth, Ps. ci. 2, to walk singularly and exactly in all things in the perfect way, that so he might please God and men, shining out before them in an holy, glorious conversation in the midst of his family. And as by their example, so by their authority, they use to bring all under them to outward obedience at the least, which bringeth a blessing to the family. Because, when grace is once kindled in the master, he will see all at least come to outward conformity. They cannot work grace in them; but as the prophet speaks, they may compel them to use the means, or else not to suffer a wicked and untoward person to dwell under their shadow. We know why God said that he would not conceal his secrets from Abraham, because he knew he would instruct and teach his family in the fear of God, Gen. xviii. 19. So this may be said of every one that is an Abraham, a governor of a family. They labour to tell them all things that have done good to themselves. Therefore they are the better for living under their shadow. Nay, further, not only the governor of the family, but if there be any graciously good in the family, they do much good. Laban's family was the better for Jacob,

* Syrian.—ED.

Gen. xxx. 27; and Potiphar, he and the jailor both, prospered the better for Joseph's sake, Gen. xxxix. 5, 23; so Naaman, that great captain, fared the better for his poor maid, 2 Kings v. 3, *seq.* It is a true position. God stablisheth grace in none who are gracious for themselves merely, but for the good of others also that converse with them. Whether it be governor or servants, no man liveth to himself, and for himself only, but for the good of all within their reach.

Use 1. For use therefore, first, this shall be for encouragement to all governors of families, *to be good, if not for themselves, yet in love to those that are theirs.* It may be, some have no care of their own souls or good. But hast thou no care of thy children, of thy wife that lieth in thy bosom, or of thy servants? If thou hast not a heart of stone or marble, surely thou wouldst desire that for them, that thou dost not for thyself. Think of this, at least thou wouldst have thy children good and prosper. Labour then, if we would have all prosper who come under our roof, that our families may be little churches of God, that all who come under our shadow may revive and return. Therefore, out of love to those that belong to us, let us labour to be good. Is it not a pitiful thing, that some who are governors of others, they look to them as to beasts, and use their service as a man would use the service of his beast? They feed their bodies, and think they have no charge of their souls. Now this is one reason why all that come under the shadow of a good governor are the better; because they take care for their instruction and best good; that they live in obedience to God's ordinances, and not like wild creatures, ruffians, vagabonds, Cains, and the like. What a strange thing is this, to have a care of the body, the worser part, and neglect the more excellent part, their souls!

Use 2. Make we also this use, of trial. Art thou a good and a gracious governor indeed? *Then grace in thy heart is communicative.* It will spread over thy family. Thou wilt labour to make thy children and thy servants good; to make all good that come under thy roof. Other things are not always communicative. Gold is a dead thing, and other goods thou mayest keep by thee, which do not spread. But if thou hast the best good, faith and love, with a gracious heart, this is like oil, or like fire, which will not be held in, but out; and shew themselves they will, and shine in their kind. So grace is a spreading, communicative thing. All that comes therefore under the shadow of a gracious family, are said to return and be the better for it. Make this therefore an use of trial, whether thou be a gracious governor or not. If thou canst say with Joshua (when he called the people together, saith he, Do what you will, I know what I will do, 'I and my house will serve the Lord.' If you will be, idolaters, or so and so; 'but I and my house will serve the Lord,' Josh. xxiv. 15). So certainly there is no man who in truth of heart fears the Lord, but he is able to say, 'I and my house will serve the Lord.'

Use 3. Lastly, for terror, *let us behold the dangerous and cursed estate of those that dwell out of Christ's shadow,* the church, and good means; who lie open to the indignation of God and storm of his wrath; who howsoever they may bless themselves in a thing of naught, yet it is a fearful thing to lie under a curse; and that soul must needs be barren where the dew of grace falls not, for God usually derives* spiritual and heavenly things by outward means. 'They that dwell under his shadow shall return.' They shall return to God; and by returning to him, return as it were and revive; as when in a swoon, a man's spirits return again, he is said to revive. But the ground

* That is, 'communicates.—G.

of returning is, that they shall return to God, and come under his roof in the church. But more immediately this is true, 'they shall return,' and shall quicken and revive in returning; which we spake of in the beginning of the chapter. Only this shall be added to that, that a wicked man, out of judgment of the danger of his estate, may make a stop; but turning is more than so. In this case a man turns his face to God and heavenwards; to good things formerly neglected, on which he turned his back formerly. What is turning, but a change of posture, when the face is turned towards that the back was to before? So it is in this spiritual turning to God. When heavenly things are in our face, when God and Jerusalem, the church, are in our eyes, still minding heavenly things and not earthly, then we are said to return. And therefore these converts mentioned in Jeremiah are thus described in their conversion, 'asking the way to Zion, with their faces thitherward,' Jer. l. 5. Whereas before in the days of our corruption, we turned our backs to God; now when we return, 'we set the Lord always before us,' Ps. xvi. 8, in everything. This is properly to return, to revive and flourish also in returning. Thus we have heard how all who live under the shadow of Christ do return, and what use we should make of it.

THE NINTH SERMON.

They that dwell under his shadow shall return; they shall revive as the corn, and grow as the vine: the scent thereof shall be as the vine of Lebanon. —HOS. XIV. 7.

OUR desire of good things is not so large as God is bountiful in satisfying our desires, and going beyond them, as we see in this chapter. Their hearts were too narrow to receive all that good which God intended them. 'Receive us graciously.' This was their petition: whereunto God answers, 'That he would be as the dew unto them; that they should grow as the lily, and cast forth their root as Lebanon, and their branches shall spread:' that they should grow in all dimensions, upwards and downwards, and spread in beauty and smell. 'Their beauty shall be like the olive, and their smell like Lebanon.' And because he would be God-like, like himself, that is, thoroughly and abundantly gracious and merciful, he doth not only, as we have heard, promise a blessing to Israel himself, but unto all near unto him, and belonging to him. 'Those that dwell under his shadow shall return; they shall revive as the corn.'

We are all too shallow to conceive either the infinite vastness of God's justice to impenitent sinners, or his boundless mercy and goodness to his poor church and children. Therefore God, to help our weak conceit in this kind, borroweth all the excellencies of nature, and makes use of them in grace. He takes out of the book of nature, into his book, what may instruct our souls; and therefore sets down the growing estate of a Christian, by all excellent comparisons that nature will afford; many whereof we have gone over. The last we spake of was, that mercy which God superabundantly shews unto the friends and servants of the church, 'Those that dwell under his shadow shall return.' Now, those that shall thus return, they revive in returning; for they turn to the fountain of life, to the Sun of righteousness. They come under God's grace. Therefore they must needs return and revive in vigour, as they return to God: which vigour is especially meant here, when he saith, 'Those that dwell under his shadow shall return.'

'They shall revive as the corn.'

Now, how doth the corn revive? Not to speak of that comparison that the godly are corn, and not chaff, as the wicked are, who are driven to and fro, Ps. i. 4, without any solidity, which, though true, is not here especially aimed at. For it is supposed that they who are good and gracious, have a substance, solidity, usefulness, and goodness in them, like corn, not being empty chaff which the wind blows away. This is useful to mention; but to come to the scope indeed* by the prophet.

1. 'They shall revive as the corn.' In this, first, that as the corn when unsown, it lies dead in the granary, fructifieth not, but when it is sown springs up to an hundredfold, as we read of in Isaac's time, who received so much increase, Gen. xxvi. 12. So it is with converted Christians. Before they were under any gracious means, or in a good place, they lay as it were dead, and did not spring forth. But afterwards, being planted and sown under gracious means, in good company, in a good family, then they increase and grow up and multiply. 'They revive like the corn.'

2. And then again, as it is with the corn, though it seem to die, and doth indeed die in some sort, covered with winter storms, ere it spring out from the oppressions of frost and snow, and hard weather, as if it were altogether perished; yet, notwithstanding, it is all the while a-preparing for springing up again more gloriously. So it is with the church, which seems to die often in regard of spiritual mortification by afflictions, whereby it is dead to the world; yet all this while there is a blessed life in the spirit, preparing the soul, under the hard pressures of all weathers, to a glorious springing up again. Therefore the church hath no hurt by afflictions, no more than the corn hath by the winter, which is as necessary for it as the spring-time or summer. For else, how should the earth be ripened and prepared? How should the worms and weeds be killed, if it were not for hard weather? So it is with a Christian: those afflictions that he suffers, and under which he seems to be buried, they are as useful to him as all his comforts. Nay, a Christian is more beholden to afflictions for his graces and comforts than he is to outward blessings. One would think that the goldsmith were a-spoiling his plate when he is a-burning of it, when all that while the dross is but a-consuming out of it; and the vessel so hammered and beaten out, is but a-preparing to be a vessel of honour, to stand before some great man. So it is with a Christian: an ignorant person looking but one way, thinks God neglects such a one; and that if God cared for such a one, or such a one, would or could such and such things befall them? they conclude hence, as the Psalmist saith, 'God hath forsaken him,' Ps. lxxi. 11, and forgotten him. And as Christ the head of the church was thought to be forgotten and neglected, even when he was most dear and precious unto God, so even they all this while. The Spirit of God is working an excellent work in them, preparing and fitting them for grace and glory. Therefore, in that respect also, 'They shall revive as the corn.'

3. Thirdly, 'They shall revive as the corn' in regard of fructification. It is true both of the church and of particular graces. We see one grain of corn, when it is almost perished and turned to froth, nothing in a manner; presently out of it springs a stalk, and thence an ear, and in that many ears, God giving it a body sixty or a hundredfold, as he pleaseth. So it is with a Christian: when he is planted, he will leaven others, and

* Qu. 'intended?'—ED.

those, others and others. A few apostles leavened the whole world, scattering the gospel like lightning all over the same. So it is true of grace in God's children; it is like a grain of mustard-seed at the first, yet it grows up and fructifies, Mat. xiii. 31, from knowledge to knowledge, faith to faith, and grace to grace; from virtue to virtue, from strength to strength, from one degree to another; nothing less at first, and nothing more great or glorious in this world in progress of time; nothing so admired of God, and pleasing unto man, as this which makes one all glorious and without spot.

Oh, what can be said more to encourage us to come under gracious means, to love God and his ordinances, good company, and the communion of saints—considering they are such happy people! 'Those that are under their shadow shall return,' revive, and be vigorous. 'They shall revive as the corn,' which doth, when it seemeth to be dead, notwithstanding all weathers, grow up and multiply. And whereas it seemed dead before and lay hid, being sown it grows. So being planted in the church, we shall grow. For there is a hidden virtue in the least grace, in the least of God's ordinances, more than we are aware of. Saith Christ, 'Where two or three are gathered together in my name, there am I in the midst of them,' Mat. xviii. 20. Much more is this made good in great congregations and families. But this is not all; he saith,

'They shall grow as the vine.'

Howsoever, the church which is the mother church grows before in the former words: the new church that comes under her shadow, shall grow in the same manner. 'They shall grow as the lily; their branches shall spread;' and more, it is said here, 'They shall grow as the vine.' It is a comparison delightful to the Holy Ghost, to compare Christ to a vine; the church to a vineyard, and Christians unto vines, but such as draw all their moisture and fatness in them from Christ the true vine, their sweetness being a derivative sweetness,

'They shall grow as the vine.'

1. The vine we know is a fruitful plant, as we read in the Judges, ix. 9, 13. The olive and the vine would not forsake their sweetness to be a king; for it is said by them, that they revive God and man, being pleasing to them. So every true Christian is like a vine for fruitfulness. He is a tree of righteousness; a plant of God's own planting; a vine that spends himself in bearing fruit.

2. Again, as it is fruitful, so it is exceedingly fruitful, abounding in fruit, So Christians are vines, not only for a little fruit that they bear, but because they are abundantly fruitful, which is premised, that if they do as they should do, they shall be vines abundant in the work of the Lord.

3. And further, the vine as we know is never a whit the worse for pruning; but is pruned and cut, as our Saviour speaks, 'that it may bring forth the more fruit,' John xv. 2. So the church and people of God are never a whit the worse for afflictions; for as the best vines need dressing and pruning, the best ground ploughing, the best linen washing, the best metal the fire, to consume away the dross, the best things we use having something amiss, so the best Christians need dressing and purging from the great Husbandman, whereby they are not the worse, but the better; having thereby much corruption purged away from them. As the pruning of the vine makes it not the worse, but draws wild things from it, which would draw away the strength of the vine, a Christian is the better for his afflictions, wherein the glory of the church especially consists. For the church never thrived better than in Egypt, where they laboured to crush

and to cut the vine. God brought his vine out of Egypt for all this, maugre all the malice of the enemies. The church was never more glorious in its own seat than it was in Babylon under the captivity. How glorious then was the church in Daniel and others!

4. Again, to the outward appearance, the vine is a rugged, unseemly plant, being not sightly and beautiful to look on; yet it is abundantly fruitful under that unsightliness. So if we look to the outward state and face of the church, it is nothing else to look to but a deformed company, defaced by affliction, lifeless here, as it were, 'having their life hid up with God in Christ,' Col. iii. 3, as the apostle speaks. Their life here is covered over with many afflictions, crosses, infirmities, and disgraces, whereunto they are subject, like unto other men. Therefore as it was the state of the Head to have no outward form or beauty, though inwardly he was all glorious, so the beauty of the church is inward; for outward show, it being unsightly like the vine, crooked and uneven, there being nothing delightful in it, unless it be in regard of the fruit that comes from it. So it is with the church of God and particular Christians; who, though in outward government they have not that policy and outward glory other governments have, yet there is an inward secret work of God's government of the church by contraries which exceeds all other policies, wherein he brings glory from shame, life by death. He brings down and lifts up. When he is about his excellent work he humbleth first. This is an ordinary way. Therefore we must not take offence at any outward deformity that we see in the church, and in God's children, when they seem to be trampled upon. They are but as vines, unsightly to the eye; they have a life, though it be a hidden one.

It is excellently set down by Ezekiel, Ezek. xv. 3, what the vine is of itself. It is serviceable for nothing. We cannot make a pin of it. It is such a brittle wood, as is good for nothing but to bear fruit. So, take a Christian that professeth religion, if he be not fruitful in his place, of all men he is the worst; of all men he is either the best or the worst. As the vine, if it bear fruit, it is the best, though it be an unsightly tree; but otherwise it is fit for nothing but the fire. Therefore let no man glory in his profession, that he is baptized, hears sermons, and reads. But where is thy fruit? Wherefore serves the dressing and pruning of the vine but for fruit? If there be no fruit, a Christian is the worst man that lives; worst, in regard that he is bad under good means; and in condition, he is the worst of all men, his torment is the greater. Those that are barren and unfruitful under means, the time will come that they will wish they had never enjoyed such a testimony against themselves.

5. And further, a vine is so weak that it must be propped and supported along, or else it will lie on the ground. Such is the estate of the church, which must have something to fence it and underprop it. God is the strength of the church. It is a wondrous weak plant. The children of God are wondrous weak, and exposed to a wonderful deal of misery. In regard whereof, and of the injuries and weaknesses they are exposed to, they must have support. A Christian is compared to the shiftless things, sheep, lambs, and doves; and in the plants they are compared to the vine, which needs a strong support. And, as Solomon saith of the conies, though 'they are a weak people of themselves,' Prov. xxx. 26, yet notwithstanding they have a strong rock over their heads, where they are safe; though they be as weak as the vine. So God's people, though they be weak of themselves, yet they have a strong support to uphold them. God, by the

ordinances of magistracy and ministry, especially by his Spirit, keeps them up and supports them, that they spread in largenses and in fruitfulness.

Use 1. Is this so? Then let us examine ourselves, what our fruit is. If we be vines, what is our fruit? what comes from us? Certainly if we do not shew forth that fruit we should, in our lives and conversations, in our speech, carriage, and actions, when we are called to it, it is an argument that as yet the dew of God's grace hath never fallen upon us, so as it must before we come to heaven. As was said before, a man may endure a dead plant in his ground, but in his orchard he will not. He may endure weeds in pastures, in neglected grounds, but not in his garden. If we be lilies in God's garden, and vines in his orchard, we must be fruitful and grow, or else God will not endure us. Of all woes, the greatest woe lies upon them who enjoy plentiful and abundant means, and yet are not fruitful, Mat. xi. 21.

Use 2. That we are vines, and God's vines, it is in the next place an use of comfort, that God therefore will have a care of us if we be fruitful. He will have a special care of that place where his vines are planted. If we see many gracious persons and families, who are conscionable in their practice and conversation, we may rest assured that God the great husbandman will have a special care of those choice vines, and the places they live in. They carry the blessing of God with them wheresoever they go, with a shadow and protection, making every place the better for them. For God will care for those vines which bring forth much fruit; as it is in Isaiah, 'Spoil it not, for there is a blessing in it,' Isa. lxv. 8. If a Christian be fruitful, and labours to be more fruitful, God gives a prohibition—'He is my vine, do him no harm.' 'Touch not mine anointed, nor do my prophets no harm,' Ps. cv. 15. Satan himself, and all creatures in heaven and in earth, have a prohibition to touch his vines no further than shall be for their good. Will a man suffer men to come into his orchard to break down his vines? He will not. Surely though the sins of this nation be very great, yet one thing ministereth hope; God hath a great many vines under his shadow and protection, many conscionable magistrates, ministers, and people of other professions, governors of families and the like, which walk holily. God will spare the vineyard, even for the vines that bear fruit. A notable place amongst others we have, Cant. ii. 15, 'Take us the foxes and the little foxes that spoil the vine; for our vines have tender grapes.' There is in every church not only gross papists, and foreign enemies, that would root out all, if it were in their power, but subtle foxes also; men that pride themselves in devilish policy, to undermine the church and children of God; who wheresoever they see vine or grapes, they malice that. Both the means, and grace wrought by the means, is the object of their cruelty. Subtle foxes they are; who account it a great deal of glory to be accounted politic men; to do mischief secretly and closely in the church. Will God suffer these foxes? No; he will not. 'Take us the foxes, the little foxes that destroy the vines,' Cant. ii. 15. God hath young growing vines, so as he will not only care for the great vines, but for the tender vines also. Christ hath a care of his lambs; as he said to Peter, 'Lovest thou me,' &c., 'Then feed my lambs,' my little ones, John xxi. 15. So Christ speaks in the gospel of these little ones. 'I tell you (of a truth) that the angels of these little ones behold the face of my Father,' &c., Mat. xviii. 10. And so he speaks in another place. 'A bruised reed will he not break, and smoking flax will he not quench, until he bring forth judgment unto victory,' Isa. xlii. 1, 2. So likewise he promiseth, 'that he will carry the lambs in his bosom, and gently lead them that are with young,' Isa. xl. 11.

Use 3. The next use shall be for encouragement unto weak ones. Should tender and weak Christians then be discouraged, for whom God is so careful? Surely no. Put case they bring forth but little fruit; yet, O destroy it not, for a blessing is in it. Therefore let us not be discouraged, if we be God's vines; which is known and discovered, not by the abundance of fruit only, but by the kind of our fruit also. If it come from the Spirit of God, and relish of the Spirit, though it be not in such plenty, yet a vine is not a thorn. A Christian is not to be discouraged, though he bring not forth abundance of fruit at the first. There are different degrees and tempers of soil, and of ages in Christianity; which is spoken to encourage those that are good; and yet are discouraged, because it is not with them, as with some other Christians of their acquaintance. Know, that there is no set measure of grace necessary to salvation, but truth. God doth assign us a measure of grace according to his good pleasure, and according as he hath purposed to make us profitable to others in the use of means. Those whom he means to use for suffering or doing of great matters in the church, those he fits suitably for that he means to call them to; others have not that abundance of grace, out of God's wisdom, who knows best how to dispense his own graces to his own glory. If we allow not ourselves in our weaknesses, but groan under them, hate them, and strive against them, reaching towards perfection; in this case our weaknesses shall not hurt our salvation, but God will perfect his power in our weakness, 2 Cor. xii. 9.

So we see it is not the multitude of fruit, but the sincerity of it. If it be true, that makes a Christian. If there be truth of grace, it will out and spread the branches; it shall not always be so with us. Sincerity and endeavour to grow, with a desire and thirst after growth, makes a man a Christian. Therefore, as was said, we must not be discouraged, though our growth and spreading be not like others. Every Christian hath his measure. Though every one be bound to go further and further, from faith to faith, and grace to grace; yet there is a blessing in a little, and a promise also to him that useth it well. 'To him that hath, it shall be given,' Mat. xiii. 12. Christ hath a care that the foxes do not hurt the little tender grapes. Let none therefore be discouraged for their non-proficiency in the ways of God, so as to go back and leave off. He knows best, when and how to take away the baits, snares, and temptations that are set to catch them and discourage them. Let God alone with his own work, who is the great vine-dresser. Do thou thine own work; attend upon good means; wait upon God; and then let the malice of the world and the devil be what they will, he will have a care of his vines; and the more care, the more young and tender they are, &c.

These considerations may affect us, not only to take good by the vine for our bodies, but for our souls also, and so the same thing may cherish both body and soul. A Christian by grace hath an extracting virtue to draw holy uses out of everything; as the Holy Ghost here compares us to a vine, to teach us these and the like things now unfolded. The last thing promised is,

'The scent thereof shall be as the vine of Lebanon.'

This Lebanon was a mountainous place, on the north side of Judea, wondrous fruitful in all kind of trees, in cedars, and goodly vines; so it did abound in spice, and all goodly things. Therefore, to shew that a Christian should be the best of his rank, he fetches comparisons from the best things in nature.

'The scent thereof shall be as the vine of Lebanon.'

Now the vine of Lebanon had a sweet scent in it, both to draw to the liking, and then to delight in the taste and taking thereof. So it is with the graces of God in his children, they carry, as it were, a sweet scent with them, both to draw others to delight in, and taste of the same things.

Quest. But how comes it to pass that Christians send forth so sweet as cent?

Ans. Because they are in Christ, in whom the ointment and all sweetness is in fulness. From him the Head, first, and from thence it is derived unto the members; all who* must partake of this ointment. As it is said of the head of Aaron, that that ointment which was poured on his head ran down to his skirts, and all his rich attire about, Ps. cxxxiii. 2. So that sweetness in Christ is poured on the skirts, all along upon his members; even the meanest Christian receiveth 'grace for grace,' John i. 16, sweetness from Christ. The virgins, that is, such as defile not themselves with idolatry, and such other lewd courses, they follow after Christ in the smell of his sweet ointments, Cant. i. 3. It is spoken of Christ, who carrieth such a sweet smell with him, as 'all his garments smell of myrrh, aloes, and cassia,' &c., Ps. xlv. 8. So sweet is the smell of Christ, when he is unfolded in his benefits and offices, that the pure and holy virgin souls of the saints follow after it. 'His name is as an ointment poured out,' Cant. i. 3; that is, himself is his name, and his name is himself, as the Hebrew proverb is: Christ made known in the unfolding of the word, that is, his name. When the box is opened, all in Christ is like ointment. In the preaching of the word, all is sweet, and nothing but sweet in Jesus. Now a Christian, being a member of Christ, and a virgin soul following Christ, must needs draw sweetness from him, casting out that scent unto others, drawn from him, because they partake of Christ's anointing. What is the name of a Christian, but a man anointed with Christ's ointment, one anointed to be a king and a priest in some sort? Rev. i. 6. Therefore they carry the favour of him wheresoever they go. Aaron the high priest had sweet garments, Exod. xxxix. 26, which made a savour where he went, having bells and sweet pomegranates at the bottom of his garment. He had not only bells to discover him, but sweet pomegranates also. So it is with every Christian. Not only the minister, but every Christian, is a priest under the New Testament, and carrieth a savour with him; graces that spread and cast a sweet scent in all places wheresoever, which they exercise upon all good occasions. As St Paul expresseth it, 'They savour the things of the Spirit,' Rom. viii. 5. Those who are in Christ, they have the Spirit of Christ, or they are none of his. And having the Spirit of Christ, they savour of the things of the Spirit; that is, their thoughts, speeches, actions, and conversation are savoury. Those 'that are in the flesh,' saith the apostle, 'cannot please God,' Rom. viii. 8, they are unsavoury. A carnal man hath no savour in his speeches. They are either worldly or civil, without spiritual savour; because he hath nothing of the Spirit of Christ to savour of. 'His heart,' saith Solomon, 'is little worth,' Prov. x. 20. The like we may say of his thoughts, actions, and affections; they are unsavoury and little worth. He hath a dead heart to goodness; and thence whatsoever goodness cometh from him is forced, and against the hair, as we say. But a Christian having the Spirit of Christ, and therewith communion with Christ, all his discourses and actions are for the most part savoury; those he acteth

* That is, 'all of whom.'—ED.

as a Christian. Therefore from his communion with Christ, it is said here, 'His smell shall be as Lebanon.'

'The scent thereof shall be as the vine of Lebanon.'

Delightful both to God and holy, blessed spirits, likewise to the church and to the angels which are about us, and pleasing to our own spirits; for there issueth a wondrous contentment even to the conscience of a person, which is fruitful and abundant in goodness. That soul receiveth an answerable proportion of comfort. As it is with heat, that accompanieth fire alway, so there is a kind of heat of comfort which naturally accompanieth the heat of any good action. There remaineth a sweet relish to the conscience of the performer, reflecting, with humility upon himself, with thankfulness to God, from whose dew, as we have heard before, cometh whatsoever is good. Reflecting on this with an eye to the principal cause, it breeds a great deal of comfort to the soul. As it was said of Josiah, the memory of Josiah was like the ointment of the apothecary; whereas, on the contrary, it is said, 'The remembrance of the wicked shall rot,' Prov. x. 7. God threateneth the Jews that they should be a hissing to all nations, and that they should be abominable to all kind of people, Deut. xxviii. 37 (for what is so odious now as the name of a Jew?), yet certainly this whole promise shall be verified even of them, this whole chapter having an eye unto the calling of the Jews. The time will come that the scent of these odious people, who are now the object of hatred unto all people, 'shall be as the vine of Lebanon.'

Use 1. If this be so, it cuts off a carnal exception of senseless persons, that think they can stop men's mouths with this, I cannot make so much show as you, but I hope I have as good a heart to God as you or as the best. But a Christian is a vine that brings forth grapes and much fruit, and casts a scent from him, as 'the scent of Lebanon,' upon all fit occasions; for his words should be 'as the apples of gold set with pictures of silver,' Prov. xxv. 11. He is seasonable in his actions of consolation, and bringeth forth his fruit in due season, as the promise is, Ps. i. 3; for Solomon sheweth that everything is made beautiful in his season, Eccles. iii. 11. Those, therefore, that have not a good word to speak, but rather express the contrary, rotten, unsavoury discourse, vain in their conversation, savouring nothing that is good, how have they as good a heart to God as the best? No; this is not to be a Christian, who should savour like Aaron's garments, or like these graces coming from his Head to him; who should spread abroad his sweetness unto others, 'shining out as a light,' Philip. ii. 15, amongst others. Therefore, away with this base plea. A rotten speech argueth a rotten heart. What can come out of a vessel but such as is within it? If the issues be naught, what is the vessel but naught? If all be unsavoury outward, what is there but a rotten heart within?

Use 2. Again, if Christians should cast a scent and savour, this should move and stir them up, if they will answer their title to be Christians, sweet, anointed persons, priests to God, to labour more and more to be spiritual, and savour the things of the Spirit, and to labour for more and more communion with Christ in the use of all sanctified means, that they may have the Spirit of Christ in their conversation, shewing forth the humility, patience, love, and obedience of Christ. As Peter speaks and exhorteth us, 'to shew forth the virtues of him who hath called us from darkness into his marvellous light,' 1 Pet. ii. 9. Then we answer our title, and 'cast forth a scent like Lebanon,' when inwardly and outwardly all things join to make us fruitful and savoury before God and man.

Quest. What will come of it if we be fruitful and savoury?

Ans. 1. God will be more pleased in all our actions, and will 'smell a sweet savour of rest,' as it is said of Noah, Gen. viii. 21, after his coming out of the ark; for God delights in his own graces, which he admireth in us. As he said to the woman of Canaan, 'O woman, great is thy faith, be it unto thee as thou wilt,' Mat. xv. 28. God, as it were, stands admiring his own graces, he is so delighted with the faith, love, prayers, and patience of his children, which is further excellently expressed in the Canticles, 'Who is this that cometh up out of the wilderness like pillars of smoke, perfumed with myrrh and frankincense, and all the spices of the merchant?' Cant. iii. 6. Christ there is brought in admiring* at his church and children, conflicting through all the miseries and incumbrances of this world, which hinder and oppose their journey to heavenwards, wherein they thrust forth all the practice of their holy graces, which smell like spices. Then let us not envy God, the saints, and holy people the sweetness of our graces, but let our scent smell abroad to the content and comfort of all, that they may delight in these graces that come from us, in our humility, patience, faith, love, sincerity, and all these graces wherein we resemble Christ and shew forth his holy virtues. Therefore, for our own comfort and delight of all, and to assure ourselves of heaven and of the love of God whilst we live here, let us labour to be fruitful in our conversation, and to cast forth a scent in regard of others, which hath an attractive, drawing force. For when they see a holy, fruitful, and gracious conversation, it casts forth a scent, and makes others like religion. So God is glorified, and religion is adorned. What greater ornament to religion than to see a fruitful, gracious Christian, who hath ability and a heart to do good upon all occasions, with an humble, meek, peaceable spirit, taught of God to be so for the good and love of others?

There must be pomegranates with bells, a sweet conversation with words, a little whereof will do more good to others than a great many words. A good conversation is sweet, and hath a kind of oratory joined with it. Therefore, if neither for God, or Christ, or others, yet for our own sakes, and the reflection of that good scent upon ourselves, let us be fruitful. A man cannot grow in fruitfulness but he must needs grow in comfort, peace, and joy. Nothing cheereth and solaceth the heart of a Christian more than this, the conscience† that God honoureth him to be fruitful, to do good, and cast a sweet savour, to draw others to good things. This will comfort us upon our deathbeds more than all other things. Therefore, in all these respects, for love of God, others, and ourselves, which are delighted with the expressions of our graces, let us labour to be fruitful trees in God's garden, and to bring forth much fruit, that we may send forth 'a scent like Lebanon.'

Now, who would not be in such an estate and condition as this, as to have title to all these gracious promises, for 'the dew' of grace to fall upon him, 'to grow as lilies' in height, and to spread as other plants do, to grow upwards and downwards, to be 'rooted as cedars' and 'fruitful as vines'? The Spirit of God sets himself here to shew spiritual things by earthly comparisons, to make us the more capable of them. The misery of the contrary condition may well stir us up to seek after the forementioned. For what a misery is it to have the curse of God upon one's soul, to have it like the barren wilderness, void of all grace and comfort that may delight others, or is spiritual, savoury, or savingly good. So all these promises tend

* That is, 'wondering.'—G. † That is, 'consciousness.'—ED.

to encourage us to be in the condition of God's children, that when we are in that estate we may comfort ourselves, and be able to claim our part, portion, and interest in these excellent promises.

Thus, by God's blessing, we have passed over the particulars of God's gracious promises to his church and all that shall come under the church, all which should encourage us to go to God, and do as the church doth here, 'take words to ourselves,' and desire God 'to take away all iniquity, and heal all our backslidings,' and that we may renounce all vain confidence, as the church doth here, who is taught to trust horses no longer, 'Asshur shall not save us.' And then let us, as was said, cleave unto the blessed promises, that we may improve them and make them our own every day more and more. Therefore, let us have in the eye of our soul the excellency of growth, or else we shall not value these promises. Let us consider what an excellent condition it is to grow, flourish, and be fruitful, having a due esteem of all these promises beforehand. Do but consider how excellent a Christian is that groweth above others, what a majesty he hath in his carriage, how undauntedly he walks in all oppositions whatsoever, as a lion in his courses, Prov. xxviii. 1; how he overlooks hell, wrath, death, damnation, and all; what a sweet communion he enjoyeth with God in all the disconsolations that the world puts upon him. He carrieth his heaven in his heart and a paradise within him, which is planted with all graces; whereas another man carrieth his hell about him.

Wherefore, let us take such courses to help ourselves as the church doth here, trust in God, and not in man or in the arm of flesh, and be encouraged, from all that hath been said, to have a good conceit* of God, to be fruitful, and draw on others to goodness, that God, his saints, and angels may be delighted with the scent of our graces, and ourselves comforted; that we may rejoice in our portion and lot that God hath dealt so graciously to us, and glory more that he hath made us members of Christ and heirs of heaven than in any condition of this world. O the incomparable, excellent state of a Christian, above all the glory of this world! who not only groweth, but shall grow to heavenwards still; and as he hath begun to hate sin, shall hate it more and more. God hath undertaken it shall be so. Ephraim, after all these sweet promises and dew of grace, shall say, 'What have I any more to do with idols?' &c., the prosecution whereof must be referred † until the next time.

THE TENTH SERMON.

Ephraim shall say, What have I any more to do with idols? I have heard him and observed him: I am like a green fir-tree: from me is thy fruit found. —Hos. XIV. 8.

WE have heard at several times heretofore, how God, out of the largeness of his goodness, goeth beyond those desires which he putteth into his people's hearts. They briefly entreat him to 'do good' to them, and to deal graciously with them; and he answereth them largely, 'That he will be as the dew to them, that they shall grow as the lily, and cast forth their roots as Lebanon.' All set out by most excellent comparisons, helping grace by nature, our souls by our bodies, and our spirits by our senses. As we have

* 'That is, 'conception.'—G. † That is, 'delayed.'—G.

souls and bodies, so God applieth himself to both: 'His branches shall spread; his beauty shall be as the olive, and his smell as Lebanon.'

Then in the seventh verse, his gracious promise reacheth unto those who dwell under the church. 'Those that dwell under his shadow shall return, they shall revive as the corn, and grow as the vine,' &c. The new church that shall come under the shadow of the old, shall flourish as the ancient did. 'They that dwell under his shadow,' that is, under Ephraim's and Israel's shadow, 'shall return,' and be partakers of the same dew of grace.

Now this eighth verse containeth a further gracious promise to Ephraim, upon his repenting and former resolutions. Ephraim said, 'Asshur shall not save us, we will not ride upon horses: neither will we say any more to the work of our hands, Ye are our gods.' Now what saith God here, repeating the words of Ephraim? Ephraim 'shall say' is not in the original; but only set down to express what the meaning is; whereas Ephraim said, 'What have I any more to do with idols?' Ephraim shall have this answer, 'I have heard him, and observed him, I am like a green fir-tree: from me is thy fruit found.'

As though the Lord had said, let not Ephraim think that when he hath forsook idols, he hath forsaken his comfort, as though there were no comfort in walking according to the rule of my word and laws. Let him know, that instead of these poor and base comforts, either in gross idolatry, or other more cunning idolatries whatsoever, which formerly took him up, that now he shall exchange them for more solid and substantial comforts. For 'I have heard him and observed him.' So that let him see what he loseth in parting with base corruptions, worldly lusts, pleasures, and the like, he shall find it more abundantly supplied in a far more excellent manner in me, and in the fruits and effects of my love unto him; so as he shall find that there is nothing lost by entering strictly into my service. And whereas formerly he walked in a vain shadow, in relying on 'Egypt, Asshur, and the works of his own hands;' now he shall have a far more excellent shadow, which no storm, nor rain, nor injury of weather can pierce through. 'I am like a green fir-tree unto him.' Not such a shadow as those his idols were, who could not keep off the storm of God's wrath from him; nor such a shadow as Jonah's gourd was, which flourished for one day, and was nipt the next, Jonah iv. 7. No; I will be constant and permanent as myself, 'I will be as the green fir-tree;' a constant shadow to keep back all annoyance whatsoever; not like the cursed noisome shadow of idols, under which Ephraim rested before. But 'I will observe and regard him, and be like a green fir-tree unto him.' I will not only be a shadow and shelter of defence unto him from injury and molestation, that he may rest quietly; but he shall be also fruitful. Though the fir-tree be not so fruitful, yet 'from me is thy fruit found.' Whatsoever he is in himself, yet this shall not be matter of discouragement unto him. I am all-sufficient, there is enough in me to supply him with; 'from me is thy fruit found.' But to take them in order.

'Ephraim shall say, What have I any more to do with idols,' &c.

Some think the words come upon Ephraim's observing and hearing of him; so as when God is seen in his most excellent majesty and glory, and observed as he is just, merciful, and wonderful, terrible in himself, that this manner of hearing and observation causeth flesh and blood so to stoop and reform, as they yield themselves, and resign up all unto God; seeing htat miserable condition they are in, and what an infinite distance there is betwixt their impurity and God's most excellent holiness. As we read of Isaiah, when he had seen God in his throne of majesty, 'Woe is me!' saith he, 'for I am undone; because I am a man of unclean lips, and I dwell in the midst of a people of unclean lips: for mine eyes have seen the King, the Lord of hosts,' Isa. vi. 5. And so of Job, 'I have heard of thee by the hearing of the ear, but now mine eye seeth thee; wherefore I abhor myself, and repent in dust and ashes,' Job. xlii. 5, 6. Which, indeed, is true in the general, that a man then truly repenteth and turneth unto God, when he knoweth God and himself to purpose, and never effectually until then; for Christ, who cannot lie, and is truth itself, calleth this kind of knowledge eternal life. 'This is life eternal, to know thee to be the only very God, and whom thou hast sent, Jesus Christ,' John xvii. 3. But, though this be a general truth, yet we take it here rather for an encouragement unto Ephraim, as before, that nothing is lost by cleaving unto God's ways, and forsaking of sin. Now whereas, 'Ephraim shall say, what have I any more to do with idols?' In the words we may consider.

1. *The manner of expression, with a great indignation of soul*, 'What have I any more to do,' &c.

2. *The matter so hated with indignation, is idolatry*, their former idols, 'Ephraim shall say, What have I any more to do with idols?'

Ephraim, we see, renounceth idolatry. But in what manner is this done? with an high indignation of zeal and hatred: 'What have I any more to do with idols?' He doth not say, Now that Ephraim hath left idolatry, I will supply all these comforts that they had by idols. But Ephraim loathes idolatry. Therefore he saith, 'What have I any more to do with idols?' It is a figurative question, implying a strong denial with a strong indignation. 'What have I any more to do with idols?' I have had too much to do with them: I have now nothing to do with idols. It is a negation and denial, with as great aversation * and abomination as can be possibly expressed: for in such questions, the denial is set forth more strongly by a negation, and with a greater emphasis, than by any affirmation is possible to express. So elegant is the Spirit of God, in setting forth spiritual things in a heavenly and transcendent manner.

'Ephraim shall say, What have I any more to do with idols?' &c.

Hence, in that Ephraim shall say thus, and say it with such vehemency of spirit and indignation, we may observe in general,

There is excellent use of the affections.

God hath planted the affections in us, to be as the wind, to carry the soul to and fro, forward or backward: for affections are planted in the soul, answerable to things aimed at by it. For, as in the nature of things, there be good and bad, delightful and hateful, hurting or pleasing; so answerably God hath framed the soul to the nature of things. For good things, God hath planted affections in us to join, clasp, embrace them and welcome them; as love, joy, delight, and such like. And for evil things, he hath planted affections to avoid them; as indignation, hatred, and the like. Indeed, religion is mainly in the affections, whereof there is excellent use. Take away them, and take away all religion whatsoever. A man, were it not for his affections, is like *mare mortuum*, the dead sea that never stirreth. Therefore it is but a doting, idle conceit of these rigid men, that take away affections; much like the folly of them, who, because they have been drunk with wine, do therefore cut up all the vines. But the way were, to moderate the excess, not to cut up the vines. So for the affections, we

* That is, 'aversion.'—G

must not root them up, or cut them down, but order them aright. For what doth the first commandment require, Thou shalt have no other gods but me; but a right ordering of all the affections of the soul, joy, delight, trust, and fear, and the whole frame of them to be carried to God? For the inward worship of God is nothing else but the excellent working of these affections suitably to the law, with the detestation of the contrary. It is not knowledge that makes a man a good man, but the affections. The devil and wicked spirits know much; but they have no love, joy, or delight in them. Therefore we must value ourselves and things, as we are in our will and affections; for so God valueth us, and we should value others thereby. This well done would bring us a wondrous deal of comfort, and stop our too much and rigid judging and censuring of others.

'Ephraim shall say, What have I any more to do with idols?'

Now in particular we see here, that Ephraim not only leaveth idols, but there is planted in him a sound indignation against them; whence we may learn,

That it is not enough to leave sin, but we must loathe sin also.

A notable place to this purpose, we have in the prophecy of Isaiah, what they should do after their conversion, in the case of hatred to idolatry. 'Ye shall defile also the covering of thy graven images of silver, and the ornament of thy molten images of gold: thou shalt cast them away as a menstruous cloth; thou shalt say unto it, Get thee hence,' Isa. xxx. 22. There is a hatred and a strong loathing indignation against sin, when it is discovered in the pollution and vileness thereof; which affection of hatred, God hath planted to draw the soul away from anything that is truly hurtful to it. It is not enough to leave sin for some by-ends, as fear of punishment, shame, and the like; but we must loathe it also. The prophet David, when he professeth his love to the law, how proveth he it? 'I hate and abhor lying,' Ps. cxix. 163. And so again, 'Do not I hate them, O Lord, that hate thee? and am not I grieved with those that rise up against thee? I hate them with perfect hatred, I account them mine enemies,' Ps. cxxxix. 21. Here is hatred, and perfect hatred with abomination.

Reason 1. The reason is, because God is a Spirit, John iv. 24; *and looks to the bent of our spirits*, seeing what we love and what we hate. Therefore the strength of this consideration draweth the soul to hate and love, with God, as he hates and loves; and as much as may be, to hate sin as he doth.

Reason 2. And then again, *he requireth our heart especially*. 'My son, give me thy heart.' Give me thy love in that which is good, and hate that which is ill. What ill we leave, we must hate first; and what good we do, we must first love, or else we shall never do either of them acceptably to purpose. What the heart doth not, is not done in religion. If it hath no hand in the avoiding of ill, it is not avoided. If it have no hand in the doing of good, it is not done before God. Therefore in true conversion, there must be a loathing of sin.

Reason 3. Thirdly, because in all true conversion there *is a new nature put in us*. Now the new creature, which partaketh of the divine nature, whereby we resemble God, it hath an antipathy to the greatest ill, which is sin, the cause of all other evils whatsoever; which maketh us opposite to God, defileth the soul, and hindereth our sweet communion with him. A new creature, we know, hath a new disposition, and is opposite to the works of the flesh; they are contrary to one another. So that we see it clear, that we must not only leave but loathe sin.

Quest. But how may we know, discern, and try this true hatred of sin?

Ans. First, true hatred is *universal.* He who hates ill truly, hates in universally in the whole kind. As we see in wicked men and devils, who hate God and all goodness. So on the contrary, those that are good hate all ill whatsoever, whether it pleasure or displeasure them; they stand not upon it, they hate the very nature of all ill. Those whose obedience and affections are partial, they hate some evils, but not others, which is not true hatred wrought by the Spirit of God, for that is universal to the whole kind.

2. Then also, wheresoever true hatred is, *it is unplacable and unappeasable.* There's no true end of sound hatred, but by the abolishing altogether of that thing it hates; as we see the hatred of Satan to the church and people of God is unappeasable and unquenchable. Nothing in the world can stay Satan's hatred, nor the hatred of his instruments, who hate the remembrance of God's people. Therefore the very name of Calvin and Luther must be put out of their books, to satisfy their hatred, not only when they are dead, burn their bones, but abolish their memory, if they can, (*m*). So there is the like disposition in God's people to that which is ill. A godly disposition, it hateth sin even to the death, and is not quiet until all sin be abolished. Whereupon it is never quiet in this life, but desires heaven, not enduring patiently the least relics and rags of sin; desiring that that which it so hateth, might have no being at all. Those who mince and cull things, who are so gentle and tender towards their sins and corruptions, in themselves and others; is this that hatred which is unappeasable, and never rests, till it see either a thorough reformation, or abolishing of what it so hateth? Wherein it is a more rooted affection than anger. For hatred is a rooted offensive displeasure, against persons and things; and so rooted, as that nothing in the world can root it out. Anger may be appeased. It is appeased in God, and it may and must be in men. But hatred is implacable, aiming at the annihilation of the thing so hated.

3. Again, where true hatred and indignation is, there *the nearer the ill is to us, the more we hate it, &c.* As we hate it in itself, so we hate it the more, the nearer it is to us. As a toad or any venomous thing, the nearer it is to us, we loathe and abhor it the more, so certainly, whosoever hates and abhorreth sin as sin (as it is a hateful thing to a renewed soul), so he hateth sin more in himself than in others, because it is nearest in his own bosom. Every man hates a snake more in his bosom than afar off, because it is more likely to do him harm there. Therefore those that flatter their own corruptions, and are violent against others, as Judah against Tamar, 'She shall be burned, bring her forth and burn her,' when himself had gotten her with child, Gen. xxxviii. 24. So many are severe in punishing of others, as if they were wondrous zealous; but what are they in their own breast? Do they reform sin in their own hearts and lives? He that truly hates sin, he hateth his own sin more than others, because it is near him.

4. And so, in proportion, he that hates sin truly *will hate it in his own family, children and servants, more than in others abroad.* It was a great fault in David, that he cockered* up Adonijah, and others in his own house, whilst he was more strict abroad. Can men think to redress and hate sin in the commonwealth, and yet suffer it in their families? True hatred is most conversant in its strength near hand. Those who suffer deboistness† and profaneness in their families, and never check it in their children and servants, they hate not sin. Whatsoever countenance they may take upon

* That is, 'indulged.'—G.

† That is, 'debauchery.'—G.

them, of reformation abroad, it cometh out of by-respects, and not out of true hatred.

5. Again, he that hateth sin truly as sin, *will hate the greatest sin in the greatest measure*, because he hates it as it is hateful. Now in the nature of things, the greatest sin deserveth the greatest abomination, and aversation* from it. Therefore he who truly hateth sin, he hates the greatest sin most of all. Those therefore that are very nice in less matters, and loose in greater things, it is but hypocrisy. For he who truly hates sin as sin, where the greatest sin is, thither he directs the edge of his hatred, which is the strongliest carried against the strongest ill. And such a one will not respect persons in evil, but wheresoever he findeth it, if he have a calling, there will be an answerable hatred of it. Therefore if one be a minister of the word of God, he will do as good Micaiah did, and will not balk† Ahab for his greatness, 1 Kings xxii. 9, *seq.*; and like good John Baptist, he will tell Herod of his faults. Because he hates sin as sin, therefore, where he hath a calling to it, he will hate it proportionably in the greatest measure. Good Eli in this case was too indulgent over his sons, 1 Sam. ii. 27, *seq.*; but we must love no man so nearly, as to love the ill in them.

6. Again, a man may know that he truly hates sin, *if he can endure admonition and reproof for sin.* He that hates a venomous plant which troubleth the ground, will not be displeased if a man come and tell him that he hath such a plant in his ground, and will help him to dig it up: surely he cannot be displeased with the party. So here, if a man do truly hate sin, will he be angry with him that shall tell him that he is obnoxious to such an evil, which will hurt him dangerously, and damn his soul if it be not helped? Surely no. Therefore let men pretend what they will, those who swell against private reproof, they do not hate sin as sin. Only add we this caution: a reproof may be administered with such indiscretion, out of self-love, and with a high hand, as that a man may dislike the carnal manner of reproving; but if it be done in a good manner, he that hates reproof, because he loveth himself and his sin, pretend what he will, he hates not sin.

7. So, *if a man love to be flattered in his sin, it is a sign he hates not sin truly.* For there is naturally a great deal of self-love in man, which makes him that he loves to be flattered in his sins; whereupon he comes to be abused to his own destruction, especially great men. Now, it is a sign of an ill state of soul to be subject to be abused by flattery, and to hate instruction. Saith Paul, 'Am I your enemy, because I have told you the truth?' Gal. iv. 16.

8. Again, we may know what our hatred to sin is, *by our willingness or unwillingness to talk of it or mention it, or to venture upon the occasions thereof.* Where hatred is, there is outward aversation. We fly from what we hate, and shun to frequent places where we may receive offence. Whatsoever hath an antipathy to nature, that we hate and run away from. Therefore those that present themselves to the occasions of sin, upon no calling, say what they will, they feed sin, and live according to the flesh. Those that hate a thing will never come near it if they can choose. Therefore, those that present themselves willingly to places infected, where there is nothing religious, but scorning of religion, your common representations of abomination, pretend what they will, their intent is to strengthen their own corruption, against the good of their souls. This is the issue. Those that hate sin will hate all that which may lead to it, the representations of

* That is, 'aversion' = turning from.—G. † That is, 'avoid.'—G.

sin also. Can a man hate sin and see it acted? Wickedness is learned when one seeth it acted, as one of the ancients saith well. Therefore let us by these and the like trials take notice what our hatred to sin is.

Only this our zeal and indignation to sin must have a mitigation and be regulated, lest, like an exorbitant river, it exceed the bounds. Therefore, not to follow the school niceties in the exactness of differences, we will touch the mark a little, how this zeal and hatred to sin, in reproof especially, must be qualified; wherein we must consider divers things.

1. First, *our calling must be respected*. For howsoever we must carry an universal hatred to sin thus far, that we must not do it, yet in the discovery of hatred and dislike to others, we must consider what calling we have, and how far we go.

2. And it must be done *with a sweet temper*, keeping our distance, and reserving the due respect unto those in whom we shew our dislike. As we see Nathan, when he came to tell David of his fault, how he doth it, what art he useth! It must so be done as that it may appear to be done out of pure zeal, that it is no wild-fire nor no heat of nature; but that it cometh merely from the Spirit, and in much love, with mildness and pity, in which case it carrieth a wondrous authority. The discovery of hatred to the faults either in a minister or in a magistrate, though they must be truly dealt with, and have their faults told them, yet there must be respect had to their place, by reason of the weakness of men. As it is with the body, great men have their physicians as well as meaner, only their physic must be more costly, because perhaps of the tenderness of their constitutions; but as for their bodies, they must not be suffered to perish, nor will not. So for their souls, they must have that which other men have to help them, but it must be done with reservation and respect; as Paul, speaking to Festus the governor, calleth him 'most noble Festus,' &c., Acts xxvi. 25. Pressing also goodness in some sort upon king Agrippa, 'O king Agrippa, believest thou the prophets? I know thou dost,' Acts xxvi. 26. So we see how we may examine whether our hatred to sin be true or not.

Let every one therefore make use of it in their calling. Those that are entrusted with God's message, let them know that God's ambassadors are to be faithful in their message, for they serve a greater Lord than is upon the earth; and let them shew their true hatred of ill, and the danger of sin, wheresoever they find it. And for those that are governors of others, let them not think that they hate sin in themselves except they hate sin also in all that belongs to them, and reform it. For we see here an evidence of conversion. When Ephraim was converted, 'What have I any more to do with idols?' and, 2 Cor. vii. 11, there is an excellent description of the nature of repentance, by many parcels. The Corinthians had repented: how is this evidenced? 'Oh, behold,' saith he, 'this selfsame thing, that ye sorrowed after a godly sort, what carefulness it wrought in you; yea, what clearing of yourselves; yea, what indignation; yea, what fear; yea, what vehement desire; yea, what zeal; yea, what revenge!' What revenge and indignation against sin! A kind of extremity of hatred, a hatred quickened and kindled, the height of hatred. What indignation! Insinuating that wheresoever there is the truth of conversion, there will be indignation against sin in ourselves. As David confesseth of himself, having sinned, 'So foolish was I, and ignorant: I was as a beast before thee,' Ps. lxxiii. 22. When he suffered such a thought to lodge in his breast, that it was better with the children of the world than with the church of God, he was troubled for it. But when he went into the church of God, and saw the end of wicked men, then he saw his own foolishness in being so deceived, and speaks against himself with indignation. So wheresoever there is true conversion, there is hatred with indignation against ourselves. As in that place before alleged, they shall say unto their idols, 'Get thee hence,' Isa. xxx. 22, what have I any more to do with you? Which is a phrase of speech shewing a disposition of hatred to the utmost extension, 'Get you hence.' So Christ to the devil, 'Get thee behind me, Satan.' This is the right temper of a truly converted Christian, expressed by divers phrases in Scripture: by a denial of our lusts, by killing and crucifying, by pulling out the eye, and cutting off the right hand. Which phrases, do they not imply a great strength of hatred and indignation, when we must, as it were, pull out our own eyes; that is, our beloved sins, which are as dear to us as our eyes, and as useful as our right hands unto us? Yet these must be cut off, mortified, crucified, and denied, Col. iii. 5. Therefore let us not deceive ourselves; but let us judge of the truth of our conversion by our true hatred to sin in ourselves and others, and in all who are committed to our charge.

If this be so, what shall we judge of a cold, lukewarm temper? It is the nature of cold, to gather heterogeneal bodies together. As we see in the ice, there are straws, and stones, and heterogeneal things incorporated, because the cold congeals them together; but where there is fire, there is a separating of the dross from the good metal. So where the Spirit of God is, it is not so cold as to jumble sin and sin, this and that together; but it purgeth away that which is ill, and that which is good it makes better. For in what proportion the fire of God's Spirit stirs up that which is good, in that proportion there is a hatred of that which is ill. They are unparalleled affections. Those that love God, they hate evil. Those that are alike to all things, do shew that they have not this active true hatred against sin. No! 'Ephraim shall say, What have I any more to do with idols?'

Quest. But now, How shall we come to get this hatred against sin, and holy revenge and indignation against ourselves for that which is amiss in us?

Ans. First, we must every day labour to get a *clearer sight of the excellency of that which is good, and a nearer communion with God by prayer and meditation.* And then, when we have been with God, it will work an abomination of whatsoever is contrary unto him. Thus Moses, when he had talked with God in the mountain, at his return, seeing them dancing and sacrificing to the calf of gold, Exod. xxxii. 19, what did Moses? He brake the tables asunder. So it is with those that have communion with God, who is 'light itself, and in whom is no darkness,' 1 John i. 5, who is holiness and purity itself. Those who have effectually conversed with God in his ordinances, meditation, prayer, and the like, when they look upon sin, which is contrary to God, they look upon it with a more perfect hatred. So Isaiah vi. 5. When God appeared to the prophet, and touched his tongue* with a coal from the altar, saith he, 'Woe is me, for I am undone, because I am a man of unclean lips,' &c., 'for mine eyes have seen the King, the Lord of Hosts.' Thus, when once he had communion with God, he began to loathe himself. So, if we would hate evil, let us labour more and more to be holy, and to increase in that divine affection of love. For in what measure we love that which is good, in that measure we hate the evil: as it is, Ps. xcvii. 10, 'Ye that love the Lord, hate evil;' insinua-

* Lips.—G.

ting, that all that love the Lord hate evil. All those that are near unto God, they hate all sin. The more they grow into communion with God, the more they grow in the hatred of all that is contrary. Let us therefore never talk of love to God, and of piety, and such like; for if there be any grace or communion with God, we hate all sin in that measure as God hateth. He who hath no zeal to reform that which God hateth, he hath no love at all.

2. Again, the way to stir us up to hate sin in ourselves and others, and out of that hatred to reform it, is to set before us, *what it is in itself;* that it is the loathsomest thing in the world, worse than the devil himself: for it is sin which makes him a devil. That corruption, pride, worldliness, and profaneness, which we cherish, is worse than the devil himself, because this made him a devil. Let us make sin therefore as loathsome as we can, and then we shall hate it: and let us present it to our souls, as the most dangerous thing of all, the ill of ills, which bringeth all other evils upon us. This may appear more ugly in our sight, in that the foulness thereof could not be expiated but by the death of the Son of God. And consider what great torments he hath prepared for that which we so cherish. This proud, sinful, and carnal disposition of ours, so opposite to all goodness, God hath appointed to punish it with eternal separation from his presence. It maketh God hate his own creatures. 'Go, ye cursed, into everlasting fire, prepared for the devil and his angels,' Matt. xxv. 41.

3. And to stir us up to reform sin in all that belong unto us, we must consider *the dangerous condition that they live and die in, in whom this is not reformed.* Eternal torments, and separation from God. These things may help to work in our hearts a hatred of sin: and from this hatred, a reformation of it, with a zeal and indignation. Therefore let us labour more and more for this temper of soul, that we may be like God, and carry the characters of the children of God in us. There is no affection will distinguish us from hypocrites more than hatred, which cometh of love, which is the first-born and breeding affection of all others. For why do we hate any thing, but because it is opposite to that we love? Why do we hate ill, but because it is opposite to God and to Christ, whom we love? Amongst others, take we along this consideration with us, that it is the spear which wounded our blessed Saviour; and that it is that he hates most which we love most. Consider the holiness of God, that he would punish it in his own Son, ere it should not be punished.

4. And consider that *it is the bane of all our comfort, this which we so cherish, and that it embitters all things to us.* We cannot rejoice, no, not in the good blessings of God, whilst we are guilty of sin; neither can we pray comfortably whilst our hearts regard it, Ps. lxvi. 18. In this case, that which should rejoice the heart, communion with God, is terrible to us. What have I to do to take his name in my mouth, when I embrace such sins? Ps. l. 16. The day of judgment is terrible also; for how can a man think comfortably thereof, if therewith he expect a heavy doom for his sins he liveth in? So we may say of the day of death. None of these can be thought upon without terror, when therewithal it cometh to one's mind, the cutting off from their sins, and the 'terror of the Lord' against all sin whatsoever, 2 Cor. v. 11. It should be the joy of our hearts to think of these happy times: therefore, there must needs be a great deal of sin and atheism in our hearts when we cannot think comfortably of them. For either we believe not these things, and so are plain atheists; or else, if we believe them, we are exceeding foolish to lose future joys for the poor 'pleasures of sin for a season.'

5. Let us labour to *grow in grace more and more;* for the more we grow in the love of God and good things, the more we shall hate sin. For, whatsoever may be said for the growth in love, and cherishing of it to good things, the same may be said for the hatred of ill, in a contrary sense.

6. The last place shall be, *to place and drive our affections a contrary way, to translate and place them on a contrary object, when they are stirred up to evil attempts.* As, when hatred is stirred up, direct it to its proper object, sin; when love is irregular, think with ourselves, that God hath not planted this affection for this object, but to carry me another way; I must love God above all, and all that he loveth, for his sake. Hath God put love and hatred into my heart, to hate my brother whom I should love, and to love the devil, and hate God? Oh no! I should love God above all, and my brother as myself; and hate the devil and all his works, whom I have renounced in my baptism. Therefore, in distempers of the affections, make a diverson, and turn them the right way. As physicians use to do, when the distempered blood runs dangerously one way; if they cannot stop that, they open a vein to drive the course of the blood another way. So it is Christian policy, when the affections run dangerously one way, then to reflect thus upon ourselves: Aye, But is this the end why God hath placed this affection in me? Certainly no! He hath planted this affection in me for another purpose. Therefore, I will hate that which I should hate; sin in general, and my own sin most of all, which makes me hate my brother. This should be our daily task and study, to take off the affections where they should not be placed, and to fix them where they should be placed; and there to let them go amain, the faster the better; restraining them where they should not run out.

Thus we ought to temper ourselves, and to work in ourselves as much as may be, a sound hatred to all sin, not only of the second table, but of the first also. The church here saith, 'What have I any more to do with idols?' Now I hate all vain inventions. And think not, with Gallio, that this belongeth not to us; if we be magistrates, and called to do it, to stand for the cause of the church and true religion.

'What have I any more to do with idols?'

The last thing to be observed from Ephraim's manner of expressing his indignation is—

Obs. That where love is not well contracted and begun, it will not hold to the end, but will end in eternal hatred.

The serpent and Eve* had some poor acquaintance together, as the issue proved. What did it end in? 'The seed of the woman shall break the serpent's head,' Gen. iii. 15. This association and acquaintance ended in everlasting war and breach. So all covenants, leagues, and associations with those we should not join with, can never soder† handsomely together, but will end in everlasting hatred. What a strict league was in former times betwixt Ephraim and idols! But when Ephraim's eyes are opened to see his idols devils, he detests and loathes all abominations, and is of another mind. 'What have I any more to do with idols?' He abominates them, as the word importeth.

Let us therefore beware with whom we join in intimate league. For what makes miserable so much, as the renting‡ of the affections from that they were strongly placed on? when love is rent from the thing beloved? If we place our affections, for some by-respects, upon wicked persons, this

* Printed 'Hevah.'—G. † That is, 'solder.'—G. ‡ That is, 'rending.'—G.

will cause so much the more torment and indignation against ourselves, that were so foolish to suffer our affections to enter so deeply where they should not. Those that glory in their league with antichrist, and wonder at the beast, Rev. xvii. 8, *seq.*, thinking him a demi-god: will this be alway so? Oh, no; when God opens the eyes of any of his people, they shall hate them for ever. So wicked persons, that now are led on to this and that wicked course: shall this be always so? Woe to thee, if it be! But the time may come that thou shalt say, 'What have I any more to do with idols,' or with such an one's acquaintance? I cannot endure to look on him: he tainted me, and misled me, and tempted me. Now we must be two, part we must, and I would we had never met together. Therefore, before we place our affections on any, consider who they be, whether we be likely to live with them for ever or not; whether there be any evidence of grace in them. If not, let them be two to us. For whatsoever vanity is in the things or persons we love, if we belong to God, we must be separate from them, unless we will be damned. Therefore we must be wise to prevent the danger betimes. Ephraim might have known before the danger of idolatry, had he been wise and prudent; but it is well he knows it now at length, which causeth him so to abominate idols. 'What have I any more to do with idols?' Thus much is spoken, because of the lukewarmness and cold temper, neutrality and halting of a great many in the world, having so many sinful combinations and associations one with another, as if these things were not material.

Now, let men consider what a disposition this is, and how it stands with that disposition which must be in those that are members of Christ, and look for heaven. Let a Christian always remember what he is, and what he hopes for, and this will put him in a right temper. 1. What he is: a king, and an heir of heaven, &c. After which he should reason with good Nehemiah, 'Shall such a man as I fly?' shall such a man as I do this? I am redeemed from my sins, and advanced to be a king to rule over my lusts, to be an heir of heaven and eternal happiness in the world to come, to reign with Christ; and shall I do thus and thus? Doth this stand with my new temper, this sin, this filthiness, this base action and thoughts that I am tempted to and encumbered with? Shall such a man as I follow these base actions, ways, and companions? Consider we this well, and then it will breed Ephraim's resolution, 'What have I any more to do with this base lust?' What hath it to do with me, or I with it? Is this and this action befitting a king, and an heir of heaven, and a new creature? And if a man be in authority, then let him consider what Mordecai said to Esther, 'What if thou be called to the kingdom for such a purpose?' Esther iv. 14. What if thou be called to this place or dignity for this purpose, to reform such and such abuses? Think with thyself, not only in particular what thou art, but in thy place, what if thou be called to reform such abuses; such unsound doctrines; to stand for God and for the truth. This will breed this resolute indignation of Ephraim in us, 'What have I any more to do with idols?' All which is for the manner of Ephraim's indignation: a strong negation of an abominated thing. 'What have I any more to do,' &c. The next, which is the substance and matter abominated—idolatry—must be reserved for some other time.

THE ELEVENTH SERMON.

Ephraim shall say, What have I any more to do with idols? I have heard him, and observed him: I am like a green fir-tree: from me is thy fruit found.—Hos. XIV. 8.

WE have heard at several times heretofore how graciously God deals with his people, alluring them by many free and gracious promises to his service; the particulars whereof we heard heretofore at large.

This 8th verse hath reference unto that which went before, ver. 3. There Ephraim renounceth his former idols. 'Asshur shall not save us,' &c.; and here, 'Ephraim shall say, What have I any more to do with idols?' Unto which the answer is, 'I have heard him, and observed him: I am like a green fir-tree unto him: from me is thy fruit found.' Now, in that 'Ephraim shall say, What have I any more to do with idols?' this in sum is only the first part of the third verse, repeated in another manner: That Ephraim shall and will go on in abominating idols, be constant in his former resolution. Therefore, in that Ephraim shall, by the Spirit of grace, go on in renouncing all false confidence, God sheweth here that Ephraim shall lose nothing by it, for he intends here the continuance of time. 'I have heard him,' and I do hear him, and I will hear him, and respect him, and be like a shady green fir-tree to shade him, causing him also to be abundant in fruit. 'From me is thy fruit found.'

'Ephraim shall say, What have I any more to do with idols?' Here we considered the manner of expression, and then the matter itself.

'Ephraim shall say, What have I any more to do with idols?'

To come, therefore, to the matter itself specified, idolatry, against which Ephraim's indignation is directed:

'What have I to do with idols?'

In handling whereof we must take in all these four together, that is—

1. *False doctrine*, which is the foundation of *idolatry*.

2. *Idols themselves;* or,

3. *Idolatry*, which they tend to (for he which hates idols, hates them because he hates idolatry); or,

4. *Idolaters;* as if he had said,

What have I any more to do with idolatrous doctrines, opinions, or conceits, or with idols framed according to these conceits, or with idolatry or idolaters? For these go together. No man worships idols, but because he is poisoned in his conceits; and idols are forbidden, because idolatry is dangerous; and communion with idolaters is forbidden, because of idolatry. So that the doctrine, idols, idolatry, and communion with them, all these are objects of Ephraim's abomination and indignation.

'Ephraim shall say, What have I any more to do with idols?'

It were to misspend precious time, appointed for better uses, to tell you of the abominable distinctions of the papists, of *Latria* and *Dulia*, (*n*) or to insist upon a discourse of heathenish idolatry; truths, but not so profitable for us to spend time in. Therefore, we will rather come to shew the reasons why Ephraim so abhorreth idolatry, idols, and conceits of all.

1. To begin, in the first place, with idols. When Ephraim is truly converted, he hates them, because idols *are abominable to God*, unto whom

Ephraim is now converted. Ephraim hates idols, for idolatry is spiritual adultery. Religion is, as it were, a conjugal act of marriage; so that a breach in religious worship is a breach of spiritual marriage. Now, the worshipping of idols being a breach of the conjugal act of marriage betwixt God and the soul, spiritual adultery, it must needs be abominable. For adultery is an abominable, filthy thing; much more spiritual adultery. Therefore, saith Ephraim, 'What have I now any more to do with idols?'

2. And then again, idolatry *frameth base conceits of God*. Whereas, on the contrary, we should elevate and raise up our hearts unto him; idolatry pulls him down, and conforms him to our base conceits. Were it not a wrong to man to make him like a swine, or an ape, or some such ridiculous creature? Who, in this case, would think himself well used? There is not such disproportion betwixt any creature and man as there is betwixt the great God of heaven and earth, and the best creature that can be made to resemble him. Therefore, it is an abominable abuse and dishonour to the great majesty of God to be represented any kind of way.

3. Again, *consider the opposition between any representation of God, and God*. They are corruptible things; God is incorruptible. They are visible; God is invisible. They are vain and nothing; God a being of himself, who giveth being unto all things. God is the living God, and the cause of all life. To be brief: the Scripture, to shew God's hatred of them, calleth them dunghill-gods, and Abel, as it is in this book, vanity, nothing, a name to alienate the affections from them. (*o*)

4. Yea, further, because *God is a jealous God*, Exod. xxxiv. 14, and will not give his glory to another. Ephraim, therefore, as soon as he cometh to know God, he hateth idols; because he knows God, being a jealous God, could not endure them, Isa. xlii. 8.

Now, idolatry is committed when either we set up false gods in place of the true God, or when we worship the true God in a false manner.

Quest. But now another question may be moved, Whether the papists be idolaters or not? For we live amongst many of them; therefore we cannot be too wary of them.

Ans. The answer is affirmative. They are idolaters, and worse in some sort than the heathen idolaters were. Only change the names of the popish saints which they in popery worship, and the names that the heathen worship, and they will be all one. Now, names be no realities.

How may this be cleared?

First, *they give the honour due to God to others*, which is idolatry. The religious worship only due unto God, they give unto other things. Christ, when he said, 'Him only shalt thou serve,' Mat. iv. 10, excepted the least divine worship from the creature. The devil, we know, would have have had him fall down before him; but Christ's answer is, 'Him only shalt thou serve;' that is, him only shalt thou religiously prostrate thyself unto. So that religious worship is proper to God only. Now, this they give to saints; for they pray to them, which is religious worship.

Obj. But they object, that they pray not directly to them, but to them as mediators, that they may pray to Christ for them.

Ans. 1. First, *they raise them above their degree, to make them mediators*, and so dethrone Christ of his office of Mediator, at least join copartners with him.

2. But this is not all. *They pray directly to saints* to help them against several ills, as they have several saints for several evils. Whatsoever they

say, who are not ashamed of lying to further their designs, yet their books and writings do testify the contrary.

3. Then again, *they vow to saints*, as in the form of their vows is seen. I vow to the Virgin Mary, &c. Now, a vow is a religious act. They vow to saints, and burn incense unto them, erect temples, and set apart days for their worship, and so break all the four commandments of the first table. In a good fashion, it is not unfit to remember them, that their memorial may be kept; but we are not to worship them.

4. And, besides saints, *they have other false gods;* for their head of the church is an abominable idol, unto whom they ascribe that which is proper unto Christ, to be the head of the church, which hath no influence from him, but all from Christ, the spiritual head thereof. Therefore the apostle complaineth of such 'who hold not the head,' &c., Col. ii. 19. Those of the Romish Church 'hold not the head,' hold not Christ, because they attribute that to saints and men which is proper to Christ only. They make the pope judge of all controversies, who must give authority to the word, and determine Scripture to be Scripture. What a shameful thing is this, to make him judge of the Scriptures, which must judge him at the last day. A pitiful thing it is to see 'a man of sin' go about to judge the righteous law of God, and to determine of that which must ere long determine him unto eternal torments, without particular repentance. Yet, being spiritually drunk, this folly they are given to, that they will be judge of that which must be judge of them. Many ways they make him an idol, ascribing that to him which is proper to Christ.

5. So likewise, *they make their sacraments to be idols.*

For, 1, they ascribe to the *water in baptism* power of conferring grace.

Now, grace is God's creature only; for all the creatures in heaven and earth cannot confer the least dram of grace. It is a thing of God's making. Now, to raise an element to confer grace, and then to trust in it, *ex opere operato*, for the conferring of it, is to make an idol of it.

2. And for *the bread*. None of all the heathens ever had such an abominable idol as the mass, a breaden god, for they worshipped living creatures, and there is not the worst living creature but it is better than a piece of bread; and yet they worship that, for, by their own confession, if the intention of the priest be not to the action, there is nothing but bread. How may the minds, then, of men be tormented when they may or shall think perhaps the priest hath no such intention, and so are in danger of idolatry. For, saith the psalmist, 'their sorrows shall be multiplied that hasten after another god,' &c., Ps. xvi. 4. So certainly the sorrows and scruples of those that are idolaters shall be multiplied. They cannot but be much tormented in soul sometimes. Coster (*p*), himself a forward Jesuit, acknowledgeth 'that if, upon the words of consecration, the bread be not turned and transubstantiated into the body of Christ, we are the most abominable idolaters of the world.' But we make the minor and assumption, long since proved by the late worthies of our church * (*q*), but there is no such transubstantiating of the bread into the body of Christ. Therefore, by their own consent, they are the most abominable idolaters of the world, worse than the heathen.

8. And in their *equalising traditions*, which are but the inventions of man's brain, *with the Scriptures*, they commit idolatry, in that they make their very church an idol. But what should we speak of their church,

* B. Jewel, D. Rainolds, D. Fulk, D. Whitaker, D. Willet, Perkins, &c. See Note *q*.—G.

when they have the pope, who is their church virtually? for what is said of the one may be said of the other. When they come to the issue, the church is nothing but the pope. Whatsoever their church or councils say, he is the whole church. Many ways they are gross idolaters, especially the common people. For though they say they give not *Latria*, worship to the image, but *Dulia*, service, but can the common people distinguish, who give worship to all alike? To say we worship not the image, but God before the image, was the heathen's excuse, as we may see in Arnobius (*r*). Can the common people distinguish? No; for they are ignorant images themselves. In this they are worse than the heathens, because they have more light, and still the more light the more sin. For they have been foretold that the whore of Rome should be the mother of all fornications, the spiritual Babylon, Sodom, and Egypt in regard of idolatry, the mother of all these abominations, Rev. xvii. 5. Now, for them who have been forewarned hereof, and in so much light still, to continue idolaters, and persist in false worship, is to be worse than the heathens, who had not the like light and warning.

Ques. But what is the reason that they are so impudent and audacious?

Ans. 1. First, to answer with the Scriptures, *they are drunk with the whore's cup*, Rev. xvii. 2; and we know a drunken man dares do anything.

2. And then, again, as the psalmist speaks, because those who worship idols *become blockish and stupid like unto them*, for an idol is a blockish, dead thing, so idolaters are stupid, dead things in a sort, who are seldom converted, partly because they are drunk, and partly because they are stupid, like the idols they worship, Ps. cxv. 8.

Use 1. If this be so, as it is too true to the eye of the whole world, then *how ought we to bless God, who hath brought us out of this palpable Egyptian darkness, out of spiritual Sodom*, as Lot was out of that Sodom! Gen. xix. 17. Oh, we cannot be thankful enough, nor ought we to desire to return to Sodom again, or unto Egypt. Where, then, is place left for neutrality? Those neuters, that will be of neither religion! Is such a disposition from the Spirit of God, which maketh Ephraim say here, 'What have I any more to do with idols?' Ephraim would not be a neuter. Therefore, what shall we say unto them that present themselves to Masses, in their travels especially? Is this to say with Ephraim, 'What have I any more to do with idols?' We must 'believe with the heart, and confess with the mouth, to salvation,' Rom. x. 9. If a man might escape with having his heart to God-wards, and his body prostrate, where were confession? In Elias's time, God told him, that there were left seven thousand in Israel, who had not bowed the knee to Baal, that is, who made no bodily prostration, 1 Kings xix. 18. Therefore, as the papists do not join with us, so neither ought we with them, if we hold the contrary religion false. In this case we should not present ourselves with them in any service.

Use 2. Again, if this be true, *what do we think of reconcilers of religion?* A thing impossible, as the apostle sheweth. 'For what communion hath God with Belial? Christ with antichrist?' 2 Cor. vi. 14, 15. What communion? The question is a strong negation, as that of Ephraim here. 'What have I now any more to do with idols?'

Obj. But some may say, We differ from them only in circumstance.

Ans. We may ask any man who hath his brains in his head, *whether idolatry be a circumstance or not?* it being clear that they are as great idolaters as the heathens, in many instances. If any affirm that idolatry is a circumstance, there is no disputing with such a one. That which is the sin, which makes God abhor and desert his own people, is that a circumstance? Is that a circumstance, which is the chief sin against the first table? Granting that they are idolaters, that the pope is 'antichrist,' and Rome to be 'Babylon' (*s*), and Babylon to be the 'mother of all fornication,' this must needs follow, that there can be no reconciling of these two religions. We may come near them, and become papists, but they will never come near us, to be good Christians.

Use 3. Again, if this be so, that popery be idolatry, and that we must beware of all idolatry, let us take heed, therefore, *that we have nothing to do with them more than we must needs.* Converse with them in our callings, we may; because, as an ancient father saith, we be compossessors of the world, and not of religion. We must go out of the world, if we will not have to do with them sometimes in the places where we live; but amity is very dangerous with such. The Scripture runs much upon it. Should we love them whom God hates? It was Eve's fault, that without a calling she ventured to talk with the serpent. We should therefore shun conversing and parley with them as much as may be. As there were rails set about Mount Sinai, to keep off the people from touching the mountain; so God hath set hedges about the second commandment, to keep us off from offending in it, as it was usual with God in this kind. As, when he would keep them far from murder, he forbade them to kill the dam with the young, Deut. xxii. 6, and not to seethe a kid in his mother's milk, Exod. xxiii. 19; only to restrain them from murder, that abominable sin. Such precepts the Jews call 'the hedges of the commandments' (*t*). So for idolatry, the Scripture would have us 'hate the garment spotted with the flesh,' Jude, verse 23; 'to defile the coverings of the images, to account them as a menstruous cloth,' &c., Isa. xxx. 22; and 'to have nothing to do with the unfruitful works of darkness,' Eph. v. 11; [and] to hate all monuments of idolatry. As Augustine saith of monuments, 'Any monument moves and stirs up the mind;' so anything that may move or stir us to idolatry, we should abhor, and keep afar off from it.

And therefore the commandments are set down in the highest pitch of the sin, to shew that we should avoid all the degrees under that which leads to so great a breach, and that we should hate all those steps and leadings to the sin itself. We should therefore beware of popish writers, and do with them as was done with the magic books in the Acts, burn them all, lest they corrupt ourselves and others, Acts xix. 19. Learn we this of the papists, who hate our books, burn them, or lock them up safe; yea, hate the very names of Luther and Calvin, much more their books.

In this case it is with the soul of man as with water, that relisheth of that soil through which it runs, if it run through a hot soil, as baths through a sulphury soil, it tastes of that. So the spirit of a man tastes of those authors he runs through. Therefore such who converse much in popish writings, unless ministers who have a calling that way to confute them, are in danger to be ensnared by them.

Use 4. And then, again, if we must hate all idolatry, *we must take heed of occasions.* Not like some looser Christians, which make no matter of crucifixes. How doth the spirit of Ephraim here agree with such? A crucifix is but a teacher of lies, representing only the outside, and that falsely; for there is no expression in Scripture, what kind of man Christ was. And if there were, yet the apostle sheweth, 'that we must now no more know him any more after the flesh,' 2 Cor. v. 16. Not as such a man, as tall and fair, &c.; but know him as the Mediator, as king of heaven and earth, avoiding all lewd, base conceits of him. People in this kind are too bold, and run too near popery. A father saith well, 'No man is safe that is near danger.' We are commanded to 'fly from idolatry,' 1 Cor. x. 14. We must not come near the pit's brink, lest we fall in. Run and fly from it as from a serpent, dally not with the occasions.

But to leave this gross idolatry, to speak of something which more nearly concerneth us, and which we are prone to. Though we hate the gross idolatries, yet there be some we are more nearly addicted to; as,

First of all, there is a proneness in us, in our worship, *to conceive false conceptions and ideas of God;* and so in place of worshipping God, we worship an idol of our own brain.

Quest. It may be said, How shall we conceive of God when we worship him?

Ans 1. First of all, negatively, do not dishonour God *in imagining any character of an infinite incomprehensible God*, but conceive of him as an infinite essence.

2. And then, *conceive not absolutely of God*, but of God distinguished in three persons, the Father, Son, and Holy Ghost; or else we conceive an idol. For there are three persons in one common nature; and in our prayers we must not conceive the nature without the persons.

3. In the third place, we must not in our prayers conceive of God, *without Christ the Mediator*. For even as God was only to be known and spoken to towards the tabernacle; so Christ is the tabernacle now, where God manifests his gracious presence, and will be worshipped in him the Mediator. For God, considered out of Christ, is a 'consuming fire;' without Christ, no converse with God. Let us therefore take Christ along with us, when we go to God. Go to him by God in our nature, our Immanuel; and so we shall conceive of God aright, and not worship an idol of our own brain.

4. Again, there is another thing which is a common abuse among Christians, wherein they come near to idolatry, *when they transform God to be like themselves in their affections*, as it is the property of all unregenerate men to do so. Idolatry is so natural, it cannot but transform God to be like itself. As for instance, a man that is not a gracious man, in the pride of his sinful course, thinks that God is like unto him. 'Thou thoughtest that I was like unto thyself; therefore I will come against thee,' &c., Ps. l. 21. As oppressors, and such who grow great by ill courses, they justify thus much. Would God let me alone if he did not approve of my courses? So they make God like themselves. And so the good fellows of the world, they make God to allow all their dissoluteness, because he lets them alone. So those that are fierce and cruel by nature, who delight in cruelty, vexation, and blood, they transform God, as though he delighted in such things, and make him a God of blood. So others transform God to be all mercy. This is to make God an idol, and as ill as if they transformed him into this and that creature; worse than the heathens, in regard of their light under the gospel; yet this is the disposition of many Christians now-a-days.

Quest. What was the reason why the heathens worshipped Bacchus and Venus, such abominable gods?

Ans. They, to countenance their lusts and drunkenness, deify them: an abominable sin of the heathen, for which God gave them up to other sins. Doth not our sin come near theirs, when we make God to countenance our sin, and cite Scripture for it, as if God can countenance sin in his word?

This is to transform God into our own abominable conceits. Those, therefore, who bless themselves in any sinful course, they are guilty of idolatry in the worst kind that may be; for it is as ill to transform God to allow of such courses, as to transform Christ to die for such who go on in their sins without remorse, or to transform him into the likeness of such and such vile creatures.

5. Further, there is another sort of idolatry Christians are subject unto—*to set up somewhat in their hearts higher than God.* There is no man without grace, but he doth so until his conversion. Nay, when a man is converted, he is prone to this, to idolize and set up something above that which should be in the heart. Hereupon Paul, Col. iii. 5, calleth covetousness, idolatry; because a covetous man placeth those affections upon his own wealth, which should dwell in God: for, 'he saith to the wedge of gold, Thou art my confidence,' Job xxxi. 24, thinking his wealth shall bear him out in any ill cause whatsoever. And then, again, that time which he should spend in thinking of God and of a better life, he buried those thoughts in his muck and wealth, toiling and moiling in the world, when he should serve God. Thus the covetous man is an idolater.

6. And there are some guilty of idolatry, likewise, in another kind, *such as have men's persons too much in admiration*, that deify them, especially if they be in great place: such who will offend God before they will offend them; and whereas for God's glory they should deny themselves, they deny themselves, and make themselves fools, for men; and to please them by whom they hope to rise, deny both wit and honesty. This is abominable idolatry, and such are as far from heaven and salvation, as those that fall before an idol, if they repent not. Oh, if these men that study to please men, and deny themselves for them, would be as careful to please God, as they have been to please men, how happy, and what excellent Christians would they be! As a great man-pleaser in his time said, 'If he had served God as well as he had served his master the king in that time, God had not left him so in his old years' (*u*).* To set up any man so high in our affections, as for him to deny ourselves, crack our consciences, and do things unlawful, will be misery in the end. 'If I please men,' saith Paul, 'I am not the servant of Christ,' Gal. i. 10. He meaneth sinful pleasing, for there ought to be service and respect. Due honour must be given unto those who carry God's image, our governors, yea, great respect and honour, and nothing in this kind can be too much; but to go beyond our bounds herein, is to commit idolatry. As the heathen did, when the government of Rome was turned into an empire, some of their emperors were made gods by them after Augustus's time, wherein they could not have devised to have done them greater wrong, for they came most of them to fearful ends (*v*). It is ill for any man to have God his co-rival; for no greater misery can befall a man, than to be set up in God's room, so to rule a man's honesty, will, and conscience at his pleasure; for God is a jealous God, and will not endure such idolatry.

7. And so, in the next place, they frame Christ an idol, *in taking him without his cross.* They will be of the true religion; but when they come to suffer anything, if it be but a frown, a reproach or disgrace, they give out and fall back. Such, they frame to themselves an idol, a false Christ; for the knowledge of Christ is never without the cross, some cross or other, some persecution or other in some kind. 'All who will live godly in Christ, shall suffer persecution,' 2 Tim. iii. 12. A man may live godly,

* A Scottish Regent before his execution. See Note *u*.—G.

and not suffer persecution ; but he that will live godly in Christ, so as he sheweth his nature to be altered, carrying an antipathy against all false courses, and so as the world may conceive that he is such an one, it is impossible that he should live in the world without persecution, because he shall meet with those that are of an opposite disposition. Therefore, to frame a smooth Christ, all comfort, is to frame a false Christ, and a false religion,—to frame an idol that hath no truth in it, that never was, nor never will be to the end of the world.

8. Again, unconverted persons especially are prone to another idolatry, *to set up their own wits and wills instead of God's.* So as there is not a greater enemy to religion than our own conceits and wills, which will have a model of religion of our own brain, which must stand, let what will come of it. This is the fault especially of great learned persons, who take upon them conceits and apprehensions of things, and then doat upon these brats of their own brain. And so for will, to have our own will in all things ; as the speech is, 'My mind to me a kingdom is.' I will have my will, whatsoever come of it. This is idolatry ; for whosoever will come to heaven must deny his will. The first lesson in Christ's school is self-denial, Mat. xix. 21, 24 : denial of wit and will, to have no more wit and wisdom, especially in divine things, than God will teach us ; and no more will, which is distinct and opposite to Christ's will, but to bring our wills to his in all things. When men will go about great affairs, and set upon things in their own wit and strength, never praying nor depending upon God for a blessing, this is a kind of idolising of parts to work out things by policy, strength, wits, and parts. As that heathen atheist could say, 'Let cowards pray, if they will ;' but his success was answerable. So is it not the common atheism of the world ? They go about things in confidence of their wit and parts, and so hope to attain a glorious issue ; whereas God, who overthrows Babels, takes delight to confound all their devices. It is his daily practice 'to send the rich empty away, and exalt the humble and meek,' Luke i. 52. Those who set upon things rashly without prayer, as though they were lords of all, and without dependence upon God, promising themselves good success, they make idols of themselves. As a proud man is an idol, 'he worships himself,' whilst he leans to his own wit, plots, and parts. Carnal men thus idolise themselves.

9. Again, you have some who are none of the worst who commit this great sin of idolatry, *by trusting to the outward performances and tasks of religion*, thinking that God must needs be bound unto them, when they have done so many tasks, read, and prayed, or heard so many sermons, or done a good deed. But here lieth the spiritual subtlety, in that they set up these things too high, when, if they find not that success they look for, then they inwardly murmur against God ; when rather all these things should be done with a spirit of humility and subjection, using them only as means whereupon we expect God's blessing, craving his assistance and strength to do them in a holy and a self-denying manner. When we do otherwise, and trust to the outward tasks and performances we do, we make them idols. And you have many that go along with outward performances who never come to a dram of grace, because they trust to the outward performances, and look not to the life and soul of them, which is the Spirit of God assisting, quickening, strengthening, blessing them. The life of a Christian is a perpetual dependence upon God in the use of means, and not an idolising of them, to be careless when he hath done his task.

10. But a more subtle idolatry than this is of another kind, *when we trust too much to the work of grace, and rely not upon God in Christ,* in the matter of justification and acceptation to life everlasting, which is a fault, both,

1. Before conversion.
2. After conversion.

First, *before conversion.* When we think we have not done so much good, and been sufficiently humbled, and therefore that God will not be merciful to us, as if Christ must take us with dowry of good deeds, or else he cannot; whereas all grace is promised upon our entry and coming into the covenant of grace, upon our believing, when we come with empty hearts and hands. 'The poor,' saith Christ, 'receive the gospel; and those that are lost, Christ is sent to save them, and to call in the weary and heavy laden,' Mat. xi. 5, ix. 13, xi. 28.

2. And *after conversion.* Those that are in the state of grace oftentimes want that comfort in the main point of justification and acceptation to life everlasting, which they should have, because they look into their imperfections, seeing this and that want, and so are swallowed up of discomfort; whereas, if we had all the graces in the world, yet we must live by faith, relying upon the merits of Christ. For our good works bring us not to heaven, as a cause, but only are helps and comforts to us in our walking to heaven. For if we had all the sins of all men, yet Christ's all-sufficient righteousness is sufficient for to do them all away, if we can go out of ourselves, and cleave to that. Therefore, in trouble of conscience we must not look either to our good or our ill, but to God's infinite mercy, and to the infinite satisfaction of our blessed Saviour the Lord Jesus Christ; there, as it were, losing ourselves, seeing our sins as mountains drowned in the infinite sea of his mercy. The blood of Christ! That will pacify and stay the conscience. Nothing else can give rest to our souls. If we look to our works and to the measure of our sanctification, what saith holy Paul in the like case? 'Yea, doubtless, and I count all things but loss, for the excellency of the knowledge of Christ Jesus my Lord, for whom I have suffered the loss of all things, and do count them but dung, that I may win Christ,' Phil. iii. 8, even his righteousness and best works. Therefore there is no regard to be had of them in that case. Wherefore when we would speak comfort to a distressed conscience, we must not look to his ill or good, but to the command, 'This is his command, that we believe,' 1 John iii. 23. And look to the all-sufficiency of God in Christ, and the promises, whereby we honour God in giving him the glory of his truth, and depart with comfort. Therefore, though we hate gross idolatry, yet we see there are many ways wherein the soul may be seduced, whereby we may come very near that sin which our soul hateth, by trusting too much to something out of God.

Use 5. If then the case be thus, *how shall we come to reform it,* for a use of direction, so as to fly from all idolatry, and to say with Ephraim, 'What have I now any more to do with idols?'

First of all, *do but consider God's hatred unto all sorts of idolaters;* for he accounts such to hate him, and so accordingly punisheth them. In the second commandment, those that are given to idolatry in any kind, are such as hate God, which is a horrible thing; and yet, notwithstanding, this is the disposition of all such as are idolaters. So far forth as they are idolaters, they hate God, for the more we know God, the more we shall hate all idols, 'What have I now any more to do with idols?'

2. Labour *to grow in the sound knowledge of God and of Christ, and of their all-sufficiency.* Mark St Paul's method, Col. ii., and in other places, when he would draw us from all outward things, he speaks gloriously of the fulness of Christ, 'In him dwelleth all the fulness of the Godhead bodily,' Col. ii. 9; and, 'In him you are complete.' When he would draw them from 'touch not, taste not, handle not, worshipping of angels, and from counterfeit humility,' Col. ii. 21, &c., he labours to dispossess them of these idolatrous conceits, and to possess them of the fulness of Christ. If in him we have fulness, why should we look for any thing out of him? If we be complete in him, if all fulness be in him, why do we seek any thing out of that fulness? Thus the holy apostle shutteth up his first epistle, 'Babes, keep you from idols,' 1 John v. 21. What is promised there? Christ is eternal life, all is in him; whereupon presently comes this, 'Babes, keep you from idols?' If life and happiness, and all be in Christ, if we be complete in him, and the fulness of all be in him, why should we go out of him for anything? When God would persuade Abraham to leave all idolatry, Gen. xvii. 1, and all things else, to depend wholly upon him, what doth he first possess him with? 'I am God all-sufficient,' &c. Know God in covenant all-sufficient, and Christ in the fulness of his high perfections as Mediator, in whom is all fulness and life eternal, in whom we are complete; we shall then be so far from going out of him for any thing, as we shall be of the same mind with Ephraim, 'What have I now any more to do with other intercessors and mediators?' what have I to do with will-worship? what need I go to other cursed means, when God is all-sufficient? It is the scope of the new covenant of grace, that we should glory in God only, who hath made Christ unto us 'wisdom, righteousness, sanctification, and redemption,' 1 Cor. i. 30. And all this, because that whosoever glorieth in him, should not go out of him for any thing. The more we know therefore the fulness of Christ, and God's mercy in him, the more we shall abhor all idolatry, with the kinds and degrees of it.

3. Another help and means to cure this disposition in us is, *to know that we are naturally wondrous prone to it in one degree or another.* It is reckoned up, Gal. v. 20, as a work of the flesh; and, naturally, man hath a working fancy, to set up somewhat in his heart and understanding above, and besides God, imaginations to adulterate things. Men live by sense, and imagination is next to sense, so that naturally all men are idolaters before conversion, in one kind or other, and doat so upon their own, that they will not be driven out of themselves unto God in Christ, without a great deal of grace. As men naturally love the child of their own body, so men love the children of their own brain.

Quest. What is the reason that it is so hard to convert a papist?

Ans. Because it is will-worship, a device of their own brain, suiting their natural will and appetite. And what makes them so furious, as all idolaters are cruel: though they be mild of their own nature, yet as idolaters, they are cruel. It is because it is a device of their own brain, a brat, a child of their own begetting, wherefore they strive to maintain it, because it is their own. Let us therefore conceive thus much, that it is no easy matter to free the soul from idolatry, and all the degrees of this cursed disposition. This will make us beg earnestly the Spirit of God, by which only we shall subdue this idolatrous proud conceit, Rom. viii. 5, and lay ourselves open to Christ, to be disposed of as he pleaseth. Beg the Spirit only, whereby we shall mortify the cursed deeds of the flesh, for nature will never subdue nature. The Spirit of God therefore is that which can, and must free us from all dregs and tainture of this cursed disposition, which the Jews were so scourged for, and hardly* driven from.

4. Again, consider *God's punishments in this kind.* As we see, Rev. ix. 20, where the Turk is said to be raised up against all these idolaters, that would not be kept from worshipping the devil and the image of the beast; yet for all this, it is said, 'they did not repent.' And so the Jewish church was still punished with enemies raised up against them for their idolatry. And it is to be expected that the idolatry of these western churches will at length pull down antichrist himself, which must be before the conversion of the Jews. For what hinders their conversion now? The world is full of idolaters, even Christians; and therefore there must be a confusion of antichrist's idolatrous worship before the conversion of the Jews, who will not return whilst that scandal is in their eye. Therefore, that we may help forward that glorious work, let us labour as much as we can to purge the church of this, in drawing others from idolatry, that we may help to make way for those glorious times a-coming; for this Scripture specially hath relation unto the calling of the Jews, not to be fulfilled till then, when 'Ephraim shall say, What have I now any more to do with idols?' with that for which we have been so plagued for in former times.

5. And withal let us consider this, that the end of all false worship, when it is left, *is grief and shame, befooling and shaming of ourselves for it.* 'Ephraim at length shall say, What have I any more to do with idols?' to cherish pride and self-conceit? which, if ever I come to heaven, I must renounce, hating myself for my own pride and folly.

6. And so for idolaters themselves, why *should we consort ourselves with these, of whom we shall say one day, What have we any more to do with them?* We must be separated from them here, or in hell live with them for ever. What will then be the hell of hell? Mutual cursing of one another. Thy familiarity and acquaintance, thy provocations and allurements, brought me into these torments! If we belong to God, late or soon, there must be these speeches, 'What have I now any more to do with such and such lying vanities?'

Therefore let us not think will-worship a slight matter; for, we see, popery is nothing else but a bundle of man's devices. We see in Scripture, when the dearest friends of Christ came unto him with devices of their own, and good intentions, Christ notwithstanding saw the devil in them. Peter made a great confession, 'Thou art the Son of the living God,' Mat. xvi. 16, and then he came 'Master, spare thyself,' ver. 22; whereunto Christ replied, 'Get thee behind me, Satan,' ver. 23. God is never more provoked than when men think to honour him with their own devices; stablishing a false, and neglecting his own true, worship. And there is usually little amendment of these kind of persons, because they carry with them a show of wisdom, as Paul saith, Col. ii. 23, and great humility; which things being so carried with a show of some grace and wisdom (though they be desperate folly in the conclusion), men hardly will part withal. As we see of corporal adultery, few of them are reclaimed, because it hath a bewitching, alluring power; which is most true of the spiritual adulterers. There are few of them reclaimed, until God, by some severe judgment, alter and bring down the proud imagination to serve him as he will be served; so as to say with Ephraim here, 'What have I now any more to do with idols?'

Well, that we may abhor idolatry the more, consider two or three direct

* That is, 'with difficulty.'—G.

places. 'Who required these things at your hands?' saith God, Isa. i. 12. When we think to please him with voluntary devised things, this will strike them dumb then. The things that God requires being so easy and so few, yet we to omit them all, and to devise new things of our own, our reward shall be, 'Who required these things at your hands?' And then again saith God, 'In vain they worship me, teaching for my precepts the devices of men,' Mat. xv. 9. See then the vanity of idolaters, who, though they would do nothing in vain, yet do all their will-worship in vain. It is not only idolatry, but obstinate idolatry, the Romish doctrine. 'We would have cured Babel, but she would not be cured,' Jer. li. 9. Is this a light cause of our coming out of Babylon? Do we leave them for trifles, when they stand guilty of abominable idolatry? You may see here, if so be Ephraim out of holy affection say, 'What have I now any more to do with idols?' what to think and judge of those that would bring God and idols together. If Ephraim had been of the temper that many men now are, he might have said, 'Tush! what need we care for idols, crucifixes, and the like? There is not such a distance betwixt them and us, why may not both religions stand together? This new-fangled niceness is but the distempered devices of some few giddy-headed men, who know not what they would have.' This is the wisdom of many men in our times, who reckon that there is not an eternal, irreconcilable distance between light and darkness, the service of God and that of idols. 'We cannot serve two masters,' saith Christ, Mat. vi. 24. Yes, they say, we may serve two masters, Antichrist and Christ, God and Belial. Oh! but what saith Ephraim? 'What have I now any more to do with idols?' There can be no mixture, you know, where there is abomination. That church, Rev. iii. 15, which was neither hot nor cold, may parallel many now in our times, who are neither hot nor cold, papists nor protestants, but politic atheists, who will be both or neither, whatsoever may best serve and advance their worldly ends. How doth God look upon such? Saith he, 'I will spue them out of my mouth.' God hates such most of all: 'now I would thou wert either hot or cold.' If this be the affection of God's people toward idols and idolaters, an utter aversation; and shall we think to jumble and mingle contrary things together, to serve God and the devil, Christ and antichrist?

Thus we see what to think of the temper of these men. In lighter matters indeed we may enjoy our own private opinions in some things. As St Paul saith in lesser things, 'If any man be otherwise minded, God shall reveal it unto him,' Phil. iii. 15. But when he comes to the point of justification by Christ in God's worship, what saith he? 'If any man be otherwise minded, God shall reveal it?' No. But 'if I, or an angel from heaven, teach otherwise, let him be accursed,' Gal. i. 8. Now, when men teach another doctrine and worship, joining with gross idolaters in that worship, there we must be of Paul's spirit, 'If I, or an angel from heaven, teach otherwise, let him be accursed.' The Holy Ghost at first appeared in the form and shape of a dove, Mat. iii. 16, which is a meek and mild creature, that hath no talons to hurt with. Yet notwithstanding, at another time, he appeared in 'fiery tongues,' Acts ii. 3, to shew that the same Spirit that in lesser things maintaineth peace and love, when it is set against any sin, especially against that sin of sins, idolatry, which brings God's vengeance upon kingdoms and states, and roots them out; there the Holy Ghost must appear in fire. That element must be in the hearts of people against sin. That, though to persons that have their slips, and in lesser matters, there must be the spirit of a dove, yet there must be in men the spirit of courage, indignation, abomination, and hatred unto the idolatry of the times, that we may say from our hearts with Ephraim, 'What have I now any more to do with idols?'

Therefore, *let us join with those that we shall live for ever with in heaven*, and go in the best courses, and we shall never need to fear separation, nor want encouragements to well-doing. Thus shall we neither grieve nor be ashamed to say with Ephraim, 'What have I now any more to do with idols?' At the length the kings of the earth, who adore the whore, they shall come and eat her very flesh, Rev. xvii. 16. So it will be the end of those that reign in other men's consciences, and in a manner will be accounted gods, that all which is gotten with wrong to God, shall be renounced with grief, shame, and detestation of the persons of those that make idols of others, and will be made idols in the hearts of others; thinking themselves not enough respected, unless they command the conscience. The end of such cannot be good. All this must end in loathing, shame, and detestation. 'What have I now any more to do with idols?' said Ephraim; and what have I now any more to do with such and such profaneness, hypocrisy, double-dealing, and the like? shall such persons, thus sinful, say one day, with shame and horror of conscience. Wherefore, let us meet God betimes, and renounce our idols of all sorts, that God may come 'to hear us, observe us, and be as a green fir-tree unto us,' &c. Whereof, if God please, we shall hear more the next time.

THE TWELFTH SERMON.

Ephraim shall say, What have I any more to do with idols? I have heard him and observed him: I am like a green fir-tree: from me is thy fruit found.—Hos. XIV. 8.

THE words, as we heard heretofore, are a gracious answer unto the prayer which God himself, by his Spirit, had dictated to Ephraim: as likewise a reward of Ephraim's reformation. Aided by grace, Ephraim shall say, 'What have I now any more to do with idols?' 'God will hear him and observe him, and be like a green fir-tree unto him.' For, saith God, 'from me shall Ephraim's fruit be found.' Whereby we see, that whensoever God doth alter the soul by his grace, there he also breeds divorce and division between it and all idolatry; a disposition in some sort like himself, having those sympathies and antipathies he hath towards sin and goodness. Now, because God is a jealous God, and cannot abide idols; therefore Ephraim, being sanctified by the Spirit of God, is minded as God is, 'What have I any more to do with idols?'

1. God hath framed the soul, *that it may enjoy the chief good*, and avoid the chief ill especially; for petty goods and petty ills are not so behoveful. Yet notwithstanding, God will have us avoid all ill, and embrace all good, and he hath made the soul into an answerable condition. Therefore hath he planted affections therein tending to good; as love, and joy, and delight, especially made for the embracing of the main good, thereby to go out of itself, and close with that main chief good, in closing wherewith it may be happy.

2. And then, *to avoid the chief ill, sin and damnation*, he hath planted affections of aversation, abhorring, hatred, grief, and the like. Thus hath he framed the soul for these main ends, without which affections the soul were as *mare mortuum*, that dead sea. The affections are the wings and the wind of the soul, that carry it unto all which it is carried unto. Especially, when the wind of God's Spirit blows upon it, then it is carried out of itself; for of itself it cannot love or hate as it should; but God must raise the affections, and lay them down again. We have not the management of our hearts. Grace teacheth us to do all.

The particular then here is, *indignation and hatred*. 'What have I now any more to do with idols?' So that the proper affection in God's children, which should be conversant about that which is ill, and sinfully ill, is hatred and indignation. Here is hatred with indignation, the extent of the affection.

Reas. 1. The reason whereof is, when God's children are once converted, *they have a new nature put into them*, like unto Christ, whose Spirit they have. What he hates, they hate. He hates all sin, and nothing but sin. He hates the devil himself for sin, and no further.

2. Then, again, when once they are God's children, *they have a new life put into them*, which hath antipathy to all that is contrary to it. Every life in any creature hath antipathy to every enemy thereof. There is antipathy in doves to birds of prey; and in the lamb to the wolf, because they are enemies to the life and being of them. So in the soul of a Christian, so far as grace is renewed, there is an antipathy, aversation, and abhorring of that which is contrary. What have I to do with sin in any kind? When grace hath altered the disposition of a man's heart, then sin and he are two; two indeed, in the most opposite terms that may be. What have I any more to do with my former delightful sins? We are two now, for we were before nothing but sin. And, indeed, where this hatred is not, there men may leave sin, because sin leaves them; but this is not enough, God would have us to hate it with indignation. 'What have I now any more to do with it?'

Quest. But how should we come to have this true hatred of sin, as Ephraim should have?

Ans. 1. Amongst those helps formerly named, this is a main one, to represent to the soul (as the soul is quick and nimble in such apprehensions) *the odiousness of sin*, that it is a truly hateful thing; and therefore, that our affection of hatred cannot be better set nor employed upon any object than that of sin. For let us consider that it is not only ill in itself, defiling the soul and hindering communion with God; but it is also the cause of all ills, being the ill of ills, as God is the good of goods. For our troubles and terrors of conscience, we may thank sin, and for all that we suffer every day in our conditions of life. What is all, but the fruit of our own ways? 'Wherefore suffereth living man?' saith the prophet; 'man suffereth for his sin,' Lam. iii. 39. 'Thine own inventions have brought these things upon thee; therefore they are bitter unto thee, they shall pierce thy bowels,' Jer. iv. 18. Shall we not, therefore, hate that which is the cause of all mischief to us? If we had an enemy, especially if he were a soothing false enemy, that under pretence of love should seek our bane and ruin, and join with our worst enemies, would we not hate such an enemy? Sin is the greatest enemy which we have in the world, and doth us more harm than the devil himself; for it betrays us to the devil, and, under pretence of favouring and pleasing our nature, betrays us. It is a false, deceitful enemy, which cometh not in an ugly shape, but closes with the soul in a kind of conjugal love, Delilah-like enticing and alluring us, whereby it hath the more advantage and strength, in that it appears in a lovely, pleasing, and not in an imperious, commanding manner. Therefore, it should be the more hateful to us. Shall we not hate such an enemy as always dogs us, and hinders us? hinders us from doing anything well, and puts us on to all that is ill. It is such an enemy, that we cannot go about to pray, or do any good thing, but it hangs upon us, and clogs us in all our performances. If a man knew that such an one as made love to him and all his were his great grand enemy, aiming at his destruction, would a man ever love such a man? Thy base, false, revengeful, covetous, worldly heart, it joins with Satan, without which he could not hurt thee. Shall a man cherish that which betrays him to his worst enemy, the devil? and then, should he cherish that which makes a breach betwixt him and his best friend? If a man saw one so maliciously evil towards him, as to sow dissension by all means he could betwixt him and his best honourable friend, by whom he was maintained in all things, would not a man hate such a one? What doth sin else but breed division and enmity betwixt God and us? And further, when it hath moved us to do ill, it crieth for vengeance against us at God's hands. Conscience, soundly awakened, is always clamorous to pull somewhat from God against us. Are not sinners justly called fools? Either men must be atheists to deny all, or else, if they cherish sin, they must needs be fools, and stark mad, if they confess this, that they join with that which is their chief enemy. Therefore, learn to be wise to salvation; make not with Solomon's fool a sport of sin, Prov. x. 23, of swearing, of defiling ourselves and others, seeing God threateneth damnation unto such.

Ans. 2. And then again, *avoid all parley and intercourse with sin in the first suggestions*, or with wicked persons that may draw us away. Use sin ruggedly and harshly, as they do here. 'What have I to do with idols?' Do but entertain parley with it, and it is of such an insinuating nature, that it will encroach daily, and spread over the soul suddenly, betraying it to the devil. Therefore, use it hardly in the first beginnings, and avoid Satan in the first suggestions, if we love the peace of our souls; as Ephraim here, 'What have I any more to do with idols?' For as we say in case of honesty, they come too near that come to have the refusal. They should not have so much hope from a chaste person. There should be such a modest carriage as should not give any one the boldness to adventure in that kind. So if a man carry himself remotely from sinful courses, he shall have a great deal of peace from wicked men, who dare not so much as adventure to draw away such a one. They know he is resolved. Therefore, constant resolution against all sin and wicked men will breed a great deal of peace, so as to say with Ephraim, 'What have I any more to do with idols?'

Ans. 3. And *we must know that this hatred comes from the life of God in us.* Therefore we must by all means maintain spiritual life; and then, as we grow spiritual, we shall grow in the detestation of sin, a sense of joy in good things, with a hatred of all that is contrary. A man can never hate sin till he hath the Spirit of Christ in him. For there be three queries, whereof this is the last.

1. The first is set down, 'No man said, What have I done?' Jer. viii. 6. When conscience in a man is awakened once, he saith, Oh! what have I done? what case am I in?

2. The second query of a wakened conscience is, 'What shall I do?'

As that, 'Men and brethren, what shall we do to be saved?' Acts ii. 37. He that truly saith, 'What have I done?' if conscience be awakened, will also say, 'What shall I do?' You shall not need to drive him when the question is answered, 'What shall I do to be saved?' that is, by casting myself upon God in Christ.

3. We need not put the question, he will say of himself, 'What have I any more to do with that which is contrary to that which saves me?' 'What have I to do with idols?' This comes in in the last place. 1. A man is awakened out of his natural condition. 2. Then he goes to God in Christ. And then, 3. There is a spiritual life wrought in him, which stirs him up to hate all that is contrary unto it. 'What have I now any more to do with idols?'

'For I have heard him and observed him.'

'I have seen and observed him,' some read the words, but very few (*w*); which is thus a very good and pious construction of them. 'What have I now any more to do with idols?' As if Ephraim should say these words, 'I have seen him and observed him;' that is, because I have seen him and observed; therefore, 'What have I now any more to do with idols?' As soon as a man comes to hear God speak, and to observe God, down goes all idols; for, indeed, the respect to idolatry, and anything that is naught, it falls down in the soul, as the knowledge of the true God is lifted up, and as affection to good things are raised up in the soul. 'What have I to do with idols any more?' 'I have seen and observed him.' As Job said of himself when he had seen God, 'I abhor myself, and repent in dust and ashes,' Job xlii. 6; much more all false courses. I abhor them all, now that 'I have seen and observed him.'

This is a safe, pious, and good sense; but the words, under correction, are fitliest applied unto God himself, as if God rather than Ephraim said thus, 'I will hear him and observe him;' I will do thus and thus; 'I will be as a green fir-tree,' to shade him from danger, and to make him fruitful.

Obj. But you will say, Ephraim cannot cast away idols till God respect him first. Therefore, this is promised in the second place. 'Ephraim shall say, What have I to do with idols?' And God shall say, 'I have seen him, heard him, and observed him,' when he hath cast away idols.

Ans. To this the answer is: Indeed, in the order of nature, God doth first stir us up to pray to him, and promiseth us respect and hearing of our prayers, after which we cast away idols; but the experience of it is after we have done the deed. After that we have found God experimentally gracious, protecting and hearing of us, then we cast away idols. So this experience a Christian finds when he abominates and rejects ill ways. Then he finds God all-sufficient, as indeed God is never fully felt and known till we renounce all other helps. So the general point is,

Obs. That nothing is lost by renouncing idolatry and carnal confidence in any worldly thing.

For God makes a supply in himself. 'I will hear him and observe him.' Nothing is lost, for God will be true of his promise. 'Seek ye first the kingdom of God and his righteousness, and all other things shall be ministered unto you,' Mat. vi. 33. The truth of God, and then his mercy, makes this good. Is not God merciful to his children when they renounce all false confidence? In regard of the truth of his promise and mercy, he will make good this, that nothing is lost by cleaving to him. We read in the story of our own times, in King Edward the Sixth's reign, the same day that there was reformation of idolatry in London, purging of churches from roods* and idols, the same day was that noble victory and conquest in the north parts over the enemies (x). So God answered their care in reforming things amiss with good success.

On the contrary, when we go on with favouring abuses and corruptions, yet expecting good success, it is in vain. Let Ephraim come to say, 'What have I to do with idols?' and see then whether God will respect him or not. Do nations or persons think that God will respect them or bless them, whilst they do that which is abominable to him? No; when Ephraim saith, 'What have I to do with idols?' then presently comes, God 'will hear and observe him, and look to him;' as you have it in that gracious promise, 'The eyes of the Lord are open unto all them that fear him, and his ears are open to their prayers,' Ps. xxxiv. 15. His eyes and his ears. Indeed, God is all eye and all ear. The best friend in the world cannot have his eye always upon us. The mother's eye cannot be always upon her child. She must have a time to sleep, when neither her eyes nor ears are open to her child's prayers. It may cry, and die in crying sometimes, before she can help it. But if we renounce sin, we have a gracious Father 'who will hear us, observe us, and see us,' and not only hear and see, but, as the Scripture phraise s, do that that follows all this. Where he sees, he will pity and relieve; and where he hears, he will pity and protect.

'I have heard him, I have observed him.' God will hear, when once we renounce sin. 'If I regard iniquity in my heart, God will not hear my prayers,' Ps. lxvi. 18, saith David. But when I do not regard iniquity, God will hear my prayers. Then a man may know that God will hear him, when once he hath renounced sin, and comes with clean hands and heart to God. As it is in Isaiah, they were corrupted in their course, and yet came to God, Isa. i. 11, *seq*, but he rejects all; so in the last of that prophecy, he accounts of their sacrifices as of the cutting off of a dog's neck, because their hands were full of blood, and they were full of sin, Isa. lxvi. 3. Reform abuses, let there be personal and national reformation; and then come and reason the matter with God, and see whether he will regard us or not. The Spirit, it is said, makes requests for the saints, and 'God knoweth the meaning of the Spirit, because it makes request according to the will of God,' Rom. viii. 27. The same Spirit that stirs us up to amend our lives, and fly idolatrous courses, the same Spirit stirs us up to pray to God, according to the will of God; and then God hears the desires of his own Spirit. Of all judgments in the world, this is the greatest, to pray and not to be heard; for when we are in misery, our remedy is prayer. Now when that which should be our remedy is not regarded, what a pitiful thing is that? Now, here is an excellent blessing set down, to pray, and for God to hear, 'I will hear him, and observe him.' Because then, God and Ephraim were of one mind, and join in one, therefore God cannot but hear and regard Ephraim, being of his mind, to love and to hate what he loves and hates. As soon as ever the prodigal began to hate his former courses, the father came out to meet him, Luke xv. 20, *seq.*; and so of David, 'I said I will confess my sins to God,' Ps. xxxii. 5. I said, that is, in my heart, I resolved to confess to God, and thou forgavest mine iniquity. God heard his resolution. We cannot else entertain a full purpose to go to God, unless there be a cessation from sin. The prodigal, for all his contrition, was afraid to be shaken off his father, for his dissolute life. Oh, but the father provides a banquet. So it is when we turn to God, and re-

* That is, 'crosses,' as in Scotland, Holyrood = holy cross.—G.

solve a new life, to cast away our idolatries, and former abominations; presently, 'God hears us, and observes us,' and is ready to meet us.

There is an excellent place, even touching Ephraim himself. 'I have surely heard Ephraim bemoaning himself: Thou hast chastised me, and I was chastised, as a bullock unaccustomed to the yoke: turn me to thee, and I shall be turned; thou art the Lord my God, &c. Is Ephraim a dear son? is he a pleasant child? for since I spake against him, I do earnestly remember him still; therefore my bowels are troubled for him: I will have mercy upon him,' Jer. xxxi. 18. If Ephraim begin to bemoan himself for his folly, presently follows, that God's bowels are turned to him; so it is said of Ephraim here. After he had renounced idols, God's bowels are turned towards him, 'I have heard him, and observed him.' Which yields us a sweet and comfortable consideration, *to turn to God from all our sinful courses*, because God is so ready to forgive, and to forgive great sins. What if our sin be idolatry, the grand sin of the first table? Yet if Ephraim say, 'What have I do with idols?' (though it be spiritual adultery), yet if Ephraim begin to renounce idolatry, God will say, 'I have heard him, and observed him.' If your sins were 'as red as crimson,' saith God, 'I will make them as white as wool,' &c., Isa. i. 18. Crimson sins, double-dyed sins, it is no matter what they are, if we come to God. There is more mercy in him than sin in us. If Ephraim say, What have I to do with my former evil courses, 'God will hear him, and observe him.'

It is never better with a Christian, than when he hath renounced all wicked courses, (though he thinks himself undone if he leaves his former Delilah delights). But there is no such matter, for we shall find an hundredfold more in God, as Christ speaks, 'Whosoever leaves father or mother, brother or sister, house or kindred for me, shall have a hundredfold in this world,' Mat. xix. 29; that is, they shall have it in contentment and grace, in peace of conscience, and perhaps in the things of this life in another kind. What lost Abraham when he obeyed God, and forsook his father's house? God was all-sufficient for him. He grew a rich man. And what lost he by giving Isaac to God? He received his son again, of whom there came an innumerable seed. And what lost holy David, in waiting for the time that he should come unto the kingdom, without making haste? He came quietly to the possession of the crown; whereas Jeroboam, who made more haste, after God had told him he should reign, he was cursed in his government, and none of his posterity came to good. There is nothing lost by depending and waiting upon God, and renouncing of carnal confidence. We think naturally we are undone. Oh, there is no such matter, as David speaks, 'When my father and mother forsaketh me, yet the Lord taketh me up,' Ps. xxvii. 10. As we know in the gospel, when the blind poor man was excommunicated and cast out, after he had spoke somewhat stoutly to the Pharisees, 'Will ye also be his disciples?' John ix. 27, yet then Christ takes him presently into his company, being expelled by them. What lost he by this? So when Israel had lost all their fleshpots in Egypt, they had no loss, for God provided them manna from heaven, and what lost they by that? They had angels' food instead of their garlic and onions.

'I have observed him.'

That is, I will have a special eye to him; I will look to him in all conditions and states whatsoever. God never slumbers nor sleeps. Like the master of the house in the parable, who, when the poor man came for bread, Luke xi. 5, all the rest being asleep, is awaked, and raised up by the importunity of the poor man. So the great master of the family of heaven and earth, that governs all, he wakes day and night, and never sleeps; herein going beyond the care of the dearest friends we have in the world, for they must have a time to sleep. The mother, though she love the child as her own bowels, yet notwithstanding she must have a resting time, and perhaps in that time the child may miscarry; but God always observes; his eye is always upon his children, they are before him, written 'in the palms of his hands, he hath them in his eye,' Isa. xlix. 16: as in Exodus, you have there God brought in observing the children of Israel. 'I have seen, I have seen the affliction of my people Israel,' Exod. iii. 7. They thought themselves neglected of God, but he tells Moses, 'I have seen, I have seen,' I know it very well; he adds knowledge to sight. So there is no affliction in this world to God's children, but God in seeing sees. As before, he hears the groans and sighs; so he sees the most intimate inward affliction whatsoever that afflicts the soul; as they were grieved in very soul at the tyranny of Pharaoh. Oh, but God in seeing he sees, whose eyes are ten thousand times brighter than the sun! This is a consolation, when one thinks that no man sees and regards; alas, what shall become of me! Why should any man say so, that hath God to go to, who is all eye, and all ear! God hears and sees; his ears are always open, as it is often shewed, especially, Ps. xxxiv. 15.

It is said, 'His ears are open to their prayers, and his eyes to see their afflictions.'

Quest. But with what kind of eye doth God see the afflictions of his children?

Solution. He sees them with a tender, compassionate eye; for he aboundeth in those affections which he hath put into a father and mother. There is no mother would suffer her child to miscarry, if she could help it. God sees surely* some afflictions are for our good, or he would relieve us; for as he hath a compassionate eye, so he hath a tender heart, and a powerful hand. He sees wicked men also; but his eyes in regard of them are 'like a flame of fire,' not only because he is quick-sighted, but because he sees with a revengeful† eye; and as his eyes are like a flame of fire, so likewise he hath feet of brass to tread them to powder, Rev. i. 14, 15.

Use 1. And this likewise is no little part of our comfort; for when we suffer anything in this world, it is from ill men for the most part, except it be in those afflictions wherein we more immediately deal with God, as in sickness, &c. But in persecution in the world, our trouble lies with men. Therefore it is our comfort, God sees our trouble, and their malice; and as he is ready to help the one, so he is to revenge the other.

Use 2. And as it is a point of comfort, so of great encouragement to be bold in God's cause. What! shall we be baser than the base creatures? Take but a dog in his master's sight, you see how he will fight. Take the meanest and basest creature, when it hath a superior nature to itself, that it ‡ is wiser and greater, that encourageth and sets it on, that it knows will see it take no harm, these base creatures will be courageous; which otherwise if it had none to set it on, had no courage at all, at least not so much. And shall we in the sight of God, and when we are set in his quarrel, and have his encouragement and his command, with promise of his presence and assistance, flinch and fly off then? It argues a great deal of atheism and infidelity of heart. God sees me and looks on me while I fight, and while I stand for his cause. God's cause is true and just, God

* That is, 'assuredly.'—G. † That is, 'avenging.'—G. ‡ Qu. 'it knows?'—ED.

sees me, and he sees who opposeth me. In regard of the eye of God therefore, let us be courageous in these things that are agreeable to the mind of God, whatsoever they be, whether matters of justice or piety.

Use 3. Again, if God have such an ear to hear us, let us have an ear to hear him, and an eye to look to him. Let us have Moses' eye to look on him who is invisible, Heb. xi. 26. His eye is upon us, and let our eye be to him; both may be together. When these two eyes meet; when my heart tells me that God seeth me, and that I see God looking upon me, this makes courageous. Therefore as God hears and sees us, so we must have an eye to see him that is invisible. And so we pass from these words, 'I have heard him and observed him;' and what the prophet's meaning is. 'I have heard him, and will hear him; I have observed him, and will observe him.' For they contain a perpetual action in God; not that he hath, and will not do it now, but what he hath done and will do. That he sets down here in borrowed speeches, for he saith also,

'I will be like a green fir-tree to him: from me is thy fruit found.'

God will be 'like a green fir-tree' in regard of shadow. A fir-tree is a high tree, a goodly, smooth tree, barren in regard of fruit, but it hath thick leaves, which hinders rain from falling upon those who rest under the shadow thereof, and likewise keeps the sun from annoying them. So it is a fit tree for shadow, and the fitter, because it hath no fruit. For usually those trees which spend not themselves this way, they spend themselves in leaves, and have a perpetual greenness, which is supplied with that which should be fruit in fruitful trees. Therefore he sets it down by this comparison of a fir-tree, that so God will keep back all showers, tempests, and storms, and all annoying heat, and he will do it perpetually, as the fir-tree hath a perpetual greenness; and he will do it with pleasure and delight, as it is a delightful shadow. But because the fir-tree hath no fruit on it, God will not only be a shadow to his children to keep ill from them, but he will be a fruitful tree to them. 'From me,' saith God, 'shall thy fruit be found;' that is, whatsoever good thou doest, thou shalt have it from me. All fruitful comfort comes from me, and all grace. Whatsoever is good for thee, for prosperity of soul or body, all is from me. So we see how God conveyeth himself and his mercy here by sweet comparisons, dealing very familiarly with us, and speaking to us in our own language. We will take both in order as they lie.

God will be as a fir-tree in regard of shadow to the passenger, and keeping off of storms. The great God, and the good God, who is goodness itself, hath provided in this world not only good for us, but hath also promised defences against all annoyances. In the comparison itself, we will observe somewhat concerning the goodness of God; for as in this life we are subject to many inconveniences, wants, and necessities; so God hath supply for all, even outward necessities. We are subject to cold, for that we have the element of fire; we are subject to storms, he hath provided garments, and skill to make them; so in our travels, he hath provided some trees especially to shelter us. We cannot name any inconvenience of this life, but the rich God in his goodness hath provided a suitable supply. Doth God take care for this fading, perishing life, which is but as a vapour? and hath he good things for it, and fences from the ill and annoyances of it, till we have fulfilled our pilgrimage upon earth? And will not that God have a care of our best life of grace that shall end in glory, that we shall have all things necessary for life and godliness, which hath the promise, not of this life only, but of a better, 1 Tim. iv. 8. He that is so good to this natural life, will be much more in things concerning a better life, which he would have us mind more. 'I will be as a green fir-tree unto him.'

God will be as a fir-tree, especially in regard of shadow, to keep from all annoyance both of storm and of the sun; for the sun in those hot countries annoys them very much, as the spouse complains of her blackness, 'because the sun had shined upon her, Cant. i. 5, 'to be black as the tents of Kedar,' &c. Whence we may observe by the way,

There is not the most comfortable refreshing creature in the world, but take it in excess, it harms and annoys.

What more comfortable than water? yet if it prevail and abound, it is a destroying creature, as we see in the deluge and divers inundations. What more comfortable than fire? and what more terrible if it exceed? What more cherishing, refreshing, and quickening than the sun? Yet in the excessive heat thereof, it scorcheth and parcheth things. So in the sun of prosperity and all other good things in the world, it is best to have and enjoy all things with moderation; for if we have grace to qualify them, all things are good; otherwise the excess hurts us. Therefore beg of God wisdom to temper and moderate the best good in this world, which otherwise hurts us. For even the excessive heat of the sun in those countries makes them glad of the shadow of the fir-tree.

Thus God doth not only give a shadow, but a comfortable shadow and defence to his people, which is therefore called 'the shadow of his wings.' 'How oft,' saith Christ to Jerusalem, 'would I have gathered thee, as the hen gathereth her chickens under her wings?' Mat. xxiii. 37. It is not only a shielding from hurts, and dangers, and storms, but a sweet defence, with rest and quiet. As those that are weary compose themselves to rest under a shadow, so in God is our rest; 'Come unto me,' saith Christ, 'all ye that are weary and heavy laden, and ye shall find rest to your souls,' Mat. xi. 28. All rest is in Christ, and in God's mercy in Christ. We see, then, after we have forsook idolatry, God is to us instead of all the good we had by idols. We lose nothing by it. 'God will be as a green fir-tree.'

Whence the point is, *there is a protection, rest, and defence provided for God's people, when once they have renounced their idolatry and sinful courses.*

Those who refuse the shelter of idols, God will be a shelter unto them, 'a green fir-tree unto them,' another manner of shelter than that which idols or any other creature can give them. Every man will have some shelter, shield, or other to cover him, this or that great man to shield or shelter himself under. A rich man, he hath riches; another, this or that defence. Every man that hath any wit about him will have some shelter, and not lie open to all storms when they come. But the only true shelter is God himself to a Christian. All other refuges are but shadows, that is, they are nothing, but like Jonah's gourd, which may shelter for a time, but there is a worm of vanity that will eat them out. Riches and the favour of men may shelter for a time, but there is a worm at the bottom which will root them out. Death will consume them and those they depend upon. But God is a true shelter to his people, an everlasting habitation, as it is written, 'Thou art our habitation from generation to generation, Ps. xc. 1. We dwell in him as in our rock and castle. He is an everlasting habitation, not only a shadow, but a tower and a castle to dwell in. Therefore the only wise man is the Christian. For, as Noah, when the flood came upon the old world, and swept them away, had an ark to save himself in, so have all God's children a house to get over their heads in the worst times, which is God's blessed protection, in whom they are safe. Let us think often of these things. What a blessed thing it is to be in the state of a Christian, that hath alway a certain and sure protection, quiet, and rest in God! And what a fearful thing is it to be as the Ahithophels of this world! to be as Cain, Judas, or Saul! who are shrewd in counsel and policy, and yet, when conscience is awakened by the storm of God's wrath, want a shelter, whilst he who is above conscience, and should be a shelter to them, frowns upon them. What a pitiful state is this! The wickedest man in the world, though he have never so great dependence, parts, and strength from human helps, yet when the storm of God's wrath comes, he is as a naked man in the midst of a storm, and knows not whither to go. Therefore let us be wise to have God for our shelter, if we would not be like these miserable politicians and worldlings.

Now, from this, that the shadow is comfortable in those hot countries, where the sun is directly over their heads, comes these sweet phrases in the Psalms and other Scriptures: 'Thou shalt keep me under the shadow of thy wings. As the apple-tree amongst the trees of the forest, so is my beloved amongst the sons. I sat down under his shadow with great delight,' &c., Cant. ii. 3. The church speaks of Christ, 'I sat under his shadow with great delight, and his fruit was sweet to my taste.' The like you have in many places in the Psalms. I will name one or two, more pregnant than the rest, to help our memories, and to breed a deeper impression of so comfortable a point. Ps. lxiii. 7. There the psalmist speaks of resting under the shadow of God's wings. And so in that other sweet and excellent psalm, in the greatest extremities of God's people, 'He that dwelleth in the secret place of the Most High,' that is, God, 'shall abide under the shadow of the Almighty,' Ps. xci. 1. He says after, 'I will say of the Lord, He is my refuge and fortress;' for where God tells a man that he is a hiding-place and a shadow, there faith adds the application presently; and then he goes on, speaking of himself, 'He shall cover me with his feathers; under his wings will I rest; his truth shall be my buckler. Thou shalt not be afraid of the terror by night; nor of the arrow by day; nor of the pestilence that walketh in the dark. A thousand shall fall,' &c., vers. 4–7. So that we see how God doth that to our souls and conditions that the fir-tree, which is God's good creature, doth to the body in the time of storm and heat, that is, he doth refresh us under the shadow of his wings. He is a sweet, comfortable, and gracious God unto us. This, you see, is a clear truth; yet, because it is so comfortable, we will enlarge it further. Look what God speaks, 'The Lord will create upon every dwelling-place of mount Zion, and upon her assembly, a cloud and smoke by day, and the shining of a flame of fire by night; for upon all the glory shall be a defence,' Isa. iv. 45. See what a comfortable shadow God is! He saith, 'He will create.' If they want the comfort of the fir-tree, and such like shadows, he says, 'God will create,' that is, make them of nothing. He will 'create upon every dwelling-place of mount Zion,' where his children dwell, and upon their assemblies, 'a cloud and a smoke by day;' that is, when they are annoyed by the sun, God will create a cloud to keep the rage and the scorching heat of the sun from them, and then a 'shining flame of fire by night,' because in the night we need light, for 'upon all the glory shall be a defence,' that is, upon all the glorious saints of God. They are glory, for there is a Spirit of glory put into them, 1 Pet. iv. 14. The people of God, in whom God will glorify himself, are glorious, and shall be further glorified, and they shall in the mean time have a defence by day and by night from all dangers whatsoever.

Thus it is clear that God will be a shadow to his people, as the fir-tree, which is an allusion to that grand passage of his providence in conducting the children of Israel out of Egypt, where God, to guide them, provided a 'cloud by day, and a pillar of fire by night,' Exod. xiv. 20. The same pillar which was lightsome to the Israelites, was dark to the Egyptians, which cloud and pillar of fire continued, God conducting them, till they came into the land of Canaan. He shadowed them by day with a cloud, and lighted and heated them by a pillar of fire at night, thus conducting them till they came to Canaan. So we, passing through the wilderness of this world till we come unto our celestial Canaan, heaven, God will be a 'cloud' by his gracious special providence, to keep all ill whatsoever from us, and a 'pillar of fire' to lighten and direct us till we come to our heavenly Canaan, where he will be all in all, when we shall need neither sun nor moon, nor have anything to annoy us, Rev. vii. 16. There the noonday shall not burn us with heat of the sun, nor the fire by night. When we are in heaven there shall be no annoyance of the creature. There shall be no more want of light, because we shall have all light and refreshing there for ever and ever. For, as it is written, then 'all tears,' all sorrow, and cause of sorrow, shall be for ever wiped away, an allusion whereunto we have comfortably set down, Ps. cxxi. 7. The more we shall enrich and refresh our memories with thinking of these things, the more comfort will sink into our hearts. The 121st psalm is all spent on comfort in this kind. 'I will lift up mine eyes to the hills, whence cometh my salvation. My help cometh from the Lord, who made heaven and earth,' all my help is from him. 'He will not suffer my foot to be moved; he that keeps Israel will neither slumber nor sleep.' 'He will not slumber;' that is, his eyes are always open to see, as his ears to hear. 'Behold, he that keepeth Israel doth neither slumber nor sleep. The Lord is thy keeper, thy shadow, so that the sun shall not smite thee by day, nor the moon by night. The Lord shall preserve thy going out and thy coming in, from this time for ever.' Thus we see this Scripture is a large gloss and commentary upon this truth, that God, with a special providence and protection, cares for his children, to keep them from all ill. He will be as the fir-tree to them in regard of shadow. Whence we observe in special,

That this life of ours, whilst we come to heaven, is subject to scorchings and many annoyances, and those both outwardly and inwardly, from ourselves and from others.*

First, for *outward annoyances*, how many of them is our poor life subject unto! and for inward terror and boiling heat of conscience, when God in anger discovers himself unto us, and sets our sins in order before us. Oh then, if we have not a shadow; if God in mercy through Jesus Christ be not a shadow to keep that boiling heat from us, what will become of the poor conscience? especially if Satan adds his poisoned fiery darts, poisoning, inflaming the conscience with temptations to despair, Ps. l. 21, as if God had forsaken and were angry; or when God seems angry, then he seems like a consuming fire. Oh, who can abide it, when all these fiery temptations are joined with God's anger! Yet the dearest of God's saints are subject to these inward boiling heats of God's anger. 'My God, my God, why hast thou forsaken me,' said the head of the church himself, Matt. xxvii. 46; and see how Job complains, 'Thou hast set me as a butt to shoot at,' Job xvi. 12. And, in regard of this spiritual desertion, David complains much throughout the Psalms. So this our life is subject to out-

* That is, '*until.*'—ED.

ward and spiritual annoyances from God, from Satan, and from ourselves and the world; every way annoyed with scorchings and heat, what need [of] a shadow, a protection, a defence else? That supposeth this.

If this be so, then consider how fearful the condition of those people is, that are not under the shadow of the Almighty; who have not God as a fir-tree to shadow and cover them; that he is not a cloud by day to, and a pillar of fire by night; that have not him for a hiding-place to spread the wings of his mercy over them. What is the state of such people? surely howsoever God feed them, and fills their belly with good things in this world for a time; yet their case will be fearful, when God lets loose conscience, and Satan's fiery darts against them. Judge then hereby what our state is by nature without God. The same sun which cherisheth and comforteth, also tortures and scorcheth us: so God is a sun, a quickening sun to his children, Mal. iv. 2, yea, a vigorous sun, who hath healing under his wings; but to the wicked he is a scorching and consuming fire, Heb. xii. 29. 'It is a fearful thing to fall into the hands of the living God,' Heb. x. 31, who is so dreadful. He will not be a shadow to the wicked in an excellent manner. He indeed permits them to have many shadows in this world, many sweet comforts, and keeps them also from many dangers; but they have not that worthy portion which Hannah had from her husband, 1 Sam. i. 5, love at the hour of death. And in time of temptation, when these comforts leave them, what shadow have they then? none at all, but are as naked men in a storm, subject to the fury of God's eternal wrath. The things which are most comfortable to God's people are most terrible to them, as it is said in one of those plagues poured out upon antichrist (for all the vials there spoken of tend to the punishing of antichrist), there is a vial poured forth upon the sun, Rev. vi.; which reflecting and lighting upon them, causeth them to blaspheme, they were so scorched with it. The sun, by probable interpreters, is said to be the word of God, which, when it is opened, is sweet and comfortable to God's people, but shining upon men that are naught, especially at the hour of death, in affliction and in distress, it speaks no comfort to them, but causeth them to despair, rage and storm. Nay, profane men, when they are at the best, they rage and storm at the direction of the sun, because it discovers to them that which they would not have known.

Use 1. Now, what use should we make of this? Will God be a shadow to his people to keep them from all evil, as his promise was to Abraham in the covenant of grace: 'I will be thy buckler,' to keep ill from thee, and 'thy exceeding great reward,' Gen. xv. 1. And in the Psalms, God promiseth to be a sun for good, and a shield to keep off all ill, Ps. lxxxiv. 11. Will God bestow good, and keep off ill from us? Then labour to come willingly under the shadow of the Almighty, to serve him, and to make God in covenant our God, that he may be a 'shield and a hiding-place' unto us, and a shadow in all extremities whatsoever. Those that attend upon great persons, they do it upon this hope: Oh, if I belong to such a great person, he will shelter me, that every base person shall not wrong me; I shall now have some prerogatives. Doth carnal policy teach poor creatures who are subject to abuse it, to get some shelter of great, noble men to be privileged? and shall not spiritual wisdom teach us to get under the great God, under the shadow of his wings? None can come near to annoy us without his special will and leave, as in the story of Job. The devil durst not annoy him, Job i. 12, nor enter into the swine, Mat. viii 31, much less hurt God's children. Shall we not, therefore, get under the service of our God? can any man shelter us better? There is no service to that of a king; but is there any service to the King of kings, and Lord of lords? Will he suffer his children to be abused in his own sight, or his followers disgraced? Surely no. Therefore make this use of it, to get into the service of the great God, which is a rich, secure, and safe service.

Use 2. Again, it yields us an use of resolution, for to obey God, and to go boldly on in a good course. What should we fear, when God is our master? He will shield us, and keep us safe, and give his angels charge over us, to shew that he hath a care over us. Indeed, he hath many keepers under him, but he is the grand keeper, who sets all a-work. For angels, magistrates, ministers, and our friends keep us; but God's Spirit within us, and his gracious good providence without us, are our chief keepers. Therefore let all our care be to serve God, and to be in his ways. He will keep us in his ways. What an encouragement is this to be in good courses, where we may look for the shadow of the Almighty God, without tempting of him! If a man be in an ill way and course, he cannot look that the Almighty should shadow him. His heart will tell him, now God may withdraw his shelter and wing from me; he may leave me naked to the devil and to the malice of men; he may strip me of all comfort in my soul and conscience, and give me up to terrors of heart out of his way. If I trust him now, I tempt him, because he will be a defence only in his own ways. Therefore let us labour always to be in those ways, and then God will be as a green fir-tree unto us.

Use 3. And, last of all, let it be an use of comfort unto us, for all the time of our life to come. Whatsoever may come, we yet pass under a buckler. Let a whole shower and shot of arrows* fall upon us, we have a buckler. 'Thou, Lord, art my buckler; thou, Lord, art my defence, my hiding-place, my castle,' Ps. xviii. 1, 2. We are subject to a world of dangers whilst we live here, but we have God instead of all, to keep off all. He is a buckler, a shield, a shadow, and a hiding-place. Let what ill soever be presented to our thoughts, there is in God some fence against it. For this purpose we have many excellent passages in Ps. xviii., which was made after a great deliverance. 'I love the Lord, my buckler, my shield, my defence,' as if he should say, I have in my lifetime been annoyed with many troubles, but I have found experience of God in all. 'He is my buckler, my shield, my fence,' everything to me. So let us comfort ourselves in this. Let come what will come, all shall come well to God's children. He will keep them, if not outwardly, yet in that they most desire to be kept in. He will preserve their spirits 'from every evil work,' 2 Tim. iv. 18, from doing ill, and from desperate falling from God; and he will guard them inwardly, 'by the peace of God which passeth understanding,' Philip. iv. 7. It shall guard their hearts; they shall have inward peace in the midst of all the troubles of this world: a great comfort! What a rejoicing is it to a poor passenger, when he passeth by the highway side in a hot, burning day, or in a storm, to see a goodly high tree, with spreading boughs, that he may hide and repose himself under it from the storm or heat. This pleaseth him marvellously, as Jonah's gourd did him. Do these outward poor contentments so refresh us in this world? and shall we not think that God, which provides such poor contentments for this sorry life in this world, will he not provide a shadow in regard of the main dangers? Surely he will, if we trust him, and shew our trust by casting ourselves upon him in obedience suitable to our calling. Saith the apostle,

* Qu. 'a whole shower of shot and arrows?'—G.

'I am persuaded that neither things present, nor to come, nor life, nor death, nor anything, shall be able to separate us from the love of Christ Jesus our Lord,' Rom. viii. 38, 39. Therefore let us be afraid of nothing that can befall us. God will be a shield and a buckler, and all in all to us in a good way. We have abundance of comfort everywhere in Scripture, and want nothing but faith to apply it home in practice. Therefore we ought to beg of God so to enlarge our faith, that as his promises and comforts are very large, so may our vessels be to retain all these excellent comforts and sweet promises.

All other comforts in the world are but like Jonah's gourd; for all other shadows yield only a shadow for a while, and then the sunshine or east wind is like a worm to nip them asunder. Never trust, then, or lean to such shadows as these be, of friends, riches, &c., which are shadows men ordinarily rely upon. I have such and such a friend, a place, and the like, my mountain is thus and thus strong. All these are Jonah's gourds. There is a worm of vanity will be at the root of all, and consume all. All other shadows are but mere shadows. What is more transient than a shadow? But God's shadow is like a green fir-tree. It never fails nor forsakes us, as all other shadows and contentments do whatsoever. But God saith, 'He will be like a green fir-tree unto thee.' Yet this is not all, nor enough, for after this he adds,

'From me is thy fruit found.'

God is not only to his children a fir-tree in regard of shadow, that tree abounding in leaves very thick, whereby we are kept from annoyance of scorching heats of troubles and terrors of conscience and persecution, &c. This is not all, but he saith also,

'From me is thy fruit found.'

A fir-tree, though it be for thickness of the leaves a very good shade, yet it is a barren, fruitless tree; but God is such a tree as hath both shadow and fruit. In God there is a supply of all wants whatsoever. All the scattered excellencies of all creatures being united in God, and eminent in him, it is in him, and in him in a divine, gracious, eminent, and comfortable manner. All the creatures, as they come from God, are his creatures, neither is there any creature but hath somewhat of God in it. Therefore, God vouchsafes to take names from the creatures. To be a rock of salvation, he is as a rock to build on; to be a shadowing tree, because he is a defence from ill; and to be a fruitful tree, because he yields good, and comfort, and grace, as he doth fruit. When we see anything that is useful, we may say, this we have from God in an eminent manner, this preservation and comfort. Do I in my passage to heaven find such comfort in the creature? When I am passing through a wild place, have I such comfort in the shadow of a tree? or when I am hungry, am I so refreshed by a fruitful tree? What comfort, then, is there in God, in heaven, in glory, when there are such comforts in the way of my pilgrimage in this world? Therefore, God is said here, both to be a fir-tree and a fruitful tree. For then the passenger travelling through a wild, barren place, thinks himself made when he can retire from the scorching of the heat, and also therewithal find fruitfulness. Shade and fruit concurring, he thinks himself marvellously happy. This is the state of a Christian that hath God for his God, being in covenant with him. He is not only a strong protection and defence from all annoyance (as God shadows us, and is a buckler from all evils, both inward and outward, from Satan, and all kind of evils and wrath), but he is also a fruitful tree too. 'From me is thy fruit found.'

THE THIRTEENTH SERMON.

I am like a green fir-tree; from me is thy fruit found.—Hos. XIV. 8.

THIS holy prophet, as we heard heretofore, did prophesy more than sixty years among the ten tribes, even until the time immediately preceding their captivity and misery, in like manner as Jeremiah and Ezekiel did to the other Jews. Now, because in the worst times God always had a remnant, and yet hath, therefore it is the prophet's care, in this chapter which we have gone over, to instruct them in divers particulars of reformation, as we have heard at large, 'to return to the Lord,' 'to take words to themselves,' which words, as we have heard, are also taught them, backed with many sweet promises and encouragements in God's answer to their petitions: the last whereof insisted and stood upon was this, that God promiseth to be like a green fir-tree unto Ephraim, who personated all the ten tribes. Ephraim thought before to shadow and fence himself by idols, and league with other idolatrous nations, which were like Jonah's rotten gourd unto them, poor shadows and defences; but saith God, 'I will be a fir-tree' for shadow to Ephraim, to defend him from all dangers whatsoever; and then in the next place he adds,

'From me is thy fruit found.'

A fir-tree is a green tree, but it hath no fruit. The excellencies of the creatures are applied to God, but not the defects. Therefore, when comparisons are taken from the creatures and given to God, we must always except the defects, supplying the same by some other clearing comparison. So God is not only a fir-tree for shelter and defence, but he is a fruitful tree. So a fir-tree is not; and therefore without comparison, God hath more in him than any creature hath. For all that excellency which is in all the creatures is in him, and that in a far more eminent manner; therefore, he is both a shelter and fruit. If a passenger in distress have not only a fir-tree to shelter him and shadow him, but a fruit-tree also to feed him, he thinks he is made when God thus comforts him. So a Christian, he hath not only shelter from the wrath of God, but he hath also a place of rest and quiet, the mercy of God to keep him, and the word and sacraments to feed him. God is a fruit-tree as well as a fir-tree.

'From me is thy fruit found.'

That is, whatsoever is graciously or comfortably good to us, in us, or issues from us, is all from God. Hence first of all we observe for our instruction,

From a man's self comes nothing that is graciously good.

Whatsoever is savingly good is altogether from God. 'Without me,' saith Christ, 'you can do nothing,' John xv. 5. Saint Paul was wondrous chary* of this point. 1 Cor. xv. 10 he saith 'he laboured more abundantly than they all: yet not I' (he recalls himself), 'but the grace of God in him that did all;' and of myself, as of myself, I cannot so much 'as think a good thought.' It is from God that we have means to make us fruitful, and from the gracious working of his Spirit comes it that they are effectual. That we think a good thought, or open our mouths to speak a good word, it is from God's Spirit enabling us thereto. 'Open thou my mouth,' saith the psalmist, 'and my lips shall shew forth thy praise.' We are tongue-

* That is, 'wary' = circumspect.—G.

tied and our lips sealed unless God open them. We cannot speak one savoury, seasonable word to further our accompt. We may speak empty words, but never a word comes from the heart that is gracious and good, but it must be by the Spirit of God. It is he who works all our works in us and for us. 'He begins the good work in us, and perfects it to the day of the Lord,' Isa. xxvi. 12, Phil. i. 6. The truth of this is wondrous clear.

If this be so, then undoubtedly the differences in the graces of men, it is from another, merely from God and God's Spirit. There is indeed difference in men, but this is originally fetched from the grace of God's Spirit. The good use of freedom, that we talk so much of, it is from God, as well as the endowments of it. We have free will, but the use of it is not in our power, to use this or that at our pleasure; for 'it is God which gives the will and the deed,' Phil. ii. 13, of his good pleasure. Not only the deed, but the will too; we should make the will an idol else. For so many wills, so many idols, if we think one man in himself can difference himself by his will.

Again, in that God saith, 'From me is thy fruit found,' we may learn hence,

That fruit that is gracious comes from us and from God too.

It is our fruit and God's, so that there is a subordination of gracious works under God. The fruit we have is from God, yet it is our fruit too.

Quest. How can this be?

Sol. Yes, easily. We speak the words, but it is God that opens our lips. We believe, but it is God that gives us grace to believe. We do the action, but God gives us grace to do it. God opened the heart of Lydia to believe, Acts xvi. 14, so that God and we meet together in the same action. We have parts, understanding, will, affections, bodies and souls. Therefore the actions are said to be ours, because God works in us as understanding creatures; but God sets the wheel a-going, so that the actions are originally his, and ours subordinately under him, 'From me is thy fruit found.'

If so be that God and man join in one action ('From me is thy fruit found;' as though he should say, Whatsoever thou hast or sayest that is good, it is from me; here we see how, and why good works cannot merit, though they come from God, as all goodness doth), yet in regard they come from us too, we add some tainture thereunto from our corrupt nature. What God and Christ himself doth, is absolute and perfect, as justification; but what fruit he works in us, there is somewhat of the old Adam in us, which taints the beauty of the work. It is God's fruit, coming from him, and yet our fruit also, coming from us; which being so much tainted should humble us, in that we add nothing to the truth of God's work in us, but abasement and defilement by our corruptions. 'From me (saith God) is thy fruit found,' so much as is supernaturally good; but because our nature is not altered on the sudden, but still tastes of the 'old leaven,' 1 Cor. v. 7, therefore there can be no meriting of salvation by any works we do, because they are not perfectly good.

Use 1. The clearing of these points, in our judgment, *they serve to work in us a deep humiliation*, seeing that we have nothing in ourselves but stains and defilements, all that is good in us coming from God, 'From me is thy fruit found.' What is from ourselves then, if all good in us comes from God? We are a barren and a cursed soil, nothing that is good can come from us. Even as the earth was cursed after Adam's fall, and brought forth nothing but briers and thorns, so our soul naturally is a cursed soil in itself, and brings forth nothing but weeds and thorns. Our hearts are like the barren wilderness, full of evil, noisome lusts and affections. Therefore this serves to abase us, that we be not lifted up with any good in us; for as that is altogether from God's Spirit, so likewise we of ourselves add nothing to it, but somewhat which may diminish the value thereof.

Use 2. Here, again, for matter of judgment, *you have a difference between the state of nature and the state of grace*, I mean of innocent nature, for in Adam we had a standing in ourselves, being trusted with our own good; but now under the second covenant, under the second Adam, Christ Jesus, we have many graces to fit us for heaven, and many good works we do, but all the fruit we have and yield is from God. So that now this is a grand difference. Adam, as it were, had the keeping of his own happiness locked up in himself; but we have our happiness, graces, and whatsoever is good for us, shut up in Christ as the spring and fountain, which is the reason of the perpetual stability and permanent condition of God's children, once his and ever his. And put the case, we want this or that help, yet this prejudiceth not the perpetuity of the condition of God's children, because those graces which come immediately from God's Spirit, may be conveyed sometimes without means, as well as with them. Therefore, whatsoever decay is in the branches that are grafted into this noble Vine, Christ Jesus, in whom we bear all the fruit we bear, yet notwithstanding there is life everlasting for us in the root, which is by little and little distilled into us. The leaves may fall, outward things may decay, but there is life alway in the root of a Christian, because he is in Christ, and hath his fruit from him; he cannot want fruit, no more than Christ can want influence and vigour, John xv. 5. Which shews us the excellent state of a Christian under the new covenant of grace, that now we fetch all out of ourselves, and it is happy for us that we do so. For without Christ we can do nothing. As without the soul the body can do nothing, so without the Spirit of Christ we can do nothing; from him is all. This is the reason why we must not trust to any grace in ourselves, that comes from us, because grace comes from God in Christ. Trust God, the spring whence it comes, whose the fruit is: God the Father in Christ, from whom all fulness comes, and is derived unto us, or else we make but an idol of grace, if we trust too much to grace. Look to the spring whence all comes to us. 'From me is thy fruit found.'

Quest. Again, for further instruction, What is the reason that some have more grace than others, and more comfort, some having grace and comfort in one degree, and some in another?

Sol. Hence it is: 'From me is thy fruit found.' It comes from the freedom of God in Christ, who according to his good pleasure gives the will and the deed, whence we have grace sometimes in the vigour, sometimes in a weaker and lesser degree, the fault being in ourselves too. Yet, notwithstanding, there is a liberty in the Spirit of Christ, to give a more or less measure of grace, to shew that our good we do springs not from ourselves. Which also is the reason of the difference betwixt Christians, because God will shew that he is the disposer and the dispenser of his own graces and comforts. And that is the reason also why we must perform this duty of waiting upon God in the use of means, though we find no sense of grace and comfort from him for the present, 'From him our fruit is found.' Wait his leisure. He suspends grace and comfort until a fit time, in regard of the degree; but yet there is alway some grace left, though he suspends the increase thereof until a fit time, because he would have us know that it is of his giving. Christians who are acquainted herewith, they will not tie God to their time, but humbly go on in the use of means, who though they find not their spirits and their comforts enlarged so as at other times, nor so great, nor as other folks are ; yet can say, Lord, thou givest the will and the deed according to thy good pleasure, all comes from thee; therefore I will use the means and depend upon thee because I have all from thee freely. God gives a spirit of prayer, and then the thing we pray for, all is from him, 'From me is thy fruit found.' Do we find the ordinances fruitful, the preaching of the word to open our understandidgs, to kindle our affections, to enlighten our judgments? It is the Spirit of God that joins with the means, that are dead of themselves, to make them fruitful. What are the ordinances without God, but empty conduit-pipes of themselves? Therefore, 'From me is thy fruit found.'

Use 3. This should teach and direct us also *in all things to look up to God in all use of means.* Lord, I may read, hear, and use helps and means long enough, to little or no purpose, unless thou give a blessing. Paul may plant and Apollos may water, but if thou give not fruit from heaven, all is to no purpose, 1 Cor. iii. 6. We forget this, and therefore prosper accordingly. We think we can work fruit out of the means, by our own wit. Oh! it is not so! Whatsoever is comfortable or gracious in the use of means, it is merely God's blessing. And therefore seeing all our fruit whatsoever, that is good, comes from God, let us stir us up to practise the spiritual worship of God, to adore God, to beg of his fulness in Christ Jesus, and likewise to resign ourselves in all conditions unto him. Lord, I put myself upon thee; all my fruit is from thee; thou canst sanctify any condition unto me. This adoration and resignation are parts of the spiritual worship of God. And likewise the service of the Lord in fear and reverence, that inward service of the Spirit; all depends upon this, that all our fruit is from God. Therefore I must serve him, and serve him as he must be served, in spirit and truth, John iv. 24. What makes a man reverence another? I depend upon him; without him I sink. Will this make a man serve man? And will it not make us serve God, and serve him with fear? What breeds an awful fear? This, that if he withdraw his influence, I fall into sin, despair, and discomfort. So that the ground of all fear of God, and service springing from this fear, it is from hence, that from him all my fruit, all my grace and comfort, is found; therefore I must have grace to serve him, as a God in fear. For if the soul be not possessed and seasoned with this heavenly doctrine, that all comes from him, then surely where is God's service? What becomes of it? . Where is that adoration and magnifying of God in our hearts? Where's that putting off ourselves upon him in all conditions?

Use 4. Again, this enforceth another part of God's spiritual and heavenly worship, *cleaving to God in our affections*, especially these two, in our faith and love; that as all comes from and by Jesus Christ, so thereby we may draw from him the fruit of grace and comfort. So that this spiritual cleaving and uniting of our souls to Christ, it comes from this, that I have all from him, therefore I must cleave to him; seeing whatsoever is spiritual, holy, and comfortable I must have from him. Therefore if we would worship God in spirit and truth, as we should do, and set him up in his due place in the soul, let us labour to have our judgments sanctified in this, that all comes from God. If we were surely grounded in the goodness, mercy, and riches of God's grace, and knew that all our fruit comes and is from him, this would make us to conclude that therefore it is reason that we should worship him and depend upon him strictly. As the prophet speaks of idols, that they can neither do us good nor harm, Jer. x. 5, enforcing that they should not fear them, so we may say of all other things distinct from God, they can neither do good nor harm, except God enable them. Will you be slaves to men? They cannot do good nor harm, but as God uses them, whose creatures they are. Therefore the worship of God is also founded hence, that God does all good or harm. If men do it they do it from him, he gives them leave; as it is said of Shimei, God bid him rail on David, 2 Sam. xvi. 10. If they do us good, they are his conduits, whereby he deriveth good to us; therefore all is from him. We see then how all the true and hearty worship of God comes from this, 'From me is thy fruit found.'

Use 5. This should make us likewise, as to worship God in spirit and in truth, so *to be resolute in good causes*, whatsoever come of it. Look for a ground, and then be resolute; because all comes from God, who will stand by us in his own cause and quarrel.

But if I forsake this and that support, I shall lay open myself to injuries and wrongs.

Mark what the Spirit of God saith, 'Ye that love the Lord, hate that which is evil,' Ps. xcvii. 10. But if I hate that which is evil, idols, &c., as Ephraim here doth, I shall be despised and trampled upon. No! saith he, 'God preserves the souls of his; he will be a shield and a buckler; a sun and a shield; and no good thing shall be wanting to them that lead a godly life,' Ps. lxxxiv. 11. God will be a sun for all good, and a shield to keep off all ill; therefore let us be resolute in good causes. Whence comes all shifting, halting, imperfect walking, and inconstances in the ways of God, but from this, that men know not where to have men? They are not grounded on this, that whatsoever is fruitful and good comes from God, who will give whatsoever is fruitful and good in depending upon him. This made the three children in Daniel courageous. They knew they should have fruit from God; that is, grace, comfort, and peace, the best fruit of all. And therefore 'know, O king, that we will not worship thine idol, nor fall down before it,' Dan. iii. 18. So holy Esther, being well grounded, could say, 'If I perish, I perish,' Esth. iv. 16. I know the cause is good; and if all help in the creature be removed and taken away, yet I shall have fruit in God.

Let us therefore carry this about us, as a principle of holy life, to know that our good is hid up in God, and not in the creature; so that if all help were taken away, yet we have it immediately, purer and better in the fountain. What if there were not a creature in the world to help me? What if all were against me? Yet God may make all their powers and endeavours fruitful. There is such fruit from God, that he can make the worst things which befalleth us fruitful when he pleaseth. There is a blessing in curses and crosses, a good fruit in them! Who can do him harm that God turneth the bitterest things he suffers to his good? Let none be daunted in a good cause, but go on resolutely, seeing God hath all in himself. Was not Moses forty days without any earthly comfort on the mount? Exod. xxxiv. 28. And Christ also without natural sustentation so long? Mat. iv. 2. Did not God give light without a sun in the first creation? We are tied to means, but he is not. We think if such friends and helps be taken away, that then all is gone; but what were they? Were not they means which God used at his good pleasure, and cannot he give comfort without them? Yes, certainly! The greatest comfort and grace is ofttimes given immediately from God, when he salutes the soul by his own Spirit, as he did Paul and Silas in the dungeon; who, in the midst of discomfort, had their spirits enlarged to sing hymns at midnight, Acts xvi. 25, God reserving that comfort for that time. Therefore seeing all comfort is from God, and he is not tied to this or that means, nay, can bless all contrary means, is not this a ground of resolution?

Use 6. Therefore now make a use of comfort of it, seeing all fruit is from God, who is in covenant with his children in Jesus Christ, and who will improve all his attributes for their good, his wisdom, goodness, power, and mercy. Let them therefore *take comfort to themselves, that howsoever the world may take their friends from them, riches, liberty, and what you will, can they take God and fruit from them?* No! 'From me is thy fruit found.' If they could take away the Spirit of God, grace, and comfort from us, it were something; but can they do that? No! The worst they can do is to send us to heaven, to the fountain of all grace and comfort; so that in this world they cannot cast us into any condition wherein we cannot have communion with God, in whom all the scattered excellencies of the creature are gathered together, meeting as it were in a centre. It is he that comforts us in our friends, that shews bowels to us in our mothers, wisdom and care towards us in our parents. The bowels of a mother, the care of a friend, the strength of wise assistance, hath he not all in himself, if all be taken away? He hath all. Therefore let Christians comfort themselves, that they can never be in a condition wherein fruit shall be taken from them. The poor worldling labours all his life for fruit, riches, and friends; and when he dies, then his fruit faileth him and falls, his leaf withereth. What becometh of his fruit then? He laboured for that which yields him nothing but vexation and death. But a Christian doth otherwise; he labours for grace and comfort to keep his communion and peace with God; and when all is taken away, either by the injury and wrongs of men, or by the extremity of the times, or as all will, in the hour of death, his fruit is most after, in death, and after death, more than can be by our narrow hearts conceived in the excellency thereof. Oh! the excellent estate of a Christian! Imagine such a one to have a tree that grows in heaven, and sends forth fruit and branches to him in whatsoever state he is in. And so indeed God reacheth fruit from heaven to the soul, being in prison and misery. He reacheth from thence the fruit of grace, of spiritual strength and comfort: a blessed estate! Therefore let Christians comfort themselves in their condition, 'that all their fruit is from him;' and that God especially will then shew himself abundant when they stand most in need of him. Other trees bear no fruit in winter and in storms, but God giveth fruit most in the worst times. He is a God that comforteth the abject. As it is 2 Cor. vii. 6; and here is said, that 'in him the fatherless findeth mercy.' We have most fruit from him in the worst times. Then especially he delighteth to shew himself a God, when no comfort can be had from the creature.

Therefore do not despair, but lay up this against evil times; never fear for the time to come. Let the mountains be cast into the midst of the sea, and let the earth and all rage, as the psalmist says, and let things run upon a head; come what can come, God is where he was, and God's children are where they were, in regard of the main comfort, Ps. xlvi. 2. They cannot be in such a condition, as that they can be deprived of their God, and of his assistance: 'From me is thy fruit found.' Therefore care not for any condition that thou art in, this or that, thou shalt have that condition which shall be comfortable to thee, though many like beasts go on, and look for no fruit from God.

Use 7. And let this also be an encouragement, *to walk with God sincerely and uprightly in all times*, not fearing any creature, or danger from the creature, because our fruit is from God. What if we lose this or that? We know what was said to Amaziah by the prophet. But what shall become of the hundred talents? saith he. God is able to give thee much more, 2 Chron. xxv. 9. So in the loss of friends, having this and that took* from us, let us comfort ourselves. Aye, but God is not taken from us. He who derives† comfort by this or that friend, can supply it better by his own Spirit. And whatsoever we part with in a good cause, let us remember what Christ saith. 'He that parts with father or mother, with house or land for my sake, shall have a hundredfold in this world, and afterwards life everlasting, Mat. xix. 29. He shall have all made up in grace, which is a hundred times better than anything that is here. He shall have contentment, which is better than the things themselves. Sometimes he shall, missing one worldly comfort, have more friends stirred up; but howsoever, in want of one, he shall be supplied in another comfort that he never dreamt of in this world. So that God is abundant to them that stick close to him in sincerity; he shall find him abundant in the things of this life, in one comfort or other.

Therefore, by these mercies of God here mentioned, let us be entreated to be in love with the condition of a Christian life, and say, as Ephraim here, 'What have I any more to do with my former corrupt courses, or idols?' Give a peremptory answer to all sinful courses and suggestions, either from others or from our own corrupt nature. 'What have I any more to do with you?' No; God shall be my God: for if I can resign myself wholly to God, and renounce the creature and all things else, God will be as a 'green fir-tree,' and hear me. I shall lose nothing by it. Be then in love with a Christian course; for it is the sweetest and the safest course, and never wants comforts from heaven: and it is the most honourable course that can be, for it will hold our communion and peace with the great God of heaven and earth; for though we break with others, we shall be sure of him. In which case take heed of that base suggestion which the devil himself was ashamed to own, 'that we serve God for nought,' Job i. 9. What! shall we renounce idolatry and wicked courses, and think that God will not have fruit for us? Shall I think, if I leave my sinful gain, that I or my posterity shall beg or starve for it? Do we serve a God that hath no fruit, that is a dead tree, or a barren wilderness? No; we serve a God that had all in himself before he made the world, and hath all the excellency in himself contained in the creatures. It is not in vain to serve him. 'Doth Job serve God for nothing?' said the devil. Therefore it is a suggestion worse than Satanical, to think we serve God for nothing, or to think, like those hypocrites mentioned by the prophet, that God regards not our fasting or our devotion, Isa. lviii. 3. No; we shall not lose a good word for God. Not a tear, but he hath a bottle for it, Ps. lvi. 8; not a sigh, or a groan, or a farthing, not a minute's time well spent shall be lost. He will pay us for every ill word we endure for his sake, for every disgrace, loss, or cross. Do we serve that God there is no fruit in? 'From me is thy fruit found.'

Whatsoever our condition be in the world, let us comfort ourselves with these things, and think that it is not in vain to serve the Lord; for we

* That is, 'taken.'—G. † That is, 'conveys.'—G.

cannot serve a richer, nor a more kind master and Lord. First of all, he gives us opportunity and means whereby fruit may be wrought in us, and then he works the fruit of grace and comfort in us, and afterwards rewards and crowns his own fruit. But we add imperfections and inventions of our own, and so mar or stain all. But we deal with a gracious God in covenant, who pities us as a father doth his children, accepts and rewards what is his, and pardons what is our own. Therefore let thus much be effectual for the guiding of our lives, and comforting of us in a good course. If we take ill courses, we must look for no fruit from God, but fruits of his displeasure; if we eat of the forbidden tree, we shall eat and reap 'the fruits of our own ways,' bitter fruits. For in this case, Jesus Christ, who is a sweet Saviour, will be a judge to us; and he who is 'the Lamb of God,' will be angry, so as we shall reap the fruit of his indignation. In the Revelation, divers are brought in desiring 'the hills and mountains to fall upon them, to cover them from the presence of the Lamb,' Rev. vi. 16. Let us not, therefore, turn a sweet Saviour to a rigorous Judge, by adventuring upon courses wherein we cannot look for fruit; but let us commend 'our souls in well-doing unto him, as unto a faithful Creator and Redeemer,' 1 Pet. iv. 19. And as it is, 'Let us acknowledge him in all our ways,' Prov. iii. 6; for it is good to acknowledge and look to him, that is, look to him for strength, quickening, success, grace, and light to direct us: acknowledge him in all our ways, and treasure up this comfort, that 'all fruit is found from God.' If we take good courses, we shall ever be fruitful, and have fruit from him, 'out of his fulness; for, saith he, 'From me is thy fruit found.'

THE FOURTEENTH SERMON.

Who is wise, and he shall understand these things? prudent, and he shall know them? for the ways of the Lord are equal, the just shall walk in them: but the transgressors shall fall therein.—HOS. XIV. 9.

THESE words seal up the whole prophecy; for the prophet, immediately before prophesying of the captivity, discovers to them at length their sins, as we heard, their idolatry, adding new idols to their former idols, Baal to the calves. The princes removed the bounds, old orders and laws; the prophets they were fools, and did not see the judgments of God hanging over their heads; and none of them all could see their 'grey hairs,' Hosea vii. 9, that is, the signs of their own ruin. After which, out of a Christian love, care, and conscience of his duty, by direction of the Spirit of God, he prescribes an excellent way how they should carry themselves, by returning to the Lord. 'Take words unto yourselves,' renounce all false confidence in Asshur, and all domestic helps at home, horses and the like, and fly to God as your best sanctuary. Then he shews what God will do to them, answer all the desires he had put into their hearts. 'I will heal their backslidings, and love them freely,' &c.

Now, because these were great matters of great consequence, to make them either happy in the observing them, or miserable in neglecting them, you see how he shuts up all in a most weighty close. 'Who is wise, and he shall understand these things? prudent, and he shall know them? for the ways of the Lord are equal,' &c.

Wherein the scope of the prophet is to stir up a holy regard of what hath been spoken. He would not have all lost for want of attention or application; and therefore he here stirs them up to a holy use of all, which stirring up is excellently and figuratively clothed with an *epiphonemy*, or acclamation, 'Who is wise, and he shall understand these things?' &c. He doth not say, Let men understand these things, but 'Who is wise, and who is prudent?' let them consider of these things; and then the exhortation is backed with many reasons.

1. *It is wisdom and prudence* to regard these things I have spoken. 'Who is *wise?* and who is *prudent?*'

2. And then again, *they are the ways of God* that are spoken of, and they are straight and equal in themselves. 'For the *ways*,' &c.

3. And they lead *to happiness directly, without winding and turning.* A man is sure to attain his journey's end in them; and if they will take example of those who only are exemplary to them, he tells them, 'the just shall walk in them.' They shall not walk alone; they shall have the company of 'a cloud of witnesses,' who prosper and walk on cheerfully in this way, and attain happiness in the end.

4. Then the last argument is taken from the *contrary end of all them who cavil and snarl at God's ways and truth*, that think themselves witty to pick quarrels with somewhat in God's book, as it is a common fashion now-a-days to have a divinity of men's own. 'Transgressors,' such as are opposite to God's ways, 'they shall fall in these ways;' that is, they take offence at these ways, and so fall into sin, and by falling into sin, fall into misery, till at last they fall into hell, which is the end of all quarrellers with divine truths. They fall and dash themselves upon them, and so eternally perish.

Now, these are strong and forcible reasons to enforce care and attention of what hath been spoken. It is 'wisdom and prudence;'. and 'the ways of the Lord' here 'are straight,' and then 'all godly people walk in them,' 'and those that stumble at them are sure to perish,' and do perish in them; not that they are a cause of their perishing, but by reason of the malice of men, finding fault and picking quarrels with them, they fall first into sin, and then into misery. Thus we have the scope of the words.

'Who is wise, and he shall understand these things.'

First of all, we must know that the prophet here in this figurative speech makes a kind of exclamation, 'Who is wise!' He doth, as it were, secretly mourn at the apostasy and fewness of those that be truly wise; as if he had said, I have given you many directions, and shewed you what sins lead to destruction; I have shewed what course ye are to take, and the bounty of God to those that return; but 'who is wise and prudent to regard these things?'

In the words, therefore, in regard of the speaker, the prophet, we may observe this ere we come particularly to them, *the character of a holy, merciful, gracious, and wise man;* that when he hath spoken things to excellent purpose, he would not have those things lost, but out of mercy and compassion, mingled with a great deal of heavenly wisdom, would have the best fruit of all he hath spoken. Which was the custom of the men of God in the Scriptures, the Spirit of God leading them to strike the nail home; when they taught truths, to lay the word close upon the conscience, as much as they could. What is the whole book of Deuteronomy, as the word signifieth,* but a repeating of the former laws? Moses thought all to

* Deuteronomy, *i.e.*, Δευτερονόμιον = the Law again or repeated.—G.

no purpose, unless he repeated laws, and fastened them upon the soul. So our Saviour Christ still when he had spoken excellent things, saith, 'Let him that hath ears to hear, hear,' Mat. xi. 15. So saith Jeremiah, 'Who is wise to consider these things?' Jer. ix. 12; and the conclusion of that excellent psalm is just thus, 'Who is wise to consider these things?' Ps. cvii. 43. And saith Moses, 'O that they were wise, that they would think of these things,' &c., Deut. xxxii. 29. So everywhere in Scripture you have such fastening of things, where truths have been spoken, in application of them; which doth justify the course of God's messengers in bringing the word home unto men's consciences, because that which is spoken loosely in general, no man applieth in particular to himself. We who are messengers of God must therefore bring things home to the conscience. 'Who is wise, and he shall understand these things,' &c.

But that which more nearly concerneth us is, whereas first of all he propounds this exhortation, to regard these things under this holy acclamation, 'Who is wise, and who is prudent?' we see, first of all,

Obs. That there are but few who are truly wise and prudent.

Few that enter the right way; for our Saviour sheweth that 'narrow is this way, and few there be that find it,' Mat. vii. 14. The point needs not much proof, it is so plain and well known; wherefore it is now touched only, making way to other things. The reason hereof is clear.

Reason. Most men, we see, live by sense, will, and passion, and not by faith, whereby they enthral the wisdom they have, and make it prisoner to sinful passions and affections, rejecting thoughts of their own future happiness; and though it behove them in this world to be broken of their will, yet they will have it here, though they perish and be damned for it hereafter. This is the state of the unbroken heart of man, till he have grace in him. Yea, it is the state of all men, especially those that are puffed up, either by their own place, humour, or the flattery of others. They will have their will. *Mens mihi pro regno*, as one said. Now, this being the proud, poisonful nature of man, we must not think it a strange thing that there are so few wise and prudent; for a man cannot be wise and passionate; for his passion transforms him to be a beast, a devil. Now, because most men live by sense and by humour, which is a life they are nuzzled* in (especially those that are subject to flatterers), therefore few come to be truly wise and prudent, to have so much steadiness and sobriety of spirit as to deliberate what is to be done. They will not in cold blood give leisure to their humours (but feed them), to consider what is best. This being the humour of the world, no wonder that there be so few prudent and wise.

Use 1. Since things are thus, learn this of it. If there be so few prudent and wise, as the prophets complain in all times, 'To whom is the arm of the Lord revealed? and who hath believed our report?' &c., Isa. liii. 1, then *take heed of living by example*, that we be not led away with the sway and error of the times; for seeing there are few 'wise and prudent,' it is better and safer to follow one man reformed by judgment than a thousand others. One man is worth a thousand, who is led with judgment and by the Spirit of God.

Use 2. And likewise *take no scandal† if you see men run upon heaps in the broad and worst way*, for that men have always done. It is the complaint of all the prophets in all times, calling the better sort few. 'As the grapes after the vintage, like a few scattered ears of corn after harvest,' Isa. xvii.

* That is, 'nursed.'—G. † That is, 'let it not be a stumbling-block.'—G.

5, 6. 'One of a city, and two of a tribe, a few of all,' Jer. iii. 14. Therefore now let us seal this truth with this exhortation.

Use 3. That we labour *to be of that few that are truly wise and prudent.* Examine, are we of those few or not, and what have we in us that may secure us to be of this small number? for if we be not, we shall never be saved. For Christ's flock 'is a little flock,' Luke xii. 32; and few there be that shall enter in at that strait gate. What hast thou, then, which may discover unto thine own soul that thou art of that number, and not of the common multitude that shall be damned? It is a thing worth the inquiring of our souls. What have we in us that may characterise us to be God's true servants, Christ's true children, and members of the church? and never rest in a common persuasion of common grace, which castaways may have as well as we. We must strive for some distinct grace, that reprobates cannot attain unto.

'Who is wise, and he shall understand these things? prudent,' &c.

But to come more particularly to the words, 'Who is wise, and he shall understand these things?' The holy man of God here in his exhortation, naming wisdom, singling out 'wise and prudent' men, 'Who is wise, and who is prudent?' he toucheth men upon the quick, right vein; for who is there that would not be thought wise and prudent? A corrupt man naturally rather desires to be thought sinful than weak; judge him as you will, so you judge him not to be an unwise, an unprudent man. A proud man, till he be subdued and humbled, had rather be thought dishonest than simple, because if he be dishonest, he thinks it is out of choice; but to be simple, this argueth imperfection, and not freedom and bravery of spirit. Therefore, it being the natural desire and instinct of all men to be thought wise and to be so, he endeavours to work upon that affection in them, 'Who is wise?' &c. Well, saith he, I know you all desire to be thought 'wise and prudent men.' Would you make it good that you are so indeed? Believe my sayings! This is the way; whosoever is wise, let him understand these things; and he that is prudent let him hearken to these things that I have spoken.

Man at first, when he had communion with wisdom itself, was a wise creature till he hearkened to Satan, and so lost all, 'becoming as the beasts which perish,' Ps. xlix. 12. Yet in that glorious building, since the corruption of nature, this amongst that rubbish is reserved, that above all things there is a desire to be happy and wise, which two desires are naturally the leading desires in men, to desire to do well, and to be wise. Therefore, the prophet here, upon that which is left in man's nature, takes advantage to build true wisdom and knowledge indeed.

To come, then, in brief, to shew what this wisdom and prudence is; for there is some distinction between wisdom and prudence. *Wisdom* is a heavenly light set up in the soul by the Spirit of God, whereby it discerneth the general truths concerning God, ourselves, the state of the church, the privileges of Christianity, and such like. In sum, it is a right, divine apprehension of spiritual truths.

And *prudence:* this is a kind of sharpness of spirit, whereby the Spirit of God directs the soul, knowing the right general principles, to particular cases. Prudence is an application of the general knowledge of general things to particulars, and is an ordering of the life in particular exigencies and cases in a right order, according to the direction of the Spirit, as we have it, Prov. viii. 12, 'I wisdom dwell with prudence.' Divine wisdom, wheresoever it is, dwells with prudence; that is, where God doth enlighten the understanding to conceive aright of the mysteries of salvation, there it dwells with prudence; that is, it directs the soul to an orderly carriage of life towards God and man, and in regard of itself, every way as it should do, in all estates, times, and conditions. That is meant here by prudence, a particular gift whereby a man is fit to consult and deliberate of things in particular to be done, in particular cases of conscience, and the like. Now, wisdom and prudence, they are both together in God's people, howsoever perhaps one is more excellent than another. Some are wiser, who have a deeper search of truths in general; and some are more prudent in their ways, that are weaker Christians for the main general truths. Yet there is not a good Christian but he hath so much prudence as will bring him to heaven. But God giveth extraordinary wisdom to some, because they are leaders of others. Yet though in God's dispensation there be a difference, yet in every Christian they are joined together. There is no Christian but he is wise for himself, which is prudence. This is, as it were, the salt which seasoneth all other graces and knowledge whatsoever; for what is knowledge without discretion but a foolish humour? what is patience but blockishness if a man do not discern how, why, and upon what ground to be patient? what is religiousness without this but superstition? and what is zeal but an indiscreet heat, if it be not seasoned with this prudence? yea, and what is constancy itself but an indiscreet rigour and stiffness without wit? So that it is the seasoning of all other graces whatsoever, that which puts bounds and measure unto all. Therefore, he joins it with wisdom, 'Who is wise? and who is prudent?' Good, as we say, consists of a whole, entire cause, unto which must be occurrence* of all circumstances together. One defect may make it to be sinful. So this is prudence, to observe a due order, clothed with circumstances of the manner and season of every good action and duty. Therefore, he joins here prudence, 'Who is wise, and he shall understand these things? prudent, and he shall know them?'

Now, these be the two graces that lead and guide a man's life. There must be first a general understanding and light of the soul, and then there must be a particular light to apply this general to particulars. Prudence is, as it were, the steward of the soul, which dispenseth the light thereof, according to particular occasions.

Now, for wisdom and prudence, we will not insist long on them, only we will draw towards a right discerning of them, squared and proportioned to our understandings by resemblances of other things. For a man may know what they are in divine things by some proportion to human things, what they are there as to give a little light to it.

1. He is a wise, prudent man in the world that will be sure to make *the greatest his friend*. So God, being the greatest of all and most able to do us good, he is a wise and prudent man that makes him his friend, and cares not who he break with, so he break not with God.

2. And we account him also a wise and prudent man in the world, that, like the wise steward in the gospel, *provides for the worst times*. What course did he take for himself herein? He provides for, as he foresees, danger, Mat. xvi. 3. So spiritual wisdom and prudence will direct a man what is best for his latter end, his eternal rest and happiness in another world. Heavenly wisdom prefixeth to† a man a full view of his latter end, and that which followeth thereupon in another world, and so makes him provide beforehand and direct all things to that end. A wise man will not have things to seek when he comes to make use of them, like the foolish virgins, who had their oil to seek when they should have had it ready,

* That is, 'concurrence.'—G.

† That is, 'sets before.'—ED.

Mat. xxv. 8. He is truly spiritually wise towards his latter end, that, as he knows there is a state to come, so is truly prudent to have all things ready against that time, that, considering the uncertainty of this life, he may not be surprised unawares, like those glorious* virgins who had a lamp without oil.

3. And amongst men he is also counted a wise and prudent man *that makes a right choice;* for this is wisdom when a man discerneth a difference, and answerably makes his choice. *Simile mater erroris,* saith one, Likeness is the mother of error (*y*). There is a likeness between good and bad in the world, and between truth and error. Now, he is a wise man who is not catched with these resemblances, but discerneth a difference between temporal and eternal things, shadows and substances, realities and appearances of things, and suitably chooseth eternals before temporals, the favour of God before the favour of men, and, in a word, those things which concern everlasting happiness before those that are perishing. Wisdom is seen in choice. By these few instances named, we may see what heavenly wisdom and prudence is, by proportion of wisdom and prudence in earthly things. Now, considering that there is a better state in another world than in this, he must needs be a wise man that orders things so as that he may not lose eternity. Most men in the world are penny-wise and pound-foolish, as we say, wise to a particular end, to get particular favours and riches, so to satisfy their intentions; but for the main, which is wisdom indeed, to look to their last estate and happiness, and to fit their actions and courses that way, how few are wise to purpose! How few provide for eternity! Therefore, no marvel the prophet saith, 'Who is wise? and who is prudent?' because men live by sense, and not by faith.

'Who is wise, and he shall understand these things? prudent, and he shall know them?'

Obs. Now, the next thing to be observed hence is this, *that the wise and prudent only know these things.* There must be wisdom and prudence before we can know divine truths, and make use of them.

Obs. And then observe further, *that true wisdom and prudence carries men to God's word.* 'Who is wise to understand these things?' By divine truth we grow wise and prudent, the Spirit joining with the same, and then we come to make a right use of them. There must be first a spiritual wisdom and prudence, enlightened by the Spirit, ere we can make use of the word aright, to taste and relish it. Because, though the word be light, yet light alone is not sufficient to cause sight, but there must concur unto the outward light an inward sight. Grace must illuminate the understanding, and put a heavenly light into the soul. As by the light within meeting with the light without, the eye being the instrument of sight, applying itself to the thing, thence comes sight. So there be divine truths out of us, wherewith, when the Holy Ghost puts an inward light into the soul, sanctified wisdom and prudence, then the inward light meeting with the light without, we see and apprehend. The Spirit, therefore, must join to work wisdom and prudence. Naturally we are all dead, and have lost our spiritual senses. Therefore the Spirit of God must work in us spiritual senses, sight, and taste, that we may see, discern, and relish heavenly things, which, ere we can do, there must be an harmony betwixt the soul and the things; that is, the soul must be made spiritual, answerable to the heavenly things pitched upon, or else, if the soul be not set in a suitable frame, it can never make a right use of them.

* That is, 'over-confident.'—ED.

Now, when the understanding of a man is made wise by the Spirit of God, it will relish wisdom and prudence. For the Spirit of God, together with the Scripture, takes the scales off the eyes of the soul, subdues rebellious passions in the affections, especially that rebellion of the will, putting a new relish in all, so as they come to love, affect,* and joy in heavenly things. Now, when these scales of spiritual blindness are fallen off the eyes of the soul, and when rebellion is removed from the will and affections, then it is fit to join and approve of heavenly things, else there is a contrariety and antipathy betwixt the soul and these things. As the body, when the tongue is affected with some aguish humour, cannot relish things, though they be never so good, but affecteth and relisheth all things suiting that distemper; so it is with the soul. When it is not enlightened it judgeth all things carnally, there being an antipathy between the soul and divine truths brought home unto it. Perhaps a soul not enlightened or sanctified will apprehend the generalities of truth very well, but when they are pressed home to practice, then, unless the soul be changed, it will rise up and swell against divine truths, and reject the practice of them. Without subduing grace, to alter and change the soul, the affections thereof are like the March suns, which stir up a great many humours, but not spending them, they breed aguish humours and distempers. So the light of the word in a carnal heart, it meets with the humours of the soul, and stirs them; but if there be not grace in the soul to subdue these affections, it stirs them up to be the more malicious, especially if they be pressed to particular duties in leaving of sinful courses. So that the Spirit of God must alter the understanding, and subdue the will and affections, ere there can be a conceiving of divine truths savingly. Therefore, before these acts, he joins these graces. 'Who is wise? and who is prudent?' &c.

Use. The use hereof is thus much: Not to come to the divine truth of God with human affections and spirits, but to lift up our hearts to God. Why, Lord, as things themselves are spiritual, so make me spiritual, that there may be a harmony between my soul and the things; that as there is a sweet relish in divine truths, so there may be a sweet taste in me, to answer that relish which is in divine truths; that the wisdom of thy word and my wisdom may be one! Then a man is wise. There is not the commonest truth, or practical point in divinity, but it is a mystery, and must be divinely understood, and must have prudence to go about it as we should do. Repentance and the knowledge of sin, it is a mystery till a man be sanctified in his understanding. He can never know what spiritual misery is till the inward man be enlightened and sanctified, to know what a contrariety there is between sin and the Spirit of God. As no man can know thoroughly what sickness is but he that hath been sick; for the physician doth not know sickness so well as the patient who feels it; so it is with a holy man, sanctified with the Holy Ghost. Tell him of sin, he feels it, and the noisomeness of it, the opposition of it to his comfort and communion with God. Only the spiritual enlightened man can tell what repentance, sin, sorrow for sin, and the spiritual health of the soul is. Therefore it is said here, 'Who is wise? and who is prudent? and he shall understand these things.'

* That is, 'choose' = cherish.—G.

THE FIFTEENTH SERMON.

Who is wise, and he shall understand these things? prudent, and he shall know them? for the ways of the Lord are right, the just shall walk in them: but the transgressors shall fall therein.—HOS. XIV. 9.

AT length, by divine assistance, we are come unto the conclusion of this short chapter, wherein the Holy Ghost, from God, hath shewed such bowels of mercy and tender compassion unto miserable sinners, encouraging them to return unto the Lord by many and several arguments, being formerly insisted upon. Our last work was to shew you what wisdom and prudence was, the difference of them, and how that none, without these endowments, are able to know and make use of divine truths and mysteries of religion. 'Who is wise, and he shall understand these things? prudent, and he shall know them?' &c.

We came then to shew, that there must be prudence and wisdom, before we can understand divine truths; there must be an illumination within. It is not sufficient to have the light of the Scripture outwardly, but there must be a light of the eye to see; there must be wisdom and prudence gathered from the Scriptures. Now, wisdom and prudence, if they be divine, as here is meant, it is not a discreet managing of outward affairs of our personal condition, but an ordering of our course to heavenward. Wherefore a man may know whether he be wise and prudent by his relishing of divine truths, for otherwise he is not wise and prudent in these things which are the main.

Now, having shewed that only the wise and prudent can conceive and make a right use of these great things delivered, he comes to shew and defend the equity of God's ways, how crooked soever they seem to flesh and blood. These things ought to be hearkened unto, because they are the ways of God.

'The ways of the Lord are right.'

By *ways* here, he understandeth the whole law and gospel, the whole word of God; which he calleth *right*, not only because,

1. They are righteous in themselves; but,
2. Because they reform whatsoever is amiss in us, and rectify us; and
3. Work whatsoever is needful for our good and salvation.

Now more particularly, God's ways are,

1. Those ways wherein he walks to us; or,
2. The ways that he prescribes us to walk in; and,
3. Our ways, as they are conformable to his.

Any of these are the ways of God; of all which more hereafter.

1. *The ways wherein he walks to us*, because many of them are untraceable, as unsearchable to us, are not here meant; as those of election, predestination and reprobation; the reasons whereof, if we take them comparatively, cannot be searched out. Why God should take one and not another, it is an unsearchable way. But take a man single, out of comparison, the ways of God will appear to be right, even in that harsh decree which many men stumble so much at. For none are ever brought in the execution of that decree to be damned, but you shall see 'the ways of the Lord right,' who a long time together offers them a great deal of mercy, which they refusing, and resisting the Holy Ghost, taking wilfully contrary courses, work out their own damnation. So that at length the issue of those unsearch-

able ways will appear to be right in every particular; howsoever the comparative reason at the first, why God singles out one man and not another, will not appear.

2. As for the *ways of his providence*, in governing the world, and ruling of his church, this is the way of God which is right; all which ways, though we cannot in all particulars see in this world, yet in heaven, in the light of glory, we shall see what cannot now be seen in the light of grace and nature. For there be mysteries in providence. Who can tell the reason why, of men equally good, one should be sorely afflicted, and the other should go to heaven without any affliction in a smooth way? None can give a reason of it; but we must subscribe to the hidden wisdom of God, whose ways are unsearchable in his providence. Yet are they most right, though they be above our conceit. If we could conceive all God's ways, then they were not God's ways; for in his ways to us, he will so carry them, as he will shew himself to be above and beyond our shallow conceits.

But the ways especially here meant, are the ways which he prescribes us to walk in; and they are,

1. What we must believe; and then,

2. What we must do. There is,

First, obedience of faith, and then obedience of life.

These are God's ways prescribed in the word, and only in the word.

3. Now *our ways*, when they join with *God's ways*, that is, when our life, purposes and desires of the inner-man, in our speeches, carriage, and conversation, agree with God's ways, then in some sort they are God's ways, 'the just shall walk in them.' They shall walk in these ways, that is, in those ways which God prescribeth. As for those ways wherein God walks to us, we have not so much to do here to consider them. But by walking in the ways which he prescribes, we shall feel that his ways to us will be nothing but mercy and truth. 'The ways of the Lord are right,' Ps. cxlv. 17. Those ways that he prescribes to men to be believed and done, they are right and straight, that is, they are agreeable to the first rule of all. Right is the judgment and will of God. He is the first truth and the first good; the prime truth and good, which must rule all others, *mensura mensurans*, as they use to speak in schools; the measure that measures all other things. For all other things are only so far right, as they agree to the highest measure of all, which is God's appointment and will. So the ways of God are said to be right; because they agree to his word and will. They are holy and pure, as himself is just, pure, and holy.

'The ways of the Lord are right.'

Right, as they agree to that which is right and straight; and right likewise, because they lead directly to a right end. We know a right line is that which is the shortest between two terms. That which leads from point to point, is the shortest of all other lines. *So God's ways are right and straight.* There are no other ways which tend directly to happiness, without error, but God's ways; all other ways are crooked ways. So God's ways are right, as they look to God, and as they look unto all other inferior courses. They are right to examine all our ways by, being the rule of them. And they are right, as they look to God's will, and are ruled by him.

'The ways of the Lord are right.'

Hence observe we in the first place, that the first thing we should look to in our conversation, must be to know this for a ground.

Obs. That man is not a prescriber of his own way, and that no creature's will is a rule.

We must embrace, therefore, no opinion of any man, or any course enjoined or prescribed by any man, further than it agrees with the first truth and the first right. God's ways are right; right as a standard, that is, a measure to measure all other measures by. So God's will and truth revealed is a right rule, and the measure of all other rules whatsoever. Directions therefore, which we have of things to be believed and done from men, must be no further regarded than as they agree with the first standard. Therefore they are mistaken, and desperately mistaken, that make any man's will a rule, unless it be subordinate to that which is higher, at which time it becometh all one with the higher rule. When a man subordinates his directions to God's, then God's and his are all one. Otherwise without this subordination, we make men gods, when we make their will a rule of our obedience. 'The ways of the Lord are right.' But of this only a touch by the way; the main point hence is.

Obs. The word of the Lord is every way perfect, and brings us to perfection.

As we may see at large proved, Ps. xix. 7, &c., where whatsoever is good, comfortable, profitable or delightful, either for this life or the life to come, is all to be had from thence. And the wise man saith, 'Every word of God is pure,' &c., Prov. xxx. 5: a similitude taken from gold, which is fined till it be pure, as it is expressed in another place, 'The words of the Lord are pure words, as silver tried in a furnace of earth, and purified seven times,' Ps. xii. 6. And so the apostle to Timothy. 'All Scripture is given by inspiration of God, and is profitable for doctrine, for correction, for reproof, for instruction in righteousness, that the man of God may be perfect, throughly furnished unto all good works,' 2 Tim. iii. 16.

Use 1. Since then the ways of God are so right, just, pure, and perfect, *this is first for reproof of them that add hereunto;* as our Romish adversaries, who do herein, by their traditions and additions, condemn God either of want of wisdom, love, and goodness, or of all. So as all defects charged upon the word, are charged upon God himself, who did not better provide and foresee for his church what was good for it. But the wise man condemneth this their audacious boldness, where he saith, 'Add thou not unto his words, lest he reprove thee, and thou be found a liar,' Prov. xxx. 6. They bar reading of the Scriptures, or to read them in English especially, lest the people become heretics. They think it safe to read their own books and idle dreams, but reject the word of God, and then, as Jeremiah speaks, 'What wisdom is in them?' Jer. viii. 9. Surely none at all; for the only wisdom is, to be governed by God's most holy word.

Use 2. Again, *it is for instruction unto us, to rest and rely upon this so holy, right, pure, and perfect word.* Since it is so sure and firm, we are to rest upon the promises, and tremble at the threatenings, though we see not present performance of them, because not one of them shall fail. For, saith Christ, 'Heaven and earth shall pass away, but one jot and tittle of the law shall not fail,' Matt. v. 28. What maketh so many judgments to overtake men, but their unbelief? what made their carcases to fall in the wilderness, so as they could not enter into the land of Canaan, but their unbelief? for, saith the text of them, 'They could not enter, because of unbelief,' Heb. iii. 19. Infidelity, and not believing God, is the root and cause of all our woe. It began with our first parents, and it cleaveth too close unto us, even unto this day. This cometh from our atheism and self-love; that if a mortal man promise or swear unto us, we believe him, and rest upon his word; but all that the great God can do unto us by promises, commandments, threatenings, allurements, and gracious examples, will not make us give credit to his word, but rather believe Satan, and our own false and deceitful hearts. As, for instance, God hath promised, that 'if our sins were as red as scarlet, yet he will make them whiter than the snow,' Isa. i. 18; though they be never so strong for us, yet he hath promised 'to subdue them,' Micah vii. 19. If our wants be never so great, yet if we will trust in God, he hath promised to relieve us, and hath said, 'that he will not fail us nor forsake us,' Isa. l. 10; Heb. xiii. 5, if we cast our care upon him. So, for the threatenings, we must believe that there is never a one of them but they shall come to pass, as sure as the promises shall be made good. If these thoughts were firmly settled in us, that 'the ways of the Lord are right,' and therefore must be all accomplished in their time, it would make us restless to fly from sin, and the punishments threatened, which all 'lie at the door,' Gen. iv. 7, and will quickly be upon us, if they be not avoided by sound and hearty repentance.

Use 3. Lastly, if every commandment be right, sure, and just, then when God commandeth do it, though the apparent danger be never so great, and though it be never so contrary to flesh and blood, pleasure, profit, or preferment, yet *know it is firm and sure, and that our happiness stands in doing it, our misery in disobeying it*,—as we know it was with Adam. What a sudden change did his disobedience work in himself, all the world since being leavened with that miserable contagious fall of his! And for the whole world this is a general, we never want any good, but for want of love and obedience unto it. 'Great prosperity shall they have,' saith David, 'who love thy law, and no evil shall come unto them,' Ps. cxix. 165. And we never had nor shall have any hurt, but from our unbelief and disobedience to the holy, pure, and perfect word of God, which is attended with comfort and prosperity here, and endless glory hereafter.

'The ways of the Lord are right.'

In the next place, if the ways of the Lord be right and straight, so straight that they lead directly to the right end, then it is clear,

Obs. That the best way to come to a good and right end, is to take God's ways. For it is a right way, and the right way is always the shortest way. Therefore, when men take not God's ways, prescriptions, and courses, they go wide about, and seldom or never come to their intended end. God's way is the right way, and therefore brings a man to his right end. Sometimes men will have their turnings, their *diverticula*, and vagaries, but they find by experience that God's ways they are the right ways, so as they never attain to comfort and peace until they come again into those ways. God until then suffereth them to be snared and hampered, and to eat the fruit of their own ways, and then they see the difference of God's ways and theirs, and that God's ways are the best, and the straightest ways unto true happiness.

Indeed, God suffers sometimes men that will have their own ways to come quickly to them, as some men hasten to be rich, and God suffers them to be rich hastily: yet they are none of God's ways which they take, but climb up by fraud and deceit. Aye, but that is only a particular end which God suffereth them to attain by byeways; but what will be the upshot? Where will all these ways end at length? Surely in hell. For when a man goes out of the right, and straight, and direct way, to be great in the world, he is like a man who goes out of his way, which is further about; who yet, when he is in that way, goes on through thick and thin, because he will gain some way. He goes on through thickets and hedges, fair and foul, where he gets many scratches, brushes and knocks. Doth any think in the world to attain his particular ends without* the direct ways of God? God may suffer him to attain his particular end, but with many flaws, knocks, and brushes upon his conscience, which many times he carrieth with him unto his grave; and finds it a great deal better, both to attain unto his particular ends by God's ways, and to have no more of anything in the world than he can have with a good conscience. For, though they be good men, ofttimes God suffers such men to have bruises in their conscience all their days, that they and others may know that the best way is the straight and right way, which at last will bring us best to our end.

Having thus made it good, 'that the ways of the Lord are right,' now, for conclusion of all, the prophet begins to shew the divers effects these right ways of God have in two sorts of people, the godly and wicked.

I. The just shall walk in them:

II. That the transgressors shall fall therein.

I. *The just shall walk in them.* Who be the just men here spoken of? Such are just men who give to every one their due; that give God his due in the first place, and man in the second place, whereby it is framed. 'The just shall walk in them;' that is, they shall proceed and go on in them till they be come to the end of their race, the salvation of their souls. And, more particularly,

(1.) Just men first, are such, *who have respect unto all God's commandments*, Ps. cxix. 6. Though in their disposition they find some more hard to them than others, yet they do not allow themselves to break any, but strive so much the more earnestly and constantly to observe them, as they find their natures opposite to them. Now hypocrites, howsoever they do many things in show, yet, like Herod and Judas, their hearts run in a wrong channel; they allow themselves to live in, and like of some sin. The young man in the gospel had not a respect unto all God's commandments, though Christ loved his amiable parts, Mat. x. 21. To this purpose James saith, 'Whosoever shall keep the whole law, and yet offend in one point, he is guilty of all,' James ii. 10. That is, he who alloweth himself in any one sin, he is guilty of all. Ask Judas, Is murder good? He would have said, no: but he was covetous, and allowed himself in it, and so drew upon him the guilt of all the rest. God is he who forbids sinning against them all. He who forbids one, forbids all; and being rightly turned to God, the same authority makes us leave all. It is not sin, but the allowance of it, that makes an hypocrite.

(2.) Again, *they do things to a good end*, the glory of God, and the good of man. For want hereof, the alms, prayers, and fasting of the scribes and Pharisees (because they did nothing out of love to God or man, but for vainglory and carnal respects), are condemned of Christ. So some are brought in at the last day, saying, 'Lord, Lord, have we not in thy name prophesied, and in thy name cast out devils, and in thy name done many wonderful works,' Mat. vii. 22; and yet Christ professeth not to know them, but calleth them 'workers of iniquity.' They had gifts and calling, and delivered true doctrine, &c. But here was their failing, 'They prophesied *in* his name, but not *for* his name.' Their actions were good in themselves, and for others, but the end of them was naught, and therefore both they and their works are condemned. Yet this is not so to be understood, but that God's children have some thoughts of vainglory, which accompanieth and creepeth into their best actions; but they do acknowledge this

* That is, 'outside of.'—ED.

for a sin, confess it, and desire the Lord to pardon and subdue it, and then it shall never be laid to their charge. Because having of infirmities is not contrary to sincerity, but allowing of them, and living in them; in which case the Lord is more pleased with our humiliation for our sin, than the motions to vainglory did offend him.

(3.) Thirdly, *a desire to grow in grace, and to become better and better*, is a sign of uprightness. Christian righteousness, as it sees still need, so it still desires more grace and less sin; because he who hath a true heart, seeth both the want and worth of grace, and feeleth his want. A man feels not the want of faith, humility, and love, till he have it in some sort, as it is said, Philip. iii. 15, 'As many as are perfect are thus minded,' to wit, so many as are upright: all is one.

(4.) Lastly, this just uprightness is known *by love of the brethren*. 'By this we know we are translated from death to life, because we love the brethren,' 1 John iii. 14. Contrary to which is that disposition which envieth at all things which suits not with their humours: as James speaketh of those who prefer men, and have their persons in admiration, in regard of outward things, despising inferiors, James ii. 2.

Use 1. If therefore we will ever be counted righteous persons, let us keep these rules set down here, have a respect to all God's commandments, do all things to the glory of God, desire to grow in grace, and love the brethren.

2. And so it is also for consolation unto such who are thus qualified; for unto them belongeth all the promises of this life, and of that to come. They are in a blessed estate, for 'all things are theirs,' 1 Cor. iii. 21, because they are Christ's. Therefore it is their bounden duty, having an upright heart, to rejoice in God, as the prophet speaks: 'Rejoice in the Lord, ye righteous, for praise is comely for the upright,' Ps. xxxiii. 1; lii. 9. None have cause to rejoice but upright men.

1. Because they of all others have title and right to joy. 2. Because they have command to do it, seeing heaven is theirs. All the promises are theirs, and they are heirs of all things. It is a comely service, and the work of heaven.

Obj. Against this some object. Oh, but I find many sins, passions, and infirmities in myself; how then can I joy in God?

Ans. To this we answer briefly, that the passions and infirmities of God's servants are not contrary to Christian uprightness and righteousness; for St James saith, that 'Elias was a man subject to like passions and infirmities as we are,' James v. 17, yet he was a righteous man, though a man subject to the like passions as we are. Therefore the passions of Christians are not contrary to Christian, but to legal, righteousness. But 'we are not under the law, but under grace,' Rom. vi. 15. The first covenant of works bids us have no sin; the other covenant bids us allow no sin. Thus much is for that question, What is meant by *just men?* It remains now that we should further inquire into that mystery, how it is that just men walk in the ways of God, and prosper therein, when yet wicked men, called 'transgressors,' fall therein. But this being a mystery, by your patience we will take time to unfold what we have to speak hereof the next time, if God be so pleased.

THE SIXTEENTH SERMON.

The ways of the Lord are right: the just shall walk in them; but the transgressors shall fall therein.—HOS. XIV. 9.

GOD's children have their times of deadness and desertion, and again their times of quickening and rejoicing. Weeping doth not always remain unto them for their portion, 'but joy cometh in the morning,' Ps. xxx. 5. In the worst times the saints have always some comforts afforded them, which supporteth them against all the storms and tempests they endure. They have always a Goshen, Exod. ix. 22, to fly to. Others shall perish in that way, wherein they shall walk and escape.

'The just shall walk in them, but the transgressors shall fall therein.'

Thus far we are now come in the unfolding of this chapter, having shewed God's rich and incomparable mercies to miserable and penitent sinners; how ready God is to embrace such, as this rebellious people named were, with all the arguments used to make them return unto the Lord. We are now come at last unto the upshot of all, a discovery of the several effects and works God's word hath upon both sorts of people here named and aimed at.

'The just shall walk in them, but the transgressors shall fall therein.'

These were very bad times; yet there were just men, who walked in the ways of God: so that we see—

In the worst times, God will have always a people that shall justify wisdom.

God will have it thus, even in the worst times, that 'the just shall walk in them.' Though before he saith, 'Who is wise? and who is prudent?' yet here he shews that there shall be a number who shall 'walk in God's ways,' who though they go to heaven alone, yet to heaven they will. Though they have but a few that walk in God's ways with them, they will rather go with a few that way, than with the wicked on the broad way to hell. Alway God hath some who shall walk in his way; for if there were not some alway who were good, the earth would not stand; for good men they are the pillars of the world, who uphold it. It is not for wicked men's sake that God upholds the frame of the creatures, and that orderly government. We see all is to gather together the number of his elect, of whom in some ages there are more, and in some less, of them born, thereafter as God breathes and blows with his Spirit. For according to the abundant working of the Spirit, is the number of the elect. Yet in all ages there are some, because it is an article of our faith, to believe 'a holy catholic church.'* Now it cannot be an article of faith, unless there were alway some that made this catholic church; for else there should be an act of faith, without an object. Therefore we may always say, I believe that there are a number of elect people that walk in the ways of God to heaven-wards.

And what is the disposition of these some? To have a counter motion to those of the times and places they live in. Some are foolish, not caring for the ways of God, cavilling at them. But the 'just shall walk in them,' that is, they take a contrary course to the world, that slights wisdom. Thus in all times it is the disposition of God's children to go contrary to the world in the greatest matters of all. They indeed hold correspondency, in outward things, but for the main they have a contrary motion. As we say of the planets, that they have a motion contrary to the wrapt motion.

* Creed, Article IX. Cf. Pearson and Smith, *in loc.*—G.

Being carried and hurried about every twenty-four hours with the motion of the heavens, they have another motion and circuit of their own, which they pass also. So it is with God's people: though in their common carriage they be carried with the common customs and fashions of the times, yet they have a contrary motion of their own, whereby being carried by the help of God's Spirit, they go on in a way to heaven, though the world discern it not. They have a secret contrary motion, opposite to the sins and corruptions of the age and times they live in. Therefore, in all ages it is observed for a commendation to go on in a contrary course to the present times. Noah in his time, Lot in his time, and Paul in his time, who complains, 'All men seek their own,' Philip. ii. 21. It is a strange thing that Paul should complain of all men seeking their own, even then when the blood of Christ was so warm, being so lately shed, and the gospel so spread; yet 'all men seek their own.' And he speaks it with tears; but what became of Paul, and Timothy, and the rest? 'But our conversation is in heaven, from whence we look for the Saviour, the Lord Jesus Christ,' &c., Philip. iii. 20. Let all men seek their own here below, as they will, we have our conversation contrary to the world. 'Our conversation is in heaven,' &c. So that they hold out God's truth in the midst of a crooked and perverse generation, that is, when every man takes crooked ways and courses in carnal policy; yet there are a company that notwithstanding walk in the right ways of God, clean contrary to others. The just will walk in the right ways of God. As holy Joshua said, 'Choose you what you will do, but howsoever, I and my father's house will serve the Lord,' Josh. xxiv. 15. So when many fell from Christ for a fit, because his doctrine seemed harsh, Peter justified that way. When Christ asked him, Will ye also leave me with the rest who are offended? 'Lord,' saith he, 'whither shall we go?' We have tasted the sweetness of the word, and felt the power thereof: 'Whither shall we go, Lord? thou hast the words of eternal life,' John vi. 68. So God's people have an affection, carriage, and course, contrary to the world.

Reason. The reason is taken from their own disposition; they are partakers of the divine nature, 2 Pet. i. 4, which carrieth them up to Godwards against the stream and current of the time.

Use. The use hereof, shall be only a trial of ourselves in evil times, whether or not then, *we justify God's ways and the best things*. If we do, it is a sign we are of the number of God's elect, to defend and maintain good causes and right opinions, especially in divine truths, which is the best character of a Christian. Others in their own sphere have their degree of goodness, but we speak of supernatural divine goodness. A man may know he belongs to God, if he justify wisdom in the worst times, if he stand for the truth to the utmost, thinking it of more price than his life. It is the first degree to religion, 'to hate father and mother, wife and children, and all for the gospel,' Luke xiv. 26. Now when a man will justify the truth, with the loss of anything in the world, it is a sign that man is a good man in ill times.

Therefore, in ill times let us labour to justify truth, both the truth of things to be believed, and all just religious courses, not only in case of opposition being opposed, but in example, though we say nothing. Noah condemned the world, though he spake not a word, by making an ark, Heb. xi. 7; so Lot, Sodom, though he told not all Sodom of their faults. So a man may justify good things, though he speak not a word to any man, for such a one's life is a confutation and sufficient witness for God against the world. Therefore it is good, though a man do not confront the world in his speeches, yet notwithstanding, at least to hold a course contrary to the world in his conversation. We have need of a great deal of courage to do this; but there is no heavenly wise man, but he is a courageous man. Though in his own spirit he may be a weak man, yet in case of opposition, grace will be above nature, he will shew then his heavenly wisdom and prudence, and of what metal he is made, by justifying wisdom in all times, 'The just shall walk therein.' But to come more directly to the words,

'The just shall walk in them.'

A just and righteous man that is made just by them, shall walk in them. Hence we may observe,

Obs. That first men must have spiritual life, and be just, before they can walk. Walking is an action of life. There must be life before there can be walking. A man must first have a spiritual life, whereby he may be just, and then he will walk as a just man. For, as we say of a bowl,* it is Austin's comparison, it is first made round, and then it runs round; so a man is first just, and then he doth justly. It is a conceit of the papists, that good works do justify a man. Luther says well, that 'a good man doth good works.' Good works make not the man. Fruit makes not the tree, but the tree the fruit. So we are just first, and then we walk as just men. We must labour to be changed and to have a principle of spiritual life; then we shall walk and have new feet, eyes, taste, ears, and senses; all shall then be new.

Again, in the second place, the necessity of it appears hence, that there must be first spiritual life in the inward man, ere a man can walk, because there will not else be a harmony and correspondency betwixt a man and his ways. A man will not hold in those ways that he hath an antipathy to; therefore, his nature must be altered by a higher principle, before he can like and delight in the ways of God. This is that which God's children desire first of God, that he would alter their natures, enlighten, change and quicken them, work strongly and powerfully in them, that they may have a sympathy and liking unto all that is good; first they are just, and then they walk in God's ways.

'The just shall walk in them.'

Obs. In the next place, we may observe hence, *that a just man, he being the prudent and wise man, he walks in God's ways.* That is, spiritual wisdom and prudence, together with grace, righteousness, and justice, they lead to walking in obedience. Let no man therefore talk of grace and wisdom or prudence altering him, further than he makes it good by his walking. He that is just, walks as a just man; he that is wise, walks wisely; he that is prudent, walks prudently. Which is spoken to discover hypocrisy in men, that would be thought to be good Christians and wise men, because they have a great deal of speculative knowledge. Aye, but look we to our ways, let them shew whether we be wise or foolish, just or unjust. 'If a man be wise, he is wise for himself,' Prov. ix. 12, as Solomon saith, to direct his own ways; 'The wisdom of the wise, is to understand his own way that he is to walk in,' Prov. xiv. 8. If a man have not wisdom to direct his way in particular, to walk to heavenward, he is but a fool. For a man to know so much as shall condemn him, and be a witness against him, and yet not know so much as to save him, what a miserable thing is this? Now all other men that know much, and walk not answerable, they know so much as to condemn them, and not to save them. Our Saviour

* That is, a 'ball' for bowling.—G

Christ he calleth such 'foolish builders,' Matt. vii. 27, that know and will not do; so unless there be a walking answerable to the wisdom and prudence prescribed, a man is but a foolish man.

Therefore let it be a rule of trial, would we be thought to be wise and prudent, just and good? Let us look to our ways. Are they God's ways? Do we delight in these ways, and make them our ways? Then we are wise, prudent, and just.

'The just shall walk in them.'

As the just shall walk in them, so whosoever walks in them are just, wise, and prudent; for is not he prudent, who walks in those ways that lead directly to eternal happiness? Is not he a wise man, that walks by rule in those ways where he hath God over him, to be his protector, ruler, and defender? Is not he a wise man, who walks in those ways that fits him for all conditions whatsoever, prosperity or adversity, life or death, for all estates? He that walks therefore in God's ways, must be the only wise man.

Now, what things doth this walking in the ways of God imply?

1. First, *perspicuity*. Those who walk in the ways of God, they discern those ways to be God's ways, and discern them aright.

2. Then when they discern them to be God's good ways, answerably *they proceed in them from step to step;* for every action is a step to heaven or to hell. So a just man, when he hath discovered a good way, he goes on still.

3. And then *he keeps an uniform course*, for so he doth who walks on in a way. He makes not indentures* as he walks, but goes on steadily in an uniform course to a right end. So a just man, when he hath singled out the right way, he goes on in that steadily and uniformly.

4. And likewise where it is said, the just walks in them, it implies *resolution to go on in those ways* till he come to the end, though there be never so much opposition.

But how shall we know whether we go on in this way or not?

First, he that goes on in a way, the further he hath proceeded therein, looking back, *that which he leaves behind seems lesser and lesser in his eye;* and that which he goes to greater and greater. So a man may know his progress in the ways of God, when earthly profits and pleasures seem little, his former courses and pleasures seeming now base unto him. When heaven and heavenly things seem near unto him, it is a sign he is near heaven, near in time, and nearer in disposition and in wisdom to discern, because the best things are greatest in his eye and esteem. In this case, it is a sign that such a one is removed from the world, and is near unto heaven, having made a good progress in the ways of God.

It implies likewise in the *second* place, *an uniform course of life.* Such a one doth not duties by starts now and then, but constantly. Therefore we must judge of men by a tenure of life, what their constant ways are. Sometimes though they be good men, they may step away into an ill way, and yet come in again. Sometimes an ill man may cross a good way, as a thief when he crosseth the highway, or a good man steps out of the way; but this is not their way, they are both out, and to seek, of their way. A wicked man when he speaks of good things, he is out of his way; he acts a part and assumes a person he is unskilful to act; therefore he doth it untowardly. But a man's way is his course. A good man's way is good, though his startings be ill; and an ill man's way is naught, though for passion, or for by-ends, he may now and then do good things. Therefore, considering

* That is, 'zig-zags.'—ED.

that the walking in the ways of God is uniform and orderly; let us judge of ourselves by the tenure of our life, and course thereof. And let those poor souls who think they are out of the way, because they run into some infirmities now and then, comfort themselves in this, that God judgeth not by single actions, but according to the tenure of a man's life, what he is. For oftentimes God's children gain by their slips, which makes them look the more warily to their ways for ever after that. He that walks in the way to heaven, if he be a good man, he looks to make surer footing in the ways of God after his slips and falls. He labours also to make so much the more haste home, being a gainer by all his slips and falls. Let none therefore be discouraged, but let them labour that their ways and courses may be good, and not only so, but to be uniform, orderly, and constant, and then they may speak peace to their own souls, being such as are here described, 'The just shall walk in them.'

Third, again, he that will walk aright in God's ways, he must be *resolute against all opposition whatsoever*, for we meet with many lets, hindrances, and scandals,* to drive us out of the way. Sometimes the ill lives of those who walk in these ways, sometimes their slips and falls, sometimes persecution, and our own natures, are full of scandals, subject to take this and that offence, and then we are ready to be snared on the right hand, or feared and scared on the left. And our nature, so far as it is unsanctified, is prone to catch, and ready to join with the world; therefore we have need of resolution of spirit and determination. As David, 'I have determined, O Lord, and I will keep thy laws; I have sworn that I will keep thy righteous judgments,' Ps. cxix. 106. This is a resolute determination.

Fourth, and then again, pray to God with David that he *would direct our ways*. 'Oh, that my ways were so directed to keep thy laws!' Ps. cxix. 3. I see that my nature is ready to draw me away to evil, and perverse crooked courses. I see, though I determine to take a good course, that there is much opposition; therefore, good Lord, direct me in my course, direct thou my thoughts, words, and carriage. Therefore, that we may walk stedfastly, let us resolve with settled determination, praying to God for strength; otherwise resolution, with dependence on our own power, may be a work of the flesh. But resolve thus, these are right ways and straight, they lead to heaven, happiness, and glory; therefore I will walk in them, whatsoever come of it. We have all the discouragement which may hinder us in the ways of God. For as we are travellers, so we are soldiers, warfaring men that meet with many rubs, thorns. Therefore to walk amidst such dangerous ways we must be well shod with the preparation of the gospel of peace, that is, patience, and reasons taken from thence. God hath provided spiritual armour in the word against all oppositions that meet with us, so that by resolution and prayer to him, using his means, we may go through all.

Now for a further help for us to walk constantly and resolutely in the ways of God.

1. Take first *the help of good company*. If we see any man to walk in a good way, let him not walk alone, but let us join ourselves with those that walk in God's ways; for why doth God leave us not only his word to direct us which way to go, but likewise examples in all times, but that we should follow those examples? which are like the pillar of fire which went before Israel unto Canaan. We have a cloud and a pillar of examples before us, (unto which he alludes, Heb. xii. 1), to lead us unto heaven, not only the word, but examples in all times. 'Walk, as you have us, for an example, Philip.

* That is, 'stumbling-blocks.'—G.

iii. 17, saith Paul. Therefore it is a character of a gracious disposition to join with the just, and those who walk in the ways of God. We see there is in all the creatures an instinct to keep company with their own kind; as we see in doves, sheep, geese, and the like. So it comes from a supernatural gracious instinct of grace, for the good to walk and company with the good, helping them on in the way to heaven. It is therefore a point of special wisdom to single out those for our company, who are able to help us thither, as it is for travellers to choose their company to travel with.

2. Again, if we would walk aright in the ways of God, *let us have our end in our eye, like unto the traveller.* Look on heaven, the day of judgment, those times either of eternal happiness or misery, which we must all come to. The having of these in our eye, will stern* the whole course of our life; for the end infuseth vigour in our carriages, and puts a great deal of life in the use of the means, breeding a love of them, though they be harsh. Therefore we must pray and labour for patience, to conflict with our own corruptions, and those of the times we live in. This is unpleasant to do; but when a man hath his aim and end in his eye, this inspires such vigour and strength in a man, that it makes him use means and courses contrary to his own natural disposition, offering a holy violence unto himself. As thus, it is not absolutely necessary that I should have this or that, or have them all, or in such and such a measure; but it is absolutely necessary that I should be saved, and not damned; therefore this course I will take, in these ways I will and must walk which lead to salvation. Let us therefore with Moses have in our eye, 'the recompence of the reward,' Heb. xi. 26; and with our blessed Saviour, the head of the faithful, have before our eyes 'the joy that was set before him,' which will make us pass by all those heavy things that he passed through. Let us with the holy men of ancient time, have 'the prize of that high calling' in our eye, to make us, notwithstanding all opposition, press forward towards the mark.

3. And then again, because it is said indefinitely here, 'They shall walk in these ways,' remember always *to take wisdom and prudence along with you in all your walkings.* It is put indefinitely, because we should leave out none. For, as we say in things that are to be believed, Faith chooseth not this object, and not another; so obedience chooseth not this object; I will obey God in this, and not in this, but it goes on in all God's ways. Therefore, if we would walk on aright in God's ways, there must be consideration of all the relations as we stand to God. *First, what duties we owe to God in heavenly things,* to please him above all, whomsoever we displease, and to seek the kingdom of heaven and his righteousness before all, that all things may follow which are needful for us, Mat. vi. 33. So, in the *next* place, when we look to ourselves, to know *those ways which are required of us in regard of ourselves;* for every Christian is a temple wherein God dwells; therefore we are to carry ourselves holily, to be much in prayer and communion with God in secret. A man is best distinguished to be a good walker by those secret ways betwixt God and his soul, those walks of meditation and prayer wherein there is much sweet intercourse betwixt God and the soul. Therefore, in this case a man makes conscience of his communion with God in his thoughts, desires, affections, using all good means appointed of God to maintain this communion.

4. Then we should look to our own carriage in the use of the creatures, *to carry ourselves in all things indifferently,* because wisdom and prudence is seen in those things especially, to use things indifferent, indifferently;

* That is, 'steer, guide, regulate.'—G.

not to be much in the use of the world, in joy or sorrow, but in moderation to use these things, being sure to set our affections upon the main.

5. And so in things indifferent, not to do them *with offence and excess;* but to see and observe the rule in all things of indifferency.

6. And for our carriage to others in those ways, let us consider what we owe *to those above us*, what respect is due to governors, and what to others; what to those who are without; what to those who are weak. We owe an example of holy life unto them, that we give no occasion of scandal; and also to walk wisely towards them that are without, that we give no occasion for the ways of God to be ill spoken of.

7. And for all conditions which God shall cast us into, remember *that those be ways which we should walk seemly in.* If prosperity, let us take heed of the sins of prosperity, pride, insolency, security, hardness of heart, and the like. If adversity, then let us practise the graces thereof, take heed of murmuring and repining, dejection of spirit, despair, and the like. This is to walk like a wise man in all conditions, in those relations he stands in.

8. *For our words likewise and expressions to others,* in that kind of our walking, that they may be savoury and to purpose, that we labour to speak by rule, seeing we must give an account of every 'idle word' at the day of judgment, Mat. xii. 36. So that in all our labours, carriage, and speech, we must labour to do all wisely and justly. These are the ways of God, and 'the just shall walk in them.'

Negatively, what we must avoid in all our walking.

Remember in general, we must never do anything against religion, against conscience, against a man's particular place and calling, or against justice. Let us not touch upon the breach of any good thing, especially of religion and conscience. Thus a man shall walk in the ways of God, if with wisdom and prudence he consider what ways are before him to God, to himself, to others; in all conditions and states of life, to see what he must, and what he must not do, and then to walk in them answerably.

For our encouragement to walk in God's ways in our general and particular callings.

1. Know first, *they are the most safe ways of all.* Whatsoever trouble or affliction we meet withal, it is no matter, it will prove the safest way in the end. For as it was with the cloud which went before God's people, it was both for direction and protection; so the Spirit of God, and the ways of God, as they serve for direction, so they serve for protection. God will direct and protect us if we walk in his ways. Let him be our director, and he will be our preserver and protector in all times.

2. Again, they are *the most pleasant ways of all.* All wisdom's ways are paved with prosperity and pleasure; for when God doth enlarge and sanctify the soul to walk in them, he giveth withal a royal gift, inward peace of conscience, and joy unspeakable and glorious, with an enlarged spirit. God meets his children in his own ways; they are therefore to walk there. Let a man start out of God's ways, he meets with the devil, with the devil's instruments, and many snares. But in God's ways he shall be sure to meet with God, if he walk in them with humility and respect to God, looking up for direction and strength, and denying his own wisdom. In this case a man shall be sure to have God go along with him in all his ways. In God's ways expect God's company. Therefore they are the safest and the most pleasant ways.

3. And they are the *cleanest and holiest ways of all;* having this excellent property in them, that as they lead to comfort, so they end in comfort;

they all end in heaven, Ps. xix. 9. Therefore let us not be weary of God's ways, of Christianity and our particular callings; wherein what we do, let us do as God's ways, having sanctified them by prayer, and do it in obedience to God. They are God's ways when they are sanctified. God hath set me in this standing, I expect his blessing therein, and what blessing I find, I will give him the praise. God hath appointed that in serving man I serve him; therefore we must go on in our particular ways, as the ways of God, doing everything as the work of God, and we shall find them the comfortablest and pleasantest ways which end in joy, happiness, and glory.

Use 1. The use hereof may be first reprehension unto those *who can talk but not walk,* that have tongues but not feet, to wit, affections; that come by starts into the narrow way; but yet be never well till they turn back again into the world, that broad way which leads unto destruction.

Use 2. Secondly, it is for instruction, *to stir us up to walk in God's ways;* as Ps. i. 1, 2, 'Blessed is the man that walketh not in the counsel of the ungodly, &c. But his delight is in the law of the Lord, and in that law doth he meditate day and night.'

Use 3. Thirdly, this is for consolation; if this be our walk, *then God will walk with us, and the angels of God shall have charge of us to keep us in all our ways,* Ps. xxxiv. 7; and though, like David, we slip out of the way, yet this not being our walk, we come to the way again. Though God's children miss of their way, yet their resolution, choice, and endeavour was to walk in the way; therefore such are still in a blessed estate, and keep their communion with God. A man is not said to alter his way till he alter his choice and resolution. The best man may have an ill passion, and miss the way, but he will not turn from it willingly. And the worst man may have a good passion, and come into the way, but never continue in it to make this walk.* From all which it appeareth that they are only righteous persons who continue to walk in the ways of God. It is therefore consolation unto them who take that course. Though all the world go another way, yet they must imitate just men. And for us, we must imitate these just men, though they be never so few in the world and despised. If we would be counted the servants of God, we must imitate those that walk in those paths.

II. Now it is said that the other sort, wicked men, the ways of God shall have quite a contrary course in them.

'But the transgressors shall fall therein.'

As one and the selfsame cloud was both light to the Israelites and darkness unto the Egyptians, Exod. xiv. 20; so the same ways of God prove both light and darkness, life and death, to the godly and wicked. As the apostle speaks, unto 'the one they are the savour of life unto life, and unto the other the savour of death unto death,' 2 Cor. ii. 16. Therefore now here is the conclusion of all. If no warning will serve the turn of all what hath been given and said, yet the word of God shall not return empty, it shall effect that for which it was sent, Isa. lv. 11; one work or other it will do, even upon the most perverse.

'The transgressors shall fall therein.'

Obs. Whence we see and may observe, *that the same word which is a word of life and salvation to the godly, is an occasion of sin and perdition unto the wicked.* The same sun which makes flowers and herbs to smell sweet, makes carrions to smell worse. The same word which made the apostles believe and confess Christ, did also make many others of his disciples go

* Qu. 'to make it his walk?'—G.

back from him, saying, 'This is a hard saying, who can bear it?' John xiii. 60. So, Acts xiii. 48, the same word which made the unbelieving Jews blaspheme, did make 'as many as did belong unto eternal life believe.' And when Christ preached, many blasphemed, and said he had a devil; others trusted and defended him. So saith Paul, the same word to some is, 'the savour of death unto death, and to some the savour of life unto life,' 2 Cor. ii. 16; and so in another place he speaks of the same word, 'But we preach Christ crucified, unto the Jews a stumblingblock, and unto the Greeks foolishness; but unto them which are called, both Jews and Greeks, Christ the power of God, and the wisdom of God,' 1 Cor. i. 23, 24. To this purpose, Peter speaks of Christ, 'Unto you therefore who believe, he is precious; but unto them which are disobedient, &c., a stone of stumbling, and a rock of offence, even unto them who stumble at the word, being disobedient, whereunto also they were appointed,' 1 Pet. ii. 7, 8. The reasons are,

Reason 1. Because 'The natural man perceiveth not the things of the Spirit of God: for they are foolishness unto him; neither can he know them, because they are spiritually discerned; but he that is spiritual judgeth all things,' &c., 1 Cor. ii. 14.

Secondly, 'Because they who do evil hate the light,' John iii. 19, and therefore, cannot love what they hate. 'This,' Christ saith, 'is the condemnation, that light is come into the world, and men loved darkness better than light, because their deeds were evil.'

Thirdly, Because they are blinded, 2 Cor. iv. 4; therefore they are led away by the god of this world, Satan, so that they cannot perceive anything that is spiritual, for God hath not given them a heart to perceive, &c., Deut. xxix. 4.

Fourthly, Because they want faith, which is called 'the faith of God's elect,' Tit. i. 1; and we know, 'without faith it is impossible to please God,' Heb. xi. 6; for it is said that 'the word profited not those unbelieving Jews, because it was not mingled with faith in those who heard it,' Heb. iv. 2.

Fifthly, Because the word is like the sun, which causeth plants to smell sweet, and a dunghill to smell stinking. So it works grace in some, and extracts the sin and foul vapours out of others.

Use 1. The use is, first, reproof unto them who *stumble at the wholesome doctrines of the word;* of election, reprobation, predestination, and the like. Such indeed stumble at Christ himself. He is a stumblingblock unto them, as Peter speaketh, 1 Pet. ii. 8. They stumble at Christ who stumble at his word.

Use 2. Secondly, *not to love the word the worse, because evil men be made the worse by it;* which shews rather the mighty power of the word which discovereth them, and will not let them be hid, unmasking hypocrites to themselves and others. As we must not like the sun the worse, because it makes carrion smell; nor the fan, because it winnoweth away the chaff; so must we not fall out with the word, because it hath these effects upon wicked men.

Use 3. Lastly, it is for consolation unto them that, when their sin is reproved, *fall not out with the word, but with their sin.* When they are excited to duty, they hate their corruption, and do endeavour to walk honestly without reproof. This shews the word is not the savour of death unto death to them, but the savour of life unto life; which St Paul makes a sign of election, 'When they receive the word of God, as the word of God, with thanksgiving,' 1 Thes. ii. 13. This indeed is a matter of praise, to give God thanks for his good word, which saves our souls, and comforts us here in the way of all our pilgrimage, till we arrive at heavenly glory.

For conclusion of all, what then remaineth on our part to be done? Surely, to hearken no more to flesh and blood, to the world or the devil; but to hear what God saith in his most holy word, Ps. xxxii. 10, and to frame our hearts with a strong resolution to this '*returning*,' here exhorted to. Oh, if we knew the many miseries and sorrows which attendeth wretched and miserable sinners, and sinful courses here and hereafter, it would be our first work to follow God's counsel to his people; to return from our sinful ways; to meet so gracious and merciful a God; that he may, as his promise is, 'heal our backslidings,' and be 'as the dew unto us,' to make us fruitful and abundant in every good and perfect work.

What can be said more for our encouragement than that which hath been delivered in this chapter? God, the party offended, who is Jehovah, God all-sufficient, exhorts us to return unto him, who is able and willing to help. And he also, out of his rich goodness, forewarneth us of the dangerous estate a sinner is in; who, being 'fallen by his iniquity,' ought therefore to pity himself. Return and not run on in a further course of disobedience and backsliding. And words are put in our mouths, dictated by God himself, which needs must be very prevailing with him. What an encouragement is this! Yea further, as we have heard, these petitions are all answered graciously and abundantly, above all they did ask; wherein God surmounteth our desires and thoughts, as we heard at large. Whereby we also may be confident to have our petitions and suits in like sort granted; if we go unto God with his own words and form prescribed. If we 'take with us words' of prayer, we shall be sure to vanquish all our spiritual enemies; for faithful prayer works wonders in heaven and earth, James v. 17. And that God doth not bid us be religious to our loss, he sheweth that we shall lose nothing by following his counsel, and walking in a religious course of life; having abominated our idols, 'He will observe us, and see us,' and be a shelter unto us, having a derivation of fruitfulness from his fulness. 'In me is thy fruit found.'

Lastly, we have heard who can make right use of these things delivered. Only 'the wise and prudent;' such only can understand heavenly things to purpose. 'His secret is with them that fear him,' Psa. xxv. 14; and 'wisdom is only justified of her children,' Mat. xi. 19. When others have no heart given them to perceive God's ways aright, as Moses speaketh, 'transgressors' fall in God's 'right ways,' whilst the just walk comfortably in them. O then let us hate sin every day more and more, and be in love with religion and the ways of God; for that is the true good, which is the everlasting good, that better Mary's part, which shall never be taken away, Luke x. 42. 'Whosoever drinks of this living water shall never thirst again,' John iv. 14. The best things of this world have but a shadow, not the substance of goodness. Let us then be wise for ourselves, and pity ourselves in time, 'whilst it is called to-day,' because, as our Saviour speaks, 'the night approacheth, wherein no man can work,' John ix. 4. O then let us often examine our hearts and covenant with them, let us see our sins as they are, and God's goodness as it is; that our 'scarlet sins' may be done away as a mist from before him, Isa. i. 18. O banish away our atheism, which, by our sinful conversation, proclaimeth us to be of the number of those fools, who have said in their heart that there is no God, Psa. xiv. 1. This serious consideration always makes first a stop, and then a returning; to believe indeed that there is a God who made the world, and a judgment to come. This, God by Moses, calleth true wisdom indeed, 'To remember our latter end.' 'Oh,' saith he, 'that they were wise, that they would think of these things,' Deut. xxxii. 29. Of which things? The miseries which attend sin here and hereafter; and the blessings and comforts which follow a godly life both here and hereafter, 'That they would remember their latter end,' the neglect whereof, Jeremiah sheweth, was the cause 'that they came down wonderfully, and had no comforter, because they remembered not their latter end.'*

Therefore, let us study this point well, that there is a God, and a judgment to come; and this will compel us, even out of self-love, to return from our sinful courses, and make a stop. By this means, we shall not need a Philip's boy (*z*) to cry to us every day, we are mortal and must die; if our meditations once a day be both in heaven and hell. These strong considerations (aided with strong rational reflectings on ourselves) will keep us within compass, overawe us, and make us quake and tremble to go on in sin; which is worse than the devil in this, that thereby he became a devil. This will drive us to fly unto God, that he may 'heal our backslidings,' who is described 'with healing under his wings,' Mal. iv. 2; who, in the days of his flesh, healed all miserable and 'returning backsliders,' who ever came unto him. Therefore, let us lay to heart these things, that so we may be kept in soul and body, pure and unspotted, holy and without blame in his sight, until the day of redemption, 'When our mortality shall put on immortality, and our corruptible incorruption, to reign with God for ever and ever,' 1 Cor. xv. 54, *seq*.

* Qu. Isaiah? and the reference, xlvii. 7.—G.

NOTES.

(*a*) P. 256.—'Return,' &c. It is very emphatical and significant in the original. Cf. Ackerman (*Prophetæ Minores*. . . . . Vienna, 1830); and Henderson (8vo, 1845), the latter especially, confirmatory of Sibbes.

(*b*) P. 286.—'It was well done by Luther, who, in a Catechism,' &c. See his '*Catechesis*' in Opera, *in loc.*

(*c*) P. 287.—'We have some bitter spirits (Lutherans they call them . . . . therefore to be in the sacrament).' The reference is to the well-known dogma of *consubstantiation* as contrasted with, and even opposed to, the papists' *transubstantiation*. Both are explained in the following sentence from Barrow (Serm. 31, Vol. II.): 'It may serve to guard us from divers errours, such as are that of the Lutheran *consubstantialists*, and of the Roman *transubstantiators*, who affirm that the body of our Lord is here upon earth at once present in many places (namely), in every place where the host is kept, or the eucharist is celebrated.' Cf. Richardson, *sub voce*.

(*d*) P. 296.—'It was well spoken by Lactantius,' &c. The thought is found several times in his *De Divino Præmio* and *De Opificio Dei* and *De Falsa Religione*. Cf. Edition by Aldus, 1515, pp.240, 304, and 1, *seq*.

(*e*) P. 297.—'As the Jews call them, he hath hedges of the commandments.' Consult Kalisch ('Historical and Critical Commentary on the Old Testament . . . Exodus [8vo, 1855]); on Exodus xxiii. 19; and Maurer there; and on Deuteronomy xxii. 6.' For Rabbinical and other lore on the subject, Works of John Gregory, 4to, 1665, pp. 90–98.

(*f*) P. 303.—'And so we might go on in other resemblances.' To all wishing to see the analogy carried out with wealth of quaint thought and illustration, we would commend the 'Soul's Sickness' of Thomas Adams (Works, Vol. I., pp. 471–506); also, as not at all inferior, and indeed abounding in even more recondite lore and unexpected flashes of wit, Bishop Gr. Williams, 'Of the Misery of Man,' in his 'Seven Golden Candlesticks.' (Folio, 1635, pp. 565–661.)

(*g*) P. 337.—'As we see now in these wars of Germany.' Cf. Memoir, Vol. I., pp. lvii.–viii. The 'now' from 1620–21, onwards.

(*h*) P. 347.—'Man is, as it were, a sum of all the excellencies of the creatures; a little world indeed.' This idea will be found worked out in quaint fashion by Bishop Earle, in his 'Micro-cosmography,' and by Capt. T. Butler, in his 'Little Bible of Man.' 1649.

(*i*) P. 349.—'The word in the original is a "standard-bearer,"' Titus iii. 8. . . . Cf. Ellicott, *in loc.*, together with extracts and illustrations given in Kypke, Observ. ii. 381; Loesner, Obs. p. 430. The word is προϊστημι. The noun, προστάτης = a leader, champion. Wycliffe renders it 'Be bisie to be abouen other in good werkis' (Hexapla . . . . Bagster); and, perhaps, 'standard-bearer' catches the idea, if it departs from the exact wording.

(*j*) P. 350.—'The fragrancy of the smell is smelt of passengers as they sail along the coast.' One of Richard Sibbes's hearers, John Milton (see our Memoir, Vol. I., p. liii.), has finely put this:—

' . . . . As when to them who sail
Beyond the Cape of Hope, and now are past
Mozambique, off at sea north-east winds blow
Sabean odours from the spicy shore
Of Araby the blest.'—*Paradise Lost*, B. IV., 159–163.

(*k*) P. 351.—'The church of God riseth out of the ashes of the martyrs, which hitherto smells sweet, and puts life in those who come after, so precious are they both dead and alive.' The sentiment is preserved by the poet, concerning the 'actions of the just,' in the familiar lines:—

' . . . . The actions of the just
Smell sweet and blossom in the dust.'
(*James Shirley*, 'Death's Final Conquest').

Shirley was a 'student' of Catharine College, Cambridge.

(*l*) P. 355.—'Monica, St Austin's mother, ... he was converted *after* her death.' &c. This is a somewhat singular blunder on the part of Sibbes. Augustine was 'converted' *before* his mother's death, as the touching narrative in the 'Confessions' has made immortal. Cf. B. VIII., 30; B. IX., 17, *et alibi.*

(*m*) P. 370.—'Calvin and Luther . . . . burn their bones,' &c. If this does not apply literally to Calvin and Luther, it yet holds good of many like-minded. Every one remembers what was done to Wycliffe's 'bones,' and also Fuller's characteristic conceits upon the scattered ashes, to which none will refuse Dr Vaughan's approving 'Well-spoken—Honest one!' Cf. Vaughan's John de Wycliffe, D.D., a monograph (4to. 1853), pp. 521, *seq.* To Wycliffe may be added Bucer, concerning the 'burning of whose bones I take the following verses from Faithful Teat's rare 'Ter Tria' (18mo. 1669, 2d edition, pp. 142, 143).

'What though revengeful papists burne
Dear Bucer's bones? still hope's his urne,
Till's ashes to a phœnix turne,
And live afresh.' (From 'Hope.')

(*n*) P. 377.—'The abominable distinctions of the papists of *Latria* and *Dulia.*' That is, λατρεία and δουλεία, commonplaces in the popish controversy. Cf. Faber, 'Difficulties of Romanism,' and almost any of the standard treatises *pro* and *con.*

(*o*) P. 378.—'Calleth them dunghill-gods, and Abel, as it is in this book, vanity,' &c. The allusion of Sibbes in the former is perhaps to Beelzebub, worshipped by the Philistines of Ekron = the fly-god, *i. e.*, dunghill-bred fly. 'Abel' means 'vanity,' and the reference is not to Abel—the proper name of Adam's second-born son—but to Hosea xii. 11.

(*p*) P. 379.—'Coster himself, a forward Jesuit.' That is, John Costerus or Costerius in his 'Comment . . . . pro Catholicæ Fidei Antiquitate et Veritate,' (Paris, 1569).

(*q*) P. 379.—'Late worthies of our church.' The following are the principal works on the popish controversy, by the eminent writers enumerated:—

1. Bishop Jewel.—(1.) 'Apologia Ecclesiæ Anglicanæ,' 1562. (2.) 'An Apology for Private Mass; with a learned annswere to it by Bishop Jewell,' 1562. (3.) Various 'Answers' to Hardinge and others.

2. John Rainolds, D.D.—'The summe of the Conference betweene John Rainoldes and John Hart, touching the Head and Faith of the Church,' &c., &c., 1584, and various editions.

3. William Fulke.—Very many works. For list, consult Watt's Bibl. Brit. *sub nomine.*

4. Dr William Whitaker.—Cf. our Memoir of Sibbes, pp. lxxxi–ii.

5. Andrew Willet.—His great work is his 'Synopsis Papismi,' 1600; but he is author of other masterly, if somewhat vehement, treatises on the controversy. Consult Watt *sub nomine.*

6. William Perkins.—His 'Works' abound in confutations of popish errors, written with great intensity. He has one special treatise of rare merit, 'The Reformed Catholike; or a Declaration shewing how neere we may come to the present Church of Rome in sundrie points of Religion; and wherein we must for ever depart from them.' (Cambridge, 1597.)

(*r*) P. 380.—'To say we worship not the image but God . . . so we may see in Arnobius.' Arnobius here referred to was one of the apologists of Christianity in the African church during the third century. His 'Disputationum Adversus Gentes Libri' (ex Editione Fausti Sabæi, Rome, 1542), remains a still vital book. It has passed through many editions. Again and again the question of image-worship comes up in it.

(*s*) P. 381.—'Rome to be Babylon.' Cf. Canon Wordsworth's conclusive little work, 'Babylon; or the question considered, "Is the Church of Rome the Babylon of the Apocalypse?"' 12mo.

(*t*) P. 381.—'Hedges of the commandments.' Cf. note *e*.

(*u*) P. 383. 'As a great man-pleaser,' &c. Sibbes places in his margin, 'A Scottish Regent, before his execution.' This must refer to the Earl of Morton, Regent of Scotland, beheaded in 1581, on a very doubtful charge of treason. It is difficult to explain Sibbes's use of 'man-pleaser,' in relation to Knox's illustrious friend. But 'man-pleaser' was a favourite term of reproach with the Puritans, which John Squier, in his extraordinary introduction to his sermon from Luke xviii. 13, thus sarcastically notices, 'If my text should lead me to avouch the dignity and authority of the superiours in our clergy, I should not escape that brand, behold a time-servant and a *man-pleaser*' (4to, 1637, page 2). Better example far he might have taken from his contemporary, Shakespeare. I refer to the famous saying of Wolsey, (Henry VIII. iii. 2)—

'. . . . . O Cromwell, Cromwell!
Had I but serv'd my God with half the zeal
I serv'd my king, he would not, in mine age,
Have left me naked to mine enemies.'

(*v*) P. 383.—'Were made gods . . . came . . . to fearful ends.' This holds of nearly all the Cæsars. For ample proof, consult Smith's Dictionary of Greek and Roman Biography and Mythology, under the respective emperors, especially Caligula and Nero.

(*w*) P. 392.—'"I have seen and observed him," some read the words, but very few.' Cf. authorities cited in note *a*.

(*x*) P. 393.—'The same day was that noble victory and conquest in the north parts over the enemies.' The allusion is to the Battle of Pinkie, on September 10. 1547, between the English, under the Earl of Hertford, Protector. and the Scotch, when the latter were totally defeated. It was one of the most decisive victories, with least loss to the conquerors, of any in history. There fell scarcely two hundred of the English; while, according to the lowest computation, above ten thousand Scots perished, besides fifteen hundred taken prisoners. 1547 (and according to Sibbes, 10th September) is usually reckoned as the 'completion' of the English Reformation, although the reformed religion was not established until the accession of Elizabeth, in 1558.

(*y*) P. 415.—'Simile mater erroris.' This is a principle which is very often stated, in various forms, in the writings of Bacon.

(*z*) P. 433.—'We shall not need a Philip's boy.' The allusion is to the (I suppose), apocryphal story of Philippus II., father of Alexander the Great, having a boy appointed for the purpose of reminding him, by a daily repetition of it, of his 'mortality.' So sensual and volatile a nature was very unlikely to do so wise a thing.

G.

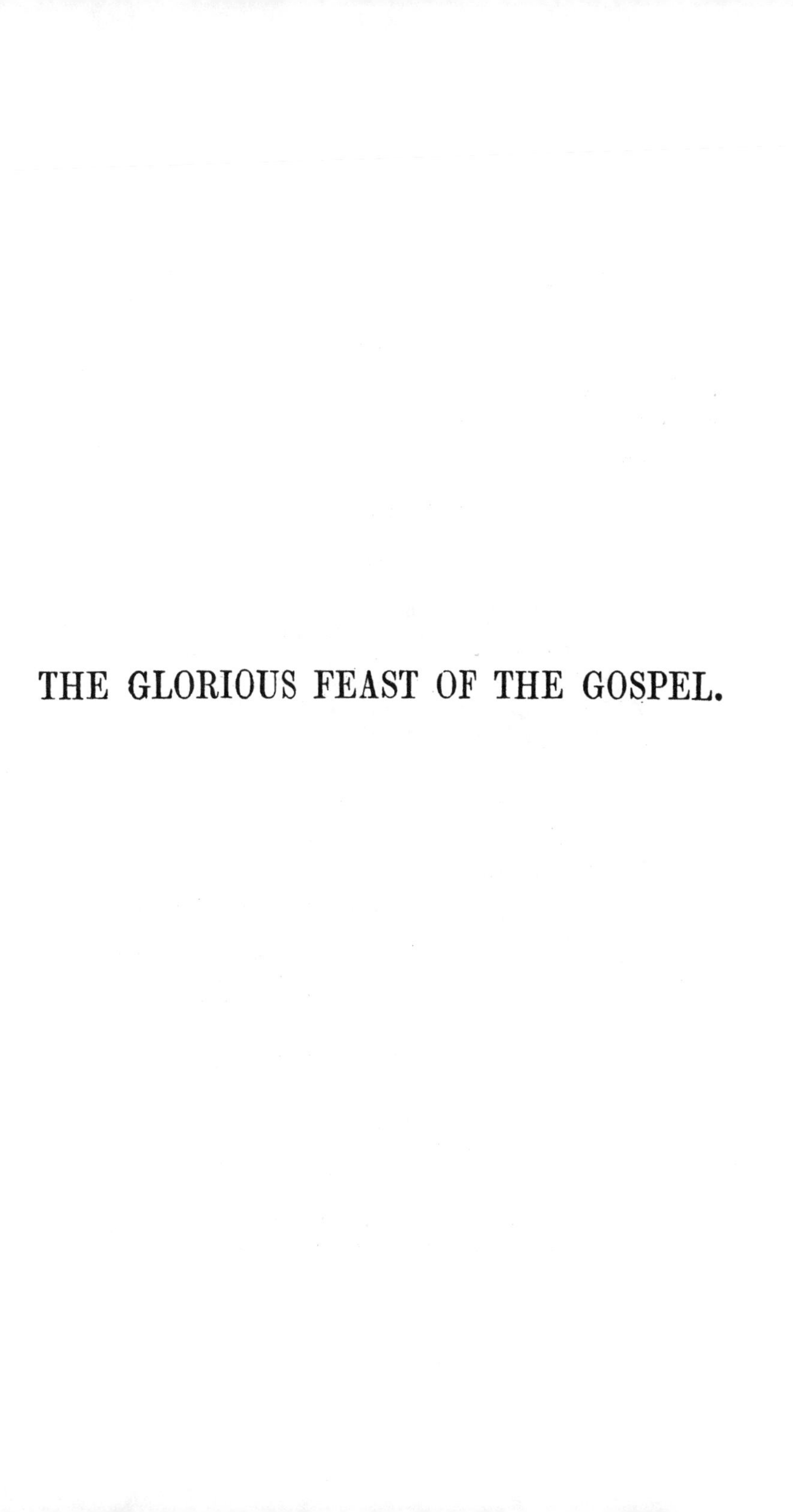

THE GLORIOUS FEAST OF THE GOSPEL.

THE GLORIOUS FEAST OF THE GOSPEL.

NOTE.

'The Glorious Feast' was published in a thin quarto in 1650. The title-page is given below.* For various mistakes in the pagination of the original edition, consult bibliographical 'List' in our last volume. G.

* Title-page :—

THE
GLORIOVS FEAST
OF THE
GOSPEL.
OR,
Christ's gracious Invitation and royall
Entertainment of Believers.
Wherein amongst other things these comfortable
Doctrines are spiritually handled:

Viz
1. *The Marriage Feast between Christ and his Church.*
2. *The vaile of Ignorance and Vnbeliefe removed.*
3. *Christ's Conquest over death.*
4. *The wiping away of teares from the faces of God's people.*
5. *The taking away of their Reproaches.*
6. *The precious Promises of God, and their certaine performance.*
7. *The Divine Authority of the Holy Scriptures.*
8. *The Duty and comfort of waiting upon God.*

Delivered in divers Sermons upon *Isai.* 25 Chap. 6, 7, 8, 9 Verses,
BY
The late Reverend, Learned and faithfull Minister of the Gospell,
RICHARD SIBBS, D.D. Master of *Katharine-*
Hall in *Cambridge*, and Preacher at Grayes-Inne, *London.*

Prov. 9. 1, 2, 3, 4, 5.

Wisdome hath builded her house; she hath hewen out her seven Pillars.
She hath killed her beasts; she hath mingled her wine; she hath also furnished her Table.
She hath sent forth her Maidens; she cries, &c.
who so is simple let him turne in hither, &c.
Come eate of my bread, and drink of my wine that I have mingled, &c.

Perused by those that were intrusted to revise his Writings.

London, Printed for *John Rothwell* at the Sun and Fountaine in *Pauls*
Church yard, neare the little North-doore. 1650.

TO THE READER.

So much of late hath been written about the times, that spiritual discourses are now almost out of season. Men's minds are so hurried up and down, that it is to be feared they are much discomposed to think seriously as they ought, of their eternal concernments. Alas! Christians have lost much of their communion with Christ and his saints—the heaven upon earth—whilst they have wofully disputed away and dispirited the life of religion and the power of godliness, into dry and sapless controversies about government of church and state. To recover therefore thy spiritual relish of savoury practical truths, these sermons of that excellent man of God, of precious memory, are published. Wherein thou art presented.

I. *With an invitation to a great and wonderful feast, the marriage feast of the Lamb.* An admirable feast indeed; wherein Jesus Christ, the eternal Son of God, is the bridegroom, where every believer that hath 'put on' the Lord Jesus, Rom. xiii. 14, 'the wedding garment,' Mat. xxii. 11, is not only the guest, but the spouse of Christ, and the bride at this wedding supper. Here Jesus Christ is the master of the feast, and the cheer and provision too. He is the 'Lamb of God,' John i. 29, the 'ram caught in the thicket,' Gen. xxii. 13. He is the 'fatted calf,' Luke. xv. 23. When he was sacrificed, 'wisdom killed her beasts,' Prov. ix. 2. At his death, 'the oxen andf atlings were killed,' Mat. xxii. 4. 'Αληθῶς βϱῶσις καὶ ἀληθῶς πόσις. His 'flesh is meat indeed, and his blood is drink indeed,' John vi. 55. And that thou mayest be fully delighted at this feast, Christ is the 'rose of Sharon,' the 'lily of the valley,' Cant. ii. 1. He is a 'bundle of myrrh,' Cant. i. 13, a 'cluster of camphire,' Cant. i. 14; his name is 'an ointment poured out,' Cant. i. 3, and 'his love is better than wine,' Cant. i. 2. In Christ are 'all things ready,' Mat. xxii. 4, for 'Christ is all in all,' Col. iii. 11. And great is the feast that Christ makes for believers, for it is the marriage feast which the great King 'makes for his Son,' Mat. xxii. 2; the great design and aim of the gospel being to exalt the Lord Jesus Christ, and give 'him a name above every name,' Philip. ii. 10. Great is the company that are bid, Luke xiv. 16, Jews and Gentiles. God keeps open house, 'Ho, every one that thirsteth, come,' Isa lv. 1, and 'whosoever will, let him come, and freely take of the water of life,' Rev. xxii. 17. Great is the cheer that is provided. Every guest here hath Asher's portion, 'royal dainties and bread of fatness,' Gen. xlix 20. Here is all excellent best wine, 'wine upon the lees well refined,' Isa. xxv. 6. Here is 'fat things,' yea, 'fat things full of marrow,' Rev. ii. 17, the 'water of life,' Rev. xxii. 17, and the fruit of 'the tree of life which is in the midst of the paradise of God,' Gen. ii. 9. All that is at this feast is of the best, yea, the best of the best.

Here is variety and plenty too. Here is 'bread enough and to spare.' Caligula and Heliogabalus their feasts, who ransacked the earth, air, and sea to furnish their tables, were nothing to this. And above all, here is welcome for every hungry, thirsty soul. *Super omnia vultus accessere boni.* He that bids thee come, will bid thee welcome. He will not say eat when his heart is not with thee. The invitation is free, the preparation great, and the entertainment at this feast—suiting the magnificence of the great King—is full and bountiful. All which is at large treated of in these excellent sermons, which are therefore deservedly entitled, 'The marriage Feast between Christ and his Church.' We read of a philosopher that, having prepared an excellent treatise of happiness, and presenting it unto a great king, the king answered him, 'Keep your book to yourself, I am not now at leisure,' (*a*). Here is an excellent treasure put into thy hand; do not answer us, I am not now at leisure. Oh, do not let Christ stand 'knocking at thy heart, who will come and sup with thee,' Rev. iii. 20, and bring his cheer with him. Oh, let not a 'deceived heart turn thee any longer aside to feed upon ashes,' Isa. xliv. 20; feed no longer with swine 'upon husks,' Luke xv. 16, while thou mayest be filled and satisfied 'with bread in thy father's house,' Luke xv. 17.

But this is not all; if thou wilt be pleased to peruse this book, thou wilt find there are many other useful, seasonable, and excellent subjects handled besides the marriage-feast.

II. Jesus Christ hath not only provided a feast, but because he is desirous that all those for whom it is provided should come to it (which only they do that believe), *he takes away the veil of ignorance and unbelief from off their hearts;* and here you shall find this skilful preacher hath excellently discoursed what this veil is, how it naturally lies upon all, and is only removed by the Spirit of Christ. And if the Lord hath 'destroyed this covering from off thy heart,' we doubt not, but the truth of this heavenly doctrine will shine comfortably into thy soul.

III. Jesus Christ, to make his bounty and mercy further appear in this feast, *he hath given his guests the 'bread of life,' and hath secured them from the fear of death.* They need not fear. There is no *mors in ollâ* at this feast. We may feast without fear. Jesus Christ by his 'tasting of death hath swallowed it up in victory,' 1 Cor. xv. 54. Christ doth not make his people such a feast as it is reported Dionysius the tyrant once made for his flatterer Damocles, who set him at a princely table, but hanged a drawn sword in a small thread over his head.* But Christ would have us triumph over the king of fears, who was slain by the death of Christ, and we thereby delivered from the bondage of the fear of death, Heb. ii. 14, 15.

At other feasts they were wont of old to have a death's head served in amongst other dishes, to mind them in the midst of all their mirth of their mortality (which practice of the heathens condemns the ranting jollity of some loose professors in these times). *Κατῆλθεν εἰς θάνατον ἀθάνάτος, καὶ τῷ θανάτῳ καθεῖλε θάνατον.* But here, Christ serves in death's head, as David 'the head of Goliah,' 1 Sam. xxxi. 9, the head of a slain and conquered death. Our Sampson by his own death 'hath destroyed death, and hath thereby ransomed us from the hand of the grave, and hath redeemed us from death,' Hos. xiii. 14, and the slavish fear of it. All which is at large handled in these following sermons for thy comfort and joy, that thou mayest triumph in his love, through whom thou art more than conqueror.

* For this well-known anecdote, consult Cicero (*Tusc.* v. 21.), and Horace (*Carm.* iii., l. 17).—G.

IV. Because 'it is a merry heart that makes a continual feast,' Prov. xv. 15, and that this feast might be a gaudy-day* indeed unto thy soul, Christ doth here promise, 'to wipe away all tears from off the faces of his people,' Isa. xxv. 8. The gospel hath comforts enough to make glad the hearts of the saints and people of God. The 'light of God's countenance' will refresh them with 'joy unspeakable and glorious,' 1 Pet. i. 8, in the midst 'of the valley of the shadow of death,' Psa. xxiii. 4. A truly godly person can weep for his sins, though the world smile never so much upon him; and though he be never so much afflicted in the world, yet he can and will 'rejoice in the God of his salvation,' Hab. iii. 18. In these sermons thou hast this gospel-promise sweetly opened and applied; wherein thou shalt find directions when, and for what, to mourn and weep, and the blessedness of all true mourners, 'whose sorrow shall be turned into joy,' John xvi. 20.

V. In these sermons you shall further find, *that though Jesus Christ respect his people highly, and entertain them bountifully, yet they have but coarse usage in the world, who* are wont to revile them as 'fools' and 'madmen,' as 'seditious rebels,' 'troublers of Israel,' 'proud and hypocritical persons.' But blessed are they that do not 'stumble at this stone of offence,' Rom. ix. 32, that wear the 'reproaches of Christ as their crown,' and by 'well-doing put to silence the ignorance of foolish men,' 1 Pet. ii. 15; for let the world load them with all their revilings, yet 'the spirit of glory rests upon them,' 2 Cor. xii. 9, and in due time he will roll away their reproach, 'and bring forth their judgment as the light, and their righteousness as the noon-day,' Ps. xxxvii. 6.

VI. And because a Christian here hath more in hope than in hand, more in reversion than in possession, 'walks by faith' rather than sense, and 'lives by the word of God, and not by bread alone,' Mat. iv. 4, thou shalt have here, Christian reader, a sweet discourse *of the precious promises of Christ* which he hath left us here to stay the stomach of the soul, till we come to that feast of feasts in heaven; that by this glimpse we might in part know the 'greatness of that glory which shall be revealed,' 1 Peter v. 1; that the first fruits might be a pawn of the harvest, and the 'earnest of the Spirit,' Ephes. i. 14, a pledge of that full reward we shall have in heaven, where we shall be brimful of those 'pleasures that are at God's right hand for ever,' Ps. xvi. 11. Christ hath given us promises to uphold our faith and hope, till faith be perfected in fruition, and hope end in vision, till Jesus Christ, who is here the object of our faith, be the reward of our faith for ever.

VII. Now because the comfort of the promises is grounded in the faithfulness of him that hath promised, this godly and learned man, hath strongly asserted *the divine authority of the holy Scriptures*, proving that they are *θεόπνευστοι*, that they are the very word of God, that they are *αὐτόπιστοι* and *ἀξόπιστοι*, worthy of all acceptation, and belief, for their own sakes; a truth very seasonable for these times, to antidote thee against the poisonfull errors of blasphemous anti-scripturists.

VIII. Lastly, because that God often takes a long day for performance of the promise, thou shalt find herein the doctrine *of waiting upon God*, excellently handled; a duty which we earnestly commend unto thy practice, as suitable to these sad times. Say, O say with the church, 'In the way of thy judgments, O Lord, we have waited for thee,' Isa. xxvi. 8; and with the prophet, 'I will wait upon the Lord that hideth his face from the

* That is, = a 'day of rejoicing.'—G.

house of Jacob, and I will look for him,' Isa. viii. 17. And rest assured, that 'none of the seed of Jacob shall seek him in vain,' Isa. xlv. 19; he will not 'disappoint their hope, nor make their faces ashamed that wait for him,' Isa. xlix. 23.

Thus we have given you a short prospect of the whole, a brief sum of that treasure which these sermons contain. We need say nothing of the author; his former labours 'sufficiently speak for him in the gates,' Prov. xxxi. 23; his memory is highly honoured amongst the godly-learned. He that enjoys the glory of heaven, needs not the praises of men upon earth. If any should doubt of these sermons, as if they should not be truly his, whose name they bear, let him but observe the style, and the excellent and spiritual matter herein contained, and he will, we hope, be fully satisfied. Besides, there are many ear-witnesses yet living, who can clear them from any shadow of imposture. They come forth without any alteration, save only some repetitions (which the pulpit did well bear), are here omitted.

The Lord make these, and all other the labours of his servants, profitable to his church. And the Lord so 'destroy the veil' from off thy heart, that thou mayest believe, and by faith come to this feast, the joy and comfort whereof may swallow up all the slavish fear of death, dry up thy tears, and roll away all reproach. And the Lord give thee a waiting heart, to stay thy soul upon the name of the Lord, to believe his word, and his faithful promises, that in due time thou mayest 'rejoice in the God of thy salvation.' This is the earnest prayer of

ARTHUR JACKSON.*
JAMES NALTON.†
WILL. TAYLOR.‡

LONDON, *April* 19. 1650.

* Jackson, like Sibbes, was a native of Suffolk, having been born at Little Waldingfield, in 1593. He won the respect of even Laud. It is told that when the 'Book of Sports' was commanded to be publicly read, he refused compliance, and was complained of for his contumacy to the Archbishop, but that prelate would not suffer him to be molested. 'Mr Jackson,' said he, 'is a quiet and peaceable man, and therefore I will not have him meddled with.' Sheldon manifested like esteem for him. At the Restoration, when Charles II. made his entrance into the city, Jackson was appointed by his brethren to present to him a Bible, as he passed through St Paul's Churchyard, which was in his parish; when he addressed the king in a congratulatory speech, which was graciously received. He was also one of the Commissioners of the Savoy. He died, Aug. 5. 1666, one of the most venerable of the 'ejected' two thousand. Consult 'Nonconformist's Memorial,' vol. i. pp. 120–124; also 'Memoir' prefixed to his 'Annotations,' vol. iv.

† This 'man of God,' beloved by Richard Baxter, and all his like-minded contemporaries, was called 'The Weeping Prophet,' because of his peculiarly tender and tearful nature. He also was one of the 'two thousand,' but died shortly afterwards in 1663. In a copy of Sedgwick's 'Bowels of Tender Mercy Sealed in the Everlasting Covenant' (folio 1661), in our possession, is the following inscription, Mary Nalton, her book, given by her dear husband, Ja. Nalton, Sept. 14. 1661.' Consult 'Noncf. Mem.,' vol. i. pp. 142–144.

‡ This 'William Taylor,' was probably the author of a sermon in the 'Morning Exercises,' and the same for whom Dr Spurstowe preached a remarkable funeral sermon. He died in 1661. G.

THE MARRIAGE FEAST BETWEEN CHRIST AND HIS CHURCH.

In this mountain shall the Lord of hosts make unto all people a feast of fat things, a feast of wines on the lees; of fat things full of marrow, of wine on the lees well refined.—Isaiah XXV. 6.

In the former chapter the holy prophet having spoken of the miseries and desolation of the church, in many heavy, sad, and doleful expressions; as 'the vine languisheth, the earth is defiled under the inhabitants thereof, because they have transgressed the laws, changed the ordinance, and broken the everlasting covenant; therefore the earth shall be accursed, and they that dwell therein shall not drink wine with a song,' &c. Here you see all sweetness and rejoicing of heart is departed from them; yet even in the midst of all these miseries, God, the God of comforts, makes sweet and gracious promises to his church, to raise it out of its mournful estate and condition. And therefore the prophet, in the former part of this chapter, speaks of blessing God for the destruction of his enemies, and for his great love to his church. And when he had spoken of the ruin of the enemy, he presently breaks out with thanksgiving, breathing forth abundant praises to his God; as it is the custom of holy men, guided by the motion of the blessed Spirit of God, upon all occasions, but especially for benefits to his church, to praise his name, not out of ill affection at the destruction of the adversaries, but at the execution of divine justice, for the fulfilling of the truth of his promise; as in the first verse of this chapter, 'O Lord, thou art my God; I will exalt thee, I will praise thy name; for thou hast done wonderful things; thy counsels of old are faithfulness and truth.' When the things that were promised of old were brought to pass, the church was ever ready to give God the glory of his truth. Therefore, rejoice not when thine enemies fall; but when the enemies of the Lord are brought to desolation, then we may, nay, we ought to sing, 'Hallelujah' to him that liveth for ever and ever.

I will now fall upon the very words of my text. 'In this mountain shall the Lord of hosts make unto all people a feast of fat things,' &c. These words they are prophetical, and cannot have a perfect performance all at once, but they shall be performed gradually. The promise of 'a new heaven and a new earth,' 2 Pet. iii. 13, shall be performed. The conversion of the Jews, and the bringing in of the fulness of the Gentiles, shall gradually be brought to pass. All the promises that ever God hath made, before the second coming of Christ to judgment, shall be accomplished. God hath made his peace with us in the gospel of peace; and when all these promises shall be fulfilled, then all imperfection shall be done away, and we shall never be removed from our Rock; but our joy shall then be full. Nay, even in this life we have some degrees of perfection. We have grace, and the means of grace; the ordinances of Christ, and a testimony of everlasting glory.

'In this mountain will the Lord of hosts make a feast.'

In these words ye have set down a glorious and a royal feast; and the *place* where this feast is to be kept is 'Mount Zion;' the *feast-maker* is 'the Lord of Hosts;' the *parties invited*, are 'all people;' *the issues of it, and the provision* for the feast, are 'fat things,' and 'wine' of the best; a feast of the best of the best, a feast of the fat and of the marrow, a feast of 'wine on the lees well refined.'

Here you may see that God doth veil heavenly things under earthly things, and condescends so low as to enter into the inward man by the outward man. For our apprehensions are so weak and narrow, that we cannot be acquainted with spiritual things, but by the inward working of the Spirit of the Almighty.

This 'mountain' is *the place* where this feast is made, even 'mount Zion;' which is a type and figure of the church, called in Scripture, 'the holy mountain.' For as mountains are raised high above the earth, so the church of God is raised in excellency and dignity above all the sorts of mankind.

Obs. 1. *As much as men above beasts, so much is the church raised above all men.* This mountain is above all mountains. The 'mountain of the Lord' is above all mountains whatsoever. 'Thou, O mountain, shalt stand immoveable,' when all other mountains shall smoke, if they are but touched. This is the mountain of mountains. The church of God is most excellent in glory and dignity, as ye may see in the latter end of the former chapter, how the glory of the church puts down all other glories whatsoever. 'The moon,' saith the prophet, 'shall be confounded, and the sun ashamed, when the Lord of Hosts shall reign in Mount Zion, and in Jerusalem, and before his ancients gloriously.' So that the brightness of the church shall put down the glory of the sun and of the moon. Thus you see the church of God is a mountain.

Reason. First, *Because God hath established it upon a stronger foundation than all the world besides.* It is founded upon the goodness and power and truth of God. Mountains of brass and iron are not so firm as this mountain. For what sustains the church but the word of God? And being built upon his word and truth, it may very well be called a mountain, for it shall be as mount Zion, which shall never be removed, Ps. cxxv. i. It may be moved, but never removed. Thus, in regard to the firmness and stability thereof, it may rightly be termed a mountain.

Obs. 2. Again, *we may here speak in some sort of the visibility of the church.* But here will arise a quarrel for the papists, who when they hear of this mount, they presently allude* it to their church, Their church, say they, is a mount; so saith the Scripture.

I answer, *Firstly,* We confess in some sort their church to be a mount (though not this mount), for Babylon is built on seven hills; but if this

* That is, = 'make it refer to.'—G.

prove her a church, it is an antichristian church. *Secondly*, That the Catholic Protestantial* church had always a being, though sometimes invisible. The apostle, writing to the Romans, exhorts them 'not to be high-minded, but fear;' for, saith he, 'if God hath broken off the natural branches, perhaps he will break off you also,' Rom. xi. 21, 24. And, indeed, for their pride and haughtiness of mind, they are at this day broken off. Christ, that 'walks between the seven golden candlesticks,' Rev. i. 12, did never say that the church of Smyrna or Ephesus should always remain a visible church to the eyes of the world, neither were they; for to this very day they lie under bondage and slavery to the Turk. The mount hath been always visible, though not always alike gloriously visible. For there will be a time when the church shall fly into the wilderness, Rev. xii. 6. Where, then, shall be the glorious visibility of the church? There is a time when all shall follow the beast. The papists themselves confess that in antichrist's time the church shall scarce be visible. The essence of a thing and the quality of a thing may differ. The church is a church, and visible, but not always equally, and alike gloriously visible; yet those that had spiritual eyes, and did look upon things with the spectacles of the Scripture, they could always declare the church was visible; for, from the beginning of the world, the church had always lustre enough sufficient to delight, and draw the elect, and so shall have to the end of the world, though sometimes the church may have a mist before it, as Austin speaks: 'It is no wonder that thou canst not see a mountain, for thou hast no eyes.' But the papists have seen this mountain. As they have always been bloody persecutors of the church, they have seen enough to confound them. For we have nothing in our church, but they have the same; only ours is refined, and freed from idolatry. We have two sacraments, they have seven. We have Scripture, they have traditions, which they equal with it. We have Scriptures pure, they, corrupt. So that our church was in the midst of theirs, as a sound and more uncorrupt part in a corrupt body.

This mountain is the church. 'The Lamb standeth upon mount Zion, and with him a hundred forty and four thousand, having his Father's name written in their foreheads,' Rev. xiv. 1. Christ standeth in the church, and standing in mount Zion he is accompanied with those that his Father hath given to him before the world was. Therefore those that belong to this holy mountain, they are Christ's. 'And in this mountain shall the Lord of hosts make a feast for all people.' And this feast is a royal feast, a marriage feast, wherein the joy and comfort of God's people are set down by that which is most comfortable among men. *The founder of the feast* is 'the Lord of hosts.' It is only he that is able to prepare a table in the wilderness, that is mighty and of ability to feast his church with a spiritual and holy banquet. We all live at his table for the feeding of our bodies, but much more in regard of our souls. He can make a feast for the whole man, for he is Lord of the conscience; and he is to spread a table for the whole world. Nay, more, if there were so many, he can furnish a table for ten thousand worlds. He is the God of all spiritual comforts, and the 'God of all consolation.' He is infinite, and can never be drawn dry, for he is the fountain of eternal life. All graces and comforts in the Scripture are called the comforts and graces of the Holy Spirit, because God is the giver of them by his Spirit. Who can take away the wound of a guilty conscience, but he that hath set the conscience in the hearts of men? He, if he pleaseth, can take away the burden of a grieved conscience, and supply

* That is, 'Protestant.'—G.

it, instead thereof, with new and solid comforts. He knoweth all the windings and turnings of the soul, where all the pain and grief lieth; and he cannot but know it, because he only is above the soul. He is therefore the fittest to make the soul a feast. He only can do it, and he will do it.

'In this mountain shall the Lord of Hosts make a feast.'

Why is he called the 'Lord of Hosts?'

It is an usual term to set forth the glory of God, to make his power and the greatness of his majesty known amongst the children of men.

'He shall make a feast for all people.'

Those that are invited to this glorious feast are 'all people.' None excepted, none excluded, that will come to Christ! Some of all sorts, of all nations, of all languages! This hath relation to the time of the gospel. The church at first had its being in particular families, but afterwards more enlarged. The church at the first was of the daughters of men, and the sons of God. The children of the church mingled with a generation of corrupt persons, that would keep in no bounds; but after Abraham's time there was another generation of the church, that so it was a little more enlarged. Then there was a third generation, a divided generation, consisting of Jews and Gentiles. So that, when Christ came into the world, the bounds of the church began to enlarge themselves more and more, so that now it is in this happy condition, 'Come ye all unto me, all that are heavy laden,' Mat. xi. 28. Both Jews and Gentiles, all are invited, whosoever they are, 'nothing is now unclean,' Acts x. 15. Christ is come, and hath made 'to all people a feast of fat things.' It must be a feast, and of fat things, for all the world shall be the better for it. The Jews shall be converted, and the fulness of the Gentiles shall come in. And yet it is no prejudice to any particular man, because the things ye are to taste of are spiritual. Go to all the good things in the world: the more one hath of them the less another must have, because they are earthly, and so are finite. But in spiritual things all may have the whole, and every man in particular. Every man enjoyeth the light of the sun in particular, and all enjoy it too. So the whole church, and only the church, enjoys the benefit and comfort of this feast; but under the name of this church come all the elect, both Jews and Gentles, and therefore it must be the Lord of Hosts that can make such a feast as this is, a feast for all people. No other is able to do it.

This feast is 'a feast of fat things, full of marrow and of wine on the lees well refined,' *the best that can be imagined, the best of the best.* A feast is promised, a spiritual feast. The special graces and favours of God are compared to a feast made up of the best things, full of all varieties and excellencies, and the chief dish that is all in all, is Christ, and all the gracious benefits we by promise can in any wise expect from him. All other favours and blessings, whatsoever they are, are but Christ dished out, as I may speak, in several offices and attributes. He is the original of comfort, the principle of grace and holiness. All is included in Christ. Ask of him and ye shall obtain, even the forgiveness of your sins, peace of conscience, and communion of saints. Ask of Christ, as of one invested with all privileges for the good of others. But yet this is by his death. He is the feast itself. He is dished out into promises. Have you a promise of the pardon of sins? It is from Christ. Wouldst thou have peace of conscience? It is from Christ. Justification and redemption? It is from Christ. The love of God is derived to us by Christ, yea, and all that we have that is good is but Christ parcelled out.

Now, I will shew why Christ, with his benefits, prerogatives, graces, and comforts, is compared to a feast.

First. In regard *of the choice of the things.* In a feast all things are of the best; so are the things we have in Christ. Whatsoever favours we have by Christ, they are choice ones. They are the best of every thing. Pardon for sin is a pardon of pardon. The title we have for heaven, through him, is a sure title. The joy we have by him is the joy of all joys. The liberty and freedom from sin, which he purchased for us by his death, is perfect freedom. The riches of grace we have by him are the only lasting and durable riches. Take anything that you can, if we have it by Christ, it is of the best. All worldly excellencies and honours are but mere shadows to the high excellencies and honour we have in Christ. No joy, no comfort, no peace, no riches, no inheritance to be compared with the joy, peace, and inheritance which we have in Christ. Whatsoever we have by him, we have it in a glorious manner. And therefore he is compared to fat, to 'fat things full of marrow,' 'to wine, to wine on the lees,' that preserveth the freshness of it; the best wine of all, that is not changed from vessel to vessel, but keepeth its strength. And, indeed, the strength and vigour of all floweth from Jesus Christ in covenant with us.

The love of Christ is the best love, and he himself incomparably the best, and hath favours and blessings of the choicest.

Second. Again, as in a feast, besides choice, *there is variety*, so in Christ there is variety answerable to all our wants. Are we foolish? He is wisdom. Have we guilt in our consciences? He is righteousness, and this righteousness is imputed unto us. Are we defiled? He is sanctification. Are we in misery? He is our redemption. If there be a thousand kinds of evils in us, there is a thousand ways to remedy them by Jesus Christ. Therefore, the good things we have by Christ are compared to all the benefits we have in this world. In Christ is choice and variety. Are we weak? He is meat to feed us, that we may be strong. He will refresh us. He is the best of meats. He is marrow. So, are our spirits faint? He is wine. Thus we have in Christ to supply all our wants. He is variety.

There is a plant among the Indians called by the name of *coquus;** the fruit thereof serveth for meat and drink, to comfort and refresh the body. It yieldeth that whereof the people make apparel to clothe themselves withal, and also that which is physical,† very good against the distempers of the body. And if God will infuse so much virtue into a poor plant, what virtue may we expect to be in Christ himself? He feedeth our souls to all eternity, puts upon us the robes of righteousness, heals the distempers of our souls. There is variety in him for all our wants whatsoever. He is food, physic, and apparel to clothe us; and when we are clothed with him, we may with boldness stand before the majesty of God. He is all in all. He is variety, and all. There is something in Christ answerable to all the necessities of God's people, and not only so, but to their full content in everything.

Third. Again, as there is variety in a feast, so there is *sufficiency, full sufficiency.* 'We beheld the only begotten Son of God, full of grace and truth,' John i. 14. And being full of grace, he is wise, and able to furnish this heavenly banquet with enough of all sorts of provisions fit for the soul to feed upon. There is abundance of grace, and excellency, and sufficiency in Christ. And it must needs be, because he is a Saviour of God's own sending. 'Labour not therefore for the meat that perisheth, but for the

* That is, 'cocoa.'—G. † That is, 'medicinal.'—G.

meat that the Son of God shall give you; for him hath God the Father sealed,' John vi. 27; that is, sent forth for this purpose, to 'feed the church of God,' 1 Pet. v. 2. As there is an all-sufficiency in God, so in Christ, who by the sacrificing of himself was able to give satisfaction to divine justice. Therefore saith he, 'My flesh is meat indeed, and my blood is drink indeed,' John vi. 55; that is, spiritually to the soul he is food indeed, and can satisfy God's justice. If we consider him as God alone, he is a 'consuming fire,' Heb. xii. 29; or as a man alone, he can do nothing; but considered as God-man, he is meat indeed, and drink indeed. And now the soul is content with that which divine justice is contented withal. Though our conscience be large, yet God is larger and above our consciences. Therefore, as there is variety of excellency, so is there sufficiency and fulness in Christ. What he did, he did to the full. He is a Saviour, and he filleth up that name to the full. His pardon for sin is a full pardon; his merits for us are full merits; his satisfaction to divine justice a full satisfaction; his redemption of our souls and bodies a full redemption. Thus all he did was full.

Fourth. A feast is for *company*. It is *convivium*. There is converse at it. So Cicero prefers the name of *convivium* among the Latins before the Greek name συμπόσιον (*b*). And this feast is not for one. We are all invited to it. The excellency of Christ's feast consisteth in the communion of saints; for whosoever takes part of it, their spirits must agree one with another. Love is the best and chiefest dish in this feast. The more we partake of the sweetness of Christ, the more we love one another. Christ by his Spirit so works in the hearts of the children of men, that, bring a thousand together of a thousand several nations, and within a little while you shall have them all acquainted one with another. If they be good, there is agreement of the spirit and sympathy between them. There is a kindred in Christ. He is the true Isaac. The death of Christ and the blood of Christ is the ground of all union and joy and comfort whatsoever. The blood of Christ sprinkled upon the conscience will procure that peace of conscience that shall be a continual feast unto the soul. This feast must needs be wonderful comfortable, for we do not feast with those that are like ourselves, but we feast with God the Father, and the Holy Spirit, sent by Christ, procured by the death of Christ. The angels at this feast attend us; therefore, it must needs be joyful. No joy comparable to the joy of a feast. This is not every feast. This is a marriage feast, at which we are contracted to Christ. Now, of all feasts, marriage feasts are most sumptuous. This is a marriage feast for the King's Son, for Christ himself; and therefore of necessity it must be full of all choice varieties, and of the sweetest of things, of the most excellentest of things, and of the quintessence of things. Here is all joy that belongeth to a feast. Here it is to be had with Christ. What acquaintance can be more glorious than that which is to be had between Jesus Christ and a Christian soul? when we have hope of better things to come, then we find the sweetness of this communion. No harmony in the world can be so sweet as the harmony maintained between Christ and the soul. When we have this, and are made one with God in Christ, our joy must needs then be unspeakable. When the contract is once made between the soul and Christ, there cannot but be abundant joy. When the soul is joined with Christ by faith, it cannot but solace itself in a perpetual jubilee and a perpetual feast in some degrees.

Fifth. Again, for a feast ye have *the choicest garments*, as at the marriage of the Lamb, 'white and fine linen,' Rev. xix. 8, which is the righteousness of the saints. When God seeth these robes upon us and the Spirit of Christ in us, then there is a robe of righteousness imputed, and a garment of sanctity, whereby our souls are clothed. So this is a feast that must have wonderful glorious attire; and when this marriage shall be consummated, we are sure to have a garment of glory put upon us.

Sixth. This was signified in old time by the Jews.

1. In the feast of the passover (not to name all resemblances, but only one or two). *The lamb for the passover*, you know, was chosen out of the flock from amongst the rest four days before the time appointed for that feast. So Christ is the true Paschal Lamb, chosen of God before the foundation of the world was laid, to be slain for us.

2. Again, *manna* was a type of Christ. It came from heaven to feed the hungry bodies of the Israelites in the wilderness. Even so came Christ, sent from God the Father, to be the eternal food and upholder of the souls and bodies of every one of us. Manna was white and sweet; so was Christ, white in righteousness and holiness, and also sweet to delight the soul. Manna fell upon the tents in the night; and Christ came when darkness was spread over all the world. God gave manna freely from heaven; so Christ was a free gift, and he freely gave himself to death, even to the cursed death of the cross, for us. All, both poor and rich, they gathered manna. Christ is a common food for king and subject. All take part of Christ. Neither Jew nor Gentile are exempted, but all may come and buy freely without money. Of this manna he that had least had enough. So here he that hath least of Christ, though he take him with a trembling hand, yet he shall have enough, for Christ is his. Whosoever hath the least grace, if it be true and sound, hath grace enough to bring him to eternal life. The Jews wondered at the manna, saying, What thing is this? (*c*). So it is one of Christ's names to be called 'Wonderful,' Isa. ix. 6. Grace and favour from Christ is true spiritual manna to the soul. Manna fell in the wilderness: even so must we remain in the wilderness of this wretched world until we come to heaven. Christ is manna to us, and very sweet in the conveyance of his word and sacraments. When the Israelites came into the land of Canaan the manna ceased, not before. So when we come to heaven, the elect's purchased possession, we shall have another kind of manna for our souls. We shall not there feed on Christ, as in the sacrament; no, but we shall see him 'face to face, and know as we are known,' 1 Cor. xiii. 12. In the wilderness of this world it is fit God should convey this heavenly manna to the soul whatsoever way he pleaseth. Manna could not fall until the Israelites had spent all the provision they brought with them out of Egypt; and we cannot taste of that heavenly manna of our Father until our souls are drawn away from all worldly dependences and carnal delights. Then, indeed, manna will be sweet and precious.

What is this heavenly manna, what is Christ and his Father, what is the word and sacraments, to a depraved, vicious heart, stuffed full with earthly vanities? Alas! it loatheth all these. As none tasted of manna but those that came out of Egypt, so none shall taste of Christ but those that are not of the world, that are come out of Egypt, out of sin and darkness. Manna fell only about the tents of Israel, and in no other part of the world, but only there, that none might have the privilege to eat of it but God's peculiar, chosen ones. Christ falls upon the tents of the righteous, and none shall taste of this blessed, spiritual food but such as are the Israel of God, such as are of the church, such as feel the burden of sin and groan under it. Oh! the very taste of this heavenly manna is sweet to their souls, and to none but them. Thus ye see the feast that Christ maketh for us in mount Zion, and that this manna doth typify Christ with all his benefits.

3. Again, *the hard rock in the wilderness*, when it was strucken* with the rod of Moses, presently water gushed out in abundance, which preserved life to the Israelites; so Christ, the rock of our salvation, the strength of his church, the rock and fortress of all his saints, when his precious side was gored with the bloody lance upon the cross, the blood gushed out, and in such a manner and such abundance, that by the shedding thereof our souls are preserved alive. He is both manna and the rock of water. Manna had all in it, so had the rock; and all necessities are plentifully supplied by Christ. The church of God hath always had bread to satisfy spiritual hunger. It never wanted necessary comforts. It is said, Rev. xii. 6, 'When the church fled into the wilderness, God fed her there,' alluding to the children of Israel fed by manna. The Jews did not want in the wilderness, nor the church of God never wanted comfort, though in the midst of the persecution and oppression of all her enemies. When Elias was in the wilderness, he was fed,' 1 Kings xvii. 4, 6. The church of God shall not only be fed in her body, but in her soul, for Christ hath hidden manna for his elect. This doth typify the exceeding joy of the church, the hidden manna, 'that neither eye hath seen, nor ear heard of, neither can it enter into the heart of man to conceive of those joys,' 1 Cor. ii. 9, that the church of God shall have when the marriage shall be consummated. Joy in the Holy Ghost, and peace of conscience, they are hid from the world, and sometimes from God's people themselves, though they shall enjoy them hereafter.

4. *All the former feasts* in times past were but types of this. The feast of tabernacles, the feast of the passover, the spiritual manna, and all other holy feasts, were but to signify and to shew forth this feast by Christ. But there is this difference between the type and the thing signified. By the type, the passover lamb was quite eaten up; but this passover, Christ, that was slain for sin, can never be eaten up. We feed upon him with our souls. He cannot be consumed as the passover lamb, nor as manna, which was gone when the sun arose. Yea, that manna that was laid up for a remembrance before the ark, became nothing, but Christ is in heaven for evermore for the soul to feed upon. Though these were resemblances, yet these failed, as it is fit resemblances should fail, that is, come short of the body of the thing itself. Thus you see the spiritual comforts of a Christian may well and fitly be compared to a feast.

5. Thus you see God provideth a feast, and inviteth all. *In the sacrament you have a feast*, a feast of varieties, not only bread, but wine—to shew the variety and fulness of comfort in Christ. He intendeth full comfort. As for our adversaries the papists, they have dry feasts. They give the people the bread, but the wine they keep for themselves. But God in Christ intendeth us full comfort. Whatsoever Christ did, it was full. His merits are complete, and his joy was full. He is fulness itself; and, therefore, whatsoever comes from him must needs be, as he himself is, both full and sweet. He intendeth us full consolation.

Use. Therefore, we ought to be prepared to partake of this feast, in such a manner as that we may have full joy, and full comfort; for there is in Christ enough to satisfy all the hungry souls in the world, he himself being present at this heavenly banquet. 'All fulness dwells in him,' Col. i. 19, from which 'we have all received, and grace for grace.' Therefore,

* That is, 'struck.'—G.

1. *Let us labour to have large hearts:* for as our faith groweth more and more, so we shall carry more comfort and more strength from this holy feast. As the poor widow, if her vessels had not failed, the oil had not ceased; if there had been more vessels, there had been more oil, 2 Kings iv. 6. Our souls are as these vessels. Let us therefore labour, and make it our great business to have large souls, souls capable to drink in this spiritual oil of gladness; for as much faith as we bring to Christ, so much comfort we shall carry from him. The favours of God in Christ being infinite, the more we fetch from him, the more glory we give unto him. But if they were finite, we should offend his bounty, he might soon be drawn dry, and so send us away with an uncomfortable answer, that he was not able to relieve us. But Christ is infinite, and the more we have from him, the more we may have. 'To him that hath shall be given,' Mat. xiii. 12. The oftener we go to Christ, the more honour and glory we bring unto him. This is a banquet to the full.

We are now come to the banquet, and Christ is the founder of it; nay, he is the feast itself. He is the author of it, and he it is that we feed upon.

Use 2. Let us labour not to be straight* receivers of the sacrament, but suck in abundance from Christ with a great deal of delight, that we may come together not for the worse but the better, considering what a great deal of strength and grace is required as very necessary for the maintaining of spiritual life.

THE SECOND SERMON.

In this mountain shall the Lord of hosts make unto all people a feast of fat things, a feast of wines on the lees; of fat things full of marrow, of wines on the lees well refined.—Isaiah XXV. 6.

I have shewed that Christ and his benefits are compared to a feast, and in what respects they are fitly resembled by a feast, and have pressed that we should prepare for it, first by getting large hearts. Now, in the second place, that we may have comfort at this feast, *we must labour for spiritual appetite;* for to what end and purpose is that man at a feast that hath no stomach? I shall therefore shew what means we are to use to get eager stomachs and holy appetites after this feast.

(1.) *The appetite is raised with sour things,* as anguish of spirit and mournfulness of heart for sin. If we will ever relish Christ aright, we must labour to have a quick apprehension of our sins. We must do as the Jews did at the passover. They ate it with sour herbs, that they might thereby have the sharper stomachs. So must we. We must cast our eyes into our own hearts, and consider what vile wretches we are, how full of sin and vanity; and this will be as sour herbs to the Paschal Lamb. We must join the sweet benefits and privileges that we have in Christ with the consideration of our own wretched and miserable condition, and then this heavenly ordinance cannot but be sweet and comfortable to our souls. I beseech you, enter into your own souls, and consider seriously under what guilt you lie, and this will whet your appetite. 'A full stomach despiseth the honeycomb,' Prov. xxvii. 7; but in this appetite there is sense of emptiness, and from that sense of emptiness pain, and from pain an earnest desire of satisfaction. Thus it is in spiritual things. We want Christ, and all the spiritual comforts that flow from him. There is an emptiness in us, and we

* Qu. 'strait?'—Ed.

see a need every day to feed upon the mercies of God in Christ. There is an emptiness in our souls, and there must be a sense of that emptiness, and pain from that sense, which must stir up a strong endeavour to follow after that that we do desire. Then Christ indeed is sweet, when we find our souls hungering and thirsting after him.

(2.) Again, if so be we would have that appetite of spirit that is fit for this feast, *we must purge our souls from the corruptions of flesh and spirit*, 'perfecting holiness in the fear of God,' 2 Cor. vii. 1. We must cleanse our souls from those lusts and passions that daily cleave unto them. All crudities must be taken away, that the edge of the stomach may not be flatted:* for while these earthly carnal corruptions lie upon the soul, we can expect no spiritual appetite to heavenly things. Let us therefore examine ourselves, what filth lies upon our souls, and what corrupt inclinations are there, that so they may be purged, and our desires be carried fully after Christ in the sacrament.

(3.) Another means to get appetite is *to consider thoroughly what is required of a Christian, well to maintain the trade of Christianity*. It is another manner of thing than we take it for, to entertain communion with God, to perform holy duties in an holy manner, to bear the yoke as a Christian should do. Here is a great deal of strength required; and because corruptions will mix themselves amongst our best performances, there must be a great deal of mercy from God to pardon them. And whence is all this but by the death of our blessed Saviour Jesus Christ? For his sake, God hath a forbearing eye. Now, if we consider what a degree of spiritual strength and vigour we should have to go through with these duties, this would sharpen our stomachs and spiritual appetites, to furnish ourselves with grace from Christ to go through with these holy services. There must be an exercising of all the duties of Christianity, which is an estate that must be maintained with a great deal of charge and labour. A man can do no service acceptable to God but by grace; and grace must feed the soul with fruitful knowledge in the power of faith. And when the soul feeleth a necessity of grace, Oh! then, beloved, it hungers and earnestly thirsteth after the love of God in Christ. We need to every trade a great deal of knowledge. Then surely the calling of Christianity needeth a great deal. A Christian must expect much both in prosperity and adversity, as the apostle saith, 'I have learned to want and to abound, to be in honour and to be in disgrace, and I can do all things through Christ that strengthens me,' Philip. iv. 12. Now, because there is so much goings so, out for the maintenance of Christianity, we must also bring in much grace, and faith, and love, and holiness, or else we shall never be able to uphold this condition. Where there is an exercise of Christianity, there will be an appetite to heaven; that is our best calling. For when that we have done all that we can, that, that we must have comfort from, is Christianity. Therefore, labour with all labour to be holy and able Christians. All other callings are but for this present life; but that that is for eternity is this calling of Christianity. And this is only to fit us here in this world for an everlasting condition of glory in the world to come.

(4.) Again, if we would have a desire and appetite to heavenly things, *we must labour to get acquaintance, and constantly converse with those that are good*. The old proverb is, 'Company will make a man fall to,' especially the company of those that are better than ourselves. For very emulation, men will be doing as others do. When men live amongst those whose

* That is 'flattened,' = appetite destroyed.—G.

hearts are framed this way, they must be equal. Conversation with those that have good relish of spiritual things, and shew forth grace in their lives, setteth an appetite upon our desires, to desire the same things that they do. Thus St Paul writeth to the Gentiles to stir up the emulation of the Jews. Therefore receive this likewise for the procuring of a spiritual appetite. To go on.

(5.) The next thing that may stir up our desires to get an appetite to the best things, is seriously to consider, *that we cannot tell how long we have to live, or may enjoy the benefit of the means of grace.* Those that sit at table and discourse away the greatest part of dinner time in talk, had need at last to fall to so much the faster, by how much the more negligent they had been before in eating. We cannot tell how long we may enjoy this spiritual feast that God makes for us. Therefore, be stirred up to get spiritual appetites; for we know not how long God will spread a table for us. We know not how long we shall enjoy our lives; and if we be surprised on the sudden, we may suffer a spiritual famine, a famine of the soul, if we have nothing to comfort us beforehand; and of all famines, a spiritual famine is most grievous, most fearful. Therefore do as Joseph did, and be wise. He in the seven years of plenty gathered for seven years of famine that was to come upon the land of Egypt, Gen. xli. 36, *seq.* Alas! if we have nothing laid up beforehand, what will be our end? We shall lie open to God's wrath and anger. Nothing can support our souls in the evil time. Wherefore, as you desire at that day to have comfort of those things ye shall stand most in need of, labour to get a good appetite. For to perish and starve at a feast is a shame; to famish in the liberty of the gospel and plenty of spiritual meat, is shameful and dishonourable. Thus you see, beloved, not to be large in the point, how you may procure such an appetite as is fit for such an holy feast. First, by getting a sense of sin; secondly, by seeing a necessity of Christ; thirdly, by purging out those lusts that lie upon the soul; fourthly, by conversing with those that are spiritually minded; and lastly, by considering the time to come.

Use 3. It is not enough to have a stomach, but we must have *a spiritual disposition of soul to heavenly things, as we have to outward things.* Labour to have a taste of good things, and a distinguishing taste of heavenly things from other things. God is the God of nature, and hath furnished us with five senses; and as he hath given us sense to apprehend, so he hath furnished the creature with varieties of excellences, suitable to all our several senses. He will not have objects in the creature without sense, nor sense in man without objects. He hath furnished man with senses, and variety of senses, and given fit and proportionable objects for those senses. The soul also hath her sense. Wheresoever there is life, there is sense. God having given spiritual life to the soul, he doth maintain that life with spiritual food. As in a feast there is sight, and the eye is not only fed there with rich furniture, but with variety of dainties; the ear likewise and the smell is satisfied, the one with music, the other with sweet savours. So in this feast there is to delight both the ear and the smell of the soul, the one with hearing the gracious promises of Jesus Christ, and the other in receiving the sweet savour of that sacrifice that was offered up once for all. Nothing so sweet to the soul as the blessings of Christ. He is sweet in the word, as the vessel that conveyeth him into our souls. Thus you see in this feast all the senses, the sight, the smell, the taste, and hearing, all are satisfied, and a great care had, in the provision for the feast, that our outward man may be pleased. And shall the Lord of Hosts make a feast, and not content the whole man? He is for our sight, if we have spiritual eyes to see; the ear, if we have ears to hear. All the senses are exercised here. What is the reason why carnal men cannot relish a pardon for sin, and justification, and sanctification, and holiness, nor go boldly to God? It may be they have good, sweet notions of these, but they have no spiritual taste or relish of them, and all because they want spiritual life. None but a Christian can have spiritual taste answerable to a spiritual life. Taste is a kind of feeling, one of the most necessary senses; and a Christian cannot be without relish and feeling. Yea, it is the very being of a Christian to have a taste of spiritual things. Of all other senses, there is a stronger application in taste. The other senses fetch their objects afar off; but as for taste, there is a near application in it, and therefore most necessary. Every life is maintained by taste. 'Taste and see how good the Lord is,' Ps. xxxiv. 8.

Now, taste doth two things; it doth relish that that is good, and disrelish the contrary. There must be a spiritual taste to discern of differences. There can be no spiritual taste but it must know what is good and profitable for the soul, and what is not. Because God will not have our tastes to be wronged, ye see what course he takes. First, the eye seeth what things we taste on, and if the eye be displeased, so also is the smell. Thus God layeth before us spiritual things, knowledge of good and bad, and giveth us many *caveats*, and all because he would not have us to taste things hurtful for the soul, nor poison instead of meat. Now, when we have tasted that which is good, let us take heed it be not a taste only, lest we fall into the sin against the Holy Ghost.

Use 4. Again, beside taste, *there must be a digesting of what we taste, and that thoroughly, in our understandings.* When we apprehend a thing to be true and good, it must be digested thoroughly into the affections. Love to the best things must be above all other love whatsoever; yet this must be digested. Men oftentimes have sweet notions, but, alas! they are but notions; they do not digest them into their affections. It is the last digestion that nourisheth; and when any spiritual truths are understood thoroughly, then comes in spiritual strength; and hereupon the soul comes and sucks in that virtue which is for the nourishment of it. Thus it is in the soul; upon digestion there is nourishment.

Again, there must be a faculty to retain what we have received, that it may be digested. Ye have many that love to hear, but they do not digest. If there be nothing in the soul, nothing can be extracted; and therefore we must learn to retain necessary truths, that so upon occasion they may come from the memory into the heart. Though, indeed, they are not in their proper place when they are in the memory only, yet notwithstanding, if they are there, they may with ease be brought down into the soul.

Use 5. Then *we must labour to walk in the strength of spiritual things.* For what is the use of this feast but to cherish both soul and spirit? The use of spiritual things which we have through Christ is to cherish and enliven. It conveyeth strength to us, that we may walk in the strength of Christ, as Elias did forty days in the strength of his food, 1 Kings xix. 8. And consider, though in our consciences and conditions we have variety of changes, yet in Christ we have several comforts suitable to all our several conditions. If so be our sins trouble us, we should watch over ourselves, that we be not over much cast down, but feed upon spiritual things in consideration of pardon for sin in the blood of Christ. This is the grand issue of all that Christ hath traced out in the forgiveness of sins. He is not, he cannot be divided. Where he pardons sins, he sanctifieth; where he sanctifieth, he writes his law in their hearts. So that there is a chain of spiritual favours. Where the first link is, all the rest follow. Where forgiveness of sin is, there is the Spirit, and that Spirit sanctifieth, and comforts, and is an earnest of everlasting life. Therefore, feed especially upon the favours of God, and get forgiveness of sins, and then all the rest of the chain of grace and spiritual life will follow.

Sometimes we stand in need of present grace and comfort, and we are undone if comforts and grace are not at hand, never considering the promises that are to come; as that promise of Christ, 'I will be with thee to the end of the world, fear not,' Mat. xxviii. 20. No temptation shall befall us, but we shall have an issue out of it, and it shall work together for the good of all those that fear God. This is *aqua vitæ* to the soul of man. Therefore the gracious promises of Christ and his Holy Spirit we should ever remember to get into our souls; for when all other comforts fail, then cometh in the comforts of the Spirit, who will be with us and uphold us in all extremities. If we had nothing in this world to comfort our spirits, yet let us rejoice in hope of glory to come. 'Our life is hid with Christ,' Col. iii. 3. We have 'the hidden manna,' Rev. ii. 17. 'In him we rejoice in hope of glory,' Rom. v. 2. And the way to maintain a Christian, holy life, is to make use of all the privileges of Christianity, and of those promises that convey these privileges to our souls.

Now that we may the better do this, observe continually what it is that hinders us, that we cannot feed upon spiritual things as we should do. Whatsoever it is, we must labour constantly to remove it.

Now, what must follow after this feast? (1.) *Why! spiritual cheerfulness!* If we find this in our duties of Christianity, it is a sign we have fed upon spiritual things. The nature of a spiritual feast is to empty the soul of sin, and to fill it full of gracious thoughts and actions. Instead thereof it moderates all things. It makes us use the world as if we used it not. When we can do this, we may certainly know that our souls have tasted of abundance of benefit by this feast.

A man that hath no spiritual joy is drowned for the most part in the contentments of the world, drowned in riches and honours; and these are like to strong waters immoderately taken, instead of cheering the spirits, [they] exhaust and kill them. He that hath the joy of heaven here by faith, is mortified to all other base delights, 'he only mindeth the things above, where Christ is,' Col. iii. 1. And therefore the exhortation, or rather command, 'Seek the things that are above,' hath this promise in fit method annexed to it, 'and then all other things shall be cast in upon you,' Mat. vi. 33. Riches and honours in the world; and if not them, yet so much as is necessary, and mortification of our sins, and the lusts of the flesh.

Again, if we have fed upon spiritual things for our souls, (2.) we shall *be thankful.* That man that hath tasted how good and gracious the Lord hath been to him in this world, and how full of joy and comfort he will be to him in another world, in consideration of this, his soul cannot choose but be thankful to God.

Here we see how to make this spiritual food fit for our souls, that Christ provideth for us. And if there be such joy as we have said there is in spiritual things, what use should we make further of them, but labour from hence (3.) *to justify the ways of godliness against our own false and carnal hearts, and against the slanderous imputations of the world.* When our hearts are ready to be false to us, and hanker after the contentments of the world, and are ready to say the best contentments that they can enjoy is in the things below; let us answer our base and false disputing hearts, that the ways of wisdom, the ways that God directs us to, they only are the ways of pleasure. And religion is that that makes the hearts of the children of men joyful; and 'a good conscience only makes a continual feast,' Prov. xv. 15, so long as man liveth. But especially at the hour of death, when all the comforts of the world cease, then conscience standeth our friend.

Obj. But the world's objection is, that of all kind of men in the world, those that profess religion are the most melancholy.

Ans. But if it be so, it is because they are not religious enough. Their sins are continually before their eyes. They have pardon for sin, and freedom from the guilt of sin, but know it not. They have good things, and do not know them. And so in regard of spiritual comforts, God's people may have spiritual joy, and inward consolation, and yet not know of it. There may be such a time when they may be sad and droop, and that is when they apprehend God doth not look pleasantly upon them. But the true character of a Christian is to be cheerful, and none else can be truly cheerful and joyous. Joy is usurped by others. There is no comfort in them that can be said to be real. All the joy of a man that is a carnal man is but as it were the joy of a traitor. He may come to the sacraments, and feast with the rest of God's people, but what mirth or joy can he have so long as the Master of the feast frowns upon him? Where Christ is not, there God is not reconciled. No joy like that joy of him that is assured of the love of God in Christ. A man may sometime through ignorance want that joy that belongeth to him. 'Rejoice, ye righteous, and be glad,' Ps. xxxiii. 1. It belongeth to those that are in Christ and to the righteous to rejoice, for joy is all their portion. They only can justify the ways of God against all reproaches whatsoever. But the eyes of carnal men are so held in blindness, that they can see no joy, no comfort in this course. As it is said of Austin before his conversion, he was afraid to turn Christian indeed, lest he should want all those joys and pleasures that the world did then afford him; but after he was converted, then he could cry, 'Lord, I have stayed too long from thee,' and too long delayed from coming in to taste of the sweetness of Jesus Christ.*

Take a Christian at the worst, and he is better than another man, take him at the best. The worst condition of God's children far surpasseth the very best condition of graceless persons. The issue of things shall turn to his good that is a member of Christ, a child of God, an heir of heaven. The evil of evils is taken away from him. Take him at the worst, he is an heir of heaven; but take the wicked at the best, he is not a child of God, he is a stranger to God, he is as a branch cut off, and as miserable a wretch as ever Belshazzar in the midst of his cups, trembling and quaking with fear and astonishment, when he saw the writing on the wall, Dan. v. 24, *seq.* When a man apprehends the wrath of God hanging over his head, though he were in the greatest feast in the world, and amongst those that make mirth and jollity, yet seeing vengeance ready to seize upon him, it cannot but damp all his joy and all his carnal pleasures; and therefore only a Christian hath a true title to this feast.

I beseech you, let us labour earnestly to have our part and portion in the things above. But what shall they do, that as yet apprehend no interest in Jesus Christ? Why! let them not be discouraged, for all are compelled

* See footnote p. 89.—G.

to come into this feast, both blind and lame. The servants are sent to bring them in. The most wretched people of all, God doth invite them. All are called to come in to this feast that are sensible of their sins; and that, God requires at our hands, or else we can have no appetite to taste of this feast. God saith, 'Come all,' Isa. lv. 1. Aye, but, saith the poor, sinful soul, I have no grace at all! Why! but yet come, 'buy without money;' the feast is free. 'God's thoughts are not as thy thoughts are;' 'but as heaven is high above the earth, even so are his thoughts above thy thoughts,' Isa. lv. 8, 9. Poor wretch! thou thinkest thou hast led a wicked life, and so thou hast! Aye, but now come in, God hath invited thee, and he will not always be inviting thee. Therefore come in, and study the excellencies of Christ. When such persons as these see they need mercy, and grace, and reconciliation, and must either have it or else be damned for ever, now they are earnest to study the favour and love of God in Christ; now they bestir themselves to get peace of conscience and joy in the Holy Ghost; now they see salvation to be founded only on Christ, and all other excellencies belonging to Christianity; and therefore he goeth constantly provided with grace and holiness, so in this life that he may not lose his part in glory in the life to come. Think of this and pray for it, as they in the gospel. 'Lord, evermore give me of that bread,' John vii. 34. Here is hope that thou mayest be saved, because thou art invited to come in. To what end is the ministry of the gospel, but to entreat thee to be reconciled? Oh! let this work upon our souls when we hear of the excellencies of these things! And together with them, consider of the necessity that is cast upon us to obtain them, and that we must have them or else be damned eternally. We must do as the lepers did, who said one to another, 'Why sit we here till we die? If we say, We will enter into the city, why, the famine is in the city, and we shall die there: and if we sit still here, we shall also die.' Now, what course took they? 'They said one to another, Let us enter into the camp of the Syrians, there is meat to feed us,' 2 Kings vii. 3, 4. So saith the soul, If I go into the city of the world, there I shall be starved; if I sit still, I shall also perish. What shall I now do? I will venture upon Jesus Christ; he hath food that endures to eternal life, and if I perish there, I perish. If I have not Christ I must die, the wrath of God hangeth over my head, and I cannot escape. Alas! poor soul, now thou seest thy wretchedness, cast thyself upon him, and come in. If thou venturest, thou canst but die! Adventure therefore, put thyself upon God's mercy, for he is gracious and full of compassion.

Those that have given up themselves to Christ, let them study to honour God and Christ, by taking those comforts that are allotted to them. When any man inviteth us to a feast, he knoweth if we respect him we will fall to. God hath bestowed his Son upon us, and will he not with him give us all things? Let us not therefore dishonour the bounty of our good God, but come in, and labour to have our hearts more and more enlarged with the consideration of the excellency of these eternal comforts. The fulness of Christ is able to satisfy the soul, though it were a thousand times larger than it is. If it were possible that we could get the capacity of angels, it could not be sufficient to shew forth the fulness of pleasures that are provided for a Christian. Let us therefore labour with all labour to open our hearts to entertain these joys, for we cannot honour God more than of his bounty to receive thankfully what he freely offers. To taste plentifully in the covenant of grace, of these riches, and joy, and hope of things to come, glorious above all that we are able to think of; I say, this is the way to honour God under the gospel of hope. Of things that are infinite, the more we take, the more we may take, and the more we honour him that giveth. Let us therefore enter deeply into our special sins, there is no fear of despair. Think of all thy wants, and of all thy sins; let them be never so many, yet there is more to be had in Christ than there can be wanting in thee. The soul that thinks itself full of wants is the richest soul, and that that apprehendeth no want at all, no need of grace or Christ, is always sent empty away. Grieve therefore for thy sins, and then joy that thou hast grieved, and go to God for the supply of all thy wants. The seeds of joy and of comfort are sown in tears and grief in this world; but yet we know we shall reap in joy in the world to come.

Remember this, we have we know not what to go through withal in this valley of tears. That speech of Barzillai was good and excellent, who being by David himself invited to the court, answered, 'I am now grown old, I am not fit for the court, for my senses are decayed and gone,' 2 Sam. xix. 32, *seq.* Even so the time will come when our sense of relishing earthly pleasures will utterly be lost. We are sure to go to our graves, and we know not what particular trouble we may meet with in this world and go through, if we live to a full age. Alas! what are all comforts here to the comforts of eternity? When our days are spent on earth, then comes in the eternity of pleasure or everlasting sorrow. Oh then if, when we shall leave all behind us, we have the joy of the Holy Ghost in our hearts, it will advance us above all the suggestions of sin or Satan, and bring us cheerfully above to the tribunal seat of Christ. Labour therefore to have a spiritual relish of soul, to grow in grace and comforts of the Holy Ghost; for the time will come when we shall wish that we had had more than we have. Every one will repent of looseness and slackness in the ways of holiness. Therefore let us labour earnestly to be good husbands for our souls for the time to come.

THE THIRD SERMON.

And in this mountain shall the Lord of hosts make unto all people a feast, &c. And he will destroy in this mountain the face of the covering cast over all people, and the veil that is spread over all nations.—ISAIAH XXV. 6, 7.

I HAVE heretofore spoken of the feast that God makes to his church, specially in the latter times, which was specially performed at the first coming of Christ, when the Gentiles came in; but the consummation and perfection of all will be at the day of judgment. Then God will spread a table for his to all eternity.

We have spoken heretofore at large of the resemblance of spiritual good things, by this comparison of a feast. God sets out spiritual things by outward, because we cannot otherwise conceive of them; the best things in grace, by the best and sweetest things in nature. And thus God enters into our souls by our senses, as we see in the sacrament.

But we have spoken at large of this. Our care must be to have a special taste, a spiritual appetite to relish this feast that God provides. Naturally we are distasteful. We relish not spiritual and heavenly things; we savour not the things of God. And the Spirit of God must alter our savour and taste, as he doth. Wheresoever there is spiritual life, there is spiritual relish of heavenly truths.

Now let me add this further, *that though it be made by God, yet we must bring something to this feast.* Christ feasteth with us, as ye have, Rev. iii. 20. He sups with us, not that we have grace from ourselves, or can bring anything; he bringeth his own provision with him when he suppeth with us; but yet by the covenant of grace whereby he enters into terms of friendship with us, we must sup with him, we must have grace to entertain him, though it is at his own cost; yet we must have something. He doth not require us to pay our debts, but he giveth us wherewith. Secretly he bids us come, but giveth a secret messenger to draw us; he sends his Spirit certainly. Certainly he will have us bring something when we come to feast, but it is of his own giving. And that we are to bring is humble and empty souls, wherein we are to delight ourselves in sense of our unworthiness; and the spirit of faith to believe his promises. That pleaseth him, when we can honour him with a spirit of faith, and then a spirit of love, and new obedience springing from a spirit of faith and love. These be the things Christ requires we should have. Our souls must be thus furnished that Christ may delight to dwell with us; and therefore it is a good importuning of God, 'Lord, I desire thou shouldst dwell in me, and prepare my soul as a fit temple;' vouchsafe me the graces thou delightest in, and delightest to dwell in. So we may beg of God his Holy Spirit to furnish our souls, so as he may dwell and delight in us.

But we have spoken largely of the former verse. I will now speak of the next that followeth.

'And I will destroy in this mountain the face of covering cast over all people, and the veil spread over all nations, to swallow up death in victory; the Lord will wipe away tears from all faces; and the rebukes of his people shall be taken from the earth, for the Lord hath spoken it.'

These depend one upon another, being the several services of the feast. He promiseth a feast in the sixth verse. And what be the several services? He will destroy in this mountain, this church, the face of covering cast over all people, &c. He will take away the veil of ignorance and unbelief, that they may have special sight of heavenly things, without which they cannot relish heavenly things; they can take no joy at this feast.

And then, because there can be no feast, where there is the greatest enemy in force and power, he swallows up death in victory. Death keeps us in fear all our lifetime. That that swalloweth up all kings and monarchs, the terror of the world, death, shall be and is swallowed up by our head, Christ, and shall be swallowed up by us in victory. In the mean time we are subject to many sorrows which cause tears; for tears are but drops that issue from that cloud of sorrow; and sorrow we have always in this world, either from sins or miseries, or sympathy in tears of that kind. Well, the time will come that tears shall be wiped away, and the cause of tears; all sorrow for our own sins, for our own misery, and for sympathizing with the times wherein we live. Our time shall be hereafter at the day of resurrection, when all tears shall be wiped from our eyes. God will perform that office of a mother to wipe the children's eyes, or of a nurse to take away all cause of grief whatsoever, else it cannot be a perfect feast.

Aye, but there are* reproaches cast upon religion and religious persons! It goeth under a veil of reproach, and the best things are not seen in their own colours; nor the worst things; they go under vizards here.

But the time will come that the rebukes of his people shall be taken away. The good things, as they are best, so shall they be known to be so; and sin, and base courses, as they are bad, and as they are from hell, so they

* Misprinted 'is.'—G

shall be known to be. Everything shall appear in its own colours; things shall not go masked any longer. And what is the seal of all this? The seal of it is, 'The mouth of the Lord hath spoken it.' Truth itself hath spoken it, and therefore it must needs be. Jehovah, that can give a being to all things, he hath said it.

We have heard why the church is called a mountain. He will destroy, or swallow up,* as the word may signify, the face of covering, or the covering of the face; the veil which is the covering of the face, and particularly expressed in that term always; the veil that is spread over all nations.

God will take away the spiritual veil that covers the souls of his people, that is between them and divine truths. It hath allusion to that of Exod. xxxiv. 34, 35, about Moses when he came from the mount. He had a veil, for the people could not behold him. He had a glory put upon his face, that they could not look upon him with a direct eye, and therefore he was fain to put a veil upon his face, to shew that the Jews could not see, as Paul interprets it, 2 Cor. iii. 15, 'To this day,' saith he, 'when Moses is read, there is a veil put upon their hearts.' They could not see that 'the law was a schoolmaster to bring to Christ,' Gal. iii. 24, the ceremonial law and the moral law. God had a blessed end, by the curse of it, to bring them to Christ. They rested in the veil, their sight was terminated in the veil, they could not see through to the end and scope of it. Nevertheless, when they shall turn to the Lord, the veil shall be taken away.

1. From the words, consider first of all, *that naturally there is a veil of ignorance upon the soul.*

2. Secondly, *God doth take away his† veil;* and God by his Spirit only can do it.

3. Thirdly, *that this is only in his church.* And where this veil of ignorance is taken off, there is feasting with God and spiritual joy, and delight in the best order; and where it is‡ taken off there is none of it.

First of all, by nature, *there is a veil of covering over all men's spirits.* To understand this better, let us unfold the terms of veil a little. There is a veil either upon the things themselves that are to be seen, or upon the soul which should behold them.

(1.) The veil *of things themselves* is when they be hidden altogether, or in part; when we know part, and are ignorant of part. And this veil upon the things ariseth from the weak apprehension of them; when they are not represented in clear expressions, but in obscurity of words or types; when we see them only in types or obscure phrases, which hideth sometime the sight of the thing itself. The manner of speech sometimes casteth a veil on things; for our Saviour Christ spake in parables, which were like the cloud, dark on the one side, light on the other, dark towards the Egyptians, light towards the Israelites. So some expressions of Scripture have a light side, that only the godly see, and a dark side, that other men, good wits, as natural men, see not.

(2.) Again, there is a veil *upon the soul and upon the sight.* If the things be veiled, or the sight veiled, there is no sight. Now the soul is veiled when we be ignorant and unbelieving; when we are ignorant of what is spoken and revealed, or when we know the terms of it, and yet believe it not.

(3.) Now, this veil of ignorance and unbelief continueth in all unregenerate men *until grace takes away the veil.* Besides, before a thing can be seen, the object must not only be made clear, and the eyesight too, but

* 'Swallow.'—Dr J. A. Alexander in his 'Commentary' adopts the rendering of Sibbes here.—G.

† Qu. 'this?'—ED.

‡ Qu. 'is not?'—ED.

there must be *lumen deferens*, a light to carry the object to the eye. If that be not, we cannot see. As the Egyptians, in the three days of darkness, had their eyes, but there wanted light to represent the object, and therefore they could not go near one to another. It is the light, and not sight. If there be sight and no light to carry and convey the object, we cannot say there is sight.

That which answereth to this veil is the veil of Scripture, whereby heavenly things are set out by a mystery. A mystery is, when something is openly shewed and something hidden.

When something is concealed, as in the sacrament, they be mysteries. We see the bread, we see the wine, but under the bread and wine other things are intended, the breaking of the body of Christ, and the shedding of his blood, and in that the love and mercy of God in Christ, in giving him to death for us, and Christ's love to give himself to satisfy divine justice. These be the things intended, which only the soul sees and apprehendeth. And so all things in the church, indeed, are mysteries, the incarnation of Christ, the union of both natures, that Christ should save the world by such a way as he did, that he should bring us to glory by shame, to life by death, to blessing and happiness by being a curse for us. It is a mystery to bring contrary out of contrary: that so glorious a person as God should be covered with our weak and sinful nature. It was a mystery, the Jews stumbled at it. Light came, and the darkness could not comprehend the light. And, as Christ was a mystery himself, so the church is a mystery. That God should so much delight in a company of poor men, the off-scouring of the world, to make them temples of his Holy Spirit, and heirs of heaven, men that were under the scorn of the world, this is a mystery. So all is mystical, the head, the members, the body, the church, and every particular point of religion. There is a mystery in repentance. No man knoweth what sorrow for sin is but the true gracious person. No man knows what it is to believe but he that hath an heart to believe. No man knoweth what peace of conscience and joy of the Holy Ghost is but those that feel it. So that is a mystery. And therefore 'great is the mystery of godliness,' saith the apostle, 1 Tim. iii. 16. Not only in the points themselves, but even the practice of religion is a mystery too. Repentance and faith, and new obedience and love, and the comforts of religion, are all mysteries. There is a veil upon them in all these points, that a carnal man cannot see them.

You see, then, in what sense there is a veil of the things, and in what sense there is a veil on men's hearts; that is, either the things themselves are hid, or if the things be open, they want sight and light of knowledge, and they want faith to believe. Beloved, we live in times that the object is clear to us, the things themselves are made clear; as who knoweth not what Christ is, and the notion of the incarnation, and of the union with him. We know them notionally. They be opened and revealed to us very clearly, all the articles of faith, and mysteries of religion, so that there is no obscurity in the object. The things are clear, specially in these places of knowledge. But yet, notwithstanding, there is a veil upon the soul. The soul of every man that is not graciously wrought upon by the Spirit of God hath a veil of ignorance and unbelief.

First of all, *of ignorance*. There is a vale* of ignorance in many, and in all men naturally a veil of ignorance of spiritual things. For, unless they be revealed, they can never be known to angels themselves. The angels

* Qu. 'veil?'—ED.

themselves know not the gospel till it be opened, and therefore they be students in it continually, and the best men in the world know nothing in the gospel further than it is revealed. But there is a veil of ignorance upon them that know these things notionally, because they do not know them as they should know them; they do not know them in *propria specie*, spiritual and heavenly things as spiritual and heavenly things. They do not know spiritual things as spiritual things, they have a human knowledge of spiritual things. Those that want grace, they know the grammar of the Scripture and divinity, and they know how to discourse as schoolmen do, from one thing to another, and to argue. They know the logic and rhetoric of the Scripture, but they stick in the stile. There is something they are ignorant of; that is, they have not an eye of knowledge, as we call it. They do not see the things themselves, but only they see things by another body's spirit, and they have no light of their own. And so no man knoweth naturally but the children of God what original sin is, what corruption of nature is, nor knows sin in its own odious colours, to be filthy, and to be dangerous as it is. To draw the curse and vengeance of God upon it, this is not known, but by the Spirit revealing the odiousness of sin, that the soul may apprehend it, as Christ did when he suffered for it, and as God doth. A gracious man seeth it as God seeth it, because by the Spirit of God he seeth the filthiness and odiousness of it, and the danger it draweth after it.

Second. And so in any points of religion naturally, *a man sees not them spiritually, as they are, and as God sees them, but he seeth them by a human light*. He seeth heavenly things by a human light, notionally, and merely to discourse of them. He seeth not intritively* into the things themselves. He seeth them *sub aliena specie*, under another representation than their own. Only a godly man seeth spiritual things as the Spirit of God, and seeth them as they are, knows sin as it is, knoweth grace to be as it is, and knoweth faith. What it is to believe, what it is to have peace of conscience, and the pardon of sins. He knoweth these things in some sense intritively, though not so as he shall do when he shall see these things in heaven, when he shall see face to face. There is a great difference in it. He sees them intritively in respect of the knowledge of other men, though he sees but in a glass in regard of the knowledge he shall have in heaven. As St Paul saith, 'For we see but as in a glass.' But he that sees in a glass seeth more life than he that sees the dead picture of a man. So, though we see but in a glass heavenly things, yet we see them better than those that see them in a dead notion. Though it be nothing to the knowledge we shall have in heaven, yet it is incomparable above the knowledge of any carnal natural man upon the earth.

Third. Again, naturally men have veils of ignorance *upon the most divine things*. Of spiritual things, such as is union, and as is the communion between Christ and us, and the mystery of regeneration in the new creature, such as is the joy in the Holy Ghost, the inward peace of conscience. I will not name the particulars to insist on them, but give you only an instance. Though they know the notion of these things, yet they are altogether ignorant of them. Their knowledge is a mere outward light. It is a light radicated† in the soul. It is not as the light of the moon, which

* Qu. 'intuitively,' or 'interiorly?'—G.; or, 'introitively?'—ED.

† There seems to be a confusion here, as if a sentence had been left out. It must be the knowledge, not of 'natural,' but of 'gracious,' men, that is as a light radicated or rooted in the soul.—ED.

receiveth light from the sun, but it is a light radicated and incorporated into the soul, as the light of the sun is, by the Spirit. It is in the soul. It is not only upon the soul, but in the soul. The heart sees and feeleth, and knoweth divine truths. There is a power and virtue in the sight and knowledge of a gracious man. There is none in the knowledge of a carnal man. The light of a candle hath a light in it, but no virtue at all goeth with it; but the light of the sun, and the light of the stars, they have a special virtue, they have heat with them, and they have an influence in a special kind on inferior bodies working together with the light. So it is with heavenly apprehension and knowledge. It actually conveyeth light. But with the light there is a blessed and gracious influence, there is heat and efficacy with that light. But though a carnal man know all the body of divinity, yet it is a mere light without heat, a light without influence. It is not experimental. As a blind man can talk of colours, if he be a scholar, and describe them better than he that hath his eyes, he being not a scholar. But he that hath his eyes can judge of colours a great deal better. Oftentimes, by book, a scholar can tell you foreign countries better than he that hath travelled, yet the traveller that hath been there can tell them the more distinctly. So he that is experienced in that kind, though a stranger, can measure another man's ground better than himself. He can tell you here is so many acres. But he that possesseth them knows the goodness of them, the worth of them, and improveth them to his own good. And so it is with many. They can measure the points of religion, and define and divide them. Aye, but the poor Christian can taste, can feel them, can relish and improve them. His knowledge is a knowledge with interest, but other men's knowledge is a knowledge with no interest or experience at all. So that there is naturally a veil of ignorance on the heart of every natural man.

Christianity is a mystery. Till conversion there is a mystery in every point of religion. None know what repentance is but a repentant sinner. All the books in the world cannot inform the heart what sin is or what sorrow is. A sick man knoweth what a disease is better than all physicians, for he feeleth it. No man knoweth what faith is but the true believer. There is a mystery also in love. Godliness is called a mystery, not only for the notional, but the practical part of it. Why do not men more solace themselves in the transcendent things of religion, which may ravish angels? Alas! there is a veil over their soul, that they do not know them, or not experimentally. They have no taste or feeling of them.

And so there is a veil of unbelief. There is no man without grace that believeth truly what he knoweth; but he believeth in the general only, he believeth things so far forth as they cross not his lusts. But when particular truths are enforced on a carnal man, his lusts do overbear all his knowledge, and he hath a secret scorn arising in his heart, whereby he derideth those truths and goeth against them, and makes him think certainly these be not true, and therefore he believeth them not. If a man by nature believed the truths he saith he knoweth, he would not go directly against them. But the ground of this is, there is a mist of sinful lusts that are raised out of the soul, that darkens the soul, that at the present time the soul is atheistical and full of unbelief. For there is no sin but ignorance and unbelief breatheth it into the soul, and maketh way for it; for if a man knew what he were about, and apprehended that God saw him, and the danger of it, he would never sin. There is no sin without an error in judgment, there is a veil of ignorance and unbelief. What creature will run into a pit when he seeth it open? What creature will run into the fire, the most dull creature? Man will not run into that danger that is open to the eye of the soul, if there were not a veil of ignorance, at least unbelief, at that time upon the soul. All sin supposeth error.

And this should make us hate sin the more. Whensoever we sin, specially against our conscience, there is atheism in the soul at that time, and there is unbelief. We believe not the truth itself. No sinner but calleth truth into question. When he sinneth, he denieth it or questioneth it; and therefore there is a veil on every man naturally over his heart by ignorance and unbelief. The truths themselves are clear. God is clear, and the gospel is light, *mens, lux;* you know they know things in the object, but in us there is darkness in our understandings; and therefore the Scripture saith not we are dark only, but 'darkness itself,' 2 Cor. vi. 14. The clouds that arise are like the mists that do interpose between our souls and divine things, arising from our own hearts; and the love of sinful things raise such a cloud, that we know not, or else believe not, what is spoken. To proceed.

Obs. 2. *God only can reveal and take away the veil of ignorance and unbelief from off the soul.* I will speak specially of this veil.

Reason 1. The reason is, there is such a natural unsuitableness between the soul and heavenly light and heavenly truths, that unless God opens the eye of the soul, and puts a new eye into the soul, it can never know or discern of heavenly things. There must be an eye suitable to the light, else there will never be sight of it. Now, God can create a new spiritual eye to discern of spiritual things, which a natural eye cannot. Who can see things invisible? Divine things are invisible to natural eyes. There is no suitableness. He that must reveal these and take away the veil must create new light within as well as a light without. Now, God, and only God, that created light out of darkness, can create light in the soul. 'Let there be light.' He only can create a spiritual eye, to see the things that to nature are visible.*

There be four things in sight. 1. The object to be beheld. 2. The light that conveyeth it. 3. The organ that receiveth it. 4. And the light of the eye to meet the light without. So it is in the soul. Together with divine truths, there must be light to discover them; for light is the first visible thing that discovers itself and all things else. And then there must be a light in the soul to judge of them, and this light must be suitable. A carnal, base spirit judgeth of spiritual things carnally like himself, because he hath not light in his own spirit. The things are spiritual, his eye is carnal. He hath not a light in his eye suitable to the object, and therefore he cannot judge of them, for the Scripture saith plainly 'they are spiritually discerned,' 1 Cor. ii. 14. Therefore, a carnal person hath carnal conceptions of spiritual things, as a holy man doth spiritualise things by a spiritual conception of them.

There be degrees of discerning things. The highest degree is to see things 'face to face' as they be in heaven; the next to that is to see them in a glass, for there I see the motion and true species of a man, though not so clearly, as when I see him face to face; therefore we soon forget the species of it in a glass. We have more fixedness of the other, because there is more reality. We see things put into water, and that is less; but then there is a sight of man in pictures which is less than the rest, because we see not the motion. It is even so; a carnal man scarce sees the dead resemblance of things. In Moses's time they saw things in water, as it were blindly, though true; but we see things in a glass of truth as clearly as

* Qu. 'invisible?'—ED.

possibly we can in this world. In heaven we shall see face to face, snall see him as he is. And then will be the joy of this excellent feast, and the consummation of all sweet promises, which here we can but have a taste of.

Reason 2. So that is the first reason of it, that God is only* the taker away of the veil, which ariseth from the unsuitableness between the soul and divine truths.

There is nothing in the heart of man but a contrariety to divine light. The very natural knowledge, that is contrary. Natural conscience, that only checketh for gross sins, but not for spiritual sins. Obedience and civil life, that makes a man full of pride, and armeth him against self-denial and against the righteousness of Christ and justification. There is nothing in the soul but, without grace, riseth against the soul in divine things.

Reason 3. Again, *there is such disproportion between the soul, being full of sin and guiltiness, and heavenly things, that are so great, that the heart of man will not believe unless God convinceth the soul, that God is so good and gracious, though they be great and excellent, yet God will bestow them upon our souls;* and therefore he sendeth the Spirit, that overpowers the soul, though it be full of fear and guilt that sin contracts.

Though we be never so unworthy, he will magnify his grace to poor sinners; and without that the soul will never believe there is such an infinite disproportion between the soul and the things, between the sinful soul and the Spirit, so that God must overpower the soul to make it believe.

The Scripture is full of this. As we are naturally ignorant and full of unbelief, so God only can overpower the soul and take away the veil of ignorance.

Reason 4. *All the angels in heaven, and all the creatures in the world, the most skilful men in the world, cannot bring light into the soul, they cannot bring light into the heart.* They can speak of divine things, but they understand them little. But to bring light into the heart, that the heart may taste of them and yield obedience to believe, that they cannot do. And therefore, all God's children, they be *theodidactoi*,† taught of God. God only hath the privilege to teach the heart, to bend and bow the heart to believe.

So that God only by his Spirit takes away the veil of ignorance and unbelief.

Obs. 3. Now, the third thing is, *that this is peculiar to the church and to the children of God*, to have the veil taken off. '*In this mountain*,' saith the Scripture, 'the veil of all faces shall be swallowed up or taken away.'

I partly shewed in the former point, that it is peculiar to God's children to have the veil taken off. There is a veil in all things. Either the things be hid from them, as amongst the Gentiles, or if the things be revealed, there is a veil upon the heart; their lusts raise up a cloud, which, until God subdue by the Holy Spirit, they be dark, yea, darkness itself. Goshen was only light when all Egypt was in darkness; so there is light only in the church, and all other parts in the world are in darkness. And amongst men in the church there is a darkness upon the soul of unregenerate men, that be not sanctified and subdued by the Spirit of God. And all godly men are lightsome, nay, they be 'lights in the world,' Phil. ii. 15. As wicked men are darkness, so gracious men, by the Spirit of God, are made lights of the world from him that is the true light, Christ himself.

It is peculiar to the church to know the greatest good, and the greatest evil. It is nowhere but in the church, who are the people of God. None

* That is, 'God only is.'—G.

† That is, θεοδίδακτοί. Cf. John vi. 45; 1 Thess. iv. 9.—G.

but God's elect can know the greatest evil, that is, sin, which the Spirit of God revealeth; and the greatest good, that is, God's mercy in Christ, and sanctifying grace. The same Spirit doth both. As light doth discover foul things as well as fair; so the same Spirit of God discovers the loathsomeness of sin, and the sweetness of grace. Where the one is,* there is never the other; where there is not truly a deep discerning of sin, there is never knowledge of grace; there is none but in the church. Those that have the spirit of illumination, they have sanctification likewise.

We shall make use of all together. You see, then, what naturally we are, and that God's grace must take away the veil; and this is from all them within the church, and in the church those whom God is pleased to sanctify.

Obs. In the fourth place. *Where this veil is taken off from any, there is with it spiritual joy and feasting,* as here he joineth them both together. 'I will make a feast of fat things, and will take away the veil,' ver. 7.

Reason. The reason of the connection of this, is, that same Spirit that is a Spirit of revelations, is a Spirit of comfort; and the same Spirit that is the Spirit of comfort, is a Spirit of revelation. All sweetness that the soul relisheth cometh from light, and all light that is spiritual conveyeth sweetness, both together. Beloved, there is a marvellous sweetness in divine truths. In Christ is all marrow, and in religion forgiveness of sins, and inward peace, and joy, and grace, fitting us to be like to Christ, and for heaven. They be incredibly sweet, they be all marrow. Aye, but they are only so to them that know them. Now God's Spirit, that revealeth these things to us, doth breed a taste in the soul. The Spirit of illumination to God's children, is a Spirit of sanctification likewise; and that sanctification alters the taste and relish of the will and affections, that with discovery of these things, there is a taste and relish of them. It is *sapida scientia,* a savoury knowledge they have. And therefore where he maketh a feast, he taketh away the veil; and where he takes away the veil, he makes a feast. What a wonderful satisfaction hath the soul, when the veil is taken off, to see God in Christ reconciled! to see sin pardoned! to see the beginnings of grace, which shall be finished and accomplished in glory! to discern that 'peace which passeth understanding,' &c., Philip. iv. 7. What a marvellous sweetness is in these things!

They cannot be revealed to the knowledge spiritually, but there is a feast in the soul, wherein the soul doth solace itself; so both these go together.

And therefore we should not rest in that revealing that doth not bring a savour with it to the soul. Undoubtedly, that knowledge hath no solace and comfort for the soul, that is not by divine revelation of heavenly truths.

We see the dependence of these one upon another. Then let us make this use of all:

Use 1. Since there is a veil over all men by nature, the work of ignorance and unbelief, and since God only taketh it away by his Holy Spirit, and since that only those that be godly and sanctified have this taken off: while this is, there is a spiritual feast, joy, and comfort, and strength; then *let us labour to have this veil taken off; let us labour to have the eyes of our understandings enlightened, to have our hearts subdued to believe; let us take notice of our natural condition.* We are drowned and enwrapt in darkness, the best of all. It is not having knowledge what we are by nature; it is not any knowledge that can bring us to heaven; there must be a revelation,

* Qu. 'is not?'—ED.

a taking away of the veil. How many content themselves with common light of education, and traditionary knowledge! So they were bred and catechised, and under such a ministry! But for spiritual knowledge of spiritual things, how little is it cared for! And yet this is necessary to salvation. There is great occasion to press this, that we rest not in common knowledge. If religion be not known to purpose, it is like lightning, which directs not a man in his way, but dazzles him, and puts him quite out of his way. Many have flashes of knowledge that affect them a little; but this affection is soon gone, and directs them not a whit in the ways of life. And therefore labour that the will and affections may be subject. Beg of God a 'fleshy heart,' 2 Cor. iii. 3, an heart yielding to the truth. We know ear-truths will harden, as none is harder than a common formal Christian. A man had better fall into the hands of papists, than into the hands of a formal hypocritical Christian. Why? They pride themselves in their profession. No persecutors worse than the Scribes and Pharisees, that stood in their own light. They were more cruel than Pilate. And therefore if we be informed, but not truly transformed, to love the truth we know, and hate the evil we know, it maketh us worse.

And then it enrageth men the more. The more they know, the more they be enraged. Men when truths be pressed, which they purpose not to obey, they fret against the ordinance, and cast stones, as it were, in the face of truth. When physic doth raise humours, but is not strong enough to carry them away, they endanger the body; and where light is not strong enough to dispel corruption when it raiseth corruption, it enrageth it. When men know truth, and are not moulded into it, they first rage against it, and then by little and little fall from it, and grow extreme enemies to it. It is a dangerous thing, therefore, to rest in naked knowledge. Beg then of God that he would take away the veil of ignorance and unbelief, that light and life may go together, and so we shall be fit to feast with the Lord.

Means. Now that we may have true saving knowledge, first, we *must attend meekly upon God's ordinances*, which be sanctified to this end to let in light to the soul.

1. Will we know sin and our state by nature, and how to come out of it; then together with this revelation *must come an heavenly strength into the soul, a heavenly taste and relish;* and therefore attend upon the ordinances, and labour for an humble soul, empty of ourselves; and do not think to break into heavenly things with strength of parts. God must reveal, God must take away the veil only by his Holy Spirit in the ordinance. The veil is taken away from the object, in opening of truths; but the veil must be taken away from the object, and from the heart too. There must be knowledge of the object, as well as an object. The object must be sanctified and fitted to the persons, else divine truths will never be understood divinely, nor spiritual truths spiritually. Labour to be emptied of yourselves. In what measure we are emptied of our self-conceitedness and understanding, we be filled in divine things. In what measure we are emptied of ourselves, we are filled with the Spirit of God, and knowledge, and grace. As a vessel, in what measure it is emptied, in that measure it is fit to be filled with more supervenient liquor; so in what measure we grow in self-denial and humility, in that measure we are filled likewise with knowledge. He will teach an humble soul that stands not in its own light, what it is to repent, to believe, to love; what it is to be patient under the cross; what it is to live holily, and die comfortably. The Spirit of God will teach an humble, self-denying soul all these things; and therefore

labour for an humble, empty soul, and not to cast ourselves too much into the sins and fashions of the times, as the apostle, 'Be not conformed to this world, but be ye transformed by the renewing of your mind,' &c., Rom. xii. 2.

2. *When a man casteth himself into the mould of the times, and will live as the rest do, he shall never understand the secrets of God, and the good pleasure of God;* for the world must be condemned. The world goeth the broad way. And therefore we must not consider what others do, but what God teacheth us to do.

3. And add to this, *what we know, let us labour to practise.* 'But he that doth the will of my Father, shall know of every doctrine, whether it be of God or no,' John vii. 17. We must do, and we shall know.

Quest. But can we do before we know?

Ans. The meaning is this, that we have, first, breeding and education, and some light of the Spirit* turneth it presently to practice, by obedience to that knowledge. And then you shall know more. He that doth these things, he shall know all. They shall know that do practice what they know already. 'To him that hath shall be given,' Mat. xiii. 12; that is, to him that hath some knowledge, and putteth in practice what he hath, God will increase the talent of his knowledge; he shall know more and more, till God revealeth himself fully in the world to come.

4. And therefore *be faithful to ourselves, and true to the knowledge we have, love it*, and put it into practice. When divine truths are discovered, let the heart affect them, lest God giveth us up to believe lies. We have many given up to this sin. Because when truths are revealed, they give way to their own proud scornful hearts, they know not the love of the truth. God knoweth what a jewel the truth is; and since they despise it, God giveth them up to believe lies. And take heed, practise what we know, and love what we know, entertain it with a loving affection.

A loving affection is the casket of this jewel. If we entertain it not in love, it removes from us its station, and being gone, God will remove us into darkness.

And remember it is God that taketh away the veil of ignorance and unbelief. And therefore make this use of it.

2. *To make our studies and closets, oratories*,† not to come to divine truths, to out-wrestle the excellency of them with our own wits; but to pray to God, as you have Ps. cxix. 18, 'Open mine eyes, and reveal thy truth.' And St Paul prayeth for the 'spirit of revelation,' Eph. i. 17. And so desire God to reveal and take away the veil from us, that he will open divine truths to our souls; that since he hath the key of David, that 'opens, and no man shutteth,' Rev. iii. 7, that he would open our understandings to conceive things, and our hearts to believe. He hath the only key of the soul. We can shut our souls, but cannot open them again. So we can shut our hearts to divine truths, we can naturally do this; but open them without the help of the Spirit we cannot. He can open our understandings, as he did the disciples'. He can open our hearts to believe; he can do it, and will do it. If we seek to him, he will not put back the humble desires of them that fear him. And therefore for heavenly light and heavenly revelation, all the teaching of the men of the world cannot do it. If we know no more than we can have by books, and men that teach us, we shall never come to heaven; but we must have God teach the heart, as well as the brain. He must teach not only the truths themselves, as they be discovered, but the love of them,

* Qu. 'of the spirit; turn, &c.?'—ED.

† That is, 'places of prayer.'—G.

the faith in them, the practice of them; and he only can do this, he only can teach the heart, he only can discover the bent of the heart, and Satan's wiles that cast a cloud upon the understanding. The Spirit only can do it; and therefore in all our endeavours, labour to get knowledge, and join holiness and divine grace, and pray to God that he would reveal the mystery of salvation to us.

Quest. But how shall we know whether we have this heavenly light and revelation or no? whether the veil be yet upon our hearts or no? I will not be long in the point.

Ans. 1. We may know it by this. The apostle Peter saith to express the virtue of God's power, 'He hath called us out of darkness to his *marvellous* light,' 1 Pet. ii. 9. The soul that hath the veil taken from it, *there is a marvelling at the goodness of God, a wondering at the things of faith.* And the soul sets such a price upon divine things, that all is 'dung and dross' in comparison of the excellent knowledge of Jesus Christ, Philip. iii. 8. Wherefore is it that thou wilt reveal thyself to us, and not unto the world? as admiring the goodness of God. What are we? What am I, that God should reveal these things to me, and not to the world? that many perish in darkness and shadow of death, though they hear of divine things, yet they, teaching rebellion and unbelief, are not moulded to them, and so perish eternally? There is a secret admiration of the goodness of God to the poor soul, and a wonderment at spiritual things. 'O! how sweet is thy law,' saith David, Ps. cxix. 103. And teach me the wonders of thy law, and joy unspeakable and glorious, and peace that passeth understanding, Philip. iv. 7. These things be high to the soul.

Ans. 2. By the taste of what they have, they wonder at that little, and at that they look for, *and are carried with desire still further and further, which is a farther evidence.* They that have any spiritual knowledge, they be carried to grow more and more, and to enter further and further into the kingdom. Where there is not a desire still, till they come to the full measure that is to be had in Jesus Christ, there is no knowledge at all. Certainly a gracious soul, when once it sees, it desires still to feel the power and virtue of Christ in it, as Paul counted all dung in comparison of this knowledge, to know myself in Christ, and feel the power of his death in dying to sin, and virtue of his resurrection in raising me to newness of life. It was Saint Paul's study to walk still to the high price* of God's calling, and where that is not, no grace is begun.

Ans. 3. And again, where divine light is, and the veil taken away, *it is the sanctified means;* for God works by his own instruments and means, and they be able to justify all courses of wisdom. 'Wisdom is justified of her children,' Mat. xi. 19. By experience they be able to say the word is the word. I have found it casting me down, and raising me up, and searching the hidden corners of my heart. I have found God's ordinances powerful, the word and sacrament. I have found my hope, faith, strength, and spiritual comfort, and therefore I can justify them; for I have found, tasted, and relished of these things, which worketh that upon the soul which Christ did on the body. I find mine eyes, I find my deaf ears opened. I can hear with another relish than before. I find a life and quickening to good things, though it be weak. I had no life at all to them before. I find a relish which I knew not before. So that there be spiritual senses whereby I am able to justify that these things be the things of God. So that they that have divine truths can justify all the ordinances of God by their own

* The old way of spelling 'prize.'—G.

experience. As Peter answered when Christ asked him, Will you be also gone? Be gone! said Peter; 'Whither should we go? thou hast the words of eternal life,' John vi. 68. I have found thy words efficacious to comfort and strengthen and raise, and shall I depart from thee, who hast the words of eternal life? And so take a soul that the Spirit of God hath wrought upon. Ask whether they will be careless of means of salvation, not to pray, or hear, or receive the sacrament. By these have I eternal life conveyed. God hath let in by these comfort, and strength, and joy, and shall I leave these things? No; I will not. 'Whither shall I go? thou hast the words of eternal life.' Are we able to justify these things by the sweetness we have found in them? Then certainly God hath shined upon the soul, and, together with strength and light, conveyed sweetness to the soul.

Ans. 4. A godly man *seeth things with life, his sight worketh upon him.* It is a transforming sight. As the apostle saith, 'We all behold the glory of God, and are changed,' 2 Cor. iii. 18. Sight of light and life goeth together with a Christian; as Christ saith, 'he is the light of the world,' John ix. 5, and 'the life of the world,' John i. 4. First light, for life cometh with light, and light conveyeth life. All grace is dropped into the will through the understanding; and wheresoever Christ is life, he is light, because true knowledge is a transforming knowledge. But if religion be not known to purpose, it hardens and makes worse.

We are now by God's good providence come to farther business, to partake of these mysteries;* yet it should be the desire of our souls that our eyes may be opened, that in these divine and precious mysteries he would discover hidden love, which is not seen with the eyes of the body. They may see and taste and relish his love and goodness in Jesus Christ; that as the outward man is refreshed with the elements, so the inward man may be refreshed with his Spirit, that they may be effectual to us; that we may justify the course God takes, so far as to come charitably and joyfully to them.

THE FOURTH SERMON.

I will destroy in this mountain the face of the covering cast over all people, and the veil that is spread over all nations. He will swallow up death in victory, &c.—ISA. XXV. 7, 8.

WE have heretofore at large spoken of the spiritual and eternal favours of God, set out in the former verse, 'In this mountain will the Lord of Hosts make a feast of fat things.' While our soul is in the body, it is much guided by our fancy. Spiritual things are therefore presented by outward, and conveyed to the soul that way; only we must remember that there is a far greater excellency in the things themselves than in their representation. For what is all banquets, fatness with marrow, wine on the lees, to the joy and sweetness of religion, begun here, and accomplished in the world to come?

In Christ there is nothing but all marrow and sweetness in religion, that may refresh a man in the lowest condition, if he can but have a taste of it.

Now because the spiritual things of Christ do us no good, as long as they are hid, therefore the Holy Ghost setteth down a promise, 'that God will

* In the margin, 'Application of this to the sacrament.'—G.

take away the covering cast on all people, and the veil spread over all nations.'

But there be some things that will damp all mirth. Now here is security against them, that our joy may be complete; and this in the next verse, to which I now come, 'He will swallow up death in victory, he will wipe away tears from all faces.' The prophet having spoken of a great feast before, an excellent feast, sets forth here the services of that feast. What is it that accompanies it?

First of all, there shall be light to discover the excellency of the feast; the veil is taken away, and a knowledge given to know divine things in a spiritual manner.

Then, which will damp all feasts, the fear of death is taken away. 'He will swallow up death in victory, and wipe away all tears,' that is, all sorrow. The effect is put for the cause. This is an excellent promise, an excellent service in this spiritual banquet. Suppose a man were set at a feast furnished with all delicates, royally attended, clothes suitable, and had a sword hung over his head ready to fall upon him, it would cast such a damp on his spirit, as would spoil the joy of this feast. So to hear of spiritual excellencies, and yet death, and hell, and damnation coming along, alas! where is the comfort you speak of. And therefore to make the feast more perfect, there is not only light and knowledge, but removal of it ever may damp the feast. So this must needs come in to comfort all the rest. 'He shall swallow up death in victory, and wipe away tears from all faces.' Death is here represented to us under the word victory, as a combatant, as one that we are to fight withal, a captain.

And then here is the victory of him, Christ overcomes him, and overcomes him gloriously. It is not only a conquest, but a swallowing of him up. Usually God useth all sorts of enemies in their own kind. He causeth them that spoil to be spoiled, them that swallow up to be swallowed up. So death the great swallower shall be swallowed up.

Beloved, death is the great king of kings, and the emperor of emperors, the great captain and ruling king of the world; for no king hath such dominion as death hath. It spreads its government and victory over all nations. He is equal, though a tyrant. As a tyrant spares none, he is equal in this. He subdueth young and old, poor and rich. He levels sceptres and spades together. He levels all. There is no difference between the dust of an emperor and the meanest man. He is a tyrant that governeth over all. And so there is this equity in him, he spares none.

He hath continued from the beginning of the world to this time; but he is a tyrant brought in by ourselves, Rom. v. 19, *seq.* Sin let in death. It opened the door. Death is no creature of God's making. Satan brought in sin, and sin brought in death. So that we be accessory ourselves to the powerful stroke of this prevailing tyrant. And therefore sin is called the cause of death. Sin brought in death, and armeth death. The weapon that death fights with, and causeth great terror, it is sin. The cause is armed with the power of the wrath of God for sin, the fear of hell, and damnation. So that wrath, and hell, and damnation, arming sin, it bringeth a sting of itself, and puts a venom into death. All cares, and fears, and sorrows, and sicknesses, are less and petty deaths, harbingers to death itself; but the attendants that follow this great king are worst of all, as Rev. vi. 8, 'I saw a pale horse, and death upon it, and after him comes hell.' What were death, if it were not for the pit, and dungeon that followeth it? So that death is attended with hell, and hell with eternity. Therefore here is a strange kind of prevailing. There is no victory where there is no enemy, and therefore death must needs be an enemy, yea, it is the worst enemy, and the last enemy. Death is not planted in the forlorn hope, but it is planted at last for the greatest advantage, and is a great enemy. What doth death? It depriveth us of all comfort, pleasure, communion with one another in this life, callings or whatsoever else is comfortable. The grave is the house of oblivion. Death is terrible of itself, even to nature, as Augustine saith, where it is not swallowed up of Christ; for it is an evil in itself, and as I said, armed with a sting of sin, after which follows hell.

Now this death is swallowed up. When the Scripture puts a person upon death,* it is not uncomely for us to speak as the Scripture doth. The Scripture puts a person upon death, and a kind of triumphing spirit in God's children over death. 'O death, where is thy sting? O grave, where is thy victory?' 1 Cor. xv. 55. Death is the greatest swallower, and yet it is swallowed up by Christ. Death hath swallowed up all, and when it hath swallowed up, it keepeth them. It keeps the dust of kings, subjects, great and small, to the general day of judgment, when death shall be swallowed up of itself. It is therefore of the nature of those that Solomon speaks of, that cry, 'Give, give,' Prov. xxx. 15, and yet is never satisfied, like the grave, yet this death is swallowed up in victory.

But how cometh death to be swallowed up? Christ will swallow up death in victory, for himself and his.

Reason. First of all, because sin brought in death, our Saviour Christ became sin, a sacrifice to his father's justice for sin. He was made sin for us, he was made a curse for us, to take away the curse due to us; and sin being taken away, what hath death to do with us, and hell, and damnation, the attendants on death? Nothing at all. Therefore, Col. ii. 10, upon the cross Christ did nail the law, and sin, and the devil. There he reigned over principalities and powers, which were but executioners let loose by reason of our sins. And God being satisfied for sin, the devil hath nothing to do with us, but to exercise us, except it be for our good. So that he hath swallowed up death, because by his death he hath taken away sin, and so the power of Satan, whose power is by sin. And therefore it is excellently set down, Heb. ii. 14, 'He also took part of flesh and blood, that through death he might destroy him that had the power of death, that is, the devil.' So Christ by death overthrew Satan, that had the power of death, because by death he took away sin, the sins of all, and bore our sins upon the cross, and was made sin for us, that knew no sin. He is ours, if we believe. For then Christ is given to a particular man when he believes. Beloved, Christ upon the cross did triumph over all our spiritual enemies, sin, and death, and all. It was a kingdom of patience. You know there is a double kingdom of Christ; a kingdom of patience, and a kingdom of power.

1. Christ on the cross suffering punishment due to sin, overcame the law, and the devil, and sin, which is the kingdom of patience.

2. The kingdom of power he hath in heaven. If Christ were so able in his kingdom of patience to conquer our greatest enemies, what will he do in his kingdom of power? As Paul reasoneth, 'If by his death we are saved, much more now he triumphs in heaven, and appears for us, is he able to convey greater matters to us,' Rom. v. 21.

If Christ in the days of his flesh did conquer, how glorious will his conquest be at the day of judgment! *Now*, Christ hath conquered all in his own person, as our head; *then* he will conquer for us in his mystical body.

* That is, 'personifies.'—ED.

What is now done in his person, shall be done in his members. In the mean time, faith is our victory, his conquest over death our victory; his victory over all our spiritual enemies is our victory. Every one that believeth is a conqueror of death, though he die, because he sees it conquered in Christ his head; and as it is truly conquered in him, so Christ will conquer it in all his members. For as Christ in his natural body is gone to heaven, there to appear in our behalf, so shall mystical Christ be wholly in glory. He will not leave a finger. We shall all triumph over all our spiritual enemies. As Christ's natural body is glorious in heaven as our head, so shall also his mystical body be.

You see then how death is swallowed up by Christ as our surety, as the second Adam upon the cross; and truly swallowed up in him. And by faith this victory is ours, and time will come when in our own persons it shall be swallowed up in victory.

This might be enlarged, but I haste to make use of it.

Mark, I beseech you, how death is swallowed up by Christ in his own person for our good. He gave a great way to death, for death seized on him upon the cross. Death severeth soul from body. Death had him in his own cabinet, his grave, for three days. Nay, this great king and tyrant death, had a great conquest over Christ himself. But here was the glory of this victory! When death, this great conqueror of the world, had Christ upon the cross, and in his own dominion, in the grave, where he rules and reigns, consuming and swallowing up all, death was fain to give up all; and Satan thought to have had a great morsel when he devoured Christ, but there was an hook in his divine power that catched him, that when he thought to have swallowed up Christ, was swallowed up himself. His head was then broken. He never had such a blow, as by Christ on the cross, when he was overcome, being a scorn of the world visibly, yet invisibly in God's acceptation of that sacrifice, and in a spirit of faith. Christ triumpheth over Satan. Death was subdued even in his own kingdom, and that makes the victory great.

Death by seizing on Christ without right, Christ hath freed us from the evil of death when it had right to us. Death hath lost all its right by fastening on Christ, and so is become as a drone* without a sting. So the great swallower of all is swallowed up itself at last by Christ.

Use 1. Now for comfortable use of it. First, let us consider *that God oftentimes giveth a great deal of way to his greatest enemies.* God useth a stratagem of retiring; he seems to retire and give liberty to his enemies, but it is to triumph and trample upon them with greater shame. He will tread them to dust afterward. Christ gave death a great deal of liberty. He was crucified and tormented, then had† to the grave, and there he lay. And this was to raise a greater triumph over this great prevailer, over the world and death itself.

It is continued so in the church. Doth not he give way to the enemies of the church? They may come to say, Aha, aha, so would we have it. Now the poor children of God are where we would have them, but then comes sudden destruction. God, to make his victory more glorious, and more to discover their cruelty, comes upon them when they be in the top of pleasure, and the church in the bottom of abasement. Then God swalloweth up all in victory, as Christ did death when it seemed to have been itself victorious.

This is a very comfortable consideration, for if death be overcome when

* That is, the 'drone' bee.—G.

† That is, 'taken.'—G.

it seemed to overcome Christ, what need we fear any other enemy? Christ hath broken the net, as an eagle or great bird, and the rest escape by him.

You may enlarge this in your own meditations. He will swallow up death in victory. This is said for the time to come, he *will* swallow up death. But Paul saith it is also past, and swallowed up already. Faith saith it is done; and so it is in our head. Were it not comfortable now to all true-hearted Christians, to hear that the church fareth better, and that the enemies were swallowed up, for they be but the instruments of this inferior death? Let us get the spirit of faith, and see them all conquered, for certainly they shall have the worst at last. He that hath swallowed up death in victory, will swallow up all that be the cause of death. And therefore the Scripture speaks of these things as past, 'Babylon is fallen, as a millstone cast into the bottom of the sea,' Rev. xviii. 21.

Get a spirit of faith, and we shall never be much troubled with Babylon; for all the enemies of Christ, and adherents to that man of sin, must down, and partake of the judgments threatened in the Revelations. Heaven hath concluded it, and all the policy of Rome and hell cannot disannul it. They be already swallowed up to faith, and Christ will rule till he hath put them all under his feet, Ps. cx. 1; which shall be done, not only to destroy them, but to raise himself higher, in giving them up to their confusion.

Use 2. Again, if death be swallowed up in victory, labour *to be one with Christ crucified, for union with him.* Begin with union with Christ crucified. The first union is with Christ abased, and then with Christ glorified. And therefore labour to see sin, that brought in death, subdued by the power of Christ's death in some measure, and then we shall have comfort in his death glorified. For in my 'holy mount' death is swallowed up, that is, the true church of Christ. Labour to be members of Christ, otherwise death will come as a tyrant indeed, armed with a terrible sting, in his full force to assail you. It is the most terrible thing to see death come armed with the wrath and anger of God, and attended with hell and damnation. Labour, therefore, to be one with Christ crucified, to get our sins crucified, and ourselves partakers of his death; and then no damnation, no fear of death to them that are in Christ. They may die, but they are freed from eternal death, and they shall rise again, even as Christ's body rose, to glory.

Get, therefore, into Christ, and desire the power of his death subduing sin. In what measure we grow in that, we grow in boldness and joy, and whatsoever privileges follow Christ.

Use 3. Again, when we be in Christ, true members of him, then *let us be thankful to God for this victory, thankful to Jesus Christ that hath given us victory.* When we think of death, of sin, of judgment, of hell, of damnation, let us be framed as a Christian should. Now let him that hath the most terrible and fearful things in the world as conquered enemies, say, Oh, blessed be God for Christ, and blessed be Christ for dying for us, and by death disarming death of his sting! That now we can think of it in our judgments quietly; now we can think of all these as conquered enemies: this is the fruit of Christ's death. They are not only enemies, but friends in Christ. Sin, the remainder of it—(the guilt of it, that bindeth over to damnation, is taken away)—the remainders of it serve to humble us, make us feel the power of pardon, and to desire another world, where we shall be all spiritual. So that death is a part of our jointure. 'All things are yours, life and death,' 1 Cor. iii. 22. Death doth us many excellent services. It is a door and passage to life. Death is the death of itself, destroyeth itself. We never truly live till we die, and when we die, we are past fear of death. So that sin dieth, misery dieth, death dieth. Though it takes us from comforts, and employments, and friends here, yet it is a change to a better place, and better company, and better employments, and better condition, to be in a glorious condition to eternity; and therefore we have cause to bless God in Christ, that took our nature, and in our nature disarmed our greatest enemy, sin, and so disarmed death, and freed us from the wrath of God, and hell, and damnation. Oh, we can never be thankful enough for this!

Use 4. Again, if death be swallowed up in victory, *let us be ashamed of the fear of death*, because Christ saith he will swallow him up, as he hath already in his own person. Shall we be afraid of an enemy that is swallowed up in our head, and shall be swallowed up in every one of us? If we cherish fear, we shew we look not for an interest in this promise; for it is a promise, that 'in this holy mountain death shall be swallowed up in victory,' and why should we fear a conquered enemy? None will fear an enemy that is conquered.

Obj. But how came Christ to fear death, and we not to fear?

Ans. Christ had to deal with death armed with a terrible sting, with sin, and the wrath of God for sin. And, therefore, when he was to die, 'Father, let this cup pass from me,' Matt. xxvi. 39. But death is disarmed to us. He had to encounter with sin and the wrath of God, and death in all its strength. But we are not so. We are to deal with death like the brazen serpent, that hath the shape of death, but no sting at all. It has become a drone ever since it lost its sting in Christ. Life took death, that death might take life, as he said. The meaning is, Christ's life itself took death, that we that were so subject to death, that we were death itself, might take life. Oh blessed consideration! Nothing comparable to the consideration of the death of Christ! It is the death of death.

And then again we are sure of victory. It is conquered in our head, and shall be in us. But you say we are to conflict with the pangs of death, and many troubles meet in death. It is true, but it is conquered to faith, and in Christ our head. We must fight. Christ traineth us to overcome death ourselves by faith, and then we are sure of victory. Join these two together. It is conquered in Christ our head, and shall be conquered of us. Death keeps our dust, and must give them all again.

Obj. But in the mean time we die.

Ans. 'Tis so, but we are sure of victory. He will protect us in our combat, that hath conquered for us. We fight against death and the terror of it, in the strength and faith of his victory. Join these three together.

He that hath been our Saviour in life, will be so to death, and not exclusively, then to leave us, but to death, and in death, for ever; yea, most ready to help us in our last conflict. Indeed, to wicked men death is terrible, for he sendeth the devil to fetch them out of the world; but for those that be his, he sendeth his angels to fetch them, and he helps them in their combat. We must not therefore fear over much. There is a natural fear of death. Death wrought upon Christ himself, God-man; not only death, but such a death. He was to be left of his Father, and lie under the sense of the wrath of God; the separation of that soul from the body he took upon him was terrible; and therefore he saith, 'If it be possible, let this cup pass from me:' that was nature, and without it he had not been true man. But that I say is, that grace may be above nature. Death is a time of darkness. It strips us of earthly comforts, friends, callings, employments; but then comes the eye of faith to lay hold of the victory on Christ in time to come, when death shall be only swallowed up in victory; and then the glorious state to come, to which death bringeth us. So that here faith must be above sense, and grace above nature, and therefore I beseech you, let us labour for it.

There be two sorts of men to whom I would speak a little.

First. Those that in a kind of bravery seem to slight death; men of base spirits, as we call them; fools, vain-glorious spirits, empty spirits. Is there any creature, unless in Christ, able groundedly* to slight so great an enemy as death, armed with a sting of sin, and attended with hell and damnation? The Romish and devilish spirits are terrible; but if thy sins be not pardoned, it is the most terrible thing in the world to die, for there is a gulf afterwards. What shall we say, then, of single combatants, that for vain-glory are prodigal of their lives, that for a foul word, a little disgrace, will venture on this enemy, that is armed with sin, and if they die, they die in sin.† And which is the miserable condition of him that dies in sin: his death opens the gate to another death, which is eternal. They say they have repented, but there is no repentance of a sin to be committed. Canst thou repent of a sin before it be committed? that is but a mockery of God. And what saith the Scripture? Is it not the most terrible judgment under heaven to die in our sins? A man that dies in sin dies in hell: he goeth from death to hell, and that eternal.

I wonder, therefore, that the wisdom of flesh and blood should take away men's wit, and faith, and grace, and all, so much as to slight death, and repentance, as if it were so easy. Now, beloved, death is a terrible thing. It hath a sting, and thou shalt know it. If thou hast not grace to feel the sting of it whilst thou livest, when thou diest the sting will revive; then thy conscience shall awake in hell. Drunkenness and jollity take away sense of sin; but sin will revive, and conscience will revive. God hath not put it into us for nought. Death is terrible, if not disarmed beforehand. And if thou go about to die without disarming it before, it will not be outfaced. It is not an enemy to be scorned and slighted. And, therefore, be Christians in good earnest, else leave profession, and perish eternally. For we must all die; and it is a greater matter than we take it. But if we be true Christians, it is the sweetest thing in the world, an end of all misery, a beginning of true happiness, an inlet to whatsoever is comfortable. Blessed are they that are in the Lord by faith, and them that die in the Lord. Their death is better than the day of life. Our birthday brings us into misery; and therefore let me speak to true Christians, and bid them be ashamed of fearing death too much, which, of an enemy is become a reconciled friend.

Second. This may in the next place *yield great consolation to those that are in Christ Jesus,* that death by Christ is swallowed up in victory; and the rather, because the Holy Ghost meaneth more than a bare victory over death. Death is not only subdued, but is made a friend to us, as Ps. cx. 1, it is said 'his enemies shall be his footstool.' Now a footstool is not only trampled upon, but an help to rise. And so death is not only subdued, but it advanceth God's children, and raiseth them higher. It is not only an enemy, but a reconciled friend; for he doth that which no friend in the world can do. It ends all our misery, and is the inlet into all happiness for eternity. And whatsoever it strips us of here, it giveth us advantage of better in another world. It cuts off our pleasures, and profits, and com-

* That is, 'on good grounds.'—G.

† In the margin, 'of [the] duellist.'—G.

pany, and callings here; but what is that to our blessed change afterward, to our praying of God for ever, to the company of blessed souls, and the profits, and pleasures at the right hand of God for evermore? And therefore it is not only conquered, but to shew the excellency of his power, he hath made it a friend of an enemy, and the best friend in the world. It indeed separates soul from body, but it joineth the soul to Christ; so that the conjunction we have by it is better than the separation, if the conjunction makes us partake of our desire. 'I desire to be dissolved,' saith St Paul, Philip. i. 23, but that is not well translated. 'I desire to *depart*, and to be with Christ, which is best of all.' So that it is not only not an enemy, but a friend. And therefore the apostle makes it our jointure, part of our portion, all things are yours. Why? 'You are Christ's, and Christ is God's,' 1 Cor. iii. 22. What are ours? 'Things present, things to come, life, death,' 1 Cor. iii. 22, 23. And well may death be ours, because sin is our enemy; that remainder, that is kept in our nature to exercise us, and humble us, and fit us for grace. As Austin saith, I dare be bold to say, it is profitable for some to fall, to make them more careful and watchful, and to prize mercy more. So that not only death, but sin and the devil himself is ours; for his plots are for our good. God over-shooteth him in his own bow. 'He will give them over to Satan,' saith the apostle, 'that they may learn not to blaspheme,' 1 Tim. i. 20. Yet though they have a spirit of blasphemy by the humbling of their bodies, they be taught not to blaspheme; so that not only death, but sin, and he that brought sin into the world, the devil, are become our friends.

This being so, it may be for special comfort that we fear not the king of fears. The devil hath great advantage by this affection of fear, when it is set upon this object death. Overcome death, and all troubles are overcome. Who will fear anything that hath given up himself to God? 'Skin for skin, and all that a man hath, will he give for his life,' Job ii. 4. The devil knoweth that well enough. Therefore 'fear not,' saith Christ, 'them that can kill the body,' Mat. x. 28. Fear causeth snares, saith Solomon, Prov. xxix. 25, snares of conscience. But if a man hath overcome the fear of death once, what more is to be done? What if they take away life, they cannot take away that that is better than life, the favour of God. If we die in the Lord, we die in the favour of God, which is better than life; and we shall be found in the Lord at the day of judgment, and shall be for ever with the Lord in heaven; and therefore this is a ground of resolution in good causes, notwithstanding all threats whatsoever, because death itself is swallowed up in victory.

The worst the world can do is to take away this nature of ours. When they have done that, they have done all they can; and when they have done that, they have done a pleasure. That is not to be feared, saith Tertullian, that frees us from all that is to be feared (*d*). What is to be feared in the world? Every sickness, every disgrace? Why, death frees us from all. We do see every day takes away a piece of one's life, and when death cometh it overthroweth itself; for the soul goeth presently to the place of happiness. The body sleepeth a while, and death hath no more power.

'He that believeth in me,' saith Christ, 'he shall not see death, but is passed from death to life,' John v. 24. He shall not see spiritual death; but as he lives in Christ, shall die in Christ, and rise again in Christ. He that hath the life of grace begun, shall have it consummate without interruption. It is a point of wonderful comfort, that death is so overcome that we be in heaven already. And it is no hard speech, but stands with the truth of other points; for are not Christ and we all one? His body is there, and is not he the head of his mystical body? He that carried his natural body, will not he carry his mystical body thither too? will he be in piecemeal in heaven? Therefore we are in heaven already the best part of us. We are represented in heaven, for Christ represents us there as the husband doth the wife. He hath taken up heaven for us.

Christ cannot be divided, as Austin saith. 'We sit in heavenly places already with Christ,' Eph. i. 3. And what a comfort is this, that while we live we are in heaven, and that death cannot hinder us from our resurrection, which is the restoring of all things. And therefore, as the apostle saith, 'Comfort one another with these things,' 1 Thess. iv. 18. These things indeed have much comfort in them.

Let us labour then to be comfortable: this use the apostle makes of it; and fruitful in our places, upon consideration of the victory we have by Christ. 1 Cor. xv. It is an excellent chapter that largely proveth Christ's victory, as the cause of our victory, because he is the first fruit that sanctifieth all the rest. 'Finally, my brethren, be constant, immoveable, always abounding in the works of the Lord, knowing that your labour is not in vain in the Lord.' He raiseth that exhortation of fruitfulness and constancy from this very ground of the victory Christ hath gotten by death. 'O death, where is thy sting? O grave, where is thy victory? Thanks be to God through Jesus Christ.' 'And therefore be constant, immoveable, always abounding in the work of the Lord, knowing that your labour shall not be in vain in the Lord,' 1 Cor. xv. 58. Make that use the apostle doth of fruitfulness to God for Christ, that we can think of death, and sin, the devil, and all his malice, and not be afraid; yea, think of them all with comfort, that we be not only freed from their tyranny, but they be our friends.

Christ hath the key of hell and death; a saying taken from the custom of governors that carried the key. He hath the government and command of hell and death. Now if Christ hath command of death, he will not suffer death to hurt his members, or triumph always over them. He will keep them in the grave. Our bodies are safe in the grave. The dust is fitted for a heavenly, for another manner of body than we have now; and Christ that hath the key will let them out again. Therefore trust a while till times of restoring come, and then we shall have a glorious soul, and glorious body, as the apostle saith, 1 Cor. xv. 43. I beseech you, think of these things, and get comfort against the evil day. And to that end, be sure to get into Christ, that we may be in Christ, living, and dying, and be found in Christ. For what saith the Scripture? 'Blessed are they that die in the Lord,' Rev. xiv. 13. It is an argument of blessedness to die for the Lord, but if it be not in the Lord, it is to no purpose. If there is granted this happiness of dying for the Lord, it is well; 'but blessed are they that die in the Lord.' Why? 'They rest from their labour.' Death takes them off from their labours. All their good works go to heaven with them. So saith the Spirit, whatsoever the flesh saith. And there is no resting till that time. Their life is full of troubles and combers,* and therefore labour to get assurance that we are in Christ, that we be in Christ, and die in Christ, and then 'there is no condemnation to them that are in Christ.'

How besotted are we to put away preparation of death till it comes! He that forgets Christ and getting into Christ, all his lifetime, it is God's just judgment that he should forget himself in death. We see how a villain that hath no care of his own life, may have power of another man's life.

* That is, 'cumbers,' cares.—G.

And therefore labour to be engrafted into Christ by faith; and that we may know it by the Spirit of Christ prevailing in us over our natural corruptions more and more. As the apostle saith, 'There is no condemnation to them that are in Christ;' for the spirit of life, 'the law of the spirit of life which is in Christ, hath freed me from the law of sin and death,' Rom. vi. 7, *seq.*, the condemning law of sin. If the law of the spirit of life which is in Christ the head, be in us in any measure, it frees us from the condemning law of sin, that it carrieth us not whither it would. Then we may say with comfort, 'There is no condemnation to them that are in Christ;' for the law of the spirit of life in Christ hath freed us from the condemning, tyrannizing law of sin and death,

Sin hath no law. It is in us as a subdued rebel, but it sets not up a throne. Some hope to be saved by Christ, and yet they set up sin a throne in the soul. Sin biddeth them defile themselves, and they must obey it. This is a woeful estate! How can they expect to die in the Lord, but such as are freed by the law of the spirit of life? New lords, new laws. When kings conquer, they bring fundamental laws; and when we are taken from Satan's kingdom into the kingdom of Christ, the fundamental laws are then altered. Christ by his Spirit sets up a law of believing, and praying, and doing good, and abstaining from evil. The law of the spirit of life frees us from the law of sin and death.

I beseech you, enlarge these things in your thoughts. They be things we must all have use of beforehand, against the evil day. It should be comfortable and useful to us all, to hear that our enemy, our greatest enemy, death, is swallowed up in victory. And yet there is more comfort in the text.

THE FIFTH SERMON.

And all tears shall be wiped away from all faces.—Isa. XXV. 8.

Not only death shall be swallowed up in victory, but God 'will wipe away all tears from all eyes.' Religion shall be religion; good things shall be good things. Nothing shall go under false notions. All tears shall be wiped away. We have now many causes of tears. In the world there is continual raising of clouds, that distil into drops of tears. Had we nothing without us to raise a vapour to be distilled in tears, we are able to raise up mists from our own mists, from our own doubts and conflicts within.

As we should weep for our own sins, so for the sins of others. As we may see in Jeremiah, where the prophet saith, 'O that my head were a fountain of tears, that I might weep continually for the sins of my people,' Jer. ix. 1. And indeed good men are easy to weep, as the heathen man observeth (*e*). They are easy to lament, not only for their own sins, but the sins and misery of another.

Our blessed Saviour himself, we never read that he laughed. We have heard that he wept, and for his very enemies, 'O Jerusalem, Jerusalem,' Mat. xxiii. 37. He shed tears for them that shed his blood. Tears were main evidences of Christ's sweetness of disposition; as that he would become man, and a curse, and die for us, and that he would make so much of little children, and call all to him that were weary and heavy laden, that he never refused any that came to him. He that wept specially for the miseries and afflictions, this shewed his gracious and sweet disposition. And that in heaven, he is so full of sympathies in glory, that when Paul persecuted the church, 'Why dost thou persecute me?' Acts x. 4; so, though he is free from passion in heaven, he is not free from compassion, from sympathy with his church. And so every child of God is ready, not only to grieve for his own sins, and the misery that followeth them, but the sins and miseries of others. 'Mine eyes gush out with rivers of tears,' saith the prophet David, Ps. cxix. 136, when he saw that men brake the law of God, whom he loved.

A true natural child takes to heart the disgrace of his father. If we be not grieved to see our father disgraced, we are bastards, not sons. They that make sport of sin, what are they? Alas! they have not one spark of the spirit of adoption. They are not children, who rejoice at that at which they should grieve.

So St Paul, 'I have told you often, and now tell you weeping, there be many enemies of the cross of Christ,' Philip. iii. 18. When he saw some men preach against, and others enemies of the cross of Christ, whose end is damnation, he telleth them of it weeping.

We have cause, therefore, to mourn for the sins of others, and for the miseries of others, whether we respect God, or the church, or ourselves.

First, the love of God moveth us to weep when we see him dishonoured.

Second, if we love the church, we should mourn for any sins that may prejudice their salvation.

Doth it not pity any* man to see an ox go to slaughter? to see a man of parts otherwise, by sinning against conscience, going to slaughter? to see an ordinary swearer, an unclean person, a profane wretch, covering himself with pride as a garment, scorning God, and the world, and all? Can a Christian look upon this, see flesh and blood, like himself, under the gospel, under a cursed condition unavoidable, without serious repentance, and not be affected with it? Can a man see a poor ass fall under a burden, and not help to take it up, and yet see man falling to hell, and not be affected with it? Thus we see we have cause enough of tears. And as there is cause, so we should be sensible. We ought to take to heart the afflictions of Joseph. He is a dead man that hath not sense in this kind. If we go to the body and state, or anything about a man, there is cause of grief. Hath not every member many diseases? and is not our lives a kind of hospital, some sick of one thing, some of another? But as there is cause we should be sensible of it, we are flesh and not stones, therefore it is a sottish opinion, to be stockish and brutish, as if to outface sorrow and grief were a glory.

Use 1. When our Saviour was sent into the world, *Christi dolor, dolor maximus, there were no patience without sensibleness.* Away, then, with that iron, that flinty philosophy, that thinks it a virtue to be stupid; † and as the apostle saith, 'without natural affections,' Rom. i. 31. He counteth it the greatest judgment of God upon the soul, yet they would have it a virtue. Why should I smite them any more? saith God; they have no sense, no feeling, Isa. i. 5.

The proud philosopher thought it was not philosophical to weep, a proud stoical humour,‡ but Christians desire it.

And therefore we ought to labour to be more sensible, that we might make our peace, and reverence the justice of God, and be more sensible of

* That is, 'draw pity from any man.'—G. † That is, 'insensible.'—G.

‡ One of the commonplaces of *Stoicism*.—G.

him afterwards. It is most true, that *Sapiens miser, plus miser;* the more wise any man is, the more sensible of misery. And therefore of all men, the best men have most grief, because they have most quick senses. They be not stupified with insensibility and resoluteness, to bear it bravely, as the world; but they apprehend with grief, the cause of grief And as they have a more sanctified judgment than other men, so they have a more wise affection of love, and a quicker life of grace. Where life is, there is sense; and where there is a clear sight or cause of grief, there is most grief. Therefore the best men have most grief, because they be most judicious, most loving.

Then they have most grace to bear it out of all others. Therefore, considering there is cause in ourselves and in others of grief continually, we ought to labour to be sensible of it, else it were no favour to have tears wiped away.

So that there is cause of tears, and tears is a duty of Christians, sensible of the cause both of sin and misery upon one and another.

Use 2. And as it is an unavoidable grief, *so it is good we should grieve.* We must stoop to God's course, we must bring our hearts to it, and pray (that since our necessities and sins do call for this dispensation, that we must under correction, he will make us sensible of his rod), that he would make good his covenant of grace, 'to take away our stony hearts, and give us hearts of flesh,' Ezek. xi. 19, that we may be sensible.

Most of graces are founded upon affection, and all graces are but affections sanctified. What would become of grace, if we had not affections? Therefore, as there is cause of grief, and tears from grief, we ought to grieve. It is a condition, and a duty: a condition following misery, and a duty following our condition.

Take heed of that which hinders sensibleness of troubles and judgment, that is, hardness of heart, forgetfulness, studying to put away sorrow with sin. For we ought to be sensible, and ought to labour to be sensible, to know the meaning of every cross in ourselves and others.

But suppose we have crosses, and we must be sensible of them, then it followeth, 'God will wipe away all tears from our eyes.' Is there nothing for the present, no ground of comfort? Yes. As we ought to be sensible of grief, so we ought to be sensible of matter of joy for the present, specially if we consider the time to come. The life of a Christian is a strange kind of life. He ought to grieve, and he ought to joy. He hath occasion of both, and he ought to entertain both; for that that we ought to aim at specially is joy, and if we grieve, it is that afterwards we might joy. We must be sensible of any affliction, that we might joy afterwards, and we ought to labour for it. For is not the joy of the Lord our strength? Are not we fit to do service, when our spirits are most enlarged? And is it not a credit to religion, when we walk in comfort of the Holy Ghost? Is it not a scandal, when we droop under the cross? We ought to be sensible, yet not so as to forget matter of joy and comfort. And therefore, as we ought to grieve, so we ought, when we have grieved, to keep up the soul with consideration of joy for the present as much as we can, yea, to pick out matter of comfort from the very cross. That is the heart of a Christian, not only to joy in other matters, but to pick comfort out of grief. God suffers me to fall into this or that condition. It is a fruit of his fatherly love. He might suffer me to run the broad way, to be given up to a reprobate sense and hard heart, but he doth not do so. Pick out matter of comfort from grief.

Then consider the presence of God in it. Indeed, I have matter of grief, but I find God moderating it. It might be far worse, it is his mercy I am not consumed; I find God by it doing me good, I find myself better by it, I cannot well be without it. Who would not labour to be sensible of a cross, when he looketh up to God's cross, and justice, and mercy? He hath rather cause to joy, than to grieve in the very cross itself.

But specially mark what the Holy Ghost saith here. We ought not to be cast down overmuch with any cross, considering God 'will wipe away all tears from our eyes,' that is, all natural tears, and the miseries of this life. There shall be no more misery, no more sickness, no more trouble.

And then all tears that arise from consideration of sin, and misery following sin. Death is the accomplishment of all mortification. It is a comfort we shall not always lead this conflicting life, but the war between the flesh and spirit will be taken up; the sense will be removed. We shall be out of Satan's reach, and the world's reach one day, which is a great comfort to consider. Whatsoever the cause is, the cause shall be removed ere long. If the cause be desertion, for that God leaveth us comfortless, we shall be for ever hereafter with the Lord. If the cause be separation from friends, why we shall all meet together ere long, and be for ever in heaven. If the cause be our own sins, we shall cease hereafter to offend God, and Christ will be all in all. Now sin is almost all in all. Sin and corruption bear a great sway in us. If the matter of our grief be the sins of others, and the afflictions of others, there is no sin in heaven, 'no unclean thing shall enter there,' Rev. xxi. 27. The souls of perfect men are there, and all are of one mind. There is no opposition to goodness, there all shall go one way; there, howsoever they cannot agree here, all shall have mutual solace and contentment in one another: they in us and we in them, and that for ever. You cannot name them, or imagine a cause of tears, but it shall be removed there. Nay, the more tears we have shed here, the more comfort we shall have. As our troubles are increased here, our consolation shall increase. That we suffer here, if for a good cause, will work our 'eternal and exceeding weight of glory,' 2 Cor. iv. 17. We say April showers bring forth May flowers. It is a common speech, from experience of common life. It is true in religion. The more tears we shed in the April of our lives, the more sweet comfort we shall have hereafter, If no tears are to be shed here, no flowers are to be gathered there. And, therefore, besides deliverance from trouble, here is comfort, God will take away all cause of grief, and all kinds of grief whatsoever.

And therefore thus think of it.

The next thing to be considered is the order. First, we must shed tears, and then they must be wiped away. After a storm, a calm; after sowing in tears, comes reaping in joy. What is the reason of that order?

Reason 1. The reason is *our own necessity*. We are in such a frame and condition since the fall, that we cannot be put into a good frame of grace without much pain. The truths of God must cross us, and afflictions must join with them. For the sins contracted by pleasure, must be dissolved by pain. Repentance must cost us tears. We may thank ourselves if we have brought ourselves to a sinful course. For the necessity of this order, a diseased person must not be cured till he feel some smart of the wounds.

Reason 2. Again, consider it is *for our increase of comfort afterwards*, that God will have us shed tears; and then to have our tears wiped away, because we be more sensible of joy and comfort after sorrow. We cannot be sensible of the joys of heaven, unless we feel the contrary here. And therefore of all men, heaven will be the most heaven to them that have had their portion of crosses and afflictions here. First, therefore, shed tears, and then they must be wiped away, because joy is most sensible. As it is with the wickedest of all men, they be most miserable that have been happiest, because their soul is enlarged by their happiness, to apprehend sorrow more quickly and sensibly. So they that have been most miserable here, shall have most joy hereafter.

Use 1. Now for use. Here is not only the mercies of God in Christ, but the tender mercy; that whereas our life is full of tears, which we have brought upon ourselves, yet God stoops so low as to wipe our eyes, like a father or mother. His mercy is a sweet and tender mercy. And, as the psalmist saith, when we are sick 'he maketh our beds in our sickness,' Ps. xli. 3. Christ will come and serve them that watch and serve him; nay, he will attend them, and 'sup with them,' Rev. iii. 20. He is not only mercy and goodness, but there be in him bowels of mercy. He not only giveth matter of joy and comfort, but he will do like a tender-hearted mother, wiping away all tears from our eyes. We cannot apprehend the bowels in God's love, the pity and mercy of God towards them that be his, and afflicted in the world, specially in a good cause. Though they be never so many, if they be penitent tears, he will wipe them all away.

And whereas we must shed tears here, that we may be comforted hereafter, take heed that we do not in this life judge by sight, but by faith. 'If we live by sight, we are of all men most wretched,' 1 Cor. xv. 19. In the world the children of God are most miserable, and of the children of God, the best saints. Who hath more cause of tears than the best saints? It is but seed-time here. While seed-time continues, there be tears. The husbandman, while it is seed-time, cannot do his office but with trouble. The minister cannot do his office, but he is forced to take to heart the sins of the times, to see his work go backward. Governors of families and such, they carry their seed weeping. Yea, the best men cannot do good sometimes, but they do it with trouble in themselves, and with conflict of corruptions. There is no good sown here, but it is sown in tears; yet take no scandal at this, 'God will wipe away all tears.'

The Head of the church, our blessed Saviour, and all his gracious apostles, what a life did they live! The glorious martyrs that sealed the truth with their blood! And therefore, as the apostle saith, 'If our happiness were here only, we were of all men most miserable,' 1 Cor. xv. 19. If we judge by sight, we shall condemn the generation of the righteous. We live by sight, when we see any cast down with sight of sin, sense of temptation, distress of conscience, [and] we think him forlorn. Oh, take heed of that! For those that shed tears here, God will wipe them all away. 'Woe to them that laugh now, for they shall mourn hereafter,' Luke vi. 25. Though we weep here, yet matter of joy enough shall spring up hereafter. 'Afflictions will yield a quiet fruit of righteousness to them that are exercised thereby,' Heb. xii. 11. We may not see their fruits presently, but afterwards. And therefore be not discouraged for anything we can suffer here, or for the church, if we see her under pressure. As darkness is sown for the wicked, the foundation of their eternal torment is laid in their joy; so the ground and foundation of all a godly man's joy is laid in tears. 'Blessed are they that mourn, for they shall be comforted,' Mat. v. 4. Yet for the present there is more matter of joy than grief, if we look with both eyes; as we ought to have double eyes, one to be sensible of our grief, as we must be, the other of our comfort, that we may not be surprised with grief. There is a sorrow to death, an overmuch sorrow. It is unthankfulness to God to forget our comforts, as it is stupidity to forget our sorrow. Take us at the worst, have not we more cause of joy than sorrow? Mark Rom. v. 1, *seq.*: 'Being justified by faith, we have peace with God, and rejoice under hope of glory.' Nay, afterwards, saith he, 'we rejoice in tribulations.' And why? upon what ground? 'Knowing that tribulations bring experience, and experience hope, and hope maketh not ashamed.' Now we rejoice in God reconciled in Christ. So that as we ought to look with one eye upon the grief, that we may have ground to exercise grace, which we are not capable of without sensibleness, so we must look to grounds of joy. Our life is woven of matter of sorrow and joy; and as it is woven of both, affections should be sensible of both, that they may be more apprehensive of the grounds of comforts.

When the day of persecution approacheth, this will make us comfortable, for our life is a valley of tears; and shall not we go through this valley of tears, to this mount where all tears shall be wiped away from all eyes? When we be dejected with the loss of any friend, they say as Christ said to the women, 'Weep not for me,' Luke xxiii. 28. They be happy, 'and all tears are wiped away from their eyes.' And therefore as it is matter of comfort while we live, so ground of comfort when we die. For there is occasion of sorrow in death, parting with friends and comforts of this world. Then tears are shed in more abundance, and then we bethink ourselves of former sins, and there is renewing of repentance more than at other times; yet then are we near the time of joy, and nearest the accomplishment of the promise that 'all tears shall be wiped away.'

And so you have the whole state of a Christian life, an afflicted condition. Aye, but it is a comfortable condition. The more afflictions here, the more comfort here, but specially hereafter. The life of a carnal man is all in misery. If he falls to joy, he is all joy; if to sorrow, he is all sorrow. He hath nothing to support him. He is like a Nabal, he sinketh like a piece of lead to the bottom of the sea, 1 Sam. xxv. 37, 38; like Ahithophel, down he goeth, 2 Sam. xvii. 23. When he is upon the merry pin, he is nothing but joy. But a Christian's state and disposition are both mixed. He hath ground of sorrow for his own sins, and for the sins and miseries of the times. So he hath matter of comfort for the present, in the favour of God, in the pardoning of sins, in the presence of God, in delivering him from trouble. He hath special ground of joy in hope of glory in time to come. Therefore, as we have a mixed state, labour for a mixed disposition, and labour to be in a joyful frame, so to grieve, as out of it to raise matter of joy. And when we would joy, grieve before, for joy is sown in grief. The best method of joy is for to take away all that disturbeth our joy. Search the bottom of the heart! see what sin is unconfessed, unrepented of! Spread it before God, desire God to pardon it, to seal the pardon! When our souls are searched to the bottom, then out of that sorrow springeth joy; and out of these sighs and groans that cannot be expressed, cometh joy unspeakable and full of glory. If a man will be joyful, let him labour to weep first, that the matter that interrupteth his joy may be taken away. Those that will be joyful, and not search to the bottom, must needs with shame be brought back to sorrow. When we will joy to purpose, let us judge ourselves, that we may not be judged of the Lord; mourn for our sins, and then lay hold upon the promise, that 'all they that mourn for sin shall be comforted,' Mat. v. 4. And blessed are they that shed tears here, for all tears shall be wiped away.

We are subject to wrong ourselves, both good and bad: for the good think, if they be in misery, they shall be ever so; the bad, if they be in prosperity, they shall always be so, and they bless themselves in it. Now the joy of the hypocrites is as the 'crackling of thorns,' Eccl. vii. 6, and the grief of the godly is but short. And therefore let not the wicked fool themselves with groundless hopes, nor the godly vex themselves with needless fears; but put off conceitedness of the long continuance of troubles. Time is but short, and ere long God 'will wipe away all tears from our eyes.' No mists, no clouds, shall be extended to heaven. The state in heaven shall be like the state of heaven, and there is no cloud there, but all pure, all serene. Therefore in Christianity consider not their beginning but their ends. 'Mark the end of the upright, for the end of the upright is peace,' Ps. xxxvii. 37. Ways have their commendation from the term in which they end. 'If by any means I may attain the resurrection of the dead,' saith Paul, Philip. iii. 11. Through thick and thin, fair and foul, rugged winds, dry or bloody death; if by any means I may come to the resurrection of the dead, the first degree of glory, all is well. It is a good way that ends well. *Non quâ, sed quò.* Consider not what way he brings us to heaven, but whither he brings us. If he bring us to heaven through a valley of tears, it is no matter; for in heaven 'all tears shall be wiped from our eyes.' And therefore Christianity is called wisdom. 'And this wisdom is justified of her children,' Mat. xi. 19. What is the chiefest point of wisdom? To look home to the end, and to direct all means to that end. He is wise that is wise for eternity. The wicked will have their payment here. 'But woe to them that laugh, for they shall mourn,' saith Christ, Luke vi. 25. They will not stay for ground of joy hereafter, but will have present payment. But though the ways of Christians be foul, and wet with tears, yet blessed are they; for God 'will wipe away all tears from their eyes.' 'Comfort one another with these words,' 1 Thess. iv. 18.

THE SIXTH SERMON.

And he shall swallow up death in victory; and God will wipe away tears from all faces; that the rebukes of his people may be taken away from off the earth: for the Lord hath spoken it.—ISA. XXV. 8.

YOU have heard heretofore of a *feast* provided for God's people, the *founder* of it being God himself, who only can indeed comfort (that which is specially to be comforted) the soul and the conscience, he being above the conscience. The *place* where the feast is kept is 'mount Zion,' the church of God. The delicacies are described by 'fat things, wine refined on the lees,' &c. The best of the best that can be thought of, which is Christ with all his benefits; who is bread indeed, and drink indeed, that cherisheth and nourisheth the soul to life everlasting. And because there should be nothing to disturb the solemnity of the feast, he promises to 'destroy the face of covering,' 'to take away the veil spread over all nations,' the veil of ignorance and infidelity, to shine upon the soul, and fill it full of knowledge and heavenly comfort. And because there can be no comfort where death is feared, being the greatest enemy in this life, therefore he will 'swallow up death in victory,' and all that makes way for death, or attends death. And when this is taken away, all the attendants vanish with it, 'God will wipe away all tears from all faces.' Because the best things have not the best entertainment in the world, nor the best persons, God promiseth that the rebukes of his people shall be taken away from off the earth; what they are they shall be known to be. These be very great matters, and therefore there is a great confirmation, they have a seal, and what is that? 'The Lord hath spoken it.'

The last day I shewed that God's children shall shed tears, and that they have cause to do it. I will now enlarge it a little.

It is the condition of men since the fall. In paradise before there was no cause of tears, nothing was out of joint, all in frame. There was no sin, therefore no sorrow, therefore no apprehension of sorrow. And so in heaven there shall be no tears, because no cause of it; they shall be as far from heaven as the cause. This life is a valley of tears, a life of misery, and therefore we shed tears here. And we want no cause of it as long as sin is in the world, and sorrow, and misery that followeth sin; our own sins and the sins of others, our own miseries and the miseries of others. And surely a child of God finds this the greatest cause of mourning in this world, that he hath a principle in him always molesting him in the service of God. He cannot serve God with that cheerfulness. His unfeelingness, that he cannot be so sensible of God, dishonoured by himself and others, is his burden. He is grieved that he cannot grieve enough. He can find tears for other things, matter of this enough, as the heathen man could say (*f*). A man loseth his estate, and hath tears for them; but forceth tears for other things which are the true ground of grief. A child of God hath a remainder of corruptions, which puts him on to offend against God, and hinders him in his service, in the liberty and cheerfulness of it. And this he complains of with Paul and others, 'Miserable man that I am,' not for his affliction, though that was much, but 'who shall deliver me from this body of death?' Rom. vii. 24.

Case 1. I will here add a case. *Some say they cannot weep, but they can grieve; whether then is it necessary or no to weep?* Tears are taken for the spring of tears; grief, all grief, shall be taken away. Tears are but the messengers of grief; and oftentimes the deepest apprehension, that takes things deeply, cannot express it in tears. In some the passages fetching the conceit to the heart are made more tender that they can weep. Now, the grief of a Christian is a judicial* grief; a rational grief, not only sensible tears must have sensible grief, but a Christian's grief is a sensible, judicial grief. He hath a right judgment of things that cause sorrow, willeth it, and tears are only an expression of it.

But how shall I know whether grief be right or no? There be tears God hath no bottle for. 'Thou puttest my tears into thy bottle,' Ps. lvi. 8. He makes much of them. They be *vinum angelicum*, as he saith. God is an angel to his people, to wipe away their tears. But some tears God hath no bottle for, hypocritical tears, Delilah's tears, tears of revenge and anger, Esau's tears. And therefore the true tears that God will wipe away, are such as first of all follow our condition here, our misery. God will wipe them away. If we speak of tears from a judicial ground,

1. The spring of true tears *is the love of God, and of Christ, and of his church, and the love of the state of Christianity.* Tears spring from love, these tears specially.

Oh! a Christian takes to heart that God should be so ill used in the world; that Christ, the Saviour of the world, should find such entertainment, that he should have anything in him that should offend such a

* That is, 'judicious.'—ED.

Saviour! This unkindness stingeth him to the heart. He takes it grievously that God should be abused. *Lætitia habet suas lachrymas*, there is not only grief that is the immediate cause of tears, but another cause beforehand; that is, love. Joy likewise hath its tears, though they be not here meant specially.

2. Again, tears are good and sound when we weep *for our own sins as well as the sins and miseries of others*. And I will add more, we must weep for the sins of others as well as for our own. For it is a greater sign of the truth of grace to take to heart the sins of others more than our own. You will say this is a kind of paradox, for often a man may take to heart his own sins as matter of terror of conscience; not his sins, as contrary to God, having antipathy to him, being opposite to the state of the soul, not as sin is properly sin, but to be grieved and vexed for sin as it hath vexation and terror of conscience. When a man can take to heart the sins of another, and that truly as it is an offence of his good God, and a crucifying again of his sweet Saviour, these be true tears indeed. It is more sign of grace than to weep for a man's own sins.

Some are taken up with terrors of conscience, that let their children, family, and friends alone. Their heart is eaten up with self-love, and they be near eaten up with their own terrors of conscience. But here is true grief and an hatred of sin in a right respect, when it exerciseth itself upon others as well as upon ourselves.

3. Again, tears arise from the right spring, from true grief, *when we can weep in secret*. Oh! saith Jeremiah, if you do so and so, 'My soul shall weep in secret for your pride,' Jer. xiii. 17. Here was a good soul indeed. Many will have tears of comfort in public, &c. Aye, but when they can weep in secret for their own sins and the sins of others, it is an evidence of a right spring of grief.

4. Again, when tears tend *to reformation of what they grieve for;* for else they be *steriles lachrymæ*, barren tears. Do they tend to reform what we weep for? Do they tend to action? Affections are then good when they carry to action; as grief, love, joy, they are all for action. When we weep and grieve, and reform withal, it is a good sign. I will name no more. You see then that grief is sound when it springeth from the love of God, and is for the sins of others as well as our own, and our own as well as others; when it stirs up to reformation; when it is in secret; and therefore let us examine our grief by these and the like evidences. It will be a good character of a gracious soul. Then God will carry himself as a sweet nurse, or loving mother to her child, that sheddeth tears. God will 'wipe away all these tears.' Oh! the transcending love of God! His love is a tender love. The love of a mother, the love of a nurse! It is not love, but the bowels of love, the bowels of mercy and compassion. How low doth he stoop to wipe away the tears of his children! 'God will wipe away all tears.'

I will propound one question more, and then proceed. But we are bid to rejoice always. Why then is it required that we weep and mourn? Can two contraries stand together?

Case 2. I answer, very well. For we may grieve, as we have matter of grief, and are in a condition of grief; and we may rejoice, and ought to rejoice, as we look to the promise that God 'will wipe away all tears.' When we think of the present cause, we cannot but grieve; but when we look beyond all troubles, we cannot but joy; it hath influence of joy into our heart. Nay, for the present we may joy and grieve, without looking to eternity sometimes. If we consider that we have offended God, done that that grieveth his Spirit, that is matter of grief. But when we consider we have Christ at his right hand, that speaketh peace for us, and makes our peace by virtue of his mediation, that giveth comfort. So that we have cause of joy, and cause of grief, about the same things at the same time.

We are never in such a state of grief here, but if we look about us, look forward, look upward . . . . .* A Christian, that is, a good Christian, is a person that hath many things to look after, that he may manage his estate of Christianity wisely. He is to look to himself and his sins, to the mercies of God in Christ, to the constancy of it, that it is answerable to the fruit of it in peace and joy here, and happiness hereafter, which are constant too. His grace, as himself, is constant, the fruits of it constant. Therefore 'rejoice evermore.' And, saith the apostle, 'I know what I say, I am well advised, 'evermore rejoice,' Philip. iv. 4. So that the life of a Christian is a mixed life, nay, the ground of our joy is our sorrow and grief, and joy is sown in grief. If we will rejoice indeed, let us mourn indeed. True joy ariseth and springs out of sorrow.

I proceed to the next. 'And the rebukes of his people shall be taken away from off the face of the earth.' Another benefit that makes the feast sweet and comfortable is this: 'He will take away the rebukes of his people.' And here is the same method to be used, *that God's children, his church, and people, are under rebukes, and under reproach.*

We need not stand to prove the truth of it. It is true, *first, the head of the church, and the church itself, and every particular member, they go under rebukes.* For the head of the church, we should spend the time to no purpose to prove it. What was Christ's life? It was under a veil. He appeared not to be what he was. You know he was esteemed the chief of devils, an enemy to his prince, to Cæsar. I will not spend time in clear truths.

For the church itself, you see in the book of Esther, iii. 8, 'There is a strange people that acknowledge no law, they be against the laws of the prince.' They pass under the imputation of rebels. The poor church, that had thoughts of peace, the meek church of God, they counted as enemies of the state, as Christ, the head, was. And so the church in Babylon, under what rebukes was it? They reproached them, 'By the waters of Babylon we sat down and wept, when they said, Sing us one of the songs of Zion,' Ps. cxxxvii. 1. The church sitteth by the waters of Babylon all this life. The world is a kind of Babylon to God's people, and then sing us one of your songs. Where is now your God? say the hearts of wretched people, when they saw the people of God in disgrace. Tully could say of the nation of the Jews, 'It sheweth how God regardeth it; it hath been so often overcome.'† Thus the heathen man could scorn the state of God's people. You see how the psalmist complains in the name of particular Christians, 'Where is his God? he trusted in him, let him save him,' Ps. xxii. 8. Oh, this was daggers to David's heart. 'It pierced to my heart when they said, Where is thy God?' Ps. xlii. 10. To touch a Christian in his God, as if God had no care of him, it is more than his own grief and affliction. So when a child of God is rebuked and affronted, when religion must suffer by it, so that the head of the church, the members of the church, are under rebukes, as it may be proved, if I carry you through all stories.

At this day, the church of the Jews, you see what it is come to: the nation of the Jews, under what reproach it is. And surely this prophecy

* This sentence is left thus unfinished.—G.

† Cicero Orat. Pro Flacco, c. 28. See footnote, vol. I., p. 303.—G.

aimeth partly at the conversion of the Jews. It shall be accomplished at the resurrection, when all tears shall be perfectly wiped away. But it hath relation to the conversion of the Jews. In what state are they now? Are they not a word of reproach? Moses's speech is verified of them, 'They shall be a hissing to all nations,' 2 Chron. xxix. 8. And is not it a proverb, Hated as a Jew?

Reason. But what is the reason of it? Not to stand long upon the point, you know there be two seeds in the world, the seed of the serpent and the seed of the woman; and the enmity between them is the true ground, and the antipathy in the hearts of carnal men to goodness. There is a light shineth in the life of them that be good, and them that be ill hate the light, as discovering themselves to themselves, and to the world, not to be that they seem to be. There is a saltness in the truth. It is savoury, but it is tart, whether in the word preached, or howsoever truth layeth open what is cross to corruption. And hereupon pride and self-love in carnal men studieth how to overcast all they can the names of those that be better than themselves with a cloud of disgrace. It is the property of vile men to make all others vile, that they may be alike. Men cannot abide distinctions of one from another. The Scripture distinguisheth the 'righteous man, more excellent than his neighbour,' Prov. xii. 26; but they will not have that. The hatred of distinction is the cause they make all as bad as they can. And hereupon it is that good things were never clothed in the right habit, nor ill things neither, but do pass under a veil. Take away the true garment of grace and holiness and goodness, and put a false veil upon it, it passeth not under that that it is in this world, because wicked men will not suffer it, but will raise up the credit of other things, of empty learning, or empty things, or vain courses, and cry up the credit of worldly things, that they may seem to be wise, and not fools, that are carried to those things. The best things had never the happiness to pass under their own names; but they had other coverings. Truth goeth always with a torn and scratched face; it is a stranger in the world, and hath strange entertainment.

Use 1. If this be so, we ought to take heed *of laying a scandal or reproach upon religion.* Salvian complains in his time that wickedness had gotten that head, that those that were good and honourable, *mali esse volunt, ne a malis abhorreantur* (*g*), they that were good studied to be vile, that they might not be vilified of others. 'Oh,' saith he, 'how much is Christ beholden to the world, that those that own him, and own goodness, and own his cause, should be therefore base, because they be his friends.' Take heed of taking scandals.

Use 2. We had need be wise, that we be not taken in this snare of Satan, *to mistake error for truth, and good for evil.* Satan and his agents make things pass under contrary representations. Superstition goeth for religion, and religion for superstition, schism, and heresy. It hath always been so. Therefore seek wisdom to discern aright. The devil hath two properties, he is a liar and a murderer; the one makes way for the other, for he could not murder unless he did lie. The devil himself will not be an open murderer if he can help it. The fraudulent persecution is worse than the violent. If he can bring to hell by fraud and lying, he will never do it by violence. He is a liar, that he may be a murderer; for when he can raise an imputation upon the church and children of God, that they be rebels, enemies of state, then he may *cum privilegio* be a murderer. When he hath tainted God's people in the conceit of the world, then they find that entertainment not which they deserve, but which they be apprehended to deserve, when the conceit of other men towards them is poisoned. 'Oh, this sect is spoken against everywhere,' say they to Paul, Acts xxviii. 22. Therefore we had need be wise; for if the instruments of Satan, led with his spirit, had not hoped that slanders should take, they would never have been so skilful in that trade. But they know they shall find some shallow fools that will believe them, without searching into the depths of them, and take up persons and things under prejudice. It is enough for them that this is said of them. They have neither wit nor judgment, nor so much patience, from following their lusts, as to examine them; and that makes them so mad as they are. *Calumniare audacter, aliquid hærebit*, slander stoutly, something will stick, they are sure of it. That which hath raised and ruined many a man, is that of Haman's casting of jealousy upon those that are better than themselves. That was Haman's trick, and so will be the practice of the wicked, as it hath been from the beginning, so to the end of the world. 'Thou art not Cæsar's friend,' say they, and it is enough to Pilate, John xix. 12. Thus it has been, and will be to the end of the world. Therefore we had need to be wise, that we be not misled. Men will never leave to speak ill till they have learned to speak better, till the Spirit of God hath taught them.

Now, it is said that Christ will take away the rebukes of his people. That is the promise. As they are, they shall be known to be. He will set all in joint again. Harmony is a sweet thing, and order is a sweet thing. Time will come when things that are now out of order to appearance, shall be all set in their due order again. Those that are basest shall be lowest, and those that be excellent shall be highest. This is a-working and framing now. In this confusion we must look to the catastrophe, the conclusion of all. He will 'take away the rebukes of all.' God is the father of truth, and truth is the daughter of time. Time will bring forth truth at last. And those that be honourable indeed shall be honourable. It is as true as God is just; for goodness and holiness are beams of God; and will he suffer it always to pass under a false veil? There is not an attribute of God but shall shine forth gloriously, even all his excellency and dignity. There is nothing shall be above him and his excellency. No; though he seems for a while not to rule in the world, or have power, but suffers them to go away with it that are his enemies, he is working another thing by suffering them, he is working the glory of his children, and confusion of his enemies. There is nothing in God but shall gloriously shine, and nothing in his children, no beams of God, but shall gloriously shine, to the confusion of the world. They that are good shall be known to be good, God will bring their righteousness to light. The witnesses that vexed the world, and had base entertainment, they were slain and disgraced, but they rose again, and were carried to heaven, Rev. xi. 12, *seq.*, as Elias. So there will be a resurrection of name, a resurrection of reputation. That that is good shall be good, and that that is bad shall be bad. It shall be known to be as it is. This is for comfort.

Use 1. You hear, therefore, what course to take under disgrace. What shall we do when the church passeth under disgrace, as it is now? A protestant is worse than a Turk or a Jew amongst the railing papists. Among ourselves we see under what reputation the best things go. It is too well known to speak of. And the scandal taken from hence doth extremely harden. It keeps men from religion, it draweth many from religion that have entered into it, because they have not learned so much self-denial as to venture upon disgrace. And surely where no self-denial is, there is no religion. Christ knew what doctrine he taught when he taught self-denial in this respect.

What shall we do, therefore? 1. Labour first of all for *innocency*, that if men will reproach, they may reproach without a cause.

2. Then labour for a *spirit of patience* to serve Christ with. 'Great is your reward when men speak evil of you,' Mat. v. 12, for a good cause. It is the portion of a Christian in this life to do well and suffer ill. Of all, certainly they are best, that, out of love to goodness, are carried to goodness, without looking to rewards or disgrace; that follow with a single eye. Labour, therefore, for patience, and not only so, but,

3. For *courage*. For the moon goeth its course, and lets the dog bark. We have a course to run, let us keep our course constantly; pass through good reports and bad reports; be at a point what the world thinks. We seek applause at another theatre than the world.

4. Again, then, labour for *sincerity under rebukes*, that we have a good aim, such an aim as Paul had, 'If I be mad and out of my wits,' 1 Cor. v. 13, 14. He being earnest for his master, Christ, they count him out of his wits. If I be out of my wits it is for Christ. 'If I be sober, it is for you, the love of Christ constraineth me to be so,' 2 Cor. v. 14. Get the love of Christ, and that will make a man care for nothing. If I go beyond myself, it is to God. As David said, when he was mocked by Michal, 'It is to the Lord,' when he danced before the ark,' 2 Sam. vi. 20, 21. *Bonus ludus*, a good dance, where Michal scoffeth, and David danceth. Where gracious men magnify God, and have Michals to scoff at them, it is *bonus ludus*. God will look upon them, for it is to the Lord. Labour that our aims be good, and it is no matter what the world judgeth of them.

5. And when all will not do, *commend our credits to God by prayer*. As we commend our souls and conditions, so our reputations, that he would take care of them, that he would bring our righteousness to light, that it should shine out as the noonday. So David doth, he complains to God, and commendeth all to him, prayeth him to take part against his enemies, to right his cause. And when we have done that, we have done our duty. Yet withal hope for better things, be content to pass under the world as unknown men, and to be inwardly worthy, and pass as unknown men. Rich men, if truly rich, they will applaud themselves in their bosoms, though the world disgrace them, yet at home I am thus furnished. And so a Christian that knoweth his worth, that he is a child of God, heir of heaven, that he is attended upon by angels, that he is a jewel to God in his esteem, [he thinks this] to be absolutely the best thing in the world. He knoweth the worth of a Christian, and his own worth as being a Christian. He applauseth* and comforteth himself, in that he knoweth he hath a hidden life, a state of glory hidden in Christ. Now it is covered with disgrace and disrespect in the world, scorned and reproached, but what is that to him? It is an hidden life, and for the present he knoweth his own excellency, and, therefore, can pass through good report and bad report. 'I care not for man's day,' saith Paul, 'there is another day to which I must stand,' 1 Cor. iv. 3.

And thus if we do, as Peter saith, 'There is a spirit of glory shall rest upon us,' 1 Pet. iv. 14. The ground we have of comfort under rebuke and disgrace, there is a spirit of glory. What is that? A large spirit enlarging our hearts with inward comfort, inward joy, inward love of God. 'A

* That is, 'applaudeth.'—G.

spirit of glory shall rest upon you,' and shall continue with you as long as disgrace shall continue. He opposeth this to all disgrace he meeteth with in the world.

God putteth sometimes a glory and excellency upon his children under disgrace and ill usage in the world, that he will daunt the world, as Stephen's face did shine as the face of an angel, which came from a spirit of glory that rested upon him, and expressed himself to be the servant of God. He that takes away from our good report, if we be good, he addeth to our reward. Our Saviour Christ saith as much, 'Blessed are you when you be ill spoken of, for great is your reward,' Mat. v. 11, 12.

THE SEVENTH SERMON.

And the rebukes of his people shall he take away from all the earth: for the mouth of the Lord hath spoken it.—ISA. XXV. 8.

Use 3. This is a great promise, *and I pray you be comforted with it.* For of all grief that God's people suffer in the world, there is none greater than reproach, disgrace, and contumely. *Movemur contumeliis plus quam injuriis*, we are more moved with reproaches than injuries. Injuries come from several causes, but disgrace from abundance of slighting. No man but thinks himself worthy of respect from some or other. Now, slanders come from abundance of malice, or else abundance of contempt; and therefore nothing sticks so much as reproaches, specially by reason of opinion and fancy, that raiseth them over high.

Our Saviour, Christ, 'endured the cross and despised the shame,' Heb. xii. 2. That shame that vain people cast upon religion and the best things, they despise that and make that a matter of patience. They knew the cross would not be shaken off, persecution and troubles must be endured, and therefore they 'endured the cross, and despised the shame.' Now, to bear crosses, take the counsel of the holy apostles, look up to him, consider Christ; and whatsoever disgrace in words or carriage we shall endure, we are sure, though we shall never know it till we feel it by experience, 'the spirit of glory shall rest upon us,' and rebuke shall be taken away.

Ere long there will be no glory in heaven and earth but the glory of Christ and of his spouse, for all the rest shall be in their own place, as it was said of Judas, that 'he went to his place,' Acts i. 25. Their proper place is not to domineer, but to be in hell, and ere long they shall be there. Heaven is the proper element of the saints; that is the place of Christ, the head, and where should the body be but with the head? where the spouse but with the husband? I say this shall come to pass, that all the wicked shall be in their place, and all the godly in theirs with Christ, and then shall the rebukes of God's people be taken away. A great matter, and therefore it is sealed with a great confirmation, 'The Lord Jehovah hath spoken it.' Therefore it must and will be so. 'The mouth of the Lord hath spoken it.' This is not in vain added, for the Lord knoweth well enough we need it to believe so great things, that there is such a feast provided, and that there is such a victory over death, our last enemy, and that there will be such glory, that all the glory shall be Christ's and his spouse's, that the wicked that are now so insolent shall be cast into their proper place with the devil, by whose spirit they are led. They be great matters, and there is great disproportion between the present condition and that condition in heaven;

and infidelity being in the soul, it is hard to fasten such things on the soul, that so great things should be done. But they are no greater than God hath said, and he is able to make good his word. 'The Lord hath said it,' and when God hath said it, heaven and earth cannot unsay it. When heaven hath concluded it, earth and hell cannot disannul it. 'The mouth of the Lord hath spoken it;' that is, truth itself hath spoken it that cannot lie. A man may lie and be a man, and an honest man too. He may sometimes speak an untruth; it taketh not away his nature. But God, who is pure truth, unchangeable truth, truth itself, cannot lie.

When we hear of great matters, as matters of Christianity be great matters, they be as large as the capacity of the soul, and larger too, and yet the soul is large in the understanding and affection too; when we hear of such large matters, *we need a great faith to believe them.* Great faith needeth great grounds, and therefore it is good to have all the helps we can. When we hear of great things promised, great deliverances, great glory, to strengthen our faith, remember God hath spoken them. He knoweth our weakness, our infirmity, and therefore helps us with this prop, 'The mouth of the Lord hath spoken it.' Let us therefore remember those great things are promised in the word of God, in the word of Jehovah, that can make them all good, that gives a being to all his promises. He is being itself, and gives being to whatsoever he saith. He is able to do it. Set God and his power against all opposition whatsoever from the creature, and all doubts that may arise from our own unbelieving hearts, 'The mouth of the Lord hath spoken it.'

Quest. But ye will say, the prophet Isaiah saith it, whose words they were.

Ans. I answer, Isaiah was the penman, God the mouth. The head dictateth, the hand writeth. Christ the head dictates, and his servant writeth. So that holy men write as they were inspired by the Holy Ghost, a better spirit than their own. 'Why do ye look on me?' saith Isaiah. Think not it is I that say it; I am but a man like yourselves; but 'the mouth of the Lord hath spoken it.'

We should not regard men, nor the ministry of men, but consider who speaks by men, who sendeth them, with what commission do they come. Ambassadors are not regarded for themselves, but for them that send them. And therefore Cornelius said well, 'We are here in the presence of God to hear what thou wilt speak in the name of God,' Acts x. 33. And so people should come with that reverend* expression, We are come in the presence of God the Father, Son, and Holy Ghost, in the presence of the blessed angels, to hear what thou shalt say in the name of God, by the Spirit of God. We are not to deal with men, but with God. And therefore he saith, 'The mouth of the Lord hath spoken it.'

Quest. 2. Hence may this question be easily answered, Whence hath the Scripture authority?

Ans. Why, from itself. It is the word; it carrieth its own letters testimonial with it. Shall God borrow authority from men? No; the authority the word hath is from itself. It hath a supreme authority from itself. And we may answer that question about the judge of all controversies, What is the supreme Judge? The word, the Spirit of God in the Scriptures. And who is above God? It is a shameless, ridiculous impudency of men that will take upon them to be judges of Scripture, as if man would get upon the throne, and as a judge there judge. The Scriptures must judge all ere long, yea, that great antichrist. Now an ignorant man, a

* That is, 'reverent.'—G.

simple man, that perhaps never read Scriptures, must judge of all controversies, yea, that that is judge of all and of himself, the word, which is from the very mouth of God,

Quest. 3. You will ask me, How shall I know it is the word of God if the church tells us not?

Ans. A carrier sheweth us these be letters from such a man, but when we open the letter, and see the hand and seal, we know them to be his. The church knows the word, and explaineth it; and when we see and feel the efficacy of the word in itself, then we believe it to be the word, for there is that in the word that sheweth it to be the word:

1. *The majesty that is in it.*

2. The matter that is *mysterious*, forgiveness of sins through a mystery, forgiveness of sin,* victory over death, life everlasting in the world to come, great matters, 'which eye hath not seen, nor ear heard, nor entered into the heart of man,' 1 Cor. ii. 9. If it had not been revealed, it could not have entered into the heart of angels, it containeth such glorious, transcending mysteries. And then again,

3. The word to all them that belong to God *hath the Spirit of God*, by which it passeth, rightly accompanying it, witnessing to the soul of man that it is so; and, 4, *by a divine efficacy* it is mighty in operation. What doth it in the heart? (1.) It *warmeth the heart* upon the hearing, and speaking, and discoursing of it, as when the disciples went to Emmaus, Luke xxiv. 32. (2.) It hath a heat of Spirit going with it to affect the heart *with heavenly joy and delight;* it hath power going with it by the Spirit to raise joy unspeakable and glorious; it hath a power to pacify the soul amidst all troubles. When nothing will still the soul, the Spirit of God in the word will do it by its divine power. (3.) Yea, it will *change a man* from a beastly or devilish temper to a higher and happier estate, as you have it, Isaiah xi. 6–9. It makes lions lambs, leopards kids. And what is the ground of all? In that very place 'the earth shall be full of the knowledge of the Lord.' The knowledge of God reconciled is such a powerful knowledge that it hath a transforming virtue to alter men's dispositions. What was Paul before conversion? and Zaccheus? Therefore, it is the word, because it hath divine operation to heat the soul, and raise the soul, and change the soul, and (4.) *cast down the soul*, as low in a manner as hell, in sense of its own misery. It will make a Felix to tremble, a man that it doth not effectually work upon. The truths of it are so moving that it will make a carnal man to quake. When Paul spake of judgment to come, of giving account of all that is done in the flesh, when a possibility of it was apprehended, it made Felix to quake. It makes mountains level, and it fills up the valleys. The word can raise up the soul; when man is as low as hell, and looketh for nothing but damnation, the Spirit with the word will fetch him from thence; as the jailor, Acts xvi. 31, there was little between him and hell, 'What shall I do to be saved? Why, believe in the Lord Jesus.' And with these words there went out an efficacy. He believed, and he afterward was full of joy.

The first gospel ever preached in pardon was by God himself. Never was any creature so near damnation as our first father Adam, cast from the greatest happiness, *miserrimum est fuisse felicem;* for he that enjoyed before communion with God and his angels, having sinned, and having conscience of his sin, considering his great parts, and apprehension of the state he had been in, this must needs affect him deeply; and being in this condition,

* Probably a misprinted repetition.—G.

the promise of the 'seed of the woman to break the serpent's head,' revived him.

There is a strange efficacy in the gospel. The Roman empire was the greatest enemy that the church ever had The ten persecutions you see what they were;* and yet notwithstanding the word grew upon them and never rested, the spreading of the gospel, and the Spirit with it, till the cross got above the crown, as it did in the time of Constantine, and so it continueth.

5. And must not this be a divine word which hath this efficacy, to revive, comfort, change, cast down, raise up again, *search secrets, search the heart to the bottom?* A poor idiot† that comes to hear the word of God, when he hears the secrets of his heart laid open by the word, he concludes certainly, 'God is in you, and you are God's ministers,' 1 Cor. iv. 25. The word 'divideth between the marrow and the bone,' Heb. xv. 12; it arraigneth the heart before God's tribunal seat. Those that are saved, it hath these effects in them that I have named. And if you ask how they know whether the word be the word? A man may answer, I have found it to be so, raising me up, comforting me, and strengthening me. I had perished in my affliction if the word had not raised me. *Principles are proved, you know, from experience,* for they have nothing above them. There is no other principle to prove the word, but experience from the working of it. How know you the light to be the light, but by itself, and that fire is hot, but by itself? Principles prove themselves only by experience; and this principle is so proved by itself, that there is no child of God but can say by experience, that the word is the word.

6. *If a man might go to reason, one might bring that which could not be easily answered for the satisfaction of an atheist.* Let him but grant there is a God, he will grant one thing in religion or another. But let him grant there is a God and a reasonable creature, then there must be a service, a religion; and this service must be according to some rules prescribed; for the superior will not be served as the inferior pleaseth. He must discover what good the superior intendeth, and what duties he expects. This must be revealed in some word. God and the reasonable creature, and religion, make a necessity of a word, and that must be the word we have, or another; and what word in the world is probable to be the word but this?

Obj. You will say it may be corrupt.

Ans. The Jews looked to the Old Testament, that it should not be corrupted; for they knew every syllable in it, and preserved every letter. It is one part of their superstition, and God blesseth that superstition to take away all such cavils. For the New Testament the Jews cared not for; but heretics on their side watch over it that there should be no corruption; they will so observe one another. But what are these reasons to those which the soul of a gracious Christian knoweth by the operation of the word upon the heart?

Use 1. And, therefore, *let us regard it as the word of God;* hear it as the word of God; read it as the word of God. A company of profane wretches you shall have, the scums and basest of the people, that will discourse, and to grace their discourse, they must have Scripture phrases; but whose word is it? It is the word of the great God. Eglon was a heathen king, and yet when a message came from God, he arose up and made obeyance,‡

* See Note *b*, vol. I. p. 384.—G. † See Note *e*, vol. I. p. 290.—G.

‡ This interpretation of the 'rising up' of Eglon anticipates Bishop Patrick *in loc.*—G.

Judges iii. 20. We should never read the word but with reverence, considering whose book it is, and that we must be judged by it another day.

Use 2. If it be the word, I beseech you consider what we say, and *know that God will make every part of it good.* There shall not a jot of it fail, nothing of it shall miscarry. God speaketh all these words. And, therefore, if you be blasphemers, you shall not carry it away guiltless. God hath said it. If you continue not to obey, you are under God's curse. Unless you repent you shall perish. Every threat God will make good. You must repent and get into Christ, else perish eternally. God hath said it, and we may confirm it in the unfolding and reading of it. The time is coming for the execution of it, and then God is peremptory. Now God waiteth our leisure, and entreateth us, but if we will not repent, we shall have that arrow in our sides that will never be gotten out till we die in hell. Whose sins are condemned in Scripture, they are condemned by God; and whom we shut heaven to, by opening the Scriptures, God will shut heaven to. The opening of the Scriptures is the opening of heaven. If the Scripture saith, a man that liveth in such a sin shall not be saved, heaven shall be shut to him; he is in a state of death, he is strucken, and remaineth in danger till he repenteth. How many live in sins against conscience, that are under the guilt and danger of their sins. They be wounded, they be struck by the word. There is a threat against their sins, although it be not executed; and they be as much in danger of eternal death as a condemned traitor, only God suffers them to live, that they may make their peace. They have blessed times of visitation. Oh, make use of it! It is the word of God; and know that God will make every part of his word good in threats as well as in promises.

Use 3. Take occasion from hence likewise to shame ourselves for our infidelity* in the promises. When we are in any disconsolate estate, we are in Job's case. Being in trouble, the consolation of the Almighty seemed light to him, Job. xv. 11. These be the comforts of God. When we come to comfort some, though the sweet promises of the gospel be opened, yet they do not consider them as being the word, the consolations of the Almighty, and therefore they seem light to them. But it should not be so. Consider they be the comforts of the word, and therefore we should hear them with faith, labour to affect† them, and shame ourselves. Is this God's word that giveth this direction, that giveth this comfort, and shall I not regard it? Is it the consolation of the Almighty, and shall not I embrace it? Therefore we should be ashamed, not to be more affected with the heavenly sweet things promised of God than we are.

A man that refuseth heavenly comforts to embrace comforts below, how should he reflect upon himself with shame? Hath God promised such things, God that cannot lie? and shall I lose my hope of all these glorious things, for the enjoying of the pleasures of sin for a season? I profess myself to be a Christian, where is my faith? where is my hope? A man must acknowledge either I have no faith; for if I had faith believing God speaking these excellent things, I would not venture my loss of them to get the enjoyment of poor temporary things here, for the good things promised in another world. Labour, therefore, to bring men's hearts to believe the word, and desire God to seal it to our souls that it is so.

Means. I will give one direction. *Labour for the Spirit of God, that writ the word, that indited the word.* Beg of God to seal to our souls that it is the word, and that he would sanctify our hearts to be suitable to the

* That is, 'disbelief,' or 'unbelief.'—G. † That is, to 'love' them.—G.

word, and never rest till we can find God by his Spirit seasoning our hearts, so that the relish of our souls may suit to the relish of divine truths, that when we hear them we may relish the truth in them, and may so feel the work of God's Spirit, that we may be able to say, he is our God. And when we hear of any threatening, we may tremble at it, and any sin discovered, we may hate it. For unless we, by the Spirit of God, have something wrought in us suitable to the word, we shall never believe the word to be the word. And therefore pray the Lord, by his Spirit to frame our hearts to be suitable to divine truths, and so frame them in our affections, that we may find the word in our joy, in our love, in our patience, that all may be seasoned with the word of God. When there is a relish in the word, and in the soul suitable to it, then a man is a Christian indeed to purpose. Till then men will apostatize, turn papist, turn atheist, or any thing, because there is a distance between the soul and the word. The word is not engrafted into the soul. They do not know the word to be the word by arguments fetched from the word, and therefore they fall from the power of the word. But if we will not fall from divine truths, get truth written in the heart, and our hearts so seasoned by it, and made so harmonious and suitable to it, that we may embrace it to death, that we may live and die in it.

To go on:

'In that day shall it be said, Lo, this is our God; we have waited for him.'

Here is a gracious promise, that shutteth up all spoken before. He spake of great things before. And now here is a promise of a day, wherein he will make all things promised, good to the soul of every believing Christian.

'In that day it shall be said, This is our God; we have waited for him; he will save us.'

It is an excellent portion of Scripture to shew the gracious disposition that the Spirit of God will work in all those that embrace the gracious promises of God. The time shall come when they shall say, 'Lo, this is our God; we have waited for him, and now we enjoy him.'

The points considerable are these:

1. First of all by supposition that there be *glorious excellent things promised to the people of God;* rich and precious promises of feasting, of taking away the veil, of conquest over death by victory, of wiping away tears and removing rebukes. Great things, if we go no farther than my text.

2. Secondly, *these have a day when they shall be performed*, which is not presently; for the end of a promise is to support the soul till the performance. God doth not only reserve great things for us in another world, but to comfort us in the way, doth reach out to us promises to comfort us till we come thither. There is a time when he will perform them, and not only a time, but there are likewise promises of performance. At that time the promises of these great things shall be performed.

3. The next thing is, *that God will stir up in his children a disposition suitable*. That is, the grace of waiting. As great things were promised before, so the soul hath a grace fit for it. 'We have waited for thee.'

4. And as they wait for them, while they are in performing, *so they shall enjoy them.* 'We have waited for thee, and we will be glad in thy salvation.' We shall so enjoy them, that we shall joy in them. Good things, when they be enjoyed, they be joyed in.

5. Again, 'we shall rejoice in our salvation, we shall glory in our God.'

After they be a while exercised in waiting, then cometh performance, then they be enjoyed, *and they be enjoyed with joy, in glorying in God*. For that is the issue of a Christian, when he hath what he would enjoy, when he enjoyeth it with joy, when the fruit of it is that God hath his glory, and therefore the heart can rejoice in his salvation.

Then there is a day, as for the exercising of his people here by waiting, so there is a day of performing promises. 'In that day.' That is, a day of all days. When that day cometh, then all prophecies and promises shall be accomplished to the uttermost.

But before that great day, there is an intermediate performance of promises assisted by waiting, to drop comfort to us by degrees. He reserveth not all to that day. There be lesser days before that great day. As at the first coming of Christ, so at the overthrow of antichrist, the conversion of the Jews, there will be much joy. But that is not that day. These days make way for that day. Whensoever prophecies shall end in performances, then shall be a day of joying and glorying in the God of our salvation for ever. And therefore in the Revelations where this Scripture is cited, Rev. xxi. 4, is meant the conversion of the Jews, and the glorious estate they shall enjoy before the end of the world. 'We have waited for our God,' and now we enjoy him. Aye, but what saith the church there? 'Come, Lord Jesus, come quickly.' There is yet another, 'Come, Lord,' till we be in heaven. So that though intermediate promises be performed here, yet there is another great day of the Lord to be performed, which is specially meant here.

6. The last thing considerable in the words is the manner of expression. They are expressed full of life, and with repetition, to make them sure and more certain, 'In that day it shall be said, This is our God; we have waited for him; he shall save us.' He bringeth them in speaking these words of affection.

Indeed, when we come to enjoy the performance of God's gracious promises, if we should live to see the fulness of the Gentiles come, and Jews called, we should speak of it again and again. Affections are large, and few expressions will not serve for large affections. It will be no tautology to say, 'This is our God; we have waited for him.'

Beloved, times are yet to come which may much affect the hearts of the children of God. Howsoever we may not live to see the performance of these things, yet we shall all live to see that day of judgment, and then we shall say, 'This is our God; we have waited for him.' We now see God in the promises, and then we shall see him 'face to face,' whom we have waited for in the promises, and we shall see him in heaven for ever.

'Lo, this is our God; we have waited for him.' While we live here we are in state of waiting, we are under promises, and a condition under promises is a waiting condition; a condition of performance is an enjoying condition. We are in a waiting condition till our bodies be raised out of the grave; for when we die we wait for the resurrection of our bodies. We may say as Jacob when he was dying, 'I have waited for thy salvation.' We are in a waiting condition till body and soul be joined together at the day of judgment for ever.

And there we should labour to have those graces that are suitable for this condition. The things we wait for are of so transcending excellency, as glory to come, that they cannot be waited for, but* the Spirit, by the things waited for, fitteth us to wait for them. A man cannot wait for glory of soul

* That is, 'unless.'—ED.

and body, but the Spirit that raiseth up faith to believe, and hope to wait, will purge, and fit, and prepare him for that glorious condition. 'He that hath this hope purifieth himself, as he is pure,' 1 John iii. 3. Oh, it is a quickening waiting, and a purging waiting. It is efficacious by the Spirit to fit and purify his soul suitable to that glorious condition he waits for. Where that is not, it is but a conceit. A very slender apprehension of the glory to come will make men better. He that hath hope of heaven and happiness under glory, it will make him suitable to the place he looketh for.

THE EIGHTH SERMON.

He shall swallow up death in victory; and the Lord God will wipe away tears from off all faces; and the rebukes of his people shall he take away from off all the earth: for the Lord hath spoken it. And it shall be said in that day, Lo, this is our God; we have waited for him, and he will save us: this is the Lord; we have waited for him, we will be glad and rejoice in his salvation.—ISA. XXV. 8, 9.

To come closer to the particulars. 'It shall be said in that day, Lo, this is our God.' The mouth of the Lord hath spoken gracious things before, hath promised a feast, and an excellent feast. God's manner is first of all to give promises to his church. Why? His goodness cometh from his goodness, his goodness of grace cometh from his goodness of nature. 'He is good and doth good.' Now the same goodness of disposition which we call bounty, that reserveth heaven and happiness for us in another world, the same goodness will not suffer us to be without all comfort in this world, because the knowledge and revelation of the glory to come hath much comfort in it. Therefore in mercy he not only intendeth performance of glory, but out of the same fountain of goodness he intendeth to reveal whatsoever is good for his church in the way to glory. So that promises of good come from the same goodness of God by which he intendeth heaven. For what moved God to come out of that hidden light, that no man can come into, and discover himself in his Son? The word in his promises to reveal his mind to mankind, and make known what he will have us to do, and what he will do to us. But only his goodness is the cause of all. And therefore the end of promises in God's intention is to comfort us in the way to heaven, that we may have something to support us. They are *promissa, quasi præmissa*. They are promises and premises, and sent before the thing itself.

Now here it cometh that the glory to come is termed the joy of heaven and the glorious estate to come. 'You have need of patience, that you may get the promises.' Heaven and happiness is called the promises, because we have them assured in promises. The blessings of the New Testament are called promises; as the children of the promise, yea, the heirs of glory; because all is conveyed by a promise, therefore all happiness is conveyed by a promise.

Now the promises are of good things. They are for the spring of them, *free*, from God's free goodness; for the measure of them, *full*; for the truth of them, *constant*, even as God himself that promiseth. And therefore we may well build upon them.

Use. Before I go any farther, I beseech you let us account the promises of the good we have *to be our best treasure, our best portion, our best riches*, for they be called precious promises, 2 Pet. i. 4; not only because they be precious in themselves, but because they are from the precious love of God in Christ to us. They are likewise for precious things. They are laid hold of by precious faith, as the Scripture calleth them, and therefore they are precious promises. Let us not only account of our riches that we have; for what is that we have, to what we speak of, to that we have in promise? A Christian is rich in reversion, rich in bills and obligations. Christ hath bound himself to him, and he can sue him out when he pleaseth. In all kinds of necessity, he can sue God for good. He can go to God and say, 'Remember thy promise, Lord, wherein thou hast caused me thy servant to trust,' Ps. cxix. 49; and can bind God with his own word.

But I take this only in passage as the foundation of what I am to speak.

From the mouth of God you see the great promises delivered; and now we have waited for them. That which answereth promises is expectation and waiting.

The second thing, therefore, between the promises, wherein God is a debtor, and the performance, is, that *there is a long time, a long day*. Oftentimes God takes a long day for performing of his promise, as four hundred years Abraham's posterity went to be in Egypt. And it was four thousand years from the beginning of the world till the coming of Christ, which was the promise of promises, the promise of the seed, a great long day. And therefore Christ is said to come in 'the latter end of the world.' Abraham had promise of a son, but it was not performed till he was an old man. Simeon had a promise to see Christ in the flesh, but he was an old man, ready to yield up the ghost, before it was performed. God taketh a long day for his promises; long to us, not to him, 'for to him a thousand years are but as one day,'

Reason 1. The promises of God are long in performing; for *to exercise our faith and our dependence to the full;*

Reason 2. *To take us off from the creature;* and

Reason 3. *To endear the things promised to us*, to set the greater price upon them when we have them. Many other reasons may be given, if I intended to enlarge myself in that point. A Christian hath a title to heaven. As soon as he is a Christian, he is an heir to heaven. Perhaps he may live here twenty or forty years more before God takes him up to glory. Why doth he defer it so long?

Reason 4. The reason is, *God will fit us for heaven by little and little*, and will perfume us as Esther was perfumed before she must come to Ahasuerus, Esth. ii. 12. There were many weeks and months of perfuming. So God will sweeten and fit us for heaven and happiness. It is a holy place; God a holy God. Christ is that holy one; and for us to have everlasting communion with God and Christ in so holy a place, requireth a great preparation. And God, by deferring it so long, will mortify our affections by little and little, and will have us die to all base things here in affection before we die indeed. David had title to the kingdom as soon as ever he was anointed; but David was fitted to be an excellent king, indeed, by deferring the performance of the promise till afterward. So in our right and title and possession of heaven, there is a long time between.

Our Saviour Christ was thirty-four years before he was taken up to heaven, because he was to work our salvation. And he was willing to suspend his glory for such a time, that he might do it; to suspend his glory due to him from the first moment of his conception. For by virtue of the union, glory was due to him at the first; but because he had taken upon him to be a Mediator, out of love he would suspend his glory due to him, that he might suffer. And so God, by way of conformity, will suspend the glory due to us, that we may be conformed to Christ. Though we have right to heaven as soon as we are born,* yet God will suspend the full performance of it; because he will by correction and by length of time subdue by little and little that which maketh us unconformable to our head.

And can we complain for any deferring of heaven when we are but conformed to our glorious head, who was content to be without heaven so long?

But to go on. As there be gracious and rich promises, and they have long time of performance to us, and 'hope deferred makes the soul languish,' Prov. xiii. 12; so God vouchsafeth a spirit to fit that expectation of his, a spirit of hope and waiting. And this waiting hath something perfect in it, and something imperfect. It is a mixed condition. There is good, because there is a promise; for a promise is the declaration of God's will concerning good. But because it is a promise of a thing not performed, there is an imperfection. So there is a mixture in the promise, and a mixture in the grace. Hope and expectation and waiting is an imperfect grace. That there be glorious things, it is perfection of good; that we have them not in possession, that is the imperfection. So that hope is something, but it is not possessed; a promise is something, but it is not the performance; a seed is something, but it is not the plant.

Thus God mixeth our condition here of perfection and imperfection. He will have us in state of imperfection, that we may not think ourselves at home in our country, when we are but in our way. Therefore he will have us in a state of imperfection, that we may long homeward; yet he will have it a state of good, that we may not sink in the way.

And not only promises; for in the way to heaven God keeps not all for heaven. He lets in drops of comfort oftentimes in the midst of misery. He doth reveal himself more glorious and sweet than at other times. There is nothing reserved for us in another world, but we have a beginning, a taste, an earnest of it here, to support us till we come to the full possession of what remaineth. We shall have full communion of saints there; we have it here, in the taste of it. We know what it is to be acquainted with them that be gracious spirits. We have praising of God for ever there. We know the sweetness of it here in the house of God, which made David desire this one thing, 'that he might dwell in the house of God, to visit the beauty of God,' &c., Ps. xxvii. 4. There we shall have perfect peace; here we have inward peace, unspeakable and glorious, 'a peace that passeth understanding,' Philip. iv. 7, in the beginning of it. There we shall have joy without all mixture of contrariety; here we have joy, 'and joy unspeakable and full of glory,' 1 Peter i. 8. There is nothing in heaven that is perfect, that is sweet, and good, and comfortable, but we have a taste and earnest of it here. The Spirit will be all in all there; there is something of it in us now. More light in our understandings, more obedience in our wills, more and more love in our affections, and it is growing more and more.

And therefore all is not kept for time to come; we have something beginning here besides promises. There is some little degrees of performance. So that the state between us and heaven is a state mixed of good and imperfection.

Now God hath fitted graces suitable to that condition, and that is ex-

* That is, 'born again.'—G.

pectation or waiting, a fit grace and a fit disposition of soul from* imperfect condition, that is afterwards to be perfected; for fruition is the condition of perfect happiness, not of waiting; for waiting implieth imperfection.

This waiting carrieth with it almost all graces. Waiting for better times in glory to come, it hath to support it. It is a carriage of soul that is supported with many graces. For, first, we wait for that we believe. We have a spirit of faith to lead to it. And then we hope before we wait, and hope is the anchor of the soul, that stayeth the soul in all the waves and miseries of the world. It is the helmet that keeps off all the blows. This hope issues from faith; for what we believe, we hope for the accomplishment of it.

So that all graces make way for waiting, or accompany it. The graces that accompany the waiting for good things in time to come are *patience*, to endure all griefs between us and the full possession of heaven; then *long-suffering*, which is nothing else but patience lengthened, because troubles are lengthened, and the time is lengthened. So there is patience, and patience lengthened, which we call long-suffering; and then, together with patience and long-suffering, there is *contentment*, without murmuring at the dispensation of God; something in the soul that he would have it to be so. He that hath a heart to rise, because he hath not what he would have, he doth not wait with that grace of waiting that issueth from a right spring.

God reserveth joy for the time to come, for our home. We should be content to have communion with God and the souls of perfect men; and not murmur though God exerciseth us with many crosses here. And therefore the Scripture calleth it a *silence*, 'In silence and in hope shall be your strength,' Isa. xxx. 15. The soul keepeth silence to God in this waiting condition, and this silence quells all risings in the soul presently; as David, 'My soul kept silence unto the Lord,' Ps. xxxix. 2. It will still all risings of the heart, issuing from a resignation of the soul to God, to do as he will have us to do. So it implieth patience and longsuffering, contentment, holy silence, without murmuring and repining.

And then it implies *watchfulness* over ourselves, till we come to the full accomplishment of the promises, that we carry not ourselves unworthily in the mean time; that we should not spend the time of our waiting in wickedness, to fetch sorrow from the devil, and the world to comfort us, or to be beholden to Satan. This is no waiting, but murmuring and rebellion, when in crosses and discomforts we cannot be content, but must be beholden to the devil, so there must be watchfulness; and not only so, but *fruitfulness* in waiting. For he waits that waiteth in doing good, that waiteth in observance. He waiteth for his master's coming, that is doing his duty all the time in a fruitful course of observance and obedience; else it is no waiting. Waiting is not merely a distance of time, but a filling up of that time with all gracious carriage, with obedience, and with silence, with longsuffering and contentment, and watchfulness [that] we take not any ill course, and observance, and with fruitfulness, that we may fill up times of waiting till performance, with all the graces, that we may have communion with God.

It is another manner of grace than the world thinks. What is the reason of all the wickedness of the world, and barrenness, and voluptuousness, but because they have not learned to wait? They hear of good things, and precious things promised; but they would have present payment, they will have something in hand. As Dives, 'Son, son, thou hast had thy good

* Qu. 'for?'—ED.

things here,' Luke xvi. 25, they will have their goods things here. And what is the reason of wickedness, but because they will have present pleasures of sins? We must prefer the afflictions of Christ before the pleasures of sin, Heb. xi. 25. Now that shortness of spirit to have reward here is the cause of all sin. They have no hope, nor obedience, nor expectation to endure the continuance of diuturnity.* Where then is patience, and hope, and contentment?

The character of a Christian is, that he is in a waiting condition, and hath the grace of waiting. Others will have the pleasures of sin, their profits and contentments, else they will crack their consciences, and sell Christ, God, heaven, and all.

A Christian, as he hath excellent things above the world, so he hath the grace of expectation, and all the graces that store up and maintain that expectation till the performance come.

And therefore it is an hard thing to be a good Christian, another thing than the world taketh it to be. For mark, I beseech you, what is between us and heaven, that we must go through, if ever we will come there. Between us and heaven, the thing promised, there be many crosses to be met withal, and they must be borne, and borne as a Christian should do. 'Through many afflictions we must enter into the kingdom of heaven,' Acts xiv. 22. Besides crosses, there be scandalous offences, that be enough to drive us from profession of religion, without grace. Sometimes good men by their failings, and fallings out, they fall into sin, and fall out; and that is a scandal to wicked men. Oh, say they, who would be of this religion, when they cannot agree among themselves? This is a great hindrance and stop. It is a scandal and rub in the way, not so much in themselves. We are full of scandal ourselves, catch at anything that we may except against the best ways. There is a root of scandal in the hearts of all, because men will not go to hell without reason.

Now because we are easy to take offence, rather than we will be damned without reason, it is not easy to hold out. Besides this, Satan plies it with his temptations from affliction, and from scandal; he amplifies these things in the fancy. Who would be a Christian? You see what their profession is. And so he maketh the way the more difficult.

And then again, look at our own disposition to suffer, to hold out, to fix. There is an unsettledness, which is a proper† infirmity in our natures since the fall. We love variety, we are inconstant, and cannot fix ourselves upon the best things, and we are impatient of suffering anything. We are not only indisposed to do good, but more indisposed to suffer any ill. The Spirit must help us over all this, which must continue all our life long. Till we be in heaven, something or other will be in our way. Now the Spirit of God must help us over all these afflictions. We shall never come to heaven to overcome afflictions, and scandals, and temptation, which Satan plies us here withal. And then to overcome the tediousness of time, this needeth a great deal of strength. Now this grace of expectance doth all. And therefore it is so oftentimes stood upon in Scripture. In Isaiah, and in the Psalms, how often is it repeated; Ps. xxxvii. 7. 'Wait on the Lord; if he tarry, wait thou.' The Lord will wait for them that wait for him; and it is the character in Scripture of a Christian. Moses, he saith, such as waited for the consolation of Israel, Gen. xlix. 18, before Christ came in the flesh, such a one is one that 'waiteth for the consolation of Israel,' Luke ii. 25. To have a gracious disposition, and a grace of waiting was the character of

* That is, 'long continuance.'—G. † That is, 'natural.'—G.

good people. Now since the coming of Christ, the character of the New Testament is, to wait for Christ's appearance. 'There is a crown of glory for me, and not only for me, but for all them that love his appearance,' 2 Tim. iv. 8. That is an ingredient in waiting, when we love the thing we wait for. And so Titus ii. 12, 'The grace of God that teacheth to deny ungodliness and worldly lusts, and to live holily, and justly, and soberly in this present evil world, looking for and waiting for this glorious appearing of Jesus Christ.'

So that looking with the eye of the soul partly on the first coming of Christ, which was to redeem our souls, and partly upon the second, which is to redeem our bodies from corruption, and to make both soul and body happy, it makes a man a good Christian. For the grace of God on the first, teacheth us to deny ungodliness; and looking for Christ's appearing, maketh us zealous of good works. You have scarce any epistle, but you have time described for looking for the coming of Christ, as Jude, 'Preserve youselves in the love of God, and wait for the coming of Christ.' So that as there be gracious promises, and a long day for them, God vouchsafeth grace to wait for the accomplishment of them.

Now as God giveth grace to wait, so he will perform what we wait for; as they say here, 'We have waited.' That is the speech of enjoying. God will at length make good what he hath promised; and what his truth hath promised, his power will perform. Goodness inclineth to make a promise, truth speaks it, and power performeth it, as you shall see here.

'We have waited,' &c.

In God there is a mouth of truth, a heart of pity, and an hand of power. These three meeting together, make good whatsoever is promised. 'He will fulfil the desires of them that fear him,' Ps. cxlv. 19. The desires that God hath put into his children, they be kindled from heaven; and he will satisfy them all out of his bowels of pity and compassion. He will not suffer the creature to be always under the rack of desire, under the rack of expectation, but he will fulfil the desire of them that fear him. And therefore learn this for the time to come.

Though we wait, God will perform whatsoever we wait for. And therefore, 'Lo, we have waited for him.' As there is a time of promising, so there is a time of performing; as there is a seedtime, so there is a time of harvest. There is a succession in nature, and a succession in grace; as the day followeth the night, and the Sabbath the week, and the jubilee such a term of years; and as the triumph followeth the war; and as the consummation of marriage followeth contract; so it is a happy and glorious condition, above all conditions here on earth. Therefore in this text you have not only the seedtime of the Christian (we may sow in tears, and in expectation, as in sowing), but here is likewise the harvest of a Christian. As there is time of sowing, so there is time of reaping; as time of waiting, so of enjoying. We have waited, and now, lo, we have what we waited for.

But why doth not the Holy Ghost set down a certain time, but leaveth it indefinite, 'In that day.' God keeps times and seasons in his own power; the point of time in general he leaveth it. There is a day; but the point and moment of time he keepeth in his own power. It is enough to know there is a day, and a day that will come in the best season. God's time is the best time. When judgments were threatened upon the wicked, they say, 'Let us eat, and drink, for to morrow we shall die,' 1 Cor. xv. 32. So Saul, 'To-morrow thou shalt die,' 1 Sam. xxviii. 19, and was he the better? So where there is a certain time of God's coming in judgment, godly men would not be the worse, and wicked men never the better. Therefore God reserveth it indefinite, 'In that day.'

There is a day, and it is a glorious day, a day of all days, a day that never will have night, a day that we should think of every day, 'That day,' by way of excellency. And before that day there be particular days in this world, wherein God sheweth himself, and fulfils the expectation of his children, to cherish the grand expectation of life everlasting. As in times of trouble they expect of God, and wait for deliverance in God's time, and they must be able to say, 'Lo, we have waited.' Because it is a beginning and pledge of the great performance that shall be consummate at that great day, and of all the miseries that shall then be removed; so there is a day when the Jews shall be converted, and the fulness of the Gentiles brought in, and the man of sin discovered, and consumed by the breath of Christ. And when the church of God seeth them, they may say, 'Lo, we have waited for the Lord,' and lo, he is come; that we looked for is now fulfilled. So that God reserveth not the fulfilling of all the promises to the great day of all days, but even in this life he will have a 'that day.'

And it were very good for Christians in the passages of their lives to see how God answereth their prayers, and delivereth them. Let them do as the saints in the Old Testament, that gave names to places where they saw God, as Peniel, Gen. xxxii. 30, he shall see God, and Abraham, 'God will be seen in the mount,' Gen. xxii. 14. So Samson and others they gave names to places where they had deliverance, that they might be moved to be thankful. A Christian taketh in all the comforts of this life to believe the things of the last great day. 'Lo, we have waited for him.'

That shall be a time of sight and fruition, of full power and full joy, which is reserved for heaven; then we shall say, 'Lo! behold, this is the Lord.' The more we see God here, the more we shall see him hereafter. There be many ways of seeing, so as to say, 'Lo, this is the Lord!' We may say, from the poorest creature, 'Lo, this is the Lord!' Here are beams of his majesty in the works of his justice and mercy, 'Lo, here is the Lord!' The Lord hath brought mighty things to pass, the Lord is marvellous loving to his children. 'Behold and see the salvation of the Lord!' We may say, 'Lo, here,' and see something of God in every creature. No creature but hath something of God. The things that have but mere being have something of God; but the things that have life have more of God. And so in some there is more, in some less of God.

But in the church of God specially, we may see his going in the sanctuary. Lo, this God hath done for his church. And in the sacraments, we may say, I have seen the Lord, and felt the Lord in his ordinance by his Holy Spirit. We do all this before we come to see him in heaven. But that is not meant specially.

We shall say, 'Lo, this is the Lord!' when we shall see him in heaven. All sight here leadeth to that sight. Faith hath a sight here, but it is in the word and sacrament, and so imperfect; but the sight in heaven is immediate and perfect, and therefore opposed to faith. We live by faith, and not by sight. In heaven we shall live by sight; not that we live not by sight here in some degree, for the lesser sight leadeth to the greater sight. But in comparison of sight in heaven, there is no sight. The Scripture speaketh of sight of God comparatively. Moses 'saw God,' that is, more than any other; and Jacob 'saw God,' that is, comparatively more than before, but not fully and wholly. We can apprehend him, but not comprehend him, as they say. We may see something of him, but not wholly.

But in heaven we shall have another sight of God, and then we shall say, 'Lo, this is the God we have waited for!' We shall see Christ face to face.

Beloved, that is the sight indeed. And if ye will ask me whether we shall see God then or no, consider what I said before. This is the God we have waited for in obedience, and fruitfully.

If we shall be ravished with the sight of God, surely if we see him here, we may see him there. We see him with the eye of faith, we see him in the ordinance, we have some sight of God that the world hath not. God discovereth himself to his children, more than to the world; and therefore they say, 'Thou revealest thyself to us, not unto the world,' John xiv. 22. A Christian wonders that God should reveal his love, and mercy, and goodness to him, more than to others. And therefore, if we belong to God, and shall see him hereafter, we must see him now. As we may see him, we must have some knowledge of him. And if we see God any way, all things in the world will be thought of no request, in comparison of the communion of God in Christ, as, 'We have seen the Lord, and what have we to do with idols?' Hosea xiv. 8. The soul that hath seen Christ, grows in detestation of sin, and loatheth all things in comparison.

And then, again, if we shall ever see God in glory, in this glorious and triumphing manner, 'This is the Lord,' this sight is a changing sight. There is no sight of God, but it changeth, and alters to the likeness of God, when he calls to look up to him, and he looks on us in favour and mercy. The best fruit of his favour is grace, of peace, and joy, for these be beams that issue from him, grace, as beams from the sun. But wherever God looks with any favour, there is a conformity to Christ, a gracious, humble, pitiful, merciful, obedient disposition, which is an earnest of the Spirit of Christ.

And there is a study of purity, of a refined disposition from the pollutions of the world. 'The pure in heart shall see God,' Mat. v. 8. They that hope to see God for ever in heaven, will study that purity that may dispose and fit them for heaven. And there is such a gracious influence in it, that they that hope for heaven, the very hope must needs help to purify them.

As there is grace suitable to waiting, so there is an influence from the things hoped for, to give vigour to all grace. As all the graces of a Christian fit and enable him for heaven, so hope of heaven yields life to all grace. There is a mutual influence into these things. God vouchsafeth discovery of these glorious things, to help us to wait, to be patient, and fruitful, and abundant in the work of the Lord. And the more we wait fruitfully, and patiently, and silently, the more we see of heaven. So that as in nature, the seed bringeth the tree, and the tree the seed; so in the things of God, one thing breeds another, and that breeds that again. So that waiting and grace fit us for heaven, and the thought of heaven puts life and vigour into all the graces that fit us for heaven. What is our faith to those glorious things we shall see hereafter? What is patience, but for consideration of that? What is hope, but for the excellency of the object of hope? And what were enduring of troubles, if something were not in heaven to make amends for all? They help us to come to glory, and the lively, hopeful thoughts of those things, animate and enliven all the graces that fit for heaven. If ever we shall hereafter possess heaven, and say, 'Lo, this is he we have waited for,' we must see him here, so as to undervalue all things, to see him with a changing sight; for the object of glory cannot be revealed, but it will stir up a disposition suitable to glory. If this be not, never hope for a sight of him in heaven.

And therefore let me entreat and beseech you, with the apostle Paul, to 'look to the end,' look to the main chance that can come in this world, and that shall come hereafter. It is wisdom to look to the end. A man that buildeth an house will think of the end, that is, dwelling and habitation, that he propoundeth. We are for everlasting communion with God; we are to be perfect, as in grace, so in glory. Heaven is our element; we rest not till then,—we are in motion till then,—that being our station. Then think often of this, never to rest in any intermediate condition, because we are in waiting till we come to that condition. Let us so carry ourselves, that we may say, this we waited for; it is the glory we expected. It is our wisdom often to have the end of our lives in our eyes, that we may be helped to wait patiently, cheerfully, and comfortably, till the consummation come, when all promises shall end in performance, when all that is ill and imperfectly good shall be removed—a consumption of ill, and a consummation of all good.

Oh, have that day in our eyes, that day of all days, and the very thoughts of it will fit us for the day. The thoughts of our end will fit and stir us up to all means tending to that end. Physic is good, if it tend to health. The very thoughts of that prescribes order and means. We read, 'Seek the kingdom of heaven first, and all other things shall be added to you,' Mat. vi. 33. The thought of the end prescribes order to all means, and it prescribes measure, 'How to use the world, as though I used it not,' 1 Cor. vii. 31, for the thoughts of my end stir me up to use all our courses suitable to that end. And therefore the best wisdom in Christians is often to prefix the end, and to be content in no grace nor comfort, as it is in a way of imperfection, but to look upon every grace, every comfort, every good, as it tends to perfection. David desired not to dwell in the house of God for ever, because he would terminate his desire in the house of God here, but he aimeth at heaven. And so when the saints of God bound and terminate their desires and contentment, it is with reference to the last day, the rest of a Christian, beyond which they cannot go, even communion with God himself.

THE NINTH SERMON.

And it shall be said in that day, Lo, this is our God; we have waited for him, and he will save us: this is the Lord; we have waited for him, we will be glad and rejoice in his salvation.—Isa. XXV. 9.

In the worst age of the church, that the church may not be swallowed up with fear, in the worst times, God doth prepare promises for his people. It was the case of our blessed Saviour himself to his poor disciples, that they might not be overwhelmed with sorrow. Therefore he addeth sacraments to passover, and the New Testament to the Old, and all to confirm faith, knowing that our hearts are very subject to be daunted.

The Lord promiseth here a feast of fat things, and all things pertaining to a feast, the best of the best, and removal of all that may hinder joy, as taking away the veil, which hinders them from the sight of it. And then death is swallowed up in victory, as it is already in our Head, who is gloriously triumphing in heaven; and then all tears shall be wiped from all faces. There is a vicissitude of things. They are now in a valley of tears, but it will not be always thus. Time shall come when all tears shall be wiped away, and the cause of all tears are sorrow. The rebukes of his people shall be taken away, the scandal that lieth upon the best things shall be taken away. The worst things go under a better representation, and the best things under a veil; but one day, as things are they shall be. The God of truth will have truth to be clear enough. And all this is sealed up with the highest authority, that admits of no contradiction. 'The Lord of hosts hath spoken it.'

We came the last day to these words, 'Lo, this is our God,' &c.; wherein we may consider first of all, *that God hath left to his church rich and precious promises*, such as is spoken of before: a feast, and removal of all hindrances whatsoever. He not only vouchsafeth heaven when we die, and eternal happiness; but in this world, in our way, he vouchsafes precious promises to support our faith, that we may begin heaven upon earth. What these promises are we shewed the last day.

The second observation was, in that God's people are here *in a state of expectation*, it shall be said, 'Lo, we have waited for him.' We are in a condition of waiting while we live in this world, because we are not at home. Our state requires waiting; heaven requires settledness and rest. There all appetites, all desires shall be satiated to the full. Our estate here is a passage to a better estate, and waiting is a disposition fit for such a condition.

And in this there is good and imperfection. Good, that we have something to wait for; imperfection, that we are to wait for it, that we have it not in fruition; and till we be in heaven we are in a state of waiting. In the Revelations, 'Come, Lord Jesus, come quickly,' Rev. xxii. 20, there is a glorious state of a church set forth; but while all is done, it hath not what it would have. We cannot be in such a state in the world; but there is place for a desire, namely, immediate and eternal communion with Christ in heaven. And therefore 'it shall be said in that day, Lo, this is our God; we have waited for him.'

I will add a little to this state of waiting before I go farther. God will not have our condition presently perfect, but have us continue in a state of waiting.

Reason 1. First of all, it is his pleasure that *we should live by faith, and not by sight*. We have sense and feeling of many things; he reserveth not all for heaven. How many sweet refreshments have we in the way! But the tenor of our life is by faith, and not by sight. God will have us in such a condition.

Reason 2. Again, *we are not fitted for sight of the glory to come here*. Our vessels are not capable of that glory. A few drops of that happiness so overcame Peter in the transfiguration, that he knew not himself,

Reason 3. God is so good to us that *he would have us enjoy the best at the last*. The sweeter is heaven, by how much the more difficult our way thither is. Heaven is heaven, and happiness is happiness, after a long time of waiting. For waiting enlargeth the capacity and desires of the soul to receive more; it commendeth the happiness afterwards. And therefore God keepeth the best for the last, because he will never interrupt the happiness of his children. When they be in heaven, there is a banishment of all cause of sorrow. He will have a distinction between the church militant and triumphant. He will train up his children here before he bringeth them to heaven. He will perfume his spouse, and make her fit for an everlasting communion with him in heaven.

The third thing is, that as there be promises, and these promises are not presently fulfilled, which put us in a state of waiting, *so God giveth grace to uphold in waiting.* Waiting is not an empty time, to wait so long, and no grace in the mean time; but waiting is a fitting time for that we are to receive afterwards.

We see in nature, in the winter, which is a dull time to the spring and harvest, and the times are very cold; yet it ripens and mellows the soil, and fits it for the spring. There is a great promotion of harvest in winter. It is not a mere distance of time. So between the promise and heaven itself, it is not a mere waiting time, and there is an end; but it is a time which is taken up by the Spirit of God in preparing the heart, in subduing all base lusts, and in taking us off from ourselves, and whatsoever is contrary to heaven. The time is filled up with a great deal of that which fits us for glory in heaven. The gracious God that fits us for heaven, and heaven for us, fits us with all graces necessary for that condition. As faith to believe, patience to wait for, and to depend on that which he seeth not, to be above sense; a grace of hope to wait for that which he believeth, to be an anchor to his soul in all conditions whatsoever. And then a grace of patience to wait meekly all the while. And then long-suffering, patience lengthened out. As the tediousness is long between us and heaven, so there be lengthening graces. We would have all presently, 'How long, Lord, how long?' Rev. vi. 10. We are so short, even David and others; and therefore God giveth grace to hold out and lengthen our spiritual faith, and hope, and perseverance, and constant courage to encounter with all difficulties in the way. When the spirit of a man beholds heaven, and happiness, and God, it makes him constant, in some sort as the things he beholdeth, for the Spirit transformeth him to the object. Now, he beholds a constant covenant; and as faith looks upon a constant God, constant happiness, and constant promises, it frameth the soul suitable to the excellency of the object it layeth hold upon.

And then the Spirit of God in the way to heaven subdueth all evil murmurings and exceptions, in suffering us not to put forth our hands to any iniquity. Though we have not what we would have, he keeps us in a good and fruitful way; for to wait is not only to endure, but to endure in a good course, fitting us for happiness, till grace end in glory.

In the fourth place, *God will perform all his promises in time.* As the church saith here, 'This is the Lord; we have waited for him.' Now, he hath made good whatsoever he hath said.

To enlarge this point a little. As there is a time of waiting, so there will be a time when God's people shall say, 'Lo, this is the Lord, we have waited for him.' Why?

Reason 1. *God is Jehovah.* A full and pregnant word! A word of comfort and stay for the soul is this word Jehovah! He is a God that giveth a being to all things, and a being to his word, and therefore what he saith he will make good. He is Lord of his word. Every man's word is, as his nature, and power, and ability is, the word of a man, or the word of an honest man, but being the word of a God, he will make all good.

Reason 2. And then he will make all good, because *he is faithful.* God, he saith it, and he will do it.

Reason 3. You need no more reason *than pity to his people,* his bowels of compassion. The hearts of people would fail if he should stay too long;

And therefore out of his bowels in his time, which is the best time, not only because he is faithful, but because he is loving and pitiful, he will make good all his promises. And then he will do it.

Reason 4. *For what is grace, but an earnest of that fulness we shall have in heaven?* What is peace here but an earnest of that peace in heaven? And what is joy here but an earnest of fulness of joy for evermore? And will God lose his earnest? Therefore we shall enjoy what God hath promised, and we expect, because we have the earnest. It is not a pledge only, for a pledge may be taken away, but an earnest, which is never taken away, but is made up in the full bargain. Grace is made up in glory, as beginnings are made up with perfection. Where God layeth a foundation, he will perfect it. Where God giveth the first-fruits, he will give the harvest.

But it will be a long time before, because he will exercise all grace to the uttermost. You see how Abraham was brought to the last. In the mountain God provideth for a sacrifice, when the knife was ready to seize on Isaac's throat, Gen. xxii. 12, 13.

We should answer with our faith God's dealing; that is, if God defer, let us wait, yea, wait to the uttermost, wait to death. He is our God to death, and in death, and for ever. If God perform his promise at the worst, then, till we are at the lowest, we must wait.

And, therefore, one character of a child of God from others is this. Give me the present, saith the carnal, beastly man, the world; but God's people are content to wait. He knoweth what he hath in promise is better than what he hath in possession. The gleanings of God's people are better than the others' harvest. The other cannot wait, but must have present payment. God's child can wait, for he liveth by faith. And therefore we should learn patiently to wait for the performance of all God's promises.

And to direct a little in that, remember some rules, which every man may gather to himself, as,

1. *God's time is the best time. Deus est optimus arbiter opportunitatis*, the best discerner of opportunities. And 'in the mountain will God be seen.' Though he tarry long, he will come, and not tarry over long; and then all the strength of the enemy is with God. *Robur hostium apud Deum.* The strength of the enemy is in his hand; he can suspend it when he pleaseth.

2. Then, though God seems *to carry things by contrary ways to that he promiseth*, which makes waiting so difficult, yet he will bring things about at last. He promiseth happiness, and there is nothing but misery. He promiseth forgiveness, and opens the conscience to cry out of sin. Aye, but Luther's rule is exceeding good in this case. *Summa ars*, the greatest art of a Christian is, *credere credibilia*, &c., and *sperare dilata*, to hope for things a long time, and to believe God when he seemeth contrary to himself in his promise.

But though God doth defer, yet *in that day* he doth perform. It is set down indefinitely, for it is not fit we should be acquainted with the particular time. And therefore he saith, 'in that day.' He sets not down a particular time, but 'in that day,' wherein he meaneth to be glorious in the performance of his promise. There is a time, and a set time, and there is a short time, too, in regard of God, and a fit time. If the time were shorter than God hath appointed, then it were too short; if longer, too long. 'My times,' saith David, 'are in thy hands,' Ps. xxxi. 15. If they were in the enemy's hands, we should never be out; if in our own, we would never enter; if in our friends', their goodwill would be more than their ability. 'But my *times*;'—he saith not, 'my time,' but—'my times are in thy hands;' that is, my times of trouble and times of waiting. And it is well that they be in God's hands, for he hath a day, and a certain day, and a fit day to answer the waiting of all his people.

And when that day is come, you see how their hearts are enlarged, they will say, 'This is the Lord, we have waited for him.'

When God meaneth to perform his promise, either in this world or in the world to come, the world to come specially, when there shall be consummation of all promises, God shall enlarge the hearts of his people. 'This is the Lord; we have waited for him.' 'This is the Lord.' He repeats it again and again.

Our soul is very capable, being a spiritual substance; and then God shall fill the soul, and make it comprehend misery, or comprehend happiness, when every corner of the soul shall be filled; and then having bodies too, it is fit they should have a part; so the whole man shall express forth the justice or mercy of God.

For the nature of the thing, it cannot be otherwise. Every member of the body shall be fit to glorify God. What the psalmist saith of his tongue, 'Awake, my glory,' he may say of every member, Do thy office in glorifying the Lord, and rejoicing in the Lord. *Pectus facit disertos.* The heart makes a man eloquent and full. So the performance of any promise fills the heart so full of affections, the affections are so enlarged; and therefore we must not have affections to a court-kind of expressions, as they in old time, and the like court-eloquence, when men might not speak fully. But when joy possesseth the heart to the full, there be full expressions. 'This is the Lord, this is the Lord; let us rejoice in him.' And therefore there seemeth so many tautologies in the Psalms, though they be no tautologies, but mere exuberances of a sanctified affection.

Oh! beloved, what a blessed time will that be when this large heart of ours shall have that that will fill it; when the best parts of us, our understanding, will, and affections, shall be carried to that which is better and larger than itself, and shall be, as it were, swallowed up in the fulness of God. And that is the reason of the repetition of the word, 'This is the Lord, this is the Lord.'

And it followeth, 'We will rejoice and be glad in his salvation.' When a gracious heart is full of joy, how doth he express that joy? A wicked heart, when it is full of joy, is like a dirty river that runs over the banks, and carrieth a deal of filth with it, dirty expressions. But when a gracious heart expresseth itself, being full of joy, it expresseth itself in thanks and praises, in stirring up of others. 'Lo, this is our God; we will rejoice and be glad in his salvation.' 'Is any merry?' saith the apostle Saint James, 'let him sing,' James v. 13. God hath affections for any condition. 'Is a man in misery? let him pray.' This is a time of mourning. Doth God perform any promise, and so give cause of joy? let him sing. There is action for every affection, affection for every condition. And this may stir us up to begin the employment in heaven on earth here. We shall say so in heaven, 'Lo, this is the Lord; we have waited for him.'

For every performance of promises, be much in thankfulness. 'Our conversation is in heaven,' saith the apostle, Philip. iii. 10. And what is the greatest part of a Christian's conversation, but in all things to give thanks. Here the holy church saith, their matter of praise was too big for their soul, and therefore they brake out in this manner. And so oftentimes a child of God. His heart is so full, that it is too big for his body in the expression of matter of praise. But it is his comfort that in heaven he shall have a large heart, answerable to the large occasion of praise. I will not enlarge myself in the common-place of thanksgiving.

In this condition we can never be miserable; for it springs from joy, and joy disposeth a man to thankfulness, and upon thankfulness there is peace, and can we be miserable in peace of conscience? Therefore, saith the apostle, 'In all things give thanks, and let your requests be made known to God,' Philip. iv. 6; and what will follow upon that, when I have made known my requests, and paid my tribute of thanks? 'Then the peace of God which passeth understanding shall guide your mind,' Philip. iv. 7. When we have paid to God the tribute we can pay him, then the soul, as having discharged a debt, is at peace. I have prayed to God, I have laid my petition in his bosom, I am not in arrearages for former favours, 'therefore the peace of God which passeth all understanding shall keep your hearts and minds.' Hannah had prayed once, went not away, but prayed again, 1 Sam. ii. 1, *seq.* The happiness of heaven followeth the actions of heaven. Praisings being the main employment of heaven, the happiness and comfort of heaven followeth.

And howsoever these promises be fulfilled in heaven, yet they have a gradual performance on earth. For he speaks certainly of the state of the Jews yet to come, wherein there shall be accomplishment of all these promises.

'We have waited for him; he will save us.' Experience of God's performance stirs them up still to wait for him, and rejoice in his salvation. Experience stirs up hope. The beginning of a Christian, and midst, is to hope for the end; and surely our beginning should help the latter end! All a Christian's life should help the end. All former things should come in and help his latter.

Beloved, we are too backward that way to treasure up the benefit of experience. There be few of years but might make stories of God's gracious dealings with them, if all were kept; the comforts past, and for time to come, and all little enough. It was David's course, 'Thou art my God from my mother's womb, and upon thee have I hanged ever since I was born; fail me not when I am old,' Ps. xxii. 10. Go along with God's favours, and use them as arguments of future blessings. As former victories are helps to get the second victory, every former favour helpeth to strengthen our faith.

In the next, God is an inexhausted fountain, and when we have to deal with an infinite God, the more we take of him the more we offer him. It is no good plea to say, you have done courtesies, therefore do them still. But we cannot honour God more than from former experience to look for great things from the great God.

'We have waited for him, he will save us; we have waited for him, and we will rejoice in his salvation.' That which a child of God gives thanks for and rejoices in, and labours for, is more and more experience of his salvation. 'We will rejoice in his salvation.' There is not a stronger word in all the Scripture, not in nature. He doth not say rejoicing in this or that benefit, but in his salvation, that is, in deliverance from all evil. We will rejoice in his preservation, when he hath delivered us, we will rejoice in his advancement of us, and we will rejoice in his salvation. And therefore, when the wisdom of heaven would include all in one word, he useth the word Jesus, all happiness in that word, that pregnant, full word, a Saviour.

So that God's carriage towards his children is salvation. He is the God of salvation, or a saving God. And God sent his name from heaven, and the angels brought it, the name of Jesus. Therefore look to the full sense of it. We have a Saviour that will answer his name; as he is Jesus, so he will save his people from their sins, Mat. i. 21. And therefore we will rejoice in his salvation. God dealt with us like a God, when he delivered us from all misery, from all sins, and advanced us to all happiness that nature is capable of. As he said before, he will wipe away all tears from all faces, and take away the rebukes of all people. He will punish the wicked with eternal destruction. And if he advanceth a people he will be salvation, than which he can say no more.

And this sheweth that the children of God rejoice, more than in anything else, in salvation, because it is the salvation of God, and because God is salvation itself. Heaven were not heaven, if Jesus and God in our nature were not there. And therefore the apostle saith, 'I desire to depart,' not to be dissolved, 'and to be with Christ, for that is better.' The sight of God, specially in our nature, God the second person taking our nature, that we might be happy, will make us happy for ever. In loving God, and joying in God, and enjoying God, makes full happiness; but that is not the cause of joy in heaven, but the cause of all is God's influence into us. Here in the world happiness is mediate, in God's revealing of himself to us by his Holy Spirit, in the use of means, in his dealings and deliverances, letting us see him by his grace, to see him, and joy and delight in him for ever. It is no good love that resteth in any blessings of God for themselves. It is an harlotry affection to love the gift more than the giver. So the saints of God they do all desire to see him as they may, and to joy in God, and enjoy God himself, and to see God in our nature, and to be with him for ever. Before he spake of a feast, and if the feast-maker be not there, what is all? In a funeral feast there is much cheer, but the feast-maker is gone. In heaven there is joy, but where is God, where is Christ, he that hath done so much, suffered so much for us, that hath taken possession of heaven, and keepeth a place for us there? What is heaven without him? Salvation, severed from him, is nothing.

We shall say when we are there, Lo, here is David, Abraham, St John, here the martyrs! Aye, but here is Christ, here is God, here is our Saviour, the cause of all, and the seeing of him in them, that he will be glorious in his saints, that maketh us rejoice. We shall see all our friends in heaven. There we shall see the excellency of the happiness of Christ, his love, his grace, his mercy.

The words are expressed with a kind of glorying, 'Lo, this is our God.' So that the joy of a Christian endeth in glory, and in the highest degree of glory, as you have it, Rom. v. 3, 'We glory also in tribulation, we glory in hope of glory,' nay, we glory in God as ours reconciled. And if we glory in him now as a God reconciled, what shall we do in heaven? Can a worldling glory in his riches, his greatness, his favour from such a man, as Haman did? And shall not a Christian glory in his God? and make his boast in his God? And therefore in this world we should learn to glory, before we come to that glory in heaven, specially when we be set upon by anything that is apt to discourage us. Glory then in our Head. Perhaps a Christian hath no wealth, no great rents to glory in, aye, but he hath a God to glory in, let him glory in him. The world may take all else from him, but not his God. As the church, in Cant. v. The virgins put the church to describe her beloved, 'What is thy beloved more than another beloved? My beloved is white and ruddy, the chiefest of ten thousand.' Then she goeth on in particulars, 'my beloved is thus and thus;' and if you would know what my beloved is, 'this is my beloved.' So a Christian that hath a spirit of faith should glory in God here, for heaven is begun here, and he should glory in Christ his Saviour, and should set Christ against all discouragements and oppositions. If you will know what is my beloved, 'this is my beloved, the chief among ten thousands.' Ps. cxv. 3. 'Our God is in heaven, and doth whatsoever he pleaseth, in heaven, and earth, and the deeps,' yea, we make our boast of God, saith the psalmist, when there is occasion. 'This is the Lord, this is our God; we have waited for him,' specially in times of afflictions; and what is the reason? This will hold out to eternity. 'This is our God.' As in the Revelations, it is a plea, and a glory for ever; for God is our happiness. As the schoolmen say, he is our *objective* happiness, and our *formal* happiness; he is our happiness, as he is ours, and he is ours in life and death, and for ever. So there is always ground of glory, only God doth discover himself to be ours by little and little, as we are able to bear him. He is ours in our worst times. 'My God, my God, why hast thou forsaken me?' Yet *my* God still, Mat. xxvii. 46.

He is our God to death, and he is ours in heaven. 'This is our God; we will rejoice in him.' And therefore well may we boast of God, because in God is everlasting salvation. If we boasted in anything else, our boasting would determine with the thing itself; but if we rejoice in God, we rejoice in that which is of equal continuance with our souls, and goeth along with the soul to all eternity.

And therefore we should learn to rejoice in God, and then we shall never be ashamed. It is spoken here with a kind of exalting, a kind of triumphing over all oppositions, 'Lo, this is our God.' Beloved, this, that God is our God, and Christ is ours, is the ground of rejoicing, and of all happiness. All joy, all comfort is founded upon this our interest in God; and therefore,

1. We must make this good *while we live here, that God is our God*, and that we may do so, observe this. Christ is called *Emmanuel*, God with us. God, in the second person, is God-man, and so God with us, and the Father in Emmanuel is God with us too. So we are God the Father's, because we are his. 'All things are yours,' saith the apostle, 'whether Paul or Apollos, things present, things to come. 'Why?' Because you are Christ's,' 1 Cor. iii. 22. Aye, but what if I be Christ's, Christ is God's? So we must be Christ's, and then we shall be God's. If Christ be ours, God is ours, for God is Emmanuel, in Christ, Emmanuel, God is with us in Christ, who is with us. God is reconciled to us in God and man, in our nature. And therefore get by faith into Christ, and get union, and get communion; by prayer open our souls to him, entertain his speeches to us by his word and Spirit and blessed motions, and open our spirits to him, and so maintain a blessed intercourse.

2. Make it good that God is our God *by daily acquaintance*. These speeches at the latter end are founded upon acquaintance before. 'This is our God.' Grace and glory are knit together indissolubly. If God be our God here, he will be ours also in glory; if not here, not in glory. There is a communion with God here, before communion with him in glory, and therefore make it good that God be our God here first, by union with

him. And then maintain daily acquaintance with him, by seeing him with the eye of faith, by speaking to him, and hearing him speak to us by his Spirit, joining in his ordinances, and then he will own us, and be acquainted with us. In heaven we shall say, 'Lo, this is our God.' We have had sweet acquaintance one with another: he by his Spirit with me, and I by my prayers with him. Our Saviour Christ will not be without us in heaven. We are part of his mystical body, and heaven were not heaven to Christ without us. With reverence be it spoken, we are the fulness of Christ, as he is the fulness of his church. And if he should want us, in some sort he were miserable, he having fixed upon us as objects of his eternal love. In what case were he if he should lose that object? And therefore, as we glory in him, he glorieth in us. 'Who is this that cometh out of the wilderness?' Who? 'His beloved,' Cant. iii. 6. And, 'Woman, is this thy faith?' Mat. xv. 28. He admires the graces of the church, as the church admires him. 'This is the Lord.' The church cannot be without him, nor he without the church. These words are spoken with a kind of admiration. 'Lo, this is the Lord, we will rejoice in him.' So I say, as there is thanks and joy, so there is admiration, 'Lo, behold!' This is a God worthy beholding, and so he wonders at the graces of his children. Beloved, there is nothing in the world worthy admiration. *Sapientis non est admirari*. It was a speech of the proud philosopher, a wise man will not admire, for he knoweth the ground (*h*). But in heaven the parts are lifted up so high that there is nothing but matter of admiration, things 'that eye hath not seen, nor ear heard, nor hath entered into the heart of man to conceive of,' 1 Cor. ii. 9. They be things beyond expression, and nothing is fit for them but admiration at the great things vouchsafed to the church.

And as with admiration, so with invitation. That is the nature of true thankfulness. There is no envy in spiritual things. No man envieth another the light of the Scriptures, but lo, behold with admiration and invitation of all others, 'This is the Lord.'

Let us therefore rejoice beforehand, at the glorious times to come, both to ourselves and to others; be stirring and exciting one another to glory, and rejoice in God our salvation.

1. And, therefore, learn all to be stirred up from hence, *not to be offended with Christ, or with religion*. Be not offended, saith Austin, with the parvity* of religion. Every thing to the eyes of the world is little in religion. A Christian is a despised person, and the church, the meanest part of the world, in regard to outward glory. But,

2. Consider with the littleness, and baseness, and despisedness of the church, *the glory to come*. Time will come when we shall rejoice, and not only see, but boast with admiration, to the stirring up of others, 'Lo, this is the Lord.' And, therefore, say with our Saviour Christ, 'happy is he that is not offended with me,' Mat. xi. 6, nor with religion. There is a time coming, that will make amends for all. Who in the world can say at the hour of death, and day of judgment, Lo, this is my riches, this my honours! Alas! the greatest persons must stand naked to give account; all must stand on even ground to hold up their hands at the great bar. We may say to the carnal presumptuous man, Lo, this is the man that put his confidence in his riches. And none but reconciled Christians can say, 'Lo, this is our God.' Therefore take heed of being offended with anything in religion.

3. Again, if time to come be so transcendently glorious, *let us not be afraid to die*, let us not be overmuch cast down, for it shall end in glory. And

* That is, 'insignificance, smallness.'—G.

let us be in expectation still of good times, wait for this blessed time to come, and never be content with any condition, so as to set up our rest here. We may write upon every thing, *hic non est requies vestra*. Our rest is behind; these things are in passage. And therefore rest content with nothing here. Heaven is our centre, our element, our happiness ; and every thing is contentedly happy, and thriveth in its element. The birds in the air, the fish in the sea, beasts on the earth, they rest there as in their centre. And that that is our place for ever, it is heaven, it is God. The immediate enjoying of God in heaven, that is our rest, our element, and we shall never rest till we be there. And therefore he is befooled for it, in the gospel, that setteth up his rest here. Whosoever saith I have enough, and will now take contentment in them, he is a fool. 'There is a rest for God's people,' Heb. iv. 9, but it is not here.

4. Neither *rest in any measure of grace, or comfort*. What is faith to sight? We have hope, an anchor, and helmet, that keepeth up many a soul, as the cork keepeth from sinking. What is this hope to the fruition of what we hope for? Here we have love, many love tokens from God. Aye, but what is love to union? Ours is but a love of desire. We are but in motion here, we lie in motion only; and our desires are not accomplished. What is this love to the accomplishing of the union with the thing beloved for ever? Here we have communion of saints. But what is this communion of saints to communion with God for ever? We have infirmities here, as others, which breedeth jealousies and suspicion. Aye, but we shall have communion in heaven, and there shall be nothing in us to distaste others, but everlasting friendship. Yea, our communion shall be with perfect souls. Our communion of saints here is our heaven upon earth, but it is communion with unperfect souls. Peace we have, aye, but it is peace intermixed, it is peace in the midst of enemies. There we shall have peace without enemies. Christ doth now rule in the midst of enemies. In heaven he shall rule in the midst of his friends. So that we can imagine no condition here, though never so good, but it is imperfect. And therefore rest not in anything in the world, no not in any measure of grace, any measure of comfort, till we be in heaven, but wait for the time to come, 'and rejoice in hope by which we are saved,' Rom. xii. 12. Wait still, and though we have not content here, yet this is not our home, this is a good refreshment by the way. As when the children of Israel came from Babylon, they had wells by the way, as in *Michae*,* they digged up wells. So from Babylon to Jerusalem we have many sweet refreshments; but they be refreshments far off the way. God digs many wells ; we have breasts of consolation to comfort us, aye, but they are but for the way. And therefore let us answer all temptations, and not take contentment with anything here. It is good, but it is not our home. *Cui dulcis peregrinatio, non amat patriam.* If we have† eternity, love heaven, we cannot be overmuch taken with anything in the way.

5. And so for the church, *let us not be overmuch dejected for the desolation of the church*, but pray for a spirit of faith, which doth realise things to the soul and presents them as present to the soul, seeth Babylon fallen, presents things in the Scripture phrase, and in the words, 'Babylon is fallen,' forasmuch as all the enemies of the church fall. Mighty is the Lord that hath spoken, and will perform it, and, as the angel saith, 'it is done,' Rev. xix. 17.

* *Sic* . . . But qu. 'Micah' and the reference, Micah i. 4?—G. Or 'Baca?' Ps. lxxxiv. 6.—ED.

† Qu. 'love?'—ED.

So time will come ere long when it shall be said, 'It is done.' The church shall be gathered, and then, 'Lo, this is our God.'

It was the comfort of the believing Jews that the Gentiles should come. And why should it not be the comfort of the Gentiles that there be blessed times for the ancient people of God, when they shall all cry and say, 'Lo, this is our God; we have waited for him long, and he will save us.' Therefore, be not overmuch discouraged for whatsoever present desolation the church lieth under. If it were not for this, 'we were of all men most miserable,' as Paul saith, 1 Cor. xv. 19. But there be times to come when we shall rejoice, and rejoice for ever, and make boast of the Lord. If it were not, 'we were of all men most miserable.' Howsoever happiness is to come, yet of all persons he is most happy that hath Christ and heaven. The very foretaste of happiness is worth all the world. The inward peace of conscience, joy in the Holy Ghost, the beginnings of the image of God and of happiness here, is worth all the enjoyments of the world. Ask of any Christian whether he will hang with the greatest worldling, and be in his condition; he would not change his place in grace for all his glory. And therefore, set heaven aside, the very first fruits is better than all the harvest of the world. Let us therefore get the soul raised by faith to see her happiness. We need it all, for till the soul get a frame raised up to see its happiness here, specially in the world to come, it is not in a frame fit for any service, it will not stoop to any base sin. Where the affections are so possessed, they look upon all base courses as unworthy of their hope. What! I that hope to rejoice for ever with God in heaven, that am heir of heaven, that have the image of God upon me, that am in covenant with God, to take any bestial course, to place my happiness in things meaner than myself, that have God to delight in, a God in covenant, that hath taken me into covenant with himself. So I say in all solicitations to sin, get ourselves into a frame that may stand firm and immoveable.

In all troubles let us know we have a God in covenant, that we may joy in him here, and rejoice with him in heaven for ever hereafter.

NOTES.

(*a*) P. 440.—'Keep your book to yourself.' Thomas Brooks in his 'Epistle Dedicatory' to his 'Apples of Gold,' thus introduces the anecdote. 'I hope none of you, into whose hands it may fall, will say as once Antipater, King of Macedonia, did, when one presented him with a book teaching of happiness. His answer was (*ou scholazo*), οὐ σχολάζω, 'I have no leisure.'

(*b*) P. 448.—'Cicero prefers the name of *convivium*.' The allusion is to Cicero de Sen, 13 *fin*, which may be here quoted:—'Bene majores nostri accubitionem epularem amicorum, quia vitæ conjunctionem haberet, convivium nominarunt, melius quam Græci, qui hoc idem tum compotationem, tum concœnationem, vocant.'

(*c*) P. 449.—'The Jews wondered at the *manna*, saying, What thing is this?' 'Manna,' meaning 'What's this?' itself expresses and records their wonder.

(*d*) P. 477.—'That is not to be feared,' saith Tertullian, 'that frees us from all that is to be feared.' This is taken from Tertullian de Testimonio animæ § iv., Non est timendum, quod nos liberat ab omni timendo.'

(*e*) P. 479.—'Good men are easy to weep, as the heathen man observeth.' Cf. Juvenal, xv. 133.

(*f*) P. 486.—'He can find tears,' &c. Cf. Seneca de Consolatione ad Polybium, 4, § 2, larga flendi et adsidua materia est.'

(*g*) P. 489.—'Salvian complains in his time,' &c. The thought is found in Salvianus de Gubernat. Dei., lib. 4, p. 74 (edition 1669), ... 'mali esse coguntur, ne viles habeantur.'

(*h*) P. 515.—'A wise man will not admire,' *i.e.*, wonder. Cf. Horace, Epist. lib. i. p. 6, v. 1;—'Nil admirari,' &c. The maxim is ascribed to Democritus.

G.

END OF VOL. II.

THE WORKS OF
RICHARD SIBBES

THE WORKS OF
RICHARD SIBBES

VOLUME 3

An Exposition of 2nd Corinthians
Chapter One

Edited by
Alexander B. Grosart

THE BANNER OF TRUTH TRUST

THE BANNER OF TRUTH TRUST

Head Office
3 Murrayfield Road
Edinburgh, EH12 6EL
UK

North America Office
610 Alexander Spring Road
Carlisle, PA 17015
USA

banneroftruth.org

The Complete Works of Richard Sibbes
first published in 7 volumes 1862-64
This reprint of volume 3 first published by
the Banner of Truth Trust 1981
Reprinted 2001, 2023

*

ISBN
Print: 978 0 85151 329 4

*

Printed in the USA by
Versa Press Inc.,
East Peoria, IL.

EXPOSITION OF 2D CORINTHIANS CHAPTER I.

EXPOSITION OF SECOND CORINTHIANS CHAPTER I.

NOTE.

The 'Exposition' of 2d Corinthians chapter i., was published in a handsome folio, under the editorial supervision of Dr Manton. The original title-page is given below.* Prefixed to the volume is a very fine portrait of Sibbes, after the same original evidently with that earlier engraved for 'Bowels Opened,' and other works, in quarto and smaller size, but in the style of Hollar. The admirers of Puritan literature will find it no less interesting than rewarding, to compare the present 'Exposition' of Sibbes with that of a man of kindred intellect and character, viz., Anthony Burgesse, 'Pastor of Sutton-Coldfield, in Warwickshire.' His 'sermons' on the same portion of Holy Scripture bear the following title, 'An Expository Comment, Doctrinal, Controversal [*sic*], and Practical, upon the whole First Chapter of the Second Epistle of St Paul to the Corinthians' (London, folio, 1661). Our copy has the rare autograph of the excellent Bishop Beveridge, on the title-page, with a note of its price, '*pret* 12. s.' **G.**

* Original title :—

A Learned
COMMENTARY
OR
EXPOSITION
UPON
The first CHAPTER of the Second Epistle of *S. Paul*
to the *CORINTHIANS.*
BEING
The Substance of many SERMONS formerly
Preached at *Grayes-Inne, London,*
By that Reverend and Judicious Divine,
RICHARD SIBBS, D.D.
Sometimes Master of *Catherine Hall,* in *Cambridge,* and Preacher
to that Honourable Society.
Published for the Publick Good and Benefit of the Church
of *CHRIST.*
By *Tho. Manton,* B. D. and Preacher of the Gospel at *Stoake-Newington,* near *London.*
——————— *Vivit post funera virtus.*
Psalm 112. 6.
The Righteous shall be in everlasting remembrance.
2 Pet. 1. 15.
Moreover, I will endeavour that you may be able after my decease, to have these things always in remembrance.
LONDON,
Printed by *F. L.* for *N. B.* and are to be sold by *Tho. Parkhurst,* at his Shop
at the sign of the three Crowns over against the Great Conduit, at
the Lower end of Cheapside. 1655.

TO THE READER.

Good Reader,—There is no end of books, and yet we seem to need more every day. There was such a darkness brought in by the fall, as will not thoroughly be dispelled till we come to heaven; where the sun shineth without either cloud or night. For the present, all should contribute their help according to the rate and measure of their abilities. Some can only hold up a candle, others a torch; but all are useful. The press is an excellent means to scatter knowledge, were it not so often abused. All complain there is enough written, and think that now there should be a stop. Indeed, it were well if in this scribbling age there were some restraint. Useless pamphlets are grown almost as great a mischief as the erroneous and profane. Yet 'tis not good to shut the door upon industry and diligence. There is yet room left to discover more, above all that hath been said, of the wisdom of God and the riches of his grace in the gospel; yea, more of the stratagems of Satan and the deceitfulness of man's heart. Means need to be increased every day to weaken sin and strengthen trust, and quicken us to holiness. Fundamentals are the same in all ages, but the constant necessities of the church and private Christians, will continually enforce a further explication. As the arts and slights of besieging and battering increase, so doth skill in fortification. If we have no other benefit by the multitude of books that are written, we shall have this benefit: an opportunity to observe the various workings of the same Spirit about the same truths, and indeed the speculation is neither idle nor unfruitful.

There is a diversity of gifts as there is of tempers, and of tempers as there is of faces, that in all this variety, God may be the more glorified. The penmen of Scripture, that all wrote by the same Spirit, and by an infallible conduct, do not write in the same style. In the Old Testament, there is a plain difference between the lofty, courtly style of Isaiah, and the priestly, grave style of Jeremiah. In Amos there are some marks of his calling* in his prophecy. In the New Testament, you will find John sublime and seraphical, and Paul rational and argumentative. 'Tis easy to track both by their peculiar phrases, native elegances, and distinct manner of expression. This variety and 'manifold grace,' 1 Pet. iv. 10,† still

* That is, a 'herdsman.'—G.

† Ubi Vulgat. Dispensatio multiformis gratiæ. The more accurate rendering from the Vulgate is, 'Unusquisque, sicut accepit gratiam, in alterutrum illam administrantes, sicut boni dispensatores multiformis gratiæ Dei.'—Ed. Paris, 2 vols. 12mo. 1851.—G.

continueth. The stones that lie in the building of God's house are not all of a sort. There are sapphires, carbuncles, and agates, all which have their peculiar use and lustre, Isa. liv. 12.* Some are doctrinal, and good for information, to clear up the truth and vindicate it from the sophisms of wretched men; others have a great force and skill in application. Some are more evangelical, their souls are melted out in sweetness; others are sons of thunder, more rousing and stirring, gifted for a rougher strain, which also hath its use in the art of winning souls to God. 'Twas observed of the three ministers of Geneva, that none thundered more loudly than Farel, none piped more sweetly than Viret, none taught more learnedly and solidly than Calvin.† So variously doth the Lord dispense his gifts, to shew the liberty of the spirit, and for the greater beauty and order of the church; for difference with proportion causeth beauty; and to prevent schism, every member having his distinct excellency. So that what is wanting in one, may be supplied by another; and all have something to commend them to the church, that they may be not despised; as in several countries they have several commodities to maintain traffic between them all. We are apt to abuse the diversity of gifts to divisions and partialities, whereas God hath given them to maintain a communion.‡ In the church's vestment there is variety, but no rent. *Varietas sit, scissura non sit.*

All this is the rather mentioned, because of that excellent and peculiar gift which the worthy and reverend author had in unfolding and applying the great mysteries of the gospel in a sweet and mellifluous way; and therefore was by his hearers usually termed *The Sweet Dropper*, sweet and heavenly distillations usually dropping from him with such a native elegance as is not easily to be imitated. I would not set the gifts of God on quarrelling, but of all ministries, that which is most evangelical seemeth most useful. 'The testimony *of Jesus* is the spirit of prophecy,' Rev. xix. 10. 'Tis spoken by the angel to dissuade the apostle from worshipping him. You that preach Jesus Christ and him crucified and risen from the dead, have a like dignity with us angels that foretell things to come, your message is 'the spirit of prophecy;' as if he had said, This is the great and fundamental truth wherein runneth the life, and the heart-blood of religion.

The same spirit is breathing in these discourses that are now put into thy hand, wherein thou wilt find much of the comforts of the gospel, of the sealing of the Spirit, and the constant courses of God's love to his people, fruitfully and faithfully improved for thy edification.

* Varia gemmarum genera propter varia dona quæ sunt in Ecclesia.—Sanct[ius].

† Gallica mirata est Calvinum Ecclesia nuper; quo nemo docuit doctius. Est quoque te nuper mirata Farelle tonantem; quo nemo tonuit fortius. Et miratur adhuc fundentem mella Viretum; quo nemo fatur dulcius. Scilicet aut tribus his servabere testibus olim, aut interibis Gallia.—*Beza.* (Poemata et Epigrammata, p. 90, 32mo, Ludg. Bat., 1614).—G.

‡ Tunc bene multiformis Dei gratia dispensatur, quando acceptum donum etiam ejus qui hoc non habet, creditur, quando propter eum cui impenditur sibi datum putatur.—*Gregor.* Moral., lib. xxviii., c. 6.

Let it not stumble thee that the work is *posthume*,* and cometh out so long after the author's death. It were to be wished that those who excel in public gifts would, during life, publish their own labours, to prevent spurious obtrusions upon the world, and to give them their last hand and polishment, as the apostle Peter was careful to 'write before his decease,' 2 Pet. i. 12–14. But usually the church's treasure is most increased by legacies. As Elijah let fall his mantle when he was taken up into heaven, so God's eminent servants, when their persons could no longer remain in the world, have left behind them some worthy pieces as a monument of their graces and zeal for the public welfare. Whether it be out of a modest sense of their own endeavours, as being loath upon choice, or of their own accord to venture abroad into the world, or whether it be that being occupied and taken up with other labours, or whether it be in a conformity to Christ, who would not leave his Spirit till his departure, or whether it be out of an hope that their works would find a more kindly reception after their death, the living being more liable to envy and reproach (but when the author is in heaven the work is more esteemed upon earth), whether for this or that cause, usually it is, that not only the life, but the death of God's servants hath been profitable to his church, by that means many useful treatises being freed from the privacy and obscureness to which, by modesty of the author, they were formerly confined.

Which, as it hath commonly fallen out, so especially in the works of this reverend author, all which (some few only excepted†) saw the light after the author's death, which also hath been the lot of this useful comment; only it hath this advantage above the rest, that it was perused by the author during life, and corrected by his own hand, and hath the plain signature and marks of his own spirit, which will easily appear to those that have been any way conversant with his former works. This being signified (for further commendation it needeth none), I 'commend thee to God, and to the word of his grace,' which is able to build thee up, and to give thee an inheritance among the sanctified, remaining

Thy servant in the Lord's work,

THOMAS MANTON.‡

* That is, 'posthumous.'—G.

† 'Some few only excepted,' viz., those which form vol. I. of this collective edition of his works.—G.

‡ It were supererogatory to annotate a name so illustrious in the roll of Puritans as is that of Thomas Manton. His memoir will appear as an introduction to his works in the present series, by one admirably qualified for doing it justice. But it may be here noticed that he was born at Lawrence-Lydiard (now Lydeard, St Lawrence), Somersetshire, in 1620, and died on October 18. 1677. Consult 'Life,' by Harris, prefixed to Sermons on 119th Psalm, and 'Nonconformists' Memorial,' i., pp. 175–179, 426–431. He was one of the 'ejected' of 1662.—G.

A COMMENTARY

UPON

THE FIRST CHAPTER OF THE SECOND EPISTLE OF ST PAUL TO THE CORINTHIANS.

Paul, an apostle of Jesus Christ, by the will of God, and Timothy our brother, unto the church of God which is at Corinth, with all the saints which are in all Achaia: Grace be to you, and peace, from God our Father, and from the Lord Jesus Christ.—2 Cor. I. 1, 2.

The preface to this epistle is the same with other prefaces. Our blessed apostle had written a sharp epistle to the Corinthians, especially reproving their tolerating of the incestuous person.* That, his first epistle, took effect, though not so much as he desired, yet it prevailed so far with them, that they excommunicated the incestuous person, and likewise reformed divers abuses. Yet notwithstanding, it being a proud, factious, rich city, where there was confluence of many nations, being an excellent port, and mart-town,† there were many proud, insolent teachers, which thought basely of St Paul; and thereupon he writes this second epistle: the scope whereof is partly apologetical, partly exhortatory.

(1.) Apologetical—to defend himself. Exhortatory—to instruct them in several duties, as we shall see in the passages of it.

The general scope of it is this, to shew that the ministerial labour is '*not in vain in the Lord*,' 1 Cor. xv. 58. The fruit of the first Epistle to the Corinthians is seen in this second; the first Epistle took effect. Therefore we should not be discouraged, neither we that are ministers of the church, or those that are ministers in their own families, as every man should be. Be not discouraged at unlikelihood. There is alway some success to encourage us, though not so much as we look for in this world, because there is a reprobate generation that are alway set upon cavilling, and opposing; yet some success there will be, as there was here.

A second thing in general out of the whole scope is this, to teach us *to vindicate our credit, when the truth may be wounded through us*, as the apostle stands here upon his reputation, and labours to free, and to clear himself from all imputations. But especially he doth this by his life, for that is the best apology. But because that would not serve, it would not speak loud enough, therefore he makes an excellent apology in this epistle. But to come to the particulars.

* Cf. 1 Cor. v. 1, *seq.*—G. † That is, 'market-town' =commercial city.—G.

'*Paul, an apostle of Jesus Christ, by the will of God, and Timothy our brother.*' This chapter is *apologetical*, especially after the preface. He stands in defence of himself against the imputations: first, *that he was a man neglected of God*—he was so persecuted, and oppressed with so many afflictions. And the second is the imputation of *inconstancy*—that he came not to them when he had made a promise to come. This chapter is especially in defence of these two.

In an excellent heavenly wisdom, he turns off the imputation of afflictions, and inverts the imputation the clean contrary way. And he begins with thanksgiving, 'Blessed be God, the Father of our Lord Jesus Christ, the Father of mercies, the God of all comfort, who hath comforted us in all our tribulations:' as if God had done him a great favour in them, as we shall see when we come to those words.

For the preface, it is common with all his epistles, therefore we make it not a principal part of the chapter. Yet because these prefaces have the seeds of the gospel in them, the seeds of heavenly comfort and doctrine, I will speak something of it. Here is an inscription, and a salutation.

In the inscription, there are the parties from whom this epistle was written, 'Paul, an apostle of Jesus Christ by the will of God, and Timothy our brother.' And the persons to whom: 'To the church of God at Corinth, and all the saints in Achaia.'

The salutation: 'Grace and Peace;' in the form of a blessing, 'Grace and peace.'

From whom: 'From God the Father, and from our Lord Jesus Christ.'

'*Paul an apostle*,' *&c.* In this inscription he sets down his office, 'an apostle,' and 'an apostle of Jesus Christ.' How apostles differ from other ministers, it is an ordinary point. St Paul was called to be an apostle by Christ himself, 1 Cor ix. 1. 'Am I not an apostle? have I not seen Christ?' It was the privilege of the apostles to see Christ. They were taught immediately by Christ, and they had a general commission to teach all, and they had extraordinary gifts. All these were in St Paul eminently. And this was his prerogative, that he was chosen by Christ in heaven, in glory. The other were chosen by Christ when he was in abasement, in a state of humiliation. 'Paul an apostle of Jesus Christ.'

'*By the will of God.*' By the appointment of God, by the designment* of Christ; for every man in his particular calling is placed in it 'by the will of God. St Paul saith, he was an apostle 'by the will of God, not by the will of man.' This is the same word as is in the beginning of the Epistle to the Philippians.†

In a word, it teacheth us this first observation, *That we should think ourselves in our standings and callings to be there by the will of God.*

And therefore should serve him by whose will we are placed in that standing. Let every man consider, who placed me here? God. If a hair cannot fall from my head without his providence, Mat. x. 30, much less can the disposing of my calling, which is a greater matter; therefore I will seek his glory, and frame myself and courses answerable to the will of him by whose will I am in this place.

Men have not their callings only to get riches, and to get preferment. Those are base ends of their own to serve themselves. God placeth us in our particular callings, not to serve ourselves, but to serve him; and he

* That is, 'designation.'—G.

† This is a slip for Ephesians.—G.

will cast in those riches, honour, preferment, dignity, and esteem, so much as is fit for us in the serving of him in our places.

The other party* in the inscription, from whom the epistle is, is,

'*Timothy our brother.*' He sends his Epistle from Timothy as well as from himself. This he doth to win the more acceptance among the Corinthians, by the consent of so blessed a man as Timothy was, who was an evangelist. Unity by consent is stronger. And there is a natural weakness in men to regard the consent and authority of others, more than the things themselves. And indeed, if God himself in heavenly love and mercy condescend to help our weakness, much more should all that are 'led by the Spirit of God,' Gal. v. 18. We are subject to call in question the truths of God. Therefore he helps us with sacraments, and with other means and allurements; and although that be truth that he saith, yet because he would undermine our distrustful dispositions by all means, he useth those courses. So St Paul, that they might respect what he wrote the more, as from a joint spirit, he writes, 'Paul, and Timothy our brother.'

It was an argument of much modesty and humility in this blessed apostle, that he would not of himself seem, as it were, to monopolize their respect, as if all should look to him, but he joins Timothy with him; so great an apostle joins an inferior.

There is a spirit of singularity in many; they will seem to do all themselves, and carry all themselves before them; and they will not speak the truths that others have spoken before them without some disdain. As a proud critic said, 'I would they had never been men that spake our things before we were, that we might have had all the credit of it' (*a*). Oh, no! Those that are led with the Spirit of God, they are content in modesty and humility to have others joined with them; and they know it is available† for others likewise; they will respect the truth the more.

And thus far we yield to the papists when we speak of this, whether the church can give authority to the word of God or no. In regard of us, the church hath some power, in regard of our weakness; but what is that power? It is an inducing power, an alluring power, a propounding power, to propound the mysteries of salvation. But the inward work, the convincing power, is from the evidence of the Spirit of God, and from the Scripture itself. All that the church doth is to move, to induce, and to propound this, *quoad nos*. It hath some power in the hearts of men.

The church thus far gives authority to the Scriptures in the hearts of men, though it be an improper phrase to say it gives authority; for, as the men said to the woman of Samaria, 'Now we believe it ourselves, not because thou toldest us,' &c., John iv. 42. The church allures us to respect the Scriptures; but then there is an inward power, an inward majesty in the Scriptures, and that bears down all before it.

Again, here is a ground why St Paul alleged human authority sometimes in his epistles, and in his dealing with men; because he was to deal with men, that would be shamed the more with them. Anything that may strengthen the truth in regard of the weakness of those with whom we have to deal, may be used in a heavenly policy. 'One of your own prophets,' saith St Paul, towards the end, i. 12. And so in the Acts of the Apostles, xvii. 28, he quotes a saying out of an atheist (*b*).

* This use of 'party' = person, which is not uncommon in Sibbes and his contemporaries, shews that it is not the modern vulgarism (so-called) which precisians would make it.—G.

† That is, 'advantageous.'—G.

'*Timothy our brother.*' 'Brother:' he means not only by grace but by calling. As we know in the law and other professions, those of the same profession are called before brethren; so Timothy was St Paul's brother, not only by grace, but by calling; and two bonds bind stronger. Here is a treble bond, nature, grace, calling. They were men, they were fellow Christians, and they were teachers of the gospel. Therefore he saith, 'Timothy our brother.' Timothy was an evangelist, yet notwithstanding it was a greater honour to him to be a brother to St Paul than to be an evangelist. An hypocrite may be an evangelist; but a true brother of St Paul none but a true Christian can be. All Christians are brethren. It is a word that levels all; for it takes down the mountains, and fills up the valleys. The greatest men in the world, the mountains, if they be Christians, they are brethren to the lowest. And it fills up the valleys. The lowest, if they be Christians, are brethren to the highest; howsoever in worldly respects, they cease in death; as personal differences, and differences in calling, they all cease in death. All are brethren; therefore he useth it for great respect. St Paul was a great apostle; Timothy an inferior man, yet both brethren, 'Timothy our brother.'

'*To the church of God at Corinth.*' We have seen the persons from whom, 'Paul and Timothy.' Now here are the persons to whom, 'to the church of God at Corinth.' Corinth was a very wicked city, as, where there is a great confluence of many people, there is a contagion of many sins of the people; and yet notwithstanding in this Corinth there was a church. For as Christ saith, 'No man can come to me, except my Father draw him,' John vi. 44; so where the Father will draw, who can draw back? Even in Corinth God hath his church. He raiseth up a generation of men, a church, which is a company of creatures differing as much from the common, as men do from beasts. And yet such is the power and efficacy of the blessed gospel of salvation, having the Spirit of God accompanying it, that even in Corinth, a wretched city, this word and this Spirit raised up a company of men, called here by the name of a church, and saints. And such power indeed hath the word of God with the Spirit, not only in wicked places, but in our wicked hearts too.

Let a man have a world of wickedness in him, and let him come and present himself meekly and constantly to the means of salvation, and God in time by his Spirit will raise a new frame of grace in his heart, he will make a new creation. As at the first he created all out of nothing, order out of confusion; so out of the heart, which is nothing but a chaos of confusion, of blindness, and darkness, and terror (there is a world of confusion in the heart of man); God by his creating word (for his word of the gospel is creating, as well as his word was at the first in the creation of the world; it hath a creating power) he raiseth an excellent frame in the heart of a man, he scatters his natural blindness, he sets in order his natural confusion, that a man becomes a new creature, and an heir of a new world.

Let no people despair, nor no person; for God hath his church in 'Corinth.'

But what is become of this church now? Why, alas! it is under the slavery of the Turks, it is under miserable captivity at this day. At the first, Corinth was overthrown by Numeus,* a Roman captain, for the abusing the Roman ambassadors; it was ruinated for the unfit carriage to the ambassadors, who would not suffer themselves to be contemned, nor the

* Qu. 'Mummius?'—Ed.

majesty of the Roman empire. But Augustus Cæsar afterwards repaired it (c). And now for neglecting of God's ambassadors, the preachers of the gospel, it is under another misery, but spiritual; it is under the bondage, I say, of that tyrant.

What is become of Rome, that glorious city? It is now 'the habitation of devils, a cage of unclean birds,' Rev. xviii. 2. What is become of those glorious churches which St John wrote those epistles to in his Revelation? and which St Paul wrote unto? Alas, they are gone! the gospel is now come into the western parts. And shall we think all shall be safe with us, as the Jews did, crying, 'The temple of the Lord, the temple of the Lord?' Jer. vii. 4. No, no! unless we respect Christ's blessed gospel of salvation, except we bring forth fruits worthy of it, except we maintain and defend it, and think it our honour and our crown, and be zealous for it. If we suffer the insolent enemies of it to grow as vipers in the very bosom of the church, what is like to become of us? If there were no foreign enemies to invade us, we would let slip the glorious gospel of salvation. God will not suffer this indignity to this blessed jewel, his truth; he will not suffer the doctrine of the gospel to be so disrespected. You see the fearful example of the church of Corinth. Let those whom it may concern, that have any advantage and authority, let them put in for God's cause, put in for the gospel, labour to propagate and to derive* this blessed truth we enjoy to posterity, by suppressing as much as they may the underminers of it. It is an acceptable service. 'To the church of God at Corinth.'

'*And all the saints in Achaia.*' Corinth was the city, Achaia the country wherein Corinth was. There were then saints, holy men in all Achaia. And St Paul writes to 'all saints,' to weak saints, to strong saints, to rich saints, to poor saints; because every saint hath somewhat that is lovely and respective† in them, somewhat to be respected. The least grace deserves respect from the greatest apostle. And all have one head, all have one hope of glory, all are redeemed with the same 'precious blood of Christ,' 1 Pet. i. 19 (and so I might run on). The many privileges agree to all. Therefore, all should have place in our respect. 'To *all* saints,' that the least should not think themselves undervalued. Weakness is most of all subject to complaining if it be disrespected. Therefore, in heavenly wisdom and prudence, the apostle puts in '*all* saints,' in all Achaia whatsoever. Besides the mother city, the metropolis of that country, which was Corinth, there were saints scattered. God in heavenly wisdom scatters his saints. As seed, when it is scattered in the ground, it doth more good than when it is on heaps in the barn; so God scatters his saints as jewels, as the lights of the world. Here he will have one to shine and there another. Here he will have one fruitful to condemn the wicked world where they are, and by their good example, and their heavenly and fruitful conversation, to draw out of the wicked estate of nature those with whom they are. Therefore he will have them scattered here and there, not only at Corinth, but 'saints in all Achaia,' besides scattered in other places.

But we must know, by the way, that these saints had reference to some particular church: for though it be sufficient to make a Christian to have union with Christ (there is the main, the head); yet notwithstanding, he must be a branch, he must be a member of some particular congregation. Therefore we have it in Acts ii. 47: 'God added *to the church* such as should be saved.' Those that are added to salvation must be added to the

* That is, 'transmit.'—G.

† That is, 'respect-worthy.'—G.

church; a man must be a member of some particular church. So, though these were scattered, they were members of some church. God's children are as stones in some building; and there is an influence of grace comes from Christ, the Head, to every particular member, as it is in the body. God quickens not straggling members, that have no reference to any particular church. That I note by the way. 'To the church of God at Corinth, and all the saints in Achaia.'

'*Saints.*' *Quest.* The apostle calls them saints. All believers are called saints. Are they so? Are all in the visible church saints? Yes, say some, and therefore they say that our church is not a true visible church; because many of them are not saints, say some that went out from among us.

Ans. I answer, *all are, or should be saints.* St Paul wrote here to those that were sacramental* saints, and such as by outward covenant and profession were saints; not that they were all of them inwardly so; but all should be so done. He calls them so, to put them in mind of their duty. To clear this point a little.

1. Sometimes the church of God in the Scripture hath its name *from the commixtion of good and bad in it.* So it is called a field where there is a mixture of good and bad seed, Mat. xiii. 19, 20; so it is called a house wherein there are vessels of honour and vessels of dishonour, 2 Tim. ii. 20; because there is such a mixture in the visible church.

2. Sometimes the church hath the name from the better part, and so it is the spouse of Christ, the love of Christ, 'a peculiar people,' 'an holy nation,' 1 Pet. ii. 9, and 'saints,' as it is here. Not that all are so, but it hath the denomination from the better part; all should be so, and the best are so, and it is sufficient that the denomination of a company be from the better part. As we say of gold ore: though there be much earth mixed with it, yet in regard of the better part we call it gold, we give it that name; so, in regard that the best are saints, and that all should be so, therefore he calls them all saints.

Quest. Should all in the visible church be saints by profession, and by sacrament? Should all that are baptized, and receive the communion, enter into a profession of sanctity? What say you then to a profane, atheistical generation, that, forsooth, make a show of holiness, and therefore we must look for none of them?

Ans. I say all profane persons are gross hypocrites. Why? for are you members of the church or no? Yes, will every one say; will you make me an infidel? will you make me a pagan? Well, take your own word then. What is it to be a member of the church but to be a saint? Must thou be a saint? Doth not thy profession, as thou art a member, bind thee to be a saint? In baptism, was not thy promise to 'renounce the devil, the world, and the flesh?' In renewing thy covenant in the communion, dost not thou purpose to cleave to God in all things? Thou that takest liberty, therefore, in the church of God, under the profession of religion, to live as a libertine, thou art a gross hypocrite, and this aggravates thy sin, and makes it worse than a pagan's. Thou which art in the bosom of the church, in the kingdom of saints, as it is in Dan. vii. 18, 'the people of the saints of the Most High,' the people of God in the church wherein thou art a professed member; and yet dost thou take liberty grossly to offend God?

Quest. What doth make a saint?

Ans. In a word, to the constitution of a true saint, there is

* That is, 'professed.' 'avowed.'—G.

A separation, dedication, qualification, conversation.

1. There is a *separation* presently. When a man is a saint, he is separate from the confused company of the world, from the kingdom of Satan. Therefore those that have all companies alike, that carry themselves indifferently in all companies, as men that profess a kind of civility, that are taken up with the complement* of the times, men that learn the language of the times, that are for all sorts, they know not what belongs to the high profession of Christianity.

There is a due to all, I confess; there is a benevolence and a beneficence to all; but there is a kind of complacency, a sweet familiarity, and amity which should be reserved to a few, only to those in whom we see the evidences and signs of grace. If there be not a separation in respect of grace, there is no holiness at all; a saint must be separated. Not locally, but in regard of amity, in regard of intimate friendship. As we see it is in outward things, in some of our houses. There is a court where all come, poor and rich; and there is the house where those of nearer acquaintance come; and then there is the innermost room, the closet, where only ourselves and those which are nearest to us come. So it is in the passages of the soul. There are some remote courtesies that come from us, as men, to all, be they what they will; there are other respects to others that are nearer, that we admit nearer, that are of better quality; and there are other that are nearest of all, that we admit even into the closet of our hearts: and those are they with whom we hope to have communion for ever in heaven, the blessed people of God, termed here 'saints.' It is an evidence of our translation from a cursed estate to a better when we love such. 'Hereby we know,' saith St John, 'that we are translated from death to life, because we love the brethren,' 1 John iii. 14. There must be a separation.

2. And withal there must be a *dedication of ourselves to the service of God.* A Christian, when he knows himself by the word of truth and by the work of the Spirit, to be God's child, he dedicates himself to better services than before. He thinks himself too good, he thinks too highly of himself to be a base blasphemer, or swearer, to be a filthy person. He considers himself as 'the temple of the Holy Ghost,' 1 Cor. iii. 16, and he useth himself to better purposes, to better studies, to do good.

3. And then with dedication, there is *an inward qualification* to inable† him with light never to forget the image of God. Herein this saintship stands, especially in this inward qualification, whereby we resemble Christ the King of saints. All our sanctification comes from him. As Aaron's ointment went down from his head to his beard, and so to his skirts, Ps. cxxxiii. 2, so all our sanctification is from Christ. Every saint is qualified from the Spirit of Christ. 'Of his fulness,' John i. 16, we receive this inward qualification, that we have another judgment of things than this world hath; what is good and what is bad, what is true and what is false, what is comfortable and what tends to discomfort. He hath another conceit of things. He hath another light than he had before, and than other carnal men have. He hath a heavenly light. He hath another language. He gives himself to prayer and to thanksgiving. He is given to savoury discourse. He hath other courses in his particular calling and in his general calling than other refuse‡ company have, or than himself had before his calling. This is from his qualification.

4. And this qualification and *conversation go together.* He hath a new

* That is, 'compliment' = fine manners.—G. † That is, 'enable' = endow.—G.
‡ That is, 'worthless.'—G.

conversation. He carries himself even like to him that 'hath called him out of darkness into marvellous light,' 1 Pet. ii. 9. So a true saint, as every professor of religion ought to be, he is dedicate to God, and he is qualified in some degree, as Christ was, by his Holy Spirit. He is a new creature. 'He that is in Christ is a new creature,' 2 Cor. v. 17, and he shews this by his conversation, or else he is no saint.

Quest. How shall we know a saint from a mere civil* man? (as there be many that live and die in that estate, which is to be pitied; and one main end of our calling is not only to reduce profane men to a better fashion of life, but to shew civil men their danger.)

Ans. A mere civil man looks to the second table. He is smooth in his carriage and conversation with men, but negligent in his service to God. A civil man he looks to his outward carriage, but he makes no conscience of secret sins. He is not 'holy in all manner of conversation,' as St Peter saith, 1 Pet. i. 15. 'Be ye holy in all manner of conversation,' in private, in public, in your retired carriage. He makes no conscience of his thoughts, of his speeches, of all.

You may know an hypocrite so, that carries himself smoothly and acceptably in the eye of the world; but he makes no conscience of his thoughts, he makes no conscience of his affections, of his desires, of his lusts, and such things. He makes no conscience of lesser oaths, nor perhaps of rotten discourses. No; they are all for this, that they may pass in the world, that they may carry themselves with acceptance. As for what belongs to the 'new creature,' to saints, they care not; for they have vain conceits of these, and judge them as hypocrites. Because such a one knows himself should be an hypocrite, if he should do otherwise than he doth, therefore he thinks that others that are above his pitch are hypocrites, and they make a show of that that is not in them; because if he should make show of that, his heart would tell him that he were an hypocrite.

A true saint differs from an hypocrite in many respects; but in this one mainly, that a true saint of God is altered in the inward frame and qualification of his soul. He is a 'new creature.' Therefore there is a spring of better thoughts, of better desires, of better aims in him than in other men. And he labours more after the inward frame of his heart than after his outward carriage. What he is ashamed to do, he is ashamed to think, he is ashamed to lust after. What he desires to do, he desires to love in his heart. He labours that all may be true in the inward man; because grace, as well as nature, begins from the heart, from the inward parts.

An hypocrite never cares for that. All his care is for the outward parts. He is sale-work. So his carriage be acceptable to others, all his care is taken. He lives to the view. Therefore he looks not to the substance and the truth, but to the shadow and appearance.

Now I come to the salutation itself.

VERSE 2.

'*Grace be unto you*,' &c. 'Grace' doth enter into the whole conversation of a Christian, and doth sweeten his very salutations. Which I observe, because many men confine their religion to places, to actions, and to times. There is a relish of holiness in everything that comes from a Christian; in his salutations and courtesies. St Paul salutes them,

* That is, 'moral.'—G.

'Grace and peace from God,' &c. And the use of holy salutations are *to shew [and] win love.*

To shew love and respect. Therefore he salutes them; and by shewing love, to gain love; for there is a loadstone in love. And thirdly, the use of salutations is by them to convey some good. For these salutations are not mere wishes, but prayers, nay, blessings. God's people are a blessed people, and they are full of blessing. They carry a blessing in their very speeches.

Quest. What is a blessing?

Ans. A blessing is a prayer, with the application of the thing prayed for. It is somewhat more than a prayer, 'Grace be with you, and peace.' It is not only a mere wish, I desire it; nay, my desire of it is with an applying of it. 'Grace shall be with you, and peace,' and the more because I heartily wish it to you. It is no light matter to have the benediction and salutation of a holy man, especially those that are superiors; for the superiors bless the inferiors. There is a grace goes even with the very salutations, with the common prayers of a holy man. It is a comfortable sign when God doth enlarge the heart of a holy man to wish well to a man.

And surely the very consideration of that should move us to let them have such encouragement from our carriage and demeanour, that they may have hearts to think of us to the throne of grace, to give us a good wish, to give us a good desire. For every gracious desire, every prayer, hath its effect when it comes from a favourite of God, especially from such a man as St Paul was; from a minister, a holy man in a calling, a man of God. They have their efficacy with them. They are not empty words, 'grace and peace.'

The popes think it a great favour when they bestow their apostolical benediction and blessing. Their blessing is not much worth. Their curse is better than their blessing. But surely the blessing of a man rightly called, those that are true ministers of Christ, they are clothed with power and efficacy from God. 'Grace be with you, and peace;' it is no idle compliment.

And here you see likewise what should be the manner of the salutation of Christians. As they ought to salute, to shew love, and to gain love, so all their salutations should be holy. There is a taking the name of God in vain in salutations ofttimes, 'God save you,' &c., and it must be done with a kind of scorn; and if there be any demonstration of religion, it becomes them not, that which should become them most. What should become a saint, but to carry himself saint-like? And yet men must do it with a kind of scorn, with a kind of graceless grace. That which in the religious use of it is a comfortable and sweet thing, and is alway with a comfortable and gracious effect in God's children; either it hath effect, and is made grace to them to whom it is spoken, or returns to them that speak it. As Christ saith to his disciples, 'When you come into a house, pronounce peace to them; and if the house be not worthy, your peace shall return to you,' Mat. x. 13. So the salutations of a good man, if they be not effectual to the parties, if they be unworthy, rebellious creatures, they return again to himself; they have effect one way or other. Let it not be done, therefore, with a taking the name of God in vain in a scornful manner, but with gravity and reverence, as becometh a holy action. There is some limitation and exception of this. Salutations, in some cases, may be omitted.

1. *As in serious business,* 'salute no man by the way,' as Christ saith to his apostles, Luke x. 4. A neglect sometimes is good manners, when

respect is swallowed up in a greater duty. As it was good manners for David to dance and to carry himself, as it were, unseemly before the ark, 2 Sam. vi. 14; because he was to neglect respect to meaner persons, to forget the respect he was to shew to men. Being altogether taken up with higher matters, it was a kind of decency and comeliness. And overmuch scrupulousness and niceness in lesser things, when men are called to greater, is but unmannerly manners. In these cases, these lesser must give way and place to the greater. 'Salute no man by the way.' Despatch the business you are about; that is, if it may be a hindrance in the way, salute not. This is in respect of time.

2. And as for time, *so for persons*. A notorious, incorrigible heretic, salute not. To salute such a one would be, as it were, a connivance or an indulgence to him. 'Salute him not' (*d*). The denying of a salutation many times hath the force of a censure. The party neglected may think there is somewhat in him for which he is neglected in that manner. In these cases, salutations may be omitted sometimes. But I go unto the particulars.

'*Grace be unto you and peace*.' These are the good things wished. We see the apostle, a blessed man, that had been 'in the third heaven' rapt up, 2 Cor. xii. 2, that had been taught of Christ what things were most excellent, and had himself seen 'excellent things which he could not utter,' 2 Cor. xii. 4, when he comes to wishes, we see out of heavenly wisdom and experience he draws them to two heads, all good things to 'grace and peace.' If there had been better things to be wished, he would have wished them, but grace and peace are the principal things.

Quest. What is meant by grace here?

Ans. Grace, in this place, *is the free favour and love of God from his own bowels;* not for any desert, or worth, or strength of love of ours. It is his own free grace and love, which is shed by the Holy Ghost, and springs only from his own goodness and loving nature, and not from us at all. This is grace. It must be distinguished from the fruits of it; as the apostle doth distinguish them, 'grace, and the gifts of grace,' Rom. v. 15. There is favour and the gifts of favour, which is grace inherent in us. Here especially is meant the fountain and spring of all the favour of God, with the manifestation of it, with the increase of it, with the continuance of it. He wisheth these things, the favour of God, with the manifestation of it to their souls; that God would be gracious to them, so that he would shew his grace; that he would discover it, and shine upon them; and to that end that he would give them his Holy Spirit, to shed 'his love into their hearts,' Rom. v. 5. This shining of God into the heart, this shedding of the love of God into the heart, is the grace here meant; God's favour, with the manifestation of it to the soul, and with the continuance of it, and the increase of it still. 'Grace unto you.' As if he should have said, I wish you the favour of God, and the report of it to your souls; that as he loves you through his Christ, so he would witness as much by his Holy Spirit to your souls. And I wish you likewise the continuance of it, and the increase of it, and the fruits of it likewise (for that must not be excluded), all particular graces, which are likewise called graces. They have the name of favours, because they come from favour; and favour is the chief thing in them. What is the chief thing in joy, in faith, in love? They are graces. They cannot be considered as qualifications, as earthly things in us. They proceed from the grace and love of God, and have their especial value from thence. So I wish you the manifestation, the continuance and increase of favour, with all the fruits of God's favour, especially such as concern a better life. The word is easily understood after the common sense. Grace is the loving and free respect of a superior to an inferior ; the respect of a magistrate to such as are under him. Such a one is in grace with the prince, we say. We mean not any inherent thing, but free grace. So in religion it is not any inherent, habitual thing, grace ; but it is free favour, and whatsoever issues from free favour. This must be the rather observed, this phrase, against the papists. We say we are justified by grace, and so do they. What do they mean by being justified by grace ? That is, by inherent grace. We say, No ; we are justified by grace ; that is, by the free favour of God in Jesus Christ. So is the acception * of the word.

But, to come to the point, that which I will now note is this, that

Doct. A Christian, though he be in the state of grace and favour with God, yet still he needs the continuance of it.

He stands in need of the continuance of God. St Paul here prays for grace and peace, to those that were in the state of grace already. Why? The reason of it is, that we run into new breaches every day, of ourselves. As long as there is a spring of corruption in us, a cursed issue of corruption, so long there will be some actions, and speeches, and thoughts, that will issue, that would of themselves break our peace with God, or at least hinder the sweet sense of it. Therefore, we have continual occasion to renew our desires of the sense and feeling of the favour of God, and to renew our pardon every day, to take out a pardon of course, as we have now the liberty to do. So oft as we confess our sins, 'he is merciful to forgive us,' 1 John i. 9. And to win his favour, we have need every day still of grace. I list not to join in conflict here with the papists concerning their opinion. I will but touch it by the way, to shew the danger of it. They will not have all of mere grace. But Christians are under grace while they are in this world, as St Paul saith, all is grace, grace still: nay, at the day of judgment, 'The Lord shew mercy to the house of Onesiphorus at that day,' 2 Tim. i. 16, at the day of judgment. Grace and mercy must be our plea, till we come to heaven. They stand upon grace to enable † us to the work; and then by the work we may merit our own salvation, and so they will not have it of grace, of gift; but as a stipend, a thing of merit, directly contrary to St Paul, Rom. vi. 23, Eternal life is χάρισμα. The word comes of χάρις, of gift. 'The gift of God, a free gift through Jesus Christ our Lord.' So from the first grace, to eternal life, which is the complement of all, all is grace.

As for the New Testament, it is the covenant of grace. The whole carriage of our salvation is called the covenant of grace ; because, God of grace doth enter into covenant with us. He sent Christ of grace, who is the foundation of the covenant. The fulfilling of it, on our part, is of grace. He gives us faith. 'Faith is the gift of God,' Eph. ii. 8. 'He puts his fear in our hearts that we should not depart from him,' Jeremiah xxxii. 40. And when he enters into covenant with us, it is of grace and love. It was of grace that he sent Christ to be the foundation of the covenant; that in the satisfying of his justice he might be gracious to us, without disparagement to his justice. Of grace he fulfils the condition on our part. We are no more able to believe than we are to fulfil the law; but he enables us by his word and Spirit, attending upon the means of salvation, to fulfil the covenant. And when we have done all, he gives us of grace, eternal life ; all is of grace.

* That is, 'acceptation.'—G. † That is, 'qualify.'—G.

There is nothing in the gospel but grace. Therefore in the Ephesians, i. 6, it is stood upon by the apostle, 'To the praise of the glory of his rich grace.' From election to glorification, all is to the glory of his grace.

We ought to conceive of God as a gracious Father, withholding his anger, which we deserve to be poured upon us; by the intercession of Christ, withholding that anger, and the fruits of it. And, notwithstanding we are in grace, if we neglect to seek to God the Father, if we neglect to seek to Christ, who makes intercession for us, then, though we be in the first grace still, we are not cast away yet; we are *filii sub ira*, sons under wrath; we are under anger, though not under hatred.

Therefore, every day we should labour to maintain the grace of God with the assurance of it. It is a great matter to carry ourselves so, as we may be under the sense and feeling of the grace of God. It is not sufficient to be in the grace of God, but to have the report of it to our own hearts, have it to shine upon us.

Quest. How should we carry ourselves so, that we may be in [a] state of grace? that is, in such a state as we may find the sweet evidence and comfortable feeling continually, that we are God's children.

Ans. First of all, there must be *a perpetual, daily practice of abasing ourselves, of making ourselves poor;* that is, every day to see the vanity of all things in the world out of us; to see the weakness of grace in us; to see the return of our corruptions that foil us every day; that so we may see in what need we stand of the favour of God: considering that all comforts without are vanity, and that all the graces in us are stained with corruption; considering, besides the stains of our graces, that there is a continual issue of corruption. These things will make our spirits poor, and make us hunger and thirst after the sense and feeling of free pardon every day. This will enforce us to renew our patent, to renew our portion in the covenant of grace, to have daily pardon. This should be our daily practice, to enter deeper and deeper into ourselves.

This is to 'live by faith,' Gal. ii. 20. As God is continually ready to shew us favour in Christ, not only at the first in acquitting us from our sins, but continually doth shew us favour upon all occasions, and is justifying and pardoning, and speaking peace continually to us; so there must be an action answerable in us, that is depending upon God by faith, living by faith. This we do by seeing in what need we stand of grace. 'God resists the proud, but gives grace to the humble,' James iv. 6.

2. Then, again, that we may walk in the grace of God, and in the sense of it, let us every day labour *to have our souls more and more enriched with the endowments and graces of God's Spirit,* that we may be objects of God's delight. Let us labour to be affected to things as he is affected. Two cannot 'walk together except they be agreed,' Amos iii. 3. Let us hate that which God hates, and delight in that which God delights in, that we may have a kind of complacency, and be in love with the blessed work of the Spirit of God more and more. Let us labour to delight in them that grow in grace, as the nearer any one comes to our likeness, the more we grow in familiarity with them. Labour also to preserve a clear soul, that God may shine upon us. God delights not in strangeness to us. His desire is that we may walk in the sense and assurance of his grace and favour.

Quest. How shall we know that we are in a state of grace with God?

Ans. I answer, that we do not deceive ourselves;

1. We must look *to the work of God's grace.* God's grace is a fruitful grace. His favour is fruitful. It is not a barren favour; it is not a winter sun.

The sun in the winter, it carries a goodly countenance, but it heats not to any purpose; it doth not quicken. But God's grace, it carries life and heat where it comes. Therefore, if we be in a state of grace and favour with God, we may discern it.

But in times of desertion, though a person be in grace and favour with God, yet many times he thinks he is not so.

It is true. Then, we must not always go to our feeling at such times, and the enlargement of our hearts by the Spirit of comfort, but go to the work of grace. For,

2. Where grace and favour is, there are *the graces of the Spirit.* As it is not a bare favour in regard of comfort, so it is not a barren favour in regard of graces; for every heart that is in favour with God hath some graces of the Spirit. God enriches the soul where he shews favour. His love-tokens are some graces. Therefore, if the witness and comfort of the Spirit cease in case of desertion, let us go to the work of the Spirit, and by that we may know if we be in grace with God. For God's people are a 'peculiar people:' and God's children have always some peculiar grace. Some ornaments, some jewels the spouse of Christ hath, which others have not.

Therefore, examine thy heart, what work of God there is, and what desire thou hast after better things, what inward hatred against that which is ill, what strength thou hast against it. Go to some mark of regeneration, of the 'new creature,' and these will evidence that we are in a state of grace with God, because these are peculiar favours. And though we feel not the comfort, yet there is a work, and that work will comfort us more than the comfort itself will do.

3. And this is one thing whereby we may know we are in favour with God, when we can comfort ourselves, *and can go to the throne of grace through Christ. When we can go boldly to God it is a sign of favour.* When we can call upon him, when we can go in any desertion to prayer, when in any affliction we can have enlarged hearts, it is a sign of favour with God. A mere hypocrite, or a man that hath not this peculiar grace, he trusts to outward things; and when they are gone, when he is in trouble, he hath not the heart to go to God. His heart is shut up, he sinks down, because he relied upon common matters. He did not rely upon the favour of God and the best fruit of it, which are graces, but upon common favours. Therefore, he sinks in despair.

But a sound Christian, take him at the worst, he can sigh to God, he can go to him, and open his soul to him. 'By Christ we have an entrance to the Father,' Eph. ii. 18; 'We have boldness through faith,' Eph. iii. 12. Every Christian hath this in the worst extremity, he hath a spirit of prayer. Though he cannot enlarge himself, yet he can sigh and groan to God, and God will hear the sighs of his own Spirit; they are loud in his ears. David, at the worst, he prays to God; Saul, at the worst, he goes to the witch, 1 Sam. xxviii. 7, *seq.*, and from thence to his sword's point, 1 Sam. xxxi. 4. But usually, the usual temper and disposition of a man in the state of grace is joy; for, as one saith, grace is the begetter of joy; for they both have one root in the Greek language. There is the same root for favour and for joy (*e*). So favour is usually and ordinarily with a sweet enlargement of heart. We may thank ourselves else, that do not walk so warily and so jealously as we should.

The reward that God gives his children that are careful is a spirit of joy. 'Being justified by faith, we have peace with God, and joy in tribulation,' Rom. v. 1. For, even as it is in human matters, the favour and countenance of the king, it is as a shower of rain after a drought, it comforts his subjects. There is a wondrous joy in the favour and grace of great persons alway; and as the favourable aspect of the heavens upon inferior bodies promiseth good things,* and men promise themselves from that favour and good, so the favour and grace of God enlarge the soul with joy and comfort. And there is that measure of joy in those that are in the free favour of God, that they will honour God freely, to cast themselves upon his mercy.

And it is with a disesteem of all things in the world besides. It is such a joy as works in the soul a base esteem of all things else. St Paul esteemed all dross, 'in comparison of the knowledge of Christ,' Philip. iii. 8, and the favour of God in Christ. So in Ps. iv., David saith of some, 'There be many that will say, Who will shew us any good?' ver. 6. *Any* good! It is no matter. But saith the Holy Spirit in David, 'Lord, lift up the light of thy countenance upon me,' ver. 6. He goes to prayer. He saith not, 'Who will shew us any good?' It is no matter what, or how we come by it, any earthly good worldly men desire. No; saith he, 'Lord, shew us the light of thy countenance.' He desires that above all things, so he saith, 'The lovingkindness of the Lord is better than life itself,' Ps. lxiii. 3. Life is a sweet thing, the sweetest thing in the world; but the grace and favour of God is better than that. For in this, when all comforts fail, the children of God have assurance, that 'neither life, nor death, nor things present, nor things to come, nor anything, can separate us from the love of God in Christ,' Rom. viii. 38, which shews itself better than life itself. When life fails, this favour shall never fail. Nothing shall be able to separate us from the favour of God in Christ. It is an everlasting favour, and therefore everlasting because it is free. If it were originally in us, it would fail when we fail; but it is an everlasting favour because it is free. God hath founded the cause of love to us in himself. So much for that, 'Grace be unto you.'

'*And peace.*' All that I will say of peace in this place is this, to shew,

Obs. That *true peace issues from grace.*

It is to be had thence. Peace, we take here for that sweet peace with God, and peace of conscience, and likewise peace with all things, when all things are peaceable to us, when there is a sweet success in all business, with a security in a good estate. It is a blessed thing when we know that all will be well with us. This quiet and peaceable estate issues from grace, peace of conscience especially. I observe it the rather [because] it hath been the error of the world to seek peace where it is not, to seek peace in sanctification, to seek it in the work of grace within a man, not to speak of worldly men, that seek peace in outward contentments, in recreations, in friends, and the like. Alas! it is a poor peace. But I speak of religious persons that are of a higher strain. They have sought peace, but not high enough. True peace must be selected from grace, the free favour in Christ. This will quiet and still the clamours of an accusing conscience. God reconciled in Christ will pacify the conscience; nothing else will do it. For if our chief peace were fetched from sanctification, as many fetch it thence in error of judgment, alas! the

* That is, according to (the now exploded, but in time of Sibbes accredited system of) astrology. Even Bacon and Milton believed in the influence of the stars. —G.

conscience would be dismayed, and always doubt whether it had sanctification enough or no. Indeed, sanctification and grace within is required as a qualification, to shew that we are not hypocrites, but are in the state and covenant of grace. It is not required as a foundation of comfort, but as a qualification of the persons to whom comfort belongs. Therefore, David, and St Paul, and the rest, that knew the true power and efficacy of the gospel, they sought for peace in the grace and free favour of God.

Let us lay it up to put it in practice in the time of dissolution, in the time of spiritual conflict, in the time when our consciences shall be awakened, and perhaps upon the rack, and Satan will be busy to trouble our peace, that we may shut our eyes to all things below, and see God shining on [us] in Christ; that we may see the favour of God in Christ, by whose death and passion he is reconciled to us, and in the grace and free favour of God in Christ we shall see peace enough.

It is true, likewise, besides peace of conscience, of all other peace, peace of success and peace of state. That all creatures and all conditions are peaceable to us, whence is it? It is from grace. For God, being reconciled, he reconciles all. When God himself is ours, all is ours. When he is turned, all is turned with him. When he becomes our Father in Christ, and is at peace with us, all are at peace besides. So that all conditions, all estates, all creatures, they work for our good. It is from hence, when God is turned, all are turned with him. He being the God of the creature, that sustains and upholds the creature, in whom the creature hath his being and working, he must needs therefore turn it for the good of them that are in covenant with him. All that are joined in covenant with him, he fills them with peace, because they are in grace with him.

This should stir up our hearts, above all things in the world, to pray for grace, to get grace, to empty ourselves of self-confidence, that we may be vessels for grace, to make grace our plea, to magnify the grace of God.

We must never look in this world for a peace altogether absolute. That is reserved for heaven. Our peace here is a troubled peace. God will have a distinction between heaven and earth. But when our peace is interrupted, when the waters 'are come into our souls,' Ps. lxix. 1, what must be our course? When we would have peace, go to grace, go to the free promise of grace in Christ. 'Grace and peace.'

'*From God our Father, and the Lord Jesus Christ.*' The spring of grace and peace are here mentioned.

After the preface, he comes to the argument which he intends; and begins with blessing.

One part of the scope of this blessed apostle is, to avoid the scandal* of his sufferings; for he was a man of sorrows, if ever man was. Next Christ, who was a true man of sorrow, the blessed apostle was a man of miseries and sorrow. Now, weak, shallow Christians thought him to be a man deserted of God. They thought it was impossible for God to regard a man so forlorn, so despicable as this man was. What doth he? Before he comes to other matters, he wipes away this imputation and clears this scandal. You lay my crosses, and sufferings, and disgraces in the world to my shame! It is your weakness. That which you account my shame is a matter of praise. I am so far from being disheartened or discouraged from what I suffer, that,

* That is, 'to take away the stumblingblock.'—G.

VERSE 3.

'*Blessed be God, the Father of Christ, the Father of mercies,*' *&c.* That which to the flesh is matter of scandal and offence, that to the spirit and to a spiritual man is matter of glory, so contrary is the flesh and the spirit, and so opposite is the disposition and the current of the fleshly man to the spiritual man. Job was so far from cursing God for taking away, that he saith, 'Blessed be the name of God,' not only for giving, but for taking away too, Job i. 21.

What ground there is in troubles and persecutions to bless God we shall see in the current and passages of the chapter.

To come, then, to the very verse itself, where there is a blessing and praising of God first; and in this praising consider

The act, object, reasons.

1. *The act*, 'Blessed be God,' which is a praising.

2. *The object* is 'God the Father.

3. *The reasons* are enwrapped in the object, 'Blessed be God the Father of our Lord Jesus Christ.'

(1.) Because he is the God and Father of Jesus Christ, therefore blessed be he. Another reason is,

(2.) Because he is the 'Father of mercies.' Another reason is,

(3.) From the act of this disposition of mercy in God, he is the 'God of all comfort,' and as he is comfortable, so he doth comfort. 'Thou art good and doest good,' saith the psalmist, Ps. cxix. 68. Thou art a God of comfort, and thou dost comfort. For as he is, so he doth. He shews his nature in his working, 'Blessed be God, the Father of our Lord Jesus Christ, the Father of mercies, and God of comfort,' of which I shall speak when I come to them.

'*Blessed be God, the Father,*' *&c.* We see here the heart of the blessed apostle, being warmed with the sense and taste of the sweet mercy of God, stirs up his tongue to bless God; a full heart and a full tongue. We have here the exuberancy, the abundance of his thankfulness breaking forth in his speech. His heart had first tasted of the sweet mercies and comforts of God before he praiseth God. The first thing that we will observe hence is, that

It is the disposition of God's children, after they have tasted the sweet mercy and comfort and love of God, to break forth into the praising of God and to thanksgiving.

It is as natural for the new creature to do so as for the birds to sing in the spring. When the sun hath warmed the poor creature, it shews its thankfulness in singing; and that little blood and spirits that it hath being warmed after winter, it is natural for those creatures so to do, and we delight in them.

It is as natural for the new creature, when it feels the Sun of righteousness warming the soul, when it tastes of the mercy of God in Christ, to shew forth itself in thankfulness and praise; and it can no more be kept from it, than fire can keep from burning, or water from cooling. It is the nature of the new creature so to do.

The reason is, every creature must do the work for which God hath enabled* it, to the which God hath framed it. The happiness of the

* That is, 'qualified.'—G.

creature is in well-doing, in working according to its nature. The heathen could see that. Now all the creatures, the new creature especially, is for the glory of God in Christ Jesus. All the new creature, and what privileges it hath, and what graces it hath, all is, that God may have the glory of grace. Why then, it must needs work answerable to that which God hath created it for. Therefore it must shew forth the praise and glory of God. 'Blessed be God,' saith the apostle, Eph. i. 3; and the blessed apostle Peter begins his epistle, 'Blessed be the Father of our Lord Jesus Christ, who hath begotten us to an inheritance immortal and undefiled, which fadeth not away, reserved for us in heaven,' 1 Pet. i. 3.

I shall not need to set down with the exposition of the word 'blessed:' how God blesseth us, and how we bless God. His blessing is a conferring of blessing; our blessing is a declaring of his goodness. It is a thing well enough known. Our blessing of God is a praising of God, a setting out what is in him.

Only one thing is to be cleared. What good can we do to God in blessing of him? He is blessed, though we bless him not; and he is praised, whether we praise him or no. He had glory enough before he made the world. He contented himself in the Trinity, the blessed Trinity in itself, before there were either angels, or men, or other creatures to bless him; and now he can be blessed enough, though we do not bless him.

It is true he can be so; and he can have heaven, though thou hast it not, but be a damned creature; and he will be blessed, whether thou bless him or no.

1. Our blessing of him *is required as a duty*, to make us more capable of his graces, 'To him that hath shall be given,' Mat. xiii. 12. To him that hath, and useth that he hath to the glory of God, shall be given more. We give nothing.

The stream gives nothing to the fountain. The beam gives nothing to the sun, for it issues from the sun. Our very blessing of God is a blessing of his.

It is from his grace that we can praise his grace; and we run still into a new debt, when we have hearts enlarged to bless him.

We ought to have our hearts more enlarged, that we can be enlarged to praise God.

2. *And to others it is good*, for others are stirred up by it. God's goodness and mercy is enlarged in regard of the manifestation of it to others, by our blessing of God.

3. Yea, this good *comes to our souls*. Besides the increase of grace, we shall find an increase of joy and comfort. That is one end why God requires it of us. Though he himself, in his essence, be alway alike blessed, yet he requires that we should be thankful to him alway; that we should bless and praise him even in misery and affliction. And why, then?

1. *Because, if we can work upon our hearts a disposition to see God's love, and to praise and bless him, we can never be uncomfortable.* We have some comfort against all estates and conditions, by studying to praise God, by working of our hearts to a disposition to praise and bless God; for then crosses are light, crosses are no crosses then. That is the reason that the apostles and holy men so stirred up their hearts to praise and thanksgiving, that they might feel their crosses the less, that they might be less sensible of their discomforts. For undoubtedly, when we search for matter of praising God in any affliction, and when we see there is some mercy yet reserved, that we are not consumed, the consideration that there is alway

some mercy, that we are yet unthankful for, will enlarge our hearts; and God, when he hath thanks and praise from us, he gives us still more matter of thankfulness, and the more we thank him and praise him, the more we have matter of praise.

This being a truth, that God's children, when they have tasted of his mercy, break forth into his praise, it being the end of his favours; and nature being inclined thereto, this should stir us up to this duty. And that we may the better perform this holy duty, let us take notice of all God's favours and blessings. Knowledge stirs up the affections. Blessing of God springs immediately from an enlarged heart, but enlargement of heart is stirred up from apprehension. For as things are reported to the knowledge, so the understanding reports them to the heart and affections. Therefore it is a duty that we ought to take notice of God's favours, and with taking notice of them,

2. *To mind them, to remember them, forget not all his benefits.* 'Praise the Lord, O my soul, and forget not all his benefits,' Ps. ciii. 2, insinuating that the cause why we praise not God is the forgetting of his benefits.

Let us take notice of them, let us register them, let us mind them, let us keep diaries of his mercies and favours every day.* He renews his mercies and favours every day, and we ought to renew our blessing of him every day. We should labour to do here, as we shall do when we are in heaven, where we shall do nothing else but praise and bless him. We ought to be in heaven, while we are on the earth, as much as we may. Let us register his favours and mercies.

Quest. But what favours?

Ans. Especially spiritual, nay, first spiritual favours, without which we cannot heartily give thanks for any outward thing. For the soul will cast with itself, till it feel itself in covenant with God in Christ, that a man is the child of God.

Indeed I have many mercies and favours. God is good to me. But perhaps all these are but favours of the traitor in the prison, that hath the liberty of the tower, and all things that his heart can desire; but then he looks for an execution, he looks for a writ to draw him forth to make him a spectacle to all. And so this trembling for fear of a future ill which the soul looks for, it keeps the soul from thankfulness. It cannot be heartily thankful for any mercy, till it can be thankful for spiritual favours.

Therefore first let us see that our state be good, that we are in Christ, that we are in covenant of grace, that though we are weak Christians, yet we are true, [that] there is truth in grace wrought in us. And then, when we have tasted the best mercies, spiritual mercies; when we see we are taken out of the state of nature (for then all is in love to us), when we have the first mercy, pardoning mercy, that our sins are forgiven in Christ, then the other are mercies indeed to us, not as favours to a condemned man.

And that is the reason that a carnal man, he hath his heart shut, he cannot praise God, he cannot trust in God; because he staggers in his estate, because he is not assured. He thinks, it may be God 'fattens me against the day of slaughter,' Jer. xii. 3. Therefore I know not whether I should praise him for this or no. But he is deceived in that. For if he had his heart enlarged to bless God for that, God would shew further favour still; but the heart will not yield hearty praise to God, till it be persuaded of God's love. For all our love is by reflection. 'We love him, because he

* 'Diaries.' As a fine specimen of, and counsels in regard to, this kind of diary, see Beadle's 'Diary of a Thankful Christian,' 12mo, 1656.

loved us first,' 1 John iv. 19, and we praise and bless him, because he hath blessed us first in heavenly blessings in Christ.

Let us take notice of his favours, let us remind them, let us register them, especially favours and mercies in Christ. Let us after* think how we were pulled out of the cursed estate of nature, by what ministry, by what acquaintance, by what speech, and how God hath followed that mercy with new acquaintance, with new comfort to our souls, with new refreshings; that by his Spirit he hath repressed our corruptions, that he hath sanctified us, made us more humble, more careful, that he hath made us more jealous, more watchful. These mercies and favours will make others sweet unto us.

And then learn to prize and value the mercies of God, which will not be unless we compare them with our own unworthiness. Lay his mercies together with our own unworthiness, and it will make us break forth into blessing of God, when we consider what we are ourselves, as Jacob said, 'less than the least of God's mercies,' Gen. xxxii. 10.

We forget God's mercies every day. He strives with our unthankfulness. The comparing of his mercies with our unworthiness, and our desert on the contrary, will make us to bless God for his goodness and patience, that he will not only be good to us, in not inflicting that which our sins have deserved. 'Blessed be God, the Father of our Lord Jesus Christ.'

And, to name no more but this one, above all, *beg of God his Holy Spirit.* For this blessing of God is nothing else but a vent from the Spirit. For as organs and wind instruments do never sound except they be blown, they are dead and make no music till there be breath put into them; so we are dead and dull instruments. Therefore it is said, we are 'filled with the Holy Ghost,' Acts ix. 17. All God's children, they are filled with the Spirit before they can praise God. The Spirit stirs them up to praise him, and as it gives them matter to praise him; for so it gives the sacrifice of praise itself. God gives to his children both the benefits to bless him for, and he gives the blessing of a heart to bless him. And we must beg both of God; beg a heart able to discern spiritual favours, to taste and relish them, and to see our own unworthiness of them; and beg of God his Holy Spirit to awaken, and quicken, and enlarge our dead and dull hearts to praise his name.

Let us stir up our hearts to it, stir up the Spirit of God in us. Every one that hath the Spirit of God should labour to stir up the Spirit. As St Paul writes to Timothy, 2 Tim. i. 6, and as David stirs up himself, 'Praise the Lord, O my soul: and all that is within me, praise his holy name,' Ps. ciii. 1, *seq.*, so we should raise up ourselves, and stir up ourselves, to this duty.

And *shame ourselves.* What! hath God freed me from so great misery? And hath he advanced me to so happy an estate in this world? Doth he put me in so certain a hope of glory in the world to come? Have I a certain promise to be carried to salvation? that neither 'things present, nor things to come, shall be able to separate me from the love of God in Christ Jesus'? Rom. viii. 38. Doth he renew his mercies every day upon me? And can I be thus dead, can I be thus dull-hearted? Let us shame ourselves. And certainly if a man were to teach a child of God a ground of humiliation, if a child of God that is in the state of grace should ask how he might grow humble and be abased more and more, a man could

* Qu. 'often?'—Ed.

give no one direction better than this, to consider how God hath been good continually; how he hath been patient and good, and upon what ground we hope that he will be so; and to consider the disposition of our own drooping, drowsy souls. If this will not abase a soul that hath tasted the love and mercy of God, nothing in the world will do it. There never was a child of God of a dull temper and disposition, but he was ashamed that, being under such a covenant of favour, that he should yet not have a heart more enlarged to bless God.

To stir us up to this duty, for arguments to persuade us, what need we use many?

1. It should be our duty in this world *to be as much in heaven and heavenly employment.* 'Our conversation is in heaven,' saith the apostle, Phil. iii. 20. How can we be in heaven more than by practising of that which the saints and angels, and the cherubins and seraphins, spend all their strength in there? How do they spend all that blessed strength with cheerfulness and joy, that are in that place of joy? How do they spend it but in setting forth the praise of God, the wonderful goodness of God, that hath brought them to that happiness? Certainly that which we shall do for ever in heaven, we ought to do as much as we may do on earth.

2. And it is, as I said before, in all afflictions and troubles the only special way to mitigate them, *to work our hearts to thankfulness for mercies and favours that we enjoy.* We have cause indeed at the first to be abased and humbled; but we have more cause to rejoice in working our hearts to comfort, in blessing of God. It will ease the cross, any cross whatsoever. I will not dwell further upon the point. I shall have occasion oft to digress upon this duty.

The object of praise here is God, clothed with a comfortable description; not God simply, for, alas! we have no hearts to praise God, take God only armed with justice, clothed with majesty. Consider God thus, indeed he deserves glory and praise, but the guilty soul will not praise him thus considered, and abstracted from mercy, and goodness, and love. Therefore saith he, 'Blessed be God.' God how considered? 'Blessed be God, the Father of our Lord Jesus Christ.'

First, he is Father of Christ, and then Father of mercies, and God of comfort. God, so considered, be blessed!

Obs. God, as he is to be prayed unto, so he is to be praised, and only God.

This sacrifice, this perfume, this incense, it must not be misspent upon any creature. We have all of his grace, and we should return all to his glory. That is a duty. But consider him as he is described here, first, 'the Father of Christ,' and then the 'Father of mercies, and God of all comfort.' And it is not to be omitted, that first begins with this.

1. '*Blessed be God, the Father of our Lord Jesus Christ.*' Not the Father of our Lord Jesus Christ only as he is God, but the Father of our Lord Jesus Christ as he is man. For God being the Father of whole Christ, being Father of the person, he is Father of the manhood, taken into unity with that person. So he is Father both of God and man. They cannot be divided in Christ. He being the Father of whole Christ, he is the Father of God and man. And he is first the Father of Christ, and then the Father of us, and the Father of mercies. For, alas! unless he had been the Father of Christ, God and man, mediator, he could never have been the Father of such cursed creatures as we are. But because he is the Father of Christ, of that blessed manhood, which Christ hath taken into

unity of person with the Godhead, therefore he is the Father of us, who by union are one with Christ.

The point then is, that,

Doct. God, thus considered, as the Father of Jesus Christ, is to be praised.

Here is the reason of blessing and praising him, in this, that he is the Father of Jesus Christ, for thence he comes to be our Father. It is a point that we think not oft enough on, but it is the ground of all comfort; for we have all at the second hand. Christ hath all first, and we have all from him. He is the first Son, and we are sons. He is the first beloved of God, and we are beloved in him. He is filled first with all grace, and we are filled from him: 'of his fulness we receive grace for grace,' John i. 16. He was first acquitted of our sins, as our surety, and then we are justified, because he was justified from our sins, being our surety. He is ascended into heaven, we shall ascend. He sits at the right hand of God, and we sit with him in heavenly places. He judgeth, we shall judge.* Whatsoever we do, Christ doth it first. We have it in Christ, and through Christ, and from Christ. He is the Father of Christ, and our Father.

Use 1. *Therefore we ought to bless God for Christ*, that he would predestinate Christ to be our Head, to be our Saviour; that he would take the human nature of Christ and make it one person with his divine nature, and so predestinate us, and elect, and choose us to salvation in him. Blessed be God, that he would be the Father of Jesus Christ!

Use 2. And as this should stir us up to bless God for Jesus Christ, so likewise *it should direct us to comfortable meditations, to see our nature in Christ first, and then in ourselves.* See thy nature abased in Christ, see thy nature glorified in Christ, see thy nature filled with all grace in Christ, and see this, that thou art knit to that nature, thou art flesh of Christ's flesh, and bone of his bone, and thou shalt be so as he is. In that Christ's nature was first abased, and then glorified, this nature shall first be abased to death and dust, and then be glorified. Christ died, 'and rose again,' Rom. xiv. 9. Thou art predestinated to be conformable to Christ. For as his flesh was first humbled and then glorious, so thine must be first humble, and then glorious. His flesh was holy, humble, and glorious, and so must ours be. Whatsoever we look for in ourselves, that is good, we must see it in Christ first.

And when we hear in the gospel, in the articles of the creed, of Christ crucified, of Christ dying, of Christ rising, ascending, and sitting at the right hand of God; let us see ourselves in him, see ourselves dying in him, and rising in him, and sitting at the right hand of God. For the same God that raised Christ natural, will raise Christ mystical. He will raise whole Christ; for he is not glorified by pieces. As whole Christ natural, in his body and members, was raised, so shall whole Christ mystical be. Therefore in every article of the creed bless God, bless God for abasing of Christ, bless God for raising him up, bless God for raising us up. 'Blessed be God, who hath raised us up to an immortal hope, by the resurrection of Christ,' saith St Peter, 1 Peter i. 3. Bless God for the ascension of Christ, that our head is in heaven. Let us bless God, not for personal favours only, but go to the spring. Bless God for shewing it to Christ, and to us in him.

This point the apostle had learned well. Therefore he begins with praise, 'Blessed be God, the Father of our Lord Jesus Christ.' If the Virgin Mary thought herself blessed, 'and all generations should call her blessed,' Luke i. 48, for bearing our Saviour in her womb, and so being his mother, then

* 'Him' is added here, an evident misprint.—G.

all generations must needs do this duty to call God blessed, because he is the Father of Christ. So God the Father is to be blessed as the spring of favours; for he gave Christ. All generations call the Virgin Mary blessed, because she was the mother of Christ: but that was in a lower degree than God was his Father. This point ought to take up our meditations, to think we have all in Christ first. To think of ourselves in Christ, it is comfortable; and Christ shall have more glory by it. God the Father and the Son shall have glory by it, and we shall have comfort.

The second consideration of God is, not only as he is the Father of Christ, but as he is

2. '*The Father of mercies.*' God is the Father of Christ, and our Father, 'and the Father of mercies.' But as I said before in this method, he is first the Father of Christ, and then our Father, and then 'the Father of mercies.' For he could never be the Father of mercies to us, except he were the Father of Christ. For mercy must see justice contented.* One attribute in God must not devour another. All must have satisfaction. His justice must have no wrong. Nor it hath not now. It is fully satisfied by Christ.

Therefore God is the Father of Christ, that Christ in our nature might die for us, and so he might be our Father notwithstanding our sins, having punished our sins in our surety, Christ. So being the Father of Christ, and our Father, he is the Father of mercies; his justice hath no loss by it.

If God had not found out a way, out of the bowels of his mercy, how he might shew good to us, by reconciling mercy and justice in the mediator Christ, in punishing him for our sins, to set us free, he had never been a Father of mercy; if he had not been the Father of Christ first. For we being in such contrary terms as God and we were, he being holiness, and we nothing but a mass of sin and corruption; without sufficient satisfaction of an infinite person there could be no reconciliation. Therefore he is the Father of Christ, who died for us. He took our nature upon him to satisfy God's justice, and then Father of us, and so Father of mercy to us.

He may well be the Father of mercies now, being the Father of Christ, of our nature in Christ: for, as I said, he is the Father of Christ as man, as well as he is God. Being the Father of our nature, being taken into the unity with his own Son's nature; for both make one Christ, he becomes 'the Father of mercies.' He is a Father to him by nature, to us by grace and adoption. 'The Father of Christ, and Father of mercies.' It is a necessary method, for God out of Christ is a fountain indeed, but he is a 'fountain sealed up.' He is a God merciful and gracious in his own nature, but there is sin that stops the fountain, that stops the current of the mercy. There must be therefore satisfaction to his justice and wrath, before there can be reconciliation, before there can any mercy flow from him. He is first the Father of Christ, and then the 'Father of mercies.' We have all from Christ. If he were not the Father of Christ, he should be the Father of nobody; for immediately† no man is able to appear before God without a mediator.

'Father of mercies.' By Father, which is a kind of hebraism (*f*), is meant he is the original, the spring of mercies, he is the 'Father of mercies.' He doth not say the Father of one mercy, but the 'Father of mercies.' His mercy is one; it is his nature, it is himself. As he is one, so mercy in him is one. It is one in the fountain, but many in the streams. It is one

* That is, 'satisfied.'—G. † That is, = 'in himself.'—G.

in him, one nature, and one mercy. But because we have not one sin, but many sins, we have not one misery, but many, that lies upon this frail nature of ours. Therefore according to the exigencies of us wretched creatures, according to our sins and miseries, his mercies stream out. They are derived* and run out to all kind of sin and misery whatsoever.

'The Father of mercies.' If all mercies were lost, they must be found in him. He is 'the Father of mercies.' They are his bowels, as it were, and mercy pleaseth him as a man is pleased with his own natural child.† 'The Father of mercies.' He doth not say the Author of mercies, but the Father of them. He gives them the sweetest name that can be. He doth not say the Father of revenge, or of judgment, though he be the Father of them too; but to his children the Father of mercies. A sweet name under which none should despair!

But to shew some reasons why he is so styled.

1. There is good reason. Being the Father of Christ, *his justice being fully contented*, sin being taken away that stopped the current of his mercies, he being naturally merciful, his mercies run freely. 'Father of Christ, and Father of mercies.' It follows well. He is the Father of mercies, because he is the Father of Christ; and because his justice is satisfied in him, and he being naturally merciful, what hinders but that mercy may run amain, freely, and abundantly upon those that are in covenant with him in Chrst, that are members of Christ. That is one reason, because his justice is satisfied.

2. And because he is *naturally merciful*, therefore he is the 'Father ot mercies.' The sea doth not more naturally flow, and is moist, and the sun doth not more naturally shine, the fire doth not more naturally burn, heavy bodies do not more naturally sink to the centre, than God doth naturally shew pity and mercy where his justice is satisfied; for it is his nature, it is himself.

The apostle doth not name other attributes, for, alas! other attributes would scare us. As, for example, if the guilty conscience consider him as a God of justice, it will reason thus: What is this to me? I am a sinner, and he will be just in punishing. If he consider he is a God of wisdom, the conscience considers he is the more wise to find out my windings and turnings from him, and my covering of my sins; he is the more wise to find me out in my courses, and to shame me. He doth not say, he is a God of power, the father of power. The guilty conscience then would reason, he is the more able to crush me and to send me to hell.

Indeed, there is no attribute of God, but it is matter of terror, being secluded from mercy; but considering God the Father of mercies, then we may consider sweetly and comfortably of all other attributes. He is merciful and good to me; therefore his wisdom, that shall serve to do me good, to devise good things for me; his power shall serve to free me from mine enemies; his justice to revenge my quarrel; and so all other attributes shall be serviceable to my comfort. They may be thought upon sweetly, where mercy is laid claim unto before. Therefore, here he is called 'the Father of mercies,' and not the Father of other attributes.

'*Of mercies.*' To unfold the word a little, 'mercy' is here the same with grace to a person in misery. Mercy is but free favour shewed to a miserable person. Grace shews the freeness of it, and mercy shews the state of

* That is, 'transmitted.'—G.

† That is, = 'marriage-born, not in the modern sense, in Scotland, of illegitimate.'—G.

the person to whom it is shewn. Alway where mercy is, either there is present or else possible misery.

There was mercy shewed to angels that stood, to free them, to give them grace to stand. They might have fallen as the devils did when they were angels. None are the subjects of mercy, but such as either are in misery, or are possible to fall into misery. Now, when God keeps and upholds the creature from falling into that which he is subject to fall into (he being a creature taken out of nothing, and therefore subject to fall to nothing without assistance), to hold him from that whereto he would fall without being upheld, this makes him the object of mercy, whatsoever the misery be, spiritual or outward.

Thus God is the Father of mercy; he upholds his children from that which else they would fall into continually. He is 'the Father of mercy,' before conversion, offering and enjoining mercy to them, that as they will be good to their souls, they would receive mercy. He joins his glory and his mercy together, that he will be glorified in shewing mercy; and he presseth it upon us. What a mercy is this, that he should press mercy upon us for our own good? 'Why will ye die, O house of Israel,' Jer. xxvii. 13. And, 'Come unto me, all ye that are weary and heavy laden,' Mat. xi. 28. There is mercy before conversion. And there is mercy in prolonging his wrath, in not punishing; and there is mercy in pardoning sin freely, in pardoning all sin, the punishment and the guilt, and all. And when we are in the state of grace, and have our sins pardoned, still it is his mercy to forbear the punishments due to us, in mitigating his corrections, and in seasonable corrections. For it is a mercy for God to correct his children seasonably. 'Therefore we are corrected of God, that we should not be damned with the world,' 1 Cor. xi. 32.

It is a mercy to have seasonable correction. It is a mercy to have correction mitigated and sweetened with some comforts. It is a mercy after we are in the state of grace, besides this, to have the continuance of outward blessings.

God renews his mercies every day. His mercies fail not,' Lament. iii. 22. His mercies are renewed continually upon us.

So he is Father of all kind of mercies; privative* mercies, in freeing us from ill; and positive mercies, in bestowing good. Pardoning mercies, healing mercies, preserving mercies, all mercies come from this Father of

I will not stand to unfold them in particular; for indeed every thing that comes from God to his children, it is a mercy. It is as it were dipt in mercy before it comes to us. It is a mercy, that is, there is a freedom in it, and a pity to his creature. For the creature is alway in some necessity and in some dependence. We are in a state of necessities in this life, in some misery or other, and that, as I said, is the object of mercy.

Besides, we are dependent for the good we have. It is at God's mercy to continue or to take away any comfort that he gives us. Every thing is a mercy. And in every thing we take from God we ought to conceive a mercy in it, and to think this is a mercy from God. If we have health, it is a mercy; if we have strength, it is a mercy; if we have deliverance, it is a mercy. It comes in the respect and relation of a mercy, all that comes from God. He is not said to be the father of the thing; but the 'Father of mercies.' There is a mercy contained in the thing. They come from the pity and love of God, and that is the sweetest. Therefore, he is said to be the 'Father of mercies.'

* That is, = 'negative.'—G.

Quest. What use may we make of this, that God is the 'Father of mercies'?

Ans. It is a point full of sweet and comfortable uses, to those that are not in the state of grace, and to those that are in the state of grace.

Use 1. *To those that are not in the state of grace, they should see here a haven to flee to; a city of refuge to flee unto.* Do but consider, thou wretched soul, how God is styled a 'Father of mercies' to thee, a God of bounty. All is to allure thee to repentance, to allure thee to come in. He is not merciful by accident, but he is naturally merciful in himself. He hath bowels of mercy in himself. 'Mercy pleaseth him,' Micah vii. 18.

Therefore, despair not, thou drooping soul, whosoever thou art that are under the guilt of sin! come to the Father of mercies! cast thyself into this sea of his mercy! hide thyself in these bowels! be not an enemy to thine own mercy! As Jonah saith, 'Refuse not thy own mercy,' Jonah ii. 8, that is offered. There is mercy pressed upon thee, mercy with threatening if thou believe not mercy, now thou art called to receive it. The wrath of God hangs over thee as a weight, or as a sword ready to fall upon thee. As Christ saith, 'The wrath of God hangs over us,' John iii. 36, if we do not receive mercy offered us.

Allege not thy sins against mercy. Thy sins are the sins of a creature; God is the 'Father of mercies.' He is infinite. Christ thy Saviour hath made an infinite satisfaction, and thy sins are finite, and in that respect there is mercy for thee if thou wilt come in, if thou apprehend and receive mercy.

'One deep calls upon another deep,' Ps. xlii. 7. The depth of thy sins and misery draws unto it, and calls upon the depth of mercy. 'The mercy of God is above all his works,' Ps. cxlv. 9. It is not only above all his works to cover them all, and under them to uphold them, but it is beyond them all. His mercy exceeds all other attributes to the creature. It is above his works, and upon his works, and under his works, and it is above thy works too. He is more glorious in his mercy than in any other attribute. He doth all for the glory of his mercy, both in the creation and in the gospel. His mercy, therefore, is above his own works, and above thy works if thou come in.

Oil is of a kingly nature. It swims above all other liquids. So the mercy of God, like oil, it swims above all other attributes in him, and above all sin in thee, if thou wilt receive it.

'Father of mercies.' In a corrupt estate the special mercy is forgiving mercy. If it were not for forgiving mercies, all other gifts and mercies were to little purpose. For it were but a reserving of us to eternal judgment, but a feeding the traitor to the day of execution, a giving him the liberty of the prison, which is nothing unless his treason be pardoned. So the forgiving mercy leads to all the rest. Now these forgiving mercies, they are unlimited mercies, there is no bounds of them. For he being the Father of Christ, who is an infinite person, and having received an infinite satisfaction from an infinite Person, he may well be infinitely merciful; and himself is an infinite God. His mercies are like himself. The satisfaction whereby he may be merciful is infinite. Hereupon it is that he may pardon, and will pardon all sin without limitation, if they be never so great, never so many.

This I observe, the rather to appease the conscience of a sinner when it is suppressed* with terror and fear of the greatness of his sins. Consider

* Qu. 'oppressed?—G.

how God hath set down himself, and will be known and apprehended of us, not only as merciful, but a 'Father of mercies,' and not of one mercy, but of all mercies, not only giving, but, forgiving especially, 'Which forgiveth all thy sins, and healeth all thy infirmities,' Ps. ciii. 3. This I observe against a proneness in us to despair. We are not now proner in the time of peace to presume, than when conscience is awakened, to despair; we are prone to both alike. For here is the poison of man's corruption. Is God so merciful? Surely, I may go on in sin, and cry God mercy, and there is an end. God is merciful, nay, the Father of mercies.

Now, in the time of peace, sin is nothing with us. Swearing is nothing, rotten discourse is nothing, going beyond others in our dealing and commerce is nothing, getting an estate by fraud and deceit is nothing. 'The bread of deceit is sweet,' Prov. xx. 17. Loose, licentious, libertine life, is nothing. And those that do not follow the same excess, and are [not] dissolute, it is a strange matter with us, they are strange people. We think it strange that others do not so, and if they be better than we, it is but hypocrisy. Men measure all by themselves. So all is nothing. Great, gross swearing is nothing. Men glory in it, and to make scruple of it, it is thus and thus. They have terms for it. And what is the bawd* for all this? Oh! God is merciful, and Christ he is wondrous merciful; he took our nature that he might die for us, &c.

It is true indeed. But when the conscience is awakened, then the conscience will tell thee another lesson. The conscience will set God as just, and Satan will help conscience with accusations and aggravations. It is true, it is too true. The conscience will take part with God and with his word. It is true thou hast done thus and thus. These are thy sins, and God is just.

And especially at the hour of death, when earthly comforts fail, and there is nothing but sin set before a man's eyes, the comforts that are set before him can do him no good. Then the conscience will hardly† receive any comfort: especially the consciences of such as have gone on in a course of sin, in spite of good means. A conscience of such a man as either refuseth or rejects the means, because it would favour itself in sin; or a conscience that being under means, having had its sins discovered to it, that conscience will hardly admit of any comfort. And there is none, but they find it another manner of matter than they think it. Sin is a blacker thing than they imagine. Their oaths that they trifle with, and their dissolute and their rotten discourse, when they should be better affected‡, upon the Sabbath, and such like. Therefore we ought to look to it.

Well! to press this point of presumption a little further, now I am in it, we are wondrous prone to abuse this mercy to presumption, and after to despair.

I consider this beforehand, that however God's mercy be unlimited, as iudeed it is in itself, it is so unlimited to those that repent, and to those that receive and embrace mercy, and mercy in one kind as well as another. It is so to those that repent of their sins. For God is so the 'Father of mercy,' as that he is the 'God of vengeance' too, Deut. xxxii. 5. He is a just God too.

The conscience will tell you this well enough, when the outward comforts, that now you dally with and set as gods in the room of God, and drown yourselves in sensuality and idolatry with the creature, and put them

* *Sic* Qu. 'bode?' = bid, meaning bait.—G.

† That is, 'affectioned' = disposed.—G.

‡ That is, 'with difficulty.'—G.

in the place of God,—when they are taken away, conscience will tell you that God is merciful indeed; but he is just to such that refuse mercies.

Therefore, though his mercy be unlimited to such as are broken-hearted to such as repent of their sins (for he will glorify his mercy as he may glorify his other attributes), he is wisely merciful. If he should be merciful to such as go on in sin, he should not be wisely merciful.

Who among men, if he be wise, would be merciful to a child or servant without acknowledgment of the fault?

Was not David over-merciful to Absalom? Yes; it was his fault. Yet, out of wisdom, he would not admit him into his presence till he was humbled for his fault and made intercession, though he doated upon him, 2 Sam. xiv. 28. God is infinitely wise, as he is merciful. Therefore, he will not be merciful to him that goes on in wickedness and sin. This cannot be too often pressed, for the most of the auditors, wheresoever we speak, the devil hath them in this snare, that God is merciful, &c. And doth he not know how to use it? He is so indeed, but it is to repentant souls that mean to break off their course of sin.

Otherwise, if the mercy of God work the other way, hearken to thy doom, 'He that blesseth himself,' saith God by Moses, and saith, 'These curses shall not come to me,' he that blesseth himself and saith, Oh, all shall be well, God is merciful, &c., 'my wrath shall smoke against him,' Deut. xxix. 16, 20, and I will not be merciful to him that goes on in his sins. God will 'wound the hairy scalp of him that goes on in sin,' Ps. lxviii. 21. As the apostle saith, he that abuseth the bounty and patience of God, that should lead him to repentance, 'he treasureth up wrath against the day of wrath,' Rom. ii. 5. The Scripture is never in any case more terrible than this way. In Isa. xxviii. 15, 'You have made a covenant with hell and death,' with God's judgments; but hell and death hath not made a covenant with you. You make a covenant, and think you shall do well; but God is terrible to such. His wrath shall smoke against such as make a covenant with his judgments, and treasure up wrath against the day of wrath.

Take heed. If the proclamation of mercy call thee not in, if thou stand out as a rebel and come not in, but go on still, then justice lays hold on thee, God's wrath shall smoke against thee, as we see in Prov. i. 26, 'I will laugh at your destruction,' speaking of those that would not come in and as* it is in Isa. xxvii. 11, 'He that formed them and made them will have no mercy on them, nor shew them favour.' He will have no delight in them. They are ignorant sots, and will not labour to know God and his will, to do and obey it. 'He that made them will have no delight in them, and he that formed them will reject them.' It is a pitiful thing when God, that made them and formed them in their mother's womb, whose creatures they are, shall have no delight in them; when he that made them, his heart shall not pity them, Ezek. xviii. 18. He that goes on in a course of sin presumptuously and doth not repent, God's eye shall not pity him. 'He that made him will have no delight in him.'

Therefore the apostle, because we are disposed and prone to abuse the goodness and longsuffering of God and the mercies of Christ, he saith, 'Be not deceived, be not deceived' (he oft presseth this), 'for neither the covetous nor licentious persons shall enter into heaven,' 1 Cor. vi. 10.

Though God be merciful, if thou live in these sins, be not deceived,

* By a strange misprint, the words 'and as,' appear in the unmeaning form of '*Chidas*,' in the folio. It is plain that 'and as' was intended by Sibbes.—G.

thou shalt never enter into heaven. God will not be merciful to the most of those that even now live in the bosom of the church, because they make mercy a band to their sinful courses. God will harden himself. He will not bless such. He hath no mercy for such. To such he is a God of vengeance.

His mercy is to such as are weary of their sinful courses. As I said, he is merciful, but so as he is wise.

What prince will prostitute a pardon to one that is a rebel, and yet thinks himself a good subject all the while? He is no rebel; cares he for a pardon? and shall he have a pardon when he cares not for it? Those that are not humbled in the sight and sense of their sins, that think themselves in a good estate, they are rebels, that have not sued out their pardon. There is no mercy to them yet. 'He that made them will not pity them,' because they are ignorant, hardened wretches, that live in blasphemy, in swearing, in corrupt courses, in hardness of heart, that live in sins, that their own conscience and the conscience of others about them know that they are sins, devouring sins, that devour all their comfort; and yet, notwithstanding, they dream of mercy. Mercy! Hell is their portion, and not mercy, that make an idol of God.

Thus it is with us; we are prone to presume upon God's mercy. I speak this that we should not surfeit of this sweet doctrine, that God is the 'Father of mercies.' He is so to repentant sinners, to those that believe. To those mercy is sweet. We know oil is above all liquors. God's mercy is above all his own works and above our sins. But what is the vessel for this oil? This oil of mercy, it is put in broken vessels; it is kept best there. A broken heart, a humble heart, receives and keeps mercy.

As for proud dispositions, as all sinners that go on in a course of sin, the psalmist terms them proud men; he is a proud man that sets his own will against God's command. 'God resists the proud,' James iv. 6. It is the humble, yielding heart, that will be led and lured by God, that is a vessel to receive mercy. It must be a deep vessel, it must be a broken vessel, deep with humiliation, broken by contrition, that must receive mercy. And it must be a large vessel laid open, capable to receive mercy, and all mercy, not only pardoning mercy, but healing mercy, as I said out of that psalm, 'That forgiveth all thy sins, and healeth all thy transgressions,' Ps. ciii. 3.

Therefore those that have not grace and mercy, to heal their corruptions, to dry up that issue in some comfortable measure, they have no pardoning mercy; and those that desire not their corruptions to be healed, they never desire heartily their corruptions to be pardoned. Those mercies go together.

He is not the 'Father of mercy,' but of all mercies that belong to salvation, and he gives them every one, and he that desires the one, desires the other.

Let us consider how the sweet descriptions of God, and how his promises work upon us. If they work on us to make us presume, it is a fearful case. It is as bad a sign as may be, to be ill, because God is good, 'to turn the grace of God into wantonness,' Jude ver. 4.

But as we are thus prone to presume; so when conscience is awaked we are as prone to despair. Therefore if they work with us this way, 'there is mercy with God, therefore I will come in;' 'therefore I will cast down my weapons at his feet,' 'I will cease to resist him,' 'I will come in, and take terms of peace with him,' 'I will yield him obedience for the time to come;' 'therefore I will fear and love so good a God.' If it work thus, it is a sign of an elect soul, of a gracious disposition. And then if thou come in, never consider what thy sins have been; if thou come in, God will embrace thee in his mercy. Thy sins are all as a spark of fire that falls into the ocean, that is drowned presently. So are thy sins in the ocean of God's mercy.

There is not more light in the sun, there is not more water in the sea, than there is mercy in the 'Father of mercy,' whose bowels are opened to thee if thou be weary of thy sinful courses, and come in, and embrace mercy.

In the tabernacle, we know, there was a mercy-seat. We call it a propitiatory. In the ark, which this mercy-seat covered, was the law. Now in the law there were curses against all sinners.

The mercy-seat was a type of Christ, covering the law, covering the curse. Though thou be guilty of the curse a thousand times, God in Christ is merciful. Christ is the mercy-seat. Come to God in Christ. There is mercy in Israel notwithstanding thy great sins. If we cast away a purpose of living in sin, and cast away our weapons, and submit ourselves to him, he is the Father of mercies. That is, he is merciful from himself, he is the spring of them, and hath them from his own bowels. They are free mercies, because he is the Father of them.

For he is just by our fault, he is severe from us, he takes occasion from our sins; but he is merciful from his own bowels. He is good from himself. We provoke him to be severe and just. Therefore be we never so miserable in regard of sin, and the fruits of sin, yet he is the Father of mercy, of free mercy; mercy from himself. 'Mercy pleaseth him,' Micah vii. 18. He is delighted in it.

Now that which is natural comes easily, as water from the fountain comes without violence, and heat from the fire comes without any violence, because it is natural. A mother pities her child, because it is natural. There is a sweet instinct of nature that moves and pricks forward nature to that affection of love that she bears to her child. So it is with God. It is nature in him to be merciful to his, because they are his. Mercy is his nature. We are his. We being his, his nature being merciful, he will be merciful to all that are his, to such as repent of their sins, and lay hold of his mercy by a true faith.

His word shews likewise his mercy. There is not one attribute set down more in Scripture than mercy. It is the name whereby he will be known, Exod. xxxiv. 6, where he describes it, and tells us his name. What is the name of God? His longsuffering, and mercy, &c. There is a long description of God in that place. David, in Ps. iii., besides that which is in every prophet almost, hath the same description of God, to comfort God's people in his time. In Ps. lxxxvi., ciii., cxlv., there is the same description of God as there is in Moses. He is merciful and longsuffering, &c. He describes himself to be so, and his promises are promises of mercy. At what time soever a sinner repents, and without limitation of sins, all sins shall be forgiven. 'The blood of Christ purgeth us from all sin,' 1 John i. 7.

If there be no limitation of persons whomsoever, of sins whatsoever, or of time whensoever, here is a ground that we should never despair. 'God is the Father of mercies.'

It is excellent that the prophet hath, to prevent the thoughts of a dejected soul, 'Let the wicked forsake his way, and the unrighteous man his thoughts, and return to the Lord, and he will have mercy upon him, and to our God, for he will abundantly pardon,' Isa. lv. 7.

Obj. Aye, but I have abused mercy a long time; I have lived in sin, and committed great sins. Well, notwithstanding that, see how he answers it: 'My thoughts are not your thoughts.' You are vindictive. If a man offend you, you are ready to aggravate the fault, and to take revenge, &c. 'But my thoughts are not as your thoughts, nor my ways as your ways,' saith the Lord; 'for as far as the heaven is above the earth, so are my thoughts above your thoughts, and my ways above your ways,' Ps. ciii. 11. We have narrow, poor thoughts of mercy, because we ourselves are given to revenge, and we are ready, when we think of our sins, to say, Can God forgive them? can God be merciful to such? &c. 'My thoughts are not as your thoughts, nor my ways as your ways.'

It is good to consider this, and it is a sweet meditation; for the time undoubtedly will come, that unless God's mercy and God's thoughts should be, as himself is, infinite, unless his ways should be infinitely above our ways, and his thoughts infinitely above ours in mercy, certainly the soul would receive no comfort.

The soul of a Christian acquainted with the word of God knows that God's mercy is, as himself is, infinite, and his thoughts this way are, as himself is, infinite. Therefore the Scripture sets down the mercies of God by all dimensions. There is the depth of wisdom, but when he comes to speak of love and mercy, as it is in Eph. iii. 18, 'Oh, the depth, and breadth, and height of this!'

Indeed, for height, it is higher than the heavens; for depth, it fetcheth the soul from the nethermost deep. We have deep misery, 'Out of the deep I cried to thee,' Ps. cxxx. 1; yet notwithstanding, his mercy is deeper than our misery. O the depth of his mercy! There is a depth of mercy deeper than any misery or rebellion of ours, though we have sunk deep in rebellion. And for the extent of them, as I said before, 'his mercy is over all his works,' Ps. cxlv. 9. It extends to the utmost parts of the earth. The Scripture doth wonderfully enlarge his mercy beyond all dimensions whatsoever. These things are to good purpose; and it is a mercy to us that he sets forth himself in mercy in his word, because the soul, sometime or other when it is awakened, as every one that God delights in is awakened, first or last, it needs all that is, it is all little enough.

God is merciful to those that are heavy laden, that feel the burden of their sins upon their souls. Such as are touched with the sense of their sins, God still meets them half-way. He is more ready to pardon than they are to ask mercy. As we see in the prodigal, when he had wasted all, when he was as low as a man could be, when he was come to husks, and when he had despised his father's admonition, yet upon resolution to return, when he was stung with the sense of his sins, his father meets him and entertains him; he upbraids him not with his sin, Luke xv. 20, *seq*.

Take sin, with all the aggravations we can, yet if we repent and resolve upon new courses, there is comfort, though we relapse into sin again and again. If we must pardon ten times seven-times, as Christ saith, Luke xvii. 4,* certainly there cannot be more mercy in the cistern than there is

* With reference to a former note (vol. I. page 231), Sibbes's phrase should have been printed 'seventy seven-times.' The question to our Lord was, 'till seven-times?' 'Yes,' he replied, 'till seventy seven-times,' which is = seventy times seven. Sibbes's quotation above is a slip.—G.

in the fountain; there cannot be more mercy in us than there is in the 'Father of mercies,' as God is.

Take sin in the aggravations, in the greatness of it, Manasseh's sin, Peter's denying of his Master, the thief on the cross, and Paul's persecution! Take sin as great as you will, he is the 'Father of mercies.' If we consider that God is infinite in mercy, and that the Scripture reveals him as the 'Father of mercies,' there is no question but there is abundance, a world of comfort to any distressed soul that is ready to cast itself on God's mercy.

Use 2. *For those that are converted, that are in the state of grace*—Is God 'the Father of mercies?' *let this stir us up to embrace mercy, every day to live by mercy, to plead mercy with God in our daily breaches;* to love and fear God, because there is mercy with him that 'he might be feared,' Ps. cxxx. 4. It is a harder matter to make a daily sweet use of this than it is taken for. Those that are the fittest subjects for mercy, they think themselves furthest off from mercy. Come to a broken soul, who is catched in the snare; whose conscience is on the rack, he thinks, alas! there is no mercy for me! I have been such a sinner, God hath shewed me mercy before, and now I have offended him again and again. Those that are the subjects of mercy, that are the nearest to mercy, when their conscience is awakened, they think themselves furthest off, and we have need to press abundance of mercy, and all little enough to set the soul in frame. There is none of us all, but we shall see a necessity of pressing this one time or other, before we die. David when he had sinned, he knew well enough that God was merciful. Oh, but it was not a slight mercy that would satisfy him, as we see, Ps. li., how he presseth upon God for mercy, and will a little serve him? No! 'according to thy abundant mercy,' ver. 1. He presseth mercy, and abundance of mercy, a multitude of mercies; and unless he had seen infinite mercy, abundant mercy in God, when his conscience was awaked with the foulness of his sin (there being such a cry for vengeance, his sin called and cried); if the blood of Christ had not cried above it, 'Mercy, mercy,' and abundance of mercy, multitudes of compassion, the soul of David would not have been stilled.

So other saints of God, when they have considered the foulness of sin, how odious it is to God, they could not be quieted and comforted, but that they saw mercy, and abundance of mercy. As the apostle St Peter saith, 'Blessed be God, the Father of our Lord Jesus Christ, who, of his abundant mercy, hath begotten us again to a lively hope, by the resurrection of Jesus Christ, to an inheritance, immortal,' &c., 1 Pet. i. 3.

'God is the Father of mercies.' For faith will not have sufficient footing, but in infinite mercy. In the time of despair, in the time of torment of conscience, in the time of desertion, it must be mercy, and 'the Father of mercies,' and multitudes of compassions, and bowels of love; and all little enough for faith to fix on, the faith of a conscience on the rack. But when faith considers of God set out—not as Satan sets him forth, a God of vengeance, a 'consuming fire,' Heb. xii. 29,—when faith considers God pictured out in the gospel, it sees him the Father of Christ and our Father, and the Father of mercies and God of comfort, faith seeing infinite mercy in an infinite God; and seeing mercy triumph against justice, and all other attributes, here faith hath some footing, and stays itself, or else the converted, sanctified soul, seeing the odiousness of sin, and the clamorousness of sin, such that it will not be satisfied, but with abundant mercy; and God must be presented to it as a 'Father of mercy' and compassion, before it can have peace.

Therefore, if so be at any time our conscience be awakened, and the devil lays hard to us, let us think of God as he hath made himself known in his word, as a 'Father of mercies and God of comfort,' represent him to our souls, as he represents himself in his word. Times of desertion, when we seem to be forsaken of God, will enforce this. Times of desertion will come, when the soul will think God hath forgotten to be merciful, and hath shut up his love in displeasure. Oh, no! he is the Father of mercy, he never shuts up his bowels altogether, he never stops the spring of his mercy. He doth to our feeling, but it is his mercy that he doth that; it is his mercy that he hinders the sense of mercy. He doth that in mercy. It is to make us more capable of mercy afterward.

Therefore, saith the Father, when he comes to us in his love, and the sense of it, it is for our good; and when he takes the sense of his love from us, it is for our good. For when he takes away the sense of his love from us, it is to enlarge our souls to be more capable of mercy after, to prize it more, to walk warily, and jealously, to look to our corruptions better. Therefore in the time of desertion think of this, when God seems to forget us. 'Can a mother forget her child?' Isa. xlix. 15. Suppose she should be so unnatural as to do it, which can hardly be believed, that a mother should forget her child, 'Yet notwithstanding I will not forget you;' you are 'written upon the palms of my hands,' ver. 16, that is, I have you alway in my eye. So that if there were no mercies to be found in nature, no bowels to be found in a mother (where usually they are most abundant), yet notwithstanding there is mercy to be found in 'the Father of mercies' still. Therefore in such times let us make use of this.

And another thing that we ought to learn hence is this, if God be so in Christ Jesus, for we must alway put that in, for he is merciful with satisfaction. And yet it is his mercy that he would admit of satisfaction. His mercy devised a way to content justice. His mercy set all on work. Mercy is above justice in the work of salvation. Justice hath received contentment from mercy. But that by the way, to make us have higher thoughts of mercy, than any other attribute of God in the doctrine of the gospel, in that kingdom of Christ. It is a kingdom of grace *and mercy*, if we have hearts to embrace it.

Let this encourage us to come to God, and to cast ourselves into the arms of this merciful Father. If we have lived in other courses before, let the mercy of God work upon our souls. In Rom. ii. 4, it is pressed there excellently. 'This mercy of God should lead us to repentance,' it should encourage us. What makes a thief or a traitor come in, when there is proclamation out against him? If there be a pardon sent after him, it makes him come in, or else he runs out still further and further, while the hue and cry pursues him. But hope of mercy and pardon will bring him in again. So it is that that brings us in again to God, the very hope of mercy and pardon. If we be never so ill, or have been never so ill, do not put off, but take this day now; 'Now is the time,' now, 'while it is called to-day,' Ps. xcv. 7, 8, take the present time. Here is our error, if God be 'the Father of mercy,' I will cry him mercy at the hour of death. Aye, thou mayest go to hell with mercy in thy mouth. He is merciful to those that truly repent. But how dost thou know that thy repentance on thy deathbed will be true? It is not sorrow for sickness, and grief for death, and fear of that. But there must be a hatred of sin. And how shall conscience tell thee now thou hast repented, that it is a hating of thy sinful courses, rather than the fear of damnation? that is rather from the sense of grief. Conscience will hardly be comforted in this, for it will upbraid. Aye, now, now you would have mercy.

We see by many that have recovered again, that have promised great matters in their sickness, that it is hypocritical repentance, for they have been worse after than they were before *(f*)*. It is not a sufficient matter to yield thee comfort, that thou art much humbled in thy sickness, and at the hour of death; for it is hard for thee to determine whether it be true repentance, or mere sorrow for sin as it brings judgment. Fear of damnation is not sufficient to bring a man to heaven. Thy nature must be changed before thou come to heaven. Thou must love righteousness because it is righteousness. Thou must love God because he is good. Thou must hate sin because it is sin.

How canst thou tell, when thou hast been naught before affliction, whether affliction have wrought this, that thou repentest only out of hatred of judgment, to shun that, or out of hatred of sin, because it is sin? Therefore now a little repentance in thy health, and in the enjoying of thy prosperity, a little hatred of ill ways now, will more comfort thee than a thousand times more prayer and striving will then. Although, if thou canst do it truly then, yet the gate of mercy is open, but thy heart will scarce say it is truly done, because it is forced.

Then, again, perhaps thou shalt not have the honour of it, thou shalt not have the mercy. Thou that hast refused mercy, and lived in a loose, profane course, thou that hast despised mercy all the while, God will not honour thee so much as to have a good word, or a sorrowful word, that even very grief shall not extort it from thee. But as thou hast forgotten God in thy life, and wouldst not own his admonitions, thou shalt forget thyself in death, and be taken away suddenly, or else with some violent disease that shall take away the use of the parts that God hath given thee, as inflammation of the spirits, or the like, that shall take away the use of sound reason. It is madness, and no better, to live as the most live, to cry God is merciful, &c. Thou mayest go to hell for all that. Repentance must be from a true hatred of sin; and that that must comfort thee, must be a disposition for the present, for then it is unforced.

Therefore all these sweet comforts are to you that come in and leave your wicked courses. If you have been swearers, to swear no more; if you have been deceivers, to deceive no more; if you have been licentious, to be so no more, but to break off the course of your sins as God shall enable you. Or else this one thing, think of it, that you now daub your conscience withal, and go on in sin with that, will be most terror to you, even mercy. Nothing will vex you so much as mercy afterward. Then thou shalt think with thyself, I have heard comfortable [tidings] of the promises, and of the nature of God, but I put off and despised all, I regarded my sinful courses more than the mercy of God in Christ, they were sweeter to me than mercy. I lived in sins, out of the abundance of profaneness that did me no good; I lived in sins, out of the superfluity of profaneness that I had neither profit nor pleasure by, and neglected mercy. The consideration of mercy neglected, with the continuing in a wretched course, it will more aggravate the soul's torment.

Let us be encouraged to come in. Such as intend to leave their sinful courses, let them remember that then they come to a Father of mercy that is more ready to pardon than you are to ask it, as you see in the prodigal son, which I instanced in before; it is a notable, sweet story. I have a Father, saith he, when he had spent all, and was come to husks, Luke

xv. 16. Affliction is a notable means to make us to taste and relish mercy. I have a Father, and there is plenty in his house; and he comes and confesseth his sin. He had no sooner resolved, but his Father, he doth not stay for him, but he meets him, and kisseth him, Luke xv. 20, *seq*.

Let us consider of this description of God, the Father of mercy. It should move any that are in ill and lewd courses before, 'In my Father's house there are good things,' and in his heart there are bowels of mercy. I have a Father, and a Father of mercy. I will go home, and submit myself to him, and say to him, I have been thus and thus, but I will be so no more. You shall find that God, by his Spirit, will be readier to meet you than you are to cast yourselves at the feet of his mercy, and into the arms of his mercy. He will come and meet you, and kiss you. You shall find much comfort upon your resolution to come in, if it be a sound resolution.

The son fears his father's displeasure; but saith the father, 'My thoughts are not as your thoughts.' Oh! I fear he will not receive me! Yes, yes, he is willing to embrace you. Mercy pleaseth him; 'and why will you perish, O house of Israel?' Jer. xxvii. 13.

Again, 'God is the Father of mercies' This should stir us up to an imitation of this our gracious Father; for every father begets to his own likeness, and all the sons of this Father are like the Father. They are merciful. 'The kings of Israel are merciful kings,' 1 Kings xx. 31, saith the heathen king Benhadad; and the God of Israel is a merciful God, and all that are under God are merciful. His sons are 'merciful as their heavenly Father is merciful, Luke vi. 36. Therefore, if we would make it good to our own hearts, and the opinion and judgment of others of us, that we are children of this merciful Father, we must put on bowels of mercy ourselves as in Col. iii. 12, 'Now, therefore, as the elect of God,' as you will make it good that God hath elected you, 'put on the bowels of mercy.' Whatsoever we have from God, it comes in the respect of a mercy, and so it should do from God's children. Everything that comes from them to them that are in misery, it should be a mercy. They should not only bestow the thing, but a sweet mercy with the thing. A child of God he pours out his bowels to his brother, as Isaiah saith, 'Pour out thy bowels,' &c., Isa. lxiii. 15. There is some bowels, that is, there is an affection in God's children. They give not only the thing, the relief, but mercy with it, that hath a sweet report to the soul. There is pity, that more comforts a sanctified soul than the thing itself. We must not do works of mercy proudly (*g*). It is not the thing that God stands on, but the affection in the thing. His benefits are with a fatherly pity. So should ours be with a pitiful respect, with a tender heart. 'The very mercies of the wicked are cruel,' Prov. xii. 10. If they be merciful, there is some pride of spirit, there is some taste of a hard heart, of an hypocritical spirit. Somewhat is not as it should be. Their mercies are not mercies. We must in our mercy imitate the Father of mercies.

Alas! it is the fault of our time. There is little mercy to those that are in misery. What a cruel thing is it that so many, I would I could say Christian souls, I cannot say so, but they are a company of men that have the image of God upon them, men that live miserable poor, such as, for aught I know, God's mercy hath purchased with the blood of his Son, and may belong to God's kingdom. They have the image of God upon them, yet they live without laws, without church, without commonwealth, irregular persons, that have no order taken for them, or not executed at the least, to repress the sturdy of them, and to relieve those that are to be relieved for age or impotency (*g**).

It is a pitiful thing and a foul blemish to this commonwealth, and will bring some ill upon wealth, and plague it from such irregular persons. He will plague the commonwealth for such enormities. How do they live? As beasts, and worse. They submit themselves to no orders of the church. They have none, and submit to none. Here is an object of mercy to those that it concerns.

And likewise, mercy ought to be shewed to the souls of men, as well as to their miserable and wretched estates. Is popery antichristian? What mercy is it to suffer poisoners? What a mercy were it in a commonwealth to suffer men that are incendiaries to have liberty to do what mischief they would? or men that should poison fountains, and all that should refresh and nourish men? Were this any policy for the body? And is it any policy to suffer those to poison the judgments of people with heresies to God, and treason to their prince? to draw the affections of men from religion and the state, where is mercy all the while?

Oh! is it a mercy to them not to restrain them? Mercy! Is it mercy to the sheep to let the wolves at liberty? No. If you will be merciful, to shew mercy to the souls of these men is to use them hardly, that they may know their error. They may now impute the liberty they have to the approbation of their cause; and so they are cruel, not only to others, but to their own souls.

I speak this the rather, [that] it may be a seasonable speech at this time, to enforce good laws this way. It is a great mercy. Mercy to the soul, it is the greatest mercy; and so cruelty to the soul is the greatest cruelty that can be.

What should I speak of mercy to others? Oh, that we would be merciful to our own souls! God is merciful to our souls. He sent his Son to 'visit us from on high,' in bowels of compassion. He sent Christ, as Zacharias saith, Luke i. 68, and yet we are not merciful to ourselves. How many sinful, wretched persons pierce their hearts through with covetousness, and other wicked courses, that are more dangerous to the soul than poison is to the body! They stab their souls with cares, and lusts, and other such kind of courses. What a mockery is this of God, to ask him mercy, when we will not be merciful to our own souls! and to entreat others to pray for us, when we will not be merciful to ourselves! Shall we go to God for mercy, when we will not shew mercy to ourselves? Shall we desire him to spare us, when we will not spare ourselves? It is a mocking of God to come and offer our devotions here, and come with an intent yet to live in any sin. God will not hear us, if we purpose to live in sin. 'If I regard iniquity in my heart, God will not hear my prayer,' Ps. lxvi. 18. As we ought to be merciful to the souls of others, and to the estates of others, so we should to our own souls.

How can they reform evils abroad, those that are governors, when they do not care to reform themselves? Can they be merciful to the souls of others, that are cruel to their own? They cannot. Let mercy begin at home.

This is that that the Scripture aims at. Mercy and the right use of it, is the way to come to salvation; and the abuse of it is that that damns; and they are damned most that abuse mercy. Oh, the sins against the gospel will lie upon the conscience another day. The sins against the law, they help, with the gospel, to see mercy; but sins against mercy prefer our sins above mercy; and in temptations to despair, to extenuate mercy, hereafter it will be the very hell of hell, that we have sinned against mercy, that we have not embraced it with faith, that we have not repented to be capable of it.

Use 3. But to end the point with that which is the most proper use of all, which is *an use of comfort in all estates, to go to God in all*. 'He is the Father of mercy.' And when all is taken from us in losses and crosses, to think, well, our fathers may die, and our mothers may die, and our nearest and dearest friends that have most bowels of pity, may die; but we have a Father of mercy, that hath eternal mercy in him. His mercies are tender mercies, and everlasting mercies, as himself is. We are everlasting. Our souls are immortal. We have an everlasting Father, that is the 'Father of mercies.' When all are taken away, God takes not himself away. He is the Father of mercy still.

Now that we may make ourselves still capable of mercy, still fit for mercy, let us take this daily course.

1. Let us labour every day, *to have broken and deep souls*. As I said before, it is the broken heart that is the vessel that contains mercy, a deeper heart that holds all the mercy. We need, therefore, to empty ourselves by confession of our sins, and search our own thoughts and ways, and afflict our souls by repentance; and when* we shall be fit objects for God the Father of mercy to shed mercy into misery. It is the loadstone of mercy, misery left discerned and complained of. Let us search and see our misery, our spiritual misery especially; for God begins mercy to the soul in his children, he begins mercy there especially. General mercy he shews to beasts, to all creatures; but special mercy begins at the soul. Now, I say, misery being the loadstone of mercy, let us lay before God by confession and humiliation, the sores and sins of our souls. And then make use of this mercy every day; for God is not only merciful in pardoning mercy at the first, in forgiving our sins at the first, but every day he is ready to pardon new sins, as it is Lam. iii. 23, 'He renews his mercies every day, every morning.' God renews his mercies not only for body, but for soul. There is a throne of grace and mercy every day open to go to, and a sceptre of mercy held out every day to lay hold on, and a 'fountain for Judah and Jerusalem to wash in every day,' Zech. xiii. 1. It is never stopped up, or drawn dry. The fountain is ever open, the sceptre is ever held forth, and the throne is ever kept.

God keeps not terms. Now the Court of Chancery is open, and now it is shut. But he keeps court every day. Therefore Christ in the gospel enjoins us to go to God every day. Every day we say the Lord's prayer, 'forgive us our trespasses,' Luke xi. 4, insinuating that the court of mercy is kept every day to take out our pardon. Every day there is a pardon of course taken out, 'at what time soever a sinner repents,' &c., 1 Kings viii. 38, *seq*.

Quest. How shall we improve this mercy every day?

Ans. 1. Do this; when thou hast made a breach in thy conscience, every day believe this, that God is 'the Father of mercies,' and he may well be merciful now, because he hath been sufficiently satisfied by the death of Christ. 'He is the Father of Christ, and the Father of mercies.' This do every day.

2. And withal consider our condition and estate is a state of dependence. 'In him we live and move and have our being,' Acts xvii. 28. This will

* Qu. 'then?'—Ed.

force us to mercy, that he would hold us in the same estate we are in, and go on with the work of grace, that he would uphold us in health, for that depends upon him; that he would uphold us in peace, for that depends upon him: he is 'the God of peace,' 1 Cor. xiv. 33, that he would uphold us in comfort and strength, to do good and resist evil. We are in a dependent state and condition in all good of body and soul. He upholds the whole world, and every particular. Let him take away his hand of merciful protection and sustaining from us, and we sink presently.

3. And every day consider how we are environed with any danger. Remember, we have compassing mercies, as we have compassing dangers, as it is, 'Mercy compasseth us round about,' Ps. xxxii. 10. Every day, indeed, we have need of mercy. That is the way to have mercy. Here is a fountain of mercy, 'the Father of mercy,' bowels opened. The only way to use it is to see what need we have of mercy, and to fly to God; to see what need we have in our souls, and in regard of outward estate, and to see that our condition is a dependent condition.

Use 4. And lastly, *to make a use of thankfulness*, 'Blessed be God, the Father of mercy,' *we have the mercy of public continued peace, when others have war*, and their estates are consumed. 'Blessed be God, the Father of mercy, we sit under our own vines, and under our own fig-trees,' Micah iv. 4. If we have any personal mercies, 'Blessed be God, the Father of mercies,' this way. If he shew mercy to our souls, and pardon our sins, 'Blessed be God, the Father of mercies,' in this kind; that he hath taken us and redeemed us out of that cursed estate, that others walk in that are yet in their sins. Oh! it is a mercy, and for this we should have enlarged hearts.

And withal consider the fearful estate of others, that God doth not shew mercy to, and this will make us thankful. As for instance, if a man would be thankful, that hath a pardon, let him see another executed, that is, broken upon the wheel or the rack, or cut in pieces and tortured, and then he will think, I was in the same estate as this man is, and I am pardoned. Oh! what a gracious Sovereign have I! The consideration of the fearful estate out of mercy, what a fearful estate those are in that live in sins against conscience, that they are ready to drop into hell when God strikes them with death; if they die so, what a fearful estate they are in! and that God should give me pardon and grace to enter into another course of life; that though I have not much grace, yet I know it is true I am the child of God; the consideration of the misery of others, in part in this world without repentance, and especially what they shall suffer in hell; to consider the torment of the souls that are not in the state of grace, this will make us thankful for mercies, for pardoning and forgiving mercies, for protecting mercies, that God hath left thousands in the course of nature, going on in a wilful course of sin. This is that that the apostle here practiseth. 'Blessed be God, the Father of mercies.' The other style here is,

'*The God of all comfort.*' The life of a Christian is a mystery; as in many respects, so in this, that whereas the flesh in him, though he be not altogether flesh, thinks him to be a man disconsolate, the spirit finds matter of comfort and glory. From whence the world begins discouragement and the flesh upbraiding, from thence the Spirit of God in holy St Paul begins matter of glory. They thought him a man neglected of God, because he was afflicted. No! saith he, 'blessed be the God of all comfort.' Our comforts are above our discomforts. As the wisdom of the flesh is enmity to God and his Spirit in all things, so in this, in the judgment of the cross; for that which is bitterest to the flesh is sweetest to the spirit. St Paul therefore opposeth his comforts spiritual to his disgraces outward; and because it is unfit to mention any comfort, any good from God without blessing of him, that is the spring and fountain from whence we have all, he takes occasion, together with the mention of comfort, to bless God, 'the God of all comfort.'

The verse contains a wise prevention of scandal at the cross. St Paul was a man of sorrows if ever any was, next to Christ himself, and that [he] might prevent all scandal at his crosses, and disgraceful afflicted usage, he doth shew his comforts under the cross, which he would not have wanted to have been without his cross. Therefore he begins here with praising of God.

We praise God for favours, and indeed the comforts he had in his crosses were more than the grievance he had by them; therefore had cause to bless God; 'Blessed be God,' &c.

'The God of all comfort.' 'The God of comfort, and the God of all comfort.' We must give St Paul leave to be thus large, for his heart was full; and a full heart, a full expression. And he speaks not out of books, but from sense and feeling. Though he knew well enough that 'God was the Father of mercy and God of all comfort,' that way; yet these be words that come from the heart, come from feeling rather than from the tongue. They came not from St Paul's pen only. His pen was first dipped in his heart and soul when he wrote this. 'God is the Father of mercy, and God of all comfort.' I feel him so; he comforts me in all tribulations.

'The God of all comfort.' To explain the word a little. Comfort is either the thing itself, a comfortable outward thing, a blessing of God wherein comfort is hid, or else it is reasons; because a man is an understanding creature, reasons from which comfort is grounded; or it is a real comfort, inward and spiritual, by the assistance and strength of the Spirit of God, when perhaps there is no outward thing to comfort. And perhaps reasons and discourse are not present at that time, yet there is a presence of the Spirit that comforts, as we see ofttimes a man is comforted with the very sight of his friend, without discourse. To a man endued with reason, whose discomforts are spiritual, for the most part, in the soul, the very presence of a man that he loves puts much delight into him. What is God then? 'The God of comfort.' His very presence must needs comfort. Comfort is taken many other ways, but these are the principal, to this purpose.

1. First, *comfort is the thing itself.* There is comfort in every creature of God, and God is the God of that comfort. In hunger, meat comforts; in thirst, drink comforts; in cold, garments comfort; in want of advice, friends comfort, and it is a sweet comfort. 'God is the God of *all* comfort;' of the comfortable things. But besides the necessary things, every sense hath somewhat to comfort it. The eye, besides ordinary colours, hath delightful colours to behold; and so the ear, besides ordinary noise and sounds, it hath music to delight it; the smell, besides ordinary savours, it hath sweet flowers to refresh it; and so every part of the body, besides that which is ordinary, it hath somewhat to comfort it. Because God is nothing but comfort to his creature, if it be as it should be, he is God of these comforts, 'the God of all comfort,' of the comfort of outward things, of friends, &c.

2. So he is the God of the second comfort, *of comfortable reasons and arguments*. For a man, especially in inward troubles, must have grounds of comfort from strong reasons. God ministereth these. He is the God of these. For he hath given us his Scriptures, his word; and the comforts that are fetched from thence are strong ones, because they are his comforts. It is his word. The word of a prince comforts, though he be not there to speak it. Though it be a letter, or by a messenger, yet he whose word it is, is one that is able to make his word good. He is Lord and Master of his word. The word of God is comfortable, and all the reasons that are in it, and that are deduced from it, upon good ground and consequence, they are comfortable, because it is God's word. He is the God of all. And those comforts in God's word, and reasons from thence, they are wonderful in the variety of them. There is comfort from the liberty of a Christian laid out there, that he hath free access to the throne of grace; comfort from the prerogatives of a Christian, that he is the child of God, that he is justified, that he is the heir of heaven, and such like; comforts from the promises of grace, of the presence of God, of assistance by his presence. These things out of the word of God are wondrous plentiful. Indeed, the word of God is a breast of comfort, as the prophet calls it: 'Suck comfort out of the breasts of comfort,' Isa. lxvi. 11.

The books of God are breasts of comfort, wells of comfort. There are springs of comfort.

God's word is a paradise, as it were. In paradise, there were sweet streams that ran through; and in paradise stirred the voice of God, not only calling, 'Adam, where art thou?' terrifying of him, but the voice of God promising Adam the blessed seed, Gen. iii. 9.

So in the word of God, there is God rousing out of sin, and there is God speaking peace to the soul. There is a sweet current of mercy runs from the paradise of God; and there is the 'tree of life,' Rev. ii. 7, Christ himself, and trees of all manner of fruit, comforts of all sorts whatsoever. And there is no angel there, to keep the door and gate of paradise with a fiery, flaming sword. No! this paradise is open for all. And they are cruel tyrants that stop this paradise, that stop this fountain, as the papists do. As God is the God of comfort, so he is the God of comfort in that respect.

But this is not enough, to make him the God of comfort. We may have the word of God, and all the reasons from thence, from privileges and prerogatives, and examples, and yet not be comfortable, if

3. We have not the God of comfort, with the word of comfort, *the Spirit of God*, that must apply the comfort to the soul, and be the God of comfort there.

For there must be application, and working of comfort out of God's word upon the soul, by the Spirit. The Spirit must set it on strongly and sweetly, that the soul may be affected.

You may have a carnal man—he for fashion or custom reads the Scriptures, and he is as dead-hearted when he hath done as when he began. He never looks to the Spirit of comfort. There must be the Spirit of God, to work, and to apply comfort to the heart, and to teach us to discourse and to reason from the word; not only to shew the reasons of the word, but to teach us to draw reasons from the word, and to apply them to our particular state and condition. The Spirit teacheth this wisdom. And therefore it is well called the Comforter. 'I will send you the Comforter,' John xiv. 26. The poor disciples had many comforts from Christ, but because the Comforter was not come, they were not comfortable, but heavy. What was the reason? Because 'the Comforter was not come.' When the Holy Ghost was come, after the resurrection and ascension of Christ, when he had sent the Comforter, then they were so full of comfort, that they rejoiced that they 'were thought worthy to suffer anything for Christ,' Acts v. 41; and the more they suffered, the more joyful, and comfortable, and glorious they are.

You see what a comfort is. It is the things themselves, and the word, and reasons from it, and likewise the Spirit of God with the reasons, and with presence. Sometimes without any reasons, with present strength, God doth establish the soul. Together with reasons, there is a strengthening power of the Spirit, a vigour that goes with the Spirit of God, that joins with the spirit of the afflicted person. So whether it be the outward thing, as reasons and discourse, or the presence of the Spirit, God joining with our spirit, God is the God of that comfort, the 'God of all comfort.'

A comfort is anything that allays a malady, that either takes it away, or allays and mitigates it. A comfort is anything that raiseth up the soul. The comforts that we have in this life, they are not such as do altogether take away sorrow and grief, but they mitigate them. Comfort is that which is above a malady. It is such a remedy as is stronger to support the soul from being cast down over much with the grievance, whether it be grievance felt, that we are in the sense of such a grievance as is feared. When the soul apprehends anything, to set against the ill we fear that is stronger than it; when the soul hath somewhat that it can set against the present sense of the grievance that is stronger than it, though it do not wholly expel it, but the discomfort remains still in some degree, it may be said well to be a comfort.

The reason why I speak of this mitigation is, because in this life God never so wholly comforts his children, but there will be flesh left in them; and that will murmur, and there will be some resistance against comfort. While there are remainders of sin, there will be ground of discomfort, by reason of the conflict between the flesh and spirit.

For instance, a man hath some cross on him: what saith the flesh? God is mine enemy, and I will take such and such courses. I will not endure this. This is the voice of the flesh, of the 'old man.' What saith the spirit? Surely God is not mine enemy. He intends my good by these things. So while these fight, here is the 'flesh against the spirit,' Gal. v. 17. Yet here is comfort, because the spirit is predominant. But it is not fully comfort, because there is the 'old man' in him, that withstands comfort in the whole measure of comfort.

Therefore we must take this degree. We cannot have the full comfort till we come to heaven. There all tears shall be wiped from our eyes. In this world we must be content to have comfort with some grief. The malady is not wholly purged.

Sometimes God removes the outward grievance more fully. God helps many times altogether, as in sickness to health perfectly. But I speak not of that. Comfort is that which is opposite to misery, and it must be stronger, for there is no prevailing but by a stronger. When the agent is not above the patient, there is no prevailing. There is a conflict till one have got the mastery.

'The God of *all* comfort.' 'All,' that is, of all comfortable things, and of all divine reasons. It must be most substantial comfort. The soul in some maladies will not be comforted by philosophical reasons. Saith the heathen, 'The disease is stronger than the physic,' when he considers Plato's comforts and the like. So we may say of the reasons of philosophical men, Romanists, and moralists. When they come to terror of conscience, when they come to inward grievances, inward stings that are in a man, from a man's conscience (as all discomforts usually when they press hard, it is with a guilty conscience), what can all such reasons do? To say it is the state of other men, and it is in vain to murmur, and I know not what, such reasons as Seneca and Plato and others have, it will scarce still the conscience for a fit. They are ignorant of the root. Alas! how can they tell the remedy, when they know not the ground of the malady?

It must be God, it must be his word, his truth. The conscience must know it to be God's truth, and then it will comfort. God is the God of comfort, of the things, and of the reasons. They must be his reasons.

And he also is the author of that spiritual presence; he is with his children. When 'they are in the fire, he goes with them into the water,' as it is in Isa. xliii. 2. He is with them 'in the valley of death,' Ps. xxiii. 4. They shall find God with them to comfort them. So there is a kind of presence with God's comforts, and a banishing of all discomfort.

And this comfort is as large as the maladies, as large as the ills are. He is a God of comfort against every particular ill. If there be diverse ills, he hath diverse comforts; if they be long ills, he hath long comforts; if there be strong ills, he hath strong comforts; if there be new ills, he hath new comforts. Take the ills in what extent and degree you will, God hath somewhat to set against them that is stronger than they, and that is the blessed estate of God's children. He is the 'God of all comfort.'

St Chrysostom, an excellent preacher, yields me one observation upon this very place (*h*). It is the wisdom of a Christian to see how God describes himself, there being something in God answerable to whatsoever is ill in the world. The Spirit of God in the Scripture sets forth God fitting to the particular occasions. Speaking here of the misery and the disgraceful usage of St Paul, being taught by the Spirit of God, he considereth God as a 'Father of mercies' and a 'God of comfort.' Speaking of the vengeance on his enemies, the psalmist saith, 'Thou God of vengeance, shew thyself,' Ps. xciv. 1. In God there is help for every malady.

Therefore the wisdom of a Christian is to single out of God what is fitting his present occasion. In crosses and miseries, think of him as a 'Father of mercies;' in discomforts, think of him as a 'God of comfort;' in perplexities and distress, think of him as a God of wisdom; and oppression of others, and difficulties which we cannot wade out of, think of him as a God and Father Almighty, as a God of vengeance; and so every way to think of God appliable to the present occasion. And though many of us have no great affliction upon us for the present, yet we should lay up store against the evil day; and therefore it is good to treasure up these descriptions of God, 'the Father of mercies, and God of all comfort.'

To explain the word a little. What doth he mean by 'God' in this place?

That he is the God of comfort, that hath a further comfort in it, in the very title that is called the God of comfort. In that he is called the *God* of comfort, it implies two things.

1. First, it shews that *he is a Creator of it;* that he can work it out of what he will, out of nothing.

2. And then, that he can *raise it out of the contrary*, as he raised light out of darkness in the creation, and in the government of this world he raiseth his children out of misery. As he raised all out of nothing, order out of

confusion, so in his church he is the God of comfort. He can raise comfort out of nothing; out of nothing that is likely to yield comfort. Put the case that there be neither medicine, nor meat, nor drink, nor nothing to comfort us in this world, as we shall have none of these things in heaven, he is the God of comfort that shall supply all our wants. As he shall then be all in all, so in this world, when it is by the manifestation of his glory. When Moses was forty days in the mountain, he wanted outward comforts; but he had the God of comfort with him, and he supplied the want of meat and drink and all other comforts, because he is the God of all comfort. In him are all comforts originally and fundamentally; and if there be none, he can create and make them of nothing.

God, as a God properly, makes something of nothing. That is to be a God; for nothing but God can make something of nothing. Gods upon earth call men their creatures, in a kind of imitation of God; but that is but a phrase that puffs them up. They are but gods in a kind of sense, and the other are but creatures in a kind of sense; because, perhaps they have nothing in them, and in that sense, deservedly creatures. But it is proper to God, to make somewhat of nothing; and so he is the '*God* of comfort.' Where there is no comfort at all, he can raise comfort, as he made the world of nothing by his very word.

And which is more, it is the property of God as God, it is peculiar to God to make comfort out of that which is contrary. Therein he shews himself most to be a God of all. He can raise comfort out of discomfort, life out of death. When Christ had been three days in the grave, he raised him. As it is with the head of comfort, with the head of believers, so it is with every particular Christian. He raiseth them out of death. Those that sow in sorrow, they reap in joy. What cannot he do that can raise comfort out of discomfort? and discomforts oftentimes are the occasions of the greatest comforts. Let a Christian go back to the former course of his life, and he shall find that the greatest crosses that ever he suffered will yield him most comfort, and who did this? Certainly it must be God, that can raise all out of nothing, and that can make comfort not only out of comfortable creatures that are ordained for comfort; but he can draw honey out of the lion's belly. 'Out of the eater came meat, and out of the strong came sweetness,' saith Samson in his riddle, Judges xiv. 14. When a honeycomb shall come out of the lion's belly, certainly this is a miracle, this may well be a riddle. This is the riddle of Christianity, that God who is the God of comfort, he raiseth comforts out of our chiefest discomforts. He can create it out of that which is contrary.

Therefore Luther's speech is very good, 'All things come from God to his church, especially in contraries;' as he is righteousness, but it is in sin felt. He is comfort, but it is in misery. He is life, but it is in death. We must die before we live. Indeed, he is all, but it is in nothing, in the soul that feels itself to be nothing. There is the foundation for God to work on. Therefore the God of comfort can create comfort. If none be, he can make comfort. If the contrary be, he can raise contraries out of contraries. He is the 'God of all comfort.' Every word hath emphasis and strength in it.

'The God of all comfort.' Amongst divers other things that flow from hence, mark the order. He is the 'God and Father of Christ' first, and then the 'Father of mercy,' and 'the God of comfort.'

Take him out of this order, and think not of him as a God of comfort, but as a 'consuming fire,' Heb. xii. 29. But take the method of the text, now he is the 'God of comfort after he is the Father of Christ.' This being laid as a ground, the text itself as a doctrine, what subordinate truths arise hence?

First of all, if God be 'God of all comfort,' there is this conclusion hence; that, *whatsoever the means of comfort be, God is the spring of it.*

Christ is the conduit next to God; for he is close to God. God is the God of Christ, and the Holy Ghost is usually the stream. The streams of comfort come through Christ the conduit; from God the Father, the fountain, by the graces of the Spirit. But I speak of outward comforts. 'Blessed be God the Father, Son, and Holy Ghost.' All are comforters! God the Father is the father of comfort; the Holy Ghost is the comforter; Christ Jesus likewise is the God of comfort. Whatsoever the outward means be, yet God the Father, Son, and Holy Ghost are the comforters. Take them together. That is the conclusion hence.

I observe it the rather, to cure a disposition to atheism in men that look brutishly to the thing. They look to the comfort, and never look to the comforter, even for outward comforts. Wicked men, their bellies are filled with the comforts of God, but it is with things that are comfortable, that are abstracted from the comforter. They care not for the root, the favour and mercy of God. So they have the thing, they care not.

Therefore they are not thankful to God, nor in their wants, they go not to the God of comfort. Why? They think they have supply enough, they have friends, they have riches, that 'are their stronghold,' Ps. lxxxix. 40, and if they have outward necessaries to supply and comfort them, that is all they care for. As for the '*God* of comfort,' they trouble not their hands* with him.

A Christian, whatsoever the comfort be, if it be outward, he knows that the God of comfort sends it, and that is the reason he is so thankful for all outward comforts. If they be the necessaries for this life, in meat he tastes the comfort of God, in drink he tastes the comfort of God, in the ornaments of this life he tastes the comfort of God. It is God that heats him with fire, it is God that clothes him with garments, it is God that feeds him with meat, it is God that refresheth his senses in these comforts.

Therefore the heathen, out of their ignorance, they made every thing a god that was comfortable, out of which they received comfort. They made a god of the fire, and of the water. These are but instruments of the God of comfort, but the heathen made gods of them. A Christian doth not so, but he sees God in them, and drives† these streams from the fountain. God is seen to be the God of comfort in them all.

Again, considering that God is 'the God of all comfort,' this should teach us as thankfulness to God, so prayer in the want of any comfort, that he would both give the thing, and the comfort of the thing. We may have the thing and the wrath of God with it. But thou that art the God of comfort, vouchsafe the outward comforts to us, and vouchsafe comfort with them. Thou that art the God of every thing, and of the comfort of the thing, vouchsafe both.

Again, if God be the God of all comfort whatsoever, then here is a ground of divers other truths; as, for instance, that if we look for any comfort from the things, or from reasons and discourse, or from God, we should go to God in the use of the thing, before the use, after the use, at all times. Before the use, that God would suggest, either by reading, or hearing, &c.,

* Qu. 'heads.'—G.

† Qu. 'derives?' = traces.—G.

reasons of comfort. In the use, that he would settle and seal comfort to our souls. Lord, I hear many sweet things. I read many comfortable things. These would affect a stone almost; yet unless thou set them on my soul, they will never comfort me. Thou art the God of comfort. The materials are from thee. But except with revelation and discovery thou join application, all will not comfort, unless with revelation and application thou open my soul to join with these comforts.

3. In the third place, *There must be a discovery and application, and an opening of the soul to them.* As there be divers flowers that open and shut with the sun, so the soul, by the Spirit of God, it opens to comforts. Though comforts be put close to the soul, if that do not open to them, there is no comfort given; for all is in the application. There is a double application, of the thing to the soul, and of the soul to the thing. God must do all.

Quest. What is the reason that many hear sermons, and read sweet discourses, and yet when they come to suffer crosses and afflictions they are to see?*

Ans. They go to the stream, they cut the conduits from the spring, they go not to the well head, they see not the derivation of comfort. It is necessary for the deriving of comfort to the soul, to take the scales from the eye of the soul. They see not the necessity of a divine presence to apply it, and to lay it close to the soul, and to open the soul, to join the soul to those comforts. 'God is the God of all comfort.' If anything will stir up devotion much to pray to God, undoubtedly this will be effectual, that whatsoever the comfort be, whether it be outward things or reasons and discourses whatsoever, we may go to God that he would give it.

Well, this being so, if God be the 'God of all comfort,' the well of comfort, the Father of comfort, and hath remedies for every malady, then you see here whither to go. You see a Christian in all estates hath ground of comfort, for he is in covenant with the God of comfort.

Quest. You will say to me, What is the reason that Christians are no more comfortable, having the 'God of comfort' for their God?

Ans. I answer: 1. It is partly *from ignorance.* We have remainders of ignorance, that we know not our own comfort. Satan doth veil the eye of the soul in the time of trouble, that we cannot see that there is a well of comfort. Poor Hagar, when she was almost undone for thirst, yet she had a fountain of water near hand; but she saw it not, she was so overtaken with grief, Gen. xxi. 15, *seq.* Ignorance and, 2, *passion* hinder the sight of comfort. When we give way so much to the present malady, as if there were no God of comfort in heaven, as if there were no Scripture that hath breasts of comfort, that is as full as a breast that is willing to discharge itself of comfort. As if there were no matter of comfort, they feed upon grief, and delight to flatter theirselves in grief, as Rachel, 'that mourned, and would not be comforted,' Mat. ii. 18. So out of a kind of ignorance, and passion, and wilfulness they will not be comforted.

And again, 3, *aggravating the grievance.* As Bildad saith, 'Are the comforts of God light to thee?' Job xv. 11. These are good words, but my discomforts are greater, my malady is greater. So the comforts of the Holy Ghost, the comforts of God's Spirit, seem light to them. Ignorance, and passion, and dwelling too much, makes us neglect comfort. It makes us to see comfort to be no comfort in a manner. Mary, when Christ was before her eyes, they were so blubbered with tears, with fear that her Lord

* Qu. 'seek.'—G.

was lost, that she could not see him, even when he was before her, John xx. 15. So grief and passion hinder the soul so much from seeing God's comforts, that we see them not when they are before us, when they are present. So men are guilty of their own discomfort. It is their own fault.

4. Again, ofttimes *forgetfulness*. As the apostle saith, 'Have ye forgotten the consolation that speaks?' Heb. xii. 5. Have ye forgotten that every son that God chastiseth not is a bastard? Have ye forgotten? Insinuating that, if they had remembered this, it would have comforted them. 'Have ye forgotten?'

5. And then one especial cause is, that I spake of before, *the looking to things present*, forgetting the spring, the well-head of comfort, God himself; the looking too much to the means. Oh! say some, if they be in distress, if I had such a book, if I had such a man to comfort me, certainly it would be otherwise with me, I should be better than I am. Put case he were with thee, alas! he is not at the spring! It is the God of comfort that must comfort thee, man, in all thy distresses whatsoever. Therefore if thou attribute not more to God than to the creature, nay, than to an angel, if he were to comfort thee, thou shalt find no comfort. 'I, even I, am he that comforts thee,' Isa. li. 12. I am he that pardons thy sins, which is the cause of all discomfort. That is comfort! That is the sting of all. 'I am he that pardons thy sins.'

We, as criers, may speak pardon to the soul; but God must give it. We may speak comfort, but God must give it. He must say to the soul, 'I am thy salvation,' Ps. xxxv. 3. When men idolise any discourse in books, or any particular man over much (though we may value those that are instrumental above others, there may be a difference of gifts, but), the resting too much in the creature, it is an enemy to comfort; and some grow to that wilfulness in that kind, that they will neglect all because they have not that they would have, whereas if they would look to God, meaner means would serve the turn ofttimes, if they would go to the God of comfort.

VERSE 4.

'*Who comforteth us in all tribulation.*' Afflictions and crosses, as they are irksome in suffering, so they are likewise disgraceful; and as it was in the cross of Christ, there were* two things, torment and shame. The one he felt himself, the other he had from others; those two. Disgrace is proper to the cross. So it is in all the crosses that we suffer, there is some disgrace with it. Therefore St Paul, to prevent the scandal and disgrace of the cross, as I said before, he doth here begin with praising God even for crosses in the midst of them. 'Blessed be God, the Father of mercies, the God of all comfort; who comforteth us in all tribulations,' &c.

'Who comforteth us in all tribulation.' These words contain a making good of the former title, 'He is a God of comfort, and doth comfort; he is good, and doth good.' He fills up his name by his works. He shews what he is. The Scripture doth especially describe God, not in all things as he is in himself; but as he is, and works to his poor church. And they are useful terms, all of them. He is 'the Father of mercy,' because he is so to his church. He is the 'God of comfort,' because he

* Misprinted 'was.'—G.

is so to his people. Therefore he saith here, as he is 'the God of comfort;' so he doth comfort us in all tribulation. He doth not say, who keeps us out of misery. Blessed be the God of comfort, that never suffers us to fall into discomfort! No! but 'blessed be the God of comfort, that comforts us *in all tribulation.*' It is more to raise good out of evil, than not to suffer evil to be at all. It shews greater power, it manifests greater goodness, to triumph over ill, when it [is] suffered to be, and so not to keep ill from us, but to comfort us in it.

He doth not say for the time past, which hath comforted us, or which can comfort us if it please him. No! He doth it. It is his use.* He doth it alway. It springs from his love. He never at any instant or moment of time forgets his children. And he saith not, he doth comfort us in one or two, or a few tribulations; but he comforteth us in '*all tribulations,*' of what kind or degree soever.

Obj. It may be objected, to clear the sense a little, he doth not alway comfort: for then there could be no time of discomfort.

Ans. I answer: He doth alway comfort in some degree; for take a Christian at the lowest, yet he hath so much comfort as to keep him from sinking. When he is at the depth of misery, there is a depth of mercy lower than he. 'Out of the deep have I cried unto thee, Lord,' Ps. cxxx. 1; and this is a comfort that he hath in the midst of discomforts, that he hath a spirit of prayer; and if not a spirit of prayer, yet a spirit of sighing and groaning to God, and God hears the sighs and groans of his own Spirit in his children. When they cannot distinctly pray, there is a spirit to look up to God. 'Though thou kill me, yet will I trust in thee,' saith Job, Job xiii. 15, in the midst of his miseries. So though God, more notoriously to the view of the world, sometime doth comfort before we come to trouble, that we may bear it the better, and sometime he doth comfort more apparently after we come out; yet notwithstanding, in the midst of discomforts, he doth alway comfort so far as that we sink not into despair. There is somewhat to uphold the soul. For when Solomon saith, 'A wounded spirit, who can bear?' Prov. xviii. 14; that is, none can bear it; it is the greatest grief. Then I would know, what keeps a wounded spirit from sinking that it doth not despair? Is it not a spirit stronger than the wounded spirit? It is† not God that is greater than the wounded conscience? Yes! Then there is comfort greater than the discomfort of a wounded conscience, that keeps it from despair. Those that finally despair, they are none of God's. So that, take the words in what regard or in what sense you will, yet there is a sweet and comfortable sense of them, and the apostle might well say, he is the 'God of all comfort, that doth comfort us in all tribulation.'

It is here a ground supposed, that *God's children are subject to tribulation.* We are subject here to tribulation of all kinds, for God comforts us in all our tribulations. We are here in a state, therefore, needing comfort, because we are in tribulation.

And the second is that God doth answer our state. *God doth comfort his children in all tribulation.*

And the ground is from himself. 'He is the God of comfort.' He doth but like himself, when he doth it. The God of comfort shews that he is so, by comforting us in all tribulations.

First, It is supposed that *in this world we are in tribulations.*

Indeed, that I need not be long in. We must, at one time or other, be

* That is, his 'wont.'—G.

† Qu. 'is it?'—Ed.

in tribulation, some or other. For though, in regard of outward afflictions, we are free from them sometimes, we have a few holidays, as we say; yet notwithstanding, there is in the greatest enlargements of God's children in this world, somewhat that troubles their minds. For either there is some desertion, God withholds comfort from them in some measure, he shews himself a stranger, which humbles them much; or else they have strong temptations of Satan, to sin by prosperity, &c., which grieves them as much as the outward cross; or else their grievance is, that they cannot serve God with that cheerfulness of spirit. Is there nothing, whoever thou art, that troubles thee as much as the cross in the day of affliction? Certainly there is somewhat or other that troubleth the soul of a Christian. He is never out of one grievance or other.

The life of a Christian is as a web, that is woven of good and ill. He hath good days and ill days; he hath tribulations and comforts. As St Austin saith very well, between these two, tribulation on our part, and comfort on God's part, our life runs between these two. Our crosses and God's comforts, they are both mingled together.

There is no child of God, but knows what these things mean, troubles either from friends or enemies, or both, domestical or personal, in body or mind, one way or other. That is supposed, and it were not an unproper argument to the text; for when he saith 'in all tribulations,' it is laid as a ground that every man suffers tribulation one way or other. But I shall have fitter occasion after to enlarge this.

Again we see here, that *God comforts his children in all tribulation.*

And his comforts are answerable to their discomforts, and beyond them. They are stronger to master all opposites whatsoever, and all grievances. There could be no comfort else. Alas! what are all discomforts, when God sets himself to comfort? When he will be a God of comfort, one look, one glance of his fatherly countenance in Jesus Christ, will banish all terrors whatsoever, and make even a very dungeon to be a paradise. 'He comforteth us in all tribulation.'

And this he doth, as you may perceive by the unfolding of the words, either by some outward thing applied to the outward want or cross, or by some inward reasons, that are opposite to the inward malady, or by an inward presence. His comforts are appliable to the tribulation, and to the strength, and length, and variety of it. We may know it by his course in this life. What misery are we subject to in this life! but we have comfort fit for it? So good is God.

We may reason thus very well. If so be that in our pilgrimage here, in this life of ours, which is but the gallery, as it were, to heaven; if in this short life, which is but a way or passage, we have, both day and night, so many comforts: in the very night, if we look up to heaven, we see what glorious things there are towards the earth here, on this side the heaven, the stars of the light,* &c. And if so be upon the earth there be such comforts, especially in the spring and summer time, if the very earth, the basest dregs of the world, yield such comfort and delights to all the senses, then a man may reason very strongly, what comforts shall we have at home? If God by the creatures thus comforts us in our outward wants, what are the inward comforts of his Spirit here to his children? and what are the last comforts of all, the comforts reserved at home, when God 'shall be all in all?' 1 Cor. xv. 28.

Now there are some drops of comfort conveyed in smells, some in gar-

* Qu. 'the light of the stars?'—Ed.

ments, some in friends, some in diet; here a drop, and there a drop. But when we shall have immediate communion there with the God of comfort himself, what comforts shall we have there? God comforts us here, by providing for us, and giving us things that are comfortable.

Or by giving reasons and grounds of comfort, which are stronger than the reasons and grounds of discomfort, reasons from the privileges and prerogative of Christians, &c. The Scripture is full of them.

But likewise, which is the best of all, and most intended, the inward inspring of comfort, with the reasons and grounds, he inwardly conveys comforts to the soul, and strengtheneth and supports the soul. And he doth this not only by the application of the reasons, and the things that we understand, to the soul, but by opening the soul to embrace them. For sometime the soul may be in such a case as it may reject comfort, that 'the consolation of the Almighty,' Job xv. 11, may seem light to it. Sometime there may be such a disposition of soul, that the chiefest comforts in Scripture yield it no comfort. They are not embraced. The soul is shut to them. God provides reasons and grounds of comfort, and likewise he applies these comforts by his Spirit to the soul, and he inwardly warms and opens the soul to embrace comfort. He opens the understanding to understand, and the will and affections to embrace, or else there will be no comfort.

Many are like Rachel. Her children were gone, and it is said of her, 'She would not be comforted,' Mat. ii. 18. God is the 'God of comfort.' As he gives the matter and ground of comfort, and reasons out of his holy word above all discomforts; so by his Spirit he frames and fits the heart to entertain these, to take the benefit of them.

'He comforts us in all tribulation.' To comfort is to support the soul against the grievance past, or felt, or feared.

There may be some remainders of grief for what is past. Grief present presseth most, and grief feared. Now God comforteth, whatsoever the grievance is, by supporting the soul against it, as I said before.

We are in tribulation in this life, and yet in all tribulations God doth comfort us. To add to that I said before of this point, let us therefore go to God in all the means of comfort, because he is the God of it, and he must comfort us.

Therefore, when we send for divines, or read holy books, for we must use all means, we must not set God against his means, but join them together: to add that caution by the way.

We may not, therefore, necessitate the God of comfort, that because he comforts us, therefore we will neglect reading and prayer, and conference with them that God hath exercised in the school of Christ, who should speak comfort to the weary soul by their office.

No, no! *God and his means must be joined together*. We must trust God, but not tempt him. To set God against his means is to tempt him; that because he is the God of comfort, therefore we will use no means, no physician for the body or for the soul. This is absurd. He is the God of comfort in the means. He comforts us 'in all tribulation,' by means, if they be to be had.

If there be no means to be had, he is the God of comfort, he can create them; and if it be so far that there be no means, but the contrary, he is a God that can comfort out of discomfort, and can, as I said, make the greatest grounds of comfort out of the greatest discomforts. But he is a God of the means, if they be to be had. If there be none, then let us go to him, and say, Thou God of comfort, if thou do not comfort, none can comfort; if thou help not, none can help; and then he will help, and help strongly. It is necessary to look to God, whatever the means be. It is he that comforts by them. Therefore let him have the praise. If we have any friend, any comfort of the outward man, or any solace of the inward man, by seasonable speech, &c., blessed be the 'God of comfort' who hath sent this comforter; who hath sent me comfort by such, and such, let him have the praise. Whatsoever the means be, the comfort is his.

And that is the cause that many have no more comfort. They trust to the means over much, or neglect the means.

Again, if 'God comfort in all tribulation,' let Christians be ashamed to be overmuch disconsolate, that have the 'God of comfort' for their God, 'who comforteth in all tribulation.' 'Why art thou so cast down?' Ps. xlii. 11. 'Is there no balm in Gilead for thee? Jer. viii. 22. 'Is there not a God in Israel?' 1 Sam. xvii. 46. It is the fault of Christians; they pore too much on their troubles, they look all one way. They look to the grievance, and not to the comfort.

There is a God of comfort that answers his name every way in the exercise of that attribute to his church. Therefore Christians must blame themselves if they be too much cast down; and labour for faith to draw near to this God of comfort.

It should make them ashamed of themselves that think it even a duty, as it were, to walk drooping, and disconsolately, and deadly, to have flat and dead spirits. What! is this beseeming a Christian that is in covenant with God, that is the 'God of comfort,' and that answers his title in dealing with his children, that is ready to comfort them in all tribulation? What if particular comforts be taken from thee, is there not a God of comfort left? he hath not taken away himself. What if thou be restrained, and shut up from other comforts, can any shut up God's Spirit? can any shut up God and our prayers?

Is not this a comfort, that we may go to God alway? and he is with us in all estates and in all wants whatsoever? So long as we are in covenant with the 'God of comfort,' why should we be overmuch cast down?' 'Why art thou so troubled, O my soul?' Ps. xlii. 11. David checks his soul thrice together for distrust in God. He is thy God, the God of all comfort.

Quest. What course shall we take that we may derive to ourselves comfort from this God of comfort, who comforteth us in all our tribulations?

Ans. 1. Let us consider *what our malady and grievance is*, especially let us look to our spiritual grievance and malady, sin: for sin is the cause of all other evils. Therefore it is the worst evil. And sin makes us loathed of God, the fountain of good. It drives us from him, when other evils drive us to him; and therefore it is the worst evil in that sense too.

2. Again, in the second place, *look to the discomforts of sin*, especially in the discomforts of conscience of those that are awakened; and Satan useth that as a means to despair in every cross.

(1.) Therefore let us search and try our souls *for our sins;* for our chief discomforts are from sin. For, alas! what are all other comforts? and what are all other discomforts? If a man's conscience be quiet, what are all discomforts? and if conscience be on the rack, what are all comforts? The disquiet and vexation of sin is the greatest of all; because then we have to deal with God. When sin is presented before us, and the judgments of God, and God as an angry judge, and conscience is awaked and on the rack, what in the world can take up the quarrel and appease conscience, when we and God are at difference, when the soul speaks nothing but discomfort?

In this case remember that God doth so far prevent objections in this kind from the accusations of conscience, that he reasons that he will comfort us, from that that conscience reasons against comfort. He doth this in the hearts of his children to whom he means to shew mercy: as we see in the poor publican. 'Lord, be merciful to me a sinner,' saith he, Luke xviii. 13. God taught him that reasoning. Nature would have taught him to reason as Peter did, 'Lord, depart from me, I am a sinful man,' Luke v. 8, and therefore I have nothing to do with God.

So our Saviour Christ, 'Come unto me, all ye that are weary and heavy laden,' Mat. xi. 28. They think, of all people they ought to run from God, they are so laden with sin, they have nothing to do with God. 'Oh, come unto me,' saith Christ. Therefore, when thy conscience is awakened with the sense of sin, remember what is said in the gospel, 'Be of good comfort, he calleth thee,' Mark x. 49; be thou of good comfort, thou art one that Christ calls, 'Come unto me, ye that are weary and heavy laden;' and 'Blessed are those that mourn,' Mat. v. 4.

That which thou and the devil with thy conscience would move thee to use as an argument to run away, our Saviour Christ in the gospel useth as an argument to draw thee forward. He comes for such, 'to seek, and to save the lost sinners.' This is a faithful saying, saith St Paul, that 'Christ came to save sinners.' Therefore, believe not Satan. He presents God to the soul that is humbled, and terrified in the sight of sin, as cruel, as a terrible judge, &c. He hides the mercy of God from such. To men that are in a sinful course he shews nothing but mercy. Aye, but now there is nothing but comfort to thee that art cast down and afflicted in the sense of thy sins; for all the comforts in the gospel of forgiveness of sins, and all the comforts from Christ's incarnation, the end of his coming in the flesh, the end of his death, and of all, is to save sinners.

Look thou, therefore, to the throne of mercy and grace, when thy conscience shall be awakened with the sense of sin, and Satan shall use that as an argument to draw thee from God. Consider the Scripture useth this as an argument to drive me to God, to allure me to him. 'Come unto me, all ye that are weary and heavy laden.' And 'Christ came to seek and to save that which was lost.' Luther, a man much exercised in spiritual conflicts, he confessed this was the balm that did most refresh his soul, 'God hath shut up all under sin, that he might have mercy upon all,' Rom. iii. 19. He shut up all under sin as prisoners, to see themselves under sin, and under the curse, that he might 'have mercy upon all;' upon all those that are convinced with the sense and sight of their sins. He hath shut up all under sin, that he might have mercy upon all those that belong to him.

This raised up that blessed man. Therefore, let us not be much discomforted, but 'be of good comfort, Christ calls us.'

For such as are sinners, that are given to the sins of the tongue, and of the life, to rotten discourse, to swearing and such like, to such as mean to be so, and think their case good. Oh! God is 'the God of comfort!' To such, as I said before, I can speak no comfort, nor the word of God speaks none. They must have another word and another Scripture; for this word speaks no comfort to such that are sinful and wretched, and will be so, and justify themselves to be so.

All the judgments in the Scripture are theirs. Hell and damnation and wrath, that is their portion to drink.

We can speak no comfort to such, nor the word of God that we unfold. It hath not a drop of comfort for them. God will not be merciful to such as go on in wicked, rotten, scandalous courses, that because hell hath not yet taken them, they may live long, and so make a 'covenant with hell and death,' Isa. xxviii. 18, and bless themselves.

Oh! but thou hast made no covenant with God, nor he hath made none with thee; and hell and death have made no covenant with thee, though thou hast made one with them. But there are two words go to a covenant. Death and hell shall seize upon thee, notwithstanding thy covenant.

Those that will live in sin in despite of the ministry, in spite of afflictions, there is no comfort to such. I speak only to the broken heart, which are fit vessels for comfort. God is 'the God of comfort' to such. What shall we say, then, to such as, after they have had some evidence of their good estate, that they are Christians, are fallen into sin? Is there any comfort for such?

Yes. Doth not St Paul, in 2 Cor. v. 20, desire such to be 'reconciled to God?' 'We are, as ambassadors of Christ, desiring you to be reconciled,' if you have sinned. So God hath comfort for those that have sinned. Christ knew that we should every day run into sins unawares. Therefore, he teaches us in the Lord's prayer to say every day, 'Forgive us our debts, our trespasses,' Mat. vi. 12. There is 'balm in Gilead,' there is mercy in Israel, for such daily trespasses as we run into.

Therefore, let none be discouraged, but fly presently to the 'God of comfort and Father of mercies.' And think not that he is weary of pardoning, as man is, for he is infinite in mercy; and though he be the party offended, yet he desires peace with us.

Caution. But yet, notwithstanding that we shall not love to run into his books, he doth, with giving the comfort of the pardon of sin, when we fall into it, add such sharp crosses, as we shall wish we had not given him occasion to correct us so sharply. We shall buy our comfort dear. We had better not have given him occasion.

God forgave the sin of David after he had repented, though he were a good man before; but David bought the pleasure of his sin dear. He wished a thousand times that he had never given occasion to God to raise good out of his evil, to turn his sin to his comfort. Yet God will do this, because God would never have us in a state of despair.

2. For *other grievances* besides sin, the comforts that we are to apply are more easy, and they are infinite, if we could reckon the particular comforts that God comforts his children withal.

It is good to have general comforts ready for all kind of maladies and grievances, and* this poor, wretched life of ours, in our absence from God, is subject to.

(1.) As, for instance, that general comfort, *the covenant of grace.* That is a spring of comfort, that God is our God and Father in Christ. What can come from a gracious and good God in covenant with us but that which is good?—nothing but what is favourably good, I mean. For the covenant is everlasting. When God takes once upon him to be our Father in covenant, he is so for ever. *Dum castigas pater, &c.* While he corrects, he is a Father; and when he smiles upon us, he is a Father.

God in the covenant of grace takes upon him a relation that ever holds.

* Qu. 'that?'—ED.

As he is for ever the Father of Christ, so he is for ever the Father of those that are members of Christ; and whatsoever comes from the Father of mercy, whether he correct or smile, whatsoever he doth, is in mercy.

(2.) Again, in the midst of any grievance remember *the gracious promise of mitigation*, 1 Cor. x. 13. 'God will not suffer us to be tempted above our strength, but he will give an issue to the temptation.' He will give a mitigation, and either he will raise our strength to the temptation, or he will bring the temptation and trial to our strength. He will fit them, and this is a comfort.

(3.) There is comfort, likewise, in all troubles whatsoever, *of the presence of God*. God will be present with us if once we be in covenant with him. He will be present in all trials to assist us, to strengthen us, to comfort us, to raise our spirits. And if God be present, he will banish all discomforts; for God is light, and where light is, darkness vanisheth. Now God, being the Father of light, that is, of all comfort, where he is present he banisheth discomfort in what measure he is pleased to banish it. Therefore David often reasoneth from the presence of God to the defiance of all troubles, Ps. iii. 6, 'If God be with me, I will not fear ten thousand that are against me.' And in Ps. xxiii. 4, 'Though I walk in the valley of the shadow of death, I will not fear, for thou art with me.' And 'if God be with us, who can be against us?' Rom. viii. 33, 34. 'And when thou passest through the fire, I will be with thee,' &c., Isa. xliii. 2. I will be with thee, not to keep thee out, but to uphold thee, as he did the martyrs. There was a fire of comfort in them above that fire that consumed their bodies; and, as we see, he was with the three children. There was 'a fourth, like the Son of God,' Dan. iii. 25.

So in all tribulations there is another with us, that is, the Spirit of God, that comforts us in all, and is present with us in all. The goldsmith, when he puts the wedge into the fire, he stands by till the dross be consumed. So God is with his children in the furnace of affliction. He brings them into affliction; he continues with them in affliction; and he brings them at last out of affliction. The presence of God is a main and a grand comfort in all tribulation.

(4.) Besides, in all that befalls us whatsoever, *consider the end*. All is for a good end. 'All things work together for the best to them that love God,' saith St Paul, Rom. viii. 28. Why do we endure physic? Because we know the physician is wise, and he is our friend, and he doth it to carry away burdensome, hurtful humours. We shall be better and lighter afterwards. Do we do this in our common course in the things of this life? Grace will much more certainly teach us to do it; to reason, It is from a father, and it is for my good. Let us look whence it comes and what it tends to, with the promise of mitigation and of God's presence in our troubles. These are main comforts, if we could think of them, if the devil did not take them out of our memory.

(5.) And for the fifth* ground of comfort that God doth comfort us withal in all tribulations, it is the promise of *final deliverance and final comfort* for ever. If none will raise our souls, that will, when we shall consider that it will not be long.

'The short afflictions in this world bring an eternal weight of glory,' 2 Cor. iv. 17. There will be a final deliverance. Life itself, that is, the subject that receives affliction, that is short. Our life is but a moment, 2 Cor. iv. 17. Therefore, our afflictions must be short.

* Misprinted 'first.'—G.

Life is longer than discomforts. There is but a piece of our life subject to miseries; and if that be but a vapour, but a moment, and as a point between eternity before and eternity after, what are the miseries of this life? Certainly they are but for a moment.

Therefore, the promise of final deliverance, when all tears shall be wiped from our eyes, this should comfort us, if nothing else would. This is the way, therefore, whereby God usually comforts, by suggesting the heads and springs of comfort.

And, indeed, there is a daily method of comforting, whereby we may comfort ourselves in all crosses, if we would use that daily method and order of comfort. As there is a kind of diet to keep the body in temper, so there is a kind of spiritual diet to keep the soul in temper, in a course of comfort, unless it be when God takes liberty to cast down for some special end, as we see in Job.

Therefore, let us take this course; for God, as he comforteth us, so he comforts us as understanding creatures, he useth our understanding to consider how we should comfort ourselves; and after we are once in a state of comfort, if we be not wanting to ourselves, there is no great difficulty to keep our comfort. There are means to keep daily comfort. God hath provided them, and he will be present to make good all his comforts. Grant it, therefore, that we are in the covenant of grace, that God is our Father in Christ, and we take him to be our God, to be all-sufficient, then, to keep ourselves in a daily temper for comfort,

[1.] Every day *keep our souls tender*, that we may be capable of comfort; keep the wound open, that we may receive balm, that there grow not a deadness upon the heart, considering that while we live here there is alway some sin in us, that must be wrought out by some course or other. Let us try and search our souls, what ill is in the wound; let us keep it open and tender, that there may be a fitness for mercy, to receive the balm of comfort, which will not be if we slubber over. Certainly it is an excellent course every day to search our hearts and ways, and presently to apply the balm of comfort, the promise of pardon. Take the present, when we have searched the wound, to get pardon and forgiveness daily. As we sin daily, Christ bids us ask it daily.

This will make us fit for comfort, by discerning the estate of our souls, and the remainders of corruption. That which sharpens appetite and makes the balm of God to be sweet indeed, is the sense of, and the keeping open of our wound. A daily search into our wants and weaknesses, a daily fresh sight of the body of sin in us, and experience how it is fruitful in ill thoughts, and desires, and actions, this will drive us to a necessity of daily comfort.

And certainly a fresh sight of our corruptions, it is never without some fresh comfort. We see St Paul, Rom. vii., he sets himself to this work, to complain of his indisposition, by reason of sin in him; and how doth he end that sight and search into his own estate? He ends in a triumphing manner, 'Thanks be to God, through Jesus Christ our Lord: There is no condemnation to them that are in Christ Jesus,' verse 25; after he had complained, 'Oh, miserable man that I am! who shall deliver me from this body of death?' There can be no danger in a deep search into our ways and hearts, if this be laid as a ground before, that there is more supply and heavenly comfort in God, and the promises of God, than there can be ill in our souls. Then the more ill we find in ourselves, the more we are disposed to fetch grounds of comfort from God.

[2.] And together with this searching of our souls, and asking daily pardon, let us for the time to come *renew our covenant with God*, that we may have the comfort of a good conscience to get pardon for our sins past, and renew our resolutions for the time to come.

[3.] And withal, that we may use an orderly course of comfort, let us every day *feed on Christ*, the food of life; let us every day feed upon something in Christ. Consider the death of Christ, the satisfaction he hath made by his death, his intercession in heaven. His blood runs afresh, that we may every day feed on it.

We may run every day into new offences against the law, to new neglect of duty, into new crosses; let us feed upon Christ. He came into the world 'to save sinners,' 1 Tim. i. 15, to make us happy, with peace of conscience here, and with glory afterward. Let us feed on Christ daily. As the body is fed with cordials, so this feeds, and comforts, and strengthens the soul.

This is to live by faith, to lead our lives by faith, to feed on Christ every day.

[4.] And likewise, if we will keep our souls in a perpetual temper of comfort, let us every day *meditate of some prerogatives of Christians*, that may raise our souls; let us single out some or other. As for example, that excellent prerogative to be the 'sons of God,' 1 John iii. 2. What love! saith the apostle, that we, of rebels and traitors, in Christ should be made the sons of God! That of slaves, we should be made servants; of servants, sons; of sons, heirs; and of heirs, fellow-heirs with Christ: what prerogative is this, that God should give his Son to make us, that were rebels, sons, heirs, and fellow-heirs with Christ! Gal. iv. 7. And to consider what follows upon this liberty, that we have from the curse of the law, to go to God boldly, to go to the throne of grace through Christ, our elder Brother, by prayer; to think of eternal life as our inheritance; to think of God above as our Father. Let us think of our prerogatives of religion, adoption, and justification, &c.

Upon necessity we are driven to it, if we consider the grievances of this world, together with our corruptions. Our corruptions, and afflictions, and temptations, and desertions, one thing or other, will drive us to go out of ourselves for comfort, to feed on the benefits by Christ. And consider what he hath done. It is for us, the execution of his office, and all for us; what he is, what he did, what he suffered, what procured, all is for us. The soul delighting itself in these prerogatives, it will keep the soul in a perpetual estate of comfort. Therefore the Scripture sets forth Christ by all terms that may be comfortable. He is the door to let us in. 'He is the way, the truth, and the life,' John xiv. 6, the water and the bread, &c. In sin, he is our righteousness; in death, he is our life; in our ignorance, he is our way; in spiritual hunger and thirst, he is the bread and water of life: he is all in all. And if we cannot think of some prerogative of Christianity, then think of some promise. As I said before, think of the covenant of grace. There is a spring of comfort in that, that God in Christ is our God to death, and for ever; and that promise I speak of, that 'All things shall work for the best,' Rom. viii. 28.

Let us every day think of these things, and suggest them to our own souls, that our souls may be affected with them, and digest them, that our souls and they may be one, as it were.

[5.] And every day stir up our hearts *to be thankful*. A thankful heart can never want comfort; for it cannot be done without some comfort and cheerfulness. And when God receives any praise and glory, he answers it with comfort. A thankful heart is alway comfortable.

[6.] And let us stir up our hearts *to be fruitful in the holy actions.* The reward of a fruitful life is a comfortable life. Besides heaven, God alway in this life gives a present reward to any good action. It is rewarded with peace of conscience. Besides, it is a good foundation against the evil day. Every good action, as the apostle saith to Timothy, it 'lays up a good foundation,' 1 Tim. vi. 19. The more good we do, the more we are assured that our faith is not hypocritical, but sound and good, and will hold out in the time of trial. It will be a good foundation that we have had evidence before, that we have a sound and fruitful faith.

What do wicked men, careless, sinful creatures, that go on in a course of profaneness and blasphemy, &c.? They lay a ground of despair, a ground of discomfort, to be swallowed up in the evil day. Then conscience will be awaked at the last, and Satan will be ready to join with conscience, and conscience will seal all the accusations that Satan lays against them; and where is the poor soul then? As it is with them, so, on the contrary, the Christian soul that doth good, besides the present comfort of a good conscience, it lays a good foundation against the time to come; for in the worst times, it can reason with itself, My faith is not fruitless, I am not an hypocrite. Though the fruits of it be weak, and mixed with corruptions, yet there is truth in them. This will comfort us when nothing else will.

Therefore let us every day be setting ourselves in some good way; for comfort is in comfortable courses, and not in ill courses. In God's ways we shall have God's comforts. In those ways let us exercise the spiritual strength we have; let us pray to God, and perform the exercise of religion with strength, shew some zeal in it; let us shew some zeal against sin, if occasion be, if it be in God's work, in God's way. Let a man set himself upon a good work, especially when it is in opposition; for the honour of God, and the peace of his conscience. Presently there is comfort upon it.

[7.] And that we may not be discouraged with the imperfection of our performances, one way of daily comfort is, *to consider the condition of the covenant of grace between God and us.* In the covenant of grace, our performances, if they be sincere, they are accepted; and it is the perfection of the gospel, sincerity. Sincerity will look God in the face with comfort, because he is with the upright. So much truth in all our dealings, so much comfort.

[8.] And with sincerity labour *for growth*, to grow better and better. God in the gospel means to bring us to perfection in heaven by little and little. In the law there was present perfection required; but in the gospel God requires that we should come to perfection by little and little, as Christ by little and little satisfied for our sins, and not all at once. In the condition of the covenant of grace, we must live and grow by grace, by little and little, and not all at once. The condition of the covenant of grace is not to him that hath strength of grace in perfection. But if we believe and labour to walk with God, if there be truth of grace, truth goes for perfection in the covenant of grace. We should labour for sound knowledge of the covenant of grace, that now we are freed from the rigour, as well as from the curse of the law; that though we have imperfections, yet God will be our Father, and in this condition of imperfection he will be a pardoning Father, and looks on our obedience, though it be feeble, and weak, and imperfect, yet, being the obedience of children in the covenant of grace, and he accepts of what is his own, and pardons what is ours.

[9.] And every day labour *to preserve the comforts of the Spirit* that we have, not to grieve the Spirit; for comfort comes with the Spirit of God, as heat accompanies the fire. As wheresoever fire is, there is heat; so wheresoever the Spirit of God is, there is comfort; because the Spirit of God is God, and God is with comfort. Wheresoever comfort is, God is; and wheresoever God is, there is comfort. If we would have comfort continually every day, let us carefully watch that we give way to the Spirit of God, by good actions, and meditations, and exercises.

And by no means grieve the Spirit, or resist the Spirit, for then we resist comfort. If we speak any thing that is ill, we lose our comfort for that time. Conscience will check us. We have grieved the Spirit. If we hear any thing with applause, and are not touched with it, we lose our comfort; conscience will tell us we are dead-hearted, and not affected as we should be. There is a great deal of flesh and corruption that is affected with such rotten discourse. And so if we venture upon occasions, we shall grieve the Spirit, either if we speak somewhat to satisfy others that are nought,* or if we hear somewhat that is ill from others. Want of wisdom in this kind, doth make us go without comfort many times: want of wisdom to single out our company, or else if we be with such, to do that that may please them, and grieve the Spirit, and hinder our own comfort.

[10.] These and such like directions, if we would observe, we might walk in a course of comfort. The God of comfort hath prescribed this *in the book of comfort*. These are the courses for God's children, to walk in a comfortable way, till they come to heaven. More especially, if we would at any time take a more full measure of comfort, then take the *book of God into your hand*. Those are comforts that refresh the soul. Single out some special portion of Scripture, and there you shall have a world of comfort, as, for example, let a man single out the Epistle to the Romans. If a man be in any grievance whatsoever, what a world of comfort is there, fitting for every malady! There is a method how to come to comfort.

There St Paul, in the beginning, first strips all men of confidence of any thing in themselves, and tells them that no man can be saved by works, Jews nor Gentiles, but all by the righteousness of God in Christ. 'All are deprived of the glory of God,' Rom. iii. 19, Jews, and Gentiles, everybody. And when we are brought to Christ, he tells us, in the latter end of the third chapter, that by Christ we have the forgiveness of all our former sins whatsoever. 'He is the propitiation for our sins.' In the fourth chapter he comforts us by the example of Abraham and David, that they were justified without works by faith, not by works of their own, but by laying hold of the promises of comfort and salvation merely by Christ. And all that St Paul saith is 'written for us,' 1 Cor. x. 11. But in the first chapter especially, because all the miseries of this life come from the 'first Adam.' Because we are children of the 'first Adam,' death and misery comes from that. He opposeth the comfort in the 'second Adam,' and he shews that there is more comfort by the second Adam, than there is discomfort by the first. Righteousness in the second Adam 'reigns to life everlasting,' Rom. v. 17, and glory. Sin and misery came by the first, but there is the pardon of all sin by the second Adam. He doth excellently oppose them in the latter end of that chapter. In the beginning of the fifth chapter he shews there the method, and descent of joy, 'Being justified by faith, in Christ, we have peace with God,' Rom. v. 1. Considering that by the righteousness of Christ we are freed from sin, 'We have peace with

* Qu. 'naught?'—Ed.

God through Jesus Christ our Lord,' Rom. v. 1. And 'we have boldness to the throne of grace, and we rejoice in tribulation: knowing that tribulation brings forth patience; and patience, experience; and experience, hope,' Rom. v. 4. He sets himself there of purpose to comfort in all tribulation, and he saith, in these things we rejoice, 'We rejoice in tribulation.'

Aye, but for our sins after our conversion, after we are in the state of grace, what comfort is there for them? There is excellent comfort in the fifth of the Romans. 'If when we were enemies he gave his Son for us:' if he saved us by the death of Christ when we were enemies, much more, Christ being alive, and in heaven, he will keep it for us; and keep us to salvation now, when we are friends, seeing he died for us when we were enemies. Aye, but the remainders of corruption in this world trouble us. That troubles our comfort, the combat between the flesh and the Spirit. Would you see comfort for that? You shall see it in Romans vii. 24, 25. 'Oh, miserable man, who shall deliver me from this body of death? Thanks be to God through Jesus Christ our Lord.' So he shews there what way to have comfort in the combat between the flesh and the spirit, to search into our corruptions, to lay them open to God by confession.

And then, in the beginning of the eighth chapter, saith he, 'There is no condemnation to them that are in Christ Jesus,' ver. 1. Though there be sin, yet there is no condemnation; though there be this conflict between the flesh and the spirit. So he comforts them. And for the afflictions that follow our corruptions in this life, there is a treasure of comfort against them in that chapter; for doth he not say, 'if we suffer with him, we shall reign with him,' ver. 17. And the same 'Spirit helps our infirmities, and teacheth us how to pray?' ver. 26. We can never be uncomfortable if we can pray; but there is a promise of the Spirit that stirs up sighs, and 'groans that cannot be expressed,' ver. 26, and a Christian hath alway a spirit of prayer, at the least of sighs and groans; and God hears the sighs of his own Spirit.

And what a grand comfort is that, that I named before, verse 28, 'All things work for the best to them that love God.' And 'if God be with us, who can be against us.' ver. 33. And he sends us to Christ. If Christ be dead, 'or rather risen again, who shall lay anything to our charge?' Christ is 'ascended to heaven, and makes intercession at the right hand of God,' ver. 34. Though Satan lay our sins to our charge, Christ makes intercession in heaven at the right hand of God. He makes continual intercession for our continual breaches with God. Who shall lay anything to our charge? Aye, but all that power of hell and sin! and all labour to separate us from God, to breed division between God and us. In the latter end of that chapter he bids defiance to all, what shall 'separate us from the love of God in Christ?' ver. 35. It shall separate his love from Christ first. God's love is found in Christ. He shall cease to love Christ if he cease to love us. Aye, but we may afterward fall into an uncomfortable case. For that he saith, 'neither things present, nor things to come, shall be able to separate us,' ver. 38.

What an excellent spring of comfort is there in that reasoning, verse 32, 'If God spared not his own Son, but gave him to death for us all, how shall he not with him give us all things else.' How many streams may be drawn from that spring! 'If God spared not his own Son, but gave him to death for us all, how shall he not with him give us all things else' in this world necessary, grace, provision, and protection, till he have brought us to heaven? If he have given Christ, he will give all. Whatsoever is written, is written for our comfort. I name* this epistle, because I would name one instance for all. 'All is written for our comfort,' as he saith after in the same epistle, xv. 4. The written word, or the word unfolded; the end of preaching, is especially to comfort. The chirurgeon opens a wound, and the physician gives a purge, but all is to restore at the last. All that the chirurgeon aims at, is to close up the wound at the last. So all our aim is to comfort. We must cast you down, and shew you your misery that you are in, and shew you, that if you continue in that course, hell and damnation belongs to you. But this is to make you despair in yourselves, and to fly to the God of comfort. The law is for the gospel. All serve to bring the soul to comfort.

Therefore go to the word of God, any portion, the Psalms or any special part of the Scripture; and that, by the Spirit of God, will be a means to raise the soul. The Spirit in the word, joining with the Spirit in us, will make a sweet close together, and comfort us in all tribulation.

[11.] And *have recourse daily to common principles.* All the principles of religion serve for comfort, especially the articles of the creed. 'I believe in God the Father Almighty.' What a spring of comfort is in that! What can befall from a father, but it shall turn to good, and by a Father Almighty? Though he be never so strongly opposed, yet he will turn it to good. He is a 'Father Almighty.' And the articles of Christ, every article hath ground of daily comfort, of his abasement. In Christ, I see myself. He is my surety, 'the second Adam.' I see my sins crucified with him. This is the way to reap comfort when the conscience is disquieted. When I look upon my sins, not in my own conscience, but take it out there, and see it in Christ dying, and crucified, in the articles of abasement to see our sin, and misery, all in Christ.† For he stood there as surety, as a public person for all. What a comfort is this! When I see how Christ was abased, I see my own comfort, for he was my surety. If my sins being laid on him, who was my surety, could not condemn him, or keep him in the grave, but overcame sin that was laid to his charge, surely‡ I shall overcome my corruptions. Nothing that I have shall overcome me, because it could not overcome Christ my surety. His victory is mine.

And so, if the soul be in any desolation and discomfort, all the articles of his 'glorification and exaltation.' His rising again acquits the soul. Therefore my sins are satisfied for, because my surety is out of prison. And his ascending into heaven shews my triumph. He led captivity captive. And the enemies that are left are for the trial of my faith, and not to conquer me. For Christ hath 'led captivity captive,' Ps. lxviii. 18, and is ascended into heaven. He led all in triumph, and sits at the right hand of God, to rule his church to the end of the world. He sits for me to overcome my enemies, as St Paul saith excellently, Rom. viii. 33, 'Who shall lay anything to the charge of God's people? It is Christ that died, or rather, that is risen again, who sits at the right hand of God.'

And if we be troubled for the loss of a particular friend, there is comfort in that article of the 'communion of saints.' There are those that have more grace, and that is for me. If my own prayers be weak, 'I believe the communion of saints,' and have the benefit of their prayers. Every one that saith 'Our Father' brings me in, if I be in the covenant of grace, and of the communion of saints. If I have weaknesses in myself, 'I believe in the Holy Ghost,' the comforter of God's elect, and my comforter. If I

* Misprinted 'mean'.—G.
† Articles I. and IV., and *infra* IX.—G.
‡ That is, 'assuredly.'—G.

fear death, 'I believe the resurrection of the body.' If I fear the day of judgment, 'I believe that Christ shall be my judge.' He shall come to judge the quick and the dead. In all the miseries of this life, considering that they are but short, 'I believe the life everlasting.' So that indeed if we would dig to ourselves springs of comfort, let us go to the articles of our faith, and see how there are streams of comfort from every one answerable to all our particular exigencies and necessities whatsoever.

And to close up this point, remember, whatsoever means we use, what prerogative soever we think of, whatsoever we do, remember we go to the God of comfort, and desire him to bless his word in the ministry, and desire him to work in the communion of saints, with his Spirit to warm our hearts. Alway remember to carry him along in all, that we may have comfort from 'the God of comfort, who comforteth in all tribulations.'

Next words are,

'*That we may able to comfort them which are in any trouble.*' These words shew the end why God doth comfort us in all tribulation. One main end is, *that we should be comforted in ourselves.* That is the first. And then, that we, being comforted ourselves, from that ability *should be able to derive** *comfort to others.* 'We are comforted in all tribulations, *that we should be able to comfort them that are in any tribulation.*'

It is not St Paul's case only, and great men in religion, ministers and the like. It is not their lot and portion alone to be persecuted and troubled, but

Obs. We are all in this life subject to disquiets and discomforts.

Every one, 'whosoever will live godly in Christ Jesus, must suffer persecution,' 2 Tim. iii. 12. Therefore the apostle saith not only our† tribulation; but that 'we may be able to comfort them that are in any trouble.' Trouble is the portion of all God's children one with another. I do but touch that by the way. But that which I shall more stand upon, it is the end, one main end why God comforteth, especially ministers: it is, *that they should be able to comfort others* with the comforts that God hath comforted them withal. 'That we may be able,' &c. Now you must conceive that this ability, it is not ability alone without will and practice, as if he meant, God hath given me comfort that I might be able to comfort others if I will. That is not God's end only, that we may be able, but that we may exercise our ability, that it may be ability in exercise; as God doth not give a rich man riches to that end that he may be able to relieve others if he will. No! But if thou be a child of God, he gives thee ability and will too, he gives an inward strength. So the meaning here is, not that we may be able to comfort others if we will, but that we may be both able and willing to comfort others.

And to comfort others not only by our example, that because we have been comforted of God, so they shall be comforted. It is good, but it is not the full extent of the apostle's meaning; for then the dead examples should comfort as well as the living. And indeed that is one way of comfort, to consider the examples of former times. But the apostle's meaning is, that I should comfort them not only by my example of God's dealing with me, that they should look for the like comfort. That is but one degree. His meaning is further therefore, that we should be able to comfort them by sympathizing with them; as indeed it is a sweet comfort to those that are in distress when others compassionate their estate.

* That is, 'communicate.'—G † Qu., 'one?'—Ed.

And not only so, by our example and sympathy with them, but likewise that we may be able to comfort them by the inward support, and strength, and light that we have found by the Spirit of God in ourselves. That is that that will enable us to comfort others, from that very support and inward strength that we have found from God; by those graces, and that particular strength and comfort that we have had. When there is a sweet expressing of our inward comfort to them, shewing something in our comfort that may raise them up, in the like troubles that we were in, then the comfort will not be a dead comfort, when it comes from a man experienced. Personated comfort, when a man takes upon him to comfort, that only speaks comfort, but feels not what he speaks, there is little life in it. We are comforted that we may comfort others, with feeling, having been comforted ourselves before, with feeling, and comfortable apprehensions in ourselves. The point considerable in the first place, to make way to the rest, is this, that

Doct. God's children, they have all of them interest in divine comforts.

St Paul was comforted, that he might comfort others. Divine comforts belong to all. They are the portion of all God's people. The meanest have interest, as well [as] the greatest. There is the same spiritual physic for the poorest subject, and the greatest monarch. There is the same spiritual comfort for the meanest, and for the greatest Christian in the world. St Paul hath the same comfort as St Paul's children in the faith. What is the reason that they are communicable thus to all? that they lie open to all?

Reason 1. God is the God and Father of *all light and comfort.* Christ is the Saviour of all. All the privileges of religion belong to all equally. All are sons and heirs, and all are alike redeemed. 'The brother of low degree, and the brother of high degree,' James i. 9. They may differ in the references and relations of this life, but in Christ all are alike.

Reason 2. Besides, *it is the nature of spiritual privileges and blessings.* They are communicable to all alike without impairing. The more one hath, the less another hath not. All have an equal share. Every one hath interest entire; every one hath all, without loss or hindrance to others. As for instance, the sun, every particular man hath all the good the sun can do, as well as all the world hath. It is peculiarly and entirely every man's own. Every man *in solidum* hath the use of it. The sun is not one man's more than another. As a public fountain or conduit, every man hath as much right in it as another. So in religion, the graces, and privileges, and favours, they lie open as the prerogatives and privileges of all God's children; and that is the excellency of them. In the things of this life it is not so. They are not common to all alike. There is a loss in the division. The more one hath, the less another hath. And that is the reason why the things of this life breed a disposition of pride and envy. One envies another, because he wants that that another hath; and one despiseth another, because he hath more than another hath; but in the comforts of God's Spirit, and the prerogatives that are the ground of those comforts, all have interest alike.

Only the difference is in the vessels they bring. If one man bring a large vessel, a large faith, he carries more; and another that brings a less faith carries less, but it lies open to all alike. As St Cyprian saith, we carry as much from God as we bring vessels. But all have interest alike in divine comforts.

Therefore among Christians there is little envy, because in the best things, which they value best, all may have alike; and that which one desires, another may have as much as he. He knows he hath never the less.

Use. The point is *comfortable to all, even to the meanest*, and to them especially, that howsoever there be a difference between others and them in outward things, that cease in death (for all differences shall cease ere long between us and others), yet the best things are common. In this life those things that are necessary, they are common, as the light, and the elements, fire, and water, &c.; and those are necessary* that are not common. But especially in spiritual things, the best things are common. Let no man be discomforted, if he be God's child. Comfort belongs to him, as well as to the greatest apostle. The chiefest comforts belong to him as well as to the chiefest Christian. Therefore, let us envy none, nor despise none in this respect.

In the next place, we may observe here, hence, that *though these comforts be common, yet God derives these comforts commonly by the means of men.*

This is God's order in deriving these comforts to the soul. He comforts one, that another may be comforted. Not that the comforts themselves that join with our spirits come from men, but that, together with the speech and presence of men whom we love and respect, and in whom we discern the appearance of the Spirit of God to dwell, together with the speech of persons in whom the Spirit is strong and powerful, the Spirit of God joins, and the Spirit raiseth the soul with comfort. So the Spirit comforteth, by comforting others, that they may comfort us.

This is not only true of ministers, but it is true of Christians, as Christians. For St Paul must be considered, in something as an apostle, in something as a Christian, in something as a minister of Christ. As an apostle, he had the care of 'all the churches,' &c., 2 Cor. xi. 28. As a Christian, he comforted and exhorted others. One Christian ought to comfort another. Therefore he would have done it as a Christian, if he had not been an apostle. And in something he is to be considered as a minister of Christ, as a teacher and ambassador of Christ, a teacher of the gospel. He was somewhat as an apostle, somewhat as a minister, somewhat as a Christian. Therefore it concerns us all to consider how to comfort one another as Christians. We are all members of the same body whereof Christ is the head. Therefore whatsoever comfort we feel, we ought to communicate.

The celestial bodies will teach us this. Whatsoever light or influence the moon and the stars receive, they bestow it on these inferior bodies. They have their light from the sun, and they reflect it again upon the creatures below. In the fabric of man's body, those official parts, as we call them, those parts and members of the body, the heart and the liver, which are both members and official parts, that do office and service to other parts, they convey and derive the spirits and the blood to all other parts. They receive strength, partly for themselves first, and then to convey it to other members. The liver is fed itself with some part of the blood, and it conveys the rest to the veins, and so to the whole body. The heart is nourished itself of the purest nourishment, the spirits are increased, and those spirits are spread through the arteries.

The stomach feeds itself with the meat it digests, and with the strength it hath. Being an official part, it serves other parts, and strengtheneth other parts; and if there be a decay in it, there is a decay in all the parts of the body. So a Christian ought to strengthen himself, and then strengthen others. No man is for himself alone. And although whatso-

* Qu., 'not necessary?'—Ed.

ever the means be, the comfort comes from God, yet he will have comfort to be conveyed to us by men this way.

Reason 1. Partly *to try our obedience*, whether we will respect his ordinance. He will have us go to men like ourselves. Now, if we will have comfort, we must look to his ordinance, we must have it of others, and not altogether from ourselves. And that is the reason why many go all their lifetime with heavy, drooping spirits. Out of pride and neglect, they scorn to seek it of others. They smother their grief, and bleed inwardly; because they will not lay open the state of their souls to others. Although God be 'the God of comfort,' he hath ordained this order, that he will comfort us by them that he hath appointed to comfort us. He comforteth others, that they may comfort us. Though God be the God of comfort, yet he conveys it, for the most part, by the means of others. I say for the most part; for he ties not himself to means, though he tie us to means, when we have means. Occasion may be, when a man is shut from all earthly comforts, as in contagious diseases, and restraint, &c. A man may be shut from all intercourse of worldly comforts; but even then, a Christian is never in such an estate, but he hath one comfort or other. Then God comforts immediately, and then he comforts more sweetly and strongly; then the soul cleaves to him close, and saith, Now thou must comfort or none, now the honour is all thine.

Now the nearer the soul is to the fountain of comfort, the more it is comforted, but the soul is never so near to God as in extremity of affliction. When all means fail, then the soul goes to the fountain of comfort, and gives all the glory to him. But I say, when there is means, God hath appointed to derive his comfort by means; when we may have the benefit, of the communion of saints, of the word, &c. God will not comfort us immediately in the neglect of the means. 'He comforteth us, that we might comfort others.' And as he doth it to try our obedience,

Reason 2. So partly, *to knit us in love one to another*. For is not this a great bond to knit us one to another, when we consider that our good is hid in another? The good that is derived to us, it is hid in others. And this makes us to esteem highly of others. How sweet are the looks and sight of a friend! and more sweet the words of a friend, especially of an experienced friend, that hath been in the furnace himself.

Thus God, to knit us one to another in love, hath ordained that the comfort that he conveys, it should be conveyed by the means of others. Other reasons there may be given, but these are sufficient.

Use. If this be so, then we ought from hence to learn, *that whatsoever we have we are debtors of it to others*, whatsoever comfort we have, whether it be outward or inward comfort.

And even as God hath disposed and dispensed his benefits and graces to us, so let us be good stewards of it. We shall give account of it ere long. Let every man reason with himself, why have I this comfort that another wants? I am God's steward; God hath not given it to me to lay up, but to lay out. To speak a little of outward comforts. It is cursed atheism in many rich persons, that think they are to live here only to scrape an estate for them and their children; when in the mean time their neighbours want, and God's children want, that are as dear to God as themselves, and perish for want of comfort. If they were not atheists in this point, they would think I am a steward, and what comfort shall I have of scraping much? That will but increase my account. Such a steward were mad that would desire a great account. The more my account is, the more I have to answer for, and the more shall be my punishment if I quit not all well.

Now men out of atheism, that do not believe a day of judgment, a time of account, they engross comforts to them and theirs, as if there were not a church, as if there were not an afflicted body of Christ. They think not that they are stewards. Whereas the time will come, when they shall have more comfort of that that they have bestowed, than of that that they shall leave behind them to their children. That which is wisely dispensed for the comfort of God's people, it will comfort us, when all that we shall leave behind will not, nay, perhaps it will trouble us, the ill getting of it.

And so whatsoever inward comforts we have, it is for the comfort of others. We are debtors of it. Whatsoever ability we have, as occasion is offered, if there be a necessity in those that are of the same body with ourselves, we ought to regard them in pity and compassion. If we should see a poor creature cast himself into a whirlpool, or plunge himself into some desperate pit, were we not accessory to his death, if we should not help him! if we would not pull one out of the fire? Oh, yes! and is not the soul in as great danger? and is not mercy to the soul the greatest mercy? shall we see others ready to be swallowed up in the pit of despair, with heaviness of spirit? shall we see them dejected, and not take it to heart? But either we are unable to minister a word of comfort to them, or else unwilling: as if we were of Cain's disposition, that we would look to ourselves only; 'we are none of their keepers,' Gen. iv. 9.

It is a miserable thing to profess ourselves to be members of that body whereof Christ is the head, to profess the communion of saints, and yet to be so dead-hearted in these particular exigencies and occasions. It lies upon us as a duty, if God convey comforts to us from others; and his end in comforting us any way, of putting any comfort in our hands outward or inward, it is to comfort others. If we do it not, we are liable to sin, to the breach of God's command, and we frustrate God's end.

But if this lie upon us as a duty to comfort others, then it concerns us to know how to be able to do it.

That we may be able to comfort others, let us,

(1.) Be ready *to take notice of the grievance of others;* as Moses went to see the afflictions of his brethren, and when he saw it, laid it to heart, Ex. iv. 31.

It is a good way to go to 'the house of mourning,' Eccles. vii. 2, and not to balk and decline our Christian brethren in adversity. God 'knows our souls in adversity, Ps. xxxi. 7; so should we do the souls of others, if they be knit to us in any bond of kindred, or nature, or neighbourhood, or the like. That bond should provoke us; for bonds are as the veins and arteries to derive comfort. All bonds are to derive good, whether bonds of neighbourhood, or acquaintance, &c. A man should think with himself, I have this bond to do my neighbour good. It is God's providence that I should be acquainted with him, and do that to him that I cannot do to a stranger. Let us consider all bonds, and let this work upon us: let us consider their grievance is a bond to tie us.

(2.) And withal let us labour *to put upon us the bowels of a father and mother*, tender bowels, as God puts upon him bowels of compassion towards us. So St Paul, being an excellent comforter of others, in 1 Thess. ii. 7, he shews there how he carried himself as a father, or mother, or nurse to them. Those that will comfort others, they must put upon them the affections of tender creatures as may be. They must be patient, they must be tenderly affected, they must have love, they must have the graces of communion.

What be the graces of communion? The graces of Christian communion to fit us in the communion of saints to do good, they are a loving, meek, patient spirit. Love makes patient. As we see mothers and nurses, what can they not endure of their children, because they love them? And they must be likewise wise and furnished. They that will comfort others must get wisdom and ability. They must get humility, they must abase themselves that they may be comfortable to others, and not stand upon terms. These be the graces of communion that fit us for the communion of saints.

What is the reason that many are so untoward to this duty, and have no heart to it, that they cannot indeed do it?

The reason is, they consider not their bonds: they do not 'consider the poor and needy,' Ps. xli. 1. They have not the graces of communion, they want loving spirits, they want ability, they are empty, they are not furnished, they have not knowledge laid up in store, they want humble spirits. The want of these graces makes us so barren in this practice of the communion of saints. Therefore we should bewail our own barrenness when we should do such duties, and cannot. And beg of God the spirit of love and wisdom, that we may do things wisely, that we may speak that which is fit. 'A word in season is as apples of gold with pictures of silver,' Prov. xxv. 11. And let us beg a humble spirit, that we may be abased to comfort others. As Christ in love to us he abased himself, he became man, and when he was man, he became a servant, he abased himself to wash his disciples' feet, talk with a silly woman, and such base offices. And if the Spirit of Christ be in us, it will abase us to offices of love, to support one another, to bear one another's burthens,' Gal. vi. 2.

(3.) Again, if we would comfort others as we should, let us labour *to get experience of comfort in ourselves*. God comforteth us that we might be able to comfort others. He will easily kindle others that is all on fire himself, and that is comforted himself. He can easily comfort others with that comfort he feels himself. Those that have experience can do it best.

As we see in physicians, if there be two physicians, whereof the one hath been sick of the disease that he is to cure in another; the other perhaps is more excellent than he otherwise, but he hath never been sick of it; the patient will sooner trust himself with the experienced physician than with the other; for undoubtedly he is better seen in that than the other, though perhaps the other may be a greater booked* physician than he. As it is with the physicians of the body, so it is with the physician of the soul: the experienced physician is the best. What is the reason that old men, and wise men, are the mercifulest of all? Because they have had experience of many crosses and miseries. A wise man knows what crosses are; he understands them best.

The way, then, to comfort others, is to get experience of divine comforts ourselves. And that we may get experience of God's comforts, let us mark what was said before of the rules of comfort, and work upon our own hearts whatsoever may be comfortable to others; that we may not be empty trunks to speak words without feeling.

He that is well may speak very good things to a sick man, but the sick man sees that he speaks without pity and compassion. Those that have

* That is, 'book-learned.'—G.

been sick of the same disease, when they come to comfort, they do it with a great deal of meekness and mildness. Those that are fit to comfort others must be spiritual themselves first, as the apostle saith, Gal. vi. 1. Saith the wise and holy apostle, 'If any man be overtaken,' as, alas! we are all overtaken with some corruption or other, 'ye that are spiritual, restore such a one,' set him in joint, as the word is (*i*), 'with the spirit of meekness, knowing that thou thyself mayest be tempted.'

The Spirit of God is a Spirit of comfort. The more we have of the Spirit, the fitter we are to comfort others. We see many men will speak very good things, but they do but personate sorrow, and personate comfort. It comes from them without feeling. As he saith, If thou didst believe these things that thou speakest, wouldst thou ever say them so? He that speaks good things without experience, he speaks as if he did never believe them. Those that speak things with experience, that have wrought them upon their hearts and spirits, there is such a demonstration in the manner of their speaking, of a spirit of love and meekness, and compassion, that it prevails marvellously. It is so true that our Saviour Christ himself, that he might have the more tender bowels of compassion towards us, he made it one end of his incarnation, as it is pressed again and again in Heb. ii. and Heb. iv. The apostle dwells upon it, 'It became him to be man, to take upon him our infirmities, that he might be a merciful Redeemer, a merciful high priest,' Heb. ii. 17. It was one end of his incarnation that he might not only save us, but that he might be a merciful Redeemer, that he might have experience of our infirmities. Of persecution, he was persecuted himself; of want, he wanted himself; of temptation, he was tempted himself; of wrath, he felt it himself, 'My God, my God, why hast thou forsaken me?' Mark xv. 34.

Here is the comfort of a Christian soul, that Christ hath begun to him in all. Therefore it became him to be man, not only to redeem us, but to be a merciful high priest, a comfortable high priest.

The way, then, you see, how to comfort others, is, to get our own hearts sensible of spiritual comfort. Two irons, if they be both hot, do close together presently, but unless both be hot, they do not join together handsomely. So that that makes us join together strongly is, if two spirits meet, and both be warm; if one godly man comfort another godly man; if one holy man labour to breed an impression of heat in another, there is a knitting of both spirits, they join strongly together. Therefore we ought to labour to get experience, that we may comfort others, seeing none can comfort so well as experimental Christians.

Quest. Why is experience such an enabling to spiritual comfort?

Ans. 1. I answer, *because it brings the comfort home to our own souls.* The devil knows comfort well enough, but he feels none. Experience helps faith, it helps all other knowledge. Our Saviour Christ is said to learn by experience, for 'he learned obedience in that he suffered,' Heb. v. 8. Experience is such a means of the increasing of knowledge, as that it bettered the knowledge of Christ, that had all knowledge in him. He had knowledge by looking upon God, being the 'wisdom of God,' 1 Cor. i. 30, yet he learned somewhat by the experience, he bettered himself by experience. He knew what to bear the cross was by experience. He knew what infirmities were by experience. He knew what he could suffer by experience. So it added to his knowledge as man. And so the angels themselves are continual students in the mysteries of the gospel. They get experimental knowledge to the knowledge that they have inbred, and that knowledge that they have by the presence of God. To that they add experimental knowledge.

So then, if it bettered the knowledge of our blessed Saviour, and increased it, [if] it was a new way increased by experience, and it adds to the knowledge of the angels, much more to ours.

2. Then, again, *it gains a great confidence in the speaker;* for what we speak with experience, we speak with a great deal of boldness.

3. Again, experimental comforts, those that we have felt ourselves, and have felt likewise the grievance, *we speak them with such expressions as no other can do*, in the apprehension of the party whom we comfort, so well as an experienced person. For he goes about the work tenderly and gently and lovingly, because he hath been in the same himself. And that is the reason that the apostle St Paul, in the place I named before, Gal. vi. 1, presseth this duty upon spiritual men, especially because themselves have been tempted, and may be tempted. Those that have been tempted, and think they may be afterward, this doth wondrously fit them for this work of comforting others. But to add a little in this point, to shew how to comfort others by our own experience and skill, I spake before of an art of comforting ourselves. There is a skill likewise in comforting others. Even as we comfort ourselves, in that method we must comfort others. When we comfort ourselves, we must first consider our need of comfort, search our wounds, our maladies, have them fresh in our sight, that so we may be forced to seek for comfort; and as we ought to do this daily, so when we are to comfort others,

(1.) We ought not only to comfort them, *but to search them as much as we can*, what sin is in them, and what misery is upon them, and acquaint them with their own estate that they are in, as far as we can discern. We may judge of them partly by ourselves. For we must not prostitute comforts to persons that are indisposed, till we see them fitted. God doth comfort, but it is the abject. Christ heals, but [it] is the wounded spirit. He came to seek, but it is those that are lost. He came to ease, but it is those that are 'heavy laden.' Therefore, that we may comfort them to purpose, we ought to shew, and discover to them, what estate they are in, that we may force them to comfort, if they be not enemies to comfort and to their own souls.

He is an unwise physician that administers cordials before he gives preparatives to carry away the noisome humours. They will do little good. We ought therefore to prepare them this way, if we intend to do them good.

(2.) And then when we see what need they stand in, *bring them to Christ and the covenant of grace.* That is the best way to comfort them, to bring them to see that God is their Father, when we discern some signs of grace in them. For this is the main stop in all comfort, that there is none but they shall find by experience. They are ready to say, You teach wondrous comforts, that there is an inheritance in heaven that God hath provided; and on earth, there is an issue of all for good, and there is a presence of God in troubles! This is true; but how shall I know this belongs to me? This is the cavil of flesh and blood, that turns the back to the most heavenly comforts that are. The main and principal thing therefore in dealing with others, and with our own hearts, is to let them see that there are some signs and evidences that they are in the covenant of grace, that they belong to God. Unless we see that, all the comfort we can give them is to tell them that they are not yet sunk into hell, and that they have space to repent. But as long as men live in sinful courses, that they are not in a state of grace, we can tell them no comfort, except they will devise a new Scripture, a new Bible. If they do so, they may have comfort. But this word of God, God herein speaks no comfort to persons that live in sin, and will do so. We should labour therefore to discern some evidence that they are in the state of grace.

And ofttimes those are indeed most entitled to comfort that think it furthest from them. Therefore we should acquaint them with the conditions of the covenant of grace, that God looks to truth. Therefore if we discern any true, broken, humble spirit, a hungering and a thirsting after righteousness, and a desire of comfort, 'Blessed are those that hunger and thirst,' Mat. v. 6; it belongs to them, we may comfort them. If we see spiritual poverty, that they see their wants, and would be supplied, 'Blessed are the poor in spirit,' Mat. v. 3; 'Be of good comfort,' Christ calls such, Mat. x. 49. If they see and feel the burden of their sins, we may comfort them. Christ calls them, 'Come unto me, ye that are weary and heavy laden,' Mat. xi. 28. If we discern spiritual and heavenly desires to grow in grace and overcome their corruptions, if we discover and discern this in their practice and obedience, 'God will fulfil the desires of them that fear him,' Ps. cxlv. 19. And he accepts the will for the deed.

There is a desire of happiness in nature that comforts not a man. It is no sign of grace to desire to be free from hell and to be in heaven. It is a natural desire. Every creature wishes well to heaven. But if there be a desire of the means that tend to heaven, a desire of grace, these are evidences of grace. These are the pulses that we may find grace by; when they see their infirmities, and groan under them, and would be better, and complain that they are not better, and are out of love with their own hearts. There is a combat in their hearts, they are not friends with themselves. When we see this inward conflict, and a desire to better, and to get victories against their corruptions, though there be many corruptions and weaknesses, a man may safely say, they are in a state of grace, they are on the mending hand. For 'Christ will not break the bruised reed, nor quench the smoking flax,' Mat. xii. 20. 'And where he hath begun a good work, he will perfect it to the day of the Lord,' Philip. i. 6. He will cherish these weak beginnings, therefore we may comfort them on good ground.

(3.) Then, besides that, in our dealing with them, when we have discovered, by some evidence, that they belong to the covenant, that we see, by some love to good things, and to God's image in his children, and by other evidences, then we may comfort them boldly; *and then to fetch from our own experience*, what a comfort will it be to such! When we can say, My estate was as yours is; I found those corruptions that you groan under; I allowed not myself in them as you do not. When a man can say from his own experience, that notwithstanding these I have evident signs of God's Spirit that I am his, then he can comfort others by his own experience.

(4.) And what a comfort is it *to go to the experiments* of Scripture!* It is an excellent way. As now, let a man be deserted of God, David will comfort him by his experience, Ps. lxxvii. 2, 8, 10, where he saith he found God as his enemy; and as Job saith, 'the terrors of God drank up his spirit,' Job vi. 4. Be of good comfort! David would come and comfort thee if he were alive. If the terror of God be against thee for sin, that thy conscience is awakened, be of good comfort! Christ, if he were on earth,

* That is, 'experiences' = examples.—G.

would shew thee by his own example that he endured that desertion on the cross: 'My God, my God, why hast thou forsaken me?' Mark xv. 34. If thou be molested and vexed with Satan, Job will comfort thee by his example. His book is most of it combating and comfort. And so for all other grievances, go to the Scriptures. Whatsoever is 'written, is written for our learning,' Pray to God, and he will hear thee as he did Elias.

Obj. Oh! but Elias was an excellent man.

Ans. The Scripture prevents* the objection: 'he was a man subject to infirmities,' James v. 17. If God heard him, he will hear thee. Believe in Christ, as Abraham did, 'the father of the faithful,' in the promised Messiah, and he will forgive thee all thy sins.

Obj. Oh! but he had a strong faith.

Ans. What hath the Scripture to take away this objection? In Rom. iv. 23, 'This was not written for Abraham only, but for those that believe with the faith of Abraham.'

Obj. Aye, but I am a wretched sinner, there is little hope of me.

Ans. Yes! St Paul will come and comfort thee by his example and experience: 'This is a faithful saying, that Jesus Christ came into the world to save sinners, of whom I am the chief,' 1 Tim. i. 15.

Obj. Aye, he came to save such sinners as St Paul was.

Ans. Aye, saith St Paul, 'and that I might be an example to all that shall believe in Christ, to the end of the world,' 1 Tim. i. 16. He takes away that objection. And the apostle is so heavenly wise, that where he speaks of privileges, he enlargeth it to others. 'There is no condemnation to them that are in Christ Jesus,' Rom. viii. 1. 'And what shall separate us from the love of God?' ver. 35. But when he speaks of matter of abasement, that we may see that he was, in regard of his corruptions, as much humbled as we, then he speaks in his own person: 'O wretched man that I am! who shall deliver me from this body of death?' Rom. vii. 24. Therefore his comforts belong to thee. Now, as these examples in Scripture, and the experiences of God's children there, be applicable to us, so much more the experience of God's children that are alive. Therefore we should be willing to do offices of comfort in this kind.

Those that are of ability, either men or women, they will have in their houses somewhat to comfort others, they will have strong waters, and cordials, and medicines; and they account it a glory to have somewhat that their neighbours may be beholden to them for. And though they bestow it freely, yet they think and account it a sufficient recompence that they can be beneficial to others. People do this for things of this life, and think they deserve a great deal of respect for their goodness in this kind. Surely, if we consider, there is a life that needs comfort more than this fading life, and there are miseries that pinch us more than the miseries of the body! Every one should labour to have in the house of his soul somewhat, some strong waters of comfort, that he may be able to tell others, This refreshed my soul, this hath done me good; I give you no worse than I took myself first. This wondrously commends the comfort in the party that gives it, and it commends it to the party that receives it, to take benefit by the comforts of other men. For is it not a strengthening to our case when another shall say to our comfort, It was my case? Is it not sealed by the evidence of two? Surely it is a great assurance when we have another to tell us his experience.

Use 1. Again, if this be God's order, that he will convey comfort to us

* That is, 'anticipates.'—G.

by others, then *we ought to depend upon God's ordinance*, we ought to expect comfort one from another, especially from the ministers, who are messengers of comfort. I speak it the rather, because in what degree we neglect any one means that God hath ordained to comfort us, though he be the God of comfort, yet in that measure we are sure to want comfort. And this is one principal ordinance, the ministry, and the communion of saints.

Some there be that will neglect the means of salvation. They have dead spirits, and live and die so, for the most part. They have much ado to recover comfort. Those men that retire themselves, that will work all out of the flint themselves, they are commonly uncomfortable. God hath ordained one to help another, as in an arch one stone strengtheneth another. The ministry especially is ordained for comfort.

2. And likewise God hath ordained *one Christian to comfort another*, as well as the ministers. Let us therefore regard much the communion of saints. Let one Christian labour to comfort another, and every one labour to be fit to receive comfort from others, labour to have humble and willing spirits. It is so true that God doth convey comfort, even by common Christians as well as the ministers, that St Paul himself, Rom. i. 12; he desires to see the Romans, 'that he might receive mutual comfort from them.' For a minister may have more knowledge and book-learning perhaps than another Christian that may have better experience than he, especially in some things; and there is not the meanest Christian but he may comfort the greatest clerk in the world, and help him by his experience that God hath shewed to him, by declaring how God shewed him comfort at such a time, and upon such an occasion. The experience of God's people, the meanest of them may help the best Christians. Therefore he will have none to be neglected.

There is never a member of Christ's body, but hath some ability to comfort another; for Christ hath no dead members. God will have it so, because he will have one Christian to honour another, and to honour them from the knowledge of the use and necessity that one hath of another. If God should not derive comfort from one to another in some degree, and from the meanest to the greatest, one would despise another. But God will not have it so. He will have the communion of saints valued to the end of the world. What will one Christian regard another, what would weak Christians regard the strong, and what would strong Christians regard the weak, if there were not a continual supply one from another? Therefore God hath ordained that by the ministry, and by the communion of saints, we should comfort one another.

Let us not think that this doth not concern us. It concerns us all. Therefore when we have any trouble in mind, let us regard the communion of saints, let us regard acquaintance. And let us know this, that God will hold us in heaviness till we have used all the means that he hath appointed. If one help not, perhaps another will; perhaps the ministry will help, perhaps acquaintance will help. But if we find not comfort in one, let us go over all. And, would you have more? Christ himself, did he not take two disciples into the garden with him when his spirit was heavy? Did not he know that God had ordained one to comfort another? 'Two are better than one,' Eccles. iv. 9. If one be alone, he shall be a-cold, but if there be two, they heat one another. If there be one alone, there can hardly be true spiritual heat. If two be together, if one fall, 'the other may raise him up,' Eccles. iv. 10, but if one be alone and fall, who shall raise him up? It is meant spiritually, as well as bodily and outwardly by Solomon.

We cannot have a better president* than our blessed Saviour. Solitariness in such times in spiritual desertion 'it is the hour of temptation.' When did the devil set on Christ? When he was alone. It was the fittest time to tempt him when Christ was severed. So the devil sets on single persons when they are alone, and tempts them, and presseth them with variety of temptations. 'Woe to him that is alone,' Eccles. iv. 10. Christ sent his disciples by two and two, that one might comfort another, and one might strengthen another, Mark vi. 7.

Now, though in particular it belong to ministers in a more eminent sort; yet let every one lay it to heart, you ought to have abilities to comfort others, and to receive comfort of others. And consider it is an angelical work to comfort others. We imitate God himself, and the most excellent creatures the angels, whose office is to comfort. Even our very Saviour, they came to comfort him in his greatest extremity. A man is a god to a man when he comforts. When he discomforts, and directs, and withdraws, he is a devil to a man. Men are beasts to men, devils to men, that way. But he that is an instrument to convey comfort, he is a god to a man. God is the God of comfort. Thou art in the place of God to a man when thou comfortest him, thou shalt save thyself and others. God honours men with his own title when they comfort. Not only ministers, but others save men. Thou shalt 'gain thy brother,' by thy admonition and reproof. What greater honour can ye have than God's own title, to be saviours one of another? It is the office, I say, of angels. They were sent to comfort Christ. It is their duty to pitch their tents about God's children, to suggest holy thoughts, as the devil suggests evil, and to be about us, though we think not of it. Nay, it is not only an angelical work, but it is the work of God's Spirit. The sweetest style of the Holy Ghost is to be a 'comforter.'

What shall we think of cursed spirits that insult over others' misery, that give them gall to eat, and vinegar to drink, that add affliction to the afflicted? What shall we say to barren spirits, that have not a word of comfort to say, but come in a profane and dead manner, I am sorry to see you thus, and I hope you will better. Barren soul, as the wilderness! What! a member of Christ, of the communion of saints, and no way furnished, no word of comfort to a distressed soul! We may know the comfort we have ourselves to be comfort indeed, and from the grace and favour of God, when we have hearts enlarged to do good to others with it.

How do gifts and grace differ, to add that useful distinction? And a man may have a great many gifts and be proud, and full of envy, and have a devilish poisonful spirit to draw all to himself, and not be good, but be carried with self-love, and die a devil, notwithstanding his excellent parts. Why? Here are such gifts, and parts, but there is a bitter root of self-love to draw all to himself, to deify himself, to make an idol of himself. But grace with gifts works otherwise. That turns all by a spirit of love and humility to the good of others.

There is no envy in a gracious heart. So far forth as it is gracious there is no pride, no scorn to do good to others. How shall we distinguish men of excellent parts, whether they be Christians or not Christians? They have both of them wit and memory, they have both courage. Aye, but whether of them improve their parts and abilities most to the good of others? Whether of them hath the most humble spirit, the most loving

* That is, 'precedent.'—G.

spirit, the most discreet spirit, to be witty to do good to others upon all advantages. There is the Christian that hath God's grace with his gifts. But for the other, 'Knowledge puffeth up,' saith the apostle, 1 Cor. viii. 1. What edifies and builds us? 'Love edifieth,' 1 Cor. viii. 1. Knowledge gathers many materials, stone, and timber, &c. What builds the house, the body of Christ? It is a loving and humble spirit.

Therefore let us think that we have nothing in Christianity, by any parts we have, of memory or wit, or reading, &c., unless we have a humble spirit, that we can deny ourselves and debase ourselves to do good to others upon all the best advantages; or else we have not the spirit of Christ, that sweet spirit of Christ that denied himself to do good to us.

Where grace is established once, and is in the right nature, there is a public mind; and it is one of the best signs of a heart that is fashioned to the image of Christ, who denied himself, and became all in all to us, to have a public mind, to have self-love killed, to think I have nothing to purpose as I should have, except I can make use of it to the good of others. Therefore let us be willing to do good in this kind.

And as I said, let us make use of comfort from others. Think that they are reserved to the times and place where thou livest, that thou mightest make use of them. Therefore those that need comfort should not flatter themselves in their grief, but humbly depend upon the means that God hath ordained. And let every man think, what if God have hid my comfort in another man? What if he have given him 'the tongue of the learned,' Isa. l. 4, to speak a word in season unto me? Let no man think to master his trouble and grief by himself. We are members of the body, and the good that God will convey to us, must be from and by others. Therefore it is a mutual duty. Those that have comfort ought to comfort others; and those that do need comfort, ought to repair to others. It is the ordinance of God, as Job saith, for one of 'a thousand to shew a man his righteousness,' Job xxxiii. 23. Though a man be never so wise, yet sometimes he knows not his own comfort. He knows not that portion of comfort that belongs to him, till some others discover it to him. Physicians will have others to heal themselves, to judge of their diseases; and certainly one reason why persons that are excellent in themselves, have passed their days in darkness, it hath been this, that they think to overmaster their heaviness and distraction of spirit with their own reason, &c., which will not be. God, what he will do, he will do by his own means and ordinance.

Use 3. Let us therefore learn, hence, *to see the goodness of God*, that besides the ministry that he hath ordained, and the salvation that he keeps for us, and the promises that he hath given us, and the angels that attend us, &c., he doth even ordain others, that are men, and have bodies with ourselves, other fellow-Christians, to be instruments to convey comfort. He trains them up, that they may be able to comfort, and do good to us; and he hides the good he intends to us in them, and conveys it to us by them. It is a special goodness of God, that everything should tend to our good. Thus all things are for us. The sufferings of others tend to increase our comfort, and the comfort of others is for our comfort. There is such a sweet prudence in directing us to heaven, that God makes everything help; not only our own troubles that we suffer ourselves, but he doth sweetly turn the troubles of others, and the comforts of others to our good.

It ministereth an argument of praising and blessing of God; and that we should answer him in the like, that as he hath devised all the ways that may be of comforting us, of turning all to our good, that that we suffer ourselves, and that that others suffer; so we should study by all means and ways to set forth his glory, and no way to grieve the Spirit of so gracious a God, that thus every way intends our comfort.

VERSE 5.

'*For as the sufferings of Christ abound in us, so our consolations also abound by Christ.*' Here the blessed apostle shews the reason why his heart was so enlarged, as we see in ver. 3, in the midst of his troubles and persecutions, to bless God. There was good reason; for as his afflictions, so his consolations abounded. It is a reason, likewise, of his ability to comfort others, the reason why he was fitted to comfort others, because he found comfort abound in himself in his sufferings. So they have a double reference to the words before. But to take the words in themselves,

'*As the sufferings of Christ abound,*' *&c.* It is an excellent portion of Scripture, and that which I should have a great deal of encouragement to speak of, if the times and disposition of the hearers were for it; for it is a text of comfort for those that suffer persecution, that suffer affliction for the gospel. Now, because we do not suffer, or at least we suffer not any great matter (except it be a reproach, or the like, which is a matter of nothing, but a chip of the cross, a trifle), therefore we hear these matters of comfort against the disgrace of the cross of Christ, with dead hearts. But we know not what we are reserved to; therefore we must learn somewhat to store up, though we have not present use of it. The several branches of divine truths, that may be observed from these words, are first this, *That the sufferings of Christians may abound.* They are many in this world, and they may be more still. 'For as the sufferings of Christ *abound in us,*' &c.

Secondly, *what we ought to think of those sufferings, what judgment we are to have of them.* 'They are the sufferings of Christ.'

Thirdly, that being the sufferings of Christ, *he will not destitute* us of comfort*; but we have our comfort increased in a proportion answerable to our troubles. 'So our consolations,' &c.

The fourth point is, *by whom and in whom all this is.* This strange work is by Christ. The balancing of these two so sweetly together, crosses and comforts, they come both from one hand, both from one spring, 'the sufferings of Christ,' and the comforts of Christ, and both abound. Our troubles are for him, and our comforts are by him. So here is sufferings and comfort, increase of suffering, increase of comfort, sufferings for Christ, and comfort by Christ. You see them balanced together, and you see which weighs down the balance. Comfort by Christ weighs down sufferings for Christ. The good is greater than the ill. It is a point of wondrous comfort. The ark, you know, mounted up as the waters mounted up, when the waters overflowed the world. So it is here in this verse. There is a mounting of the waters, a rising of the waters above the mountains. Afflictions increase, and grow higher and higher; but be of good comfort, here is the ark above the waters, here is consolation above all. As our sufferings for Christ increase, so our consolations, likewise, by Christ increase.

For the first, I will be very short in it.

Doct. The sufferings of Christ abound in us.

* That is, 'deprive.'—G.

There is nobody in this world, but first or last, if they live any long time, they must suffer; and as a man is in degrees of goodness, so his sufferings must abound. The better man, the more sufferings. Sufferings abounded in St Paul. It doth not abound in all. That was personal in St Paul, to abound in sufferings. It doth not go out of the person of St Paul, and such as St Paul was. All must suffer, but not in a like measure. There are several cups. All do not abound in sufferings, as all do not abound in grace and strength. Those that are of a higher rank, their sufferings abound more. God doth not use an exact proportion in afflictions, but that which we call geometrical, a proportion appliable to the strength of the sufferer. Christ, as he had more strength than any, so he suffered more than any; and St Paul, having an extraordinary measure of strength, he suffered more than all the apostles. The sufferings of Christ abounded in him; but all must suffer.

What is the reason of it? What is the reason that troubles abound thus? Surely if we look to God, the devil, the world, ourselves, we shall see reasons enough.

Reason 1. If we look to *God and Christ, we are ordained to be conformable to Christ.* We must be conformable to Christ in sufferings first, before we be in glory. It is God's decree, we are called to sufferings, as well as to be believing. We must answer God's call. Every Christian must resolve to take up his cross every day, some degree of the cross or other. Reproach for Christ's sake is a suffering. The scorn of the world is the rebuke of Christ. We are called to suffering, as well as to glory. It is part of our effectual calling, it is an appendix, an accessory thing to the main. We must take grace with suffering, and it is well we may have it so too. It is well that we have the state of grace here, and glory hereafter, with suffering.

Reason 2. If we look *to the devil, there must be suffering.* Satan is the prince of the world. He is the prince of an opposite kingdom.

Reason 3. If we consider *what place we live in when we are taken out of the world to the blessed estate of Christians,* to be members of Christ and heirs of heaven. The world is strange to us, and we are strangers to it. Crosses and afflictions are necessary for them that are travellers. We would think else that we were at home, and forget our country. Considering the condition we live in, we must have sufferings. If we consider the disposition of the parties among whom we live, they are people of an opposite spirit. Therefore they malign us, because we are taken from among them; and though there be no opposition shewed to them, yet it upbraids enough their cursed estate when they see others taken from them. That speaks loud enough that their course is naught, that they see others mislike it. The world, that is led by the spirit of Satan, maligns them that are better than themselves. There is opposition between the seed of the serpent and the seed of the woman. So long as there are wicked men, that are instruments and organs of the devil, God's children must be opposed. While there is a devil suffered to be 'the god of the world,' 2 Cor. iv. 4, and so long as he hath so strong a faction in the world as he hath, 'the children of disobedience,' Eph. v. 6, in whom he rules, God's children shall never want suffering.

Reason 4. If we *regard ourselves,* we have always in ourselves good and bad. That which is good, we have need of sufferings to exercise it and to know it; for if there were no sufferings, how should we know what good we have?

(1.) Is it not a great comfort to a Christian, when he knows by suffering that he hath more patience than he looked for, that he hath more faith than he thought he had, that he hath more love to God, that he can endure to suffer more for God than ever he thought he could, that he hath more resigning of his heart and giving up of himself than he thought of, that he can deny the world, which he thought he could not have done? What a comfort is it to a Christian when he knows by suffering what he can do and what he cannot do. It is good, therefore, and necessary in regard of ourselves, that we may know our strength.

(2.) In regard, likewise, of the evil that is in us, suffer we must. For there must be a daily purging; and the best instruments to scour us are wicked men, the devil's instruments. It is unfit for God's children to take that base office on them, for one Christian to fall upon another. It is good there should be an opposite faction in the world, that there should be wicked men, in regard of the ill that is in us. There is somewhat to be scoured and purged out. So we see, whether we look upward or downward, to God, or to the devil, or to the faction of the devil in the world, or to ourselves, for good or evil, it is necessary that there should be some afflictions.

And to speak a little more home to us, there must be sufferings in this regard, because the church alway hath corruption and soil, especially in prosperity. If a man look to the churches in Germany, that have suffered much of late,* and mark what reports hath been given of them, how cold and dull they were in the possession of the gospel, how indifferent they were, how they valued not that invaluable pearl, a man shall see that suffering was needful to scour them. If a man look to the state of this city, though there be many good people (the Lord increase the number of them), yet, if a man consider with what cold affections the blessed truth of God is entertained, which I say is above all, what is all that we enjoy? What is our peace to the gospel of peace? What is our prosperity, and what is all, to the blessed truth of salvation? If we had not that, wherein were not the Turks as good as we? For all other things, were not other nations as good as we? Certainly yes. For policy, and other beauty, and ornaments, and rarities, what have we to lift up our excellency but the continuance of the blessed doctrine of salvation, whereby our souls are begotten to God, to 'an inheritance immortal, undefiled, reserved in the heavens?' 1 Peter i. 4. Now, the cold esteem of this certainly will enforce in time a national suffering, unless there be a national repentance. It is true of every particular Christian. As we see, when the rain and the heat join together, they breed as well weeds as corn, so prosperity and the blessings of God, they have brought up in us much weeds as well as good corn; and there must be a time of weeding and purging in regard of our state in this world. We are gathering soil every day. There must be a suffering one time or other.

Obj. But some will say, What! do you talk of suffering? Now is a time of peace. We live among Christians, and not pagans and Turks; and for our adversaries, though they be many, yet they do not shew themselves.

Ans. St Austin answers this in himself. Do but begin to live as a Christian should, and see if thou shalt not be used unchristianly of them that are Christians in name, but not in deed. A suffering from Christians is more sharp than that of enemies. Those that are fleshly will be ready to be injurious; those that are carnal, formal professors, will be ready to offer some disgrace or other to those that are more spiritual than themselves.

There is a threefold suffering in the church since Christ's time. The first was of doctrine concerning the natures of Christ. There was persecution about that; for there were Arians that denied the Godhead, and others

* That is, 1624–5. Cf. note *o**.—G.

that denied the manhood of Christ,* and such like great enemies of the church. Afterward, in popery, they set on Christ's offices, and divided his kingly and priestly and prophetical office, to the pope, to saints, to works, and such like, encroaching upon them, and persecuting with fire and faggot all those that gave all to Christ, and did not sacrilegiously give anything to the creature.

But there is a persecution as ill as any of these, where the nature and offices of Christ are well enough understood, where the power of religion is opposed by others, when so much religion as is necessary to bring a man to heaven is opposed; for it is not the knowledge of the nature, and offices, and benefits by Christ, but it is a knowledge that hath obedience with it that must bring us to heaven, a knowledge with self-denial, a knowledge with selling and parting with all our lusts and wicked courses, that will not stand with the gospel.

Now, where this is, this cannot be brooked by any means, and it goes under as great disgrace, as heresies did in former times. So that it is matter of reproach to have so much religion as is necessarily required of a man before he can be saved. That which the world disgraces is necessary to every man before he can be saved, that is, a strict giving up of himself to God, and a watching over his ways as much as human frailty will permit, a conscionable† endeavour in all things to please God, out of conscience and thankfulness to God. We must not think to come to heaven without that. It will not be. 'Without holiness none shall see God.' This despised holiness, this maligned holiness, is that which is necessary to bring us to heaven, and so much as is necessary to bring us to heaven is disgraced everywhere.

Those that resolve to be Christians in good earnest, and would have comfort on their deathbed and in the times of persecution, they must endure to be set light by, to bear the reproach of Christ. They must resolve on this beforehand, that when these things come to pass, we be not offended.

Use. Well, then, to make a little use of this. Since there must be troubles and crosses, and they must increase if we will be Christians, let this teach us *to judge aright of those that are ill thought on in the world ofttimes*, when we see nothing but good in their carriage. Oh, what imputations are laid on them! You may see what an indiscreet man he was, you may see that he lacked wisdom and policy, else he might have kept himself out of this trouble. I would ask such a party, Had not Christ as much wisdom as thee? He was the 'wisdom of the Father.' Did he keep out of reproaches? Was he not reproached as a troublesome man, as an enemy to Cæsar, and taxed for base things, as a 'winebibber,' &c., Mat. xi. 19, and one that 'had a devil,' Mat. xi. 18, and many other ways? Was not St Paul as discreet as we are, who in our understanding and conceit are ready to conceive distastefully of men that suffer anything for the gospel? And yet, notwithstanding, all his wisdom kept him not from the cross, 'but the cross abides me,' saith he, 'everywhere,' 2 Cor. i. 5. The devil and the cross follow God's children wheresoever they go. All their wisdom and holiness cannot keep them from it, because God hath decreed it and called them to it, and they must be conformable to Christ.

Therefore, let us take heed that we do not suffer men to suffer in our conceits, when they suffer in a good cause, the cross of Christ, reproachful things, base death, &c. Afflictions are therefore called the cross, because there is a kind of baseness with them, and as it is so, so carnal men esteem it.

* That is, the Gnostics.—G.

† That is, 'conscientious.'—G.

Presently with the suffering there goes a taint, and an abasing in their conceit, of those men that suffer in a good cause. There is a diminishing conceit goes in carnal men of that which should be their glory. 'Our crosses abound,' 2 Cor. i. 5. But what ought we to judge of these crosses?

Doct. They are the sufferings of Christ.

Quest. Why? Christ suffers nothing; he is in heaven, in glory. How can he suffer? This is to disparage his glorious estate, to make him suffer anything.

Ans. I answer, the sufferings of Christ, they are twofold. The sufferings of Christ's person, that which he suffered himself, which were propitiatory and satisfactory* for our redemption; and the sufferings of Christ in his mystical body, which likewise is called Christ. For Christ in Scripture is taken either for Christ himself, or for the members of Christ. 'Why persecutest thou me?' saith he to Saul, Acts ix. 4; or for the whole body mystical with the head, 1 Cor. xii. 27. 'So is Christ.' Christ, Head and members, is called Christ. Now, when he calls the sufferings of the church the sufferings of Christ, he means not the sufferings of Christ in his own person; for he suffers nothing; he is out of all the malice of persecutors; they cannot reach to heaven to Christ; but he means the sufferings of Christ in his mystical body. These are called 'the sufferings of Christ.'

Quest. Why are these called the sufferings of Christ?

Ans. (1.) Partly, because they are the *sufferings of mystical Christ*, the body of Christ, the church. For the church, the company of true believers, are the fulness of Christ, they make up the mystical body of Christ. Therefore when they suffer, he that is the head suffers.

(2.) Again, they are called the sufferings of Christ, those that his members and children suffer, *because they are for Christ*, they are in his quarrel, they are for his truth, for his cause, and by his appointment he calls us to suffering. It is for his cause. In our intendment we intend to suffer for Christ, to maintain his cause. They are the sufferings of Christ likewise in the intent of the opposites and enemies. They persecute us for some goodness they see in us. They persecute the cause and truth of Christ in us. So they are the sufferings of Christ both ways.

(3.) Especially, they are the sufferings of Christ *by way of sympathy;* because Christ doth impute them to himself. 'The sufferings of Christ.' It is a phrase that springs from the near union that is between Christ and his members, the church; which is as near or nearer than any natural union between the head and members. Hereupon it comes that we are said to suffer with him, to die with him, to be crucified with him, to ascend with him, to sit in heavenly places with him, to judge the world with him, to do all with him by reason of this union. And he is said to suffer with us, to be afflicted in us, to be reproached with us. He was stoned in Stephen, he was persecuted by Saul, he was beheaded in Paul, he was burned with the martyrs, he was banished with the Christians, and he suffers in all his children. Not that he doth so in his own person, but because it pleaseth him, by reason of the near communion that is between him and us, to take that which is done to his members, as done to himself. Therefore they are called 'the sufferings of Christ.' He suffers when we suffer, and we suffer when he suffers.

The difference is, all the comforts in our sufferings, it comes from communion in his sufferings, because he is our surety. For why are we encouraged to suffer by way of sympathy and communion with him? Be-

* That is, 'satisfying.'—G.

cause he in love died for us, and was crucified for us, and abased for us, and shamed for us. And when is the soul encouraged to suffer afflictions for Christ? When it hath a little felt the wrath of God that Christ suffered for it. Oh, how much am I beholden to God for Christ, that endured the whole wrath of God? They are 'the sufferings of Christ.' This is a wondrous comfortable point; and it is a notion that doth sweeten the bitterest crosses, that they are the sufferings of Christ. Not only that we are conformable to Christ in them, we suffer as he did, but they are 'the sufferings of Christ,' he imputes them as done to him, he suffers with us.

(4.) And another reason, why they are the sufferings of Christ, it is because he not only takes it as done to himself, *but he is present with them.* He was with St Paul in the dungeon, he was with the three young men in the fiery furnace. There were three put in, and there was a fourth, which was Christ, the Son of God (*j*). He goes with the martyrs to the prison, to the stake. He is with them till he has brought them to heaven. He is present with them when they suffer.

Here I must, before I come to make use of it, distinguish between the crosses, and sufferings of Christ, and of ordinary sufferings as men.

[1.] Something in this vale of misery *we suffer as creatures:* as being subject to mutability and change, because this is a world of changes. In this sublunary world there is nothing but changes. Thus we suffer as creatures. All creatures are subject to vanity, and complain and groan under it.

[2.] Somewhat we suffer *as men.* It is the common condition of men. This nature of ours, since the fall, is subject to sicknesses, to crosses, and pain, and casualties. Every day brings new crosses with it. This we suffer as men.

[3.] Now the sufferings of Christians, *as religious holy men,* those are here meant, those are 'the sufferings of Christ.' Yet notwithstanding the sufferings as men, by the Spirit of God, help our conformity to Christ, by them the flesh is purged, and the Spirit strengthened, and weaning from the world is wrought, and a desire to heaven.

By the daily crosses we suffer as men, not for religion, we are much bettered; and those in some sort may be called the sufferings of Christ, because by them we are conformed to Christ more in holiness. We grow more out of love with the world, and more heavenly minded. This distinction is necessary to know which are best, the sufferings of Christians as good men.

Use. It is a point, I say, of wondrous comfort. That we should be conformable in our sufferings with our head Christ Jesus, our glorified head in heaven, is it not a wondrous comfort? Nay, is it not a glory? It is a wondrous glory that God will set us apart to do any thing, that God will take any thing of us, much more that he will single us out to be champions in his quarrel, and more, that he will triumph in us, that the comfort shall abound.

To give an instance. If a monarch should redeem a slave, a traitor from prison, and take him to fight in the quarrel of his own son, to be his champion, were it not an honour? So the very sufferings for Christ are an encouragement. The disgraces, and whatsoever they are that we suffer in a good cause, they are ensigns of honour, they are badges of honour of Christian knighthood. If a golden fleece, or a garter,* or such things, be accounted so highly of and glorified in, because they are favours, &c., much more should the sufferings for Christ be glorified in, as ensigns of the love of God, and of our Christian profession. When we fight under Christ's

* That is, the knightly 'orders' so designated.—G.

banner, we are like to Christ. We are conformable to him. He went before, and we follow his steps; 'and if we suffer with him, we shall be glorified with him,' Rom. viii. 17.

Therefore be not discouraged. That which we think to be matter of discouragement, it should be our crown. It is our crown to suffer reproach in a good cause. It is a sign God favours us, when he takes our credit, our goods, or our life to honour himself by. Is it not an honour to us? Doth he take anything from us but he gives us better? He takes our goods, but he gives us himself. He takes our liberty, but he gives us enlargement of conscience. He takes our life, but he gives us heaven. If he take anything from us, for to seal his truth, and stand out in his quarrel, as Christ saith, he 'gives an hundredfold' in this world, that is a gracious spirit of contentment and comfort.

We have God himself. Hath not he more that hath the spring than he that hath twenty cisterns? Those that have riches, and place, and friends, they have cisterns; but he that suffers for God, and for Christ, he hath Christ, he hath God, he hath the spring to go to. If all be taken from him, he hath God the spring to go to. If all particular beams, he hath the sun. It is durable, wondrous comfort to suffer for Christ's sake.

Therefore, let it encourage us in a good course, notwithstanding all the opposition we meet with in the world; let us here learn what is our duty. Let the malicious world judge, or say, or do what they will; if God be on our side, 'who can be against us?' Rom. viii. 33, 34. And if we suffer anything for Christ, he suffers with us, and in us, and he will triumph in us over all these sufferings at last.

I will add no more, to set an edge upon that I have said, than this, [as] 'they are the sufferings of Christ,' we should be many ways encouraged to suffer for him. For did not he suffer for us that, which if all the creatures in heaven and earth had suffered, they would have sunk under it, the wrath of God? And what good have we by his sufferings? Are we not freed from hell and damnation? and have we not title to heaven? Hath he suffered in his person so much for us, and shall not we be content to suffer for him, and his mystical body, that in his own body suffered so much for us?

Again, when we suffer in his quarrel, we suffer not only for him that suffered for us, but we suffer for him that sits at the right hand of God, that is glorious in heaven, 'the King of kings, and Lord of lords.' Our sufferings are sufferings for him that hath done so much for us, and for him that is so able now to over-rule all, to crush our enemies; for him that is so able now to minister comfort by his Spirit. This is a notable encouragement, that they are the sufferings of Christ, that is, so glorious as he is, and that will reward every suffering, and every disgrace. We shall be paid well for every suffering. We shall lose nothing.

And will not this encourage us likewise to suffer for Christ's sake, because he will be with us in all our sufferings. He will not leave us alone. It is his cause, and he will stand by his own cause. He will maintain his own quarrel. He will cause comfort to increase. Is it not an encouragement to defend a prince's quarrel in his own sight, when he stands by to abet us? It would encourage a dull mettle. When we suffer for Christ's cause, we have Christ to defend us. He is with us in all our sufferings to bear us up. He puts his shoulder under, by his Holy Spirit, to support us.

We cannot live long in this world. We owe God a death. We owe nature a death. The sentence of death is passed upon us. We cannot enjoy the comfort of this world long. And for favour and applause of the world, we must leave it, and it will leave us, we know not how soon. And this meditation should enforce us to be willing, however it go with us, for anything here, for life, or goods, or friends, or credit and reputation, or whatsoever, to be willing to seal the cause of Christ with that which is dearest to us. 'If we suffer with him, we shall be glorified with him,' Rom. viii. 17.

The very sufferings of Christ are better than the most glorious day of the greatest monarch in the world that is not a Christian. It is better to suffer with Christ, than to joy with the world. The very abasement of St Paul was better than the triumph of Nero. Let Moses be judge. He judged it the best end of the balance, Heb. xi. 26. The very sufferings and reproach of Christ, and of religion, is better than the best thing in the world. The worst thing in Christianity, is better than the best thing out of Christ. The best thing out of Christ is the honour of a king, the honour of a prince, to be a king's son, &c. But the reproach of Christ for a good cause is better than the best thing in the world. I say, let Moses be judge, if we will not believe it ourselves till we feel it. The worst day of a Christian is better than the best day of a carnal man; for he hath the presence of God's Spirit to support him in some measure.

Therefore let us not be afraid beforehand. 'Fear nothing,' saith the apostle, 'that thou shalt suffer,' Acts xxvii. 24. And with Moses, let 'us not be ashamed of the rebuke of Christ,' Heb. xi. 26; but 'let us go out of the camp with Christ, bearing our reproach,' Heb. xiii. 13. And because we know not what God may call us to, let us entertain presently a resolution to endure whatsoever in this world God calls us to; to pass through thick and thin, to pass through all kinds of ways to the 'hope of our glorious calling,' Philip. iii. 14; if by any way, by any means,' saith St Paul, 'I may attain the resurrection of the dead,' Philip. iii. 11: if by any means I may come to heaven, by fair death, or by violent death. He scorned reproach, if by any means he might be happy.

And for others, it is a wondrous quailing to the spirits of men that offer any wrong, if it be but a disgrace. A scoff is a persecution to a Christian for a good cause. When wicked men oppose a Christian in a good cause and course, let us learn what they do, they 'kick against the pricks,' Acts ix. 5. Do they know what they do? When they reproach Christians, it is the 'reproach of Christ,' Heb. xi. 26. What was Ishmael's scorning? A persecution, Gal. iv. 29 Christ is scorned in his members. Will he endure this at their hands? When good causes are opposed, Christ is opposed, and Christ is scoffed. This doth enable* our suffering, being an abasing of itself, that Christ accounts it done to him.

Base men of the world, they think when they scoff at goodness, and wrong the image of God in his children, they think they deride and despise a company of weak creatures, that they scoff at silly persons meaner than themselves. But they are deceived. They scoff Christ in them, and he takes it so, 'Saul, Saul, why persecutest thou me?' Acts ix. 4. The foot is trod on the earth, and the head speaks from heaven. It is the reproach of Christ; and it will be laid to thy charge at the day of judgment, that thou hast scoffed, and persecuted, and reproached Christ in his members. It will be a heavy indictment. Men should not regard what they conceive of things; but what he that must be their judge will conceive of things ere long; and he interprets it as done to his own person. It is true both of good and ill. Whatsoever good we do to a Christian as a Christian, to a disciple in the name of a disciple, Christ takes it as done to himself,

* That is, 'strengthen us in suffering.'—G.

'Inasmuch as you have done it to these, you have done it to me,' Mat. xxv. 40.

It should animate us to do good offices to those that are Christ's. What we do to them, we do to Christ. Let us be willing to refresh the bowels of Christ in his members, at home or abroad, as occasion serves; to maintain the quarrel of Christ as much as we can, to relieve Christ. He comes to us in the poor, and asks relief. He that shed his blood for us, he that died for us, he that hath given us all, asks a little pittance for himself; that we for his sake would be so good to him in his members, as to do thus and thus; that for Jonathan's sake we would regard poor, lame Mephibosheth, his son, 2 Sam. ix. 1, *seq.* Christ, though he be gone, he hath some Mephibosheths, some poor, weak members; and what offices we do them, he accounts done to himself. It runs on his score. He will be accountable for every good word we speak in his cause, for every defence, for every act of bounty. It is a point of large meditation to consider, that the crosses and afflictions of Christians, they are the sufferings of Christ.

Do but consider the Spirit of God intended in this phrase, to dignify all disgraces and indignities that are put upon us in a good cause and quarrel. Could he have said more in few words? He calls them not disgraces, or losses, or death; but he puts such a comfortable title upon them, that might make us in love with suffering anything, and set us on fire to endure anything in a good cause. They are the 'sufferings of Christ.'

'As the sufferings of Christ abound, so our consolations,' &c. The third general point is, *that our consolations are proportionable to our sufferings.* 'Our consolations abound.' We suffer in this world. That is hard. Aye, but they are the sufferings of Christ. There is sweetness. And then another degree is, our consolations abound as our sufferings abound. Consolation is, as I shewed before in the unfolding of the word, an inward support of the soul against trouble felt or feared; and it must be stronger than the grievance, or else the action of comfort will not follow. There is a disproportion between the agent and the patient, in all prevailing actions, or else there is no prevailing. If the comfort be not above the malady, it is no comfort. And therefore no comforts but divine comforts will stand at length, because in all other comforts *sedet medicinum morbo*,* the malady is above the remedy. They make glorious pretences, as the philosophers do, Plutarch and Seneca, and the rest. But they are as apothecaries' boxes. They have goodly titles, but there is nothing within.

Alas! when there is trouble in the conscience, awakened with the sight of sin, and the displeasure of God, what can all those precepts compose and frame the soul in petty troubles? They have their place; and surely the neglect of them many times is that that makes the cross heavier. But alas! in divine troubles, in terror of conscience, it must be divine comfort. It must be of like nature, or else the effect of comfort will never follow; and those be the comforts that he means here. As our troubles and afflictions abound, so our consolations, our divine supports, they abound. The point is this, that

Doct. Our comforts are proportionable to our sufferings.

What did I say, proportionable? It is above all proportion of suffering. As it is said, 'the afflictions of this life are not worthy of the glory that shall be revealed,' Rom. viii. 18. And indeed in this life the consolations abound as the sufferings abound. For God keeps not all for the life to come. He gives us a taste, a grape of Canaan, before we come to Canaan.

* Qu. '*cedit medicina morbo?*'—Ed.

As the Israelites, they sent for grapes to taste the goodness of the land, and they had them brought to them by the spies, by which they might guess of the fruitfulness and sweetness of the land itself. So the taste and relish that God's children have of that fulness which is reserved in another world, it is answerable and proportionable to their sufferings; and in the proportion, the exceeding part is of comfort. There is an exceeding, if not for the present, yet afterwards. The ark did rise together with the water, and comforts rise together with matter of suffering.

But what is the reason of the proportion? Why the greatest comforts follow the greatest sufferings? What is the ground of it? They are many.

Reason 1. To name some: first of all, this is a ground *that the more capable the soul is of comfort, the more comfort it receives.* But great troubles bring a capacity and capableness of soul, fitting it to receive comfort. How is that? Troubles do humble the soul, and humility is a grace, and the vessel of all grace, and of comfort too. A low and meek spirit is a deep spirit, and the lower and deeper, and the larger the spirit is, the more capable it is to contain heavenly comfort. We know the more empty a man is of himself, the more fit he is for comfort; but crosses and afflictions empty us of ourselves, to see that there is nothing in us, that what we are we must be out of ourselves; and the less we are in ourselves, the more we are in God. And that is the reason that St Austin saith, that nothing is more strong than a humble, empty spirit; because it makes the creature to go out of itself to him that is strength itself, and comfort itself. Now, that which makes us go out of ourselves to strength, that is strong. But this doth crosses and afflictions. That is the main reason why the proportion holds.

Reason 2. Again, another reason is this, *troubles, and afflictions, and crosses do exercise graces;* and the more grace is exercised, the more comfort is derived, for comfort follows graces. The comforts of the Spirit follow the graces of the Spirit, as the heat follows the fire, or as the shadow follows the body. Now, the more grace, the more comfort; the more affliction, the more exercise of grace; the more exercise of grace, the more grace itself; as we see, the deeper the root the higher the tree. After the sharpest winter usually there is the sweetest spring, and the fruitfulest summer and autumn; because in the sharpest winter the ground is mellowed most, and the seed sinks the deepest; and the ground is inwardly warmed, the soil, the earth is prepared for it; and thereupon, when the outward heat comes to draw it forth, it comes to be abundantly fruitful. We see it in nature, that that we call *antiperistasis,** the environing of one contrary with another increaseth the contrary. Whatsoever is good is increased, being environed by the contrary ill, because they are put to the conflict.

So it is with the soul. It is the showers of affliction that bring the sweet flowers of comfort after. The soul is prepared and manured for them. The soul is exercised, and enlarged, and fitted for them every way. 'In the multitude of my sorrows, thy comforts refreshed my soul,' saith David, Ps. xciv. 19. Answerable to our discomforts, God's comforts refresh our souls.

Reason 3. And *God is so wise, that before we enter to suffer any great matter, he will give us more grace answerable to the greatness of our suffering*, and after great suffering he will give great comfort. God is so infinitely loving and wise, that he will not call us to suffer great troubles till he give us some grace answerable. As a captain will not set a fresh-water soldier in a

* That is, 'ἀντιπερίστασις, opposition or counteraction of the surrounding parts; in rhetoric as explained above.'—G.

sharp brunt, but some experienced man. Whatsoever wisdom is in man, it is but a drop in regard of that infinite wisdom that is in God. He proportions our strength before we suffer, and in suffering he doth increase it; and after suffering, then comfort comes following amain. Indeed, especially after a little while waiting, for God's time is the best time.

Reason 4. And we shall have most experience *of the presence of Christ and his Holy Spirit* at such times. The nearer to the spring of comfort, the more comfort. But in the deepest and sharpest afflictions, we are near to God. Therefore the more comfort.

How is this proved? The more we are stripped of outward comforts, the more near we are to God, who is styled the 'God that comforteth the abject,' Job xxix. 25; and the nearer to God, the nearer to comfort itself. For all comfort springs from him; and when outward means fail that should convey comfort to us, then he conveys it immediately by himself. I confess he is present at all times; but when the comfort is conveyed by the creature, by man, it is not so sweet as when God joins with the soul immediately, as in great crosses he doth. Such occasion, and such extremity may be, that none can comfort a man but God, by his Spirit. When Christ comes to the soul immediately, what abundance of comfort is there then! As a king that doth not send a messenger, but comes immediately in his own person to visit one in misery, what a grace is it! So what a grace is it to a soul afflicted and deserted, to have Christ immediately present! As the martyrs found, when no other creature could comfort them, there was a fire within above all the outward fire and torment, which abated and allayed the torments that were without. The divinest comforts are kept for the harshest and the worst times. We shall have the presence of Christ in the absence of all other creatures, and he will minister comfort. They may keep outward comforts from us, they can never keep the God of comfort from us; and so long as a Christian soul and God can close together, it cannot want comfort.

Reason 5. Another reason why comforts increase, *because we pray most then.* When we pray most, we are most happy. But in our greatest sufferings we pray most, and most ardently. Therefore then we feel most comfort. When God and a Christian soul can talk together, and have communion, though he cannot speak to God with his tongue, yet he can sigh and groan to God. He can pour forth his spirit to God, and as long as we can pray we can never be miserable; as long as the heart can ease itself into the bosom of God, there will alway be a return of a sweet answer. Of all the exercises of religion, that exercise that hath most immediate communion with God is prayer. Then we speak familiarly to God in his own language and words, and call upon him by his own promises. We allege those to him, and this cannot be, we cannot speak, and confer, and converse with the God of comfort without a great deal, without a world, of comfort. Great crosses drive us to this, and therefore then we have great comfort.

Use 1. What use may we make of this? First, for ourselves, *we should* not fear nor faint, neither faint in troubles nor fear troubles.* Faint not in them. We shall have comfort proportionable; and let us not fear troubles before they come, or any measure of them. Proportionable to the measure of our afflictions shall be our comfort. Let us not fear anything we shall suffer in this world in a good cause; for as we suffer so we shall receive from God. We fear our own good. For it is better to have the comfort we shall have in suffering anything for a good cause, than to be exempted

* Mis rinted 'would.'—G.

from the suffering and to want the comfort. There is no proportion. The choice is much better, to have comfort with grievance than to want the comfort together with the grievance. St Paul would not have chosen immunity from suffering, he would not have been exempted from the cross to have wanted his comfort.

For the disproportion is wide and great. The comforts are inward and sweet, the crosses, for the most part, are outward. What are all the crosses and sufferings in this world? Set aside an afflicted conscience, it is but brushing of the garment, as it were; some outward thing in the outward man, but the comforts are inward and deep.

But what if there be inward grievances too? Then we have deeper comforts than they. The cross is never so deep but the comfort is deeper. 'Oh the depth of the wisdom and love of God!' Rom. xi. 23. There is the part and dimension of God's love, the depth of it! There is a depth in crosses. 'Out of the deep have I cried to thee,' Ps. cxxx. 1. But there is a deeper depth of comfort, there is a hand under to fetch us up at the lowest. 'Thy right hand is upon me, and thy left hand is under me,' Song of Sol. ii. 6, saith the church to God. There is comfort lower and deeper than the grievance, though it be inward, spiritual grievance. Nay, of all grievances (I know what I speak a little of mine own experience, and it is true in the experience of all ministers and Christians, that) there is none that have more help than they that are exercised with spiritual temptations of conscience. They are forced to search for deep comforts. Shallow comforts will not serve their turn! And when they have them, they keep them, and make much of them. They have more retired and deep thoughts of Christ, and of comforts than other people, who as they are strangers to their crosses, so they are strangers to their comfort. There is no degree of proportion between the crosses and the comforts. The crosses are momentary, the comforts are growing. The crosses make us not a whit the worse, and the comforts make us better. Fear nothing therefore; but go on in the ways of religion, and never be discouraged to suffer in a good cause for fear of men, to think, Oh this will come, and that will come. No, no; if the sufferings grow, the comforts shall grow with it, be of good comfort.

Use 2. Again, another use may be, *that we judge aright of those that are disgraced in the world, if their cause be good;* that we should not have distasteful conceits of them, as indeed suffering breeds distaste naturally in men. They love men in a flourishing estate, and distaste them suffering; but that is corruption of men. But God is the nearest to them then, nearer than ever he was, and their comforts increase with their crosses. In the conjunction between the sun and the moon, as by experience we see, in the space between the old and new moon, there is a time of conjunction. We think the moon to be lost in that time, because we see her not; but the moon is more enlightened then, than ever she was in herself. But here is the reason, the light part of the moon is turned to the sunward, to heavenward, and the dark part is turned toward the earth. So a Christian in crosses and abasement seems to be a dark creature, but he is more enlightened then, than ever before? Why? His light part is to Godward, it is not seen of the world. The world sees his crosses, but they do not see his comforts. And as the moon is nearer the sun at that time than at other times; so the soul hath to deal with God in afflictions. It is nearer to God, and his dark side is toward the world. As the world sees the moon's eclipse, so the world sees our darkness, but not our inward comfort. Therefore we should judge aright of others in this case.

Use 3. Another use shall be *of thankfulness to God*, that besides the comforts of heaven (which are not to be spoken of, and which we shall not know till we come to feel them), besides the great comfort we have to be free from hell, that we have a measure of comfort here in this world, in our pilgrimage, and absence from heaven, such a measure of comfort, as may carry us with comfort along. We ought to be thankful to God, not only for redemption and glorification, but that God comforts us in our pilgrimage, that he mingles crosses with comforts; nay, that in this world our comforts are more than our crosses.

Obj. Some may object, Aye, but my crosses are more than my comforts?

Ans. Are they so? Dost thou suffer in a good cause or no? If thou dost, thy comforts are more than thy crosses, if there be not a fault in thee.

Quest. What shall I do therefore?

First, Take this direction in suffering, *pull out the sting of sin*, though we suffer in never so good a cause, for in one suffering, God aims at divers things. God in thy suffering aims at thy correction, as well as at the exercise of thy grace and at thy comfort. Therefore, let affliction have the correcting and amending part first, and then the comforting part will follow. Though the cause be good, yet God's children ofttimes want comfort till afterward. Why? They have not renewed their repentance, and cleansed their souls. They have not pulled out the sting. When they have repented of their personal sins that lie upon them, and gone back to the sins of their youth, and then renewed their covenant with God, and their purposes for the time to come, then comes comfort, and not before. Therefore it is no disparagment to a good cause, that sometimes Christians find not present comfort. They have personal sins that hang on them, that are not repented of, which God intends to amend them of, as well as to honour them by suffering in his cause.

Second. Again, if God's children complain, that their sufferings are above their strength, and above measure, and desire God to weigh their afflictions, they are so great, as Job saith,—*it is the speech of sense and not of faith*, it is the speech of the fit, and not of the state. There is a fit and a state. It is no matter what they say in their fit, then the flesh and sense speak, and not grace and faith at that time. If they judge by sense, then they judge so, but we know that reason corrects the errors of sense, and faith corrects the errors of reason. But what do they say in their constant state? Their comforts are answerable to their crosses, either in suffering or afterwards, though not alway at the same time. So much for that.

But this will be abused by carnal persons. We speak of abundance of comfort, but it is to those that have interest in it. The book of God speaks no comfort to persons that live in sin, and will do so. We speak comfort to those that are broken-hearted for their sins, that are content to endure the reproach of religion in despite of the world, that will bear the cross of Christ. For the other, as their jollity increaseth in the world, so their crosses and troubles shall increase. As it is said, Rev. xviii. 17, of mystical Babylon, the Church of Rome, that hath flourished in the world a great while, and sat as a queen and blessed herself, 'As she glorified herself, and lived deliciously, so much torment and sorrow give her.' So it is true of every wicked man that is in an evil course, and will be, and as the Scripture phrase is, 'blesseth himself in an evil course,' they shall be sure of the curse of God, and not of comfort. For in what proportion they have delighted themselves in this world in sin, in that proportion they shall have torment of conscience, if conscience be awaked in this world; and in that proportion they shall have torment in the world to come. As sin is growing, so rods are growing for them. Wicked men, saith St Paul, 'they grow worse and worse,' 2 Tim. iii. 13. The more they sin, the more they may. They sink in rebellion, and the more they sink in rebellion, the more they sink in the state of damnation. They fill up the measure of their sins, and treasure up the wrath of God against the day of wrath. Whosoever thou art that livest in a sinful course, and will do so in spite of God's ordinance, in spite of the motions of the Spirit, that hast the good motions of the Spirit knocking at thy soul, and yet wilt rather refuse comfort than take comfort, together with direction, go on still in this thy wicked course, but remember, as thy comforts increase in this world, so thy torment is increasing. And here is the disproportion between God's children and others. They have their sufferings first, and their comfort afterward; but others have their pleasure first, and their torment after. Theirs are for a time, but others for ever. Thus we see what we may comfortably observe from this, that comforts increase as crosses increase.

A word of the fourth and last point.

How comes this to pass, that *as our afflictions abound, so our consolations abound?*

Doct. They abound by Christ, saith the apostle, God the Father, he is the God of comfort; the Holy Ghost is the comforter. But how comes this to pass, that we that are not the objects of comfort, but of confusion, should have God the Father to be the 'God of comfort,' and the Holy Ghost 'to be our comforter?' Oh, it is that Jesus Christ, the great peace-maker, hath satisfied God, and procured the Holy Ghost; for the Holy Ghost is procured by the satisfaction and death of Christ, and he was sent after the resurrection and ascension of Christ. Therefore Christ is called 'the consolation of Israel,' Luke ii. 25, and those that waited for Christ waited for the consolation of Israel. All comfort is hid in Christ. He is the storehouse of comfort. 'We have it through him, and by him, and in him.' For that God is the 'Father of comfort,' it is because Christ is our mediator and intercessor in heaven; that the Holy Ghost is 'the comforter,' it is because Christ sent him. And the comforts of the Holy Ghost are fetched from Christ, from the death of Christ, or the ascension of Christ, from some argument from Christ. Whatsoever comforteth the soul, the Holy Ghost doth it by fetching some argument from Christ, from his satisfaction, from his worth, from his intercession in heaven. Something in Christ it is. So Christ by his Spirit doth comfort, and the reasons fetched by the Spirit are from Christ. Therefore it is by Christ.

What is the reason that a Christian soul doth not fear God as 'a consuming fire,' Heb. xii. 29, but can look upon him with comfort? It is because God hath received satisfaction by Christ. What is the reason that a Christian soul fears not hell, but thinks of it with comfort? Christ hath conquered hell and Satan. What is the reason that a Christian fears not death? Christ by death hath overcome death, and him that had the power of death, the devil. Christ is mine, saith the Christian soul. Therefore I do not fear it, but think of it with comfort, because a Christian is more than a conqueror over all these. What is the reason that a Christian is not afraid of his corruptions and sins? He knows that God, for Christ's sake, will pardon them, and that the remainder of his corruptions will work to his humiliation, and to his good. 'All shall work for the best to them that love God,' Rom. viii. 28. What is the reason that there is not any thing in the world but it is comfortable to a Christian? When he thinks of God, he thinks of him as a Father of comfort; when he thinks of the Holy Ghost, he thinks of him as a Spirit of comfort; when he thinks of angels, he thinks of them as his attendants; when he thinks of heaven, he thinks of it as of his inheritance; he thinks of saints as a communion whereof he is partaker. Whence is all this? By Christ, who hath made God our Father, the Holy Ghost our comforter, who hath made angels ours, saints ours, heaven ours, earth ours, devils ours, death ours, all ours, in issue.

For God being turned in love to us, all is turned. Our crosses are no curses now, but comforts; and the bitterest crosses yield the sweetest comforts. All this is by Christ, that hath turned the course of things, and hid blessings in the greatest crosses that ever were. And this he did in himself, before he doth it in us. For did not his greatest crosses tend to his greatest glory? who ever in the world was abased as our head Christ Jesus was? that made him cry, 'My God, my God, why hast thou forsaken me?' Mat. xv. 34. All the creatures in the world would have sunk under the sufferings that Christ endured. What abasement to the abasement of Christ? and what glory to the glory of Christ? 'He humbled himself to the death of the cross; wherefore God gave him a name above all names, that at the name of Jesus every knee should bow, both of things in heaven, and things in earth, and things under the earth,' Phil. ii. 8. Now as it was in our head, his greatest abasement ushered in his greatest glory; so it shall be in us,—our greatest crosses are before our greatest comforts. He is our president.* He is the exemplary cause as well as the efficient working cause. It is by Christ all this, that consolations abound in us. It was performed first in him, and shall be by him, by his Spirit to the end of the world.

Use. The use that we are to make of this is, that in all our sufferings, before we come to heaven, *we should look to Christ.* He hath turned all things. Let us study Christ, and fetch comfort from him. Our flesh was abased in him. Our flesh is glorified in him now in heaven, in his person. And so it must be in our own persons. Our flesh must be abased, and then as he is glorious in heaven, so shall we be in ourselves. That very Spirit that raised and advanced him at the lowest, that very Spirit (there being but one Spirit in the head and members) in our greatest abasement shall vouchsafe us the greatest advancement that we can look for, to sit at the right hand of God, to reign with Christ; 'for if we suffer with him, we shall reign with him,' Rom. viii. 17.

And hence you may have a reason likewise why Christians have no more comfort. They do not study Christ enough. They consider not Christ, and the nearness wherein Christ is to them, and they to Christ, that both make one Christ. They do not consider how Christ hath sweetened all. He hath turned God, and turned all to us. He hath made God our Father, and in him all things favourable unto us. So that now the fire is our friend, the stone, and the gout, and all diseases, disgrace and temptation, all are at peace and league with us; all is turned in the use and issue to good, to the help and comfort of God's children (*k*). 'All things are yours, and you are Christ's, and Christ is God's,' 1 Cor. iii. 23. There is not the worst thing but it is at peace with us; because the malignant power it hath, in order to damnation, is taken away. Now it doth not hurt us, but there is a sovereign curing power to turn it to good.

I confess God's children are discomforted, but then they wrong their principles, they wrong their grounds, their religion, their Saviour. They

* That is, 'precedent' = exemplar.—G.

wrong all the comforts they have interest in, because they do not improve them when occasion serves, as Job is checked, 'Hast thou forgot the consolations of the Almighty?' Job xv. 11, or why dost thou forget them? So if we have consolations and forget them, and doat and pore upon our grievance, it is just with God to leave us comfortless; not that we want any comfort, but we flatter our grievance and forget our comfort. Let us change our object, and when we have looked upon our grievance, and been humbled in the sight of our sins, let us look upon the promises, let us look upon Christ in glory, and see ourselves in heaven triumphing with him.

What can terrify a soul? not death itself, when it sees itself in Christ triumphing. Faith sees me as well triumphing in heaven, and sitting at the right hand of God, as it doth Christ, for it knows I am a member of Christ, and whatsoever is between me and that happiness, that is reserved for me in heaven, I shall triumph over it.

Christ triumphed in his own person over death, hell, sin, the grave, the devil, and he will triumph in me his mystical body. What he hath done in himself, he will do in me. This faith will overcome the world, and the devil, and hell, and all that is between us and heaven. A Christian that sees himself sitting at the right hand of God with Christ, triumphing with him, he is discouraged at nothing; for faith that makes things to come present, it sees him conquering already.

Let us be exhorted to joy, 'Rejoice, and again I say rejoice,' Philip. iv. 4. We have reason to do so, if we look to our grounds. But when we yield to Satan, and our own flesh, we rob God of his glory and ourselves of comfort, but we may thank ourselves for it.

But I come to the sixth verse, wherein the apostle enlargeth himself, by shewing the end of his sufferings in regard of them, by setting down both parts, both affliction and comfort.

VERSE 6.

'*Whether we be afflicted, it is for your consolation and salvation: or whether we be comforted, it is for your consolation and salvation.*' It is much in everything, how the mind is prepared to receive what is spoken. The apostle, therefore, to make way for himself in their hearts, he removes scandal from his sufferings, and he shews that it was so far that they should take offence at it, that they ought to do as he did, to bless God for it; for as the sufferings of Christ abounded in him, so his comfort abounded. And because they should think themselves no way hurt by his sufferings and base usage in the world, he tells them in the verse that all was for their good. No man should be offended at his own good. They had no reason to take scandal at that which was for their good; but, saith he, if you think basely of me for my sufferings, you think basely of your own comfort: for my sufferings are for your good, and my comforts are for your good. Whether I suffer or be comforted, it is for you.

The cross is a distasteful thing to us, and likewise the cross in others is a distasteful thing, not only distasteful and bitter to us, but shameful. St Paul knowing this, because he would, as I said, work himself into their good conceit, that he might prevail with them for their good, saith he, you ought not to think a whit the worse of me for this, for all is for you. So you see the scope of the words, 'Whether we be afflicted, it is for your consolation,' &c.

But first he speaks of affliction alone, and then of comfort alone. If we be afflicted, it is for your good; and if we be comforted, it is for your good. His reason is, because sometimes afflictions appear without comfort. Therefore he saith not, 'If we be comforted only, it is for your good;' but 'If we be afflicted, it is for your good.' Sometimes comfort is before our afflictions. That we may endure it the better, God cheers us to it. Sometimes God sheds his Spirit in affliction, that there is abundance of comfort in it. But for the most part it comes after, after we have waited; but in it there is always such a measure of comfort that supports us, that we sink not. Yet the special degree of comfort usually comes after. Therefore he speaks of affliction in the first place. 'If I be afflicted, it is for you,' &c.

The point is easy, that

Doct. The afflictions of the saints are for the good of others.

The afflictions of God's church are God's people's, especially the afflictions of pastors and leaders of God's army. God singles out some to suffer for the good of others; the good especially of consolation and salvation, for these two goods.

Quest. How can this be, that the afflictions of God's people are for the consolation and salvation of others?

Ans. I answer, many ways, as we shall see afterwards more particularly: but only now to make way.

1. Afflictions are for the good and comfort of others, *because we have their example in suffering, to train us up how to suffer.* Example is a forcible kind of teaching. Therefore, saith the apostle, our afflictions are for you, to lead and teach you the way how to suffer. Words are not enough, especially in matter of suffering. There must be some example. Therefore Christ from heaven came, not only to redeem us, but to teach us, not only by words, but by example, how to do, and suffer willingly, and cheerfully, and stoutly, in obedience to God, as he did.

2. Again, afflictions do good to others, *by ministering occasion to them to search deeper into the cause.* When they see the people of God are so used, they take occasion hereby to inquire what is the cause, and so take occasion to be instructed deeply in matters of religion; for man's nature is inquisitive, and grace takes the hint off anything. What is the matter that such and such endure such things? Hereupon, I say, they come to be better grounded in the cause, and little occasions ofttimes are the beginnings of great matters; by reason that the spirit as well as wit is of a working nature, and will draw one thing from another. We see what a great tree riseth of a little seed! how a little thing, upon report, worketh conversion. Naaman the Assyrian had a servant, and she told him that there was a prophet in Jewry that was a famous man, that did great matters, and if he would go to him, he should be cured of his leprosy. That little occasion being ministered, Naaman comes to the prophet, and he was cured of a double leprosy, both of soul and body, and went home a good man, 2 Kings v. 1, *seq.* So by way of ministering occasion of inquisition, the sufferings of others do good.

3. And then, seeing the constant and resolute spirits of those that suffer, it *doth them good, and comforts them:* for, first, it makes them conceive well of the cause: certainly these men that suffer constantly, and cheerfully, it is a good cause that they suffer for, when they see the cause is such a resolution and courage in the sufferers. And it makes them in love with, and begin to think well of, the persons, when they can deny themselves. Surely these men care not for the pleasures and vanities of the world, that can endure to suffer these. So Justin Martyr saith when he

saw Christians suffer; he thought they were men that cared not for pleasures; for if they had, they would not suffer these things (l).

4. Besides, *they can gather from the presence of God's Spirit emboldening the sufferers, what they may hope for themselves if they should suffer.* They may reason thus: Is God by his Spirit so full and so strong in these that are flesh and blood as we are? Is he so strong in women, in young men, in aged men, that neither their years, nor their sex, nor their tenderness, can any kind of way hinder them from these kind of abasements and sharp sufferings? Surely the same Spirit of God will be as strong in me, if I stand out in the same cause, and carry myself as they do. And there is good reason, for God is the same God, the Spirit is the same Spirit, the cause is the same cause. Therefore it is no false reasoning. I may, upon a good presumption, hope for the presence and assistance of the Spirit of God to enable and strengthen me as he did them; for the same Spirit of God will be strong in all.

5. And this is partly likewise *in the intent of them that suffer.* There is a double intent. It is the intent of God to single them out to suffer for the good of others; and it is their intent to suffer that others may have good. This is one reason why they are willing rather to suffer shame, or bodily punishment, than they will hinder others of the good they may take by their suffering. So it is God's end, and their end. It is for your consolation, in God's intent, and in my intent and purpose, and in the event itself. Thus you see how afflictions, suffered in good cause, help for the consolation and salvation even of others. The example of those that suffer flow into the mind, and insinuate into the judgment and affection, of the beholders many ways.

And this the factors of antichrist know very well; for if ever there be any persecution again, we shall hardly have fire and faggot, that they may not give example. They will come to gunpowder plots and massacres, and such violent courses, to sweep away all. They know if it come to matter of example once, the grace of God in his children, and the presence of his Spirit, that shall appear to others, it is of a wondrous working force. They are wise enough to know that. The devil teacheth them that wit, when he hath been put by all his other shifts.

If it be so that the sufferings of God's children are for the good of others, then to make some use of it.

Use 1. Let us not take offence at the cause of religion for suffering. We ought not to have an ill conceit of a cause for suffering, but rather think the better of it. I speak it in this regard, we have many that will honour the martyrs that are dead, that are recorded in the book, but if any suffer in the present view, before their eyes, they are disgraceful to them. This should not be. For, first of all, if the cause be good, the end of good men (by the help of the Spirit of God) is for thy good. Was it not a cruel thing in Saul to strike at David when he played on his harp, when he sought his good and easement? 1 Sam. xviii. 10, 11. To kill a nightingale in singing, it is a barbarous thing. God's children, by all that they suffer, intend the good of others. Now, to hurt and malign them in doing good, to persecute them that endure ill for our good, or that labour and do anything for our good, it is a barbarous, savage thing. All is for the elect. 'I suffer not* for the elect's sake,' saith St Paul in 2 Tim. ii. 10; so my sufferings are for you. We may know we are elected of God, if we take good by the sufferings of others; if we take no scandal and offence, and do not add

* Qu. 'all?'—Ed.

affliction to the afflicted, for all is in God's intent, and in their intent, for our good.

For instance (a little to enlighten the point, because it is not usually stood on, and it is a notion that may help our conceits of the excellent estate of God's children), reprobation, to go as high as we may, it is for their good, to shew mercy to them, to set by and neglect so many, and to single them out. The creation of the world is for their sakes. God's providence directs all for their good. For why doth he suffer wicked men? It is that they may be instruments to exercise them that are good. It is by reflection, or some way for the cause of the good, that the wicked are suffered to be upon the earth. The administration of the world, it is not for the rebels that are in it, it is for those that are God's children; and he tosseth and tumbleth empires and monarchies. The great men of the world, they think they do great matters; but, alas! all this is for the exercise of the church, this is reductive to the church, by God's providence. All their attempts are for the little flock, for a few that are a despised company, that he means to save, if we had eyes to see it.

So likewise his ordinances are to gather this church, which he hath chosen from all the world to himself. The ordinances of the ministry, and of the sacraments, the suffering of ministers, the doing and suffering of Christians, all is for their good, as we see in this place, 'I suffer for your consolation and comfort.' Heaven and earth stands for them. The pillars of heaven and earth would be taken asunder, and all would come to a chaos, an end would be of all, if the number of them were gathered that are the blessed people of God, for whom all things are. The doings and sufferings of God's people, we do not know indeed, that are ministers, who belong to God and who do not, but our intent is to do good to those that are God's, and the issue proves so. The rest God hath his end in it to harden them, and bring them to confusion, to take excuse from them; but the real good of all our pains and suffering is the elect's.

Let us examine what good we take by ordinances of God, and by the sufferings of the present church, and the sufferings of the former church. Do their examples animate, and quicken, and encourage us to the like courses? It is a sign we are elected of God. There is no greater sign of a good estate in grace, than a gracious heart, to draw good out of the examples of others, and to draw good out of everything that befalls us, because God's end in election, and his manner of providence, is to guide all to their good.

Use 2. Again, we learn another thing likewise, *how God overrules in his providence the projects of carnal men, of the devil and his instruments, and agents and factors.* God overrules all things, that which in itself is ill, and in the intendment* of the inflicter is ill, yet God turns it to the good of others, and the good of them that suffer too. Satan intends no such matter, as it is said, Isa. x. 5. Nebuchadnezzar thinks no such thing. 'Asshur, the rod of my wrath,' he intends no such matter. They intend not the consolation of God's when they wrong the saints of God, and so exercise their patience and grace. No! they intend their hurt and confusions. It is no matter what they intend; but God at the first created light out of darkness, and in his providence doth great matters by small means. In his providence over his church, he doth raise contraries out of contraries; he turns the wicked projects of men to contrary ends, and makes all serviceable to his own end.

* That is, 'intention.'—G.

In state policy, he is accounted the wisest man that can make his enemies instrumental to his own purpose, that can make others serve his own turn, to work his own ends by others that are his opposites; and he had need of a great reaching head that can do so. The great providence of heaven doth thus. God is the wisest politician in the world. All other policy is but a beam from that Sun. He can make instrumental and serviceable to him his very enemies. And this is the torment of Satan, that God overshoots him in his own bow. He overreacheth him in his own policy. Where he thinks to do most harm he doth most good. In those afflictions whereby he thinks to quell the courage of the church, God doth exceeding good to them, and enlargeth the bounds of the church this way.

It is an ordinary speech, 'The blood of the martyrs is the seed of the church' (*m*). The word of God is the seed of the church; how then is the blood of the martyrs and sufferers the seed of the church? Thus the word of God is the seed of the church, how? As it is in the Bible, in the book? No! As it is published in preaching, much more as it is published in confession, and much more as it is published and sealed in martyrdom, by suffering. The word of God is so laid open, as not only spoken but confessed and practised in life; and not only so, but sealed by enduring anything. Thus it is the seed, and works strongly.

God overrules all inferiors. Though they have contrary motions in their own intent to his, yet he brings them about to his end. As we see the heavens have a contrary motion to the first heaven, that carries the rest, the *primum mobile*, yet they are turned about by another motion, contrary to the bent of themselves. They go one way, and are carried another.* As we see in the wheels of the clock, one runs one way, another another; all make the clock strike, all serve the intent of the clockmaker; so one runs one way, and another, another. Carnal men offer disgrace and disparagement to God's people; their intent is to otherthrow all, to disgrace and to trample on the cause of religion; but God useth contrary wheels, to make the clock strike. All turns in the issue to his end. Therefore though we say in our common speech, that the devil is the god of this world, it is the Scripture phrase, 2 Cor. iv. 4; and it is so in regard of the wicked that are under him, yet he is a god under a God. There is but one monarch of the world. He is a god that hath not power over swine further than he is suffered, Mat. viii. 30, *seq*. It is a point of wondrous comfort, that though we be thus used, yet there is an active providence, there is one monarch, one great king, that rules all.

It is a ground of patience and contentment in whatsoever we suffer, not to look to the next instrument, but [to] look to the overruling cause, that will turn all in the issue to our good. This Joseph comforted his brethren with. You sent me, and of an ill mind too; but God turned it to good. It was no thank to them, yet it was no matter. He comforted them in this, that God turned their malice to his good, and to their good too, for he was sent as a steward to provide for them.

And it is one ground why to think more moderately in regard of anger, fierceness, against wicked men, it is ground of pitying of them; for, alas! poor souls, what do they! Though they intend it of malice, they are but instruments, and shall be overruled to do good contrary to their meaning, as St Paul saith here, 'Whether I be afflicted, it is for your consolation and salvation.' The worst intents and designs of the enemies of religion,

* This frequently-recurring illustration is drawn from the Cartesian system of astronomy, which Newton's discoveries had not yet superseded.—G.

was for the consolation and salvation of the Corinthians. It is good to think of this beforehand. It is a ground of patience; and not only so, but of comfort and joy, which is a degree above patience. God overrules all thus. Therefore we should quietly cast ourselves wholly upon him, willing to do and suffer whatsoever he will have us, knowing that he will direct all to the good of the church, to our comfort, and his own glory.

Use 3. Again, a further use may be this, *to teach us to communicate our estate to others, because it is for their good.* Good is diffusive, saith St Paul. All that I do or suffer, it is for your good, to join comfort and suffering together. 'If I be comforted,' it is for you; and if I suffer, it is for you. It must be by their taking notice of it, and that is not all that they ought to take notice, but we ought to let them take notice as much as we can, 'Come, children, and I will teach you the fear of the Lord,' Ps. xxxiv. 11. 'Come and I will tell you what the Lord hath done for my soul.' 'The righteous shall compass me about,' saith David, Ps. cxlii. 7. As when a man hath some great matter to tell, there will be a ring of people about him, desirous to hear what he saith; so saith David, the righteous shall compass me about. When David had sweet matter of experience, to tell what God had done for him; how he had been with him in his affliction, and delivered him, 'the righteous shall compass me about,' I will declare it to others. For God's children make others' case their own. They comfort them as they would be comforted of them again.

As they ought to do so, so we should take notice of their troubles and deliverances, how God sanctifies them to them. These things tend to edification. There is the same reason to one saint of God as to all, and God is the same to all in the like case. Experiments are made much of in other things in physic, and judged cases in law, and such like. Tried things in all professions are good. So tried truths should be valued. Now when a man teacheth another his experiment,* it is a judged case, a tried truth. It is not every truth that will stay the soul in the time of a great temptation, but a truth proved, a tried truth. Therefore it is good for parents and governors, for friends and for all degrees of men, to make it one way to spend their time fruitfully, to discourse with others of the blessed experiments which they have had of God's gracious providence, in the passages of their life. 'Abraham will teach his children,' Gen. xviii. 19, I will tell it to him therefore, saith God. It is a means for God to reveal many things sweetly to us, when he knows we are of a communicative, spreading disposition. God gains by that means. His glory is spread. Our grace is increased. The good of others is multiplied.—To go on.

'*It is for your consolation and salvation.*' Whether we be afflicted, or whether we be comforted, all is for your consolation and salvation. I will not trouble you here with the diverse readings of copies. Some Greek copies want the word salvation, but the most that the translations follow have both consolation and salvation. Some have consolation and salvation in the first, but they repeat it not in the second. 'Whether we be comforted, it is for your consolation and salvation.' But because the more current have both, therefore we will join both, 'it is for your consolation and salvation' (*n*).

For *huper*† in the Greek it hath a double force. It signifies either to merit; *hupon*,‡ to procure and merit salvation; and so we do not under-

* That is, 'experience.'—G. † That is, ὑπὲρ = over, above.—G.
‡ Apparently a misprint.—Ed.

stand it. Or *huper** for your good, a final cause. It includes either a meritorious deserving cause, or a final cause. 'Whether I be afflicted, it is for your consolation and salvation,' not by merit and desert;—so Christ's suffering was—but to help it forward in the execution of it.

I speak this to cut the sinews of a popish point, as I meet it, which is a cozening point of their religion, which indeed is not a point of religion, but a point of Romish policy, a point of cozenage; as most of their religion is but a trick for the belly. They have devices forsooth of the pope's treasury. He being the treasurer of the church, hath a treasury; and what must that be filled with? With the merits of saints, with the superabundance. For they can deserve and procure heaven for themselves, and more than obey. There is an overplus of obedience. The superabundance of that is laid in a treasury. And who should have the benefit of that but the treasury of the church and the pope? But how shall the church come by this abundant satisfaction and merit? They must buy them by pardons, and they come not to have pardons for nought, but by purchasing of them, and hence come popish indulgences. That is nothing but a dispensing of the satisfaction and merits of the saints, which they did, say they, for the church, abusing such phrases as these. When they had more than their own obedience, they did good to others, and others had benefit by it.

A shameful opinion, bred in the dark night of popery, when the Scriptures were hid, and when people did lie in ignorance; and it was merely to advantage their own selves. For indeed the Scripture saith that God's children did suffer for the church; but that was not for satisfaction for the church, but for the good of the church. Only Christ's death was satisfactory. Christ is the only treasury of the church, and the satisfaction of Christ. They think they merit by their sufferings, when they suffer for their merits. And they think they merit not only for themselves, but for others too, which is a diabolical sarcasm. The devil mocks them that way; he makes them ignorant of themselves. Alas! that a silly, sinful man should think to do enough for himself, and more than enough, enough for others! The wise virgins had but oil enough for themselves; they had none for others. But these wise virgins have more than for themselves; they have for others too. It is not worth the standing on, to hinder better and more comfortable things. The phrase runs in this sense, when it is meant of Christ. Christ suffered for our satisfaction, for our redemption. And Leo the pope, one of the best of their popes, and in his rank, a holy man in his time, he saith excellent well for this, *sanctorum preciosa mors, &c.* The death of the saints is precious; but the death of no saint is a propitiation for others. Their death is sanctified, but not propitiatory to others. Therefore *singularis singulis.* All the saints, their death was for themselves. It is an excellent speech *solus Christus, &c.* (*o*). Every other besides Christ, their death was singular. It went not out of their persons to do others good, otherwise than by an exemplary course, as St Paul speaks here. But only Christ it is, in whom all died, in whom all are crucified, in whom all are raised, in whom all ascend, in whom all are glorified. As public Adam, his death was for all. He was not considerable in his death, as one man, but as a 'second Adam,' who by his public obedience, as the first public person, by his disobedience infected all; so he by his obedience and satisfaction, by his passive obedience, especially when he shut up his obedience in death, all died in him. It was as much as if all had died, as if all

* That is, ὑπὲρ = for the realization of.—G.

had been crucified, and risen in him. The meaning is therefore, 'Whether we be afflicted, it is for your consolation and salvation,' to help it forward, to help forward your comfort, by way of example, and not by way of satisfaction and merit any kind of way.

Do but consider this one reason, and so I will end the point. There was no saint that ever merited heaven by his own satisfaction, therefore he could not do good to others by way of satisfaction. How do you prove that? By that excellent speech, in Rom. viii. 18, 'The sufferings of this world are not worthy of the glory that shall be revealed.' All that they suffered was not worthy of the glory to be revealed; therefore they could not by any satisfaction of their own merit heaven for themselves. What should we speak of others then, to do any good to others, I mean, by way of satisfaction? But he shews this in the next words more clearly, how good is done to others, 'Whether we be afflicted, it is for your consolation and salvation.

'*Which is effectual in enduring the same sufferings that we also suffer.*' It is read in the margin, and most go that way, and the oldest interpreters too (*p*). Some translators have a word as fit in the margin as in the text ofttimes, and they leave it to the readers to take which they will. It is good and useful both ways, but the most go that way, and it is more clear. The meaning is this, 'Whether we be afflicted, it is for your consolation and salvation,' which salvation of yours is wrought out, 'in enduring the same sufferings that we also suffer.' If it be read 'effectual,' as it is in the text, and not in the margin, then it is thus, 'If we be afflicted, it is for your consolation and salvation, the assurance whereof in you is effectual, to make you endure the sufferings that we suffer.'

Now here must be a thing clear.

How salvation is wrought by affliction?

I answer, salvation is wrought by Christ, by way of merit and procurement, and purchase and satisfaction to divine justice; but salvation, in regard of the profession of it, is wrought by afflictions, that is, we come to have it by this way. We might consider salvation in purchase and title, and salvation in possession and investing into it. Salvation in title and purchase is wrought by the death and sufferings of Christ, who hath this pre-eminence, to be called and styled a Saviour; but though it be gotten by him, it is not possessed but by a certain way and course. That salvation, the title whereof we have by Christ, it is not possessed or entered into, but by a course of suffering and doing. God hath measured out so many holy actions for every Christian to do, and so many things for every Christian to suffer, so many grievances, if he be of years of discretion. God hath a way to save children which lean to his wisdom, but this way God saveth men. They have a cup measured to them, they have so many afflictions to suffer, before they be possessed of that which Christ hath purchased. So it is wrought in regard of possession, in suffering the same afflictions that others suffer.

There are two ways, doing good, and suffering for good, that are the beaten way to obtain salvation, which salvation is wrought by the satisfaction of Christ. Mark here, he saith our sufferings tend to your comfort and salvation. How? Because it helps you to endure the same suffering. By seeing others suffer, and by enduring the like, we come to the possession of salvation in the end, because by seeing them suffer, we are encouraged to suffer. The point hence is this, that,

Doct. Whatsoever good we take by the sufferings of any, it is by stirring up and strengthening some grace in us.

Whatsoever good we take by any,—set Christ aside, from whom we take good likewise by way of example, as well as merit; but in a singular respect by way of merit,—but for others, whatsoever good we take, it is not direct, it is not immediate, but only by stirring up some grace, by strengthening some grace in us. There is no good derived from others to me but by confirming and strengthening some grace. So I come to have good by them, saith St Paul here, 'My sufferings increase your salvation.' But it is because my sufferings stir you up to suffer the same afflictions. You learn of me by my carriage and example to suffer, and so by suffering that which I suffer you come to salvation.

This is sufficient to convince that idle opinion that I spoke of before, that the sufferings of the saints are not conveyed by way of pardon to the ignorant people, that know not what saint, or pardon, or suffering, or merit is. But the way of comfort by the suffering of others, is by confirming and strengthening some grace, of patience, or comfort, &c., in them. All the good that is in the father cannot help the son, except he tread in his father's steps. If we go not in the same way as others do to heaven, in the same graces, all their sufferings will do us no good, but serve to condemn us. The point is clear; because it serves to enlighten other points, I do but name it. But that which I will a little more stand on is, that salvation is wrought by suffering.

Doct. We come to the possession of salvation by patience.

Faith of salvation by Christ stirs us up to suffer, till we come to the possession of that that we have title to. Mark how these hang together. First, a Christian knows that God will save him by the merits, and satisfaction, and obedience of Christ, his surety. The assured persuasion of this salvation that he hath title to by Christ, because the possession of it is deferred till the next world, and there is a distance of time, and that time is encumbered with afflictions, hereupon comes a necessity of some special grace to carry us along till we be fully invested into that that we have title to by Christ. There must be some grace between faith and the possession of heaven. I am assured of the possession of heaven in my first conversion; but I am not invested into it. It is deferred. There is a distance of time which is afflictive; for hope deferred maketh the heart faint. A thing that we have right and title to, deferred, afflicts the soul, and the deferring of good hath the respect of ill. Good deferred puts upon it the consideration of ill; for it is a grievance to want a good I have a right unto. Now it is not only deferred, but my life is an exercised life, with many actions and sufferings. What grace must bear me up between me and heaven, and in the tediousness of the time prolonged? Especially the grace of enduring. Therefore faith in Christ, by which I have a title to heaven, that stirs up hope, and hope stirs up patience, and that helps me in the way to heaven. It helps me to bear crosses and afflictions, and likewise to endure the tediousness and length of time till I come to heaven. So salvation is wrought by suffering. We come not to the possession of it but by suffering and enduring. 'You have need of patience,' saith the apostle, Heb. x. 36.

Give me leave to clear the point a little. How doth patience enter into this great work of helping our salvation? Patience in enduring affliction, it helps many ways.

1. *They work salvation, not by way of merit, for that were to disable the*

title we have by Christ, but by way af evidence. It helps the evidence of the title. For I have title by Christ. But how do I know that my evidence to that title is good? Afflictions, and the patient suffering of them. Not afflictions alone, but afflictions joined with the grace of patience to endure them; for else they do no good. Afflictions are evil in themselves. For thus it increaseth my evidence. Every heir is a son. For heaven is the inheritance of sons; and every son must be corrected; and I am corrected and afflicted in this life; and God doth give me grace to endure them, and to see my good in them. These afflictions, therefore, mingled with patient enduring of them, do evidence that I am not a bastard. In Heb. xii. 8, the apostle proves this. Every one that hath not some affliction or other, 'he is a bastard and not a son.' It increaseth my evidence that I am the child of God, especially if I suffer for a good cause. 'If we suffer with him, we shall reign with him,' Rom. viii. 17. Here the evidence is increased. By this I know I am in the way which is strewed with crosses and afflictions. We must enter into heaven this way. I know it for the way, so it furthers my salvation. It gives me assurance that my evidence is good.

It is the Scripture's manner to say things are done, when the knowledge of the thing is increased: as to say we are saved, when we know more assuredly that we shall be saved; to say we are in the kingdom of heaven when we know we are in the state of the kingdom of heaven, as in 2 Pet. iii. 18. Saith he, 'grow in grace,' &c., for by this means, 'a further entrance shall be ministered unto you, into the kingdom of God,' 2 Pet. i. 11. The knowledge of a man's estate in grace is a further entrance into the kingdom of God, that is begun here in this life. The knowledge that I am an heir of heaven, is to be in heaven before my time. Thus afflictions joined with patience help salvation, because they help the evidence of salvation. They shew that we are sons, and not bastards. It is an evidence of our adoption.

2. And then sufferings, joined with the grace of enduring, *help forward salvation by way of qualification.* There is a qualification and disposition of soul, which is necessary before we come to heaven; 'because no unclean thing shall ever come to heaven,' Rev. xxi. 27.

Now suffering, joined with patience, having a mighty and blessed work this way, to purge us of that soil that we cannot carry to heaven with us. We may not think to carry our unmortified pride and lusts, and base earthly affections, and our pleasures and riches ill gotten, to heaven with us. Oh, no! the presence of heaven is a more pure presence than so, and the place will not endure such defilements. We must be cleansed therefore.

Now, because afflictions endured with patience, have a blessed power to subdue that which by nature is powerful in us, to purge out those base affections, that are contrary to the glorious estate we look for; therefore they help us to heaven, they help the qualification of the person, not the merit and desert of it.

They help likewise the qualification, by removing that which corruption feeds on; for affliction endured removes that which corruption works on, and strengthens itself by. Affliction is either in removing riches, or honours, or pleasures, somewhat that corruption feeds on; for all corruption is about those idols, greatness, or pleasure, or profit of the world. Now sufferings crossing us in our reputation, or estates, or body, one way or other, they withdraw the fuel that feeds our corruptions, and so help mortification and purgation, and so fit us for heaven. They help our repentance. They make the favour of God sweet, and sin bitter. It is a bitter thing to offend God. We feel it by the afflictions that are laid on us.

3. Again, *many positive graces are required before we come to heaven.* Affliction endured helps all graces whatsoever. The only time for grace to thrive in is the time of affliction, for affliction endured helps our zeal, our love. We have experience of the patience of God, and they stir up prayer. All graces are set on work in affliction. 'Out of the deep have I cried,' Ps. cxxx. 1. Prayers are cries in affliction. They are not cold dull things, but set on fire; they set the spirit on work to cry to God with earnest, frequent, and fervent prayer.

4. Then again, *afflictions endured, they work salvation and help us to heaven, because they whet and sharpen our desire of heaven;* for when we find ill usage here below in our pilgrimage, we have a great desire to be at home at rest; and that is one main end why God sends afflictions, to help salvation this way by sharpening our desires. For were it not for afflictions, and the enduring of them, would we ever say, 'Come, Lord Jesus, come quickly'? Rev. xxii. 20. Would we not be of Peter's mind, 'It is good for us to be here'? Mark ix. 5. Would we ever be weary of the world, before we be fired out of it and pulled out of it, as Lot out of Sodom? No. They help our desire and earnestness. The creature groans, Rom. viii. 21, 22. 'Those that have received the first fruits of the Spirit, they wait for the adoption of the sons of God.' Those that have the beginnings of grace, they wait for the accomplishment. What makes this but afflictions and troubles of the world? They desire a state wherein all tears shall be wiped from their eyes.

So we see, these and many other ways, but these are the principal, how afflictions, endured as they should be, they help salvation, they work our salvation. Though they work not the title of it, yet they help us in the way.

First, because they assure us that we are the sons of God, and so have evidence that we are in a good state; and then they remove the hindrances and purge us of our sins. And then they help us in all graces, they cherish all graces, and they sharpen and whet the edge of our desires to be out of this world.

And all this must be in every Christian before he come to heaven; for God never brings a man of years to heaven but he gives him cause to see why he would be out of this world, either by long sickness or affliction, or by one thing or other. He makes them see that it is better to be there than here; and if it were not for crosses, who would be of that mind?

Therefore, have we not cause to suspect ourselves that we are in smooth ways and find no crosses? God doth give respite to his children. They have breathing times. They are not alway under crosses. He is merciful. Perhaps they have not strength enough. He will not bring them to the lists,* to the stage, because they are not enabled, they have not strength enough. But they that have a continual tenor of prosperity may well suspect themselves. If one have direction to such a place, and they tell him there are such ways, deep waters, that except he take heed he will be drowned, and step into holes, and they are craggy ways; and if he meet with none of these, he may well think he is not in his way. So the way to heaven, it is through afflictions. We must endure many afflictions, saith the apostle here, 'Salvation is wrought by enduring the same afflictions

* That is, 'barriers.' Cf. Richardson, *sub voce*—G.

that you see in us.' Now, if I suffer and endure nothing, if I cannot endure so much as a filip, a disgrace, a frown, a scorn for Christ, if the way be over-smooth, it is not the way to heaven certainly. The way is not strewed with roses. We must have our feet 'shod with the preparation of the gospel,' Eph. vi. 15. They must be well shod that go among thorns; and they had need to be well fenced that go the way to heaven. It is a thorny, rugged way. But it is no matter what the way be, so it brings us to heaven; but certainly, if the way be too smooth, we ought to suspect ourselves.

Now, because it may be objected, many will say, alas! What do we suffer? and, therefore, our case is not good.

I answer, every Christian suffers one of these ways at one time or other, nay, at all times, either by sympathy with the church [or otherwise.]

1. Put the case we have no afflictions of our own, do we not *sympathise with the church beyond the seas?* When thou hearest ill news, if thou be glad to hear it, certainly thy case is bad. There is a suffering by sympathy, and that suffering is ours.

2. Then again, there are afflictions and sufferings *that arise upon scandals*, that men run into before our eyes, which is a great grief. 'Mine eyes gush out with rivers of waters, because men keep not thy law,' saith David, Ps. cxix. 136. Is it not a matter of suffering to a Christian soul to see that he would not see, and to hear blasphemies and oaths that he would not hear? to have the understanding forced to understand that he would not, living in a world of iniquity, in the kingdom of the devil? It is a great grievance. 'Woe is me that I am forced to dwell in Meshech, and to have my habitation with the tents of Kedar,' Ps. cxx. 5. It is a pitiful affliction to the saints of God, to him that hath the life of grace in his heart, to have the wicked as 'goads and thorns,' as the Scripture saith the Jebusites should be to the Israelites, Num. xxxiii. 55; to have thoughts forced upon us and things forced upon our souls that we would not see nor think nor hear of, that which shall never be in heaven.

3. Again, *every one suffers the burden of his calling*, which is a great suffering. A man need not to whip himself, as the Scottish papists do (*q*), if he be but faithful in his calling. It is a notable means of mortification. God keeps a man from persecution many times because he hath burdens in his calling to exercise him. He hath many crosses in his calling. God hath joined sweat to labour, and trouble, and pains; and there is no man that is faithful in his calling as he should be, but he shall find many crosses.

4. And then, that which afflicts most of all, the affliction of all afflictions, *the inward combat between the flesh and the spirit*, which God usually takes up in persecution and outward troubles. God's dear children in persecution find little molestation from their corruptions, because God will not lay more upon them than he will give them strength to bear; and now, when he singles them out to outward crosses, he subdues their corruptions, that they do not vex them as before.

In the time of peace he lets loose their corruptions, sometimes anger, sometimes pride, sometimes one base affection, sometimes another; and think you this is no grief to them? Oh, yes; it grieves them, and humbles them more than any cross would do. St Paul was grieved more at this than at all his sufferings. It made him cry out, 'Oh, wretched man that I am, who shall deliver me from this body of death?' Rom. vii. 24. He doth not say, Oh, wretched man, who shall deliver me from crosses and afflictions? Though they made him wretched in the eye of the world, yet he rejoiced in those. But his grief was, that he could not do the good that he would; and that made him cry out, 'O wretched man that I am,' &c. It is God that ties up our corruptions, that they run not so violently on the soul at one time as they do at another, for he hath the command of them by his Spirit. There is no Christian but one of these ways he suffers in the greatest time of peace. Especially this way God exerciseth them, that he makes them weary of their lives by this spiritual conflict. If they know what the life of grace means, he makes them know what it is to be absent from heaven. He makes them know that this life is a place of absence; and all this is to help our disposition to salvation, by helping mortification and by helping our desire to heaven. Those that go on in a smooth course, that know not what this inward combat means, and are carried away with their sins, they are so far from taking scandals to heart, that if they see evil men, they are ready to join with them, to join with blasphemers and wicked persons; and instead of sympathising with the church of God, they are ready to join with them that censure them, and so add affliction to the afflicted.

But to proceed.

'*Whether we be comforted, it is for your consolation and salvation.*' Of 'comfort' I spake in the former verse. Only that note that I will briefly commend you to is this, that

Doct. God's children, hap how it will, they do good.

Cast them into what estate you will, they do good. They are good, and do good. If they be afflicted, they do good by that; if they have comfort, they do good to others by that. No estate is amiss to God's children; and that is the reason of their perfect resignation. The child of God perfectly resigns himself into God's hand. Lord, if thou wilt have me suffer, I will suffer; if thou wilt have me afflicted, I yield myself; if thou wilt have me enjoy prosperity, I will. I know it shall be for my good, and for the good of others.

There is an intercourse in the life of a Christian. He is now afflicted, and now comforted, not for his own sake only, but for the good of others; and when he shall be afflicted, and how long, and what comfort he shall have, how much, he leaves it to the wisdom of God. It is a blessed estate, if we could think of it, to be a Christian, that we need to care for nothing but to serve God. We need to care for nothing, but study to keep a good conscience. Let God alone with all our estate; for God will enable us to want and to abound in our own persons, and likewise he will sanctify our estate for the good of others.

And a Christian will be willing to be tossed, and to be 'changed from vessel to vessel,' Jer. xlviii. 11, from state to state, for the good of others. If his afflictions may do good to the church, he is content that God should withdraw his blessings from him, and humble him with crosses. If his example may be good to others, he is likewise joyful; when God gives him rest, and causeth an inward comfort, he knows that this is good for others. He hath learned in his first entrance into Christianity, self-denial, not to live to himself, but for the glory of God and the good of others, as much as he may.

Use. We should labour therefore to content ourselves in all conditions, knowing that all is for the best, not only to ourselves, and God's glory, but for the good of others. God, when he takes things from us, and afflicts us, and when he comforts us, he intends the comfort of others. So we should reason when we endure anything, and when we are comforted, certainly

God intends the good of others by this; therefore I will have a special care in suffering, to carry it decently and exemplarily, knowing that the eyes of many are upon me. I will carry myself so, that God may have glory, and others may have edification and comfort, knowing that I am but God's steward, to convey this to others, that are of the same body with myself. Therefore in our communion we have with others, upon any good occasion, we ought to express the blessed experience of the comfort of God upon us. This is the practice of holy men in their meeting with others, to shew them the comforts of God to their souls. 'Come, and I will shew you what God hath done for my soul,' Ps. cxlii. 7, saith the psalmist. All are the better for a good man. He doth good to all; and therefore Solomon saith, 'When a righteous man is advanced, the city rejoiceth,' Prov. xi. 10. They have cause, for he hath a public mind. Nothing doth more characterise, and is a better stamp of a true Christian, than a public mind.

A carnal man out of self-love may grieve at his own sins, and may labour to comfort himself; but a Christian thinks others shall take good by me. It is the mind of Christ, and it is the mind of all the members of Christ, when a man thinks he hath nothing, except he have it to improve for the good of others.

A dead, sullen, reserved spirit, is not a Christian's spirit. If by nature we have such, we must labour to help it with grace; for grace is a diffusive, communicating thing, not only in the ministers of God, but in every Christian. Grace will teach them to make savoury their conversation to others, this way, that whatsoever they are, or whatsoever they can do, or whatsoever they suffer, they study to improve all to the good of others.

And mark the extent of the loving wisdom and providence of God, how many things he doth at once. For in the same affliction ofttimes, he corrects some in his children, in the same affliction he tries some grace, in the same affliction he witnesseth to his truth in them, in the same affliction he doth good to others besides the good he doth to them. In the same affliction that others inflict, he hasteneth the ruin of them that offer it; at one time, and in one action, he hasteneth the destruction of the one, by hastening the good of the other; he ripens grace in his children, making them exemplary to others, and all in the same action, so large is the wise providence of God.

It should teach us likewise to follow that providence, and to see how many ways anything we suffer any kind of way may extend, that if one way will not comfort, another may. When we suffer, and are grieved, let us consider withal that he that doth the wrong, he hastens his ruin and judgment. As Pharaoh, when he hastened the overthrow of the children of Israel, he hastened his overthrow in the Red Sea. So a pit is digged for the wicked, when they dig a pit for the godly, Ps. vii. 15. And consider, to comfort thyself, thou hast some sin in thee, and God intends not only to witness this truth, but to correct some sin in thee, and thou must look to that. Thou hast some grace in thee, and he intends the trial of that. Look to these things. This shews strong heavenly-mindedness, when there is self-denial. Let us consider what God calls us to; for God looks to many things in the same act. Wherefore doth God give us reason and discourse, but to be able to follow him in his dealing, as far as we can reach to?

But I go on to the next verse.

VERSE 7.

'*And our hope of you is stedfast, knowing that as you are partakers of the suffering, so you shall be also of the consolation.*' This verse is nothing but a strengthening of what he said before. He had told them that whatsoever he suffered, it was for their comfort too; and now he repeats it again, and sets a seal upon it, 'Our hope of you is stedfast, knowing that as you are partakers of the sufferings, so you shall also be of the consolation.' In these words he shews that they shall share in the good with him as well as in the ill; that the Spirit of God in them should help them to take all the good they could, both by his sufferings and by his comfort. For as he by the help of the Spirit of God intended the public good, intended their good and comfort in all, whether he were afflicted or comforted; so he saith here, he was assured that as they were partakers of his sufferings, so they should be of his comforts likewise.

Here is the truth, and the seal of the truth.

The truth, that they were 'partakers of his sufferings,' and should be 'partakers of his consolations.'

And *the seal* is in the manner of affirming these truths, 'Our hope of you is stedfast.' And in this order I will speak of them. First,

Doct. God's children are partakers of the sufferings of others.

The Corinthians were partakers of the sufferings of St Paul.

God's children are partakers of the sufferings of others many ways.

First. By way of sympathy, taking to heart the estate of the church and children of God abroad. It grieved the Corinthians to hear that St Paul was afflicted; for even as it is in the natural body, so likewise in the mystical body, there is a sympathy between the members.

Second. Likewise they partake of the sufferings of others *by way of proportion.* They suffered in their kind and proportion as he suffered; though perhaps not in the same very individual kind. There is a portion of suffering in the church. Some suffer one way, and others another; but all partake of sufferings in some degree or other.

3. Then again, they did partake of St Paul's sufferings *in preparation and disposition of mind.* Howsoever now they did not suffer as much as he, yet, saith he, I know as far as the Spirit of God is in you, you are prepared to suffer; and what we are prepared to do, that we do. Christ saith we 'sell all for the gospel,' when upon serious examination of our hearts we find we can part with it. When we set ourselves to examination, what cannot I part with for Christ? Can I part with my goods? Can I part with my life? If we can once come to resolution, it is done, as Abraham is said to sacrifice his son, because he resolved to do it, Heb. xi. 17; and David is said to build the temple, because he intended to do it, 1 Kings viii. 18. God looks upon us in our resolutions and preparations. What we resolve to do, that is done. So, saith he, you are partakers of my sufferings, not only by sympathy, and in proportion of sufferings, but you are prepared, he speaks charitably and lovingly, to suffer whatsoever I suffer, if God call you to it.

Reason. And the ground of Christians partaking of the sufferings one of another, it is the *communion that is between Christians.* They are all members of one body. If the hand suffer, the head suffers. The head thinks itself wronged when the hand or the foot is wronged, by reason of the sympathy between the members, as I said; and so it is in the mystical body of Christ.

There are these three unions which depend one upon another.

1. *The union of Christ with our nature*, which is inseparable. It is an eternal union. He never lays that blessed mass of our flesh aside which he took, which is the ground of all our comfort; for God is now at one with us, because God hath taken our nature on him, and satisfied the wrath of God his Father.

2. Next the union of Christ with our nature, *is the union of Christ mystical.* Christ and his members when they suffer, Christ suffers. Their sufferings are the sufferings of Christ.

3. The third *is the union of one member with another*, that what one member suffers, another doth suffer. Therefore the Corinthians were partakers of Christ, because their sufferings were the sufferings of Christ; and they were partakers of St Paul's sufferings, because his sufferings were their sufferings.

They were partakers of Christ's sufferings, because of the communion between the head and the members; and they were partakers of St Paul's sufferings, because of the communion of one member with another. And surely there is not a heart that was ever touched with the Spirit of God, but when he hears of any calamity of the church, whether it be in the Palatinate (*r*), in France, in the Low countries, or in any country in the world, if he hears that the church hath a blow, it strikes to the heart of any man that hath the Spirit of God in them, by a sympathetical suffering. It is one good sign to know whether a man be of the mystical body or no, to take to heart the grievance of the church. As good Nehemiah did; he would not take comfort in the pleasures of a court, in the king of Babylon's court, when it went not well with his country. When the church was in distress, he took their grievance to heart. So Moses, the very joys of Pharaoh's court could not please him, when he considered the abasement of his countrymen, and he joined with them; and it is called the 'rebuke' of Christ.

So it is with all the people of God. There is a communication of sufferings. 'As you are partakers of the sufferings, so you shall be also of the consolation.'

Wherein two things are observable.

First, *that a necessary precedent condition of comfort is sufferings.*

And then the consequent of this, *that those that suffer as they should are sure of comfort.* These two things unfold the meaning of the Spirit of God here.

Before there be comfort, there must be suffering; for God hath established this order. Even as in nature, there must be a night before the day, and a winter before a summer; so in the kingdom of Christ, in his ruling of the church, there is this divine policy, there must be suffering before comfort. God will sooner break the league and the covenant between day and night, than this league of suffering and comfort: the one must be before the other. It was so in our head, Christ. He suffered, and then entered into his glory. So all his members must be conformable* to him in suffering, and then enter into their glory.

The reasons of this are divers.

Reason 1. First of all, this method and order is, first, suffering, and then comfort, *because God finds us in a corrupt estate;* and something must be wrought out of us, before we can be vessels to receive comfort. Therefore there must be a purgation one way or other, either by repentance, or if not,

* Misprinted, 'comfortable.'—G.

by repentance, by affliction, to help repentance. There must be suffering before comfort. The soul is unfit for comfort.

Secondly, *this order commends and sweetens comfort to us.* For fire is sweet after cold, and meat is sweet after hunger; so comfort is sweet after suffering. God fits us to comfort by this, by purging out what is contrary to comfort. And he endears comfort by this. Those that have felt the cross, comfort is comfort indeed to them. Heaven is heaven indeed to him that hath had a hell in his conscience upon earth, that hath been afflicted in conscience, or outwardly persecuted. It set a price and value upon comfort.

Partly likewise to sharpen our desire of comfort; for suffering breeds sense, and sense that stirs up desire, and desire is eager. Now suffering, it makes comforts precious, and sets us in a wondrous strong desire after them.

And by this means, likewise, God comes to his own end, which is that our comforts may be eternal. Therefore we have that which is ill, in the first place. Woe to us, if it should be said to us, as to Dives in the gospel, 'Son, son, thou hadst thy good here, and now thou must have thy ill,' Luke xvi. 25. God intends not to deal so with his children; but they taste the worst wine first, and better afterward. Because he intends eternal happiness to them, he observes this method, first ill, and then good, the best at last.

Use 1. If this be so, *then why should we be offended at God's order?* Why should we not take it, not only gently and meekly, but joyfully, the afflictions that God sends to prepare and fit us for happiness, to sharpen our desire to happiness, to make it precious to us? Certainly it is a ground, not only of patience and meekness, but of joy and comfort, in all the things we suffer. Will a patient be angry with his chirurgeon for searching of his wound? He knows that that is the way to cure him. Will any man take offence at the goldsmith for purging his mass? They know that is the way to purify it, and fetch out the dross.

This is the method in nature. The ground must be ploughed and prepared, and then comes the harvest. Let us be content with this method, and rejoice in any suffering, knowing it will have a blessed issue; and not to think much at suffering anything for a good cause in ourselves, or by way of sympathy or support with others, because this is the highway to a better estate. If we suffer with the church, or for the church, any kind of way, we shall be comforted with the church. It is that which sweetens the cross, that we are under hope of better still. Who would not endure a little grievance in the way, to have honour in the end? to have ill usage in an inn, and to go to a kingdom? All our discomforts and afflictions are but by the way here; and crosses are necessary for travellers, and here we are but in a travelling estate. It should, I say, encourage us not to take offence at anything that God exerciseth us with in this world, nor to take scandal at the afflictions of the church.

Use 2. And then *it should strike terror to those that will not endure so much as a scratch, a scoff, a word, a chip of the cross, that will endure nothing.* Do they know that this is God's order? Do they avoid crosses in any degree? and do they think to have comfort? No! God will not change his order for them. He hath established this order, and heaven and earth shall fail, rather than God's order shall not be sure. If we will have comfort, we must suffer. If we will avoid suffering, and think to go to heaven another way than God hath ordained, we may take our own way, but we must give him leave to take his way in comforting and advancing whom he will, and that will not be us, because we will not frame ourselves to his order. We must not look for his dignity. 'If we will not suffer with him, we shall not reign with him,' Rom. viii. 17.

The next thing observable in the order is this, that

Doct. Those that suffer as they should are sure of comfort.

There is a threefold conformity with Christ, in *suffering*, *grace*, *glory*.

Those that are not conformable to him in suffering, they cannot be conformable to him in grace; and if they be not in grace, they shall not in glory. He took upon him our nature abased first; and our nature purified, and our nature glorious, he hath now in heaven. So our nature in us must keep this order. First, it must be abased, as our flesh was in him, and then filled with grace, by little and little, and then glorions, as our nature is in him. If we will not suffer our flesh to be abased and exercised with afflictions, and let God work his own good work as he pleaseth this way, we are not conformable to Christ, who was first abased, and then advanced. What was wrought in his blessed flesh, must be wrought in his mystical body, in all his members, by little and little. Therefore those that are tender and wayward to endure anything, when God calls them to it, they are enemies to their own comfort. God hath set down this order, if they do not partake of the sufferings of the church, they shall not partake of the comfort.

Oh, it is a cursed estate to be out of the condition of God's people, and it is a comfortable thing to have part with those that are good, yea, even if it be in suffering with them. It is better to have communion with God's people in suffering, than to have communion with the wicked in the world, in reigning and triumphing.

And that is the reason that the Spirit of God in the prophet made him desire, 'Deal with me, Lord, as thou usest to deal with those that fear thy name,' Ps. cxix. 124. He knew he deals well enough with them. 'Visit me with the salvation of thy children,' Ps. cvi. 4. He knew that was a special salvation. So to have God deal with us, as he deals with his, and to visit us in mercy and love, as he visits his own, it is a special favour. It is better to bear the cross with them, that we may partake with them in the comfort, than to have all the comforts that the wicked have, and to share with them in the misery afterward. Therefore let us be content to share with God's people in their suffering. When we hear of any that suffer for a just cause, though we have no sufferings of our own, let us bear a part with them, and with the bond of the communion of saints, help what we may.

And it is as true on the contrary, if we partake with the wicked in their sins, we shall partake with them in their punishment. Therefore the Scripture saith, 'Come out of Babylon, my people, lest if you partake of her sins, so you partake of her punishments,' Rev. xviii. 4. Now, atheistical people think it nothing to enter into league, and amity, and society with profane people, that are professedly so, not only by weakness, but those that are stigmatized. But what saith the Scripture?—and the Holy Ghost doth not trifle with us.—'Come out of Babylon, my people, lest you partake of her plagues;' which is not meant so much locally to come out of the place, as in disposition to come out in respect of liking, and converse, and secret intimate communion. Lot's sons-in-law, they thought it was but trifling. They gibed as atheists do now, when they hear the ministers encourage people to make much of religion, and to set against those that are opposite. They think they are enforced to it, and it is upon mistake, &c., though it be as palpable as the light of the sun. They deal as Lot's sons-in-law, when he warned them to come out of Sodom, and he was pulled out. They would believe nothing till fire came down from heaven, and destroyed them all. It was too late then. Therefore let us hearken to the counsel of the angel, let us not make this a matter of scorn, a light matter; but as we desire to have no part in their confusion, so avoid their courses. The Scripture is terrible to those that, after the breaking out of the light, will be such. There is not more direct Scriptures against any kind of men, than those that wilfully cleave to antichrist. Therefore we should not esteem it a light matter, but think of it seriously indeed.

And not only in respect of them, but all wicked society. Were it not pity that men should be severed from them hereafter, whose company they will not be severed from now? If thou see an adulterer, a blasphemer, a wicked, licentious, atheistical person, and thou runnest into the same excess of riot with him, thou wilt not be drawn by any persuasions, ministerial or friendly, or by thine own light, which knows his course to be naught, to retire from his society,—dost thou not think to share with him afterward in his judgment? As you are all tares, so you shall be bound in a bundle, and cast into hell together, Mat. xiii. 30. As the wheat shall be gathered into heaven, so the tares, a cursed company, that will cleave together though they be damned for it. As they clave together as burs and tares here, so they shall be cast into hell together. That is the end of dissolute, unruly creatures, that nothing will sever them from those who in their own consciences they know their courses to be naught.

'*Our hope of you is stedfast.*' There is a double certainty, a certainty of the truth of the thing, and a certainty of the estate of the person. The certainty of the truth is this, *those that suffer with Christ and his church, shall be glorified with Christ and his church.* The certainty of the truth is more certain than heaven and earth. Now, besides the certainty of the truth, or thing, there is interposed a certainty of the persons, that as they were interested in the sufferings, so they should be in the comforts. And this is true as well as the former. For God's promises are not mere ideas wanting truths, that have no performance in the persons; but if the thing be true, it is true in the person to whom the truth belongs. Suffering goes before glory. Therefore if we suffer we shall be glorified. But this is the condition, if they suffer with Christ. Then St Paul takes it for certain that they shall be glorified with Christ. There is not the same certainty of the persons as of the truth itself. The truth is certain by a certainty of faith, but the certainty of the persons is the certainty of a charitable persuasion. I am persuaded that you will suffer with me in sympathy, and therefore I am persuaded in the certainty of charity that you shall of a certain have the comfort.

'Our hope of you is stedfast.' St Paul, you see, hath a good conceit of them, that he might encourage them to sympathise and take to heart his crosses, and to take good by them. A good hope of others hath a double efficacy.

1. It hath one efficacy in the party that hath the good hope of another. It stirs him up to be diligent to take all courses that may be for the good of another. As the speech is, Hope stirs up to work; it stirs up endeavour; so it doth in the husbandman, and in every kind of trade. Hope quickens endeavour. A man will never sow upon the sands. He

loseth his cost. A man will never bestow his pains upon those that he thinks are desperate. And what is it that dulls and deads endeavour? I despair of ever doing such a man good. When those despairing thoughts enter into the soul, there is a stop of all endeavour. And surely Christians are much to blame that way. When they might have ground, if charity were in them, at least of hope of others; upon some hard, despairing conceits they cast off hope, and so neglect all endeavours of doing good to others. The Spirit of God is witty* in the hearts of his children to observe all advantages of doing good. Therefore it is willing to entertain all offers of good in others. If they be but willing to hear reproof, if they be willing to hear comfort, and to hear good discourse, it will make a good construction of their errors, if it may be, except it be those that are maliciously obstinate. It will impute it to passion, or to ill company, to one thing or other. As far as possible it will admit of a good construction. Love in God's children will admit of it; and love stirs up to hope, and hope stirs up to deal with them for their good.

I know that charity is not sottish; but yet it is willing to think the best. Where there is probability of good for the present, or where there is a tractableness, where there is a willingness to entertain communion, where there is any propension,† we must be of our blessed Saviour's disposition, 'who will not quench the smoking flax, nor break the bruised reed,' Mat. xii. 20. We must draw all, and drive none away. This is one special fruit and effect that hope hath in the party that doth hope toward another.

Now, as it is good for the speaker to be well conceited; so it is a good preparative in the hearer. It hath a winning power in the party hoped of. It is a great attractive; for we willingly hear those that conceit good of us. St Paul here works upon the natural disposition in all, which is, that they love to be well thought of; and natural dispositions are strong. It is the natural disposition for every man to love where he is well thought of; and it is not sinful, unless it be in vainglory, to desire to have good place in the esteem of others. And there a man will labour to carry himself answerable to the good conceit had in him.

There is a conflict in the worst man. Where he is well conceited of, he labours to maintain it, except it be those that are mightily enthralled, as some wretches are, to blasphemy, and to a cursed life, that they care not. But else if they be well thought of, it will stir them up to maintain it. He is a dissolute man, he is not a man, so far as he is careless of this, he is brutish and senseless. St Paul, in saying 'our hope is stedfast concerning you,' he wins himself into their good opinion; and so by that means he hoped to prevail with them for greater matters. So hope, it stirs up men to do good, and it makes the other willing to receive good. For it makes them willing to content them that hope well of them. St Paul was led with this heavenly wisdom, and that which made him so industrious, was hope of prevailing; and that which made him prevail with others, was the good conceit he had of them. He would gather upon every one. When he saw Agrippa come on a little, 'Agrippa, believest thou the Scriptures?' Acts xxvi. 27. I know thou believest. 'Almost thou persuadest me to be a Christian,' saith he, ver. 28; and so he comes in a little. It is good, as much as may be, to have hope of others.

But what is his degree of hope? 'Our hope of you'—is stedfast.

He had a stedfast hope, that if they were sufferers, they should be partakers of the comfort.

* That is, 'wise.'—G.

† That is, 'inclination.'—G.

The observation may be this, that

Doct. Divine truths are such as we may build a stedfast hope on the performance of them.

Divine truths, divine comforts, they are of that nature, that though we do not yet enjoy them, yet we may build certainly upon them. I hope stedfastly, that if you be partakers of the sufferings, you shall be partakers of the comforts. A man cannot say so of any thing else but divine truths. A man cannot say of any other, or of himself, I hope stedfastly to be rich, I hope stedfastly to be great, or I hope stedfastly to live long. The nature of the thing is uncertain. The state of the world is vanity; and life itself, and all things here, will not admit of a certain apprehension. For the certainty in a man's understanding, it follows the certainty of the thing, or else there is no adequation.* When there is an evenness in the apprehension to the thing, then it is true; but if we apprehend anything that is here, that either riches or life, or favour will be thus, or thus long, it is no true apprehension. We cannot build a certain hope upon an uncertain ground. But of divine truths, we can say, if we see the one, undoubtedly the other will follow; if we see the signs of grace in any man, that he is strong to endure any disgrace for religion, any discomfort, then we may say, certainly, as you partake of the afflictions of Christ, and of the afflictions and sufferings of his people, his body mystical; so undoubtedly you shall be partakers of the comfort of God's people: heaven and earth shall fail, but this shall never fail.

Is not this a comfort to a Christian, that when he is in the state of grace, he hath something that he may build on, when all things else fail? In all the changes and alterations of this life, he hath somewhat unalterable,—the certainty of divine comforts, the certainty of his estate in grace, though he be in an afflicted estate. As verily as he is afflicted, so verily he shall be comforted. 'If we suffer with Christ, we shall be glorified with him,' Rom. viii. 17.

Upon what ground is this certainty built, that if we suffer we shall be glorified?

It is built upon our union with Christ. It is built upon the communion we have with the church of God. We are all of one body. And it is built upon his own experience. As verily as I have been afflicted, and have comfort, so shall you that suffer be comforted: what I feel, you shall feel.

Because in things necessary there is the like reason from one to all; if one be justified by faith, all are justified by faith; if one suffer and receive comfort, all that suffer shall receive comfort. Divine comforts are from one to all, from the head to the body, from the body to every member. If Christ suffered, I shall suffer, if I be of his body; if Christ was comforted, I shall be comforted. Divine truths they agree in the head and the members. If it be true in one, it is true in all. St Paul felt it in his own person; and, saith he, as I have felt afflictions increase, and comforts increase, so it shall be with you; you shall be partakers of the comforts now, or hereafter. And it is built likewise upon God's promise, which is surer than heaven and earth. 'If we suffer with him, we shall be glorified with him,' as the apostle saith, Rom. viii. 17. All these are grounds to found this stedfast hope on. And then the nature of God: he is a just God, a holy God, and when we have taken the ill, we shall find the sweet, as in

* That is, 'proportion.' This is a superior example of the use of the word to that given by Richardson, *sub voce* from Fuller—G.

2 Thess. i. 6. 'It is just with God, to render to them that afflict you trouble, and to you comfort.' God hath pawned his justice upon it, and he will observe this order. Where he begins in trouble, he will end in comfort. It is just with God, and therefore I may be persuaded.

It should be a special comfort to all that are in any sanctified cross, whether it be for a good cause or no. If a man find that he stands out for a good cause, then there is more matter of joy. It is matter of triumph then. But if they be crosses common to nature, if a man find them sanctified, (as they are only to God's children, they learn humility by them, they learn heavenly-mindedness, they learn patience, they learn more carefulness by their afflictions, if it be thus sanctified), then a man may say to such a one, 'As you partake of the sufferings, so you shall partake of the comfort,' though you feel it not for the present.

Is it not a comfort for a patient to have his physician come to him, whom he knows to be wise, and speaks by his book, to say to him, Be of good comfort, you shall never die of this disease; this that I give you will do you good: there was never any that took this potion but they recovered. Would not this revive the patient? Now when the physicians of our souls shall come and tell a man, by discerning his state to be good, by discerning signs of grace in his abasement, Be of good comfort, there is good intended to you; your sufferings shall end in comfort, undoubtedly; we may well be persuaded of this, God will never vary his order. Therefore, when we are in any trouble, and find God blessing it to us, to abate our pride, to sharpen our desire, to exercise our graces, when we find it sanctified, let it comfort us, it shall turn to our further comfort. We find a present good that it is a pledge of a further good. It will make a bitter potion to go down, when the physician saith, it will do you good. How many distasteful things do poor creatures endure and take down to cure this carcase! It were offensive to name what distasteful things they will take to do them good (*r**).

Let us take this cup from God's hand, let us endure the cross patiently, whatsoever it be. It is a bitter cup, but it is out of a Father's hand, it is out of a sweet hand. There may be a miscarrying in other physic, but God's physic shall certainly do us good. God hath said it, 'All things shall work for the best to those that love him,' Rom. viii. 28. He hath said it beforehand. We may presume, and build our persuasion upon this issue, that all things shall work for our good. What a comfort is this in all the intercourses and changes of this life, when we know before, that whatsoever we meet with, it hath a command from God to do us good, it is medicinable, though it seem never so ill, to do us good, to work ill out of us, by the blessing of God. But to proceed.

VERSES 8, 9.

'For we would not, brethren, have you ignorant of our trouble which came to us in Asia, that we were pressed out of measure, above strength, insomuch that we despaired even of life: But we had the sentence of death in ourselves, that we should not trust in ourselves, but in God which raiseth the dead.'

Here St Paul comes to the particular explication of what he had generally spoken before. He had generally said before, that he had both comfort and affliction; but now he specifies what afflictions they were. 'I would not have you ignorant of the troubles which came to us in Asia,' &c.

'*I would not have you ignorant of!*' He knew it was behoveful for them to know: therefore, to insinuate into their respect the more, he tells them of it. Indeed, to know both together is very sweet and comfortable, to know both the afflictions of God's people and their comforts, as here, he tells them what ill he endured in Asia, and how God delivered him: to see how these are linked together in God's people, is very comfortable. Therefore 'I would not have you ignorant.'

Now, that they might not be ignorant, he sets before their eyes the particular grievance that he suffered in Asia. And see how he doth raise himself by degrees, and represent it to them most lively.

First of all, saith he, 'We were pressed out of measure.' There is one degree, 'we were pressed.' It is a metaphor. 'We were pressed,' as a cart is pressed under sheaves, as a man is pressed under a burden; as a ship that is over laden is pressed deep down with too much burden. So it was with us, we were pressed with afflictions. Afflictions are of a depressing nature, they draw down the soul as comfort raiseth it up.

'Out of measure.' There is the second degree; they were not only pressed, but pressed 'out of measure.'

'Above strength.' Above my strength, above ordinary strength. And he riseth higher still. The waters rise higher, 'insomuch that we despaired of life.' We despaired of any escaping out of trouble at the present encounter, nay, we did not see how we should escape for the time to come.

Nay, it was so great, in the first place, that we passed 'the sentence of death upon ourselves.' It is a speech taken from malefactors that are condemned; for even as they, having the sentence pronounced upon them, we account them dead men, they esteem themselves so, and so do others esteem them, the sentence being passed upon them; so I even passed the sentence on myself, seeing no evasion or escape out of the troubles I was in, the sentence of death passed upon me. 'We had the sentence of death in ourselves.' It was not passed by God, nor by the world; for they had not decreed to kill him, but he passed it upon himself when he saw no way to escape. He was deceived, though, as ofttimes God's children are, for he died not at that time.

And then afterwards he sets down the end why all this was, a sweet end, a double end, 'That we should not trust in ourselves.' What should we trust in then? 'But in God that raiseth the dead.'

First to speak of his grievance, and then of the reason why God did thus follow him.

'*We would not have you ignorant.*' He prevents all scandal by this. 'I would not have you ignorant.' I am so far from caring, or fearing, or being ashamed, that you should know of my affliction that I suffer, that 'I would not have you ignorant of it.' For know this, that when you know my afflictions you shall know my deliverance also. St Paul was wondrous scrupulous at this, lest they should take any offence at his sufferings. Indeed it is the state of God's children; their worst cross. Sometimes are censures upon them for the cross, the harsh censures of others in their troubles. It was the last, and the greatest of Job's troubles, that, and his wife together. When his house was overthrown, his children killed, his goods taken away, himself stricken with boils, then for his indiscreet friends to become 'miserable comforters,' those that should have comforted him, to become censurers and judges of him, as if he had been a man deserted and forsaken of God, as if all had been from God as a punishment for his sins, this was his greatest cross, as it was his last, when his wife in his bosom, she that should have comforted him most, should solicit him to ill, and his friends by their rash and vile censures to make his cross heavier. So it is with God's children in the world. They cannot endure hardness in the world, they cannot be used otherwise than their cause deserves. But they must also undergo hard censures; that grieves them more than the cross itself. It was the case of this blessed apostle. The Spirit of God in him therefore sets him to mention his affliction with boldness and confidence, yea, with comfort and joy. 'I would not have you ignorant,' I am not of the mind of carnal men, that would* have it concealed, nay, I would not have you ignorant, I pray understand it. He lays it open to their view, that they might be affected with it, as he was; for those things that we are affected with, we are large in the discourse of them. He shews that the misery, though it were past, and were off, yet he was affected with it. 'We were pressed out of measure above strength.'

Obj. This seems to thwart another place of Scripture in 1 Cor. x. 13, 'God is faithful, and will lay no more upon you than you shall be able to bear;' and yet here he saith, 'we were afflicted above strength.' How can these hang together?

I answer, God will not suffer his children to endure anything above strength, above that they are able to bear, especially in spiritual evils, but for sickness and persecution or such, sometimes he may lay more upon them than they have present strength to bear.

But, put the case that St Paul speaks of, inward grievance, and outward afflictions too, as both usually accompany one another. St Paul's meaning is here undoubtedly, 'We were pressed above strength,' that is, above ordinary natural strength, that unless God had made a supply by a new supernatural strength, we had never been able to endure it. Therefore take it so, above ordinary natural strength; for extraordinary crosses must have extraordinary strength, and crosses with grievance of spirit must have more than natural strength to bear them.

Obj. Again, where it is said, 'Insomuch that we despaired of life,' as if he had cared much for his life,—this seemeth to cross another place, Phil. i. 23, 'I desire to be dissolved, and to be with Christ;' and here he seems to be very careful, in a strait, lest he should die.

Ans. I answer, we must take St Paul in diverse considerations and respects. As St Paul hath finished his course, and done his work, so 'Henceforth is laid up for me the crown of righteousness,' 2 Tim. iv. 8; so he thinks of nothing but life and glory; he cares not for his life. But take St Paul in the midst of his course, and so he had a care to his charge. Take St Paul as he looked to glory, so he desired to be dissolved; take him as he was affected to edify the church, so he laboured to live by all means, and so he saith he despaired of life, as desiring to live to do good to the church.

Obj. Again, it may be objected against the last, 'We received the sentence of death in ourselves.' St Paul died not now, and he had the Spirit of God in him, to know what he spake; how doth this agree then that he had the sentence of death passed?

Ans. I answer, St Paul spake according to the probability of second causes, according to the appearance of things; and so he might pronounce of himself without danger, as being no sinful error, that indeed I am a dead man, I see no hope of escaping. If I look to the probability of second causes, all my enemies are about me, I am in the lion's mouth, there is but

* 'Not' inserted here by a self-correcting misprint.—G.

a step between me and death. He doth not look here to the decree of God, but he looks to the disposing of present causes. So God's children are often deceived in themselves in that respect. It is no great error; for it is true what they speak in regard of second causes, though it be not true in regard of God's decree.

The objections being satisfied, we may observe some points of doctrine.

And out of the first part of St Paul's trial, which some take it to be that in Acts xix., [when] at Ephesus, Demetrius the smith raised up a trouble against him, when they cried out, 'Great is Diana of the Ephesians.' But those are but conjectures. It may be it was some great sickness; it may be some other affliction. The Scripture is silent in the particular what it was. To come then to the points themselves. In the first part, this is considerable in the first place, that

God suffers his children to fall into extreme perils and dangers.

And then secondly, that *they are sensible of it.*

For the first,

God suffers his children to fall into great extremities. This is clear here, we see how he riseth by degrees. 'We were pressed above measure, above strength, that we even despaired of life, we received the sentence of death in ourselves.' He riseth by five steps, to shew the extremity that he was in. This is no new thing, that God should suffer his children thus to be exercised.

It is true in the head, it is true in the body, and it is true of every particular member of the body.

It is true of our head, Christ Jesus himself. We see to what exigencies he was brought, in what danger of his life ofttimes he was, as when they would have cast him down from the mount, Luke iv. 29, and when, in apprehension of his Father's wrath, he sweat 'water and blood' in the garden, Luke xxii. 44; and on the cross cried out, 'My God, my God, why hast thou forsaken me?' Mark xv. 34. None was ever so abased as he was. He 'humbled himself to the death of the cross,' Philip. ii. 8, nay, lower than the cross; he was in captivity in the grave three days. They thought they had had their will on him there, they thought they might have trampled on Christ; and no doubt but the devil triumphed over the grave, and thought he had had him where he would. But we see afterward God raised him again gloriously.

Now, as the head was abased, even unto extremity; so it is true of the whole body of the church from the beginning of the world. The church in Egypt was in extremity before Moses came; therefore, a learned Hebrician Capne (*s*), that brought Hebrew into these western parts, was wont to say, When the tale of brick was doubled, then comes Moses, that is, in extremity. When there was no remedy, then God sent them deliverance. In what a pitiful case was the poor church and people of God in Esther's time. There was but a hair's-breadth between them and destruction. It was decreed by Haman, and they had gotten the king's decree too. They were, as it were, between the hammer and the anvil, ready to be crushed in pieces presently, had not God come between. And so in Babylon the church was in extremity, insomuch as that when deliverance was told them, 'they were as men that dream,' Ps. cxxvi. 1, as if there had been no such matter; they wondered at it. And so in the times of persecution, God hath suffered his church to fall into extreme danger, as now at this time the church is in other parts. I might draw this truth along through all ages. It is true of the whole body of the church. It is true likewise of the particular members. Take the principal members of it. You see Abraham, before God made good his promise, he was brought to a dry body, and Sarah to a dead womb, that they despaired of all second causes. And David, though God promised him a kingdom, yet he was so straitened that he thought many times he should have died. 'I said in my haste, All men are liars,' Ps. cxvi. 11. They tell me this and that, but there is nothing so. He was hunted as a 'partridge in the wilderness,' 1 Sam. xxvi. 20.

It was true of St Paul. We see what extremity he was brought unto, as the psalmist saith, Ps. cxviii. 18, 'I was afflicted sore, but I was not delivered to death,' even as we say, only not killed. It is and hath been so with all the members of the church from Abel to this day. Sometime or other, if they live any long time, they shall be like Moses at the Red Sea. We see in what a strait he and his company was there. There was the Egyptians behind them, the mountains on each side of them, the Red Sea before them. What escaping was here for Moses? So it is with the poor church and children of God ofttimes. There are dangers behind them, and perils before them, and troubles on all sides. God brings them so low as death's door, sometimes by sickness, as there is an instance in Ps. cvii. 18, of those that go down to the sea in ships. 'He brings them to death's door,' saith the psalmist.

What is the reason that, by persecution and afflictions, by one grievance or another, God brings his children to such a low ebb?

The reasons are many.

Reason 1. The first may be, *he will thus try what mettle they are made of.* Light afflictions, light crosses, will not try them thoroughly; great ones will. Jonah, that slept in the ship, he falls a-praying in the whale's belly. He that was pettish out of trouble, and falls a-quarrelling with God himself in trouble, he falls to praying when he was in the bottom of hell, as he saith himself. Little afflictions may stand with murmuring and repining, but great ones try indeed what we are. What we are in great afflictions, we are indeed.

Reason 2. Again, *to try the sincerity of our estate*, to make us to know ourselves, to make us known to the world and known to ourselves, what good we have and what ill we have. A man knows not what a deal of looseness he hath in his heart, and what a deal of falseness, till we come to the cross and to extremity. Whereas before I thought I had had a great deal of patience, a great deal of faith, and a great deal of heavenly-mindedness; now I see I have not that store laid up as I thought I had. And sometime a man is deceived on the contrary. I thought I had had no goodness in me; and yet in extremity such a one goes to prayer, he goes to the word of God, to the communion of saints, he delights in good things, and only in those. Extremity makes him discern and know himself for ill and for good, and makes others to know him too. That is another end.

Reason 3. Again, God suffers us to fall into extremity, *to set an edge upon our desires and our prayers*, to make us cry to him. 'Out of the deep I have cried unto thee, O Lord,' Ps. cxxx. 1. When a man is in the deep, it is not an ordinary prayer will serve, but he must cry. God loves to hear his children speak to him. He loves the voice of his children. It is the best music that he delights in. Therefore, he will take a course that he will be sure to hear from them; and rather than they shall neglect prayer, he will suffer them to fall into some rousing sin, into such a state and condition, that they may dart up prayers, that they may force prayers out of the anguish of spirit, that their prayers may be violent, that will take no denial, that they may be strivings with God, that they may wrestle with

God, as we see in Jacob and the woman of Canaan, that they may be importunate, and never leave him, nor take any denial.

Reason 4. Again, God suffers his children to fall into this extreme peril and danger, not only to try them, what good they have in them, but when he hath tried it to exercise it, *to exercise their faith and their patience.* St Paul had a great deal of grace in him, and God would be sure to have a great deal of trial and exercise of it; and therefore he suffered him to fall into extreme dangers, that so all the patience and all the faith he had might be set on work. And so it was in Job. God had furnished his champion with a great measure of patience, and then he singles him out to the combat; he brings him into the lists to encounter with Satan, and to triumph over Satan and all the evils he suffered whatsoever.

Reason 5. Again, *it is to perfect the work of mortification,* to let patience have her perfect work, and faith and prayer to have their perfect work, to perfect all graces, and so to perfect the work of mortification. For in extreme dangers he weans us perfectly from the world as much as may be; nothing will do it if these will not. St Paul came to many cities, and there he thought ofttimes to have great matter of entertainment; and instead of that, he was whipped and misused. God used the matter so to mortify pride and self-confidence in St Paul. He scoured him so from pride, that he should not go out of the city but he should be well scoured first by misusage. So, rather than God will suffer his children to go to hell, and rather than he will suffer them to live in the world here without glory to their profession, without manifesting of grace, to mortify and subdue their base, earthly affections, he will scour them, to subdue their pride and to subdue their earthly-mindedness. We might prevent the bitterness of the cross if we would. We might prevent his mortifying of us by afflictions, by the mortification of the spirit; but because we are negligent in that work, to perfect the work of mortification he is forced to lay here many crosses and extreme dangers upon us.

Reason 6. Lastly, God doth this for another end, *that he might be sure by this means to prepare us for greater blessings;* for in what deep measure we are humbled by any deep affliction, in that measure we are prepared for some blessing. Humility doth empty the soul, and crosses do breed humility. The emptiness of the soul fits it for receipt. God therefore doth empty us by crosses, that we may be fit vessels to receive some larger measure of grace and comfort. For, as it is said before, 'As our tribulations increase, so our comforts increase.' Therefore, it is a good sign that God intends much spiritual good to any man, when he lays some heavy load upon him in this world. All is to prepare for some greater comfort and some greater measure of grace.

Why doth the husbandman fall upon his ground, and tear and rend it up with the plough, and the better the ground is, the more he labours to kill weeds? Is it because he hath an ill mind to the ground? No. He means to sow good seed there, and he will not plough a whit longer than may serve to prepare the ground. It is the Holy Ghost's comparison, Isa. xxviii. 24. So likewise the goldsmith, the best metal that he hath, he tempers it, he labours to consume the dross of it, and the longer it is in the fire, the more pure it comes forth. So God keeps his children under crosses, and doth plough them. They neglect to plough themselves, and he is fain to set ploughers that will do it indeed,—some ill-minded men, or some cross. If they would plough themselves and examine themselves, they might spare God the labour. But when they are negligent, God takes the labour into his own hand, and sets others on work that will do it to purpose. But all is to prepare them for heavenly seed, for grace and comfort, that in what measure we have been depressed, as he saith here, 'we were pressed above measure,' in that measure he means to lift us up by heavenly comfort.

And, which is a clause of that, *that we might set a price upon the comforts when they come;* for when he hath so prepared us for it, and then we receive it, then comfort is comfort indeed. Comfort in itself is all one, and glory in itself is all one, first and last; but it is not all one to the person. Comfort is endeared to a person that hath been kept under and been dieted before. Then when it comes he sets a great value upon it, when he hath been without it so long.

Our nature is so, that we value things by the want of them rather than by the present enjoying of them. After we have wanted it, and have been long time prepared for it, then when it comes it is welcome indeed. For these and many such like ends we must be willing to approve of God's holy and wise dispensation in this, in ordering matters so with his children, in bringing them to great dangers of body, in danger of life, sometimes to spiritual desertions, leaving them to themselves, as if he had no care of them. But St Paul speaks especially here of outward crosses. You see the reasons of it.

Use 1. The use of it, is first, *that we should not pass a harsh, unadvised, rigid censure upon ourselves, or others, for these respects,* for any great affliction or abasement in this world. The world is ready to pass their verdict presently upon a man. Oh, such a one, you see what a kind of man he was, you see how God follows him with crosses. So uncharitable men judge amiss of 'the generation of the righteous.' Whereas they should set the court in their own hearts, and begin to censure there, and to examine themselves, they go out and keep their court abroad. But I say, pass not a harsh censure upon others, or on thyself, no, not for extreme dangers. For God now is making way for great comfort. Let God go on his way, without thy censuring of him.

Use 2. Again, this should teach us, *that we should not build overmuch confidence on earthly things, on the things of this world,* neither on health of body, or on friends, or on continuance of life. Alas! it is God's ordinary course, to strip us of all in this world. We think of great reputation; but, saith God, I will take that from you; you shall learn to trust in me. You think you have strong and vigorous bodies, and you shall live long, and therefore you will venture upon such and such courses. Aye, but God suffers his children to come to extreme dangers and hazards, that they think the sentence of death is passed upon them.

And since this is God's course with the body, and with the members, and with our head Christ himself, shall we think to have immunity, and to escape, and not look to God's order?

The church is in great misery, and we are negligent in prayer; we think there are many good people, and there is strong munition, &c., as if when God's people are in security, and forget him and his blessings, it were not his course to strip them of all, to suffer them to fall into extreme dangers. Have we not the church before our eyes to teach us? Let us trust, therefore, in nothing in this world.

So much for that point.

The second thing in the first part is this, that

Doct. As God's children are brought to this estate, so they are sensible of it.

They are flesh and not steel, 'they have not the strength of steel,' as Job saith, Job vi. 12. They are men, they are not stones. They are Christians, they are not Stoics. Therefore St Paul, as he was in extremity, so he apprehended his extremity; and with all his heart he would have escaped if he could. He looked about to all evasions how he might escape death. God's children are sensible of their crosses; especially they are sensible of death, as he speaks here of himself, 'We despaired even of life itself.' The word is very significant in the original. We were in such a strait that we knew not how to escape with life, so that 'we despaired of life' (*t*). We would have escaped with our lives, but we saw no way to escape. To make this clear, there are three things in God's children.

There is *grace*, *nature*, corrupt nature, nature with the tang* of corruption.

Grace, that looks upward, to glory and comfort. Nature looks to the present grievance, nature looks not to things to come, to matters revealed in the word, to supernatural comforts: nature looks to the present cross, even nature without sin. Corrupt nature feels, and feels with a secret murmuring and repining, and heaviness and dulness; as indeed corrupt nature will alway have a bout† in crosses; it will alway play its part, first or last. There are alway these three works in the children of God, in all extremities. Grace works, and that carries up, up still. 'Trust in God.' It looks to heaven, it looks to the end and issue, that all is for good. Nature it fills full of sense and pain, and makes a man desire remedy and ease. Corrupt nature stirs a man up to fret, and say, what doth God mean to do thus? It stirs a man ofttimes to use ill means, indirect courses.

St Paul was sensible, from a right principle of nature; and, no doubt, here was some tang* of corruption with it. He was sensible of the fear of death. Adam in innocency would have been affected, and exquisitely sensible, no doubt, if his body had been wronged; for the more pure the complexion,‡ the more sensible of solution. As physicians say, when that which should be knit together, if anything be loosed by sickness, or by wounds, that should by nature not be hurt, but continue together, it breeds exquisite pain, as to cut that which should not be cut, to disjoin that which should be together. This is in nature.

The schoolmen say (*u*), and the reason is good, that Christ's pains were the greatest pains, because his senses were not dulled and stupified with sensuality, or indirect courses. He had a body of an excellent temper, and he was in the perfection of his years when he died. Therefore he received such an impression of grief in his whipping, and when he was crowned with thorns. That was it that made him so sensible of grief, that when he sweat, he sweat drops of blood, and upon the cross it made him cry out, 'My God, my God, why hast thou forsaken me?' Mark xv. 34.

God's children, out of a principle of nature, are sensible of any grievance to this outward man of theirs, to the body, especially in death, as we see here St Paul. And there is most patience where there is most sense. It is stupidity and blockishness else.

Quest. Why are God's children so sensible in grief, especially in death?

Ans. Oh, there is a great cause. Indeed, in some regards, they are not afraid of it; for death is an enemy to nature, it is none to grace. But when I speak not of grace and glory, but of nature,

* That is, = 'taint,' or 'touch.'—G. † That is, 'turn,' 'part.'—G.
‡ That is, = 'conjunction,' or 'union.'—G.

Reason 1. *Hath not nature great cause to tremble at death, when it is an enemy to nature, even to right nature?* It is the king of fears, as Job saith, Job xviii. 14. It is that tyrant that makes all the kings of the earth to tremble at him. When death comes, it is terrible. Why? because it strips us of all the contentments of this life, of all comforts whatsoever we have here. Nature without sin is sensible of earthly comforts that God hath appointed for nature; and when nature sees an end of them, nature begins to give in, and to grieve.

Reason 2. Again, *death parts the best friends we have in this world, the body and the soul*, two old friends; and they cannot be parted without exquisite grief. If two friends that take contentment in each other, common friends, cannot part without grief, how shall these bosom friends, these united friends, body and soul, part without grief? This marriage between the soul and the body cannot be disunited without exquisite pain, being old acquaintance.

Reason 3. Again, nature abhors death, [because] *it hinders us of all employment.* It hinders of all service of God in church and commonwealth. And so grace, which is beyond nature, doth a little desire the continuance of life.

But nature, even out of no sinful principle, it sees that now I can serve God no longer, I can do God no more service, I can do good no longer in this world. And therefore it takes it to heart. Our Saviour saith, 'While you have light, walk: the night cometh, when no man is able to work,' John ix. 4, the night of sickness and death. So it breeds discomfort, and is terrible that way.

Reason 4. Again, in death *we leave those that cast their care upon us*, we leave ofttimes wives and children, without husband or father; those that had dependence upon us. And this must needs work upon nature, upon a right principle of nature. Indeed the excess of it is with corruption alway.

Reason 5. Again, in death, *there is great pain.* They say, births are with great pangs, and so they are. Now death is a birth, the birth of immortality. No wonder then if it have great pangs. Therefore nature fears it even for the pangs, the concomitants that are joined with it.

Reason 6. And then in death, nature considers *the state of the body presently after death*, that that goodly body, that strength and vigour I enjoyed before, must now be worms'-meat. I must say 'to the worm, Thou art my brother, and to corruption, Thou art my mother,' and the like, as it is in Job, Job xvii. 14. That head, that perhaps hath ruled the commonwealth, the place where I lived, it must lie level with others; and that body that others were enamoured with, it must now be so forlorn, that the sight of it will not be endured of our best friends. Nature considers what the estate will be there, that it shall turn to rottenness ere long; that the goodliest persons shall be turned to dust, and lie rotting there till the day of the resurrection.

Faith and grace looks higher; but because we have nature as long as we are men, these and such like respects work upon nature, and make death grievous.

Reason 7. But besides the glass of nature, and these things here in the world, look upon it *in the law of God*, in that glass; and so nature trembles, and quarrels at death. Death! what is it? It is the 'wages of sin,' Rom. vi. 23, it is the end of all comfort; and nature cannot see any comfort after that. It is beyond nature. Nature teacheth us not that there will be a resurrection of the body, nature teacheth us not that the soul goes to God. Here must be a great deal of grace, and a great deal of faith, to convince the soul of this. Nature teacheth it not.

Now, when besides this, the law of God comes and saith, death came in by sin, 'and sin is the sting of death,' 1 Cor. xv. 56, death is armed with sin, and sin comes in with the evidences of God's anger. Here, unless there be faith and grace, a man is either as Nabal, a stone and a sot in death, or as Judas and Cain, swallowed up with despair. It is impossible for a man that is not a true Christian, that is not a good man, but that either he should be as a stone, or desperate in sickness and death, without grace. He must be one of them. If he be a wise man, he cannot but despair in the hour of death. For is it a matter to be dallied with, or to be carried bravely out, as your Roman spirits and atheists think? They account it a glory to die bravely, in a stout manner. Is the terrible of terribles so to be put off? When all the comforts in this world shall end, and all employments cease, when there is eternity before a man; and, after death, hell, and eternal damnation of body and soul, are these matters to be slighted? It would make a man look about him. If a man have not faith and grace, he must either despair or die like a stone. None but a good Christian can carry himself well in the hour of death. Nay, a good Christian is sensible of death; and till he see God's time is come, he labours to avoid it by all means, as St Paul doth here.

Reason 8. But St Paul had another ground beyond nature to avoid death. *He knew himself ordained for the service of the church;* therefore he desired to escape, that he might serve God a longer time for the good of his church.

Use 1. Are God's children sensible of death, and the danger of it, and out of a principle of nature and grace too? *How then should carnal, wretched men look about them,* that have not made their accounts even with God? The report of death to them should be like the handwriting upon the wall to Belshazzar, Dan. v. 24. It should make their knees beat together, and make their countenance pale. It should strike them with terror; and, like Nabal, make their hearts to die as a stone within them.

Use 2. But it is a use of comfort to *poor, deluded Christians.* They think, alas! can my estate be good? I am afraid of death, I tremble and quake at the name of death, I cannot endure to hear of it, but it most of all affects me to see it. Therefore I fear I have no grace in me, I fear I have no faith in me.

Be not discomforted, whosoever thou art, that sayest so, if thou labour to strengthen thy faith, and to keep a good conscience; for thou mayest do thus out of a principle of nature. Nature trembles at death.

A man may do two things from diverse principle, from diverse repects, and both without sin. For example, in fasting, nature without sin desireth meat, or else fasting were not an afflicting of a man's body; but grace, that hath another principle, and that desires to hold out without sustenance, to be afflicted. So here is both a desire, and not a desire, and both good in their kind. So a man in the time of sickness and death, he may by all means desire to escape it, and tremble at it out of a principle of nature; but out of a higher principle he may triumph. 'O death, where is thy sting? O grave, where is thy victory?' 1 Cor. xv. 55; and 'they that believe in Christ shall never die,' John xi. 26. 'We are in heavenly places together with Christ,' Eph. i. 3. We are as sure of heaven as if we were there. So out of such kind of principles we may triumph over death, by faith and grace.

So let none be discouraged. Nature goes one way, and faith and grace another. A man may know when it is nature, and when it is grace. When grace subdues nature, and subordinates it to a higher principle, a man need not be much troubled.

Christ himself our head, he was afraid of death when he looked on death as death; but when he looked upon death as a service, as a redemption, as a sweet sacrifice to God, so 'with a thirsting I have thirsted,' saith he, Luke xxii. 15. He thirsted after death in that respect. Looking to his human nature, to the truth of his manhood, then saith he, 'O that this cup might pass from me,' Mat. xxvi. 39; but in another consideration, he willingly gave his soul a sacrifice for sin to God.

The desire is as the objects are presented. Let heaven and happiness be presented, so death is a passage to it, so death is the end of misery, and the beginning of happiness, so God's children 'desire to be dissolved, and to be with Christ,' as St Paul did, Philip. i. 23. But look upon death otherwise, as it is an enemy to nature, as it is a stop of all employment in this world, and of all service to the church, that we can do God no longer service; and so a man may desire to live still, and be afraid of death, if he look upon death in the glass of nature, and in the glass of the law, likewise that it comes in as a punishment of sin, so indeed it is terrible, it is the king of fears. But look upon it in another glass, in the glass of the gospel, as it is sweetened and as it is disarmed by Christ, and so it is comfortable. 'Better is the day of death than the day of birth,' Eccles. vii. 1; for in our birth we come into misery, in death we go from it. So upon diverse considerations we may be diversely affected, and have diverse respects to things; for the soul of man is framed so to be carried to the present objects, and therefore in a good man in some respects, at some time, death is terrible; he trembles at it, which upon higher considerations and respects, he embraceth willingly.

Indeed, it is a sign of a wise man to value life. It is the opportunity and advantage to honour God. After death we are receivers, and not doers. Then we receive our wages. But while we are here, we should desire even for the glory that is reserved for us, to do all the good we can, because the time of life is that blessed advantage of doing good and of taking good. It is to be in heaven before our time to do others good, and to get evidence of heaven for ourselves. This is the second thing, that as God's children are suffered to fall into extreme dangers, so they are very sensible of them, especially in matter of death, which is the last enemy. There the devil sets upon them indeed. He knows that that is the last enemy, and that there he must get all or lose all; and he labours to make death more terrible than it is or should be.

The way not to fear death, and not to let nature have overmuch scope, is to disarm death beforehand, to pluck out the sting of it by repentance; weaken it beforehand, that it may not get the better, even as we do with our enemies. The way to overcome them is to weaken them, to weaken their forces, to starve them if we can, to intercept all their provision. What makes death terrible and strong? We put stings into it, our sins, our sins against conscience. The time will come when conscience will awaken, and it will be then, if ever, to our comfort; and then our former sins will stare in our faces, the sins of our youth, the sins that we have before neglected soundly to repent for. Therefore let us labour this way to make death less terrible.

Again, that we may not fear it overmuch, let us look upon it in the glass of the gospel, as it is now in Christ, as it is turned clean another way. Now, it hath sweet names. It is called a dissolution, a departure, a sleeping, a going to our Father's, and such like. God doth sweeten a bitter thing, that it may enter into us with less terror. So it must be our wisdom to sweeten the meditation of it, by evangelical considerations, what it is now by Christ.

And withal to meditate the two terms, from whence and whither. What a blessed change it is if we be in Christ! It is a change for the better, better company, better employment, a better place, all better. Who would be grieved at, and afraid of, death? Let us recall the promise of the presence of God. He will be with us to death, and in death. 'Blessed are those that die in the Lord,' Rex. xiv. 13. And especially faith in Christ will make us, that we shall not fear death, when we shall see him our head in heaven before us, ready to receive us when we come there; and to see ourselves in heaven, already in him; as verily in faith and in the promise, as if we were there. 'We are set in heavenly places' with Christ already. Let us have these and such like considerations to sweeten the thought of death.

But to touch this, which is an appendix to that formerly mentioned, that *Obs. God's children are deceived concerning their death ofttimes.*

The time of death is uncertain. St Paul thought he should have died when he did not; he was deceived. There is a double error about death. Sometimes we think we shall not die, when indeed we are dead men. Sometimes we receive the sentence of death, we pass a censure upon ourselves, that we cannot live, when God intends our escape. So it is uncertain to us the hour of death. Sometime we are uncertain when it is certain; sometime we think it certain when it falls not out so. Both ways we are deceived, because God will have us, while we live here, to be at an uncertainty for the very moment of death. 'Our times are in his hand.' Our time of life is in his hand. We came into the world when he thought good. Our time of living here is in his hands. We live just as long as he will have us. Our time of death is in his hand. The prophet saith not only, my time is in thy hands, but 'my times,' my time of coming into the world, my time of living in the world, and my time of going out of the world shall be when thou shalt appoint me. Therefore he will have us uncertain of it ourselves, till the moment of death come. St Paul was deceived, 'He received the sentence of death in himself,' but he died not at that time.

So that the manner and circumstances of death are uncertain, whether it shall be violent or fair death, [whether] it shall be by diseases or by casualties, whether at home or abroad. All the circumstances of death are hidden from us, as well as death itself and the time of it.

And this is out of heavenly wisdom, and love of God to us, that we should at all times be provided, and prepared for our dissolution and change. It is left at this uncertainty, that we might make our estate certain, to be fitted to die at all times. Let us make that use of it to provide every day. Oh, it were a happy thing if we could make every day, as it were, another life, a several life; and pass sentence upon ourselves, a possible and probable sentence; it may be this day may be the last day. And let us end every day as we would end our lives. How would we end our lives? We would end them with repentance for our sins past, with commending our souls into the hands of God, with resolution and purpose to please God in all things, with disposing all things wisely in this world. Let us end our days, every day so, as much as possible may be; let us set everything right; let us set the state of our souls in order, set all in order as much as may be every day. It were a blessed course if we could do so.

And this is one part, one main branch of our corruption, wherein it shews itself strongly, that we live in an estate that we are ashamed to die in. Come to some men, and ask them, how it is with you? have you repented of your sins past? have you renewed your purposes for the time to come? Yes; we do it solemnly at the communion. But we should renew our repentance, and renew our covenants every day, to please God that day. Do you do so now? If God should seize upon you now, are you in the exercise of faith? in the exercise of repentance? in the exercise of holy purposes, to please God? are you in God's ways? do you live as you would be content to die? But Satan and our own corruption bewitcheth us with a vain hope of long life, we promise ourselves that, that God doth not promise us; we make that certain that God doth not make certain. Indeed we are certain of death, but for the time, and manner, and circumstances we know them not. Sometimes we think we shall die when we do not, and sometimes we die when we think we shall not.

Oh, will some say, if I knew when I should die, I would be a prepared man, I would be exact in my preparation. Wouldst thou so? thou art deceived. Saul knew exactly he should die. He took it for exact when the witch in the shape of Samuel told him that he should die by to-morrow this time, and yet he died desperately upon the sword's point for all that. He did not prepare himself. It must be the Spirit of God that must prepare us for this. If we knew never so much, that we should die never so soon, we cannot prepare ourselves. Our preparation must be by the Spirit of God. Let us labour continually to be prepared for it.

And let no man resolve to take liberty a moment, a minute of an hour to sin. God hath left it uncertain the day of death. What if that moment and minute wherein thou resolvest to sin should be the moment of thy death and departure hence? for it is but a minute's work to end thy days. What if God should end thy days in that minute? Let no man take liberty and time to sin, when God gives him no liberty in sin. If God should strike thee, thou goest to hell quick, thou must sink from sin to hell. It is a pitiful case, whenas eternity depends upon our watchfulness in this world. But to come to the end and issue, why he was thus dealt with by God, carrying him through these extremities.

'*That we might not trust in ourselves, but in God that raiseth the dead.*' Here is the end specified that God intended, in suffering him to be brought so low, even to death's door, that there was but a step between him and death. The end is double, 'That we should not trust in ourselves, but in God that raiseth the dead.' It is set down negatively and positively. First, 'That we should not trust in ourselves,' and then that we should 'trust in God.' And the method is excellent. For we can never trust in God till we distrust ourselves, till our hearts be taken off from all confidence in ourselves and in the creature; and then when our hearts are taken off from false confidence, they must have somewhat to rely on, and that is God or nothing; for else we shall fall into despair. The end of all this was, that 'we might not trust in ourselves, but in God that raiseth the dead.'

The wisdom of heaven doth nothing without an end proportionable to that heavenly wisdom; so all this sore affliction of the blessed apostle, what aimed it at? To pull down, and to build up; to pull down self-confidence, 'That we might not trust in ourselves;' and to build up confidence and affiance in God, 'but in God that raiseth the dead.'

We being in a contrary state to grace and communion with God, this order is necessary, that God must use some way that we shall not trust in ourselves; and then to bring us to trust in him. So these two are subordinate ends one to another. 'We received the sentence of death, that we might not trust in ourselves.'

From the dependence this may be observed, that

Doct. The certain account of death, is a means to wean us from ourselves, and to make us trust in God.

The sentence of death, the assured knowledge that we must die, the certain expectation and looking for death, is the way to wean us from the world, and to fit us for God, to prepare us for a better life. You see it follows of necessity, 'We received the sentence of death, that we should not trust in ourselves,' &c.

The looking-for of death therefore, takes away confidence in ourselves and the creature. Alas! in death, what can all the creatures help? What can friends, or physic, or money help? Then honours, and pleasures, and all leave us then.

This the rather to note a corrupt atheistical course in those that are to deal with sick folk, that are extreme sick, that conceal their estate from them, and feed them with false hopes of long life. They deserve ill of persons in extremity to put them in hope of recovery. Physicians that are not divines in some measure, what do they? against their conscience, and against their experience, and against sense, Oh, I hope you shall do well, &c. Alas! what do they? they hurt their souls, they breed a false confidence. It is a dangerous thing to trust upon long life, when perhaps they are snatched suddenly away, before they have made their accounts even with God, before they have set their souls in that state they should do.

Therefore the best way is to do as good Isaiah did with Hezekiah, 'set thy house in order, for thou must die,' 2 Kings xx. 1, that is, in the disposition of second causes, thou shalt have a disease that will bring thee to death, and God had said so. God had a reservation, but it was more than Isaiah knew at that time. 'Set thy house in order, for thou must die.' So they should begin with God, to tell them, as we say, the worst first. It is a pitiful thing that death should be accounted the worst, but so it is, by reason of our fearfulness. Deal plainly with them, let them 'receive the sentence of death,' that so they may be driven out of themselves and the creature altogether, and be driven to trust in 'God that raiseth the dead.' Put thy soul in order. You are no man of this world; lest they betray their souls for a little self-respect perhaps, because they would not displease them.

It may be in some cases discreet to yield, to make the means to work the better; but where there is nothing but evident signs of death, they ought to deal directly with them, that they may receive the sentence of death. It wrought with St Paul this good effect, 'I received the sentence of death, that we might not trust in ourselves, but in God that raiseth the dead.'

It is God's just judgment upon hypocrites, and upon many carnal wretched persons, that are led with a false confidence all their life, that trust in the creature, trust in friends and riches, that will not trust in God, and will not be taught to number their days in their lifetime. It is just with God [toward those who], to their very death [are filled] with false confidence, when they come to death, to suffer them to perish in their false confidence, and so to sink into hell. It is just with God to suffer them to have atheists about them, or weak persons that shall say, Oh, you shall do well enough, and then even out of a very desire to live, they are willing to believe all, and so they die without all show of change; and as they live, so they die, and are wretched in both. The life of a wicked man is ill, his death worse, his estate after death worst of all; and this is one way whereby God suffers men to fall into the snare of the devil, when he suffers not those that are about them to deal faithfully. St Paul received the sentence of death, that it might force him not to trust in himself, but in God that raiseth the dead.

The second thing that is observable hence out of this first part, which is the negative part, is this, that,

Doct. God's children are prone to trust in themselves.

The hearts even of God's dear children are prone in themselves, if they be left to their own bent and weight, to self-confidence, and will not hold up in faith and affiance in God further than they are lifted and kept up by a spirit of faith, which God puts into them. It was not in vain that God used this course with blessed St Paul. Here is an end set down, that he 'might not trust in himself.' What, was he in peril to trust in himself? Alas! St Paul, though he were an holy excellent man, yet he was a man; and in the best man there is a double principle, a principle of nature, of corrupt nature, and a principle of grace; and he works according to both principles. There is an intermixture of both in all his actions, and in all his passions too, in his sufferings. Corruption shews itself in his best deeds, and his best sufferings, in everything. 'That we should not trust in ourselves,' that is, in anything in ourselves, or out of ourselves, in the creature; it is all one. We see by the example of St Paul that the best are prone to trust in themselves. All this hard usage of St Paul, that he received the sentence of death, it was that 'he should not trust in himself.' What, was there danger in St Paul to trust in himself? a man that had been so exercised with crosses and afflictions as he had been, no man more, one would think that he had been scoured enough of pride, and self-confidence! the whippings and misusings, the stocks, the dungeons, &c., would not all this work pride, and self-confidence out of the apostle? No! So deeply it is invested into our base nature, our trusting to present things, that we cannot live the life of faith, we cannot depend upon God, whom we cannot see but with other eyes than nature hath. It is so deeply rooted in our nature, that the blessed apostle himself must have this great help, to be taught to go out of himself, and to depend upon God. We see in what danger he was, in another place, to be lifted up with the revelations. He was fain to have a 'prick in the flesh, a messenger of Satan to buffet him,' 2 Cor. xii. 7.

Hezekiah, his heart was lifted up, as the Scripture speaks, in his treasures, that he shewed to the King of Babylon's ambassadors, as if he were such a rich prince. And so holy David, in numbering the people, to shew what a mighty prince he was. It was his vain confidence. Therefore God put him to a strange cure. He punished him in that that he gloried in. He took away so many of his people. And so Hezekiah was punished in that he sinned in. He was fain to have a purge for it. His treasure was taken away and carried to Babylon. 'I said in my prosperity,' saith holy David, 'I shall never be moved,' Ps. xxx. 6. The best are subject to false confidence to trust in themselves.

One reason partly, because there is a mixture of corruption in us while we live here, and corruption looks to this false principle in us, that will never be wrought out with all the afflictions in the world. Till death make an end of corruption, there will be a false trust in ourselves and in the creature. We cannot trust God perfectly as we should do.

Reason 1. Again, the reason is, *because the things of this life are useful and commodious unto us, and we are nouzelled* up in the use of them,* and when Satan doth amplify them in our fancy to be greater in goodness than they are; and opinion sets a greater worth on them, if there were no devil. But he presenting these things in all the lustre he can, he helps the imagination, which he hath more to do with than with all the parts of the soul. And the soul looks in the glass of opinion upon these things, and thinks they are goodly, great matters, learning and wisdom, honour and riches. Looking upon them as they are amplified by the false fancy of others and the competition of the world wherein we live, every man is greedy and hasty of these things. All men have not faith for better things. Therefore, they are mad of these. So the competition of others and the enlarging our conceits upon them above their worth, these make us put greater confidence in them, and then we come to trust in ourselves and in them, and not in God.

Reason 2. *Naturally we cannot see the nothingness of the creature,* that as it came out of nothing, so it will turn to nothing. But because it is sensible, these good things are sensible, and present, and necessary, and useful; and naturally we live by our senses. Therefore, we place our delight in them, that when they are taken away all the soul goes with them. As he that leans upon a crutch, or anything, when that is taken away, down he falls, so it is with a man by nature; he trusts to these things, and when they go, his soul sinks together with the things. Even as it is with those that are in a stream, when they are in a running stream they are carried with the stream, so all these things go away, they are of a fleeting condition. We see them not in their passage. When they are gone, we see them past. We see not ourselves vanish by little and little out of this life. We see not the creatures present, we see not death, and other things beyond death, as we should by the eye of faith. So things pass, and we pass with them; the stream and we run together. It must be a great measure of faith that must help this. We are prone to trust to sensible things naturally. We know what it is to live by sense; but to live by faith it is a remote thing, to lead our lives by reasons drawn from things that are not seen, to live by promises, it is a hard thing, when things that are sensible cannot work upon us. When we see men die, and see the vanity of things sensible, it will not work upon us; how then do we think that things that are supernatural, which are remote† far above sense, should work on us? It is a hard thing not to trust to ourselves, we are so addicted to live by sense; and there is some corruption in St Paul, in the best men, to trust to present things.

Who doth not think but he shall live one day longer, and so trusts to life? As the heathen man could say, 'There is not the oldest man but he thinks he may live a little longer, one day longer' (*v*). Who makes that use of mortality and the uncertain, fading condition of this life as he should? And all because of a false trust; as in other things, so in the continuance of life. We see we are prone to trust, to put base, false confidence in somewhat or other while we live in this world.

Reason 3. Again, *our nature being prone to outward things, and sunk deeply into them, it can hardly be recovered;* it cannot be sober without much ado

* That is, 'nourished.'—G. † That is, 'removed.'—Ed.

and brought from trusting of present things. You have some men that have things at will in this world. They never know what faith means. All their life they live by sense. Their conscience is not awaked, and outward afflictions seize not on them and supply of earthly things they have. What religion means, and what God and heaven means, they have heard of them perhaps, but throughly and inwardly what it means they never come to know in this world, without there be some alteration and changes. They must have some changes. 'The wicked have no changes,' saith the prophet, Ps. lv. 19. But while they be as they are, they know not God, nor themselves, nor the vanity of earthly things. We speak the truth of God to a company ofttimes that are besotted with sensuality, and that have perpetual supply of earthly things. Speak to them of faith, and of things that are remote from sense, &c., they hear them as if they were in a dream. Nature is prone to trust in present things, even in the best, in St Paul himself.

Use 1. Now, our proneness to it *doth justify God's dealings in many things, as* (1.) *Why doth God humble great ones with great afflictions?* Why doth he humble great men, great and excellent Christians, with great falls? That they might not trust in themselves; no, not in their own present graces. God will not bring a man to salvation now by grace in himself to give him title to heaven. His graces must only be to help his evidence that he is not an hypocrite, and to give evidence to others, that others 'may see his good works,' &c., Mat. v. 16. But if he come to trust in them once, to set them in Christ's stead, God will abase his pride by suffering him to fall, that he may go out of himself, to be saved by Christ, and to seek for mercy in Christ.

(2.) And this is the reason why God in his providence *doth great things by small means, without means, and against means sometimes.* When he crosses and curses great means, it is that we might not 'trust in ourselves.' We are prone to self-confidence; and because God will cure it, for we must not carry it to heaven with us, therefore he is forced to take this kind of dispensation.

Proud flesh will always devise something but that which it should do, to uphold itself withal. It will not be driven from all its holds; God hath much ado to work it out from all its holds. If it have not wealth, it will have wit and policy; or if it have not that, it will have civil life, and outward works to trust to, and to swell it with. But to come and give God the glory of salvation only by mercy, and to depend only on God, and to see an insufficiency in any thing we do, it can hardly be brought to pass. Insomuch that that article of justification by the obedience of Christ only, it is merely a spiritual thing, altogether transcending nature.

No marvel if we find such opposition from the Church of Rome, and all, unless it be the true church; they understand not the main article, of salvation only by mercy, because nature is so desperately prone to self-confidence.

Use 2. Let us *take heed of false confidence in the things of this life,* of confidence in any thing but God.

But to come to some trials. You will say, how shall we know whether we put over much confidence in them or no?

(1.) It is an easy matter to know it. We trust them too much when we grow proud upon any thing, when our spirits are lifted up. 'Charge rich men that they be not high-minded,' 1 Tim. vi. 17, insinuating that they are in danger to be high-minded. 'If riches increase, set not your hearts upon them,' saith the Psalmist, Ps. lxii. 10. There is great danger when the heart is set on them, and lifted up, when men think themselves so much the better as they are greater. Indeed, if they weigh themselves in a civil balance it is so, but the corrupt nature of man goes further, and thinks a man intrinsically better, and more beloved of God for these things. It is a dangerous sign that we trust too much to them.

(2.) Again, *overmuch grief, if they be taken away any of them, or if we be crossed in them.* The grief in wanting betrays the love in enjoying. It is a sign that Job had gotten a great measure of self-denial, not to trust in himself or his riches, though he were a rich man, because when they were taken away, 'Blessed be God,' saith he, 'thou gavest them, and thou hast taken them away,' Job i. 21. He that can stand when his stay is taken from him, it is a sign he trusts not too much to his stay. He that is so weak that when his stay is taken away, down he falls, it is a sign he leans hard. Those that when these things are taken from them, when their friends are taken away, or their honours, or riches are taken away, yet they can support themselves out of diviner grounds, it is a sign they did not overmuch trust these things. Nature will work something, but overmuch grief betrays overmuch love always.

Again, which is but a branch of the other, we may know that we overmuch set by them, *by fretting to be crossed in any of these things.* A man may know Ahithophel trusted too much to his policy and wit: when he was crossed he could not endure it. We see he made away himself for very shame, 2 Sam. xvii. 23. When a man is crossed in his wit and policy, when he is crossed in those projects he hath laid; when he is crossed in his preferment, or riches, or friends, then he is all amort,* he frets, which is more than grieving; when he not only grieves, but with Ahithophel he goes to ill courses. It is a sign he trusted too much, and too basely to them before.

(3.) Again, when the enjoying of these things *is joined with contempt and base esteem of others,* it is a sign that we rest too much in them. There is more trust put to them than they should bear. We should not, in the enjoying of honour, or riches, or pleasures, or any thing, think the meaner of others.

(4.) Especially, *security shews that we trust too much in them,* when we bless ourselves, I shall do well. 'Soul, soul, thou hast goods laid up for many years,' Luke xii. 19, saith the fool, and he was but a fool for it, to promise certainty for uncertainty. A man cannot stand in that which cannot stand itself. To promise life in a dying condition, to promise any thing in this world, when the very nature of them is uncertain, 'Thou fool,' saith the Scripture. If his soul had been so full of faith as his barns were of corn, he would never have said, 'Soul, soul, take thy rest,' for these things; but he would have trusted in God. It is a sign we trust too much to these things, when we secure ourselves all will be well, and bless ourselves, as the Scripture speaks.

(5.) Again, it is a sign we trust too much to these things, *when upon confidence of these things we go to ill and unwarrantable courses, and think to be borne out by these things.* As when the younger sort shall pour forth themselves to vanity, and are careless of swearing and licentiousness, that they care not what to do, they shall live long enough to repent, &c. This is a diabolical trust, that God will give them no security in. So when men

* That is, 'spiritless,' 'inanimate.' This from Sibbes supplements excellently Richardson, *sub voce.*—G.

that have riches will venture on bad causes, and think to carry it out with their purse, they trust in matter of oppression, and think to bear out the matter with their friends, or with their place, or with their wits; this is false trust. 'Thy wisdom hath caused thee to rebel,' as the prophet saith concerning Babylon, Isa. xlvii. 10. They thought they had reaching heads, and so ventured upon rebellious courses. When any of these outward things draw us to unwarrantable, unjustifiable courses, it is a sign we plant too much confidence in them: and it is a sign, if we belong to God, that he intends to cross us in them. The very confidence in these things hath drawn many to ill courses, to do that that they should not do, as good Josiah, Hezekiah, David, and the rest.

Thus we see how we should examine ourselves, whether we trust too much in these things or no.

Now, since we are thus prone to this false confidence, and since we may thus discern it; if we discern it in ourselves, how shall we cure it? That in the next doctrine:—*That we might not trust in ourselves.* From whence observe,

Doct. It is a dangerous state to trust in ourselves.

This ill disposition, to trust in ourselves, or anything out of ourselves, but only in God, in whom we should trust, it is dangerous. For a man may reason thus from the text: That which God is forced to take such desperate courses for, as to bring such an excellent man as St Paul to such extremity, and all that he should not trust in himself, that he was not only prone to, but it was a dangerous estate for him. But God brings him to death's door, that he 'received the sentence of death, that he might not trust in himself,' that he might see the nothingness of all things else. Therefore it was a dangerous estate for him to trust in himself.

It is ill in respect of I. *God*; II. *ourselves.*

I. *In respect of God.* To trust to ourselves, or the creature, is

1. *To idolize ourselves, or the creature.* We make an idol of the thing we trust in. We put God out of his place, and set up that we trust in, in God's room; and so provoke God to jealousy. When men shall trust their wits in matters of religion, as in popery they do (they serve God after their own inventions), what a dishonour is it to God? as if he were not wise enough to prescribe how he will be worshipped. 'Go after me, Satan,' saith Christ to Peter, Mat. xvi. 23. He calls him devil. Why? what hurt was it? He came with a good intention? That which papists* think they please God most in, they are devils in; and these things that they teach are 'the doctrines of devils,' 1 Tim. iv. 1. 'But the wisdom of the flesh is death; it is not subject to the law of God, nor can be subject,' saith the apostle, Rom. viii. 7. So it is dangerous, because it is offensive to God. 'There is a way that seemeth right in a man's own eyes: the issues whereof are the issues of death,' Prov. xiv. 12. It is idolatry in regard of God.

2. And it is *spiritual adultery.* For what should take up our affections? Should we not place our joy, our delight, which follows our trust alway; for trust carries the whole soul with it: what should take up our joy and delight? Should not God, and heaven, and heavenly things? should not these things have place in our hearts, as they have in their own worth? When we take these affections from God, and place them upon the creature, they are adulterous affections. When we love riches or pleasures better than God that gave us all, it is an adulterous, whorish love. 'Oh ye

* Misprinted 'popery.'—G.

adulterers and adulteresses,' saith blessed St James, 'know ye not that the love of this world is enmity with God?' James iv. 4.

3. It is likewise *falsehood*. For it makes the creature to be that that it is not, and it makes God that which he is not. We despise him, and set up the creature in his room. There is a false witness alway in false confidence. Indeed there are many sins in it.

4. There is *ignorance;* not knowing the creature to be so vain as it is. There is ignorance of God, not knowing him to be 'all in all,' Col. iii. 11, as he is.

5. And there is *rebellion*, to trust in the creature, when God will not have it trusted in.

6. And there is *impatience*. When these supports are taken away, then men grow to murmuring. There is almost all sins hidden in self-confidence and self-sufficiency. You see the danger of it to God.

II. Besides that, it is dangerous *to ourselves*. It brings us *under a curse*. 'Cursed is the man that maketh flesh his arms,' Jer. xvii. 5, that trusts in anything but God. It brings us under a curse, as I said, because it is idolatry and spiritual adultery. And then again, because leaning to a false prop, that being taken away that shored us up before, down we fall, with that we leaned on.

Now all things but God being vanity, we, relying upon that which is vain; our trust is vain, as the thing is vain. We can hope for no better condition than the things we trust to. They are vain, and we are vain; so there is a curse upon them.

Therefore we have great cause to hate that upstart religion, that hath been devised for their own ends, for their own profit, because it would bring us under a curse. They would have us to trust to our own works in matter of salvation, to trust to our own satisfaction to be freed from purgatory, &c. They would have us to trust to creatures, to something besides God; to trust in the mediation of saints, to be our intercessors, &c. And what doth this false trust? It breeds despair at length.

What is the reason that a well-advised papist, that knows what he doth, cannot but despair, or else renounce popery? Because popery carries the soul to false props in matter of justification. They renounce their own religion at the hour of death, as Bellarmine did (*w*). They live by one religion, and die by another, which would not be if their religion were good. For their hearts tell them that they have not done so many works that they may trust in them, and they have not been so well done that they may trust in them. It is a dangerous thing. 'Cursed is he that trusts in man,' or in anything in man.

Nay, we must not trust our own graces, as they are in ourselves, not by way of merit; no, not by way of strength. We must not trust our present graces to carry us out, without new supply to further us. It was Peter's fault. 'Though all men deny thee, yet will not I,' Mat. xxvi. 35. He trusted to his present strength; he forgot that if he had not a new supply from the spring of grace, that he should miserably miscarry, and so he died.* All our righteousness to trust to, it is a 'broken reed,' Isa. xxxvi. 6. It is somewhat, if we place it in the due place, to give us evidence that we are true Christians; but to trust in it by way of merit, the devil will pick so many holes in that kind of title, and conscience will see so many flaws in it, if we bring no better title, than either the holiness in us, or the works from us, the devil and our own conscience will spy so many flaws and

* That is, spiritually, and for the moment of his backsliding.—G. Qu. 'did?'—Ed.

cracks in it at the time of death, that we shall not dare to trust in it, but we must run out of ourselves to Christ, or else we die in desperation. Let us know these things. All things but God, the more we know them, the less we trust in them. But it is clean contrary of God, the more we know him, the more we shall trust in him. The more we meditate, and enlarge our hearts in the consideration of his divine essence every way, the more we shall trust in him. 'They that know thy name, will trust in thee,' Ps. ix. 10. Let us trust in no outward thing.

No! not in the humanity of Christ. I add that further. We are very prone to trust in things sensible; and the apostles, because Christ was present with them, and comfortable among them (as indeed he was sweet and loving, bearing with their infirmities, and encouraging them upon all occasions); O they were loath to part with him. He tells them that he must leave them, but they should not fare the worse, he would 'send them the Comforter.' 'The flesh itself profits nothing,' John vi. 63, without the Godhead, saith he.

Trust not in the sacraments above their place. It is a dangerous thing to put too much in any creature (God is extremely offended at it), as not only our adversaries the papists, but proud persons among us, that are weary of the doctrine of the church, and will not submit, in their pride, to riper judgments. They attribute too much to the sacraments, as some others do too little. They attribute a presence there. They make it an idol. They give it such reverence as they will not do to God himself, and from a false conceit. Oh, there is I know not what presence. Therefore the Lutherans must needs in a great degree be idolaters, by their consubstantiation; and the papists by their transubstantiation, by their real presence. Coster saith, and saith truly, if Christ be not there, we are the greatest idolaters in the world (*x*).

But there is a more subtle kind of attributing to the sacraments, that alway God gives grace with the sacraments, the sacraments convey grace alway. As a plaster it hath a kind of power to eat out the dead flesh, and as physic hath a power to carry away the ill humours, so the conveying of grace is included in the sacraments. So they tie God's grace to these things.

Indeed, there is grace *by* them, though not *in* them. God gives grace to the humble receiver; but otherwise, to him that comes not with an humble, believing heart. They are seals to a blank. There is no validity in them. All the good use they have is to strengthen faith; and if there be not something before to be strengthened, and confirmed, and assured, they are but seals to a blank. It is in these things according to our faith, and according to our preparation; and then God in the holy, and humble, and faithful use of them blesseth his own ordinance, for the increase, and confirming of our faith, and for the increase and strengthening of all grace.

So that there is not anything in the church, but the proud, naughty heart of man will take hurt by it, rather than submit to the pure, and powerful truth of God. It will have by-ways to have 'confidence in the flesh,' Philip. iii. 4, one way or other.

And many men, rather than they will trust to sound repentance and humiliation for sin, they will trust to the words of absolution without it, and when they are said, go to hell with a pardon about their necks. The false heart will trust to outward things though it be damned for it. In their place they are good, if they be used only as helps in their kind. We lay more weight upon outward things, upon the sacraments, and upon the words of the minister than they will bear, and never care for the inward powerful work of grace. Everything of God is excellent in their order and kind, but our corrupt hearts bring an ill report upon the things.

You see then, it is a dangerous disposition to trust any too much. It is to idolise them, and to wrong God, to take the honour from God. It is to hurt ourselves, and bring ourselves under a curse; and to wrong the things themselves, to bring an evil report upon the things. It is universally true. You shall never see a false, bitter heart, that will not stoop to God's plain truth (they will have by-ways of their own), but in some measure or other they are barren of great matters, and given up to some sensible bitterness, to self-conceitedness, and self-confidence. They are alway punished in that kind with a spiritual kind of punishment.

We must take heed therefore of trusting too much to anything but God himself. God is jealous of our trust. He will have us trust in nothing but himself in matters of salvation. No; not in matters of common life, not in matters politic and civil. We must not build our trust in any creature so much as to think ourselves happy by them, or to think they cannot deceive us. They are creatures of nothing. Therefore they are prone to deceive. They are prone to turn to nothing. Therefore we must not build upon them overmuch, no not in civil matters.

Indeed, if we see the image of God in any man, we may trust him: if we see him faithful, and loving, and good. Yet trust him as a man alway, that is, as such a one as may deceive, and yet he may be a man and a good man. So in other creatures, in the use of physic, and wars, and arms, &c. In danger we may in some subordinate consideration trust to them; but we must use them as means, that is, as such as God hath free liberty to use to good to help us, and free liberty not to use. We must use them, but not trust to them. 'Some trust in chariots, and some in horses; but our trust is in the Lord,' Ps. xx. 7. And, 'Trust not in princes,' Ps. cxlvi. 3, as the psalmist saith. Trust not in anything.

If we trust in anything, it must be subordinate to our trust in God. It must not be co-ördinate, as we say, that is, not in the same rank, much less above God. As worldlings trust in their wealth, they trust in their friends above God; they trust not so much in heaven and happiness there, they think not themselves so happy for that as they do for earthly things. Nay, they trust against God in confidence of their friends and of their purse. A carnal man makes riches 'his stronghold;' he trusts them above God, and against God. We must neither trust them with God, in a co-ordinate proportion with him, nor above God, much less against God. What makes base flesh and blood devilish in that respect, to attempt cursed means, against the truth, and against good causes?

They bear themselves out with these things; perhaps the truth crosses them in their designs, and shames them, and frets them. What makes them undermine good causes, and go desperately to kick against the pricks, to dash themselves against wrath which is stronger than they? They think to bear themselves out with their greatness, with their friends, with some carnal support or other. This is to trust against God, which is worst of all.

And this makes that harlot of Rome so confident against the church of God. 'I sit as a queen,' saith Babylon, Rev. xviii. 7; not only outward Babylon, that was the type, but spiritual Babylon, 'I sit as a queen.' I shall be hereafter as I am now. Therefore saith God, 'Thy destruction shall come in one day,' Rev. xviii. 8. Thy destruction shall come unrecoverably and suddenly, because she blest herself in an ill course; as now at this day they think all is sure.

If we trust anything but God, we must trust them as instruments, as helps in their rank and place which God hath set them; so much and no more. 'Let a man esteem of us as ministers of Christ,' saith St Paul, 2 Cor. vi. 4. If they esteem of us more, it is too much; if less, it is too little, just so much; as ministers, but 'as ministers of Christ.' So there is a due to everything. No more; for then you wrong God; no less; for then you wrong the thing and God too. Just so much as God would have it, and then we shall have just the grace that God intends.

Seeing there is such a danger in false confidence, let us take heed of it by all means.

'*That we may not trust in ourselves.*' That is, in any earthly thing in ourselves, or out of ourselves, wit, honour, riches, learning, or whatsoever, but God and his truth and promises. Let us labour to have a sanctified judgment in everything; to judge of things in their nature and order and rank as we should do, and be not carried with opinion of things. Judge of them as the Creator of things judgeth of them, as God judgeth, and the Scripture judgeth.

Now, of all outward things that we are prone to trust in, how doth the Scripture judge of them? How doth God judge of them? They are uncertain riches. 'Riches they have wings,' Prov. xxiii. 5. They are nothing, as the prophet saith. 'Wilt thou set thy heart upon that which is nothing?' Job vii. 17. They are vanity; they are of nothing, and they tend to nothing.

When the hour of death comes, what, will all these do good? They are uncertain, and weak, and inefficacious for that for which we trust them. They will not make us happy. They commend us not a whit to God. He hates us no more if we want them. He loves us no more if we have them. They make us not the better in ourselves, but the worse. They make us more indisposed to good things.

We say of those that are intoxicate with any kind of frenzy or lunacy, twice as much physic will not serve their turn as will serve another, because of the distemper of their brain, and the inflammation of their blood and spirits. Certainly it is true of those that are spiritually drunk with the conceit of the creature, with honour, with riches, &c. Three times, many times so much means, will not serve the turn, to bring them to goodness, as will serve meaner men.

What is the reason the poor receive the gospel?

Because there is a lesser distance between them and the blessed truths of God than in others, though perhaps they belong to God too; for the things of this life will work a little.

We say of weak brains, that strong drink doth much weaken them; and so weak stomachs, hard meat will not digest in them, it will overcome them. And weak brains, though strong water overcome them not, yet it will weaken them. So in these things, great parts and great place set a man further off from the gospel. A great deal of corruption cannot be overcome and digested without a great measure of grace. The proportion of grace it must be great, it must be treble to men that have great matters in this world; it must be greater than to poorer men, who [are] in a less distance from heaven.

Hence we may see the reasons of God's dispensation, why God doth seldom work by great means. I say seldom, sometimes he doth, to shew that they are good means. As it is said and observed by an ancient father, that seldom he saw any good come by General Councils. Why? They are good in themselves, but men trust too much upon them, and therefore God disappoints them of that they trust to. Because the naughty nature of man puts too much trust in these things, therefore God will not give that issue that we look for, but, on the contrary, a curse.

Why doth not God bless great preparations, many times, to war? &c. Because we put too much trust in them. Here are too many, saith God to Gideon, Judges vii., *et alibi*. Take away some, here are too many to go to war. What is the reason that God, where the greatest excellencies are, adds some imperfection to balance them? Because they should not trust in themselves.

What is the reason that in the church God chooseth men of meaner parts and sufficiencies, the disciples fishermen? If they had been great men, men would have said place had carried it; if they had been scholars, men would have said that their learning had carried it; if they had been witty* men, they would have said their wit had carried it. It had been no marvel if they should win the world. But when they saw they were mean men, fishermen, sitters at the receipt of custom (and perhaps their parts were not great), then they might attribute it to the divineness of the gospel, to the divineness of God's truth, and to God's blessing upon it.

What is the reason that God suffers excellent men to fall foully sometimes, St Peter himself, and David? &c. Because they should not trust in themselves, not trust in their grace, not trust in anything, no, not in the best things in themselves.

What is the reason that God goes by contraries in all the carriage of our salvation? 'That we should not trust in ourselves.' In our calling he calls men out of nothing. 'He calls things that are not as if they were,' Rom. iv. 17. In justification, he justifies a sinner, he that despairs of his own righteousness. That no man should trust in anything he hath, or despair if he want any perfection, God justifies a sinner that despairs of himself. In sanctification, God sanctifies a man when he sees no goodness in himself. Most of all, then, he is a vessel fit to receive grace. And he doth sanctify him sometimes by his falls. He makes him good by his slips, which is a strange course to make a man better by. Saith St Austin, 'I dare say, and stand to it, that it is profitable for some men to fall; they grow more holy by their slips' (*y*). As Peter, he grew stronger by his infirmity. This strange course God takes. Why so? That we should not trust in ourselves. In our calling, in our justification from our sins, 'that we should not trust in ourselves,' nor despair.

In sanctification. Nay, he takes a course that we shall grow better by our falls, that we may be ashamed of them, and be more cautelous† and humble, and more watchful for the time to come. In glorification he will glorify us, but it shall be when we have been rotten in our graves before; we must come to nothing. So in every passage of salvation he goes by contraries, and all to beat down confidence in ourselves, and that we should not distrust him in any extremity; for then is the time for God to work his work most of all.

'That we might not trust in ourselves.' To help us further against this self-confidence, let us labour to know ourselves well, what we are, distinct from the new creature, distinct from grace and glory. Indeed, in that respect we are something in God. If we go out of ourselves and see what

* That is, 'wise.'—G.

† That is, 'cautious.'—G.

we are in Christ, we are somebody. For we are heirs of heaven, we are kings and rulers over all, all things are subject to us, hell, and sin, and death. We are somebody there. But in that wherein our nature is prone to put over much confidence, what are we? What are we as we are strong, as we are rich, as we are noble, as we are in favour with great ones? Alas! all is nothing, because ere long it will be nothing. What will all be in the hour of death, when we must receive 'the sentence of death?' What will all favours do us good? They will be gone. What will all relations, that we are styled by this and that title, what good will it do? Alas! these end in death; all earthly relations shall be laid in the dust. All the honours in the earth, all riches and contentments, all the friends that we have, what can they do? Nothing! All shall leave us there. And for us to trust in that which will fail us ere long, and which being taken away, we receive a great foil* (for he that leans to a thing, if that be taken away, down he falls), what a shame will it be?

As the heathen man said, that great emperor, 'I have been all things, and nothing doth me good now,' when he was to die (*z*). Indeed, nothing could do him good. 'Let not the rich man glory in his riches, nor the wise man glory in his wisdom, nor the strong man in his strength,' saith the prophet; 'but let him that glorieth, glory in the Lord,' Jer. ix. 22.

Consider what the best thing is that we have of inward things, our wisdom. Wisdom, if it be not spiritual, it is only a thing for the things of this life, and we are ofttimes deceived in it. It makes God to disappoint us ofttimes to make us go out of ourselves. An excellent place for this we have in Isa. l. the last verse, 'Behold, all ye that kindle a fire, and compass yourselves about with sparks, walk in the light of your own fire,' &c. (it is a kind of *ironia*†), 'and the sparks that you have kindled; this you shall have of my hand, ye shall lie down in sorrow.' Walk in the light of your own fire, walk according to your own devices and projects; this ye shall have at my hand, ye shall lie down in sorrow. God catcheth the wise in the imagination of their own hearts; he disappoints the counsel and the projects of Ahithophel. God takes a glory in it, to shame the policies and projects of those that will be witty in a distinct way against God. The best policy is to serve God and to walk uprightly.

'*That we should not trust in ourselves, but in God who raiseth the dead.*' This is the other branch, what we should trust in, in God. All this humbling of the blessed apostle, even to death's door, that 'he received the sentence of death,' it was first to subdue carnal confidence in himself. He was prone to think himself stronger than he was, or that he should be upheld, that something or other should keep him from death. That he might subdue this carnal confidence, and then that he might trust in God, it was all for these two ends, 'that we might not trust in ourselves (or in any means), but in God that raiseth the dead.'

Was St Paul to learn to trust in God, that had been so long a scholar in Christ's school, nay, a master in Israel? Was he to learn to trust in God?

Yes; doubtless, he was. It is a lesson that is hardly learned, and it is a lesson that we shall be learning all our life, to go out of ourselves and out of the creature, and to go further into God, to rely more and more upon him. It is a lesson that we can never learn as we ought. Therefore, weak Christians ought not to be discouraged when they find defects and weakness

* That is, 'fall.'—G. † That is, 'irony.'—G.

in their trust. Our hearts are false, and prone to trust outward things; but do they groan under their corruptions? Do they complain of themselves? Do they go out of themselves? Their estate is good. The estate of a Christian, it is a growing, it is a conflicting estate. He comes not to full trust and confidence in God till he have gathered many experiments,* till God have exercised him to the proof throughly; therefore, let them not be discouraged. A Christian is not alway like himself; he is in a growing estate. There is a weak faith and a strong faith. 'O, ye of little faith,' Mat. vi. 30. The disciples had a little faith as well as Abraham, 'that was *strong* in faith. As long as we are on the complaining hand, and on the striving hand, and growing hand, all is hopeful. St Paul himself still strived against self-confidence, and still learned to trust in God more and more.

But mark the order. First, God doth all this, 'that we should not trust in ourselves.' But that is not the thing he doth mainly aim at, but another thing, that we should trust in God who raiseth the dead.' Whence we may observe, that

Doct. God, to make us trust in himself, is fain to cast us out of ourselves.

His proper work is not to drive us out of ourselves, that is a work subordinate to a higher. But the furthest and last work is, that we should 'trust in him,' as the prophet saith. 'God doth a strange work,' Isa. xxviii. 21. He doth a work strange to himself, that he may do his own work. He doth a work that doth not concern him so properly, that he may do his own work, as he is God, that is, to confirm and settle us upon himself. But that he may do this, he must set us out of ourselves by crosses and afflictions. That is not his own proper work, to afflict us, and to bring us low; for he is the 'Father of mercies.' But that he may do his own work, to bring us to him, and then do good to us, he must take this in his way, and do this first. To make it clear. A carpenter, he pulls down a house, he takes it in pieces. His art is not to pull down houses, but to build them up. But he doth that which doth not belong to him properly, that he may do that which doth belong to him; for he will not build upon a rotten foundation. So neither 'will God build upon a rotten foundation.' He will not build upon carnal confidence, upon carnal trust, upon pride, and covetousness; but he will demolish that rotten foundation with afflictions and crosses. He will use such means that we shall have small joy to trust in sin. He will by crosses and afflictions force us to go from our sins. He will demolish that rotten foundation, that he may raise up an excellent edifice and frame of the new creature, that shall endure to everlasting. The work of a physician is to cure nature, and not to weaken it. It is not his work to make people sick, but to make them sound. If the body be distempered, it must be weakened. He must carry the burden of ill and noisome humours before it be strengthened. To make people sound he must give them strong purgations, that shall afflict them and affect them as much as the disease for a while. But all is to make them lighter and stronger after, when they are eased of the burden of noisome humours: and so it is in every other trade. So God shews his skill in this great matter in bringing us to heaven this way. He doth that work which doth not properly concern him, to work at last his own blessed good work. He afflicts us to drive us out of ourselves, that we may come at last to trust in him, in whom is all our happiness and good.

The reason of it is clear. For in a succession of contraries there must

* That is, 'experiences.'—G.

be a removing of one contrary before another can be brought in. If a vessel be to be filled with a contrary liquor, the first must have a vent; it must be emptied of the worse, that the better may come. So it is with us. We are full of self-confidence, as a vessel of naughty liquor. Out must that go, that better things may come in. So it is in ploughing, and in everything else. This is taken as a principle in nature. The order generally is this, that we should not trust in ourselves, that we might be brought to trust in God. He brings us low, to 'receive the sentence of death,' to drive us out of ourselves, that he may bring us to rely on him.

Use 1. The use we should make of it, among many others, is this, *that we should not take offence at God when he is about this strange work*, as we think. When he is making us sick with physic, with afflictions, and troubles, let us not think that he hates us. Doth the physician hate the patient when he makes him sick? Perhaps he stays a good while from him till his physic have wrought throughly, but he doth not hate him, but gives it time, and suffers it to have its work, that so he may recover himself. Doth the goldsmith hate his precious metal when he puts it into the fire, and suffers the fire to work upon it? What is lost? Nothing but the dross. What is lost in the body by sickness? The ill humours that load the body and distemper the actions and functions of it, that it cannot work as it should. There is nothing lost but that that may well be spared. So when God goes about his work, he afflicts thee and follows thee with losses and crosses. He takes away friends and credit, this outward thing and that. All this is to give thee a purge. He works a strange work, that he may work his own work, that he may bring thee to himself.

Therefore let us be far from murmuring at this blessed work of God: let us rather bless God for his care this way, that he will not suffer us to perish with the world. God might have suffered us to rot upon our dregs, that we should have no changes, as the world hath not. But he hath more care of us than so. The husbandman will not plough in the wilderness. The heathy ground shall go unploughed long enough. He loves it not so well as to sow good seed there. So when God takes pains, and is at cost with any man; when he purgeth him, and ploughs him, and hammers him; all this is to consume that which is naught, to plough up the weeds, to fit him for the blessed seed of grace, to fit him for comfort here and glory in another world. Why then should we murmur against God? Let us rather be thankful, especially when we see the blessed issue of this, when we see our earthly-mindedness abated, when we see ourselves more heavenly-minded, when we see ourselves weaned from the world, when we see ourselves take more delight in communion with God. Then, blessed be God for crosses and afflictions, that he hath taken the pains, and would be at the cost with us to exercise us. It is a ground not only of patience, but of thankfulness, when God humbles us. Be not discontent, man! Grudge not! murmur not! God doth a work that seems strange to thee, and which is not his own proper work, that he may do his own work, that he may bring thee nearer to himself. Why dost thou murmur at thy own good?

The patient cries out of the physician that he torments him. He hears him well enough, but he will not be advised by his patient. He means to advise *him*, and to rule *him*. He would fain have comfort. He is in pain, and cries for ease. But his time is not yet come. So let us wait, and not murmur under crosses. God is doing one work to bring to pass another. He brings us out of ourselves, that he may bring us nearer to himself.

Use 2. And another use that we may make of it, let us examine ourselves *whether our afflictions and crosses have had this effect in us, to bring us to trust in him more.* If they have, all is well. But if they make us worse, that we fret and murmur, and feel no good by them, it is an ill sign; for God doth bring us low, that we may not trust in ourselves, but in him. *Quem præsentia mala non corrigunt*, &c. Whom the presence of ill and grievance amends not, they bring to eternal grievance. 'This is Ahaz,' saith the Scripture, 2 Chron. xxviii. 22: a strange man, a wicked king, that notwithstanding God followed him with judgments, yet he grew worse and worse. This is Ahaz! He might well be branded. When a man belongs to God, everything brings him nearer to God. When a man is brought to be more humble, and more careful, and more watchful every way, to be more zealous, more heavenly minded; it is a blessed sign that God then is working a blessed work, to force him out of himself, and to bring him nearer himself, to trust in him. This we cannot too much consider of.

Use 3. It should teach us likewise this, *that we judge not amiss of the generation of the righteous, when we see God much humbling them.* When we see him follow them with sickness, with troubles and disgraces in the world, perhaps with terror of conscience, with desertions, be not discouraged. If he be thy friend, censure him not; add not affliction to his affliction. Is not his affliction enough? Thou needest not add to* thy unjust censure, as Job said to his friends. The more we are afflicted of God, the more good he intends to work to us. The end is to bring us from ourselves to trust in him.

It is a wicked disposition in men that know not the ways of God. They are ignorant of the ways that he takes with his children. When they see men that are Christians, that they are humbled and cast down and troubled, they think they are men forsaken of God, &c. Alas! they do not know God's manner of dealing. He casts them down that he may raise them up. They 'receive the sentence of death' against themselves, that he may comfort them after, that he may do them good in their latter end. Let this therefore keep us from censuring of other men in our thoughts for this hard course which God seems to take with them.

Use 4. And let us make this use of it, when we are in any grievance, and God follows us still, *let us mourn and lament the stubbornness of our hearts, that will not yield.* God intends to draw us near to him, to trust in him. If we would do this, the affliction would cease, except it be for trial, and for the exercise of grace, and for witness to the truth. When God afflicts, sometime for trial and for witness, there is a spirit of glory in such a case, that a man is never afflicted in mind. But, I say, when God follows us with sickness, with crosses, with loss of friends, and we are not wrought upon, let us censure our hard hearts, that force God to take this course.

And 'justify God in all this,' Job i. 22, *et alibi.* Lord, thou knowest I could not be good without this, thou knowest I would not be drawn without this; bring me near to thyself, that thou mayest take away this heavy hand from me. The intemperate man that is sick makes the physician seem cruel. It is because I set my affections too much on earthly things, that thou followest me with these troubles. We force God to do this. A physician is forced to bring his patient even to skin and bone. An intemperate patient sometimes, that hath surfeited upon a long distemper, he must bring him to death's door, even almost to death, because his distemper is so settled upon him, that he cannot otherwise cure him. So it is with God, the physician of our souls. He must bring us wondrous low. We are so prone,

* Qu. 'to it?'—Ed.

so desperately addicted to present things, to trust to them, and to be proud of them, and confident in them, that God must deal as a sharp physician. He must bring us so low, or else we should never be recovered of our perfect health again, and all is that we might trust in God.

Observe we from hence another point, that

Doctrine. God in all outward things that are ill, intends the good of the soul.

He takes liberty to take away health, and liberty, and friends, to take away comforts. But whatsoever he takes away, he intends the good of the soul in the first place. And all the ills that he inflicts upon us, they are to cure a worse ill, the ill of the soul; to cure an unbelieving heart, a worldly, proud, carnal heart, which is too much addicted to earthly things. We see here how God dealt with St Paul. All was to build up his soul in trust and confidence in God, all was for the soul.

The reason is; other things are vanishing, the soul is the better part, the eternal part. If all be well with the soul, all shall be well otherwise at last. If it be well with the soul, the body shall do well. Though God take liberty to humble us with sickness, and with death itself, yet God will raise the body and make it glorious. A good soul will draw it after it at last, and move God to make the body glorious. But if the soul be naught, let us cherish and do what we will with the body; both will be naught at last.

This life is not a life to regard the body. We are dead in that while we live. 'The sentence of death' is passed. We must die. We are dying every day. 'The body is dead because of sin,' Rom. viii. 10. We are going to our grave. Every day takes away a part of our life.

This is not a life for this body of ours. It is a respite to get assurance of an eternal estate in heaven. God takes our wealth, and liberty, and strength, &c., that he may help our souls, that he may work his own blessed work in our souls, that he may lay a foundation of eternal happiness in our souls.

Therefore, hence we should learn to resign our bodies and estates to God. Lord, do with me what thou wilt! only cure my soul, only strengthen my faith. I give thee liberty with all my heart to take what thou wilt, so thou save my soul. Give me not up to an unbelieving heart, to an hypocritical, false heart, to false confidence, to trust in false grounds, and to perish eternally; for my estate and body, do what thou wilt. We should be brought to this. Why? Because indeed the state of the soul is the true state either in good or ill. If all be naught with that, all will be naught at last. We shall try it to our cost.

And therefore let us even rather thank God, and desire God to go on with his work. Lord, rather than thou shouldst give me up to a hard heart, to a stubborn heart, and perish and have no sound change, rather than suffer me to perish thus, use me as thou wilt.

And thank him when we find any degree of goodness or faith. Lord, thou mightst have followed me with outward blessings, and so have given me up in my soul to hypocrisy, and to pride, that I should never have felt the power of grace, that I should never have known thee, or myself throughly, or the vanity of outward things. But this thou hast not done, thou hast not given me liberty in outward things, that thou mightest do good to my soul, blessed be thy name. Let us not only take it well, but thankfully at God's hands. To proceed,

'That we might trust in God that raiseth the dead.'

Obs. The soul must have somewhat to trust to. The foundation must be laid;

for the soul is a creature, and a dependent creature. Somewhat it must have to rely on; as all weak dependent things have somewhat to depend on. The vine is a weak plant. It must have the elm or somewhat to rely on. It will sink else, it will become unfruitful and unprofitable. All things that are weak, are supported by somewhat that is stronger. It is an inclination and instinct in things that are weak, to look for supply from things that are stronger than themselves to support them; and it is their happiness to be so. The creatures that are unreasonable* are guided by those that have reason, by men; and the creatures that are reasonable are guided by superiors, by God, and by angels that are above them, and have the care and charge over them. It is the happiness of weaker things to be under the supportation of that which is stronger. And some support it will have, good or bad.

The soul, if it have not God, it will have pleasures, it will have profit. The worst of men, that think there is little for them in heaven, by reason of their blasphemy, and filthy courses; they will have base pleasures to go to, that they will trust to, and carnal acquaintance to solace themselves withal. The worst of men will have some dirty thing or other, to give their souls to, to support themselves withal; something the soul will have.

God loves the soul, and hath made it for himself; and as he hath made it for himself, to join with himself, to solace himself in it ('My son, give me thy heart,' Prov. xxiii. 26) so when he takes it from outward things, he will not have it empty, to rely upon nothing, but he takes it to himself. All this is to take our hearts from ourselves, and from self-confidence, that we may trust in him. God is for the heart, and that is for him; as I said, he calls for it, 'My son, give me thy heart,' give me thy affection of trust, of joy, of delight. All the affections, they are made for God, and for heaven, and heavenly things. Our affections that we have, they are not made for riches. Our souls are not made for them. The soul is larger than they. They will not content the soul. The soul is a spiritual substance, and they are outward things. The soul is large, they are scanty in their extent. They are uncertain, and momentary; the soul is an eternal thing. It outlives those things. And thereupon the soul is not made for them, and they are not made for the soul.

They are to give contentment to the outward man for a while here. They are made for our pilgrimage, to comfort us in the way to heaven; but the soul is not for them.

The soul is the chamber, and the bed, and, as it were, the cabinet for God himself, and Christ to rest in only.

All outward things must be kept out of the heart. We may use them; but we must keep them out of the heart. It is not for them. We must not joy in them, and solace ourselves, and delight in them over much, further than we seek God in them, and enjoy God in them. But as they are sensible† things, the heart is not for them. Therefore God takes the heart from self-confidence, and from other things. He suffers it not to wander; but he takes it to himself, that we may trust in him.

The next thing, then, that we may observe is, that when we go out of ourselves, we must have somewhat to rely on, which is better than all things else. We lose not by the change; but when we are stripped of ourselves, and of all earthly things, we have God to go to.

Doctrine. God is the object of trust.

God is the proper object of trust of the Christian soul. He is the object of trust, as well as the author of it. He is the cause and worker of it by

* That is, 'without reason.'—G.

† That is, 'outward.'—G.

his Spirit, and he is the object of it. If we trust to other things, it must be as they are God's instruments, as they are God's means. But if we trust anything, either wealth, or friends, or anything, to neglect the worship of God, or to please ourselves in it, to put our hands to ill courses, in confidence of the creature, in confidence of men, or anything else, to take any false cause in hand, this is to trust them above their respect. We must trust to them as instruments, as voluntary instruments, which God may use when he pleaseth, or not use when he pleaseth. When we use them otherwise, we forget their nature. Then we use them not as instruments, but as the chief. We forget the order.

God is the object of trust. We must rest on him for grace and glory; for the best things, and for the things of this life, as far as they are good.

So far as we trust to anything else to move us to security, to rest in them, or to sin for them, it is a sinful trust. Other things we may trust; but in the nature of vain instruments, changeable instruments, that God may alter and change. He that is rich to-day, may be poor to-morrow. He that hath a friend to-day, may have him taken away to-morrow. And so all outward things, they are changeable and mutable. But we may trust God all times alike. He is eternal. He is infinitely able, and infinitely wise, to know all our grievances. We may trust him with our souls, with our hearts. He is faithful, and loving, and eternal, as our souls are. He gives eternity to the soul. Therefore at all times we may trust in him, in all places, everywhere. He knows our hearts, he knows our grievance everywhere. He hath all grounds of one that may be trusted to. He hath power and goodness, and mercy and wisdom. He is the object of trust.

But how considered, is he the object of trust, God out of Christ, Mediator?

Oh, no! God in covenant with us in Christ,—he is the object of our trust, or else there is such a distance and contrariety between man's nature and God, that he is a 'consuming fire,' Heb. xii. 29. Since the fall from the covenant of works, we cannot be saved by that: but he hath vouchsafed to be ours in a better covenant in Christ, in whom 'all the promises are yea and amen,' 2 Cor. i. 20. This good comes from God to us by Christ. Christ first receives it, and he derives* it to us, as our elder Brother, and as our head. All the promises are made in him, and through him. He receives it for us. We receive it at the second hand. God hath filled him first. 'And of his fulness we receive grace for grace,' John i. 16.

'Without him we can do nothing,' John xv. 5. With him we can do all things. So we trust in God reconciled; God made ours in the covenant of grace in Jesus Christ, who hath made our peace. Else God is a 'sealed fountain.' He is a fountain of good, but a sealed fountain. Christ hath opened this fountain. His love is open to Christ, and derived to Christ, in whom our flesh is. He is 'bone of our bone, and flesh of our flesh,' Eph. v. 30, that we might be bone of his bone, and flesh of his flesh by being united with him. So now we trust in him, as God, the Father of Christ, reconciled. 'I believe in God the Father Almighty,' as it is in the creed. God thus considered is the object of trust. There are two ojects of trust: God the Father, Son, and Holy Ghost; and Christ Mediator.

Use. If this be so, that God reconciled now is the object of trust, for all things that are good, not only for salvation, but for grace, and for all com-

* That is, 'transmits.'—G.

forts, to bring us to heaven, then *we see the vanity of all other confidence whatsoever*, as I touched before.

And is it not a blessed thing that God will be trusted, that he hath made himself such a one as we may trust him? Now blessed be God for Christ, that he having received satisfaction to his justice by him, he may be trusted, and desires that we should trust him; that now in Christ he hath made himself a Father, that we should not fear him, nor run away from him. It is a great favour that God will be trusted of us, that he will honour us so much.

He accounts it an honour when we trust him, but indeed it is an honour to us that we have a throne of grace through Christ to go to; that he hath devised a way that we might trust him, and not run from him; that we may go to him in Christ, who sits at his right hand, who is our intercessor, who hath redeemed us with his precious blood. It is our happiness that he hath made himself a gracious and loving Father, that he calls us to him, and thinks himself honoured by our trusting in him.

Again, we see here that,

Doct. Trust in God is a main duty.

He is the object of trust, and it is a main duty. It is a spring of duty out of which all comes; for we see here all doth aim at this. Afflictions they come to mortify our self-confidence. Self-confidence is subdued that we may trust in God. Our trust must be carried to him. He is the object of it. And this trust in God is a main duty, which in this world we ought to labour for. It is that that God doth aim at, and it is that that we should aim at. God doth aim at it in exercising of us; and we should aim at it on our part, in our hearing, in our receiving the sacrament, in everything, that our trust and affiance and confidence may be in God, and that we may grow more and more and more in it.

Well, since God is the object of trust, and trust is such a necessary grace, that God doth all to bring us to trust in him, let us come to search ourselves, how shall we know whether we trust in God or no? And then to direct us, how to come to trust in him, to give some means and helps.

1. He trusts in God reconciled in Jesus Christ *that flies to him in extremity.* That a man trusts unto, that when he is pinched he flies unto. How shall a man know that he is a covetous worldling? If he be in extremity, he goes to his purse, he makes a friend of that. How shall a man know that he trusts to the arm of flesh, that he trusts his friend too much? In extremity he runs to him, presently he goes to a friend he hath. What we run to, that our trust is in. A Christian, he runs to his God; and happy is that Christian that is in covenant, that he hath a God to run to in all extremities, in sickness, in death, at all times. He is happy that he hath a God, when all fails, to trust in.

Wilt thou know therefore whether thou trustest in God or no? Whither goest thou? A carnal man, he goes to one earthly prop or other. If God answer him not presently, then he goes with Saul to the witch, to the devil himself perhaps. If God do not send him present help, he goes to one carnal help or other, to fetches* of his wit, to policy, to crack his conscience, to bear out things with impudence. He hath not learned to trust in God, and he runs not to him, but to some wicked course or other.

All that go not to God in the use of good means (for we must put that in, we must go to God in the use of his means, in the use of good means only), they trust not God; for God will not be tempted, but trusted. We

* That is, 'devices.'—G.

must go to him by prayer, and in the use of lawful means, and only of lawful means; or else, if we trust him and do not use the means, we tempt him. We must serve God's providence in using the means.

2. Therefore, secondly, he that trusts in God *useth his means*. He that trusts God for a harvest must plough, and sow, and do all that belongs to the providence of God.

So a merchant that will increase his estate, he must get a ship and other provision to do it with, for we must serve God's providence as well as trust God's providence. When we neglect good and lawful means, and run into ill courses, and use ill means, we serve not God, nor trust him. Those that grow rich by calling 'evil good, and good evil,' Isa. v. 20, they have not learned to trust in God. Those that think except they leave their posterity great they shall not be happy, and therefore they will neglect the Sabbath, and neglect all, to scrape an estate;—is this to trust in God? Have they learned to trust in God, when sacrilegiously they take away the time dedicated for the salvation of their souls and the service of God? Is this one means that God hath ordained to trust him in? They that flatter and serve men's humours when they know them to be in a naughty and ill way, is this to trust God, when they go out of his means and way, and make an idol of flesh and blood to serve their own turn?

Alas! we need not name these things. If men had learned what it is to trust in God, and depend upon him in the use of lawful means, and would rather be content to want in this world than to have anything with a cracked conscience!

I beseech you, let us examine our own hearts in this. There are many that think they trust in God when they do not. They trust their policy, they trust flesh and blood, and by consequence they trust the devil, if they trust not in God.

3. In the next place, he that trusts in God, *his mind will be quieted in some comfortable measure, when he hath used the means that are lawful, and cast himself upon God*. He will be quiet, and let God work then. When he hath taken pains in his calling lawfully, and desired God's blessing, if God send wealth, so it is; if not, he is not much troubled. He knows that all shall be for the best to them that trust in God. When he cannot have it in the use of lawful means, he is quiet. He that trusts a physician, when he hath used the direction of the physician, he is quiet. He thinks he is a wise man, an experienced physician, and now he will not trouble his mind any longer. If a man vex himself, and think all will not be well, he doth not trust his physician. And so in other professions we trust to a man's counsel, if we think him wise and honest. We follow his direction, and then we will be quiet.

Now, God is infinitely wise. When we have used lawful means, and commended the means to God; for as he will be trusted in, so he will be sought unto. 'I will be sought to by the house of Israel for this,' Ezek. xxxvi. 37. For except we pray to him, he is not trusted. But when we have prayed to him, in the use of lawful means, let us be quiet, let us not be distracted with dividing cares about this and that, as if there were not a God in heaven that had care of us, that had a providence over things below. Certainly he hath. Do thou do thy work, and let him alone with his work. The care of duty belongs to thee. When thou hast done thy duty, rest thou quiet, or else thou honourest him not as a God, thou trustest him not, thou dost not make a God of him. It is a great dishonour to God.

A man thinks himself dishonoured when he is not trusted; when we see he hath alway been faithful to us, and is so reputed, and yet we call his credit in question, and will not be quiet. We should do as children do. They follow their books, and let their father take care for all provision for meat and drink, and clothes and such things. They beat not their heads about it. They know they have a father that will take care for that. If we were true children of God, and have the disposition of heavenly children, we will do so. If we trouble ourselves, and beat our heads, it is a sign that we fear that God is not our Father. Therefore I add that to other signs, a resting of ourselves quiet. When we are quiet, God will do more than when we vex ourselves. 'Be still, and see the salvation of the Lord,' saith Moses at the Red Sea, Exod. xiv. 13. So let us be still and quiet, and see the salvation of God. He will work wonders.

4. Again, it is a sign that we trust in God, *when there are no means, yet notwithstanding we will not despair, but hope and trust in God*. When we see nothing in the eye of flesh and blood, no means of recovery, yet we trust in God. He can work his way though we see not how; he can make a passage for us. When God is thus honoured he works wonders. This is to make a God of him, when there is no means, to believe that he can work against means. If my life shall be for his glory and my good, he can recover my life though the physician say I am a dead man. If he have employment for me in this world, he can do it. He can work with means, or against means, or without means. And so in desperate troubles, if God see it good for me, he can deliver me though there be no means. He is the Creator of means. Do not tie him to his own creature. If all be taken away, he can make new.

5. Again, he trusts in God that labours *to make God his friend continually;* for he whom we trust unto we will not provoke. Certainly we will not provoke a man whom we mean to make our friend. Those that live in swearing, in defiled courses, in contempt of God and holy things, of the ordinances of God, of the day appointed to holy and religious uses, those that 'wax stubborn against God,' 1 Tim. v. 11, as the Scripture speaks, do we trust him against whom we walk stubbornly? Will a man trust him that he makes his enemy by wicked courses? Thou makest God thy enemy, and provokest him to his face, to try whether he will pour vengeance upon this* or no. He tells thee thou shalt not be unpunished if thou 'take his name in vain,' Exod. xx. 7; yet thou wilt be stubborn, and not make conscience of these things. Dost thou trust him? No! thou provokest him. Thou mayest trust him; but it must be to damn thee, to give thee thy reward with rebels; thou mayest trust him for that. But for good things thou doest not, thou canst not trust him in wicked courses.

Who will trust his enemy, especially he that hath made his enemy by his ill course of life? A man that goes on in an evil course, he cannot, he doth not trust in God.

6. He that trusts in God's promise *will trust in his threatening*. Where there is an evangelical faith, there is a legal faith alway. He that believes that God will save him if he trust in Christ, he believes that if he do not believe in Christ he will damn him, if he live in his natural course without repentance.

There is a legal faith of the curse, as well as an evangelical of the promise. They are both together. If thou do not believe God's curse in wicked courses, thou wilt never believe him for the other. Therefore, I will add this to make up the evidences of trust in God. True trust looks to

* Qu. 'thee?'—ED.

God's truth, and promise, and word in one part of it as well as another. Thou trusts God for thy salvation and the promises of that; but thou must trust him for the direction of thy life too. Faith doth not single out some objects; I will believe this, and not that. Faith is carried to all the objects, it believes all God's truths. Therefore, if I believe not the threatenings and directions, to be ruled by them, I believe not the promises. In what measure thou believest the promise of mercy to save thy soul, in that measure thou believest the directions of God's word to guide thy soul. He that receives Christ as a Priest to save him, he must receive him as a King to rule him.

All the directions, and all the threatenings, and all the promises must be received and believed.

A man hath no more faith and trust in God than he hath care to follow God's direction; for faith is carried to all divine truths. All come from the same God. Thousands go to hell, and think, Oh, God is a merciful God, and I will trust in him! But how is thy life? Is it carried by God's directions? Thou art a rebel. Thou livest in sins against conscience. Thou wilt trust in God in one part of his word, and not in another. Thou must not be a chooser.

7. Again, the last that I will name at this time, if thou trust God for one thing, *undoubtedly thou will trust him for all.* If thou trust him with thy soul, certainly thou wilt trust him with thy children. Some men hope to be saved by Christ. Oh, he will be merciful to their souls; and yet even to their death they use corrupt courses to get an estate and to make their children rich; and except they have so much, they will not trust in God. If they have nothing to leave them, they think not that there is a God in heaven who is a better Father than they. Put case thou hast nothing, hast thou not God's blessing? Canst thou trust thy soul with God, and canst thou not trust him with thy family? Is he not the God of thy seed? Hath he not made the promise to thy posterity as well as to thyself? If thou trust him for one thing, thou wilt trust him for all. Wilt thou trust him for heaven, and wilt thou not trust him for provision for daily bread? Wilt thou not trust him for this or that, but thou must use unlawful means? He that trusts God, he trusts him for all truths and for all things needful, with his family, with his body, with his soul, with all. And so much for the trials, whether we trust in God or no.

Let us not deceive ourselves. It is a point of infinite consequence, as much as the salvation of our souls. What brings men to hell in the church? False confidence. They trust to false things, or they think they trust in God, when indeed they do not.

The fault of a ship is seen in a tempest, and the fault of a house is seen when winter comes. Thy trust, that is thy house that thou goest to and restest in, the fault of that will be seen when thou comest to extremity. In the hour of death, then thou hast not a God to go to, then thy conscience upbraids thee; thou hast lived by thy shifts* in carnal confidence and rebellion against God, and how canst thou then willingly trust God, whom thou hast made thine enemy all thy lifetime?

To go, then, to some helps. If upon search we find that we do not so trust in God as we should, let us lament our unbelieving hearts, complain to God of it, desire God, whatsoever he doth, that he would honour us so much as that we may honour him by trusting in him; for it is his glory and our salvation.

* That is, 'expedients.'—G.

But because I will not go out of the text, the best way is that which follows, to know God as he is.

How come we to trust a man? When we know his honesty, his fidelity, his wisdom, and his sufficiency, then we trust him. Therefore, St Paul adds here that we should 'trust in God that raiseth the dead,' that is, 'in God Almighty.' From whence I raise this general, that

The best way to trust in God is to know him as he is.

We know his attributes by his principal works. We know his nature by his works, as here is one of the principal set down, he is God 'that raiseth the dead.' A sound, sanctified trust in God is by knowing of him. 'They that know thy name will trust in thee,' Ps. ix. 10.

There are three ways of the knowledge of God:

His nature, promises, and works—

To know what he hath engaged himself in, in all the promises that concern us; and then to know his strength, how able he is to make good these promises; and then to know his works, how his nature hath enabled him to make good those promises.

1. Especially *his nature;* as to consider his goodness and his wisdom. Every attribute, indeed, doth enforce trust, for he is good freely, he is good to us of his own bowels. We may trust him that hath made himself a Father, out of his own mercy in Christ, when we were enemies. His goodness and wisdom is infinite as himself, and his power and his truth. As the Scripture saith ofttimes, 'Faithful is God that hath promised,' Heb. xi. 11.

St Bernard, a good man in evil times, saith he, 'I consider three things in which I pitch my hope and trust, *charitatem adoptionis*, the love of God in making me his child; and *veritatem promissionis*, the truth of God in performing his promise. His love is such, to make me his child; his truth is such, to perform his promise. Thirdly, I consider his power, that is able to make good that that he hath promised' (*w*).

This threefold cable is a strong one. His love in adoption, his truth in performing his promise, and his power in making good all this. This threefold cable will not easily be broken. Let my sottish flesh murmur against me as long as it will. As the flesh will murmur, who art thou, that thou darest trust in God? What is thy merit, that thou hopest for such great glory? No, no, saith he; 'I know whom I have believed,' 2 Tim. i. 12, as St Paul saith. I answer with great confidence against my sottish, murmuring flesh, 'I know whom I have trusted.' He is able, he is good, he is true. This that holy man had to exercise his faith.

I name it, because it is the temper of all believing souls that are so in truth. The believing heart considers the nature of God, the promise of God, and though the murmuring, rebellious flesh say, What art thou? how darest thou that art flesh and blood look to God? Oh! he is faithful, he is good and gracious in Christ. He hath made himself a father. I know whom I have believed. God is all-sufficient.

Trust and confidence doth grow in the soul, in what measure and proportion the knowledge of him whom we trust in grows, and as his strength grows. The more rich and strong a man grows, in whom I trust, and the more gracious and good he grows, and the more my knowledge of him is increased with it too, that I see he is so able, so true, so loving a man, a man so affected to me, the more he grows, and my knowledge of him, the more my trust is carried to him. So a Christian, the more he considers the infiniteness of God's love, of his wisdom and goodness, the more he is carried in trust, and confidence to it.

Not to trouble you with many places, the 42d Psalm is an excellent psalm for trust and confidence in God. The whole psalm is to that purpose, to stir up himself to trust in God; for that follows knowledge; when upon knowledge we rouse up our hearts. 'God is my rock, and my salvation, and defence.' Is he so? Then, my soul, 'trust in God.' He chargeth it upon his soul, 'Therefore I will trust in God.' And then he blames his soul, Is God so? Why art thou so disquieted, O my soul?'

This is the exercise of a Christian heart, when, upon sound knowledge, he can charge his soul to trust in God, and check his soul, 'Why art thou cast down? Still trust in God.' Why dost thou not trust in him? Is he not true? Is he not wise? He is the 'God of my salvation.' And in ver. 8, 'Trust in God at all times,' in prosperity, in adversity. Why? 'God is my refuge.'

There he sets forth his nature. If our troubles be never so many, there is somewhat in God that is answerable; as in Ps. xxviii. 7, 'He is a rock and a shield.' He hath somewhat in him that is opposite to every ill.

And withal, 'pour out thy heart to God;' for where there is trust there is prayer. 'Trust in God at all times, and pour out thy heart before him, for he is our refuge.'

And so, 'trust not in oppression and robbery. If riches increase, set not your heart upon them; for God hath spoken once, and twice, that power belongs to God,' Ps. lxii. 11. Trust not any other thing but God. Power and mercy belong to him. This is a notable way to trust in God, to know that power and mercy belong to him. If another man love me, hath not God another man's heart in his hand? 'The king's heart is in his hand,' Prov. xxi. 1. Therefore trust in God for the favour of men. Hath he not all the power? That that another man hath that affects me, it is but a derived power from him. He hath inclined him to do good to me. All mercy and love, it is from God; and he turns and disposeth it as it pleaseth him. As it is the Scripture phrase, the language of Canaan, the heart is in God's hands; he inclined the heart of such a man. The knowledge of God, with prayer and stirring up ourselves to trust in God, and checking our souls for the contrary, it is a notable means to trust in God.

And though we feel no present comfort from God, trust him for his word, trust him for his promise, though he seem now to be a God hidden. As a child in the dark he holds his father fast by the hand. He sees not his father, but he knows his father's hand is strong. And though he see him not, yet he believes it is his father, and holds him though it be in the dark.

Men they cast anchor in the dark, at midnight. Though they cannot see, yet they know that the anchor will hold fast. Cast anchor upon God in darkness and temptation. Hold God fast in the dark night, although we see nothing. We shall alway find this, that he is a God able to fulfil his promise, that he is a true and faithful and able God. Cast anchor in him therefore. Though thou feel or see nothing, be sure in all extremities to trust in God.

2. Besides other things, trust in God is properly and primarily wrought *by the promises*. Trust in God so far as he hath discovered himself to be trusted. I can trust a man no farther than I have a writing or a word of mouth from him, or a message from him.

Now, what have we from God to trust him for? We have his word written, and that is sealed by the sacrament. The way to trust in God, therefore, is to know the promises.

(1.) The *general promises* that do concern all Christians and all conditions and estates of men. 'God will be a sun and a shield;' a sun for all good, and a shield to keep away all evil. 'And no good thing shall be wanting to him that lives a godly life,' Ps. lxxxiv. 11. Again, general promises for issue. 'All things shall work for good to them that love God,' Rom. viii. 28. And, 'He will give his Spirit to them that ask him,' Luke xi. 13. It is a general promise to all askers whatsoever, that they shall have the Spirit of God, which is a promise that hath all particular graces in it. For the Spirit is the fountain of all grace. It is the Spirit of love, of faith, of hope. All are in the promise of the Spirit, and God hath promised this. Let us trust in God for these general things.

(2.) And for *particular promises*. He hath made a promise to be 'a husband to the widow, and a father to the fatherless,' Ps. lxviii. 5. He will 'regard the cause of the widow,' Ps. cxlvi. 9; and he is a God 'that comforteth the abject,' 2 Cor. vii. 6. He hath made promises to those that are afflicted, to all estates and conditions of men. Trust in God for these.

But how? He hath made these with conditions in regard of outward things. Let us trust him so far forth as he hath promised, that is, he will either protect us from dangers or give us patience in dangers. He will give us all outward things, or else contentment, which is better. Take him in that latitude. Trust in him as he will be trusted to. For outward things, he will either give the things or give the grace, which is better. He will either remove the grievance, or he will plant the grace, which is better. If he remove not the evil, he will give patience to bear it. And what do I lose if he give me not the good thing, if he give me contentment? I have grace to supply it, which makes me a better man.

If he give me the thing without the grace, what am I the better? A carnal reprobate may have that.

So let us trust him, as he will be trusted. For grace and spiritual things, all shall be for our good without fail; but for the things of this life, either he will give them, or else graces.

Let us trust God, therefore, as he will be trusted in his word and promises.

Now this trusting of God (to speak a little to the present purpose, because St Paul was now in great affliction. When he learned to trust in God, he was in fear of death), let us see how we are to exercise this trust in great crosses, and in the hour of death. St Paul was in these two.

The point is very large, and I will take it only according to the present scope.

How doth a Christian exercise trust in extremity, in extreme crosses? for then he must go to God; he hath none else to go to.

1. *He is beaten from the creature;* and, as I said before, the soul will have somewhat to go to. The poor creatures, the silly conies, they have the rocks to go to, as Solomon saith, Prov. xxx. 26. The soul that hath greater understanding, it is necessitated to trust in God in afflictions. Then the soul must say to God, 'Lord, if thou help not, none can,' as Jehoshaphat said in 2 Chron. xx. 12, 'We know not what to do, but our eyes are to thee.' In great afflictions we exercise trust, because we are forced.

2. And because then we are put to this, *we put the promises* in suit, the promises made to us for extremity.

(1.) He hath promised to be with us 'in the fire, and in the water,' Isa. xliii. 2. There is a promise of *God's presence*, and the soul improves that. Lord, thou hast promised to be present in great perils and dangers, as there are two of the greatest specified, fire and water. Thou hast promised thou wilt be present with us in the fire, and in the water. Now, Lord, make good thy promise, be thou present. And when God makes good this promise of presence, then the soul triumphs, as in Ps. xxiii. 4, 'Though I walk in the valley of the shadow of death, I will not fear, because thou art with me, Lord.' So in Ps. xxvii. 1, he begins triumphantly, 'The Lord is my shield, whom shall I fear? of whom shall I be afraid?' Let us exercise our trust this way in extremity. 'God is with us, and who can be against us?' saith the apostle, Rom. viii. 31. Thus the Christian soul lives by trusting in God. In all extremity of crosses whatsoever, the soul is forced to God, and claims the promises of presence.

And not only the promise of his presence, but

(2.) The promise *of support and comfort, and of mitigation.* There is a promise in 1 Cor. x. 13, 'God is faithful, and will not suffer us to be tempted above our strength.' Here faith is exercised. Lord, I am in a great cross now, I am in affliction; thou hast promised that thou wilt not suffer me to be tempted above that I am able to bear.

Now make good this promise of thine, be present, and be present by way of mitigation; either pull down the cross, and make it less, or raise up my strength, and make that greater. For thou hast promised that thou wilt not suffer us to be tempted above our strength.

3. And then the soul lives *by faith of the issue in great extremities.* I am in great extremity, but I know all shall end well. Thus we trust in God in all extremity of afflictions whatsoever; in the hour of death, when we receive the sentence of death, how do we then exercise trust in God! In Ps. xvi. 9, 'My flesh shall rest in hope, because thou wilt not suffer thy Holy One to see corruption.' Because God did not suffer Christ to see corruption, who is our head, therefore my flesh likewise shall rest in hope, when I die. Our Head triumphed over death, and is in heaven, and I die in faith; I trust in God that raised him from the dead, who was my Surety. I know my debts are paid; my Surety is out of prison. Christ, who took upon him to discharge my debts, he is out of the prison of the grave, he is in heaven, therefore my flesh shall rest in hope. [We could not thus speak] if it were not for this, that Christ were risen. When we have the sentence of death, we overlook the grave, we see ourselves in heaven, as David saith, 'I should utterly have failed, but that I looked to see the goodness of the Lord in the land of the living,' Ps. xxvii. 13. Then faith looks beyond death, and beyond the grave. It looks up, and with Stephen it sees Christ at the 'right hand of God,' Acts vii. 56. We see Christ ready to receive our souls.

Then we trust in God that raiseth the dead; nay, we see ourselves, as it were, raised already.

Use. Thus we see *how we should trust in God, in great crosses, and in the sentence of death.* This, in a word, should be another ground of patience, and not only of patience, but of contentment, in extreme crosses, in the hour of death, that all that God doth is for this, that we may exercise trust in him. And if the soul clasp to him, who is the fountain of life, the chief good, it cannot be miserable. But this it doth by trust. Our trust makes us one with him. It is that which brings us to God; and afflictions, and death itself, force us to exercise faith in the promises, and drive us to him. So God hath overpowered all crosses, extreme crosses, even death itself, that he hath sanctified them to fit us to trust in him; and who can be miserable that trusts in God?

What construction should we make of crosses and afflictions? Surely this is to take away false confidence; this is to drive me to God. Shall I be impatient and murmur at that which God hath ordained to bring me nearer to himself, to trust in him, to take away all false confidence in the creature?

No! This should cut the sinews of all carnal confidence, and make us patient and thankful in all crosses; because God now is seeking our good, he is drawing good out of these crosses. He labours by this to bring us nearer to himself. Blessed is that cross, blessed is that sickness, or loss of friends whatsoever, that brings us nearer to God! Why doth God take away our dear friends? That we might cling nearer to him, because he will have us to see that he is all-sufficient.

What doth a man lose when he trusts in God, though he lose all the world? Hath he not him that made the world at the first, and can make another if he please? If a man lose all, and have God, as he hath that trusts in him, and in his word; for God will not deny his word and truth. He that trusts in God hath him, and if he have him, what if he be stripped of all? He can make another world with a word of his mouth. Other things are but a beam to him; what need a man care for a beam, that hath the sun?

All the afflictions of this world are to draw or to drive us to God, whether we will or no. As the messengers in the gospel, to force the guests to the banquet with violence, Luke xiv. 23; so afflictions they are to force us to God. This blessed effect they have in all God's children.

But those that do not belong to God, what do they in the hour of death and in extremity? They are either blocks, as Nabal was, senseless creatures; or raging, as Cain, Ahithophel, and Judas; either sots, or desperate in extremity. Saul in extremity goes to the witch, to ill means. David in all extremity he goes to prayer, he goes to his rock and shield; to God who was his 'all in all.' He knew all this was done to drive him to trust in God. 'Why art thou disquieted, O my soul? why art thou vexed in me? trust in God,' Ps. xlii. 11. All this is to make thee trust in God. He checks and chides his own soul. A child of God doth check himself. When his base heart would have him sink and fall down, and go to false means, then he raiseth himself up, 'Trust in God, O my soul.'

But such as Saul, proud, confident hypocrites, when all outward things are taken away, they go to the witch, to the devil, to one unlawful means or other, and at the last to desperate conclusions, to the sword itself.

As we desire to have evidence of a good estate in grace, that we belong to God, so let us desire God that we may find him drawing us so near to him by all crosses whatsoever, that we may see in him a supply of whatsoever is taken from us; if we lose our friends, that we may trust God the more. As St Paul speaks of the widow, 1 Tim. v. 10, *seq.*, when her husband was alive, she trusted to him; but now she wants her former help to go to, she gives herself to prayer, she goes to God, she trusts in God. So it should be with all. When friends are taken away we should go to God. He will supply that which is wanting. Those that are bereft of any comfort, now they should go to God. What do we lose by that? We had the stream before, now we have the fountain. We shall have it in a more excellent manner in God than we had before.

And that makes a Christian at a point in this world. He is not much discouraged whatsoever he lose. If he lose all, to his life, he knows he shall have a better supply from God than he can lose in the world. Therefore he is never much cast down. He knows that all shall drive him nearer to God, to trust in God. As St Paul saith here, 'We received the sentence of death, that we might not trust in ourselves, but in God that raiseth the dead.'

One means to settle our trust the better in God reconciled to us, in the covenant of grace through Christ, his beloved, and our beloved, is the blessed sacrament. And therefore come to it as to a seal sanctified by God for that very purpose, to strengthen our trust in God. How many ways doth God condescend to strengthen our trust? because it is such an honour to him. For by trusting in him we give him the honour of all his attributes, we make him a God, we set him in his throne, which we do not when we trust not in him. How many ways doth he condescend to strengthen our trust!

(1.) We have *his promise*, 'If we believe in him, we shall not perish, but have everlasting life,' John iii. 15.

(2.) We have *a seal of that promise*, the sacrament; and is not a broad seal a great confirmation? If a man have a grant from the king, if he have his broad seal, it is a great confirmation. Though the other were good, yet the seal is stronger. So we have God's promise, and in regard of our weakness there is a seal added to it.

(3.) If that be not enough we have more, we have *his oath*. He hath pawned his life. 'As I live, saith the Lord,' &c., Ezek. xviii. 32. He hath pawned his being. As he is God, he will forgive us if we repent. We have his promise, seal, and oath. Whatsoever among men may strengthen trust and faith, God condescends unto to strengthen our faith, because he would not have us perish in unbelief.

(4.) Besides that, he hath given us *earnest*. A man's trust is strengthened when he hath earnest. Every true Christian hath a blessed earnest, that is, the Comforter. He hath the Spirit in him, the first fruits. Where God gives an earnest, he will make good the bargain at the last. Where he gives the first fruits, he will add the harvest. God never repents of his earnest. Where 'he hath begun a good work, he will finish it to the day of the Lord,' Philip. i. 6. An earnest is not taken away, but the rest is added.

(5.) And the same Spirit that is an earnest is also a *pawn and pledge*. We will trust any runagate, if we have a pawn sufficient. Now God hath given us this pawn of his Spirit. Christ hath given us his Spirit, and hath taken our flesh to heaven. Our flesh is there, and his Spirit is in our hearts, besides many evidences that we have in this life as pawns.

Indeed, in extremity sometimes we must trust God without a pawn, upon his bare word. 'Though he kill me, yet will I trust in him,' saith Job, chap. xiii. 15; but God ordinarily gives us many pawns of his love.

The sacrament is not only a seal of the promise, but likewise it hath another relation to strengthen our faith. It is a seizon (*x*), as a piece of earth that is given to assure possession of the whole. As a man saith, Take, here is a piece of earth, here is my land; here are the keys of my house; so in the promises sealed by the sacrament, here is life, here is favour, here is forgiveness of sins, here is life everlasting. What can we have more to strengthen our faith? God hath condescended every way to strengthen us, if we will come in, and honour him so much as to trust him with our souls, and our salvation. Therefore let us come to the sacrament with undoubted confidence. God will keep his credit. He will not deceive his credit. 'He will never forsake those that trust in him.' Ps. ix. 10. But to answer an objection.

Obj. Oh! all these are confirmations indeed, if I did believe and trust in God, but my heart is full of unbelief. Indeed all these are made to some that believe already in some measure. They have this seal, and oath, and earnest, and pawns, and first fruits, and all, if they believe; but I cannot bring my heart to trust in God.

Ans. What hinders thee?

I am a wretched creature, a sinful creature.

Dost thou mean to be so still? It is no matter what thou hast been, but what thou wilt be. The greater the sickness, the more is the honour of the physician in curing it; the greater thy sins, the more honour to God in forgiving such sins. Retort the temptation thus upon Satan. God works by contraries, and whom he will make righteous he will make them to see their sins; and before he will raise us up he will make us rotten in our graves; before he will make us glorious he will make us miserable. I know that God by this intends that I should despair in myself. God intends that I should despair indeed, but it is that I should despair in myself, as the text saith here, that 'we should not trust in ourselves,' when we have a sight of the vileness of our sins; 'but in God that raiseth the dead,' that raiseth the dead soul, the despairing soul, that it should trust in him. Therefore retort the temptation upon Satan, because I see my sins, and despair in myself, therefore I trust in God, 'He that is in darkness and sees no light, let him trust in the Lord his God,' Isa. l. 10.

Mark for thy comfort, the gospel calls men who in their own sense and feeling think themselves furthest off; he that is poor, and sees his want, 'Blessed are the poor in Spirit.' Mat. v. 3. But I have no grace, Oh that I had grace! 'Blessed are they that hunger and thirst,' Mat. v. 6. If thou mourn for thy sins, 'Blessed are they that mourn,' Mat. v. 4. Thou findest a heavy load of thy sins, 'Come unto me all ye, that are weary, and heavy laden, and I will ease you,' Mat. xi. 28. The gospel takes away all the objections and misdoubtings of the unbelieving heart, God is so willing to come to him. Therefore stand not cavilling, interpret all to the best. God will have us to despair in ourselves, that we may trust in him; and then we are fittest to trust in God, when we despair in ourselves; then we make God all in all. He hath righteousness enough, holiness enough, satisfaction enough, he hath all enough for thee.

And for men that are not yet believers, how wondrously doth God labour to bring such men to a good hope! If they yield themselves and come in, there is an offer to every one that 'will come in and take the water of life,'

There is a command. He that hath commanded, 'Thou shalt not murder, Thou shalt not steal,' he lays a charge on thee that thou believe, 1 John iii. 23, 'This is his command, that we believe in the Son of God.' And think with thyself, thou committest a sin against the gospel, which is worse than a sin against the law; for if a man sin against the law, he may have help in the gospel. But if he sin against the gospel there is not another gospel to help him. God offers thee comfort. He commands thee to trust in him. And thou rebellest, thou offendest him, if thou do not believe.

Is not here encouragement, if thou be not more wedded to thy sinful course, than to the good of thy soul? If thou wilt still live in thy sins, and wilt not trust in God, then thou shalt be damned. There is no help for thee if thou believe not, 'the wrath of God hangs over thy head,' John

iii. 36. 'Thou art condemned already,' John iii. 18, by nature. If thou believe not, thou needest no further condemnation, but only the execution of God's justice.

Naturally thou art born the child of wrath, and God threateneth thee, to stir thee up, and to make thee come in. He useth sweet allurements, besides the commands and threatenings, 'Come unto me, all ye that are weary and heavy laden, and I will ease you,' Mat. xi. 28. And 'Why will ye perish, O house of Israel,' Jer. xxvii. 13. And, 'O Jerusalem, Jerusalem, how oft, &c.,' Mat. xxiii. 37? God complains of thee, he allures thee, he sends his ambassadors. 'We are ministers in Christ's name to beseech you to be reconciled,' 2 Cor. v. 20, to come in, to cast down your weapons, your sins, to believe in God, and trust in his mercy, and to hope for all good from him. What should keep thee off? He is willing to have thee believe.

Obj. 'Oh, if I were elected,' &c.

Trouble not thyself with dark scruples of his eternal decree! Obey the command, obey the threatening, and put that out of doubt. If thou yield to the command, if thou obey the threatening, if thou be drawn by that, undoubtedly thou art the child of God. Put not in these doubts and janglings, things that are too high for thee till thou believe. Indeed, when thou believest, then thou mayest comfort thyself; I believe, therefore I know I shall be saved. 'Whom he hath chosen, them he calls; and whom he calls, he justifies,' Rom. viii. 30. I find myself freed from the sentence of condemnation in my heart, therefore I know I am called, I know I am elected. Then with comfort thou mayest go to those disputes. But not before a man obeys. Put those cavils out, and obey the gospel, when salvation is offered, when Satan puts these things to thee, when thou art threatened and commanded.

How shall this justify God at the day of judgment against damned wretches, that have lived in the bosom of the church, and yet would not believe. They will believe after their own fashion; if God will save them, and let them live in their sinful courses. But they will rather be damned than they will part with them. Are they not worthy to be damned? judge thyself, that rather than they will alter their course, and receive mercy with it, rather than they will receive Christ, whole Christ, as a king and a priest, to rule them as well as to satisfy for them—they will gild over their wicked courses, and will have none of him at all. They will rather be damned than take another course; their damnation is just.

If thou take whole Christ, and yield to his government, he useth all means to strengthen thy faith after thou believest, and he useth all means to allure thee to believe. It is a point of much consequence, and all depends upon it. It is the sum of the gospel to trust in God, in Christ. Therefore I have been a little the longer in it. Till we can bring our hearts to this we have nothing.

When we have this, then when all shall be taken from us, as it will ere long, all the friends we have, and all our comforts; yet our trust shall not be taken from us, nor our God in whom we trust shall be taken from us. We shall have God left, and a heart to trust in God. That will stand us in stead when all other things shall fail. 'That we might not trust in ourselves, but in God which raiseth the dead.'

These words have a double force in this place.

First, St Paul might reason thus, I am brought to death, as low as I can be, even to receive the sentence of death; but I trust in God, who will raise me when I am dead. Therefore he can raise me out of sickness. Though there be no means, no physic, he can do it himself. Or if it were persecution, he might reason, I am now persecuted; but God will raise me out of the grave; therefore he can raise me out of this trouble if it be for my good. It hath the force of a strong argument that way.

And it hath another force, that is, put case the worst, 'I received the sentence of death,' that is, if I die, as I look for no other, yet I trust that God that raiseth the dead, he will raise me; the confidence of the resurrection makes me die comfortably. As we sleep quietly, because we hope to rise again; and we put our seed into the ground, with comfort, Why? we hope to receive it in a more glorious manner in the harvest. So though my body be sown in the earth, it shall rise a glorious body. I trust in God, though 'I receive the sentence of death,' yet I shall sleep in the Lord. As when I go to sleep, I hope to rise again; so I trust when the resurrection shall come, that my body shall waken and arise. 'I trust in God that raiseth the dead.' Because he raiseth the dead, he can recover me if he will. If not, he will make this body a glorious body afterward. So every way it was a strong argument with St Paul, 'I trust in God that raiseth the dead.'

The apostle draws an argument of comfort from God's power in raising the dead. And it is a true reason, a good argument. He that will raise the dead body out of the grave, he can raise out of misery, out of captivity. The argument is strong. Thus God comforts his people in Ezek. xxxvii., in that parable of the dry bones that he put life in. So the blessed apostle St Paul, he speaks of Abraham, 'He looked to God who quickeneth the dead, who calleth things that are not, as though they were,' Rom. iv. 17. What made Abraham to trust in God, that he would give him Isaac again? he considered if God can raise Isaac from the dead, if he please he can give me Isaac back again; and though Isaac were the son of promise, yet he trusted God's word, more than Isaac the son of his love. Why? He knew that God could raise him from the dead, though he had sacrificed him. He trusted in God, 'who quickeneth the dead.'

Doct. The resurrection, then, is an argument to strengthen our faith in all miseries whatsoever.

It strengthens our faith before death, and in death. I will not enter into the common-place of that point concerning the resurrection; it would be tedious and unjust, because it is not intended here, but only it is used as a special argument. Therefore I will but touch that point.

Doct. God will raise us from the dead.

Nature is more offended at this, than any other thing. But St Paul makes it clear, that it is not against nature, that God should raise the dead, 1 Cor. xv. 35, *seq.* To speak a little of it, and then to speak of the use the apostle made of it, and of the use that we may make of it. Saith the apostle in that place, speaking to witty atheists, that thought to have cavilled out the resurrection from the dead, Thou fool, thou speakest against nature, if thou think it altogether impossible.

Look to the seed, do we not see that God every spring raiseth things that were dead. We see in the silk-worm, what an alteration there is from a fly to a worm, &c.? We see what men can do by art. They make glasses, of what? Of ashes. We see what nature can do, which is the ordinary providence of God. We see what it can do in the bowels of the earth. What is gold, and silver, and pearl? Is it not water and earth, excellently digested, exquisitely concocted and digested? That there should be such excellent things of so base a creature! We see what art and nature can do. If art and nature can do so great things, why do we call in question the power of God? If God have revealed his will to do so, why do we doubt of this great point of God's raising the dead?

The ancients had much ado with the pagans about this point. They handled it excellently, as they were excellent in those points which they were forced to by the adversaries, and indeed they were especially sound in those points. I say they were excellent and large in the handling of this: but I will not stand upon that. It is an article of our creed, 'I believe the resurrection of the body.'* Indeed, he that believeth the first article of the creed, he will easily believe the last. He that believes in 'God the Father Almighty, maker of heaven and earth,' he will easily believe the resurrection of the body.

But I will rather come to shew the use of it. God will raise the dead. Therefore, God's manner of working is, when there is no hope, in extremity, as I touched before. He raiseth us, but it is when we are dead. He doth his greatest works when there is least hope. So it is in the resurrection out of troubles, as in the resurrection of the body. When there is no hope at all, no ground in nature, but it must be his power altogether that must do it, then he falls to work to raise the dead.

Use. Therefore *our faith must follow his working*. He raiseth the dead. He justifies a sinner. But it is when he is furthest from grace, a sinner despairing of all mercy. Then he hath the most need of justification. He raiseth the dead, but it is then when they are nothing but dust; then it is time for him to work to raise the dead. He restores, but it is that which is lost. God never forgets his old work. This was his old manner of working at the first, and still every day he useth it, 'he made all of nothing,' order out of confusion, light out of darkness. This was in the creation; and the like he doth still. He never forgets his old work. This, St Paul being acquainted with, he fasteneth his hope and trust upon such a God as will raise the dead. Therefore make that use of it that the apostle doth. When the church is in any calamity, which is as it were a death, when it is as in that 37th of Ezekiel, 'dry bones,' comfort yourselves. God comforted the church there, that he would raise the church out of Babylon, as he raised those dead bones. The one is as easy as the other. So in the government of the church continually, he brings order out of confusion, light out of darkness, and life out of death, that is, out of extreme troubles. When men think themselves dead, when they think the church dead, past all hope, then he will quicken and raise it. So that he will never forget this course, till he have raised our dead bodies; and then he will finish that manner of dispensation. This is God's manner of working.

We must answer it with our faith, that is, in the greatest dejection that can be, to 'trust in God that raiseth the dead.' Faith, if it be true, it will answer the ground of it. But when it is carried to God, it is carried to him that raiseth the dead. Therefore, though it be desperate every way, yet notwithstanding I hope above hope. I hope in him whose course is to raise the dead, who at the last will raise the dead, and still delights in a proportion to raise men from death, out of all troubles and miseries.

Well! this God doth, and therefore carry it along in all miseries whatsoever, in soul, in body, or estate, or in the church, &c.

God raiseth from the dead, therefore we must feel ourselves dead before we can be raised by his grace. What is the reason that a papist cannot be

* Article XI.—G.

a good Christian? He opposeth his own conversion. What is conversion? It is the first resurrection, the resurrection of the soul. But that which is raised must be dead first. They account not themselves dead, and therefore oppose this resurrection. And so, when we are dead in grace or comfort, let us trust in God that raiseth the dead. And so for outward condition in this life and the estate of the church.

The conversion of the Jews, which seems a thing so strange. When a man thinks how they are dispersed, and thinks of their poverty and disgrace, he thinks, Is this a likely matter? Remember what God hath said, he will raise the dead. And because this is a work that seems as hard as the raising of the dead, therefore their calling and conversion is called a kind of resurrection, Rom. xi. 15. Let us hope for that. He that raiseth the body will raise that people, as despicable as they are, to be a glorious people and church.

And so for the confusion of the 'man of sin.' The revelation of the gospel, when it came out of the grave of darkness, out of the Egyptian darkness of popery, was it not a raising of the dead?

When Luther arose for the defence of the truth, a man might have said to him, What! dost thou set thyself against the whole world? Go to thy cloister, and say, 'Lord, have mercy upon us.' Dost thou hope to reform the world against all the world? Alas!* he trusted in God 'that raiseth the dead,' that raiseth men to conversion when he pleaseth, and that raiseth the church when he pleaseth, even from death. He raised the church out of Babylon, and he will raise the Jews that now are in a dead state. Why should we doubt of these things, when we believe, or profess to believe the main, the resurrection from the dead?

And every day in the church God is raising the dead spiritually. The dead hear the voice of Christ every day. When the ministry is in power, when there is a blessing upon it, conveying it to the heart, then he is raising the dead. So 'wisdom is justified of her children,' Mat. xi. 19. The gospel is justified to be a powerful doctrine, having the Spirit of God clothing it, to raise people from the dead, those that are dead in sin.

There are none that ever are spiritually raised, but those that see themselves dead. And that is the reason why we are to abhor popery, because it teacheth us that we are not dead in ourselves, and then there can be no resurrection to grace; for the resurrection is of the dead. The more we see a contrariety in nature to grace, the more fit objects we are for the divine power of God to raise. 'He raiseth the dead.'

Thus we see how to go along with this. In all troubles God will raise the dead, therefore he will bring me out of this trouble, if he see it good. Therefore in extremity let us thus reason with ourselves. Now I know not which way to turn me; 'there is but a step between me and death,' 1 Sam. xx. 3. If God have any purpose to use my service further, he that raiseth the dead will raise me from the grave; 'to him belong the issues of death,' Ps. lxviii. 20. He can give an evasion and escape if he will; if not, if he will not deliver me, then I die in this faith, that he will raise me from the dead.

This is that that upholds a Christian in extremity. This made the martyrs so confident. This made those three young men so resolute that were cast into the fiery furnace. What was their comfort? Surely this, God can deliver us if he will, say they. He is able to deliver us now; but if he

* 'Alas!' The peculiar use of this interjection by Sibbes has elsewhere been noted. It will be frequently met with thus used in the present volume.—G.

will not do this for us, he will raise our bodies. If he will not deliver them here, there will be a final deliverance at the resurrection.

So in Heb. xi. 16, those blessed men, 'they hoped for a better resurrection,' and this made them confident.

This makes us confident to stand out against all the threatenings and all the crosses of the world, that we may hold our peace with God, notwithstanding all the enticements and allurements to the contrary, because we trust in God that raiseth the dead.

Again, let us learn to extract contrary principles to Satan out of God's proceedings. What doth he reason when we are dead, either in sin or in misery? What hast thou to do with God? God hath forsaken thee. No! saith faith, God is a God raising the dead. The more dead I am in the eye of the world, and in my own sense, the nearer I am to God's help. I am a despairing sinner, a great sinner; but the more, God will magnify his mercy, that 'where sin hath abounded, grace may abound much more,' Rom. v. 20. Retort home the argument, draw contrary principles to him. This is a divine art which faith hath.

Oh, but then you may presume, and do what you list.

Not so, retort the argument again upon him; if I do so, God will bring me to death, he will bring me to despair; and who is it that delights to have that course taken with him, to be brought so low? So every way we may retort temptations from this dealing of God. If I be careless, he will bring me as low as hell. I shall have little joy to try conclusions with him.

And if thou be low, despair not, thou art the fitter object. God raiseth the dead, therefore I will not add to my sins legal. I will not add this evangelical sin, this destroying sin of despair and unbelief; but I will cast myself upon the mercy of God, and believe in him that raiseth the dead; and desire him to speak to my dead soul, which is as rotten as Lazarus's body, which had been so long in the grave, that he would say to it, 'Come forth' of that cursed estate. It is but for him to speak the word, to bless his word, and then it will come out by faith. It is the art of faith to draw contrary arguments to Satan, and those that belong to God do so in all temptations. But those that do not, they sink lower and lower, having nothing to uphold their souls. They have not learned to trust in God that raiseth the dead.

God is the God that raiseth the dead. Therefore let us oft think of this; think what God means to do with us, that we may carry ourselves answerably, 'I trust in God that raiseth the dead.' Therefore let us honour God while we live, with that body that he will raise; let us be fruitful in our place. St Paul draws this conclusion, 1 Cor. xv. 58, from the resurrection, 'Finally, my brethren, be constant, unmoveable, alway abounding in the work of the Lord, knowing that your labour is not in vain in the Lord.' Especially considering that he will raise the dead bodies after a more glorious manner than they are now, he will make a more glorious body. For alway God's second works are better than his first. He raiseth the dead, and will make our bodies like the glorious body of Christ.

But the point of the resurrection is very large, and perhaps I shall have better occasion to speak of it afterward. I only apply it to the present purpose, how it strengthens faith in misery and in the hour of death.

A man is strengthened in his faith when he thinks, now I am going 'the way of all flesh,' Josh. xxiii. 14, I am to yield my soul to God, and death is to close up mine eyes; yet I have trusted in God, and do trust in God that will raise my body from the grave. This comforts the soul against the horror of the grave, against that confusion and darkness that is after death.

Faith seeth things to come as present, it sees the body, after it hath a long time been in the dust, clothed with flesh, and made like the glorious body of Christ. Faith sees this, and so a Christian soul dies in faith, and sows the body as good seed in the ground in hope of a glorious resurrection.

And that comforts a Christian soul, in the loss of children, of wife, of friends, that have been dearest and nearest to me. I trust 'in God that raiseth the dead,' that he will raise them again, and then we shall all be for ever with the Lord. It is a point of singular comfort. For the main articles of our faith they have a wondrous working upon us, in all the passages of our lives. It is good to think often upon the pillars of our faith, as this is one, 'that God will raise us from the dead.'

But I go on to the next verse.

VERSE 10.

'*Who delivered us from so great a death, who doth deliver us; in whom we trust that he will yet deliver us.*' St Paul sets down his troubles to the life, that he might make himself and others more sensible of his comforts, and of God's grace and goodness in his deliverance. These words contain his deliverance out of that trouble, his particular deliverance out of a particular trouble. And this deliverance is set down by a triple distinction of time. As time is either past, present, or to come; so God, who is the deliverer for all times, 'he hath delivered us' for the time past, 'he doth deliver us' for the present, 'in whom we trust that he will deliver us' for the time to come.

Who delivered us from so great a death.' After St Paul had learned to trust in God, after he had taken forth that lesson, a hard lesson to learn, that must be learned by bringing a man to such extremity, I say, after he had learned 'to trust in God that raiseth the dead,' God gave him this reward of his diligence in the blessed school of afflictions. He delivered him, 'who hath delivered us, and who doth deliver us' continually. He will not take his hand from the work, and for the time to come I hope he will do so still.

St Paul here calls his trouble a death. It was not a death properly. It is but his aggravation of the trouble that calls it a death; because God's mercy only hindered it from being a death. It was only not a death. It was some desperate trouble, some desperate sickness. The particular is not set down in the Scripture. We know what a tumult there was about Diana of Ephesus, Acts xix, and in 1 Cor. xv. 32, 'He fought with beasts at Ephesus (which is in Asia), after the manner of men.' Whether it were that, or some other, we know not. Whatsoever it was, he calls it a death. He doth not call it an affliction, but a death; and a great death, to make himself the more sensible.

Wherefore have we souls and understandings, but to exercise them in setting forth our dangers, and the deliverances of God? to consider of things to affect us deeply? The apostle here to affect himself deeply, he sets it down here by a death.

And ofttimes in the Psalms, the psalmist in Ps. xviii. 4, and Ps. xi. 6, he calls his afflictions death and hell, and so they had been indeed, except

God had delivered him. But to come to the points that are considerable hence. First of all we may observe this, that

God, till he have wrought his own work, he doth not deliver; he brings men to a low ebb, to a very low estate, before he will deliver.

Secondly. *After God hath wrought his own work, then he delivers his children.*

Thirdly. *He continues the work still, 'he doth deliver me.'*

Fourthly. *That upon experience of God's former deliverance, God's children have founded a blessed argument for the time to come.* 'He hath, and he will deliver me.' God is alway like himself. He is never at a loss. What he hath done, he doth, and will do, reserving the limitations, as we shall see afterward.

Doct. 1. *God doth not at the first deliver his children.*

He delivered St Paul, but it was after he had brought him to 'receive the sentence of death,' and after he had learned not to trust in himself, but 'in God that raiseth the dead.' God defers his deliverance for many reasons. To name a few.

Reason (1). God doth defer his deliverance when we are in dangers, partly, as you see here, *to perfect the work of mortification of self-confidence*, to subdue trust in any earthly thing. St Paul by this learned not to trust in himself.

2. And then to *strengthen our faith and confidence in God;* when we are drawn from all creatures to learn to trust in him.

3. And to *sweeten his deliverance when it comes, to endear his favours;* for then they are sweet indeed, after God hath beat us out of ourselves. Summer and spring are sweet after winter. So it is in this vicissitude and intercourse that God useth. Favour after affliction and crosses, is favour indeed. That makes heaven so sweet to God's children when they come there, because they go to heaven out of a great deal of misery in this world.

4. And partly likewise God defers it *for his own glory*, that it may be known for his mere work; for when we are at a loss, and the soul can reason thus, God must help or none can help, then God hath the glory. Therefore in love to his own glory he defers it so long.

5. Again, he useth to defer long, that he might *the more shame the enemies at length;* for if the affliction be from the insolency and pride of the enemies, he defers deliverance, till they be come to the highest pitch, and then he ariseth as 'a giant refreshed with wine, and smites his enemies in the hinder parts,' Ps. lxxviii. 66. He is as it were refreshed on the sudden. And as it is his greatest glory to raise his children when they are at the lowest; so it is his glory to confound the pride of the enemies when it is at the highest. If he should do it before, his glory would not shine so much in the confusion of them, and their enterprises against his children. One would think he should not have let Pharaoh alone so long; but he got him glory the more at the last, in confounding him in the Red Sea. So Haman came very far, almost to the execution of the decree he had gotten by his policy and malice; and then God delivered his church and confounded Haman. These and the like reasons may be given to shew that God in heavenly and deep wisdom doth not presently deliver his children.

Use. The proper use of it is, that we should learn *not to be hasty and short-spirited in God's dealing*, but learn to practise that which we are often enjoined, to wait on God, to wait his good leisure.

Especially considering that which is the second point, let that satisfy us, that *Doct.* 2. *After God hath done his work, he will deliver.*

Let us wait, for he will deliver at length. Perhaps his time is not yet that he will deliver; but usually when all is desperate, when he may have all the glory, then he delivers. He delivered the three young men, but they were put into the fire first, and the furnace was made seven times hotter, that he might have the glory in consuming their enemies. So he delivered Hezekiah in his time, but it was when the enemy was even ready to seize upon the city, Isa. xxxvii. 14, *seq.* He promised St Paul that not one man should perish in the ship, but yet they suffered shipwreck, they went away only with their lives, Acts xxvii. 24, 44. God doth so deliver his, that he doth not suffer them to perish in the danger.

Use. Therefore let us *stay his time, and wait.* It may be it is not God's time yet.

When shall we know that it is God's time to deliver, that we may wait with comfort?

(1.) God knows his own time best; but usually it is when *we are brought very low*, and when our spirits are low. When we are brought very low, both in regard of human support, and in regard of our spirits, when we are humble, when our souls 'cleave to the dust,' Ps. cxix. 25. 'Help, Lord,' for we are brought very low. 'Help, Lord, for vain is the help of man,' Ps. lx. 11.

When the church can plead so, it is a good plea. When we are at the lowest, and the malice of the enemy is at the highest, when the waters swell, 'Help, Lord, for the waters are come into my very soul,' Ps. lxix. 1; when we are very low, and the enemies very high, as we see in Pharaoh; and so in Herod, when he was in the height of his pride, when he was in all his glory, God takes him there.

Thus God delivers his, and confounds his enemies. I join them both together, for the one is not commonly without the other. The annoyance of God's children is from their enemies. Therefore when he delivers the one he confounds the other. When the malice of the one is at the highest, and the state of the other is at the lowest, and their spirits are afflicted and cast down with their estate, then is the time when God will deliver.

(2.) Again, *when our hearts are enlarged to pray*, when we can pray from a broken heart. As you see here, he joins them together. God will deliver me, but it must be by your prayers. When we have hearts to pray, and when others have hearts to pray for us, that is the time of deliverance. Usually there goes before deliverance an enlarged heart to pray to God, as we see in Daniel, chap. ix., a little before they came out of Babylon, he had a large heart to pray to God. And when we can plead with God his promise, 'Remember, Lord, thy promise wherein thou hast caused us to trust,' Ps. cxix. 49; when we can cast ourselves upon God's mercy with prayer, and plead with God to remember his promise, it is a sign God means to deliver us. When the heart is shut and closed up, that it cannot speak to God, when there is some sin or other that doth stifle the spirit, that it cannot vent itself with that liberty to God, it is a sign that it is not the time yet of God's deliverance.

God will at the length deliver. Therefore from both these, that he doth defer deliverance, and that he will deliver at length, let us infer this lesson of waiting; let us wait therefore, and wait with comfort. Let us remember these principles.

First, God hath a time, as for all things, so for our deliverance.

Secondly, that God's time is the best time. He is the best discerner of opportunities.

Thirdly, remember that this shall be when he hath wrought his work upon our souls, specially when he hath made us to trust in him. As here, when St Paul had learned to trust in God, then he delivered him. And why should we desire to do our bodies good, or our estates good, till God hath wrought his cure on our souls? for God intends our souls in the first place. Our souls, they are the whole man, in a manner. The welfare of the soul draws the welfare of the body, and the welfare of the estate after it. The body shall do well, if the soul do well.

Therefore we should desire rather that the Lord would let the affliction stay, than that it should part without the message for which God sends it. Every affliction is God's messenger. We should desire the Lord to let it stay for the answer for which he hath sent it.

And indeed, it will never part without the answer for which God sends it, till it have humbled us, till it have brought us to trust in God, till we be such as we should be. And a Christian soul rather desires to be in the furnace, to be under the affliction, to be purged better yet, than to have the cross and affliction removed, and not to be a whit the better for it. Therefore, considering that there will be a time, and that God's time is the best time, and that this time will be when he hath fitted us, we should learn to wait in any cross, and not to be over hasty.

Again, consider, though the time be long, yet he will deliver at length by death. Death will end all miseries.

And consider, that how long soever we endure anything, yet what is that that we endure here, to that that we are freed from by Christ? We are freed from misery, from all misery, from the wrath of God, from damnation. And what is that that we can suffer here, to the glory and joy that remains for us in heaven? What is all that we can suffer here, to that that Christ hath endured for us? What is all that we can endure here, to that that we have deserved? Considering, then, what we are delivered from, what God hath reserved for us, what Christ hath endured, and what we deserve, it will make us wait, and wait with patience. Especially considering, as I said before, that God is working his good work for our good. Though we at the first, perhaps, for a while do not see the meaning of the affliction, the meaning of the cross, we cannot read it perfectly, yet in general we may know it is for our good. God of his infinite wisdom will not suffer a hair to fall from our heads, without his providence. 'And all shall work together for the best to those that love him,' Rom. viii. 28.

It is long then, we see, ere God deliver; and why? and at the last he will deliver one way or other; and therefore let us wait quietly. And this the saints of God have practised in all ages. 'Yet, my soul, keep silence to the Lord,' Ps. lxii. 5. He had a shrewd conflict with himself, when he saw how good causes were trampled on, and he saw the insolence of wicked persons, how they lift up their heads, 'Yet, my soul, keep silence to the Lord.' So he begins, 'Yet God is good to Israel,' Ps. lxxiii. 1, for all this. And God chargeth it upon his people that they should wait, 'If I tarry, wait thou,' Hab. ii. 2. And the blessing is promised to those that can wait and not murmur, as in Ps. cxlvii. 11. It is a duty that we are much urged to, and very hardly brought to the practice of. Therefore we are to hear it pressed the more, 'The Lord taketh pleasure in them that fear him, in those that hope in his mercy,' Ps. cxlvii. 11, in those that trust in his mercy.

The like you have in many places: 'Therefore will the Lord wait, that he may be gracious to you; therefore he will be exalted, that he may have mercy upon you: he is a God of judgment, blessed are all that wait for him,' Isa. xxx. 18. So in Lam. iii. The church still waits upon God.

How oft doth David charge himself, 'Wait, and trust in God, O my soul,' Ps. xlii. 5. Let us learn this upon these grounds, that God is long ere he deliver, but at last he will deliver; and that is sufficient to force this, to wait still upon God with patience and silence.

Well, thus we see God doth deliver, 'who delivered us,' &c. What will he do for the time present? He hath delivered, and doth deliver, and he will deliver. From all jointly together, you see that

Doct. God's people in this world stand in need of deliverance alway.

They have always troubles. When one is past, another is present. Deliverance supposeth dangers.

1. *There have been dangers, there are dangers, and there will be dangers.* Our life is a warfare, a temptation. We are absent from God. We are alway exposed to dangers. We live in the midst of devils and of devilish-minded men. We have corruptions in us that expose us to sin, and sin draws on judgments. We are alway in danger one way or other while we live in this world. But our comfort is, that as there have been dangers, and are dangers, and will be dangers; so there hath been deliverance, there is deliverance, and there will be deliverance. It is a trade that God useth. It is his art. 'God knoweth how to deliver his,' as St Peter saith, 2 Peter ii. 9. He hath alway exercised it, he is excellent at it. He hath delivered his church, he doth deliver his church, and he will deliver his church; and so every particular member, he hath, and doth, and will deliver them.

Wonderful is the intercourse that God useth with his people and their estate. Even as in nature there is a change and intercourse of day and night, of light and darkness, of morning and evening, of summer and winter, of hot and cold; so in the life of a Christian there are changes, dangers, and deliverances. There is a 'sowing in tears, and a reaping in joy,' Ps. cxxvi. 5. There is a night of affliction, and a morning of joy and prosperity: 'Heaviness may be in the evening, but joy cometh in the morning,' Ps. xxx. 5.

And thus we go on till we end our days, till we be taken to heaven, where there shall be no change, where 'all tears shall be wiped from our eyes.'

If we had spiritual eyes, eyes to see our danger, to see how full the world is of devils! And then to consider how many dangers this weak life is subject to, how many casualties! We cannot go out of doors, we cannot take a journey, but how many dangers are we subject to! We are environed with perpetual dangers. The snares of death compass us almost everywhere, abroad and at home, in our greatest security.

But our comfort is, that God doth compass us with mercy, as it is, Ps. xxxii. 6. As dangers are round about us, so God is a 'wall of fire about us.' We have dangers about us, devils about us. We have a guard about us, we have God about us, we have angels about us, we have all his creatures about us. 'All things are yours,' saith the apostle, 2 Cor. iv. 15, &c.

It is God that hath delivered us, that doth deliver us. Who restrains the devils from having their wills of us? They are enemies not only to our souls and to our salvation, but to our bodies. They are enemies to our health, as we see in Job. We live in the midst of lions; ofttimes in the midst of enemies. Who restrains their malice? We are preserved from dangers day and night. Who shuts in the doors, who watcheth over us, but he that keeps Israel? It is God that delivereth us. Without his deliverance all deliverances were to little purpose. All shutting in were to little purpose, except he shut us in that shut Noah into the ark. He must watch over us. It is God that delivereth us.

But doth he deliver us only outwardly?

2. No! *He hath delivered, and he doth deliver, us spiritually.* He hath delivered us from the power of hell and damnation. He doth deliver us from many sins that we should commit; and when we have sinned, he delivers us from despair. He delivers us from presuming, by touching our hearts with saving grief for sin. If we belong to him, one of the two ways he delivers; either from the sin or from the danger of the sin; either from the committing of the sin, or from despairing for the sin, or presuming in a course of sin.

Who delivereth us from our inbred corruptions? Should we not run every day into the sins that we see others commit? Who cuts short our lusts, and suppresseth them, that we are not swearers, that we are not licentious persons, that we are not godless persons? Are we not hewn out of the same rock? Who keeps us from sin? Is it any inbred goodness? Are we not all alike tainted with original sin, children of wrath? Who puts a difference between us and others? It is God that hath delivered us, and that doth deliver us.

It is his mercy that we do not commit sin, it is his preventing deliverance; and when we have committed sin, it is his mercy to pardon it. There is his preserving deliverance from despair after the committing of sin.

All are beholden to God for deliverance. Those that have committed sin, that he delivers them from the wrath to come, from the damnation that they deserve; and those that have the grace not to commit sin, they are beholden to him, that he delivers them from that which their corruptions else would carry them to, if he should take his government from their hearts.

We have an inward guard as well as an outward, an invisible guard, 'We are kept by the Spirit of God through faith to salvation,' 1 Pet. i. 5. We have a guard that keeps us from despair, from sinking. God delivereth us from ourselves by this inward guard. There is not the vilest atheist that lives, but let God open his conscience, and let loose himself upon himself, to see what he deserves, to see what he is ready to sink into, if he see not God's mercy to deliver him, if he see not an intercessor, a mediator to come between God and him, what would become of him? Therefore saith St Paul in Philip. iv. 7, 'The peace of God which passeth all understanding shall "guard" your hearts and minds;' for so the word is in the original, 'shall guard your hearts and minds.'*

We have not only a guard outward, but we have a peace in us, the Spirit of God, the strengthening power of God, the sight of the love of God. God delivers us, as from all others, so from ourselves. Judas had no enemies. God let him loose to himself. What became of him? Ahithophel had no enemy. God let him loose to himself too; and then we see what a desperate conclusion he came to.

So, whosoever thou art that comtemnest religion, that makest anything of greater moment and respect than that, if thou hadst not an enemy in the world, but all were thy friends, as Judas had all to be his friends. The Pharisees were his friends. He had money of them. But God opened

* See note *k*, vol. i. p. 334.—G.

his conscience, and he could not endure the sight of it. It spake bitter things to him, when God opened an inward hell in his conscience. So God doth deliver us outwardly and inwardly, and the inward is double; partly from despair, partly from the rage of corruptions, as I said before. Is it not God that ties up our corruptions? There is such a world of sin in the heart of a man, as often he finds the experience of it, when he meets with a fit temptation to his disposition, that God's children complain of themselves that the sins of their hearts have deceived them. So God delivers men from the rage of lusts. He ties up their corruptions, and delivers them from them. And when we fall, and are ready to despair for them, he delivers us from despair. He doth deliver, he is perpetually delivering. It implies that we alway stand in need of deliverance.

Therefore, we should alway look up to God. He is the breath of our nostrils; 'In him we live, and move, and have our being,' Acts xvii. 28. In him we stand, and in him we are delivered in the midst of all our enemies. It should stir up our hearts thankfully to depend upon God. He that hath delivered us, he doth deliver us. If he should not continue his deliverance, we should be continually in extreme danger.

'*Who hath delivered us, and doth deliver us,*' *&c.* A Christian is never in so great perplexity but God is delivering of him, even in trouble. So the church saith, Lam. iii. 22, 'It is God's mercy that we are not all consumed.'

The church was in a pitiful estate then. One would have thought they were as low as almost they might be. Yet, notwithstanding, the Spirit of God in those blessed men that lived in those times, they saw that they might have been worse than they were; and they saw that there was some danger from which they were delivered, 'It is thy mercy that we are not all consumed.' God delivered them from extremity.

Nay, in troubles God doth deliver so as there may be a distinction, for the most part, between his and others. 'When I gather my jewels, it shall be known who serves me, and who serves me not,' Mal. iii. 17. God continually delivers, more especially at some times.

As we say of providence, providence is nothing but a continued act of creation. And it is true. The same power that created all things of nothing, the same power sustains all things. God upholds all things with his right hand.

For even as it is with a stone which is upheld by a man's hand, let him withdraw his hand, and down it falls. So naturally all things, as they are raised out of nothing, so they will fall to their first principles except they be sustained by that continual act of creation which we call providence, to maintain them in the order wherein they were set at the first. So there is a continual act of deliverance till we be delivered out of all troubles, and set in a place where there shall be no more annoyance at all, either from within us or without us. God doth still deliver.

Use. Oh! let this move us to a renounce* of the eye and majesty of the great God, of the presence of God. Who will willingly provoke him of whom he stands in need to deliver him?

Let God withdraw his deliverance, his preventing deliverance, or his rescuing deliverance. For, as I said, there is a double deliverance. He prevents us from trouble, he delivers us that we do not fall into it; and

* That is, 'renunciation.' And yet this can hardly be what Sibbes intended here. Query, does he use it etymologically, as = to report, and by inference, recognise?—G.

when we are fallen into it he rescues us. If God should not thus deliver us, there is no mischief that any others fall into but we should fall into the like were it not for his preventing deliverance.

As St Austin saith well, A man that is freed from sin ought to thank God as well for the sins that he hath not committed as for the sins that he hath had forgiven; for it is an equal mercy that a man fall not into sin as for his sin to be pardoned. And so for troubles too. It is God's mercy to prevent troubles as well as to deliver out of trouble when we are fallen into it.

Who would not reverence this great God? What miscreant wretches are they that inure their tongue to swearing, to tear that majesty, that if he should withdraw his deliverance and protection from them, what would become of them?

Where there is perpetual dependence upon any man, how doth it enforce reverence and respect even amongst men? It is atheism, therefore, for men to inure their tongues to speak cursed language, to inure their hearts to entertain profane thoughts of God, and to neglect the consideration of his majesty. Holy men in Scripture are said to walk with God, that is, to have God in their eye in all times, in all places, as he had them in his eye to delight in them, to prevent troubles, and to deliver them from troubles when they were in them.

We should take notice of God's special providence in this kind, that God by deliverance often gives us our lives, and it should teach us to consecrate our lives to God, 'who doth deliver us.'

'*In whom we hope*,' or trust, or have affiance, '*that he will yet deliver us*.' The holy apostle doth take in trust here the time to come. He speaks as if he were assured of that as of anything past; and he doth found his hope for the time to come upon that which was past and present. As he saith in Rom. v. 4, 'Experience breeds hope,' so it doth here in the blessed apostle, 'He hath delivered, and he doth deliver,' and why should I not trust in so good a God for the time to come? I hope he will deliver me. And surely so may we do.

Doct. A Christian may rely on God for the time to come.

Upon what ground, upon what pillars is this confidence built of the holy apostle?

1. *Upon the name of God, the name of his nature*, 'Jehovah,' 'I am,' which signifies a constant being, 'I was, I am, and am to come.'

There was danger, there is danger, and there will come danger. There was a God, there is a God, and there will be a God, Jehovah, I am. If there be a flux, a perpetual succession of ill, there is a perpetual being and living of the living Jehovah. So Christ is proved to be Jehovah, because he calls himself, Rev. i. 8, 'He that was, and is, and is to come,' Jehovah, alway like himself.

Now, if God be Jehovah, alway like himself, then if he have delivered, if he doth deliver, he will deliver. He is I AM in himself.

2. Now, as his name is, *so is his nature and properties*. He is 'I AM' in his love to his church. He is alway in the present tense. 'Whom he loves, he loves to the end,' John xiii. 1. He is unchangeable. 'I, the Lord your God, change not; therefore, you are not consumed,' Mal. iii. 6. The reason why, notwithstanding our many provocations of him, that we are not consumed, it is because his love to us is unchangeable. Though we are up and down, 'he cannot deny himself,' 2 Tim. ii. 13; and there is

the foundation of our comfort, that though we change oft, yet he never changeth. There is no outward thing can change him; for then that were God, and not he. There is no inward thing can change him; for then he were not perfectly wise. So there is nothing either in himself or in the creatures that can change God. He is alway like himself. Therefore, this is a ground of confidence for the time to come.

3. Likewise *his covenant and promise*. The covenant that he hath made with his children is an everlasting covenant, that he will be their God to death, and for ever; and the gifts and graces of God, his inward love, they are without repentance, and their union with Christ is an everlasting union.

4. And also *experience built upon these grounds*, that God is Jehovah. What he hath done he will do; and his properties are answerable to his name; he is unchangeable, and his promise and covenant are unchangeable. Therefore, experience from the time past comes to be a good argument from these three grounds: because he is Jehovah, 'I AM;' and because he is unchangeable, being Jehovah; and because his covenant is everlasting, because he is unchangeable.

For the foundation of all comfort is the name and being of God, Jehovah. From his being, issue and flow his properties, and they are like him unchangeable and eternal, and from his properties comes that to be unchangeable that comes from him, his word, and promise, and covenant. Considering then that his name and being is such, that his properties are such, that his covenant is such, issuing from his nature and properties, experience then of trust in the love and mercy of God, is an unanswerable argument against all temptations. He hath loved, he doth love, and he will love; he hath delivered, he doth deliver, and he will deliver, and will 'preserve us to his heavenly kingdom,' 2 Tim. iv. 18.

It is a good argument that God that is Jehovah, that God that is unchangeable, that God that is in covenant with me, that is my God, and I his, that God of whom I have had experience for the time past, that he hath been my God. Why should I doubt for the time to come? Unless I will call in question the very being of God, the very properties of God, and the truth of God in his covenant, and overturn all, I may as well trust him for the time to come, as for the time present; 'He hath delivered me, he doth deliver me, and he will deliver me.'

Obj. But it may be objected, God doth not deliver alway, and therefore it seems not to be a current truth. How doth God deliver his children, when we see how they miscarry in troubles and persecutions, both the church in general and particular Christians, as there be many instances. It seems God doth not deliver his. They die martyrs. St. Paul himself died a bloody death. Therefore, how is this true that we may build a certain confidence upon it, 'he hath delivered, he doth deliver, and he will deliver?'

Ans. I answer, we must take it in the latitude, this deliveranee.

1. God delivers them so as stands with their desires to be delivered; for there may cases come wherein God's children will not be delivered, as we see the three young men when they were cast into the fire, they would not be delivered *out of* the fire, but they were delivered *in* it. And so in Heb. xi. 35, there is a notable example. 'Tender women receive their dead again raised to life, and others likewise were tortured, and would not accept of deliverance.' They would have none upon ill terms. So sometimes God doth not deliver his children, no, nor they will not be delivered,

because perhaps their deliverance is promised upon ill terms; that they may redeem their lives if they will by denying God and religion; an ill bargain (*cc*).

2. Again, I answer that howsoever God doth not deliver his from trouble, yet he delivers them in trouble, as in Isaiah xliii. 2, he promiseth to be with them, and to deliver them in 'the fire, and in the water.'

God did not keep the martyrs out of the fire, but God was with them in the fire, and in the water, to support them by the inward fire of his Spirit, that they might not be overcome of the outward fire and flame. So God delivers them in trouble, though not out of trouble.

There is an open deliverance visible to the world, and a secret, inward, invisible deliverance. There is an open glorious deliverance, as we see in the deliverance of the three young men, and many other examples. And there is an invisible deliverance, which is only felt of them, and of God, who delivers them. He delivers them in the inward man. He delivers them from the ill of troubles, from sin and despair; that they put not their hands to sinful courses. He supports them inwardly with comfort, and supports them inwardly in a course of obedience. And that spiritual, inward deliverance is the best, and that which God's people more value than deliverance out of trouble. He doth not deliver them from suffering ill, he delivers them from doing ill, as in that notable place, 2 Tim. iv. 17, 18, 'I was delivered out of the mouth of the lion, and the Lord shall deliver me from every evil work.' He doth not say, God shall deliver me from death, and from suffering evil works of tyrants; no, but he shall deliver me from carrying myself unseemly and unbefitting such a man as I am, that I may not disgrace my profession. 'He shall deliver me from every *evil work*.' And that is that which the saints and martyrs and all good people desire, that God would deliver them, that they may not sink in their minds, that they despair not, that they carry not themselves uncomely in troubles, but so as is meet for the credit of the truth which they seal with their blood (*dd*). 'He hath delivered me, and he will deliver me from every evil work.' And what saith he afterwards? 'He shall preserve me to his heavenly kingdom.'

He doth not say, he shall preserve me from death. He knew he should die. But, 'he shall preserve me to his heavenly kingdom.' So put the case that God do not deliver *from* death, yet he delivers *by* death.

There is a partial deliverance, and a total deliverance. There is a deliverance from this and that trouble, and there is a deliverance from all troubles. God delivers us most when we think he delivers least; for we think how doth he deliver his children when we see them taken away by death, and ofttimes are massacred?

That is one way of delivering them. God by death takes them from all miseries. They are out of the reach of their enemies. Death delivers them from all miseries of this life, both inward of sin, and outward of trouble. All are determined in death. Therefore, God when he doth not deliver them from death, he delivers them by death, and takes them to his heavenly kingdom.

God oft-times delivers his by not delivering them out of trouble; for when he sees us in danger of some sin, he delivers us into trouble to deliver us from some corruption. Of all evils God's children desire to avoid the delivering up to themselves, and to their own lusts, to their own base earthly hearts, to a dead heart. He delivers them into trouble therefore to deliver them from themselves.

God will deliver us for the time to come, so that we depend upon him, and humble ourselves, and be like ourselves. When God delivereth us at the first, it may be we are like ourselves, but perhaps afterward we grow prouder, and self-confident, and will not do that we formerly did. Therefore, God sometimes though he put us in hope of deliverance, yet he will not deliver us, because we are not prepared, we are not thoroughly humbled. As we see in Judges xx. There the Israelites were to set on the Benjamites. They go the first time, and had the foil.* They go the second time, and are foiled. The third time they set on them with fasting and prayer, and then they had the victory.

What was the reason they had it not at the first time? They were not humbled enough; they did not flee to God, with fasting and prayer. It may be there is some sin, some affection unmortified, of revenge and anger. When God hath subdued that, and brought it under, and brought us to fasting and prayer, then God will deliver us; as at the third encounter they carried away the victory. When we have not made our peace with God, we may come the first and second time, and not be delivered; but when we are thoroughly humbled, and brought low, then God will deliver us.

And then, we must know that alway these outward promises have a reservation to God's glory, and our eternal good. 'God hath delivered me,' and he doth, and will deliver me, if it may stand with his glory and my good. And therefore the soul saith to God, with that reserved speech of him in the gospel, Lord, 'if thou wilt, thou canst heal me,' Mat. viii. 2. If thou wilt, thou canst deliver me. If it be for thy glory, and my eternal good, or for the church's good, thou wilt do it. And neither the church nor the particular members of the church, desire deliverance upon any other terms. But when it may be for the glory of God, and for the church's good; when they may be instrumental by long life to serve God, and to serve the church; and when it is for their own advantage to gather further assurance of their salvation, then he hath, and doth, and will deliver still. This is enough to build the confidence of God's children upon, for their deliverance for the time to come.

God will deliver his church and children, and he will deliver them out of all. He will 'deliver Israel out of all his troubles,' Ps. xxv. 22. He will not leave a 'horn or a hoof,' as Moses said, Exod. x. 26. He will not leave one trouble. He will deliver us at the last out of all, and advance us to his heavenly kingdom. His bowels will melt over his church and children; he is a father, and he hath the bowels of a mother. This may serve to answer all objections that will arise in our hearts, as indeed we are ready to cavil against divine truths and comforts; especially in the time of trouble and temptation, our hearts are full of complaints and disputes; therefore I thought good to answer this.

But what is the argument of the apostle here? Especially experience; 'He hath delivered, he doth deliver, and he will deliver me.'

Doct. As God will deliver his church for the time to come, so this is one main argument that he will do it, experience of former favours and deliverances.

This St Paul useth familiarly, 'I was delivered out of the mouth of the lion,' and 'the Lord shall deliver me from every evil work, and preserve me to his heavenly kingdom,' 2 Tim. iv. 17, 18—a blessed arguing. So David argues, 'God delivered me from the bear and the lion, and therefore he will deliver me from this uncircumcised Philistine,' 1 Sam. xvii. 37.

So Jacob pleads, that God would deliver him from Esau. He had had

* That is, = 'defeat.'—G.

experience of God's mercy till then, and therefore he trusted that God would deliver him from Esau.

It is a good argument, to plead experience to move God to care for us for the time to come.

It was used by the Head of the church, by the body, the church, and by every member of the church.

1. It was used by *the Head*, Ps. xxii., which is a psalm made of Christ, 'I was cast on thee from my mother's womb, therefore be not far from me.'

It was typically true of David, and it was true of the Son of David.

2. So *the church pleads with God* in divers places, in Isa. li. 2, God calls to his people to make use of former experience. 'Look to Abraham your father, and to Sarah that bare you,' &c. Look to former times, 'to the rock whence you were hewn, and to the hole of the pit whence you were digged.' He that was your God then, is your God now. 'Look to Abraham, your father,' and from thence reason till now. So in Isa. lxiii. 7, 'I will mention the lovingkindness of the Lord, and the praise of the Lord, according to the great goodness of the Lord bestowed upon us.' 'In all their afflictions he was afflicted,' &c. He speaks of former experience: 'In love he bare them, and carried them all the days of old.' So in Ps. xliv. 1, 'Our fathers have told us' this and this. So both the Head of the church and the church itself, plead with God from former experience, and God calls them to former experience: 'Remember the rock whence you where hewn.' And he upbraids them, because they forgat the works done to their fathers, in Ps. cv., and divers others. He objects to them that they did not make use of God's former favours, 'They forgot their Saviour, that had done great things in Egypt,' &c., Ps. cvi. 11, 12. They forgat his former favours. And in the 13th verse of that psalm, 'They soon forgat his works, and waited not for his counsel.'

And so it is with every particular saint of God. They have reasoned from experience of God's favours, from the time past to the time to come. The Psalms are full of it. Among the rest, 'I remembered the days of old, and meditated on all thy works; I mused on the works of thy hands,' Ps. cxliii. 5. And in Ps. cxvi. 3, 'The sorrows of death,' (as the apostle saith here, 'I was delivered from so great a death,') 'the sorrows of death compassed me, the pains of hell took hold on me. I found sorrow and trouble. I cried unto the Lord: O Lord, I beseech thee, deliver my soul. The Lord preserveth the simple: I was brought low, and he helped me.' What doth he build on that? 'Return unto thy rest, O my soul; the Lord hath dealt bountifully with thee. Thou hast delivered my soul from death, mine eyes from tears, and my feet from falling.' What will he do for the time to come? 'I will walk before the Lord in the land of the living.' Thus we see how we may plead with God, as the psalmist doth excellently in Ps. lxxi. He goes along with God there from the beginning of his days, in verse 5. 'Thou hast been my hope, Lord, and my trust from my youth; by thee I have been held from the womb; thou tookest me out of my mother's bowels: my praise shall be continually of thee.' What doth he plead from this now, when he was old? In verse 9, 'Cast me not off in the time of my old age; forsake me not when my strength faileth.'

Why? Thou hast been my God from my youth; thou hast held me from the womb: therefore cast me not off in my old age, forsake me not when my strength faileth. So he pleads with God, verse 17, 'Lord, thou hast taught me from my youth; now when I am old and grey-headed, forsake me not, till I have shewed thy strength to this generation, and thy power to every one that is to come.'

Thus we see how the Spirit of God in his children makes a blessed use of former experience, to reason with God for the time to come; and it will afford us arguments in all kinds. We may reason from former spiritual favours to spiritual favours. As for instance, God hath begun a good work in us, therefore 'He will finish it to the day of the Lord,' Phil. i. 6. 'His gifts and graces are without repentance,' Rom. xi. 29. And we may reason from spiritual favours past to all favours to come that are of a lower nature, Rom. viii. 32, 'He that spared not his own Son, but gave him to death for us all, how shall he not with him give us all things?' It is a strong reason. He hath done the greater, therefore he may well do the less. We may reason from one favour to another. Thus, from temporal to temporal. He hath delivered me, therefore if it be for his glory and my good he will deliver me. We may reason from once to all of the like, Ps. xxiii. 1, 'God is my shepherd,' &c. 'He hath been with me in the valley of death,' ver. 4. He hath shewed himself to be my shepherd in all my troubles. What doth he build on that, for the time to come? 'Doubtless the loving-kindness of the Lord shall follow me all the days of my life,' ver. 6.

Use 1. This should teach us then, this holy practice, *to lay up observations of God's dealing*, and to take them as so many pawns and pledges to move God for the time to come to regard us. It is wondrous pleasing to him. It is no argument to prevail if we come to men, to say, you have done this for me, therefore you will; because man hath a finite power which is soon drawn dry. But God is infinite. He is a spring. He can create new. What he hath done he can do, and more too. He is where he was at the first, and will be to the end of the world. He is never at a loss. Therefore it is a strong argument to go to God, and say, 'Lord, thou art my God from the womb,' thou hast delivered me from such a danger, and such an exigence. When I knew not what to do, thou madest open a way. I see by evident signs it was thy goodness, thou art alway like thyself, to be the same God now. Therefore we should treasure up observations of God's dealing with us.

Use 2. And *consider with them the promises*, and see how God hath made good his promise by experience, and then join both together, and we may wrestle with God. Lord, thou hast promised thus and thus, nay, I have had the performance of this promise in former times. And now I stand in need of the performance of that promise which before I have had experience of.

Use 3. And *desire God by his Spirit to sanctify our memories*, that we may remember fit deliverances, and fit favours, that when the time shall come we may have arguments from experience. What is the reason that we sink in temptation? that we are to seek when troubles come? It is from baseness of heart, that though God have manifested his care and love to us by thousands of experiments,* yet we are ready upon every new trouble to call all into question, as if he had never been a good God to us. This is base infidelity of heart; and our neglecting to treasure up blessed experiments of God's former favour.

It should be the wisdom of every Christian to be well read in the story of his own life, and to return back in his thoughts what God hath done for him, how God hath dealt with him for the time past, what he hath wrought in him by his Holy Spirit. Let us make use of it, both in outward and in inward troubles, in disconsolations of spirit, and in inward desertions; let

* That is, 'experiences.'—G.

us call to mind what good soever hath been wrought in us, by such a means, by such an ordinance, by such a book, by such an occasion.

Let us call to mind how effectually God hath wrought in us in former times, and make use of this in the midst of the hour of darkness, when God seems to hide his face from us.

I see not the sun in a cloudy day, yet notwithstanding the sun is in the sky still. At midnight we hope for the morning. The morning will undoubtedly come, though it be midnight for the present. So David comforted himself in Ps. lxxvii. 11, 'I will remember the works of the Lord; surely I will remember thy wonders of old, I will meditate of all thy works, and talk of thy doings,' &c. See his infirmity. When he was in trouble of mind, his sins began to upbraid him that God had left him. 'I said in my infirmity, God hath forgotten me, &c., and hath God forgotten to be gracious? hath he shut up his tender mercies in displeasure? then saith he, this was my infirmity, but I will remember the years of the right hand of the Most High,' &c. And the same he hath in many other places, as Ps. cxliii. 4, 5.

It argues the great weakness of our nature, which is ready to distrust God upon every temptation of Satan, as if God had never dealt graciously with us, as if God were changeable like ourselves. Let us labour to support ourselves in the time of temptation with the former experience of God's gracious goodness, and his blessed work upon our souls. He that delivered us from the power of Satan, and keeps us from him still, that we sink not into despair, he will keep us for the time to come, so that 'neither things present, nor things to come,' as the apostle saith, 'shall be able to separate us from the love of God in Christ,' Rom. viii. 35. And let us, as it were, make diaries of God's dealing to us. This is to be acquainted with God, as Job speaks, Job xxii. 21; this is to walk with God, to observe his steps to us, and ours to him. It is a thing that will wondrously strengthen our faith, especially in old years, in gray hairs. What a comfortable thing is it when an aged man can look back to the former part of his life, and can reckon how God hath given him his life again and again! how God hath comforted him in distress! how God hath raised him up in the midst of perplexity, when he knew not which way to turn him, how God comforted him when he was disconsolate! All these meeting together, in our last conflict, when all comfort will be little enough, what a comfort will it be!

And those that disfurnish themselves by their negligence and carelessness of such blessed helps, what enemies are they to their own comfort!

Therefore consider God's dealing, remember it, observe it, think of it, and desire God's Spirit to help your minds and memories herein, that nothing may be lost. For, I say, all will be little enough, the comforts of others, our own experience, the promises of Scripture, our hearts are so ready to sink, and to call in question God's truth, and Satan will ply us so in the time of temptation.

Especially those that are old and grow into years, they should be rich in these experiments, and able even to have a story of them. We should be able to make a book of experiments from our childhood. God's care to every man in particular, it is as if there were none but he, and there is no man that is a Christian but he observes God's ways to him, that he can say, God cares for me as if he cared for none but me. Let us, therefore, treasure up experiments. We see one notable example in David, how he pleads with God, Ps. lxxi. 3, from his former experience, 'Be thou my habitation, wherein I may continually rest: thou hast given command to save me; for thou art my rock and my fortress.' Whatsoever is comfortable in the creature, God hath taken the name of it to himself, that in all troubles we might fly to him as the grand deliverer; for it is he that delivers, whatsoever the means be, whether it be angels or men. It is he that sets all on work. Therefore he is called a 'rock' and a 'fortress,' &c. 'Thou hast given command to save me,' Ps. lxxi. 3, that is, God hath the command of all creatures. He can command the fish to give up Jonah. He can command the devils to go out. Christ did it when he was on earth in the days of his flesh. Therefore much more now he is in heaven. He can command winds and storms, and devils and all troubles. He hath the command of all, as he saith to Elias, 'Behold, I have commanded a widow to feed thee,' 1 Kings xvii. 9. 'The hearts of kings are in his hand, as the rivers of waters,' Prov. xxi. 1. He that commands the creatures can command deliverance, 'Thou hast commanded to save me,' for the time past. What doth he say for the time to come? 'Deliver me, O God, from the wicked: thou art my hope and trust from my youth, &c. Cast me not off in mine old age; when my strength faileth me, forsake me not.' It is a good argument, 'Thou hast been my God from my mother's womb, therefore cast me not off in my old age.'

Well! we see here the practice of God's children in all times. Let it be a pattern for our imitation, that we 'do not forsake our own mercy,' as Jonah saith, ii. 8.

When God hath provided mercy, and provided promises to help us with experience, let us not betray all through unbelief, through base despair in the time of trouble. If we had but only God's promise that he will be our God, that he will forgive our sins, were not that enough? Is it not the promise of God, of Jehovah, that is truth itself? But when he hath sweetened his promise by experience, and every experience is a pledge and an earnest of a benefit to come, what a good God have we, that is content, not only to reserve the joys of heaven for us, but to give us a taste, to give us the assurance and earnest of the time to come, and, besides his promise, to give us comfortable experience, and all to support our weak faith!

But remember withal that this belongs only to God's children, and in a good cause. For wicked men to reason thus, 'He hath, and therefore he will,' it is a dangerous argument. They must not trust former experience. We must hope that God will continue as he hath been, upon this ground, that we are his, or else the ground of the ruin of wicked men is presumption that God will bear with them as he hath done. 'The king of Sodom' and his people were rescued out of trouble by Abraham and the army that he raised; yet they were pitifully consumed, not long after, by fire from heaven. Pharaoh was delivered by Moses's prayer. God delivered him from ten plagues. They made not a good use of it, and they perished after miserably in the Red Sea. Rabshakeh comes and tells of the former prosperity of Sennacherib, 'Where are the Gods of Hamath and Arpad,' &c. 2 Kings xviii. 34. Hath not my lord overcome all? Aye, but it was immediately before his reign.* Herod, he prospered, and had good success in the beheading of James, and therefore he would set upon Peter. He thought to trust to his former success. He was flushed in the execution of James. He thought God hath given me success, and blessed me in this. He thought God was of his mind, as it is, Ps. l. 21, 'Thou thinkest me to be like thyself,' thou thinkest I hate those that thou hatest, that are my

* Qu. 'ruin?'—Ed.

dear children. Therefore Herod presumed to go on and lay hold on Peter. But the church falls a-praying, and God smites Herod with a fearful death. He was eaten up with lice, with worms bred in his body, Acts xii. 23.

So I say it is no good argument to say, I have prospered in wicked courses, I do prosper, and therefore I shall prosper. I have gotten a great deal of goods by ill means, and I have kept such ill company; and though some mislike my courses, yet I hope to-morrow shall be as to-day, &c. Take heed, bless not thyself. 'God's wrath will smoke,' Deut. xxix. 20, against such. 'Treasure not up wrath unto thyself against the day of wrath,' Rom. ii. 5. Argue not so upon God's patience. It is an argument for God's children. He hath been my God, he is my God, and he will be my God. It is a sophism else for others, and as the prophet Amos saith, 'He that hath escaped the lion shall fall into the hands of the bear,' v. 19. So the wicked that escape one danger shall fall into another at length. It is no good argument for them to hope for the like of that they have had.

Nay, rather it is the worst outward sign in this world of a man in the state of reprobation, of a man hated of God, to prosper and have security in ill courses. God blesseth him, and lets him go on in smooth courses. As the streams of Jordan go on smooth and still, and then enter into the Dead Sea; so many men live and go on in smooth, easy courses, and we see at length they either end in despair, as Judas, or in deadness of heart, as Nabal. So that of all estates it is the most miserable when a man lives in a naughty course, and God interrupts him not in his course with some outward judgment. It is a reason only for the children of God to support themselves with, in a good cause, wherein they walk with a good conscience. Then they may say truly, God, that hath been my God till now, will be my God to the end of my days.

Use. Is God so constant to his children in his love, and in his fatherly care and providence, that whom he hath delivered, he doth deliver and will deliver? *Let us be constant in our service, and love back again.* Let us return the echo back again, and say, I have served God, I do serve God, and I will serve God; because he hath loved me, he doth love me, and he will love me. He hath delivered me, he doth deliver me, and he will deliver me. As he is constant in love to me, so will I be constant in respect, in reverence and obedience to him.

Therefore we see the saints of God, as God loves them from everlasting to everlasting, being Jehovah, as he never alters in his nature, so not in his love to them; so they never alter in their love to him. Therefore it is a clause in Scripture expressed by holy men, 'To whom be praise for ever,' Ps. cxi. 10. As they knew that he was their God for ever and for ever, so they purposed to be his people, and to praise him for ever and for ever. And because they cannot live here alway themselves, they desire that there may be a generation to praise him for ever and for ever, and they lay a plot and ground so much as they can, that God's name may be known, that religion may be propagated for ever. They know God is their God for ever. They know he is constant in love to them, and they are constant in their love to him, and for his glory, 'To whom be glory for ever.'

See here the happiness of a true Christian that is in covenant with God; he can say, I have had my happiness and my portion, I have it, and I shall have it for ever. Take a worldling, can he say so? He cannot. God will confound his insolence if he should say so. I have been rich, I have prospered in my course, I have attained to this and that means, I yet thrive, and I shall thrive, Aye, is it so? No! Thou buildest upon the sands. Howsoever God hath done, and howsoever he doth, thou canst not secure thyself for the time to come. Only the Christian that makes God his rock and his fortress, his shield and strong tower of defence, he may say he hath had that which is certain, he enjoys that which is immutable and constant. God is his portion, his eternal portion. He hath been good, he is good, and he will be good to eternity. No man else, that hath a severed happiness out of God, can say so.

A sound Christian, take him in all references of time, he is a happy man. If he look back, God hath delivered him from Satan, from hell and damnation, and many dangers. If he look to the present, he is compassed about with a guard of angels, and with the providence of God. God doth deliver him. He hath a guard about him that cannot be seen but with the eye of faith. The devil sees it well enough, as we see in Job, 'Thou hast hedged him about,' Job i. 10. How can I come to him? He looked about to see if he could come into Job, to see if the hedge had any breach, but there was none. God's providence compassed him about. God hath and doth deliver. And if he look to the time to come he will deliver, he seeth that 'neither things present, nor things to come, shall be able to separate him from the love of God,' Rom. viii. 38.

And this is not only true of outward dangers, but especially in spiritual. God hath been gracious. He hath given Christ. 'How shall he not with him give us all things?' Rom. viii. 32. A Christian is in the favour of God now, how shall he be* so for ever? He hath eternity, world without end, to comfort himself in, that God, as long as he is God, he hath comfort. As long as he hath a soul, so long Jehovah, the living God, will be his God, both of his body and soul. He is the 'God of Abraham,' therefore he will raise his body. He is the God 'that raiseth the dead,' and he will for ever glorify both body and soul in heaven.

Look which way he will, a Christian hath cause of much comfort. Why should he be dismayed with anything in the world? Why should he not serve God with all the encouragement that may be, when he hath nothing to care for but to serve him? As for matter of deliverance and protection, it belongs not to us, but to him. Let us do that that belongs to us, and he will do that that belongs to him, if 'we commit our souls to him as to a faithful Creator in well-doing; he hath delivered us, he doth deliver us, and he will deliver us, and preserve us to his heavenly kingdom.'

VERSE 11.

'*You also helping together by prayer for us.*' In these words the holy apostle sets down the subordinate means that God hath sanctified to continue deliverance to his children. 'He hath delivered, he doth deliver, and he will deliver us for the time to come.' Was this confidence of St Paul a presumption without the use of means? He will deliver us, 'you also helping together by prayer for us.' The chief cause doth not take away the subordinate, but doth establish it. And though God be the great deliverer, and 'salvation belong to the Lord,' Ps. iii. 8, as the Scripture speaks, salvation and deliverance it is his work; yet notwithstanding he hath, not for defect of power, but for the multiplication and manifestation of his goodness, ordained the subordinate means of deliverance; and as he will deliver, so he will deliver in his own manner and by his own means.

* Qu. 'not be?'—G.

He will deliver, but yet notwithstanding you must pray: 'you also helping together by prayer for us.'

The words have no difficulty in them, 'you helping together,' that is, you together joining in prayer with me. I pray for myself, and you together helping me by prayer, God will deliver me.

The points considerable in these words are these:—

First of all, that in the time of peril, or in the want of any benefit, the means to be delivered from the one, and to convey the other, *it is prayer.* God will do this, 'you praying.'

The second is this, *that God's children can pray for themselves.*

The third is, that notwithstanding, though they can pray for themselves, *yet they require* the joint help of others,* and they need the help of others.

The fourth is, *that our own prayers, and the prayers of others joining all together, is a mighty prevailing means for the conveying of all good, and for the removing of any ill.* God will 'deliver me, you helping by your prayers.'

Doct. Prayer is a means to convey all good, and to deliver from all ill.

Because God hath stablished this order, 'Call upon me in the day of trouble, and I will deliver thee,' Ps. l. 15. He joins deliverance to calling upon him. So in Ps. xci. 15, a notable place; besides others. Indeed, the psalms are wondrous full in this kind. 'He shall call upon me, and I will answer him; I will be with him in trouble, I will deliver him, and honour him.' Mark it, 'He shall call upon me, and I will deliver him;' and more than so, for God's benefits are complete, he doth not only deliver, but he honours, 'I will deliver him, and advance him,' Ps. xci. 15. God doth not only deliver his children by prayer, but he 'delivers them from evil works, and preserves them to his heavenly kingdom.' He delivers them and advanceth them together. He doth not do his work by halves. 'The eyes of the Lord are over the righteous, and his ears are open to their cry,' Ps. xxxiv. 15. His eyes are upon them, to see their miseries and wants. Aye, but though his eyes be open, his ears must be open too, to hear their cry. If his eyes were open to see their wants, if his ears be not open to hear their cry, his children might be miserable still.

Sometimes God delivers wicked men. He preserves them. But the preservation of a wicked man is but a reservation of him for future judgment, to feed him for the slaughter; and that deliverance is not worth the speaking of. But for his children, his eyes are open on them, and his ears to hear their cry. As they be in misery that he sees them, so they must cry that he may hear them. God hath stablished this order. He will deliver, but prayer is the means.

Now, the reason that he hath established this order,

It is for *his glory* [*and*] *our own good.*

Reason 1. *It is for his own glory;* because prayer gives him the glory of all his attributes. For when we go to him, do we not give him the glory of his omniscience, that he knows our hearts and knows our wants? Do we not give him the glory of his omnipotence, that he can help us? Do we not give him the glory of his omnipresence, that he is everywhere? Do we not give him the glory of his truth, that he will make good his promise which we allege to him and press him with? What a world of glory hath God by prayer.

Reason 2. And then *for our sakes* he hath established this order to convey all by prayer, to

(1.) Shew *our dependence on him.* For we being in such a low distance

* That is, = 'seek.'—G.

under God, it is good that we should know from whom we have all. Therefore, he will have us to pray to him. He commands it. Prayer is an act of self-denial. It makes us to look out of ourselves higher. Prayer acknowledgeth that we have that which we have, not of ourselves, but from him. Prayer argueth a necessary dependence upon him to whom we pray; for if we had it at home, we would not go abroad.

(2.) And then, again, it doth us good, because, as it gives God all the glory, so likewise *it exerciseth all the graces in a man.* There is not a grace but it is put into the fire, it is quickened and kindled by prayer. For it sets faith on work to believe the promise. It sets hope on work to expect the things prayed for. It sets love on work, because we pray for others that are members of the church. It sets obedience on work, because we do it with respect to God's command. Prayer sets humility on work. We prostrate ourselves before God, and acknowledge that there is no goodness or desert in us. There is not a grace in the heart but it is exercised in prayer.

The devil knows it well enough, and therefore of all exercises he labours to hinder the exercise of prayer, for he thinks then we fetch help against him; and, indeed, so we do. For in one prayer God is honoured, the church is benefited, grace is exercised, the devil is vanquished. What a world of good is by prayer? So that God hath established this order upon great reasons, fetched from our own comfort and good, and from his glory.

Since God hath established this order, away with idle suggestions, partly carnal and partly devilish. God knows what we want, and God knew before all time what we have need of, and he may grant it if he will. Aye, but that God that decreed, at the same time that he decreed to convey good, at the same time he decreed to convey it this way by prayer. Therefore, let us not disjoin that which God hath joined. Christ knew that God decreed all, and yet spent whole nights in prayer. And who knew God's love more than he? Yet because as he was man he was a creature, because as he was man he received good from his Father, to shew his dependence he continually prayed, he sanctified everything by prayer. And all holy men of God from the beginning, the more certain they were of anything by promise, the more eager, and earnest, and fervent they were in prayer. It was a ground of prayer. They knew that this was God's order. Therefore, if they had a promise, they turned it into prayer presently.

The means of the execution of God's decree, and the decree itself of the thing, they fall under the same decree. When God hath decreed to do anything, he hath decreed to do it by these means. So prayer comes as well within the decree as the thing prayed for. In Ezek. xxxvi. 37, 'I will do this, but I will be inquired of by the house of Judah.' I will do it, but they shall ask me, they shall seek to me first. So there is a notable place, Phil. i. 19, 'I know that this shall turn to my salvation through your prayers.' We must not, then, so reason as to make the chief cause to take away the subordinate means; but let us serve God's purpose and providence, let us serve God's order. He hath stablished this order and course, let us serve it. This is the obedience of faith, the obedience of a Christian.

Doct. 2. The second thing is, that

God's children are enabled to pray for themselves. I observe this the rather because the vilest men that live, when they are in trouble, as Pharaoh, Oh, go to Moses, let him pray for me! He could not pray for himself. He was such a desperate, wretched creature, he knew that God would not regard him. Therefore he saith, Go to Moses. And so Simon Magus, who was a wretch, yet when Peter denounced a judgment against him, 'Pray thou that none of these things light upon me,' Acts viii. 24. You are accepted of God; my conscience is so full of terror and horror, and so full of sin, that I dare not pray. A wicked man may desire others to pray for him; but, alas! his conscience is surprised with horror for his sins, and his purposes are so cruel, so earthly, and so base, that he knows he cannot pray with acceptance for himself. God's children, as they desire the prayers of others, so they can pray themselves. They do not desire that others should do all, but that they would 'help together with their prayers.'

Reason. Now, the reason of this, that God's children can pray for themselves, and must pray for themselves, it is because they are children; and as soon as ever they are new born, they are known by their voice, by crying. A child, as soon as he is born, he cries. A new-born child cries as soon as he is new born. He cries, 'Abba, Father.' He goes to his Father presently. In Acts ix. 11, as soon as Paul was converted, he cries, he goes to God by prayer. Therefore God, when he directs Ananias to him, saith he, Go to such a place, and there thou shalt find Paul, 'he is praying.' As soon as he is converted he is praying.

God's children have the spirit of adoption, the spirit of sons. God is their Father, and they exercise the prerogative and privilege they have. They go to their Father, and cry to him. In Zech. xii. 10, you have there a promise 'that God would pour the Spirit of supplication' upon his children. They cannot pray of themselves, but God pours a Spirit of supplication into their hearts; and his Spirit being poured into them, they can pour forth their prayers to him again.

Use. The use of this is, not to content ourselves to turn over this duty of prayer to the minister and to good people, 'Oh, pray you for us.' Aye, we do so; but pray for thyself. If thou wilt have another man's prayers do thee good, thou must help with thy own prayers, be good thyself.

Men turn it off with slight phrases and speeches, 'You must pray for us,' &c.

Alas! what will our prayers do thee good if thou be a graceless, blasphemous, carnal, brutish person? If thy conscience tell thee by the light of nature (for the word of God it may be thou dost not care for) that thou art so, what can our prayers do thee good? If thou mean to be so, though Noah, Daniel, and Job, saith God, should stand before me for this people, I would regard them for themselves, I would not hear them for this people, Ezek. xiv. 14. Let us be able and willing to help ourselves, and then we shall pray to some purpose.

God loves to hear the cries of his children. The very broken cries of a child are more pleasing than the eloquent speech of a servant. Sometimes the children of God have not the Spirit of prayer as at other times; and then they must do as Hezekiah did, they must 'mourn as a dove, and chatter as a swallow,' Isa. xxxviii. 14. And as Moses at the Red Sea, he cried, and the Lord heard his prayer, though he spake never a word. So in Rom. viii. 26, 'The Spirit teacheth us to sigh and groan.'

When we cannot pray, we must strive with ourselves against unbelief, and deadness of heart, by all means possible. Sighs and groans are prayers to God, 'My groans and my sighs are not hid from thee,' saith the prophet David, Ps. xxxviii. 9. And so in Lam. iii. 56, the church being in distress, saith she, 'Thou hast heard my voice, hide not thine ear at my breathing.' Sometime the children of God can only sigh, and breathe, and groan to God; for there is such a confusion in their thoughts, they are so amazed at their troubles, they are so surprised that they cannot utter a distinct prayer; and then they sigh, and breathe, and groan; they help themselves one way or other. If thou be a child of God, though thou be oppressed with grief, yet cry and groan to God, strive against thy grief all thou canst; and though thou canst not cry distinctly, yet mourn as well as thou canst, and God knows the groans of his own Spirit, and those cries are eloquent in his ears, they pierce heaven. But this being but supposed as a ground, the third observation is, as God conveys all blessings by prayer, and God's children have a spirit of prayer; so *God's children desire the prayers of others, and it is the duty of others to pray for them.* 'You also helping by your prayer for us.'

Doctrine 3. *Christians ought to help one another by prayer.*

The holy and blessed apostle was sure of God's love to him, and of his care of him; yet notwithstanding he was as sure that God would use both the prayers of himself and others to continue this his goodness to him; and therefore the greater faith, the greater care of prayer. And where there is no care of prayer, either of our own or of others for us, there is no faith at all.

There is an article of our faith, which, I think, is little believed. Though it be said over much, and heard often, yet it is little practised, 'I believe in the communion of saints.' Is there a communion of saints? wherein doth this communion stand? Among many other things, in this, that one saint prays for another.

This is one branch of the communion of saints, as they communicate in privileges; for they are all the sons of God, they are all heirs of heaven, they are all members of Christ, they are all redeemed by the blood of Christ; and so all other privileges belong to all alike. As there is a communion in privileges, so there is a communion in duties one to another. One prays for another. There is a mutual intercourse of duty. And those that truly believe the communion of saints, do truly practise the duties belonging to that blessed society, that is, they pray for one another. I mean here on earth. Here we have a command, here we have a promise, here we have mutual necessities. I have need of them, and they have need of me. We have need one of another.

In heaven there is no such necessity; yet there may be, as divines grant, a general wish for the church, because the saints want their bodies, and because they want the accomplishment of the elect.

Where there is want of happiness, there will be a general desire that God would accomplish these days of sin; but for any particular necessities of ours, they cannot know them. 'Abraham hath forgotten us, and Israel knows us not,' Is. lxiii. 16. There is a communion of saints, and this blessed communion and society trade this way in praying for one another. God commands that we should 'pray one for another,' James v. 13, 14.

Every Christian is a priest and a prophet. Now the priest's duty was to pray, and the prophet's duty was to pray. Now, as the priest carried the tribes on his breast, only to signify that he had them in his heart, and that he was a type of Christ, who hath us in his heart alway in heaven, to make intercession for us; so in some sense, every true Christian is a priest. He must carry the church and people of God in his heart. He must have a care of others. He must not only pray for himself, but for others, as he himself would have interest in the common prayer, 'Our Father,' as Christ teacheth us. Not that a Christian may not say, 'My Father,' when we have particular ground and occasion to go to God. But Christ being to direct the Church of God, he teacheth us to say, 'Our Father.' There is therefore a regard to be had by every true Christian of the estate of others.

Reason. The reason is, God's children sometimes cannot so well pray. Though they have alway a spirit of prayer, that they can groan to God, yet in some cases they cannot so well pray for themselves, as in sickness. Affliction is a better time to pray in than sickness; for affliction gathers and unites the spirits together. It makes a man more strong to pray to God. But sickness distempers the powers of the soul. It distempers the instruments that the soul works by. It distempers the animal spirits which the understanding useth. They are inflamed, and distempered, and confused. Now the spirits, that are the instruments of the soul, being troubled with sickness, sickness is not so fit a time for a man to pray for himself. Though God hear the groans of his Spirit, as David saith, 'My sighs are not hid from thee,' Ps. xxxviii. 9; yet notwithstanding it is good at this time to send for those that can make a more distinct prayer, though, it may be, they be great Christians. Therefore, saith St James, 'Is any man afflicted? let him pray; is any man sick? let him send for the elders of the church, and let them pray for him,' James v. 13, 14; not that he is not able to pray for himself, but let them help by joining together with him to God, 'And the prayer of faith shall save the sick, and the Lord shall raise him up.'

Nay, I add more, for the illustration of the point, it is so true that God regards the prayers of one for another, that he regards the prayer of weak ones, for grand ones. Great Christians are helped by mean ones; yea, pastors are helped by the people. St Paul, a man eminent in grace and place, a grand Christian, and for place an apostle, yet he was helped by the prayers of the weak Corinthians. So that a weak Christian in grace and place, may help a greater Christian than himself, both in grace and in place. Parents are helped by the prayers of their children. Magistrates by those that are under them. The rich are helped by those that are poor. The ministers by the prayers of the people, 'You helping by your prayers.' The prayers of the people prevail for the ministers; for though there be a civil difference which shall all end in death, yet notwithstanding in the communion of saints, there is no difference. 'A poor man may be rich in faith,' as St James saith, ii. 5, and one may have as much credit in the court of heaven as another. As St Austin saith well, God hath made the rich for the poor, and the poor for the rich: the rich to relieve the poor, and the poor to pray for the rich; for herein one is accepted for another.

St Paul stands much upon the virtue and efficacy of the prayers of the Corinthians, for himself a great apostle. And so in Rom. xv. 30, 'I beseech you for the love of Christ, and for the blessed work of the Spirit, strive by prayer together with us.' As ever you felt Christ do good to you, and as ever you felt the efficacy of the Spirit, strive with God, wrestle by prayer for me; and so in every epistle he begs their prayers.

And ministers need the prayers of people to God, as well as any other, or rather more; for, as God conveys much good to others by them, so Satan maligns them more than other men. 'Aim not at small nor great, but at the King of Israel,' 1 Kings xxii. 31, pick out him. So the devil aims not at small nor great, but at the guides of God's people, at the leaders of his army. 'I will smite the Shepherd, and the sheep shall be scattered,' Zech. xiii. 7.

Therefore pray for them, that they may have abilities, that they may have parts and gifts, and that they may have a willing mind, a large heart to use them, that they may have success in using them, that they may have strength of the outward man, that they may have protection from unreasonable men, 'Pray for us, that we may be delivered from unreasonable and absurd men,' 2 Thess. iii. 1, 2. 'Absurd men;' for none but absurd men will wrong those that God conveys so much good by, as he doth by the ministry. It is their lot to be vexed with such men ofttimes; and, therefore, pray for us.

What is the reason of this, that mean Christians may help great Christians by their prayers?

God will have it thus. Great Christians have not the spirit of prayer alike at all times. Though it be supposed they have it, yet the more help there is, the more hands are put to the work, the sooner it is despatched. As in the removing of a burden, the more join together, the sooner it is removed; and so in the drawing of anything, the more hands, the speedier despatch.

So when we would draw blessings from heaven, the more prayers there be that offer violence to God, the more we draw from him. If it be a judgment that hangs over our heads, the more there be that labour to put away the judgment by prayer, and to remove the cloud that hangs over our heads, the sooner it passeth by. Many help much, as many brands make a great fire; and many little rivers running into a common channel, they make the river swell greater; so prayer is strong when it is carried by the spirits of many; yea, those that are not, perhaps, so well experienced.

But, as I said, sometimes men not only great in place, but great in grace, need the help of others. The spirit of prayer is not in a like measure in them. Sometime they are too secure, sometime they are too presumptuous, sometime too negligent and careless, in stirring up the grace of God in them, sometime they are prone to be lifted up too much, sometime to be cast down too much.

If this be so, what a benefit is this then to have the help of others? when ofttimes a man meaner in gifts may have as great a measure of the spirit of prayer as another.

Prayer, it is not a work of gifts, but of grace. It is a work of a broken heart, of a believing heart.

And in prayer there be divers gifts which are far more eminent in one than in another, yet all excellent good in their kind. Some have the gift to be fluent, to be large in words, in explication of themselves. Some men have not so much in that, but they have a broken heart. Some again have it in zeal and earnestness of affections. So that there is something in the very action of prayer which helps in many. One helps with his ability, with his large gift of speech; another with his humble and broken spirit; another with his zeal and ardency to wrestle and strive with God to get a blessing.

Moses was a man of a stammering tongue, and yet Moses was a man for prayer. Aaron and Hur were silent, and were fain to hold up his hands, but Moses must pray; and yet Moses was no man of eloquence, and he pretends that for his excuse when he was to go to Pharaoh, Exod. iv. 13.

Therefore it is a matter of the heart, a matter of grace, of humility, of strong faith, and not a matter of words, though that be a special gift too.

Reason 1. God will have it thus in his wise dispensation, *because he will have every man esteemed, and because he will have no man to be proud.* He will humble his own to let them know that they stand in need of the prayers of the weakest. Every man in the church of God hath some gifts, that none should be despised; and none have all gifts, that none should presume over-much and be proud. In the church of God, in the body of Christ, there is no idle member. In the communion of saints there is none unprofitable. Every one can do good in his kind.

Reason 2. God will have this, because *he will have none despised.* It was a fault in St James's time, 'The brother of high degree,' James i. 9, did despise the brother of low degree, that is, the rich Christians despised the poor Christians. But saith St James, 'Hath not God chosen the poor in the world, rich in faith?' James ii. 5. Now faith is the ground of prayer. It is a fault in all times. Men have swelling conceits against the meaner sort, and undervalue them. God will not have it so. He will have us see that we stand in need of the meanest Christians; and by this he will raise up the dejected spirit of weak Christians.

What a comfort is it then, that I should be able to help the greatest man in the world? That he should be beholden to me for that duty? So it abaseth the greatest, that they stand in need of the meanest; and it raiseth the meanest, that the greatest are helped by them, and it knits all into a sweet communion. For when a great Christian shall think, yonder poor Christian, he is gracious in the court of heaven! Howsoever he be neglected in the world, he may do me good by his prayers. It will make him esteem and value him the more, and it will make him value his friendship. He will not disparage him. He will not grieve the spirit of such a one, whose prayer may prevail with God, and draw down a blessing for him. We see here the Corinthians help the apostle by their prayers.

You see the reason of it, that God will knit Christians together; and humble them that think themselves great, and that he might comfort every mean Christian.

Use 1. Therefore *let no Christian slight his own prayers, no, not those that are young ones.* That great divine Paulus Phagius, who was a great Hebrecian in his time, and one that helped to restore the gospel in England (*ee*), it was a good speech of him, he was wont to say, 'I wish the prayers of younger scholars; for their souls are not tainted with sin, and God often hears the poor young ones (that are not tainted, and soiled with the sins of the world, as others are) sooner than others. A weak Christian, that hath not a politic head and a devilish spirit, meaner persons that are but young ones, they have more acquaintance, many times, with God than others.' Despise not the prayer of any. And let none despise his own prayer. Shall I pray to God, will some say? I pray! do you pray for me. Why dost thou not pray for thyself? I am unworthy. Unworthy? Dost thou so basely esteem of it, when God is not only willing that thou shouldst pray for thyself, but requires thee to pray for others? Hast thou so base an esteem of this incense? 'Let my prayers be directed in thy sight as incense,' saith David, Ps. cxli. 2. God esteems this as odour, and wilt thou say, I am not worthy? Abase not that which he hath vouchsafed so to honour. God esteems so highly of it, that he will not only hear thy prayers for thyself, but for others.

Use 2. Again, *there is no pretence for any man to be idle in the profession of religion.* Thou hast not riches, thou canst not give; thou hast not place, thou canst not shew countenance to others; but if thou be a child of God, thou hast the Spirit of prayer, the Spirit of adoption, the Spirit of a son in thee, which enables thee to pray for thyself and others. There is no Christian but he may do this, 'You also helping together by your prayers for me.'

The fourth and last observation out of these words is, that

Doct. 4. *Prayer is a prevailing course with God.*

It prevails for the removing of ill, or for the preventing of ill, or for the obtaining of good, 'I shall be delivered,' I shall be continued in the state of deliverance; but yet you must pray. Your prayers will obtain and beg this of God.

Reason 1. Prayer is a prevailing course, because, as I said, it is obedience to God's order. He bids us call upon him, and he will hear us. Prayer binds him with his own promise. Lord, thou canst not deny thyself, thou canst not deny thy promise, thou hast promised to be near all those that call upon thee in truth; and though with much weakness, yet we call upon thee in truth; therefore we cannot but be persuaded of thy goodness that thou wilt be near us. So it is a prevailing course, because it is obedience to God's order.

Reason 2. And *it is a prevailing course,* because likewise it sets God on work. Faith, that is in the heart, and that sets prayer on work, for prayer is nothing but the voice of faith, the flame of faith. The fire is in the heart and spirit, but the voice, the flame, the expression of faith, is prayer. Faith in the heart sets prayer on work. What doth prayer? That goes into heaven, it pierceth heaven, and that sets God on work; because it brings him his promise, it brings him his nature. Thy nature is to be Jehovah, good and gracious, and merciful to thine! thy promise is answerable to thy nature, and thou hast made rich and precious promises. As faith sets prayer on work, so prayer sets God on work; and when God is set on work by prayer (as prayer must needs bind him, bringing himself to himself, bringing his word to him; every man is as his word, and his word is as himself), God being set on work, he sets all on work. He sets heaven and earth on work, when he is set on work by prayer. Therefore it is a prevailing course. He sets all his attributes on work for the deliverance and rescue of his church from danger, and for the doing of any good. He sets his mercy and goodness on work, and his love, and whatsoever is in him.

You see then why it is a prevailing course, because it is obedience to God, and because it sets God on work. It overcomes him which overcomes all. It overcomes him that is omnipotent. We see the woman of Canaan, she overcame Christ by the strength that she had from Christ. And Moses he overcame God, 'Let me alone,' Exod. xxxii. 10, why dost thou press me? 'Let me alone.' It offers violence to God, it prevails with him; and that which prevails with God, prevails with all things else. The prayer of faith hath the promise. 'The prayer of a righteous man,' in faith, 'it prevails much,' saith St James, v. 16. Consider now, if the prayer of one righteous man prevail much, what shall the prayer of many righteous men do? As St Paul saith here, my prayers and your prayers being joined together must needs prevail.

For instances, the Scripture is full of them, how God hath vouchsafed deliverance by the help of prayer. I will give but a few instances of former times, and some considerations of later time.

For former times: in Exod. xvii., you see when Amalek set upon the people, Moses did more good by prayer than all the army by fighting. As long as Moses' hands were held up by Aaron and Hur, the people of God prevailed: a notable instance to shew the power of prayer. In 2 Chron xiv., Asa prayed to God, and presseth God with arguments, and the people of God prevail. In 2 Chron. xx., there you have good king Jehoshaphat. He prays to God, and he brings to God his former experience. He presseth God with his covenant, with his nature, and the like arguments spoken of before ; and then he complains of their necessity, 'Lord we know not what to do, our eyes are towards thee,' 2 Chron. xx. 12. And God's opportunity is when we are at the worst, and the lowest. Then he is near to help, 'We know not what to do, but our eyes are towards thee,' saith that blessed king, and then he prevailed.

So the prophet Isaiah and Hezekiah, they both join together in prayer to God, and God heard the prophet, and the prayer of the king. They spread the letter before the Lord, and prayed to God, when Rabshakeh railed against God, and they prevailed mightily, Isa. xxxvii. 14.

Esther was but a woman, and a good woman she was. The church was in extremity in her time. She takes this course. She fasted and prayed, she and her people ; and we see what an excellent issue came of it, the confusion of proud Haman, and the deliverance of the church. In Acts xii., Herod having good success in the beheading of James, being flushed with the blood of James, he would needs set upon Peter too. The church, fearing the loss of so worthy a pillar, falls to praying. See the issue of it, God struck him presently. Woe be to the birds of prey, when God's turtle mourns! When God's turtle, the church, mourns, and prays to God, woe be to those birds that violently prey on the poor church! Woe be to Herod, and all bloody persecuting tyrants! Woe be to all malignant despisers of the church, when the church begins to pray! For though she direct not her prayers against them in particular, yet it is enough that she prays for herself, and herself cannot be delivered without the confusion of her enemies. You see these instances of old.

I will name but some of later times. What hath not prayer done? Let us not be discouraged. Prayer can scatter the enemies, and move God to command the winds, and the waters, and all against his enemies. What cannot prayer do, when the people of God have their hearts quickened, and raised to pray? Prayer can open heaven. Prayer can open the womb. Prayer can open the prison, and strike off the fetters. It is a pick-lock. We see in Acts xvi., when St Paul was cast in prison, he prayed to God at midnight, and God shakes the foundations of the prison, and all flies open, Acts xvi. 26. So St Peter was in prison, he prays, and the angel delivers him, Acts v. 19. What cannot prayer do? It is of an omnipotent power, because it prevails with an omnipotent and almighty God.

Oh that we were persuaded of this! But our hearts are so full of atheism naturally, that we think not of it. We think not that there is such efficacy in prayer ; but we cherish base conceits, God may if he will, &c., and put all upon him, and never serve his providence and command, who commands us to call upon him, and who will do things in his providence, but he will do them in this order. We must pray, first to acknowledge our dependence upon him. If we were thoroughly convinced of the prevailing power of prayer, what good might be done by it, as there hath been in former times! Certainly we would beg of God above all things the spirit of supplication. And if we have the spirit of prayer, we can never be miserable. If a man have the spirit of prayer, whatsoever he want he causeth it from heaven. He can beg it by prayer. And if he want* the thing he can beg contentation,† he can beg patience, he can beg grace, and beg acquaintance with God ; and acquaintance with God it will put a glory upon him.

It is such a thing as all the world cannot take from us. They cannot take God from us, they cannot take prayer from us. If we were convinced of

That is, 'be without' = denied.—G. • That is, 'contentment.'—G.

this we would be much in prayer, in private prayer, in public prayer, for ourselves, for the church of God.

The church of God now abroad, you see, is in combustion. If the Spirit of God in any measure and degree be in our breasts, we will sympathize with the state of the church. We wish them well, it may be; but wishes are one thing, and prayer is another. Dost thou pray for the church? If we could pray for the church, it would be better. We should do more good with our prayers at home than they shall do by fighting abroad; as Moses did more good in the mount by prayer than they did in the valley by fighting. Undoubtedly it would be so.

We may fear the less success, the spirits of men are so flat and so dead this way. The time hath been not long since that we have been stirred up more to pray, upon the apprehension of some fears, to pray with earnestness and feeling, expressing some desire in wishing their welfare; but now a man can hardly converse with any that have so deep an apprehension as they have had in former times.

Now therefore, as we desire to have interest in the good of the church, so let us remember to present the estate of the church to God. And let us present the church of God to him as his own, as his turtle, as his love.

You know when they would move Christ, they tell him, 'Him whom thou lovest is sick,' Lazarus 'whom thou lovest,' John xi. 3. So, Lord, her whom thou lovest, the church, whom thou gavest thy Son to redeem with his blood; the church to whom thou hast given thy Spirit to dwell in; the church wherein thou hast thy habitation amongst men; the church that only glorifieth thee, and in whom thou wilt be eternally glorified in heaven, that church is sick, it is weak, it is in distress, it is in hazard.

Let us make conscience of this duty, let us help the church with our prayers. St Paul saith, 'I shall be delivered, together with the help of your prayers,' Philem. 22. Without doubt the church should be delivered, if we had the grace to help them with our prayers. And God will so glorify the blessed exercise of calling upon him, that we, I say, shall do more good at home than they shall do abroad. Let us believe this; it is God's manner of dealing.

In the book of Judges, in that story of the Benjamites, concerning the wrong done to the priest's concubine, the rest of the tribes of Israel, when they set on the Benjamites, they asked counsel of God twice, and went against them, and were discomfited; but the third time they come to God, Judges xx. 26, 'Then all the children of Israel came to the house of the Lord, and wept, and sat there before the Lord; and fasted that day till the evening.' They thought because they had a good cause, they might without fasting and prayer, and without seeking to the Lord, prevail, and therefore they went against them twice, and were shamefully foiled, to their great loss. But when at the last they came and humbled themselves before God, and fasted, and inquired of God the cause of that ill, after that they had a glorious victory.

Christ tells his disciples that there were some kind of devils that will not be cast out by fasting and prayer, Mat. xvii. 21. So there are some kind of miseries, some kind of calamities, some kind of sins, that will not be overcome, and which God will not deliver the church from, but by fasting and prayer.

And so for private Christians, they have some sins that are master-sins, personal sins. It is not a slight prayer and a wish that will mortify them. There must be fasting, and prayer, and humiliation; and that way those devils are cast out. I would we were persuaded of it, that it is such a prevailing thing, holy prayer, to help ourselves in sin, and to help us in misery, to help the church of God.

Use. Well, since the prayers even of the meanest Christians are so prevailing, let us learn *to respect them;* for, as they can pray, so their prayers will prevail. And take heed we grieve not the Spirit of God in any poor saint, that so they may pray for us with willingness and cheerfulness. Do but consider what a blessing it is to have a stock going, to have our part in the common stock. As there is a common stock of prayer in the church, every Christian can pray, and pray prevailingly. What a blessing is it to be a good Christian, to have a portion in the prevailing prayers of others! That when a man is dead and dull, and unfit himself, this may comfort him, that others have the spirit of zeal, and will supply his want. It is a blessed thing! Let us consider the excellency of this duty of prayer, from the prevalency of it, to whet us on to the exercise of it. It is a happiness to have a part in it. It is a blessing whereby we can do good to others. We can reach them that are many hundred miles off, those that be at the farthest end of the world. When we cannot reach them other ways, we can reach them by prayer. We cannot speak to them, they are far off, but we can speak to God for them; and he can convey that good to them that we desire. What a blessed condition is this!

Quest. But some man may say, How shall I know that I can pray, that I am in a state to help the church of God, and to prevail for it by my prayers?

1. I answer, first of all, thou shalt know it *if thou be as willing to help otherwise, if thou canst, as well as by prayer.* St James speaks in his time of certain men that would feed the poor people of God with good words, James ii. 16. Now good words are good-cheap; but they will do nothing. They will buy nothing, they will not clothe, nor feed. So St James tells them, that that is but a dead faith.

So there are a company that will only pray for the church when they are able to do other ways, when they have countenance, and estate, and riches, and friends, and place, and many things that they might improve for the good of others, and for the good of the church. Some will be ready to say, I pray for the church, and I will pray. Aye, but art thou not able to do somewhat else? St Paul when he wishes them to pray for him, he means not only prayer, but that duty implies to do all that they pray for, to help their prayers, or else it is a mocking of God. If thou pray aright for the church, thou art willing to relieve them; if thou pray for thy friend, thou art willing to help him, and succour him; if thou pray for any, thou art willing to countenance them. That is one trial, which discovers many to be hypocrites. If their prayers were worth anything, and the times stood in need of them, it is likely they should not have them, because they only give good words, and nothing else.

2. Again, he that is in a state of prayer, he must be such a one *as must relinquish in his purpose all wicked, blasphemous, scandalous, unthrifty courses whatsoever.* He that purposeth to please God, and to have his prayer accepted of God, he must leave all. For as the Psalmist saith, 'If I regard iniquity in my heart, the Lord will not hear my prayer.' For a man to come with a petition to God, with a purpose to offend him, is to come to practise treason in the presence-chamber; to come into the presence of God, and to have a purpose to stab him with his sins. Dost thou purpose to live in thy filthy courses, in thy scandalous evil course of life, to be a

blasphemer, a swearer, and yet dost thou think that God will hear and regard thy prayer? 'If I regard iniquity in my heart, the Lord will not hear my prayer,' Ps. lxvi. 18. That is another thing that thou mayest know it by, whether thou be in such an estate as that thou mayest pray successfully for thyself, and for others.

3. In Prov. xxviii. 9, there is a third discovery, 'He that turns his ear from hearing the law, even his prayer shall be abominable.' Thou mayest know it by this, if thou be in such an estate as that God will regard thy prayers for thyself or for others, that they may be prevailing prayers; how standest thou affected to God's truth and word? how art thou acquainted with the reading of the Scriptures, and with hearing the blessed word of God unfolded and broken open by the blessed ordinance of God? How doest thou attend upon God? Wouldst thou have him who is the great God of heaven and earth to hear thee, and to regard thee, when thou wilt not hear and regard him? Thou wouldst have him to regard thy prayers, and thou regardest not him speaking by the ministry of his word. Thou despisest his ordinance which he hath left with thee. He hath left thee the mysteries of his word, and thou regardest them not, but spendest thy time altogether either about thy calling, or about some trifling studies, and neglectest the main, the soul-saving truth; will he hear thy prayer? No, saith the wise man; 'He that turns his ear from hearing the law, that man's prayer shall be abominable.'

Since prayer is so prevailing a thing, so pleasing to God, so helpful to the church, and so helpful to ourselves, who would be in such a case that he cannot pray, or if he doth pray, that his prayer should be abominable, that God should turn his prayer into sin? It is a miserable case that a man lives in, that is in league with sin, that allows himself in any wicked course, in rebellion to God's ordinance. Such men are in such a state that God doth not regard their prayers for themselves or for others. Some do so exalt and lift up their pride against God, that they do not regard the very ordinance of God. No, not while they are hearing it, but set themselves to be otherwise disposed at that very time. How can such expect that God will regard them? This shall be sufficient to press that point. Saith Saint Paul, 'I shall be delivered by your prayers.'

Obs. God will deliver the ministers by the people's prayers.

God will be good to the ministers for the prayers of the people. This concerns us that are ministers. Prayer is prevailing even for us. And as it is our duty to give ourselves to preaching and prayer, so it is the people's duty to pray for us likewise, and for these particulars, as I named.

To pray for ability,—to pray for a willing mind to discharge that ability,—to pray for success of that discharge. For we must be able to preach to the people of God, and we must be willing, and there must be success. It doth much discourage God's people, and those that are ministers, when they find no success of their labours. Isa. xlix. 4, saith the prophet, 'I have laboured in vain.' Elias was much discouraged in his time, Romans xi. 4, 1 Kings xix. 18; and Isaiah and Elias were good men, yet they were much discouraged. They saw little fruit of their labour. Therefore let us help the ministers with our prayers in this respect, that God would enable them; that God would enlarge their hearts with willingness. For there are many that are of ability, but they are so proud, and so idle, that they think themselves too good to preach to them, whom God and the church hath called them to bestow their labours on. They have ability, but they want a large heart. And those that have both ability and a large heart, they want success, they see little fruit; because the people pray not for them; and they perhaps are negligent in the duty themselves; their labours are not steeped in prayers.

Again, a fourth thing that we ought to pray for for them, *is strength and ability of the outward man;* and all that fear God, and have felt the benefit of the ministry, they do this, and God doth answer it.

Likewise to pray *for protection and deliverance from unreasonable men,* to pray for strength of spirit, and likewise for protection. For, as St Paul saith, 'All men have not faith. Pray for us, that we may be delivered from unreasonable, absurd men: all have not faith,' 2 Thess. iii. 2. Men that believe not God's truth, that believe not God's word, that are full of atheism, full of contempt and scorn, they are 'absurd men.' Though they think themselves the witty* men of the world, yet they are unreasonable and absurd men. 'Pray for us, that we may be delivered from unreasonable men.'

Likewise from him that *is the head of wicked men, the Devil.* He sees that the ministers they are the standard-bearers, they are the captains of God's army. They stand not alone, and they fall not alone. Many others fall with them. There is no calling under heaven by which God conveys so much good, as by the dispensation of his ordinance in the ministry; therefore we should help them by our prayers. There are no men better if they be good, nor none more hurtful if they be bad; none worse. As Christ saith, 'They are the salt of the earth,' to season the unsavoury world, 'and if the salt have lost the savour, it is good for nothing but to be cast on the dunghill,' Luke xiv. 34, 35. Therefore pray that God would deliver them from the devil, who maligns them. They are the butt† of his malice, by his instruments.

There are many that come to hear the word to carp, and to cavil, and to sit as judges to examine, but how few are there that pray for the ministers! and surely, because they pray not, they profit not. If we could pray more, we should profit more. I beseech you in the bowels of Christ, put up your petitions to God, that God would teach us (that are inferior to you in other respects, setting aside our calling) that we may teach you, that we may instruct his people. As John Baptist saith, 'The friends of the bride learn of the bridegroom,' John iii. 29, what to speak to the spouse. So we learn from prayer, and from reading, we learn from Christ what to teach you. If you pray to God to teach us that we may teach you, you shall never go away without a blessing.

And therefore, as I said, we see how the apostle desires the Romans to strive and contend with him in prayer. He useth all protestations, and obtestations, 'For the love of Christ and of his Spirit,' &c., Romans xv. 30. And, pray for us, 'that the word may have a free passage, and be glorified,' 2 Thess. iii. 1. In every epistle still he urgeth, 'Pray for us.' The blessed apostle was so heavenly-minded, that he would neglect no help that might further him in the ministry. So if we have Christian hearts, we will neglect no helps, not the help of the meanest Christian that we are acquainted with. When he that was a great apostle saith, 'Pray for us, strive in prayer for us,' he prays for the help of others' prayer. So the more gracious we are, and the nearer to God, the more we understand the things of God, the more careful we shall be of this Christian duty of prayer, for the ministers, and for ourselves, and others. Upon this ground, that it is God's ordinance; and there is nothing established by God that shall

* That is, 'wise.'—G. † That is, 'mark.'—G.

want a blessing. Therefore if we have faith, we will pray; the more faith the more prayer; the greater faith the greater prayer. Christ had the greatest faith, and he prayed whole nights together. St Paul was mighty in faith; he was mighty in prayer. Where there is little faith, there will be little prayer; and where there is no faith, there will be no prayer. 'You also helping together by prayer for us.'

Mark the heavenly art of the apostle. He doth here insinuate and enwrap an exhortation by taking it for granted that they would pray for him. It is the most cunning way to convey an exhortation, by way of taking it for granted, and by way of encouragement. 'The Lord will deliver me.' He doth not say, therefore I pray help me by your prayers; but the Lord will deliver me if you help me, and I know I shall not want your prayers. He takes it for granted that they would pray for him; and granted truths are the strongest truths. It is the best way to encourage any man, if we know any good in him, to take it for granted that he will do so; and so 'I shall be delivered, you helping together by your prayers.'

'*That, for the gift bestowed upon us by the means of many persons, thanks may be given by many on our behalf.*' After he had set down the means that God would convey the blessing by, which was prayer, then he shews the end, why God would deliver him by prayer. For the gift of health and deliverance bestowed upon me, by the means of many prayers of many persons, 'likewise thanks shall be given by many on our behalf;' that is, on my behalf. Yea, as many shall be ready to thank God for my deliverance and health, as before many prayed to God for it. So that in this regard, God in love to his own praise and glory will deliver me by your prayers, because he shall gain praise, and praise of many.

'That for the gift bestowed,' &c. And first for the words somewhat.

'For the gift bestowed on us.' Deliverance and health is a gift, *charisma*,* a free gift. If health be a gift, what are greater things? They are much more a free gift. If daily bread be a gift, certainly eternal life is much more a gift. 'The gift of God is eternal life,' Rom. vi. 23.

Away with conceit of merit! If we merit not daily bread, if we merit not outward deliverance, if we merit not health, what can we do for eternal life? It is a doting conceit, a mere foolish conceit then, to think that the beggar merits his alms by begging, prayer being the chief work we do. What doth the beggar merit by begging? Begging, it is a disavowing of merit. Health, you see here, it is a gift bestowed by prayer, that 'for the gift bestowed upon us,' &c.

Things come to be ours either by contract or by gift. If it be by contract, then we know what we have to do. If it be by gift, the only way to get a thing by gift is prayer. So that which is gotten here by prayer, it is called a gift, not only a gift for the freeness of it, but because health, and deliverance out of trouble, is a great and special gift. For, as it seems, St Paul here was desperately sick (I rather incline to that than any other deliverance), 'I received the sentence of death,' &c.

Is not health a gift? Is it not the foundation of all the comforts of this life? What would riches comfort us? What would friends comfort us? Bring all to a sick man, alas! he hath no relish in anything, because he wants the ground of all earthly comforts, he wants health. Therefore you know the Grecians accounted that a chief blessing. If they had health, they were contented with any estate (*ff*). A poor man in a mean estate,

* That is, 'χάρισμα.'—G.

with a little competency, is more happy than the greatest monarch in the world that is under sickness and pain of body.

Health! it is comfort itself, and it sweetens all other comforts.

Therefore it is a matter that especially we should bless God for, both for preventing* health (God keeps us out of sickness), and likewise for delivering us out of it, for both are like favours. And they that have a constant enjoyment of their health should as well praise God, as they that are delivered out of sickness. It is God's goodness that they do not fall into sickness. There is the ground of sickness in every man. Though he had no outward enemy in the world, yet God can distemper the humours; and when there is a jar and disproportion in the humours, then follows a hurting of the powers, and a hindering of the actions, &c. We should bless God for the continuance of health. It is a special gift. 'For the gift bestowed.'

'By the means of many persons.' God bestowed health on St Paul, but it was by the means of many prayers of many persons.

Quest. Would not God have bestowed health upon St Paul if he had not had their prayers?

Ans. Yes, doubtless. But yet notwithstanding when there are many prayers, they prevail much more. Many streams make a river run more strongly, and so many prayers prevail strongly. Health is such a blessing as may be begged by others.

Therefore it is a good thing in sickness, and in any trouble, to beg the prayers of others, that they may beg health and deliverance of God for us. The good Corinthians here, they pray St Paul out of his trouble. And God so far honours his children, even the meanest, that they are a means to beg health and deliverance for others, even to pray them out of this or that trouble.

And what a comfort and encouragement is this, that a Christian hath so many factors for him! He hath all the saints in the world that say, 'Our Father,' praying for him. He must needs be rich that hath a world of factors, that hath a stock going in every part of the world. A Christian hath factors all the world over. He is a member of the mystical body, and many prayers are made for him. It is a great comfort.

And it is a great encouragement for us to pray for one another, considering that God will so far honour us. St Paul's health here, it was a gift by the prayers of many.

Obj. But thou wilt object: I am a weak Christian, a sinful creature. What, should God regard my prayers? Alas! my prayers will do you little good.

Solution. Yes, they will do much, not only for thyself, but for others. What are prayers? Are they not incense kindled by the fire of the blessed Spirit of God? Are they not in themselves good motions, stirred up by the Spirit? Themselves in their nature are good, though they be imperfect and stained. The Spirit that stirs them up is good, the good Spirit of God. 'We know not how to pray,' Rom. viii. 26, but the Spirit teacheth us. The Mediator through whom they are offered, who mingles his odour with them, Rev. viii. 3, 'He is the angel that mingleth odours with the prayers of the saints,' and makes them acceptable to God. The person likewise that offers them is good. What is he? Is he not God's child? Do not parents love to hear the voice of their children? If, therefore, the person be good, though weak, and the prayer be good, and the Spirit good,

* That is, = keeping off ill health.—G.

and the Mediator so good, then let no man be discouraged, not only to pray for himself, but to pray for others. God would hear the Corinthians, though they were stained with schism, and many other weaknesses. They were none of the most refined churches that St Paul wrote to, as we may see in the first epistle; yet saith St Paul, my health and deliverance is a gift, and a gift by the prayers of many, weak and strong joining together.

Obj. It is the subtilty of Satan, and our own hearts join with him in the temptation. What should I pray? My conscience tells me this and that.

Ans. Dost thou mean to be so still? Then indeed, as it is, 'If I regard iniquity in my heart, the Lord will not hear my prayer,' Ps. lxvi. 18. But if thou have repented thee of thy sins, and intendest to lead a new life for the time to come, God will hear thy prayers, not only for thyself, but for others. God will bestow gifts upon others, by means of thy prayers.

To go on.

'Thanks may be given by many persons.' God's end in delivering St Paul by prayer, was that he might have many thanks for many prayers, when they were heard once. 'That thanks may be given by many on our behalf,' that is, because we are delivered, and restored to health and strength again, to serve the church as we did before. You see here how

Obs. Praise follows prayer.

Many prayers, and then many praises; these follow one another. Indeed this is God's order; and we see in nature, where there is a receiving, there is a giving. We see the earth, it receives fruit, it yields fruit, as Christ saith of the good ground, sixty-fold, many-fold. You see bodies that receive the sun, they reflect their beams back to the sun again.

The streams, as they come from the sea, so by an unwearied motion they return back again to the sea. And men do eat the fruit of their own flocks, they reap the fruit of their own orchards and gardens. In nature, whatsoever receives, it returns back again. The influence and light that those heavenly bodies, the stars, and the planets, &c., have from the sun, who is the chief light of all, they bestow it upon the inferior bodies. You see it in nature, much more is it in grace. What we receive from God by gift, obtained by prayer, he must have the praise for it. Many prayers, many praises. As soon as ever a benefit is received, presently there is an obligation, a natural obligation, and a religious obligation. Upon the receipt of a benefit, there must be some thought of returning something presently.

It teacheth us what a horrible sin ingratitude is. It is the grave of all God's blessings. It receives all, and never returns anything back again. As those lepers, they never came back again to thank Christ, but only the tenth, a poor Samaritan, Luke xvii. 17. Men are eager to sue to God, restless till they have that they would have, but then they are barren and unfruitful, they yield nothing back again. After prayer, there must be praise and thanksgiving. It condemneth our backwardness and untowardness in this kind. Like little children, they are ready to beg favours, but when they come to thanksgiving, they look another way, as if it were irksome to them. So it is with our nature. When we go about this heavenly duty, we give God a formal word or two, 'Thanks be to God,' &c. But we never work our hearts to thankfulness. 'That thanks may be given *by many.*'

As the prayers of many are mighty with God to prevail, so likewise the praises of many are very grateful and acceptable to God, even as it is with instruments. The sweetness of music ariseth from many instruments, and from the concord of all the strings in every instrument. When every instrument hath many strings, and are all in tune, it makes sweet harmony, it makes sweet concord. So, when many give God thanks, and every one hath a good heart set in tune, when they are good Christians all, it is wondrous acceptable music to God, it is sweet incense; more acceptable to God than any sweet savour and odour can be to us. That is one reason why God will have many to pray to him, that he may have many praises.

God doth wondrously honour concord, especially when it is concord in praising of him. It is a comely thing for 'brethren to live in unity,' as it is Ps. cxxxiii. 1. If to praise God be a comely thing, and if concord be a comely thing, then when both meet together, it must needs be wondrous beautiful, and wondrous acceptable to God, when many brethren meet and join to praise God. Therefore it is said, in the church's new conversion, 'They met all together as one man,' Acts ii. 46, they were of one heart and one soul, and they were given to prayer and to praising of God. A blessed estate of that beginning church! They were all as one man, of one heart, of one spirit, of one soul.

As the blessed angels and blessed spirits in heaven, they all join together, as it is in Rev. xiv. 2, 3. The blessed man heard a voice in heaven as the voice of many waters, and of great thunder; and he heard the voice of harpers, 'and they sang a new song.' There were many harps, but one song, one thanksgiving, one heart, one spirit in all, wondrous acceptable to God.

This should make us in love with public meetings. Severed thanksgiving is not so acceptable a thanksgiving. God doth bestow all good upon us in the body, as we knit ourselves not only in thanksgiving to him, but in love to the church. As all things are derived from God to us in the body, so let our praise return to God in the body as much as we may.

It shews what a hateful thing schism and division is in the church. Besides many other inconveniences, God wants glory by it. God loves to be praised by many joining together. As the apostle saith here, 'Thanks shall be given by many,' &c. Many! not as they are many persons, but as they are many godly persons that are led by the Spirit of God.

Use. Therefore, if the praise of many be so acceptable, it should first be an encouragement to union. In John xvii. 21, saith our Saviour Christ there, 'I pray that they may be one, as we are one.' It was the sum of that heavenly prayer, the unity of the church to the end of the world, 'That they may be one, as we are one.' The Trinity should be the pattern of our unity. Because, I say, all good is in union, and all that comes from us that is accepted of God, it must be in peace and union.

God so loves peace, and a quiet disposition inclinable to peace, that he neglects his own service till we have made peace one with another, Mat. v. 24, 'If thou have any offence with thy brother,' if thou have done him any wrong, or he thee, 'go and be reconciled to him, and then come and bring thy offering.' God will stay for his own offering; he is content to stay for his own service, till we be at peace one with another. Whether it be prayer or praise, if we be not at peace, it is not acceptable. Again, this should teach us to stir up others, when we praise God, and others have cause as well as we, 'that thanks may be given by many.' When we are in trouble, call upon others; and as it is the common and commendable fashion, desire others to pray for us, that prayer may be made by many; and when we receive any favour, any deliverance from any great danger, acquaint others with it, that thanks may be given by many. It was the practice of David, in Ps. lxvi. 16, 'Come! I will tell you what the Lord hath done for my soul.' And in Ps. xxxiv. 4, and in Ps. cxlii. 7, 'Bring my soul out of trouble, that I may praise thy name,' and what shall others do? 'Then the righteous shall compass me about, for thou hast dealt bountifully with me:' shewing that it is the fashion of righteous men, when God hath dealt graciously with any of his children, they compass him about, to be acquainted with the passages of divine providence, and God's goodness towards them, 'The righteous shall compass me about, for thou hast dealt bountifully with me.'

Holy David, in Ps. ciii. 20–22, he stirs up every creature to praise God, even the creatures of hail, of storms, and winds, and everything, even the blessed angels, as we see in the latter end of that psalm, as if thanksgiving were an employment fit for angels; and indeed so it is. And, as if all his own praise were not enough, except all the creatures in heaven and earth should join with him in that blessed melody to praise God; the angels, and all creatures praise God. Let us stir up one another to this exercise.

How do the creatures praise God? They do praise God by the tongue. Although they have a kind of secret praise which God hears well enough, for they do their duty in their place willingly and cheerfully; but they praise God in our tongues. Every creature gives us occasion of praising God.

'That thanks may be given by many,' &c.

Many give thanks here for one, St Paul, for the minister. We see here God's end, that many should praise God, not only for themselves, but for others, especially for those by whom God conveys and derives good unto them, whether outward or spiritual good. The apostle exhorts us 'to pray for all men,' 1 Tim. ii. 1, 2; 'for kings,' yea, though they were persecuting kings at that time. And surely if we ought to pray to God for all mankind, we ought to praise God for all sorts of men, especially for governors and ministers, &c., because God by them bestows his greatest blessings. Obey the magistrate. 'Let every soul be subject to the higher powers; for the powers that are, are ordained of God, and he is the minister of God for thy good,' Rom. xiii. 1. So the governors and ministers of God are for our good. We ought therefore, as to pray for them, that they may execute their office for our good, so to praise God for the good we have by them. You know David stirred up the people to mourn for Saul, though a tyrant. 'He clothed you and your daughters,' saith he, 'with scarlet,' 2 Sam. i. 24. If they should praise God for a persecuting king, and mourn for him when he was gone, much more should we for those that are good.

And so likewise for pastors, we ought to praise God for them, and all that have good by them will pray to God, and praise God for them. And undoubtedly it is a sign of a man that hath no good by them, that prays not for them, and that praiseth not God by them. We ought to praise God in that proportion, as well as to pray to God one for another.

And this should stir us up to be good to many, that many may praise God, not only for themselves, but for us. If it be our duty to pray for those that we derive good by, and to praise God for them, then let us labour to be such as may communicate to others. Good is diffusive, and good men are like the box in the gospel, that when it was opened, all the house smelled of it, John xii. 3.

The heathen philosopher said that a just man, a good man, is a common good, like a public stream, like a public conduit, that every man hath a share in. Therefore, as the wise man saith, 'When good men are exalted, the city rejoiceth,' Prov. xi. 10, many rejoice. Who would not, therefore, labour in this respect to be good, to have a public disposition, to have a large heart, to do all the good we can, that so we may not only have more prayers to God for us, but we may have more praise to God for us, that God may gain by it, 'that thanks may be given by many on our behalf?'

Let us take notice of our negligence in this kind, and be stirred up to this blessed duty. And, therefore, consider wherein it consists.

1. It consists in our *taking notice of the favours of God to ourselves and others*, and in valuing the good things that we praise God for, to esteem them. The children of Israel, they did not bless God for the manna, they did not value it, 'This manna, this manna,' in scorn, Num. xi. 6. So in Ps. cvi. 7, 'They neglected God's pleasant things, they set light by them.' Hos. viii. 12, 'He gave them the great things of his law, and they accounted them as slight, as strange things,' not worthy to be regarded.

2. Praise consists *in taking notice*, and not only in taking notice, but in *remembering and minding them*, as in Ps. ciii. 2, 'My soul, praise the Lord, and forget not all his benefits.'

3. And likewise *in an estimation of them;* and likewise,

4. *In expressing* this thankfulness in words, 'Awake, my glory,' Ps. lvii. 8. Our tongues are our glory, especially as they are instruments to praise and glorify God. We cannot use our language better than to speak the language of Canaan in praising of God.

5. Likewise, praise consists in doing good, which is real praise, though we say nothing. Moses cried to God, though he spake not a word. Evil works have a cry, although they say nothing. Abel's blood cried against Cain, Gen. iv. 10. And as evil works, so good works have a cry. Though a man praise not God with his tongue, his works praise God. Job saith, 'The sides of the poor blessed him,' Job xxxi. 20. What! could their sides speak? No; but there was a real thanksgiving to God. Their sides blessed God. So our good works may praise God as well as our tongues and hearts. The heavens and the earth, they praise God, though they say nothing, because they stir us up to say something. 'Let men see your good works,' Mat. v. 16, that they may take occasion from thence to bless God, saith Christ. Or else your praising of God is but a mere complimenting with God; to give him thanks with the tongue, and after to dishonour him with your lives, Ps. l. 16, 'What hast thou to do to take my name into thy mouth, sith thou hatest to be reformed?' What hast thou to do to take my name into thy mouth, either in prayer or in praise, when thou hatest to be reformed? 'High words are unseemly for a fool,' saith the the wise man, Eccles. v. 3, x. 14. And what higher words than praise? Therefore, praise for a man that lives in a blasphemous course of life, in a filthy course of life, praise is too high a word for a fool. We must praise God in our lives, or else not at all. God will not accept of it. It consists in these things.

Now some directions how to perform it for ourselves and others.

1. If we would praise God for ourselves, or for any, then *let us look about us, let us look above us and beneath us, let us look backward, look to the present, look forward.* Everything puts songs of praise into our mouth. Have we not matter enough of our own to praise God for? Let us look about us, to the prosperity of others. Let us praise God for the ministry, praise God for the magistracy, praise God for the government wherein we live. There

are many grievances in the best government, but a Christian heart considereth what good he hath by that government, what good he hath by that ordinance, and doth not only delight to feed on the blemishes, as flies do upon sores. It is a sign of a naughty heart to do so. Although a man should not be insensible of the ills of the times (for else how should we pray against them?), yet he is not so sensible as to forget the good he hath by them. If we would praise God, let us look to the good, and not so much upon the ill.

Look up to heaven, look to the earth, to the sea. David occasions praise from every creature. Every creature ministers matter of praise, from the stars to the dust, from heaven to earth, from the cedar to the hyssop that grows by the wall. Is there not a beam of God's goodness in every creature? Have we not use of every creature? We must praise God not only for the majesty and order that shines in them, but for the use of them in respect of us.

And so let us look to the works of providence, as well as to the works of creation. Look to God's work in his church, his confounding of his enemies, his deliverance of his church, the churches abroad, our own church, our own persons, our friends. Thus we should feed ourselves, that we may have matter of praising God. God gives us matter every day. He renews his favours upon the place wherein we live and upon us, as it is Lam. iii. 22, 'It is his mercy that we are not all consumed.' Let us look back to the favours that we have enjoyed; let us look for the present. What doth he do for us? The apostle saith here, 'God doth deliver us.' Doth he not give deliverance, and favour, and grace, inward grace for the time to come? Hath he not reserved an inheritance, immortal and undefiled, in the heavens for us? Wherefore doth he bestow things present, and wherefore doth he reveal things laid up for us for the time to come, but that we should praise him, but that we should praise him for that which he means to do afterwards? 'Blessed be God the Father, who hath begotten us to an inheritance, immortal and undefiled,' &c., saith St Peter, 1 Pet. i. 4. God reveals good things that are to come, that we are heirs-apparent to the crown of glory. This is revealed that we might praise him now, that we might begin the employment of heaven upon earth. Let us look upward and downward, let us look about us, look inward, look backward, look to the present, look forward. Everything ministereth matter of praise to God.

Yea, our very crosses. Happy is he whom God vouchsafeth to be angry with, that he doth not give him over to a reprobate sense to fill up his sins, but that he will correct him, to pull him from ill courses. Happy is he that God vouchsafeth to be angry with in evil courses. There is a blessing hid in ill, in the cross. '*In all things* give thanks,' saith the apostle, Eph. v. 20. What! in afflictions? Aye, not for the affliction itself, but for the issue of it. There is an effect in afflictions to draw us from the world, to draw us to God, to make us more heavenly-minded, to make us see better into these earthly things, to make us in love with heavenly things. 'In all things give thanks.' When we want matter in ourselves, let us look abroad, and give thanks to God for the prosperity of others.

2. And withal, in the second place, when we look about us, *let us dwell in the meditation of the usefulness of these things, of the goodness of God in them, till our hearts be warmed.* It is not a slight 'God be thanked' that will serve, but we must dwell upon it. Let our hearts dwell so long on the favours and blessings of God till there be a blessed fire kindled in us. The

best bone-fire* of all is to have our hearts kindled with love to God in the consideration of his mercy. Let us dwell so long upon it till a flame be kindled in us. A slight praise is neither acceptable to God nor man.

3. And then let us consider *our own unworthiness, let us dwell upon that.* 'I am less than the least of all thy favours,' saith good Jacob, Gen. xxxii. 10. If we be less than the least, then we must be thankful for the least. Humility is alway thankful. A humble man thinks himself unworthy of anything, and therefore he is thankful for anything.

A proud man praiseth himself above the common rate. He overvalues and overprizeth himself, and therefore he thinks he never hath enough. When he hath a great deal, he thinks he hath less than he deserves, and therefore he is an unthankful person; and that makes a proud man so intolerable to God. He is alway an unthankful person, a murmuring person. A humble man, because he undervalues himself, he thinks he hath more than he deserves, and he is thankful for everything. He knows he deserves nothing of himself. It is the mere goodness of God whatsoever he hath.

The best direction to thanksgiving is to have a humble and low heart. Therefore David, 1 Chron. xxix. 14, when he would exercise his heart to thankfulness, when the people had given liberally, saith he, 'Who am I, or what is this people, that we should be able to offer willingly after this sort? All comes of thee, and all is thine own that we give.' What am I, or what is this people, that we should have hearts to give liberally to the temple? See how he abaseth himself. And Abraham, 'I am dust and ashes, shall I speak to my Lord?' Gen. xviii. 27. And Job, 'I abhor myself in dust and ashes,' xlii. 6, when he considered God's excellency and his own baseness. A humble heart is alway thankful, and the way to thankfulness is to consider our humility. 'What am I?' saith David. He had a heart to be thankful. 'Of thine own I give thee.' Not only the matter to be thankful for, but of thine own I give thee; when I give thee thanks, thou givest me a thankful heart.

As the sacrifice that Abraham offered was found by God, so God must find the sacrifice that we offer, even a thankful heart. Of thine own, Lord, I give thee, even when I give thee thanks.

Therefore you may make that a means to have a thankful heart, to pray for a thankful heart. And when we have it, bless God for it, that we may be more thankful. God must vouchsafe the portion of a thankful heart with other blessngs. He that gives matter to be thankful, must give a heart to be thankful.

4. Again, to make us more thankful, do but consider *the misery of ourselves if we wanted the blessings we are thankful for, and the misery of others that have them not.* Thou that hast health, if thou wouldst be thankful for it, look abroad, look into hospitals, look on thy sick friends that cannot come abroad. Thou that wouldst be thankful for the liberty of the gospel, look beyond the seas, look into the Palatinate, and other countries, and certainly this will make thee thankful, if anything will. If we would be thankful for spiritual blessings, consider the misery of those that are under the bondage of Satan, how there is but a little step between them and hell, that they are ready to sink into it. There is but the short thread of this life to be cut, and they are for ever miserable. If we would be thankful for any blessing, let us consider the misery to be without it. If we would be

* That is, 'bon-fire,' = boon-fire, or fire of joy, voluntarily kindled. Cf. Richardson, *sub voce.*—G.

thankful for our wits, let us consider distracted persons. What an excellent engine to all things in this life, and the life to come, is this spark of reason! If we want reason, what can we do in civil things? What can we do in matters of grace? Grace presupposeth nature. If we would be thankful for health, for strength, and for reason, if we would be thankful for common favours, consider the misery of those that want these things.

Would we be thankful for the blessed ordinance, consider but the misery of those that sit in darkness, and in the shadow of death, how they are led by Satan and want the means of salvation. Those that would be thankful for the government we have, let them consider those that live in anarchy, where every man lives as he lists, where a man cannot enjoy his own. The consideration of these things it should quicken us to thankfulness, the consideration of our own misery if we should want them, and the misery of those that do want them.

5. And let us *keep a catalogue of God's blessings*. It will serve us, as in regard of God to bless him the more, so in regard of ourselves, to establish our faith the more; for God is Jehovah, alway like himself. Whom he hath done good unto, he will do good to. He is constant in his love. 'Whom he loves, he loves to the end,' John xiii. 1. God shall have more thanks, and we shall have more comfort.

Again, to add some encouragements and motives to thankfulness, which may be a forcible means to make us thankful, do but consider.

(1.) *It is God's tribute, it is God's custom.* Do but deny the king his custom, and what will come of it? Deny him tribute, and you forfeit all. So you forfeit all for want of thankfulness.

What is the reason that God hath taken away the gospel from countries abroad, and may do from us if we be not more thankful? Because they were not thankful. It is all the tribute, all the impost he sets upon his blessings. 'I will give you this,' but you shall glorify me with thanksgiving. It is all the honour he looks for. 'He that praiseth me honoureth me,' Ps. l. 23. And 'now, O Israel, what doth the Lord require of thee,' for all his favours, but 'to serve him with a cheerful and good heart?' Deut. x. 12, to be thankful.

What is the reason that the earth denies her own to us, that sometimes we have unseasonable years? We deny God his own. He stops the due of the creature, because we stop his due.

When we are not thankful he is forced to make the heavens as iron, and the earth as brass. We force him to make the creature otherwise than it is, because we deny him thankfulness.

The running of favours from heaven ceaseth when there is not a recourse back again of thankfulness to him. For unthankfulness is a drying wind. It dries up the fountain of God's favours. It binds God. It will not suffer him to be as good as his word. If ever God give us up to public judgments, it will be because we are not thankful to God for favours and deliverances, as that in '88, by sea,* and from the gunpowder treason by land.† Was it not a sick state after Queen Mary, when Queen Elizabeth received the crown? The church and commonwealth were sick. Now if we be to praise God for our particular persons, when we have recovered our health, much more should we praise God, when the state, when the church is delivered, as it was at the coming in of Queen Elizabeth, and afterward in '88; and of late time, and continually he doth deliver us. And if we look that

* That is, from the Armada, 1588. See note, vol. I. p. 318.—G.

† 'Treason.' See note *e*. vol. I. p. 315.—G.

he should deliver us, not only our persons, but the state wherein we live, let us pray to God that he would do so, and praise God for his former deliverance.

(2.) Again, this is another motive, the praising of God for former deliverances, *it invites him to bestow new blessings.* Upon what ground doth the husbandman bestow more seed? Upon that which hath yielded most in time past. Will any man sow in the barren wilderness where it is lost? No; but where he looks to reap most, and hath done formerly. Where he sees a soil that is fruitful, he will sow it the more; and where the heart is a barren wilderness, that it yields nothing back again, he takes that away that he gave before.

You know there is a debt in giving. There must be a returning of thanksgiving alway; and kindness requires kindness. There is an obligation. And where benefits are taken, and men are thankful, that is the way to get more, to be thankful for that we have. For God minds his own glory above all things, and he will especially be bountiful to those from whom he sees he hath most glory. Therefore alway those that have been richest in grace, and in comfort, they were most in thankfulness, as we see in David, 'a man after God's own heart,' 1 Sam. xiii. 14, Acts xiii. 22, and in divers others. Let this encourage us.

First, if we be not thankful, it stops the current of benefits.

Secondly, if we be thankful God will give us more mercies and deliverances. When we praise him in our hearts, in our lives, in our bounty to others, in real thankfulness, when we are ready to good works, then he is ready to bestow new still.

(3.) Again, to stir us up to this duty of praising God for ourselves and others, consider *it is the beginning of heaven upon earth.* What a happiness is it, that when our persons cannot go to heaven till we die, till our bodies be raised, yet we can send our ambassadors, we can send our prayers and thanksgivings to heaven; and God accepts them, as if we came in our own persons. 'Let your conversation be in heaven,' saith the apostle, Philip. iii. 20. How is that? By praising God much. I pray, what is the employment of heaven, of the angels, and blessed spirits? They praise God continually for the work of creation, and for the work of redemption. That is their especial task in heaven. Our duty is to be much this way, in praising God. Self-love forceth prayer ofttimes; but to praise God comes from a more heavenly affection.

(4.) Again, do but consider, *that no creature in the world is unthankful*, but devils only, and devilish men; and good men, only so far as they are corrupt and hold correspondency with their corruptions. For every creature praiseth God in his kind, set the devil aside, who is full of envy and pride and malice against God. Therefore, except we will be like the devil, let us be thankful. God hath made all creatures to praise him, and to serve us, that we may praise him; and when they praise him, shall we blaspheme him? May not the swearer think with himself, every creature blesseth God, even the senseless creatures, and shall I dishonour God by my tongue which should be my glory, to glorify him? Shall I blaspheme him, and be like to the devil? Shall I be more base than the senseless creatures? What glory hath God by many men that live in the church, that blaspheme God; and their whole life is a witness against God, as the whole life of a Christian, after he is in the state of grace, is a witness for God, and a praising of him. His whole life is a thanksgiving. So the whole life of wicked and careless creatures, is a dishonour of God, it is a witness against God. There are none but devils, devilish-minded men, but they praise God, even the very dumb creatures. Let us labour to have a part in that blessed music and harmony to praise God. If we do not praise God here, we shall never do it in heaven.

But we must remember, by the way, that this thankfulness it must be a fruitful thanksgiving. As for us to pray to God to bless us, and then to do nothing, it is a barren prayer; so to thank God, and then to do nothing, it is a barren thanksgiving. Our deeds have words, our deeds have a voice to God. They speak, they pray. There is a kind of prayer, a kind of thanks in our works. Works pray to God. They have a kind of cry to God, both ill works and good works. And if good works have a cry to God in prayer, they will have a voice in thanksgiving. This fruitful, this real thanks, is that which God stands upon.

And therefore it is alway joined with a study how to improve the things that we thank God for to the best advantage. If we thank God for health, and recovery, and deliverance, we will labour to improve it to God's glory. If we be thankful to God for riches, for peace, we will improve that to grow in grace, to do good to others. There is never a thankful heart, but it studies to improve that which it is thankful for really, that God may have the glory, and it the comfort, and benefit by it; or else it is but a lip-labour, but a lost labour.

Let us shame ourselves, and condemn ourselves for our unthankfulness; and that will be done by comparing our carriage to men with our carriage to God. If so be that a man do us a little courtesy, how are we confounded if we have not returned some thanks? And yet, notwithstanding, from God we have all that we have, all that we are, all that we hope to have; and yet how many benefits do we devour, and do not return God thanks?

This disproportion will shame the best Christian, that he is not so quick in his devotion to God to be thankful there, as he is sensible of small kindnesses done by men. This is a good way to make us more thankful.

And now when we come to the sacrament, let us bless God. The Eucharist is a thanksgiving. Where there are many, there should be thanksgiving. Where there is a communion there is many; and thanksgiving should be especially of many met together to thank God for Christ, and for the good we have by him. For if many joined together in praise for St Paul that was but a minister, that was but an instrument to set out the praise and the doctrine of Christ, much more should we be thankful to God for Christ himself, which is the gift of all gifts, and for which he gives us all other gifts. If he give us him, can he deny us anything? If we be thankful for the health of our bodies, as indeed we should, if we be thankful for the peace of our humours, much more should we be thankful for the peace of our consciences, when our souls are set in tune, when God and we are friends, when the soul by the Spirit of God is set at peace, and is fit for the praise of God, and is fit to do good; when it is a healthful soul.

As in the body, it is a sign it is sick when the actions are hindered; so it is likewise with the soul.

We should bless God for ability to do good, for any health in our souls, more than for health of body. Do but consider, if we are to thank God for the instruments of good, much more are we to thank him for the good things themselves. If we should thank God for the ministers (for now I stand upon that, many prayers and praises were given to God for St Paul) much more should we be thankful for that which we have by the ministry, that is, for all the blessings of God, for grace and glory, for life and salvation. It is the ministry of life, 'and the power of God to salvation,' Rom. i. 16. We should be thankful to God for peace, 'we are the messengers of peace,' Eph. vi. 15. We should be thankful to God for grace, and for his Holy Spirit; the Spirit is given with it. We should be thankful especially for spiritual favours. A man cannot be thankful to God for health and liberty, unless first he know God to be his, that he can bless God for spiritual favours. 'Blessed be God, the Father of our Lord Jesus Christ, who hath blessed us with all spiritual blessings in Christ, Eph. i. 3. We should be thankful for Christ, and all the benefits we have by Christ, much more than for any other blessings whatsoever.

Therefore, now seeing we are a communion, let praise be given by many.* We have greater matters than the health of a minister (or any particular person, either ourselves or others) to be thankful for. We have greater cause, being to bless God for the greatest gift that ever he gave, even for Christ. The disposition in a feast is to be joyful, and cheerful, to praise God. Now we are to feast with God, and with Jesus Christ. Christ is not only the food, but he invites us, he is with us. What will we do for Christ if we will not feast with him? What a degree of unthankfulness is it, when we will not so much as feast with him? when we will not willingly receive him? What will he do for Christ that will not feast with him? How unfit will he be to praise God, and praise Christ, that when Christ makes a feast of himself, and gives himself together with the bread and wine, representing the benefit of his body and blood, broken, and shed for us, and all his benefits? If we will not feed upon himself, when he stoops so low as to give himself for us, and to feed us with himself, what will we do? How can we be thankful for other blessings, when we are not thankful for himself? And how can we be thankful for himself, when we will not come and partake of him?

Let us stir up our hearts and think now to take the communion; as for matter of repentance and sorrow, it should be despatched before. It is the Eucharist, a matter of thanksgiving. We should raise our hearts above earthly things. We should consider that we are to deal with Christ, and these are but representations.

When the bread is broken, think of the body of Christ; and when the wine is poured out, think of the blood of Christ. And when our bodies are cheered by these elements, think how our souls are refreshed by the blood of Christ by faith. If we should be thankful to God for bodily deliverance, how much more should we thank him for our souls, being delivered from hell by the blood of Christ, which is the grand deliverance? Let us dispose our hearts to thankfulness. It is a fit disposition for a feast.

And, as I said, take heed of sin. It chokes thankfulness. Therefore examine thy purposes, how thou comest. If thou come with a purpose to live in sin, thou art an unfit receiver. The place we stand in is holy, the business is holy, we have to deal with a holy God; and therefore if we purpose not to relinquish wicked courses, and to enter into covenant with God, to abstain from sin, we come not aright. 'When thou comest into the house of God, take heed to thy feet,' saith the wise man, Eccles. v. 1. Take heed to thy affections; consider with whom thou hast to deal. But if thou hast renewed thy repentance, and thy purposes with God for the time to come, come with cheerfulness, with a thankful disposition. Thankfulness

* Margin-note here, 'It was a sacrament day.'—G.

is a disposition for a feast. If it be a disposition for bodily deliverance, it is much more for the deliverance of the soul; and much more for Christ, and the blessings we have by him, who is 'all in all.' 'That thanks may be given by many on our behalf.'

VERSE 12.

'*For our rejoicing is this, the testimony of our conscience*,' &c. St Paul in these words doth divers things at once.

1. *He shews a reason why many should pray for him, and give thanks on his behalf.* You have cause, saith he, 'for our rejoicing is this, the testimony of our conscience,' &c. Therefore if many of you give thanks to God for me, it is your duty. My conscience bears me witness that I have carried myself well towards you. You have cause to pray for us, and to praise God for our deliverance, for you have received much good by us. God conveys much good by public persons to those that are under them. Therefore there ought to be many prayers, and many thanks, for them.

2. And again, they ought to pray and give thanks for him, *because they should not lose their labour, they should not lose their prayers, their incense;* because it should be for a man that was gracious with God, that had the testimony of his conscience that he walked in simplicity and godly sincerity, as he saith, 'Pray for us, for we are assured that we have a good conscience,' Heb. xiii. 18. So they are a reason of the former.

3. Another thing that he aims at is, *the preventing* of some imputations.* He was accused in their thoughts at least, and by the words of some false teachers, that were his worst enemies, as you have no enemy, next to the devil, to a minister, like a minister. If a man would see the spirit of the devil, let him look to some of them. St Paul had many enemies, many false brethren, that laid false imputations upon him to disparage him in the thoughts of others, in the thoughts of his hearers. They accounted him an inconstant man, that he came not to them when he promised; and that he suffered affliction, and it was like enough for some desert. They accounted him a despicable man. He suffered afflictions in the world. He wanted discretion to keep himself out of the cross. Nay, saith he, whatsoever you impute to me, and lay upon me, 'our rejoicing is this, the testimony of our conscience,' &c.

4. Again, he aims at this, *to lay the blame upon those false brethren who deserved it.* They think I am a deceiver, they think I am wily. No! I do not walk so, I do not walk in fleshly wisdom as they do that seek themselves, and not you. So I say, St Paul aims at divers things in bringing in these words.

We see here, first of all, that

Doct. The more eminent a man is for place and gifts, the more he should be prayed for, and the more thanks should be given for him.

You have cause, saith St Paul, to do it for me; for our rejoicing is this, that 'we have walked in simplicity and sincerity, &c., and more abundantly to you-ward.' St Paul was a brother as he was a Christian. He was a father, in regard he had called them to the faith; and he was an apostle. In all regards they ought to praise God for him; because he was a father, because he was the father of them, 'you have not many fathers,' saith he,

* That is, 'anticipating.'—G.

and because he was an apostle, a man eminent, by whose means God conveyed a world of good to the church.

To make way to the main thing, observe this in general, that

Obs. Christians are often driven to their apology.

Especially ministers, the fathers of Christians. Holy men in the church are driven to their apology and defence; because those that shine in their own consciences, wicked men labour to darken them in their reputation, that their own wickedness may be the less seen and observed. It hath alway been the policy of Satan, and of wicked men, that so all might seem alike, to lay aspersions upon those that were better men than themselves. St Paul is forced to make his apology, to retire to the testimony of his conscience. 'Our rejoicing is this, the testimony of our conscience,' &c.

Use. Therefore make this use of it, *not to think it strange if we be driven to our apology.*

Quest. But some may say, Is not the life the best apology? as St Peter saith, 'that you may stop the mouths of gainsayers.'

Ans. Yes, of all apologies life is the best, to oppose to all imputations; but notwithstanding it is not enough.

A man is cruel if he make not his apology and defence sometimes. Because his imputations* tend to the hurt of others, being public persons, especially ministers, who have so much authority in the hearts of people, as they can gain by their good life and desert. And if any imputation lie upon them, they are to clear it in words. Their life will not serve the turn, but they must otherwise make their apology, if it be needful, for themselves, as St Paul doth here. It is not only lawful, but expedient sometimes, to speak by way of commendation of ourselves.

In what cases?

1. Not only in case of thankfulness to God, to praise God for his graces in us.

2. And likewise in case of example to others, a man may speak of God's work in him, he may tell what God hath done for his soul, and in his soul, that God may have glory, and others may have benefit.

3. But likewise in the third place, and it was St Paul's case here, a man may speak of himself, by way of apology and defence, that the truth suffer not. It is a kind of betraying the cause, for a man to be silent when he is so accused. Though, as I said, a good life be the best apology, and except there be a good life the verbal apology is to little purpose, yet the apology of life ofttimes in public persons is too little. In these cases we must speak of ourselves, and of the good things of God in us.

Quest. But another query† may be here, May a man glory in that which is in him, of the grace of God that is in him? Our glorying should be in Christ, in the obedience and righteousness of Christ, and in God reconciled through Christ. Can a Christian glory in anything that is in him, which is imperfect?

Ans. I answer briefly, St Paul doth not here glory in the court of justification, but in the court of a Christian conversation. Therein a man may glory in the work of grace in him, in those inward works, and the works that flow from them. When a man is to deal with men, he may set forth his life, nay, when a man is to deal with God, he may set forth his sincerity, not, I say, in the court of justification, but in the court of sanctification, and a holy life. There good works are the ornament of the spouse. They are her jewels. But come to the court of justification, all are dung, as the

* That is, imputations against him.—G.

† Spelled 'quere.'—G.

apostle saith, 'all are dung and dross,' Philip. iii. 8; not worthy to be named. They are not able, they are not strong enough. All that comes from us, and all that is in us, it is not able to bear us out in glorying in the court of justification. 'All are stained as menstruous cloths,' Isa. xxx. 22.

But mark, St Paul speaks of glorying before men, of a sanctified life. He glories not in his conversation and sincerity as a title, but he glories in it as an evidence that his title is good. That whereby he hath his title, is only by the righteousness of Christ. That he hath heaven, and is free from hell, that is the title. But what evidence have you that Christ and his righteousness is yours? There must be somewhat wrought in you, and that is sincere walking. So he allegeth it as an evidence of his state in grace, that that was good. So we see in what case he gloried in his sincerity.

To come to the words.

For the words themselves, they contain the blessed temper of St Paul's spirit in the midst of disgraces, in the midst of imputations. The temper of his spirit it was joyful, glorying.

'Our rejoicing is this.' The ground of it is, 'the testimony of our conscience.'

The matter whereof conscience doth witness and testify, it is conversation. That is the thing testified of.

And the manner positively, 'in simplicity and godly sincerity.' 'In simplicity.' You would think this to be a simple commendation, to commend himself for simplicity; but it is a godly simplicity, whereby we are like to God, to be simple without mixture of sin and hypocrisy, without mixture of error and falsehood. That simplicity that is despised by carnal wretches that stain and defile their consciences, and call them what you will, so you account them not simple. They despise the term of an honest, simple man.

Simplicity is not here taken for a defect of knowledge, as the word is commonly used, but for an excellency whereby we resemble God; that is, free from all mixture of sin and ignorance. 'In simplicity and godly sincerity.' And then negatively, 'not in fleshly wisdom.'

And then, because this setting out of himself might seem to be ostentation, to set down his glorying in his conscience, and in his simplicity, here is a qualification of it likewise. Indeed I glory in my simplicity, and sincerity, that is, in my conversation; but it is by the grace of God. By the grace of God my conversation hath been in godly sincerity, and not in fleshly wisdom. For St Paul was wondrous jealous of his heart, for fear of pride; not I, saith he, 'I laboured more than they all; O, not I, but the grace of God that was in me,' 1 Cor. xv. 10. He was afraid of the least insinuation of spiritual pride, and so he saith here 'Our rejoicing is the testimony of our conscience, that in simplicity and sincerity, by the grace of God.'

And then the extent of this conversation, thus in simplicity and sincerity, in regard of the object. It hath been thus, 'In the world, towards all men that I have conversed with. They can say as much, wheresoever I have lived; 'And more abundantly to you-ward.' My care and conscience hath been to carry myself as I should, 'more abundantly to you-ward,' with whom I have lived longest. This is an excellent evidence of a good man, that he is best liked where he is best known. Now St Paul had lived long amongst them, and he was their father in Christ; and therefore, saith he, my conversation is known, especially to you-ward.

Many men are best trusted where they are least known. Their public conversation is good and plausible, but their secret courses are vile and naught, as those know that are acquainted with their retired courses. But you, saith the apostle, with whom I have lived longest, with whom I have been most, you can bear witness of my conversation, that I have lived so and so in the world, and more abundantly to you-ward.

'This is our rejoicing,' &c. We see here the temper and disposition that St Paul was in. He was in a glorying, in a rejoicing estate. We see then that

A Christian, take him at the worst, his estate is a rejoicing estate.

'Our rejoicing is this.' The word in the original is more than joy, for it is καύχησις, a glorying. 'Our glorying' is this, which is a joy manifesting itself in the outward man, when the heart and the spirit seem as it were to go outward, and, as it were, to meet the thing joyed in. A Christian hath his joy, his glorying, and a glorying that is proper to himself. It is a spiritual joy, as it follows after, 'Our rejoicing is the testimony of our conscience.'

So good is God, that in the worst estate he gives his children matter of rejoicing in this world. He gives them a taste of heaven before they come there. He gives them a grape of Canaan, as Israel. They tasted of Canaan, what a good land it was, before they came thither. So God's children, they have their rejoicing. St Paul swears and protests it, 1 Cor. xv. 31, 'By our rejoicing in Christ Jesus I die daily.' As verily as we joy in all our afflictions, so this is true that I say, that I die daily.

Use. Therefore we should labour *to be of such a temper, as that we may glory, and rejoice.* A Christian hath his rejoicing, but it is a spiritual rejoicing, like his estate. Every creature hath his joy, as St Chrysostom speaks. We do all for joy. All that we do is that we may joy at length. It is the centre of the soul. As rest is to motion, so the desire of all is to joy, to rest in joy. So that heaven itself is termed by the name of joy, happiness itself, 'Enter into thy master's joy,' Matt. xxv. 21. Every creature hath his joy proper to him. Every man hath his joy. A carnal man hath a carnal joy, a spiritual man hath a holy joy.

1. First, he joys in his *election*, which was before all worlds, that his name is written in heaven, as it is, Luke x. 20, 'Rejoice in this, that your names are written in heaven, and not that the devils are subject unto you.'

2. And then, he joys in his *justification*, that he is freed from his sins, Rom. v. 1, 'Being justified by faith we have peace with God through Christ, and we rejoice in afflictions.' Being justified first. There is the way how this joy comes in. A Christian being justified by faith, and freed from the guilt of his sin, it worketh joy.

3. And then, there is a joy of *sanctification*, of a good conscience, of a holy life led, as we see here, 'Our rejoicing is this, the testimony of our conscience, '&c.

4. And then, there is a joy *of glory to come*. 'We rejoice under the hope of glory,' saith the apostle, Rom. v. 2. So a Christian's joy is suitable to himself.

There is no other man that can glory, and be wise, because all men but a Christian, 'they glory in their shame,' Philip. iii. 19, or they glory in vanishing things. A Christian is not ashamed of his joy, of his glorying, because he glories not in his shame. Therefore the apostle here justifies his joy. Our rejoicing is this, I care not if all the world know my joy, it is the 'testimony of my conscience.' As if he should say, Let others rejoice in base pleasures which they will not stand to avow; let others rejoice in riches, in honours, in the favour of men; let them rejoice in what they please, my joy is another kind of joy. 'I rejoice in the testimony of my conscience.' A Christian, as he hath a joy, so he hath a joy that he will stand to, and make it good. There is no other man but he will blush, and have shame in his forehead, that joys in anything that is baser than himself, that joys in outward things. He cannot stand to it, and say, This is my joy. But a Christian hath the warrant of his conscience for that which he joys in, and therefore he is not ashamed of it. Another man dares not reveal his joy.

All the subtilty of the world, is to have the pleasures that sin will afford; and yet withal they study to cover it, that it may not appear. Where is the joy of the ambitious?

His study, his thought, and his joy is to have respect, Haman-like; and yet he studies to conceal this. He dares not have it known. He dares not avow it. 'This is my rejoicing;' for then all the world would laugh at him for a vain person.

Again, the joy of the base-minded man, is in his pleasure, but he dares not avow this. He dares not say, my rejoicing is this; for then every man would scorn him as a beast. The rich man, he joys in his riches, but he dares not be known of this, for he would then be accounted a base earthly-minded man. Every man would scorn him. He studies to have all the pleasure, and all the comfort that these things will afford, and yet to cover them. Because he thinks, that there is a higher matter that he should joy in, if he were not an atheist.

A Christian is not ashamed of his joy, and rejoicing. 'I rejoice in this,' saith he. For,

1. *It is well bred.* It is bred from the Spirit of God witnessing that his name is written in the book of life, witnessing that his sins are forgiven, witnessing that he lives as a Christian should do, witnessing that he hath the evidences of his justification, that he hath a holy life, the pledge likewise of future glory. His joy is well bred.

2. Likewise *it is permanent.* Other men's joy and rejoicing is but as a flash of thorns, as the wise man calls it, as it were, a flame in thorns; as the crackling of thorns, which is sooner gone. And it is an unseemly glorying and rejoicing, for a man to glory in that which is worse than himself, and in that which is out of himself. As all other things are out of a man's self, and worse, and meaner than a man's self; therefore a man cannot rejoice in them, and be wise. It is a disparagement to the wisdom of a man, to glory in things that are meaner than himself, and that are out of himself. A holy Christian hath that in himself, and that which is more excellent than himself, to glory in. 'This is our rejoicing, the testimony of our conscience.'

All other rejoicing it is vain glory, and vain rejoicing. Therefore in Jer. ix. 23, saith he, 'Let not the wise man glory in his wisdom, let not the strong man glory in his strength, let not the rich man glory in his riches;' but if a man will glory, 'let him glory that he knows the Lord to be his,' and that he knows himself to be the Lord's. When he knows the Lord to be his, and himself to be God's by faith, and a good conscience, then there is matter of glorying.

Of all kind of men, God doth hate proud boasters most of all; for glory is the froth of pride, and God hates pride. He opposeth pride, and sets himself in battle array against it, and who can thrive that hath God for his enemy? Boasting and pride in any earthly thing it is against all the commandments almost. It is idolatry, it makes that we boast, and glory in, an idol; whereas we should glory in God that gives it.

And it is spiritual adultery, when we cleave in our affections to some outward thing more than to God. It is false witness. Pride is a false glass. It makes the things and the men themselves that enjoy them to seem greater than they are. The devil amplifies earthly things to a carnal man in a false glass, that they seem big to him; whereas if he could see them in their true colours, they are false things, they are snares and hindrances in the way to heaven, and such names they have. The Scripture gives an ill report of them, 'They are vanity and vexation of spirit,' Eccles. i. 14; because we should be discouraged from setting our affections on these things, and from glorying in them.

Therefore let us take heed of false glorying. If we will glory, we see here what we are to glory in. 'This is our rejoicing, the testimony of our conscience,' &c. And this we may justify and stand by that. It is good. It is the 'testimony of conscience.'

'This is our rejoicing, the testimony of our conscience.'

The testimony of conscience, it is a matter and ground of joy to a true Christian. Here we are to consider these things.

First, to consider a little *the nature of conscience.*

And then, *that conscience bears witness;* that there is a testimony of conscience.

And that this conscience bearing witness *is a ground of comfort.*

For the first,

Every man feels and knows what conscience means. There be many rigid disputes of it among the schoolmen that had leisure enough; and of all men knew as little, and felt what it was, as any sort of men, living under the darkness of popery and superstition, and being in thraldom to the pope, and to the corruptions of the times they lived in. They have much jangling about the description of it, whether it be the soul itself, or a faculty, or an act.

In a word, conscience is all these in some sort, in divers respects. Therefore I will not wrangle with any particular opinion.

1. *For what is conscience, but the soul itself reflecting upon itself?* It is the property of the reasonable soul and the excellency of it, that it can return upon itself. The beast cannot; for it runs right forward. It knows it is carried to the object; but it cannot return and recoil upon itself. But the soul of the reasonable creature, of all even from men to God himself, who understands in the highest degree, though he do not discourse as man doth, yet he knows himself, he knows and understands his own excellency. And wheresoever there is understanding, there is a reflect act whereby the soul returns upon itself, and knows what it doth. It knows what it wills, it knows what it affects, it knows what it speaks, it knows all in it, and all out of it. It is the property of the soul. Therefore the original word in the Old Testament that signifies the heart, it is taken for the conscience (*gg*). Conscience and heart are all one. I am persuaded in my soul, that is, in my conscience; and the Spirit witnesseth to our spirit, that is, to our conscience. Conscience is called the spirit, the heart, the soul; because it is nothing but the soul reflecting and returning upon itself.

Therefore it is called conscience, that is, one knowing joined with another; because conscience knows itself, and it knows what it knows. It knows what the heart is. It not only knows itself, but it is a knowledge of the heart with God. It is called conscience, because it knows with God;

for what conscience knows, God knows, that is above conscience. It is a knowledge with God, and a knowledge of a man's self.

And so it may be the soul itself endued with that excellent faculty of reflecting and returning upon itself. Therefore it judgeth of its own acts, because it can return upon itself.

2. Conscience likewise in some sort may be called *a faculty*. The common stream runs that way, that it is a power. It is not one power, but conscience is in all the powers of the soul; for it is in the understanding, and there it rules. Conscience is it by which it is ruled and guided. Conscience is nothing but an application of it to some particular, to something it knows, to some rules it knows before. Conscience is in the will, in the affections, the joy of conscience, and the peace of conscience, and so it runs through the whole soul. It is not one faculty, or two, but it is placed in all the faculties.

3. And some will needs have it *an act, a particular act*, and not a power. When it doth exercise, conscience, it is an act. When it accuseth, or excuseth, or when it witnesseth, it is an act. At that time it is a faculty in act. So that we need not to wrangle whether it be this or that. Let us comprehend as much in our notions as we can; that it is the soul, the heart, the spirit of a man returning upon itself, and it hath something to do in all the powers; and it is an act itself when it is stirred up to accuse or to excuse; to punish a man with fears and terrors, or to comfort him with joy, and the like.

Now conscience is a most excellent thing, it is above reason and sense; for conscience is under God, and hath an eye to God alway. An atheist can have no conscience therefore, because he takes away the ground of conscience, which is an eye to God. Conscience looks to God. It is placed as God's deputy and vicegerent in man. Now it is above reason in this respect. Reason saith, you ought to do this, it is a comely thing, it is a thing acceptable with men amongst whom you live and converse, it becomes your condition as you are a man to carry yourself thus, it agrees with the rules and principles of nature in you. Thus saith reason, and they are good motives from reason. But conscience goeth higher. There is a God to whom I must answer, there is a judgment, therefore I do this, and therefore I do not this. It is a more divine, a more excellent power in man than anything else, than sense or reason, or whatsoever. As it is planted by God for special use, so it looks to God in all.

Therefore the name for conscience in the Greek and Latin signifies a knowledge with another (*hh*); because it is a knowledge with God. God and my own heart knows this. God and my conscience, as we use to say.

There are three things joined with conscience.

1. *It is a knowledge with a rule, with a general rule.* That is alway the foundation of conscience in a man (*ii*). For there is a general rule.—Whosoever commits murder, whosoever commits adultery, whosoever is a blasphemer, a swearer, a covetous, corrupt person, 'he shall not enter into the kingdom of heaven,' as the apostle saith, 1 Cor. vi. 9, *seq.* Here is the general rule. Now conscience applies it, but I am such a one, therefore I shall not enter into heaven. So here the conscience it practiseth with a rule. It is a knowledge of those particulars with a general rule. And then,

2. *It is a knowledge of me, of my own heart.* I know what I have done, I know what I do, and in what manner, whether in hypocrisy or sincerity; I know what I think. And then,

3. *It is a knowledge with God;* for God knows what conscience knows.

He knows what is thought or done. Conscience is above me, and God is above conscience. Conscience is above me and above all men in the world; for it is immediately subjugated to God. Conscience knows more than the world, and God knows a thousand times more than conscience or the world. It is a knowledge with a general rule; for where there is no general rule there is no conscience. To make this a little clearer. All have a rule. Those that have not the word, which is the best rule of all, yet they have the word written in their hearts; they have a natural judicature in their souls, their conscience excusing, or accusing one another. They have a general rule. You must do no wrong, you must do that which is right.

In the soul there is a treasure of rules by nature. The word doth add more rules, the law and the gospel. And that part of the soul that preserves rules is called intellectual, because it preserves rules. All men by nature have these graven in the soul. And therefore the heathen were exact in the rules of justice, in the principles which they had by nature, grafted and planted in them.

Now because the copy of the image of God, the law of God written in nature, was much blurred since the fall, God gave a new copy of his law, which was more exact. Therefore the Jews, which had the word of God, should have had more conscience than the heathen, because they had a better general rule. And now we having the gospel too, which is a more evangelical rule, we should be more exact in our lives than they.

But every man in the world hath a rule. If men 'sin without the law, they shall be judged without the law,' Rom. ii. 12, by the principles of nature. If they sin under the gospel, they shall be judged by the word and gospel. So that conscience, it is a knowledge with a rule, and with the particular actions that I have done, and a knowledge with God.

In a word, to clear this further concerning the nature of conscience, know that God hath set up in man a court, and there is in man all that are in a court.

1. There is a *register* to take notice of what we have done. Besides the general rule (for that is the ground and foundation of all), there is conscience, which is a register to set down whatsoever we have done exactly. The conscience keeps diaries. It sets down everything. It is not forgotten, though we think it is, when conscience is once awaked. As in Jer. xvii. 1, 'The sins of Judah are written with a pen of iron, and with the point of a diamond' upon their souls. All their wit and craft will not rase it out. It may be forgotten a while, by the rage of lusts, or one thing or other; but there is a register that writes it down. Conscience is the register.

2. And then there are *witnesses*. 'The testimony of conscience.' Conscience doth witness, this I have done, this I have not done.

3. There is an *accuser with the witness*. The conscience, it accuseth, or excuseth.

4. And then there is *the judge*. Conscience is the judge. There it doth judge, this is well done, this is ill done.

5. Then there is *an executioner*, and conscience is that too. Upon accusation and judgment, there is punishment. The first punishment is within a man alway before he come to hell. The punishment of conscience, it is a prejudice* of future judgment. There is a flash of hell presently after an ill act. The heathen could observe, that God hath framed the

* That is, 'pre-judgment.'—G.

heart and the brain so as there is a sympathy between them, that whatsoever is in the understanding that is well and comfortable, the understanding in the brain sends it to the heart, and raiseth some comfort. If the understanding apprehend dolorous things, ill matters, then the heart smites, as David's 'heart smote him,' 1 Sam. xxiv. 5. The heart smites with grief for the present, and with fear for the time to come.

In good things, it brings joy presently, and hope for the time to come, that follows a good excusing conscience.

God hath set and planted in man this court of conscience, and it is God's hall, as it were, wherein he keeps his first judgment, wherein he keeps his assizes. And conscience doth all the parts. It registereth, it witnesseth, it accuseth, it judgeth, it executes, it doth all.

Now you see in general, what the nature of conscience is, and why it is planted in us by God.

One main end among the rest, besides his love to us to keep us from sin, and then by smiting us to drive us to conversion and repentance, to turn from our sins to God, another main end, is to be a prejudice,* to make way to God's eternal judgment; for therein things are judged before. When God lays open the book of conscience, when it is written there by this register, we shall have much to do to excuse ourselves, or to plead that we need many witnesses; for our conscience will accuse us. We shall be self-accusers, self-condemners, as the apostle saith. Conscience will take God's part, and God will take part with conscience. And God hath planted it for this main end, that he might be justified in the damnation of wicked men at the day of judgment.

Now I come to the second particular, that conscience gives evidence or witness. 'This is the evidence or testimony of our conscience.' The witness of conscience it comes in this order. Upon some general rules, that the conscience hath laid up in the soul, out of nature, and out of the book of God, the conscience doth apply those generals to the particulars.

First, *in directing*. This is such a truth in general, you ought to carry yourself thus and thus, to do this, saith conscience.† So it directeth, and is a monitor before it be a witness. Well, if the monitions of conscience be regarded and heard, from thence comes conscience to witness, that the general rule that directs in particulars hath been obeyed; and so after it hath done its duty in directing, it comes to judge and to witness, this I have done, or this I have not done. So the witness of conscience comes in that manner.

Now if you would know what manner of witness conscience is. It is, 1. A witness that *there is no exception against*. It is a witness that will say all the truth, and will say nothing but the truth. It is a witness that will not be bribed, it will not be corrupted long. For a time we may silence it, but it will not be so long, nor in all things. Some sins may be slubbered over, but there are some sins that by the general light in nature are so known to be naught‡ that conscience will accuse. Therefore it is a faithful judge and witness; especially in great sins, it is an uncorrupt witness. It is a true register. It is alway writing and setting down, though we know not what it writes for the present, being carried away with vanities and lusts. Yet we shall know afterward, when the book of conscience shall be laid open.

It is a witness that we cannot impeach. No man can say, I had nobody

* That is, 'pre-judgment.'—G. † Margin-note here, 'Joseph's brethren.'—G.
‡ That is, 'naughty, wicked.'—G.

to tell me. Alas! a man's own conscience will tell him well enough at the day of judgment, and say to him when he is in hell, as Reuben said to his brethren, when they were in Egypt in prison, 'Did not I tell you, hurt not the boy?' Gen. xxxvii. 22, *seq*, meddle not with him. So conscience will say, Did not I witness? did not I give you warning? Yes, I did, but you regarded it not. It is a faithful witness. There is no exception against it.

2. And then it is *an inward witness*, it is a domestic witness; a chaplain in ordinary, a domestical divine. It is alway telling us, and alway ready to put good things into us. It is an eye-witness, and an ear-witness; for it is as deep in man as any sin can be. If it be but in thought, conscience tells me what I think; and conscience tells me what I desire, as well as what I speak, and what I do. It is an inward and an eye-witness of everything. As God sees all, and knows all, who is all eye; so conscience is all eye. It sees everything, it hears everything. It is privy to our thoughts.

As we cannot escape God's eye, so we cannot escape the eye of conscience. 'Whither shall I flee from thy presence?' saith David. 'If I go to heaven, thou art there; if I go down into hell, thou art there,' Ps. cxxxix. 7. So a man may say of conscience, Whither shall I flee from conscience? If a man could flee from himself, it were somewhat. Conscience is such a thing as that a man cannot flee from it, nor he cannot bid it begone. It is as inward as his soul. Nay, the soul will leave the body, but conscience will not leave the soul. What it writes, it writes for eternity, except it be wiped out by repentance. As St Chrysostom saith, whatsoever is written there may be wiped out by daily repentance.

You see, then, it is a witness, and how and what manner of witness conscience is.

Use. Therefore, we should not sin in hope of concealment. What if thou conceal it from all others, canst thou conceal [it from] thy own conscience? As one saith well, What good is it for thee that none knows what is done, when thou knowest it thyself? What profit is it for him that hath a conscience that will accuse him, that he hath no man to accuse him but himself? He is a thousand witnesses to himself. Conscience is not a private witness. It is a thousand witnesses. Therefore, never sin in hope to have it concealed. It were better that all men should know it than that thyself should know it. All will be one day written in thy forehead. Conscience will be a blab. If it cannot speak the truth now, though it be bribed in this life, it will have power and efficacy in the life to come. Never sin, therefore, in hope of concealment. Conscience is a witness. We have the witness in us; and, as Isaiah saith, 'Our sins witness against us.' It is in vain to look for secrecy. Conscience will discover all.

Use. Again, considering that conscience doth witness, and will witness, let us labour *that it may witness well*, let us labour *to furnish it with a good testimony*. Let us carry ourselves so in all our demeanour to God and men that conscience may give a good testimony, a good witness. It will witness either for us or against us.

1. Therefore, first of all, labour *to have good rules to guide it,* and then labour to obey those rules. Knowledge and obedience are necessary, that conscience may give a good witness. Now, a good witness of conscience is twofold: a true and honest witness, and then a peaceable witness follows on it; that it may witness truth, and then that it may witness peace for us.

That conscience may witness truly and excuse us, conscience must be rightly instructed; for naturally conscience can tell us many things. The heathen men, philosophers, we may read it to our shame, they made conscience of things which Christians, that are instructed by a further rule than conscience, that have the book of God to rectify the inward book of conscience, yet they make no conscience of. How many cases did they make scruple of, to discover faults to the buyer in their selling, and to deal truly and honestly, for the second table especially! It should make Christians ashamed.

But besides that rule, we have the rule of the Scriptures, because men are ready to trample upon and to rase out the writing of conscience, but the book of God they cannot; therefore, that is added to help conscience. And God adds his Spirit to his word to convince conscience, and to make the witness of the word more effectual; for although the word say thus and thus, yet till the Spirit convince the soul, and set it down that it is thus, till it convince it with a heavenly light, conscience will not be fully convict. That conscience, therefore, may be able to witness well, let us regard the notions of nature, preserve them. If we do not, God will give us up to gross sins. Let us labour to have right principles and grounds, to cherish principles of nature common with the heathens, and to lay up principles out of the word of God, to preserve the admonitions, and directions, and rules of the word.

And especially the sweet motions of God's blessed Spirit. For conscience alway supposeth a rule, the rule of nature, the rule of the word, and the suggestions of the blessed Spirit with the word.

Therefore, to note by the way, an ignorant man can never have a good conscience, especially a man that affects ignorance, because he hath no rule. He labours to have none. It is not merely ignorance, but likewise obstinacy with ignorance.

He will not know what he should, lest conscience will force him to do what he knows. What a sottish thing is this! It will be the heaviest sin that can be laid to our charge at the day of judgment, not that we were ignorant, but that we refused to know, we refused to have our conscience rectified and instructed.

And those that avoid knowledge because they will not do what they know, they shall know one day that their wilful ignorance will be laid to their charge as a heavy sin.

Labour to have right principles and grounds. What is the reason that commonly men have such bad consciences? They have false principles. They conclude, May I not do what I list? may I not make of my own what I will? and every man for himself, and God for us all. Diabolical principles! And so, commonly if a man examine men that live in wickedness, they have false principles, God sees not, God regards not, and it is time enough to repent. The cause that men live wickedly is false principles. Therefore they have so vile consciences as they have. Their hearts deceive them, and they deceive their hearts. They have false principles put into them by others. They are deceived, and they deceive their hearts. They force false principles upon themselves. Many study for false grounds to live by for their advantage.

There are many that are atheistical, that live even under the gospel, and what rule have they? The example of them by whom they hope to rise. They study their manners. They square their lives by them. This is all the rule they have.

And again, the multitude. They do as the most do, and custom, and other false rules. These rules will not comfort us. To say, I did it by such an example, I did as others among whom I live did, or I did it because it was the custom of the times; these things being alleged will comfort nothing. For who gave you these rules? Doth God say anywhere in his word, You shall be judged by the example of others, you shall be judged by the custom of the times you live in?

No; you shall be judged by my word. The word that Moses spake, 'and the word that I speak, shall judge you' at the last day, John xii. 48. They that have not the word shall be judged by the word written in their hearts. 'Those that have sinned without the law' shall be judged by that, 'without the law of Moses,' Rom. ii. 12.

God hath acquainted us with other rules. We must take heed of this, therefore, that we get good rules. Take heed that they be not false rules. For the want of these directions men come to have ill consciences. Where there is no good rule, there is a blind conscience; where there is no application of the rule, there is a profane conscience; and where there is a false rule, there is an erroneous, a scrupulous, a wicked conscience.

A papist, because he hath a false rule, he cannot have a good conscience. The abomination of popery is, that they sin against conscience; and conscience, indeed, is even with them, for it overthrows the most of their principles. They sin against conscience many ways, I mean not against their own conscience, but they sin against the conscience of others. For what do they? That they may rule in the consciences of men (for that is the end of their great prelate, the tyrant of souls), they have false rules, that the pope cannot err. Their rule is the authority and judgment of him that cannot err; and he, for the most part, is an unlearned man in divinity, that never read over the Scriptures in all his life, and he must judge all controversies. Where this is granted, that the pope cannot err, he sits in the conscience to do what he list. And he makes divine laws; and cursed is he, saith the Council of Trent, that doth not equalise those traditions with the word of God (*jj*).

From this false rule comes all, even rebellion itself. If he give dispensation from the oath of allegiance because he cannot err, therefore they ought to obey him, and rebel against their governors. All rebellion is from that rebellious rebellion that comes from false principles. These men talk of conscience, and they come not to church for conscience sake. What conscience can they have when they have false rules? To equivocate and lie,—sins against nature. And other rules, that give liberty against the word; that children may disobey their parents, and get into a cloister, &c.

The most of popery, though there were no word of God, it is against nature, against conscience, which God hath planted in man as his deputy, his tenant.

And as they sin against conscience, so, as I said, conscience is even with them. For let a man trust to his conscience, and he can never be a sound papist: except he leave that, and go upon base false grounds, because other great men do it, and because his predecessors have done it, &c. I appeal to their own consciences, if any man at the day of death think to be saved by his merits, doth not Bellarmine (after long dispute of salvation by merits) disclaim it?* doth he not put away merits, for the uncertainty of his own righteousness? So their own consciences do wring away the testimony of trusting to merits.

* See Note *g*, vol. I. p. 313.—G.

Again, that original sin is no great sin. It is but the cause of sin, and it is less than any venial sin. Oh, but when conscience is awaked to know what a corrupt estate it is, it will draw from them that which it drew from St Paul, 'O wretched man that I am, who shall deliver me from this body of death?' Rom. vii. 24. Conscience, when it is awaked, will tell them that it is another manner of sin, and that it is the fountain of all sin.

And so for justification by works. Conscience itself, if there were no book of God, would say it is a false point. And then they plead for ignorance. They have blind consciences. Their clergy being a subtle generation, that have abused the world a long time, because they would sit in the conscience where God should sit, they 'sit in the temple of God,' 2 Thess. ii. 4, and would be respected above that which is due to them—they would be accounted as petty gods in the world. Therefore they keep the people from the knowledge of the true rule, and make what they speak equal with God's word. Now if the people did discern this, they would not be papists long; for no man would willingly be cozened. Let us labour therefore for a true rule.

2. And when we have gotten rules, *apply them;* for what are rules without application? Rules are instrumental things; and instruments without use are nothing. If a carpenter have a rule, and hang it up by him, and work by conceit, what is it good for? So to get a company of rules by the word of God (to refine natural knowledge as much as we can), and then to make no use of it in our lives, it is to no purpose; therefore when we have rules, let us apply them.

In this, those that have the true rule, and apply it not, are better than they that refuse to have the rule, because, as hath been said, an ignorant man that hath not the rule, he cannot be good. But a man that hath the rule, and yet squares not his life by it, yet he can bring the rule to his life. There is a near converse between the heart and the brain. Such a man, he hath the rule in his memory, he hath it in his understanding; and therefore there is a thousand times more hope of him that cares to know, that cares to hear the word of God, and cares for the means, than of sottish persons that care not to hear, because they would not do that they know, and because they would not have their sleepy, dull, and drowsy conscience awaked. There is no hope of such a one. It should be our care to have right rules, and in the application of them to make much of conscience, that it may apply aright in directing, and then in comfort. If we obey it in directing, it will witness and excuse; and upon witness and excuse, there will come a sweet paradise to the soul, of joy and peace unspeakable and glorious.

The last thing I observe from these words is this, that

Doct. The testimony and witness of conscience is a ground of comfort and joy.

The reason of the joining these two, the witness of a good conscience, and joy, it is that which I said before in the description of conscience; for

1. *Conscience first admonisheth, and then witnesseth, and then it excuseth, or accuseth, and then it judgeth, and executeth.** Now the inward execution of conscience is joy, if it be good; for God hath so planted it in the heart and soul, that where conscience doth accuse, or excuse, there is alway execution. There is alway joy or fear. The affections of joy or fear alway follow. If a man's conscience excuse him, that he hath done well, then conscience comes to be enlarged, to be a paradise to the soul. to be a jubilee,

* In the margin, 'From the office of conscience.'—G.

a refreshing, to speak peace and comfort to a man. For rewards are not kept altogether for the life to come. Hell is begun in an ill conscience, and heaven is begun in a good conscience. An ill conscience is a hell upon earth, a good conscience is a heaven upon earth. Therefore the testimony of a good conscience breeds glorying and rejoicing.

2. Again, conscience when it witnesseth, *it comforts, because when it witnesseth, it witnesseth with God;* and where God is, there is his Spirit, and where the Holy Spirit is, there is joy. For even as heat follows the fire, so joy and glorying accompany the Spirit of God, 'the Spirit of glory,' 1 Pet. i. 14. Now when conscience witnesseth aright, it witnesseth with God; and God is alway clothed with joy. He brings joy and glory into the heart. Conscience witnesseth with God that I am his.

3. And *it witnesseth with myself that I have led my life thus,* 'Our rejoicing is the witness of *our* conscience.' It is not the witness of another man's conscience, but my own. Other men may witness, and say I am thus and thus, but all is to no purpose, if my own conscience tell me I am another man than they take me to be. But when a man's own conscience witnesseth for him, there follows rejoicing. A man cannot rejoice with the testimony of another man's conscience, because another man saith, I am a good man, &c., unless there be the testimony of my own conscience.

Now it is a sweet benefit, an excusing conscience, when it witnesseth well. Let us see it in all the passages of life, that a good conscience in excusing breeds glorying and joy.

It doth breed joy *in life, in death, at the day of judgment.*

1. *In life,* in all the passages of life, in all estates, both good and ill.

(1.) *In good,* the testimony of conscience breeds joy, for it enjoys the pleasures of this life, and the comforts of it with the favour of God. Conscience tells the man that he hath gotten the things well that he enjoys, that he hath gotten the place, and advancement that he hath, well: that he enjoys the comforts of this life with a good conscience, and 'all things are pure to the pure,' Titus i. 15. If he have gotten them ill, conscience upbraids him alway, and therefore he cannot joy in the good estate he hath. If a man had all the contentments in the world, if he had not the testimony of a good conscience, what were all? What contentment had Adam in paradise, after once by sin he had fallen from the peace of conscience? None at all. 'A little that the righteous hath, is better than great riches of the ungodly,' Prov. xvi. 8, because they have not peace of conscience.

(2.) And so for *ill estate,* when conscience witnesseth well, it breeds rejoicing.

[1.] In false imputations, and slanders, and disgraces, as here, it was insinuated into the Corinthians by false teachers, and those that followed them, that St Paul was so and so. Saith St Paul, You may say what you will of me, 'my rejoicing is this, the testimony of my conscience,' that I am not the man which they make me to be in your hearts by their false reports. The witness of conscience is a good and sufficient ground of rejoicing in this case. Therefore holy men have retired to their conscience in all times, as St Paul you see doth here.

So Job, his conscience bare him out in all the false imputations of his comfortless friends that were 'miserable comforters,' Job xvi. 2. They laboured to take away his sincerity from him, the chief cause of his joy. 'You shall not take away my sincerity,' saith he, Job xxvii. 6. You would make me an hypocrite, and thus and thus, but my conscience tells me I am otherwise, therefore 'you shall not take away my innocency from me.' And in Job xxxi. 35, 'Behold, it is my desire, that the Almighty would answer me, and that my adversaries would write a book against me, I would take it upon my shoulder, I would take it as a crown unto me.' Here was the force of a good conscience in Job's troubles, that if his adversaries should write a book against him, yet he would bind it as a crown about him, xxxi. 36. And so David, in all imputations this was his joy, when they laid things to his charge that he had never done: he takes this for his joy, the comfort of his conscience. So St Paul, he retires to his conscience, and being raised up with the worthiness of a good conscience, he despiseth all imputations whatsoever. He sets conscience up as a flag of defiance to all false slanders and imputations that were laid against him, as we see in the story of the Acts, and in this place and others. Saith he in one place, 'I pass not for man's sentence,' 1 Cor. iv. 3, I pass not for man's day. Man hath his day, man will have his judgment-seat, and will get upon the bench, and judge me that I am such and such. I care not for man's day. There is another judgment-seat that I look unto, and to the testimony of my conscience, 'My rejoicing is the witness of my conscience.'

Holy men have cause to retire to their own consciences, when they would rejoice against false imputations. So holy St Austin, what saith he to a Donatist that wronged him in his reputation? 'Think of Austin what you please, as long as my conscience accuseth me not with God, I will give you leave to think what you will' (*kk*).

If so be that man's conscience clears him, he cares not a whit for reports; because a good man looks more to conscience than to fame. Therefore if conscience tell him truth, though fame lie he cares not much; for he squares not his life by report, but by conscience. Indeed he looks to a good name, but that is in the last place.

For a good man looks first to God, who is above conscience; and then he looks to conscience, which is under God; and then, in the third place, he looks to report amongst men. And if God and his conscience excuse him, though men accuse him, and lay imputations upon him, this or that, he passeth little for man's judgment. So the witness of conscience, it comforts in all imputations whatsoever.

[2.] Again, *it comforts in sickness.* Hezekiah was sick. What doth he retire unto? 'Remember, Lord, how I have walked uprightly before thee,' Isa. xxxviii. 3. He goes to his conscience.

In sickness, when a man can eat nothing, a good 'conscience is a continual feast,' Prov. xv. 15. In sorrow it is a musician. A good conscience doth not only counsel and advise, but it is a musician to delight. It is a physician to heal. It is the best cordial, the best physic. All other are physicians of no value, comforts of no value. If a man's conscience be wounded, if it be not quieted by faith in the blood of Christ; if he have not the Spirit to witness the forgiveness of his sins, and to sanctify and enable him to lead a good life, all is to no purpose, if there be an evil conscience. The unsound body while it is sick, it is in a kind of hell already.

[3.] Again, *take a man in any cross whatsoever, a good conscience doth bear out the cross, it bears a man up alway.* Because a good conscience, being a witness with God, it raiseth a man above all earthly things whatsoever. There is no earthly discouragement that can dismay a good conscience, because there is a kind of divinity in conscience, put in by God, and it witnesseth together with God. So that in all crosses it comforts.

So likewise in losses, in want, in want of friends, in want of comforts, in want of liberty; what doth the witness of a good conscience in all these? In want of friends, it is a friend indeed; it is an inward friend, a near friend to us. Put the case that a man have never a friend in the world, yet he hath God and his own conscience. Where there is a good conscience, there is God and his Holy Spirit alway. In want of liberty, in want of outward comforts, he hath the comfort of a good conscience.

A man on his death-bed, he sees he wants all outward comforts, but he hath a good conscience. And so in want of liberty, when a man is restrained, his heart is at liberty.

A wicked man that hath a bad conscience, is imprisoned in his own heart. Though he have never such liberty, though he be a monarch, a bad conscience imprisons him at home, he is in fetters, his thoughts make him afraid of thunder, afraid of everything, afraid of himself; and though there be nobody else to awe him, yet his conscience awes him. Where there is a conscience under the guilt of sin unrepented, [though] there is the greatest liberty in the world, there is restraint; for conscience is the worst prison. Where there is a good conscience, there is an inward enlargement. A good man in the greatest restraint hath liberty. Paul and Silas, Acts xvi., in the dungeon, in the hell of the dungeon, in the worst place of the dungeon, in the stocks, and at the worst time of the day, of the natural day, I mean, at midnight, and in the worst usage, when they were misused, and whipped withal, they had all the discouragements that could be; and yet they sang at midnight, these blessed men, Paul and Silas. Because their hearts were enlarged, there was a paradise in the very dungeon.

As where the king is, there is his court, so it is where God is. God in the prison, in the noisome dungeon, by his Spirit so enlarged their hearts, that they sang at midnight. Whereas if conscience be ill, if it were in paradise, conscience would fear, as we see in Adam, Gen. iii. 8. St Paul in prison was better than Adam in paradise, when he had offended God. Adam had outward comforts enough; but when he had sinned, his conscience made him afraid of him from whom he should have all comfort; it made him afraid of God, and hide himself among the leaves. Alas, a poor shift! We see then, conscience doth witness, and the witness of it when it is good doth cause the soul to glory and rejoice, not only in positive ills, in slanders and crosses, but in losses, in want of friends, in want of comforts, in want of liberty.

And so for the time to come, in evils threatened, a good conscience is bold: 'It fears no ill tidings,' Ps. cxii. 8. 'My heart is fixed, my heart is fixed,' saith David. 'Wicked men are like the trees of the forest. Wicked Ahaz,' his heart 'did tremble and shake as the leaves with the wind,' Isa. vii. 2. The noise of fear is alway in their ears. An ill conscience, when it is mingled with ill news, when there are two fears together, it must needs be a great fear.

2. And a good conscience, when it hath laid up grounds of joy in life, in the worst estate and condition of life, *then it makes use of joy in death;* for when all comforts are taken from a man, when his friends cannot comfort him, and all earthly things leave him, then that conscience that hath gone along with him, that hath been a monitor, and a witness all his lifetime, now it comes to speak good things to him, now it comforts him, now conscience is somebody. At the hour of death, when nothing else will be regarded, when nothing will comfort, then conscience doth. 'The righteous hath hope in his death,' as the wise man saith, Prov. xiv. 32. Death is

called the king of fears, because it makes all afraid. It is the terrible of terribles, saith the philosopher ; but here is a king above the king of fears. A good conscience is above the king of fears, death. A good conscience is so far from being discouraged by this king of fears, that it is joyful even in death ; because it knows that then it is near to the place where conscience shall be fully enlarged, where there shall be no annoyance, nor no grievance whatsoever.

Death is the end of misery, and the beginning of happiness. Therefore a good conscience is joyful in death.

3. And after death, *at the day of judgment*. There the witness of conscience is a wondrous cause of joy ; for there a man that hath a good conscience, he looks upon the Judge, his brother : he looks on him with whom he has made his peace in his lifetime before, and now he receives that which he had the beginnings of before, then he lifts up his head with joy and comfort. So you see how the witness of conscience causeth glory and joy in all estates whatsoever, in life, in death, after death. It speaks for a man there. It never leaves him till it have brought him to heaven itself, where all things else leave a man.

Therefore, how much should we prize and value the testimony and witness of a good conscience ! And what madness is it for a man to humour men, and displease conscience, his best friend ! Of all persons and all things in the world, we should reverence our own conscience most of all. Wretched men despise the inward witness of this inward friend, this inward divine, this inward physician, this inward comforter, this inward counsellor. It is no better than madness that men should regard that everything else be good and clean, and yet notwithstanding in the midst of all to have foul consciences.

Obj. But to answer an objection, and to unloose some knots. It may be said, that when the hearts of people are good, yet there a good conscience concludes not alway for comfort. Where there is faith in Christ, and an honest life, conscience should conclude comfort. Here is the rule, this I have obeyed, therefore I should have comfort.

Now this we see crossed ofttimes, that Christians that live exact lives are often troubled in conscience. How can trouble of conscience stand with joy upon the witness of conscience ?

Ans. I answer, the witness of conscience, when it is a good conscience, it doth not alway breed joy.

1. *It is because our estate is imperfect here*, and conscience doth not alway witness out of the goodness of it. Sometime conscience is misled, and so sometimes good Christians take the error of conscience for the witness of conscience.

These things should be distinguished. Conscience sometime in the best errs, as well as gives a true witness.

If we take the error of conscience for the witness of conscience, there will come trouble of conscience, and that deservedly, through our own folly.

Now conscience doth err in good men, sometimes when they regard rules which they should not, or when they mistake the matter and do not argue aright. As for instance, when they gather thus, I have not grace in such a measure, and therefore I have none, I am not the child of God.

What a rule is this ? This is the error of conscience ; and therefore it must needs breed perplexity of conscience. A good conscience, when it is right, cannot witness thus, because the word doth not say thus. Is a nullity and an imperfection all one ? No ; there is much difference in the whole kind. A nullity is nothing. An imperfection, though it be but a little degree, yet it is something. This is the error of conscience, and from thence comes trouble of conscience, which makes men reason ill many ways. As for instance, I have not so much grace as such a one hath, and therefore I have no grace. Now that is a false reasoning; for every one hath his due measure. If thou be not so great a rich man as the richest in the town, yet thou mayest be rich in thy kind.

2. Again, when conscience *looks to the humour*. You are to live by faith, and not by the humour of melancholy. When the instrument of reason that should judge is distempered by melancholy, it reasons from thence falsely. Because melancholy persuades me that I am so, therefore conscience being led by the humour of the body, saith I am so. Who bade thee live by humour? thou must live by rule. Melancholy may tell thee sometime when it is in strength, that thou art made of glass, as it hath done some. It will deceive thee in bodily things, wherein sense can confute melancholy, much more will it if we yield to it in matters of the soul. It will persuade us that we are not the children of God, that we have not grace and goodness when we have.

3. Again, hence it is that conscience doth not conclude comfort in God's children, *because it looks to the ill*, and not to the good that is in them; for there are those two things in God's children. There is good and ill. Now in the time of temptation they look to the ill, and think they have no good, because they will not see anything but ill. They fix their eyes on the remainders of their rebellious lusts, which are not fully subdued in them, and they look wholly on them. Whereas they should have two eyes, one to look on that which is good, that God may have glory and they comfort.

Now they, fixing their eyes altogether on that which is naught, and because they do not, or will not, see that which is good, therefore they have no comfort; because they suffer conscience to be ill led that it doth not its duty.

And conscience in good men, it looks sometimes to that that it should not in others, in regard of others. It looks to the flourishing of wicked men, and therefore it concludes, 'Certainly I have washed my hands in vain,' since such men thrive and prosper in the world, Ps. xxxvii. 35, *seq.*, and Ps. lxxiii. 13. Who bade thee look to this, and to be uncomfortable from thence, that thy estate is not good, because it is not such an estate? 'So foolish, and as a beast was I before thee,' saith David, because I regarded such things, Ps. lxxiii. 22. No marvel if men be uncomfortable that are led away by scandals. Look to faith, go to the word, to the sanctuary. 'I went to the sanctuary,' saith he, 'and there I saw the end of these men,' ver. 17. So conscience must be suffered to have its work, to be led by a true rule.

4. Again, conscience sometimes concludes not comfort, when there is ground of comfort, *from the remainders of corruptions and infirmities*; whereas we should be driven by our infirmities to Christ. And conscience sometimes in good men doth not exercise its work. It is drawn away with vain delights, even in the best of men.

And conscience, of its own unworthiness, and of the greatness of the things it looks for, being joined together, it makes a man that he joys not when he hath cause. As for instance, when the soul sees that God in Christ hath pardoned all my sins, and hath vouchsafed his Spirit to me, and will give me heaven in the world to come, to such a wretch as I am; here being a conflict between the conscience and sense of its own unworthiness, and the greatness of the good promised, the heart begins to stagger, and to doubt for want of sound faith.

Indeed, if we look on our own unworthiness, and the greatness of the good things promised, we may wonder; but alas!* God is infinite in goodness, he transcends our unworthiness; and in the gospel, the glory of God's mercy, it triumphs over our unworthiness, and over our sins. Whatsoever our sin and unworthiness is, his goodness in the gospel triumphs over all.

In innocency God should have advanced an innocent man; but the gospel is more glorious. For he comes to sinners, to condemned persons by nature, and yet God triumphs over their sins and unworthiness. He regards not what we deserve, but what may stand with the glory of his mercy. Therefore we should banish those thoughts, and enjoy our own privilege, the promises of heaven, and happiness, and all comforts whatsoever. So much for the answer of that objection.

Now if we would joy in the witness of a good conscience, we must especially in the time of temptation live by faith, and not by feeling, not by what we feel for the present. But as we see Christ in his greatest horror, 'My God, my God, why hast thou forsaken me?' Mark xvii. 34, he goes to *my God* still, we must 'live by faith and not by sense,' 2 Cor. v. 7.

And then if we would rejoice in extremities, remember that God works by contraries. God will bring us to heaven, but it must be by hell. God will bring us to comfort, but it must be by sense of our own unworthiness. He will forgive our sins, but it must be by sight and sense of our sins. He will bring us to life, but it must be by death. He will bring us to glory, but it must be by shame. God works by contraries; therefore in contraries believe contraries. When we are in a state that hath no comfort, yet we may joy in it if we believe in Christ. He works by contraries.

As in the creation he made all out of nothing, order out of confusion; so in the work of the new creation, in the new creature, he doth so likewise; therefore be not dismayed.

Remember this rule likewise, that in the covenant of grace God requires truth, and not measure. Thou art not under the law, but under the covenant of grace. A little fire is true fire as well as the whole element of fire. A drop of water is water as well as the whole ocean. So if it be true faith, true grief for sins, true hatred of them, true desire of the favour of God, and to grow better; truth is respected in the covenant of grace, and not any set measure.

What saith the covenant of grace? 'He that believes and repents shall be saved,' Mark xvi. 16, not he that hath a strong faith, or he that hath perfect repentance. So St Paul saith, as we shall see after, 'This is our rejoicing, that in simplicity and sincerity we have had our conversation among you,' 2 Cor. i. 12. He doth not say, that our conversation hath been perfect. So if we would have joy in the testimony of conscience, we must not abridge ourselves of joy, because we have not a perfect measure of grace; but rejoice that God hath wrought any measure of grace in such unclean and polluted hearts as ours are. For the least measure of grace is a pledge of perfection in the world to come.

'*This is our rejoicing, the testimony of our conscience,*' *&c.* Hence we may gather clearly, that

Obs. A man may know his own estate in grace.

* See note, p. 169.—G.

I gather it from the place thus, 'Our rejoicing is this, the testimony of our conscience, that in simplicity,' &c.

Where there is joy, and the ground of joy, there is a knowledge of the estate; but a Christian hath glorying, and a ground of glorying in himself, and he knows it. He hath that in him that witnesseth that estate. He hath the witness of conscience; therefore he may know and be assured of it. If this testimony were not a true testimony, it were something. But all men naturally have a conscience; and a Christian hath a sanctified conscience. And where that is, there is a true testimony, and true joy from that testimony. Therefore he may be assured of his salvation, and have true joy and comfort, a heaven upon earth before he come to heaven itself.

If conscience testify of itself, and from witnessing give cause of joy, much more the Spirit of God coming into the conscience, 'The Spirit bears witness with our spirits.' If our spirit and conscience bear witness to us of our conversation in simplicity and sincerity, and from thence of our estate in grace, much more by the witness of two. 'By the witness of two or three everything shall be confirmed,' Matt. xviii. 16; but our spirits, and conscience, and the Spirit of God, which every child of God hath, witnesseth that we are the children of God, Rom. viii. 14, *et alibi*. 'The Spirit witnesseth with our spirits that we are the sons of God.' Therefore a Christian may know his estate in grace.

The spirit of a man knows himself, and the Spirit of God knows him likewise, and it knows what is in the heart of God; and when these two meet, the Spirit of God that knows the secrets of God, and that knows our secrets, and our spirit that knows our heart likewise, what should hinder but that we may know our own estate? It is the nature of conscience, as I told you, to reflect upon itself and upon the person in whom it is, to know what is known by it, and to judge, and condemn, and execute itself, by inward fear and terror, in ill; and in good, by comfort and joy in a man's self. It is the property that the soul hath above all creatures, to return and recoil upon itself. If this be natural to man, much more to the spirit of a man. For if a man know what is in himself naturally, his own wit, and understanding, which is alway with him, bred up with him, much more he knows by his spirit the things that are adventitious, that come from without him, that is the work of grace.

If a man, by a reflect knowledge, know what naturally is in him, in what part he hath it, and how he exerciseth it; if he know and remember what he hath done, and the manner of it, whether well or ill; then he may know the work of the Spirit that comes from without him, that works a change in him.

We say of light, that it discovers itself and all other things; so the soul it is lightsome, and therefore knows itself and knows other things.

The Spirit of God is much more lightsome. Where it is it discovers itself, and lighteneth the soul. It discovereth the party in whom it is. As the apostle saith, 1 Cor. ii. 12. 'We have the Spirit, whereby we know the things that we receive of God.' It not only worketh in us, but it teacheth us what it hath wrought. Therefore a Christian knows that he is in the state of grace, he knows his virtues, and his disposition; except it be in the time of temptation, and upon those grounds named before.

Therefore we should labour to know our estate, to 'examine ourselves whether we be in the faith or no, except we be reprobates and castaways,' as the apostle speaks, 2 Cor. xiii. 5. A Christian should aim at this, to understand his own estate in grace upon good grounds.

Obj. But it may be objected; how can we know our estate in grace, our virtues are so imperfect, our abilities are so weak and feeble.

Ans. I answer, the ground of judging aright of our estate, it is not worthiness or perfection, but sincerity. We must not look for perfection. For that makes the papists to teach that there may be doubting, because they look to false grounds; but we must look to the ground in the covenant of grace, to grace itself, and not to the measure. Where there is truth and sincerity, there is the condition of the covenant of grace, and there is a ground for a man to build his estate in grace on.

The perfect righteousness of Christ is that that gives us title to heaven; but to know that we have right in that title, is the simplicity and sincerity in our walking, in our conversation, as the apostle saith here, 'This is our rejoicing,' &c. Therefore Christians, when they are set upon by temptations of their own misdoubting hearts, and by Satan, they must not go to the great measure of grace that is in others, that they have not so much as others, and therefore they have none; nor to the great measure of grace that they want themselves, but to the truth of their grace, the truth of their desires and endeavours, the truth of their affections. 'Hereby we know that we are translated from death to life, because we love the brethren,'

Use. This should stir us up *to have a good conscience, that we may rejoice.* Why should we labour that we may rejoice? Why? what is our life without joy? and what is joy without a good conscience?

What is our life without joy? Without joy we can do nothing. We are like an instrument out of tune. An instrument out of tune it yields but harsh music. Without joy we are as a member out of joint. We can do nothing well without joy, and a good conscience, which is the ground of joy. A man without joy is a palsy-member that moves itself unfitly, and uncomely. He goes not about things as he should. A good conscience breeds joy and comfort. It enables a man to do all things comely in the sight of God, and comfortably to himself. It makes him go cheerfully through his business. A good 'conscience is a continual feast,' Prov. xv. 15. Without joy we cannot suffer afflictions. We cannot die well without it. Simeon died comfortably, because he died in peace, when he had embraced Christ in his heart, and in his arms, Mat. ix. 36. Without joy and the ground of joy we can neither do nor suffer anything. Therefore in Psalm li. 12, David, when he had lost the peace and comfort of a good conscience, he prays for the free Spirit of God. Alas! till God had enlarged his heart with the sense of a good conscience in the pardon of his sins, and given him the power of his Spirit to lead a better life for the time to come, his spirit was not free before. He could not praise God with a large spirit. He wanted freedom of spirit. His conscience was bound. His lips were sealed up. 'Open my lips, and my mouth shall shew forth thy praise,' Ps. li. 15. His heart was bound, and therefore he prays to have it enlarged. 'Restore to me thy joy and salvation,' Ps. li. 12; intimating that we cannot have a free spirit without joy, and we cannot have joy without a good conscience sprinkled with the blood of Christ, in the pardon of our sins.

If it be so, that we cannot do anything nor suffer anything as we should, that we cannot praise God, that we cannot live nor die without joy, and the ground of it, the testimony of a good conscience; let us labour, then, that conscience may witness well unto us.

Especially considering that an ill conscience, it is the worst thing in the world. There is no friend so good as a good conscience. There is no foe so ill as a bad conscience. It makes us either kings or slaves. A man that hath a good conscience, that witnesseth well for him, it raiseth his heart in a princely manner above all things in the world. A man that hath a bad conscience, though he be a monarch, it makes him a slave. A bad conscience embitters all things in the world to him, though they be never so comfortable in themselves. What is so comfortable as the presence of God? What is so comfortable as the light? Yet a bad conscience, that will not be ruled, it hates the light, and hates the presence of God, as we see Adam, when he had sinned, he fled from God, Gen. iii. 8.

A bad conscience cannot joy in the midst of joy. It is like a gouty foot or a gouty toe covered with a velvet shoe. Alas! what doth it ease it? What doth glorious apparel ease the diseased body? Nothing at all. The ill is within. There the arrow sticks.

And so in the comforts of the word, if the conscience be bad, we that are the messengers of comfort, we may apply comfort to you; but if there be one within that saith thus, It is true, but I regarded not the word before, I regarded not the checks of conscience, conscience will speak more terror than we can speak peace. And after long and wilful rebellion, conscience will admit of no comfort for the most part. Regard it, therefore, in time; labour in time that it may witness well. An ill conscience, when it should be most comforted, then it is most terrible. At the hour of death we should have most comfort, if we had any wisdom. When earthly comforts shall be taken from us, and at the day of judgment, then an ill conscience, look where it will, it hath matter of terror. If it look up, there is the Judge armed with vengeance; if it look beneath, there is hell ready to swallow it; if it look on the one side, there is the devil accusing and helping conscience; if it look round about, there is heaven and earth, and all on fire, and within there is a hell. Where shall the sinner and ungodly appear? 'If the righteous scarcely be saved, where shall the sinner and ungodly appear,' 1 Pet. iv. 18, at that time?

O let us labour to have a good conscience, and to exercise the reflect* power of conscience in this world; that is, let us examine ourselves, admonish ourselves, judge ourselves, condemn ourselves, do all in ourselves. Let us keep court at home first, let us keep the assizes there, and then we shall have comfort at the great assizes.

Therefore, God out of his love hath put conscience into the soul, that we might keep a court at home. Let conscience, therefore, do its worst now, let it accuse, let it judge; and when it hath judged, let it smite us and do execution upon us, that, 'having judged ourselves, we may not be condemned with the world,' 1 Cor. xi. 32.

If we suffer not conscience to have its full work now, it will have it one day. A sleepy conscience will not alway sleep. If we do not suffer conscience to awake here, it will awaken in hell, where there is no remedy.

Therefore, give conscience leave to speak what it will. Perhaps it will tell thee a tale in thine ear which thou wouldst be loath to hear, it will pursue thee with terrors like a bloodhound, and will not suffer thee to rest; therefore, as a bankrupt, thou art loath to look in thy books, because there is nothing but matter of terror. This is but a folly, for at the last conscience will do its duty. It will awaken either here or in hell. Therefore, we are to hope the best of them that have their consciences opened here. There

* That is, 'reflex.'—G.

is hope that they will make their peace with God, that 'they will agree with their adversary while they are in the way,' Mat. v. 25. If thou suffer conscience to be sleepy and drowsy till it be awaked in hell, woe unto thee! for then thy estate is determined of; it will be a barren repentance. Now thy repentance may be fruitful, it may force thee to make thy peace with God. Dost thou think it will alway be thus with thee? Thou besottest thy conscience with sensuality, and sayest, 'Go thy way, and come another time,' as he said to St Paul, Acts xxiv. 25. I will tell thee, this peace will prove a tempest in the end.

Conscience of all things in the world deserves the greatest reverence, more than any monarch in the world; for it is above all men, it is next unto God. And yet what do many men? Regard the honour of their friends more than conscience, that inward friend that shall accompany them to heaven, that will go with them to death and to judgment, and make them lift up their heads with joy when other friends cannot help them, but must needs leave them in death. Now, for a man to follow the humours of men, to follow the multitude, and to stain conscience, what a foolish wretch is he! Though such men think themselves never so wise, it is the greatest folly in the world to stain conscience to please any man, because conscience is above all men.

Again, those that follow their own humours, their own dispositions, and are carried away with their own lusts, it is a folly and madness; for the time will come that that which their covetous, base lust hath carried them to, that shall be taken away, as honours, riches, pleasures, which is the fuel of that lust which makes them now neglect conscience; all shall be taken away in sickness or in the time of despair, when conscience shall be awaked. Now, what folly is it to please thy own lust, which thou shouldst mortify and subdue, and to displease conscience, thy best friend! And then when thy lust is fully satisfied, all that hath been fuel to it, that hath fed it, shall be taken away at the hour of death, or some special judgment, and conscience shall be awaked, and shall torment thee for giving liberty to thy base lusts and to thyself. And those eyes of thy soul that thy offence delighted to shut up, there shall some punishment come, either in this life or in that to come, that shall open those eyes, as Adam's eyes were opened after his sin. Why? Were they not open before? He had such a strong desire to the apple, he did not regard them; but his punishment afterward opened those eyes, which his inordinate desire shut. So it shall be with every sinner. Therefore, regard no man in the world more than thy conscience. Regard nothing, no pleasure, no profit, more than conscience; reverence it more than anything in the world. Happy is that man that carries with him a good conscience, that can witness that he hath said, nor done nothing that may vex or grieve conscience. If it be otherwise, whatsoever a man gains he loseth in conscience, and there is no comparison between those two. One crack, one flaw in conscience, will prove more disadvantageous than the rest will be profitable. Thou must cast up the rest again. 'They are sweet bits downward, but they shall be gravel in the belly,' Prov. xx. 17.

We think when we have gained anything, when we have done anything, we shall hear no more of it, as David said to Joab, when he set him to make away Uriah, 'Let not this trouble thee,' 2 Sam. xi. 25. So, let not this ill gain, let not this ill speech or this ill carriage, trouble thee, thou shalt hear no more of this. We take order to stop and silence conscience, thinking never to hear more of it. Oh, but remember, conscience will have its work; and the longer we defer the witness and work of conscience, the more it will terrify and accuse us afterward.

Therefore, of all men, be they never so great, they are most miserable that follow their wills and their lusts most; that never have any outward check or inward check of conscience, but drown it with sensual pleasures. As Charles the IXth, who at night, when conscience hath the fittest time to work, a man being retired, then he would have his singing boys, after he had betrayed them in that horrible massacre,* after which he never had peace and quiet; and as Saul sent for David's harp when the evil spirit was upon him, 1 Sam. xvi. 23, so wicked men, they look for foreign helps. But it will not be; for the greatest men with their foreign helps are most miserable.

The reason is, because the more they sink in rebellion and sin against conscience, the more they sink in terrors. It shall be the greatest torment to those that have had their wills most in the world. The more their conscience is silenced and violenced in this world, the more vocal it shall be at the hour of death, and the day of judgment. Therefore judge who are the most miserable men in the world (although they have never so much regard in the world besides), those that have consciences, but will not suffer them to work, but with sensuality within them, and by pleasing, flattering speech of those without them, they keep it down, and take order that neither conscience within, nor none other without, shall disturb them; if they do, they shall be served as Ahab dealt with Micaiah, 2 Kings xxii. 24. These men that are thus at peace in sinful courses, of all men they are most miserable. They enjoy their pleasure here for a little time, but their conscience shall torment them for ever; and shall say to them, as Reuben said to his brethren, 'I told you this before, but you would not hearken to me, and now you shall be tormented.'

Conscience is an evil beast. It makes a man rise against himself. Therefore of all men, those that be disordered in their courses, that neglect conscience, and neglect the means of salvation, that should awaken conscience, they are the most miserable. For the longer they go on, the more they sink in sin; and the more they sink in sin, the more they sink in terror of conscience; if not now, yet they shall hereafter.

If we desire therefore to have joy and comfort at all times, let us labour to have a good conscience that may witness well. And therefore let us every day keep an audit within doors, every day cast up our accounts, every day draw the blood of Christ over our accounts, every day beg forgiveness of sins, and the Spirit of Christ to lead us, that so we may keep account every day, that we may make our reckonings even every day, that we may have the less to do in the time of sickness, in the time of temptation, and in the time of death, when we have discharged our consciences before by keeping session at home in our own hearts.

This should be the daily practice of a Christian, and then he may lay himself down in peace.

He that sleeps with a conscience defiled, is as he that sleeps among wild beasts, among adders and toads, that if his eyes were open to see them, he would be out of his wits. He that sleeps without a good conscience, he is an unadvised man. God may make his bed his grave, he may smite him suddenly. Therefore let us every day labour to have a good conscience, that so we may have matter of perpetual joy.

A good conscience especially, is an evangelical conscience; for a legal

* That is, of Bartholomew. The after-dread of Charles IX. is recorded by all his historians and biographers. See footnote, vol. i. p. 149.—G.

good conscience none have; that is, such a conscience as acquits a man that he hath obeyed the law in all things exactly. A legal complete good conscience none have, except in some particular fact; there is a good conscience in fact. As the heathen could excuse themselves, they were thus and thus, Rom. ii. 15; and God ministereth much joy in that. But an evangelical good conscience is that we must trust to; that is, such a conscience that though it knows itself guilty of sin, yet it knows that Christ hath shed his blood for sinners; and such a conscience as by means of faith is sprinkled with the blood of Christ, and is cleared from the accusations of sin.

There is an evangelical conscience when, by faith wrought by the Spirit of God, in the hearing of the gospel, we lay hold upon the obedience and righteousness of Christ. And such is the obedience and righteousness of Christ, that it pacifieth the conscience, which nothing else in the world will do. The conscience, without a full obedience, it will alway stagger.

And that is the reason that conscience confounds and confutes the popish way of salvation by works, &c. Because the conscience alway staggers, and fears, I have not done works enough, I have not done them well enough; those that I have done they have been corrupt and mixed, and therefore I dare not bring them to the judgment-seat of God, to plead them meritorious. Therefore they do well to hold uncertainty of salvation; because, holding merit, they must needs be uncertain of their salvation. A true Christian is certain of his salvation, because his conscience lays hold on the blood of Christ, because the obedience whereby he claims heaven is a superabundant obedience, it is the satisfaction of Christ, as the apostle saith in that excellent place, Heb. ix. 14, 'The blood of Christ, which offered himself by the eternal Spirit (that is, by the Godhead), shall cleanse your consciences from dead works to serve the living God.' The blood of Christ that offered himself, his human nature by his divine, to God as a sacrifice, it shall purge your consciences from dead works. The blood of Christ, that is, the sacrifice, the obedience of Christ, in offering himself, fully pacified God, and answered the punishment which we should have endured; for he was our Surety. 'The blood of Christ speaks better than the blood of Abel,' Heb. xii. 24. It speaks better than our sins. Our sins cry vengeance, but the blood of Christ cries mercy.

The blood of Christ out-cries our sins. The guilty conscience for sin cries, Guilty, guilty, hell, damnation, wrath, and anguish; but the blood of Christ cries, I say, mercy, because it was shed by our surety in our behalf. His obedience is a full satisfaction to God.

Now, the way to have a good conscience is, upon the accusations of an evil conscience by the law, to come to Christ our surety, and to get our consciences sprinkled by faith in his blood, to get a persuasion that he shed his blood for us, and upon that to labour to be purged by the Spirit. There are two purgers, the blood of Christ from the guilt of sin, and the Spirit of Christ from the stain of sin; and upon that comes a complete good conscience, being justified by the blood of Christ, and sanctified by the Spirit of Christ. Therefore Christ came not by blood alone, or by water alone, but by water *and* blood; by blood in justification, by water in sanctification and holiness of life.

Quest. Why do we allege this now for the sacrament?

Ans. We speak of a good conscience, 'which is a continual feast,' Prov. xv. 15. How comes a good conscience to be such a continual feast?

An evangelical conscience is a feast indeed; because it feeds on a higher feast: it feeds on Christ. He is the Passover lamb, as the apostle applies it, 1 Cor. v. 7. He is the 'Passover, slain for us;' and there is represented in the sacrament, his body broken and his blood poured out for our sins. He came to feast us, and we shall feast with him.

Hereupon, if we bring repentance for our sins past, and faith whereby we are incorporate into Christ, then our consciences speak peace; and as it is in 1 Pet. iii. 21, the conscience makes a good demand. 'It is not baptism, but the demand of a good conscience.' When the conscience hath fed on Christ, it demands boldly, as it is Rom. viii. 33, of Satan and all enemies, 'Who shall lay anything to our charge? It is God that justifieth. It is Christ that died, or rather that is risen again.' It boldly demands of God, who hath given his Son. The bold demand of conscience prevails with God, and this comes by faith in Christ. Now, this is strengthened by the sacrament. Here are the visible representations and seals that we are incorporate more and more into Christ; and so feeding upon Christ once, our conscience is pacified and purged from all dead works, and we come to have a continual feast.

Christ is first the Prince of righteousness, the righteous King, and then 'Prince of peace;' first he gives righteousness, and then he speaks peace to the conscience. 'The kingdom of God is righteousness, peace, and joy in the Holy Ghost,' Rom. xiv. 17.

So that all our feast and joy and comfort that we have in our consciences, it must be from righteousness. A double righteousness: the righteousness of Christ which hath satisfied and appeased the wrath of God fully; and then we must have the righteousness of a good conscience sanctified by the Spirit of Christ. We must put them together alway. We can never have communion with Christ, and have forgiveness of sins; but we must have a spirit of sanctification. 'There is mercy with thee, that thou mayest be feared,' Ps. cxxx. 4. Where there is mercy in the forgiveness of sin, there is a disposition to fear it ever after. Therefore if for the present you would have a good conscience, desire God to strengthen your faith in the blood of Christ poured out for you; desire God to strengthen your faith in the crucified body of Christ broken for you; that so feeding on Christ, who is your surety, who himself is yours, and all is yours, you may ever have the feast of a good conscience, that will comfort you in false imputations, that will comfort you in life and in death, and at the day of judgment. 'This is our rejoicing in all things, the testimony of our conscience;' first purged by 'the blood of Christ,' and then purged and sanctified by the Spirit of Christ, that we have had our 'conversation in simplicity and sincerity,' &c.

'*Our rejoicing is this, that in simplicity and sincerity.*' This is the matter of this testimony of conscience, that is simplicity and sincerity. St Paul glories in his simplicity and sincerity. And mark that by the way, it is no vain glorying, but lawful upon such cautions as I named before. But to add a little,—a man in some cases may glory in the graces of God that are in him; but with these cautions.

First, if so be that he look on them *as the gifts of God.*

Secondly, if he look on them *as stained with his own defects,* and so in that respect be humbled.

Thirdly, if he look upon them *as fruits of his justification,* and as fruits *of his assurance of his salvation,* and not as causes.

And then, if it *be before men that he glories: not when he is to deal with*

God. When men lay this and that imputation upon a man, he may rejoice, as St Paul doth here, in the testimony of his conscience, 'in simplicity and sincerity.'

The matter of the testimony of conscience wherein he glories is 'simplicity and godly sincerity,' or, as the words may well be read, 'in the simplicity and sincerity of God,' such as proceeds from God, and such as aims at and looks to God, and resembles God. For both simplicity and sincerity come from God. They are wrought by God; and therein we resemble God. And both of them have an eye to God, a respect to God. So it is in the original, 'in the simplicity and sincerity of God' (*ll*).

There is not much difference between simplicity and sincerity. The one expresseth the other. If you will have the difference, simplicity especially respects men, our conversation amongst men. Simplicity hath an eye to God in all things in religion, opposite to hypocrisy in religion. 'Simplicity,' that is opposed to doubleness. Where doubleness is, there is alway hypocrisy, opposed to sincerity; and where simplicity is, there is alway sincerity, truth to God. But it is not good to be very exact and punctual in the distinction of these things. They may one express the other very well.

'Simplicity.' St Paul's rejoicing was, that his conscience witnessed to him his simplicity in his whole conversation in the world, his whole course of life, which the Scripture calls in other places a 'walking,' Acts ix. 31. St Paul means this first of himself; and then he propounds himself an example to us.

Quest. How was St Paul's conversation in simplicity?

Ans. Not only if we consider St Paul as a Christian, but consider him as an apostle, his conversation was in simplicity. It was without guile, without seeking himself, without seeking his own; for rather than he would be grievous to the Corinthians, the man of God he wrought himself. Because he would not give any the least scandal to them, being a rich people, he had rather live by his own labour than to open his* mouth. He did not seek himself. In a word, he did not serve himself of the gospel. He served Christ. He did not serve himself of Christ.

There are many that serve themselves of the gospel, that serve themselves of religion. They care no more for religion than will serve their own turn. St Paul's conversation was in simplicity. He had no such aim. He did not preach of envy, or of malice, or for gain, as he taxeth some of the Philippian teachers, 'Some preach Christ,' not of simplicity and sincerity, 'but of envy,' &c., Philip. i. 18.

Then again, as an apostle and a teacher, his conversation was in simplicity; because he mingled nothing with the word of God in teaching. His doctrine is pure. 'What should the chaff do with the wheat?' Jer. xxiii. 28. What should the dross do with the gold? He did not mingle his own conceits and devices with the word: for he taught the pure word of God, the simple word of God, simple without any mixture of any by-aims. So the blessed apostle was simple both in his doctrine and in his intentions; propounding himself herein exemplary to all us, that, as we look to hold up our heads with comfort, and to glory in all estates whatsoever, so our consciences must bear us witness that we carry ourselves in the simplicity and sincerity of God.

Now simplicity is, when there is a conformity of pretension and intention, when there is nothing double, when there is not a contradiction in the spirit of a man, and in his words and carriage outwardly. That is simplicity,

* Qu. 'their?'—G.

when there is an exact conformity and correspondence in a man's judgment and speech, in his affections and actions. When a man judgeth simply as the truth of the thing is, and when he affects as he judgeth, when he loves and hates as he judgeth, and he speaks as he affects and judgeth, and he doth as he speaks, then a man is a simple man.

Simple, that is properly, that hath no mixture of the contrary. As we say, light is a simple thing; it cannot endure darkness: fire is a simple body; it cannot endure the contrary with it: so the pure majesty of God cannot endure the least stain whatsoever. So it is with the holy disposition of a Christian. When he is once a new creature, there is a simplicity in him. Though there be a mixture, yet he studies simplicity; he studies to have nothing opposite to the Spirit of God; he studies not to have any contradiction in him; he labours that his heart may not go one way, and his carriage another; that his pretensions be not one, and his intentions another. He bears the image of Christ. You know Christ is compared to a lamb, a simple creature, fruitful to men, innocent in himself. So the Holy Ghost appeared in the shape of a dove, a simple creature, that hath no way to avoid danger but by flight; a harmless creature.*

The devil takes on him the shape of a serpent, a subtle, wild creature. The Holy Ghost appeared in the shape of a dove. You see then what simplicity is. It is a frame of soul without mixture of the contrary.

1. We must not take simplicity *for a defect;* when a man is simple because he knows not how to be witty. Simplicity is sometimes taken in that sense for a defect of nature, when a man is easily deluded; but here it is taken for a grace. A man that knows how to double with the world, how to run counterfeit, how to be false in all kinds; but he will not. He knows the world, but he will not use the fashions of the world. So simplicity here is a strength of grace.

2. Likewise, simplicity and plainness, it must not be taken *for rudeness* and unnecessary opening of ourselves; for that is simplicity in an evil sense, profane rudeness.

You shall have some that will lay about them, they care not what they speak, they care not whom they smite; but, as Solomon's fool, they throw 'firebrands,' Prov. xxvi. 18. They speak what they list, of whom they list, against whom they list. Here simplicity and plainness is no grace. This is no virtue. This is but an easing of their rotten, corrupt, and vile heart.

We know there are two kinds of sepulchres, open and shut sepulchres. They are both naught.† But yet, notwithstanding, your hidden sepulchre is less offensive. That which is open stinks that none can come nigh. That is very offensive. An hypocrite, that is a hidden sepulchre, a 'painted sepulchre' without, and nothing but bones within, he hath a naughty, rotten heart: yet, notwithstanding, he is not so offensive as the open sepulchre, which offends all that come near it. So these men that say they cannot dissemble, and they have a plain heart, though they will swear, and dissemble, and detract, and throw firebrands against any man; is this a plain heart? It is an open sepulchre, that sends a stench to all that are near.

3. Again, let us take heed, that we do not for simplicity *take credulity.* 'The simple man,' saith Solomon, 'will believe everything,' Prov. xiv. 15. This is simple credulity. A man must not believe everything, for there is much danger comes by credulity. Jeremiah, and Gedaliah, and others,

* Cf. 'Bowels Opened,' vol. II., pp. 76–79.—G.

† That is, 'naughty' = filthy.—G.

they were much harmed by credulity. It is a good fence not to be too hasty to believe; for incredulity and hardness to believe is a good preservative; and he is a wise man that will not believe everything. So you see there are some things that come near this simplicity, as defect, rudeness, and credulity, which yet are not that simplicity that St Paul saith he walked in.

And this simplicity may well be called the simplicity of God; because God is simple. 'He is light, and in him there is no darkness at all,' 1 John i. 5. There is no mixture of fraud, or contrariety. He is pure, simple, and sincere. And as he is in his nature, so he is in his carriage to men every way. There is a simplicity that he doth in his word testify. And indeed he hath shewed that he loves us. Would we have a better evidence of it than his own Son? There is no doubling in God's dealing to men. And therefore as it comes from God, so this simplicity it resembleth God.

For alas! if God had had by-respects, what would the creature yield him? Doth he stand in need of us, or doth he need anything we have? All counterfeiting, and insincerity, and doubling, is for hope of gain, or for fear of danger. Now what can God have of the creature? What cause hath he in us of his dealing toward us? In his giving, in his forgiving, in all his dealing, he is simple.

So every one that is the child of God, he hath the virtue of simplicity. Simplicity is such a grace as extends to all the parts of our conversation As the apostle saith here, 'My conversation in the world hath been in simplicity.'

By nature man is contrary to this simplicity, since the fall. God made him right and straight, and simple, but as the wise man saith, 'he sought out many inventions,' Eccles. vii. 29. So that a man without grace is double in his carriage. And that from self-love, from self-ends, and aims.

And hereupon he must be double; for there must be something that is good in him. For else evil is destructive of itself. If there were not some thing good, men could never continue, nor the place could never continue. And if all were good, and all were plain, and honest, that would destroy the ill which men labour to nourish. Men have carnal projects to raise themselves, to get riches, and this must be by ill means. There is an idol in their hearts which they serve, which they sacrifice to. Their self-love, either in honour, or in riches, or in pleasure, they set up something. Therefore a man without grace, he studies to be strongly ill; and because he cannot be ill except he be good, for then all the world would see it; hereupon comes doubling. Good there must be to carry the ill he intends the more close; ill there must be, or else he cannot have his aim. And hence comes dissimulation and simulation, the vices of these times, both opposite to simplicity, and such vices as proceed from want of worth and want of strength.

For when men have no worth to trust to, and yet would have the profit of sin, and the pleasure of sin, and would have reputation, then they carry all dissemblingly. Where there is strength of worth, and of parts, and reputation, there is less dissembling alway. It is a vice usually of those that have little or no virtue in them. A man of strength carries things open and fair.

This dissimulation it comes from the want of this grace of simplicity, both

Before, *in*, [and] *after* the project.

1. *Before*, as you see in Herod. He intends mischief, when he pretends he would be a worshipper of Christ, Mat. ii. 8. And so Absalom, he pretends he had a vow to make, when he intends murder, 2 Sam. xv. 7; a dissimulation, pretending good when there is an intention of ill before.

2. So there is a dissimulation *in* the project for the present, which comes from this doubling; when men carry things fairly outwardly to those with whom they live, and yet notwithstanding have false and treacherous hearts; as Judas had all the while he conversed with Christ. He covered his ill with good pretexts, a care for the poor, &c.

3. So *after*. When the ill is done, what a world of doubling is there to cover ill, to extenuate it, and excuses, and translations! This is the simplicity that reigns among men where there is no strength of grace. Where there is want of simplicity there is this dissembling.

And with dissimulation there is simulation, that is, when we make ourselves sometimes worse than we are; when we are better than we seem to be. Sometimes that wins on us too. Then we carry not ourselves simply.

For if we were good, we would be good everywhere. But a man that useth simulation, if he be in evil company he fashioneth himself to the company, he speaks that which his conscience checks him for, he carries himself vainly and lightly, he holds correspondence with the company. So that by dissimulation and simulation, there is a fault committed against simplicity, which yields the testimony of a good conscience.

It is a base fault this simulation, which we think to be a lesser fault than the other, which is dissimulation. For whom do we serve? Are we not the sons of God? Are we not the sons of our heavenly Father, the sons of the great King? and for us to carry ourselves not to be such as we are in the midst of the wicked world, it is a great want of discretion. St Paul would discover who he was, even before the bar; David 'would speak of God's righteous testimonies even before princes, and not be ashamed,' Ps. cxix. 46.

And this is that which Christ saith, 'He that is ashamed of me before men, of him will I be ashamed before my heavenly Father,' Mark viii. 38. Let us take heed of dissimulation and simulation, which are opposite to this simplicity.

Again, this simplicity is opposite to curiosity, and fineness. And thus the apostle! Both in his calling and conversation, St Paul conversed in simplicity, as a Christian, and as an apostle.

As an apostle, he was not overcurious in words. He reproveth those foolish, vainglorious spirits, that were so among the Corinthians. He delivered the word plainly, and plainness is best in handling the word of God; for who will enamel a precious stone? We use to enamel that that hath not a native excellency in itself, but that which hath an excellency from something without. True religion hath this with it alway, that it is simple; because it hath state enough of its own.

The whore of Babylon hath need of a gilded cup, and pictures, and what not, to set her out; but the true religion is in simplicity.

Christ himself when he was born, he was laid in a cratch.* He was simple in his carriage, and his speeches. It was a common speech in ancient time, when the chalices were gold, the priests were wood. In religion, fineness and curiosity carry suspicion of falsehood with them.

Those that overmuch affect fineness of speech, they are either deceived

* That is, 'crib or manger.'—G.

or will deceive. That which is not native, and comes not from within, it will deceive. Some falsehoods carry a better colour than some truths; because men set their wits on work to set some colour upon falsehood alway.

And here take notice of the duty of ministers, that they should utter divine truth in the native simplicity of it. St Paul as a minister, delivered the plain word plainly.

And as a Christian in our common course of life, as we should take heed of doubling, so of too much curiosity. For too much curiosity in diet or apparel, it implies too much care of these things, which hinders our care of better things, as our Saviour Christ saith to Martha, 'Martha, thou art troubled about many things,' Luke x. 41.

The soul is finite, and cannot be set about many things at once. Therefore, when there is overmuch curiosity in smaller things, it implies little or no care in the main. What is more than for decency of place, it argues carelessness in the main. Therefore the apostle, labouring to take off that, he bids women that they should not be 'decked with gold and broidered hair,' &c.; but to look to the 'hidden man of the heart,' 1 Tim. ii. 9. And therefore Christ took off Martha from outward things, because he knew it could not be without the neglect of better things. Seriousness in heavenly things, it carries a carelessness in other things. And a Christian cannot choose but discover a mind that is not earthly and vain. When he is a true believer, he regards other things as poor petty things, that are not worthy estimation.

A Christian when he hath fixed his end, to be like to God, to be simple as God is, he still draws toward his end; and therefore he moderates his carriage in all things. What is unnecessary he leaves out. His end is to be like God, and like Christ, with whom he shall live hereafter. Now the best things are the most simple, as the heavens, the sun, and the stars, &c. There is diversity, but no contrariety. There is diversity in the magnitude of the stars, but they are of the same nature. So in a Christian there are many graces, but they are not contrary one to another. So that a Christian hath his main care for better things; he cares not for the world, nor the things thereof. And therefore he accounts them, in comparison of better things, as nothing; and that is the reason that he is careless and negligent of those things that he did formerly regard, as having better things to take up his thoughts.

We see then that simplicity, as it is opposed to doubling, so it is opposed to fineness and curiosity.

And usually where there is a fineness and curiosity, there is hypocrisy; for it is not for nought when men affect anything. Affectation usually is a strain above nature. When a man will do that which he is not disposed to by nature, but for some forced end, it is hypocrisy. So the Corinthian teachers argued* the falseness of their hearts by the fineness of their teaching. They had another aim than to please God and convert souls. Usually affectation to the world is joined with hypocrisy towards God.

Again, this simplicity is contrary to that corruption in popery, namely, equivocation. What simplicity is that, when they speak one thing, and mean another? when there is a mental reservation, and such a reservation, that if that were set down that is reserved, it were absurd.

Or else there may be a reservation: a man may reserve his meaning. A man may not speak all the truth at all times, except he be called to it, in judgment, &c. Otherwise truth, as all good actions, it is never good but

at is, 'proved.'—G.

when it is seasonable; and then it is seasonable when there is convenient furniture of circumstances, when a man is called to it. For there may be a reservation. A man is not bound to speak all things at all times, but to wait for a fit time. One word in a fit time is worth a thousand out of time. But mental reservation, to speak one thing, and to reserve another, it is absurd and inconsequent, and so is dissimulation. There is a lie, in fact. A man's life is a lie, that is a dissembler. Dissimulation is naught.*

A man may sometimes make some show to do something that he intends not. Christ made as though he would have gone further when he did not mean it, Luke xxiv. 28 (*mm*). But dissimulation is that which is intrinsically naught.*

Obj. But some man will say, Except I dissemble, I shall run into danger.

Ans. Well! it is not necessary for thee to live, but it is necessary for thee to live like an honest man, and keep a good conscience. That is necessary.† For come what will upon true dealing, we ought to deal truly, and not dissemble. Those that pretend a necessity, they must do it, they cannot live else, they cannot avoid danger else, unless they dissemble: saith Tertullian very well, There is no necessity of sin to them, upon whom there lies no other necessity but not to sin (*nn*). Christians, they are men that have no necessity lies upon them but not to sin. It is not necessary they should be rich, it is not necessary they should be poor, it is not necessary they should have their freedom and liberty. There is no necessity lies upon them, but that they be good, that they do not sin. Can he pretend I must sin upon necessity, who hath no necessity imposed upon him by God, but to avoid all sin?

As for lying, which is against this simplicity that should be in speech, all kinds of lies, officious‡ lies, or pernicious lies. Officious lies, to do a good turn to help ourselves or others with a lie, it is a gross sin. It is condemned by St Austin in a whole book, which he wrote against lying.§ Therefore I pass it. I shall have occasion to speak somewhat of it afterward. It is intrinsically ill every lie, because it is contrary to the hint|| of speech. God hath made our reason and understanding to frame speech, and speech to be the messenger and interpreter of reason, and of the conceit.¶ Now when speech shall be a false messenger, it is contrary to the gift of speech. Speech should be the stream of understanding and reason. Now when the fountain is one, and the spring is another, there is a contradiction. It is against nature, so it is intrinsically ill. It is not only against the will of God, but it is against the image of God, which is in truth. It is ill, not by inconvenience or by inconsequence, but a pernicious lie is inwardly ill. Jesting lies, pernicious lies, officious lies, all lies, let them be what they will, they come from the father of lies, the devil, and are hated of God, who is truth itself.

Besides that, it is a sin opposite to society, and therefore by God's just judgment it is punished by society. All men hate a liar, a false dissembler, as an enemy to society, as a man that offends against that bond whereby God hath knit men together.

Now, to move us the better to this simplicity, this direct course of life, that there may be a conformity and harmony between the outward and inward man, in the thoughts, speeches, and actions, that they may be one.

1. Consider, first of all, that this simplicity, *it is a comely thing*. Come-

* That is, 'naughty' = bad.—G.

† See note *l*, vol. I. p. 210.—G.

‡ That is, 'o fficial.'—G.

§ That is, his '*De Mendacio*.'—G.

|| That is, 'end.'—Ed.

¶ That is, 'conception.'—G.

liness and seemliness, it is a thing that is delightful to the eyes of God, and to a man's own conscience; and it stands in oneness and proportion. For you know where there is a comely proportion, there all things suit in one; as in a comely body, the head and all the rest of the members are suitable. There is not a young green head upon an old body, or a fair face on a deformed body, for then there is two; the body is one, and the complexion another. Beauty and comeliness is in one, when there is a correspondency, a proportion, a harmony in the parts.

In Rev. xiii. 11, *seq.*, you have a cruel beast there with the horns of a lamb. There is two, there is a goodly pretension and show, but there is a beast that is hid within. Dissimulation is double, and where there is singleness and doubleness, there is deformity alway. It is an ugly thing in the eyes of God, it is a misshapen thing, it is a monster: Jacob's voice, and Esau's hands: words 'as smooth as oil, and war in the heart.' Prov. v. 3, Ps. lv. 21. It is a monstrous thing. Even as there be monsters in nature, so there be in disposition. Where there is such a gross mixture, the devil and an angel of light, outwardly an angel of light and inwardly a devil; to hide a devil in the shape of an angel of light, there is a horrible deformity.

It is a comely thing, therefore, when all things hold conformity and correspondence in our lives, when they are even amongst men, when we labour to have sanctified judgments of things, and speak what is our judgment, and have outward expressions answerable to the inward impressions wrought by the Spirit of God every way, then a man is like himself, he is one. There is not a heart and a heart. Adam at the first was every way like himself, but after falling from God to the creature, the changeable, corruptible creature, to have his corruptible end, he fell to this doubleness.

2. And as St James saith, 'A double-minded man is *unconstant in all his ways.*' That is another reason to move us to simplicity of disposition; for where doubling is, a man is unconstant in all his ways. What doth St James mean by this, where he saith, 'A double-minded man is unsettled?' Because a double-minded man, he looks with one eye to religion, and to those things that are good, and with another part of his heart to the world; and hereupon he can never be settled any way. Why? Because having unsettled intentions, having false aims, double aims, he will be crossed continually. Please God he would, he would be religious. That is one intention. But now comes the world and religion to dash one against another, and then he must be inconstant, because he hath not simplicity, he hath not a 'single eye,' as Christ saith, 'If the eye be single, then the body is light.' He hath not a right intention, a right judgment of things; he judgeth too high of the world, and not high enough of grace and goodness. And hereupon it comes, that when the world comes to cross his good intentions, having his mind on earthly things, because it is cross to religion, his mind is unsettled.

Again, by terrors of conscience, a double-minded man, that will please God, and yet be a worldling, is inconstant in all his ways. If his eye were single, then all his body would be light; that is, if a man had a single judgment to know what is right, to what in life, and in death to stick to, all would be single. The judgment and intentions go together. When a man's judgment is convinced of the goodness of spiritual things, upon judgment follows intention. When a man desires and resolves to serve God, and to please him in all things, then all the body and his affections are lightsome. His affections and his outward man goes with a single eye. A man that hath a false, weak judgment, and thereupon a false, weak, double intention, his body is dark, he hath a darksome conversation. A double-minded man is inconstant in all his ways. Therefore we should labour for this simplicity in all our conversation.

3. Again, we should the rather labour for this simplicity, because *it is part of the image of God*. Therein we resemble God, in whom is no mixture at all of contraries: but all is alike.

4. And as it resembles God, so it bears us out in the presence of God, and our own conscience; as he saith here, 'Our rejoicing is this, the testimony of our conscience, that in simplicity,' &c. Now God is greater than conscience. A man that carries himself in simplicity, and in an uniform, even manner to God, and to men, that man hath comfort in his conscience, and comfort before God.

And of all other sins, the time will come that none will lie heavier on us than doubling, both with men and with God, when it will appear that we have not been the men that we carried ourselves to be.

The reason is, the more will there is in a sin, and the more advisedness, the greater is the sin; and the greater the sin is, the greater the terror of conscience; and the greater that is, the more fear and trembling before God, that knows conscience better than we do.

Now where there is doubling, where a man is not one in his outward and inward man, in his conversation to men, when there is a covering of hatred, and of ill affections with contrary pretences, there is advisement, there is much will and little passion to bear a man out, to excuse him; but he doth it, as we say, in cool blood, and that makes dissimulation so gross, because it is in cool blood. The more will and advisement is in any sin, the greater it is, so the aggravation of sin is to be considered; and where temptations are strong, and the less a man is himself, so there is a diminution, and a less aggravation; as when a man is carried with passion, with infirmity, or the like. But usually when men double they plot.

David he plotted before and after his sin. He doubled before and after his sin. That was laid to his charge more than all that ever he did in his life. He was a man 'after God's own heart, except in the matter of Uriah,' 1 Kings xv. 5. Why? Because in that he plotted. We see before what many shifts, and windings, and turnings he had to accomplish it. He sends Uriah to Joab, and gives him a letter to place him in the fore front, and useth many projects.

And after it was committed, how did he cover it? And when it was hid from men, he would have hid it from God a great while, till God pulled him from his hiding-place, and him* confess roundly, Ps. xxxii. 3, till he dealt directly with God, 'My bones were consumed, and my moisture was turned into the drought of summer.' He hid it from men, and would have hid it from God. Therefore, because there was much plotting in that sin, that is set down as the only blemish in all his life. He 'was a man after God's own heart, except in the matter of Uriah.' Many other faults are recorded in the Book of God of David; but because there might be some excuse, they were from infirmity, or out of passion, or oversight, &c., they are not so charged on him. But this was with plotting. It was in cold blood. There was much will and advice in it; therefore this is doted† for a great sin.

And if it be in our dealing amongst men, we should consider who it is we deceive, who it is we go beyond in doubling, who it is that we circum-

* Qu. 'made him?'—Ed. † Qu. 'noted?'—G.

vent, and who it is that doth it. Are we not all Christians? We are or should be all new creatures. And who do we do it to? To our fellow-members and to our brethren. Therefore, in Eph. iv. 25,* when the apostle dissuades the Ephesians from this, from double dealing, and double carriage to men, saith he, 'You are members one of another.' Let us consider who we are and whom we deal with.

Now there be some persons, and some courses, that are likelier and more prone to this doubling than others, for want of this grace of simplicity.

Where there is strength of parts, there is ofttimes a turning of them against God, and against our brethren. Where grace hath not subdued strong imaginations, strong thoughts, and brought all under it, there is a turning of those parts against God, and against our brethren. And as it is in particular persons, so some callings are more prone to double-dealing, to this carriage that is not fair and commendable before God, nor comfortable to the conscience. As we see now a-days it reigns everywhere, in every street.

We see amongst men of trade, merchants and the like, there is not that direct dealing. They know one thing, and pretend another.

So likewise in the laws there are many imputations, I would they were false, that men set false colours upon ill causes; to gild a rotten post, as we say, to call white black and black white. There is a woe in Isaiah pronounced against such as justify hard causes, such 'as call evil good, and good evil,' Isa. v. 20. It is a greater sin than it is usually taken for.

So, go to any rank of men. They have learned the art of dissimulation in their course; they have learned to sell wind, to sell words, to sell nothing, to sell pretexts, to overthrow a man by way of commendations and flattery. Such tricks there are, which are contrary to this simplicity. To cover hatred with fair words, to kill with kindness, as we say, to overthrow a man with commendations; to commend a man before another who is jealous of the virtues he commends him for; to commend a man for valour before a coward; to commend a man, and thereby to take occasion to send him out of the way; to commend a man, and then to come in with an exception, to mar all; to cover revenge and hatred with fair carriage, thereby to get opportunity to revenge—such tricks there are abroad, which ofttimes discover themselves at length. For God is just. He will discover all these hidden windings and turnings; for plotting makes it more odious. Of all men doublers are most hateful.

How shall we come to attain this grace, to converse in the world in simplicity?

First of all, take it for a rule, though many think it no great matter to be a dissembler, *our nature is full of dissimulation since the fall* The heart of man is unsearchable. There is a deep deceit in man. Take a child, and see what dissimulation he learns. It is one of the first things he learns, to dissemble, to double, to be false. We see the weakest creatures, what shifts, what windings and turnings they have to save themselves?

It is a virtue to be downright; for therein a man must cross himself. It is no thanks for a man to shuffle, and to shift in the world. Nature teacheth this, to dissemble, to turn and wind, &c. A man need not to plough to have weeds. The ground itself is a mother to them, though it be a stepmother to good seed. So we need not teach men to dissemble. Every man hath it by nature. But it must be strength of grace that makes a man downright. Take that for a ground.

* Misprinted '1 Thess. iv.'—G.

There are a company of sottish men, that take it for a great commendation to dissemble; and rather than they will be known not to dissemble in business, they will puzzle clear business. When a thing is fair and clear, they will have projects beyond the moon, and so carry themselves in it as if they desired to be accounted cozeners and dissemblers. Alas! poor souls. Nature teacheth men to be naught in this kind well enough. Know therefore, whosoever thou art that studiest this art of dissembling and doubling, thy own nature is prone enough to this, and the devil is apt to lead thee into it. This being laid for a ground, how may we carry ourselves in the world in holy simplicity, that may yield comfort to our conscience in life and in death?

1. First consider, that the time will come *that we shall deal with that that will not dissemble with us.* Let the cunningest dissembler hold out as long as he can, he shall meet with sickness, or with terror of conscience, he shall meet with death itself, and with the judgment of God, and hell torment. Although now he carry himself smoothly, and dance in a net, as we say, and double with the world, though he make a fair show, yet ere long thou shalt meet with that that will deal simply with thee, that will deal plain enough with thee. Thou shalt be uncased, and laid open to the world ere long (*oo*). Let us consider this.

We see a snake or serpent, it doubles, and winds, and turns when it is alive, till it be killed, and then it is stretched forth at length. As one said, seeing a snake dead, and stretched out, so, saith he, it behoved you to have lived. So the devil, that great serpent, that ancient 'old serpent,' Rev. xii. 9, he gets into the snake, into the wily wit, and makes it wind and turn, and shift and shuffle in the world. But then some great cross comes, or death comes, and then a man is stretched out at length to the view of the world, and then he confesseth all, and perhaps that confession is sincere when it is wrung out by terror of conscience, then he confesseth that he hath deceived the world, and deceived himself, and laboured to deceive God also.

If we would have comfort in the hour of death, labour we to deal plainly and directly; and of all other sins, as I said before, remember this is that which will lie the heaviest on us, as coming nearest the sin against the Holy Ghost. For what is the sin against the Holy Ghost? When men rush against their knowledge in malice to the truth known. Where there is most knowledge, and most will, there is the greatest sin. Now in lying and dissembling, and double-dealing, a man comes near to the sin against the Holy Ghost; for he knows that he doth ill, he plots the ill that he knows; and when there is plotting, there is time to deliberate; a man is not carried away by passion.

Consider, the time will come when you will be uncased, when you will be laid open and naked; and then at that time, of all sins, this will lie heavy on thee, thy dissembling in the world. Therefore every one in his calling, take heed of the sins of his calling, among the rest, of this one of double-dealing.

2. And therefore that we may avoid it the better, *labour for faith, to live by faith.* What is the reason that men live by shifts, and by doubling in the world? They have not faith to depend upon God, in good and plain downright courses. Men are ready to say, If I should not dissemble and double, and carry things after that manner, how should I live? Why, where is thy faith? The righteous man lives by his faith, and not by his shifts, not by his wits. God will provide for us. Are we not in covenant

with God? Do we not profess to be God's children? Do children use to shift? No; a child goes about to do his father's will and pleasure, and he knows that he will maintain him. It is against the nature of the child of God, as far as he knows himself to be a child of God, to use any indirect course, any windings and turnings in his calling. Let us depend upon God as a child depends on his father; and of all others God will provide most for them that in simple honesty, in plain downright dealing, depend on him in doing good.

For God accounts it a prerogative to defend and maintain them that cast themselves on him. He will be their wisdom that can deny their own wisdom, and their own shifts by nature, and in conscience labour to deal directly. He will be wise for them and provide for them. It is his prerogative to do so, and not to suffer his children to be deserted. A little faith therefore would help all this, and would make us walk in simplicity. If we could make God our all-sufficiency once, then we should walk uprightly before God and men.

For what makes men to double?

This certainly makes men to double. They think they shall be undone if they be direct; for if they deal directly, they shall lose their liberty, or their lives, or their opportunity of gaining, &c. Well; come what will, deal thou directly, and know this for a rule, thou shalt have more good in God's favour, if thou be a Christian, than thou canst lose in the world, if upon grounds of conscience thou deal directly in what estate soever thou art.

If thou be a judge, if thou be a witness, deal directly, speak the truth. If thou be a divine, speak directly in God's cause, deal out the word of God as in God's presence, come what will, whatsoever thou losest in thy wealth, or liberty, &c., thou shalt gain in God. Is not all good in him? What is all the good we have, is it not from him? And the nearer you come to him, the more your happiness is increased; the more you are stripped of earthly things, the more you have in God. Hath not he men's hearts in his hands? When you think you shall endanger yourselves thus and thus by plain direct dealing without doubling, if you be called to the profession of the truth, &c.; hath not he the hearts of men in his hands to make them favour you when he pleaseth? In Prov. x. 9, 'He that walketh uprightly, walketh boldly.' He that walketh uprightly, not doubling in his courses, he walketh safely. God will procure his safety. God that hath 'the hearts of men in his hand as the rivers of water,' Prov. xxi. 1, he can turn them to favour such a man.

A man's nature is inclined to favour downright-dealing men, and to hate the contrary. You see the three young men, when they were threatened with fire, come what will, 'O king, we will not worship the image of gold which thou hast set up,' Dan. iii. 14, *seq.* They would be burned first. What lost they by it?

Howsoever, if we should lose, as it is not to be granted that we can lose anything by direct dealing, 'For the earth is the Lord's, and the fulness thereof,' Ps. xxiv. 1, and the hearts of men are his. But suppose they do, yet they gain in better things, in comfort of conscience, and expectation and hope of better things. Faith is the ground of courage, and the ground of all other graces that carry a man's courage in a course of simplicity in this world.

Therefore, if we would walk simply, and have our conversation in the world in this grace, let us labour especially for faith to depend upon God's promises, to approve ourselves to him, to make him our last and chief end, and our communion with him, and to direct all our courses to that end. This is indeed to set him up a throne in our hearts, and to make him a God, when rather than we will displease him or his vicegerent, his vicar in us, which is conscience (that he hath placed in us as a monitor and as a witness), we will venture the loss of the creature, of anything in the world, rather than we will displease that vicar which he hath set in our hearts. This, I say, is to make him a God; and he will take the care and protection of such a man. St Paul here, in all the imputations, in all crosses in the world, he retires home, to himself, to his own house, to conscience; and that did bear him out, that 'in simplicity he had his conversation in the world.' The next particular is,

'In sincerity.' The apostle adds to simplicity, this 'godly sincerity.' And he may well join these two together, for plainness and truth go together. A plain heart is usually a true heart. Doubleness and hypocrisy, which are contrary, they always go together. He that is not plain to men will not be sincere to God. Simplicity respects our whole course with men. Sincerity hath an eye to God, though, perhaps, in matters and actions towards men. Sincerity is alway with a respect to God; and so it is opposed to hypocrisy, a vice in religion opposite to God.

Now this sincerity that the apostle speaks of, it is *a blessed frame of the soul, wrought by the Spirit of God, whereby the soul is set straight and right in a purpose to please God in all things (and in endeavours answerable to that purpose), and to offend him in nothing.*

I make a plain description, because I intend practice. There may be some nicer descriptions.

But, I say, it is a blessed frame of the soul, wrought by the sincere Spirit of God, whereby the soul is set straight and right to purpose, and to endeavour all that is pleasing in God's sight; and that with an intention to please God, with an eye to God, or else it is not sincerity. It is such a disposition and frame of soul that doth all good, that hates all ill, with a purpose to please God in all, with an eye to God.

And therefore it is called 'sincerity of God,' or 'godly sincerity;' and it is called so fitly: because God is not only the author of it, but God is the aim of it, and the pattern of it; for he is the first thing that is sincere, that is simple and unmixed. God is the pattern of it. It makes us like to God, and he is the aim of it. A man that is sincere aims at God in all his courses: wherein he aims not at God he is not sincere. It comes from God, and it looks to God. For naturally we are all hypocrites. We look to shows. Therefore sincerity is from God.

And it is the sincerity of God especially, because, where this sincerity is, it makes us aim at God in all things, it makes us have respect to him in all things, as the creature should have respect to the Creator, the servant to the master, the son to the father, the subject to the prince. The relations we stand in to God should make us aim at him in all things.

The observation from hence is this,

Doct. A Christian that hopes for joy, must have his conscience witness to him, that his conversation is in the sincerity of God.

As the apostle saith here, 'This is the testimony of our conscience, that in simplicity and godly sincerity we have had our conversation,' &c.

Now to go on with this sincerity, and lay it open a little. Sincerity, it is not so much a distinct thing, as that which goes with every good thing. Truth and sincerity, it is not so much a distinct virtue, and grace, as a truth joined to all graces; as sincere hope, sincere faith, sincere love, sincere repentance, sincere confession. It is a grace annexed to every grace. It is the life and soul of every grace, and all is nothing without it.

Therefore it behoves us to consider of it, I say, not so much a distinct thing from other graces, as that which makes other graces to be graces, without which they are nothing at all. So much sincerity, so much reality. So much as we have not in sincerity, we have nothing to God. It is but an empty show, and will be so accounted.

In philosophy, you know, that which is true, only hath a being and consistence. All truth hath a being, all falsehood is nothing. It is a counterfeit thing. It is nothing to that it is pretended to be. An image is something, but St Paul calls it nothing, because it is not that which it should be, and which the idolater would have it to be. He would have it to be a god, but it is nothing less. All is nothing without sincerity. Therefore let us consider of it. And that we may the better consider of it, let us look upon it in every action.

All actions are either good, ill, indifferent.

How is sincerity discovered in good actions?

1. Sincerity is tried in good actions many ways.

(1.) First of all, a man that is sincere in the doing that which is good, *he will have a mind prepared to know all that is good;* to know the good he stands disposed to, to know good, and to learn by all good means. Therefore he hath a heart prepared with diligence to be informed in the use of means. So far as a man is careless and negligent in coming to the means of knowledge, and to be put in mind of good duties, so far a man is an hypocrite and insincere.

(2.) Again, in regard of good duties, a true, sincere Christian *hath an universal respect to all that is good.* He desires to know all, and, when anything is manifested to him, he intends to practise all. 'We are here in the presence of God,' saith Cornelius, 'to practise all things that shall be taught us by God,' Acts x. 33. 'I will have respect to all thy commandments,' Ps. cxix. 6, one and another.

The ground of it is this, sincerity looks at God. Now God, he commands one thing as well as another; and therefore, if a man do anything that is good, in conscience to God, he must do one as well as another. As St James saith excellently to this purpose, 'He that offends in one is guilty of all,' ii. 10. Because, abstaining from one sin, and doing one good for conscience, he will do all for conscience if he be sincere.

Therefore it is true in divinity,—a man that repents of one sin, he repents of all, if he repent of any sin as it is a sin, because all sins are of one nature. We must not single out what pleaseth us, and leave what doth not please us. This is to make ourselves gods. The servant must not choose his work, but take that work that his master commands him; therefore sincerity is tried in universal obedience.

Partial obedience is insincere obedience. When a man saith, This sin I must keep still, herein 'God be merciful to me,' this stands with my profit, I must not leave this; this sin I am affected to, as we see in Saul,—this is insincerity. It is as good as nothing to God-ward. It may keep a man from shame in the world, &c., but to God it is nothing. A man must have respect to all God's commandments. It is not done to God else.

(3.) More particularly, he that is sincere, *he will have regard of the main duties, and he will have regard likewise of the lesser duties, and especially of the lesser*, such as are not liable to the censure of men, or to the censure and punishment of the law; for there a man's sincerity is most tried. In great duties, there are great rewards, great encouragements; but for lesser duties, there are lesser encouragements. But if a man do them, he must do them for conscience sake.

Therefore this is sincerity, to practise good duties though they be lesser duties, and though they be less esteemed in the world, and less countenanced; to practise them though they be discountenanced by the devil, and by great ones; yet to practise them, because they be good; and to love good things that the world cares not for, because they be good.

The practice of private prayer morning and evening, it is a thing we are not expressly bound to, but as conscience binds us. Therefore if a man be sincere he will make conscience of that, as well as any other duty, because God bids us 'pray alway,' 1 Thess. v. 17. So, to fear an oath for conscience sake, not to swear common or lighter oaths,—for I count him not worthy the name of a Christian, that is an ordinary swearer; but—lighter oaths a Christian makes conscience of, because he looks to God. Now God looks to little sins as well as to great; and there is no sin little indeed that toucheth the majesty of God.

The practice of all duties, therefore, is a notable evidence of sincerity. Herod did many things, but he had a Herodias, that spoiled all. And so if thou obey in many things, and not in all, thou hast a Herodias, a main sin. Alas! all is to no purpose! thou art an hypocrite.

(4.) Again, for good things, one that is sincere in respect to God, he is *uniform in his obedience*, that is, he doth all that is good, and he doth it in one place as well as another, and at one time as well as another. He doth it not by starts.

Therefore there is constancy required in sincerity. Where sincerity is, there is constancy to do it in all times, in all places. Or else it is but a humour. It is not sincerity when a man doth it but in good moods, as we say. Therefore a man that is sincere, he makes conscience of private duties as well as of public; of personal duties between God and his own soul, as well as of the duties that the world takes notice of; in one place as well as another. He is holy not only in the church, but in his closet; not only in his calling as he is a Christian, but when he is about his particular business. He considers he is in the presence of God in every place, at all times.

St Paul everywhere laboured to have a good conversation. When he was at the bar, he remembered where he was, and he laboured to convert others. In the prison he converted Onesimus, Philem. 10. When he had his liberty, he spread the gospel everywhere.

So in all places he was uniform like himself, which shewed that he had a good conscience. And therefore he doth not say, I do now and then a good action, but my course of life, 'my conversation, is in sincerity.' So there must be sincerity in our walking, our whole conversation. Thus we see in good actions how to try our sincerity.

(5.) A sincere man in the very performance of good duties, *he is humble;* because he doth all things in the eye of God. He doth it in sincerity with humility. He doth all good with reverence, because he doth it to God.

Humility, and reverence, it is a qualification of sincerity; because whatsoever we do, we do it in the eye of God. Therefore we are reverent in our very secret devotions in our closets. We carry ourselves reverently;

because when no eye seeth us, the eye of heaven seeth us, in one place as well as another. A sincere christian, is a reverent, and humble Christian, and this reverence accompanies all his good actions.

(6.) And when he hath done all, a sincere Christian that doth them to God, he is humble, *and then he is thankful;* for he knows that he hath not done it by his own strength, but by God, and therefore God hath the glory.

He is humble, because *they are mixed with some infirmities of his.* A sincere Christian is alway humble, having an eye to God. Though to the eye of the world he hath done excellent well, yet he knows that God seeth* as he seeth. He seeth some defects, God seeth more, and that humbleth him. As we see David, 1 Chron. xxix. 14. Saith he, 'Who am I? or who is this people, that we should be able to offer willingly after this sort? All things come of thee; of thine own I have given thee.' So he humbled himself in thankfulness to God.

2. For ill actions, (1.) a true sincere Christian beforehand *he intends none.* He regards none in his heart. Ps. lxvi. 18, 'If I regard iniquity in my heart, the Lord will not hear my prayers.' His disposition is to regard none. He is in league with none. If he were, his heart were false, his conscience would tell him he were an hypocrite. He is subject to infirmities, but he doth not respect them, he doth not regard them. He intends not in his heart to live in them.

(2.) Again, if he fall into any sin, *he is sincerely grieved for them.* His heart is tender, and he sincerely confesseth them, without guile, Ps. xxxii. 2. 'Blessed is the man in whose spirit there is no guile,' who when he sees he hath sinned, he doth not guilefully cloak and extenuate his sin. As we see Saul, he had many evasions, and excuses for himself, 1 Samuel xiii. 12. A true Christian will lay open his sin with all the aggravations that his conscience tells him of. As David saith, what a fool, 'and what a beast was I,' Ps. lxxiii. 22; what an unthankful creature was I to sin against so many benefits and favours! He will be ashamed and confounded in himself.

(3.) And of all sins, a sincere Christian is most careful *to avoid his personal sins.* You may know sincerity by that. He that takes not heed to that which he is most inclined unto, he shall be tripped in it.

An hypocrite and false-hearted man, he doth good, but it is with a purpose to be favoured in some sin wherein he strengtheneth himself. He will do something, that God may be favourable to him in other things.

But a true sincere Christian, though he be inclined by temper of body, or by his calling, or by the former custom of his unregenerate life, to some sin more than another, and he hath not shaken some sin wholly off, he hath not purged himself wholly of the dregs of it, but he finds still a propenseness in his nature to it; yet as far as he is sincere, he gets strength, especially against that. A false-hearted man favours himself, especially in those sins; and will swell if he be found out in them. He will not bear a reproof. But a Christian that is sincere, that intends amendment, that intends to be better, he would reform his heart if it be amiss, and is willing to be discovered in his most particular and personal sins that he is prone to.

We may try ourselves by this, not only by hating sin in general and at large, but how we stand affected, especially to those particular sins we are most prone to. Sincerity, as it hates all wicked ways, so it hates those sins

* Qu. 'seeth not?'—G.

that are most sweet, that we are most prone to, as well as any other, nay, more than any other; because those especially endanger the soul. A child of God will abstain from all evil. He will be careful, not only that others abstain from sin, but he will abstain from sin himself most of all. Noisome things we hate them always, but we hate them most when they are nearest us. As a toad, we hate it afar off, much more when it is near. So a sincere Christian hates sin most in his own breast.

(4.) Now because sincerity hath an eye to God, *I must hate all sin as well as any*, or else I am not sincere.

A man that hath the point of his soul to God-ward, he will hate all manner of ill, little ills as well as great; because all sin agrees in this,—all sin is against God. It is contrary to the mind of God; and all sin is pernicious to the soul. All sin is against the pure word of God, and considering it is so, therefore I must hate all sin, if I hate any; because God hates all, and all sin is contrary to the image of God; and not only contrary to the image of God, but contrary to the revealed will of God, contrary to my soul's comfort, contrary to communion with God, and contrary to the peace of my conscience. Those regards come in every sin. Every sin hinders that.

(5.) Again, where the soul and conscience is sincere, there will be *a special care for the time to come of the sins we have been overtaken withal.* So we see how this sincerity may be tried, in abstaining from evil, as well as in the good we do.

3. For actions that are of a more common nature, *that in themselves are neither good nor ill, but as the doer is, and as the doer stands affected*, a true Christian may be tried by them thus—

(1.) For the actions *of his calling*, though they be good in their kind, yet they be not religious, thus he stands affected if he be sincere,—he doth them as God's work. Common actions are as the doer is affected. A sincere man considers what he doth as God's work. He is commanded to serve God in his calling as well as in the church; and, therefore, he will not do it negligently. 'For cursed is he that doth the work of the Lord negligently,' Jer. xlviii. 10.

He will not do it falsely. He will not profane his calling. I will not prostitute my calling to serve my lust, or to serve my gain. Doth not God see it? is not he the author of my calling? is it not his work, saith conscience? Yes! and therefore he doth common actions with an eye to God, and so he makes them good and religious actions. For the grace of God is a blessed alchymist! Where it toucheth, it makes good and religious. Though the actions be not so in their own nature, it raiseth the actions, it elevates them higher than themselves.

It makes the actions of our calling, that are ordinary actions, to be holy, when they are done with an eye of sincerity to God. As St Paul saith, the very servant serves God in serving his master.

(2.) And so for actions that we account most indifferent, *as recreations and liberty to refresh ourselves.* A sincere man considers of them as a liberty bought to him by the blood of Christ, and considers himself in the presence of God. And, therefore, whatsoever he doth, 'whether he eat or drink.' &c., 1 Cor. x. 31, he still useth his refreshings as in the presence of God, and doth all as in the sight of God. His conversation, that is, his whole course, whatsoever he doth, is sincere with an eye to God. He knows his corruption is such that it most watcheth him in his liberties; for the more lawful a thing is, the more we are in danger to be entangled in it.

In excess, in open ills, there is not so much danger as in things that seem indifferent, lawful recreations, &c. Recreations, and such things, are lawful; but to spend whole nights unthriftily, basely, scandalously this way, it is not only against religion, but against civility. In a civil man's judgment, it is a scandal to the place and person. Therefore he that hath any truth of grace in him, he will look to himself, and look to God in the most free actions of all. You see then how we may judge of our sincerity whatsoever we do. A sincere Christian stands thus affected in some measure, in some degree, in the good he doth, in the ill he abstains from. Whatsoever it be, he thinks he hath to deal with God.

Use 1. Now to stir us up to this blessed state, to labour for this frame of soul, to be sincere, to have our conversation in sincerity, what needs be added more than this, that without it all is nothing.

1. *All our glorious performances are mere abominations, without sincerity.* God will say, you did it not to me, you did it for vainglory, you did it for custom or out of education, for vain and by-respects, and not to me, and do you look for a reward of me? You did it not for conscience; for conscience alway looks to God. And what we do not in conscience and obedience to God, in our general or particular calling, it stands not on our reckoning with God. It is as good as if it were not done, in regard of God, and of the life to come. 'You have your reward,' saith Christ, Mat. vi. 2. It is no matter what your respects be here. If you carry yourselves carefully in your place, to have the credit of men, to gain the favour of men, you have your reward. Will you look for a reward from God, when what you did, you did it to the world?

What a pitiful thing is this, that a man should do many things, many years together, and yet do nothing that may further his day of account, because it was not done out of conscience of his duty? His conversation was not in sincerity to God. Now, if we have not truth we have nothing in religion. St Paul saith, as I said before, 'Of an idol, it is nothing,' Why! it is a piece of wood, or a piece of gold, the materials of it is something, but it is nothing to that which it should be. If a man be not true in religion, he is nothing in that. He is a true hypocrite, but a false Christian. He is nothing in Christianity. He is something in hypocrisy, but that something is nothing.

All the shows in the world, and all the flourishes, they are nothing. What is the reason that excellent clerks,* men of excellent parts, die comfortless many times? Why! God is not beholden to them for all that they did. They sought their own praise. As the prophet Isaiah saith, 'When you fasted, did you fast to me?' Zech. vii. 5. When you did good works, did you do them to me? may God say. There was no truth in it. So much simplicity, so much comfort. Sincerity is all that we can come to in this world. Perfection we cannot attain to. Christ is perfection for us. Truth is all that we can reach to, and without that all is nothing. Therefore we ought to regard it especially.

2. Again, on the other side, this is a great encouragement to be sincere, to be true-hearted in all our courses and actions; *because it gives acceptance to whatsoever we do;* and it is that by which God values us. God values us not by perfection, not by glorious shows, but by what we have in truth. So much truth, so much worth. A little pearl is worth a great deal of rubbish.

A little sincerity, because it is God's own creature, it is 'the sincerity of God,' it is wrought by him, it is his stuff. There is an almighty power to

* That si, = 'ministers of the gospel.'—G.

work truth in us; for by nature we are all false. God gives to some men to carry themselves more civilly than others; but it is nothing worth except God change a man by grace; because God accepts us according to sincerity. God values us by truth. So much truth, so much esteem of the God of truth.

And where this sincerity is, God bears with many infirmities. As in marriage, the husband that is discreet, that knows what belongs to marriage, if the heart of the wife be true, though she have many woman-like infirmities, he passeth by them as long as the conjugal knot is kept unviolate. So a Christian, if his heart be true, that he looks to God in all things, though he have many infirmities, God passeth by them. As we see in Asa; how many faults had he committed? He trusted in the physicians, he used the prophet hardly, and many other faults, and yet it is said that his heart was upright all his days, because he had truth in him. It was in passion that he did this or that otherwise. So Hezekiah, although he had many infirmities, yet he could say that he 'had walked uprightly before God,' Isa. xxxviii. 3; and God did well esteem him for it. And when he speaks of those that were to come to the passover, 'Be merciful to those that prepare their hearts,' 2 Chron. xxx. 19, those that have true hearts, though they have many weaknesses.

Now, if the heart be false, though a woman have many virtues, yet if she want the main, if she have a false heart to her husband, what is all the rest? So the soul that is married to God, that hath sweet communion with God, if the heart and soul be naught, what are all the shows in the world? They are nothing. Let us take it to heart, therefore, and labour to approve our hearts and souls to God in all that we do, more than our lives and outward conversations to the world. Let them think what they will, so God approve of our hearts, and intentions, and purposes; we are not to 'pass what the world judgeth,' as St Paul saith of himself, 1 Cor. iv. 3.

3. Again, this should encourage us to labour for sincerity and truth, because wheresoever that is, *there is a growing to perfection.* 'To him that hath shall be given,' Mat. xiii. 12. 'If we order our conversation aright,' as the psalmist saith, Ps. l. 23, and labour to please God in all things, the more we do, the more we shall have grace to do; and the more we have, the more we shall have. 'To him that hath shall be given;' that is, he that truly hath, and doth not seem to have, but [he that] hath not indeed, that seemeth to have goodness, and hath none indeed, that which he hath shall be taken from him.

A true Christian is alway on the mending hand. It is a blessed prerogative. He is alway mending and bettering by God's blessing. For where God gives in truth, if it be but a little, if it be but a grain of mustard-seed, if it be true, he will cherish it till it come to be a tree. He will add grace to grace, one degree of grace to another. Where there is truth, it is alway honoured with growth. It is not only a sign of truth, but where truth is there will be an endeavour of growth. It is a prerogative. Where God bestows truth, he will always add the grace of growth, though not at all times alike. Yet if Christians sometimes do not grow, their not growing and their failings shame them, and makes them grow more afterward, and recover their former backwardness. A true Christian is alway on the mending hand. An hypocrite grows worse and worse alway, till he be uncased altogether, and turned into hell. These and such like considerations may stir us up to labour to have a conversation in simplicity and godly sincerity.

Use 2. Now, how shall we come to carry ourselves in sincerity, that we may have comfort in all estates?

That we may carry ourselves in sincerity,

1. First, *we must get a change of heart.* Our nature must be changed. For by nature a man aims at himself in all things, and not at God. A man makes himself his last end. He makes something in the world, either profits, or pleasures, &c., the term that he looks unto. Therefore, there must be a change of heart. A man must be a good man, or else he cannot be a sincere man. Such as we are, such our actions will be. Therefore, we cannot be sincere till we have our hearts changed.

2. No man can aim at God's glory, but he *that hath felt God's love in himself.* Therefore as a particular branch of that, labour to get assurance of the love of God in Jesus Christ; for how can we endeavour to please him unless we love him? And how can we love him unless we be persuaded that he loves us in Christ? Therefore let us stablish our hearts more and more in the evidences of his love to us; and then knowing that he loves us, we shall love him, and labour to please him in all things. These are grounds that must be laid before we can be sincere; to get assurance of God's love to us in the pardon of our sins. 'Our conscience must be purged from dead works, to serve the living God,' as the apostle saith, Heb. ix. 14; that is, we cannot serve God to our comfort till our consciences are sprinkled with the blood of Christ, which assures us of the pardon of our sins. Therefore saith Zacharias, 'We are redeemed, that we might serve him in righteousness and holiness before him all the days of our life,' Luke i. 75. So that unless a man be redeemed, he cannot serve him in righteousness and holiness 'before him' all the days of his life; that is, he cannot serve God in sincerity.

For who will labour to please his enemy? Therefore the papists maintain hypocrisy when they say we ought not to be persuaded of the love of God, for then we ought to be hypocrites. For how shall we seek him with the loss of favour, and of credit, and of life itself, if we know not that his favour will stand us in stead, if we lose these things for him?

3. Again, that we may be sincere, let us labour *to mortify all our earthly affections to the world;* for how can we be sincere when we seek for honours and pleasures, and riches, and not for better things? Therefore we must know that there is more good to be had in truth, in a downright Christian profession, than in all worldly good whatsoever. And if we be hypocrites in our profession, there is more ill in that than in anything in the world. This will make us sincere, when we can be persuaded that we shall get better things by being sincere in religion than the world can give us, or take away from us. For why are men insincere and false-hearted? Because they think not religion to be the true good. They think it is better to have riches than to have a good mind. These things therefore must be mortified; and a man must know that the life of a Christian is incomparably the best life, though it be with the loss of liberty, yea, with the loss of life itself.

Simon Magus grew to false affections in religion, because he thought to have profit by it. So the Pharisees, they had naughty hearts, and therefore they had no good by religion. No man can profit by religion so long as his heart is naught, so long as there is some idol in his heart. A good Christian had rather have a large heart to serve God, and rather grow in the image of God, to be like him, than to grow in anything in the world, and that makes him sincere out of a good judgment; because Christian excellency is the best excellency incomparably. For he knows well what all else will be ere long. What! will all do good, riches, honours, friends? What good will they do in the hour of death? There is nothing but grace, and the expression of it in the whole conversation, that will comfort us. Therefore he undervalues all things in the world to sincerity and a good conscience.

4. Again, that we may have our conversation in sincerity, let us labour in everything we do *to approve ourselves to the eye of God*. We see the Scripture everywhere shews, that this hath made God's children conscientious in all their courses; even when they might have sinned not only securely, but with advantage. What kept Joseph from committing folly with his mistress? 'Shall I do this, and sin against God?' Gen. xxxix. 9. And so Job in chap. xxxi., he shews what awed and kept him from ill-doing; in ver. 3, 'Doth not he see my ways, and account all my steps?' This was it that kept him in awe. So the church of God, Ps. xliv., being in great distress, they kept themselves from idolatry, and from the contagion of the times wherein they lived. Upon what ground? You shall see in verse 21, 'If we had done thus and thus, shall not God search it out? for he knows the very secrets of the heart.' So a Christian being persuaded of the eye of God upon him, it makes him sincere. The eye of God being ten thousand times brighter than the sun, he being light itself. He made the heart, and he knows all the turnings of the heart. The consideration of this will make us sincere in our closets, in our very thoughts; for they all lie open and naked to his view.

What is the reason that men practise secret villany, secret wickedness, and give themselves to speculative filthiness? Because they are atheists. They forget that they are in the eye of God, who sees the plots and projects of their hearts, and the nets that they have laid for their brethren. Therefore David brings them in saying, 'Tush! God sees us not,' Isaiah xxix. 15. And that is the reason they are unconscionable in their desires, in their hearts, in their secret thoughts. It is from a hidden atheism. For if we did consider that the eye of God sees us in all our intents and actions, and sees us in what manner we do all, and to what end; that he sees every action, with the circumstances, the aims, and ends; if the heart did well ponder this, it would prevent a great deal of evil.

Conscience is the witness of our conversation, a witness that will keep us from offending. If there were a witness by, and that witness were a great person, a judge, &c., it would keep us in our good behaviour. Now when a man shall consider, I have a witness within me, my conscience; and a witness without, which is God, who is my Judge, who can strike me dead in the committing of a sin, if he please: this would make men, if they were not atheists, to fear to sin.

Let us labour therefore to approve our hearts to God, as well as our conversations to men; set ourselves in the presence of God, who is a discerner of our thoughts as well as of our actions; and that which we should be ashamed to do before men, let us be afraid to think before God. That is another means to come to sincerity.

5. Another direction to help us to walk sincerely is, *especially to look to the heart*, look to the beginning, to the spring of all our desires, thoughts, affections, and actions, that is, the heart. The qualification of that is the qualification of the man. If the heart be naught, the man is naught. If that be sincere, the man is sincere. Therefore look to the heart. See what springs out thence. If there spring out naughty thoughts and desires,

suppress them in the beginning. Let us examine every thought. If we find that we do but think an evil thought, execute it presently; crush it: for all that is naught comes from a thought and desire at the first. Therefore let us look to our thoughts and desires. See if we have not false desires, and intents and thoughts answerable.

God is a Spirit, and he looks to our very spirits: and what we are in our spirits, in our hearts and affections, that we are to him. Therefore, as a branch of this, what ill we shun, let us do it from the heart, by hating it first. A man may avoid an evil action from fear, or out of other respects, but that is not sincerity. Therefore look to thy heart, see that thou hate evil, and let it come from sincere looking to God. 'Ye that love the Lord, hate the thing that is evil,' saith David, Ps. xcvii. 10: not only avoid it, but hate it; and not only hate it, but hate it out of love to God. And that which is good, not only to do it, but to labour to delight and joy in it. For the outward action is not the thing that is regarded, but when there is a resolution, a desire and delight in it, then God accounts it as done. And so it is in evil. If we delight in evil, it is as if it were done already. Therefore in doing good, look to the heart, joy in the good you do, and then do it; and in evil, look to the heart, judge it to be evil, and then abstain from it.

This is the reason of all the errors in our lives. Because we have bad hearts, we look not to God in sincerity. Judas had a naughty heart. He loved not the Lord Jesus Christ, and therefore he had a naughty conclusion. What the heart doth not, is not done in religion. Thus we see how we may come to have our conversation in sincerity, that we may rejoice in the testimony of our conscience.

Use. Therefore now, to make an use of exhortation, *we should labour for sincerity, and esteem highly of it, because God so esteems of it*. Truth is all that we can allege to God. We cannot allege perfection. St Paul himself saith not, I have walked exactly or perfectly: no, but he saith, 'This is our rejoicing, that we have walked in sincerity.' So, if a man's conscience can excuse him of hypocrisy and doubling, though it cannot free him from imperfections, God in the covenant of grace looks not so much at perfection as at truth.

Obj. Here I might answer an objection of some Christians. Oh, but I cannot pray without distraction, I cannot delight so in good things, &c.

Ans. Though a Christian's heart cannot free him from this, yet his heart desires to approve itself to God in all things; and his heart is ready to say to the Lord, as David said, 'Lord, try me, if there be any way of wickedness in me,' Ps. cxxxix. 23. And therefore he will attend upon all means to get this sincerity. He will be diligent in the word of God, for therein the mind of God is manifestly seen. The word of God, it is a begetting word, it makes us immortal, it makes us new creatures. It is truth, and the instrument of truth. Truth will make truth. The true sincere word of God, not mingled with devices, it will make what it is. The word of God, being his word who is Almighty, it hath an almighty transforming power from him. It is accompanied and clothed with his Almighty Spirit. Truth will cause truth. Such as it is in itself it will work in our hearts.

In that mongrel, false religion, popery, they have traditions, and false devices of men, and so they make false Christians. Such as they are they make. Strain them to the quintessence, and they cannot make a true Christian. Truth makes true Christians. Therefore attend upon God's ordinance with all reverence, and it will make thee a sound heart. It is a transforming word. Those that desire to hear the word of God, and to have their consciences to be informed by the hearing of it, they are sincere Christians; and those that labour to shut up the word of God, that it may not work upon the conscience, they are false-hearted.

A heart that is sincere, it prizeth the word of God that makes us sincere. The word of God hath this effect, especially being unfolded in the ministry of it, that a man may say, as Jacob did, 'Doubtless God is in this place,' Gen. xxviii. 17. It is all that is ours. Nothing runs upon our reckoning but sincerity. For what I have not done truly, conscience saith I have not done to God, and therefore I can expect no comfort for it; but what I have done to God, I look to have with comfort: for I know that God regards not perfection, but sincerity. He requires not so much a great faith, as a true faith; not so much perfect love, as true love, and that I have in truth, as St Peter said, 'Lord, thou knowest that I love thee,' John xvi. 30.

This will make us look God, who is the Judge, in the face. It gives us not title to heaven, for that is only by Christ; but it is a qualification required of us in the gospel. Nothing is ours but what we do in truth.

And again, consider that it will comfort us against Satan at the hour of death. When Satan shall tempt us to despair for our sins, as that he will do, we may comfort ourselves with this, that we have been sincere. We may send him to Christ, for that must be the way, who hath fulfilled God's will, and satisfied his Father's wrath. Satan will say, This is true; it is the gospel, and therefore it cannot be denied; but it is for them that have walked according to the Spirit, and not according to the flesh; for those that have obeyed God in all things. Now when our conscience shall join with Satan, and say, we did nothing to God, we have not obeyed him, how can we answer him? we must needs yield to the tempter. But when we can say with Peter, 'Lord, thou knowest that I love thee,' thou knowest I have laboured to approve my heart to thee, and that I have prosecuted this desire with endeavours; this will comfort a man in the time of temptation. Therefore let us labour to have our conversation in sincerity.

It will afford us much comfort in this life, as it did St Paul. St Paul here was in some grievous sickness, even to death, and he was disgraced as a person that regarded not his promise of coming to them. Now what doth he do in all this sickness and disgrace? what doth he answer to them? He comforts himself in this, 'My rejoicing is, that my conscience doth testify my sincerity.' He runs to God, and to his sincerity, as his stronghold. He approves himself to God. Something we shall have in this life first or last; afflictions, or disgraces, and troubles will come. What is then the stronghold of a Christian? Then he runs to his sincerity. What would Hezekiah have done when he received the 'sentence of death,' [if it had not been] that he had walked before God in uprightness and sincerity? Sincerity then is worth more than the world. And he that will not labour for that which is worth more than all the world, it is a sign he is ignorant of the worth of it. A man at the hour of death he would lose all the world if he had it, for sincerity.

Therefore let us not part with our sincerity. Let us not offend against sincerity and truth by falsehood in our carriage, and in our tongues, or conversations any manner of way, since it will yield us so much comfort in temptations, and afflictions, and at the tribunal and judgment-seat of Christ.

Let us not have false aims and ends, and do things in a false manner.

It is not action only that God requires, but the manner. If we regard not the manner, God will not regard the matter. The matter of the Pharisees' performances was very good for stuff, but their hearts being naught, God regarded it not. Let us look to the manner of doing all that we do, that we do them to God, that we do them in sincerity, in a holy manner. The Scripture requires this, receive the sacrament, but thus, 'Examine yourselves,' 1 Cor. xi. 28. 'Take heed how you hear,' Mark iv. 24. Let your conversation be in the world, but thus, 'in simplicity and godly sincerity.' St Paul doth not say that he rejoiced in miracles, or in the great works that he had done, in converting of nations, &c., which yet were matters of joy; but when he comes to joy indeed, here is his joy, that his conversation had been in 'simplicity and godly sincerity.'

And Christians must take heed that they reason not against sincerity another way, that is, to conclude they have no goodness, because they see a great deal of corruption and imperfections; for imperfections may stand with truth. Asa, as I said, had many infirmities in his life, yet notwithstanding it is said, that he walked in sincerity. So Hezekiah, it is said he 'walked before God uprightly,' yet he had many infirmities and imperfections. Nay, a man may well retort this upon such poor souls, that are witnesses with Satan against themseves, in the sight of their sins, that their sins being known by them, especially with hatred of them, it is a sign of sincerity.

Again, others are ready to say, I am not sincere, because God follows me with afflictions and distresses. Reason not so, for he therefore follows thee with afflictions, because he would have nothing but sincerity in thee. He would make thee wholly sincere, and purge thee as metal is purged in the fire from the dross. Therefore take heed thus of sinning against sincerity. Do nothing in hypocrisy. And when we are once sincere, let us not sin against it by yielding to the devil. This comforted Job, when his friends alleged his corruptions. 'Well,' saith he, 'you shall not take away my sincerity from me,' Job xxvii. 6. He looked to the eye of God, that saw him, to whom he approved his heart; and that consideration made him sincere, and thence he comforted himself. So let us comfort ourselves in our sincerity against Satan's allegations; as a condition of the covenant of grace, which respects not perfection but truth.

To add one thing more. As there is an order of other graces; so there is an order in this sincerity which we should labour for. There is this order to be kept.

1. *We must dig deep.* We must lay a sincere foundation. What is that? A deep search into our own hearts and ways by sound humiliation. We say of digestions, if the first be naught, all are naught; if the first concoction in the body be naught, there can never be good assimilation, there can never be good blood. So if there be not a good, a sincere foundation, there can never be a sincere fabric. Therefore many mistake, and build castles in the air, comb-downes, as we say (*pp*). They build a frame of profession that comes to nothing in the end; because it is not sincere in this order. They were never truly humbled. They had a guileful heart, in the confession of their sins. They never knew what sin was throughly, and feelingly. 'Blessed is the man in whose spirit there is no guile,' Ps. xxxii. 2. The psalmist especially means and intends there, in regard of downright dealing with God in the confession of sins. For he himself when he did not deal roundly and uprightly with God in the confession of his sins, with detestation, and with resolution never to commit the same again, he

was in a pitiful plight both of soul and body; his moisture was turned into 'the drought of summer,' Ps. xxxii. 4.

2. But when without guile he laid open his soul to God, then he came from sincere humiliation, and sincere confession, *to sincere faith*. Therefore, for the order, let us first labour to be sincere in the sight of that which is ill in us, in the confession of our sins, and then we shall be sincere, the better to depend upon God's mercy in Christ by faith.

3. And from thence we shall come to *sincere love*. When we believe that God is reconciled in Christ, we shall love him. Our love is but a reflection of his love to us. When once we know that he loves us, we shall love him again.

The spring of all duty is sincere love, coming from sincere faith; as sincere faith is forced out of the sincere sight of our sins, of the ill and miserable estate we are in. A man will not go out of himself, so long as he sees any hope in himself; and therefore sound knowledge of the evil condition we are in, it forceth the grace of faith, which forceth a man to go out of himself. And then when he is persuaded of God's love in Christ, he loves him again.

Love is that which animates, and quickens, and enlivens all duties. What are all duties, but love? Christ reduceth all to love. It is a sweet affection that stirs up and quickeneth to all duties. It carries us along to all duties. All are love. What need I stand on sincere patience, sincere temperance, sincere sobriety, &c.? If a man have sincere love to God, it will carry him to all duties. Remember this order.

Especially every day, enter into your own souls, and search impartially, what sin there is there unconfessed, and unrepented of, and make your peace with God by confession. And then go to sincere dependence on God by faith in the promises. And then stir up your hearts to love him; and from the love of him to love one another in sincerity, not in hypocrisy. Thus we have the manner of the blessed apostle's carriage in the world, whereupon his rejoicing was founded. 'Our rejoicing is this, the testimony of our conscience, that in simplicity and godly sincerity,'

'*We have had our conversation in the world.*' I will speak a little of those words, before I come to the negative part, 'Not in fleshly wisdom.'

'Our conversation.' By 'conversation,' *anastrophe*,* he means the several turnings of his life, in what relation soever he stood to God, to men, as a minister, as a Christian, as a friend, as a neighbour, at home or abroad, in all estates, in all places, and at all times. His conversation was 'in simplicity and sincerity.'

'In the world,' that is, wheresoever he had lived. And mark how he joins them together. His conversation in the world amongst men, it was with sincerity to God. It was that that did rule his conversation in the world. And so it should be with us wheresoever we are, or whatsoever we do in the world, our carriage here must be directed by a higher aspect. The ship while it is tossed in the sea, it is ruled by the pole-star. That must guide it. So in our conversation in the world. The stuff of our conversation may be the business we have in the world, but the rule, the regiment† of all must be from heaven, with an eye to God. I touch that from the knitting of these together.

Now where he saith, that his conversation was in simplicity and sin-

* That is, ἀναστροφή, turning about, = manner of life.—G.

† That is, 'government.'—G.

cerity, you may see here then that all the frame, all the passages of his life were good. This makes good that which I touched before, which hath its proper place here, that

Sincerity extends itself to all the frame of a man's life.

He that is sincere, is sincere in all places, and at all times; in all the turnings and windings and passages of his life; or else he is not sincere at all. His conversation must be sincere, wheresoever he lives, or whatsoever he doth, in prosperity or adversity, at home or abroad.

The veriest hypocrite in the world, hath he not pangs sometimes? Take an oppressor, he thinks that he should not die so, he thinks, I must be called to an account if I do thus. Doth not Ahab lie upon his sick-bed sometimes? Is not Herod sometimes troubled in conscience? Hath not a wicked man sometimes twitches of conscience which the world sees not, secret checks of conscience? Oh, yes! There is not the vilest man living, but he hath his good fits, he hath pangs of goodness. But what is this to a conversation? Our conversation must be in sincerity in all the turnings and passages of it.

God judgeth us by the tenor of our life, and not by single particular acts. A good man may be ill in a particular act; and an evil man may be good in a particular act. But I say, God doth not judge us by a distinct severed passage, but by the tenor of our life. Uniformity, equability, and evenness of life, it is an undoubted evidence of a good man.

Because he is a new creature, and being a new creature, he hath a new nature; and nature works uniformly. Art works differently, and enforcedly. Teach a creature somewhat that is against nature, it will do something, but a lion will have a lion's trick, and a wolf will have a wolf's trick. Teach them never so much, a lion will be a lion in all places; a wolf will be a wolf, and an eagle will be an eagle. Every creature will observe its own nature, and be like itself.

A Christian, as far as he is good, as far as he is a Christian, is uniform. His conversation is good, he is like himself, in all places, in all times, upon all occasions, in prosperity, in adversity. The very word shews that the universality of a man's course must be in sincerity, wheresoever he is. God is everywhere, and sincerity hath an eye to God. It makes a man good everywhere; or else it doth nothing to God. Doth not God see everywhere, abroad, and at home in our closets? If we plot villany, there sees he it as well as abroad. Therefore if I do it anywhere, I regard not the eye of God.

Again, where he saith, 'our conversation,' it implies constancy, as well as uniformity. He was so in all places and in all times. But that I noted before, therefore I pass it. 'Our conversation *in the world*.'

That is, amongst other men, wheresoever I was, and have lived. Whence we see, that

Obs. Christianity may stand with conversing abroad in the world.

Men need not be mued*up in a cloister, as the foolish monks in former times. They thought that religion was a thing confined to solitariness; whereas ofttimes it requires greater strength of grace to be alone than to be in company. We know the proverb, 'Woe to him that is alone,' Eccles. iv. 10. A good Christian converses in the world, and that in simplicity and sincerity. We need not, I say, cloister ourselves up to be good men, to be sincere Christians. We may converse in the world in sincerity if we have St Paul's spirit.

* That is, 'mured,'= immured.—G.

But that which I will press more, is this, that

Obs. True religion, where it is in strength, doth carry a man in the world, and yet he is not tainted with the world.

St Paul conversed in the world in sincerity. The world is an hypocrite, as he said of old. The whole world acts a part. It is an hypocrite, and a cruel opposer of sincerity and truth. St Paul lived abroad in the world, amongst men that had aims of their own, and abused themselves in the world, and yet he walked in 'simplicity and sincerity.' He was a good man for all that. A man that is not of the world, but begotten to be a member of a higher world, he may carry himself in the world without the corruptions of the world, he may carry himself so in the world that he may not be carried away of the world. We see St Paul did so.

Noah was a good man in evil times, 'a good man in his generation,' Gen. vi. 9. Enoch, in evil times 'walked with God,' Gen. v. 22. In Acts xiii. 22, 'David in his generation served the purpose of God;' and his generation was none of the best. For you know there was Ahithophel, and Doeg, which were bad companions, yet in his generation he served the purpose of God. So every man in his time may live and converse in the world, and yet not be carried away with the corruptions of the times.

What is the reason?

Reason. The reason is, that a true Christian hath a spirit in him above the world. As St John saith, 'The Spirit that is in you is stronger than he that is in the world,' 1 John iv. 4. The child of God hath a spirit in him, a new nature, that sets him in a rank above the world. Christians are an order of men that are above the world. They are men of another world. And therefore having a principle of grace that raiseth them above the base condition of the world, they can live in the world, without the blemishes and corruptions of the world. They are men of a higher disposition.

Even as sickness in the body hurts not the reasonable life, so anything that a Christian meets with in the world, it hurts not his Christian life, which is his best life, because it is a life of a higher respect, of a higher nature. St Paul's 'conversation was in heaven,' Philip. iii. 20, it was above the snares here below. He was 'crucified to the world,' Gal. vi. 14. He was a dead man to all that was evil in the world, and to that which was good and indifferent in the world. For pleasures, for honours, for meat and drink, and such necessaries; the counsel that he gave to others, he practised in himself, for worldly callings, and refreshings, and the like, 1 Cor. vii. 29. 'The time is short, let us use the world as though we used it not.' He used indifferent things in the world, which are good or evil as they be used, as if he had not used them. He lived in the world, as a traveller or passenger. He knew he was not at home. He knew he had another home to go to. 'Here we have no continuing city,' Heb. xiii. 14, and therefore he used the world as though he used it not. As a traveller useth things in his way as far as they may further him; but let his very staff trouble him, he throws it away. So a Christian useth indifferent things in the world, which are good or evil according as himself is, he useth them well; because 'all things are pure to the pure,' Titus i. 15. He useth them so as that he doth not delight in them, because he hath better things to solace himself in. He doth not drown himself in these as worldlings do.

And for the ills of the world, a Christian in a good measure is crucified to the world, and the world to him. And he hath his conversation in heaven, 'But our conversation is in heaven,' Philip. iii. 20. Many serve their bellies, 'whose end is damnation, but our conversation is in heaven.'

Now his conversation being heavenly, that is the reason that he can converse in the world in sincerity, though the world be of another strain.

So you see then that a Christian is of a higher nature, of a higher condition than the world; and he is crucified to the world; and he knows himself to be a passenger and a traveller in the world, and therefore he useth the world as though he used it not. And withal he hath his employment above the world. The birds that have the air, as long as they are there, they are not catched with snares below; and Christians that have their conversation above, they are not ensnared with the things of the world as other men are. We see St Paul conversed in the world in sincerity.

I observe it the rather, because it is the common exception of weak, and false spirits.—We must do as the world doth, or else we cannot live. He that knows not how to dissemble, knows not how to live. And the times are naught; so that which is naught and grounded in themselves, they lay all the blame of it upon the times.

Indeed the times are naught, like themselves. As he said, There is a circle of human things. The times are but even as they were. Things come again upon the stage. The same things are acted. The persons indeed are changed, but the same things are acted in the world to the end of the world. The times were naught before, they are naught, and they will be so. Villany is acted upon the stage of the world continually. The former actors are gone, but others are instructed with the same devices, with the same plots. The corruption of nature shews itself in all. Only now we have the advantage for the acting of wickedness in the end of the world; because, besides the old wickedness in former times, we have the new wickednesses of these times. All the streams running into one, make the channel greater.

Men say, Alas! alas! the times are ill. Were they not so in Noah's time? Were they not so in David's time? Were they not so in St Paul's time? Men pretend conformity to the world upon a kind of necessity. They must do as others do.

If they were true Christians it would not be so; for Noah was good in evil times. Nehemiah was good in the court of the king of Babel.* Joseph was good, even in Egypt, in Pharaoh's court. This can be no plea. For a Christian hath a spirit to raise him above the corruption of the times he lives in; he hath such a spirit likewise as is above prosperity or adversity, which will teach him to manage both, and to govern himself in all occasions and occurrents† of the world. 'I can do all things,' saith St Paul, 'through Christ that strengtheneth me!'

As we say, the planets have one course whereby they are carried with the first mover every twenty-four hours, from east to west, as the sun is, whereby he makes the day. But the sun hath a course of his own back again. And so by creeping back again he makes the year in his own course. So the moon hath one course of her own; but yet she is carried every day another course by the first mover.

So, a good Christian that lives in the world, he is carried with the world in common things; he companies, and traffics, and trades, and deals with the world. But hath he not a motion of his own contrary to all this at the same time? Yes; though he converse in the world, yet notwithstanding he is thinking of heaven, he is framing his course another way than the world doth. He goes a contrary course, he swims against the stream of the world.

* That is, 'Babylon.'—G.

† That is, 'occurrences.'—G.

There are some kind of rivers, they say, that pass through the sea, and yet notwithstanding they retain their freshness. It seems as an emblem to shew the condition of a Christian. He passeth through the salt waters, and yet keeps his freshness, he preserves himself. Therefore, I say, it is no plea to say that times are naught, and company is naught, &c. A man is not to fashion himself to the times. An hypocrite, chameleon-like, can turn himself into all colours but white; and as the water, which we say hath no figure of its own, but it is figured by the vessel that it is in (if the vessel be round, the water is round; if the vessel be four-cornered, the water is so), it being a thin, airy, moist body. It hath no compass of its own, but is confined by the body it is kept in.

So some men they have no religion, they have no consistence, no standing, no strength or goodness of their own; but such as their company is, such they are, and they think this will serve for all. I must do as others do; it is the fashion of the world. If they be among swearers, they will swear; if they be among those that are unclean, they will pollute themselves. They frame themselves to all companies. They will be all, but that which they should be. This will not serve the turn.

A Christian may pray for the assistance of God to keep him in the world; and he may know that God will. What ground hath he? Our Saviour Christ, saith he, 'Father, I pray not that thou shouldest take them out of the world, but that thou keep them in the world,' John xvii. 15. He prays for his apostles and disciples, that God would keep them in the world from the contagion of sin, and from the destruction of the world. St Paul, you see, lived and conversed in the world, wheresoever he was, in sincerity and simplicity. He was not carried away with the stream, and errors of the times wherein he lived.

Nay, to add more, it doth unite the power of grace together, and make a man the better, the worse the company or the place is where he lives. We know in nature, the environing of contraries increaseth the contrary; and holy men have been better ofttimes in the midst of temptation, and have gathered their forces and strength of grace together, more than when they have been more secure. The envy and malice of the world is quick-sighted, and the more they live amongst those that are observers of them, the more cautelous* they are of their carriage. You know it is the apostle's reason, 'Redeem the time, because the days are evil,' Eph. v. 16. Be you the better, because the days are evil. Witness for God in an 'evil generation,' in evil times. He doth not say, Do you sin, because the days are evil. God's people do always witness for him.

Let me add this likewise, to give farther light, that we must not take occasion hence, to conform and fashion ourselves to any company, to cast ourselves into evil company when we need not. We must not tempt God; for then it is just with God to suffer us to be soiled with the company. And by our carelessness in this kind, we offend the godly, that easily hereupon take us to be worse than we are. And as we grieve the Spirit of God in them, so in ourselves; and we build up and strengthen wicked persons. And, therefore, this living in the world 'in simplicity and sincerity,' it must be when our calling is such, that we live in the world, that we need not any local separation to sever ourselves. But when in the world, we are cast on men without grace, by our callings, and occasions, we may presume that God will keep us by his Spirit.

Let us not be weary of hearing of this point. For ere long we must all

* That is, 'cautious.'—G.

appear before God, and then what an honour will it be for us, that we have witnessed for God in this world! that we have stood for God and good causes in the midst of the world, and 'shined as lights in the midst of a crooked generation'! Philip. ii. 15. That we have managed the cause of God, and stood for religion, and held our own in the midst of papists and atheists, and profane persons, and witnessed for the best things in spite of all, when we have been called to it. We are not to thrust ourselves into unnecessary troubles, no, not for the best things, unless we be called to it; but when we are called, and can witness for the best things, what an honour will it be for us!

And on the contrary, saith Christ, 'He that denies me, and is ashamed of me before men, of him will I be ashamed before my heavenly Father,' Mark viii. 38. What a fearful thing is this! Let us look to God in simplicity and sincerity, and God will keep us that the world shall not hurt us.

Obj. What will become of us? will some say, this trouble we shall come into, and that persecution will befall us.

Ans. It is not so. Christ was opposed when he was here upon earth; but till his hour was come they could not do anything. Every man hath his hour, every man hath his time allotted to serve God in here. God hath measured out his life; and till his hour be come, that God will take him out of the world, God will bind up the endeavours of men. Their plots shall be to no purpose. God will keep them, and watch over them that are downright. 'Because thou hast kept my word, I will keep thee,' Rev. iii. 8–10, saith God. Let us keep the word of God in evil times, and God will keep us; let us stand for God, and he will stand for us.

It is no plea to say, I shall run into this danger, and that danger. 'God will be thy buckler and thy shield,' Ps. xci. 4, if thou stand for him. And that which brings danger is too much correspondence with the world. When men forsake their sincerity in the world, when men will be on both sides, they carry things unhappily, and unsuccessfully. A downright atheist will carry things with better success than a halting Christian. For his policy and subtlety will carry him to actions inconvenient; but then comes his conscience after, when he is in the midst of them, and damps him that he cannot go forward nor backward. Therefore the only way is to resolve to live in the world in simplicity and sincerity. If we do so, we may carry holy businesses strongly. God will assist us therein. He will increase our light, and make our way plain and clear to us.

But if a man be not sincere, but double, and carnal, and pretend love of religion, and yet take courses and do actions that are not suitable to religion, it will not succeed well. God will curse it. He will strike him with amazement. He will strike his brain with errors in judgment, &c. There is no pretence therefore to make us live falsely, and doubly in the world; but we ought to live as St Paul did, let the world be as bad as it will, or as it can be, 'in simplicity and sincerity.' God will shew himself strong for those that walk uprightly. He will be wisdom to such. But if we walk doubly, and falsely, and make religion our pretence, God will shew himself our enemy.

Where be your neuters then? Where be your politicians in religion, that will keep their religion to themselves? St Paul conversed in the world, wheresoever he was, in sincerity. He made show what he was. He walked not according to carnal wisdom, as he saith afterwards. Where be your *Nullifidians** then, that are of all beliefs, and yet are of no belief? that fashion themselves to all religions? And if they be of the true religion, yet it is their wisdom to conceal it. St Paul did not so. But I shall have occasion to touch that in the negative part afterward, 'not in fleshly wisdom,' &c.

Again, where he saith, 'My conversation hath been thus in the world,' he means, in this life my conversation here hath been sincere. I will give you a touch on that. Though it be not the main aim here, yet notwithstanding it may well be touched, that,

Obs. We must, while we live here in this world, converse in simplicity and sincerity.

We must not turn it off to live as we list, subtlely, politicly, and carnally, and then think to die well. No; we must live 'soberly, righteously, and justly in this present world,' Tit. ii. 12. Do you think to begin to live well when you are gone hence? No; that is a time of reward, and not a time of work. This world is God's workhouse; here you must work. This is God's field; here you must labour. This is God's sea; here we must sail. Here we must take pains. We must sweat at it. Here we must plough and sow, if ever we will reap.

Dost thou think to carry thyself subtlely, to have thy own ends in everything here, and then when death comes, a 'Lord, have mercy upon me' shall serve for all? No; thou must converse as a Christian while thou livest here in this world, 'in simplicity and sincerity.' God must have honour here by thee. Thou must have a care of thy salvation here. Dost thou think to have that in another world which thou dost not care for here? Dost thou think to have glory in another world, which thou didst not think of here? Dost thou think to reap in another world that which thou didst not sow here? Let us in this world stand for the glory of God, openly and boldly, and for the example of others, for the exercise of our own graces. A true Christian hath his conversation in 'sincerity in this world;' the more blame to the world then to deprave their dealing! Why? Because they are lights in the world, and they serve the world to good purpose, if the world would take benefit by them. They shine in the world to lead them the way to heaven. But the world is willing to let them go to heaven alone if they will.

But if the carriage of God's children be like St Paul's, as it is true, for they are all of one disposition, they 'converse in simplicity and sincerity wheresoever they are,' wicked, slanderous, malicious, depraving persons are to blame, that lay to their charge hypocrisy, and this and that, when it is nothing so. They deserve well of the wicked unthankful world, and God upholds the world for their sakes. 'When the righteous are exalted, the city rejoiceth,' saith Solomon, Prov. xi. 10. Because wheresoever they live, they live not only in simplicity and sincerity, but they live fruitfully. The city, the whole community, all the people are the better. They make the times and the places the better wherein they live, because a good man is a public good. The Spirit of God, when it makes a good man, it puts him out of himself, and gives him a public affection. It teacheth him to deny himself. It teacheth him to love others. It teacheth him to employ and improve all that is in him, that is good, for the service of God and of men; to serve God in serving men in the place he lives in. Therefore malicious and devilish is the world to deprave such kind of men as live in the world in simplicity and sincerity, that serve God and the world by all the means

* That is, 'no-faith's.'—G.

they can. 'Our conversation hath been in simplicity and sincerity in the world.'

'*But more abundantly to you-ward.*' Why? Was it in hypocrisy to others, and in sincerity to them only? No; that is not the meaning. But thus, that wheresoever he had lived in the world, in what estate soever he was, he carried himself in 'simplicity and sincerity;' but to you I have made it more evident than to any other. Why? Because he had lived longer with them; and they were such as he was a Father unto in Christ. Therefore, saith he, I have evidenced my 'simplicity and sincerity more abundantly to you than to any other.' Whence we may observe, that

Obs. A sincere Christian is best where he is best known.

It is a note of a truly good and sincere man to be best where he is best known, as I touched when I opened the words. It is otherwise with many. Their carriage abroad is very plausible; but follow them home: what are they in their familes? They are lions in their houses. What are they in their retired courses and carriage? They do not answer the expectation that is raised of them abroad. They never pray to God, &c. Those that know them best will trust them least. It is not so with a Christian. My conversation in the world hath been good wheresoever it hath been. But among you, with whom I have conversed more familiarly, who have seen my daily carriage and course of life, among you my conversation was best of all. It is a note of a man that is sincere, that the more he is seen into, the more he shines. The godly are substantially good, and therefore where they are best known, they are best approved.

For Christians they are not painted creatures, that a little discovery will search them to the bottom, and then shame them. They are not gilded, but gold; and therefore the more you enter into them, the more metal you shall find still. They have a hidden treasury. The more you search them, the more stuff you shall have still. Their tongues are as 'fined silver,' and their heart is a rich treasury within them. A Christian he labours for a broken heart still. He labours to get new grace, and new knowledge of the word of God still; and the more you converse with him, the more you see him, the more you shall approve and love him, if you be good as he is. Therefore saith the apostle, I have carried myself well to all, but especially to you with whom I have lived longer.

Use. Therefore, as we would have an evidence of our sincerity, which is the best evidence that we can have in this world, that we may be able to say that we are sincere and true Christians, which is better than if a man could say he were a monarch, that he were the greatest man in the world, let us labour *to carry ourselves in our courses to those that know us best, and in our most retired courses, like to Christians.* And not to put on the fashion of religion, as men put on their garments: their best garments, when they go abroad, and so to make good things serviceable to our purpose. But to be so indeed at home amongst our friends, among those that know us, when we are not awed, as there is a great deal of liberty amongst friends. Wheresoever we are, let us remember we are alway in the eye of God; and labour to approve ourselves most to them that know our courses most.

God knows more than men, therefore let us chiefly labour to approve ourselves to him. And next to God, let us approve ourselves to conscience. Fear conscience more than all the monarchs in the world; because that knows most, and will be most against us.

And then again, for others that know our conversations, good men that converse with us, let us approve ourselves to them most that have the best and the sharpest judgments.

A true Christian, as he loves goodness, so he loves it most that it should be in his own heart. He lives more to God and to conscience, than to fame and report. He had rather be than seem to be. And as he hates all ill, so he hates even secret ill. The nearer corruption is, the more he hates it, as a man hates toads and venomous creatures ; and the nearer they are, the more he hates them. The most retired carriage of a Christian is most holy, and best of all.

Again, where he saith, 'My conversation hath been in simplicity, &c., to you-ward,' here is a good note for preachers, that if they look to convert any by their doctrine, they must win them by their conversation likewise in simplicity and sincerity. St Paul being to gain the Philippians to Christ, he doth it not by words only, by arguments of logic, and by persuasions only, to convince the understanding of the truth of that which he taught ; but he demonstrates to them how they should live. 'Walk as you have me for an ensample,' Philip. iii. 17. I shew you that that which I teach is possible, by my practice. I shew to high and low, how I carry myself. 'My conversation hath been in simplicity and sincerity.' Those that I would convert by my doctrine, I labour by my conversation to gain them. So I say, ministers have here a special direction how to carry themselves.

And others likewise that have a gaining disposition, as indeed we should not stand upon terms of this and that, but every one labour to gain others. Would you work upon others, and gain them from popery, &c.? Then not only shew them arguments to convince their judgments, which must be done, that is certain ; but likewise let them see that the things that you speak are possible things, things that you are persuaded of. And if you be not good, and press them to goodness, you cannot persuade them of the truth of that you speak. They will think it is not possible ; for then you would act it yourselves. But when they see one go before them, and demonstrate it to their eyes, how they should carry themselves, this is the way to teach them to be sound Christians indeed. But I hasten to the negative part.

'*Not in fleshly wisdom*,' *&c*. Here is a secret wipe, a secret taxing of the false apostles and teachers. 'My conversation hath been in simplicity and sincerity,' whatsoever you think of me. 'Not in fleshly wisdom,' as theirs is.

'Not in fleshly wisdom.' To distinguish it a little.

1. There is a *natural wisdom* planted in the soul of man, even as there is a natural light in the eye, to see both things that are hurtful, and that are good, for the outward man. So in the soul of man, which is his eye, there is an inbred light of natural wisdom, a common light to discern of things and of creatures ; a natural kind of wisdom, which may be polished and advanced to a higher degree by experience and art. As the eye of the body, it sees better when it is helped with an outward, with a foreign light. This is natural wisdom.

2. There is likewise a *politic or civil wisdom*, gotten by observation, and increased by observation ; and withal, it is a gift of God, though it be a common gift, as Ahithophel's. It was not merely carnal wisdom that was in him, but he had a gift of policy. So some men, though they be not

truly religious, yet God gives them a gift of politic wisdom, to be able to discern the difference of things, to lay states and commonwealths together, to be able to judge, and resolve, and to execute wisely, and politically, and prudently. It is an especial gift of God. This the apostle doth not aim at; neither natural nor civil wisdom, though it be a gift of God, I say, which is increased by observation and by other means.

3. Besides this, there is *a spiritual, a heavenly wisdom*, whereby the soul having a right end and aim set and prefixed to it, it directs all its courses to that end; whereby the soul is able to deliberate, to consult, and to resolve on heavenly things, and what hinders heavenly comfort; and to resolve upon good duties, and to resolve against that which is ill, to resolve upon all advantages of doing good to the church, and of all hindrances of ourselves, and of the church, and of the places we live in. It is a heavenly kind of prudence to guide our own ways, yea, and to guide others too.

4. But besides all these, there is another wisdom which is here the '*wisdom of the flesh;*' which because the flesh hath correspondency with Satan, it is also a devilish wisdom, for the most part. For the devil ploughs with our heifer. The most mischief that he hath done in the world, it is by the correspondency that he hath with our flesh, our enemy within. The flesh and Satan do join together, and work all strongly with the mischievous policy of the world: and therefore it is called likewise 'worldly wisdom.'

And hereupon Christians that are mere professors, and not Christians soundly, some are called flesh, because they are ruled of the flesh. And they are called the world, because they frame themselves to the wisdom and to the courses of the world. And if you would anatomize them, there is nothing but the world in them, worldly pride and worldly ends. And they are called devils too, as Judas was called a devil, John vi. 70. They plot with Satan by carnal wisdom. They yield to Satan. They savour not the things of God.

Men have their name and denomination in the Scripture, by that which they are ruled by. When they are ruled by the flesh, they are called flesh; when they are ruled by the world and the evil examples thereof, they are called the world. And when they are ruled by Satan, so far as they are ruled by him, they are called Satan. 'One of you is a devil,' saith Christ.

'Not in fleshly wisdom.' What is meant here by 'fleshly wisdom?' If it be fleshly, why is it wisdom? Wisdom is but one. There is but one wisdom. Wisdom we know, in itself, it is a knowledge of principles and grounds, and deductions and conclusions from principles. A wise man knows both the grounds and principles, and he knows what may be raised from thence; and likewise a man that is truly wise, he not only knows them, but he knows how to act them, how to work and act his principles and conclusions to an end. He hath principles, and conclusions, and workings out of his brain; and when he hath done all in the brain, when he hath framed the aim of his principles, and the manner how to act them, then he goes about to work; and a wise man can work answerable to his end and rules.

Now there is a carnal wisdom that initiated this; for carnal wisdom hath aims, and ends, and principles, and it hath conclusions from those principles, and it acts to an end. A true Christian he hath his ends. His aim is supernatural: to please God in all things, to be happy in another world, to enjoy God, to have nearer acquaintance with him while he lives here. Many such subordinate ends, besides the main end, he hath. And some principles likewise he hath out of the word of God concerning this end; and then he hath directions out of the word of God suitable to those principles. And then he sets on working, and all that he works is in order to his end, and in virtue of the end he propounds. As a man that travels, every step that he goes in his journey, every step is in virtue and strength of his first intention, and the end that he propounds, though he think not of his end in every step, and he consults and asks about the way, and all to that end.

So it is with a carnal man too, he that walks after carnal wisdom. Carnal wisdom hath its end, and that is a man's self; for a carnal man himself is the idol, and the idolater. His end is himself, either in his honours, or in his pleasures, or riches, &c. Himself is the centre into which all the lines of his life fall. And he hath rules. Seek thyself in all things. Love thyself above all. And what then? If thou love others, love them for thyself, as far as they may serve thy turn. Care for no man further than thou canst make use of him for thyself. Respect him so far, and no further.

But it may be there are many that stand in the way. Then again he hath principles. Undermine them, ruin them, make way to thine own ends by the ruin of as many as thou canst. And if another man's light over-shine thine, that thou art nobody to him, carnal wisdom bids thee deprave him, slander him, backbite him. The more he seems to be vile, the less thy nakedness shall appear. Here is carnal wisdom.

There is no envy in goodness, in strength and ability. They would have all to be so; but baseness is joined with much envy. When it sees another overshadow it, it labours to eclipse him with slanders and base reports. This is a principle of carnal wisdom. And hence comes all that working and undermining, secret conveyances, and laying nets for others, as the prophet speaks.

All carnal wisdom hath carnal ends, and carnal rules, and carnal courses answerable. It consults upon the attaining of its end. It deliberates and consults, and shrewdly too; for it is whetted by Satan. And then it goes with the stream of the world, and therefore it is carried very strongly towards its end. And then it resolves strongly; because fleshly wisdom usually is with the times. And then it executes. God suffers it oft-times to come to execution, and to enjoy its plots and projects. And therefore in regard that it hath the same passages, though in a contrary kind, with other wisdom, it is called wisdom, though indeed it be not wisdom. And thereupon it hath a diminishing term here, it is 'fleshly wisdom.'

Now this wisdom is called 'fleshly,' because it is led with reasons from the flesh, and it tends to the maintenance of the flesh. It comes from it, and it tends to it.

I take not 'flesh' here, for one part of a man, his body; but for the unregenerate part, which is carried to changeable things, to the creature, and sets up some creature to be an idol, instead of the Creator, 'blessed for evermore.'

And that from this reason, because the creature, the things below are near to us, and pleasant to us; and because we are brought up in these delights of the creature that are sensible; and therefore the flesh, the baser part, is ready to draw away the soul to the delights of it; because the delights of it are pleasant, and we are trained up in them from the beginning of our life to the end of it. Now these things below, the profits, and pleasures, and honours, they work first upon the senses, upon the outward man; and from the senses they ascend to the fancy, and imagination, and that being carnal by nature esteems more highly of them than there is cause, and esteems of the contrary to these as the greatest ills. Oh! poverty is worse than hell to a carnal man! and he had rather be dead than be disgraced. He had rather damn his soul, than to be denied of his pleasure. Imagination makes them such great things, and the devil helps imagination. He hath much affinity with that part, with the imagination; and imagination, when men have strong conceits of these things, that labours to draw the will and affections to itself, to sway that part, So that the will, the commanding part of the soul, for the most part it yields to these imaginations of base things. It conceives of them highly, and the contrary to be vile and base. And hereupon the will comes to approve of these things, and to choose these things; yea, and the understanding part itself, that blessed spark of wisdom that is left in us, capable of better things, and fit for the image of God. Yet that, by our corruption, being stripped of the grace it had in the creation, and now being under original corruption, being under the law of sin, it is led by a carnal will and imagination, and by sense, and is ruled by them. So that that which should rule all, is ruled by base, earthly things.

The soul of man, while we live here, is between things better than itself, and worse than itself, meaner than itself. Now by corruption it cleaves to things meaner than itself. It is witty to devise them. It is willing to choose them. It delights in them. It bathes itself in them. So that whereas it should rule the body, the body and the lower parts rule the soul. When it yields to that which is better than itself, to the sanctifying Spirit of God, and to the word of God, and is clothed with the image of God, when it yields to better things, then they raise it to a degree of excellency even above itself when it was at the best. For a man that is in Christ, that hath the image of Christ upon him, in some sort, is better than Adam was in innocency. His estate is more sure; and the dignity he is advanced to by Christ is greater than he should have had if he had stood still in Adam. This is the condition of the soul. An excellent creature, it is capable of the image and likeness of Christ, and of God, capable of all grace.

Again, if it submit itself to base creatures, it becomes even as them; and therefore men are called 'the world.' They are called 'flesh.' They are called after that which leads them. The very soul itself, as it were, is flesh, For, as the very body of a holy man in some sort is spirit; and everything in him is spirit; as it shall be at the day of judgment, as St Paul saith, 'it shall be raised a spiritual body,' 1 Cor. xv. 44; because it shall be subject to the motions of the Spirit of God in all things; and it shall not be supported by bodily means. Now the very soul is bodily and carnal. Such a degeneration is wrought in man since the fall. He makes his soul that was given to guide him in this world, and which is made apprehensive of better things, of the things of another world. This soul he makes it the bawd to serve his base lusts and pleasures.

'Not in fleshly wisdom.' Now wisdom is a middle word. It may be either spiritual or carnal, as the man is in whom it is. If a man have moral honesty in him, and good things in him that way, it makes him a good politician, a wise man, useful in his place. Though he be not a sound Christian, yet he may be a wise man in his place; and God useth such kind of men in the world, and they have their reward here, they are advanced, &c.

But if it is light in a devilish nature, in a crooked, oblique nature, then it is malicious, devilish wisdom.

And, note this by the way. All men that have flesh in them, have not fleshly wisdom; for some are carried with the flesh, with the rage of fleshly lusts. As the swine in the gospel were carried headlong into the sea, they are carried by their lusts to hell, as your common swaggerers and roarers; so that they may escape the danger of the laws, they care not for God nor man—irregular, wild persons. These have flesh, they are ruled by the flesh, but they have not so much as 'fleshly wisdom;' for they take courses to overthrow themselves in the world, to overthrow their names, and their bodies and all. They have not so much as policy in them, their lusts so reign in them. Such wretches we have ofttimes amongst us, that think themselves somebody, but they have not so much as carnal wisdom in them to carry themselves better than a devil.

Now, in other men the flesh hath a wisdom that carries them not after this fashion; but it whets their wits, and they are as bad in another kind. As, take the same man, when he is young he is carried by his brutish lusts, without any wisdom at all, even as the hurry of his lusts carry him, and transport him: when he grows old he is carried subtlely with the wisdom of the world. He is alway under lusts, alway under the flesh. When he is young he is carried with base lusts; and when he is old he is under the flesh, and fleshly wisdom still. He is carried with slavish covetousness to the world, as formerly he was subject to base lusts in his youth. All this is naught.

Where these differ in the subject, in the person, usually the base lust serves the witty. Those that are carried with base lusts, they are subject, and enthralled, and overruled by those that are carried with the wisdom of the flesh. As your subtle men, your usurers, and subtle oppressors, great witty men, they make other men serviceable to their turn. Other men are slaves to them.

But to come nearer that that I mean to stand on.

'My conversation hath not been in fleshly wisdom.' You may see by the coherence, which I will not dwell on, what to judge of 'fleshly wisdom.'

Observ. Fleshly wisdom is, where there is no simplicity nor sincerity: because he opposeth them here. Where 'fleshly wisdom' is, there is neither 'simplicity' nor 'sincerity.' For take a subtle wise man, he is all outside, and there is no simplicity in him. He that is not wise to God, but to the world, he wraps himself in ceremonies in matters of religion, and studies the outside of things to approve himself to the world, and to attain his own ends; but there is no simplicity or sincerity. He that is wise to the world hath no respect to God.

Sincerity hath an eye to God; and a sincere man, as far as he is sincere, hath an eye to God, and he doth this and that because God seeth him, and because God is pleased with it; but he that works according to fleshly wisdom, he hath aims contrary and distinct to that. Therefore the apostle saith, 'We walk in the sincerity of God' (as it is in the original*), 'and not according to fleshly wisdom.'

So you may know from the opposition, that fleshly wisdom is where there is no sincerity. Where there is no love to God or to men, there is

* That is, '*εἰλικρινείᾳ Θεοῦ*.'—G.

no simplicity, all is for show; and where there is all for show, there is double carriage, not in simplicity aiming at God's glory. There is 'fleshly wisdom.' That for the connection.

But the point of doctrine proper to the place is this, that

Doctrine. God's children have another manner of rule to live by than the world: the rule that a godly wise man goeth by, is not fleshly wisdom.

A man that looks for any joy, that looks to be in the blessed estate that St Paul here was in, he must not be ruled by fleshly wisdom. 'Our conversation,' saith he, 'in the world hath not been in fleshly wisdom.' St Paul, no question but he had flesh in him, and likewise he had 'fleshly wisdom:' because flesh is in all parts, and it mingles itself with all graces. In the understanding there is light and darkness; in the will there is rebellion and pliableness to God. So St Paul had the stirrings of fleshly wisdom in him. When he was in danger, no doubt but the flesh would stir in him, you may avoid it by shifts if you will. And when he was before great ones, you may flatter and betray the truth if you will.

No doubt but St Paul, as he expressed himself, Rom. viii., as he had a conflict in himself in other regards: so there was a conflict between wisdom and wisdom. The wisdom of the flesh did stir against the wisdom of the spirit. Aye, but it is one thing to have fleshly wisdom in us, and it is another thing to make it our rule. It is one thing to have flesh in us, and another thing to 'be in the flesh,' as the Scripture phrase is.* This conflict wondrously afflicted St Paul. No doubt but it was one sharp conflict.

No question but carnal wisdom set St Paul to shift for himself many times; but by the power of the Spirit he checked it and kept it under. It was not his rule.

Now, the reasons of this doctrine, that the godly guide not themselves by fleshly wisdom, which hath worldly aims, and carnal means to bring those aims to pass, they are,

Reason 1. First, because God's children *will not cherish that in them, and make that their rule, which is contrary to God, which is enmity to God.* But this carnal wisdom, which prowls for the world, and looks for ease, and profit, and pleasure, it is 'enmity to God,' Rom. viii. 6–8. The apostle proves it at large. They being subject to God, children of God, being under him in all kind of subjection, as servants, as children, as spouses, they will not cherish that which is rebellion to God, which is not subject to God, neither can be. As we may say, a papist that is jesuited, he is neither a good subject, nor can be; so the wisdom of the flesh, neither is it subject to God, nor can be subject. In the nature of it, it is rebellion. It is God's enemy; it withstands all the articles that he hath given us to believe. Fleshly wisdom hath some opposition against all truth. It opposeth every command that God gives us to obey. There is something in flesh and blood to withstand every command. It is the greatest enemy that God hath.

2. And as it is an enemy to God, so it is to us. It is contrary to our good. It is death, 'the wisdom of the flesh,' Rom. viii. 4. Saith the apostle, Rom. vii. 8, 'The flesh deceived me and slew me.' There is no wise man will cherish that which is death, and which is God's enemy, and his own too. The wisdom of the flesh, as it is opposite to God's Spirit, a rebel and an enemy to him, so it is death to a Christian, and therefore he will not frame his course of life by it.

* Cf. 2 Cor. xii. 7; Gal. ii. 20; Philip. i. 22.—G.

It brings us to eternal death, it betrays us to Satan. Sampson could have had no harm had not Delilah betrayed him; so the devil could not hurt us unless it were for fleshly wisdom. The devil is not such an enemy to a man as his own fleshly wisdom.

Reason 2. Again, a Christian knows, that as it is contrary to God and contrary to his good, *so it is base and unworthy, as well as dangerous.* It is base and unworthy for a Christian, that is an heir of heaven, that is raised to be a child of God, to abase his wits, to prowl for the world. How base and unworthy is it for him to seek the things below, that is born again 'to an inheritance, immortal and undefiled, that is reserved for him in heaven?' 1 Pet. i. 4.

How unworthy is it for him that hath his understanding and all his inward parts and powers dedicated and consecrated to God, to make his understanding a bawd for the base purposes of the flesh! The high indignity of the thing makes the child of God ashamed to be ruled by the flesh, to prostitute the strength of his soul to the flesh; to make his soul, that should carry the image of God, to carry the image of the devil; to make his wit and understanding a bawd to accomplish earthly things, which God hath sanctified to attain grace and comfort in this world, and to live as a Christian should do, that he may die with comfort, and enjoy heaven.

Reason 3. Again, God's children will not be ruled by that which they should *mortify and subdue.* But this wisdom of the flesh is the object of mortification. They are redeemed from it.

A Christian, as he is redeemed from hell and damnation, so he is redeemed from himself. He is redeemed and set at liberty from the slavery of his soul to Satan, to the world, and worldly projects. He is redeemed from the base conversation he was in before. What hath he to do to be ruled by him from whom he is redeemed? These things might be amplified at large; but you see the truth evident, what ground a Christian hath not to be ruled by fleshly wisdom.

Reason 4. But to make it a little clearer. A Christian hath no reason to be ruled by earthly wisdom, for the yielding to it *doth all the mischief in the world.* It is the cause of all the misery in the world, unto Christians especially. God catcheth 'the wise in their own craftiness,' Job v. 13, though they be politic and wise. Especially if a Christian give way to carnal politic wisdom, God will universally shame him. I never knew a Christian thrive in politic courses. When he hath secret conveyances for the world, God crosseth him every way, in his reputation, in his projects, and purposes.

But consider, to amplify that which I gave in a branch before, what reason hath a Christian to be ruled by 'fleshly wisdom,' when it hinders him from all that is good, if he yield unto it, and keeps him in imperfect good?

I speak especially now to those that are not in the state of grace. What reason hath any one of you to be ruled by fleshly wisdom, when it keeps you in the state of unregeneracy? It keeps you perhaps in some good, but it is imperfect good. You think you are good enough, and that all is sure, and God will be merciful, &c., whenas a reprobate may go beyond you.

It hinders from good actions with pretences, for fleshly wisdom will tell us there will be danger, you shall be reproached if you do this and that, you shall be accounted thus and thus, and run into obloquy.

It hinders from doing good. 'There is a lion in the way,' Prov. xxvi. 13.

It forecasts this and that danger. It keeps us in imperfect good that will never save us. It objects dangers. The sluggard that will not set on his spirit to labour, he thinks himself wondrous wise in forecasting dangers. Oh, I shall want myself, &c.

It dulls and distracts us in good. He that hath a carnal protecting head, it eats up his soul, that when he comes to pray, or to hear, or to meddle with spiritual matters, the marrow and strength of his soul is eaten up with carnal projects, and he doth things by halves.

Nay, carnal wisdom, as far as it is in us unmortified, it sets itself against good by depraving good, that we may seem to be mischievous, and ill, and wicked with reason. Men are loath to go to hell without reason. There was none that ever went to hell yet without wisdom, a great deal of wisdom. And how doth their wisdom bring them to hell? As in other respects, which I named before, so in this; it whets the poisonfulness of their nature to invent and to raise scandals, or to be willing to take scandals when they are offered.

A carnal wise man, when he knows that such a degree of religion is contrary to his carnal projects, he fasteneth all the disgrace on it that he can, that he may be the less observed. Religious he would be, but with a limitation, with a reservation and restraint, as far as may stand with his carnal projects and purposes; and so much religion as goes beyond that, and discovers him to be false and halting, so much he opposeth. The wisdom of the flesh is bitter and sharp against all the opposers of it, and stirs the cursed nature of man to the opposing of that which is contrary to it.

Take a carnal man, either in magistracy or ministry, if he be not humbled with pains in his calling and with the word that he teacheth, what doth he most hate in the world? What doth he oppose? Is there anything but saving grace? Is there anything but that which God loves most, and which is best for his soul, that is the object of his spite and of his poison and malice?

To be led by this is even as if a man should be led by a pirate, by a thief, by an enemy. And what can become of that man, to be led 'as the fool to the stocks,' as Solomon saith, Prov. vii. 22. He is in the way of death. 'There is a way that seemeth good to a man in his own eyes, but the issues of it are death,' saith Solomon, Prov. xiv. 12; and that is the way that carnal wisdom dictates to men.

It hinders also from the reforming of ill. Policy overthrows policy, as we say. Policy overthrows commonwealths. Tell a man that is in place, You ought to reform this abuse and that abuse. He is ready to think, Oh, if I be not wary, others will inquire into my life too, and find me out.

So this cursed policy, this carnal wisdom, it makes men unfruitful in their places, by forecasting dangers; and so it hinders from doing good, and from reforming gross abominations and abuses.

So it hinders from suffering when God calls to it. It forecasts: if you be religious, you must suffer, it will bring your good name in question, it will bring your life in question, it will hazard your estate. Whereas, indeed, all the world is not worth tho truth of God; and a man loves not his life that will not hate it in such a case; if it come to case of confession, and standing for the truth in a good quarrel.

But here fleshly wisdom objects this and that danger; as we see in Spira and others. And thus man, yielding to fleshly wisdom, he grows desperate at length (*qq*).

There are two men in a man, as it were. There is the flesh and the spirit. The flesh saith as Job's wife said, 'Curse God and die,' or 'Bless God and die,' read it whether you will (*rr*). There is the murmuring part in the cross that bids us curse God; and as Peter said unto Christ, 'Oh! save yourselves, this shall not befal you,' Mat. xvi. 22; pity yourself, have regard of yourself.* The flesh when we are to suffer saith as Eve to Adam, as Job's wife to him, or as Peter to Christ, Oh spare yourself, be wise, be wise. And to colour the matter the more, there must be a pretence of wisdom; whenas it is the greatest folly in the world to redeem any earthly commodity, even life itself, with the cracking of conscience, with the breach of that 'peace which passeth understanding,' Philip. iv. 7, and perhaps with the loss of our souls. It is the greatest folly in the world; it is to be penny wise and pound foolish. So we see whensoever we are about to suffer, carnal wisdom hinders us. As it hinders us from good, and in good, and hinders us from reforming evil; and in suffering when we are called to it. So it provokes us to evil. And that we may swallow down the evil with the greater pleasure, and more deeply, it colours ill with good. We may thank this politic carnal wisdom, that truth and goodness ever goes with a scratched face, that it goes under disgrace, that it goes in a contrary habit; and that hypocrisy goes in its ruff, in its colours. I say we may thank carnal wisdom; for if truth were presented in its own view, it would stir up approbation from all. And if men could see vice and wickedness uncased, if they could see it in its own hue, they would all detest it. Carnal wisdom sees that this is not for the advancing of the projects it hath, and therefore it disgraceth that which is good, and sets false colours on that which is ill.

I say, it stirs up to ill, and it keeps us in ill. Carnal wisdom saith, You may do this, you may continue thus long. It deceives us with vain hopes of long life.

I might enlarge the point. You see then what reason God's children have, not to be ruled by fleshly carnal wisdom.

By the way, let me give this caution, *that oftentimes that is accounted carnal wisdom that is not.* The weaker sort, they are to blame ofttimes to lay imputations upon those that God hath given greater gifts to; and they account that carnal wisdom that is not so, but is spiritual prudence. I must needs add that caution by the way. As for a man to keep his mind, and not to speak against evil in all places. 'The prudent man shall keep silent,' saith the prophet, Prov. xii. 23. The times and the place may be such, that the prudent man may keep silence. It is best to do so.

And likewise to be cautelous to prevent danger so far as it may be without breach of a good conscience. St Paul, you know, when he was called before the Sadducees and the Pharisees, he escaped by a shift.* It was not a sinful shift. He said he was a Pharisee, and so he set them together, and they falling into contention, St Paul in the mean time escaped, Acts xxiii. 7. Many things might be done, if we would take heed of carnal wisdom, and that with a great deal of wisdom and approbation too.

Jeroboam might have settled his kingdom, and yet he need not have set up the two calves in that cursed policy. It was foretold that he should have those tribes, but he would be wiser than God, and he would devise a way of his own, 2 Chron. xiii. 8, *et alibi.*

David might have escaped from Achish the king of Gath. He need not have made himself a fool. Ahithophel might have provided well for himself under David his old master. He need not have proved a rebel.

* See Note *g*, vol. II., p. 194.—G. † That is, 'expedient.'—G.

There is nothing that carnal wisdom doth, but heavenly wisdom will do it better if men could light on it; and God would give them better success in their carriage. But there is a way for heavenly prudence, I say, and that must not be accounted carnal wisdom.

It is for want of this that people are too credulous. Gedaliah, he trusted too much, he was too credulous to trust. Considering that men are subject to infirmities, and subject to falseness, it is good to be doubtful, to be suspicious sometimes; and it is no carnal wisdom neither. The very loadstone of a lie is credulity. What emboldens people to deal falsely with men? They know them to be credulous and weak. They will believe anything.

But for the most part the error is on the contrary, over-much jealousy. Your carnal politicians are over-jealous. Jealousy is good, suspicion is good, considering that we live in a false world; but not to be over-jealous. We see Herod, he thought, Oh! Christ is born; and out of jealousy he kills a number of poor infants, and his own among the rest. Alas!* Christ came not to take away his kingdom, but to give a heavenly kingdom. So the Jews they were very jealous that if Christ were not condemned, the Romans would come and take away their kingdom, John xi. 48; but that which wicked men fear, out of such jealousy, shall come upon them. And so the subtlest and most devilish men in late times, that grounded the persecution of the poor Protestants, upon jealousy, absurd jealousy; for they, by the rules of their religion, walk in sincerity. It ties them from plotting. And yet out of fear and jealousy, they exercised a world of cruelty against them.

And if any man shall but consider and read Stephen Gardiner's letters (a man of a devilish jealousy), to see out of his wit he projected what hurt would come by suffering the gospel to remain, it will seem strange (*ss*). Alas, poor man! the commonwealths beyond the seas and our own nation never prospered better than by entertaining the gospel. Yet this devilish-witted man, whose wit was set and sharpened by the devil, was in fear and jealousy of the gospel. And God usually punisheth it this way, that those subtle heads that are jealous of those that mean them no harm, but all the good that may be, usually, they are over-credulous in another kind. They trust those that deceive their trust, they trust those that the weakest, the very dregs of the people, will not trust, they trust those that are notoriously false. God strikes their brains and besots them, that they trust men that all the world know to be underminers; notwithstanding where they should trust, and cast themselves into the bosom of their true-hearted friends, there they are all full of fear and jealousy. But this caution by the way.

You see the thing proved, that godly men when they give their names to God, they ought to be ruled by God, and not by carnal policy or fleshly wisdom. You see the reasons of it.

Use 1. The use that we will make of it *shall be to stir us up to imitation of the blessed apostle St Paul.* I speak to them that their breeding and parts have raised many of them I hope from base filthy lusts; so that the danger is now of 'fleshly wisdom.' The devil is more in the brain than in the heart, as he said of a cursed politician. Many men have the devil in their head. He is not altogether in the heart and affections, but in the brain; and there he works his engines. And politic subtle men, they are the great engineers of Satan; and that which he cannot do by himself, he doth it by them.

Therefore, I beseech you, let us not be instrumental to Satan, who was

* See Note p. 159.—G.

the first author of this carnal wisdom; for by his temptation we offended God, and then came all shifts upon it. You see what shifts came presently upon Satan's temptation.

Man did naturally affect wisdom; to know good and evil. What wisdom did he get after he had fallen? He had wisdom to flee from God. There was his wisdom, to run from God. So all the wisdom of a man that hath not grace, it is to shift, to run away from God, and to have helps and supports against God. A foolish thing it is, as if he could do it! And then, another shift of Adam was, to cover himself with fig-leaves, a silly shift. And then to translate his fault upon another. So, this shifting of carnal wit it came presently upon the fall. Take heed, therefore, of carnal wisdom; it is devilish: presently upon yielding to the temptation of the devil it came in.

And that you may not make it your rule, and live by carnal wisdom, consider seriously what I said before, how it hinders you from all that is good; how it hinders you from reforming that which is ill in your places and callings; how it stirs up to all that is ill; how it stirs you up to cover ill. It teaches you wit to do ill, and to cover ill when it is done. As we see in David's adultery, what a deal of wit there was to practise it. And then what a many windings and turnings there were to cover it. But God laid him open, and brought him to shame in this world, being a good man.

And as I said, who will be ruled by his enemy? If a man be on the land, and be ruled by a thief that will lead him out of his way, it is extremity of sottishness. Or if he be on the sea, and be guided by a pirate, what good can come to that man that is ruled by those that seek his ruin? Now if a man be ruled by carnal wisdom, he is ruled by his enemy; and if all the enemies in the world should plot to do a man that mischief that his own head and carnal wit doth him, he would cry out of them. In Isa. xlvii. 10,* 'Thy wisdom hath made thee to rebel.' It is wisdom that makes men to rebel against God. Too much trusting to tricks and shifts of carnal wisdom, it makes men take contrary courses to God, and so provoke him. 'Are we wiser than he? are we stronger than he?' 1 Kings xx. 23, 25. Doth he not daily and continually make those the butts† of his displeasure and wrath, that adventure their wisdom and policy against his wisdom? Yes, surely! God delights to catch the wise in their own craftiness; he delights to overturn the builders of Babel. It is but a building of Babel to rear anything by politic wisdom, contrary to the rules of religion, and contrary to the practice of piety. To do anything against conscience and honesty; to do anything against the truth by politic shifts, it is to build a Babel that will fall upon our own heads. It is like the foolish fire that leads a man out of his way.‡ This foolish fire of carnal wisdom, it leads men to hellish strength: it makes them forsake God's light, and the light of his Spirit and word, and follow a false light of their own imagination and invention. And therefore you see what the prophet Isaiah saith of the people that were in those times, Isa. l. 11, that did much plod in tricks of policy, 'Behold, all ye that kindle a fire, that compass yourselves about with sparks: walk in the light of your fire, and in the sparks that ye have kindled: this ye shall have of my hand, ye shall lie down in sorrow.' So, consider this, it falls out ofttimes, that God suffers a man to walk in the light of his own fire that he hath kindled, and in his own comforts. He will have comforts, and a distinct way from God's ways; and he will

* Misprinted 'Jeremiah.'—G.

† That is, 'marks.'—G.

‡ That is, the *Ignis fatuus.*—G.

have distinct rules from God's rule. Well, well! you have kindled a fire; walk in the light of your own fire, but be sure you shall lie down in sorrow.

It is the greatest judgment that God can shew in this world, to give us up to our own wits, to our own devices; for we shall wind, and turn, and work our own ruin. And that is the hell of hell in hell, when the soul there shall think with itself, I brought myself hither. God will be exceedingly justified when men by their own wit shall damn themselves; when God hath revealed to man, and taught them, this is the way, 'O man, I have shewed thee what is good, and what doth the Lord require of thee,' Deut. x. 12. He hath revealed it in his word, do this and do that, and he hath given conscience to help; and yet out of policy to contrive thy own pleasures, and profits, and advantages in the world, thou hast done the contrary. When a man's soul shall reason thus, My own wit brought me hither; I am damned by wit, I am damned by policy. A poor policy it is that brings a man to damnation!

Therefore we should beg of God above all things, that he would not deliver us up to ourselves. As St Austin hath a good speech, 'Lord, free me from myself, from my own devices and policy' (*tt*). The devil himself is not such an enemy, as I said, as our own carnal wit; for it is that that betrays us to Satan. Satan could do us no harm unless he had a friend within us. Therefore beg of God above all things, Lord, give me not up to my own brain, to my own devices (for man is a beast by his own knowledge); but let thy wisdom and thy will be my rule.

Use 2. Again, if so be that we ought not to make this carnal, fleshly wisdom the rule of our life, then let us have *a negative voice ready presently for it.* Whensoever we find any carnal suggestion in our hearts, say nay to it presently, deny it presently, have a jealousy presently. When any plot ariseth that is not warrantable by the word of God, and that is contrary to conscience and to simplicity and sincerity, presently deny it; consult not with flesh and blood, as St Paul saith of himself, 'I consulted not with flesh and blood,' Gal. i. 16.

And when you have anything to do, considering that this is not the rule you are to live by, or when you have anything to resist, when you have anything to suffer, consider what God requires; consider what is for the peace of conscience; consider what is for the good of yourselves, and for the good of the church; consult with these advisers, with these intelligencers, and not with flesh and blood. Consider not what is for your profit, for your pleasure, for your ease; but resolve against them. Get the truth of God so planted in your hearts that it may carry you through all these impediments, and all these suggestions whatsoever.

Use 3. And because we cannot do this without a change, we cannot have a disposition contrary to carnal wisdom without a change (for except a man be born anew, except he be a new creature, he cannot have holy aims), you must labour therefore more and more *to have the spirit of your mind renewed, and to grow in assurance of a better estate.* For what makes men carnally to project for this world? They are not sure of a better. They reason thus with themselves: It may be I may have heaven, it may be not. I am sure of the pleasures present, of the profits present, although, alas! it be but for a short time. Whereas, if thy soul were enlightened with heavenly light, and thou wert convinced of the excellent estate of God's children in this world in the state of grace, that a Christian is incomparably above all men in the first-fruits of heaven, in the peace of conscience, and 'joy in the Holy Ghost,' Rom. xiv. 17, which is above all prosperity, and all profit whatsoever; and that in heaven, which is above our capacity and reach, every way they shall be happy. If men were convinced of this, certainly they would not prostitute their pates to work so worldlily. If they were sure of heaven, they would not so plod for the earth.

Let us therefore labour to grow daily in the assurance of salvation; beg of God his Spirit to have your minds enlightened.

Use 4. And withal, to join both together, *to see the vanity of all earthly things, which set carnal wisdom on work.* For, first, outward things they work upon the sense, upon the outward man. Profits and pleasures are outward things, and therefore they work upon sense, they work upon opinion. In opinion they be so, as indeed worldly things are more in opinion than in truth. A carnal wordly man, he thinks poverty a hell, he thinks it is such a misery. It is not so.

Labour to have a right judgment of the things of the earth, that set carnal wisdom on work, to avoid poverty, to avoid suffering for a good cause. The devil inflames fancy. Fancy thinks it is a great hurt to be in poverty; fancy thinks it is a great good to be in honour, to be in credit, to have great place, that other men may be beholden to us. Alas! get a sanctified judgment to see what these things be that set our wits on work. What are all these things? 'Vanity, and vexation of spirit,'

Let our meditations walk between these two. Often think of the excellent estate of a Christian in this world, and in the world to come; and that will set heavenly wisdom on work. It will make you plot, and be politic for heaven. And then withal see the vanity of all other things, of pleasures, and honours, and profits, and whatsoever, that we may not prostitute our souls to them which are worse than ourselves; that our souls may not set themselves on work to project and prowl for these things that are worse than themselves.

Let this be your daily practice. The meditation of these two things is worthy to take up your cogitations every day. To consider the vanity, the vexation, and uncertainty that accompanies all these things, when you have got them; as we see in Ahab, when he had gotten the vineyard. Besides the vanity of them, consider how you have gotten them, and how miserable will you judge yourselves presently! How doth God meet the carnal wits of men in the attaining of things! 'The wicked man shall not roast that which he took in hunting,' Prov. xii, 27. He hunted after preferment, he hunted after riches, to scrape a great deal for his posterity; how doth God deal with such? He overthrows them utterly; and his posterity, perhaps they spoil all. Himself roasted not that which he took in hunting. Ahab got much by yielding to the carnal wisdom of Jezebel, 'Hast thou gotten, and also taken possession,' 1 Kings xxi. 19. What became of Ahab with all his plots and devices?

Ahithophel and others, God may give them success for a while, but afterward he gives them the overthrow. Herod, he had success a while in killing of James, and, therefore, he thought to work wisely and get Peter too; God struck him with worms, Acts xii. 23. Pharaoh, in the overthrow of God's people, saith he, 'Let us work wisely,' Exod. i. 10. How wisely? They were overthrown and drowned themselves. Their wisdom brought them into the midst of the sea. Consider the vanity of earthly things. And then consider how just it is with God to cross them either in their own time; as the rich fool in the gospel, when he had riches for many years, 'This night shall they take away thy soul!' Luke xii. 20. That we may not walk according to the false rules of fleshly wisdom, let us oft think of these things.

And to add another thing out of the text. You see here that St Paul rejoiced in this, that his conscience could witness that he had not walked in 'fleshly wisdom;' so if you do not walk according to the rules of fleshly wisdom, you shall have this benefit, *your conscience shall glory in it.*

To make it clear to you,—take in your thoughts a politician upon his deathbed, that hath striven so much for riches, that hath striven to root himself by policy, to attain to such and such places, to obtain his pleasure and delights in the world; what glory, what comfort hath he in this? There is nothing more opposite to comfort than plotting; for, as I said before when I spake of simplicity, the more will there is, the more deliberation and plotting there is in sin, the more is the sin; because it is done coolly, as we say. So of all persons usually, if their wits be their own, the greatest plotters die most desperately. For then their conscience tells them, that they have set their wits on the rack, to do this mischief and that mischief; and here his comfort is cooled, his peace of conscience is broken. What comfort can there be, when that which he sinned for, that which he broke the peace of his conscience for, that is gone, and he must be taken and hurried away from that. But the wound of conscience, the crack of conscience, that remains for ever; when he shall think, that for which I sinned is vanished, but my terror abides for ever.

A man therefore that walks after the rules of fleshly wisdom, he can never say with St Paul, 'I rejoice.' But on the contrary, let a man be able to witness to himself, as St Paul could; at such a time my fleshly, subtle wisdom would have discouraged me from doing good; and the wisdom of flesh and blood in others would have discouraged me from reforming such and such abuses; but I knew it was my duty, and I did it. Here now is comfort. At such a time I was moved to such evil by flesh and blood in myself, or perhaps in others (as a man shall never want the devil in his friends. The devil comes to us in our nearest friends). But I had the grace to withstand it. I was not led by such and such rules, by my acquaintance, or by my own devices; but I had grace to resist such motions. What a wondrous comfort is this?

There is nothing so sharp in conflict as this. To resist carnal wisdom, it is the shrewdest temptation that is from carnal wisdom; and as the temptation is the strongest, so the comfort is answerable. When Jezebel shall be offered with her enticements, with her colours, with her paint; and a man can dash her in pieces, and cast her out of the window, when a man can maintain sincerity and honesty, what a comfort is this! The greater and stronger the temptation is that is resisted, the more is the comfort, when we come to yield our souls to God, when we come to our account. Therefore, be not discouraged when you are set upon by carnal wisdom, by strong reasons of others, or subtle reasons of your own. Is it against the rule? Is it against conscience? Is it against the word? withstand it! That which is sharpest in the conflict, will be sweetest in the comfort.

Use 5. Again, if so be that carnal, fleshly, worldly wisdom (for it is all one, for the flesh is led by the world, and both conspire together, and hold correspondence to betray the soul, if it) be such an enemy, that it hinders our joy and comfort, and that if ever we will joy, we must not be led by carnal wisdom; then we ought in our daily courses *to repent, not only of gross sins, but to repent even of carnal devices,* and carnal designs. Why? It is the motion and the counsel of God's enemy, and of our enemy.

Therefore, as David, Ps. xxxvii. and Ps. lxxiii., when fleshly wisdom did suggest to him carnal motions of doubting of the providence of God, that he began to think well of the ways of the wicked, that they prospered that were led altogether by fleshly wisdom, he censures himself (it is the drift of both Psalms), 'So foolish was I, and as a beast before thee,' Ps. lxxiii. 22; as indeed, 'Man is a beast by his own knowledge,' as Jeremiah saith, x. 14. For all carnal men sympathise either with beasts in base lusts, or else with devils in politic lusts; either they are like devils, subtle, or like beasts, brutish in all their courses.

Therefore, when any base thought, opposite to the majesty of God and his truth, and to the Spirit of God moving our hearts, ariseth in our hearts, think, this is the motion of mine enemy, of an enemy that lurks in my bosom, of God's enemy, of a traitor; let us renounce it, and be abased, and censure ourselves for it, as holy David did, 'So foolish was I,' &c. Crush all thoughts and devices of carnal wisdom in the beginning.

We see that the godly, they ought not, nor do not lead their lives by fleshly wisdom; nay, take it in the best sense, take it for the rules of reason, they do not lead their lives altogether by the light of nature, but only in those things wherein the light of nature and reason may be a judge. For the light of reason, the principle of reason, is given us as a candle in the dark night of this world, to lead us in civil and in common actions, and it hath its use. But yet natural reason, it becomes carnal reason in a man that is carnal. 'All things are impure to him that is impure, even his very light is darkness,' Tit. i. 15; Mat. vi. 23. Not that the light of nature, and that reason, which is a part of the image of God, is in itself evil. It is good in itself, but the vessel taints it. Those that have great parts of learning, that have great wits, and helps of learning as much as may be, what do they? They trust in them, and so they stain them. Therefore, Luther was wont to say, 'Good works are good, but to trust in good works is damnable' (*uu*). So nature, and reason, and learning, they are good in themselves; but trusting in them they become carnal, when a man neglects better rules for them. When men scorn religion, as your politicians usually do, then natural reason, in regard of this tainture, it becomes carnal. 'Not with fleshly wisdom,' or not with natural wisdom, as it is a higher rule of life.

What then shall become of a Christian, when he hath renounced that which is in him by nature? when he hath denied his wit and his will? when he hath renounced a bad guide, shall he have no guide at all? Yes! For a man is never lawless. He is always under some guide or other. A man is alway under one kingdom or other. When he ceaseth to be under the kingdom of Satan, he comes under the kingdom of Christ; and when he is not led by the flesh, he is led by the Spirit. God's children, when they have renounced natural, carnal wisdom, they have not renounced all wisdom. They are wise still; but they are wise by a supernatural light, they are wise in supernatural things. Yea, and in natural things after a supernatural manner. They are new creatures, advanced to a higher rank and order of creatures. So their wisdom is a gracious wisdom, when they are Christians.

When a Christian hath renounced carnal wisdom, God leaves him not in the storm in the world as a ship without a stern.* He leaves him not as having no pole-star to guide his course by, but he gives him better direction. He hath the word of God, he hath the Spirit of God, he hath

* That is, 'helm.'—G.

the grace of God to guide him. Therefore, after the negative here, 'Not in fleshly wisdom,' the holy apostle tells us how the child of God is led in his own person, but

'*By the grace of God.*' It is good for inferiors alway to be under the government of superiors, and so God hath framed the world. For beasts, because they have no wisdom of their own, they are led and guided by men: and man, because he is, as I said before, 'a beast by his own knowledge,' and hath but a finite, a limited understanding, he is guided by a larger understanding, he is guided by God if he be good. And it is the happiness of the creature to be under the guidance of a better wisdom. All things in the world are guided to their end. Things without life are guided to their end without their privity. We see there is an end in everything. There is nothing in nature but it hath its end; whereupon comes that saying of the philosophers, which is good, that the work of nature is a work of deep understanding. Not so much as the leaves, but they serve to shelter, and cover the fruit from the sun, and the storms, that it may thrive the better. There is nothing in nature but it is of great use. The work of nature is a work of deep understanding. Now man, because he hath a principle of understanding in himself, he is so guided by the wisdom of God to his end, as that he understands his own end himself. He is so led by the wisdom of God, as that God hath created a work of wisdom in himself, that he together with God is carried to his end. Now, as I said, when we are out of the regiment and government of the flesh, we come under the gracious government of God. Therefore the apostle saith here, 'Not in fleshly wisdom, but by the grace of God.'

The holy apostle means here especially, the particular grace opposite to fleshly wisdom, that is, spiritual wisdom.

Quest. But why should the apostle here not say thus, 'Not with fleshly wisdom, but with spiritual wisdom?' Why should he not say so, rather than thus, 'Not with fleshly wisdom, but by the grace of God?' Why should he put grace instead of wisdom?

Ans. I answer, he doth it for heavenly ends.

1. First, to shew that that wisdom whereby we are governed, it is not from ourselves, *but it is a grace.* He considers wisdom, not so much as it is in ourselves, in the conduit; but as it is in the spring, in the free love of God. It is a divine consideration, to consider all habitual graces in us, not as they are streams derived to us, and resting in us, but as they are knit to a spring which is never drawn dry; which besides is a free spring. Therefore they are graces.

And that is the reason of the comfort of a Christian. He knows he shall never be destitute of necessary strength, of necessary comfort, of necessary direction and grace to lead him to heaven; because those things that are necessary in him, he considers them as graces, not as habits, as it was the proud term of the philosophers to call them (*vv*).

We must consider them not as things in us invested in our nature, but as things that have their original from the free, constant, and eternal love of God; as, what is so free as grace? So a Christian looks on his disposition wrought by grace, and on every particular grace he hath; as love, wisdom, patience, he looks to all as graces, as they come from the free love of God that is constant; for 'whom he loves, he loves to the end,' John xiii 1. And his joy is more in the spring than in the stream; it is more in the sun, in Christ himself, than in grace from him. Therefore the apostle, instead of the abstracted distinct grace of wisdom, or any such thing, he saith, 'grace.' There is a savour in the very terms of Scripture, a sweet taste in the very language of the Holy Ghost.

2. And then to shew that we are not only governed by wisdom, but by other graces, *to shew the connection of it with other graces*; therefore he saith, 'We have had our conversation, not in fleshly wisdom, but by the grace of God.'

3. To shew likewise, *that where wisdom fails in us, it is supplied by grace*; for the wisdom of God *for* us, is larger than the wisdom of God *in* us. The wisdom that God works in us by his Spirit, it teacheth us to avoid dangers, and teacheth us how to lead our lives; but we are led by a higher wisdom. The grace of God for us, it is higher than that which is in us.

The wisdom of God for us, it watcheth over us, it keeps us from more evil, and doth more for us, than that which is in us, although that be spiritual and heavenly. Therefore the apostle here, he names not distinctly 'gracious wisdom,' which he mainly intends, as we see by the opposition, 'Not by fleshly wisdom, but by gracious wisdom;' why doth he not say so, but 'by grace?' Because our Christian conversation it is not only by wisdom in us, but by grace and love, partly in us and partly for us.

For indeed there is a watchful providence, there is a waking love about the guiding of a Christian in his course to heaven, that keeps him in, more than any grace that is in him. And a Christian at the hour of death, and at the day of judgment, will be able to say with experience, that the wisdom of God for me hath been more than any wisdom he wrought in me: though by the wisdom in me, he enabled me to discover many discouragements, to see many wants, and to take many good courses that he blessed for me.

But his wisdom for me was greater in preventing occasions above my strength, in offering means that I never dreamed of, in fitting occasions and opportunities to me.

The wisdom of God about and toward a Christian is more than any wisdom that is in him. For, alas! having to do with the devil and with malicious spirits, and with the world, the stream whereof is against grace, it is hard for that beam of wisdom in us, that little wisdom we have, though it be an excellent, spiritual, divine thing. Yet notwithstanding there is a heavenly wisdom that watcheth for us, and gives issue and success to all the good we do, and turns away all evil that is above the proportion of grace and strength in us. Therefore, saith he, our conversation is in the grace and favour of God, not only *in* me, but *for* me. I find experience of grace; not only the grace that is in me, but of grace every way for me in all my courses.

And that is the reason why weaker Christians are sometimes the safer Christians. Another Christian that is wiser, he meets with troubles perhaps.

Aye, but God knows that he hath but a little proportion in him, and therefore God's wisdom is more for him without him. God doth wondrously for infants and weak persons. The lack in them is supplied by his heavenly wisdom.

And that makes Christians confident, not to take thought what they shall speak, or how to carry themselves, more than is meet; not to have distracted thoughts, I mean, to be discouraged in a good cause. He thinks I have not only a promise of grace to direct and guide me, but likewise the wisdom of heaven for me, to discourage others, to take away occasions of discouragement from me, to offer me encouragements, and to lift up my spirit when occasion serves.

This is the comfort of a Christian, that God is his strength. 'He hath wrought all our works for us,' saith the prophet, Isa. xxvi. 12. He not only works gracious works in us, but he works all our works for us.

In that the apostle mentions grace, when his meaning is of the particular grace of wisdom, as the opposition shews, the first thing that I will observe from it is this, that

Obs. A Christian stands in need of wisdom.

When he is out of the fleshly government of fleshly wisdom, he stands in need of another wisdom, and that is grace, the wisdom of God.

We stand in need of wisdom; for, alas! what can we do in this world without wisdom? what can we do without light? For bodily inconveniences we have a bodily light, an outward light to shew us what is noisome; for reasonable inconveniences that our common wits apprehend, we have the light of reason.

1. But there be many inconveniences, *many dangers to the soul.* Now there must be a light of wisdom answerable. We need a heavenly wisdom to avoid devilish inconveniences and dangers to the soul, which without wisdom we cannot avoid.

2. Again, there is a necessity of wisdom that is heavenly, when we have renounced carnal wisdom, *there is such a likeness between that which is good, and that which is evil, between truth and falsehood.* 'Likeness is the mother of error.'* Falsehood is wondrous like truth. Evil is wondrous like good ofttimes, in show, when a sophister hath the handling and the propounding of it. Though there be as much distance between them as between light and darkness; yet to the appearance of man, to his shallow judgment, they are wondrous like one another. Here is need of wisdom to discern, and distinguish between these.

3. Again, there is wondrous need of wisdom, because *there are a great many hindrances from the doing of that which is good.* It is good to have wisdom to see how to remove those hindrances. There are a great many advantages to help us to do good. There is much wisdom requisite to take all the helps and advantages to do that which is good; and unless we have wisdom we cannot take the advantages to do good, as we should.

4. Again, *good is not good without wisdom.* Virtue is not virtue without discretion, when to speak, and when not to speak. 'A fool speaks all his mind at all times,' saith the wise man, Prov. xxix. 11. Now to do things in season, to be trees of righteousness to 'bring forth fruit in season,' Ps. i. 3. 'To speak a word in season it is like apples of gold with pictures of silver,' Prov. xxv. 11. One word in season is worth ten thousand out of season. Good is such a thing, that it is never good indeed except it be clothed with all convenient circumstances. One inconvenience in the circumstance mars the good things. And a world of wisdom there needs to see the things that are about good actions to help them, or to hinder them; and if there be helps and advantages, to know how to use them, there needs a great deal of heavenly light. So we stand in need of wisdom. As we stand in need of our eyes to walk in our common ways, so much we need a heavenly eye in our souls, a heavenly light of wisdom.

5. Again we see, by the policy of Satan, that that which is good, the best good, *it is hid under evil.* The best wisdom goes under the name of folly, and unnecessary niceness; and the vilest courses go under policy and wis-

* See Note *y*, vol. II. page 435.—G.

dom. Now there is need of much wisdom to discover things, and to see them in their right colours, when things are thus carried. In a word, such difference there is of things, that there needs a great deal of discerning and heavenly wisdom, and a greater light than a man hath by nature, to guide him to heaven. I need not stand to multiply reasons; you see a man hath need of a great deal of wisdom. And, which is the second branch, as he needs it,

So *he may have wisdom.*

He may have this heavenly wisdom. As St Paul saith here, 'I walk not according to fleshly wisdom, but by the grace of God.' The grace of wisdom he means, according to heavenly wisdom. As he needed it, so he had it. St James tells you how you may have it, 'If any man lack wisdom,' to guide his life either in prosperity or adversity, how to abound without pride, and how to bear afflictions; how to make his prosperity that it be not a snare to him, 'If any man lack wisdom, let him ask it of God,' James i. 5, who is the fountain of wisdom; let him light his candle at God's light. Carnal wisdom lights its candle at hell-fire. A carnal man, rather than he will miss of his ends, he will go to hell, he, and his riches, and policy, and all. It is otherwise with heavenly wisdom. We have need of wisdom, and wisdom we may have.

The vessel that we must fetch it in is faith, and the vent of faith is prayer. Faith sends its ambassador prayer to God. 'If any man lack wisdom, let him go to God.'

And surely thus Solomon did. He is an example of that. He saw he lacked wisdom to govern so great a people as was committed to his charge. God was so well pleased with his petition, that he gave him wisdom, and wealth, and honour too.

Use. Make this use of it. Let us consider what relation we stand in, in what rank God hath set us; let us consider what good we are advantaged to do by the place we are in, what helps we have to do it, and what mischiefs, and inconveniences may come; and let every man in his place and standing consider what good he may do, and what evil he may avoid, *and let us go to God for wisdom.*

He that is a magistrate, let him do as Solomon did, desire God above all things to give him wisdom to rule as he should, 2 Chron. i. 10, that God would give him a public heart for a public place, and he will do it. And those that in their families would have wisdom to go in and out before them, let them go to God for wisdom, that they may avoid the snares that are incident to family-government, distrustfulness, worldliness, unfaithfulness in their particular calling. And so for personal wisdom, to guide and manage our own persons, let us desire wisdom of God, to know the hidden abominations of our own hearts, the deceits and subtleties of our own hearts, which is out of measure deceitful. To know our particular sins, to know what hurts us, and to know how to avoid it, and how to carry ourselves in our particular ways, to order 'our conversation aright' every way. We see here St Paul led his life and conversation by that wisdom. As it was needful for him, so he had it; and we must go all to the same spring for it: we must go to God.

And we must know that God will not only make us 'wise to salvation,' 2 Tim. iii. 15, that he will not only give us wisdom in things that merely concern heaven; but the same love, the same care that gives us wisdom that way, will give us wisdom in our particular callings, to take every step to heaven; the same Spirit of God doth all. He gives us grace necessary to salvation, and he gives us grace likewise for the leading of a Christian life.

Therefore it is an abominable conceit to distinguish religion from policy and government, as if the reasons of religion were one and the reasons of state were another; and as if these were distinguished one against another. It is an abominable atheistical conceit; for the same heavenly Spirit of God that reveals the mysteries of salvation, reveals likewise to men the mysteries of state.

Christ hath the keys of heaven, of the mysteries of God; and he hath the keys of all earthly policy whatsoever. He hath the greater; hath he not the less? Doth he guide us by his Spirit in heavenly mysteries; and then for matters of policy, and government of states and commonwealths, are we to be guided by the devil, by devilish, carnal wisdom? No! He gives all wisdom in its due place, even wisdom for common things.

Therefore consider, when men will not be ruled by God, by wisdom from above, in the regiment and government of their lives, how fearfully and shamefully they miscarry! Partly by reason of the accidents of this life, and the variety of business. You know wisdom, as it governs our life about the things of this world, it deals with things unstable, uncertain, and vain. As Solomon saith, they continue not long in the same state. Therefore, if a man have not a better wisdom than his own, he shall be mightily to seek. Partly because of the imperfection of his wisdom. The things are imperfect; and the wisdom, without it be guided from heaven, is much to seek ofttimes.

Take the wisest man, when he leaves heavenly wisdom once. As we see in Solomon, he thinks to strengthen himself by combination with idolaters that were near to him. Did he not miscarry foully? And hath not God made the wisest men that ever were in the world exemplary for gross miscarriages, because they had too much confidence in their parts, and neglected the guidance of God in the course of their lives? Who was more fool than Ahithophel? Who was a greater fool than Saul, and than Herod?

The emperors had great conceits. Constantine the Great, a good Christian emperor, he had a conceit, if he could stablish a new seat at Byzantium (Constantinople it was called afterwards), he would seat the empire there; he would rule Rome by a viceroy, by another, and he would be there himself and rule all the eastern parts of the world. A goodly conceit he had of it; but this proved the ruin both of east and west. For hereupon, when he was absent from Rome, the pope of Rome he came up and grew by little and little. The emperors they thought they did a great matter to advance the pope, who was Christ's vicar, a spiritual man. They consulted with carnal wisdom, and he came and over-topped them, and ate them out, and out-grew them, as the ivy doth the tree that nourisheth it. The pope never left growing till he had over-topped them. So men, when they go to carnal wisdom, and neglect prayer, and neglect the counsel of God and the wisdom of God, to guide them in the matters of this life as well as for the life to come, they come to miscarry grossly.

Therefore let us take St James his counsel. We all lack wisdom, let us every day beg it of God; desire God every day that he would 'make our way plain before us,' Prov. xv. 19, in our particular goings in and out; that he would discover to us what is best.

Use. And here I might take occasion *to reprove sharply the atheism of many* that would be accounted great statesmen, that bring all religion to reasons of state. They bring heaven under earth, and clean subvert and overthrow the order of things; and therefore no wonder if they miscarry. They care not what religion it be, so it may stand with peace. Whether it be false or true, if it may stand with the peace of the state, all is well. Give me leave to touch it but in a word. It is a most abominable conceit. Religion is not a thing so alterable. Religion is a commanding thing. It is to command all other things, and all other things serve that. And it is not a matter of fancy and opinion, as they think out of their atheism, to keep men in awe. It is stablished upon the same ground as that there is a God: that upon the same ground that we say God is, upon the same ground we may say religion is. It teacheth us that, that God is to be observed; and that Christ is equal to him as God, and inferior to him in regard of his humanity, &c. So that there is the same ground that there is a God, and that there is a religion.

And so again, by the same reason that there is one God, by the same reason there is but one religion. And it is not any religion that will serve the turn. For that one God will be worshipped his own way. 'There is one God, one truth.' And that one religion must needs be that in which that one God discovers and reveals himself, and not that which man deviseth. For will any master be served with the device of his servant? And will God suffer his creature to devise a religion to serve him? Therefore there is of necessity, as one God, so one religion; and that one religion must be that which that God hath left in his word.

Therefore those that are to govern states, as they will answer to that one God, they are to establish that religion that he hath left to the world in his word, and not any religion: not that which men have devised. To go a little further.

In that one religion that is left by him, there must be a care had, that the people live by the rules of that one. For this is a rule in nature. Nothing in religion will help him that will not live according to the rules of it. Therefore it concerns all that are not atheists to labour to stablish one religion, and obedience to that one.

And every particular man, as he looks for good by his religion, is not to live by the rules of fleshly wisdom, but by the rules of religion.

And here a man might deplore the misery of poor religion above all other things, above all other arts and trades. In other arts and trades he is accounted nobody that works not according to his trade, and that hath not, besides some speculative skill and rules in his head, that hath not skill to work. He is accounted nobody but a talker, except he *doth*. But in religion men think it is enough to know. Practice it goes under base names. Any common conscience, any common care, and obedience to the rules we must be saved by, is reproached and rejected. Religion will not do a man good, except he be ruled by it. Wherefore serves the rule, but to bring things to it? But I will not stand on this point longer.

There is a necessity of wisdom, And this wisdom may be had. And this wisdom it leads not only to salvation, but it reacheth to the state. And it leads every man in his calling. Well! we may see, to touch that by the way, in the third place,

Obs. True wisdom toucheth conversation.

'My conversation hath been by the grace of God,' that is, in wisdom. He puts the general for the particular. There were other graces besides; but together with them there was this wisdom. So wisdom tends to conversation.

Mark what I said, wisdom is not in word, but in work. A man that will be master of his trade must work. When a man can work well, he is master of his trade, and not till then. Religion tends to practice. You know what Christ saith, 'If you know these things, happy are ye if ye do them,' John xiii. 17. He entails happiness to doing, 'If you know these things,' he saith not, you are happy if you know them: no! 'If you know these things, happy are you if you do them.' For indeed true wisdom is not only speculative. This wisdom, understanding, and knowledge, when it is true and spiritual, it alway tends to practice; and practice is never sound but when it springs from wisdom, from things known. Every article in the creed it tends to practice in a Christian's life, and quickens practice [of] every article.* So wisdom tends to conversation.

Now, besides that main wisdom which properly concerns salvation, there is another wisdom which is more particular, that tends to conversation, which is called spiritual prudence, for particular actions. This comes from the Spirit of God, 'I wisdom dwell with prudence,' Prov. viii. 12. Wheresoever there is wisdom to salvation, there is prudence to the guidance of a Christian's life.

Use. But in a word, if so be that wisdom tend to conversation, and is joined with it, *you may see that all naughty livers are nobodies in religion;* they are fools in religion. Wherefore serves knowledge? wherefore serves light, but to walk by? wherefore serves an instrument, but to work by? wherefore serves wisdom, but to guide our lives by? Is it to be matter of discourse and talk? Therefore this doth demonstrate clearly to any man that thinks there is any religion, or any heaven, who be the best Christians, even those that by the Spirit know the wisdom that God hath revealed in his word, and apply it in their lives and conversations to be ruled by it, to work to that end. Wisdom prefixeth an end alway, and those that work to that end, they are wise men. He is a wise man that works to attain his end. Now there is no man that can attain his end by mere knowledge. He attains his end by working, by doing. Therefore the wisest Christian, he sets himself to converse wisely and holily; and he shews his religion in his particular calling, in everything. 'If any man be religious, let him shew it in holy conversation, let him be unspotted of the world,' James i. 26, 27. So much for that.

'But by the grace of God.' To give a little further light to the words. Grace is either—

1. *The free favour of God in himself*, issuing from his goodness, whereupon we have forgiveness of sins, and acceptation through Jesus Christ to life everlasting. This is grace resting in the breast of God, but is only entertained of us, and works no change in us of itself. Or else,

2. Grace is *something from that favour*, from that free grace of God wrought in us. And that grace wrought in us is—

(1.) First, *the grace of a whole, universal change;* for whomsoever God accepts graciously to life everlasting, he gives them the gifts of grace, with his favour; he changeth their nature, that they may be fit to entertain fellowship with him. For when by grace he accepts us to favour, if he should not alter our natures, alas! what a case were we in! were we fit for communion with God? No! Therefore, that we may have communion with God, he alters our dispositions, that we may be holy as he is holy. This change is the first change in Christianity.

(2.) Now in this gracious change, which is a work of the gracious Spirit,

* Qu. 'practice quickens every article?'—Ed.

derived to us by Christ, in whom our nature is filled with all grace, and in whom we receive 'grace for grace,' there are *graces wrought:* as—

[1.] *A heavenly light* to see a further end than ever we saw before; a heavenly convincing light to see the love of God, to see life everlasting, to see glorious things.

[2.] And withal comes the *grace of love* to carry the whole inward man to the things that we see.

[3.] Then there is the *grace of hope* to expect, and *patience* to endure all till we be possessed of that which our understandings are enlightened to see.

[4.] And *faith* persuades the soul where to have it, and relies on the promise. So particular graces are wrought. Therefore that is one reason why the apostle names not wisdom in particular, when he saith, 'We have not led our conversation according to carnal, fleshly wisdom, but by grace.' His meaning is that a Christian, when he hath heavenly wisdom, he hath all graces and wisdom together. There is a connection, a combination of graces, as I said. So he leads his life by all graces; for all graces are necessary to a Christian life. Therefore instead of wisdom, he puts the word grace.

(3.) Now besides these, besides the favour of God accepting us in Christ; and besides the working of these graces in us, in and after our conversion, there is another degree of grace requisite, *which is a particular exciting, applying, strengthening grace*, which is required to every good act, to act every good work, and resist every evil, and to enjoy good things as we ought to enjoy them. I say, there is a grace necessary to withstand temptations in all evil, besides graces habitual that are wrought in us, of faith, and love, and hope, &c. These, except they be actuated and enlivened by the continual work of the Spirit, except they be brought to act, and a new strength put into them, they are not sufficient for a Christian life. Therefore St Paul here by grace, means not only the graces of the Spirit, habitual graces; but the power of the Spirit acting, enlivening, quickening, and strengthening him against every evil in particular, and to every good work in particular.

'But by the grace of God.' In that the apostle here, though he principally mean wisdom, yet he means grace, the next point I will observe is this, that

Doctrine. All the wisdom that we have it comes from grace.

All the wisdom we have comes from grace, merely from grace. And this grace is not wanting to us when we have renounced our fleshly wisdom. Heavenly wisdom comes altogether from grace. To make this a little clear. Whatsoever is spiritual it comes from Christ. Since the fall we have nothing but by especial grace. God being reconciled by Jesus Christ, he hath placed all fulness of grace in him: he hath enriched our nature in him with wisdom, and all graces whatsoever. 'All the treasures of wisdom are in him,' Col. ii. 3, and all other graces. God the Father, and our Saviour Christ, they send the Spirit, they communicate the Spirit, which takes of Christ, and doth enlighten, and quicken, and guide all those that are members of Christ. All in particular, all inward things come from grace. Grace comes from the Spirit, the Spirit from Christ, and this is the descent of grace and wisdom.

Thereupon they are taken indefinitely in Scripture, sometimes to 'walk wisely,' Eph. v. 15, to walk graciously, sometimes to 'walk in the Spirit,' Rom. viii. 1, sometimes to 'walk in Christ,' Col. ii. 6. It is all one. Sometimes to be in Christ. 'Whosoever is in Christ,' &c., 2 Cor. v. 17.

And to walk in the Spirit, and by the Spirit, to pray in the Spirit, and in wisdom, and in faith, or to live by faith, or to live by grace, or in grace, they are all one, because they are subordinate. For Christ is the treasure of the church. All that is good for the church is laid up in him, 'wisdom,' and whatsoever. 'Of his fulness we receive grace for grace,' John i. 16. Grace, answerable to the grace that is in him. He vouchsafes us his Spirit.

Now the Spirit guides us not immediately, but it works a habit in us, as we call it, it works somewhat in us to dispose us to that which is good. And when that is wrought, the Spirit guides us to every particular action. These things that the Spirit works in us are called graces: because they come from out of ourselves by the Spirit. So wisdom is called grace, because it comes from the Spirit. The Spirit comes from Christ, and Christ hath grace, not only grace in himself, but he infuseth grace into us. He hath not only abundance, but redundance; not only grace flowing in himself, but redundant, overflowing to all his members. This St Paul means, when he saith, 'We have had our conversation by the grace of God,' that is, by such blessed habits of wisdom, faith, love, &c., as are wrought by the Spirit of God; which Spirit is given us by Jesus Christ our head.

Hence we learn, that everything that is necessary to bring us to heaven, it is a grace, that is, it comes from without us. Adam had it within him. He was trusted with his riches himself. But now in Jesus Christ we have all of grace: we have all out of ourselves. Christ is the Sun. We have all our beams from him, all our light, all our life from him. He is the head. All our motion is from him. And this is not only true of habits, as we call them, that is, a constant work, or disposition wrought in God's children, which for the most part they carry about with them; but likewise in all the particular passages of their life. They have need of grace for every particular action. And herein the soul is like to the air. The air stands in need of light, and if it be not enlightened by the sun, it is presently dark. So a man is no wiser in particular actions than God will make him on the sudden. Put case he be a man of a wise spirit for the most part, that he passeth for an understanding man, and is so: yet except he have the grace of God's Spirit, except he have wisdom to guide him in particular, he is no wiser than God at that time will make him to be. You see all motion in the body it comes from the head. Let the spirits in the head be obstructed never so little, and there follows an apoplexy, there will be no motion. So all our wisdom, all the direction that we have to lead our lives as becomes Christians, it comes from Christ, it comes from grace; not only the disposition, but likewise every particular action. For we need grace continually to assist us, to excite and stir up our powers, and to strengthen them against oppositions; and if the opposition be strong, we have need of a stronger grace.

There is never a good work that we do, but it is opposed from within us, from without us. From within us, by carnal wisdom, as I said before, and by carnal passions and affections. From without us, by Satan, by the world, and by men that are led by the spirit of the devil. Therefore there is need of a strength above our own. Besides the grace that is in us ordinarily, there needs a new particular strength and light, to particular actions.

Use. Doth all come from God and from his grace? Let us take heed when we have anything, of sacrilegious affections, of attributing anything to ourselves, to our own wisdom, and let us give all presently to grace. Mark the phrase of St Paul here, 'Not by fleshly wisdom, but by the grace of God.' He doth not say, by any habit in myself. He doth not say, by any wisdom that is in me. But he chooseth that which is in God, grace and favour; because he would not rob God of any honour. It was a proud term the philosophers had, as I said, sometimes they called their moral virtues habits (*ww*); and if we consider them merely as they are in the person, they are habits; but indeed they are graces. The Scripture gives them a more heavenly term, 'grace,' those things that we guide our lives by, as wisdom, love, temperance, sobriety. Grace is a fitter word than habit, because then we consider them as they come from God freely. They are graces. They come from grace and favour. And when men differ one from another in wisdom, they differ in grace and favour. He gives more light, he opens the understanding of one more than another. Therefore St Paul was wise, and careful this way, when he speaks of that he had done himself, lest he should rob God. 'Not I, Oh not I,' 1 Cor. xv. 10, 'but the grace of God that was in me; that was all in all.' For indeed we are what we are, and we do what we do, by grace. Even as by ourselves we are men, we are what we are, and we do what we do, by our souls, by our reason and understanding. So it is with spiritual grace. We are what we are out of ourselves by spiritual grace, and we do what we do by spiritual grace. And when that ceaseth, when God suspends the blessed motions of his Spirit to humble us, alas! we are dark. A man is a confused creature, he is at a loss, he is in darkness for the particular managing of his life. He knows not what to do, he knows not what to speak, he is puzzled in every particular action. And therefore when he hath spoken, or done that which is fit, he should consider it as a grace.

'My conversation hath been in the grace of God,' saith the apostle. Therefore let us sanctify God in our hearts this way. And when we stand in need of any direction, desire God of his grace to give us wisdom, and to give us the grace that we stand in need of. This is for the phrase. The point as I told you was this, that

All wisdom comes from grace, and God is ready to give us his grace.

For saith St Paul, 'My conversation' hath been in grace, which God did minister to me, and hath ministered to me to lead my life by.

The reason is this—*Christ hath undertaken to give us grace if we be his.* Men under grace shall never want grace to lead a Christian life. For Christ hath undertaken to be our head, to be our husband, to be our guide in our way to heaven. As our head, he is to give us motion, to move us as his members. As he is our shepherd, as he saith, 'I am the good shepherd,' John x. 11, so he is to lead us in our ways and passages, in his paths, to conduct us to happiness. And as he is our husband, so he is to be the head of his wife. To guide us, it is his office. And he works according to his own office. He is a king to subdue in us whatsoever is contrary to his good Spirit, to subdue our rebellions, and to bring all our imaginations under his Spirit; as well as to be a priest to make peace between God and us. He is a king to rule us, and to overrule in us whatsoever is ill. And he is a prophet to teach us and to guide us. He is the angel of the covenant, the great counsellor, that hath the spirit of counsel in him, Isa. ix. 6, not for himself only, but for his church.

Therefore as all things that we need come from grace, and from the favour of God; so we need not doubt of the grace of God in Christ. Being reconciled, he is willing to give us grace.

This I observe, to cut off all cavils of flesh and blood, and to arm us against all discouragements.

There are two things that greatly hinder us from a Christian course,—presumption and despair.

Presumption, to set upon things, without asking grace of God, without depending upon his direction, by the strength of natural parts, of natural wit.

And then *despair*, when a man saith, What should I go about these things? I shall never bring them to pass. No. First, consider thy standing, thy place and calling; and then consider the abilities that God hath given thee. Consider thy parts, consider thy duty that thou art to do. And beg of God assistance and strength; and if it be a thing that belong to thee, go on, set on all the duties that belong to thy place, in this confidence that thou shalt have grace.

Go to the fountain, to Christ, for grace for the direction of thy life. He is the light of life, he is the way, he is 'all in all' to bring us to heaven.

Wherefore serves all the promises, not only of life everlasting, but even of grace? but to encourage us to set on holy duties in confidence, that if we have a will to be out of Satan's kingdom, and if we have a will to be out of 'fleshly wisdom,' God will take us into his kingdom, and into his government. 'He will give the Spirit to them that ask him,' Luke xi. 13. Now the Spirit is a Spirit of direction, a Spirit of assistance, a Spirit of strength and comfort. It serves all turns. How many promises are wrapped in that promise of the Spirit? In want of direction he shall be our counsellor; in want of strength, to assist us. In perplexities, when we know not which way to turn us, to advise us. In extremities, when we are ready to sink, to comfort us. He will give us his Holy Spirit to supply all our defects in a fit time if we ask him; if we find our need, and if we will renounce our carnal wisdom. Therefore set on those duties that God calls you to.

And withal, do as St Paul doth here (he sets the negative before the affirmative), renounce carnal wisdom, be not guided by that; trust perfectly to the word of grace, and to the Spirit of grace. For the word of grace and the Spirit of grace go together. And then you shall find that God will do 'abundantly above all that you are able to ask or think,' Eph. iii. 20. Luther when he set on the work of reformation, those that saw him at the first might have said, 'Get thee into thy cloister,' and say, 'Lord, have mercy upon thee,' for thou settest on a work impossible. But he saw the parts that God had given him, that he had wit to understand the abuses of the times, and he had given him courage. He saw by his profession he was called to be a divine. His conscience was awakened to see the abominations of the times, and he set on to discover these things. Did Christ leave him? No! He did not, but gave success to him to be admired* of all. When all the world was set against one man, yet he prevailed against them all; even because he walked as St Paul did here, 'in sincerity and simplicity,' that is, he looked to the truth of the cause, and not to his own honour, or profit, or pleasure. He was content to be no wiser than the book of God would have him to be; to be no richer or greater in the world than God would have him; but committed himself to God 'in simplicity and sincerity.' How did God maintain him? Wondrously, to admiration! I instance in him to shew how base distrust causeth things to be no better carried than they are.

Now to encourage you to go to the grace of God, to go to the fountain, and not to be held under carnal wisdom, under these pretexts, Oh! if I do not

* That is, 'wondered at.'—G.

hearken to carnal wisdom, I shall be a beggar, I shall never rise, I shall never do this or that in the world, I shall never escape this and that danger. Fie upon those base conceits. St Paul here renounceth the regiment of carnal wisdom. What became of him? Did he want a guide? Grace took him up. 'Not by carnal wisdom, but by the grace of God.' When we come under the government of God, we come under the government of grace. And we shall want nothing either for heaven or earth that is for our good.

Whatsoever we had that was good before we were gracious, that we keep still, and it is under a better guide. Were we learned before? were we wise before? had we authority before? were we noble before? We lose none of these when we come under Christ; but he advanceth and elevates these, he makes them better. If we were wise, he makes us graciously wise; if we were learned, if we were noble, he makes us doubly noble. We lose nothing, but we are under a sweeter government, the government of grace, which is a mild government; a government that tends to the advancing of us above ourselves, that advanceth us to be the spouse of Christ and the heirs of heaven.

Those that are in Christ Jesus, and are led by his Spirit, they are his. In Rom. viii. 1, *seq.*, there is excellently set down the prerogatives that they have. Those that lead their conversation 'in simplicity and sincerity,' those that are in Christ, and in the Spirit, and in grace, there is 'no damnation to them.' And then again, if they suffer anything, saith he, 'The afflictions of this world are not worthy of the glory that shall be revealed,' Rom. viii. 18. If they have any infirmities, saith he, 'the Spirit helps our infirmities,' ver. 26. The 'Spirit teacheth us how to pray,' ver. 26, when we know not how to pray. If we suffer any evil, God 'turns all to good.' 'All things shall work together for the best to them that fear God,' ver. 28. For infirmities in other things we have Christ, and he makes intercession in heaven. 'Who shall lay anything to the charge of God's people' that are in Christ, ver. 33, that are in grace, that are in the Spirit, such as St Paul was here? 'It is Christ that is dead, or rather that is risen again, and makes intercession for us,' ver. 34. And 'if he have given us Christ, shall he not with him give us all things else?' ver. 32. If he have given us Christ, he will give us grace to bring us to heaven. See the excellent estate of a Christian that is under the regiment of Christ, that is led by the Spirit. That chapter may serve instead of all.

And see the sweet combination here, how he knits these things together. 'My rejoicing is this, that I have not had my conversation in fleshly wisdom, but by the grace of God.' Here is a knitting together of divers things that seem to differ, as here is 'wisdom' *and* 'simplicity.' I have had my conversation by the grace of God, by wisdom, and yet in simplicity. For it is wisdom to be simple. When a man hath strength of parts, it is wisdom to bring them parts of simplicity.

It is wisdom to be simple concerning that which is evil; for a man to be simple there is his best way. There is 'wisdom' joined with his 'simplicity.' Then, again, besides wisdom and simplicity, here is 'our conversation' and 'God's grace,' both joined together. St Paul by grace guided his conversation. So God stirs us to do all that we do. We see, but he opens our eyes to see; we hear, but he opens our ears; we believe, but he opens our hearts to believe.

This I speak to reconcile some seeming difference. Doth God's Spirit do all, and we do nothing? We do all subordinately; we move as we are moved; we see as we are enlightened; we hear as we are made to hear; we are wise as far as he makes us wise. We do, but it is he that makes us do.

St Paul here led his conversation, but it was grace that moved him to lead it graciously. Well, then, he that joins simplicity and wisdom together, the wisdom of the serpent and the simplicity of the dove; he that trusts in God and grace, and yet in trusting to grace doth all that he can, and goes on in a Christian course, he shall rejoice. 'Our rejoicing is this, that we have had our conversation in simplicity, and according to the rule of grace, not by fleshly wisdom.'

Consider seriously of it, what a joy will this be, that we have led our lives by a rule different from the world, that we have led our lives and courses according to the motion of God's blessed Spirit! This must needs bring joy and rejoicing with it in what estate soever.

The world join these together, simplicity and sincerity of life, where they see them, that they may slander them, that they may lay imputations upon them. They see they are courses opposite to theirs, and they lay loads on them. But what doth God? Where there is simplicity and wisdom and a holy conversation, he adds his Spirit, he joins the Spirit of grace, which is a Spirit of joy always. As light and comfort go with the sun, so the Spirit of joy and comfort go alway with the Spirit of grace. St Paul here, in regard of the world, was afflicted, 'he received the sentence of death,' he was slandered and misused; yet to God-ward, saith he, 'Our rejoicing is this, that we have led our conversation according to grace,' according to the motion of God's blessed Spirit, and 'not with fleshly wisdom.'

If this be so, that the joy of God's Spirit goes with the grace of God's Spirit, and that those that lead their conversation by grace have a rejoicing above all imputations and slanders whatsoever, let this be an encouragement to us to lead a godly life. We all seek for joy. Every creature seeks for joy. If we would have joy within us, if we would have a spring of joy, let us labour to lead a conversation by this rule, by grace, by the motion of God's Spirit, which is ready to guide us if we commit ourselves to his guidance.

'But by the grace of God.' To come then to make an use of trial, whether we lead our lives by this gracious wisdom or no, and not by carnal wisdom. And then to come to direct us how to lead our lives by the grace of God, which is the ground of all joy and comfort, as St Paul saith here.

Quest. How shall a man know whether he lead his life by this spiritual, gracious wisdom, or no?

Ans. I answer, mark the opposition here, 'Not with fleshly wisdom, *but by the grace of God.*' He then doth lead his life by the 'grace of God,' that doth renounce carnal and fleshly wisdom. Carnal wisdom is a false rule, and it cannot stand together with grace; they one expel another. 'A double-minded man,' saith St James, 'is inconstant in all his ways,' James i. 8, that is, he that hath two strings to his bow; he that will be content to be led by the grace of God, and by the word of God, which is the 'Word of his grace,' and yet notwithstanding he will have carnal policies, he will have shifts too, he is a double-minded man; he is now under the government of grace, he halteth, as the prophet tells the Israelites, 'Why do you halt?' 1 Kings xviii. 21. So he halteth between carnal and heavenly wisdom. He is loath to renounce carnal wisdom. No, he thinks if he do, he shall be a fool, he shall lose this way of getting, and that way of rising.

But he that is under the Spirit of God; that is under grace, and is guided by it, he will renounce the motions and stirrings of carnal wisdom. When carnal wisdom, like to Eve, or like Job's wife, or like Peter, shall suggest, Oh, spare yourself, why will you do this? why will you go on in these courses? yet notwithstanding he is able to renounce it.

The most of God's judgments in this world, on his children, it is for this halting. They have much carnal wisdom in them; and God, to work it out of them, is forced to cross them sharply in their projects and courses; and all to bring them to rely on grace, to rely on his government in the use of good means; for we must serve God's providence in the use of good means.

A man may know by God's afflicting of his children, that they deal too much in carnal wisdom; for if it were not for carnal wisdom, if we would submit ourselves to his sweet and easy guidance, and use the lawful means that he hath discovered in a lawful calling; if we would observe lawful courses; alas! we should see a clear light, and an easy passage. We need not to use these shifts. But because we cannot do so, we are loath to trust him. But we are double-minded. We will be ruled by him a little, but we will be politic and subtle. Therefore he sends crosses upon crosses upon our carnal ends and projects; especially those that are his children, he will not suffer them to prosper in ill courses.

Sign 1. That is one sign, those that are led by the grace of God, *they will not be led by God's enemy, and the enemy of their own souls*. Now God and our own souls have not a worse enemy than carnal, fleshly wisdom. That is evident from the opposition.

Those that deny carnal wisdom, that deny themselves, and put themselves upon God, it is a good evidence. And as it is a sign, so it is a cause. You see in holy Abraham, when he had put himself on God, and left his country, and his father's house, God guided him, God took him into his government. 'I am God all-sufficient, walk before me, and be perfect,' Gen. xvii. 1. God means this, that by leaving all other things, and cleaving to me, thou shalt lose nothing, thou shalt have all in me, I will be 'all-sufficient;' therefore 'walk before me, and be perfect,' be sincere. A man shall never know what God will do for him till he put himself upon him, and cease to try him, and begin to trust him; trust him once, honour him of his word; have not a double eye, partly to carnal means, and partly to him, but have a single eye to his wisdom, and know that he will reward thee and keep promise. It is an excellent thing to deny carnal wisdom.

How many cavils might blessed Noah have had, before he built the ark? The world would scorn him as an old doating man, that would go about to be wiser than all the world besides. But he denies all carnal reason, and rejects the scorns of sinful persons, and obeys God; and we see how God protected him, and went on with him. And so in David, and St Paul.

And to add a little to that I touched before, God usually strangely crosses carnal wisdom, because men will not deny their carnal will, and their carnal wit. There was never any politician in the world that ever was, but complained of it, if he lived any time in the world, that God went beyond him. Saith the heathen man Tully, 'I thought myself wise, but I never was so;' (*xx*) and so they may all take up the same complaint. God dashes the imaginations of the proud. They build a Babel, a confusion to themselves and others, that are led by carnal wisdom, that will not trust to the grace of God.

Let no man flatter himself, but trust in God, and not rely upon carnal wisdom, and such courses. Those that will bring religion to reasons of state, and policy; and subject the highest thing in the world to the basest thing, which is carnal wit, as I said before, we see what they do. The nature of man infinitely desireth the accomplishment of their will. We see that where corruption may have the greatest advantage in greatness, let them have their will, they will overthrow a world to have it; their wit is bent to serve their will.

All witty men, that account it a heaven upon earth to have their will, instead of law, and conscience, and all, they set their wits on the strain to serve their will, and so set themselves against God. Is it not God's honour to set himself against them? 'Was there ever any fierce against God and prospered?' saith Job, ix. 4. Denial of fleshly wit, and will, and wisdom, it is both a sign and evidence of grace; and it is a means likewise why* God's grace will lead us. When we deny that which is strong in us, God will make a supply by his grace. We are no losers by it.

Sign 2. Again, you see here in the text, where the life is led by the grace of God, by the Spirit of God stirring us, acting us, leading, moving, and strengthening of us, there *a man's courses are in simplicity and sincerity*. The soul that is under grace will put itself simply upon God. That soul will be no wiser than the word of God makes it to be. It will be no happier, no richer than God makes it. It will use no other means than what God allows. This is plainness, and singleness, and simplicity of heart.

Again, it will be in sincerity. Where a man leads his life graciously, his actions are sincere. This grace, as it comes from God, so it tends to God. Sincerity looks to God: it doth things as to God. So that where grace is, it carries a man above himself, to seek the glory of God, and life everlasting, to have spiritual and heavenly ends, to seek God in all things. The grace of God in St Paul guided him to lead his life in the simplicity and sincerity of God, that is, sincerity that looks to, and aims at, God in all things.

And indeed, a gracious man, and only a gracious man, can look out of himself to an end above himself; only a gracious man can aim at God's glory, at the pleasing of God. Why? Because only a gracious man knows that he hath better things in God than in the world. A worldly man makes himself his term,† he makes himself his last end; because he knows not better out of himself than in himself. He dares not venture upon God's favour, to put all upon that. He knows not whether he be his friend or no. He thinks he is his enemy, as he may well enough, by his ill courses. Only the gracious man can put himself upon God. He knows he is redeemed out of a miserable condition into a glorious estate; and if he should be denied of all the world, yet he knows he hath more happiness in him than he can look for here. He knows he would be all-sufficient for him. He is assured of his salvation. Therefore he hath higher ends, he is sincere in all things.

God when he is honoured by trusting of him, when in sincerity we make him our wisdom, and make his word our rule, and the happiness that he hath promised our chief happiness that we aim at, and rest in him; when we honour him so far, then he makes a supply of all other things. But I spake of sincerity to the full before, only I bring it now, to shew how it is a note of a man that makes the grace of God his guide—he walks sincerely, he seeks the glory of God.

Sign 3. Thirdly, He that walks by the grace of God, and in the grace of God; by it as a rule, and in it as a principle: he that walks in it, and by

* Qu. 'whereby?'—Ed.

† That is, = 'termination, end.'—G.

it, and through it: you shall see it *by the ability that is in him above nature, by the things that he doth, that other men cannot do, that walk not by grace.* Therefore you have a trial of a man that converseth by grace, from hence. He can cross the common corruptions of the place, and of the time he lives in. He is not a slave, he is not enthralled to common fears, to common hopes, to the common joys and delights that the world is carried withal. But as grace is a thing that is mighty, and strong, and powerful of itself, it is a Spirit (the Spirit is like the wind, as Christ tells Nicodemus, John iii. 8); it is a mighty, powerful, strong thing: so it makes him strong, it enables a man's spirit to do above himself, above that which he could do, if he had not grace. It makes him deny himself in matter of pleasure, in matter of profit; it will make him cross himself in matter of revenge, as David spared Saul, when he had him in his power, 1 Sam. xxiv. 4. It will make him triumph over all estates. He can abound, and he can want, as St Paul saith, Philip. iv. 12.

Other men are changeable with their condition; they are cast down in adversity, they are puffed up in prosperity, they can deny themselves in nothing; they are always enthralled to their base pleasures, and profits, and honours; they are always swayed with some carnal end or other. Grace, it raiseth a man above nature. He can do that which another cannot do; he can endure that which another man cannot endure. He can die, he can endure shame, he can resist that which another man cannot resist.

Sign 4. In a word, you may know grace in a man *that hath great parts of nature.* How shall we distinguish grace from nature in him? Thus, you shall have him *subdue his parts unto grace, and to the rules of religion.* If he have a strong wit, he will not make show of the strength of it, as though he would break through business with his wit; but he will consult with conscience. You may know a man that is led by grace, especially where there are great parts; he can deny not only his corruptions, but other things, if they stand not at that time with the will of God; he forbears ostentation of learning when he sees it is hurtful, when it is rather to shew himself, than to get glory to God, or to win souls. When a man sees that such and such courses might crush another, and advance himself; yet if it touch upon conscience, he will not do [it]. Here is a conflict between parts, and the grace of God, and goodness. Now when a man in this can deny himself, it is a sign that a man makes grace his guide.

It is not so easy in weaker dispositions; for men seem sometimes to be good, when it is defect of parts; but in men of ability, it proceeds not from defect, or want of parts, but it is the power of grace only whereby they are swayed. Such a man dares not do it. He wants not ability or skill; but he dares not offend God, he dares not seek himself, he dares not give scope to his wit, and to his vain mind; he knows what spirit in him moves such things, and he suppresseth them presently, and yields to the motions of God's blessed Spirit.

But yet in weaker men a man may know when such a one is ruled by grace. Thus, when a man sees something in him that strengthens nature, as, grace takes not away nature, but betters it. When you see a man that otherwise is simple, yet he is wondrous skilful in resisting a temptation, skilful in giving advice, skilful in keeping the peace of his conscience, skilful in giving reproof, even above himself: a man may know that he hath a better schoolmaster: that the Spirit of God, the Spirit of grace, is his schoolmaster.

So that whether a man have strong or weak parts, a man may know whether he be led by grace or no. In the weaker, it raiseth him above himself; in the stronger, when the exercise of his parts of nature and grace cannot stand together, it makes him deny himself. That he may be led by the one, he denies the other altogether. This is gracious wisdom.

Sign 5. Again, a man may know that he leads his life in gracious wisdom, or by gracious wisdom, *when he fetcheth reasons for his actions, not from things below, but from religion, from conscience, from spiritual things.* He doth not fetch the reason of his actions from this, that this will profit me, or I shall advantage myself thus and thus; but he fetcheth the reasons and ground of his actions higher: this is pleasing to God, this is according to the peace of my conscience, this is for the good of the church, for the good of the state I live in, this is for the good of my Christian brethren. The strongest reason of a Christian is that that makes for religion, and for conscience. If he may gain in his own particular one way, and gain to the state or religion another, he considers not, what will it advantage me? but, what is it for religion? It is the chief prevailing reason, how he may gain to religion, and the glory of God. He will not redeem his life to impeach the glory of God and religion. This is a man that leads his life by grace.

Sign 6. Again, where grace is, *there graces are together.* There is a sweet linking of them. Therefore St Paul, instead of wisdom, names 'grace of God,' all grace. A man, therefore, may know that he is led by grace, when there is no solitary grace; for where grace is solitary, it is not at all, it is but a shadow.

For there is not one grace, but it is of special use in the managing of a Christian's life and conversation; therefore St Paul, instead of wisdom, puts grace here. For instance, there is a great necessity of seeing by a light above nature, things above nature. If a man lead a life above nature, there is a necessity of heavenly illumination, and conviction that there is a better happiness than the world affords. And then there is a need of love to carry the soul to that happiness that is discovered. But then there are a world of impediments between us and heaven and happiness, that is discovered to us in the gospel by Christ Jesus. There must be heavenly wisdom, therefore, to discover the impediments, and to remove them. And there are many advantages how to attain our end. We must use this and this means, these and these helps that God hath ordained. Here must be heavenly wisdom to use the advantages, and to avoid the hindrances. But there is a world of troubles between our end and us, between heaven that is discovered, and us. Therefore saith the apostle, 'Ye have need of patience.' And patience, that is sustained by hope. Hope casts anchor in heaven, and assures us of happiness there; and then patience sustains us in whatsoever befalls us in this world. Therefore the apostle saith not, I lead my life by wisdom, but by grace; by wisdom, as it hath a connection with all other graces.

Therefore a man that, out of hearing of the word, or reading, &c., hath it discovered, that there is a better way than he takes, and yet notwithstanding hath not love to carry him to it, nor wisdom to remove the impediments, he works not towards his end; there is no grace at all. There is illumination, but it is not sanctified illumination, but a mere common work of the Spirit; because where true wisdom is, there is love, and patience, and hope, and all other graces, to carry the whole soul to that happiness that is discovered.

Therefore by this you may know a gracious wise man, he works to his end always. Another man hears and wishes, Oh! it were well if I could attain heaven. But carnal policy and base affections hold him in a beastly course of life, that he works not to that end. Only he hears such things, and thinks God will be merciful, and Christ hath died; and when he cannot enjoy the world longer, he will have good words that way. But that will not serve the turn. A man must lead a life in grace, that will die, and be saved by grace. He must work, and carry the whole man with it; and not only have knowledge, but faith, and love, and all. A man must work with it.

Who is a wise man in outward matters? Is he a wise man that only talks of state matters, out of books he hath read? No! but he that, when he comes to a business to negotiate in the world, can remove hindrances, and attain his end, and overthrow the plots of his enemies, when it comes to particular actions. Here is a wise man, that can attain his end by working; that doth work to his end, till he have attained it. So he proves graciously wise in religion, that works to his end; or else he is a foolish man, a foolish builder. As Christ saith, 'If ye know these things, and do them not,' Mat. vii. 26, you are as a man that builds on the sands; your profession will come to nothing.

Sign 7. Again, a man may know that he is guided by grace, that he doth everything by gracious wisdom, *when he doth provide for himself best in the best things, out of a sanctified judgment*, when he doth judge aright of differences; when he considers that there is a difference between the soul and the body, between this life and eternal life. There is a main difference between the glorious eternal life in the world to come, and this fading life which the soul communicates to the body in this world. When a man judgeth the difference between true riches and these things that we are so set upon, that are but lent us for a little while; when he judgeth between the true honour to be the child of God, and the fading honours of this world that shall lie down in the dust with us, and shall all depart and be gone, it appears then he hath a sanctified judgment; he 'discerns of things that differ,' Heb. v. 14.

And according to this, if he lead his life in gracious wisdom, he makes his provision. He makes his provision as his judgment leads him. His judgment leads him to the best things, therefore he provides for the best things. As Christ saith of the children of this world, 'they are wise' in their courses, 'in their generation.' They provide against beggary, they make friends beforehand, as we see in that unjust steward, Luke xvi. 8. So a Christian provides for his soul, he looks to that, he 'makes him friends of his unrighteous mammon,' xvi. 9; he makes him friends of his earthly things, that is, he doth deserve well of men that they pray for him, and so help him to heaven. He daily makes his account ready, he cuts off impediments that he meets with in the way, he troubles not himself with impertinences, he spends not more time than needs about worldly things; he useth them as they may help his work to be better and better in grace, to be fitter and fitter for glory. As he discerneth differences, so he makes his provision answerable; he provides for the best in the first place. Or else he were a foolish merchant, a foolish builder, a foolish man every way. The Scripture saith he is no better that cannot discern the difference, and provide well for himself when other things fail.

The Scripture doth well call wicked men fools. They have no judgment, they do not provide for themselves; they prefer these things, say what they will, before better things; they are fools in their provision. Ahithophel, he made provision, he set his house in order, and what became of him after? He hanged himself. He made much provision for the world, and at last he knew not how to forecast and provide for his soul. The Scripture calls the rich man in the gospel, 'a fool,' Luke xii. 20. He was wise enough to contrive for himself, yet he was but a rich fool. 'The fool,' as the wise man saith, 'knows not the way to the city,' Eccles. x. 15; so a wicked man he knows not the way to heaven, he discerns not the difference, he provides not, he knows not the way thither. He cannot do one thing that is gracious, not one action that may further his account.

I might be very large in the point. It is profitable, because we do infinitely deceive ourselves in that point, which is of more consequence than the whole world; for the man is, as the rule that he is led by is. Carnal men are led by carnal rules; gracious and holy men guide their lives by heavenly wisdom, by a gracious rule.

Now if you find yourselves defective, for a good Christian may be defective in this; but if he have hearkened to carnal wisdom, if he have forgotten himself, if he have troubled himself too much about the world, he will come to his centre again, he will come to his old way again, he will not be long out of it; his way and course is by grace. Sometimes he may have a policy that is not good, as David had, yet his way is gracious. I say, if you find yourselves defective, I will shew some helps how we may guide ourselves, 'not by fleshly wisdom, but by the grace of God,' that is, by gracious wisdom, by the Spirit.

Now the Spirit leads us not immediately, but works graces in us, and stirs up those graces in us. The Spirit guides a godly man, by working grace in him, by making him better, by using those graces in him. Sometimes the Spirit of God moves a wicked man, but it makes him not better. He puts conceits into his head, and makes him do that which otherwise he would not; but he is not bettered. The Spirit guides a good man by making him better, he works a gracious disposition, a gracious bent in him, that his judgment concurs with God's, his affections concur with the Holy Spirit, and make him holy and pure. There is a disposition wrought in a good man like to the Spirit that sanctifies him, and like to the disposition of Christ to whose image he is renewed.

Now that we may guide our lives by the Spirit working in us spiritual and gracious wisdom,

First of all, *consider what I said before of fleshly wisdom.* There are none but they have one of these two guides, either the flesh, and by consequent the devil; for the devil dwells in our carnal reason: that is his fort, that is his tower, his castle. Carnal, fleshly imaginations is the devil's forge: there he works all his tools, all his instruments. For the devil works not so much immediately, as by carnal men that are led with him.

Our wit and policy, and carnal wisdom, it is the shop, the forge of the devil, wherein he works all his mischief to overthrow us. It is the devil's workhouse, where he engines with all his tools and instruments.

Then considering that there are but two guides, the flesh, the world, and Satan, which alway go together in one, or God's Spirit and grace, 1. Let us be willing *to submit our thoughts and desires, to submit our projects and our aims, and all to the Spirit of grace;* submit to the word of grace, and to the motions of the word; the word of God having the Spirit of God accompanying of it. The word of grace accompanied by the Spirit of grace, is forcible, as the apostle saith, 1 Cor. x. 4. It beats down strongholds, 'strong imaginations.' Satan fortifies himself in strongholds, as the Scripture calls them, in high thoughts, working discoursive thoughts. Now when we come to hear the word, which teacheth the simple, sincere truth of God, that teacheth us how we should be saved, and how we should guide our lives; if we will be guided by grace, if we will yield to God's simple truth, let him erect a throne in us, let us lay down all. When we come to hear the word, let us think, I come to hear the wisdom of heaven itself, I come to hear that word that shall make me wise to salvation; I will not entertain projects, I will not entertain a wisdom that is contrary to it; when they rise in my soul contrary to the direction of the Spirit, and of the word, down they shall, I will not own them. This is the wisdom of a man that intends to make grace his rule.

Now a carnal hearer, a carnal reader, a common Christian, he brings his naughty, proud heart, he brings his high conceits to the hearing and reading of the word, he comes as a censurer, as a judge, he comes to talk of what was said in this passage and in that passage, he comes not as to hear God speak in his ordinance, he comes not as a humble man; he comes not to hear it as the ordinance of God with reverence; and that makes him come and go out again as a beast. As the beasts that went out of Noah's ark, they went out as they came in; so many come into the church and go out again as beasts. They go out worse than they came in, because they bring not hearts to submit themselves to God and to his word. O! a spirit of subjection, it is a blessed thing.

Self-denial is some help to this. Be content in the guiding of your common life, and in the guiding your way to salvation, to be no wiser than God's Spirit, and God's word will make you, to have no will nor no wisdom contrary to his will and wisdom. But you will live as men that have nothing of their own, nothing different from God, no distinct will, no contrary will and wit to God, but you will let God take the guidance of you himself; and whom he guides must needs come to a happy end, as the psalmist saith excellent well, 'Thou wilt guide me by thy counsel, and after bring me to glory,' Ps. lxxiii. 24. Those that submit themselves to be guided by God's counsel, he will bring them to glory.

2. Serviceable to this is that which is pressed everywhere in the Scripture, humility. God gives grace to the humble, that is, he gives them not only forgiveness of sins, and acceptation to life, but he gives them grace for the regiment of their lives; 'He gives grace to the humble.' Those that humble their wits to God (for there is a humiliation of the wit as well as of the affections), that they care not for the 'depths of Satan,' Rev. ii. 24, they care not for school tricks; they care to know nothing but 'Christ and him crucified,' as St Paul saith, 1 Cor. ii. 2. God's word is of power and majesty enough to save me, I need not bring my wit for my acceptance to God. It is truth that is accepted, not a strong brain to cavil. 'God gives grace to the humble.' Those that bring their understandings to be led and taught by God, he gives grace to them.

3. Again, in the third place, if we would have our thoughts guided by counsel, *let us have a high esteem of wisdom,* above all precious stones and pearls. Solomon presseth it, Prov. iv. 7, *et alibi;* have a high estimation of wisdom, of the government of God's Spirit as the best government. And be out of love with carnal reason, with carnal affections and their guidance; account them as base things, not worthy to come into the esteem of a Christian heart. Those that highly prize wisdom, God will lead them by it; those that sell all for the pearl shall have it, Mat. xiii. 46. There must be a

high price set on the guidance of God's Spirit, and on grace, as indeed it is worthy of it, and then we shall have it.

4. Again, if we would lead our lives according to spiritual and heavenly wisdom, according to grace, and gracious wisdom; let us learn, as it is, Job xxii. 21, *to be more and more acquainted with God by prayer;* for grace comes not from within us. Grace is in Christ as in the root, as in the spring, as in the sun; we have it but as the beam, as the stream. Therefore let us learn to be acquainted with God, and with Christ by prayer and meditation, and search into his word by reading, and by hearing him speak to us, and let us often speak to him.

Let us acquaint ourselves with him by prayer, and by hearing his word, and then we shall have his grace to guide us. For grace is a fruit of his peculiar love. He gives grace to his own peculiar people. How do you think, shall he have a peculiar delight in us, if we labour not to be more and more acquainted with him? by often speaking to him, by often hearing of him, by coming into his presence, and attending as much as we can upon his holy ordinances, by conversing as much as we can in the holy things of God. Those that will be warm, they come under the beams of the sun; those that would have the Spirit work effectually, they must come where the Spirit is effectual, where the Spirit works. Now the Spirit is effectual in the word preached. The Spirit fell upon Cornelius and the rest when they were hearing of St Peter, Acts x. 44. And the Spirit is where there is conversing in good company. 'Where two or three are met together, I will be in the midst of them,' saith Christ, Mat. xviii. 20. 'If we walk with the wise, we shall be wiser,' Prov. ix. 9.

It must be the heavenly wisdom of a Christian, if he would lead his life by grace, to attend upon all the means of grace. Because the Spirit of God is effectual by his own means, he works by his own means; therefore use the means that the Spirit hath sanctified for the working of grace. I do wonder at a company of vain sottish creatures, that carry themselves according to their vain conceits, according to the whirling of their own brain, in toys* and baubles that come into their heads! They care not for the hearing of God's blessed truth. Either they abstain altogether, or else they hear it carelessly, as if it were a thing that concerned them not. Oh, but those that will lead their lives by grace, they come to it by the Spirit, and the Spirit is only effectual in holy ordinances. It must be our wisdom therefore, to bring ourselves under some means or other, that the Spirit may be effectual.

The wisest and the best men in the world are no longer gracious than they are wise this way. If they neglect good company, good acquaintance, if they neglect the hearing of the word, if they neglect prayer, they will grow dead, and dull, and carnal-minded; they will be possessed with base thoughts. How do men differ one from another? Not so much by any habitual grace that is in them, as by avoiding all that might prejudice them in a Christian course, and by using all means whereby the Spirit of God may be effectual.

5. Again, the way to be under the grace of God's Spirit *is often to meditate of the grace of God, the free love of God in Jesus Christ:* for so it comes first. The first grace of all is God's free love in the forgiving of our sins, and accepting us to life everlasting; and then he doth alter and change our natures more and more, he transforms us more and more. When we find therefore any defect of grace in our hearts, when we find coldness, and

* That is, trifles.—G.

deadness, and dulness, go to the first fire, to the first Sun, to the free grace of God in Christ, pardoning all our sins, and accepting us to life everlasting, and promising us grace to lead our lives in the mean time. If you have fallen into any sin by the temptation of Satan, or your own weakness, beg not first grace to alter your course, to sanctify your life; but renew every day your interest in the first grace, in the forgiveness of sins, and your acceptation to everlasting life. For till God have pardoned your sins, and have witnessed to your souls that you stand reconciled, he will not give the best fruit of reconciliation, which is grace.

Therefore every day examine your lives, if you have offended God, in what terms you stand with God, and if you stand in ill terms, that there is any sin against conscience, the best way is not presently to amend that; for that will not be, except the heart be warmed with God's love and favour in the pardon of your sins first, and in the acceptation of you in Christ, notwithstanding your sins; as he justifieth us every day, not only in the first act of conversion, but daily. He acquits our consciences daily from our sins. And therefore in the Lord's prayer Christ teacheth us every day to say, 'Forgive us our sins,' Mat. vi. 12. And then, after forgiveness of sins, to beg the particular graces for our lives that we want. I would this were better thought on.

6. *Challenge likewise the covenant of grace.* We have a promise of all grace, and the spring of all grace. We have a promise of love. God will teach us to 'love one another,' John xiii. 34. We have a promise of fear. He hath promised that 'he will put his fear into our hearts, that we shall never depart from him,' Jer. xxxii. 40. We have a promise of the Holy Spirit. Let us challenge these promises every day. So much for the directions how to lead our lives by grace.

'But by the grace of God.' St Paul here makes it the ground of his rejoicing, that he led not his life by 'fleshly wisdom, but in simplicity and sincerity,' and 'by the grace of God;' and all that are led by St Paul's spirit live thus.

There is a religion in the world that bears itself very big, on high terms of universality, succession, antiquity, &c., and they will have it thought to be a spiritual and holy religion. Well! if a man be a carnal man that is led with fleshly wisdom, and not by the grace of God, that religion must needs be a naughty religion that hath only the support and the foundation of it in fleshly wisdom, which is an enemy, and opposite to the grace of God, and to simplicity and sincerity.

But popery is this. Take it in the regiment and government of it, take it in the worship, take it in the opinions: you may draw all to one of those three heads.

1. *For the government of it.* There is a wisdom, a wondrous wisdom, a fine subordination to one head, the pope, to hear all controversies; and under him the cardinals, and under them the generals, and all at Rome; and they have their provincials under them. Here is a wondrous fine subordination; but all this is by 'fleshly wisdom.' For this 'beast' riseth out of the earth, and out of the sea, out of the tumult of the people, out of base earthly respects. Therefore it is said in the Revelation, when the bishop of Rome became pope, and was at the highest, that a star fell, Rev. ix. 1. He fell when he rose. When he was at the highest, he was at the lowest. Why? Because his rising was carnal and earthly; or lower if you will, it was hellish and devilish.

Their government is opposite to Christ's government, and being so, it must needs be mightily opposed by him again; and therefore it must needs down, the fabric of it being opposite to the frame of Christ's government, though it be wondrous witty. Therefore in the Revelation, 666 is the 'number of a man.' If you mark the frame of the Romish policy, it is wondrous accurate, it goes smoothly, by tens and by hundreds, 666. This Babylon is the number of a man; a fine policy! But it is but the number of a man. It is the device of carnal wisdom itself. Therefore it is devilish wisdom. Thus it is in the government of it.

2. *And their worship* is according to the wisdom of the flesh. Some wisdom there is in not going to God immediately, but by saints and angels. What! is it not wisdom in the prince's court, first to go to the favourite, and by him to the prince? So, is it not wisdom not to go directly to God? It is bold rashness to come immediately to God, but by saints and angels. This is the wisdom of a man, this is the wisdom of the flesh, Col. ii. 8, *seq.*, this is carnal wisdom. It is opposite against the truth.

Doth not Christ bid us come all to him? Do angels love us better than he? Is not he the great Favourite of heaven? I will not enter into controversy, but only shew how they work by 'fleshly wisdom.' Here is wisdom, when we cannot raise ourselves up to God, to bring him down to us. As in the sacrament, they shew carnal wisdom. Oh! it is a fine thing that Christ's body and ours should be joined together! It seems to be a fine point, that Christ should be hid in the bread, &c. But here is no spiritual wisdom.

The union that the Scripture speaks of is by faith, ascending into heaven, laying hold on Christ there; and going back to the cross, and seeing Christ crucified there, and so 'he is meat indeed, and drink indeed,' John vi. 55, as we see him crucified, and satisfying God's wrath for us, for our sins.

And so again, is it not a pretty wisdom to draw men by pictures, and likenesses? Are not men delighted with the images of their friends and of their parents? And therefore is it not a good religious policy to have pictures of Christ, and pictures of God the father? Here is wisdom correspondent to the dealing and affairs of men, but all this is fleshly wisdom. The Scripture speaks mightily against making of images, the word of God is directly against it. This is fleshly wisdom. Grace doth not rule here.

So, that the souls when they go out of this world being very unclean, that they should be purged, that there should be some satisfaction, some purgatory, &c., here seems to be wisdom. But wherefore serves the blood of Christ then? That is the only purgatory, that purgeth from all sins, mortal sins, venial sins, all sins.

Again, is it not a seeming wisdom to come to heaven by our own works, by our own merits, that so we may set the people on to good works? or else we dull their spirits and endeavours. Aye, but this is 'fleshly wisdom,' this is devilish wit, and so it will prove in the end; for the Scripture goes only to Christ, only Christ. 'We are saved by faith,' Eph. ii. 8, only by Christ. I will not enter into the point, I only shew you what a seeming wisdom they have; but it is not heavenly, but merely carnal.

3. And that their religion is carnal, do but consider *that all the points wherein they differ from us, may be resolved either to belly-policy, or to state-policy; either to ambition, and riches, or the belly.* Wherefore is their monarchy, all their great preferments, but to increase their ambition? Wherefore are their pardons, and indulgences, but to get money basely, as

some of their own writers confess? And their purgatory, &c.? These things be for carnal ends. It is a religion fitted for their own ends. They make what they list to serve them. Religion, nature, reason, conscience, whatsoever is good, they make all stoop to interest their own cause in. Their orders, that is, their spiritual good, must be their advancement. It is but a colour put upon carnal ends. The spiritual good is their own advancement. They aim at their own peculiar interest in all their villanies; as if God stood in need of our lie, as if God's glory were advanced by the devil.

As well their government as their religion is lies. It is defended by lies, by equivocation, and rebellion, by withdrawing the allegiance of subjects, and murdering of princes. Laws, and religion, and all must stoop to their wisdom, under pretence of *bonum spirituale*. These things are known. I do but touch them, to breed a deeper hatred of this religion, which is altogether fleshly and carnal. And so far as they are led by carnal wisdom, they are not led by the grace of God. Wherefore is their lying for advantage? their dispensations, and horrible allowing of anything? Is it not merely carnal wisdom?

In a word, their religion is merely policy, if it be not too good a word for it. It is merely carnal policy. It came not from heaven, but from the 'bottomless pit,' Rev. ix. 2.

Then they fell from heaven when they grew to their highest, when they were in their top. This I thought good to touch collaterally from the text, which doth characterise a true Christian indeed in his temper, that he is joyful when he is as he should be; and the ground of it is from a good conscience, and that good conscience ariseth out of a course of life and conversation led in simplicity and sincerity to God. For religion hath majesty enough in itself, without far fetches and devices. And the principle from whence, 'By the grace of God,' in the evidence of the Spirit, and not according to fleshly and carnal wisdom.

In a word therefore, labour that from the evidence of the Spirit, having your souls sanctified by the Spirit, you may reflect on yourselves, and look into your lives, and say truly, as St Paul doth here. My care in my course of life and conversation hath been in simplicity, I have cast myself upon God and his government, and not looked to the world; and in sincerity I have aimed at God in all things, I have had no false and by-aims, I have not spared even my life by any carnal end: I have not served myself either in religion, or in my course of life, but I have laboured to serve God in serving my brethren, and have led my life by the grace of God, and by the word of grace, which I laboured to know that I might follow. Let us be able, in some measure, in truth to say thus. And then we may say further with St Paul, that 'this is our rejoicing, the testimony of our conscience.' We shall never want joy. And then let the world judge of us as it will, there is such a strength and power, such a prerogative, and majesty in Christian comfort, when a man can, as I said, reflect thus on himself, that though in a weak measure, yet in truth, his conversation and course of life hath been, though his tidings* have been something, 'in simplicity and sincerity,' that nothing can daunt it in this world.

It is above all discouragement, above all eclipse of good name, the testimony of conscience, which hath God's testimony with it.

The witness of two is a strong witness. The witness of God, and conscience, it will so settle our souls, that neither ill reports nor any usage in

* Qu. 'failings?'—Ed.

the world shall daunt us; we shall have comfort in all the passages of our lives, be they what they will. Whereas other men that lead not their lives in a constant course of holy simplicity and sincerity, they are as the prophet saith, 'like the leaves of the forest,' Isa. vii. 2, shaken with every alteration, with every rumour of ill news. But a sound Christian in the worst alteration, there may be combustions, there may be alteration of state, yet his 'heart is fixed,' Ps. lvii. 7, he is not moved.

Likewise, in the hour of death he can say with Hezekiah, 'Thou knowest, Lord, I have led my life in simplicity,' Isa. xxxviii. 2, that I have served thee 'with a perfect heart,' that is, in sincerity. I have desired, and endeavoured to grow better, which is all the perfection we have in this world. Sincerity witnessed by growth, and strength against the contrary, this will comfort us in all the alterations and changes in this world, which is as a sea full of trouble, and at the hour of death likewise, and at the day of judgment. This is that only that will make us able to look Christ in the face.

Truth hath a divinity in it, this simplicity and sincerity, more than any earthly thing. It hath that in it that is real and spiritual.

A man that hath the grace of God in the truth of it, there is a great deal of majesty in it. There is the greatest majesty in heavenly things when they appear most simple, because of their excellency. There is something of God's in sincerity. So much as a man hath in truth, so much of God's. He partakes of the divine nature, as St Peter saith, 2 Peter i. 4, so much as he hath in truth, though it be never so little. And being a branch of God, it will make him look upon God in the day of judgment. Why? Because he knows he is in the covenant of grace, that he hath title to heaven by Christ.

When a man's conscience can tell him that he hath led his life, not by carnal wisdom, but in the truth of grace, it will make him out-look Satan, and all the troubles of the world, and look unto Christ with comfort. Who would not be in such a state? Thus we see a Christian leads his life, 'Not in fleshly wisdom, but by the grace of God.' I will add one thing more, and so finish the verse.

We may see hence, *that the most religious men are the best statesmen.*

I know proud, carnal Machiavellian dispositions make a scorn at these positions. They think them to be austere and poor principles, till they come to death; as that wretch said himself, when he came to die, 'That he had provided for all things but for death' (*yy*). But while they are in their ruff, they think they can manage states, and do all, when, indeed, they bring the vengeance of God upon their own persons, and upon the state they live in; for God is neither in them, nor with them. He is not *in* them; for they want grace, they are led by carnal wisdom altogether. And he is not *with* them. God will not give them good success, unless it be to increase their judgment. He will not give good success to those projects that they take up contrary to his rule.

Therefore, those that will be guided by reasons of religion, and submit themselves to the guidance of God's blessed Spirit, they are best for the state of their own souls, and best for the public estate. For doth not God know the mysteries of state better than any man? Is not he a better politician than any Ahithophel in the world? If they have any state policy that is worth the naming, is it not from him? Is it not a beam from that sun? Yes! why then, who is the better? the difference of parts excepted. But take them alike, a gracious man, and another that is not so; let the one fetch his counsel from hell, from darkness, and the other be ruled by reasons of conscience and religion, there is no comparison.

God will cross and curse their projects that are for their own ends, both in themselves, and in the state too.

As for the other that are under grace, and the government of grace, God will be wise in them by his Spirit, and he will be wise for them. 'Whatsoever a good man doth, it shall prosper,' Ps. i. 3. It is a large promise. How wondrous happy and wise were the children of Israel, when they kept the covenant of God. 'This is your wisdom, to keep the commandments of God,' Deut. iv. 6; and their wisdom made them happy. How happy were they in David's time, who made the statutes of God, 'the man of his counsel,' Ps. lxxiii. 24. How happy was the state in Solomon's time, till Solomon did warp and bend to carnal counsel to strengthen himself. How happy was his government till that time, but never after that. They were environed with enemies round about. But, alas! who could hurt the people of God, so long as they submitted themselves to the government of grace! they were alway happy.

Therefore it is an idle thing to suppose that there will be any good success by carnal projects; no, the only good statesman is the religious man. And it was never better with the church of God, before or since the time of Christ, than when those were in the stern.* Do but think of this oft, as St Jude saith, 'God only wise,' ver. 25. We must all of us light our candle at that fire.

All wisdom, even this poor spark of reason that God enlighteneth 'every man that comes into the world' withal, it comes from Christ Jesus. 'In him are all the treasures of wisdom, God, and God-man, only wise,' Col. ii. 3. There is no wisdom without him, therefore let us submit ourselves to his government; let us pray to him, and seek for wisdom of him in all things. But I go on to the next verse.

VERSE 13.

'*For we write none other things unto you than what you read or acknowledge, and I trust you shall acknowledge even to the end.*' Here St Paul strengthens himself by another course. First, he retires to his own heart and conscience, 'My rejoicing is this, the testimony of my conscience,' &c.; and he sets this as a bulwark against all the slanders and detractions of his opposers whatsoever. He sets it as a flag of defiance, the testimony of his own conscience.

But to set himself the more upright in their hearts, whom he was to deal withal, knowing what a great advantage it was to have the good opinion of them, and to wipe away all imputation, he passeth from his conscience to their conscience. For my own conscience my rejoicing is this, that you cannot accuse me that I have led my life by carnal false principles, but by reasons of religion, and by the blessed motions of God's Spirit. Nay, I can go further than so. For what I say of mine own conscience, I dare say you can say too; for 'I write no other things than what you read or acknowledge.'

'What you read.' Some take it, 'what you know or acknowledge,' because these are distinct things. The word *anaginoskein*,† signifies to know or to read; but usually, to read. We may well, therefore, take it so as

* That is, = 'helm.'—G. † That is, from ἀναγινώσκω. Cf. Robinson, *sub voce*.—G.

most translate it here, 'I write no other thing,' concerning my simplicity, 'but what you read or acknowledge.' I write of my simplicity simply. I speak not of my sincerity insincerely, but what I write, you read or acknowledge; because St Paul knew he had a place in their conscience, they could not but acknowledge what a man he was; for the Spirit was wondrous effectual by his ministry in their hearts; and they were his epistle, as he saith in another place, 2 Cor. iii. 2. And, therefore, he appeals to their acknowledgment, to their conscience, 'We write no other thing,' &c. And for the time to come, 'I trust you shall acknowledge to the end.'

So he doth appeal to their conscience for the present, and he doth take in trust the time to come, what their thoughts shall be of him, and what his estate shall be. You shall have grace to think well of me to the end, because you shall have ground to think well of me for my constancy. 'I hope you shall acknowledge to the end;' and you shall have wisdom, and experience of my goodness to acknowledge to the end.

I will give a touch on these things, because they be useful; and but a touch, because I stood somewhat on them before, and shall have fit occasion for them severally after.

Obs. 'We write no other things than what you read.'

This seemeth strange. Why, how could they read other things than what he wrote? Yes! If he had written falsely, if he had not expressed his thoughts in his writings, then they had read one thing and he had been another. As a woman that is painted, there is *prosopon* and *prosopeia;* * there is the visage and the true natural countenance. She is not the woman she appears to be, her face is one and herself is another; but I am as I express myself. His meaning is, I speak of my simplicity and sincerity, simply and sincerely. I speak not of my virtues to go beyond you, but I speak sincerely; what I speak you read. For I think not that he means his former epistle, but what he wrote concerning himself and the leading of his life. That which I speak concerning myself, that you read; and what you read that I speak (*zz*). It yields me this observation, which though I had occasion to speak of when I handled simplicity, yet I shall now touch it, that

A Christian man is one man, he doth act one man's part.

He hath not a heart and a heart, he is not a man and a man. There is a harmony between his thoughts and resolutions, between his speeches and his actions. They all sweetly accord together. What he thinks and resolves on, that he speaks; what he speaks, that he writes; what he writes and speaks, that he doth; he is one man in all, he doth not deal doubly.

It is the easiest thing in the world to be politic, to be naught, to double. The nature of man teacheth a man to be false. Man's heart is full of naughtiness. It is a hard thing for a man to be one; and till a man be a gracious man, he shall be a double man.

Therefore you must take heed of a fault, which is called the abuse of signs, of such signs as serve to express what a man is inwardly. Let your inward disposition and the signs that express it accord. The signs of expression that come from one man to another are speech, writing, countenance, and the like.

A man should not be one thing within, and his speech another. He should not be one thing, and his writing another. He should not be one thing, and any other expression another.

* That is, πρόσωπον, = a face, visage; and προσωπεῖον, = a personification.—G.

This abuse of signs and expressions, when they are one way, and the heart another, besides the odiousness of it to God (as being contrary both to his nature and to his word, it is contrary to his nature; for he is simple and sincere, he is one in all, 'there is no shadow of change in him,' James i. 17, there is no mixture. As it is contrary to his nature, so it is contrary to his word, that bids us not 'dissemble nor lie one to another,' Col. iii. 9), it makes a man most like the devil, who never appears in his own shape, but always in another. He comes in our friends as 'an angel of light,' 2 Cor. xi. 14. He never discovers himself in his own colours. Besides all these and such like respects, it is the overthrow, it cuts the sinews, of human society; for what is the band of human society but the intercourse by speech, and writing, and the like? Now, if there be abuse of these signs, that they are one thing and we another, that we do not express what is the true thought and impression of our hearts, all society is dissolved.

Therefore we cannot too much hate popish principles, of not keeping fidelity with heretics, as they call them. It is the custom of them to deal so. As you know in a war of theirs with the Turks—the story is well known—when the cardinals had broken their promise, after they had in a manner gotten the victory, the Turks even cried to Christ that he would revenge their treachery; and the Turks came again upon them, and overcame them, and gave them a mighty overthrow (*aaa*). Their gross principle of equivocation, and the like, which stands in the abuse of expressions and signs! Yea, their abuse of the blessed sign and seal, an oath, which is the sign of all truth between man and man. Their abuse of the sacrament too! They have abused all God's signs, and all to ill purposes, to swear with private reservations; whereas the old principle of Isidore is constantly and everlastingly true (*bbb*), 'Conceive the oath as you will, it must be understood as he to whom it is sworn understands it, and not as he that swears.' Therefore undoubtedly popery must fall every day;* and judicious men, though they be not gracious, they see it must fall. It should make us hate them deeply, because the courses they take are the overthrow of society. This abuse of expressions, of that excellent gift that God hath given, namely, the tongue, whereby what is in my heart another man may understand; and also writing, whereby a man may convey his mind many hundred miles. Now, these excellent gifts that God hath given for society, for men to turn them against God, and against society, it must needs provoke the majesty of God.

And as it is a sin against society, so it is a sin that is punished by society. All men must needs hate them that do so. Those that have no other argument against popery, they have argument enough from their equivocation. Those that are not subtle-headed to see other things, when they look to the gunpowder treason and to their equivocation, there is argument enough for any plain, simple man to hate popery.

Therefore let us be like ourselves in all that we do to God or to men. I had occasion to press the point when I spake of simplicity, therefore I will not dwell further on it.

'*I write no other thing than what you read or acknowledge.*' He means, they acknowledged it in their heart and conscience. What I write of my conversation, that which you have heard, it is no other than that you read, and you acknowledge it too; for they had felt the power of his ministry. Whence first of all observe, that

* Qu. 'way?'—Ed.

Obs. Where the minister converseth by the grace of God, and not by carnal wisdom, God is not only wise in him, but for him.

He is gracious and good for him, he gives him success in the hearts of others. When a man is led by the Spirit of God, the same Spirit that guides him in speaking, guides his auditors in hearing, and gives a sweet and a strong report in their hearts of what he saith, What I write of myself you acknowledge, that my conversation hath been in sincerity; and not only my conversation, but my doctrine; every way you have acknowledged me. The same Spirit that guided me to do so, wrought in you an acknowledgment of it in your conscience.

Therefore, if you would have the speeches of the ministers to take effect, you should desire God not only to guide them in what they are to say, but likewise with the same Spirit to work in the hearers; and when the same Spirit works in both, what a glorious success is there! As we see here, St Paul carried himself in his own person, and in his ministry graciously, in simplicity, and sincerity; for it is meant of both. He taught simple doctrine without any glossing, without any far-fetched beauty from wit, or eloquence, or the like; and he looked to God in his life and conversation; and as God guided him, so he stirred them up to pray for him: as the word and prayer they are alway joined together. The word had a report in their hearts, as it had in his own, 'What I speak, you acknowledge,' &c.

It is not for us to deliver our minds, and there an end; but when we are to speak, we ought beforehand to look up to God, and desire his Spirit to be effectual in us, that we may speak in the wisdom and grace of the Spirit; and likewise that it may be effectual to them, that they may acknowledge it, that they may feel in their souls and consciences the power of what we speak and feel in ourselves. So you see the truth of what I said before, that God was not only wise in St Paul, but he was gracious and good for him in those that he was to deal with.

And there is the glory of a good minister that is a humble man, and denies carnal wisdom: that God will delight to honour himself by using him as an instrument to do good to others. God usually will give report of what he saith to the hearts of others.

Proud men, that speak what they speak by carnal projects, and carnal wisdom, and seek themselves, usually the hearts and consciences of other men give no report to them. For man naturally is proud, and when he sees that the most excellent man in the world hath by-aims, he will not be gone beyond by him, say what he will. If a man set up sails for himself, he doth not win upon others. But he that discovers himself, that he seeks the glory of God, and the good of the souls that he deals with, and denies himself in that which otherwise he could do, that useth not the strength of parts which he hath, because he would discover the simple word, which is most majestical in simplicity, God seeing this simple and sincere desire, he honours and crowns the ministry of such a man with success in the hearts of the people. Therefore saith St Paul here, 'I write no other thing' concerning myself, but God hath honoured me with the issue of it in your hearts likewise, that you 'acknowledge' what I say.

'You acknowledge.' *Acknowledge* is a deep word. It is more than to 'know.' It is more than a conviction of the judgment. It is when the heart and affections yield, when the inward Spirit upon experience yields, I feel and acknowledge this is true. It is more, I say, than knowledge. The next point then that I observe is this, that

Obs. God doth give his children that love him in simplicity and sincerity, a place in the conscience of men.

He gives them place in the consciences of those that have conscience: for there are some that have no science,* and therefore they have no conscience: as popish superstitious persons, &c. But those that deal faithfully, that live in the church, and see the glory of God, God gives them a place in the conscience of those that they live amongst and deal with. And they seek more to have place in their conscience, than in their fancy, than in their opinion, and imagination, and humour. A carnal man, so he may have the humour, the fancy, and imagination of his hearers delighted, he regards not what inwardly they may feel from him: he regards not how he warms their hearts, and conscience, and how they acknowledge him within; and therefore, perhaps, if he have a good word for the present, Oh, a glorious man, &c., it is all he cares for; but he hath no place in their conscience, because they feel him not working there, and he hath no aim to be there. A good man seeks to edify, and build up the conscience in sound principles, in good courses, in the faith of Christ, in holy obedience: things that will hold out in life and death. If I were to speak to ministers, I would enlarge the point further.

Use. Let us all in our conversations labour rather *to approve ourselves to the consciences of men*, that they may acknowledge us to be honest, downright, faithful men, rather than to please their humours and fancies; for, as Solomon saith, 'he that tells a man the truth, shall have more favour at the last, than he that dissembleth,' Prov. ix. 8, xxiv. 25, *et alibi:* for his conscience will witness that he hath dealt rightly, and faithfully with him, that he is an honest man, and goes on in the same principles still.

Let us therefore first look to our own conscience, and then to the conscience of others; and if we cannot approve ourselves to our own conscience, and to the conscience of others, alas! what will become of us? how shall we approve ourselves to God and to Jesus Christ at the day of judgment? There is no man but a sound Christian that approves himself to the conscience of another man. For any other man, it is just with God in his judgment to find him out first or last. He may wind himself into the conscience for a time, as the superstitious papists do, but first or last he is found out to be a dissembler, and to bring false wares.

And so for civil conversation, there is none that will have place in the conscience of other men, to think them and their courses good, but those that are sound Christians. For the most, those that are not led by the grace of God's Spirit, all mens' consciences condemn them. They are smitten, and censured there, and judged there. Besides, their own conscience, which perhaps they will not give leave to tell them somewhat in their ear that they would be loath to hear, this you are, this you did, and this you spake amiss: they will not suffer conscience to speak, but drown it in sensuality, and stifle it. They take this course, they think they are well enough, and they would never be themselves. A carnal man will hardly give conscience leave to speak, till it will, whether he will or no, at the hour of death, and the day of judgment, when God lets it loose upon him. But let them take this course as long as they will, yet in the conscience of other men they have no place: for they live not, as St Paul saith here, 'in simplicity and sincerity, not by carnal wisdom, but by the grace of God.'

This is the benefit that a good man hath in this life, that howsoever he

* That is = 'knowledge'.—G.

have the ill words of carnal men sometimes, and their humour is against him: yet notwithstanding if they be in the church, and have any illumination, any judgment, he hath their conscience for him. Nay, I say more, they cannot but think reverently of a man of God, of a good Christian (I speak not of ministers only), they cannot but think reverently of them, and reverence them in their consciences, do what they can. For it is not in men's power to frame what conceits they will, to frame what opinions they will of men; but as there is a necessity of reason, as the principles we say are so strong, that a man cannot say they are false, do what he can, because the light is visible to the understanding; as a man cannot say the sun shines when it is night, when it is dark, because it is a sensible falsehood; so a man cannot deny the principles of any art, if they be principles; because there is such a light of truth that overpowers him, and as it were compels the inward man. So it is here: there is such a majesty in grace, and good courses of a Christian, that another man that lives a wicked life he cannot think of him what he would. He may force himself to speak what he list, and force odd* opinions of him, but when he is sober himself, he must needs if he have any relics of conscience in him, if he be not altogether a sot, he must needs think well in his conscience of such a man's courses. This is the majesty and honour of good things, that however they may have the humour, and passion, and fancy of men against them, yet they have their conscience for them; yea, of wicked men when they are themselves.

Take the wickedest man at the hour of death, if he have himself at command, that his spirits be not disturbed, and ask him whether he justify the courses of such and such men? he will answer, Oh yes! I would I had led them myself. What is that that besots them? Sensuality, and such courses; for men that are not led by the grace of God, are led with outward things which besot the judgment for a time; but when that dulness is past, when a wicked man is stripped of all, and is best able to judge, then he likes such courses.

If the worst men shall in their conscience acknowledge the best persons, and the best things one day, nay, they do now, if they will suffer themselves to be themselves, then let us take such courses as our own consciences may justify, as St Paul saith here, 'This is my glorying, the testimony of my conscience;' and likewise the conscience of those I live with, 'I write no other thing,' but what you acknowledge in your consciences yourselves.

'*And I trust you shall acknowledge to the end.*' This word, 'Trust,' doth not imply, as usually it doth in common speech, an uncertainty of a thing, a moral conjecture, I trust, or hope it may be so; it may be otherwise, but I hope well. It is not an uncertain conceit with the fear of the contrary; but the word implies a gracious, dependent disposition upon God, 'I trust in God,' as it is so expressed in some other places.†

Now you acknowledge me, and 'I trust in God you shall acknowledge me to the end.' So here St Paul sets down what he resolved to be by the grace of God, and what in the issue he should be; because holy resolutions are seconded with gracious assistance.

And likewise he sets down what they should judge of him to the end; I trust as you acknowledge me now, so to the end you shall have grace so to

* That is 'singular, extraordinary.'—G.

† Cf. Philip. ii. 24; Philem. 22; Heb. xiii. 18; 2 John 12.—G.

do, and I shall have grace so to be; I shall be as I am, and have been; I have led my life 'in simplicity, and sincerity;' and as you have acknowledged me to be such a one, so you shall have grace still to acknowledge me, 'I hope, or trust.' I will not enter into any common place, only I will speak that which the text puts to me.

'I trust you shall acknowledge to the end.' Here he begins with his hope of their judging of him, to continue so to the end.

Saint Paul here takes a good conceit, a good opinion of his children whom he had begotten to the faith in Corinth. I hope as you are, and as you do judge of me, so you will judge of me to the end.

Why hath St Paul such a trust of them as of himself?

Reason 1. Among many reasons this is one, *He knew that where God had begun a good work, he would finish it.* He saw that he had begun a good work in them, and therefore he knew that he would go on with it.

Reason 2. And then again, God planted in him a good hope and trust of them; *because hope and trust stir up endeavour to the thing hoped for.* Desperation doth quell all courage, and cool all endeavour. Now God, because he would have us constant in our carriage, and in the expressions of our love to other men, he stirs up in us a trust that all shall be well with them.

Reason 3. Likewise St Paul sets down his hope that God had put into his heart of them, *for his own comfort;* for it is a great comfort to a minister, or to a Christian, when he is to deal with such as he trusts are good, and will be good. It is a heaven upon earth, and therefore God doth plant good conceits of other men in us for this end; partly, to stir up our endeavour to do all good to them, and partly to comfort us. For if the final estate of any man were discovered to us, that God had no delight in them concerning their salvation, who would do any service of love for them? or who would have comfort in conversing with them? But when God stirs up in our hearts a good opinion of them, partly it is good for them, to stir up our endeavour to do all good for them; and it is good for us, it is a great comfort.

And again, it was an encouragement to them when they heard of Saint Paul's trust of them to the end, that they should continue as they were. For to have a good conceit and opinion of another man, especially the good conceit of a pastor, it is a great encouragement. And the best Christians in the world have need of it ofttimes. Besides the judgment of themselves, which is sometimes shaken by Satan, that they give a false witness of their own estate. Oh! it is comfortable that a man have the judgment of a man that looks without passion, and temptation on him; you have been thus, and my trust and confidence is in God, and the promise of God, looking to your former course, that you will be so to the end; he gives not a false witness.

Saint Paul speaks thus to stir up his own endeavour to do good to them; and to comfort them, that so great an apostle should have so good an opinion of them.

Therefore let us labour, I say, to entertain as good a conceit of them among whom we live, as their carriage will bear. Two things usually are the object of our hope and trust. While men are here, before their estate be determined of in hell, God may have mercy on them, and deliver them out of the snares of Satan. That hope should stir up some endeavour to pray for them; seeing their estates are not desperate, they are not yet sunk into hell (*ccc*). Or else if we see them in the state of grace, we should express our love in the services and offices of love, because God hath already set his stamp on them.

There is no man living but we may trust, and hope of him one way or other. Those that we see no grace in, as the apostle saith, 2 Tim. ii. 24, we may have 'patience towards them,' seeing if at any time God will have mercy on them to deliver them out of the 'snare of the devil.'

It is not good to cast off all conceit, and all hope of any man living. The worst sign is, when we see men malicious, and oppose known truths, because it comes near the sin against the Holy Ghost; but because we may err in that, it is good to take the safest way. But where we see evidences of grace, though in never so little a measure, let us entertain and cherish a good hope; because it will cherish that which we are all bound to, to love one another. We are bound to love one another, and to shew all the offices of love. Now that which stirs up love and all the offices of love, is hope. Faith works by hope, as well as by love. Faith works by love in all duties; and it works by hope in this duty. If we hope that God will have mercy on them, that will stir up our endeavour; but we are not much in this error: we are rather ready to conceit over-well, than too ill of men.

'I trust you shall acknowledge to the end.' Saint Paul here, besides his good conceit of them to the end, doth imply his own resolution and purpose to hold on in good courses to the end. My trust in God's grace is, that you shall acknowledge to the end what I have written to you of mine own courses. As if he had said, I am Paul now, and you shall find me Paul hereafter; you shall find me always an honest man like myself; for as he whom I have trusted 'is yesterday, to-day,' to-morrow, 'and the same for ever,' so likewise by God's grace I hope to be the same that I have been, I hope I shall be like myself.

The grounds of St Paul's trust that he should be so, is partly the act itself, together with the endeavour, 'I trust' I shall be so 'to the end;' because I trust in God to the end, and God is good to them that trust in him. How often is it repeated in the Psalms! 'He is the God of them that trust in him,' Ps. xxxvii. 3; 'he is a sun and a shield,' Ps. lxxxiv. 11; he is all that is good, and he keeps away all evil. All the promises are entailed to trusting in God. Now because I have confidence in it that God will do so, I stir up my endeavour to shew that it is not a presumptuous trust. I trust in him that will perform the conditions of the covenant which is made to them that honour him by trusting in him.

St Paul knew what God had done. He knew that he that had bestowed the first fruits, he would make up the harvest; he knew that he that had laid the first stone, he would set up the roof; he knew that God had begun a good work in him by experience, and that he would finish his own work. That he knew by former experience.

And then he knew the promises of God, the promises of the covenant. Many such grounds St Paul had to bear him up that he should continue to the end in a course of simplicity and sincerity, and in the grace of God.

But withal St Paul did add a holy and heavenly course to come to this end, together with his trust. What course did St Paul take?

St Paul, that he might hold out constantly in holy resolutions to the end,

First, he did judiciously consider what might hinder him, between that and the end of his race and course. He balanced all things that he possibly could suffer; and he laid in the other balance the things that he had in hope and promise; and he resolves, all that I can suffer that should shake me off from my course, it is not 'worthy of the glory that shall be revealed,' Rom. viii. 18. Saith he, if you balance both, you will conclude this.

There are many things that may shake us in our Christian course. St Paul thought of all Satan's snares, 'I am not ignorant of his enterprises,' 2 Cor. ii. 11, saith he. And then for the world, that might cast trumpery in his way, saith he, 'I am crucified to the world, and the world is crucified to me,' Gal. vi. 14. And for anything that might happen to him, he knew that the issue of all things should work for the best to them that love God. He includes himself, Rom. viii. 28. Saith he, we know it beforehand, we believe, before troubles or evils come; come what will, the issue of all things is in the regiment and power of God, and as he pleaseth all shall work for the best to those that love God; and therefore as I am, so I will be. What should hinder? if all things help me, nothing can hinder me.

And then St Paul took this course, he looked forward still, 'I press forward to the prize of the high calling,' Philip. iii. 14. He forgat that which was behind, and he resolved to go forward. He had a mind to grow better and better alway, and this comforted him that he should hold out to the end. For it is the reward of a growing Christian to have a sweet sense of his present state of grace in God's favour, and to hold out to the end. Such a man is like the sun that grows* up still, till he come to high noonday, as Solomon saith, Prov. iv. 18. St Paul took this course. He strove for perfection, he had a crown in his eye, a crown of righteousness and glory, and that will not suffer a man to be idle and cold that hath such a thing in his eye. St Paul, to whet his endeavour, not only looked forward, but to glory; for as Christ looked to 'the glory, and despised the shame,' Heb. xii. 2; so St Paul looked to the crown, and despised all his sufferings.

Then besides, St Paul was conscious of his own sincerity; for grace carries its own witness with itself, as he saith here, I know my conversation. 'This is the testimony of my conscience, that in simplicity and sincerity I have walked before you.' He knew that sincerity is accompanied with constancy and perseverance. It is a rule that alway constancy and perseverance are companions with simplicity and sincerity. I have begun in sincerity hitherto, now I am sincere, and have expressed to you the truth of my heart, and of my courses; and as I am, so I mean to be; therefore, having begun in sincerity, I know I shall end in perseverance and constancy.

Truth of grace is accompanied with constancy. All other things are but grass, they are but shows, they will vanish; but sincerity, the truth of grace, is a divine thing. 'The word of the Lord,' that is, grace wrought by 'the word of the Lord, that endures for ever,' 1 Pet. i. 25. Where there is truth of grace, though it be but as a grain of mustard-seed, there is perseverance to the end. St Paul knew this well, and therefore he builds his trust on these things, on these courses that he took.

We should all take the like course, look to St Paul's grounds, and take his courses. Those be they that will hold out to the end. Judicious consideration of all the difficulties, to put into the balance what impediments we shall have from the world, and what will be great to us when it is balanced with the glory to come! And withal, to aim forward still, as St Paul did. And take another course that he took likewise, to depend upon grace continually. He knew there was a throne of grace open to him alway for the time to come, as well as for the time past, and present. He knew that Christ in heaven was alway full of grace; he knew he should not want in any exigent when he should go to him; he knew that God would not des-

* Qu. 'goes?'—Ed.

titute or forsake any of his children, them that he hath called to see the necessity of wisdom, and of courage, and comfort. Let us do therefore as St Paul was answered from heaven, say, 'His grace is sufficient for us,' 2 Cor. xii. 9; if not to keep us from all sin, yet to keep us in comfortable courses, to keep us in sincerity and simplicity. The grace of God is sufficient to bring us to heaven.

Let us persuade ourselves, that if we go on in Christian courses, in that confidence, God will give us grace to bring us to heaven. This was St Paul's confidence, therefore he saith, 'I trust you shall acknowledge to the end,' because I know that I shall continue in simplicity and sincerity to the end. God will keep me, I shall have grace to beg, and he will give me grace; for his gifts in this kind can never be repented of.

Let us take from St Paul this course, and this comfort: this course to trust in God for the time to come; to have constant resolutions for the time to come, to cleave to God, and to good courses.

Let us every day renew our covenants in this kind, and our resolutions to do nothing against conscience, to go on in Christian courses; let it be our constant course. For as God's children know they shall continue to the end, so it is wrought from resolution so to do; and this resolution stirs them up to depend upon God by prayer, that he would 'knit their hearts to him, that they may fear his name,' Jer. xxxii. 40; that he would give them grace sufficient, &c., that he would establish their hearts, as David prays.

This resolution, it drives them to prayer, and to all good courses, that God would stablish them in every good work, in every good thought and desire, and that he would knit their hearts nearer to him. Resolve, therefore, every day, in dependence upon God, to take good courses, that so whensoever any judgment of God shall come, or when the hour of death shall light on us, it may not come as a snare, that it may take us in good resolutions. It is no matter how we die in outward respects, if we die in good resolutions.

As we resolve, so we are; for our resolutions are full of will. Wishes and resolutions: they carry the whole man with them; and God esteems a man by his will. For if there be impediments that are not impossible to man, resolution will break through all. God judgeth men by their resolutions: 'Teach me, O Lord, thy statutes, and I will keep them even to the end. I have sworn, and I will perform it, that I will keep thy righteous judgments,' Ps. cxix. 106. Every day take we these promises to ourselves, and bind ourselves with them to God.

In vows, be chary. I do not speak of them now, I speak of purposes and resolutions, alway take in God with them. I trust in God, depend upon God in good courses (that God do not punish us, and give us into desertion for our presumption), and then we may know that our state is good. Look to St Paul, and see the property of a good conscience. It looks back, it looks to the present, and to the time to come. 'Our rejoicing is this,' that we have had our conversation hitherto well. Is that enough for a good conscience? No! you have acknowledged me to be as I have written, to have a good conscience in my ministerial course, and in my conversation; and you shall acknowledge me still.

This is the glory of a good life, that whether a man look above him, he hath God to witness for him. Or whether he look to the world, to right judging persons, he hath them to judge for him. He dares appeal to their conscience. Or whether he look within him, he hath a good witness from his own conscience. Which way soever he looks he hath comfort. 'You have acknowledged me,' and you shall acknowledge: I know God will not leave me for the time to come. So that which makes up a complete good conscience, is the looking to the time to come, as well as to the time past and present. A good conscience that is purged by the blood of Christ from the guilt of former sins, shall alway have grace to stablish the heart in good resolutions. For where there is a cleansing from the guilt, where there is pardon of sin, there is alway given a power against sin for the time to come.

We usually say in divinity, that the grace of God, and a purpose to live in any sin, cannot dwell in one heart; and it is true, if there be not a purpose to obey God in all things, to 'leave every wicked way,' Isa. lv. 7, if there be an inclination to any iniquity, the heart and conscience is not good. A good conscience gives testimony of the time past, present, and to come.

And always, as I said, remember to take God in all your resolutions, or else you are liable to St James his exception in a higher degree. 'Go to now, ye that say, We will do this, to-day and to-morrow,' James iv. 13, and that in strength and confidence of your own, not remembering the uncertainty of human events, how many things may fall out that God may cross it. If it be a presumptuous speech in matters of this life, how much more in matters of grace for the time to come, which God only hath in his keeping, and 'gives the will and the deed according to his good pleasure,' Phil. ii. 13. Therefore we should 'make an end of our salvation with fear and trembling,' Eph. vi. 5.

Let us do as St Paul did, trust in God. My trust and dependence on God is this, that I shall do so; because I have a constant resolution to be so to my life's end.

Therefore join them both together. Every day renew our dependence on God, and his promises. The life of a Christian is a life dependent. Salvation is wrought out of us by Christ, procured by him: and our carriage to salvation is wrought out of us by grace coming from Christ. He keeps the fountain, and he lets out the streams more or less as we humbly depend on him. So that both salvation is out of us, and the carriage to salvation is of grace; all is out of us. How should this make us carry ourselves humbly, in a dependence on Christ for salvation, and the carriage of it! And therefore resolve not to offend God in anything, but to trust in God, and to look to his word. To trust in God and his word is all one, Ps. cxxx. 5. Thus we should take St Paul's course, to trust in God, and renew our purposes every day.

And then take St Paul's comfort to yourselves, persuade yourselves, that 'neither things present, nor things to come,' as St Paul saith, Rom. viii. 38, nothing shall intercept your crown. For what he said here beforehand, that he experimentally saith of himself, 2 Tim. iv. 7, *seq.*, a little before he died (which was the last epistle that ever he wrote), he saith here, they should acknowledge him to the end; and there, when his end was come, what saith he of himself? 'I have fought a good fight, I have kept the faith, I have run my race; now henceforth is laid up for me a crown of righteousness,' &c. Before this time, I depended upon God, that he would carry me to my end, as he hath done; and now I am to close up my days, and my sun is to set: all this I have done; God, that was with me from the beginning, is with me to the end: I have done all this, and what remains now but a crown of righteousness?

Therefore, I beseech you, take in trust the time to come, as well as any time past; resolve well, and trust with your resolution; live by faith and obedience—join them both together, the one to be the evidence of the truth of the other: then, take in trust for the time to come all the good that you can promise yourselves from God. You cannot honour him more.

'I trust you shall acknowledge to the end.' St Paul saith of himself, that the grace of God should lead him to his end, and that they should acknowledge it. You shall not acknowledge me to the end to be rich, or to be in favour, &c., but this you shall acknowledge, that I shall be the like man. It is uncertain for anything in the world. We cannot promise ourselves, nor others cannot promise for us; but you shall acknowledge this, that I will be as I have been to the end. 'You have acknowledged, and you shall acknowledge,' &c.

Seeing acknowledging is repeated twice as an evidence of a good Christian, to approve of the image of God in another, and to acknowledge it, therefore often examine your hearts what you acknowledge. Do you acknowledge that the abstaining trom evil courses, from fraud and cunning in your callings, that the abstaining from sensual living, from carnal policy, is good? Why then, take that course, resolve upon it. Are the courses of God's children good? Why will you oppose them? St Paul gives an excellent rule, Rom. xiv. 22, 'We should not condemn ourselves in that which we allow.' Do you allow in your judgment and in your conscience the best courses? as, indeed, you will do one day. Then do not condemn yourselves in the present for them. 'Happy is the man that condemneth not himself in that which he alloweth,' saith the apostle, Rom. xiv. 22.

Examine ofttimes seriously, how your judgment stands in the ways of God; how it is built, whether upon human fancy, to please any man, or upon divine directions, the word of God. If it be so, take heed that you do not condemn yourselves in those courses, and those persons that you allow. Do you in your soul justify such persons? Why do you not join with them? Why do you not walk their ways? Are such courses good? Why do you not take them? Your justifying them in the end will be little to your comfort, if you condemn them all your life against your conscience; for afterwards it is not so much a work of grace for you to justify good courses, and to acknowledge good things. In most men it is not so much a work of grace as it is the evidence of the thing. And when the cloud of sensuality, and the fume that riseth out of worldly pomp is taken away, then the natural conscience comes to see clearly better things, not from the love of them, not that it is changed and transformed with the love of them; but God so discovers it to them, to make them justify his sentence of damnation the more. He discovered to them better courses than they took: it shall justify their damnation.

We are deceived ofttimes in men's ends. They acknowledge good ways and good courses; and on the other side some of God's good children they pronounce the contrary. But let none trust to that. Good courses are so evident and clear, that if men be not atheists, they must acknowledge them, especially when the impediment that hindered them before is taken away. You must acknowledge, therefore 'acknowledge' now; not in your hearts only, but acknowledge them in laying aside your opposition, in casting away your weapons, and by joining with them in good courses. Set not your hands against good courses and good persons; set your tongues to speak for their good. Take God's part; stand on God's side. It is the best side. If you allow it only hereafter, it will be a barren allowance, it will be no comfort to you; it often falls out to be so.

O beloved! whatsoever courses else you take, they will sink and fall. They will sink first in your own souls, and none will be readier to condemn you than your own conscience. When God shall make you wiser, you will censure yourselves, What folly was it! How was I deluded with this ill company and with that! As wicked company is wondrous powerful to infuse ill conceits: as the spies they infused discouragement by the oration they made of the giants in the land, &c., they altered the mind of the whole people, Numb. xiii. 33. It is a dangerous thing to converse with naughty persons. The devil slides together into the soul with their carnal reasoning, and alters the judgment for the time, that they are not so wise as conscience would make them, and as they might be, if they did not hearken to the hissing of the serpent.

First, if you take any course but good, *your own conscience is by, and will be the first that will find you out.* For sin is a base thing, a work of darkness. It must be discovered. It is a madness. It must be manifest to all men. Popery and all their sleights must be discovered, and the whore must lie naked and stink. Nothing shall be so abominable as popery and popish persons ere long.

Truth will get the victory in the consciences of people; and good courses will get approbation. Therefore, if you approve them not, first you shall be unhappy in this life, and everlastingly hereafter. This shall be the principal torment in hell, that you saw better courses than you lived in, and you would not give your judgments leave to lead you. There was something better, conscience told you, but you gave way to your lusts, and to the insinuations of wicked men, instruments of the devil, rather than to the motions of conscience, and of God's Spirit, that awakened conscience.

This I say will more ease* your torment of hell that you might have done otherwise if you had had grace. But you willingly betrayed yourselves, you silenced conscience, you willingly condemned yourselves in the things that you acknowledged were naught, you did that which you condemned, and you did not practise that which your judgment did allow.

God will have little to do at the day of judgment with most men in the church, to condemn them; for, alas! their own consciences will condemn them, the consciences of all will condemn them that their courses were naught.

And that makes wicked men so cruel, especially if they get into place of authority. They know they are not allowed, they are not acknowledged in the consciences of those that are judicious, they know they are condemned there, and they fret and fume, and think to force another opinion of themselves upon others, but it will not be; and that makes them that they cannot endure the sight of them that are of a contrary judgment; they think themselves condemned in the hearts of such men, and that makes them cruel. Especially those that have some illumination. They cannot abide their own conscience to take its course, they cannot abide to see themselves. They think themselves condemned in the judgment of others; and those that think they have the prejudice† of others that their courses are naught, they carry an implacable hatred. It is a desperate case.

Hast thou knowledge that they think thy courses naught, and on good

* Qu. 'increase?'—Ed.

† That is, = pre-judgment.—G.

ground, and dost thou hate them? And hate to be reformed thyself? Will this alway hold out? No! As I said before, truth is eternal! That which thou acknowledgest must continue. It will be acknowledged. It will get the victory at the day of judgment by men and angels. Truth will have the victory. It is eternal. Take that course for the present, that thou mayest be good for the present, and hold out to the end, as we see the Corinthians here, 'You do acknowledge me, and you shall acknowledge me to the end,' and testify to the world that you acknowledge the best things, and the best persons, that you may be one with them by love here, and in heaven for ever hereafter.

'I trust you shall acknowledge to the end.' To shut up this point. Let me seal it up with this, make this *query** to yourselves, What estate you are in when you come to the communion, whether it be well with you or no? If not, why will you live any whit at all, in the uncertainty of our lives, and the shortness of them, and the danger of the wrath of God, when there is so little between you and eternal damnation, in a doubtful, in a dangerous, estate? Are you resolved to be naught then? No! If you be not atheists you will not say so. Do you intend to be good, and come and make your covenant with God? Yes! Why, then, resolve to be so.

A good conscience looks not only back to sins past, to repent of them; but for the time to come it resolves to please God in all things, and to hold out to the end.

Some make a mockery of the holy things of God. One part of the year they will be holy; a rotten, foolish affection of people that are popish. In Lent they will use a little austerity, oh! they will please God wondrously! but before and after they are devils incarnate. So they make that part of the year as a good parenthesis, in an unlearned and unwitty speech. A good parenthesis is unseemly in a wicked speech, and a good piece is unseemly in a ragged garment; so their lives that make a good show then (and there are few that do so, they are scarce among us; men are such atheists that there is not outward reformation, but if there be), if they give themselves leave to be civil, and to respect holy things a little time, afterward they return to their looseness again. Doth this patching out of a holy life please God? No, no! 'I have sworn, and I will perform it, that I will keep thy righteous statutes,' saith David, Ps. cxix. 106. And St Paul, 'I have resolved to be so to the end;' I will be myself still. So where grace is, there is a resolution against all sin for the time to come. If you entertain not this resolution, to walk 'in holiness and righteousness all the days of your life,' Luke i. 75, acknowledge no benefit by Christ's redemption, and come not near the holy things of God.

This is the honest heart that the Scripture speaks of, that receives the seed deep into it; that hates sin above all miseries and ills, and that loves grace above all other good things. Therefore if any infirmity come, he can say it is against his resolution. I purposed not this, I plotted it not, I do not allow myself in it. Here is an honest heart. The word is fixed deeply in such a heart. It comes with an honest resolution. If you come to the sacrament, and purpose to live in sin, you profane the holy things of God. The word of God will do you no good. It will never take deep root to save you. So much for St Paul's resolution for the time to come, 'I trust you shall acknowledge to the end.'

* Spelled 'quære.'—G.

VERSE 14.

'*As also you have acknowledged us in part, that we are your rejoicing, even as ye are ours in the day of the Lord Jesus.*' You have acknowledged us in part, now since you have repented; for when he wrote the former epistle to them, they had many corruptions among them in doctrine and in conversation about the sacrament, many corrupt opinions they had; and in 'conversation' they endured the incestuous man among them, without casting of him out; and many of them doubted of the resurrection. Now, when he wrote the first epistle, it took a blessed effect in their hearts; they repented, and began to acknowledge St Paul, notwithstanding they were distasted of him by reason of the bad information of some presumptuous teachers. Saith he now again, 'You have acknowledged us in part that now we are your rejoicing,' &c. Observe this, which I touch by way of coherence,

Obs. It is a sign of a repentant man, of a man that hath repented of his sins, and is in a good estate, to acknowledge him that hath told him of his sins, to acknowledge his pastor.

For a false heart swells against the reproof. If the Corinthians had not been sound-hearted, they would never have endured St Paul's sharp epistles. But now he tells them their own plainly (as indeed it is a very sharp epistle in many passages), yet now they acknowledge him to be a good and gracious man, a faithful teacher.

Use. Let it be a trial of your estate, can you endure a plain, a powerful, an effectual ministry? More particularly, can you endure a plain, effectual friend, that brings that which is spoken by the minister more particularly home to your hearts? It is a sign of a good heart, of a repentant heart, that would be better. But if not, it is a sign you have a reserved love to some special sin that will be your bane; it is a sign your souls have not repented. As you see after in another chapter of this epistle, where he sets down the fruits of repentance, vii. 9, 10. And here is one sign, 'You have acknowledged us in part,' &c.

In the words,

First, *there is the thing itself*—'acknowledgment.'

Secondly, *the object-matter of it*, 'that we are your rejoicing, and you are ours.' There is a mutual intercourse of rejoicing.

And then *the time is set down*, 'the day of the Lord Jesus,' the second coming of Christ.

To speak a little of 'acknowledgment.'

'Acknowledgment' is more than knowledge; for knowledge is a bare, naked apprehension, and acknowledgment is when the will and affections yield to the entertaining and the owning of the thing known. As a father not only knows his son, but acknowledgeth him; a king acknowledgeth his subjects, and the subjects their prince. It is not only a knowledge of such men, but an acknowledging of them, acknowledging a relation to them. So you acknowledge us; that is, in the relation we stand to you, to be faithful and good ministers, and good men too.

What doth St Paul mean by saying, 'You have acknowledged us? Doth he mean himself?

No; not altogether; but you have acknowledged me in my faithful preaching of Christ to you. Wheresoever the minister is acknowledged as a minister, Christ is acknowledged. For what are we? We are but the ministers of Christ, no more, nor no less. Saith St Paul, 'Let a man esteem of us as of the ministers of Christ,' 1 Cor. iv. 1. If they think of us more than ministers, that we can make and coin things of our own, they think too much of us; if they think meanly and basely of us, they think too little of us. 'Let a man think of us as of the ministers of Christ,' no more, nor no less. It is enough that they acknowledge us so as the ministers of Christ. So they are never acknowledged, but Christ is acknowledged by them; for they have a relative office, they are the ministers *of Christ*.

How shall we know then whether we acknowledge the minister or no?

If we acknowledge Christ first by him.

How shall we know that we acknowledge Christ?

1. *To acknowledge Christ, God-man in his natures, that we have a great deal of love to him, that he would be born for us; and a great deal of reverence, in that he is God.* We must not think of him but with a great deal of reverence, and meddle with nothing of him but with much love; he is God-man, God incarnate. He acknowledgeth Christ in his priestly office, that doth not despair, that doth believe his full satisfaction to God; and doth not mingle other things, popish satisfaction, and purgatory for venial sins. He acknowledgeth Christ's priestly office, that goes boldly to God through Christ's intercession in heaven, and boldly trusts in the satisfaction of Christ in the clamours of conscience, and the accusations of Satan. This is to acknowledge Christ a priest in our boldness and liberty to God, and confidence in our conscience of the forgiveness of sins. To acknowledge Christ as a King, is to yield subjection to his word, and to suffer him to rule us. To acknowledge him as a prophet, to be instructed, and guided by him.

But now such as are ruled by their own lusts, and by the examples of others, and care not for the spiritual leading of Christ, they do not acknowledge him. 'Let not this man reign over us,' Luke xix. 14. They shake off his bands, they are 'sons of Belial,' Judg. xix. 22, without yoke. And they shall be reckoned at the day of judgment among them that know not Christ; because to know him, and not to acknowledge him, is to no purpose. As God knoweth us well enough; but if he know us not, and acknowledge us to be his, what will become of us at the day of judgment? 'I know you not,' Mat. xxv. 12, saith he, that is, he acknowledgeth them not to be his. So, if our knowledge be to know Christ generally, so as not to give up ourselves to be ruled by him, to be directed by him, this is not to acknowledge him; and to know him, and not to acknowledge him, will be no comfort for us; as it will be no comfort to us for him to know us, and not to acknowledge us. They that acknowledge Paul, or any minister, they are brought to acknowledge Christ by him.

2. And then, to give you a familiar taste of these things, they do acknowledge the minister, *that acknowledge the word to be the word of God, to be from him.* What is that? When they are cast into the form and mould of the word, and are willing to be framed, to be such as the word would have them, to be pliable to it; if it threaten, to be terrified; if it comfort, to be raised up; to be fashioned every way to the word. Then they acknowledge the word, then they feel it to be God's word. Why? For they feel it leavening the soul, making all the powers holy and comfortable. As leaven changeth the whole lump, so the word of God, when we are cast into it, and embrace it, it frames and fashions the whole man to be holy, as the word is holy.

This is to acknowledge the word of God, to hear it as the word of God, to hear it with reverence, as we would hear something from a great potentate, from a judge, from a man that hath to do with us. We know the word of God, and acknowledge him in the minister, when we tremble at it, and hear it with obedience. As Cornelius saith, 'We are all here in the presence of God, to hear whatsoever shall be commanded us of God,' Acts x. 33, 'whatsoever,' without distinction, and turning over, and declining the word, and shifting. When there is a willing yielding to everything that is told us, and a meaning to obey it, this is to acknowledge the word of God, or else we do not.

St Paul saith comfortably to the Thessalonians, 'That they received the word of God, as the word of God,' that is, they acknowledged the word of God, because they heard it with such reverence, and obedience, and respect.

So you may know that you acknowledge the minister, if you acknowledge Christ, if you acknowledge the preacher, and the word that he preacheth; and you acknowledge him when you will be directed by him; when he speaks in the name of Christ, to esteem highly of the 'consolations of the Almighty,' Job xv. 11, in his mouth, to suffer the strongholds of sin to be beaten down by his ministry. This is to acknowledge the minister. There is no good taken by God's ordinance, where* it is not only known, but acknowledged.

Christ comes to us in his ministers as well as by the poor, and it shall be known one day that we have rejected, not poor men like ourselves, but Jesus Christ. For we are joined with Christ in acceptation, or in neglect and contempt. What we do in our ministry faithfully, we are joined with Christ in our acceptance. We accept Christ, when we accept and esteem of the minister; or we reject Christ, when we reject, and refuse, and set light by the ministers of Christ.

The hypocrisy of man's heart is not discerned almost so much in anything as in this. Let any command come from great men that have power of our bodies or estates to advance us, or debase us, Oh! there is much astonishment, and much heed taken. Wondrous heed of penal laws and statutes, that we run not into the dint of them! Now God by his ministers threatens hell, and damnation, hardness of heart, and to throw us from one sin to another; we hear these things as judges, forsooth, as if they concerned us not. It shall one day be known that they are God's ministers, and that it is God's word, if we have grace to acknowledge them as speaking from God. This is to acknowledge the minister, to be directed by him, and to hear that that he speaks in the name of God. 'We are ambassadors of God,' saith St Paul, 'and entreat you, as if Christ himself were on earth he would entreat you, to be reconciled to God,' 2 Cor. v. 20. Therefore when you refuse our entreaty, you refuse Christ that comes with us. Those that will not hear him here shall hear that sentence hereafter. They must not think to be regarded of him then. But of that I shall speak hereafter.

'As ye have acknowledged us in part.' You acknowledge us ministers, you acknowledge our doctrine, you acknowledge Christ by us.

How do these Corinthians acknowledge St Paul in part?

'*That we are your rejoicing, even as ye are ours, in the day of the Lord Jesus.*' 'You have acknowledged us, that we are your rejoicing.' What

* Qu. 'but where?'—Ed.

is the meaning of that? You have acknowledged us, that you have cause to rejoice much, to the day of judgment, and then you shall rejoice to purpose, that ever I was your apostle, that ever you had grace to hearken to me; that ever you had such a sincere downright apostle, that would tell you the truth, and gain you to Christ.

'That we are your rejoicing.' Whence we may observe, that—

Doct. A faithful minister is the rejoicing of the people.

Those people that are good, and have any grace in them, and not only here, but they will be so at the day of judgment.

Why?

Reason. Because a faithful minister brings to them him that is the cause of all joy; him that is Isaac, 'laughter,' Christ Jesus, at whose very birth there was a message of joy from heaven.

For all joy and all glory is originally and fundamentally in God reconciled. That is certain. There is our joy in God reconciled. For naturally, before God be reconciled, our hearts are full of confusion; they are so far from joy and glory, that they are full of horror. Now God is reconciled by Christ's satisfaction and obedience, his full satisfaction witnessed by his resurrection; and thereupon comes our glorying, to be in Christ, who hath brought us to be at one with God, with the God of glory. 'Blessed be God, the Father of our Lord Jesus Christ,' saith St Peter, 'that hath begotten us to a lively hope through the resurrection of Jesus Christ,' &c., 1 Pet. i. 3. Now we have a lively hope, we have a glorious hope, we may glory in it, in the resurrection of Christ; considering that his resurrection is an evidence that the debt is paid, our Surety being out of prison, he being risen again.

But all this must be opened to us, and offered to us, and applied to us, by the ministry. What Christ hath done, and what he will do, it must be opened to us, and offered to us; to receive Christ thus graciously bringing us to God. And faith must be wrought in us, to join us to Christ; and this is by the ministry.

Now in the next place, when the ministry doth this, *it doth teach us that God is reconciled by the satisfaction of Christ, and teacheth the nature and offices of Christ, and the benefits we have by Christ.* It unfolds 'the unsearchable riches of Christ,' Eph. iii. 8. The ministry offers Christ; and God by his Spirit works grace in the ministry, to believe, and to walk worthy of Christ. Hereupon comes glorying in the ministry; in the preaching of Christ faithfully, crucified and risen, and teaching us to walk worthy of Christ.

So it is not that any man should glory in the minister for himself; but in that he brings us to Christ, which Christ brings us to God, in whom is all our glory. So we see the ground of it, how St Paul was the rejoicing of the Corinthians, because he brought them to Christ.

The office of the minister is to be wooers, to make up the marriage between Christ and Christians' souls. Now herein is the rejoicing in a good minister, when we are brought to Christ; and then see the riches of our husband unfolded by the ministry. Here is matter of joy, especially at the day of judgment. Then we shall joy indeed that ever we knew such a minister, that ever we knew such a holy man, that was a means to bring us to Christ, and to God.

Hereupon it is that the ministers are said to be a special gift of God, Eph. iv. 11. 'Christ when he ascended on high, he led captivity captive, and gave gifts to men.' What gifts? 'Some apostles, some prophets, some pastors, some teachers, to the end of the world, for the building of his church.' Christ when he went in triumph, after his resurrection, when in his ascension he went triumphantly to heaven (as the great emperors, on the day of their triumph, they scattered money, so), he scattered gifts; and they were not mean gifts, money, and such trifling things; but when he went in his triumphant chariot to heaven, he had no better gifts to leave to the world, than to give such kind of gifts as these—he left ministers, apostles, to found a church; he left pastors and teachers to the end of the world. These were the gifts that Christ gave when he went in triumph to heaven; therefore well may they joy in the ministers as a special gift of God.

So there is a notable place, Jer. iii. 14, 15. There is a promise, if they would turn to God, and be a gracious people, what he would do. 'I will give you pastors according to my own heart, and feed you with knowledge and understanding,' insinuating that it is a special blessing; it is a blessing above all blessings in this world, indeed, none comparable. To live in a place where all solaces are, where all worldly contentments; yet to be there where the sound of the gospel is not, where the best things are not, it is but a dead place. What is it to be fatted to destruction? what life to the life of grace? and how is the life of grace begun and strengthened, but by the means of salvation? When God gives pastors according to his own heart, to feed his people with understanding and judgment, it is a great blessing, and so it is matter of rejoicing and glorying. For may not the soul reason thus?—Who am I? that when thousands sit in darkness, and in the shadow of death, God should send his ambassadors to me, to offer Christ Jesus with all his riches to me; and by his Holy Spirit effect it, by such and such a ministry working grace in me, to give me the first fruits of glory, the pledge of salvation, the beginning of grace here, when millions of other people sit in darkness? Thus a Christian rejoiceth in God first, and then rejoiceth in the minister. He rejoiceth in everything that is an occasion to bring him to heaven.

What is the reason God brings us to heaven by the ministry of men, and doth not send angels, or do all by his Spirit without help?

Amongst the rest, this is one, he would have one to glory in another, he would tie one to another. Therefore, it ties one man to another, this relation to see the need of God's ordinance, and that people might rejoice one in another as the gift of God. Therefore, he calls man by man, to knit man to man, and that they may see God's love to them in men. They saw Christ's love to them in St Paul. St Paul saw Christ's love to him in them, in their obedience. This is the reason that God useth men to call men.

Therefore, those that neglect the ordinance of God, let them never think of glory by Christ, that glory not in the minister that brings them to Christ. Therefore, 2 Cor. v. 19, they are excellently joined together, 'God was in Christ reconciling the world to himself.' What then? What need the ministry if God be reconciled to the world in Christ? God is merciful, and Christ died, and there is an end. No; he hath put to us apostles, and after us to pastors and teachers, 'the word of reconciliation,' and we, 'as ambassadors, entreat you in Christ's stead to be reconciled to God.' So there is no word of reconciliation effectual to any but we must have the efficacy of it by embassage, it must be offered by the ministry.

This ministry, contemned by the world, must be the means to bring us to Christ. We have no benefit brought to us from God unless it be by the word of reconciliation.* Neglect the word, neglect reconciliation itself. Therefore it is called, 'the word of the kingdom,' 'the word of grace,' 'the word of life,' insinuating that if we neglect the word unfolded by God's ordinance in the church, we neglect grace, we neglect life, we neglect [the] kingdom, and all; because we see they are joined together. I will not be long in this point in this place.

Use. Only this, when God doth vouchsafe any abroad wheresoever, or to any of us, to partake of his ordinance in an effectual, holy manner, *to joy in it*. As Solomon saith, Prov. xix. 14, 'Inheritance comes by parents, but a good wife is the gift of God.' So a good minister, or a true Christian friend, is the gift of God that he bestows on men, a special gift; because it is in order to eternal happiness. It is such a gift as Christ gave when he ascended into heaven. So much for that point, 'We are your rejoicing.'

'As also ye are ours.' There is an intercourse of joy. We are your rejoicing, 'and ye are ours,' in the day of the Lord.

How were they St Paul's rejoicing?

They were St Paul's rejoicing as they were gained to God and to Christ by his ministry. When he looked on them, he looked on them as people given him by God. As God said to him of them in the ship when they suffered shipwreck, 'I have given thee all their lives,' Act xxvii. 23, *seq*.

It was a great honour to St Paul that God should give him the lives of all that were in the ship, but more honour that God gave him so many souls. Thou shalt have the honour of saving so many souls. Therefore, they were his rejoicing, in the day of the Lord especially, but now they were his rejoicing, because by faith he apprehended that they should be his special rejoicing when he and they should stand together before the judgment seat of Christ. For faith makes things to come present. 'Ye are our rejoicing, because you shall be our rejoicing then more especially. This is the nature of faith, to present things absent. For blessed St Paul, now in heaven, when at the day of judgment he shall stand before Christ with all the rank about him of Corinthians, Ephesians, Philippians, &c., and all the churches he converted,—when he shall be environed with them as so many brought in triumph under the kingdom of Christ, and pulled from the bondage of Satan (as what a world of people did he bring to God, what triumph did he make over Satan and the corruption of men, bringing men into captivity to Christ!)—when all these shall be set before him, what a glory will this be for holy St Paul, when he shall look on all these blessed people as conquered and brought under Christ's government by him! And so for all the apostles, St Peter and the rest; and so for every minister, when he shall say, 'Here I am, and the souls that thou hast given me,' John xvii. 12. Thou hast honoured me so much as to be an instrument to gain them to Christ, to bring them to heaven, a special glory. The point of doctrine or truth I observe hence is this, that

Doct. The people's proficiency in grace is the minister's joy.

The people's good estate in grace is the minister's joy, and will be, especially after the day of judgment. 'Ye are our rejoicing.' As he saith, Philip. iv. 1, 'Ye are our crown and our glory.' And so, 1 Thess. ii. 19, 'What is our crown and rejoicing? Is it not you?'

In every epistle almost, those good and gracious people, he makes them his hope, and joy, and crown, and rejoicing.

In what sense?

1. Because they were the *objective matter of his joy*. When he looked

on them, he looked on such as yielded him comfort. He could not present them to his thoughts, but he thought of them as matter of joy. Here be the people that God hath honoured me to do much good unto. He could not think of them but as the object of his rejoicing. The word is *Cauchema*,* 'our rejoicing,' that God had given them to him to bring to heaven.

Love descends, we know, and the workman looks upon his work with a kind of complacency. St Paul could not look upon those that he was used as a blessed instrument to do good upon, without a special kind of delight. They were the object matter of his joy.

2. Then, again, they were not only the matter of his joy and rejoicing, presenting to his soul comfortable considerations, but also they *were some means to increase his joy in heaven*; for 'those that convert souls shall shine as the stars in the firmament,' Dan. xii. 3. Those that are honoured of God so far as to bring souls to God, 'they shall shine as the stars in the firmament,' especially those that convert souls shall have a degree of honour above others, though the substantial glory be by Christ. It is not to be denied that the accidental increased glory comes by the increase of the fruit of the ministry; and so Christians, those that are fruitful Christians, that do much good, they shall have much glory. St Paul shall have more rejoicing than others that did not so much good as he. 'Ye are our rejoicing,' because you shall be a means of my greater rejoicing. They were the object of his joy and the means of his joy.

3. Then in the third place, they were his rejoicing, because they were the *seal of his ministry, that he was a sound minister*. How was it known whether St Paul were a good minister or no? Behold his works! see how he wrought on such and such people! how many he gained to God! When he looked on them, he looked on them as a seal of his ministry, that he was a good minister, and in that regard they were his rejoicing.

4. And in some regard likewise in the fourth place, that their gaining *was an evidence to his soul that he was a good man*. Ordinarily (though God convert men by ill men, as Judas no question might convert some, yet) for the most part God honours his servants; and he that is heat himself, can kindle another. Those that are not heat with grace, they cannot speak of the efficacy and power of the things they feel not in their own hearts, as others do. Therefore no question but it comforted him in the state of Christianity, that God honoured him to be a means to bring others in to Christ. So in many respects the people's goodness is the minister's joy.

Use. If this be so, let those that are under the ministry not deny themselves that comfort, or the ministers that joy to be good. There are many poisonful, spiteful spirits that are in love with damnation, that will cherish the corruptions of their naughty nature, in spite of God and all. Rather than they will acknowledge to be wrought on by such and such, to be their children, they will be as they are; they will be broken in a thousand pieces before they will bend to any minister, upon such weak resolutions to yield to a poor ordinance of man. Here is the devilish pride and poison of man's corrupt nature. Can we set light by that, but that at the same time we must set light by our own comfort and salvation?

How were the Corinthians St Paul's joy? Were they not their own joy first? They were matter of joy to St Paul, because he saw he had gained them to Christ. The good was especially theirs. It reflected on him only by consideration. When he looked on them he was comforted; but

* That is, καύχημα.—G.

they were more comforted a great deal. They had more comfort in his rejoicing than he. His was but by reflection of their goodness, a comfort that came by consideration. They had the main comfort of their goodness.

It is little comfort for any to carry themselves so, as that those that are over them in Christ Jesus, when they think of them, can but sigh, when they hear their blasphemies; when they cannot so much as gain of them to leave courses that the very light of nature condemns. The filthy discoveries of a rotten heart, their vile words, and their offensive carriage, can this be a grief to the minister, and not for the damnation of their souls together? And they shall find it a heavy and bitter thing to grieve the Spirit of God in others, as well as they wound their own conscience. Both are joined together.

What a happiness is this, that the more a man is interested in the good of another man, the more glory, if he be a means of any good in him! He shall have good, and you shall have glory.

The best things in nature are communicative and diffusive. The sun gives light to the whole world. So the best man is most fruitful, and communicative. He labours to gain all men by his acquaintance. He knows this, that he is not for himself. He is redeemed for the honour of Christ. And then he knows that another's good will be my glory. It will increase my glory, and be the object of my glory.

On the contrary, we see a company of wretched, despicable creatures, (let their outward estate be as glorious as it will; but I speak of them as Christian eyes judge and esteem of them), that draw others on to the same course with them. If they be blasphemers themselves, they glory to make others so; if they be given to sensuality, they labour to make others sottish as themselves; if they be given to filthiness, they draw others to communion with themselves. Well! will these people be much for their rejoicing in the day of the Lord, think you? What will they do when they think of others, such as they have neglected altogether, that God gave them charge of? The very thought of them, instead of making them rejoice, it will make them astonished. I betrayed his soul,—he was my friend,—or my servant,—I let him live in such sins. Good neglected will torment us hereafter. But then ill infused, by example, and by word, I poisoned him; suppose I have repented myself, but perhaps the person that I have drawn to communion in my sin, hath not repented; what a torment will this consideration be! Good neglected will be matter of torment, much more evil infused, poison infused. When we shall see at the day of judgment, instead of a company that we have gained to God, and been a means to further their salvation, we shall see a company that we have infected with our ill example, and our evil persuasions, this will be in hell an increase of torment.

One will curse another, and say, You brought me hither. The father will curse the son. To get riches for you I cracked my conscience, and lost my soul. And the son shall curse the father. By your riches that you left me, I lived a base and sensual life, whereas perhaps I might have trusted to my good endeavours otherwise. So here shall be cursing. The friend shall curse his friend. You might have told me of this, you strengthened me in evil courses.

As it will be our glory when we shall see such and such, as God hath used as instruments to do good unto; so it will be a torment indeed to think, such and such I neglected and betrayed, such and such I corrupted. I beseech you, therefore, take heed of it.

And would you have matter of joy in this world, that should joy you when nothing else will joy you? (as St Paul was in affliction oft) what comforted St Paul? First, his own conscience, that he was a good Christian, an heir of heaven, a good apostle. But when he wanted joy, what would he do? when he had no liberty, but was imprisoned, when he had nothing, then he considered, how hath Christ dignified me to do good to others? This honouring of him to do this, it comforted him more than all his imprisonment, and abasement, and reproaches could discourage him; the conceit that God did use him as an honourable instrument for his honour and service, to do good to others.

So the testimony of our conscience, that God hath used us to do good to others, not only to make me to gain heaven, but to be an instrument to gain others, this will comfort us in the world, come what will.

Use. This should stir up those that have to deal with the souls of others, (not only ministers, but all others), that have any committed to them, that they should labour to make them good, to work upon them for the good of their souls, that they may have them as matter, and objects, of their joy at that day. If they do not, as I said, when they are presented to them as persons whom they have neglected and betrayed negligently for want of instruction, and reformation of their lives, and as persons whom they have infected with their ill example, which is worse, alas! what matter of horror will they be. They will not say of them as St Paul saith here, 'You are my joy, and my crown, and my glory,' but they will be matter of horror. These be they that I have betrayed, and neglected, and infected, and brought to hell, to this cursed condition with myself. It will be an increase of the torments of hell at that day, all those whom we have hurt any kind of way.

But what shall it be then of those that have opposed goodness? that have not only betrayed others by neglect, but have maligned good where they have seen it? What will become of them, that are so far from making others good, that they have despited the image of God in others, and have exercised their bitterness upon Christ in his members and ministers?

To add one thing more.

What! these Corinthians, that had so many abuses, and such weaknesses, were they the matter of St Paul's joy?

Yes! why, therefore people must take heed how they leave churches that have corruptions in them. Schism ofttimes is a greater fault than the fault upon which they pretend separation. The things for which they pretend a rent, are not so great a fault in the church, as the want of charity in them to do so. If St Paul would have taken occasion to leave them, what good occasion had he? Alas! how many corruptions had they in doctrine, and in manners too. But yet, notwithstanding, as ill as they were, he saw what good was in them, and looked not to the evil: he knew that God would perfect the good things that were in them; and, saith he, notwithstanding all their infirmities, I see you were ready to reform when I wrote an epistle to you, therefore I doubt not but you will be 'our rejoicing.'

'*In the day of the Lord Jesus.*' This is the time. It must be taken inclusively, 'I am your rejoicing, and you are mine, to the day of the Lord Jesus, and in the day of the Lord.' So he means here. It is laid as a ground here, that

Obs. Jesus Christ hath a day.

It is his day by way of eminency and excellency. Jesus Christ hath many days, two especially; the day of his first coming, and the day of his second coming. The first coming of Christ was the day of the gospel, when he came to work our salvation. His second coming is to accomplish our salvation. In his first day he came to be humbled, and to be judged, to be a sacrifice for us. In his second, he is to come gloriously to judge the quick and the dead. In the first, he came to gain a church to himself; by his second he shall come to accomplish the marriage. Now is the contract; there is the Sabbath. After the six days of this life the day of the Lord shall appear, the Sabbath day, the day of jubilee, the solemnisation of the marriage, the solemn triumph over all enemies. The first day was to save our souls, especially from the thraldom of sin and Satan. The second day, this that we speak of here, shall be to save our bodies from the rottenness and corruption in which they have lain rotting in the grave till that day of Christ. As he raised his own body, so at that day he shall raise our bodies, and make them 'like his glorious body,' Phil. iii. 21. That is the main day, the day of all days, for then he will come to accomplish all. That day shall never have a night, it shall be day for ever.

As the cloud that went before the Israelites to Canaan, that side toward the Egyptians was dark, but the other side was lightsome toward the Israelites; so this day, it shall be a dark day, it shall be both a day of vengeance and a day of glory.

St Paul saith here, 'You shall be my rejoicing,' and I yours at that day. But those that do not believe the gospel, and obey the ministry of it, it shall not be a day of rejoicing to them. It shall be a glorious day when all other glory shall vanish. All other glory in the world shall be eclipsed, even as the stars are not seen when the sun appears in the firmament. All the glory at that day shall be the glory of Christ, and of his church. To omit other things that may be spoken out of other places of Scripture, the point I will observe hence is this, that,

Doct. The measure of a Christian's rejoicing in this world in anything, it is the consideration of what it will be at the great day of judgment.

I say, the rule whereby a Christian judgeth things, and that measure whereby a Christian measures things, to be thus or thus in their excellency and worth, it is as they will be esteemed at that day of the Lord Jesus Christ. Here St Paul saith, 'I am your rejoicing, and you are ours at the day of the Lord Jesus.' What! is this a vain glorying to commend him? Oh! he is a worthy learned rabbi, a great learned apostle; and then that they were such and such people! No, no! They had grace wrought in them; and St Paul saw such evidences of grace in them, that at that day they should look upon Christ with boldness, because they were sincerely gained to the gospel. So then this must be the rule of the worth of anything, to esteem it as it will be then at that day; which is a day when all our estates will be determined of, for eternal happiness or eternal misery.

To explain it a little.

We do not value things of short continuance, because they are short, as flowers that are fresh in the morning, and cast away at night; but we esteem things that will hold out. So our rejoicing, and glory, and comfort, we should consider of it how it will hold out, 'Riches avail not in the day of wrath,' Prov. xi. 4. Things have that degree of goodness or evil in them, they have that degree of vanity, or seriousness, as they will stand out at that day. What are riches in the day of wrath, even in this world? What will riches be then at the day of the Lord Jesus? Therefore a Christian values them not; they are not the good of a Christian; he esteems not the applause of men. And pleasures are nothing, they are momentary, they avail not when conscience is awaked. They leave a man, and not only so, but they leave a sting behind them.

If all the good things in the world will stand us in no stead then, then what will the sins do that thou hast made so much of? What will the sins do that thou hast betrayed and damned thy soul for? Thy filthiness, and thy betraying of goodness, what will that do? How wilt thou look the Judge in the face, whenas nothing in the world that is excellent will hold out and avail at that day?

But what then will avail at that day when Christ shall come to judge both the quick and the dead?

Why, this; that thou hast submitted thyself to acknowledge Christ as thy king, and thy priest, and thy prophet; and by means of the ministry thou hast been wrought on, and the work of the new creature is begun in thee, true and sincere grace that thou darest look on Christ, that thou art in the state of grace, this will comfort thee in the day of judgment.

By this you may discern who take the wisest course: he that measures his life by a right measure and rule. Who judgeth aright of persons and things? He judgeth aright of things, that values and labours to interest himself in those things that will comfort him in this world, and stand by him in the world to come; he hath a right judgment and esteem of things.

What be those things?

Grace, a holy, humble, gracious, believing carriage and disposition. When a man gives himself to Christ, and renounceth the world, and sees the vanity of all things but the estate of Christianity, he hath those things in some little measure that shall be perfected at that day. Who take the wisest course? Those that seek to please the humour of men, those that seek to feed their own corruptions and the corruptions of others, those that will have some present glory in the flesh? Aye, but what will they have at the day of the Lord Jesus? Surely, those that labour to approve themselves in sincerity and truth to Christ Jesus in all things. And so that they may approve their hearts to him, they care not what the world judgeth of them, as St Paul saith, 'I pass not what ye judge of me,' 1 Cor. iv. 3. If there be a day of the Lord, when he shall be judge, then those are the wisest and the best courses that will hold out at that day. And those that will not, we shall be ashamed of them all.

And that is the reason that many men of excellent parts and endowments are comfortless in the time of temptation. They did not think to do things with reference to Christ, in sincerity to please him; for then they might hold up their heads at that day.

There is a great deal of atheism in our hearts. We frame our courses to present contentments, by reason that we have little belief for the time to come.

I beseech you, let us often have in our thoughts the second coming of Christ. The best things are behind. Our chief rejoicing is behind. Our rejoicing now is our hope that we shall rejoice then. The Corinthians were St Paul's joy now, because he knew they should be his main rejoicing then. If we rejoice in anything now, let it be that our names are written in heaven, in the testimony of our conscience that we are God's, that our hearts are rought on, that we have something that Christ will acknowledge when he sees his stamp and image on us. When he shall look on us, and see his own image upon our hearts, there will be matter of joy in that day.

There will be joy in ourselves, and joy in all the blessed instruments that are under Christ. The ministers, they shall rejoice likewise in us, and all of us shall join in joying in Christ, all shall meet there. For their joying in St Paul, and he in them, it was that Christ was theirs. And 'Christ shall come,' as it is in 2 Thess. i. 10, 'to be glorified in his saints;' not only in himself, but in his believing members; for his glory shall reflect upon them as the sun reflects upon light bodies. All light bodies are made light by the sun. So the 'Sun of righteousness' shall come, and all them that have glory it shall be by reflection from him; they shall be glorious in him. So he is both the minister's joy and the people's. They shall all glory in Christ, whose glory is their glory. He shall come 'to be glorious in his saints.' Therefore frame your courses that way to have glory then, to have comfort in the hour of death, and at the day of judgment. And to end the point,

Let us labour to be acquainted with him now before that day. We shall never have comfort in the day of the Lord Jesus, except we be acquainted with him, and acknowledge him in the ministry now, and in the sacraments; for none shall ever be acquainted with him there, that have not been acquainted with him, and known him in this world.

How do we come to be acquainted with Christ?

To be present where he is present; and he is present where two or three are met together in his name. He is present now in our meetings, he is present when we hear the word. He is present in the sacrament more especially; we have his very body and blood. As verily as we take the outward signs, so verily Christ is present to our hearts; at the same time from heaven, he reacheth us himself with all the benefits of his passion. When the minister reacheth the bread, he reacheth his body. As our outward man is refreshed with the elements, so our souls are refreshed with the spiritual presence of Christ. Now he is excellently present in heaven, he is present to our senses in the sacrament, and by his Spirit in the word.

Would you have him then at his appearing come and own you, and say then, 'Come, ye blessed?' Mat. xxv. 34; be acquainted with him now upon all occasions, hear the word, receive the sacrament, and come to the sacrament as acknowledging him there.

How is that?

Why, then, you acknowledge the bread and wine to be seals of him, and of all the blessings by him, when you come prepared, when you come to them as his. Or else you do not acknowledge them. You know them to be such and such things, but you acknowledge them not to be set apart for such a holy use, except you come with prepared hearts.

Will anybody acknowledge him to go to a great person, when he goes deformed and in rags? Do you know whither you go? would some say to him. He considers not whither he goes, that comes to the sacrament in his old sins. Come acquainted therefore with Christ, to acknowledge him that shall be your judge at the latter day; therefore come prepared.

And then, because the sacrament is a means to seal to us all the benefits we have by Christ, and to incorporate us more nearly into Christ, he that comes to the sacrament as he should, must come with joy. Is it not a joyful thing to be united to Christ, and to have further assurance of all the good things by him? Yes! it is a matter of great joy. Therefore, when you have repented of your sins, come with joy.

And come with holiness. The things are holy, as our liturgy hath it; let us give holy things to holy persons. Here is presented holy bread and wine, and here you are to deal with Christ. Therefore come with holy reverence in the whole carriage of the business.

And come with faith and assurance, and then you shall acknowledge Christ in this ordinance, in the sacrament. You shall acknowledge that he deals not complimentally with you, to feed you with empty signs; but you shall have himself with his signs; you shall have the Lord himself in the word, and in the sacraments. With the field you shall have the treasure in the field, as the wise merchant had, Mat. xiii. 44. With the word you shall have Christ wrapped in the word. And in the sacrament you shall have Christ and all his benefits. Trust to it, make it your weapon against Satan, he will tempt you to doubt of your interest in Christ. Think with yourselves, Had I grace to receive Christ? to be incorporate nearer into him? why should I doubt to renew my covenant? And though I have fallen by weakness, yet I have a gracious intercessor in heaven that makes my peace continually. Come in faith. Know that God in good earnest here offers Christ with all his benefits.

And come with a purpose and resolution to be led by him. You come to renew your covenant. Here is the covenant, when Christ is given to you, and you give yourselves to Christ. Therefore, as I said, if you come with a purpose to live in sin, come not at all. Christ will not live in a heart where there is a purpose to sin. Therefore resolve to leave all sin, or else you cannot receive him.

To move you to come, and to come thus, do but consider that it will be your joy in this world, and in the world to come, before Christ, that you have been thus acquainted with him here on earth, acquainted with him in the ministry, acquainted with him in the sacrament, in private prayer, and meditation, in all the blessed means that he hath appointed: and then he will look on you as upon his old friends.

But now he that is a rebel, that goes away, or else comes, not acknowledging with whom he hath to deal; him that shall be his judge ere long, the great God of heaven and earth, that shall come in glory and majesty with thousands of his angels. Then he shall be 'wonderful' indeed, as his name is, Isa. ix. 6; and as the apostle saith, 2 Thess. i. 10, where he useth the word, 'he shall be wonderful in his saints.' Then all the world shall wonder at the glory of a poor Christian, when he shall put down the sun, and all the creatures in glory. Consider with whom you have to deal, him that ere long shall be wonderful in his saints. Therefore come prepared, come joyfully, come faithfully, come reverently and holily, and you shall find a blessing answerable. This I thought good to touch concerning the occasion of the sacrament. 'Ye are our rejoicing.'

'At the day of the Lord Jesus.' St Paul esteemed of nothing but that which would comfort him at that day. Therefore let us oft think of the day of the Lord Jesus. Why? What will make us digest labour, and pains, in dealing with the souls of others, in doing good, and being fruitful in our places? The consideration of that day. There is a day will come that will make amends for all, and that is the day of the Lord Jesus.

And considering that there is such a day, let us make much of the day of the Lord that is now left us. What is that? This day. 'The Lord's day.' It is called 'The Lord's day,' Rev. i. 10. And as I said, labour to be acquainted with that Lord that must be judge of quick and dead then.

The Lord hath a day now wherein we may be acquainted with him; by hearing his word, by yielding obedience to his truth unfolded to us; therefore let us make much of this day, if we would have comfort at that day. 'Ye are our rejoicing in the day of the Lord.'

VERSE 15.

'*And in this confidence I was minded to come unto you before, that you might have a second benefit, or grace.*' 'In this confidence.' In this assurance, in this persuasion, 'I was minded to come to you.'

'That you might have a second benefit,' saith the last translation (*ddd*). It doth diminish the strength of the word. Therefore go from the text to the margin. You have ofttimes a fitter word in the margin.

*Charis.** The word is pregnant in the original. It signifieth grace. If it signify a benefit at all, it signifies a benefit that issues from grace and favour. 'Benefit' is a weaker word. Grace, though it be not so common, is a fit word, and reaches to the strength of the word in the original, to the meaning of the apostle. So it is better to read it so, 'That you might have a second grace.'

St Paul in this verse sets down *what intention he had to come to them.*

And likewise, *the end of his intention.*

In the next verse he sets down, *the manner how he would come to them.*

Fourthly, he shews *why he came not to them;* it was 'to spare them,' as he saith afterward.

Here in this verse he shews what his intention was. 'My intention was to come to you.' 'In this confidence I was minded to come to you.'

To what end? 'That you might have a second benefit.'

His intention is set down by the inward moving cause, his 'confidence.' 'In this confidence I was minded to come to you.'

I will speak of his intention and purpose of coming; and of the end of it. And in his purpose of coming, of the moving cause, his 'confidence.'

'*In this confidence.*' What is that? 'In this confidence,' because I am assured that you are my rejoicing, and I yours in the day of the Lord Jesus; in this confidence that you will be so to me, and I to you. 'In this confidence.'

St Paul had a good opinion of them. The inward moving cause of St Paul to come, it was a good conceit of them.

Obs. It is good, as far as possibly we can, to cherish a good judgment, and conceit of others.

Let others have as good place in our affections as possibly may be.

Why?

Reason 1. *If they be good, we wrong them else even in our conceit.* We do not only wrong men in our speeches and actions, but in our sinister judgments, in the censures of our minds. Therefore we should have as good conceit of men as possibly we can in that regard.

Reason 2. And likewise, *because confidence and assurance that they have something in them that is good, and it will be better with them after in the day of the Lord, this will be a means to stir us up to deserve well of them.* Hope stirs up will. We have no mind to a thing that we have not hope of. And likewise hope stirs up endeavour, and hope keeps in endeavour. What

* That is, 'χάρις.'—G.

makes a man so long in endeavouring the good of others? He hath some hope. They are good, and will be better. So it stirs up our will. The bent of it, it stirs. It stirs up endeavour upon will; and it keeps us in endeavour when we hope for good at men's hands.

And therefore we ought not to cast off men, especially those that are young, for imperfections. The Corinthians were weak, and carnal, as you may see in the former epistle, yet in this confidence that they had repented of their ill usage of St Paul, he was minded to come to them. Persons that are the subjects of hope are not free from infirmities. Novices cannot have that perfection that grown Christians have, at the first. Consider further what is of passion, and what is of the poison of nature; consider what is of infirmity, and what is of malice; consider what sins they have been longer accustomed to, and how hardly such sins are suddenly broken off. These considerations would mitigate something where we see any degree of goodness.

Oh! this pleaseth now some vicious disposed persons. They think this makes for them.

Not at all; what I speak is, where there is any ground to hope well of. St Paul had some ground, for he wrote a sharp epistle to them, and he saw they were amended on it. He saw they yielded, they acknowledged, that is, they reformed by his ministry, and by his epistle. So where we discern reformation, that there is a willingness of amendment, we must hope of such, though they be sometimes overtaken. And if they be overtaken, we must construe it to the best. The temptation perhaps was great, and they were not watchful at that time. The subtlety of the opposition and the malice of men was great, and their caution was not so great. Thus we may construe to bear with them, if upon the discovery of their fault they become pliable. But otherwise, if they arm themselves with malice and bitter poison, and resolve to be so still, there is no hope, no confidence of such. St Paul's confidence here was with evidence from their carriage. They gave him some cause to be so confident.

Therefore it is in vain to think that we are too censorious when we tell you of your faults. That very conceit that you think bitterly, and arm yourselves with resolutions, rather to vex those that inform you than to amend that which is amiss, that is as ill a disposition, as ill a state as can be. We can hope for no good of such. Yet notwithstanding we ought so far to hope of them, as not to give them over, as St Paul saith, 2 Tim. ii. 25, 26, 'To prove if at any time God will shew mercy to them, to deliver them out of the snare of the devil.' They are in the devil's snare; yet we ought still to take pains with them. For we know not whether it will please God at that time, or at any time, to have mercy on them, and deliver them out of the snare of Satan.

If God bear with them, we ought to bear with them as well as teach them; but to have a good conceit of them, when we see them maliciously bent against those that tell them of their faults, we cannot.

Use. If this be so, it should be an encouragement for all those that are under others that inform and instruct them, to give them some good occasion and ground to hope well of them. You would have us hope well of you. What ground do you give? What is your company? Shall we think you are good because you converse with those that are swearers? with vicious and carnal company? Would you have us blind? Charity indeed interprets the best, but it is not blind. What shall we judge of you by your outward demeanour and carriage, that is ofttimes scandalous and offensive? when your speeches are filthy and corrupt, joined with blasphemies and oaths, daring God, as it were, whether he will suffer you to carry it away unrevenged and unpunished or not. Where this abominable corruption of heart discovers itself outwardly in the tongue, how can we entertain good conceits of you? You think we wrong you by not conceiving thus and thus of you. What ground have we? what hold have we from anything that is in you or from you so to conceit? Resolve on this, there cannot be grievance offered to the minister, but you must reward ill to your own souls. If you be not his joy, it will be your sorrow. You will have the worst of it. And therefore study as much as may be to have the good hope and confidence of others. This will stir up willingness, and stir up endeavour, as it did in St Paul. The good hope he had of them by their repentance, and reformation, and pliableness, it stirred up his diligence. They gained by it. But I mean not to stand on that.

'In this confidence,' that you will be my joy, and I yours, in the day of Lord.

'*I was minded to come unto you.*' St Paul was minded to come unto them. You see then that

Obs. Personal presence hath a special power and efficacy.

Personal presence hath more efficacy than writing. For there the holy things that are delivered, they are, as it were, acted to the life. Men are wondrously affected when they see gracious things delivered with life and feeling: it hath a wondrous lively working. Therefore St Paul tells the Romans, Rom. i. 15, that besides his learned and worthy epistle he wrote to them, he was desirous also to preach the gospel to them.

But some object: reading is preaching, say they, some kind of preaching. But not that which the apostle meant; for then St Paul's epistle was preaching, some kind of preaching. But I speak not to sophisters. But, saith St Paul, I desire to preach the word to you by vocal teaching: it hath a special efficacy. It is wondrous good praying for others, and writing to others; but presence, when the minister is the mouth of God with them and to them, their mouth to God, to pray together with them, and God's mouth, to speak to them, this presence is of a wondrous efficacy; therefore St Paul saith, 'I purposed to come to you.'

Use. It should stir up in our hearts an esteem of the ordinance of God of preaching; or else we slight it with the prejudice of our own souls. For doth God appoint it for anything but for our own good? There is a common objection, which (because it is raised out of this epistle, and may be answered out of this epistle) I will answer.

Obj. Oh! say some, a lively voice hath not alway that energy, that operation, that writing and reading have; for we see St Paul's epistle was more terrible than his presence. It is the objection of men that content themselves in their own idleness, wresting off such places as this. Among the rest, 2 Cor. x. 10, say they, 'His bodily presence is weak, and his speech contemptible,' but his letters seem terrible. Therefore this is not alway true, that bodily presence hath more efficacy than writing.

Ans. I answer briefly,—St Paul compares not here his bodily presence with his letters, as if his letters were more efficacious than his bodily presence; but he compares his mild dealing, being present, with his sharp dealing, being absent; his letters, indeed, were sharper than his presence. But to take away such cavils, he tells them after that they shall know, if they reform not, that his presence shall be as sharp as his writings. Let such a one think this, 'such as we are in word being absent, such will we be when we are present.' We will be as sharp, if you reform not, in our presence, as we were absent. So he compares the sharpness of his letter with the sweetness of his presence. It is not to be taken in that sense, that his letters were more effectual of themselves than his presence; for he saith the contrary, You shall know that my presence shall be as sharp as my letter was. Therefore, it is but a cavil to think there is more efficacy in reading, than in preaching.

'*That you might have a second grace.*' I come now to St Paul's end. His intention and purpose was 'to come.' The end of his coming was 'to bestow a grace on them' by his presence. In general observe here, that

Obs. Holy men are set on work from holy moving causes, and holy aims.

Holy aims are the winds that carry them to their business, and they are the water that drive their mill. I come with a holy confidence that you will be my joy; here is my moving cause. What is my aim in coming? It is this, to bestow a grace on you. Holy men have holy aims for holy actions; they have holy grounds, and holy moving causes.

When two men do the same thing, yet it is not the same thing; perhaps their aims differ, their moving causes differ. St Paul comes here to do a good thing from a good end, from a good moving cause. 'In this confidence I was minded to come,' to bestow a grace on you.

Use. Let us look in all our actions, therefore, to our moving cause, and to our aims. And especially ministers, their aim it should not be for the fleece, it should not be to gain respect, or any advantage to themselves, but to bestow some spiritual good thing. As the apostle saith, 'To bestow some good thing upon you,' Rom. i. 11, some grace, as he calls it. This should be their aim, not to receive good from them, so much as to do them good. Ministers are fathers, they should have that tender disposition. Parents do not think of receiving much (they look to that in the second place, that must be maintained); but, especially, they look to their children's good. 'I come to bestow a grace on you.' How this is observed, I list not to speak, therefore I leave it, and come to that which concerns us all. 'I was minded to come to you.'

'To bestow a grace on you.' We see then, that

Doct. The preaching of the gospel is a special grace.

It is a free and bountiful benefit of God. Grace implies freedom, and mercy, and bounty. It is a free mercy of God to have the gospel.

Why?

Reason. Because this is the means to work all that is savingly good in us. This is a means to open to us God's love in Christ, and to work in us a disposition answerable to his love. Therefore it must needs be a grace. Heaven is a grace, life is a grace, reconciliation a grace, and such like. Therefore the word must needs be a grace, by which all these are communicated. Therefore the word hath the name of these things. It is the word of the kingdom of heaven. It is called the kingdom of heaven, the preaching of the gospel, because it puts us into the state of the kingdom of heaven. And the word of reconciliation, because by it we know our reconciliation with God. It is offered, and wrought in our hearts, and faith to apply it by this word. 'It is the word of life,' Acts xx. 32; the life of grace, and the life of glory, all come by this word. 'I commend you to God, and the word of his grace,' saith the apostle. All grace and spiritual life is wrought in us by the word; therefore the word preached, it is a special grace and favour of God.

St Paul here calls his coming to them to strengthen and confirm them, 'a grace.' For all means come under the same decree of God's eternal love with the decree itself. When God out of grace resolves and sets down that he will bring such a one to heaven, of his free love, he doth out of the same grace fit him with opportunities of persons and means; he accommodates him with all means; for he intends in such a way to bring him to heaven.

And therefore St Austin doth well define predestination; it is an ordaining to salvation, and a preparing of all means tending thereto (*eee*). Therefore all fall in the compass of grace, both the free favour of God, setting a man down to make him happy; and likewise by sending men that have an outward calling, and inwardly furnishing them with gifts, and whatsoever,—all is of grace. The preaching of the word is a grace.

Use. It concerns us therefore so to esteem it. Do not many sit in darkness, and in the shadow of death? Is it not a grace therefore that we partake of the means of salvation? What is in us by nature better than in Turks and Pagans? or than many other people under Satan, and under popish teachers, and so rot away in their ignorance? Nothing. We differ only by the grace of God. Therefore let us esteem it as a grace.

How shall we esteem it as a grace?

Receive it thankfully, as a largess and bounty, and free grace of God; receive it as a bounty with thankful hearts. Grace begets grace, it begets thankfulness. So to receive it as a grace, is to receive it with thankful minds, to be more thankful for the means of salvation, than for any outward thing.

How shall we come to be thankful?

Never, unless we find some grace wrought by the word of grace. Therefore to receive it as a grace, is to receive it as a free, loving gift of God, and to yield to it; when by it holy motions are stirred in our hearts, not to suppress and quench holy motions, but to yield to them; not to quench and resist the Spirit, but to yield ourselves pliable to the word. This is to acknowledge it a grace, to be thankful for it, because you find your hearts wrought to holy obedience by it. Give it way in your souls, that it may be an ingraffed word; that all the inward and outward man may be seasoned with it, and relish of it; that the word may season your thoughts, and speeches, and desires, and season your course of life; that what you think may be in the relish and strength of the word, in the strength of some divine truth, and the guide of your actions may be divine truth, or some motives from it. Then you will give thanks for what is wrought on you, when it is an ingraffed word in your souls, and all relish of it, your speeches and actions, and your whole course; when a man may know by your carriage that there is something invested and ingraffed in your souls, that gives a blessed relish to all the expressions of the outward man. Such a one indeed will account the word a special grace, by a sweet experience wrought in his heart. I will not press that point any further.

Again, whereas St Paul saith, he would come to bestow a second grace on them, we see here that—

Doct. Those that are in the state of grace already, they need a second grace.

Those that have initial grace to be set in a good course, they need confirming and strengthening grace. St Paul had planted them before. Aye, but he must come to water them. There is alway somewhat left for the minister to do, till he see their souls safe in heaven. He hath alway somewhat to do to the Christian souls under him. For he must not only get them out of Satan's kingdom into a good estate, but he must labour to build them up. He must water them, and fence them, and strengthen them against all discouragements.

A man is never safe till he be in heaven. Therefore he saith, 'I will come to you,' but I will come 'to bestow a second grace on you;' you have need of it, and my love is such to you, that you shall have it. To enforce this a little: because we set terms to our growth, and go on plodding in a course, and many years after we are no better than we were at the first; and some out of a profane fulness, out of a Laodicean temper, they think they have enough, they are rich, when indeed they are empty, and miserable, and wretched, and poor; and if temptations set upon them, they have nothing in them, Rev. iii. 17.

To let you see that we stand in need of a second grace, and of a third grace, and of a fourth grace, that we need continual building up.

Reason 1. First, *look within, what opposition there is to saving goodness within!* what rebellion of lusts! what ignorance, and blindness, and darkness, and indisposition! what head the flesh makes in us against the word of God. Let a man a little continue out of the means, and he shall see what growth of corruptions there will be; a distasting of all means, that a man shall be ready to begin anew with them almost. Having a double principle in them, of grace and corruption, there needs continually strengthening and stablishing grace.

Reason 2. Consider *outwardly what discouragements from the ill examples, and allurements, and seducing of others, from the disgrace that is put on good things; what discouragements and scandals from without!*

Reason 3. Again, *are there not ofttimes new and great temptations*, that a man must have a new measure of grace to resist? There is continual occasion of new spiritual strength to oppose new temptations, and new spiritual strength to endure new crosses, and to enjoy new benefits. In all the passages of our life, there is a necessity of more grace, of further supply of grace. A man with that proportion of strength which he had before, he cannot encounter with new temptations; and therefore there must be new grace, and fresh attending upon the means while we live here.

Reason 4. Again, *unavoidable times will come*, when there must be strength of grace: sickness will come, temptations to despair will come, conflicts with Satan will come. We need not say, put the case such and such; but it is an unavoidable case. They will come, wherein a great strength of grace will be necessary. Therefore we cannot be too much careful in attending upon the means of salvation, to be confirmed and strengthened.

Reason 5. Again, do we not need a great measure of strengthening grace continually? *Doth not the devil envy goodness and good actions?* When we go about to pray, when the best men are about the best actions, what a deal of distraction is there! how doth Satan confound them with distractions! What a deal of confirming grace need we to every good work! When a Christian is taken out of the kingdom of Satan, he is the butt, the object of his malice, and the malice of those that are his instruments. We must pull every good work, as it were, out of the fire. We must use violence to nature, to temptations in every good duty, to perform them strongly. We need a second and a third grace, many degrees of grace.

Reason 6. Then again, *we are capable of more grace;* for our understanding is such that we may know more still, and our will is such that it affects* more still, and the more holy truths are made known to us, the more the will is enlarged to cleave to them; the more we know, the more we may know. Our understandings are wondrous large. There is a great capacity in them, and our adhesion and cleaving to truths is more and more. The more we know, the more the will cleaves to it; as it is, Acts xi. 23, 'They exhorted them, that with full purpose they would cleave fast to God.' We must cleave and adhere fast to the truth and to God; every day go deeper, get nearer and closer to God, and labour to be established in good things. St Paul prays that they might be established more and more; and David prays that he might be established in good thoughts, and desires, and resolutions in good purposes, to be stablished in everything that is good. Grace is a state that we may grow in, and our souls are fit to be enlarged; for there is a great capacity in the soul. Till we come to heaven, it is not full. We may grow in every grace stronger and stronger. As in the examples of holy men in Scripture, it was never well with them but when they were growing. There is a necessity of growing.

Use 1. If this be true, *let us set no pitch to ourselves, and abhor, abhor even as the temptation of the devil, the conceit of fulness and of self-sufficiency;* to think, I know enough, what should I know more for? or, perhaps, I could read at home, as I said before. It is God's ordinance, and cursed is all private study when it is done in contempt of the ordinance of God. Take heed of such suggestions of fulness and standing at a stay. No; we need a second, we need many degrees of confirmation and strength, and all little enough. There was never any that repented of the careful use of the means. Strengthening, and proficiency, and growth in this kind is a pledge of perfection, that God will perfect more and more that that he hath graciously begun. I beseech you, take it to heart, that we may alway need a further degree of strengthening grace while we live in this world.

The strongest Christians are most desirous of strength. Who have you that doth most hunger after the means of salvation? Surely those that have the greatest measure of grace, because with grace the capacity of the soul is enlarged to receive more. The soul is so framed by God that the more it hath, the more it hungers after; and 'blessed are those that hunger, they shall be satisfied.' Who care least for the means? Debauched, shallow creatures, those that are popishly conceited, such as are ill bred, such as take scandal at all things in the communion of saints, at holy exercises, the frequenting of public and private duties, the making conscience of calling upon God. A Christian that knows what it is, he thinks all the means little enough, he will not omit one of them that may be a means of his growth and strength; he thinks if he neglect one means, he decays in all. Therefore, he joins to all means, private duties, and then public, of hearing the word; and he hears out of season when he finds himself indisposed. As the ministers are to 'preach in season and out of season,' 2 Tim. iv. 2, so he hears in season and out of season. And therefore, of all men, he that is the most careful of his growth is the great, the strong Christian. The better he is, the more he hungers after it.

Use 2. *Take this as a trial, if you do not desire to be strengthened in good things more and more, you have no goodness at all.* I will press the point no further at this time, but go on. Saith St Paul, 'I was minded to come to you, that you might have a second benefit, a second grace,' that is, a

* That is, = seeks.—G.

confirming, strengthening grace. We all need, then, a second grace, a confirming grace. Here I might make some use to ministers; I will but touch it, to shew what their duty is to those that are under them. Every man is, as it were, a minister in his place to strengthen another, and to exhort one another, and to bestow grace upon one another. But ministers should do it especially. They are like those that repair the sea banks. The sea gets over ofttimes, and eats out the banks; they must be repaired continually, they will impair else. The minister's pains, it is like the labour of the husbandman. When he hath sown, he must weed; and when he hath weeded, he must fence, to keep it from the birds of prey and the violence of beasts, &c., and he must live by faith till the grain be ready. So the minister, after he hath planted, he must water, and weed, and fence, and all little enough; he must look to the banks, and many times that which he getteth in one day he loseth in another; nay, ofttimes the pitiful condition of a minister is this, that at the week's end he hath all to do again. Another man sees an end of his work, but in this the devil and corruption hath undone all again. We enforce good things on people on the Lord's day; but within one day, ill company and employment in worldly business overthrows all. The sea banks are down; they must be new repaired. Therefore, there is a necessity laid on us of the ordinances to our lives' end, till our souls be in heaven; there is a necessity of repairing them. We cannot be too diligent in our places. And those that have the oversight of others, let them make conscience of it; it is needful. And mark here, in the next point,

Doct. The language of Canaan, the language of the Spirit of God, that he puts the name of grace upon every benefit, especially those that concern a better life. Grace usually we take to be nothing but a gracious frame of heart, the new creature, as we call it; but indeed, in the language of the Holy Ghost, every free gift of God that concerns our souls any way is a grace. The very ministry is a grace. It is the grace and free love of God to give us the ministry. The very heart to embrace it, and to hear it, is a grace. The very heart to give alms is a grace. Saith St Paul, 'Thanks be to God for this unspeakable gift,' 2 Cor. ix. 15, for this unspeakable grace that you had a heart to give; so that everything that is good, it is a grace, a gift of God.

St Paul conceived of his coming to them as a grace. Indeed the grace of God moved and directed St Paul to come to them. It is grace that God directs the preacher to speak to the people. It is a grace that the minister speaks gracious things. It is a greater grace when you close with and entertain that which is spoken,—all is of grace. Your ready minds to do good, it comes of God, it is a grace; your acceptance of God, as well as eternal life, all is of free grace.

The ground of it is this, as Austin, as I said, defines predestination well, it is a destinating and ordaining to a supernatural end, to everlasting salvation in the world to come, and a preparing of all means to that end.* Why, now as it is a grace that God pulls out some men to an eternal estate of salvation in heaven, to a supernatural estate, that they could never attain without his especial grace; so the preparing of all means to that end, it falls within the compass of predestination, within the grace.

So when we have any means prepared to bring us to that end, the offer of the word, and the Spirit of God disposing us to embrace the word, this preparing of the means to that end, it falls within the compass of predes-

* Cf. note *eee*.—G.

tination, we may gather our election by it. When we see the word sent in favour, and have gracious hearts to receive it, this is a preparation wrought to bring us to heaven, a man may know his election by it. All is of grace that falls within the decree of grace. When God decrees to bring a man to heaven, all that helps to the main must needs be grace. The minister is a grace, the word a grace, opportunities to do good a grace, the communion of saints a grace, all that helps a man forward is a grace. A gracious heart sees God in everything, it sees God's love in everything; it considers of everything that befalls it as a grace. Why? From this disposition especially, because with the grace there is grace to make a blessed use of, and to improve everything.

Use. If this be so, *let us look upon every benefit that concerns salvation, though it be remote, even the very direction of good speeches to us, account it a grace.* It is the grace of God that I have this opportunity, especially the public ministry. St Paul calls it 'a grace;' let us think of it as a grace. And as we do in clocks, we go from the hammer that strikes, to the wheels, and from one wheel to another, and so to the weights that make it strike: we go to the first weight, the first wheel that moves all, and leads all. So when we see good done, look not to the good done only, but go to the wheels, to the weights, that move it, and make it strike. What sets all agoing? The grace and free love of God. When good things are spoken, when any good is done, go higher to the first wheel that sets all agoing, to the grace and free love of God. This is the language of the Scripture and of the Spirit of God. Thus we must speak and think, to the end that God may have the glory of his grace in whatsoever good is done or offered.

When Abigail met David, and diverted him from his bloody intention to kill Nabal, and gave him counsel another way, 'O blessed be God, and blessed be thou, and blessed be thy counsel,' 1 Sam. xxv. 32–34. So when opportunities are offered to do good, and to hinder us from evil intentions, 'O blessed be thou, and blessed be thy counsel.' When a benefit is done, if it be a benefit of this life, take it as a grace coming freely from God. So a poor man, his alms is a grace. 'Thanks be unto God for this unspeakable gift,' saith St Paul, 2 Cor. ix. 15. It is grace in him that hath it, that God should respect him so much as to relieve him. It is grace in the party that gives it, that he hath a heart enlarged to do it. So when anything outward or spiritual is done that is good, look on it as a grace, put that respect on it, and that will make you holy-minded to give God his own.

Our life should be a praising and blessing of God. We should begin the employment of heaven while we are on earth. How should we do that? 'In all things give thanks,' Eph. v. 20. Every good thing from God, take it as a grace, as a largess; not as due, not as coming by chance, but as a grace. And this will make us improve it as a grace for the best. It will make us to give God the glory, and improve it to our own good, when we are thankful for grace, that we may have cause to account it a grace. Our hearts would not be so full of atheism, and our tongues so full of blasphemies, if we had learned this lesson; our lives would be a praising of God.

And that we may not want matter to feed a thankful spirit, alway consider, what good things we have are of grace. We deserve not so much as a crumb of bread; therefore we pray, 'Give us this day our daily bread,' Mat. vi. 11. Everything is a grace, especially the things of a better life.

How shall I know that the minister is a grace, or a good speech from a minister to be a grace, as St Paul saith here, I intended you a 'second grace,' that is, to speak gracious things to you?

I shall know it, if by that gracious means, by those gracious speeches, God distil into me a spirit to improve them to gracious purposes. As indeed, God turns all to a gracious end to his children: he gives them a principle of grace to work good out of everything; they see grace in everything: in affliction they see the love of God. In the worst things, grace will pick out somewhat, and make use of it. As God by his providence intends all to good, so his Spirit, by a provident eye to the word, works good out of everything. But those that have not grace, they are not grace to them, but tend to their further hardening.

To end this point; when you come to the communion, come to it as a grace. It is the grace of God that he hath ordained us to salvation. It is the grace of God that he hath sent his word. It is the grace of God that he hath sent his sacrament to seal that word, and all little enough. He knows us better than we know ourselves. He knows we have need of all, to confirm and help us, the word and the sacraments, even to the end of our days. As the apostle saith, Eph. ii. 22, 'To build us up.' The means of grace are not only necessary for the planting, but for the building up of the church. And therefore come with this purpose, to have grace confirmed, and receive it as a grace of God with thankfulness, that God will condescend to our infirmity, to give us helps, to support our weak faith. It is a true proverb, grace begets grace. It begets thankfulness, where it is apprehended as a grace. Therefore come with a thankful disposition to the sacrament; embrace every ordinance of God with thankfulness. Alas! do not thousands 'sit in darkness, and in the shadow of death?' They do; and therefore those that find the benefit of God's ordinances, they are disposed by the same Spirit that works any good in them, to return thankfulness to God again.

'That you might have a second grace.' Saint Paul's purpose was to come to them, to bestow 'a grace,' not to take from them; to bestow good and gracious speeches on them, which he knew the Spirit of God would make effectual to work some good in them.

Obs. A gracious man is a vessel of grace, and he should take all occasions to vent that which is good.

When St Paul saith, he intended to bestow a second grace, his meaning is, that he would utter things that were gracious, that the Spirit of God should seal to the souls of them that heard him, and make them effectual.

Therefore every Christian should have this disposition. St Paul did it as a holy man, as well as a minister. Do we think ourselves vessels of grace, as the Scripture calls the elect, children of God, or no? Yes! God forbid else. Now God's children, God hath appointed some to be vessels of gold, some of silver, as the apostle saith to Timothy, some for this use, and some for that: all for good use, 2 Tim. ii. 20. A vessel is to be filled with something, and to be used for something; therefore set abroach* some good thing when you have the advantage of it, when you are called to it; not unnecessarily to thrust forward yourselves. Let the desire of your hearts be to do good upon all occasions. A vessel of grace must not be an empty vessel. A Christian he is a member of Christ, and he hath a part in the communion of saints, and he hath gifts for that end. There is no Christian, but he can comfort, or instruct, or dissuade from ill when it is moved. There is no Christian, but he is furnished as a member ought to

* That is, 'cause to flow.'—G.

be, in some competent measure. There is no man that hath benefit by the communion of saints, but he hath grace to fit him for that blessed communion. He is fitted to comfort, upon occasion; and he hath some grace, some knowledge to correct. He that hath not is a dead member, not fit for that communion. Therefore we should bestow grace where we come; and not leave an ill scent behind us, to infect others with filthy speeches, and blasphemous oaths, to open the rottenness of our own hearts in their presence, and so be conscious of that which is ill in them, because we strengthen it by our example, and by our words. St Paul was a good man. 'I come to bestow a second grace,' that is, to speak that which is gracious, that God's gracious providence shall direct to do you special good. For God's word is inspired by the Spirit; and the same Spirit that breathed the word of God into the penmen of it, the same Spirit is with the word in the uttering of it. When it is done by a gracious heart, to a gracious man, it works graciously, it hath a blessed operation with it.

Therefore we should upon all good occasions speak gracious things. Divine truths, they will have a wondrous efficacy. If men would set on it, and be more fruitful in this kind, they should have occasion to bless God. But, alas! the life of a Christian is little known in the world. We have but naked, shallow conceits of the glory of heaven, and of the state of a Christian, and how he lives in this world; and that makes men live such stained, such base lives, that will not stand with comfort in this world, or glory in the world to come. But a Christian should be such a one as frames his disposition to do good wheresoever he comes; and he hath ability if he be a sound Christian. How graciously did God bless Abigail's word to David? yet she was a mean woman. How dost thou know, but that by uttering gracious words in company, in season (as discretion must guide all our actions, all our words), how dost thou know but that thou mayest divert another man from sin, by a word in season?

I beseech you carry this disposition about you, as you desire to be thought vessels of grace here, and of glory hereafter, to be thought vessels of gold and silver, for the use of God, labour to be employed by the Spirit of God to good purposes, that you may leave a good savour where you come; that others that are acquainted with you in the 'time of their visitation,' 1 Pet. ii. 12, they may bless God, that ever they were acquainted with such a friend. Blessed be God that I knew him. As it will be our joy at that day, so it will be one another's joy here; for God blesseth the exhortations and comforts of friends one to another, as well as the ministerial ofttimes. So I come to the 16th verse, how he meant to come to them to Corinth. Saith he, 'I was minded to come to you.'

VERSE 16.

'*And to pass by you into Macedonia, and to come again out of Macedonia unto you, and of you to be brought on my way to Judea.*' See what a circuit the blessed apostle fetched. Indeed, he was industrious after his conversion. He made amends for his harsh* conversion by his speedy labours. For he spread the gospel like lightning, through all the world almost. His course was like the course of the sun; he went every where spreading the gospel. We see his circuit here, 'to pass by you into Macedonia, and to come again from Macedonia to you, and by you to be brought on my way to Judea.'

* Qu. 'hard?' = long delayed.—G.

There is little to be observed here. Because it is a passage to other things, and circumstantial, I will not dwell on it. Only this by the way: we see here, that

Obs. It is a commendable custom among the people of God to bring one another on their way, by way of honour and respect.

Partly it was for his security and safety; but especially for the honour of his person. And they knew that it would not be a barren courtesy; for they knew that he was a man of a blessed spirit, so thankful, that he would deceive* all the tediousness of the journey by his heavenly discourse. And he intended their good as well as his own. You may see, therefore, religion establisheth courtesy. Saith the apostle to the Philippians, chap. iv. 8, 'Whatsoever things are of good report, whatsoever things are lovely (he goes over many instances), think of these things.' The same command of God that urgeth, and presseth love, it commands all the expressions of love, and all the means to kindle love.

Now this, their carrying of him, and going on the way with him, which was for honour and respect of so excellent a person, that he deserved so well of them, it was an expression of their love, and a means to preserve it. I shall not need to prove it, it is taken for granted. Those compliments that express and maintain love, they are good, when the outward expression and the inward affection go together.

I speak this by the way, to shew that religion doth not countenance incivility. Therefore those that affect unnecessary sternness, and unnecessary retiredness, it is not out of religion. Religion stablisheth whatsoever is good, 'whatsoever is of good report,' whatsoever may maintain love. So much as a man is defective in this, he is defective in religion; unless his affections and intentions at that time be deeply taken up by serious things. For then lesser things must give way to the greater, or else there is no excuse. For religion is a thing of a large extent, even duties of civility and courtesy, and whatsoever may express and maintain love, is established by religion. We see in Gen. xviii. 16, when Abraham entertained the angels, he led them on their way. And so in Acts xx. 4, 36, *seq.*, 'The company sent them on their way.' And we see in Scripture many common courtesies.

But I do but touch it by the way: because this whole verse is but a passage to another thing. Therefore I come to the seventeenth verse.

VERSE 17.

'*When I therefore was thus minded (to come unto you), did I use lightness? or the things that I purpose, do I purpose according to the flesh, that with me there should be yea, yea, and nay, nay?*' The apostle still goes on to prevent scandal.† 'Woe to the world because of offences,' Mat. xviii. 7, saith our blessed Saviour, especially offences taken. Because our nature is so corrupt, that it is subject to take offence where none is given, it will pick quarrels enough to go to hell. Proud men that have only nature in them, they will not be damned without reason. Tush! I had been good, say they, but for such and such. Now St Paul was a man much exercised with the cross. He wipes away scandal from that, as we heard in the first part of the chapter. He saith, 'As his crosses' for Christ abounded, so his comforts in Christ abounded. He lost nothing by it.

* That is, = 'make them be inobservant of.'—G.

† That is, 'offence.'—G.

Again, they took offence that he promised to come to them, and did not; especially some that were not well-willers to him: therefore he labours to satisfy that.

And *first*, that he might the better satisfy them that he was no inconstant man, no unsettled man, he premiseth a description of his own disposition and course of life, he appeals to his own conscience, 'This is our rejoicing, the testimony of our conscience,' &c.

And *then he appeals to their conscience.* A manifest note of a man confident, that dares appeal to his own conscience, and to the conscience of another. Obnoxious men are always afraid, not only of their own conscience, lest it should tell them that which they would be loath to hear, but they are afraid of the consciences of others likewise. St Paul appeals to their conscience, 'I write no other things than what you read and acknowledge,' &c.

And so he comes more directly to satisfy their suspicion of him for his not coming to them. In this verse he labours to remove their false imputation, 'When I was thus minded to come unto you, did I use lightness?

Wherein you have St Paul's purgation of himself. Here is a prevention of an objection of suspicion, that the flesh will move in them that have doubtful suspicious minds. Why! if you intended to come, why did you not? Saith he, 'When I was thus minded, did I use lightness?' First, Observe hence in general, that

Obs. Men are wondrous prone to jealousy and suspicion.

It is the state of God's children here in this world to have suspicions raised of them. They are obnoxious to slanders and imputations, and they are forced to their apologies. Men are prone to suspicion, yea, and good men too: as here, they took his not coming in the worst part, by the wrong handle.

That is suspicion, when there are two handles of a thing, two apprehensions of a thing, and there is a proneness in the mind to the worst part; to take things in an ill sense. They might have construed it many ways better than thus; but they thought the worst of him: he is light in his promises; he will say, and unsay again: he is off and on. This is in natural men, yea, in Christians: as far as they have old Adam in them, they are prone to suspicion.

Whence is this?

1. Partly out *of the poison and malice of man's nature in many*, esteeming others by themselves; for the worst natures are alway most suspicious, out of a privity of their own indisposition in themselves. Usually those that deserve worst are most jealous, because there is most cause. Conscience of a man's own imperfections and weakness makes him think others to be as he himself is.

2. And again, *there is envy in man's nature toward excellent persons especially.* The malice of man's nature cannot abide eminency in others. The false teachers among the Corinthians they saw that Paul stood in their light, therefore they labour to eclipse and obscure him all they could. Hence it is, that men are willing to entertain willingly any suspicion. For not being willing out of baseness to rise to their greatness and excellency, they labour to bring them down by their suspicion to their baseness and meanness, that all may be ill alike. Therefore baseness is subject to suspicion, and the fruit of suspicion, that is, slander; to take every thing in suspicion, and to utter it in words; because they would have men of eminency brought down to their meanness; and if they cannot do it indeed,

they will bring them by reports as low as they can, that they speak, and unspeak, and are inconstant as other men. There are many causes of this; and therefore St Paul seeing the baseness of it, he stands the more upon it.

Quest. How shall we arm ourselves against this suspicion, and the fruit of it? How shall we carry ourselves against this disposition of men among whom we live?

Ans. I answer briefly, first, *labour for innocency*, that if they will speak maliciously, yet they may speak falsely. Saith St Ambrose, '*Et nobis malus*,' &c. (*fff*). Our care must be that no man speak ill of us without a lie. Let us live so that no man may believe them; labour for innocency therefore. But that will not do.

2. Therefore *patience* in the next place. For innocency could not fence Christ himself, who was innocency clothed with our flesh. If innocency will not prevail to make men hold their tongue from speaking their suspicious minds, then labour for patience.

3. But that will not do neither, but men go on still; then *prayer*. That was David's course: that God would defend our innocency, and take our cause into his hands, and bring forth our innocency as the light, to judge for us.

4. And when nothing else will serve the turn, neither innocency nor patience, &c., then *just apology and defence*, as we see the apostle doth here defend himself. For it is not for public persons to dissemble* slanders; and especially for them not to suffer ill suspicions to rest in the hearts of those that are under them. Therefore the apostle is enforced through Christian prudence to his apology, to wipe away the imputation. 'When I was thus minded, did I use lightness?' saith he. This I observe in general.

Quest. Now, because suspicion is a doubtful thing, it is either good or evil, how shall we know when suspicion is naught and evil?

Ans. 1. First of all, *when it is out of misconstruction*. When it is from weak grounds, or doubtful grounds, then it is ill for the ground.

2. Or it is ill likewise *when it ill affects, and sways, and disposeth the mind;* if it dispose the affections to malice, to the suppression of love; if it discover itself to come to slander. As here in this place, they thought presently it was lightness in him. Here was a misconstruction, here was a false ground. What did this incline them to do? From inconstancy presently they fly to his disposition, from suspicion to slander his disposition. They enter into God's throne: his purposes and projects, certainly they were naught. Carnal, proud man will enter into God's throne, and judge a man's thoughts, and purposes, and intentions. Then a man may know his suspicion is not right when it enters too deep, when it riseth from false grounds, from suspicious grounds, and brings men from actions, to go to the disposition. 'Did I use lightness? or the things that I purpose, do I purpose according to the flesh?' that is, carnally, as they thought: this entered to his disposition.

3. Then again, *when it stirs us up to speak in slander, when we speak without cause or ground*. Then when it inclines a man from an error in one thing, to go to the habitual disposition in all things. As here now, because in one thing the apostle was inconstant, and did not come to them, they went to his habitual disposition in all things. Nay, you may see what he is, you see what we are like to have from him in other things, he doth but

* That is, = 'conceal.'—G.

purpose things according to the flesh; he hath his own aims, I warrant you. So when from one thing we presently judge that he purposeth other things according to the flesh, that is a bad suspicion: when a man goes from one thing to the habitual disposition.

'*When I was thus minded, did I use lightness?*' The more to convince them of their suspicion and hard surmises, he cites them, and propounds as it were interrogatories to them. I pray answer me, saith he, 'When I was thus minded, did I use lightness,' as you imagine? 'or the things that I purpose, do I purpose according to the flesh?' &c. After he had cleared his purpose before, and cleared his conscience, now he comes to propound it to their conscience; because he would have them to think, that if he were such a man as he shewed himself before, that he had a good conscience in all things, and a good affection to them, that they should not have had a misconstruction of that particular failing, that he came not to them when he purposed; for particular actions must be construed according to a man's habitual carriage and affection. You see how I have laboured in all things to have a good conscience; and for you, you acknowledge that I purposed to come to you; therefore you should construe my actions according to that intention. Now, having cleared my disposition and intention to you, you see your error in misconstruing my not coming to you. So he comes to it in good season, after he had freed himself to them.

'When I was thus minded, did I use lightness?' &c. These things he declines:

1. *Lightness or inconstancy.*
2. *Purposing or deliberating according to the flesh.*
3. And then *inconstancy in his speeches*, that they should be 'Yea, yea, Nay nay.

The point that I observe from the first concerning lightness is, that

Doct. Every Christian, especially ministers and public men, should labour by all means to avoid the just imputation of lightness and inconstancy.

The imputation of lightness is especially to be avoided of those that are in place. Lightness and inconstancy! what is that? When a man hath not pitched his resolutions and purposes to one thing, when a man doth not stand in his purposes.

Now, a man must avoid imputations of lightness, especially persons of quality.

Why?

Reason. Not to speak all that might be said in the point, especially for this end, *to preserve authority*. Authority is that that furnisheth a man in place, in magistracy or ministry, wondrously to prevail, to do good. I take not authority here for that which the king puts on them, or the chief magistrate; but authority is that high respect that the people have of the eminency of their parts and honesty, an impression of somewhat more than ordinary in them. This is that authority, a beam of excellency that God doth infuse, for the strengthening and fortifying of his own ordinance. What reason is there else that a thousand should be subject to one man, but that God doth put a majesty upon his own ordinance, and upon the persons in it? And this respect to it must be maintained by a uniform, constant carriage. Now, when people shall see that they are, as in their place, so in their disposition, great, and serious, and weighty, and firm in their resolutions; that they may build on them, and know where to have them as we say, it breeds authority, and maintains authority. For then what they say is regarded. And how their affections stand: if it be love, it is much sought after; if displeasure, it is much feared. For they are men of a fixed disposition, it gains wondrous respect.

Let men be never so great, if they be such as St Paul here declines from himself, that they use lightness, they lose their authority. Authority is the special help that governors have to rule, and that ministers have to prevail. Now, nothing weakens esteem and authority more than when men are tossed between the waves of contrary affections; when men are such as we know not where to have them; as we say, off and on, fast and loose, one while sitting, another standing: no man will build on them, or much regard their love or hatred.

Now you know authority is a beam of majesty, and God hath put it upon magistrates above others; and imprinted likewise the respect of it in the people's hearts, to maintain the world. 'The pillars of the earth will shake else,' as the psalmist saith, Ps. lxxv. 3. What would become of the pillars of government, if it were not for authority in them that are above, and respect of that authority, an impression of it in them that are under.

Now there are many grounds of authority, as success, when God blesseth them with it wonderfully to admiration, and good parts, &c.; but one main ground of authority is constancy and firmness. This raiseth a high respect in the hearts of the people.

I will not multiply reasons why those that are in place should avoid the imputation of lightness. Ministers especially should take heed of it, because they are ministers of God's truth; and if they take not heed of it, people will be ready to go from their moral civil carriage to their doctrine, and think there is an uncertainty in that they speak, because they do not regard what they say.

But let me add this by the way, *Mater erroris similitudo*, Likeness is the mother of error. So there is somewhat like constancy in governors, and others, when they are nothing less, but merely refractory and obstinate; to maintain the reputation of constancy, they will run into the fault of wilfulness. Such as are subject that way, had need of strong wits to rule their strong wills, to guide them, or else woe be to those that have to deal with them. That I thought good to add, lest we mistake.

We should all labour to avoid inconstancy and lightness in our resolutions, in our purposes, and affections.

If we ought to avoid it, how shall we come to know it? What is the ground of lightness? The grounds are many.

1. Sometimes *from the temper of the body*. Some are of a moveable temper, of a moveable, quick spirit, that they cannot out of their constitution fix long, except they set weights upon nature. I am by disposition thus; but my resolution shall be otherwise: as where grace and wisdom is, it will fix the temper, and fix the resolution, and the thoughts. This I could not do, if I should yield to my own disposition; but this I will do, and I should do. There are many resolutions, as in the younger sort, and some out of their very temper are more fixed and resolved.

2. But now consider it as it is in religion, lightness comes out of the disposition of the mind.

(1.) *Inconsideration ofttimes is the ground*, when we do not see the circumstances of a thing that we promise or purpose. You know there is nothing comes to action, but it is beset with circumstances. There are advantages of it, and there are stops and hindrances of it: somewhat may fall out. Everything that comes to action is besieged with circumstances. Circumstances, you know, have their name of standing about a business, about a thing. Now when the things that are about, the impediments, and the hindrances, and lets are not weighed, a rash man sees not the things, he considers not the things that he enters upon; he resolves without considering the circumstances that beset the thing; he never considers what oppositions he may meet with, or what advantages there be which perhaps he neglects; but he thinks of the thing, it is good, and suitable to his purpose; he resolves, and never considers the circumstances about a thing, but runs on in confidence of his own wit and parts, and thinks to rule all by the strength of his wit, not foreseeing, not casting in his mind, to prevent beforehand what may fall out. It is just with God to shame such men. Frustration of their purposes, it is a just reward of their folly. Therefore we should take heed of inconsideration, and have our eyes in our heads, to set the soul to foresee what possibility there is of the business, and what may fall out. This is the right way, if we would avoid imputation of lightness.

(2.) Again, another ground of lightness, and of that decay in authority and respect that comes from it, *is the passion of men.* Therefore they are light. They are carried with the hurry and wind of their passion. And Satan joins with passion. A passionate man is subject to Satan more than a man that is led by reason, or with grace. For that is a beam of God. Even reason itself, judgment, it is an excellent thing, and it prevents many temptations.

Give not way to passion, for those are unreasonable things. As we see Saul in his passion, Satan, the evil spirit, mingled with his passion of anger. So let men be in any passion, over joy, or be over angry; let them give the reins to unruly passion, and they give advantage to Satan, that we cannot settle our souls in any good resolution.

(3.) Again, *in the things themselves there is cause of lightness and inconstancy, from the nature of things;* and then it is not so great a fault to change. Then it is not properly inconstancy. But it is inconstancy when the things are mutable and variable, and we do not think of it as we should.

Now the things of this life are variable and uncertain; the event of things in this life is wondrous variable. Grace and glory, they are certain things, and the way that God directs us to heaven, they are certain promises, and certain grounds; but the things of this life are subject to much change. God takes a great deal of liberty in altering things in this world, they fall out divers ways.

(4.) But now therefore we must take heed that we take not inconstancy for that which is not. Every change of opinion and purpose is not lightness. It is not inconstancy for a man to change his mind and purpose, when it is from the things. Men are men, and the things that we deal with in the world are subject to variety and inconstancy; and for a man to alter according to the variety of things, it argues no inconstancy, if the aim be good.

As for example, a mariner, a seaman, he is not inconstant, when one time he strikes sail, and another time he hoisteth up sail. When he makes indentures,* and goes with a side wind, he goes on his way, and his aim is still to come to the haven. He is not inconstant, because he changeth not

* That is = circuits.—G.

his star. He alway aims at the right star, and to his compass and card that he sails by. He varies not from his rule. He varies from the things, because the winds and the seas vary, because he deals with variable objects. The things vary, but he doth not vary. He comes to his project, to the haven, and hath his direction from the North Pole, &c.

So the husbandman, sometimes he sows, sometimes he harrows, sometimes he reaps. Is he inconstant and varies? No! the matter about which he is varies. So in governors, sometimes they do this, and sometimes that. They are about variable matters, yet here is no variableness nor lightness of disposition, because they deal with mutable, with variable objects.

So God in managing his church's affairs, in his dispensation in that point; you see he used one dispensation before Christ, and another since Christ. God changeth not, but the times are changed. In the infancy of the church one dispensation was requisite, and now another. Therefore it is not inconstancy for a man to change on good ground, or when the things themselves change.

Therefore this should have made them thought well of St Paul. His affection was not changed to them, but the business was changed, as we shall see after. Other things let* him. So a good man, his honest resolution should not change. His aim to serve God and his country, and to deserve well of mankind, this should be constant; but the manner how, the circumstance of time and place, and ordering of these things, they are variable. They do not change, but maintain their constancy and resolution, in the variety of occasions that fall out; for we cannot frame our life otherwise than it is, to be unvariable. When a man is guided by a certain principle, though the things of this life be uncertain, and he vary sometimes according to his principle, and aim, and end, yet it is no inconstancy. And it will excuse a man's conscience exceedingly, when his aim is good, and the rules and principles he goes by are good and honest, if things fall out otherwise than he aims at, though there be a change of his course, because his heart tells him his rules and his purposes were good.

3. One other main cause of lightness and sinful inconstancy, *it is irreligion;* casting ourselves upon future things, without a dependence on divine providence. An atheistical independence, when we project things to come, and never call upon God to assist us, and never have divine reservations as we should have, but boast, This I will do; and sometimes negatively, This I will not do, I have time enough to do it; as if we had future times at our command. St James excellently taxeth such people, James iv. 13, 'Go to now, you that say, To-day and to-morrow we will go to such a city, and buy, and sell, and get gain.' 'Go to now:' see here how he shames them by a kind of ironical permission. 'Go to now.' You will do great matters! 'whereas,' saith he, 'you know not what shall be to-morrow.' God that hath given us the time present to repent in, and to do good, the time to come he hath reserved in his own power. We know not what shall be to-morrow. Where he shews the ground of this atheism, and rushing upon business without dependence; they forget the condition of this life, that it is a vapour. 'What is your life? it is even a vapour that appeareth for a little while, and then vanisheth away.' Your life is inconstant. God is the Lord of your purposes. He is the Lord of your life, and of all opportunities and circumstances. 'Your life is but a vapour.' Here all things fall under his providence and guidance. You consider not this, and there-

* That is, 'hindered.'—G.

fore you project so for the time to come. 'What is your life? it is even a vapour,' &c.

Then he comes to direct them how they should entertain resolutions for the time to come, 'Ye ought to say, If the Lord will;' or if we live, we will do this and that. 'If the Lord will,' in whose power are our intentions, and resolutions, and affections. He guides the inward man, and all the things in the world, to the falling of a hair from our head, to the falling of a sparrow to the ground, even the least things, Luke xii. 7. You should say thus.

And he calls it 'vain boasting.' What makes God confound insolent attempts? as indeed he triumphs over insolent attempts of kings and captains, or whatsoever, that set up great business in high conceits, they will do this and that. Saith St James, 'You rejoice in your boasting,' James iv. 16. They boast they will do this and that. That makes God confound them so, because they will be gods to themselves. Man is a dependent creature. Everything is God's, and we are dependent. 'In him we live, and move, and have our being,' Acts xvii. 28.

Man being a dependent creature, yet he resolves to do this and that, as if he had the guidance of his own thoughts and purposes. This provokes God to jealousy, when he makes himself a god, and sets not God before him in his actions. He sets upon things without dependence, without prayer, or reservation, if God permit this. Because God rejoiceth to confound these bold attempts, therefore they never thrive in such attempts.

Therefore a true Christian joins modesty for the time to come. He will attempt nothing but what he may expect to have God's protection in. He that thinks God may cross him will do nothing ill that he fears God will cross him in; he will be modest. The best Christians are the modestest. They consider the uncertainty of the things of this life, and the weakness of man in foreseeing things. They see a dependence of all things on the majesty of God, even to the least things; that he guides things that are most casual; and that 'he rules even the hearts of princes,' as Solomon saith, 'as the rivers of water,' Prov. xxi. 1. They are guided by him; they are in his hand. Hereupon a wise Christian becomes modest for the time to come in his resolutions: he undertakes all with a holy dependence on God, if God will, and if God permit. He will undertake nothing for the time to come, but with warrant, that he may without tempting of God look for his assistance. For to go to God to bless us in ill projects, is to make God the patron of that which is bad, which is contrary to his nature. Therefore he learns to depend upon God for the time to come, and will entertain or enter upon no business but such as he may safely, without tempting of God, depend upon him for his assistance. This is the disposition of a modest Christian.

You see in Ps. ii. how the Psalmist there insults over those that threaten to do this and that. 'Why do the heathen rage, and the people imagine a vain thing, &c., against the Lord, and against his Anointed?' As if they would swallow up the church, and Christ the anointed: why do they do this and that? God that sits in heaven, he laughs them to scorn. You see the grounds of lightness, so far forth as is needful. I will name no more.

The way to prevent it may be in observing these grounds of constancy, especially this:—

1. *Stablish your thoughts with counsel for the time to come*; consult, go not rashly and headlong about matters. It is not with our common life

as with those that run in a race; for their swiftness gets all. But in matters of government in commonwealth, there the most staid get all; those that weigh things, and then execute upon mature deliberation; that ripen things first, and go not rawly, and indeliberately about it. This every man takes for granted, but it is not thought on.

2. Then again, *labour to suppress passion in anything that comes from us.* Speak nothing in passion; for one of these things will follow. If we execute it, we are in danger for the things in passion, and inconsiderately spoken; if not, we shall have the shame of being frustrate. We undergo the shame of lightness, that we speak that in our passion and heat that we retract after. One of these inconveniences will follow: either you will do it, and then it will be dangerous; or you will not do it, and then you will be ashamed, a fit reward of rashness.

God gives us passions to be guided and ruled, and not to rule us. They are good servants and only servants, that should be raised up, and stirred up, only when reason and judgment raiseth them, and not otherwise. But to go on.

3. Another cure of this rashness *is holy dependence on God by prayer, and by faith, to commit our ways to him, our thoughts to him for the time to come.* Leave all to him, entertain nothing wherein we cannot expect his gracious assistance. The best Christian is the most dependent Christian. That is the first thing the apostle declines.

What is the second thing?

'*Or the things that I purpose, do I purpose according to the flesh?*' They thought he was a politician; as this is the lot of God's children sometimes. If so be that God hath given them parts, either of nature or breeding, carnal, devilish men that are led altogether by plots themselves, esteem them by themselves. 'The things that I purpose, do I purpose according to the flesh?' He propounds this interrogatory to their conscience, not idly; but he knew that they had a prejudice in them, by his co-rivals, false apostles. There he labours to wipe away that imputation likewise, that he did not purpose and consult of things according to the flesh.

What is flesh here?

'Flesh' is the unregenerate part of man, whereof fleshly wisdom is the chief; for that guides the 'old man,' that is the eye of old Adam. Carnal wisdom, it is the flesh's counsellor in all things; therefore especially he means that.

But why is it called flesh?

For many reasons. Among many this is one, that the soul, so far as it is sinful, it is led with things that are fleshly, that are outward; and thereupon a man is called flesh. And the soul itself is called flesh, because it cleaves in its affections and desires to earthly things; and because the poor understanding now, which ruled all, and should rule all, is become an underling to the carnal will and carnal lusts. Therefore itself is called flesh likewise, 'The wisdom of the flesh is enmity with God.' For now it is swayed even which way carnal fancy, and opinion, and the flesh, lead it.

The reason is, it is betwixt God and heavenly things, and betwixt earthly things. And if it were in its right original as it came out of God's hands, being a Spirit, it should be led by God, and by God's Spirit, and God's truth, by better things than itself (as every infirm thing is guided by that which is better than itself; as brute creatures are guided by men, and weaker persons by magistrates, that are, or should be, better); but now since the fall, without grace renew a man, the understanding part of man's soul, instead of lighting its candle from heaven, it often lights it from hell, and is ruled by Satan himself, and takes advices even from things meaner than itself, and plots, and projects altogether for things worse than itself. It was not given for that end, God knows that gave it, this soul of ours, to prowl for earthly things; for the ease, and honour, and profits, and pleasures of the world. That excellent jewel that all the world is not worth, it was not given for that end. No! it was given to attain a higher end than this world, to attain communion with God. But now since the fall it is thus with it, that it is a slave. Carnal wit is a slave to carnal will, and that carnal will is drawn by carnal affections. Affections draw the will, and the will draws the wit, and makes it plot and devise for that which it stands for; for carnal lusts and affections which whet the wit that way. Therefore the whole soul is called flesh, even reason itself.

And hereupon wicked men are called 'the world.' Why the world? Because they are led with the things of the world, with the guise and fashion of the world.

A man, in the language of the Scripture, is termed by that which he cleaves to; therefore if the heart and soul cleave to the flesh, and the things of the flesh, it is flesh; if it be led with the world, and the things of the world, it is called the world. Wicked men are the world, because the best thing in them is the love of worldly things, and their wit is for worldly things. All the inward parts of their soul are spent upon worldly things; therefore they are called flesh, and the world. And sometimes 'Satan' himself. A man, as far as he is carnal, is called Satan, yea, good men; 'Go after me, Satan,' saith Christ to Peter, Mat. xvi. 23.

A man as far as he yields to anything, he is named from that which he yields to. When fleshly things rule a man, he is called 'flesh;' when worldly things rule him, profits and pleasures, a man is the 'world;' when a man yields to Satan, he is 'Satan.'

Use. This should make us *take heed by whom we are led*, under whose government we come. Saith St Paul, 'Do I purpose according to the flesh?' That is, according to the profits, and pleasures, and honours which the flesh looks after. Are those my advisers, my intelligencers, my counsellors in the things I take in hand? what may make for my honour, my pleasure, my estate, my worldly ease here? No! saith he, 'I purpose not according to the flesh.' The rule from hence is this, that,

Obs. A Christian man ought by all means to avoid the imputation of carnal policy.

Every Christian, much more a Christian man in authority and place, a minister, or magistrate, ought by all means to avoid it? St Paul here declines it, 'Did I purpose things according to the flesh?' Was I politic? I had just occasion to speak largely of it in the former verse concerning fleshly wisdom, therefore I will speak the less of it now. We ought by all means to decline the imputation of it, and much more the conscience of it, than the report of it; to be holily wise, and to be accounted so too.

Reason. The reason is, *it is God's enemy, and our enemy.* Should a Christian consult and deliberate with his enemy? to take his enemy to be his judge, and his friend, and counsellor? A man that hath his enemy to guide him to a place, that hath a pirate to guide him in a ship, how can he come to good? He that is led by the flesh he consults with his enemy, when he looks what is for his profit, or his pleasure, &c. These things we should renounce as we promised in baptism, when we gave our names to

Christ. If we live and deliberate 'according to the flesh, we shall die,' saith the apostle peremptorily. It is a dangerous enemy; death is the issue of all the counsel of the flesh, Rom. viii. 2, *seq.*

Again, it is *a secret enemy, a domestic enemy.* It is in all the powers of the soul. We cannot be too jealous against it. It is a perpetual enemy that accompanies us continually, in all our consultations, in all places; in prosperity, in adversity. It hinders us from all good, it keeps us from the reformation of anything that is ill.

If a magistrate be suggested by any other, or by a good motion of his own, do this, reform this, Oh! I shall run myself into danger, I shall incur censure! So ill is done, and is unreformed, only by consulting with the flesh; and good is neglected,—I shall be accounted an hypocrite, if I do this.

So there is flesh and blood to hinder in every good thing. The flesh will be foisting bad ends, or bad moving causes, and the flesh will be ready to keep us from reforming ill from fear of danger. And if we do ill, and be in ill, it will be ready to keep us in ill. Oh! it is time enough to repent, &c. A thousand such policies the flesh hath to keep us in ill till we be in hell itself. Who would be advised, and take counsel by such an enemy?

Use. Therefore, let us take heed. We have it in us, *but let it live in us only, and not rule in us.* Although it will be in us as long as we live, yet let us not be ruled by it; let us not admit it to counsel, but suppress it, and keep it under. Especially those that are magistrates, that are called to public business, let them not bring private respects to public business, but bring public hearts to intend the good of religion, and of their country, before any private interest whatsoever. And not consult according to the flesh: If I do this, I shall displease such and such. That is no matter. If it were not for religion, if a man have a public mind, such as the very heathens had, he would lay aside base respects in public business. Therefore, I humbly desire such to examine deeply their intentions and purposes, what they aim at; whether to serve God, and the church, and their country, or to serve themselves; that if so be they may be safe, they care not what befall their country, or religion, or whatsoever. That is it that moves God to indignation, to cross their intentions; for when God sees they set earth above heaven, the world present before the world to come; and the dirt of the world, base respects before those that are greater, that they invert the order of things, he crosseth them in that they aim at, because they cross him in neglecting their duty. Therefore, as we would have things succeed well, let us labour to consult, not according to the flesh, for our private advantage; but for what may make most first for religion, and then for the public good.

Again, we may learn from hence, that

Obs. A ground of lightness is to purpose things according to the flesh.

To purpose according to carnal reason, and affection, it is a ground of lightness. For mark the reason of it, when a man is carried in his deliberations by carnal respects, this will be for my profit, this will incline such a man to me, by this I shall get such a place, &c., when he is led by low and base respects, it makes him light with God, though he be never so good otherwise. Because carnal respects build on outward things that are uncertain; therefore all resolutions built on outward things, and carnal respects, are uncertain. He that takes fleshly wisdom for his counsellor, and adviser, and intelligencer, what doth he? He is led with by-respects, with one of the three idols of the world, some honour, or pleasure, or base profit, now when the rule of deliberation is the flesh, and the flesh carries to outward things that are variable. A man is alway light and inconstant, that propounds the deliberation of things according to the flesh.

What is the reason that a wicked man (though he be not notoriously, outwardly wicked; but a shrewd man, that is for himself, that makes himself the end of all his projects), what is the reason that such a man can never be a sound friend? He is never a sound friend; he is only a friend, so long as it makes for himself; so long as he gets to his own in all things. As the Jesuits use to say, so it is true of every natural man, they do all they do, and consult in an order to spiritual things; they do this, and that, and overrule kings and states, and this is for the good of society, and in an order of spiritual things. A man that hath not grace in him above nature, and above respects of nature, he can never be a sound friend; for when fleshly advantages come, of pleasures, and profits, and honours, when these rise one way or other, there he leaves the bonds of friendship; because there is a nearer bond between him and the things of this life; he is led with the flesh, and deliberates according to the flesh.

And that is the reason likewise why such a man can never be a good Christian. He can never go through the variety of times. Why? Because he consults of things according to the flesh, and as long as religion stands with his aims, that he may enjoy his riches, and his greatness, and the contentments of this life with religion, so long he is content to be religious; if religion cross him in these, he hath not learned to deny himself, and therefore he is not constant.

Or if times do not fall out so cross, he is not constant in his disposition; and God looks on him as he is in his disposition, and so he will judge him at that day. Now being led with the flesh, his disposition alters, and varies.

How shall I know whether I consult according to the flesh or no?

In a word, examine two things: (1.) the ground, and (2.) the aim of our actions, whence they rise, and what they aim at. Spring they from self-love? Aim they at our self-contentment and private interest? Then a man is led with the flesh.

To use a familiar instance. In marriage, when a man looks more to wealth than to religion, he adviseth according to the flesh. And so for a minister to respect his living more than anything that might weigh with his conscience otherwise, if he were good; he is led with respects according to the flesh. Those that leave their former good acquaintance, and choose such as they only hope to gain by, and forsake those acquaintance that they cannot gain by, though they be never so good otherwise, they are led according to the flesh.

How shall we know that we do not things, and consult not of things according to the flesh?

1. Some men may know it easily; as when men are of pregnant parts, when the strength of their wit leads them one way, *and religion leads them another way*, yet in the awe of God they do not go that way that politic respects would carry them. They could be as errant politicians as the best, but they dare not. Here now is a man that is 'led by the Spirit,' when it is not for want of parts, but out of conscience, he doth not so miscarry by his enemy. Many times an honest man could be rich by ill means as well as another. He knows the way. It is not for want of wit, but because he dares not. The awe of conscience and the awe of God lead him to better rules and aims. So it is easily discerned in eminency of parts.

2. And likewise *in fitness of opportunities*, if there be not parts, when a man hath all outward advantages to satisfy the flesh, to yield to it, to have

his aims, and yet he will not. If a man have power, and yet doth not revenge himself, he consults not with flesh and blood; for he might be revenged if he would. So I say, when there is something that might sway us another way, and yet notwithstanding out of mere conscience, and better rules, we will not, it is a sign we purpose not, we advise not things according to the flesh, but according to the Spirit; we are led with better rules than the world is.

In strong suggestions, a Joseph can say, 'How shall I do this and offend against God?' Gen. xxxix. 9. 'Doth not God see it?' saith Job, xxxi. 4. So a Christian in the strength of temptations, and solicitations, and opportunities to do ill, he considers, 'Doth not God see? How shall I do this, and offend against God?' Shall I break the peace of my conscience for the gaining of this, and this? Why no. Then a man is not led with carnal wisdom.

3. Again, we may know this, that we are not led by the flesh, and advised by the flesh, *when we are humble in all our consultations*. It is a perpetual concomitant of carnal wisdom to be proud. Knowledge mingled with corruption puffeth up.

Quest. But how shall we labour to overcome this, because we have the flesh ready by us, in all our consultations? We have this counsellor alway ready at hand, as St Paul complains, Rom. vii. 19, 'that when we would do well, evil is present.' It is present at our elbow; nay, it is nearer, the flesh is mingled in all the powers of our souls; and with heavenly wisdom there is a mixture of carnal wisdom; how shall we do that we may not be tainted with it?

I will give a direction or two.

Ans. First of all, have a prejudice of it, *Cave, time*, &c., saith the holy man St Austin. 'Take heed of the evil man thyself' (*ggg*); take heed of carnal reason; be jealous of it. It is an enemy, and the issues of the ways it adviseth to are death. 'There is a way that seems good to a man in his own eyes, the issues whereof are death,' Prov. xiv. 12, not temporal only, but eternal death. It is a deadly enemy; have a prejudice of it, and conceit of it to be as it is; have a jealousy of it, and of our own selves, especially in things that concern ourselves. What is the reason that a man is an incompetent judge in his own cause? This, because there is natural self-love and flesh that draws all to itself. Consult not with it therefore; consult with higher rules, and principles, what may make most for the chief end, for the glory of God, for the assurance of our comfort while we live here, and a better estate hereafter, that which may make most for the common good; let us labour to live by right rules and principles: God will value us by that.

Put the case a man by passion be led another way, what is his rule? what is his aim? His aim is not carnal. He may fall by passion, &c. God judgeth not by passion, but by the tenor of our life. God esteems us not by a single particular exorbitant act that by passion or incogitancy a man falls into, but by the tenor of our life. Therefore let us labour to have our rules and aims good, though we fail in particular, yet that our way may be good; though we step awry, yet our way may be good; that when judgment shall come, when death shall come, it may not find us in an ill way, in an ill course. Therefore let us consult with God, consult with his word, consult with those that are led by the Spirit of God; labour to be under the government of God's blessed Spirit, to be guided by the Spirit of God, and by the word of God. This should be our care, to labour that God would guide us by his good Spirit in those ways that may lead to our comfort, that of all other enemies in the world, he would not give us up to our own flesh to guide us, but that he would take the guidance of us to himself, that as he hath right to us by his covenant, so he would take us into his government. And desire Christ that as he is our priest to die for us, so likewise he would be our prophet to instruct us, to subdue all in us. And let divine truth be our counsellor, to bring our inner man into subjection, as it is, 2 Cor. x. 4, 'The weapons of our warfare are mighty,' to bring all into captivity, to subject all high devices and reasonings.

How shall I do this? I shall miss of my ends, I shall miss of my projects. O! but religion when it comes and brings down all, it makes not a man to cast away reason, but brings reason under, and brings the soul under God. A man may keep his wisdom and understanding safe still, so he keep it under, and let divine truth sway and bring all in us into captivity to itself.

But, alas! the scope of the world is contrary! Instead of bringing the soul into captivity to God's truth, to be led by him, to have no thoughts, no aims contrary to God's will, they make God's truth a captive and prisoner to their own base affections; as St Paul saith, Rom. i. 18, 'They hold the truth,' they withhold it as a prisoner under base affections. And whereas all should serve the main end, and intend better things, they make a counterfeit loving of good things to serve their carnal ends, they make heaven serve earth, they make God serve man, the Spirit serve the flesh: they invert the order of things clean, which is as contrary to nature as if they had wisdom to consider it, as that the heaven should be under the earth, and the water above the air. It overturns all in religion, when we suffer carnal wisdom to rule all, to imprison that light that God hath put into the heart and conscience, and the light of his word to base affections, and not to bring all into captivity to the Spirit and the word.

When we come to hear God's word, we should consider that we come not for recreation; but we come to a counsellor, to that that should sway and direct all our ways and words, to that that is not only our comfort in the time of affliction, but our counsellor. As David saith, 'it was the man of his counsel,' Ps. lxxiii. 24, *et alibi.* So we come here to be counselled, to hear that which must direct us in the way to heaven. We must come with a purpose to be guided by that, to be taught. As Cornelius saith, 'We are here in the presence of God, to hear what shall be said to us from God,' Acts x. 33. St Paul gives this direction, 1 Cor. iii. 18. If a man will 'be wise in heavenly things, let him be a fool first.' It is a strange thing, 'Let him be a fool,' that is, let him be content to be esteemed so, let him be content to lose his reputation of wisdom, 'that he may be wise.' When he knows others to be fools, let him take a substantial course, that the vain world may think him wise.

It is hard counsel; for of all imputations in the world, many and the most had rather be accounted wicked, than be accounted fools. Account them the veriest fools which are unfit to speak; think of them in the highest degree of ill you can, Oh! they have wit enough for that, they have learning, and parts for that; take not away their learning, and parts, account them not fools, account them what you will. Religion masters this base opinion. Saint Paul saith, 'Let a man be a fool, if he will be wise.' Let no man deceive himself, and think, let poor men be so, and so; religion is the private man's good, and let them make conscience of such things; but for us that are in place and authority, we must rule by policy, and he knows not how to rule that is not a politician. Let no man deceive himself; there is no man, great or small, but if he will be wise for heaven, 'let him be a fool,' let him take courses that are conscionable, though he be accounted a fool for his pains.

Let us be jealous of our own hearts in private and public, let us take heed to our own hearts that the flesh come not in. Let us labour to be acquainted with Christ, that he may be our counsellor and our guide in all things.

Specially now when we come to the communion. We now renew our covenant with God, and our acquaintance with Christ Jesus; we come to feast with him. Do we think to have any good by him, any benefit by his death, except we make him our king and prophet, to rule and guide us, except we make him our counsellor? Therefore let us think beforehand, we cannot come as we ought to receive the communion, unless we intend beforehand to renounce the flesh, Christ's enemy. Can you be welcome guests, and resolve after to be led and ruled by his enemy? If you will have good by Christ's death, as a priest to reconcile you to God: (as this sacrament seals the benefits of his death, the breaking of the bread, and the pouring out of the wine,) come with a purpose to be ruled, and guided by this counsellor in all things. He is the great Counsellor, Isa. ix. 7, that is willing to advise us by his word and Spirit in all the particular passages of our lives; and the more we enter into acquaintance with him by the sacrament, and maintain it by private prayer, and by all sacred means, the more ready he will be to do the office of a friend, and counsellor, in all the passages of our lives to advise us what is best. I had occasion in verse 12th to speak at large of fleshly wisdom, therefore I pass it.

'*That with me there should be yea, yea, and nay, nay.*' This sets down the manner of inconstancy, the form of it, 'yea, yea,' to be on the affirmative part once; and then 'nay, nay,' the negative; to be of one mind, and peremptory in it, and then to be of another mind, and peremptory in that. This is the issue of carnal wisdom, and follows on it, 'The things that I purpose, do I purpose according to the flesh, that with me there should be yea, yea, and nay, nay?' insinuating, that those that purpose things according to the flesh, they are 'yea, yea, and nay, nay.' Whence first we may observe, (which I touched before a little, but it issues more properly hence from the dependence) that

Obs. Carnal men are alway inconstant men.

For a fleshly man, led with the flesh, being led with the things of the world, and they being inconstant, he must needs be as that which he is ruled by. A man cannot stand safe upon the ice, because itself is not safe. A man cannot stand in a thing that stands not, that hath no consistence. Now a carnal man he hath no prop to hold him but the things below. He cleaves to them, and they are inconstant, and variable, and uncertain. He that purposeth according to the flesh is 'yea, yea, nay, nay.' Therefore his love is 'yea, yea, nay, nay.' If he may have good by you, he is 'yea, yea,' he is for you; but can you do him no good, he is 'nay, nay,' he will not own you then.

Therefore one way to be constant, is not to be ruled according to the flesh, which I spake of before, for they that are, are 'yea, yea, nay, nay.'

Therefore take heed how you trust carnal men, in near intimate society, as in marriage. Or in near friendship, never take a man that hath his own aims and ends. For he will respect you no more than he can advance his own ends by you. 'Trust not the wife of thy bosom,' saith the prophet, Deut. xiii. 6; if she be carnal, she will have her own ends. So a friend that is carnal, he will have his own ends. The idol that he respects more than thee, or than anything in the earth, is his own fleshly wisdom, and his own ends. Every carnal man makes himself his god. He reduceth all to himself. His own ends is his idol; therefore have no intimate society with such.

'That with me there should be yea, yea; nay, nay.' Observe again in this place, that

Obs. Carnal men are vehement.

They are vehement in either part. If they be 'yea,' they are 'yea, yea,' and yet they will be 'nay, nay,' naught at the same time. The soul of man will admit of contraries, and yet be still the same in the general; 'yea, yea,' at one time, and 'nay, nay,' at another time. And usually they that are vehement in business one way, are vehement another, if they be carnal. A carnal man is vehement one way in the pursuit of things, and he is vehement on the contrary if he be crossed.

What is the reason that men that are carnal, some stand against religion and some for religion with like eagerness? The one is 'nay, nay,' as much as the other is 'yea, yea.' Both are flesh, and if those that are 'yea, yea,' were where the other are, they would be 'nay, nay.' For instance, a man is religious only for carnal respects, he is 'yea, yea.' O! he will have the religion of the times. Why? He could not be safe else, he cannot have his ends else, he was bred up in it, &c. Another, on the contrary, is as much for the opposite religion. What is the reason? He was bred in it, it stands for his ends. If a man be religious not for religious respects, he is peremptory, and contrary to him of the opposite religion; and yet they are equally naught.

A common protestant hath no better ground for his religion than a papist hath for his. The same reason that a papist hath, the same such a protestant hath; he was bred in it, and the king is of that religion, and he shall attain his ends by it. Hath a papist other reasons? Except a man be truly changed and altered, he shall be 'yea, yea,' and 'nay, nay,' sometime one, sometime another, peremptory in one and peremptory in another, and all naught.

As, for instance, the sea, sometimes it ebbs, sometimes it flows, sometimes it flows one way, and then flows back another way; yet it is alway salt and brinish, the nature of it is not changed. So some men are peremptory, 'yea, yea,' they run one way amain, and then they ebb again, yet they alway keep their nature brinish. They are peremptory for good sometimes, and when it stands for their ends they are peremptory against it. Such a cause is so; it is 'yea' if it help their advantage, and it is not so if it help not that, as if truth itself in their judgment were flexible and alterable. Thus a carnal man, he alters, and yet he is never good in his judgment. St Paul declines this; he was not 'yea, yea, nay, nay,' because he did not purpose things according to the flesh.

To come to the point itself. This declining of inconstancy, of 'yea, yea,' 'nay, nay,' it came in St Paul from hatred of inconstancy and falsehood. For 'yea' and 'nay,' when a man is of one mind and another, it comes from one of these two grounds in a carnal man:

Either because *he is inconstant*, that he is now of one mind and now of another;

Or because *he is false and means to dissemble.*

Now, both are dispositions that are contrary to a Christian man; he should neither be light, nor be false and untrue.

Now, St Paul doth much more decline the imputation of falsehood and dissembling, that he should be 'yea,' when he meant not 'yea,' but 'nay,' when he had declined the imputation of lightness; for a man may truly say he will, and yet change his mind after. But for a man to say he will, and yet mean it not, that is falsehood and dissembling, which is worse. St Paul intends much more to decline the suspicion of that.

Dissemblers are 'yea, yea,' 'nay nay,' not at divers times, but at the same time; they make yea and nay all at once. We say contradictions cannot be true, for a thing to be and not to be at the same time; but dissemblers would have contradictions true. They make as if they loved when indeed they hate.

God is the God of truth, the word is the word of truth, and Christ is the truth, and the devil is 'the father of lies,' John viii. 44. Therefore, as we would be like to God, and as we would be unlike Satan, let us labour for truth in all things. St Paul here labours to avoid the opinion of dissembling.

How would he think, then, of equivocation, when there is yea and nay at a breath? They are not at divers times inconstant, but yea and nay at once, to speak one thing and mean the contrary, to have reservations of the contrary. It is so odious that I will not spend time to speak of it,—only this.

1. If it were allowable, as the best of their writers allow it and practise it (however, if they do not allow it, their practice is so, but they do allow it), *by this means the devil himself should never be a liar*, there would be no lie at all. And it were in vain for God to make prohibitions against lying if there might be equivocation, for there is no lie in the world but it may be salved up with reservations. Therefore, that course that brings the devil from being a liar, that frustrates God's course, and that makes men that they shall not lie, whatsoever they do, it is abominable such a conceit, and odious to God. But to maintain equivocation, is to do all this; for with absurd reservations, what in the world may not be justified?

2. Then, again, we are exhorted to suffer martyrdom, to stand for God's cause. Now, to allow equivocation *is to avoid suffering*. Where is the honour of martyrdom and suffering for God's cause, when men shall speak untruths and justify themselves by a lie? It is contrary, I say, to the whole tenor and stream of Scripture.

3. Then again, *they may call it equivocation to mince it, but it is a lie to speak one thing and reserve another*. For what is a lie? To speak falsehood with a purpose and intention to deceive another. Now, they speak false and with a purpose to deceive. A lie must be esteemed as it is esteemed by another that hears it, not him that speaks it, as it is with an oath. Isidore saith (*hhh*), 'An oath is to be esteemed as he that I speak to esteems it, not as I in my sense esteem it; as God esteems it, and he to whom I speak.' So a lie is to be judged as he judgeth it that I speak to, because God forbids lying as a breach of charity to others, because he would not have others deceived. If I salve it up in my own thoughts and deceive others, it is a breach of charity and a lie, because it is a speech of untruth which another thinks to be a truth; it is an untruth, and to deceive him. But these men will have yea and nay at a breath; they will say, 'Yea,' and yet have a reservation of nay, at once. St Paul would much more decline and abhor this, if he were alive now, when he so declined the imputation of inconstancy, of 'yea, yea,' and 'nay, nay,' at

divers times. Indeed, St Paul reserved this. He promised to come to them if God did permit, with a divine reservation. We may say in all the business we are to do, This I will do, if God permit, and if God will. And, indeed, God hindered his journey. But I say for equivocation, the matter is so odious and palpable, that if it were not that *nondum satis odimus*, &c., we hate not these men enough, I would not have spoken of it. Their religion is so abominable and odious, we do not yet hate it enough; and, therefore, it is good on all occasions to uncase them, and all little enough. But I go on.

VERSE 18.

'*As God is true, our word to you was not yea and nay.*' The apostle in the former verse having laboured to clear himself from the imputation of lightness and inconstancy, that he did not come to them as he had promised; and from an imputation likewise of policy for himself, that he did purpose things according to the flesh, which is the cause of inconstancy, 'of yea, yea, and nay, nay,' he comes now to that which he more intended than those particulars. For he was content to be thought to have disappointed them in the matter of his journey; but that which he aims at was to stablish them in this, that his doctrine was sound, 'As God is true, our word to you was not yea and nay.' Perhaps I promised to come, and did not. It is true. But my preaching was not 'yea and nay.' All that I taught was sound and certain. You may build your souls on it. It was 'yea.' He labours to draw them to be persuaded of the certainty of his ministry, as being very unwilling that a defect in his promise about a business of the world should weaken their faith in the truth that he delivered as a minister.

'*As God is true, our word to you was not yea and nay.*' He seems to make a difference between yea and nay in civil things and in divine. There is a difference when a holy man speaks of the things of this life and when he speaks of divine truths. St Paul promised to come to them; he meant it honestly, and did intend it, but it was subject to alteration, because God stops our purposes in this life, yea, our good purposes, many times. Good things may have variety. One good thing may be more convenient than another. And the cause why he came not to them was not his inconstancy, but their unfitness. It was from their corruption in manners and in doctrine. They were not ready. As he saith after, 'he came not, *to spare them*.' They were unfit till they were humbled with his former epistle, and then, when they were humbled, he purposed to come. But now in divine truths, what things he spake to them concerning grace and glory, that was certain. 'Our word to you was not yea and nay.'

Quest. A question may be moved briefly, how St Paul could be deceived in his journey and not in his doctrine. Being so good a man, led by the Spirit of God, how could he promise to come, and yet did not?

Ans. I answer, the difference is much between these two. St Paul had three persons* on him.

He was a *man*, a *Christian man*, an *apostle*.

As a man, he was subject to all things that men are subject unto, that is,

* In the sense of the Latin *persona*, a character which one represents, or part which he acts.—ED.

he desired in truth of heart to come and visit his friends; he purposed a journey, with a reservation that God might hinder him; and so as a man he might have a 'Yea,' that is, a purpose to do a thing; and afterward a 'Nay,' upon the uncertain event of the things of this life. So, as a man he purposed to come. Nay, as a *holy man* he purposed a journey to a good purpose, to stablish them; but with a reservation, if God permit; God might stop his journey. But as *an apostle*, he taught other things, than speaking of journeys. That he spake of only as a man, and as a holy man, alway supposing the condition of human things, and under permission, if God permit. But as an apostle he was not yea and nay. There he was certain. As an apostle he spake divine truths, and was guided infallibly by the Spirit of God; he delivered truths without all conditions and exceptions. As an apostle, he did not admit of any such uncertainty. There is an eminency and excellency in divine truth. It is stable, and firm, and not subject to variety and inconstancy. So his doctrine as an apostle was always 'Yea.'

For his journey, and coming to them, he promised his journey *in veritate propositi*, in the truth of a good purpose of a friend; but as he spake of divine truths, he spake of them in the certainty of the divine Spirit. In the one, he spake in the certainty of truth; in the other, in the truth of affection. As a man, he spake in the truth of a good affection he bare to them; but as an apostle, he spake in the certainty of divine truth.

And you must know this, that God, as he used the apostles and excellent men to write his book, to write the word of God, to be his penmen, yet he hindered them not to be men. As he hinders not godly men to be men, but at once they may be saints and men; so St Paul as a good man, desired to see them, with a reservation; but as an apostle, he was guided by a certain infallible assistance of divine truth.

Nathan, as he was a man, gave David liberty to build the temple. He was overshot in it something. But then he goes to God, and consults with him, whether he should or no; and then Nathan gives David another advice.*

So the prophets and apostles, as men, they might be alterable without sin. For God will allow men to be men, and subject to mistakes. For *nescience*, not knowing the possibility of things to come, is no sin in man; because it is an unavoidable infirmity. So that St Paul, as his usual manner is, in promising things to come, things of that nature, he promiseth them under reservation and permission, if God permit, if God will; and he doth not sin, though he be frustrate of his intention.

It is not the only part of a wise man to divine what will be. St Paul had not providence to see whether his journey should be crossed or no; but out of a Christian intention, he resolved to come, if God did not cross him; that was as a man, and a good man. But as an apostle, his doctrine was without ifs and ands, without exception, as we say, 'if God permit,' &c. 'No,' saith he; 'as God is true, our word to you was not yea and nay.' So in the apostles, we must consider a difference of divine truths that they delivered as apostles, from those things that they purposed as men, and as holy men. Those were subject to be crossed, and without sin too. For God will have men to be men, that is, variable creatures, and such as cannot promise themselves for the time to come any certain thing.

It is God's prerogative to know things to come. We may know them by their causes; we may know when there will be an eclipse a hundred

* Cf. 2 Sam. vii. 3, with 4–11.—G.

years hence; but to know what weather there shall be, as we may know the eclipse, we cannot; because there is nothing in the cause. I say, God will have men to be men. St Paul may promise holily, with a reservation to God, as a man, and as a holy man, and without sin too; but as an apostle, in his doctrine he was not so; but 'as God is true, our word to you was not yea and nay,' but constant as God himself. That shall suffice to satisfy that. Therefore St Paul makes the difference, I promised to come, but I did not; but 'as God is true, our word to you was not yea and nay.'

Our voyage to heaven, and the reference we have to a better life, stands not on uncertainties, as the things here in this world. St Paul's journey to Corinth might be frustrate; but St Paul had another course to heaven; his religious course stood not on uncertainties. Whatsoever he taught in a religious course, it was 'yea;' as he saith in the next verse, 'Christ the Son of God whom we preach, was not yea and nay, but yea;' that is, infallibly true, perpetually true, necessarily, eternally true.

'As God is true, our word to you was not yea and nay.' St Paul labours to establish them therefore in a good conceit of his ministry; and that made him indeed so much decline the suspicion of inconstancy in other things: because carnal men are prone to think a man in his calling, even a preacher in his doctrine, to be inconstant, if he be so in his common course.

St Paul knew their corruption was such, that from a suspicion of lightness in his carriage and common course, they would rise to a suspicion of his doctrine; therefore he was so curious to avoid the imputation of lightness in his journey, because he would avoid any imputation of lightness in his doctrine. That is it which he more aims at. He stands not on the imputation of lightness in his journey, or such matters; but he knew the corruption of men is such, that if a man fail in common things, presently they think he is so in his calling. Full of false surmises and suspicions is the nature of man; and as a man is once, they gather him to be so alway. Therefore he deceiving them in not coming, they might think he would do so at other times too. That makes the apostle labour to clear himself, but especially his doctrine, from all suspicion.

'As God is true, our word to you was not yea and nay.' Here is a truth; and the seal of it.

His averring the truth is this, 'Our word, our preaching,' as it is in the margin (*iii*). 'Our word,' as it was unfolded, it was not 'yea and nay,' it was not uncertain.

And the proof and seal of it, 'God is true,' as it is in the original, which is made up in the English tongue, 'As God is true,' it is in our translation; but in the original it is, 'God is true;' and as he is true, and constant, and faithful, so our word is constant and faithful; you may build on it (*jjj*). 'As God is true,' as God is to be credited and believed, so my word to you is to be credited as 'yea,' as a certain doctrine that is not 'yea and nay.' It is a kind of an oath.

'As God is true.' The apostle here seals it with an oath.

What is an oath?

An oath is a religious calling of God to witness, or to be a judge in doubtful things.

It is in doubtful things a calling of God to be a witness of the truth we speak, and to be a revenger if we speak not true. It is to call God to witness and to judge, to make him *testis et vindex*. St Paul here calls God to witness, 'God is true,' and as verily as he is true, 'our word to you was not yea and nay.'

You know oaths are either, as we say, *assertory*, to aver a thing; or *promissory*, for the time to come to do this or that; and they are either imposed or voluntary. Now this is an *assertory* oath, not a *promissory*. He avers and avoucheth peremptorily, that as God is true, his word to them was not 'yea and nay,' but yea.' And it was a voluntary oath; for nobody exacted it of him. But he saw there was a necessity to stablish them in the certainty of the doctrine he taught, to seal it with an oath, that they should as well doubt of the truth of God, as of his doctrine. 'As God is true, my word is true.'

Jeremiah the prophet hath three conditions of an oath, 'It must be in truth, in righteousness, and in judgment,' Jer. iv. 2.

In truth. We must speak and swear true things.

And *in judgment;* necessary things, with discretion.

And *in righteousness.*

Now St Paul observed the conditions wondrous well here. For St Paul doth it in a true matter, and in judgment; for he was forced to it.

An oath is never good but when it is necessary; not to seal up every idle discourse, as if men would make everything they say to be as true as an oath. Indeed, the life of a man should be an oath. The life of an honest man is an oath, as true; but we must not call God to question for every idle impertinent thing. St Paul saw it necessary to call God to witness; it was true and necessary.

I will not enter into a large discourse of an oath, because afterward I shall have better occasion to speak of it. Only thus much at this time: St Paul here useth it. He thinks it to be necessary, to establish their minds the better in his ministry, and a good conceit of it that it was constant. 'God is true, our word to you was not yea and nay.'

Therefore, in such a case we may not make scruple of an oath, if it be

In *charity, piety, necessity.*

In charity; in matters of controversy of civil life.

In piety; to establish matters of religion.

And in *matters of necessity*, that cannot be determined otherwise, there is no scruple to be made of it.

And where we are bid 'not to swear at all,' Mat. v. 34, that is, not in ordinary course; or not to swear by creatures; but if we do swear, it is a part of God's service, we must swear by him. And, indeed, it is a service of God, and to good purpose, when Christians swear to stablish and determine truths that otherwise are doubtful.

They were doubtful of St Paul's doctrine and his person. Saith he, To put you out of doubt of the truth I speak to you, I dare call God to witness it is true and sound. The apostle doth so once after in this chapter. Therefore I reserve the further handling of an oath to verse 23d, because the word there is more infallible,* 'I call God to record upon my soul,' &c.

The next thing I observe hence is this, that

Obs. The believing that God's word is God's word, and is certain, it is a matter of great consequence.

It is of great consequence, for God's people that look to be saved, to be stablished in their opinion and judgment of divine truth, that it is certain, and not flexible and mutable, according to our wills, and conceits, and dispositions, but is 'yea,' alway the same, as God himself, the author of it.

* That is, 'explicit, unmistakeable.'—G.

For laying this for a ground, that I said before, that St Paul takes God to witness, he would not interpose an oath, but in a matter of great consequence; therefore, it is a matter of great consequence to be settled in this, that the Scripture is divine truth, unalterable and unchangeable.

An oath is never good, as I said, but when it is necessary. It must not only be in truth, but there must be a necessity. It must not only be taken in righteousness, but in judgment; a man must do it in discretion, when the thing is not determinable any other way, Therefore it is a matter of great consequence, that men take the word of truth not to be as the oracles of Apollo and of the devil, true one way, and false another (*kkk*). The devil would escape the imputation of a lie, though he be a liar; but God's oracles be divine, they be 'yea.' And it is good that we think them to be so, to be constant, undoubted, certain, and unmovable. Therefore the apostle seals it with an oath. He would not seal a slight truth by an oath, but saith he, 'As God is true, our word to you was not yea and nay,' &c.

And St Paul saw a disposition in them to suspect the truth of God, as indeed, we are proner to believe the lies of our own hearts, and the suggestions of Satan, and the counsel of politicians, of carnal friends, than to believe God himself. Therefore, partly for the indisposition in us; and partly for the great exigence and necessity of the thing, to believe that God's word is his word, that it is truth, he seals it with an oath, 'God is true.' It is a point of great consequence.

Reason. The reason is, God can have no service else, and we can have no comfort.

If we do not believe the word of God to be undoubtedly true, in great temptations and assaults, what armour of proof shall we have? We can have no comfort nor grace. For sometimes subtle and strong temptations to evil come, if the word of God be not more undoubted to me, than the present profit, or pleasure, or whatsoever; if the temptation be ready, and I be not built on, and settled on some grounded truth that I know to be true as God is true. When the temptation is strong, and our faith weak, where are we? A man presently yields to base lusts and temptations.

And so in matter of danger and despair. When a man is tempted to despair, if he cannot build on this, 'God is true,' and his word is as true as himself, 'He wills not the death of a sinner,' &c., Ezek. xviii. 32, here a man is swallowed up.

It is no matter how strong the foundation be, if the building on that foundation be weak. If a strong man stand in a slippery place, down he falls; if a man stand slippery, and have a weak standing on a strong place, on a strong foundation; if he have a weak building on a strong foundation, he shall soon be cast off. So, the word of God is true in itself: but if we be not persuaded so, that it is infallibly true, that it is alway 'yea,' we shall be shaken with temptations. When we are tempted to sin, the temptation is present, we are sure of the temptation. If we be not more sure of somewhat against the temptation, somewhat out of the word to beat back the darts of Satan, when we are tempted to sin, and to despair for sin, down we go; and, therefore, it is a matter of infinite consequence to be persuaded of divine truth.

What makes many as they are, in courses that are corrupt in their callings? Nothing but this: they stagger, whether it be true or no that there shall be a judgment; they stagger, whether it be true or no that the Scripture saith. If they were persuaded that it were 'yea,' as true as God is in heaven, as true as they have souls, so their souls must be called to judgment for that they speak and do, would they do as they do? Therefore St Paul stablisheth them by an oath, 'God is true, and as God is true, our word to you was not yea and nay.'

Use. Therefore take in good part with thankfulness the means that God hath ordained to strengthen our faith and assurance of the word of God, and the promises of God. Therefore he hath appointed the sacrament for that purpose. I say there is nothing in the world so strengthened as the soul of a Christian, if he give himself to God's truth to be ruled by it. For if we will believe God, we have his promise, that 'whosoever believes in Christ shall not perish, but have everlasting life,' 2 Pet. iii. 9; rich promises, 'precious promises,' 2 Pet. i. 4, as the Scripture calls them. We have not only promises, but they are sealed with an oath. Now an oath is an unchangeable thing, Heb. vi. 16. We have promises and oath, that we might have 'strong consolation.' Whatsoever might secure man we have. Besides his oath we have his seal, his sacrament. It was his love to condescend to make any covenant with sinful creatures, that upon any terms he would give them life everlasting. It was a higher degree of love to set Christ to be the foundation of this peace, and of this covenant, that now God and we may be at peace with satisfaction to divine justice, that he is the foundation of the peace between God and us. Now God may be merciful without wrong, without impeachment to his justice; that is a higher degree of mercy, to enter into covenant, and to give Christ to be the foundation of all. And then it is a higher degree than that to secure us of the covenant, that Christ is ours, to seal the word with an oath, and with the sacrament which is the seal of the covenant; what could God do more?

What a horrible sin therefore is unbelief, that we should tremble at, to call God's love and truth in question! But yet we are prone to it; or else why did Christ ordain the sacrament to strengthen and stablish our faith, and to confirm us, but that he knew our propenseness to unbelief?

In the time of ease and prosperity, it is easy to think, God is merciful, and Christ died; but in the time of temptation, all is little enough to shore and prop up the faith of a drooping Christian. Therefore God, out of heavenly wisdom, and love to us, hath appointed these ordinances for the strengthening of our faith. And all is to no purpose, unless our faith be strong in the promises, as St Paul takes an oath, to build them on the promises he taught them. And so all is little enough, oath, and promises, and seal, &c. Therefore we should with all reverence attend upon God's ordinances for the strengthening of our faith. But to come to the words themselves.

'As God is true, our word to you was not yea and nay.' Take the words out of the form of an oath, and the proposition is, that

Doct. God is true and faithful.

In this link of the sentence, 'God is true'—First, it is true that *God* is. He is truly God. His nature is true; his properties true. Likewise God is true and faithful, not only in his nature and properties, but in his free decrees, in the things that freely come from him. It was free for him to make promises of salvation or no, as it was free for him to make a world or no, and whether he would redeem mankind or no; but when he had promised, except he should deny himself and his truth, he must send Christ. So in all the free promises of forgiveness of sins, and life everlasting by Christ, if we believe in him, we say they are certainly true, because God that is true hath promised. God is true in his nature, and true in his free promises, and threatenings; he is true in his works, true in his word, every way true. He is true in his nature, all is true within him, and without him. If anything could change him from within, he were not himself, he were not God. And from without there is nothing can change him; for there is nothing stronger than God. God is true in all his purposes, true in his free and voluntary decrees. It was free for him to decree, but having decreed, there is a necessity of performing. It is of the necessity of his nature as he is God. He is true in his free decrees. They are not free in regard of the event, but in regard of the original, as I said. He might have made a world at the first or no, and have redeemed mankind or no; but having made these decrees, of necessity as he is God he must be true in his free decrees.

There is a subordination of truths, whereof one is the cause of all the rest. Now all depends upon this grand truth, *God is*. It is the first truth that ever was of all truths in the world, in heaven and earth, that there is a God, that there is such a thing, such an excellency as God, the Author of all things in nature, the Author of all things in grace and glory. I shall not need to prove this fundamental truth, this truth of truths, that God is. It infers all other truths. For grant this, that God is, and a man must needs grant that that follows upon it, that God is as a God should be, that is, unchangeable, eternal, immutable, almighty, all-sufficient, and all the blessed attributes, that he is the Author of all good in the creature. That must needs follow. God is the first truth; and then God is so and so, as becomes a God. And then this must follow in the next place, that he is a God immutable and unchangeable. He must be so in all the manifestations that come from him, in his free decrees, and in the outward manifestations by promises, and threatenings, and whatsoever; and therefore God is true, immutably and unchangeably true, or else he were not God. He cannot be otherwise, and be God. A man may say of a man, he is a liar, and yet he may be a man. A man may be a man, and a good man, and yet be inconstant and changeable, because he is a creature. But to say a God, and not to be true, is to say a God, and not a God. Of the necessity of his nature he must be true. It is not of the necessity of the nature of man to be true. He may be a man, and be a liar ('Every man is a liar,' Ps. cxvi. 11), because it is not of the essence of man to be true. But God is true out of the necessity of nature. He cannot be God if he be not true, because God cannot deny himself. Man is changeable, because he is a creature, as Damascene's speech is (*lll*), 'All things created are mutable, and man as a creature is changeable.' A man therefore may be alterable, and false, and be a man; but God cannot be so, and be God.

Obj. It will be objected, that God hath threatened oft, and hath not performed; as we see in the Ninevites, and Hezekiah in his sickness, and so in many others.

Ans. But the answer is easy. God is true in all these; for God's promises that come from his truth, they are either absolute or conditional. The absolute are those that have nothing annexed to them, but shall certainly be. As God would have sent Christ without all conditions, Christ should have come without all peradventure, as we say. But now some promises have conditions annexed to them: if a nation repent of their sins, God will repent of the evil he hath threatened, as it is in Jer. xviii. 8. Now those threatenings that are on condition of repentance, if the condition be performed, the sentence is reversed. All the promises are made with exception of the cross; all must suffer before they come to heaven and be glorified. Now all the promises, with the exception of the cross, are conditional. So God is true, both in his absolute promises that are made without condition, and he is true in his conditional promises; because where he performs the condition, he will perform likewise that that is tied to the condition. He changeth his sentence sometimes, and his threatening, but not his decree; for his purpose and decree is to forgive and reverse the sentence, if we repent. I say, it is a clear truth that God is true, unchangeably and immutably true.

And it is the prime truth of all truths, that God is, and God is true. As we say of the heavens, unless the heavens were moved, there would be no motion in the earth. For if the sun had not a motion in the zodiac up and down, where were summer and winter? If he had not his course, where were night and day? the vicissitude and intercourse of all earthly things? If the heavenly motion were not, *nisi moverentur, &c.*, if those did not move, we could not move, because we depend upon that. So, unless it were true that God were, there is a God, and God is unchangeably true, there would be nothing true in the world; for all truth is therefore true, because it is answerable to that exemplar truth that is true in God, answerable to God's conceit and decree of things.

This I observe the rather, because it is a fundamental thing. It doth wondrously stablish our faith in divine truths, when we know it comes from God that is true. If we would seek for evidences of our faith, then we must go within us, and see what love, and what hope, what combat between the flesh and spirit there is; but if we look for anything to stablish our faith, go out of us, consider the unchangeable truth of God, whose truth it is.

God as God creating a reasonable creature, he must give him some revealed truth, he could not be worshipped else. How must we know this revealed truth whereby he will be worshipped by the reasonable creature (for no man will be served by his servant as he pleaseth)? How shall we know these certain truths? Because they come from his nature. God is true; and as God is true, 'so our word to you was not yea and nay,' that is, it was true. There is the same ground of the certainty of evangelical truth as there is of God himself to be true.

To add a little further in the point, consider the truth of God every way, the faithfulness of God, as it signifies in the original, 'as God is faithful.' Consider what relations God hath put upon him in his divine truth, how he will be thought on. And then bring those relations to his nature; for there we must pitch at last. What is he to us? and how hath he revealed himself to us? Thus and thus. What is he in his nature? So and so; and there we must rest.

For instance, the Lord hath made many promises. Who is it that hath made them? He that is true and unchangeably true. There the soul rests in the nature of God. But what relations hath he put upon him? He is a God, and a Lord, and a Judge, and a Father, &c.

Now, as he is God, he is true: therefore he will do all things that a true God should do. He will uphold his creature, while he will have his creature continue; he will give it life, and being, and motion.

And as a Lord he will do with his own what he list, and it is not for us to contend with him why he will do this or that, why he makes one rich and another poor. He is Lord of all, and a true Lord. Therefore we must give authority to this true Lord.

And then, as he is a Judge, he corrects men for sin, and rewards them for the good they do. As a Judge, sometime he punisheth them inwardly in conscience, sometimes outwardly. All the good we have is from this, that he is a faithful and true God; therefore there we must rest. He is a true Judge, he 'rewards every man according to his works, whether they be good or evil,' Mat. xvi. 27.

And so in the relation of a Father, he is a true Father, he corrects when time serves, he rewards and encourageth when time serves, he gives an inheritance to his children, and hath pity and compassion on his children when time serves. He is a true Father. Other fathers do this and that out of passion, not out of truth and goodness; but he doth. So when we consider God in his relations, consider of the attribute of his truth.

All truth, in his word, comes from this, God is true. This truth is sealed by this, that our truth to you, our word to you, was not 'yea and nay,' uncertain. God's truth is not uncertain and variable. There is no 'shadow of change in him,' James i. 17, and his word is like himself. We say usually, in the word of an honest man, and that is something. *In verbum Sacerdotis*, in the word of a priest, it was accounted in former times a great matter. It should be so indeed. In the word of a king is a great matter. But when God saith in the word of a God, 'The word of the Lord hath spoken so,' Jer. x. 1, it is not yea and nay, it was not flexible, and doubtful, because it is the word of him that hath the command of all that he saith. It is his word that is Lord of heaven and earth. Now when he that saith a thing is the Lord of heaven and earth, he is Lord of his own word, therefore what he saith is not 'yea and nay,' uncertain; for he can make good what he saith. There is the same ground of evangelical truth, as there is of God himself to be true. I will speak no more in the unfolding of the point. It is plain that God is true.

Is this true, that God is true, that he is truth itself? Then many things issue from hence. It is a ground of many other truths. It was the ground of all the uses that St Paul makes of the word of God. It is profitable every way. I will name some principal, to avoid multiplicity in a plain point.

Use 1. God is true, and his word is true. *Hereupon the threatenings of God must needs be true*, even as true as God himself. If this be so, then unless we will make another Scripture, another word, this word is 'yea.' That word that threatens sin, that idolaters, and covetous, and wantons shall never enter into the kingdom of heaven, ('Be not deceived,' saith the apostle, 1 Cor. vi. 9,) that word is 'yea.' It is true. God is true. This must follow, therefore, that whatsoever he saith is true; therefore his threatenings are true. It is a truth that hath influence into all other truths whatsoever. That which is prefixed here by St Paul, not only as an oath, 'as God is true,' so his word is not yea and nay, but certain. But I say it hath influence into all other truths whatsoever; threatenings, promises, directions, all are therefore true, because God is true.

Therefore those that shuffle off the threatenings, and think they shall do well, and bless themselves, God's wrath shall 'smoke against them,' Deut. xxix. 20; for God must alter his nature, and his word must be altered, or else his judgments must stick on them death and damnation without repentance. If God should not be avenged on ordinary swearers and blasphemers; if adulterers should live in such sins, and ever come to heaven, they must have another God, and another word of God. This hath said, they shall not enter into heaven that live in these sins. If it be true as God is true, what horrible atheism is in the hearts of men, to think that God will change his nature, though they do not change their course, and that the word of God shall alter, though they will not alter? What hope can profane, blasphemous persons have, that make but a trifle of swearing, when God hath said they shall not go unpunished? and those that live in a filthy course, when God hath said, 'Whoremongers and adulterers God will judge'? without horrible atheism how can these men hope for favour from God, when he hath sealed his word with this, that as he is true, and truth itself, his word is true, they shall never enter into heaven?

Use 2. So again, if this be true, that God is true, and his word thereupon is not yea and nay, *it serves to comfort us many ways.*

When we are oppressed in the sense of sin, 'If we confess our sins, he is merciful to forgive our sins,' 1 John i. 9. He that is true hath said it, whose word is not yea and nay, but yea. Trust to it. If we doubt of perseverance for the time to come, he that hath 'begun a good work will perfect it to the day of the Lord,' Philip. i. 6. He is yea, and his word is yea; he is true, and his word is true.

Use 3. Again, hence for our judgment we learn this truth, that the word of God hath the same ground of truth as God himself. Therefore it is the judge of all controversies. Of all things questionable in religion, the word of God is judge; because it is not 'yea and nay, but yea,' and 'it is true, as God is true.' And it is judge of this controversy too, whether it be the word of God?

The question between the papists and us is, whether the epistles and the prophets be the word of God, or no? whether is it or no?

I answer, from apostolical testimony, St Paul saith, 'As God is true,' his word is true, the true word of God; and 'All Scripture is given by inspiration,' 2 Tim. iii. 16. The word of God therefore is the judge of all divine truths, because it is most certain, even as certain as God himself.

What are the properties of a chief judge?

He must be true, without error; authentical, without appeal, such as can from himself without a higher determine. He must be infallible, without peril of error. All these belong to God's truth.

It is yea, it is true without error, it is alway yea. And then it is authentical. There is nothing higher but God himself, whose word it is, and it hath the same authority that himself hath, 'As God is true,' so it is true. It is authentical without all appeal. We cannot go higher than God himself in his word. We cannot call God or Christ from heaven. He hath left us his word, and therefore it is to be credited of itself.

And it is infallibly true, without danger of error. One depends upon another, 'As God is true, so our word is true.' If God be true infallibly, this issues by consequence, that the Scripture is the judge, and infallibly true without danger of error.

Hence we may know what to judge of that Romish assertion. There are no other judges in the world can be said to be 'yea' alway.

Councils are not alway yea: they are 'yea and nay.' What one council hath set down, another hath reversed. In the council of Basle, the pope was above the council. In another council, that is above the pope.

So one pope's decrees thwart another. The popes are 'yea and nay,' and not yea; for many hundred years they laboured to cross and thwart one another. So councils and popes are 'yea and nay,' and not alway 'yea.'

Traditions of the fathers are 'yea and nay,' and not alway 'yea.' They thwart themselves. St Austin, the best of the fathers, to whom the church is most chiefly beholden of all the rest, he was 'yea and nay.' Doth he not retract? He wrote a book of retractations of his former opinions (*mmm*).

Then he was 'yea, and nay,' and yet a holy man. That which is the judge of controversies must be yea, that is, infallibly true, authentically true, that there be not a higher. From all others, from fathers and councils, there may be appeal to Scripture, but from Scripture to none; because it is the voice and word of God. All things else are yea and nay, they are changeable, and they may be so without prejudice to the being of them. A council may be a good council, and inconstant in many things. Fathers may be holy fathers, and uncertain. It is only the prerogative of God to be infallible like himself, unchangeable in his nature; and his word is like himself.

Use 4. Hence likewise issues this, that *whatsoever agrees not with the word of God, which is not yea and nay, is false and naught.* Therefore those opinions of the Church of Rome, that say they cannot err, if they be not yea with this yea, then they are not yea; for only the word of God is not 'yea and nay, but only yea,' that is, only certain and true. All other religions that are not divine, are yea and nay. Popery is not grounded upon the word of God, because it is 'yea and nay,' that is, it is uncertain. See how they cross many ways this word of God, that is always yea, and true as God himself is true.

Is it 'yea,' that they saw no image of God, and therefore they must make and worship no image? 'Nay,' saith the Church of Rome. They have a nay for this yea; they will make images and worship them, the image of Mary, and other saints. 'Yea,' saith the Scripture, 'drink ye all of this.' 'Nay,' saith the Church of Rome. They have a 'nay' for this 'yea;' only the priest must drink the wine. 'Let the word dwell plenteously in you,' is the 'yea' of Scripture. The Church of Rome hath a 'nay' for this 'yea.' It is dangerous for the people to read the Scripture, and therefore they are forbidden it. We must pray with the understanding as well as with a good affection, 1 Cor. xiv. 15, that is, we must know how we pray. It is proved at large excellently. Nay, understand, or not understand, so the intention be good, saith Rome; pray in Latin, or howsoever. There is their nay to this yea. 'Let every soul be subject to the higher powers, is the 'yea' of God's book. Therefore the souls of the clergy, and whosoever. The Church of Rome hath a 'nay' for this 'yea.' Therefore their doctrine is bad; for only God is true, and his word is only 'not yea and nay, but alway yea,' infallible. Therefore that which is contrary to it must needs be false. If only yea be true, then that which is contrary to it must needs be false (*nnn*).

And likewise again, if God's word be not 'yea and nay,' that is, not inconstant, then whatsoever is inconstant, and thwarts itself in contradictions, is not God's word. Popery is full of inconstancy, full of contradictions to itself.

1. First, besides inconstancy, and uncertainty, *it is full of contradictions;* it is 'yea *and* nay.' For a body to be in many places at once, and yet a true body; to be in a hundred, in a million of places at once, as they would have Christ's body to be in the sacrament, here is to be, and not to be; a body and no body, for it hath not the properties and quantity of a body; for a body can be but in one place at one time. Here is yea and nay.

For Christ to be a perfect Redeemer, and yet notwithstanding to need the help of other mediators and intercessors, here is yea and nay. It is a contradiction.

That the church of Rome is the catholic church; if it be Roman, it is not catholic. The universal catholic Roman church, it is as much as the 'universal particular church.' It is a contradiction. One thing overturns another.

The sacrifice of the mass, an unbloody sacrifice; a sacrifice is the killing of a thing that was alive; a sacrifice is with blood. The offering of Christ in the bread, is an unbloody sacrifice; a sacrifice, and not a sacrifice. Here is yea and nay, a contradiction. So that besides their thwarting of Scripture, they thwart and contradict themselves in their fundamental points, they are 'yea and nay.'

2. And then *they are full of uncertainties*, they are not undoubtedly 'yea.' There is no papist in the world would end his days so, if he be not drunk, if he be advised, if he be not surprised with passion, if he do not forget himself. Come to a papist, and ask him, what are the main points of popery that you believe always yea? Can you say when you confess your sins, that you confess all? No. Can you then say then you have a perfect absolution, that depends upon your confession? No! it is an uncertain thing. What an absurd thing is popish religion? It wrecks* the conscience of people.

Can you say that the priest intends consecration in these words, 'This is my body?' No! and if the priest's intention be not there, then Christ is not there, and then you are idolaters. Can you tell certainly that transubstantiation depends upon his consecration? No! How full of uncertainties and contradictions is popery! You cannot say the points of popery are always yea. Perhaps they are yea in life, but are they yea in death? It is yea in life, that they merit salvation by works, but is it yea in death? No! Bellarmine disclaims it.† It is safe not to trust in our own merits for danger of vainglory, &c., but to trust only in the mercy of God in Christ. So their doctrine it is yea in life, to sin by, to live riotously by, but then it is nay in death. They reverse it if they belong to God. They disclaim their works, and other things, and cleave only to Christ, and there is hope of them that have grace truly to do so. So their doctrine is not yea, that in life and death they can stick to.

To go on a little further, to lay open the grossness of their tenets,‡ and the danger of their religion. We are better bottomed than they are, which make the word of God our rule and ground, that is not yea and nay, but yea. The canonisation of saints. The pope, he makes Garnet, a traitor, and Thomas of Becket, saints (*ooo*). How can he know that these were saints that he canoniseth? He that makes a saint must know the hearts of men, and search the heart; for the truth of grace is there. Now, it is the privilege of God to know the heart. So that popery is full of uncertainties and pitiful perplexities.

Indeed, they maintain the doctrine of doubting, that we must doubt; as if our nature were not sufficiently prone to doubt, but we must get arguments to make us doubt; as if it were needful to have infirmities to stablish grace in us. Alas! we are too prone to doubt, and the devil is ready to make us stagger in the time of temptation.

Again, the invocation of saints it is a point wondrous full of uncertainties. Can they know and say certainly that the saints hear them? They cannot know that one saint, having a finite power, should hear a hundred petitions at once. A finite creature hath but a finite power to hear one thing at one time distinctly. How can they be persuaded that a finite saint

* Qu. 'racks?' See page 367, line 19 from top.—G. † Cf. note *w*.—G.

‡ Spelled 'tenent,' as in the 'Bloody *Tenent* [*i. e.*, Tenet] Washed' of John Cotton, 4to, 1647.

in heaven at one time distinctly should hear many thousands that put up their petitions at once? Can a man that is but a capable creature, though glorified, as Peter or Mary, &c., distinctly consider a thousand petitions that are made? They cannot. How then can they think that a certain truth, the invocation of saints?

The main ground of all their religion is 'yea and nay.' The pillar of it, what is that? The infallible judgment of the pope. But how can they tell when he speaks *ex cathedra?* For nine or ten exceptions and tricks they have, when he speaks, to be built on, and when not. How can poor souls know when he speaks so, that the people may infallibly build on his judgment? Because many times he is an illiterate man, that knows nothing in divine things wherein he is to judge. So the very foundation of popery is yea and nay; that is, a most uncertain thing.

And then the ground of that, that he is the successor of Peter, there is no place of Scripture for it, neither dare they bring any. It is but a tradition. It is somewhat uncertain whether ever Peter were at Rome (*ppp*). That he was bishop there, is more uncertain. But that the pope should be his successor, is most uncertain and impossible of all.

So indeed the religion of popery is a rack to conscience, especially to conscience that is awaked, and knows what religion means at all. Why is it a rack to them? There is no certainty in it, in the main tenets of it.

It is not only contrary to God's 'yea,' but it is 'yea and nay,' uncertain in itself. Now, here the apostle, he frees his preaching from this imputation, 'our word to you was not yea and nay;' and he calls God to record, 'God is true,' and as he is true, 'my word to you was not yea and nay,' but was certainly 'yea.' Thus you see what use we are to make of it for confutation and conviction of our own judgments.

Quest. It may be moved by some perhaps, How doth it appear, how shall we know, by what argument, that it is yea, and not yea and nay? I answer,

Ans. 1. The testimony of St Paul here is, that it is so; and his appeal to God, with an asseveration, 'as God is true.'

2. But our own experience doth tell us that the word of God is certain and true, if we belong to God; for we stand convict in judgment by many arguments, which I will not now repeat.

Quest. But how shall any man certainly know* it is yea? [that] the word is the undoubted word of God, unchangeable wheresoever it is? In a word, you may know† it is so.

Ans. 1. He thinks it is so, *if he yield obedience to it*, as to such a word, absolute obedience to God's truth without questioning. When once a thing is clear to be agreeable to God's truth, [and] he yields obedience to it, then it is 'yea.' If it be a duty, he must do it; if it be a threatening, he must avoid it by repentance; if it be a promise, he must believe it. This is absolute obedience.

2. Likewise *reverence in hearing it*, as Cornelius did, Acts x. 33. To hear it as the word of God. 'To tremble at the word of God,' as it is Isa. lxvi. 2. To tremble at it as men do at thunder. The thunder is said to be 'the voice of God.' 'The voice of God shakes the cedars of Lebanon,' Ps. xxix. 8. So it is with the voice of God's word. 'Shall the lion roar, and the beasts of the forest not tremble?' Isa. vii. 2. Shall

* This seems to be a misprint for 'shew;' at least the answers direct in regard to *shewing* rather than *knowing*.—G.

† If this should not also read 'shew,' then the meaning is, = he knows it is so who yields obedience.—G.

God threaten for sins that we are obnoxious to, and shall we not tremble at his threatenings? Therefore howsoever we hear it as if it were yea and nay, yet it is yea; therefore let us not think to go on in sin, and escape, and do well enough. No! it will not be so. He that thinks it is the word of God, he trembles at his word, and hath answerable affections to all the parts of God's word. If God direct, he follows; if God threaten, he trembles; if he promise, he believes; if he command, he obeys. He hath a pliable disposition to every passage of divine truth, or else we do not believe it.

What shall we say then of those that come not so far as the heathen man did? We know Felix, 'when he heard of justice, and temperance, and judgment to come, he trembled,' Acts xxiv. 25. When he heard of things that he was loath to hear, that he should be called to a reckoning for the course of his life, he trembled and quaked. If we hear these things, and live in a course perhaps worse than he, and do not tremble, where is our faith that the word of God is yea, that it is undoubtedly true?

Let us therefore examine ourselves what power and efficacy the word hath. It is a word that changeth and altereth the whole man. It transforms the whole man. It is a word of life. If we find it hath so altered and changed us, we can from experience say it is 'yea.'

And likewise from particular promises. If we observe God's promises made good to us, if we find peace of conscience upon the confession of our sins, we can say God's word is 'yea.' If upon committing of sin we find God punishing and correcting us, we can say God's word is yea; and it is a bitter thing to offend God.

I find carefulness is the best course to please God. He finds me out in my sins, and it is a bitter thing to offend God. This is the best way to say in truth, without hypocrisy, that God's word is 'not yea and nay, but yea.'

Thus we see this truth, that God is true, and what follows thence. His word is true as himself, and not inconstant, yea and nay. Besides all this that I have said, let us make this use of it, *not to think God's word to be too good to be true, but yield obedience to it; yield the obedience of faith to it in the promises*. Here is a foundation for faith. The foundation of faith is without us. The evidences of faith are within us, by love, by purging our hearts, and stirring us up to pray, &c. But the foundation is out of ourselves. Here is a foundation and pillar for faith to lean on. God is true, and his word is true, and not yea and nay. It is eternally true. Therefore apply all the promises in the Old and New Testament to thyself. It was not yea to Abraham, and not to thee. God's promises of forgiveness of sins were not yea to David, and not to thee. They were not yea to Manasseh, and not to thee. But God's truth is yea, eternally yea. 'Whatsoever was written heretofore, was written for our comfort,' Rom. xv. 4; and we are now the Davids, and the Manassehs, and the Abrahams of God; we are now the beloved of God. For every one in their age are as they were in theirs; and as the promises of God were yea to them, and saved their souls, because they trusted on them, so certainly every promise of God is a shield for those that will have recourse to it. 'The name of God is a strong tower,' Prov. xviii. 10; and his word is his name whereby he will be known in his promises. Have recourse to it on all occasions, rely on the word, wrestle with him when his dealings seem contrary, though his dealings with us seem to be yea and nay. We have been God's children, he hath assured us that we were in the state of grace; but now he deals with us as if we were not his children, he afflicts us, he suffers Satan to be let loose on us to tempt us. Here flesh and blood is ready to say, Certainly I am not God's child, can I be? thus and thus followed as I am. No, no! God's 'gifts are without repentance,' Rom. xi. 29. Hadst thou ever grace? God hath said it, who is truth itself, that his 'gifts are without repentance.' Build on it therefore. If thou hadst ever any grace, where he hath begun he will make an end. 'Where he hath begun a good work, he will perfect it to the day of the Lord,' Philip. i. 6.

Therefore wrestle with God in all temptations. When things seem contrary, yet allege God's nature to him; and his word, for both are true; and one is true, because the other is true.

He is true in his nature and true in his word, and free in his decree, whatsoever his actions seem to be. Yet, Lord, thou canst not deny thyself, thou art unchangeable, thou art truth itself. And thy word that hath promised regard and respect to humble sinners that repent and come to thee, it is unchangeably true as thyself. Therefore, Lord, 'I will not leave thee, though thou kill me,' as Job saith, xiii. 15. Here is a ground of wrestling as Job did. Allege the nature of God and the word of God against his dealing. Let his dealing be what it will, his nature is true, and his word is true. Therefore his promises are true, which is a branch of his word, that if we repent, and confess our sins, he will be merciful to us.

Therefore let us not forsake our own mercy. This will uphold us, as in all temptations, so in divine temptations, when God seems to forsake us: so Christ himself, our blessed head, did. We cannot have a better pattern. When God left him on the cross, and left him to his human nature, to wrestle with the devil's temptations, and the pains of his body, and the sense of his wrath; 'My God, my God, why hast thou forsaken me?' Mark xv. 34; yet he upheld himself that God was his God still; and so likewise in the former example of Job. I say it is a special comfort, that God's word is not 'yea and nay.' As I said, it is not doubtful as the oracles of the Gentiles, the oracles of the devil; but God's word is certain. Whatsoever it was to any saint of God heretofore, it is to every believing, to every humble afflicted soul now, and shall be to the end of the world. So much for that.

VERSE 19.

'*For the Son of God, Jesus Christ, who was preached among you by us, by me, and Silvanus, and Timotheus, was not yea and nay, but in him is yea.*' In the words the apostle shews in particular what he preached among them, and we have in them these particulars briefly to be unfolded:

First, That Christ Jesus, in his nature and his offices, is the chief and main object and subject matter of preaching.

Secondly, That to make him profitable to us, he must be preached.

Thirdly, That consent of divines and preachers helps faith.

Fourthly, That Jesus Christ, being preached by the apostles, is an undoubted 'yea,' that is, an undoubted ground and foundation to build on, in all the uncertainties of this life, in all the uncertainty of religion. Jesus Christ preached by St Paul and other holy men of those times, was not 'yea and nay, but yea.'

Doct. 1. *First, Christ Jesus is the main object of preaching.*

It were impertinent here to stand on particulars, to shew you how Christ is the Son of God; for he is brought in here as the object of preaching. Only in a word, we must of necessity believe that Christ Jesus is the Son of God. For how wondrously doth this stablish our faith when we believe in a Saviour that is God; the Son of God, Jesus Christ by eternal generation. In a word, here are these prerogatives of Christ's generation from all other sons whatsoever. Other fathers are before their sons, this Son of God was eternal with his Father. Other fathers have a distinct essence from their sons, the father is one, and the son another; they have distinct existences; but here there is one common essence to the Father and the Son. Other fathers beget a son without them, but this Father begets his Son within him. It was an inward work. So it is a mystical divine generation, which indeed is a subject of admiration rather than of explication, that Jesus Christ is the Son of God and the Son of man. This was typified in the ark. The ark was a type of Christ. The ark had wood, and gold that covered that wood. Christ's human nature was the wood, and his divine nature that contained it, that is the gold. But I should be too large, and besides* the scope of the text, if I should unfold this point. I only touch it by the way. Christ Jesus in his natures as he is God and man, and in his offices as Jesus Christ, that is, anointed as king, priest, and prophet, and in his estates of abasement, and advancement, is the main subject matter of preaching. For what can we say, but it must be reductive, and brought to Christ? If we open men's consciences by the law, and tell them what a terrible estate they are in, what do we but drive them to the physician. What is the law, but as John Baptist was to Christ, to prepare the way, to level the soul, to pull down the high thoughts and imaginations, to make way and passage for Christ? And then in Christ, when we preach Christ, we preach his natures, God and man, and his offices, as king, priest, and prophet, as he is predestinate, and sealed, and anointed by God the Father for that purpose, that we may have a strong Saviour, strong in himself, and authorised by his Father. And we preach his estates of abasement, as he was crucified and suffered for our sins; and his estate of exaltation, as he arose and ascended into glory. These things belong to the preaching of Christ.

And then the benefits we have by him, reconciliation to his Father by his death, and peace of conscience, and joy in the Holy Ghost, and such like wondrous benefits we have by him.

And then our duty to him again, which is faith, and a conversation worthy; to embrace all that is offered by Christ, that it be not lost for want of apprehending. Christ Jesus is the subject matter of our preaching, in his natures, in his offices, in the benefits we have by him, in the duties we owe to him, in the instrument of receiving all,—faith. For in preaching, that faith which we require to lay hold on Christ, is wrought.

For preaching doth not only manifest the benefits we have by Christ, but is a potent instrument of the Spirit of God to work this qualification, to make Christ profitable to us. Now all that we preach of holy duties, is either to humble us if we have them not, to make us fly to Christ by faith; or when we believe, to make us walk answerable to our faith. So whatsoever we preach is reductive to Christ; either to prepare us, or to furnish us to walk worthy of Christ. Indeed, Jesus Christ is all in all in our preaching, and he should be so in your hearing. Of all things you should desire to hear most of Christ. The apprehension of your sinfulness should drive you to Christ. The hearing of duties should be to make you adorn your

* That is, 'beside.'—G.

Christian religion you have taken on you. Naturally men love to hear flashes, witty conceits, and moral points wittily unfolded; but all these in the largest extent do but civilize men. It must be Christ unfolded, and God's love, and mercy, and wisdom in him reconciling mercy and justice together: the wondrous love of God in Christ, and his justice, and mercy; and the love of Christ in undertaking to work our redemption; and the benefits by Christ, his offices, estates, and conditions. These things work faith and love. These things do us good.

All other things, take them at the best, they do but fashion our carriage a little; but that which enlivens and quickens the soul is Jesus Christ.

Use. Therefore we should of all other things *be desirous to hear of Jesus Christ.* It is a point that the very angels are students in. For the ark, which I named before, it had the law, and the mercy-seat in it, the mercy-seat to cover the law. Now Christ hath satisfied the law, and reconciled his Father, he hath freed us from the curse of the law, and hath given full satisfaction to the law. He is the mercy-seat, by whom we have access to God the Father.

Now the angels were upon the mercy-seat, interviewing one another, and prying down upon the mercy-seat, insinuating, that the reconciling of God's justice and mercy by that infinite wisdom of God in Christ; that our sins should be punished in him, and yet he be merciful to us; that he should punish our surety for us; that he should join these attributes together; that all the creatures in heaven and earth could not devise it, is a matter for angels to pry into. The very frame of the ark signified this. And shall not we be students in those mysteries, that the angels themselves desire every day more and more to understand? If Christ be the main thing we are to stand on, let us labour more and more to understand 'Christ, and him crucified;' let us see our nature in him advanced now in heaven, to make us heavenly-minded; let us see our nature in him punished; let us see our sinful nature in him cleansed and purged by his death and abasement; let us see our nature in him enriched.

Let us consider him as a public person, and see our interest in his humiliation, and exaltation in glory; because he is the 'second Adam.' These things should raise up our thoughts wondrously to think of his humiliation, and his exaltation, and of the love and mercy of God in him. And then think of what you will, nothing is discouraging; think of death, of hell, of the day of judgment; think of Satan, of the curse of the law; they are terrible things. Aye, but think of the Son of God, of Christ anointed of God the Father to satisfy the law, to satisfy his justice, to overcome Satan, to crush his head, to be our Saviour as well as our Judge at the day of judgment; these things will make all vanish. Things that are most terrible to the nature of man without the consideration of Jesus Christ the Son of God, all are most comfortable when we think of him. Now when we think of Satan, we think of one crushed and trod under foot, as he shall be ere long. When we think of judgment, we think of a Saviour that shall be our Judge. When we think of God, we think of God reconciled in Christ. We have access by Christ to the throne of grace. He is now in heaven, and makes intercession for us. When we think of death, we think of a passage to life where we shall be with him, 'I desire to be dissolved, and to be with Christ,' Philip. i. 23. So the things that are most uncomfortable, yet bring the consideration of them to Christ exalted in heaven, having triumphed over all these in our nature, and sits at God's right hand. The thoughts of these things are comfortable meditations.

Nay, think of that which is the most terrible of all, the justice of God, his anger for sin, it is a matter of comfort above all other. God is just to punish and revenge sin; what then? Because he is just he will not punish one thing twice; but his justice is fully satisfied, and contented in his Son Christ Jesus, whom he hath anointed, and predestinate, and sent himself; and he must needs acknowledge that satisfaction that is done by him, that he hath sent himself. Hereupon we come to think comfortably of God's justice.

God out of Christ is a 'consuming fire,' Heb. xii. 29. There is nothing more terrible than God without Christ; but now in Christ we can think of the most terrible thing in God with comfort. Therefore St Paul makes it the main scope of his preaching, and so should we of ours; and you should make it your main desire in hearing, and the main subject matter of your meditating, something concerning Christ. Let us often think of our nature in him now exalted in heaven, and that we shall follow him ere long. Our head is gone before, and he will not suffer his body always to rot in the earth. Let us think of his natures, and his offices, and all the blessed prerogatives that we have by him, and all the enemies that are conquered by him, that in him we have God reconciled, and the devil vanquished, we have heaven opened, and hell shut; we have our sins pardoned, and our imperfections by little and little cured; in him we have all in all.

There are four things that the apostle speaks of, which includes all, 1 Cor. i. 30. 'Of him are ye in Christ Jesus, who of God is made to us wisdom, righteousness, sanctification, and redemption.' Christ Jesus is all in all. If we be ignorant, he is our 'wisdom;' if we want righteousness and holiness to stand before God, 'he is our righteousness.' We stand righteous, being clothed with his righteousness. If we want grace, 'Of his fulness we receive grace for grace,' John i. 16. He is sanctification to us. If we be miserable, as we shall be to our sense, our bodies shall be turned to rottenness, 'he is our redemption,' not only of the soul, but of the body. He shall make our bodies 'like his glorious body,' Philip. iii. 21. As he makes our souls glorious, by his Spirit conforming them to his own image here, he means here redemption of our bodies from corruption, as well as of our souls from sin. 'He is all in all.' In sin, he is sanctification; in death, he is life; in ignorance, he is wisdom. There is nothing ill in us, but there is abundant satisfaction and remedy in Christ. I speak this the rather to shew what reason St Paul had to stand on this, that all his preaching was to bring Christ Jesus among them. I go on.

'*The Son of God, Jesus Christ, preached among you.*'

Doct. 2. *All the good we have by Christ is conveyed by the ministry.*

Despise that, and despise Christ himself. Therefore whatsoever benefits we have by Christ, they are attributed to preaching; they are attributed to the gospel as it is preached and unfolded; therefore it is called 'The gospel of the kingdom,' 'The word of reconciliation,' 'The word of life,' 'The word of faith.' All these are by Christ. But it is no matter, whatsoever we have by Christ, we must have it by Jesus Christ unfolded in the ministry of the word. Despise the ministry, that is contemptible to flesh and blood, and despise Christ himself, despise the kingdom, and life, and all; for Christ preached is that we must rely on, Christ unfolded. The bread of life must be broken, the sacrifice must be anatomized and laid open, Christ Jesus the Son of God must be preached. He profits not but as he is preached. His riches must be unfolded, 'the unsearchable riches of Christ,'

Eph. iii. 8. Therefore God, that hath appointed us to be saved by Christ, hath appointed and ordained preaching, to lay open Jesus Christ among us.

But, to come to the third point.

Doct. 3. *Consent of ministers a help to faith.*

Why doth he bring in consent to help? 'By me, and Silvanus, and Timotheus.' Would not his own authority serve the turn?

I answer, no; it would not sometimes. In itself it will, but in regard of the weakness of men, it is necessary to join the consent of others. St Paul was an apostle of Christ, but he knew that they were so weak, that they would regard his testimony the more for the joint testimony of 'Timotheus and Silvanus,' and the rest.

God considers not so much what is true in itself, as how to stablish our faith in it. As in the sacrament, would not God give Christ and his benefits? is he not true of his word? Yes! but he gives the sacrament for us. His promises are sure enough, yet he condescends to our weakness, to add sacrament, and oath, and all the props that may be. So the men of God, that are led by the Spirit of God, though their own authority were sufficient, yet they condescend to the weakness of others. Therefore St Paul allegeth with himself, 'Silvanus and Timotheus,' to strengthen them the better.

Then again, consent is a lovely thing, and proceeds from love. How sweet a thing is it for brethren to dwell together in unity; therefore we ought to stand much upon consent, if it may persuade us. But as Cyprian saith well, 'it must be consent in the truth' (*qqq*). Consent that is not in the truth, is not properly concord, but conspiracy; consent in a lie, in falsehood. The builders of Babel they had a consent among themselves when they came for a wicked purpose, as we see ofttimes in Scripture. Consent must be in the truth, in that which is good, or else it is not consent, but conspiracy. By reason of our weakness, consent is useful, and that is the reason why in doubtful cases we may allege antiquity; not that the word is not sufficient in itself, but to help our weakness, to shew that we do not divert from the truth, but that it is a truth warranted by others before. In doubtful cases this is warrantable. He brings it likewise to enforce obedience the more, when it was a truth brought to them by so many. But that is not a thing I mean to stand on, a touch is enough.

That which I will spend a little more time in, is the next thing, that is, that

Doct. 4. *Evangelical doctrine now is most certain.*

Something I spake of it before in the former verse, but I have reserved something to speak of it now. The Son of God preached by St Paul, with the consent of these blessed men, it was not 'yea and nay,' it was not unconstant. Evangelical truth is not yea and nay; and the preachers of it, the apostles, were not 'yea and nay' in the delivering of it. As it is true in itself, so it was true in the delivery of it. They were constant in it, they sealed it with their blood some of them.

Quest. How shall we know the doctrine of the gospel concerning Christ to be yea, undoubtedly true?

Ans. 1. I answer, *how do we know the sun shines?* I know it by its own light, and by a light that I have in my eye. There is an inward light joined with the outward light. So it is in this business, how do we know divine truth out of the book of God to be divine? By the light in itself, by the majesty of the Scriptures, by the consent of the Old and New Testament, by the opposition of the enemies, and the confusion of them at the last that have been opposers of it, by the miraculous preservation of it, and the like; but especially by the powerful work of it on the heart, by the experience of this blessed truth. I know this to be an undoubted truth, I find it quelling my corruptions, changing my nature, pacifying my conscience, raising my heart, casting down high imaginations, turning the stream of nature another way; to make me do that which I thought I should never have done, only because I have a strong light of divine truth and comfort. There is this experience of Christ, that a man finds in his soul. It sets him down that he can say nothing, but that it is divine truth, because he finds it so (*rrr*).

Ans. 2. Besides this, *the testimony of the Spirit of God, and the work of the Spirit in him.* For as to see, there is an outward light required, and an inward light in the eye; so to see divine truth there must be a light in itself, a divine sparkle in God's book, in every passage; but yet I must have an eye to see too. I cannot see it except God witness to my soul, that these things are divine, that they are yea, that they are certainly and infallibly true.

There is a great difference between us and our adversaries. I can but touch it, and I need but touch it. They say we must believe, and we must believe because of the church. I say no. The church, we believe, hath a kind of working here, but that is in the last place. For God himself in his word, he is the chief. The inward arguments from the word itself, and from the Spirit they are the next. The church is the remotest witness, the remotest help of all. For the church is but to propound God's truth, to lay it open; to be as it were the candlestick. Now the candlestick shines not, but upholds the candle while that shines. So the church is but to propose, to set up divine truth, that of itself being set up will enlighten well enough. The church is to set out the word, and to publish it by the ministry, which word of itself will shine. That work which the church hath therefore is the last, and the inferior; for the Spirit of God, and the inward majesty of the word, is of more force.

If a messenger come, and bring a relation, or bring a letter from one, and he tells me many things of the man; aye, but I doubt him, because he may be false for aught I know; but when I see his hand and seal, and his characters and style, that shews such a spirit to be in him, I know by his own characters certainly this comes from the hand of that man. Now, the messenger brings it and gives it, but I believe it, because I see the characters and hand and seal of such a one, that it is a truth. So the church propounds. It is the messenger that brings the truth of God to us; but when a Christian soul hears the truth, and sees God's seal upon it, there is a majesty and power that works on the soul. Now, we believe not for the messenger, but for the thing itself. Here is the difference. We believe the Scripture for the seal of divinity that is in itself; they believe it for the messenger, as if a doubtful messenger should come that is not certain, and a man should believe the things he brought for him, for his sake. We believe and entertain the messenger for the message sake, not the message for the messenger's sake. Our faith is better built than theirs.

Obj. But they say, This all comes to this at the last, God speaks by the church as well as by the Scriptures; therefore, the church is to be believed more than the Scripture itself.

Ans. I answer, God speaks indeed in his church by his Spirit and by his word; but his speaking by his word is the cause of his speaking in the church. For what is the church but begotten by the seed of the word? How is the church a church but by the word? Therefore, he speaks first by the Scriptures. There is a majesty and a spirit in the Scriptures. And then he speaks by the church, as cleaving to the Scriptures, in a secondary manner. He speaks by the church mediately, because that goes to the word which speaks immediately. The word was written by men led immediately by the Spirit of God; and the church relying on that, he speaks by them in the church, but primarily by his word. Having just occasion, I thought to touch this.

Undoubtedly, there are none that are not led with partiality, but incomparably they see our faith is built on a better foundation than theirs. They have a rotten foundation. They talk of a church, and when all comes to all, the church their mother is nothing, but the pope their father. What is their church but the pope himself? For they run from the church essential to the church representative. They run to councils, and when we force them with councils that they may err, then the pope, he is the church virtually. So, I say, the church their mother is nothing but the pope their father; and what manner of men they have been; histories tell us well enough. We see on what ground they build.

Jesus Christ, that is, the gospel by him, is not 'yea and nay, but yea;' that is, it is certainly, and infallibly, and eternally true.

Quest. Hereupon we may answer that curious question that hath been, and now is, everywhere, how we may know that our church was before Luther's time or no,* as they idly say, how we may know that the faith that we profess is the ancient faith.

Ans. I answer hence, Take these grounds:

First. There is but one faith. Men have varied, but faith hath not varied, as St Austin saith well. For there is but one faith, as there is one God, one heaven, and one happiness. There was one faith from Adam. The times vary, but not the faith of the times; the same fundamental truth hath been in all times. Sometimes it hath been more explicated and unfolded, as we have the canon enlarged now in the time of the New Testament in many books. There is not a new faith, but a larger explication of the old faith. Divine truth is alway the same. It was one faith from the beginning of the world, from the first promise to Adam in paradise, till now. Abraham believed as we do now. So they were all saved by faith, Heb. xi.

Even as there is one catholic church, consisting of all the members, the triumphant being the greater part, from the beginning of the world to the end of the world, so there is one faith. Take that for a ground. Indeed, the church varies as a man varies when he is a child and when he is a man. He hath one manner of clothes when he is a child, and another when he is a man. So the church varies in clothes. It was clothed with ceremonies then, which were cast off in Christ; but this is but a variation of garments. The church had one faith.

Second. Hereupon comes a second, *there is one catholic church, that is built on that one faith*, one essential church, one catholic company that believe in Christ, from the beginning of the world to the end of the world, which we believe in the apostles' creed. Well, then, this being so, as it is undeniable that it is so, what church is built upon that one faith that was 'yea' in the apostles, and was 'yea' before then, as the apostle saith here, 'Our preaching was yea,' certain and true, you may build on it, what

* See note *d*, vol. ii. p. 248; and see *sss*.—G.

church builds on that? That church all the while hath been; for there is but one faith and one truth that runs along in all ages, which is the seed of the church. Therefore, there must be a church in all ages that is a branch of the catholic church. Why? The church must be built upon that one faith; therefore, all particular churches before us, that were branches of the general church, were built upon that preaching of the apostle, which he saith was 'yea.' There is but one faith, and therefore all churches that are true are built upon that one faith. If we can prove that the apostolical doctrine agrees with our times, that ours hath consanguinity with the apostles' doctrine, then our church was before we were, ever since the apostles. It hath been alway yea, for there is but one truth.

The church is built upon the foundation of the prophets and apostles; and Christ saith, Mat. xvi. 18, when Peter said to Christ, 'Thou art the Son of God,' &c., saith he, 'Thou art Peter, and upon this rock,' that is, upon this confession of thine, 'will I build my church.' So the confession of faith is the rock of the church. Now there is alway one rock of the church that is alway yea. If our church be built upon that rock, then it is founded upon apostolical doctrine, upon the prophets and apostles. It was before we were. And if there were any church, then it was ours, which professeth that one faith.

If we conjure the papists, they are silent, they dare say nothing. Dare they say their doctrine is nearer apostolical than ours? They dare not say but ours is nearer. Why, then, our church is built upon the foundation of the apostles. Why so? All the churches since have been built upon one foundation, because there is one faith and one church. Unity of faith makes the unity of the church.

The seed of the church is the gospel, is divine truth. Now, if divine truth hath been alway, there hath been a church alway; and if there hath been a church alway, there hath been divine truth that hath been 'yea' alway. Now, it is an article of our faith in all times to believe a catholic church. Therefore, there is a certain truth that is always yea, to be the seed and foundation of that catholic church. Therefore, we must search out what that 'yea' was, what was the apostolical doctrine, the positive doctrine in those apostolical times, in the virgin-times of the church, before the church was corrupted. The church was not long a virgin, as the Father said. What was the yea of those truths? Some there must be alway that held apostolical truths in all ages. Our church holds that positive truth that the apostles held: for directly in so many words, we defend the apostolical faith out of the apostles. Therefore, we say our church was before Luther, because our doctrine is apostolical, and the church continually hath been apostolical, because it was built upon the apostles' doctrine.

Our church hath no doctrine in the positive fundamental points of it contrary; therefore our church hath continued. Put case we cannot name the men, as idly and ridiculously they urge, what is that to the purpose? Shall we go from ignorance of particular men, to ignorance of the church? We must believe that there is a catholic church; and there must alway be a positive doctrine and truth, the seed of that church.

Obj. The papists cavil with us, and say we possess a negative religion. Ye cut off our opinions, say they, but what have you of your own? what affirmatives have ye?

Ans. It is most certain, that all our affirmatives have been ever since the apostles' time; for we and the papists differ not in affirmatives, only they add patcheries* of their own. Religion stands most in affirmatives, that is the ground first. For we believe negatives, because they agree not to affirmatives: we believe a lie to be a lie, because it is contrary to positive truth, and the truth is before a lie; the affirmation is before the negation; a thing is, before the contrary is not. This laying for a ground, affirmatives being truths, our positive truths that we hold have been held in the apostles' times, before and since, even in the Church of Rome a thousand years after; and even now the affirmatives that we hold.

Do not they believe the Scriptures to be the word of God? Yes! But they add patcheries of their own, the Apocrypha, and their own traditions, to be the word of God too.

Do not they believe that Christ is Mediator? Yes! But he is the only Mediator for redemption, and not for intercession. They join others with him, saints and angels.

We are saved by faith, that is the affirmative, and so say they. But they add of their own, that we are saved by faith and works.

Then again, we say there are two sacraments, baptism and the Lord's supper; and so say they, but they add five of their own. So I might run over all their opinions. Whatsoever we hold, they hold. Therefore in their own confessions, our affirmatives have been ever since the apostles' times. If they had any church, we had a church, because our foundations are included in their religion. All that we say, they say; but then again they say many things that we do not. Therefore they account us heretics, because we make not that that they hold to be our yea too.

Again, the negatives that they believe, and we do not believe, they are but novelties in experience, they are not of the ancient apostolical faith. That the apocrypha should be had in equal authority with the word of God in Scripture, alas! such a conceit was not thought of for six hundred years after the apostles. That the people should not read the Scriptures, it was but since the other day. Transubstantiation, since the Council of Lateran, a thousand years since Christ. That the pope should be supreme, and depose princes, such a thing was not heard of a thousand years after Christ. That he should have authority to canonize saints, it was but since the other day. Equivocation, but of late time. And so their idle babbling of divine service in Latin, and twenty other trumperies. So the things that we deny that are gross and abominable in the judgment of every man that knows anything, they were but since the other day; they were not yea in the apostles' times. Then the apostolical church being not built on them, they must be devised after. As, indeed, a thousand years after Christ the most of these were never heard of. The most of the points of popery wherein they differ from us, nay, not any of them, were never established by a council till the Council of Trent, except transubstantiation, by the Council of Lateran, which was a thousand years after Christ (*ttt*).

The affirmatives that we hold, and they hold too, we say they are constant from the apostles' time; they have been in all ages maintained and affirmed.

Our positive points that we ground out of St Paul, and out of the Scriptures: we seek the 'old way,' and the 'best way,' as Jeremiah adviseth us, Jer. vi. 16. There was none of the popish trash in Abraham's time, in the patriarchs' time, in Christ's and his apostles' time, or in many hundred years after. They came in by little and little, for their own advantage; a

* That is, patches.—G.

mere policy to get money, and to abuse people. I say, they hold all our positive truths; but their error is in addition.

Quest. Now this question may be made, whether their additions may be dangerous or no? Because it may be supposed that some among them will say that heresy is not in addition, but in contrariety to the faith, and detracting; but when one holds more than they should, that is no heresy, because there is somewhat superabounds; now we hold the truth, and more too.

Ans. I say it is gross and false; for if additions did not overthrow the foundation, there should never be any idolatry, nor never any heresy in these times. What was idolatry, especially in the church of God? Among the Jews was there not the worshipping of the true God? Yes! but before an image, their additions, their false manner overthrew the true. There is none of them fundamental points, as we call them, though they make them fundamental. They make their traditions of as much authority as the word of God; and their fooleries as the articles of faith. They overthrow the main foundation. They are such additions as are destructive, to join with the word of God traditions. To worship God under another species and kind, is to be an idolator. Though they worship the true God, if it be after a false manner, it is prohibited. St Paul saith, and with a commination, Gal. i. 8, 'If I or an angel from heaven teach otherwise.' Beside, put case it be not plainly and directly contrary, if he teach other things that are not necessary to be believed, 'let him be accursed.' We ought not to go from the Scriptures in any fundamental point of faith, under pain of a curse. Therefore popery is a cursed religion, in respect of their very additions.

Doth not St Paul tell the Galatians they were 'fallen from Christ,' Gal. v. 4, if they added circumcision to Christ? He doth not say if they did that which was directly contrary to faith: no! but in adding circumcision and works to Christ, they were fallen from Christ. Whole Christ, or no Christ. In some cases additions are heresies, and overthrow the foundation.

Quest. If this be so, we may answer another question easily: the apostolical doctrine you see is only yea: whether then it be safer to be a papist or a protestant, considering that whatsoever we hold they do hold?

Ans. I answer, to be a Protestant it is safer in any man's judgment; because all that we say, themselves say: it hath been apostolical. We can prove in all ages of the church our affirmatives, we have a catalogue of witnesses in all ages of them that held what we say. It was founded in the apostles, and then came down to all ages. But what they say distinct, and differing from us, they have not the like testimony for: for indeed they are so beaten that Bellarmine hath this, 'The authority of all councils and fathers, and all depends upon the authority of the present church.' Bring to them councils and fathers! Tush! tush! all authority depends upon the present church. What authority gives the present church, when twenty years after the church varies? What certainty is there, when all authority of former times shall depend upon the present church?

In those things wherein they differ from us, and that we deny, any understanding, reasonable man may see that they are novelties and corruptions. As for the pope to depose princes, if a man have but his naturals,* he may see it abominable. To pray in a 'strange tongue,' to debar the people of the wine, when Christ saith, 'Drink ye all of it,' 1 Cor. xi. 25, who that hath ordinary discretion but will think it absurd? There is nothing that

* That is, = the understanding he has as a man.—G.

we differ from them in, but a man that hath but his naturals will condemn. Therefore ours is safer a great deal by their own confession, the learnedest of them, that it is enough to believe as we do. Do we not believe the articles of the creed? Do we not believe the first four general councils? We do. Who then will not say that these are sufficient, being understood and believed, to make a man that he be no heretic?

Quest. I may answer hence another question, whether a papist may be saved or no? It is a curious question, you will say; but it is so ordinary that somewhat I must say.

Ans. I answer, no doubt but many of them are saved. How comes that to pass? They reverse their false grounds, and stick to those positive truths that they and we hold together; they reject their own works, and help of saints, and go to Christ only; for, as I said, popery is full of contradictions. Now a papist, when he comes to have his conscience awakened, he leaves the pope's indulgences, their five sacraments, justification by works, and then embraceth only Christ, and then he comes to our part. They live by their religion, and die by ours. So the question is, whether living or dying? Luther saith, If they live and die peremptorily in all the points professed in the Tridentine Council, they cannot (*uuu*). But no doubt many of them the Lord hath mercy on, to open their eyes to see the vanity of their works and of all their fooleries, which those that are wise and have their consciences enlightened turn off then, and so may be saved, but it must be with reversing the grounds of their religion, and sticking to ours, which is agreeable to the word.

Nay, to speak a little more of it, I say, we do more safely believe. We are more safe, and on better grounds led into some less errors, than they do believe main truths. It may seem strange, but it is most true.

For if so be a sound protestant maintain an error, it is because he thinks it is in the Scripture, that it is in the word; if it be discovered out of the word of God to be an error, he leaves it. As St Cyprian and other fathers, blessed saints in heaven, they held some errors; but if they saw the Scripture held otherwise, they had prepared minds to believe otherwise. Therefore, holding the main fundamental truths, though they held particular errors, they were saved.

The papists maintain fundamental truths with us. They believe the word of God, they believe in Christ, and to be saved by mercy; but upon what grounds? They believe the truth upon heretical, devilish grounds. As upon what grounds do they believe the articles of the faith to be so, and the Scriptures to be so? Because the church saith so. Who is the church but the pope? And what man is the pope ofttimes? A man, if we believe their own writers, led with a devilish spirit: some of them have been magicians. If they believe the truth, they do it not as divine truth. They believe the truth for matter; but the grounds of believing those truths are human, nay, worse, many times devilish. For you know in the Revelation, the beast is inspired with the spirit of the dragon, with the spirit of the devil, and teacheth the doctrine of devils, 1 Tim. iv. 1. Now, to teach that which is materially true, upon reasons that are diabolical or human (at the best, it is but human), as the testimony of the church is, what an unsafe thing is this!

Nay, I say, it is the most horrible witchery, the most horrible abomination that ever was since the beginning of the world, this principle, that their church cannot err: that is the reason of the believing of all divine truths. Hereupon they come to practise most abominable treacheries, hereupon they defend lies, hereupon they kill princes, and dissolve the bonds of allegiance that subjects owe to princes. And all human and divine things, all the light of nature and Scripture, all becomes a nullity. Why? Because the church cannot err. And this they have from their holy father the pope. He is above all councils and all, and cannot err. We know if principles be false, all other things are false. An error in principles is a dangerous error. An error in the ground is the worst thing in the world. As to maintain treason to be lawful, it is worse than to be a traitor; for his judgment is convinced already; but he that maintains a false principle, he is a dangerous man indeed. So, to have this abominable principle, that the church, that the pope cannot err, hence come all those dangerous practices in this commonwealth ever since the beginning of Queen Elizabeth's time.

Who would have thought, but that God gave up bitter, proud, poisonful spirits, vain spirits that rejected the word of God, that men of parts and understanding should ever be so sotted to believe such a thing, that a wretched ignorant man should get into the chair, and he should judge infallibly of the truths that he never knew in his life, being of another profession, as some are canonists, and not divines? But I leave that point.

To touch one thing more that borders a little upon this, that divine truth is of an inflexible nature, whatsoever men think of it. And that crosseth another rule of theirs, that they will give what sense they will of Scriptures, and the current of the present church must judge of all former councils. Now doth truth vary according to men's judgments, according to the present church? Must we bring the rule to the crooked timber, or the timber and the things to be measured to the rule? Shall the judgment of any man be the rule of truth? shall it be the rule in one time, and not in another? Shall present men interpret it thus, and say it is so now; and others that succeed say, whatsoever it was now, thus it must be believed?

Hereupon likewise, if it be the constant nature of truth alway to be believed; hereupon it comes to cross another thing, their dispensation. No man can dispense with God's law; truth is truth indispensable. Laws divine and natural are indispensable, because they are alike in all things. Reason is reason in Turkey as well as here. The light of nature is the light of nature in any country as well as here. Principles of nature vary not as languages do: they are inbred things.

If the principles of nature be invariable and indispensable, much more divine principles, saith the heathen. Filthiness is filthiness, whether thou think it to be so or no. Opinion is not the rule of things, but the nature of the thing itself.

Therefore whatsoever is against nature none can dispense with. 'God cannot deny himself!' 2 Tim. ii. 13. What was naught in one age is naught in another, and is for ever naught. Whatsoever is divine or natural is indispensable. No monarch in the world can dispense with the law of nature, or the divine law, the word of God; for the opinion of any man in the world is not the rule of his course, but the undoubted light of God, whether the light of nature or the light of divine truth.

I speak this the rather to cross base parasites, that when God calls them to stand for true causes, what do they make their rule? Not God's constant '*Yea*,' but they bend and bow to opinion, as if the opinion of any man in the world were the rule of their faith and obedience. This is to make men, and no men. Is not the written word of God the word of God? Is not the law the law? (Politic laws I speak not of.) Shall a man yield to men's opinion, especially if the word do not warrant it? Shall he yield to any man living that is inconstant by his disposition? There is truth which is certain, that a man must maintain to the death. He is not only a martyr that maintains religion. John Baptist was a martyr that stood out in a matter that was not against heresy, but for the standing out against Herod. He did not yield, as many thousands would have done in such a case. 'Thou must not have thy brother Philip's wife;' it is unlawful, Mark vi. 18.

Men ought to suffer for the truths of nature, and not deny truth whatsoever, because it is a divine sparkle from God. If it be any truth whatsoever, it must be stood in, because it is constant; and it is the best thing in the world next to divine and saving truth.

Use. If this be so, that the gospel and divine truth be 'yea,' and that the church at all times hath been built on that, and that whosoever is saved is saved by that yea, let us labour to have a faith answerable to our truth. We say, and distinguish well. There is a certainty of the thing, and a certainty of the mind apprehending the thing. It is certain the sun is bigger than the earth; but you shall never persuade a simple countryman that it is so. There is a certainty of the object, but not of the subject. He will never believe it, because it is against sense. But now there must be both in a Christian. The apostle's doctrine, the truth he doth believe, the truth in the Scripture is 'Yea,' that is, it is certain and true, and not 'yea and nay,' it is not flexible. It is not as the heathen oracles were, that is, doubtful and wavering. Let our assent be answerable to the truth; let us build soundly on a sound foundation.

As a ship that is to rest in the midst of the waves, there is a double certainty necessary, that the anchor-hold be good in itself, and that it be fastened upon somewhat that is firm. If it be a weak anchor, or if it be fastened upon ground that will not hold, the ship is tossed about with waves, and so split upon some rock or other. So our souls require a double certainty. We must have an anchor of faith as well as an object of faith; we must have an anchor of hope as well as an object. For the object we may cast anchor there. It is divine truth which will hold. There is no doubt of that. It is yea. But then our anchor must be firm, our faith and affiance. Let us labour to build soundly and strongly upon it. It should be our endeavour continually to stablish our faith, to stablish our hope, that we may know on what terms we live, and on what terms to die.

Do but consider the difference between an understanding, strong Christian and another. A Christian that is judicious and understanding, ask him in what estate he is. Why, comfortable! What is the ground of his faith? Why, thus: I live in no known sin, I confess my sins to God, my doctrine is 'yea,' and I labour to bring my life to my doctrine.

Ask another, What do you mean to live so loosely and carelessly? Why will you stand thus? Will you be content to die so? Perhaps he doth not know sound doctrine, or if he do, it is confusedly; he doth not build on that rock, on that foundation.

Oh! let us labour to build stronger and stronger on the truth. Our building strongly makes us eternal. God's truth is eternal truth, because it makes us eternal. Is it not a strange thing that man, that is chaff, and vanity, and smoke, whose life passeth as a tale that is told, that yet notwithstanding if he build on this yea, which is certain and infallible, the doctrine of the gospel, it will make him a rock, a living stone, it will make him eternal? 'All flesh is grass, but the word of God endures for ever,' 1 Pet. i. 25.

What a comfort is this, our life being a vapour, and vanity, and growing to nothing, that the time will shortly come when we shall be no more, no more in this world; then to have divine truth that will make us eternal! Ps. xc. Moses, a good man, he saw men drop away. Saith he, 'Thou art our eternal habitation from generation to generation.' What is the meaning of that? That is, we dwell in thee. Here in our pilgrimage to Canaan we drop away, but 'thou art our habitation from generation to generation.' So when a Christian considers his life is uncertain, all things are vanity that support this life, yet notwithstanding I have a 'yea' to build on, the divine truth. 'The word of the Lord endures for ever,' and it will make me endure for ever. It is a rock itself, it makes me a rock; it will make me a living stone, built on that foundation, that all the gates of hell shall not prevail against my faith and hope.

What a comfort is this! We have nothing without this 'yea.' We are 'yea and nay,' and our happiness is 'yea and nay.' We are so happy now, as we may be miserable to-morrow. Let us labour to build on divine truth, which is like itself, that in all the changes of the world we may have somewhat that is unalterable, that is as unchangeable as God himself. As St Paul here brings God himself, 'as God is true, my word to you was not yea and nay, but yea.' So much shall suffice for that verse. I go on to the 20th verse.

VERSE 20.

'*For all the promises of God in him are yea, and in him amen.*' This comes in after this manner, My preaching to you, saith he, was invariable and constant, because Christ himself is alway 'yea.' If Christ, the matter of my preaching, be always 'yea,' and I preach nothing but Christ, then my preaching is invariable and constant. How doth he prove the *minor?* How doth he prove that Christ is alway 'yea?' 'All the promises of God in him are yea, and in him amen.' Christ is invariable, and my preaching of him was not 'yea and nay.' Christ is not 'yea and nay,' because 'all the promises of God in him are yea and amen.'

'The promises of God in him are yea,' that is, they are constant; 'and in him they are amen.' There is some diversity in reading the words (*vvv*). But most constantly the best expositors have it as this translation hath it, 'all the promises of God in him are yea, and in him amen.' The literal meaning is this, 'all the promises of God in Christ are yea,' that is, they are certain, they are made in him; 'and in him they are amen,' that is, they are accomplished in him. In him they are made, and in him they are accomplished.

I might spend a great deal of time to shew the acception* of the word 'amen,' but it is not pertinent to my purpose.

'Amen' is here certain, undoubtedly certain, as it is here to make way to that which is to be understood.

There are three main senses of 'amen.' It signifies that a thing is positively so, and not no, it is so. 'Yea and amen' signify that such a thing is; as, 'let your yea be yea,' Mat. v. 37, such a thing is. But now 'amen'

* That is, 'acceptation.'—G.

is more, not only that a thing is, but it is so truly, and so unchangeably; it is 'yea *and amen.*' The promises are 'yea,' they are made in Christ; and then they are true in him, undoubtedly, eternally, unchangeably true.

So take it in the strictest, in the strongest, sense you can; all the promises of God in Christ they are so true, that they are invariably, constantly, eternally true in him, they are made in him, and performed in him; 'they are yea in him, and amen in him.' So the whole carriage of the promises is only in Christ.

The truths we are to deliver out of the words are these:

First of all we must know, that since the fall of man it hath pleased the divine nature, the three persons in Trinity, *to stablish a covenant of grace, and so of salvation in Jesus Christ; and to make him a second principle, a second Adam, by whom mankind is restored to a better estate than ever we had in the first Adam.* God now since the fall takes another course to bring us back again to him. He doth not leave us as he left the angels that fell, in a state of perdition for ever; but as we fell by infidelity and distrust of him, so now we are recovered again by promises, and by faith in them.

There can be no intercourse between God and man but by some promise on his part.

Obs. God deals with man by promises.

Reason 1. The reason is this, *how can man dare to challenge anything of the great majesty of God without a warrant from himself?* How can the conscience be satisfied? The conscience looks to God. It is a knowledge together with God; how can conscience rest but in that it knows comes from God? Therefore for any good that I hope for from God, I must have a promise.

Reason 2. For this *is God's constant dispensation, while we live in this world we are alway under hope.* We are children of hope. 'We are saved by hope,' Rom. viii. 24: 'we rejoice in the hope of glory,' Rom. v. 2: and hope looks to the promises, whereof some part is unperformed. How doth heaven and earth differ? Heaven is all performance. Here is some performance to encourage us, and there is alway some promise still unperformed. We are alway under some promise; and therefore the manner of our apprehending God in this world differs from heaven. Here it is by faith and hope, there by vision. Vision is fit for performance. Faith and hope looks to the promise alway here. Therefore God rules his church by promises; partly, I say, to secure the soul of man. We cannot have any thing from God but by the manifestation of his own good will. How can we look for any thing from God but by promise? Can we look for anything from God by our own conceits? That is a fool's paradise.

Further, God will have his church ruled by promises in all ages, to exercise faith, and hope, and prayer, and dependence upon God. God will try of what credit he is among men, whether they will depend upon his promise or no; so that knowing he is true, by promise, it may be certain to them, they shall have performance in time. He gives men promises to see if they will trust him.

Reason 3. God will have this manner of dispensation to rule his church by promises, *to arm us in this world against fears and discouragements;* therefore we have alway some promise. He might have done us good, and have given us no promise; but now having given us promises, he will try the graces that are in us, and arm us against all discouragements and difficulties, till the thing promised be performed. For we must know that a promise is a divine thing, better than any earthly performance. Let

God give a man never so much in the world, if he have not a promise of better things, all will come to nothing at the last. Therefore God supports the souls and spirits of his children with promises, to arm them against all temptations on the right hand and on the left, that would draw them from trusting in his promise. He will have them live by faith, and that hath alway relation to the promise.

Quest. This is a general ground then, that God now in Christ Jesus hath appointed this way to govern the church with promises. Now what is a promise?

Ans. A promise is nothing but a manifestation of love, an intendment of bestowing some good, and removing some ill. A manifestation of our mind in that kind is a promise of conferring of a future good, or removing of a future ill; therefore it comes from love in the party promising.

There are three degrees of loving steps, whereof a promise is the last. The first is inward love; the second is real performance; and the third is a manifestation of performance intended before it be; and this, I say, is a degree of love. For love concealed, it doth not comfort in the *interim*, in the time that is betwixt. Now God, who is love, doth not only love us, and will not only shew his love in time, but because he will have us rest sweetly in his bosom, and settle ourselves on his gracious promises, in the mean time, he gives us rich and precious promises. He is not only love, and shews it in deed, but he expresseth it in word. And we may well build on his word, as verily as if he had performed it in deed; for whatsoever he saith is 'Yea, and Amen.' This is the nature of a promise. It is not only love, and the expression of love in deed, but the expression of it in word, when he intends to solace, and comfort, and stablish, and stay the mind of man till the good promised be performed.

Therefore, even from this we see how God loves us, that not only he hath an inward love in his breast, and doth good to us, but he manifests it by word. He would have us, as I said, live by faith, and stablish ourselves in hope.

Faith and hope are two graces altogether from promises. If there were no promise there could be no faith nor hope. What is hope? Nothing but the expectation of the things that the word saith. And what is faith, but a building on the word of God? Faith looks on the word that God will give such a thing, and hope looks upon the thing that the word promiseth: as the distinction is good, faith looks to the word of the thing, and hope looks to the thing in the word: faith looks to the word promising; hope looks to the performance of the thing promised. Faith 'is the evidence of things not seen,' Heb. xi. 1, because it sets the things that are absent as if they were present; hope is for the accomplishment of that. If there were no promise to hope, what needed hope? and where were a foundation for faith? Now God being willing to exercise faith and hope, feeds them both, and satisfies both, that we may be heavenly-wise in trusting and believing, and not foolish as men in the world. Therefore God hath given us promises, and sealed them with an oath, as we shall see afterward.

Now all promises coming from love, what love can there be in God to us since the fall, but it must be grounded on a better foundation than ourselves? If God love us, it must be in one that is first beloved: hereupon

Obs. 2. *Comes the ground of the promises to be Jesus Christ, God-man.* For all intercourse between God and us, it must be in him that is able to satisfy God. God will so in the covenant of grace entertain covenant and league with us, as that he will have his justice have full content,* he will be satisfied; and therefore he that will be the foundation of intercourse between God and us, he must be God-man, perfectly able to satisfy divine justice; he must be a friend of God's and a friend to us. Hereupon the promises must come from God's love in Jesus Christ; and he must first receive all good for us, and we must have it at the second hand from him. Hereupon it is said here, that 'all the promises of God *in him* are yea and amen.'

1. It is a rule, the first in any kind is the cause of all the rest. Now *Christ is the first beloved thing;* therefore in Col. i. 3, he is called 'the Son of God's love.' Christ being the only begotten Son of God, he looks on him first, before he looks on anything else; and whatsoever is lovely he looks on it as it is in him in whom his love is first, because he being his only begotten Son, he is the first object of all the respect that God hath. Therefore, whatsoever is beloved, it is as it hath a consistence in Christ. Therefore Christ he must first be loved, and then we in him; consider him as the Son of God.

2. Consider him *as man.* He is the first beloved, being a holy man above all other men; for the nature of man hath a subsistence in the second person in Christ. Therefore, Christ as man is beloved before all others, having a subsistence in his Godhead which is first beloved. He is the prime and most excellent creature as man. God looks first upon Christ as his only begotten Son, and upon Christ as man secondarily: upon the church in the third place as united to Christ; and all other creatures in reference to the church. And, therefore, there was never anything in the world, nor shall be, that ever was or shall be loved, but in the first-beloved Christ Jesus.

3. Again, Christ is first, because Christ *is the mediator between God and man by office.* Consider what relation he hath between God and man, and we may easily see that God first respects him, and us for him. For Christ being *God* and *man,* and *Mediator,* therefore, between God and man, he is loved of both. He is a friend to both, to bring both together. He is first regarded as Mediator, and then we for whose cause he is Mediator.

4. Then again, consider Christ, not as he is between God and us, *but as he is to us,* so he is first beloved. To God, he is his first begotten; to God and us a mediator. *To us a head, to us a husband, to us a brother;* a head from whence there is all influence of life and motion; a husband from whence we have all riches. He is all in all to us in the relations he stands in to us. Therefore he is first in all things, as the apostle saith, 'In all things he must have the pre-eminence,' Col. i. 18; and it is fit it should be so.

Especially since the fall. Leave the consideration of Christ, and this may be a reason. Consider us since the fall, as we are in the mass of corruption, are we fit objects for God's love? Are we not fuel for consuming fire? Is not he a 'consuming fire,' Heb. xii. 29, and we stubble for his wrath? Is not our nature defiled and tainted, and can it otherwise be amiable, than considered as knit to him that is first amiable, that is Christ? It cannot be. So look to Christ as the Son of God's love, whether as God or as man; look to his office as mediator, look on him as in relation to us as our husband and head; look on us without him, you may see that God's love is first founded in Christ, and then in us.

I mean in regard of execution in the passages of our salvation. For at

* That is, 'satisfaction.'—G.

first it was a free love that gave Christ to us, and us to Christ, 'So God loved the world, that he gave his Son,' John iii. 16. That was the first that set all the world in execution; but in the execution from predestination to glorification, before all worlds he loved us in Christ to everlasting. From the everlasting in election, to everlasting in glory, all is in Christ in regard of execution. We subsist in him, we are sanctified in him, we are justified in him, his righteousness is ours, we are glorified in him, we are loved in him; God blesseth us with all spiritual blessings in him, 'God hath made us accepted in his beloved,' Eph. i. 5, 6; in him who is his beloved Son, in whom he is well pleased; not only 'with whom,' but 'in whom,' in him and all his, in him as mystical Christ, head and members. God now looks upon our nature as it is united to the person of his only begotten Son; and thereupon our nature is lovely in the eyes of God, and enriched, and honoured, and advanced in Christ.

Even as a base woman by marriage with a great person is advanced; so our nature being mean of itself, taking our nature when it was defiled with sin (though that particular mass was sanctified by the Holy Ghost), it was much advanced and ennobled, by having a subsistence in the second person. So God looks on us in Jesus Christ, and loves us in him, and bestows all spiritual blessings in Christ.

Therefore whatsoever we have, Christ must have it first for us; whatsoever is done to us, must be done first to Christ. Christ is first predestinate, as it is, 1 Peter i. 2. He is the predestinate Lamb of God. He was ordained before all worlds, to be a sacrifice for us, and to be the head of his church. He was ordained before we were ordained. Christ is first beloved, and then we are beloved in his beloved. He is well pleased in him, and then in us. He is first loved, and then we. He is predestinate, and then we. He is the Son of God's love by nature, therefore we are sons of God's love by adoption and grace. What we are by adoption, he is by nature first of all. Therefore we are said to be elected in him, and sanctified in him. He first of all removes all ill, and then we have it removed, because he hath removed it. He is first justified from our sins, he is first quitted and freed from our sins, when he took them upon himself, and on the tree satisfied the wrath of God. 'He bore our iniquities, and by his stripes we are healed,' Isa. liii. 5. If he had not been freed from our sins, we had for ever lain under them. Therefore saith St Paul, 'If Christ be not risen, you are yet in your sins,' 1 Cor. xv. 13, *seq.* We are free from our sins, because Christ our surety is out of the prison of the grave. He is in heaven.

He must first rise from the dead. 'He is the first fruits of them that sleep; the first begotten from the dead,' Rev. i. 5; 1 Cor. xv. 20. For though some rose before, yet it was in the virtue of Christ, who rose altogether by his own strength. Therefore he hath made a 'living way' to heaven. 'We are born again to a lively hope by the resurrection of Christ from the dead,' 1 Peter i. 3. We have a lively hope, a hope that makes us lively in good works, because our surety is in heaven. Now we hope for an inheritance immortal and undefiled. Because he is risen, we shall rise. He is ascended, therefore we shall ascend. We do ascend in the certainty of faith now, and shall ascend indeed hereafter.

Whatsoever we do, he doth it first; and whatsoever we have from God, it is at the second hand. He hath it first, and conveys it to us; the natural Son to the adopted sons. Therefore all the promises come to be made in him, and not directly to us alone abstracted from Christ.

Use. It is a point we should often think of, and seriously consider of;

for it doth wondrously stablish our hearts. Doth God love me, and doth he do good to me abstracted from Christ, myself alone? No; for then, alas! I should fly from his presence; but he looks upon me, and considers me as I am in his Son. Therefore in John xvii. 24, in that blessed prayer of Christ, saith he, 'That thou mayest love them with the same love wherewith thou lovest me.' God loves us with the same love that he loves his Son with. 'That the love wherewith thou lovest me, may be in them.' He loves him first, and then he loves us with that love that he loves him. Here is the reason that God looks on us with a forbearing eye, notwithstanding all the matter of anger and wrath in us. He looks on us in his Son, as members of his Son. His love to us is founded on his love to his Son.

Hereupon back again is our boldness to God the Father, that we go to him in his beloved Son, and present his Son to him. Lord, look on thy Son that thou hast given for us, in whom we are members. We are not as in ourselves, but in thy beloved. For as all things descend from God to us, so our souls should ascend to him. All descends from God to us, in his Son. Why! all our comfortable considerations of God must be in his Son Christ. Thereupon we have boldness to God through him, not in ourselves but in and through Christ. Let us bring 'Benjamin,' Gen. xlii. 36, *seq.*, with us, bring Christ, and then we shall be welcome. If we come in the garments of our Elder Brother, then we shall get the blessing.

But of ourselves God cannot endure to look on us; therefore this is a heathenish conceit in our prayers, to presume to go to God otherwise than he hath clothed himself with the comfortable relation of a Father in Christ. If we consider him as a just God, as a God of vengeance, as a holy God, the more it makes to our terror, if we be not besotted. But go to him as he is now in his Son Christ, and go boldly. The heathens otherwise conceived wavering and doubtingly of a God; alas! conceiving him out of Christ, he was nothing but a 'consuming fire' to them, Heb. xii. 29.

How dares that man that knows himself, and that knows God, how dares he think of God? He thinks basely of God, that can think of him, and not think of him as he is to him in Christ. Darest thou think of God who is a 'consuming fire,' and not think of him as he is pleased and pacified in thy nature in Christ, that hath taken thy nature to be a foundation of comfort, to be a 'second Adam,' a public person for all that are in him, and members of him? To see God fully appeased in him who is God-man, thou mayest think of him with comfort then. Never think of the promises of grace or comfort, or anything without Christ.

Therefore St Paul saith, 'Now to Abraham and his seed was the promise made; he saith not to seeds, as to many, but to thy seed,' Gal. iii. 16; as speaking of one, even Christ. All the promises of good to us are made to Christ, and conveyed from Christ to us; the promises, and likewise the things promised. 'He hath promised to us eternal life, and this life is in his Son,' 1 John v. 11; and so grace, and whatsoever, it is in him. The promises and the things promised they are conveyed from God to Christ, and so to us. They are a deed of gift. We have them from and by Christ. Why are the angels attendants upon us? The angels attend upon Jacob's ladder, that is, Christ. It is he that knits heaven and earth together; so the angels, because they attend upon Christ first, they become our attendants. Whatsoever we are, whatsoever privileges we have, it is in Christ first. It belongs to us no further than we by faith are made one with Christ. Thus we see whatsoever we have from God, it is by promises. And these promises are not abstracted from love, for they are the fruits of love; and this love is seated in Christ, who hath satisfied God's justice. We have promises, and promises in Christ.

Obs. 3. In the third place, *the apostle saith that all the promises of God in him are yea.* They are constant and sure in him; they shall be performed.

All promises are either Christ himself, or by Christ, or from Christ, or for Christ. All promises that ever were made to God's people, they were either of Christ himself, when he was promised, or such as were promised for Christ. The promise of Christ himself is the first grand promise, that he should be made man, the promise in his own person. But whatsoever promise was made by the prophets and apostles, they were made by his Spirit, they were made for him, for his sake, and in him, and they were made to those that are in him too. For as God's love is founded in him to those that are in him mystically as the Son of his love, so the promises are made and given over to him of all good. He takes all the promises of good from God for us, and then they are made to us as we are in him.

He himself is the first promise that runs along in all the Scripture; and all the promises of Christ are 'yea;' for whatsoever was promised of Christ before he came, it was fulfilled when he came. For all types were fulfilled in him, and all prophecies, and all promises, they were all accomplished in him.

I. *All types, whether personal or real.*

1. For *personal types*, he was the 'second Adam.' Adam was a type of him. He is the true Adam. He was the true Isaac, the ground of laughter.* He is the true Joseph, advanced now to the kingdom, to the right hand of God. He is the steward of his church, to feed his church here, and bring her to heaven with himself afterward. He is the true Joshua, that brought Israel out of the wilderness to Canaan. He brings us from Moses, from the law, to heaven. He is the true Joshua, that brings us through Jordan, from death and miseries in this world to heaven. He is the true Solomon, the prince of peace.† So all personal types of kings and priests, as Aaron was a type of him, &c., they were yea in him, they were fulfilled in him.

2. And all *real types*.‡ He is the true 'mercy-seat' wherein God would be heard and prayed unto, for he covers the law, the curse of it, as the mercy-seat did. He is the true 'brazen serpent,' that whosoever looks on him with the eye of faith, 'shall not perish, but have everlasting life,' John iii. 15. He is the true 'manna,' the bread of life. That type had its 'yea' in Christ. He is the true sacrifice, 'the passover lamb,' the lamb of God 'that takes away the sins of the world,' John i. 29. If our hearts be sprinkled with his blood, the destroying angel hath nothing to do with us. The passover hath its 'yea' in him. Therefore that which is affirmed of the passover is affirmed of him, 'Not a bone of it shall be broken,' Ps. xxxiv. 20. That is attributed to Christ that was performed in the type. That is applied to Christ that was spoken of the passover; to signify the identity of the type, and the thing signified. He was the yea of that, and of all comfortable types that were real, and personal, all have their 'yea' in him.

Therefore saith our Saviour Christ, the last words of his almost upon the cross, 'All is finished,' John xix. 30, all the types real and personal.

II. And *all promises and prophecies have their 'yea' in Christ.* The first

* That is, the name Isaac means 'laughter.'—G.
† That is, the name Solomon means 'peace.'—G.
‡ That is, 'typical *things*.'—Ed.

promise, what was it but Christ? 'The seed of the woman shall break the serpent's head,' Gen. iii. 15. It was nothing but Christ, it was 'yea' when he was born; and when he died he crushed the serpent's head. 'By death he overcame him that had the power of death, that is, the devil,' Heb. ii. 14. So the promise that was renewed to Abraham, 'In thy seed shall all nations of the earth be blessed,' Gen. xii. 3, that is, in Christ. And so to David, that he should come out of his family. And that particular promise of Isaiah, 'that a virgin should conceive,' Isa. vii. 14. And the Baptist points him out, 'Behold the Lamb of God,' John i. 29. All the particular things that befell Christ in time, they were prophesied of before, and Christ was the 'yea' of all, that is, all had their determinate truth in Christ when he came. This is one reason why St Paul saith, 'All the promises in Christ are yea.' Whatsoever was promised concerning Christ, or foretold, it was 'yea' in him, concerning his birth, and the place of it; concerning his death, and the manner of it; concerning his resurrection and ascension; concerning his offices, all was foretold. As we see in Scripture, in the New Testament, it is the foot of divers verses, that 'it might be fulfilled;' so this that was foretold in the Old, it was fulfilled in the New. So Christ is the first promise, and whatsoever was said of him is 'yea and amen.' Whatsoever was spoken of Christ, it was 'yea' in the Old Testament and 'amen' in the New; it was made to them in the Old Testament and performed in the New.

And what is the Old and New Testament but this syllogism? He is the blessed seed, that is, the Son of the Virgin Mary, born in Bethlehem, that shall come in the end of Daniel's weeks, that shall come when the sceptre shall be departed from Judah, &c. He is the true Messiah, the true Christ, saith the Old Testament. Here is the 'yea.' 'Amen,' saith the New Testament to this. But Christ is the Son of the Virgin Mary, he suffered these things that it might be fulfilled. So all is 'amen' in the New Testament. I say, this is the main reason that all is built on. He in whom all these agree is the true Messiah. But, saith the New Testament, all these are 'amen' in Christ. Therefore Christ, the Son of the Virgin Mary, he is the true Messiah. We see whatsoever was prophesied concerning Christ himself, was 'yea.'

III. And not only so, *but all the prerogatives and good things that come by Christ are 'yea.'* They are undoubted in Christ, and they were 'yea' before he was. He profited before he was. He was 'yea' to Adam. Because, however he that was the seed of the woman came not till the latter end of the world, till four thousand years after the beginning or thereabouts, yet the faith of Adam and of Abraham made him present. Abraham 'saw Christ's day, and rejoiced,' John viii. 56. There was a virtue from Christ to all former ages. They all had benefit by Christ, as it is proved at large, Heb. xi. And in Acts xv. 11, 'We hope to be saved by Christ, as well as they,' insinuating that they hoped to be saved by Christ as well as we. So he was 'yea' for comfort to all that were before him, as well as now. All the promises were 'yea,' even to the patriarchs and prophets.

Even as if a man should undertake three or four years hence to pay a debt that is due by one that is subject to be carried to prison, and on that condition that this man shall be freed. I undertake at such a time to pay such a debt. So though the debt be paid three or four years hence, he is let go free that was obnoxious to go to prison for the debt, though it be to be paid after. So it was with Christ. He, the second person in the Trinity, undertook, being so appointed by God the Father. The blessed Trinity stablished this, that Christ should pay the debt by death; the debt to divine justice should be satisfied by the cursed death of the cross, that those that before should have gone to hell else for the debt, should be all freed that had any part and interest by faith in Christ, who should pay the debt afterwards. Christ undertook at such a time to be incarnate, and to pay it for us. God the Father to whom we were obnoxious, that was the creditor for the payment of that, four thousand years after, let them go. So Christ was yea to them, they had benefit by Christ's death.

Hereupon the prophets spake of him as a thing present, 'To us a Son is born, to us a child is given,' Isa. ix. 6. Faith mounts over many years, six hundred years before Christ in the prophet it mounted, and made the time of Christ's coming and his death to be present; because they had benefit by him as if he had been present. Only with this difference, in the time present when Christ came in the flesh they had some comfortable enlargement of grace. When he came in the flesh, I say, there was a new world as it were, there was grace poured out in abundance.

So you see that all the promises concerning Christ, they were performed; they were 'yea and amen,' and the good things by Christ. St Paul saith excellently, Heb. xiii. 8, 'Christ yesterday, to-day, and the same for ever.' Yesterday to the patriarchs, to-day for the present time he is 'yea,' and for the time to come he is 'yea,' the same alway.

He is yea to all ages. He is yea to us as well as to those that were in Christ's time. Christ is then crucified to thee, when thou believest in Christ crucified. If we now by faith look to Christ, crucified and sent from his Father to take our nature on him, we have as much benefit by Christ as those that beheld him crucified. As they before looked forwards by the eye of faith, so we look backward. We have benefits by Christ. He is 'yesterday, to-day, and the same for ever.' 'All the promises are yea in him,' that is, they are constantly 'yea' for all ages. The promises of Christ, as the spirits in the body, they run through all ages of the church. Without him there is no love, nor mercy, nor comfort from God. As I said before, God cannot look on our cursed nature out of Christ; therefore whosoever will apprehend anything merciful in God, must apprehend it in Christ the promised seed. 'All the promises in him are yea.'

He is called *Logos*, the word. Why is he so? Both actively and passively. Actively, 'the word,' because how should we ever have known the mind in the breast of God, hidden and sealed there, unless Christ had been the *Logos*, the word? For a word is expressed from reason, and there is a word that is essential, that is reason, *Logos;* and so the word coming from it, speech, the issue of reason. So Christ is the essential word, by nature and by office the word, to discover the inward will and purpose of God to us. All the promises of God are discovered by Christ, as the Angel of the covenant. And passively he is the word, *Logos*, of whom all the prophets spake, as Peter saith, Acts iii. 18, who was fore-signified by all the types, as I shewed. Christ he is truly all in all.

Use. It is a comfortable way to study Christ this way; to see him foretold in the Old Testament, and to see the accomplishment in the New; to parallel the Old and New Testament. It is an excellent way of studying the gospel. For we know men are delighted to know divers things at once. When a man's knowledge is enriched divers ways at once, it delights him, as when a man knows the history of a thing, and the truth with it; when he knows a promise, and the truth; a type, and the truth, how doth it delight! When a man sees the type in the Old, and the truth in the New, the history there, the promise and the accomplishment here, it is a wondrous delightful thing. For why doth proportion delight the eye, but because it is an agreement of different things, a sweet harmony of different things? Why doth music so please the ear? Because it is a harmony of different things. When we see a type different from the truth performed, and a promise different from the performance, and yet a sweet agreement, from agreement a man is delighted. A man is not delighted with colours as colours, but as they hold proportion with the rest of the body; he is not delighted with a limb as a limb, but as it holds proportion with the man; if there be no proportion and comeliness, it delights not. So in this case it is good to consider both together. God therefore for this end and purpose would have truths conveyed in the Old Testament, by way of types, and prophecies, and promises, that it might delight us now to hear them, and to study them the more; for, as I said, when we know many things at once, it is delightful.

That is the reason why comparisons and allusions are so delightful, because we know the comparison, and the thing to which it is compared. And that is the reason why our Saviour Christ, besides types and figures, and promises and prophecies, is set out by whatsoever is excellent in nature in the Scriptures. There is nothing in nature that is excellent, but there is something taken from it to set forth the excellency of Christ. He is the 'Sun of righteousness;' he is the 'water,' he is the 'way,' he is the 'bread,' he is the 'vine,' he is the 'tree of life.' Whatsoever is excellent in nature, either in heaven or earth, it serves to set forth the excellency of Christ. Why? To delight us, that we may be willing and cheerful to think of Christ; that together with the consideration of the excellency of the creature, some sweet meditation of Christ, in whom all those excellencies are knit together, might be presented to the soul. When we see the sun, oft to think of that blessed Sun that quickens and enlivens all things, and scatters the mists of ignorance. When we look on a tree, to think of the Tree of righteousness; on the way, to think of him the Way; of life, of him that is the true Life. When we think of anything that is excellent, think of God's love in Scripture to set out Christ, that he would shadow him in all; for he is the true Sun. All creatures must vanish ere long, and whatsoever is excellent in the creature; and what will stand then? Only he in whom all these excellencies are comprised in one. 'All the promises in him are yea and amen.'

If this be true then, that the promise of Christ himself, who is the chief good promised, is in the New Testament 'amen,' all of him is 'yea and amen,' then comes this as a deducted truth, all other promises must needs be 'yea and amen.' For God, he that performed the grand promise in giving Christ in the fulness of time, will for Christ's sake perform all other promises. Therefore the incarnation, the life, the death, and resurrection of Christ our blessed Saviour, it is a pawn and pledge to us of the performance of all things to come.

God promised to the Jews that they should come out of Babylon, he promised that he would deliver them from the enemy; and he usually prefixeth this promise, 'A virgin shall conceive and bear a son,' Isa. vii. 14; and 'to us a child is born, and a son is given,' Isa. ix. 6; to signify, that therefore they should have deliverance, because God would give them a better thing than that. He would give them Christ, in whom all the promises are 'yea and amen;' and because Christ should come of that people, they should not miscarry in captivity under their enemies; for then how should Christ come of them?

Therefore because 'a virgin should conceive,' and because 'a Child shall be born, and a Son given,' therefore you shall have outward deliverance. All other things are 'yea and amen' for Christ, as St Paul divinely reasons, 'If he spared not his only begotten Son, but gave him to death for us all, how shall he not with him give us all things else?' Rom. viii. 32. All other promises are made in Christ and performed for him. And since the grand promise itself is now 'amen,' that Christ is come, it is a pledge of all other things that are to come. Is Christ come in the flesh according to the promise? Hath he done all and suffered all according to the prophecies, as it was written of him? Then why shall we not look for the accomplishment of all that are to come, on the same ground? Have we not a pledge? Why shall we not look for the resurrection of the body, for the day of judgment, for the second coming of Christ? Is not his first coming a pledge of it?

When God is become man, and was mortal, why should we doubt that man being mortal should be immortal? Is not the greater performed already? Is it not a greater matter for God to become man, and to die in our nature, than for we that are mortal to become immortal by Christ? Why should we not expect that which is to come, since the greater is done? Why should we doubt that we shall be taken up to God, since he is come down to man? Therefore, since it is upon the same ground, let us look for the performance of all to be 'yea and amen.'

Since the coming of Christ, many promises have been performed in the church, and many yet remain. Some have been performed, as the calling of the Gentiles, and the discovery* of antichrist foretold by St Paul, and the consuming of him in part. There is somewhat unfulfilled: the conversion of the Jews, the confusion of antichrist, the resurrection to glory with Christ, &c. Why should we doubt of them that are to come, having such a pledge of truth of God and Christ in the real performance of that which is past? Let us not doubt of it; for in Rev. xvi. 17, *et alibi*, when he speaks of the destruction of antichrist, 'It is done, it is done,' saith the angel. As Christ said when he was on the cross, all was finished, so it is as true of his adversaries, all is done; it is as sure as if it were done already.

Therefore the church and people of God should comfort themselves for the time to come, in the destruction of the implacable, malicious enemies of the church, that glory in the flesh, that set up an outward religion that is opposite to the power of Christ, that the time shall come that all shall be done to them, and that all other promises shall be finished. For as in the first coming of Christ all was finished for the working of our salvation, so in his second coming there will be a time when it will be said, all is finished, for the accomplishment of that which was done in his first coming. Therefore let us stablish our souls in the expectation of the blessed promises, for 'all the promises in Christ are yea and amen,' and shall be for ever.

All the promises are infallibly true, as God and Christ himself is true. Christ shall as soon fail, and God shall as soon fail, as any promise that we have made us in the gospel, if we apprehend it in Christ, and believe it in Christ.

Use 1. Then here you see for the direction of our judgment, what to think of a rotten opinion that some have that are unacquainted with divine truth, and the all-sufficiency of Christ, and the mercy of God in Christ, that consider

* That is, 'manifestation.'—G.

not the vileness of our nature, and the infinite majesty of God. They will have the Gentiles saved by the light of nature, and the Jews by the law of Moses, and Christians by the gospel of Christ; as if there were some other means to come to heaven, and to the favour of God, than by Christ. Whereas now all that we have must be by promises, and all the promises we have are in Christ. They are all yea in him. Without him there is no intercourse between the majesty of God and us. Therefore 'there is no name under heaven whereby we can be saved, but by the name of Jesus,' Acts iv. 12; which not only confutes the devilish opinion and conceit that some have, but also the charitable error of others, that think the heathens that never heard of Christ shall be saved. I leave them to their Judge. We must go to the Scriptures. All the promises are in Christ, in him they are 'yea,' in him they are made; in him they are 'amen,' in him they are performed. Out of him we have nothing, out of the promises in him we have nothing.

Use 2. How we are *to magnify God that we live in the sunshine of the gospel*, that in Christ we have precious and rich promises! A precious Saviour we have, and precious faith to lay hold on him, and precious promises; all precious, both promises to be believed, and our Saviour in whom they are apprehended. He is 'a precious stone,' 1 Pet. ii. 6; and the faith that lays hold on him is 'precious,' 1 Pet. i. 7. How are we to bless God that we have these advantages! that we have Christ laid open, and precious and rich promises, whereby we may have precious faith to lay hold on these precious promises? We are much to bless God for it.

Use 3. Again, are all the promises of God in Christ, and in him yea and amen? *This should direct us in our dealing with God, not to go directly to him, but by a promise;* and when we have a promise, look to Christ in whom it is performed. Go to God in the blessed promises that we have for Christ's sake, that he would perform all. 'If we ask anything of God in Christ's name, we shall receive it,' 1 John v. 14, because the promises are in him. If we thank God for anything, it must be in Christ, for that we have in him.

What a comfort is this, that we may go to God in Christ, and claim the promises boldly; because we see out of the love he bears to Christ, he loves us, and hath made us promises in him, and as verily as he loves him, so he loves us, and will perform all his gracious promises to us? If we lay fast hold on Christ, I say, he can as soon alter his love to Christ as to us; for he loves us with the same love that he loves Christ with, he loves us in his beloved. He hath 'blessed us with all spiritual blessings in him,' Eph. i. 3, he hath made us sons in him that is the natural Son; and as his love is unchangeable to his Son, so it is to us in Christ.

If a prince's love to any man be founded and grounded upon the love he bears to his son, if he loves his son he loves such a man, because his son loves him. Surely he may have great comfort that it will hold! Because his affection is natural and unalterable, he will alway love his son. Therefore he will love him whom his son loves alway. Now Christ is the Son of God, he loves us in his Son; he hath given us rich promises in his Son. He hath given him the first promise, and all other promises of forgiveness of sins, and life everlasting in and through him. As long as he loves Christ, he will love us, and as sure as he loves Christ, he will love us.

Nothing in the world can separate his love from his own Son, and nothing in the world can separate God's love from us, because it is in his Son. Christ loves his mystical body as well as his natural body; and God loves the mystical body of Christ as he loves his natural body. He hath advanced that to glory at his right hand, and will he leave his mystical body the church? Will he not advance that? Doth he not love whole Christ? Yes! God loves whole Christ. Our nature that he hath taken to him, it is the chief thing, the most lovely thing in heaven or earth, next to God; and he loves all that are in him, his mystical body. For indeed he gave us to Christ. He hath sealed and anointed him. He is anointed by God the Father for us.

Upon what an unchangeable, eternal ground is the love of God built, and the faith of a Christian! How can the gates of hell prevail against the faith of a Christian, when it carries him to the promises, and from the promises to the love of God, and from thence to Christ, upon whom the love of God is founded? Before the faith of a Christian can be shaken, the promises must be of no effect, they must be 'yea and nay,' and not 'yea.' And if the promises be shaken, the love of God must be uncertain, and Christ uncertain. Heaven and earth must be overturned to overturn the faith of a Christian. There is nothing in the world that is so firm as a believing Christian, that casts himself on the promises, that are alway 'yea;' and to make them 'yea,' they are founded on Christ, the Son of God's love.

Well, these promises, coming from such love, may be ranked into divers ranks. I will touch some of them, to shew how we are to carry ourselves, to make comfortable use of this, that 'all the promises are yea and amen in Christ.'

(1.) There *are some universal promises*, for the good of all mankind; as that God would never destroy the world again. Or (2.) promises that concern *more particularly his church*. And those are promises either of outward things, or of spiritual and eternal things, of grace and glory.

Now, for the manner of promising, they admit of this distinction: all the promises that God hath made to us, either (1.) they are *absolute*, without any condition. So was Christ. God promised Christ, let the world be as it will, Christ did and would have come. And so the promise of his glorious coming, he will come, let men be as they will. There will be a resurrection. Some promises (2.) be *conditional* in the manner of propounding, but yet absolute in the real performance of them. As, for example, the promises of grace and glory to God's children. The promise of forgiveness of sins,—God will forgive their sins if they believe, if they repent. They are propounded conditionally, but in the performance they are absolute, because God performs the covenant himself; he performs our part and his own too. For since Christ, though he propounded the promises of the gospel with conditions, yet he performs the condition; he stirs us up to attend upon the means, and by his Spirit in the word he works faith and repentance, which is the condition. Faith and repentance is his gift.

He 'writes his law in our hearts,' Jer. xxxi. 33, and teacheth us how to love. So, though they be conditionally propounded (for God deals with men as men by way of commerce,—he propounds it by way of covenant and condition), yet in the covenant of grace, which is truly a gracious covenant, he not only gives the good things, but he performs the condition, by the Spirit working our hearts to believe and to repent.

Again, there are promises not only propounded conditionally, of grace and comfort, *but of outward things*. All outward things are promised conditionally, as thus: God hath promised protection from contagious sicknesses, from war, and troubles. General promises there are of protection everywhere. 'God will be a hiding-place,' Ps. xci. 2, and he will deliver his children. There are private promises, and then positive promises, that he will do this and that good for them; but these are conditional, so far forth as in his wise providence he sees it may serve spiritual good things, grace and the inward man. For God takes liberty in our outward estate, and in our bodies to afflict them, or to do them good, as may serve the main.

For do what we will, these bodies will turn to dust and vanity, and we must leave the world behind us; but God looks to the main state in Christ, to the new creature. Therefore as far as outward blessings may encourage us, and as far as deliverances may help the main, so far he will grant them, or else he denies them. He takes liberty in outward things.

Therefore that sort of promises they are conditional, with exception of necessary affliction. For we cannot have the blessings of this life positive or privative, we cannot be delivered always, and have blessings, but our corrupt nature is such, that except we have somewhat to season them, we shall surfeit of them: we cannot digest them, and therefore they are all with the exception of the cross.* As Christ saith, he that doth anything for him, he shall have 'an hundredfold here,' Mat. xix. 29, but with affliction and persecutions; he shall be sure of that; whatsoever else he hath, let him look for that. All the crosses we have in the world are to season the good things of this life. Many other distinctions and differences we might have to lay open the kinds of promises in Scripture; but this shall suffice to give you a taste. Now, all these are made in Christ, and performed in Christ, so far forth as is for our good.

Use. Are all the promises, of what kind soever, spiritual or outward, temporal and eternal—are they all made to us in Jesus Christ, and are they certain, yea and amen in him? Then make this use of it, *let us renew our former exhortation, get into Christ by all means;* for out of him we have nothing savingly good.

Obj. But you will say, Doth not God do many good things to them that are out of Christ? Doth not the rain fall upon the ill as well as the good? And doth not he 'fill the bellies of the wicked with good things?' Ps. xvii. 14.

Ans. Yes, he doth, he doth! But are they blessings? No! they are not. But as God saith to Moses, if you do this and this ill, 'I will curse you in your dough, I will curse you at home and abroad, I will curse you in your children,' &c., Deut. xxvii., xxviii. They are cursed in their blessings, Mal. ii. 2. There is no man that is a carnal, brutish man, but though he live and have revenues and pleasures, he is cursed in his blessings. For what? Is he made for this life only? No! he is but 'fatted on to the day of destruction;' they are 'snares' to him, Josh. xxiii. 13. How do you know they are snares? Because they make him secure and careless of the worship of God; they make him profane, they make him despise the power of religion. A man may see by his conversation they are snares. They are not promises in Christ, for then they would come to him out of God's love. Therefore get into Christ, rest not in anything abstracted from Christ. Let us not rest in any blessing except we have it in God's love in Christ.

And I may know that I have anything in this world, any deliverance from ill, or any positive good thing from God's love in Christ, if I have it with a heart wrought on to the best things, to value Christ, and to account all dung in comparison of him. When I esteem my being in Christ above all beings, above being rich, or honourable, or in favour, alas! this I know

* That is, the cross is to be always on the other side of the balance.—Ed.

is fading; but my being in Christ is 'yea and amen,' that will stand by me when all these beings will fail. This is comfortable, if I can do this, and have other things, I have them with the love of God and Christ. Let us get into Christ therefore.

For this purpose, *attend upon the means of salvation*, that the word may be effectual, by his Spirit accompanying his own ordinance, to open the excellencies of Christ to us, to make us love him, and get our affections into him. How are we in Christ? By knowing him; and then knowledge carries our hearts. For our wills cleave to that that we know to be excellent and necessary. Christ is discovered as excellent and necessary, and so the will cleaves to him as a good so discovered; and the affections follow the will. When the will cleaves to Christ as excellent and necessary, then I love him, then I rest on him, then I have peace in him. I may know that I am in Christ, upon my knowledge of him and cleaving to him, and finding peace in my conscience. For he that is in Christ hath rest. Faith in Christ hath a resting, stablishing power. If I be in Christ, my soul rests; for I know that all is 'yea and amen in him.' My soul rests in him. Whatsoever I find in the world to unsettle me; things are amiss, and otherwise than I would have them; but I rest in the love of God in Christ. Let us get into Christ by knowledge; let the will follow that, and our affections follow that; and then we shall find the rest and peace that will secure us that indeed we are in Christ.

Alas! what is a man out of Christ? As a man in a storm, that hath no clothes to hide his nakedness, to cover him from the violence of the storm: as a man in a tempest, that is out of a house to hide him: as a stone out of the foundation, that is scattered here and there as neglected: as a branch out of the vine, out of the root, what shape is in such a branch? It will be cast into the fire afterwards. A man out of Christ, that is not clothed with him, that is not built on him, and settled on him, and planted in him, he is a man destitute. We pity such men's cases in the world; but if we had spiritual eyes to look on these men, on profane civil wretches, that pride themselves in a little morality, and have scarce that perhaps, and neglect grace, and the mystery of Christ, such a man deserves pity. There is but a step between him and hell, if he be out of Christ, and live and die so; and at the day of Christ he will account him so.

Oh! saith St Paul, Philip. iii. 8, 'I account all dung and dross in comparison of Christ, not having my own righteousness, but to be found in him,' having the righteousness of God in Christ. O happy man in death, and at the day of judgment, that is found in Christ, and not in himself, not in his own righteousness; though that there must be, not to give us title to heaven. The best thing is to be found in Christ, to have his righteousness and obedience. That is so excellent that St Paul accounted all 'dung and dross' in comparison of that, to be found in that. Get into Christ by all means; for in him all the promises are 'yea and amen;' not out of him.

Use. If so be all the promises be 'yea and amen' in Christ, then here again see the stability of a Christian's estate, that hath promises to uphold him. Compare it with a man that hath present things only, with an Esau that hath the things of this life, Heb. xii. 16. The men of this world, as the psalmist calls them, they have present things, they have performance; he gives them their portion here, as he saith to Dives, 'Thou hadst thy good,' Luke xvi. 25; that which thou caredst for, thou hadst it here; and Lazarus had pain, and misery, and poverty here. Now the case is altered: he is advanced, and thou art tormented.

A Christian, as a Christian, he hath a great many promises. Some of them are performed; for God is delivering him, and comforting him, and protecting him, and speaking peace to his conscience; but the greatest part are yet to be performed, the perfection of grace and glory to come. He is a child of the promise, a son of the promise, here is his estate. Another man hath present payment, and that is all he cares for; he hath something, and he swells in the conceit of that, that he is somebody. What is the difference? what hath the one but a great deal of nothing? what saith Solomon, that had tried all the world? 'All is vanity and vexation of spirit,' Eccles. i. 2. All is uncertain, and we are uncertain in the use of them, if we have no better life than the life of nature. But the promises they are 'yea,' they are certain, they contain undoubted certain good things, that will stick by us when all else will leave us.

A Christian, take him, and strip him in your thoughts from all the good things in the world, he is a happier man than the greatest monarch in the world out of Christ. Why? He hath nothing but present things, with a great deal of addition of misery: and his greatness makes him more sensible of his misery. It makes him more tender and apprehensive than other men. The other he wants many comforts of this life, he wants the performance; he is rich in bills and bonds. God is bound to him, he hath promised he 'will not forsake him,' Deut. iv. 31; but he will be his God in life, to death, and for everlasting. He hath title to all the promises, 'Godliness hath the promises of this life, and of that which is to come,' 1 Tim. iv. 8. Happy man! he hath so much performance for the present, as is useful for his safe conduct to bring him to heaven! He shall have daily bread: he that will give him a kingdom, will not deny him bread; he that will give him a country, will give him safe conduct. And besides that he hath here by performance, he hath rich and precious promises, and they are all 'yea and amen,' they are certain.

His life is uncertain, his estate in the world is changeable here, his life is as a vapour; and the comforts of life are less than life. When life itself, the foundation of these comforts, is but a vapour, so uncertain, what are all the comforts of life? yet a Christian hath comfort here, the promises are invested into him, and lodged in his heart, and made his own by faith. Faith hath a wondrous peculiarising virtue. It makes a man own that which is generally propounded in the gospel. Now faith making the promises his own, and they are certain. A Christian, take him at all uncertainties, he hath somewhat to build on, that is 'yea and amen,' that is undoubtedly constant and certain, that will stick by him when all things fail him.

I speak this, to commend the estate of a believing, repentant Christian, to make you in love with it. In all the changes and varieties in this world, a Christian hath somewhat to take to. And likewise in all the dangers of this life, he hath a rock to go to, a hiding-place. God hath chambers of providence, as it is, Isa. xxvi. 20, he bids the church 'come into thy chambers.' God hath a hiding-place, and secret rooms to hide children in, when it is good for them, in the time of pestilence and war, in the time of public disturbance; when there is a confusion of all things, 'come into thy chambers.' God is a resting-place and a hiding-place. He is styled so everywhere in the Psalms: Ps. xviii. 2, 'my rock and my shield,' as if David had said, I have many troubles in the world, but in God is my defence; for he is my rock, my shield, and all. Whatsoever is defensive, I have it in him.

What a comfort is this in all dangers! a Christian knows either he shall be safe here or in heaven; and, therefore, he doth rest. 'He dwells in the secret of the Almighty,' Ps. xci. 1, that is, in the love and the protec-tection of God Almighty; and as Moses saith, 'Thou art our habitation from everlasting to everlasting,' Ps. xc. 1, that is, God is a dwelling-place for him that builds on his promise; for God and his word are all one. 'Thou art our dwelling-place,' &c. He saw they dropped away in the wilderness by the wrath of God, as we do now by the pestilence,* and Moses made that psalm. He took occasion to meditate of the frailty of man's life. We are as grass, as a tale that is told; but what is our estate in God, in the promises? 'Thou art our habitation from everlasting to everlasting,' Ps. xc. 2. We dwell not long in the world, sickness may come and sweep us away, but 'thou art our habitation.' We dwell in God when we are dead, when we are out of the world; we dwell in God in Christ for ever. Our estate in Christ is an everlasting estate. Therefore in Psalm cxii. 7, the Psalmist saith of the righteous man there, 'that he is not troubled for ill news.' He is not senseless, he is very sensible; but yet notwithstanding he is not shaken from his rest, from his rock and stay for no ill news or tidings, why? The Psalmist gives the reason, 'his heart is fixed.' Upon what foundation? Upon the promises and providence of God. God hath promised to provide for him. He is his Father; and, therefore, he is not afraid of ill tidings.

What a blessed estate then is it to be in Christ, and to have promises in Christ to be protected and preserved here, so as is for our good, and to have such a state in God, for him to be our habitation and hiding-place from everlasting to everlasting! If our hearts be fixed here, let us hear of ill tidings, of war, of this sickness and contagion, let it be what it will, if our hearts be fixed, blessed men are we. But if we have nothing to take to when trouble comes, we are, as I said before, as a man in a storm without a hiding-place. Now every word of God, saith the Psalmist, 'is a tried word, as silver tried in the fire,' Ps. xii. 6. The promises are tried promises that we may rest on them, and as we are Christians, what are we but men of promise? The best is behind, and what is our comfort in this world? God lets down his love to us in gracious promises; and he gives us a taste of the performance. As children have somewhat of their inheritance in their nonage to keep them, so somewhat of heaven to comfort our souls we have, but the main is to come, and the performance is left till then; therefore we cannot too much consider of this comfortable point. Consider how many promises we have in the word; the certainty of them, that they are 'yea and amen;' and in whom they are founded, in him that is 'Amen' himself; for Christ is 'Amen, the true and faithful witness,' Rev. iii. 14. These are comfortable considerations.

Are the promises of God in Christ 'yea and amen? Let us divide men who may make any use of them. All men, they are either such as are in Christ, or such as are not in Christ.

Quest. All the promises being made in Christ, what comfort or what good can those that are not yet in Christ have by the promises?

Ans. I answer, till they be in Christ, none at all; for a man out of Christ is out of the favour of God. God cannot look on such a man but as the object of his wrath, and as fuel for his vengeance; and, therefore, there is no hope for such a man till he be in Christ. All other things in the world cannot comfort such a man; for, alas! his being in the world,

* In the margin, 1625. See note *r*.—G.

his being rich, his being in favour with such or such, what are they? Fading beings that fail, and himself with them. He stands on the ice. They slip and he slips with them. What are all beings in death, if a man have not a more stable being in Jesus Christ.

Quest. What comfort is there then for such a man by the promises in Jesus Christ?

Ans. This, that while there is life, there is hope to get into Christ, and so to get interest in the promises; for the promises are free, the word is *evangelia*,* free promise. It is not a promise on this or that condition; but a free promise out of mere love, a mercy. Then though thou be yet in the state of corruption in old Adam, yet the promise is free.

Obj. But I have no worthiness in me, thou wilt say; I have no faith, no grace in me at all.

Ans. But remember the promise is free, the condition is only if thou wilt receive Christ, which is not properly a condition of worth in thee. It is not propounded by way of condition of any worth, but thou must come with an empty hand, with a receiving hand; as a man must let fall what he hath, before he can hold and take anything. A man must let go other things, he must let go his hold of the creature; he must not be so proud of the creature, and so confident in it as he was; he must see the emptiness of the creature, and of all things in the world; thou must see that, if thou be not in Christ, thou art a wretched, damned creature. The hand of thy soul must be empty, and then a sight of thy unworthiness is all that is required before thou come to Christ, and the promises, a sight of thy unworthiness and a coming to grasp with Christ and the promises; for what is faith but a beggar's hand, empty of all things, coming to receive a benefit? They are most unworthy † that find themselves most unworthy.

Obj. But you will say, the promise is made to the poor in spirit, and to those that hunger and thirst.

Ans. It is true, but it is by way of preventing an objection of these men that are cast down in the sight of their unworthiness. As if Christ had said, you think these men the unworthiest men in the world, that are poor, and hungry, and thirsty, you think you are destitute and have nothing; but you are 'blessed,' you have interest in Christ, and in the promises, they are for you. Let no man therefore be discouraged, the promises are free. Therefore be not rebellious, stand not out against God's command. God lays a command upon thee. Though thou be not in Christ, and hast no right to the promises, he lays a command on thee to believe.

Quest. Thou wilt ask, what ground, or title, or right hast thou to believe, to claim Christ and the promises?

Ans. This right thou hast, thou hast the offer of God's love in Christ. And thou hast not only God's offer, but his command. God commands thee to do it. As St John saith, 1 John iii. 23, he hath commanded us to believe in his Son Christ, as well as not to commit adultery, or murder. And thou art guilty if thou break this command, as if thou break the other of murder or adultery. And men that live under the hearing of the gospel, they shall be damned more at the day of judgment for disobeying this command, for not receiving of Christ, than for the other; for the breach of all other commands may be forgiven if this were obeyed. Therefore there is an offer of Christ, with a command to receive him, and a promise if thou

* That is, εὐαγγέλια. But Sibbes appears to have quoted from memory; for the word in the text is the cognate and nearly synonymous one ἐπαγγελία.—G.

† Qu. 'worthy?'—G.

receive him all shall be well, all thy sins shall be forgiven; is not here encouragement enough?

And then there is an invitation, 'Come unto me, all ye that are weary and heavy laden,' Matt. xi. 28. And put case thou hast nothing, yet notwithstanding, 'come and buy without silver,' saith the prophet, Isa. lv. 1. If thou say thou hast nothing, yet all is free here, 'Come whosoever will, and drink of the water of life.'

And he threatens damnation if thou wilt not, the wrath of God hangs on thee if thou do not come in.

Aye, but I am a sinner.

But where sin hath abounded, 'Grace shall more abound,' Rom. v. 20. So if a man stand out of Christ, and come not in to him, there are many encouragements for him to come, and terrible denunciations of wrath if he come not. 'The wrath of God hangs over his head,' John iii. 36. For if he be not in Christ, he sinks into hell when this short life is ended.

So there is this to encourage a man, there is God's command, and his sweet invitation, 'Come unto me.' And add to that his beseeching, 'We are ambassadors in Christ's name, to beseech you to be reconciled to God,' 2 Cor. v. 20, to come to Christ, to come out of the state of nature, and out of the curse of God that you are under, to come out of the uncertain condition that the world affords. We beseech you to be reconciled to God, to cast away your weapons whereby you are enemies to God; he seeks to you for your love. And if you have nothing, come and buy without money; have you a will to come? If you be besotted, and will continue in your estate, then be damned, and rot in your estate; but if you will, 'come and drink of the waters of life freely,' Rev. xxi. 6.

Let none be discouraged: Christ and the promises are open to all. Therefore how will God's vengeance be justified at the day of judgment, when these courses have been taken, and yet men will not come in? As Christ said to the Jews, 'You will not believe in me, that you might have life,' John v. 40. Men will not. Men are in love with the profits and pleasures and fading things: they will not embrace the promises that are 'yea and amen.' It is nothing but wilful rebellion that keeps men off, that rather than they will leave their sins, and come under the government of Christ, they will reject the offers of mercy; if they cannot have Christ with their sins, away mercy. If they can have him to lead them to hell, to swear, and cozen, &c., then welcome Christ: if he will come on those terms, he is welcome; but rather than they will have him upon his own terms, they reject him.

So there is great reason for God to justify the damnation of wretched hard-hearted persons, that rather than they will alter their course, they will reject mercy, and Christ, and all. If they may have half Christ, they will. They will have him with mercy to forgive them, but they will not have whole Christ as a King to govern them. So there is ground for those that are not yet in the state of grace to come to Christ. If they will receive him upon his own terms, to take him as a King as well as a Priest, to take him as a King to rule them, as well as a Priest to reconcile them to his Father. Nay, God, as I said, in the ministry entreats them to receive Christ, to cast away the weapons of their rebellion, to come under his government, and all shall be well with them.

But for them that are in Christ, that have embraced and clasped him in some comfortable measure, what comfort is it for them that all the promises in Christ are 'yea and amen?'

I answer, when we are once in Christ, and believe in Christ, all the Scripture speaks comfort to us. If we come in, and receive him as he is offered, upon his terms, to be our governor, our king, our priest, and prophet, then all the promises are 'yea and amen' to us.

As for instance, forgiveness of sins: if we receive Christ, God will forgive us our sins, and be reconciled to us for Jesus Christ's sake. 'We have an advocate with the Father, and he is the propitiation for our sins,' 1 John ii. 2. 'The blood of Christ shall cleanse us from all sins,' 1 John i. 7. These promises shall be 'yea and amen' to thee; if thy sins trouble thee, they shall be done away. How many promises to this purpose have we of the forgiveness of sins!

Again, if so be thou find want of grace, all the promises in Christ are 'yea and amen.' He hath promised his Holy Spirit to them that ask him, Luke xi. 13. There is a promise shall be 'yea and amen,' if thou beg it. He hath promised the fundamental graces. 'He will put his fear in our hearts, that we shall never depart from him,' Jer. xxxii. 40. 'He will teach us to love one another,' John xiii. 34. You are taught of God to love one another. He hath promised private blessings in this kind, 'to circumcise, and cut off the foreskin of our hearts,' Jer. iv. 4. If a naughty and stony heart vex thee, 'he will take away that and give thee an heart of flesh,' Ezek. xi. 19, a tender heart. So these promises in Christ shall be 'yea and amen,' if we apply and believe them, to take away our corruption, and subdue that; and to give and plant graces,—he hath promised to do this. Therefore make use of them, not only of the promises of pardon and forgiveness of sins, but of grace necessary.

Art thou sensible of thy imperfections, that thou canst not go about the duties of religion, and of thy particular calling? What saith Moses? 'Who gives a mouth?' Exod. iv. 11. Is it not God that gives a mouth? And, 'Be not afraid,' saith Christ, 'you shall have speech,' Mark xiii. 11, and a spirit given you that all shall not be able to withstand. Be not afraid, God that calls us he will enable us.

You have a promise of sufficiency of gifts. 'If any man lack wisdom, let him ask it of God,' James i. 5. If any man lack wisdom, to manage his affairs, to bear crosses and afflictions, let him ask it of God; a rich promise in that kind.

And so, art thou doubtful for the time to come what shall befall thee? God in Christ Jesus hath made a promise, that where he hath begun he will make an end, 'He that hath begun a good work will finish it to the day of the Lord,' Philip. i. 6. Christ is 'Alpha and Omega,' too, Rev. i. 8; and 'What shall separate us from the love of God in Christ? Neither things present, nor things to come, nor anything else,' Rom. viii. 35, *seq.* Why? Because it is the love of God in Christ. God's love is founded in Christ, and he will love thee eternally. There is a ground of perseverance. Therefore be sure to take in trust the time to come, as well as the present: he will be thy God for the time to come, as well as for the present; he will be thy God to death. Jesus Christ 'is yesterday, to-day, and to-morrow, and the same for ever,' Heb. xiii. 8. 'He was, and is, and is to come,' Rev. i. 8. He was good to thee before he called thee; he is good to thee now in the state of grace, and he will be for ever. Why shouldst thou stagger for the time to come? Take in trust all that shall befall thee for the time to come, as well as for the present; for he is 'yea and amen' himself, and 'all his promises are yea and amen.' Christ is 'Amen,' the true witness. 'Thus saith Amen,' Rev. i. 18, and all his promises are like himself, 'amen.'

Obj. Oh but I may fall away, my grace is weak, I stagger often!

But are the promises founded upon thee? No! the promises are founded in Christ. Christ receives grace for thee, and he is a King for ever, and a Priest for ever, to make intercession for thee, and he is faithful. He is beloved for ever, and as long as he is beloved, thou shalt be beloved, because thou art in him. God is in Christ, and thou art in Christ, how canst thou miscarry? God is in Christ for ever, and thou art in Christ. Will he lose a limb? Will he lose a member? No! the promises in him are 'yea and amen,' and not in thee. They are in thee 'yea and amen,' thou hast the benefit of them, because they are in him 'amen' first.

Aye, but for the troubles of this world, for afflictions, and crosses, what promises have we to build on for them?

God in Christ is 'yea and amen' to us; and the promises are 'yea and amen' in that kind, in all things necessary for this life. 'Let your conversation be without covetousness: for he hath promised he will not fail thee nor forsake thee,' Heb. xiii. 5. It is taken along from Joshua's time. It was a promise made to Joshua, and is enlarged to all Christians. He hath promised, he will not fail thee, nor forsake thee.' Therefore 'let your conversation be without covetousness,' insinuating the reason why men are covetous, because they do not trust that promise, 'I will not fail thee, nor forsake thee.'

For if men in their calling, as they should do, would trust in God, without putting forth their hands to ill means, their conversation would be without shifting and covetousness. Therefore covetous men are faithless men. They believe not the promise, that God will not fail them nor forsake them; for then they would not live by their wits and by their shifts, but by faith in this very promise, which is 'yea and amen' to all that believe it.

'God is a sun and shield,' Ps. lxxxiv. 11, 'and no good thing shall be wanting to those that lead a godly life.' Would you have more? He is a sun, for all good; he is a shield, to keep from all ill. 'I am thy buckler, and thy exceeding great reward,' saith God to Abraham, Gen. xv. 1. 'I am thy buckler,' to keep thee from all ill; 'and thy exceeding great reward,' to bestow all good. Having these promises, why should we stagger? They are 'yea and amen' in Christ; God is all-sufficient in Christ.

For the issue in our labours, Oh! what will become of it? We take pains to no purpose, we rise early, and go to bed late, what will become of all in the issue? What saith St Paul? 1 Cor. xv. 58, 'Be constant, alway abounding in the work of the Lord: be ye abundant in the work of the Lord, knowing that your labour is not in vain in the Lord.' Therefore abound you in the work of the Lord: let the issue go to God, you have a rich promise, 'Knowing this, that your labour is not in vain in the Lord.' Therefore you know, when Peter had fished all night, and had caught nothing, when Christ bids him cast the net into the sea, saith he, 'We have fished all night, and catched nothing,' Luke v. 5, to what purpose should I cast it? yet in thy word, in thy command I will cast it. He obeyed, and he drew so many, that the net brake again with the fish. So, I say, it is thy command, Lord, that I should go on in the duties of my calling, that I should do that that belongs to me; and in welldoing to commit myself to thee 'as to a faithful Creator,' 1 Peter iv. 19, and a gracious Redeemer, and to cast myself on thy promises, do what thou wilt: you shall see then, as the apostle graciously speaks, 'Your labour shall not be in vain in the Lord,' 1 Cor. xv. 58. 'Cast your care on him; for he cares for you,' 1 Peter v. 7.

Aye, but when we have done, there are so many imperfections cleave to that we do, that they discourage us. Why, look, the promise is 'yea and amen' for acceptance, 'a cup of cold water is accepted,' Mat. x. 42. Offer that thou doest in the mediation of Christ, God will pardon that which is faulty, and accept that which is good. So we have promises of acceptance in Christ, 'God will pardon, and spare us as a father spares his child,' Ps. ciii. 13. Doth not a father accept the endeavour of his poor child, and pardon his weakness, when he cannot do as he would? God looks on us as a father on his children. Therefore let us not fear this. We have a promise of acceptance of what we do, though it be weak, and maimed, and lame obedience. If we cannot do as much as others, yet bring 'two turtles,' Lev. v. 7. They that could not bring an ox, a great sacrifice, a less was accepted, two pigeons. If thou canst not do as much as others, a little sacrifice shall be accepted.

Oh! that we had faith! we might run through all the passages of our life, justification, sanctification, perseverance for the time to come; the duties of our calling, the issue of our labours, whatever you can imagine. There is no passage of our life but our souls would be supported, if we could think that these promises are 'yea and amen' in Jesus Christ. There is no estate that we are in but there are promises made to it. We want no good, but we have a promise of supply; we are under no ill, but we have a promise, either for the removal of it, or for the sanctifying of it, which is better.

We may enlarge it likewise to posterity. If the promises in Christ be 'yea and amen,' that is, true to us, and to them that succeed us; for as I said, Christ 'is yesterday, to-day, and the same for ever.' He was yesterday to our ancestors, to-day to ourselves, to-morrow to our posterity. Therefore saith Peter to the believing Jews, Acts ii. 39, 'The promise is made to you, and to your children;' your children are in the covenant, and God is the 'God of thee and of thy seed;' for the 'promises in Christ are yea and amen,' they are constant to us, and to our children, to the end of the world.

It is a comfort to parents that can leave their children no inheritance: they leave them God in covenant, and he is a good portion. 'I will be thy God,' Jer. vii. 23; for the grand promise is the promise of the Father, Son, and Holy Ghost. God hath promised to be a Father, and the Father gives his Son, and the Father and Son give the Holy Ghost. Well then! God is the God of us and of our children; he is the Father of us and of our children; Christ is the Christ of us and them; the Holy Ghost is the Spirit that sanctifies us and them. Is not this a comfort to those that can leave their children nothing else, that they leave them God in covenant?

And this is a comfort for children, if they have good parents, that they may say when they pray, 'O God of my father Abraham,' Gen. xxiv. 12. And as David, Ps. cxvi. 16, 'I am thy servant, and the son of thy handmaid;' I am thy servant myself, and the son of one that was thy servant. Is not this a comfort to a Christian to say, I am thy servant, and the son of thy servant, therefore there is a double bond why thou shouldest respect me? I cast myself on thee, and I am the son of a believing father, of a believing mother. Oh! it is a blessed thing to be in covenant with God, that those that can leave their children little else, can leave them a place in the covenant by their own goodness and faith.

Wicked parents are cruel. They damn their own souls, and they are cruel to posterity. Jeroboam hurt his posterity more than all the world besides. For his sin God cursed his posterity. 'They walk in the ways of Jeroboam,' 1 Kings xv. 34. God many times will not punish men themselves, but their posterity. Wicked kings, God spares them themselves sometimes, but he punisheth their posterity. Jeroboam was spared for his own life, but his posterity was punished. When wicked men die, others applaud their wisdom. They die thus and thus, &c., and their posterity applaud their wisdom. God therefore curseth their posterity, walking in their ways. Jeroboam's children, I say, had cause to curse their father. They had a prejudice in his example. They thought him a very wise man, that by setting up the calves he could make such a rent, but it turned to their destruction. I say, parents are cruel to posterity; for God revengeth their sins on their posterity. Let this be a strong motive to men to believe in Christ, that they may leave a good posterity, a posterity in covenant with God.

Men are very atheists in this point; for they are more careful a great deal to leave them rich, to leave them great, than to leave them good; and so they leave them a little goods perhaps, but they leave the curse and vengeance of God with it. I beseech you, therefore, enlarge this comfort, that the promises of God concerning all good things are made in Christ, they are yea and amen to ourselves, and to all ours, to our posterity.

Thus I have laboured to lay open a little to you the promises. You may enlarge them yourselves. Therefore take this course:

First, consider your present estate, if you would make use of this portion. It is our portion. Our best inheritance are the promises, and indeed they are a good child's portion. Though the world take all from us, though God strip us of all, if he leave us his promises, we are rich men. Therefore the psalmist calls them his portion, and his inheritance; and indeed so they are: because they are so many bonds whereby God is bound to us; they are so many obligations.

And if a wretched exacting man think himself as rich as he hath bonds, though he have not a penny in his purse; he that hath a thousand pounds in bonds, thinks himself richer than he that hath a hundred pounds in money, and he thinks he hath reason to be so, because he hath good security; certainly, a Christian that hath rich faith in the rich promises, he is a rich man, because he hath many bonds; and when he pleaseth he can sue his bonds, and God is well pleased with it. Therefore indeed there is little difference between a Christian in poverty and a rich Christian; only the one hath more for the present, but God is the riches of the other. As for a worldling, he hath but a cistern when he hath most; the other hath the spring, he hath God in covenant, and God's promises.

Let us therefore consider every day the exigents* we are in, whether in want of grace, or want of assistance and necessaries, or want of comfort; and according to that, let us consider what we are to do. Are we at our wits' end now? Is there no hope for this in Israel? Yes! God hath left us rich and precious promises. Let us look to them.

In the next place, then, *from our wants look to the promises, and proportion the promises to our wants;* rank the promises. It were a good work. Oh, that we should have so many promises, and yet have them to seek when the devil besiegeth us. He layeth siege to shake our consciences, and we are to seek in the time of temptation. Let us remember the promises answerable to our necessities.

If we be troubled with sin, call to mind the promise of forgiveness. If

* That is, 'exigencies.'—G.

we be troubled with want, call to mind the promise of supply. If we be troubled with fear for the time to come, call to mind the covenant of grace, the marriage for everlasting. 'God, whom he loves, he loves to the end,' John xiii. 1. God loves us in Christ. He loves Christ for ever. Therefore he will love us for ever. So, as I said before, suit the promises to our present estate.

And from the promises have a higher rise yet: *go to him in whom they are made.* They are rich promises indeed, good promises; but how shall I know they shall be performed? In whom are they made? In whom? God loves thee in Christ. What is he? God and man. He is God, and therefore able to perform them: he is man, and therefore he loves thee as his own flesh, and therefore he will perform them. He is 'the Son of God's love.' God for his sake, as Mediator, will perform them. Heaven and earth shall conspire for thy good, rather than thou shalt miss of the performance of the least promise. Therefore from thy wants go to the promises, and from the promises go to Christ, and consider him. He is anointed of God for thee. He is anointed that he might be thy Christ, and thy Jesus, that he might be thy Saviour, 'Immanuel, God with us,' Isa. vii. 14, that he might reconcile God in us, that in office he might be so, that he might bring God and us together. Consider him.

And then go *to God, and consider what relation in Jesus Christ God hath put upon him.* In Christ God is a Father, and what can a father deny to his adopted son in Christ, whom he looks on in his natural Son Christ?

Yea, and to settle our minds the more, let us consider *the relations that God and Christ have put upon them, and the relations we stand in;* and the many promises we have in Christ, who is anointed and sealed by God the Father to be our Saviour, and to bestow good upon us. God is become our Father. What a world of promises is in that word Father? What will a father deny to his son? What if God had not left particular promises in Scripture, if he had left but the relation of a father, it had been promise enough. What can a father deny his child?

And then Christ, what relation hath he taken on him? He is our husband. What a world of promises is there in that? What can a loving husband deny his spouse, that he hath given himself for?

He hath taken upon him to be our head. What want of influence can there be from such a head, that hath taken all upon him for the body? The head sees, and hears, and doth all for the body; so Christ hears, and sees, and doth all for us. What a world of promises is in this relation of a head, if there were no particular promise?

Again, Christ styles himself sweetly our brother. What a world of promises are in these relations! God the Father is ours, Christ is ours. Here is the grand promise, 'I will be your God,' and will give you my Son.

And then, in the third place, he hath promised his Spirit. He will 'give his Spirit to them that beg him,' Luke xi. 13. What a world of promises is in that promise of the Spirit! It is a comforting Spirit, a sanctifying Spirit, a quickening Spirit, a strengthening Spirit, all is in the Spirit. As our soul doth all that the body doth, so it is by virtue of the Spirit, all the grace, and all the comfort we have. God hath promised himself, and Christ, and the Spirit, the whole Trinity. There is the grand promise: I will be your God, Christ shall be your Christ, and I will give you my Spirit. If we had not other promises, what a world of comfort have we in these!

Now in what relation stand we to these? We are children, we are heirs, we are 'temples of the Holy Ghost,' &c., 1 Cor. iii. 16. Put case our memories do not serve to call to mind particular promises, in the time of trouble, consider in Christ how God loves thee: he is thy God in Christ; how Christ loves thee: he hath taken thy nature on him to be thy husband; he makes love to thee, and desires thee to be reconciled. And the Spirit is given thee by Christ; he hath promised to give him if thou ask him: the Holy Spirit is the 'Spirit of promise,' Eph. i. 13. Think therefore of the general, of the covenant of grace, and these relations that have the force of promises; for sometimes particular promises may not come to our mind perhaps, and these will stablish a man against the gates of hell, and against all particular temptations.

This course we ought to take, then, to feed our thoughts with the promises. The promises are the food of faith. Let not our faith languish and famish for want, for want of meditations of God and Christ, what relations they have put upon them: and for want of meditating on particular promises in all kinds. How well-thriving might our faith be, if we would oft think of these things?

And to make us the more to think of these things, consider that all other things, alas! what are they, when we have not a promise of them in Christ? They are all vain, fading things; they will all come to nothing. That which we have by promise, grace, and comfort, and glory, they are ours for ever. God is ours for ever, Christ is ours for ever, the Spirit is ours for ever, the relations we are in are for ever. All other things are nothing, they will come to nothing ere long. This course we ought to take, then, that we may have comfort by the promises.

Again, in the next place, if we look to the kinds of the promises, whether to the promises for this life, or the promises of grace.

1. If they be promises of this life, take heed *we abuse not ourselves in them*. There have been gross miscarriages even from the beginning of the world, and will be to the end of the world, in the false application of outward promises. We see the Jews cried, 'The temple of the Lord, the temple of the Lord,' Jer. vii. 4, as if God had tied himself to that by a perpetual promise. 'Trust not to lying words,' saith the prophet, Jer. vii. 4. You think you are God's people, and that he will always keep you out of captivity; challenge not temporal promises without reservation and subjection to God's will, as he shall see good. Babylon saith, 'I sit as a queen, and I shall for ever.'

So mystical Babylon in the Revelation saith, 'I sit as a queen,' Rev. xviii. 7, till her judgment and destruction come in one day; because she trusted to her present temporal estate. Let no man promise himself that that God doth not promise in his word, immunity from the cross; for whatsoever promise of protection and provision we have, all is with the exception of the cross; remember therefore to construe the promises aright.

2. Then again, another rule about the promises is, *that it is usual with God to perform them in a wonderful manner*, that men know not how. He doth perform them notwithstanding. Take that for a rule. How is that? As Luther was wont to say, God's carriage is by contrary means; he performs them wonderfully.

He promised Abraham a child, but his body was dead in a manner first, and Sarah's womb. He promised Joseph to raise him up so high; but alas! the iron entered into his soul first. He promised that Christ should come, but all was desperate first, 'The sceptre was departed from Judah,' Gen.

xlix. 10. So he hath promised, that we shall rise from the dead, but we must rot in our graves first. He hath promised forgiveness of sins, that he will be merciful to us, but he will waken our consciences to see our desperate estate, that we are forlorn creatures first, and unworthy of any respect from him. He hath promised us happiness. We that are Christians are the happiest creatures in the world, yet in the sense and eye of the world for the present we are the most forlorn creatures that are. Yet he performs his promise with comfort here, and at last will fully manifest his love to us. So at the last his promises shall be wonderfully performed.

God doth not perform his promises according to human policy; he will not do thus, because we look he should do thus and thus. He will cross our expectation, and yet perform his promise. St Paul looked to come to Rome, Rom. i. 15, but he thought not of coming to Cæsar by whipping, and peril, and shipwreck. Moses knew he should come to see Canaan, did he think to have such a conflict in the wilderness? Alas! he thought not of it. God doth wondrous strangely perform his promises by contraries; he crosseth our imaginations and conceits directly, and yet he is true of his promise.

3. Another branch of this is, that though God's promises be 'yea and amen' in his time, *yet he usually defers his promises for a time*, and why? Among many other reasons, to mortify self-confidence, to fit us for his blessings! for except he deferred them, we should not be fit for them. He defers them, that we may be fitted for them long before they come; that we might mortify self-confidence, to see that he immediately and graciously performs his promise. And in the mean time, to exercise faith and repentance, and desire, and prayer, therefore he defers them; but they are amen at last, though he defer.

God's time is better than ours, he knows better than we. The physician knows his time better than the patient. Hereupon comes a duty consequently upon this dispensation of God. If he perform his promises wondrously, and unexpectedly, and perform them in delay; let thy duty be answerable to his dealing, *wait, wait upon God*, tie him not to such and such courses. He can transcend, and go beyond thy imagination, and do more than thou art able to conceive, as the apostle saith. Therefore wait his good time, 'He that shall come will come,' Heb. x. 37, stay God's leisure, prevent him not, run not before him.

And as he doth things by contraries, so when thou art in contraries look for contraries. When thou art in sin, and feelest it on thy conscience, believe that he is made righteousness to thee. He hath promised it. It is 'yea and amen' in Christ. When thou shalt be turned to dust in the grave, believe that he will raise thy body. This promise is 'yea and amen,' and as a pledge of it Christ is gone to heaven. When thou art miserable, remember the promise, thou shalt be glorious with Christ as he is glorious. 'All his promises are yea and amen.' In contraries believe contraries; because in contraries he performs contraries; and say as Job doth, 'Though he kill me, yet will I trust in him,' Job xiii. 15. I know thou canst not deny thyself, and thy 'promises are yea and amen.'

In the worst estate that befalls us, let us learn to wrestle with God in the promises, and implead his promises. Why! Lord, thou hast promised forgiveness of sins to them that ask it; thou hast promised grace, and mercy, and favour; remember thy promise, thou canst not deny thyself, thou canst not deny thy gracious promise, thy word is thyself, thou art Amen, and thy word is 'yea and amen,' only give me grace to wait thy good leisure ; yet I will not let thee depart without a blessing, I will hold thee till I have received a gracious answer, as Jacob wrestled with him till he had the blessing, Gen. xxxii. 24, *seq.* Let us labour to answer the promise with our faith, and labour to bring our souls to be like his promises. They are 'yea and amen.' Though they be not presently performed, let us constantly believe a constant promise, let us cleave to God, let us have an 'amen' for God's 'amen.' Are the promises amen? Amen let the soul say. Lord, 'So be it,' so it shall be, I will seal thy amen in thy promise, with my amen in my faith. So let us have an amen for Christ's amen. They are all, and will be all amen in Christ in fit time; all the gracious promises will be 'yea and amen;' let our souls echo, and say, Amen. For our faith must answer the promises. Faith and the promises be correlatives; for the promise is not except it be applied. Let faith answer the promise. Let us labour to be established in the promises in God's word.

Shall we have certain promises, and *shall we waver and stagger?* Therefore let us complain, Lord, thy promises are sure and certain as thou hast said, what is the reason I cannot build on them? Oh my unfaithful heart! Let us condemn our unbelieving, our lying hearts, that call the truth of God into question, and make that which is 'yea and amen' to be 'yea and nay.' We make truth a lie, and do rather believe our own lying hearts than God's immutable and unchangeable promises. Therefore let us see the fulness* of our hearts, and complain of them to God, and desire him to cure it and redress it, and he will do it.

This is *to give glory to God indeed.* We cannot honour God more than to believe his promises, and build on him. This will breed love, when we feel the comfort of the promises. Foolish men think to honour God by compliments, by dead performances. Silly men consider that the principal honour in the world. To God, [it] is to seal his truth, that thou shouldst not make him a liar. Hath he promised all things in the world? Get faith. That will honour him, and he will honour thy faith.

What makes God honour faith so much? He that believes he will bring him to heaven. Faith honours him. It gives him the glory of his truth, the glory of his goodness, of his mercy, of his truth, &c. As it honours him, he honours it.

The believer shall come to heaven, when the idle fashionable Christian shall vanish with his conceits, that thinks to serve God with empty vain shadows. Honour God with the obedience of faith, man. Cast thyself upon him, trust in him, in life and death, and then thou givest him the honour that he requireth at thy hands. For as the honour of his mercy is the greatest honour he will have in this world, more than that in the creation, so thou honourest him more in the gospel, to cast thyself on him for forgiveness of sins, and life everlasting, and for the guidance of thy daily course of life; thou honourest him more than by looking on the creature, or by doing him any service. He is honoured more by faith in Christ than by any other way. Let faith go to him; as faith honours him, so he will honour it, 'Let it be according to thy faith,' Mat. xv. 28.

Let not all be lost, let us bring vessels for the precious promises, the vessel of a believing heart. Shall all this be lost for a vain heart that will not lodge up these promises? Shall we have a rich portion, and neglect it? Shall we have so many promises, and not improve them, and make use of them?

* Cf. Ezek. xvi. 49.—G. Qu. 'foulness?'—ED.

Therefore I beseech you, let it be our practice continually every day, of all portions of Scripture make the promises most familiar to us; for duties follow promises. If we believe the promises with our heart, they are quickening promises. We will love God, and perform other duties. 'Faith works by love,' Gal. v. 6. If we believe, love will come kindly off. Therefore he saith here, 'All the promises are yea and amen,' insinuating that all is included in the promises.

Let us empty our hearts of confidence in anything, and fill them with the promises in Christ that are 'yea and amen.' Let us stablish our hearts with the promises, let us warm, and season, and refresh our hearts every day with these.

In these times of infection, what do we? Those that are careful of themselves, that go abroad in dangerous places, they have preservatives, they take something to preserve their spirits, and to strengthen them against the contagion abroad; and it is wisdom so to do, it is folly to neglect it, and to tempt God, not to be careful in this kind: it is very well done. But what is this, if thou do not fence thy soul and thy spirit, and take a draught of the promises every day afresh? Let us take out our pardon of course every day, of the forgiveness of sins. We sin every day, let us go for our pardon. 'If we sin, we have an Advocate with the Father, Jesus Christ, and he is the propitiation for our sins. And the blood of Jesus Christ shall purge us from all sin,' 1 John ii. 1. And he is in justifying us still every day, he is acquitting our souls; and there is a pardon of course to be taken out every day. Let us renew and refresh our hearts with the promises of pardon and forgiveness of sins every day. Let us strengthen our souls with renewing the promises of grace for that day to walk comfortably before God, that he will keep us by his Spirit from sin, that he will be a shield and a sun to us, that he will give us wisdom to carry ourselves as we should; and he will give us his Holy Spirit if we beg it.

Let us every day take these promises to be cordials in these dangerous times; and then come life, come death, all shall be welcome. Why? Because we are in Christ, and have embraced the promises and Christ; and all in Christ is 'yea and amen:' it shall go well with us. What a wondrous comfortable life would a Christian's life be, if he could yield the obedience of faith answerable to the promises! What a shame is it, that having such rich promises we should be so loose, so changeable, that we should be cast down with crosses, and lift up with prosperity? It is because we believe not the promises of better things, therefore we are proud of present things, and cast down with present crosses, and are fast and loose. Now we have good things for the present, afterward the devil comes between us and the promises, and makes us let go our hold. Religion stands on this, which makes me to press it the more. If this were well taken to heart and digested, we should know what religion means; if we know Christ and the promises, all other things will come off. All others are but formalities. They will never comfort without the consideration of knowing God in Christ, and the rich promises to us in Christ.

Likewise, if this be so, that the promises of God in Christ are 'yea and amen,' this teacheth us how *to make use of all former examples of others, and of all former goodness to ourselves*. Was God merciful to Abraham and to David? 'Our fathers trusted in thee, and were not confounded,' Ps. xxii. 4. Therefore he reasons, if I trust in God I shall not be confounded; for the 'promises are yea and amen.' They are true to one as well as another. And 'whatsoever was written afore, was written for our comfort,' Rom. xv. 4.

And this is a singular good use we may make of reading of the stories of the Scripture, and of holy men, that the same God he lives for ever, 'his arm is not shortened, he that was, is, and is to come,' Isa. lix. 1; and therefore we should read histories with application. Did God make sure his promises to them? Surely he will make sure his promises to us. Had David forgiveness of sins upon his confession? Surely so shall we. 'Abraham believed, and it was accounted to him for righteousness,' Gal. iii. 6, and so it shall to us if we believe. It is alleged for that end. And St Paul prefixeth his example to all posterity, 'God was merciful to me, and not so only, but to all that believe in him,' 1 Tim. i. 16.

This is an use that we may make likewise of the story of our own lives, as well as the story of others; for, consider the former times, why, Lord, thy promises heretofore have been 'yea and amen,' thou hast delivered me from such and such dangers, thou hast been so good, and so good to me, thou art not changed. Let us store up experience out of the story of our own lives. God is 'Yea and Amen,' and 'his promises are yea and amen,' constant to all his children, and to their children; and they are alike in all ages 'from generation to generation,' as Moses saith, Ps. xc. 1, 'Thou art our God from generation to generation for ever.'

Thus we see how to make use of the promises; for promises, we must know, are either directly to particular persons, or implied. A promise made to any directly, to any in particular, is an implied promise to me in the general equity in matter of grace, and glory, or the removal of some true misery. What was made to Joshua, is applied to all the church, Heb. xiii. 10, *seq.*; that which was directly promised to him, is an implied promise to all that will make use of that example.

Again, if so be that all the promises of God be 'yea and amen,' that is, certain and constant in Christ, this should comfort us *when men deal loosely with us, and fail in their promises*, whereon perhaps we have builded too much, when men deal falsely with us. And indeed, there is nothing that makes an honest heart wearier of this wicked world, than the consideration of the falsehood of men in whom they trust. Oh! it is a cruel thing to deceive him, that unless he had trusted he had never been deceived by thee. It is a treacherous thing, but this world is full of such treacherous dealing, that a man can scarce trust assurances, much less words. But there are things thou mayest trust, if thou have a heart concerning the best good, there are promises that are 'yea and amen;' there is a God that keeps covenant. It is his glory to do so from generation to generation. Here is the comfort of a Christian, when he finds falseness in the world, to retire to his God, and hide himself there.

And in the uncertainty of all things below, in all changes, as this world is full of changes—now poor, now rich; now in favour, now out of favour—why, what hath a Christian to cast himself on? The promises of God in Christ, they are 'yea and amen;' they are promises that never fail. They that know thy name will trust in thee, Ps. ix. 10. What is the reason? It follows, 'Thou never failest those that trust in thee.' Therefore in the vicissitude and intercourse of all earthly things under the moon, that are like the moon, changeable, let us stablish our souls upon that which is unchangeable, and that will make us unchangeable, if we build on it, 'For the word of the Lord endures for ever,' Isa. xl. 6, which is alleged by Peter, 1 Peter i. 25, 'All flesh is grass, and as the flower of the grass,' that is, it fades as the grass, and as the flower of the grass; all the excellency of wit and learning, it is but as the flower of the grass, but 'the word of the

Lord endures for ever.' How doth the word of the Lord endure for ever? St John expounds it, 1 John ii. 17. A true Christian endures for ever by the word of the Lord. He that believes in the word, he endures for ever, because his comforts endure for ever; they are 'yea and amen.' His grace endures for ever. God's love endures to him for ever. Therefore by building upon that which is certain, we make ourselves certain too. When the word is ingraffed (it is St James his phrase), when it is ingraffed into our hearts, it turns our hearts to be like itself, it is eternal itself, and it makes us eternal. 'He that doth the will of the Lord abides for ever, saith St John. 'The world passeth, and the lust thereof, but he that doth the will of the Lord abides for ever,' 1 John ii. 17. And 'the word of the Lord abides for ever,' as it is in another place, 1 Peter i. 25. The one expounds the other, that is, we, by believing, and doing the word of the Lord, abide for ever.

To stir us up to rely constantly upon this word, the promises, and the grace of God brought to us by the promises. As I said before, shall we have certain promises of God that never lie, and shall we not build on them? What is there in the world to build on, if we cannot build on this? And yet the froward heart of man will believe anything rather than God's truth. The merchantman he commits his estate, his goods, to the sea. He hath no promise that they shall come again. It is only in the providence of God. He hath made no promise for it. The husbandman commits his seed to the ground, though he have nothing left of his seed; and though he sow in tears, yet he commits all to the earth in hope of a return; and yet he hath no promise for this, but God's ordinary providence, that may sometimes fail.

Are we in such hope when we commit our seed to the ground, and when we commit our goods to the sea, to the waves, and yet have not a promise for this, but God's ordinary providence, which ofttimes fails, having not bound himself that it shall be alway so, because God will shew himself the God of nature, that he can command nature? And shall we not trust him when we have his providence and his promise too? when he is bound by his promise, when he hath made himself a debtor to us? when the free God, who is most free, hath made himself a debtor by his promise, and hath sealed his promise by an oath and by sacraments?

Alas! God hath made all things faithful to us. Therefore we trust them. But we trust not him that hath made other things so, and is so faithful to us. Therefore let us build on these promises in Jesus Christ.

Now to direct us a little further, to train ourselves up to make use of the promises of God in Jesus Christ,

1. Observe every day, *how God fulfils his promises in lesser matters.* Parents train up their children by education, that they may trust them for their inheritance. So God trains us up to believe his providence, that he will provide for us, without cracking our consciences by ill means. Will we believe his promises for these things, and will we not believe him for life everlasting? No! certainly we cannot. Therefore let us exercise faith to believe the promises for provision, that 'he will not fail us, nor forsake us,' but be with us in our callings, using lawful means for the things of this life.

2. Sometimes again take another method. When faith begins to stagger for the things of this life, quicken it *with the grand promises.* Will God give me life everlasting? and hath he given me Christ? are his promises in him 'yea and amen?' will he give me the greater, and will he not give

me the less? Sometimes by the lesser, be encouraged to hope for the greater; sometimes quicken our deadness and dulness in believing the lesser, with the undoubted performance of the great. Will God give me life everlasting, and will he not give me provision in my pilgrimage till I come there? undoubtedly he will. 'Fear not, little flock, it is your Father's will to give you a kingdom,' saith Christ, Luke xii. 32. They were distrustful for the things of this life. Do you think, saith he, that he will not give you the things of this life, that keeps a kingdom for you? 'Fear not.'

3. Again, when we hear any promise in the word of God, *turn it into a prayer*, put God's bond in suit, as it were. His promises are his bonds. Sue him on his bond. He loves to be sued on his bond; and he loves that we should wrestle with him by his promises. Why, Lord, thou hast made this and this promise, thou canst not deny thyself, thou canst not deny thine own truth; thou canst not cease to be God; thou canst as well cease to be God, as deny thy promise, that is, thyself. So let us put the promises into suit, as David, Ps. cxix. 49, if it be his (*www*), 'Lord, remember thy promise, wherein thou hast caused thy servant to trust,' as if God had forgotten his promise; 'Lord, remember thy promise,' I put thee in mind of thy promise, 'wherein thou hast caused thy servant to trust.' If I be deceived, thou hast deceived me. Thou hast made these promises, and caused me to trust in thee, and 'thou never failest those that trust in thee.'

What makes a man faithful? Trust to a man makes him faithful. So when God is honoured with our trusting of him, it makes him faithful. Let us therefore put in suit his promises of provision and protection every day in the way of our calling; and for necessary grace and comfort, that he will not fail us in any necessary grace to bring us to heaven, considering that he hath filled our nature with all grace in Christ.

4. Again, let us take this course, when we hear of rich and precious promises that are made, *labour to know them*. What? shall we have an inheritance, a portion, and not labour to know it? Let us labour to know all our portion, and to know it of those that search the word of God, to be glad to hear anything concerning the privileges and prerogatives of a Christian. Those that dig the mines of the Scripture, which is the office of the ministers, let us labour to know all our privileges.

Let not Satan rob us of one privilege. Every promise is precious. They are rich promises. Yet they are no more than God thought necessary for us. He thought all little enough to stablish our faith. Let us not lose one. We cannot be without one. Let us labour to know them.

And when we know them, work them upon our hearts by meditation, and shame ourselves upon it: say, is it true, are these promises so? Is it true that God hath revealed these things in his word? To whom hath he made them? to angels or to beasts? No! to men, to sinners, to men in the world to comfort them. They are their provision, their inheritance, as David saith, Ps. cxix. 57, 103, 'Thy word is my inheritance, and my portion; they are sweeter than the honey and the honeycomb.' Are they so? Do I believe this, or do I not believe it? Yes! I do. If I do, can I believe them, and be so uncomfortable? Let us shame ourselves. Do I believe the promises of life everlasting, the promises of perseverance, the promise that God will hide me in danger, that he will be my habita ion and my hiding-place? and do I look to unlawful means? Do I live without God in the world, as if there were no promise? What a shame is this! There is a weakness in my faith certainly. When a branch withers, there is a fault in the root. So there is a defect in the radical grace, that it draws not juice out of the promises as it should. There is a defect in my faith. Therefore I will look where the defect is, and strengthen my faith.

Thus we should shame ourselves. Can I hear these promises, and be no more joyful, and be no more affected? Can I use indirect means, and yet believe that God is all-sufficient to me in the covenant? Certainly I cannot.

Therefore let us come to the trial, to some few evidences, that a man doth believe in the promises.

He that believes the promises of God in Christ to be 'yea and amen,' doubtless he will be affected, answerable to the things promised. Saith David, 'Thy statutes they are the joy of my heart,' Ps. cxix. 11.

1. The promises *will be the joy and rejoicing of our heart.* He that can hear of promises, and not be affected, certainly he believes them not. When a man thinks of his inheritancee, and of his evidences, that they are clear, that he shall enjoy it without suit, or trouble, it comforts him, he cannot think of it without comfort. Cannot a man think of a little pelf of the earth without comfort, when he knows he hath assurance to it? and shall we think of heaven and happiness, and not rejoice? Will not these be the joy of a man's heart? Certainly they will affect him. When good things are apprehended by faith, will they not work upon the affections? Certainly they will.

2. Again, where the promises are believed, they will *quicken us to all cheerful obedience.* Certainly, if God will assist me with strength and comfort if I go on in his ways, and in the end of all give me life everlasting, this will quicken me to all obedience. Therefore those that go deadly and dully, as if they had no encouragement here, nor promise of glory after, they believe not the promises. For God doth not set us on work as Pharaoh set the children of Israel to make brick without straw; but when he bids us do anything, he promiseth us grace, and gives us his Spirit, and after grace he gives glory. If men did believe this, they would go about God's work without dulness and staggering. So far as we are dull, and stagger in the work of God, so far our faith is weak in the promises of God.

3. Again, as they quicken in regard of comfort, *so they purge in regard of holiness;* for they make men study mortification and sanctification, 2 Cor. vi. 18, and the beginning of the viith, 'Having these promises, let us purge ourselves from all filthiness of flesh and spirit, perfect sanctification in the fear of God.' 'Having these promises.' So that the promises, as they have a quickening, so they have a purging power; and that upon sound reasoning. Doth God promise that he will be my Father, and I shall be his son? and doth he promise me life everlasting? and doth that estate require purity? and no unclean thing shall come there? Certainly these promises being apprehended by faith, as they have a quickening power to comfort, so they purge with holiness. We may not think to carry our filthiness to heaven. Doth the swearer think to carry his blasphemies thither? Filthy persons and liars are banished thence: there is 'no unclean thing.' He that hath these promises purgeth himself, 'and perfecteth holiness in the fear of God.' 'He that hath this hope purifieth himself, as he is pure,' 1 John iii. 3. So these promises affect, and quicken, and purge.

4. And then the promises *they do settle the soul,* because they be 'yea and amen:' they make the soul quiet. If a man believe an honest man on

his word, he will be quiet; if he be not quiet, he doth not believe. So much faith, so much quiet. 'Being justified by faith, we have peace with God through Jesus Christ our Lord,' Rom. v. 1. So much faith, so much peace. 'In nothing be careful, but let your desires be known to God in prayer, supplication, and thanksgiving,' Philip. iv. 6; and when you have done this, 'The peace of God which passeth all understanding, shall preserve your hearts and minds in Christ Jesus,' ver. 7. So where there is prayer, and thanksgiving, and doing of duty, the peace of God which passeth all understanding, will keep the mind in Christ; and where there is not quiet and peace to preserve the heart and mind, there is neglect of duty before, not committing ourselves to God's promises to build on them.

5. Again, where there is a believing the promises, there is not only a staying of the soul in general, *but when all things are gone, when all things are contrary*. That is the nature of faith in the promises. Put the case, that a Christian that is of the right stamp, have nothing in the world to take to, only God's word and promises; surely he knows they are 'yea and amen.' It is the word of God all-sufficient; he is Jehovah; he gives a being to his word, and to all things else; therefore he hath the name Jehovah. Therefore thinks the soul, though I have nothing, yet I have him that is the substance of all things. All other things are but shadows; God the Father, Son, and Holy Ghost, are the substance that give all things a being; and therefore I will cast myself on God. Here now is the triumph of faith. When there is nothing else to trust to, nay, when all things else are contrary, when it is faith against faith, and 'hope against hope;' when there is such a conflict in a man, that he sees nothing but the contrary; here faith will shut the eye of sense, and not look to present things too much. Though I see all things contrary, though I see rather signs of anger than otherwise, yet I will hope and believe in God, for this or that. Here is the wisdom of a believing Christian that believes the promises—he will shut his eyes, and not look on the waves, on the troubles. They will carry him away, and dazzle him. But he looks to the constant love of God in Christ, and to the constant promises of God. His nature is constant, and his truth is as his nature. He cannot deny himself and his own word, when he hath made himself a debtor by his promise, and bound himself by his word.

Therefore in contraries say as Job, 'Though he kill me, yet will I trust in him,' Job xiii. 15. True faith when it is in strength will uphold a man when all fails; nay, it will hold a man when all is contrary. This our Saviour Christ, in whom 'all the promises are yea and amen,' did excellently teach us by his own example. For when all was contrary, and our blessed Saviour felt the wrath of God, which made him sweat drops of blood, and made him cry out, 'My God, My God, why hast thou forsaken me?' Mark xv. 34; yet here faith wrestled with 'My God, my God,' still, even under the wrath of God. He brake through the seeming wrath of God, into the heart of God.

Faith hath a piercing eye. It will strive through the clouds, though they be never so thick, through all the clouds of temptation. Christ had so piercing a faith, it brake through all. He saw a Father's heart under an angry semblance. So a Christian triumphs by faith in oppositions to faith. When all is contrary to faith, yet notwithstanding he can say 'My God' still. This is an evidence of a strong faith in the promises.

6. Again, an evidence of faith in the promises is *faithfulness in ourselves, in our promises to God;* for surely the soul that expects anything of God,

that he should be faithful, it studies to be faithful in the covenant, Ps. xxv. 10, 'All the ways of God are mercy, and truth.' All his dealings to his children are mercy and truth, 'to them that keep his covenant.' For you know, the promises have conditions annexed; and where God fulfils his promise, he gives grace to perform the condition, to walk before him, to allow ourselves in no sin. For if we allow ourselves in any sin, we perform not the covenant on our part. Now God will give grace to perform the covenant where he will perform his own. Therefore those that are unfaithful in their covenant, and yet think God will be faithful to them, it is presumption.

When we come to the communion, we think we do God a great deal of service; but we must consider we enter into covenant with God, as well as he binds himself to us. He gives us Christ, and all his blessings. He reacheth forth Christ with all in him, if we will receive him. Aye, but we bind ourselves to God, to lead a new life, and to be thankful, and to shew it in obedience. And so in baptism; we do not only receive in the sacraments, but we yield, we bind ourselves to God. And we must be careful of what we promise to God, as well as expect that which he promiseth to us. If we expect his truth, we must be faithful, and careful of performing our covenants to him.

Quest. Oh, but how shall I do that? saith the distressed soul. I have no grace.

Ans. God knows that well enough; therefore he that promiseth, he promiseth grace to perform the condition; that is one part of the covenant, to give grace to fulfil the covenant. For he that saith, If we believe and repent, &c., he will give us hearts to repent, if we ask them; he hath promised to circumcise our hearts, to give us new hearts, and to give us his Holy Spirit if we ask him. Why, Lord, thou knowest I have no grace in myself to fulfil the covenant; no, but thou must perform both parts; thou givest the grace, and good thing promised, and grace to keep the covenant too; therefore let none be discouraged.

Many things are required, it is true; but the things are promised that are required, if in the use of means we depend on him by prayer. For the promises are legacies as well as promises. What is the difference between a legacy and a covenant? A covenant is with condition, with stipulation; a legacy is an absolute thing, when a man gives a thing freely without any condition. So, though the promises be propounded by way of covenant, with stipulations to and fro in the passages of them, as a covenant; yet in regard of God's gracious performance, to them that depend upon him, all the promises are legacies.

Therefore God's promises, and God's covenant they are called a testament, as well as promises. They are called a will. A will, shewing what God will give us freely in the use of means, as well as what our duty is in the covenant. Therefore our estate is happy in Christ, if we depend upon God in the use of means. He will give us all things that are necessary that he hath promised; nay, he will give grace to fulfil the covenant, if we beg it.

If a man be careless and live in sins against the covenant, he cannot perform the covenant; and let him not allege this, that he cannot, for God will give grace to them that are careful to fulfil it. Let such a man as neglects the performance on his part, expect no good from God while he is so, let him expect vengeance; *for all the threatenings of God* are 'yea and amen,' *as well as his promises*, to them that live in sins against conscience. Those that will not expect grace to serve him for the time to come, all the threatenings are 'yea and amen.' There is no comfort for such.

I beseech you therefore consider, it is a terrible thing to live in a state without God, and without Christ; to have no care of the performance of that that we have bound ourselves to God by the sacrament, and in our particular vows; for his threatenings are effectual as well as his promises. In Zech. i. 5, there he tells the Jews of the prophets that had threatened many things. The prophets are dead, saith he, that threatened your fathers; but for all that, the threatenings lighted on them. 'The prophets, where are they?' They were but men, but when they were gone, the threatenings lighted on your fathers. Jeremiah died, but the captivity that he threatened, it did not die; they were carried captive seventy years. So we threaten the vengeance of God on obstinate sinners, that will not come in to the gospel; we are not 'yea and amen' in regard of our being, we die; but our threatenings are 'yea.' If they be not reversed by repentance, the threatenings are 'amen,' as well as the promises. It is an evidence therefore we do not believe, if we have not care to make good the covenant on our part.

7. Again, another evidence of a child of the promises, of a man that believes the promises, *it is inward opposition of the flesh, and hatred of fleshly men;* for as it is, Gal. iv. 29, 'The son of the bondwoman persecuted the son of the freewoman.' A true, downright believer is a son of the freewoman, a son of promise; and the flesh in us opposeth it, like Ishmael, like Job's wife, and like Sarah, that laughed when the promise was made. We have an Ishmael and a Sarah in us. Aye, can this promise of life everlasting when I am rotten, and this promise of forgiveness of sins, and that goodwill, be good to me if I crack not* my conscience? If I take this and that course, shall these promises be performed? Here is opposition. We cannot believe the promises without much opposition.

So carnal men, 'they mock and deride the counsel of the poor,' as the psalmist saith, Ps. xiv. 6. The children of the promise that depend upon God's mercy in Christ, they are persecuted by fleshly justiciaries, and they that look to be saved by themselves without a promise, they will not be beholden to God so much. Their proud, swelling hearts rise against Christians that honour God by trusting in his promises, and will be saved by promises.

A proud popish person, his heart riseth against a holy Christian that is a son of the promise; he scorns him. You intend to be saved by the righteousness of another. No! we will not be so much beholden to God, we will satisfy for ourselves; we will merit heaven ourselves. God shall not be beholden to us to trust in him, we will bring somewhat ourselves, we will buy it out. Can these men have humble hearts? Nay, can they have any other than malicious, persecuting hearts against humble, believing Christians, that honour God by trusting in his promises?

You know Isaac was 'a son of the promise.' How was he born? Not according to the course of nature. Sarah's womb was dead. Christ was the Son of the promise. How was he born? Not according to the course of nature, for his mother was a virgin. So a Christian is a son of the promise. He is begotten where there is nothing in the course of nature likely, where there is breeding for sin, no works, no righteousness, then he believes in Christ. Isaac was a notable type of Christ and a son of promise. He was begotten besides the course of generation. So a Christian is not

* Qu. 'crack?'—ED.

begotten as a proud justiciary, by works; but he shews himself therein to be a true believer. He is begotten against the course of nature when he sees a barren heart, and sees as little disposition in his heart to be a Christian as was in the virgin's womb for Christ to be born.

How was the promise made to the virgin? She could not conceive how this should be since she knew not man. It was replied again, 'The Holy Ghost shall overshadow thee,' Luke i. 35. Her heart closed with that speech, and Christ was conceived then. So the barren heart of a Christian if it can believe, his sins shall be forgiven, and he shall have life everlasting,—if he can honour God in believing that he will keep him in life and death. Let the heart close with these promises, and a Christian is begotten. He is a son of the promise.

As for the proud justiciary that will have something in himself to vaunt of, and will persecute others that are true Christians, he relies on no promise. A Christian when he sees nothing to rely on but the promise, he closeth with the promise, and Christ is begotten in him at that very instant. To name no more evidences, you see how we may examine ourselves whether we trust in and cast ourselves upon the promises of God or no. If we do, we shall find them 'yea and amen.'

Consider it therefore, and be glad of these promises; and when you have them, go to God in Christ for the performance of them. Take the counsel of that blessed man, that in these latter times brought the glorious light of religion to light, Luther, I mean (to whom we are beholden for the doctrine of free grace more than any other divine of later times). Go to God in Christ in the promises. Christ is wrapped up in the promises. The promises are the swaddling-clothes wherein Christ is wrapped, as he saith (*xxx*). We must not think of God out of Christ. There is, saith he, God absolute in himself; so, he is 'a consuming fire,' Heb. xii. 29. But there is God incarnate, go to God incarnate, to God making good his promises in Christ incarnate; go to Christ sucking his mother's breast, lying in the manger, living humbly, talking with a sinful woman, inviting sinners to come to him, conversing with sinful creatures, altering and changing their natures, that never refused any that came to him.

Go not to God absolute. He is a 'consuming fire.' Go to Christ incarnate, God-man; go to him abased, and there is sweet converse for thy faith; for 'all the promises are made in him yea and amen.'

I beseech you, therefore, be acquainted with the mystery of Christ more and more. We have the promises in him. And you must know besides, that the Father and the Holy Ghost, they have a part, a hand in Christ's abasement; for Christ did all by his Father's appointment, and therefore it is as much as if the Father had been abased; for Christ was anointed to be so. Therefore think, that God the Father allures and invites you when Christ doth it, because he is anointed to invite you. Think that the Father is as peaceable as Christ was, because Christ was so by his Father's appointment, by his anointing. See all the three Persons, the Father, Son, and Holy Ghost in Christ. See God incarnate making all the promises before, and as the ground of all that is made good to us. See the wondrous love of God incarnate. And then go and see Christ raising that flesh that he was abased in; see him ascended into heaven, and sitting in it at the right hand of God. Then think of God in Christ glorious, think of Christ a public person, and we all in him. So as Leo saith, 'Only Christ was he that died, in whom all died; he was crucified, in whom all were crucified; and he rose again, in whom all rise, he being a public person; other particular men died, and themselves died only.'* Let us look upon God incarnate, and see ourselves in him, see God in Christ, see Christ a public person; for therefore the second Person took the manhood, that he might be a public person.

Christ took not our persons, but our nature; that our nature being knit to the second person, he might be a public person; as Adam was a public man for all mankind. Therefore think of all the promises in Christ as God-man, that he was the man Christ, made man for us. This is wondrous comfortable, let us solace ourselves with it.

Take away Christ, and the promises in Christ, and what is there in the world? Nothing but idolatry and superstition, staggering and wavering, and darkness and blindness, and popery and devilishness. Who reigns in the world but the devil and antichrist, heathenism and paganism, and all filthiness? Take away Christ, the sound knowledge of Christ incarnate, and the sound knowledge of the promises, the clear, settled promises in Christ, and what is the life of man but a horrible confusion, even a hell upon earth? Where Christ is not known, what are the lives of men, the utmost quintessence of them, but only projecting for an estate here in this world, and then to slip into hell? To live a civil life, as morality perhaps may fit a man for that, and then to be cast into hell.

Out of Christ there is no salvation, no certain comfort, no life, no light, nothing to be reckoned on out of Christ, and the promises in Christ. Therefore let us love them, and build on them, and make much of the truth we have, and get into Christ; for 'all the promises in him are yea and amen.' God hath no commerce with us immediately but by Christ the mediator, through whom he looks on us, and in whom he conveys all good to us.

The Scripture is termed a paradise. It is like a paradise, wherein we have the streams of the water of life, and the tree of life, Jesus Christ, and wherein we have the promises of life; and there is no angel to keep the door, or gate, or entrance of this paradise, but rather we are allured to come to it to refresh ourselves. There is God himself walking, there is Christ himself the tree of life. Therefore, we should make the Scriptures wondrous familiar to us, especially single out the promises, make use of them. Learn what it is to live by faith in the promises, for 'all the promises in Jesus Christ, in him are yea and in him amen.'

'*To the glory of God by us.*' The end of all this, that God will engage himself by promises, that he will stablish these promises so sure in Christ Jesus the Mediator, God and man, that he will make them 'yea and amen' in him, it is for his own glory, and 'to the glory of God' by us ministers; for we preach these promises to the people, and people believe them, and they believing give glory to God.

Obs. God's glory is manifested in the gospel, especially when it is believed in the promises.

What wondrous glory hath God in the promises in Christ!

More a great deal than in the creation. In the creation man was made according to God's image. Now, in the gospel we are created according to Jesus Christ, God-man. There God added light to light, comfort to comfort. He made man good, and would have continued him good. But here is the glory of his mercy and goodness in Christ. Here he doth good to sinners. He raiseth a sinner to mercy. He doth not add light to light, but he brings light out of darkness. In the gospel mercy strives with

* See the passage from Leo, in foot-note, vol. I. page 369.—G.

misery, and strives with sin, and overcomes all our ills. It is God's will in the gospel to do good to sinners. Mercy is added to sinful men, contrary against contrary, God's goodness triumphing over the misery of man.

The righteousness that Adam had, it was the righteousness of a creature, of a man; but the obedience we have in Christ, it is the obedience of God-man. Therefore, that being imputed to us, it is a more exquisite righteousness. It brings us to God and entitles us to heaven. It is infinitely more than Adam's was. God manifests greater glory than in the creation. There is greater love, and greater mercy, and greater goodness manifested in the gospel than to Adam in innocency.

Our estate in Christ is more perfect. His estate was not 'yea and amen,' for it was 'yea' to-day and 'nay' to-morrow. He stood but a while. But in Christ the 'promises are yea and amen.' He had no promise, we have. Our estate by promises in Christ is better than ever Adam's was, as we are in a better root than he, for he was not in Christ the Mediator. We by faith are united to Christ, Mediator; and by virtue of the promise, God, where he begins, he will make an end; where he is Alpha, he will be Omega. What a glory is this to God, that he can repair man to a better estate than ever he had at the first, as God's mending is ever for the better. The state of grace and glory is better than ever the state of nature was; spiritual is better than natural. Therefore, it is much for the glory of the wisdom of God that he can in Christ reconcile justice and mercy, and shew more mercy than ever he did in making man out of the dust of the earth, and all is to the glory of God. These attributes especially are glorious in the promises in Christ.

His justice is glorious in punishing sin in Christ. There sin is odious in the punishing of Christ, God-man; if we speak of justice, there is justice.

If of mercy, to put it upon our surety, for God to give his Son for us, there is transcendent mercy and transcendent justice in the punishing of our sin. How could it be punished greater?

And then the glory of his wisdom, to bring these together, infinite mercy and infinite justice, in Christ.

Infinite power, for God to become man, and, without sin, to be so far abased; a humble omnipotency, to descend so low that God could be mortal, and then to raise himself again.

And then the glory of his truth, that whatsoever was promised to Abraham, to David, to the prophets, all was performed in Christ, all the types. Here is glory by Christ of mercy, justice, wisdom, truth; for all are 'yea and amen' in Christ. Therefore, he may well say all this is 'to the glory of God.'

Therefore, consider how the glory of God shines in the face of Jesus Christ, as the apostle saith. If you would see God, see him shining 'in the face of Jesus Christ,' 2 Cor. iv. 6, see his mercy shining in Christ, and his justice in the punishing our sin in Christ; see his truth, his power, his wisdom, shining in Christ, and shining more than in the creation, or in anything in the world besides.

Can you honour God more than in believing the gospel? Can you dishonour him more, than to call his truth into question, that is 'yea and amen?' If you believe the gospel, you 'set to your seal that God is true,' John iii. 33. What an honour is this, that God will be honoured by you! In setting to your seal that he is true, you give him the glory of all his attributes. In not believing, what a dishonour do you do to God! You deny his mercy, his wisdom, his justice, his truth, you deny all his attributes, 'you make God a liar,' 1 John v. 10. What a horrible sin is unbelief!

Therefore fortify your faith. The devil layeth siege to our faith above all other things. If he can shake that, he shakes all: for holy life goes when faith goes. Who will love God, or obey God, when he knows not whether he be his God or no? Let faith flourish, and it will quicken life in the heart. Let the promises grow in the heart, and the word be grafted in the heart, and all will flourish in a Christian's life. All will come off clearly and freely. Obedience will be cheerful and free, when we see God reconciled in Christ. Then love will be full of devices. When I see God's love to me, what shall I do to shew love again, to shew thanks to God? Where is there any that for God's sake I may do good unto? How shall I maintain the truth, and resist all opposers of the truth? Can I do too much for him that hath done so much for me? Love quickens. The devil knows if he can shake faith he shakes all. Let us fortify faith, and we glorify God more than by anything else. He is glorious in the gospel, and how shall he be so by us, except we set our hearts to believe him? Therefore let us seal God's truth by our faith, and 'set to our seals that God is true.' God vouchsafes to be honoured by weak sinful men believing of him: and that faith that honours him he will be sure to honour.

'By us.' By us ministers. How? When the gospel is preached, God is carried in triumph, as it were, and his banner is set up, and the promises displayed, and sinners called unto him; and God is glorified by the discovery of these things, and faith is wrought in people to whom they are discovered; and they glorify God when they believe: they bless God that ever they heard these tidings. So every way God is glorified.

The ministers they open, as it were, the box of sweet ointment, that the savour of it may be in the church, and spread far. They lay open the tapestry, the rich treasure of God's mercies: they dig deep, and find out the treasure. Therefore these promises in Scripture being so made and performed in Christ, they tend to God's glory, but by us, by our ministry. God, to knit man and man together, will convey the good he means to convey by the despised ministry.

The enemies, therefore, of the ministry of the gospel, what are they? Here is a double prejudice against them: they are enemies of the glory of God, and of the comfort of God's people, for they glorify God in the sense of his mercy. When it is unfolded to them, God gets glory, and they comfort.

What do we think then of Popish spirits, that feed the people only with dead and dull ceremonies? But let them go. I go on to the next verse, having dwelt somewhat long on this.

VERSE 21.

'*Now he that stablisheth us with you in Christ is God, who hath anointed us,*' &c. As the riches of a Christian consisteth in the promises of God, which, as we have heard, in Christ 'are all yea and amen;' so unless he be stablished and built upon this strength, all is nothing. What if a man stand on a rock, if he be not built on it! What if the foundation be never so strong, if he be not stablished thereon! It is not sufficient that the promises be stablished, but we must be stablished upon them. The promises of God are indeed 'yea and amen,' might the soul say, but what is that to me? Therefore the apostle addeth, He that gives the promises, will stablish us upon the promises.

'*Now he which stablisheth us with you in Christ is God.*' The first thing that I will observe, before we come to the particular handling of the words, shall be only this in the general, from the connection and knitting together of this verse with the former, viz.,

Obs. That there must be a double amen.

1. There is an amen in the promises. They are in themselves true. There must be an amen likewise in us. We must say amen to them, that is, we must be stablished upon them. There must be an echo in a Christian's heart unto God; that as God saith, these and these things I promise, and they are all amen; so the soul by faith must echo again, these things are for me, I believe them.

For, as we say in the schools to good purpose, there is a double certainty, a double firmness; a certainty of the object, and a certainty of the subject; there is a firmness of the promises in Jesus Christ; and there must be a firmness in us upon those promises. It is no matter what the certainty of the thing be that we are to build upon, if there be not a certainty in the person, if there be not a building on that thing. God shall lose the glory of his truth, and we the comfort, unless we be certain, as well as the promises are certain. It is no matter what the garment be, if it be not put on. It is no matter, as I said before, how firm the rock be, if we plant not ourselves upon it; and therefore besides the writing of God's word on tables, unless he write it likewise in our hearts, unless our hearts be stablished on that truth that in itself is certain, that it may be certain to us, all is to no purpose.

You see therefore, *the absolute necessity of the application of the soul unto those truths which are certain and sure in themselves.* There must be a stablishing of us, as well as a stablishing of the promises. There is a necessity of the application of the promises to ourselves, that they be true to us. Christ is a garment. We must put him on then. He is the robes that we appear glorious before God in; but we must put him on by faith. Christ is the food of life. He is so indeed, but then he must be digested. Meat, except it be applied, except the stomach work nourishment out of it by application, and so digest it to all the parts, the body hath not nourishment from it.

Christ is the foundation of his church, aye, but there must be application. We as living stones must be built on him. Let the foundation be never so strong, if the stones be not laid on the foundation, the stones cannot stand. Though Christ be the spouse of the church, and be never so rich, there must be application and consent; we must strike up the bargain and match between Christ and us. There must be our consent to tie ourselves to him, to give up ourselves to him. So look to all the comfortable relations that our blessed Saviour hath taken upon him in the book of God, they all enforce application.

The ground, I say, is this, that though there be never so much certainty in the thing, yet if there be not a certainty in the person to found application upon, all is to no purpose.

These two therefore must go together, and they are sweet relatives, promises on God's part, and faith on our part. The promises and Christ are nothing without faith. For there must be a touch to draw virtue. If faith have never so little touch of Christ, it will draw virtue; but there must be a touch, there must be application.* Christ is nothing without faith, and faith is nothing without Christ and the promises.

For what is the difference between faith and presumption? Presumption is an empty, groundless, fruitless conceit. Faith builds on the promises of the word; we can allege the promise. It is nothing for a madman to assume himself to be king of another country. Why? He hath no promise. He that made account that all the ships that came to the haven were his, it was but a frantic part of him, and so he was accounted. So a man that thinks his estate is good, and builds not himself upon the promise, that hath no ground for it out of God's word, it is but a presumptuous frantic conceit. The promises are nothing without faith, and faith is nothing without the promises. There must be application. This I thought good to observe first in the general. To come now more particularly to the words themselves.

'He that stablisheth us with you,' &c. In the words you have, *first*, a gracious act of building, or stablishing.

Secondly, the basis, the foundation of that stablishing or building, and that is Christ.

Thirdly, the author of this stablishing—God.

Lastly, the persons who are built and stablished on that foundation 'with you.' 'He that stablisheth us with you in Christ is God.'

The first thing *is the act* 'stablishing.'

The point is this, first, that,

Obs. Stablishing, settling grace is necessary.

It is necessary that there be a stablishing, confirming grace. It is not sufficient that we be brought out of the kingdom of Satan; for when we are gotten out of his hands and strength, he pursues us with continual malice. Therefore there must be the same power to stablish us still in grace, that first brought us into the state of grace. For as providence is a continual creation, so stablishing grace is the continuance of the new creature; the same grace that sets us in the state of the new creation in Christ, the same stablisheth us. Stablishing grace is necessary. It is necessary many ways. Man of himself is an unstable creature. Take him at the best, but a creature. God found no stability in the angels. Take the best of creatures, even as creatures they are unstable. For God will have a creature as a creature to be a dependent thing upon the Creator, who is a being of himself, Jehovah. There is no stability in any creature. Man in his best estate was an unstable creature. Since, we are very unstable, ready to be carried away in our judgment to the wind of any false doctrine, ready to be blown over with every little temptation. Nay, now in the state of grace, in ourselves we are very unstable, ready to fly off presently; and therefore we have need to be established of God.

Reason 1. It is necessary in regard *of the indisposition of our nature to supernatural truths*. We are an unprepared subject for them in ourselves. The law indeed, we have some principles of it; but of the gospel there are in us no seeds at all of it; and that is the reason there are so many heresies against the gospel: there are none against the law. And therefore divine truths being contrary to our disposition, as there must be a supernatural beginner, so there must be a supernatural strengthener. He that is Alpha must be Omega. As there must be a mighty subduing of the heart to be a vessel to receive these truths, an almighty power to lay the soul on this foundation, because of the contrariety of the truth to the natural heart of

* Cf. Mark v. 25-34.—G.

man, so there is need of no less than of a divine and supernatural stablishing. Our natures are very inconstant, and unsettled, and wayward. Take us at the best, before the fall, you see how soon we fell, being left to ourselves, and having no stablishing grace. Much more now since the fall is there a necessity of divine stablishing. When we come to know the truth, we are subject to fall away. Like little children, that are ready to sink, if they be not upheld by their parents or nurse, God must uphold and prop us, and shore us up: we presently sink else. Moses was but in the mount a while, and we see how soon the Israelites fell to idolatry. Paul did but leave the Galatians a little, and they were removed presently from Christ to false teachers, Gal. iii. 1. The nature of man is wonderful unstable, very loose and unsettled. Divine truths are supernatural. We have need of stablishing therefore.

2. Again, stablishing grace is necessary, *in regard of those oppositions that are made against us after once we be in Christ.* For with what malice doth Satan pursue a Christian, when he is once taken out of his kingdom! And the world runs a clean contrary bias in the several examples thereof. How many scandals do there arise daily even in the very church itself! How many things are in our natural disposition joining with them! All which will make a man fly off, and unsettle him, if he be not stablished in grace.

And indeed what is the difference between one Christian and another that lives in the bosom of the church? between a temporiser and another? The difference is but in their radication, in their stablishing. For all have the general knowledge of the truth. But here is the difference,—the true Christian is radicated and rooted in the truth, a false Christian is not. And thereupon when temptations come, either from within, from conscience, or from without, from Satan and the world, he falls away, because he is not rooted; but the other holds on, because he is established.

3. And the best of us all have need of stablishing; for there *be degrees of truths, degrees of faith, in all the parts of faith.* There is conjecture, a certain suspicious knowledge; and there is opinion, which is with fear of the contrary; and there is knowledge; and there is faith, which is founded upon the authority of the speaker: and yet this faith, though it be founded upon the word of God, it may receive further and further strength in all the parts of it. In assent, there may be a higher degree; in affiance, there may be a higher degree, &c.; and therefore the best of us all have need of strengthening.

But where shall we have it?

Christ is the basis, the foundation, of all our stability. Now, in the covenant of grace, we are stablished in him, not in ourselves. The point is this, that

Obs. Christ is the ground of our firmness.

As all the promises are made to us in Christ in regard of the execution, so God he brings us Christ. All is conferred to us in Christ. As the promises are made, so they are executed. God stablisheth us in Christ. He draws us to Christ. 'None come to me, but God the Father draws,' John vi. 44. Therefore God doth reveal Christ to us in our conversion, and our stablishing is in him. Therefore our salvation is so certain, because it is laid upon one that is so certain in himself, Jesus Christ.

And happy it is, that we are stablished in him that loves us so well, that is both a low high priest, that will pity us; and a great high priest, equal with God, able to do all things to God for us, and between God and us. Adam, we know, had his strength in his own keeping, and being left to himself, we see what became of him. The angels had their strength in their own keeping, and we know how soon they fell. But since the fall, we are founded and bottomed upon a surer foundation. Now we stand not by our own strength, but we are established in Jesus Christ. We are surer than the angels were before they fell, surer than Adam was in paradise; for now we are stablished in Christ the Mediator, God and man. And because we could not keep our stability in ourselves, we are stablished in him that wrought it for us, and that possesseth it for us in heaven, and that keeps it for us; and as it is laid up and kept for us, so we are kept for it. 'You are kept by the power of God to salvation,' 1 Pet. i. 5. And, therefore, as there be many differences which advance the state of grace above the state of nature, so this is one, that our state in grace is more stable and firm, as being stablished upon a better ground, even upon Jesus Christ the second Adam. God never mends, but he mends for the better; and he never restores, but he restores for the better. The new heaven and the new earth shall be better than the first, so the new creature, the new Adam, is more glorious than the first; and as that which we recover in Christ is more and better than that we lost in Adam, so the certainty and security of our estate in grace, is far beyond the other, this being stablished in Christ.

But what in us is stablished in Christ? and in Christ how considered?

1. First of all, *our judgment*, that is stablished in evangelical truths, concerning the natures and the offices of Christ, concerning the privileges that we have by him; and this is the ground of all other stablishment. We cannot firmly cleave to that with our will and affections, which we do not clearly apprehend with our understandings. When we have a clear and judicious apprehension of things, then follows a firm affection to them. The adhering and cleaving of the will and affections, it comes from the discerning of the understanding; and, therefore, as we say of the first concoction, if that be naught, all is naught; and if that be good and sound, it makes way for all concoctions after; so if things be well digested in the judgment, if there be a sound illumination and apprehension of divine truths, it makes way for a constant and firm adhesion; therefore the first stablishing is of our judgments.

2. Secondly, as our judgments, *so our wills* are stablished in cleaving unto Christ, making choice of him above all things in the world; that as he became man to sue unto us for our love, and to become our husband, so we then marry him, when upon judging what an excellent person he is, and how fit for us, we choose him and cleave unto him constantly without all separation, for better, for worse, in our joy, in our love and delight. For, indeed, he is the only excellent object, and most fittest for our affections to be placed on. Whatsoever other things besides, we place our affections on too much, they make us worse than ourselves. Only he can advance us to a better state than we are in, that can raise us higher.

3. In a word, the whole soul, judgment, will, *and affections*, and all the inward man, for so the apostle takes it in that latitude, Eph. iii. 16, is stablished in Christ, and this carries the outward man with it. We are stablished in Jesus Christ, not in ourselves.

Now when we are stablished in Christ, whatsoever Christ hath, or is, is ours. It is a most excellent condition to be in Christ, and to be stablished in him; for to be established in Christ, is to be in a firm estate, in an everlasting estate. Once Christ's, and for ever his. It is a glorious state, for he hath conquered over all enemies whatsoever, and his conquest is ours.

Well then, we see the foundation of the church, and of every particular Christian, Christ Jesus. Whence comes the stability and firmness of the church, 'that the gates of hell shall not prevail against it'? It is built upon the rock, upon Christ. So all the stablishing that a Christian hath, it is from this rock, his being built upon Jesus Christ. If we were built upon man, we could not stand; if we were built upon angels, we could not stand; if we were built upon anything in the world, we could not stand; but being built upon Jesus Christ, who is 'all in all' to a soul that is stablished in him, there must needs be an everlasting stablishing.

It is a fond* objection of some, and unlearned, against the principles of divine truth, that we may fall, as well as Adam in paradise, as well as the angels in heaven; as if there were not a wide and broad difference between the state of grace and the state of nature. A Christian hath more strength than the angels in heaven, or than Adam in paradise ever had; he hath a more firm consistence, because he stands by grace. 'By grace we stand,' as the apostle saith, Heb. xiii. 9. A Christian hath promises of perseverance, Adam and the angels had none. And, therefore, to fetch a reason of falling away from grace, from the proportion we have to that condition, is a mere sophism, not rightly discerning the disparity. It is not alike with the angels, and Adam, and us, for we stand by grace, out of ourselves, being stablished in one another.†

We have not only a promise of happiness, as the angels and Adam had happiness and a blessed estate, but they had no promise to stand and be confirmed. A poor weak Christian hath a promise to be stablished and confirmed. Therefore those proud sectaries that are between us and the papists, and join rather with them than us, that trouble the church so much, they make an idle objection concerning falling away from grace, to say, Did not Adam fall away? What is that to the purpose? Was Adam under the same covenants as we are now in Christ? Is there not a new promise made to us in Christ, better than ever Adam could attain to?

Besides, we are founded upon a better Adam, upon the 'second Adam,' God-man. We have not only a better foundation, but better promises, that Adam and the angels themselves wanted. And, therefore, the covenant of grace is said to be 'an everlasting covenant.' 'I will marry thee to myself for ever,' Hosea ii. 19.

A Christian is not to be considered abstractively, or alone; for then, indeed he is a weak creature, as weak as other men are; but consider him in his rock on whom he is built; consider him in his husband to whom he is united and knit; consider him in his head, Christ; look upon him as he is thus founded and stablished, Oh he is an excellent person!

See him in the difference betwixt him and others. Those that are not stablished by a firm judgment, and will, and affection, and so by faith in Jesus Christ, what confidence, what stability have they? Those who have the firmness they have in the favour of men, it is but vanity; those that have the firmness they have in riches, what are they? how soon do they leave it all? those that have the firmness they have in dependence upon any creature, be it never so great, alas! they are nothing, they are all vanity. Both we ourselves in depending, and the things we depend upon, are vanity. Therefore we are vanity, because we fasten upon that which is vanity. Things have no more firmness than that hath upon which they lean. Those that have but a weak prop to support them, when that falls, they fall together with it. Now those that are not founded upon Christ by knowledge and love, and united to him by faith, alas! what standing have

* That is, 'foolish.'—G.

† Qu. 'in another?'—Ed.

they, when all things else besides God are vain! For nothing hath a being but God, and a Christian so far as he leans upon God. Were not all things taken out of nothing? and shall not they all turn to nothing? must not this whole world be consumed with fire?

There must be a new world, 'a new heaven and a new earth,' 2 Pet. iii. 13; but this and all the excellencies in it, as they were raised out of nothing, so they shall come to nothing. God, he is, 'I am that I am,' saith he, Exod. iii. 14; and Christ he is 'yesterday, to-day, to-morrow, and the same for ever,' Heb. xiii. 8. A man cannot say of any creature in the world, that it was yesterday, and shall be to-morrow and for ever. We may say it of Christ, 'he is Alpha and Omega, the first and the last, he was, and is, and is to come,' Rev. i. 8; and, therefore, those that are founded upon him, that have their happiness in him, they are firm as he is firm; and those that build upon any other thing, they vanish as the thing vanisheth. There is nothing in the world hath such a being, but it is subject in time not to be. It is only a Christian that is in Christ, who is as firm as Christ is; and Christ can never be but that which he is; for of necessity God must be always like himself. He is Jehovah, 'I am, I am' at all times; and Christ he is Jehovah. A Christian therefore, and none but a Christian, hath a firm stablishing in Christ. Without this stablishing in Christ, what are we? what are wicked men? Chaff, that the wind blows away! They are grass, &c., things of nothing, carried away with every blast. But a Christian is a stone, a rock, built upon Christ Jesus.

But to come to the person, who is it that stablisheth? 'He that stablisheth us in Christ, is God.'

Wherein we may consider these two branches:

God must stablish.

God will stablish.

Can none stablish the soul upon Christ but God?

No! For God is the only maker of the marriage between Christ and the church. The same God that brought Adam and Eve together in paradise, brings the church and Christ together. And as he gives Christ to the church, and hath sealed and appointed him to be 'wisdom, righteousness, sanctification, and redemption,' 1 Cor. i. 30 (being made of God unto us for that purpose, as the apostle saith), so he works the consent of the church, a consent in heart and spirit to take and embrace Christ. Now it is God only that can work the heart to Christ. 'None can come unto me, except God the Father draw him,' John vi. 44. It is God that gives Christ to be the husband of the church, and that brings the spouse, the church, to Christ.

1. For first, it is God by his Spirit that discovers *to the soul its hideous, desperate, and woful estate without Christ; and by the Spirit in the ministry of the word, lays open the riches and excellency that is in Christ, and the firmness and stability that is to be had in him;* and so draws us with the cords of a man, with reasons, discovering an absolute necessity of getting into Christ, and of having him to be our husband, except we will lie under the wrath of God and be damned; and, withal, discovering the fulness and excellency that is in Christ.

2. Again, it is God only that must *stablish the soul, all the parts of it, both judgment and conscience.* For, I beseech you, what can any human creature, what can anything under God, work upon the soul? I mean so firmly as to stablish it; and, therefore, our controversy with the papists is just and good.

We say the reason and ground of our believing the word of God to be the word of God must not be the testimony of the church and the authority thereof; for, alas! what can the judgment of man, what can the judgment of the church, do? It may incline and move the will by inducing arguments, and so cause a human consent; but to establish the soul and conscience, and to assure me that the word of God, which is the ground of my faith, is the word of God, it must be God by his Spirit that must do it; the testimony of the church will never do it. The same Spirit that inspired holy men to write the word of God, works in us a belief that the word of God is the word of God. The stablishing argument must be by the power of God's Spirit. God, joining with the soul and spirit of a man whom he intends to convert, besides that inbred light that is in the soul, causeth him to see a divine majesty shining forth in the Scriptures, so that there must be an infused establishing by the Spirit to settle the heart in this first principle, and indeed in all other divine principles, that the Scriptures are the word of God.

3. And, to go on a little further, this is a fundamental error in our practice; *for what is the reason we have so many apostates?* What is the reason so many are so fruitless in their lives? What is the reason that men despair in death, but even this, because men are not built and stablished aright? God's Spirit never stablished their souls in divine truths. For, first, concerning apostasy, ask them what is the reason they are of this or that religion, they will say they have been taught so, they have been brought up to it, the company with whom they have conversed have been devout men, and have been always led with this opinion, and they see no reason to thwart it.

Is that all? Hath not the Spirit wrought these things in thy heart? hath he not given thee a taste of them? hath he not convinced thee in thy judgment that it is so? hast thou not found the power of the Spirit working upon thy soul, changing of thee, raising of thee, drawing of thee out of the world nearer to God? hast thou not, I say, felt the power of the Spirit this way?

No; but thus I was catechised, and thus I have been bred, and thus I have heard in the ministry. And no otherwise? Alas! it will never hold out, there will be a falling away; for when a man believes not that which he believes from the Spirit of God, he will be ready, when dangerous times come, when there is an onset made by the adversaries, to fall, and to fall clean away, as we see it was in the time of popery; for whatsoever is not spiritual, whatsoever knowledge is not divine and from the Spirit of God, never holds out. Therefore, I beseech you, what is the reason that you have many illiterate men that set upon the truth and hold out to the end, and, on the contrary, many great seeming scholars, that are skilful in school-learning and in other authors, do not? The reason is, the one hath the truth from the Spirit, discovering all the objections that the heart of man can make against it, and the strength that is in the truth to answer and silence all those objections. The other man hath only a discoursing knowledge, an ability to gather one thing from another, and to prove one thing by another, by strength of parts. But the Spirit of God never discovered the sleights and the corruptions of his heart, never fastened and settled his heart upon the truth, he never had experience of the truth. For, indeed, nothing doth stablish so much as the experience of the truth on which we are stablished.

4. Again, what is the reason of that *unfruitfulness that is amongst men*, but because truths were never settled in the soul by the Spirit of God?

That which men know out of the word of God concerning Christ and the privileges by him, they were never persuaded of it in their hearts; therefore, they come not to a fruitful conversation. It is impossible but that men should be abundantly fruitful that have spiritual apprehensions of divine things, of evangelical truths. Hence comes all our unthankfulness and undervaluing of the gospel. The gospel of itself is an unprized thing. However we esteem of it, God values it highly. We value it not, because our apprehensions of it are customary and formal, gotten by breeding, and education, and discourse, and not by the Spirit; we feel not the spiritual and heavenly comforts of those truths we think we know.

5. How comes likewise *despair in time of temptation, and in death*, but only because men want this stablishing by the Spirit of God? Men go on in evil courses, trusting to a formal, dead, human knowledge, gotten by human means, and not settled in them by the Spirit of God, that hath not sealed the truth in their hearts; and hereupon, when sharp trials come, they despair, because they have no feeling of the truths of the gospel; and so when conscience is awakened and smarts, it clamours and cries out upon all their formal and human knowledge. For they having not a spiritual sense of the mercies of God in Christ, and the persuasions of comfort are not so near to support the soul, as the temptations, and vexations, and torments are, how can they but despair? Now who can still the conscience, but the Spirit of God? Why now, if the knowledge that men had were spiritual and heavenly, in all accusations of conscience, it would set conscience down and still it. I am a sinner indeed, I am this and this, but I have felt the sweet mercies of God in Christ; God hath said to my soul, 'I am thy salvation,' Ps. xxxv. 3; he hath intimated to my spirit, by a sweet voice, 'Son, thy sins are forgiven thee,' Mark ii. 5. Where there is, I say, a knowledge and an apprehension of these evangelical truths wrought by the Spirit, it sets down conscience and stills it, though the heart rage at the same time. There are thousands in the very bosom of the church that miscarry because of this, resting in a literal, outward, formal knowledge, gotten only by discourse, and by reading, and commerce with others, and never labour to have their hearts stablished in Christ by God's Spirit.

You see here, then, a necessity of God's writing his truth in our bowels. He saith in the covenant of grace, 'I will write my law in their inward parts,' Jer. xxxi. 33, that is, I will teach their very hearts: that knowledge that they have shall be spiritual.

For, beloved, the knowledge that must save us must not only be of divine things, but it must be divine; it must not only be of spiritual things, but it must be spiritual. The light that we have of spiritual things must be answerable to the things; we must see them by their own light. We cannot know spiritual and heavenly things by a human light; but as the things themselves are spiritual, so we must have the Spirit of God, that by it we may come to know spiritual things spiritually.

Desire God therefore to vouchsafe us his Spirit, that it may teach us, and convince us of the truth of those things which we read and hear. God must do it, he must persuade and bow the heart, and will, and affections; and so he will do it, and doth it to those that rely upon him. And this is the second branch.

Obs. As God must do it, so God will do it.

What is the reason of that?

1. It is this: he will do it, *because he is constant.* Where he 'begins a

good work, he will finish it to the day of the Lord,' Philip. i. 6. He will do it, because in the covenant of grace he hath undertaken both parts, both his own and ours. He undertakes his own part, which is to give us eternal life, and to give us Christ; and he undertakes our part too, which is to believe, and to cleave unto Christ, &c. He makes this good himself. He works this in the heart by the Spirit; for therefore it is called the covenant of grace, because God himself is graciously pleased to do both parts, which must be comfortably remembered against an objection that flesh and blood will make. I might indeed come to God and Christ, but I am an unworthy, empty creature, I have no faith.

Come and attend upon the means; the gift of application, and confirming, and stablishing, is part of the covenant. The covenant that God makes with thee, is not only to give thee life everlasting and glory, but to give thee grace likewise. 'Faith is the gift of God.' He that stablisheth us, and confirms us upon that which is certain in itself, is God.

Lay it up against a time of temptation for a pillar and ground of your faith, that here God doth both. He gives us promises, and gives us Christ whereon the promises are founded; and likewise establisheth us, and seals us, &c. He doth all. So that as none can stablish the soul, but God by his Spirit, so he will do it. It is an excellent reason of the apostle in Rom. v. 10, 'If when we were enemies, God gave us his Son to reconcile us, how much more now shall we be saved!' If we were saved by the death of Christ when we were enemies, much more shall we be preserved by his life, he now living in heaven! So I say, if God, when there was nothing in us, but we were in a clean opposite estate, did begin spiritual life in us, much more will he stablish that which he hath begun in us.

And this stablishing, as well as the beginning of grace, comes likewise from God; for take grace in the whole latitude and extent of it, take all that can be in grace, all comes graciously from God: the offer of it, the beginning of it. This manner of it, that it should be strong, the strengthening of grace, it comes from God. He strengtheneth us in grace, as well as begins it. So that grace itself, and this *modus*, this manner, that it is strong and firm, that it should hold out, all comes from God.

A Christian needs not only converting grace, but stablishing grace. God that converted him must stablish him, and build him up, and confirm him. Peter was in the state of grace, and yet when God did not stablish him, you see how he fell. So David was an excellent man, but when God did not stablish him, you see how he fell. The weakest, with the stablishing grace of God, will stand: and the strongest, without the stablishing grace of God, will sink and fall.

The apostle doth not say, he hath done, but he doth 'stablish' us. This must be considered, that the life of a Christian is a perpetual dependent life: not only in his conversion he lives by faith, he hath his first life; but ever after he lives by faith, that is, dependence on God for assistance, and protection, and strength in the whole course of his life.

The ignorance of this makes us subject to fail; for when we trust to grace received, and do not seek for a new supply, we fall into Peter's case, 'Though all men forsake thee, yet will not I,' Mat. xxvi. 35. Hereupon Peter fell foully. He had too much confidence in grace received.

Therefore God is fain to humble his children, to teach them dependence; and usually therefore in Scripture, where some special grace is given, he hath somewhat joined with it, to put them in mind that they do not stand by their own strength. In the same chapter where Peter makes a glorious confession, 'Thou art the Son of the living God,' Mat. xvi. 16, and he was honoured of Christ by that confession; yet Christ calls him Satan in the same chapter, ver. 23, and he forsakes his Master. A strange thing! to teach us, that we stand not of ourselves. When we are strong, it is by God; when we are weak, it is by ourselves.

Jacob wrestled, and was a prevailer with God, but he was fain to halt for it. He was struck with halting all the days of his life: though he had the victory, and overcame God, taking upon him, as I said before, the person of an enemy to strive with him. Yet God, to put him in mind that he had the strength whereby he prevailed from him, and not of himself, he made him limp all his days. We need perpetual dependence upon God.

Therefore let us set upon nothing in our own strength, as Hannah saith comfortably, 1 Sam. ii. 9, 'No man is strong by his own strength.' God is all our sufficiency. Man's nature doth affect a kind of divinity; he would be a god to himself: but God will teach him that he is not a God, but a dependent creature. He affects a divinity. Thus he will set upon things in confidence of his own wisdom, without prayer, and thinks to work things with the strength of his own parts, to compass things with his own wit, to bring things to a good issue. O no! it will not be so. In Prov. iii. 6, 'Acknowledge God in all thy ways,' that is, acknowledge him in thy enterprises in anything; acknowledge him in the progress, that thou needest stablishing grace; acknowledge him in the issue, that thou needest his blessing upon all thy endeavours; acknowledge God in all our ways.

Therefore, what do we but make ourselves gods, when we set upon business, especially weighty, without invocation and dependence? A Christian is wondrous weak, a man is vanity in himself; but take him as he is built upon the promises, and as he is in the love of God and Christ, he is a kind of almighty man; then 'I can do all things in Christ that strengtheneth me,' Philip. iv. 13. A Christian is omnipotent if he depend upon the promise, and commit his ways to God; but he is impotent and weak in himself. It is God that must stablish us. A man that is vanity, he makes him firm; a man that is weak, he makes him strong; a man that is unsettled, he settles him. The word is a firm thing, and God that builds us on the word is as firm; and Christ in whom we are built is as firm. Peter when he built on the word he was wondrous firm, he was a rock too. A man that stands on a rock is firm. Now in believing the gospel, and in being built on the gospel, upon the prophets and apostles, upon apostolical truth, now we that are weak in ourselves are firm.

The weakest creatures have the strongest shelters; and weakness is turned by God to be a help; for conscience of weakness makes us seek for strength out of ourselves. You know the conies, as Solomon saith, 'they hide themselves in the rock,' Prov. xxx. 26, they flee to their burrows. The birds, because snares are laid for them below, they build their nests on high, to secure themselves that way. We see the vine, a weak plant, it hath the elm to prop it. Weak things must have a strong support. So man, being weak in himself, weak in judgment, weak in affections, he is stablished by God, God herein triumphing in our weakness over strength. For when we have strong adversaries, and we are weak, Satan is a strong enemy. God himself puts upon him the vizor of an enemy sometimes, as in Job's case, and Christ's on the cross; when God personates an enemy, and the devil is a real enemy; and the devil's instruments, heretics and seducers, are strong, strong in wit and parts every way, and we are weak to encounter with God, to wrestle with him; and we are weak to encounter with 'principalities and powers,' Eph. vi. 12, and with men of stronger parts, that are besotted and intoxicated with Satanical temptations, and labour to draw all into the snare of the devil with themselves. Now when God in weakness shall triumph over strength, here is glory to God, in stablishing us. It is God that must stablish us.

And as God must only do it, so he is ready to do it; for in the covenant of grace it lies upon him. God hath promised there to confirm it; and therefore the apostle, 1 Thess. v. 24, binds it with the faithfulness of God, 'Faithful is he that hath promised, who also will do it.' God is content that our confirmation should lie upon his faithfulness; and therefore when he accepts us into the covenant of grace, he performs our part as well as his own. 'God is faithful,' saith the apostle, 1 Cor. i. 9, 'who hath called us to the fellowship of Christ,' who will confirm us to the end. He is content to hazard his reputation, as it were, and to be counted unfaithful else; so that strengthening grace is of God. He hath bound himself by his faithfulness to confirm and to stablish those that are his.

Mark here by the way, before I come to handle the doctrine of perseverance, what an invincible argument you have to prove that a man that is once in Christ can never fall away.

Say they, indeed, God for his part is ready to maintain us, to do this; but we for our part are subject to fall away: as if the carrying of us along in the course of grace to salvation did not lie upon God and Christ. God is faithful to confirm us to the end. We being once in the covenant of grace, he doth our part and his own too: how can those then that are in the state of grace ever finally fall away?

Now God doth confirm us, by working such graces in us by his Spirit, by which we are stablished. As for instance, 'I will put my fear into their hearts, that they shall never depart from me,' Jer. xxxii. 40; he stablisheth us by fear. 'Make an end of your salvation with fear and trembling, for it is God that works in you both the will and the deed,' Philip ii. 12. He puts a spirit of jealousy into a man over his corruptions; and a reverential filial fear, which keepeth him from presuming.

And likewise he preserveth us by wisdom, as it is, Prov. ii. 10, 11. 'When wisdom entereth into thy heart, discretion shall preserve thee, and understanding shall keep thee.'

And by faith, 'you are kept,' saith the apostle, 'by the mighty power of God through faith to salvation.'

And by peace of conscience, which is wrought in the heart by the Spirit. 'The peace of God which passeth all understanding shall guard (for so the word signifieth) your hearts and minds,'* that is, a true believer that is once in Christ, he finds such joy in the Holy Ghost, such inward peace of conscience, as preserves and guards him from despair, from the temptations of Satan, from the seeming wrath of God. So that God as he stablisheth us, so he stablisheth us as it becometh Christians, as it becomes men, by sanctifying our understandings, by working grace in our hearts, the grace of fear, of wisdom, of faith, of peace, &c. So that a Christian now cannot presume, save in a holy kind of presumption, that God will finish his own good work. But of this, I say, I shall have fitter occasion to speak hereafter.

To conclude therefore—God you see must stablish, and God will stablish. It is a point of great comfort every way; comfort from the foundation and root in whom we are stablished; and from him that hath taken

* Cf. note *k*, vol. I. p. 334.—G.

upon him to stablish us, God by his Holy Spirit. If a Christian should fall, God must be unstable; or Christ the foundation must be unstable; or the Holy Spirit by which we are stablished must be unstable; but it were blasphemy to think thus.

I come now to the last thing, the subject, or the persons that are stablished, 'us with you.'

'He that stablisheth *us with you.*' We should have honourable conceits of all Christians. There is an ointment runs down upon the very skirts of Aaron's garment, Ps. cxxxiii. 2. There is not the lowest Christian, but he receiveth something from Christ the head. Perhaps thou hast one grace in an eminent manner. It may be he hath another more eminent than thou hast. Thou mayest have more knowledge, he may have more humility; thou mayest have more strength of judgment, he may have more sense of his own wants. There is somewhat in every Christian that is valuable, that is estimable and precious, not only in the eye of God, who valued him so as to give his Son for him, but should be so also in the eye of stronger Christians. Therefore St Paul here, a strong Christian, out of the sweetness of his spirit, joins 'us with you.' He saith not, you with us, but as if they were as firmly set in Christ as himself, he saith, 'us with you;' he puts them together with himself; for indeed, all of us, one with another, weak Christians and strong Christians, fetch all that we have from one fountain, draw all from one spring, are led all by one Spirit.

You have here also the character of a sound Christian; he loves and values all Christians. A carnal man may value excellent Christians, that have excellent parts, of whom he hopes for kindness in some peculiar regard, but he loves not all the saints. Love to all Christians as they be Christians, because they have some anointing of the Spirit, some earnest, somewhat they have to be valued, is a note of a good and sound Christian.

Another reason why he joins 'us with you,' is, to shew that the working of the Spirit it is not in the members severed from the body, but as they are in the body. The Spirit works in us, but in us with you, and in you with us; that is, as all the spirits come from the head and heart to the several members of the body, so they must be united, they must be in the body, before they can have the benefit of the spirits. There must be an union with Christ the head and with the rest of the members before we can have the Spirit to strengthen us and anoint us. Those that rend themselves from the body, cannot hope for stablishing from the head.

This should be a bond to tie us to the communion of saints. We have all that we have in the body; we all grow in the body; we are all stones in one building, whereof Christ is the foundation; therefore as stones in an arch strengthen one another, so should we. Let us look for grace to be given in the communion of saints. It is an ill sign when any man will be a solitary Christian, and will stand alone by himself. As we are knit to Christ by faith, so we must be knit to the communion of saints by love. That which we have of the Spirit is had in the communion of saints. It is worth observing, the better to cherish Christian lovingness.

Thus you see the parts of this sentence in which we have the grace itself here spoken of, 'stablishing.'

In whom we are stablished—'In Christ.' *By whom?*—'By God.' And *who those are that are stablished*—'Us with you.'

To make now some application of all.

Use. If it be God that stablisheth us, let us make this use of it, *let God have the glory of our stablishing.* If we have it in dependence upon God by prayer, let us return all by praise and thanksgiving. All comes of his mere grace, let all return to his mere glory. 'Not unto us, but unto thy name give the praise,' Ps. cxv. 1. It is the song of the church on earth, and the song of the church triumphant in heaven, that all glory be to God in all the whole carriage of salvation. The promises are his, stablishing is his, that he would make a covenant, it is his; that he will perform his covenant to us, it is his; that he will enable us to perform the covenant, it is by his strength; all is his. Therefore both the church here, and the church in heaven, our song should be, Great, and gracious, and merciful is the true God, that is so gracious and righteous in all his promises.

Let us labour, I beseech you, for stablishing, especially in these times. Is it not a shame that we have gotten no more ground now than we had threescore years ago? Nay, that we rather call principles into question? The pope hath been antichrist; and traditions hath been accounted traditions, and not equal with the word. What shall we now stagger in the foundation? Is here our progress? Oh, beloved, labour to be stablished in the present truth, that you may not be a prey for every subtle man.

And here especially I would speak to the younger sort, that they should labour for this stablishing betimes, before they be engaged in the world, and before other businesses possess them over-deeply; for falsehood hath more correspondency, and suits better with our corruption, specially if it be forced from subtle wits. It prevails much with unstable dispositions. Those that are uncatechised and ungrounded, they are soon led away; and, therefore, with other studies we should study the truth, and remember that our best calling is to be a Christian, and our best honour to be able to stand for the truth we profess.

Labour to have fundamental graces established, and then all will be stablished. If the root be strengthened, the tree stands fast; radical graces must be strengthened.

First, *Humility*. The foundation of religion is very low, and humility and abasing is in all parts of religion. Every grace hath a mixture of humility, because our graces are from God; they are dependencies. Now humility is an emptying grace, and acknowledgeth, that in myself I am nothing. Spiritual poverty with humility acknowledgeth that I in myself am a dependent creature. If God withhold his influence, if God withdraw his grace, I shall be as other men, as Samson when his hair was cut. Our strength is in God altogether. Let us pray that we may be humble; 'God gives grace to the humble,' James iv. 6. 'When I am weak,' saith blessed St Paul, 'then I am strong;' that is, when I am humble, and feel, and acknowledge my weakness, 'then I am strong,' 2 Cor. xii. 10; or else a man is not strong when he is weak, but when he feels and acknowledgeth his weakness. Therefore let us labour to grow in humility and self-denial, and we shall grow in strength.

2. Then again, another radical grace to be stablished is *Faith*. Depend upon God altogether; for considering our strength is out of ourselves, and faith being a grace that goes out of ourselves, and lays hold of that that is out of ourselves, faith is necessary to our stablishing, 'Believe, and ye shall be stablished,' saith the prophet, 1 Pet. v. 10.* Though the promise be sure in itself, yet we must be established by faith. How doth God stablish us? By working a spirit of faith; therefore strengthen faith, strengthen all other graces. All have their issue from faith.

3. And faith comes from *sound knowledge*; knowledge therefore hath the

* Qu. 'Isa. vii. 9?'—Ed.

name of faith. 'This is eternal life, *to know thee*,' 1 John v. 20; strengthen and increase knowledge. Historical faith is nothing but knowledge; when we know the word of God to be as it is; and that is the ground of justifying faith and dependence. For the more I know God in covenant as he hath revealed himself, and the more I know the promise, and the more I know Christ, the more I shall depend upon him, and trust in him. 'They that know thy name will trust in thee,' Ps. ix. 10.

Therefore let us labour for certainty of knowledge, that we may have certainty of faith. What is the reason that our faith is weak? Because men care not to increase their knowledge. The more we know of God, the more we shall trust him. The more we know of a man that we have bonds from, that he is an able man, and just of his word, we shall trust him more, and the more our security upon his promise and bond is increased. So the more we know of God as he hath revealed himself in his word, and his voluntary covenant he hath made with us, and performed in the examples of Scripture, the more we know him, the more we shall trust him.

And this must be a spiritual knowledge; not only a bare, naked reading, but it must be spiritual, like the truth itself. We must see and know spiritual things in their own light. To know them by their own light is to know them by the Spirit. You know the Spirit dictated the Scripture to the prophets and apostles, the Spirit did all: they wrote as they were acted by the Spirit. Now the same Spirit must inform our understanding, and take away the veil of ignorance and infidelity, I say, the Spirit must do it: we must know spiritual things in their own light.

Therefore a carnal man can never be a good divine, though he have never so much knowledge. An illiterate man of another calling may be a better divine than a great scholar. Why? Because the one hath only notional knowledge, discoursive knowledge, to gather by strength of parts one thing from another. Divinity is a kind of art, and as far as it is an art to prove one thing by another; so a natural man may do wonders in it, and yet know nothing in its own spiritual light. That is the reason the devil himself knows nothing. He is a spirit of darkness, because he knows nothing spiritually and comfortably; therefore as there must be humility and faith for our stablishing, so there must be spiritual knowledge.

It is said here, that God stablisheth us. The same God that stablisheth us, must give us faith whereby we are stablished, and he must give us knowledge. Beg of God that he would vouchsafe us his Spirit. When we read the Scriptures, beg of God that he would open our understanding by his own Spirit, that as there is light in the Scriptures, so there may be in us.

You know an eye must have light before it can see the light. Light is full of discovery of things in itself. I can see nothing except there be light in my eye too. There must be a double light. So there must be a Spirit in me, as there is a Spirit in the Scripture before I can see anything. God must open our eyes, and give us spiritual eye-salve, to see, and then the light of the Scripture, and our light together, is sufficient to found a saving faith, as stablishing faith, on.

What is the reason that a Christian stands to his profession, though he be weak, when the greatest learned men in the world flinch in persecution? The knowledge of the one is spiritual and heavenly: he hath light in him; the other hath no divine, spiritual light. When light is joined with light, the light in the soul with the light in the Scripture, it makes men wondrous confident.

1. To this end, labour *to be acquainted with God's word.* Study the Scrip-

tures and other treatises of that kind, that you may be able to hold fast the truth, that it be not wrung from you upon any occasion. And in reading, it is a good course to observe the main, principal, undeniable truths, such dogmatical truths as are clear and evident, and to lay them up; and oft make queries to ourselves, Do I understand this or no? Yes, I do, this I know is true. Build on it then, and bottom the soul upon it. And so if it be matter of promises; these promises are undeniable true, I will stay my soul upon them. And so when we meet with plain evidences in the Scriptures that cross our corruptions, that meet with our known sins, then consider of those places as jewels, and lay them up that you may have use of them as occasion serves.

All things have not an equal certainty in Scripture to us; some things we may have an implicit faith in; but the main we must have a clear apprehension of. There are some things that concern teachers more to know than others, by reason of their standing in the church. It is sufficient that in preparation of mind we be ready to embrace further truths that shall be discovered; but in fundamental truths it is not so. We must have our hearts stablished upon them, that as they are certain in themselves, so they may be certain to us. And often let us examine ourselves, would I die in this, and for this? would I stand in the defence of this against any? This will make us make much of so much truth as we know, and labour to grow in truths in that kind.

2. And *take no scandal* to hear that any shrink from the profession of the truth, and the maintaining of it, that are of great reputation.* Was Christ the worse for Judas betraying of him, and for Peter's denying of him? was Paul's truth the worse because he had many enemies, Elymas the sorcerer and others? Is the truth the worse because there are many that have carnal outward dependence, that seem to shrink when they should stand out? The truth is not the worse. It is the same truth still. Truths are eternal in themselves, and in the good they bring, if they be believed. The word of God endures for ever. It is not variable, as man is. And therefore be not discouraged, though men discountenance it; remember whose truth it is, and for whose good it is given. The word of God, it is a soul-saving truth.

3. And *retain the truth in love.* Love is an affection with which we should receive the truth; or else God will give us over to uncertainties. They in 2 Thess. ii. 10, had the truth, 'but because they received not the love of the truth,' therefore God sent them 'strong delusions,' that they should believe a lie. Oh, how lovely is the truth! The certainty of our estate in Christ; the glorious privileges that come by him; that the gifts of God are without repentance; that God looks on us, not for foreseen faith or works, but such as he had decreed to work himself,—how comfortable! how lovely are these truths, being the word of God, notwithstanding some seek to shake them! These very truths should be retained in love. And indeed, the truth is not in its own place, till it be fixed in the heart and affections, and in a good conscience, which St Paul makes likewise the vessel of the truth; and those that care not for that, they make shipwreck of the truth.

4. And what truths you know, *labour to practise,* and then you shall be stablished. 'If any man do the will of my Father,' saith our Saviour, John vii. 17, 'he shall know of the doctrine, whether it be of God, or whether I speak of myself.' Be true to known truths; be not false in disobeying

* That is, 'offence,' = let it not be a stumbling-block.—G.

them. 'To him that hath shall be given,' Matt. xiii. 12. We have a little stablishing; by an uniform obedience to the truth we shall have more; God will increase it. I say, let us be faithful to the truths we have, and not cross them in any sinful course; let us not keep the truth prisoner to any base affection; as those in Rom. i. 21, *seq.*, that had but the light of nature, yet because they imprisoned it, and held it in unrighteousness, and lived in sins contrary to that light that God had kindled in them, though I say it were but the light of nature, God gave them up to sins not to be named; much more will he do to us if we withhold the light of the gospel. Take heed therefore that we enthral not the truth to any base lust whatsoever, and that is a means to be stablished in the truth.

5. And *be oft in holy conference with others.* Conference, if it be rightly used, is a special means to stablish. That is most certain, which is certain after doubting and debate; because that which is doubted of at the first, we come to be resolved of at the last, comparing reason with reason, remembering always that of St Ambrose, that there must not be striving for victory, but for truth (*yyy*). And then when we have tried all, we must keep that which is good, and not be always as the iron between two loadstones, haled this way and that way, always doubting and never resolved; there must be a time of resolution. This the apostle observes to be an excellent way of stablishing, oft to confer of things doubtful.

6. And labour *to get experience of the truth in ourselves;* nothing stablisheth more than experience. Our Saviour Christ, in John vi. 68, when many left him out of dulness, not understanding the spiritual things that he taught (as many whose wits will serve for matters of the world, and to make them great amongst men, but when they come to heavenly things they have no understanding, they cannot apprehend them) he asks his disciples, 'Will you go away also?' John vi. 67. Peter, who had his heart opened by the Spirit of God, saith he, 'Lord, whither shall we go? thou hast the words of eternal life;' insinuating, that the experience that he had of the power of that truth that Christ taught, did so establish him in the present truth, that with a holy kind of indignation at the question, he replies, 'Whither shall we go? thou hast the words of eternal life.' I have found thy words to have a spiritual life in them. So when we come once to have an experimental knowledge of the truths we learn, then our hearts are stablished. Indeed, then it is an 'ingraffed word,' as St James saith, i. 21, then the word is true leaven, when it altereth and changeth the soul. In such a case there is no separating from fundamental truth, when it is one with ourselves, and digested into us.

7. And *pray to God oft,* as David did, Ps. lxxxvi. 2, *seq.*, *to knit our hearts to fear his name.* Lord, my heart is loose and ready to fall off of itself, Oh, knit my heart! It is unsettled, Oh, settle my unsettled heart! settle my judgment and affections. This should be our meditation.

8. And because it is God that stablisheth, *alway maintain spiritual poverty in the soul,* that is, a perpetual dependence upon God. See the insufficiency that is in ourselves, that we cannot stand out. What is the reason that God suffers great men to fall from the defence of the truth, and from the profession of it in their lives, as we see it in the case of Peter? To shew, that we stand not by our own strength. Therefore we should be always in this temper of spiritual poverty, to know that as Samson's strength was in his hair, so our strength is in God. God is my strength, of myself I have no strength. And therefore upon every new defence of the truth, when we are called to it, we should lift up ejaculations, and dart up strong desires to

God, that God would strengthen and stablish our souls, that we may not be traitors to the truth, but that we may stand to it; for in his own strength shall no man be established.

9. And *grow every day more and more in detestation of a lukewarm temper.* Your *Ancipites*, as Cyprian calls them (*zzz*), your doubtful flatterers of the times, that have their religion depending upon the state and the times, that are neither fish nor flesh, bats, as we say, that are neither mice nor birds, but of a doubtful religion, that out of carnal policy are fit to entertain anything; Oh, this is a devilish temper! Howsoever we, in our lukewarm disposition, value the truth, God values it highly. It was purchased by Christ's blood, and sealed by the blood of martyrs, and shall not we transmit it to our posterity, as safe and as firm, and retain it, come what will? Let us grow into dislike of this temper, a temper that we should as much hate as God hates it; such a temper as is in popery, they are in an *adiaphorisme** temper in religion, a lukewarm, cold temper, a temper of religion according to reasons of flesh and reasons of policy; this will make us be spued out of God's mouth at the last. Do we think to lose religion alone? Oh no; never think to part with religion alone. It came with peace and prosperity, and if we keep not this *depositum*, this truth delivered to us, God will take it away, and that which we betray it for, peace and plenty.

Use 1. Let us labour, therefore, *to be radicated in our judgment, in our affections, in our love, in our faith, in our whole inward man, in the truth revealed.* To be stablished in the truth, it is our best inheritance, it is that will stand by us when all leaves us.

What consistence hath a man out of the truth? Are you rich or honourable? Death will drive you out of all your riches and honours in the world, and strip you of all. What stablishing hath any man but in Christ, in the truth? Take a man that is not bottomed, that is not fastened on Christ, he is the changeablest creature in the world, he is vanity, he is nothing.

Oh! love this state, that we may say, though I be variable here, though I be not so rich as I was, or have not that favour of great ones that I have had; or it is not with me as it hath been, but in all changes I have somewhat that is unchangeable; my soul is settled upon Christ, and upon the truth in him, which is certain. As it is a glorious being to be found in Christ, so it is an eternal and an everlasting being: once Christ's, and for ever his; he will never lose a member. Labour we therefore to be stablished in Christ in all the changes and alterations in the world, and then we shall have something that is unchangeable to fix and stay ourselves upon, even in the hour of death.

Use 2. Again, in the second place, to make an use of examination, I beseech you, *examine yourselves whether you find this stablishing in your hearts or no?* whether your hearts be thus settled or no by the Spirit of God? For, beloved, it is worth the labour and pains to get this grace, and to be assured that you have it. Stablishing in Christ is most necessary, and we stand in need of a great deal of spiritual strength. Do we know what times may come? If dangerous times come, if we be not stablished, what will become of us? Oh! it is a happy estate, a Christian that is stablished in the sound knowledge and faith of Christ! I beseech you therefore consider of it. To give you an evidence or two whereby you may discern whether your hearts be settled and stablished.

1. A man hath the grace of stablishing, and confirmation, *when it is upon the word*, when God doth stablish him upon the promises.

* That is, = 'adiaphorous,' from ἀδιαφορος, indifferent.—G.

2. And then, again, *by the effect of it.* A man is stablished by the Spirit of God when his temptations are great, and his strength little to resist, and yet notwithstanding he prevails. Satan is strong. If we prevail against Satan's temptations, we are stablished. God is strong, too strong for us. If we can break through the clouds when he seems an enemy, as Job, 'Though thou kill me, yet will I trust in thee,' Job xiii. 15: here is a prevailing, a stablished faith. In great afflictions, when clouds are between us and God, when we have faith that will break through those clouds, and see God through them shining in Christ, here is a strong, a stablished faith; because here is mighty temptations and oppositions.

The strength is known by the strength of the opposition, and the weakness of the party. In the times of martyrdom, there was fire and faggot, and the frowns of cruel persons; who were the persons that suffered? Children, women, old men sometimes, all weak. Children, a weak age; women, a weak sex; old men, a withered, melancholy, dry age, fearful of constitution. But when the Spirit of God was so strong in young ones, in weak women, in old withered men, as to enable them to endure the torment of fire, to enable them to endure threatenings, and whatsoever, as we see, Heb. xi. 35–37, here was a mighty work in weak men. A man may know here is stablishing grace, because, except there were somewhat above nature, where were a man in such a case? Then a man may know especially that there is stablishing grace, when he sees somewhat above nature prevailing over the temptation, and confirming the weak nature of man. That is the best evidence we have of God's stablishing grace. Sometimes, them that are stronger at some times are weaker at other times; but, as I said before, that is to teach them that they have their strength from God.

Use 3. Again, if your hearts be soundly bottomed and founded and grounded on Christ, and the promises of God in him, then *you will be freed at least from all victory and thraldom to base fears, and to base cares, and base sorrows, and base passions.*

A man that hath no settled being on Christ, he is tossed up and down with every passion: he is full of fears and cares for the world, which distract the soul upon every occasion, full of unseasonable and needless sorrows and griefs, which vex and perplex the soul continually. Oh! how he fears for the time to come! what shall become of me if such a thing happen? how shall I be able to live in such a time, &c.? If he were settled upon God in Christ, that he were his Father: if he were stablished upon the promises of God in Christ, 'I will not fail thee nor forsake thee,' Heb. xiii. 5. 'Fear not, little flock, it is the Father's will to give you the kingdom,' Luke xii. 32; and 'Why do you fear, O you of little faith?' Matt. vi. 30. And, 'He that provides for the birds of the air, for the sparrows, for the lilies of the field, for the poorest creature, will he not much more for you?' Matt. vi. 25, *seq.* If, I say, we were thus stablished upon Christ, and the promises, there would be no disquietness. Those [are the] fears and griefs that usually perplex and enthral the minds of men; but where there are these distracting cares, and vexing sorrows, and needless fears, it argues a heart unsettled, though perhaps there may be some faith notwithstanding.

Let us often examine ourselves in this particular: how it is with us when such thoughts arise? what if trouble should come? what if change and alteration should come? He that hath truly settled his heart will say, If they do come, I am fixed, I know whom I have believed; I know I am a member of Christ, an heir of heaven, that God is reconciled to me in his Son; I know God hath taken me out of the condition I was in by nature, and hath advanced me to a better condition than I can have in the world; and when the world shall be turned upside down, I know, when all things fail, I shall stand.

He that his heart can answer him thus, is firm. A good man, saith the psalmist, 'shall not be afraid of evil tidings,' Ps. cxii. 7. Why? His heart is fixed, trusting in the Lord; and again, in ver. 8, 'His heart is stablished, therefore he shall not be afraid.' If our hearts be established, then we shall not be afraid of evil tidings, nor afraid of wars, nor of troubles, nor of loss of friends, nor of loss of favours, or the like. A righteous man is afraid of no evil. He that hath his heart stablished in Christ, and that hath peace of conscience wrought by the Spirit of God in the promises, his heart is fixed. In all alterations and changes, he hath somewhat that is unchangeable. Even when he ceaseth to be in this world, he hath a perpetual, eternal being in Christ. If he die, he goes to heaven. He hath his being there, where he enjoys a more near communion with Christ than he can have in this world. So that all is on the bettering hand to him that is stablished in Christ; for it is not an act of one day to be stablished in Christ. God doth it more and more till death, and then comes a perfect consummation of this stablishing. 'We shall be for ever with the Lord,' saith the apostle, 1 Thess. iv. 17. A man then that is stablished in Christ, he is fixed, he is built on a rock; come what can come, he is not afraid.

Alas! others that are not so, they are as wicked Ahaz, in Isa. vii. 2: he was boisterous out of trouble, but in trouble he was as fearful. His heart shook 'as the leaves of the forest,' as the leaves of the forest when the wind comes. They are shaken, because they are not seemly knit to the tree, because they have no stability.

All those whose hearts are not firmly settled in the knowledge of Christ, and the excellent prerogatives that come by him, when trouble come, they are as the leaves of the forest; or, as you have it in Ps. i. 4, 'As the chaff that the wind driveth to and fro;' because it hath no consistence, it is a light body, or as 'the dross,' Ps. cxix. 119. 'God shall destroy the wicked as dross.' See how the Scripture compares men, not only for their wickedness, but for their misery, that have no certain being, but on earthly things, though they be never so great, and, as they think, deeply rooted, when troubles come, they are as dross, they are as chaff that hath no firmness before the wind; when the wind of judgment comes, they are as stubble presently wasted and brought to nothing.

I beseech you therefore, without deceiving of our own hearts, let us enter into our own souls, and examine, for our knowledge first, and then for our boldness.

What dost thou know in religion that thou wouldst die for, or die in? We are stablished in no more to purpose, than we would die for. Are those truths thou knowest so firmly wrought in thee by the Spirit of God? Hast thou such experience of them, such spiritual sense and taste of the goodness of them, that thou wouldst be content to part with thy life, rather than to part with them? Thou art stablished then by the Spirit of God in Christ. I do not speak of every little truth. It needs not that a man should die for that; but I speak of fundamental truths. Canst thou prove them so out of the Scripture? and dost thou find the testimony of Jesus Christ witnessing to thy heart that they are true? Then thou art confirmed and stablished in these truths. I beseech you, let us often examine upon what grounds, and how firmly we know what we know. For, have we not many that, if the adversaries should come, would conform to popery, and join themselves to Rome, because they cannot back their principles with Scriptures, and because they have not a spiritual understanding and apprehension of divine truths? Now he that is stablished stands firm against temptations and against arguments; he will not be won away from his faith, but remains unmoveable.

Therefore, I say, let us often examine ourselves in this particular. I believe this and this against the papists and others. Aye, but how shall I stand out for this? If trials should come, am I able to prove this from the Scriptures so clear as if it were written, as he saith, 'with a sunbeam?' The temptation and assaults of the devil, by men's subtle wits and arguments, will shake our judgments, will hurt more, and if time should come, try us better than fire and fagot. Those spies that brought an evil report upon the land of Canaan, we see that though the land, when it was won, was fruitful enough, and the conquest of it honourable, &c., and therein those spies discovered their own weakness; yet when they had made that shrewd oration, and brought subtle arguments to the eye of flesh and blood, we see, I say, how the people were discouraged, and how they staggered, Num. xiii. 33, *seq.* So a man that is not stablished, he may sometimes have shrewd men to deal withal, perhaps atheists, papists, Jesuits, and the devil joining with them to unsettle men; and they will prevail if men be not well settled and stablished before.

4. And so *for the course of our life and conversation amongst men, we should examine how we are stablished in that;* for we are not only to stand firm in cases of religion, but for causes of honesty. John Baptist was as good as a martyr, though the cause he died for was not religion, but a bold telling of Herod, when he thought he took an unlawful course in keeping his brother's wife, Mark vi. 18.

An honest man may die and suffer much for civil matters. Therefore examine yourselves in this. I have undertaken this cause, upon what ground? in what confidence? how far would I willingly go in it? could I be content to lose the favour of great ones? to die in the quarrel if need be? So far as a man is stablished by God's Spirit, so far is he settled also in this.

You have had heathen men, that would stand out firmly even to the death, against all disfavours, against all losses and crosses for evidence of civil truths, as you have it storied of Papinian, an excellent lawyer, that in the defence of right stood forth to the loss of his life (*aaaa*); and many other the like examples have been. But much more doth the Spirit of God stablish men. This I understand, this is good, this I will stand in, come what will, when I am called to it.

Let us oft call ourselves to an account, what we believe, and upon what ground; what we do, and upon what ground we undertake it; whether on grounds of conscience, or out of spleen and passion. When a man undertakes things on natural grounds, in great temptations, if God do not assist him, he will sink. Take the strongest courages that are, if they have no more but nature, though they may stand out sometimes, to the shame of Christians, yet in some cases they will shew themselves to be but mere natural men.

And therefore labour for the Spirit to stablish us. It is not necessary that we should enjoy our wealth, nor the favour of men, nor our life itself;

but it is necessary that we should keep a good conscience, it is necessary that we should be saved, it is necessary that we should look upon our Judge with confidence at the day of judgment.

It becomes Christians who, besides the light of nature, have the Spirit to stablish them, to be settled in their courses, to look that the conscience be good, the cause good, the aim good. If such a one give over when the cause is clear and good, it is a sign that his heart is not stablished by the Spirit of God in Christ. He hath either corrupt aims, or else he is weak, and understands not the grounds of religion, and the vanity of this life as he should do.

There are none that flinch and give over in a good quarrel, but either it is from hypocrisy, that he pretends to believe in Christ, and life everlasting, and yet he doth not; or else it is from extreme and wonderful weakness, which, if he belong to God, he shall recover, as Peter did, and shall stand more strongly another time.

It is but a forced, a false encouragement and stablishing, when a man that hath not the Spirit of God shall set light by death, though perhaps he die in a good quarrel, and with some comfort. For when a man shall know that after death there is a judgment, and that God hath many things to lay to his charge, when his conscience shall tell him that he is guilty of a thousand deaths, if he be not in Christ, and his pardon sealed by the Spirit of God in the blood of Christ: is it not madness to be courageous in that which he cannot conquer? It is good for a man to be courageous in time of conquest. It is a dastardly thing for a Christian to be cowardly, because he hath death and hell conquered, and everything is made serviceable to help him to heaven. But for another man to set light by these things, it is mere madness. No man but a Christian can be stout and courageous, except it be from a false spirit; especially in things that are above man's natural power, as death, it is eternal, and what man can stand out against the eternal wrath of God?

And therefore those that put on a Roman stoutness and courage, though they seem to have strong spirits, it is but false; either they are besotted with sensuality, or else with a spirit of pride. When they look before them, and see eternity, and see their sins, and that they must all appear at the day of judgment, they cannot be strong. Let us labour therefore to have our hearts stablished by the Spirit of God; and try ourselves often, by propounding queries, how we do things? With what minds and upon what grounds?

5. Again, another evidence whereby we may know that we have spiritual strength and stability in Christ wrought in us by the Spirit of God, is this, *when it makes us desire the coming of Christ;* when it makes us think of death, and of the time to come with joy and comfort; and that for the present it gives us boldness to the throne of grace in extremities. He that in extremity can go to God in Christ, it is a sign his heart is established.

Hypocrites in extremity fly to desperate courses, as Saul and Ahithophel did; but in extremity the soul that is stablished goes to God. 'My God, my God,' saith Christ, Mark xv. 34; so Job, 'Though he kill me, yet will I trust in him,' Job xiii. 15. I say, it is an evidence of a soul stablished upon Christ by the Spirit of God, to have 'boldness to the throne of grace,' Eph. iii. 12, in extremity; nay, when God seems to hide himself, which is the principal extremity of all, as in divine temptations, when God seems to be an enemy. Then for a man to fight and wrestle with God, and tug with the temptation, and not to let God go, though he kill him, this is a true Israel, a conqueror of God; this is a heart fortified by the Spirit.

It is an argument of a heart established, when, besides for the present, for the time to come, he can cheerfully and boldly think how it will be with him when death shall come, that he shall go to Christ, that the match shall be fully made up that is begun by God between Christ and him (for the contract is in this world, but the nuptials are celebrated in heaven), and in confidence hereof can say, 'Come, Lord Jesus, come quickly,' Rev. xxii. 20.

A heart that is not stablished saith, Oh! come not. 'Wherefore art thou come to torment us before our time?' Mat. viii. 29, say the devils to Christ; so an unstablished heart, at the hour of death, is afraid it shall be tormented before the time: and therefore Come not, come not, saith such a soul. But the soul that is stablished upon Christ, and upon the promises in Christ of forgiveness of sins, and life everlasting by the Spirit of Christ, that saith, 'Come, Lord Jesus, come quickly.'

I have been larger upon this point than I intended. These unsettled times moved me to speak a little more than ordinary, that we might labour to have our hearts stablished, that whatsoever comes, we may have somewhat that is certain to stick to; that our estate in Christ may be sure, whatsoever becomes of our state in the world otherwise.

VERSE 22.

'*Who hath anointed us, and also sealed us, and given the earnest of the Spirit in our hearts.*' The apostle having formerly laid open the riches of a Christian, in this verse he cometh to shew his strength. His riches consisteth in the promises of God in Christ; his strength, in being stablished upon those promises. Now that which he had spoken of more generally in the word 'stablishing,' he unfolds in three borrowed terms, 'anointing,' 'sealing,' 'earnest,' implying therein the manner of the Spirit's establishing a Christian. 'He who stablisheth us,' how is that wrought? By the Spirit 'anointing,' by the Spirit 'sealing,' and by 'the earnest of the Spirit;' which three terms do all argue assurance. For you know, that in the old law, kings, priests, and prophets were anointed, that is, they were authorised and confirmed in their places. And for sealing, writings among ourselves are 'sealed' for security. And an 'earnest' secures contracts and bargains. So that whatsoever may serve to strengthen a Christian's faith and assurance, is here laid down. God, to help our souls by our senses, fetcheth it from human affairs, applying words borrowed from earthly commerce, by a heavenly anagogical* sense to spiritual things.

First, the sure estate of a Christian is set down in the general, by 'stablishing;' and then in particular, we are 'anointed and sealed,' and have 'the earnest of the Spirit.'

God, in the covenant of grace, doth our part and his own too. He gives faith, and strengthens faith, and seals us. He gives us promises, he doth stablish us upon those promises, and works our hearts to an embracing of them. He anoints us, and seals us, and gives us 'the earnest of the Spirit.' All in the covenant of grace depends upon the faithfulness of God; and not upon ours, but upon ours dependently, as he is faithful in stablishing us. Now, because the holy apostle would have us settled in the excellency of

* That is, 'ascending.'—G.

the state of a Christian in the covenant of grace, you see how large-hearted he is. He useth four words implying one and the same thing, 'stablishing,' 'anointing,' 'sealing,' and giving 'earnest;' all of them words used in ratification amongst men.

God is pleased to stoop to speak to us in our own language; to speak of heavenly things after an earthly manner; and, therefore, he sets down the certain estate of a Christian by borrowed speeches. This is a gracious condescending of God, stooping, as it were, lower than himself; and, indeed, so he always abaseth himself when he deals with man, coming down far below himself.

To come to the words in particular.

'*And hath anointed us.*' This word hath a double reference. The Holy Ghost carries our minds, first, to the relation and proportion that is between the graces of the Spirit of God, and the ointment with which in former times they were anointed in the Jewish polity. And it hath reference likewise, and relation, to the persons that were anointed. The persons were kings, priests, and prophets.

Now God hath anointed us in Christ. The order is this:

First, Christ himself, as Mediator, is 'anointed with the oil of gladness above his fellows,' Ps. xlv. 7, but *for* his fellows. The ointment is first poured on the head of spiritual Aaron, and then it runs down to all the skirts of his garment, that is, to the meanest Christian. Even as the least finger and toe is actuated, and enlivened, and moved by the soul and spirits, that the head and the chief vital parts are; so every Christian, though he be but as the toe or the foot, yet all have communicated by the Spirit, from Christ the head. So that the third person, the Holy Ghost, that sanctified the human nature of Christ, that filled and enriched it with all grace, and anointed Christ; the same Spirit enricheth all his mystical members. As there is one Spirit in Christ, and that sacred body he took on him; so there is in the mystical body but one Spirit quickening and enlivening, and moving the head and the members. He is a head of influence, as well as a head of eminence. 'Of his fulness we have all grace for grace,' John i. 16. He is first anointed, and then we are anointed in him.

We will first speak of it as it hath reference to anointment; and then, as it hath reference to the persons anointed.

In the *first* place then, why are graces here called anointing?

I answer, they are called 'anointing,' from reference to that composed ointment in Exod. xxx. 22, *seq.*, where you have the composition of the holy oil laid down.

But in particular, you may observe these five particulars in which the relation standeth.

1. *First*, ointment *is a liquor supereminent:* it will have the highest place, it will have the eminency, and be above all other liquors, and in that respect it is a royal liquor. So the graces of God's Spirit, they are of an eminent nature. Spiritual gifts are above the gifts of nature; and spiritual blessings are above earthly things. The grace of God is a supereminent, a royal thing. It will be above all, even above our parts of nature. If a man have by nature a strong wit, grace will subdue his wit, so that he shall be only witty* to salvation, he shall be only strong to defend the truth, and to do nothing against it: he will subjugate and subordinate his parts and whatsoever excellency he hath by nature to grace, cast all at Christ's feet, 'count

* That is, 'wise.'—G.

all as dung, in comparison of the excellent knowledge of Christ,' Philip. iii. 8. And so again, grace is above corrupt nature, above all our corruptions. It will bring them under, it will subdue corruptions, temptations, afflictions; any thing, what you will, that is either natural or diabolical; for grace is spiritual, and that which is spiritual is above all that is below. Grace is of an invincible nature. It will bear sway by little and little. It is little in quantity, but it is mighty in operation. And it is above any outward excellency whatsoever. If a man be a king, if he have this anointing, it makes him better than himself. He is better in that he is a Christian, that he hath this sacred anointing, than for any other created excellency under heaven whatsoever, yea, though he were an angel. Grace hath its derivance* and influence from Christ, who is higher than all, and will be above all; and so will grace. That is the first. Other liquors, the best of them will be beneath, but oil, it will be above all.

2. It is compared to ointment in the *second* place, because that ointment *is sweet and delightful*. So was the ointment that was poured upon our Saviour by the woman in the gospel. Therefore the spouse in Cant. i. 3, speaking of Christ, 'Because,' saith she, 'of the savour of thy good ointments, thy name is an ointment poured forth, therefore do the virgins love thee.' The graces that are in Christ are so sweet, that they draw the virgins, they draw all believers after him. So grace in a Christian, it makes us sweet; it sweetens our persons and our actions. It sweetens our persons to God. God delights in the smell of his own graces. It makes us delectable for Christ and his Holy Spirit to lodge in our souls as in a garden of spices. It makes us sweet to the church, to the communion of saints. A gracious man, that hath his corruptions subdued, is wondrous sweet. His heart is as fine silver, every thing is sweet that comes from him. When the woman poured the box of ointment upon Christ, the whole house was filled with the smell thereof, John xii. 3; so the whole church is filled with the savour of the graces of good men, that either do live in the present times, or have left their graces in writing to posterity.

A wicked man is an abomination to God, and so are all his actions. He that is in the flesh 'cannot please God,' Rom. viii. 8. A civil man that hath not this anointing, all that he doth is abominable to God. 'All things are unclean to the unclean,' Rom. xiv. 14: even their best actions have a tincture of defilement from their corruption. Without this ointment we are not sweet, neither to God nor to others. Therefore the Scripture terms men in the state of nature, swine and goats, stinking creatures; and so indeed they that have not this anointing, they are stinking goats, and shall be set at Christ's left hand, except they have grace to sweeten their understandings and affections, and to draw them higher than nature can.

Likewise grace is full of sweetness to a man's self. It sweeteneth our nature and our actions to ourselves. A 'good conscience' being privy to itself of the work of grace, 'is a continual feast,' Prov. xv. 15. The conscience of a Christian, once renewed by grace, enlargeth the soul, and fills it with sweet peace and joy in believing.

3. Thirdly, the graces of the Spirit are called anointing, *because anointing strengthens*. Therefore, usually warriors and combatants, among the heathen, that were to encounter, were first anointed. So there is a spirit of strength in all those that are true Christians, which they have received from God, whereby they are able to do that that worldlings cannot do. They are able

* That is, 'derivation.'—G.

to deny themselves, to overcome themselves in matters of revenge, &c., they are able to want and to abound, to bear crosses, to resist temptations, and, as the apostle saith, 'able to do all things,' Philip. iv. 13. Nothing can stand in the way of a gracious man, no, not the gates of hell. He that is in him, grace is stronger 'than he that is in the world,' 1 John iv. 4. The least measure of grace, though it be but as a 'grain of mustard seed,' is stronger than the greatest measure of opposition, though strengthened with all the power of hell.

4. In the fourth place, ointment *makes the joints of the body nimble.* So this spiritual anointing it oils the joints of the soul, as I may say, and makes them nimble and ready to serve God 'in newness of Spirit, and not in the oldness of the letter,' Rom. vii. 6. God's people are called 'a willing people,' Ps. cx. 3, and a cheerful people, ready to every good work. And there is good reason for it; for they have an inward spiritual anointing, that makes them active and nimble in everything they do. That Spirit that sanctifieth them, that spirit telleth them what Christ hath done for them, that 'there is no damnation to them,' Rom. viii. 1, that God is reconciled to them, that they are freed from the greatest dangers, that all is theirs, and so their joy and nimbleness is from good reason, and there is a spirit of love in them unto God and Christ, which makes them nimble. When a man is without grace, he goes lumpishly and heavily about the service of God. He is drawn and forced to prayer, and to hearing, and to conference and meditation: he is dead and dull, and frozen to good works. But when a man hath received this sweet anointing of the Spirit, his heart is enlarged to all duties whatsoever, he is prepared to every good work.

5. Again, *oil makes cheerful.* So doth grace. It makes cheerful in adversity, cheerful in death, cheerful in those things that dismay the spirits of other men; so much grace, so much joy. For even as light and heat follow the fire, so the spirit of joy doth follow this spiritual anointing. Conscience of the interest he hath in the favour of God in Christ, and the evidences of grace stamped upon his heart, and an assurance of a better estate in the world to come, wonderfully enlarge the soul with spiritual joy. That which makes a man lumpish, and heavy, and earthly, is not the Spirit of God. The Spirit of God is a Spirit of joy, and it puts a gracious cheerfulness in the heart of a Christian. If there be mourning, it is that it may be more cheerful; for 'light is sown to the righteous,' Ps. xcvii 11, sometimes in mourning. 'God loves a cheerful giver,' 2 Cor. ix. 7, and a cheerful thanksgiver; all must be sweetened with cheerfulness. Now this comes from the Spirit of God; and he that is anointed with the Spirit, in some measure partakes of spiritual joy and cheerfulness.

6. Again, ointment, you know, *is of a healing nature*, as balm and other sweet ointments have a healing power and virtue. The Scripture makes mention of the 'balm of Gilead,' Jer. xlvi. 11; so grace hath a healing power. Repentance! That is of a purging, spiritual joy, of a healing nature. There must, you know, be first a cleansing, and then a healing and strengthening; so some graces are purgative and cleansing, some again are strengthening and healing. Repentance is a good purgation. It carries away the malignant and evil matter. But the cordial that strengthens the soul is joy. 'The joy of the Lord is your strength,' Neh. viii. 10. And so the grace of faith and love tend to cherish and corroborate the soul, so that, I say, these graces, this balm of the Spirit, hath a special sovereign power to heal us, to heal us both from the guilt of sin, and from the

dominion, and rule, and filthy stain of sin. It hath both a purging and a cordial virtue.

Thus you see, that upon good grounds the graces of God's Spirit that he communicates to the elect, and only to them that are in Christ, they are called 'anointing;' and they will have the effect of an ointment in us, if we receive this anointing.

Let us therefore try ourselves by these, whether we be anointed or no. What cheerfulness is there? What joy? What strength? What nimbleness to that which is good? What sovereignty hath grace in our hearts? You have a company that profess religion, but make it serve their own turn, that make heaven to come under earth, that make the service of God to stoop to other ends. Beloved! grace it is a superior thing, and religion makes all subordinate. Grace, and religion, wheresoever it is in truth, is of a ruling nature; and so it is sweet, and it is strong wheresoever it is. It is curing, and purging, and cleansing wheresoever it is. Therefore, I beseech you, let us not deceive ourselves.

I need say no more of the point; you may enlarge it in your own meditations. I come to the persons.

As this anointing hath reference to the ointment, so it hath relation to *the persons that were anointed.*

Now the persons anointed were first dedicated by anointing; they were consecrated to God, and separated from the world. And as they were dedicated and separated, so they were dignified by this anointing. It raised them above the common condition. And likewise with this anointing God gave them qualifications suitable.

You have three eminent persons that were anointed, and so raised above the common condition of other men.

Prophets, to teach the people.

Priests, to offer sacrifice.

Kings, to govern them.

Now Christ is principally all these. He is the principal Prophet of his church, 'the Angel of the covenant,' Gen. xxxii. 24, 25–29. He is 'Logos,' the Word, John i. 1, because as the inward word, the mind of a man, is known by the outward word, so Christ is called the Word, because, as a Prophet, he discovers his Father's mind, and makes known his Father's will unto us.

And he is the great High Priest. He makes atonement between God and us; he stands between his Father and us.

And he is the great King of his church, that rescues it from all its enemies, to protect and defend it.

But as Christ hath received this anointing primarily, and 'above his fellows,' Ps. xlv. 7, yet, as I said before, he hath received it *for* his fellows. Every Christian hath his anointing from Christ's anointing: all our graces and all our ointment is derived from him. 'He,' saith the apostle, Rev. i. 5, 'hath loved us, and washed us in his blood.' He loved us first, which is the cause of all, and then he washed us in his blood. He did not only shed his blood for us, but he 'washed us in his blood.' He hath applied his blood to our souls, and by applying that and sprinkling it upon our souls, 'he hath made us kings and priests to God his Father,' Rev. i. 6. And indeed, the great King of heaven and earth, he is and will be attended upon by none but kings and priests. He hath no servants but such as are anointed. He is followed of none but eminent persons, such as are separated from the world, and dignified above all other people; for the glory of his followers tends to his honour. Therefore those whom God chooseth to be his attendants, he qualifies them, gives them the hearts of kings, royal qualifications, and the hearts of priests, and the hearts of prophets. But this in the general.

To shew it therefore in particulars.

A Christian is *anointed:* he is a person severed from the world, dedicated to God; and dignified above others, and that from good reason, because God hath given him an inward qualification, which is the foundation of all.

1. And first, he is a *true prophet*, for he hath received 'the anointing' of the Spirit, 1 John ii. 27, whereby he is enabled to discern of things. He knows what is true honour, to be the child of God; he knows what is true riches, grace; he knows what is true nobility, to be 'born of God,' 1 John ii. 29; what is true pleasure, 'peace of conscience, and joy in the Holy Ghost,' 1 Thess. i. 6; he can discern between seeming and real things, and only he that hath received this 'anointing of the Spirit.'

And again, as a prophet, he knows not only the things, but the doing of the things. He hath with the anointing of the Spirit ability to do that which he knows. The grace of God teacheth him not only the duty, that he should live 'justly, and soberly, and godly,' Tit. ii. 12, but teacheth him to do the things. For God writes his laws in his bowels, that is, in his affections. He can love and joy in God, and hate sin, and overcome revenge, &c. The Spirit sheweth him divine things by a divine light. He sees heavenly things with a heavenly light; and divine and spiritual knowledge is a working knowledge, of the same nature with the things known. The poorest Christian in the world, having this anointing, sees good things with such a convincing light, and evil things with such a convincing hatred, that he is doing and acting; whereas a Christian that hath not the Spirit, he may know heavenly things by a natural light, by a discoursive knowledge. He may know what he should do, and so perhaps he may talk, but he cannot do; he may talk of death, but he cannot die; he may talk and discourse of suffering, but when it comes, he cannot suffer; he may speak much of patience, but he cannot act patience when occasion is. A true Christian hath the knowledge of doing things.

And likewise he is able 'to speak a word in due season,' 2 Tim. iv. 2, to reprove, to admonish, to comfort. Every member in the communion of saints hath some qualification in regard of knowledge, when he is put to it.

But especially he hath received this anointing as a priest and a king.

2. As a *priest*, to stand before God, and to offer up prayers for himself and others. Every Christian is a favourite in heaven. He hath much credit there. He hath God's ear open at all times, and he improves it for the good of the church, for the good of others as well as for his own. And as to pray for ourselves and others, so to bless ourselves and others, that was one part of the priest's office, and so, as the Scripture saith, we are called unto blessing; and therefore those that are given unto cursing are not priests.

And again, a Christian that hath received this anointing as a priest, he keeps himself 'unspotted of the world,' James i. 27. You know, the priests were to touch no unclean thing, nor to defile themselves with any manner of pollution. So every Christian in some measure is enabled to abstain from the common pollutions of the times, to hate 'even the garment spotted with the flesh,' Jude 23. He is not carried with the stream of the times;

he will not converse amiably with those that may stain him, but as his calling leads him, lest he contaminate his spirit.

And likewise a Christian hath his heart always as the 'holy of holies,' that so he may offer up thanks and praise to God. There is a disposition in him always to praise God. As the fire in the sanctuary must never go out, so the fire that is kindled by the Spirit of God in the heart of a Christian, it never goes out. The Holy Ghost maintains it continually. He is ready to praise God upon all occasions; ready to offer up himself unto God as a sacrifice. The sacrifices of a Christian are a broken heart; and as in the law, the sacrifices for sin must first be killed, and then offered, so now in the gospel, it is the work of every Christian, to mortify, to kill, and slay those beasts, those corruptions that are in him contrary to God. A Christian must not offer himself to God as a sinner, but he must first slay his corruptions. He must mortify his sins, and then offer up himself slain to God.

Therefore our care must be to mortify every corruption, every faculty of the soul, and every part of the body. We must circumcise our eyes, that they behold not vanity; and our ears, that they hear not, and delight not in unchaste things; and our thoughts and every part, our wills and affections, and then offer up soul and body as a living sacrifice unto God, that all may be dedicated and sanctified unto him: and then it is a sweet sacrifice. Then, when a Christian hath dedicated himself to God, it is an easy matter to give him his goods when he calls for them, then he will be ready to let all go, as the apostle saith of the Corinthians,* 'they first gave themselves to God, and then to others,' 2 Cor. viii. 5. Other sacrifices will follow when we have first given ourselves to God. Therefore the first sacrifice is to kill our corruptions, to offer ourselves to God, and then we shall be ready to offer our estates, and to have nothing but at God's disposing. O Lord! of thy hand I have my body and my life, and my goods and all, I give them unto thee; if thou wilt have me to enjoy them, I do; but if thou wilt have them sacrificed, I am a priest, I am willing to offer myself as a burnt-sacrifice to thee even to the death, and all other things when thou shalt be pleased to call for them; and, indeed, all other sacrifices of our goods, and thankfulness in words, they will easily come off when we have offered ourselves, as I said before.

What is the reason that men will not part with a penny for good uses? They have not given themselves as sacrifices unto God; therefore in the Scripture we are pressed to give ourselves unto God first; and it useth arguments to that purpose; as that 'we are not our own, but bought with a price,' &c., 1 Cor. vi. 20.

And so for the kingly office.

3. Every Christian by this anointing *is made a king*, Rev. i. 6, 'He hath loved us, and washed us, and made us kings,' &c.

But how are we kings? To take away an objection that ariseth in the hearts of carnal men. Oh, say they, they talk that they are kings, when perhaps they have not a penny in their purse; they talk they are kings, when in the mean time they are underlings in the world. Here are kings indeed, think profane, conceited persons.

Indeed, all other things are but shadows; these be realities. This is a kingdom to purpose. Thou livest by sense and by fancy, or else, if thou hadst the spiritual eye-salve, if thou hadst thine eyes open to see the dignity of a Christian, thou wouldst judge him to be the only king in the world; and,

* The 'Macedonians,' not Corinthians.—G.

therefore, I do not enlarge the point to set colours upon matters, but indeed I rather speak under. There is no excellency that we can think of in this world that riseth high enough to set out the state of a Christian; he is indeed a king.

For, I beseech you, what makes a king? Victory and conquest, that makes a king. Is not he a conqueror that hath that in him that conquers the world and all things else? Others, that are not Christians, they are slaves to lusts and pleasures. A Christian is chief conqueror in the world, he conquers the world in his heart, and all temptations are inferior to him; he sees them as things that he hath gotten the mastery of; he subdues the principal enemy. A Christian fears not death, he fears not judgment, he fears not the wrath of God. He knows God is reconciled in Christ, and so all things are reconciled with him. God being at peace, all things else are at peace. So he is a conqueror. He hath a kingdom in himself. Others have kingdoms out of themselves, and in themselves they are slaves. He is such a king as hath a kingdom in himself. He hath peace and joy, and rest from base affections and terror of conscience.

Is not he a king that is lord and master of all things? A Christian is master of prosperity. He conquers it, he can make it serve his turn—to be thankful to God, to be ready to distribute. He is master of adversity. 'I can want and I can be abased, I can do all things through Christ that strengtheneth me,' saith blessed Paul, Philip. iv. 12, 13. He is an omnipotent king in some sense, 'he can do all through him that strengthens him.' He hath conquered the king of fears—death. That that makes the greatest monarch in the world to shake and tremble, a Christian can think of with comfort. He can think of God's wrath with comfort appeased in Christ, staunched with his blood. He can think of the day of judgment with comfort, that then his Saviour shall be his judge, and that he shall stand at the right hand of God. He can think of afflictions with comfort; he is sanctified to all things, and all things are sanctified to him, and 'all things shall work for his good,' Rom. viii. 28; 'nothing shall be able to separate him from God's love to him in Christ, neither things present nor things to come,' Rom. viii. 38. That which amazeth the Belshazzars of the world, and makes their knees smite one against another, as that handwriting did him; that which makes others quake to think of, a revenging God, before whom they must appear, and answer for all their miscarriages, and their neglect of precious time, and abuse of their places, they can think of with joy and comfort.

He hath conquered himself and his own heart: he can subdue the carnal part of him, and bring it under the Spirit. All others, though kings, if they be not Christians, are slaves to some reigning lust or other.

He is a king likewise in regard of possession, which is a second thing which makes a Christian an excellent person. As he is a great conqueror, so he is a great possessor; for 'all is yours,' saith the apostle, 'things present and things to come, life and death, afflictions and crosses, and all is yours,' 1 Cor. iii. 22. How? To help him to heaven. Things present are his; comforts are his, if they be present; afflictions are his, to purge him and fit him for heaven; things to come are his, heaven is his, and terrors to come, all serve him. Even evil things are his in advantage and success. Though in disposition they be not his, but have an hostile disposition in them, they are all overpowered by the love of God; and Christ, the king of heaven and earth, overrules all to the good of his. And so all good things are his, though not in civil possession, but as far as the great governor of all things sees fit. What a king is this! And, therefore, the word is not too great, to say a Christian is a king. He is indeed the most excellent person in the world.

And he hath likewise a kingly spirit, that is, he doth things with love and freedom of spirit that others do upon compulsion, for he hath the royal law of love, as the apostle saith, written in his heart, James ii. 8. What is that? The royal law of love is this, when a man doth that which he doth from love and from a princely spirit,—when he is not compelled. That which others do not at all, or by force is wrung from them, he doth out of a princely spirit that is in him, because his spirit is enlarged and anointed by the Spirit of God to every good work.

These things might be enlarged, but a taste of them is sufficient, and they are very useful to raise our hearts to consider that there is another manner of state than the world thinks of. There are spiritual and excellent kings and priests; and this will stand by us when all other excellencies fail, 'All flesh is grass, and as the flower of the grass,' 1 Peter i. 24. But this dignity, this anointing which we have by the Spirit and by the word of God, it endures for ever, and abides to all eternity.

Now, not to go on in more particulars, but to make some use of this. Surely this is true in some degree of every Christian, that he is a prophet, 'to discern of things that differ,' Heb. v. 14; and he hath a supernatural, heavenly light answerable to the things, a spiritual light to judge of spiritual things. And he is a priest, to stand before God continually; and he is a king, by conquest, by possession, by qualification. I say this undoubtedly is true of all spiritual persons, that are anointed. As it is said of Saul, that when he was anointed he had another spirit, 1 Sam. x. 11, so God never makes a Christian but he gives him the spirit of a Christian. God's calling is with qualification. It is not a mere titular anointing, but there is another spirit goes along with this anointing than there was before calling. Though men be trained up from their infancy in the truth, yet when they are anointed by the Spirit of God there will another manner of spirit appear in them than ever was in them before, or than that which is in the world.

I beseech you therefore,—for dignity prepares and stirs up to duty; a man never so carries himself in his place and condition, as when he thinks of his condition,—oft think of the excellent estate we are advanced to in Christ. It will put us in mind of a qualification and disposition answerable; that as the apostle oft presseth it, we may 'walk worthy our calling,' Eph. iv. 1, that we may walk worthy of this dignity.

When we are tempted therefore to sin, and to base courses, let us say as good Nehemiah when he was moved to flee, 'what, shall such a man as I flee?' Neh. vi. 11. So should we say to any temptation to base courses of life, what! shall such a man as I do this? Why! if I be a Christian, if I be not only a titular Christian,—which is only sufficient to damn me, and not to do me good,—but if I be a real Christian, I must be a priest, I must keep myself unspotted of the world, and undefiled, and not touch any unclean thing; I must be in a state and condition to pray to God, 'Shall I regard iniquity, that God should not hear my prayer?' Ps. lxvi. 18.

If I be a Christian, I am a king; shall I debase myself? shall I cast my crown in the dirt? God hath raised me, and made me an heir of heaven, shall I abase myself to sins, and to base lusts, so that I cannot rule my own members, and yet profess myself to be a king? For a Christian that is a king, that hath a guard of angels about him, that is the most excellent creature in the world, for him to abase himself to the world; he that is bred from heaven, for him to have no higher thoughts than the things below, to have an earthly mind, and earthly thoughts, it is a shrewd presumption that he is but only a titular Christian, and hath not received this inward and spiritual anointing. It was a speech of the martyrs in the primitive church, when they were asked their names, they gave this answer, *Christianus sum*, I am a Christian (*bbbb*), and that satisfied all questions. So when we are basely tempted to courses unbefitting our dignity, answer them from our baptism, I am baptized into Christ, and so am become a Christian, and this is unbeseeming the profession of Christianity.

I beseech you let us remember our calling. We are called to be prophets, kings, and priests, and not only here, but in the world to come we shall be so. We must not think to be kings in heaven, except we begin it here.

It is with a Christian, as it was with David. He was anointed many years before he was actually a king upon the throne, 1 Sam. xvi. 13. While Saul lived, he did not enjoy the kingdom. So we are anointed in this world, in part we are kings while we are here; kings over ourselves, and over the world. A Christian sees all under him that is worldly, he treads the moon under his feet. But our anointing hath then especially its effect when we are in heaven, as David's anointing, it had its special effect when Saul was dead. We must now carry ourselves as those that shall be kings. Those that are not kings here, shall never be kings hereafter; those that are not priests here, shall never walk with Christ in heaven in long white robes for ever. Eternal life is begun here, in all the parts of it.

And therefore I beseech you, if our memories be so shallow that we cannot remember other bonds, let us remember our baptism, let us read our duty in our baptism. What are we baptized into? Into Christ, that is, to take the name of Christ upon us, to be Christians; which name implies these three, to be a king, priest, and prophet. What do we then when we sin? We reverse our baptism in some sort. Let it be an aggravation then when we are tempted to sin; it is treason to God, I shall leave my Captain, under whose banner I have vowed to fight against 'the devil, the world, and the flesh;' and to forsake my colours is the greatest treachery. Yea, it is sacrilege. And so God accounts it, when thou profanest thine eyes and thine ears in seeing and hearing of vanity, as you do when you frequent playhouses and the like. I say, it is sacrilegious. Kings and priests were dedicated persons, and to employ dedicated things about any other business, than to God, is sacrilege; it is a committing of folly with thy soul. Men have slight conceits of religion, and scarce a tincture of it. If they did deeply consider what religion is, that it seizeth upon the soul, that it alters and changeth it, that whosoever will have benefit by the promises, he must have an inward qualification, and be anointed with the Spirit, they would have better conceits of it than they have; and hence it is therefore that men make so little conscience of giving liberty to their ears and eyes to hear and see vanity, and defile themselves in evil courses, and cleave to the occasions of sin.

Let us oft, I beseech you, be stirred up to think of our high prerogatives, with high admiration. What love! what love! hath God shewed, 'that we should be called the sons of God,' 1 John iii. 1, that we should be made kings and priests to God the Father. And if ever you hope to have comfort by religion, you must find this anointing in yourselves, raising you above other men to holy duties, to be kings, and priests, and prophets.

'*Who hath anointed us, and sealed us,*' *&c.* You see then, a Christian is stablished this way in Christ, because he is anointed by the Spirit of God; he is dedicated and consecrated to God. Hence, before I go on to that which followeth, in that the apostle coupleth anointing, and sealing, and earnest to the promises, observe this briefly,

None have interest in the promises of mercy, none can find comfort by them, but such as find some change in themselves.

The promises of God, as I have often said, are the riches of a Christian, and his inheritance. Take all from him, you must needs leave him this. You cannot take this from him. And as an usurer thinks he is a rich man, though he have not twopence in his house, but all that he hath is in bills and bonds; so a Christian, though happily he have not much in actual possession, yet he is rich in that he hath God's bonds in the promises. But now a man cannot say that he is interested in the promises, that he can lay claim to them, if he be an unfruitful man, an unhallowed man, that hath not the sweet ointment of the Spirit, changing of him, as it is said of Saul, into another man; for God wheresoever he reconciles himself, and gives any promise of favour and mercy, there he works a qualification. Of necessity it must be so, because he is reconciled to amity. Now in friendship there must be a correspondent similitude of disposition and sympathy. Now as long as we are in our natural estate, and remain unhallowed and defiled, we are in such terms as God and we cannot meet in amity; and therefore wheresoever the promises of the favour of God and reconciliation are of force, there must be a change. God, when he intends to shew favour to any, he alters and changeth them, that they may be such as he may have content, and complacency and delight in.

We see then there is a necessity of examining ourselves in this point. If thou be anointed, examine thyself, what inward power of grace thou hast, what sweet work of the Spirit; whether thou find in thee a principle above corruption, that makes thee rule above that which the world is inthralled unto. Undoubtedly as our title to heaven it is out of ourselves, by the promises we have of salvation and reconciliation in Christ; so the evidences must be found in ourselves; there must be anointing, and sealing, and the earnest of the Spirit. Therefore I beseech you, think seriously of what I have delivered of that point before. But we shall have occasion in the particulars after to speak more of this. I go on therefore to the second word,

'Who hath sealed us.' The same God that anoints us seals us. Anointing and sealing go both together; both are to secure us our estate in Christ, both wrought by the Spirit of God.

Now Christ is the first sealed, John vi. 27, 'Him hath God the Father sealed.' Christ is sealed to be our redeemer, that is, God hath set apart Christ from others, hath distinguished him, and sealed him, and set a stamp upon him to be the Messiah; sealed him to the great work of redemption, first by the graces of the Spirit; for he is full of them, having received 'the Spirit above measure,' John iii. 34; and not only so, but he sealed him by many miracles, by the resurrection from the dead, by which he was declared to be the Son of God; by the calling of the Gentiles, and by many other things.

Christ being sealed, he sealed all that he did for our redemption with his blood; and for the strengthening of our faith, he hath added outward seals, the two sacraments, to seal our faith in this blood, and in him who is sealed of the Father.

But here in this place is meant another manner of sealing; for here is not meant the sealing of Christ, but the sealing of us, that have communion with Christ. The same Spirit that sealed the Redeemer, seals the redeemed.

What is our sealing?

Sealing we know hath this use.

1. *First* of all, *it doth imprint a likeness of him that doth seal upon the wax that is sealed;* as when the king's picture or image is stamped or sealed upon the wax, everything in the wax answers to that in the seal, face to face, eye to eye, hand to hand, foot to foot, body to body. So we are said to be sealed, when we carry in our souls the image of Jesus Christ; for the Spirit sets the stamp of Jesus Christ upon every Christian, so that there is the likeness of Christ in all things; understanding answers understanding, in proportion. As a child, you know, answers the father; it hath limb for limb, foot for foot, finger for finger, but it is not in quantity, but in proportion and likeness; so it is in the soul that is sealed by the Spirit, there is a likeness to Christ, something of every grace of Christ. There is understanding of the same heavenly supernatural truths; there is a judging of things as Christ judgeth; and the affections go as Christ's do; he loves that which Christ loves, and he hates that which he hates; he joys in that which Christ delights in. Every affection of the soul is carried that way that the affections of our blessed Saviour are carried in proportion. Everything in the soul is answerable to Jesus Christ; and there is no grace in Christ, but there is the like in every Christian in some small measure. The obedience of Christ to his Father even to the death, it is in every Christian. The humility whereby Christ abased himself, it is in every Christian. Christ works in the soul that receiveth him, a likeness to himself.

And this is an undoubted character of a Christian. The soul that believes in Christ doth not only believe in him for his own sake, to be forgiven of his sins; but together with believing, feeling the forgiveness of his sins, and that Christ hath so loved him, and done such things for him, he is ambitious to express Christ in all things; and it stirs him up with desire to be like him; for, thinks he, is there such love in Christ to me? and is there such grace and mercy in God to me? and was Christ so good as to do and to suffer such things for me? Oh! how shall I improve things for him! Oh! that I might be like him! lovely in his eyes! This, I say, must needs be so. These desires are undoubtedly universally in the souls of all those that partake of Christ. It is the nature of the thing to be so. We shall desire to be transformed more and more to Christ; every way to bear the image of the 'second Adam,' who is, as the apostle saith, from heaven, heavenly; and so shall we be heavenly-minded as he was heavenly-minded on earth, talking and discoursing of the kingdom of heaven, and fitting people for the kingdom of heaven, and drawing others from this world to meditate of a better estate. There is a likeness to these in the soul of every believer; and that is the reason that Christ's offices are put together in all those that he saves, that look, whosoever he is a priest to, to die for their sins—to them he is a prophet to teach them, and a king to subdue their corruptions, and to change them, and alter them, and to rule them by his Spirit.

You have carnal men in presumption, which leads them to destruction; they sever things in Christ. They will take benefit by Christ, but they care not for his likeness; they will have him as priest, but they respect him not as a king. Now all that are Christ's have the stamp of the Spirit upon them. There are desires wrought in them by the Spirit of God to that purpose; and a Spirit of sanctification that makes them every way like Christ in their proportion.

And that is an evidence of the sealing of such a soul, because the soul of itself hath no such impression: for the soul of itself is a barren wilderness, a stone that is cold and incapable of impression. When, therefore, the soul can command nature, being stiff, and hard, and dead, we see an impression of a higher nature, a man may know that undoubtedly the Spirit of God hath been in his soul; for we see a loving spirit, an humble spirit, a gracious, a believing, a broken spirit, an obedient spirit to every commandment of God, the soul can yield itself wholly to the will of God in all things. Certainly, I say, the Spirit of God hath been here, for these things grow not in a natural soul. A stone, you know, is cold by nature, and if a man feel a stone to be hot, a man may undeniably gather, certainly, the sun hath shined upon this stone. Our hearts are very cold by nature; undoubtedly, when they are warmed with the love of God, that they are made pliable to duties, the Sun of righteousness, Christ, hath shined on this cold heart. God's Spirit can work on marble, can work on brass, as Jeremiah saith, Jer. vi. 28. It was the commendations of one of the fathers that he could work on brass. God can work on our souls, which are as brass, and make an impression of grace there; and therefore when a man sees an impression upon such hard metal, certainly he may know that the finger of God's Spirit hath been there. So that the work of sanctification is an undoubted seal of the Spirit of God.

2. A second use of a seal is *distinction*. Seals are given for distinguishing; for, you know, sealing is a stamp set upon some few out of many. So this sealing of the Spirit, it distinguisheth Christians from others, as we shall see more at large afterwards.

3. Then again, a seal, it serves for *appropriation*,' for men seal those things that are their own. Merchants seal those wares that they either have or mean to have a right unto. Men seal their own sheep and not others, and stamp their own wares and not others. God here stoops so low as to make use of terms that are used in human matters and contracts: and by sealing he shews that he hath appropriated his own to himself, chosen and singled them out for himself to delight in.

4. Again, sealing further serves *to make things authentical, to give authority and excellency to things*. Magistrates and officers go with their broad seal, and deliver things that they would have carried with authority sealed, and the seal of the prince is the authority of the prince. So that a seal is to make things authentical, to give validity to things answerable to the value and esteem of him that seals.

These four principal uses there is of sealing. Now, God by his Spirit doth all these: for God by his Spirit sets the stamp and likeness of Christ upon us; he distinguisheth us from others, from the great refuse of the world; he appropriates us to himself, and likewise he authoriseth us and puts an excellency upon us to secure us against all. When we have God's seal upon us we stand against all accusations. 'Who shall separate us from the love of God?' Rom. viii. 35. We dare defy all objections and all accusations of conscience whatsoever. A man that hath God's seal, he stands impregnable, it so authoriseth him in his conscience; for it is given us for our assurance, and not for God's. God seals not because he is ignorant; he '*knows* who are his,' 2 Tim. ii. 19.

But what? Is the Spirit itself this seal, or the graces of the Spirit, or the comforts of the Spirit? What is this seal? for that is the question now, whether the Spirit itself, or the work of the Spirit, or the comfort and joy of the Spirit?

I answer, Indeed, the Spirit of God where it is, is a sufficient seal to us that God hath set us out for his: for whosoever hath the Spirit of Christ is his, and whosoever hath not the Spirit of Christ is none of his; but the Spirit is the author of this sealing, and the sealing that is in us is wrought by the Spirit, so that except you take the Spirit for that which is wrought by the Spirit, you have not the right comprehension of sealing: and so the Spirit, with that which the Spirit works, is the seal, for the Spirit is alway with his own seal, with his own stamp. Other seals are removed from the stamp, and the stamp remains, though the seal be gone; but the Spirit of God dwells and keeps a perpetual residence in the heart of a Christian, guiding him, moving him, enlightening of him, governing him, comforting him, doing all offices of a seal in his heart, till he have brought him to heaven, for the Holy Ghost never leaves us. It is the sweetest inhabitant that ever lodging was given to. He doth all that is done in the soul, and he is perpetually with his own work in joy and comfort. Though he seems sometimes to be in a corner of the heart, and is not discernible, yet he alway dwells in us; the Spirit is always with the stamp it sets upon the soul.

What is that stamp, then? to come to the matter more particularly, what is that that the Spirit seals us with, especially,—what is that work?

I answer, The Spirit works in this order, for the most part, and in some of these universally:

1. *First*, the Spirit doth, together with the word, which is the instrument of the Spirit, the chariot in which it is carried, *convince us of the evil that is in us, and of the ill estate we are in by reason thereof.* It convinceth us that we are sinners, and of the fearful estate that we are in by sin. This is the first work of the Spirit on a man in the state of nature,—it convinceth us of the ill that is in us, and of the ill due unto us, and thereupon it abaseth us. Therefore, it is called 'the Spirit of bondage,' Rom. viii. 15, because it makes a man tremble and quake till he see his peace in Christ.

2. When the Spirit hath done that, *then it convinceth a man by a better, by a sweeter light, discovering a remedy in Christ,* who is sealed of God, to reconcile God and us. And as he enlighteneth the soul, convinceth it of the all-sufficiency that is in Christ, and the authority that he hath, being sent and sealed of God for that purpose, so he works on the affections, he inclines the heart to go to God in Christ, and to cast himself on him by faith.

Now, when the soul is thus convinced of the evil that is in us, and of the good that is in Christ, and with this convincing is inclined and moved by the Holy Spirit, as, indeed, the Holy Spirit doth all, then upon this the Spirit vouchsafeth a superadded work,—as the Spirit doth still add to his own work,—he adds a confirming work, which is here called 'sealing.' That seal is not faith, for the apostle saith, '*After* you believed, ye were sealed,' Eph. i. 13. So that this sealing is not the work of faith, but it is a work of the Spirit upon faith, assuring the soul of its estate in grace.

But what need confirmation when we believe? Is not faith confirmation enough, when a man may by a reflect act of the soul know that he is in the state of grace by believing?

It is true, as the natural conscience knows what is in a man, as the natural judgment can reflect, so the spiritual understanding can reflect; and when he believes, he knows that he believes, without the Spirit, by the reflect act of the understanding, except he be in case of temptation. What needs sealing then?

This act of ours in believing, and the knowledge of our believing, it is oft terribly shaken; and God is wondrous desirous, as we see by the whole passage of the Scripture, that we should be secure of his love. He knows that he can have no glory and we can have no comfort else. And, therefore, when we by faith have sealed to his truth, he knows that we need still further sealing, that our faith be current and good, and to strengthen our faith, for all is little enough in the time of temptation. And, therefore, the single witness of our soul by the reflect act, knowing that we do believe when we do believe, it is not strong enough in great temptations, for in some trials the soul is so carried and hurried that it cannot reflect upon itself, nor know what is in itself, without much ado; therefore, first the Spirit works faith, whereby we seal God's truth, John iii. 33, 'He that believes hath put to his seal that God is true.' When God by his Spirit moves me to honour him by sealing his truth, that 'whosoever believes in Christ shall be saved,' John iii. 18, then God seals this, my belief, with an addition of his Holy Spirit. So that this sealing is a work upon believing; and as faith honours God, so God honours faith with a superadded seal and confirmation.

But yet we [are] not come particularly enough to know what this seal is. When we honour God by sealing his truth, then the Spirit seals us; certainly then the Spirit doth it by presence, by being with us in our souls. What then doth the Spirit work when we believe? How shall we know that there is such a spiritual sealing?

I answer, the Spirit in this sealing works these four things:

First, a secret voice or witness to the soul, that we are 'the sons of God.'

Secondly, a voice or speech in us again to God, causing us to have access to the throne of grace 'with boldness.'

Thirdly, a work of sanctification.

Fourthly, 'peace of conscience, and joy in the Holy Ghost,' Rom. xiv. 17.

By these four ways we may know the sealing of the Spirit after we believe, and that our faith is a sound belief, and that we are in the state of grace indeed.

1. *First*, I say, *the Spirit speaks to us by a secret kind of whispering and intimation*, that the soul feels better than I can express. 'Be of good comfort, thy sins are forgiven thee,' saith he to the soul, Matt. ix. 2, 'I am thy salvation,' Ps. xxxv. 3. There is, I say, a sweet joining, a sweet kiss given to the soul. 'I am thine, and thou art mine,' Cant. vi. 3. God by his Spirit speaks so much. There is a voice of God's Spirit speaking peace to his people upon their believing.

2. And then, *Secondly, the Spirit of adoption stirs up the speech of the soul to God, that as he says to the soul, Because thou believest, now thou art honoured to be my child; so the Spirit stirs up in the soul a spirit of prayer to cry, 'Abba, Father.'* It can go boldly to God as to a Father; for that 'Abba, Father,' it is a bold and familiar speech.

There are two things in a prayer of a Christian that are incompatible to any carnal man: there is an inward kind of familiar boldness in the soul, whereby a Christian goes to God, as a child when he wants any thing goes to his father. A child considers not his own worthiness or meanness, but goeth to his father familiarly and boldly: so, I say, when the Spirit of God speaks to us from God, and tells the soul, 'I am thine,' 'I am thy salvation,' 'thy sins are forgiven thee, be of good comfort:' and when the soul again speaks to God, when it can pour forth itself with a kind of familiar boldness and earnestness, especially in extremity, and in time of trouble, and can wait in prayer, and depend upon God,—this spiritual speech of God to the soul, and of the soul to God, it is a seal of the Spirit that indeed we are true believers, because we can do that that none can do but Christians. God speaks to our souls, he raiseth our souls, and by his Spirit he puts a spirit of supplication into us, and helps our infirmities; for we know not what to ask, but he helps our weakness, and enables us to lay out the wants of our souls to God. These are evidences of the presence and of the seal of the Spirit.

3. In the third place, this sealing of the Spirit after we believe, is known *by the sanctifying work of the Spirit:* for, as I told you before in the unfolding of the point, the Spirit seals our spirits by stamping the likeness of the Spirit of Christ on us. So that when a man finds in his soul some lineaments of that heavenly image of Christ Jesus, when he finds some love, he may know by that love that he is 'translated from death to life,' John v. 24; when he finds his spirit subdued, to be humble, to be obedient, when he finds his spirit to be heavenly and holy as Christ was; when he finds this stamp upon the soul, surely he may reason, I have not this by nature; naturally I am proud, now I can abase myself; naturally I am full of malice, now I can love, I can pray heartily for mine enemies, as Christ did; naturally I am lumpish and heavy, now in afflictions, I can joy in the Holy Ghost; I have somewhat in me contrary to nature, surely God hath vouchsafed his Spirit, upon my believing in Christ, to mark me, to seal me, to stamp me for his, I carry now the image of the second Adam, I know the Holy Ghost hath been in my heart, I see the stamp of Christ there. 'Know you not that Christ is in you, except you be cast-aways?' saith the apostle, 2 Cor. xiii. 5. So upon search, the Christian soul finds somewhat of Christ always in the soul to give a sweet evidence that he is sealed to the day of redemption.

4. The fourth evidence that the Spirit of God hath been in a man's heart, *is the joy of the Holy Ghost and peace of conscience.* Sanctification is the ordinary seal that is always in the soul: this is an extraordinary seal, peace and joy. When the soul needs encouragement, then God is graciously pleased to superadd this, to give such spiritual ravishings which are as the very beginnings of heaven, so that a man may say of a Christian at such times that he is in heaven before his time, he is in heaven upon earth. But especially God doth this when he will have his children to suffer, or after suffering, after some special conflict, after we have combated with some special corruption, with some sinful disposition, with some strong temptation, and have got the victory: 'To him that overcometh will I give of the hidden manna, and a white stone, and a new name that none can read it, but he that hath it,' Rev. ii. 17, that is, he shall have assurance that he is in the state of grace, and the sweet sense of the love of God, and that sweet heavenly manna that none else can have. Thus God dealt with Job. After he had exercised that champion a long time, at the last he discovered

himself in a glorious manner to him. So it is usually after some great cross; or in the midst of some great cross, when God sees that we must be supported with some spiritual comfort, we sink else. Then there is place and time for spiritual comfort, when earth cannot comfort. Thus St Paul in the midst of the dungeon, when he was in the stocks, being sealed with the Spirit, he 'sang at midnight,' Acts xvi. 24, *seq*. Alas! what would have become of blessed Paul? his spirit would have sunk if God had not stamped it with 'joy in the Holy Ghost,' Rom. xiv. 17; and so David, and the 'three young men' in the fiery furnace, and Daniel in the den. God doth then, even as parents, smile upon their children when they are sick and need comfort: so above all other times God reserves this hidden sealing of his children with a spirit of joy when they need it most, sometimes in the midst of afflictions, sometimes as a reward when they come out of their afflictions; sometimes before. So our Saviour Christ had James and John with him upon the mountain to strengthen them against the scandal of suffering after. So God when he hath a great work for his children to do, some suffering for them to go through, as an encouragement beforehand, he enlargeth their spirits with the joy of the Holy Ghost. And sometimes also after a holy and gracious disposition in the ordinances of God, God doth add an excellent portion of his Spirit, a seal extraordinary: for indeed, God thinks nothing enough for his children till he have brought them to heaven, seal upon seal, and comfort upon comfort; and the more we depend upon him in the means of salvation, and the more we conflict with our corruptions, the more he increaseth the sweet comforts and the hidden manna of the Spirit.

Thus we see how the Spirit seals; I beseech you, therefore, let us examine ourselves by that which hath been spoken: after we believe, God seals those that do believe. We honour him by believing, he honours us by sealing us with his Spirit. Hath God spoken to thy soul by the witness of the Spirit, and said, 'I am thy salvation,' 'thy sins are forgiven thee?' doth God stir up thy spirit to call upon him, especially in extremity? and to go with boldness and earnestness to him? Surely this boldness and earnestness is an evidence of the seal of the Spirit; for a man that hath no seal of the Spirit, he cannot go to God in extremity. Saul in extremity he goes to the witch; and Ahithophel and Judas in extremity go to desperate conclusions. A man that hath not the Spirit of God speaking peace to his conscience, to whom God hath not given the spirit of adoption to cry, 'Abba, Father,' in all manner of exigents, he sinks as lead to the bottom of the sea. So heavy is the soul that is not raised by the Spirit of God, he hath no consistence till he come to the centre, to hell. Did you ever feel the sweet joy of the Spirit after conflict with corruptions, and getting ground of them, and in holy duties, &c.? It is a sign that God hath sealed you.

But you will say, How can that be a seal that is not always? A seal continues with the thing. God's children find not peace always. The joy of the Spirit comes after the work of the Spirit: how then can this be a seal?

I answer, Yes; for howsoever it be or not alway sensible, yet it is alway a seal. Though we have not always the joy of the Spirit, yet we have the spirit of joy. A Christian hath not the joy of the Spirit at all times, for that is moveable; but he hath always the spirit of joy, which spirit, though it be not known by joy, yet it is known by operation and working. There is the work of the Spirit, where there is not always the joy of the Spirit; and therefore when that fails, go to the work of sanctification, and see what stamp and resemblance of Christ there is; see if thy heart be humble and broken, if thou have a loving disposition in thee like to Christ, that thou hatest that which Christ hateth, that thou seest a division in thyself. I say, when the joy of the Spirit ceaseth, go to the work of the Spirit, and to this work of the Spirit, viz., the voice of the Spirit,—canst thou cry to God with prayer and supplication? and if thou canst not pray with distinct words, canst thou mourn and groan to God? This sighing and groaning is the voice of God's Spirit, and God knows the voice of his own Spirit. But for the question propounded: the soul of a Christian knows that when it finds not extraordinary comfort from God's Spirit, that God's love is constant. It can reason thus: though I find not the comfort of the Spirit, yet I have the spirit of comfort, because I had the Spirit in former times, and God's Spirit is unchangeable, and therefore though it be not with me now as in those ravishings of the Spirit, yet the love of God is the same, though my feeling be not the same; because, though I be off and on, and my feelings ebb and flow, yet His love is not so; and hereupon the extraordinary feeling of the Spirit, which is superadded as an extraordinary seal, it may be a sound seal of comfort from the constancy of God who gave it; and he gave it for this end, that we might have recourse, and retire back in our thoughts, and argue it was thus and thus with me. Then we remember the times of old, as David saith, Ps. lxxvii. 6, and help ourselves with our former feelings. He that alway hath life, is not always alike stirred. Christ may be begotten and live in us, but he stirs not always alike. So though the Spirit of sanctification be in us, and stir in us, yet his stirring is not alike so sweet; and the stirring of the Spirit, though it be not alway, yet the Spirit is alway there. So the soul may have recourse to that which is unchangeable and constant, even God himself, and his love is as himself.

But to take a Christian in his worst time, in the worst and greatest afflictions, how shall he know then that he is sealed of the Spirit? When corruption, temptation, and affliction meet together in the soul; when temptation is joined with our corruption, and afflictions yield ground to temptations (for Satan useth the afflictions we are in as temptations to shake our faith), canst thou be a child of God, and be so exercised? Is this grace? So affliction is a weapon to temptation, for Satan to help his fiery darts with. Now how shall a man know that God hath any part here?

1. He may know that he is sealed by the Spirit of God, *if he have a spirit to thwart these,* if he row against the stream, if he go contrary to all these; if he find a spirit resisting Satan's temptations, and raising himself above afflictions, and standing against, and combating with his corruptions, and checking his carnal soul when it is drawing him down. 'Why art thou discomforted, O my soul?' saith David, Ps. xlii. 11; xliii. 5. He found corruptions, and afflictions, and Satan's temptations working with them, depressing his soul downwards; hereupon, having the Spirit in him, saith he, 'Why art thou disquieted within me? Trust in God.' He first chides his soul, 'Why art thou so?' and then he lays a charge upon it, 'Trust in God.' So I say, when this is in the soul in the greatest extremity, when I can check my soul, 'Why art thou thus? yet trust in God;' whatsoever there is in the world, yet there is hope in heaven, though there be little comfort upon earth; this is a sign that I am sealed with the Spirit of God: and thus in the worst temptations that can come, and so in the worst times, a man may know that he is in the state of grace.

2. One use of a seal, I told you before, was to distinguish. If a man, therefore, find in himself *a distinguishing from the errors of the times* [he may know that he is 'sealed']. 'Many walk,' saith the apostle, 'of whom I have told you oft, their end is damnation, their belly is their god, they mind earthly things,' Philip. iii. 18, 19. But what did St Paul in the mean time? what did the Spirit work in him? 'But our conversation is in heaven,' saith he. The whole world was overspread with a deluge of sin; but what was Noah and his family? God by his Spirit distinguished them; they went a contrary course to the world; and Lot in Sodom. So a man may know that he is sealed, when the Spirit leads him another way, that he is not led with the errors of the times.

Thus we have unfolded to you the sealing of the Spirit; and you see the Spirit of God not only anoints, but seals. Now we should labour to have our hearts thus sealed by the Spirit. Can we desire and never be at quiet till our instruments be sealed, till our acquittances, till our charters be sealed? and shall we be patient not to have our souls sealed?

Let us labour by all means to have the image and likeness of Christ stamped upon our souls especially. That is wondrous comfortable when we can find somewhat in us like to Jesus Christ.

To encourage us to this, let us consider, that death and judgment will come, and God will set none at his right hand but his sheep that have his mark. Those that he sets his stamp and image upon, those he will set on the right hand in the day of judgment.

And how comfortably in the hour of death can the soul commend itself to God, when it sees itself stamped and sealed by the Spirit of Christ! when he can say to Christ, 'Lord Jesus, receive my soul,' Acts vii. 59, that thou hast redeemed by thy blood, that thou hast sealed by thy Spirit, and that thou hast set thine own stamp upon, acknowledge thine own likeness, though it be not as it should be; what a comfort, I say, hath the sealed soul at the hour of death! And so in all other extremities, and in times of trouble and danger, those in whom God sees his own image and likeness, he will own, and to those he will always shew a distinct and respective love in hard times.

What a difference is between that soul and others in the time of affliction, as in the time of pestilence and war. The soul that is sealed knows that he is marked out for God, for happiness in the world to come, whatsoever befalls him in this world; and he knows that God in all confusion of times knows his own seal. Those that are sealed, God hath a special care of, I say. Therefore in Ezek. ix. 6, they are said to be marked in their foreheads; not that there was any visible mark on them, but it is a phrase to signify what special care God had of his people, specially in times of destruction: God will as it were set them out in those times, and make special provision for them. Thus Josiah was taken away from the evil to come; and Lot was taken out of Sodom when fire and brimstone was to come from heaven; and Pella, a little village, was delivered when the general destruction came upon Jerusalem (*cccc*). So that, I say, God hath a special care of his little ones in this life; and if he take them away, yet their death is precious in his sight. He will not part with them but upon special consideration; he sees if they live it will be worse for them; he sees it is better for them to be gathered to himself, and to 'the souls of men made perfect in heaven.'*

* Cf. with Catlin's reflections on the death of Sibbes himself. Appendix to Memoir, A. vol i. pp. cxxxix–xli.—G.

And as he hath a special care of them in regard of outward miseries and calamities, so in regard of spiritual contagion and infection, as Rev. vii. 3, *seq.* There God's holy ones were sealed, so many of such a tribe, &c., which is to signify to us, that God hath always some that he will keep and preserve from the universal infection and contagion of Antichrist in the worst times. God hath always a church in the worst times, in the obscurest age of the church, eight or nine hundred years after Christ, especially nine hundred years [after], when Egyptian darkness had overspread the world, and there was little learning and goodness in the world,* God had always sealed ones, marked ones, that he preserved from the danger of dark times; and so he will always have a care of his own, that they be not led away with that soul-hurting error, popery; another manner of mischief than men take it for. The Scripture is more punctual in setting down the danger of those, especially in lighter times of the church, that are carried away with that sin, than any other sin whatsoever; they have a contrary mark. Those that have the mark of the beast, it is contrary to the mark of Christ: it is far from being the mark and seal of the Spirit, that implicit bloody faith. Theirs is the bloody church, pretend what they will, and they stand out to blood in the defence of all their cruel, superstitious, and bloody decrees. Those persons, I say, that are deeply dyed in popery, that have the mark of the beast, they are in a clean opposite condition to those that are marked with the Spirit, that Christ marks for his.

Let us not fear therefore, I say, if we have the Spirit of God stamped upon us, though in a little measure: if it be true, let us not fear death; Christ knows his own mark even in death, and out of death. And let us not fear afflictions nor evil times, Christ will know his seal. He hath a book of remembrance for those that are his, Mal. iii. 16; for those that mourn for the sins of the times, and when he gathers his jewels, those shall be his. He will gather his jewels as a man in his house gathers his jewels; he suffers his luggage to burn in the fire. So God in common calamities, he suffers luggage, wicked men to go to wreck, but he will free his own.

Let us labour therefore for this seal, to have our souls stamped with the Spirit of God, to have further and further evidence of our state in grace, that in the time of common calamity we may be free from danger, free from error and destruction.

But you will say, What shall I account of it, if there be but a little sign of grace?

Be not discouraged, when the stamp in wax is almost out, it is current in law. Put the case the stamp of the prince be an old coin (as sometimes we see it on a king Harry groat†), yet it is current money, yea,' though it be a little cracked. So, put the case the stamp of the Spirit be, as it were, almost worn out, it is our shame, and ought to be our grief that it is so, yet there are some evidences, some pulses, some sighs and groans against corruption: we mourn in our spirits, we do not join with corruption, we do not allow ourselves in sin. There is the stamp of the Spirit remaining, though it be overgrown with the dust of the world that we cannot see it.

Sometimes God's children, though they have the graces of the Spirit in them, yet they yield so much to their corruptions, that they can read nothing but their corruptions. When we bid them read their evidences, they can see nothing but worldliness, nothing but pride and envy, &c. Though there be a stamp on them, yet God holds the soul from seeing it, so that they can see nothing but corruption. This is for their negligence. God gives

* That is, the 'Middle or Dark Age,' so-called.—G. † That is, Henry VIII.—G.

them up to mistake their estates, because they will not stir up the graces of the Spirit, because they grieve the Spirit, and quench the Spirit, by doing that which is contrary to the Spirit.

Let us therefore, that we may have the more comfort, preserve the stamp of the Spirit fresh, by the exercise of all grace, and communion with God, and by obedience, and by faith. Honour God by believing, and he will honour thee by stamping his Spirit on thee more and more. And let this be our work every day to have the stamp of the Spirit clear. Oh! what a comfort it is to have this in us at all times! If a man have nothing in him better than nature, if he have nothing in him in regard of grace, if he have not Christ's image upon his soul, though he be a king, or an emperor, yet he shall be stript of all ere long, and be set on the left hand of Christ, and be adjudged to eternal torments.

It is the folly of the times come up of late, there is much labouring for statues, and for curious workmanship of that kind, and some pride themselves much in it, and account it great riches to have an old statue. Alas! alas! what a poor delight is this in comparison of the joy that a Christian hath by the seal of the Spirit? and what is this to the ambition of a Christian, to see the image and representation of Christ stamped in his soul? that he may be like the 'second Adam,' that he may be transformed more and more by looking on him, and seeing himself in him, to love him, considering that he hath loved us so much (for we cannot see the love of Christ to us, but we must love him the more, and be transformed into him). Now this transforming ourselves into the image of Christ is the best picture in the world; therefore labour for that every day more and more.

There is besides the common broad seal of God, his privy seal, as I may call it. It is not sufficient that we have the one, that we have admittance into the church by baptism, but we must have this privy seal which Christ sets and stamps upon the soul of the true Christian. Alas! for a man to build only on the outward seals, and outward prerogatives, (which in themselves are excellent, yet) the standing upon them betrays many souls to the devil in times of distress.

It is another manner of seal than the outward seal in the sacrament that will satisfy and comfort the conscience in the apprehensions of wrath at the hour of death or otherways. It must be this privy seal, and then comes the use of those public, open, known seals, the broad seals; then a man with comfort may think upon his baptism, and upon his receiving the communion, when he hath the beginnings of faith wrought in him by the Spirit of God. When a man finds the beginnings of faith in him, then he may make use of the broad seal to be a help to his faith.

We must not be so profane as to think slightly and irreverently of God's ordinances. They are of great and high consequence; for when Satan comes to the soul, and shakes the confidence of it, and saith, Thou art not a Christian, and God doth not love thee; why! saith the soul, God hath loved me, and pardoned my sins; he hath given me promises, and particularly sealed them in the sacrament; here is the excellency of the sacrament, it comes more home than the word, it seals the general promise of God particularly to myself. I am sealed in the sacrament, and withal I find the stamp of the Spirit in my heart; and therefore having the inward work of the Spirit, and God having fortified the inward work, and strengthened my faith by the outward seal, I can therefore stand against any temptation whatsoever. They are excellent both together, but the special thing that must comfort, must be the hidden seal of the Spirit.

Let us labour therefore to be sealed inwardly, and observe God's sealing-days, as we use to speak, which though it may be every day if we be in spiritual exercises, yet especially on the Lord's day; for then his ordinance and his Spirit go together.

Now as there is a sealing of our estates that we are the children of God, so there is of truths, and both are in the children of God; as for instance, this is a truth, 'Whosoever believes in Christ shall not perish, but have everlasting life,' John iii. 16. Now the same Spirit that stirreth up the soul to believe this, seals it in the soul, even to death, and in all times of temptation; and likewise there is no promise but upon the believing of it; it is sealed by the Spirit upon the soul; for those truths only abide firm in the soul which the Spirit of God sets on.

What is the reason that many forget the comforts and consolations that they hear? Because the Spirit sets them not on, the Spirit seals them not. What is the reason that illiterate men stand out in their profession to blood, whereas those that have a discoursive kind of learning they yield? The reason is this, the knowledge of the one is sealed by the Spirit, it is set fast upon the soul, the Spirit brings the knowledge and the soul close together; whereas the knowledge of the other is only a notional swimming knowledge; it is not spiritual.

Those therefore that will hold out in the end, and not apostatise, those that will stand out in the hour of death against temptation, and those that will hold out in the time of life against solicitations to sin, they must have a knowledge suitable to the things they know, that is, they must see and know heavenly things by a heavenly light, spiritual things by the Spirit of God.

And therefore when we come to hear the ministers of God, we should not come with strong conceits, in the strength of our wit; but with reverent dispositions, with dependence upon God for his Spirit, that he would teach us together with the ministers, and close with our souls, and set those truths we hear upon our souls; we shall never hold out else. And it must be the Holy Ghost that must do this; for that which must settle and seal comfort to the soul, must be greater than the soul, specially in the time of temptation, when the terrors of the Almighty are upon us, and when the hell within a man is open, when God lays open our consciences, and 'writes bitter things against us,' Job xiii. 26, and our consciences tell us our sins wondrous near; they are written as it were 'with a pen of iron, and the point of a diamond, upon our souls,' Jer. xvii. 1; now I say, those truths that must satisfy conscience that is thus turmoiled, must be set on by that which is above conscience. The Spirit of God who is above our spirits, can only set down our spirits, and keep them from quarrelling and contending against the truth, and quiet the conscience; and this the Spirit doth when it sets the truth upon the soul.

And therefore when our souls are disquieted and troubled, and we hear many comfortable truths, let us lift up our prayers to God, let there be ejaculations of spirit to God. Now Lord, by thy Holy Spirit set and seal this truth to my soul, that as it is true in itself, so it may be true to me likewise.

This is a necessary observation for us all. Oh, we desire all of us in the hour of death, to find such comforts as may be standing comforts, that may uphold us against the gates of hell, and against the temptations of Satan, and terrors of conscience; why! nothing will do this but spiritual truths spiritually known; nothing but holy truths set on by the Holy Spirit of God.

But what course shall we take when we want comfort ? when we want joy and peace ?

In the first [Epistle] of John, v. 7, 8, there are 'three witnesses in heaven, and three in earth,' to secure us of our state in grace, and the certainty of our salvation. The three witnesses upon earth are 'the Spirit, the water, and the blood, and these three agree in one;' and the 'three that bear witness in heaven,' are 'the Father, the Word, and the Holy Ghost;' and the three on earth, and these three in heaven agree in one (*dddd*).

Now the Spirit is the feelings and the sweet motions of the Spirit. The water may well be that washing of the Spirit, sanctification. The blood is the shedding of the blood of Christ, and justification by it. When therefore we find that part of the seal, that extraordinary seal that I spake of before, the joy of the Spirit of God, that it is not in us, what shall we do ? Shall we despair ? No ; go to the water. When we find not spiritual joy and comfort, when the witness of the Spirit is silent, go to the work of the Spirit in sanctification.

Aye, but what shall we do if the waters be troubled in the soul, as sometimes there is such a confusion in the soul that we cannot see the image of God upon it in sanctification, we cannot see the stamp of God's Spirit there, there is such a chaos in the soul ? God can see somewhat of his own Spirit in that confusion, but the spirit itself cannot.

Then go to the blood of Christ ! There is always comfort. The fountain that is opened for 'Judah and Jerusalem' to wash in is never dry. Go therefore to the blood of Christ, that is, if we find sin upon our consciences, if we find not peace in our consciences, nor sanctification in our hearts, go to the blood of Christ, which is shed for all those that confess their sins, and rely on him for pardon, though we find no grace. For howsoever as an evidence that we are in Christ, we must find the work of the Spirit ; yet before we go to Christ it is sufficient that we see nothing in ourselves, no qualification ; for the graces of the Spirit they are not the condition of coming to Christ, but the promise of those that receive Christ after. Therefore go to Christ when thou feelest neither joy of the Spirit, nor sanctification of the Spirit ; go to the blood of Christ, and that will purge thee, and wash thee from all thy sins.

This I only touch for a direction what to do when our souls want comfort, when perhaps we cannot see the seal of the Spirit in sanctification so clearly.

To go on now to the next.

'*And given us the earnest of the Spirit.*' Here is the third word borrowed from human affairs, to set out the work of the Spirit in our souls. 'Anointing' we had before, and 'sealing'; now here is 'earnest.'

The variety of the words shews that there is a great remainder of unbelief in the soul of man, that the Spirit of God is fain to use so many words to express God's dealing to the soul to bring it to believe, to be assured of salvation. And indeed so it is, howsoever we in the time of prosperity, when all things go well with us, we are prone wondrously to presume, yet in the hour of death, when conscience is awakened, we are prone to nothing so much as to call all in question, and to believe the doubts and fears of our own hearts, more than the undoubted truth and promise of God. Therefore God takes all courses to stablish us. He gives us rich and precious promises, he gives us the Holy Spirit to stablish us on the promises, he seals us with his Spirit, and gives us 'the earnest of the Spirit,' and all to settle this wretched and unbelieving heart of ours.

So desirous is God that we should be well conceited of him, he loves us better than we love ourselves. He so much prizeth our love, that he labours by all means to secure us of his love to us, because except we know his love to us, we cannot love him again, and we cannot joy in him, &c. But that only in the general.

Here is earnest, and 'the earnest of the Spirit,' that is, in plain terms, he gives us the Spirit with the graces and comforts of it, which doth in our hearts that which an earnest doth amongst men.

But what is the Spirit an earnest of?

It is an earnest of our inheritance in heaven, of our blessed estate there. We are sons now, but we are not heirs, invested into the blessed estate we have title to. God leaves us not off in the mean time while we are in our pilgrimage. He keeps not all for heaven, but he gives us somewhat to comfort us in our absence from our Husband, from our Lord and King, Christ. He gives us the earnest of the Spirit, that is, he gives the Holy Ghost into our hearts, which is the earnest of that blessed, everlasting, glorious condition which we shall have in heaven hereafter. That is the meaning of the words.

In what regard is the Spirit called an 'earnest?'

1. *First of all*, an earnest is for *security of bargains and contracts*. So the Holy Ghost assures the soul of salvation, being present with his graces and comforts; the Holy Ghost is given for security.

2. *Secondly*, an earnest is *part of the whole bargain*. Though it be a very little part, yet it is a part; and so the Spirit of God here, and the work of the Spirit, and the graces and joy of the Spirit, it is a part of that full joy and happiness that shall be revealed. The Spirit dwells not fully in any one. He dwelleth no further than he sanctifieth and reviveth. But that is an earnest for the time to come, that the Spirit shall be all in all, wherein we shall have no reluctancy, nor nothing to exalt itself against the sure regiment* of the Spirit.

3. *Thirdly*, an earnest is *little in comparison of the whole bargain*. So the work of the Spirit, the comforts, the joy, the peace of the Spirit, it is little in comparison of that which shall be in heaven, in regard of the fulness of the Spirit which we shall have there. An earnest, though it be little in quantity, yet it is great in security and assurance. A shilling may secure a bargain of a thousand pounds perhaps; so the Spirit, it is little in quantity it may be, but it is great in assurance. And as we value an earnest, not for the bigness of the piece; for, alas! it may be it is but little; but we value and esteem it for that which it is an earnest of. So the work of the Spirit, the joy and peace of the Spirit, the comforts of the Spirit, though they be little, yet they are great in security, and are to be prized according to that excellent bargain and possession, of which they are an earnest.

4. *Fourthly*, an earnest is given *rather for the security of the party that receives it, than in regard of him that gives it;* so God gives 'the earnest of the Spirit,' grace and comfort; this is not so much in regard of God, for God meaneth to give us heaven and happiness. (He hath passed his word, and he is master of his word, he is 'Jehovah,' that gives a being to his word as well as to every other thing.) But, notwithstanding, having to deal with doubtful, mistrustful persons, he doth it for our security, he regards not himself so much, but us. He works answerable to his own

* That is, 'government.'—G.

greatness, strongly; but he speaks according to our weakness; and therefore here is the term of 'earnest' borrowed for this purpose.

5. And *lastly*, an earnest *is never taken away, but it is made up with the bargain.* So it is with the Spirit of God; the graces and comforts of it are never wholly taken from a Christian, but accomplished in heaven. 'I will leave you the Comforter,' saith our Saviour Christ, 'that shall abide with you for ever,' John xiv. 16.

So that in these and such like other respects, the Spirit of God by itself, together with the graces of it, and the comforts it bringeth, for they go both together, are called an 'earnest.'

Hence then, having thus cleared the words, we may observe some particular doctrines. As first, I observe from the first property of an earnest, that it secures the whole bargain, this, that

Obs. A Christian ought to be, and may be assured of his estate in grace.

Because, as I said before, an earnest is given for security, and that not so much for God's sake, as for our sakes; this then must needs follow, either none have this earnest, or those that have it may be assured, or else God is fickle and plays fast and loose with his children, which is blasphemy to affirm. If none have this earnest, then the apostle speaks false, when he saith here, he 'stablisheth us, and gives us the earnest of his Spirit, and us with you,' both together. Ordinary Christians as well as grand ones, as well as Paul, may be assured of their salvation. And if this be so, then either those that have this earnest, this seal of the Spirit, they may be assured or no; and if not, where is the fault? Doth not God mean in good earnest to them when he gives them this? Undoubtedly he doth. And why is it given but for assurance? He is desirous that we should be persuaded of his love in all things, and therefore God's children they may and they ought to be assured of his love in this world.

It is a point that we have often occasion to meet with in other portions of Scripture. I speak it therefore here only as a ground out of this place, in that the Spirit of God, together with the graces and comforts, are called an 'earnest,' I say therefore from hence, *that we may be assured of our salvation.*

I beseech you, what is the aim of the Epistles to the Romans, to the Ephesians, of the Epistle of St John, but a stirring of them up to whom they wrote to be persuaded of God's love to them, and to shew what excellent things we have by the love of God in Christ? And St John's Epistle* it is for nothing else, in respect of the substance of it, but to give evidences how we may know that we are the sons of God. Wherefore did God become man? Wherefore was Christ himself sealed by the Father, Son, and Holy Ghost to his office, when he was baptised? And wherefore did he die and rise again? And wherefore doth he make intercession in heaven? That we should doubt of God's love, when he hath given us that which is greater than salvation, that which is greater than all the world, his own Son? Would we have a greater pledge of his love? Is not all this, that we should not doubt of his love to us, if we cast ourselves upon him by faith? Christians may, and ought, and have had assurance. These here had assurance, and the Scripture speaks of such as had it. They have had it, we may have it, because the Spirit is a seal and an earnest; and we ought to have it, because God hath framed both his word and his sacraments, and all his dealing to man so as to persuade us of his love.

Caution. Yet add this caution, *that Christians have not at all times a like assurance of their salvation;* neither all Christians at all times have it not,

* That is, the 1st Epistle.—G.

nor the best have it not at all times. For there is an infancy of grace, when we know not our own estate and condition; and there is a time of temptation after infancy, when likewise we stagger in our assurance. There be times likewise of desertion, when God, to make us look better to our footing, leaves us a little, as if he would forsake us, when indeed he leaves us to draw us after him, to cleave more closely to him; for this shaking is to settle us deeper. So there be times and seasons wherein though we be assured, yet we cannot then know our own assurance. And this assurance differeth in Christians; for some have more, some less; even as the constitution of the body, some are of a melancholy constitution, that helps Satan in his temptations, and they are subject to fearing and misdoubting: and so as there is a difference in regard of tempers, some are more hardly brought to be persuaded than others, so there is a difference likewise in care and diligence; for those that use more care and diligence have more assurance. There is a difference likewise in growth and continuance in Christianity, some are fathers, and some are babes. Answerable to the difference of constitution, and of care and diligence, and of age and growth in Christianity, so is the difference of assurance.

Nay, it is possible that for a long time God's child may want this act of assurance, for there is a double act of faith.

(1.) An act whereby the soul *relies upon God as reconciled in Christ*, and relies upon Christ as given of God, and relies upon the promise. And then;—

(2.) There is a *reflect act*, whereby, knowing we do thus, we have assurance. Now, a man may perform the one act and not the other. We may do that deed that may found our assurance, if the waters of the soul were not troubled; that is, we may believe and yet want assurance, because that is another distinct act that followeth upon our casting of ourselves upon God. And so, many of the dear children of God, sometimes they can hardly say that they have any assurance, but yet, notwithstanding, they can say, if they do not belie themselves and bear false witness against themselves, that they have cast themselves upon God's mercy, they have performed the first act of faith, and this faith is not fruitless altogether.

Now, there be many things that may hinder this other act, viz., that act of faith whereby I am assured of my state in grace. Sometimes God, together with my believing, will present such things to the soul as wholly take it up, so that a man cannot have definitive thoughts upon that that God would have him think of. As when God will humble a man for his boldness in adventuring upon sin, he takes not away the spirit of faith, but God, to humble him throughly, he sets before him his anger, sets before him terror, even hellish terrors, that will make him in a state little different from a reprobate for the time, so that he is far from saying that he hath any assurance at that time; yet, notwithstanding, he doth not leave off, he casts himself upon God's mercy still. Though God 'kill him, yet he will trust in him,' and yet he feels nothing but terror. And this, I say, God doth to school him, and to humble him, and to prepare him for the feeling of assurance after.

These things we must observe, that we give not a false evidence of ourselves, that though we have not such assurance as we have had and as others have, yet, I say, alway there is some ground in us, whereupon we may be assured that we are God's, if we could search it. Such ought to labour for assurance, and such will in time come to assurance. And, therefore we should be far from allowing that doctrine, which is as if a man should light a candle before the devil, as we use to say, to help him against our hearts by a doctrine of doubting, as if our naughty hearts were not ready enough of themselves to doubt.

It is the profaneness of the world—they will not use the means that God hath appointed to this end; nay, they had rather stagger, and take contentment and assurance in their own ways. If God will love me in a loose course, so it is; but 'to give diligence to make my calling and election sure,' 2 Peter i. 10, I had rather believe the popish doctrine that I ought to doubt, and only to be of a good hope; whereas we ought constantly to labour to be assured of our state in grace, that God may have more honour, and that we may have more comfort from him again, and walk more cheerfully through the troubles and temptations that are in the world.

A carnal, proud person, he swells against this doctrine, because he feels no such thing, and he thinks what is above his measure is hypocrisy. He makes himself the measure of other Christians, and therefore he values and esteems others by his dark state; for a carnal man's heart, it is like a dungeon. A man in a dungeon can see nothing, because he hath no light, but he that hath the light, he can see the dungeon. The heart of a Christian hath a light in it,—there is the Spirit in him,—and therefore he can see his own estate, and he can tell what is in him upon due search. Now, in a carnal man all is dark. He sees nothing, because his heart is in a dungeon, his eye is dark, his heart is full of darkness; all is alike to him, he sees no difference between flesh and Spirit, and therefore he holds on in a doubting hope and confused disposition and temper of soul. But a Christian that labours to walk in the comforts of the Holy Ghost, he is not content with such a confused state; and therefore we ought to abhor that doctrine by all means, and to justify this doctrine, that we ought, and that we may, have assurance of salvation in this world.*

The *second* thing which I observe, and which I join to the former, is *the doctrine of perseverance*. An earnest, you know I told you, is made up with the bargain, but it is never taken away, so that the point is this, that God's children, as they may be assured of their salvation, so

Obs. They may be assured that they shall hold out to the end.

I think many of you think these two points to be so clear that it is unnecessary to divide them; for if we be assured of our salvation, there must needs be perseverance to the end, for what kind of assurance is it to be in the state of grace to-day, and not to be to-morrow?

But if you ask some degenerated followers of Luther, that leave him in his sweet and comfortable doctrines, and take up some errors of his, and some others that would divide these, hot they are against the papists for denying the doctrine of assurance of salvation; but when they come to perseverance, they hold that a Christian may fall away altogether. These things cannot stand together, for undoubtedly it is most sure and just and right that these truths follow one the other, assurance of salvation and perseverance. And, therefore, if they maintain that we ought to be assured of salvation, and not doubt of God's love, surely then they cannot, with the same spirit and the same ground, doubt that God, that hath begun a work, will finish it to the day of the Lord. There is no question but that the one follows the other, because an earnest, as it assures us of salvation, so it assures of perseverance. Herein an earnest differs from a pawn or pledge. A pledge, it is given, but it is taken away again; but an earnest, when it is once given, is never taken away again, but as it is a part of the bargain, so it is

* Cf. Richard Blachynden's exhaustive treatise, 'Whether a Certainty of being in a State of Salvation be Attainable,' &c. 1685.—G.

filled and made up with the bargain. So grace is a part of glory, and is never taken away, but made up with perfection of glory.

From this we see, then, that he that is in the state of grace is undefeasible, he perseveres to the end, because he hath the earnest of the Spirit. If God should take away his Spirit from him, he should take away his earnest, and if he takes away his earnest, he takes away that for which he gives it, assurance of salvation, and so should overthrow all. But God never repents of his earnest. Man ofttimes repents of his earnest, and wisheth he had not made such a fruitless bargain ; but God never doth, but where he gives the first-fruits, he makes up the harvest ; where he lays the foundation, he makes up the building ; where he gives earnest, he makes up the bargain ; where he begins a good work, he finisheth it to the day of the Lord ; once his, for ever his. We cannot be so sure of anything as we may be of God's love for the time to come. We have a common speech amongst us, I know what I have, but what I shall have I know not. It is an ill speech. Thou knowest not what thou hast, for these worldly things, a man hath them so to-day as they may take to themselves wings and be gone to-morrow, for they are but vanity. I may be as rich as Job in the morning, and as poor as Job at night. So that a man knows not what he hath ; but for the time to come for grace and glory he may say, Though I know not what I have, or how long I shall have it, I know what I shall have, 'I know that neither things present, nor things to come, shall be able to separate me from the love of God in Jesus Christ,' Rom. viii. 38.

So that you see here a foundation of the sweet and comfortable doctrine of perseverance. Grace is the earnest of glory, and it doth but differ in degrees. The beginning of glory is here in grace, the consummation of it hereafter. We are anointed kings here, we shall be kings in heaven. We are sons here in this world, we shall be heirs in heaven. We shall be adopted there in soul and body, here we are adopted in soul. For in this life Christ's first coming was for the soul, his second coming is for body and soul. Therefore the resurrection is called the 'day of regeneration,' Mat. xix. 28, because then it shall be perfected: here regeneration is only begun.

So that in respect that the work of the Spirit, the graces of the Spirit are called an 'earnest,' we may know and be assured of perseverance in grace, and that that which we have now in the beginning shall be accomplished. *

O ! how should this set us upon desires to have the blessed work of the Spirit upon us, to have the Spirit to set his seal upon us, to be Christ's, to have this earnest, and to get more and more earnest till we have the full bargain accomplished in heaven.

Thirdly, I told you that an earnest is part of the whole : they therefore that have not the earnest cannot look for the bargain. The observation hence is, that—

Obs. Those that look to be happy, must first look to be holy.

This point I mean to touch very briefly. I am loath to pass it by, though it be not the principal thing I aim at, because it may serve *for a kind of trial, whether a man have any right to heaven or no.*

It is the ordinary presumptuous error of common Christians, to think to go to heaven out of unclean courses, with 'Lord, have mercy upon us ;' but miserable wretches are they that have not this 'earnest' of the Spirit in them, an earnest of heaven beforehand, in grace, and peace, and joy. We must all read our happiness in our holiness ; and therefore it is that

* Cf. Stafford Brown's 'Truth on both Sides ; or, Can the Believer Finally Fall.' 1848. 12mo.—G.

happiness in heaven and holiness here, which is happiness inchoate, have both one title, to shew that we cannot have the one without the other. We must enter into heaven here in this life.

The stones, you know, they were hewed before they were brought to the building of the temple, they were all made and fitted beforehand; and so all that shall be stones in heaven, they must be hewed, and prepared, and fitted here; there must be no knocking and fitting of them there.

So then you see these three things touched, that the Holy Spirit, together with the graces and comforts of it, are called an 'earnest,' and therefore that it is a part of the whole, an assurance of the whole, and that it shall never be taken away.

Now for the fourth, that an 'earnest' is little in regard of the whole; (and indeed the holy apostle aims at this partly as well as at any other thing else) an earnest is little, perhaps we have but a shilling to secure us of many pounds. So then the point is this, that—

Obs. Howsoever we may be assured of our estate in grace, and likewise that we shall hold out, yet the ground of this assurance is not from any great measure of grace, but though it be little in quantity, it may be great in assurance and security.

As we value an earnest not for the worth that is in itself, but because it assures us of a great bargain; we have an eye more to the consummation of the bargain, than to the quantity of the earnest: so it is here, grace is but an earnest; yet notwithstanding though it be little as an earnest is, yet it is great in assurance of validity, answerable to the relation of that it hath to assure us.

There is nothing less than a 'grain of mustard-seed,' but there is nothing in the world so little in proportion, in a manner, that comes at length to be so great, as the graces of God, and the work of the Spirit is. The crocodile, a huge creature, comes of an egg, and the oak, it riseth to that greatness from an acorn. But what are these to the wondrous work of the new creature, to be the 'heir of heaven,' rising from so little, despised beginnings, from a little light in the understanding, from a little heat in the affections, from a little strength in the will, compared for the littleness thereof to a grain of mustard-seed!

Indeed, grace grows, a man knows not how. As Christ saith of the seed sown in the earth, it grows up first 'to a blade, and then to a stalk, and then to an ear, and then to be corn,' Mark iv. 28, but a man cannot tell how; so it is with the work of grace and the comforts of the Spirit: when the Spirit together with the word works upon the soul, there is a blade, a little, and then a stalk, and then corn.

First a babe in Christ, little at the first; and as it is little, so it is much opposed. As we see the sun when it is weak in the rising in the morning: there gather a great many vapours to besiege the sun, as it were, as if they would put out the light of it, till it comes to fuller strength, and then it spends them all, and gloriously shines in heaven. So it is with the work of the Spirit of grace. When it first ariseth in the soul, there gather about it a great many doubts and discomforts; the flesh riseth and casteth up all the dirt and mud it can, to trouble the blessed waters of grace, till it have gotten fuller and fuller strength to spend them all, as it is when a man comes to be a strong Christian. But yet as little as it is, seeing it is an 'earnest,' and 'the first fruits,' as the apostle saith, which were but little in regard of the whole harvest, yet it is of the nature of the whole, and thereupon it comes to secure. A spark of fire is but little, yet it is fire as well as the whole element of fire; and a drop of water, it is water as well as the whole ocean. When a man is in a dark place,—put the case it be in a dungeon,—if he have a little light shining in to him from a little crevice, that little light discovers that the day is broke, that the sun is risen. Put the case there be but one grape on a vine, it shews that it is a vine, and that the vine is not dead. So, put the case there be but the appearance of but a little grace in a Christian, perhaps the Spirit of God appears but in one grace in him at that time, yet that one grace sheweth that we are vines, and not thistles, or thorns, or other base plants, and it shews that there is life in the root.

The Spirit of God appears not in all graces at once, it appears some time or other in some one grace. We see in plants, the virtue of them appears diversely. In winter the virtue of them lies in the root; in the spring-time, in the bud and the leaf; in the summer, in the fruit: it is not in all parts alike. So it is with the Spirit, as it is an 'earnest,' it appears not in all graces in a flourishing manner at the first. Sometimes it appears in the root, in humility, sometimes in faith, sometimes in love, sometimes in one grace, sometimes in another. Though the Spirit be in every grace, yet in appearance to a man's self and others, it appears but in one. An 'earnest' is little, especially at the first.

Weak Christians therefore should not be discouraged. 'Despise not the day of little things,' Zech. iv. 10. There is cause of mourning. We that have received the 'first-fruits' of the Spirit, we mourn because we have but the first-fruits, and we would have the full harvest; but as there is cause of mourning because we have but the first-fruits, so there is cause of comfort, because it is the first-fruits. It is an 'earnest' only, and not the whole bargain, therefore we have cause of mourning that it is so imperfect, that it is so weak as it is; yet there is cause of comfort, because though it is not the whole, yet [it] is a part, and secures us of the whole.

And therefore Christians should labour to mingle duties, and let one grace qualify another; for indeed a Christian is a mixed creature, his comforts are mixed, and his mourning is mixed. With a carnal man it is all otherwise, if he mourn he is all a mort,* because he hath no goodness; if he joy, he is mad, his mirth is madness.

A Christian joys indeed, sometimes he hath 'joy unspeakable and glorious,' 1 Peter i. 8, because he looks to his hope, and the accomplishment of it, and yet he mourns, because he hath but the 'earnest,' because he hath but the beginnings, because he hath but the first fruits here.

Use 2. And therefore again, as it should comfort us, if we have anything; so it should exhort us to examine rather the truth, than the measure of any grace. We have examined the truth, it is the truth of this 'earnest,' the truth of grace and comfort. It is an excellent speech of our Saviour Christ, in Rev. iii. to the church of Philadelphia, in verse 8, 'Because thou hast a little strength, and hast kept my word, and hast not denied my name.' There is a great promise made to the church of Philadelphia; and why? 'Because thou hast a little strength.' How is that discovered? 'Thou hast kept my word, and hast not denied my name.' So then, if that little be true, God respects not that little as it is little in quantity, but as he means to make it ere long. He looks upon the 'earnest,' as he means to make up the bargain; he looks upon the foundation, as he means to rear up a goodly building; he looks upon the first-fruits, as he means to add the harvest; and therefore, Eph. i. 4, and other places, 'We are

* That is 'dead,' = 'deeply sunken'.—G.

elected to be holy and blameless in his sight.' So Eph. v. 27, 'He purgeth the church, that she may be presented to him without spot.' So Christ looks upon his Church as he is purging and washing, till he have made it holy in his sight. We are elected, not to 'earnest,' not to 'first-fruits,' but to be 'unblameable;' we are elected to perfection. It is the comfort of Christians, that God looks upon his, not as they are imperfect here, but as they are in beginning, and as they are growing, and as he intends to bring them to perfection afterwards. For all things are present, we know, to him, the time to come, what we shall be; he considers us as if we were in heaven already; we are in our degree, and in our faith. So now 'we sit in heavenly places,' Eph. i. 3; therefore as he looks on us as we shall be, so faith answers his looking, when we are framed by the Spirit to comfort; faith looks not upon the weak 'earnest,' the poor beginnings, but as we shall be after in heaven, 'without spot and wrinkle,' Eph. v. 27.

Aye, but how shall we know the truth of his 'earnest,' that it is true, though it be little? To speak a word or two of that for trial.

Where the Spirit of God is, with the relation of an 'earnest,' he is an 'earnest' by way of grace and comfort; for those two ways the Spirit discovers himself in us, to sanctify our nature, or by comfort, and peace, and joy, and such like.

1. Then it doth stir up the soul *to mourn that* [it] *is but an 'earnest,'* as I said before, and to wait for the accomplishment, as the apostle saith in Rom. viii. 23, 'We that have received the first-fruits of the Spirit, mourn in ourselves, that it is no better with us than it is;' and withal.

2. '*We wait for the redemption of the sons of God*,' the adoption of the sons of God, we wait for the accomplishment hereafter. It is the nature therefore of the Spirit of God, as it is an earnest, to stir up the spirits of God's children to mourn something, and likewise,

3. To *wait patiently, to wait for the full accomplishment hereafter;* and as a fruit of their waiting, to endure quietly, patiently, and comfortably that which is between the earnest, and the accomplishment of it. And therefore God gives them the grace of hope and constancy, and of perseverance, till all be accomplished; for there is the tediousness of time, between which is irksome, hope deferred, and a tediousness of deferring, and besides many afflictions withal.

Now God's children that have the earnest of the Spirit, they have a spirit likewise to wait; and that they may be strengthened to wait, they have,

4. The *spirit of constancy*, a spirit of patience to endure trouble, and to persevere, and to hold out in regard of the tediousness of the time. So that they may not give over religious courses, though they have it not fully here, but go on still, and wait. And likewise those that have the earnest of the Spirit, that have the Spirit, as it hath this qualification upon it of an earnest, it stirs them up,

5. *To frame themselves, answerable to the full accomplishment;* for 'He that hath this hope,' saith the apostle, 'purgeth himself,' 1 John iii. 3. He that finds some little beginnings of grace and comfort, the beginnings of heaven upon earth, he frames himself to the perfect state in heaven; for it is the nature of faith and hope, wheresoever they are, to frame the disposition of the person in whom those graces are planted by the Spirit, to the condition of that soul that believes and hopes, for it is in the nature of the thing it should be so. For doth not hope in any man that hopes to appear before some great person, make him alter his attire, and fashion his carriage and deportment, as may be plausible before the person whom

he goes to? and doth not faith and hope of better things, where they are in truth, fashion and dispose every man to be such as may be fit for heaven? The title to heaven we have indeed by Christ; but the soul knows there must be a qualification, 'No unclean thing shall enter into heaven,' Rev. xxi. 27; and therefore where the 'earnest' is, there is a continual desire to be better, a continual relinquishing of corruption more and more, a perfecting of the work of mortification, and the work of grace more and more; for the same Spirit that is an earnest, and gives us any beginning of a better life, it likewise stirs us up, it fits and prepares us for that state that is kept for us. It is impossible it should be otherwise. In what strength the 'earnest' is, in that strength sanctification and mortification are; and therefore persons that live in sins against conscience, that defile their tongues, and defile their bodies, let them talk what they will, it is but a presumptuous conceit. It is not the voice of God's Spirit, but of carnal presumption; for wheresoever the Spirit is an 'earnest' of heaven, it is always preparing and fitting the soul for that glorious and happy estate. And wheresoever likewise this earnest of the Spirit is, wheresoever this grace is begun in truth,

6. There *is a desire of accomplishment*, an earnest desire of the coming of Christ to finish all, to finish the bargain. Rev. xxii. 17, 'The Spirit and the spouse say, Come;' that is, the spouse by direction of the Spirit, where the spouse is guided by the Spirit; and so far as the spouse is guided by the Spirit, she saith, 'Come, come, Lord Jesus, come quickly,' Rev. xxii. 20.

Cautions. Except in two cases, (1.) Except the Christian *hath grieved and wounded his conscience, grieved the Spirit*, and then it is loath to go hence. (2.) Unless likewise the spirit of a Christian *be careless, and would settle things in better order before he go to Christ;* for this is the fruit of presumption, and carelessness, that it grieves the Spirit of God, and the Spirit being grieved, grieves them. He makes that which should be their comfort, their going to Christ by death, he makes it terrible; for as we see a weak eye cannot endure the light, so a galled guilty conscience trembles to think of Christ's coming. Though the 'earnest' be there; yet if the soul tremble, that the soul be wounded, stay a while, 'O stay!' saith the psalmist, 'before I go hence, and be no more seen.' When the wife hath been negligent, she would have her husband stay;* but when she hath been diligent, then the wife is willing her husband should come; but perhaps things are not settled as they should, and therefore she doth not desire his coming as at other times.

But take a Christian in his right temper, he is willing to die; nay, he is willing, and glad, and joyful to go to Christ. Then he knows the earnest shall be accomplished with the bargain; then he knows what God hath begun, he will perfect; then he knows, all the promises shall be performed, when all imperfection shall be removed, and all enemies shall be conquered, &c. A carnal man doth not say as the Spirit in the spouse speaks, 'Come, Lord, come;' but stay, Lord, stay;† and as the devil that possessed that person, 'What have we to do with thee? Art thou come to torment us before our time?' Mat. viii. 29. They think of it with quaking. For otherwise they that have the earnest of the Spirit, have joyful thoughts of it, and wishes answerable to those thoughts.

7. Again, wheresoever this earnest is in truth, the earnest of the Spirit, *there is growth;* for it is the nature of things imperfect to come to their per-

* and † That is, 'stay *away*.'—G.

fection, that they may encounter with whatsoever is contrary to them, and that they may do their functions that they are fitted by for God.

Now God having fitted the new creature to serve him, and to go through all the impediments in this world, and all the crosses, where he hath begun this work, it will labour to come to perfection. As in the natural body we are not content to live; but when we have life, we desire health; and when we have health, we are not content with that, but we desire strength; not only health, but strength to perform that we should do. So where the spiritual life is begun, the living soul is not content to live, to find an 'earnest,' a little beginnings, but if he have that, he would have health, he would not have any spiritual disease to lie on the soul, that might hinder it in the functions of it; and together with health, it desires fuller and fully strength, because it hath many temptations to encounter with, many corruptions to resist, many actions to do, many afflictions perhaps to bear, all which require a great deal of strength. Wheresoever grace is in truth, it is always with a desire of growth, and answerable to that desire will be the use of all the means of growth. Again, to name one or two more, and so end:

8. Wheresoever the Spirit is as an 'earnest,' it doth as the seal doth, spoken of before, that as it hath a quieting power, an assuring power, *it quiets the soul.* Wheresoever it is, it is given to stay the soul, to comfort it, that the whole shall be performed in time; and therefore the soul that hath the 'earnest of the Spirit,' so far forth as he hath this 'earnest,' it quiets and stays the soul. A man may know true faith from false, and true earnest from presumption by this, as we know other things; I say, it stills and quiets the soul, and

9. *It will endure the trial.* We say of alchemy* gold, *it is counterfeit*, it will not strengthen the heart. True gold hath a corroborating power to strengthen the heart (whether it be so or no, let the alcumists look to it); but it is true, that true 'earnest,' the beginnings of faith, though it be but in a little measure, it hath a quieting, a stilling, a strengthening power, to strengthen and corroborate the soul, for it is given for that purpose. And a man that hath the least grace will endure the search, as true gold will endure the touchstone, the false will not. And it is a sign that a man hath true grace in him, although it be with much imperfection, that desires *to be searched in preaching:* hearing searching sermons, and desiring to be searched in conference, and that doubts not his conscience, but would be searched throughly. When men fret at the searching of their sins, they will not be searched, and are content to go on in presumptuous courses, and think all is well, it is a sign there is not so much as an 'earnest.' But not to go further, that in the Revelation shews the truth of a little grace; what saith he? 'Thou hast a little strength.' What doth that little strength move the church of Philadelphia to do? 'Thou hast kept my word, and hast not denied my name.'

10. Where there is a little strength, *there will be a keeping of the word in obedience*, a keeping of it in conversation; where is not a regard to God's word, a moulding of the soul into it in obedience of it, there is not so much as a little strength of grace, and therefore those that live in rebellious courses, have not so much as an earnest to them; yet, 'Thou hast kept my word,' and withal, 'thou hast not denied my name.'

11. Where a little strength is, there they will not deny Christ's name, *they will hold out* in the profession of the truth, and confess it if occasion

* Spelled 'alcumy,' and a little onward 'alcumists.—G.

serve. And therefore where any are slight in their profession, that give in if they be ready to dash upon any displeasure of any one; if they be to venture their estates or so, then they are ashamed of Christ, and that profession which they took upon them; they deny his name, at least they do not own it, they have not so much as a little strength, if they do not recover. Peter was in such a temptation, but he recovered his strength, and got more strength, and a firm standing upon it: the shaking of Peter was for the rooting of him.

So God to shame his children, suffers them sometimes to have dastardly spirits, but they recover themselves, they are ashamed of it. But those that are common politicians in this kind, that will not stand out in a good cause to maintain their truth and profession, when God thrusts his cause into their hands, specially at such times when God saith to them, 'Who is on my side? who?' 2 Kings ix. 32, now is the time to appear then. If they have not a word for God, they will not own the quarrel and cause of God and religion, they have not a little strength; for they that have a little strength here, keep the word and have not denied the name. Those therefore that can fashion themselves to all religions, to all companies, they will have a religion mutable and flexible to their occasions; where is the earnest of the Spirit? The Spirit, as much as he is, is strong and vigorous, and powerful. These men have not so much as a little strength, that are as water which is fashioned to the vessel it is in, like to the Samaritans, as Josephus* the historian of the Jews writes of them (*eeee*). When the Jews prospered, oh! then they would be Jews; when the Jews had ill success, then they were great enemies to the Jews; so you have many that are no friends to the afflicted, to the disgraced truth; but as long as the cause of religion is carried out with the countenance of the State, with the favour of great ones, so far they will own it; but if Christ once comes to be abased, they will not know Christ, nor his cause.

I beseech you, let us take notice of it. It is a sign there is no grace at all, where there is such an habitual disposition without shame or grief, or repentance; for God's children sometimes may be overtaken with a spirit of dastardliness, which afflicts them sore afterwards, that they gather more strength. A man may know if he be God's child in such a state; for it is universally true, God's children are never overtaken with a spirit of cowardliness and fear, but they regain it, and grow more strong upon it; as we see in Cranmer and others (*ffff*). God purposeth sometimes to let them see what they are in themselves without his support and strength; but afterwards they gather new resolutions, new purposes to stick firmer to the truth than e'er before. I might add many other things, but I go on to that which follows.

You see here now how we may try, if we have any true 'earnest' in us at all or no.

Now I beseech you, let us labour *to have this 'earnest,'* if we have it not, to have this assurance especially. Let me desire those of the younger sort to labour to have the seal of this Spirit, and the 'earnest' before they be further and further engaged into the world, and before they be so hardened that they will not receive a contrary stamp to their corruptions. It is a wondrous advantage that gentlemen, and others that are young, before the world hath soiled them, and before their understandings be darkened, and their affections are crooked, and carried away much with the stream and errors of the time, they have much advantage above others, for they have spirits fitter for grace, fitter to receive the impression of this seal of the Spirit,

* Spelled 'Joseph.'—G.

and fitter for the 'earnest.' Let us labour for this earnest betimes. What a comfortable thing will it be to carry along with the 'earnest' an assurance of a better estate from our youth to our age, and from our age to our old age, and so to heaven with us! What a deal of comfort do young ones deprive and rob themselves of, that will not be gracious betimes! Let us labour to have the stamp of the Spirit set on us in our prime time, in the strength of our years. But I will press the point, if the time will give leave, afterwards.

Now we must know, that God gives this earnest *not for himself, but for us*, to secure us; and that is one reason why it is called an earnest.

There is besides bargaining another state and condition that 'earnest' is applied unto, which perhaps the apostle aims at, as marriage; whatsoever was before the consummation of the marriage, was a kind of *Arrah*,* a kind of 'earnest,' to assure the affection of the contracted person and persons that loved one another, till the consummation of the marriage.

So Christ now contracts us on the earth, and having love to us, and taking our nature on him, that he might woo us in our own flesh, and in our own nature, taking upon him the 'earnest' of our flesh, he gives us the 'earnest' of his Spirit; and to assure us that he loves us, and that he means to make up the bargain afterwards, he sends us love tokens, graces, and comfort and joy. Even as Isaac when he was to marry Rebecca, he sent by his servants bracelets and jewels, and such things, to secure† her of his love, Gen. xxiv. 53.

So Christ in heaven intending the consummation of the match, he sends us here graces and comforts of the Spirit, and all to secure us: all is for us, I say, which I observe the rather, because I would raise your hearts to hate unbelief and distrust exceedingly, because God labours to undermine it by all means possible.

Wherefore doth he use so many terms here, of 'sealing,' 'anointing,' and 'earnest,' with words and sacraments, and all whatsoever may confirm you? The Holy Ghost applies it to us. All this is that we may not doubt of the favour of God: and therefore when we find any goodness in us, let us account that to give false witness against ourselves is a horrible sin; it is to make God a liar. God stands upon his credit; and therefore take heed what we say (specially if we have found the work of grace in former time, any 'earnest'), that we have no grace. God doth this for our assurance. All his dealing of word and sacraments, of earnest and oath, and all that may be to assure us; and therefore we should not cross the goodness of God, so as to cherish such a disposition as is most contrary to him, that he labours to undermine by all means.

And, therefore, here is the poison of popish religion, that it maintains doubting, and leaves men doubting. Indeed they do well to maintain it in their doctrine, for indeed they false-found a man upon satisfaction, they false-found him upon purgatory and merits, and the foundation they have of a Christian soul is uncertain; and therefore they may well teach doubting: it suits with the course that they take. But I say it is very corrupt, for God useth all means that we should not doubt; and therefore it is idly objected, God for his part will, but for our part we have reason to doubt. Why! he in all things stoops to us, he labours to secure us; and therefore in the covenant of grace he doth his part and ours too.

* That is, ἀῤῥαβών = earnest, pledge. The Scotch '*arles*,' or earnest-money seems to preserve this, and is a curious example of an unexpected etymology.—G.

† That is = assure, make her certain of.—G.

But I hasten to that which follows, because I would end with the time. To touch that a little distinctly by itself, that the Spirit doth all, the 'earnest of the Spirit:' for indeed, though Spirit be not added to stablishing, yet the Spirit stablisheth by Christ, and the Spirit anoints, and the Spirit 'seals to the day of redemption,' and 'the earnest of the Spirit.'

So it is the Holy Ghost doth all. Here you have the three Persons in the Trinity. We have three grand enemies, 'the world, the flesh, and Satan.' Now here are the three Persons in the Trinity stronger than all our enemies. 'He which stablisheth us, is God the Father, by his Spirit:' upon whom? upon Christ, 'in Christ,' and gives 'us the earnest of his Spirit.' You have, I say, the three Persons of the Trinity here. But why doth the Spirit give us the earnest? why doth the Spirit give us grace and comfort, seal us, and doth all, and stablish us?

1. I answer, first of all, because now since the fall *we have no principles of supernatural good*, and therefore it must be a principle above our nature to work both grace and comforts in our barren hearts.

2. Again, as there is no principle to that which is supernaturally good, *so there is opposition to that which is supernaturally good;* and therefore there must be somewhat to overpower the corruptions of our nature.

(1.) But why the Spirit, rather than the Father and the Son? *He comes from both;* and proceeding from both he is fit to witness the love of both. For the Holy Ghost is in the breast of the Father and the Son, and proceeds from both, and he knows the secret love of the Father to us, and the love of Christ Jesus Mediator to us.

Now the Spirit knowing the secrets of God, as a man's spirit, saith the apostle, knows his own secrets, he knows his love, and he knows whom he loves! So the Spirit of God knowing the affection of the Father, and the affection of Jesus Christ to us, is fit to be an 'earnest,' fit to be a 'seal.'

Indeed all things are wrought by the Spirit in grace for application; the desert* is from the Son, originally from the Father; but in regard of application of what is wrought by the Son, all is by the Holy Ghost. Both graces and comforts the Holy Ghost takes from Christ; for if grace be wrought, it is with divine reasons from the love of God in Christ. If grace be wrought, it is from the wondrous love of God reconciled in Christ, wherein heaven is opened, hell is vanquished. It is by reasons fetched from Christ; and so 'he takes of mine,' as Christ saith, 'He shall take of mine, and give to you,' John xvi. 15. He takes reasons from Christ,—the Holy Ghost,†—whereby he makes all. The application is altogether by the Spirit.

(2.) And it must be by the Spirit again, because the Spirit of God, and no less than the Spirit, *can quiet our spirits*. For when the soul is distempered, it is like a distempered lock that no key can open: so when the conscience is troubled, what creature can settle the troubled conscience? can open the ambages‡ of a troubled conscience in such perplexity and confusion? and therefore to settle the troubled conscience aright, it must be somewhat above conscience; and that which must quiet the spirit, must be such a Spirit as is above our spirits. This is excellently set down in this epistle, in the third chapter, the work of the Holy Ghost in this kind. But I cannot stand upon it now at this time. I go on.

* That is, 'merit.'—Ed.
† That is, 'He, the Holy Ghost, takes reasons from Christ.'—G.
‡ That is, 'winding-passages,' = subterfuges, evasions.—G.

Likewise in the first Epistle to the Corinthians, the second chapter, and 11th verse, that one place shall stand instead of all. 'What man knows the things of a man, but the spirit of a man that is in him? So the things of God no man knows but the Spirit.'

Now, 'We have received the spirit, not of the world, but the Spirit of God, to know the things that are freely given us of God.' If our spirits were in the heart and soul of another man, in the breast of another man, we should know what another man thinks. If a man had a spirit in another man's spirit, surely he would know all his thoughts and all his affections.

Now the Holy Spirit of God is in the breast of the Father, and the Son, and he knows our spirits better than we know our own spirits; he searcheth, he is a 'searcher,' as the word is in the original (*gggg*). The Spirit is a searcher. He searcheth our own hearts, and he searcheth the secret love of God to us, that is, the Spirit must stablish us.

Well then, if the Spirit doth all, how shall we know then that we have this Spirit? A note or two, and so go on.

1. If we have this Spirit of God to seal us, and to be an earnest (I will not speak all that may be, but a little; for indeed all comes from the Spirit), even as in our souls, how may a man know that he hath a soul? *by living and moving, by actions vital*, &c., so we may know a man hath the Spirit of God by those actions that come only from the Spirit, which is to the soul, as the soul is in the body: for as all beauty and motion comes from the soul to the body, so to the soul from the Spirit, all comes of the Spirit, and therefore every saving grace is a sign that the Spirit is in us.

2. In a word, the Spirit is in us in the nature of fire, as in other things, so in this, *in transforming*. Wheresoever the Spirit dwells, he transforms the soul, he transforms the party like himself holy and gracious. Those therefore that find the Spirit transforming and changing them in the use of the ordinance of the word, they may know that they have the Spirit sealing them, and being an earnest to them.

3. They may know likewise, that they have it wrought by the Spirit, for every one grace, you may know spiritual graces are *with conflict;* for what is true, is with a great deal of resistance of that which is counterfeit.

Comforts and graces that are not the earnest of the Spirit, are with little conflict; but where there are true comforts and graces of the Spirit wrought by the Spirit, it is with much conflict with Satan and with himself; for there is a great deal of envy in the devil against the man that walks in the Spirit. Thinks he, what! such a base creature as this is to have the 'earnest' of heaven, to walk here as if he were in heaven already, and to defy all opposite powers! Nay, I will trouble his peace, he shall go mourning to heaven, if he go there. This is the reasoning of the cursed spirit, and hereupon he labours to shake the assurance and persuasion; and the grace and comfort of a Christian,—it is with much conflict and temptation, not only with Satan, but with his own heart.

Our hearts misgive us, when we are guilty of some sins, as always there is guilt on the soul,—so much guilt, so much doubt. Till the soul be free from guilt, it will never but be casting of doubts; and therefore there is always resistance in us, and there must be a higher power than the heart and soul of a man to set the heart down and quiet it; it is always in conflict.

4.* And the graces and comforts of the Spirit wrought by the Spirit, are

* In margin, 'By supernatural obedience.'—G.

always in the use of means, holy means; and it carries a man *above the strength of nature*, it carries a man to the practice of that which he could not do by nature, to pardon his enemies, to pray for them, to overcome revenge, and to enjoy prosperity without pride, in a comfortable measure; and it enables him to practise the last commandment, that he shall be content with his estate, and not lust after others; and the first commandment. The graces of the Holy Spirit enables a man to love God, and to rejoice in him above all as his best portion. It makes his joy spiritual, and it makes him delight in all connatural things that are like the Spirit; as whatsoever is spiritual is connatural to the Spirit.

If a man have the graces of the Spirit, he joys in spiritual company, he joys in the presence of God, he hates sin as being contrary to the 'earnest of the Spirit,' he hates terror of conscience, and the way unto it. He will look on good things as God looks on them, and as the Spirit looks on them, and everything that is spiritual he relisheth, 'he favours the things of the Spirit,' Mark viii. 33.

Now because I will not detract* your thoughts, there are some six or seven properties of the Spirit in one chapter, that you may have them all together in Rom. viii. I will not name all, but such as are easy.

5. First of all, it is said in the 9th verse, that the Spirit where it is, *it dwells* as in a house. Now, wheresoever the Spirit is, he is dwelling and ruling; for the Holy Ghost will not be an underling to lusts, and he repairs and makes up the breaches of the soul. Where the Spirit dwells, all the breaches are made up. Ignorance to knowledge, he begets knowledge, and affection, and love; he prepares all, he prepares his own dwelling, and it is familiar and constant to the Spirit. A dwelling implies familiarity and constancy. He is not in us, as he is in wicked men that have the Spirit. As Austin saith, 'The Spirit of God knocks at their hearts, but he doth not dwell there' (*hhhh*).

To go on, that is the first. The Spirit dwells in us, if we have the Spirit.

6. And then the Spirit *doth subdue the contrary;* for the Spirit, when it comes into a man, it pulls down all the 'strongholds,' it makes way for itself; and, therefore, it is said to 'mortify the deeds of the flesh,' ver. 13. If you mortify the deeds of the flesh by the Spirit, you are led by the Spirit. Those, therefore, that by the help of the Spirit, by spiritual reasons, subdue their corruptions, they are led by the Spirit; those that cherish corruptions, or mortify them, not by spiritual reasons, but out of civil respect, to carry authority among men, and, therefore, they would be free from aspersions, as might disable their reputation, they have not the Spirit.

7. Thirdly, as many as are led by the Spirit, *are the sons of God;* the Spirit *leads them.* As the angel that went before the Israelites from Egypt unto Canaan; so the Spirit of God, like the angel, goes before us, and leads us the way, and removes the lets.† It doth lead us, I say, sweetly, and not violently, as the devil leads his that are possessed with his spirit. So that those that have the Spirit working grace and comfort in them, sweetly he leads them, and yet strongly too; for it is strongly, because it is against corruption and opposition from without; but yet sweetly, preserving the liberty and freedom of the soul. We by nature are like children or blind men; we cannot lead ourselves, and, therefore, the Spirit leads us. Those therefore that have the Spirit, it leads them, they submit themselves to the guidance and leading of the Spirit. That is another evidence.

* Qu. 'distract'? or perhaps = divert, turn aside.—G.

† That is, hindrances. Cf. note *d*, vol. I. p. 101.—G.

8. A fourth is this, That *it is a spirit of adoption*. It assures us that we are the sons of God; it gives us assurance of our adoption, that we are the sons of God. The same Spirit that sanctifieth us, it witnesseth to us, it makes us holy. It witnesseth to us that we are the sons of God.

9. And then again, the Spirit *stirs up* 'sighs and groans that cannot be expressed,' Rom. viii. 26, when we are not of ourselves *able to pray*. This is an evidence of the 'earnest' of the Spirit, when we can send our sighs and groans to God. I say, God will hear the groans, the voice of his own Spirit. For whence come those sighs and groans to God? Why! should we not rather sink in despair in troubles, but because the Spirit is in us? Those therefore that in extremity, having nothing to comfort them, and yet are able to send forth sighs and groans to God, they may certainly know that they have the Spirit.

10. And, likewise, the Spirit makes us *mourn and wait for the adoption* of the 'sons of God.' Those that mourn and wait, have the evidence of the Spirit; for a worldling doth not mourn for his imperfections, for his corruptions: he doth not mourn that he is absent from his Saviour, neither doth he wait for the accomplishment of that that shall be bestowed on saints, because he hath his portion here. Therefore, those that can mourn for their corruptions, for those things which the world is not able to tax them for, because they cannot serve God with enlargement of the Spirit as they would; and they wait also without despair, or without discouragement, till God have finished their course, they are led with a better Spirit than the world.

Though I should name no more, what a many sweet evidences are here to manifest a soul truly acted, and guided, and led by the Spirit. But these shall be sufficient for this time.

Well then, if the Spirit doth all, if the Spirit anoint and seal, and give 'earnest' of grace, and comfort, and all, till he bring us to heaven, being Christ's Vicar (for Christ hath no other vicar on earth but his Spirit); if the Spirit doth all, as indeed he doth all for God to us, and from us to God (whatsoever God doth to us it is by the Spirit; he anoints, and seals, and sanctifieth by the Spirit; and whatsoever we do to God, it is by the Spirit, or else it is not acceptable; we sigh and groan in the Spirit, we pray in the Holy Ghost, saith Jude, ver. 20, and that God doth to us immediately from the Spirit, and all that we do to God, is in the Spirit). Is this so, then is it an undoubted truth, oh then! we should labour by all means for this Spirit of God. To give some directions in a word, and so to end.

1. Labour, I say, to have the Spirit, and to groan in the Spirit; and to this end, because the word is the chariot of the Spirit, in which the Spirit is carried, *attend upon the ordinances of God, and use all kind of spiritual means*, wherein the Spirit is usually effectual; for the Spirit will only work with his own means. All those bastard inventions and devices fetched from the Church of Rome, human devices in God's service, they are naught. God's Spirit will not be effectual with popish devices; and, therefore, Rome is 'the habitation of devils,' Rev. xviii. 2. God's Spirit hath nothing to do there, because they have set up a worship contrary to God's worship, they have set up a covenant contrary to Christ's covenant, they have set up the covenant of works, and deny, in a manner, a covenant of grace. Christ is not taught as he should be there.

Now, wheresoever the Spirit is, it is with the clear teaching of the gospel. 'Received you the Spirit by hearing of the law, or of faith preached?'

Gal. iii. 2. Therefore, let us attend upon the unfolding of Christ Jesus in the gospel; for the Spirit is given with a clear and true unfolding of Christ; and omit no spiritual means, wherein the Spirit is effectual, as meditation, reading, &c.

For as a man working in a garden, though he think not of it, perhaps he draws a sweet scent of the flowers, there is a tincture from the air that is round about him.

So the word of God being indited by the Spirit of God, we being in holy company, being led by the same Spirit, a man shall either by reading of the word, or in holy company, or conversing in good books, he shall draw a spiritual sweetness from the word, or from those that he hath to deal with.

The spirit of a man is like water that runs from minerals. As we see baths have their warmth from minerals that they run through, they have a tincture from them to be hot in this or that degree, in this or that quality; so it is with the soul, when it runs through holy things, when it hath to deal with good books, and good company, &c., it draweth a spiritual tincture. And, therefore, if we would have the Spirit of God to guide us, let us be much in those things that the Holy Ghost hath sanctified us for that end, at all times, when we have liberty from our callings.

2. And withal, take heed that *we grieve not the Holy Ghost any way*, if we will have the Spirit to 'seal' us, to increase our earnest.

How do we grieve the Holy Ghost?

(1.) By *cherishing contrary affections, and lusts, and desires*. And resist not the Holy Ghost; as now when you hear the word of God, if you shut your resolutions, if you shut your hearts, and resolve not to give way to any instruction that shall be delivered, this is a resisting of the Holy Ghost. God now knocks at the hearts of those that are here, by his word and Spirit; and therefore we should 'open the everlasting doors, and let the King of glory come in,' Ps. xxiv. 7, 9.

We should lay open all to the Spirit. Oh, when the Spirit, when Christ is so willing to give the Spirit, it cannot be any but our fault, if we be no more spiritual than we are; for indeed there is nothing in a manner required to be spiritual, but not to resist the Spirit.

The Holy Ghost presseth upon us in the word such reasons of heavenly-mindedness, of despising of earthly things, of purging ourselves from the corruptions in the world, such reasons to be good, that indeed none are damned in the bosom of the church, but such as set a bar against the Spirit of God in their hearts, with a cursed resolution that they will not be better, that they will not part with their cursed lusts. Therefore they are damned, because they will be damned, that, say the preachers by the word, and Spirit, what they will, they think it better to be as they are, than to entertain such a guest as will mar and alter all that was there before. Take heed therefore of resisting of the Spirit, and of grieving of the Spirit by any thing in ourselves, or by conversing with company that will grieve him.

He that hath the Spirit of God in him, cannot endure carnal company; for what shall he hear, what shall he draw in at his senses? but that which will be vexation of spirit to him. Therefore it is said of Lot, 'His righteous soul was vexed with the unclean conversation of the Sodomites,' 2 Pet. ii. 7. It is an undoubted sign of a man that hath no grace, not to care for his company that hath grace.

(2.) Likewise *yield all obedience and subjection to the Spirit*, and to all the motions of the word and Spirit; bring our hearts into subjection, lay ourselves, as it were, before the Spirit, suffer ourselves to be moved, and fashioned, and framed by it; for God gives his Holy Spirit to them that obey him.

(3.) And *beg the Spirit* also as the principal thing. 'God gives the Spirit,' saith Christ, 'to them that ask him,' Luke xi. 13; and by Christ's manner of speaking there, he insinuates, as if he should say, What can I give you better than the Holy Ghost? and yet this will I give you, if you ask him, that is the good thing that God gives; for indeed, that is the seed of all graces, and of all comfort; and therefore a world of promises are included in that promise, that he 'will give the Spirit to them that ask him.'

Labour by these and such like means for the Spirit; and then if you have the Spirit, the 'earnest' of the Spirit, and the 'seal' of the Spirit, then mark what will come of such a temper of soul. That will go through all conditions whatsoever, come what will; for the Spirit is above all, and the comforts of the Spirit are above all earthly comforts; and the graces of the Spirit are able to encounter with all temptations.

So that a man that hath the Spirit, stands impregnable. The work of grace cannot be quenched, because it is the effect and the work of the Spirit. All the powers of all the devils in hell cannot stir it. God may hide his comfort for a time, to humble us; but to quench the work of the Spirit once wrought in the heart, all the power of all the devils in hell cannot quench the least spark of saving grace. It will carry us through all opposition whatsoever.

Let a man never baulk or decline in a good cause, for anything that he shall suffer; for the 'seal' and the 'earnest' of the Spirit is never more strong than when we have no other comfort by us but that: when we can draw comfort from the well-head, from the spring; therefore we should labour for the earnest of the Spirit; for it will fit us for all conditions whatsoever.

What makes a man differ from himself? What makes a man differ from another? Take a man that hath the 'earnest' of the Spirit, you shall have him defy death, the world, Satan, and all temptations. Take a man that is negligent in labouring to increase his earnest, you shall have him weak, and not like himself.

The apostle Peter, before the Holy Ghost came upon him, the voice of a weak damsel astonished him; but after, how willing was he to suffer any thing! Therefore let us not labour much to strengthen ourselves with the things of this life, or to value ourselves by our dependence upon others. If thou hast grace, thou hast that that will stand by thee when all other things fail; for all other things will be taken away, but the Comforter shall never be taken away; it goes along with us continually.

1. First, *it works 'earnest' in us*, and then it stamps upon us his own mark; and then it leads us from grace to grace; and in the hour of death, then especially it hath the work of a Comforter, to present to us the fruits of a good and holy life, and likewise the joys of heaven. When we are dead the Spirit watcheth over our bodies, because they were 'the temples of the Holy Ghost,' and at the day of judgment the same Spirit shall knit both body and soul together, and after, the same Spirit that hath done all this, shall be all in all to us in heaven for ever, and then our very bodies shall be spiritual, whereas now our souls, even the better part of them, is carnal. Even as the fire when it possesseth a piece of iron, it is all fire; so our bodies shall be all spiritual.

What a blessed thing is this, to have the Spirit! What are all friends to the Holy Ghost, which will speak to God for us! The Spirit will make request with sighs and groans, and God will hear the voice of his own Spirit.

What prison can shut up the Spirit of God? Above all, labour to have more of the Spirit of God. This will make us more or less fruitful, more or less glorious in our profession, more or less willing to die. Labour to increase this 'earnest,' that the nearer we come to heaven, the more we may be fitted for it.

Consider but this reason, if you want this, alas! we can never be thankful to God for anything, if by the Spirit we have not assurance that our state is the state of grace. For otherwise we might think that God gives us all in anger, as a carnal man, he always fears that God fats him as an ox to the slaughter. What a fearful case is this, that a man cannot be thankful for that he hath!

2. Labour for the Spirit, *that we may be thankful to God for everything*, that we may see the love of God in everything, in every refreshing we take; that that love of God that fits us for heaven, and that fits heaven for us, it gives us daily bread. The earnest of the Spirit will make us thankful for everything.

3. Again, labour for the 'earnest' of the Spirit, *that we may be joyful in all conditions*. How can a man suffer willingly, that knows not that he is sealed with the Spirit; that knows not that God hath begun a good work in him? Alas! he is lumpish and heavy under the cross.

What makes a man bear the cross willingly, but this assurance? what makes him deny himself in temptations, and corruptions? Oh! saith the child of God, the work of the Spirit is begun in me, sealing me up to life everlasting, shall I grieve and quench this Spirit for this base lust? But a man that hath not the Spirit, saith, I had as good take this pleasure, as have none at all; for aught I know, I shall have none; he sees no greater pleasure than the following of his lust.

So that none can resist temptations, but he that hath the Spirit giving him earnest in a comfortable measure; and it is a good sign when we resist temptations for spiritual reasons, that the Spirit works it.

4. Again, unless we have this earnest of the Spirit in our hearts, we can never *be content to end our days with comfort*. He that hath the earnest of the Spirit is glad of death when it comes. There shall be then an accomplishment of all the bargain. Then the marriage shall be consummate, then shall be the year of Jubilee, the Sabbath of rest for ever. Then is the triumph, and 'then all tears shall be wiped from our eyes,' Rev. vii. 17.

But now let a man stagger and doubt whether he be the child of God or no, that he cannot find any mark of the child of God in him, that he cannot read the evidences of a Christian state in his soul, they are so dim, he sees nothing but corruption in him, he sees no change, no resistance of corruption, he hath no earnest. Alas! what a miserable case is such a man in when he comes to die! Death, with the eternity of misery after it, who can look it in the face, without hope of life everlasting, without assurance of a happy change after death? Therefore we should labour for the Spirit, that howsoever we grow or decay in wealth and reputation, let God alone with that; but above all, beg of God that he would increase in us, and renew the earnest, and the stamp of the Spirit, that we may have somewhat in our souls, wherein we may see the evidences of a Christian estate.

I might add many things to this purpose, but this is sufficient to any judicious Christian, to encourage us to labour for the Spirit above all things in the world. All other are but grass, but fading; but grace and glory, grace, and peace, and joy, nay, the very 'earnest' of the Spirit, is better than all earthly things; for the earnest of it is 'joy unspeakable, and glorious, and peace that passeth all understanding,' 1 Pet. i. 8.

If the promise and the earnest here be so, I beseech you, what shall the accomplishment of the promise be? If the promises, laid hold on by faith, so quicken and cheer the soul, and if the giving a taste of heaven lift a Christian's spirit above all earthly discouragements, what shall it be when the Spirit shall be all in all in us, if the earnest be so comfortable? But I go on to the next verse.

VERSE 23.

'*Moreover, I call God to record upon my soul, that to spare you, I came not yet to Corinth.*' In this verse the apostle labours to remove suspicion of levity and inconstancy. There were jealousies in the minds of the Corinthians, which were also fomented by some vain-glorious teachers amongst them, that laboured to undermine St Paul in the hearts of the Corinthians, as if he had not loved the Corinthians so well as they did. Therefore he is so careful to clear himself in their thoughts, from suspicion of inconstancy, and want of love to them; because suspicion grounded upon the lightness in his carriage, might reflect upon his doctrine.

He knew well enough the malice of man's nature, and therefore he is very curious, and industrious, to make a clear passage for himself into the hearts of these Corinthians by all means possible, as we heard in part out of the 17th verse.

'*Moreover, I call God to record,*' *&c.* St Paul is here purging himself still, to clear himself.

First, he labours to clear himself from the suspicion of inconstancy, and want of love to them in not coming.

Secondly, he sets down the true cause why he did not come: 'I came not, to spare you.'

You were much to blame in many things, and among the rest of the abominations among you, you cherished the incestuous person, and many of you doubted of the resurrection. I should have been very severe, if I had come, therefore 'I came not, to spare you,' hoping that my letter would work upon your spirits, so that I need not be severe to you; therefore do not suspect that for any ill mind I came not, for it was to spare you, that I might not be forced to be severe.

Then the *third* thing is, the sealing of this speech with a serious oath, 'I call God for record upon my soul, that I came not, to spare you.' So here is the wiping away of suspicion, and the setting down the true cause why he did not come, and the ratifying and confirming it by an oath: he makes his purgation here by an oath. These three things I will briefly touch.

First of all, you see here he *avoids* suspicion of lightness* which the Corinthians had of him, partly by the false suggestion of proud teachers among them, who fomented their suspicious dispositions, because they would weaken St Paul's esteem among the Corinthians. They had a conceit he

* That is, 'frees himself from.'—G.

was an uncertain man: he promised to come, and did not; now here he declines that suspicion.

Where, first, observe these two things briefly.

First, that the nature of man is inclined to suspicion.

And *secondly*, that it is *the duty of men to avoid it as much as may be, and to wipe it away, if it cannot be avoided.*

Obs. Man's nature is prone to suspicion.

Man's nature is prone to suspect ill of another, though never so good. Christ could not avoid it. Because he conversed sociably with other men, he was thought to be a 'wine-bibber,' 'a companion of sinners.' And God himself was suspected of Adam in innocency. The devil is so cunning, that he calls God himself into question, as if he had not meant so well to him. What will that impudent spirit do, that will bring the creature in suspicion of him that is goodness itself? 'God knows that when you eat, your eyes shall be open, and you shall be as gods, knowing good and evil,' Gen. iii. 5. Do you think that he intends you any good, in forbidding you to eat, &c.? He did not spare Christ, innocency itself, clothed with man's flesh; and will he spare to bring uncharitable suspicions upon others? Surely he will not. And then man's nature of itself is prone to suspect and think ill of another, from many grounds—

1. Sometimes, out of experience of *the common infirmities* that men meet with in the world; out of the experience of the falsehood of men, they are many times prone to suspicion.

2. But most commonly it is *out of guiltiness* that men think ill of others, because others have cause to think ill of them. None are so prone to suspicion as those that are worst themselves, because they judge others by their own hearts.

The better sort of people think of others as they are, and as they deserve themselves; but others, because they are naught, they think others are so. Because they deserve ill, they think others have deserved an ill opinion of them. So many times it comes of guilt, because we are not as we should be.

Then again, it ariseth from a guilty conscience in another respect. We think, because men have cause, though they have no wrong to themselves; yet because our own hearts tell us we are ill, we suspect them. So from an uncharitable disposition, and guiltiness of conscience, it ofttimes comes.

3. Then again, sometimes from *the concurrence of probabilities*, the suiting of circumstances that makes things somewhat probable, whereupon suspicion may be fastened. Sometimes when there is a concurrence of probabilities of the likelihood of things, their suspicion is prone to rise; for suspicion is not a determining of a thing, it is but a slight kind of conceit. It is more than a fear, and less than judgment of a thing. It is more than fear; for he that fears, suspects not. Suspicion is a degree to judgment. It doth not fully judge, for then it were not suspicion. It is more than fear; suspects not, but fears. It conceives slightly that such a thing should be done, and yet he dares not say it is done.

Suspicion is nothing else but an inclination of the soul to think and imagine ill of another; a looking curiously under a thing, or person. As we use to say, envy pries into things. An envious person searcheth. So, a suspicious person looks under to see if he can see matter of ill to fasten his ill soul upon. So it inclines the soul to think ill upon slight grounds. Now this ofttimes ariseth, and is fed with seeming probability. Christ conversed with wicked men. Here was some colour for them to conjecture him so.

We say, things have two hands, a right hand, and a left. Now suspicion takes hold of the left hand always. If things will admit of a double construction, suspicion alway takes hold of the worst, suspicion takes hold of the ill part. That is the nature of a diseased soul, to take things by the wrong hand. We see then it is a disposition that we are subject unto naturally; and it is cherished by Satan, and Satan's instruments, wicked men.

And why doth the devil so cherish suspicion, and a jealous disposition?

Oh, it hath been wondrous instrumental to Satan! I daresay, there is no disposition or frame of soul that hath been the occasion of more bloodshed, of more injustice in the church and state from the beginning of the world, than a jealous disposition, especially in great ones. Therefore the devil labours, as to breed jealousies of God, so of God's church and children from the beginning. Was it not ever the disposition of ill-minded men to put jealousies into the hearts, especially of those that were in authority concerning men far better than themselves? Was it not Haman's policy? when the Jews had angered him, oh, they are a people that care not for the laws, &c. Perhaps they were more obedient than himself. Had it not been the occasion of their ruin, if God had not been more merciful?

Herod had a jealousy and suspicion, that Christ when he was born would turn him out of his kingdom; and all Jerusalem was in an uproar, Mat. ii. 3. Alas! Christ came to give a heavenly kingdom, and not to take away earthly; yet this jealousy cost the lives of the poor infants.

So in the primitive church, there were wicked men put jealousies concerning the Christians, into the heads of the emperors, when alas! they reverenced the emperors, next God, above all. Yet alway there were wicked instruments that sought to domineer, and have their own ends under the emperors. They conveyed jealousies; and thence came so much bloodshed. In later times in popish countries, if a man read the stories, whence came that bloodshed? This was one chief cause, jealousies, and suspicions cast into the heads of popish princes by wicked men about them, set on work by Satan himself. O! they are such as will turn you out of your state; a people that are rebellious, and unquiet.

This was the policy among us in former times. We may consider of later times; to see the disposition of a man, that was a great statesman in his time, and a man of great parts and learning, but of a very fierce and cruel disposition; I mean Stephen Gardiner.* The chief hurt that was done in that magnanimous prince's time,† it was done by him. And how? By jealousies, as appears by his letters, &c. Oh, if these things prevail, this and that will come! He cast such jealousies that did affright that great prince. Oh, other princes will fall out with you, if you maintain not these things, they will break with you! And so upon his death-bed; this doctrine of justification, if the people once know it, all is gone.

God shows, that all these jealousies are but follies; for all that he feared came to pass. In good Queen Elizabeth's time, religion that he was so jealous of, was established: and she cared not for princes' correspondency, that were of other religions, further than might stand with reasons of state; and did not she flourish, and her people in quiet all her time, notwith-

* Cf. note *ss*.—G.

† That is, Henry VIII. It is curious to find Sibbes anticipating the eulogy of Froude.—G.

standing all former jealousies, as if religion established could not stand with peace? So that the event proved what kind of jealousies these were.*

Do we think then that a great deal of hurt is not done among particular persons, when in states there is such a world of hurt done by Satan, and his instruments? Well! let us take notice therefore of our disposition, and of the inclination of men this way, that we may the better prevent it, and that will appear in the second thing, that,

Obs. We should labour by all means to avoid suspicion, and to decline it as much as we can.

It should be the care of ministers, and others (it generally belongs to all Christians), to free themselves from any ill suspicion in the hearts of others as much as they can; as St Paul did here the suspicion of inconstancy, and lightness, and want of love to them that he did not come among them.

Suspicion is a canker that eats into the soul where it is, and it will consume and waste all love. It is the very venom of love and friendship. A little thing will breed it, but will not work it out. Therefore we ought first of all to take great heed that we give no ground of suspicion at all; or if we do, that we be careful to get it out as soon as we can; for usually where it takes place, it boils till it break out into words, and then words when they are discovered, breed strangeness, and that breeds other inconveniences.

And the rather we should labour to avoid it, because, *quod suspectum*, &c., that which is suspected, is made unprofitable; for a man when he unwarrantably suspects another thing, it is unprofitable to him. We take little good by those that we suspect are ill, or ill-affected to us, and then we do little good to them; for love is much daunted by the ill conceit we have taken against them. A man cannot do that good that he might, when he is suspected. There lies a bar in the way; ill suspicion in the other party, which is an obstruction between him, and the good he might do. Therefore even for the love of others we ought to avoid suspicion as much as may be, that they may receive good from us.

As we ought not uncharitably to suspect others, that we may do good to them; so we ought to avoid by all means suspicion from them, lest it be a bar for that good we might do towards them. Let us labour to clear ourselves from all suspicion of want of love, and ill carriage what we may, that so there may be nothing between our spirits and theirs that may hinder the good that might come from us to them, but that all may pass clear. You see how curious holy men have been in all times, to avoid suspicion as much as they could.

Even God himself,—we cannot have a more glorious pattern,—what course hath he taken from the beginning of the world with mankind? He hath condescended, and stooped to man's weakness, to clear himself of suspicion of unkindness to man, that man might not cherish suspicion that he doth not love him. For there is that poison in the cursed nature of man, that do God what he can, he will lay imputations upon God, to bear himself out in stubborn courses, as if God delighted not in him, nor regarded him. And as you have it in Ezek. xviii, 2 *seq.* I am punished for other folks' sins, God deals hardly with me, and brings the sins of my fathers upon me; and, 'the fathers have eaten sour grapes, and the children's teeth are set on edge.' God knows the cankered disposition of man since the fall. Satan lies upon the disposition of man, and broods upon it, to make it like him-

* Cf. Sir Philip Sidney's famous Letter to Elizabeth on her fears of isolation in Europe. It will be found in 'Life' of Sidney, by Bourne, and by Lloyd, both recently issued.—G.

self, malicious even against God himself. God, as it were, puts himself to his purgation, even with no less than an oath. 'As I live, saith the Lord, I will not the death of a sinner,' Ezek. xviii. 23. You think I am severe to you; and men they will rather impute it to God's severity, than their own sin. That is the pride of man's nature.

A sinner is wondrous proud till he come to destruction itself, and the book of conscience be opened. Sin will have something to shelter itself with: sin is a proud thing. God purgeth himself by an oath. 'As I live, saith the Lord, I will not the death of a sinner.' If you die, you may thank your own sins. Though you be so bad, if you will repent, 'I will not the death of a sinner, but rather that he return, and live.' Yet notwithstanding, man to countenance himself in sin, he will fly perhaps to the decree of God. God perhaps doth not delight in me. Whereas the rule of our life is, 'He hath shewed thee, O man, what is good,' Micah vi. 8, to do good, and abstain from evil, and then that question will be out of question, whether thou be God's or no. But man will force upon himself, that God doth not regard him, that he may sin with more freedom.

As the unfaithful servant, 'I knew thou wert a hard master, that exactest that that thou hadst not given,' Mat. xxv. 24,—and therefore I hid my talent. The bad servant forceth upon himself hardness in his master, when he was not so,—that he might be idle. So men force upon themselves somewhat in God to be hard; God's dealings to be so and so, that they may take more liberty. For if God be so loving, and so gracious, as he hath discovered himself to be, their hearts would melt, they would never live in such courses, but rather put all to the venture, than to clamour upon God's justice. Therefore God himself purgeth himself from a disposition of unkindness, and unmercifulness. 'As I live, saith the Lord, I will not the death of a sinner.' So his whole course is to shew that he loves us.

And what is our Saviour Christ's whole course, but to free men from suspicion of want of love? Did he ever turn any back from him, but those that went away of themselves? Did he not shed tears for those that shed his blood, so merciful and gracious was he? If so be that holy men of all times have laboured to clear themselves to others, we ought not to rage against the ill dispositions of men. If we were as good as God, and as Christ, men would have false suspicion of us. It is no innocency in the world that will free a man from suspicion; the wicked, poisonful disposition that the devil stirs up against him. Therefore rage not against it, but bear it with a spirit of moderation.

And let us decline as much as we can, and free the hearts of people from evil suspicion; and if we cannot avoid it, yet to bear it without discontent, considering it is the lot of God's children to be suspected, as we see here St Paul was.

'*To spare you, I came not to Corinth.*' St Paul besides his labouring to remove suspicion, he sets down here the true cause of his not coming to them. It was not lightness and inconstancy, it was 'to spare you.' They had many abuses among them, and amended they must be, that was a conclusion. But the question is *de modo*, whether by gentle means, by writing an epistle, and staying a while, or afterwards by coming, and telling them their sin to their face, and by being severe, and terrible among them? Now he concludes, I came not among you, for this very cause, that I might not be so severe, and terrible among you, as by office I should have been, if you had not amended before I came; as indeed they did, for they cast out the incestuous person, and reformed other abuses comfortably. They prevented St Paul's severity, with their reformation. They had not at the first cast out the incestuous person, and they had factions among them; they had atheists among them that doubted of the resurrection, many abuses were crept in among them. St Paul wrote a former epistle upon a desire to reform those, and there was a blessed reformation wrought. St Paul did not delight in austerity; therefore he deferred his coming, that he might have more joy and contentment than sorrow.

'To spare you, I came not.' Before I come to the points, take this for a ground,

Obs. Sin must be judged and censured when it is committed.

It must be undone by repentance, or by eternal punishment in hell. It must be censured here or hereafter.

For it is against God's nature and God's word. 'The soul that sinneth shall die,' Ezek. xviii. 4. It must be repented of, of necessity, or eternally punished in hell. Censured it must be, one way or other, it is of such a contrary nature, so opposite to the holiness of God. That is a ground.

Now this being laid as a ground, the question is, What is the best way to take away sin, whether by means gentle or severe? By gentle means, it may be; if not, then by severe. St Paul would not have spared them, if he had come, if they had not amended. So the points are two.

First of all, that the best way for the redressing of sin, *is by gentle means, if it may be.*

Secondly, if that will not, *then by severe,* if men would not have men damned.

'I came not, to spare you,' because I desired that gentler courses might prevail. So I say, the first point is this, that

Doct. If gentler courses will prevail, they ought especially, and in the first place, to be taken.

It should be the care both of ministers, and of all those that deal with others, first of all to use mild, and winning, and gaining courses.

Now to prove this.

Reason 1. *First, they are more suitable to the nature of man*; for the nature of man is best wrought on by rational courses suitable to his nature, suitable to his principle. Man is a reasonable creature, therefore rational courses will prevail with a rational man, a course of persuasion and discovery. A man that is not beast-like, tell him but the danger of his sin, tell him the peril of it in gentle words, and he will amend, if so be he be not hardened by God to destruction; or if God do not reserve him to a more severe redress. Gentle courses ought first to be used, because they are agreeable to the nature of man.

2. Again, *they suit most to God's disposition;* for 'God is love,' 1 John iv. 8, and his course to man is love. If he take any course contrary to love, it is not his own work; as he saith, to punish man it is not his own work, he is forced to that alway. To shew love and mercy, that is his work, that that comes from his own principle, from his mercy, 'he is love.' He doth not say, he is justice, or rigour, but he is love. It agrees with the nature of God to deal mercifully. If he deal otherwise, it is forced from us.

3. *It suits with the whole carriage of our salvation,* these courses of love, and gentleness first of all; for we are saved by a manner of love. We are saved by God giving his Son, and by his Son giving himself. We are saved by a course of entreaty. The ministers of God are ambassadors to

desire us to be 'reconciled to God,' 2 Cor. v. 20. God having saved us by a manner of love, he will have us taught by a manner of love, in the gospel especially; because God's aim is to gain our love, and which way can that be, but by a way of love?

For the nature of man is such, that it will never love till it know it be loved first. Therefore God stoops to a way of love, because he would have our love; which he would never have by other courses, because they are contrary to our nature.

4. *It is the practice of God.* His custom is answerable: for first, he deals by gentle means always, and then after, if those will not prevail, he goes to severe means, and in severe means he takes degrees; first less, and then more violent, and then violent indeed. God would never descend to sharper courses, if milder would serve the turn. You know he bade his own people, before they set in hostile manner upon any, to give them fair warning, to give them conditions of peace: so it is his course to offer conditions of peace. So he did to the old world, and so he doth to us. Before he corrects, he offers conditions of peace. You see how sparing Christ was, and how full of love, 'O Jerusalem, Jerusalem,' &c., Mat. xxiii. 37.

5. Again, *they are courses that promise best success ordinarily:* for the proud nature of man will raise itself up, and will harden itself against severe courses. Man naturally, as I said, will be led, and not forced. His nature will rise against forced violent courses, therefore for the event itself it is the best.

6. Again, *they are courses that are more lasting.* That that is gained by love, is constant; that that we prevail with men for by reason, it will hold. Other courses are not so faithful, they will not hold. What we gain on men by fear, there is shame in it, that a man should be forced to anything, and nature will break out; but it will hold best, that is gained by way of love and reason.

Use. Therefore *let us imitate God in this,* when we are to deal with any, not to take violent courses in the first place, but to deal with men as men, deal with them by love and reason, and not stand upon our own stomach and greatness, and take delight, as it were, in the commanding of others; that we have a destructive power, a power that can quash, and crush men, and shew it to the utmost, and pride ourselves in it. If God should deal so with such, where were those proud creatures? If God were not a forbearing, indulgent, sparing God?

Therefore you may see what disposition those are of, that all are for fire, for violent courses, rigorous courses. That is not the way that God useth. It is not the way that Christ used. It is not the way that ministers do use that have the Spirit of God.

You have some kind of people, that if a man be not always in matters of damnation, his sermon is nothing. So you have some that in their courses are so violent, that they know nothing that is moderate, (and yet perhaps they are good too, but) they cherish too much a violent disposition. Now St Paul, though he were a very zealous, holy man, yet notwithstanding he would not put himself upon violent courses but when there was great necessity. He is rather a butcher than a physician, that loves to torment his patient. You see what course is first to be taken. I need not be long in so clear a point; therefore I will spend no more time in it, but come to the second, that is more generally useful. Because indeed men are so, that gentle means will hardly prevail with them, what must be done then? 'not spare them.'

Doct. When gentle means will not serve the turn, then we must not spare.

St Paul came not, that he might 'spare them.' Now, if they had not amended, what would have St Paul have done, think you? Would he have suffered them to have cherished the incestuous person among them? that wicked person that had committed that which was intolerable amongst the heathen? Would he have cherished proud factious men amongst them, that would disgrace St Paul's doctrine, to win authority to themselves? Would not he have told them to their face the danger of their sin, and have made them ashamed? Undoubtedly he would: he would [not] 'have spared.' So I say, if gentle means will not prevail, men must not be spared; neither minister nor magistrate must spare; especially in dangerous courses that are prejudicial to the souls of others.

Why?

Reason. We must spare none, that God may spare all. We that are ministers must spare no sin, that God may spare all. 'Lift up thy voice like a trumpet,' saith God, 'and tell Israel of their sins,' Isa. xviii. 58. If gentle means will not reform them, 'lift up thy voice like a trumpet.' Cast out Jezebel with her painted face. Though sin paint and colour itself, it must be cast out. Jonah must out of the ship, the ship will perish else. Achan must be stoned. We must tell men of their danger, not with hatred of their persons, but to prevent an eternal punishment.

You know well that preventing justice is better than executing justice. Is not discipline better than execution? Is it not better to hear of our faults roundly, when other means will not prevail, than to cherish that that will be for our eternal destruction? Is not searing and cutting better than killing? Is it not better that a limb be seared and cut, than that all be clear cut off, and the whole body perish? Is not the pain of chirurgery, or physic that makes a man sick for a while, better to be endured than the pains and terrors of death itself? These preventing courses are the best courses: therefore we must spare none, but tell them of their danger faithfully.

Only, liberty of speech must not be a cover for boisterousness, or a cover for the venting of evil humours, as sometimes it is. For flesh will never prevail with flesh. Flesh, and pride in the speaker, will never prevail with pride in the hearer; but it must be a spiritual kind of severity, discovering the danger to them we speak to, with a spiritual holy affection, and a spirit of love, though with severity: for there is a severity of love and gentleness, it will prevail when it comes from such a spirit. But if there be a discovery of flesh, not only in ministers, but in those that deal with others, flesh will rise against flesh. A man may sometimes find fault with another with greater corruption than the thing he finds fault with in another; he may be more to blame for his dealing than the other for his fault. 'I came not, to spare you.'

Use. Therefore, when ministers are plain in discovering the danger of the times, the danger of the persons, and places where they are to deal, *people must hear them as they love their own souls.* If they have any quarrel, let them quarrel with their master; for what we speak is from the word of God. We come as his ambassadors and servants, and should be considered as ambassadors. Therefore, considering whose message we bring, they must take it in good part to be told of their sins in a good manner. As St Austin saith very well. Christ, saith he, speaks to the sea, and it was quiet: Christ said, 'Be still,' the sea heard, and the waves were still; but he speaks to us in the ministry to stay our violent courses in sin, and we puff and swell when we are told of our faults (*iiii*). Is this good, think you? No. If we do so, it is a sign that God intends to seal us to destruction. As we know, Eli's sons, when they did not hearken to their father, God had appointed them to destruction. Those that will not hearken to ministerial reproof, it is a sign that God hath sealed them over to destruction.

If we would not have either ministers or others to be severe in telling us, let us be severe to our own sins first. Men are like to children; first they foul and defile themselves, and they cry when they are washed: so men soil themselves with sins, and cry when they should be purged from them. If we cannot endure to be told of our faults, how shall we endure to be tormented for our faults in hell? Those that are so tender, that they will not endure a word contrary to their dispositions, how will they endure that sentence, 'Go ye cursed,' when they shall be turned into hell? Consider what will come of it, if we live in sin.

I beseech you therefore, suffer the word of exhortation at our hands. Our salvation lies upon it. If we discover not the danger of the sins of people to whom we speak, if we discern them, we shall perish for it, because we are unfaithful in our embassage. Therefore for your own souls; and likewise that we may discharge our duty as we should, patiently and quietly sit under exhortation and reproof, not only public, but private, if occasion be.

O beloved! at the latter day it will be a matter of vexation that we were cherished too much in our courses. Do you not think that the damned spirits in hell wish, O! that we had been told! O, that we had been dealt with violently, that we had been pulled out of this flame! There is an excellent place in Jude's epistle, 'Have *mercy* upon some.' Use some gently that are of tractable dispositions; and pull 'some out of the fire with fear,' with threatening eternal damnation, with terrible courses, that they may have cause to fear; first with admonitions, and if that will not prevail, with suspension, with further censure; and if that will not prevail, with excommunication, cast them out of the church, as this incestuous Corinthian, 'that their souls may be saved in the day of the Lord,' verse 23.

There is a threefold correction, or finding fault, that are gradual one after another, and they should be of vigour in the church in all times.

1. *First, a friendly telling of a fault*, between man and man, if we see any thing dangerously amiss.

2. Then, *when a man takes another man before company*, when he takes him before those that he respects, when privately he will not amend. Then

3. *Correction*, if admonition of friends will not do, '*tell the church*,' Mat. xviii. 17, rather than suffer his soul to perish.

These steps and degrees were observed in the best times of the church, and if they were observed now, many souls would be saved. This is that that St Jude speaks of, 'Save some, pulling them out of the fire,' that is, snatch them out by violent means, by excommunication, that 'their souls may be saved in the day of the Lord.' Those that are in hell wish that they had been pulled out with fear, with violent courses. O! that we had been told of our filthy courses, of our swearing, of our injustice, that we had had violence offered us rather than to have come into this place of torment. O! those will bless God another day for that gracious violence. And those that are let alone will curse all another day; ministers, friends, and parents, they will curse all, that there were not more violent courses taken with them, to stop them in their way to hell: to deal plainly with them. It is the best mercy that can be shewed, to be faithful in this kind.

Therefore while it is time, suffer the word of exhortation, and reproof; the time will come else that you shall condemn yourselves that you were so impatient, and shall wish, O! that we had had those that would have dealt more violently with us! It is cruel pity as can be in ministers, to be flatterers, and to daub; or in parents and governors of others, to dissemble with them in their courses, and not to tell them of it. It is the most cruel pity of all; it is betraying of them to eternal torments. For sin, as I said, it must be judged and censured here, or hereafter; if it be not here, there is more reserved for the time to come, when God will open the treasures of his wrath. We put into his treasury fast enough; and the time will come of opening all the treasuries of his vengeance, when he will pour out the vials of his wrath upon sinners that are not reformed. So much for that point.

'*I call God for a record upon my soul.*' St Paul to purge himself from suspicion, seals all this with an oath. Herein he doth shew his great love to them, and his care over them, that he would so seriously purge himself to gain their love, and good opinion of him. It was an argument of the great esteem he had of them. He was willing they should think he was very desirous of their love, and of their good opinion, for whose sake he would swear, and clear himself by an oath. As God esteems man's love much, when he will condescend so far as to seal his love, and promise with an oath; God would have us to think that he values, and esteems our respect very much, so St Paul would have them think he esteemed them much, that he would make such a solemn oath for their sakes. Now to speak of an oath a little.

An oath, as we know, is either in judgment before a magistrate; or in particular cases between private persons. And it is either assertory of a thing past, or promissory of a thing to come. Now this oath of St Paul's is an assertory oath of a thing that was past, to secure them that he did not come to them upon this ground, that he had a mind to spare them. It was no promise of anything to come, but an assertion of a thing that was past. An oath is either an assertion or a promise, with a calling of God to be a witness and a judge; to be a witness of the truth, or a judge if he say false. You have the description of an oath in this text. I say, it is either an assertion of a thing past, or a promise of a thing to come, a sealing of this by calling God to witness of the thing we say, and to avenge the falsehood if we say false. As St Paul here, 'I call God to record,' that what I say is true, 'and upon my soul,' if I say false.

Many conclusions concerning an oath might be raised out of the text.

1. *First of all*, concerning the person that makes an oath, *he should indeed be a gracious, a holy, and a good man.* As St Paul saith, 'I call God to witness, whom I serve in my spirit,' Rom. i. 9. A man is scarce fit to swear, which is a part of God's worship, that is not good otherwise. Will he care for the religion of an oath, that hath no religion in him? He whose oath should be taken, should be such a man as St Paul, in some degree, whose oath should be taken. The Turks are careful of this,—to the shame of Christians,—they will not take an oath of an ordinary swearer. It must be a man that hath somewhat in him, that shall have his oath regarded.

2. Again, we see *by whom an oath should be taken:* by the name of God. We ought not to swear by creatures, but by God himself; nor to swear by any idol, as the mass, and by Mary, and such like. It is a taking God to witness. An oath is a part of God's service, a part of divine worship, as it

is, Deut. xxix. 12, and other places. Now we ought to serve God only; therefore we ought not to use the name of any creature in an oath. He that we swear by must know the heart, whether we speak true or no. Now who knows the heart but God? therefore we must swear only by the name of God. These things are easy, therefore I do but name them.

3. We see here again, *the two grand parts of an oath;* besides assertion, or promise of the truth, there must be a calling God to witness, and imprecation. Though these be not always set down, they are implied. Sometimes the Scripture sets down the one part; but always the other is implied. There is imprecation in every oath. Sometimes imprecation implies both, as God do so and so. Sometimes there is a calling God to witness without imprecation, yet it is always implied. For whosoever swears, calls God to witness of the truth, and if it be not true, that God would punish him.

These three go together in an oath. God that can discover it, he knows my heart whether I say true or no. And he is judge, and thereupon a revenger. In an oath, God is considered not only as *judex,* but as *judex* and *vindex;* not only as a discoverer, but as a judge and revenger, if it be false. Therefore it is a part of divine worship, because it is with prayer; and imprecation is alway implied, if it be not expressed. So we see in this text what an oath is, and by whom it is to be taken, and the parts of it.

4. Again, we see here in the text, *that an oath ought to be taken in serious matters.* The rule of an oath is excellently set down by Jeremiah, iv. 2. I know no one place of Scripture more pregnant, and therefore I name it. 'Thou shalt swear,'—how?—'The Lord liveth, in truth, in judgment, and in righteousness.'

(1.) We must swear *in truth,* that is, that not only the thing be true that we swear; we must look to that, but we must think it so too. The thing must be true, and we must apprehend it so. 'We must swear *in truth.*'

(2.) And then *in judgment,* that is, with discretion. We must understand throughly the matter whereof we swear, and what an oath is. Therefore persons under years ought not to take an oath, because they cannot swear in judgment, to know what the weight and validity of an oath is; and when it is a fit time to take it. It must be taken in serious business, as St Paul here to clear himself to the souls of the Corinthians whom he laboured to edify; when he saw their ill conceit of him hindered their edification, therefore he clears himself by an oath.

(3.) Thirdly, it must be *in justice,* that is, we must not bind ourselves by an oath to anything that is ill: it is a rule a long time past. Herod bound himself by an oath in that kind, Mat. xiv. 9. But an oath must never be a bond of injustice, but it must be taken in righteousness.

Therefore here is condemned the equivocation and reservation of the papists. They will swear before a magistrate, but with equivocation. This is not in righteousness; for it is a rule that an oath must be taken in that sense as he to whom we swear takes it; that is a constant rule among all divines, because it is to persuade him of the truth that we swear. It is for his and others' sakes; and as he and others take it, so it must be took. Therefore equivocation with absurd reservations are wicked, because they are absurd if they be expressed. He will swear that he is not a priest: he means after the order of Melchizedec. It is a mocking and profaning of an oath, it is not to swear in justice and righteousness. But it is so foul and abominable a course, that it is not fit to be spoken of almost; and ey are ashamed of it themselves. St Paul's oath was all this. He sware in truth; he was truly persuaded of the truth of his own affections toward them. And then in judgment; it was done in discretion; for being not able otherwise to clear himself, having no witness in earth, he goes to heaven for a purger, he goes to God himself for a witness; he fetcheth strength from heaven. There was none on earth that knew St Paul's affection, but the Spirit of God and his own spirit; and he thought his own spirit was not sufficient. My own spirit tells me that 'I came not, to spare you;' but if you would know my mind better, 'I call God to witness,' and to be a revenger, if I speak false, that I came not, for this end, that I might spare you, to prevent the rigour and severity that I should have used toward your sin.

An oath should be true and weighty; but that is not enough, it must be in matters indeterminable. For if a thing may be determined without an oath, we should never use it. The end of an oath is to end controversies; for if St Paul could have persuaded them of his gracious and loving heart, that he stood affected as he did, he would not have used an oath; but having no other means to do it, he goes to heaven for a witness.

It were but misspending of time to shew that an oath is lawful. Have we anabaptists among us, that call this into question? No! we have many atheists. It is dangerous atheism in the anabaptists to question whether they may take an oath. We have the example of St Paul, we have the example of God himself; shall we think it unlawful when God himself swears, and the angel swears, and Christ swears, and the apostle swears?

Where it is forbidden that we should not swear, it is meant that we should not swear in our ordinary talk, where we need not seal every light speech with the solemnity of an oath. Men will not put on their best apparel every day; so men ought not to use solemn matters upon every occasion, but only upon holy and grand occasions.

Our Saviour Christ forbids swearing, first by the creature at all, and swearing in ordinary talk at all. 'Whatsoever is more than yea and nay,' in ordinary talk, is sin, Mat. v. 37. Therefore, considering that St Paul doth it in a serious matter, we ought to learn not to swear, except it be in great matters: when we are called before a magistrate, or when we are to purge ourselves from evil suspicion of our Christian friends; as we see here St Paul doth to the Corinthians: he calls God to witness against his soul, if it were not true.

Obj. But you will say, Men will not believe me except I swear, and therefore I swear so oft.

Ans. Then live better for shame, that men may believe thee for thine honest life. If thy honest life be not better than thy oath, they will not believe thee for swearing; for he that swears oft swears false, and 'in many words there cannot want iniquity,' Prov. x. 19, much more in many oaths there cannot want iniquity; and he that swears much, out of doubt he oft forswears.

Obj. Oh! it is my custom, and I cannot break a custom.

Ans. Use that apology to a judge. Though malefactors be none of the modestest creatures, will any of them say, It is my custom to rob and steal? Will not the judge say it is his custom to cut them off? Thou sayest it is thy custom. It is God's custom to damn such persons. Therefore that is an aggravation of thy sin.

But here we that are ministers may take up a complaint, that when we have to deal with the wretched disposition of men in things concerning their souls and a better life, do what we can, we cannot prevail with them to leave that that they have no profit nor no good by; they are not put upon it by any fear. It is only out of superfluity of pride and malice against God, out of the abundance of profaneness.

Can we think to prevail with men to deny themselves in greater matters, to forsake their unlawful gains, or to venture the suffering ill for a good cause, and to renounce pleasures that are lawful, do we think to gain upon men for these things, when we cannot for superfluities that they are not forced to by any violence, that they have no gain nor credit by, except it be among a company of debauched men like themselves? Yet it is our case; we deal in the world with a company of persons to leave that that they have no gain by, except it be the wrath of God, and yet we cannot prevail.

Obj. Oh, but you will say, I live with such company that I must swear.

Ans. What a shame is it for thee that carnal company should prevail more with thee than the vengeance of God, and the authority of God in the ministry! What a heart hast thou that a base person like thyself should move thee to do that that God himself and the authority of his ordinance cannot move thee to forbear! It is an argument of a base nature. How darest thou look God and Christ in the face another day, when for his sake thou wilt not leave a superfluous, profane oath? Thou regardest a wicked companion more, because thou wilt not be mocked of him; thou wilt swear for company, or because thou wilt please him, that he may think thee to be so and so, a companion fit for him; to please him, thou wilt displease God and Christ, before whom thou shalt be judged ere long. If people were not mad and sold to destruction, they would consider these things.

Indeed, these things are so clear, and so odious in themselves, that we need not press them. We should spend that little time we have to preach of more sublime matters than to come to dissuade men from swearing. Alas! under the glorious gospel that we have lived so long, have we gained so little that we are forced to spend our time to dissuade men from swearing? We should look to the mysteries of religion, and draw men to further perfection; but such times we are fallen into, and we must be content with it, and I would we could gain anything by discovering the danger of these things.

An ordinary course of swearing, it argues a very vile heart wheresoever it is: bear it out as boisterously as they will. It argues this venom in the heart: Well! I cannot offend against the second table, but the laws of the kingdom will hamper me! I cannot steal, or murder, but somewhat I can do in despite of God himself, and the worst that can come, it is but a trifling matter. What venom is in the hearts of men, that where there is but the least damage, they will be restrained; and here, because there is not present execution upon a sinner in this kind, they profane and abuse the glorious name of God!

1. When God's name is abused by swearing and blasphemy, usually the original of it, among other things, *is atheism*. If we thought that God were so as the Scripture shews, we would not dally so much. They that lead others into bad courses, it is from the height and depth of atheism. Make the best of it, it is a great degree of irreverence to the glorious Majesty of God. For when God shall say, 'He that takes my name in vain, shall not carry it away guiltless,' Exodus xx. 7: What will he do, think you, to him that swears idly, and profanely, when the vain taking of God's name in vain without an oath, the vain trifling with the name of God, shall not

escape? When men do not reverence and fear an oath, as it is, Eccles. ix. 2, it argues much irreverence.

And, indeed, it is worse in the principle than in the thing itself. Though the words be heinous, yet the principle whence it ariseth is worse, that is, infidelity and atheism, and alway irreverence and want of fear of the glorious Majesty of God, this ground makes it more odious. Therefore, those that are subject to it, if they would amend it, let them remove the ground.

2. Sometimes, again, *it is cherishing too much passion.* So, because they cannot be sufficiently revenged upon their poor brethren, God must smart for it; they will tear his glorious name that never did them wrong. What a mad passion is this; hath God done them any wrong? Therefore, I say, let us labour to remove the ground of it; and labour to plant the contrary in our hearts, the true fear of God, that we may fear an oath. Let us labour to subdue unruly passion.

3. Again, in some others *affectation is the cause.* Many of the frothy sort, they think it a thing commendable to fill up their discourse with these parentheses, with oaths; which perhaps doth them a service to knit their wounded discourse together. So this foolish and sinful affectation is one cause. Men desire to be thought to be somebody, by swearing. They would have the world to think that they are valorous men, that can be so bold with God himself; therefore let other men take heed how they meddle with them, when God smarts for it, as if he that could swear most, had most courage.

4. And in many *it is out of a sinful shame,* because they will hold correspondence with the company, and they are afraid to be thought to be strict; and that they may be thought to be free from suspicion of overmuch conscionableness* in their ways, they will not let the world see that they shall not think that they are men that make any conscience of strictness, but they can be bold with the name of God: so, because they would have others think that they are men that do not stand upon terms of conscience and strictness, they will swear they are men for the world, they are serviceable for any purpose. Men that make conscience of anything, make conscience of all; but a man that makes conscience of an oath, or any such thing, he is a stiff man, he is not serviceable, he is not for the turn. Now, because men would be thought of others not to be of that strain, to make any conscience, hereupon they break out to the profaning of the name of God. How shall such persons, that out of sinful weakness labour and apply themselves more to satisfy sinful men, than the great God, how dare they look God in the face? Jesus Christ saith, 'He that is ashamed of me before men;' he that is ashamed to own religion, nay, to own justice, to own even common good behaviour, rather than he will offend others: he that is ashamed of me in such mean things as these, 'I will be ashamed of him before my Heavenly Father,' Mark viii. 38.

If other reasons will not move us to leave this sin, let the love of the state and kingdom we live in do it. Jeremiah saith, 'for oaths the land shall mourn,' Jer. xxiii. 10. Indeed, there is a mulct for this, but that men slight it. And God, I hope, will be merciful to the state, for the censure of the state upon profanation, it is a very worthy act (*jjjj*). But if that be not executed, or men grow not to make more conscience, the land will

* That is, 'conscientiousness.'—G.

mourn for it; because where the magistrates cease to do their office, God will do his office. Where sin is punished, God will not punish. Where the magistrate spares, God will not spare. He will punish. Therefore this sin where it is not censured and punished, the land shall mourn for it.

If the care of the kingdom will not move them, yet the care of their own houses and families should. In Zech. v. 1, the prophet speaks of a flying book of judgments that should come upon the house of the swearer, and consume the posts of his house. And the wise man saith in Ecclesiasticus (though it be apocryphal), 'The plague shall not depart from the house o the swearer,' iii. 11.* God's vengeance accompanies even the very family and house of the swearer.

And, for avoiding of this, I would there were more conscience made of those oaths that border upon gross oaths. I will not dispute the matter. Take it for granted they be no oaths, but asseverations, as to call their truth in question, and their confidence in matters of religon; who will lay a thousand pound to pawn for a matter of sixpence? Who, if he be discreet and considerate, will lay his faith and religion to pawn for every trifle in common talk? Faith is the most precious thing in the world: for a man to lay a great matter for a twopenny or sixpenny debt, it is odious among men. Certainly, it is idle at the best among men, to lay asseverations of religion without ground, upon every trifle. He that will avoid danger must not come near it; he must avoid all that borders upon it. I would therefore more care were had, even of these.

I will only add one thing more. Whereas he calls God 'for a record upon his soul,' that those that are overmuch given to rash calling upon the name of God, to rash swearing, let them know this, as I said, that there is an imprecation implied in every oath: they do as it were curse themselves. If the thing be not true, their damnation is sealed under a curse: they call God to record upon their souls against themselves.

Let us so live that our life may be a kind of oath: the life of a Christian should be so. An oath is a calling God to witness, a calling God to curse if it be not so. A Christian should live so, as he may call God to witness for every action he doth; to bring himself to an oath, under a curse ofttimes, as it is in Ezra, and oft in Scripture, 'If I do not so and so,' vii. 23, &c. Because our nature is unstable, it starts† from holy duties, we should bring ourselves to duties with an oath, under a curse.

It is an excellent thing when we can live as in God's presence; to do all we do in the presence of God. God is a witness whether we call him or no. Therefore we should so carry ourselves, that we might call God to witness the sincerity of our aims, and whatsoever we do. He is a witness, and he will be our judge: therefore, whether we formally in the manner of an oath call him or no, that is not the matter, but let us know and think that he is, and will be so.

I beseech you consider the sweet comfort that will arise out of it, that he that will live and think and affect,‡ and speak in the presence of God, that he may call God to record of the sincerity of his intentions, of all that he speaks, and thinks, and doth; how comfortably shall he live, and give his account to God, that hath lived as in the presence of God all his days! He that hath presented to his soul, as it were, the bar of Christ in his lifetime, that hath lived as one that could give an account and reckoning,

* Cf. footnote, vol. II. page 351.—G.

† That is, 'turns aside.'—G.

‡ That is, 'choose, love.'—G.

when he comes to the point that he must give up his account, how joyfully and comfortably will he do it! So much for that verse.

I come now to the last verse of the chapter.

VERSE 24.

'*Not that we have dominion over your faith, but are helpers of your joy; for by faith ye stand.*' St Paul is yet in his clearing, he is yet in his apology. 'Not that we have dominion over your faith,' &c. I do not tell you, I came not yet to 'spare you,' as if I meant to domineer over your faith when I came. Because those words, 'I came not yet, to spare you,' might seem to carry some highness, some lordliness with them, as if the apostle would have taken much upon him; therefore he corrects those words in this verse, 'Not that we have dominion over your faith,' &c. So that in these words he removes a suspicion of spiritual tyranny over them. Because he had said before, 'he came not, to spare them,' they might think, What would he have done if he had come? would he have enforced us? Oh no! Indeed your reformation hath spared me a labour, and you a chiding; but if I had reproved you sharply, it should have been for your good.

Then he sets down the true cause, 'We are helpers of your joy.' If I had come, and told you of your faults, if I had not spared you, it should have been to help your joy; and now I come not to you, it is to help your joy: my scope in all is to be a furtherer of your joy. So these words are a reason of the former, why he did not come to domineer over their faith, 'For by faith ye stand.' You stand by faith, and you stand out by faith against all oppositions whatsoever; therefore your faith must not lean on me; I must not domineer over that you stand by; if your faith should rely on me, I am but a man. Faith must rely on God. It must have a better pillar than myself. You must stand upon Divine strength: therefore 'you stand by faith;' and if you stand by faith, we have no reason to have dominion over your faith.

These words are declined by many interpreters (*kkkk*). They know not what the dependence is: but this is the best dependence of the words, 'We domineer not, or rule not over your faith;' because by faith you stand as upon a bottom; you stand against all adverse power by faith. Therefore you had need to have it well founded, you had need to plant your faith well, by which you stand against all opposite power, and against all human authority. For a man may be a liar, and do good in many things. A man hath a deceitful nature, as far as he hath a corrupt principle in him. He may deceive, and yet be a good man too; in particular cases he may shew himself a changeable creature. But there must be no falsehood nor uncertainty in faith; for it is a grace that must have truth and certainty: it must have immoveable and unchangeable truth to build on. Therefore we domineer not over your faith. God forbid we should do so; for faith is the grace whereby you stand; if you should build upon us as men, you could not stand alway. The point is clear, that,

Doct. No creature can have dominion over the faith of another.

The faith of a man is only subject to the Spirit of God, to God, and to Christ. And by the way, St Paul taxeth* those false apostles and false teachers, that laboured to creep into the consciences of people, to have higher place in the hearts of people than they should have, that so they might rule the

* That is, 'chargeth, accuseth.'—G.

people as they list. Now that should not be the scope of the minister, to have dominion over the faith of others ; for the ministry is a ministry, not a magistracy. A minister, so far as he is a pastor, he is a minister ; that is, he is to deliver things from God that may stablish the soul, not to domineer over men's faith, as if he would prescribe what men should believe.

Now to unfold this point, I will first shew what it is to have no dominion over men's faith. And then what it is to have dominion and rule over other men's faith, and who are guilty of this.

1. Not to have dominion over another man's faith, it is not when a church doth force prescribing* to the articles of religion. That is not to have dominion over the faith of others, to draw people to conformity of the same religion in the substantials of it (as some that seek extravagant liberty, lay that imputation perhaps). It is used in all churches.

2. Again, it is not to domineer over faith, to suppress that that they call of late in neighbour-countries, a liberty of prophesy (*llll*), to suppress a liberty of preaching when men list; that men should have an unbridled licence. We see in Poland,† and other countries, what abundance of heretics there are, where there is more liberty to preach, and to publish what men list. Those countries are like Africa‡, where, they say, there are alway new monsters. Or like to Egypt ; when *Nilus* overflows it leaves a slime behind, and when the sun works upon that slime it breeds many imperfect strange creatures. So those countries where there is liberty of religions, there are always some strange novel opinions, some monsters. Experience of foreign countries shews it too true ; therefore to hinder that extravagant liberty is not dominion over faith.

Nay, to force men to the means of faith, it is not to domineer over faith. St Austin himself was once of this mind, that people were not to be forced (*mmmm*). It is true. But they may be compelled to the means, though they cannot be compelled to believe. Men may be compelled to the means by mulcts, and other courses of state. And it is a happy necessity when people are forced to the means, under which means, by God's blessing, they may be reduced to a better habit and temper of soul.

Therefore it is cruelty to neglect this care, to leave people to their own liberty to attend upon the means, or not to attend on them. Therefore our State is, and may be justified well, for those violent courses to recusants. And many of them after, bless God they have done it, and they have cause. For there is a majesty in the ordinances of God. If people were brought under the means, God's Spirit would make the means effectual. And there is not a greater snare of the devil, whereby he holds more in the Romish church in perdition, than by persuading them that it is a dangerous thing to come to our prayers, and to attend upon the means of salvation; whenas in our liturgy there is nothing that may justly offend. Therefore to force to the means, it is not to domineer over faith ; because it is only a drawing from outward inforcement to the use of means.

3. Again, it is not a ruling over faith, nor a base slavery, when men hear the word of God opened directly and clearly, when men shall persuade others according to their own judgment, that this is so, and when others shall yield. There is some faith that may be called in some degree implicit faith and obedience, that is not sinful, but good and discreet. As when men by their standing in the church, and by their experience and holiness of life, are thought to be men that speak agreeable to the ground

* That is, 'subscribing, subscription.'—G.
† Spelled 'Polonia.'—G.
‡ Spelled 'Africk.'—G.

of Scripture, though they have not a direct rule and place of Scripture for it, other men's conscience may follow what they say. I have been directed by such men at such times, that by reason of their calling have opportunity to advise.

But this frees it from base service, that it must be with reservation, till it appear otherwise by some place of Scripture, or till better counsel may be yielded. Obedience to others with reservation, and counselling with others, this is no domineering, because it is with reserving ourselves to a further discovery, and a further light. That, the moralists use to call the opinion of an honest man. Where the law speaks not, it is much to be esteemed; especially an honest discreet Christian, when the law of God speaks not directly. Then he that speaks out of conscience, and some light, he may persuade another man, with this reservation, till further light be discovered; this is no domineering over faith.

I might take away many things that might breed a suspicion, as if we domineered over the faith of others when we do not.

But to come to shew you this positive truth, what this tyranny over the faith of others is, and where it is practised.

1. Those tyrannise over the faith of others *that do equalise men's traditions, some canons of their own, with the word of God*, and press them with equal violence, perhaps more; because they are brats of their own brain. Those that will devise a voluntary worship of God, and so entangle people, and tell them, This you must do, when there is no ground for it in the word of God; it is will-worship. God loves willing worship, when we worship him willingly; but he loves not will-worship, when it is the device of our own brain how we will serve him. As if a servant or a slave must devise how his lord will be served; what impudency is this, if we consider what God is! They tyrannise over people's consciences, that equalise their own dotages, though they account them witty devices, and their own inventions with the worship of God; that jumble all together, as if conscience were equally bound to any device of their own, as to God's word.

2. Again, those do tyrannise over the faith of others, *that think they can make articles in religion to bind conscience*. Those that think to free themselves from the danger of error, as if what they said were infallible, they tyrannise over others. Those that for trifles excommunicate whole churches, because they hold not correspondency with them in their errors, they tyrannise over the faith of others: those that withhold the means of knowledge, that so in a dark time all their fooleries may be more admired. As we see masks, and such like overly* things, they must have the commendation of some light that is not so glorious as the sun to win admiration of men; so those that would win admiration of their fooleries, they shut people, as much as they may, in darkness, that they may have their persons, and all other things in admiration. This is to tyrannise over faith, and to hinder them from that that is the means to reform them better.

Quest. But who are guilty of all this?

Ans. We see what church especially is guilty of this of domineering over the faith of others, that is, the church of Rome.

1. The Council of Trent equaliseth traditions with the word of God. They divide the word of God into the written and unwritten; and under a curse they pronounce that all must be received with the same reverence.

2. And then they have devised a will-worship of their own, and follow,

* That is, 'over-lying,' = concealing, disguising.—G.

and force their will-worship with greater violence, than the worship of God; and they set God's stamp upon all their fooleries, to gain authority under the name of Christ's church, and the word of God: they carry all.

3. Again, you know, they hold the church to be infallible. They hold the judgment of the pope, the 'man of sin,' to be infallible, he cannot err; and hereupon whatsoever he saith, it must bind conscience, because he is in his chair and cannot err; whatsoever he saith is the scope of God's word, infallible. And this is a fundamental error, as we call it, a first lie, a leading lie. This is moving to error, this is the mover that moves all other errors under it.

For whereupon is all the abominations of popery justified? They are justified by this, though they seem ridiculous, gross, and blasphemous, they came from the church, and the church is virtually in the pope. An absurd position, that the whole church should be virtually in one man; yet that is the Jesuitical opinion; and the church cannot err: therefore it is good, because these tenets come from him whose judgment is infallible. That is the error that leadeth to, and establisheth all other errors under it: it is the first lie. And in lies, there is a leading, one goes under another, they never go alone; so this is the leading lie of all popery, that the pope cannot err; by this means they domineer over the faith of others, and make the people even beasts indeed.

But to see the indignity of this, that the pope cannot err, it is the greatest error of all, and the prevention of all amendment on their side. Do you think that they will ever amend their opinion, when they hold this that is a block in the way of all reformation, that the pope can err? for deny that, and you call all the fabric of their religion in question; and grant that, it stops all reformation on their side. What reformation may we hope for on their side that hold this position, that they cannot err? Hence come all their treasons, and rebellions; they have some dispensation from the pope, and he cannot err, though he prescribe rebellion and treason.

4. Another opinion they have, *that the church is the judge of all controversies*, in which the faith of men must be resolved at last; but it is the pope that the Jesuits mean. Now this is indeed to domineer over the faith, to make a man of sin to be a judge over all points of faith, and faith to be resolved at last into that, into the judgment of the church.

The church hath an inducing power, a leading power, persuading to the belief of the Scriptures, and to hear what God saith in his word, but after, there is inward intrinsical grounds in the word, that make us to know the word without the church. Now they would have the authority of the word depend upon the church, and so overrule men's consciences in that case. Whereas all that the church hath, is a leading, inducing, persuading to hear the word, under which word and ordinance we shall see such light and majesty in the Scriptures, that from inward grounds we shall be persuaded that the word of God is the word of God. Therefore the church is the first inducer to believe the word of God, not the last object to which all is resolved. For they themselves cross it in their tenets when they speak discreetly. Is this opinion so, and so? The church holds it. But what authority hath the church to maintain it? Where is the authority of your church? Then they bring some place of Scripture; 'I will be with you to the end of the world,' Mat. xxviii. 20. And, 'he that heareth you, heareth me,' &c. Luke x. 16. I do but a little discover to you the danger of this error. They make the word of God to be believed, because the church saith so; they make truth to be believed, because their man of sin, whom they depend upon, saith so. Do we believe the Trinity, or that Christ is our Redeemer, because the church saith so? Should we not believe it except the church say so? What if the church teach the 'doctrine of devils,' 1 Tim. iv. 1, as they do? They cannot shake it off. We must believe because the church saith so. So upon equal grounds they shall teach the doctrine of devils, and the doctrine of Christ, because the church saith so.

As it was said anciently, he that believes two things, the one for the other, he believes not two, but one in effect; because he believes the one for the other. So in effect they believe nothing but the church; that is, themselves believe the truth to be divine, because they say so; so they may believe any devilish error, because they say so; so any treason, or rebellion must go current, because they say so, because they cannot err. You see how they domineer over the faith of others; shall not Christ be Christ, nor God be God, nor the devil be the devil, except the church say so?

5. Again, *in the very matters themselves, in the points that themselves do not urge*, the church of Rome domineers, and tyranniseth over the souls of people. For example, they hold that *the intention of a minister in the sacrament makes it effectual.* What a fear doth this breed in the souls of men, that they know not whether they be baptized or no, because it must be in the intention of the minister?

And then *in confession*, they must confess all. What a tyranny is this to the souls of people, when perhaps there is somewhat that they have not confessed, and so their confession is of no worth?

And *in satisfaction*, perhaps I have not made satisfaction enough by their injunction laid on me, and therefore I must satisfy in hell; what a rack is this to conscience?

So, what a rack to conscience is that opinion, that the pope cannot err; when I cannot tell, perhaps, whether he be the right pope or no. If he came in by simony, or is not *in cathedra* (*nnnn*), and many conditions they have to solve that point. If any of those conditions be not observed, he is not the man he should be; what tyranny do they force upon people over their faith? Therefore they are called in the Revelations, 'scorpions,' Rev. ix. 3, 10; indeed they are spiritual scorpions, that sting the soul of God's people.

The devil is the king of darkness; and is not he the prince of darkness that maintains ignorance of the word of God, that all his old tenets and opinions may have the better sway, that he may sit in the blind and dark consciences of people? It is said that he 'sits in the temple of God,' 2 Thess. ii. 4, that is, in the church; nay, he labours to have another temple, to sit in man's soul, which is the temple of the Holy Ghost. It is not sufficient for him that is the man of sin to have any other place, he must sit in the very souls and consciences of men.

Satan hath a special malice to sit in the place of God. Since he was turned out of heaven, and cannot come thither, he will come to that place, if he can, upon earth where God should be; and where will God be? God will especially be in the hearts of his people, in the souls and consciences of his people. Conscience is God's throne. Satan being thrust out of heaven, labours to stablish his throne there. Now they that are Satan's vicars, led with his spirit, they are of the same mind. Let them be what kind of great ones they will, they desire to sit in God's throne, in the conscience; and if a man will not tie his conscience to them, he is nobody to them. This is the property of antichrist in the highest degree; as far as any are addicted to this, that they will not be satisfied, but the consciences of men must be tied to them, they must deny all honesty, and justice, and law, and all to please them, and to gratify them with particular kindness; so far they are led with the spirit of antichrist, and of the devil himself, who labours to sit in God's throne, that is, in the hearts and consciences of people. And therefore, as I said, they labour to keep people in darkness for this very purpose, that people may let them into their consciences, and rule them as they please.

As Samson, when they had put out his eyes, they led him to base services; so do they with God's people, they put out their eyes, and then they lead them to grind in the mill, to all the base services they can, Judges xvi. 21. It is not to be spoken of the brutish slavery and ignorance that is in Spain and other countries where that devilish inquisition reigns, which is a great help to popish tyranny.

What should I speak of the state of the Romish Church? Indeed the main scope of it is to subdue all to them, to subdue all kings and kingdoms to them. That is the grand scope of the greatest of them. Others have their particular scope for their bellies and base ends; but those among them that have brains, that are governors, their scope is to bring all under their girdle; and how shall they do this? They cannot bring their persons, but they must bring their consciences; for where the conscience is, the person will follow presently. Therefore they labour to lay a tie upon the conscience of prince and people, upon all, that so they may domineer and rule over their consciences. And for that end, they labour to nourish them up in blindness; for by blindness they rule in the conscience; and ruling their conscience, they may rule their persons and kingdoms. This is their main scope, this hath been their plot for many hundred years.

So that the Romish religion indeed is nothing but a mere carnal devilish policy, to bring others to be subject to them; and to make not only kings and princes, but to make God, and Christ, and the Scriptures, whatsoever is divine or human, to make all to serve their aims. What do they with Christ, but under the name of Christ serve themselves? What do they with the church, but under the name of the church, carry their own ends? What do they with the names of saints and angels, Peter, Mary, &c., but under a plausible pretence carry their own ends, and set up a visible greatness in this world, answerable to the Cæsarian monarchy? This is plain and evident to all that will see, that it is so; and one main way to attain their ends is to rule over the conscience.

And that they may help all the better forward, they have raised in the church a kind of faith which they call an implicit and infolded faith, that people must believe what the church teacheth, though they know not in particular what the church teacheth, and so they lead people hoodwinked whither they please themselves.

To make some use of it briefly.

Use. Let us labour *to bless God that hath freed us from this spiritual tyranny.* O! beloved! it is a great tyranny when conscience is awaked, to be racked and tormented, and stung by scorpions; to have conscience tormented with popish errors; as in the point of satisfaction, the most of them, if their eyes be open, they die with terror. O! it is a blessed liberty that we are brought out of antichristian darkness, that we know we believe, and upon what terms we believe; and are taught to submit our conscience only to the blessed truth of God; that the soul it is the bed, as it were, only for Christ, and his Holy Spirit to dwell in, and to lodge in; and that no man may force the conscience with any opinion of his own, further than it is demonstrated out of the word of God. What a sweet enlargement of spirit do we live in now! and our unthankfulness perhaps may occasion God to bring us in some degree of popish darkness again.

I beseech you, let us stand for the liberty of Christ, and the liberty of our consciences against the spiritual tyrant of souls. Let us maintain our liberty by all we can, by all laws and execution of laws; by all that may uphold our spiritual liberty; for there is no bondage to that of the soul. Do but a little consider the misery of the implicit faith that the popish sort are under, that infolded, inwrapped faith, wherein they are bound to believe, without searching, what the church determines. Hereupon they swallow in all doctrines that tend to superstition, that tend to rebellion, that tend to treason. They swallow up all under this implicit faith, as if God had set an ordinance and ministry in the church against himself; as if he had advanced any ministry against his own ordinance.

When you think of popery, consider not so much particular dotages, as about images, and transubstantiation, and relics, &c., but consider the very life and soul of popery in this opinion, the leading error of all others, the tyranny over souls of people, and holding them in blindness and darkness. It is not a device of mine. Do but read the Council of Trent in some editions. There the late Pius Quartus that sat there daily, he made more articles than the apostles, distinct, not proved by Scripture; he made articles of his own to be believed. People were tied upon the necessity of salvation to believe them, and to believe them with that faith that is due to Scripture (*oooo*).

And it is a common tenet among them, Every man is bound to be under the authority of the church of Rome, under peril of damnation. There is the grand error, that it is a matter necessary to salvation to be under their tyranny.

Hereby they excommunicated all the Eastern churches, and all former times wherein they were not under the Roman tyranny, for that is but of late, six hundred years since. They condemned St Cyprian's time, and other times. And they made articles of religion, and established them with this censure, that upon pain of damnation men must believe these things as well as the articles of the creed, as transubstantiation, invocation of saints, purgatory, and such things. They are so many articles, indeed, as I say, they have more articles than the twelve articles of the apostles.*

We say, an error in the foundation, it is not mended after: and the first concoction, if it be naught, all after are naught; if there be not good concoction in the stomach at the first, the blood is naught, and all is naught. So this is a fundamental error, and a ground of all errors, that they hold they cannot err; and hereupon they come to tyrannise over the consciences and souls of people.

Therefore, I say, let us bless God that hath set our souls in spiritual liberty, that now we see God in the face of Christ, now we see the means of salvation. We see the bread of life broken to us, we see Christ unveiled, we see what to found our consciences upon. We cannot be sufficiently thankful for this. Thankful we may be for the peace of the kingdom that we have so long a time enjoyed, and for the outward prosperity we have so long had; but, above all, be thankful for the peace of religion, for the peace of conscience, for the liberty of soul, that we enjoy. And, as I said, if anything move God to strip us of all, it will be our unthankfulness, and our

* The reference here and above, is to 'The Creed,' which is commonly called the Apostles'. Cf. Nichols' Pearson, (8vo, 1854).—G.

practice witnessing our unthankfulness, by valuing no more the blessed estate of the gospel we enjoy.

'*Not that we have dominion over your faith.*' This disposition to domineer over the faith of others, from abominable grounds it ariseth:

Partly from pride and tyranny, that they would set themselves in the temple of Christ, where he should rule in the hearts of his people.

And partly out of idleness. They raise the credit of their own traditions, that they may not be forced to take the labour of instructing the people. Therefore, they fasten a greater virtue upon outward things than there can be, only to avoid the labour of instruction.

And then it riseth partly from guilt. They are so in their lives, especially if they be looked inwardly into, as that they cannot endure the knowledge of people. They are afraid that people should know much, lest they know them too well, and their courses and errors. So, partly from pride, and partly from idleness and sloth, and partly from guilt, they domineer over the faith of God's people.

'*But are helpers of your joy.*' The end of the ministry is not to tyrannise over people's souls, to sting and vex them, but to minister comfort, to be helpers of their joy; that is, to help their salvation and happiness, which is here termed joy, because joy is a principal part of happiness in this world and in the world to come. Now, the end of the ministry is to set the people's hearts into a gracious and blessed liberty, to bring them into the kingdom of grace here, and to fit them for the kingdom of glory, to help forward their joy.

This is the end, both of the word and of the dispensation of the word, in the ordinances of salvation, in the sacraments, and all, that our joy may be full; as our blessed Saviour saith, 'These things have I spoken, that your joy may be full,' John xv. 11. It is the end of all our communion with the Father, Son, and Holy Ghost, and with the ministry, and one with another; as it is, 1 John i. 4, 'These things have I written that your joy may be full;' you have communion with the Father, Son, and Holy Ghost, and with us, 'that your joy may be full.' All is for spiritual joy.

'We are helpers of your joy.' The meaning is, we are helpers of your faith, from whence joy comes more especially; for he doth not repeat the word again, 'We have not dominion over your faith, but are helpers of your faith;' but, instead of that, he names joy, as that that doth accompany true faith.

The points considerable in this clause are these:

1. *That joy is the state of Christians, that either they are in, or should labour to be in*, because the apostle names it for all happiness here. All that have given their names to Christ should labour to rejoice. Either they do rejoice, or they should labour to come to it. That is supposed as a ground. I will be the shorter in it.

2. The second is, *that the ministers are helpers of this blessed condition.*

3. The third is, *they are but helpers.* They are helpers, and but helpers. They are not authors of joy, but helpers. 'We are but helpers of your joy,' saith the apostle. These three things I will speak of briefly out of these words. First,

Doct. 1. *Joy is that frame and state of soul that all that have given their names to Christ either are in, or should labour to be in.*

For this doctrine is fetched from the principle of nature. We do all with joy. All in our callings is done with joy. What do men in their trades, but that they may have that that they may joy in when they have it? It is an old observation of St Chrysostom, 'We do all, that we may joy.' Ask any man why he doth take so much pains, and be a drudge in his place? It is that he may get somewhat to rejoice in in his old days. So, out of the principle of nature, this ought to be the scope of all, to joy.

Now, those that are Christians, God requires it at their hand as a duty, 'Rejoice alway, again I say, rejoice,' Philip. iv. 4. And he doth prepare and give them matter enough of joy, to those that are Christians.

(1.) For whether we consider *the ills they are freed from*, the greatest ills of all. They are freed from sin and the wrath of God, they are freed from eternal damnation, they are freed from the sting of death, from the greatest and most terrible ills.

(2.) Or whether we regard *the state that God brings them in* [to] *by believing:* being in the favour of God, they enjoy the fruits of that favour, 'peace and joy in the Holy Ghost,' Rom. xiv. 17. And then for the life to come, they are under the 'hope of glory.' The state of a Christian is a state of joy every way, whether, I say, we regard the ill he is freed from, or the good he is in for the present, or the hope of eternal good for the time to come. A Christian, which way soever he look, hath matter of joy. God the Father is his, Christ is his, the Holy Ghost is his Comforter, the angels are his, all are his, life or death, things present or things to come, all are his, 1 Cor. iii. 22. Therefore, there is no question of this, that every one that hath given his name to Christ is in a state of joy, if he answer his calling, or he should labour to be in it; he wrongs his condition else.

Why should they labour to be in that state?

Reason 1. Among many reasons, one is, that God that gives them such matter of joy, may have glory from them. For what should the life of a Christian be, that is freed from the greatest ill, and advanced to the greatest good? His life should be a perpetual thanksgiving to God; and how can a man be thankful that is not joyful? Joy is, as it were, the oil, the anointing. It makes a man cheerful, it makes the countenance of his soul to be cheerful.

Reason 2. It makes him active in good, when he is anointed with the oil of gladness. Now every man should have a desire to be good, to be diligent and expedite* in all that is good. Therefore we should labour for this spiritual anointing, that we may be ready for every good work, 'Vessels of mercy prepared for every good work,' Rom. ix. 23.

Reason 3. And then for suffering, we have many things to go through in this world. How shall a man suffer those things that are between him and heaven, with joy, unless he labour to bring himself to this temper of joy?

Reason 4. And then for others, every man should labour to encourage others. We are all fellow-passengers in the way to heaven. Therefore even to bring on others more cheerfully, we ought to labour to be in a state of joy. Those that do not rejoice, they bring an ill report upon the way of God, as if it were a desolate, disconsolate way. As the spies brought an ill report upon the land of Canaan, whereupon the people were disheartened from entering into it; so those that labour not to bring their hearts to spiritual joy, they bring an ill report on the ways of God, and dishearten others from entering into those ways. Which way soever we look, we have reasons to encourage us to joy, that God may have more glory, and that we may do him more service; that we may endure afflic-

* That is, 'active.'—G.

tions better, and encourage others, and take away the reproach of religion from those that think it a melancholy course of life; which indeed do not understand what belongs to the state of a Christian, for the state of a Christian is a state of joy.

And if a Christian do not joy, it is not because he is a Christian, but because he is not a Christian enough, because he favours the worse principle in him, he favours himself in some work of the flesh.

God in the covenant of grace is all love and mercy. He would have us in our pilgrimage to heaven to 'finish our course with joy,' Acts xx. 24; and he knows we can do nothing except we have some joy. It is the oil of the soul, as I said, to make it nimble and fit for all actions, and for all sufferings. It gives a lustre and grace to whatsoever we do. Not only God loves a cheerful performer of duties, but it wins acceptance of all others, and makes the worker himself wondrous ready for any action. This I mention only as a ground. A Christian that hath given his name to Christ, is either in a state of joy, or else should labour for it.

The second, which is the main, is that—

Doct. 2. The word of God, as it is unfolded, is that that helps this joy.

'We are helpers of your joy,' we ministers. St Paul spake of himself as a minister. The word of God is a helper of joy, especially as it is unfolded, considered as it is dispensed in the ministry. You know the word of God it is called 'the word of reconciliation,' 2 Cor. v. 18, because it doth unfold the covenant between God and us. It is called 'the word of the kingdom,' the 'word of life,' &c., which all are causes of joy; therefore the word breeds joy, Ps. xix. One commendation of the statutes of God is, that 'they comfort the heart,' Ps. xix. 8, and refresh the heart. He follows the commendation of the word at large, 'The statutes of God are perfect, converting the soul; the testimonies of God are sure, making wise the simple,' Ps. xix. 7, 8, 9. And among the rest of the commendations, as a commendation issuing from the rest, 'The statutes of God are right, rejoicing the heart.' The word of God is a cordial, especially to refresh and solace the heart.

St Paul, Rom. xv. 4, makes it the scope of the word: 'Whatsoever was written aforetime, was written for our learning, that we, through patience and comfort of the Scriptures, might have hope,' So likewise, 'He that prophesieth speaketh to men to edification, to exhortation, and to comfort,' 1 Cor. xiv. 3, 4. 'He that prophesieth,' that unfoldeth the word, 'he speaketh to men to edification, to exhortation, and to comfort.' So the end of the word, and the end of prophesying, the ministry of the word, is to help our joy, our comfort, to support us against all ills either felt or feared, by greater arguments than the ill is. For that is to comfort and rejoice, to make any to joy. It is to support the soul against all grievance, either spiritual or outward, either felt or feared, and that from stronger arguments than the grievances are. If they be equally poised, it is no comfort; if the comfort be inferior, it is no comfort.

As the heathen man complained of those comforts he had, I know not how it is, but the physic I have to cure the grievance of my mind, it yields to the malice of the disease, the disease is above the cure. So it is true of all philosophical comforts, that are fetched out of the shop of nature, the physic yields to the disease; the malady or disease exceeds the remedy, therefore there is no comfort. Comfort is, when the inward support is greater and stronger than the grievance is, whatsoever it be.

Now such comfort must only be fetched out of the word. The Scripture is a common treasury of all good and comfortable doctrines; but especially as it is dispensed in the ministry, as it is divided by the ministers of God; thereafter as they see the necessity of God's people, and the exigents* they are brought to, accordingly they should draw comfort out of this common treasury. Thereupon that that Christ saith of himself, 'Thou hast given me the tongue of the learned, to speak a word in season to the weary soul,' Isa. l. 4, it is true of all the true ministers of Christ, that have that spiritual anointing, that have the same Spirit that Christ had. 'God hath anointed them, that they might speak a word in season' to poor distressed souls. God hath given them the tongue of the learned, for this very end and purpose. God hath given them a healing tongue for a wounded soul. Indeed, they carry physic in their tongues; and the very leaves, the very words, have a medicinal force.

When those that are true ministers speak a word in season to a wounded, distressed soul, the Spirit goes with the word, and it hath wondrous efficacy for the comfort and raising up of the soul. Experience shews this.

Now to give a few instances how it is done, how the ministers do it, how they are 'helpers of our joy.'

1. They do it *first* of all, *by acquainting people with the ill estate they are in;* for all sound comfort comes from the knowledge of our grief, and freedom from it. They acquaint people with their estate by nature, that they are in the state of damnation, that they are under the 'curse' of God, under the 'wrath of God,' that they are in a 'spiritual bondage;' they labour that they, together with the spirit of bondage, may make people to see their state of bondage. For they must plough before they sow, and the law must go before the gospel. The law shews the wound, but the gospel heals the wound. Now they must know the wound; the commanding part, all the threatening part of the word. They must know what they are, before they can know their comfort. Therefore John Baptist he came before Christ, he made way for the sweet doctrine of Christ that came with blessing in his mouth, 'Blessed are the poor in Spirit;' 'Blessed are they that hunger and thirst;' 'Blessed are those that suffer persecution,' &c., Mat. v. 3, 6, 10. Even as to Elias there was a strong wind came before the still voice, 1 Kings xix. 12, so there must be somewhat to rend, and to open the heart, before this oil of comfort can be poured in. Now that is the first thing, the ministers help people to comfort, by helping them to understand themselves, what they are in the state of nature. They labour to search the wound first, to cure the soul as much as they can of all guile of spirit, that the soul may not be guileful to misunderstand itself.

2. And when they have done this, then they breed joy, *by propounding, and shewing the remedy which is in Jesus Christ;* then they open the riches of God's love in Christ, then open the sweet 'box of ointment' in Christ, they shew to man his righteousness. As you have an excellent place in Job, chap. xxxiii. 14, *seq.*, of the whole force of the ministry; it is followed at large what the minister doth to bring a man to joy. He begins, verse 14, 'God speaks once and twice, but man perceives it not; in visions and dreams by night, when deep sleep falls upon them; then he opens the ears of man, and seals instruction,' &c. 'He chastiseth him with pain upon his bed, and the multitude of his bones with strong pain; so that his life abhors bread.' He speaks of a man, that is brought down by the sight of sin. 'His flesh is consumed away, it cannot be seen, his bones stick out,' &c.

* That is, 'exigencies.' Cf. footnote, vol. I. p. 412.—G.

A strange description of a man in a disconsolate estate. His 'soul draws near to the grave, and his life to the destroyers.' What of all this? what is the way to bring him out of this? 'If there be a messenger with him, an interpreter, one of a thousand, one that hath the tongue of the learned, to shew a man his righteousness, then God is gracious to him, and delivers him from going to the pit. I have found a ransom,' &c. The messenger, 'one of a thousand,' the man of God, that hath 'the tongue of the learned,' he hath showed him where his ransem is to be had, he hath shewed him his righteousness.

Thus did St Peter, after he had brought them to 'Men and brethren, what shall we do to be saved?' Acts ii. 37, 38; then he points them out to Jesus Christ. Therefore the ministry is called 'the ministry of reconciliation,' 2 Cor. v. 18, and the 'ministry of peace,' Eph. ii. 17; they are called 'messengers of peace.' You know joy comes from reconciliation with God in Christ, joy comes from peace. Now the ministers they are messengers of reconciliation, and messengers of peace, and therefore messengers of joy, 'They bring glad tidings of joy,' Luke i. 19. You see how ministers are helpers of joy, by shewing to man his ill, and then by shewing to man his good, and comfort in Jesus Christ; they shew, that 'where sin hath abounded, grace abounds much more,' Rom. v. 20. They dig the mine, to let people see what riches, what treasure they have in the word of God, and what comfort they have there.

3. And then in the continual course of life, they are 'helpers of joy.' For what do ministers, if they be faithful in their places, but *advise in cases of conscience what people should do?* so their office is to remove all scruples, and hindrances, and obstacles of spiritual joy, by advising them what to avoid, and what to do (*pppp*).

We know that *light* is a state of joy. The ministry of the gospel is light. It sets up the light of God's truth. It shews them the way they should go in all the course of their life; and thereupon it rejoiceth them. The word of God is a lanthorn, especially in the ministry.

Spiritual liberty, and freedom, that doth make people joyful. But the end of the ministry is to set people more and more at liberty; both from the former estate that I named, and likewise daily by office, to set them at liberty from corruptions, and temptations, and snares; to bring them to an enlarged estate.

Victory, and triumph is a state of joy. Now the ministers of God teach God's people, how to fight God's battles, how to handle their weapons, how to answer temptations, how to conquer all, and at length how to triumph. Therefore in that regard they are helpers of their joy. They encourage them against discouragements, against infirmities and afflictions, against Satan's temptations, shewing them grounds of joy out of the Scriptures.

4. Then they are 'helpers of their joy,' by *forcing it as a duty upon them*, 'Rejoice evermore, and again I say, rejoice,' saith St Paul, Philip. iv. 4. They are as guides among the rest of the travellers, that encourage them in the way to heaven, 'Come on,' let us go cheerfully. As the apostles in all their epistles, they stir up to joy and cheerfulness; so should those do that are guides to God's people. Travellers they need refreshments of wine, &c. Now thus the ministers of God help the people of God in their spiritual travel to heaven. If the people of God faint at any time, then as it is, Cant. ii. 5, they refresh them with 'apples and wine,' with the comforts of the Holy Ghost. They are ready to support and comfort them in all their spiritual falls, when they are ready to sink.

We see by experience in all places where the ministry of the word is established, how comfortably people live, and die, and end their days above other people 'that sit in darkness, and in the shadow of death,' Mat. iv. 16. So we see this is true, that the ministers help joy, because they help that that breeds joy, not only at the first, but continually help the joy of the people of God, even to death.

5. And then *in death itself*, the end of the ministry is to help joy, to help them to heaven, to help them to a joyful departure hence, to give them a good and comfortable loose* out of this world, drawing comfort out of the word for this purpose; for whatsoever the minister doth, it is by drawing comfort out of the word, shewing them that the sting of death is taken away, that now death is reconciled, and become a friend to us in Christ; that it is but a passage to heaven, that now it is the end of all misery, and the beginning of all happiness, 'Blessed are those that die in the Lord,' Rev. xiv. 13. So they assist, and help them in those last agonies.

There is special use of the dispensation of the word in all conditions while we live, and at the hour of death. You see it is clear, I need not further enlarge the point, that the ministers by reason of the word, which indeed is the main thing that comforts, they are helpers of the joy of God's people.

Obj. But you will say, They help God's people to sorrow, and they vex and trouble them ofttimes.

Ans. Indeed, carnal men think so, as the two witnesses in the Revelations, it is said, 'They vexed the men upon the earth,' Rev. xi. 10. So indeed, the faithful witnesses of God, they vex the earthly-minded, base men; as Ahab said of Elias, 'Thou art he that troubleth Israel,' 1 Kings xviii. 17. He accounted him as one that troubled Israel, when it was himself that troubled Israel. These ministers, they are accounted those that mar all the mirth in the world; that a man that is given to pleasures and delights, he trembles at the sight of them, as men opposite to his delights and carnal course: he cannot brook the very sight of them; so it is with a carnal man.

But we may make an use hence, to judge of what spirit they are that judge and think so, they are not true believers; for there is no man that hath given his name to Christ, and makes it good by his life that he is a good Christian, but he accounts the ministers 'helpers of his joy.' Those that do not so, are in an ill course; and which is worse, they resolve to be in an ill course.

Therefore, let us make much of the ordinances of God, as that which is the joy of our souls; not only make much of the word of God, but of the word of God in the ministerial dispensation of it; for ofttimes we find that comfort by the opening of the word of God, that our own reading and private endeavours could never help us to: experience shews that. We see when the eunuch was to be converted, it was he that read, but Philip was sent to open the word to him, and then 'he went away rejoicing,' Acts viii. 39. And so the poor jailer, when the word was opened and applied to him, then he rejoiced, Acts xvi. 33. Therefore, as we intend our own comfort, let us regard the ministry.

Obj. Many object that, that Naaman the Assyrian did, I can have as much comfort by reading.

Ans. I would they were so well occupied. But God gives a curse to private means, when they are used with neglect of the public. And joy comes

* That is, 'loosening,' = departure. Cf. note *a*, vol. I. p. 350.—G.

from God's Spirit. God will not attend our pleasure to give us joy and delight in what we single out, but in his own course and way. And if Naaman the Assyrian,* that thought the rivers of Damascus were as good as Jordan, and, therefore he thought it a fond† thing to wash there; if he had not yielded to the counsel of his servants, he had gone a leper home as he came; but he was wiser, 2 Kings. v. So those that cavil at the ordinance of God, they may live and die lepers for aught I know, except with meekness of spirit they attend upon the ordinance.

Obj. But you will say, Those that are true Christians and good men, they are ofttimes cast down by the ministry, and brought to pangs of conscience; therefore, what joy can there be? how are they 'helpers of their joy?'

Ans. If they do so, yet it is that they might joy. St Paul did bring the Corinthians here to sorrow, but he brought them to sorrow that they might joy; as you have it excellently set down. 'For though I made you sorry with a letter, I do not repent, though I did repent,' 2 Cor. vii. 8. I was sorry that I was forced to be so bitter against you; for I perceive that the same epistle made you sorry, though but for a season; 'now I rejoice, not that you were made sorry' (here is a sweet insinuation), but that you were sorry to repentance; 'for you were made sorry after a godly manner, that you might receive damage by us in nothing.' So the sorrow that is wrought by the ministry in the hearts of the people, it is a sorrow to repentance, a sorrow tending to joy.

We say of April, that the showers of that month dispose the earth to flowers in the next; so tears and grief wrought in the heart by the ministry, they breed delight in the soul; they frame the soul to a delightful, joyful temper after.‡ And that is part of the scope of this very text, 'we are helpers of your joy,' and, therefore, if I had not spared you, but had come in severity, all had been for joy: so whether the minister open comfort or direction, it is for their joy. If they see them not in a state fit, then [it is their office] to discover to them their sin and danger, and to tell them that they must be purged by repentance, before they can receive the cordial of joy; but all is for joy in the end.

A physician comes, and he gives sharp and bitter purges; saith the patient, I had thought you had come to make me better, and I am sicker now than I was before. But he bids him be content, all this is for your health and strength, and for your joyfulness of spirit after; you will be the better for it. So in confidence of that, he drinks down many a bitter potion. So it is with those that sit under the ministry of God, though it be sharp and severe, and cross their corruptions, yet it is medicinal physic for their souls, and all will end in the health of the soul, in joy afterwards.

Obj. It will be objected again, The word of God, and the dispensation of it, it is for doctrine, 'to teach and to instruct,' and not especially to joy: that should not be the main end; for we see in Rom. xv. 4, 'Whatsoever was written, was written for our learning.' So in 1 Cor. xiv. 3, he that speaks, speaks to 'edification and exhortation,' as well as to comfort.

Ans. It is true; but all teaching, and all exhortation, and all reproof, they tend to comfort: even doctrine itself tends to comfort. For as it is with divers kinds of food, they have both a cherishing virtue in them to strengthen, and a healing virtue to cure. So it is with the word of God,

* That is, 'Syrian.'—ED. † That is, 'foolish.'—G.

‡ See this comparison beautifully stated by Adams (Practical Works, vol. III. p. 299).—ED.

the doctrinal part of it hath a comforting force. And, indeed, doctrine is for comfort; for what is comfort but a strengthening of the affections, from some sound grounds of doctrine imprinted upon the understanding, whereof it is convinced before? The understanding is convinced thoroughly, before the soul can be comforted thoroughly. Therefore the Scripture tending to doctrine, that being one end of it, tends likewise to comfort, because that is the issue of doctrine; for what is comfort, but doctrine applied to a particular comfortable use?

As in plants and tree, what is the fruit of the tree? nothing but the juice of the tree applied and digested into fruit; so, indeed, doctrine is that that runs through the whole life of a Christian, and the strength of doctrine is in comfort. Comfort is nothing but doctrine sweetly digested and applied to the affections. He will never be a good comforter, that doth not first stablish the judgment in some grounds of doctrine, to shew whence the comfort flows. So that howsoever there be many things in Scripture that are doctrinal, yet in the use of them those doctrinal points tend to joy and comfort. As, I said, in meat there is the same thing, something* that both nourisheth and likewise refresheth, as a cordial; so the word of God both nourisheth the understanding, and is as a cordial to refresh and comfort; and it is a kind of joy to the soul, to have it stablished in sound doctrine: that is the ground of comfort. So that notwithstanding any thing that can be objected, the end of the word of God, especially in the dispensation of it, is to joy and comfort.

Use. Which should teach people to regard the ministry in this respect, that it is a helper of their comfort, that they do not grieve those that help their comfort; for what is the end of a minister, as a minister, but to make others joy? that both God in heaven, and the angels, and ministers, and all may rejoice together in the conversion of a Christian.† Now, for people to vex those that, by virtue of their calling, labour to help forward their joy, is very unkind usage; yet it was the entertainment that our blessed Lord and Master himself found in the world; and St Paul himself saith, 'The more I love you, the less I am loved of you,' 2 Cor. xii. 15.

And then it should move people to lay open the case of their souls to their spiritual physicians upon all good occasions. People do so for the physicians of their bodies; they do so in doubtful cases for their estates. Is all so well in our souls that we need no help nor comfort? no removing of objections that the soul makes, no unloosing of the knots of conscience? Is all so clear? Or are men in a kind of numbness, and deadness, and atheism, that they think it is no matter that they put all to a venture, and think all is well? It were better for the souls of many if they had better acquaintance with their spiritual pastors than they have; for their calling is to help the joy of the people; and how can they help it except they lay open their estates to them upon good occasion? What do they herein but rob themselves of joy? They are their own enemies.

I pass to the third,

Doct. 3. *They are helpers of joy, and but helpers.*

They do but utter and propound matter of joy, grounds of joy from the word of God; but it is the Spirit of God that doth rejoice the heart, 'The fruit of the lips is peace,' Isa. lvii. 19. It is true, but it is when the Spirit of God speaks peace to the soul together with the lips, 'God creates the fruit of the lips to be peace,' saith Isaiah. The fruit of the lips is peace,

* Misprinted 'sometime.'—G.

† That is, 'of a sinner converted *into* a Christian.'—G.

but God creates it to be so. So the ministers are comforters, but God saith, 'I, even I, am thy comforter,' Isa. li. 12. We speak matters of comfort and grounds of comfort, but God seals them to the heart by his Holy Spirit. God is the comforter himself, 'He is the Father of comfort, and the God of all consolation,' Rom. xv. 5. And the Spirit is called 'the Comforter,' to shew unto us that however in the ordinances the materials of comfort be set a-broach* to God's people, yet notwithstanding that that speaks peace to the heart, and sets on those comforts to the soul and conscience, it is the Spirit of God, God himself. So there is the outward preaching and the spiritual preaching. He hath his chair in heaven that teacheth the heart, as St Austin saith (*qqqq*). St Paul speaks, but God opens the heart of Lydia; he hath the key to open the heart.†

Therefore, you have all attributed to the Spirit of God. In John xvi. 5, *seq.*, 'I go hence, but I will send you the Comforter,' the Holy Ghost; and what shall the Comforter do? 'He shall convince the world of sin, of righteousness, and judgment.' Do not pretend, therefore, your own inability, that you are unable to comfort, or to cast down, or to seal unto people their righteousness; do you that that is your duty, propound grounds of direction, and casting down, and of righteousness, and of judgment, of holy life after; and then the Holy Ghost shall go with you; the Comforter shall do this to the hearts of people; the Holy Ghost shall convince. 'What is Paul, or what is Apollos, but ministers?' 'Paul may plant, and Apollos may water;' but if God give not the increase, what is all? 1 Cor. iii. 6.

Therefore, Christ promiseth his disciples, that the Holy Ghost should accompany their teaching. They might have objected, Alas! we shall teach the world, that they are Gentiles, that they are obstinate persons, hardened in superstition. Do not fear, saith he, 'I will send the Holy Ghost.' He shall fall upon you and furnish you. Now when the Holy Ghost was in them, and the Holy Ghost in their auditors too, together with the word inspired by the Holy Ghost: when the Spirit meets in these three, there are wonders wrought. When the Spirit of God is in the teacher, and the Spirit of God in the hearers, and the Spirit of God in the word: I say, when there is one Spirit in the teacher, and in the hearers, and in the word, there are wonders wrought of conversion and comfort.

It is the Spirit that must do all. We are nothing but ministers. 'Let a man conceive of us as ministers and dispensers of the gospel,' 1 Cor. iv. 1. Ministers of comfort we are, and but ministers; just so we are 'helpers of your joy,' but we are but helpers. Those that account us not helpers of joy, know not our calling; and those that account us more, that we are able to comfort people by the word, they turn the preaching of the word to magic, to a charm. We can speak the word; but God must speak to the heart at the same time.

As it is with physical water; there is the water, and there are many strong things in it. What! doth the water cure or purge? It is a dead thing, it hath no efficacious quality, but to cool, &c. Whence comes the efficacy? There are some cool herbs, some strong things in it, and then it doth wonders. So what is the infusion of the word but water, but *aqua vitæ*, water of life, the dew of heaven, *rosa solis?* Whence is it so? As water? No; but there is a divine influence and vigour in it, that refresheth and

* That is, 'broached' = opened.—G.

† 'Lydia's Heart Opened,' is the title of one of Sibbes's minor writings.—G.

quickeneth the soul. It doth not do it of itself, but it hath a divine influence of the Spirit.

So we see, though ministers be helpers of joy, they are but helpers. They are but the conduits that convey that that comes from the Spirit of God. They are instruments of the Spirit.

1. You see it clear then, *that God only speaks comfort*; because the Spirit of God only knows our spirits thoroughly. The Spirit of God can only comfort, because he knows all the discomforts of our hearts, he knows all our griefs, all the corners of our hearts. That the minister cannot do. The minister may speak general comforts; but the Spirit of God knows all the windings and turnings of the heart, and all the disconsolate pangs of the heart and soul; every little pang and grief, the Spirit of God knows it. Therefore, the Spirit of God is the Comforter. He strikes the nail, and seals the comfort to the soul: we are but helpers.

2. Then again, the Spirit of God must do it, *because the soul must be set down with that that is stronger than itself.* It must be so convinced and set down, that it must have more to say against the grief or temptation, than can be alleged by the devil himself. The soul, before it be comforted, it must be quieted and stilled. Now who is above the soul, and Satan that tempts the soul? Let Satan be let loose to tempt the soul, and the soul hath a hell in itself, if God let it alone. Who is above those unspeakable torments of conscience, if they be not allayed by the Spirit of God? Who is above the soul, but the Spirit of God? Will the soul allay itself? No, it will never. Therefore the Spirit of God, that is stronger and wiser than the soul, and is the Spirit of light and strength, it must set down, and quiet, and calm the soul, that it hath nothing to say against the comfort it brings, but quiets itself, and saith, I must rest, I must see this is from heaven, I am quiet. This the Spirit doth.

Use. Therefore make this use of it, that in all our endeavours to procure peace to our consciences, and spiritual balm to the wounds of our souls, *let us go to this heavenly Physician:* not depend overmuch upon the ministry, or reading, or any outward task; but in the use of all things lift up our hearts to God, that he would comfort us by his Spirit, that he would send the Comforter into our souls.

Though the disciples had comfort upon comfort by Christ, yet till the Comforter came, whose office it was to do it, to seal his word to their souls, alas! they were dead-hearted people; but after the resurrection, when the Comforter came, and refreshed their memories, and convinced their understandings, then they could remember all the sweet comforts that our blessed Saviour had taught them before. So it is with us,—we hear many sweet comforts day after day out of God's book, comforts against sin, comforts against trouble, outward, and inward, and all; but till the Comforter come, till God send his Holy Spirit, we shall not make use of them. Therefore let us labour to have more communion with God before we come to hear the word; and after we have heard it, let us have communion with God again, that he would seal whatsoever is spoken to our souls, and make it effectual to us.

Therefore we must learn to give the just due to the ordinance of God, and not to idolize it; to make it the means of comfort, not to make it the chief Comforter, but the Spirit of God by it. What is Paul or Apollos? what are we but ministers of faith? and by consequent, ministers and helpers of comfort, but not the authors of comfort.

Oh! if I had such and such here, I should do well, I should be so and so.

Alas! all is to no purpose, unless thou hast the Holy Ghost, the Spirit of God. That can help by weak means. Therefore we must not tie comfort and joy to this or that means; but in all means look to the ground of comfort, and the spring of all, the Holy Ghost.

The reason why men do not profit more, that they are not more cheered and lift up with the ministry of the word (which is a word 'of reconciliation,' and of joy and comfort), it is because they are more careful in the use of means, than in going to God for his Spirit to bless the means. Now these must go together: a care of using the means, and a care to pray to him that he would give us wisdom, and strength, and blessed success in the use of all means. Then if we would join religiously and conscionably* these two together, the use of all means conscionably, and in the use of all to lift up our hearts to God to bless them, we should find a wondrous success upon the ministry, and all other good means likewise. So much for that. I go on to the last clause of the chapter.

'*For by faith ye stand.*' Why doth the apostle vary the word, 'We have not dominion over your faith, but are helpers of your joy,' whereas the consequence, it seems, might run thus: 'We do not domineer over your faith, but are helpers of your faith?' He puts joy instead of faith; and afterward he brings in faith again: 'for by faith ye stand.'

This is one main reason: because joy riseth from faith, therefore he names it instead of faith; for the Holy Ghost is not curious of words, but when the same Spirit works both, he names that which he thinks will fittest suit the purpose.

Obs. Faith breeds joy.

How is that?

1. Because faith, first of all, doth shew to us the freedom from that that is the cause of all discomfort whatsoever, *it takes away all that may discourage.* For it takes away the fear of damnation for our sins; it shews our reconciliation in Jesus Christ. Faith shews liberty and deliverance; and so discovering deliverance by a Mediator, it works joy. Is not a prisoner joyful when he is set at liberty?

2. Then likewise faith discovers to us the face of God shining to us in Jesus Christ: *it shews not only deliverance, but favour.* It shews us the ground of all, the righteousness and obedience of our Saviour, whereby we are delivered, and brought into favour.

Now from this comes peace: from the knowledge of our deliverance and acceptance with God, founded upon the obedience of God-man, a Saviour, there comes in peace, and peace breeds joy; because faith discovers all these, the ground of reconciliation with God in Jesus Christ, and thereupon peace, therefore it causeth joy.

For this is the pedigree and descent of joy, as the apostle hath it, 'The kingdom of God is in righteousness, and peace, and joy,' Rom. xiv. 17. There must be righteousness first, of a Mediator, to satisfy the wrath of God, and procure his favour. From righteousness comes peace, peace with God, peace of conscience. From peace comes joy. There is no joy without peace, no peace without righteousness.

And this whole pedigree of joy, as it were, is excellently set down, 'Being justified by faith, we have peace with God through Jesus Christ our Lord,' Rom. v. 1, and have access to the throne of grace, by which grace we stand, and not only so, but rejoice. So there is justification by the

* That is, 'conscientiously' = with conscience.—G.

righteousness of Christ, and thereupon peace with God; and from peace, boldness and access to God, and thereupon joy. So we see how faith brings in joy, because it shews the spring of joy whence it comes, it shews peace, and peace riseth from reconciliation, and reconciliation from [the] righteousness of Christ, Mediator, whereupon we are delivered from all that we may fear, and set in a state of true joy, God being our friend. When God is reconciled, all is reconciled, all is ours; have we not cause of joy then? Therefore the apostle saith, 'The God of peace fill you full of joy in believing,' Rom. xv. 13, shewing that faith is the cause of all spiritual joy. And the same you have in 1 Pet. i. 8, 'In whom ye rejoiced, after ye believed, with joy unspeakable and glorious.' In whom, after ye believed, that is, in Christ, 'you rejoiced with joy unspeakable and glorious.' And therefore you see the apostle might well substitute joy instead of faith, because it springs and riseth from faith in Jesus Christ, the Mediator.

Use. Hereupon we may come to make this use of trial, how we may know whether our joy be good or no. Among many other evidences, this is one.

1. That spiritual joy is good, *if it spring from the word of faith;* if it spring from the ordinance of God unfolded in the word, shewing us the ground of believing. For he that truly joys, can shew the ground of his joy.

Herein joy differs from presumption, from presumptuous swelling conceits. True joy, that is, not the joy of an hypocrite, it doth shew from whence it comes, it riseth from grounds out of divine truth.

2. Then again, this joy *doth more immediately spring from faith in the word,* from assurance that God is ours, and that Christ is ours; that God is at peace with us, and that we are at peace with him. It ariseth from peace that is wrought by faith.

3. Then again, this joy, if it be sound, it is such a joy as St Peter saith is an unspeakable and glorious joy. Joy arising from the word of God, and from faith and peace, *it is above discouragement,* because we have in the word of God matter of joy above all discouragements and all allurements whatsoever. It is a joy above the joy of riches, or pleasures, or profits. Why? Because the word shews matter of joy above all these. The prophet David rejoiced in the word of God above gold and silver, 'as one that had gotten great spoils,' Ps. cxix. 162. You see how oft he repeats it. 'It was sweeter to him than the honey and the honeycomb,' Ps. xix. 10. It puts his soul out of taste with all other things. This joy of the Spirit, it puts such a relish in the soul that it makes it undervalue all other things whatsoever. The price of other things falls down when a man joys in the Holy Ghost, because it ariseth from the grounds of faith, from peace and righteousness.

And, likewise, if it look forward, from the hope of life everlasting and the favour of God, the ground of all, it riseth from things that are above all other contentments, 'the lovingkindness of the Lord' (that faith apprehends, that is the ground of joy), 'it is above life itself,' Ps. lxiii. 3. Now, life is the sweetest thing upon earth; but the lovingkindness of God is better than that.

Therefore, those that lose their souls in base contentment, and joy in the dirty things of this life, that are not fit for the soul to fasten on, to place contentment in, but are only to be used as those that take a journey to refresh them; but those that are swallowed up in these things, they know not what spiritual joy is, that ariseth from the word of God, from divine truth, that ariseth from faith; for if they did, this joy would raise them higher, above all earthly contentments whatsoever.

4. Then again, where this joy is, this spiritual enlargement of soul, which is called joy, it is from true grounds, *it is with humility;* for the same word that discovers matter of joy, discovers matter of humility and grief in ourselves, by reason of the remainders of sin and of our own deservings. So true joy, it is a tempered and qualified joy. It is not joined with pride and swelling, because it riseth from those grounds that teach us what we are in ourselves. Alas! such, that we need not be proud in ourselves, but if we will glory, 'we must glory in God,' 1 Cor. i. 31. Well! it is not that that I mean principally to stand on, but only I speak of it because it is placed here for faith, as it springs from faith. 'We are helpers of your joy.' To hasten, then, to that that follows.

'For by faith ye stand.' This principally depends upon the first words, 'We have not dominion over your faith,' because faith is such a grace as you stand by in all conditions. Now, what you stand by must be firm, it must be on a good bottom; and what is firm must not be human, but divine. Therefore, we have no dominion over your faith, 'for by faith ye stand.'

Standing is a military word (*rrrr*). 'By faith ye stand,' that is, first of all faith gives a standing, a certain standing, before any conflict. It gives a standing in Christianity, it sets the soul in a frame, in a standing.

Nay, faith helps us; we stand by faith, not only in a frame of Christianity, and furnished with spiritual strength, but then we are fit to encounter opposition. By faith we stand to it, and stand against all opposition. We stand, and stand to it, by faith.

And standing likewise implies continuance in managing Christianity, and opposing all enemies whatsoever. By faith we stand, and continue standing; we hold out in all opposition.

Standing likewise, in the next place, implies a kind of safety, together with victory at length. 'By faith ye stand.' You stand so as you are not wounded to death; you stand so as you are kept safe, especially from mortal wounds, and altogether safe so far as you use faith as a shield, till you have got perfect victory, and faith end in triumph. So faith is that grace whereby we stand, whereby we are in a frame of religion fit to stand, and whereby we, so standing, encounter oppositions, and continue so encountering, and preserve ourselves safe, till victory be obtained. This is the full expression and comprehension of the word, 'By faith ye stand.'

Quest. Now, why is it by faith that we have this standing?

Ans. Because faith, it is that grace in the new covenant that makes the soul go out of itself. It empties the soul of all things in itself, and goes out to somewhat else, whereupon it stands. For in the new covenant, since Adam's fall, all our strength is in the 'second Adam,' our Head; we fetch it there.* And faith is the hand of the soul.

Now, because faith in the new covenant is an emptying grace, and likewise because, as it is a grace that empties the soul, so it fastens upon another thing, whereupon it relies; for faith is an uniting grace as well as an emptying grace. Now, faith emptying and uniting, so it makes us stand.

And likewise faith as it draws. It hath a drawing virtue, an attractive force. It is a radical grace. It is like a root; when it knits to Christ, it sucks out and draws virtue from him. Every touch of faith draws

* That is, 'thence.'—Ed.

spiritual strength and virtue; so it causeth us to stand by the attractive virtue it hath.

And then it is the force of faith, likewise, to make things present; for therein it differs from hope. Hope looks upon things as absent. Now, the things that hope looks on as things remote and distant in time and place, faith makes them present; therefore, it is said to be 'the evidence of things not seen,' Heb. xi. 1. Now, that that makes the soul to be strong and able to stand, it must be somewhat present. However the full possession of things be reserved, not for faith, but for vision, for comprehenders in heaven, where faith ends and determines, yet notwithstanding faith draws so much for the present. It sets things to come so far present with such evidence and force, as it upholds the soul and makes it stand. 'It is the evidence of things not seen;' and thereupon it hath a kind of omnipotent power to make things that are not, to be. Heaven, and glory, and happiness, they are not for the present; but faith, looking on them in the authority of God and the divine promises, faith makes them present by a kind of almighty power that it hath, laying hold on an Almighty power; and hereupon it upholds the soul, it is the prop and stay of the soul, as in Heb. xi. i. *seq.*, it signifies to stay up, to hold up as a pillar; even from this virtue it hath to make things to come present.

You see, then, what it is to stand, and how faith is fitted for this purpose, because, as I said, it is the grace of the new covenant emptying us and drawing us to Christ, from whom we draw all virtue, and because it makes things to come as present.

By faith we are set in a right frame and condition again, as by want of faith we fell. The same grace must set us right, for want of which we fell.

How came we to fall at the first? You know Adam hearkened to his wife Eve, and she hearkened to the serpent. They trusted not in God, they began to stagger at the promises, to stagger at the word of God. Satan robbed them of the word. He observes, and continues the same art still, to take the word from us, and to cause us to stagger and doubt whether it be true or no. He comes between us and our rock, the word of God. So Adam fell. Now we must be restored by the contrary to that we fell. We fell by unbelief and distrust, by calling God's truth in question; we must learn to stand again by the contrary grace, by faith. Thus you see the terms something unfolded. 'By faith ye stand.'

To clear it a little further. There be four degrees of assent that the soul hath to anything.

1. The *first* is *a slight assent*, that we call opinion, that is, with some fear that it may be otherwise. That is a weak, a pendulous* assent. It is a wavering assent, it yields not a certain assent. Opinion is a weak thing: it may be so: aye, but it may not be so. It is with a fear of the contrary.

2. The *second* degree of assent is that that hath a better ground, *that is the assent to grounds of reason.* A man hath reason to yield and assent to, and those reasons satisfy the soul, and rest the soul something† thereafter as the strength of them is. And that assent we call knowledge, science.‡ This is founded upon grounds of reason.

3. There is a *third* kind of assent and yielding that the soul hath, *that we call believing*, which is merely upon the credit of him that speaks, though we know no reason why the thing should be so; but only the person, it may

* That is, 'swaying.'—G. † That is, 'somewhat.'—G.

‡ Cf. Dan. i. 4, and 1 Tim. vi. 20.—G.

be, is a person of credit, and wisdom, and knowledge; and thereafter as we conceive well of him, thereafter we fasten our faith and assent to his authority; so that assent to the authority of the speaker, we call belief.

4. The *fourth* degree of assent is, when we do not only assent to the thing because we have reason so to do, and arguments, or because we have some man to confirm it by authority; but because we feel it to be so *by experience and by taste.* As a man assents that fire is hot, and that sweet things are so, not from reason altogether, or from the speech or rehearsing of another man, but because he feels it so indeed; he assents to it from experience.

Now you will say, How come we then to stand by faith?

As faith especially relies upon the authority of God, upon God's word, so we stand by faith, because it assents to an authority. But God's word gives reasons too; therefore faith assents to the authority of God's word first; and then we see divine reason enough too, when we once believe God.

And then experience in divine things too. After we believe there is an incredible sweetness in divine things, there is a knowledge with a particular taste. There is never a divine truth but it hath an evidence in it, when a man believes it once, that a man may say, 'I know whom I have believed,' 2 Tim. i. 12, from experience. Let the speakers of the things be what they will, let them apostatize from that that they have spoken; after a man believes, he will see the things themselves have divine reason in them, as well as divine authority stablishing of them.

Some divine truths are altogether upon divine authority. We see no other reason but that God hath said it; but some truths are both credible and intelligible. Credible, because God hath said it, and there is reason to prove it; as a man may prove by divine reason, that 'all shall work for the best,' Rom. viii. 28. Why? The apostle saith, 'We love God, and God hath called us according to his purpose,' Rom. viii. 28. Therefore all things shall work for them that God hath called, to them that answer his divine call. There is both reason and comfort. So it is credible as it hath divine truth, and intelligible as it hath comfort. There are homogeneal reasons with divine authority. God doth not only press us with authority, but he gives us reasons.

Besides this, there is experience; for the doctrine of divine providence, and of the corruption of nature, and the doctrine of comfort in the Mediator Christ altogether, the doctrine of faith, the doctrine of the issue of all troubles for good, we find these by experience. However the teacher that teacheth them, perhaps, may have no sense of them himself, let him apostatize and do what he will, our faith stands upon them, partly because God saith so, that is the chief; and because there is reason for them; and because we find it so by experience. In many divine things, these three, both reason, authority, and experience, concur in faith. But to come a little further.

Quest. What doth faith itself stand most on, by which we stand? That which we stand on must stand itself. Let us examine a little what faith itself stands on, by which we stand.

Ans. I shewed you before partly: by divine authority and experience, which gives some light to it; but we will follow it a little further. That faith by which we stand must stand itself; therefore it cannot be opinion, it must be faith. It must not be bare science neither, it must be science that hath faith; faith must come in. Now faith looks to divine revelation especially, it looks to truth revealed from God. Now faith looking to the word of God, it builds, and pitcheth, and bottoms itself upon divine truth, divine authority, divine revelation, which we call the first truth, the first verity.

And not only so, but faith, that it may stand the better, hath, together with the word of God, the seals; for God hath added sacraments as seals to the word, that helps the word. To us at least, God's word is true enough of itself in regard of him; but he condescends to us, and therefore that faith may stand the better, that we may build upon his word, there are his sacraments. There are seals together with his word, and his oath too.

Again, that his word may be the better foundation for faith, it is conceived under the manner of a covenant, the evangelical part of it, the covenant of grace, wherein God in Christ promiseth to forgive our sins, to accept us to life everlasting, if we believe in Christ. It is a gracious covenant. God condescends to make a covenant that faith may stand; shall not I believe him that hath made a covenant, and bound himself by covenant that he will do so? Nay, in the covenant of grace, faith lays hold upon this, that he will fulfil and perform both conditions himself, both his part and our part. For the same truths that are a covenant, are a 'testament' too in the gospel. A testament bequeaths things without a covenant, and therein it differs from a covenant. A testament is, I bequeath, and give this. Now, whatsoever Christ in the covenant requires, because that in the gospel he makes good, the covenant, is* a testament, 'If we believe and repent,' John iii. 36. Now he hath promised to give repentance and belief in the covenant of grace to all that attend upon the means, and expect the performance of the covenant from him.

For we can no more perform the conditions of the covenant of grace of ourselves than the covenant of the law. Nature cannot do it, because it must be done by the Spirit altogether. Now here is a foundation for faith to stand on. God so far condescends, as he gives his word, and his seal, and his oath with his word, to convey that word by way of a covenant, and to make that covenant a testament and will to us, that he will do this: and to seal that will with his own blood: for 'a testament is of no force till the testator be dead,' Heb. ix. 17. His own blood hath sealed the testaments. You see here what ground there is for faith to stand upon.

Then, again, the sweet relation that God hath taken upon him in Christ. He is our Father. Faith builds not on naked God, divested of his sweet relations (for then he is a 'consuming fire,' Heb. xii. 29); but upon God a Father in Christ. What a sweet thing it is to consider God a Father! In Christ the nature of God is fatherly to us, and our nature is sweet to him. We are sons in Christ. His nature is sweet to us, and ours to him. He will surely perform his relations. For in Christ he is a Father, not in creation only, but in the covenant of grace. Faith relies upon the word of God, upon the covenant, and testament, and upon God himself, altered and changed in the covenant of grace to be a sweet Father.

But what is a further ground of this? The nature of God himself who is a Father: for if God himself were not clothed with properties that might satisfy faith, and satisfy the soul fully, though he were a Father, it were not a sufficient ground for faith. But now who hath taken the relation of a father upon him? God, who is infinitely good, infinitely merciful above all our sins. It must be infinite mercy. Faith would not have footing else. For the soul will so upbraid in the sense of sin, that if God

* Misprinted 'as.'—G.

were not a Father, and a Father infinite in mercy, nothing but infinite mercy will satisfy the soul when conscience is awaked, and infinite power to subdue all enemies, and infinite wisdom to go beyond the reach and subtlety of all the devils in hell. God is such a Father, as in his nature is of infinite mercy, and wisdom, and power. Here is a foundation for faith to lay hold upon indeed, to have a Father, and such a Father that is Jehovah. There we must rest in his essence; he is 'Jehovah, I am;' he is eternal and immutable, an eternal being of himself, and he gives being to all; and all things have their dependence upon him. The devils in hell, and wicked men, he can quell them all, and subtract their being, and turn them to their first nothing from whence they came.

You see if we resolve all to 'Jehovah, I am,' to the eternity of God; and then to his nature, clothed with power, and wisdom, and mercy; and then to his relation of a Father: and then how he condescends to convey himself sweetly by way of covenant and testament, I beseech you, is not here a foundation for faith to build upon in the word of God, when God hath thus opened himself to us? You see what this standing is, and how by faith we stand, and what faith stands on, and may well stand on. To come to some observations, then,

First of all, observe hence, that,

Obs. The foundation of faith must be out of a man's self.

That bottom that a man must lay his soul upon, must be out of himself: it must be divine, it must be God. For the soul rests not till it come to God.* And if the word were not God's word, it would not rest on that. God must open himself by his word. It must be divine revelation that the soul must stand upon, and at last resolve to pitch, and build, and rest there. It must not be human authority, therefore, not the authority of any creature that the soul must stand on; because that that the soul stands on, must stand itself. Now nothing hath a firm consistence, but that which is divine: which I prove thus, there is no creature, but though it be true and good, yet it is changeably true, and may be otherwise than it is, and yet be a creature still, and a good creature. There is no man but he is changeable, and is changeable as a creature, and as a creature severed from the consideration of sin he is changeable. The very angels are changeable as they are creatures. All things created are mutable. It is the observation of Damascene.†

Now that that is the foundation of faith must not only be true, but infallibly and unchangeably true: there must be no danger of error in that that faith lays itself upon. It is an old rule, falsehood cannot be under faith, because faith must lie upon truth, infallible and immutable truth; and who is so but God? and what revealed truth is so, but divine truth? Therefore faith only relieth upon the first good, and the first truth, upon God and his truth.

Therefore we may see what to judge of that controversy between us and our adversaries, that would have our faith to be resolved into the authority of the church, and not of the Scriptures, and by consequent, not to the authority of God himself.

The question is, Who hath the best standing, the papists or we? We say we stand by faith, therefore we stand better than they. They say they stand by faith too, but how? Their faith is resolved into the authority of the church at length, and there they rest. But I say, even by the confession of themselves, or of any reasonable man, the word of God is

* See Note *h*, vol. I. p. 294.—G. † See note *jjj*.—G.

more divine than the authority of the church can be. For the authority of the church is therefore infallible and true, because the word of God saith so, that 'he will be with the church,' &c., and save his church. The ground is determined upon the word.

Now the word to which they have recourse, to prove that they cannot err, that must be trusted before them. If they have credit from the word, the word must be believed before them, before men; for there is no man, if God speak by him, but he speaks by him so far as he understands the Scripture, and builds upon the Scriptures first. Therefore we must first found ourselves upon the Scriptures, and upon men as far as they agree to the Scriptures.

If the Scriptures were not the word of God indeed, they could not be the foundation of faith, we could not stand upon them; but they are the word of God indeed, for men wrote as 'they were inspired by the Holy Ghost,' 2 Tim. iii. 16. Now that that comes from men it is not infallibly the word of God; but if they speak anything that is good, it is so far as it is agreeable to the first truth, the word of God.

Indeed, the resolution of their faith is very rotten and unsound, and bewrays what their church is; for they come at length in the grand point of all, to mere traditions. What is the present church? The pope is the church virtually. How do they know that he cannot err? He is Peter's successor! How do they know he is so? The Scriptures saith not so. It is tradition. So that the foundation of their religion is mere tradition, a thing from hand to hand, that is questionable and uncertain. That is the foundation of all their religion. What a resolution of faith is this!

We stand upon this against the gates of hell, and against all temptations and trials whatsoever. We believe, and fasten our souls upon this truth. Why? It is the word of God. How do we know it is the word of God? Indeed the church first of all hath an inducing, leading power, persuading to read, and to hear the word of God, and to unfold the word by the ministry; and that is all that the church doth. But when we hear this, there is a divine intrinsical majesty in the word itself, by which I know the word to be the word. How do I know light to be light? From itself. It gives evidence from itself. So divine light in the Scriptures gives light of itself to all those for whom the Scripture was penned. For whom was the Scripture penned? For God's people. To all that have gracious hearts, the word carries its own evidence with it. As light carries its own evidence, it discovers itself and all things else; so doth the Scriptures, 'You have a sure word of the prophets,' 2 Pet. i. 19.

Our Saviour Christ himself founds what he teacheth upon the word. Shall not we therefore ground our faith upon the word, when he that was the head of the church brings all to the word in his teaching? Therefore we have a better resolution for our faith than they have.

For indeed to say the truth, as we may say of their kind of prayers, when they pray to saints, &c., 'They worship they know not what,' John iv. 22. So we may say of their faith, they believe they know not what, they believe in a sinful man; for the present pope is all their church, which is an ignorant man, many times, in the Scriptures, perhaps he never read them; and he must determine controversies, and get into the chair, and judge that that shall judge him ere long. He must judge the Scripture that must be his judge, and the judge of all mankind. I list not to be large in this point; a little discovery is enough.

I hasten to something more practical. We see then that faith hath an establishing power; to stand by faith. Then hence we may see these truths, which I will but touch.

1. *First*, that faith *is certain*. It is a certain thing, and makes the soul certain. It is not a weak apprehension.

2. Again, in that it is said here, 'By faith ye stand,' we see here *the perseverance of faith*.

But you will say, that faith whereby we stand is changeable, and therefore we may fall. No; St Peter makes a comment upon this place. 'We are kept by faith to salvation;' and 'receiving the end of your faith, the salvation of your souls,' 1 Pet. i. 5, 9. We are kept through faith to salvation. So God by his power keeps that faith that keeps us. There is a divine power that keeps faith, that faith may keep us; so we stand by faith, and that faith stands to salvation, because it hath a firm bottom to stand on, and because it is kept by God himself. 'We are kept by the power of God through faith to salvation.' Mark how it runs along to salvation. Salvation is not only certain in itself, but that faith that lays hold on salvation is sure. 'By faith we stand;' not only for the present, but we continue by faith, and stand even to the death.

3. Again, in the *third* place, which follows from the other, *faith is a certain thing in itself*, and we are assured of our continuance. We are assured that we shall be saved; he that believeth may be assured that he shall be saved. First, faith is a certain thing in itself, laying hold upon a strong foundation, the word of God. And it is sure to continue, it builds upon the rock. Therefore a man may believe, and he may know that he shall be saved; he may know that he shall continue in a sure faith. There is a latitude, a breadth in faith; and sometimes there is doubting, and sometimes faith, but yet there is always faith, more or less. There is a little and a great faith, but there is always faith. 'By faith we stand.' These things need no further enlargement. I only shew how they spring from this text.

4. In a word, hence we learn, *that it is by faith that we stand, and withstand all opposition whatsoever;* for faith is our victory. 'That is your victory, even your faith,' 1 John v. 4. By faith we overcome the world, by it we stand, and stand against all opposition whatsoever.

To make it a little clear.

The reason is, partly because faith *doth present to the soul greater good than the world can*, therefore nothing on the right hand can shake the soul of a believing Christian. Shall pleasures, and profits, and the honours of the world draw a Christian from his faith, when faith presents better honours, better pleasures at the right hand of God, 'pleasures for evermore'? Ps. xvi. 11. No, they cannot; for there is nothing in the world, but there is better in religion, incomparably better. There is no comparison of the pleasures of religion and of the world; between the honour of being a child of God, and the honours that the world can give. Therefore there is nothing on the right hand in the world that can overcome the faith of a Christian, but he can stand against all, though it be a kingdom. 'Moses refused to be called the son of Pharaoh's daughter.' Why? Faith presented him greater honours in the church of God. He accounted the very 'reproach,' the worst thing in the church, better than the best thing in the world, 'the reproach of Christ better than the treasures of Egypt,' Heb. xi. 26.

Let discouragements be offered to faith by Satan and the world, let them come with all the terrors and threatenings they can, faith is victorious, and triumphant against them all, it stands against them all; because it sets before the soul greater good than the ill that the world can inflict; and sets before the soul greater ills if it apostatise than the world can inflict. Saith the world, If you do not thus and thus, you shall be cast into prison, or perhaps you shall lose your life. O! but saith the soul, if I yield to the temptations of Satan, and my own vile corruptions, I shall be cast into hell; is not that worse? There can nothing be presented to the soul that is terrible, but faith will present to it things more terrible; therefore if there be faith in the soul, it will stand against all those terrors whatsoever. 'Fear not them that can kill the body, when they have done their worst;' if you will needs fear, I will tell you whom you shall fear, 'Fear him that can cast both body and soul into hell,' Mat. x. 28.

So, if we be forced to suffer the loss of any thing that is good in the world, or be cast into any ill condition, what saith St Paul? 'The troubles and afflictions of the world are not worthy of the glory that shall be revealed,' Rom. viii. 18. Let us set that glory before us, and that will prevail against all that the world can threaten, or take from us. What is all to it? Nothing. Therefore, 'by faith we stand,' we keep our own standing, and withstand all oppositions whatsoever.

Quest. Oh! but what if there come more subtle temptations, and the Lord himself seems to be our enemy: that we have sin, and God is angry; and we see he follows us with afflictions that are evidences of his anger; how shall we stand now, and keep ourselves from despair?

Ans. This is a fiery dart of Satan, when a man hath sinned, and conscience is awakened, to make him sink in despair. O, but faith will make the soul to stand in these great temptations against those fiery darts; faith puts a shield into the hand of the soul, to beat back all those fiery darts. For faith will present Christ to God. Indeed I have been a sinner, but thou hast ordained a Saviour, and he is of thine own appointing, of thine own anointing, a Saviour of thine own giving, and thou hast made a promise, that 'whosoever believeth in him shall not perish, but have everlasting life,' John iii. 36. I cast myself upon thy mercy in him. Hereupon faith comes to withstand all such fiery temptations whatsoever, nay, against God himself: Lord, thou canst not deny thine own Saviour, thou seemest to be an enemy, and though I be a sinner, and have deserved to be cast into hell, yet I come to thee in the name of thy Son, that is at thy right hand, and pleads for me by virtue of his blood shed for me; I come in his name, thou canst not refuse thy own Son. For all temptations, when a man hath faith in him, it will send Satan to Christ to answer for him. Go to Christ, he is my husband, he hath paid my debts, he hath satisfied for my sins. So that whatsoever the temptation be, make it as subtle as you will, there is a skill in faith to stand against it, and to beat back all the fiery darts of Satan.

Therefore, to end all, we see here *what an excellent estate a Christian is in above all others,* that he hath a better standing than others have; not only a better standing in religion than the papists have, but in the profession of religion, he hath a better standing than common professors. Why? He stands by faith, by sound faith. He stands not upon opinion, or because he hath been bred so; he stands not upon his wit, because he sees reason for it; he stands upon faith, and faith stands upon divine authority. He stands partly upon his own experience, that seconds faith.

Those then that care not for religion, what standing have they? Those that stand only in pleasures and profits, and in the favour of great men, what standing have they? They stand, as the psalmist saith, 'in slippery places,' Ps. lxxiii. 18. There is no man, but if he have not faith he stands slippery; though he be never so great, if he be a monarch, alas! what is it to stand a while? All these things are but uncertain. Though they yield present content, they are but uncertain contentments. The wise man saith, they are but 'vanity,' Eccles. i. 2. They are like 'the reed of Egypt,' 2 Kings xviii. 21, that will not uphold. They will not sustain the soul in the time of trouble. There is nothing that a man can stand upon, and fasten his soul upon, if he be not religious, that will hold scarce the fit of an ague, that will hold in the pangs of death, even in the entrance of it, that will hold in terrors of conscience.

How little a trouble will blow away all those that stand on so weak a foundation as an earthly thing is! For they have but an imaginary good to speak of, and that imagination is driven out by the sense of the contrary. Let contrary troubles come, and all their fools' paradise, and their happiness they had before, is at an end; it goes no deeper than imagination.

All the things in this world stablish not the heart. Those that do not stand by faith in the favour of God in Christ, let their standing be what it will, it will soon be overturned by any temptation; they can stand out against nothing.

Therefore let us labour, above all things in the world, to have that faith strengthened by which we stand; and let us often be encouraged to strengthen our faith by all means, that we may stand the better upon it; and try our faith, before we trust it. It is that that we must trust to, and stand to in life and death.

Therefore let us often think, Is my faith good? is it well built? Let us oft put this query to our souls, I believe the religion I profess, but upon what grounds? I believe the truths in the word of God, but upon what grounds? Have I a clear understanding of them, because they are divine? Doth the Spirit of God open them, and shew a light in the Scripture that is divine? Doth the Spirit of God give me a relish of the Scriptures above all the pleasures in the world? Do I find God speaking to my heart in the word? Do I find the Spirit of God with his ordinance? Then my knowledge and my faith will hold out, I can stand by that faith in the word that is wrought by the Spirit, and fastened upon the word with the Spirit. But if I believe the religion I profess only because the State doth so; and if the king and State should do otherwise, I would change my religion; or if it be because my parents were so, or my friends and patron is of that religion, whom I depend upon; or because I see greater seeming reason for this than for the other; I can hold argument for this, and not for the other. Alas! this will not hold. But labour to know the truth of the word of God by experience as much as we can, and by the Spirit of God giving evidence to our souls, from the inward grounds of Scripture, that it is the word. 'I know whom I have trusted,' 2 Tim. i. 12. I know the promises are good; I have felt them in my soul; the Spirit hath reported them to my soul; they are sweeter than all the things in the world. It is a sure word; I bottom upon it; I have found the comfort of it before, therefore I will build upon it.

We can never stand, unless we can make our knowledge spiritual. It is but acquisite* knowledge else.

We fall in three things vilely, [unless] we labour that our knowledge of

* That is, 'acquisitive' = acquired.—G.

religion be spiritual, and fetched divinely out of the word of God, together with the Spirit.

1. We fall into sin from this very ground; for why do men fall into sin? Because at that time they stand not upon the word of God, revealed by conscience to be the word of God. Ask them why they swear? if they did believe the truth, the word saith, 'I will not hold them guiltless that take my name in vain,' Exod. xx. 7. But I am not convinced by the Spirit assuring my soul that it is the word of God. If men did believe it, would men bring a curse upon themselves?

And so whoremongers. The word of God saith, 'Whoremongers and adulterers God will judge,' Heb. xiii. 4. Would men, if they did believe this truth, live in these sins? But they have only an opinion of these things, I hear that these things are divine, perhaps they are not so, and the knowledge that we have is not divine; faith is not mingled with the Spirit.

2. Then again, from sin, we fall into despair for sin at last. Why? Because our knowledge of divine truths is not spiritual, nor from inward grounds of Scripture felt by experience, the Spirit sealing the Scripture to my heart by some spiritual experience; and thereupon men fall into despair for sin at length. For Satan plies them with temptations from their own guilty conscience. The grounds of their fears are present, and the grounds of their terrors are present to their souls; for they are there, as it were, sealed, and branded in their very souls; but their comforts are overly,* the promises are overly, the word is not rooted in their hearts by faith, it is not sealed there by the Spirit of God, the sanctifying Spirit never brought the word and their souls together. Hereupon they fall into desperation, when their terrors are present, and their comforts are overly.

If a man had never so sound a foundation, if he stand not, but float upon it, he may fall, and sink. If a man be never so weak, if he lie on a rock, the strength of the rock is his. So in our temptations, if we have a strong foundation, if we do not rest on it, the foundation will not uphold us. Now how can those rest on it that stagger in it? that were never convinced by the Spirit that these things are so? and that have had no spiritual experience? Satan draws thousands of souls to perdition, because their terrors are present, and their comforts are overly. They are not built upon divine truth by the Spirit of God.

3. Again, for apostasy, in the times of the alteration of religion; why do men alter as the State alters? They are ready to have every month a new faith, if the times, and government alter. Why? Because they were never convinced by the Spirit of God of divine truths. They had it from foreign arguments. The former state of things countenanced this way, now another state countenanced another opinion, therefore I will be of the safest. This is because the soul was never convinced of the truth.

Therefore I beseech you, labour to have arguments from the experience of the power of the word in your souls, and arguments from the Spirit of God to your spirits that it is the word of God. I will stand to divine truth, I find such a majesty, such a humbling, pacifying, satisfying power in it to all my perplexities and doubts, that it cannot but be the word of God, it stays my soul in all oppositions, in all temptations, and corruptions: it gives a stay and foundation to my soul, that no truth in the world else can do. When the soul is brought to such a frame, such a soul will not fall into gross sins while it is in such a frame, much less will it despair for sin; and if there be altering of religion a thousand times, it stands as a rock

* That is, 'lying over, superficial.'—G.

unmoveable, because it knows from inward grounds, from the word of God itself, sealed by the Spirit to my spirit, that it is the word of God. Such a soul will hold out, and only such a soul.

We should labour therefore by all means to have our faith strengthened; and amongst other means, by the use of the sacrament, whereby God sweetly conveys himself to us, by way of a banquet strengthening our faith in Christ. He presents Christ to us as the food of our souls to refresh us, even as the bread and wine doth. Our blessed Saviour is wiser than we. He knows what we stand in need of, that we have need to strengthen our faith. For we have need to strengthen that that must be our strength, which is faith. And what is the ordinance of God to strengthen faith, is it not the sacrament? The proper use of the sacrament is to strengthen faith; which the sacrament doth, being a visible sermon to us; for here we see in the outward things Christ's body broken, and his blood shed. It is a lively representation, a visible crucifying of Christ, a breaking of his body, and pouring out of his blood. And withal here is an offer of Christ to us in the elements, sealing of what it represents to our souls, if we come prepared.

God feeds us not with empty signs, but together with the outward things themselves, he gives the spiritual to the soul that is a worthy receiver.

Therefore come with a humble stooping to God's wisdom in appointing these ordinances to this end, to strengthen faith. And come with a desire to have faith strengthened. That will uphold us against all temptations to sin, or to despair for sin.

Oh, beloved! if we knew what good our faith must do us ere long, we would labour to have it strengthened by all means. What will become of us in the hour of death, and in great temptations? We shall be as chaff driven with the wind. If we have no consistence, and stability in divine truth, if our souls be not built on that, if we have not faith whereby our souls may be rooted in Christ, we shall be but a prey for Satan. Therefore considering that faith is of such wondrous consequence, it is the root of all other graces whatsoever; as the apostle saith here, 'By faith ye stand.' He doth not say, by patience, or by hope, or the like. They are drawn from faith. Strengthen that, and strengthen all other that are infused from it.

As a tree, we cast not water on the branches, but on the root. All the branches are cherished by the root. So strengthen faith. We strengthen love, and hope, and all, if we strengthen faith, and assurance of God's love in Christ. Thus I have at length gone over this fruitful portion of Scripture.

TRIN-UNI DEO GLORIA!

NOTES.

(*a*) P. 9.—'As a proud critic said, "I would they had never been men that spake our things before we were, that we might have had all the credit of it."' This seems to be a kind of paraphrase of the saying, 'Pereant qui ante nos nostra dixerunt,' which, if I err not, belongs to the younger Scaliger.

(*b*) P. 9.—'And so in the Acts of the Apostles, xvii. 28, he quotes a saying out of an atheist.' It may be well to give here the original . . . ὡς καί τινες τῶν κάθ' ὑμᾶς ποιητῶν εἰρήκασιν Τοῦ γὰρ καὶ γένος ἐσμέν. Γένος οὖν ὑπάρχοντες τοῦ Θεοῦ. . . . The quotation has been traced to two of the Greek poets, viz.,

(1) Aratus. Phenomena, 5. Τοῦ γὰρ καὶ γένος ἐσμεν = For we are also his offspring.

(2) Cleanthes. Hymn to Jupiter. Ἐκ σου γὰρ γένος ἐσμεν = For we are thy offspring.

Cf. 'The New Testament Quotations collated with the Scriptures of the Old Testament, in the original Hebrew, and the Version of the LXX; and with other writings, Apocryphal, Talmudic, and Classical, cited or alleged so to be. By Henry Gough. 8vo. 1855.' The whole of this masterly and standard work is valuable; but the division headed 'Quotations from Greek Poets,' with the relative 'Notes,' is of the last interest.

(*c*) P. 11.—'Corinth. . . . But Augustus Cæsar afterwards repaired it.' For a very full and vivid description of ancient and more modern Corinth, I would refer readers to Conybeare and Howson's 'Life and Epistles of St Paul,' in any of its editions. Cf. also Alford, Webster and Wilkinson, Hodge and Stanley, in their respective introductions to the 'Epistles.' Dr Stanley will especially reward. Dr Smith's 'Dictionary of the Bible,' and Herzog, contain much excellent elucidation of the topography.

(*d*) P. 16.—'Salute him not.' For the significance of the Eastern 'salutation' cf. Rom. xvi. 5, 7, 10, 11, 13, 16, 21, 22; and the present Epistle (2 Corinthians), xiii. 13. Also with another reference, 2 Kings iv. 29. One of the few post-apostolical traits preserved of John, represents him in the well-known anecdote as refusing to reciprocate the 'salutation' of a heretic who had met him in the public baths.

(*e*) P. 19.—'Grace is the begetter of joy; for they both have one root in the Greek language. There is the same root for favour and for joy.' That is, χάρις is grace, favour, and χάρμα is joy, delight.

(*f*) P. 28.—'By Father, which is a kind of Hebraism,' &c. The original is ὁ πατὴρ τῶν οἰκτιρμῶν, on which consult Dean Stanley, *in loc.* (2d ed. 1858). Webster and Wilkinson prefer 'Orientalism' to 'Hebraism.' Cf. *in loc.* (Greek Testament, vol. ii., 1861.)

(*f**) P. 39.—'We see by many that have recovered again, that have promised great matters in their sickness, that it is hypocritical repentance, for they have been worse after than they were before.' For startling illustrations of this, consult 'The Prison Chaplain: a Memoir of the Rev. John Clay, B.D., late Chaplain of the Preston Gaol, &c. &c. By his son, the Rev. W. L. Clay, M.A. Cambridge (Macmillan). 8vo. 1861;' also his 'Annual Reports,' and other occasional publications. Of '*reprieved*' criminals who, in the shadow of the gallows, had manifested every token of apparent penitence and *heart*-change, the number whose subsequent career gave evidence of reality is as 1 to 500, perhaps as awful a fact as recent criminal statistics reveal.

(*g*) P. 40.—'We must not do works of mercy proudly.' Lowell has finely put this:—

> '*Not that which we give, but what we share,*
> *For the gifts without the giver is bare:*
> *Who bestows himself with his alms feeds three,*
> Himself, his hungering neighbour, and me.'
>
> *The Vision of Sir Laurifal.*

(*g**) P. 41.—'What a cruel thing is it . . . without Church,' &c. This touching expression of Sibbes's feeling for the neglected 'masses,' the *home*-heathen, deserves a place beside the excellent Alleine's and Baxter's like-minded early setting forth of the claims of the *foreign* heathen. Consult Stanford's 'Joseph Alleine,' pp. 207–208.

(*h*) P. 47 —'St Chrysostom, an excellent preacher, yields me one observation upon this very place.' This seems to be a very vague recollection of the father's sentiment in his 'Homily' on the Epistle, under the verse. Nor have I met with anything nearer elsewhere in his writings.

*** Having omitted a letter of reference to the following in its place, I add it here:—

P. 66, line 4th from bottom.—'As St Cyprian saith, 'We carry as much from God as we bring vessels.' The original is 'Nostrum tantum sitiat pectus et pateat. Quantum illuc fidei capacis afferimus, tantum gratiæ inundantis haurimus."—*Epist. I. ad Donatum.*

(*i*) P. 71.—'If any man be overtaken . . . . set him in joint, as the word is,' Gal. vi. 1. The word is καταρτίζω = to refit, mend. Cf. Liddell and Scott, and Robinson, *sub voce.*

(*j*) P. 83.—'There were three put in, and there was a fourth, which was Christ, the Son of God.' Cf. Daniel iii. 25. Our English version with its capitals has placed this among the *memorabilia* of Scripture, and of Christian experience. Few texts are oftener used to cheer the afflicted, while in the '*furnace* of affliction.' It is perhaps allowable as an accommodation to do so, but the original does not seem to warrant our interpreting the '*fourth*,' as THE Son of God = the Lord. As in the case of the 'den of lions,' Jehovah sent his 'angel,' in Scripture phrase '*a* son of God,' Job. xxxviii. 7.

(*k*) P. 92.—'So that now the fire is our friend, the stone,' &c. Compare Thomas Adam of Wintringham's very remarkable 'thanks' to God for 'the stone,' in his 'Private Thoughts,' than which few modern books contain so much uncommon and suggestive thinking. Bishop Wilson has worthily edited the priceless little volume.

(*l*) P. 95.—'So St Justin Martyr saith when he saw Christians suffer,' &c. His words are worth giving (Apolog. ii. 12), 'I myself, when I took pleasure in the doctrines of Plato, and heard the Christians slandered, seeing them to be fearless of death, and of everything else that was thought dreadful, considered that it was impossible that they should live in wickedness,' &c. &c.

(*m*) P. 97.—'The blood of the martyrs is the seed of the church.' This familiar apophthegm originated with Tertullian; but runs more literally, 'Blood is the seed of Christians.' (*Apologeticus adversus Gentes*, c. l.) The original is 'Plures efficimur quoties metimur a vobis; semen est sanguis Christianorum.'

(*n*) P. 98.—'Some Greek copies,' &c. Cf. Alford, *in loc.* (Greek Testament, vol. ii.)

(*o*) P. 99.—'It is an excellent speech, solus Christus.' For the passage, see vol. I. footnote, page 369.

(*p*) P. 100.—'It is read in the margin, and most go that way,' &c. Cf. Alford, as in note *n*.

(*q*) P. 104.—'A man need not to whip himself, as the Scottish papists do.' The reference is probably to the *over*-zeal of the Scottish papists at the period contemporary with Sibbes, which manifested itself in a morbid observance of the extremest austerities of popery.

(*r*) P. 108.—'When he hears of any calamity of the church, whether it be in the Palatinate, in France, in the Low Countries,' &c. Sibbes, as stated in our Memoir, took the deepest interest in the 'foreign' Protestants, and especially in the persecutions in the Palatinate. Cf. 'Memoir,' c. vii., and 'Sword of the Wicked, vol. I. pp. 115, 116.

(*r**) P. 114.—'It were offensive to name what distasteful things they will take to do them good.' In Stehelin's 'Rabbinical Literature; or, the Traditions of the Jews, contained in the Talmud and other mystical writings, &c. &c. (2 vols. 8vo, 1748); Dr Wotton's 'Miscellaneous Discourses relating to the Traditions and Usages of the Scribes and Pharisees in our Blessed Saviour Jesus Christ's Time;' &c. &c, (2 vols. 8vo, 1718), and scattered throughout Lightfoot's 'Talmudic,' and other 'Illustrations,' will be found many singular confirmations of the text of Sibbes in relation to Scripture; while Timothy Bright's 'Treatise, wherein is declared the 'Sufficience of English Medicines for cure of all Diseases' (1615). preserves, with all the quaint wit of his 'Melancholie' (the prototype of Burton's great book), the 'distasteful things' to which Sibbes's contemporaries submitted. Consult also the various histories of the early 'Materia Medica.'

(*s*) P. 117.—'A learned Hebrician Capne,' &c. John Reuchlin, one of the foremost names of Germany, alike in relation to the Reformation and the Restoration of Letters, has recently received the splendid eulogium—enriched with accumulated 'testimonies'—of Sir William Hamilton. Consult his 'Discussions on Philosophy and Literature,' &c. &c. (2d edition, 1853), pp. 212, *seq.*, 216, 237, 239, *seq.* His student-visitors will remember how Sir William was wont to exhibit, as one of the greatest prizes of his collection, the interesting holograph letter of Reuchlin, first published in above; and with what glowing appreciation he expatiated upon its writer. Sibbes calls him by his later name of Capne. He translated, in the fashion of the day, his guttural German into the more euphonious Greek,—both signifying the same thing, viz., 'smoke' (*Der rauch* and καπνος), as Philip Schwartzerde became Philip Melancthon. He was born at Pforzheim, 1450; died, 1522. He was the preceptor of Melancthon; and Luther acknowledged to him that 'he only followed in his steps,—only consummated his victory, with inferior strength, indeed, but not inferior courage, in breaking the teeth of the Behemoth.' Epist. ad. Reuchl., lib. ii., sig. C. iii., and in De Wette's Luther's Briefe, i. 196.

(*t*) P. 121.—'The word is very significant in the original,' &c. The expression is intensive, ἐξαπορηθῆναι = to be utterly at a loss, or absolutely without a way (πόρος) of escape. Cf. Dr Charles Hodge, *in loc.*

(*u*) P. 121.—'The schoolmen say,' &c. Query, Aquinas? He speaks of the 'Magnitudo doloris Christi' as arising from his body being 'optime complexionatus.' Leigh, in his 'Body of Divinity,' so cites it, and gives as the reference 'Aq. Part 3. Quæst. 46., Art. 6.'

(*v*) P. 129.—'As the heathen man could say,' 'There is not the oldest man but he thinks he may live a little longer, one day longer.' The 'heathen man' is Cicero, who says, 'Nemo enim est tam senex, qui se annum non putet posse vivere.' De Senectute, c. vii. § 24.

(*w*) P. 133.—'They renounce their own religion at the hour of death, as Bellarmine did.' The authority for this statement is Bellarmine's own work on Justification, lib. v. c. 7. After defending the Romish doctrine on this subject in opposition to the Protestant Evangelical, he makes this concession, which speaks more for his piety than his consistency: 'Propter incertitudinem propriæ justitiæ et periculum inanis gloriæ, tutissimum esse in sola misericordia Dei et benignitate fiduciam suam reponere.' If I err not, a like confession is made in his 'Last Will.'

(*x*) P. 134.—'Coster saith, and saith truly, if Christ be not there, we are the greatest idolaters in the world.' Cf. Note *p*, vol. II. p. 434.

(*y*) P. 137.—'Saith St Austin, 'I dare say, and stand to it, that it is profitable for some men to fall; they grow more holy by their slips.' The sentiment will be found in the following quotations:—

(1.) 'Audeo dicere, superbis continentibus expedit cadere,' &c.—*De Divers. Serm.* cccliv. cap. ix, tom v. col. 1378. Bened. ed. fol. Par. 1679 *sqq.*

(2.) 'Audeo dicere, superbis esse utile cadere in aliquod apertum manifestumque peccatum, unde sibi displiceant, qui jam sibi placendo ceciderunt.'—*De Civ. Dei.* xiv. 13.

Cf. footnote vol. I. 324, and Jeremy Taylor, 'Sermon on Lukewarmness and Zeal; or Spiritual Fervour.' Edition of Works by Eden, iv. 149.

(*z*) P. 138.—'As the heathen man said, that great emperor, "I have been all things, and nothing doth me good now," when he was to die. "Omnia fui, nihil expedit' is ascribed to the emperor Septimus Severus on his deathbed (A.D. 211).

(*aa*) P. 149.—'St Bernard, a good man in evil times,' saith he, 'I consider three things in which I pitch my hope and trust, *charitatem adoptionis*, the love of God in making me his child; and *veritatem promissionis*, the truth of God in performing his promise,' &c. Sibbes paraphrases the following: 'Tria igitur considero, in quibus tota spes mea consistit, charitatem adoptionis, veritatem promissionis, potestatem redditionis.'—Sermon iii., *de panibus*, 8.

(*bb*) P. 154.—'It is a seizon, as a piece of earth,' &c. Sir William Blackstone ('Commentaries,' b. ii. c. 20.) explains this: 'This livery of *seisin* is no other than the pure feodal investiture, or delivery of corporeal possession of the land or tenement; which was held absolutely necessary to complete the donation.'—Cf. also Richardson, *sub voce.*

(*cc*) P. 170.—'Deliverance is promised upon ill terms; that they may redeem their lives if they will, by denying God and religion—an ill bargain.' The 'persecutions' of the early Christians furnish many illustrations of the text. They were called merely to 'sprinkle a little incense on the altar' (*i. e.*, of the gods), and a free pardon would ensue. The stern 'Covenanters' of Scotland, under Charles II. and James II., were repeatedly offered their 'lives,' if they would say, 'God save the king.' Neither earlier nor later was the 'ill bargain' acceded to.

(*dd*) P. 170.—'That they carry not themselves uncomely in troubles, but so as is meet for the credit of the truth which they seal with their blood.' The pleasant message of the proto-martyr of the Reformation, John Rogers, to Hooper—who was confined in another apartment—on the night before his death, is perhaps the most striking illustration of the text in English history. There is abundant evidence of the 'credit' his stout-hearted bearing brought to 'the truth.' Rogers' most recent biographer observes: 'To the other condemned preachers still in prison, the news of Rogers' constancy came like a sudden burst of sunlight from a heavy cloud. If they wavered under the doom that threatened them, they did so no longer. He had set them an example worthy of imitation, and whither he had led the way, they could now more confidently follow. We find Bradford, in a letter to Cranmer, Ridley, and Latimer, written four days after Rogers' death, rejoicing that their 'dear brother' had 'broken the ice valiantly.' Ridley writes thus to Bradford: 'I thank our Lord God and Heavenly Father by Christ, that since I heard of our dear brother Rogers' departing and stout confession of Christ and his truth, even unto the death, my heart, blessed be God, so rejoiced of it, that, since that time, I say, I never felt any lumpish heaviness in my heart, as I grant I have felt sometimes before.'—Cf. Chester's 'Life of John Rogers,' pp. 213–14. 8vo. 1860.

*** P. 182.—'As St Austin saith well, God hath made the rich for the poor, and the poor for the rich: the rich to relieve the poor, and the poor to pray for the rich; for herein one is accepted for another.' The words are, 'Fecit Deus pauperem, ut probet divitem; et fecit Deus divitem, ut probet illum de paupere.' In Psalm cxxiv. *Enarrat in fine.*

(*ee*) P. 184.—'That great divine Paulus Phagius, who was a great Hebrecian,' &c. Paulus Fagius was born 1504, died 1550. The words quoted by Sibbes form part of his "Concio valedictoria," which will be found both in German and Latin, in Melchior Adam's Lives of German Theologians, page 209. The German begins thus, 'Ihr jungen bittel Gott,' &c. The Latin thus, 'Vos juniores orate Deum. Forte enim vos facilius exaudiet quam qui plus peccatorum admiserunt.'

(*ff*) P. 191.—'Therefore you know the Grecians accounted that a chief blessing.' Sibbes probably refers to the many praises of ὑγίεια, and to the axiomatic summary of every 'blessing,' ἡ περὶ το σῶμα καὶ την ψυχὴν ὑγίεια, (Isocrates, 234 B) which has passed into the Latin (*mens sana in corpore sano*), and all other civilized languages. Hygieia, the goddess of health, received abundant 'worship.'

(*gg*) P. 208,—'The original word in the Old Testament that signifies the heart, it is taken for the conscience.' Cf. Gesenius, *Thesaurus* (preferable to his 'Lexicon'), under לֵב and its synonymes, with Liddell and Scott, and Robinson, under καρδία and συνείδησις.

(*hh*) P. 209.—'Therefore the name for conscience in the Greek and Latin signifies a knowledge with another.' That is συνείδησις = a knowing with one's self, consciousness; and *conscientia* (con-scio) = joint knowledge. Cf. Note *gg* above.

(*ii*) P. 209.—'It is a knowledge with a rule, with a general rule,' &c. See this principle brought out with power and pungency, by Professor Sewell of Oxford, in the following remarkable pamphlet, now unhappily 'out of print,' and only to be met with at an extravagant price, 'The Plea of Conscience for seceding from the Catholic Church to the Romish Schism in England. . . . A Sermon preached before the University of Oxford, Nov. 5. 1845. To which is added an Essay *on the Process of Conscience.* Oxford: J. H. Parker. 1845. Pp. xxvii. and 53.

(*jj*) P. 214.—'Cursed is he, saith the Council of Trent, that doth not equalize those traditions with the word of God.' Cf. History of the Council of Trent, by L. F. Bungener (1853. Crown 8vo.); Tradition, book ii. pp. 83, 88, 89, *et alibi;* also Memoirs of the Council of Trent, &c., &c., by Joseph Mendham, M.A. (1834. 8vo); and Buckley's 'History,' (1852.)

(*kk*) P. 217—'So holy St Austin, what saith he to a Donatist that wronged him in his reputation,' &c. The reference is to the following, 'Senti de Augustino quidquid libet, sola me in oculis Dei conscientia non accuset.' *Lib. Secund. contra Manich.*

(*ll*) P. 229.—'So it is in the original, "in the *simplicity* and sincerity of God." The word is ἁπλότης = *singleness* of mind, the opposite of duplicity. Cf. Deans Alford and Stanley as to the *readings.*

(*mm*) P. 234.—'Christ made as though he would have gone further,' &c. The Evangelist is *describing the attitude* of the Lord *as he appeared to the 'two disciples.'* He was '*going on*' (προσεποιεῖτο). Assuredly he *would* have gone on had he *not* been solicited to 'abide.' His 'going on,' or 'remaining,' was contingent on their request, . . . only a lesser operation of the great law of all our spiritual 'blessings' being contingent upon prayer, upon our 'asking.' It seems somewhat perilous then to concede with Sibbes and our translators, that the Lord made a 'show to do' what he did not 'mean' to do. He *was* 'going on,' intended to 'go further,' but was '*constrained*' to 'abide,' (ver. 29). This explanation is surely more satisfactory than Sibbes's concession, and than that which resolves it into a 'speaking after the manner of men.' Jeremy Taylor and others, 'he *pretended*,' is exceedingly unguarded.

(*nn*) P. 234.—'Saith Tertullian very well, There is no necessity of sin to them, upon whom there lies no other necessity but not to sin.' The passage is in the treatise *De Coronâ Militis*, as follows:—'Nulla est necessitas delinquendi, quibus una est necessitas non delinquendi.'

(*oo*) P. 238.—'Thou shalt be uncased.' One of Thomas Adams' most wonderful 'sermons' is entitled 'The White Devil; or, The Hypocrite *Uncased*,' (*i.e.*, Judas). See 'Practical Works' in the present series, II. p. 221, *seq.*;

(*pp*) P. 251.—'Comb-downes,' as we say. The Rev. Dr Bonar of Kelso kindly informs me that he met with the word 'comb-downe' in an old English poet as = sky-fort. That is, 'comb or coomb,' old English and Scotch for sky (coomb-ceiled = sky-roofed, *i. e.*, arch-roofed, concave) and down = dun, *i. e.*, fort or castle. According to this, 'comb-downe' resolves itself into our 'sky-castles = castles in the air.' I regret that Dr Bonar has not been able to recover the reference. I venture to query if in 'comb-downe,' we have not the origin of our word, '*down-come*' or 'come-down' = great fall, as from prosperity to poverty.

(*qq*) P. 267.—'As we see in Spira,' &c. Consult Gribaldus. 'Historia Francisci Spiræ' (1548), which, translated into English by Aglionby, as follows: 'A notable and maruailous epistle concerning the terrible judgment of God upon hym that for feare of men denyeth Christ and the knowen veritie; being the case of Francis Spera or Spira, an Italian, with a preface of Dr Caluine' (1550), has ever since been a popular chap-book.

(*rr*) P. 268.—'Curse God,' &c. Cf. Rev. A. B. Davidson's 'Job' *in loc.*, (vol. i. 1862). He says, '*Renounce* בָּרֵךְ, the usual word in these chapters. Some prefer taking the word here, however, in its usual sense. *Bless* (with sarcastic intonation and in irony), bless this God of yours (i. 21) again, and die! &c. &c. (page 28).

(*ss*) P. 269.—'Stephen Gardiner's letters,' &c. There does not appear to be any collected edition of the 'Letters' of this notorious Prelate: but various were published singly, and others are met with in collections. Nearly all are in the library of the British Museum; and also among the MSS. there.

(*tt*) P. 271.—'As St Austin hath a good speech, "Lord, free me from myself, from my own devices and policy."' This is a reminiscence of an often-recurring apophthegm of the 'Confessions.'

(*uu*) P. 274.—Therefore Luther was wont to say, 'Good works are good, but to trust in good works is damnable.' This is a frequent saying of the Colloquia Mensalia, which in the great folio of Captain Henrie Bell (1652), was a special favourite with the Puritans. Our copy bears the autograph of the famous 'Puritan' worthy and statesman Sir Nathaniel Barnardiston, a presentation copy to his son, 'Ex dono T. B. meo filio.' Sibbes seems to have derived the greater number of his Luther quotations from the 'Colloquia Mensalia.'

(*vv*) P. 275.—'Graces, not as habits, as it was the proud term of the philosophers to call it.' The reference appears to be to the Greek term ἦθος, a custom, but taken to signify a virtue—hence *ethics*. So also the Latin term *mos*.

(*ww*) P. 284.—'It was a proud term . . . . . *as I said*.' Cf. page 275, and note *vv* as above.

(*xx*) P. 288.—'Saith the heathen man Tully, "I thought myself wise, but I never was so."' This must be a vague recollection of Cicero. I have not been able to trace it.

(*yy*) P. 209.—'As that wretch said himself, when he came to die, "That he had provided for all things but for death."' See note *z* above.

(*zz*) P. 301.—'For I think not that he means his former epistle,' &c. Modern scholarship agrees with Sibbes. Cf. Deans Stanley and Alford.

(*aaa*) P. 302.—'As you know in a war of theirs with the Turks, the story is well known,' &c. The Turk was Amurath. He made a treaty of peace for ten years with Ladislas, king of Hungary. Julian, the pope's legate, persuaded Ladislas to break the peace, absolving him from his oath. Amurath was engaged in another war, and was thus taken at a disadvantage. A battle was fought at Varna, 10th November 1444. At first the victory inclined to the side of the Christians; upon which Amurath, seeing his great danger, plucked from his bosom the treaty which had thus been broken, and holding it in his hands, with eyes upraised to heaven, made the following appeal: 'Behold, thou crucified Christ! this is the league that thy Christians in thy name made with me; which they have without any cause violated. Now, if thou be a God as they say thou art, and as we dream, revenge the wrong now done unto thy name and me, and shew thy frown upon thy perjured people, who by their deeds deny thee their God.' An attack was immediately made, and the battle, which was almost lost to the Turks, was restored. The Hungarian king was killed, and his head placed upon a spear. Two-thirds of the Christian army perished; and yet the Turks lost 20,000 men, so dreadful was the slaughter. I find above abstract of Sibbes's reference, in the Life of the great Huniades of Hungary, who was taken prisoner in this battle, and who afterwards became regent during the minority of Ladislas, the successor of Ladislas IV.

(*bbb*) P. 302.—'The old principle of Isidore is constantly and everlastingly true, "Conceive,"' &c. Isidore (Hispalensis) died 636. 'Quacunque arte verborum quis juret, Deus tamen, qui conscientiæ testis est, hoc accipit sicut iste cui juratur intelligit.'—Libri duo Synonymorum, lib. ii.

(*ccc*) P. 306.—'That hope should stir up some endeavour to pray for them, seeing their estates are not desperate,' &c. Cf. note *c*, vol. I. page 171. In a long, very characteristic (unpublished) letter of John Newton, addressed to the late Professor Lawson of Selkirk, in our possession, the following paragraph occurs, and is a beautiful commentary upon Sibbes's counsel. He is speaking of the sudden death of Robinson of Cambridge, in the house of Dr Priestly, and says:—'I think Dr Priestly is out of the reach of human conviction; but the Lord can convince him. And who can tell but this unexpected stroke may make some salutary impression upon his mind? *I can set no limits to the mercy or the power of our Lord, and therefore I continue to pray for him. I am persuaded he is not farther from the truth now than I was once.*'

(*ddd*) P. 327.—'"That you might have a second benefit," saith the last translation.' 'The last translation' was our present or King James's version, first issued in 1611. We find 'benefit' in the text, and 'grace' in the margin, as described by Sibbes.

(*eee*) P. 331.—'Therefore St Austin doth well define predestination; it is an ordaining to salvation, and a preparing of all means tending thereto.' The original is as follows:—'Hæc est Prædestinatio sanctorum, nihil aliud; præscientia scilicet et præparatio beneficiorum Dei, quibus certissime liberantur, quicumque liberantur.'—De Dono Perseverantiæ, c. xxv.

(*fff*) P. 340.—'Saith St Ambrose, "Et nobis malus,"' &c. I have failed to discover the saying in Ambrose. Sir Philip Sidney uses it with great effect (without naming Ambrose), in his memorable Letter to Elizabeth, dissuading her from her proposed marriage.

(*ggg*) P. 350.—'Cave, time, &c., saith the holy man St Austin.' One of the *memorabilia* of the 'Confessions.'

(*hhh*) P. 354.—'Isidore saith, "An oath is to be esteemed as he,"' &c. Cf. note *bbb*.

(*iii*) P. 357.—'"Our word, our preaching," as it is in the margin.' See note *ddd*. The word is ὁ λογος, probably of purpose indefinite, so as to embrace both his personal communications and his 'preaching.'

(*jjj*) P. 357.—'"As God is true," it is in our translation, but in the original it is, "God is true."' The original is πιστὸς δε ὁ Θεος, ὁτι ὁ λόγος ἡμων, &c., which Dean Stanley thus puts, 'So true as it is that God is faithful, so true is it that my communications are not variable.' Cf. xi. 10; Rom. xiv. 11.

(*kkk*) P. 359.—'The oracles of Apollo . . . . . . true one way, and false another.' Consult Schmitz's article on 'Oracles,' in Smith's Dictionary of Greek and Roman Antiquities, (2d edit. 1859, 8vo).

The following paragraph, from *Horne's Introduction*, gives a clear view of the matter:—

. . . . . When no means of evasion remained, the answers given by the heathen oracles were frequently delusive, and capable of quite contrary interpretations; and the most celebrated of them concealed their meaning in such ambiguous terms that they required another oracle to explain them. Of this ambiguity several authentic instances are recorded. Thus, when Crœsus consulted the oracle at Delphi relative to his intended war against the Persians, he was told that he would destroy a great empire.—*Κροισος 'Αλυν διαβὰς μεγάλην ἄρχην καταλυσει.* This he naturally interpreted of his overcoming the Persians, though the oracle was so framed as to admit of an opposite meaning. Crœsus made war against the Persians, and was ruined; and the oracle continued to maintain its credit. The answer given as to Pyrrhus, King of Epirus, many ages after, was of yet more doubtful interpretation, being conceived in terms so ambiguous, that it might be either interpreted thus:—*I say that thou, son of Æacus, canst conquer the Romans. Thou shalt go, thou shalt return, never shalt thou perish in war;* or thus, *I say that the Romans can conquer thee, son of Æacus. Thou shalt go, thou shalt never return, thou shalt perish in war.*

Aio te Æacida Romanos vincere posse:
Ibis redibis nunquam in bello peribis.

Pyrrhus understood the oracle in the former sense; he waged an unsuccessful war with the Romans, and was overcome; yet still the juggling oracle saved its credit. Another remarkable instance of the ambiguity of the pretended prophets occurs in 1 Kings xxii. 5, 6. Jehoshaphat, king of Judah, and Ahab, king of Israel, having united their forces against the Syrians, in order to recover Ramoth-Gilead, the latter monarch gathered the false prophets together, about four hundred men, and said unto them, "Shall I go up against Ramoth-Gilead to battle, or shall I forbear?" And they said, "Go up, for the Lord shall deliver [it] into the hands of the king." It is to be observed that the word *it* is not in the original, and that the reply of the pseudo-prophets is so artfully constructed, that it might be interpreted either *for* or *against* the expedition; as thus.—the Lord will deliver *it* (Ramoth-Gilead) into the king's (Ahab's) hand; or, the Lord will deliver (Israel) into the king's hand; that is, into the king's hand, that is, into the hands of the King of Syria. Relying upon this ambiguous oracle, the monarchs of Judah and Israel engaged the Syrians, and were utterly discomfited.—*Horne's Introduction*, vol. i. ch. iv. sec. 3, pp. 274–5 (10th ed. 1856).

This subject is well treated by Henry Smith, in his "God's Arrow against Atheists."

(lll) P. 361.—'Man is changeable, because he is a creature, as Damascene's speech is.' The speech is the following:—*πᾶν γαρ γενητὸν, τρεπτόν ἐστιν. ὧν γὰρ ἡ ἀρχὴ της γενέσεως ἀπὸ τροπῆς ἤρξατο, ἀνάγκη ταῦτα τρεπτὰ ἐιναι.* Damasc. De Fide Orthodoxa, cap. xxvii.

(mmm) P. 364.—'St Austin. . . . . . He wrote a book of retractations of his former opinions.' This father's magnanimous 'retractations' are found in all the collective editions of his works.

(nnn) P. 365.—'If only yea be true, then that which is contrary to it must needs be false.' All Sibbes's hits at popery have long formed the commonplaces of the controversy, and are introduced into all the standard works *pro* and *con*.

(ooo) P. 366.—'The pope he makes Garnet, a traitor, and Thomas of Becket, saints.' Henry Garnet was a 'priest,' notorious as having been 'privy' to the 'Gunpowder Plot.' He was born 1555, and was executed May 3. 1606. His plea for not revealing the infamous 'Plot' was that it had been made known to him in 'confession,' an extenuation that intensified the national abhorrence of the whole system of popery. Sibbes speaks of the pope making him a 'saint.' While going to the block, he was told by his friends that he would be regarded as a 'martyr;' but exclaimed, 'Me martyrem! O qualem martyrem!' Concerning Becket, it is only necessary to refer to 'Becket, Archbishop of Canterbury; a Biography. By J. C. Robertson. 1 Vol. 8vo. 1859. (Murray.)

(ppp) P. 367.—'It is somewhat uncertain whether ever Peter were at Rome.' For a full and scholarly examination of this matter, consult 'The Question, "Was St Peter ever at Rome?" Historically Considered. By Augustus Scheler.' (1 Vol. 12mo. 1849. Nisbet.) Scheler's conclusive treatise, which returns a negative to the question, is at once an expansion of the 'Ist Petrus in Rom und Bischof der römischen Kirche gewesen,' and a gathering together of data scattered through the writings of Scaliger, Salmasius, Spanheim, Bost, and Malan.

(qqq) P. 373.—'But as Cyprian saith well, "It must be consent in the truth."' Perhaps the following may be the passage referred to: 'Quare si solus Christus audiendus est, non debemus attendere quid alius ante nos faciendum esse putaverit, sed quid qui ante omnes est, Christus prior fecerit. Neque enim hominum consuetudinem sequi oportet, sed Dei veritatem.'—Ep. 63, Ad Cœcilium de Sac. Dom. Cal

(*rrr*) P. 374.—'It sets him down that he can say nothing, but that it is divine truth, because he finds it so.' On the force of personal 'experience' as an 'evidence' of the truth of Christianity, consult the excellent treatise of Wardlaw thereupon—worthy son of a worthy sire.

(*sss*) P. 375.—'How we may know that our church was before Luther's time or no.' Cf. Note *d*, vol. II. p. 248. I take this opportunity of giving the exact title-page of Logie's rare tractate:—'Cum Bono Deo. Raine from the Clouds upon a Choicke [*sic*] Angel: or, A returned Answere to that common Quæritur of our Adversaries, Where was your Church before Luther? Digested into several Meditations, according to the difference of Points, Extorted off the Author, for stilling the incessant and no lesse clamorous coassation of some Patmicke Frogges, against the lawfulnesse of our Calling. Aberdeene. Imprinted by Edward Raban, Dwelling upon the Market-place, at the Townes Armes, 1624, cum privilegio.' 4to. 1634, in Note *d*, vol. II. is a misprint for 1624. A copy of this singular tractate is preserved in Peterborough Cathedral Library; and I have to acknowledge the kindness of the Rev. Thomas Hutton, M.A., Rector of Stilton, in securing to me unrestricted access to its treasures, of which privilege after-volumes will shew the benefit.

(*ttt*) P. 377.—'The most of the points of popery, wherein they differ from us, nay, not any of them, were never established by a council till the Council of Trent, except transubstantiation, by the Council of Lateran, which was a thousand years after Christ.' The Councils of Lateran were held in the Basilica of the Lateran, at Rome. Of these Councils, there were five. The 'fourth,' on church affairs generally—attended by 400 bishops and 1000 abbots—was held in 1215. Innocent III. presided.

(*uuu*) P. 379.—'Luther saith, If they [the papists] live and die peremptorily in all the points professed in the Tridentine Council, they cannot [be saved].' Cf. Note *uu*.

(*vvv*) P. 382.—'There is some diversity in reading the words.' Cf. Alford *in loc.*

(*www*) P. 412.—'As David, Ps. cxix., if it be his.' Consult S. F. Thrupp's 'Introduction to the Study and Use of the Psalms' (2 vols. 8vo, 1860). He accepts Bishop Jebb's suggestion of Daniel being the author of this the most splendid tribute to the Word of God anywhere to be found. See vol. II. pp. 244–256.

(*xxx*) P. 417.—'Take the counsel of that blessed man . . . Luther, I mean, . . . Go to God in Christ, in the promises.' From the 'Colloquia Mensalia.' See Note *uu* concerning this storehouse of quotable sayings.

(*yyy*) P. 436.—'Remembering always that of St Ambrose, that there must not be striving for victory, but for truth.' See note *fff*.

(*zzz*) P. 437.—'Your *Ancipites*, as Cyprian calls them, your doubtful flatterers of the times.' Cyprian seems to employ the vivid word in its etymological sense of having two heads, two natures, double = undecided, changeable. Lucan speaks of '*ancipites animi*' (9, 46).

(*aaaa*) P. 440.—'As you have it storied of Papinian, an excellent lawyer.' For an interesting notice of Papinian, consult Mr Long's article in Dr Smith's 'Dictionary of Greek and Roman Biography and Mythology;' also Dio. Cass., lib. lxxvii., with note from Spartianus, Caracc. c. viii.

(*bbbb*) P. 451.—'They gave this answer, *Christianus sum*, I am a Christian.' This is recorded in all the early 'Apologies,' *e. g.*, Justin Martyr, Tertullian (Apolog. c. ii.).

(*cccc*) P. 460.—'Pella, a little village, was delivered when the general destruction came upon Jerusalem.' Pella was the place whither the Christians fled before the destruction of the 'Holy City.' Cf. Eusebius H. E. iii. 5; Epiphanius de *Mens. et Ponder*, p. 171; Reland, Palaestina, p. 924; also Croly's 'Salathiel.'

(*dddd*) P. 464.—'1 John v. 7, 8.' With reference to the 'Three Witnesses' of the present passage, it is only necessary to refer to Orme's admirable and well known 'Memoir' of the 'Controversy' (1830, 12mo); and to the works of Travis, Burgess, Middleton, and Wiseman in favour of, and Porson, Marsh, and Turton against, the retention of the disputed clause. It is now usually enclosed in our Greek Testaments in brackets; and perhaps it were well if it were similarly marked in our English Bibles. Cf. Webster and Wilkinson *in loc.*, and Tregelles in Horne, iv., c. xxxvi. (10th ed., 1856).

(*eeee*) P. 475.—'Like to the Samaritans, as Josephus, the historian of the Jews, writes of them. When the Jews prospered, oh! then they would be Jews,' &c. The passage will be found in the 'Antiquities,' Book ix., c. xiv. § 3, 'When they [the Cutheans or Samaritans] see the Jews in prosperity, they pretend that they are changed, and allied to them, and call them kinsmen, as though they were derived from Joseph, and had by that means an original alliance with them; but when they see them falling into a low condition, they say they are no way related to them, and that the Jews have no right to expect any kindness or marks of kindred from them, but they declare that they are sojourners that come from other countries.' Cf. also xi. c. viii. § 6, and xii. c. v. 5.

(ffff) P. 475.—'As we see in Cranmer and others.' The good Archbishop's early faltering, and subsequent recantation and martyr-death, are historic.

(gggg) P. 478.—'The Holy Spirit searcheth. . . . He is a "searcher," as the word is in the original.' Cf. 1 Cor. ii. 10 The verb is ἐρευνάω, = explore; *i.e.*, accurately and thoroughly know. Hodge, and Webster and Wilkinson, *in loc.*, will reward consultation.

(hhhh) P. 479.—'As Austin saith, "The Spirit of God knocks at their hearts but he doth not dwell there."' This is a frequently-recurring saying of the 'Confessions' and *De Civitate*, with varying phraseology, as all readers of this father are aware is common with him.

(iiii) P. 491.—'As St Austin saith very well. Christ, saith he, speaks to the sea, and it is quiet,' &c. Cf. Augustine on Mark iv. 39. It is found also in Theophylact.

(jjjj) P. 497.—'God, I hope, will be merciful to the state; for the censure of the state upon profanation, it is a very worthy act.' There were multiplied 'proclamations' at this period against '*profaneness*,' as also during the reign of Charles II. The rigidness of the 'laws,' and the laxity of the practice, suggest much.

(kkkk) P. 499.—'These words are declined by many interpreters.' Consult Hodge, Dean Stanley, and Webster and Wilkinson *in loc.*

(llll) P. 500.—'It is not to domineer over faith, to suppress that that they call of late in neighbour countries a *liberty of prophecy*.' Cf. Bishop Jeremy Taylor's magnificent vindication of this 'liberty' in his 'ΘΕΟΛΟΓΙΑ 'ΕΚΛΕΚΤΙΚΗ; or, A Discourse of the Liberty of Prophesying, with its just Limits and Temper: shewing the Unreasonableness of prescribing to other men's faith, and the iniquity of persecuting differing opinions.' (Works, ed. 1849, by Eden. V. pp. 339–605.)

(mmmm) P. 500.—'St Austin himself was once of this mind, that people were not to be forced.' His words are, 'Ad fidem quidem nullus est cogendus invitus.' *Contra Ep. Petiliani Donatistæ*, lib. ii. c. lxxxiii.

(nnnn) P. 503.—'If he came in by simony, or is not *in cathedra*.' Ranke supplies abundant examples of the former, and the latter denotes that the pope is infallible only while he acts in his official character, *e.g.*, propagating a bull or making a decision. *Extra cathedram*, or as a *private* man, he is held by papists to be liable to err.

(oooo) P. 505.—'Council of Trent and Pius IV.' Cf. note *jj*, and Ranke under Pius IV. and Trent.

(pppp) P. 510.—'Ministers . . . . advise in cases of conscience.' Sibbes's contemporaries, and indeed the whole of the leading theologians before and after him, occupied themselves with drawing up 'resolutions' of 'cases of conscience.' It is only necessary to name the great 'Ductor Dubitantium' of Jeremy Taylor, and the pungent 'Treatise' of William Perkins.

(qqqq) P. 514.—'He hath his chair in heaven that teacheth the heart, as St Austin saith.' The words are, 'Cathedram habet in cœlo, qui corda docet in terris.' *In 1 Epist. St Johan.* Tr. iii. § 13. Cf. also his *De Disciplina Christiana.*

(rrrr) P. 518.—'Standing is a military word;' *i.e.*, ἵστημι, opposed to φεύγω. Cf. Eph. vi. 13.

A. B. G.

AN

ALPHABETICAL TABLE

DIRECTING THE READER TO THE READY FINDING OUT THE PRINCIPAL POINTS AND MATTERS HANDLED IN THIS BOOK.*

* This 'Alphabetical Table,' prepared by Dr Thomas Manton, it has been deemed proper to retain, and accommodate to the pagination of our reprint. It does not furnish those minuter details and references that belong to an Index *proper*, such as will be given with the closing volume of this edition of the Works; but as the 'Commentary' is extensive, it will prove acceptable as an interim guide to the 'treasures, new and old,' of this Treatise.

This 'Commentary,' it is necessary to observe, is *not* a fragment of an intended Exposition of the entire Epistle, but a Treatise on the 'Apology of St Paul,' complete within itself, according to the design of the author. Cf. page 528, last line.—G.

END OF VOL. III.

THE WORKS OF
RICHARD SIBBES

THE WORKS OF
RICHARD SIBBES

VOLUME 4

Edited by

Alexander B. Grosart

THE BANNER OF TRUTH TRUST

THE BANNER OF TRUTH TRUST

Head Office
3 Murrayfield Road
Edinburgh, EH12 6EL
UK

North America Office
610 Alexander Spring Road
Carlisle, PA 17015
USA

banneroftruth.org

The Complete Works of Richard Sibbes
first published in 7 volumes 1862-64
This reprint of volume 4 first published by
the Banner of Truth Trust 1983
Reprinted 2001, 2023

*

ISBN
Print: 978 0 85151 371 3

*

Printed in the USA by
Versa Press Inc.,
East Peoria, IL.

PREFATORY NOTE.

As a fitting sequel to Vol. III., which contains the Exposition of 2 Corinthians chap. i., the present will be found to bring together all Sibbes's Treatises and Sermons founded upon other texts or portions of the Two Epistles to the Corinthians. A. B. G.

CONTENTS.*

A CHRISTIAN'S PORTION; OR, THE CHRISTIAN'S CHARTER.

* Abridged from the original Tables. The Indices in our closing volume of the works will preserve all the minuter details here omitted.—G.

PAGE

THE SPIRITUAL MAN'S AIM.

JUDGMENT'S REASON.

A GLANCE OF HEAVEN; OR, A PRECIOUS TASTE OF A GLORIOUS FEAST.

THE EXCELLENCY OF THE GOSPEL ABOVE THE LAW.

THE CHURCH'S RICHES.

A CHRISTIAN'S PORTION;

OR,

THE CHRISTIAN'S CHARTER.

A CHRISTIAN'S PORTION; OR, THE CHRISTIAN'S CHARTER.

NOTE.

'The Christian's Portion' was published originally in 1637, and forms a tiny volume of 67 pages. It is very imperfect. Its title-page is given below.* This, the *first* edition, was superseded in the following year, by a much 'enlarged' and 'corrected' one, from evidently fuller and more accurate 'notes.' The latter is followed in our reprint. Its title-page will also be found below.† Prefixed to it is Marshall's smaller portrait of Sibbes. G.

* The
Christians
Portion.
Wherein is unfolded the
unsearchable *Riches* he hath by
his interest in *Christ*. Whom in-
joying hee possesseth all
things else.

By *R. Sibbs* D.D. and Preacher
to the Honorable Society of *Grayes-*
Inne, and Master of *Catherine*
Hall in *Cambridge*.

Published by
T. G. and P. N.

London.
Printed by John Norton
for John Rothwell, and
are to be sold at the Sunne in *Pauls*
Church-yard. 1637.

† The Christians
Portion, or,
The Charter of a
Christian, (so stiled by
the Reverend Author.)
Wherein are laide open
those unsearchable riches and
priviledges, he hath by his inter-
est in Christ: whom enjoying,
he possesseth all things else.

By the Reverend Divine
R. Sibbs, D.D. and Preacher
to the Honourable society of
Graies Inne, and Master of
Katherine Hall in *Cambridge*.

Corrected and enlarged.

Published by T. G. *and* P. N.

Christ is all in all.

LONDON.
Printed by *J. O.* for *John Rothwell*,
and are to be sold at the Sunne in
Paules Church-yard. 1638.

*** The T. G. and P. N. on both of these title-pages were Dr Thomas Goodwin and Philip Nye. Cf. Vol. II., page 3, but for Hanburg read Hanbury. G.

THE EPISTLE TO THE READER.

Good Reader! didst thou ever yet read over thy own heart and life, and mend in some degree what was amiss in both? If not, what comfort can this treatise afford thee? If so, what comfort can it not? This short discourse lays open a great matter. It is a counterpane of a Christian's charter. The author himself styles it 'The Christian's Charter.'

If thy life be good, thy tenure is large; yea, larger than that of the Corinthians. The apostles, as Paul, Apollos,* and Cephas were theirs; so they are thine. And besides them, all that have succeeded them, the faithful ministers of the gospel, and all their studies and writings. The reverend author of this treatise is thine, and this book is thine; thine to shew thee how much is thine. Let me be thine also to commend this work to thee, and to pray for thee, that as the Lord opened the eyes of Elisha's man to see the mountain full of horses and chariots, and more with them than against them, 2 Kings vi. 17, so he would open thine, to see thy great riches and privileges in Jesus Christ. The want of sight makes us think we want. Post over the two great volumes of heaven and earth, and thou shalt find thyself wealthy.

Man hath this excellency above all inferior creatures, to know what he is and what he hath above others. The brute beasts are better than plants, but they know it not; and so plants are more excellent than the elements, &c. They have worth, but understand it not. Man hath this added to his dignity, to know it. And this is given him, as a schoolman saith, that he may rejoice in that he hath, and him that gave it (*a*). The sun rejoices not in its own beauty, because it knows it not. As there is *ignoti nulla cupido*, so *nulla delectatio*. We can as little delight in what we know not, as desire it.

He therefore must needs be rich that hath the 'blood of Christ,' which purchased the world. When all losses, either in goods or children, befall such a man, yet he hath enough besides. When man says all is gone, Christ says all is his. This should make him hold up his head, but not too high. It should make him cheerful, but not withal scornful.

Men are still apt to run into extremes. Tell men of the heinous nature of sin, and for the most part they either stop short and do not bewail it, or step beyond and quite despair. Obstinacy is the low extreme like the earth, hard also and rocky as it is. Despair is as much too high, as it were in the element of fire, which scorches up the spirit. The middle region of air and water, of sighs and tears, is the best. Thus when we treat of a godly man's privileges, some will overween them as fast as others undervalue them. Christian virtues are *in medio* as well as moral; but generally men seem to promise to themselves, as Jonathan to David, 1 Sam. xx. 36, either to shoot short or beyond. Men will either overdo or do nothing. The Mediator teaches us a middle way. St Paul, when the viper hung upon his hand, was thought some notorious malefactor;

* Spelled 'Apollo.'—G.

when he shook it off without harm, was a god, Acts xxviii. 3, *seq.* The first was too bad, and the last too good. The middle had been best: if they had said, he is some good man.

This causes many differences in religion. Men run so far one from another, some to one side and others to the other side of the circumference, that whilst they stand *è diametro oppositi*, they leave the truth behind them in the centre. Some will give too much to this or that ordinance, because others give too little; and some will give too little, because others give too much. It is a spirit of opposition that causes divisions. Two spheres will but touch in a point; and so when men are swollen with pride and anger, they gather up one from another, and resolve not to adhere so much as in one point.

The apostles were given to the church to rejoice in, but neither to despise nor deify; they might neither glory over them, nor glory in them. It is the sin of these times; look it, reader, that it be not thine. Some men fall out with the whole tribe, and thereupon begin to lay aside the principles of sobriety. But should I tell thee what is said by Baronius (*b*) and some others, and what might be said of the honour of that calling, this discourse would rather want an epistle than be one, for the length. Indeed, some have gone too far, and made the priesthood more than it is. A Latin postiller upon that in Exod. xxx. 31, where it is said, 'Thou shalt anoint Aaron and his sons,' &c., because it is said, ver. 32, 'upon man's flesh it shall not be poured,' thence infers, in an hyperbolical sense, that priests are angels, not having human flesh. Some kind of postils and glosses are like antique flourishings about a great capital letter, which is not so much adorned by them as darkened. Such is this. We have a dignity indeed, but no deity. Therefore in the words following the text here handled, chapter the fourth, verse the first, says the apostle, 'Let men so account of us, as the ministers of Christ, and stewards of the mysteries of God.' As the ministers of Christ, we are not to be abased, and as but ministers, not to be adored; as stewards, not to be magnified, and as stewards of the mysteries of God, not to be vilified. Consider the Lord's messengers both as 'earthen vessels' and as having a treasure in them. But there are those that set some too high, and depress others too low. This partiality hath brought many miseries upon the church, and diverted many men from the church. It hath sent many a *renegado* bound for Rome. Discontent is a dangerous thing, when the occasion is just.

In a word, I desire thee to weigh well one passage, and not to misdeem it, which the worthy author hath, page 16, concerning the right of wicked men to earthly things. He says it is a mistake to think they have no right to them. And so it is indeed, Ps. xvii. 14. They have their portion in this life. A man must needs have some right to his portion. What Ananias had, Acts v. 4, was his own, whilst he had it, as Peter tells him; and yet Satan had filled his heart. We are to do good to all, but especially the household of faith, Gal. vi. 10. Therefore we may do good, and distribute to those that are not of the household of faith. But what needs this, if earthly things belong not to them? If in giving them we shall make them usurpers, we had better not give to them. If a covetous man hath no title to his goods, when sentence of condemnation is passed upon him, he may say, Why am I condemned for not giving, when I had nothing to give? Besides it will follow, that no man shall be condemned for want of liberality in not giving, but only for want of justice in not restoring. The earth was to bring forth to Adam fallen, or for Adam, though thorns and thistles. The sons of Adam have the earth, though the curse with it. A title therefore they have, though not the same title with the righteous. The godly have them as from a loving Father, the wicked as from a liberal Lord, who out of goodness makes the 'sun to shine both upon the just and unjust,' Mat. v. 45. Therefore a Christian's right doth not exclude, but excel theirs.

Let not therefore a godly man trouble himself to argue them out of their good things here received; they are all they shall have. Let the wicked make much of what they have, for they shall have no more. The servant of the Lord must seek his portion in another life. The greatest part of the things he hath here is the least part of the things he shall have hereafter.

But then take the right course, and first make God thine, and then all shall be thine. But before God can be thine, Christ must be thine; and before him, faith must be thine; and before faith, the word must be thine. Therefore so order thy affairs as to hear, and so order thy hearing as to believe, and so thy faith as to find Christ in thy heart; and then thou shalt find God in Christ, and all in God.

But I entreat thee for the mercies of Christ, if thou undertakest a Christian profession, walk answerably to it; and to a good profession, add a good confession. 'Oh! that men would praise the Lord for his goodness, and declare the wonders that he doth for the children of men,' Ps. cvii. 8. Bless God for all thou hast and shalt have; yea, for this work, &c., the man that indited it: a man, for matter always full, for notions sublime, for expression clear, for style concise; a man spiritually rational, and rationally spiritual; one that seemed to see the insides of nature and grace, and the world and heaven, by those perfect anatomies he hath made of them all. But his work needs no letter of commendation from any, much less from one so unworthy as I am. Therefore pardon me, and read him, and try thyself, and glorify God. Farewell. J. B.*

* These initials probably represent Jeremiah Burroughs, than whom none of the Puritans more nearly resembled Sibbes either as a man or as a writer. He died November 14. 1646. He is one of Fuller's 'Worthies.' For a short memoir, consult Brook's Lives of the Puritans, III. pp. 18–25.—G.

A CHRISTIAN'S PORTION;

OR,

A CHRISTIAN'S CHARTER.

Therefore let no man glory in men: for all things are yours; whether Paul, or Apollos, or Cephas, or the world, or life, or death, or things present, or things to come; all are yours; and ye are Christ's; and Christ is God's.—1 Cor. III. 21–23.

One man is prone to idolise and set up another man in his soul higher than is fit, which is never without great danger and derogation from Christ. Men, for the love of that good that is in others, whom they reverence overmuch, take in ill, and all. We are very prone to this fault when we look too much to persons who are subject to like infirmities with ourselves. That is the reason why the apostle is so careful in this chapter to abase man in the beginning of this 21st verse. 'Let no man glory in men;' that is, so far as to depend upon them in matters of faith. This, therefore, is the principal scope of the apostle, in this place, to cut off faction and overmuch dependence upon men. There were some vainglorious teachers that had crept into the consciences of people (as it is their use),* and drew factions, and so set up themselves instead of Christ. The apostle, to prevent this, saith, 'Let no man glory in men.' Do not glory in your teachers; they are but your servants and Christ's servants; 'for all things are yours.' By means of those vain-glorious teachers the people grew divided, and began to set up one and cry down another. To redress this, the apostle saith, 'All things are yours;' whether Paul, meaning himself, or Apollos,† another excellent man; yea, Cephas, Peter himself. Paul with all his learning, Apollos with his eloquence, Peter with his vehemency of spirit; what he is, and what he hath, all his endowments are for the good of the church.

So that here we have, *first*, a *dehortation:* 'Let no man glory in man.' Then a *reason of it;* 'For all things are yours.'

He sets down the reason, first, in gross in the whole, 'All things are yours.'

And then parcels it out, as it were, by retail: 'whether Paul, or Apollos,

* That is = 'custom, way.'—G.

† Again, and throughout, spelled Apollo.—G.

or Cephas, or the world, or life, or death, or things present, or things to come.' And so by induction of particulars he lays open and unfolds this tapestry, that they may see the riches of this 'all,' and then he wraps up all again, 'all are yours.' Those things that I have named are yours, nay, things that are most unlike, 'life and death are yours.' What need we doubt of other things, when death is ours? He that hath the power of death, the devil, is not excluded; 'he is ours.'

Here is also a gradation: 'All is ours.' Is there a full point there? No. 'We are Christ's, and Christ is God's. The gradation is upwards and downwards. God descends to us. 'All' is from the Father, and from Christ mediator, to man, and for man's sake to the creature. The gradation up again is, 'We are Christ's, and Christ is God's.' Which makes a blessed concatenation, or chaining and linking of things from the wise and great God. All things hang on him, and are carried to him again; and as they come from one, so they end in one. As a circle begins and ends in one point, so all comes from God and ends in God.

In the reason we have the 'Charter of a Christian,' the dowry that the church hath by her marriage with Christ. He is the greatest king that ever was, and she is the greatest queen; for Christ, he is Lord of heaven and earth, and of all things; and her estate is as large as his. 'All things are yours,' &c., even from God to the poorest thing in the world. God passeth over himself to his children; he is theirs, Christ is theirs. Therefore angels are theirs; for angels ascend and descend upon Jacob's ladder, that is, Christ.

Having set down this general, 'all things are yours,' to discourage them from glorying in men, he parcels that general into particulars: 'Paul, or Apollos, or Cephas, or life, or death,' &c.

1. *All persons* are yours.
2. *All things* are yours.
3. *All events* are yours.

Persons: 'Paul, Apollos, Cephas.'

Things: 'The world, or life, or death.'

Events: Whatsoever can come, for the present, or for time to come, 'all is yours.'

For persons: 'Paul, Apollos, Cephas are yours.' Therefore Peter is not the head of the church. He is named here in the third place, among the rest, and after the rest: 'Whether it be Paul, or Apollos, or Cephas, he is yours.' You know who ground all their religion on this. Peter is the head of the church, and they are the successors of Peter. But Peter is the church's, and therefore cannot be the head and commander. The pope pretends that he is Peter's successor, and yet he will be head of the church. But you see Cephas is a servant of the church's, as well as Paul and Apollos. You see the hypocrisy of him, by the way. He will call himself *servus servorum Dei*, the servant of the servants of God, as if he would justify this blessed speech. Cephas and Paul are servants of the church, and I, that am Peter's successor, am so; but yet he stamps in his coin, 'THAT NATION AND COUNTRY THAT WILL NOT SERVE THEE, SHALL BE ROOTED OUT' (*c*). And so, while he pretends to be servant of servants, he will be lord of lords; he tyranniseth over the church, and overthrows this text that saith, 'All things are for the church, and we must glory in no man,' so as to let him be the author of our faith in anything. That man of sin and his adherents, the faction of Rome, wrong the church two ways especially.

1. *First of all*, in that they have of their own brain, without Christ, the

head of the church, *ordained a world of idle ceremonies*, which they will have to have supernatural effects, and to confer grace.

2. And then, *secondly*, in that they *make laws to bind the conscience, without reference to Christ*, and their traditions must have the same authority with the word of God; so they sit in the temple of God; and that is the reason why popery prevaileth so. Whereas, indeed, no man is lord of the faith of another man. The chiefest men in the world are but servants of the church: Paul, and Apollos, and Cephas. 'The woman must not usurp authority over the man,' 1 Tim. ii. 12, nor must the church be above Christ.

To go on; not only all persons, but the whole world, is the church's.

The world natural, the civil world, and the ecclesiastical world.

(1.) *First, the world natural is the church's;* that is, the frame of heaven and earth. All things are made for man, and he is made for God. As a wise philosopher could say, that man is the end of all things in a semicircle *(d)*; that is, all things in the world are made for him, and he is made for God. The world is ours, all things in the world are our servants; for they mourn in black, as it were, for our miseries since the fall, and in our restoring again they shall be restored. They wait for the day, as it is Rom. viii. 21, 'For the glorious liberty of the Son of God.' They have their happiness and misery together with men. The world stands for the elect. If all the elect were gathered out of the world, there would be an end of all things; all would be in confusion presently.

(2.) And so *for the civil world*, all states are for the church. The commonwealth is for the church. Therefore St Paul bids us 'pray for kings and princes,' &c. Why? That under them we may live a godly and peaceable life,' 1 Tim. ii. 2. If it were not for the gathering of the church, God would take little care for commonwealths. They stand because the church is mingled with them. Take church from the commonwealth, and what is it but a company of men that make the world their god? Kingdoms and commonwealths are but hospitals and harbours for the church. Though they despise the church, and account of it as Christ was accounted, a stranger that they will not acknowledge, yet notwithstanding, those few despised ones are the substance of the kingdom. God intends the church as the considerable part of the world, though men think not so. The rest that are not the church, they are for the church. As we say of a field of wheat, the ploughing, the rain, the stalk, the ear, the husk, all is for the wheat; so the standing of the world, the government of it, the parts and gifts of men, all are for the church, to do good to it. Were it not for the service they owe to the church, they should not continue.

(3.) And *in the church* all that ever is good is for the elect's sake. As we stand under Christ in great terms, ambassadors, &c., so we stand to the church as servants. 'We preach ourselves servants for Christ's sake,' 2 Cor. iv. 5. 'Let a man esteem of us as of the ministers of Christ,' 1 Cor. iv. 1. No greater nor no less, but as the ministers of Christ. Persons and ministry, calling and gifts, all are for the church, as it is Eph. iv. 11, *seq.*, at large; when he ascended up on high, he 'gave some to be apostles, some pastors,' &c., all for the good of the church. 'I suffer all for the elect's sake,' saith St Paul, 2 Tim. ii. 10. Therefore it forceth very well; we should not glory in the ministers, nor in any creature. They are for us. But if a man will glory, let him glory in him who hath made all things his, that is, in Christ.

(4.) Further, *the world is ours, take it in the worst sense;* the world of wicked men, all their plots, and the 'prince of the world' are the church's.

How is this? He and all his instruments are under the command of him that turns all his designs contrary to his own intention. This is a hell to Satan, and one of the chief torments that he hath; that as his malice is above his power, so God overpowers him in his power. God overshoots him in his own bow. Whatever he designs against the head Christ, and against his members the church, it is overturned for the good of the church. In the apostles' times some were 'given over to Satan, that they might learn not to blaspheme,' 1 Tim. i. 20. It is a strange thing that Satan should teach not to blaspheme, who is the author of blasphemy; yet by consequence, he afflicting their bodies, thereupon they came to be wise, and learned to be moderate and sober, and to be Christianly minded, and not to blaspheme. So the prince of the world is ours in this by an over-commanding power, that turns all to good against his intentions. For there is but one grand monarch in the world; every kingdom is under a higher kingdom. There is but one to whom all are subject. There is one grand wheel that turns all the others. And therefore Satan himself is serviceable to God's end, whether he will or no.

And then for the world of wicked men, all their designs, though for the present they seem to be against the church, yet they are serviceable to the church. For wicked men are but the launderers of the church, to wash the church, to purge it, to do base services that God intends for the refining of the church. And all their hatred is for the good of the church. For God suffers the world to hate his children, that his children might not love the world, because it would be a dangerous love. The church is a strange corporation; it is such a corporation as hath greatest benefit by enemies. The enemies of the church are the promoters of the greatest good of the church. The very world is the church's, take it in the worst sense, for the 'wicked world that lies in mischief.' But I will not dwell upon that. To go on.

As all things in general, so *life* especially is the church's. Why doth God prolong the life of good pastors and good people, but that they may be blessed instruments to convey truth to posterity? As St Paul saith, Phil. i. 23, 24, 'It is for your sake that I am not with Christ. It were best for me to be dissolved, and to be with Christ,' a great deal; but for your sake, for your good, I must remain still. So, for the life of pastors and good Christians, by communion with whom we have benefit. For their particular it were best for them to be in heaven, to be gathered to the triumphant church, to their friends, to Christ, to the saints, the souls of just men made perfect, there is no question of it; but for the church's sake they are made to want their glory for a time. Paul was content to be without the joys of heaven for a while, to want his crown of glory, to live in the church, to do good. So the life of other able worthy men it is for the church, and it is the calamity of the church when God takes them away.

And so the life of good magistrates, it is for the benefit of the church. It were better for them to be in heaven. But as it is said of David, Acts xiii. 36, 'He served God in his own generation.' So every magistrate hath his generation, time, allotted, a generation to stand up in the church and state, and to serve God in, and then God takes him away.

And then our own life is ours, while we live in order to a better life (for all must be understood in order to happiness), which is the only life. This present life is nothing but a shadow, yet we have a world of advantage in this life, to get assurance of a better. This life, indeed, is but a little spot of time between two eternities, before and after, but it is of great consequence, and it is given us to get a better life in, that glory may be begun in grace, and that we may have a further and 'further entrance into the kingdom of heaven here,' as Peter saith, 2 Peter i. 11.

Again, life is ours, because the time we live here is a seed time. This life is given us to do a great many of good things in, the crop and harvest of which is reserved for the world to come; and when we have done the work that God hath given us to do, we are gathered to our fathers.

And life is a special benefit, because by the advantage of life we further our reckonings after death. A good Christian, the longer he lives, the larger good accounts he hath, the more he soweth to the Spirit. It is therefore a blessed thing for a godly man to live long, for a good man to be an old man. All his sins are wiped away; they shall never be laid to his charge. He may say, he hath lived long, and sinned a long time, yet his sins are forgiven, and all his good deeds shall be upon the file,* and be set on the score, even to 'a cup of cold water,' Mat. x. 42, and he shall be rewarded. There is not a sigh, not a tear but it is registered. The longer a man liveth, if he should live Methuselah his days, the richer he should be in good works; and the richer he is in good works, the more he shall have his part and share in glory after. The longer he lives, the happier the times are in which he lives; for a good man makes the times happy, and it is happier for himself. The more rich he is in good works, the more rich he shall be in glory after, the heavier his crown, and his reward shall be in heaven. The richer shall be his harvest, the larger his seed-time hath been.

Use. These things being so, *we should bless God, and be very thankful that he yields to us this life;* for besides an advantage of doing good, it is a preparative to a better. This life is, as it were, the seminary † of heaven. Heaven indeed is the true paradise of all the plants of God, but they must have a seminary to be planted in first; and therefore the church is called the kingdom of heaven, because we are first planted here. Therefore we should bless God for this life, and not wish ourselves dead out of murmuring, but in subjection yield ourselves when God will. Oh, this life is a blessed time. It is our seed time. The longer we live the more opportunity we have to do good, to grow in grace, and to do good to others, and to enlarge our own accounts and reckonings to the end. The next thing to speak of is death.

'Or death.'

He doth well to join these two together, for if life be not ours for good, death will never be ours. He that doth not make a good use of life, never hath death to be his comfort; but instead of an entrance into heaven, it shall be a trap-door to hell. But if life be ours, and we have made a blessed improvement of it, then death also shall be ours. And 'blessed are they that die in the Lord,' Rev. xiv. 13.

It is a strange thing that death should be ours, that is a destroying hostile thing to nature; the king of fear as the Scripture calls it, Job xviii. 14; and that terrible of all terribles, as the philosopher saith, (*e*) 'the last enemy,' as Paul saith, 1 Cor. xv. 26. Death is ours many ways. It is a piece of our jointure, for these words contain the jointure of the church. The church is Christ's spouse. 'All things are Christ's,' and therefore all things are the spouse's; and among other particular gifts given to the church, death is one.

But this death in the gospel is turned to another thing. It is a harmless

* Cf. Note *b*, Vol. I., page 289.—G. † That is, 'seed-plot.'—G.

death. The sting is pulled out. It hath lost all his venom in Christ. That which is malignant and hurtful in death is taken away. What is the poison and sting of death? It is sin. Now that is forgiven in Christ. But that is not enough for God's bounty, that death should not hurt us. No; it is ours, it tends to our benefit many ways.

First, It unclothes us of these rags, these sick, weak, and untoward bodies of ours, that occasion so much disquiet to our souls; these mud walls. It takes down the tabernacle, it puts off our old rags, and puts on a new robe of immortality, and garments of glory. It ends all that is ill. All is determined in death. It is the last evil. It puts an end to all our labours, to all our troubles, and sorrows. Then the cursed labour of all our sins (that are the cause of sorrow) shall have an end. 'Blessed are they that die in the Lord, they rest from their labours,' Rev. xiv. 13. There is no rest till we be dead. Death is the accomplishment of our mortification.

And there is an end of the labour and toil in our callings, and the miseries and afflictions that accompany them. It frees us from all labours whatsoever. For death is a sleep, and all labours end in sleep. And as after sleep the spirits are refreshed; so after death we are more refreshed than we can conceive now. Death is ours because it is our resting-place. After our bodies are weary and worn out in toiling, then comes death, and then we rest in our graves.

It frees us from wicked men, and sets us clear out of Satan's reach. This world is the kingdom of Satan, but when we are gone hence, he hath nothing to do with us. Sin brought in death, and now death puts an end to sin; we shall be no more annoyed with Satan or his temptations, which is a great privilege.

And then death is a passage to another world. It is the gate of glory and everlasting happiness. It is the beginning of all that is good, that is everlastingly and eternally good. Our death is our birthday. Indeed, death is the death of itself; death is the death of death (*f*). For when we die, we begin to live, and we never live indeed till we die. For what is this life? Alas! it is a dying. Every day we live, a part of our life is taken away. We die every day, 1 Cor. xv. 31. The more we have lived, the less of our life we have to live.

The life in heaven begins at death. Death is the birthday of that life of immortality, and that is the life which can only truly be called life. When Christ came by dying to purchase life, it was not this sorry life on earth, but the life in the world to come, that life of immortal glory; and death's day is the birthday of this life. And for our bodies, they are but refined by death, and fitted, as vessels cast into the fire, to be moulded, to be most glorious vessels after.

Death is ours every way. It is our greatest friend under the mask of an enemy. So that, whatsoever Satan may suggest to the contrary, death is ours; our friend that was our enemy; a good thing that was an ill. Our fancy in a temptation may make us apprehend those things that are useful and good to be terrible and ill, and those things that are truly dangerous to us as if they were the only good. Satan abuseth our imagination, by amplifying the good of evil, and the evil of good. But, indeed, death, and all that makes way unto it, sickness, and misery, they are ours; they do us good, they fit us for heaven. Sickness, it fits us for death; it unlooseth the soul from the body. As for the profits, and pleasures, and honours of the world, what do they? They nail us faster to the world, and do us hurt. Therefore, death is ours. It is a good messenger; it brings good tidings when it comes. Hereupon it is that the wise man saith, 'The day of death is better than the day of birth,' Eccles. vii. 1. When we are born, we come into misery; when we die, we go out of misery to happiness. It is better to go out of misery than to come into it. If the day of death be better than the day of birth to a Christian, certainly then death is theirs. It makes a short end of all that is miserable, and it is a *terminus* from whence all good begins. There is nothing in the world that doth us so much good as death. It ends all that is ill both of body and soul, and it begins that happiness that never shall have an end. Therefore, 'blessed are they that die in the Lord, saith the Spirit,' Rev. xiv. 13, 'A voice from heaven' saith so, and therefore, 'Write,' saith he. It may be written if the Spirit saith it: it is testimony and argument enough. 'Blessed are those that die in the Lord: they rest from their labours; and their reward follows them.' For they rest from all that is evil, and from that only. All that is good, 'their works follow them.' So that if all evil cease, and all good follows, I hope death may well be said to be ours, and for our good.

Use. If death be ours, and all that makes way to death, sickness, &c., the curse of them being taken away, and in the room a blessing hid in them, then why should we startle and be affrighted too much at the message of death, as if it were such a terrible thing? Why should we be afraid of that that is a part of our portion? Why should we be afraid of that which is friendly to us and doth us so much good? What, to be a Christian that lives in the household and family of faith, and to want faith so far as not to believe the glorious estate after death, or that it is not his, or that death lets him not into it!

Nature will be nature, and death is a dissolution, and so the enemy of nature, the last enemy. Therefore nature cannot but in some measure be affrighted with death; but then grace and the Spirit of God in his children should be above nature, and cause them to look beyond death to that happy condition which death puts them in possession of. Death is like Jordan. We go through the waters and waves of it to Canaan, the land of promise and happiness. Faith would let us see this; and so grace would subdue nature, though nature will have a bout* with the best, death being the terrible of terribles, and the king of fear, as I said before. Therefore I speak not this that we should be senseless, but that we may see how far the meditation of these things, of this blessed prerogative, and this one part of our charter, should strengthen us.

I beseech you, therefore, let us lay up this against those dark times wherein death will be presented unto us an ugly and grim thing. It is so to nature indeed, but to faith, death is become amiable.† Indeed, as I said, there is nothing in the world that doth us so much good as death, for it is the best physician. It cures all diseases whatsoever of soul and body. And indeed—for to shut up this point—death is the death and destruction of itself; for after death there is no more death. It consumes itself. By death we overcome death. 'We can never die more,' Rom. vi. 9. We are freed from all death. Therefore, to be afraid of death, is to be afraid of life, to be afraid of victory; for we never overcome death till we die. Lay up these considerations against the time of need. When death comes, there will be a confluence of a world of grief, when conscience, being guilty

* That is, 'one turn,' 'one trial.'—G. † That is, 'lovely.' Cf. Ps. lxxxiv. 1.—G.

of sin, shall be arraigned before God; when there will be sickness, and diseases of body, and a deprivation of all the comforts and employments of the world. They will all meet in a centre, in a point, at death; but a man had need to gather the greater comfort against that hour; and what shall comfort us then? There is a sweet comfort in Rom. viii. 38, 39, that neither life, nor death, nor things present, nor things to come, shall be able to separate us from the love of God in Christ. It is a sweet comfort, that nothing shall separate us; but this is a greater comfort, that death is ours. It shall not only not separate us from God and from happiness, but it shall bring us to nearer communion with God and Christ, for it is a separation that causeth a nearer conjunction; the separation of soul and body causeth the conjunction of the soul to Christ for the present, and afterwards an eternal conjunction of soul and body in this blessed fruition of him. Now, blessed be God for Jesus Christ, that hath made in him even death, the bitterest thing of all, to be sweet unto us.

'Or things present.'

Whatsoever is present, good or ill. The good things present are ours, for our comfort in our pilgrimage and passage towards heaven. God is so good unto his children, as that he doth not only reserve for them happiness in another world, but the very gallery and passage to heaven by the way is comfortable. Things present are theirs. They may enjoy them with comfort; they have a liberty to all things, for refreshings, &c. 'All things are pure to the pure,' Titus i. 15. 'Every creature of God is good, so it be received with thanksgiving and prayer,' 1 Tim. iv. 4. We have a liberty to use them, but it must be with prayer and thanksgiving. Though a man hath a liberty and right to any thing, yet there must be a suing it out, there must be some passage in law to put him in possession. So, though we have a freedom to 'present things,' there must be somewhat to make a sanctified use of them. We must go to God by grace to use them well; all must be sanctified by prayer and thanksgiving.

And as good things, so ill things present are ours. Afflictions are ours, because they fit us for a happier state; they exercise what is good in us, and mortify what is ill. They are sanctified to subdue that which is ill, and to increase that which is good, and to make us more capable of glory. Who is so capable of glory as he that hath been afflicted in this world? To whom is heaven heaven indeed but to the man that hath led an afflicting life, a conflicting course with the world and his own corruptions? Heaven is a place of happiness indeed to him. Therefore, evil things are ours, because they sweeten happiness to come, and make us more capable and more desirous of it. So both good and evil things present are ours. God governing the world, and all things coming from him as a father, nothing shall come to us for the present but what he means to guide for our good.

Use. Therefore *we should take them thankfully at God's hands.* 'In all things be thankful,' 1 Thes. v. 18. 'In all things rejoice,' Phil. iv. 4. Because evil, though it be grevious for the time, yet it hath 'the quiet fruit of righteousness,' Heb. xii. 11. It quiets the soul after in that good we have by it. There are divers good things that we never have but by evil. There was never man yet could say he had patience but by suffering. So things present, whether they are good or ill, they are ours, to help us in the state of grace, and to fit us for the state of glory. But the most difficulty is in

'Things to come.'

For what assurance have we of things to come? Yet 'things to come are ours,' whether they be good or evil.

For good. The remainder of our life, that is ours to do good in. Death is to come, and that is ours. And judgment, that is ours; for our Brother, our Head, our Saviour, and our Husband, he shall be our judge, 1 Cor. vi. 2; and at the day of judgment, 'we shall judge the world.' And then after judgment heaven is ours; immortality and eternity is ours; communion with the blessed company in heaven is ours. 'All is ours' then.

Indeed, the best is to come; for if we had nothing but what we have in this world, 'we were of all men most miserable,' 1 Cor. xv. 19. Alas! what have we, if things present only are ours? But the best is behind. That for which Christ came into the world is behind. That which he enjoys in heaven is ours. He will take his spouse where himself is, into his own house, and he will finish the marriage, which is begun in contract, and then 'we shall be for ever with the Lord,' 1 Thes. iv. 17. 'The things to come' are the main things, that which our faith lays hold on. That which we raise ourselves and comfort ourselves by, are especially the things to come, especially the promises of happiness and glory, and exemption and freedom from all ill. Whatsoever is to come is ours, and ours for eternity. Indeed, here I am swallowed up; I cannot unfold to you what is ours in that sense. For 'if neither eye hath seen, nor ear hath heard, nor hath entered into the heart of man to conceive, what God hath prepared for his children in this world,' 1 Cor. ii. 9, that peace of conscience and joy in the Holy Ghost, how can we conceive here of that glory that is to come? Indeed, it is to be in heaven to conceive of it. It is a part of heaven to know them; and therefore the full knowledge of them it is deferred for that time till we come there.

And evil things to come are ours also. They cannot do us harm, they cannot 'separate us from Christ,' Rom. viii. 35. Nothing for the time to come shall be prejudicial, to unloose that blessed union that is between our soul and Christ; as St Paul, Rom. viii., in that heavenly discourse of his, towards the latter end of the chapter, Rom. viii. 38, 39, saith triumphantly and divinely, 'Nothing shall separate us from Christ; neither life, nor death, nor things present, nor things to come.' We have the word of God for it, 'that nothing to come shall hinder us.' Whatsoever is to come, be it never so ill, it shall further us, as the apostle saith in the same chapter: Rom. viii. 28, 'All things shall work together for the best to them that love God.' Therefore, if nothing to come can hinder us, and all things that are to come shall further us, then all things to come must be ours. In 1 Pet. i. 5, 'We are kept by the power of God, through faith, to salvation.' Salvation is laid up for us, and we are kept through faith, by the power of God, to salvation. Therefore all things to come are ours.

It is a great comfort that nothing shall separate us; no, not death itself. But this text affords an exuberancy of comfort above that, that death is ours; and in being so, it shall not only not separate us from Christ, though it separate soul and body, but join us to him.

I beseech you, take it as a notion that may help against the terror of that doleful separation of soul and body. It parts two old friends, but it joins better friends together, the soul and Christ.

Farther, all things to come are ours; even all things in the largest sense, the bitterest of all things.

The very judgment of the wicked, and the eternal sentencing of them, is the church's. Why? It adds a lustre to God's mercy in advancing his own, as it is Rom. ix. 23. God magnifies his mercy to 'the vessels of mercy,' by punishing a company of reprobates, in whom he hath no delight, by reason of their sins. His mercy appears much by that, even by the eternal sentence and punishment of wicked men. So all serves to set out the glory and excellency of God's people.

Use. The use that the apostle mainly intends is, that a Christian is as sure of the time to come as of the time past or present. We are sure of what we have had, and what we have; but a Christian is in so firm a condition and state that he may be sure of what is to come: because God and Christ are not only 'Alpha, but Omega' also; Christ is not only he 'was, and is,' but 'is to come,' Rev. i. 8. He is 'Jehovah, the same for ever,' Heb. xiii. 8. And therefore, as things past could not hinder us from being elected and called; and things present cannot hurt, but they are ours: so are things to come; because God, and Christ, who is the mediator under God, hath the command of all things to come. And therefore we may be as sure of things to come as of things present. What a comfort is this to a Christian, when he is casting what should become of him, if times of trouble and public calamity should come! Presently he satisfieth himself with this, come what will come, all shall be for the best, 'all things to come are ours,' even all things whatsoever.

'All things are yours.'

But yet we must understand this with some limits. We therefore unloose some knots, and answer some cases.

Case 1. *First,* it may seem *there is no distinction of propriety,** *if all be a Christian's.*

Obj. And if every Christian may say, 'All is mine,' then what is one man's is another's, and there will be no propriety.

Ans. I answer, undoubtedly there is a distinction of properties in the things of this life. 'All is ours,' but it is in another sense. 'All is ours,' to help us to heaven; 'all is ours' in an order to comfort and happiness; but for propriety, so all things are not ours. For you know the distinction: some things are common *jure naturæ,* by the law of nature, as the sun and air, and many such like things; and some *jure gentium,* by the law of nations. It is but some things are thus common. But then there are some that by particular municipal laws are proper.

The distinction is established both by the law of God and the law of man.† Therefore, not to stand long in answering this question, the Scripture stablisheth the distinction of master and servant; and therefore it establisheth distinction of goods. The Scripture establisheth bounty and alms. If there be not a distinction of property, where were alms? Solomon saith, 'The rich and the poor meet together: God is the maker of both,' Prov. xxii. 2. He means, not as men only, but as poor and rich.

If riches be of God, then distinction of properties is of God; for what is riches but a distinction of properties? If God make poor and rich, then there must be poor and rich. The poor you have always with you,' Mat. xxvi. 11. Therefore the meaning is, 'All is yours;' that is, all that we possess, and all that we need to help us, is ours in that order and carriage of things that may help us to heaven. And so the want of things is ours, as well as the having of them. The very things which a Christian wants are his; not only the grace of contentment to want, but when God takes away those things that are hurtful for him, that may hinder him in his

* That is, 'property.'—G.

† In margin here, 'Read Judges xi. from ver. 12 to 20.'—G.

course to heaven, that is his. It is a part of this portion, not to have things, if God see it good. The want of things is a part of this 'all.'

Obj. That which is so commonly alleged to the contrary, in Acts ii. 44, 'All things were common,' will easily receive answer.

Ans. 1. For, *first, it was partly upon necessity*. If all things then had not been common, they had all been taken from them.

2. And then, *secondly, it was arbitrary also*.* 'Was it not thine own?' saith Peter, Acts v. 4. Thou mightst not have parted with it, if thou wouldst. It was arbitrary,* though it was common.

3. And then, *thirdly, all things were not common* (*g*). Some good men kept their houses. Mary had her house, Acts xii. 12.

4. And then, *fourthly*, all things were common, but how? To distribute as they needed; not to catch who would and who can. But they were so common as they had a care to distribute to every one that which they needed.

Case 2. *Obj*. Another case is this; all is the church's, all is good people's, and therefore if a man be naught,† nothing is his. There is a great point of popery grounded upon this mistake. For therefore say the Jesuited papists, the pope may excommunicate ill princes, in order to spiritual things, *in ordine ad spiritualia*. He is the lord and monarch of all. They are evil governors; nothing is theirs, all is the church's.

Ans. But we must know that political government is not founded upon religion; that if a prince be not religious, he is no king; but it is founded upon nature and free election, so that the heathen that have no religion, yet they may have a lawful government and governors, because it is not so built upon religion; but where that is not, yet this may be, and God's appointment to uphold the world. So that, let the king be anything or nothing for religion, he is a lawful king.

Obj. But it is further objected, that they succeed Christ, &c., and he was the Lord of the world, and they are the vicars of Christ; and therefore they may dispossess and invest whom they will.

Ans. But you must know, Christ as man had no government at all: but Christ as God-man, mediator; and so he hath no successor. That is incommunicable to the creature. Christ as man had no kingdom at all, for he saith, 'My kingdom is not of this world,' John xviii. 36. And St Austin saith well, 'Surely he was no king, that feared he should be a king' (*h*). For when they came to make him king, 'he withdrew himself and went away,' John vi. 15. And now Christ governs all things in the church. How? As God, as mediator, as God-man; not as man, but as God-man; and so he hath no substitute. They are all vain, impudent allegations, as if all were theirs, because all is the church's to dispose; and the pope takes himself virtually to be the whole church.

'All things are ours.'

Case 3. Doth not this hinder bounty? It is mine, and therefore I do not owe any bounty unto others; as Nabal said, 'Shall I give my bread, and my water, and refreshing,' &c., 1 Sam. xxv. 11. He was too much upon the pronoun 'mine.'

Ans. However all that we possess is ours in law, yet in mercy many times it is the poor's, and not ours. The bonds of duty, both of humanity and religion, are larger than the bonds of law. Put case, in law thou art not bound to do so, yet in humanity, much more in Christianity, thou art. That that thou hast is the church's, and the poor's, and not thine. It will

* That is, 'uncontrolled' = of choice.—G. † That is, 'naughty' = wicked.—G.

be no plea at the day of judgment to say, it was mine own. Thou mayest go to hell for all that, if thou relieve not Christ in his members. Therefore 'all things are ours' now, not to possess all we have, but to use them as he will have them used, that gives them. And when Christ calls for anything that is ours, we must give it. And though we bé not liable to human laws, if we do not, yet we are liable to God's law; and alms and works of mercy, is justice in God's account; for we ought to be merciful to Christ's. And in the royal law, the works of love and mercy are justice, and we withhold good from the owners, if we be not merciful. For in religion, the poor, that by God's providence are cast on us to be provided for, have a right, and that which we detain from them is theirs. And therefore, as St Ambrose saith very well, 'If thou hast not nourished one, howsoever in the law thou art not a murderer, yet before God thou art' (*i*). It is a breach of that law, 'Thou shall not steal,' not to relieve. The very denial of comfortable alms is stealth in God's esteem; and therefore, though 'all be ours,' yet it is so ours, as that we must be ready to part with it when Christ in his members calls for it; for then it is not ours.

Case 4. Again, here is another question; if all be ours, we may use a liberty in all things, what, and how we list, because all is ours.

Ans. I answer: The following are good consectaries hence. 'All is ours;' and therefore with thankfulness we may use any good creature of God. 'All is ours;' and therefore we should not be scrupulous in the creatures, we should not superstitiously single out one creature from another, as if one were holier than another. 'All is ours;' and therefore with a good conscience we may use God's bounty. But hereupon we must not take upon us to use things as we list, because 'all is ours.' There is difference between right, and the use of that right. God's children have right to that which God gives them, but they have not the use of that right at all times, at least it may be suspended. As for example, in case the laws forbid the use of this or that, for the public good of the nation. Also in case of scandal. A man hath right to eat, or not to eat; but if this eating 'offend his brother,' he must suspend the use of his right. 'Whatsoever is sold in the shambles, that eat,' saith St Paul, 'asking no question,' 1 Cor. x. 25; that is, freely take all the creatures of God, without scruple. 'For the earth is the Lord's, and the fulness thereof,' Ps. xxiv. 1. God, out of his bounty, spreads a table for all creatures, for men especially. 'The eyes of all things look up unto thee, and thou givest them meat in due season,' Ps. cxlv. 15, 16. 'The earth is the Lord's, and the fulness thereof.' Make no scruple therefore. But mark, in verse 28, he restrains the use of that liberty upon the same text of Scripture: 'But if any man say, This is offered to an idol,' and take offence, 'eat not, for his sake that shewed it, and for conscience sake;' till he be better satisfied. 'For the earth is the Lord's, and the fulness thereof.'

Quest. Can the same reason be for contraries?

Ans. Yes. That is, for thyself, when thou art alone, take all things boldly. God envies not thy liberty. Take any refreshment, yet needest thou not to eat 'to offend thy brother;' God having given thee variety of creatures, even in abundance, and hath not limited thee to this or that creature; so that the same reason answereth both. 'The earth is the Lord's, and the fulness thereof.' Use it then alone, and not to the scandal of thy brother. 'For the earth is the Lord's, and the fulness thereof.' Why shouldst thou use this creature, as if there were no more but this?

And therefore in case of scandal and offence, we should suspend our liberty, though all be ours.

Again, though all be ours, yet notwithstanding we have not a sanctified use, but by the word and prayer. 'Every creature of God is good, if it be received with prayer and thanksgiving,' 1 Tim. iv. 4. His meaning is, though we have a right to all things to our comfort, to help us to heaven, to cheer us in our way, to be as it were chariots to carry us; yet in the use of that right, we must do it in faith, that we may apprehend our right, that we do not use them with a scrupulous conscience, and sanctify them by prayer. We must take them with God's leave. A father gives all to his son that he needs, and promiseth his son that he shall want nothing; but he will have his son seek to him, and acknowledge him. You shall have all, but I will hear from you first; you shall have all, but I will reach it to you from my hand. So God deals with his children. They have a right to all, but he reacheth it to them in the use of means. We must have a civil right by labour, or by contract, &c., and then we must have a religious right by prayer. We must not pull God's blessings out of his hands. For though he give us a right in the thing, yet, in the use of that right, he will have us holy men.

Case 5. If you ask, What is the reason that good men oft fall to decay, and have a great many crosses in the world?

Why surely (not to enter into God's mysteries), when they have God's blessings they sanctify them not with prayer; they venture upon their right with scandal and offence to others.

Case 6. Again, 'all things are ours.' Therefore truth, wheresoever we find it, is ours. We may read [a] heathen author. Truth comes from God, wheresoever we find it, and it is ours, it is the church's. We may take it from them as a just possession. Those truths that they have, there may be good use of those truths; but we must not use them for ostentation. For that is to do as the Israelites; when they had gotten treasure out of Egypt, they made a calf, an idol of them. So we must not make an idol of these things. But truth, wheresoever we find it, is the church's. Therefore with a good conscience we may make use of any human author. I thought good to touch this, because some make a scruple of it.

'All things are ours.'

Use 1. Now to make some use of this point, 'all things are ours.' We see then that a Christian is a great man, a rich man indeed; and only he is great and rich. It is but imagination and opinion that makes any worldly man great. Can we say that all is his? No. A spot of earth is his, and not his neither; for it is his but to use for a time. He shall be turned naked into the grave ere long, and then he shall be stripped of all. But a Christian is a great man; though he be as poor as Lazarus, 'all is his.'

Obj. But you will say these are great words, 'all is his.' Perhaps he hath not a penny in his purse.

Ans. It is no great matter. God carries the purse for him; he is in his non-age, and not fit for possession. He hath much in promises; he is rich in bills and evidences. Again, let a Christian be never so poor, others are rich for him. Solomon saith there are some kind of oppressing rich men, 'that gather for those that will be good to the poor,' Prov. xxviii. 8. God hath given gifts to wicked men for the good of the church. They themselves are not the better for them. They want love and humility to make use of them. But all things are ours, as well what we want as what we have. For it is good for us that we should want them. A man hath riches when he hath a spirit to want riches. Is not he richer that hath a heart subdued by grace to be content to want, than he that hath riches in the world? For outward things make not a man a whit the better. But he that hath the Spirit of God to support him, that he can submit to God, he is truly rich. It is the mind of a man that makes him rich, and not his purse. Now there is no child of God, but he is master of all things. Though he be poor, he is master of riches, because he can want them, and be without them. Grace teacheth him to want and to abound, as St Paul saith of himself, 'through Christ that strengtheneth him,' Phil. iv. 13. He hath grace to master poverty and whatsoever is ill, and to be content to be what God will have him to be. In want he hath contentment, and in suffering patience. I appeal to the conscience of any man that hath a conscience, is it not better to want temporal things, when we have supply in grace, in faith, &c., than to have great possessions as snares, for so they are to a carnal heart? Is not a Christian better in his wants, than another in his possessions. Who would be as many great ones are and have been alway, though they be invested into much greatness, both of authority and riches? Who would not rather choose the state of a Christian? Though he be poor, yet he hath grace. [Who would choose] rather to be great without grace and to be left of God to their corruptions, to abuse that greatness and riches to their own destruction, and the destruction of many others?

Therefore a Christian is a happy man, a great man, take him as you will; greater than the greatest man in the world without grace; for what he hath, he hath with a curse, as God gave Israel a king in his rage, Hosea xiii. 11. You know what Moses saith, Deut. xxviii. 17, 'Cursed shalt thou be in thy blessings.' A man may have a great many things, and be cursed in them. He doth not say he will curse them in the want of riches, that they should be poor, but he will curse them in their good things; they should have the vengeance of God with them. A Christian may want these things, but he hath the grace of God to want them, and he hath comfort here and assurance of better hereafter. Therefore all things are his, even the worst, because all things have a command to do him good. All things have a prohibition that they do him no harm. As David said of Absalom, 'Do the young man no harm,' 2 Sam. xviii. 5, so God gives all things a prohibition that they do his children no harm, nay, they have a command on the contrary to do them good. If they do them not good in one order, they do it in another; if they do it not in their outward man, they do it in their inward; and God's children by experience find him drawing them nearer to himself, both by having and wanting these things. So though they be not in possession theirs, yet in use, or, as we say, by way of reduction. The worst things are God's children's. For God brings all things about to their good. And when God's children shall be on the shore hereafter, and shall be past all and shall set their foot in heaven once, then they shall see by what a sweet providence God guided it, 'that all things wrought for their good,' Rom. viii. 28.

Quest. But you will say this or that particular is not mine, nor possessed by any of the saints.

Ans. All things are not ours by possession, but by some kind of use or other. We see and behold and meditate upon such things as are possessed by others, and exercise our thoughts profitably about God's providence in disposing these things as he pleaseth; as also we hereby stir up within us the graces of patience, contentedness, and thankfulness for what we have. Thus what we possess not may be ours, and in a better and more profitable use of it to us than to them that possess it.

A Christian therefore, I say again, is a great man, above other men. And this is the reason that carnal men, that have the spirit of the world in them, do so bitterly envy and malign them. Certainly, they secretly think, this man is greater than I am; there is that in him that I have not. A Christian is above other men, and is able to judge them; and knoweth what they are, even miserable in their greatest heights. 'The spiritual man is judged of none,' 1 Cor. ii. 15. Men judge him poor and wretched, but it is false judgment, for he is ever truly rich and noble and happy. He fixeth a true judgment on them, but they cannot of him; for he is in a rank of creatures above them. 'The saints shall judge the world,' 1 Cor. vi. 2. Those that are despised now shall judge others ere long; they shall be assessories in judging the world. No marvel wicked men secretly malign God's people. The wicked cannot but judge them better and happier than themselves. As the life of grace is a higher thing, in the nature of the thing, than the life of reason, so those that have a gracious spiritual life, they are in a rank of creatures above all other men in the world whatsoever.

We see then what a great man a Christian is. He is master of what he hath, and of what he hath not. And is not this a wonderful prerogative that a Christian hath, that turn him to what condition you will, raise him or cast him down, kill him or spare his life, you cannot harm him? If you spare his life, this life is his; if you kill him, 'death is his.' Kill him, save him, enrich him, beggar him, his happiness is not at your command. There is a commanding power to rule all things for the good of God's people. It is not at the devotion* of any creature in the world, either devils or men. God overturns and overpowers all, and all is and shall be theirs.

The state of grace is higher than any earthly condition, therefore it cannot be tainted or blemished by earthly things. Nothing that sense suffers hath power over reason, for it is above sense. If a man be sick he hath the use of reason; if health, reason also manageth it. No inferior thing can manage a superior. Let a man's estate be what it will, grace will master it, because it is a condition above, a ruling commanding condition.

Use 2. [1.] *What a comfort is this in all troubles, that God will sanctify all conditions to us, and us to them.* Who would be disconsolate in any condition whatsoever? Who would be disconsolate to live, when he knows that life is his? If God had not good to do by his life, he would take him away. Who would grieve when death comes, when he knows that death is his? So that a Christian may say, if poverty, if disgrace be good; if the order of evil things will help me; if cross winds will blow me to heaven, I shall have them. For the world and the miseries of the world, the persecutions and afflictions, 'all are ours.' The worst things are commanded to serve for our main good. Therefore let us comfort ourselves. We cannot be at loss in becoming religious and true Christians, for then 'all things are ours.' He loseth nothing that, by losing anything, gaineth all things.

[2.] *For grace*: for seeing 'all things are ours,' *this should teach us to use all things to the honour of him that hath given us all things, not to be servants to anything, not to be subject to any creature*, as St Paul saith of himself, 'I will not be in bondage to anything,' 1 Cor. vi. 12. Why? A Christian is master and lord over all. What a base thing is it for a man to be enthralled to such poor things? As you have some in bondage to a weed.† Some are in bondage

* That is, 'the option.'—G. † That is, 'tobacco' = smoking.—G.

to this affection and some to that, some to an idle custom. For a man to be as Rachel, 'Give me my children, or I die,' Gen. xxx. 1; I must have wealth, I must have pleasure, or else I cannot live; as you know that wretched man Amnon, he pined away to have his will; and so Ahab, who pined away himself because he had not that he would have—are these men masters? No. They bring themselves in slavery and subjection to the creature. Can they say as Paul, 'All things are ours; things present or to come'? when they put themselves in subjection, and those blessed souls of theirs, they make slaves to their servants, to things worse than themselves, that they trample on. If all things be ours, let us bring ourselves in subjection to nothing; but labour rather to have grace to subdue and use all things to right ends.

Use 3. Again, this *should increase in us the grace of thankfulness*. Hath God thus enriched us? Hath he made all things ours to serve our turn (in such a way as he accounts service); that is, that whatsoever we have shall help us to heaven and hath a blessing in it? Though it be sickness, or want, it is ours, and for our benefit. Lord, do what thou wilt, so thou bring me to heaven. If thou wilt have me poor, if it will do me good, let me be so; if thou wilt have me abased, I am content, only sanctify it to bring me to heaven. How thankful should we be to God, that hath placed us in this rank, that he hath put all things under us, and made all things our servants! It was at his liberty to have made us men or not, and when we were men, to make us Christians or not. But being made, we are made lords over all; all things are put under our feet, being one with Christ, as Ps. viii. 6. In the thoughts hereof our hearts should rise up to the Lord thankfully, and say, as he doth there, 'Lord, how wonderful is thy name in all the world.'

Use 4. And fourthly,* it should teach us, for matter of judgment, though it be a shame for us to be taught it, *that there is a God and a wise God*. There are a company, yea, a world of things in the world of different ranks and natures, as evil and good, &c., and yet you see how one thing is disposed for another. The sun shines upon the earth; the earth is fruitful for the beasts; the beasts serve man; and we are Christ's, and Christ is God's. Where there are many things, and things that understand not themselves, and yet there is subordination, there must needs be a wise God that made all things, and sets all in this frame and order. And as it shews there is a God, so that this God is one, because all tend to one. There are a world of things, but all are for man. There are a world of Christians, but all are for Christ, and Christ is for God. Where there are variety of things, and all ordered to one, there must needs be one eternal, wise God. It helps and stablisheth our faith in that grand point, to know that there is a wise, understanding, gracious, powerful God, that rules and marshals all the creatures, otherwise than themselves can do. If there be order in things that have no understanding, surely the ordering of them must come from an understanding. The work of nature, as we say, is a work of intelligence: as in bees, there is planted a wonderful instinct, and in other things, but they understand it not themselves. Therefore the work of the creature, being a work of understanding, it must needs come from him that is a higher understanding, that orders these things. If all these things, good and evil, creatures, states, and conditions, serve God's children, and they are for God, then certainly there is a wise God that orders these things out of goodness to us. And we finding all

* Misprinted 'thirdly.'—G.

things ordered to us, should order ourselves to God. If there be a God that hath ordained variety of things, and of his goodness hath placed us in this rank of things, that all should be our servants, we ought to refer all our endeavours, what we are, and what we can do, to the glory of this God. And this indeed is the disposition of all those that can speak these words with any comfort, 'All things are ours, Paul, and Apollos, magistrates, ministers, life, and death, things present or to come; all are ours.' Those that can speak these words with comfort, are thus disposed; finding all things theirs, they refer all to the glory of him who hath made all things serviceable to them. But to proceed.

I come now to the next branch.

'Ye are Christ's.'

It pleaseth us well to hear that 'all things are ours.' Aye, but we must know further, that there is one above to whom we owe homage, and of whom we have and hold all that we have. 'Ye are Christ's.' This is the tenure we hold all things by, because 'we are Christ's.' Whatsoever the tenure *in capite* be amongst men (which you are better acquainted with than myself*), I am sure it is the best tenure in religion, 'All is ours,' because 'we are Christ's.' We hold all in that tenure. If we be not Christ's, nothing is ours comfortably. 'We are Christ's,' and therefore 'all is ours.'

Quest. But what say you then of those that are not Christ's? Are not the things theirs that they have, because they are not Christ's; or have wicked men nothing that may be called theirs?

Ans. I answer, they have. And it is rigour in some that say otherwise, as that wicked men are usurpers of what they have. They have a title, both a civil title and a title before God. God gave Nebuchadnezzar Tyrus as a reward for his service; and God gives wicked men a title of that they have. And they shall never be called to account at the day of judgment for possessing of what they had, but for abusing that possession. And therefore properly they are not usurpers, in regard of possession; but they shall render an account of the abuse of God's good bounty.

It is in this as it is in the king's carriage to a traitor. When a king gives a traitor his life, he gives him meat and drink that may maintain his life, by the same right that he gives him his life. God will have wicked men to live so long, to do so much good to the church; for all are not extremely wicked that are not Christ's members, that go to hell. But there are many of excellent parts and endowments, that God hath appointed to do him great service. Though they have an evil eye, and intend not his service, but to raise themselves in the world, yet God intends their service for much purpose, and he gives them encouragement in the world, as he will not be behind with the worst men. If they do him service, they shall have their reward in that kind, Ps. lxii. 12. If it be in policy of state, they shall have it in that; and they shall have commendations and applause of men, if they look for that; and if he give them not heaven, they cannot complain, for they care not for that; they did it not with an eye for that. Now if God use the labour and the industry and the parts and endowments of wicked men for excellent purposes, he will give them their reward for outward things: 'Verily, you have your reward,' saith Christ, Mat. vi. 2.

Obj. But the apostle saith, 'All things are yours,' because 'ye are Christ's;' as if those that have not Christ have nothing.

Ans. It is true, howsoever, in some sense, men that are out of Christ, that

* The auditory being at 'Gray's Inn.'—G.

have not his Spirit, have title by virtue of a general providence to what they have; yet they have not a title so good and so full as a godly man, as a Christian hath. They have not this tenure to hold all things in Christ. Therefore their tenure is not so good, nor so comfortable, in three respects.

[1.] *First,* they have them not *from the love of God in Christ.* They have it from God *and* Christ, as the governor and ruler of the world, and making all things serviceable to the church. Therefore he gives these gifts even to wicked men; for the good of others, as the governor of the world; but he bestows them on his children out of love.

[2.] And then, *secondly,* they have them not from God, *as a father in covenant.* They have no title as children of God; for so a Christian is the heir of the world. The first-born was to have a double portion. A true Christian hath a double portion. 'All things are his' here; and heaven is his when he dies. 'Things present are his' while he lives; and 'things to come are his,' when he goes hence.

[3.] And then, *thirdly,* in regard to the end, *to wicked men they do not further their salvation.* They have them not from God with grace to use them well. But God's children, as they have them from his love, and from God as a Father in covenant, so it is for their good. Wicked men they have *donum Dei sine Deo,* they have the gifts of God without God; without the love and favour of God, as Bernard saith well (*j*). But God's children have the gifts of God with God too. Together with the gifts and good things from him, they have his favour, that is better than his gift. For all the good things we enjoy in this world, they are but conduits to convey his favour. God's love and mercy in Christ is conveyed in worldly things; and the same love that moved God to us in heaven, and happiness in the world to come, it moves him to give us daily bread. There is no difference in the love, as the same love that moves a father to give his son his inheritance, moves him to give him breeding and necessaries in the time of his non-age. We are here in our non-age, and God shares out such a state to us; and from the same love that he gives us these things, he gives us heaven afterwards. Now wicked men have not this full degree of title. Yet they have a title, as I said before; and they shall never answer for the possession of what they have, but for the wicked use of that possession.

Case 4. Again, a little further to clear one case I touched before.* If all things be ours because we are Christ's, may we as are Christians use all things as we list?†

Ans. There is a fourfold restraint in regard of the use.

[1.] There is a restraint, *first, of religion.* Though all things be ours in regard of conscience: we may eat and drink, and use any creature of God without scruple; yet there is a restraint put upon it sometimes in religion: that it be no prejudice to the worship of God. In the Lord's day we may refresh ourselves, but not so as to hinder the worship of God: here is a higher restraint put upon our liberty.

[2.] And then, *secondly, sobriety,* it puts a restraint upon our liberty. 'All things are ours' in Christ. We must not take liberty, therefore, to exceed sobriety. *Licitis perimus omnes,* it is an ordinary speech, we all perish by lawful things (*k*). Howsoever, 'all things are ours,' for our use; yet we must use them soberly, and not exceed.

[3.] And then, *thirdly, charity* puts another restraint.‡ It must be

* Cf. page 16.—G. † That is, 'as we choose.'—G.

‡ In margin here, 'See Case 4 before.'

without offence to others. We must not think to have a free use of that may offend others. In that case there is a restraint. Therefore St Paul saith, 'I will never eat flesh whilst I live, rather than I will offend my brother,' 1 Cor. viii. 13.

[4.] And in the *last place*, in case of *obedience*. There is a restraint upon 'all things' we have; that is, in outward things. Howsoever no man may meddle with the conscience; yet the magistrate may restrain this or that creature. 'All things are ours,' because we are Christ's. This may satisfy in some doubts.

Now to come more directly to this branch, to shew how 'we are Christ's.'

We are Christ's in all the sweet terms and relations that can be. Name what you will, 'we are Christ's.' We are his subjects, as he is a king: we are his servants, as he is a lord; we are his scholars, as he is a prophet. If we take Christ as a head, we are his members; if we take Christ as a husband, we are his spouse; if we take Christ as a foundation, we are the building; if we take Christ as food, he incorporates us to himself; if we be temples, he dwells in us. There is no relation, nor any degree of subjection and subordination, but it sets forth this sweet union and agreement between Christ and us. So that 'Christ is ours,' and 'we are Christ's' in all the sweet relations that can be. We are his members, his spouse, his children: for he is the 'everlasting Father,' Isa. ix. 6. He is all that can be to us, and we are all that can be to him, that is lovely and good.

But yet all relations are short.* They reach not to set out the excellency and the truth and reality of this, that 'we are Christ's.' For what is a head to the body (which is one of the nearest)? Can the head quicken the dead body? No. But Christ can, *agere in non membrum;* he can work in a dead member, that that is not a member, to make it one. Can a husband change his spouse? Moses could not. He married a blackamore. He could not alter her disposition or her hue (*l*). But Christ can alter his spouse. He is such a foundation as makes all 'living stones.' Therefore, in St John xvii. 21, because there is no manner of union in the world, that can serve to set out the nearness we have to Christ, saith Christ, 'Father, I will that they may be one, as thou and I am one.' He sets it out by that incomprehensible union. He goes divinely above earthly things, to set out the reality of this, how we are Christ's and Christ ours. We are Christ's in the most intimate nearness that can be; we are so Christ's, as nothing in the world else is, when we believe once. Though all things are Christ's, yet the church is Christ's in a more peculiar manner. There is a peculiarity in this that we are Christ's; that is, we are in the nearest bonds, nearer to Christ than the very angels. For they are not the 'spouse' of Christ; they are not the 'members' of Christ. They are ministering spirits to Christ, and so to us. There is no creature under heaven, no, nor in heaven, that is Christ's, as we are. We are his 'portion,' his 'jewels,' his 'beloved.' We are Christ's in all the terms of nearness and dearness that can be.

And this nearness is mutual. We are Christ's, and Christ is ours. He dwells in us and we in him. He abides in us, and we in him. He is in us as the vine is in the branches, and we are in him as the branches in the vine. And as it is intimate and mutual, so it is eternal; we are Christ's for ever.

But to come more particularly: By what title are we Christ's?

(1.) The *first* title that Christ hath to us is the same that he hath to all

* That is—they fall short of the relation between Christ and his people.—Ed.

things else. All things are God's and Christ's *by creation* and preservation: all things consist in Christ.

(2.) But, *secondly*, there is a more near title than by creation; namely, *by gift*. For the Father hath given us to him. For all that are God's by election, he gave them to Christ, to purchase for them* 'by his blood.'

(3.) And, *thirdly*, he hath title to us '*by redemption*.' We cost him dear. We are a spouse of blood to him, the price of his blood, Exod. iv. 25. He died for us. We could not be Christ's, but he must redeem us out of the hands of our enemies. And God would have his justice satisfied, that grace and justice might meet and kiss one another. God's justice must be satisfied before Christ would have us: for however there was *amor benevolentiæ*, a love of good will, that gave us to Christ, yet till Christ redeemed us, and made us his own, there was not *amor amicitiæ*, a love of friendship between God and us. So all friendship comes upon title of redemption.

(4.) Then, *fourthly*, upon redemption, there is a *title of marriage* that Christ hath to us. God, that brought Adam to Eve in paradise, he brings Christ and us together. And

(5.) We *give consent on our part*, as it is in marriage, to Christ. He is our husband, and we give our consent to take Christ to be so, that he shall rule and govern us, and we take him for better for worse in all conditions. Thus we see how Christ comes to be ours, and we to be Christ's. Now, the points that arise from this branch, 'And ye are Christ's,' are these,—

First, That 'all things are Christ's.'

Secondly, That 'we are Christ's.'

Thirdly, That 'all are ours, because we are Christ's.'

The connection of the text is this: 'All things are yours.' Why? Because 'you are Christ's.' How follows that? Because all things are Christ's. If all things were not Christ's and we Christ's, the argument would not hold. So that all are Christ's first. All the promises are made to Christ first, and all good things are his first. All the 'promises are yea in him,' 2 Cor. i. 20; they are made in him, and they are 'amen,' they are performed in him. I need not stand much upon this. All things in the world are Christ's, for he made all, as it is Col. i. 16, and he hath reconciled all. All things are Christ's, especially by the title of redemption, as he redeemed man. And indeed we could not be Christ's unless Christ had subdued all things to himself. Unless he had possessed all good and subdued all that is ill, how could he have brought us out of the hands of our enemies? Therefore, in St John xvii. 2, our Saviour Christ speaks there of the 'power that his Father had given him over all things.' But this was upon consideration of his resurrection. After his resurrection, he saith, 'All power is given to me in heaven and earth,' Mat. xxviii. 18. Christ, as mediator, had title to all things by virtue of the union. As soon as the human nature was knit to the divinity, there was a thorough title to all things. But it was not discovered,* especially till the resurrection was past, when he had accomplished the work of redemption.

He was also to ask. 'Ask of me and I will give thee the heathen for thy possession,' Ps. ii. 8. God would not let his Son have anything (though he redeemed the church, and all things, in some sort) without asking. Shall any man then think to have anything without prayer, when all things were conveyed to the Son of God by asking?

Further, Christ is 'the heir of the world,' Heb. i. 2. Therefore, all

* Qu. 'to purchase them'?—Ed. † That is, 'manifested.'—G.

things must be his as the heir. This is a clear point, and I do but name it, because it hath a connection with the truths I am now to speak of.

Hereupon it comes, that 'all things are ours, because Christ is ours.' Christ is said 'to be the first-born of many brethren,' Rom. viii. 29; and the 'first-begotten of every creature,' Col. i. 15; and 'the first-begotten from the dead,' Col. i. 18. All these shew the priority of Christ, that Christ is first, that he should have the pre-eminence in all things. For Christ is the prime creature of all; he is God's masterpiece. That is the reason why nothing can be ours but it must be Christ's first. He is the first-begotten of every creature, both as God and man. He is the 'first-begotten,' because he is more excellent in order and dignity than any other whatsoever. So he is the 'first-begotten from the dead,' 'the first fruits' of them that sleep, because all that rose rose by virtue of him. Hereupon it is that we can have nothing good but we must have it in Christ first.

Use 1. Therefore we must know this to make a right use of it, *whatsoever privilege we consider of as ours, we ought to see it in Christ first.* Our election is in Christ first. He is chosen to be our head. Our justification is in Christ first. He is justified and freed from our sins being laid to his charge as our surety, and therefore we are freed. Our resurrection is in Christ first. We rise, because he is the 'first-begotten from the dead.' Our ascension is in Christ, and our sitting at the right hand of God in him first. All things that are ours, they are first his; what he hath by nature we have by grace. Why do the angels attend upon us, and are ministering spirits to us? We are Christ's, and he is the Jacob's ladder upon whom the angels ascend and descend. All the communion those blessed spirits have with mankind is because we are Christ's. They are ministering spirits to Christ first, and then to us, because we are Christ's.

Therefore it is a good meditation, fitting the gospel, never to think of ourselves in the first place, when we think of any prerogative, but to think of it in our blessed Saviour, who began to us in all. He was the first in everything that is good. As the elder brother, it was fit it should be so. And he must have the prerogative in all things. Therefore,

Use 2. *Let us glorify Christ in everything.* When we think of our title to anything, think, this I have by Christ: be it of our justification or glorification, this I had by Christ and in Christ.

This is another use we are to make of it, the rather because it sweetens all things we have. If all things should come immediately from God, they were comfortable, but whenas all shall be derived from God by Christ, we have God's and Christ's love together. There is not the least good thing we have, but we must think, This I have by Christ, this victory over ill, and this conversion of ill to good. The thing is sweet, but the love of Christ is sweeter. The thing itself is not so good as the spring whence it comes. It pleaseth God we have a triple comfort at once in every good thing: comfort in God the Father, that we have it from his love, and comfort in the Son of God, and comfort in the creature. Therefore, let us not be swallowed up in the creature, but reason thus: This is a sweet comfort, but whence have I it? Oh! it is from Christ, and the love of Christ, and I have Christ from the Father. There is Christ, and God the Father, and the thing, and the love of Christ, and the Father, which is sweeter than the thing itself. As in the gifts from friends, the gift is not so sweet as the love it comes from. The love and favour of God is better than the thing itself. This is indeed a comfortable observation to know, that 'all things are ours, because we are Christ's.' For why is Paul, and

Cephas, and the ministers ours? They are the ministers of Christ first. 'We are the ministers of Christ, and your servants, for his sake,' saith the apostle, 2 Cor. iv. 5.

Why is life and death ours? Because Christ hath conquered death first; and it was the passage of Christ to his glory. He conquered the ill of it. He took away 'the sting of it;' and thereupon it is so good and useful to us. He hath the 'key of hell and death;' that is, he hath the government of it, having overcome it. And 'things present and to come.' Heaven, which he now possesseth, it is his, and thereupon it comes to be ours. Therefore, let us think of Christ in all things, and think of the sweetness of all things from this, that they come from Christ.

To enlarge this point a little further. We have all from Christ, and in Christ, yea, and by Christ, and through him.

[1.] *First*, We have all we have in Christ, *as a head*, as the first, as our 'elder brother,' as a root, as the 'second Adam.' We have all in him, by confidence in him. We have whatsoever is good in him.

[2.] And, *secondly*, we have all by and through him, *as a mediator*, for his sake. We have title to all, because Christ, by redemption, hath purchased a right to all, in and through him.

[3.] *Thirdly*, We have all by him, by a kind of working *as the efficient cause*, because we have the Spirit of God to extract good out of all. For, being reasonable creatures, God will make all ours, as becomes understanding creatures; that is, by sanctifying our understanding to extract the quintessence out of every thing. For a Christian hath the Spirit to let him see that God is leading him by his Spirit to good in all. And whence comes the Spirit? From Christ. Christ hath satisfied the wrath of God the Father. And now the Father and Christ, both as reconciled, send the Spirit as the fruit of both their loves. So Christ, as the efficient cause, makes all ours, because the Spirit is his, by which Spirit we make all ours.

[4.] And, *fourthly*, Christ is an *exemplary cause*. We have all in him, and through him, and by him, as an exemplary pattern. The same Spirit that subdued all to him subdues all things to us. To make this clear a little. There was in Christ *regnum patientiæ*, a kingdom of patience, as well as *regnum potentiæ*, a kingdom of power and glory. There was a kingdom of patience; that is, such a kingdom as Christ exercised in his greatest abasement, whereby he made all things, even the worst, to be serviceable to his own turn and the church's. So in every member of his, there is a kingdom of patience set up, whereby he subjects all things to him. To make it yet clearer.

When Christ died, which was the lowest degree of abasement, there was a kingdom of patience then. What! When he was subdued by death and Satan, was there a kingdom then? Yes, a kingdom. For though visibly, he was overcome and nailed to the cross; yet invisibly, he triumphed over principalities and powers. For by death he satisfied his Father; and he being satisfied, Satan is but a jailor. What hath he to do when God is satisfied by death? Christ never conquered more than on the cross. When he died he killed death, and Satan, and all. And [did] not Christ reign on the cross when he converted the thief? when the sun was astonished, and the earth shook and moved, and the light was eclipsed? Who cares for Cæsar when he is dead? But what more efficacious than Christ when he died? He was most practical when he seemed to do nothing. In patience he reigned and triumphed; he subjected the greatest enemies to himself, Satan, and death, and the wrath of God, and all. In the same manner all things are ours, the worst things that befell God's children, death, and afflictions, and persecutions. There is a kingdom of patience set up in them. The Spirit of God subdues all base fears in us, and a child of God never more triumphs than in his greatest troubles. This is that that the apostle saith, Rom. viii. 37, 'In all these things we are more than conquerors.' How is that, that in those great troubles we should be 'conquerors and more'? Thus the spirit of a Christian, take him as a Christian, reigns and triumphs at that time. For the devil and the world labour to subdue the spirits of God's children and their cause. Now to take them at the worst, the cause they stand for, and will stand for it; and the spirit that they are led with is undaunted. So that the Spirit of Christ is victorious and conquering in them, and most of all at such times.

It is true of a Christian indeed that one speaks of a natural man—but he speaks too vaingloriously—he subdues hope and fear, and is more sublime than all others. A Christian is so *dum patitur vincit*, &c.; when he suffers he conquers, nay, more then than at other times; for the spirit gets strength, and the cause gets strength by suffering, and answerable to his suffering is his comfort and strength. So that all things are his. The Spirit that subdued all things to Christ, subdues them to him. Nay, he makes all advantageous for the time to come; as St Paul saith, 'These light afflictions that we suffer, work unto us an exceeding weight of glory,' 2 Cor. iv. 17; because they fit and prepare our desires for glory. And answerable to that measure that we glorify God, shall our reward be in heaven; and the more we suffer, the more 'entrance' we have into heaven in this world; we enter further into the kingdom of grace, and by consequent into the kingdom of glory. So that there is a kingdom set up in a Christian, as there was in Christ, in patience in suffering. So we see that 'all things are ours,' because 'we are Christ's,' and what we may observe from thence.

To shut up this point with some use.

Use 1. *Let us be stirred up to study Christ, and in Christ to study our own excellency.* St Paul accounted all 'dross and dung, in comparison of the excellent knowledge of Jesus Christ,' Phil. iii. 8. And indeed we cannot study Christ but there will be a reflection upon the soul presently; it is a transforming study. The study of the love of Christ must needs make us love him again. The study of the choice that Christ hath made of us, it will make us choose him again, and to say, 'Whom have I in heaven but thee?' Ps. lxxiii. 25. If we study the grace and mercy of Christ, we cannot but be transformed in marvellous respect to him again. Therefore let us raise up our thoughts more to think of Christ, and the excellencies of Christ, with appropriation to ourselves, 'All things are yours, and you are Christ's.' We should not study Christ and any excellency in him, but we should also think, This is mine, this is for me. The more the spouse hears of the riches and advancement of her husband, the more she blesses herself, and saith, This is for me. And the more we think of Christ, the more we think of our own advancement and excellency. Therefore we should be willing to hear 'the unsearchable riches of Christ' unfolded to us; for these serve to kindle the love of the spouse to Christ.

The ministers are *paranimphy*,* friends of the bridegroom, that come between the spouse and Christ, to make up the match between them; and one blessed way whereby they do it, is to unfold to the church her own

* That is, *παρανυμφιοι*.

beggary, and the riches she hath by Christ; her own necessity, and the excellency that she hath in Christ. The main scope of the ministry is to shew us our beggary in ourselves, and our danger: that we are more indebted than we are worth; that we are indebted to God's justice for body, and soul, and all; and as we are indebted, so we must have supply from the riches of another of necessity, or else we go to prison and perish eternally.

Now Christ doth not only pay our debts—for that we may look for out of self-love—but he is 'the chief of ten thousand,' Cant. v. 10, he is an excellent person in himself. Now the unfolding of the excellencies in Christ is a means to procure the contract and marriage between the church and Christ. And let us labour by all means to be one with Christ, to study further union and communion with Christ, because upon this term and tenure 'all things are ours,' if we be Christ's; if not, nothing is ours but damnation. And considering that the more union we have with him, the more we shall know our own prerogative, that 'all things present and to come are ours,' therefore we should labour to know him more. There are three graces tending to union:

Knowledge, faith, and love.

The more we know him, the more we shall trust him. 'They that know thy name will trust in thee,' Ps. ix. 10. And the more we trust in him, the more we shall love him. Knowledge breeds trust, and trust breeds love. Therefore let us labour to grow in our knowledge, and trust, and love to Christ.

And to that end, as I said, to take all occasions to hear of the excellencies of Christ, to study them ourselves, and to hear of them from others, especially in the ministry. In Cant. v. 9, those that were not converted, the daughters of Jerusalem, they ask the church, 'What is thy beloved more than another's beloved?' 'My beloved,' saith the church, 'is white and ruddy, the chiefest of ten thousand;' and thereupon she sets him out from top to toe, in all his excellencies, and saith, 'This is my beloved;' and thereupon she that before asked in slighting, 'What is thy beloved more than another's beloved?' in the 6th chapter saith, 'Where is thy beloved, that we may seek him with thee?'* So when we know Christ and his excellencies, the next *query* will be, 'Where is thy beloved?' Of all arguments in divinity we can study, we hear of nothing more comfortable than of Christ and the benefits we have by him; for God will be glorified in nothing so much as in that great mystery of Christ. Therefore let these things be more and more sought after.

Quest. But how shall I know that Christ is mine, or that I am in Christ, or no? For all depends upon this tenure, that we are in Christ.

Ans. Ask thine own heart. (1.) Hast thou given thy *consent*, and contracted thyself to Christ, or no? This is one way, as I said, whereby we are Christ's, by giving our consent. Our own hearts will tell us whether we have given our consent to take Christ to be a head, a governor, and a king to rule us, as well as for a priest to die for us. If thou be content to come under the government of Christ, to be ruled by his Spirit, thou mayest say, I am Christ's; I have given up myself to him; I am content to take him. We know what hath proceeded from our own will, and there are none that have given up themselves to Christ, but they may know it. Therefore let us consider whether we have passed our consent to Christ, or no. I fear it is yet to do with many; for instead of contracting themselves to Christ, they have yielded to their own lusts.

* Cf. Vol. II., page 132, *seq.*—G.

(2.) Again, *secondly*, consider *by what spirit thou art guided*, whether by the Spirit of Christ or no. 'He that hath not the Spirit of Christ is none of his,' Rom. v. 8. Christ is a husband that will rule his spouse. He will rule in his own temple and house. He is a head that will rule his own members. Consider what spirit guides and actuates thee, whether the Spirit of Christ or the spirit of the world. If the Spirit of Christ rule in us, it will work as it did in Christ, that judgment of things that Christ had, heavenly things to be the most excellent, and the same judgment of persons to esteem of those that Christ esteems of. It will work the same carriage to God, to men, to enemies, to Satan. If we have the Spirit of Christ, it will transform us to be like Christ in our judgment and dispositions and affections every way, in some degree, according to our capacity and measure. Therefore let us not deceive ourselves; if we be led by the spirit of the world, and not by the Spirit of Christ, we cannot say with comfort, I am Christ's. When every one shall come to challenge their own, the devil will say, Thou art mine, thou wert led by my spirit. But if we yield ourselves to be guided by the blessed truth of God, when that challenge shall come, 'Who is on my side. Who?' Christ will own us for his in evil times.

(3.) *Thirdly*, He that is Christ's will stand for Christ upon all occasions, and stand for religion. He will not be a lukewarm neuter. If we be Christ's, it is impossible but we should have a word to speak for him and for religion. If we be Christ's, we will be strong for Christ; we will be true to him; we will not betray Christ and the cause of religion that is put into our hands. But, by the way, let us take heed of making this a name of faction, as the Corinthians did, to say 'I am of Paul, and I am of Apollos, and I am of Christ;' as some that say they are neither papists nor protestants, but Christians. But in times wherein profession is required, a man must shew his religion here. Not to say, I am Christ's, is to be an atheist. In case of confession and profession of religion, we must own the side of Christ and say we are Christ's indeed.

It is said in the Revelation, that so many hundreds and thousands were sealed with a 'seal in their foreheads,' Rev. vii., *throughout*. For even as the slaves of antichrist are sealed in the hand, they have a mark in their hand; that is, they are bold for antichrist; so all God's children are sealed in their foreheads. That is the place of confession and profession, the forehead being an open place. Christ carries God's broad seal. He seals all that come to heaven in the forehead. He seals them first in their hearts to believe the truth, and then he seals them in the forehead, openly to confess. 'With the heart we believe, and with the mouth we confess to salvation,' Rom. x. 10. Therefore those that are not bold to confess and profess religion when they are called to it, they are none of Christ's 'sealed ones,' for he seals them to make them bold in the profession of religion. Let this be one evidence whether thou art Christ's or no; if the question be, 'Who is on my side?' to own Christ's side, to stand for Christ and the religion reformed and stablished. If a man do not this, he cannot say I am Christ's; but his heart will give his tongue the lie, if he stand not boldly for the cause of Christ. 'He that is ashamed of me before men, I will be ashamed of him before my heavenly Father,' Mark iii. 38.

It is a comfortable consideration, if upon trial we find ourselves Christ's, that we own the cause of Christ and his side. It is the best side, and we shall find it so in the hour of death and the day of judgment. If we find ourselves to be Christ's, what a comfort will this be? Of all conditions in the world, it is the sweetest and the safest condition to be in Christ. It is to have all below us ours, and all above us too to be ours; to have God the Father ours, and God the Holy Ghost; to have all in heaven and earth to be ours, 'things present and things to come.' What a comfortable consideration is this in all storms, to be housed in Christ, to dwell in Christ, to be clothed with Christ! When the storm of God's anger shall come upon a nation, and at the day of judgment to be found in Christ, 'not having our own righteousness,' Philip. iii. 9, and in the hour of death to die in Christ! If we be Christ's, we live in him and die in him, and shall be found in him at the day of judgment. If we be Christ's, we are in heaven already in Christ our head. We sit in heavenly places together with him. In all the vicissitude and interchanging of things in the world, which are many, 'life and death, and things present, and things to come,' there is a world of vicissitudes; but in all, in life and death, look backward, or forward, or upward, or downward, if a man be in Christ, he is upon a rock. He may overlook all things as his servants. All things shall be commanded by God to serve for his good, and to bring him to heaven, to yield him safe conduct. We study evidences and other things. This is worth our study more and more, to make this sure, that we are Christ's, and Christ is ours. The more we grow in knowledge, and faith, and love, the more we shall grow in assurance of this.

Use 2. Again, if we be Christ's, *why then should we fear want, when all things are ours, and we are Christ's?* Can a man want at the fountain? Can a man want light that is in the sun? Can a Christian that hath all things his; and in this tenure his, all things are his, because Christ is his, —can anything be wanting to him? It should comfort us against the time to come, if we be stripped of all, yet we have the Fountain of all. We must be stripped of all at the hour of death, whether we will or no; but if we be Christ's, and Christ be ours, all things are in him in an eminent manner. It is a wonderful comfort for the present, against all fears and wants; and it is a comfort for the time to come, that when all things shall be taken from us, yet he that is better than all things, that is better than the world itself, will remain to us. Therefore let us think of these things. It is wondrous comfortable to be Christ's, and to be his in such a peculiar manner.

Use 3. And, *thirdly, let us learn, as we are advised*, Ps. xlv. 10, 'to forget our father's house,' to forget all former base acquaintance, and to be contented with Christ. What saith our blessed Saviour in the Gospel? 'Those that hear my words, they are my brother, and sister, and mother,' Mark iii. 35. Are they so? And shall not we, for Christ's sake, that is nearer than any in the world, 'hate father and mother,' &c., Luke xiv. 26, that is, not regard them for Christ. If we be so near Christ, and he will stick to us when all will leave us, then let us answer Christ's love. He is to us instead of all kindred; let him be so, if we cannot have their love upon other terms than to forsake Christ. Thus we see what we may observe from this, that 'we are Christ's.' Now it is said here besides, that

'Christ is God's.'

Here is a sacred circle that ends where it begins; for all things come out from God at the first, and all things go back again to God and end in him. 'All are yours, and you are Christ's, and Christ is God's.' Man is, as it were, the horizon of all things; that hath one half of the heavens below, divided and terminated, and the other above. A holy man is between all things, above him and under him. All things are his below him. They serve his turn and use, to help him to heaven, as a *viaticum*. And all things above him are his; that is the cause that all things below are his. Now to come to this last branch.

'And Christ is God's.'

In what sense is Christ God's? Was he not the Son of God? Yes! That is true. He was the eternal Son of God. But that is not here meant. Christ is God's, as Mediator. The Father, the first person of the Deity, is the fountain; and the Mediator comes from him in a double sense.

First, Because the Father, the first person, was offended; therefore he must appoint a mediator. Now, by what bonds is Christ God's? By all the strong terms that can be devised. God sent him into the world: 'He sent his Son,' Rom. iii. 25. God set him forth as a propitiation: 'Him hath the Father sealed,' John vi. 27. He came forth with God's broad seal. God sealed him to be Mediator in his baptism, and by his working of miracles, and raising him from the dead. God the Father sealed him, and set his stamp upon him to be his. He sent him, and set him forth, and sealed him: 'He was anointed with the oil of gladness above his fellows,' Ps. xlv. 7. He was anointed to shew his authority. Kings, and priests, and prophets were anointed. So God the Father hath appointed him to be king, priest, and prophet of his church. He is anointed in all these terms: 'It pleased the Father that in him should all fulness dwell,' Col. i. 19. And Mat. xi. 27, 'All power is given to me of my Father, in heaven and earth.' So when he was to ascend, saith he, 'All power is given to me in heaven and earth,' Mat. xxviii. 18. He came out from the Father with all authority. The Scripture is marvellous pregnant in this point, to shew with what authority Christ came from the Father. The points here considerable are, first of all, that all things are Christ's, and therefore we are Christ's; so

All things are the Father's.

This is the highest degree. We can go no further. There is the centre wherein we must rest: 'All things are the Father's.' All things are of God, that made all of nothing, and can turn all to dust at his pleasure. 'All things are of him, and by him, and through him,' as it is Romans xi. 1, *seq.*, divinely set forth. There is no question of this. It were to add light to the sun to shew that all things are the Father's; and hereupon Christ is the Father's in the first place. And then 'all things are ours,' because 'Christ is ours,' and 'Christ is the Father's.' The point that is more material, and worth standing on, is this, that

Though all things come from the Father, yet not from the Father immediately, but they come from Christ.

Christ is the Father's, and we are the Father's in Christ; and all things are ours in Christ. There is no immediate communion between us and the Father, but Christ comes between God and us.

Why is this needful?

For many undeniable reasons.

Reason 1. *First, Because there is no proportion between God the Father and us, but a vast disproportion.* He is holiness and purity, and a 'consuming fire' of himself. What are we without a mediator, a middle person, without Christ coming between? Nothing but stubble, fit fuel for his wrath. So that all love and good that comes from the first Person, it must come to us through a middle person: 'You are Christ's, and Christ is God's.' We cannot endure the brightness of the majesty of the Father. It is too great a presence: 'He dwells in that height that no man can attain unto,' as the apostle saith, 1 Tim. vi. 16. Therefore there must come a person between, invested in our nature. God in our nature comes between the Father and us, and all things come from God to us in him. As the salt waters of the sea, when they are strained through the earth, they are sweet in the rivers, so the waters of majesty and justice in God, though they be terrible, and there be a disproportion between them and us, yet being strained and derived* through Christ, they are sweet and delightful; but out of Christ there is no communion with God. He is a friend to both sides: to us as man, to him as God. All things come originally from the fountain of all, God. They are God's; and you know the three persons meet, in one nature, in God the Father, Son, and Holy Ghost. Ay; but, as I said, the holy God doth not convey immediately good things to us, but by the mediation of Christ. For God would have it thus since the fall, that having lost all, we should recover all again by the 'second Adam,' that should be a public person, a mediator between him and us; and so through Christ we should have access and entrance to the Father, and that by him we should have boldness. And that God again downward might do all things with due satisfaction to his justice; because, as I said, we are as stubble, and God 'a consuming fire.' Were not Christ in the middle, what intercourse could there be between the Lord and us? No other than between the fire and the stubble: majesty on his side, and misery and sin on ours. There must be a mediator to bring these two contraries together. So all comes downward through Christ from God to us. God doth all in Christ to us. He chooseth us in Christ, and sanctifies us in Christ; he bestows all spiritual blessings on us in Christ, as members of Christ. To Christ first, and through him, he conveys it to us. He hath put fulness in him, and of his fulness 'we receive grace for grace,' John i. 16; for Christ is complete, and in him we are complete.

Reason 2. Then again, *secondly*, God will have it thus, as it is fit it should be so, *because Christ is fitted for it*. He is the Son by nature; and it is fit that we, that are sons by adoption, should have communion with the Father in the Son by nature. He is beloved of the Father first: 'In him I am well pleased,' Mat. iii. 17. We come to have communion with God in him in whom he is well pleased. Christ is *primum amabile*, the first beloved of all; for God looks on Christ as the first begotten of him. He is the first Son by nature, and beloved of God. Hereupon God comes to delight in us that are sons by adoption, that are heirs, because we are 'fellow heirs with Christ.' He delights in us, because we are one with Christ, in whom he beholds us.

Reason 3. Again, *thirdly*, God doth this, not only to keep his state in remoteness from us, and his greatness, *but he doth it in mercy*. He hath appointed Christ to come between, that now we might not be afraid to go to God by the middle person, appointed by himself, 'who is bone of our bone, and flesh of our flesh.' Now, we go to God, who is bone of our bone and flesh of our flesh; God not simply and barely considered, but God incarnate. There is no going to him in ourselves, but God being bone of our bone, and flesh of our flesh; as Bernard saith, I go willingly to a Mediator made bone of my bone, my brother (*m*). It was a comfort to Joseph's brethren, that they had Joseph their brother the second man in the kingdom. And is it not a sweet comfort to Christians that they have one that is the second person in the Trinity, that is their brother, that is the high steward of heaven and earth? Is it not a comfort to the

* That is, 'communicated.'—G.

spouse that her husband is advanced over all, and is nearest to the king? Is it not a comfort to every one that is in relation to another to have one that may stand for them, that is both able and willing? Now, Christ is able as God, and willing as our brother; and therefore is a fit person to come between God and us. He can do us good, because he is God; and he will do us good, because he is 'bone of our bone, and flesh of our flesh.' So we see that Christ is God's, and why there must be a third person come between God and us; and Christ is fitted to be the middle person.

Now, to confirm it by a place of Scripture or two. The Scripture is everywhere full of this argument: 'It pleased God to reconcile all to himself in Christ, in whom we have obtained the inheritance, that in the fulness of time he might gather together in one all things in Christ,' Eph. i. 10, *seq.* It is a recapitulation, a bringing all to one again. God the Father, in Christ, brought all to a head again; he brought all to himself again; for without Christ we are scattered, and severed, and distracted* from God. But in Christ God brought in all† one head again, both that are in heaven and in earth. And so in Col. i. 19, 'It pleased God that in Christ all fulness should dwell, and in him to reconcile all things in heaven and earth.'

The use of this is manifold, and very comfortable.

Use 1. *First of all*, do all things come from God the Father to us in Christ, a middle person? As all things below us are ours in Christ, so all things above us: God the Father is ours in Christ. Then it should teach us *to direct our devotion upward to God, as God comes downward to us.* All things come down from God in Christ. God is the Father of Christ, and Christ is the Father of us. As nothing comes immediately from the Father down to us, so let us not go mediately up but in Christ to the Father; that is, let us offer all our prayers to God in the mediation of his beloved Son, the Son of his own appointing, Jesus Christ. We must ask all in his name. 'Whatsoever ye ask the Father in my name,' &c., John xiv. 13, 14. 'Do all in the name of Christ,' Col. iii. 17. It is ignorant presumption, arrogant, and fruitless, in any of our devotions and prayers to God, to go to God in our own name, to think of God without a relation of a Father in Christ. Though we do not alway name Christ, yet we must think of God in the relation of a Father, in which Christ is implied; for how comes he to be a Father but in Christ? He is Christ's first, and ours in him. Let us not consider of a bare naked God, but of God invested with a sweet relation of a Father in Christ, by whom he is become our Father. Therefore, Lord, we come not to thee in our own name, and in our own worth and desert, which is none at all; but we come to thee in the merits of Christ, in the mediation of Christ, in that love thou bearest to him, and that for his sake thou bearest to us that are his members. This is the way of intercourse between God and us. To think of God out of Christ, out of the mediator, it is a terrible thought, nothing more terrible: but to think of God in Christ, nothing more sweet; for now the nature of God is lovely, coming to us in Christ, and the majesty and justice of God are lovely. When it comes through Christ to be satisfied, it is sweet; for, Lord, thou wilt not punish the same sin twice. And the majesty and greatness of God is comfortable. Whatsoever is God's is ours, because Christ is ours. God in his greatness, in his justice, in his power. All things being derived and passing through Christ, are sweet and com-

* That is, 'separated' = violently.—G. † Qu. 'all in'?—Ed.

fortable to us. Therefore, seeing 'Christ is God's,' and all things come from God in Christ, let it direct us to perform all to God in Christ.

Use 2. Again, *secondly*, if so be that God be ours, and all things ours in Christ, then, when we are to deal with God the Father, or to deal with Satan, or to deal with others soliciting us, then let us make use of this, *Christ is God's, and I am God's through Christ.* When we have to deal with God the Father, that seems angry for our sins, and our consciences are wakened and terrified, say, Lord, Christ is thine; I have nothing to bring thee myself but a mediator of thy own setting and sending forth; of thine own anointing and sealing; and thou wilt not refuse the righteousness and obedience of a mediator of thine own. Christ is God's. Let us carry our elder brother with us whensoever we would have anything of God. When we have offended him, come not alone, but bring our Benjamin with us; come clothed with our elder brother's garments. God will not refuse the very name of his Son; it is a prevailing name with his Father. It is thine own Son; he is a mediator of thine own: though I have nothing of my own to bring thee, yet I bring thee thine own Son. I beseech you, let us think of this when we have offended God, and our consciences are troubled; let us go to God in the sweet name of his Son.

Use 3. Again, *thirdly*, if so be that Christ is God's, and nothing comes from God but through Christ, *let us give Christ the greatest pre-eminence.* Christ is of God's own appointment, and all things are ours because Christ is ours; nay, God is ours, because Christ is ours. Therefore let no man set up themselves in our consciences but Christ and God. The conscience is for Christ, for our husband. Christ is ordained of God to be our head, and to be all in all to us of God the Father. Therefore, in the solicitations of our judgment, to judge thus and thus, let us think what saith Christ my husband, who is God's. God will have us hear him: 'This is my beloved Son, hear him,' Mat. iii. 17. He comes with authority from God the Father; what saith he? If it be not the judgment of Christ, who shall sit in my conscience but Christ? Shall the pope? Shall any man usurp by an infallibility of judgment to say it is so; you must, upon pain of damnation, believe it? I cannot but speak a little of it by the way. The modestest and learnedest Jesuit of late times, speaking of this argument of Christ: bringing an objection that some may make against the pope's authority: saith he, If the pope say otherwise, his authority were more to me than the definition of all the holy fathers; nay, saith he, I say with Paul, 'If an angel from heaven should come and say it,' and the pope should say otherwise, I would believe the pope before I would believe an angel from heaven (*n*). Such a place hath that 'man of sin' in the conscience of those great learned men. This is intolerable. We are Christ's; he is our husband. Christ comes with authority from the Father. We must hear him; he is God's. Therefore let no man prevail in our consciences that brings not the word of God and of Christ.

Use 4. Again, *fourthly*, if Christ be God's, and all things come to us from God by Christ, then *we see a rest for our souls.* We can go no farther than God, and in God to the first person in trinity. The Christian religion pitcheth down a centre for the soul to rest in, a safe pitching place, a safe foundation. It shews our reconciliation with the great God now. Christian religion shews that all is ours, and we are Christ's, and Christ is God's; and there it sets down a rest for our souls. In Mat. xi. 28, Christ, after he had said, 'All things are given me of my Father,' saith he, 'Come unto me,' therefore, 'all ye that are weary and heavy laden, and I will ease you.'

What encouragement have we to come to him? 'All things are given me of the Father.' 'Christ is God's.' Therefore ye may boldly come unto me. 'Ye shall find rest to your souls in me.' Ay, but is Christ the last rest? No; the Father is the last rest: for in Christ I know the Father is well pleased. Ye shall find rest in Christ, because he hath satisfied the Father. So all solid comfort must be terminated in God, in the first person in the Trinity. We can go no further than God, the first person, the fountain of the Trinity. So you see in that we are Christ's, and Christ is God's, there the soul hath footing for itself in God the Father.

Quest. But may we not rest in Christ?

Ans. Yes. Because he is authorised of God the Father; and we can go no further; for the party offended first of all by our sins is God the Father, and he hath found out this remedy, this mediator. And therefore why should we suspect anything, to trouble our souls, to run in a maze, but go to God in the name of Christ upon this very ground? Lord, thou that art the party offended, and out of the bowels of mercy hast found out this mediator, I rest in him, because he came out from thee. And therefore here is a solid rest for the soul, when the soul goes back to God the Father, and rests in him. We say of a circle, it is the strongest of all figures, because it is a round figure: it strengtheneth itself; whereas a straight line is weak. As we see those round bodies that are made arches, &c., they are the strongest figures, because every stone strengthens another; so this is the strongest reflection of all, that as all things come from God the Father, so when we go to him and rest there, who can make a rupture? It is the strongest of all. The soul stays not in the way in this and that thing: all are false rests; but it goes to Christ. And to satisfy the soul the more, when it rests in Christ, it rests in the Father. Therefore when I deal with Christ, and think of Christ, I must think I have to deal with the Father. Christ was incarnate; it was as much as if the Father had been incarnate; for it was by his authority. Christ suffered, but God 'gave him to death for us all.' See the Father in all, and there the soul will rest.

We see herein the wondrous strong salvation of a Christian. It is not only founded in the good will of the Son, or of the Father, but it is founded in the love of both, and upon the authority of Christ coming from the Father. For 'God was, in Christ, reconciling the world to himself,' 2 Cor. v. 19. So our salvation is founded and built upon the mutual love of the Father and of the Son to us. The Son loves us as from the Father, and the Father in the Son, so strong is our salvation built.

Use 5. Then again, *fifthly, for comfort.* If Christ be God's, appointed by God a Saviour, and to make all things ours, to bring us back again, shall not we reason with the apostle, Rom. viii. 32, 'If he hath not spared his own Son, but given him to death for us all, how shall he not with him give us all things else?' That place is a proof of the text in hand. How shall we prove that 'all things are ours' for our good? Because 'God hath not spared his own Son,' that is better than the world. Therefore God will rather create another world, than we shall want anything that is for our good. If he have 'given his Son for us all, how shall he not with him give us all things?' as much as shall be conduceable for our good.

Use 6. Now for an use of *duty.* Since God hath ordained and anointed Christ for our good, let us thank God for Christ, as the apostle doth: 'Blessed be God the Father of our Lord Jesus Christ,' Eph. i. 3. We forget it. We see it is the beginning of every epistle almost of Paul and Peter. 'Blessed be the Lord and Father of Christ,' 1 Peter i. 3. Alas!

how had he been our Father if he had not been the Father of Christ first? And where had been our anointing, if Christ had not been anointed first? Where had been our inheritance, if he had not been the heir first? And where had been his love to us, if he had not loved him first? For there could be no communion between the holy God and us without that middle person. Therefore 'blessed be God, the Father of Christ.'

We bless God for our meat and drink, for the comforts of this world, for everything; but do we remember to bless God for Christ? We bless God for petty things, as indeed we cannot be too much in thanksgiving; it is the employment of heaven. Oh! but let us bless God especially for him, in whom we have all in this world and in another world. Blessed be God for anointing Christ. So 'God loved the world, that he gave his Son,' John iii. 16. He could not express how much. 'Christ is God's.' Therefore bless God for Christ above all other things whatsoever.

Use 7. And now, *seventhly, to go boldly upon all occasions to the throne of grace.* Now in Christ there is good terms between heaven and us. So long as we have our flesh sitting at the right hand of God to plead for us, to be an intercessor and advocate for us, let us go boldly in all our necessities to the throne of grace in the mediation of Christ. 'Christ is God's,' and with God at his right hand in all glory and majesty making request for us, nothing can be thought of more comfortable. Indeed, without these considerations, what is our religion? What is all mortality* without knowing God in Christ? 'This is eternal life, to know thee, and whom thou hast sent, Jesus Christ,' John xvii. 3. It is the beginning of heaven, as Christ saith. It is not only the way to bring us to heaven, but it is initial salvation. The knowledge of God the Father, and the knowledge of Christ coming from the Father with a commission to work all for our good, it is eternal life.

Thus we see what we may observe out of this, that Christ is God's. We can go no further. We cannot take up our rest better than in this. 'All is ours, and we are Christ's, and Christ is God's. Therefore let us end with that in Rom. xi. 36, 'Of him, and by him, and through him are all things: therefore to him be glory for ever, and for ever.' If all things come from the Father, by and through the Father in Christ, to the Father therefore be all glory for ever and ever. Amen.

* Qu. 'morality'?—G.

NOTES.

(*a*) P. 3.—'Man hath this added to his dignity, to *know it*. And this is given him, as a schoolman saith, that he may rejoice in that he hath, and him that gave it.' This sentiment occurs with even more than his ordinary grandeur of expression in the 'Thoughts' of Pascal, who has clothed with new splendour many of the incidental observations of the Schoolmen. Pascal was of course much later than Sibbes; but their reading lay in the same directions. Cf. Pascal by Pearce after Faugère; 'Thoughts on Religion,' c. iii. iv.; Disproportions or Inequalities in Man; The Greatness and the Misery of Man (1850).

(*b*) P. 4.—'But should I tell thee what is said by Baronius and some others, and what might be said of the honour of that calling' [the ministry], &c. . . . Cæsar Baronius (or Baron) was a cardinal of the Church of Rome. A list of his numerous ecclesiastical and controversial writings will be found in Watt's Bibliotheca Britannica, *sub voce*. Throughout he extols, rather exaggerates, the office of, not the ministry as Sibbes understood it, but the priesthood. This he does in common with all the papist controversalists, who in proportion as they degrade THE PRIEST, exalt the priests. Pity the Romish writers are so oblivious of the Epistle to the Hebrews.

(c) P. 7.—'Cephas and Paul are servants of the church, and I that am Peter's successor am so; but yet he stamps in his coin "That nation and country that will not serve thee, shall be rooted out.'" This legend is found on a coin of Pope Julius III., about 1557, as follows:—'GENS. ET. REGNUM. QUOD. NON. SERVIERIT. TIBI PEREBIT.' A representation of one of these coins is given by Elliot in his *Horæ Apocalypticæ* (II. page 474, 5th ed., 1862). It is understood to have had special reference to the invasion of England by the Spanish Armada in the following year.

(d) P. 8.—'As a wise philosopher could say, that man is the end of all things in a semi-circle.' That is, probably, the final cause, for whose sake the inferior creatures exist.

(e) P. 10.—'That terrible of terribles, as the philosopher saith' [of death]. Sibbes usually employs the historic formula of *the* orator = Cicero; *the* philosopher = Aristotle. His present reference is probably therefore to the familiar παντων τῶν φοβερῶν φοβερωτατος of Aristotle. The phrase is frequent in the Latin classics also.

(f) P. 11.—'Indeed, death is the death of itself; death is the death of death.' Dr John Owen has appropriated these words as the title of one of his most striking books, viz., 'The Death of Death in the Death of Christ; or a Treatise of the Redemption and Reconciliation that is in the Blood of Christ' (1642. 4to).

(g) P. 16.—'And then, all things were not common.' Sibbes is probably inaccurately reported here. The thought may be thus brought out. 'All' [did not make the] things (or property) [which they possessed] common. Without this caveat Sibbes would seem to contradict Acts ii. 44, than whom none would have shrunk with greater horror from so doing. Perhaps the following paraphrase renders the statement of the original: 'All that believed who were together, had all things common;' *i. e.*, the associated Christians as distinguished from the permanent residents in Jerusalem.

(h) P. 16.—'And St Austin saith well, "Surely he was no king that feared he should be a king.'" The words of St Augustine are, . . . 'Quid enim? Non erat rex qui timebat fieri rex? Erat omnino' (Tract. xxv. in Joan vi.). Sibbes appears to have read the sentence without the note of interrogation.

(i) P. 17.—'And therefore, as St Ambrose saith very well, "If thou hast not nourished one, howsoever in the law thou art not a murderer, yet before God thou art."' This sentiment occurs again and again in the writings of St Ambrose, and is dwelt upon in his treatise on Ahab and Naboth's vineyard; but the actual expression has not been found.

(j) P. 23.—'As Bernard saith well, Donum Dei sine Deo, they have the gifts of God, without God; without the love and favour of God.' The passage referred to is probably the following, 'Neque enim quæ habemus ab eo, servare aut tenere possumus sine eo.'—*Bern. in Ps.* xc., *Serm.* I.

(k) P. 23.—'Licitis perimus omnes, it is an ordinary speech: we all perish by lawful things.' This is probably a recollection of Gregory's fuller statement: *Solus in illicitis non cadit, qui se aliquando et a licitis caute restringit* (Moral. lib. v. et Homil 35 in Evang.).

(l) P. 24.—'Moses . . . . . married a blackamore. He could not alter her disposition,' &c. This, which is a common illustration in Sibbes's age, is surely unwarranted, at least if by 'blackamore' he intended what we understand thereby, viz., a thick-lipped negress. Shakespeare makes a similar mistake respecting Othello.

(m) P. 33.—'As Bernard saith, I go willingly to a Mediator made bone of my bone, my brother.' The following are the words of Bernard:—Ut ex aequo partibus congruens mediator, neutri suspectus sit, Deus filius Dei fiat homo, fiat filius hominis; et certum me reddit in hoc osculo oris sui. Securus suscipio mediatorem Dei filium quem agnosco et meum. Minime, plane, jam mihi suspectus erit. Frater enim et caro mea est. Puto enim, spernere me non poterit os de ossibus meis, et caro de carne meâ.—*Bern. in Cant. Cant. Ser.* II.

(n) P. 35.—'The modestest and learnedest Jesuit of late times, speaking of this argument,' &c. A very similar passage from Bellarmine is quoted in Vol. I. p. 313.

G.

THE SPIRITUAL MAN'S AIM.

THE SPIRITUAL MAN'S AIM.

NOTE.

'The Spiritual Man's Aim' was originally published in a small volume (less than 18mo) in 1637. Its title-page is given below.* Prefixed to it is Marshall's smaller portrait of Sibbes, which is found in 'The Christian's Portion' and elsewhere. A second edition, which is our text, appeared in quarto in 1656. Its title-page is likewise given below.† The initials T. G. and P. N. represent the well-known Dr Thomas Goodwin and Philip Nye. Cf. Vol. II. page 3, but for Hanburg read Hanbury. G.

† The
SPIRITUALL-MANS
AIME.
Guiding a *Christian* in his
Affections & Actions, through the
sundry passages of this Life. So that
God's glory and his Salvation may be
the maine end of all.

By the faithfull and Reverend
Divine, R. Sibbes, D. D. and some-
time *Preacher* to the Honourable
Society of *Graies Inne*.
Published by
T. G. and P. N.

London,
Printed by E. G. for John Rothwell,
and are to be sold at the Sunne in
Paul's Church-yard. 1637

† THE
SPIRITUALL
MANS AIME.
GUIDING
A Christian in his *Affections* and
Actions through the sundry passages of
this Life. So that God's glory, and his own
Salvation may be the maine end of all.
BY
The faithfull and Reverend Divine,
Richard Sibbs, D. D. and sometime
Preacher to the Honourable Society
of *Graies Inne*.
Published by
T. G. and P. N.
LONDON,
Printed by *W. H.* for *John Rothwell*, at the
Sign of the Beare and Fountaine in
Cheapside, 1656.

THE SPIRITUAL MAN'S AIM.

It remaineth, brethren, the time is short: let those that have wives be as if they had none; and they that weep, as though they wept not; and they that rejoice, as though they rejoiced not; and they that buy, as though they possessed not; and they that use this world, as not abusing it: for the fashion of this world passeth away.—1 Cor. VII. 29–31.

The blessed apostle, in the former part of this chapter, had given direction in cases of conscience, being a man that had the tongue of the learned to speak a word in season to the weary, Isa. l. 4; whereupon, having in his eye greater matters, as his use is almost in every epistle, he calls them from particular cases, that they should not overmuch trouble themselves about them, but mind the main, 'The time is short: let those that are married be as if they were not,' &c. But yet, notwithstanding,

He gives satisfaction to the particular cases. For as, in travelling, it is not enough to know that a man's way lies east, or west, or north, or south, but he must know the turnings and windings, the particularities of the way; so in religion it is not enough to know that we must serve God above all, and love our neighbour as ourself, &c. Those generalities atheists will embrace, and in pretence of them shake off all further study of religion. Our knowledge must stand in clearing particular cases also, which, being cleared, the way is smoother to heavenward. Yet, notwithstanding, we must not dwell too much upon particulars, for here you see the apostle calls them off, 'Finally, my brethren, the time is short;' it remains that we look to the main, &c. 'For the fashion of this world passeth away;' wherein we considered* two points in general, which I will only name, and hasten to that which followeth.

The first was this, that,

Doct. 1. *A very good way to satisfy cases of conscience in particular, is to have in our mind the main.*

For there be many that puzzle themselves all their life about this and that particular, and forget the main in the mean time. Let a man look to the main, and he will soon resolve in such particulars as these whether it be good to redeem time to hear a sermon now and then. He will do the thing, and not stand making a case of it; for when he considers how it

* From this reference it would appear Sibbes had delivered sermons that have not been preserved, from the present text.—G.

helps to the main, the saving of his soul, &c., for which he came into the world, he will easily be resolved.

And so for sanctifying the Lord's day entirely; many have scruples and keep ado, but if they had the love of God in their souls, and did look to the main, they would see it to be an idle question. For how much conduceth it to the main?

And so for conversing with company, are they such as are comfortable and cheerful? Are they such as we may profit by? Why do I entangle myself and hinder the main? So we see Paul, in resolving the particulars, he calls them to the main: 'Brethren, the time is short,' and therefore be in these things as if ye were not (as we shall see anon in the particulars), 'for the fashion of this world passeth away.' This is the reason why none but a true Christian can carry himself moderately in the things of this world. Why? Because none but a sound Christian hath a main, and a chief end that sways the stern* of his whole life; he looks to heaven and happiness, and how it shall be with him afterwards, and he considers particulars thereafter; when another man of necessity must err in particular cases, because he hath not a gracious aim. You have no man but a Christian, but he loseth himself in the things of this world.

The second thing is this; you see that,

Doct. 2. *Religion meddles with all matters.*

With the world, with marriage, with buying, and possessing, as we shall see afterwards. Saith an atheist that stomachs it, that his ways should be hindered from that commanding skill of religion which hath to do in all things, What hath the minister to do with our callings, with lawyers, with tradesmen, or statesmen? What hath the minister to do with these things?

It is true, not with the materials, with the particular matters of those callings. That is left to those that are artists, and that have skill in the particulars of their professions in each kind. But a minister and a Christian, and religion in any man, hath to deal with these things, as they help to further the main. For religion is a skill that fits a man for a further end, for his last end, for heaven.

Now, being such a skill, it must direct everything so far as it helps or hinders that. State knowledge, we say, is a commanding knowledge. Why? Because it meddles with all trades. How? Hath a statesman skill in this or that trade? No; not in the particular mystery, but he hath skill so far as he sees what may serve for the public good. Let the safety of the commonwealth be the law of all trades. The state knowledge is the supreme knowledge, which is for the good of the whole; therefore he cuts off particulars if they be mischievous to the whole. So all trades must be told of their faults, as they are blemishes to religion, for we must not be so in this or that trade, as that we forget we are Christians, and therefore we must hear meekly the word of God when it meets with our particular callings. We see Paul meddleth with buying and selling, with marriage, &c. How? As far as they might hinder the main: 'Finally, my brethren, the time is short, and the fashion of this world passeth away.' Therefore be not overmuch in these things.

It is the *suprema ratio*, &c., it is the main reason that makes for religion: as I said before of state knowledge, it is *suprema lex*. Yet though that be supreme in regard of inferiors, yet there is one above that, the chief reason of all that makes for religion; there be many particular reasons that make

* That is, as the 'helm' placed in the 'stern,' ruling the ship.—G.

for this and that. Ay, but religion saith the contrary, and then that must rule, that is the *suprema ratio*. Now I come to unfold the particulars. The apostle here stands upon five directions and bounds. Those five directions with three reasons :—

'Let those that are married be as if they were not.'

'Those that weep, as if they wept not.'

'Those that rejoice, as if they rejoiced not.'

'And they that buy, as though they possessed not.'

'And they that use this world, as not abusing it.'

How are these five directions enforced?

They are enforced from three reasons :—

The *first* is in the front of the text : 'The time is short.' Therefore be moderate in all things here.

The *second* is in the shutting up of the text : 'For the fashion of this world passeth away.'

The *third* reason is a main reason too, that is, from their state and condition in Christ : 'Why, brethren,' saith he, 'partakers of the heavenly calling,' Heb. iii. 1, as he saith in another place, 'Partakers of better things,' 2 Cor. i. 7, and by being 'brethren,' 'brethren in Christ,' 'members of Christ.' He is the knot of the brotherhood, being born again 'sons of God;' 'brethren of Christ,' not brethren only among yourselves, but 'brethren in Christ,' and so sons of God and heirs of heaven. What! for you to be immoderate in the things of the world. Paul wraps up a moving reason, not only to insinuate to gain their affections, 'Oh! my brethren,' but to add a force of reason likewise. 'Brethren, the time is short.' And, brethren, 'the fashion of this world passeth away.' So add these three reasons to the five directions, and see how strongly Paul backs his directions. Indeed, it was needful for Paul so to do. We are so desperately set on the things of this world, we are so hardly taken off, that there must be reason upon reason; for the Holy Ghost, the Holy Spirit of God, loves not waste of reasons, to spend them where there is no use. And therefore we must think it is a weighty point, and of great equity, that we give ear to these directions.

We must remember that every one of these reasons has a force in every direction. You that have wives, be as if you had none, for the 'time is short,' and 'the fashion of the world passeth away.' And so you that 'weep, as if you wept not,' 'for the time is short, and the fashion of the world passeth away.' And you are 'brethren,' you that 'use the world, as not abusing it,' for 'the time is short, and the fashion of the world passeth away.' So that all these reasons must be thought on in every particular direction that I speak of, only in general. I will speak a little of the first reason, 'The time is short.'

What time?

(1.) *The time of the world.* There is but a little time before the day of judgment. Christ is at hand to judge the quick and the dead. The time between this and that is short. It was short then, it is shorter now. 'The time is short.' We are fallen into the latter end of the world. But that is not all.

(2.) The time is short *of our little world;* our particular judgment is near at hand. It shall be with us at the latter day as it is when we die. Our time is short; the time of our particular life is short, and that is more forcible to persuade us 'the time is short.'

(3.) *The season of the time,* which is the prime time. The season and opportunity of time is shorter than the time of life; for we have not opportunity of time all our life. 'The time is short;' that is,

[1.] *The advantage of doing good and of taking good is short.* All the year is not harvest or seed-time. It is not always tide; it is not always sunshine. And as it is in nature, so it is in the spiritual state of things; we have not always advantages and opportunities; we have not always gales. Opportunity therefore is shorter than time, as our time is shorter than the time of the world. 'The time is short;' the opportunity and season of time is shorter.

[2.] Ay, and *uncertain;* we cannot tell how short. If it were told any of us here that within two days he shall die, it would startle us, the best of us all; it would make us look about us: but who of us all knows certainly that he shall live two hours? The time, as it is short, so it is uncertain, and here is the wondrous folly of our nature, that we will take so much time to come in trust, as though we should live so long, and make a covenant with death. But one party cannot make a covenant. God and the time to come make no covenant with us. Therefore it is extremity of folly to say, I will live so long, and so long. 'Thou fool,' saith God, when he projected for a long time and had treasure laid up for many years, 'Thou fool, this night they shall take thy soul,' Luke xii. 20. A man is a fool when he makes account of continuing that he hath no promise of. And therefore the time being short, and uncertain too, take it while we may catch hold of it, especially the opportunity of time.

[3.] And in the *third* place, *it is irrecoverable* when it is gone. There is no recalling back of time when it is past. In all these respects we must be good husbands; we must be thrifty of our time, and not take care how to drive away that, that flies away of itself so fast. It is a precious thing, precious for great purposes. What is this little time given us for? To provide for eternity, world without end. And we trifle it away about this thing and that thing to no purpose; we fill it up with vanity, and with sin, which is worse. In this little time we do that, that in a long time we cannot undo again. That is our madness and folly. Therefore 'the time being short,' let us take heed what we do in it. We may do that in a little time that we may rue for eternity. We may do that good, and get that good in a little time, that may stand by us world without end. Those that have but a little plot of ground, they will husband it so, as not to lose a handful of it; so those that have but a little time, let them husband it well, sow to the Spirit, that our harvest may be eternal life; that we may say, Oh! it was a great blessing, that God gave me a little time to get into Christ, to repent of my sins, &c. Beloved, there are three main parts of this little time:

Past, present, to come.

(1.) The time that is gone; *let us repent of it,* if it have not been spent well. That is the best use we can make of the time past; for there is nothing to be done in the time that is past. But if things have been done ill, repent.

(2.) The time present *is to do good in;* and for the time to come, it is out of our power; and therefore even for the present we must work. The time past; the best use we can make of it, is to comfort ourselves, as Hezekiah, in our sincerity, Isa. xxxviii. 3, or to repent if anything have been done amiss. But look to the present, put not off, do the work for which we came into the world, presently. 'The time is short,' the journey is long, the business is great. It is a great journey from earth to heaven; it is a great matter to get from earth to heaven.

(3.) Now having such business as to go to heaven, let us, I beseech you, *consider the weight of the business, and give our eyes no sleep, nor our eyelids slumber, till we are gotten into such a state and condition as is not liable to time;* let us make this special use of precious time. Those that are young, let them be advised to take time along with them, which is to be esteemed far above gold, and consecrate the prime and the flower of their time to God and to the best things; especially considering, that we have no assurance of this time. And those that are old, that through age are going into the grave, let them not neglect their time. A young man, as we say, may die soon; an old man cannot live long. And therefore let those that are stricken in years be put in mind to think that their time is shorter than others'. All men's times are short, old men's shortest. Let those therefore think of this, 'The time is short.' Our folly is this, we make it shorter than it is by our 'Vanity, vanity.' It were well if it were only vanity. By sinful and intemperate courses many shorten their days, and so are felons upon themselves; or by their wickedness, they give God occasion to shorten them. 'A bloodthirsty and cruel man shall not live out half his days,' Ps. lv. 23. God meets with him. So 'the time is short,' and we make it shorter. We are guilty of the shortness of it. Let us take heed of that. But I have been over long in this point; only because it is the prime reason, set before all the particulars, I beseech you consider, 'the time is short.' If we do not make use of it we are worse than the devil himself; he makes use of the shortness of his time. What doth he? 'Because the time is short,' he doth all the mischief he can, Rev. xii. 12. He fills up his time to increase his kingdom; he doth all the mischief he can, for this reason; because his time is short. Let us learn somewhat of the worst of spirits. But that which it serves for in particular here, is this; we have many things to do, and the time being short, let us be sure we do the main thing that we come for, and other things as they help the main, and not hinder it. The time is short, and we have many businesses to do; let us be sure that we do our business, so as that we leave not the main undone. That is the thing he aims at here. 'The time is short.'

'It remains that those that have wives be as if they had none.'

1. That is the first particular; for before they had asked him cases of conscience about marriage, and that makes him speak of it. All the particulars have dependence one upon another. Those that marry will have occasion to weep, that is next, for there will be cause. There will be loss of husband, or wife, or child, and there is somewhat always; family crosses attend upon marriage. And therefore he adds weeping after marriage.

And then because there is joy. 'A woman brings forth in sorrow, but she joys when a man child is born,' as Christ speaks, John xvi. 21. There is joy in children, and there is a mutual joy in that sweet conjugal friendship, there is much joy; and therefore as there is weeping, so there is joy in marriage.

'And those that buy, as if they possessed not.' There must be buying where there is wife and children; there must be looking to posterity; and then all this enforceth, 'using of the world.' And men when they enter into that estate, they enter into the world; as we use to say, they begin the world anew. They enter into the world; for there are many things necessary to maintain that society. Therefore we see one thing depends upon another. He joins all together, aiming especially at one thing, at that kind of life especially.

Now in every one of these particulars, he gives a liberty to do the thing. You may marry, you may weep, you may joy, you may buy, you may use the world. But as there is a liberty, so there is a danger; you may, but you may not go too far. And therefore with a liberty he gives a restraint. Do them, but take heed you overdo them not. And this restraint is backed with reason; he hath reason for his restraint. 'The time is short;' and therefore there is danger, lest you shoot yourselves too far, lest you pass too deep into these things. 'And the fashion of this world passeth away;' all things here pass away. Therefore it is in vain for you to be overmuch in those things that are passing things.

And then you are, brethren, called to greater matters; so there is a liberty, a danger, and a restraint upon the danger; and likewise a reason to back it in every particular.

(1.) *The liberty:* We may marry. It is not questioned. There is not only a liberty, but it is an honourable estate, and necessary; honoured in paradise, honoured by Christ's presence; a liberty by which the church is upheld, heaven is increased. It was the devil that brought in a base esteem of that honourable condition. In popery, they rather will be the members of an harlot, than the head of a wife. It was the devil that brought in those abominable opinions and writings to disparage that honourable condition, and so it must be thought.

(2.) But there *is a danger;* and that is the main thing. You that have wives, 'be as if you had none.' There is a great danger in a double respect. A danger in the things, and a peril if we go too far in them. That is, there is a great hazard, and we shall go overfar in that condition, and a danger that it tends to.

For instance, those that have wives, have they not been drawn away by their wives, as Solomon was, to idolatry? 1 Kings xi. 4. Is there not a danger of being drawn away? And in being drawn away is there not a hazard to our souls? Did not sin come in that way? Was not Adam led away by his wife? And how many men perish by being too *uxorious*,* by being too flexible in that kind? If they had remembered the apostle's precept to marry as if they had not, they would not have been so drawn away. Because there is a danger, there is a restraint: 'Let those that have wives be as though they had none.' What! to use them as if they had none? To care for them as if they had none? No; that is not the meaning; 'but to be as if they had none.' That is, let them be as resolute for God's truth, as if they had no wives to hinder them; let them be as willing to suffer crosses, if God call them, as if they had none; let them be as ready to good duties, if it fall within their calling, as if they had none; let them avoid distracting cares, and worldly incumbrances, as if they had none; let them not pretend their marriage for baseness and worldliness, and for avoiding of crosses and afflictions when God is pleased to call them unto them; let them not pretend marriage for their doubling in religion and dissembling, 'I shall undo my wife and children,' 'Let them be as if they had none,' for Christ hath given us direction to hate all for Christ. A man is not worthy of Christ and of religion, that undervalues not wife and children and all, for the gospel. If things stand in question, whether shall I stick to them or to Christ, my chief husband; I must stick to Christ. The reason is, the bond of religion is above all bonds. And the bond that binds us to Christ it abides when all bonds cease; for all bonds between husband and wife, between father and children, they end in death; but the

* That is, 'wifely' = wife over-loving.—G.

bond of Christ is eternal. Every bond must serve the main bond; and therefore we must not pretend this and that to wrong Christ and religion, which is the main bond. We must so labour to please others, that we displease not our chief husband. For the time will be, when we shall neither marry, nor be given in marriage, but we shall be as the angels, Mat. xxii. 30; and that time shall be without bounds and limits, for eternity; and we must look to that. And therefore those that marry, 'let them be as if they were not married.' You know how it fared with them in the gospel, that pretended this, for his not coming to Christ; he that was married saith, 'I cannot come.' His excuse was more peremptory than the rest, 'he could not.' Could not this excuse him?* And will pretending this excuse men when they are called to duties? There is that disproportion so much between Christ, our chief husband, and any other, though it be the wife of our bosom, or the children of our loins (the one having redeemed us, and is our best husband, a husband for eternity in heaven), that no excuse will serve the turn for a man to wrong the bond of religion for any bond whatsoever. And therefore you know the peremptory answer to him that pretended that excuse, 'You shall never taste of my feast,' Luke xiv. 24.

'And those that weep, as though they wept not.'

2. *It is lawful to weep*, not only for sin—that should be the main—but likewise to weep for the miseries of the time and state we live in. There is a liberty here, 'Oh that my head were a fountain of tears,' saith Jeremiah, ix. 1. He thought he could not weep enough; and therefore he wished that his head were 'a fountain.' He thought his tears would soon be dry. 'Oh that my head were a fountain,' so that there is a liberty to weep. Nay, men are bound to weep. There are tears of sympathy for the misery of the state and time we live in. And so for family losses and crosses. We are flesh, and not spirit; and God hath made us men, and hath given us sensible apprehensions of grief; and it is a cursed temper to be without natural affection. We may weep, and we may grieve; nay, we ought to grieve.

Now grief is as it were a cloud from whence the shower of tears comes, and weeping is but a distillation of that vapour.

If we may grieve and ought to grieve for the times; and it is a stupid temper not to apprehend the miseries of the state and times we live in; if we may grieve, we may weep. That is put for the spring whence weeping comes. For grief itself, there is a liberty, no question of that; we may weep, but we must weep as if we wept not: for there is a danger in weeping over-much for any crosses. Here is a danger, for we may flatter our grief too much for wives and children. God takes it ill; he takes it unkindly; that when Christ himself is a perpetual husband, and God is an everlasting Father, that we should weep and grieve too much for the loss of father, or of wife, or of child. For is not God worth all? So there is a danger that naturally we are prone to over-grieve, when we do grieve, as we are to over-joy when we do joy. For our nature can hardly keep bounds; and God takes it unkindly when we do so, when we over-grieve; for it is a sign we fetch not that comfort from him that is the spring and fountain, that we should do. And therefore let those that weep be as if they wept not. That is, not over-much. 'For the time is short.' Dost thou lose any friend, or any thing? 'The time is short,' we shall meet again. There is but little time between this and the latter judgment, 'and the fashion of

* Qu. 'This could not excuse him'?—G

this world passeth away.' There will be a new world, a new heaven, and a new earth. And then we shall 'live for ever with the Lord.'

And then, my 'brethren.' Why? 'Brethren' should not be without hope of the resurrection, as the Gentiles are. They may weep that never think to see one another again. But a Christian, a brother, that hath hope of meeting again, let not him weep as without hope; 'so let us weep, as if we wept not.' So he lays a restraint upon that; nay, though our weeping be for sin, there must be a moderation in that, for we may over-grieve. We are bound to joy in the Lord, and alway to rejoice. And therefore we must weep for sin, so as we must remember to joy. We must with one eye look upon our sins to humble us, and to look upon our hearts to grieve; but with the other eye we must look upon God's mercy in Christ to comfort us again. The best grief of all, that must be moderate; much more, grief for any earthly thing.

Now, when we are tempted to over-grieve for any earthly thing, the best way is diversion.* Do I grieve for these? Ay, but is my soul as it should be? Let me weep over my dead soul, as Christ wept over Lazarus when he was dead. Let me weep over my dull soul, let me weep over that.

As physicians, when the blood runs too much one way, they give an issue another way; so let us turn our grief the right way. How is it with us? Is the life of grace there? Is reckonings even between God and my soul? Am I fit to end my days? Am I in a state fit for heaven? Then we shall weep for something. It is pity such pearls as tears should be lost. God hath no bottles for tears that are shed over-much for the things of the world. But if they be for our sins, and the sins of the time we live in, and for the ills and miseries of the state that are on us, and hang over our heads, then let us weep to purpose; turn our grief the right way; and then let us grieve amain, if we will, so our grief run in that channel.

'Those that joy, as if they did not.'

3. *Joy we may and we ought;* for God envies not our joy. He hath given us wherewith in this life to joy, abundance of comforts of all sorts for all our senses, flowers and colours, &c. We have nothing in soul or body but it hath objects to delight in. God hath made himself for the soul to delight in, and there is somewhat to delight us in every creature. So sweet is God, we may and ought to rejoice. God gives us wife and children to rejoice in: 'Rejoice in the wife of thy youth,' Prov. v. 18. There is no question of a liberty in these things.

But then there is a danger, especially in sweet affections. There is danger, because we are like to over-joy. And poison is the subtlest conveyed in sweet things. We are prone to over-joy. There is a danger; therefore there must be a restraint. 'We must joy as if we rejoiced not;' that is, so joy, in any thing here, as considering that 'the time is short,' I cannot enjoy it long. Shall I joy in that I cannot enjoy? 'The time is short.' I cannot enjoy them. If a man cannot enjoy a thing long, he cannot joy. 'The time is short;' you must go. The things must go, and both must go. 'And the fashion of this world passeth away.' All the frame of things pass away; marriage passeth away; callings and friends pass away; and all pass away. I beseech you, let us learn to joy as if we rejoiced not. The prophet calls Nineveh a rejoicing city, Jonah iii. 3, and we live in a jovial age. Men eat and drink as they did in the days of the old world, in Noah's time; they marry and give in marriage, Mat. xxiv. 37; and therefore we had need to lay some restraint upon our joy: especially

* That is, 'turning away from.'—G.

when God calls us to mourning as well as joy, as he doth if we look round about us. If we look upon the time, we shall see cause to joy as if we did not. We must not always be on the merry pin, as we say, but we must temper and qualify our joy.

Now, considering that the apostle adds, weeping, grieving, and joy, you see that

Religion is especially in moderating the affections.

Religion is purging the affections from the evil that is in them, and moderating them, if they be lawful and good; and therefore think not that you are religious enough if you know a great deal, as many Christians are very greedy of knowing, and yet if you look to their lives, their grief and joy is intemperate; they have not learned to bridle and to school their affections. You see that religion is in moderating of grief and joy in earthly things. Let us see men shew the power of religion in bearing of crosses, so that 'they weep as if they wept not;' and in bearing prosperity so as they can learn to abound, to joy as if they rejoiced not. That man hath learned religion to purpose; for religion is especially about the affections. For we are good if we joy well and grieve well, but not if we know much. The devil knoweth more than we. Therefore, especially labour, that God would vouchsafe grace to govern the affections, that we may know how to grieve and how to joy; as naturally indeed we do not.

And then we see here another point, which now I add, that

The affections of God's people are mixed.

They so weep as that it is mingled with joy, and their joy is mingled with weeping. 'They weep as if they wept not,' 'they joy as if they joyed not.'

A carnal man is in simples altogether. If he joy, he thrusts the house out of the window, as we say. If he be merry, he is mad; he hath no bounds. If he be sorrowful, if somewhat restrain him not, he sinks like a beast under his sorrow, as Nabal did, 1 Sam. xxv. 37, 38, for he hath no grace to temper his sorrow and to temper his joy; and, therefore, he is over-sorrowful or over-jocund. Ah! but grace, considering that we have objects of both, doth temper the affections. A Christian, when he joys, he doth not over-joy, for he hath cause at that time to mourn for somewhat; and when he grieves, he doth not over-grieve, for he hath somewhat then to joy in; for Christ is his, and heaven is his, and the providence of God to direct all for good is his still; he hath somewhat to joy in at the worst. And therefore all his affections are tempered and qualified. So much for that point.

'And they that buy, as if they possessed not.'

4. *It is lawful to buy.* It is lawful to make contracts; and propriety* is lawful. Every man ought to have his own. There were no theft if there were no propriety, nor there could be no works of mercy Now, if propriety and dominion of things be lawful, that we may possess things as our own, then buying is lawful. That is one way of contract of making things our own; there is no danger in that. But there is a danger in the manner of buying. Men buy to perpetuate themselves: 'They call their lands after their names,' Ps. xlix. 11, and they think to continue for ever. God makes fools of them; for how few have you that go beyond the third generation? How few houses have you that the child, or the grandchild can say, This was my grandfather's and my great-grandfather's? How few houses have you, that those that are now in them can say, My ancestor

* That is, 'property.'—G.

dwelt here, and these were his lands? Go over a whole country, few can say so.

Men when they build, together with building in the earth, they build castles in the air; they have conceits. Now I build for my child, and for my child's child. God crosses them. Either they have no posterity, or by a thousand things that fall out in the world, it falls out otherwise. 'The time is short, and the fashion of this world passeth away;' that is, the buildings pass away, the owning passeth away, all things here pass away: and therefore buy as if you possessed not, buy so as we neglect not the best possession in heaven, and so possess these things, as being not possess[ed] and commanded of them.

In Lev. xxv. 8, there you see the year of Jubilee was that all possessions might return again, if men would. God trained them up by this, to teach them that they should not think of inheriting things long that they bought, for it returned in the year of Jubilee, in the fiftieth year. So we must learn that we cannot possess things long. Though we possess them ourselves, we may be thrust out by fraud or tyranny. Therefore 'let those that buy be as though they did not possess.' Jer. xxii. 23 he saith, 'Thou makest thy nest in the cedars,' and thinkest it shall be thus and thus with thee. Oh! beloved, let us not build and dwell in our hopes and assurance upon that which will yield no certain hope and assurance in this world. 'For the fashion of this world,' as we shall see hereafter,' 'passeth away.'

And then for 'brethren' that have an inheritance in heaven; for them to buy as if they should live here for ever! 'Brethren,' that is a reason to take them off. 'Brethren, buy as if you possessed not.' Thus much of the four directions.

'They that use the world, as not abusing it.'

5. *We may use the world*, while we are here in it, for we cannot want the things of this life. We are members of two worlds while we are here. We are members of this world, and we are heirs of a better; we have relation to two worlds.

Now while we live in this world we must use the things of this world. How many things doth this poor life need while we are in this world! While we are passengers we must have things to help us in the way to heaven. Passengers must have necessaries; there is no question of that. And therefore we must use the world many ways.

'As not abusing it.'

There is danger in using the world; there is a danger of cleaving in your affections to the things of this world, so much as that we forget a better world; and therefore we should use it as not abusing it.

How should we use it?

Why, use this world as laying a foundation for a better world. While we live here, use the world as we may further our reckonings for a better. Use the things of the world as we may express some grace in the using of it. Use the world as that the using of it may comfort us when the thing passeth. The 'world passeth.' But let us use the world, as that the grace that we express in the use of it may continue. Use the world to the honour of God, to the good of others, to the increase of our reckoning; abuse it not to the dishonour of God; fight not against God with his own blessings. That is to abuse the world. Forget not God the giver. Were it not an unkind thing if a man should invite strangers, if they should turn their kind friend that had invited them out of doors? And so it is to use the things of the world so as to turn God out of our hearts that gives all.

Turn not the things of this world against God, or against others, to make them weapons of injustice, to be great to ruin others. Abuse them not to wrong, and to pierce our own souls, as the apostle saith, 'with cares and the like,' 1 Tim. vi. 10. This is to abuse the world, when we dishonour God and wrong others, or to pierce our own souls. God hath not given us the things of this world for this end, to hurt ourselves with them. And therefore together with the things, let us desire a gracious use of them, for it is better than the thing itself. Labour to use them as not abusing them, as we shall if we have not grace to use them well. Many have the gifts of God without God, because they have not his grace. When we have the gifts of God, desire grace to manage them well. To his children God gives this with the other; he never gives them anything, but he gives them grace to make a sanctified use of it. They are sanctified to all things, and all things are sanctified unto them. 'Use the world as not abusing it.' The reason is strong, 'The time is short.' Why should we be overmuch in using the things of this world; for that is one way of abusing the things of this world. 'The time is short.' We must be pulled from them whether we will or no. And therefore let us wean ourselves. And then, 'the fashion of this world passeth away.' Why should we doat upon a perishing fashion? All things here pass away, and a new fashion comes after. You, 'brethren,' that are heirs of a better world, use this 'world as not abusing it.' 'Brethren,' he puts them in mind of a higher calling. And so I come to the last.

'For the fashion of this world passeth away.'

6. That is the *second* reason. The *schema*,* that is, the apparition of this world, the outward fashion, the outward view and hue of the things of this world, pass away. It is a notable diminishing word in the original, as if the world were not a substance, but a fashion, *schema*. As we say in philosophy, in the air there are apparitions and substances; as there are flying horses sometimes and fighting men in the air. These are not substances, but apparitions of things. It is but *phasis*, but an apparition, or shape. The substance and true reality of these things is another matter. So whatsoever is in the world, it is but an apparition. When the devil shewed Christ all the kingdoms of the world, he shewed him but an apparition, but a show of things. There is a diminishing in the word 'show' (*a*).

And then in the word 'fadeth away.'

'The fashion of this world passeth away;' or, as some translate it, 'deceives, and turns us aside' (*b*). And so it doth indeed from better things. 'The fashion of this world passeth away.' That translation is fit enough. 'It passeth away.' Now shall we be immoderate in anything that passeth away? It is but an apparition, but a show, but a pageant. The word is partly taken from a pageant, or a show that hath a resemblance of this and that. But there is no reality or substance in a pageant. From this,

Use 1. *Learn to conceive aright of the things of this life, that there is no reality in them to speak of.* They have a kind of reality. Riches are in some sort riches, and beauty is in some sort beauty, and nobility is in some sort nobility, and so possessions are in some sort possessions. But all this is but a pageant as it were, as a man that acts in a pageant, or in a play; he is in some sort a king, or a beggar for the time. But we value him not as he is then, but as he is when he is off the stage. And while we live here, we act the part, some of a rich man, some of a nobleman,

* That is, Σχῆμα. Cf. Philip. ii. 8.—G.

some of a beggar or poor man; all is but an acting of a part (*c*). And there is a less proportion between the acting of a part in this life, than there is between our life and eternity. All is but the acting of a part. We are not rich in the grave more than others. The king is as poor in the grave as the base peasant; his riches follow him not. The worm and the grave know no difference. When we go to that house there is no difference; all acting and all differences end in the grave. And therefore, considering that this world is but an apparition, but the acting of a part, why should we think ourselves the better for anything here? Doth he that acts the part of a nobleman upon the stage think himself better than another that acts the part of a poor man? No. He knows he shall go off in a short time, and then he shall be as he was before. Why are we not thus wise in better things? It is not he that acts the greatest part, but he that acts any part best. He that acts the part of a poor man may do better than he that acts the part of a rich man. It is not the greatness of the part, but the well acting of it. All is but an apparition. If a mean man honour God in his condition, and be faithful in a mean estate, he is a thousand times better than a great man that makes his greatness an instrument of injustice, as if all the world were to serve his turn, and to make men idolise him; such a man is a wretched man, and will be when he is turned off the stage. It is no matter how long he hath lived, or how great a part he hath acted, but how well. We value not men as they are when they are acting, but as they are after. If they were bad before, they are bad after; and they are praised after if they do it well. So it is no matter what a man acts. If he do it well, he is for ever happy; if he do it ill, he is for ever miserable; all here is but a pageant. If you talk of reality, it is in the things of religion. If you talk of true nobility, it is to be the child of God. If you talk of true riches, they are those that we carry to our deathbed; those that we carry to heaven; those that comfort the soul; those that enrich the soul with grace and comfort and peace; that is true riches. If you talk of true beauty, it is to have the image of God stamped upon our souls, to be like Christ, to be new creatures. If we talk of true strength, it is to stand against temptations, to be able to serve God, and to go through the world without polluting our souls, to bear crosses as we should; that is the true reality. The things of this life are all but apparitions and pageants. The greatest man in the world will say so when he lies a-dying, as that great emperor said, 'I have run through all things, and now nothing doth me good.'* The reality was gone that he thought of, and now there was nothing but a show and apparition; when the reality was gone, nothing doth me good. Come to a man that is gasping out his life, and ask him, What doth honours do you good? What doth riches do you good? What doth possessions do you good? Solomon, a wise man, wise by the Spirit of God; wise by experience, because he was a king; wise by a special gift of God, a gift of wisdom; he had all to enable him to give a true sentence; he that had run through the variety of all good things, what doth he pronounce, but 'vanity of vanities?' He cannot express himself. 'Vanity of vanities,' saith wise, holy, experienced Solomon. He that had all abilities, that no man was able to say it so well as he, yet he saith, 'Vanity of vanities;' and that which is worse, 'vexation of spirit,' if a man have not especial grace to manage them aright. And therefore I beseech you, 'brethren,' do but represent the things of this life, even under the notion here; they are but apparitions, they are but pageants. If we go to buy anything in this

* Cf. Note, Vol. III. page 531, note *z*.—G.

world, we first pull off the trappings; we pull off the mask, or else we may be cozened in the thing. So if we would judge of the things of this world as they are: what is within riches? Is there not a great deal of care? What is within government? What is within the things of this life? There is a goodly show and apparition. What is within? Pull off the mask, and then you shall see the things of this world. The more you pierce into them, and the more you know them, the worse you like them. There is emptiness, and not only so, but vexation. But in the things of heaven, the nearer you are the more you will love them, the more you will admire them. The more a man knows God, the more he may know him. The more a man knows Christ, and loves Christ, the more he may. There is a height, and breadth, and depth there, all dimensions in the love of God in Christ, and in the joys of heaven; they are beyond comprehension. The things that we have in Christ, they are larger than the soul; we cannot comprehend them. There is nothing here but we may compass it; it is inferior to our knowledge and affections. Our affections and our knowledge are larger than anything here; the things of a better life are beyond all. Shall we be taken with apparitions, that the more we know them the more we shall undervalue them?

'And the fashion of this world passeth away.'

It is a fashion, it is but a fashion; and then it 'passeth away.' Indeed, they do pass away; experience sheweth that they pass even like a river. The water passeth away; it goes, and goes along, but it never comes. So the things of this world; they pass away, but they never come again. They vanish away, and we pass away with them too. Even as men in a ship, whether they eat, or drink, or sleep, or walk, the ship goeth, and they go in it. So it is in this world, whether we eat, or drink, or sleep, we pass away to death. Every day takes a part of our life away; and every day we live, we live a day less. It is gone and past, and never returns again, as water when it is gone; and whether we walk or do anything, the time passeth. While you hear, and while I speak, the time passeth, and never returns again. So 'the fashion of this world passeth away.' All things are passing here.

We say they are moveables, and indeed those things that we call immoveables are moveables. All pass away; heaven and earth will pass away ere long, and there will be a new heaven and a new earth, Rev. xxi. 1. Kingdoms pass away, and kings pass away, and states pass away. What is become of Rome? What is become of Jerusalem? What is become of Babylon, and all those goodly cities? All are 'passed away;' they are all gone. This experience speaks as well as divinity.

Reason 1. Now, the ground of all this is, not only the nature of things —all things that are [are] made of nothing. Being therefore subject to fall to their first principles again, that is the fundamental reason why things may be moveable 'and pass away.' But that they are so, it is not a sufficient reason, for God might have suspended the mutability of things if he would; as, the heavenly angels are mutable, because they are created, but God hath suspended their mutability world without end; and therefore it is not sufficient that all things are of nothing. It shews that of themselves they may turn to nothing indeed.

Reason 2. But there is another reason; since the fall of man there is a curse upon all things. There is a sentence of mutability and change, and a sentence of 'passing' is passed upon all. All things that have a beginning shall have an end, and that this world shall be a stage of changes and alteration. There is a sentence of vanity upon the creature: 'The creature is subject to vanity; not of his own will, but because God hath subdued it to vanity,' Rom. viii. 20. Man committed treason, and therefore the creatures, which are man's servants, all mourn for their master's fall; they all mourn in black, as it were. All the creatures are subject to vanity, all the creatures under the sun are subject to mutability and change; but we may thank ourselves, we are the grand traitors that brought this misery upon the creature. That is the true reason why all things 'pass away,' and so why ourselves have the sentence of death upon us. 'We pass away,' and the things 'pass away;' and we in the use of them. Thus you see the ground of this, why things pass away in the sentence of mutability and vanity that God hath passed upon them.

Use 2. If this be so, beloved, *let us learn not to pass* much for things that will 'pass away.'* Not to pass for them, learn all the former directions: 'The fashion of this world passeth away.' Shall we grieve much for the loss of that that we cannot hold? If a glass be broke, is a man much angry? We say it is but brittle metal, and nothing lasteth always. If a friend be dead, shall a man be therefore angry? 'The fashion of this world passeth away.' A sentence is passed upon them. Shall I be moved at that that God hath set down a law for, that one generation shall go and another shall follow after, and there is a succession as in the streams of water? Shall I oppose God's sentence? God hath made all things frail, and it is but the common condition of all since the fall.

Use 3. *So it should be a use of comfort and contentment with anything in this world.* Place, or riches, or honour, I must leave them, I know not how soon; and this will breed a disposition of contentment. It is enough for him that must leave all, I know not how soon; have I little or much, I must leave all. Here is enough for him that must leave all. And therefore leave worldly things to worldly men; leave all these vain things to vain men. Shall I build a fixed hope on vain things? Oh, no! that should not be so.

Use 4. As we must learn contentment, *so it should take us off from the hopes of this world, and from promising ourselves that which we have no promise in the world for, nor experience.* Who promised thee thou shouldst enjoy thy wife long? that thou shouldst enjoy thy children long? thy place long? Hast thou a promise for this? The nature of things fight against thee. The things of the world are variable. Have we not experience of former times? And have we not scriptures to shew that all is 'vanity'? Why should we promise ourselves that which the word doth not promise us, or that we cannot see experience of in the world? Why would we have a condition severed from all men? The seeing of things in a condition of fading, as it should teach us contentment in the use of all things, so it should teach us moderation and wisdom, that we should not promise ourselves anything in this world.

Use 5. And it should teach us *to provide for stable, for certain things in changes and alterations.* Look to somewhat that may stand by us when all things are gone. Will all these things leave me, and must I leave them? How is it with me for the world without end? Shall I not therefore look for those comforts, and those graces, and for that condition that will abide when I am gone hence? What desperate folly were it! Let us labour for a sanctified use of the 'passing away' of these things, that we may provide for that which is not subject to alteration and change. The

* That is, 'put a high value upon.'—G.

favour of God in Christ is for everlasting. The graces of God's Spirit are for everlasting. The condition of God's children is for everlasting. And therefore why should we look after perishing things, and neglect better? For a Christian hath the reality of things: he hath a husband for ever, he hath matter of joy for ever, he hath a possession for ever; and then there will be a new world. All these things are but shows. The Christian hath the reality of all, that never 'passes away.' And therefore, considering that all things else 'pass away' but the things that belong to a Christian as a Christian, let Christians learn to make most of their best calling, and value themselves as they are Christians, and value others as they are Christians, not as they are rich, or as they are poor, as they are noble, or as they are great: 'The fashion of this world passeth away.' Value them by that they have of eternity. What of the Spirit is in them? What of the image of God is in them? What grace is in them? Are they new born? Are they truly noble? Are they new creatures? Value them by that, and labour to get that stamped upon our children, and upon our friends. Labour to have communion so with those that we love, that we may have eternal communion in heaven with them. Labour so to enjoy our friends that our friendship may continue in heaven, considering that 'the fashion of this world passeth away.' All friendship, all bonds, all possessions, and all that we doat of and are desperately mad on, all passeth away: 'The fashion of this world passeth away.'

It is a strange thing, beloved, that a man capable of high thoughts, of excellent thoughts, should spend the marrow of his soul, and the strength of his spirits, about these things; that he should tire his spirits, that he should crack his conscience, that he should wear out his life, about things which he cannot tell how long he shall enjoy them, and neglect these things that abide for ever. For a man this is ill; but for 'brethren,' as he saith, for 'brethren' to do so, that have an inheritance immortal; for them to be cast off the hooks for every cross, for every loss, that are the children of God and heirs of heaven; what a shame is this, that Christians are so much in joy, and so much in sorrow, for these things! It comes from these grounds:

[1.] *First*, They do not *consider and look upon things as passed.* They look not with the eye of faith upon things; these things will pass. But they look upon things in passing, and they see no alteration for the present. They should consider; ay, but what sentence is upon them? These are as good as passed; they will be gone ere long. Look upon them therefore as things passed. We are dead; our friends are dead; and the world is gone. Faith saith this. We consider not this 'ay,' and so we are carried away with them. We look upon things passing, and there we see little alteration. A man that looks upon the shadow passing, he cannot see it; but if he come two or three hours after, he shall see it past. Let us look upon things as gone. Though they be not for the present gone, see them in the eye of faith, and that will make us consider them as 'passing away.'

[2.] Again, we are deceived hence in the passing of the things of this life, *that we compare them not with eternity.* We think it a great matter to enjoy things twenty or forty years. What is this point of time to eternity? Compare this short time here, of health and strength, of honour and place and friends; what is this to eternity? What desperate folly is it to venture the loss of eternity for the enjoying of these things! Compare these things with world without end, Eph. iii. 21, and that will keep us from being deceived with these passing things. We are deceived, because we lay them not in the balance with things that are for ever.

[3.] And then the third ground is, *we are forgetful, we are not mindful of our best condition, we make not that use of our knowledge that we might.*

When a Christian is all in passion, all in joy, all in fears, or in grief; why, what is the matter at that time? What thoughts hath he of his eternal estate? of the fading condition of these things? He is forgetful and mindless. And therefore let us labour oft to keep our souls in a heavenly frame. And to draw to a conclusion, let us learn to value ourselves. If we be Christians, as we all profess ourselves to be, value ourselves. It is a poorness of spirit for a Christian to over-joy, or to over-grieve for anything that is worse than himself. Are not all things so, that are here, if we be Christians indeed? If we be not Christians, the very toads and serpents are better than blaspheming and filthy creatures, that are opposers of God's ordinances; they are better than such wretches, as many among us. The devil is almost as good as they; such are next the devil. The earth they tread on is better than they. But if a man have grace in him, all the world is inferior to him. What weakness of spirit is it therefore, and emptiness, to be put off with over-much cause of grief and sorrow for anything below that is meaner than ourselves, for anything that is fading, when we have a condition that is not subject to fade? And therefore oft think of our dignity in Christ; think of the motive here; 'brethren,' think of that as well as of the fading condition here. If we would wean ourselves from these things, oft think of the eternal estate of a Christian, that our thoughts may run upon that much; and then upon the frail condition of all things below, that we may be taken off from them, for two things mortify * a man.

The taking off of his affections from that they are set on, and to set them upon that that will fill them and satisfy them to the full; if a man do that, he doth that that a mortified man should do, who is in this world, passing to a better.

To conclude all with this.

All things here in this world are subordinate to a further end. And let us consider therefore that we use them as that we lose not the main.

All the contentments of a traveller are subordinate in the way to his journey's end. If things come amiss in his inn, will he quarrel with his host that he hath not a soft bed? He will think, I am going, I shall have better at home; and these lead me homeward. So all things below are subordinate helps to better. Shall we make them the main? Shall we make all things subordinate to them as worldlings do? subordinate religion to worldly things, and make all things contrary? They do not 'grieve as if they grieved not;' but they hear as if they heard not. They receive the sacrament as if they received it not. They pray as if they prayed not. They speak of holy things, and do them, as if they did them not. But for other things they are drowned in them. This is the policy of Satan, that labours to bring religion to be subordinate. So that if men can be religious and have the favour of such a one, if he can be religious and be great in the world, he will; but if religion itself, and the standing for it, hinder their aims, away with it; they will rather be hollow than stand for a good cause, because they have not learned to subordinate things to the main end. And the reason is, because they have not grace and heavenly wisdom to teach them in what place things should be valued; what is the main, and what

* That is, = make a man *dead* to such and such.—G.

attends upon the main; and therefore they take by-things for the main, and the main for the by. Indeed no man is wise but a sound Christian, and he is wise for his soul, and he is wise for eternity. But what is this for the sacrament? To cut off other things, it is this.*

Are these things perishing food, such as we must leave—vain and empty things? Will not this therefore make us seek the main—the food that endures to everlasting life; and labour to be in Christ more and more, labour to cherish communion with Christ, that everlasting bond? What is the sacrament but the food of our souls, our everlasting manna, that will continue for ever, and make us continue for ever? Christ, if we have him, he continues for ever, and he makes us continue for ever too. And therefore considering that all things else are vain, I beseech you let the consideration of that that hath been spoken be as 'sour herbs' to make the passover, to make Christ relish the better. Oh! Are all things vain, and shall I not labour to have my part in that that shall never die, in him that is my husband for ever, and my Lord for ever? Shall I not labour to strengthen mine interest in him that hath all good things in him? What if all the earth should fail? If I have communion with Christ, I have all. If I marry Christ, I have all with him. All is my jointure, if I have Christ once: 'All things are yours, if you are Christ's,' 1 Cor. iii. 21–23. If I have Christ, what can I want? Let this strengthen my desire to come to the sacrament. Christ is the food of the soul; all other food the sweetness of it is gone within a quarter of an hour. The sweetness is gone presently, and the strength within a day or two, of all other food that we take. But this food, Christ, the food of the soul, Christ offering himself unto death, and shedding out his blood, and giving his body to be crucified for us, this food feeds our souls to everlasting life. We cherish our faith in the assurance of the favour of God to everlasting; the sweetness, the strength, and the comfort of this food endures for ever. And therefore, considering that all other things are food that perisheth, labour for that that will feed us to everlasting life. And then we shall make a right use of the alteration and change of all things.

A heathen man can say this text, set 'brethren' aside; a heathen man could tell you, *Transit gloria mundi* (*d*), and 'The fashion of things pass away.' He sees them, and thereupon could infer the negative part. Therefore we should not be worldly. By the light of nature, a man that hath no religion may be sound in that, and therefore not to care much for earthly things, considering that we must be gone.

A heathen man could speak very sweetly this way, as Plutarch, and Seneca, and the rest. What fine speeches had they this way. Oh, but the positive part, that is, when we see all things here are vain and fading, to know what we must cleave to, that is proper to religion, to know Christ, and the good we have by Christ. When we have him we have all. He is the food of our souls. These things are proper to religion. And therefore let us arise from the consideration of the vanity of all things to the positive part, to interest ourselves in that that is better than all things. Which if we have, we have all; and then we shall make a right use of this.

* In the margin here, 'Application to the sacrament.'—G.

NOTES.

(*a*) P. 51.—'There is a diminishing in the word "show."' The 'diminution' is that spoken of at the beginning of the paragraph; that it is not said *the world*, but only *σχημα*, the *fashion*, or *show* of the world.

(*b*) P. 51.—'Deceives and turns us aside.' The verb is *παράγω* . . . *παράγει γαρ τὸ σχῆμα του κόσμου τούτου*. Cf. Ps. xxxix. 4–6, 1 John ii. 17, and Rev. xxi. 1. I have not met with the alternative translation offered; therefore cannot say who the 'some' are, intended by Sibbes.

(*c*) P. 52.—'All is but acting a part.' The whole of this passage recalls the famous 'All the world's a stage,' of the greatest of Sibbes's contemporaries (cf. *As you like it*, II. 7). It is interesting to notice those not unfrequent tacit references to Shakespeare and Bacon found in Sibbes.

(*d*) P. 57.—'Transit gloria mundi.' This saying 'Sic transit gloria mundi,' forms the beginning of a sequence of the Romish Church; and is used at the inauguration of the popes. Cardinal Wiseman, in his 'Recollections,' has described the accompanying ceremony with much pictorial beauty and effect. G.

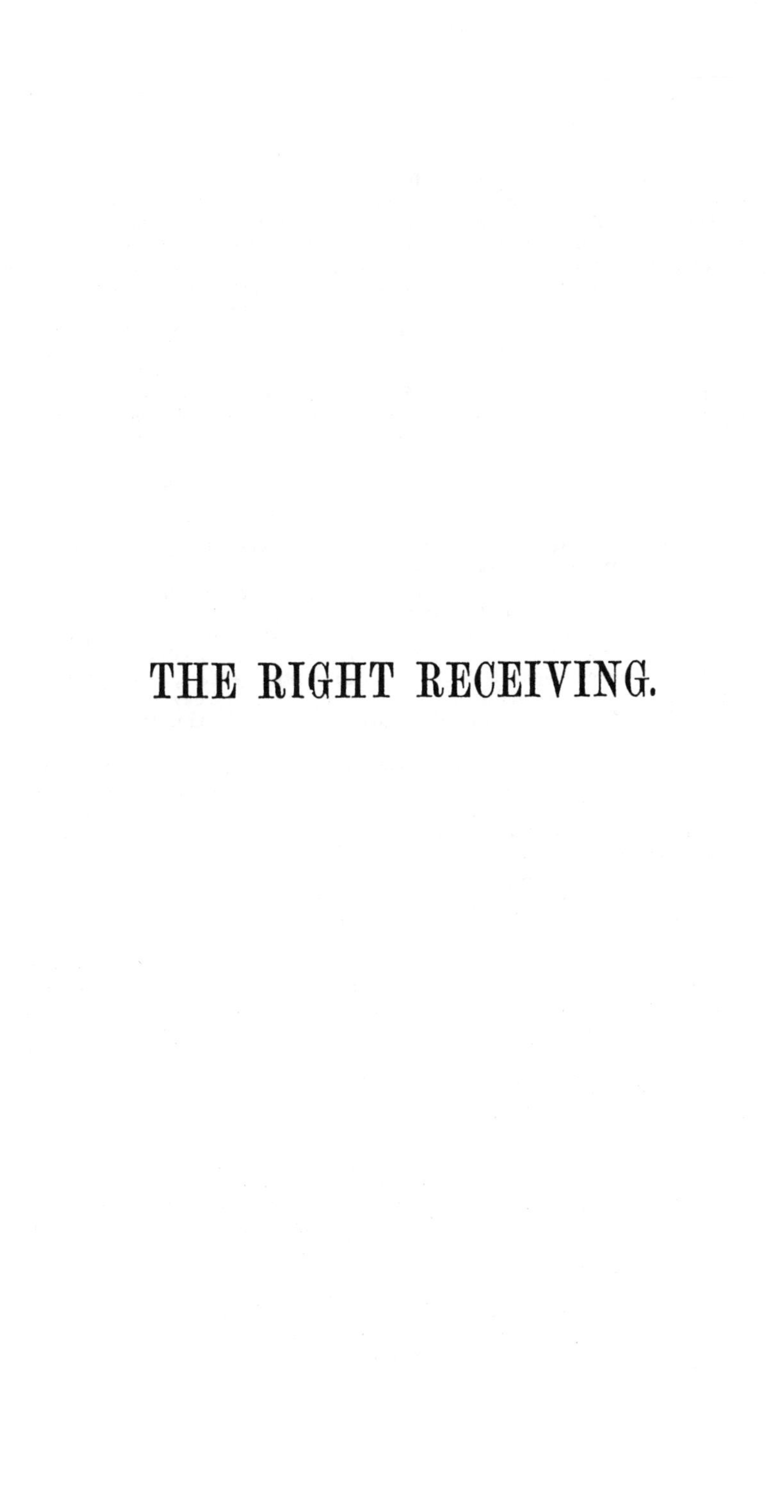

THE RIGHT RECEIVING.

THE RIGHT RECEIVING.

NOTE.

This sermon of 'Right Receiving,' from 1 Corinthians xi. 28, 29, forms No. 19 of the first edition of a folio volume, entitled 'The Saint's Cordials.' The separate title-page is given below.* This sermon was excluded from the subsequent editions of 1637 and 1658. Probably the original edition of the 'Cordials' was surreptitiously published from 'imperfect notes;' but it seems to have been revised by the author, with the result shewn in the various readings of the after editions, many of which in other of the sermons are large and important, and all interesting as shewing Sibbes' care. 'Right Receiving' was, no doubt, along with others, withheld from the editions of 1637 and 1658 because of the looseness and unsatisfactoriness of the report of it. Of the 'Cordials,' more than of any other of his works, Sibbes might well make the complaint in his 'Epistle' to the 'Bruised Reed.' Cf. Note *in loc.* As 'Right Receiving' is the first contribution from the 'Cordials' to the works of Sibbes in our edition, I subjoin the full title-page of the volume in its three editions, which will facilitate after references.† ‡ §. Throughout, in reprinting 'The Saint's Cordials,' I take for text the edition published during Sibbes' own life—1629—adding the 'various readings' of 1637 and 1658.—G.]

* THE RIGHT RECEIVING. In One Sermon. Which shews, wherein unworthy receiving consists. What it is to eate Judgement to ones selfe. The properties wherein we are to examine our selves. Divers sacramentall actions in receiving. The examination of the Heart and Affections. And what is to be done for triall of our estates in the matter of Sanctification, &c. [A wood-cut here of a 'burning candle' in an old-fashioned 'candlestick,' with the motto, 'Prælucendo Pereo.'] Vprightnes Hath Boldnes. John 6. 54, 55. Whoso eateth my flesh, and drinketh my blood, hath eternall life, and I will raise him up at the last day. For my flesh is meat indeed, and my blood is drink indeed. London, Printed in the yeare 1629.

† THE SAINTS CORDIALS. As they were delivered in svndry Sermons upon speciall Occasions, in the Citie of London, and else-where. Published for the Churches good. [Woodcut as in *.] Vprightnes Hath Boldnes. Isa. 40. 1, 2. Comfort yee, comfort yee my people, saith our God: Speake yee comfortably to Hierusalem, and cry unto her that her warfare is accomplished, that her iniquitie is pardoned; for shee hath received of the Lords hand double for all her sins. London, Printed for Robert Dawlman dwelling at the Brazen-Serpent in Pauls Church-yard. [No date, but the separate Sermons within the Volume are dated 1629.]

‡ THE SAINTS CORDIALLS; delivered in svndry Sermons at Graies-Inne, and in the Citie of London. Whereunto is now added, The Saints Safety in Evill Times, Preached in Cambridge upon speciall occasions. By Richard Sibbs D.D. Late Master of Katherine-Hall in Cambridge, and Preacher at Grayes-Inne. [Woodcut here of Time with a scythe, and the motto 'Virtus retvndit sola aciem hanc.'] My strength and my heart faileth, but God is the strength of my heart, and my portion for ever, Psal. 73. 26. London, Printed by M. F. for Henry Overton, and are to be sold at the entring in of Popes Head Alley out of Lumbard street., 1637.

§ THE SAINTS CORDIALLS, Wherein We have particularly handled, The Saints safety and hiding-place, The Saints Assurance, Christs sufferings for mans sin, The Saints Refreshing, Salvation applyed, The Churches Visitation, Christ is best, The Life of Faith, The Art of self-judging and humbling, The difficulty of Salvation, The danger of back-sliding, The ungodlies misery, With other material things. Delivered in sundry Sermons, at Graies-Inne, in the City of London, and at Cambridge. By Richard Sibbs, D.D. Late Master of Katherine-Hall in Cambridge, and Preacher at Grayes-Inne. Psal. 73. 26. My strength and my heart faileth; but God is the strength of my heart, and my portion for ever. London, Printed by M. S. for Henry Cripps, and are to be sold at the entring in of Popes-Head-Alley, out of Lumbard-street, 1658.

THE RIGHT RECEIVING.

But let a man examine himself, and so let him eat of that bread, and drink of that cup. For he that eateth and drinketh unworthily, eateth and drinketh damnation to himself, not discerning the Lord's body.—1 Cor. XI. 28, 29.

In the former words the apostle had propounded to the Corinthians the first institution of the Lord's Supper, declaring the causes why our blessed Saviour appointed these ordinances, the especial end whereof was the remembrance of the Lord's death until he came; and not only a bare remembrance thereof, but likewise the communion of the virtues of that death—for the comfort of all Christians—until his coming. And from the same the apostle in the verse going before draweth his conclusion: that seeing this holy supper is instituted by our blessed Saviour for such an end as this, so excellent, to be a lively representation of the crucifying of the Son of God, of the breaking of his body, and the pouring forth of his blood for our salvation; therefore he inferreth that all men should come with a reverend* regard thereunto, not as to a common table. Seeing the matter is thus, saith the apostle, that this is not an ordinary supper, it behoveth us not to come thither as unto an ordinary feast. We may not make any small difference betwixt this and our common banquets; but if a man cometh unworthily, that is, unbeseemingly, such a man as this, instead of comfort, reapeth unto himself judgment. If we come hand over head, without preparation; if we so eat, we shall be 'guilty of the body and blood of the Lord.' It sheweth that we make no reverend * account of it when we will come so unreverently unto the same, making no difference betwixt this heavenly manna and our ordinary food; and therefore, eating unworthily,—coming to partake of the body and blood here set, without due preparation,—shall be culpable of judgment.

Quest. But here some will say, How doth a man come unto the Lord's table unworthily? Is any man worthy? Seeing under these veils is signified, and, more than that, exhibited unto us, the body and blood of Christ Jesus, is any man worthy? It was a great thing, that the ancient people of the Jews were fed with manna. John vi. 31, 'They ate manna in the wilderness, he gave them bread from heaven to eat, and yet they died. But he that eateth the flesh of the Son of man, and drinketh his blood, hath eternal life.' Now, howsoever it be true that the body of Christ is in heaven and we upon earth, yet here is the conveyance, whereby we have interest in his body and blood; here is the seal of the great indenture.

* Qu. 'reverent'?—Ed.

God giveth us not only the great draught, which we are in possession of; not only his word, that we have an interest in his Son; but also unto his deed made unto us in his word he giveth a more propriety,* even these holy sacraments, wherein† he clappeth this broad seal, thus tendered unto us.

Ans. I answer, then, that no man is worthy to be a guest; but worthiness here is taken in another sense. A man is not said to be worthy in regard of any worthiness in himself, but in respect of his affection and preparation, and in regard of his fit and seemly receiving. As we use to say, the king received worthy entertainment in such a gentleman's house, not for that he was worthy to receive him, but because he omitted no compliments and service in his power fit to entertain him: even so I say, we are not worthy of Christ, that he should enter into our houses, that he should come under our roof. But, notwithstanding, we are said to be worthy when we do all things which are in our power, fit for the entertainment of him. If we come not in pride and in our rags, but with repentance, joy, comfort, and humility, then are we worthy.

This therefore being the ground of the exhortation, let us come to the words, 'Let a man therefore examine himself.' He that eateth unworthily procureth great hurt unto himself, therefore examine yourselves; as if he should say, Wouldst thou know how to come worthily? Examine thine own heart, and see whether all things are well within; whether thou mayest put God's seal to the grace that thou findest in thyself.

I will open it as plain as I can, 'Let a man therefore examine himself,' &c. The question is here, How a man cometh to the Lord's table worthily? The apostle saith he cometh worthily if he examineth himself; whence, in the first place, we observe this doctrine, *that the Lord hath appointed the sacrament of the supper, not as the sacrament of baptism, once to be administered, and never after, but he hath appointed it to be received often.*

The reason is apparent: it is sufficient for a man once to be born. Now baptism is the sacrament of our spiritual regeneration; therefore but once to be administered. But it is not sufficient for a man to make one dinner and no more, but we must daily eat and get strength. Now this sacrament of the supper, signifying not our new birth, but our proceeding, our strength, and obedience, is therefore, as a means to increase strength, often to be received. As he that hath a weak stomach will eat his meat often, and little at once; so we, having found our great want and weakness, must often receive this sacrament. Well! so often as we come, the apostle biddeth us to examine ourselves, if we would be good guests. Examine! Why? Saith the apostle to these Corinthians in another place, 2 Cor. xiii. 5, 'Try yourselves, whether ye be in the faith or not,' &c. Thou comest to have God's seal put unto the communion thou hast with him. Well! then God contenteth not himself with once examination for all; but he calleth Christians unto this duty often. This is worthy to be considered. There are many who in the beginning of their conversion can take some pains to sift and ransack their own hearts, to bring them unto the sight of sin. They can consider the fearful estate of sinners when they go out of the world. It may be also that they find some beginnings of repentance. Now, because this goeth against their hearts, this often examination, they would therefore post off all thus, to their first conversion. Once I have found the grace of repentance; God is unchangeable; whom he loveth once, those he loveth for ever. Now the Lord, knowing it to be dangerous for us to pitch upon this ground, doth therefore call upon us to try our title. There are many

* That is, 'property.'—G. † Qu. 'whereon'?—G.

corners in the heart of man; it is hardly sounded; it is full of hypocrisy; and he is wonderful ready to deceive his own heart. In regard whereof, seeing it is so deceitful, we must not content ourselves with once humiliation and repentance, nor suppose every light motion to be God's Spirit, but we must, as often as we eat of this bread and drink of this wine (and as any occasion is given us), try and examine ourselves, and labour to make our election sure. And if we consider the flattering of our own hearts, together with the delusion of Satan, this will be found needful. The greatest hypocrite will have a good conceit of himself, and will be ready to say with the proud Pharisee, 'I thank God I am not as other men are, an adulterer, extortioner,' &c., Luke xviii. 11. Thus he blesseth himself in his heart; and if then there be but any light motion, any common gift of God's Spirit in his heart, the devil is ready to persuade him that he is in heaven, and that all things are well with him. Now for a man to content himself with being once enlightened (with having once some tokens of God's favour come towards him) it is very dangerous. Consider this. God's children in the beginning of their conversion, their faith is weak,—small as a grain of mustard seed, which, though small, yet in time groweth great,—like the flax not always smoking. The hypocrite will shew a greater measure of profession in the sight of man than a true Christian, insomuch as a man would think he should never come to that perfection which they seem to have attained who perish with their holiness; for he groweth fast, and is quickly down again; soon ripe, soon rotten, like unto the corn which groweth upon the house-top; whereas the child of God goeth on fair and softly, soft and sure, and doth constantly proceed, in renewing the work of faith and repentance.

Use. Let this move us unto this duty, *that we often examine ourselves.* because, besides our old debts (those sins we committed before our calling), we multiply new sins, and do every day run upon a new score; for do we not know that sin is odious unto almighty God? Why? Consider it is worse for thee to continue in rebellion against God, than for a stranger who knoweth him not. A man that is dead, what works can be expected from him but dead works? But the Lord having translated thee from that death, looks to have new fruit; and for thee to bring forth sour grapes, this should trouble and grieve thee exceedingly. And this is especially to be observed of them who come unto the Lord's table. It becometh them to examine themselves, whereby they may be rightly entertained. It is much to be bewailed that this sacrament is in such small account, that men come unto it they know not how, so unpreparedly, that I am persuaded if they were to sit at the king's table, they would come with more preparation. Haman boasted of Ahasuerus his honour he had done unto him, and what was that? He accounted it a great honour that he was called to the banquet of a king, Esther v. 9; and shall we not account it a greater favour that the King of kings doth invite us to his table? Shall we come with such unwashed hands hither? Remember that the ground is holy; put off thy shoes when thou comest to this sacrament. You shall see therefore how the Lord was angry with his people when they did not respect but disgraced his sacrament, Exod. iv. 24. Moses was sent to redeem the Israelites. He being employed in this service, and being great in the favour of God, it came to pass by the way in the inn, the Lord met him, and would have killed him. A man would think that he with whom God was but even now so familiar had committed some great offence, that God should kill him. And what was it? But because he did neglect the Lord's sacrament. Ay, though Zipporah called him a bloody husband, because of the circumcision, yet the Lord would have killed him if he had not done it. And so they that receive unworthily, you may see are guilty, as 2 Chron. xxx. 3, *seq.*: the sacrament there was not wholly omitted; but because they came to it without due preparation, as the Lord required, he smote the people; for a multitude of Ephraim and Manasseh had not cleansed themselves. Yet did they eat the passover, but not as it was written. The Lord also, you see, would have killed Moses, because he administered not circumcision to his son. Many other come unto this sacrament, but they come not according unto God's ordinance.

Well, Hezekiah prayed for them, saying, 'The good Lord be merciful unto them, who prepare their whole heart to seek the Lord God, the God of their fathers, though they be not cleansed according to the purification of the sanctuary.' So that here you have a plain token, that God is displeased when a man presumeth to come with unwashen hands. Now, when a good man prayeth for mercy, for whom doth he pray? What! for him who never respecteth God, but will be constant in a wicked course? If all the hands in heaven and earth were lifted up for such a one, all possibly could do him no good. When Hezekiah prayed, the Lord, notwithstanding his ordinance was broken, was moved to be merciful. For whom? for them that had an upright heart; for them who prepared their hearts to seek him. So that here is an evidence, what a fearful thing it is for a man to come to the sacrament without this preparation. And to go no further for proof than where my text is now, ver. 29, 'He that eateth unworthily'—he that will come to this table without preparation, not addressing of his heart to entertain the Lord,—'he eateth judgment to himself.' We see, therefore, what a fearful thing it is. Now that the law, which was prepared and ordained for life, is now become unto us as death, what is the cause of this? The rebellion of thy heart hath turned the course of the law; so that that which was appointed for life is now become death. Ay, but is not this also a heavy thing, that the same is said also of the gospel? that the gospel, which was ordained for life, is now by thy negligence proved to be thy death? It is so: 'He that eateth unworthily, he eateth destruction, he eateth judgment to himself.'

Now, judgment we must not take in the terrible sense, that he that cometh unworthily shall eat judgment presently. But it is taken otherwise. Wilt thou, his enemy, eat unworthily? He will judge thee. If thou beest a child, he will whip thee; if thou beest a wicked man, he will for ever condemn thee; if his servant, he will inflict other outward judgments upon thee. So that I take it in another sense: if the child of God come unworthily, the Lord will make him smart; if the wicked man, who reviles him daily, intrude himself to the Lord's table, he shall eat damnation; so that neither the children of God nor the wicked shall escape judgment: the one shall have sentence of damnation, the other of sharp punishment. That this is the meaning of the apostle, it appeareth by the words following: 'for this cause,' when he had said 'many eat judgment,' he addeth, 'many are sick,' where in particular he setteth down that judgment whereof he spake of before. God's children, if they come without preparation, unreverently, they eat such judgment to themselves; God will send sickness upon them. For this cause it is that many of you are punished with death itself; and it followeth, ver. 31, 'But when we are punished, we are chastened of the Lord.' Why? 'Because we should not be condemned with the world.' You see judgment is opposed to condemnation. God's children eat judgment to themselves to avoid condemnation, which I stand upon, because many think that if they come unworthily, they shall be damned presently; as I have known some who have abstained seven years, because they were afraid they should eat unworthily. O! then be not damned. The apostle saith 'that we are chastised of the Lord, that we may *not* be condemned.'

For the necessity of this duty then, seeing it is necessary for a man to examine himself, as hath been shewed, it followeth now that we consider

The properties wherein a man is to examine himself.

Wherein must he examine himself? I answer, this dependeth upon the knowledge of the institution of the sacrament. Let us then consider for what end it was instituted, and let us see what that is which is done in the sacrament.

The end of a sacrament, Rom. iv. 11—speaking of one sacrament—namely, of circumcision: Abraham received the sign of circumcision, as the seal of the righteousness of that faith which he had when he was uncircumcised. In those words you have a second use for a sacrament set down. It is appointed of God, *first*, to be 'a sign of the righteousness of faith.' A sign to inform the understanding, touching the benefits we have by the communion of Christ. And *secondly*, it is not only the bare sign, as words are, but it is also a seal, that is, a thing appointed of God, to confirm that there is a difference betwixt these two. As for instance: if a man hath the picture of a king, he hath a sign of the king; but it he have a deed, confirmed with a seal from the king, this sheweth that he hath an interest in something which he receiveth from the king. Well then, the sacrament is a sign to inform the understanding of man, touching the benefits we have by Christ, and a seal to assure us of that there signified. The first use of the sacrament is, to open the mysteries of the gospel to all that have understanding; the second is, to seal the comforts which are there signified in the sacrament: for, as in the former use, it is not every one unto whom the gospel giveth knowledge, but to them that believe. So, doth this sacrament seal unto all? No; but to them who besides understanding have grace. So that then here is the point: the sacrament is a sign to declare the mysteries of the gospel unto all that have understanding; secondly, it is a seal to assure some of the comforts of Christ, and not to all, but unto them who have grace.

1. So that I must, *first*, examine myself, *whether that I have understanding;* and *secondly*, whether I have grace, whereby I must make use of it, for I must be knit to it, not by the brain, but by the affection. Otherwise, if I come to it as the Papists, to a dumb show, not bringing an understanding heart of the mysteries thereof, I shall come unworthily. Now for the *first* point. The matter to be considered is, whether thou art an ignorant body? whether thou knowest what is meant by these? That this is needful, it may appear by this: this is the Lord's table, and he inviteth hitherto his friends and acquaintance. And dost thou think that thou, which knowest neither Father, Son, nor Holy Ghost, mayest come? For thee to thrust in amongst his friends and familiars, is not this presumption? Therefore, first ye must examine yourselves. And besides this, they that are ignorant are not only strangers, but also enemies to God; yea, such as against whom the Lord will come, 2 Thess. i. 7, 8, 'in flaming fire, rendering vengeance unto them which know not God, nor obey unto the gospel of our Lord Jesus Christ.' Here you see the enemies of Christ, against whom he shall stand, are ranked into two kinds: first, they are such as know him not; secondly, they are such who have knowledge and understanding, but they have not grace, 'they obey not the gospel of Christ Jesus.'

Examine, then, yourselves. Doth the ignorance of God make you to be his enemies? Of this examine thyself; for dost thou think that ever God will endure his enemies shall come unto his table? Let all ignorant persons examine themselves; for howsoever they may come, yet it grieveth the Lord that they come. And this shall be a judgment unto them at the last, that they were so bold to come without examination. I speak not this to discourage a man from coming, for thou shalt pay for it if thou comest not; but know this, if thou come ignorantly, there standeth the angel of the Lord to keep thee, as Adam was, Gen. iii. 24, from this sacrament, or any comfort by it.

2. Another reason why the sacrament was instituted, is it not to strengthen faith? as Rom. v. 4. 'It was the seal of faith.' Well; and can there be faith without knowledge? No; Isa. liii. 11. 'By his knowledge' (speaking of his Son) 'shall my righteous servant justify many.' By faith; and this faith is expressed by knowledge, to shew that where there is no knowledge, there is no faith. The sacrament is instituted for this end. And where there is no faith, there is no worthy receiving of the sacrament. As then thou lovest thine own salvation, inform thyself in this point; please not thyself in thine ignorance. For the informing then of our understanding, two things are here to be considered; *first*, we must not here have any dumb shows, but we must understand that all these things are a gospel, preached unto our eyes. Now, the things presented to our eyes are two:

1. *Outward elements.* 2. *Certain actions done by us.*

For the outward elements, you see there are bread and wine, set apart for an holy use. The bread is broken, and the wine is poured out. All this is done before we partake. When we come to see these things done, we must bring with us looking hearts and affections to see what God hath done for us. The next thing is, we see not only bread and wine set apart, but it is given unto us, taken by us, drunk of us, and nourisheth us. It first shews us that accomplishment of our redemption by the Son of God. Dost thou see thee sanctified to this work? What, then, dost thou think is meant by the breaking? what by the pouring out of the wine? This is my body broken, this is my blood shed for many. It is the man Jesus Christ who is put before your eyes. When you come thither, there is a spectacle of Christ crucified. And it is set apart to shew that, as it was in the paschal lamb, there was a lamb to be taken out of the flock, to be separated from the rest, to shew that it was set apart for some extraordinary work. I say, what doth this shew, but that our high priest, Christ Jesus, was separated from sinners? More; thou seest the bread broken, and the wine poured forth. This should stir thee up to be in the same estate, as if thou wert upon Golgotha, at the place whereupon he was crucified, crying with a loud voice, 'My God, my God, why hast thou forsaken me;' as if thou sawest him sweat water and blood. And our affections should be like that of the blessed virgin, to whom the sight of her son in his anguish could not but be a great vexation and grief. Consider that this is a property of God's Spirit, Zech. xii. 10: 'I will pour upon the house of David, and upon the inhabitants of Jerusalem, the spirit of grace and of compassion: and they shall look upon me whom they have pierced, and they shall lament and mourn for him, and be in bitterness,' &c. Such should be thine affections, when thou seest the bread broken and the wine poured forth. Thou must consider the circumstances of Christ's breaking, and his soul poured out for sin; that God had broken him, 'then shall they look upon him whom they have crucified.' It is not sufficient for thee to say that they, speaking of the Jews, would do thus. We are ready to spit in their faces. Ay, but saith the text, 'they shall look upon him.' It is I that crucified the Lord of glory; it is we that murdered him by our sins. And this should move us in a spiritual compassion, that we have imbrued our hands in his most innocent blood. That this might move the people in the old law, you see there was an innocent beast; but before it was slain, the man that was to offer the sacrifice, was first to put his hand upon the head thereof, to signify that every one of our sins was the cause of this, Lev. i. 4, *et alibi*. This must be our mature consideration. We lay our hands upon the immaculate Lamb; we put our hands upon his head: we have murdered him. Let us then see whether this affecteth us.

You should all say, Is sin so deadly and dangerous as this, that it will seize upon the Son of God himself, rather than sin shall be unpunished? Is my sin a dart shot up into heaven to pull him down from thence? Is my sin such a thing as this? Is it so that it will make the Son of God to lie upon the ground? and have I such a hard heart that it will not make me to weep? These, and such like godly cogitations, we should make when we see the bread and wine broken and poured forth. And let us go further. Do you not esteem of an oath, of an idle word, or such like sin? This is that which made Christ to be crucified, and therefore is not to be dallied withal. There is the first thing to be considered. When thou seest the bread broken and the wine poured forth, it is a calling to mind of the sufferings of the Son of God.

The *second* point. What is meant by these actions performed by us? That is, what Christ did for us. But what is that to thee? All thy comfort standeth in the apprehending it unto thyself. Christ hath prepared a medicine in the apothecaries' shop, ministering no comfort unless we apply it to ourselves. This bread thus broken is given. Here God bringeth his Son bathed in his blood. The Father seeth him in his gore blood, and saith, Take him. What a wonderful comfort is this, that he should come and say, 'Take and eat.' Be it that God once moveth thy heart to receive him, he meaneth as plainly as the minister doth, when he saith, take the bread; he offereth him plainly and freely. This is his offer, and will not this be a great condemnation to the world? So often as it is administered, so often is condemnation read to a wicked man. Doth God offer his Son, and will not thou take him? 1 Cor. ii. 4, *seq*. The apostle there speaketh in the ministry of the gospel, that we are not to think it a mean matter that God sendeth a minister to make an offer of his Son, but we must think that this is done by God himself. The apostle, 2 Cor. v. 20, saith, 'Now then are we ambassadors for Christ, as though God did beseech you,' &c. Oh, say some, if I might hear Christ say thus much, or if I might hear but God say so, I would receive him. The case is alike; we are ambassadors for Christ, we pray you in Christ; as if God were present in person, we say, Receive him, God beseecheth you to be reconciled. It were fit for us to beseech him, but he cometh to our doors and offereth us pardon; and therefore this will be condemnation, that where mercy is brought home, we notwithstanding reject it. Well! besides the offer, there is further the actual delivery of it. Take, eat. They take, eat, and drink. What is represented by this? It representeth a further point, that we are not only in Christ, flesh of his flesh, and bone of his bone, but that Christ is actually delivered; that we seize* upon him. When we see the bread and wine taken, he meaneth that hereby we by faith do accept of Christ, and do lay

* That is, = 'take possession,' a law term. Cf. note *bb*, Vol III., p. 531.—G.

hold of him. Here is the foundation of our comfort, that a Christian man may say of Christ, that he can be assured of nothing so much which he possesseth for his own, as he may be of him. His cloak upon his back, his house he dwells in, his lands, yea, the blood in his veins, and whatsoever he hath, is not so much his; he cannot be so assured thereof as of Christ. Take him. There is delivery and seizement of Christ—as by the ring of a door—we are interested into heaven, and if he be ours, with him, we have all things.

Nay, I will go further—for the Papists will go thus far—they will say Christ is to be delivered and received; ay, but how? After a gross *caparnaicall** opinion, eaten really and bodily with the mouth. But Christ is transferred into me, and I into him, by faith; we are made one with him, flesh of his flesh, and bone of his bone; as it is John vi. 54, 'He that eateth my flesh, and drinketh my blood, dwelleth in me, and I in him.' I would not have him for a while, but for ever. Well, he is planted into thee, and dwelleth in thee; that as meat, by the wonderful work of nature, is turned into ourselves, so is Christ, by the supernatural work of grace, once being entertained, made one with us. We are one body, one flesh. He hath more assured hold of us than we have of him. We know the devil is strong, but he may not pull off a leg or an arm, or any of his members. He is stronger than all. We dwell in him, and he in us, and no man can take us out of his hands. And then that which is next, all comforts shall be ours when we have Christ. We cannot have the benefits of Christ unless we have Christ himself; and therefore, in the Lord's supper, Christ saith not, This is justification, or sanctification, but This is my body, &c. We may not look for the graces of sanctification, justification, or redemption before we have Christ. If we have him, we shall with him have all things else. The apostle, Heb. iii. 1, 14, saith, 'We are made partakers of Christ, if we keep sure unto the end, the beginning wherewith we are upholden.' The apostle useth the term of being partakers of Christ. We are made partakers of Christ if we constantly hold what we have begun unto the end. He saith not only we are made partakers of the benefits of Christ, but also of Christ himself, which is more than all the others. Now for the opening of this: will a man be nourished by bread if it be not eaten? No; but he must first eat and drink. So, faith, it is like unto an eagle that flieth up unto heaven, and there seizeth upon the Son of God; and there having thus seized upon him, then cometh remission of sins, justification, sanctification, and redemption, many blessings, and a floodgate of all graces.

These are the points which we are to consider, they are the signs to which God giveth a voice unto us; as the Lord speaketh unto Moses, Exod. iv. 8, 'So shall it come to pass, that if they will not believe thee, neither obey the voice of the first sign, yet shall they believe for the voice of the second sign.' You see to the sign is given a voice. [You see] that the sacrament, when the bread is broken, and the wine poured out, it is a voice speaking unto thee. Thou must therefore be a man of understanding to discern the same.

The next point; the sacrament is not only a sign to signify that all things are to be had in Christ, for a wicked man may know thus much; but Abraham received the sign of circumcision as a seal: it is also a seal. We must therefore examine ourselves in our knowledge as whether we have faith and grace, otherwise God sealeth no comfort unto us. But how shall a man know this?

* Probably refers to John vi. 52, a question put in *Capernaum*.—G.

There is a general life. I will touch it as briefly as I can, and so make an end. The matter to be understood is this, whether we have grace in us, whether living and regenerate. No man spreads his table for dead men. We are dead by nature, and if we find that we are dead, this banquet is not for us. We must then be regenerate. I know many come when they are dead, and therefore they abuse God and their own souls, and they put his seal to a false deed. Well, the apostle's conclusion is, 1 John v. 12, 'He that hath the Son hath life.' But the point of this examination is, namely, how a man may know whether he be dead or living, which must be the point of trial in the next place.

That matter and examination which concerneth the heart and affections.

For knowledge, with examination, is not enough to make a man a right receiver; but there must first be understanding, and then grace in the heart. For we must understand thus much of the sacrament of the supper, it never bringeth grace where it findeth none. It confirmeth that good grace which it findeth before. So that, as I have said, it always presupposeth some grace to be in the heart. When we come, we come not to receive life, but to have our strength increased. For if a man were to deal with the king, and would have him to confirm some estate unto him, it were to no end if his title and ground were not good; so, if the ground of our estate fail, if we have not some grace, faith, and the like, the receiving of the sacrament will not give them, they will not make an ill matter good. Therefore we must labour for grace in our hearts if we would have comfort. Upon this we may expect a blessing. I will touch the heads of this briefly, because it is very large. The points wherein a man must examine himself are,

1. *Whether he discerneth of the necessity of this new life: whether he discerneth that without this supply from heaven, without the body of Christ, his estate is most wretched and miserable.*

This is the *first* thing in our examination, which may be thought a thing needless to examine our conscience upon: that our estate is miserable without Christ. But it is necessary, and that course which God taketh with his children. He first makes them discern in what a miserable estate they are. And it is not every one that can discern this; for it must be the work of God's Spirit to shew a man the death of sin; because every man hath naturally pride in his heart. So the apostle Paul confesseth, Rom. vii. 9, *seq.*, before the Lord had shewed him his misery by the law. Whilst he was left to natural direction, [he] thought himself a man of worth—by his own confession—a great man. Now, therefore, before the Lord would discover unto him the riches of his grace, he applieth the law unto him; the law that told him, 'Thou shalt not lust.' Then he perceiveth his misery, as soon as the commandment came, seeing himself to be full of concupiscence. Then, when the commandment came, sin revived and appeared to be sin, saith the apostle. A man must first, therefore, discern that he is in a miserable estate. Hereupon, John xvi. 8, *seq.*, when the works of God's Spirit are set down, the first is this, 'to convince the world;' when the Spirit shall come and shall convince the world of sin. The ground of our sensible comfort in this action stands in the humiliation of our souls, when a man becometh out of love with his sin; when he, finding the body of sin about him, can say, 'Who shall deliver me from this bondage of corruption?' when this giveth him an edge to come unto Christ, for we must not think that we are thus ready to come, unless we be drawn by some scourge or other. The prodigal son, when he had wasted his goods riotously, if he might have had husks to keep his life and soul together, he would never have come home. So we, the sons of Adam, might we have but fig-leaves to cover our nakedness, we would never become suitors unto God for pardon. Here, then, examine; dost thou discern that without the receiving of his body and blood thou art like a man kept from meat and drink, and that thou art dead? If thou findest this, there is one step good; but if otherwise thou standest stoutly and thinkest that thou hast no need thereof, thou art an unworthy receiver. These are for matter of grace. The second point wherein a man must examine himself is,

2. *Whether upon the discerning of his wants, upon the discerning of that death which certainly belongeth unto him, he rely upon Christ; whether the Lord worketh upon his heart a true longing for that righteousness without* * *himself.*

When the Lord spreads his table to feast his friends, he calleth not them who have no kind of appetite, nor stomach; and therefore thou must examine thyself whether thou hast a stomach, an hungering after Christ Jesus. This is a special point, which certainly if a man find not, he may doubt whether he be sound or not. If a man have his victuals taken from him, he grows hungry and thirsty, is vexed and discontented. How then cometh it to pass that our bodily hunger is so sensible, when yet our soul's hunger is not felt of us? He that is in this estate, a-starving, and feels it, is not that man ready to die? Before we come therefore to the Lord's table, let us labour to get an appetite, for, I say, God thinketh such precious meat as this ill bestowed upon them that have no appetite unto it. We see worthy patterns in the Scriptures. David he says, 'As the hart panteth after the rivers of water, so my soul longeth after the living God,' Ps. xlii. 1. And, beloved, blessed is he that findeth this thirst, blessed are they, they shall be blessed. Contrary to this, whenas children play with their meat, it is time it should be taken from them. Their estate in this case is woful for the present. The *third* point whereupon a man must examine himself is,

3. *Whether these two grounds being laid* (that first he discerneth his misery, his death, that he is a dead man without he get Christ; and secondly, that he hungers and thirsts after him), *he setteth himself about it.*

For it is not sufficient for a man to hunger, and never go about the work; but as a hungry man is eager to feed, nothing should keep him from it. Here is the point, whether our hunger after righteousness putteth us so on that we will have it whatsoever it costs us. A man that is ready to die for hunger will give all that he hath rather than he will go without meat. Even so the soul, when it is once pinched and hunger-bit, and seeth bread in heaven, it presenteth itself before God, beggeth as for life that God would bestow his Son for cure. So that I may truly say, 'The kingdom of heaven suffers violence,' Mat. xi. 12, and nothing shall withhold the violent from taking it, when they come into the presence of God. The *fourth* point is,

4. *Whether* (upon this touch of conscience, upon this earnest hungering and thirsting after righteousness) *we presently can set forward without delay, and go to the throne of grace.*

That we consider our case is now like the case of him who had committed man-slaughter amongst the Jews, for whom there was appointed a city of refuge, unto which if he could fly before he was apprehended, he saved his life; if otherwise taken before he came thither, he was to die. Without question that man would make great haste thither. Examine then thyself

* That is, = outside of, independent.—G,

whether thy hungering after righteousness worketh this effect, that without all delay thou wilt come after Christ Jesus thy refuge and defence. It is not sufficient for thee to say, I know that without Christ I shall die ; I will do it to-morrow, when I have done other things, I will purchase his favour. Well ; boast not of to-morrow ; examine thyself whether thy hunger after righteousness be so great, that it will not suffer thee to rest or sleep till thou hast his favour. He that cometh thus affected, and that will make no delay, but be an earnest suitor unto God for his Son, that he may have Christ—though the request be great, the necessity yet is such a matter that we forget all good manners, and so presently do well ; and what do we then ? We take unto us words. Then a man cometh before the throne of grace ; but standeth he there mute ? No certainly. He that is partaker of Christ, and hath grace in his heart, standeth he there mute ? No ; but he can put up an elegant note in the ears of God, as it is said, Rom. viii. 26, 'We know not how to pray as we ought ; what shall we say then ?' Why, saith the apostle, 'If you are the sons of grace, the Spirit helpeth your infirmities, and maketh request for you with sighs and groans which cannot be uttered.' There is the point wherein we ought to examine our hearts, whether the Spirit of God hath made such an intercession in us ? that is, whether he hath made us able when we come into the presence of God, upon the consideration of his mercy, to send up a volley of sighs unto him ? whether we can fill heaven with our groans, and dart them upwards ? He that can do this, that when he presents himself before God (that knoweth the heart, who knoweth what is the meaning of his groans, what he would say, and is accepted of him) ; he that can find in himself the Spirit of prayer, that he can come before him, unwrap and shew his sores ; desire the Lord to pity him, and will never give him over till he hath graciously answered, and hath invited him—the Lord loveth such a suitor. Perhaps he will not give him a ready answer and despatch at first, but will have him attend. But if like Israel* he will still solicit him, till he have got the blessing, if he will take no denial ; the Lord hath said, and his word shall stand, 'Take my Son ;' this man may have full consolation ; this man hath grace. And then followeth,

5. *A setting of the heart upon the promises of God.*

That a man having discerned that God hath so compassed him with favour that he hath seen his misery ; that he hath seen a way to get out, and hath found a way to approach unto the throne of God ; he presently thereupon cometh unto God, looks whether or not he will hold forth unto him the golden sceptre. He seeth the Lord hath made him to beg Christ earnestly, and that he can confess his sins unto him ; then presently there cometh a setting of the heart upon the promises. Hath not God said, 'Blessed are they that hunger and thirst for righteousness : for they shall be satisfied,' Mat. v. 6. He hath given me but a cold answer ; but it is true, hath not he said, 'Come unto me, all ye that are weary and heavy laden, and I will ease you' ? Mat. xi. 28. I find but little ease, but I know that I am in his favour. He hath given unto me feet, affection, and an heart to come unto him ; and hereupon I will set mine affections. Howsoever he spurneth me, yet I know that he is just, and therefore will not be broken off. I know he is faithful, and therefore will forgive me. And hereupon the Christian setteth himself upon a settled resolution. Having considered the promise of God, he is persuaded 'that neither life nor death, principalities nor powers, things present nor things to come, shall separate him

* That is, Jacob. Cf. Genesis xxxii. 26, *seq.*—G.

from the love of Christ,' Rom. viii. 35, 38. And that man who is thus persuaded and assured by faith, though not by sense, whom God hath thus far carried, will thus reason the matter with himself. Well, I know that he that hath 'begun this good work will finish it,' Philip. i. 6. And therefore with this conclusion, I will come looking for an increase of grace. Now I see some life, some health, some strength; I will look for an increase of these; more life, more health, and more strength. Therefore I will come unto the Lord's table; this is a worthy receiver. *These concern our justification*, wherein a man must examine himself.

And take this; he that cometh without faith, that man cometh without his wedding garment, whom the master of the feast (when he cometh to take notice of the guests that are come) shall single out from the rest, and say, 'Bind him hand and foot, and cast him into everlasting torments,' Mat. xxii. 13. But a man will say, May not I read good books at home, the Bible or others? Ay, but thou shalt not have such a feast at home. He here provideth a feast; and when the feasters are set, he cometh and seeth them. Thus God is present here in these assemblies, and seeth of what disposition his guests are. Now when a man comes without his wedding garment, that putteth to the seal, but wanteth the writing, will not this make God to single him out? There is a day when he shall be mute. Know therefore, that this table is provided for God's friends, and therefore unless thou by faith canst know that thou art friends with God, thou canst have no comfort; therefore examine thyself, for before that thou findest thy heart settled, before thy sins are forgiven, thou art not fit. A man will say, Alas! I would, if I had it, give all the world for it, but alas! all is in vain; I have often sought for it; often groaned and shed many tears for it before God; and yet things go not as I would. And what then? Shall I abstain? No; if thou discernest that thou art weak, thou must come. This table is provided for them that are weak. And if thy faith be weak, if thou hast but the least grain of faith, thou must come. As the church in the Canticles, when she began to be sick, desired to be stayed with flagons, Cant. ii. 5; so when our souls are ready to faint, we must desire him to come unto us, to comfort us, to stay us. 'The Lord quencheth not the smoking flax, nor breaketh the bruised reed, Mat. xii. 20, but will make it grow to a great tree; only be thou patient, and wait the Lord's leisure. And thus much shall suffice to have spoken of the first point, wherein the affections must be examined; that is, upon the point of justification. We come now to the next point and matter, which is the grace of sanctification.

We must examine ourselves next in the grace of sanctification.

And for this, they that come must especially look unto it; for let us ask the question, Why will God provide a table? Why will he feed them? Is it not that they may do him service? Especially then examine thine own heart, whether thou art minded to serve God thyself, or the devil. Is there a man who saith, I will serve mine own turn, by hook or crook. I will get this? Is the table of the Lord, think you, provided for him? to strengthen him to do service against him? Thou that wouldst come unto the table, thou must remember thou art to be one of his family; he will have thee sit down with him. And doth he not then require that thou shouldst do him service? If then thou art ready to serve against him, if thou runnest into the camp of the enemy, to join with Satan against thy Maker, dost thou think that thou art fit to come? Nay, let me speak unto them that are profane, who break his Sabbaths and blaspheme his name. I say, that man who thus cometh with a covetous heart, if it be with resolution, I will not be broke off from it; take what sin thou wilt, if thou come with a resolution that thou wilt not part from it; when a man shall say, I will follow my course, this is a great sin. And I say that man taketh a cup of poison in his hands; I say, he that cometh with such a heart, proclaimeth war against him and killeth him, as Judas did. The Lord will not be mocked; and know this, that that man shall he be partaker of God's mercy? No; for he that partaketh of God's mercies cannot be profane. And it is as true, that that man who hath not holiness, whose heart is not set to please God, that that man shall never see God. The Papists cannot enforce this doctrine so much as we, because they be ignorant of the power and true life of holiness springing from the true ground thereof.

A wicked man, I say, shall have no benefit in the body and blood of Christ Jesus. This is a fearful saying, you will think. But it is true, that a man intending to live and die in his sin, and will not be broken off, shall have no portion in his body and blood. Was there ever any man who so much magnified the free mercy of God without works as the apostle Paul [did? yet he] saith, 'Whatsoever a man soweth, that shall he also reap. If to the flesh, of the flesh he shall reap corruption; if to the Spirit, of the Spirit he shall reap life everlasting,' Gal. vi. 7. Mark, saith the apostle, look you to this, if there be a man who soweth nothing but tares in the seed-time, and yet in the harvest will look for good corn, will we not think him mad? If thou hast sown good corn, thou mayest then expect good fruit; if otherwise, bad; accordingly as thou hast sown thou shalt reap. And will you deceive yourselves, that when you have sown to the flesh, you think to reap of the Spirit? Deceive not yourselves thus. And, Gal. v. 19, *seq.*, now, saith the apostle, 'The works of the flesh are manifest, which are adultery, fornication, uncleanness, wantonness, idolatry, witchcraft, hatred, debate, emulations, wrath, contentions, seditions, heresies, envy, murders, drunkenness, gluttony,' and such like. There is a black guard of them. Well, then, saith the apostle, do you think to reap the harvest of God's children, whilst you sow such fruits? No; I tell you now as before, they which do such things shall not inherit the kingdom of God. This shall not be reversed, but shall stand as firm as the law of the Medes and Persians, not to be revoked, Esther i. 19. Such wicked persons, as it is Rev. xxii. 15, shall be thrust out amongst the dogs, 'enchanters, whoremongers, murderers, and idolaters, and whosoever loveth or maketh lies.'

So now to come to the point: he that cometh unto the Lord's table, let him examine his heart, whether or not he be given unto these vices. Some will say, I am no Papist, no idolater; nay, I hate such; I am not envious. But the apostle here speaketh of all such things as are like them. Yea, he speaketh against such things as are accounted but petty matters, as envy, drunkenness. Oh! they say, some have not gentlemen's qualities, which cannot swear. But the apostle's words stand firm, that such shall not see God; their gentlemen-like qualities shall bring their souls to hell. When they have so malicious and quarrelsome spirits, when they have such proud contentious spirits, that men cannot live quietly amongst them, what fruit is this? What doth it argue but certainly this, that there is no grace in them, whenas their hearts are thus set against all men?

But you will say as in justification, so in this matter of sanctification, I thank God, I am not given to these gross Tyburn* matters, though mine heart telleth me that I have a great sink of corruption in me.

* That is, Tyburn, or the place of the gallows = great sins.—G.

I will then examine thee how dost thou stand affected towards sin? Hast thou shaken hands with it? hast thou shaken off familiarity with all sin, and not from some only? For so an hypocrite. But see whether there is not some sin remaining which thou wilt and dost make reckoning of. If it be to thee as a right eye, or as a right hand, Mat. v. 30, as our Saviour saith, look unto that especially, which is so dear and profitable that it bringeth in great wealth; see how thou standest affected to that. Art thou content, though it be as profitable as thy right hand, to have it chopped off? If thou findest this resolution to be in thee, thou art in a good estate; thy case is happy. This sheweth that there is good seed in thee. For it is impossible that there should be such a divorce betwixt thee and thy corruption, if grace were not in thy heart. A man then who cometh unto the Lord's table must consider and say, I have been wanting in the service of God; I have not been so careful in keeping of the Sabbath; I have not had that watchfulness over my corruptions. Well; I will now get me new strength; I will go to this table that I may be more strengthened in time to come, to fight afresh; that whereas I was weak and feeble before, I will now get strength. He that cometh with this resolution, if his heart can say, This I aim at, it is wonderful to think what profit the Lord will give unto him. If we say, we come to get strength to fight against Satan, and so forth, we shall prevail and obtain it. Would not a man think his meat ill bestowed on him whom it doth no good, who eateth and drinketh, and yet is never the better, whose meat is never seen by him. Even so he that cometh to the Lord's table, and yet thriveth not by that heavenly food there eaten, he discrediteth the same. It is with him as it was with the ill-favoured kine, Gen. xli. 1, *seq.*, who albeit they ate up seven others, yet they themselves were still so ill-favoured and lean, that it could not be seen that they had eaten anything. It is so with many poor Christians, who often feast and yet are never the better, remaining as lean as ever.

We must therefore have a care in this case that we discredit not those heavenly commons,* but we must find our strength increased. If before we could be able to beat down one sin, we must now be able to beat down three. Jonathan in the first of Samuel, when Saul was in the pursuit of his enemies, charging that they should taste no food till they had gotten the victory, hereupon saith he, 'My father hath troubled the people, because he hath forbidden them to eat, whereby their strength faileth,' 1 Sam. xiv. 19. So when God cometh to feed us, let us find strength, let us see, are not our eyes enlightened as were Jonathan's, being cleared after he had tasted a little honey? Have we not better hearts than before? Shall we not make a greater slaughter of our enemies than before? If we find this, what a hand shall we get over our enemies? Let us therefore eat, and so eat, that we labour to go 'forty days in the strength of this meat,' 1 Kings xix. 8, until we come to the full and final possession of Horeb, the mount of God; and so shall the Lord take delight to refresh us. We shall get new hearts, new courage, and we shall more and more tread down Satan under our feet; and, as the apostle speaketh, 'The God of peace shall at length tread him finally under our feet,' Rom. xvi. 20; when we shall have the blessed fruition of our dear Saviour, and the eternity of those unspeakable joys, to reign with him for ever. Which God grant, and that for Christ Jesus' sake! Amen.

* That is, 'meals.'—G.

JUDGMENT'S REASON.

JUDGMENT'S REASON.

NOTE.

The 'Two Sermons' from 1 Cor. xi. 30, 31, also appeared originally in the folio volume entitled 'The Saint's Cordials,' in the first—1629—edition of which they form Nos. 3 and 4. Their separate title-page therein is given below.* In the editions of the 'Saint's Cordials' of 1637 and 1658, they form Nos. 5 and 6, under a different title, which will also be found below.† Our text, as explained in note to 'Right Receiving,' follows the edition of 1629. Those of 1637 and 1658‡ are designated by the letters B and C respectively in the 'various readings' appended to each page. 'Readings' peculiar to C are noted by numerals 1, 2, &c. G.

* IVDGEMENTS
REASON.
In Two Sermons.
WHEREIN THAT GREAT QVESTION
IS DECIDED, AND THE AFFLICTED
SATISFIED ;

Why God sends so many crosses and troubles in this life ; both up his best Seruants ; and those who are not yet brought into the way of life.

[The woodcut of 'Right Receiving' here.]
VPRIGHTNESS HATH BOLDNES.
HEBR. 12. 10.

For, they verely for a few dayes, chastened us after their own pleasure : but hee for our profit, thot we might be partakers of his Holinesse.

LONDON,
Printed in the yeare 1629.

† The Art of
Self-Ivdging.
Delivered
In A Preparatory Sermon
To The Sacrament:
At Coleman-street Church in London.

By R. Sibbs D.D. Master of Katherine Hall in Cambridge
and preacher of Grayes Inne London.

The second Edition.
[Same woodcut as in 1629.]
Esay 57. 15.

For thus saith the high and lofty One, that inhabetith Eternity, whose Name is Holy; I dwell in the high and holy Place: with him also that is of a contrite and humble spirit, to revive the spirit of the humble and to revive the heart of the contrite ones.

London,

Printed for R. Dawlman, at the brazen Serpent in
Pauls Churchyard. 1637.

‡ The edition of 1658 is marked 'The Third edition,' and 'Printed for Henry Cripps at his shop in Popes head Alley. 1658.' It spells 'self' and 'street' with final 'e,' and substitutes a different woodcut. Cf. title-pages subjoined to note to 'Right Receiving.—G.

JUDGMENT'S REASON.

SERMON I.

For this cause many are weak and sick among you, and many sleep. For if we would judge ourselves, we should not be judged,' &c.—1 Cor. XI. 30, 31.

I nitend at this time especially to stand upon the duty of judging, as being fittest for the occasión.* But yet, by God's assistance, we† will take the words‡ in order, because I desire to speak somewhat of the other which follow.

'For this cause many are sick,' &c. After the holy apostle, the seedsman of God, had sown the seed of heavenly doctrine, Satan also by his instruments had sown his cockle of abuses among the Corinthians, of which, amongst many, this was one, to come irreverently to the holy communion. Whereupon God was forced to take them into his own hands; and lest they should be ignorant of the cause, the blessed apostle points them here, as it were with the finger, to the cause of the visitation among them, § for their irreverent and unprepared coming to the Lord's table, 'For this cause,' &c. In the words we will speak of,

1. The cause of the correction among them.
2. And then of the kinds of it: 'Many are sick, and weak, and sleep.'
3. And then of the care, if it had been used, that might have prevented those contagious sicknesses among them: 'If we would judge ourselves, we should not be judged.'

But lest God's children should despair when they are judged and sharply corrected of him, he adds, in the next place, the comfort; howsoever things fall out, our salvation is promoted. 'When we are judged,' and chastened of the Lord, 'it is that we should not be condemned with the world.'

First, *of the cause.* ‖

I will speak briefly of the former verse, but dwell most upon the next, of self-judging. 'For this cause many are weak and sick, and many sleep.' Observe here in the cause.

* That is, celebration of the sacrament. Cf. preliminary note †.—G.

† 'By . . . assistance' omitted in B, C, and for 'we' is substituted 'I.'—G.

‡ 'Text' in B, C; and the sentence, 'and speak somewhat of the other words.'—G.

§ 'Their unprepared coming,' &c., in B, C.—G.

‖ 'Observe here' in B, C, and 'I will speak . . . in the cause,' omitted.—G.

Doct. (1.) *First, when there is a cause, God will correct;* and *where there is this cause, he will correct,* that is, irreverent coming to the communion.

Doct. (2.) *Secondly, As there is a cause when God doth correct, so usually there is this or that particular cause.*

For the first, where there is cause he will correct, and where there is this cause. Where there is no cause he will not correct. 'For this cause.' There is always a cause, and a particular cause, [and a particular cause of God's judgment is]*

Quest. Why must there be alway a cause?

Ans. Because God is the judge of the world, and the judge of the world must needs do that which is right, Gen. xviii. 25. And therefore he will not judge without a cause.† We have ill in us, before we suffer ill. God is forced to mortify sins by afflictions, because we mortify them not by the Spirit, and in the use of holy means. There is a cause always.‡ God doth favours from his own bowels, and from his own nature; but he never correcteth without a cause from us. Corrections and judgments are always forced. It is a stranger[1] work to him than favours that come from his own nature as a gracious God, and therefore the cause of his judgment is always in us. But when he is beneficial to us, it comes from himself, as water comes from a fountain.

Instruction. This should teach us *in all visitations to justify God, and to take heed of that which our nature is prone to,* of swelling and murmuring, and rising up against God. Just thou art, and righteous are thy judgments. 'I will bear the wrath of the Lord, because I have sinned,' &c., as it is said, Micah vii. 9. Let us lay our hand upon our mouth, and justify God in all his visitations. There is a cause.

And not only a cause at random, but if we search ourselves there is this or that particular cause. So 2 Thes. ii. 10 it is said, 'For this cause God gave them up to strong delusions, because they entertained not the truth in the love of it.' There is a 'this;' for God shoots not his judgments, as children shoot their arrows, at random, light where they will; but he hath his aim.

Quest. How shall we find out that 'this'?

Ans. 1. *Our consciences will upbraid us.* If we be well acquainted with our consciences, we shall know it by them, as Joseph's brethren did. It was because they used their brother hardly many years before, Gen. xlii. 21.

2. Again, *what the word meets most with when we hear it.*

3. And *what our friends tell us most of.*

4. And *what our enemies upbraid us most with.*

5. *That we may know the cause, we may know the sin by the contrary.* God cures contraries with contraries. We may read ofttimes the cause in the judgment. Is the judgment *shame?* Then the cause was *pride.* Is the judgment *want?* Then our sin was in *abundance.* We did not learn to abound as we should when we had it. It is an ordinary rule, contraries are cured with contraries. Usually God meets with men, he pays them home in their own coin and kind. Those that have been unmerciful, they shall meet with those that shall shew them no mercy, &c.§ By searching into our own hearts, by considering these things, we may know what is the 'this,' the particular cause.

* The words enclosed added in B, C, intended to link on to the sentence interrupted by the question, Why, &c.—G.

† 'And therefore . . . cause,' omitted in B, C.—G.

‡ 'There is . . . always,' omitted in B, C.—G.

[1] 'Strange' in C—G.

§ The '&c.' characteristic of Sibbes's style omitted in B, C.—G.

And, if we fail in the search, then go to God, that he would teach us, as well as he corrects us, as usually he doth his children: Ps. xciv. 12, 'Blessed is the man that thou correctest and teachest.' Desire God that unto correction he would add teaching, that we may know what the meaning of the rod and of the cross is. Whatsoever it is, if we join prayer with the other means, we may know the 'this,' the particular sin that God aims at. So you see these things * clear, that there is a cause, and usually the 'this,' some particular cause.

Doct. (3.) The next point is that *where there is a cause, God will correct first or last*, and where there is this cause mentioned, irreverent coming to the communion, he will do it because he is just. If we prevent † it not by repentance, and so afflict our souls, surely we must fall into God's hands. He will lose the glory of none of his attributes. Where there is a cause he will correct. Sin is against his nature, against his truth, against his manner of dealing with us by favours and benefits, and therefore he will correct us.

For even as smoke goes before fire, and as conception goes before birth, and as seed-time goes before harvest; so sin goes before some correction or other universally, ‡ unless it be those daily infirmities that God's children fall into, those sins of daily incursion, as we call them. When we labour to knit our hearts fast and close to God, some infirmities slip from us that God overlooks; he takes not notice of every slip; § he bears with our infirmities 'as a father bears with a son that serves him,' Mal. iii. 17. And yet if we allow ourselves in any infirmity, we shall not go unpunished. ‖ Infirmities are one thing, and allowance and defence of them is another. Therefore I beseech you make this use of it. ¶

Use. Take heed of sinning upon this false conceit, We shall escape, we shall never hear of it again. No; it will be owing first or last. As we say of those that make bold with their bodies, to use them hardly, to rush upon this thing and that thing: in their youth, they may bear it out, but it will be owing them after; they shall find it in their bones when they are old. So a man may say of those that are venturous persons, that make no conscience of running into sin, these things will be owing to them another day; they shall hear of these in the time of sickness, or in the hour of death. And therefore never sin upon vain hope of concealing; for as there is a cause alway, and 'this cause,' so where there is a cause, God will correct his own children.

Again, *where there is this cause, God will visit.* What was this cause? This cause was irreverent, unprofitable coming to the holy table of the Lord. Why, is this so great a matter as to provoke God's judgment? Oh, yes! Favours neglected provoke anger most of all.

Is it not a great favour for the great God to condescend[1] to help our weakness in the sacrament? Is it not a special favour that he will stoop to strengthen our weak faith this way? And shall we, when he condescends to us, rise up in pride against him, and forget our distance, forget with whom we have to deal? No; God will be honoured of all that come near him; if not by them, yet in them. Those that come not to God now

* 'See it clear that there is a cause, and usually some particular cause' in B, C.—G.
† That is, 'anticipate.'—G.
‡ This reads more accurately in B, C: 'So some sin or other goes before correction universally.'—G.
§ 'From us' in C.—G. ‖ 'For infirmities' in B, C.—G.
¶ 'Therefore . . . use of it' omitted in B, C.—G. [1] 'To descend' in C.—G.

in Christ, a Father, they know not his goodness; and those that come irreverently, know not his greatness and majesty. Take heed, therefore, when we come before God, that we come not with strange fire, as Nadab and Abihu; that we come not irreverently and unpreparedly, with carnal affections; but that we converse in holy business with holy affections. Is it not a great pity that those things which God hath ordained for the comfort of our souls, and the help of our faith, that we by our carelessness should turn them to our hurt, as we do by an irreverent coming to the holy things of God? We procure our own judgments, and therefore we ought to help this irreverent demeanour and carriage of ourselves in the holy things of God by all means, with the consideration of his majesty, and our dependence upon him;* and such considerations, which I cannot now enter into, because I hasten. So you see these things clear, *the cause*, and the particular cause, *this cause.*

To go on *to the kinds* therefore. The kinds are set down in three degrees:

1. Some are weak.
2. And some sick.
3. And some sleep.

Nay, 'many are sick and weak, and many sleep.' Here are three degrees, like the three degrees of sin amongst them. Some are more presumptuous than other, and,

Doct. 4. *God, who made all in number, weight, and measure, dispenseth all in number, weight, and measure.* Some are weak, and some are sick, which is greater; and some sleep, that is, die.† Even as in the commonwealth, those that are discreet governors have degrees of punishment, as the stocks, the prison, and the gibbet, violent death, and the like; so God, the great Governor of heaven and earth, according to the different degrees of sin, hath different degrees of correction.

A physician loves all his patients alike, but he doth not minister sharp potions alike to all; but out of the same love there is a different carriage of the same, according to the exigent‡ of the party. So doth the wise God. 'Some are weak, and some sick, and some sleep.'

Doct. 5. Again, we may observe here, that *sickness and weakness of the body come from sin, and is a fruit of sin.* Some are weak, and some are sick, 'for this cause.' I shall not need to be long in the proof of that, which you have whole chapters for, as Deut. xxviii. 27, *seq.;* and many psalms, cvii., and others.§ It is for the[1] sickness of the soul that God visits with the sickness of the body. He aims at the cure of the soul in the touch of the body. And therefore in this case, when God visits with sickness, we should think our work is more in heaven with God than with men or physic. Begin first with the soul. So David, Ps. xxxii. 5, till he dealt roundly with God, without all kind of guile, and confessed his sins, he roared; ‖ his moisture was turned into the drought of summer. But when he dealt directly and plainly with God, and confessed his sins, then God forgave him them, and healed his body too. And therefore the best method, when God visits us in this kind, is to think that we are to deal with God. Begin the cure there with the soul. When he visits the body, it is for the soul's sake: 'Many are weak and sick among you.' We see what taber-

* 'And the like' in B, C; and 'which I cannot . . . this cause' omitted.—G.

† 'Which is greatest of all' added in B, C.—G.

‡ That is, 'exigency.'—G.

§ Cf. Mat. ix. 2, Luke vii. 47.—G.

‖ 'And' in B C.—G.

[1] 'The' not in C.—G.

nacles of dust we carry about us, that if we had no outward enemy, yet God can raise that in our own bodies that shall cast out the greatest giant, 'weakness and sickness,' that we may learn to fear God, in whose hand is both health and sickness. And it should teach us to make precious use of our health while we have it. It were a thousand times better for many persons to be cast on the bed of sickness, and to be God's prisoners, than so scandalously and unfruitfully to use the health that they have: 'many are weak and sick.'*

Doct. 6. The sin was general, and God's visitation was as general. *When sins grow general, corrections grow general.* It is an idle and vain excuse that many think to make to themselves, The world doth thus; others do thus. Oh! there is the more danger of a spreading and general visitation! Do others so? Is it a spreading sin? Take heed of a spreading and contagious punishment. We must not follow a multitude to do evil, Exod. xxiii. 2. He is not a whit the less[1] tormented that is tormented with company. The plea therefore that they make from many, that the world doth thus, it should rather, if they did wisely reason, move them to take heed. 'Many are sick and weak, and many sleep,' saith he;† that is, many even die. God takes away the life of many for the irreverent coming to[2] the holy things of God. So that sin brings with it death itself, not only at the last, but sin it shortens a man's days; and this kind of sin, irreverent coming to the holy things of God, shortens our days, and puts out our own candle, and pulls our own houses about our ears. They are felons upon themselves, soul-murderers and body-murderers, that wilfully commit sin; yea, if it be this sin in the holy things of God, not only if they commit gross sins, but if they commit this sin, if they be careless and unconscionable‡ in the performance of this holy duty. If any other did us the thousand part of that harm we do ourselves by a careless life, a loose and lawless kind of course, we would not bear them. We see here what hurt we do ourselves [what injury, what wrong we do to our own souls and bodies also];§ for 'for this cause many are weak and sick, and many sleep.'

We are the greatest enemies to ourselves. We cry out of Judas and Ahithophel that made away themselves, and we may well. Every stubborn man, that goes on in a course of sin, and forgets with whom he hath to deal, he is like Judas and Ahithophel; he is an enemy to himself, and a murderer of himself. Oh! take heed therefore of the Devil's baits; meddle not with this pitch; touch it not; hate all shows and appearances of evil.

Doct. 7. Again, it is not to be forgotten here that he saith, 'Many of *you*,' that is, 'you, believing Corinthians;' whence learn, that *God will correct sin wheresoever he finds it, even in his dearest children;* nay, he will correct them more sharply in this world, because he will save their souls in another world, than he will others. The careless, brutish‖ world, that are not worthy of correction, God lets them go on in smooth ways to hell; but 'many of you,' &c. Let none think to be exempt, and venture themselves from grace they have. No. God will look to those of his family, that are near him;¶ he will have a special eye to them, he will have his

* Not given in B, C.—G.
† 'Saith he' omitted in B, C.—G.
‡ That is, 'unconscientious.'—G.
§ Added in B, C.—G.
‖ 'Brutish' omitted in B, C.—G.
¶ 'That are near him' omitted in B, C.—G.
1 'The less' is blunderingly omitted in C.—G.
2 'Of' in C, another misprint.—G.

family* well ordered: 'You have I known of all the nations of the world,' saith he, 'and therefore I will be sure to punish and to correct you,' Amos iii. 2. Let none therefore bear themselves upon their profession, I do thus and thus, so many good things, therefore I may be bold; nay, therefore, you may be the less bold. Moses cannot so much as murmur at the waters of strife, but he must not come into Canaan, Num. xx. 2. David cannot have a proud thought of numbering the people, but he must smart for it, 1 Chron. xxi. 2. The Corinthians cannot come irreverently to the communion, 'but for this cause many are weak and sick.'

I beseech you, let us take it to heart, and let no profane person take encouragement because God so deals with his own: 'If God deal thus with the green tree, what will he do with the dry?' 'If judgment begin at the house of God, where shall the sinner and ungodly appear?' 1 Pet. iv. 18. If the godly taste of the cup of God's anger, the wicked must drink off the dregs of his wrath. And therefore let no man take offence that God follows the church with crosses, that the cross follows the poor church in the world. Alas! they carry corruptions about them continually. We see here,† 'you, many of you,' &c. Let us therefore labour to make an end of our salvation with fear and trembling, the best of us all.

Doct. 8. One thing more before I leave this; that is, *how God in justice remembereth mercy.* 'Many,' he saith not, 'all,' and 'many of you are *weak;*' he takes not all away with death. It is a mercy, then, that the correction is outward in the body, weak in body, and sick. There was not a spiritual giving up to hardness of heart. Beloved! if we consider what kind of judgments spiritual judgments are, to have a seared conscience, and a hard and desperate heart, which are forerunners of hell and of eternal judgment and damnation, we would much prize mercy in judgment. Oh! it is not so with God's church. Their visitations are in the outward man; they are weak, and sick, and die, but God is merciful to their souls, as we shall see after.[1] And it should be an art we should learn and labour to be expert in, to consider God's gracious dealing in the midst of his correction;‡ that in the midst of corrections § we might have thankful, and cheerful,‖ and fruitful hearts, which we shall not have, except we have some matter of thankfulness. Consider, doth God make me weak? He might have struck me with death, or if not taken away my mortal life, he might have given me up to a spiritual death, to a hard heart, to desperation, &c. So let us search out in the visitations that we are in, always some matter of mitigation, and we shall always find that it might have been worse with us than it is.¶ So much shall serve for that verse, that is, the cause and the kinds, 'For this cause many are weak and sick, and many sleep.' Now I come to *the cure.*

'If we would judge ourselves, we should not be judged.'

This course, if it had been used by the Corinthians, they might have prevented their weakness, sickness, and over-timely** death; and so we, if we take the course prescribed by the apostle here, may prevent the like; and perhaps God will not now, in this dispensation that he useth in the latter end of the world, outwardly visit us, for now usually his dispensation and government is more inward. And therefore we should take the more

* 'Them' in B, C.—G.
† 'As we see here' in B, C.—G.
‡ 'Corrections' in B, C.—G.
§ 'That in them' in B, C.—G.
‖ 'Cheerful' omitted in B, C.—G.
¶ 'This shall serve for the cause' in B, C; and 'So much . . . sleep' omitted.—G.
** That is, 'untimely' or 'premature.'—Ed.
[1] 'Hereafter' in C.—G.

heed to what followeth; he may give us up, I say, to blindness, to deadness, to security. He doth not usually give men up to sickness, and to death, now, for such breaches, but his government is more spiritual. Indeed then, for the terror of all, his government was more outward in the primitive times of the church. To come therefore to that I mean to speak of: *the cure of all is judging*. There is a judge set up in our own hearts. 'If we would judge ourselves, we should not be judged of the Lord.' To open the words a little.*

That which is translated here 'judging,' is by the best expositors, one and other,[1] and according to the nature of the word, 'if we would *discern* of ourselves,' 'if we would *try* ourselves,' and have our senses exercised to distinguish what is good, and what is ill in us, and then to fall upon judging, trial, and discussing. The word signifieth primarily 'to discuss,' and 'to sift,' and then 'to censure' upon that; and then after, 'To sever ourselves from the ill we censure.' The word implies all these duties.†

God hath so framed man, that he alone of all other creatures can work upon himself; he hath this reflexed act, as we call it, he can examine, judge, try, and humble himself; other creatures look straight forwards. Man, I say, can discern and put a difference; he can discern of relations; this and that hath relation to such and such a thing. The beast cannot discern of relations:‡ the beast goes to the water, and to the fodder, but knows not what relation that hath to spiritual things. But man, when he sees the sacrament, he can think of Christ; when he seeth one thing, he can think of this relation to more spiritual things. So he can discern of himself, and of the things he takes in hand, by a principle that God hath put into him peculiar to himself. Now God hath set up in a man a judgment-seat, wherein things should be judged, before they come to this scanning and judgment. We ourselves are the parties judged, and we should be the judges; we are the parties that examine, and the parties examined; we are the parties that condemn, and the parties condemned. This is the power of conscience, that God hath made his vicegerent and deputy in us. But to acquaint you with what things I mean to speak of, as the time will give leave.

Doct. 9. [1.] *First of all*, out of these words, *the cure I will shew;* that naturally we are very backward to this duty, because the Corinthians here were failing in the duty.§

[2.] *Secondly*, I will shew you the necessity, profit, and use of this self-judging.

[3.] Then of the time when we should judge especially; when we are to deal with God in holy things.

[4.] And then,‖ what to do after all, when we have judged ourselves; what course to take then. The unfolding of these things will help us to understand this great point that is so necessary.

[1.] First of all, *naturally we are wondrous backward to this duty*, as we see here in the Corinthians; they slubbered over this duty of examination and self-judging.

Quest. What is the reason?

Sol. The reason is, *it is an inward act;* and naturally we look to outward glorious things. There is no glory in it before the world; it is in God,

* 'To open . . . little' omitted in B, C.—G.

† The word is διακρίνω, on which consult Robinson, *sub voce*, and cf. Hodge and Stanley, and Webster and Wilkinson, *in loc.*—G.

‡ 'Relation' in B, C.—G.

§ 'Because . . . duty' omitted in B, C.—G.

‖ 'Then' omitted in B, C.—G.

[1] 'Another' in C.—G.

and his own soul, and usually the life of careless persons, even of Christians sometimes, it is spent outwardly; they never enter into their own souls to see what is there.

Again, *naturally we rest in the judgment of others.* Others conceive well of us, and therefore we conceive well of ourselves. Remember they are but our fellow-prisoners. What can they excuse, if God accuse and condemn us? Those things that make us most odious to God are undiscernible of the eye of man, as a proud heart, a revengeful spirit, an earthly disposition, and the like; no man can see these things.

Again, usually we rest in this, *that we have wit enough to judge others.* The proud nature of man thinks itself somebody, when it can get up and judge others perhaps better than itself. This is a poor contentment, and an easy thing for a man to spend his censures upon others, and is done usually with some glory. It is necessary sometimes to those that are under us, to discover to them what we judge of their ways, but ofttimes, I say, it is done only of self-love and pride.

Again, *we are backward to this duty.* Hence that the heart of man is a proud piece of flesh; and therefore he is loath to be conceited* of himself as there is cause. Man naturally would be in [a] fool's paradise. He knows if he enters deeply into himself, somewhat will be presented to the eye of his soul that will be an ungrateful object to him; and therefore, because he will not force upon himself other conceits of himself than he hath for the present, he is content never to examine his courses, but to go on still. As there are some creatures in the world deformed, that are loath to come to the water, because they will not see their deformity in it; so it is with the nature of man, he is loath to see his deformity, he is willing to be deceived. In other things we are loath to be mistaken, but in our state between God and us, we are willing to be deceived. We deceive ourselves, we are sophisters unto ourselves, in this great point. Thus we see that it is a duty to which we are very backward, and that it is something hard, because, I say,† it reflects upon ourselves, and requires retiring; for naturally we are slothful and idle; and then sin it loves corners, which makes it harder.

Now, what is this sifting and searching of the heart, but a searching of all the corners of the soul by the light of God's word and Spirit? A searching of all the corners of the heart. This requires much pains. Naturally we are loath to take pains with our own souls, though indeed this be a preventing pains, to shun a worse misery hereafter; there is nothing gotten by favouring ourselves. What need I be large in this point? It is clear that naturally we are loath to judge ourselves, as we shall see hereafter.‡ Oh! if the worst man had that judgment of himself, as he shall have ere long, when he shall not be besotted, but be free from his spiritual drunkenness and madness that he is in, carried with the course of the world, then he shall judge truly of himself. Oh! that he could do it in time. But naturally, I say, what for negligence, and what for pride, and resting in the conceits that others have of us, we neglect so necessary a duty.

Well, then, to go to the second point: as we are prone to neglect it, so we must know,

Doct. 10. *That it is a necessary and useful duty to judge ourselves:* for it is the ground of all repentance, Jer. viii. 6. He complains that they rushed as[1] 'a horse into the battle, and no man said, what have I done?'

* That is = to conceive.—G. † 'I say' omitted in B, C.—G.

‡ 'It is clear . . . of himself' omitted in B, C.—G.

[1] 'As,' by a misprint, not in C.—G.

Quest. What was the reason they rushed as a horse into the battle?

Sol. No man entered into himself and said, What have I done? I considered my ways, and turned my feet to thy testimonies, saith David, Ps. cxix. 59. Consideration is the ground therefore of repentance and conversion. Thus in discussing of our ways, and trial of them, and of every good work, there must be this judging, this discerning, what is spirit and what is flesh. A man cannot do a good work without the use of this principle that God hath put into him, of judging himself, and judging his ways.

And then again, *it is a duty that makes a man good in himself:* for when we do outward good duties, they are good for others. If a man be bountiful, another hath the benefit; if he be merciful, another hath the profit; but when a man judgeth himself, and sets up a court in himself, his own soul is the better for it; he is the more holy man, the more watchful man, the more clear from his sins; he is the fitter framed for holy duties; it is the better for his own self; and therefore this duty it is the spring of all other good duties, and it is most beneficial to a man's own soul.

Again, *this is such a duty as doth settle the judgment, and make us impregnable in temptation.* When we have passed a judgment upon ourselves, let this or that judgment be, we care not; for we have judged ourselves as we should by the rule. We know what we have done, we know what we have said, we are able to justify it: it makes us ready and able to give an account to God, and to the world for what we do. But what, should I go further than the text? Here is a special good use it hath: if we judge ourselves, we shall not be judged of the Lord. This judging of ourselves, it* prevents a further judgment.

Quest. How is that?

Ans. First of all, because we spare God a labour. When we judge ourselves, he need not take us in hand to judge us. His corrections and his statutes are often called judgments in the Psalms.† Now upon the neglect of his judgments‡ and statutes, we run into his judgments and corrections; yet if we were careful of our duty, we might prevent the judgments of correction.§

Then again, *things judged in one court cannot be judged in another by equity.* Now‖ the God of all justice and equity will surely strictly observe equity. When our sins are judged in an inferior court; when in the court of conscience we have cited, indicted ourselves before ourselves, and given sentence upon ourselves, before ourselves,¶ then what is** condemned in this lower court of conscience, it shall never be condemned for hereafter: and, therefore, the necessity of this duty issues hence; 'if we judge ourselves, we shall not be judged.'

Quest. What is the ground that men are judged with the judgment of correction?††

Sol. We may learn hence, that we may thank ourselves for not returning into our souls. I was careless of setting up a court in my‡‡ own heart; careless in using those abilities that God hath given me to discern, to

* The 'it,' which with other pronouns is a characteristic in this use of Sibbes, as of his contemporaries, omitted in B, C—G.

† Cf. Ps. x. 5; xix. 9; xxxvi. 6; lxxii. 1; cxix. 7, *et alibi*.—G.

‡ 'Judgments and' omitted in B, C.—G.

§ 'Yet if . . . of correction' omitted in B, C.—G.

‖ 'Now' omitted in B, C.—G.

¶ 'Before ourselves,' omitted in B, C.—G.

** 'Was' in B C.—G.

†† The question 'What,' &c., omitted in B, C.—G.

‡‡ 'Mine,' in B, C.—G.

understand my* own ways. I have been careless there; and because I did not judge myself, it is just with God to judge me. We see here the necessity from the text: when we judge ourselves, we shall not be judged; therefore, when we are judged, we have been negligent in this duty of judging ourselves.†

Well, to hasten;‡ if this be so, if it be a duty that we are backward to, and yet it is a holy and useful duty, then we come, in the next place, to some directions how to carry ourselves in it.

(1.) First, in judging ourselves, *let us call and cite ourselves before ourselves*, and fall to a reckoning both with our persons and the state wherein we stand, and likewise the actions that come from us; what is good in us, and what is ill; what omitted, and what committed; what corruption is mingled with our best performances, and such like, as we shall see after. First, call ourselves to a reckoning, and see whether we can give account to ourselves or no. And if we cannot give account to ourselves, much less can we to the all-seeing eye and justice of God. I would fain have a worldling give account to himself, why the elder he grows the more worldly he should be; he cannot give an account to himself for it. I would have a profane swearer give account to himself, why he dallies with the great and terrible majesty of God, as if he were greater than he, when he pronounceth 'that he will not hold him guiltless that taketh his name in vain,' Exod. xx. 7. I would fain know of those that spend the prime of their time and years in the service of the devil, and bring their rotten old age to God, what account they can give to their own hearts. I would have any sinner, that lives in a course of sin, give account to his own heart: thou wretched man, canst thou not give an account to thyself? God is greater than thy heart; how dost thou think to stand before the judgment-seat of God ere long? The first thing, therefore, is to arraign ourselves at our own bar. I exclude not others that have calling to examine others, but especially present ourselves.

(2.) And when we find anything amiss, *then besides this arraigning of ourselves, we must give sentence against ourselves.* That is the second thing in discussing: as David, Ps. lxxiii. 22, 'So foolish was I, and as a beast,' when he had entertained a thought that God neglected his church, and regarded it no more; he had a dishonourable thought of God raised in his heart. 'Oh,' saith he, 'I was ashamed, so foolish, and so like a beast was I.' And so you have the prodigal; and Dan. ix. 4, *seq.*, and Ezra ix. 6. *seq.*, for examples how to pass a censure upon ourselves, when we find anything amiss; and labour that those affections that are in us towards ill, as grief, and shame, and sorrow, may be stirred up in us, by setting ourselves in grief, and shame, and sorrow, as we should, to turn the stream of our affections the right way.

When we find anything amiss in our own hearts, when we have given sentence and judgment upon ourselves;§

(3.) Then proceed *to execution:* let them go together, judgment and execution. This the apostle calls an holy revenge, 2 Cor. vii. 11. If we have been proud, let us abase ourselves. If we have been base in the duties of charity and good works to others, let us now, as Zaccheus, labour for the contrary, Luke xix. 8. If we have misspent our precious time, let us labour

* 'Mine' in B, C—G.

† The sentence 'We see here,' &c., omitted in B, C—G.

‡ 'To hasten,' and 'If this be so,' not in B, C, and reads simply, 'If this be a duty,' &c.—G.

§ The sentence 'When we find,' &c., omitted in B, C—G.

now to redeem the time, to do the contrary good. This course we ought to take.

And for the things that we ought to sift, and to try, and to judge, they are not only our persons, but whatsoever comes from us: we are to judge all our actions, not only our[1] ill actions, but our good actions. There is much dross mingled with our gold: let us examine our best actions. Nay, and not only our outward, but go to the very root. When we find a fault in any outward action, follow it to the very corrupt spring. Those that have a plant, that bears venomous fruit, they dig it at the root; so when any bad fruit comes from us, go to the root, strike there at it; follow sin to its burrow, its first hatching place, to the very heart. Thus David doth, Ps. li. 5: he goes to his birth sin. What, should I speak, saith he, of the sins that I have committed? 'In sin was I conceived.' In all actual sins look to the corrupt root and puddle whence they come; as, Oh, what is this word that I have spoken? what is this action? I have a corrupt nature, that is ready to yield to an hundred such upon the like occasion; and thereupon go to the heart, and to* the soul, and censure that; for that is worse than any particular act whatsoever.

Take heed of laying the fault upon this occasion, or that occasion,† *when we find ourselves faulty.* No. Say it was thou, my proud heart! it was thou, mine angry heart! my base worldly heart! The occasion did but help; the principal was mine own heart. Let us labour, therefore, to be acquainted thoroughly with our heart, that is wondrous unfaithful. There is a mystery of deceit in it.

What is the reason that God's children sometimes fall into sins that they never thought of, and that naturally they are not prone to?

Sol. Because there is no man that sufficiently knows the depth of the falsehood of his own heart. For Moses to become an angry man, that was the meekest man on earth, it was strange, yet at the waters of strife he brake forth into passion, Num. xx. 10. For David, that had his heart touched for cutting off the lap of Saul's garment, it was strange to come to murder, 1 Sam. xxiv. 5, 2 Sam. xi. 15, *seq.* Now, who would have thought that murder had lodged in David's heart? For Peter, that loved Christ so much, to come to deny and to forswear his Master; who would have thought that forswearing had lurked in the heart of Peter? Mat. xxvi. 72. Beloved! we know not what corruption lurks in our hearts. Nay, sometimes we shall find, if we search our hearts narrowly, those corruptions therein that at other times we are not prone to, so deceitful is our heart. And therefore, in all breaches outwardly, in speech or carriage, be sure to run to the heart to condemn sin, and to strike at it there.

Well, thus we see some directions how to carry ourselves. *It is not, beloved, the having of corruption that damns men, but the affections we carry towards our corruptions.* The best of us have corruptions, but mark how we do carry ourselves towards them. A carnal man pleads for his corruptions, he strengthens them; and another man hath corruption, but it is hardly used. Corruption is differently used in the heart of a carnal and of a gracious man, for in the one it is fostered, cherished, and pleaded for: in a civil, carnal man;‡ in the other man it is indeed, but it is subdued and mortified, it is judged and condemned. As we say of a man, when judgment is passed upon him, he is a dead man, though he be not dead, because the sentence of death is passed upon him, who, when he comes to

[1] Misprinted 'for' in C.—G.
* 'To' not in B, C.—G.
† 'Upon this or that occasion' in B, C.—G.
‡ 'In a civil . . . man' omitted in B, C.—G.

be executed, by little and little he dies, till he be perfectly dead; so it is when corruption is judged by us and condemned in our hearts, it is as it were dead, because we have passed the sentence on it, we have condemned it, and because[1] we have begun the execution that shall end in death; and therefore, as we would difference ourselves from the world, let us labour more and more, that though we have corruption, yet to carry ourselves thus towards it, to make it more hateful by all means. We cannot make it too hateful to us; it doth us all the mischief in the world; it is the ill of ills. All other ills are but the fruits[2] of it; it puts a fiery, venomed sting into all things; it makes things comfortable uncomfortable: as the hour of death, that should be thought on as our entrance into heaven; and the day of judgment, the consideration whereof should be our joy. What makes these things terrible? Oh! it is sin, the sin that we cherish and love better than our souls; it is that that makes things that are most comfortable uncomfortable. What a thing is that that makes us afraid to go to God! to think of a gracious God! that hinders us in our best performances! that makes us backward and dull! Labour, by all means, to make sin odious, I say. In the best commonwealth in the world there will be lurking rebels, base people. What! doth the commonwealth bear the blame? No. The laws are against them, and they are executed when they are found out. So in the best heart there will be rebellious thoughts, evil thoughts, but let it not be laid to the charge of God's people. There are laws against them; they labour to find them out and to execute them. Here is the comfort of God's children, that though they groan under many infirmities, yet they look upon them as enemies, and as objects of their mortification.

Well, to hasten: again, in judging ourselves, *let us labour to judge ourselves for those things that the world takes no notice of;* for spiritual, for inward things: as for stirring of pride, of worldliness, of revenge, of security, unthankfulness, and such like; unkindness towards God, barrenness in good duties, that the world cannot see. Oh, let these humble our hearts! For want of judging ourselves for these, God gives us up to outward breaches, and justly too. When we make not conscience of spiritual sins, God gives us up to open sins, that stain and blemish our profession.

Again, *for the sins in good duties.* Take heed in our best performances that we be not deceived in them. Poison is dangerously taken in sweet gloves, and in sweet things, because it is conveyed in sweetness; and so in holy duties there is conveyed pride and resting in them. Take heed, lest corruption mingle some deadly thing with our best performances.

The Corinthians came to the table of the Lord; but because they thought the duty a good duty,* and that they might not sin in a good duty, they came hand over head, carelessly [unto it].† Oh, but we see how God deals with them. And therefore, let us examine, in good duties and performances, with what minds we come, with what preparation, with what aims and ends [we perform them].‡ Many thousands, we may fear, are damned even for good duties; for § duties that are not ill in themselves, because they think they may be bold there, and put off the power of grace, and rest in common civil things, [even] ‖ in outward performances. When we regard not the manner, God regards not the matter of the things we do,

* 'But because they thought the duty good,' in B, C.—G.
† 'Unto it' added in B, C.—G
‡ Added in B, C.—G.
§ 'For because they are not ill in themselves,' &c., in B, C.—G.
‖ 'Even' added in B, C.—G.
[1] 'Therefore because' in C.—G.
[2] 'Fruit' in C.—G.

but oftentimes punisheth for the performance of good duties, as we see here in the Corinthians. But to proceed.

Let us observe some helps to all this that we have spoken. To help us, let us get a *good rule.** Let the rule of our judging and discerning be digested into our hearts; let the word of God be engrafted into us; that is the word that we must judge by, that we must be saved or damned by ere long; [as]† for false rules, the practice of the world, our own imaginations, away with them. We must not judge by those, but by the truth of God; and,‡ therefore, be sure of this, that so the rule and our souls may be one, that we may have the rule as ready as any corruption and as any sin is; when anything ariseth in our hearts, that the word engrafted in our hearts may be ready to check it presently. An unlearned judge oftentimes may mar all, whatsoever the cause be, though never so good. So, when the judgment is not instructed, an ignorant person can never manage his own soul. Let us labour for knowledge, that we may be learned in this judicature and judgment§ of ourselves.

Quest. What is the reason that many good souls are ready to bear false witness against, and to condemn themselves for what they should not?

Sol. (1.) *Sometimes they condemn their state,‖ and think [that]¶ they are not the children of God, when they are.* They want judgment out of God's book. Because they have corruption in them, they conclude that they have no grace; because they have but little grace, therefore they have none at all; as if God's glory were not to shew his strength in the midst of their weakness, and so, for want of judgment out of the Scriptures, they lay a plaster upon a sound place, and a true man is condemned for a traitor. Just persons condemn themselves in their courses that are gracious, for want of a sanctified and good judgment. Let us labour to have our judgment rightly instructed out of God's word, and in the use of all good means, grow in knowledge, that we may be discerning Christians, to judge between the flesh and the spirit,[1] between good and bad, to have our senses exercised in this kind.

Sol. (2.) *And not only to have the law, but to know the gospel too.* To know in what estate Christians should be under the gospel, not to look to legal breaches altogether, but what the gospel requires; not only how short we are of the law (which we can never attain to),** but of that which we might attain to in the gospel. Let us bring ourselves to that which we might be, and which others have attained to, to the view of others better than ourselves, and this will make us to judge ourselves. But, as I said before, let us labour to know the sins against the gospel; let us know what condition of life is required under the gospel: a fruitful life and a thankful. Our whole life should be nothing but thankfulness under the gospel, and fruitfulness; we should be inflamed with the love of Christ. Oh! take heed of turning that grace of God into wantonness. Oh! would we have fresh evidence of the love of God in Christ?†† Take heed of sins against the gospel; know what the conversation of a Christian should be, to walk worthy of the gospel, worthy of the high calling of a Christain. The state of the gospel requires that we should deny all ungodliness and worldly lust, and live righteously, and soberly, and godly, &c., Titus ii. 12; that we

* 'To help . . . rule' not in B, C.—G.
† 'As' inserted in B, C.—G.
‡ 'And' omitted in B, C.—G.
§ 'And judgment' not in B, C.—G.
‖ 'Estate' in B, C.—G.
¶ 'That' added in B, C.—G.
** 'Unto' in B, C.—G.
†† 'Of his favour' in B, C.—G.
[1] 'The flesh and the spirit' not in C.—G.

be earnest, and zealous of good works. When we find ourselves otherwise, think, Oh! this is not the life of a Christian under the gospel. The gospel requires a more fruitful, more zealous carriage, more love to Christ. 'Anathema maranatha' belongs to him that loves not the Lord Jesus, 1 Cor. xvi. 22; and therefore, when we find any coldness to so gracious a God, and so blessed a Saviour, let us condemn ourselves.

Sol. (3.) *And take the benefit likewise of the judgment of others, if we would learn to judge ourselves thoroughly;* consider what others say; it is one branch of the communion of saints to regard the judgment of others. Oh, it is a blessed thing to have others tell us of our faults, and as it were to pull us out of the fire with violence, as Jude speaketh, 23; rather to pull us out with violence, with sharp rebukes, than we should perish and be damned in our sins. If a man be to weed his ground, he sees need of the benefit of others; if a man be to demolish his house, he will be thankful to others for their help; so he that is to pull down his corruption, that old house, he should be thankful to others that will tell him, This is rotten, and this is to blame; who if he be not thankful for seasonable reproof, he knows not what self-judging means. If any man be so uncivil when a man shews him a spot on his garment, to grow choleric, will we not judge him to be[1] an unreasonable man? And so when a man shall be told, This will hinder your comfort another day; if men were not spiritually besotted, would they swell and be angry against such a man? Therefore take the benefit of the judgment of others among whom you live. This was David's disposition, when he was told of the danger [in]* going to kill Nabal and his household; when Abigail, a discreet woman, came and diverted him; Oh, saith he, 'Blessed be God, and blessed be thou, and blessed be thy counsel,' 1 Sam. xxv. 32; thou hast kept me from shedding of innocent blood this day. So we should bless God, and bless them that labour by their good counsel and advice to hinder us from any sinful course, whatsoever it is.†

Sol. (4.) And then again, as a help to awaken thy conscience, *go to the house of mourning.* That will help us by awakening conscience. Consider the judgments of God abroad in the church, and consider our danger at home, and labour to have our hearts awakened; and then we will be ready to judge ourselves, when we keep our souls in a waking temper; take heed of spiritual security above all things.

Sol. (5.) *For our conversion,‡ let it not be with the world;* for then we will justify ourselves, but converse with those that are better, and the light of their excellency will abase us, and make us to judge ourselves. I have reason to be as good as they, to be as forward as they; what a shame is it for me not to do as they do! To bring ourselves to the light of good examples, it doth much good to Christians, and makes them ashamed of their backwardness and dulness. Those that have false hearts they§ shun the company of those that are better than themselves; who because they would have all alike, they besmear and sully others in their reputation, because they shall not be thought to be better than they. A base and devilish course! Whereas a Christian labours to converse with those that are better, because he would grow better than himself; take heed of a false heart in this kind.

Sol. (6.) Again, because I cannot follow the argument so fully as I

* 'In' added in B, C.—G.
‡ Qu. 'conversation'?—Ed.
† 'It is' not in B, C.—G.
§ 'They' not in B, C.—G.
[1] The words 'a spot,' &c., blunderingly omitted in C; and reads, 'If any man be so uncivil, when a man shews him to be an unreasonable man.'—G.

thought I should have done, when all these helps and directions perhaps are not sufficient, *join with this* a desire that God would help us by his own Spirit to search our hearts and judge ourselves*; and complain to him of our corruptions and weaknesses; as the virgin when she was forced, Deut. xxii. 26, if she complained, she saved her reputation and her life. So complain to God, Lord, I would serve thee, but corruption bears too great a sway in me; and desire God to help us with heavenly light and strength, so shall we escape eternal death. Corruption is his enemy. [It is]† Christ's enemy as well as ours, and Christ, if we beg of him, will help us against his enemy and ours; this should be our daily course and practice.

Obj. Now some will object, Here is a troublesome course! what a deal of do is here. What kind of life would you have the life of a Christian to be, to be thus discussing and censuring?

Sol. I answer, *it is the trouble of physic that prevents the trouble of sickness.* Is it not better to be troubled with physic, than to be troubled with a long and tedious sickness? Is it not better to be troubled with the pain of a tent,‡ than with the pain of a wound? All this is but preventing; by this course we prevent further trouble. For we must know that God hath put conscience into us, and this conscience must, and it shall have its work, either in this world or in the world to come; and therefore let us discharge it now by sifting, by examining and condemning ourselves, that it may not rise and stand against us, when we would have it our friend. Oh, carry things so that conscience may be a friend at the day of judgment, put it § out of office now, let it say what it can, stifle it not, stop it not, divert it not, let it have its full scope to say what it can. For I beseech you do but consider the fearful estate of a man that hath neglected self-examination: when he comes to die, and is in any trouble, when he sees death before him, live he cannot, and to die he is unfit; for if he look back, he looks back to a world of sin[1] not repented of; forwards he sees eternal damnation before him; if he look to God, he is offended for his rebellious course of life. Where is then the comfort of such a one, that in the glorious light of the gospel doth not practise this duty of judging himself?

Sin must be judged either in a repentant heart or [else]‖ by God, [it]‖ being against God's prerogative, for he hath made a law against it. Judged it must be: we must give account of every 'idle word,' either in a repentant heart, by afflicting our own souls for it, or at the day of judgment, Mat. xii. 36. Now what a fearful thing will this be, to have all to make account for then. Is it not a great mercy, beloved, that God hath pointed out such a course to set up a court of conscience to prevent shame? Were it not a shame for us to have our faults written in our foreheads? And yet better so, than to have all to reckon for at the day of judgment. For if all our faults were laid open, our corrupt thoughts and vile affections here—there were hope of repentance in this world; but to have them laid open to our shame and confusion in the world to come, it is a matter of eternal despair. Now God, to prevent both these, hath set up a court of conscience, that we might judge ourselves, and prevent shame here, and damnation hereafter.

Quest. And how shall this torment [wretches]¶ in hell, when a man** shall think, God put conscience in me; if I had not put it off, but suffered

* 'These' in B, C.—G.

† 'It is' added in B, C.—G.

‡ That is = ligature made '*tent*' or 'tight.'—G.

§ Qu. 'put it not'?—Ed.

‖ 'Else' and 'it' added in B, C.—G.

¶ 'Wretches' added in B, C.—G.

** 'They' in B, C.—G.

1 'Yet' in C.—G.

it to have done what it would, I might have been thus and thus, but now I have wilfully cast myself into this [misery].* It will be the hell in hell, that shall torment us more than hell,† when we shall think, I have brought myself carelessly and securely to that ‡ cursed estate such shall be then in; § therefore, I beseech you, consider the misery of a man that neglects the practice of this duty, and consider withal how happy and how sweet the condition of that man is that hath and carefully doth daily perform this duty: he is afraid of no ill tidings; if anything come, he hath made his reckoning and account with God, there is no sin upon the file ‖ unrepented of, and unjudged, and unconfessed to God. If he looks back, he considers his sins, but he hath repented of them. If he look forward, he sees nothing but God reconciled, and he can think of death and judgment with comfort. Oh, the happiness, and the peace, and the inward paradise of such a man, about ¶ another careless man that puts off his estate, because he will not trouble and afflict his own soul, and torment himself before his time.

Here is the difference between a careless and a sound Christian; what the one thinks now, the other shall ere long. But only the one is mad now, and is not his own man, but besotted with ambition and covetousness; the other is sober, and in his right wits, able to judge and to censure himself. And therefore let holy persons that are careful, pass not a whit for the censures of vain persons; they speak against what they know not; against a strict course of life. Those that truss up the loins of their souls, and are careful of their ways, they are the only sound Christians; they are the only comfortable Christians, that can think of all conditions, and of all estates comfortably. I beseech you take these things to heart, and let us be stirred up to perform this duty I speak of,** of daily trying and examining of †† our ways, that daily we may relish Christ.

Quest. What is the reason there is no more rejoicing and thankfulness for Christ?

Sol. We keep not the wound, I mean corruption, open; we see that which is unmortified, but we dry it up; and therefore we do not relish Christ. Sweet is Christ to the soul that is exercised in a search of his own heart and ways.

Quest. But at what times especially are we to examine?

Sol. At all times, every day; because we must feed on Christ every day. Therefore we ought to have these sour herbs, considering that we daily sin, that Christ may relish. Christ justifieth the ungodly every day. We have use of justification; and therefore we should daily see our corruptions, and judge ourselves for them: then Christ is Christ indeed, and Jesus is Jesus indeed to us. Every day let us do this. We have short memories; and sin when it is green it is easily rooted out. Therefore,

1. Every day, before sin be rooted, let us judge ourselves. The more we do it now every day, the less we shall have to do when we die, and when we are on our sickbeds; and therefore do it still, that we may have the less to do when we are weak. Is that a fit time to go over our life, and to censure our courses, when we are in such a case as we cannot think of earthly things? Oh, it is an ill time to get grace when we should use grace. And therefore, that we may have the less to do when we shall have

* 'Misery' added in B, C.—G.

† 'The flames' in B, C.—G.

‡ 'This' in B, C.—G.

§ 'Such shall be then in' omitted in B, C.—G.

‖ Cf. Vol. I., note *l*, p. 289.—G.

¶ Qu. 'above'?—Ed.

** 'I speak of' omitted in B, C.—G.

†† No 'of' in B, C.—G.

enough to do to struggle with sickness; and have nothing to do when we die, but to die and comfortably yield up our souls to God let us be exact in our accounts every day.

2. But more especially we should do so when we are to deal with God, as now we are to receive the communion, wherein we draw near to God.* Those that go to great persons, they will not go in rags, but put on their best attire, and make all neat and handsome, that nothing may be offensive. Have we this wisdom when we appear before any greater than ourselves? When we are to appear before God and Christ (especially† to have so near communion as we have in the sacrament), let us labour, I say,‡ to come neat and prepared. When they were to come to the passover, the lamb was singled out beforehand three days, that they might have time to prepare themselves in, Exod. xii. 6. But we ought especially§ to examine and to judge ourselves when we come near to God in holy communion, to feast with God,‖ which is here intended, when we come to receive the blessed sacrament. They should have prepared and have judged themselves.¶ Because they neglected it they were judged of God; and therefore know you that mean to receive now, now is the time when we should judge ourselves, the more especial time.** Though we should do it every day, yet this is the special time. Take heed of superstition though, to thrust all religion into one time, to the time of the communion, as many do. They turn off all their examination to a little time before the communion, and the taking of the communion to one time of the year, to Easter; and thus they think God will bear with them. Oh, take heed!†† that is superstition. As I said before, keep a daily account; every week examine how we have kept our daily account; and every month examine how we have kept our weekly account; and when we come to the communion, examine how we have kept our daily account, whether we have slubbered anything before,‡‡ especially when we come to take the communion.

Quest. But what shall we do, when we have done all? When we have examined, and judged, and passed a censure upon ourselves,§§ what shall [we] do when we have done all?

Sol. When we are condemned in one court, go to another; as a man that is condemned in the Common Law, he appeals to the Chancery. When we are condemned in the court of justice, fly to God's chancery, fly to mercy. He that hath a sentence passed in one court, he appeals to another: when we have judged ourselves, then appeal to mercy; for this is to do it in faith; and when we judge ourselves in faith, then, upon our judging, we know that God will pardon. You know he hath promised, 'If we confess our sins, he is merciful to forgive them,' 1 John i. 9. Say, Lord, I confess them, cancel thou the bond, cancel thou the debt. Therefore a Christian's plea is, when he hath judged himself, to fly to God for pardon. Saul, we know, could judge himself; and Judas could pass a sentence upon his

* 'Unto him' in B, C.—G. † 'Specially' in B, C.—G.

‡ 'I say' not in B, C; and 'much more' added after labour. Neat = pure.—G.

§ 'And ought not we' in B, C.—G.

‖ 'Him' in B, C; and 'which is here intended' omitted.—G.

¶ 'But because' in B, C.—G.

** 'The more . . . is the special time' omitted in B, C.—G.

†† 'Of such a superstitious course' added in B, C; and 'That is . . . before' omitted.—G.

‡‡ 'We have grown in grace, got ground of corruption, been exact in time, hung loose from God or not' added in B, C.—G.

§§ 'In a strict manner' added in B, C; and 'when we have done all' omitted.—G.

own act, that he had sinned; but they went no further, they did not fly to God for mercy in Christ. Therefore let us fly to the throne of grace; as we have an excellent pattern of this, Ps. cxxx. 3: saith the psalmist there, 'If thou be strict to mark what is done amiss, Lord, who shall abide it?' There he is condemned in one court. If thou be strict to mark what is done amiss, who shall abide it? There, being condemned in that court, he flies to the throne of grace: 'But there is mercy with thee, that thou mightst be feared.' Lord, if thou be strict to mark what is done amiss by me in this action and in that action, who shall abide it? But, Lord, there is mercy with thee in Jesus Christ, in whom thou hast stablished a throne of mercy;* there is mercy with thee, that thou mayest be feared. Take this course, and undoubtedly God will shew mercy; because the Son directs us to the Father in the Lord's prayer that we should ask forgiveness; and God the Father directs us to his Son, to believe his Son† for forgiveness. 'This is his commandment, that we believe in his Son Jesus Christ,' 1 John iii. 23. We cannot honour the Father more, we cannot honour the Son more, than to go to God for mercy; because God in Christ now will be glorified in his mercy.‡

Let us fetch out a pardon of course for every sin. 'If we confess our sins, he is merciful to forgive our sins.' And therefore it is our own fault if we find not the assurance of the forgiveness of them, because we deal not roundly, without a spirit of guile, with God. That is the next duty then, after we have judged ourselves, to go to mercy. And to shew you one example, how peace comes in after this judging of ourselves, Rom. vii. 24, the blessed apostle complains of his own corruptions. He had laid sore to his own charge, that the ill that he would not do, that he did; and the good that he would do, that he did not; and he breaks out, 'Oh! wretched man that I am.' What did he find presently upon this? 'Thanks be to God,' presently upon it, as if he had found peace presently upon complaining of his corruptions. Oh, miserable man, &c.§ So when we honour God by confessing and judging ourselves, he will honour us with inward peace and joy; because faith honours him by trusting and relying upon his mercy. If therefore we would find inward peace in the pardon of our sins, let us deal faithfully with our souls in spreading our sins before God; and we shall find peace presently upon it. If not, learn to wait; for undoubtedly God will make good his promise.

Quest. But what shall we do in the next place, after we have so opened the case to God, and gone to him for pardon, and forgiveness, and mercy in Christ?

Sol. Then renew our covenant with God for the time to come, of better service, and enter upon reformation,‖ upon our resolution; for this is a fruit of the former.

Quest. How shall we know that we have humbled ourselves, and judged ourselves as we should do?

Sol. When we relish the mercy of God in the pardon of our sins.

Quest. But how shall we know when God hath pardoned our sins?

Sol. When he gives us grace to renew our covenants for the time to come, not to offend him; and when he gives us strength to reform our ways; for with pardoning mercy there goeth healing mercy: Ps. ciii. 1, 'Praise the

* 'Grace' in B, C; and 'There is . . . feared' omitted.—G.
† 'In him' in B, C.—G. ‡ 'In mercy to penitent sinners' in B, C.—G.
§ 'Oh, miserable man' omitted in B, C.—G.
‖ 'Of life' in B, C; and 'Upon . . . of the former' omitted.—G.

Lord, O my soul, that forgives all thy sins, and heals all thine infirmities.' So these must go together, judging and censuring of ourselves; then pleading for mercy, and renewing of our covenants, with reformation thereupon. A Christian looks as well to the time to come as to the time past: for the time past he repents; for the time to come he resolves against all sin. A wicked carnal man could be content to be freed from the guilt of sins past, that his conscience might not twitch* him and torment him. But for the time to come he makes no conscience to entertain any vows, and purposes, or desire, that God would assist him against all sin. But† a Christian is as careful of the sin that he is in danger to commit for the time to come,‡ as a wicked man is to have the sin past off his conscience.§

As therefore we would have an evidence of our certainty,|| let us look that we renew our covenants and purposes for the time to come; an excellent pattern for this you have, Ps. xix. 12, where David prays, 'Lord, cleanse me from my secret sins' (for the sins that hung upon him, and his sins past¶), and what for the time to come? 'Lord, keep me that presumptuous sins have not the dominion over me.' So we should pray to God, 'Lord, cleanse me from my former sins, and keep me by thy Holy Spirit, that presumptuous sins for the time to come have not the dominion over me;'** and as it is in the Lord's Prayer, to join both together, 'Forgive us our debts,' and 'lead us not into temptation' for the time to come. Those that feel in their souls' assurance of pardon, they†† will entertain purposes against all sin for the time to come; they will as heartily say, Lord, lead me not into temptation, as they will say, Lord, forgive my sins.

Use 1. Well,‡‡ I beseech you, *let us lay these things to heart, to practise them.* Our peace depends upon them. Oh! how sweet is peace and rest, after we have made our peace with God, when we have dealt thoroughly and soundly with our own souls, and have not daubed with them!§§ There may be dangerous times a-coming; there is a cloud hangs over our heads; we know not how it may fall; we see all the world is in combustion. Who, when troubles come, will be the happy man? [Even]|||| he that hath judged himself, accused himself, that hath mortified his corruptions, and, according to the grace that God hath given him, renewed his covenant and laboured to reform his life, and keeps it in his purpose of heart so to do (as David prays, that he may not offend God for the time to come¶¶), he is fit for all times; whatsoever times come they shall find him in good purposes. What a fearful thing were it if death, if some terrible judgment should light on us in an evil course of life; what would become of us then? Happy man is he that is in the good way, in good purposes, in good resolutions, that the bent of his soul is to God and to heavenward; and therefore, as we would evidence to ourselves, that our state is good, that we are wise, and not fools, I beseech you let us practise this duty, and make it more familiar to

* 'Touch' in B, C.—G.

† 'But' not in B, C.—G.

‡ 'For the future' in B, C.—G.

§ 'Of his conscience pardoned' in B, C.—G.

|| 'In bliss' added in B, C.—G.

¶ 'The present sins that hung upon him, and his sins past' in B, C.—G.

** 'Have no power over me' in B, C; and the 'and' following omitted, together with 'to join both together.'—G.

†† 'They' not in B, C; neither 'for the time to come' following.—G.

‡‡ 'Well' not in B, C.—G.

§§ That is = 'have not dealt superficially.' Cf. Ezek. xiii. 10, 11, 12, 14; xxii. 28.—G.

|||| 'Even' added in B, C.—G.

¶¶ 'As David . . . to come' omitted in B, C.—G.

us than we have done; and then undoubtedly we shall find somewhat in us better than nature. Nature cannot judge itself. Corruption cannot pass a censure upon itself. It is grace, a principle above nature, that censures corruption; and therefore when we judge ourselves, it is an undoubted evidence that we are in the state of grace. Who would want such an evidence?

Use 2. Again, when we find want of grace, *go out of ourselves, go* to God and to Christ.* Naturally we stick in ourselves. Judas and Saul, they could not go to God for mercy, when their conscience was awaked with the sense of their sin. To go to God for pardon, it is an argument that there is somewhat wrought above nature in the heart; and therefore, as we would have an evidence to our souls, that there is somewhat in us above common men, *let us judge ourselves; let us spare no sin, that God may spare all,* Be severe to ourselves, that God may be merciful to us; and when we have done this, look to the abundant mercy of God in Christ. 'Where sin hath abounded, grace hath more abounded,' Rom. v. 13. Oh! mercy is sweet after we have searched into our corruptions. There is a height, and breadth, and depth of mercy, when we have felt the height, and breadth, and depth of corruption first. The Lord give a blessing to that which hath been delivered.

* 'On' inserted in B, C, and 'to' omitted.—G.

JUDGMENT'S REASON.

SERMON II.

For this cause many are weak and sick among you, and many sleep. For if we would judge ourselves, we should not be judged. But when we are judged, we are chastened of the Lord, that we should not be condemned with the world.—1 COR. XI. 30-32.

AFTER blessed St Paul had sown the seed of heavenly doctrine, Satan had sown some tares. Besides some corruption in doctrine, there was also corruption in life among the Corinthians; whereupon God was forced in mercy to visit them with some judgment: and lest they should be ignorant of the cause, the blessed apostle here doth put his finger to it, 'for this cause.' We have considered these four things in the words: *the cause* of the judgment; and then *the kinds;* and *the remedy* for the prevention, if it had been used: 'If we would judge ourselves, we should not be judged;' and *the comfort:* howsoever, 'when we are judged, we are chastened of the Lord, that we should not be condemned with the world.' Of the cause, the kinds, and the remedy we have spoken; and now we proceed to the comfort.

Mark here the text that I have read unto you. Though we do all neglect this forenamed remedy in part, yet God is wonderful merciful: 'When we are judged, we are chastened of the Lord, that we should not be condemned with the world.' We will unfold the comfort, as the text leads us. In the words consider these things especially, these general heads:—*

1. First of all, *that there is a world that must be condemned:* we shall not be condemned with the world.†

2. And then, *God's people shall not be condemned with the world.*

3. The third conclusion that ariseth out of the text is this, *that the way that God sanctifies to prevent his children from damnation, is fatherly correction and chastisement;* and therefore we are judged, that we should not be condemned with the world; in the unfolding of which course that God takes, these three things are to be touched:—

(1.) *That God's dealings with his children are but chastisements.*

(2.) *And his chastisements:*‡ 'We are chastened *of the Lord.*'

* 'These general heads' omitted in B, C.—G.

† 'We . . . world' omitted in B, C.—G.

‡ 'They are his' in B, C.—G.

(3.) *And that* they are blessed for this end, to keep us from damnation.* These things we will speak of in order.

Doct. 1. First, *There is a world that is to be condemned: God's children shall not be condemned with the world.*

What is the world in this place?

The world in this place, it is not the frame of heaven and earth; but (to avoid multiplicity of acceptions, in which were idle to spend time) by world here is meant those that Peter speaks of, the ungodly world, the world of ungodly.† As we see, 2 Pet. iii. 7, they are called the world of ungodly; so there is a world took out of the world, the world of the elect. For as in the great world there is the little world—man—so in the great world of mankind, there is a little world—the world of God's people; but here it is the world of the ungodly.

Why are they called the world?

They are called the world, *partly because they are great in the world.* They swagger in the world, as if they were upon their own dunghill there, and as if they were the only men in the world, as indeed for the most part they are. God's people are a concealed, a hidden people here. And then again, they are the world, *because they are the most of the world.* But especially they are the world, *because the best thing in them is the world.* They have their name from that they love. Love is an affection of union. What we love, that we are knit unto. Now because carnal men are in love with the things of the world, being united in their affections to it, they have their name from that they love. And indeed, anatomise a carnal man that is not in the state of grace, rip him up in his soul, what shall you find in him but the world? You shall find in his brain worldly plots, worldly policy and vanity. You shall find little of the word of God there, and scarce any thing that is good, because the best thing in him is the world; therefore he is the world.‡ But to pass from the meaning of the word to the point: *This world must be condemned.* Why condemned? Mark these four or five reasons.

[1.] First of all, *because the world doth set itself upon things that must be condemned,* upon present vanities. Why?§ All things in this world must pass through the fire ere long, the frame of heaven and earth and all in it. Now those that love the world especially, and have no better things in their souls, they must perish with the world. He that stands on ice, and on slippery things, he slips with the thing he stands on. So those that fasten their souls upon the world, upon slippery and vain things, they fall, and slip with the things themselves. Now, because the world pitched their happiness‖ in the things of this life, they are vain as the things themselves.¶ But to go on.

[2.] A second reason why the world must be condemned is this, *because they serve a damned prince,* and it is pity that the state of the subject and the state of the prince should be severed. Satan they serve; Satan rules in them according to his own lust; Satan bathes himself in their humour as it were, in their anger, in their pride [in their covetousness**], in their melancholy, in their passion. As Saul, when he was given up to an evil passion, the devil seized upon him; so the devil leads them according to the stream of their own humour and of their own lusts; they are led

* No 'that' in B, C.—G.

† 'The world of ungodly' omitted in B, C.—G.

‡ 'Therefore . . . world' not in B, C.—G.

‖ 'The worldly men pitch' in B, C.—G.

§ 'Why' not in B, C.—G.

¶ 'Are' added in B, C.—G.

** 'In their covetousness' added, and 'in their melancholy' omitted in B, C.—G.

according to the bent of the prince of the world.* Now, being led by the temptations of Satan, who knows where to have them upon any temptation, and leads them as we lead sheep with a green bough, when he presents anything to them, he knows where to have them; and he being a damned† prince and governor, all that are under him are in the same condition.

[3.] The *third* reason why the world shall be damned is this, *because the world condemns God.* It is but quittance. Carnal people in the world condemn God's ways and God's children, and the ways of religion to be nice‡ and foolish. The world hath its conceits of itself, and scorns the sweetness of religion, and accounts the word and obedience to be a weak and poor spirit. §Considering that the world passeth such censures upon God's ways, and condemns the generation of the righteous, if God condemn the world, do you wonder, when the base and slavish world, led by the devil and by their own lusts, will condemn God and his ways? And certainly, if you would see into the poisonful disposition of persons among whom we live, that are yet in the world, how malicious they are to God's courses, you will not wonder that God hath ordained such to be set on the left hand, to pass the sentence of eternal condemnation upon them; because though the light discover to them which way they should walk, yet they abhor all God's ways, and take ways of their own: as if they would teach God wisdom, and prescribe what he should do; as if they were wiser than God. All your politicians they‖ are such: they lead their lives as if they would teach God wisdom: what he should prescribe; as if they were wiser than he a great deal. Do you wonder that he condemns them [then]?¶

Obj. But you will say, 'the world?'** What do you talk? We are baptized. We hear now and then a sermon! Are we the world? The world are Pagans, and Turks, and Jews, and such; perhaps papists. Such as they are the world.

Ans. Oh no, beloved, 'Babylon is in Jerusalem,' as the father saith,†† the world is in the city of God, the world is among you. Nay, and that part of the world that shall be deepest damned is here amongst us. For our damnation shall be deeper than the Turks' or Jews'. 'You have I known of all the nations of the world, saith God; and therefore I will be sure to visit you,' Amos iii. 2. The three bad grounds,‡‡ beloved, were the world, Mat. xiii. 1, *seq.* Howsoever, all heard the word, yet there was but one good. You may be of the world, and yet live in the midst of the church, as Paul, Phil. iii. 18, *seq.*, complains of many, 'of whom, saith he, I have told you often, and now tell you weeping, they are enemies to the cross of Christ,' [they were teachers in the church; they were so far from being aliens], 'whose end is damnation, whose belly is their god, whose glory is their shame, who mind earthly things.' When the guides and teachers of the church, that should give aim at§§ salvation to other people; when they shall make 'their belly their god, and damnation their end;' shall we secure ourselves that we are in a good estate, because we are baptized, and because we hear the word; when the 'three bad grounds' did so? It is another manner of matter to be out of the world, and to be in Christ, than the world takes it for. Beloved, in holy duties there are two

* 'They are led . . . of the world' omitted in B, C.—G.
† That is, 'condemned.'—G.
‡ Cf. Note *c*, Vol. II. p. 194.—G.
§ 'Now considering' in B, C.—G.
‖ 'They' not in B, C.—G.
¶ 'Then' added in B, C.—G.
** 'The world' omitted in B, C.—G
†† Augustine de Civitate Dei.—G.
‡‡ 'Beloved' not in B, C.—G.
§§ 'Of' in B, C.—G.

things; there is the outward[1] duty, the shell, and the life and soul of the duty. A carnal worldly man may do the outward thing; he may be baptized and receive the communion; he may come to hear the word of God, but there is a life and soul in the duty; to hear as he should; to be moulded into the performance of it; to obey that we hear, and to come to receive the sacrament with reverence and due preparation; and to increase the assurance of salvation, and our comfort and joy. This is the hard part of the duty; this the world cannot do. Let us value ourselves by the practice of the inward part of the duty, the power of the duty, and not rest in the outward performance.

[4.] The next reason to shew that the world must needs be condemned, it is this, *because even in the church there are a company of men* (I beseech you, let not your thoughts go out of your* congregations and places we live in when we speak of the world) *that will be damned.* It is a strange thing; that will be damned! Who will be damned? I say, there are a company among whom we live, that resolve to be damned. Why? There are evil courses, which whosoever will take, they will go to hell; they will end in death, as in the Proverbs, Prov. viii. 35. 'He that takes such a course, hates his own soul.' God saith thus, that† is Wisdom himself; and therefore if you wilfully walk in those courses that lead to hell, it is as much as if you would‡ be damned. Indeed, there is none but would be saved, if they would be saved in the paths of the broad way, that lead to damnation; they could be content to go to heaven in a race of vanity. Who would not be saved in that sense? But the world will be damned in this sense, if they resolve to take a course to flatter their own lusts, going their own ways in spite of God, in spite of his truth, in spite of conscience, and to despite the Spirit that awakeneth them and tells them that there is another way that they should walk in, and puts them in mind, 'This is the way, walk in it,' Isa. xxx. 21; and this is not the way, avoid it; and yet they will rush on in their courses, as the horse rusheth into the battle. Say God what he will, the world will be damned. Are there not many that have been told of their pride§, of their vanities, of their lusts, of their sins that their conscience tells them they pamper themselves in? and they will not amend for all this. This, in God's construction (and this conscience will tell them another day), is because they would go on rebelliously in courses tending to damnation. Nay, which is worse, there is a generation of venomous persons, that hate the ministers, hate good people, hate the image of God, and hate anything, that may present to their hearts a dislike of the courses they are wedded to. Oh! I would they would hate the devil so; and do you wonder that these are damned, that hate the image of God, the motions of the Spirit, and raise reproaches upon religion, and make it odious as much as they can, that their vileness may the less appear, and be the less disgraced in their wicked ways? And yet this is the course of many thousands in the bosom of the church, and in the best places, that are guilty of this; whom if one tell, that this temper and frame of soul is contrary to God, and will yield nothing but desperation in the end,‖ notwithstanding they will not regard what you say. Well, beloved,¶ I must hasten. Many other reasons there are to shew that the world must be damned, as,

* 'Our' in B, C.—G.
† 'Who' in B, C.—G.
‡ 'Resolved' in B, C.—G.
§ 'And hypocrisy' in B, C.—G.
‖ 'They will nothing regard' in B, C.—G.
¶ 'Beloved' not in B, C.—G.
[1] 'Holy' in B, C.—G.

[5.] *The world, it is shut out of Christ's prayer.* They have no part in the prayer of Christ, in him that died to redeem us. And the world will not receive the Spirit, because they maintain their own lusts. Many other reasons the Scripture heaps upon this, that there are a company of men that must and will be damned. But what is the use of this?

Use (1.) *First, to pull our friends, our children, out of the world;* to get ourselves out of the world, as soon as we can. Come out of Sodom, come out of Babylon, make all haste; for, as the angel tells Lot, 'I will destroy this place,' Gen. xix. 16. The world is a place that God will destroy. It is Sodom; it is Babylon; get out of it. There is no being there, except you will reap eternal damnation with the world.

(2.) Again, *pass* not for the censures of worldly proud people, that think that they are jolly Christians,* when they are but in truth damned persons. God may recover them, but yet they are in damnable ways. Who cares† for the sentence of a damned person, till he have gotten his pardon? Such are all profane persons, that have not the work of grace wrought in their hearts in an effectual manner; they are yet in the state of damnation. Why should we pass for their censures? There are a company of weak persons, who reason as weakly, If I do this, the world will say thus and thus. What is the world? The world is a generation of unregenerate wretched people, that must be damned. Who would regard the censure of a damned person? and indeed who would follow the guise of damned persons? And yet of late such is the madness of people, that they take up the fashions, though they be condemned fashions. They‡ do not consider the vanity of it, so to take up the fashions of damned persons.§ The world is a condemned generation; therefore take not up the guise and fashion of the world.‖ The world's fashion is the worst fashion of all. I speak not of correspondency with the world in civil actions in the passages of our life. We must 'come out of the world,' as Christ saith, 'if we will not be correspondent in outward things,' 2 Cor. vi. 17; and here should be a redeeming of our peace with the world in yielding in lesser matters. But I speak of those things which concern our inward comfort and peace, and that concern the practice of holy duties; let us not stand in it, what the world judgeth or allows, but practise holy duties, though the world censure them; and abstain from wicked courses, though the world applaud them. So we shall have a seal that we are taken out of the world.

Use (2.) Let us make another use of trial, *and examine whether we be taken out of the world or no.* In brief, therefore, let us ask¶ our aims, our ends. For, those that are taken out of the world have aims beyond the world; they frame their courses to supernatural ends, to eternity; and labour so to guide themselves in this, that they may be saved in another world. We should steer and guide our actions suitable to our peace hereafter. We should have further ends than the world hath. He that is a worldling confines his thoughts within the compass of the world; he hath no further aim. Sometimes he hath by-thoughts of heaven and happiness. But he makes it not his aim, it is not his scope to which he directs his course. In the second place, answerable to our aims, let us examine what our affections are. Our affections will tell us of what city we are, whether of Jerusalem, or of Babylon, as one of the ancients saith well.**

* That is, = heed not.—G.

† That is, 'who would wish.'—G.

‡ 'And do not' in B, C.—G.

§ 'So to take . . . persons' not in B, C.—G.

‖ 'Therefore take not up their guise' in B, C.—G

¶ 'Observe' in B, C.—G.

** Augustine.—Cf. ** p. 99, *ante*.—G.

Ask thy love, Whither dost thou weigh down in thy love? Doth earthly love as a weight press thee to things below? or is it a sanctified love, that carries thee to Christ, and to the things of God? Examine thy affections of love,* of joy and delight, of what city thou art. Mere earthly actions are hypocritical; therefore the inward affections are the best discoverers of the estate of our soul, where our joy and delight is.† And ask likewise in the third place, our relish, What do we savour most? Come to a carnal man; put him to a course of vanity; he hath learned the language of the times, all your complimental phrases; he hath them exactly; all the language of the time he can speak. But come to him in matters of religion; he is out of his theme there; he savours not those things. Those that are of the world speak of the world. Talk to them of vanity, of this and that, and you put them to their proper theme; but tell them of other things, they are mere strangers; and they speak as if they had never learned anything in that element. And so those that are of the world, they converse with those that are of the same bent; doves flock to doves, and delight in those that are like themselves. Many such arguments of trial we may have, but especially think what I have said before.‡ *Look to your aims, to your affections, and to your inward relish and bent of soul*, which way your and conversation is bent,§ and how it relisheth; and these will discover to us our state, as in Rev. xiii. 11, *seq.*, and other places: there antichrist is called the beast that riseth out of the earth; because Romish religion is taken out of the earth, that is, it hath earthly aims, earthly grounds and principles. It is all for the world; it is a fallacy indeed, popery and not religion; and thereupon the pope is called the beast rising out of the earth. All the considerations that feed popery are out of the earth. Oh! a glorious monarch of the church, to have glory; and in the church to have all that may feed the senses, and that may please the outward man. Every thing, I say, is to please the outward man, to get riches, &c. They are called Gentiles; 'the outward court shall be cast to the Gentiles.' He speaks there, that antichrist with his crew that follows him, they should trouble, vex, and persecute the church, and cast it out to the Gentiles. The followers of antichrist are called Gentiles. But I speak not of them. We are earth and Gentiles, if our aims, projects, and affections be towards the earth, as the Scripture useth to speak.‖ Therefore,¶ let us examine ourselves by what I have said. I beseech you, let us consider that the world must be condemned. And before I leave it, do but think what damnation is. I beseech you,** have no slight thoughts of it. The Scripture saith, 'We shall not be condemned with the world.'

What is condemnation?

To be condemned is to be adjudged from the presence of God, and to be adjudged†† to eternal torment with the devil and his angels. It were somewhat unseasonable to enlarge this point; but I beseech you consider what is wrapped in this word 'condemned,'‡‡ '*condemned* with the world;'

* 'Love' not in B, C.—G.

† 'Where our joy and delight is' not in B, C.—G.

‡ 'But . . . before' not in B, C. After 'we may have' there is 'therefore.'—G.

§ 'Sways' in B, C.—G.

‖ The paragraph 'Everything I say' . . . to 'useth to speak' not in B, C.—G.

¶ 'I beseech you, let us examine ourselves by what I have said and considered, that,' &c., in B, C.—G.

** 'I beseech you' not in B, C . . . nor 'the Scripture saith,' &c.—G.

†† 'Cast' in B, C.—G.

‡‡ 'Condemned' not in B, C.—G.

that so if we hate the end, damnation, we may hate the way that leads to it, the ways of the world. But to go on.

Doct. The *second* general is this, *that God's children shall not be condemned with the world.*

Quest. Why?

Ans. 1. *Because they are the first-fruits dedicated to God out of the world, and Christ was condemned for them.* How can they be condemned for whom Christ himself* was condemned?

Ans. 2. And then *a godly man in the state of grace, he is in heaven already;* and who shall pull him from heaven? How can he be condemned that is in heaven already? We sit in heavenly places already. Beloved, to hold that an elect Christian may fall away, is to pull Christ himself out of heaven; we are in heaven already in Christ. A Christian being a member of Christ cannot be condemned, no more than Christ can be condemned, be it spoken with reverence to his majesty.

Ans. 3. Again, *for whom Christ is a priest, he is a king.* He is a king to rule them in this world, and to subdue whatsoever might oppose their salvation. Whom he hath bought with his blood as a priest, he rules as a king, and orders all things to help their salvation. Where Christ is a king, for those he is a priest.† Can those be condemned then?‡ And he vouchsafes them a spirit stronger than the world. God's children have a spirit in them that overcomes the world: 'Stronger is he that is in you,' saith John, 'than he that is in the world,' 1 John iv. 4. For the Spirit of God suggests reasons, and arguments, and motives that are stronger to a believing soul than the temptations of the world are; the world biasseth them one way, and the Spirit of God another way. The children of God have the Spirit of God, especially a spirit of faith, therefore they overcome the world. It presents better things in religion than the world can afford. Now those that have the Spirit of God, and a spirit of faith, by which they overcome the world, how can they be condemned with the world? And God takes a safe course with his children.

Note. That they may not be condemned with the world, he makes the world to condemn them; that they may not love the world, he makes the world to hate them; that they may be crucified to the world, he makes the world be crucified to them. Therefore they meet with crosses, and abuses, and wrongs in the world. Because he will not have them perish with the world, he sends them afflictions in the world, and by the world. Thus I might enlarge myself in the condition of God's people, of his saints;§ they shall not be condemned with the wicked world.

Use. The use of it is this, *that we should be in love with the state of God's people.*‖ Who would not be in love with this condition? I may boldly speak it, my beloved. The meanest poor soul that hath the work of grace upon it, that is taken out of the world, is in a better condition than the greatest worldling. Let a man be as happy as a world¶ can make him; if he be a condemned man, what is his condition? All the time that other men live, that are not in the state of grace, it is but the time between the sentence passing and the execution. Now, that is but a little time. The life of a carnal man, it is but the life of a man condemned at the bar, and is deferred for the execution a while. Another man, that is in the

* 'Himself' in B, C.—G.

† 'Where Christ . . . priest,' not in B, C.—G.

‡ 'Whom Christ vouchsafes a spirit,' &c., in B, C.—G.

§ 'Of his saints' not in B, C.—G.

¶ 'The world' in B, C.—G.

‖ 'Holy men' in B, C.—G.

state of grace, he is safe; he shall not be condemned with the world; he is in heaven already; he is sure of it, as if he were there. I beseech you, let this make us in love with the sincerity of religion, and let us never cease labouring till we have gotten out of this cursed state into this happy estate.* There is but a little flock of Christ. We should never give our temples† quiet, and our souls rest, till we‡ evidence to them that we are of the little number which are taken out of the world; till we see that we are a first-fruits dedicated to God; till we find the beginnings of grace wrought in our souls. Why should we defer one hour till we have gotten this assurance, considering our life is so uncertain?

Doct. 3. The third general thing is this, *the course that God takes with his children in this world, whereby they are preserved from damnation, it is corrections and chastisements.* We are chastened of the Lord, that we should not be condemned with the world; wherein, as I shewed you, there are these three branches. I will specially speak of the last.§

(1.) *First*, that *whatsoever God's dealings be with his children, it is but a fatherly correction and chastisement;* and therefore it is in mercy, in discretion; a little punishment is enough of a mother to her child. God hath the wisdom of a father, but he hath the bowels of a mother; and therefore God‖ is pitiful and merciful, because he is a Father. There is a wondrous sweet comfort wrapped in that word *Father*. The whole world is not worth this¶ that is yielded to a Christian from this, that a Christian** is the child of God, and that God is his Father. I might enlarge myself in the point, that all are but fatherly corrections. A father, when he sees his child in an evil way, he corrects him; but it is a preventing correction, it is to prevent execution after. A child set at liberty makes his mother and his father ashamed; and so if we should be set too much at liberty, if God should not meet us with seasonable correction, we should shame religion and shame Christ; and therefore God in mercy corrects us with fatherly correction. Oh! it is a wonderful comfort to think, when we are taken into the covenant of grace, all comes from God as a Father then; and having taken us of enemies to be children, will he cast off his children for infirmities? Will a mother cast off her children for breaches, for something that displeaseth her? No! But rather she will be more merciful and more pitiful. But I will not enlarge myself in this point. It is a familiar point; and, I suppose, you hear it often. But, I beseech you, do but think of it, that it may be ready in your hearts and in your memories against temptation, to have a good conceit of God. It overcomes temptation†† ofttimes to have a good conceit of God, to present God to our souls as a father, whereas the devil would present him as a judge, as one that hates us. Oh! take heed of it, this is but fatherly correction. God is our Father: 'Our Father which art in heaven,' saith Christ. Let us help our souls by presenting God to us in these colours, as a father in temptation, and all that we suffer as fatherly corrections. To speak familiarly, we know in the street,‡‡ when one child is corrected, and another is not, we know he is the father that corrects. God doth not use to correct those that are not his children; he lets them go on still, they

* 'Condition' in B, C.—G.
† That is, = bodies. Cf. 1 Cor. vi. 19.—G.
‡ 'Can evidence' in B, C.—G.
§ 'I will . . . last' not in B, C; nor 'because he is a Father.'—G.
‖ 'He' in B, C.—G.
†† 'Temptations' in B, C.—G.
¶ 'The comfort' in B, C.—G.
‡‡ 'When we see in the street' in B, C.—G.
** 'He' in B, C.—G.

are not worth correcting;* because they have abused his mercy before, he lets them go on.† When God takes us in our sinful course, and meets with us, and hedgeth our ways with thorns, he shews himself to be a Father. We are bastards, and not sons, if we have not correction, as at large it is sweetly followed, and many arguments to it,‡ Heb. xii. 7, *seq.* God shews himself a Father when he corrects us, or else we are bastards, and not sons.

Use 1. Well, *let us take all things therefore the better at God's hands, because they are but corrections;* for we need it, the best of us. The bes gardens have need of weeding, and the best metals have need of purging, and the best linen hath need of washing. God knows it well enough, and therefore he will purge us. As the Scripture saith, As gold and silver is purged, he will purge out the dross, and all in mercy. We lose nothing by any visitations of God but corruption. The fruit of all his dealing with us is to take sin from us.

2. It is said here in the *second* place, that as *they are corrections, so they are from God.* We are chastened *of the Lord.* I will but touch it in a word, and that to help our forgetfulness in a main point. In the governing of a Christian life we are carried naturally to second causes. Now all second causes are but rods in God's hands. Look therefore to the hand that smites, look to God in all. He chastiseth us, as David said in the matter of Shimei, 2 Sam. xvi. 10; and as Job, 'It is the Lord that hath given, and the Lord hath taken away,' Job i. 21. And so in benefits we should see God in all things, and think we are to deal with him. Our work lies in heaven, therefore in any visitation or cross, I beseech you, think of it. We are to deal with the great Mover of heaven and earth, that hath all second causes in his hand; that hath the hearts of kings in his hand; § and let us make our peace with him.

Quest. Why should we go to the serjeant? We should make our peace with the judge; make not peace with the second causes, but with the principal. It is God that chastiseth; let us make our peace there, ‖ and he will take off the second cause. I cannot follow the point; I beseech you think of it. We forget it in our practice, and that makes us so atheistical, as if there were not a God to govern the world, but we run presently upon second causes.¶

Let us go on; God's corrections are but chastenings, and they are from him. *And they are sanctified of him,* which is the main point, to preserve us from being damned with the world. These corrections are sanctified by God for that end.**

Quest. And how is that?

Ans. 1. *Because they embitter sinful courses to us.* When we are crossed in our sinful courses, sinful courses are embittered unto us; we grow out of love with them.

Ans. 2. And then again, *these chastisements, they help us to relish heaven and heavenly things better.* Oh! then the word of God is the word of God indeed; then Christ is Christ; then heavenly things are heavenly things;

* 'Chastising' in B, C.—G. † 'He lets them go on' not in B, C.—G.

‡ 'And many arguments to it,' with the next sentence, 'God shews,' &c., not in B, C.—G.

§ 'That hath the hearts,' &c., not in B, C.—G.

‖ 'Agree with him' in B, C.—G.

¶ 'Inferior things,' and 'I go on,' in B, C.—G.

** 'These . . . end' not in B, C.—G.

then a messenger, one of a thousand, will be heard, as Job xxxiii. 23; then welcome the man of God all that time. When a man cannot relish earthly things, when he cannot take comfort by his friends, then welcome heavenly comforts. Chastisements, therefore, they help us, that we be not damned with the world, by making us out of love with vanities, that we shall not care for them. We see they do us good, to help us to relish heavenly things. Blessed are those corrections that are sanctified that way. We hear with other ears then. When we have been in the fire, and God hath met with us by crosses, we hear with another manner of attention than at other times. Though* I might be large on the point, for it is very large, rather let us think of it to make use of it. But† first to take away all objections, that I may fasten the comfort upon our souls the better, it may be objected,

Obj. 1. Oh! *but it is such a correction as takes away my friends from me.* I cannot have the use of my friends, as sometime in a noisome contagious disease.

Ans. What if thou hast no friends but God and his angels to help thee to heaven? Whatsoever comfort God conveys by friends, he hath it in himself still; and he can convey those immediate comforts which are most sweet, when they come from the spring; when outward comforts fail, those are the best comforts. It is a greater grace for a prince to visit a sick body himself than to send a messenger to visit him. So when no man can come to us, God himself comes from heaven, and visits us by the comforts of the Holy Spirit; and what do we loose‡ then?

Obj. 2. Oh! *but it is a sharp affliction, a sharp cross.*

Ans. Oh! but it is a sweet hand it comes from. Shall not I take a cup out of a father's hand? It is a bitter cup, but it is out of a father's hand, and therefore out of a loving hand. It is from love, and it is directed to my good, and it is sweetly tempered and mixed, and moderated; and therefore if it come from love, and be directed to my good, and for the present be mixed and moderated§—why should I complain of the correction, that is for my good, to keep me that I should not be damned with the world?

Obj. 3. But *how can death itself be a correction, when it takes away life, that we have no time to be better?*

Ans. I answer, God, to his children, before he takes them out of the world, he‖ gives them his Spirit, that they sharply repent, and put much to a little time; and God requires rather truth of heart than length of time. As we see sick bodies shoot out suddenly that did not grow before, so a sick afflicted soul it shoots out suddenly. God visits it with sharp repentance, though it be short, perhaps that they call their ways to account;¶ and though he take them out of the world, yet he saves their souls.

Obj. 4. *But perhaps it is but hypocritical repentance before my death* (because many recover, and shew themselves to be hypocrites after); *and so if I should die, perhaps I should die an hypocrite.*

Ans. Oh! take heed of that. Many do so; as an ancient saith, He that is never good but under the cross (he means *only*), is never good.** He that is good under bonds is never good; if he doth it from fear, and not

* 'Though' not in B, C.—G. † 'And' in B, C.—G. ‡ Qu. 'lose'?—Ed.
§ 'By him' in B, C.—G. ‖ 'He' not in B, C.—G.
¶ 'Perhaps that . . . account,' not in B. C—G.
** This reads in B, C, 'He that is never good but under the cross, such a one is never good' in B C.—G.

from hatred of sin. But thou shalt know that it was not in hypocrisy that now thou hast repented in thy sickness, if thou desire rather the grace of God, than to recover. A soul that is sanctified had rather have pardon of sin, and strength against corruption, than to have recovery; and he desires God from his soul: Now, Lord, sanctify this sickness, and this cross before thou take it away; for the plaster would fall off if the wound were healed; and the malady would cease if there were not a ground. I beseech you therefore, those that make that objection, let them consider whether they desire the removal of the cross rather,* or to have it sanctified, before it be removed from them. A true heart doth so; and it were better that we should be under the cross all the days of our lives, and to have the cross laid more heavy upon us, than that we should grow worse under it, as many do, and are not the better for it. But say thou, 'Nay, Lord, rather sear me, and burn me, and chastise me; save my soul and do what thou wilt.' That is the disposition of a Christian; for God takes a great deal of liberty with our carcases, and in our outward estate. Such things we must leave behind us, we know not how soon; and† therefore he takes liberty to correct us in them sharply; but so he saves our souls, all is in mercy. It is a blessed correction that draws us nearer to him, that makes us hate sin more, and love the ways of God more.

Obj. 5. But it will be objected again, *but I am accessary to my own death, I have been an intemperate man, I have shortened my own days.*

Ans. Beloved, a heavy temptation at the hour of death! But be not discouraged. For so blessed Josiah shortened his own days; for he went rashly when he had counsel to the contrary; and so 'the good prophet' shortened his own days when the lion met him and slew him by the way for his disobedience, 1 Kings xiii. 24; and so the good thief. Therefore despair not at that, if the thing should be that thou shouldst fall into some course whereby thou shouldst shorten thine own days, and be accessary to thine own death; as these Corinthians, they were accessary to their own deaths,‡ and they slept before their time; they cut the thread of their own life and they put out their own candle. No question but this was heavy upon the conscience; I brought myself to it. This is the hell of hells of the damned souls; I brought myself hither. So when we are guilty of the punishment and affliction of ourselves, it is most bitter unto us. But, I say, consider the former examples, God hath strange ways to bring his children home to him, and sometimes the furthest way about is the nearest way home.§ God suffers his children to sin, and by sin to shorten their days, and all to occasion repentance and a sight of their corruption, and a hatred of themselves, and of their base courses, and to give themselves to him more thoroughly than before. So infinitely wise and gracious is God to those that belong to him. So that, notwithstanding all objections to the contrary, the position laid down before is true, that God sanctifies corrections to us, that we should not be damned with the world.

Uses of all. *Use* 1. Now to make some general use of all that hath been spoken, and so to end all.‖ Is this so? Here we might stand upon a point to instruct our judgment, to shew that *all the corrections of God's children, they come not from vindictive justice, but from a fatherly affection,*

* 'Or' in B, C.—G. † 'And' not in B, C.—G.

‡ 'They were accessary to their own deaths' not in B, C, but simply, 'who slept before their time, they cut,' &c.—G.

§ In the margin here, 'As in Israel's forty years' voyage. Cf.

‖ 'So' not in B, C.—G.

against that doctrine of popery that maintains satisfaction; that judgments are for satisfaction. A proud and damnable point. Can a man with a penny deserve a thousand pounds? Sin deserves eternal damnation. Can we with a little suffering satisfy that? 'The wages of sin is death,' Rom. vi. 23, eternal death. It is a gross position. No! They are corrections, not satisfactions; they come from fatherly affection. This is to rectify our judgment in that point.

Use 2. And then again, *to help us against Satan's temptations.* He useth afflictions as temptations to weaken our faith.

Obj. If God did love thee, he would never do so and so; God hates thee;* why doth he follow thee with his judgments, but that he hates thee and hath no delight in thee? And why should he single out thee more than others?

Ans. Retort back again, Nay! because God loves me, he deals thus with me; because he means† to save my soul, therefore he will not suffer me quietly to run the broad way to destruction. Therefore it is rather an argument of love, from that, whereby Satan would shake our faith. Doth not Satan set upon Christ with this temptation? He comes with an 'if.' 'If thou be the Son of God,' Matt. iv. 3, *seq.* If thou wert the child of God, shouldst thou be so afflicted? Whereas, indeed, because we are the sons of God, therefore we are afflicted. Beat back therefore Satan's weapons into his own bosom again. If God corrected his own Son, that is, the author of our salvation (when yet under the signs of his greatest displeasure, his Father loved him), let us think that we may be beloved of God in the signs of his greatest displeasure, as Christ upon the cross, 'My God, my God,' &c.‡ He apprehended, in the signs of greatest displeasure, God's love, and so should we. Let us answer God's dealing with the like. His dealing is this.§ In the worst condition he calls us children, and he is our father, and loves us. Therefore, in the worst condition, let us trust him, and say with Job. 'Though thou kill me, yet will I trust in thee,' Job xiii. 15.

Quest. Why?

Ans. Because thou mayest kill me, and yet be a father, and mayest do it in love. I will answer thy dealing by my faith again; therefore though thou kill me, yet will I trust in thee.

Use 3. Again, *this strengthens our judgment in the point of perseverance, that being once in the state of grace, we shall hold out still.* For rather than God's children shall fall away, God will take a course that they should not be damned with the world; he will correct them. It is most divinely set down, Rom. viii. 35. Saith he, among other things,‖ 'Neither life nor death shall be able to separate us from the love of God;' neither life, nor the vanities of this life.

Quest. And what if we give God cause to visit us with death.¶

Ans. 'Yet neither life nor death shall separate us from the love of God,' as here the Corinthians they were visited with death; yet neither life nor death shall be able to separate us from the love of God in Christ; and therefore be stablished in the truth of that point.

Use 4. Then again, for a further use, *it fenceth the soul against the scandal***

* 'God hates thee' not in B, C.—G.

† 'Meaneth' in B, C.—G.

‡ 'Still' in B, C.—G.

§ 'His dealing is this' not in B, C.—G.

‖ 'Saith he among other things' not in B, C.—G.

¶ 'As here the Corinthians were visited' inserted here in B, C.—G.

** That is, the 'stumblingblock.'—G.

of the cross, and of visitations and sicknesses and crosses that we meet withal in the world; for the scandal is this: shall we be in love with the ways of God, wherein we meet with these and these corrections? Oh, yes! take not scandal* at that which is sanctified by God to be a means to preserve us from being damned with the world. And the child of God, take him at the lowest, take him at the worst, he is better than a worldling at the best. Take no offence, therefore, at God's dispensation with his children. All is, that they may not be damned with the world. Do not only justify God, but magnify God for his corrections, and after thou shalt receive fruit by them. And we have reason, when we find ourselves more mortified to the world, and to have the quiet fruit of righteousness to magnify God. Hath the Spirit sanctified it to thee to make thee lead another course of life? Say, Blessed be God for sending this cross, for indeed we have ofttimes occasion to bless God more for crosses than for comforts. There is a blessing hidden in the worst things to God's children, as there is a cross in the best things to the wicked. There is a blessing in death; a blessing in sickness; a blessing in the hatred of their enemies; a blessing in their losses whatsoever. There is a blessing hidden in the worst things; and therefore let us not only justify God, but glorify and magnify God for his mercy, that rather than we shall be condemned with the world, he will take this course with us.

Use 5. And then here again, *you have a ground of impregnable comfort in all temptations whatsoever;* a wondrous comfort, that God will take a course with his to bring them to heaven. What a blessed course is this, that† the time to come we may take in trust of God, as well as the time past? That now in the state of grace, rather than he will condemn us, he will take one course or other to bring us to heaven? Rather than David shall live in his sin, he will send Nathan to him; rather than Peter shall not repent, Christ will look back upon him; rather than God's children shall go the broad way, God‡ will send the devil himself to annoy them, and to infest them, and to vex them. God will be sure to lose none of his. What a comfort is this? and therefore never think that we can be in such a condition wherein there is true ground of despair. No! We cannot. We are under hope in the most woeful condition in the world. We are under hope still;§ for there is more mercy in God than can be sin and evil in us; and he is infinitely wise to rule all to his own ends. What if things seem untoward? They are in his hands; he hath a powerful hand to manage the worst things‖ to good. So gloriously wise and powerful is God, that he sways the worst things. 'All things work for the best for those that love God,' Rom. viii. 28, even the worst things in this world.

Obj. Oh! but profane spirits will object and say, 'If this be so, we may be careless; if our salvation be made sure, that we shall not be condemned with the world, that God will take care even to bring us to heaven.

Ans. Oh! but the text takes away that objection of profane spirits that take liberty from this blessed truth of God. For though God do not damn his with the world, yet he sharply corrects them here.¶ By a careful sober

* 'Take no offence' in B, C.—G.
† 'For,' and 'we may trust God,' in B, C.—G.
‡ 'He' in B, C.—G.
§ 'We are under hope still' not in B, C.—G.
‖ 'All evil' in B, C.—G.
¶ 'That by,' &c., in B, C.—G.

life they might obtain many blessings, and prevent many judgments, and make their pilgrimage more comfortable. Therefore it argues neither grace, nor wit to argue so, because God will save me, therefore I will take liberty. No! Though God will save thee, yet he will take such a course that thou shalt endure such sharpness for thy sin, that it shall be more bitter than the sweetest of it was pleasant. There is no child of God that ever came to heaven, but God hath made their sinful courses more bitter to them than ever they have had benefit by them, though their souls have been safe. Put the case a man were sure not to be executed, yet to be branded, to be stigmatised, or to be disgraced in the country, would he for a paltry thing, not worth the speaking of, do wrong, because he should not be executed, and have friends to keep him from that? Who would* do such a thing as that, to bring himself to shame for a thing of nothing? So put the case thou shalt not be damned, thou art sure of that; yet thou mayest fall into such a course as God may brand thee; and thou mayest bring disgrace to religion; and mayest weaken the comfort of thine own soul; and mayest make Satan rejoice; and mayest grieve the angels about thee; and mayest vex the Spirit in thee; we may put a sting to the affliction we suffer, we may deprive ourselves of comfort in the midst of comforts for our boldness. Who, that hath the use of his wits, would do this for the pleasures of sin for a season?

Oh! therefore, when you go about to sin, consider what you go about. I go about to grieve God's Spirit, to provoke my heavenly Father; I go about to force out of his hand some rod, some correction; I go about to rejoice Satan; to grieve the angels, that are about me for my custody; to put a sting to my trouble, and to embitter it. This is the ill of ills, when a man is in affliction; my own wickedness brought me to this. Let us wisely consider this: though God save our souls, yet he will take such a course in this world, as we shall wish that we had not tried conclusions with God. David gave liberty to his lusts, but he wished (no doubt a thousand times), that he had not bought his pleasure at so dear a rate. Therefore, this I add, to fence this truth from the offence that a carnal heart takes at it. But to come to the proper and native use of it. Consider, I beseech you, how this doctrine is a fence against the rock of despair, and against the rock of presumption.

First, Against the rock of presumption. The soul may say, shall I be bold to sin? Surely I shall buy the pleasures of sin at a dear rate;† God will correct me sharply. And shall I force‡ God for such a pleasure, and for such a profit? No! I will not buy sin at that rate. So it fenceth the soul from presumption.

Again, *it fenceth the soul from despair.* Oh! but I have sinned; my own weakness hath given me the foil; and Satan he joins with my weakness and hath foiled me. Oh! but do not you yet despair, for therefore we are corrected, that we should not be condemned with the world; as I said before,§ a Christian is never so low, but mercy triumphs over the ill in him. There is more abundant mercy‖ in God, than there can be ill in us. So happy a condition it is to be in Christ, that¶ in the covenant of grace, God

* 'Could' in B, C.—G.
† 'Dearly' in B, C.—G.
‡ 'Provoke him' in B, C.—G.
§ 'As I said before' not in B, C.—G.
‖ 'Goodness' in B, C—G.
¶ 'That' not in B, C; and 'wherein God sets,' &c.—G.

sets himself to triumph over the greatest ills, over sin, and over affliction. There can be no ill so great, but it yields to his mercy in Jesus Christ, and therefore be not discouraged,* whatsoever ill we suffer. And so it keeps us from these two rocks of presumption and despair. Let us therefore for a conclusion of all take this course.

First of all, *be sure, beloved, that we get out of the world,*† *get out of Sodom, get out of the condition we are in by nature.* Trust not to a formal profession of religion. Do not deceive your souls; it will deceive you. Get out of the world, and get into Christ; get something by attending upon the means, and by prayer, and by crossing your corruptions; get somewhat in‡ you, that may evidence that you are taken out of the world, and that you are in Christ, being led with a better spirit than your own.

In the next place, *when you are in the state of grace, honour that condition.* Walk worthy of that glorious condition.§ Oh! the state of a Christian, it is a glorious state. It requires much holy wisdom to manage the state of Christianity. If we be Christians, let us carry ourselves like Christians worthily; if we will have good of our profession. Let us carry ourselves so, as that we may not go so far in religion, as may minister God more matter to damn us. What good is it to have so much knowledge, and so much profession as shall damn us the more? But if we will be religious, let us be religious to purpose,‖ and let us walk worthy of this glorious state.

Obj. Oh! but in the next place, I have not done it,¶ I have forgotten my condition, forgotten my hopes, forgotten my state, and** regarded my base lusts more; I have been surprised, and catched.

Sol. Then take this course: judge yourselves, if you have been overtaken; take the counsel of the apostle, while there is hope, and judge yourselves.††

Obj. But I see now, God is ready to take me out of the world, and I have not judged myself as I should; though I be out of love with my courses, and am in league with no evil course, yet I have been‡‡ faulty.

Sol. Oh! comfort thyself, let not Satan swallow thee up in despair; mark what the apostle saith, God sends this, that we should not be condemned with the world; and therefore presently make a covenant with him, renew thy purposes presently, as Ps. xxv. 1, *seq.* All his ways to his children are mercy and truth; his ways of correction and his ways of love, all his ways§§ are mercy. And therefore take heed that we never deny our own mercy, that we never forsake our own mercy; let not Satan prevail so much. We have need of all this, beloved, especially to remember it‖‖ in the time of temptation, in spiritual desolation, when we gasp for comfort; let us labour to learn this spiritual wisdom, to present to our own souls the promises of the gospel, and the relation that God hath put upon himself,

* 'Whatsoever . . . therefore' not in B, C; and the latter sentence 'won for a conclusion.'—G.

† 'Be sure . . . world' not in B, C.—G.

‡ 'To' in B, C.—G.

§ 'Calling' in B, C.—G.

‖ 'In deed and not in word only' in B, C; but 'and let us,' &c., omitted.—G.

¶ 'This' in B, C.—G.

** 'And' not in B, C; but with this addition, 'and walked loosely with God.'—G.

†† 'Repent speedily' in B, C.—G.

‡‡ 'Exceeding' not in B, C.—G.

§§ 'All his ways to his' in B, C.—G.

‖‖ 'To remember it' not in B, C.—G.

to be a father; his dealings to us, that they are fatherly corrections. Let not Satan wring these comforts out of our souls. But let us honour God by trusting him in life and death, and say with Job, 'Though he kill me, yet will I trust in him,' Job xiii. 15. So sweet and powerful is the death of Christ, that it turns all things, even the bitterest, to the greatest good. But this may be sufficient by the blessing of God's Spirit.

YEA AND AMEN;

OR,

PRECIOUS PROMISES AND PRIVILEGES.

YEA AND AMEN; OR, PRECIOUS PROMISES AND PRIVILEGES.

NOTE.

'Yea and Amen' forms a moiety of a little volume, which consists of it and a kindred but independent treatise. The title-page is given below.* The 'Privileges' will appear in its proper place. 'Yea and Amen,' being based upon a passage in the Commentary which fills our third volume, has unavoidable repetitions, but of such a kind as rather to excite interest than weary. The illustrations are multiplied, and new phases of the 'precious promises' developed; while the language is unusually compact. Indeed 'Yea and Amen,' for insight into the 'mind of the Spirit,' and of the sorrowful and despondent believer, and tenderness of consolation, and pathetic pleading, must take its place beside 'The Bruised Reed.' G.

* YEA AND AMEN:
OR
PRETIOUS PROMISES,
AND
PRIVILEDGES.
Spiritually unfolded in
their Nature and Use.
Driving at the assurance
& establishing of weak Believers.
By R. Sibbs, D.D. master of Katherine Hall in Cambridge, and
Preacher of Grayes-inne London.
Reviewed by himselfe in his life
time, & since perused by T. G. & P. N.
London,
Printed by R. Bishop for R. Dawlman,
& are to be sold by Humphrey Mosley
at the Princes Armes in Pauls
Church-yard. 1638.

YEA AND AMEN;

OR,

PRECIOUS PROMISES LAID OPEN OUT OF 2 COR. I. 19-23.

But as God is true, our word towards you was not yea and nay. For the Son of God, Jesus Christ, who was preached among you by us, was not yea and nay, but in him was yea. For all the promises of God are in him yea, and in him Amen, unto the glory of God by us.

The blessed apostle, that he might have the better place in the hearts of his hearers, endeavours here with all diligence to wipe off any imputation which they might have against him; that so his doctrine might come home to their souls, and have the freer access to work upon their consciences.

We have therefore in these words St Paul's apology for not coming unto the Corinthians, according to his promise. Wherein he allegeth that it was not from any inconstancy in him, but indeed from corruption in manners among them: ver. 23, 'I call God to record, that to spare you I came not.' The apostle as a man, and as a holy man, might promise many things common to this life, and might lawfully vary afterwards upon the appearance of real impediments.

But the things which he promiseth, and speaks of as an apostle, they admit of no such uncertainty. Therefore his care is to decline* all thoughts of wavering therein, and to maintain the credit of the gospel, which he had taught, to the uttermost; knowing well how ready 'false teachers' would be to persuade the people that Paul was as light in his preaching as he was in keeping his word with them. Therefore 'our word is true, as God is true,' saith he.

There is the same ground of the certainty of evangelical truths, as there is of God himself. 'Jesus Christ,' whom I preached among you, was not 'yea and nay,' saith the apostle, but 'yesterday and to-day, and the same for ever.' Whence may be observed:

Doct. 1. *That the object of preaching now in the time of the gospel, is especially Jesus Christ.* This is the rock upon which the church is built. Christ should be the subject matter of our teaching, in his nature, offices, and benefits; in the duties which we owe to him, and the instrument whereby we receive all from him, which is faith.

* That is, 'repudiate.'—G.

If we preach the law, and discover men's corruption, it is but to make way for the gospel's freer passage into their souls. And if we press holy duties, it is to make you walk worthy of the Lord Jesus. All teaching is reductive to the gospel of Christ, either to make way, as John Baptist did, to level all proud thoughts, and make us stoop to him, or to make us walk worthy of the grace we receive from him.

The bread of life must be broken; the sacrifice must be anatomised and laid open; the riches of Christ, even his 'unsearchable riches,' must be unfolded. 'The Son of God,' must be preached to all; and therefore God, who hath appointed us to be saved by Christ, hath also ordained preaching, to lay open the Lord Jesus, with the heavenly treasures of his grace and glory. But to go forward.

Jesus Christ who was preached among you by me, and Silvanus, and Timotheus, was not yea and nay.

Obs. Here observe, *that the consent of preachers in the mysteries of salvation, is an excellent means to strengthen faith in their hearers;* not in regard of the truth itself, but in regard of men. So it pleaseth God to condescend to our weakness, in adding sacraments and oath unto his promises, thereby to shew the more stableness of his counsel towards us.

By 'yea' here is meant certain, constant, invariable. The times vary, but not the faith of the times. The same fundamental truth is in all ages. Sometimes indeed it is more explicated and unfolded; as we have in the New Testament divers truths more clearly revealed than in the Old. There is not a new faith, but a larger explication of the old faith. Divine truth is always the same. If there hath been a church always, there hath ever been a divine truth. Now it is an article of our faith in all times to believe a 'catholic church.' Certainly then there must be a catholic truth to be the seed of this church. Therefore we should search out what was that 'yea,' that positive doctrine in those apostolical times of the church's purity, before it was corrupted.

The church was not long a virgin; yet some there were that held the truth of Christ in all ages. Our present church holds the same positive truths with the apostles before us. Therefore we say, 'Our church was before Luther,* because our doctrine is apostolical; as also is our church that is continued thereby, because it is built upon apostolical doctrine.' Put the case we cannot shew the men, as they ridiculously urge; what is that to the purpose? From an ignorance of particular men, will they conclude us to be ignorant of the church of Christ, which hath ever been?

Hence the true church may easily be discerned. The points of religion wherein our adversaries differ from us, be but patcheries† of their own. They were not 'yea' in the apostles' times. Their purgatory, invocation of saints, and sacraments of divers kinds, were devised by themselves afterwards. And indeed, for a thousand years after Christ, many of the differences betwixt us and the papists were never heard of, neither were they ever established by any council till the Council of Trent.‡

Our positive points are grounded upon the Holy Scriptures. We seek the 'old way' and the 'best way,' as Jeremiah adviseth us, Jer. vi. 16. There was no popish trash in Abraham's time among the blessed patriarchs, nor in Christ's time, no, nor many hundred years after. They came in by little and little, by human invention, for their own advantage; a mere policy to get money and abuse the people. Indeed, they hold many of

* Cf. note *sss*, Vol. III., p. 536.—G.

† That is, 'additions.'—G.

‡ Viz., 1545 to 1563.—G.

our truths, but they add something of their own to them. They add necessity of tradition to the Scriptures, merits to faith; they add saints to Christ in divine worship. They have seven sacraments to our two (*a*). They may safelier therefore come to us than we to them. We hold all that they should hold, only their own additions we hold not; we leave them to themselves. So much for that.

Doct. 2. To touch only another point that borders a little upon it. *Divine truth is of an inflexible nature.* This crosseth another rule of theirs; for they hold that they may give what sense of Scripture they will, and that the current of the present church must judge of all former counsels. What! doth the truth vary according to men's judgments? Must we bring the straight rule to the crooked timber for to be measured? Shall the judgment of any man be the rule of God's unerring truth? Shall present men interpret it thus, and say it is so now? And shall others that succeed after say, Whatever it was then, now it is thus? and must we believe all? God forbid.

Doct. 3. This declareth *that no man can dispense with God's law.* This written word is alike in all. Truth is truth, and error error, whether men think it to be so or no. Reason is reason in Turks as well as amongst us. The light of nature is the light of nature in any country as well as here. Principles of nature vary not as languages do, they are inbred things. And if principles of nature be inviolable and indispensable, much more is divinity. Filth is filth, we all confess. Opinion ought not to be the rule of things, but the nature of the thing itself.

Therefore, what is against nature, none can dispense withal. God cannot deny himself. What is naught in one age is naught in another, and for ever naught.* There is no monarch in the world can dispense with the law of nature, or with the divine law of God. For the opinion of any man in the world is not the rule which he may comfortably live by, but the undoubted light of Christ's written word.

I speak this the rather to cross their base practices, who, when God calls them to stand for his cause and truth, they will bend and bow the sacred truth (which is always 'yea and amen') to their own by-ends and base respects. As if the opinion of any man in the world were the rule of their faith and obedience. This is to make God no God. Is not right right? Is not the law the law! Is not the word of Christ a word that alters not but remains stedfast to all eternity?

Assure yourselves there is a truth of God that we must maintain to the death, not only in opposing heresy, but resisting of impiety wheresoever we meet it. John Baptist was a martyr when he stood out against Herod, and said, 'Thou must not have thy brother Philip's wife,' Mat. xiv. 3. He would not be meal-mouthed in reproving his sin, but cried out against the unlawfulness of it, though it cost him his life. Men ought to suffer for the truth, and not, for base ends, deny the least word of God, because it is a divine sparkle from himself.

'For all the promises of God in him are yea, and in him are amen.'

This comes in after this manner. The word that I preached, saith Paul, is invariable, because Christ himself is always yea, and I have preached nothing but Jesus Christ among you. My preaching, then, must needs be a certain and immutable truth.

There are divers readings of the words (*b*), but the most material is (as this translation and the best expositors have it), 'All the promises of God

* That is, 'naughty,' wicked.—G.

in Christ are yea;' that is, they are certain and constant in him. And then they are 'amen;' that is, in Christ they are fulfilled. In him they are made, and in him they are accomplished. The whole carriage of the promises are in Christ; for his sake they were first given, and in him they shall be performed. As Christ himself was yesterday and to-day, and the same for ever, so are all God's promises made in him, undoubtedly, eternally, and unchangeably true to all posterities.

Here are divers truths which offer themselves to our consideration.

Obs. first. Take notice, that since the fall of man, *it hath pleased our good God to establish a covenant of grace in Jesus Christ, and to make him a second Adam*, by whom we might be restored to a better estate than ever we had in the first Adam. In which happy condition there can be no intercourse betwixt God and man without some promise in his Christ, so that now God deals all by promises with us. The reason is this.

Reason 1. *How can poor dust and ashes dare to challenge anything of the great Majesty of heaven, without a warrant from himself?* How can the conscience be satisfied? (Conscience, you know, is a knowledge together with God.)* How can that rest quiet in anything but in what it is assured comes from God? And therefore, for any good I hope for from God, it behoves me to have some promise and word of his mouth for it, this being his constant course of dispensation to his people. While we live in this world we are always under hope. 'We rejoice in hope of the glory of God,' Rom. v. 2. Now, hope looks still to the promise, whereof some part is unperformed.

How doth heaven differ from earth but in this? Heaven is a place all for performances. Here we have some performances to encourage us, but are always under some promise not yet accomplished. And therefore, the manner of our apprehension of God in this world exceedingly differs from that in heaven.

Here it is by faith and hope; there it is by vision. Vision is fit for performance. Faith and hope look always to a word revealed; God therefore rules his church in this manner for their greater good. Alas! what can we have from God but by the manifestation of his own good will? May we look for favour from God for anything *in ourselves?* It is a fond† conceit.

Reason 2. Again, *God will have his church ruled by promises in all ages, to exercise the faithful in prayer and dependence upon him.* God will see of what credit he is among men, whether they will rely upon his bare promise or no. He might do us good, and give us no promise; but he will try his graces in us, by arming us against all difficulties and discouragements, till the thing promised be performed to us. Promises are, as it were, the stay of the soul in an imperfect condition; and so is faith in them, until our hopes shall end in full possession. And we must know that divine promises are better than earthly performances. Let God give man never so much in the world, if he have not a promise of better things, all will come to nothing at the last. And therefore God supports the spirits of his servants against all temptations, both on the right hand and on the left, by sweet promises. He will have them live by faith, which always hath relation to a promise. This is a general ground, then, that God now in Christ Jesus hath appointed to govern his church by way of promises.

But what is a promise?

A promise is nothing but a manifestation of love; an intendment of be-

* Cf. notes *hh*, *ii*, Vol. III., p. 532.—G. † That is, 'foolish.'—G.

stowing some good, and removing some evil from us. A declaring of a man's free engagement in this kind is a promise. It always comes from love in the party promising, and conveys goodness to the believing soul. Now what love can there be in God to us since the fall, which must not be grounded on a better foundation than ourselves? If God love us, it must be in one that is first beloved. Hereupon comes the ground of the promises to be in Jesus Christ. All intercourse between God and us must be in him that is able to satisfy God for us. The almighty Creator will have our debts discharged before he enters into a covenant of peace with us.

Now this Christ hath perfectly done, and thereby reconciled lost sinners. Hereupon the promise immediately issues from God's love in Christ to believing souls. He must first receive all good for us, and we must have it at the second hand from him. The promises in Christ are as the spirits in the body. They run through all the ages of the church. Without him there is no mercy nor comfort to be had. God cannot look on this cursed nature of ours out of Christ; and therefore whosoever apprehends any mercy from God, he must apprehend it in Christ, the promised seed. To make it clearer. Our nature since the fall is odious to God; a sinful, cursed nature remains in the best of us; and therefore that God may look peaceably upon it, he must look upon it in him that hath it undefiled, and in him whom he loves, even his only Son, like unto himself, that hath taken our nature upon him.

Now, our nature in Christ must needs be lovely and acceptable; and if ever God love us, it is for Christ alone, who was predestinated before all worlds to be a sacrifice for us, to be the head of his church, 1 Peter i. 10. He was ordained to do us good before we ourselves were ordained. Christ is the first beloved, and then we. God loves us in his beloved one. 'This is my beloved Son, in whom I am well pleased,' Mark i. 11. As if the Lord had said, I am pleased in him, and in all his; in his whole mystical body. Christ is the Son of God by nature, we by adoption. Whatever good is in us is first and principally in him. God conveys all by the natural* Son to the adopted sons. Therefore, all the promises are made to us in Christ. He takes them from God for us. He himself is the first promise, and all are 'yea and amen in him.' They are not directed to us abstracted from him; but we are elected in Christ, sanctified in him, acquitted from sin through him. 'By his stripes we are healed,' Isa. liii. 5. If Christ had not satisfied the wrath of God by bearing our iniquities upon the cross, we had been liable every moment to condemnation. If he had not been free from our sins, we had for ever lain under the burden of them. 'You are yet in your sins,' saith St Paul, 'if Christ be not risen,' 1 Cor. xv. 17. We are freed from our debts, because Christ our surety is out of prison. He is in heaven, and therefore we are at liberty.

The promises are a deed of gift which we have from and by Christ, who is the first object of all the respect that God hath to us. Why are the angels attendants on us? Because they attend upon Jacob's ladder; that is, upon Christ, that knits heaven and earth together. So that the angels, because they attend upon Christ first, become likewise our attendants. We have a promise of 'eternal life,' but this life is 'in his Son,' 1 John v. 11. God blesseth us with all spiritual blessings in him, Eph. i. 3, and makes us sons in him the natural Son. Whatsoever prerogative we enjoy, it is in Christ first, and so belongs to us; but no further than we by faith are made one with him. How darest thou think of God, who is a 'consuming

* That is, 'Son of his nature,' not at all in the modern sense of 'natural.'—G.

fire?' Heb. xii. 29, and not think of him as he is pleased and pacified with thy person in Christ, who took thy nature upon him, to be a foundation of comfort, and a second Adam; a public person, satisfying divine justice for all that are members of his body?

We may think upon God with comfort, when we see him appeased in his Christ. As long as he loves Christ, he cannot but love us. Never think to have grace, or salvation, or anything without Christ. Doth God love me? Doth he do good to my soul for my own sake, abstracted from his Son? No, surely. Then should I fly from his presence. But he looks upon me in his beloved, and in him accepts of my person. Therefore our Saviour prayeth, 'I desire thee, blessed Father, that the love wherewith thou lovest me, may be in them, and I in them,' John xvii. 23.

This should direct us in our dealing with God, not to go directly to him, but by a promise. And when we have a promise, look to Christ, in whom it is performed. If we ask anything of God in Christ's name, he will give it us, John xiv. 13. If we thank God for anything, thank him in Christ, that we have it in him. What a comfort is this, that we may go to God in Christ and claim the promises boldly, because he loves us with the same love he bears to his only beloved Son. If we get fast hold on Christ, and cleave there, God can as soon alter his love to him as alter his love to us; his love is every whit as unchangeable to a believing member, as to Christ the head of the body. The promises are as sure as the love of God in Christ is, upon which they are founded, and from which 'nothing can separate us,' Rom. viii. 35. For promises being the fruit of God's love, and God's love being founded first upon Christ, it must needs follow, that all the promises are both made and made good to us through him.

If a prince should love a man, and his love should be founded upon the love he bears to his own son, surely such a one may have comfort: that love will never fail him, because it is an affection natural, and therefore unalterable. He will always love his son, and therefore will always delight in him in whom his son delighteth. Now Christ is the everlasting Son of the Father—his dear and only Son, in whom he is ever well pleased, and through whom he cannot be offended with those that are his. So surely as God loves Christ, so surely he loves all that are united to him. There is nothing in the world can separate his love from his own Son; neither is there anything able to separate his love from us that are one with him, Rom. viii. 35. God loves Christ's mystical body, as well as his natural body. He hath advanced that to glory at his right hand in heaven; and will he, think you, leave his mystical body, the church, in a state of abasement here on earth? No certainly. God loves every member of his Son? for as he gave us to Christ, so him hath he sealed and anointed to be a Saviour for his people.

This is the reason why God looks upon us with a forbearing eye, notwithstanding the continual matter of displeasure he finds in us: he looks on us in his Son; his love to us is grounded on his love to Christ. And hereupon comes our boldness with God the Father, that we can go to him in all distresses with comfort, and say, 'Lord, look on thy Son whom thou hast given for us, and in him behold his poor members now before thee.' 'In ourselves we have dread, but in thy dearly beloved we have joy in thy presence.' If we come in the garments of our elder brother, we are sure to get a blessing; but in ourselves, God cannot endure to behold us. If we bring Benjamin to our father, if we carry Christ along with us, then come and welcome.

Upon what unchangeable grounds is the love of God and the faith of a Christian builded? How can the gates of hell prevail against the faith of a true believer, when it is carried to the promise, and from the promise to God's love? The love of God to Christ shall as soon fail, as the faith of a sincere Christian shall be shaken. The promises else should be of no effect; they should be 'yea and nay,' and not 'yea and amen.'

If the promises could be shaken, the love of God and Christ should be uncertain. Overturn heaven and earth, if we overturn the faith of a true, persevering Christian. There is nothing in the world of that firmness as a believing soul is; the ground he stands upon makes him unmoveable. Our union with the Lord Jesus makes us like 'mount Sinai, that cannot be shaken.' But we must know there are three degrees or steps of love, whereof a promise is the last:—

1. *Inward love.*
2. *Real performance.*
3. *A manifestation of performance intended before it be done.*

Love concealed doth not comfort in the interim. Therefore God, who is love, doth not only affect* us for the *present*, and intend us mercy hereafter; but because he will have us rest sweetly in his bosom, and settle ourselves on his gracious purposes, he gives us in the mean time many 'rich and precious promises,' 2 Pet. i. 4. He not only loves us, and shews the same in deeds now, but he expresseth his future care of us, that we may build on him, as surely as if we had the thing performed already.

By this we see how God loves us. He hath not only an inward liking and good will to us in his breast, but manifests the same by word. He reveals the tenderness of his bowels towards us, that we may have the comfort of it beforehand. God would have us live by faith, and establish ourselves in hope, because these graces fit us for the promise. If there were no promises, there could be no faith nor hope.

What is hope but the expectation of those things that the word saith? And what is faith, but a building on the promise of God? Faith looks to the word of the thing; hope to the thing in the word. Faith looks to the thing promised; hope to the possession and performance of it. 'Faith is the evidence of good not seen,' Heb. xi. 1, making that which is absent as present to us. Hope waits for the accomplishment of that good contained in the word. If we had nothing promised, what need hope? and where were the foundation of faith? But God being willing to satisfy both (that we may be heavenly-wise, in relying upon a firm foundation; and not as fools, 'trust in vanity,' Ps. iv. 2), in mercy gives us promises, and seals them with an oath for our greater supportment. That love which engaged the Almighty to bind himself to us in 'precious promises,' 2 Pet. i. 4, will furnish us likewise with grace needful till we be possessed of them. He will give us leave to depend upon him, both for happiness and all quieting graces, which may support the soul till it come to its perfect rest in himself.

Now these gracious expressions of our good God may be reduced into divers ranks. I will but touch some few particulars, and shew how we should carry ourselves to make a comfortable use of them.

First, There are some universal promises for the good of all mankind; as that God would never destroy the world again, &c., Gen. ix. 11.

Secondly, There are other promises that more particulavly concern the church. And these are promises.

* That is, 'love,' 'have an affection for.'—G.

(1.) Either of *outward things*.

(2.) Or of *spiritual and eternal things, of grace and glory*.

In the manner of promising they admit of this distinction. All the promises of God are made to us either,

(1.) *Absolutely*, without any condition. So was the promise of sending Christ into the world, and his glorious coming again to judgment. Let the world be as it will, yet Christ did come, and will come again, with thousands of angels, to judge us at the last, 2 Tim. iv. 1.

Or (2.) *Conditional;* as the promise of grace and glory to God's children, that he will forgive their sins, if they repent, &c. God deals with men (as we do by way of commerce one with another), propounding mercy by covenant and condition; yet his covenant of grace is always a 'gracious covenant.' For he not only gives the good things, but helps us in performing the condition by his Spirit; he works our hearts to believe and to repent.

Thus all promises for outward things are conditional; as thus, God hath promised protection from contagious sickness, and from trouble and war; that he will be 'an hiding-place,' Ps. xxxii. 7, and a 'deliverer' of his people in time of danger, Ps. xl. 17; that he will do this and that good for them. But these are conditional; so far forth as in his wise providence he sees they may help to preserve spiritual good things in them, and advance the graces of the inward man. For God takes liberty in our outward estate to afflict us or do us good, as may best further our soul's welfare. Because, do what we can with these bodies, they will turn to dust and vanity ere long. We must leave the world behind us. Therefore he looks to our main estate in Christ, to the 'new creature;' and so far as outward blessings may cherish and increase that, so far he grants them, or else he denies them, to his dearest ones.

For we cannot still enjoy the blessings of this life, but our corrupt nature is such, that, except we have somewhat to season the same, we shall surfeit, and not digest them. Therefore they are all given with exception of the cross; as Christ saith, he that doth for him anything, 'shall have a hundredfold here,' Mat. xix. 29, but 'with persecution.' Be sure of that, whatsoever else he hath. Let Christians look for crosses to season those good things they enjoy in this life.

Use. To come now to some use of the point. Are all the promises, of what kind soever, whether spiritual or outward, temporal or eternal, are they all made to us in Jesus Christ? And are they certainly true, 'yea and amen' in him? Then I beseech you *get into Christ betimes, strengthen your interest in him by all means, out of whom we have nothing that is savingly good*. Rest not in anything abstracted from him, so as to be accepted with God.

Obj. But you will say, Doth not God do many good things to them that are out of Christ? Doth not the sun shine, and the rain fall, upon the just and the unjust; upon the evil as well as the good? Doth he not clothe, and feed, and protect wicked men daily?

Ans. He doth indeed, it cannot be denied. But are they blessings? Are these favours to them? No; but as God saith to Moses, Deut. xxviii. 16: 'If thou sin against me, cursed shalt thou be in thy basket and thy store. Cursed shall be the fruit of thy body, and the fruit of thy land, the increase of thy kine, and the flocks of thy sheep: cursed at home, cursed abroad.' They are cursed in their very blessings. A graceless, brutish person, though he swim with worldly pleasures, and have never such revenues and comings in to maintain his bravery,* is yet an accursed creature in the midst of all. For what are we made for, think you? To live here only? Oh no. 'Then we were of all others the most miserable,' 1 Cor. xv. 19. There is an eternity of time a-coming, wherein, after a few days spent in the flesh, we shall live either in perpetual bliss, or unspeakable torment. The very best things beneath have a snare in them; they rather hinder than further our eternal welfare.

Quest. How doth that appear?

Ans. Because for the most part they make men secure and careless in the worship of God, so as to despise the power of godliness, and follow iniquity with greediness. We may see by men's conversations that outward things are snares to them. They are not promises in Christ; for then they would come out of God's love only, which alone makes mercies to be mercies indeed to us, and without which, the best of blessings will prove but a curse in the end.

If I have anything in this world, any deliverance from evil, or any positive good thing, I may know it is for my benefit, when my heart is made more spiritual thereby, so as to value grace and holiness at the highest rate; I esteeming my being in Christ above all transitory things whatsoever, above riches and honour and the favour of great persons, which at the best is fading. Our interest in him will stand by us, when all these things are withered and shrunk to nothing. Christ is a fountain never drawn dry; his comforts are permanent. The good in the creature soon vanisheth and leaveth the soul empty. Therefore get into Christ speedily, it concerns thee nearly.

For this purpose *attend upon the means of salvation*, and beg of God that he would make his own ordinances, by his Spirit accompanying the same, effectual to thy soul; that he would open the excellencies of Christ to thee, and draw thy affections to close with him.

Quest. How are we in Christ?

Ans. When, by knowing of him, our knowledge carries our hearts unto him, John xvii. 3. When our wills cleave to that which we know to be excellent and necessary for us, when I firmly adhere to Christ as the only good for me, then I love him, then I rest on him, then I have peace in him.

I may discern that I am in Christ, if upon my knowledge of him, my heart is united to him, and I find peace of conscience in him. Faith hath a quieting and establishing power. If I be in Christ, my soul will be cheered and satisfied with him alone. I know all is yea and amen in him; therefore my soul rests securely here. However our outward condition be various and perplexed, yet our estate in Christ is firm and constant.

Quest. What is a man out of Christ?

Ans. As a man in a storm that hath no clothes to hide his nakedness, or to shelter his body from the violence of the weather. As one in a tempest, that hath not house nor harbour to cover him. As a stone out of the foundation, set lightly by, and scattered up and down here and there. As a branch out of the root; what sap is there in such a thing, it being good for nothing but to be cast into the fire?

A man that is not built up in Christ, planted in him, nor clothed with him, is the most destitute, despicable creature in all the world; and if we look with a single eye, we shall so discern him. Such a man's case is deeply to be bewailed. Had we but hearts to judge righteously, we would prefer the meanest condition of God's child, before the greatest estate of

* That is, 'grandeur.'—G.

any earthly monarch, be their flourishing felicity never so resplendent. Oh! the miserable and woeful plight that all profane wretches are in, who neglect grace and the mysteries of Christ, to gratify their base lusts. Such an one, there is but a step between him and hell; he hath no portion in the Lord Jesus. 'I account all dung and dross,' saith St Paul, 'in comparison of Christ, to be found in him, not having on mine own righteousness,' Philip. iii. 8. Happy is that man at the day of judgment, who thus appears.

Use 2. Again, if so be that all promises are 'yea and amen in Christ,' then here *take notice of the stability of a Christian, that hath promises to uphold him.* Compare him with a man that hath present things only, with an Esau that abounds with worldly goods; and how great is the difference? God gives them their portion here, as he saith to Dives, 'Thou hadst thy good things,' Luke xvi. 25, *seq.:* that thou chiefly caredst for, thou hadst them here, but Lazarus had pain, misery, and poverty. Now therefore the case is altered; he is advanced, 'and thou art tormented.'

A believing Christian enjoys the sweetness of many promises in this life (for God is still delivering, comforting, and perfecting of him; renewing of his spirit, and supplying him with inward peace); but the greatest part is yet to be accomplished. Perfection of grace and glory is to come. He is a child, he is a son. The promise here is his chief estate.

Another man hath present payment, and that is all he cares for; he hath something in hand, and swells with a conceit of happiness thereby. Alas! what are we the better to have a great deal of nothing? Solomon, that had tried all the world, resolves it to 'vanity and vexation of spirit,' Eccles. i. 14. All things below are uncertain, and we are uncertain in the use of them. If we have no better a life than a natural one, eternal joy appertains not to us. Take a Christian and strip him in your thoughts from all the good things in the world, he is yet a happier man than the greatest worldly favourite out of Christ; for the one hath nothing but present things, with a great deal of addition of misery, which his ease and contentment makes him more sensible of; as being more tender and apprehensive of an evil than other men. The other, though he want many comforts of this life, and enjoys not present performances; yet he is rich in bills and bonds. God is bound to him, who hath promised he 'will never forsake him, but be his portion for ever,' Heb. xiii. 5. He hath a title to every communicable good. 'Godliness hath the promise of this life, and that which is to come,' 1 Tim. iv. 8. A happy man! Whatever is most useful for his safe conduct to heaven, he is sure to have it. He that will give us a kingdom, will not deny us daily bread; he that hath prepared a country for us, will certainly preserve us safe, till we come there.

Besides that we have here in performance, we have many excellent promises of a greater good in expectation, which in Christ are all 'yea and amen.' They are certain, though our life be uncertain, and the comforts of our life, less than life itself, mutable and perishing. If life, the foundation of outward comforts, be but a vapour, what are all the comforts themselves, think you?

It is a Christian's rejoicing in the midst of all changes beneath, that he hath promises invested into him from above that are lodged in his heart, and made his own by faith, which have * a wondrous peculiarising virtue to make that a man's own that is otherwise generally propounded in the gospel. A Christian, take him at all uncertainties, he hath somewhat to build on, that is 'yea and amen,' undoubtedly sure, that will stick by him.

* Qu. 'hath'?—Ed.

I speak this to commend the estate of a believing Christian; to make you in love with it, seeing in all the changes and varieties of this world he hath somewhat to take to. In all the dangers of this life he hath a rock and chamber of providence to go unto, as it is Isa. xxvi. 20. God hath secret rooms to hide his children in in times of public disturbance, when there is a confusion of all things. God hath a safe abiding place for thee. 'I have many troubles,' saith David, 'but God is my defence continually,' Ps. lxxxviii. 4. He is my 'shield and strong tower;' whatsoever I want I have it in him. What a comfort is this!

A Christian knows either he shall be safe here or in heaven, and therefore rests securely. 'He that dwells in the secret place of the most High, shall abide under the shadow of the Almighty,' Ps. xci. 1, 2; that is, in the love and protection of God above. As Moses saith, 'Lord, thou hast been our habitation from everlasting to everlasting,' Ps. xc. 1; that is, thou art our sure help in the greatest extremity that can befall us in any age of the world.

Therefore build on his promise, for God and his word are all one. If we have nothing to take to when troubles come, woe unto us! In ourselves considered, we are even as grass, and as a tale that is told, soon vanishing. But our estate in God is durable. We have here no continuing city; sickness may come, and death may environ us the next moment. Happy are they that have God for their habitation. We dwell in him when we are dead. When we leave this world we shall live with God for ever. 'The righteous is not troubled for evil tidings,' Ps. cxii. 7. He is not shaken from his rock and stay. He fears no danger, because 'his heart is fixed,' ver. 8.

What a blessed estate is it to be in Christ, to have promises in him, to be protected and preserved, not only whilst we are in this vale of tears, but when this earthly tabernacle shall be dissolved, even to all eternity. If our hearts be fixed on God, let us hear evil tidings of war, or famine, or pestilence, let it be what it will, blessed men are we. 'Every word of God is tried as silver in the fire,' saith the psalmist, Ps. xii. 6. The promises are tried promises; we may safely rest upon them. But if we have nothing to take to when troubles arise, we are as a naked man in a storm, without any shelter, encompassed round with distress and misery.

The promises are our inheritance, yea, our best inheritance in this life. Though the Lord should strip us naked, and take away all things else, yet if the promises remain ours, we are rich men, and may say with the psalmist, 'My lot is fallen into a good ground; thy testimonies are better unto me than thousands of gold and silver,' Ps. xvi. 6. For the promises are as so many obligations, whereby God is bound to his poor creature. And if wretched men think themselves as rich as they have bonds, though they have never a penny in their purses, much more may a true Christian, who hath the promises of Christ for his security, esteem himself a wealthy person; as having many bonds whereby not man, but God, is engaged to him, and that not only for temporal good things, but for heavenly favours and spiritual blessings, for all which he may sue God at his pleasure, and desire him to make good his word of truth.

There is little difference betwixt a poor Christian and him that abounds in this world's riches; only this, the one hath wealth in his own possession, the other hath it in God's bond; the one hath it in hand, the other in trust. As for the worldling, he hath but a cistern when he hath most; whereas every faithful soul hath the spring-head, even God himself to fly unto in all distresses, who will never fail him, but be a 'sun and a shield,' to defend us from all evil and preserve us in all goodness all our days. But I go on.

'Now he which stablisheth us with you in Christ, and hath also anointed us, is God.'

Obs. 1. Here observe, *that the Christian needs not only converting but establishing grace.* He that hath begun any good work in us must perfect it. The God of strength must give up his promise to support our weakness, without which we cannot stand. Peter was in the state of grace, and yet when God did not stablish him, we see how he fell. The weakest believer with the establishing grace of God will stand; and the strongest Christian, without divine assistance, will sink and fall away.

Obs. 2. Whence this may be further considered, *that the life of a Christian is a perpetual dependent life.* He not only lives by faith in his first conversion, but ever after. He depends upon God for protection and strength throughout his whole course. God doth establish us in Christ. The ignorance of this makes men subject to backsliding. For when we trust to grace received, and seek not for new supply, we are straight of Peter's condition, 'Though all forsake thee, yet will not I,' Luke xxii. 33, which occasioned his shameful fall. He had too much confidence in grace received.

God is therefore fain to humble his children, to teach them dependence. And usually where any special grace is bestowed upon sinners, God joins something therewith to put them in mind that they do not stand by their own strength. Peter makes a glorious confession, 'Thou art Christ, the Son of the living God,' Mat. xvi. 17, 18, 19; and Christ honoured him exceedingly, saying, 'Upon this rock will I build my church.' But yet by and by we see he calls him, 'Satan, get thee behind me,' Mat. xvi. 23, to teach us that we stand not by our own power. When we are strong, it is of God; and when we are weak, it is of ourselves. Jacob wrestled with the Almighty, and was a prevailer, but he was fain to halt for it. Though he had the victory, and overcame at last, yet he was stricken with lameness all his days. God did this to mind him that he had that strength whereby he prevailed out of himself.

Use. A Christian then should set upon nothing in his own strength. Hannah saith comfortably, 'No man shall be strong in his own might,' 1 Sam. 2, 9. God is all our sufficiency. Man naturally affects* a kind of divinity, and will set upon things in confidence of his own abilities, without prayer and seeking of God's help. He thinks to compass great matters, and bring things to a good issue by his own wit and discretion. Oh! delude not yourselves. This cannot be. 'Acknowledge God in all thy ways, and he shall direct thy paths, Prov. iii. 6. Seek unto the Lord in every enterprise thou goest about; acknowledge him in the beginning, progress, and issue of all thy employments. What do we but make ourselves gods, when we set upon business without invocation and dependence? A Christian is wondrous weak, even vanity of himself; but take him as he is built upon the promises, and as he is in God, and then he is a kind of almighty person, 'He can do all things through Christ that strengthens him,' Philip. iv. 13. A Christian is in sort omnipotent whilst he commits his ways to God, and depends upon the promise; otherwise he is weakness itself, the most impotent creature in the world.

Let God, therefore, have all the glory of our establishing, and depend on him by prayer for the same. As all comes of his mere grace, so let all

* That is, 'pretends' = *chooses* to appear.—G.

return to his mere glory. 'Not to us, Lord, not to us, but to thy name be given the praise,' Ps. cxv. 1. It is the song of the church militant on earth, and it is the song of the church triumphant in heaven, that *all* glory is to God in the whole carriage of our salvation. The promises are in him. He only made the covenant, and he must perform it to us: without him we can do nothing. Labour, therefore, to be wise in his wisdom, strong in his strength, to be all in all in Christ Jesus.

Obj. How shall we know that a man hath establishing grace?

Ans. His assurance is firm when his temptations are great, and his strength to resist little; and yet notwithstanding he prevails over them. Satan is strong and subtile. Now if we can stand against his snares, it is a clear evidence of greater strength than is in ourselves. In great afflictions, when God seems an enemy, and clouds appear between him and us, if then a man's faith can break through all, and in the midst of darkness see God shining in Christ upon him, and resolve, 'Though thou kill me, yet I will trust in thee,' Job xiii. 15; here is a strong establishing.

In the times of martyrdom there was fire and faggot, and the frowns of bloody men; but who were the persons suffering? Even many children, old men and women, the weakest of creatures. Notwithstanding the Spirit of God was so strong in these feeble ones, as their lives were not precious to them; but the torments and threatenings of their cruel persecutors were cheerfully undergone by them, as Heb. xi. 34, *seq.* Here was God's power in man's infirmity. If we have not something above nature, how is it possible we should hold out in great trials?

Means to obtain establishing grace.

By what means may a Christian obtain this stablishing grace?

First, Labour for fundamental graces. If the root be strengthened, the tree will stand fast.

(1.) Humiliation is a special radical grace. The foundation of religion is very low. Abasement of spirit is in all the parts of holiness. Every grace hath a mixture of humility, because they are all dependencies on God. Humility is an emptying grace, and acknowledgeth that in ourselves there is nothing. If God withhold his influence, I am gone; if he withdraw his grace, I shall be like another man, as Samson was when his hair was cut off. Self-emptiness prepares for spiritual fulness. 'When I am weak,' saith blessed Paul, 'then I am strong;' that is, when I feel and acknowledge my weakness, then my strength increases; otherwise a man is not strong when he is weak; but when he is sensible and groans under the burden of his infirmities, then he is inwardly strong.

(2.) Another fundamental grace is *dependence upon God;* for considering our own insufficiency, and that faith is a grace that grows out of ourselves, and lays hold of the righteousness of another to justify us, nothing can be more necessary to quiet the soul. 'Believe, and you shall be established:' as the promises are sure in themselves, so should we repose firm confidence in them.

Obj. But how doth God establish us by faith?

Ans. By working sound knowledge in us: 'This is life eternal, to know thee,' John xvii. 3. When we know the truth of God's word aright, we have a firm ground to depend on; for the more a man knows God in covenant, the more he knows Christ and the promises, the more he will trust and rely upon them. 'They that know thy name will trust in thee,' Ps. ix. 10, saith the prophet. Therefore labour for certainty of knowledge, that thou mayest have a certainty of faith. What is the reason our faith is weak? Because we are careless to increase in knowledge. The more we know of God, the more we shall trust in him. The more we know of a man that he is able and just of his word, the more safely we put confidence in him. So the more our security is in God's promises, as his bonds increase, so our trust will be strengthened.

(3.) Thirdly, if thou wouldst have establishing grace, *beg it earnestly of God*. Our strength in him is altogether by prayer. Bind him, therefore, with his own promise; beseech him to do unto thee according to his good word. He is the God of strength, desire of him the spirit of strength; allege to him thy own weakness and inability without him, and that if he helps not, thou shalt soon be overcome; lay open thy wants in God's presence; shew him how unable thou art of thyself to withstand temptations, to bear crosses, to perform duties, to do or suffer anything aright; turn his gracious promises into prayers; desire God that he would stablish thee by his grace; that he would prop and uphold thy soul in all extremities.

Quest. What is the reason that Christians are so daunted, and fly off in time of danger?

Ans. They have no faith in the promise. The righteous is as mount Sinai, that shall not be moved. He builds on a foundation that can never be shaken, for the heart is never drawn to any sinful vanity, or frighted with any terror of trouble, till faith lets go its hold. Out of God there is nothing for the soul safely to stay itself upon.

No marvel to see men fall that rest on a broken reed. Alas! whatsoever is besides* God, is but a creature; and can the creature be other than changeable? The comfort that we have in God never fadeth; it is an abiding, lasting comfort, such as contents the soul, and satisfies all the wants and desires of it, which things beneath can never accomplish.

We see that the heavens continue; and the earth, without any other foundation, hangs in the midst of the world by the bare word of the Almighty. Therefore well may the soul stay itself on that, when it hath nothing else in sight to rely upon.

In this case Christians should look, *first*, that their principles and foundations be good; and, *secondly*, builded strongly upon them. For the soul is as that which it relies on: if upon empty things, itself becomes poor and empty; which the devil knowing, strives to unloose our hearts from our Maker, and draw us to rely upon false objects. He sees full well, that whilst our souls cleave close to God, there is no prevailing against us by any malice or subtilty of men or devils. The saints, in him, are bold and undaunted in the midst of troubles and torments. Indeed, the sweetest communion with God is, when we are beaten from other helps: though misery upon misery encounters us below, yet there is still succour issuing from above to a believing soul. If God hath it in heaven, faith will fetch it down and enjoy the sweetness of it here. That man can never do amiss that hath his dependency upon the Almighty; there being no communion like that of a faithful heart with the Lord.

It is the office of faith to quiet our souls in all distresses; for it relies upon God for heaven itself, and all the necessary provision, till we come thither. Strengthen faith, therefore, and you strengthen all. What can daunt that soul, which in the sorest affliction hath the great God for his friend? Such a spirit dares bid defiance to all the powers of darkness. Satan may for a time exercise, but he can never wholly depress a gracious heart. True believers can triumph over that which others are slaves unto.

* That is, 'beside,' as elsewhere 'sometimes' for 'sometime.'—G.

They can set upon spiritual conflicts, and endure fiery trials, which others tremble to think of. They can put off themselves, and be content to be nothing, so their God may appear the greater; and dare undertake or undergo anything for the glory of their Maker. Considering they are not their own, but have given up themselves to Christ, 'they count not their lives, or anything that is theirs, dear for him,' Acts xx. 24.

He that stablisheth us with you is God, who hath anointed us, &c.

Messiah signifies 'anointed.' Our nature is enriched in Christ with all graces: 'He is anointed with the oil of gladness above his fellows' for us, Ps. xlv. 7, that we might have a spring of grace in our own nature; that God and Christ being one, and we being in the Lord Jesus, might have all our anointing of the first anointed, for 'of his fulness we receive grace for grace,' John i. 16.

Quest. What are those graces which we receive from Christ's fulness?

Ans. (1.) *First,* The grace of *favour and acceptance;* for the same love that God bears to Christ, he bears to all his, though not in so high a degree.

(2.) Secondly, The grace of *sanctification,* answerable to the grace of sanctification in him. Every renewed work in us comes from Christ.

(3.) Thirdly, *The rich privileges and prerogatives* that issue to persons sanctified. We have dignity for dignity, favour for favour, gracious qualifications for gracious qualifications in Christ. God anoints us all in his Son. As the ointment that was poured upon Aaron ran down to 'the skirts of his garment,' so the weakest Christian is stablished with grace by Christ. Grace runs from the Head to the poorest member, 'the hem of the garment.' Every one that doth but touch Christ, draws virtue and strength from him.

Quest. Why is it called here an anointing?

Ans. Because, as the holy anointing, Exod. xxx. 31–33, was not to be applied to profane uses, so neither are the graces of the Spirit (God being the author of them) to be slighted and undervalued by the professors* of them.

Quest. What are the virtues of this ointment?

Ans. First, It hath a *cherishing power;* it revives the drooping soul, and cheers a fainting spirit. When men are ready to sink under the burden of their sins, this easeth them.

Second, Anointing hath a *strengthening power.* It makes our limbs vigorous. So doth grace fortify the soul, nothing more. Our life is a combating life with Satan, and temptations of all sorts; therefore we need continual anointing to make us nimble and active in resisting our enemy. Oil hath a suppling quality; so the Spirit of God makes pliable the joints of the soul. It supports us with hidden strength, and enables us to encounter great oppositions, and to be victorious through Christ over all.

Grace is little in quantity, but it is mighty in operation. It carries the soul through difficulties; nothing can stand in the way of a gracious man, no, not the gates of hell. The spirit of grace that is in a Christian is stronger than he that is in the world. 'A grain of mustard seed,' the very least measure of true holiness, is stronger than the greatest measure of opposition. A Christian's strength lies out of himself. He never overcomes by his own power: 'He can do all things through Christ assisting him,' Philip. iv. 13. Otherwise he is a most impotent creature, unable to

* Qu. 'possessors'?—G.

do or suffer anything, ready to give over at the least trouble, and sink under every pressure of affliction.

Third, Again, ointment *doth excellently delight and refresh our spirits;* as we see the box in the gospel, when it was opened, the whole house smelled of it, John xii. 3. So grace is a wondrous sweet thing. Before we are anointed with the Spirit of Christ, with stablishing grace, what are we but a company of nasty, abominable persons in the eyes of God? All things are accursed to us, and we are accursed in whatever we do. God cannot look on us but as loathsome creatures; as the prophet saith, 'I would not so much as look on thee, if it were not for Jehoshaphat's sake,' 2 Kings iii. 14.

That which makes a man sweet is grace. This makes our nature, that is noisome and offensive in the nostrils of the Almighty, in itself, to become pleasant and amiable. A wicked man is a vile man, an ulcerous, deformed creature. Grace is of a healing nature wheresoever it is. This cures our spiritual distempers, beautifying the inner man, and making the whole frame of a Christian's carriage sweet and delectable.

(1.) *First*, to *God*, who loves the scent of his own grace, wheresoever he finds it.

(2.) *Secondly*, to *angels*. The conversion of sinners rejoiceth them, Luke xv. 10. When our custody is committed to their charge, how are they delighted with the beauty of holiness shining in us! The graces of God in his saints are a feast to them. The very name of a godly and gracious man 'is as a sweet ointment' everywhere, Cant. i. 3.

(3.) Holy men, when they are read of in stories, *what a savour do they cast in the church!* So far as a Christian is a 'new creature,' it makes him in love with himself, scorning to be so undervalued as to defile himself with base services. So far as a man is gracious, he gives himself to honourable employments. Being a vessel of grace, he improves his abilities to glorious uses, esteeming things below too mean for him.

Grace is a wondrous pleasant thing, offensive to none but to wicked men, that have no savour of God or goodness. It sweetens the soul, makes it delectable for Christ and his Holy Spirit to lodge in, as in 'a garden of spices.' A gracious man, that hath subdued his corruptions, is wondrous amiable, both to himself and to the communion of saints. His heart is 'as fine silver.' Everything is sweet that comes from him. Grace is full of comfort to a man's own conscience, the sense of which enlargeth the soul to all holy services.

Fourthly, An ointment hath another property, *it consecrates persons to holy uses*. Anointed persons are raised above the ordinary rank. The graces of God's Spirit elevate men above the condition of others with whom they live. Anointed persons are sacred persons, they are inviolable: 'Touch not mine anointed, and do my prophets no harm,' Ps. cv. 15. We wrong the 'apple of God's eye,' Zech. ii. 8, we offer indignity to Christ himself, if we hurt these. Indeed, nothing can hurt them; but God, by his over-ruling power, turns all for their good.

Lastly, *An ointment is a royal liquor*. It will be above all. So the graces of God's Spirit, where they are, will be uppermost, they will guide and govern all. As if a man have excellent parts, grace will rule these and make them serviceable to Christ his truth and members. If we have weakness and corruption, grace will subdue it by little and little, and never leave conflicting till it hath got the victory.

What are our souls without God's anointing? Dead, stinking, offensive to God, to good men, and to ourselves. We cannot see with peace the visage of our own souls. Who can reflect seriously into his heart and life without horror, that hath no grace? A man that sees his conscience awakened without this anointing, what is he? Surely as the body without the soul. It is not all the excellencies of the soul laid upon a dead body, or all the goodly ornaments that bedecked it, can keep it from stinking, and being a loathsome object, because it wants the soul to quicken and enliven it to good employments. Of itself it is but a piece of earth. All the vigour and life that the body hath is communicated from the soul. They are beholden to our souls for many things. Put the richest ornaments whatsoever upon the body, and not the Spirit of grace upon the soul (to cherish and refresh the same, that it may appear lovely in God's sight), all is to no purpose.

Likewise this anointing hath relation to the persons anointed: kings, priests, and prophets. Christ is primarily anointed, and all our grace is derived from him. He teacheth us divine things by a divine light. The poorest Christian in the world, whose heart is right with God, sees good things with such convincing love, that he embraces them, and ill things with such a convincing hatred, that he abhors them. A man that lives without God in the world may talk, but he cannot do; he may speak of death, but he dares not die; he trembles to think of the last tribunal, and of resigning his soul into the hands of his Maker. Such an one may discourse of suffering, but when it comes to the point, his heart fails him. Oh! how he shrinks when danger approacheth. What indirect courses will he take to save his skin! How hardly is corrupt self brought under! How heavily do men come off in this point of doing and suffering for Christ, laying down all at his feet, and resolving to be disposed of at his pleasure in everything. Men speak much of patience and self-denial, but they do not practise them. These virtues shine not forth in their conversation, which is the shame of religion. Only a true Christian hath the right knowledge of the doing of things, and is able to speak a word 'in due season,' Isa. l. 4, to reprove, to admonish, to comfort. Every member in the communion of saints hath some qualification for the good of the whole body.

A faithful man is likewise spiritually anointed a priest to stand before God Almighty. He pours out his soul for himself and for others, having God's ear open at all times to his suits. Every sincere Christian is a favourite in heaven. He hath much credit there, which he improves for the welfare of the church here below. And he keeps himself as a priest, unspotted of the world. A true Christian is taught of God, and knows the meaning of that law of his, which prohibiteth priests so much as to touch defiled things. Therefore he studies innocency; he runs not after the course of the multitude, neither is carried away with the streams of the times. He will not converse familiarly with those that may stain him but so far as his calling leads him, lest he should thereby contaminate his spirit. A Christian priest hath his heart always to the 'holy of holies,' that so he may offer up thanks and praise to God, and offer himself a sacrifice to him. His endeavour is to kill and slay those beasts, those lusts, that lurk in his heart, contrary to the Almighty.

Lastly, He that is anointed by the Spirit is a king in regard of his great possessions, for all are ours. 'Things present, and things to come, life and death, prosperity and adversity,' all help us to heaven, Rom. viii. 38. Evil things are ours in advantage and success, though in disposition they be not ours, but have a hostile disposition in them. God overpowers the evil of things, and gives a Christian a living principle of grace, to suck sweet out of sour, and draw good out of evil. What a king is this, that even the most terrible things are at his command, and work for the best unto him! He conquers and brings under his greatest enemies, and fears neither death or judgment, nor the vengeance to come. Knowing God in Christ to be his reconciled Father, he rests assured all things else will be at peace with him. Others have kingdoms out of themselves, but in themselves they are slaves. Every lust leads them away captive. A Christian is such a king as hath a kingdom within himself. He hath peace and joy and rest from base allurements, and terrors of conscience. He walks by rule, and therefore knows how to govern all. The glory of his Maker is the chief thing he eyes, and to that he refers every action.

'Who hath anointed us, and sealed us.'

Anointing and sealing go together. The same God anoints us doth also seal us. Both are to secure us of our happy condition. Now Christ is the first sealed: John vi. 27, 'Him hath the father sealed.' God hath set Christ apart from others, hath distinguished him, and set a stamp upon him to be the Messiah by the graces of the Spirit, whereof he was richly beautified, and by many miracles, whereby he shewed that he was the Son of God; by his resurrection from the dead, by his calling of the Gentiles, and many other things.

Christ being sealed himself, he sealed all that he did for our redemption with his blood, and hath added for the strengthening of our faith outward seals, the sacraments, to secure his love more firmly to us.

But in this place another manner of sealing is to be understood. For here is not meant the sealing of Christ, but the sealing of us that have communion with him. The same Spirit that seals the Redeemer seals the redeemed.

Quest. What is the manner of our sealing by the Spirit?

Ans. (1.) Sealing we know hath divers uses. First of all, *it doth imprint a likeness of him that doth seal.* When the king's image is stamped upon the wax, everything in the wax answers to that in the seal, face to face, eye to eye, body to body. So we are said to be sealed when we carry in our souls the image of the Lord Jesus; for the Spirit sets the stamp of Christ upon every true convert. There is the likeness of Christ in all things to be found in him. As the child answers the father, foot for foot, finger for finger in proportion, but not in quantity, so it is in the sealing of a believer. There is a likeness in the soul that is sealed by the Spirit to the Lord Jesus. There is understanding of the same heavenly supernatural truths; there is a judging of things as Christ judgeth, a loving of that which he loves, and a hating of that which he hates; a rejoicing to do that which he delights in, and a grief to commit anything that displeaseth his majesty. Every affection of the soul is carried that way that the affections of our blessed Saviour are carried, in proportion; everything in the soul is answerable to him in its degree.

There is no grace in Christ, but there is the like in every Christian in some measure. The obedience of Christ to his Father, even to the death, is to be found in every true Christian. The humility whereby Christ abased himself, it is in every renewed heart. Christ works in the soul that receives him a conformity to himself. The soul that believes that Christ hath loved him, and done such great things for him, is ambitious to express Christ in all his ways. Being once in Christ, we shall delight to be transformed more and more unto him. To bear the image of the 'second Adam' upon our breasts, to make it appear that Jesus Christ lives in us, and that we 'live not to ourselves, but to him that died for us,' 2 Cor. v. 15; to be meek and heavenly-minded as he was, talking and discoursing of spiritual things, going about doing good everywhere; active for God, fruitful in holiness, doing and receiving all the good we are able, drawing others from this world to meditate of a better estate, labouring for the advancement of God's kingdom, and approving ourselves to him. This is one use of sealing, to imprint a likeness.

(2.) A *second* use of the seal is *distinction*. Sealing is a stamp upon one thing among many. It distinguisheth Christians from others, as we shall see after.

(3.) Again, it serves for *appropriation*. Men seal those things that are their own. Merchants, we see, set their stamp on those wares which they have or mean to have a right unto. It pleaseth God thus to condescend unto us, by applying himself to human contracts. He appropriates his own to shew that he hath chosen and singled them out for himself to delight in.

(4.) Sealing further serves to make things *authentical*, to give authority and excellency. The seal of the prince is the authority of the prince. This gives validity to things, answerable to the dignity and esteem of him that seals.

These are the four principal uses of sealing; and God by his Spirit doth all these to his. He stamps his own image upon us; he distinguisheth us from others, even from the great refuse of the world. God by his Spirit appropriates us to himself; he makes us to be his, and shews that we are his. He likewise authoriseth us, and puts an excellency upon us, to secure us against all temptations. When we have God's seal on us, we stand firm in the greatest trial. 'Who shall separate us from the love of God?' Rom. viii. 35. We dare defy all objections of Satan, and accusations of conscience whatsoever. A man that hath God's seal stands impregnable in the most tempestuous season; for it is given for our assurance, and not for God's. The Lord knows who are his.' He seals not because he is ignorant, but for our comfort and establishment.

Quest. Whether is the Spirit itself this seal, or the work of the Spirit, and the graces thereof wrought in us?

Ans. I answer, the Spirit of God, where it is, is a sufficient seal that God hath set us out for himself; for whosoever hath the Spirit of Christ, the same is his. He is the author of our sealing; so that, except you take the Spirit for that which is wrought by the Spirit, you have not the comprehension of sealing, for that which the Spirit worketh is the seal. The Spirit goes always with his own mark and impression. Other seals, when they are removed from the stamp, the stamp remains still. But the Spirit of God dwells and keeps a perpetual residence in the heart of a Christian, guiding him, moving him, enlightening him, governing him, comforting him, doing all offices of a seal in his heart, till he hath brought him to heaven. The Holy Ghost never leaves us. It is the sweetest inhabitant that ever lodging was given to. He doth all the saving good that is done to the soul, and is perpetually with his own work in joy and comfort. Though he seem sometimes to be in a corner of the heart, and is not easily discerned, yet he always dwells in his sealed ones.

Quest. What is the stamp that the Spirit seals us withal?

Ans. 1. The Spirit works in this order for the most part. First of all, the Spirit doth, together with the word (which is the instrument, and the chariot wherein it is carried) convince us of the ill that is in us, and the misery attending on us for the same. *It convinceth us of sin*, and the fearful estate we are in by that, and abaseth us thereupon. Therefore it is called the 'spirit of bondage,' Rom. viii. 15, because it makes a man tremble and quake, till he see his peace made up in Christ.

Ans. 2. When he hath done this, then he *convinceth us of righteousness*, by a sweet light discovering the excellencies of the Lord Jesus, and the remedy in him provided for sinners. God opens the eye of the soul, to see the all-sufficiency of his Son's sanctification,* and inclines the heart to cast itself by faith upon him.

Ans. 3. When we are thoroughly convinced of the ill that is in us, and of the good that is in Christ, and are moved by the Holy Ghost to go out of ourselves, and embrace reconciliation in the Lord Jesus, then a superadded work is vouchsafed unto us; *for the Spirit daily perfecteth his own work.* He adds, therefore, after all, his seal, to confirm us; which seal is not faith; for the apostle saith, '*After* you believed, *you were sealed*,' Eph. i. 13, where we see the work of faith and sealing distinguished. First, the soul is set in a good estate, and then follows assurance and establishment.

Quest. But what needs confirmation when we believe? Is not faith confirmation enough: when a man may know by a private reflect act of the soul that he is in a state of grace?

Ans. This act of ours in believing is oft terribly shaken, and God is wondrous desirous that we should be secure of his love. He knows he can have no glory, nor we any solid peace else. Therefore when we by faith have sealed to his truth, he sees that we need further sealing that our faith be current and good; for all is little enough in the time of temptation; the single witness of our soul is not strong enough in great assaults. For sometimes the Spirit is so tossed and disquieted with temptations, that we cannot reflect aright on ourselves, nor discern what is in our own breasts without much ado. Therefore God first works faith to apply the promise, Whosoever believes in Christ shall be saved,' Acts ii. 21. I believe in Christ, therefore I shall be saved; and then sealeth this belief with an addition of his Holy Spirit; for this sealing is a work upon believing, an honouring of faith with a superadded confirmation.

Quest. How shall we know that there is such a spiritual sealing in us?

Ans. (1.) I answer, when we truly believe, the 'Spirit of adoption,' Rom. viii. 15, *reveals unto us that we are the 'sons of God'* by a secret whispering and intimation to the soul (which the believing heart feels better than I am able to express), saying, 'Be of good comfort, thy sins are forgiven.' There is a sweet kiss vouchsafed to the soul: the Lord refresheth it with the light of his countenance, and assures it that all enmity is now slain. I am thy salvation. Thou art for ever mine, and I am thine. Because thou believest, behold thou art honoured to be my child.

Ans. (2.) Again the 'Spirit of adoption,' *quickens and fills the soul with heavenly ejaculations to God;* it stirs up fervent supplications to cry, 'Abba, Father.' The soul when it truly believes, hath a bold and familiar speech to God.

There are two things in the prayer of a Christian that are incompatible with a carnal man: there is, first, an inward confidence; and secondly, an earnestness in the soul, whereby he goes to God as a child to his loving father, not considering his own worthiness or means, but the constant love that is borne to him.

This spiritual speech of God to the soul, and of the soul to God, is an evident demonstration of our truth in grace, because we can do that which no hypocrite in the world can attain to.

Ans. (3.) *Thirdly*, This sealing of the Spirit after we believe, *is known by*

* Qu. 'satisfaction'?—Ed.

the work of sanctification which it effecteth in us. The Holy Spirit seals our spirits, by stamping the likeness of Christ upon us; so as when a man finds in his soul some lineaments of the heavenly image, he may know thereby that he is 'translated from death to life,' Col. i. 13. When he finds his heart subdued to humility and obedience, to such a holy and gracious frame as Christ's was, he may clearly discern that he hath something more than the 'old man' in him. When a man can say, Naturally I am proud, but now I can abase myself; naturally I am full of malice, now I can love and pray heartily for my enemies; naturally I am lumpish and dead-hearted, now I can joy in the Holy Ghost; naturally I am apt to distrust the Lord, and be discontented with my condition, now I can rest securely upon his promise and providence; sin hath been my delight, now it is my sorrow and heart-breaking; I find somewhat contrary to corruption in me, I carry the image of the 'second Adam' about me now; I say, whosoever hath this blessed change, may rest assured of his right to happiness. 'Know you not that Christ is in you, except ye be reprobates?' saith the apostle, 2 Cor. xiii. 5. A Christian that upon a thorough search finds something of Christ always in his soul, can never want a sweet evidence that he is 'sealed to the day of redemption.'

Ans. (4.) The *fourth* way is *by the joy of the Spirit;* which is the beginning of heaven as it were, and a possessing of glory before our time. There are few of God's children, but in the course of their pilgrimage, first or last, have this divine impression wrought in them, enlarging and ravishing their souls to joy in the Almighty.

Yet this is especially seen after conflict, when the soul hath combated with some strong corruption or temptation. 'To him that overcomes will I give of the hidden manna,' saith Christ, 'and a white stone, which none can read but he that hath it,' Rev. ii. 17; that is, he shall have assurance that he is in the state of grace, and the sweet savour of goodness itself shall be his portion. Usually God gives comfort after we have conflicted with some sinful disposition and have got the victory, as we see in Job. After God had exercised that champion a long time, at the last he discovered himself in a glorious manner to him, Job xlii. 12.

In the midst of afflictions, when a Christian is under great crosses, and God sees he must be supported with spiritual strength, or else he sinks, then he puts in with supply from above. When the creature cannot help us, the Creator of all things will. Thus Paul in the midst of the dungeon, being sealed with the Spirit, 'sang at midnight' when he was in the stocks, Acts xvi. 24, *seq.:* and so David in the midst of persecution; Daniel in a lion's den; the three children in the fiery furnace, &c. God doth as parents, smile on their little ones when they are sick and dejected. He reserves his choicest comforts for the greatest exigents.* When God hath a great work for his children to do, or some sharp suffering for them to undergo, as an encouragement beforehand, he oft enlargeth their spirits that they may be able to go through all; as our Saviour Christ had James and John with him upon the mountain, to strengthen them against his ensuing suffering.

Let us then examine ourselves by that which hath been delivered. Hath God spoken to thy soul, and said, 'I am thy salvation,' 'thy sins are remitted,' and thy person received into my favour? Doth God stir up thy spirit to call upon him, especially in extremity, and to go with boldness and earnestness to his throne? Surely this is an evidence of the seal of the Spirit; for whoever wants this cannot look God in the face when

* That is, 'exigencies.'—G.

distress is upon him. Saul in this case goes to the witch, and Ahithophel to desperate conclusions. Judas in extremity, we see what becomes of him. So every one that hath not this sealing of the Spirit (to whom God speaks not peace, 'by shedding abroad the love of Christ in his heart,' Rom. v. 5), must needs sink as lead in the bottom of the sea, which hath no consistence, till it come to the centre, to hell. Did you ever feel the joy of the Spirit in holy duties, after inward striving against your lusts, and getting ground of them? This is a certain sign that God hath sealed you.

Quest. But you will say, How can that be a seal? A seal continues with the thing, but the joy of the Spirit comes after the work of the Spirit, and abides not with us.

Ans. I answer, though we have not always the joy of the Spirit, yet we have the Spirit of joy; which, though it be not known by joy, yet may be discerned by its operation and working. A Christian may have a gracious work of the Spirit in him, and yet want the delight and joy of the Spirit. Therefore when that fails, look to thy sanctification, and see what resemblance of Christ is formed in thee. See if thy heart be humble and broken; if thou have a heavenly disposition like to thy Saviour. When the joy of the Spirit ceaseth, go to the work of the Spirit, and from the work of the Spirit to the voice of the Spirit. Canst thou cry to God with strong supplications? or if thou canst not pray with distinct words, canst thou mourn and groan? 'The Spirit helps our infirmities, when we know not what to ask,' Rom. viii. 26. This sighing and groaning is the voice of God's Spirit, which he will regard wheresoever he finds it. This made Job in his distress to swim above water.

If one be in the midst of extremity, and can seriously seek to God, it is an undoubted sign that such a one is sealed, especially when the corruption of his soul joins with Satan's temptations the more to afflict him. For a sinner in the midst of storms and clouds of darkness, then to cast anchor, and quiet his soul in Christ, argues great faith. So when a temptation closes with our corruption, and affliction yields ground to further the temptation, then to pray and rely securely upon God is a gracious sign. For Satan useth the afflictions we are in as temptations to shake our faith, as thus, Canst thou be a child of God, and be so exercised, so vilified, so persecuted? Didst thou belong to Christ, would ever these crosses and losses and miseries have befallen thee? Deceive not thyself! Thus affliction is a weapon to temptation, for Satan to help his fiery darts with, he having such a dangerous party in us—as our own corruption—doth us the more harm continually.

Quest. How shall a man know whether God hath a part in him?

Ans. I answer, If he can run against the stream; if he find his soul resisting Satan's temptations, and raising him above afflictions, standing out and combating with corruptions to the uttermost. When he can check his carnal heart that draws him downwards, saying, 'Why art thou cast down, O my soul? and why art thou disquieted within me? Ps. xlii. 5, it is a good sign.

David found inward corruptions and outward afflictions joining with Satan's temptations, to depress his spirit; hereupon he chides his own soul, 'Why is it thus with thee? why art thou dejected in this manner?' And then he lays a charge upon it, 'Trust in God,' ver. 11. Whatsoever hardship we meet with in the world, yet there is hope in God still. Though we can find little comfort below, yet there are rivers of consolation above. It argues a gracious heart to quiet one's self in God in the worst times.

Use 1. I beseech you *let us labour to have our souls sealed with the Spirit of God*, to have further and clearer evidence of our estate in grace. It is a blessed thing to have Christ live in us. The enemies of our salvation are exceeding many, and how soon death or judgment may seize us, we know not. God will set none at his right hand but his sheep, those that have his own image on them. His best sheep have no outward mark, but an inward. The world sees not their beauty; 'The king's daughter is all glorious within,' Ps. xlv. 13.

How comfortably will the soul commend itself to Christ, when it finds itself stamped with the Spirit of Christ; when he can cheerfully say, Lord Jesus, receive my soul,' Acts vii. 50. Thou that hast redeemed me by thy blood, and sealed me by thy Spirit, acknowledge thine own likeness in me. Though it be not as it should be, yet there is somewhat of thine in me.

Beloved, we must not give false evidence of ourselves, as we must not against others. What a comfort hath a sealed soul in the hour of death, and in all extremities. What a difference is there between such a soul and others in the time of affliction, as in the time of pestilence, war, and persecution for Christ. The soul that is sealed knows that he is marked out for happiness in the world to come. Whatsoever befalls him in this life, he knows that God in all confusion of times knows his own seal, and that his destroying angel shall spare and pass over those that are marked, Ezek. ix. 4, *seq*. And though our bodies escape not, yet our souls shall.

Josiah we see was taken away from the evil to come; and Lot was delivered from the judgment of the Sodomites. If we partake not of the sins of the wicked, we shall never partake of their plagues. God hath a special care of his 'little ones' in this life; and if he take them away, yet their death is precious in his sight, Ps. cxvi. 15. He will not part with them but upon special consideration. He sees if they live it will be worse for them. Their precious souls are in continual danger. He sees it is best for them to be gathered to God, and the souls of perfect ones in heaven; therefore he provides a shelter to free them from all storms on earth.

And as he hath an eye over them in regard of outward miseries, so in respect of spiritual corruption and infection, as Rev. vii. 3. God's holy ones were 'sealed,' so many of such a tribe, and so many of such a tribe, to signify that God hath always some that he will keep and preserve from the leprous contagion of sin and antichrist; even in evil times God hath his 'little flock' still.

In the obscure ages of the church, nine hundred years after Christ, when there was little learning and goodness in the world, and Egyptian darkness had overspread the earth, God had always sealed ones, marked out for himself, whom he preserved from the danger of dark times. Why then should we be afraid of evil tidings? Let any affliction, or death itself, come, Christ will know his own stamp in us. He hath a book of remembrance for those that are his; and when he gathers his jewels, they will be highly set by, Mal. iii. 17. God in common calamities suffers his luggage, wicked men, to go to wreck; but he will secure his jewels, his darlings, whatever come of it. Labour therefore to be a sealed person.

Quest. But you will say, What shall I account of myself, if there be but a little sign of grace in me?

Ans. Be not discouraged. You know in wax, though the stamp be almost out, yet it is current in law notwithstanding. Put the case the stamp of the prince be an old coin, is it not current though it be cracked? Suppose the mark of the Spirit should be dim and blurred, scarce discernible in us (this ought to be our shame and grief), yet some evidences of grace are still remaining; there are some sighs and groans against corruption, which may continually support us. If we mourn in our spirits, and do not join with our lusts, nor allow ourselves in them, this is a divine impression, though it be, as it were, almost worn out. The more comfort we desire, the fresher we should keep this seal of comfort.

Use 2. And labour to *grow in faith and obedience, that we may read our evidence clearly ; that it be not overgrown with the dust of the world, so as we cannot see it.* Sometimes God's children have the graces of the Spirit in them, yet they yield so much to fears and doubtings, that they can read nothing but their corruption. When we bid them peruse their evidences, they can see nothing but worldliness, nothing but pride and envy, because they grieve the Holy Spirit by their negligence and distrust. Though there be a stamp in them, yet God holds the soul from it, and gives men up to mistake their estates, for not stirring up the graces of his Spirit in them.

Honour God by believing, and he will honour thee by stamping his Spirit more clearly on thee. What a comfort is it to have the evidence of a gracious soul at all times. When a man carries about him the mark of the Spirit, what in the world can discourage such a soul ? On the contrary, if a man have not something above nature in him, when death and judgment comes, how miserable is his condition ? If a man be a king or an emperor of the world, and have not an interest in Christ's righteousness, ere long he shall be stripped of all, and adjudged to eternal torments. Oh, the excellency of man's soul ; a jewel more to be prized than a prince's diadem.

It is the folly of the times to set up curious pictures, but what a poor delight is this in comparison of the ambition of a true Christian, to see the image of Christ stamped in his soul, to find the joy of the Spirit, and God speaking peace to his inner man.

The transforming of ourselves into the image of Christ is the best picture in the world. Therefore we should labour for the 'new creature,' that as we grow downward one way, we may grow up towards heaven another; that as the life of nature decays, so the spiritual life may be more active and working. It should be our daily study, while we live in this world, to attain that 'holiness, without which no man shall ever see God,' 2 Cor. vii. 1, *et alibi.*

There is besides the common broad seal of God, his privy seal. What is the reason that many proud-hearted persons are damned ? The truth is, they are all for external contentments, and despise the ordinances of God. For though they stand upon their admission into the church, upon the common seals and prerogatives (which in themselves are excellent), yet relying on these things over-much betrays many souls to the devil in the time of distress. It is another manner of seal than the outward seal in the sacrament, that must settle peace in the conscience. When once the beginnings of faith are wrought in us, then we may with comfort think upon our receiving of the communion; but the special thing to be eyed is the hidden seal. If the external means work no inward sanctification in our hearts, we shall be the worse rather than the better for them ; yet we must not be so profane as to think slightly of God's ordinances ; they are of great consequence.

For when Satan shakes the confidence of a Christian, and saith, Thou art an hypocrite, God doth not love thee, these help us to hold out. Why, saith the soul, I can speak by experience that I have found the contrary; the Lord hath removed my fears, he hath pardoned my sin and accepted my person; he hath given me many precious promises to support my spirit. Here is the excellency of the sacrament. It comes more home to me; it seals the general promises of God particularly to myself; for finding the inward work of the Spirit in my heart, and God having strengthened my faith by the outward seal, I can defy Satan with all his accusations, and look death in the face with comfort. We should labour therefore to observe God's sealing days, when he uses to manifest himself to his people; which though it may be every day (if we be spiritually exercised), yet it is in the Lord's day more especially; for then his ordinance and his Spirit go together.

Now there is a sealing of persons, and of truths, besides the sealing of our estates, that we are the children of God. There is a sealing of every particular truth to a Christian. For where there is grace to believe the truth, God seals those truths firmly to that soul by the comforts of his Spirit. For example, this is a truth, 'Whosoever *believes* in Christ, shall not perish but have everlasting life,' John iii. 15. Now the same Spirit that stirs up the soul to believe this, seals it fast upon the conscience even to death. There is no promise, but upon our believing the same, it is sealed by God upon us; for those truths only abide firm in the soul which the Holy Ghost sets on. What is the reason that many forget their consolations? The reason is, they hear much, but the Spirit settles nothing on their hearts.

Quest. What is the reason that unlettered men many times stand out in their profession to blood, whereas those that are more able and learned yield to anything?

Ans. The reason is, the knowledge of the one is set fast upon the soul; the Spirit brings his seal and this man's knowledge close together; whereas the learning and abilities of the other, is only a discoursive thing, swimming in the brain without any solid foundation. Their knowledge of truths is not spiritual; they see not heavenly things by heavenly, but by a natural light. Those that would not apostatise must have a knowledge suitable to the things they know; they must see spiritual things by the Spirit of God. Therefore when we come to hear the word, we should not come with strong conceits of our own, to bring all to our wits, but with reverent dispositions and dependence upon God, that he would teach us together with his ministers, and close with his ordinances so as to fasten truths upon our souls; else shall we never hold out; for that which must stablish and quiet the soul, must be greater than the soul.

In time of tentations, when the terrors of the Almighty encompass us, when God lays open our conscience, and writes bitter things against us, those truths that most satisfy the soul at such a time must be above the natural capacity of the soul. Therefore, saith the apostle, 'It is God that establishes,' and God by his Spirit that seals us up unto the day of redemption; because divine truths of themselves in the bare letter cannot stir up the heart. It is only the blessed Spirit (which is above our spirits) that must quiet the conscience in all perplexities. The Lord can soon still the soul when he settles spiritual truths upon it. Therefore go to him in thy distress and trouble of mind. Send up ejaculations to God, that he would seal the comfort revealed in his word to thy soul, that as it is true in itself, so it may be true to thee likewise.

This is a necessary observation for us all. Oh, we desire in the hour of death to find some comforts, that be standing comforts, that may uphold us against hell and judgment. Know that nothing will do this but spiritual truths spiritually known; but holy truths set on by the Holy Ghost upon the soul. Oft therefore enter into thine heart, and examine upon what grounds and motives thou believest. Consider well what it is thou believest, and upon what evidences, and with what light; otherwise expect not to find solid peace.

Quest. What course may a Christian generally take when he wants comfort and inward refreshing?

Ans. There are, in 1 John v., 'three witnesses in heaven and three in earth,' to secure us of our estate in grace, The three witnesses in heaven are, 'the Father, the Word, and the Holy Ghost.' And the three witnesses in earth are, 'the Spirit, the water, and blood;' and these three on earth, and those three in heaven agree in one.* Now by the Spirit here is meant the feelings and sweet motions thereof. The water may well be the laver of sanctification; and by blood is understood the sufferings of Christ for our justification.

When therefore we find that extraordinary seal I spake of before—the joys of the Spirit of God—that it is not in us, what shall we do? Shall we despair then? No. Then go to the water. When the witness of the Spirit is silent, go to the work of the Spirit; see what gracious dispositions are found in thee.

Quest. Ay, but what shall we do if the waters be troubled in the soul, as sometimes there is such a confusion that we cannot see the image of God upon it in sanctification.

Ans. Then go to the blood. There is always comfort. Go to the 'fountain set open for Judah and Jerusalem to wash in,' Zech. xiii. 1. That is never dry. If we find much sin upon our consciences, and no peace in our hearts, apply the blood of sprinkling. That will give rest.

When thou findest nothing but corruption and filthiness in thy soul, when thou seest neither joy nor sanctification of spirit, go to the Lord Jesus, and he will purge thee from all guilt, and wash thee with clean water. But to go on.

Who hath sealed us, and given us the earnest of his Spirit in our hearts.

This is the third word, borrowed from human contracts, to set forth God's gracious work in the soul. Anointing we had before, and sealing. Now here is 'earnest.' The variety of expression shews there is a great remainder of unbelief in the soul of man, which causeth the blessed Spirit to use so many words to manifest God's mind, and assure the soul of salvation; stablishing, anointing, sealing, and earnest.

And indeed so it is. Howsoever we in the time of prosperity, when all things go well with us, are apt to presume our estate is good, yet in the hour of death, when conscience is awaked, we are prone to nothing so much as to call all in question, and believe the lies and doubts and fears of our own deceitful hearts, more than the undoubted truth and promise of God. Therefore the Lord takes all courses to establish us. He gives us rich and precious promises; he gives us the Holy Spirit to confirm us in those promises, he seals us with that Spirit, and gives us a comfortable 'earnest' thereof, and all to settle these wretched and unbelieving hearts of ours. So desirous is God that we should be well conceited of him, that he loves us better than we love ourselves. He prizeth our love so much, that he labours by all means to secure us of our eternal welfare; as knowing, that

* Cf. Note *dddd,* Vol. III. page 536.—G.

except we apprehend his love to us, we can never love him again, nor delight in him as we ought to do.

Now the Spirit is an 'earnest' of our inheritance in heaven. We are sons here indeed; but we are not heirs invested into the blessed estate we have title to. God doth not keep all our happiness till another world, but gives us somewhat to comfort us in our absence from our husband. He gives us the Holy Ghost in our hearts, as a pledge of that glorious condition, which we shall one day have eternally with him. This is the meaning of the words.

But to shew you more particularly in what regard the Spirit is called an 'earnest.'

(1.) *First* of all, you know an earnest is used *for security of a contract.* So the Holy Spirit doth secure us of the blessed estate we shall have in heaven for ever.

(2.) *Secondly,* An earnest *is part of the bargain, a part of the whole which is secured.* Though it is a very little part, yet it is a part. So it is with the Spirit of God in its gracious work upon our hearts. The joy of the Spirit is a part of that full joy and happiness which shall be revealed hereafter to us.

(3.) *Thirdly,* An earnest is *little in comparison of the whole.* So the Spirit, in the work and graces thereof, is little in regard of that fulness which we shall have in heaven. But though an earnest be small in itself, yet it is great in security. A shilling secures a bargain of a thousand pounds, we see. We value an earnest not for its own worth so much as for that which it is a pledge of: for the excellent bargain and rich possession which it doth interest us into. So the Spirit of God with its blessed effects in the soul, the joy and peace of the Spirit, cheering and reviving perplexed sinners; this earnest, I say, though it be little in itself, yet it is great to us in respect of the assurance that we have by it.

(4.) Again, it hath the term of an earnest, because an earnest is given *rather for the security of the party that receives it, than in regard of him that gives it.* So God gives *us* the 'earnest of the Spirit,' grace and comfort in this life, not so much for God. For he means to give us heaven and happiness when we are dissolved. As he hath passed his promise, so he will undoubtedly perform the same; he is Lord and Master of his word. He is Jehovah that gives a being to his word, as well as to every other thing. But notwithstanding, having to do with mistrustful, unbelieving men, he is pleased to condescend to our weakness; he stoops to the lowest capacity, and frames his speech to the understanding of the simplest soul, for which purpose this term of earnest is here borrowed.

In these respects the Spirit of God, together with the graces of it, and the comforts it brings (for they are not divided) is called an 'earnest.' And thus having cleared the point, we will observe this doctrine for our further instruction.

That a Christian ought to be, and may be assured of his interest in God; because, as I have said before, an earnest is given not so much for God's sake, as for our sakes. This then must needs follow from hence. Either none have this earnest, or else those that have it may be assured of their comfortable condition. Otherwise God is fickle, and plays fast and loose with his children, which is blashemy to affirm. Besides, if none have this earnest, then the apostle speaks false when he saith, 'God hath stablished us, and given us the earnest of his Spirit,' which is horrible impiety once to conceive.

Quest. If this be so, then either such as have this seal and earnest of the Spirit may be assured of their estate in grace or not. And if not, where is the fault? Will not God really and truly vouchsafe unto his people this earnest of the Spirit in their hearts?

Ans. Undoubtedly he will. He is desirous that we should be persuaded of his love in all things, and therefore we may and ought to be assured of his favour towards us. St John's whole epistle * contains little else but sundry marks and evidences how we may know that we are the children of God. Wherefore was Christ himself sealed of the Father to the office of Mediator? wherefore did he die and rise again? and wherefore doth he still make intercession for us in heaven? That we should doubt of God's love, whenas he hath given us that which is greater than salvation, yea, greater than all the world, even his own Son? No, certainly. Can we desire a more ample testimony of his favour than he hath already bestowed upon us? Is it not the errand of all God's mercies to bring us nearer to himself, that we should not doubt of his love, but rest securely upon him? Why then do we distrust the Almighty, who is truth itself, and never failed any?

Yet we must know that Christians have not at all times alike assurance of their interest; for there is an infancy of grace, where we are ignorant of our own condition. And there is a time of desertion, whenas God, to make us look better to our footing, leaves us a little, as if he would forsake us quite; when indeed he only withdraws his assistance for a while to make us cleave the closer to him. There be also certain seasons, wherein, though we are assured of God's favour, yet we have no feeling or apprehension of the same, which differeth in Christians much, according as they are more or less sensible of their estates. Some again use not that care and diligence in the use of means which God requires, whereupon they are justly deprived of that inward peace and comfort which others enjoy. There is a difference likewise in growth and continuance in Christianity. Some are strong Christians, and some weak; answerable whereunto is the difference of assurance of God's love usually in the hearts of his people. Nay, it is possible that for a long time the Lord's jewels, his redeemed ones, may want this blessed comfort.

For we must conceive there is a double act of faith.

First, An act whereby a poor distressed sinner casts himself upon God as reconciled to him in Christ.

Secondly, There is a reflect act, whereby knowing that we rely upon the truth and promise of the Almighty, we have assurance of his favour. Now a man may perform the one act and not the other. Many of the saints sometimes can hardly say that they have any assurance; but yet, notwithstanding, they will daily cast themselves upon the rich mercy and free grace of God in Jesus Christ.

Besides, There are many things which may hinder this act of assurance, because (together with believing) God may present such things to my mind as may so damp and disquiet my soul, that I cannot have any definitive thoughts about that which God would especially have me to think upon.

As when God would humble a man, he takes not away the Spirit of faith wholly from him, but sets before such a sinful creature his anger and sore displeasure, together with the hellish torments and pains of the damned as due to his soul, which makes him for the present to be in an estate little differing from the reprobate. So that he is far from saying he hath any

* Viz., 1st Epistle.—G.

assurance at that time. Yet, notwithstanding, he doth not leave off nor renounce his confidence, but casts himself upon God's mercy still. 'Though the Lord kill him, yet will he trust in him,' Job xiii. 15, although he sees nothing but terror and wrath before him. This God doth to tame our presumption, and to prepare us for the enjoyment of his future glory. If we feel not sense of assurance, it is good to bless God for what we have. We cannot deny but God offers himself in mercy to us, and that he intends our good thereby; for so we ought to construe his merciful dealing towards us, and not have him in jealousy without ground. Had we but willing hearts to praise God for that which we cannot but acknowledge comes from him, he will be ready in his time to shew himself more clearly to us. We taste of his goodness many ways, and it is accompanied with much patience. And these, in their natures, should lead us not only to repentance, but to nearer dependence on him. We ought to follow that which God leads us unto, though he hath not yet acquainted us with his secrets.

These things we must observe, that we give not a false evidence against ourselves. Though we have not such assurance as we have had, yet always there is some ground in us whereupon we may be comforted that we are God's children, could we but search into it. Let us not then be negligent in labouring for the same, and in the Lord's good time we shall certainly obtain it. It is the profaneness of the world that they improve not those helps which God hath afforded for this purpose.

Nay, they had rather stagger, and take contentment in their own ways, saying, If God will love me in a loose, licentious course, so it is; but I will not 'give diligence to make my calling and election sure,' 2 Peter i. 10; I will never bar myself of such profits and delights, nor forsake all, chiefly to mind spiritual things.

Whereas we ought constantly to endeavour for assurance of grace, that God may have honour from us, and we the more comfort from him again, that we may live in the world above the world, and pass cheerfully through the manifold troubles and temptations which befall us in our pilgrimage.

A man in his pure naturals will swell against this doctrine, because he feels no such thing, and thinks what is above his measure is hypocrisy. He makes himself the rule of other Christians to walk by, and therefore values and esteems others by his uncertain condition. But the heart of a Christian hath a light in it; the Spirit of God in his soul makes him discern what estate he is in.

In a natural man, all is dark. He sees nothing, because his heart is in a dungeon. 'His eye being dark, the whole man must needs be in blindness,' Mat. vi. 22, *seq.* All is alike to him; he sees no difference between flesh and spirit, and therefore holds on in a doubting hope, in a confused disposition and temper of soul, to his dying day.

But a Christian, that labours to walk in the comforts of the Holy Ghost, cannot rest in such an unsettled estate; he dares not venture his eternal welfare upon such infirm grounds. What! To depart this life, and be tossed in uncertainty, whether a man goes to heaven or to hell! What a miserable perplexity must such a soul needs be in! Therefore, he is still 'working out his salvation,' Phil. ii. 12, and storing up of grace against the evil day.

And well may this condition challenge all our diligence in labouring for it, because it is neither attained nor maintained without the strength and prime of our care. For the sense of God's favour will not be kept without keeping him in our best affections, above all things else in the world besides; without keeping of our hearts constantly close and near to him; which can never be done without keeping a most narrow watch over our loose spirits, which are ever ready to stray from him, and fall to the creature.

It cannot be kept without exact walking, and serious self-denial. But what of that? Can we spend labours to better purpose? One sweet beam of God's countenance will requite all abundantly. A Christian indeed undergoes more trouble and pains, especially with his own heart, than others do; but what is that to his gains? One day spent in communion with God is sweeter than a thousand without it. What comforts so great as those that are fetched from the fountain! Oh, woe to him that savours not these heavenly, but lingers after carnal comforts. It cannot but grieve the Holy Spirit, when the 'consolations of the Almighty' are either forgotten, or seem 'nothing to us,' Job xv. 11.

Quest. But why doth the Spirit thus establish and seal us, and convey grace to our souls? Why doth that do all?

Ans. 1. Because since the fall we have no principles of supernatural good in us; and there must be a principle above nature to work grace in our barren hearts.

Ans. 2. Again, there is still remaining in us an utter averseness to that which is spiritually good in the best. Therefore there must be somewhat to overpower their corrupt disposition.

Quest. But why the Spirit rather than the Father or the Son?

Ans. He comes from both, and therefore is fit to witness the love of both. The Holy Ghost is in the breast of the Father and the Son; he knows their secret affections towards us. A man's spirit is acquainted with his inmost thoughts. The blessed Spirit is privy to the hidden love of God, and of Jesus Christ to us poor creatures, which we are strangers unto. Therefore none so fit to cheer and revive us.

Indeed, the love originally is from the Father; but in regard of application of what is wrought by the Son, all proceeds from the Holy Ghost; he receives grace from Christ for us. It must needs be so, because no less than the Spirit of God can quiet our perplexed spirits in time of tentation. For when the conscience of a guilty person is affrighted, what man can allay its fears? That which must settle a troubled spirit must be a spirit above our own; it being no easy thing to bring the soul and God together after peace is broken. We have both wind and tide against us in this business, grace being but weak, and corruption strong in the best of us.

We should labour therefore for heavenly spirits, and get something more than a man in us. There can never be any true peace attained till the Spirit from above settle it in our souls. An unsanctified heart is an unpacified heart. If there be a neglect of holiness, the soul can never be soundly quiet. Where there is not a clear conscience, there cannot be a calm conscience. That is a general rule. Sin, like Jonah in the ship, will raise continual storms both within and without a man. Take away God once, and farewell all true tranquillity. Spiritual comforts flow immediately from the Spirit of comfort, who hath his office designed for that purpose.*

Quest. But how shall we know that we have the Spirit? How may a man know that he hath a soul?

Ans. 1. By living and moving, by actions vital, &c. Even so may a man know he hath the Spirit of God by its blessed effects and operations.

* That is, 'The Comforter' (Παρακλητος) —G.

It is not idle in us, but as the soul quickens the body, so doth the Spirit the soul. Every saving grace is a sign that the Spirit is in us. Wheresoever the Spirit dwells, he transforms the soul, and changes the party, like himself, to be holy and gracious. This is an undoubted symptom of the Spirit's habitation.

Ans. 2. *Secondly*, All spiritual graces are *with conflict;* for that which is true is with a great deal of resistance of that which is counterfeit. 'The flesh still lusts against the Spirit,' Gal. v. 17, and Satan cannot endure to see any man walk comfortably to heaven. What, thinks he, such a base creature as this is to have the earnest of salvation, to live here as if he were in heaven already; and to defy all opposite powers! Sure he shall have little peace this way. I will disquiet and vex his spirit. If he will go to heaven he shall go mourning thither.

This is the reasoning of the cursed spirit, whereupon he labours to shake our assurance and follow us with perplexities. The grace and comfort of a Christian is with much conflict and temptations, not only with Satan, but with his own heart; which, so long as guilt remains, will ever be misgiving and casting of doubts. There must, therefore, be a higher power than the soul of man to quiet and allay its own troubles.

Ans. 3. *Thirdly*, The Spirit enables us *to the practice of those duties which by nature we are averse unto*, as to love an enemy, to overcome our revenge, to be humble in prosperity, and contented with any estate. It draws our affection heavenward, and makes us delight in God above all as our best portion. He that hath the Spirit joys in spiritual company and employment; he hates sin, as being contrary to that blessed 'earnest' which he hath received. He looks on things as God doth, and approves of the same, as he is made more or less spiritual thereby, and so is brought nearer to that fountain of goodness—God himself. By them he esteems his best being to be in Christ, and therefore labours more and more to be transformed into his likeness. He values nothing in the world further than it conduceth to his spiritual welfare. If all be well for *that*, he accounts himself happy, whatsoever else befalls him. Indeed, where the Spirit hath taken up his firm abode, that soul will little set by any outward change. Nothing can be very ill with a man that hath all well within him.

But that I may not distract your thoughts, you shall find divers properties of the Spirit of God in Rom. viii. 1, *seq.*, which I will briefly touch. *First*, it is said that the Spirit where it is '*dwells*' in that heart, as in a house; it '*rules*' wherever it comes. The Holy Ghost will not be an underling to our lusts. It repairs and makes up all our inward breaches. The Spirit prepares his own dwelling, he begets knowledge and acquaintance of God within us. He is not in us as he is in the wicked; he only knocks at their hearts, but hath not his abode there.

Secondly, When the Spirit comes into a man, he *subdues whatsoever is contrary to it, and makes way for itself by pulling down all strongholds which oppose it.* Therefore we are said 'to mortify the deeds of the flesh' by the Spirit, ver. 13. Those that by help of the Spirit have got the victory of sin, can in no wise be led as slaves by the flesh; as, on the contrary, he that cherishes corruption and crucifies it not (by spiritual reasons, but out of civil respects to be freed from aspersions, and to uphold his reputation or the like) is a mere * stranger to the Holy Ghost's working.

Thirdly, As many as are 'led by the Spirit of God are the sons of God.' As the angel went before the Israelites from Egypt into Canaan, so the

* That is, 'altogether.'—G.

Spirit of God goes along with his in all their ways, removing all lets and strengthening against all impediments in their Christian race. It conducts us sweetly, not violently, as the devil doth those that are possessed with the Spirit.* We are led strongly indeed, because it is against corruption within us, and opposition from without us; but yet sweetly, to preserve the liberty and freedom of the soul still. We are all by nature like children or blind men. We cannot lead ourselves. The Spirit must be our conduct[or], or we shall wander and go aside presently. Those therefore that enjoy the same, submit themselves to its guidance and direction in all things.

Fourth, Again, The Spirit stirs up sighs and groans, that cannot be expressed. When we are not able to pray, or lay open the griefs of our souls, if we can but send our sighs and groans to heaven, they shall be accepted; for God will hear the voice of his own Spirit, from whence these sobs and complaints come. How should we be overwhelmed with despair, did not the Spirit support us? Those, therefore, that in extremity have nothing to comfort them, yet are able to send forth holy desires to the Lord, may certainly conclude that the Spirit is in them.

Fifth, Again, The Spirit makes us mourn and wait for the adoption of sons. The same Spirit that sanctifies a sinner, witnesses to his soul that God is his. Worldlings grieve not for their absence from Christ, neither at all long they for his blessed appearing, because their heaven is here. They mourn not for the hidden distempers and secret imperfections of their souls; whereas the godly are much in condemning themselves for that which no creature can tax them of. Want of communion with their Maker, straitness of spirit, distraction in duty, that they cannot obey as they would—these exceedingly deject them, yet wait they will without despair till God have finished their course. There is such a divine power in faith, as a very little beam of it, having no other help than a naked promise, will uphold the soul against the greatest discouragements, and keep it from utter sinking.

Indeed, 'waiting' is a difficult duty, both in regard of the long day which God usually takes before he performs his promise, as also by reason of the untowardness of our natures, being ready to be put off by the least frown, did not God by a Spirit of constancy preserve the soul immoveable in all conditions, whether present or to come, so as it fails not before him: and why? Because it knows full well that God, in whom it rests, is unchangeably good.

Alas! we are at the best but light and vain creatures, till the divine Spirit fix and settle us. The firmer our union is here, the surer will be our standing in all danger; for what can daunt that soul, which in the greatest troubles hath made the great good to be his own? Such a person dares cheerfully encounter any opposition, as having a Spirit higher than the world about him; and seeing all but God far beneath him. Though I might name more, what a many sweet evidences are here to manifest a soul truly acted and led by the Spirit of God!

Quest. How may a man obtain this blessed guest, to lodge in his soul and rule over him?

Ans. First, Attend upon the teaching of the gospel. 'Received ye the Spirit by the hearing of the law, or of faith preached?' saith the apostle, Gal. iii. 2. The Spirit is usually given with a clear unfolding of Christ.

Secondly, Omit likewise no means wherein the Spirit is effectual; for as a man walking in a garden, though he think not of it, draws a sweet scent of the flowers, so the word of God, being dictated by the Spirit, leaves a

* Qu. 'his spirit'?—Ed.

heavenly savour in such as converse with it. The spirit of a man is like water that runs through minerals. We see baths have their warmth from minerals that they run through. So it is with the soul in its holy employments. When it hath to deal with good books and good company, it draweth a spiritual tincture from these things, and is bettered by them.

Thirdly, Withal, *take heed that thou* 'grieve not the Holy Ghost,' for that will cause an estrangement of his presence in thy soul.

Quest. How is that done?

Ans. By cherishing contrary affections and lusts to his blessed motions, as when we hear the word, but resolve never to obey it. When God knocks at our hearts for entrance, oh how readily should we set open these everlasting doors to receive him! If Christ be willing to give us his Spirit, it must needs be our own fault if we remain carnal; there being nothing in a manner required to be spiritual, but not to resist the Spirit. What greater indignity can we offer to the blessed Comforter, than to prefer our base lusts before his motions, leading to happiness? What greater unkindness can a man do his friend, than to slight his loving direction, and embrace the counsel of a professed enemy? The Holy Ghost presses such forcible reasons upon us of heavenly-mindedness and despising earthly things, that it is more than evident none are damned in the bosom of the church but those that set a bar against the Spirit of God in their hearts. Such are damned because they will be damned, that, say the preacher whatever he will, think it better to be as they are, than to entertain such a guest as will mar and alter all that was there before.

Take heed, therefore, of resisting the Spirit in the least kind; sad* not his blessed motions, but make much of the same by yielding subjection thereunto. Lay thy soul often before the Spirit; suffer thyself to be moulded and fashioned by his gracious working. Oh consider how high the slighting of a gracious motion reaches, even to the contemning of God himself. Certainly as we use these, so would we use the Spirit himself, were he [not] invisible to us.

And converse not with carnal company; for what wilt thou gain there but sorrow to thine heart, if thou belongest to God; and as holy Lot, vex thy righteous soul with the unclean conversation of these Sodomites? It is an undoubted sign of a man destitute of grace, not to care at all what company he frequents.

Fourthly, Seeing the Holy Ghost is promised to them that ask it, *beg earnestly, for it is at God's hands.* This is the 'good thing' that God gives. Christ seems to insinuate as much, saying, What can I give you better than the Holy Ghost? Yet this 'will I bestow on them that ask it,' Mat. vii. 7, *seq.;* for indeed that is the seed of all grace and comfort. A world of promises is included in the promise of giving the Spirit.

Labour therefore, above all gettings, to obtain this high prerogative. The comforts of the Spirit are above all earthly comfort, and the graces of the Spirit enable to encounter the greatest temptations whatsoever. A man that hath this stands impregnable. God may withdraw his favour for a time, to humble us; but to quench the work of the Spirit, once wrought in the soul, all the power of all the devils in hell cannot stir it. This will carry us through all oppositions and difficulties in our Christian race. Let a man never baulk or decline a good cause for anything that he shall suffer; for the seal and earnest of the Spirit is never more strong than when we are deprived of all other comforts save that alone.

* That is, 'sadden,' as elsewhere 'dead,' for 'deaden.'—G.

What makes a man differ from himself and from other men but this? Take a Christian that hath the 'earnest of the Spirit,' you shall have him defy death, Satan, the world, and all. Take another that is careless to increase his 'earnest,' how weak and feeble will you find him, ready to be overcome by every temptation, and sink under the least burden.

The apostle Peter, before the Holy Ghost came upon him, was astonished with the voice of a weak damsel; but after, how forward was he to suffer anything.*

Labour not then to be strengthened in things below, neither value thyself by outward dependences. Alas! all things here are perishing. If thou hast grace, thou hast that which will stand by thee when these fail. The Comforter shall never be taken away. What are all friends in the world to the Holy Ghost! This will speak to God for us when no creature dares look him in the face. The Spirit will make requests with 'sighs and groans' in our behalf; and we may be sure we shall be heard when that intercedes for us. What prison can shut up the Spirit of God? Oh gain this, whatever thou losest; prefer it to thy chief treasure. The very 'earnest' of the Spirit is far more precious than the creature's full quintessence. If the promises laid hold on by faith quicken and cheer the soul, what shall the accomplishment of them do! If the giving a taste of heaven so lift our souls above all earthly discouragements, how glorious shall we shine forth when the Spirit shall be all in all in us! This will make us more or less fruitful, more or less glorious in our profession, and resolute in obedience through our whole course.

If we want this, we can never be thankful for anything; for it is the love of God that sweetens every mercy to us; and indeed is more to be valued than any blessing we enjoy besides: which if we eye not or are ignorant of, what can we expect but wrath and displeasure in all that befalls us? Oh it is sweet to see favours and benefits issuing from grace and love. They do not always prove mercies which men ofttimes esteem to be so. We can have no solid comfort in any condition, further than God smiles upon us in it. What a fearful case must that then be, wherein a man cannot be thankful for what he hath.

Every condition and place we are in should indeed be a witness of our thankfulness to God. We must not think life was given only to live in. Our life should not be the end of itself, but the praise of the Giver thereof. It is but fit that we should refer all that is good to his glory, who hath joined his glory to our best good, in being glorified in our salvation; which while we question and doubt of, it is impossible ever to be cheerful towards him.

Besides, how can a man suffer willingly, that knows not that God hath begun any good work in him? How lumpish and dead is he under the cross without this assurance! It is worth the considering, to see two men of equal parts under the same affliction, how quietly and calmly the one that hath interest in Christ will bear his grievances, whereas the other rages as a fool, and is more beaten. A man will endure anything comfortably, when he considers it proceeds from his Father's good pleasure. This breeds a holy resigning of ourselves to God in all estates; as Eli, the 'will of the Lord be done.' His will is a wise will, and ever conduceth to his people's good.

Fearest thou danger? Cry unto God, 'I am thine,' 'Lord, save me.' I am the price of thy Son's blood, let me not be lost. Thou hast given me

* Cf. Mat. xxvi. 71 with Acts v. 41.—G.

the earnest of thy Spirit, and set thy seal upon me for thine own, let me neither lose my bargain nor thou thine.

Hence it is that God's child can so easily deny himself in temptations and allurements which others sink under. Oh! saith he, the Holy Ghost hath 'sealed' me up 'to the day of redemption,' shall I grieve and quench the same for this base lust? It is a great disparagement to prefer husks before the provision of our Father's house. When we give content to Satan and a wretched heart, we put the Holy Ghost out of his office.

Again, without this we can never comfortably depart this life. He that hath the earnest of the Spirit in his heart, may laugh Satan in the face, and rejoice at death's approaching, as knowing there will be an accomplishment then of all the bargain. Then the marriage will be perfectly consummate; then shall be the great year of jubilee, the Sabbath of rest for ever. He that lives much by faith will find it no hard matter to die in it. But let a man stagger and doubt whether he belong to God or no, what a miserable case will he be in at the time of dissolution! Death, with the eternity of torment after it, who can look it in the face without the assurance of a happy change? This makes men, that see no greater pleasure than the following of their lusts, resolve of swimming in worldly delights still. Alas! say they, I had as good take this pleasure as have none at all; what shall become of me hereafter, who knows?

NOTES.

(*a*) P. 117.—'They have seven sacraments to our two,' viz., (1) The Supper, (2) Baptism, (3) Marriage, (4) Penance, (5) Confession, (6) Extreme Unction, (7) Orders.

(*b*) P. 117.—'There are divers readings of the words.' Instead of 'all the promises,' the Greek is 'as many promises.' Cf. Dr Hodge *in loc.* for exposition, and Alford and Webster and Wilkinson for 'variations' of text. G.

A GLANCE OF HEAVEN;

OR,

A PRECIOUS TASTE OF A GLORIOUS FEAST.

A GLANCE OF HEAVEN.

NOTE.

'A Glance of Heaven' was first published in 1638. Its title-page is given below.* It is among the rarest of Sibbes's books. Prefixed to it is an engraving by Marshall representing the Table of the Lord 'spread' for the supper. At the top is placed, 'Wisdom hath built her house, she hath hewn out seven pillars, and furnished her table, Prov. ix. 1, 2.' Beneath the table, 'Compare Prov. ix. 1, 2, and Isa. xxv. 6 with 1 Cor. ii. 9. Secrets which the gospel reveals, election, redemption, justification, peace of conscience, joy unspeakable, faith, love. A feast prepared for them that love God in heaven consummated.'

* A
GLANCE
OF HEAVEN.
OR,
A PRETIOVS TASTE
of a glorious Feast.

Wherein thou mayst taste and see
those things which God hath prepared for them that love him.

The secrets of the Lord are with them that
feare him, &c. Psal. 25. 14.

Ry R. Sibs, D.D. Master of *Katherine Hall,*
and preacher of *Grayes Inne London.*

LONDON
Printed by *E. G.* for *I. R.* and are
to bee sold by *Henry Overton,* at
the entring in of Popes head Palace out
of Lumbard street. 1638.

TO THE CHRISTIAN READER.

Beloved! it is grown a custom that every book whosever, or of whatsoever subject, must be presented to you in state; with some prescript purposely. Were it not that custom is a tyrant, this labour might now be spared. Such matter from such an elder as here follows, needs no 'epistle of recommendation.' The reverend author is well approved to be 'a man of God,' a 'seer in Israel,' by those things which, without control, have already passed the press. Might I have my wish, it should be no more but a 'double portion' of that Spirit of God which was in him. The divine light, which radiated into his breast, displays itself in many other of his labours, but yet it is nowhere more condensed than in this following. It is truly said of Moses, by faith 'he saw him that was invisible,' Heb. xi. 27.

And St Paul prays for the Ephesians, 'that they might know the love of that which passeth knowledge,' Eph. iii. 19. These things imply a contradiction. Yet in like phrase I fear not to say of this father and brother, he saw those things 'which eye hath not seen,' spake those things which 'ear hath not heard,' and uttered those things 'which have not entered into the heart of man to conceive,' 2 Cor. ii. 9. This knot needs no cutting. He that rightly understands the text will easily look through this mystery without the help of an hyperbole. His scope was to stir us up to love God; his motive to persuade is taken from the excellency of those things which God hath prepared for them who love him. That excellency is expressed in a strange manner; by intimating it cannot be expressed, no, nor so much as comprehended by any natural ability of the body or mind. Yet it is expressed in the doctrine of the gospel sufficiently. So as here, as in a glass, we may 'behold the glory of God,' and in beholding, be 'changed from glory to glory,' 2 Cor. iii. 18. What duty more necessary than to love God? What motive more effectual than the gospel? For what is the gospel but a revelation of such things as natural men could never invent? Such things, that is, so precious, so useful, so comfortable to us; so divine, admirable, and transcendent in themselves. Many of us are like the angel of Ephesus, 'We have lost our first love,' Rev. ii. 4; yea, as our Saviour prophesied, Mat. xxiv. 12, 'The love of many waxes cold.' One reason may be, because to see-to,* we reap so little fruit of our love. Were it so, that we had nothing in hand, no present pay, that we served God altogether upon trust, without so much as an earnest, yet there is something 'prepared.' Let us believe that, and our hearts cannot but be warmed. We shall then be 'fervent in spirit, serving the Lord,' Rom. xii. 11. Be we persuaded of that, 'God is not unrighteous to forget your work and labour of love, which you have shewed towards his name,' Heb. vi. 10, and then we may triumphantly insult† with Paul, 'Who shall separate us from the love of Christ?' Rom. viii. 35. There is this difference between natural sight and spiritual. The one requires some nearness of the object, the other perceives things at greatest distance. As faith makes

* That is, = outward appearance.—G.

† That is, = exult, boast.—G.

future things present, so it makes remote things near, and things 'prepared' to affect as if they were enjoyed. But what hath God prepared? If I could answer this, it might not only satisfy, but inebriate. 'Such as eye hath not seen,' &c. It seems to be a proverbial form of speech, whereby the rich plenty of the divine blessings and benefits which God intendeth to us in and by Christ, according to the gospel, is shadowed forth. The words are to see-to* as a riddle, but here is 'one of a thousand, an interpreter,' Job xxxiii. 23, at hand, to unfold them. I could say much to invite you, but that the matter itself is as a loadstone. My testimony will add little weight, yet, having some care committed to me by Mr P. N.,† whom this business chiefly concerned, I could do no less than let you understand here is one rich piece of spiritual workmanship, wrought by a master builder, very useful for the building up and beautifying of God's temples. The blessing of God Almighty be with it, and upon the whole Israel of God.—So prays L. SEAMAN.‡

* Cf. *ante*, = sense.—G. † That is, Philip Nye. Cf. Vol. II. p. 3.—G.

‡ Dr Lazarus Seaman was one of the 'Ejected,' having been at the time in Alhallows, Bread Street, to which he had been presented by Laud in 1642. He died in September 1675. Jenkyn preached his funeral sermon. See the Noncf. Mem., I. 80–83.—G.

HIDDEN SECRETS REVEALED BY THE GOSPEL.

But, as it is written, Eye hath not seen, nor ear heard, neither have entered into the heart of man, the things which God hath prepared for them that love him.—1 Cor. II. 9.

The holy apostle St Paul, the trumpet of the gospel, 'the vessel of election,' was ordained to be a messenger of reconciliation, and to spread the sweet savour of the gospel everywhere. And answerably to his calling, he makes way for the excellency of his embassage into the hearts of those he had to deal with. This he doth by the commendation of his function. And that he might the better prevail, he removes all objections to the contrary. There were some that would debase his office, saying that the gospel he taught—Christ crucified—was no such great matter. Therefore, in the 6th verse of this chapter, he shews that the gospel 'is wisdom, and that among them that are perfect;' among the best and ablest to judge. St Paul did not build, as the papists do now, upon the blindness of the people. But it were not popery if they did not infatuate the people. St Paul saith to this effect:—We dare appeal to those that are the best, and of the best judgment, let them judge whether it be wisdom or no; the more perfect men are, the more able they are to judge of our wisdom.

It might be objected again, You see who cares for your wisdom, neither Herod, nor Pilate, nor the great men and potentates, the scribes and pharisees, great, learned men, and withal men of innocent lives, notable for carriage. Therefore, saith he, 'We speak not the wisdom of this world, or the princes of this world, that come to nought.' Do not tell us of such men's wisdom, they and their wisdom will come to nought too. We teach wisdom of things that are eternal, to make men eternal. As for the princes of the world, they and all that they know, their thoughts and all their plots and devices, perish. But 'we speak the wisdom of God in a mystery;' that is, the wisdom of God's revealing, a deep wisdom, a mystery that 'God ordained before the world;' ancient wisdom, not a yesterday's knowledge, though lately discovered. The preaching of the gospel is the discovery of that wisdom that was hidden before the world was.

And to invite you, and make you more in love with it, it is a wisdom 'to your glory.' God hath a delight to shew himself wise in devising a plot to glorify poor wretched man.

As for the words themselves, they are a proof of what he had said before, why none of the princes of the world knew this great mystery. If so be that the 'eye of any man hath not seen, nor the ear of any man hath heard, nor the heart of any man hath conceived,' what do you tell us of the wise men, which were not all, nay, what should I speak of men? The very angels (as we know by other places) are excluded from a full knowledge of these mysteries. Therefore it is no marvel though none of the princes of this world knew them. They are universally hidden from all natural men. This I take to be the sense of the words. They are taken out of Isaiah lxiv. 4. St Paul delights to prove things by the prophets. But here it is not so much a proof as an allusion, which we must observe to understand many such places. For Isaiah there speaks of the great things God had done for his church, such as eye had not seen, nor ear heard. And the apostle alludes to it here, and adds somewhat. This clause, 'nor hath entered into the heart of man,' is not in that place, but it is necessarily understood. For if the eye doth not see, and the ear hear, it never enters into the heart of man. For whatsoever enters into the heart of man, it must be by those passages and windows, the gates of the soul, the senses.

And whereas St Paul saith, 'for them that love him,' it is for them that 'expect him,' as in Isaiah. The sense is all one. Whosoever love God, they expect and wait for him. Where there is no expectation, there is no love.

This is the apostle's drift. If God did do such great matters for his church, as 'eye hath not seen, nor ear heard,' according to the prophet Isaiah, what shall we think he will do in the kingdom of grace here and of glory hereafter?

The words then, as we see, contain the excellency of the mysteries of the gospel, described first by the hiddenness of it to men at first.

Secondly, By the goodness of the things revealed, such as 'neither eye hath seen,' &c.

The hiddenness and excellency of the gospel in that respect is set forth by way of negation. 'Eye hath not seen, nor ear heard, nor heart conceived.' And indeed this is the way to set forth excellent divine things. God himself is set out by way of denial; by removing imperfections: he is invisible, immortal, &c. And so heaven, that is near to God, as being prepared by him, it is set out by way of denial, as St Peter saith, 'It is an inheritance immortal, undefiled,' &c., 1 Peter i. 4.

So here positive words could not be found sufficient to set out the excellency of the things that God hath prepared.

As for the knowledge of the mystery of salvation in Jesus Christ, we neither can come to it by natural invention nor by natural discipline. All the things that we know naturally, we know by one of these two ways; but divine things are known neither way.

Where could there have been any knowledge of Christ, if God had not opened his breast in the gospel, and come forth of his hidden light, and shewed himself in Christ, God-man; and in publishing the gospel established an ordinance of preaching for this purpose—where had the knowledge of salvation in Christ been?

To prove this we have here a gradation. The eye sees many things, but we hear more things than we see. Yet 'neither eye hath seen nor ear heard.' Ay, but the conceits of the heart are larger than the sight of the eye or the hearing of the ear. Yet neither eye hath seen, nor ear hath heard, 'nor hath entered into the heart of man to conceive,' &c. The philosopher saith, there is nothing in the understanding, but it came into the senses before: (*a*) and therefore it cannot enter into the heart of man, if it enter not by the eye or by the ear.

The things here spoken of be especially the graces, and comforts, and privileges to be enjoyed in this life, and the consummation and perfection of them in heaven. Christ brings peace and joy, justification and sanctification, and the like; and even in this life. The perfection of these is in heaven, where the soul and the body shall be both glorified, in a glorious place, together with glorious company; the Father, Son, and Holy Ghost, innumerable angels and just men. These are those things that 'eye hath not seen,' &c.; the beginnings here, and the perfection and consummation of them hereafter. Having thus far unfolded the words, I come to the points considerable.

Doct. First, God hath a company of beloved children in the world, that he means a special good unto.

The *second, God hath prepared great matters for them.*

1. If great persons prepare great things for those whom they greatly affect,* shall we not think that the great God will prepare great things for those that he hath affection to, and that have affection to him? If God be a friend to the elect, and they be his friends, surely he will answer friendship to the utmost. Answerable to the great love he bears his children, he hath provided great things for them.

If that be excellent that is long in preparing, then those things which belong to God's children must needs be excellent; for they were preparing even before the world was. Solomon's temple was an excellent fabric; it had long preparation, 1 Chron. xxii. 5. Ahasuerus made a feast to a hundred and twenty-seven provinces, Esther i. 1, *seq.* It was long in preparing. Great things have great preparation. Now these things that God intends his children have been preparing even from everlasting; and they are from everlasting to everlasting. They must needs be excellent. But before I dwell on any particular point, here is a question to be answered.

Quest. If the things that God hath prepared for his children be secret and excellent, how then come we to know them at all?

We come to know them (1.) *By divine revelation.* God must reveal them first, as it is in the next verse, 'God hath revealed them by his Spirit.'

The Spirit reveals them by way of negation, and indefinitely; as also by way of eminence. Whatsoever is excellent in the world, God borrows it to set out the excellency of the things that he hath provided for his children in grace and glory.

A feast is a comfortable thing. They are called a feast. A kingdom is a glorious thing. They are called a kingdom. Marriage is a sweet thing. They are set forth by that; by an inheritance; and adoption of children, and such like. So that all these things are taken to be shadows of those things. And indeed they are but shadows; the reality is the heavenly kingdom of grace and glory, the heavenly riches, the heavenly inheritance, the heavenly sonship. When all these things vanish and come to nothing, then comes in the true kingdom, sonship, and inheritance.

Again (2.) We know them in this world *by way of taste.* For the things of the life to come there are few of them but God's children have some experimental taste of them in this world. God reserves not all for the life to come, but he gives a grape of Canaan in this wilderness.

(3.) Thirdly, *by arguing from the less to the greater.* If peace of conscience be so sweet here, what is eternal peace! If a little joy here be so

* That is, 'love,' 'choose.'—G.

pleasant and comfortable that it makes us forget ourselves, what will be that eternal joy there! If the delights of a kingdom be such that they fill men's hearts so full of contentment that ofttimes they know not themselves, what shall we think of that excellent kingdom! So by way of taste and relish we may rise from these petty things to those excellent things, which indeed are scarce a beam, scarce a drop of those excellencies.

If Peter and John, when they were in the mountain, were not their own men,—when they saw but a glimpse, but a little glory of Christ manifested in the mount, Mat. ix. 6,—what shall we think when there is the fulness of that glorious revelation at the right hand of God, where there is 'fulness of pleasures for ever'? Ps. xvi. 11. How shall our souls be filled at that time! Thus by way of rising from the lesser to the greater, by tasting, feeling, and by divine revelation, we may know in some measure the excellency of those things prepared for us.

Now to clear this thing more fully, know that there are three degrees of revelation.

First, There must be a revelation of the things themselves, by word, and writing, or speech, and the like; as we know not the mind of a man but either by speech or writing. So there must be a revelation of these things, or else the wit of angels could never have devised how to reconcile justice and mercy, by infinite wisdom, by sending a mediator to procure peace, God-man, to work our salvation. Therefore we could not know them without a revelation and discovery outward. This is the first degree, that we may call revelation by Scripture, or by the doctrine of the gospel. Who could discover those things that are merely supernatural, but God himself?

Second, Then again, When they are revealed by the word of God, and by men that have a function to unfold the unsearchable riches of Christ by the ministry of the gospel, yet notwithstanding they are hidden riddles still to a company of carnal men. Put case the veil be taken off from the things themselves, yet if the veil be over the soul, the understanding, will, and affections, there is no apprehension of them. Therefore there must be a second revelation, that is, by the Spirit of God. Of necessity this must be; for even as the apostle saith in this chapter, 'None knoweth the mind of man but the spirit that is in man,' ver. 11, so none knoweth the mind of God but the Spirit of God. What is the gospel, without the Spirit of Christ to discover the mind of God to us? We know not the good meaning of God to us in particular. We know in general that such things are revealed in Scripture; but what is that to us if Christ be not our Saviour and God our Father? unless we can say as St Paul saith, 'He loved me, and gave himself for me,' Gal. ii. 20. Therefore you see a necessity of revelation by the Spirit.

But this is not all that is here meant. There is,

Thirdly, A higher discovery, and that is in heaven. That that is revealed here is but in part; and thereupon if we believe, we believe but in part, and we love but in part. If our knowledge, which is the ground of all other graces and affections, be imperfect, all that follows must needs be imperfect also. Therefore St John saith, 'We know that we are the sons of God, but it appears not what we shall be,' 1 John iii. 2. What we shall be in heaven it doth not appear now. There must be a further revelation, and that will be hereafter, when our souls shall be united together with our bodies. And then, indeed, our eyes shall see, our ears hear, and hearts shall conceive those things that while we are here in the womb of the church we neither can see, nor hear, nor understand, more than the child in the womb of the mother can conceive the excellencies in this civil* life. Thus we see these truths a little more unfolded. I will now add somewhat to make use of what hath been spoken.

Use 1. *First* of all, therefore, for *matter of instruction.* If it be so, that the things of the gospel be such, as that without a revelation from God they could not be known, then we see that *there is no principle at all of the gospel in nature.* There is not a spark of light, or any inclination to the gospel, but it is merely above nature. For he removes here all natural ways of knowing the gospel, eye, ear, and understanding. Therefore the knowledge of it is merely supernatural. For if God had not revealed it, who could ever have devised it? And when he revealed it, to discover it by his Spirit, it is supernatural; but in heaven much more, which is the third degree I spake of. Therefore, by the way, you may know the reason why so many heresies have sprung out of the gospel, more than out of the law and the misunderstanding of it. There are few or no heresies from that, because the principles of the law are written in the heart. Men naturally know that whoredom, and adultery, and filthy living, &c., are sins. Men have not so quenched nature but that they know that those things are naught. Therefore there have been excellent law-makers among the heathens. But the gospel is a mere 'mystery' discovered out of the breast of God, without† all principles of nature. There are thousands of errors that are not to be reckoned, about the nature, the person, and the benefits of Christ; about justification and sanctification, and free will and grace, and such things. What a world of heresies have proud wits continually started up! This would never have been but that the gospel is a thing above nature. Therefore, when a proud wit and supernatural knowledge revealed meet together, the proud heart storms and loves to struggle, and deviseth this thing and that thing to commend itself; and hereupon comes heresies, the mingling of natural wit with divine truths. If men had had passive wits to submit to divine truths, and to work nothing out of themselves, as the spider out of her own bowels,‡ there had not been such heresies in the church; but their hearts meeting with supernatural truths, their proud hearts mingling with it, they have devised these errors; that I note in the first place.

Use 2. Then again, if the things that we have in the gospel be such divine truths, above nature altogether, *then we must not stand to look for reason too much, nor trust the reason or wit of any man, but divine authority especially.* For if divine authority cease in the gospel, what were it? Nothing. The law is written in men's hearts; but we must trust divine authority in the gospel above all other portions of Scripture, and not to the wit of any man whatsoever.

The Church of Rome, that is possessed with a spirit of pride and ignorance and tyranny, they will force knowledge on them that be under them from their sole authorities. The church saith so, and we are the church; and it is not for you to know, &c., and Scriptures are so and so. But is the gospel a supernatural mystery above the capacity of any man? and shall we build upon the authority of the church for these truths? Oh, no! There must be no forcing of evangelical truths from the authority or parts of any man. But these are not things that we stand in so much need of.

* That is, 'outward life.'—G. † That is, 'outside of.'—G.

‡ This is a comparison constantly used by Bacon, in his *Novum Organum*, and elsewhere.—Ed.

Therefore I hasten to that which is more useful. 'Eye hath not seen, nor ear heard,' &c.

Use 3. Here then we have an use of direction *how to carry ourselves in reading and studying holy truths; especially the sacred mysteries of the gospel.* How shall we study them? We think to break into them with the engine of our wit, and to understand them, and never come to God for his Spirit. God will curse such proud attempts. 'Who knows the things of man, but the spirit of a man? and who knows the things of God, but the Spirit of God?' Therefore in studying the gospel, let us come with a spirit of faith, and a spirit of humility and meekness. There is no breaking into these things with the strength of parts. That hath been the ground of so many heresies as have been in the church. Only Christ 'hath the key of David, that shutteth, and no man openeth; and openeth, and no man shutteth,' Rev. iii. 7. He hath the key of the Scripture, and the key to open the understanding. And to press this point a little. If 'eye hath not seen, nor ear heard, nor hath entered into the heart of man to conceive, the things of the gospel,' without the revelation of the Spirit, then we must come with this mind when we come to hear the things of the gospel. Lord, without thy Holy Spirit they are all as a clasped book; they are hidden mysteries to me, though they be revealed in the gospel. If my heart be shut to them, they are all hidden to me.

We see men of excellent parts are enemies to that they teach themselves, opposing the power of the gospel. Whence is all this? Because they think only the opening of these things makes them divines, whereas without the Holy Ghost sanctifying and altering the heart in some measure to taste and relish these things, that as they are divine in themselves, so to have somewhat divine in the heart to taste these things, it is impossible but that the heart should rise against them; and so it doth. For when it comes to particulars, you must deny yourself in this honour, in this pleasure, and commodity; now you must venture the displeasure of man for this and that truth. The heart riseth in scorn and loathing of divine truth. When it comes to particulars they know nothing as they should. For when is truth known, but when in particulars we stand for it; and will neither betray it nor do anything that doth not benefit* a Christian? If we have not the Spirit of God to relish truths in particular, they will do us no good. And except the Spirit sanctify the heart of man first by these truths, the truth will never be understood by the proud natural heart of man.

Therefore the course that God takes with his children is this. Those that he means to save, he first inspires into their hearts some desire to come to hear and attend upon the means of salvation, to understand the gospel; and then under the means of salvation he shines into the understanding by a heavenly light, and inspires into the will and affections some heavenly inclination to this truth of the gospel, to justification, sanctification, self-denial, and the like, and works a new life; and new senses, and upon them, wrought under the means, comes the soul to relish, and to understand these mysteries; and then the ears and the eyes are open to see these things, and never before. A holy man, that hath his heart subdued by the Spirit of God in the use of the means, oh he relisheth the point of forgiveness of sins; he relisheth the point of sanctification; he studies it daily more and more, and nearer communion with God; he relisheth peace of conscience and joy in the Holy Ghost; they are sweet things, and all the duties of Christianity, because he makes it his main

* Qu. 'befit'?—Ed.

business to adorn his profession; and to live here, so as he may live for ever hereafter. And this must be of necessity; for mark out of the text: if the natural eye and ear and heart can never see nor hear, nor conceive the things of God, must there not be a supernatural ear and eye and heart put into the soul? Must not the heart and all be new-moulded again? If the former frame be not sufficient for these things, of necessity it must be so.

Use 4. From hence learn *to arm yourselves against all scandals.** When ye see men of all parts and account, and such there may be, men of deep apprehensions and understanding in the Scripture for the matter of notion, and for the language of the Scripture exquisite, and yet to be proud, malicious, haters of sanctity, next to devils, none greater, consider what is the reason. Either they have proud spirits that despise and neglect the means of salvation altogether; or if they do come, they come as judges; they will not submit their proud hearts to the sweet motions of the Spirit. Stumble not at it, if such men be both enemies to that they teach themselves, and those that practise it. The reason is, because their proud hearts were never subdued by the Spirit to understand the things they speak of. For such a teacher understands supernatural things by a natural light, and by human reason; that is, to talk, and discourse, &c., but he sees not supernatural things by a supernatural light, divine things by a divine light. Therefore a poor soul that hears the things published by him, understands them better by the help of the Spirit than he that speaks them; better indeed for his use and comfort. As we see, there are some that can measure land exactly; but the man that owneth the land measured, he knows the use of the ground and delights in it as his own. The other can tell, here is so much ground, &c. So some divines, they can tell there are such points, and so they are raised; and they can be exquisite in this; but what profit have they by it?

The poor soul that hears these things, by the help of the Spirit he can say, These are mine, as the man for whom the ground is measured. As it is with those that come to a feast, the physician comes and says, This is wholesome and good, and this is good for this and that, but eats nothing. Others that know not these things, they eat the meat, and are nourished in the mean time. So when such men discourse of this and that, a poor man that hath the Spirit, he relisheth these things as his own. The other goes away, only discourseth as a philosopher of the meat, and eats nothing.

And therefore when you read and hear these things, content not yourselves with the first degree of revelation. No; that is not enough. When you have done that, desire of God to join his Spirit, to give you spiritual eyes and hearts, that you may close with divine truths, and be divine as the truths are; that there may be a consent of the heart with the truth. Then the word of God will be sweet indeed.

Use 5. Again, here we see this divine truth, *that a man when he hath the Spirit of God knows things otherwise than he did know them before, though he did not know them by outward revelation of hearing and reading, &c.* And he believes them otherwise than he did before; he sees them by a new light. It is not the same knowledge that an unregenerate man hath with that he hath after, when God works upon his heart, 1 Cor. ii. 14, 15; for then it is a divine supernatural knowledge. And it is not the same faith and belief. The Spirit of God raiseth a man up in a degree of creatures above other men, as other men are above beasts; he gives new eyes, new ears, and a new heart; he moulds him anew every

* That is, 'stumbling-blocks.'—G.

way. Therefore you have good men sometimes wonder at themselves, when God hath touched their hearts, that they have had such shallow conceits of this and that truth before. Now they see that they were in the dark, that they were in a damp before, that they conceived things to be so and so, and thought themselves somebody. But when God opens their eyes, and takes away the scales, and lets them see things in their proper light, heavenly things by a heavenly light, and with a heavenly eye, they wonder at their former foolishness in divinity, especially so far as concerns the gospel. For there is more in the Scripture than pure supernatural divinity; there are many other arts in the Scripture.

The gospel, I say, is a knowledge, not of natural men, or great wits, but of holy sanctified men. Therefore we must not think that these things may be known by nature, &c. It is a sacred knowledge, so much as will bring us to heaven; it is a knowledge of holy men, that have their hearts brought to love and taste, and relish that they know. Therefore it is no wonder, though a company of men of great parts live naughtily. They are no true divines, because they have no true knowledge. The devil is no divine, nor a wicked man properly. Though he can discourse of such things, yet he is not properly a divine; because he knows not things by a divine light, or heavenly things by a heavenly light. The knowledge of the gospel, it is a knowledge of sanctified, holy men. But to come nearer to our practice.

Use. 6. If eye hath not seen, nor ear heard, nor hath entered into the heart of man to conceive those things that God hath prepared for his, then *let us make this the rule of our esteem of anything that is good, or anything that is ill; make it a rule of valuation.* The apostle here, you see, hath a rank of things above the sight of the eye, or the hearing of the ear, or the conceiving of the heart of man. If there be such a rank of things above this, then the greatest ills are those that eye hath not seen, nor ear heard, nor hath entered into the heart of man; and indeed they are so. We grieve at the ague, and at the stone, and at the gout; they are grievous things indeed. Oh, but what be these things that we feel and see, to those in another world, that we cannot apprehend for the greatness of them! The torments of hell, we cannot conceive and understand them here; for it is indeed to be in hell itself to conceive what hell is. And therefore when God enlargeth men's spirits to see them, they make away themselves. And so for the greatest good. These goods here, this outward glory, we can see through it. Christ could see through all the glory in the world that the devil shewed him, Mat. iv. 8. And these are things that we can hear of, and hear the utmost that can be spoken of them. Therefore surely they are not the greatest good. There are more excellent things than they. Because the eye sees them, the ear hears of them, and the understanding can conceive of them. But there be things that the eye hath not seen, nor ear heard, nor the soul conceived; and these be the joys of heaven. And thereupon, to descend to practice, if this be a rule to value things that the best things are transcendent, beyond sense and comprehension, then shall I for those things that I can see, and can hear, and feel, and understand, shall I lose those excellent good things, that 'neither eye hath seen nor ear heard,' &c.? Is not this desperate folly, to venture the loss of the best things, of the most transcendent things, that are above the capacity of the greatest reaches of the world? Shall I lose all for petty poor things that are within my own reach and compass?

How foolish, therefore, are those that are given to pleasures! They feel the pleasure indeed, but the sting comes after. They delight in those ill things that they can hear, and hear all that can be spoken of them, and never think of the excellent things that the eye hath not seen, nor ear heard, &c.

Let this make us in love with divine truths in the Scripture, with the gospel, that part of the Scripture that promiseth salvation by Christ, and all the graces and privileges of Christianity. They are above our reach. We study other things. We can reach them. We can reach the mysteries of the law by long study, and the mysteries of physic, and to the mysteries of trades by understanding, and when men have done all they may be fools in the main—Solomon's fools. They may do all these things, and be wise for particular things, by particular reaches of that which eye hath seen, and ear heard, &c.; and then for the best things that are above the capacity of men, they may die empty of all, and go to the place of the damned. To be wise to salvation is the best wisdom.

What a pitiful case is this, that God should give us our understandings for better things than we can see or hear in this world, yet we employ them in things of the world wholly. Let us not do as some shallow, proud heads, that regard not divine things. The holy Scriptures they will not vouchsafe to read once a-day, perhaps not once a-week; nay, some scarce have a Bible in their studies. For shame; shall we be so atheistical, when God hath provided such excellent things contained in this book of God, the Testament? Shall we slight these excellent things for knowledge that shall perish with us? as St Paul saith before the text. The knowledge of all other things is perishing, knowledge of perishing men. Learn on earth that that will abide in heaven, saith St Austin. If we be wise, let us know those things on earth, that the comfort of them may abide with us in heaven. Therefore let us be stirred up to value the Scriptures, the mysteries of salvation in the gospel; they are things that 'eye hath not seen, nor ear heard,' &c. Nay, I say more, that little that we have here, by hearing truths unfolded, whereby the Spirit of God slides into our hearts, and works with them. There is that peace that a man hath in his heart, in the unfolding of the point of justification or adoption, or any divine comfort, that it breeds such inward peace and joy as is unspeakable and glorious. All that we have in the world is not worth those little beginnings that are wrought by the hearing of the word of God here. If the first fruits here be joy ofttimes 'unspeakable and glorious,' 1 Peter i. 8, if the first fruits be 'peace that passeth understanding,' Phil. iv. 7, what will the consummation and perfection of these things be at that day?

Again, here you see a ground of the wonderful patience of the martyrs. You wonder that they would suffer their bodies to be torn, and have their souls severed so violently from their bodies. Alas!* cease to wonder; when they had a sense wrought in them by the Spirit of God of the things that eye hath not seen nor ear heard. If a man should have asked them why they would suffer their bodies to be misused thus, when they might have redeemed all this with a little quiet? Oh, they would have answered presently, as some of them have done: We suffer these things in our bodies and in our senses, for those that are above our senses; we know there are things laid up for us that eye hath not seen, nor ear heard, &c. What do you tell us of this torment and that torment? We shall have more glory in heaven than we can have misery here. For we can see this, and there is an end of it; but we shall have joy that 'eye hath not seen, nor ear heard, &c. As St Paul most divinely, in divers places in Rom.

* Another example of Sibbes's unusual use of 'alas.'—G.

viii. 18, the things that we suffer here are not 'worthy of the glory that shall be revealed.' Therefore let us not wonder so much at their patience as to lay up this ground of patience against an evil day when we may be drawn to seal the truth with our blood. By the way learn what popery is. They think to merit by their doings, but especially by their sufferings, though they be ill doers, and suffer for their demerits; this is their glory. Shall those stained good works (put case they were good works, they be defiled, and stained, and as menstruous cloths, as it is, Isa. xxx. 22), shall they merit the glory to be revealed, that is so great that eye hath not seen? &c. What proportion is there? In merit there must be a proportion between the deed done and the glory. What proportion is there between stained imperfect defiled works, and the glory to be revealed? Should not our lives be almost angelical? 'What manner of men should we be in all holy conversation,' 2 Pet. iii. 11, considering what things are laid up in heaven, and we have the first fruits of them here? Can men be too holy and exact in their lives, that look for things 'that eye hath not seen, nor ear heard?' &c.

I wonder at the stupidity and hellish pride and malice of men's hearts, that think any man can be too exact in the main duties of Christianity, in the expression of their love to God, in the obedience of their lives; in abstinence from the filthiness of the world, and the like. Can a man that looks for these excellent transcendent things be too careful of his life? I beseech you yourselves be judges.

THE END OF THE FIRST SERMON.

THE SECOND SERMON.

As it is written, Eye hath not seen, nor ear heard, &c.—1 Cor. II. 9.

The apostle sets out the gospel here with all the commendations that any skill in the world can be commended by. From the author of it, 'God.' From the depth of it, it is 'wisdom;' in a mystery, 'hidden wisdom.' From the antiquity of it, 'it was ordained before the world was.' From the benefit and use of it, 'for our glory.' *God is content his wisdom should be honoured in glorifying us, such is his love.* And then when it was revealed, that none of the 'princes of the world' (he means not only commanding potentates, but, he being a scholar himself, esteemed philosophers, Pharisees, and learned men to be princes, because the excellency of a man is in the refined part of man, his soul), none of these princes of the world, for all their skill and knowledge, knew this.

In this verse he shews the reason why 'eye hath not seen, nor ear heard,' &c. He removes knowledge, by removing the way and means of knowledge. The means of knowledge in this world is by the passage and entrance of the senses. Now, this heavenly mystery of the gospel, it is such a knowledge as doth not enter into the soul by the senses.

The points we propounded were these: 1. *That God hath a people in the world, whom he favours in a special manner.*

Then, secondly, *for these that he accounts his friends, he hath prepared great matters.* Kings prepare great matters for those they mean to advance; what shall we think then God will do for his friends?

Now, these things prepared, they are great matters indeed; for, in the third place, they are such as *eye hath not seen, nor ear heard, &c.*

And then, in the fourth place, *the disposition and qualification of those for whom God hath prepared such great matters.* It is for those 'that love him;' not for his enemies, or for all men indifferently, but for those that love him.

Of the first and second I spake in the former; and I will not now stand to speak of them, but enlarge myself in the two last.

The things that God hath prepared for them that love him, are such excellent things as neither eye hath seen, nor ear heard, &c. He means the natural eye, and ear, and understanding, or heart of man.

There be three degrees of discovery of heavenly things:

First, In the *doctrine of them;* and so they are hid to them that are out of the church.

And then, secondly, in the *spiritual meaning of them;* and so they are hid to carnal men in the church.

And then, thirdly, in regard of *the full comprehension of them*, as they are indeed; and so they are reserved for heaven. We have but a little glimpse of them, a little light into them in this world. Now, in this place is meant the things that are discovered in the gospel, especially as they are apprehended by the Spirit, together with the consummation of them in heaven. For they differ only in degree, the discovery of the heavenly things in the gospel here; the privileges, and graces, and comforts of God's children, and the consummation of them in heaven. And we may reason from the lesser to the greater, if so be that a natural man—though he have natural eyes, and ears, and wits about him—cannot conceive the hidden mysteries of the gospel spiritually with application; much more unable is he, and much less can he conceive, those things of a better life. Now the things of the gospel, the privileges, the graces, and comforts which Christ, the spring and head of them all, in whom all are, and whence we have all, cannot be comprehended by a natural man. He can discourse of them as far as his natural wit conceives them, but not understand heavenly things in their own light as heavenly things, as the things of the gospel. They can talk of repentance—that we commonly speak of, which is a mystery—but notwithstanding who knows repentance by the light proper to it, but he that by the Spirit of God hath sin discovered to him in its own colours! He knows what it is to grieve for sin.

The sick man knows what it is to be sick. The physician knows it by definition, by books, and so he can enlarge it; but if he be not sick, the sick patient will speak to better purpose. So there is a mystery in the common things of the gospel, repentance and grief for sin. A holy man feels it another matter, because he feels sin discovered by the Spirit of God. And so in faith, in the love of God, and every grace of the gospel is a mystery. If one come to the Schoolmen, they will tell you of faith, and dispute learnedly of it, and deduce this from that; but when he comes to be in extremity, when the terrors of the Lord are upon him, when he comes to use it, he is a mere stranger to it; to cast himself, being a sinful creature, into the arms of God's mercy, he cannot do it without a further light of the Spirit discovering the hidden love of God to him in particular; and so for other graces. Therefore they do but speak of these things—men that are unsanctified—as a blind man doth of colours. They inwardly scorn the truth they speak of; and those to whom they speak, if by the power of God's Spirit they come to profit by the things they teach, if themselves be carnal, they hate them. A carnal man believes not a whit of what he saith; he hath only a common light for the good of others, a common illumination to understand and discover things, and a doctrinal gift to unfold things for others, and not for themselves. For themselves they scorn them in their hearts, and in their lives and conversations, and they will speak as much when it comes to self-denial in preferment, in pleasures, in anything that is gainful. Tush! tell him what he hath taught, or what he knows out of the book of God, he cares not, he knows them only by a common light; but for a particular heavenly light with application and taste to himself, springing from an alteration by the Spirit, he never knows them so. Therefore content not thyself with a common light, for together with our understanding God alters the taste of the whole soul; he gives a new eye, a new ear, to see and hear to purpose, and a new heart to conceive things in another manner than he did before.

But you will ask, How can a godly man know them at all, seeing 'eye hath not seen, nor ear heard,' &c.?

I answer, *first*, the things of another life, as we see here, *are known by negation*, as God is, by way of removing imperfections. The natural eye sees them not, nor the natural ear hears them not, &c. No; nor the spiritual eye nor ear in a full measure. So things transcendent, that are above the reach of man, are described in the Scriptures by the way of denial, which is one good way of knowledge.

That 'ye may know the love of God that is above knowledge,' saith the apostle, Eph. iii. 19; that ye may know it more and more. But it is above all knowledge in regard of the perfection of it. As a man may see the sea, but he cannot comprehend the sea. He may be much delighted in seeing the sea, but he sees neither the bottom nor the banks; he cannot comprehend such a vast body. He may see the heavens, but he cannot comprehend them. So a man may know the things when they are revealed, but he cannot comprehend them; apprehension is one thing, and comprehension is another. There may be apprehension in a poor degree, suitable to the capacity of the soul here; but, alas!* it is far from the comprehension that we shall have in heaven. That is one way of knowing them, by way of negation and denial of imperfections to them.

And then, *secondly*, they are known, as we call it, by way of *eminence*; that is, by comparing them with other things, and preferring them before all other excellencies whatsoever; as we may see the sun in water by resemblance. For God borrows from nature terms to set out grace and glory, because God will speak in our language. For they are called a 'kingdom' and a 'feast,' and a 'crown' by way of comparison. Shallow men think there is a great deal in a kingdom; and indeed so there is, if there were no other. There is great matters in a 'crown,' in 'the feasts' of kings, and the like. But alas! these be shadows; and there is no rhetoric or amplification in this, to say they be shadows. A shadow is as much in proportion to the body as these are to eternal good things. The true reality of things are in the things of another world, for eternity. If we talk of a kingdom, let us talk of that in heaven; if of a crown, of that wherewith the saints are crowned in heaven. If we talk of riches, they are those that make a man eternally rich; that he shall carry with him when he goes out of the world. What riches are those that a man shall outlive, and die a beggar, and not have a drop to comfort him, as we see Dives in hell had not? Luke xvi. 19, *seq*. Here are riches indeed. So if we talk of beauty, it is the image of God that sets a beauty on the soul, that makes a man lovely in the eye of God. True beauty is to be

* Cf. footnote, page 163.—G.

like God. And to be born anew to that glorious condition is the birth and inheritance. All these poor things are but acting a part upon a stage for a while, as the proudest creature of all that is invested in them will judge ere long; none better judges than they. This is one way of knowing the things of the gospel, by naming of them in our own language. As if a man go into a foreign country, he must learn that language, or else hold his peace: so God is forced to speak in our own language, to tell us of glory and happiness to come, under the name of crowns and kingdoms, and riches here. If God should set them out in their own lustre, we could not conceive of them.

But, *thirdly*, the most comfortable way whereby God's people know the things of heaven, and of the life to come, *is in regard of some taste;* for there is nothing in heaven but God's children have a taste of it before they come there in some measure. They have a taste of the communion that is in heaven, in the communion they have on earth: they have a taste of that eternal Sabbath, by some relish they have of holy exercises in these Christian Sabbaths. A Christian is as much in heaven as he can be, when he sanctifies the holy Sabbath, speaking to God in the congregation by prayer, and hearing God speak to him in the preaching of the word. That peace that we shall have in heaven, which is a peace uninterrupted, without any disturbance, it is understood by that sweet peace of conscience here 'that passeth all understanding,' Eph. iii. 19. We may know, therefore, what the sight of Christ face to face will be, by the sight we have of Christ now in the word and promises. If it so transform and affect us, that sight that we have by knowledge and faith here, what will those sights do? So that by a grape we may know what Canaan is: as the spies, they brought of the grapes of Canaan into the desert. We may know by this little taste what those excellent things are.

The *fourth* way is by *authority and discovery*. St Paul was rapt up in[to] the third heaven; he saith, they were such things that he saw, that could not be spoken of, strange things, 2 Cor. xii. 4. And Christ tells us of a kingdom. Christ knew what they were. And the word tells us what they are. Our faith looks to the authority of the word, if we had not the first fruits, nor any other discovery. God that hath prepared them, he saith so in his word, and we must rest in his authority. And there are some that have been in heaven. Christ our blessed Saviour, that hath taken into a perpetual union the manhood with the second person, which he hath knit unto it, he knows what is there; and by this means we come to have some kind of knowledge of the things to come.

Fifthly, Again, *by a kind of reasoning likewise from the lesser to the greater*, we may come to know not only the things, but the greatness of them. As, is there not comfort now in a little glimpse, when God shines upon a Christian's soul, when he is as it were in heaven? Is there such contentment in holy company here, what shall there be in heaven? Is there such contentment in the delights of this world, that are the delights of our pilgrimage? (They are no better; our houses are houses of pilgrimage; our contentments are contentments of passengers.) If the way, the gallery that leads to heaven, be so spread with comforts, what be those that are reserved in another world! A man may know by raising his soul from the lesser to the greater. And if the things that God hath provided in common for his enemies as well as his friends (as all the comforts of this world, all the delicacies and all the objects of the senses, they are comforts that are common to the enemies of God, as well as his friends): if these things be so excellent, that men venture their souls for them, and lose all to be drowned in these things, Oh what peculiar things are they that God hath reserved for his own children, for those that love him, when those that are common with his enemies are so glorious and excellent! These kind of ways we may come to know them by the help of the Spirit.

Those unmixed joys, those pure joys, that are full of themselves, and have no tincture in heaven, are understood by those joys we feel on earth; the joy of the Holy Ghost, which is after conflict with temptations, or after afflictions, or after hearing and meditating on good things. The heavenly joys that flow into the soul, they give us a taste of that full joy that we shall have at the right hand of God for evermore. That comfort that we shall have in heaven, in the presence of God, and of Christ, and his holy angels, is understood in some little way by the comfortable presence of God to the soul of a Christian, when he finds the Spirit of God raising him, and cheering him up, and witnessing his presence; as ofttimes, to the comfort of God's people, the Holy Ghost witnesseth a presence, that now the soul can say, God is present with me, he smiles on me, and strengtheneth me, and leads me along. This comfortable way God's children have to understand the things of heaven, by the first fruits they have here. For God is so far in love with his children here on earth, and so tender over them, that he purposes not to reserve all for another world, but gives them some taste beforehand, to make them better in love with the things there, and better to bear the troubles of this world. But alas! what is it to that that they shall know? as it is 1 John iii. 2, 'Now we are the sons of God, but it appears not what we shall be.' That shall be so great in comparison of that we are, that it is said not to appear at all. It appears in the first fruits in a little beginnings; but alas! what is that to that glory that shall be! 'Our life is hid with Christ in God,' Col. iii. 3. It is hid. There is no man knows it in regard of the full manifestation; because here it is covered with so many infirmities, and afflictions, and so many scorns of the world are cast upon the beauty of a Christian life; it is hid in our head Christ. It is not altogether hid, for there is a life that comes from the root, from the head Christ to the members, that quickens them; but in regard of the glory that shall be, it is a hidden life.

Reasons. Let us consider the reasons why God will have it thus, to make it clear, before I go further. We must be modest in reasons when we speak of God's counsels and courses. I will only name them to open our understandings a little.

1*st Reason.* (*First.*) *It is enough that God will have it so.* A modest Christian will be satisfied with that, that God will have a difference between heaven and earth. God's dispensation may satisfy them.

(*Second.*) *God will have a difference between the warring church and the triumphing church.*

This life is a life of faith, and not of sight. We walk and live by faith. Why? Partly to try the truth of our faith, and partly for the glory of God, that he hath such servants in the world here that will depend upon him, upon terms of faith, upon his bare word; that can say, There are such things reserved in heaven for me, I have enough. What a glory is it to God that he hath those that will trust him upon his bare word! It were no commendation for a Christian to live here in a beautiful, glorious manner, if he should see all and live by sight. If he should see hell open, and the terrors there, for him then to abstain from sin, what glory were it! The sight would force abstinence. If we should see heaven open, and the joys of it present, it were no thanks to be a good man, for sight would force it.

2d *Reason.* The *second* reason is this, *that God will have a known difference between hypocrites and the true children of God.* If heaven were upon earth, and nothing reserved in faith and in promise, every one would be a Christian. But now the greatest things being laid up in promises, we must exercise our faith to wait for them. Now, there are none that will honour God in his word but the true Christian. That there are such excellent things reserved in another world, in comparison of which all these are base, there is none but a true Christian that will honour God upon his word, that will venture the loss of these things here for them in heaven, that will not lose those things that they have in reversion and promise for the present delights of sin for a season! Whereas the common sort, they hear say of a heaven, and happiness, and a day of judgment, &c. But in the mean time they will not deny their base pleasures and their rebellious dispositions, they will cross themselves in nothing. Do we think that God hath prepared heaven for such wretches as these? Oh let us never think of it! God therefore hath reserved the best excellencies for the time to come, in promises and in his word, if we have grace to depend upon his word, and in the mean time go on and cross our corruptions. It is an excellent condition to be so. It shews the difference that God will have between us and other men.

3d *Reason.* Again, *thirdly, our vessels could not contain it.* We are incapable; our brain is not strong enough for these things. As weak brains cannot digest hot liquors, so we cannot digest a large revelation of these things. As we see St Peter was not himself in the transfiguration; he forgot himself, and was spiritually drunk with joy, with that he saw in the mount. He wot not what he said, as the scripture saith, when he said, 'Master, let us make three tabernacles,' &c., Mark ix. 5. Nay, St Paul himself, the great apostle, when he saw things in heaven above expression, that could not nor might not be uttered, could not digest them, 2 Cor. xii. 4. They were so great, that if he had not had somewhat to weigh him down, to balance him, he had been overturned with pride. Therefore there was a 'prick in the flesh' sent to Paul himself, to humble him, 2 Cor. xii. 7. Are we greater than Paul and Peter, the great apostles of the Jews and Gentiles; when these grand apostles could not contain themselves? When they see these heavenly things, and but a glimpse of them, the one did not know what he said, and the other was humbled, by way of prevention, with a prick in the flesh; and shall we think to conceive of these things? No! we cannot; for that is to be in heaven before our time. These and the like reasons we may have to satisfy us in this, why we cannot conceive of the things to come as they are in their proper nature. God saith to Moses, when Moses would have a fairer manifestation of God, 'No man can see me and live,' Exod. xxxiii. 20. If we would see God as he is, we must die. If we would see heaven, and the joys of it as it is, we must die first. No man can see the things that the apostle here speaks of, in their proper light and excellency, but he must die first.

They are not proportionable to our condition here. For God hath resolved that this life shall be a life of imperfection, and that shall be a perfect estate of perfect glory. Alas! our capacities now are not capable, our affections will not contain those excellent things. Therefore God trains us up by little and little to the full fruition and enjoying of it. Thus we see how we come to have some knowledge of them, and why we have not a full knowledge of them here.

Use 1. Well, to leave this and go on. If this be so, *then let us oft think of these things.*

The life of a Christian is wondrously ruled in this world by the consideration and meditation of the life of another world. Nothing more steers the life of a Christian here than the consideration of the life hereafter; not only by way of comfort, that the consideration of immortal life and glory is the comfort of this mortal base life, but likewise by way of disposition and framing a man to all courses that are good. There is no grace of the Spirit, in a manner, but it is set on work by the consideration of the estate that is to come; no, not one.

What is the work of faith? 'It is the evidence of things not seen,' Heb. xi. 1. It sets the things of another world present before the eye of the soul, and in that respect it is victorious. It conquers the world, because it sets a better world in the eye. Where were the exercise of faith, if it were not for hope of such an estate which feeds faith? The excellency of faith is, that it is about things not seen. It makes things that are not seen to be seen; it hath a kind of omnipotent power; it gives a being to things that have none, but in the promise of the speaker.

And for hope, the very nature of hope is to expect those things that faith believes. Were it not for the joys of heaven, where were hope? It is the helmet of the soul, to keep it from blows and temptations. It is the anchor of the soul, that being cast within the veil into heaven, stays the soul in all the waves and troubles in this world. The consideration of the things to come exerciseth this grace of hope. We look within the veil, and cast anchor there upward, and not downward; and there we stay ourselves in all combustions and confusions by the exercise of hope, Heb. vi. 19.

And where were patience? If it were not for a better estate in another world, a Christian 'of all men were most miserable,' 1 Cor. xv. 19. Who would endure anything for Christ, if it were not for a better estate afterwards?

And so for sobriety. What forceth a moderate use of all things here? The consideration of future judgment, that made even Felix to tremble, Acts xxiv. 25. The consideration of the estate to come, causes that we surfeit not with the cares of the world and excess, but do all that may make way for such a glorious consideration.

What enforceth the keeping of a good conscience in all things? St Paul looked to the resurrection of the just and of the unjust; and this made him exercise himself to keep a good conscience.

And so purity and holiness, that we take heed of all defilements in the world, that we be not 'led away with the error of the wicked,' 2 Peter iii. 17; but 'keep ourselves unspotted,' James i. 27. What forceth this but the consideration of a glorious condition in another world! 'He that hath this hope purgeth himself,' 1 John iii. 3. There is a purgative power in hope; a cleansing efficacy, that a man cannot hope for this excellent condition, but it will frame and fit the soul for that condition. Can a man hope to appear before a great person, and not fit himself in his deportment and attire beforehand, to please the person before whom he appears? So whosoever hopes to appear before Christ and God, of necessity that hope will force him to purge himself. Let us not stand to search curiously into particulars, what the glory of the soul or of the body shall be (the apostle discovers it in general, we shall be 'conformed to Christ our head in soul and body'), but rather study how to make good use of them; for therefore they are revealed beforehand in general.

Use 2. And withal *to humble ourselves, and to say with the psalmist*, 'Lord, what is man, that thou so far considerest him?' Ps. viii. 4; sinful man, that hath lost his first condition, and hath betrayed himself to thine and his enemy; to advance him to that estate, 'that neither eye hath seen, nor ear heard,' &c. This consideration will make us base in our own eyes.

Shall not we presently disdain any proud conceits? Shall we talk of merit? What can come from a creature that shall deserve things that 'eye hath not seen nor ear heard;' that such proud conceits should enter into the heart of man? Surely grace never entered into that man's heart, that hath such a conceit to entertain merit. Shall a man think by a penny to merit a thousand pounds; by a little performance to merit things that are above the conceit of men and angels? But a word is enough that way.

Use 3. And *with humiliation, take that which always goes with humiliation, thankfulness, even beforehand.* When the apostle St Peter thought of the 'inheritance immortal and undefiled,' &c., he begins, 'Blessed be God, the Father of our Lord Jesus Christ,' &c., 1 Peter i. 3, 4. He could not think of these things without thankfulness to God. For we should begin the life of heaven upon earth, as much as may be; and what is that but a blessing and praising of God? Now we cannot more effectually and feelingly praise God, than by the consideration of what great things are reserved for us; for faith sets them before the soul as present, as invested into them. Now if we were in heaven already, we should praise God, and do nothing else. Therefore faith making them sure to the soul, as if we had them, sets the soul on work to praise God, as in Eph. i. 3, and in 1 Peter i. 3. St Peter and Paul, they could never have enough of this. Thus we should do, and cheer and joy our hearts in the consideration of these things in all conflicts and desolations. We little think of these things, and that is our fault. We are like little children that are born to great matters, notwithstanding not knowing of them, they carry not themselves answerable to their hopes. But the more the children grow into years, the more they grow in spirit and conceits,* and carriage fitting the estates they hope for.

So it is with Christians at the first; when they are weak they are troubled with this temptation and with that, with this loss and with that cross; but when a Christian grows to a full stature in Christ, every petty cross doth not cast him down. He thinks, What! shall I be dejected with this loss, that have heaven reserved for me? Shall I be cast down with this cross, that have things that 'eye hath not seen nor ear heard,' &c., prepared for me? He will not. He makes use of his faith to fetch comfort from these things that are reserved for him, that are inexpressible and inconceivable.

Use 4. And *let us comfort ourselves in all the slightings of the world.* A man that hath great hopes in his own country, if he be slighted abroad, he thinks with himself, I have other matters reserved elsewhere, and I shall have another manner of respect when I come home. The world it knows not God, nor Christ, nor us. Shall not we be content to go up and down as unknown men here, when God the Father and Christ our Saviour are unknown? There are better things reserved at home for us. Therefore let us digest all the slightings and abusage of carnal men. And let us not envy them their condition that is but for term of life, use it as well as they will; that hath a date that will be out we know not how soon. Alas! all

* That is, 'conceptions.'—G.

their happiness it is but a measured happiness; it is within their understandings; their eyes can see it and their ears can hear it, and when they can neither see nor conceive more in this world, then there is an end of all their sensible * happiness. Shall we envy, when they shall shortly be turned out naked out of this world to the place of torment? We should present them to us as objects of pity, even the greatest men in the world, if we see by their carriage they be void of grace; but not envy any condition in this world. But what affection is due and suiting to the estate of a Christian? If we would have the true affection, it is admiration and wonderment. What is wonderment? It is the state and disposition of the soul toward things that are new and rare and strange; that we can give no reason of, that are beyond our reach. For wise men wonder not, because they see a reason, they can compass things.† But a Christian cannot but wonder, because the things prepared are above his reach. Yea, when he is in heaven, he shall not be able to conceive the glory of it. He shall enter into it; it shall be above him; he shall have more joy and peace than he can comprehend. The joy that he hath there it is beyond his ability and capacity, beyond his power; he shall not be able to compass all. It shall be a matter of wonder even in heaven itself, much more should it be here below. Therefore the holy apostles, when they speak in the Scriptures of these things, it is with terms of admiration and wonderment, 'joy unspeakable and glorious,' 1 Peter i. 8, and 'peace that passeth understanding,' Philip. iv. 7; and when they speak of our deliverance out of the state of darkness into the state of grace, they call it a being 'brought out of darkness into his marvellous light,' 1 Peter ii. 9. And so 'God loved the world,' he cannot express how, John iii. 16. 'Behold what love hath the Father shewed us, that we should be called the sons of God,' 1 John iii. 1. To be called, and to be, is all one with God; both beyond expression.

Use 5. Again, if this be so that God hath provided such things as neither 'eye hath seen nor ear hath heard,' &c, *beg of God first the Spirit of grace to conceive of them as the Scripture reveals them, and then beg of God a further degree of revelation*, that he would more and more reveal to us by his Spirit those excellent things. For the soul is never in a better frame than when it is lift up above earthly things. When shall a man use the world as though he used it not? When he goes about his business in a commanding manner, as seeing all things under him; when he is raised up to conceive the things that are reserved for him above the world. That keeps a man from being drowned in the world. What makes men drowned in the world to be earth-worms? They think of no other heaven but this; they have no other thing in their eye. Now by the Spirit discovering these things to them that have weaned souls, it makes them go about the things of the world in another manner. They will do them, and do them exactly, with conscience and care, considering that they must give an account of all; but they will do them with reserved affections to better things. Therefore let us oft think of this, and labour to have a spirit of faith to believe them that they are so, that there are such great things; and then upon believing, the meditation of such excellent things will keep the soul in such a frame as it will be fit for anything without defiling of itself. A man that hath first faith that these things are so, and then that hath faith exercised to think and meditate what these things are, he may be turned loose to any temptation whatsoever. For first of all, if there be any solicitation to any base sin, what will he think? Shall I for the pleasures of sin for a season,

* That is, 'sentient,' = sense-derived.—G. † Cf. note *h*, Vol. II. p. 518.—G.

if not lose the joys of heaven and happiness that 'eye hath not seen,' &c., yet surely I shall lose the comfort and assurance of them. A man cannot enjoy the comfort of heaven upon earth without self-denial and mortification. Shall I lose peace of conscience and joy in the Holy Ghost for these things? When Satan comes with any bait, let us think he comes to rob us of better than he can give. His bait is some present pleasure, or preferment, or contentment here. But what doth he take from us? That which 'eye hath not seen, nor ear heard,' &c. He gives Adam an apple, and takes away paradise. Therefore in all temptations consider not what he offers, but what we shall lose; at least the comfort of what we shall lose. We shall lose the comfort of heaven, and bring ourselves to terrors of conscience.

Religion is not so empty a thing as that we need to be beholding to the devil for any preferment, or riches, or contentment, or pleasure. Hath God set up a profession of religion, and do we think that we must be beholding to his, and our enemy, for any base contentments? No. It is a disparagement to our religion, to our profession and calling, and to our Lord and Master we serve, to think that he will not provide richly for his. You see here he hath prepared things that 'eye hath not seen,' &c.

And by this likewise we may judge of the difference of excellencies; the difference of degrees of excellencies may be fetched from hence. The things that the eye can see they may be excellent good things, but if the eye can see them there is no great matters in them. The thing that the ear hears by reports are more than the eye sees. We may hear much that we never saw, yet if we can hear them and conceive of them upon the hearing, they are no great matters, for the soul is larger than they. We conceive more than we can hear; the conceit is beyond sight and hearing. If we can conceive the compass and latitude of anything, it is no great matter, for it is within the reach, and model, and apprehension of man's brain; it is no wondrous matter. Ay, but then the things that are most excellent of all they are above sight and beholding and hearing and conceit, that the soul cannot wholly compass and reach them. Those are the excellent things of all. The rule of excellency is to know what we can conceive, and what is beyond our comprehension. The wit of man can conceive all things under the heavens. All the knowledge we have comes within the brain of man; the government of states and the like. Oh but the things that God hath provided for his never came wholly within the brain of man, and therefore they are the most excellent!

And so by way of contraries for ills; what are the greatest ills? Those that the eye can see, that we can feel, and hear of, and conceive? Oh no. The greatest ills are those torments that never eye saw, that ear never heard of. It is to be in hell to know these things. They are beyond our conceit. 'The worm that dies not, fire unquenchable,' Mark ix. 43, the things above our apprehension are the most terrible things. It is not the gout or the stone. Men feel these things, and yet suffer them with some patience. These are not the greatest ills, but those of another world that are reserved for God's enemies; as the best things are those that are reserved for his friends.

Therefore let us make use of our understandings in laying things together, and make use of God's discovery of the state of Christianity, the excellencies of religion. Why doth God reveal these things in the word? That we should oft meditate of them, and study them, that we may be heavenly-minded. For there are none that come to heaven but they must have a taste of these beforehand. There are none ever enjoy them in perfection. When the day of revelation shall come (the gospel now is the time of revelation, but the day of revelation is the time of judgment), then shall we be revealed what we are. But in the mean time there is a revelation by the Spirit in some beginnings of these things, or else we shall never come to have the perfection of them in heaven. If we know not what peace, and joy, and comfort, and the communion of the saints, and the change of nature is here in sanctification, we shall never know in heaven the fulfilling of it.

And those that have the first fruits here, if they be in a state of growth, that they desire to grow better continually, they shall, no question, come to the perfection; for God will not lose his beginnings. Where he gives earnest, he will make up the bargain.

Therefore let us all that know a little what these things are by the revelation of the Spirit, let us be glad of our portion. For God that hath begun, he will surely make an end.

The affection and bent and frame of soul due to these things is admiration, and not only simple hearing. If these things in their beginnings here be set out by words of admiration, 'peace that passeth understanding,' and 'joy unspeakable and glorious,' what affection and frame of spirit is suitable to the hearing of those things that are kept for us in another world! If the light that we are brought into here be admirable, great (we are brought out of darkness into admirable wonderful light), if the light of grace be so wonderful to a man that comes out of the state of nature, as it is indeed (a man comes out of a damp into a wonderful clear light), what then is the light of glory! Therefore let us often think of it. Those that are born in a prison, they hear great talk of the light, and of the sun, of such a glorious creature; but being born in prison, they know not what it is in itself. So those that are in the prison of nature, they know not what the light of grace is. They hear talk of glorious things, and have conceits of them. And those that here know not the glory that shall be after, when they are revealed, that affection that is due to them is admiration and wonderment. 'So God loved the world, that he gave his only begotten Son,' John iii. 16; and 'Behold what love the Father hath shewed to us, that we should be called the sons of God,' 1 John iii. 1. What love! He could not tell what, it is so admirable; and to know the love of God, that is above all knowledge! Who can comprehend the love of God, that gave his Son! Who can comprehend the excellency of Christ's gift! The joys of heaven by Christ, and the misery of hell, from which we are delivered and redeemed by Christ! These things come from the gospel, and the spring from whence they come is the large and infinite and incomprehensible love of God. And if it be so, what affection is answerable but admiration? Behold what love! If God have so loved flesh and blood, poor dust and ashes, so as to be heirs of heaven, and of such glory as eye sees not, nor cannot in this world; nor ear hears not; nor hath entered into the heart of man, till we come fully to possess them; let us labour to admire the love of God herein.

And labour to know more and more our inheritance, as we grow in years, as children do. They search into the great matters their parents leave them, and the nearer they come to enjoy them, the more skill they have to talk of them. So should we: the more we grow in Christianity and in knowledge, the more we should be inquisitive after those great things that our Father hath provided in another world. But to go on.

How shall we know whether these things be prepared for us or no? whether we be capable of these things or no? God hath prepared them, and he hath prepared them for those that love him; but how shall we know that God hath prepared them for us?

In a word, *whom God hath prepared great matters for, he prepares them for great matters.* We may know by God's preparing of us, whether he hath prepared for us. God prepared paradise before Adam was created: so God prepares paradise, he prepares heaven before we come there. And we may know that we shall come to possess that, if we be prepared for it. What preparation? If we be prepared by a spirit of sanctification, and have holy desires and longing after those excellent things; for certainly there is preparation on both sides. It is prepared for us, and us for it. It is kept for us, and we are kept for it. Whom God keeps heaven for, he keeps them for heaven in a course of piety and obedience. We may know it by God's preparing of us, by loosing us from the world, and sanctifying us to himself. Thus a man may know whether those great things be prepared for him or no.

But the especial thing to know whether they be provided for us or no is love. God hath prepared them for them that love him: not for his enemies. He hath prepared another place, and other things for them; those torments that 'eye hath not seen, nor ear heard, nor hath entered into the heart of man,' for those that are his enemies, that would not come under his government; but these things are prepared 'for those that love him.'

'For those that love him.' Especially that love is all in all, in the disposition of a holy man. All graces are one in the spring, which is love. They are several in the branches, but they are one in the root.

Thus you have heard the use we are to make of this, that there is a reservation of a glorious condition for the people of God so great that neither 'eye hath seen,' &c.

But who be the parties that God hath prepared these things for?

'For them that love him.'

This is the fourth part, the disposition of the parties for whom, 'for them that love him.'

Quest. 1. *Why not for those that God hath elected?* Why doth he not go to the root of all? The great things that God hath prepared for those that he hath chosen to salvation? No. *That is out of our reach.* He would not have us to go to heaven, but rather go to our own hearts. We must search for our election, not above ourselves, but within ourselves.

Quest. 2. *Why doth he not say, to them that believe in him, because faith is the radical grace from whence the rest spring?*

Ans. But faith is a hidden grace many times; and the apostle's scope is to point to such a disposition, that every one may know, that is more familiar. Sometimes faith is hidden in the root, and it is shewed in the effect more than in itself, in love. A poor Christian that is in the state of grace, that saith, 'Oh, I cannot believe,' ask him if he love God. Oh yes; he loves the preaching of the word; he loves good people and good books, and the like. When he cannot discover his faith, he can his love. Therefore the Holy Ghost sets it out by the more familiar disposition, by love rather than faith.

Quest. 3. *Why doth he not say, For those that God loves?* God's love is the cause of our love.

Ans. Because God's love is manifested more familiarly by our love to him; for that is always supposed. Wheresoever there is love to God, and good things, there is God's love first. For our love to God is but a reflection of that love he bears to us. First, he shines on us, and then the beams of our love reflect upon him. Therefore he need not say, whom God loves (though that be the cause of all), but who love God; and know thereby that he loves them.

Quest. 4. *But why for them that love him more than for any other thing?*

Ans. Because all can love. Therefore he sets down this affection. There is no man living, not the poorest *lazar** in the world, that hath a heart and affections, but he can love. He doth not say, that are prepared for this great Christian, and that learned Rabbi. No. But for all that love him, be they poor or rich, great or small, all those that love him. Therefore he sets down that to cut off all excuses. Yea, and all that love him, be they never so many, are sure to have these great things prepared for them. God hath 'prepared these things for those that love him.'

To come therefore to some observations. The first general thing is this, that

Obs. God doth qualify all those in this world, that he hath prepared heaven and happiness for in another world.

The cause of it is his free love. But if you ask me what qualifications the persons must have? They are such as 'love him.' This is not the proper cause why, but the qualification of the persons for whom these things are. There must be an inward disposition and qualification, before we come to heaven. All those that hope for heaven without presumption must have this qualification, they must be such as 'love him.'

Why?

Reasons. The Scripture is plain, (1.) *No unclean thing shall enter into heaven.* No whoremonger, or drunkard, or filthy person. Be not deceived, saith the apostle, you think God is merciful, and Christ died, &c., but neither such, nor such as you are (and your consciences tell you so) shall ever enter into heaven, 1 Cor. vi. 9, *seq.* We must not think to come *è cœno in cœlum*, out of the mire and dirt of sin into heaven. There is no such sudden getting into heaven; but there must be an alteration of our dispositions, wrought by the Spirit of God, fitting us for heaven.

(2.) Another is, that that I touched before, that *heaven and earth differ but in degrees, therefore what is there in perfection must be begun here.*

(3.) Then again, *thirdly, it is impossible for a man, if he be not truly altered, to desire or wish heaven as it is holy.* He may wish for it under the notion of a kingdom, of pleasure, and the like; but as heaven contains a state of perfect holiness and freedom from sin, he cares not for it. A man that is out of relish with heavenly things, and can taste only his base sins, whereon his affections are set and exercised, cannot relish heaven itself. A common, base sinner, his desires are not there. There must be some proportion between the thing desired, and the desire. But here is none. He is not for that place, being an unholy wretch.

Therefore his own heart tells him, I had rather have this pleasure and honour that my heart stands to, than to have heaven, while he is in that frame of desire. Therefore there is no man that can desire heaven that is not disposed aright to heaven before. Beetles love dunghills better than ointments, and swine love mud better than a garden. They are in their element in these things. So take a swinish base creature, he loves to wallow in this world. Tell him of heaven: he hath no eyes to see it, no ears to hear it; except he may have that in heaven that his heart stands to (which he shall never have), he hath no desire of heaven. Therefore in these and the like respects, of necessity there must be a disposition wrought before we come there. These things are prepared for those that 'love God.'

* That is, 'diseased beggar like Lazarus.'—G.

Use 1. If this be so, *let us not feed ourselves with vain hopes.* There are none of us but we desire, at least we pretend that we desire, heaven; but most men conceive it only as a place free from trouble and annoyance; and they are goodly things they hear of, kingdoms, crowns, and the like. But except thou have a holy, gracious heart, and desirest heaven that thou mayest be free from sin, and to have communion with Christ and his saints, to have the image of God, the divine nature perfect in thee, thou art an hypocrite, thou carriest a presumptuous conceit of these things; thy hope will delude thee; it is a false hope. 'Every one that hath this hope purgeth himself,' 1 John iii. 3. Every one, he excludes none. Dost thou defile thyself, and live in sinful courses, and hast thou this hope? Thou hast a hope, but it is not this hope; for every one that hath this hope purgeth himself. No, no; however in time of peace, and pleasure, and contentment that God follows thee with in this world, thou hast a vain hope; yet in a little trouble, or sickness, &c., thy own conscience will tell thee another place is provided for thee, a place of torment, that neither 'eye hath seen nor ear heard, nor hath entered into the heart of man to conceive' the misery of it. There is not the greatest man living, when he is troubled, if he be a sinful man, whose greatness can content him. All his honour and friends cannot pacify that poor conscience of his. But death, 'the king of fears,' will affright him. He thinks, I have some trouble in this world, but there is worse that remains; things that he is not able to conceive of. Let us not therefore delude ourselves. There is nothing will stand out but the new creature, that we find a change wrought by the Spirit of God. Then we may without presumption hope for the good things which neither 'eye hath seen,' &c.

Use 2. Again, we see in the second place *God's mercy to us; the qualification is within us, that we need not go far to know what our evidence is.* Satan abuseth many poor Christians. Oh I am not elected, I am not the child of God! Whither goest thou, man? Dost thou break into heaven? When thou carriest a soul in thy breast, and in that soul the affection of love; how is that set? Whither is thy love carried, and thy delight, and joy, those affections that spring from love? Thy evidence is in thine own heart. Our title is by faith in Christ. His righteousness gives us title to heaven. But how knowest thou that thou pretendest a just title? Thou hast the evidence in thy heart. What is the bent of thy soul? Whither is the point of it set? Which way goeth that? Dost thou love God, and divine things, and delight in them? Then thou mayest assure thyself that those things belong to thee, as verily as the Scriptures are the word of God, and God a God of truth. When thou findest the love of God in thy heart, that thy heart is taught by his Spirit to love him, then surely thou mayest say, Oh blessed be God that hath kindled this holy fire in my heart. Now I know that 'neither eye hath seen, nor ear heard, nor hath entered into the heart of man, those excellent things that are laid up for me.'

THE END OF THE SECOND SERMON.

THE THIRD SERMON.

Eye hath not seen, &c.—1 Cor. II. 9.

Saint Paul, as we heard before, gives a reason in these words, why the 'princes of this world' (not only the great men, that ofttimes are not the greatest clerks,* but the learned men of the world, princes for knowledge), why they were ignorant of the mysteries of the gospel.

Now the fourth is the disposition of those for whom he doth all this; the quality he infuseth into them, they are such as 'love him.'

1. *He hath prepared them before all eternity.* He prepared happiness for us before we were; nay, before the world was. As he prepared for Adam a paradise before he was; he created him, and then brought him into paradise: so he prepared for us a kingdom with himself in heaven, a blessed estate before we were; *i. e.*, in election, before the heavens were. And then in creation he prepared the blessed place of the happy souls of happy persons hereafter, where he himself is. He prepared it for himself, and for all those that he means to set his love upon from the beginning to the end.

2. And then, *secondly*, he prepared them *more effectually in time.* He prepared these things when Christ came in the flesh, and wrought all things for us, in whom we have all. Of these things thus prepared he saith, 'Eye hath not seen, nor ear heard them,' &c. In what sense it is meant we heard before. Now take the whole of the matter; the meaning is, *the matters of grace, the kingdom of grace, and the kingdom of glory, they are but one.* For (to add this by the way) the kingdom of heaven in the gospel includes three things.

First, The doctrine of the gospel, the publishing of it.

And then, *secondly*, Grace by that doctrine.

And *thirdly*, Glory upon grace, the consummation of all.

So the mysteries of salvation is, *first*, the doctrine itself. That is the first degree of the kingdom. The doctrine itself is a mystery to all those that never heard of it; for what creature could ever conceive how to reconcile justice and mercy, by devising such a way as for God to become man, to reconcile God and man together? That Immanuel, he that is 'God with us,' should make God and us one in love, this could be no more thought of, than Adam could think of himself to be made a man when he was dust of the earth. Could man when he was worse than dust, in a lost, damned estate, think of redemption? It is impossible for a man that cannot tell the form and the quintessence, that cannot enter into the depth of the flowers, or the grass that he tramples on with his feet, that he should have the wit† to enter into the deep things of God, that have been concealed even from the angels themselves till God discover them. I add this to illustrate what I said before. Therefore the doctrine itself, till God discover it out of his own breast, was concealed to the angels themselves; and since the discovery, they are students in it, and look and pry into it, 1 Peter i. 12. But where the doctrine is no mystery, but is discovered, there the application and spiritual understanding, to those that have not the light of the Spirit, is such a thing as 'eye hath not seen nor ear heard.' And therefore we must have a new light, a new eye, a new ear, and a new heart, before we can apprehend the gospel, though we understand it for the literal truth. As for the things of glory, we have no conceit of them fully, but by a glimpse and weak apprehension; as a child conceives of the things of a man, by some poor weak resemblances. As St Paul saith, 'When I was a child I spake as a child, I thought as a child,' 1 Cor. xiii. 11. So when we are now children, in comparison of that perfect estate we shall attain in heaven, we think and speak as children, of these holy and heavenly things that shall be accomplished in another world.

* That is, = 'scholars.'—G. † That is, 'wisdom.'—G.

And observe this too, that when we would understand anything of heaven, and see anything, say, 'This is not that happiness I look for,' 'I can see this, but that is not to be seen.' And when we hear of anything that is excellent, 'I can hear this, it is not my happiness.' And when we comprehend anything, 'I can comprehend this;' therefore it is not the happiness I look for, but those things that are above my comprehension, that are unutterable and inexpressible.

Moreover, *let us be stirred up to think it a base thing for a Christian to lose the comfort and assurance he hath of these things* 'that eye hath not seen nor ear heard,' *for any earthly thing whatsoever.* We account it a poor thing of Esau to sell his birthright for a mess of pottage, Heb. xii. 16. And we all smart for Adam's ill bargain that he made, to sell paradise for an apple. And it was a cursed sale that Judas made, that sold Christ himself for thirty pieces of silver. Surely it is that that every carnal man doth; and howsoever we cannot lose heaven, yet it should be our endeavour to enjoy heaven upon earth, to enjoy the assurance of this condition. When we do anything to weaken our assurance, and to weaken our comfort, what do we but with Adam lose heaven for an apple, and with Esau part with our birthright, as much as the assurance and comfort of it is, for a mess of pottage? Therefore let us account it a base thing to be over-much in love with any earthly thing, whereby we may weaken (though we could* lose) the comfort and assurance of this happy condition, which is so transcendent. All wicked men, and indeed all men whether good or bad, as far as they fall into sin, are fools; the Scripture terms them so.† There is none wise indeed but the true Christian, and that Christian that preserves the sense, and feeling, and assurance of his happy condition.

'For those that love him.'

The disposition of the parties is, they are such as 'love God.' He saith not, such as are elected, because that is a thing out of our reach to know; but by going upward, by going backward, to go from our grace to our calling, and from thence to election; nor such as believe, because that is less discernible than love; nor the love of God to us, for that is supposed when we love him. Our hearts being cold, they cannot be warm in love to him, but his love must warm them first. Love is such an affection as commands all other things, therefore he names that above all. And love is such a thing as every one may try himself by. If he had named either giving or doing of this or that, men might have said, I cannot do it, or I cannot part with it, but when he names love, there is none but they may love. The point considered was, that

There must be a qualification of those that heaven is provided for.

They must be such as love God, such as are altered, and changed, and sanctified to love him; because no unclean thing shall enter in thither; because we cannot so much as desire heaven without a change. We cannot have communion there with Christ and those blessed souls without likeness to them, which must be by a spirit of love; our natures must be altered. Therefore it is a vain presumption for any man to think of heaven unless he find his disposition altered. For we may read our eternal condition in heaven by our disposition upon earth. The apostle Peter saith, 1 Pet. i. 3, 'Blessed be God, the Father of our Lord Jesus Christ, that hath begotten us to a lively hope of an inheritance immortal and undefiled, reserved in heaven.' So that the inheritance in heaven, we are begotten to it; we must be new born; we must have a new birth before we can

* Qu. 'should not?'—Ed. † Cf. Psalm xiv. 1; Prov. xviii. 7; Luke xii. 20.—G.

inherit it; 'He hath begotten us to an inheritance immortal,' &c. He that is not a child may not think of an inheritance. Put case there be never so many glorious things in heaven that 'eye hath never seen nor ear ever heard,' &c., if our names be not in Christ's will, that we are not his, and prove ourselves to be his, by the alteration of our dispositions, what are all those good things to us, when our names are not contained there!

It is called a hope of life, 'a lively hope,' 1 Pet. i. 3; because he that hath this 'hope purgeth himself.' It makes him vigorous and active in good. If his hope of life make him not lively, he hath no hope of life at all. Therefore those that will look for heaven (that Satan abuse them not by false confidence), let them look whether God have altered their hearts; that the work of grace be wrought in some measure. For God hath not ordained these great things for his enemies; for blasphemers, that take God's name in vain; that run on in courses contrary to his will and word; that live in sins against the light of nature; do you think he hath provided these great matters for them? He hath another place for them. Therefore let us not be abused by our own false hearts to think of such a happy condition. Unless we find ourselves changed, unless we be new born, we shall never enter into heaven.

'Lord, Lord,' say they. Christ brings them in pleading so, 'Lord, Lord;' not that they shall say so then, that is not the meaning; but now they cherish such a confidence. Oh we can speak well, and we can pray well, 'Lord, Lord.' Oh thou vain, confident person, thy confession and profession, 'Lord, Lord,' shall do thee no good. I will not so much as own thee; 'Away hence, thou worker of iniquity,' Mat. xxv. 41. Thy heart tells thee thou livest in sins against conscience. Away, avaunt, I will none of thee. God in mercy to us will have the trial of the truth of our evidence in us. The ground of all our salvation is his grace, his free favour, and mercy in his own heart; but we cannot go thither; he would have us to search within ourselves, and there we shall find 'love.'

'God hath prepared for those that love him.'

Obs. In particular, therefore, *those that God hath provided so excellent things for, they are such as love him.* They are such, first of all, that are beloved of him; and shew that they are beloved of him by their love to him. Therefore, when the papists meet with such phrases, they think of merit. He hath provided heaven for them that love him, and shew their love in good works. But we must know that this is not brought in as a cause why, but as a qualification of the persons who; who shall inherit heaven, and who shall have these great things. It is idle for them to think that these things are prepared for those whom God foresees would do such and such good works. It is as if we should think he hath provided these happy things for those that are his enemies. For how could he look for love from us in a state of corruption, when the best thing in us was enmity to him? Is it not a vain thing to look for light from darkness? to look for love from enmity and hatred? Therefore how could God foresee anything in us, when he could see nothing but enmity and darkness in our dispositions by nature?

And then (as we shall see afterward) this love in us it must be with all our heart, and soul, and might. It is required and commanded; and when we do all this, we do but what we are bound to do. But they abuse such places upon so shallow ground, that indeed it deserves not so much as to be mentioned.

To come then to the point itself, *the disposition of those that shall come to heaven then is, they must be such as love God.* Now he names this because these two go always together. There goes somewhat of ours together with somewhat of God's, to witness to us what God doth. There goes our choice of God, with his choosing of us; our knowing of God, with his knowledge of us; our love to him, with his love to us. Therefore, because these are so connexed and knit together, he takes the one for the other; and to make it familiar to us, he takes that which is most familiar to us, our love to him.

Now he names this above all other affections, because love is the commanding affection of the soul. It is that affection that rules all other affections. Hatred, and anger, and joy, and delight, and desire, they all spring from love; and because all duties spring from love both to God and man, therefore both tables are included in love. And when the apostle would set down the qualifications of those that shall enjoy these things, he saith they are for those 'that love him.' Because it stirs up to all duty, and adds a sweet qualification to every duty, and makes it acceptable and to relish with God. It stirs up to do, and qualifies the actions that come from love to be accepted.

All duties to man spring from love to man, and love to man from love to God. It is the affection that stirs up the duty, and stirs up the affection fit for the duty; it stirs up to do the thing, and to do all in love. Whatsoever we do to God or man, it must be in love. All that God doth to us it is in love. He chooseth us in love, and doth everything in love; and all that we do to God it must be in love. Therefore he names no other affection but this, because it is the ground, the first-born affection of the soul. Therefore Christ saith it is the great commandment to love God, John xv. 12. It is the great commanding commandment, that commands all other duties whatsoever; it is the first wheel that turns the whole soul about.

Again, it is such an affection as cannot be dissembled. A man may paint fire, but he cannot paint heat. A man may dissemble actions in religion, but he cannot affections. Love is the very best affection of truth. A man may counterfeit actions; but there is none that can love but the child of God. 'God hath prepared these things for those that *love him.*'

Then again, without this, all that we do is nothing, and we are nothing. We are nothing but an empty cymbal. Whatsoever we do is nothing; all is empty without love. 'My son, give me thy heart,' Prov. xxiii. 26; that is, if thou wilt give me anything, give me thy affections, or else they are still-born actions, that have no life in them. If we do anything to God, and do it not in love, he regards it not. That is the reason why he mentions love instead of all. It is so sweet an affection, and so easy; what is more easy than to love? It is comfortable to us to consider that God hath made this a qualification of those that he brings to heaven; they are such as 'love him.'

Quest. But why doth he set down any qualification at all, and not say, *for Christians?*

Ans. Because *profession must have expression.* When God sets down a professor of religion, he sets him down by some character that shall discover him to be as he is termed. How dost thou know thou art good? Dost thou love God, or call upon God? as it is in other places, 'To all those that call upon his name,' 1 Cor. i. 2, to let us know that religion and holiness is a matter of power. Wouldst thou know what thou art in religion? Dost thou love God, or call upon God?

It is not to be tolerated, to be Christians, to profess as Demas, 2 Tim.

iv. 10. Oh no! but they must be such as from the heart-root are good, 'such as love God.'

Therefore, dark disputes of election and predestination, at the first especially, let them go. How standest thou affected to God and to good things? Look to thy heart whether God have taught it to love or no, and to relish heavenly things. If he hath, thy state is good. And then thou mayest ascend to those great matters of predestination and election. But begin not with those, but go first to thine own heart, and then to those deep mysteries afterward. If a man love God, he may look back to election, and forward to glorification, to the things that 'eye hath not seen nor ear heard,' &c. But see first what God hath wrought in thy heart, what affection to heavenly things; and thence from thy affections to go backward to election, and forward to glorification, there is no danger in it.

To come therefore to express more particularly this affection of love, which is the disposition that God requires and works in all those that he intends heaven to. Let us search into the nature of this love to God. What it is to love we need not be taught, for all men know it well enough. It is better known, indeed, by the affection than by discourse. What it is to love is known by those that love better than by any books or treatises whatsoever, for it is the affection that is in all men. Natural love, it is in those that have no grace at all, and civil love in those that are evil men. They know what it is to love by reason of that wild fire, that carnal love that is in them, that transports them. A man may see the nature of it in those as well as in any; for set aside the extravagant nature of it in such kind of persons, we may see the nature of it. Therefore I will not meddle with that point; it is needless. I come therefore to this love of God, to shew how this stream of affection should be carried in the right channel to God, the right object of it, who only can make us happy by loving of him. Other things, by loving of them, they make us worse, if they be worse than ourselves; for such as we love, such we are. Indeed, our understandings make us not good or ill, but our love doth. By loving God and heavenly things we become good. Our affections shew what we are in religion.*

There be four things in this sweet affection in true natural love.

1. *There is an estimation and valuing of some good thing, especially when the love is to a better, when it is not between equals.* Now there is a great distance between God and us. There is a high esteem in common love; love will not stoop to nothing. There cannot be love maintained but upon sight of a supposed excellency; love will not stoop but where it sees somewhat worth the valuing. Therefore there is a high esteem of somewhat as the spring of it. And that is the reason that we say a man cannot be wise and love in earthly things, because love will make a man too much to value those things that he that apprehends better would not.

2. In the *second* place, *there is a desire to be joined to it, that we call the desire of union.*

3. In the *third* place, upon union and joining to it, *there is a resting, a complacency and contentment in the thing to which we are united,* for what is happiness itself but fully to enjoy what we love? When we love upon judgment and a right esteem, to enjoy, that is happiness and contentment indeed.

4. In the *fourth* place, where this true affection is, *there is a desire of contentment to the party loved, to please him, to approve ourselves to him, to displease him in nothing.* Every one knows that these things are in that affection by nature.

* Cf. President Edwards' treatise on 'The Religious Affections.'—G.

Look to carnal self-love, a man may know what it is to love; the affection is all one in both. Take a man when he makes himself his idol, as till a man love God he loves himself above all, he is the idol and the idolater; he hath a high esteem of himself, and those that do not highly esteem him he swells against them. Again, self-love makes a man desire to enjoy himself, and to enjoy his content, to procure all things that may serve for his contentment.

Now, when the Spirit of God hath purged our hearts of this carnal idolatry of self-love, and self-seeking, and sufficiency, and contentment in himself, then a man puts God instead of himself; grace, and the Spirit doth so; and instead of highly esteeming of himself, he esteems highly of God, and of Christ, and religion. Then, instead of placing a sufficiency in himself and the things of this life, and resting in them, there is a placing of sufficiency in God all-sufficient. And instead of seeking his own will and content in all things, *mens mihi pro regno*, my mind is to me a kingdom,* then a man seeks to give contentment to God in all things, and 'to be a fool, that he may be wise,' 1 Cor. iii. 18, and to have no will and no delight in anything that cannot stand with the pleasure of and obedience to God.

Thus a man, by knowing what his own natural corruption is, he may know what his affection is to better things.

First of all, *there must be an estimation, an esteem of God and Christ*; for to avoid misconceit, we take both these to be one: God, our Father in Christ, and Christ. Whatsoever Christ did for us in love, he did it from the love of the Father who gave him. And when we speak of the love of God, we speak of the love of Christ to us. Therefore there must be a high esteeming, and valuing, and prizing of God above all things in the world, and of his love.

(1.) Now, this must needs be so; for where grace is, it gives a sanctified judgment; a sanctified judgment values and esteems things as they are. Now the judgment, apprehending God and his love to be the best thing to make us happy, prizeth it above all: 'Whom have I in heaven but thee? and what have I in earth in comparison of thee?' Ps. lxxiii. 25. He prizeth God and his love above all things in the world.

Now, if we would know if we have this judgment, we may know it by our choice. This valuing it is known by choice: for what a man esteems and values highly he makes choice of above all things in the world. What men make choice of is seen by their courses. We see it in holy Moses, Heb. xi. 26, *seq.* He had a high esteem of the estate of God's people, that afflicted people. As afflicted as they were, yet he saw they were God's people, in covenant with him, and more regarded of him than all the people in the world besides; and upon his estimation he made a choice: 'he chose rather to suffer afflictions with the people of God, than to enjoy the pleasures of sin for a season.' His choice followed his esteem. So if we value and esteem God and religion, and love God above all things, we will make choice of the Lord. As St Peter saith, John vi. 68, *seq.*, when Christ asked them, 'Will ye also forsake me?' saith he, 'Lord, whither shall we go?' We have made choice of thee; 'whither shall we go? thou hast the words of eternal life.' Let us do that in truth that he for a time failed to do, when he said, 'Though all forsake thee, yet will not I,' Mat. xxvi. 33. If we make this choice of Christ from the truth of our hearts, this shews our esteem.

* This Latin apophthegm forms the burden of Byrd's classic little poem.—G.

What is thy choice? Is it religious ways and religious company? Is it the fear of God above all things? 'One thing have I desired, that I may dwell in the house of God for ever, and visit his temple,' Ps. xxvii. 4. Hast thou with Mary made choice of the better part? Dost thou value thyself as a member of Christ, and an heir of heaven, as a Christian above all conditions in this world (for what a man esteems he values himself by)? Then thou art a true lover, thou hast this love planted in thy heart, because thou hast a true esteem. You see Paul accounted 'all dung and dross in comparison of the excellent knowledge of Christ,' Philip. iii. 8. Oh that we could come to that excellent affection of St Paul, to undervalue all things to Christ, and the good things by Christ and religion! Certainly it is universally true, where Christ is loved, and God in Christ, the price of all things else fall in the soul. For when we welcome Christ, then farewell all that cannot stand with Christ.

(2.) Again, our esteem is known *by our willing parting with anything for that that we esteem;* as a wise merchant doth sell all for the pearl, Mat. xiii. 46. We may know therefore that we esteem God and his truth; for they go together, God and his truth and religion. We must take God with all that he is clothed with, wherein he shews himself unto us. If we sell all for the truth of God, and part with all, and deny all for the love and obedience of it, it is a sign we have an esteem answerable to his worth, and that we love him.

Those therefore that will part with nothing for God, nor for religion and the truth, when they are called to it, do they talk of love to God? They have no esteem, they value not God. If they did esteem him, they would sell all for the pearl. Therefore those that halt in religion, that care not which way religion and the truth goes, so they may have honour and pleasures in this world, where is their esteem of the gospel, and of the truth of Christ and of God? They have no love, because they have no estimation.

(3.) Again, what we esteem highly of *we speak largely of.* A man is always eloquent in that he esteems. It will put him, to the extent of his abilities, to be as eloquent as possible he can be. You never knew a man want words for that he prized, to set it out. Therefore when we want words to praise God, and to set out the value of the best things, it is an argument we have poor esteem of them. All go together, God and the things of God. What! do we talk of loving God, and despise Christians and religion? They are never severed. If a man esteem the best things, he will be often speaking of them. If a man set his affections upon a thing, it will suggest words at will. Therefore those that are clean out of their theme, when they speak of good things, are to seek, Alas! where is the affection of love? where is esteem? Esteem it makes a readiness to speak.

(4.) Esteem likewise *carries our thoughts.* Wouldst thou know what thou esteemest highly? What dost thou think of most and highest? Thou mayest know it by that. We see the first branch, how we may know we love God, if we have a high esteem and valuing of God, by these signs.

Secondly, Where there is true love and affection, *there is a desire of union;* of knitting and coupling with the thing loved. Of necessity it must be so; for love is such a kind of affection, it draws the soul all it can to the thing loved. It hath a magnetical force, the force of a loadstone. Every one knows what this means.

This affection of love makes us one with that we love. If a man love the world, he is a worldling, a man of the world, because affection breeds union. Though a man be never so base in choosing, whatsoever a man loves he desires union with it; and being so, he hath his name from that he loves. He that loves the world is a worldling, an earthworm. Now, if there be the love of God, as in covenant, as a Father in Christ, for so we must conceive of God, there will be a desire of fellowship and communion with him by all means, in the word and sacrament, &c. If a man desire strangeness, that he cares not how seldom he receive the sacrament or come into God's presence, is here love? How can love and strangeness stand together? Thou art a strange person from God, and the things of God; thou hast no joy in his presence. Where thou mayest enjoy his presence here in holy things in this world, if thou delight not in his presence and in union with him, how canst thou say thou lovest him?

Can a man say he loves him whose company he cares not for? Thou carest not for God's company. Thou mayest meet him in the word and sacraments, and in good company: 'Where two or three are gathered together, I will be in the midst,' Mat. xviii. 20. Dost thou pretend thou lovest God if thou carest not for these? Thou hast no fellowship in this business; all that relish not heavenly things, they do not love.

Now, to try whether we have this branch of love, that is, a desire of union. Where therefore there is a desire of union with the party loved, of uniting to that person (for we speak of persons), there will be a desire of communion.

(1.) *A desire of union will breed a desire of communion;* that is, there will be a course taken to open our minds. If we have a desire of communion with God, we will open our souls often to him in prayer, and we will desire that he will open himself in speaking to our hearts by his Spirit. And we will desire that he will open his mind to us in his word. We will be careful to hear his word, and so maintain that sweet and heavenly commerce between him and our souls by this intercourse of hearing him and speaking to him: 'Where two or three are gathered together, I will be in the midst.' Therefore those that make no conscience either of hearing the word, or of prayer public and private, and of using the glorious liberty that we have in Christ, of free access to the throne of grace, that do not use this prerogative and privilege to cherish that union and communion they may have with God, they love not God and Christ. Strangeness is opposite to love, and it dissolves and disunites affections. Therefore when we are strange to God, that we can go from one end of the week to the other, and from the beginning of the day to the end of it, and not be acquainted with God, and not open our souls to him, it is a sign we have no love; because there is no desire of union and communion with him.

(2.) Again, where we love *we consult and advise, and rest in that advice, as coming from a loving person,* especially if he be as wise as loving. So in all our consultations, we will go to God and take his counsel; and when we have it, we will account it the counsel of one that is wise and loving.

Those therefore that trust to their own wits, to policy and such like, what do they speak of love when they make not use of that covenant that is between God and them? They consult not with him; they make not his word the 'man of their counsel,' Ps. cxix. 24; they go not to him by prayer for advice; they commit not their 'ways' to him, as the psalmist speaketh, Ps. xxxvii. 5.

(3.) And this distinguisheth a good Christian from another man: *a good*

Christian he is such a one as acquaints himself with his God, and will not lose that intercourse he hath with God for all the world. As Daniel, he would not but pray; they could not get him from it with the hazard of his life, Dan. vi. 11.

(4.) Again, where this desire of union and joining is, *there is a desire even of death itself, that there may be a fuller union, and a desire of the consummation of all things.* Therefore so far as we are afraid of death, and tremble at it, so far we want love. When the contract is once made between Christ and the soul of a Christian, for him to fear the making up of the marriage, when we are now absent from the Lord, to fear the sweet eternal communion we shall have in heaven, where we shall have all things in greater excellency and abundance, it is from want of faith and love. Therefore we should be ashamed of ourselves when we find such thoughts rising in our hearts, as they will naturally, to be basely and distrustfully afraid of death. St Paul saith, 'I desire to be dissolved, and to be with Christ;' that is good, nay, it is much better for me, Philip. i. 23. Nay, it is best of all to be with Christ. Therefore, you see, it stirred up his desire: 'I desire to be dissolved, and to be with Christ.' 'Come, Lord Jesus; come quickly,' saith the church, Rev. xxii. 20. And the Spirit in the spouse stirs up this desire likewise: 'Come; the Spirit and the spouse say, Come,' Rev. xxii. 17. And we should rejoice to think there are happier times to come, wherein there will be an eternal meeting together that nothing shall dissolve, as the apostle saith, 1 Thes. iv. 17, 'when we shall be for ever with the Lord.' Oh those times cheer up the heart of a Christian beforehand!

Now where these things possess not the soul, how can we say that we love God? In Cant. i. 1 the church begins, 'Let him kiss me with the kisses of his mouth.' She desires a familiar communion with Christ in his word and ordinances, 'Let him kiss me,' &c. Let him speak by his Spirit to my heart. In this world Christ kisseth his church with the kisses of his mouth. But in the latter end of the Canticles, 'Make haste, my beloved,' viii. 14, she desires his second coming, thinks it not enough to have the kisses of his mouth; 'Make haste, my beloved, and be as the young roes upon the mountains of spices;' that is, come hastily from heaven, the mountain of spices, and let us meet together, my beloved. These things be somewhat strange to our carnal dispositions, but if we hope ever to attain to the comfort of what I say, we must labour that our hearts may be brought to this excellent condition, to desire the presence of Christ. That is the second property of love.

The *third* is *to rest pleased and contented in the thing when we are joined with it;* so far as we are joined with it to place our contentment in it. And it is in the nature of that affection to place contentment in the thing we desire to have, when we have it once.

Now we may know this our contentment whether we rest in God or no by the inward quiet and peace of the soul in all conditions, when whatsoever our condition be in this world, yet we know we have the light of God's countenance, and can rest and be content in it more than worldly men in their corn and wine and oil, as David saith, Ps. iv. 7, 'I rejoice more in the light of thy countenance, than when they have their corn and wine and oil;' when we can joy and solace ourselves with the assurance of God's favour and love in Jesus Christ. 'Being justified by faith, we have peace with God,' and rejoice in God, as it is Rom. v. 1; we rejoice in God as ours.

Therefore those that go to outward contentments, that run out to them as if there were not enough in God and divine things to content their souls, but they must be beholding to the devil and to the flesh, this is not to rest in God. He is over-covetous whom God cannot content. If we be in covenant with him, he is able to fill our soul, and all the corners of it; he is able to satisfy all the delights and desires of it; he is a gracious Father in Christ. Whither should we go from him for contentment? Why should we go out of religion to content ourselves in vain recreations and pleasures of sin for a season, when we have abundance in God?

And where there is contentment, there will be trusting in him and relying upon him. A man will not rely upon riches, or friends, or anything; for where we place our contentment, we place our trust. So far as we love God, so far we repose affiance and trust in him; he will be our rock and castle and strength. Wouldst thou know whether thou restest in him or no? In the time of danger, whither doth thy soul run? To thy purse if thou be a rich man? or to thy friends if thou be a worldly-minded man? Every man hath his castle to fly to. But 'the name of the Lord is a strong tower,' Ps. lxi. 3. He that is a child of God flieth thither for refuge, and there he covereth himself, and is safe. He enters into those chambers of divine providence and goodness, and there he rests in all troubles.

Therefore ask thy affections whither thou wouldst run if there come a confusion of all things. When men are apt to say, Oh what will become of us! and they think of this and that, a good Christian hath God to rest in. He hath God reconciled in Christ, and in his love he plants himself in life and death. He makes God his habitation and his castle, as it is Ps. xviii. 2, 'I love the Lord dearly, my rock and my fortress.' And Moses in Ps. xc. 1, *seq.* (for his psalm it is), 'Thou hast been our habitation from everlasting to everlasting.' We dwell in thee. Though in the world we are tossed up and down, and live and die, yet we alway dwell with thee. So a Christian hath his contentment and his habitation in God; he is his house he dwells in, his rock, his resting-place, his centre in which he rests. 'Come unto me, and ye shall find rest to your souls,' Mat. xi. 28. When a man is beat out of all contentments, he may know by this whether he love God or no. As David when he was beat out of all, and they were ready to stone him; but 'he trusted in the Lord his God,' Ps. xxvi. 1, *et alibi*. So in losses and crosses hast thou contentment in God, thou wilt fetch what thou losest out of the love of God, and what thou art crossed in thou wilt fetch out of God's love. Thou wilt say, This and that is taken from me, but God is mine; I can fetch more good by faith from him than I can lose in the world. A soul that is acquainted with God, when he loseth anything in the world, he can fetch it out of the fountain and spring. He is taught to love God; he is skilful this way to pitch his hope and affiance in God, where he hath enough for all crosses. Let us labour to bring our souls more and more to this, and then we shall know what it is to love God by this placing of our contentment in him. 'Take all from me,' saith holy Austin, 'so thou leave me thyself' *(b)*. So a Christian can say, Take all from me, so I have God.

Indeed, where shall a man have comfort in many passages of his life, if he find it not in religion? What will become of a man in this uncertain world, if he have not somewhat where he may place his content? Oh, he will find before he die that he is a wretched man. He knows not where to find rest and contentment before he dies; he will be beat out of all his holds here either by sickness or one thing or other.

The *fourth* and last is, *where the true affection of love to God is, it stirs* *up the soul to give all contentment to God, to do all things that may please him.* This is the nature of love. It stirs up to please the party loved. Isaac's sons saw that their father loved venison, therefore they provided venison for him, Gen xxv. 28. Those that know what God loves will provide what they can that that God may delight in. He loves a humble and a believing heart. 'Thou hast wounded me with one of thine eyes,' Cant. iv. 9—the eye of faith, when the soul can trust in the word, and humbly go out of itself. His delight is in a broken yielding heart, that hardens not itself against his instructions, but yields. A broken heart that lies low, and hears all that God saith, Oh 'it is a sacrifice that God is much delighted in,' Ps. li. 17, *et alibi.* A humble spirit is such a spirit as God dwells in. 'He that dwells in the highest heavens dwells in a humble spirit,' Isa. lvii. 15. Doth God delight in a meek, broken, humble spirit? Oh then it will be the desire of a Christian to have such a spirit as God may delight in. A meek soul is much esteemed; 'the hidden man of the heart,' 1 Pet. iii. 4, is much prized. Search in God's word what he delights in, and let us labour to bring ourselves to such a condition as God may delight in us, and we in him. And then it is a sign we love him, when we labour to procure all things that may give him content. You know that love where it is, it stirs up the affections of the party to remove all things that are distasteful to the party it loves. Therefore it is a neat* affection; for it will make those neat that otherwise are not so, because it will not offend; much more this divine heavenly affection, when it is set on a right object, upon God, it is a neat, cleanly affection. It will purge the soul; it will work upon the soul a desire to be clean as much as can be, because God is a pure, holy God, and it will 'have no fellowship with the works of darkness,' Eph. v. 11. Therefore as much as human frailty will permit, it will study purity, to keep itself 'unspotted of the world,' James i. 27. It will not willingly cherish any sin that may offend the Spirit. Those therefore that are careless of their ways and carriage and affections, that make nothing of polluting, and defiling their affections and their ways, there is not the love of God in their hearts. It stirs up shame to be offensive in the eyes of such a one, especially if they be great. There is both love and respect met together. Where it is a reverential love with respect, there is a shame to be in a base, filthy, displeasing condition. God hates pride and idolatry, &c. Therefore a man that loves God will hate idols and all false doctrine and worship that tends this way. His heart will rise against them, because he knows God hates it, and all that take that course. He observes what is most offensive to God, and he will avoid it and seek what is pleasing to him.

God and Christ are wondrously pleased with faith. 'Thou hast wounded me with one of thine eyes.' Faith, and love from faith, wounds the breast of Christ: therefore let us labour for faith. 'O woman, great is thy faith,' Mat. xv. 28. It is such a grace as binds and overcomes God, it honours him so much. Let us therefore labour for faith, and in believing, for all graces. They are things that God loves. Therefore let us labour to be furnished with all things that he loves. Especially those graces that have some excellency set upon them in the Scripture we should most esteem. Isaac, when he was to marry Rebecca, he sends her jewels beforehand, that having them, she might be more lovely in his eye, Mat. xv. 28. So Christ, the husband of his church, that he might take more delight and content in his church, he sends her jewels beforehand; that is, he enricheth

* That is, = nice, clean, opposed to filthy. Cf. Vol. II. p. 80—G.

his church with the spirit of faith, meekness, humility, and love, and all graces, that he may delight and take content in his spouse. Those that have not somewhat that God may delight in them, they have not the spirit of love. Those, therefore, that rebel instead of giving God content; that resist the Spirit, and the motions of it, in the ministry, and in reprehensions, and the like: those that live in sins directly against God's command, that are common swearers, and filthy persons, neglecters of holy things, profane, godless persons, do they talk of the love of God and of heaven? You may see the filthiness of their hearts by the filthiness that issues from them. God keeps not such excellencies for such persons. The love of God, and living in sins against conscience, will not stand together. A demonstration of love is *exhibitio operis*, the exhibition of somewhat to please God. Shew me in thy course what thou doest to please God. If thou live in courses that are condemned, never talk of love. It is a pitiful thing to see in the bosom of the church, under the glorious revelation of divine truth, that men should live apparently* and impudently in sins against conscience, that glory in their shame. It is a strange thing that they should glory in their profaneness and swaggering; that they should glory in a kind of atheistical carriage. As they have been bred, so they will be still. Many are marred in that; they are either poisoned in their first breeding, or neglected in it.

To see under the glorious gospel of Christ, that those that think they have souls eternal, that they should live in impudent base courses, void of religion and humanity, only to satisfy their own lusts, instead of satisfying and obeying God; men that live in the bosom of the church as beasts, and yet hope to be saved as well as the best; Oh, but the hope of the hypocrite, the hope of such persons, will deceive them.

Oh let us labour therefore to have this affection of love planted in our hearts; that God by his Spirit would teach us to love him, and to love one another. This affection of love must be taught by God. It is not a matter of the brain to teach that, but a matter of the heart. God only is the great schoolmaster and teacher of the heart. He must not only command us to love, but teach our affections by his Holy Spirit, to enable our affections to love him.

Where love is in this regard likewise to give content, there will be love of all those whom the party we approve ourselves to loves. Is there any of Jonathan's posterity, saith David, that I may do good to them for his sake? 2 Sam. ix. 1. The soul that loves God and Christ saith, Is there any good people, any that carry the image of God and Christ? It will be sure to love them. It will do good to Jonathan's posterity. Those that hate them that carry the image of God and Christ, that their stomach riseth against good men, how do they 'love him that begets, when they love not him that is begotten?' 1 John v. 1. There cannot be the love of God in such a man. Undoubtedly if we love God, we shall love his children, and anything that hath God's stamp upon it. We shall love his truth and his cause and religion, and whatsoever is divine and toucheth upon God. We shall love it, because it is his. It is such an affection as sets the soul on work to think, Wherein may I give content to such a person? It is full of devices and inventions to please. Therefore it thinks, Can I give consent in loving such and such? As Christ saith, he that respects these little ones, it is to me, it is accountable on my part, I will see it answered, Matt. xviii. 5. If the love of Christ be in us, we will

* That is, 'openly.'—G.

regard this, because we will think: Christ will regard me for the good I do for his sake, and in his name, to this and that party. Thus we see how we may try this sweet affection, and not deceive our own souls.

And therefore, where there is a desire of giving content, there will be a zeal against all things; to remove all things in our places and callings that may offend. It will carry us through all difficulties. To please him, it will make us willing to suffer. I will please him, by suffering some indignity for his cause. I will do it, that I may engage his affection to me. Therefore the disciples gloried in this, when they were thought worthy to suffer for Christ's sake, Acts v. 41. Where there is a desire to please God, it is so far from being ashamed or afraid to suffer, that it joys in this. Oh, now there is occasion given to shew that God respects me more, if I, for his sake, stand out in his quarrel, and break through all difficulties.

It will make us please him in all things that we are capable, in all things that we can do any way in our standings; as Christ describes it out of Moses, to 'love God with all our mind, with all our soul, and with all our strength,' Deut. vi. 5. Where love is, it sets all on work to please and give content. It sets the mind on work to study, Wherein shall I please God? And it will study God's truth, and not serve him by our own inventions. We must serve and love God after his mind; that is, as he hath commanded. It will set the wits on work to understand how he will be served, and to love him with all our soul, and with all our heart; that is, with the marrow and strength of our affections, with all my strength, be a man what he will be. If he be a magistrate, with the strength of his magistracy; if he be a minister, with the strength of his ministerial calling. In any condition I must love him, with all that that condition enableth me to. For it is a commanding affection; and being so, it commands all within and without to give content to the person loved. It commands the wit to devise, and the memory to retain, good things. It commands joy and delight; it commands anger to remove hindrances; and so all outward actions, love commands the doing of all things; it sets all on work. It is a most active affection. It is like to fire. It is compared to it. It sets all on work, and commands all that man is able to do. Therefore those that study not in all their endeavours according to their callings and places, according to every thing that God hath entrusted them with, to please God and to honour him in their conditions, they love not God.

What a shame is it, that when God hath given us such a sweet affection as love, that he should not have our love again, when we make ourselves happy in loving him? He is happy in his own love, the Father, Son, and Holy Ghost; but when he intends to make us happy, it is a shame that we should not bestow our affections upon him.

Much might be said to this purpose for the trial of ourselves, whether we love God or no. Let us not then forget these things; for it is the command both of the Old and New Testament; they run both upon love. 'I give you a new command,' saith Christ, John xv. 12; and yet it is no new command, but old and ordinary. But it is commanded now in the gospel; that is, it is renewed by new experiments* of God's love in Christ, 'that we should love him, as he hath loved us,' John xiii. 34, which is wonderfully; that we should love him, and 'love one another.' And all this is in this affection, as we see when the Holy Ghost would set out the disposition and qualification of such as those great things are prepared for,

* That is, 'experiences' = 'manifestations.'—G.

that 'neither eye hath seen, nor ear heard, nor hath entered into the heart of man,' he sets it down by this, 'They are for those that love him.'*

THE END OF THE THIRD SERMON.

THE FOURTH SERMON.

As it is written, Eye hath not seen, nor ear heard, nor hath entered into the heart of man, the things that God hath prepared for them that love him.—1 COR. II. 9.

That which hath already been said should force us to beg the Spirit of God to teach the heart, to teach us the things themselves, the inside of them. For a spiritual holy man hath a spiritual knowledge of outward things of the creatures; he sees another manner of thing in the creature than other men do. As another man hath a natural knowledge of spiritual things, so a holy man hath a spiritual knowledge even of the ordinary works of God; and raiseth and extracts a quintessence out of them, that a worldly man cannot see, to glorify God, and to build up his faith in the sense of God's favour, &c. This I add by the way to that.

But the highest performance of this, that there are things provided for God's people that 'neither eye hath seen nor ear hath heard,' &c., it is reserved for another world. For the promises of the gospel have then their fulfilling indeed. These words are true of the state of the gospel here now, but they have their accomplishment in heaven. For whatsoever is begun here is ended there. Peace begun here is ended there. Joy that is begun here it shall be ended there. Communion of saints that is begun here it shall be ended there. Sanctification that is begun here it shall be ended there. So all graces shall be perfect, and all promises performed then. That is the time indeed when God shall discover things that 'neither eye hath seen nor ear heard,' &c. In the mean time let us learn to believe them, and to live by faith in them, that there are such things.

And God reserves not all for another world, but gives his children a taste of those things beforehand to comfort them in their distresses in this world, as indeed there is nothing in this world of greater use and comfort to raise them, than the beginnings of heaven upon earth. A little peace and joy in the Holy Ghost will make a man swallow all the discontents in the world. Now God is so far good to us, as that he lets us have some drops of these things beforehand to raise up our spirits, that by the taste we may know what great things he hath reserved for us. But of these things, and the use of them, I spake before.

We come then to speak of the qualification of the persons.

'For them that love him.'

Not that we love God first, and then God prepares these things for us; but God prepares them, and acquaints us what he means to do with us, and then we love him. A Christian knows before what title he hath in Christ to heaven, and then he works. He knows Christ hath wrought salvation for him, and then he works out his salvation in a course tending to salvation. For there must be working in a course tending to the pos-

* At close of this sermon is placed 'Finis,' and the 4th follows on a separate pagination. Probably *it* was given to the publisher after the others had been printed.—G.

session of salvation. That Christ hath purchased; we must not work and think by it to merit heaven. We know we have heaven, and those great things in the title of Christ, and then we fall on loving and working. There is a clean contrary order between us and those mercenaries. They invert the order of God; for, for whom God hath prepared these things, he discovers them to the eye of faith, and then faith works by love. This I add by the way.

Now he sets down this description of those persons for whom these excellent things are prepared, by this affection of love, by this grace of love, as being the fittest for that purpose to describe a Christian. Faith is not so fit, because it is not so discernible. We may know our love when we cannot know our faith. Ofttimes those that are excellent Christians, they doubt whether they believe or no; but ask them whether they love God and his truth and children or no? oh yes! they do. Now God intending to comfort us, sets out such an affection as a Christian may best discern; for of all affections we can discern best of our love. But to come to the affection itself, there are three things in love.

There is the affection, passion, grace of love. We speak of the grace here.

The affection is natural.

The passion is the excess of the natural affection when it overflows its bound.

Grace is the rectifying of the natural affection, and the elevating and raising it up to a higher object than nature can pitch on. The Spirit of God turns nature into grace, and works corruption and passion out of nature, and elevates and raiseth that which is naturally good, the affection of love to be a grace of love. He raiseth it up to love God (which nature cannot discover), by spiritualizing of it. He makes it the most excellent grace of all. So that while I speak of the love of God, think not that I speak of the mere affection, but of the affection that hath a stamp of grace upon it. For affections are graces when they are sanctified. And indeed all graces (set illumination aside, which is in the understanding) spring from this. What is true grace but joy, and love, and delight in the best things? And all others spring from love. What do we hate but what is opposite to that we love! And when are we angry, but when that we love is opposed and wronged? Then there is a holy zeal. So that indeed all grace is in the affections, and all affections are in this one primitive affection, this first-born and bred affection, love. I speak of it then as a special grace. Now the way of discerning of it we heard partly before. The way to discern of this sanctified affection, this grace, is to know what we esteem, for love, it is from an estimation. And likewise, in the second place, esteem breeds a desire of union. And desire of union breeds content in the thing when we have it. And contentment in the person breeds desire of contenting back again. These things I stood on, and will not press further.

Let us examine and try ourselves oft by our affections, how they stand biassed and pointed, whether to God and heavenward, or to the world; for we are as we love. For what we love, we, as it were, marry; and if we join our love to baser things, we marry baser things, and so debase ourselves. If we join in our affections to things above ourselves, to God, and spiritual things, we become spiritual as they are. So that a man stands in the world between two goods, somewhat that is better than himself, and something that is meaner; and thereafter as he joins in his affections, thereafter he is. For the affection of love to God and to the best things makes him excellent; and his affection to baser things makes him base. Let a man be never so base in the world, if his affections be base, he is a base person. Therefore we have the more need to try our affections.

But to answer some cases briefly.

1. It will be objected, may we not love anything but God and holy things? May we not love the creatures, because it is here specified as a note of those, that these things are 'prepared for those that love God'?

Yes. We may love them as we see somewhat of God in them, as every creature hath somewhat of God in them. Whereupon God hath the style of every creature that hath good in it. He is called a 'Fountain,' a 'Rock,' a 'Shield,' everything that is good, to shew that the creatures every one hath somewhat of God. He would not have taken the style of the creature else. We may love the creature as it hath somewhat of God in it, a being, or comfortable being, or somewhat; and as it conveys the love of God to us, and leads us back again to God. There is no creature but it conveys some love, and beams, and excellency of God to us in some kind, and leads us to God. So we may love other things. We may love men, and love God in them, and love them for God, to bring them to God, to leave a holy impression in them, to be like God. There is no question of this. But the love of God, that is the spring of all.

But it will be said by some weak conscience, How shall I know I love God, when I love the world and worldly things? I love my children, and other things, perhaps that are not ill; I fear I love them more than God.

We must know for this, that when two streams run in one channel they run stronger than one stream. When a man loves other good things, nature goes with grace. So nature, going with grace, the stream is strong. But when a man loves God, and Christ, and heavenly things, there is grace only; nature yields nothing to that. When a man loves his children or his intimate friends, &c., nature going with grace, it is no wonder if the stream be stronger when two streams run in one. So corruption in ill action ofttimes carry the affections strong. As in many of our loves there is somewhat natural that is good, yet there is some corruption, as to love a man for ill. Here nature and corruption is strong, but in supernatural things grace goes alone.

Then again, we must not judge by an indeliberate passion, by what our affection is carried suddenly and indeliberately to; for so we may joy more in a sudden thing than in the best things of all, as in the sight of a friend there may be a sudden affection. But the love of God, it is a constant stream. It is not a torrent, but a current that runs all our lifetime. Therefore those affections to God and heavenly things, in a Christian, they are perpetual. They make no great noise, perhaps, but they are perpetual in the heart of a Christian. A sudden torrent and passion may transport a man, but yet he may have a holy and heavenly heart. I speak this for comfort.

2. Ay, but my love to God is faint and little.

Well, but it is a heavenly spark, and hath divinity in it. It is from heaven, and is growing, and vigorous, and efficacious; and a little heavenly love will waste all carnal love at length, it is of so vigorous and constant a nature. It is fed still by the Spirit; and a little that is fed and maintained, that is growing, that hath a blessing in it (as the love of God in the hearts of his hath; for God continually cherisheth his own beginning), that little shall never be quenched, but shall overgrow nature at length, and eat out corruption, and all contrary love whatsoever. Though for the present we see corruption overpower and oppress grace, yet the love of God being a divine spark, and therefore being more powerful, though it be little, than the contrary, it hath a blessing in it to grow, till at length it consume all. For love is like fire; as in other properties so in this, it wastes and consumes the contrary; and raiseth up to heaven, and quickens, and enlivens the persons, as fire doth. And it makes lightsome dead bodies; it transforms them all into fire like itself. So the love of God, by little and little, transforms us all to be fiery; it transforms us to be lovers. These cases needed a little touching, to satisfy some that are good and growing Christians, and must have some satisfaction.

3. But it may be asked again, as indeed we see it is true, what is the reason that sometime meaner Christians have more loving souls than great scholars, men of great parts? One would think that knowledge should increase love and affection?

So it doth, if it be a clear knowledge; but great wits and pates* and great scholars busy themselves about questions and intricacies, and so they are not so much about the affections. A poor Christian ofttimes takes those things for granted that they study, and dispute, and canvass, and question. There is a heavenly light in his soul that God is my Father in Christ, and Christ, God and man, is my Mediator. He takes it for granted, and so his affections are not troubled. Whereas the other, having corruption answerable to his parts, great wit and great corruption, he is tangled with doubts and arguments. He studies to inform his brain; the other to be heated in his affections. A poor Christian cares not for cold niceties, that heat not the heart and affections; he takes these for granted if they be propounded in the Scripture. Instead of disputing, he believes, and loves, and obeys; and that is the reason that many a poor soul goes to heaven with a great deal of joy, when others are tangled and wrapped in their own doubts. So much for satisfying of these things. To go on, therefore, to give a few directions how to have this heavenly fire kindled in us, to love God, considering such great things are provided for those that love God. It is a matter of consequence: as we desire heaven, we must desire this holy fire to be kindled in us.

Let us know for a ground, as it were, that it is our duty to aim at the highest pitch of love that we can, and not to rest in the lowest. The lowest pitch of loving God, is to love God because he is good to us. That is good. The Scriptures stoops so low as to allow that God would have us love him and holy things for the benefit we have by them. But that is mercenary if we rest there. But God stoops to allure us by promises and favours, though we must not rest there. But we must love God, not for ourselves, but labour to rise to this pitch, to love ourselves in God, and to see that we have happiness in God, and not in ourselves. Our being is in him. We must love ourselves in him, and be content to be lost in God; that is, so to love God, that if he should cast us away (his kindness is better than life), do others what they will, we will love him, and ourselves for his excellencies, and because we see ourselves in him and are his children. We must labour to rise to that, and that is the highest pitch that we can attain to. We must know that for a ground.

And know this for another, that when we speak of the love of God, we speak of love incorporate into our conversations and actions; not of an abstracted love and affection, but of love in our places, and callings, and standings, love invested into action. Therefore the Scripture saith, we

* Qu. 'parts'? If 'pates,' = heads.—G.

must love God 'with all our mind, with all our heart, with all our power and strength,' Deut. vi. 5; that is, in our particular places. To make it clear. When we speak of love to God, we speak of love to him in our particular callings. He loves God that is a magistrate and executes justice for God's sake; and he that is a minister, and teacheth the people conscionably for God's sake, and shews them the way to heaven. He loves God as a man in the commonwealth, a statesman, &c., that in that place seeks the glory of God, and the good of the church and religion. Shall men talk of love to God, and their affections are stirred up I know not whereabout? No. It is an affection that is discovered in actions.

How can we love God with all our might, except as far as our might extends, our love extends? How far doth thy activity, thy power, thy sphere, that thou canst do anything, stretch? So far must thy love; and thou must shew thy love in all the powers and abilities that God hath furnished thee with.

For a man that hath great place and opportunity to do good, and to think it enough only to love God in his closet, &c., this is not the love we speak of. A man must love God with all his might, as he stands invested in relation this way or that way.

The love of God in a private man will not serve for a magistrate or a public man. He must shew his love in his place by standing in the gap, to hinder all the ill, and to do all the good he can. Every man must do so, but such a one more especially, because God hath trusted him with more. Well, these things premised, to come to some directions how to come to love God.

First of all, the way to love God *is to have a heavenly light to discover what we are in ourselves and our emptiness;* for being as we are, we can never love God till we see in what need we stand of his favour and grace, that we are damned creatures else.

Now when we come to have our eyes opened to see our sinfulness and emptiness, we will make out to God, and make out to his mercy in Christ above all things. Indeed, the first love is the love of dependence, before we come to a love of friendship and complacency with God; a love to go out to him, and to depend upon him for mercy and grace and all. A love that riseth from the sense of our misery, and goes to him for supply.

There is a sweet concurrence of misery and mercy; of emptiness and fulness; of beggary and riches.

Now when we see our own misery, and beggary, and sinfulness; and then a fulness in God to supply; of riches to enrich us every way; then this breeds a love. This is the way to all other loves that follow. And where this is not premised, and goes before, a man will never delight in God. In Luke vii. 47 that good woman she loved much. Why? Much was forgiven her; many sins were forgiven her.

So when the soul shall see what need it hath of forgiving mercy, of pardoning mercy, and how many great debts God hath forgiven us in Christ, there will be a great deal of love, because there is a great deal forgiven. And we must begin indeed with seeing the infinite mercy of God before any other attribute of God, and then we shall love him after. This is the first thing. There is no soul that ever loves God so, as the poor soul that hath been abased with the sense of sin and its emptiness, that it is empty of all goodness; and then sees a supply in the mercy of God in Christ. Those souls love God above all.

Another way to love God is to consider of his wonderful goodness, to meditate and think of it. He is good and doth good. It is a communicative goodness. Let us think of his goodness, and the streaming of it out to the creature. The whole earth is full of the goodness of the Lord. What are all the creatures but God's goodness? We can see nothing but the goodness of God. What is all the creatures but *Deus explicatus*, God unfolded to our senses? He offers himself to our bodies and souls; all is God's goodness.

And then see this goodness fitted to us. It is a fit goodness that comes from God. He is good and doth good, and so fitly he proportions his goodness. For he hath fitted every part of us, soul and body, with goodness; all the senses with goodness. What do we see but goodness in colours? What do we hear but his good, in those delights that come that way? We taste and feel his goodness. Against the cold we have clothing; in hunger we have food; in all necessities, in all exigencies, we have fit considerations of God for all necessities whatsoever outward.

But then for our souls, what food hath he for that? The death of Christ, his own Son, to feed our souls. The soul is a spiritual substance; and he thought nothing good enough to feed it but his own Son. We feed on God's love in giving Christ to death; and on Christ's love in giving himself to death.

The soul being continually troubled with the guilt of some sin or other, it feeds on this; it is nourished with Christ every day more and more, especially at the sacrament. Thus we see how God hath fitted his goodness to us. And then in particular dangers how he fits us with several deliverances; so seasonably as we may see God's love in it.

Then as God's goodness is great and fit, so it is near us. It is not a goodness afar off, but God follows us with his goodness in whatsoever condition we be. He applies himself to us, and he hath taken upon him near relations, that he might be near us in goodness. He is a father, and everywhere to maintain us. He is a husband, and everywhere to help. He is a friend, and everywhere to comfort and counsel. So his love it is a near love. Therefore he hath taken upon him the nearest relations, that we may never want God and the testimonies of his love.

And then again this goodness of God, which is the object of love, it is a free goodness, merely from himself; and an overflowing goodness, and an everlasting goodness. It is never drawn dry; he loves us unto life everlasting. He loves us in this world, and follows us with signs of his love in all the parts of us, in body and soul, till he hath brought body and soul to heaven to enjoy himself for ever there. These and such like considerations may serve to stir us up to love God, and direct us how to love God.

Benefits will work upon a beast; as it is Isaiah i. 2, 'Hear, O heavens; and hearken, O earth: the ox knoweth his owner, and the ass his master's crib; but my people have forgotten me.'

Proud men become baser, and more brute than the very brutes; benefits will move the very brute creatures. So, I say, these favours to us in particular should move us, except we will be more brute than the brutes themselves.

Especially to move us all, consider some particularities of favours to us more than to others, for specialties do much increase love and respect.

Consider how God hath followed thee with goodness outwardly, when others have been neglected. Thou hast a place in the world, and riches, and friends, when many other excellent persons want all these. There are some common favours to all Christians; as the favour we have in Christ, forgiveness of sins, sanctification, and such other favours. But there be some specialties of divine providence, whereby it appears that God's providence hath watched over us in some particulars more than others; those be special engagements. And is there any of us that cannot say that God hath dealt specially, in giving them some mercy more than to others? I add this therefore to the rest.

Again, to help us to stir up this grace of love, *consider those examples of loving of those that have then lived in former times.* Take David, and Paul, and other holy men. David wonders at his own love: 'Lord, how do I love thy law!' Ps. cxix. 97. And have we not more cause comparing the grounds of our affection, when we have more than they in those times? What! did he wonder at his love of God's law, when the canon was so short? They had only Moses, and some few books, and we have the canon enlarged; we have both the Old and New Testament, shall not we say much more, How do I love thy law, thy gospel, and divine truths! This should shame us, when they in dark times so loved the truth of God, and we see all clear and open, and yet are cold.

Likewise it is good in this case *to converse with those that are affectionate.* As face answereth face, so spirit answers spirit; as 'iron sharpeneth iron,' so one sharpens another, Prov. xxvii. 17. Conversation with cold ones will make one cold: 'For the abundance of iniquity, the love of many shall wax cold,' Mat. xxiv. 12. Conversing with sinful, cold people casts a damp upon us. But let us labour, if we will be wise for our souls, when we find any coldness of affection, to converse with those that have sweet and heavenly affections. It will marvellously work upon our hearts.

I might say much this way to stir us up, and direct us how to love God.

But indeed nothing will so much enable us to love God as a new nature. Nature will love without provocation. The fire will burn, because it is fire; and the water will moisten, because it is water; and a holy man will love holy things, because he is holy; a spiritual soul will love spiritual things, because he is spiritual. Therefore, besides all, add this, that our natures be changed more and more, that they be sanctified and circumcised as God hath promised: 'I will circumcise your hearts, that ye may love me,' Deut. xxx. 6. There must be a circumcised heart to love God. We must be sanctified to love God; for if nature be not renewed, there cannot be this new commandment of love. Why is love called a new commandment, and an old commandment?

It is called old for the letter, because it was a command in Moses' time: 'Thou shalt love the Lord with all thy soul,' Deut. vi. 5. But now it is a new commandment, because there is abundance of spirit given by Christ; and the Spirit sanctifies us and writes this affection in our hearts. It was written in stone before, but now is written in our hearts by the Spirit. And now there are new incentives and motives to love, since Christ came and gave himself for us, new encouragements and provocations to love. Therefore it is a new commandment, from new grounds and motions, that are more a great deal than before Christ. But there must be a new heart to obey this new command of love. The old heart will never love.

Therefore we must, with all the means that may be used, beg the Spirit of sanctification especially, beg the discovery of God's love to us, for our love is but a reflection of God's love. We cannot love God except he love us first. Now, our love being a reflection of God's love, we must desire that he would give us his Spirit to reveal his love; that the Spirit being a witness of God's love to us, may thereupon be a Spirit of love and sanctification in us.

And let us labour to grow more in the assurance of God's love, and all the evidences of it. Let us dwell long in the meditation of these things. The dwelling in the meditation of God's love, it will make us to love him again. As many beams in a burning-glass meeting together they cause a fire, many thoughts of the many fruits of God's love in this world, and what he intends us in the world to come, our hearts dwelling on them, these beams will kindle a holy fire in our hearts.

Many are troubled with cold affections, and wish, Oh that they could love! They forget the way how to love. They will not meditate; and if they do meditate, they think to work love out of their own hearts. They may as well work fire out of a flint, and water out of a stone. Our hearts are a barren wilderness. Therefore let us beg the Spirit that God would alter our hearts, with meditation and all other helps; that God would sanctify us, and discover his love to us, and that he would give us his Spirit (for he doth the one where he doth the other). When God doth so, then we shall be enabled to love him. We must not think to bring love to God, but we must fetch love from God. We must light our candle at his fire. Think of his love to us, and beg the Spirit of love from him; love is a fruit of the Spirit. That is the course we ought to take, for God will teach our hearts to love.

Now, to stir us up the more, to add some motives and encouragements to labour more to get this affection. Let us consider seriously that without this love of God we are dead; and whatsoever comes from us it is still-born, it is dead. Without love we are nothing; without love all that comes from us is nothing; without love 'I am as a tinkling cymbal,' saith Paul, 1 Cor. xiii. 1. For a man to be nothing in religion, and all that comes from him to be dead and still-born, to be abortive actions, who would be in such a case? Therefore let us labour, before we do anything that is good, to have our hearts kindled with the love of God, and then we shall be somebody, and that that we do will be acceptable; for love sweetens all performances. It is not the action, but the love in the action; as from God it is not the dead favour that comes from him that comforts the soul of a Christian, so much as the love and sweetness of God in the favour. That is better than the thing itself. When we have favour from God in outward favours, consider the sweetness: 'Taste and see how gracious the Lord is,' Ps. xxxiv. 8. The taste of the love and favour of God in the blessing is better than the thing itself, for it is but a dead thing. And so from us back again to God. What are the things we perform to him? They are dead. But when they are sweetened with the affection of love, done to him as a father in Christ, he tastes our performances as sweet. Love makes all we do to have a relish, and all that he doth to us. Therefore we should labour for this sweet affection.

And withal consider, that we may be called to do many things in this world. Surely there are none of us but we have many holy actions to perform. We have many things to suffer and endure in the world, many temptations to resist. What shall or will carry us through all? Nothing but love. If we have loving and gracious hearts, this affection will carry us through all good actions, through all oppositions and temptations; for 'love is strong as death,' Cant. viii. 6. Consider therefore that there are so many things that will require this affection, this blessed wing and wind of the soul, to carry us along, in spite of all that is contrary, through all opposition; *let us labour for love, and that affection will carry us through all.* Indeed, if we have that it is no matter what a man suffers. A man can never be miserable that hath this affection of love. If this heavenly fire be kindled in him he cannot be miserable; take him in what condition you will, take him upon the rack. St Paul in the dungeon sang at midnight in the dungeon, in the stocks, at an uncomfortable time and place. When he had been misused, his heart was enlarged to sing to God out of love, Acts xvi. 25. Nay, everything increaseth it. The things we suffer increaseth this flame. Let a man love God, whatsoever he suffers in a good cause it increaseth his love, he shall find his love increased with it. The more he loves the more he can suffer; and the more he suffers the more he loves God, and the more he increaseth in a joyful expectation of the times to come. And love is alway with joy, and hope, and other sweet affections. It draws joy with it always, and hope of better things; and as joy increaseth and hope increaseth, so a man's happiness increaseth in this world. Therefore it is no matter what a man suffers that hath a gracious and loving heart, enlarged by the Spirit of God. Let him never think of what he suffereth of pain, of losses and crosses, if God discover his fatherly breast, and shine on him in Christ; and he look on God reconciled, and taste of the joys of heaven beforehand. If you tell him of sufferings, you tell him of that that encourageth him. It is an argument I might be long in, and to great purpose; for if we get this holy fire kindled once, we shall need little exhortation to other duties. It would set us on work to all. And like the fire of the sanctuary that never went out, so it is such an affection, that if it be once kindled in the heart it will never out. It is a kind of miracle in ill when we love other things besides God, baser than ourselves; it is as much as if a river should turn backward. For man that is an excellent creature, to be carried with the stream of his affection to things worse than himself, it is a kind of monster for a man to abuse his understanding so. What a base thing is it for a man to suffer such a sweet stream as love, a holy current, to run into a sink? Who would turn a sweet stream into a sink, and not rather into a garden? into a sweet place to refresh that? Our love is the best thing in the world, and who deserves it better than God and Christ? We can never return anything, but this affection of love we may again. And can we place it better than upon divine things, whereby we are made better ourselves? Doth God require our affections for himself? No. It is to make us happy. It advanceth our affection to love him; it is the turning of it into the right stream. It is the making of us happy that God requires it. For consider all things that may deserve this affection. It will keep us from all sin. What is any sin but the abuse of love? For the crookedness of this affection turns us to present things, that is the cause of all sin. For what is all sin, but pleasure and honours and profits, the three idols of the world? All sin is about them. And what are all good actions but love well placed? The well ordering of this affection is the well ordering of our lives; and the misplacing of this affection is the cause of all sin.

And to make us the more careful this way, consider that when we place our affections upon anything else, consider the vanity of it. We lose our love and the thing and ourselves. For whatsoever else we love, if we love not God in it, and love it for God, it will perish and come to nothing ere long. The affection perisheth with the thing. We lose our affections and the thing; and lose ourselves too, misplacing of it. These are forcible considerations with understanding persons. And if we would use our understanding and consideration and meditation, and our souls, as we should, to consider of the grounds and encouragements we have to love God, and the best things whereby we may be dignified above ourselves, it would not be as it is; we should not be so devoid of grace and comfort. It was a miracle that the three young men should be in the midst of the furnace, and be there as if they were in another place, no hotter, Dan. iii. 12, 13, *seq*. And it is a miracle that men should be in the midst of all encouragements that we have to love God (as there is not the like reasons for anything in the world to keep our souls in a perpetual heat of affection to love God—no motives, or arguments, or incentives; all are nothing to the multitude of arguments we have to inflame our affections), and yet to be cold in the midst of the fire. It is a kind of miracle to have dark understandings and dead affections; that notwithstanding all the heavenly means we have to keep a perpetual flame of love to God, yet to be cold and dark in our souls; let us bewail it and be ashamed of it.

What do we profess ourselves? Christians, heirs of heaven; so beloved of God as that he gave his own Son to deliver us, being rebels and enemies, in so cursed a state as we are all in by nature. Poor creature! inferior to the angels that fell, that he should love man, sinful dust and ashes, so much as to give his own Son to free us from so great misery, and to advance us to so great happiness, to set us in 'heavenly places with Christ,' Eph. i. 3, and to have perpetual communion with him in heaven; to have such encouragements, and to be cold and dead-hearted; nay, wilfully opposite in our affections, to be enemies to the goodness of God and grace, having such arguments to love God. And yet how many spirits edged by the devil oppose all that is good, and will not give way to God's Spirit? God would have them temples, they will be sties. God would marry them; nay, they will be harlots. God would have them happy here, and hereafter. No; they will not; they will have their own lusts and affections.

Let us be afraid of these things, as we love our own souls and ourselves; and consider what encouragements we have to love God for which such great things are reserved as 'neither eye hath seen, nor ear heard, nor hath entered into the heart of man to conceive.'

Imprimatur; Tho. Wykes. Aug. 1638.

NOTES.

(*a*) P. 157.—'The philosopher saith, there is nothing in the understanding but it came into the senses before.' *The* philosopher is of course Aristotle, whose suggestive fragments of philosophical thinking on mental and moral science have been systematized by Locke and Bishop Berkeley. The latter observes of him, 'That philosopher held that the mind of man was a *tabula rasa*, and that there were no innate ideas.'—*Siris*, § 308.

(*b*) P. 188.—'Take all from me,' saith holy Austin, 'so thou leave me thyself.' One of the *memorabilia* of the 'Confessions,' and frequent in this Father. G.

THE EXCELLENCY OF THE GOSPEL ABOVE THE LAW.

THE EXCELLENCY OF THE GOSPEL ABOVE THE LAW.

NOTE.

'The Excellency of the Gospel above the Law' fills a considerable volume, which was originally published in 1639, under the supervision of Goodwin and Nye. See title-page below.* G.

* THE
EXCELLENCIE
OF
THE *GOSPELL*
above the *LAW*.
Wherein the Liberty of the
Sonnes of God is shewed.
With the Image of their *Graces*
here, and *Glory* hereafter.
Which affords much Comfort and
great Incouragement, to all such as Be-
gin Timely, and Continue Constant-
ly in the wayes of God.
By *R. Sibbs*, D.D. Mr. of *Katherin*
Hall, *Cambridge*, and Preacher
Grayes-Inne, London.
Begun in his life time, and published
by T[homas] G[oodwin] and P[hilip] N[ye].†
LONDON
Printed by *Tho. Cotes*, and are to be sold by
Iohn Bartlet, at his shop, at the Signe of the guilt
Cup, neere *S. Austins* gate. 1639.

† Cf. Vol. ii. p. 3.—G.

EXCELLENCY OF THE GOSPEL ABOVE THE LAW.

Now the Lord is that Spirit: and where the Spirit of the Lord is, there is liberty. But we all, with open face beholding as in a glass the glory of the Lord, are changed into the same image from glory to glory, even as by the Spirit of the Lord.—2 Cor. III. 17, 18.

The Apostle beginneth this chapter with the commendation of his ministry, having been put upon it by their undervaluing of him; yet so as together with himself he commendeth them as his best and only testimonial and letters of commendation, ver. 2; and so maketh way for himself to fall into a more set and large commendation of the glorious gospel itself, whereof God 'hath made him so able a minister to them, ver. 6. And because the excellency of anything is best commended by comparing and setting by it something else that excels in itself, and yet is exceeded by it, therefore he carrieth along his commendation of the ministry of the gospel through the whole chapter, by comparing it with the law and the ministry of the Old Testament. This comparison is made by the apostle,

First, more briefly, in *laying down some distinct properties and prerogatives of the gospel* wherein it excelleth the law, ver. 6, as

(1.) That this was 'the ministry of the *New* Testament;' that of the law of the Old.

(2.) And 'not of the letter,' as the law was; 'but of the Spirit.'

(3.) Nor of death, 'for the letter killeth'; but of life, for 'the Spirit quickeneth.'

And then, *by inferences drawn from these properties* thus briefly summed up, the apostle *more largely illustrates the transcendent glory of the gospel, and how far it exceedeth the glory of the law;* although it be granted the law be glorious. As

[1.] If that which was but a ministration of the letter written and engraven in stone was glorious, verse the seventh; that is, if the literal notions and bare knowledge of the law, which (like so many dead words or characters) maketh no alteration at all, but leaveth their hearts hard and stony, like the tables on which the law was written, which remained stones still; if this was glorious, even the literal knowledge of the law: as it was, both in the Jews' own account of themselves and in the judgment of the nations amongst whom they lived: 'how shall not the ministration of the Spirit be rather glorious? verse the eighth; the meaning whereof is largely explained in the third verse; where the Corinthians are said to be an 'epistle written not with ink' (or dead letters), 'but with the Spirit of the living God'; which kind of writing leaveth not the heart a heart of stone, as the dead writing of the law did, but changeth it into a 'heart of flesh,' and maketh such a thorough alteration in the whole man, as the writing within, 'in the tables of their hearts,' is 'known and read of all men. So that their lives and conversations being answerable to that spiritual and gracious writing of Christ in their hearts, they are 'manifestly declared to be the epistle of Christ.' And therefore such a ministry as this is, by which the Spirit of the living God is received (and not by the law, Gal. iii. 2), which is a Spirit of glory, and worketh glorious things both in the hearts and lives of men, must needs be 'rather glorious.'

[2.] Another inference we have in the ninth verse; 'If the ministration of condemnation be glorious;' that is, if that word which 'concluded men under sin,' Gal. iii. 22, and pronounced the sentence of death upon them, 'be glorious, much more doth the ministration of righteousness exceed in glory. For it is more glorious to pardon than to condemn; to give life, than to destroy. It is the glory of a man to pass over an offence, Prov. xix. 11., and in God it is called the 'riches of his glory,' Rom. ix. 23. 'The law, which was made glorious,' in terrifying, condemning, and stoping the mouths of men, insomuch as they had not a word to say for themselves, 'hath no glory, by reason of the glory' of the gospel 'that excelleth,' even in this respect, that it bringeth such a righteousness, as by the merit whereof and satisfaction given by it, we are justified and have peace towards God, notwithstanding the utmost rigour of the law.

[3.] The apostle argueth further, ver. 11, 'If that which is done away was glorious,' as the old covenant is, which was made old by the coming of the new, Heb. viii. 8, and by it removed as a thing grown weak and shaken, Heb. xii. 27, 'much more that which remaineth,' which is the new covenant, which cannot be shaken, but shall remain, and is 'the everlasting gospel,' Rev. xiv. 6, 'is more glorious,' as God's last works exceed the former, and taketh away the remembrance of them in comparison. As when he createth 'new heavens and a new earth,' the former shall not be remembered nor come into mind, Isa. lxv. 17.

[4.] There is another excellency of the gospel above the law, which the apostle addeth, and insisteth upon it more largely than upon all the rest, and that is, *the comfortable plainness and perspicuity of the doctrine and ministry of it:* verse the 12th, 'Seeing we have such hope, we use great plainness of speech.' In which it excelled the ministry of Moses, which was in much difficulty and obscurity, and that in a threefold respect, laid down in the 13th, 14th, and 15th verses.

(1.) *The matter of it was terrible*, tending to the shame, confusion of face, and condemnation of the hearers; insomuch as they were not able to stand before him, nor stedfastly to behold his face, it was such a dazzling and amazing light that shined in his ministry.

(2.) *The manner of delivery was in obscure and dark expressions*, that 'the children of Israel could not see to the end of that which is abolished;' that is, they could not see the drift and scope of his ministry, by reason of the types and shadows, which was 'the veil he put upon his face.'

(3.) *Their minds were blinded.* There was 'a veil upon their hearts,' which is evident bv experience in the Jews at this day, who so cleave in their affection to Moses, and to the shadows and ceremonies of his ministry, that they reject the scope and end of it, which is Jesus Christ crucified. And they can do no other. For although the veil that was upon Moses's face be removed, as it is by the doctrine of the gospel, which sheweth us in all possible plainness what the drift and meaning of Moses was in all those types and ceremonies, yet until the gospel in the spirit and efficacy of it cometh home to their hearts, and taketh off 'the veil that is upon their hearts' also; that is, until their natural blindness and obstinacy be taken away, which cannot be, but is rather increased, by the law—'For although Moses be read, yet until this day remaineth the same veil untaken away,' 2 Cor. iii. 14—the Jews will unavoidably abide in their ignorance and bondage.

Now, in opposition to this darkness and obscurity of the law in all those respects, the apostle exalteth the gospel in this high and excellent privilege of it, that it is plain, and evident, and full of demonstration, and that the light of it is not terrifying and amazing, but sweet and comfortable. So that we may with much liberty and boldness of spirit look constantly upon the great and glorious things set before us in it, although it be no other but the glory of the Lord Jesus Christ.

[5.] And there is, moreover, such an efficacy and working power in this ministry of the gospel, as it will not suffer men to remain the same without alteration, as they did under Moses's ministry, though he was read daily, but it will 'change' them even 'into the image of Jesus Christ, and carry them on still in that image and likeness, from one degree of glory to another,' after a most admirable and spiritual manner of working.

This special excellency and prerogative of the gospel is laid down in the two last verses of this chapter, which are the words upon which we shall more largely insist in the following discourse.

Verse 17. 'Now the Lord is that Spirit: and where the Spirit of the Lord is, there is liberty.'

'The Lord is that Spirit' that takes away the veil that is spoken of before.

He sets down what Christ is by what he doth; Christ is 'that Spirit,' because he gives the Spirit.

And then a sweet effect of the Spirit of Christ, 'Where the Spirit of Christ is, there is liberty.'

The Spirit here is not taken for the person of God, as if the Holy Ghost had said, 'The Lord is a Spirit,' and not a bodily thing, though that be a truth.

And as it is not meant naturally,* so not personally, 'Christ is that Spirit,' as if Christ were the Holy Ghost. That were a confusion of persons. Nor as restrained to the third person. The Holy Ghost is the Spirit. Neither, as some heretofore would have it, to shew that the Spirit is Jehovah, God. It is neither to shew that Christ is God, nor that the Spirit is God, nor that Christ is the Holy Ghost. But it is meant in regard of a special dispensation. 'The Lord is that Spirit;' that is, the Lord Jesus Christ, who is the Lord of his church by marriage, office, &c., 'is that Spirit;' that is, he

(1.) Hath the Spirit in himself eminently; and

(2.) Dispenseth and giveth the Spirit unto others; all receiving the Spirit from him as the common root and fountain of all spiritual gifts.

First, He was 'that Spirit,' as *having the Holy Ghost in himself as man*. The Holy Ghost filled the human nature and made it spiritual. The Spirit

* That is, as speaking of the nature of God, or of the Holy Spirit, the third person.—G.

is all in all in the human nature of Christ; and whatsoever he doth, he doth, as it were, being full of the Spirit, in himself. He gives the Spirit as God, and receives it as man. So he both gives and receives. The Spirit proceedeth from the Father and the Son as God, but the Spirit sanctified Christ as man, as it did in the virgin's womb. The Holy Ghost sanctified that blessed mass of his body. It sanctified him, and filled him with all graces and gifts; whereupon it is said, 'He received the Spirit without measure,' John iii. 34; that is, in abundance. Christ hath the Spirit in himself in a more eminent excellent manner than all others; and it must needs be so for these reasons:

(1.) *From the near union between the human nature and the divine.* They are one person. Therefore there is more Spirit in Christ than in all creatures put them together; than in all the angels, and all men, because the divine nature is nearer to Christ than it is to the angels or to any creature.

(2.) Christ hath the Spirit without measure, *both in regard of extension and intension*, as we say. He hath all graces in all degrees, even next to an infinite. All others have it in their measure and proportion.

(3.) *The Spirit doth rest upon Christ invariably.* In other men that have the Spirit, it ebbs and flows; it is sometimes more and sometimes less. There be spiritual desertions, not only in regard of comfort, but in regard of grace, though not totally. But the Spirit rests on Christ eternally in a full measure; and therefore you have it thus in Isa. xi. 2, 'The Spirit of the Lord shall rest upon him, the Spirit of wisdom and understanding, the Spirit of counsel and might,' &c.

(4.) By reason *of his place or offices in relation to the church*, as head, husband, king, priest, prophet, &c. The head is made by nature the seat of the more noble faculties, as of seeing, hearing, understanding, judging, and is furnished accordingly with greater plenty of spirits for the ruling and governing the whole body. So Christ is the Head of the church, and the government of all the world is laid upon him, and all excellencies are derived from him unto all his members, as from the root life is derived* unto all the branches. And therefore he must needs have the Spirit in greatest abundance. His fulness of the Spirit is as the fulness of the fountain; ours is but as the fulness of the cistern. He hath grace in the spring; we have it but in the conduit. His graces are primitive; ours derivative. We have nothing but what we have received. Therefore it is said, 'He hath the oil of gladness poured upon him above his fellows,' Ps. xlv. 7.

He hath his name from anointing, 'Christ.'† He was anointed; that is, separated and ordained to the office of mediatorship, by anointing, not properly,‡ that is, with any material oil, but with the Spirit. This was in regard of his human nature only, but it was above his fellows; that is, above all kings and priests, for they are his fellows in regard of titles. He was above them all, for all have their anointing from him. Therefore he is the King of kings, and the Prophet of prophets, &c. Also above *all* his fellows. As we take his fellows for Christians, they are his fellows; 'I go to my God and your God,' &c., John xx. 17. He is the 'first-born' amongst them, and in all things he hath the pre-eminence.

(5.) *He is to be as the pattern*, we are to follow him. We are 'predestinated to be conformed to him,' Rom. viii. 29, and to grow up to that fulness which is in him. And in this respect there is cause why he should have the Spirit and all the graces of it in greater abundance, that he might

* That is, communicated.—G.

† That is, Χριστός (χρίω) anointed.—G.

‡ That is, = literally.—G.

exceed all, even Christians of greatest growth and perfection. He is to be a pattern and example to all: to the strongest as well as to the weak. Even Paul himself, who was a leader to others, for the excellency of the grace of Christ that was in him, was yet a follower of Christ. 'Be you followers of me, as I am of Christ,' 1 Cor. iv. 16.

Quest. When did this fulness of the Spirit come upon Christ? When had he it?

Ans. 1. There was a fulness of the Spirit poured out upon Christ *in the union of the human nature with the divine.* Union and unction went together. There was anointing of the Spirit, together with the union of the Spirit.

Ans. 2. There was a more full manifestation of the Spirit *in his baptism.* When the Holy Ghost fell on him in the shape of a dove, then he received the Spirit. He was to enter into the ministry of the gospel. 'The Spirit of the Lord God was upon him,' because he had anointed him to preach good tidings unto the meek, &c., Isa. lxi. 1.

Ans. 3. But the fullest degree of declaration and manifestation of the Spirit upon Christ was *after his resurrection;* after he had satisfied fully for our salvation. Then the stop of his glory was taken away. For to work our salvation, there was a keeping back of the glory of Christ from his human nature, that he might be abased to suffer for us. When he had fully suffered for us, that stay of his glory, his abasement, was taken away, and then nothing appeared but all glory and Spirit in Christ. All things were put under his feet, and he was set upon his throne as a glorious king. His priestly office appeared in his death, his prophetical office before his death. But then he appeared to be King and Lord of all in the resurrection. Thus we see how Christ is that Spirit; that is, he is full of the Spirit in regard of himself.

Secondly, He is 'that Spirit' *in regard of his dispensations towards his church and children.* 'The Lord is that Spirit;' that is, [1.] of all truths, and [2.] of all persons, to give life and quickening to them.

(1.) *First, of truths.* What is the scope of the whole Scriptures but Christ? from the first promise of the blessed seed, 'The seed of the woman shall break the serpent's head,' Gen. iii. 15, to the end of the book. What is all the Scriptures without Christ? The law is a dead letter; yea, and so is the gospel too without Christ. He is 'that Spirit' which gives life unto all the Scriptures. Moses without Christ is but a shadow without a body, or a body without a soul. Take away Christ, what was the brazen serpent? What was the ark? What were the sacrifices? What is all? Is not Christ 'all in all' these? The kings, and priests, and prophets, they were types of Christ; all the promises they were made and fulfilled in Christ. The law ceremonial aimed at Christ; the law moral is to drive us to Christ. Christ is the Spirit of all. And the Scripture without Christ it is but a mere dead thing; it is but a shell without a kernel, as it is to the Jews at this day.

(2.) Christ is 'that Spirit,' *in regard of persons,* quickening them. He is a universal principle of spiritual life, infusing it into all his church and children. Christ is always with his church from the beginning of the world, and will be to the end. It was no loss to the church that Christ in his bodily presence left it, for he left them 'the Comforter,' his Spirit, by which he wrought greater works after his ascension than he did before. He is 'anointed with the oil of gladness,' and grace 'above his fellows,' Ps. xlv. 7, but all was for his fellows. Whatsoever he is, or hath, all is for his church and children. 'For us' he was born, 'for us' he was given. He is a King, a Priest, a Prophet for us. He died for us, he rose again for us.

And he doth all he doth towards the church, as he hath the Spirit, and by the Spirit. The Father is the first in the Trinity, '*from* whom' all comes; and the Son, '*by* whom' all things are; but the Holy Ghost is the immediate worker of all things, next the creature. All things are applied *from* God the Father, *through* the Son, *by* the Spirit. What Christ wrought, and what the Father in wisdom devised, was applied by the Spirit; and so the framing of us to be fit for such a glorious condition as we have by Christ, is also by the Spirit. And this is the reason why Christ giveth the Spirit to those to whom he purposeth to give faith or love, or to work any gracious work.

For where Christ saveth, he doth it not only by merit and satisfying the wrath of God for us, but also by sanctifying and effectual working in us, that he might be a perfect Saviour. Now the essential vigour and operative principle in all things, either wrought by or from the Father or the Son, is the Spirit. As in man there is his will from which he resolveth and purposeth, there is wisdom and understanding by which he proceedeth, and then there is a vigorous power in man by which he executeth and doth all. So is it in this working of God. The Father plotteth* and determineth of what is to be done; the Son, 'who is the wisdom of the Father,' 1 Cor. i. 24, dispenseth what the Father willeth; the Holy Spirit, the power of both, finisheth and worketh all upon us, and therefore he is called the 'power of the highest,' Luke i. 35.

Whatsoever works come from God to the creature in general, and are wrought in the world, as works of creation and providence, are immediately by the Holy Spirit nakedly considered, as the third person coming from the Father and the Son. And in those special works, wrought in his church and on his children, all things cometh from the Holy Ghost, but not simply considered as the third person, but as he is 'the Spirit of Christ;' that is, first sanctifying and filling the human nature of Christ, and then sanctifying and filling us. Christ could not give the Holy Ghost immediately to us, we being in enmity with God, and separated from him through our sins; but he must first take it to himself, who having by his death and sufferings reconciled us to his Father, and purchased the Spirit *for* us, may now dispense and give forth his Spirit *to* us.

If we had stood in Adam, we should not have received grace so as now we do; for we should have received it from the first Adam but as from a man. Now we receive it not from mere man, but, which is much more, from the 'second Adam,' who is God-man. Nay, Adam himself received not his grace after so glorious a manner as we do, for he received it from the Spirit nakedly considered as the third person in the Trinity, and as all other creatures received their excellencies. But we receive it from the Holy Spirit, which doth not only proceed from the Father and the Son, but cometh, as it were, through our own nature, which was marvellously united to God the Son, and made one with him, unto us, and worketh in us.

'The first Adam was a living soul, the last Adam was a quickening Spirit,' 1 Cor. xv. 45. He quickened himself when he was dead, and he quickens all his members too. First, he receives the Spirit himself, and the same Spirit that filled and sanctified his human nature, the same Spirit sanctifieth his church, which he 'loves even as himself.' As he loveth that his own human nature, which the Holy Ghost sanctified, so doth he love

* That is, 'deviseth.'—G.

his own mystical body, his church, being mystically united to him, and sanctifieth it by the same Spirit.

Christ dispenseth his Spirit unto us, as head of his church, and this he doth in divers respects.

(1.) As he is God, by way of *immediate influence*. He poureth it out upon us as the prime and principal cause. And this he doth as God, not as man, for the manhood cannot work above itself, it cannot do the work of God, it cannot work grace or give the Spirit.

(2.) As he is man, considered as joined together with the Godhead, by way *of merit and satisfaction*. He procureth the Spirit to be given and poured out, which is done by the Father and the Son on all those who are beloved in the Son. So that the Spirit is given by Christ, with the Father, as Mediator, meritoriously. For he by suffering and satisfying procured the gift. Christ himself is the first gift, yea, the greatest that ever was given, the giving of Christ to die, to satisfy the wrath of God, and to obtain eternal life. Next to that main gift is the gift of the Spirit, in which is the seed of all gifts and graces; and this we have by his merit and mediatorship. Yet this we must likewise remember, that although Christ be said to give the Spirit, as he doth, yet the Holy Spirit giveth itself too. For there is such a unity in the Trinity of consent and nature, that though the Father and the Son send the Spirit, yet the Spirit comes of his own self. Though the Father and the Son give the Spirit, yet the Spirit giveth himself.

(3.) We have the Spirit from Christ not only by way of merit, but in some kind by way of *example*. He is the exemplary cause of all graces in us; looking to whom, we are transformed, as we shall see afterwards, 'from glory to glory.' For when we consider that Christ hath done so much for us as to save us, and redeem us, and die for us, this begetteth a love in us to Christ, and makes us often to think of him, and desirous to imitate him, as we usually do such as we love and highly esteem of.

The *dispensation of the Spirit is in most abundance* after the resurrection of Christ. As he appeared in himself then to be most spiritual and glorious after he rose again; so then being as the sun in its full height and perfect beauty, casteth his beams most plentifully abroad, and that for these reasons,

[1.] Because then he having finished the work of redemption and satisfied the wrath of God fully, and given contentment to divine justice, and accomplished all by his death, *there was nothing to hinder the blessed gift of the Spirit*. It is said that 'before, the Holy Ghost was not given, because Christ was not glorified,' John vii. 39. The gift of the Holy Ghost especially depends upon the glorifying of Christ. When he had fulfilled the work of redemption, and was raised to glory, God being pacified gave the Holy Ghost as a gift of his favour.

[2.] Then again after his resurrection and ascension, he did give the Holy Ghost more abundantly than before to his church, *because now he is in heaven*, and hath the advantage of the place, being exalted on high. As that glorious creature the sun, by the advantage it hath being placed in the heavens above us, is able to shine upon the greatest part of the earth at all times; and we need not call the sun down from its place to come into our houses, or fields, or gardens. No. Where it is seated in its proper place or orb, it hath the best opportunity, in most abundance and largest extent, to send down heat and light and influence to inferior things. So Christ doth his church more good now he is in heaven, from whence he sends the

Spirit, than he could do if he were below; because though his human nature be confined in heaven, his person is everywhere. And being 'ascended now far above all heavens,' he giveth gifts more liberally and plentifully, insomuch as he filleth all things, Eph. iv. 10. He enlargeth the tents of his gospel, and hath taken in a greater people to himself. We see in winter, when the sun is low and near the earth, all things are dead and cold; but when the sun in the spring cometh to overtop us, to be in a higher point above us, we see how all things put a new garment upon them. There is a new vigour and freshness in them. So there was more abundant vigour of the Spirit when Christ came in the flesh; his virtue appeared much more every way than before. But when this blessed Son of righteousness was advanced, and seated at the right hand of his Father, where his nature was perfectly enriched, and perfectly adorned with all kind of graces whatsoever in the highest glory of them, his influence of light and heat now beginning to be increased, and the efficacy and working of it to be felt everywhere, the glorious beams of the sun began to be scattered, and the light of the gospel to shine to a greater number of people. Now there was no respect of persons, whether Jew or Gentile, bond or free, male or female, all was one. The commission was enlarged to all, Mark xvi. 15, 'Go preach the gospel to every creature;' and with the word the Spirit went, and was received; and those that were 'added to the church,' even such as 'should be saved,' were many thousands, Acts ii. 47.

Thus have we opened the meaning of the words, and shewed 'how Christ is that Spirit,' both in respect of the Spirit's being eminently in him, and his giving of it, and spiritual gifts by it. All the vigour and life and influence we have that is spiritual and supernatural, and above the ordinary course, is from the Spirit; and whatsoever the Spirit hath, or doth for us, is done as sent from Christ, in whom the Spirit is in all fulness. Now we shall shew how many ways the consideration of these truths will be profitable and useful to us in the course of our lives, and for the comfort of our spirits.

Use 1. Christ is the Spirit of the Scriptures, of all truths, of all ordinances. We may by this be able *to reconcile the Scriptures, one place with another, where they seem to contradict.* The law is said to be 'a dead letter,' a 'ministration of condemnation,' &c., 2 Cor. iii. 6, *seq.;* but in the 19th Psalm there it is said, 'The law of the Lord is perfect, converting the soul,' &c., Ps. xix. 7. These places are thus reconciled. The law is said to be dead, so it is without Christ, without the Spirit which quickeneth; and so is the gospel too, even 'a savour of death,' 2 Cor. ii. 15. And so are the sacraments also as well as the word, dead ordinances if Christ be not in them. The law is said to be 'perfect,' and 'to convert the soul.' So it doth, when the Spirit goeth along with it, as it did ordinarily before Christ came in the flesh, as in David's time. But after Christ was come, who was the substance of those shadows, they became 'beggarly rudiments,' as in Paul's time, Gal. iv. 9. And the Spirit did not work with them, but with the gospel, 'the hearing of faith,' Gal. iii. 2.

Use 2. And we may understand likewise from hence *what the reason is that an ordinance at one time differeth so much from itself at another time in respect of the life and comfort of it,* as we often find even in our own experience; as also why the same ordinance (be it word, or sacrament, &c.) at the same time is profitable to one, and another hath no benefit at all from it. This is from the presence or absence of Christ, who is 'that Spirit.' What is the reason that wine, or *aqua vitæ,* doth more refresh and strengthen than common water? It is of the same substance, of the same colour that other water is. But there is more spirit in it. All things work answerable to the spirits that is in them. So what is the reason that the reading or hearing of the same thing affecteth one, and not another at all? The substance of the thing is the same, but the Spirit is not the same. The Spirit goeth with the one, and not with the other. We grant that our negligence in preparation and attention, our pride and earthly-mindedness, our want of faith to mingle with the word: these, or the like, may be causes why we are many times sent empty away; yet this still must be observed as a most evident truth, that all the efficacy and fruit of any ordinance dependeth upon Christ's being present in it, who is 'that Spirit' that quickeneth. The most powerful means that ever was ordained for our good will be dead and heartless if he be not there by his Spirit to put life into it. It may seem strange what John saith, chap. vi. ver. 63, 'The flesh profiteth nothing.' 'The flesh of Christ,' our nature which Christ took, and in which so much was wrought for us, which is the greatest ordinance of all, yet this flesh 'profiteth not,' nor will there be any benefit of it, if it be not applied to us spiritually. For it is not the flesh simply considered, but as by it and with it we receive the Spirit of Christ, which Spirit quickeneth and maketh the flesh of Christ 'meat indeed.' As it is with the flesh of Christ, so with all other ordinances. The Scriptures profit nothing, preaching profiteth nothing, the sacraments will profit nothing; there is none of these will be 'meat indeed,' unless the Spirit of Christ quicken them.

Therefore we ought to join with all the ordinances of God, a desire that Christ would join his Spirit, and make them effectual. We ought to come to the ordinances in a dependence upon Christ for a blessing upon them, and for his presence in them, who is the life and scope of all; and then we should not find such dulness and deadness in them. It is the sin of this age, this formality. It is the sin of those that have any thing in them. Set desperate drunkards and roarers and such wretches aside, as plainly discover themselves to be acted by the spirit of the devil. Take them that conform themselves in any fashion to religion, the killing sin that they lie under is this same dead formality. They will hear a sermon now and then, look on a book, and it may be pray morning and evening, but never look up to the living and quickening Spirit Jesus Christ. So that all they do is dead and loathsome, like salt that hath no savour. What is the best liquor if it hath lost its life and spirit, but flat and unsavoury: and blood when the spirits are out of it, what is it but loathsome gore! So are all their performances, even like sacrifices that had no fire in them. The Lord loathed such sacrifices as he did Cain's; and so he doth all our flat and lifeless services, yea and our persons too, being as Jude saith, 'fleshly, and not having the Spirit,' ver. 19.

Use 3. What need is there that *we should sanctify all we take in hand by prayer!* When we go to hear a sermon, when we take up the Bible to read a chapter alone by ourselves, or in our families, we should lift up our eyes and hearts and voices to heaven; we should say to Christ, Lord, join thy Spirit, be present with us; without thee thy word is dead, our hearts are dead, and will harden under the means, and darken in the light, and we shall fall under the heavy condemnation of these secure and formal times, if thou leavest us.

Use 4. Christ is said to be that Spirit, to send the Spirit as God, and to receive it as man, *in fulness*, and that for our sakes. It is a point of much comfort, that there is such abundance of Spirit in our nature in Christ, and for the behalf of the church, that we have a fulness to receive of. It was a comfort to Joseph's brethren, and that family, that Joseph was full of honour, and rules the second in the kingdom. Therefore they should want nothing that was good in Egypt. Is it not a comfort for Christians to know that Christ is the Spirit, that he hath the Spirit to give, the Spirit of wisdom in all straits, the Spirit of truth to keep us from all errors, the Spirit of strength for all services, the Spirit of comfort for all afflictions? He that is their Lord hath abundance of Spirit in him, and for them. Therefore, when we want any grace, or gift of the Spirit, we should go to Christ; for God doth all by Christ. Christ doth all by the Spirit. Desire Christ that he would vouchsafe his Spirit to rule us, counsel us, comfort us, and strengthen us. Therefore in our emptiness, as indeed we are empty creatures of ourselves, let us go to Christ for the Spirit. He hath received that fulness for us; desire him that out of his fulness he would vouchsafe to give unto us.

It is the reason why Christians are so dead and so dull and so dark in their spirits; they do not first consider themselves, and then go to Christ. We should all, in all exigents* whatsoever, make use of this our great high treasurer, the great high steward of heaven and earth, of this our Joseph, the second person in heaven. He is at the right hand of God, and all to fill his church with his Spirit. Our comfort is now that our strength and comfort lies hid in Christ, that is near to us as man, and near to God as God. He is between the Father and us; he is near the Father as being of the same nature with him; he is near us as being of the same nature with us. So being a mediator in office, and being so fit for a mediator in nature, what a comfort is this.

Indeed, there is no coming to God, no intercourse between God and us immediately, but between God-man and God and us, who is the mediator between God and us. He comes between. In Christ we go to God, in our flesh, in our nature; and in Christ, and from Christ, and by Christ, we have all grace and comfort. From Christ we have all as God, together with the Holy Ghost and the Father; and we have all in Christ as a head and husband; and we have all through Christ as mediator by his merit. Therefore we should go to Christ every way.

Use 5. Let us labour *to be in Christ that we may get the Spirit.* It is of great necessity that we should have it. Above all things next to redemption by Christ, labour for the Spirit of Christ.

Christ is our Saviour, not only by merit and satisfaction, but by efficacy and grace, that is, as he hath purchased us for his people by his blood; so he will subdue our corruptions, and rule us by his Spirit.

For, *first*, 'He that hath not the Spirit of Christ is none of his,' Rom. viii. 13. Those that have not the efficacy of the Spirit in them to rule them, shall not have benefit by his death to reconcile them, for these go alway together, Christ as a king to rule, and as a priest to die. 'He came by blood and by water,' 1 John v. 6, to satisfy and to sanctify.

Secondly, There is a necessity of the Spirit, *that we be new creatures.* It was the Spirit's brooding upon the chaos that brought forth all, Gen. i. 2; so the Spirit must sit upon our souls before any change will be made. Now there is a necessity that we be changed, and that we be new, or else we can never be inhabitants of the new heavens and the new earth. We must have the Spirit of God. Therefore, Zech. iv. 6, as in the material temple

* That is, 'exigencies.'—G.

'it is not by might, or by power, but by the Spirit,' so in raising up spiritual temples it is not by strength of wit or parts, but by the Spirit. Therefore the Spirit is necessary for us, even as our being in grace is necessary.

The holy apostles, we know, till the Spirit came more abundantly upon them, what dark creatures they were! But when the Holy Ghost was come upon them, how full of life and light and courage they were! that the more they suffered, the more they might suffer! So it will be with Christians: the more spiritual they grow, the more lightsome and courageous; the more strong, the more lively and vigorous to all duties. The Holy Ghost is the substantial vigour of all creatures whatsoever. All the spiritual vigour of every thing comes from the Holy Spirit, and the Holy Spirit from Christ.

For nothing can work above itself. Nature cannot work above nature. That which elevates nature above itself, and sets a spiritual stamp, and puts divine qualities upon it, is the Spirit of God. That divine quality is called spirit. There is the flesh and the spirit. All in us is flesh by nature, and whatsoever is spiritual and divine cometh from the Spirit, and therefore it is called spirit. You see therefore a necessity of the working of the Spirit, even as there is a necessity to be new creatures, and to be spiritual. If we will be spiritual, we must have it from him that is first spiritual, the Spirit himself; that is the principal* and fountain of all that is spiritual.

Thirdly, We are called ofttimes to do and suffer such things as are above nature; and therefore we must have a spirit above nature. When we feel sin, to believe the forgiveness of sins; when we see death, to believe life everlasting; and when we are in extremity, to believe God present with us to deliver us, to believe contraries in contraries, is a strange almighty work of faith, by the work of the Spirit. It is above the work of nature to die, to end our days with comfort, and to resign up our souls, for nature sees nothing but darkness and desolation in the grave and destruction. Nothing can make a man comfortable in death, but that which raiseth him above nature, the Spirit of God.

Now these things, and many such like, we must do and suffer, if we be Christians; and therefore we must have the Spirit to enable us to do all. The Spirit is to the soul as the soul is to the body. What is the body without the soul? A carcase, a loathsome dead thing. What is the soul without the Spirit? A chaos of darkness and confusion.

Well, how shall we know whether we have the Spirit of Christ or no?

(1.) We may know it partly by that I said before. *The Spirit is a vigorous working thing*, and therefore all three persons take upon them the name of Spirit, but the Holy Ghost especially, because he is the spiritual vigour. The Spirit is an operative thing. The spirits are the quintessence and extraction of things, that is nothing but operation. God that is nothing but a pure act is said to be a spirit. Those that have the Spirit of God are full of act and vigour. The spirits of dull creatures are active when they are extracted. Shall the spirits of bodies be vigorous, and shall not the Holy Ghost be vigorous, that is a substantial vigour? Therefore, if a man have the Spirit of God in him, it will work in him; it is very operative.

Therefore it is compared to fire in divers respects, for,

First, Fire it is of a working nature. It is the instrument of nature. If we had not fire, what could we work? All fabrics and all things are done by fire, especially metals; they are framed and made malleable by fire. So

* Qu. 'principle?'—ED.

the Holy Ghost, it is a working thing and softeneth the heart, and makes us malleable; it makes us fit for the impression of all good.

Secondly, Fire, again, *though bodies be dark, it makes them lightsome like itself*. Iron is a dark body, but if the fire penetrate it, it makes it lightsome. We are dark creatures of ourselves: if we have the Spirit it makes us light.

Thirdly Again, fire *it makes cheerful, and ascends upwards*. If a man have the Spirit of God, his conversation will be upward, his conversation will be heavenly, he minds the things of God, he doth not grovel here below; so in divers such respects the Holy Ghost is compared to fire, and hath such effects in us. In some sort we find our understandings enlightened, and ourselves quickened, and carried up to the above nature, in holy and heavenly actions; and then it is a good sign that we have the Spirit of Christ. A part will follow the whole. As we see a part of the earth it falls to the centre, because all the earth is heavy, all the whole earth falls down to the centre, and therefore every little clod will do it; so Christ our head, that hath abundance of the Spirit, is in heaven, and if we have the Spirit we will follow him, and mind the things where Christ is.

(2.) Where the Spirit of Christ is likewise, *it convinceth*, as it is John xvi. 8, *seq.*; that is, it brings a clear evident conviction with it, that the truth of God is the truth of God. It is no doubtful thing. Therefore when a man staggers in the truth, in this and that course, whether he should do this or that, it is a sign he hath not the Spirit, or that he hath it in a very little measure, because the Spirit is a convincing thing, as light it convinceth a man. He doth not doubt of that that he seeth at noon-day. So that that a man seeth by the Spirit, he is convinced of. When a man doubts and wavers, whether he should take a good course or a bad, and wavers, it is a sign he is carnal, and hath not the Spirit of God; for if he had not the Spirit* it would convince him, and set him down, You must take this course if you will be saved. That is said to convince, that saith more for a thing than anything can say against it. Now when a man hath the Spirit of God, he can say more for God and for good things and good ways, than all the devils in hell by discouragement can say against them. Therefore, when a man cannot say anything for God, and for good causes to purpose, he hath not the Spirit of God. The Spirit of God would so convince him, that he should answer all cavils and objections. The argument is wondrous large. I give you but a taste, to know whether the Spirit of Christ be in you or no.

(3.) In a word, if Christ be that Spirit, and have infused the Spirit into us, *it will make us like him*; it will transform us into his likeness, it will make us holy and humble and obedient as he was, even to the death. These things might be largely followed, but we have occasion to speak of these in other portions of Scripture. Therefore, that ye may get the Spirit of God, take these directions.

[1.] *We must go to Christ, study Christ*. If we will have the Spirit, study the gospel of Christ. What is the reason that before Christ there was so little Spirit in comparison? There was but a little measure of the knowledge of Christ. The more Christ is discovered, the more is the Spirit given; and according to the manifestation of Christ what he hath done for us, and what he hath, the more the riches of Christ is unfolded in the church, the more the Spirit goes along with them. The more the free grace and love of God in Christ alone is made known to the church, the

* Qu. 'had the Spirit?'—Ed.

more Spirit there is; and again back again, the more Spirit the more knowledge of Christ; for there is a reciprocal going of these two, the knowledge of Christ and the Spirit. What is the reason, that in popery the schoolmen that were witty to distinguish, that there was little Spirit in them? They savoured not the gospel. They were wondrous quick in distinctions, but they savoured not the matters of grace, and of Christ. It was not fully discovered to them, but they attributed it to satisfaction, and to merits, and to the pope, the head of the church, &c. They divided Christ, they knew him not; and dividing Christ, they wanted the Spirit of Christ; and wanting that Spirit, they taught not Christ as they should. They were dark times, as themselves confessed, especially about nine hundred and a thousand years after Christ, because Christ was veiled then in a world of idle ceremonies—to darken the gospel and the victory of Christ—that the pope made, who was the vicar of Satan. These were the doctors of the church then, and Christ was hid and wrapped in a company of idle traditions and ceremonies of men; and that was the reason that things were obscure.

[2.] *Now when Christ, and all good things by Christ, and by Christ only, are discovered, the veil is taken off.* Now of late for these hundred years, in the time of reformation, there hath been more spirit and more lightsomeness and comfort. Christians have lived and died more comfortably. Why? Because Christ hath been more known. And as it is with the church, so it is with particular Christians, the more they study Christ, and the fulness that is in Christ, and all comfort in him alone to be had—'wisdom, righteousness, sanctification, and redemption,' 1 Cor. i. 30—the more men grow up in the knowledge of Christ, the more they grow spiritually; and the more spiritually they grow, the more they grow in the knowledge of Christ. Therefore, if we would have the Spirit, let us come near to Christ, and labour to know him more, who is the fountain of all that is spiritual.

[3.] Then again, if we would be spiritual, *let us take heed we trust not too much to dead things,* without Christ; to have a kind of popery in the work done; to think that reading, and hearing, and receiving the sacrament, and that the government of the church will do it, as if it were as man would have it. Put case there were all these, which are excellent good things; but what are all these without the Spirit of Christ! A man may be dead with all these. Though he hear never so much, and receive the sacrament never so often, if a man go not to Christ the quickening Spirit in this manner: Lord, these, and my soul too, are dead things without thy Spirit, therefore quicken me. Join Christ with all our performances, without which all is nothing, and then he will be spiritual to us.

[4.] And when we go to Christ for the Spirit, as we must beg it if we will have it,—God will give the Holy Ghost to them that ask him, Luke xi. 13,—*remember that we use the means carefully;* reading, and hearing, and holy communion of saints, because though these without the Spirit can do nothing, yet the Spirit is not given but by these. These are the golden conduits of the Spirit of Christ. No man is ever spiritual but they are readers, and hearers, and conferrers of good things, and attenders upon the means of salvation, because God will work by his own tools and instruments. Therefore it is said, Rev. i. 9, that John was 'full of the Spirit upon the Lord's day.' Let a Christian sanctify the Sabbath as he should do, he will be in the Spirit on the Lord's day more than on other days. Why? Because then he is reading, and hearing, and conferring, and in some spiritual course; and the more a man on the Lord's day is in a spiritual course, the more he is in the Spirit: 'John was in the Spirit on the Lord's day.' So much for these words, 'The Lord is that Spirit.'

'And where the Spirit of the Lord is, there is liberty.'

We see here what the Spirit works where it is. 'Where the Spirit of the Lord is, there is liberty.' I will name the instance that I gave before, that I may the better go on. We say the sun is heat and influence; not that it is so, for they be accidents, but the sun appears to us for our comfort in heat and influence, therefore we call it by that name. We say of a man, he is all spirit. So Christ is all Spirit. The sun is all light, and where the light and heat of the sun is there is fruitfulness. So Christ is all Spirit, and where the Spirit of Christ is there is spiritual liberty.

It were expense of time to no purpose to tell you of the divers kinds of liberty. In a word, liberty is that that all desire, but our miscarriage is in the means of it, the way to attain to it. Here we see whence to have it, from the Spirit of Christ. Liberty is a sweet thing, especially liberty from the greatest enemies of all. If outward liberty be such a sweet thing—liberty from tyranny and base servitude, it is a thing that man's nature delights in; and the contrary, man as a man abhors; and he hath not the nature of a man that doth not abhor it,—what shall we think then of the liberty of the Spirit from the great enemies that daunt the greatest monarchs in the world? Liberty from the anger of the great God; and liberty from Satan, God's executioner; liberty from the terror of conscience, from the fear of death, and hell, and judgment; what shall we think of liberty in these respects? Therefore we speak of great matters here below when we speak of liberty.

Now liberty is either Christian or evangelical.

You may think this a nice difference, but there is some reality in it.

(1.) *Christian liberty* is that that belongs to all, even to those before Christ. Though they have not the term of Christians, yet they were members of Christ. Christ was head of the church 'yesterday, and to-day, and for ever,' Heb. xiii. 8.

(2.) *Evangelical liberty* is that that is more appropriated to the times of the gospel since the coming of Christ. Now the liberty that belongs to Christians as Christians, is perpetual from those grand enemies, the greatest enemies of all, spiritual and inward liberty. In evangelical liberty, besides that, there is another outward liberty, from the ceremonial and moral law and such like; and a liberty from the restraint of the law. The Jews were under many restraints, that under the gospel in this time we are not. I speak therefore of liberty as it runs through all ages of the church, not of evangelical merely since the time of Christ. Where the Spirit is, both these liberties are now since the coming of Christ. Now in that the Holy Ghost saith here, 'Where the Spirit of Christ is there is liberty,' it supposeth that *we are in bondage before we have the Spirit of Christ.*

That is a supposed ground and truth, and indeed so it is. For out of Christ we are slaves, the best of us all are slaves. In Christ the meanest of all is a free man, and a king. Out of Christ there is nothing but thraldom. We are under the kingdom of the devil. When he calls us we come. We are in thraldom under the wrath of God, under the fear of death and damnation, and all those spiritual enemies that I need not mention. They are well enough known to you by often repetition. There is no man but he is a slave till he be in Christ; and the more free a man thinks himself to be, and labours to be, the more slave he is. For take a man that labours to have his liberty, to do what he list,* he thinks it the happiest condition in the world; and others think it the best condition to have liberty not to be tyrannised over by others. It is the disposition of man's nature without grace. They account it a happiness to have their wills over all other, but the more liberty in this, the more slavery. Why?

The more liberty that a man hath to do lawlessly what he will, contrary to justice and equity, the more he sins. The more he sins the more he is enthralled to sin. The more he is enthralled to sin the more he is in bondage to the devil, and becomes the enemy of God. Therefore if a man would pick out the wretchedest man in the world, I would pick out the greatest man in the world if he be naught,† that hath most under him; he hath most liberty, and seeks most liberty, and accounts it his happiness that he may have his liberty. This is the greatest thraldom, and it will prove, when he dies and comes to answer for it, the greatest thraldom of all. Therefore the point needs not much proof, that if we be not in Christ we are slaves, as Augustine saith in his book *De Civitate Dei*, 'He is a slave though he domineer and rule.'

A man till he be in Christ is a slave; not of one man or of one lord over him, but he hath so many lords as he hath so many lusts. There are but two kingdoms that the Scripture speaks of, that is, the kingdom of Satan and darkness, and the kingdom of Christ; all therefore that are not in the kingdom of Christ, in that blessed liberty, they must needs be shoaled‡ under the other kingdom of Satan. This is a ground. Therefore I speak shortly of it, as an incentive and provocation to stir us up, to get into Christ, to get the Spirit of Christ, that we may have this spiritual liberty, or else we are all slaves, notwithstanding all our civil liberties, whatsoever they be. Now, 'where the Spirit of Christ is there is liberty,' there is freedom from that bondage that we are in by nature, and which is strengthened by a wicked course of life. For though we be all slaves by nature, born slaves, yet notwithstanding by a wicked course of life, we put ourselves into bonds and tangle ourselves; so many sins and so many repetitions of sin, so many cords; the longer a man lives the greater slave he is. Now when the Spirit of Christ comes, it frees us from all; both from the natural and from the customary§ slavery.

Now this liberty is wrought by Christ and applied by the Spirit. What Christ works he makes it ours by his Spirit, which takes all from Christ. As Christ doth all by the Spirit, so the Spirit takes all from Christ. All the comfort it hath is from reasons taken from Christ, from grounds from Christ, and doctrines from Christ, but yet both have their efficacy—Christ as the meritorious cause, and the Spirit as the applying cause. The Spirit discovers the state of bondage we are in by nature, and it discovers withal a more excellent condition; and as it discovers, so likewise the Spirit of God brings us to this state, by working faith in that that Christ hath done for us. Christ hath freed us by his death from the curse of the law, from the wrath of God, from death and damnation, and the like. Now whatsoever Christ hath done the Spirit works faith, to make this our own by uniting us to Christ. When Christ and we are one, his sufferings are ours, and his victory is ours, all is ours. Then the Spirit persuading us of the love of God, and Christ redeeming us from that cursed slavery we were in,

* That is, 'chooses.'—G.
† That is, 'naughty' = 'wicked.'—G.
‡ That is, = massed.—G.
§ That is, = through custom, habit.—G.

that Spirit, it works love in us, and other graces whereby the dominion of sin is broken more and more, and we are set at liberty by the Spirit.

Now the Spirit doth not work liberty properly originally, but Christ is the grand redeemer. But Christ redeemeth two ways.

First, He redeems us by paying the price, and so he only* redeemeth, for he paid the price to divine justice. We are in bondage to the wrath of God under his justice; and so there must be satisfaction to justice before we can be free.

Then, *secondly, We are in bondage to Satan*, as God's executioner and jailor. Now from him we are freed by strong hand. So Christ freeth us by his Holy Spirit, working such graces in us as makes us see the loathsomeness of that bondage; working likewise grace in us to be in love with a better condition, that the Spirit discovers to us. So that the Spirit brings us out by discovery and by power. All that Christ freeth by virtue of redemption, paying the price for, all those he frees likewise by his Spirit, discovering to them their bondage, and the blessed condition whereunto they are to be brought to a state of freedom, which freedom he perfects by little and little, till he bring them to a glorious freedom in heaven.

And the reason of this,—that where Christ doth free by way of redemption, to die and satisfy God's justice for any, to those he gives his Spirit, by which Spirit they are set at liberty—the reasons are manifold. To name one or two.

[1.] *Christ doth save all that he doth save answerable to the nature of the party saved.* He saves them as reasonable persons, for he saves us that he may make us friends. He saves us as men, and redeems us as men. He doth not only pay a price for us as we buy a thing that is dead, but likewise he frees us, so as we may understand to what, and by whom we are freed, and what condition we are freed from. Therefore there must be a Spirit joined with the work of Christ, to inform us thoroughly, being creatures fit to be informed.

[2.] And God intending to come into covenant with us, that we may be friends with him, which is our glory and happiness, *he acquaints us as friends with all the favours and blessings that he hath done for us.* He acquaints us what misery he brings us out of, and what happiness he brings us unto, and what is our duty. This is the work of the Spirit, to shew us what he hath done for us, that we may be friends.

[3.] *And then it is a ground to love God.* God saveth us by a way of love in the covenant of grace. His desire is that we may love him again, and maintain love. Now how can this be, without the Spirit of God discover what God in Christ hath done for us? Therefore there must be the Spirit to shew to the eye of the soul, and to tell us, this Christ hath done for us.

[4.] Then again there must *be a fitting for heaven, for that glory that God intends us in election.* Now this fitting must be altogether by the Spirit. The same Spirit that sanctified Christ in the womb, the same Spirit that anointed Christ, anoints all those that are Christ's, that they may be fit for so glorious a head. So there must be the Spirit as well as Christ in the work of redemption and liberty.

Now this Spirit of God doth set us at liberty, in all the course and whole carriage of salvation, from the beginning to the end.

He sets us at liberty at the first in calling us.

He sets us at liberty when we are justified.

* That is, = 'alone.'

He sets us at liberty when he sanctifieth us.

And he sets us then at liberty fully in glorification.

First of all, the Spirit of God is a Spirit of liberty, *when we are first called powerfully and effectually*. For living in the church sets us not at liberty, unless the Spirit stir us up to answer a divine call. 'For many are called but few are chosen,' Mat. xx. 16. In the church there is Hagar and Ishmael as well as Isaac. There are hypocrites as well as sound Christians. There is outward baptism as well as inward. There is outward circumcision of the flesh as well as inward of the spirit. A man may have all these outward privileges, and yet notwithstanding be a slave in the bosom of the church; for Ishmael was a bond-slave though he were in the house of Abraham. Therefore the first beginning of spiritual liberty is, (1.) *When the Spirit of God in the ordinances, in the means of salvation, stirs up the heart to answer God's call as it were.* When we are exhorted to believe and repent, the Spirit gives power to echo to God, 'Lord, I believe; help thou my unbelief,' Mark ix. 24. Lord, I repent, and desire to repent more and more. When the Spirit of God in the ordinance saith, 'Seek my face, Thy face, Lord, will I seek,' Ps. xxvii. 8. Be thou mine, Lord, and I will be thine. This spiritual echo and answer of the soul comes from the Spirit of God in calling, and it is the first degree of liberty.

(2.) Now this answer of the soul, by the power of the Spirit, overpowering our corruptions, is *together with the obedience of the inward man to go out*. For man answereth the call, not only by the speech of the heart, Lord, I do it; but he doth it indeed. Therefore when by the power of the Spirit we come out of the world and out of our corruptions, and walk more freely in the ways of God, then we are set at spiritual liberty. Now the Spirit doth all this. For if it were not the Spirit that persuaded the soul, when the minister speaks, alas! all ministerial persuasions are to no purpose. If the Spirit do not stir up the soul to answer, all speech is to no purpose from men. But this the Spirit doth. In the first place he openeth the eyes with spiritual eye-salve to see our natural bondage; he openeth our eyes to see, I must come out of this condition if I will be saved, of necessity, or else I am miserable for ever. And it is enough for the soul of a miserable man if he be convinced to see his misery and bondage, what he is by nature; for let us be convinced of that once, and all the rest of the links of the golden chain of salvation will follow. Let a man be convinced that he is as the Scripture saith he is, and as hereafter he shall find to his cost, you shall not need to bid him come out of his conversation and condition, and worldly course that he is in. All this will follow where there is conviction of spirit. Therefore the first work of the Spirit in spiritual liberty is to convince us of sin and misery; and then to work, as I said, an answer of the soul, and an obedience of the whole man. This I will not be long in, being a clear point.

Second, 'Where the Spirit is, there is liberty.' Again, *in matter of justification* there is a liberty and freedom of conscience from sin and the curse of sin, and all the danger that follows upon sin, by the Spirit.

Obj. But you will say, the liberty of justification is wrought by Christ; we are justified by the obedience of Christ; and the righteousness of Christ is imputed to us.

Ans. It is true Christ is our righteousness. But what is that to us except we have something to put it on? Except we be united to Christ, what good have we by Christ if Christ be not ours? If there be not a spiritual marriage, what benefit have we by him if we have not him to pay our debt? For his riches to be ours, and our debt to be his, there must be a union first. Now this union is wrought by the Spirit. It is begun in effectual calling. From this union there comes to be a change; his righteousness is mine, as if I had obeyed and done it by myself; and my debts and sins are his. This is by the Spirit, because the union between Christ and me is by the Spirit. For whatsoever Christ hath done, it is nothing to me till there be a union. And then freedom is by the Spirit likewise, because the Spirit of God works faith in me, not only to unite and knit me to Christ, but faith to persuade me that Christ is mine, and that all his is mine, and that my debts are his. This supernatural hand of faith the Spirit works to lay hold upon Christ, and then to persuade me. For the Spirit is a lightsome thing, and together with the graces it tells me the graces it works. As reason, besides reason, it tells me that I use reason when I do. It hath a reflex act. So the Spirit of Christ it hath a reflex act upon itself; for, being above reason, it doth not only lay hold upon Christ, it doth not only do the work, but it tells me that I do so when I do. Therefore it not only tells me that Christ is mine when I believe, but it assures me that I do believe. It carries a light of its own. I know the light by the light, and reason by reason, and faith by faith, together with the reflex act joining with it. So that the reflex act joining with it, the Spirit is the cause of liberty in justification in that respect, as it is a means of union, whereupon there is a passage of all that is Christ's to be mine, and mine to be Christ's. And likewise it assures me that I do believe, when I do believe without error. For the Spirit is given me to know the things that I have by Christ, not only to know the privileges by Christ, but the graces of Christ.

And, beloved, unless the Spirit should do it, it would never be done; for the soul of man is so full of terrors and fears and jealousies, that except the Spirit of God witness to my spirit, that God is reconciled in Christ, and that Christ's righteousness is mine, I could never be persuaded of it. For the soul it alway thinks God is holiness itself, and I am a mass of sin. What reason have I to think that God will be so favourable to such a wretch, to such a lump of sin as I am, were it not that God the Son hath satisfied God the Father? God hath satisfied God; and the Spirit certifies my conscience. So the Spirit, that searcheth the deep things of God, that knows what love is in the breast of God, and therefore he searcheth the heart, he searcheth the heart of God, and he searcheth my spirit. Except the Spirit should tell me that God the Son hath satisfied (and God the Father will accept of the satisfaction of God the Son), I should never believe it. Therefore God must stablish the heart in a gracious liberty of justification, as well as that God the Son hath wrought it.

It is no wonder that men of great parts without grace are full of terrors and despair; for the more parts and wit a man hath without the Spirit of God, the more he disputes against himself, and entangles himself with desperate thoughts. But when the Spirit is brought to speak peace to the soul in Christ, and makes the soul to cast itself on him for salvation, then God's Spirit is above the conscience. Though conscience be above all things else, yet God is above conscience, and can still the conscience; and the Spirit tells us that God the Father is reconciled by the death of God the Son. And when God witnesseth what God hath wrought, then conscience is at peace. Thus we see how the Spirit sets us at liberty in the great matter of justification.

Third, So likewise in the matter *of holy life, in the whole course of a holy life*, 'where the Spirit of Christ is, there is liberty,' and freedom from the slavery of sin. For there the understanding is freed from the bondage of ignorance, and there the will is freed from the bondage of rebellion ; there the affections likewise, and the whole inward and outward man is freed. But this liberty of holiness, inherent liberty, it doth spring from the liberty that we have by justification, by the righteousness of Christ, whereby we are perfectly righteous, and freed from all the title that Satan hath in us. We are freed from the curse of God, from the law, and enabled in a course of sanctification to go on from grace to grace. The Spirit of Christ comes after justification. For whom God gives forgiveness unto, he gives his Spirit to sanctify them. The same Spirit that assures me of the pardon of my sin, sanctifies my nature. Where the Spirit is of sanctification, it breaks the ruling power of sin. Before then the whole life is nothing but a continual sinning and offending of God ; but now there is a gracious liberty of disposition, a largeness of heart which follows the liberty of condition. When a man is free in state and law from wrath, and from the sentence of damnation, then he hath a free and voluntary disposition wrought to serve God freely, without fear or constraint.

When a man is under the bondage of the law, when he is under the fear of death, being armed with a sting, whatsoever he doth he doth it with a slavish mind. Where the Spirit of God is, there is the spirit of adoption, the spirit of sons, which is a free spirit. The son doth not duties to his father out of constraint and fear, but out of nature. The Spirit alters our nature and disposition. It makes us sons, and then we do all freely. God doth enlarge the hearts of his children. They can deny themselves in a good work. They are 'zealous of good works.' It is the end of their redemption ; as it is Tit. ii. 14, 'We are redeemed to be a peculiar people, zealous of good works.' For then we have a base esteem of all things that hinder us from freeness in God's service, as worldliness, &c. What doth a Christian when he seeth his gracious liberty in Christ ? The love of the world and worldly things, he is ready to part with all for the service of God. He is so free-hearted that he can part with life itself. Paul saith of himself, 'My life is not dear to me, so I may finish my course with joy,' Acts xx. 24. As we see in the martyrs and others how free they were, even of their very blood.

What shall we think of those therefore, that if we get anything of them, it must be as a sparkle out of the flint. Duties come from Christians as water out of a spring. They are natural, and not forced to issue, so far forth as they are spiritual.

I confess that there is remainders of bondage where the Spirit sets at liberty ; for there is a double principle in us, while we live in this world, of nature and grace. Therefore there will be a conflict in every holy duty. The flesh will draw back when the Spirit would be liberal. The flesh will say, Oh but I may want ! When the Spirit would be most courageous, the flesh will say, But there is danger in it. So that there is nothing that we can do but it must be gotten out of the fire. We must resist. Yet notwithstanding here is liberty to do good, because here is a principle that resists the backwardness of the flesh.

In a wicked man there is nothing but flesh, and therefore there is no resistance. And we must understand the nature of this spiritual liberty in sanctification. It is not a liberty freeing us altogether from conflict, and deadness, and dulness, and the like ; but it is a liberty enabling us to combat, not freeing us from combat. It is a liberty to fight the battles of the Lord against our own corruptions, not freeing us from it. That is the liberty of glory in heaven, when there shall be no enemy within or without.

Therefore let not Christians be discouraged with the backwardness and untowardness of the flesh, to good duties. If we have a principle in us to fight against it, to enable us to fight against our corruptions, and to get good duties out of it in spite of it, it is an argument of a new nature. God will perfect his own beginnings, and subdue the flesh more and more, by the power of his Spirit. We see our blessed Saviour, what a sweet excuse he makes for his disciples when they were dead-hearted and drowsy, when they should have comforted him in the garden: Oh, saith he, 'the spirit is willing, but the flesh is weak,' Mat. xxvi. 41.

Indeed, there is a double hindrance in God's people when they are about holy duties, sometimes from their very mould and nature, considered not as corrupted; the very mould without the consideration.

And then consider it as it is made more heavy and dull by the flesh, and corruptions in them, as there be invincible infirmities and weaknesses in nature. Sometimes deadness, after labour and expense of spirits, creeps in invincibly, that a man cannot overcome those necessities of nature. So that 'the spirit may be willing, and the flesh weak;' the flesh without any great corruption. God looks upon our necessities; as the father saith, Free me from my necessities (*a*). As we see, Christ made an excuse for them. It was not so much corruption, though that were an ingredient in it, as nature in itself. Christ saw a great deal of gold in the ore, therefore we see how he excuseth them. Therefore when we are dull, let us strive. Christ is ready to make excuse for us, if our hearts be right: 'The spirit is willing, but the flesh is weak.' I speak this for the comfort of the best sort of Christians, that think they are not set at liberty by the Spirit, because they find some heaviness and dulness in good duties. As I said, there is sin in us while we live here, but it reigns not. After a man hath the Spirit of Christ, the Spirit of Christ maintains a perpetual combat and conflict against sin. It could subdue sin all at once if God saw it good; but God will humble us while we live here, and exercise us with spiritual conflicts. Therefore God sees it sufficient to bring us to heaven, to set up a combat in us, that we are able by the help of the Spirit to fight God's battles against the flesh. So that the dominion of sin may be broken in us, and excellently, saith Paul, Rom. viii. 2, 'The law of the spirit of life in Christ Jesus hath freed me from the law of sin and of death.' The law of the Spirit of life, that is, the commanding power of the Spirit of Christ, that commands as a law in the hearts of God's people, it frees us from the law, that is, from the commanding power of sin and death. So that the dominion and tyranny of sin is broken by the Spirit of Christ, and so we are set at a gracious liberty. In some respects we are under grace, therefore sin shall not have dominion over us, as the apostle speaks.

Again, by the Spirit of Christ in sanctification we are made kings, to rule over our own lusts in some measure; not kings to be freed altogether from them, but kings to strive against them. It is a liberty to fight, and in fighting to overcome at last. When the Israelites had a promise that God would give their enemies into their hands, the meaning was not that he would give them without fighting a blow, but I will give them into your hands. You shall fight; and be of good comfort, in fighting you shall overcome. So this liberty of sanctification, it is not a liberty that we should have no combat with our corruptions, but a gracious liberty to keep them under, till by subduing them by little and little, we get a perfect victory. What greater encouragement can a man have to fight against his enemy, than when he is sure of the victory before he fights, of final victory! You see then how the Spirit brings a liberty into the soul. It brings us out of that cursed kingdom of Satan and sin. It brings us out of the curse of God and the law in justification; and it brings us from the dominion and tyranny of sin, by a spirit of sanctification.

But this is not all that is in liberty; for the Spirit doth not only free us from all that is ill, from sin, but from that that follows it. There is some ill that follows, as fear and terrors of conscience, &c. They follow sin and death and wrath, and such like, the subjection to these. Now, where the Spirit of God is, it frees from the ill consequents, from the tail that follows sin. Where the Spirit is, it frees us from fear; for the same Spirit that tells us in justification that God is appeased, the same Spirit frees us from the fear of damnation and death and judgment; from the terrors of an evil conscience. Being 'sprinkled with the blood of Christ,' 1 Pet. i. 2, we are freed from fear.

And it frees not only from the fear of ill things, but it shews immunity and freedom to good. Liberty implies here two things: a freedom from ill, from a cursed condition, and likewise a liberty to a better; a liberty from ill, and to good. We must take it in the just latitude, because the benefits of Christ are complete, not only privative but positive; not only to free us from ill, but to confer all good to us, as much as our nature is capable of. As much as these souls of ours are capable of, they shall be made free and glorious and happy in heaven, God will leave no part of the soul unfilled, no corner of the soul empty. By little and little he doeth it, as we shall see in the next verse. When we are called out of Satan's kingdom we are not only called out of that cursed state, but we are made free of a better kingdom; we are made the members of Christ; we are enfranchised. And so in justification we are not only freed from damnation, from the justice and wrath of God, but likewise we can implead* our righteousness whereby we have title to heaven, which is a blessed privilege and prerogative. We are not only free from the curse of the law, but likewise we have other gracious prerogatives and privileges. We are not only freed from the dominion of sin, but we are likewise set at liberty by the Spirit to do that that is good. We have a voluntary free spirit to serve God with as great cheerfulness as we served our lusts before; and as we are freed from the rigour and curse of the law, so we have prerogatives to good answerable. We are now by the Spirit set at liberty to delight in the law, to make the law our counsellor, to make the word of God our counsellor. That that terrified and affrighted us before, now it is our direction. Even as he that was a severe schoolmaster to one in his under years, after, when he comes to years, becomes a wise tutor to guide and direct him; so the law that terrified and whipped us when we were in bondage, till we be in Christ,—it scares us to Christ,—that law after comes to be a tutor, to tell us this we shall do, to counsel us, and say this is the best way; and we come to delight in those truths, when they are discovered to us in the inward man. And the more we know, the more we would know, because we would please God every day better. So that besides freedom from that that is ill, and the consequents of ill, there is a blessed immunity and prerogative and privilege. That is meant here by liberty.

For God's works are complete. We must know when he delivers from

* That is, = 'use the plea.'—G.

ill he advanceth to good. His works are full works always. He doth not things by halves. Therefore we have through Christ, and by the Spirit, not only freedom from that that is ill, but advancement to all that is comfortable and graciously good.

And one thing give me leave to touch, which though it be more subtle, yet it is useful, that the text puts me to speak of. 'Where the Spirit of God is, there is liberty' of the inward man, liberty of judgment, and liberty of will. Where the Spirit of God is not, there is no liberty, no free will. A little to touch upon that.

That which we call free will, it is either taken for a natural power and endowment that God hath put upon the soul, and so the will is alway free in earth and in hell. The devil's will is free so, free to evil. There is the natural freedom; for freedom it is a dowry upon the will, invested upon the will, that God never takes from it. To do it freely, that is, upon reason that it sees, be it good or evil, so I mean not freedom; but I take freedom for ability and strength to that that is good. For any liberty and ability to that that is good is only from the Spirit; and the defence of Luther's and others (*b*), that wrote of this freedom, is sound and good, that the will of man is slavish altogether, without the Spirit of God. 'Where the Spirit is there is liberty:' liberty as it is taken for power and ability to do good. In a word, there is alway a liberty of the subject, of the person; a liberty of the understanding, but not of the object, to this or to that thing. A liberty to supernatural objects comes from supernatural principles. Nothing moves above its own sphere; nothing is acted above its own activity, that God hath put into it. Now a natural man can do nothing but naturally; for nothing can work above itself, by its own strength, no more than a beast can work according to the principles of a man. Therefore the soul of man hath no liberty at all to that which is spiritually good, without a supernatural principle, that raiseth it above itself, and puts it into the rank of supernatural things.

First, The Spirit of God puts a new life into the soul of a man; and then when he hath done that, it preserves that life against all opposition; and together with preserving that life, it applies that inward life and power it hath put into it to particular works. For when we have a new life, yet we cannot do particular actions without the exciting power of the Spirit of God. The Spirit stirs up to every particular thing, when the soul would be quiet of itself. The moving comes from the Spirit of God. As every particular moving in the body comes from the soul, so the Spirit it puts a new life, it applies that life, it applies the soul to every action. Where the Spirit of God therefore is not, there is no liberty to any supernatural action; but 'where the Spirit of God is, there is liberty.' It follows both negatively and affirmatively. There is a liberty of will to that that is good. So then this riseth from hence, again, that where the Spirit of God is efficacious and effectual in his working, there it robs not the soul of liberty, but perfects that liberty.

You have some divines, too many indeed, that hold that the Holy Ghost only works by way of persuasion upon the soul, and by way of moving, as it were, without; but he doth not enter into the soul, nor alter and change the soul; he doth not work upon the soul as an inward worker, but only as an outward entreater and persuader and allurer, propounding objects, and with objects persuasions and allurements. This is too shallow a conceit for so deep a business as this; for the Spirit works more deeply than so. It puts a new life into the soul; it takes away the stony heart and gives a fleshly heart, Ezek. xl. 19. Those phrases of Scripture are too weighty to fasten such a shallow sense upon them, only as to entreat them to be converted, as a man would entreat a stone to be warm, and to come out of its place. He might entreat long enough. But the Spirit with that speech, it puts a new life and power, and then acts and stirs that power to all that is good.

Obj. Oh, say they, which is their main objection, here is a prejudice to the liberty of the will! This is to overthrow the nature of man!

Ans. Oh, by no means! This is no prejudice to the liberty of the will; for the Spirit of God is so wise an agent that he works upon the soul, preserving the principles of a man. It alters the judgment by presenting greater reasons, and further light than it saw before; and then it alters the will, that we will contrary to that we did before, by presenting to the will greater reasons to be good than ever it had to be ill before. Then the soul chooseth freely of its own will any thing, when it doth it upon discovery of light and reason, with advisement and reason. Then the soul doth things freely, when it doth them upon the designment of reason, when judgment tells me this is good. Now when the Spirit changeth the soul, it presents such strong reasons to come out of that cursed estate I am in, and to come to the blessed estate in Christ, that the will presently follows that that the understanding presents as the chief good of all. Here the freedom is preserved, because the will is so stirred by the Holy Ghost, as that it stirs itself, being stirred by the Holy Ghost; and upon this ground it sees a better good. So that grace takes not away liberty. No; it stablisheth liberty. Though we hold that in effectual grace the Spirit of God works upon the soul throughly, yet notwithstanding we preserve liberty, because we say that the soul works of its own principles, notwithstanding grace; because the Spirit of God acts and leads the soul according to the nature of the soul. The Spirit of God preserves things in the manner of doing of things. It is the manner of doing of the reasonable creature, to do things freely. Therefore the Spirit working upon the soul, it preserves that *modus*, though it work effectually upon the soul; and the more effectually it works upon the soul, the more* the soul is; because it seeth reason to do good. Therefore the more we give to the Spirit in the question of grace and nature, the more we stablish liberty, and prejudice it not. Where these three or four rules are observed, there liberty is preserved, though there be a mighty working of the Holy Spirit; as,

First, Where the will chooseth and makes choice, and inclines to a thing with the advisement of reason. Alway that must be, or else it is not a human action. Now when the Spirit of God sets the will at liberty, a man doth that he doth with full advisement of reason; for though God work upon the will, it is with enlightening of the understanding at the same time; and all grace in the will comes through the understanding, as all heat upon inferior things it comes with light. So that though heat cherish the earth, it comes with light. So all the work upon the soul is by the heat of the Spirit. But it comes from the light of the understanding. So the freedom of the soul is preserved, because it is with light.

Second; Again, where freedom is, *there is a power to apprehend other things, as well as that it doth; to reason on both sides, I may do this or that.* For that power to reason on both sides is proper to the soul alway. Now grace takes not away that power to reason on both sides; for when a man is set at liberty from the base slavery of ill to do good, he can reason with himself, I might have done this and that if I would be damned. So that the judgment is not bound to one thing only, but the judgment tells him

* Qu. 'the more free'?—Ed.

he might have done otherwise if he would; but he sees he must do this if he will not be damned.

Third; Again, *where there is liberty and freedom, there is an enlargement to understand more things than one, or else there were no freedom;* and though the soul be determined to choose one thing, and not many, yet of itself it hath power to choose many things. To make this clear a little: some creatures are confined to one thing, out of the narrowness of the parts they have; some are confined to one thing, out of the largeness of parts. These seem contrary, but thus I will give this instance to make it clear. The creature that is unreasonable* is alway confined to one manner of working, because they want understanding to work in a diverse manner. Birds make their nests and bees make their hives always after one manner, because of their narrowness, that they have not choice.

Now when the Spirit sets a man at liberty to holy things, he is confined to good; especiall[y] this is in heaven. This is out of largeness of understanding, apprehending many goods and many ills; and that good that he conceives to be the best good, out of a large understanding he is determined to that one. So that, though the Spirit of God take away as it were that present liberty that a man cannot do ill,—it will not suffer him to be so bad as he was,—yet it leaves him in a state of good, to do a multitude of good things. And then, though it confine him to a state of happiness, that he cannot will the contrary, yet here is no liberty taken away, because it is done out of strength of knowledge, not out of narrowness; because there is no more things for him to judge, but out of largeness, telling him this is the best of all, and carries all the soul after it. The glory of heaven robs not a man of his power.

What is the reason they are determined eternally to that that is good? Is it for want of understanding that the angels choose not ill? No! They know what ill is by speculation, but there is a strength of understanding to know that that is good; and the understanding, where it hath full light, it carries the will to choose. Therefore 'where the Spirit of the Lord is, there is liberty.' Notwithstanding all objections to the contrary, the Spirit takes not away, nay, it strengtheneth, the liberty of the soul. It is an idle objection and a great stay of many that are willing to be deceived, Oh if grace confine a man, determine him, as the word is, sway him one way perpetually, that he holds on to the end, and leaves him not at liberty to his will, this confining and swaying one way it is an abridging him of his liberty, &c. No. For it comes not from weakness of understanding, but from strength of understanding; and it is perfect liberty to do well. Therefore, on the contrary, it is so far from abridging the liberty of the soul that it cannot do ill, or that it cannot but persevere to do good, that it is the strength of liberty.

For I would know whether the first Adam's liberty were greater, or the liberty in heaven, the second Adam's liberty? Our liberty in grace or that in glory? The liberty of the first man was, that he might not sin if he would; the liberty of Christ was, that he could not sin at all. Which think you was the chief? He that could not, or he that might not sin if he would? Was there not a more gracious and blessed liberty in Christ than in Adam, when he might not sin if he would? Is this a worse liberty then when a man cannot sin? So when the Spirit of God bears that sway over the soul, and takes away that potentiality and possibility to sin, that a man cannot sin, because he will not, his will is so carried by the

* That is, 'without reason.'—G.

strength of judgment, this is the greatest good. I will not move out of this circle. If I go out of this I shall be unhappy. And this is the greatest liberty of all.

What do we pray in the Lord's prayer but for this liberty? 'Thy will be done,' Mat. vi. 10. That is, take me out of my own will more and more; conform my will to thine in all things. The more I do so, the more liberty I have. The strength of that petition is, that we may have perfect liberty in serving God.

The greatest and sweetest liberty is, when we have no liberty to sin at all; when we cannot sin. It is greater chastity not to have power to resist, to be impregnable in continence and sobriety. When there is such a measure of these graces as they are not to be overcome, it is greater strength than when they may be prevailed over. So men mistake to think this the greatest liberty to have power to good or evil. That is the imperfection of the creature. Man was at the first created free to either good or evil of himself, that he might fall of himself. This was not strength, but a thing that followed the creature that came out of nothing, and that was subject to fall to his own principles again. But to have the soul stablished that it shall not have freedom to ill, it is so stablished in good. It hath the understanding so enlightened, and the will so confirmed and strengthened, that it is without danger of temptation. That is properly glorious liberty, and that is the better endowment of both, so that we see it clearly that grace takes not away liberty, but establisheth it.

Now besides this inward spiritual liberty that we have by the Spirit, there is an outward preserving liberty that must be a little touched, and that is twofold.

(1.) *A liberty of preaching the gospel; and* (2.) *A liberty of discipline, as we call it;* of government that is in the church of God; and should be at least in all places, because we are men, and must have such helps. Now these are liberties that the Spirit bestows upon the church wheresoever there is an inward spiritual liberty. Men are brought into the church by the liberty of the gospel, and preserved by government. There must be a subjection to pastors; there must be teaching and some discipline, or else all will be in a confusion. Now this inward liberty is wrought by the liberty of the gospel.

Quest. What is the liberty of the gospel?

Ans. When there is a blessed liberty in the church to have true liberty opened, the charter of our liberty.

Quest. What is the charter of our liberty?

Ans. The word of God. When the charter and patent of our liberty is laid open, in laying it open we come to have interest in those liberties. Therefore the liberty of the temple, the liberty of the church, of the word and sacraments, and some order in the church with it, it brings in spiritual liberty and preserves it. It is as it were the bonds and sinews of the church. Now where the Spirit of God is with the gospel, there is this liberty of the gospel; there are the doors of the temple and sanctuary set open, as, blessed be God, this kingdom hath had. With the spiritual liberty, there is an outward liberty of the tabernacle of God and the house of God, that we can all meet to hear the word of God and to receive the sacraments; that we can all meet to call upon God in spirit and in truth; and these outward liberties, beloved, are blessed liberties. For where God gives these outward liberties, he intends to bestow and to convey spiritual liberty. How shall we come to spiritual liberty without unfolding the charter, the word of God? Therefore Christ hath established a ministry, apostles, and doctors,* and pastors, to edify the church to the end of the world; and therefore we see where there is no outward liberty of unfolding the word, where there is no outward liberty of the ministry, there wants this inward liberty. For God by the preaching of the gospel sets us at liberty.

Again, when Christ preached the gospel first, it was the year of jubilee. Now, in the year of jubilee, all servants were set at liberty, and those that had not sold† their inheritances might recover them again if they would. This jubilee was a type of the spiritual liberty that the gospel sets us at. Those that have served sin and Satan before, if they will regard the gracious promises of the gospel, they may of slaves of sin and Satan become the free men of Jesus Christ. But in those times some would be servants still, and would not be set at liberty. Their ears were bored for perpetual slaves;‡ and it is pity but their ears should be bored for everlasting slaves, that now, in the glorious jubilee of the gospel, resolve still to be slaves. When a proclamation of liberty was made to come out of Babylon all that would, many would stick there still. So many are in love with Egypt and Babylon and slavery. It is pity but they should be slaves. But those that have more noble spirits, as they desire liberty, so they should desire spiritual liberty especially. And here you see how to come by it. 'Where the Spirit of the Lord is, there is liberty;' and where the ordinance of God is; that is, the ministry of the Spirit, there is the Spirit. Where these outward liberties are, it is a sign that God hath an intendment to set men at spiritual liberty.

Those, therefore, that are enemies of the dispensation of the gospel in the ministry, they are enemies to spiritual liberty; and it is an argument that a man is in bondage to Satan when he is an enemy any way of the unfolding of the word of God. For it is an argument that he is licentious, that he will not be called to spiritual liberty, but live according to the flesh; when he will not hear of the liberty of the Spirit, as you have some kind of men that account it a bondage, 'Let us break their bands, and cast away their cords,' Ps. ii. 3. Why should we be tied with the word and with these holy things? It is better that we have no preaching, no order at all, but live every man as he would. Though they speak not so in words, yet their lives and profane carriage shew that they regard not outward liberties; and that argueth that they are in spiritual bondage, and that they have no interest in spiritual liberty, because they are enemies of that whereby spiritual liberty is preserved.

Therefore the gospel is set out by that phrase, 'The kingdom of God.' Not only the kingdom of God set up in our hearts, the kingdom of the Spirit, but likewise where the gospel is preached, there is the kingdom of God. Why? Because with the dispensation of divine truth Christ comes to rule in the heart; by the outward kingdom comes the spiritual kingdom. They come under one name.

Therefore those that would have the spiritual kingdom of God, by grace and peace to rule in their hearts till they reign for ever in heaven, they must come by this door, by the ministry, by the outward ordinance. The ordinance brings them to grace; and grace to glory. And it is a good and sweet sign of a man spiritually set at liberty, brought out of the kingdom of Satan, and freed from the guilt of sin, and from the dominion of sin, which

* That is, 'teachers.'—G.

† Qu. 'had sold'?—Ed.

‡ Cf. Exodus xxi. 6.—G.

is broken in sanctification, when we can meekly and cheerfully submit to the ordinance of God, with a desire to have his spiritual thraldom discovered, and to have spiritual duties unfolded, and the riches of Christ laid open. When he hears these things with a taste and relish, and a love, it is a sign God loves his soul, and that he hath interest in spiritual liberty, because he can improve the charter of his soul so well. 'Where the Spirit of the Lord is, there is liberty.'

And besides this liberty in this world, there is a liberty of glory, called 'the liberty of the sons of God,' Rom. viii. 21. The liberty of our bodies from corruption, the glorious liberty in heaven, when we shall be perfectly free. For, alas! in this world we are free to fight, not free from fight; and we are free, not from misery, but free from thraldom to misery. But then we shall be free from the encounter and encumbrance. 'All tears shall be wiped from our eyes,' Rev. vii. 17. We shall be free from all hurt of body, in sickness and the like, and free from all the remainders of sin in our souls: that is perfect liberty, perfect redemption, and perfect adoption, both of body and soul. And that we have by the Spirit too; for where the Spirit of God is, there is that too in this world in the beginning of it. For, beloved, what is peace of conscience and joy in the Holy Ghost? Is it not the beginnings of heaven? Is it not a grape of the heavenly Canaan? Is it not the Spirit that we have here an earnest of that inheritance? An earnest penny; and an earnest is a piece of the bargain. It is never taken away, but is made up with the bargain. Therefore, when by the Spirit we have the beginnings of grace and comfort, we have the beginnings of that glorious liberty; and it assures us of that glorious liberty as sure as we have the earnest. For God never repents of his bargain that he makes with his children. Grace in some sort is glory, as we see in the next verse; because grace is the beginning of glory. It frees the soul from terror and subjection to sin, from the thraldom of sin. So the life of glory is begun in grace. We have the life of glory begun by the Spirit, this glorious life.

Use 1. If we have all these blessed liberties in this world and in that to come by the Spirit, then we should labour *to have the Spirit of Christ, or else we have no liberty at all;* and labour every day more and more to get this spiritual liberty in our consciences, to have our consciences assured by the Spirit that our sins are forgiven, and to feel in our consciences a power to bring under sin that hath tyrannized over us before. Let us every day more and more labour to find this spiritual liberty, and prize daily more the ordinances of God, sanctified to set us at liberty. Attend upon spiritual means, that God hath sanctified, wherein he will convey the Spirit. There were certain times wherein the angel came to stir the waters of the pool, John v. 3. So the Spirit of God stirs the waters of the word and ordinances, and makes them effectual. Attend upon the ordinances of God, the communion of saints, &c., and the Spirit of God will slide into our souls in the use of holy means. There is no man but he finds experience of it. He finds himself raised above himself in the use of holy means. The more we know the gospel, the more we have of the Spirit; and the more Spirit we have, the more liberty we enjoy. If we prize and value outward liberty, as indeed we do, and we are naturally moved to do it, how should we prize the charter of our spiritual liberty, the word of God, and the promises of salvation (whereby we come to know all our liberty, where we have all the promises opened to us; the promise of forgiveness of sins, of necessary grace; the promise of comfort in all conditions whatsoever). Therefore let us every day labour to grow farther and farther both in the knowledge and in the taste and feeling of this spiritual liberty.

Use 2. *Oh beloved, what a blessed condition it is to have this spiritual liberty!* Do but see the blessed use and comfort of it in all conditions. For if a man hath the Spirit of God to set him at spiritual liberty, in all temptations, either to sin, he hath the Spirit of God to free him from temptation; or, if temptation catch hold on him for sin, he hath the Spirit of God to fly to, the blood of Christ, to shew that if he confess his sins and lay hold on Christ, he hath pardon of sin; and the blood of Christ 'speaks better things than the blood of Abel.' It speaks mercy and peace. If he by faith sprinkle it upon his soul, if he know the liberty of justification, and make use of it: what a blessed liberty is this when we have sinned!

In restraint of the outward man. If ever God restrain us to humble us, what a blessed thing is this, that the spirit is at liberty! and that is the best part of a man. A man may have a free conscience and mind, in a restrained condition; and a man may be restrained in a free state. In the guilt of sin, bound over to the wrath of God, and bound over to another evil day, a man in the greatest thraldom may have liberty. What a blessed condition is this!

So in sickness, to consider that there is a glorious liberty of the sons of God, and a redemption of body, as well as of soul, that this base body of mine shall be like Christ's glorious body; that there is a resurrection to glory—the resurrection will make amends for all these sicknesses and ills of body—what a comfort is it to think of the resurrection to glory!

And so when death comes, to know that by the blood of Christ there is a liberty to enter into heaven; that Christ by his blood hath opened a passage to heaven.

And so in all necessities, to think I have a liberty to the throne of grace; I am free of heaven; I am free of the company of saints in earth and in heaven too; I am free to have communion with God; I have a freedom in all the promises;—what a sweet thing is this, in all wants and necessities, to use a spiritual liberty, to have the ear of God, as a favourite in heaven! Not only to be free from the wrath of God, but to have his favour, to have his care in all our necessities: what a blessed liberty is this, that a man may go with boldness to the throne of grace by the Spirit of Christ!

Beloved, it is invaluable. There is not the least branch of this spiritual liberty but it is worth a thousand worlds. How should we value it, and bless God for giving Christ to work this blessed liberty; and for giving his Spirit to apply it to us more and more, and to set us more and more at spiritual liberty. For both the Father, and the Son, and the Holy Ghost, all join in this spiritual liberty. The Father gives the Son, and he gives the Spirit; and all to set us free. It is a comfortable and blessed condition.

Use 3. *But how shall we know whether we be set at liberty or no?* Because all will pretend a liberty from the law and from the curse of God, and his wrath in justification? And though it be the foundation of all, I will not speak of that, but of that that always accompanies it, a liberty of holiness, a liberty to serve God, a liberty from bondage to lusts, and to Satan. Therefore,

(1.) Wheresoever the Spirit of God is, there is a liberty *of holiness, to free us from the dominion of any one sin.* We are freed 'to serve him in holiness all the days of our lives,' Luke i. 75. Where the Spirit therefore is, it will free a man from thraldom to sin, even to any one sin. For the

Spirit discovers to the soul the odiousness of the bondage. For a man to be a slave to Satan, who is his enemy, a cruel enemy, what an odious thing is this! Now whosoever is enthralled to any lust, is in thraldom to Satan by that lust. Therefore where this liberty is, there cannot be slavery to any one lust. Satan therefore cares not how many sins one leaves, if he live in any one sin; for he hath them in one sin, and can pull them in by one sin. As children when they have a bird, they can give it leave to fly, so it be in a string to pull it back again; so Satan hath men in a string, if they live in any one sin. The Spirit of Christ is not there, but Satan's spirit, and he can pull them in when he will. The beast that runs away with a cord about him, he is catched by the cord again; so when we leave many sins, and yet notwithstanding carry his cords about us, he can pull us in when he lists. Such are prisoners at liberty more than others, but notwithstanding they are slaves to Satan by that, and where Satan keeps possession by one sin, and rules there, there is no liberty. For the spirit of sanctification where it is, is a counter-poison to the corruption of nature, and it is opposite to it, in all the powers of the soul. It suffers no corruption to get head.

(2.) Again, where this liberty from the Spirit is, there is not only a freedom from all gross sins, but likewise a blessed freedom *to all duties, an enlargement of heart to duties.* God's people are a voluntary people. Those that are under grace, they are 'anointed by the Spirit,' Ps. lxxxix. 20, and that spiritual anointment makes them nimble. Christian is nothing but anointed.* Now he that is truly anointed by the Spirit, is nimble, and quick, and active in that that is good in some degree and proportion. One use of anointing is to make the members nimble, and agile, and strong; so the Spirit of God is a spirit of cheerfulness and strength where it is. Therefore those that find some cheerfulness and strength to perform holy services, to hear the word, to pray to God, and to perform holy duties, it is a sign that this comes from the Spirit of God. The Spirit sets them at this liberty, because otherwise spiritual duties are as opposite to flesh and blood as fire and water. When we are drawn therefore to duties, as a bear to a stake, as we say, with foreign motives, for fear, or out of custom, with extrinsecal motives, and not from a new nature, this is not from the Spirit. This performance is not from the true liberty of the Spirit. For the liberty of the Spirit is, when actions come off naturally without force of fear or hope, or any extrinsecal motive. A child needs not extrinsecal motives to please his father. When he knows he is the child of a loving father, it is natural. So there is a new nature in those that have the Spirit of God to stir them up to duty, though God's motives may help as the sweet encouragements and rewards. But the principal is to do things naturally, not for fear, or for giving content to this or that man.

Artificial things move from a principle without them, therefore they are artificial. Clocks and such things have weights that stir all the wheels they go by, and that move them; so it is with an artificial Christian that composeth himself to a course of religion. He moves with weights without him; he hath not an inward principle of the Spirit to make things natural to him, and to excite and make him do things naturally and sweetly. 'Where the Spirit of God is, there is freedom;' that is, a kind of natural freedom, not forced, not moved by any foreign extrinsecal motive.

(3.) Again, where the freedom of spirit is, there is *a kind of courage against all opposition whatsoever, joined with a kind of light and strength of*

* That is, as Christ is = anointed, *so* Christian.—G.

faith, breaking through all oppositions. A consideration of the excellent state I am in; of the vileness of the state we are moved to by opposition;—when the Spirit discovers these things with a kind of conviction, what is all opposition to a spiritual man? It adds but courage and strength to him to resist. The more opposition, the more courage he hath. In Acts iv. 23, *seq.*, when they had the Spirit of God, they opposed opposition; and the more they were opposed, the more they grew. They were cast in prison, and rejoiced; and the more they were imprisoned, the more courageous they were still. There is no setting against this wind, nor no quenching of this fire, by any human power, where it is true; for the Spirit of God, where it sets a man at liberty indeed, it gathers strength by opposition. See how the Spirit triumphed in the martyrs over all opposition, fire, and imprisonment, and all. The Spirit in them set them at liberty from such base fears, that it prevails in them over all. The Spirit of God, where it is, is a victorious Spirit. It frees the soul from base fears of any creature. 'If God be on our side, who shall be against us?' Rom. viii. 33, 34. It is said of St Stephen, that they could not withstand the Spirit by which he spake, Acts vi. 10; and Christ promiseth a Spirit that all the enemies shall not be able to withstand: so those that are God's children, in the time of opposition, when they understand themselves and that to which they stand, God gives them a Spirit against which all their enemies cannot stand. The Spirit of Christ in Stephen put such a glory upon him, that he looked as if he had been an angel, Acts vi. 15; so the Spirit of liberty, where it is, it is with boldness, and strength, and courage against opposition. Those, therefore, that are awed with every petty thing for standing in a good cause, they have not the Spirit of Christ; for where that is, it frees men from these base fears, especially if the cause be God's.

(4.) Again, where the Spirit of liberty is, *it gives boldness with God himself*, and thus it is known especially where it is: 'where the Spirit is, there is liberty.' What to do? Even to go to God himself, that otherwise is a 'consuming fire,' Heb. xii. 29. For the Spirit of Christ goes through the mediation of Christ to God. Christ, by his Spirit, leads us to God. He that hath not the Spirit of God cannot go to God with a spirit of boldness. Therefore, when a man is in affliction, in the time of temptation or great affliction, especially when there is opposition, he may best judge what he is in truth. When a man is in temptation, or opposition from the world, within or without, and can go boldly to God, and pour out his soul to God freely and boldly as to a father, this comes from the Spirit of liberty. Where the Spirit of Christ is not, though the parts be never so strong, or never so great, it will never do thus. Take another man, in the time of extremity, he sinks; but take a child of God in extremity, yet he hath a spirit to go to God, and to cry, Abba, Father; to go in a familiar manner to God. Saul was a mighty man. When he was in anguish, he could not go to God. Cain could not go to God. Judas, a man of great knowledge, he could not go to God. His heart was naught;* he had not the Spirit of Christ, but the spirit of the devil; and the spirit of bondage bound him over for his treason to hell and destruction; because he had not the Spirit to go to God, but accounted him his enemy; he had betrayed Christ. If he had said as much to God as he did to the scribes and Pharisees, he might have had mercy in the force of the thing. I speak not of the decree of God, but in the nature of the thing itself. If he had said so much to Christ and to God, he might have found mercy. So let a man be never so

* That is, 'naughty'=wicked.—G.

great a sinner, if he can go to God, and spread his soul, and lay open his sins with any remorse; if he can come, and open his soul in confession and in petition, and beg mercy of God in Christ, to shine as a Father upon his soul—this Spirit of liberty to go to God, it argues that the Spirit of Christ is there, because there is liberty to go to God. In Rom. viii. 26, speaking there of comfort in afflictions, this is one among the rest, 'that the children of God have the Spirit of God, to stir up sighs and groans.' Now, where the Spirit of God stirs up sighs and groans, God understands the meaning of his own Spirit. There is the spirit of liberty, and there is the spirit of sons; for a spirit of liberty is the spirit of a son. A man may know that he is the son of God, and a member of Christ; and that he hath the spirit of liberty in him, if he can, in affliction and trouble, sigh and groan to God in the name and mediation of Christ; for the Spirit stirs up groans and sighs: they come from the Spirit.

That familiar boldness whereby we cry 'Abba, Father,' it comes from sons. They only can cry so. This comes from the Spirit. If we be sons, then we have the Spirit, whereby we cry, Abba, Father. So, if we can go to God with a sweet familiarity,—Father, have mercy upon me, forgive me; look in the bowels of pity upon me,—this sweet boldness and familiarity, it comes from the spirit of liberty, and shews that we are sons, and not bastards.

Your strong, rebellious, sturdy-hearted persons, who think to work out [of] their misery, out of the strength of parts and friends, &c., they die in despair. Their sorrows are too good for them. But when a broken soul goes to God in Christ with boldness, this opening of the soul to God, it is a sign of liberty, and of the liberty of sons, for this liberty here is the liberty of sons, of a spouse, of kings, of members of Christ: the sweetest liberty that can be imagined. It is the liberty that those sweet relations breed of a wife to the husband, and of loving subjects to their prince, and of children to their father. Here is a sweet liberty; and 'where the Spirit of God is, there is all this sweet liberty.'

There are three degrees that a man is in, that is in the way to heaven.

[1.] *The state of nature*, when he cares neither for heaven nor hell in a manner, so he may have sensual nature pleased, and go on without fear or wit,* without grace, nay, without the principles of nature, so he may satisfy himself in a course of sin. That is the worst state, the state of nature.

[2.] But God, if he belong to him, will not suffer him to be in this sottish and brutish condition long, *but brings him under the law;* that is, he sets his own corrupt nature before him, he shews him the course of his life, and then he is afraid of God: 'Depart from me, I am a sinner;' as Adam he ran from God when he had sinned, that was sweet to him before; so a brute man, when he is awakened with conscience of sin, considering that there is but a step between him and hell, and considering what a God he hath to deal with, and that after death there is eternal damnation,—when the Spirit of God hath convinced him of this, then he is in a state of fear, and when he is in this state, he is unfit to have liberty to run to God. He useth all his power to shift from God all he can, and hates God, and wisheth there were no God, and trembles at the very thought of God, and of death, &c.

[3.] Oh, but if a man belong to God, God will not leave him in this condition (and though this be better than the first, it is better that a man

* That is, 'wisdom' = knowledge.—G.

were out of his wits almost, than to be senseless as a block); there is another condition spoken of here, that is, *of liberty;* when God by his Spirit discovers to him in Christ forgiveness of sins, the gracious face of God ready to receive him, 'Come unto me all ye that are weary and heavy laden,' Mat. xi. 28, saith Christ; and 'where sin hath abounded, grace more abounds,' Rom. v. 20; when a man hears this still sweet voice of the gospel, he begins then to take comfort to himself, then he goes to God freely. Now all in this state of freedom, take them at the worst, they have boldness to go to God. David in his extremity, he runs to God. David trusted in the Lord his God. When he was at his wits' end, what doth Saul in his extremity? He runs to his sword's point, Judges ix. 54, *seq.* Take a man under nature, or under the law, in extremity, the greater wit he hath, the more he entangleth himself. His wit serves to entangle him, to weave a web of his own despair. But take a gracious man, that is acquainted with God in Christ, in such a man there is a liberty to go to God at the lowest; for he hath the Spirit of Christ in him. What did the Spirit in Christ himself direct him to do at the lowest? 'O my God, my God,' Mark xv. 34. In the deepest desertion, yet 'my God.' There was a liberty to go to God. So take a Christian that hath the same Spirit in him, as indeed he hath, 'My God' still. He owns God and knows him in all extremity.

Many are discovered hence to have no Spirit of God in them. In trouble whither go they? To their purse, to their friends, to anything. They labour to overcome their troubles one way or other, by physic and the like, but never to go with boldness and comfort, and a kind of familiarity to God. They have no familiarity with God. Therefore they have not a Spirit of liberty.

[4.] Again, where this Spirit of liberty is, as there is a freedom to go to God, *so in regard of the creature and the things here below, there is a freedom from popular, vulgar conceits, from the errors of the times and the slavish courses of the times.*

There are alway two sorts of wicked persons in the world.

(1.) *The one who accounts it their heaven and happiness, to domineer over others;* to bring them into subjection, and to rule over their consciences if they can, and sell all to please them, conscience and all.

(2.) Another sort again, *so they may gain, they will sell their liberty, their reason and all:* if it be but for a poor thing, so they may get anything that they value in the world, to make them beasts, as if they had no reasonable understanding souls, much less grace. Between those two, some domineering and others beastly serving, a few that go upon terms of Christianity, are of sound judgment. Now where the Spirit of God is, there is liberty, that is, a freedom not to enthral our judgments to any man, much less conscience. The judgment of man enlightened by reason is above any creature; for reason is a beam of God, and all the persons in the world ought not to think to have power over a man, to say anything against his knowledge.* It is to say against God, if it be but in civil matters, be it what it will. Judgment is the spark of God. Nature is but God's candle. It is a light of the same light that grace is of, but inferior. For a man to speak against his conscience to please men, where is liberty! For a man to enthral his conscience to please another man! No man that hath the spirit of a man will be so pharisaical, to say as another man saith, and to judge as another man judgeth, and to do all as another man doth, without seeing some

* That is, power to make a man say anything that he knows to be untrue.—G.

reason himself; going upon the principles of a man himself. It is true of a man as a man, unless he will unman himself. It is much more true of a Christian man. He will not for base fears and engagements enthral his conscience, and sell heaven and happiness and his comfort for this and that; and those that do it, though they talk of liberty, they are slaves; though they domineer in the world, the curse of Cain* is upon them, they are slaves of slaves.

Therefore, where the Spirit of Christ is, there is an independent liberty. A man is independent upon any other man, further than he sees it agrees with the rules of religion; and he is dependent only upon God, and upon divine principles and grounds. The apostle saith, 'The spiritual man judgeth all things, and is judged of none,' 1 Cor. ii. 15. So far as a man is 'led with the Spirit,' Rom. viii. 14, he discerns things in the light of the Spirit. He judgeth all things to be as they are, in the light of the Spirit, and is judged of none. His meaning is not, that none will usurp judgment of him, for that they will do. The emptiest men are most rash and censorious; but he is judged of none aright. It is a fool's bolt. But the spiritual man indeed passeth a right verdict upon persons and things, as far as he is spiritual. And that is the reason that carnal men especially hate spiritual men above all things. They hate men that have a natural conscience, that judge according to the light of reason, for that is above any creature. When a man will not say white is black, that good is evil, to please any man in the world, a man that hath a natural conscience will not do this. And this is very distasteful. Where men idolise themselves they love not such, but such as are slaves to them. But much more, when a man is spiritual, he judgeth all things and censureth them and their courses; for he is above all, and seeth all beneath him. Therefore the greatest men in the world are holy men. They are above all other men, and without usurpation, they pass a censure upon the course and state of other men, though they be never so great. Howsoever the image of God is upon them, in regard of their authority and the like, yet in their dispositions they are base, and slaves to their corruptions and to Satan. They are not out of the base rank of nature. Now a man that is a child of God, he is taken into a better condition, and hath a spiritual liberty in him. 'He judgeth all things and is judged of none.' They may call him this and that; it is but malice, and a spice of the sin against the Holy Ghost; but their hearts tell them he is otherwise. He shall judge them ere long, for 'the saints shall judge the world.'† Therefore Christians should know, and take notice of their excellency. 'Where the Spirit of God is, there is liberty' to judge all things as far as they come within their reach and calling, to judge aright of all things. Therefore we should know how to maintain the credit of a Christian, that is, to maintain a liberty independent upon all but God; and other things with reservation, as far as they agree with conscience and religion. Thus we see how we may judge of this liberty. 'Where the Spirit of the Lord is, there is liberty.'

He doth not say licentiousness to shake off all government; for by too much licentiousness all liberty is lost; but 'where the *Spirit of God is, there* is liberty.' For a true Christian is the greatest servant and the greatest freeman in the world; for he hath a spirit that will yield to none. In things spiritual he reserves a liberty for his judgment, yet for outward conformity of life and conversation he is a servant to all, to do them good. Love makes him a servant. Christ was the greatest servant that ever was.

* Qu. Ham? Gen. ix. 25.—G. † Cf. 1 Cor. vi. 3; Mat. xix. 28.—G.

He was both the servant of God and our servant. And there is none so free. The greater portion of the Spirit, the more inward and spiritual freedom; and the more freedom, the more disposition to serve one another in love, and to do all things that a man should do outwardly, all things that are lawful. We must take heed of that, mistake not this spiritual liberty. It stands with conformity to all good laws and all good orders, and there is a great mistake of carnal men for want of this. They think it liberty to do as men list.* It is true, if a man have a strong and a holy understanding, to be a good leader to it, but it is the greatest bondage in the world, to have most freedom in ill. As I said before, those that are most free in ill are most slaves of all; for their corruptions will not suffer them to hear good things, to be where good things are spoken, to accompany with those that are good, their corruptions hath them in so narrow a custody. Some kind of men, their corruptions are so malignant and binding, that they will not suffer them to be in any opportunity wherein their corruptions may be restrained at all, but they hate the very sight of persons that may restrain them, and all laws that might restrain them. Now this is the greatest slavery in the world, for a man to have no acquaintance with that that is contrary to his corrupt disposition.

Well, 'new lords new laws,' as soon as ever a man is in Christ and hath Christ's Spirit, he hath another law in his soul to rule him contrary to that that there was before. Before he was ruled by the law of his lusts, that carried him whither he would; but now in Christ he hath a new Lord and a new law, and that rules him according to the regiment† of the Spirit, 'The law of the Spirit of life in Christ hath freed me from the law of sin and of death,' Rom. viii. 2.

Use 4. Again, seeing where the Spirit of God is, there is this sweet and glorious liberty, let us *take heed by all means that we do not grieve the Spirit.* When we find the Holy Ghost in the use of any good means to touch upon our souls, Oh give him entrance and way to come into his own chamber, as it were to provide a room for himself; as Cyprian saith, *Consecra habitaculum, &c.*, enter into thy bedchamber; consecrate a habitation for thyself *(c)*. So let us give him way to come into our souls when he knocks by his motions. We that live in the church, there is none of us all but our hearts tell us that we have often resisted the Holy Ghost. We might have been saved if we had not been rebellious and opposite. Grieve not the Spirit by any means.

Quest. How is the Spirit grieved?

Ans. Especially these two or three ways.

(1.) The Spirit being a Spirit of holiness, is grieved *with unclean courses, with unclean motions and words and actions.* He is called the *Holy* Spirit, and he stirs up in the soul holy motions like himself. He breathes into us holy motions, and he breathes out of us good and holy and savoury words, and stirs us up to holy actions. Now when we give liberty to our mouths to speak rottenly, to swear—I am ashamed almost to name that word—when we give liberty to such filthiness, is not this a grieving of the Spirit, if we have the Spirit at all? If we have not a care to grieve ourselves, do we not grieve all about us? Therefore take heed of all filthy unholy words, thoughts, or carriages. It grieves the Spirit.

(2.) Then the Spirit is a Spirit of love, *take heed of canker and malice.* We grieve the Spirit of God by cherishing canker and malice one against another. It drives away the sweet spirit of love. Therefore make con-

* That is, 'choose.'—G. † That is, 'government.'—G.

science of grieving the Spirit. He will not rest in a malicious heart who is the Spirit of love.

(3.) Again, the Spirit of Christ, wheresoever it is, it is joined *with a spirit of humility.* 'God gives grace to the humble,' James iv. 6. It empties the soul that it may fill it. It empties it of what is in it, of windy vanity, and fills it with itself. Therefore those that are filled with vain, high, proud conceits, they grieve and keep out the good Spirit of God; for we should empty our souls that the Spirit of God may have a large dwelling there, or else we grieve the Spirit.

(4.) In a word, *any sin against conscience* grieves the Spirit of God, and hinders spiritual liberty, because 'where the Spirit of God is, there is liberty.' Would we preserve liberty, we must preserve the Spirit. If we sin against conscience, we hinder liberty every way. We hinder our liberty to good duties. When a man sins against conscience he is dead to good actions. Conscience tells him, Why do you go about it, you have done this and that? He is shackled in his performances; he cannot go so naturally to prayer and to hearing. Conscience lays a clog upon him.;

[1.] *He is shackled, in prayer especially;* he hath not liberty to the throne of grace. How dares he look to heaven, when he hath grieved the Spirit of God, and broken the peace of his conscience? What communion hath he with God? So it hinders peace with God. A man cannot look Christ in the face. As a man, when he hath wronged another man, he is ashamed to look on him, so the soul when it hath run into sins against conscience, it is ashamed to look on Christ, and to go to God again. Therefore any sin against conscience grieves the Spirit, and hinders all sweet liberty that was before. It takes away the degree of it.

[2.] It hinders *boldness with men,* for what makes a man courageous in his dealings with men? A clear conscience. Let it be the stoutest man in the world, let him maintain any lust against conscience, it will make him so far a slave; for when it comes to the crossing of that lust once, then you shall see he will even betray all his former stoutness and strength. If a man be covetous and ambitious, he may be stout for a time, but when he comes to be crossed it will take away all liberty that a man hath, to cherish any sin.

In a word, to preserve this liberty, let us go to Christ, from whom we have this liberty; complain to him. When we find any corruption stirring, go to the Lord in the words of St Austin, and say, 'Now, Lord, free me from my necessities.'* I cannot serve thee as I should do, nor as I would do. I am enthralled to sin, but I would do better. I cannot do so well as I would; free me from my necessities. Complain of our corruptions to God. As the woman in the law, when she complained if she were assaulted, she saved her life by complaining, Deut. xxii. 25–27, so let us complain to Christ if we find violence offered to us by our corruptions. I cannot by my own strength set myself at liberty from this corruption. Lord, give me thy Spirit to do it. Set me more and more at liberty from my former bondage, and from this that hath enthralled me. So complain to Christ, and desire him to do his office. Lord, thy office is 'to dissolve the works of the devil,' 1 John iii. 8. And go to the Spirit. It is the office of the Holy Ghost to free us, to be a Spirit of liberty. Now desire Christ and the Holy Ghost to do their office of setting us at spiritual liberty. And this we must do in the use of means and avoiding of occasions, and then it will be efficacious to preserve that spiritual liberty as will tell our consciences that we are no hypocrites; and that will end in a glorious liberty in the life to come.

* Cf. Note *a.*—G.

And let this be a comfort to all poor struggling and striving Christians that are not yet set at perfect liberty from their lusts and corruptions; that it is the office of the Spirit of Christ as the King of the church; it is his office by his Spirit to purge the church perfectly, to make it a glorious spouse. At last he will do his own office. And besides this liberty of grace joined with conflict in this world, there is another liberty of glory, when I shall be freed from all oppositions without, and from all conflict and corruption within. It is called 'the liberty of the sons of God,' Rom. viii. 21, and those that look not more and more for the gracious liberty to be free from passions and corruptions here, they must not look for the glorious liberty in heaven. But those that live a conflicting life, and pray to Christ more and more for the Spirit of liberty to set up a liberty in us, these may look for the liberty of the Son of God, that will be ere long, when we shall be out of reach, and free from corruption; when the Spirit of God shall be all in all. Now our lusts will not suffer the Spirit to be all in all, but in heaven he shall; there shall be nothing to rise against him. This that hath been spoken shall suffice for that 17th verse, 'The Lord is the Spirit, and where the Spirit of the Lord is there is liberty.' I proceed to the next verse, which I purpose to dwell more on.

Verse 18. 'But we all, as in a glass, with open face behold the glory of the Lord, and are changed into the same image, from glory to glory, as by the Spirit of the Lord.'

As the sun riseth by degrees till he come to shine in glory, so it was with the Sun of righteousness. He discovered himself in the church by little and little. The latter times now are more glorious than the former; and because comparisons give lustre, the blessed apostle, to set forth the excellency of the administration of the covenant of grace under the gospel, he compares it with the administration of the same covenant in the time of the law; and in the comparison prefers that administration under the gospel as more excellent. Now besides other differences in the chapter, he insists upon three especially.

They differ in generality, evidence, efficacy.

(1.) First, in regard of the *generality*, '*We all* now with open face,' &c. Moses only beheld the glory of the Lord in the mount, but 'we all,' not all men, but all sound Christians that have their eyes opened; all sorts of believers, behold this glory. In spiritual things there is no envy. Every one may be partaker *in solidum*, entirely of all. Envy is in the things of this life, where the more one hath the less another hath. It is a matter of glory and excellency the more are partakers of spiritual things. The Jews rejoiced that the Gentiles should be called, and we now rejoice in hope, and should rejoice marvellously if we could see it effected, that the Jews should be taken in again; the more the better; 'we all.'

(2.) And then for *evidence*. 'We *behold with open face*,' that is, with freedom and boldness, which was not in the time of the law. For they were afraid to look upon Moses when he came down from the mount, his countenance was so majestical and terrible. But 'we all with open face,' freely, boldly, and cheerfully, look upon the glory of God in the gospel. The light of the gospel is an alluring comforting light; the light of the law was dazzling and terrifying.

'As in a glass.' They beheld God in a glass, but it was not so clear a glass. They beheld him as it were in the water, we behold him in crystal. We see God in the glass of the word and sacraments, but they in a world of ceremonies. Christ was to them swaddled and wrapped up in a great many types.

(3.) And then *for the power and efficacy*, the gospel is beyond the law. The law had not power to convert, to change into its own likeness; but now the gospel, which is the ministry of the Spirit, it hath a transforming changing power, into the likeness of Christ whom it preacheth. 'We are changed from glory to glory.' It is a gradual change, not all at once, but from glory to glory, from one degree of grace to another; for grace is here called glory. We are changed from the state of grace till we* come to heaven, the state of glory.

And then the cause of all. It is 'by the Spirit of the Lord.' The Spirit runs through all. It is 'by the Spirit of the Lord' that we behold. It is the Spirit of the Lord that takes away the veil. It is by the Spirit that we are changed from glory to glory.

Thus you see how many ways the administration of the covenant of grace now is more excellent than the administration of the covenant of grace was then. In a word it hath four excellencies especially, as,

First, *Liberty and freedom* from the bondage of ceremonies and of the law. In a great part they had little gospel and a great deal of law mingled with it. We have much gospel and little law. We have more freedom and liberty.

Second, And thereupon we have *more clearness*. We see Christ more clearly. 'With open face we behold the glory of the Lord.'

Third. And *thirdly*, there is more *intension of grace*. The Spirit works more strongly now, even to a change. The ministry of the gospel hath the Spirit with it, whereby we are changed from the heart-root inwardly and thoroughly.

Fourth, And *lastly*, in the *extension*. It is more large. 'We all,' Gentiles as well as Jews, 'behold,' &c.

Hence, let us seriously and fruitfully consider in what excellent times the Lord hath cast us, that we may answer it with thankfulness and obedience. God hath reserved us to these glorious times, better than ever our forefathers saw.†

There are three main parts of the text: *Our communion and fellowship with God in Christ*. 'We all now in a glass behold the glory of the Lord.' And then,

Our conformity thereupon. By beholding we are changed into the same image.

The third is *the cause of both;* the cause why we 'behold the glory of God,' and why by beholding 'we are changed from glory to glory;' it is 'the Spirit of God.'

This text hath many themes of glory. All is glorious in it. There is the glorious mercy of God in Christ, who is the Lord of glory, the gospel in which we see the grace of God and of Christ; 'The glorious gospel,' 1 Tim. i. 11, the change by which we are changed, a glorious change 'from glory to glory,' and by a glorious power, by 'the Spirit of the Lord,' all here is glorious. Therefore blessed be God, and blessed be Christ, and blessed be the Spirit, and blessed be the gospel, and we blessed that live in these blessed and glorious times! But to come to the words.

'But we all as in a glass,' &c.

The happiness of man consists especially in two things:

* Misprinted 'he.'—G.

† Cf. Introduction to Sibbes's Will, Vol. I. page cxxvii.—G.

In communion with God, in conformity to God.

The means how to attain them both are laid down in this verse.

I shall speak of them in order. *First, of our communion with the chief good;* and then *of the conformity wrought upon that communion.*

And in the communion, *first* of God's *discovering of himself by his Spirit.*

And then *of our apprehension of him by beholding.*

'We all with open face behold the glory of the Lord,' &c.

In the glass of the gospel we see Christ, and in Christ the glory of God shining, especially of his mercy.

The point then here is, that,

Doct. The grace and free mercy of God is his glory. Now in our fallen estate the glory of God is especially his mercy shining in Jesus Christ.

What is glory?

Glory implieth these things.

[1.] *First, Excellency.* Nothing is glorious but that that is excellent.

[2.] *Secondly, Evidence and manifestation*; for nothing is glorious, though it be excellent, if it appear not so. Therefore light is said to be glorious, because the rays of it appear and run into the eyes of all as it were. And therefore we call things that are glorious by the name of light, *illustrissimus* and *clarissimus*, terms taken from light, (*d*) because where glory is there must be manifestation. Thus light, it is a creature of God that manifests itself and other things.

[3.] *Thirdly, Victoriousness.* In glory there is such a degree of excellency as is victorious, and convincing that it is so indeed; conquering the contrary that opposeth it. Light causeth darkness to vanish presently. When the sun which is a glorious creature appears, where are the stars? And where are meaner men in the appearance of a glorious prince? They are hid. The meaner things are shadowed by glory.

[4.] Again, usually glory hath with it the *suffrage and approbation of others*, or else it hath not its right end; that is, Why doth God create such glory in nature as light, and such like, but that men may behold the light? and why are kings and great men glorious at certain times, but that there be beholders? If there were no beholders there would be no glory.

Now to apply this to the point in hand. 'The glory of the Lord;' that is, his attributes, especially that of grace, mercy, and love in Christ. That especially is his excellency.

And there is an evidence and manifestation of it. It appears to us in Christ, 'The grace of God had appeared,' Titus ii. 11. Christ is called grace. He is the grace of God invested and clothed with man's nature. When Christ appeared, the grace and mercy and love of God appeared.

Then again it is victorious, shining to victory over all that is contrary. For, alas! beloved, what would become of us if there were not grace above sin, and mercy above misery, and power in Christ Jesus above all the power in Satan and death!

And then they have a testimony of all that belong to God; for they have their eyes opened to behold this glory, and by beholding are transformed from glory to glory, as we shall see after.

So that whatsoever may be said of glory may be said of this glory, whence all other glory indeed is derived.

'The glory of the Lord.'

By the glory of the Lord then is meant especially the glory of his mercy and love in Jesus Christ.

The several attributes of God shine upon several occasions. They have as it were several theatres whereon to discover their glory. In creation there was power most of all. In governing the world, wise providence. In hell, justice in punishing sinners. But now to man in a lapsed estate, what attribute shines most, and is most glorious? Oh it is mercy and free grace. If grace and mercy were hid, our state being as it is since the fall, what were all other attributes but matter of terror? To think of the wisdom, and power, and justice of God would add aggravations. He is the more wise and powerful to take revenge on us, &c. Grace is the glorious attribute whereby God doth as it were set himself to triumph over the greatest ill that can be, over sin. That that is worse than the devil himself cannot prevail over his grace. There is a greater height and depth and breadth; there are greater dimensions in love and mercy in Christ than there is in our sins and miseries; and all this is gloriously discovered in the gospel.

Do you wonder then why the grace of God hath found such enemies as it hath done alway, especially in popery, where they mingle their works with grace? For the opposite heart of man being in a frame of enmity to God, sets itself most against that that God will be glorified in. Therefore we should labour to vindicate nothing so much as grace. We have a dangerous encroaching sect risen up, enemies to the grace of God, that palliate and cover their plot cunningly and closely, but they set nature against grace. Let us vindicate that upon all occasions; for we live by grace, and we must die by grace, and stand at the day of judgment by grace; not in our own righteousness, but in the righteousness of Christ, being found in him. But because it is a sweet point, and may serve us all in stead, to consider that God will honour himself gloriously in this sweet attribute, let us see a little how the glory of God shines in Christ more than otherwise; parallel it with other things a little.

(1.) *The glory of God was in Adam;* for Adam had the image of God upon him, and had communion and fellowship with God; but there is greater glory now shining in the gospel, in Jesus Christ, to poor sinners. For when man stood in innocency, God did good to a good man, and God was amiable and friendly to a friend. Adam was the friend of God then. Now to do good to him that is good, and to maintain sweet communion with a friend, this is good indeed, and it was a great glory of God's mercy that he would raise such a creature as man hereto. But now in Jesus Christ there is a further glory of mercy; for here God doth good to ill men, and the goodness of God is victorious and triumphant over the greatest misery and the greatest ill of man. Now in the gospel God doth good to his greatest enemies herein, as it is Rom. v. 10. God set forth and commended gloriously his love, that 'when we were enemies, he gave his Son for us. Therefore here is greater glory of mercy and love shining forth to fallen man in Christ than to Adam in innocency.

(2.) *The glory of God shines in the heavens.* 'The heavens declare the glory of God, and the firmament sheweth his handiwork,' Ps. xix. 1. Every creature hath a beam of God's glory in it. The whole world is a theatre of the glory of God. But what is the glory of creation, of preservation, and governing of the world, to the glory of his mercy and compassion that shines in Christ? The glory of the creature is nothing to this; for all the creatures were made of nothing; but here the glory of mercy is such in Christ that God became a creature himself.

(3.) *Nay, to go higher, to the angels themselves.* It is not *philangelia*, but *philanthropia* that outshines all.* God is not called the lover of angels. He took not upon him the nature of angels, but the nature of man; and man is the spouse of Christ, the member of Christ. Angels are not so. They are but ministering spirits for the good of them that shall be saved. Christ, as it is Eph. i. 21, when he rose again, he was 'advanced above all principalities and powers,' therefore above the angelical nature. Now Christ and the church are all one. They make but one mystical body. The church is the queen, and Christ is the king. Therefore Christ mystical, the church, is above all angelical nature whatsoever. The angels are not the queen and spouse of Christ. So the glory of God's goodness is more to man, to sinful man, after he believes and is made one with Christ, than to any creature whatsoever. Thus God hath dignified and advanced our nature in Jesus Christ. Comparisons give lustre. Therefore this shews plainly unto us Christians that the glory of the mercy and love and kindness of God to man in Christ shines more than his glory and mercy and kindness to all the creatures in the world besides. Therefore here is a glory with an excellency.

On the other side, nothing more terrible than to consider of God. Out of Christ, what is he but a 'consuming fire'? Heb. xii. 29. But to consider of his mercy, his glorious mercy in Jesus Christ, nothing is more sweet. For in Jesus Christ God hath taken upon him that sweet relation of a Father; 'The Father of mercy, and God of all comfort,' 2 Cor. i. 3. So that the nature of God is lovely in Christ, and our nature in Christ is lovely to him. And this made the angels, who, though they have not increase of grace by Christ, yet having increase of comfort and glory, when Christ was born, to sing from heaven 'Glory to God on high,' &c., Luke ii. 14. What glory? Why, the glory of his mercy, of his love, of his grace to sinful men. Indeed, there is a glory of wisdom to reconcile justice and mercy together, and a glory of truth to fulfil the promise. But that that sets all attributes for our salvation on work was mercy and grace. Therefore that is the glory of God especially here meant. For as we say in morality, that is the greatest virtue that other virtues serve, so in divinity, that attribute which others serve is the greatest of all. In our salvation, wisdom, yea, and justice itself, serves mercy. For God by his wisdom devised a way to content justice, by sending his Son to take our nature, and in that nature to give satisfaction to justice, that there might be a harmony among the attributes. To make some use of this.

Use 1. Doth God manifest his glory? I will not speak at large of glory, being an endless argument, but confine it to the glory of grace and mercy in the gospel, which therefore is called the glory of the gospel. I say, doth God shew such glorious mercy in Christ? Then, I beseech you, *let us justify God, and justify this course that God hath taken to glorify his mercy in Jesus Christ, by embracing Christ.* It is said of the proud Pharisees, 'they despised the counsel of God,' Luke vii. 30. God hath poured out mercy, bowels of mercy, in Christ crucified. Therefore, in embracing Christ, we justify the counsel of God concerning our salvation.

Do but consider what a loving God we have, who would not be so far in love with his only Son as to keep him to himself, when we had need of him: a God that accounts himself most glorious in those attributes that are most for our comfort. He accounts not himself so glorious for his wisdom, for his power, or for his justice, as for his mercy and grace, for

* That is, not φιλαγγελια, but φιλανθρωπια.—G.

his *philanthropia*, his love of man. Shall not we therefore even be inflamed with a desire of gratifying him, who hath joined his glory with our salvation? that accounts himself glorious in his mercy above all other attributes? Shall the angels, that have not that benefit by Christ as we have, shall they in our behalf, out of love to us and zeal to God's glory, sing from heaven, 'Glory to God on high'? and shall we be so dead and frozen-hearted that reap the crop, as not to acknowledge this glory of God, breaking out in the gospel, the glory of his mercy and rich grace? The apostle is so full when he falls upon this theme, that he cannot speak without words of amplification and enlargement; one while he calls it 'rich grace,' Eph. i. 7, another while he stands in admiration, 'Oh the depth of the love of God,' Rom. xi. 33. What deserves admiration but glorious things? The best testimony that can be given of glorious things is when we admire them. Now if we would admire, is there anything so admirable that we can say, Oh the height, and depth, as we may of the love of God in Christ? There are all the dimensions of unparalleled glory, height, and breadth, and depth. Therefore, I beseech you, let us often even stand in admiration of the love of God to us in Christ. 'So God loved the world,' John iii. 16. The Scripture leads to this admiration by phrases that cannot have a *podesis*,* a redition* back again. 'So.' How? We cannot tell how. '*So*' as is beyond all expression. The Scripture itself is at a stand for words. Oh base nature, that we are dazzled with anything but that we should most admire. How few of us spend our thoughts this way, to consider God's wonderful and admirable mercy and grace in Christ, when yet there is no object in the world so sweet and comfortable as this is, that the very angels pry into! They desire to pry into the mystery of our salvation by Christ. They are students therein. The cherubins, they were set upon the mercy seat, having a counterview, one upon another, implying a kind of admiration. They pry into the secrets of God's love in governing his people, and bringing them to heaven. Shall they do it, and shall not we study and admire these things, that God may have the glory? God made all for his glory, beloved; and 'the wicked for the day of wrath,' as Solomon saith, Prov. xvi. 4. And hath he not new made all for his glory? Is not the new creature more for his glory than the old creature? Therefore if we will make it good that we are new creatures, let us seek to glorify God every way, not in word alone, but in heart admiring him, and in life conversing with him.

And that we may glorify God in deed, let us glory in God's love; for we must glory in this glory. Nature, beloved, is glorious of itself, and vain-glorious. But would you glory without vanity? Go out of yourselves and see what you are in Christ, in the grace and mercy and free love of God, culling us out from the rest of mankind; and there you may glory safely over sin, and death, and hell. For being justified freely from our sins, you can think of death, of the damnation of others, of hell, without fear. 'God forbid,' saith St Paul, 'that I should glory in anything, but in the cross of Christ,' Gal. vi. 14; that is, in the mercy of God appointing such a means for satisfaction. 'Let not the wise man glory in his wisdom, nor the strong man glory in his strength,' &c., Jer. ix. 23. There is a danger in such glorying. It is subject to a curse. But if a man will glory, let him 'glory in the Lord.'

Use 2. Again, if God account his mercy and love in Christ, especially his glory, *shall we think that God will admit of any partner with Christ in the*

* Qu. 'apodosis' and 'reddition'?—Ed.

matter of salvation? If, as the psalmist saith, 'he made us, and not we ourselves,' Ps. c. 3, shall we think that we have a hand in making ourselves again? Will God suffer his glory to be touched upon by intercessions of saints' merits, and satisfaction, and free will? Grace is not glorious if we add the least thing of our own to it. Cannot we make a hair of our head, or the grass that we trample upon, but there must be a glory and power of God in it? And can we bring ourselves to heaven? Therefore away with that 'Hail, Mary, full of grace!' 'Hail, Mary, freely beloved!' is the right interpretation; and they that attribute matter of power and grace and favour to her, as in that 'Oh beseech thy Son,' &c., they take away that wherein God and Christ will be glorified, and attribute it to his mother and other creatures (*e*). I do but touch this, to bring us into loathing and abomination of that religion that sets somewhat of the creature against that wherein God will be glorified above all.

Use 3. Again, *let us stay ourselves, when we walk in darkness, with the consideration of the gloriousness of God's mercy in Jesus Christ,* here called 'the glory of the Lord.' It is no less mercy than glorious mercy that will satisfy us, when we are in distress of conscience; and if this will not, what will? Let Satan aggravate our sins as much as may be, and join with conscience in this business; yet set this glorious mercy against all our sins, make the most of them, they are sins of a finite creature. But here is infinite mercy, triumphing and rejoicing over justice, having gotten the victory over it. Oh beloved, when the time of temptation comes, and the hour of death, and conflict with conscience, and a confluence and concurrence of all that may discourage, Satan will bestir himself; and he is a cunning rhetorician to set all the colours upon sin, especially in the time of despair; be as cunning to set all colours upon mercy, glorious mercy. If God were glorious in all other attributes, and not in mercy, what would become of us? The glory of other attributes without mercy tends to despair; glorious in wisdom to find us out; glorious in justice to deal with us in rigour. These affright, but that that sweeteneth all other attributes is his mercy.

What a comfort is this to sinful man, that in casting himself upon Christ, and upon God's mercy in Christ, he yields glory to God; that God hath joined his glory with our special good; that here is a sweet concurrence between the *summum finis** and the *summum bonum* of man! The last end of man of all is the glory of God; for that is as it were the point of the circle from which all came (for he made all for his glory), and in which all ends; so is the chief good. Therefore by the way it is a vain conceit for some to think, 'Oh we must not look to our own salvation so much; this is self-love.'

It is true, to sever the consideration of the glory of God's mercy and goodness in it, but see both these wrapped and knit together indissolvable, our salvation and God's glory. We hinder God's glory if we believe not his mercy in Christ to us. So at once we wrong ourselves and him, and we wrong him not in a mean attribute, but in his mercy and goodness, wherein he hath appointed to glorify himself most of all; and therefore, I beseech you, let us yield to him the glory of his mercy, and let us think that when we sin we cannot glorify him more than to have recourse to his mercy. When Satan tempts us to run from God, and discourageth us, as he will do at such times, then have but this in your thoughts, God hath set himself to be glorious in mercy, above all other attributes. And this

* Qu. '*summum finem*'? or '*summus finis*'?—Ed.

is the first moving attribute that stirs up all the rest, and therefore God will account himself honoured if I have recourse to him. Let this thought therefore be as a city of refuge. When the avenger of blood follows thee, flee presently to this sanctuary. Think thus, Let not me deny myself comfort and God glory at once: 'Where sin abounds, grace abounds much more,' Rom. v. 20. Though sins after conversion stain our profession more than sins before conversion, yet notwithstanding go to the glorious mercy of God still, to seventy times seventy times,* there is yet mercy for these.† We beseech you be reconciled, saith St Paul to the Corinthians, when they were in the state of grace, and had their pardon before. Let us never be discouraged from going to Christ.

Oh, but I have offended often and grievously. What saith the prophet? 'My thoughts are not as your thoughts; but as high as the heavens are above the earth,' &c., Isa. lv. 8. Therefore howsoever amongst men, oft offences breed an eternal alienation, yet notwithstanding with God it is not so. But so oft as we can have spirit to go to God for mercy, and spread our sins before him, with broken and humble hearts, so often we may take out our pardon. Compare Exod. xxxiii. with Exod. xxxiv. Moses, in chap. xxxiii. 18, *seq.*, had desired to see the face of God. There was some little curiosity perhaps in it. God told him that none could see him and live. To see the face of God in himself must be reserved for heaven, we are not proportioned for that sight. But in the next chapter there he shews himself to Moses; and how doth he shew himself and his glory to Moses? 'The Lord, the Lord, gracious, merciful, long-suffering,' clothed all in sweet attributes. He will be known by those names. Now, then, if we would know the name of God, and see God as he is pleased and delighted to discover himself to us, let us know him by those names that he proclaims there, shewing that the glory of the Lord in the gospel especially shines in mercy; and as I said before, it must be glorious mercy that can satisfy a distressed conscience, howsoever in the time of ease and peace we think a little mercy will serve the turn. But when conscience is once awaked, it must be glorious and infinite mercy must allay it.

And therefore those that find their consciences anything wounded with any sin, stand not out any longer with God, come and yield, lay down your weapons, there is mercy ready. The Lord is glorious in his mercy in Jesus Christ. It is a victorious triumphing mercy over all sin and unworthiness whatsoever. Look upon God in the face of Jesus Christ; as you have it in 2 Cor. iv. 6, 'God, who commanded light to shine out of darkness, hath shined in our hearts, to give us the light of the knowledge of God, in the face of Jesus Christ.' In the face of Christ God is lovely. Loveliness and excellency is in the face above all the parts of the body.

'The glory of God.'

We are never in such a condition as we ought to be, except grace be glory to us; and when is grace glory to a sinner? Oh, when he feels the weight and burden of his sin, and languishing desires. Oh that I might have a drop of mercy! Then grace is glory, not only in God's esteem, but in the eye of the sinner. Indeed, we are never soundly humbled till grace in our esteem be glory; that is, till it appear excellent and victorious. I beseech you remember it. We may have use of it in the time of desertion.

* Cf. note *, Vol. III. p. 36.—G. † Qu. 'thee'?—Ed.

How is this grace of God in Christ conveyed to us yet nearer? By the gospel.

'As in a glass.'

The gospel is the 'good word of God,' Heb. vi. 5. It reveals the good God to us, and the good Christ. It is a sweet word. For Christ could do us no good without the word, if there were not an obligation, a covenant made between God and us, the foundation of which covenant is the satisfaction of Christ. If there were not promises built upon the covenant of grace, whereby God hath made himself a debtor, what claim could a sinful soul have to Christ and to God's mercy? But God hath bound himself in his word. Therefore the grace of God shines in Christ, and all that is in Christ is conveyed to us by the word, by the promise. The gospel then is a sweet word. You know that breeding promise of all others, Gen. iii. 15, 'The seed of the woman.' That repealed* and conveyed the mercy of God in Christ to Adam. So the continuance of that and all the sweet and gracious promises bud from that; all meet in Christ as in a centre, all are made for him and in him. He is the sum of all the promises. All the good things we have are parcels of Christ. Christ he is the Word of the Father, that discovers all from the bosom of his Father. Therefore he is named 'the Word.' The gospel is the Word from him. Christ was discovered to the apostles, and from the apostles to us, to the end of the world, by his Spirit accompanying the ordinance. So the mirror wherein we see the glorious mercy of God, is first Christ. God shines in him, and then there is another glass wherein Christ is discovered, the glass of the gospel. Thus it pleaseth God to condescend to stoop to us poor sinners, to reveal his glory, the glory of his mercy, fitly and suitable in a Saviour, God-man, God incarnate, God our brother, God our kinsman, and to do it all yet more familiarly, to discover it in a word. And then to ordain a ministry together with the word, to lay open the riches of Christ; for it is not the gospel considered nakedly, but the gospel unfolded by the ministry.

Christ is the great ordinance of God for our salvation. The gospel is the great ordinance of God, to lay open 'the unsearchable riches of Christ,' Eph. iii. 8. The casket of this jewel, the treasury of his treasure, the grace and love and mercy of God, are treasured in Christ; and Christ and all good things are treasured in the gospel. That is the rich mine; and the ministry of the gospel lays open that mine to the people. Nay, God yet goes further. He gives his Holy Spirit with the ministry. It is the ministry of the Spirit, that howsoever there are many that are not called and converted in the gospel, yet the Spirit of God is beforehand with them. There are none under the gospel but the Spirit gives them sweet motions. He knocks at their hearts, he allures and persuades them; and if they yield not, it is because of the rebellion of their hearts. There is more grace of the Spirit offered than is entertained. So that the mouths of men shall be stopped. Thus God descends, and Christ, and grace, the gospel, the ministry, the Spirit, all in way of love to us, that we may do all in a way of love to God again. It should therefore work us to do all with ingenuous hearts to him again.

The gospel is the glass wherein we see this glory. Christ indeed in some sort is the glass, for we cannot see God out of Christ but he is a terrifying sight. But in the glass Christ we can see God, as we see the sun in the water. If we cannot see the sun in his glory, that is but a creature, how

* That is, 'repealed the curse.'—G.

can we see God himself but in some glass? Therefore we must see him in Christ, and so his sight is comfortable.

And in the dispensing of the gospel, especially in the preaching and unfolding of the word, the riches of God in Christ are unfolded, and not only unfolded, but the Spirit in unfolding conveys the sense, assurance, and persuasion thereof unto us.

There is such a connection between the evangelical truth of God and Jesus Christ, that they have both one name,* to insinuate to us that as we will be partakers of Christ, so it must be of Christ, as he is revealed in the gospel, not in conceits of our own. The word is truth, and Christ is truth. They have the same name; for were there never so much mercy and love in God, if it were concealed from us, that we had nothing to plead, that we had not some title to it by some discovery of it in his will, the word and the seal of the word, the sacraments (for the sacrament is but a visible word, they make one entire thing, the word and sacraments; the one is the evidence, the other the seal), what comfort could we take in it? Now his will is in the promise, wherein there is not only a discovery of what he doth or will do, but he hath engaged himself: 'If we believe, we shall not perish, but have life,' John iii. 15; and 'Come unto me,' Matt. xi. 28, and be refreshed, saith Christ. Every one that thirsts, come and be satisfied, John vii. 37. And now we may claim the performance of what he hath spoken, and bind him by his own word. 'He cannot deny himself,' John vii. 37. So now we see him comfortably in the glass of the word and sacraments.

These three go together, the glory of God; Christ the foundation of all grace, in the covenant of grace; and then the gospel of grace, the gospel of the kingdom, the gospel of life, that discovers the gracious face of God shining in Christ. We have communion with God through Christ, with Christ through the gospel; therefore in the gospel 'we behold as in a glass the glory of God.'

This is suitable to our condition while we are here below. We cannot see divine things otherwise than in a glass. That sight of God that we shall have in heaven, immediately, without the word and sacraments, that is of a higher nature; when our natures shall be perfect. But while we live here we cannot see God but in Christ, and we cannot see him but in the word and sacraments. Such is the imperfection of our sight, and such is the lustre and glory of the object, the glory of God, that we cannot perfectly see it but in a glass. God said to Moses, 'None can see me and live.' His meaning is, none can see me as I am, none can see me immediately and live. If we would see God, and the glory of God immediately without a glass, we must see it in heaven. We must die first. We must pass through death to see God face to face as he is; then, not as he is, but more familiarly than we can now. Then God will represent himself so as shall be for our happiness, though not simply as he is; for he is infinite, and how should finite comprehend infinite? We shall apprehend him, but not comprehend him (*f*). While we are in earth, therefore, we must be content to see him in a glass, which is the gospel, especially unfolded.

Now in this word 'glass,' in which we see the glory of God, is implied both a perfection and some imperfection.

Perfection, because it is as a clear crystal glass in regard of the glass that was before; for those under the law saw Christ in a glass of cere-

* That is, λογος and ἀληθεια. Cf. John x. 35 with i. 1, and John xiv. 6 with xvii. 17.—G.

monies. And, as I said before, there is difference between one's seeing his face in water and in a crystal glass. So then this implies perfection in regard of the former state.

Again, in regard of heaven, it implies *imperfection*, for there we shall not see in a glass. Sight in a glass is imperfect, though it be more perfect than that in water. For we know out of the principles of learning and experience, that reflections weaken, and the more reflections, the more weak. When we see a thing by reflection, we see it weakly; and [when] we see it by a second reflection from that, we see it more weakly. When we see the sun on the wall, or any thing that is light, it is weaker than the light of the sun itself. When a man seeth his face in a glass, it is a weaker representation than to see face to face. But when we see the sun upon the wall, reflexing upon another wall, the third reflection is weaker than the first. The more reflections the more weak. So here all sight by glasses is not so powerful as that sight and knowledge which is face to face in heaven. That is the reason that St James saith, that he that seeth his face in a glass is subject to forget (i. 23). What is the reason that a man cannot remember himself, when he seeth his face in a glass, so well as he can remember another man's face when he seeth it? Because he seeth himself only by reflection. Therefore it is a weaker presentation to him, and the memory and apprehension of it is weaker. When he seeth another face to face, he remembers him longer, because there is a more lively representation. It is not a reflection, but face to face. So there is imperfection in this sight that we have of God, while we are here, as in a glass. It is nothing to that when we shall see face to face, without the word and sacraments or any other medium, which sight, what it is, we shall know better when we are there. We cannot now discover it. It is a part of heaven to know what apprehensions we shall have of God there. But sure it is more excellent than that that is here. Therefore this implies imperfection.

We consist of body and soul in this world, and our souls are much confined and tied to our senses. Imagination propounds to the soul greater things than the senses. So God helps the soul by outward things that work upon the senses; sense upon the imagination, and so things pass into the soul.

God frames his manner of dealing suitable to the nature he hath created us in. Therefore he useth the word and sacraments, and such things, whereby he makes impressions upon the very soul itself.

And this indeed, by the way, makes spiritual things so difficult as they are ofttimes, because we are too much enthralled to imagination and sense. and cannot abstract and raise our minds from outward sensible things to spiritual things. Therefore you have some, all the days of their life, spend their time in the bark of the Scriptures; and they are better than some others that are all for notions and outside: such things as frame to the imagination, and never come to know the spirit of the Scriptures, but rest in outward things, in languages and tongues, and such like. Whereas these things lead further, or else they come not to their perfection. The Scripture is but a glass, to see some excellencies in it. 'We see as in a glass.'

Now the use of a glass among us especially is twofold.

(1.) *It is either to help weakness of sight* against the excellency of the object. When there is a weak sight and an over excellent object, then a glass is used, or some polite* and clear body, as we cannot see the sun in itself. The eye is weak and the sun is glorious. These two meeting therefore together, we help it by seeing the sun in water, as in an eclipse.

* That is, = polished.—G.

If a man would judge of an eclipse he must not look on the sun, but see it in water, and there behold and discern these things; so to see the glory of God in himself, it is too glorious an object. Our eyes are too weak. How doth God help it? He helps it by a glass, by 'God manifest in the flesh,' 1 Tim. iii. 16, and by the word and sacraments whereby we come to have communion with Christ. To apply this more particularly.

Now that we are to receive the sacrament, conceive the sacraments are glasses wherein we see the glory of the love and mercy of God in Christ. For take the bread alone, as it doth not represent and figure better things, and what is it? and take the wine alone, as it doth not represent better things, and what is the wine? But an ordinary poor creature. Oh, but take them as they are glasses, as things that convey to the soul and represent things more excellent than themselves, so they are glorious ordinances. Take a glass as a glass, it is a poor thing; but take the glass as it represents a more excellent thing than itself, so they are of excellent use; so bread and wine must not be taken as naked elements, but as they represent and convey a more excellent thing than themselves, that is, Christ and all his benefits, the love and mercy and grace of God in Christ; and so they are excellent glasses. Therefore I beseech you now, when you are to receive the sacrament, let your minds be more occupied than your senses. When you take the bread, think of the body of Christ broken; and when you think of uniting the bread into one substance, think of Christ and you made one. When the wine is poured out, think of the blood of Christ poured out for sin. When you think of the refreshing by the wine, think of the refreshing of your spirits and souls by the love of God in Christ, and of the love of Christ that did not spare his blood for your soul's good. How doth Christ crucified and shedding his blood refresh the guilty soul, as wine refresheth the weak spirits. Thus consider them as glasses, where better things are presented, and let your minds be occupied as well as your senses, and then you shall be fit receivers, as 'in a glass.'

'We behold,' &c.

God when he made the world, this glorious frame of the creatures, and all their excellencies, he created light to discover itself, and all other excellencies. For light is a glorious creature. It discovers itself. It goes with a majesty and discovers all other things, good and bad whatsoever; and together with light God created sight in man, and other senses, to apprehend the excellency of the creation. What were all this goodly frame of creatures, the sun, and moon, and stars, and glory of the earth, if there were not light to discover and sight to apprehend it by? Is it not so in this outward creation of the old heavens and old earth that must be consumed with fire? And is it not much more in the new creation? There is excellent glory, marvellous glory, wondrous grace in* Christ, &c. Must there be light, and must not there be an eye to discover this? Surely there must. Therefore it is said here, 'We behold.'

God puts a spiritual eye by his Spirit into all true believers, whereby they behold this excellent glory, this glorious grace, that God may have the glory, and we the comfort. Those are the two main ends. God intends his own glory and our salvation. There must be a 'beholding.' How should he have glory and we comfort, unless all were conveyed by spiritual sight! Well then the Spirit creates and works in us spiritual senses. With spiritual life there are spiritual senses, sight, and taste, and feeling. Sight is here put for all, 'We behold.'

* Misprinted 'and.'—G.

There are many degrees of sight. It is good to know them. Therefore I will name some of them.

[1.] *We see God in his creatures*, for 'the heavens declare the glory of God.' They are a book in folio (*g*). There God is laid open in his creatures. That is a goodly sight. But what is this to the knowledge of him in his will to us, what he means to us? The creatures discover not what he means to us.

[2.] Besides therefore the sight of God in the creatures, there is a sight of God *in his will, in his word and promises*. There we see what he is. His grace is revealed in Christ, and what his good will to us is, and his will from us, what he will do to us, and what he will have from us again. There we see him as a spouse sees her husband in a loving letter which concerns herself. We see him as the heir sees a deed made to him with an inheritance. He sees with application. It is not a bare sight, but a sight with feeling and discovery of a favour. So the sight in the word and sacraments, it is a higher sight.

[3.] *There was a sight of Christ when he was in the flesh*. When he was covered with the veil of our flesh upon earth, it was a sweet sight. Abraham desired to see it, John viii. 56, and Simeon, when he saw it, was willing to be dissolved and to depart, Luke ii. 29. He had enough. But that outward sight is nothing without another inward sight of faith.

[4.] *There is a sight therefore of faith*, and other sights are to no purpose if they be without this, a sight of God shining in Christ. And this is perfected in heaven, in the sight of glory, when we see him as he is. Now there is a comfort in all these sights, to see him in his word and works. It was a glorious thing to see him in his bodily presence; and by faith to see God in Christ, to see his face in Christ. Oh it is a sweet and lovely sight to see God shining in Christ! Oh but what is all this to the sight of him after in glory! Now this beholding meant here especially, is the beholding of faith, in the ordinances, in the word and sacraments. 'We all behold,' as in the glass of the word and sacraments, by the eye of faith. Faith is expressed by beholding, by knowledge; for indeed faith is nothing but knowledge with application. Therefore faith includes knowledge. What is faith, but to know God and Christ, and the promises as mine? Christ in the sacrament as mine, as verily as the outward things are mine: Knowledge with application is faith. Therefore, when I say faith, I include knowledge, 'We behold.'

The knowledge of the mind is compared to the eye of the body. Knowledge and faith is compared to seeing and beholding, for many reasons.

First, Because sight *is the most glorious and noble sense*. It is the highest in situation, and the quickest in apprehension, for in a moment, presently sight apprehends its object in the highest heavens. So it is with faith. It is the most noble sight of all, and it is quick as sight is; for faith is that eagle in the cloud. It breaks through all, and sees in a moment Christ in heaven: it looks backward, and sees Christ upon the cross; it looks forward, and seeth Christ to come in glory. Faith is so quick a grace, that it presents things past, things above, things to come, and all in a moment, so quick is this eagle-eye of faith.

Second, Again, *it is the largest sense*; for we can see almost the whole hemisphere at one view. That a little thing in the eye should apprehend so much in a moment, as it is quick in apprehension, so it is large in comprehension.

Third, Again, *it is the most sure sense*—sight more than hearing; therefore that divine act of knowledge is compared to seeing; believing is compared to beholding. When faith looks upon God in the glass of the word and promises, it is as certain as the object is certain. Now, how certain is the object? The mercy and love of God in Christ, who is truth itself, is most certain.

Fourth, Then it is that sense *that works most upon the soul*, sight; for what the body seeth, the soul is affected and moved with. The affections of desire and love rise out of sight. It works upon the affections most. Therefore the knowledge that stirs up the affections, and works upon the heart, is compared to sight. It affects us marvellously, for, answerable to our faith, we love, and joy, and delight. It alters the frame of the whole man. Therefore it is expressed here by beholding. Divine, spiritual knowledge, it works upon the heart. So we see why this beholding spirituall[y] of the understanding and soul, is compared to outward sight. It is called beholding, because it is a most noble spiritual act of the soul; and it is most certain and sure. 'Faith is the evidence of things not seen,' Heb. xi. 1; and it works upon the heart and soul.

Use. Therefore, we should labour to clear this eye of the soul, that we may behold the glory of God in the glass of the gospel.

Quest. How shall we have the eye of our souls fit to behold the glory of God?

Ans. 1. *We must fix the eye of the soul;* fix our meditation upon the glory of God and the excellency of Christ. A moving, rolling eye seeth nothing. Therefore we must set some time apart, to fix our meditations upon these excellent things in the gospel.

Ans 2. Then again, *we must labour to have the hindrances removed, both within and without.*

(1.) *Sight within* is hindered by some inward suffusion. We must labour that the soul be cleansed and purged from all carnal passions and desires and base humours, that we may clearly behold this spiritual object. Unless the soul be spiritual, it can never behold spiritual things. The bodily eye cannot apprehend rational things, nor the rational eye behold not spiritual things. Therefore there must be a spiritual eye. The soul must be purged and sanctified by the Spirit. There must be some proportion between the soul and spiritual things, before the soul can behold them. Therefore, as the soul must be fixed upon this meditation, so the Spirit of God must sanctify and purge the soul.

(2.) *Outward hindrances of sight*, as dust in the eyes, and clouds, &c., they hinder sight. Satan labours to hinder the sight of the soul from beholding the glory of God shining in the gospel, with the dust of the world, as the apostle saith in the next chapter, 'The god of this world blinds the eyes of men,' 2 Cor. iv. 4, that they behold not the glory of God shining in the gospel. Therefore, if the gospel be hid, it is hid to them that perish, that are lost, in whom the god of this world hath blinded their minds, that they believe not, lest the light of the glorious gospel of Christ should shine upon them, 2 Cor. iv. 4. Therefore, take heed of too much worldly things, of fixing our souls upon the dust of the world, upon things here below. The sight of Christ, and of God in Christ, it is not gotten by looking below, by fixing the soul upon base things below. Let us look, therefore, that our souls be inwardly cleansed, and fixed upon spiritual things; and then we shall the better behold the glory of God shining in the gospel.

And we should preserve this sight of faith by hearing. Hearing begets seeing in religion. Death came in by the ear at the first. Adam hearing the serpent, that he should not have heard, death came in by the ear. So life comes in by the ear. We hear, and then we see: 'As we have heard, so have we seen,' say they in the psalm, Ps. xlviii. 8. It is true in religion, most of our sight comes by hearing, which is the sense of learning. God will have it so. Therefore we should maintain all we can this beholding of the glory of the Lord in the glass of the word; and for that end hear much.

You will ask me, What is the best glass of all to see and know Christ in?

If you ask a papist, he will shew you crucifixes, and such kind of things. Oh but to behold Christ in the glass of the word, with a spirit of faith, that is the best picture and representation that can be! It is scarce worth spending so much time, as to confute that foolery, to have any grace wrought in the heart by such abominable means as that is, as they use it. Take it at the best, it is but a bastardly help, and bastardly means breed a bastardly devotion. For will God work grace in the heart by means of man's devising? If pictures be any teachers, they are 'teachers of lies,' saith the prophet, Isa. ix. 15; and in the church of God, till pastors and teachers became idols, idols never became teachers. Then came the doctrine of idols teaching of simple people, when idols became teachers a thousand years after Christ. So that the best picture to see Christ in, is the word and sacraments; and the best eye to see him with, is the eye of faith in the word and sacraments. Keep that clear, and we need no crucifixes, no such bastardly helps of bastardly devotion, devised by proud men that would not be beholden to God for his ordinances. But a touch is almost too much for such things, that are so clear to men that have spiritual eyes. In Gal. iii. 1, see what St Paul saith his judgment was: 'Oh foolish Galatians, before whom Christ hath been painted and crucified!'(*h*) How was he painted? Nothing but by the preaching of Christ crucified in the gospel, and the riches of Christ in the gospel; and in the sacraments laid open. Do you think there were any other crucifixes in the world then?

'With open face.'

The manner of this beholding is 'with open face.' There must be a double veil taken away before we can behold the glory of God: the veil of obscurity, and the veil of slavery; the veil of ignorance and infidelity within, and the veil of the things themselves. These two veils are both taken away before we can with open face behold the glory of the Lord. The inward veil is taken away by the Spirit of God illuminating our understandings, and giving us a spirit of faith. The outward veil of the obscurity of the things is taken away by the teaching and ministry of the gospel, having that help to know the meaning of the Scriptures; so that now in these glorious times of the gospel, both the veils are taken away, that we may behold without hindrance the glory of God shining in the gospel. For now we enjoy the ministry of the Spirit. The Spirit is effectual to shine in our hearts. And then we have the gifts of men, outward gifts, whereby the veil of ignorance is taken away in regard of the things themselves, the things are unfolded.

If the things of themselves be dark; or if they be lightsome, and there be no sight within; or if there be sight, and that sight be veiled; there can be no seeing. But now to God's elect he takes away all these veils, he shines inwardly and gives outward light in the help of means; and yet notwithstanding while we live here, there is always some obscurity and darkness, for the veil of the Scriptures is not quite took* away. There is some

* That is, 'taken.'—G.

darkness of the Scriptures, and likewise the veil of ignorance and infidelity is not altogether taken away. There are some remainders of ignorance, of infidelity, and hardness of heart; but yet in a great measure it is taken away here, and shall by little and little [be] took away, till we come to see God face to face in heaven.

'With open face.'

Coverings had two uses in the Jewish state.

They had a use of *subjection*. Therefore the women had their veils in token of subjection.

And they had a use likewise of *obscurity*, to hinder the offensive* lustre of that that is glorious. Therefore Moses put a veil on his face when he came down from the mount. Now in Christ Jesus in the gospel, both these veils are taken away in some respects. The veil of subjection and slavery, so far as it is a slavery, is taken away. The Spirit of Christ works liberty. As I said before, now we serve God as sons, and not as servants any longer. The veil of subjection is taken away, only there is a spouse-like filial subjection; the servile subjection we are freed from.

And then the veil that hid the things is taken away too. So now 'with open face we behold the glory of the Lord.' Now the things themselves, Christ and the gracious promises of grace and glory and comfort, they are clearly laid open without any veil. How comes it then that we see them not? There is a veil over our hearts. The more shame for us, that when the things are unveiled we should have a veil upon our hearts, of ignorance and unbelief. Therefore if any believe not, it is because 'the God of this world hath blinded their eyes,' 2 Cor. iv. 4. Where the means of salvation are, and Christ laid open in the means, if men do not believe, the fault is not in the things; for they are unveiled, they are discovered and laid open. The fault is in us. There is a veil over the heart. There is a cloud of ignorance and unbelief, that keeps the heart from beholding the glory of the mercy of God in Christ.

'With open face.'

We see the glory of God with boldness in the gospel. We go boldly to God. Christ takes us by the hand and leads to his Father. We have boldness and access to God through Christ by the Spirit, as St Paul teacheth in divers places,† God is not terrible to us. Now in Christ, God's nature is fatherly and sweet to us. Christ in the gospel is our head. Therefore we go boldly to God in Christ; and Christ by his Spirit brings us to his Father. We may boldly lay open our souls in prayer; and all our complaints before him as to a Father. We come not as malefactors to a judge, as slaves to a lord, but as children to a father, as a wife to her spouse. 'With open face' in the gospel, we behold God, that is, with boldness we go to him. The gospel by shining upon us takes away a spirit of fear and bondage; the more we see Christ the less fear; the more love the less fear. The more we see the grace of God in Christ, it diminisheth a spirit of fear, and puts into us a spirit of love and boldness. For it presents to us in Christ, full satisfaction to divine justice, that when we offer Christ to the Father whom he hath sent and sealed for us, God cannot refuse a Saviour of his own sending and sealing, and appointing to satisfy his justice. Therefore we go boldly to the throne of grace. It is a marvellous privilege that we see God clearly in the gospel, with open face, with a spirit of boldness, the veil of ignorance being taken away. For the sight of God to a conscience that is natural, and is not convinced of the

* That is, 'offending' = injuring.—G. † Cf. Eph. iii. 12; Heb. x. 19.—G.

mercy of God by the Spirit, it is a terrible sight. A guilty conscience cannot see a man but it trembles. It cannot see a judge without trembling. And will not the trembling conscience, the guilty soul, flee from the face of God apace, that trembles at the sight of a man? What is so contrary as the nature of God to the nature of man out of Christ? The unholy, impure, and unclean nature of man, to the pure, holy nature of God? If Christ had not taken our nature and sanctified it in himself, and satisfied justice in it, what boldness could this unclean nature of ours have had to go to the holy God? Let us, I beseech you, be wrapped up in admiration of the singular love of God to us, especially in the days of the gospel, that now we see in a glass, in a clear glass, the love of God in Christ, and with open face boldly we may go to God.

Sometimes when the soul is bold in sin, it weakeneth boldness and faith, and makes us look upon that object that our sins hath deserved, upon a wise God. For howsoever we may behold his glorious face in Christ, yet if we behold sin against conscience, God will hide himself, Christ will hide his face, and hide the promises, and leave us to terrors of conscience; and the soul shall not apprehend his gracious face in Christ, but that correction that our sin hath deserved. God hath power over the soul, and makes the soul apprehend what object he will; and he presents to a bold soul that runs into sin what it deserves, hell for the present. There is no terrors to the terror of a Christian that is bold in sin, till God shine upon him in his grace again. Sins against conscience, especially wasting sins, weaken faith, that we cannot go so boldly to God. Therefore those that say when they sin against conscience, that all the cause of their grief is because they do not conceive the free mercy of God, they are ignorant of God's ways. God is wise, and though he pardon sin, as sin is pardoned in heaven, before it be pardoned in the conscience, they shall never be pardoned in thy conscience till God have made thy conscience smart for it; and God will let wrath into thy conscience, and thy faith shall stagger. It is a sin for faith to stagger, it should not do so; but it will tremble and quake, till we have humbled ourselves before God.

What is the way, after we have had boldness and sweet familiarity with God, and it hath been interrupted by sin? how shall we recover ourselves?

Surely, to apprehend our sins to be pardonable in Christ, and that God is an everlasting Father, and that the covenant of grace is everlasting, and that there is mercy in Israel for this thing; and the conceit* of mercy must work our hearts to grief and shame. That is certain; for mark in the gospel, 'Come unto me, all ye that are weary and heavy laden,' Mat. xi. 28. He calls us when we find our consciences afflicted and tormented. 'He came to save that which was lost,' Mat. xviii. 11. By the blessed power of the Spirit, the blood of Christ is as a fountain 'for Judah and Jerusalem to wash in,' Zech. xiii. 1, and the 'blood of Christ purgeth us from sin,' 1 John i. 7; and Christ bids us for daily trespasses ask pardon, Mat. vi. 12. Daily therefore conceive goodness in God still, an everlasting current of mercy; and this must work upon us grief and shame, and recover and strengthen our faith again. For God's children, after breaches, arise the stronger rather than ever they were before. But this only by the way. We see here how God's glorious grace is conveyed to us, and what is wrought in us to apprehend it, a spiritual eye to see it, in the glass of the gospel, and 'with open face we behold it,' we may go boldly to the throne of grace.

* That is, 'conception.'—G.

I beseech you, let not that privilege be forgotten, this privilege of the gospel. What is the glory of the times we live in, but God's face discovered in Christ? In the gospel faith is wrought in us to apprehend this, to see God's face openly, and that we may come boldly with Benjamin, our elder brother;* come with Esau's garments, Gen. xxvii. 23; come with Christ, and we cannot be too bold. Remember alway there must be a reverent familiarity, because he hath majesty mixed with his bowels of mercy. Both are mixed together; beams and bowels. So our carriage to him must be loving and familiar, as he is full of bowels of mercy. But then he hath majesty. A reverent familiarity is fit for a father, and for so gracious and so sweet a God. Therefore that phrase we see in the Scriptures, 'We go boldly,' and cry, 'Abba, Father,' Rom. viii. 15. Father is a word of reverence; that is, we go boldly to God in Christ, and open our wants as to a father, with love and reverence; as it is said here, 'with open face.' Let us not forget this privilege.

'We all.'

Here is the generality, 'We all.' Before, in Moses's time, he alone went into the mount and saw God; but now 'we all,' Jews and Gentiles, where the gospel is preached, 'we all.' Therefore, you see here the church is enlarged by the coming of Christ. And it was a comfort to St Paul, and to all good Christians, to think of the enlargement of the church by taking in the Gentiles, as it will be a comfort hereafter to think of the enlarging of the church by taking in the Jews again. The more the better in religion. Why is it a privilege for many, that 'we all?' Because in matters of grace and glory there is no envy at all. All may share without prejudice. All cannot be kings here upon earth, nor all cannot be great men, because the more one hath the less another hath. But in Christ and in religion all may be gracious. God respects every one, as if there were none but them. He respects all as one, and one, as if there were none but he. Every man *in solidum*, as civilians express it, entirely enjoyeth Christ, as if there were none but he. He is to all as one, and to one as if there were none but he. There is no envy, as I said, in grace and glory, where all may share alike. And that is the reason why it is alway comfortable to think of community in religion. It is joined with comfort.

And indeed so it is matter of comfort to see a communion of many in one; for what is the mystical body of Christ Jesus but many members joined in one body, under one gracious and glorious head? And therefore it is a deformed sight to see fraction and disunion. It is that the devil rules in. Divide and rule. It is fit for the devil. God and Christ rule in union. The same Spirit of God that knits the members to the head by faith, knits the members one to another in love; and all grace is derived from the head to the members, as they are united to the body. If there be therefore disunion, there is no grace conveyed so far as there is disunion. There is no grace conveyed from the head; for the body grows up as compact under one head.

Therefore let us labour to cherish union, and as we hate distraction† itself, so hate distraction and division; for dissipation causeth distraction.† Therefore by all means labour for union, especially now we are to take the communion, that is a seal of our communion with Christ by faith, and one with another. By love let us labour to bring our hearts to a holy communion.

* There seems to be a mis-recollection here. Perhaps the thought is, 'Come boldly with [our] Benjamin—[come with] our elder brother,' &c.—G.

† Qu. 'destruction'?—Ed.

None gains by disunion but the devil himself. Alway his policy is to make the breach greater where any is. Therefore let us labour by all means to be united. The more join together in the blessed mysteries of the gospel, the more comfort and the more glory. When all live and join together in holy things of God, and in sweet love one to another, it is the glory of that place and society and state. So much for that 'we all.'

'And are changed.'

I shewed before how man's happiness stands partly in communion with God, and partly in his conformity and likeness to God. And surely wheresoever there is communion there will be conformity. This conformity is here set down springing from communion. 'We all behold the glory of God.' Now, reconciled in Jesus Christ, what doth that beholding work? A conformity. We are 'changed into the same image, from glory to glory.' In these words we see,

First, A necessity of a change; changed we must be.

Then in this change there must be a pattern of conformity. We are changed into the image of Christ, who is the prototype, the first type and idea of all perfection. We are changed into the same image.

And then, how this change is wrought to the image of Christ. It is by beholding the glory of Christ in the gospel. There is a transforming power in beholding the glory of God's mercy in Christ. It is not a delighting object only, to see the mercy of God in Christ, but it is a powerful object that hath an influence upon the soul.

And then the state of man after this change, it is a glorious condition, 'We are changed from glory.'

And then it is a growing condition, 'We are changed from glory to glory.' Still, till we come to that pitch, where there can be no growth; when the soul shall be filled 'with the fulness of God,' as the apostle speaks, Eph. iii. 19; when the soul shall have all the powers that it hath to receive and retain, and comprehend, all the corners of it filled. So we grow from glory to glory till then. These things follow one another. To begin with the first.

There is a necessity of a change.

In the state we are we must be changed, as Christ tells Nicodemus, John iii. 1, *seq.* There must be a change; and such a change as is a new birth. It must be all new, as a bell; if there be but a crack in it, it must be new moulded and cast again. It is good for nothing else. So the soul of man, if there be but a flaw, but a crack, all is naught. It must be cast and moulded again anew. We must be set in tune again. All is out of tune. Before the soul can make any sweet harmony in the ears of God, there must be a change. There is no coming to heaven without a change. What need I press this, it is so easy a point in religion. 'Except we be born anew we cannot enter into heaven,' John iii. 3. But to clear from evidence of reason the necessity of a change in the whole man.

First, Because we are in a contrary state to grace and to God. We are dead. There must be life in us before we come to heaven. We are enemies, and if* enemies we must be made friends. How shall we be fit for communion else with God, wherein our happiness stands, without conformity? Communion is between friends. Before those that are in an opposite condition can be friends, there must be an alteration; and this alteration it must be on God's part, or on our part. Now who must change?

* Qu. 'of''—Ed,

God that is unchangeable, or we that are corrupt and changeable? God will not change. There is no reason he should. He is goodness itself, alway unchangeable. His perfection stands in an individual point. He cannot alter a whit. There is not a shadow of change in God. Therefore, when there is difference between God and us, the change must be on our part. We must be changed, as it is Rom. xii. 2, and other places, 'in the spirit of our minds.' We must be wholly moulded anew. Where there is a condition so opposite as the frame of our hearts is to God, he being holiness and we a mass and lump of sin, of necessity there must be a change. God intends in the gospel to bring us near himself, and Christ's end is to bring us to God, as it is 1 Pet. iii. 18. All the gospel is to bring us back to God from whom we fell. Now our nature, as I said, is defiled and unholy; and we cannot be friends with God till there be a likeness in disposition to God. Therefore our natures must be suitable to the sweet and holy and pure nature of God in some measure. We enter into a covenant with God, in the covenant of grace, and how can we maintain the covenant of grace, without some likeness to God and Christ? In that regard of necessity there must be a change; and this change must be on our part. As we see in an instrument, those strings that are out of tune are brought to them that are in, so it is we that must change and alter, and not God. God is alway unchangeable, like himself in his love; and it is our comfort that he is so unchangeable in his mercy and holiness and justice. Therefore I say the change must be on our part.

'Flesh and blood, as it is, cannot enter into heaven,' 1 Cor. xv. 50; that is, the nature of man, as it is corrupted; we must have new judgments of things, and new desires, and new esteem, new affections, new joys, new delights, new conversation, new company. All the frame of the soul must be new. There must be a new bent of soul. It must be turned another way. The face of the soul must look clean another way. Whereas before it looked to the world-ward, and to things below, now it must look to God-ward and heaven-ward. Therefore those that are in their pure naturals, that feel no change in themselves, what shall we think of them? They are not in the state of grace, for of necessity there must be a change.

There is a double change, real and gradual.

First, A real change, from ill to good.

And *then, A gradual change from better to better*, 'from glory to glory.'

The first change is from the state of nature to grace at our first conversion, when God puts the first form and stamp upon us.

And then a change in grace, 'from glory to glory,' we must be changed.

Second, Then again, *we all expect glory in heaven;* and how can we do that except we be fitted for it? The church is the fitting place for glory. We enter into heaven in the church here. We are hewn and squared here. If we be not holy here, we shall never enter into heaven. There must be a change begun here if ever it be perfected in heaven. 'No unclean thing shall come there,' Rev. xxi. 27. As soon as ever Satan, an angel of light, sinned, he was tumbled out of heaven. It will brook * no unclean thing; no unclean thing shall ever come there again. Therefore our nature must be altered suitable to that place and glorious condition, before we come to heaven. Except we be new born, we cannot enter into the kingdom of God. There is direct Scripture for it. Beloved, this is forgot. Men trust to the grace and mercy of God, and look not after a change; and this holds many from embracing the gospel in the truth of it;

* That is, 'suffer,' 'endure.'—G.

from knowing Christ as the truth is in him. They hear they must be changed, which they are unwilling to. They believe that God is merciful, and that Christ died, &c. They snatch so much of the gospel, as may serve to build them up in self-love. So far they think all is well. But when they see such grace as must teach them 'to deny ungodliness and worldly lusts,' Titus ii. 12, and such grace as must change and alter them, this they cannot brook. They are content to go to heaven if they may have it in a way to hell; in maintaining their corruptions; being proud and covetous and worldly, as they are. This must not be. Of necessity there must be a change.

Third, Nay, I say more, beside the former reasons, *the soul that truly desires mercy and favour, desires always power against sin.* Pardon and power go together, in God's gift and in the desire of a Christian's soul. There is no Christian soul but he desires the grace of sanctification to change him, as much as the grace of pardon; for he looks upon corruption and sin as the vilest thing in the world; and upon grace and the new creature as the best thing in the world. There is no man changed but he hath those apprehensions of sanctification.

Remember this against some weak conceits likewise, that would have all the change in justification. They rent * Christ's offices, as if he were all priest, and not a king to govern; as if he were righteousness, and not sanctification; as if he had merit to die for us and to give us his righteousness, and no efficacy to change our natures; as if in the covenant of grace God did not write his law in our hearts, but only forgave our sins. He doth both in the covenant of grace. And where God makes a combination, we must not break it. Efficacy and merit, justification and sanctification, water and blood, go together. There must be a change. But to follow the point a little further.

Fourth, There must be change, *because no holy action can come from an unchanged power and faculty.* Actions spring from powers and faculties. They are suitable to them. Therefore there must be a change in the powers and faculties of the soul, before there be a change in the life and conversation. These three follow in nature.

The form, and living, and being of things; and powers; and action issuing from the power. So in the life of grace and sanctification there is a power and ability to believe in God, and to be holy, and to love God; and then the actions of love spring from that power. We live, and then we have a power to move. In nature, being and life and moving go together. So if we have a being in grace, we have a power to move. I beseech you, therefore, consider the necessity of a change of the inward man, of the powers and faculties of the soul. Can the eye see without a power of seeing? or the ear hear without a faculty of hearing? Can the soul perform sanctified actions without a sanctified power? It is impossible.

And especially the alteration and change is in the will, which some would have untouched. They would have it free; those that would have no more given to grace than needs must. But grace works upon the will most of all. Divinity rules the will especially. For the bent of the will makes a good or a bad man; and the desires of the will carry the whole man with it. We are as the bent is of our will. We are as the choice of our will is. If the choice, and bent, and bias be the right way, by the Spirit, it is good. If the will be not inclined and wrought to go the best way, there is no work of grace at all. Though all grace come in through

* That is, 'rend,' = separate.—G.

the understanding enlightened, that is the first, yet it goeth into the will. It passeth through the understanding into the will, and it puts a new taste and relish upon the will and affections.

Well, you see, therefore, that the grace wrought in the gospel it is not a mere persuasion and entreaty, &c., but a powerful work of the Spirit entering into the soul and changing it, and altering and turning the bent and inclination of the will heavenward, whereas* corruption of nature turns the soul downward to things below. When the Spirit of God entereth into the soul, it is not only by mere outward persuasion to leave it to the liberty of will, but it altereth the taste of the will. The soul is carried up, and is shut to things below. It useth the world as though it used it not. We must have great conceits of the work of grace. The Scripture hath great words of it. It is an alteration, a change, a new man, a new creature, new birth, &c. We see the necessity of a change.

Fifth. Again, another reason is this: *God, where he calls and dignifies, he also qualifies*. Princes cannot qualify those they raise, but God, whom he advanceth to glory, he fits and qualifies for glory; where he bestows his mercies and favours to life everlasting, he calls to great matters, and he also changeth them. If Saul were changed when he came to be a king, in regard of a new quality, shall we think that God will call any to the participation of his glorious mercy in Christ, in pardoning their sin, and accepting them to life eternal, but he will change them? No. Whosoever he calls to glory, he changeth and altereth their dispositions to be fit for so glorious a condition as a Christian is called to. There must be a change.

Proud men love not to hear of this. It is a prejudice to their former authority. What! I that was accounted a wise man, now to be a fool! I that was accounted so and so, to alter all my frame and course, and to turn the stream another way—the world will say I go mad. I say because grace altereth and changeth all: 'Old things are passed away, and all things are become new,' 2 Cor. v. 17; those that are carnal and proud cannot endure a change, because it is some prejudice to their reputation. But it must be so if they look for salvation. Thus you see that point proved enough.

'Into the same image.'

The pattern to which we are changed is the image of Christ. It is a rule, and a true rule, the first in every kind is the measure of all the rest. It is the idea, the pattern, and platform of all the rest. Now Christ is the first, for he is the 'first-born,' the 'first fruits,' the 'first beloved.' Therefore he is the pattern of all the rest, and the measure of all other. The nearer we come to Christ, the better we are; for that is the measure of a thing, the nearer it answereth to that the better. Now Christ is the best, and our nature in Christ is joined to the Godhead in one person. Therefore we are changed to the likeness of Christ, 'the second Adam;' for as before we are changed, we are corrupted and depraved according to the likeness of the first Adam after his fall; and as before his fall, if he had not fallen, we had been born according to his likeness, that is, good and righteous; so now being fallen, as soon as by faith we are planted and grafted into the second Adam we are changed into his likeness. Christ as it were is God's master-piece, that is, the excellentest work, and device, and frame of heaven that ever was, to set up such a Mediator, to reconcile justice and mercy in bringing God and man into one person. Now Christ being God's master-piece, the best and most excellent frame of all, he is fit to be the

* A misprinted 'by' here.—G.

pattern of all excellency whatsoever. Therefore he is the image, the idea, the pattern and platform of all our sanctification.

Christ the second Adam is the image into which we are changed. We are not changed to the image of the first Adam by grace, but to the image of the second Adam. There is from him a derivation of all good, opposite to all the ill we drew from the first Adam. We drew from the first Adam the displeasure of God; by the second we obtain the favour of God by his death and satisfaction. With the wrath of God we drew corruption from the first Adam, in the second we have grace. From the first Adam we have death, and all the miseries that attend death and follow it. In the second Adam we have life and all happiness, till it end in glory. In a word, whatsoever ill we have in the first Adam, it is repaired abundantly in the second, when we are changed into his image. Therefore, when you read of the image of God in the New Testament, it must be understood of the image of God in Jesus Christ, the second Adam.

Now this image consists in knowledge, in holiness and righteousness. If we compare Col. iii. with Eph. iv., this was perfect in Christ, who was the image of his Father, and we must be like Christ the second Adam in sanctification.

Now the grounds why we must be conformable to the image of the second Adam, and not to the first, are these:

Because the second Adam is far excelling the first Adam; and as I said, we must be conformed to the best image. As we have borne the image of the first, so we must bear the image of the second, as it is in 1 Cor. xv. 49.

And then the image of God in the second Adam is more durable. For all excellencies and grace is more firmly set on Christ than ever they were upon Adam. It is set upon him with such a character and stamp as shall never be altered. When God set his image on the first Adam it was rased, and decayed, and lost, by the malice of the devil, because it was not set on so firmly, Adam being a man and a good man, yet he was a man changeable. But Christ is God-man; in one nature God hath set such a stamp of grace on the human nature, being eternally united to the Godhead, that shall never be altered. Therefore we are renewed according to the image of God as it is stamped on Christ, not as it was stamped on the first Adam.

And that is the reason why the state of God's children is unalterable, why being once gracious they are so for ever. If God set the stamp of the Spirit of Christ on them, it is firm, as it is upon Christ. It never alters in Christ, nor in those that are members of Christ. The alteration is in growth from better to better. God's children sometimes a little deface that image by sin, security, and the like. But as a piece of coin that is a little defaced, yet it hath the old stamp still, and is acknowledged for good coin, so a Christian in all desertions, in the worst state, he hath the stamp still. Though it be darkened by his carelessness, yet after it receives a fresh stamp it is an everlasting stamp. When once we are God's coin we are never reprobate silver. And all is, because we are 'renewed according to the image of Christ,' and grace is firmly set in our nature in Christ so sure that all the devils in hell cannot rase it out. And he is the 'quickening Spirit,' and therefore able to transform us to his likeness better than the first Adam was. Therefore the image of God is the likeness of the second Adam, and we are changed into that.

Now the reasons why the second Adam changeth us into his own image are many:

First, Because he is a powerful head that changeth all his members, a powerful root that changeth all his branches into his own nature, a powerful husband that changeth his own spouse. I say, he is a quickening Spirit, a public person, and the root of all believers, as the first Adam was of us all as we are natural men.

Second, Again, it is meet that brethren should be all alike; therefore, as it is in Rom. viii. 29, '*we are predestinate to be conform to Christ.*' 'He is the first among many brethren.' The chief brethren must be all alike. Therefore we being predestinate to salvation, it was fit we should be predestinate to be conformable to our elder brother, that brethren might be of one nature and disposition. It is fit that the husband and wife should be of one disposition. Christ is the husband and we are the spouse. Therefore by grace he alters, and cleanseth, and purgeth his spouse, as it is Eph. v. 25, *seq.*, 'He loved his spouse, and gave himself for it; that he might purge it, and make it a glorious spouse.' It is meet the wife should be the glory of the husband, as St Paul saith, 1 Cor. xi. 7, that is, that she should reflect the excellencies of her husband. Therefore that the church might be the glory of Christ and reflect the excellencies of Christ, she is changed to be like Christ more and more daily. There is a kind of congruity that brethren should be like, and that the spouse and the husband should be alike. Therefore God hath ordained that we should be like him in a threefold degree: in suffering, in grace, and in glory. Whosoever will be like him in glory, must be like him in grace. First God's election and ordaining must have its issue; that is, the representation of the likeness of Christ in our natures.

Third, Again, *the end of Christ's coming was 'to destroy the works of the devil,'* 1 John iii. 8, to deface all Satan's works, especially his work in us, the image of Satan in our dispositions. For every man by nature carries the image of the devil on him, till the image of Christ be stamped on, and the image of Satan rased out. For in man there is naturally an opposition to the truth, a hatred of God and of good things. Now Christ coming to dissolve the works of the devil, puts out this image, and sets his own stamp and image upon the soul. Therefore unless Christ change us to his own image he should miss of the end of his coming. These and many such reasons there are to prove that we are restored according to the image of Christ Jesus, and why Christ will change us to his own likeness. To add one more:

Fourth, The end of Christ is, *that we should enter into a sweet communion with him.* Therefore he will set such a stamp upon us as he may delight in us and be friends. Now if he should not change our natures, what correspondence could there be between Christ and us? Now when he hath altered and changed us, he looks on us as carrying his stamp and image.

Use 1. If this be so, that we are changed into the image of the second Adam, Jesus Christ, then I beseech you *let us labour every day more and more to study Christ*, that so by beholding Christ we may be transformed into his likeness. For the looking upon Christ is a transforming sight. Therefore let us look into his disposition as it is set forth in the gospel, and to his carriage, and look to his privileges, that so we may receive 'grace for grace,' grace suitable to his grace, disposition suitable to his disposition, conversation suitable to his conversation, and privilege and prerogative suitable to his prerogative, that we may be like him every way.

What was his disposition and carriage? It were too large to unfold it to you as it is in the gospel, but because we must be changed into the image of Christ, it is good to look to that picture, that we may resemble that image as much as may be. You see in the gospel how he carried himself to his friends, enemies, the devil, himself.

You see how full of love he was. What drew him from heaven to earth, and so to his cross and to his grave, but love to mankind? You see how full of goodness he was: 'He went about doing all the good he could,' Acts x. 38. How much good doth that speech savour of that Paul speaks of him, 'It is a more blessed thing to give than to receive,' Acts xx. 35. See how full of zeal he was! He whipped the buyers and sellers out of the temple, John ii. 15. He was full of goodness. It was his meat and drink to do good, John iv. 32, *seq.* It was as natural to him as for a fountain to stream out.

(1.) And as I said for his carriage toward *his friends*, to those that were good, how sweet and indulgent was he.

[1.] *Where there was any beginnings of goodness*, he did encourage it. He never sent any back again, but those that went back again of their own head, as the young man. Christ sent him not back. He was so full of sweetness to weak Christians, nay, he discovered himself most to the weakest. He was never more familiar with any than with the woman of Samaria, that was an adulteress, John iv. 6, *seq.*; and Mary that had been a sinner, how sweetly did he appear to her first, John xx. 1, *seq.* How sweet was he to sinners when they repented! how ready to forgive and pardon! See it in Peter. He never cast him in the teeth with his apostasy; he never upbraided him with it; he never so much as tells him of it, only he 'looks' upon him, and afterward, 'Lovest thou me?' &c., John xxi. 15.

[2.] *He would not* 'quench the smoking flax, nor break the bruised reed,' Mat. xii. 20, *so gentle and sweet a Saviour have we.* He was sweet to those that were good in the lowest degree of goodness; nay, where there was but a representation of goodness, as in the young man, he kissed and embraced him when he came and said, 'What good thing shall I do to inherit eternal life?' Mark x. 17. He embraced him, and made much of him. And so to the Pharisee, 'Thou art not far from the kingdom of God,' Mark xii. 34. He laboured to pull him further. He was of a winning, gaining disposition. Those that were good he loved them, and carried himself so to all as much as might be. Shall we not labour to be of his disposition, not to set people further off, but to be of a gaining, winning nature?

[3.] See how obedient he was *to his Father*, 'Not my will, but thine be done,' Mat. xxvi. 42; both in active and passive obedience, in all things he looked to his Father's will, being subordinate to him. Wheresoever there is subordination, there ought to be obedience. Now there is a subordination to God as our Father in Christ. Therefore we should labour to be obedient even to death, as Christ was. Our happiness stands in subordination. The happiness of the inferior is in subjection to the superior that may do him good. Therefore we must be obedient to God as Christ was. We see he prayed whole nights.*

(2.) *For his own particular*, how holy and heavenly was he.† He takes occasion of vines, of stones, of water, of sheep, and all things to be heavenly minded, to raise his soul upon all occasions. And when he rose from the dead, and conversed with his disciples, what was his talk? He discoursed all of matters of the kingdom of heaven. So his whole disposition was heavenly and holy in himself, and patient in wrongs done to him. He did

* Cf. Luke vi. 12: xxi. 37.

† According to the method on page 261, at bottom, this ought to have been the fourth particular.—G.

not return injury for injury. You see how meek he was. I give you but a touch of every particular. You may by proportion apply the rest. He was in his own particular holy and heavenly, and full of purity and holiness and heavenliness.

(3.) *What was he to his enemies?* Did he call for fire from heaven when they wronged him? Was he all on a heat? When his poor disciples, being more flesh than spirit, would have fire from heaven, 'You know not what spirit you are of,' saith he, Luke ix. 55. He shed tears for those that shed his blood, 'Oh Jerusalem, Jerusalem,' &c., Mat. xxiii. 37, that afterward crucified him. And upon the cross you see there to his very enemies, 'Father, forgive them, they know not what they do,' Luke xxiii. 34. So then if we will be like to Christ, consider how he carried himself to God in devotion and obedience, and how in himself he was full of purity and holiness, unspotted every way; how to his friends, to all that had any goodness in them; and how to his enemies, he prayed for his very enemies.

(4.) And *for the devil himself*. Deal with him as Christ did, that is, have no terms with him, although he come to us in our nearest friends. He came to Christ in Peter. 'Satan avoid,' saith he, Mat. xvi. 32. If the devil come to us in our wives, in our children, in our friends, 'avoid Satan.' Satan comes to us sometime in our friends, to give corrupt judgment, to maintain self causes, to do this or that that may crack our conscience. Discern the devil in our best friends; for sometime they may be the trunks* of the devil. The devil may convey his spirit through Peter. Let us imitate Christ. Discern between our friends' love and the subtilty of the devil in them, and be able to give them an avaunt, 'avoid Satan.' We see Christ when he encountered Satan, he fights not with Satan's weapons; and when he was to deal with his instruments, but with the word of God. He gives not reproach for reproach, nor sophistry for sophistry; but 'It is written,' Mat. iv. 4, *et alibi*, shewing that we must encounter Satan with God's armoury, with weapons out of the book of God.

And then when Satan would confess him, and make much of him, 'Oh thou art the Son of God,' he would have nothing to do with him. So those that are manifestly led with the spirit of Satan, and would press kindness on us, have nothing to do with them so far. As we say of the devil he is not alway a liar, but he alway cozeneth; so take those that are led by the spirit of the devil, that are Jesuited papists, they lie not in all, but there is cozening in all; for all is but snaring kindness and gifts that will hurt more. All offers from Satan, and those that are led with the spirit of Satan, we ought to suspect, as Christ we see when Satan offered him a kindness, he saw he was to be took heed of. Therefore saith he, 'away,' you and your kindness. So have nothing to do with devilish men. Those are best at ease, and prosper most that have least to do with them; those that see they are alway deceivers though they be not alway liars; those that are nearest hostility prosper best. Thus you see a taste of Christ's carriage to his friends, to his enemies, to Satan. And for hypocrites he speaks, 'Woe to them,' Mat. xxiii. 13. He hated them above all the proud Pharisees. I might spend much time in going over particulars in the gospel, to see what expressions there are of Jesus Christ.

Use 2. I beseech you, make this use of it, when in the gospel you read of any expression of his love and gentleness, of his obedience and humility, in washing his disciples' feet, and 'Learn of me for I am meek,' &c., Mat. xi. 29, and 'Come unto me, all ye that are weary and heavy laden,' Mat.

* That is, trunk or chest, = *instruments* of the devil.—G.

xi. 28, then think *this is the expression of my blessed Saviour*, 'the second Adam,' *to whose image I must be conformed, and transformed, and changed;* and therefore when you are moved and tempted to sin, from your own corruption, or from Satan, reason thus with yourselves: Would our blessed Saviour, if he were upon earth, do this? would he speak thus? would he not do thus if he were here now? would he not be ready to do this good turn? Surely he would; and I must be changed into his image and likeness. Therefore let me consider what my blessed Saviour would do in the like case. Surely our blessed Saviour would not stain and defile his body. He would not make his tongue an instrument of untruth to deceive others. He would not be covetous and injurious. Art thou a Christian or no? If thou be a Christian thou hast the anointing of Jesus Christ. That anointing that was poured on him as the head, it runs down to thee as a member, as Aaron's ointment ran down to his skirts. If thou be the skirt of Christ, the meanest Christian, thou hast the same grace if thou be a Christian. And therefore thou must express Christ, that as thou art partaker of his name, so thou must be partaker of his anointing. If thou be a Christian, why doest thou thus? Doth this suit with thy profession? Dost thou carry the image of Satan, and dost thou think to be a Christian, except it be in title and profession only? No. There is no Christian but if he be a true Christian he is changed into the likeness of Christ, into his image. Therefore it is a good thought upon all occasions, every day to think what would my blessed Saviour say if he were here? and what did he in the like case when he was upon earth? I must be 'led by the Spirit of Christ,' or else I am none of his. Therefore let us shame ourselves when we are moved by our corruptions and temptations to do anything contrary to this blessed image.

And consider, the more we grow into the likeness of Christ, the more we grow in the love of God, who delights in us as he doth in his own Son: 'This is my beloved Son, in whom I am well pleased,' Mat. iii. 17. Now the more like we are to Christ, the more he is pleased with us.

And the more we shall grow in love one to another; for the liker pictures are to the first pattern, the liker they are one to another. So the liker we grow to Christ, the liker we are one to another, and the more like, the more love.

Who keeps Christ alive in the world, but a company of Christians that carry his resemblance? As we say of a child that is like his father, this man cannot die as long as his son is alive, because he resembleth his father; so as long as Christians are in the world, that have the Spirit of Christ, Christ cannot die. He lives in them, and Christ is alive no otherwise in the world than in the hearts of gracious Christians, that carry the picture and resemblance of Christ in them.

But how are we changed into the likeness of Christ? How come we to be like him?

When once we believe in Christ, we are graft into the similitude of his death, and into the likeness of his resurrection. It is a point somewhat mystical, yet it is stood upon in the Scriptures, in Rom. vi. especially, at large.

How come we to die to sin by virtue of Christ's death? and to live to righteousness by the fellowship of Christ's resurrection? It is said we are transformed into the likeness of Christ. The phrases of Scripture shew it. But to stand upon these phrases a little.

Beloved, as it was in Christ's own person when Christ died, whole

Christ died and was crucified, but yet the death itself, the crucifying was terminate in the human nature: the human nature died and not the Godhead; yet by reason of the union, whole Christ died and was crucified: the 'Lord of glory' was crucified, as the Scripture speaks. And as it was in Christ natural, so it is in Christ mystical, whole Christ mystical was crucified, whole Christ mystical is risen again, notwithstanding the crucifying was terminate in Christ the head, not in the members. As his death was terminate in his human nature, it ended and was confined in that; so this crucifying belonged to the head, and the head rose; yet whole Christ, all believers as soon as they are one with Christ, by reason of the mystical union, they are dead and crucified in Christ their head, and risen and sit in heavenly places, in Christ their head. So then a true believer, when he is made one with Christ, he reasons thus, My corruption of nature, this pride of heart that naturally I have, this enmity of goodness, this is crucified; for I am one with Christ. When he died, I and my head did die, and this pride and covetousness and worldliness, this base and filthy carnal disposition, was crucified in Christ my head. I in my head was crucified, and I in my head now am risen and sit in heaven. Therefore now I am in some sort glorious. Therefore I mind things above in my head. And therefore because of the necessary conformity of the members to the head, I must more and more die to sin, be crucified to sin, and rise by the Spirit of Christ and ascend with him. The more I know, and consider, and meditate of this, the more I am transformed into the likeness of his death and resurrection. But to go a little further.

Quest. What things in Christ's death did especially discover themselves to us, when we once believe, to our comfort?

Ans. Three things.

In regard of us, wonderful love, that he died for us.

In regard of sin, wonderful hatred, that he would die for sin.

And *wonderful holiness and love of grace.* He shewed his hatred of sin, that he would shed his heart-blood for it; and wanting the glory of God, as it were, by feeling the wrath of God for a time, even in hatred to sin.

There were these two affections pregnant in Christ upon the cross, wondrous love for us to die for us, and wondrous hatred of sin to purge it, for which he died; and wondrous holiness, from whence hatred of sin came. Whence doth hatred of sin come, but from wonderful purity and holiness, that cannot endure sin? Thus, when the soul considers it is one with Christ, it hath the same affections that Christ had. Christ in love to us died. Can I apprehend that love of Christ when he died and was crucified and tormented for my sin, but out of love I must hate sin again? And when I consider how Christ stood affected to sin upon the cross, when he died to purge it, and to satisfy for it, can I have other affections, being one with him, than he had upon the cross? I cannot. So, whether I consider his love to me, or the hatred he bore to sin, considering myself one with him by a mystical union, I shall have the same affection of love to him, and be like him every way, to love what he loves, and to hate what he hates.

I cannot but hate sin; and, hating sin, I must act his part anew, that is, as he died for sin, so I die to sin; as he was crucified for it, so it is crucified in me; as he was pierced, so he gives corruption a stab in me; as he was buried, so my corruption is buried; and as he died once, never to die again, so I follow my sins to the grave, to death, and consumption of old Adam, that he never riseth again. So I say, the consideration of my union with

Christ, that I in Christ did die and was crucified, because my head died and was crucified. And then it puts that affection into me that was in Christ, and makes me act Christ's part, to die to sin daily more and more. These and the like thoughts are stirred up in a Christian, which St Paul aims at in Rom. vi. and other places.

So by the virtue of his resurrection I am conformable more and more to the graces in him; for as the power of God's Spirit raised him up when he was at the lowest, when he had been three days in the grave, so the Spirit in every Christian raiseth them up at the lowest to comfort, to a further degree of grace, more and more; nay, when they are fallen into any sin or any affliction for sin, the same power that raised Christ when he was in the grave, for our sins, in the lowest humiliation that could be, it raiseth them from their sins daily, that they gather strength from their sins. The power that raised Christ at the lowest raiseth a Christian at the lowest in sin and in affliction for sin; for when he is tripped and undermined by his corruptions, God by that power that raised Christ at the lowest recovers and strengthens him, and makes him afresh revenge himself upon his sin. And when he is at the lowest, in the grave, the same power will raise him, like Christ every way. So you see how we are changed to the likeness of Christ.

How shall we know then whether we have the image of Christ stamped upon us or no?

If we be changed into the likeness of Christ, we shall be changed in our understandings, to judge of things as he did. His aim was to please his Father in all things. If we have the same ends, and the same opinion and esteem of things, . . .* He judged matters of grace and of the kingdom of God above all other; for the soul is more worth than the whole world. See the judgment that he passed upon things: 'Seek ye first the kingdom of God, and all other things shall be cast upon you,' Mat. vi. 33. We must be changed in our judgment if we will have his image upon us. We must be like him in our will, in our choice, in the cleaving, and purpose, and resolution of our will. We must have the bent of our soul as his was. Our souls must be edged and pointed as his was, wholly for heaven and the kingdom of God. And so for our affections, there must be a change in them, in our love, and joy, and delight. We must love and joy and delight in whatsoever he did.

Now the way to stir us up to this is to see what image we naturally carry, and to see ourselves in the glass of the law. If a man consider thus, if Christ's image be not upon me, I carry the image of the devil, this would make him labour to get another image upon him. For, beloved, at the day of judgment Christ will not own us if he see not his image upon us. Cæsar will own Cæsar's coin if he see his image upon it. 'Whose image and superscription is this? Give unto Cæsar that which is Cæsar's,' Mat. xxii. 20. If Christ see his stamp on us, he will own us at the day of judgment, or else not. Naturally we are all opposite to Christ; naturally we are full of pride and malice; of the spirit of the world and the devil. Get out this by all means, or else Christ will not own us at the day of judgment. He will not look on us. He cannot abide to see us if we have not his image. We must bear the image of the second Adam as we did the image of the first.

Again, the law of God was written in Adam's heart, it is expressed and copied out. There see ourselves. There see all the curses. There see

* Sentence unfinished.—G.

ourselves guilty of the breach of every commandment. If we understand the law spiritually, that desire of women and revengeful thoughts are murder and adultery. Understand the law spiritually, and see ourselves in that glass, see ourselves utterly condemned. This will make us fly to the glass of the gospel, that we may be changed into the image of Christ.

There is another image that we more desire to be changed into. We are transformed into the likeness of the world, cast into the mould of the times. We labour to have those opinions that the times have, and those ways of getting and rising to preferment that the world hath, and to have that carriage and disposition every way that the world hath, and so frame to the spirit of the world in all things, that so we might not be observed by others, and crossed in our pleasures, and preferments, and profits. Well, this desire to be transformed into the likeness of the world, to have the spirit of the world, what will it come to in the end? The world shall be condemned. If we will be condemned with the world, let us labour to be transformed into the opinion of the world, and to go with the stream and errors of the time if we desire to be damned. The world must be condemned. It is the kingdom of Satan, wherein he rules. Therefore there is no image or likeness for us to be transformed into, if we will be saved and have comfort, but the image of Christ; and can we have a better likeness to be transformed into than the image of him by whom we hope to be saved? than to be like him, from whom we hope for so great a matter as salvation is?

Use 2. Again, that we may be changed into the likeness of Christ, *let us fix our meditations upon him*, and we shall find a change we know not how, insensible. As those that stand in the sun for other purposes, they find themselves lightened and heat [ed]; so let us set ourselves about holy meditations, and we shall find a secret, insensible change; our souls will be altered and changed we know not how. There is a virtue goes with holy meditation, a changing, transforming virtue; and indeed we can think of nothing in Christ but it will alter and change us to the likeness of itself, because we have all from Christ. Can we think of his humility and not be humble? Can we think, was God humble, and shall base worms be proud? Shall I be fierce when my Saviour was meek? Can a proud, fierce heart apprehend a sweet, meek Saviour? No. The heart must be suitable to the thing apprehended. It is impossible that a heart that is not meek, and sweetened, and brought low, should apprehend a loving and humble Saviour. There must be a suitableness between the heart and Christ. As he was born of a humble virgin, so he is born and conceived in a humble heart. Christ is born and conceived, and lives and grows in every Christian; and in a humble and lowly heart, made like him by his Spirit: that is the womb. The heart that is suitable, that is the heart that he is formed in.

Use 3. Again, to be changed into this image, when we are once in the state of grace, *let us look to the remainder of our corruptions*. The best of us shall see that that will make us look after Christ. Look to our worldly-mindedness, to our passions, to our rebellions, to our darkness and deadness of spirit, and then go to Christ. Lord, thou hast appointed Christ to be a head, to be a full vessel, that of his grace we might have grace for grace. He was 'anointed with the oil of gladness above his fellows,' Ps. xlv. 7, but for his fellows. I am earthly-minded, he is heavenly. I am full of rebellions, of lusts; all is at peace in him. The image of God is perfect in him, and he is a head to infuse grace, a head of influence as well as of eminence. He is not only above me, but he hath all grace for me.

Therefore, go to Christ. I need thy heavenly-mindedness, and some portion of thy meekness, of thy spiritual strength. I am weak, and dark, and dead, shine on me. Thou hast fulness for me. So go to Christ, and draw upon every occasion virtue and life from Christ our head. This is to know what is meant by being transformed to Christ our head.

There are two conformities, beloved, exceeding comfortable to us, and we must meditate on both.

First, Christ's conformity to us. He was transfigured into our likeness. He became man in love to us; not only man, but in the form of a servant, base man. He took man's nature, and man's base condition, Phil. ii. 8. Here is the ground of our comfort, that Christ took our form, he transfigured himself to our baseness; and shall not we labour to be transformed, to be like him, that out of love stooped so low to be like us? Let us but think of this, beloved! Our blessed Saviour took our nature on him pure and holy by his Spirit. He followed sin to death. He was conceived, and lived, and died without sin, to satisfy for sin; and now by his Spirit he cleanseth out sin. He pursued and chased out sin from his conception in all the passages of his life; so we should be like him. Drive away sin, get the Spirit, that our nature in us may be as it was in him: holy, and pure, and spiritual. Shall he be conformed to us, and shall not we be conform to him? Many such reasons and considerations there be to move us to be changed into the image of Christ.

Christ, in this work of changing, is all in all; for (1.) first of all, by Christ's death and satisfaction to divine justice, *we have the Spirit of God that doth all;* for the Spirit is the gift of God's love, next to Christ, the greatest. Now Christ having reconciled God, God being reconciled, gives the Spirit. Our sins being forgiven, the fruit of God's love is the Spirit. So we have the Spirit by the merit of Christ.

(2.) Again, we have it *from Christ*, as a head, derived* unto us. We have the Spirit for Christ and from Christ. Christ receives the Spirit first, and then he sends it into our hearts. So for Christ's sake, and from Christ as a head, we have the Spirit.

(3.) Again, from Christ *we have the pattern of all grace whatsoever*, to which we are changed. The pattern of all grace is from Christ. He begins to us in every grace.

(4.) Again, in the fourth place, *the reasons inducing are all from Christ.* For we are not only changed by power, but by reason. There is the greatest reasons in the world to be a Christian, and to come out of the state of nature. When our understanding is enlightened to see the horrible state of nature, with the angry face of God with it, and then to have our eyes opened at the same time to see the glorious and gracious face of God in Jesus Christ, here is the greatest wisdom in the world to come out of that cursed state to a better. Now, the reasons of this change are fetched from Christ, that by knowing Christ we know by reflection the cursed state out of him, and to see the glorious benefits by Christ's redemption and glorification. These set before the eye of the soul, and then the heart wrought upon these by reasons. If Christ gave himself for me, shall not I give myself to Christ? Paul hath his heavenly logic, 'Christ died for us, that we might live to him,' 2 Tim. ii. 11. So we have the merit of the Spirit from Christ, the derivation of the Spirit from Christ as a head, and the pattern of grace from Christ, and the inducing reasons all from Christ, in this changing to his image.

* That is, = 'conveyed.'—G.

(5.) Again, in that Christ is the image to which we are changed, *let us learn, if we would see anything excellent and comfortable in ourselves, see it in Christ first.* There is nothing comfortable in man but it is in Christ first, as the first image, the first receiver of all, Christ Jesus himself. If we would see the love of God, see the love of God in Christ our head first, in him that is God's beloved; if we would see the gifts that God hath blessed us with spiritual blessings, but it is in Christ. We have it from our head first. If we would see God's favour, 'This is my beloved Son, in whom I am well pleased,' Mat. iii. 17. I am well pleased in him, and in all his, that are one mystical body with him. If we would see comfortably our ill done away, our sins removed, see it in Christ abased, in Christ crucified, and made a curse. See them all wiped away in the cross of Christ. If we would see glory upon the removal of our sins, see it in Christ first. He is first risen, and therefore we shall rise. He is ascended, and sits in heavenly places, therefore we ascend and sit in heavenly places with him. All that we have or look to have comfortable in us, see it in the first pattern and platform in Christ. The reason is clear in Rom. viii. 29. We are elected and predestinate 'to be comformed to the image of his Son.' We are predestinate to be conformed to Christ in all things, to be loved as he is, to be gracious as he is. To rise to be glorious, to be freed and justified afterward from all our sins, as he our surety was. We are ordained to be conformable to him every way. In a word, the flesh of Christ it was holy, it was a suffering flesh, and then a glorious flesh, now it is glorious. So our nature must be like this image. It must be sanctified flesh, by the same Spirit that sanctified the mass that he was made of in the womb. It must be suffering flesh, in conformity to him; for the flesh that he took was suffering flesh, and he had a kingdom of patience before he had a kingdom of glory. So we must go through a kingdom of patience to the kingdom of glory, and then upon conformity in holiness with Christ comes our conformity in glory. When we are content to be conformed to Christ in our suffering flesh, then we shall be conformed to Christ in our glorious flesh; for our flesh must be used as his was. It must be holy and patient and suffering, and then it shall be glorious. So in all things we must look to Christ first; he must have the pre-eminence.

Beloved, of all contemplations under heaven, there is no contemplation so sweet and powerful as to see God in Christ, and to see Christ first abased for us and ourselves abased in Christ, and crucified in Christ, and acquitted in Christ. And then raise our thoughts a little higher. See ourselves made by little and little glorious in Christ. See ourselves in him rising and ascending and sitting at the right hand of God in heavenly places. See ourselves, by a spirit of faith, in heaven already with Christ. What a glorious sight and contemplation is this! If we first look upon ourselves what we are, we are as branches cut off from the tree; as a river cut off from the spring, that dies presently. What is in us but we have it by derivation from Christ, who is the first, the spring of all grace, the sum of all the beams that shine upon us? We are as branches cut off. Therefore now to see Christ, and ourselves in Christ, this transforms us to be like his image. It is the sweetest contemplation that can be.

We see this change is wrought by beholding. The beholding of the glory of God in the gospel, it is a powerful beholding; for, saith he, 'we are changed, by beholding,' to the image of Christ. Sight works upon the imaginations in brute creatures; as Laban's sheep, when they saw the parti-coloured rods, it wrought upon their imaginations, and they had lambs suitable.* Will sight work upon imagination, and imagination work a real change in nature? And shall not the glorious sight of God's mercy and love in Christ work a change in our soul? Is not the eye of faith more strong to alter and change than imagination natural? Certainly the eye of faith, apprehending God's love and mercy in Christ, it hath a power to change. The gospel itself, together with the Spirit, hath a power to change. We partake by it of the divine nature.

This glass of the gospel hath an excellency and an eminency above all other glasses. It is a glass that changeth us. When we see ourselves and our corruptions in the glass of the law, there we see ourselves dead. The law finds us dead, and leaves us dead. It cannot give us any life. But when we look into the gospel and see the glory of God, the mercy of God, the gracious promises of the gospel, we are changed into the likeness of Christ whom we see in the gospel. It is an excellent glass, therefore, that hath a transforming power to make beautiful. Such a glass would be much prized in this proud world; such a glass is the gospel.

Therefore let us be in love with this glass above all other glasses whatsoever. Nothing can change us but the gospel. The gospel hath a changing power, as you have it Isa. xi. 6, *seq.*: there the lion shall feed with the lamb,' &c. 'For the whole earth shall be full of the knowledge of the Lord,' ver. 9. The knowledge of Christ Jesus is a changing knowledge, that changeth a man even from an untractable, fierce creature, to be tractable, sweet, and familiar. So that the knowledge of God in Jesus Christ, you see, it is a transforming knowledge, and changeth us into the image of Christ, to the likeness of Christ.

Especially upon this ground, that when we look upon Christ, and God in Christ, we see ourselves there in the love of Christ, and in the love of God; and thereupon we are moved to be changed to Christ, not by seeing Christ alone, or by seeing God in Christ alone, but by seeing God's love in Christ to us, and Christ's love to us. For the Spirit of faith, which is given together with the gospel, it sees Christ giving himself for me, and sees God the Father's love in† me in Christ, and giving me to Christ. When the Spirit of faith with this appropriation seeth God, mine in Christ, and seeth Christ mine, and sees myself in the love of God, and in the love of Christ, hereupon the soul is stirred up from a holy desire to be like Christ Jesus, that loved me so much, and to be conformable to God all I can. For if the person be great and glorious, and our friend too, there is a natural desire to be like such, to imitate them, and express them all we can. Now when we see ourselves in the love of God and Christ, out of the nature of the thing itself, it will stir us up to be like so sweet, and gracious, and loving a Saviour.

There are three sights that hath a wondrous efficacy, and they go together.

God sees us in Christ, and therefore loves us as we are in Christ.

Christ sees us in the love of his Father, and therefore loves us as he sees us in his Father's love.

We see ourselves in Christ, and see the love of God to us in Christ.

These three sights are the foundation of all comfort. God gives us to Christ, and sees us as given to him in his election. Christ sees us as given of the Father, as you have it John xvii. 12; and loves us as we are loved of the Father, and then sees us as his own members. And we by a Spirit of faith see Christ, and see ourselves in Christ, and given to Christ

* Cf. Gen. xxx. 32, *seq.*—G.

† Qu. 'to'?—Ed.

by the Father. Hereupon comes a desire of imitation and expression of Jesus Christ. When we see ourselves in Christ God looks upon us in Christ, and we look upon ourselves in Christ; and when we look upon the mercy of God in Christ, it kindleth love, and love kindleth love, as fire kindleth fire. Fire hath that quality, that it turns all to itself. Now the meditation of the glorious love of God in Christ it works love, and love is an affection of changing; love transforms as fire doth. The love of God warms us, and we are fit for all impressions, as things that are warm. Iron is a dull and heavy thing, yet when it is warm it is bright and pliable, and hath as much as may be of the nature of fire imprinted upon it. So our dead, and dull, and inflexible, and unyielding souls become malleable and flexible by the love of Christ shining upon them. His love transforms them and kindles them. So here is the way how the glory of God's love in Christ transforms us, because the discovery of the bowels of mercy in God towards us kindles love to him; and that being kindled it works likeness, for love to greatness transforms us. It works a desire to be like those that are great. Where there is dependence there is a desire to be like, even among men. Much more considering that God so loves our nature in Christ, and that our nature is so full of grace in Christ as it is, the love of God in Christ, that hath done so much for us, it breeds a desire to be like Christ in our disposition, all we can.

By looking to the glory of God in Christ we see Christ as our husband, and that breeds a disposition in us to have the affections of a spouse. We see Christ as our head, and that breeds a disposition in us to be members like him.

Quest. How shall we know then that we see God in Christ, and the glory of God in the gospel comfortably?

Ans. Hath this sight a transforming power in thee, to the image of Christ, to make thee like him? If it have not a transforming power, it is a barren, empty contemplation, that hath no efficacy or comfort at all. So far as the sight of God's love in Christ breeds conformity to Christ, so far it is gracious and comfortable. See therefore whether thou art transformed to the image of Christ. If there be not a change, there is no beholding of Christ to speak of. No man ever sees the mercy of God in Christ by the eye of faith, but he is changed.

For, beloved, as there must be a change, so it is in this order, from beholding the mercy of God in Christ. For can you imagine that any soul can see itself in the glass of God's love in Jesus Christ, that it should see in the gospel Christ, and in him God reconciled unto him in particular, but that soul, out of the apprehension of God's love in Christ, will love God again, and be altered and changed? It is impossible such a sight therefore, whereby we see ourselves in this glass, as when we look in a glass, and see our own image, we see our own selves in Christ, and the love of God.* Such a sight altereth and changeth alway. It works love, and love is the worker of imitation; for what doth make one labour to express another in their disposition, carriage, and conversation? Oh it is love, as children imitate their parents. Love is full of invention, and of this kind of invention, that it studies to please the person loved, as much as it can every way. Hereupon we come to be desirous to be like Christ, because we see the glory of God's mercy shining in Christ.

The adversaries of the grace of God they fall foul upon us, because we preach justification by the free mercy and love of God in Christ. Oh, say

* Sentence unfinished.—G.

they, this is to dead the spirits of men, that they have no care of good works.

Beloved, can there be any greater incentive and motive in the world to sanctification, to express Christ and to study Christ, than to consider what favour and mercy we have in Christ? how we are justified and freed by him, by the glorious mercy of God in Christ? There cannot be a greater. Therefore we see here they depend one upon another. By seeing in the glass of the gospel the glory of God, we are transformed from glory to glory. An excellent glass the gospel is: by seeing God's love in it we are changed. The law is a glass too, but such a glass as St James speaks of, that when a man looks into it, and sees his duty, he goes away, and forgets all, i. 23. The law discovers our sin and misery. Indeed, it is a true glass. If we look there, we shall see the true picture of old Adam and of corruption; but it is such a glass as works nothing upon us. But when this glass is held out by the ministers of the word, whose office it is to hold the glass to people, when they see the love of God in Christ, this is a changing, transforming glass, to make them that were deformed and disfigured before, that bore upon them the image of Satan before, now to be transformed to be like Christ, by whom they must be saved. Is there any study in the world, therefore, more excellent than that of the gospel, and of the mercy of God in Christ, that transforms and changes men from one degree of grace to another, as it follows in the text.

Therefore, those that find themselves to be the 'old men' still, that have lived in corrupt courses, and do so still, let them not think to have any benefit by the gospel. They deceive themselves. They never knew God. For he that saith he hath communion with God, and walks in darkness, he is a liar, 1 John iv. 20. St John gives him the lie, for God is light. How can a man see himself in the love of God, and remain in a dark state opposite to love? Will it not alter a man? It will not suffer him to live in sins against conscience. Let no man that doth so, think he hath benefit by Christ. That knowledge is but a notional knowledge, a speculation, a swimming knowledge: it is not a spiritual knowledge; because wheresoever the knowledge of God in Christ is to purpose, there is a change and conversion of the whole man. There is a new judgment and new affections. The bent and bias of them is another way than they were before. There is a change which is called a turning in the Scripture.* Those things that were before them before, are now behind them; and those things that were behind them, are now before them. Whereas they turned their back upon God and good things, now they turn their faces, they look God-ward and heaven-ward, and to a better condition; for this change is nothing else but conversion. Therefore a man may say as he said, 'I am not I.' Those that have seen Christ, it makes them differ from themselves; this sight works a change.

If there were not a change, it would make God forsworn; as it is Luke i. 13, *seq.*, in Zacharias's song, 'He hath sworn that, being delivered out of the hands of our enemies, we should serve him without fear, in holiness and righteousness, all the days of our lives.' If any man, therefore, say he is delivered from his enemies, that he thinks he shall not be damned and go to hell, and yet doth not live in holiness and righteousness, he makes God's oath frustrate, for God's oath joins both together: 'He hath sworn that, being delivered out of the hands of our enemies, we should serve him without fear;' without slavish fear, but with a fear of reverence:

* That is, *στρεφεσθαι*. Mat. xviii. 3, and elsewhere.—G.

'in holiness and righteousnes all the days of our life.' Whosoever, therefore, are in a state of deliverance, have grace granted them whereby they may serve God in holiness and righteousness all the days of their life; they are changed into the same image,

'From glory to glory.'

By glory is meant especially grace here, and that which accompanies the grace of God, the favour of God. When we are persuaded of it by the Spirit, by which grace is wrought in us, upon grace in us there follows peace, and joy, and comfort, and many such things which the Scripture accounts to be glory.

We say there are four degrees of the glory of a Christian.

First, initial glory, in his first conversion, and thereupon, the knowledge of his deliverance from that cursed and damnable state that he is in; the knowledge, likewise, of his title to life everlasting. He comes to have friendship with God; he comes to have his nature renewed, that he may be friends with God. There must be an assimilation by the Spirit, like God, in a holy disposition. Now, upon the favour of God we come to be friends with God, and to have our natures altered; and hereupon comes those glorious qualifications, as peace, and joy, and consolation in all conditions, and liberty, and boldness to the throne of grace. This is glory, beloved! Is it not a glory to be friends with God, and to have God deal with us as friends? to reveal his secrets to us of his love and grace in Christ? to discover the hidden mysteries of his love to us, that was hid from the beginning of the world? We never know it till our effectual calling, till our first conversion, for God to be friends with us all our lives: Abraham was the friend of God. And then to have our nature renewed, to have our shame laid aside. Indeed, sin makes us shameful. It is the dishonour and abasement of the soul. The very change of our nature to be such as God may delight in, this is glory. The image of God is glory. Therefore in Rom. iii. 23, *et alibi*, it is said we are stripped and 'deprived of the glory of God' since the fall, that is, of the image of God, by Adam's sin, whereby we resembled God in holiness; so grace whereby we resemble God is the image and likeness of God, and that is the glory of man. If one should ask, What is the best glory of a man? that intrinsecal glory that characteriseth a man indeed? It is the stamp of Christ upon him, the image of the second Adam, in his soul to be like him.

And hereupon those glorious qualifications that follow upon it, glorious peace, and glorious joy; glorious and unspeakable comfort, above all discomforts whatsoever; as indeed the comforts of religion are comforts triumphing and prevailing above all discomforts. There are no comforts but those in religion, that are above the discomforts we meet with in this world. For what can be set against the wrath of God, against hell and damnation, but the comforts of the gospel? Now when a man is in the state of grace, and hath these glorious things following him, sweet and glorious peace that passeth understanding, that all the world, and all the devils in hell cannot shake, and joy in the Holy Ghost, and comforts above all discomforts whatsoever: and then glorious liberty he hath to come into the presence of God upon all occasions, being a friend of God—are not these things glorious, beloved? And these belong to every Christian.

Second, Now as a Christian *grows in assurance of his salvation and further friendship with God, and further peace and joy and comfort*, there is a further degree of glory. The growth of grace is glory. Therefore in 2 Pet. i. 5, *seq.*, he follows the point at large. When we add grace to grace, he saith it gives a further entrance into the kingdom of God: for the kingdom of God is begun in grace here; and the further we grow in grace, the more we enter into the kingdom of grace; and the further we enter into that, the nearer we are to the kingdom of glory.

Third, The next degree of glory is when the soul enjoys *the presence of God in heaven.*

Fourth, Then the upshot and conclusion, the closure and consummation of all, *at the day of judgment*, when body and soul shall be united again. Then is perfect glory. Here it is insinuated, when he saith we are changed from glory to glory, that is, from grace to grace, till all end in glory, which is the perfection of all in heaven, when body and soul shall be both glorious, 'from glory to glory.'

In this is considerable, first, that grace is glory: and then, that grace being glory, is growing in a continual course till it come to perfection. We grow 'from glory to glory,' from one degree of grace to another.

[1.] Grace whereby we resemble Christ is glory, and indeed so it is, *for the image and likeness of God is our glory.* What was Adam's glory but his likeness to God? He was created in God's image. And what is our glory? To be like Christ. Therefore grace is our glory.

[2.] *Man's perfection is his glory.* But the renewing of God's image in grace is man's perfection. Therefore it is his glory.

[3.] That which makes a man *terrible to all opposites whatsoever is glory.* But grace makes a man terrible to the devil and to wicked men. Both grace in one man, and grace in the church; for the church is 'terrible, like an army with banners,' Cant. vi. 4. When the ordinances of God are set up in glory, and there is glorious obedience to them in the church, it is terrible to the enemies as an army with banners; for there is a lustre and glory in all that is God's, both in the persons of believers, and likewise in the ordinances of God. Grace is glorious. As the wise man saith, 'Wisdom makes a man's face to shine,' Eccles. viii. 1. Is not wisdom a glorious thing: to see a wise understanding man able to guide himself and others? It puts a beauty upon a man, to be a wise and understanding man. Humility makes a man glorious; for it makes God put glory upon a man, when a man is glorious, and understands it not. As Moses when his face shined, he knew not that it shined himself. Many humble men are glorious and think not so. They are glorious, and they shine, though they see it not.

Is it not a glorious thing to be taken out of ourselves, to deny ourselves, to offer a holy violence to ourselves, and to our corruptions? Is not this a glorious thing, when others lie grovelling like slaves under their corruptions, to stand unmoveable in all the changes of the world, and in all intercourse of troubles to stand as a rock in the midst of all, unmoveable, founded upon the love of God in Christ, and the hope of glory after? Not to be shaken with the wind of temptations from his standing, at least not to be shook off his standing: this is glorious, to have a constant spirit.

Is it not glorious to have admittance boldly by grace; to go into the presence of God at all times; to be prevailer with God? Faith overcomes not only the world, but God himself. It binds him with his own promise. Is not faith a glorious grace, that triumphs over the great God himself, binding him with his own word and promise?

Is not love a glorious grace, that melts one into the likeness of Christ? Beloved, get love. It is the only artificial worker of imitation. It melts us into the likeness of Christ. It constrains, it hath a kind of holy violence in it. No water can quench it. We shall glory in sufferings for that we love. Nothing can quench that holy fire that is kindled from heaven. It is a glorious grace.

Hope, what doth it? When it casts anchor in heaven, it keeps us in all the waves. It purgeth our natures to be like the thing hoped for. There is no grace but it is glorious. So that grace is glory. The image of God is glory. It makes a man glorious. It makes him shine.

Beloved, do but represent to your thoughts such a one as Joseph, of a sweet, wise, and loving spirit. It is an excellent state to see a man in his place in the commonwealth. What a glorious sight is it to see a Joseph, a Nehemiah, to see a man like Paul, all on fire for the glory of God and the good of the church! The care of all the churches lay upon him. The conceit* of a man shining in grace, what a glorious representation in our thoughts is it!

And so in men now living. When we see wisdom and love tending to the common good; when we see a spirit of mortification, when we see a spirit of love, that is not for itself but for other men, a spirit of love above self-love, all for the good of others, as Christ 'went about doing good,' Acts x. 38, it makes them so lovely and glorious, as that no object in the world is so glorious, as to see a man in whom the image of Christ is; it puts a glory upon him.

Besides, it puts an inward glory upon a man, when it makes him rejoice: 'The Spirit of glory rests upon him,' Isa. lxi. i. Nay, in imprisonments and abasements, take a good man in any condition, he is glorious. His carriage is glorious. You shall not see flesh and blood, no revengeful humour. When flesh and blood is subdued, and nothing appears in a man but the image of Christ, he is a glorious creature in the greatest abasement that can be. When Paul was in the stocks, what a glorious condition was he in! When he sung at midnight, when the Spirit of glory was upon him! To see the martyrs suffer without revenge, to pray for their enemies, that they had a spirit that conquered all wrongs and fear of death, and displeasure of men; a triumphant spirit above all things below, to raise them above encouragements and discouragements, what a glorious thing was this! To see a man in his right principles, with the image of God upon him, he sees all things below, beneath him. This is glorious, to see a man that overcomes the world, that cares no more for the offers of preferment on the right hand, or for threatenings on the other hand. All is nothing to him. He breaks it as Samson did his cords. To see such a victorious spirit, is not this glorious! To see a glorious soul, that is above all earthly things whatsoever, that tramples the world under foot, as the 'woman clothed with the sun' treads the 'moon under her foot,' Rev. xii. 1. The church clothed with Christ, who is the glory of the church, tramples all earthly things under feet. Grace is victorious and conquering, prevailing over those corruptions that prevail over ordinary men. A Christian as David, when he had Saul in the cave, overcomes himself, 1 Sam. xxiv. 4, *seq*. It is an argument of a great deal of strength of grace. Christ overcame himself on the cross. He prayed for his enemies. So when the nature of man is so subject to the power of grace, that though there be rebellions in us, as there will be, while we are in this world, yet they cannot overpower the principle of grace. All this while a man is a glorious Christian, because he is not subject to the common humours and infirmities and weaknesses of men. Therefore that makes a Christian glorious, when he brings every thought and affection, and every corruption, as much as may

* That is, 'conception.'—G.

be, to the subjection of the Spirit of glory, to the Spirit of Christ in him. Though old Adam stir in him, yet he brings him down, that he doth not discover himself to the scandal of the gospel and profession, and to the weakening of the love of good things in the hearts of others. It shall not break out. He subjects these rising thoughts. Here grace is glorious.

Another man cannot do this. He cannot love God; he cannot deny himself; he cannot resist temptations, not inwardly. He may forbear an action out of fear, but a Christian can love, and fear, and delight in good things; and he can resist, and he can enjoy the things of this life, in a subordinate manner to better things. A worldling cannot do it. There is a glory upon a Christian, a derivative glory from Christ. For we shine in his beams. We are changed according to his image 'from glory to glory.'

Obj. The thing is not much questionable that grace is glorious, but it may be objected, Doth grace make one glorious? Then how comes the world to despise such as have grace? such as are like Christ?

Ans. 1. I answer it is from *blindness, from spiritual drunkenness and madness.* They cannot discern of things; they are besotted; they see no difference. Therefore they cannot discern things that are excellent. But take a man in his right principles; take a sober man, and he will see an excellency in a Christian above himself.

Ans. 2. Again, grace is not made so much of ofttimes in the world, *because it is joined with so many infirmities.* Our life 'is hid with Christ,' Col. iii. 3. It is hid under infirmities and under afflictions ofttimes; and being hidden it doth not appear so much in this world.

Ans. 3. And then again, *however men force upon themselves a contempt of grace, and of the best things, yet notwithstanding it is but forced;* for their conscience stoops at it. Witness conscience when it gives evidence on their deathbed. Take a man when he is himself, when he is sober, when he is best able to judge, when those things are taken from him, that obscured and darkened his judgment, and then you shall have him justify all things that are good, both grace and the means of grace.

Ans. 4. Again it must be so, *that we may be conformable to Christ.* The world misguideth* the state of a Christian. They think them vile and base persons. So they did Christ the head of the church. You see how Christ was esteemed. His glory was veiled with our nature and with misery a while; but it sparkled out ofttimes in his miracles. Now this was that he might suffer and perform the work of salvation. For the devil nor the wicked world would never have done that they did to him, if his glory had broken forth to the full lustre of it.

So it is with the body mystical of Christ. The world misjudgeth of them. It appears not now what they shall be hereafter, nor what they are now indeed; because God will have them conformable to Christ. If so be that the glory of Christians were discovered in the true lustre, who would wrong a Christian? If they did see him indeed to be a member of Christ and an heir of heaven, the care of angels and the price of Christ's death; if they did see him in his excellency, all the world would admire him, and make another man of him than of potentates and monarchs! But how then should he be conformable to his head in afflictions? The head was to save us by death. He must be abased. The world must take him as a strange man, and we that must be conformed to him, we must pass as unknown men in the world. But not so unknown, but that grace breaks out sometimes to admiration and imitation; and when it hath not imitation, it stirs

* Qu. 'misjudgeth'?—G.

up envy and malice in others, in the children of the devil. Therefore, notwithstanding all objections, grace is glory. It makes us like Christ, who is glorious, who is 'the Lord of glory.'

And then it draws glory with it, glorious peace and glorious comfort, and joy in the Holy Ghost, the attendants of grace in the hearts of God's people. Is it not, as I said, a glorious thing for a man to have that peace in him that passeth all understanding, that shall settle and quiet his soul in all tumults in the world? When all things are turned upside down, for a Christian to stand unmoveably built upon the rock: whence comes this glorious pitch, but from grace? Grace and peace: one follow another. Then for a man to have inward joy and comfort in the midst of afflictions and disconsolations in the world, it is a wonderful and a glorious thing. It is called 'joy unspeakable,' 1 Peter i. 8, and 'glorious grace,' 2 Cor. iii. 8. Therefore in regard of that that follows it, in this world it is glory.

Hence it is that the wise man saith, that 'the righteous is more excellent than his neighbour.' He is more glorious than another man, as pearls are above pebbles. He is more excellent in life, in death, and after death especially; for there is a growing from glory to glory. He is glorious in life, more glorious in death, when his soul shall be put into glory in heaven; and most of all glorious when Christ shall come to be glorious in his saints, as it is in 2 Thess. i. 10. So he is excellent in life, and in death, and for ever. For another man, that is but a man—a man, said I, nay, if a man be but a man, he is either like a devil in subtlety, or a beast in sensuality; he carries the image either of a beast or of the devil, besides a man. A righteous man therefore that hath the image of God stamped upon him, he is better than another man every way; for he is in a higher rank of creatures. Grace sets a man as far above other men as other men are above other creatures. At the first the creatures reverenced God in Adam. They came and took their names from him. They were subject to him. So grace is a glorious, majestical thing. Wicked men, even Herod, reverenced grace in John Baptist, Mark vi. 20, and evil men reverence it in their hearts, in God's people, though their mouths speak against it. A Christian is a spiritual man. As reason lifts a man above other creatures, so the image of God set upon a man, it lifts and raiseth him above other men.

Use 1. If grace and the image of God and Christ in us be glory, and make us excellent, *let us all labour for grace above all things*. We all, as I said before, desire liberty; and as we desire liberty, so we desire glory; but we know not the way how to come to it. In seeking liberty, we seek licentiousness; in seeking glory, we seek it from men that cannot give it. We seek glory in outward things that are nothing. What is the glory of all outward things, but the shining of a rotten piece of wood in the night time, or as a glow-worm? What is all this glory but a flash? It is nothing. If we would seek true glory indeed, as naturally all do, let us seek grace. Thereby we resemble Christ, 'the Lord of glory;' thereby we are glorious in the eyes of Christ; thereby we are glorious both without and within. Though this glory for the present be hid, thereby we are terrible to the devil and all enemies. For ever since his head was crushed by Christ, that broke the serpent's head, he is afraid of man's nature in Christ; he is afraid of Christians, as knowing that they be better than himself. And he shall be judged by them ere long. The devil shall be judged by Christians. Therefore let us study for this glory. A man is never glorious till he be a Christian.

It is said of Antiochus, that he was a vile person. What! Though he was a king (*i*)? Yes. Let a man be never so great in the world, if he be a wicked man, a man that dishonoureth his tongue, that should be his glory, that hath not the language of Canaan, that dishonours and defiles his body, that should be the 'temple of the Holy Ghost,' 1 Cor. vi. 19, a man that carries a malicious and malignant spirit, that hath the image of the devil in his soul: if he be never so great a person, he will be vile ere long, when all relations shall end in death. All excellencies must be laid down in death. Therefore seeing all other excellencies cannot keep a man from being a vile person, let us labour for that that will put a glory upon us. Labour for the image of Christ to be stamped upon our soul. There is a great humour in this age in looking to pieces of workmanship. If a man have skill to discern a piece, as they call it, it is more than ordinary. Beloved, what a vanity is this (though these pictures be lawful; they are a kind of mute poetry). But what is this to the having of the glorious image of Christ stamped upon us; to be glorious in the eye of God and in the very judgment of carnal men!

There is nothing so excellent as grace, and nothing so base as sin. Indeed there is nothing base but sin; and nothing excellent but grace. So that God's children, not only in their glorious riches and prerogatives to be the sons of God and heirs of heaven, are glorious, but they have an inward glory. 'The spouse of Christ is glorious within,' Ps. xlv. 13. Insomuch that Christ is in love with his own graces. He wonders at his own graces in his children.

Use 2. Again, *oppose this to the scorn and hatred of the world;* base-minded persons, that disgrace goodness that their illness may be the less discerned. They labour to make all alike, all they can, by slanders at least, that their illness may not appear. Oppose the judgments of God's Spirit that esteems grace glory against all the judgment of the base world. Beloved, they shall know one day, that those that they despise shall judge them; and their hearts secretly tell them so. What makes them malign men better than themselves? They have a secret conceit, he is above me. 'The spiritual man judgeth all things,' 1 Cor. ii. 15. He is a man that discerns by a spiritual eye. He judgeth and condemneth my ways, and hereafter he will judge me. A secret conscience in him makes him fear a good man. Though he deprave* and malign him, yet his heart stoops.

Use 3. Again, is grace glory? *When God sets in† on us, shall we cast our crown in the dirt?* Shall we defile and blemish our glory by sinning against conscience? We forget our excellency, that grace is glory. It teacheth us how to carry ourselves to ourselves. If there be grace in us, let us be honourable to ourselves. It is a good caveat that we should be venerable to ourselves; that is, Christians should take a holy state to themselves. What! I that am an heir of heaven; I that am a king; I that am a conqueror; I that am the son of God; I that am a freeman: should I tangle myself with these things? Shall I go and stain myself? Is it not an unsightly thing to see a golden pillar daubed with dirt? or to see a crown cast into the dirt? God hath put a crown upon me; he hath made me a king; he hath made me an heir of heaven; he hath made me his son; he hath put a glory upon me;—shall I abase myself to devilish base courses? No. I will be more honourable in my own eyes. Let us think ourselves too good for the base services of Satan. These thoughts we should take to ourselves. These are not proud thoughts, but befitting our con-

* That is, 'undervalue.'—G.

† Qu. 'it'?—ED.

dition. When we are tempted to any base course, whatsoever it is, it is contrary to my calling.

Use 4. And let us *comfort ourselves in the work of grace, though it be wrought in never so poor a measure, in all the disparagements of the world;* for those that are besotted with false vain-glory, they have the eyes of their souls put out, and dimmed and dazzled with false glory. They cannot judge of the glory of a Christian. They want eyes. Therefore let us be content to pass in the world as hidden. Christ passed concealed in the world; only now and then the beams of his glory brake forth in his miracles. So we must be content. For our glory is hid in Christ, for the most part; and it is clouded with the imputations and malice of men, and sometimes with infirmities, as it will in this world. Let us comfort ourselves with this, that we are glorious howsoever, and glorious within; and this glory will break out in a holy conversation. And it is better to be glorious in the eyes of God, and angels, and good men, and in the consciences of ill men, than to have glory from their mouths. Malice will not suffer them to glorify them with their mouths, but their consciences must needs stoop to goodness; for God hath put a majesty into goodness, that any man that is a man, that is not a beast, that hath natural principles, will reverence it; and the consciences of such men will make them speak the truth one day, and they shall say, 'We fools thought these men mad,' but 'now we see ourselves fools.' Therefore in the disparagements of worldly men, that know not where true glory lies, let us be content with this, that God hath made us truly glorious by working a change in a comfortable measure; let us comfort ourselves in this.

Use 5. Again, *by this we may know whether we have grace in us or no.* If we think grace to be glory, let us have that judgment and conceit of grace.

(1.) *Of the change of our natures,* by the Spirit of God, and the truth of God, as the Holy Ghost hath here, calling it glory. That very judgment shews that there is an alteration in our affections; that we are changed in the spirit of our minds; that we have a right conceit of heavenly things. For none but a Christian indeed can judge grace to be glory, that can truly think so. For if a man think grace to be glory truly, if he be convinced by the power of the Spirit, he will be gracious. For there is an instinct in all men by nature to glory in something. You have the gulls* of the world, they glory in something, in swaggering, beastly courses. You have devilish men glory that they can circumvent others. Rather than men will have no glory, they will glory in that that is shame indeed. Man having a disposition alway to glory in something, if he be convinced that grace is glory, he will be gracious.

Therefore, I beseech you, enter into your own souls, and see what conceits you have of the image of God, of the graces of Christianity, and then certainly it will raise a holy ambition to have that stamp set upon you.

(2.) Again, this is another evidence that a man is gracious, *if he can look upon the life of another that is better than he with a conceit that it is glory, and loving of it as glory.* Many men see grace in other men, but with a maligning eye. They see it to disgrace it. For naturally this is in men. They are so vain-glorious and ambitious, that when they see the lives of other men outshew theirs, instead of imitation, they go to base courses. They obscure and darken that light with slanders, that they will not imitate in their courses. This is in the better sort of men, the prouder, and greater sort of men. What grace they will not imitate they will defame. They

* That is, 'the deceived' = fools.—G.

will not be outshined by anything. Therefore, those that can see so far into the life of another man, as they love it, and honour the grace of God in another man, it is a sign there is some work of glory begun in them. Men can endure good things in books, and by reports, and good things of men that are dead, &c., but they cannot endure good things running in their eyes. Especially when it comes in a kind of competition and comparison, they love not to be outshined.

'From glory to glory.'

We see the state of God's children here, and the state in heaven, come both under one name; both are 'glory.' The children of God are kings here, they shall be kings in heaven. They are saints here, as they be saints in heaven. There is an adoption of grace as well as an adoption of glory, Rom. viii. 30, *et alibi*. There is a regeneration here of our souls; there is a regeneration of soul and body then. We are new creatures here; and we shall be new creatures there.

Quest. Why do all come under one name, the state of glory in heaven, and the state of grace here? Is there no difference?

Ans. Yes. But the difference is in degrees, and not otherwise. For heaven must be begun here. If ever we mean to enter into heaven hereafter, we enter into the suburbs here. We must be new creatures here. We are kings here; we are heirs apparent here; we are adopted here; we are regenerate here; we are glorious here, before we be glorious hereafter. Therefore, beloved, we may read our future state in our present. We must not think to come *de scelo in cœlum*, as he saith (*j*), out of the filth of sin to heaven, but heaven must be begun here. You see both have the same name, grace, and glory. Therefore, wouldst thou know what thy condition shall be afterwards? Read it in thy present disposition. If there be not a change and a glorious change here, never look for a glorious change hereafter. What is not begun in grace shall never be accomplished in glory. Both grace here and glory hereafter coming under the same name, it forceth this.

And likewise it is a ground of comfort; for why have we the same term here? When we are in the state of grace, why are we decked and adorned with the same title as we shall be in heaven?

It is partly for certainty. Grace is glory, as well as the perfection of it is glory, to shew that where grace is truly begun it will end in glory. All the powers in the world cannot interrupt God's gracious progress and way. What is begun in grace will end in glory. Where the foundation is laid, God will be sure to put up the roof. He never repents of his beginnings. Solomon saith that the 'righteous is like to the sun,' that grows brighter and brighter, till he come to his full strength, Prov. iv. 18. So the state of the godly grows more and more, from light to light, till he come to full strength. The state of the wicked is clean contrary. The state of the wicked is like the declining day. The sun grows down and down till it be twilight, and thence to darkness, and then to utter darkness. So they being dark in themselves, they grow from the darkness of misery and terror of conscience to eternal darkness, black, dismal darkness in hell. But the state of the godly it is like the course of the sun after midnight, that is growing up, up still, till it come to mid-day. So the state of the godly it is alway on the mending hand; it is always a growing state; it is a hopeful condition. They go from glory to glory. And therefore let us be assured of eternal glory for the time to come, as sure as we are of the beginnings of grace here wrought. You see, then, a main difference between the godly and others

Other men grow backward, *proficere in pejus*, as we say. They take degrees back from worse to worse, till they end in utter desolation and destruction for ever. But the other riseth by degrees, till they come to that happiness that can admit no further degrees. All the glory of the world ends in vanity and in nothing; but the glory of a Christian that begins in grace, you see it proceeds from glory to glory, alway growing and amending. If men were not spiritually mad, would they not rather be in a condition alway amending and growing more and more hopeful still, than to be in a condition alway declining, and most subject to decline when it is at the top. There is no consistence in any human felicity, but it is *in præcipite*, near a downfall when it is at the highest. God's children are near rising when they are at the lowest. There is a spirit of glory lights, and not only so, but rests on them. It doth not light upon them and then go away. It is not as a flash or blaze of flax or so (*k*). But the Spirit rests and grows still upon them, 'from glory to glory.' The state of a Christian it is comfortable, that is soundly converted, when he shall think every day brings me nearer my glory; every day I rise I am somewhat happier than I was the day before, because I am somewhat more glorious and nearer to eternal glory; when another wretch that lives in sins against conscience may say, I am somewhat nearer hell, nearer eclipsing, and ebbing, and declining than before. So every day brings terror to the one, and matter of comfort to the other.

'From glory to glory.'

Grace, we see, is glory, especially when it is in strength; and the more grace grows, the more glory. The more it shines, the more glory. We say of fire, the more it burns the less it smokes; the less infirmity appears that may disgrace it, the more grace. The more light and lustre, and the less infirmity. Glory belongs to the growth of grace in this world. For is not a Christian a glorious Christian when he is a grown Christian? when he sends a lustre as a pearl? when as a glorious light he shines to the example of others? when he is able, as Paul saith gloriously of himself, 'I can do all in Christ that strengtheneth me,' Philip. iv. 13, to want and to abound. Cast him into any condition what you will, he is like himself. Cast Joseph into prison, he is Joseph still; cast Paul in the dungeon, he is Paul still, and is never more glorious than in the midst of afflictions. So grace growing to some perfection is glorious; 'wisdom makes a man's face to shine,' saith Solomon, Eccles. viii. 1. So it is true of all other graces in some perfection. They make a man shine. There is nothing in the world so glorious as a Christian that is grown to some perfection. Indeed, he is so glorious, that the eye of the world, when it is cast upon him, it stirs up envy, as carnal persons, when they see a Christian man unmoveable in the midst of all motions, and unchangeable in all changes, when nothing can alter him, but he goes on, they wonder at the condition of this man, whenas indeed his grounds and resolutions are above all discouragements or encouragements that the world can afford. David was a king and a prophet, and David was a holy man, and David, for constitution of body, was ruddy and of a sweet complexion; and David, for the manner of his kingdom, was a king of a great people, There were many excellencies of David. Oh but what doth David account the prerogative of a man? 'Blessed is the man whose sins are forgiven, in whose spirit there is no guile,' Ps. xxxii. 2; that is, that is truly sanctified in spirit; that is in the state of justification; and as a witness of that, of the forgiveness of his sins, hath a spirit without guile. Happy is that man, not that is a king, or a prophet, or a strong man, or a beautiful man, or hath this endowment or that; but happy is the man whose sins are forgiven, and whose spirit is sanctified.

'From glory to glory.'

We see then that there must be an increase, a growing 'from glory to glory.' There is no stop nor stay to be made in religion. There must be of necessity a desire to grow better and better; for glory will grow still to glory. Grace will never cease till it end in glory.

[1.] Both *in our dispositions that have it wrought in us;* we shall desire it may increase in us the image of God and Christ more and more.

[2.] And *in God's purpose.* Where he begins he makes an end. Whether we look to him that will not have us in a state of imperfection,* . . . . He hath not chosen us to imperfection, but to perfection; and he hath called us not to imperfection, but to perfection. He hath elected us to perfection. He hath chosen us to be spotless, not to be conflicting with our corruptions, and to be halting alway as Jacob. We shall have perfect strength. We are called and elected to perfection. Therefore there is no standing at a stay in religion; there must be a perpetual growth. It is our disposition to desire and endeavour it still.

For, beloved, it is that that is inbred to all things that are imperfect, to hasten to perfection, till they come to their *ubi*, to their pitch. We see it in grain, weak grain. Till it come to the full growth, it breaks through clods, through harder things than itself. There is a nature in corn and seeds, that have a beginning of life in their kind in them, till those seeds come to growth, they put out themselves with a great deal of strength against opposition. So grace is of such a strong nature. Being intended by God to perfection, it will not rest in mean beginnings, but puts itself forward still, and breaks through opposition. I will not stand upon the common place of growth in grace. It is a large discourse, and I touched it upon many occasions. You see the necessity of it. There must be a growth from glory to glory.

A growth not in parts as we say. For at the first regeneration, in the first beginning, when we are gracious, there is the beginning of a new life, and there is the seeds of all graces. But especially this growth is in intension and extension. Grace grows more and more in strength, and extends and reacheth itself further and further to the use of many. Grace grows, I say, in the intension of itself, and extends and reacheth itself to the use of more. The more a Christian lives, when he is in a right state and frame as a Christian should be, he is of more strength in all particular graces, and doth the more good, and shines more in his life and conversation to others.

And likewise, as there is a growth in intension and extension, so there is a growth in the quality and purity of grace; for the longer a man lives, those graces that he hath grow more refined. When a Christian is but a new Christian, he tastes much of the old stock. As all fruit at the first will taste of the stock, so there is no fruit of righteousness that comes from a man, at his first conversion, but it tastes a great deal of old Adam. It savours of the old stock. The more he live, and grows spiritual, the more that that comes from him relisheth of the Spirit, the more refined is his wisdom, the more refined is his love, the more refined from self-love, his joy and delight is more refined.

Obj. Hence we may answer an objection by the way; an old man seems not to grow in grace. He seems not to be so good a man, not to be so zealous as when he was young; not so forward.

* Sentence unfinished.—G.

Ans. Beloved, In those that are young there is a great deal of nature joined with a little grace, and that grace in them makes a greater expression, because it is carried with the current of nature. But in age it is more refined. That that is, that knowledge they have, is more pure and more settled, and that love and affection is more refined. There is less self-love, and that zeal they have it is joined with more heavenly discretion. There is less wild fire, there is less strange fire with it. Though there be less heat of nature, that it do not work in outward demonstrations to the eye of the world, yet it is more refined and pure. So grace grows thus likewise in the purity and perfection of it; not altogether pure, for somewhat will stick to our best performances, savouring of the worst principle in nature. For as we carry flesh and spirit alway, so that that comes from them will savour of corruption; yet less in a grown Christian, that is a father in Christianity, than in another.

'From glory to glory.'

Grace is glory in regard of the state before. The least degree of grace is glory in regard of the state of nature. But grace is not glory properly till it come to a growth. Grace is not glorious, so in comparison to other Christians that are grown. In regard of the state of nature, grace is glory, take it in the lowest; for is not this a glory for a man to be taken into the fellowship of Christ? to be the son of God, and an heir of heaven? to have angels for his attendants? to be begotten by the glorious gospel, the word of God, that immortal seed? Whatsoever thing is about a Christian it is glorious. Is not he glorious that hath God the Father, and God the Son, the Lord of glory, and the Holy Ghost, the Spirit of glory, and the glorious gospel, and glorious angels for his attendants? Every thing is glorious in a Christian. In every Christian there is this. So grace is a kind of glory; but notwithstanding we must not content ourselves with that. Grace is then especially glory when it comes to growth. We must labour that grace may appear. What is glory? Properly glory is excellency and victory over the contrary with manifestation, excellency manifested. Now a man is said to be glorious in grace, when his grace comes to be excellent in view, and victorious over the contrary with public manifestation.

Use 1. Now this we ought to labour for; though grace be glory in respect of the former estate, yet in the rank of Christians *we ought to be glorious, that is, more and more gracious;* both.

In regard of God, that God may have the more glory from us. The more grace, the more esteem from him, because we resemble him.

And in regard of Christ Jesus; the more glorious we are, the more we resemble him. Let us labour to be more and more glorious, in regard likewise of the church, whom we shall benefit more. The more we grow in grace, the more we shall prevail with God by our prayers. Who prevailed more with their prayers than Moses, and such men? Again, when grace is glorious, that is, with victory and full manifestation, the more we are fit to give a lustre and light, that others seeing it may glorify God; to draw others to the love of grace, when they see grace glorious. Now grace is then glorious in us that others may be encouraged. When we can resist strong temptations, when we are not like children 'carried away with the wind of every doctrine,' Eph. iv. 14, this is a glorious thing. When a Christian can hold his own in the worst times; when it is a witty* thing to be a Christian: as Hilary said in a time of schism, 'it required a great

* That is, 'wise.'—G.

deal of wit to be a Christian' (*l*), it requires a great deal of wit and study to hold a man on in Christianity.

And for a man to be strong against temptations and the world, whether it frown or fawn, that he cares for neither, but holds his own, is not this a glorious thing? When a man shall carry himself as a lion, break through oppositions in ill times, and fall square, cast him as you will, in all conditions,—here is a glorious Christian. Therefore through grace be glory, that must not content us, but we must labour to have such a measure of glory as that we may be glorious in our own rank. Is it not a glorious thing when a man can break through doubts and fears that trouble other folk too much? As the sun is said to be in glory when he is gotten on high; there are many clouds in the morning, but when the sun is gotten to his height at noon-day, he scatters all. So a Christian is in his glory and exaltation when he can scatter doubts, and fears, and terrors that trouble other weak beginning Christians. Therefore when we are troubled with scruples, with this and that, we should labour to get out of them, that grace may be glorious; to shew that we have gotten such a light and such a convincing knowledge, and that we are so rooted in faith and grace, that the Spirit of Christ in us hath broken through all these clouds and mists, and made us glorious.

'From glory to glory.'

Our glory it is not like a torrent that runs amain for a time, and after is dried up for ever. Grace it is a continuing and an increasing thing. It continues still. As the stream that it is fed with is an ever-living spring, so is grace. It is fed with the grace in Christ, and he is a never-dying spring, a fountain. For that grace in him is fed with his divinity. Therefore there must be a perpetual spring in Christ. So where Christ hath opened a spring in the heart, he will feed that grace perpetually.

Use 2. *Let none be discouraged that have grace begun in them.* God will go on with his own grace. When he hath begun a good work, 'he will finish it to the day of the Lord,' 1 Cor. i. 8. Though grace be little at the first, yet it shall not stay there. It grows up we know not how; but at last it is glorious indeed. For till grace be grown, it is little discerned from other things: as between weeds and herbs there is little difference when they be green, till they be grown. Grace is little at the first, as a grain of mustard-seed, Mat. xiii. 31. Jerusalem is not built in a day, as we say of Rome. You have some that are a weaker sort of Christians, that are good, they would fain be in Canaan, as soon as ever they are out of Egypt, and I cannot blame them. But hereupon they are discomforted. As soon as ever they have grace in them, they would have their pitch presently, out of spiritual covetousness. Oh that I had more knowledge and more victory! &c. These desires are good; for God puts not in vain desires into the hearts of his children, but they must be content to be led from glory to glory, from one degree of grace to another. Christ himself grew more in favour with God and man. As that little stone grew to a mountain, Dan. ii. 34, so we must be content to grow from grace to grace. There is a gradual proceeding in the new creature. We must not be presently in Canaan. God will lead us through the wilderness, through temptations and crosses, before we come to heaven. Many because they see they are far short of others that are stronger Christians, therefore they think they have no grace at all.

Therefore let those that are on the growing hand, though they be short of many that are before them, let them not be discouraged with their over-little beginnings. For it is God's ordinance and course in this world, to bring his children by little and little through many stations. As they were led in the wilderness from standing to standing, and from place to place, so God brings his children by many standings to heaven. And it is one part of a Christian's meekness to [be] subject to God's wisdom in this kind, and not to murmur that they are not so perfect as they would be, or as they shall be; but rather to magnify the mercy of God that there is any change in such defiled and polluted souls; that he hath vouchsafed any spiritual light of understanding, any love of good things; that the bent of their affections are turned to a contrary course than they were before; that God hath vouchsafed any beginnings. Rather magnify his mercy than quarrel with his dispensation, that he doth not this all at once; and, indeed, if we enter into our own hearts, it is our fault that we are not more perfect. But let us labour to be meek, and say, Lord, since thou hast ordained that I shall grow from glory to glory, from one degree of grace to another, let me have grace to magnify thy mercy, that thou hast given me any goodness, rather than to murmur that I have no more. And be content in the use of means, and endeavour to grow further, though we have not so much as others have. Nay, we may not be discouraged, because of the weakness of grace, but we may not be discouraged with a seeming interruption in our spiritual growth. God sometimes works by contraries. He makes men grow by their puttings back, and to stand by their falls. Sometimes, when God will have a man grow, he will suffer him to fall, that by his fall he may grow in a deeper hatred of sin, and in jealousy over his own heart, and a nearer watchfulness over his own ways; that he may grow more in love with God for pardoning of him, and grow more strong in his resolution for the time to come; that he may grow more in humility. None grow so much as those that have their growth stopped for a time. Let none be discouraged when they find a stop, but consider that God is working grace in another kind. The Spirit appears in one grace when it doth not in another. It grows in one grace when it doth not in another. Sometime the Spirit will have us grow in humility; as the juice of the herbs runs to the root in the winter, it is in the leaves in the spring, it is in the seed in the autumn; as the life sometime appears in the plant in one part and sometime in another; so the Spirit of God appears sometime in humility, sometime in joy, sometime in spiritual strength and courage. Let none be discouraged overmuch when they find a stop; for there is no interruption of Spirit altogether, and this little interruption is like a sickness that will make them grow and shoot up more afterwards. It spends the humours that hinders growth. There is such a mystery in the carrying of men from glory to glory, that it makes men more glorious sometimes by base sins. I would have no man discouraged therefore. Indeed, God will work so, that he shall wish he had not given him occasion to shew his strength in his weakness, his glory in his shame; but God, where he hath begun he will go through with the work, and will turn all to good.

And to encourage us here, grace begun hath the same name as grace perfect. Both are glory. Why doth God call them by one name? To encourage Christians. He tells them that if it be begun it is glory, not that it is so properly, but if it be begun it shall never end till it come in heaven. Therefore God styles grace in all the latitude, from the highest to the very beginnings, by the same name, to encourage Christians. If they be within the door of the temple, though they be not so far as those that are in high and glorious places, yet they are going thither. To encourage Christians to know that unavoidably and indefeasibly they shall come to perfection of glory if it be begun. And God looks not on Christians as they are in their imperfections and beginnings, but that that in time he means to bring them to. He intends to bring them to glory. Therefore he gives grace the style of glory. As in the creatures God looked not on the seeds of trees as such, but he looked on them as seeds that he meant to make trees of; and when God looks upon his children, he looks not on them as they are children, but as they shall be perfect men. Doth the wisdom of God look on the seeds of trees as he intends to make them trees? and doth he not look upon Christians, that are babes in grace, as he intends to make them men, to come to the perfect stature of Christ? He views us at once in our beginnings and perfections. All is presented at once to him. Therefore he gives one name to the whole state of grace, grace and glory, all is glory. I beseech you therefore, if there be any goodness, any blessed change in us, let us be comforted; for he that hath brought us to the beginnings of glory will never fail till he hath brought us to perfect glory in heaven, and there our change shall rest. There is no further change there, when we are once in our element.

For even as God, when he made man, he rested from all his work upon the Sabbath; man was his excellent piece. So the Spirit of God will rest, sanctifying and altering of us. When we are once in heaven, in that eternal Sabbath, then we shall need no changes from glory to glory. We shall for ever be filled with the fulness of God, till which time there is no creature in the world so changeable as a Christian.

For, first, you see he was made in God's image and likeness in his state of standing.

After he fell there was a change, to his second state of sin.

After the state of fall, there is a change to the state of grace.

After that from one degree of grace to another in this world till he die.

And then the soul is more perfect and glorious. But at the last, when body and soul shall be united, there shall be no more change; there shall be an end of all alteration.

So we see that God intends by his Spirit to bring us to perfection, though by little and little, to perfection of glory as far as our nature is capable, and this shall be at the latter day.

Quest. Why not before? why not in this world?

Ans. Beloved, we are not capable here of that fulness of glory. Saint Peter on the mount had but a glimpse of the glory of heaven, and he was spiritually drunk as it were, he knew not what he said, Mark ix. 6. We are not capable. Therefore we must grow here from glory to glory, till we come to that perfection of glory. God that gives us the earnest could make up the bargain here if we were capable of it, but we are not.

God will have a difference between the militant and the triumphant church, and will train us up here to live the life of faith, till we come to live the life of sight, the life of vision for ever in heaven.

Doth God by his Spirit change us by his Spirit to the likeness of Christ, 'from glory to glory,' till he have brought us to perfection of glory in heaven? Oh let us comfort ourselves in our imperfections here. We are here lame Mephibosheths. He was a king's son, but he was lame. We are spiritually lame and defective, though we be kings' sons (*m*). Oh, but we shall grow from glory to glory, till all end in perfection in heaven. What a comfort is this in our imperfections, that as every day we live in this world cuts off a day of our life, for we live so much the shorter, so every day we live brings us nearer to heaven; that as we decay in the life of nature every day, so we grow up another way, 'from glory to glory,' till we come to perfect glory in heaven; is not this a sweet comfort? Let us comfort ourselves with these things.

Use 3. Again, if the state of God's people be thus sweet and comfortable, and full of well-grounded hopes, that glory shall go further on to glory, and end in glory, *then why should we be afraid of death?* For grace will but end in glory. A mean glorious estate will but even be swallowed up of a truly glorious estate. Indeed grace is swallowed up of glory, even as the rivers are swallowed up of the ocean. Glory takes away nothing, but perfects all better by death. Why should we be afraid of death? We are afraid of our glory, and of the perfection of our glory.

There be degrees of glory. There is glory begun here in grace, and there is the glory of the soul after death, and the glory both of soul and body for ever in heaven, and these make way one to another. A Christian is glorious while he lives, and he grows in glory while he lives. He is more glorious when he dies, for then his soul hath perfectly the image of Christ stamped upon it. But he is most glorious at the day of resurrection, when body and soul shall be glorious, when he shall put down the very sun itself. All glory shall be nothing to the glory of the saints, 'They shall shine as the sun in the firmament,' Dan. xii. 3. And indeed there will be no glory but the glory of Christ and of his spouse; all other glory shall vanish and come to nothing. But the glory of the King of heaven and his queen that he hath chosen to himself to solace himself eternally with, when the spiritual marriage shall be accomplished, they shall be for ever glorious together. Why then should we be afraid of death? For then there shall be a further degree of glory of the soul, and after that a further degree of body and soul, when our bodies shall be conformable to the glorious body of Christ, when they shall be spiritual, as it is in 1 Cor. xv. 44. I beseech you, therefore, let us learn this to comfort ourselves against those dark times of dissolution, when we shall see an end of all other glory. All worldly glory shall end in the dust, and lie down in the grave; when we must say that 'rottenness is our father,' and the 'worm our mother,' Job. xvii. 14. We can claim no other kin in regard of our body, yet then we shall be more glorious in regard of our souls. Christ shall put a robe of glory upon us, and then afterward we shall be more glorious still.

Therefore it is base infidelity to be afraid of our dissolution, when indeed it is not a dissolution, but a way to glory. We should rather consider the conjunction, than the dissolution. Death takes in pieces body and soul, but it joins the soul to Christ. It makes the soul more glorious than it was before. We go from glory to glory. Our Saviour Christ saith, 'He that believeth in me shall never die,' John xi. 26. What doth he mean by that?

Indeed, we shall never die, for grace shall be swallowed up of glory. As soon as ever the life of nature is gone, he lives the life of glory presently. So he never dies. There is but a change of the life of grace and of nature for the life of glory.

What that glory shall be at that day, it is a part of that glory to know; for indeed it is beyond expression, and beyond the comprehension of our minds. They cannot conceive it nor our tongues express it. Peter, as I said, seeing but a glimpse of it, said, 'It is good for us to be here.' He forgot all his former troubles and afflictions. If such a little glimpse of glory could so possess the soul of that blessed man Peter, as that it made him forget all his former miseries, and all his afflictions whatsoever, to be in love with that condition above all others, what shall the glory of heaven be then! Shall we think then of our former misery, and baseness, and trouble, and persecutions? Oh no.

Use 4. Again, let us be exhorted by this *to try the truth of grace in us, by our care to grow and proceed from glory to glory*, still to be more glorious in Christianity. Beloved, of necessity it must be so. Let us not deceive ourselves in our natural condition. Do we content ourselves that we live a sick man's life? No. We desire health. When we have health, is that all? No. When we have health, we desire strength too, that we may encounter oppositions. Is it so in nature, that life is not enough, but health; and that is not enough, but strength too? And is it not so much more in the new creature, in the new nature, in the divine nature? If there be life, there will be a desire to have health, that our sick souls may be more and more healed; that our actions that come from our faculties sanctified be not sick actions; that they be not weak languishing actions; that we may have healed souls; that God together with pardoning grace may join healing grace, to cure our souls daily more and more, that we may be more able to performances. And then, when we have got spiritual health, let us desire spiritual strength to encounter oppositions and temptations, to go through afflictions, to make way through all things that stand in our way to heaven. Let us not deceive ourselves. This will be so. If there be truth of grace, still a further and further desire of grace, carrying us to a further and further endeavour.

The more we grow in grace, the more God smells a sweet sacrifice from us; that that comes from us is more refined and less corrupt. It yields better acceptance to God.

And then for others, the more we grow in grace, the more we grow in ability, in nimbleness, and cheerfulness to do them good; and that that comes from us finds more acceptance with others, being carried with a strong spirit of love anddelight, which alway is accepted in the eyes of men.

The more we grow in grace, the more cheerful we shall be in regard of ourselves. The better we are, the better we may be; the more we do, the more we may do. For God further instils the oil of grace, to give us strength and cheerfulness in good actions, so that they come off with delight. Our own cheerfulness increaseth as our growth increaseth. In a word, you see glory tends to glory, and that is enough to stir us up to grow in it. Seeing glory here, which is grace, tends to glory in heaven, we should never rest till we come to that perfection; till the glory of grace end in glory indeed. For what is the glory of heaven but the perfection of grace? And what is the beginnings of grace here but the beginnings of glory? Grace is glory begun, and glory is grace perfected. Therefore, if we would be in heaven as much as may be, and enter further and further into the kingdom of God, as Peter saith, 2 Pet. i. 5, *seq.*, let us be alway adding grace to grace, and one degree to another. Put somewhat to the heap still, that so we may go from glory to glory, from knowledge to knowledge, from faith to faith, from one degree to another.

Obj. But it will be objected that Christians sometimes stand at a stay, sometimes they seem to go back.

Ans. In a word, to answer that, some because they cannot see themselves in growing, they think they grow not at all. It is but ignorance; for we see the sun moves, though we see him not in moving. We know things grow, though we see them not in growing. Therefore it follows not, that because we perceive not our growth from grace to grace, that therefore we grow not.

But put the case indeed that Christians decay in their first love and in some grace. There is a suspension of growth. It is that they may grow in some other grace. God sees it needful they should grow in the root, and therefore abaseth them in the sense of some infirmity, and then they spring out amain again. As after a hard winter comes a glorious spring, upon a check grace breaks out more gloriously. And there is a mystery in God's government in that kind, that God often increaseth grace by the sight and sense of our infirmities. God shews his powerful government in our weakness; for God's children never hate their corruption more than when they have been overcome by it. Then they begin to be sensible of it, that there is some hidden corruption that they discerned not before, that it is fit they should take notice of. The best man living knows not himself till he comes to temptation. That discovers himself to himself. Temptation discovers corruption and makes it known, and then stirs up hatred for it. As love stirs up endeavour, so hatred aversation* and loathing. It is profitable for God's children to fall sometimes. They would never be so good as they are else. They would not wash for spots; but when they see they are foul indeed, then they go to wash. But this is a mystery; God will have it so for good ends.

It checks the disposition of some good people. They think they have not grace, because they have but a little. This phrase shews that we have not all at once. God carries us by degrees, 'from glory to glory,' from one degree of grace to another. God's children, when they have truth of grace wrought in them, their desires go beyond their endeavour and strength. Their desires are wondrous large, and their prayers are answerable to their desires. Therefore in the Lord's prayer what say we? 'Thy kingdom come; thy will be done in earth as it is in heaven,' Mat. vi. 10. Can it be so in this world? No. But we must pray till we come to it. We must pray till we come to heaven, where prayer shall cease. So the prayers and desires of God's people transcend their endeavours. Their prayers are infinite. Hereupon, the chief thing in conversion being the desire, the turning of the stream of the will, when they find their will and their desire good, and their endeavour to fall short of their purposes, they say, Surely I have no good, because I have not that I would have, as if they should have heaven upon earth. We must grow 'from glory to glory.' And thank God for that beginning. It is God's mercy that he would work the least degree of grace in such rebellious hearts as all of us have; that he would work any goodness, any change, though never so little. God looks not to the measure, so much as to truth. For he will bring truth to perfection, though it be never so little. Let us be comforted in it. And it is God's government, to bring his children to glory by little and little, that so there may be a dependence of one Christian upon another; the weaker on the stronger: and that there may be pity, and sweet affections of one Christian to another; and that there may be perpetual experience of God's mercy in helping weak Christians; and a perpetual experience of that which is the true ground of comfort, justification; that we must needs be justified, and stand righteous before God, by Christ's absolute righteousness, having experience of our imperfect righteousness. So a little measure of grace in us is for great purpose. Therefore let none be discouraged, especially considering that God, whom we desire to please, values us by that little good

* That is, 'aversion.'—G.

we have, and esteems us by that condition he means to bring us to ere long to perfection. So long as we take not part with our corruptions, but with the Spirit of God, and give way to him, and let him have his work in us; so long be of good comfort in any measure of grace whatsoever.

Use. 5. Again, in that grace is of a growing nature, in all changes and alterations, whatsoever we decay in, *let us not decay in grace*. Beg of God. Lord, whatsoever thou takest from me, take not thy Spirit from me! take not thy stamp from me! Let me grow in the inward man although I grow not in the world. Let us labour to grow 'from glory to glory,' though we lose otherwise. That is well lost and parted with in the world that is with the gain of any grace, because grace is glory. It is a good sickness that gets more patience, and more humility. It is a good loss that makes us grow less worldly-minded and more humble by it. All other things are vanity in comparison. And that grace that we get by the loss of them is well gained. Grace is glory; and the more we grow in grace, the more we grow in glory. Therefore I beseech you labour to thrive that way, to grow up heavenward, daily more and more in our disposition. Beloved, the more grace we get the more glory; and the more like we are to Christ and to God, the more we adorn our profession; and the more we shame Satan and his instruments, and stop their mouths, the more duties come off naturally and sweetly from us without constraint. It is good for us to be grown Christians, that we need not be cumbered with corruptions. The more we grow, the more nimble and cheerful and voluntary we shall be in duty. We shall partake more of that anointing that makes us nimble in God's service. There is nothing in the world so glorious as a grown Christian. Therefore let us be in love with the state of Christianity, especially with grown Christians. Of all things, he is compared with the best. If he be a house, he is a temple; if he be a plant, he is a cedar growing up; if he be a flower, he is a lily rising and growing fresher; if he be a stone, he is a pearl. He grows in estimation and use more and more. Beloved, if we had spiritual eyes to see the state of a Christian, of a grown Christian especially, we would labour above all things to thrive in this way. Have we not many works to do? Have we not many enemies to resist? Have we not many graces to perfect? Are we not to die and to appear before God? Are we not to enjoy the blessings of God purely? and do not these things require a great deal of strength of grace? Oh they do. Therefore labour above all things in the world to behold God's love in Christ, and to behold Christ, that by this sight we may grow from glory to glory.

And this will make us willing to die. What makes a man willing to die, but when he knows he shall go from glory to greater glory? After death is the perfection of glory. Then we are glorious indeed, when we are in heaven. A weak sight here by faith changeth us; but a strong sight, when we shall see face to face, perfectly changeth us. Then we shall be like him, when we shall see him face to face.

A wicked man cannot desire death, he cannot desire heaven itself. Why? Because heaven is the perfection of grace. Glory [which] is but grace he loves not. Therefore it is a certain evidence of future glory, for a man to love grace, and to grow. I say such a man is willing to die. A wicked man, that hates grace, that loves not Christ in his image, in his children, or in his truth, he hates glory that is the perfection of grace; for peace, and joy, and comfort, they are but those things that issue from grace, and spring from grace. Grace is the chief part of heaven, the perfection of the image of God, the perfection of all the powers to be like Christ. But for peace and comfort that springs from it, a wicked man loves peace and quiet, but to have his nature altered he loves not that; and if he love not grace, how can he love glory? There is no man but a Christian that loves heaven. We are ready to drop away daily. Now to be in a state unchanged, it is a fearful thing. Unless we be changed by the Spirit of God, we shall be afraid to die. We cannot desire to be in heaven. The very heaven of heavens is the perfection of grace. To see God to be all in all, and by the sight of God to be transformed into his likeness, it is the chief thing in heaven. Therefore I beseech you let us labour more and more to grow in grace; set Christ before us. Let me add this one thing, make use of our patterns among us. Christ is now in heaven, but there will be the Spirit of Christ in his children to the end of the world; and grace is sweetly conveyed from those that we live amongst. We grow up in grace by growing in a holy communion one with another. Christ will kindle lights in every generation. Therefore let us labour to have the spirit of those we live with given to us; in conversing, to be like Christ in his members; to love the image of Christ in his children, and to converse with them; to be altered into their likeness. This will change us to the glorious likeness of Christ more and more.

Those that care not what company they keep, those that despise the image of Christ in those among whom they live, can they grow in grace?

We shall give account of all the good examples we have had. Doth God kindle lights for nothing? We should glorify God for the sun and moon and stars, and other creatures. Is not a Christian more glorious than all the creatures in the world? We should glorify God for grace in Christians, and labour to be transformed to them that we may grow the liker to Christ, that we may grow more and more glorious. I speak this to advance the communion of saints more and more, as we desire to partake more and more of this grace, and to grow 'from glory to glory.'

Use 6. Again, considering that God means to bring us, by little and little, by degrees, to perfect glory of body and soul, and condition in heaven to be like Christ, *let this make us be content to be vile for Christ in this world, as David said when he was scorned*, 'I will be yet more vile,' 2 Sam. vi. 22, 'do you think I think much to shew myself thus, for the honour of God?' When Michal scoffed, 'I will be more vile.' Let us be content to go out of the camp, and bear the reproach of Christ, Heb. xi. 26, bear the reproach of religion. Let the world scorn us for the profession of religion. God is bringing us from glory to glory, till he bring us to perfect glory; and shall we suffer nothing for him? Let us be content to be more vile, and to bear the reproach of religion. The very worst thing in religion, the reproach of Christ, as Moses made a wise choice, it is better than the treasures of Egypt, Heb. xi. 26. The most excellent things in the world are not so good as the worst thing in religion, because reproach ends with assurance of comfort, that God will take away that, and give us glory after. Therefore, let us not be discouraged from a Christian course, but go through good report and bad report, break through all, to finish our course with joy, as St Paul speaks of himself, Acts xx. 24.

Use 7. And doth God bring us from glory to glory, till he have brought us to perfection of glory? Then, I beseech you, *let us beforehand be thankful to God*, as we see in the epistles of blessed St Paul and Peter: 'Blessed be God, the Father of our Lord Jesus Christ, that hath begotten us to an inheritance immortal, undefiled, reserved in heaven,' saith St Peter, 1 Pet. i. 4; and so St Paul. Let us begin the employment of heaven beforehand. For why doth God discover to us that he will bring us to glory? why doth he discover it to our faith, that excellent state? That we might begin heaven on earth, as much as might be. And how shall we do that? By the employment of heaven. What is that? 'Holy, holy, holy, Lord God of hosts,' Rev. iv. 8. There is nothing but magnifying and glorifying of God. There shall be no need of prayer. There are praises alway; and so much as we are in the praises of God, and glorifying of God for his mercy and love in Christ, so much we are in heaven before our time. I beseech you, therefore, be stirred up in consideration of this, that we are leading on by degrees, from glory to glory, till we come to perfection. Let us even give God the praise of all beforehand. For it is as sure as if we had it. For one way, how things to come are present, is by faith. Glory to come is present two or three ways already, that may stir us up to glorify God beforehand.

(1.) The glory to come is *present to Christ our head*. We, in our husband, are in heaven. Now he hath taken heaven for us!

(2.) And in regard *of faith*, that is the evidence of things not seen. It is the nature of faith to present things to come as present. To faith, glory to come is present, present in Christ, and we are part of Christ, Christ mystical, and members. And we in our head are in heaven already, and sit there. And to faith, that makes things present that are to come, we are in heaven already.

(3.) And we have the earnest of heaven, *the first-fruits of the Spirit*. We have grace which is glory, the beginnings of glory. We have the first-fruits and earnest. Now, an earnest is never taken away, but is made up by the bargain with the rest; so the earnest of the Spirit of God, the first-fruits of peace and joy, of comfort and liberty to the throne of grace, these are the beginnings of heaven. Therefore, be much in praising God. Oh that we could be so! If we could get into a frame and disposition to bless God, we could never be miserable; no, not in the greatest afflictions, for thankfulness hath joy alway. When a man is joyful, he can never be miserable, for joy enlargeth the soul. When is a man most joyful, but in a state of thankfulness? And what makes us thankful so much, as to consider the wonderful things that are reserved in another world, the glory that God is leading us to by little and little, from glory to glory, till we be perfect?

'Even as by the Spirit of the Lord.'

'As' here is taken according to the phrase in the Greek; and there is the like word in the Hebrew. It signifieth likeness and similitude sometimes, and sometimes otherwise.* It is not here meant as if we were like the Spirit of the Lord, but this change is wrought even as by the Spirit of the Lord. That is, it is so excellent and so strong, that you may know that it is done by none but the Spirit of God.

Again, 'as by the Spirit of the Lord,' that is, so far as the Spirit of the Lord changeth us. It implieth those two things, that is, it is done by the power of the Spirit, that we may know it is done by the Spirit of the Lord; and then, as by him and no further, for we no further shine than he enlighteneth us. As the air, it is no further light than the sun shines into it; so we have no more glory, strength, comfort, and peace, or anything gracious or glorious, than the Spirit of God shines into us: therefore he saith, 'as by the Spirit of the Lord.' It is so glorious and excellent, and so far forth as he doth it. 'As by the Spirit of the Lord;' so he expresseth the meaning of that phrase.

* That is, *καθάπερ* = Hebrew, כַּאֲשֶׁר. Cf. Gen. xii. 4; Exod. vii. 6, 10; in LXX.—G.

Now you see here the doctrine is clear, that all that I have spoken of before comes from the Spirit of the Lord, and from no other cause.

The beholding, the transforming, the degrees of transforming from glory to glory, the taking away of the veil, all is from the Spirit of the Lord. To go over the particulars.

The Holy Ghost doth open our eyes to behold the glory of the Lord, and therefore he is called the Spirit of illumination. The Holy Ghost takes away the veil of ignorance and unbelief, and thereupon he is called the Spirit of revelation. The Holy Ghost upon revealing the love of God to us in Christ, and the love of Christ to us, and illuminating our understandings to see these things, he breeds love to God again, shewing the love of God to us, and thereupon he is called the Spirit of love. Now when God's love is shed into us by the Spirit of illumination and revelation, then we are changed according to the image of Christ; and thereupon the Holy Ghost, from the working of a change, is called the Spirit of sanctification, because he is not only the holy temple of that blessed person, but he makes us holy; and because this change is a glorious change, a change from one degree of grace to another, till we come to be perfect in heaven; hereupon it is called a Spirit of glory, as St Peter saith, 'the Spirit of glory resteth on you,' 1 Peter iv. 14, that is, the Spirit of peace, of love, of comfort, of joy, &c. The Spirit, in regard of this blessed attribute, working all these, he is called the Spirit of glory. The Spirit hath divers names according to the divers operations he works in the saints and people of God; as here the Spirit of illumination, of revelation, of love, of sanctification, of glory, all is by the Spirit. Whatsoever is wrought in man it is by the Spirit. All comes from the Father as the fountain, and through the Son as Mediator; but whatsoever is wrought it is by the Holy Ghost in us, which is the substantial vigour in the Trinity. All the vigour and operation in the Trinity upon the creature, it is by the Holy Ghost, the third person. As in the creation the Spirit moved upon the waters, and moving there and brooding on them, framed the whole model of the creatures; all were framed by the Holy Ghost; so the Holy Ghost upon the water of our souls frames the new creature, frames all this change 'from glory to glory,' all is by the Holy Spirit. Therefore it is here in the passive term, 'We are changed from glory to glory, as by the Spirit of the Lord.' So in the chain of salvation you have passive words in them all. 'Whom God foreknew he chose: and whom he chose he justified: and whom he justified he glorified,' Rom. viii. 30, all because they come from God, and the Spirit of God. So here we are transformed from glory to glory, all is by the Spirit of God, the third person. For, beloved, even as from God toward us all things come through the Son by the Spirit, so back again, all things from us to God must come by the Spirit and through Christ. We do all by the Spirit, as all things are wrought in us by the Spirit. God gives us the Spirit of prayer and supplication, and the Spirit of sanctification; and we pray in the Spirit, and work in the Spirit, and walk in the Spirit. We do all in the Spirit, to shew that the Spirit doth all in all. In this new creature and work of sanctification it is by no less than the Spirit of the Lord. For, beloved, as it was God that redeemed us, so it is God that must change us; as it was God that wrought our salvation and reconciled us,—no less person could do it,—so it must be God that must persuade us of that glorious work, and fit us for it by his Holy Spirit. It is God that must knit us to our head Christ, and then by little and little transform us to that blessed condition that Christ hath purchased for us. God the Son doth the one, and

God the Spirit doth the other. You have all the three persons in this place, for we see the glory of God the Father, Son, and Holy Ghost shining in Jesus Christ. Christ is the image according to which we are changed. The Spirit is he that changeth us according to that image. God shews his mercy in Christ. We knowing and apprehending the mercy of God in Christ by the Spirit, are changed by that Spirit 'from glory to glory.' So that the blessed Trinity, as they have a perfect unity in themselves in nature, for they are all one God, so they have a most perfect unity in their love, and care, and respect to mankind. We cannot want the work of any one of them all. Their work is for the good of mankind. The Father in his wisdom decreed and laid the foundation how mercy and justice might be reconciled in the death of the Mediator. Christ wrought our salvation. The Holy Ghost assures us of it and knits us to Christ, and changeth and fits us to be members of so glorious a head, and so translates and transforms us more and more 'from glory to glory.'

It is a comfortable consideration to see how our salvation and our fitting for salvation, till we be put in full possession of it, stands upon the unity of the three glorious persons in the Trinity, that all join in one for the making of man happy.

I will name two or three doctrines, before I come to that which I mean to dwell on.

As, first, that

Doct. The Spirit comes from Christ.

It is said here, 'By the Spirit of the Lord,' that is, of Christ; because Christ doth *spirare*,* as well as the Father. The Father doth *spirare*, and the Son doth breathe. The Holy Ghost proceeds by way of spiration from both. Therefore the Spirit is not only the Spirit of the Father, but of the Son, as we see here, 'The Spirit of the Lord.' Christ sends the Spirit, as well as the Father. 'I will send you the Comforter.' The Holy Ghost proceeds from the Father and the Son; and he doth report to us the love of the Father and of the Son; and therefore, 2 Cor. xiii. 14, the shutting of the chapter, 'The grace of our Lord Jesus Christ, the love of God the Father, and the communion of the Holy Ghost,' &c. As the Holy Ghost hath communion in proceeding from the Father and the Son, and knows the secrets of both; so he reveals them to us. The love of God the Father, and the Son, and the communion of the Holy Ghost; so the Holy Ghost proceeds from the Son as well as from the Father; he is called here the Spirit of the Lord.

Then again, the Spirit is a distinct person from Christ. It is said before, 'The Lord is that Spirit.' That might trouble men, how to know that 'the Lord is that Spirit.' Men might think that Christ is all one with the Spirit. No. Here the Spirit is said to be the Spirit of the Lord. He means he is another distinct person from Christ; and the Spirit is God as well as Christ, because the Spirit hath the operations of God attributed to him, to change and transform, and make new. We are changed into the same image, from glory to glory, 'even as by the Spirit of the Lord.' Creation and renovation of all new is from an almighty power. All the power in heaven and earth cannot make that that was not, to be, especially that that was contrary and opposite, to be. Now for a man in opposition and enmity to religion, to be changed to a better image, to the image of Christ, it argueth an almighty power. These doctrinal points I do but only touch. I come to that that I judge more useful; that is, that

* That is, 'breathe.'—G.

Doct. Whatsoever is good in us comes from the Spirit of God.

What need I stand upon reasons? Whatsoever is above nature it must come from God's Spirit. The Spirit is the author of all things above nature. Grace whereby we are like Christ, is above nature; therefore it must be by the Spirit of God.

Besides, that which riseth of nothing, and is opposite, and hath Satan to oppose it, it must have an almighty power to work it. Therefore whosoever works anything that is supernaturally good in us, he must be above the devil. We cannot so much as call Jesus,* with a feeling, but by the Spirit of God. We cannot think a good thought. All is by the Spirit, whatsoever is gracious and comfortable in us. I should be over-troublesome to you to be much in so clear a common argument as this is. Therefore I will hasten to make some use of it.

Use 1. And therefore put out of your thoughts, I beseech you, when you look to have any grace or comfort wrought, shut out of your hearts *too much relying upon any outward thing*. Think not that education can make a man good, or plodding can make a man good: in bodily exercise, in hearing much, in conferring much, in custom or education, or any pains of our own. These are things that the Spirit will be effectual in, if we use them as we should; but without the Spirit what are they? Nay, what is the body of Christ without the Spirit? 'The flesh profiteth nothing,' John vi. 63. What is the sacrament and the word? Dead things without the Spirit of the Lord. Nothing can work upon the soul, no outward thing in the world, but the Spirit of God; and the Spirit of God works upon the soul by the means of grace, by gracious habits and qualities wrought. For he doth not work upon the soul immediately. Before he alter and change the soul, the Spirit works upon the soul by altering, and changing of it; and when it hath altered the soul, then it joins with the soul, and alters and changeth it according to the image of Christ, more and more still.

I beseech you, in your daily practice, all learn this, that you trust not too much to any outward performance or task; to make idols of outward things. People when they would change their dispositions, and be better, they take a great deal of pains in hearing, and reading, and praying. All these are things necessary; but they are dead things without the Spirit of Christ. Therefore in the use of all those outward things, whatsoever they be, look up to Christ, that is the quickening Spirit, that sends the Spirit into our hearts. The Spirit must enliven and give vigour to all these things, and then somewhat will be done in religion, in hearing, and reading, and praying, and receiving the sacrament. Therefore in all these look to the Spirit first. He laboureth in vain that relieth not wholly upon the Spirit of God, that trusts not to a higher strength than his own. It must be a higher strength than our own that must work any good in our souls, either grace, or comfort, or peace. And therefore in the use of all things, as the proverb is, *oculos ad cœlum, &c.* Let the eye be to heaven, when the hand is at the stern† at the same time; and then we shall be transformed and changed by the Spirit of God. Know that in all means alway the Spirit is the principal, efficient, blessing, cause of all. And therefore before we set upon anything that is good, wherein we look for any spiritual good, desire God by his Holy Spirit that he would clothe what shall be said. Words are wind without the Spirit. The Spirit must go with the ordinances, as the arteries go together with the veins. You know in the veins in the body there are arteries that go with them. They convey the spirits.

* Qu. 'Jesus, Lord'?—Ed.

† That is, 'the helm.'—Ed.

The veins convey the blood. That is a dull thing, without the spirits, of itself. If there were no spirits in the arteries, what would the blood in the veins be? Nothing but a heavy uncomfortable humour. But the arteries that come from the heart, the fountain of life, being joined, and conveying the spirits, they quicken the blood that comes from the liver. So the veins and arteries join together to make the blood cheerful. The word and truth of God are like the blood in the veins. There is a great deal of matter in them, but there is no life at all. There must the Spirit go along with them to give life and quickening to the word, to clothe those divine truths with the Spirit, and then it works wonders, not else. Paul spake to Lydia, Acts xvi. 14, *seq.*, but the Holy Ghost opened her heart. The Spirit hath the key of the heart to unlock and open the heart. We speak to the outward man, but except the inward man be opened by the Spirit of God and unlocked, all is to no purpose. Therefore let us pray for the Spirit of this changing. All is by the Spirit of the Lord.

It is in mystical Christ, even as it was in natural Christ; all his grace was from the Holy Ghost as man. For though he were conceived of the Holy Ghost, he was anointed by the Holy Ghost; he was sealed by the Holy Ghost; he was led by the Holy Ghost into the wilderness; he offered himself by the Spirit; he was raised by the Spirit; he was full of the Spirit. As it was in Christ natural, so it is in Christ mystical; that is, in the church all is by the Spirit. As he was conceived in the womb by the Spirit, so we are conceived to be Christians by the Spirit. The same Spirit that sanctified him sanctifieth us. But first the Spirit by way of union sanctifieth us, by knitting us to him the head of all; and then unction comes after union; anointing after union. Then the Spirit, when he hath knit us to Christ, works the same anointing that he did in Christ. Therefore we are called Christians of Christ, not only partakers of the naked name, but of the anointing of Christ—that anointing that runs down the head of our spiritual Aaron to the skirts, to every poor Christian. All change, all comfort, all peace is from the Spirit of Christ. Therefore give him the glory of all. If we find any comfort in any truth, it comes not from us, but from his Spirit; and we must go upward to him again. As all descends from heaven, from the Father of lights and from the Spirit of God, so all must ascend again. Yield him the praise of all. And one work of the Spirit is to carry our souls up. For the Spirit, as it comes from heaven to change, so it carries us up again to view and to imitate Christ, to be where Christ is. As water when it is to be carried up, it is carried as high as the spring head, from whence it came, so the Spirit coming from Christ, it never leaves changing and altering of us till it have carried us to Christ again. Therefore as it is the work of the Spirit to carry us to Christ, so let us desire it may carry us beforehand for the good work begun in us, in thankfulness, that we may begin heaven upon earth. All is from the Spirit of Christ.

A man now in the state of grace must look for nothing from himself; for as we are saved altogether out of ourselves by Christ the mediator, so the fitting for that glorious salvation that we have purchased by Christ, it is by the Spirit. The working of our salvation is by God, and the assurance of it to our souls is by the Holy Ghost, by the witness of God sealed to us. And the fitting and preparing and changing and sanctifying of us, it is by the Holy Ghost. All is out of us in the covenant of grace, wherein God is a gracious Father in Christ. All is out of us in regard of the spring. The work indeed is terminated in us. The Spirit of God alters our understanding, will, and affections, but the spring is out of us. As in paradise those four streams that watered paradise, that ran through it, yet the head of them was out of paradise, in another part of the world. So though the work of the Holy Ghost, the streams of the Spirit, run through the soul and water it; yet the spring of those graces, the Holy Ghost, is out of us, and Christ the root of salvation is out of us. For God in the covenant of grace will not trust us, as in Adam God trusted us with grace, he had grace in his own keeping. If he would he might have stood. He had liberty of will, but God saw we were all ill husbands of grace and goodness, that he would not trust us again. Therefore he trusted God-man, the second Adam, with grace; and he sends his Spirit into us, and conveys grace 'from glory to glory' by degrees, and all by the Spirit of the Lord.

And, in the next place, this point of doctrine should marvellously comfort and stay us, and direct us.

Use 2. It should comfort us when we find no goodness at all, nor no strength at all in our natures. Doth God expect that we should have anything from ourselves? Who expects anything from a barren wilderness? Our hearts are such. God knows it well enough. There is no goodness in us, no more than there is moisture in a stone or a rock. Therefore he looks that we should beg the Spirit of him, and depend upon him for the Spirit of his Son, to open our eyes with the Spirit of illumination; to reveal his love to us, and then to sanctify us and to work us more and more to glory, and to work out all corruption by little and little. He expects that we should depend upon him for the Spirit in all things we do.

Therefore Christians are much to blame. They think to work and to hew out of their own nature the love of God, and keep ado with their own hearts, as if they had a principle of grace in themselves as of themselves; and they may long enough work that way. But that is not the way, but acknowledgment that in ourselves, as of ourselves, as Saint Paul saith, we cannot do anything, Philip. ii. 13. We cannot so much, by all the power in the world, as think a good thought. If we should live a thousand years, there cannot rise out of our hearts a good desire of ourselves. All is out of us from the Spirit of the Lord. Now thereupon we must not look for it in ourselves, but go to God for his Holy Spirit. Go to Christ for his Spirit, for the Spirit proceeds from them both, that he would enlighten us and sanctify us, as I shewed in particular before. We must not therefore presume that we can do anything of ourselves; and so we must not despair. Shall we despair when once we believe in Christ? when we have abundance of grace and Spirit in our head Christ? And he can derive* his Spirit as he pleaseth. He gives the Spirit by degrees as he pleaseth; for he is a voluntary head to dispense it as he will. He is not a natural head. Who shall despair when he is in Christ, who is complete? And in him we receive grace for grace, grace answerable for grace in him.

Let none presume that he can do anything of himself, for you see how God suffered holy men to miscarry. It was folly in this case in Peter to presume of his own strength: 'Though all forsook Christ,' Mark xiv. 31, *seq.*, yet would not he. He presumed upon his own strength. God left him to himself. You see how foully he fell. So it is with us all, when we presume upon the strength of our nature and parts. We must not come to this holy place in the strength of our own wit and parts, but come with a desire that the Spirit may join with his ordinances, and make them efficacious for our change. All change is by the Spirit of the Lord. Nothing works above his own sphere. It is above the power of nature to work any-

* That is, 'convey.'—G.

thing supernatural. Therefore if we will profit by the word, come not with presumptuous spirits, but lift up our hearts to God, that his Spirit may clothe the ministry with vigour and power, that he may convey holy truths into our hearts, and make them effectual for the changing of the inward and of the outward man. Then we come as we should. All is by the Spirit of the Lord, blessing all means whatsoever, without which all means are dead. Therefore we must open as that flower that opens and shuts as the sun shines on it *(n)*. So must we as Christ shines on us; and we ebb and flow as he flows upon us. We shine or are dark as he shines on us. As the air is no longer light than the sun shines, so we are no longer lightsome and open, and flow and are carried to anything, than Christ by his Spirit flows on us. For we do what we do, but we are patients first to receive that power from the Spirit. We hear and do good works, but the activity and power and strength comes all from the Spirit of God.

Use 3. Hence likewise we may make another use of trial, *whether we have the Spirit of Christ or no;* whether we have the Holy Ghost, which is called here the Spirit of the Lord.

I will not go out of the text for trials.

(1.) If a man have the Spirit of God, *it openeth the eyes of the soul to see in the glass of the word, the face of God shining on him in Christ.* If a man have the Spirit he sees God as a Father, by the Spirit of illumination.

(2.) Again, if thou hast the Spirit of God, *thou hast the Spirit of love.* God's Spirit manifesteth the hidden love of God, that was hid in the breast of God, to his soul; for the Spirit of God searcheth the breast of God and the secret of God, and it searcheth my heart. Now he that hath the Spirit of God knows the love of God in Christ to him; it reveals the love of God, the height, and breadth, and depth of it to our spirits. As in the text, we see the gracious love of God in Christ, and then we love him again.

(3.) And thereupon where the Spirit *is it changeth.* It is not only a Spirit of illumination, but of sanctification. Where he dwells he sanctifieth the house, and makes it a temple. It is efficacious. Where the Spirit is, it will work. It is like the wind. Where it is it will stir, it will move. Where it moves not it is not at all. Where the Spirit alters not the condition from bad to good, and from good to better, suspect that it is not there; at least it will move. As the pulses will have a drawing in, and a sending out, by stirring, so there will be some operation of the Spirit that is discernible to a judicious eye; alway some stirring where the Spirit of God is.

The papists slander us willingly: I think against many of their consciences that understand anything. Oh, say they, we will have Christians like Satan, to appear as angels of light, and blackamores in white garments, that have their teeth white, and nothing else. So your Christians put on the garment of Christ's righteousness. Let them put on that, and then though they be not changed a whit, it is no matter. Who teacheth thus? We teach out of this text, that,

First of all, the Spirit of God opens our eyes. He takes off the veil, and then we see the glory of God's mercy in Christ, pardoning our sins for the righteousness and obedience of Christ; and then that love warms our hearts, so that it changeth our hearts by the Spirit, from one degree of grace to another. There is a changing power that goes with the love of Christ, and with the mercy of God in Christ. This [is] our doctrine. The same Spirit that justifieth us by applying to us the obedience of Christ, the same Spirit sanctifieth us. Therefore their allegations and objections are to no purpose. We see here the Spirit of the Lord changeth us.

And so for your common atheistical professors, that profess themselves Christians. They partake of the name, but not of the anointing of Christ. True Christians that are anointed with the Spirit of Christ, it will enforce a change. Beloved, we cannot behold the sun, but we must be enlightened; we cannot behold the Sun of righteousness, but we shall be changed and enlightened. The eye of faith, though we think not of it, though it look upon Christ for justification and forgiveness of sins, yet notwithstanding at the same time insensibly there is an alteration of the soul. If a man look up for other ends, yet at the same time there is an enlightening by the sun. So at the same time that we look upon the mercy of God in Christ, at the same time there is a glory shines upon us, and we are altered and changed, though we think not of it. At the very instant that we apprehend justification and forgiveness of sins, in the mercy of God in Christ, at the same instant there is a glory put upon the soul. We cannot have commerce with the God of glory, but we shall be glorious. Therefore, there is no man that hath anything to do with God, that hath not some glory put into his soul, whatsoever he is.

Therefore, let no man think he hath anything to do in religion till he find the work of the Spirit altering and changing him. He hath the title of Holy Spirit, from the blessed work of sanctifying and changing: he doth change us.

(4.) And when he hath changed us, *he governs and guides us from glory to glory*. Where the Holy Ghost is, therefore, he promotes the work of grace begun. He doth not only move us but promove; he promotes the work begun. Therefore those that have the Spirit of God, they rest in no degree of grace, but grow from grace to grace, from knowledge to knowledge, from faith to faith, till they come to that measure of perfection that God hath appointed them in Christ. Those, therefore, that set up their staff, and will go no further, that think all is well, they have not the Spirit of God. For the Spirit stirs up to grow from one degree of grace to another, to add grace to grace, and to enter further and further into the kingdom of grace, and to come nearer to glory still.

(5.) For this end the Holy Spirit dwells in us, and guides us, as it is, Rom. viii. 26. He is a tutor to us. Where the Holy Ghost is in any body, it is as a counsellor. 'Guide me by thy counsel, till thou bring me to glory,' Ps. xxxi. 3, *et alibi*. It is a tutor. As noblemen's children they have their tutors, so God's children are nobly born. They have their tutor and counsellor, as well as angels to attend them. They have the Spirit of God to tell them, This do, and that do, and here you have done ill. They have a voice behind them, to teach them in particular wherein they have done amiss. They that have the Spirit, find such a sweet operation of the Spirit, the Spirit is a teacher and a counsellor to them. They that are acquainted with the government of God's Spirit, they find it checking them presently when they do ill. It grieves them when they grieve the Spirit, so it teacheth them in particular businesses, Do this, do not that. Thus may we know if we have the Spirit, if it guide and govern us from glory to glory, till we come to perfection, where the Spirit is all in all in heaven.

(6.) Another evidence is this, the Spirit where it is *it rests and abides;* because it doth not only change us at the first, but it leads us from glory to glory. As St Augustine saith, 'Wicked men have the Spirit of God knocking, and he would fain enter' (*o*); as the wickedest man, when he hears holy truths discovered, the Spirit of God knocks at his heart, and he finds sweet motions in his poisonful rebellious nature, but this is but the

Spirit knocking, that would have entrance. But God's children have the Spirit entering, and dwelling and resting there. The Spirit of God resteth on Christ, and it rests on Christ's members. How can it change them, and having done so, guide and govern them from glory to glory; but he must rest there, he must take up his lodging and residence. A Christian is not an ordinary house, but a temple; he is not an ordinary man, but a king; he is not an ordinary stone, but a pearl; he is not an ordinary tree, but a cedar; he is an excellent person. And therefore the Spirit of God delights to dwell in him. As the excellency of the body is from the soul, so the excellency of the soul is from the Spirit dwelling in him. However, in particular operations, the Spirit suspends his acts of comforting and guiding, to humble them for their presumption, alway the Holy Ghost is in the heart, though he be hid in a corner of the heart. 'I will send you the Comforter, and he shall abide with you for ever,' saith Christ, John xiv. 16. Thus we may see how we may try ourselves, whether we have the Spirit of the Lord or no. If we have not the Spirit, we are none of his, we are none of Christ's, Rom. viii. 13, 14. And then whose are we, if we be none of Christ's? Do but think of that. Therefore if we would not be men not having the Spirit, that is, men dead, led with a worse spirit than our own, let us labour to know whether we have the Spirit of Christ or no. Let us see what change there is to the likeness of Christ. For,

(7.) The Spirit, as it comes from the Lord, *so it makes us like the Lord, and we are changed by reasons from the Lord; by reasons and considerations from Christ, and from the love of. God in Christ;* because the Spirit takes from Christ whatsoever he hath: 'He shall take of mine,' &c., John xvi. 13. That is the comfort he comforts the soul with; he fetches them from his death and bloodshed, and the love of God in him. That he takes of Christ. So there is a change wrought in us by reasons fetched from the love of God in Christ, those conforming reasons. God hath given his Son, and Christ hath given himself, and we feel the love of God by the Spirit. If the Spirit work any grace or comfort by considerations fetched from Christ, this is the true Spirit. The change and alteration that it works in us is according to the image of Christ, that we may be like Christ. So Christ is the beginning and the end, and Christ is all. He works from Christ and to Christ. Let us examine therefore if we have the Spirit of Christ, whether it change us; and examine if we have the Spirit, from what reasons and grounds it changes us; and then we may upon some comfortable grounds say we have the Spirit indeed.

If we have not the Spirit, how shall we come to have the Spirit? What means must we use to get it?

In a word, this chapter excellently sets out that, for,

[1.] *The gospel is called the ministry of the Spirit;* for the opening of the love of God in Christ, which is the gospel, is the ministry of the Spirit. Why? Because God hath joined the Spirit with the publishing and opening of these mysteries. Therefore study the gospel, and hear unfolded divine evangelical truths. The more we hear of the sweet love of God in Christ, the more the Spirit flows into the soul together with it. The Spirit goes together with the doctrine of the gospel; which is called the ministry of the Spirit. Therefore let us delight in hearing evangelical points, the love of God opened in Christ.

A civil moral man, Oh he is taken mightily, if he hear a moral witty politic discourse that toucheth him; and he is in his element then. What is this to the gospel? This hath its use. Oh but the Spirit goes with the opening of the gospel, with evangelical points; and if our hearts were ever seasoned with the love of God, these points of Christ, and the benefits and privileges by Christ, they will affect us more than any other thing in the world. That is one means to study the gospel, and to hear the truths of the gospel opened where the Sprit works.

[2.] Again, the Spirit of the Lord it is given to us usually *in holy community*. The Holy Ghost fell upon them in the Acts when they were gathered together, Acts iv. 31; and surely we never find sweeter motions of the Spirit than now, when we are gathered at such times, about holy business, as this day. We never find the Spirit more effectual to alter and change our souls, than at such times. 'Where two or three are gathered together, I will be in the midst of you,' Mat. xviii. 20, but by the Spirit, saith Christ, warming, and altering, and changing the soul. For God infuseth all grace in communion, as we are members of the body mystical. Those that have sullen spirits, a spirit of separation, that scorn all meetings, they are carried with the spirit of the devil, and of the world. They know not what belongs to the things of God. It is the meek spirit that subjects itself to the ordinance of God. The Holy Ghost falls usually upon men when they are in holy communion.

[3.] And in Luke xi. 13, there God will give the Holy Ghost to all that *beg him*. *Pray for the Holy Ghost*, as the most excellent thing in the world. He shall be given to them that beg him, as if he should say, there is nothing greater than that, and God will give him to them that ask him. Therefore, come to God, and in any thing we have to do, empty ourselves and beg the Spirit; for the more a man empties him of his own confidence, in regard of holy performance of duties, the more we will desire to be filled with the fulness of the Spirit; and this sense of our own emptiness will force prayer.

Therefore, know that of ourselves we can do nothing holily, that may further our reckoning, but by the Spirit. Do all things therefore in a sense of our own emptiness, and beg the Spirit.

As likewise when we are framed by the Spirit to obedience. Those that obey the motions of the Spirit, the Spirit joins more and more closely with their souls. God gives his Spirit to them that obey him. Those that obey the first motions of the Spirit, they have further degrees. What is the reason that men have no more Spirit in the ordinances? The Holy Ghost knocks at their hearts, and would fain have entrance, and they resist it, as Stephen saith, Acts vii. 51. Now the Holy Ghost is willing to enter upon the soul, but he is resisted. Therefore if you will have him more and more, let us open our souls, that the King of glory may come in. The Spirit is willing to enter, especially in holy assemblies. Saith St John, Rev. i. 10, 'I was on the Lord's day, I was in the Spirit,' that is, as if he were drowned in the Spirit on the Lord's day. When we are about holy exercises we are never more in the Spirit than then. Let us open our souls to the Spirit, and then we shall find the Spirit joining with our souls. The Spirit is more willing to save us, and to sanctify us, than we are to entertain him. Oh that we were willing to entertain the sweet motions of the Spirit! Our natures would not be so defiled, and we so uncomfortable as we are. There are none of us all, but we find comfortable motions in holy exercises. Thus we may get the Spirit of the Lord, that doth all, that illuminates, and sanctifieth, and ruleth, and rests in us.

(8.) And let us learn, I beseech you, hence to give the third glorious person, the Holy Ghost, *his due*. Since we have all by the Spirit, let us learn to give the Spirit his due, and learn how to make use of the work of the Spirit. There are several works of the Spirit. You see here what the Spirit doth, 'We all.' The Spirit unites us together. It is a Spirit of union. It knits all together by one faith to God. All meet in God the Father reconciled; and we all are joined together by love, wrought by the Spirit, 'with open face.' Who takes away the veil? We are all veiled by nature. The Spirit takes away the veil from our eyes, and from the truth. What is the reason the gospel is so obscure? The Spirit takes not away the veil, it teacheth not by the ministry; or else it takes not away the veil from the eyes. The Spirit takes away the scales from our eyes, and the Spirit in the ministry takes away the obscurity of the Scriptures. All those that we call graces, the free gifts, the ministerial gifts, they are the gifts and the graces of the Spirit; and they are for the graces of the Spirit. Skill in tongues and in the Scriptures, and in other learning, are given to men that they may take away the veil from the Scriptures, that they may be lightsome; and then when the Spirit is given, he takes away the veil from the soul by his own work; and then with open face 'we behold the glory of the Lord.' What doth open our eyes to see, when the veil is taken off? The Spirit. We have no inward light nor sight, but by the illumination of the Spirit. All light in the things, and all sight in us, it is by the illumination of the Spirit. And then the change according to the image of Christ, this is altogether by the Spirit of Christ, it is altogether from the Holy Ghost. Christ baptizeth 'with the Holy Ghost, and with fire,' Mat. iii. 11, and Christ came 'by blood, and by water,' 1 John v. 6: by blood, to die for us; and by water, by his Spirit to change us and purge and cleanse us. All is by the Spirit. Christ came as well by the Spirit as by blood. This change, and the gradual change from glory to glory, all is by the Spirit. Therefore we should not think altogether of Christ, or God the Father, when we go to God in prayer; but think of the work of the Spirit, that the Holy Ghost may have his due.

Lord, without thy Spirit, my body is as a thing without a soul, a dead, loathsome, stiff, unapt carcase, that cannot stir a whit; and so my soul without the operation of thy Holy Spirit, it is a stiff, dead, unmoveable thing; and therefore by thy Spirit breathe upon me. As thy Holy Spirit in the creation did lie upon the waters, and brood as it were all things there; lying upon the waters it fashioned this goodly creature, heaven and earth, this *mundus*. So the Spirit of God lying upon the waters of the soul, it fashions all graces and comforts, whatsoever they are; all is wrought by the Spirit in the new creature, as all in this glorious fabric of the world was by the Spirit of God. Let the Spirit of God therefore have due acknowledgment in all things whatsoever.

And what are we to look to mainly now? The knowledge of God the Father, and his love to us shining in Christ, all is in Christ; and if we would have anything wrought in us, any alteration of our natures, let us beg the Spirit, that we may have the discovery of the love of God in Christ, and the Spirit attending upon the gospel.

And because we have all these abundantly in these latter times of the church, in the second spring of the gospel, in the reformation of religion, after our recovery out of popery, there is a second spring of the gospel. Oh, beloved, how much are we beholding to God! Never since the beginning of the world was there such glorious times as we enjoy. We see how the holy apostle doth prefer these times before former times, when the veil was upon their eyes, and when all was hid in ceremonies, and types, and such things among the Jews. 'Now,' saith he, 'we behold the glory of God, and are changed by the Spirit from glory to glory.'

To conclude all. Therefore consider that the glory of the times, and the glory of places and persons, all is from the revelation of Christ by the Spirit, which hath the Spirit accompanying it. The more God in Christ is laid open, the more the times, and places, and persons are excellent. What made the second temple beyond the former? Christ came at the second temple. Therefore though it were baser in itself, yet the second temple was more glorious than the first. What made Bethlehem, that little city, glorious? Christ was born there. What makes the heart where Christ is born more glorious than other folk? Christ is born there. Christ makes persons and places glorious. What makes the times now more glorious than they were before Christ? What made the least in the kingdom of heaven greater than John Baptist? He was greater than all that were before him; and all that are after him are greater than he. Because his head was cut off, he saw not the death and resurrection of Christ, and the giving of the Holy Ghost. He saw not so much of Christ. So that the revelation of Christ and the love of God in Christ, it is that that makes times, and persons, and places glorious, all glorious, because the veil is taken away from our eyes. We see Christ the King of glory in the gospel flourishing, and the love of God manifested, and by the Spirit of God the veil is taken away inwardly as well as outwardly. Now for a fuller discovery of Christ than in former times, comes the glory of the times. Now there are more converted than in former times, because the Spirit goes together with the manifestation of Christ. What is the reason that this kingdom is more glorious than any place beyond the seas? Because Christ is here revealed more fully than there. The veil is taken off, and here 'we see the glory of God with open face,' which changeth many thousands from glory to glory by the Spirit of God that accompanies the revelation of the gospel. Is there any outward thing that advanceth our kingdom before Turkey, or Spain, &c.? Nothing. Their government. and riches, and outward things are as much as ours, if not more. The glory of places and times are from the revelation of Christ, that hath the Spirit accompanying of it. That Spirit changeth us 'from glory to glory.' Our times are more glorious than they were a hundred years or two before. Why? Because we have a double revelation of Christ, and of antichrist. We see Christ revealed, and the gospel opened, and the veil taken off. We see antichrist revealed, that hath masked under the name of head of the church, and hath seduced the world.

Now this double revelation challengeth acknowledgment of these blessed times. What should all this do but stir us up to know the time of our visitation, and to thankfulness; to bless God that hath reserved us for these places and countries that we live in, to cast our times to be in this glorious light of the gospel to be born in. What if we had been born in those dark Egyptian times of popery? Our lives had not been so comfortable. Now we live under the gospel, wherein 'with open face' we see the glory of the mercy of God in Christ, the 'unsearchable riches' of Christ opened and discovered to us. And together with the gospel, the ministry of the Spirit, goeth the Spirit; and those that belong to God, thousands by the blessing of God are changed from glory to glory.

Certainly if we share in the good of the times we will have hearts to thank God, and to walk answerably, that as we have the glorious gospel, so we will walk gloriously, that we do not by a base and fruitless life dishonour so glorious a gospel. I beseech you let us think of the times, else if we be not the better for the glorious times, if the veil be not taken away, we are under a fearful judgment. 'The god of this world hath blinded our eyes,' 2 Cor. iv. 4. Do we live under the glorious light, and yet are dark, that we see no glory in Christ? We see nothing in religion, but are as ready to entertain popery as true religion. Is this the fruit of the long preaching of the gospel, and the veil being taken off so long? Certainly the god of this world hath cast the dust of the world into our eyes, that we can see nothing but earthly things. We are under the seal of God's judgment. He hath sealed us up to a dark state, from darkness of judgment to the darkness of hell without repentance. Therefore let us take heed how we live in a dull and dead condition, under the glorious gospel, or else how cursed shall we be! The more we are exalted and lifted up above other people in the blessings of God this way, the more we shall be cast down. 'Woe be to Chorazin,' &c., Mat. xi. 21; and Heb. ii. 3, 'How shall we escape if we neglect so great salvation?'

I beseech you let us take heed how we trifle away our time, these precious times and blessed opportunities; for if we labour not to get out of the state of nature into the state of grace, and so to be changed from glory to glory, God in justice will curse the means we have, that in hearing we shall not hear, and seeing we shall not see, and he will secretly and insensibly harden our hearts. It is the curse of all curses, when we are under plenty of means, to grow worse and duller. Oh take heed of spiritual judgments above all others, tremble at them. They belong to reprobates and castaways. Let us labour for hearts sensible of the mercies of God in Christ, and labour to be transformed and moulded into this gospel every day more and more. That that hath been spoken shall be sufficient for this time, and for this whole text.

NOTES.

(*a*) P. 222.—'As the Father saith, free me from my necessities.' The well-known apophthegm of Augustine, 'A necessitatibus meis libera me Domine.'

(*b*) P. 224.—'The defence of Luther's and others that wrote of this freedom is sound and good, that the will of man is slavish altogether without the Spirit of God.' The great Reformer's masculine treatise on 'The Bondage of the Will' (*De Servo Arbitrio*), has been repeatedly translated, though not over-exactly, into English; *e. g.*, by Cole (1823).

(*c*) P. 236.—'As Cyprian saith, Consecra habitaculum,' &c. We have not found this expression. The following is in substance equivalent:—'Denique magisterio suo Dominus secreto nos orare præcepit, in abditis et semotis locis, in cubiculis ipsis.'—*De Orat. Dom.* § iv.

(*d*) P. 240.—'And therefore we call things that are glorious by the name of light, *illustrissimus* and *clarissimus*, terms taken from light.' *Illustris* and *illustrissimus* from *lux: clarus* = clear, bright.

(*e*) P. 244.—'Hail, Mary, full of grace.' . . . . 'Oh! beseech thy Son,' &c., &c. For startling examples and confirmations of the text, consult Tyler's conclusive treatise on 'The Worship of the Virgin Mary.'

(*f*) P. 247.—'And how should finite comprehend infinite? We shall *apprehend* him, not *comprehend* him.' Have we not in this brief sentence the whole 'philosophy of the infinite,' that has been so darkened in the controversies of Sir William Hamilton, Calderwood, Mansel, Maurice?

(*g*) P. 250—'The heavens declare the glory of God, They are a book in folio.' Thus quaintly does John Cragge of Lantilio Pertholy expand the thought of Sibbes, in his 'Cabinet of Spiritual Jewels' (1657, 12mo.): 'A time there was before all times, when there was no day but the Ancient of Days: no good but God: no light but the Father of Lights: Arts were but ideas; the world a map of Providence; heavens, the book in folio: earth, water, air, and fire, in quarto: hell, the doomsday pageant: men and angels but capital letters in the margin of God's thoughts.'

(*h*) P. 252.—'Oh foolish Galatians, before whom Christ hath been painted and crucified.' Consult and compare Bagge on Galatians, *in loc.*: also Ellicott.

(*i*) P. 277.—'It is said of Antiochus, that he was a vile person,' &c. Cf. Memoir of Antiochus, in Dr Smith's 'Dictionary of Greek and Roman Biography,' with its ample authorities.

(*j*) P. 280.—'We must not think to come *de cœno in cœlum*,' as he saith, 'out of the filth of sin to heaven, but heaven must begin here.' One of Augustine's *Memorabilia*.

(*k*) P. 281.—'It is not as a flash or blaze of flax, or so.' For a fine description of the lighting and fading away of the threads of flax, on the consecration of a pope, see Cardinal Wiseman's interesting 'Recollections of the Popes,' in any of its editions.

(*l*) P. 284.—'As Hilary said in a time of schism, 'it requireth deal of wit to be a Christian.' The following is probably the passage referred to:—'Cum . . . . nec negari possit ex vitio malæ intelligentiæ fidei extitisse dissidium, dum quod legitur sensui potius coaptatur quam lectioni sensus obtemperat.'—*Hilar. De Trinitate*, lib. vii.

(*m*) P. 286.—'We are here lame Mephibosheths.' That rare little book, full of pensive and wise meditation, by a very dear friend of Dr Sibbes's—the 'Al Mondo, or Contemplatio Mortis et Immortalitatis,' of Henry, Earl of Manchester—furnishes an interesting parallel passage here—'Nature's perfection caught a fall when she was young, as Mephibosheth did, whereof she hath halted ever since' (5th edition, 1642, 18mo, page 12).

(*n*) P. 298.—'Therefore we must open as that flower that opens and shuts as the sun shines on it.' There are very many flowers of this character. The common daisy is the most familiar example. What one in particular the author refers to we cannot tell.

(*o*) P. 299.—'As St Augustine saith, 'Wicked men have the Spirit of God knocking, and he would fain enter, ... But God's children have the Spirit entering and dwelling and resting there.' A frequent sentiment in 'The Confessions' of this father. G.

EXPOSITION OF 2D CORINTHIANS CHAPTER IV.

EXPOSITION OF SECOND CORINTHIANS CHAPTER IV.

NOTE.

The 'Commentary or Exposition' upon the fourth chapter of the 2d Epistle to the Corinthians forms the larger portion of a quarto volume published in 1656. The title-page is given below.* The second of the three treatises mentioned therein is given in the present volume. The others will appear in their proper place hereafter. G.

* A LEARNED
COMMENTARY
OR,
EXPOSITION,
UPON
The fourth CHAPTER of the
second Epistle of Saint *PAUL* to
the CORRINTHIANS.

To which is added:
I. *A Conference between Christ and* Mary *after his resurrection.*
II. *The Spirituall Mans aim.*
III. *Emanuell, or Miracle of Miracles.*

Published for the advantage of those that have
them not, others may have the *Commentary* alone.
——*Virtus Cœlo beat.*

By that Reverend and Godly Divine, RICH: SIBBS D.D.
Sometimes Master of *Catherine Hall* in *Cambridge*, and
Preacher to that Honourable Society of *Grayes-Inne.*

Psalmes 37. 30. *The mouth of the righteous will speak of wisdome, and his tongue will talk of judgement.*
Vers. 31. *For the Law of his God is in his heart, and his steps shall not slide.*

LONDON,
Printed by *S. G.* for *John Rothwel*, at the *Fountain*
in *Cheap-side.* 1656.

TO THE READER.

CHRISTIAN READER, there are three ways by which a minister preaches: by doctrine, life, and writing. It may be questioned which is the hardest.

1. Truly for preaching,—the apostle's τίς ἱκανός, 2 Cor. ii. 16, 'who is sufficient?' may correct the slight apprehensions of hearers, and the hasty intrusion of teachers. Luther was wont to say, If he were to choose his calling, he would dig with his hands rather than be a minister (*a*). The disposition both of speakers and hearers, saith Chrysostom, makes this work difficult (*b*). In regard of hearers, scarce any member groans under more moral diseases than the ear. We read of an 'uncircumcised ear,' Acts vii. 51; 'deaf ears,' Rom. xi. 8, Micah. vii. 16; 'itching ears,' 2 Tim. iv. 2; 'ears that are dull of hearing,' Mat. xiii. 15. Most people come to hear as men do to a theatre, *non utilitatem sed voluptatem percepturi*, not so much to feed their faith as please their fancy. And for teachers, how many dangers do they lie open to! If they do not preach novelties, falsities, yet to preach *sana, sanè*, sound things soundly; to deliver the word, ὡς δεῖ με λαλῆσαι, Col. iv. 4, 'as it ought to be spoken.' To 'speak a word in season,' Isa. l. 4; to 'approve' themselves to God workmen that need not be ashamed; ὀρθοτομοῦντα τὸν λόγον τῆς ἀληθείας, rightly cutting the word into parts, giving every one his portion, 2 Tim. ii. 15.* And when a man hath done God's work in God's strength, to go away, with a humble heart, *hic labor*:—such a one is an 'interpreter,' 'one among a thousand,' Job xxxiii. 23.

2. But then for the life. Alas! how many think the work is done when the glass is out (*c*); how many are good in the doctrine, bad in the application, especially to themselves; how hard is it to have life in doctrine, and doctrine in life! It is easier to preach twenty sermons than to mortify one lust. It was a harder task Paul set Timothy, 2 Tim. iv. 12, when he bids him be an example to believers, in conversation, in charity, in spirit, &c., than when he bids him 'give attendance to reading, exhortation, doctrine,' ver. 13. Yet we shall often hear ministers say, They must study to preach, then study to practise. God would have the very snuffers in the tabernacle pure gold (*d*), to shew they that purge others must shine themselves. Surely they must needs be 'unclean,' that chew the cud by meditation, but divide not the hoof by practice. Lastly,

3. For writing—that hath more pre-eminency, though the two former have

* Metaphora à sacrificiis. Illyr. Perkins. [*i. e.*, William Perkins. Cf. Opera, Geneva, 1611, *in loc.*]. Metaphora à convivii apparatoribus. Gerh[ard] in Harm. Evang. [The book here cited is the 'Evangelistarum Harmoniæ Chemnitio-Lyserianæ Continuatio.' Jenæ, 1626–27.—G.]

more vivacity. There is, saith a good man,* as much difference between a sermon in the pulpit and printed in a book, as between milk in the warm breast and in the sucking bottle. Yet the convenience of it is very great. Good books are the baskets that preserve excellent lessons that they be not lost. This also wants not its difficulty; for what censures, impostures, contempt, wrestings, have the labours of the most eminent saints been exposed to, yea, the Scriptures themselves—the pandect of all truth, the testament of our Lord Jesus—how much have they suffered in all ages, besides the great difficulty, that is in other men's spirits to write truth. Yet let us bless God for the writings of his servants, for by these, 'being dead, they yet speak to us,' Heb. xi. 4. We have the prophets and apostles, in their writings, preaching to us. Their sermons were like a running banquet, refreshed many; their writings were a standing dish. Sermons are like showers of rain, wet for the present. Books are like snow-banks, lie longer upon the earth, and keep it warm in winter. It might be a problem whether professors preaching and writing, or confessors dying, have most profited the church.

Some have thought it preposterous in times of reformation to shut the pulpit against erroneous persons, and leave the press open to them, that being so compendious a way to propagate and to multiply errors; and the liberty, used more to condemn truths received, than to debate in a friendly way things indifferent. Indeed, it must be acknowledged a very sad thing, the multitude not only of vain but blasphemous treatises this age hath produced, and the great mischief they have done. But blessed be God, the press is as open to truth as error, and truth has been as nimble heeled as error. God never yet suffered any Goliah to defy him, but he raised up a David to encounter him.† Though error, like Esau, hath come out first, yet truth, like Jacob, hath caught it by the heel, and wrestled with it, Gen. xxv. 26. If God hath suffered any horn to push at his Israel, he hath presently raised a carpenter to knock it off. Let us bless God for the witnessing spirit that is abroad, though it go in sackcloth, Rev. xi. 3. Think how great a mercy it is to keep ground, though we cannot gain ground.

Let none complain of the multitude of good books. Though one bad one be too many, yet many good ones are too few; or, as one saith, 'one useless or erroneous book is too many. Many useful orthodox books are but one.'‡ All the prophets and apostles make but one Bible, upon which account we may say all the books that faithfully interpret that are but one book.

All these ways this reverend author was serviceable to the church of God while he lived; and, since his decease, the providence of God hath brought to light several tracts of his, some sooner, some later. And that in great wisdom; for our foolish nature doth many times prize the labours of those dead, whom we despised living, as the Jews, 'Their fathers killed the prophets, and their sons builded their tombs,' Matt. xxiii. 29. We may have such in these days. The spirit of man hath a more reverent opinion of things past than present, of things ancient than modern, of things farther off

* Gurnal's Ep.[istle] to his 'Christian in Compleat Armour.' [The one great *practical* work of the Conformists. . . . . a perfect storehouse of evangelical truths, and informed by a fine spirit. It was first published in 1656–62, and has since passed through many editions.—G.]

† The same day Pelagius was born here in Britain, Augustine was born in Africa.—[viz., Nov. 13. 354.—G.]

‡ Caryl. on Job v. part in the Ep[istle].

than near at hand. Another thing wherein the wisdom of God appears in the multitude of books, is, not only a discovery of the manifold gifts of the Spirit, that he pours on his servants (which could not well be seen but in variety and diversity), but also to invite us to the farther study of them by change; for the best of us have some seeds of curiosity. Now God, by the variety of gifts and graces in his servants, invites us to pass from one to another.

We shall say no more, but entreat thee to consider this treatise as a *posthume.** The notes were taken from his mouth by the pen of a ready writer, and a person of note and integrity, whose design is not to forge a piece under the author's name. The very style and matter is so like his other pieces, we hope the legitimacy of it will not be questioned. It is easier to counterfeit another man's name than another man's gifts. Had the author lived to supervise his own work, no question but it would have passed his hand with more authority and more politeness.† Thou wilt sometimes meet with some repetitions, yet with the addition of new matter. When thou meetest with it, read it as an impression which may carry force, and work more upon thy heart. In a word, the 'earthen vessel' is broken, the 'heavenly treasure' is preserved for thy use, and here offered to thee.

Now that God ‡ hath caused light to shine out of darkness, cause the light of the knowledge of the glory of God, in the face of Jesus Christ, to shine in thine and our hearts, more and more to the perfect day! So pray,

Thy souls' and thy faiths' servants in the Lord's work,

Simeon Ash.
Ja. Nalton.‖
Joseph Church.¶

* That is, posthumous.—G. † That is = more polished.—G.

‡ Qu. 'God that'?—Ed.

§ Ash was one of the most eminent of the Puritan 'worthies,' alike as a minister of the gospel and as an actor in the events of 'the Commonwealth.' He died on the evening of the memorable 'Bartholomew' of 1662; and Calamy preached his 'funeral' sermon. It will be found in the fullest and most trustworthy 'Collection of Farewell sermons' (3 vols. 12mo, 1663), Vol. i. at end. Cf. The Nonconformist's Memorial, i. 94, 95, and Hanbury, 'Historical Memorials relating to the Independents,' repeatedly.—G.

‖ See Notice of Nalton in Vol. II. page 442.—G.

¶ He was one of 'The Ejected' of 1662, having been minister of St Katherine's, Coleman Street, London. His 'Christian's Daily Monitor' is worthy to be placed beside Scudder's kindred treatise. Cf. Non. Mem. i. 137.—G.

A LEARNED COMMENTARY OR EXPOSITION

UPON

THE FOURTH CHAPTER OF THE SECOND EPISTLE OF ST PAUL TO THE CORINTHIANS.

For God, who commanded the light to shine out of darkness, hath shined in our hearts, to give the light of the knowledge of the glory of God in the face of Jesus Christ.—2 Cor. IV. 6.

In the last verse of the former chapter, the blessed apostle sets out the dignity of the gospel above the things of Moses and the things of the law. 'We all,' saith he, 'with open face, as in a glass, behold the glory of God, and are changed into the same image, from glory to glory,' &c. And hereupon, in the beginning of the next chapter, he sets out the excellency of the gospel ministry, being conversant about so excellent a mystery, and sheweth his fidelity in it. 'Therefore,' saith he, 'we faint not; but have renounced the hidden things of dishonesty, not walking in craftiness, nor handling the word of God deceitfully; but, by manifestation of the truth, commend ourselves to the consciences of all men in the sight of God.' Here he sheweth his fidelity in the ministry, and his courage, 'he fainteth not;' and likewise his sincerity, he 'labours to approve himself to the consciences of them in the sight of God.' Perhaps he had not all their good words; but it is better to have the consciences of people to give testimony of us than their words, their hearts than their mouths. Therefore the apostle knew not what they censured, but knew he had got some authority in their consciences; and therefore labours 'to approve himself to them in the sight of God,' which sheweth his sincerity. For this is the property of sincerity, to do all as 'in the sight of God;' to do good at all times, in all places, to all persons, in all actions. He that is sincere honours God in all.

Obj. Well, it might be objected, 'Many care not for the ministry nor the gospel, it is too obscure,' &c.; as it is the common course of the popish Jesuits to fall to accusation of Scripture as dark.

Ans. But, saith he, 'If the gospel be hid, it is hid to them whom the god of this world hath blinded.' And for further answer of the objection, 'If the gospel be hid from any, it is from them that perish.' And what is the cause? It is in regard of their own hardness of heart, joined with the malice of Satan. The god of the world hath thrown dust in their eyes, otherwise the gospel is clear enough. The blessed apostle was so privy to his own fair, open, free-dealing, that he dares freely say, 'If the gospel be hid, it is to them that perish.' There is no unfaithfulness, no obscurity in me. Satan hath an hand in it: 'the god of this world hath blinded their eyes.'

The god of this world. What! doth he put God out of his place? No; but the world maketh him so, namely, a god, by doing that to Satan, partly in himself and partly to his instruments, that they should do to God. They are at his beck, and run at his command; he leadeth them by worldly profits and pleasures, as a sheep is led by a green pasture. His influence acts. Wicked men are rightly styled 'men of the world,' Ps. xvii. 14; and Satan is truly called, by our apostle, 'the god of the world,' for they make him so by yielding to him in his designs.

Satan hath ruled in the church for many hundred years, yet more formerly than he doth in these times; but he did it subtilly. Great persons ruled by their friends, their friends were ruled by popish spirits; they by Jesuits, and the Jesuits by the man of sin, and he by Satan. So you see all resolved to the first principle. Satan hath a great hand in the government of the world. Doubtless the frogs that came out of the mouth of the beast, Rev. xvi. 13, are Jesuits and irksome devilish spirits. He lieth hid in a corner, and is not seen; but he is the god of the world, because by his subordination he ruleth as he list.

Use. Here you see *the malice of man, justice of God, and usurpation of Satan*. Man is the delinquent, God the judge, Satan the executioner. Man hath a hard and malicious heart against the light, he swelleth against it, and hateth nothing so much as the light. Take a worldly man that hath great parts, offer him the world,* contrary to his lusts and preferment, he will swell. Satan cavils against it. Indeed, men hate nothing so deadly as light, and this is the procuring cause of all mischief. When the truth is forced† on you, and you will have none, then God as a just judge saith, Take him, Satan; take him, Jesuit; take him, this or that profane person or vice; and how can such persons escape the blackness of darkness for ever?

And, beloved, can a man receive this glorious light of the Lord Jesus, when men are so dull and ignorant in the great point of religion? not only because they hate the light, and put off God's just judgments, but also from Satan's temptations, either immediately from himself or his instruments. And lest this should seem to be spoken something too high, 'the gospel is hid to them that perish,' &c., therefore, saith he, 'we preach not ourselves, but Christ; and ourselves your servants for his sake.' He did not speak this arrogantly, for all his ministerial function. He aimeth not at himself, but 'I serve Christ; and am your servant for his sake.' Not the servant of your lusts, for had he been the servant of men he had not been the servant of the Lord Jesus Christ; but the servant of their souls, one that would have laid his hands‡ at their feet to serve them, and would have been their servant indeed for their souls' good.

Now, the words that I have read to you shew the chief and principal cause of the glorious light of the gospel, and the means both to remove the cause of obscurity from the Scripture, and from St Paul's ministry, and shew where it is indeed.

* Qu. 'word'?—Ed. † That is, '*en*forced'.—G. ‡ Qu. 'head'?—Ed.

The principal cause of all light is God: 'God, that hath commanded the light to shine out of darkness, hath shined in our hearts,' not only outwardly in his word, but in our hearts. And to that end he gave the word, &c. So here is the chief cause of the chief end.

First, *The chief cause of all saving light that we have in the ministry of the word is God*, that shineth in our hearts by the ministry of the gospel. And,

Secondly, *The chief end is to give the light of the glory of God in the face of Jesus Christ;* not obscurely, like popish spirits, to impose darkness upon the Scriptures. Darkness is not from them; for the subject of the Scriptures declareth the image of God, not the accidental, but the real image of God the Father, who is light; and then they* oppose God, who is light in himself. But the end of the gospel is to give light, and 'the knowledge of God in the face of Jesus Christ.' If therefore the cause and matter and end be light, where is the cause of obscurity?

To come to the words:

First, You see *the cause of light, of inward light in the heart.* There is a double light—a light in the air and a light in the eye. So there is a light in the heart and a light in the truths themselves. Now, God is the cause of that inward light: '*God* hath shined in our hearts;' not only to us, but in our hearts, by his Holy Spirit.

Second, The end of this light is, not to shine in our hearts to no purpose, but to shine in our hearts *that we may shine to others;* that we may prove the light we have, that shineth to us in darkness, to convey the knowledge of God to all. What knowledge? The knowledge of Christ, and saving knowledge 'in the face of Christ.' And why doth God enlighten the ministers that they may convey light to others? That God's glory may be manifested. All is for his glory. The glory of his goodness, and justice, and his sweet attributes are manifested in Christ, which I shall speak of when I come to them.

Here he sets out God shining in the hearts of his ministers and children, by comparing of the light shining in darkness and God's commanding of light to shine out of darkness in the creation together. He ariseth from works of nature to works of grace, and from earthly things leads the Corinthians to spiritual things, in shewing an exact proportion between the things of nature and the things of grace; and therefore so should we in the matter of grace and glory.

This he doth to help our apprehensions of heavenly things, by these kind of glasses.

Therefore look how he takes things of nature to this end, and mark what he saith. He saith not Almighty God hath shined in our hearts, but he sets down that glorious attribute of God's almightiness by a word more familiar to our understandings: 'He that hath commanded light to shine out of darkness.' And thereupon sheweth the almighty power, wisdom, and goodness, that God graciously hath shined in our hearts. It is a wonderful comfort to the soul to single out of God what is fittest, either out of his attributes, his word, his works, or his creation.

But here we will speak first of that whence he raiseth his proportion, of God's commanding light to shine out of darkness; secondly, and then will shew the proportion between outward and spiritual light.

1. *The proportion of God's commanding light to shine out of darkness, and of light to shine in the soul.* The rise whence he fetcheh this is from the creation: 'God commanded light to shine out of darkness.' You know

* That is, 'the popish spirits.'—G.

there was a primitive light; *lux primogenita*, as Basil calls it (*e*); the first light, which was before the body of the sun, and after was put into the body of the sun, at the fourth day. He created the light first. God 'commanded that light to shine out of darkness.' Now, there is much ado, to no great purpose, what that light was that was created out of darkness, before the sun was made the receptacle of light. The time is short, and to spend it in unnecessary speculations is curious to search, and too rash to determine what that light was, whence it was taken, whether out of the confused mass or the purest part of it, and so lifted up to shine in the world; or whether he did create light out of darkness, taking darkness for the *terminus*, and not for the matter, to create light out of darkness, because there was nothing but darkness before; or whether God created this primitive light out of any body in the mass, or it was created out of darkness as out of a mass. But the Scripture determines it not, and therefore we will not meddle with anything in these matters without light of Scripture. Certain it is, that this light did distinguish day and night, and afterward was carried to the body of the sun. And it was created by God's commandment; for it is said, '*He that commanded light out of darkness* hath shined in our hearts.'

Now, it is said here that light is God's creature. It is out of darkness, and it is by God's command. It was but his word *fiat et fuit*, a word and a world; as it was spoken it was made, Gen. i. 3.

1. The thing created was *light;* 2. The manner how, by the *word;* 3. Out of what? From *darkness*. I will not speak distinctly* of them—it were to little purpose—but altogether: 'God hath commanded light to shine out of darkness.'

This command shews that God did it quickly and easily. It was but a word, a command; and he did it without any influence at all, by a mere word.

It was independently done of God. There was no matter to make it of, at least as good as nothing; for it was made of the mass. The mass was made of nothing.

Reason 1. Now, if you ask, Why God did create light in the first place? I answer, *It was because he might distinguish his six days' works.* If there had not been [light] to distinguish day and night, where had that distinction been?

Reason 2. And then again, *God had lost the glory of his works if he had not created light.* Light hath a heavenly quality, the principal of all qualities, the most excellent part of all.

Reason 3. And God created it first, *that it might discover itself and all other things.* It was *primum visibile*, that made all others seen. What had the beauty of the creatures been if light had not been created? They had all been covered in darkness. What end had there been of the eye and colours? Indeed, there is no quality that so much resembles God and divine things as light. The Scripture is exceedingly delighted in the using of this term light: 'God is the light of the world,' John i. 4, *seq.* 'Christ is the light of the world, that lighteth every one that cometh into the world,' John i. 9. The Holy Ghost is light, the angels light, the saints are the children of light. So that God taketh from hence those terms by which he sets out the dignity and excellency of himself, his children, and servants; and shews you the reasons of that light 'that enlightens every one that cometh into the world.'

* That is, 'separately.'—G.

Light sheweth and discovereth all the excellency of things, and distinguisheth one thing from another, and therefore Ambrose calleth it *lux prima gratia mundi* (*f*), the first grace of the world, and that ornament of the creature which sets out all other ornaments, that distinguisheth one from another.

Reason 4. Again, *it is that quality that doth quicken and enliven, and therefore the things that do quicken and enliven are lightsome;* a lively quality that puts life and cheerfulness into things. Light is sweet, Eccles. xi. 7. And it hath a quality likewise that it is not alone, for it is *vehiculum*, a conveyer of all influence from heaven. The virtue of conveying life into things on the earth is the light. Heat is but a connection. Heat cometh with light; and heat together with light, fosters and cherisheth all things in the world; as in nature, if there were not fire and heat, what could be good in nature? and if not heat and light, what would become of the world? All progressions and motions come from hence; and when light discovers good or ill, danger or commodity, this or that, thereupon the creature moves or removes from things hurtful, by benefit of the light. To be in darkness is a most hideous and irksome condition. Darkness breeds nothing but fear and terror, which weakeneth the spirit, and doth whatsoever is contrary to light. *Lux gloria creationis, tenebræ sunt opprobria.*

I might be very large in setting out the excellency of it, and all to good purpose, that we might see the excellency of the benefit thereof.

O beloved, what were our lives without it! We forget common benefits. How dark, disconsolate, fearful, terrible, and uncomfortable were our lives if they were without this quickening and solacing quality of light! and therefore we ought to take notice even of the rise of St Paul. I do but give a taste, 'For God who commanded the light to shine out of darkness, hath shined in our hearts, to give the light of the knowledge of the glory of God in the face of Jesus Christ.'

We see then that God by his authority commanded light to shine out of darkness. But what God? God the Father or God the Son? I answer, *Elohim*, the Father, Son, and Holy Ghost. All things were first from the Father, but the Son was Λόγος, and it was the Word that gave this command, Heb. i. 3. But the will of God is his word. The will of Christ is λόγος; for God created all things by the Son, who is the Wisdom of the Father. Therefore this word, 'Let there be light,' came from that Word, that Λόγος, which is the cause of all things, as John i. 3, 'By him were all things made that were made.' And the Spirit was an immediate cause; for the Spirit of God lay upon the waters. It lay upon the chaos. By it all things were made. It brooded as a hen upon the chickens, and as an eagle fluttereth upon her young ones.* The Holy Ghost did cherish and foster the primitive matter, on which all things were made. But they all agree in one.

You have the story in the first of Genesis. Elohim did it, Father, Son, and Holy Ghost. I would willingly come to some observation that may make it useful to us. Before I come to the main thing, this is worth our observing.

Obs. 1. That God commanded light out of darkness, *to shew that God is the Almighty God, gracious, wise.* We see that all things came from an almighty power. So the use of everything, the connection and subordina-

* The allusion is to Gen. i. 2; and all wishing to see Sibbes's paraphrase carried out with much quaint and not unuseful fancy, will consult Trapp and Hughes *in loc.*—G.

tion of one thing to another, it sheweth that all things came from a wise and gracious beginning. For we see that in the earth there are many beautiful things. The heavens, how glorious are they! and in the world how many excellent beauties! What were these if there were no light? and what were light if there were not an eye? Now, where there is a reference of one thing to another, and a connection of things, and a use of one thing to serve another, it sheweth that he was a God, and a wise God, that made all. This principle cannot be too much stood upon, because the weight of Christianity lieth upon it. The order, and use, and goodness of things, and connection of things, shew there is a good and a wise God. Take that for granted.

So you see what manner of worker God is in the creation, although independent, that can do all things at a word, with ease, without influence, without help. He dependeth not on matter as we do, that can do nothing without matter and subject to work upon, but he can work his own matter, can raise things out of nothing.

Use. And it is very observable, *for to help us in the dealings of our lives, to have such a conceit* of God that we should not limit God in our thoughts;* when we are in any extremity to tie him to this thing or to that thing. He can make matter out of nothing. Why should we limit the unlimited God, and so hinder our own comfort? Therefore we should infer hence, that God commandeth light *to shine out of darkness.* Observe that, when we be in dark conditions, and dark in sin, whatsoever sin and dark conditions we are in, as Isa. xlv. 7, 'I the Lord create light out of darkness,' that is, out of a darksome condition. Now light is taken for a comfortable condition, Esther viii. 16. When we be in any dark condition, limit not God. He is an independent worker. Question not how this may be and that may be. We must not bring God within the compass of our conceits and reasons. God is not as man; and therefore whatsoever our condition be, let us never limit God. God's people should never be better, the times were never worse. Where we be bad, God is good. Times are bad, God is good. He can alter all. When there is no hope of escaping, no likely issue, God can make it good. In the hardships, the exigencies of the soul, God takes occasion to shew the glory of his power, as Isa. iv. 5, God, saith he, 'created a pillar of fire, to go before the Israelites out of Egypt into Canaan.' If we want any comfort in any condition, being in covenant with such a God, if we be his children, he can create light, and can make a pillar of fire to go before his people to bring them to Canaan. See what the apostle saith, 2 Cor. i. 3, 'He is the God of *all* consolations;' not of this or that consolation, but the God of *all* consolations; that if we want he can work good out of the contrary, light out of darkness; he can draw matter of comfort out of discomfort; he can make every condition serve to his own ends; he can make 'all things work together for the good of his children,' Rom. viii. 28. The greater the power of this great God is, the greater is our comfort. We serve a God that can 'command light to shine out of darkness,' and shall we despair in any condition whatsoever? He can give rest without sleep, and strength without meat. He cannot be limited. Therefore let us not limit him.

Use 2. So again, *for the state of the church, whatsoever condition it is in, consider the creation.* 'God commands light to shine out of darkness.' The church being in darkness, God can command the light presently to shine out of darkness, as in Esther's time, Esther vi. 3, *seq.* What terrible dark-

* That is, 'conception.'—G.

ness was the church in, when Haman was commanded to destroy all the Jews! and what a terrible case was the church in in Egypt and Babylon! In a most darksome condition; and yet God brought light out of darkness, as in Esther's time.

And so of latter times; a little before Luther's time, was not the church brought low, so that darkness overspread the world? and cannot God raise up the blessed light of the truth? And also of latter times, look but the last year,* in what a dark condition the church was. But God begins to do for his church again. Who would have thought this the other year, when the enemy began to be so insolent? But God can fetch Cyrus from the east and from the north to help his people, Isa. xliv. 28; xlv. 1. God can fetch a man from the north, from this place and that place, to help his church. Therefore in no condition of the church despair; for we are in covenant with God, that can 'command light out of darkness.' 'He that is in darkness, and hath no light,' let him trust in the name of his God, Isa. l. 10. We must cast anchor at midnight, and trust in the midst of darkness. We see darkness is hideous, yet a little spark of light doth banish it, and overcome it, as a little rotten wood expelleth it in some measure, that hath shining in it. Now, beloved, is this darkness in the world, this lower darkness, driven away by a spark of light in some proportion? and shall not we think that great Light, the Father of lights, God, when he shines on the soul, will quickly banish away all darkness? It must needs be so.

Use 3. This may help us likewise *for time to come*. Great things are promised for time to come. We must help ourselves by this former work of creation. God that 'commanded light to shine out of darkness' will restore the Jews his ancient people again. St Paul calleth it the resurrection from the dead, Rom. xi. 15. It shall be a raising from the dead, as it were. He that 'commanded light to shine out of darkness' can do it, and will do it. He that did make all things out of nothing, can cause that that which is less, a resurrection. And so the fulness of the Gentiles, they be now in darkness, and in the shadow of death. What pitiful darkness are the East and West Indies in, and many of the southern countries, that serve the devil, not God? Better times are coming. The converting of the Gentiles will come, and in due time we may expect that the 'man of sin' shall be laid flat in the dust. Babylon shall fall. It is fallen exceedingly much, specially in the hearts of the people, which is the way to the last fall; but antichrist must fall together,† and then the church will be glorious, Rev. xiv. 8. He that made all things out of nothing, can make great things out of nothing. He that made of nothing glorious things, can make glorious things nothing. It is the same power to annihilate that it is to create. God, that made all things out of nothing, can bring all things to nothing. God will consume, and blast, and blow upon that 'man of sin.' Jehovah is mighty, and doth mightily. Therefore the vast world shall be consumed ere long. Comfort yourselves therefore with these things from hence, that God that made all things of nothing, can turn those things that are into nothing again.

Would you know how? 'Strong is the Lord that judgeth his,' Rev. xviii. 8. He answereth an objection. Oh, but she flourisheth, and hath many princes, emperors, potentates, and strong arms of flesh to support her. 'But strong is the Lord that hath spoken it,' and can do it. If God will consume her, who can support her? Thus we see what use to

* In margin here, 'Anno Dom. 1631.' † That is, 'altogether,' utterly.—G.

make of the foundation of St Paul: he fetcheth it from God's commanding light out of darkness.

It is a very sweet use to search the former works of God, to look back and consider what God hath done in former times. You may see in Isa. xxvii. 3, and Ps. lxxiv. 16, 'The day is thine, the night is thine.' Thou hast made distinctions between day and night: thou canst deliver thy church. It is a singular grace to make use of common things, even of the works of creation; for herein a child of God differs from another. Another takes God's common mercies, and sees the works of God, and goeth on brutishly. A fool considers not these things. Oh, but the intelligent Christian considers the great work of creation, of his commanding of all things out of nothing, and he can make no common use of things. And that is the excellency of a Christian; to support his faith, he can make use of sacraments, and word, and creation. Therefore, let us know we be God's children, by gaining glory to God by our gracious spirits, by shewing our skill by the Spirit, to let nothing pass without observing, which may support our faith and encourage our souls, as the apostle fetcheth comfort from the work of creation. Let us make use of this so great a God, who can do great things, and you can do great things with him. If a company would join in an army of prayers, it were worth all the armies in the world; it would set the great God on work. He that can raise light out of darkness, what cannot he do to his poor church, if they had a spirit of prayer to set him on work! Let us pray for the things we have promises for with much confidence: for the conversion of the Jews, and confusion of the 'man of sin.' We have the word for it. God goeth before it. The enemies begin to fall before the church. Follow God wheresoever he goeth. There is something for faith to lay hold upon, and encouragement, that he is mighty; and whatsoever he can do, he will do for the good of the church; and you see how he can do it. He doth but command, and it is done. God with his beck commands all. He can hiss for an enemy from the farthest part of the world, and have them come presently, Isa. v. 26. His finger will do great matters: what will his arm do then? When our blessed Saviour was in the days of his flesh, and said, 'Avoid, Satan,'* he must be gone presently. He commanded away the devil at a word; he rebuked fevers, sicknesses, waves, tempests: he spake but the word, and all was quiet and still; the devil and all, at his command. And is not he as strong in heaven as on earth? It is but a word, out of doubt, to deliver his church, and restore lightsome times again.

'What aileth thee, O thou Jordan, that thou gatherest thyself on heaps? The sea fell back at thy rebuke, O Lord,' Ps. cxiv. 5. He hath all things at command. A whale is commanded to receive Jonah, i. 17; a fish was at his command to bring tribute, Mat. xvii. 27; and all things in heaven and earth. Oh what a God we serve, who as he can bring out of darkness, so he can do it by his word.

Use 4. Therefore, labour from hence *for perfect resignation of our souls, and bodies, and conditions, into the hands of this God* that can do all with his word, as those three men did in Dan. viii. 16, 'God can deliver us if he will,' but we will resign ourselves into his hands. What lost they by that? And the poor man in the gospel: 'Lord, if thou wilt, thou canst make me clean,' Mat. viii. 2. Presently, 'I will, be thou clean.' If we can, in any disconsolate condition, say, If thou wilt, Lord, thou canst, we shall, in

* That is, 'depart,' or 'go away,' in the etymological sense of the word, not as now = eschew, shun.—G.

God's blessed time, have an answer, I will; therefore thou shalt be in a better condition. Leave it to him that knoweth better what is for the good of us, than ourselves do.

And therefore, I beseech you, make this use of it. Give up yourselves to God, and serve him exactly and perfectly. Will you have a rule and a ground to serve God exactly at every beck and command? Remember you have such a God as commands light out of darkness, and shall not we serve him? Shall we be slack in obedience to him that can create comforts when we want? that can bring us out of any condition, or at least, can make any condition comfortable? He can enter into dungeons, prisons, and make prisons paradises; he can by his Spirit do immediately what the creature doth; for what command is in the creature but it is in him? And he can speak that comfort to the soul that the creature can;* and therefore, shall we not walk perfectly with him that is an independent worker, that can work above means, against means, that can do all he hath done, and more than he hath done, can do all that he will do, and will do more than we can conceive he can? And shall not we resign ourselves to him, and walk perfectly with him? shall we displease him, to please men? shall we leave his subjects and children, for this and that fear? Let our condition be never so uncomfortable, he can make it comfortable, and he can make the greatest and most glorious condition in the world a hell; and therefore, let us make use of these in all the extremities of the church.

VERSE 6.

For God, who commanded the light to shine out of darkness, hath shined in our hearts, to give the light of the knowledge of the glory of God in the face of Jesus Christ.

The apostle labours, in the beginning of the chapter, to remove an imputation cast upon the gospel, as if it were not true doctrine. But if it be so, it is to them 'in whom the god of this world hath blinded their eyes.'

Secondly, he labours to remove the imputation of vain-glory, as if his preaching did such great wonders; and sheweth that the efficacy of all is from above, from God, who commanded light to shine out of darkness; and for this end, 'to give the light of the glory of God in the face of Jesus Christ.'

The words have these two *parts:* the chief and principal cause of all heavenly light in us—ministerial will not serve the turn—'*God* commanded light to shine,' &c.

For the first, 'God hath commanded light to shine out of darkness.' *There is no less work to shine in that dark heart of man, than to create the world*, to create light out of darkness. So much harder than that (though not in regard of an omnipotent power, for to that nothing is hard, but in regard of the thing itself), because there is much obscurity and rebellion in the heart. There is no help at all.

To add a little—that we may be raised up to admiration of the excellency of the new creature. There is nothing at all of it in our nature. There is something in nature to join with duty; there is a seed of it in us. But for heavenly light, for knowledge of God in Christ, there is nothing at all of it in nature. It must not be repairing and piercing, but a whole creation. And therefore there be more good lessons in the gospel than in the law, because the law hath something in it that accordeth with us, for the law and the law in

* Qu. 'cannot'?—Ed.

our hearts agree; but the gospel is altogether from without, both the truth itself, and the special grace wrought by the gospel. And therefore the proud and vain hearts of men make this and that conceit of Christ and his offices, because nature will not submit to it, it having nothing of it in itself; and therefore the gospel must raise oppositions. It bringeth in self-denial, being the first doctrine, so contrary to the will, which turneth a man out of himself. Therefore God that created light out of darkness must shine in our hearts.

And yet let me add this, we should not despair, for it is God that shineth. Come under the means wherewith God is pleased to be effectual, attend on the posts of wisdom, and God will stir the waters in his good time, John v. 3, will convey an almighty power in the use of the ordinances. Let no man therefore despair, because it is in God's power to shine in our hearts, and it is well for us that it is in the power of God to work grace, for now it is out of our own. And all immediately depend on God. Meet him, attend him there, and he will meet us; depend on him, and undoubtedly he will work grace first or last. This is God's way, and you shall find God in it.

Secondly, *the end of this light* that God commandeth to shine *in our hearts*, not in our brains. God's illumination goeth through the whole soul, alters the will and affection. They that are not altered in the course of their hearts and souls, as well as their understandings, in Scripture they are said to know nothing at all. He that knoweth not Christ so as to put off the old man, and put on the new, that hath not divine light passing through the understanding to the will, and through the whole man, he knoweth nothing in religion but what may stand with damnation.

When the light presseth on him in his courses, he is always reproving it, and therefore they be never quiet. It is a vexing light, an unprofitable light, nay, a light whereby damnation is increased, if it be not joined with sanctification and illumination overspreading the whole soul.

And the end of it is to give the 'light of the knowledge of God in the face of Jesus Christ.'

God's children they have light shining on them. No man hath grace in themselves alone; and specially it is true of ministers, who besides personal graces, have graces of office for others. And therefore 'God shineth in their hearts, to give the light of the knowledge of God, in the face of Jesus Christ.' He shineth on them that they may reflect their light on others, as the moon and stars, that have their light from the sun, that they may reflect on the earth, and inferior bodies.

1. The particulars are these: the knowledge of God is the end of all. Now that God will be glorified, especially in his attributes of mercy and love, wisdom and justice, and holiness, all these are seen specially in the gospel, but most of all the sweet attributes of grace and mercy. The glory of God is his aim, and his glory shines in these attributes, and they shine in the face of Christ.

Now Christ must be made known, his face must be shewed, and therefore there must be a light to make known the face of God in Jesus Christ. Religion is the way of God, the end especially in these sweet attributes, and these must have a ministry. God hath ability at call, to give the light of the knowledge of these excellencies in Christ.

Of the first we spake. There is one first cause of all things, and one last end, that is God; all for his glory. All things come from God, and all things must terminate and end in him. Now this glory is victorious, excellent, and manifested, and so manifested as it is apprehended by others. Now God's glory is wisdom, mercy, holiness, goodness. They are excellent in

God, and excellently victorious over the contrary; for he is so good that his goodness is above our ill, and it is with a glorious discovery, and it is glorious that we do apprehend it. For if we be Christians, our eyes be opened by the Spirit to apprehend the glory that shineth in the gospel. Therefore God sets down this excellency by way of glory. It is not ordinary grace, but glorious grace, glorious love, and glorious wisdom, to reconcile mercy and justice. It is glorious, and eminently victorious. And all Christians have eyes to see that it is no ordinary excellency, but glory in God. When God will have it excellently set out by the word, he calls it 'glory,' to satisfy a conscience awakened, which will not be satisfied but by glorious mercy and infinite mercy. When we be in health and strong to sin (as many, the Lord be merciful to them, use their wits and strength and policy to offend, running in a course of sin, and never think of these); but Satan is a cunning rhetorician; he will amplify bitter things against us at the hour of death and time of temptation. And unless we have something that is above all his rhetoric and high mercies, victorious mercies, glorious mercies above all our sins, and above Satan's malice, the conscience will not be satisfied.

And let no man object his sins at such times, for God is glorified when his mercy is received, and his goodness entertained. 'Where sin aboundeth, grace aboundeth much more,' Rom. v. 20. Where sin aboundeth in the conscience that is guilty and groaneth under it, oh grace aboundeth in such a man; grace is glorious grace to such a man. The more thy sin is, the more is the glory of grace in pardoning it.

But how is this glorious mercy and goodness of God derived* to us, God being so pure and holy, and we so unholy?

Therefore in the next place, it is the glory of God *in the face of Jesus Christ*. God will not suffer the glory of one of his attributes to devour and consume another, but he will have his justice fully satisfied. And therefore this glorious mercy is to be seen in the face of Jesus Christ, who was made a curse for us, Gal. iii. 13.

'In the face of Jesus Christ.' It is a borrowed speech, and all one with that which went before, 'Christ who is the image of God,' in the 4th verse of this chapter. He meaneth the person of Christ, incarnate, and living, and dying, and being made a curse for us: Christ made man.

Face is the person described by that face; for the face is the most known part of a man. It is the glass of the soul, wherein we may see a man's inside, his affections, love, hatred, and whatsoever is in the inward man. And so God discovers himself, and whatsoever is in him, 'in the face of Jesus Christ.' We may see his hatred of sin, his love of the elect, and whatsoever is in God. Whatsoever we see in Christ, it is in God originally.

We will unfold the point in three particulars.

1. First, We will shew that in the gospel we see the face of Christ, that is, more familiarly than others. It is a speech appropriated in some manner to the gospel.

Secondly, We see the face of God in Christ.

Thirdly, That this seeing of the face of God in Christ is a most comfortable and excellent sight and knowledge.

First of all, in the gospel, *we see the face of Christ*. Moses, and all before Christ, saw Christ, but not the face of Christ. They saw him not so plainly, clearly, distinctly, and comfortably as we do in times of the gospel.

Now we see Christ incarnate, and Christ sacrificed for us; Christ dead,

* That is, = communicated.—G.

risen, ascended, and sitting on the right hand of God. They did not. And therefore Saint Ambrose saith well, *Christus umbra in lege, imago in evangelio, veritas in cœlo;* in the law he was a shadow, the image of God in the gospel, but in heaven he is the truth (*g*). And there we shall see him most lively of all.

Now there be five or six ways of God's manifesting of himself.

1. One is more excellent than the other, that is, by speech, which is an excellent manifestation.
2. And then by vision.
3. And then by dreams, as in old time.
4. And then by miracles, of which he wrought many.
5. And by sacrifices, as the passover.
6. And last of all, by types.

All these ways God manifested himself before Christ. But, as Heb. i. 2, now God speaks to us in his own Son, that is, more familiarly, even by God in our nature; and therefore the manifestation by Christ is more excellent than all former manifestations.

Then his three offices were shadowed out by king, priest, and prophet. All the kings, priests, and prophets were shadows of this great prophet, priest, and king. And all the benefits of salvation were shadowed darkly: his election, by singling Abraham out of his father's house, Gen. xii. 1; the Israelites out of the world; his vocation, by calling of Abraham and his people, Gen. xvii. 5; his justification, by divers sacrifices, which were types of Christ; by the paschal lamb, Ex. xii. 3, *seq.;* by the brazen serpent, Num. xxi. 9, the propitiatory and the mercy seat, Ex. xxv. 17. The great work of redemption shadowed out, by their redeeming out of Babylon and Egypt, Ex. xii. 31, *seq.*; the great works of sanctification, by their washing and cleansings, Lev. xiv. 8, which were the shadow of the inward purity of the soul; and glorification, the consummation of all blessings, by the land of Canaan, Josh. i. 2, *seq.*, and 'the holy of holies,' which was the type of heaven, Ex. xxvi. 33. So that all the benefits we have of salvation were shadowed out then, but they be clear in the gospel; we see the face of Christ. In the gospel we hear Christ speaking himself. God in our nature discovers all these things to us.

Obj. But you will say, We cannot see the face of Christ, for it is gone, we cannot see him now.

Sol. Nó. But when we preach the gospel, receive the sacraments, hear the word, we see Christ. We see Christ in the gospel, the word is the glass of Christ; and so are the sacraments, wherein you may see the face of Christ. *Fides est spiritualis oculus;* faith is a spiritual eye, and seeth Christ.

But Abraham saw Christ and was glad. True. But now faith sees Christ more clearly than ever before. Nay, it is in some sort better for us to see Christ with the eye of faith in heaven than to see him on the earth walking up and down. Many reprobates saw him on earth, but now none can see him but with eyes of faith; none can speak to Christ but those that have learned his language.

And it is for our advantage that we see not Christ now. He doth more good in heaven than he could do on the earth. He is now at the right hand of God, and hath all power in heaven and earth. The sun, if it were lower, would consume the world, but it is high, that it may shine over more than half the world at once. So Christ, for the good of the church, is gone to heaven, and we have more good from him by the Spirit than if he were on earth.

Obj. But you will say, We shall not see his face till we see him in heaven.

Ans. True. Therefore, mark, 1, *the diversity of the phrase in comparing it to former times.*

We see his face in the gospel. But if we compare these times to the glorious times when he will come gloriously to judgment, we saw him but in the glass, then we shall see him face to face. So you see in what sense we see the face of Christ. What they expected and looked for, that we see. Beloved, it is happiness for us to live in these times of the church. We see Christ clearly. All the happiness of the church dependeth on the Scripture and knowledge of Christ; for he is the glory of the church, and the happiness of the church. And those times that have most of Christ are the most happy times. Now, considering we in the latter age of the world know Christ most, we are most happy. Wherein was the first temple glorious above the second? The second temple had not many things the other had. Ay, but Christ came into the second temple, and that made it glorious: 'Blessed is the eye that seeth the things that you see, and the ears that hear what you hear,' Mat. xiii. 16.

So it is our happiness that we live in a second spring of the gospel, and not when it was covered not only with Jewish ceremonies, but with fond* superstitions of their own. But now we see Christ face to face. His excellency is unveiled. It is our happiness if we be better for it, or else it will increase our damnation.

2. But it is not sufficient, *unless we see God in Christ, and the glory of God 'in the face of Jesus Christ.'* For the soul will not rest but in God. God is the last rest and stay of the soul. As 1 Peter i. 21, Christ was raised again from the dead, 'that your faith and hope might be in God.' God is the stay, and rest, and subsistence of the soul; it cannot rest but in God. So that we must see the glory of God in the face of Jesus Christ, else the soul will not be sufficiently stayed. Therefore consider in what sense 'the glory of God shineth in the face of Jesus Christ.' You must know first that Christ is the perfect image of his Father; his Father shineth in him.

There be three or four things in the Scripture that set out this great mystery. As, 1, Christ is called the character of the Father, χαρακτὴρ τῆς ὑποστάσεως, Heb. i. 3. They differ in this, that they be not the same in personal subsistence. They be Father and Son, one in essence; in love to mankind all one; only in personal subsistence they differ, the Father is not the Son.

2. Then he is the Wisdom of the Father.

3. Then he is the Word, shewing the likeness. The word is but the image of the soul. There is the inward word and the outward word; the inward is nothing but the expression of the soul, and when it is outwardly expressed, it is but the soul conveying itself outwardly. And therefore in the original tongue, we shewed that one word sheweth both reason and speech, because speech should be nothing but the issue of reason.† And therefore Christ is called λόγος.

It is not enough that the glory of God appeareth in the second person of the Trinity, that he is the character of God, and the image of God, and the Word, but we must see what he is to us, and how he discovers the word to us.

So that he is the image of God in a double sense.

1. As an invisible image of his invisible Father.

* That is, foolish.—G. † Cf. note *o*, Vol. II. page 195.—G.

2. To us-ward, he sheweth to us what the Father is; so that he is the image of God, in regard of God, and in regard of us.

We see by his discovery the wisdom of God in him, and so he is the hidden word, that is, the expression of the Father. But what is that to us, without expression to us? So that he is made to us. As a man knows what is hidden in a man's mind, by his words, so by Christ we know the hidden meaning, and good will of the Father to us, because Christ is the word in a double sense, as an expression of the Father's image, and his discovering to us the words of the Father.

So that the glory of God, especially God the Father, is now to be seen in the face of Jesus Christ, not only as Christ is the second person, *God*, but as Mediator, *God-man*. Now Christ is the image of God to us, the wisdom of God to us, and the character of the Father to us.

To come to it more particularly. 'In the glory of God to us, shining in the face of Jesus Christ.' Everything in the Father is comfortable to us, shining in Christ. God as discovered in Scripture is not comfortable to us, but as discovered to us in him.

1. *As the sweet sovereignty of God over all in Christ.* He is made King of kings, Lord of lords. So in the face of Christ we see God Lord over all, for our good, committing all to Jesus Christ: 'All power is given me from my Father,' Mat. xxviii. 18.

2. *And all the graces that are in God.* You may term them so, for indeed all the sweet excellencies in God are seen in Christ, as the wisdom of God, the justice of God. All the sweet affections of God are seen in Christ. What are those that in a high sense may be attributed to God? That is, his love and mercy; God is love, but he is so in Christ, he is 'the Father of mercy,' but it is for Christ's sake that he is so. His sweet love to mankind, see it in Christ.

3. *And then the relation he stands in.* Take one, his being our Father. How is God our Father in a comfortable sense? He is a Father to Christ; and what Christ is by nature, we are by adoption. 'I go to my Father and your Father;' therefore to your Father, because my Father, 'to your God and my God;' therefore to your God, because my God, John xx. 17.

4. Now, to go on farther, *take Christ in all his states and offices, take him in his whole dispensation of salvation, and you shall see something of the glory of the Father in all.* The Father, by his Spirit, sanctified him in the womb, gave his only begotten Son to death for us, made him a curse for us. 'To us a Son is given,' Isa. ix. 6. The Father raised him up again. See the Father in his humiliation and exaltation, see him in all the sweet offices he hath taken upon him to accomplish our salvation. The Father hath anointed him by the Spirit to be king, and priest, and prophet. Him hath the Father sealed, setting his stamp on him, to be our Saviour. The Father hath sent him; he hath his warrant and commission from the Father. The Father hath set him forth to be a propitiation, Rom. iii. 25. So that all the authority he hath in all his offices it is from the Father.

5. But more specially, *we see the love of the Father in Christ crucified and made a curse for us.* For there, as it were, the Father poured out his bowels. For how could the mercy and goodness of God appear, more than to give his own Son, equal with him? as it is at large set down, Phil. ii. 6, *seq.* That God should give his Son, the greatest gift that ever could be thought of, that could make ten thousand worlds of nothing, that he should give him to us, and take our nature into unity with his divine nature, that he might suffer in it; how could the glory of mercy shine more than

to give him to be a curse for us, to satisfy his justice in that manner? It is a mystery that requireth a large time, for herein shineth the glorious mercy of God, but especially Christ's love in giving of himself, and the Father's in giving him. So you see how the glory of God shineth in Jesus Christ.

Quest. But how doth Christ discover the Father to us?

Ans. 1. He discovers his Father to us, *in opening his Father's meaning*, as a prophet teaching us, coming to be a minister of the circumcision to teach in our nature; and to teach by his Spirit in his apostles and ministers, to the end of the world. Therefore, John i. 18, it is said, that 'the only begotten Son of God, that lieth in the bosom of the Father, hath revealed him to us.' Christ is the ἐξηγήτης, the great expositor of the Father, the λόγος, for he lieth in the bosom of his Father, which implieth an intimate knowledge, because he lieth in the bosom, he knows the secrets of God's love to every particular believing soul. It implieth likewise a high valuation of Christ, to shew that the Father loveth him and honours him.

Now 'lying in the Father's bosom,' that is, the Father being so intimate and familiar with his Son, there is knowledge of union (different from our knowledge of faith) which the human nature hath from the divine, by virtue of union, and he is fit to discover it, because he is in the bosom of the Father, highly valued and prized by the Father.

2. Again, Christ is discovered not only as lying in his bosom, as an expositor and prophet; but Christ discovers what his Father is *by his whole life and conversation*. For see Christ, and see the Father. See his meekness and humility in stooping low, his love, his fruitfulness, his goodness, as a man; for so he resembleth God, as his human nature could do, every way shewing forth the grace of God in his whole course, disposition, and conversation, he carrieth himself as the Son of God.

3. But the main way whereby Christ layeth open God the Father to us, *was in his suffering*. The Father was discovered in all that Christ did and suffered. For it was all done by the Father's authority. Christ did not only speak by words shewing what the Father was (as the son when he resembleth the disposition of the father, we say, you may in him see his father), but you may see the Father's authority in everything. So 'God loved the world, that he gave his only begotten Son,' John iii. 16. It pleased the Father to reconcile the world to himself. So you see how the face of God is discovered in Christ, and how Christ discovers himself, John i. 18; it is an excellent place. 'No man hath seen the Father at any time, but the only begotten Son he hath revealed him;' and John xiv. 11, 'Believe that I am in the Father, and the Father in me.' They both agree about the salvation of mankind. You not only see the love of the Son in our salvation, but the love of the Father in the Son. In Eph. i., Gal. i., these great mysteries are at large unfolded.

4. But one other way, and the most sweet of all, whereby Christ revealeth his Father to us, *is by his Spirit, together with the means of salvation*; for as it is excellently set down in Mat. xi. 27, 'No man knoweth the Father but the Son, and him to whom the Son revealeth him,' that is, by the Spirit. None knoweth the Father to be his Father but by the Son, who hath begot him by the Spirit. None knoweth the Son but they that be begotten by the Spirit. We must have the Spirit both from the Father and the Son before we can have the Father and the Son, and therefore it is called communion of the Spirit; because the Spirit of the Father and Son discovers the Father to be our Father, and the Son to be our Saviour.

So that add this to all other discoveries, and you have a full discovery of Christ, as the Father is laid open by Christ to every particular Christian. You see then that God the Father hath shined in the face of Jesus Christ. God the Father liveth in light that no soul can approach to but only the Son. He is come out of his hidden light. Nay, the Father hath discovered the bowels of good will to mankind, and in his Son he discovers by his Spirit his particular good will to every particular Christian. So that we may with boldness go to the Father in the name of Christ.

Three things beget boldness:

First, When the matter of disagreement is taken away.

Secondly, Likeness of disposition.

Thirdly, Acquaintance and familiarity.

1. Now Christ, by his death and suffering, hath taken away *the disagreement*, that is, our sins. He hath borne our sins, and borne them away as the scape-goat did, Lev. xvi. 8. When we believe in him, he takes our sins and carrieth them away: *Christus tibi crucifixus est, cum credis in Christum crucifixum*, Christ is then crucified to thee, when thou believest in Christ crucified. So that the sluice of mercy being open, it runneth amain on us.

2. *There must be a likeness;* because by Christ we have the Spirit to renew us, to make us savour the things of God, to love the things God loveth, to hate the things God hates. Now, a sanctified soul delights in communion with God, a carnal man hates it; the more holy anything is, the more he distastes it.

3. Again, from likeness of disposition *comes familiarity and acquaintance with God*, cherished by love, devotion, and piety; and all this we have in Christ. And therefore we go boldly, having God's justice fully satisfied, and finding the Spirit renewing our natures, and claim acquaintance with God, and pour out our souls to him as to a Father in Christ Jesus. Oh the wonderfulness of this privilege, that now in Christ we can call God Father, his Father and our Father; that we can pour out our complaints before him, as to a gracious Father, in all our necessities! The world is not worthy of this privilege that we enjoy, who in all distresses and wants can go boldly to God, the Father of our Lord Jesus Christ, and call him our Father.

Use 1. *We should value these privileges more than we do, and improve them more than we do.* Are we in God or in Christ? Then glory in God—Rom. v. 3—whence the apostle Paul makes a threefold glorying:

1. A glorying in affliction under the cross.

2. He glorieth in the hope of glory; and not only so, but

3. 'We glory in God.' How is that? That God the Father is ours. If Christ be in me, I have God with Christ: 'God is with Christ reconciling the world to himself,' 2 Cor. v. 19. 'All things are yours; you are Christ's; and Christ is God's,' 1 Cor. iii. 21, 23. If we are Christ's we have God, and all; and can we have more? 'Shew us the Father,' saith Philip, 'and it sufficeth us,' John xiv. 8; that is, shew the Father to be our Father, bring us into acquaintance with him, and what need we more? Let it be discovered to our souls that God is our Father, and that will suffice, or nothing.

Use 2. *Labour therefore to joy in this prerogative;* and when we think of God, let us not think of *Deus absolutus*, of an absolute God distinguished from Christ. If ever we go to God in prayer, look up to him 'in the face of Christ.' We must ascend to him as he descended to us. How is that?

Doth not he descend and convey all his favours in God incarnate, nay, God in our flesh? He came down in our nature, and we must go back again to him in our nature, in Christ; and therefore it is not only fruitless, but dangerous presumption, to go directly to God without a mediator. In the Law nothing must be done without a priest, who must offer all our sacrifices, and so all that are between God and us must be by mediation of our high priest Jesus Christ.

And then present ourselves to God in his name: Lord, I offer thy own Son unto thee, a Son of thine own sending, sealed, appointed, elected, and predestinated to be my Saviour. Thou canst not refuse the righteousness of thy own Son, thou gavest him to be my Saviour. Therefore taking Christ along with us, we may break through the very justice of God; for, Lord, I bring one with me that hath satisfied thy justice; therefore I go through thy justice to thy mercy-seat in Christ, in whom thy mercy is glorified. I go not with my own righteousness, but clothed with Christ.

3. And will not this *answer Satan's temptations?* Send thy soul to God in Christ, the glory of God, and he will shine in Christ. Christ is ordained to be my Saviour, and I cast myself into his arms, and put myself in the bowels of Christ.

So in all temptation I beseech you make use of this grand comfort, that the glory of God may shine in the face of Christ.

There be three of the sweetest sights that ever were thought of for poor Christians.

That is, God the Father's sight of us in his Son Christ, as members of him whom he loveth. Absolutely* we are miserable.

Again, we see God 'in the face of Christ,' and Christ sees us in his Father's good pleasure, as given to him in charge of the Father; 'Thine they were, thou gavest them me,' John xvii. 24. Christ seeth us in God's eternal purpose to save, for Christ saveth none but them whom God gave. 'All that thou gavest come to me, and thou castest them not away,' John xvii. 2. God's choice and Christ's salvation run parallel. So God's choice saveth none but such as Christ is anointed to save, and God seeth us to be saved. As he gave us to Christ, and as Christ died for us, so we by spiritual faith see ourselves in Christ, as our Father. These do so arm the soul against all discouragements, that nothing can separate it, for God's love to me is bounded in his love to Christ. God looks on me, but he looks on Christ first. Now God's love is eternally founded on Christ, therefore eternally founded on me to be one with Christ. It is excellently set down: Rom. viii. 35, 'What† shall separate me from the love of Christ?' for it is a love of God founded on Christ. God loveth Christ, and so likewise he will love me. As Christ is his 'Son in whom he is well pleased,' Mat. iii. 17; so he loveth whole Christ mystical, for he gave his Son for the body of Christ the church; and therefore whensoever we hear of the love of Christ, go to the love of the Father. Hath Christ loved me? Then see the Father's love in that love. You may enlarge these things in your own meditations, they being wonderful useful.

'The glory of God that shineth in the face of Jesus Christ.' Therefore, I beseech you, let us now value and esteem the great mystery of the incarnation and Christ crucified, because Christ is the common centre of heaven and earth, in whom we all concentre: Father, Son, and Holy Ghost meet in Christ the Mediator. The first person sees us in Christ, the second person took our nature into union with himself, and the Holy Ghost sancti-

* That is, = apart from Christ, or in ourselves.—G. † 'Who.'—G.

fieth it; so all meet together in Christ, He is the abridgment of all the elect in one, so that all the three persons, as they appeared at his baptism, met together in him. Let us mainly labour to get into Christ, and then grow up in Christ, in the knowledge of God the Father, and love of the Father, to grow more and more acquainted with the secret will of the Father to our salvation; and therefore esteem much of all the blessed means sanctified to strengthen our faith in the word and sacraments. In the sacrament see the Father. When the minister giveth the bread and wine, think that God the Father giveth his Son to every one of us in particular, and all to strengthen our faith; see God the Father together with God the Son. The Father was the person first offended, and therefore God the Father is reconciled by Christ. And it is more comfort that God the Father, the person offended, hath the chief hand in the plot of salvation; 'He gave Christ's body to be broken, and his blood to be shed for our sins,' Rom. iii. 25.

I beseech you therefore to labour to be acquainted every day more and more with these mysteries, and do not take these as any encouragement to a sinful course, because the glory of mercy shineth in Jesus Christ, and therefore turn grace into wantonness. Mark this one thing. Amongst other attributes that shine in God, there is specially his holiness and displeasure against sin, for God shewed his displeasure against sin in turning his angels out of heaven. Heaven itself could not brook* sin. It turned Adam out of paradise, and is the chiefest procurer of God's wrath; but all these are nothing to that hatred of sin that appeared in Christ. The purity of God appeared in him above all things in the world, and it will at the day of judgment appear more in sending the greatest part of the world to eternal destruction and torment. But it is not so much as in making his Son a curse. Therein we see the holiness of God, that rather than man's sins should not be satisfied for, he would set apart his own Son to satisfy it. How much then is the holiness of Christ, that offered himself for it? how much is the holiness of God, that gave his Son to take it away? Can any man now believe in God as his Father first, and in Christ as his Saviour, and live in sin?

We must look on sin as the Father when he gave the Son, and on sin as the Son did when he gave himself. Therefore if we do not look on sin as most opposite to holiness, and have not an antipathy rooted in our hearts, how can we bear God's image and the image of Christ resembling him in all things? How can we think ourselves his members when we want his Spirit? How can we say we be his, when he walks in light and we in darkness?

If that holiness be not rooted to look on sin, in some measure, as God the Father and Son [do], we can as yet have no comfort, and therefore there is no reason to 'turn the grace of God into wantonness,' Jude 4.

And then remember this one caveat more. Whatsoever I spoke of the love of God the Father, and Christ the Son, is nothing unto us, unless every [one] of us labour in particular to have the Spirit of the Father and the Son discovering to us in particular this, that the Father is our Father, and the Son our Saviour, for that is the issue of our ministry. We must not rest in the ministerial discovery of things, but if we belong to God there is a work of the Spirit, and the chief work of it is to particularise and to bring truths home to every man's soul; and therefore Christ is nothing to us, unless the mind of God to us in particular be discovered. The Spirit

* That is, 'bear.'—G.

knoweth the 'secrets of God,' and revealeth to every particular man their particular interest in God the Father and God the Son, and this should be our desire and prayer every day, together with all knowledge, that God would give his Spirit to discover to us his peculiar love in Jesus Christ, and that Christ would by his Spirit discover our interest in him. Ministerial light will not serve for comfort unless our spirits be sealed to be the sons of God. Therefore are the sacraments to seal in particular an interest in Jesus Christ. Therefore we should set our faith on work. God in particular died for me, as if for none but me, and God the Father giveth me comfort in Christ. As I taste the outward element with outward sense, so with my inward taste of faith I taste of Christ. These be the things will stand in stead against temptation. He is the Saviour of the elect; but what though? The Spirit of the Father and the Son must discover the love of the Father to us in his Son.

These words contain the chief cause of all spiritual light, which is God, who by the same power by which he 'commanded the light to shine out of darkness, hath shined into our hearts,' or rather by a greater, because here is more opposition, and no help at all from nature to spiritual things, not so much as a seed of it.

'Hath shined into our hearts.' The end of spiritual knowledge in the ministry, is especially 'to give the glory of the knowledge of God in the face of Jesus Christ.'

I propound these things.

First, *That God is glorious in his mercy, wisdom, and other attributes, his reconciling justice and mercy together.* Secondly, *That this glory of mercy is in Christ, and satisfaction of his justice by him.* Thirdly, *That the glory of God, and all his sweet attributes in the face of Christ, must be made known to others*; and that this knowledge may be, *there must be a calling.* So God hath shined into our hearts to give the light. The ministry is to give the light of the knowledge of God; knowledge leadeth us to Christ; Christ to God, in whom our faith is terminated, as in its last object.

Divers of these things we have unfolded,

As the first, *that God's mercy is a glorious mercy:* therefore called the 'glory of God in the face of Christ.' That his mercy, specially in Christ, is his triumphing attribute. The power of God shineth in creation, the justice of God in damnation; but mercy triumphs in salvation by Christ. And it is not every mercy, but glorious mercy. Mercy sets all others on work, and therefore I mean that excellent mercy that stirred up wisdom to devise a way how justice might be satisfied, and so reconciled, that a way may be made for mercy. So that there is a wonderful mystery in these things, which the very angels desire to behold. This glory 'shineth in the face of Jesus Christ.'

'None knoweth the Father but the Son, none the Son but the Father, and they to whom the Father and the Son will reveal themselves by the Spirit,' Mat. xi. 27. If the Father revealeth his Son by his Spirit, the Son revealeth the Father by the Spirit. Then they are known, but [not] else.

'The glory of God shineth in the face of Jesus Christ,' being incarnate, made God-man. I will proceed to bring this truth home, to make it more clear and comfortable.

You see then the glory of God shine in Christ, and then it shines to us. So that Christ is between God and us; the face of Christ between God and our face.

What is the reason of this order? Because God and we be in such opposition, that Christ must be between. God cannot love our nature, but as it is pure, and clean, and undefiled; and it is only so in Christ. And therefore he loveth our nature only in Christ, as being knit to Christ, and so purged by the Spirit of Christ. For there cannot be more opposite terms than between God, 'who is a consuming fire,' Heb. xii. 29, and sinners; therefore Christ cometh between. That is, the middle person of the Trinity must be the middle person for reconciliation. He that is the Son is fit to make us sons. He that is the image of God, is fit to restore us to God's image. He that is beloved, is fit to bring us in love with the Father, to give entrance and access to him. And therefore God shineth first 'on the face of Christ' before it come to us. It cometh to us at the second hand by reflection.

Then Christ is *primum amabile*, the first subject and seat of divine love, for he is the first begotten; and whatsoever God loveth he loveth in relation to his Son. If he loveth us it is in relation to him. If he loveth any before they be in Christ, it is to give them to Christ. So that all the love of God must be seated in the first subject and receptacle of his love, which is Christ. First God shines on Christ, and then on all them that be one with Christ. Therefore Christ is called ὁ ἀγαπητὸς, 'The beloved,' and the Son of God's love, 'in whom are all the treasures of wisdom,' Col. ii. 3; and therefore is truly lovely.

Whatsoever good we have, it is in Christ. For the first degree of salvation, the first link of the chain, from election to glorification, all is in Christ, seated in free grace, of which Christ is the first-fruit. For so 'God loved the world, that he gave his Son,' John iii. 16. Christ himself, and all the benefits by him, are first-fruits of the free grace of God, which was *amor benevolentiæ*, a love of good will; but then there was *amor amicitiæ*, a love of amity, which is only in Christ; and the execution of all favours is in Christ. He calleth, justifieth, sanctifieth, and glorifieth in Christ, because by our consistence* in Christ we have all benefits, even from election to glorification. The apostle runneth in this stream: Eph. i. 3, 'Blessed be God, who hath blessed you with all spiritual blessings in Christ Jesus.' We are beloved in him, as the first love. So that in all things Christ is the first. He was the first Son of God,† we sons in him. What he is by nature, we are by grace and adoption. He is first beloved, we beloved for him, as having communion and fellowship with him. He hath justified us from our sins, and therefore we are justified in him. He is our surety. If he be not acquitted, we shall never be acquitted. He is risen, therefore we rise. He is the 'first-fruits of those that sleep,' 1 Cor. xv. 20. He is the 'first-born of many brethren,' Rom. viii. 29; the 'first begotten from the dead,' Col. i. 18. He ascended, therefore we ascend. He sits in heavenly places, therefore we sit in heavenly places; for God hath elected us to be conformed to him. He is the first-fruits of God's predestination, as Austin observeth (*h*). God first made choice of him as the head of all, and of us in him. We are elected to be conformed to him in grace and comfort, in the love of God here, and in glory and perfect happiness hereafter. He is our eldest brother. Now it is fit therefore that he should have pre-eminence in all things. Christ in all things hath pre-eminency, in love and grace, in every passage of glory, resurrection, ascension, sitting at the right hand of God; and in all things hath pre-eminency.

This is a very comfortable and useful point in the great mystery of

* That is, 'standing.'—Ed.

† Qu. 'He was first the Son of God'?—G.

Christ and glorification, to know the foundation of God's love to us. It is seated on Christ first, and then it cometh to us; nay, and through Christ, in Christ, as an head, through Christ as mediator.

Use 1. Therefore let us make this use of it. *Never think of God without Christ.* And again, never think of any spiritual favour, but think of it in Christ first. If we think of any promise, think of it as given to Christ first. For all promises are made over to him, and he maketh them over to us. 'All promises are in him yea and amen,' 2 Cor. i. 20. Promises come from love. Love is first in him, and therefore must come first from him; and therefore desire God to make them good for his sake. If we think of the love of God, think of it in our flesh, in Christ first, as our head. If we think of freedom from sin, think of Christ our surety, who is first freed from it. If we think of resurrection and ascension, think of it in Christ our head. If we think of glory, think of it in Christ; we are glorious in our head. And have it as a fruit of his prayer, that 'we should be where he is,' John xvii. 24. Whensoever we think of anything that is good, think of it first in Christ, that God may have his scope and end, which is, that Christ the second person, that took our nature on him, may have his pre-eminency.

Use 2. And this should make us in our devotions *to bless God for being the Father of Jesus Christ, when we bless him for being our Father.* O blessed be God the Father of our Lord Jesus Christ, for if he had not been his Father, he had never been our Father: John xx. 17, 'I go to my God and your God, my Father and your Father.' If he had not been his God and his Father, he had never been our God and our Father. Therefore bless God for his love to Christ, and Christ for his love to us; for they both join in our salvation. As Rom. viii. 39, 'Nothing can separate from the love of God,' nor from the love of Christ. They be both together in the verse, because they be all one in Christ. See the love of the Father in Christ. See his own love in himself, together with his Father's. Therefore consider the sweet agreement of the Trinity towards the salvation of mankind; and that we come not to heaven, are elect, and saved only by the counsel of the Father, or only by the love of the Son, or only by the operation of the Holy Ghost, but all three joining together in our salvation. God looks on us 'in the face of Jesus Christ.' God loveth us, the Son loveth us, the Holy Spirit sealeth the love of both to us. So then conclude that our salvation is strongly built. It is built on the love of the Father in Christ, and on the love of Christ, together with the Father, and on the assurance of the Holy Ghost, testifying both these to our souls. God for ever loveth his Son, and God for ever must love us, for he shineth on us 'in the face of his Son.' Now what is the love of God to his Son? Pure love, tender love, bowels of love, an everlasting love, and a rich love. And is not his love to us the same? If he loveth Christ, he loveth whole Christ; not only Christ personal, but mystical Christ, and all his members. He loveth the whole body of Christ with a pure, tender, perfect, and everlasting love. And therefore as God's love can never be removed from his own Son that lieth on his bosom, so God's true love shall never be removed from any true Christian that liveth in his Son.

It is a comfortless, fond conceit to imagine any separation in that kind, because his love is founded not upon love to their persons, but on his Son. Now having an everlasting foundation, it must be an everlasting love; and this may comfort us in all conditions.

Use 3. To make another use to direct our devotions aright, *we must not go to an absolute God*, for he is 'a consuming fire,' Heb. xii. 29, *but must take Christ's name along*. We must take Christ along in all our prayers. It is an unworthy conceit to think God will be pleased otherwise than in his Son. It is God must satisfy God, and not we, that be stubble to go to the fire. It is presumption, and the end of it will be confusion. Therefore go to God in the sweet name of his Son Jesus Christ. Only so. We do not conceive worthily enough of God if we think he can have any communion with us, if his love be not conceived in the person of Christ. Therefore if we will have worthy conceits of him, go to him, that is, God made flesh in our nature, a Saviour of his own appointment, a mediator of his own sending, and sealed. And God will not refuse him, if you bring his Son before him. Therefore let it be our rule to put up our prayers in the name of Jesus Christ, our head.

Now our natures are in Christ lovely to God, because our flesh is in him pure, sanctified, and separate from all sin; so that he loveth our natures. And the nature of God, before opposite, is now lovely to us, because God dwells in our nature, as the apostle saith, bodily, that is, fully, Col. ii. 9. Now God in our nature is lovely. God out of our nature is not, because he is purity and holiness itself; but in our nature he is all love and mercy, for his justice is fully satisfied. God by his Spirit will never leave any particular Christian till he makes their nature in them like his own nature, that is divorced and separate wholly from sin, that it may be a pure glorious nature, fit for so glorious a head. Therefore go boldly to the throne of grace. There be good terms between God and us through Christ.

'We shall die, because we have seen God,' saith Manoah, Judges xiii. 22. Now we shall live because we have seen God in Christ. Out of Christ we cannot see an angel, and live; but seeing God in the face of Christ, a mediator not of our appointing, this is a sweet and comfortable sight.

I beseech you, let us make a comfortable use of these things. God thinks of us in Christ. It was a good prayer of a holy martyr, 'that God would shine on him in the face of Jesus Christ.' He was so guilty of his own sins and corruptions that he durst not look upon God, but desires God to look on his Son first, and then on him, in his Son. In Christ God can see us perfect, for Christ's righteousness is our righteousness, and we have the same spirit with Christ. For note that by the way.

As Christ, by taking our nature on him, testified by the Spirit he was the Son of God in our nature, so the same Spirit of Christ having knit us to Christ, and sanctifying our nature, we become the sons of God and Christ too. The same Spirit that sanctified the nature of Christ in the womb, will sanctify every Christian. And as the grace of union was the cause of Christ's unction, so the grace of union with Christ is the ground of all communion with Christ. And therefore labour in the first place to be one with Christ by faith, the foundation of all the comfort that I have unfolded.

To us-ward is the union with Christ by faith, that Christ and we are one; for if God look on us in the face of his Son, then we must be one with his Son: bone of his bone, flesh of his flesh, by his Spirit, as he is bone of our bone, flesh of our flesh, by our nature. He took our human nature that we might partake of his divine nature; and therefore labour for union, that we may have gracious communion with him. If we be one with Christ we are his friends, and he will be with us. 'I and the Father will sup with him, Rev. iii. 20. Rest specially in that. It was the effect of Christ's prayer, 'that we may be all one: I in them, and thou in me, and that thou mayest love them with the love thou lovest me,' John xvii. 22, 23. So intimate was Christ's love that he desires the same love to us, and in us, one with another. This is a blessed union of the Trinity in one, and of Christ with the Father, and of every Christian with Christ and the Father, one with another. This is the fruit of Christ's offering himself a sacrifice to God, 'that we may be one, as they are one: I in them, and thou in me.'

The reason of Christ's prayer for that union is, that all good is conveyed from the Father to us, 'in the face of Jesus Christ,' as we have our consistence and being in Christ, and are one with Christ; and that makes the sacraments and all holy ordinances to be means to bring us into communion with Christ, and to seal it to us, and thereby our communion with the Father and the Holy Ghost. If the Father, Son, and Holy Ghost be ours, what can we want? 'Shew us the Father and it will suffice,' saith Philip, John xiv. 8. If we have God for our Father, we need no more. Therefore make much of the means whereby our union and communion and fellowship with God in Christ is stayed, and confirmed to us. To go on.

It is said here, there must be a 'knowledge of this glory of God in the face of Jesus Christ.' And the ministry is the cause of that knowledge, for God hath shined in our hearts to give the light, &c.

Doct. So that *we must know the face of God in Jesus Christ.* Knowledge is the first thing in this new creation, as light was the first in the old creation. God by his word made light, and God by his word puts the Spirit of light in our hearts. All grace is conveyed by knowledge, grace being nothing but knowledge digested. And therefore, Col. iii. 10, the apostle maketh it the 'image of God,' which in the Eph., iv. 24, he calls 'holiness and righteousness.' But there he bringeth all under that one head, because all grace cometh by knowledge, and all comfort is conveyed by knowledge. For even as together with light from heaven comes influence and heat, so together with the divine light comes the divine influence and heat of the soul. Therefore the apostle joineth together grace and knowledge: 2 Pet. iii. 18, 'Grow in grace, and the knowledge of our Lord Jesus Christ.' So you see the reason why the glory of God in Christ must be known. For it is an axiom in divinity, no spiritual blessing doth a man good but by way of knowledge, and therefore out of the church there is no salvation, because the church being like Goshen, there is no light of knowledge out of the church. Therefore it is a gross and fundamental error of them that will have men saved in any religion, for all salvation cometh by knowledge, and that is only in the church.

Use 1. I beseech you, therefore, *labour for knowledge of God* 'in the face of Jesus Christ,' and to grow in it every day more and more. 'Without knowledge the soul is not good,' Prov. xix. 2. The soul is dark, and therefore those that be enemies of knowledge, are enemies to the salvation of God's people. They are enemies of God's glory, because God's glory shineth in the knowledge of God in the face of Jesus Christ. But this is a clear truth.

Use 2. To make it more useful; every man thinks he knoweth Christ. *But knowledge of God's glory in Christ is another matter.*

(1.) *It is a purifying knowledge, and it is a sanctifying knowledge.*

(2.) *It is a knowledge that is both full and experimental.* It is a knowledge with a taste. It is a knowledge that brings a man to salvation. He relisheth divine truths. Every divine truth hath a sweetness and a savour in it, and our souls are to relish it. If there be not relish in the palate, the relish in meat is to no purpose. And therefore God giveth knowledge *per modum gustus.* When things are to us as in themselves, then things have a sweet relish. God's favour and sonship, and grace and peace, they have sweet relish in themselves.

And as they are in themselves, so they are to every Christian. There is a harmony or suitableness in every Christian to divine truths wrought in him. If we have not a relish of divine truths, undoubtedly we know them not as we should.

Use 3. *And it is a knowledge with application of interest in the things*, when we know God to be our God, and Christ to be our Christ, heaven to be ours, and all the promises to be ours, for that is the nature of faith to make its own, whatsoever it layeth hold on. What good doth Christ, and the glory of God in Christ, if we know not Christ, and God in Christ, and make applications that God and Christ may be ours? Therefore the sacraments are ordained for the particular attaining to the knowledge of Christ, that as we are really interested in what we receive, and turn it into ourselves, so by faith we have interest in Christ, and he is one with us, and we with him.

Use 4. *And then this knowledge is a transforming knowledge*, suitable to the object. In nature, objects have an influence into the things that apprehend them. If a man look on a lovely object, it stirs up affection of love; if on hateful objects, it stirs up affection of hatred. But much more in divine things, for they have not only influences into the spirit, but a Spirit accompanying the influence to transform the soul. So that by reason of the object and the Spirit, all divine truths have a transforming force.

Therefore, he that knoweth God to be his God, transforms himself to be his Son. He that knoweth Christ as he should, transformeth himself to be like Christ, to labour for the gracious bountifulness, free obedience, and disposition of Christ. We cannot know Christ as we should, by a spiritual knowledge, without it transform us to the likeness of the thing we know. The knowledge of the glory of God in Christ, will make us glorious Christians. Apprehending glory we shall be glorious, as the apostle saith, 2 Cor. iii. 18: 'Beholding the face of God in Christ, μεταμορφούμεθα, we are changed from glory to glory,' that is, from one degree of grace to another.

Wherein is our happiness? For what is the happiness of a Christian, but to be like Christ, and in Christ like God? The very heathen could say, likeness to God, and communion with God, is the foundation of all happiness. Therefore, this transforming happiness, by which we look to be saved, which makes us more like Christ, that we must labour after, this may be sufficient to stir up our affections, to labour to know God in Christ, being that which is most excellent knowledge. The right knowledge of God in Christ is that that the very angels have a desire to look unto, 1 Pet. i. 12. It is a knowledge we should more desire than angels; for if we know God in Christ as we should do, we are above angels. Did God take the nature of angels? Are they the mystical body of Christ? No. They are the acquaintance of Christ's, but not the spouse of Christ. In both these respects we are above angels. And shall not we study that more than angels, that have more interest therein than angels? Is not the knowledge of this glorious? and shall not we study to know that, that raiseth our natures above the angels themselves? So we should do. And so we will do, if we have the Spirit of God, as Paul, Phil. iii. 7, 8: 'I count all dung and dross,' not in comparison of Christ, but διὰ τὸ ὑπερέχον τῆς γνώσεως Χριστοῦ Ἰησοῦ τοῦ

Κυρίου μου, in comparison of the *excellent knowledge* of Christ Jesus my Lord. The right knowledge of God shining in the face of Christ, with an interesting* knowledge of Christ to be my Saviour, God my Father, myself to be a temple of the Holy Ghost, a member of Christ, heir of heaven, to know I am by grace what Christ is by nature: what is all the world to this, if we had hearts to consider of it? And therefore labour to prize and value this knowledge every day more and more, to beg the Spirit of revelation, that God would reveal himself to us in Christ more and more: pray for the Spirit that knoweth the secrets of God and Christ, that we may know God to be our God, and Christ to be our Saviour. And let it be the desires of our hearts, that God would give us deep knowledge of him, in particular: not only in general, but that he would reveal his fatherly love in Christ, and Christ's sweet love to us.

Quest. But how shall we come to this knowledge?

Sol. God shines not into the brain, but into the very heart of his ministers, that they may give the knowledge of God in the face of Jesus Christ.

Doct. So that the end of God's shining on his ministry is, *that they may shine on others.*

So then, if you ask what is the sanctified means of God to come to so excellent a knowledge of the face of God in Christ, it is specially to the ministry. So God shines in them, that they may give the light of the knowledge they have to others.

And here I will unfold to you their excellency, and authority ministerial, and the necessity of the calling, they being the light of the world, the sun of the world; of whom it is said, 'As the Father sendeth me, so I send you,' John xx. 21. But these things concern our calling more.

Only it concerns all to know this, that God hath not set up an ordinance in his church in vain. As it is glorious to know 'the glory of God in the face of Christ,' so if ever we will know it, we must come to the ministry, that God hath set up as lights in his church; for they be appointed to give thee 'the knowledge of the glory of God in the face of Christ.' So that the ordinance of God is joined with access to the ministers of God. If you regard God and Christ, regard the ministry, for the grace of God, and faith, and knowledge, and the ministry of faith, are all linked together, and he that despiseth the ministers, despiseth God, and grace, and heaven and all. And therefore the word, as opened in the ministry, is called τὸν λόγον τῆς καταλλαγῆς, 'the word of reconciliation,' 2 Cor. v. 18. No reconciliation without it; τὸν λόγον τῆς ζωῆς, 'the word of life,' Philip. ii. 16; τό ἐνδοξον εὐαγγέλιον, 'the glorious gospel,' 1 Tim. i. 11; τὸν ἀνδρείον βραχίονα τοῦ Θεοῦ ἐις τὴν σωτηρίαν, 'strong arm of God to salvation;' τὴν δυνάμιν τοῦ Θεοῦ, 'the power of God,' 2 Cor. vi. 7; because God conveyed all these things by it. And they that despise it, despise glorification, reconciliation, glory, and life, and all. It is ὁ λόγος τῆς βασιλείας, the 'word of the kingdom,' Mat. xiii. 19; because we enter into the kingdom of grace here, by his ordinance, and then into the kingdom of God. Therefore to despise God's ordinance is to despise God; and Acts xiii. 46, the apostle saith, 'Seeing you account yourselves unworthy of the kingdom of heaven.' If they will not hear the gospel, it is as if they despised the kingdom of heaven.

Use. That I advise is, that every one labour *for a right apprehension of the ordinances of God.* 'Let a man esteem of us as the ministers of Christ,'

* That is, 'interested.'—G.

1 Cor. iv. 1, neither more nor less, but just so; that is, not lords over our faith, but ministers that dispense the mystery of Christ.

I need not speak much of this, because God never wrought good in any but they would have a due and right conceit of the ministers and ordinances of God. And they that have base conceits of it, it is a sign God never wrought any good in them. And therefore I speak to them that have respect to the ordinances of God, and that they [may] have more respect to it. Mark what the apostle saith, 'God shines on the heart of the apostles to give light,' &c.

Obj. But it may be objected, God shines in the hearts of his ministers that they may shine on others. Can only good men convert?

Ans. I answer first, that they have a great advantage above all others, because they have those affections and those desires to stir them up to pray to God heartily for their people. And then they have love to the people. It is love that begets grace, and so they having sanctified hearts, that way they do more good than others. But the effect of God's ordinance is not tied to the dignity of any man's person. Judas was a preacher, as bad as he was. Those that convert many shall 'shine in heaven,' if they be good, Dan. xii. 4; if they be bad they may convert others and never come thither themselves; therefore respect the ordinance of God for itself. But because a good expression of the integrity and constant sufficiency in the teacher is a good help to attention and respect, therefore we ought to be careful in the choice of these. For though God's ordinances depend not on the worthiness of the minister, yet there is much help this way.

Obj. But you will say, Can the ministry cause the knowledge of God in the face of Jesus Christ? They be but men, and God shineth in us that we may give knowledge of God.

Ans. I answer, man doth it whether they be good or otherwise, ministerially. God honours them so far as to give them his own title: Acts xvi. 14, Paul preached, God opens Lydia's heart. There must be a concurring of God with the ministry: 1 Cor. iii. 6, 'Paul may plant, and Apollos water, but God giveth the increase.' But if Paul plant and God giveth not increase, all is to no purpose. 'Be faithful in thy calling,' saith Paul to Timothy, and so thou shalt both save thyself and thy hearers, 1 Tim. iv. 16. So that God appoints calling, and giveth gifts and callings for the good of his church. The sun shineth on the moon and stars, to enlighten the world; and the light that ministers have is to shine upon others. God teacheth men by men, and it is most suitable and proportionable to our weakness. As it is a trial of our obedience to respect the word, as it comes from one subject to the same infirmity with ourselves, so it is suitable to our weakness. We could not hear God, nor an angel, therefore God giveth gifts to men for men. Beloved, it is a marvellous fruit of God's love, that he will establish such a calling, the end of which is to bring men to heaven. They be 'sent of God,' Acts xiii. 26; they be the 'salt of the earth,' Mat. v. 13, the world would be putrified without it; they be 'the light,' Philip. ii. 15, the world would be dark without it. If it were not for the gospel, what is England, that is now so glorious above other countries that sit in darkness? And therefore seeing God conveyeth all good to us this way, let it be our prayer to God 'to send labourers into his vineyard,' to set up light in dark places, and to teach his ministers, that they may teach us.

It is strange that Paul, so holy a man as he was, should desire the Romans, chap. xv. 30, 'to pray and strive with God in prayer for him.' 'I beseech you,' I conjure you, 'by the Lord Jesus Christ, and the love of the Spirit, that you strive to God for me.'

Note. The devil sets against this ordinance of God especially, for it battereth his kingdom, and is a means to draw men out of his darkness, 'into the glorious light of the sons of God,' Rom. viii. 21; as in the Acts xxvi. 18, the Lord 'sent him to bring them from darkness to light.' Therefore the devil stirs up 'unreasonable men,' malicious men, that have hurtful and evil principles, to do hurt to them that seek their good, to requite good with ill; and therefore the apostle prayeth, 'Lord let me be delivered from unreasonable men,' ἀπὸ τῶν ἀτόπων, absurd men, greedy, that are so far from faith that they have not common reason, 2 Thes. iii. 2. Now considering God conveyeth all good, specially saving knowledge this way, desire God to preserve the ministers from unreasonable men; that God would let the gospel 'run and be glorified,' 2 Thes. iii. 1; and that the ministry may be glorious, that is, that the Spirit may accompany it to get a great deal of love and strength to bear afflictions. Where the ministry is rightly received it is a glorious thing. And therefore the apostle prays that the gospel may have a free passage, and be glorified by the Spirit accompanying it, in the hearts of the people; and they that will profit most by it, must be so far from undermining it, that they must desire God to assist the teacher, that he being taught may teach others. Thus far it concerneth us all.

And this not only teacheth the ministers to shine to others, but every Christian is a prophet.* And they that have the light of God shining on them are to give the light to others. We are all anointed of God, and like good Christians we have all received the anointing of the Spirit, and in our sphere we ought to do all the good we can to every one in his place. 'You have all knowledge,' saith the apostle, 'that you may exhort and edify one another,' 1 Thes. v. 11. This must be done by the public ordinance, and by every particular Christian. And therefore every Christian may shine to others, and open to others the mystery of salvation, according to their calling, specially in their families. Our Saviour saith, 'Admonish thy brother, and thou shalt save thy brother,' Mat. xviii. 15. God maketh common Christians saviours of others. And therefore as we believe communion of saints in the creed, so we ought to labour for the grace of communion of saints, that is, for ability and love, that we may be able to do good one to another. And no man is a Christian for himself alone. Every man hath grace for the good of the body. There is no idle member of the church's body. As soon as any one is a Christian, he is a profitable member. Onesimus, as soon as he is converted, 'he is profitable,' Philem. 11. By prayer, by advice, by comforting, and counsel, he hath ability to do something to the body of Christ. As he hath good by the graces of the body, so by God's grace he is able to do some good in the body: he is no dead member, but hath some grace of communion.

And it is no vain glory, if it be not done for ostentation; if for Christ, not for his own advantage or ostentation. Breasts may be opened to give milk, which otherwise would be shut; gifts may be opened to do good. If they know anything that is good they ought to infuse it to them, whom God hath made near and dear to them, for grace is communicable.

The sun shineth on the greater part of the world at once. The more communicable the better: the more near God and Christ.

And then we may think that we have all things, the benefit and comfort

* That is, = 'teacher.'—G.

of any true gift, when we have spirits of love to communicate it to others. These be therefore two main graces of communion, humility, and love. And when we can sweetly, humbly, and by the spirit of love communicate it to others, then we be masters of what we have, else it is not given for our good. God will blast it if we do not communicate it. God will take away that he hath from the idle servant, that will not employ his talent. I would to God more conscience were made of this, that not only ministers, but every one, would be first the cistern, and then the conduit, first get something in, and then put it out, when it is seasonable, and when we have a calling to do it.

How hath a Christian a calling to comfort others, to give seasonable reproofs, to give admonitions, to strengthen others, when no minister is by? He that is not able to do it in some measure, can he believe communion of saints? Therefore labour for some spiritual ability, that ye may not be dead and idle members of the body, but shine to others in giving example to others in the way to heaven, that others may have cause to bless God. O blessed be God that ever I was acquainted with such a one. As David said of Abigail, 1 Sam. xxv. 39, so such a one gave me counsel, and it came from love, from a sweet spirit, and I shall have cause to remember it while I live.

Consider it is our calling. We are all prophets, all anointed. A Christian hath an high calling; but specially consider what we do believe by the 'communion of saints;' and what we pray for, when we say, 'thy kingdom come,' that is, that faith may reign in our hearts and minds. Shall we say, let thy kingdom come, when we are enemies of the ministry and good communion? If we use this prayer thus, we mock God. I desire God to make these things effectual.

The apostle in the former chapter, as we have heard, raiseth up the soul to the chief cause of all heavenly light in the soul, which is God, by his almighty power shining in our hearts, as he caused the light to shine at the first. By how much that light is more excellent than that light of nature, by so much the greater power is put forth for the working of it, being so opposite thereunto.

The end of this shining in the hearts of the ministers especially, is to 'give the light of the glory of God in the face of Jesus Christ.' God shineth on ministers that they may reflect that light upon others. As John Baptist saith, 'they be friends of the bride, that learn of the bridegroom,' Christ, what to do to help his spouse, John iii. 29. They labour to know the meaning of Christ, what his good will is to them that be his. They be friends on both sides, on Christ's, and the spouse's. They come between both, for the furthering of the blessed marriage between Christ and the soul.

I have spoken of the glory of God, which specially shines in his mercy and goodness. There is a greater lustre of God's attributes in the gospel than in the law.

Quest. It may be asked, Are not we for to preach the law as well as the glory of God in the face of Christ discovered in the gospel?

Ans. I yield there must be special care of that, even now in the days of the gospel; for you know there be three degrees, the state of nature, the state under the law, and the state under grace. Before we can come from nature to grace, we must come under the law; we must know ourselves thoroughly, and be humbled to purpose. Many live under the gospel, that were never yet under the law, that think themselves under Christ, and under grace, and yet were never humbled. Therefore in love to the souls of men, let the law be discovered; as God gave the law, not to damn men but in love to men, that thereby they might see the impurity of their natures, and lives, and the curse due to it, and so follow him forthwith to Christ, from Sinai to Sion, appealing from the throne of justice to the throne of grace and mercy, the Lord Christ. The Lord gave not the law purposely to damn men, but to drive them to an holy despair in themselves. They that despair in themselves, they come to see their whole hope of comfort to be in the face of God in Christ.

Therefore respectively to grace, we ought to force the law in these dull and drowsy times. For they that stick in the state of nature, as profane godless persons, swearers, loose persons, were never yet under the law. And what have they to do with Christ, that were never humbled? If their eyes were open to see what they are by nature, and what they would be if God should cut the thread of their lives, they would look about them then. The kingdom of heaven would suffer violence, if men understood their states throughly, that there is but a step between them and hell, nothing but a life full of uncertainties, without serious repentance.

Moses brought none into Canaan. That was Joshua's part. When Moses had brought them near, then he giveth up his office to Joshua. The law must give up its office to Christ. When men are cast down with apprehensions of sin, they must run into the bosom of the gospel, and shelter themselves under the wings of Jesus Christ. Though such persons may in the error of their conscience think themselves farthest off grace, yet they be nearest. For 'blessed are the poor in spirit, for theirs is the kingdom of heaven,' Mat. v. 3. 'And come to me, all ye that be heavy laden, I will ease you,' Mat. xi. 28.

Quest. Again, some will object, we must teach moral duties, teach men not to be sottish and drunken and filthy in their lives.

Ans. It is very good. I would these abominations were reformed, but if there be not a better foundation laid for the knowledge of God in the face of Christ, by the discovery of the hidden face of nature, we should make them but hypocrites, and only civilise them. Therefore the right way to make them leave these abominations is, first, to get knowledge of themselves by nature, and of their original corruptions; and then, to lead them to the knowledge of God 'in the face of Jesus Christ,' that seeing love, love may kindle love, and alter their course, and make them study to please God. If duties spring not from love, they be dead duties, and but carcases of duties. But love constraineth us to perform services by the apprehension of God's mercy in Christ.

Therefore if we will make men leave sin on good grounds, teach the gospel; else we shall bring them into a civil* compass which is good, and I would there were more of it; but we should not rest there. Holy duties, and abstaining from gross sins, is a great deal more groundedly enforced from the gospel than the law. For the reasons from thence are very demonstrative, as Paul, Titus ii. 12, 'The grace of God hath appeared, teaching us to deny ungodliness and worldly lusts; and to live soberly to ourselves, righteous to others, holily to God.'

And therefore the apostle's method is first to lay the ground and foundation of Christian doctrine, and then to build upon it Christian duties in all his epistles; as in the Romans, after he had shewed free justification, by the mercy of God in Christ Jesus, and then sanctification of our nature, then he comes to the comforts of a Christian life in predestination, and

* That is, = moral.—G.

God's free everlasting love. 'Then I beseech you, by the mercies of God in Christ, give up your bodies as reasonable sacrifices to God,' Rom. xii. 1. The ground of his exhortation is to devote and consecrate ourselves to God, and it is from the mercies of God. And so in all the rest of his epistles, he layeth foundation of a Christian life upon Christian doctrine, as Lactantius saith well, 'All morality without piety is a goodly statue without an head (*i*). [It is] the head that giveth life and influence into all duties of a Christian and the knowledge of Christ.* In a word, whatsoever we preach is either to drive to Christ, or is Christ himself, by his benefits unfolded, or an holy life, with this respect, that we may live answerable, and worthy of Christ; so that whatsoever we preach, it hath respect to Christ.

And therefore the apostle speaking of the main duty saith, 'God hath shined in our hearts, to give the knowledge of the glory of God in the face of Jesus Christ.' Certainly all will follow where this is, 'She loved much, because much was forgiven,' Luke vii. 47. She had relished the sweet love of God in pardoning her, and therefore loved much. For what is love but all duty in the root? It is one in the root, and all in the branches. All sin is one in original corruption, the root which brancheth itself many ways into particulars. So love being one in the root, when the heart is filled with that, you shall not need to dictate to it, to do this or that. Love is an affection full of invention, to please, delight, and gratify the person loved, and sets the soul on fire to all duties whatsoever.

1. Again, the knowledge of God *differenceth God's people from atheists, that know no God at all.* So to know God in Christ, that differenceth them from those without the church, that know God, but not 'in the face of Christ.' To know God in the face of Christ as he should be known, differs true Christians from popish and rotten professors, and from an hypocrite within the church. The papists know God not in the face of Jesus Christ; only they go to him by other mediators, and they will have crucifixes, and many gods, never desiring to discover the face of Christ.

But the best discovery of God is to see him 'in the face of Christ.' The best sight of Christ is, not in a crucifix or the work of an idle painter, but to see him in the word and sacrament. You have seen Christ 'crucified before your eyes,' saith Paul to the Galatians, Gal. iii. 1. God worketh grace by his own means, and not by the bastardly means of man's invention. The knowledge of God is conveyed by Christ, and no other mediator. That knowledge which comes nearest the knowledge of God in Christ is not only disciplinary, but a sound saving knowledge, that sees things in their formal, proper, spiritual light, and not only in their shell.

2. *This distinguisheth likewise them under the law.* And they see the face of God under the law, poor distressed sinners. Ay, but they see an angry face there. But if they will see God as they should do, and as true Christians, they see not his angry countenance in Moses under the law, threatening men with hell and damnation; but they see him 'in the face of Jesus Christ,' reconciling the world to himself.

In the next verse, ver. 7, the apostle preventeth an objection, as he is very curious in prevention; for he was full of love, and desired to make way for himself in the hearts of them whom he taught. When he saw anything between him and their hearts, he labours to remove it, by all the wit and policy that he could; and therefore he now preventeth an objection from the meanness of his person and condition. You speak much of preaching the gospel, what doth the world esteem of you? you

* Qu. 'The head . . . is the knowledge'?—ED.

be a poor despised man. It is true, but I carry the excellent treasures of the love of God in Christ; nay, we carry it in earthen vessels; but it is a treasure, though in earthen vessels, though conveyed by despised persons. And God hath a wise end in it. I look to God's end; which is, that in the meanness of my condition the power and excellency of what I teach may come from him, and not from me; therefore he useth mean instruments in his great work. So that the words have a prevention of an objection.

And there is a double answer to the objection.

1. We are 'earthen vessels,' but we carry a 'treasure' in them.

2. Again, God doth it 'that the excellency of the power' of my preaching 'may be of God, and not of us.' To come to the particulars.

1. That the gospel, and the knowledge of God in the face of Christ, it is a treasure.

2. And the way to come to it is by the ministry. Our ministerial dispensation of it is the way to convey it to others.

3. That ministers, as well as others, are but frail, empty vessels. Indeed, they have a treasure conveyed by the dispensation that God hath set upon his church, but it is all but by earthen vessels. These be the three things.

Then the next part is, 'that the excellency of the power may be of God, and not of us.' So that there is a power, and an excellent power, shewed in the ministry to all them that shall be saved.

There is a power in them that be reprobate wretches, and they feel it at length, to harden them more and more, to make them more bitter and worse; but in them that be saved there is a power, and excellency of power, in the ordinances of God.

This power is of God, and not of men. It is conveyed by man, but the power originally, *tanquam à fonte*, cometh from God. These be the parts.

1. 'We have this treasure in earthen vessels,' the gospel, the knowledge of God in the face of Jesus Christ. The knowledge of Christ, and of God in Christ, it is a treasure.

What is a treasure? We all know. Experience sheweth that it implieth plenty, and variety of things of price, and rare things, not common, and them of excellent and special use for the time present and to come, for ornament, or for security, or defence, or for discharge of debt and trouble, or for help and comfort. When any want lieth upon a man, he hath recourse to his treasure.

The gospel is a treasure in these and all other respects that may be comfortable.

For here is plenty, variety, rarity, price, usefulness in the highest degree; for in Christ, who is the chief thing in the gospel, we have all.

(1.) *There is plenty in Christ*, treasures of wisdom and of all good hidden in him for our good. The apostle saith, 'In him are hid all the treasures of wisdom and knowledge,' Col. ii. 3; and he is all in all, he is our riches. The particulars I have unfolded out of a portion of Scripture heretofore.* He is 'wisdom,' he is 'righteousness,' and 'sanctification,' and 'redemption,' 2 Cor. i. 30: wisdom to supply our ignorance, righteousness to supply the guilt which we stand charged before God with; and so he is righteousness to our consciences. He is sanctification to the defilement of our natures, our conditions and persons being miserable. He is redemption to us, partly of our souls in this life, and of soul and body in

* Cf. Vol. III. on 2 Cor. i. 30.—G.

the life to come. He hath all by grace of union; for our natures being so near as to be hypostatically united, and taken into one person with God. . . .*

As there be three ways of conveying excellency—union, revelation, and vision—so Christ hath it by union, we by revelation in this world, by vision in the world to come.

Now Christ hath a fulness in him, partly by virtue of this union, and partly *ratione officii*, as he is the head of the church; for where should we be but in the head? The head is wisdom for the body. All the senses are in the head. It sees, it hears, it understandeth for the body, it doth all for the body; so that the riches of a Christian is hid in Christ, but for the good of the body. Whatsoever we stand in need of, God is all-sufficient, and Christ is God-man, and we are knit to Christ by faith, so that Christ and we are all one, and therefore a Christian hath a rich treasure in Christ.

(2.) *And then he hath price and excellency in the things we have in him.* If any things be excellent, these things are. They raise our condition above the common condition of the world; nay, above angels in some sort, making us heirs and fellow-heirs with Christ. It makes us the sons of God, sets us at liberty from our cursed condition, and not only at liberty, but in a state of advancement as high as our natures can reach unto. *Liberatio à summo malo, summi boni habet rationem*, freedom from the greatest evil, which is damnation and destruction. It hath respect to the greatest good; but then, together with freedom from the greatest evil, we have advancement to the greatest good. Indeed, we can hardly conceive of the excellency of the things we have in Christ. Every grace is precious.

[1.] How precious is faith, that layeth hold of all the graces in Christ, and makes them our own!

[2.] What precious grace is love, that makes us to deny ourselves and communicate ourselves to the good of others! A world of good a loving soul can do.

[3.] And so the hope of life, what an anchor it is to stay the soul in all conditions patiently and contentedly!

And every grace is precious, and needs must every grace be precious, considering the price they cost. Things dearly bought are precious, and every grace of the Spirit, and the Spirit itself, is purchased by the blood of Christ. For the Spirit hath no communion with us till peace be made between God and us by Christ; but when God the Father is reconciled by Christ, then the Spirit, a friend of both, cometh from both, and assureth us of the love of both, discovering the secret love of God in Christ, and bestoweth all grace, to furnish and fit us for heaven. So that the graces of the Spirit are precious, and to be accounted precious, because they cost so dear as the blood of Christ.

(3.) And then *for usefulness, what use have we of every grace?* What were our lives without grace? What serve treasures for but to pay our debts? Christ paid all your debts to God the Father, to God's justice. We are all discharged. One red line of his blood drawn over the debt-book crosseth all the debt. Satan hath nothing to do with us. In him we have remission of sins, and he is now in heaven to make intercession for us, and plead our cause as our friend. At God's right hand we have a friend and brother in our nature, that maintaineth the love of God constantly to us as his members and as his spouse.

Besides, we have comfort in all distresses; and we have strength in all our weaknesses; light and direction in all our perplexities, by the Spirit,

* Sentence unfinished.—G.

and grace of the Spirit. So that in every respect Christ and the graces of the Spirit are satisfying treasures.

(4.) The gospel which revealeth this is a treasure *specially for the time to come*, for then is a treasure specially useful. Christ is a rich storehouse, and in him we have all. For the time to come we have more in Christ than here. When Christ shall be revealed, and we shall be revealed, then our treasure will appear. And before that, at the hour of death, when all comforts shall be taken from us, then comes in the treasure of a Christian, then he hath use of Christ, of the Spirit of Christ, to support him; and the spirit of faith and hope, to strengthen him with patience and willingness to go to Christ: then come in all the riches that he hath laid up, all the spiritual graces, for to help him at that hour. So that specially then in time of need comes in these treasures, Christ with his grace and Spirit. The best use of religion is in time to come. Now, we can make a shift with riches, and friends, and strength; but when all is done, we must have a better treasure, that is, Christ and the graces of Christ.

We may refer all to these two heads, Christ partly imparted and partly imputed. That that is imputed is his righteousness, by which we have freedom from hell, advancement to heaven; and the imparted and bestowed favours are the graces of his Spirit for all times and services. We have remedies for all maladies. And they are of a higher nature than all other treasures whatsoever.

Therefore, to shew the difference between this and other treasures, to raise up the estimation of Christ, and the good things in him, these treasures we have in Christ imputed and imparted.

1. They are *independent*. The comfort of them doth not depend on any inferior comfort, or things in this world, but when all comforts are taken away, then they are of special use.

2. And as they be independent, so they be *universal*. Christ and the good things in him are universally good for all turns. There is no other treasure but is for particular ends, and cannot do all things. Riches can make a man as happy as riches can do; and dainties make a man as lively as such things can do; and friends can do what friends can do; but all is limited: they cannot do more than in the sphere of their activity. But what is said of money, that it is good for all things, I am sure it is true of the grace of God in Christ. It is good for all things and all conditions: it is a universal good.

3. Then it is a treasure that is *proportionable to the dignity of a man*. It is proportionable to the soul, to satisfy the desires thereof. A man's desire is larger than any pleasure in the world. A man can spend all his contentment in an earthly thing. In his thoughts and affections he runneth through the contentment of all earthly things presently. If a man had all earthly contentments, the soul would pass through them all and see beyond them; and when he hath done, he looks on them as soiled commodities and cast things; but the treasures of the gospel in Christ are proportionable to the soul. They be spiritual, as the soul is spiritual; nay, likewise they be larger than the soul, the treasure is larger than the treasury. But of other things, the treasure is but little, the treasury large; but here the treasure is larger than the treasury, for our soul is not capable of the fulness of Christ. There is more in Christ, and more in our state of happiness than the soul can contain. The soul can never spend nor run through all the good we have, for there is still more and more. Therefore the apostle calls it, Eph. iii. 8, 'the unsearchable riches of grace.' Search more and

more, and still they be unsearchable. 'Neither eye hath seen, nor ear heard, nor hath it entered into the heart of man to conceive of the excellent things in Christ,' 1 Cor. ii. 9. They transcend the capacity of the soul, which no other treasure can do.

4. And then they have another excellency. *They make the soul and the whole person a treasure*; as God saith, Mal. iii. 17, 'I will make up my jewels.' The grace of God makes us gracious, turneth us into jewels. No other treasure can change the cask wherein it is; but these blessed things of God and of Christ, wheresoever he dwelleth, he makes the soul like himself, stamping his own image and likeness upon it. For such is the change of nature into grace that it makes us treasures.

Other treasures perhaps make us worse, as indeed they do, by reason of the proneness of our dispositions to earthly things, they soil and stain our natures. But these treasures of excellent things purify our natures, make us better, and change us into the nature of themselves; nay more, grace changeth the worst things to be good to us: that is the excellency of its virtue. They talk of the philosopher's stone, and strange things, but I am sure the grace of God is so excellent a treasure that it extracts good out of every evil, and as grace, turneth all to good, and so the sanctifying Spirit concurring with it, draweth the greatest comforts out of the greatest crosses. And is not that a rich treasure, that turneth the worst things to good? It will make every thing to guide us to the main.

5. That our affections may be raised higher. *All other treasures whatsoever they be, here we find them, and here we must leave them, whether we will or no, or they will leave us.* As the wise man saith of riches, 'they have eagles' wings,' Prov. xxiii. 5. *Peritura perituris,* we must leave perishing earthly things to perishing men. But is this treasure of that nature or no? For it makes the soul eternal, it doth raise the soul to be spiritual, the soul carrieth them to heaven with it. The earthen vessel indeed is cracked to pieces, but the treasure remaineth. The soul goeth out of this earthen vessel to heaven, and thither carrieth all the love it had, and all the graces, and the image of Christ it had. All is there perfectly, nothing is taken away. As we say of an earnest, it is part of the bargain, and not taken away again. Luke x. 42, it was said of Mary's part, that 'her part shall never be taken from her.' All other things will be taken from us. We shall be stripped of all, and turned naked into our graves, we know not how soon. As we came naked, so must we be turned naked; but Mary's part, the interest in the treasure of the gospel and the good things of Christ, shall never be taken from us, but shall be perfected in heaven. When friends are taken away, and life taken away, and all comforts taken away, yet Mary's part endures for ever. When nothing will comfort, all our treasures fail, as at the hour of death, then comes in this treasure and comforts most. So that herein it differs from all treasures: it is never taken from us, and stands us in greatest use and stead in our greatest necessity.

6. And which is of special use, *other treasures we cannot carry about us whithersoever we go*. But this is like [a] pearl rather than treasure. A Christion carrieth this treasure wheresoever he goeth; nay, he carrieth it in his heart, it is hid there, and who can take it out thence? Can the devil? No. It is hid in his affections. His love, and choice, and judgment hath gotten it and mastered it. This I have, and this I must stick to in life and death; for having got it in his heart, judgment, and affection, he carrieth it wheresoever he goeth, maketh use of it wheresoever, in prison, at liberty, abroad or at home. Let all the devils in hell conspire, they may take away

his life, but not his treasure, they must leave him the gospel. Perhaps they may take it out of the book, but can they get it out of the soul? Indeed, unless divine truths be gotten into the heart, the devil will come between us and our souls and rob us of them; but if it be in the judgment and heart, we carry it with us, and that continually and in all places, else it could not serve for all turns. You see then in what respect this treasure is so excellent.

First, that we may believe these things we must believe God, and believe his saints, and believe Christ.

(1.) *God by his Spirit saith it is so*, Prov. iii. 14, 15. The knowledge of Christ and the good things by him, nothing is to be compared to them, Mat. vi. 29. God's judgment is the rule of the goodness of things. If he saith it is so, it is so. Christ calleth it a treasure, that a wise man that hath God's Spirit in him will sell all for to obtain it. 'Lay up treasure in heaven,' Luke xii. 21. Labour to be rich in God, for that is 'true riches,' Luke xvi. 11.

(2.) And *for the servants of God, take Moses and St Paul.* What was the judgment of Moses? In comparison, the worst things that can be in Christ and religion are better than the best things that can be in the world. What are the worst things? Shame and reproach, together with poverty, and the like; but the 'reproach of Christ,' which is most insufferable to the disposition of one that is a man; but the rebukes of Christ are greater riches than all the treasures of Egypt. Nay, Moses balanceth them; he layeth the reproach of Christ in one scale, and the treasures of Egypt in the other, and the reproaches of Christ is the heavier scale, Heb. xii. 26. Take St Paul, Phil. iii. 7, 8. He puts into one scale all his excellencies whatsoever he had. He was a Jew 'of the tribe of Benjamin,' 'without reproof,' 'as to the law blameless;' after he was a Christian, he had excellent graces, abundance of the Spirit of God. No man, next to Christ, discovered a greater portion of the Spirit of Christ; and yet, not only 'I did' before my being in Christ, account of my Pharisaism, and righteousness of the law and civil life, but note, 'I do,' when I am well advised what I say, I do 'doubtless esteem all dung in comparison of the excellency of the knowledge of Jesus Christ, and to be found in him, not having mine own righteousness, but the righteousness of Christ.' *Διὰ τὸ ὑπερέχον τῆς γνώσεως Χριστοῦ Ἰησοῦ τοῦ Κυρίου μοῦ.* That is the jewel of jewels; the treasure of treasures; for thereby we come to have infused righteousness. Imputed is the most useful, and therefore the apostle so esteems that, that in regard of it he esteemed the other nothing, and thinks he hath not done enough till he hath set disgraceful terms upon it, calling it dung, offal, that which is cast to dogs.* He will suffer the loss of all righteousness, reputation, and all, that he may gain Christ. Thus, if we believe the judgment of God, and of men led by the Spirit, and of Christ, we must needs judge this an excellent treasure.

Use. Therefore *let us labour to have our parts and shares in this excellent treasure of Christ, and the good things of Christ;* to give no rest to our souls till we have union and communion with him, in whom 'all treasures are hid,' Col. ii. 3. Get the Spirit of Christ, whence all graces and comforts be derived; what will all other treasure do good, when we stand most in need? When we lie gasping for comfort, as we must ere long, what will friends and possessions do good? what will these farther you,

* *σκυβαλα* quasi *κυσίβαλον*.—*Suidas.* Intestinum quod canibus abjicitur.—*Lapide.* Significat id quod omnes aversantur.—*Zanchius in loc.* Excrementum.—G.

when you go swelling and puffing against God's ministers, and truth, and them that be better than yourselves—What will they do, you good that thus leave you? Alas! nothing at all. It will only fill your souls with despair and horror. The knowledge of God in Christ, and the Spirit of God to seal it, and to sanctify hard hearts, is the only thing that will comfort us. It will not comfort a man on his deathbed, that he hath worn gay apparel, or been acquainted with great persons, or borne so high a place, or tasted of so many dainties. Alas! when he reflecteth on these things, what good will they do? This will do him good; I remember such promises, such comforts, such precious mercies, that have been unfolded to me; the work of God's Spirit in me hath led me to such and such holy actions, as the fruits of his Spirit. I remember Christ hath been unfolded to me, that I might cast myself on his mercy. These things may comfort, but other things may be objects of discomfort, but comfort they can yield none. I beseech you, let us consider wherefore we came into the world, and wherefore God hath given men great parts. We are sent as factors* into the world to trade, being all merchants. And what do we trade for? For this commodity that we should carry to heaven with us, that we may go stored to heaven with them. If a merchant send a factor into a foreign country, and he bring nothing but baubles and trifles, can he give a good account to him that sent him? Doth God send us into the world to get a great deal of 'hard clay,' Hab. ii. 6, and of ill-gotten goods for pleasures, and to deify ourselves and others, to make ourselves much more the children of the devil than we are by nature? No. We are factors for great matters, to get the knowledge of God in Christ, to get near acquaintance with God, to get out of the state of nature, to get near to heaven; these be the ends wherefore we live in the world. This earth and this church of God is a fit place, a seminary, a nursery, wherein we grow, and are fitted to be transplanted to the heavenly paradise. Wherefore do we live, and wherefore doth God give these excellent parts by nature? Is our understanding to exercise itself in the dirt of the world? Is this heart, these wills, and affections given to cleave to baser things than ourselves? Hath he given love, so sweet, so large an affection, to cleave to things below?—which is capable of Christ, of heaven, of happiness. These excellent capacious souls of ours, which the world cannot contain, are they for anything that is meaner than ourselves? Oh no. They serve for Christ, and for these excellent treasures. Oh that we should forget the end of our creation, redemption, live here, and labour not for the things which we live in the world only to attain to but let the devil abuse us! As they catch whales, with casting empty barrels about them to play withal, so while we be playing about this and that vanity, we are made a prey to Satan. How few live to that purpose for which they are! Few fit themselves for their eternal condition, by heaping up comforts from these things, which may be true comforts. Lay these things to heart, that we may be wise to purpose, wise to salvation. This is our wisdom and our understanding.

Use 2. *Quest. But how shall we know whether we have interest and portion in these excellent treasures*, ay or no?

Ans. [1.] *We may see our interest in them, especially by our esteem of them.* If they be presented to our souls indeed as God doth, and as Christ and the word of Christ presents them, then it is an argument, that there is a tincture in our spirits whereby they are made suitable to the Spirit of Christ. If they be presented [as] excellent things—and beyond all com-

* That is = agents, servants.—G.

parison, all the things thou canst think of are not to be compared with them—do we so present them to ourselves, that we esteem of them as Moses, and Paul, and God's children do? Do we so esteem of grace, that if we were left to our wish, whether we will have anything in the world, or a greater measure of grace, of the love of God, of union with God, what choice would we make? Our estimation and choice will discover the frame of our hearts. As we esteem, so we be. If it were left to our own opinion, and wish, and desire, would we make David's choice, Ps. iv. 6, 'When many said, Who will shew us any good?' A right temper of a worldling, 'Who? it is no matter who,' let any 'shew me any good,' do but shew it, I have ways enough to get it. But saith David, 'Lord, lift thou up the light of thy countenance upon me.' Life is in the favour of God; nay, the favour of God is better than life itself. I had rather part with my life than the favour of God; saith Paul, 'My life is not dear to me, so I may finish my course with joy,' Acts xx. 24. Now do you esteem communion with God and peace of conscience higher than life? It is a good sign of interest in Christ when you have this estimation and choice on him.

Ans. [2.] Again, a sign of interest in this treasure is, *when we have grace to make use of it on all occasions;* for together with graces the Lord gives his Spirit to make use of them, in our afflictions, in our troubles. And therefore they that make not use of the Scriptures, and promises of good things they have in Christ, have no part in this treasure. What is the use of a treasure if it be not applied to our occasions; if we run to earthly contentments, and never make use of our best grounds of comfort? Christ giveth an excellent note of discerning: 'Where the treasure is, there the heart will be,' Mat. vi. 21. Wouldst thou know whether thy treasure be in earth or heaven? Where is the heart? that is, where is thy love, thy joy, delight? Ask thy soul what thou lovest most? what thou most cleavest in affection to? what thou delightest most in? There is thy heart. And therefore they that have few thoughts, and very shallow and weak thoughts of the better state to come, and of the state that they have here in Christ, and the excellencies in Christ above the world, that do not think of these things with joy and love of God, their heart is not there; therefore their treasure is not there. They have hearts eaten out with the world, if they were anatomised, you should find nothing but projects for the world. Anatomise their affections, there is nothing but the love of the world, and vanity, and emptiness, and which is worse than emptiness, much sin and evil that Satan hath brought into the world. And if nothing be found in the soul but worldly vanities and profits, alas! where is our treasure? Our treasure certainly is here, and not in heaven; for 'where the heart is, there is our treasure.'

They that have treasures, Oh they mind them. Therefore we shall see worldly men, they have nothing in them. You shall not have a savoury word of goodness. Their minds are like mines of gold and silver. They say of them, that where they are the ground is always barren, because the metal sucketh out the juice that should cherish it. And so it is with all the minds of earthly men. Enter into an heavenly discourse, it is not for them. They have not a word with them, they have no savour, no relish of it, they shew a distaste; yet if it be brought in by occasion of mortality, a short thing will serve. But they will quickly be in the old tract of the world. They be so unwilling to dwell in the meditation of these things, that they be mere* strangers to them.

* That is, 'altogether.'—G.

Ans. [3.] *A man will think of his treasure and look on it*, as a covetous man, that though he use not his gold, yet will open his chest to look on it; excellent is the colour of it.

Note. Shall a worldling joy in refined earth, and shall not a Christian delight to reflect on Christianity and his comforts in Christ, and his future estate, and what blessed conditions abide in him, and being for ever with the Lord, and having such rivers of pleasure? The oldest man, the dullest wit, will never forget where he layeth his treasure, and when we cannot call to mind this comfort, and that comfort, and things useful for us, it is a sign they be not treasures to us, for if they were we would make more of them.

I beseech you, therefore, labour more and more, that as things are in themselves, and as God who is the rule of all truth doth judge of things, so let us judge of things, let them be to us as they are to him, and as they are in themselves. If they be treasures, the blessings and comforts of God's Spirit and the good things of Christ, let them be so to us; never leave begging of God that we may have a sanctified judgment, to have the same mind of them that he hath; and to this end balance them often with other things. As Moses did, and as Paul did, lay them in the scale, and consider the emptiness and vanity of all things besides* grace and the Spirit, and the good things of Christ, and what other comforts they will afford. God hath given wit and discourse, how shall we use them better than by comparing different things, and answerable to our comparing to make choice? We should shew ourselves wise men in our wise choice, and good men in our good choice. How else should we shew ourselves to be what we would be thought to be?

There be treasures in these poor vessels of bread and wine. Now what treasures are conveyed by them, if we look on themselves? Bread is an ordinary thing, but the good conveyed to us by God is conveyed by these common easy things. Thus God delights to shew himself in common ordinary ways to us. Therefore raise up your thoughts from the commonness of the things to the excellency of the things conveyed. What is conveyed by bread? The body of Christ crucified. And what is conveyed by that? God reconciled in Jesus Christ, by the sufferings of Christ, the love of God, and mercies of God, and pardon of sins. Great good is conveyed by the bread broken, for Christ is conveyed with satisfaction to divine justice, and thence favour and reconcilement with him. And so when his comforts are represented by refreshing of our bodies, Christ's body 'is meat indeed,' Christ's blood 'is drink indeed,' John vi. 55. The benefit of Christ's blood and satisfaction are great things that are conveyed by a reverent receiving of the sacrament. If we come preparedly we have communion with Christ, in whom are 'hid all treasures,' Col. ii. 3.

VERSE 7.

But we have this treasure in earthen vessels, that the excellency of the power may be of God, and not of us.

We entered upon this verse the last day. 'But we have this treasure in earthen vessels;' where he answereth an objection, for the heart of man is full of objections against Scripture truths. God in manner of his dispensation pleaseth not the natural heart of man, especially when it thinks itself most wise, but pleaseth itself in cavilling and expostulating against

* That is, 'beside.'—G.

the word, or the dispensation of it; and therefore the apostle being desirous that these blessed things may come to the hearts of the people he hath dealt withal, takes away all objections that may stand between them and the truth.

The chief objection is the baseness of Paul's condition. He was scorned and persecuted in the world.

It is true we are 'earthen vessels,' but we have a 'treasure' in these vessels. And God is wise, and his end is good, 'that the excellency of the power may be of God and not of us.'

And then the treasurer, and the under-treasurer; Christ is the chief; we are the under-treasurers. And then the vessels which this treasure is contained in. 'Earthen vessels' are baser than the treasure itself; and then the reason of this seeming disproportion, that so excellent a treasure is in earthen vessels. These be the particulars that deserve to be unfolded. Some of them have been unfolded in part already.

I shewed that the gospel was a treasure. Soul-saving truth is a treasure. It was compared to light, the most divine quality of all, fittest to set out divine truths, which hath influence conveyed from heaven with it; and which discovers itself and all excellencies in the world besides. And now it is set out by another borrowed speech, which we highly esteem in the world, that is, a treasure. Nothing more prized than light and treasure. God speaketh in our own language to us; not that heavenly things are not better than any earthly things, but we cannot understand God if he speaks in any other language. And therefore he conveyeth the excellency of spiritual things under that which we most prize in the world, under light, and under treasure.

I came then to make a use of trial, whether we have this treasure or no.

Use 3. For further use, if so be Christ, and the good things by him discovered, are such a treasure, *then we ought to be content with him*, though God cut us short in regard of outward things; for we have a treasure, and this is one benefit we have by it. If we have Christ, we shall have all other things, as much as God shall see needful. They shall be cast into the bargain, and that is one comfort.

The little we have we shall have with a blessing. And then though we be never so poor in the world, we are rich in promises. Rich faith we have to make use of these rich promises. Precious faith, and precious promises. We have bills, and God is a good paymaster, and is content to be sued on his own bond. We cannot have a better debtor than God himself. Now, having the Spirit of God, to give us precious faith, to lay hold on the rich and precious promises we have in Jesus Christ, therefore we should not be much discontented with whatsoever befalls us in this world, for we have a rich portion.

Let us labour to understand this, and consider not only that we are rich in bills and promises, but in reversion. The best riches are laid up in heaven for us. We have some earnest and other tastes of them here, some grapes of Canaan,* but the best is to come, the true treasures are laid up in heaven. What we have here, alas! is nothing to that we shall have hereafter. Therefore having a rich God, and a rich Saviour, God-man; God having enriched our natures, and willing to enrich our persons, so far as shall concern heaven; having rich faith, and rich promises, and

* Tichbourne and Durant have appropriated the phrase 'Grapes of Canaan' for the titles of perhaps their best books. Many of the casual happy sentences of Sibbes reappear in this way in subsequent writings of his Puritan admirers.—G.

rich reversions; for matters of this world let God deal as he pleaseth. God, that gave so rich a treasure as his own Son, cannot deny anything else, as the apostle reasoneth strongly: 'If he hath not spared his own Son, but given him to death for us all, how shall not he with him give us all things?' Rom. viii. 32. He wonders that any man should call it to question, 'How can it be?'

He stands not on petty commodities, which we stand in need of, that giveth treasures. It is your Father's pleasure to give you a kingdom: *Dabit regnum, et non dabit viaticum?* He will give you a kingdom, and will not he give you safe conduct and provision to bring you to heaven?

Consider this, and often examine your faith, whether ye believe these things or no. If you believe them, why are you discontented with every petty loss and cross in the world, as if there were no better things to depend upon?

(1.) Oh labour to bring [y]our hearts *to a holy contentment, and for a Spirit of wisdom to improve this treasure.* What use is there of a treasure, if we do not employ it for a supply of our wants? And therefore make use of the riches we have in Jesus Christ. Are we sinful? He is gracious. Have we much guilt [that] lieth on our consciences? Christ hath a great deal of favour: he is 'the beloved Son of God,' Mat. iii. 17. Set that against conscience. Have we many enemies in the world? We have an intercessor in heaven. 'Doth sin abound? Grace aboundeth much more,' Rom. v. 20. Is there any want either in grace or in comfort in the things of this world? See a full and rich supply in Jesus Christ.

(2.) And then *get wisdom to make use of it.* There is a special art to make use of the good things we have in Christ every day. For a man to famish at a feast, to starve and perish with thirst at the fountain's head, it is ignorance and want of wisdom. If we be in Christ, if we have a well-head, whence we may fetch whatsoever we stand in need of, if we have faith, then* to this end beg of God a spirit of wisdom and revelation to know the excellent things we have in Christ.

(3.) And likewise labour *for a vessel of faith for to contain this treasure,* and get enlargement of faith. The larger faith we bring, the larger measure we carry from Christ. As the poor woman, that had vessels of oil, had she had more vessels, she had more oil, 2 Kings iv. 6; for the oil increased as her vessels served. If we had more faith, we might have larger oil of grace, and larger oil of comfort from God's word in Christ, and God's riches in Christ. And therefore beg with the holy apostles, 'Lord, increase our faith,' Luke xvii. 5, that as we have rich promises, and a rich Christ, and rich comforts, so we [may] have rich faith.

(4.) And because Christ is rich, not to them that are without him, but within him, as they have union with Christ, labour therefore *to strengthen this union with Christ,* that we may be nearer and nearer the fountain, nearer and nearer the well-head, nearer and nearer the treasure of all. And therefore labour in use of the word and sacraments to increase union, and so to increase communion with Jesus Christ.

(5.) And for this purpose *increase the sense of emptiness in ourselves,* for as we grow empty in our conceits, so are we fitted to be full with God's goodness. 'He sends the rich empty away,' Luke i. 53, that be rich with the windy conceit of their own worthiness. Let us search deeply into our own hearts what we want, what sin lieth on us, that we may be pardoned. What is wanting we should know, that it might be supplied.

It should be our daily task to empty ourselves, by our daily consideration

* Misprinted 'and.'—G.

of our own wants and sinfulness, and then to fetch a fresh supply from the throne of grace.

It is with a Christian's heart, as a vessel that is full of something it should not be. So when men's hearts are full of windiness and what they should not have, the more we labour to set* ourselves, the more God infuseth supernatural grace and knowledge into us. And therefore let these two go together. Know our riches in Christ, and know ourselves; know God in Christ, and Christ, and then our own baseness, and that is the way to make use of the treasure we have.

(6.) And likewise *meditate and recollect our thoughts daily of the vanity of all things here*, that our hearts run after so much. Alas, what is here we should stand so much upon as to neglect our treasure! what is here will induce the scanning of a wise man! what is worthy our spirits, our souls, our labours!

Let us wisely consider, and see through these things, and see beyond all things here, see them, and then see as much as we can into these treasures, which we can never see through, for they be larger than the soul. All other treasures are contained in a place, and the place larger than the treasure, but these riches be larger than the treasury. But see as far as we can into the dimension, and height, and depth, and breadth of these things, and seeing the vanity of all things below, the excellency of these things, using our wits this way, it will teach us how to improve this treasure.

I know these things be uncouth and strange to a carnal proud man, to advance things so much that they see not, to set such a price on things they understand not. But God is wiser than we, and if we take his word for truth, we must judge good, and conceive more than I relate to you. We must go to a skilful lapidary if we will know the price of a stone; and if we will know the price of a treasure, go to him that is able to judge. Consider not what vain foolish men think of God's ways, but ask God and Christ. Foolish creatures prize a bastardly coral more than a precious stone. So much of that doctrine.

To proceed to the next point. We are the treasurers. 'We have this treasure in earthen vessels,' we apostles and ministers. So that the riches of the gospel, they are conveyed under dispensations ministerial. And then the conditions of these, namely, 'they be earthen vessels.' God is so good that he not only conveyeth treasure to us, and giveth us rich promises, but he giveth us those that shall help us to come to the possession of, and interest in them. All the riches that we can desire are in Christ and from Christ, but then Christ must be acknowledged, and these treasures must be conveyed, and brought in; and therefore God hath ordained an ordinance to us by way of entreaty, by way of persuasion, and by all the ways the Spirit of God in Scripture useth. And hereupon the ministry of the word, from the excellent use of it, is set out many ways.

(1.) As it is with the lifting up of the brazen serpent, Num. xxi. 9, if it had not been lift up, they could not have seen it to have healed them. The ministry of the word sets up Christ that all may behold for the healing of all their spiritual diseases.†

(2.) It is the lifting up of a banner, that all may come under it. The gospel is this banner, as in Cant. ii. 4.

(3.) If treasures be never so rich and lie hid in the earth, there is no

* Qu. 'empty'?—Ed.

† A priceless expansion of Sibbes's thought will be found in John Brinsley's 'Mystical Brazen Serpent, with the magnetical virtue thereof.' (1653, 12mo.)—G.

use of them. Now therefore is a calling appointed to dig out treasures, to spread them before God's people, to lay before them 'the unsearchable riches of the gospel,' Eph. iii. 8. The use of the ministry is to lay them open to the view of God's people.

(4.) Christ hath a great love to his people, but we must have somebody to woo for him. The ministry is a wooing for Christ. It discovers the excellency of Christ, and our want, and need to be enriched by Christ. Therefore they be called παρανυμφίοι, 'friends of the bride,' to shew the riches of Christ, and the church's beggary, and so to procure the happy marriage between Christ and the church, John iii. 29, ὁ δὲ φίλος τοῦ νυμφίου. That is the use of the ministry, to handfast Christ and the church together, to make up the marriage, that so 'the church may be presented a chaste virgin to Christ, so glorious a husband,' 2 Cor. xi. 2. By them God sends his jewels and treasures to the church in this time of contract, as this world is but a time of contract between Christ and his church. As Abraham sent his servant to procure a marriage between Isaac and Rebekah, Gen. xxiv. 1, *seq.*, the faithful servant carrieth jewels to enrich her, and make her more lovely in Isaac's sight, when she was brought to him; so ministers carry those treasures, open these jewels to overcome the church, that seeing the riches in Christ, she may be more in love with Christ, so rich a husband.

(5.) The ministry is 'the salt of the world,' Mat. v. 13. Without salt, things putrify. So salt preserveth them, and eats out the corruption. It hath a cleansing, purifying power. What were the souls of God's people without it? Rotten and stinking in God's nostrils, with pride and self-conceitedness.

(6.) So we are called 'the light of the world,' Mat. v. 14. We are in darkness, and were not God's light held out, what were the world but an Egypt?* Nothing but palpable darkness. As in times of popery, when there was no ministry, but instead of it mass, and other empty things.

(7.) And therefore in the Revelations and other places they are compared to 'stars.' The church is as a firmament, and heaven. And antichrist, in opposition, is compared 'to earth.' And the 'stars in heaven' be those that be set to shine in the darkness of the night of the world, to give aim to others which way to walk.†

But I might be large in this. I only speak of it for a general use to us all, that we may better conceive of God's love, not only to give to his church rich treasures, but likewise a calling whereby these things may be unfolded to us, that our love and affection may be stirred up to them. And therefore, Eph. iv. 8, when Christ ascended to heaven in triumph, intending to leave the richest things in the world (as emperors and kings in triumph scatter gold and silver), 'he gave gifts to men.' What were these gifts? petty mean things? No. But 'some evangelists, some prophets, pastors and teachers,' Eph. iv. 11. And how long? 'To the end of the world,' ver. 13. Not only for the laying of the foundation of religion (as some will have the word only used to lay the foundation, and then to leave them to I know not what), but to edify and build them up more and more.

Therefore the greatest gift Christ in triumph will scatter to his church, is gifts, and men furnished with gifts for the service of the church, Jer. iii. ver. 15. When God promiseth to bless his people, he saith, 'I will give you pastors according to mine own heart,' as if that were a blessing of blessings. And therefore, they that live under the ministry of the gospel, let them

* Cf. Exod. x. 21.—G. † Cf. Rev. i. 16, 20, ii. 1, iii. 1, and xvi. 2.—G.

know the good things of the gospel are not only treasures, but the ordinances of God, wherein that treasure is conveyed, it is a treasure. We ministers carry this treasure in earthen vessels.

The church where means are, is as it were Goshen, a place of light, and all other places are places of darkness, Exod. x. 22, 23. How pitiful is it to live in places where means of salvation are not, that have no light shining in their hearts at all? I would enforce this point if I were to speak in another place, and to another auditory; but I cannot unfold my text without opening it in some degrees, and therefore we will hasten.

'We have these treasures in earthen vessels.'

The condition of all ministers, they be men, and carry these treasures in earthen vessels. In earthen vessels, in what sense?

First, It is true *fundamentally*. And for the matter whereof ministers and all other men consist, it is but earth.

Secondly, It is true of their *condition*. Earth is the basest of all elements, and they are counted of carnal foolish men, the basest callings of all. They be poor and despised, and thereupon 'earthen vessels' in the regard of the esteem of the world, and usage in the world. Earth in matter, earth in condition, earth in esteem, earth in usage suitable to their esteem, earthen vessels every way.

[1.] *For the matter whereof we consist, the foundation of all the rest.* It is the common condition of all. The rest are more peculiar to the ministers. We are all but 'earthen vessels.' You know the story of our creation, Gen. ii. 7. God made us of the earth; but if we had not sinned, though we had been made of the earth, we should never have been turned to the earth again, but our states should have been changed.

God's gracious power would have suspended that mortality which our nature of itself was subject to; for man being made of earth, was subject to have turned to earth again, though he had not sinned. But by the door and gate of sin, death entered into the world.

The angels were subject to fall as well as the devils, for every created thing is changeable, and so the angels, only God suspendeth that possibility of sin, and establisheth them in grace, but he withdrew his support from the devils and suffered them to fall. So man, if he had not sinned, God would have continued him in grace, that though mortal by nature, yet his mortality should have been so suspended, that the subjection to mortality should never have come to act. But since sin, the curse is on us, 'Of earth thou art, and to earth thou shalt return; dust thou art, and to dust thou shalt return,' Gen. iii. 19. We be all 'earthen vessels' in our original, and in our end, 'earth to earth, dust to dust;' as we say of ice, 'water thou art, and to water thou shalt return,' because it riseth of water, and is dissolved into water again. So a man that consisteth of earth, 'dust thou art, and to dust thou shalt return.' Thou shalt be resolved into thy first principle whereof thou wast made; so that we are but 'earthen vessels,' by reason of the curse inflicted on us since the fall.

[2.] An earthen vessel *is but a weak frame;* a little dirt concocted with the fire. And we are a more exquisite frame, knit together by a more singular art, of God, being made in a wonderful manner; and yet God compares his frame * of us to our frame * of earthen vessels, since the fall, Jer. xviii. 4.

Beloved, it is matter of experience which needeth no proof. I would we could make good use of it, rather than stand to prove it. Nothing is

* That is, 'framing.'—ED.

more apparent than the frailty of man, and yet nothing less made use of. 'The Lord remembers we are but dust,' Ps. ciii. 14, but we forget it. If we could remember we were dust, it were well, to make us less proud, and less presumptuous. The Lord knows we are but dust, to pity us, but we remember not that we are dust, to humble us. And therefore as God knows we are dust and earthen vessels, we should often think of it too, to make us humble and sober, and to take off our high thoughts from any excellency here.

And take heed lest by intemperance we break ourselves sooner than we should do. Many break themselves by intemperate courses, as candles that have thieves in them (*j*), as we say, that consume them before their ordinary time. So many by intemperate lusts and courses, they break the thread of their lives.

Indeed, let an earthen vessel be preserved never so, it will moulder to pieces, though it may be kept an hundred years, if preserved from knocks; so man will moulder of himself to an end; all the art and skill in the world cannot prevent it.

Yet notwithstanding there may be, and ought to be, care that we shorten not our own days, as many intemperate persons do, and that in sinful courses, which is more to be lamented.

Therefore let us often think of our condition, Jer. xviii. 2, 3, 4. God bids the prophet go to the potter's house and see his making of pots, and there he sees how he makes one to one use and another to another; and so we are but vessels of earth for several uses; and let us learn the use the prophet there was taught, to resign ourselves to God's dispensation. If he will make us longer or shorter, of this use or that use, let God have his will, and not quarrel with God; as the vessels never quarrel with the potter, who makes what vessels he pleaseth, and for what end he pleaseth, as the apostle makes use of it in the great point of predestination, Rom. ix. 23.

Use 1. And since the best ministers, magistrates, and all are but earthen vessels, *make what use we can of them while we have them.* Let us not rely on them. They be but 'earthen vessels;' but though we must not depend on them for our comfort, yet make use of them while we have them, for they may be knocked in pieces, we know not how soon, and then all the use we might have had is gone.

Use. 2. And to rise to a higher use, which concerneth us all, since ministers, kings, subjects, and all are but 'earthen vessels' in regard of the manner,* and seeing they may be golden vessels in regard of grace and glory, as the apostle saith, 'in a great house are vessels of gold and silver,' 2 Tim. ii. 20, *let us labour to have another manner of being than this, labour to be born again* of 'the immortal seed of the word,' 1 Peter i. 23, and then in death we shall live, then these 'earthen vessels' shall be made golden vessels for ever; for God's second work is a great deal better than his first. Now we be in the first creation 'earthen vessels,' but when God reneweth us out of dust again, if we get into Christ we shall be golden vessels in heaven for ever, born and begotten of the seed of the word; as the apostle Peter saith, 'All flesh is grass,' he compares us not only to earthen vessels, but to grass, of less substance than earthen vessels, 'but the word of the Lord endureth for ever,' 1 Peter i. 25.

Labour that we may be golden vessels under a golden head. If we be Christians we have a golden head, though earthen vessels; and having a golden head, he will make all conformable to him ere long. We shall have

* Qu. 'matter'?—ED.

bodies conformable to him, as Phil. iii. 21. He will make our earthen bodies, vile bodies, base bodies, like his glorious body, by the power whereby he is able to subject all things to himself.

And this comes by hearing the word of the Lord. That word is the seed of the new birth. 'O earth, earth, earth, hear the word of the Lord,' Jer. xxii. 29, and consider we be earth, earth, nothing but earth; for he repeats it thrice together, 'Hear the word of the Lord,' that we of earthen vessels may be made vessels of everlasting continuance.

Use 3. *And then it is no prejudice to us that we be earthen vessels, but rather a comfort;* for death, whereby we shall be knocked in pieces, will be only a consummation of our grief and trouble here, and a beginning of the happiness in another world. In the grave dust lieth a while, but we shall be made of another fashion, and receive another kind of stamp in the world to come.

Use 4. And, I beseech you, *forget not that which is the proper use of it for humility.* You may differ in outward relations, but you be all of one stuff. You be all earth; *judices terræ terram judicant,* the judges of the earth judge the earth. They judge other men that are earth, and they be earth themselves, and *filii terræ,* that is, base men. The sons of the earth, and men of the earth, that is, great men, that account all as grasshoppers in regard of themselves; though they be men and giants, yet they be but earth. We should all therefore labour to have low conceits of this life, and of all comforts of it, as Austin saith well, *Respice terram,* look to the dust; go to the grave and say, Here is the dust of the emperor, here is a rich man, here is a poor man; see if you can find them differ. Alas, no difference at all. Therefore make use of sobriety in regard of the use of things of this life, for we be all earthen vessels. And so much shall serve for this point.

But the apostle intendeth more than so, for he speaketh of their esteem; earthen vessels are not only broken, but contemptible. Look into the element, and you shall see every element and creature as the more light, it is more excellent, and as more earthly, it is more base, as the apostle before saith. We see now the water more lightsome than the earth, the air than the water, the fire more lightsome than it, and the element more pure than it, till we come to God himself, who is pure light. So everything as more light, is more excellent. What is the excellency of pearl? They have a sparkling light in them; but everything as it groweth near the earth is more base, for earth is the dregs of the world. Now ministers are more so than others, both in esteem and in usage, which followeth esteem. And what is the reason of it? Surely,

Reason 1. Because that the world *is foolish and childish, and liveth by sense and fancy; and the matters of the gospel and divine truths we speak of are spiritual things, matters of faith, far remote from sense and fancy, by which the world liveth.*

When we preach spiritual things, what are these to honours, and to riches, and to dependence, and to the goodly things of this world? Thus the fools of the world undervalue the things of God, especially when they be in their gawdes.* See a foolish man when he hath his riches, and clothes, and friends about him, his fancy is full of these things; tell him of spiritual things, what a loathing there is in the heart of a man! This is the proud carnal heart of a man, which the more carnal, the more it loatheth

* That is, gauds = trifles, toys, trumpery; and so the text means when fools are in the midst of their follies. Or is it gaudery = fine clothes?—G.

things of a higher nature, being besotted and drunken with worldly excellencies, as men's natures are.

Reason 2. Again, *divine truth is a solid thing*. Men naturally are given to superstitious conceits in religion. They will have one, but it shall be with this conceit or that conceit; as the apes, so they hug the brats of their own brains; they will have devices of their own. Religion is solid, and tells them this is God's way, and God's course; but the foolish heart of man will not yield to it. And that is the reason they cry down the solid things of God's word which have realities in them, and things to purpose. And then the world loveth their own courses, and are in love with their own way. Sin is a sweet morsel to them. Herodias is sweet to Herod. John Baptist was a good man till then, but when he meddled with that sweet morsel, then his head must off, Mat. xiv. 2, *seq.*, Mark vi. 28. And so when Christ opposed the worldly courses of the Scribes and Pharisees, he was counted a demoniac, a wine-bibber, and an enemy to Cæsar, and what not, when he took on him the office ministerial.* When Paul calleth himself an 'earthen vessel,' how did they use Paul? Tertullus, a prating orator, counteth him a pestilent fellow, Acts xxiv. 5. And his usage was base. They whipped him, put him into the dungeon. The Corinths, that were begotten by him, because he had not eloquence and gifts of ostentation, and fitting the stage, as their flaunting teachers had, they count him a mean person. The proud teachers brought him out of conceit with the Corinthians, and therefore he is fain to make apology for himself. 'He writes great letters indeed, but his presence is mean and base,' as in the 10th chapter of this Epistle, ver. 10.

There may be many reasons given why this calling is subject to base usage in the world, and esteem from the dispositions of men contrary to it, but indeed not much to follow the point. It is not so much at all times, nor in all places. God doth at some time give more liberty, and raise up a more excellent esteem of them than at other times; but ordinarily it is thus, the more faithful, the more despised of carnal people.

If you ask a reason what raised popery to be so gaudy as it is, they saw the people of the world fools, and knew that children must have baubles, and fools trifles, and empty men must have empty things; they saw what pleased them, and the cunning clergy thought, we will have religion fit for you. And because they would be somebody in the world, they devise a religion that is only outward, and such an one as dishonours God, by thinking him like to themselves, to delight in incense, and ornaments, and pictures, and the like; and hereupon came all the outside of popery, whereby they labour to ingratiate themselves to the world. They fool the world with all toys to please themselves, and they had suitable clergies: like lips, like lettuce; they had a religion suitable to their life. And hence came all that trash in popery to please the foolish heart of man. And because they will not be basely esteemed of, they get into the consciences of people by raising authority by false means and false conceits, that man can make his Maker, and turn bread into Christ's body by five words; and the pope cannot err, and whatsoever comes from him thou must obey, though with denied obedience to thy lawful prince; for they had seated themselves in the consciences of the people, and raised themselves by false means to avoid that which they saw would follow, the gospel. They knew the cross would follow the doctrine of the cross, the preaching of Christ crucified, and mortification and self-denial. And therefore they thought

* Cf. John vii. 20, Mat. xi. 19, John xix. 12.—G.

to take another way, and hence is all that forced respect they have in popery.

But it is clean contrary, where any that are won by God to the means, they have high esteems of it presently. As the jailor that had whipped and abused the apostles, Acts xvi. 33, used them very respectively,* and made them a feast. And so first [epistle of the] Cor. chap. xiv. 24, 25, When the simple man heareth the word open his sinful estate, he presently falls down at the apostles' feet, and saith, Certainly God is in you. No man is won by the blessed truth of God, but hath high conceits of the pure ordinances of God; and the more pure and close and home it is, the more he esteemeth of it. And therefore we may take an estimate of ourselves by our esteem of it.

A sanctified ear sheweth a sanctified heart, and a sanctified esteem of God's ordinance, as God's ordinance. From the power and virtue we find in it, working upon our souls, it is an argument we be wrought upon by the ministry; for though we be counted 'earthen vessels,' by base earthly-minded men, yet they that be wrought upon have other estimations of us.

Their calling is to bring men's souls to heaven, to be saviours of the people, to be God's own name, to be fathers. It is a calling that the angels may stoop under it. 'Who is sufficient for these things?' 2 Cor. ii. 16, and yet the base slight it; but I say, respect must not be won by forced means, as in popery, but by opening the mysteries of God, and the Spirit accompanying the outward ministry. This will work so effectually in the heart, as will raise the heart to a high esteem of these things, from the blessed experience they find of the Spirit of God working in them. But that will appear more in the next, where he saith, God's end of conveying heavenly things by earthen vessels is, that the excellency of the power may be of God, and not of man.

The first part of the verse we have unfolded, and have shewed,

1. That the gospel is 'a treasure.'
2. The 'treasurers,' they be the 'apostles and ministers.'

And then, 3. The 'vessels.' We carry it in 'earthen vessels,' earthly vessels for the matter and for their esteem.

Of this I will only say, that which concerneth every man.

1. *It is not a severed condition, it is the condition of all.* To be earth of itself is no such base condition. That it is a word of disgrace and frailty, it is from sin. For howsoever we be earthy, and of nothing, and so might fall to nothing, yet God would have suspended the inclination of the creature, which is prone to turn to its original, which is nothing, if Adam had not sinned. The heavens are made of nothing, and yet still continue their condition, because God preserveth them. And the angels made of nothing, and are subject to fall to nothing, as the angels that fell, they might have fallen. And they stand not by any strength of their own, but God's grace suspendeth that possibility of falling to nothing, and confirmeth them in that blessed condition. And so the baseness of the earthen vessels is from sin.

2. And add this by the way, *see the marvellous power of God.* At first, all things were nothing at all, then they were a chaos, a confused mass; out of a confused mass comes a heaven and earth, and all the creatures. Man himself falleth, and becomes worse than nothing, having sinned; and to be delivered out of that miserable condition he must be a new creature. Of an earthen vessel he makes him a vessel of glory, and never leaveth him

* That is, 'respectfully.'—G.

till he be settled in a blessed everlasting condition. So that God brings man from nothing, and worse than nothing, to a blessed and glorious condition.

Let us often think of it, that we be earthen vessels. It is a strange thing that God hath joined body and soul together, which are so wonderfully different, the soul being spiritual, the body earthly. But that he hath joined this spirit with a sinful polluted soul, that is more wonderful. But to join the Godhead with earth, that the Virgin Mary being an 'earthen vessel,' should have Christ made of her substance, that he should set his own stamp and image in a piece of earth, and take a piece of earth into union of his person, that earth should be joined with God, here is a wonder of wonders.

3. Therefore *let it tend to our humiliation*, that we be but earthen vessels: and keep us in terms of subjection, that we dash not against God, being but earthen vessels; for he hath iron sceptres for proud earth, to dash them all to pieces, Ps. ii. 9.

4. *Let us be thankful for our protection and preservation*, being earthly vessels. In the last visitation, how many of these earthen vessels were dashed to pieces in one day?* Beyond the seas, in the wars, how many dashed together in a moment? We be so frail, that if the like judgment fall on us, we turn to nothing. We are proud, womanish, and lewd, and have high thoughts, as if not 'earthen vessels;' and therefore it is a great mercy that we have been thus long preserved.

As ministers are earthen vessels, so magistrates and great men. Their souls be knit to their bodies by no sounder bonds than the meanest man's. There is as little combination, and as weak, between the strongest and greatest men in the world, as between the poorest.

5. But as it concerneth ministers especially, let me make one use further to the people that are in any relation to the ministry or magistracy, *that we do not refuse the treasure for the weakness or infirmity of the vessel.* Elias had meat brought to him by a raven; did he refuse it because so poor a creature brought him his meat? 1 Kings xvii. 6. No. But took it as a special blessing of God that he had meat at all, sent from God, to refresh him in his weariness, and therefore stands not upon the vessel, but marks the treasure whence that came. Who would refuse a pardon, because he that bringeth it may be meaner than himself? Look to the prince's hand and seal. Is it a sealed truth? Doth conscience bear witness to it, being God's privy seal? It is no matter who bringeth it. Magnify God's ordinances, that not only giveth pardon, but giveth likewise a messenger to bring it. Therefore bless God rather for his ordinances, than stumble at the weakness of his ministers.

It is no matter what the hand is, if it give a treasure. We be wise in the things of this life, and so should we be in heavenly things, considering God doth this in a wise and gracious dispensation, condescending to our weakness. We bear no proportion to messengers of an higher nature. If we cannot endure the sight of an angel, we cannot endure God himself. You know the history of Moses.† And therefore seeing God hath thus stooped to us, yield thankfully to this weak dispensation, that God conveyeth spiritual things to man by man.

Now what is the end of all this? 'that the excellency of the power may be of God, and not of us.' Wherein are these things observable.

* In margin here, 'The last great plague, anno Dom. 1624.'—G.

† Cf. Exod. xxxiii. 11; Deut. xxxiv. 10.—G.

First, *That there is a power in the ministry and dispensation of the gospel, and an excellent power.* The apostle cannot enlarge himself enough here, when he enters upon the argument of commending the gospel.

Secondly, This power, and excellency of power, it is of God, and not of man.

Thirdly, And that this may appear to be so, he useth the ministry of weak men, and earthen vessels, *that by the disproportion between the excellency of the things and earthen vessels, they may know if any good be done, it comes from him who is the highest cause of all conversion of the soul.* To bring the soul out of Satan's kingdom to the liberty of God's children, to be heirs of heaven, is so far above 'earthen vessels,' that it must needs appear to be God's work.

Doct. For the former, we shall put them both together, *that there is an excellent power in the ordinances of God, as it is dispensed under the gospel.* The Word itself, what power hath it? Are not all things by the Word in creation? Nay, is not the vigour and strength that every creature hath from the same Word? Is not the being and efficacy of all things, and the continuance of things, from the Word? As Heb. i. 3, φέρων τε τὰ πάντα τῷ ῥήματι τῆς δυνάμεως αὐτοῦ, He upholds all things by his mighty power and word. Whence comes the support and continuance of the vigour of every creature, but from God? Who doth cause the sun to shine, and to give light to inferior things, that they may bring forth fruit, for the use of every creature?

And why is the sea, that vast and unruly creature, kept within its bounds that it cannot go an inch farther; is it not God's commanding words? At first God created it, and God made bounds that it cannot go beyond its due compass. Is not an eternal law set upon every creature by the word? This you are, this is your virtue, this is the extent of it, thus far you shall go, and no farther. 'God sent forth his word,' saith the psalmist, 'and they were created,' Ps. cxlviii. 8. I speak it but by way of illustration of the point in hand. And so the excellency of the power in the great work of redemption and salvation of man is from the word, as it will appear in particulars.

(1.) *What a large power is put forth in the conversion of a man.* For is it not the bringing a man out of Satan's kingdom into the kingdom of Christ? Col. i. 13. And will Satan let a man go willingly? Is not conversion a world of miracles? How many miracles hath that one work of conversion? It was a miracle when the blind man saw, and the deaf man had his hearing restored, when the dumb man began to speak, he that had his feet together so that he could not enlarge himself, to be able to run. But to give life to a dead man is a miracle indeed.

Now in the conversion of a sinner by the ordinance of God and the Spirit accompanying it, all these are in one; for what is conversion but the opening of the sight of the soul to see its misery by nature, and a better condition in Christ than ever; and the opening of the ear to hear and to taste heavenly discourse in another manner than before? What is it but restoring feet to run [in] God's commandments, to delight in the ways that were tedious before, and that the mouth that was used to swear and to curse, in the language of hell before, now do set forth the praises of God. Is there not a world of wonders in one work? Therefore there is a power, and an excellent power, put forth in conversion. Whatsoever Christ did in the gospel to the body, that he doth to the soul in conversion, and there is greater power put forth in the one than in the other.

To enter into the heart of man, that fenceth itself against all goodness, 'to pull down strongholds, high imaginations,' 2 Cor. x. 4, rebellious oppositions against God and goodness—do not you see daily such spirits under the gospel? Do but guess therefore what is in the whole mankind. What was it when Christ sent his apostles into the world? He sent his word accompanied with his Spirit, and that word should enter into the hearts of men, and cast all the proud, high, lofty imaginations, and lay all flat before Christ. 'Men and brethren, what shall we do?' Acts ii. 37. We have been vile wretches, and now we are convinced of it. Is not the word powerful to turn a man out of himself, clean to dash him to pieces, and then to make him up new again better than ever he was? This is power indeed.

There is an excellent power in the word. First, in the ministers themselves; and secondly, by them to the people.

[1.] *There is an excellency of power to make them fit for the work, and then to go along with them in the working others' conversion.* A great power wrought on Paul, and Peter, and the rest, and a great power wrought by them on all the rest. But because I speak not to ministers, but as it concerneth all, we will speak of the power in general.

[2.] I might be very large in shewing the power of the ministry *from the success of it.* Look into the history of the church, mark Christ's time, the apostles' time, that strange fishermen, and men of low conditions, being furnished with commissions from heaven, and carried these treasures in earthen vessels; see what wonders they wrought in the world by spreading the sweet savour of the gospel. The fishermen cast their great nets into the great world, as Austin saith, and got in whole nations (*k*). And therefore Saint Paul magnificently speaks for himself and the rest of the apostles. 'I am not ashamed of the gospel of our Lord Jesus Christ, for it is the power of God unto salvation,' Rom. i. 16. As Isa. liii. 1, 'To whom is the Lord revealed and made bare?' as the word signifieth. That is, to whom is the power of the word in the ministry made bare? The ministry is the arm of God, whereby he pulleth man out of Satan's kingdom. Now God the Father draweth them to Christ in spite of corruption, in spite of sin and Satan, into his own kingdom. The cross was then set above princes' crowns, the greatest emperors that were, submitted themselves to the sceptre of Jesus Christ, and laid down their crowns at his feet. In the ten persecutions,* was there not mighty power of the gospel, that when it had catched the hearts of women, young men, old men, or children, all conditions, all the fire, all the torments that tyrants could devise, could not get Christ out of their hearts, but they were willing to sacrifice their lives, and found more comfort in the blessed gospel of Jesus Christ, that all the discouragements in the world could not make them forsake him. Such a fire was rooted in their hearts by the fire of God's word, that made them not care for all other fires whatsoever. Where this excellency of the power of the word appears in any, it armeth them against all oppositions whatsoever.

3. *We will shew the powerful work of the word in some branches of it.*

(1.) *That there is an excellency of power that enables a man against his own corruptions, against temptations from Satan, from the world, sometimes from God himself in a way of trial.* But this ordinance having God's Spirit accompanying it, enables a man against corruption, the most bosom corruptions, against all temptations whatsoever. It makes a man do that which

* For notice and list of these persecutions cf. Vol. I. page 384.—G.

is clean contrary to his nature. It will turn Jordan back, to make of Mary, a light woman, a blessed woman; to make of Paul a persecutor, Paul a preacher, to be able to subdue corruptions when they rise, that great persons lie under, to subdue their carnal wills. We see great persons are led by their wills, and countenanced by him that rules their wills, the evil spirit, and so they run rushing on, the devil joining with them, to destruction. The Christian having the power of the word and Spirit crossing his will, he is able to deny himself; and what an excellent power is that! Is it not an excellent power? Now the word giveth us strength and comfort against temptations to sin and for sin; and whether they come from Satan or from God, shewing himself an enemy. The word teacheth how to oppose God himself, when he personates an enemy, as sometimes he doth. A poor Christian then can say, Lord, remember thy promise. Thou seemest to be mine enemy, and 'writest bitter things against me;' but I believe not thou art an enemy, thou hast made rich promises, and remember them, Lord, wherein thou hast caused me to trust, Ps. cxix. 49. God is content to be bound by his word; and is not that powerful that can bind God himself, when we can sue him by his bond? Thou seemest to be mine enemy, but I will not away, I will lie at thy feet till I hear comfortable news from heaven.

For temptations on the right hand, allurements and promises, and on the left, as threats and afflictions and the like, the word sets other matters before us than these; and the word enables us to all kind of duty. A man that is tongue-tied, it enables him to call on God; and a man that hath naturally nothing to speak that is good, it enables him to speak a word of comfort to others; it enableth him to every duty that God calls him to, to trust him, and to love him above all; it enables him to live well and to die well, to perform all duties God requires. The word with the Spirit enables us to manage all in a spiritual manner.

(2.) And so *for bearing afflictions*, how doth the psalmist speak in the Old Test[ament]? The word will direct and comfort for the carrying on of our souls in troubles of all sorts; as David, 'I had perished in mine affliction, if it had not been for thy word,' Ps. cxix. 92. No affliction can befall us but we have grand comforts to support us in it, when God hath promised his gracious assistance, that he will not fail us nor forsake us, when the sting is taken out by him that hath sanctified all afflictions in his own person, that as our crosses increase, so our comforts and consolation shall increase. And the afflictions of this world are not worthy the excellency that shall be revealed.

Then no wonder there is that strength in the word that it enables us to duties of our calling, public and private; it enables us to bear afflictions. And therefore the apostle may well say, 'That the excellency of the power may be of God, and not of us.'

(3.) And so *to enjoy all things that God giveth in a right manner*. The word with the Spirit teacheth how to use the world as if not, to enjoy it as helps in our pilgrimage and way to heaven, that they be not snares to us, as they be to carnal men, who perish in these things, as wasps on gallypots.

They are drowned in riches, and drowned in pleasures, but the word and the Spirit directs the children of God to use these things in an holy and sanctified manner, and to taste them as they ought, which no man can do but they that have the word engrafted by the Spirit in their hearts.

And there is a great reason; for what doth this word oppose? Doth it not oppose greater things than the world hath? What is all preferment here to heaven? And what is all discouragement of tyrants to hell? If any one saw the joys of heaven, would not he forsake ten thousand worlds rather than lose it? If a man saw with his eyes hell opened to swallow him up if he did not alter his courses, would not he leave his courses? Now, the Lord saith, it is true that these things shall be. Let a power go with the word, and is it a wonder that he will leave his sinful courses rather than have a curse? It is no wonder that Moses should leave 'the pleasures of a court, that saw him that was invisible,' Heb. xi. 26; and that Paul, that was lift up to the 'third heaven,' and saw things that could not be uttered, 2 Cor. xii. 4, regarded not the threats of all tyrants, for he saw the right difference of things, he saw things in their right colours. So if the Lord lets us see spiritual things and earthly things in their colours, one will appear to be realities indeed, and other to be nothing but vanity. It is for want of faith and power accompanying the ordinance of God, to persuade ourselves that these things be as they are, and as we shall undoubtedly find them another day. And therefore it is no wonder the gospel findeth such power, where it is received and obeyed, because of the vast difference of conditions.

I beseech you, let us consider these things, and not be led away with a spirit of vanity and folly and error. So that there is a power, and an excellency of power, in the ministry; and you that have open understandings in the history of the church, know how it hath powerfully wrought in all times.

Quest. How do you know the word to be the word?

Ans. It carrieth proof and evidence in itself. It is an evidence that the fire is hot to him that feeleth it, and that the sun shineth to him that looks on it; how much more doth the word, that carrieth its own character and stamp with it, to them that be God's people; for it not only giveth light, but giveth that which is more than the sun can do. And that giveth light, but no eyes. The word giveth understanding to the simple, opens their eyes, Ps. cxix. 130; and a Christian can say, God hath not only shined upon me by the word, but hath wrought in my heart by it; so that in it I will live, and in it I will die. So that they need not seek arguments, for the word itself is stronger than all framed arguments. It hath a character of divine truth stamped upon it, in the heart of every believer, that mingleth it with faith that it is the word, though all the world preach the contrary, and the ministers that teach it apostatize from it. I am sure I felt it, it warmed my heart, and converted me. And that is the best trial of the word to be the word, because of the efficacy felt in the heart.

That Spirit that makes the word effectual, doth by that efficacy convince the soul that the word is the word. For the soul reasons thus: I have found this word casting me down, I have found this word lifting me up; I have found this word warming my heart when it was cold and dead. I found it enlarging my heart in loving God and praising God. I have found the Spirit of God in the word casting down strongholds, and Satan out of me, and setting up his kingdom in me, and ruling me by his Spirit, that I cannot but do what was irksome to me before, and can abstain from that which was sweet to me before; and all because I am convinced of another course than before. The soul that can say thus, if objections come, he defieth the motion. My soul hath felt the strength of the word taking root downwards, bringing forth fruit upwards, 2 Kings xix. 30, and shall I doubt it to be the word? But to leave this.

Application. I beseech you, if there be such efficacy in the word, make a use of instruction of it, that we regard it more than we have done.

Use 1. And first of all, that we may make way for instruction, do but examine ourselves *whether it be as a word of power to us, or any that have lived so long under the gospel?* The trial is very easy.

[1.] If it be a word of power to us, *certainly it will enable us to defend it, and maintain it in the worst times.* St Paul saith, 1 Thes. i. 5, 'You received the word in much affliction.' If we should live in places where holy things are disclaimed and abandoned with Ishmael's persecutions, that is, the persecutions of these times, scoffings and scornings, yet hearing divine things unfolded, we receive them, and entertain them, and that with joy and comfort, with an opposition to the poison of the times, it is a good sign that the power of the word hath caught every one of our hearts. But if every taunt of Ishmael and poisonful spirits be regarded, when in times of poverty a little thing will discourage us and make us flinch, where is the power? Alas! whatsoever profession we make, we deny the power of it; for if it did work upon us, we should receive it, in the midst of opposition, with joy and comfort.

(2.) The apostle saith in another place, 'Receive the word, as the word of God,' 1 Thes. ii. 13. Now if a man receive divine truths, he will acknowledge that it is a word of power, and excellent power. What is it then to receive the word as the word? To receive divine truths with a great deal of reverence, as blessed truths, that come from the bosom of God, and likewise with a great deal of subjection, submitting the soul to them. It is God's truth delivered by Jesus Christ in the ministers, and therefore I do receive it as God's truth, and submit my conscience to it. Though there be discovery of some rebellion, yet if I allow of no risings against the power of the word, it is a sign we have felt the power of the word, when we regard it as the word.

You see then some particular evidence how we may know if the word hath wrought upon us.

Add the particulars named before, by way of trial.

(3.) *What power have you to help you against temptations?* What power have you against temptations from the word and divine truth? What power have you to bear crosses, and afflictions, to comfort you in sickness, losses, and crosses in the world? Can you fetch comfort from truths heard and read out of this book of God's word? It is a sign then that the Spirit of God, with the word, hath wrought a blessed change in your hearts. Can you use the world moderately? Can you perform duties in a spiritual manner? Undoubtedly, you may comfort yourselves, though with much conflicts and oppositions, both without and within.

If on trial we find these things not so, I beseech you own * not yourselves one minute of an hour, for that minute may be the minute of our destruction, and may cut off the thread of our lives. Rest not one minute, for howsoever we may bless ourselves, as all proud hearts do against God, and the ordinances of God, and godly ways, in a scorn, as if they had a heart distinct from God and the word, and needed not to be beholding to God for direction.† They can go home, and there they have means and friends, and they can do well enough. God sets himself to laugh at the destruction of such; and that word that they cast behind them, and would have nothing to do withal, now that will stick by them to the hour of death, and they shall carry it with them in their own consciences to hell, and their

* That is, do not regard yourselves as Christians.—Ed.

† The sentence is left thus unfinished. Cf. 'To the Reader,' Vol. I. p. 38.—G.

consciences shall say, God told these truths to thee, and I told them to thee; I heard this from God's word, and thou regardedst me not. And therefore when your consciences be awakened with divine truths, know, that conscience shall be one day revived, and you shall hear it. What you now slight, you shall regard. You regard now no command, no duty, but you shall think of them when it is too late. Therefore seeing this is the time, labour to find the power of God in the heart, rest not.

But how shall we carry ourselves, so that the word may be effectual to us?

[1.] *Labour to have humble, teachable souls*, attending on God's divine dispensation in his ordinances meekly. You know what David saith, Ps. xxv. 9, 'The humble he will teach.' Come with teachable hearts, and God will reveal mysteries to us. He will teach secrets, so that we shall say, I never thought there had been such light, such sweetness in the word. Come with humble souls, and you shall find him opening the secrets of heaven, especially if you desire the Lord to give the Spirit of revelation, and to take off this veil of darkness and corruption, that he would back his Spirit with his own ordinance,* and make it effectual, that as things are in themselves holy, and heavenly, and excellent, and as they are to God's children, so they may be to us. God's word is a word of power to all elect children. Oh that I might find it a word of power to me! that I might get myself to be God's elected child.

[2.] *Join with the means a spirit of prayer*, as God shall enable you, and 'to him that hath shall be given,' Mat. xiii. 12. Labour to wait for this. If God speak not at first, the good hour is not yet come; wait till the waters be stirred, as it was in the pool of Bethesda, John v. 3. Wait till he give the Spirit of revelation, and at length we shall find such a change as Isaiah speaks of, 'The lion and the lamb shall dwell together, and the leopard and the kid, for the earth shall be full of the knowledge of the Lord,' xi. 6. The knowledge of the Lord maketh lions lambs, and leopards kids, makes them fit to live together, though their dispositions be never so cross. If we have grace to wait God's leisure, we shall find a transforming, changing power in the word to alter us perfectly, and to mould us to a holy frame of spirit.

The apostle, as we heard heretofore, laboureth in the former chapter, as likewise in this, to set out the dignity of the ministry of the gospel above the ministry of the law, and answereth, as we have heard, all objections; and lest he should seem to savour of too high a spirit, as Saint Paul to attribute so much to his ministry, in the sixth verse, he giveth all to God; 'God who commanded light to shine out of darkness, hath shined in our hearts.' So that whatsoever light is conveyed by the ministry, is conveyed by God, and by an almighty power in God, even by the same that was used in the creation, and in some sort above it. Now the end of the knowledge kindled in the heart especially of the ministers is, 'that the light of the knowledge of the glory of God may be seen in the face of Jesus Christ.' God shineth on the ministers, not only upon their understandings, but upon their hearts; and to what end? Not to shine in ourselves only, but to reflect the light, whereby God shineth upon us, to others. Then he shews the end of the ministry is especially to set out God in Christ, and the glorious mercy and goodness and bounty of God in Christ Jesus.

* Qu. 'with his Spirit his own ordinance'?—Ed.

And what is the end of this? That God will have such an excellent treasure, as is in the dispensing of the mysteries of Christ, out of earthen vessels, that the excellency of the power may be of God and not of us.

Wherein is considerable, first of all, that there is a power, and an excellency of the power, in the sweet truths of God, discovered in the gospel, especially in the dispensation of it by weak vessels; so powerful, so excellently powerful it is, that it may be known that it is of God. It is of God, but that it may 'appear to be of God;' for things are said to be when they appear in regard of men. Now that it may appear to all, that the power and efficacy of the ministry of the gospel is of God, and not of man, God would have such a disproportion between the vessels and the treasure. The treasure shall be rich and heavenly, the vessels shall be earthly, that whatsoever is good, it may appear it cometh not from the vessels, but from the treasure itself.

That there is a power, and excellent power, in the truths of God, especially dispensed by the ministry, we have in part shewed heretofore, but we will follow the point. God hath furnished everything in the world with power. Every creature hath power, together with being. The heavens have a power of influence; the dull earth hath a power to put forth what it receiveth from the influence of heaven, into this and that creature, being the common mother of many excellent things, but all the power is from God. God hath put a power into the creatures, which we call an eternal law. Besides the law made to man, there is a statute given to the creature. Heaven shall move, and by moving limit time, and heaven shall bestow influence upon inferior bodies. There is a law for the sea that it shall ebb and flow, and not pass the bounds God hath set it; and by the law of God there is a centre immoveable on which the earth shall stand. These keep the statutes and the laws that God hath given them eternally. God to shew a miracle can make the sun stand still, or the earth move, or the sea to overflow. But the power we are to speak of is another manner of power, a spiritual power, and excellency of power.

There is a power, then, in the ordinance of God, and a spiritual power. There is in every ordinance of God something that hath an heavenly relish. There is in the word, in the sacraments, that that maketh a heavenly relish. And God, by the word and the ministry, doth create spiritual sense suitable to the relish that is in spiritual things. Had we not by the word created in us spiritual sense to relish those heavenly things in the ordinances, they were to no purpose; God should lose his glory, and man should lose his benefit thereof. God createth spiritual eyes to see, and spiritual taste connatural and homogeneal to spiritual things. As there is a sweet taste in the word, so God altereth the taste of the soul, that the word should be found better than the appointed food, sweeter than the honey-comb. Nothing so sweet as divine promises to a sanctified soul; because God, that hath put a sweet taste into the ordinances, altereth the relish of the soul, the taste, and sight, and spiritual feeling of all divine truths. The spiritual heart feeleth the comforts of the sacrament in strengthening faith, and tasteth the goodness of God in Christ in giving his body and shedding his blood, so that there is a relish and virtue in the things themselves, and by them the soul is fitted to take the benefit that is hidden in the things.

There is in divine ordinances not only a light to convince, but likewise a power, together with the light, to open the eyes. There is light and power to open the eyes of the soul together. What if all were light? If there were not the eye to see, the light would be of no use at all. There is power in the ordinances not only to offer light, but it hath a spirit accompanying it to open the eyes of the soul to see that light, so that there is extraordinary power in God's ordinances. What light can give sight, and what meat can give relish to him that wanteth it? There is therefore an excellent power in the ordinances.

Now, there is a power *φυσει et φήσει*, there is a power of a thing in nature, and there is a power by institution. Now the power of the ordinances and the ministry is drawn from God's institution, who hath appointed it and sanctified it to have such power, where he will accompany them with his Holy Spirit.

Now this power that is in the ordinances of God, it is set out and illustrated by many speeches and comparisons that are very clear and excellent for that purpose.

(1.) As the word and ministry is called '*the salt*,' Luke xiv. 34. Now the power of salt is to season, to make sweet, to relish, to consume the superfluous humours, to preserve, and keep long. So the word hath the power of salt to eat out the corruptions, and to preserve the soul to make it relish God. The souls of men, without divine truths accompanying them, they are, to speak with reverence, but carrion souls and dead souls, ever stinking in the nostrils of God; howsoever they bear it out in the world to be godly persons, yet if they have not souls sanctified by divine truths, they have but rotten hearts, and are good for nothing.

(2.) The dispensing of it is compared to '*the arm of God*.' Isa. liii. 1, 'To whom is the arm of the Lord revealed?' Now a man's power is in his arm. The ordinance is not only 'the finger of God,' but 'the arm of God' to pull men out of Satan's kingdom and their wicked courses, by shewing them the vengeance of God, and better things than the world can, or Satan can. The word, the power of the Spirit accompanying it, is the arm of God 'made bare,' as the word signifieth in the original.* God revealeth and maketh bare his arm in the ministry when he pulleth men out of Satan's kingdom and their wicked courses.

(3.) And so likewise the truth of God in the dispensation of it is the '*sword of the Spirit*,' Eph. vi. 7, and cuts on both sides. It is no leaden dagger, as the papists blasphemously term it (*l*). It hath a force in it to cut as it goeth, and they shall feel it one day that will not feel it now; and therefore it is compared, together with the Spirit, '*to wind*,' which hath a mighty power to carry and transport things, John iii. 8.

(4.) And the ministers of God's holy truths, in regard of the efficacy of the ministry, have excellent terms. They are,

[1.] 'Stars,' because they give light, Rev. i. 16.

[2.] They are 'ambassadors,' as they have commission from God, Luke ix. 2.

[3.] They are, in regard of the excellency of the truth, 'angels,' Rev. ii. 1.

[4.] They are, in respect of the necessity of God's people, 'saviours.' So were Moses and Joshua.

God saveth by the ministry ordinarily those whom he doth save; so that there is a power and efficacy of power in the ministry, as appears by the terms by which it is set out.

(5.) Again, God is able to give efficacy to whatsoever he will. As he giveth power to every creature according to its own natural working, so he

* In margin here—'נִגְלָתָה Nigletah (*sic*) from Galah *manifestatus fuit; de* revelatione absconditorum propriè dicitur.'—Amos iii. 7.—G.

giveth power to those things that have institution from him. He is able to do it, to make them effectual for the end for which he hath appointed them, for he is the supreme power himself. All power is resident in him as the head; and therefore he furnisheth and clotheth this ordinance of his with a power.

(6.) The word is compared to 'seed,' Mat. xiii. 3, *seq*. Now, in seed there is a power to put forth itself, to grow and breed seed like itself, and it will break through clods till it comes to its ripeness and maturity. So there is a power in the word. When it is so in the believer's heart, it will bring forth a disposition like itself, as seed doth. As it is a holy word and a pure word, it will make the heart that receiveth it suitable. Therefore James* calleth it the 'engrafted word,' James i. 4, comparing divine truths to a syance† engrafted into a plant, that turns the juice of the plant into its own nature. So when the word is engrafted, it altereth the heart, that the inward man doth relish of divine things, thinketh in power of what he heareth, and speaks in power of what he heareth, and understandeth, and worketh, and doth in power of what he knoweth; so that divine truth is like a syance† engrafted into the heart. Therefore there is a power, and an excellency of power in it, not only in truth itself, but in the dispensation of it. God setteth not up an ordinance but he giveth a blessing upon it. There is an excellency of power as a power. Is there not a power and excellency of power to level mountains and to fill up valleys? It filleth the valleys. Poor dejected souls are filled with comfort. Is there not power and excellency of power to make a camel to go through a needle's eye? That is, to strip a man of self-conceitedness of his own worth, so far that being a camel, a swelling person before, he shall now be humble and low in his own sight. It is difficult as for a camel, so for a cable too (*m*). There needeth much extenuation to make a cable to go through a needle's eye, and much to humble a Christian; and is not this an excellent power? Sure it is. Therefore there is a power, and an excellency of power.

I will shew you this in particular.

1. The power of the ordinance of God is first seen in that *it discovers to men their natural conditions*, sheweth what they are by nature; for which end it useth the law, to shew that we be dead men, carnal men, under a fearful bondage, and the Spirit going along with it, convinceth the soul that we are dead, and thereupon the soul is amazed and cast down with fear and terror.

2. And then the word hath a power likewise *to shew and discover the mercies of God in Christ Jesus*, to pull us out of Satan's kingdom, to drive the strong man out of our hearts by higher reasons, by higher comforts, Mat. xii. 29.

3. And then the word, together with the ministry of the Spirit, *hath a converting power*, a changing power, to alter the very frame of the soul. All the words in the world, all philosophy, all education, all the best helps that can be given, cannot stamp the image of God upon the soul, or frame holiness in the soul, but only the blessed truth of God, especially in the dispensation of it. So that the image of Christ in the 'second Adam' is stamped upon the soul, by the Spirit accompanying the ordinance.

And when the Spirit of God in the ordinance hath set a stamp of holiness in the soul, and made it like to Christ, it worketh in the soul, and by the soul. When the soul is altered and changed, it is a fit instrument of the

* Misprinted Paul.—G. † That is, scion = graff.—G.

Spirit, together with the ordinance, to pray, to do any service, to trust in God, to love God.

4. And to shew more particularly wherein the power of God's word is seen *after conversion*, I will shew it in four or five particulars.

(1.) First of all, when it hath altered and changed men's frame, and pulled them out of Satan's kingdom, it is seen *in enabling them to perform duty in a right manner*, which a natural man cannot reach unto; as the soul altered by the power of the word and Spirit, can love God, can deny itself, can hate that it formerly loved, can pray—which no carnal man can do—can have communion with God, can perform spiritual duties and actions above the rank of nature. This the Spirit of God, together with the ordinance, raiseth the soul to do. A man may do many things that a Christian man doth, a common Christian may do many things that a sincere Christian doth, but self-respect* enters into all he doth. He doth it either of slavish fear and terror, or to be thought well of, or to redeem some inward quiet to his tormented conscience; but he hath not the Spirit of God altering the relish of his soul, to love divine truths, and out of love and obedience to do what he doth. An holy man, if there were no enforcement out of God's word, he loveth the truth because it is truth, and hath a suitableness to his sense. If there were no hell, no torment at all, yet there is that excellency in divine truths, his soul being altered and changed suitable to divine truths, that he obeyeth heavenly truths out of love to heavenly truths, and obeyeth God out of love to God, because it is best in his judgment to do so, and not only out of fear, though that is a useful way too.

(2.) Again, as there is a power enabling a man to do, so there is a power in the word enabling a man *to resist temptation*; for the word breedeth faith, and faith knitteth the soul to Christ, and draweth virtue from him to resist Satan. By faith we overcome the world, temptations of honours, pleasures, temptations from within and from without. The Spirit of God working faith to lay hold on better things, enableth us to resist all temptations on the right and on the left hand. 'This is your victory, even your faith,' 1 John v. 4. 'Faith cometh by hearing,' Rom. x. 11. Faith presenteth to the soul such excellent good things, such terrible evil things, that it overpowereth the soul to embrace better good, and to avoid greater evil, notwithstanding all temptations from the world. The good the world affordeth is nothing so good, and for the evil there is nothing so evil. Now faith apprehending this by divine light, it overcometh the world.

(3.) And as the power is seen in enabling to do duties above another man, and enabling to resist temptations, so likewise it is seen *in shewing our corruptions that we be naturally prone to*. A man by the power of grace is so altered that he falleth out with his most beloved sins, and laboureth to get strength against that above all other sins. The word maketh division between his Spirit and sin. Jordan is driven back with him. That stream of nature that was carried amain one way, now is carried another way. Though he hath corruptions which sometimes foil him, yet faith getteth spiritual strength, whereby he at last not only subdueth them, but at last expelleth them; and therefore the Scripture calls it self-denial. He hath a self that denieth itself, he hath a self wrought by the Spirit and word, by which he denieth himself, that is, his carnal self, Titus ii. 12. When his corruptions would have such a thing, his other self saith no, it shall not be; when it stirreth him up to revenge, no, it shall not be. I owe no

* That is, respect to self.—G.

service to my flesh. And he hath a principle in him, whereby he subdueth what before was wonderfully powerful in him, which setteth him above himself.

(4.) There is a power, and excellency of power, in the word, *to comfort us, to raise the soul in all dejections, in all discomforts.* Therefore it is called 'the word of faith,' 1 Tim. iv. 6, an instrument to beget faith in the promises. Faith relieth upon better things, and sets the soul above all inferior things. And so for comfort, it setteth the soul upon a rock, higher than all trouble; it setteth the soul upon God's infinite goodness and power and truth, and promises; it setteth the soul upon the things promised, heaven and happiness to come. What are these things to the glory to come? So faith carrieth the soul to heaven, to God, to Christ, to the promises; it pitcheth the soul upon such a foundation, as no discomforts here below can shake the soul; it is above the reach of any trouble. A soul that pitcheth itself on the word and Spirit of God, and so upon God himself (for God and his word are one), it is above the reach of all discomforts whatsoever, so far as it believeth; and therefore it comforteth a man. The comforts of God's word, having the Spirit of God with them, are called 'the consolations of the Almighty.' 'Despisest thou the consolations of the Almighty?' Job xv. 11. We will instance a little in a few promises. Let the soul be in want, it pitcheth itself on the promises in the word. God hath promised 'he will not leave thee nor forsake thee,' Heb. xiii. 5. Let a man be in some weakness and disability, he cannot perform his duty. God hath promised his 'Holy Spirit to them that beg it,' Luke xi. 13. We are in many miseries and crosses, 'all things shall work together for the best to them that love God,' Rom. viii. 28. God is working my good by this cross, and shall I be angry with God for working my good? No. Let me by faith see the issue of things in this promise. God will turn all to the best, and how will this stay the soul! God sheweth himself as a Father, and it is for my good, and I shall receive 'the quiet fruit of righteousness,' Heb. xii. 11. And so you may see how the soul is stayed in all afflictions whatsoever. 'I had perished,' saith the psalmist, 'in mine afflictions, but that thy statutes were my comforts,' Ps. cxix. 92. They were my supports. Thus you see in some particular things how there is a power in the word, and an excellent power many ways, enabling us to duty, sustaining us in all crosses whatsoever.

(5.) Again, there is a power, an excellency of power, in the ordinances, whereby *we are above all good things that the world affords to us.* By the word, we know we have lawful use of the blessings, prosperity, peace, and plenty, God giveth us. We may use them as God's creatures, being in covenant with God. And by the word we come to manage them, and not to be slaves to them, as to make them our masters that are our servants. By the word, and by the Spirit accompanying of it, we have a sanctified use of all. All conditions are sanctified to us, and we sanctified to all conditions; not only to afflictions, but to prosperity and everything. By the Spirit of God we are raised above prosperity, which subdueth more than adversity doth. There is an excellent place, Phil. iv. 12, 13: saith St Paul, 'I have learned'—in Christ's school, not at the feet of Gamaliel—'to want, and to abound; I can do all things in Christ that strengthens me.' But a carnal man, that hath not let the word into his heart by the Spirit of God, he can neither want without murmuring, nor abound without pride and licentiousness. Every thing turneth to his bane, because he giveth not way to the Spirit. But where the Spirit getteth place in the heart, it advanceth the heart above all conditions. Thus you see, in particular, wherein the excellency of the power in the ordinance of God appeareth.

Now all this is from God, not from us; and therefore saith the apostle excellently, 2 Cor. x. 4, 'The weapons of our warfare are mighty through God to beat down strongholds' of corruptions, and to beat back temptations. So the weapons of the ministry of the word, they are 'mighty,' but 'through God;' being 'strong in the Lord, and by the power of his might.' I have learned, saith Paul, 'to want and to abound,' but it is through Christ. The gospel is a dead letter, the word is dead letters without the Spirit, which is the infusion. Take water without infusion, it is dead; but a drop of *aqua vitæ*, which hath such spirits, is more than a pint without spirits: that is flat and dead. So take the Spirit from God's ordinances, they are the massy substance, but they want infusion. There is the bread, but the staff of bread is gone; the staff of all the infusion is from God, and not from us. You may see this in the Acts, chaps. i. ii. When the Spirit of God did fall down upon the apostles, what extraordinary men were they! It carried them through all oppositions, through all abasements, whips, scourges, imprisonments. It wrought mightily, nay, by help of the Spirit it did greater things than Christ. We may speak it with reverence, for Christ saith, 'You shall do greater things than these,' John xiv. 12, speaking of the mighty power of the Spirit, that should fall on them after his ascension. He never converted so many at once as Peter, who converted three thousand, and yet might have preached three thousand sermons and not have converted one man, if it had not the Spirit to accompany it. He cast the net, and caught three thousand souls, and all because the Spirit was mighty in the ordinance, Acts ii. 42. What maketh the age of the church bad or good, but because there is more and less of the Spirit? Why were the eight hundred, nine hundred, and thousand years so dead? Because Christ was not known as he should be; or so the Spirit was not given in that measure, and therefore they were dead and dull times. So that it is the Spirit of Christ accompanying the ordinance, that maketh it effectual. 'I, even I, am thy comforter,' saith the prophet, Isa. lvii. 15. Men must speak comfort, but God must comfort the heart. 'I create the fruit of the lips, peace, peace,' ver. 19. The fruit of the lips it cometh by the ordinance, but I will create it, and make it to be so. What is the fruit of the lips, if God create it not? 'Paul may plant, and Apollos may water,' and if men had the tongue of men and angel, if the Spirit did not accompany them, all were nothing. 1 Cor. iii. 6. Nay, miracles are nothing without Christ. Israel saw the wonders of God in Egypt, yet because God gave them not an heart, they were not effectual. Nay, the miracles of Christ did no good. Nay, the doctrines of Christ did no good, without the Spirit. The Jews were not converted, because the Holy Ghost was not so abundantly given, as afterwards. Afflictions and crosses will not work without the Spirit. As it is said of Ahaz, 'This is Ahaz,' 2 Chron. xxviii. 22. The more God humbled him, the worse he was; and Pharaoh, after ten plagues, was ten times worse than before. Nothing will humble, neither word nor work, but by the power of the Spirit. Therefore as there is power and excellency of God in God's ordinance, so it is all from God, for all operation is from the Holy Ghost. God the Father and the Son work by the Spirit. Power is originally in the Father, and it is conveyed to Christ God-man, mediator, for to be the treasure and fountain of all power, and riches, and goodness. But the Holy Spirit doth take it from the Father and the Son, as the third person being near to us, and working in us. And so by the Spirit is meant the Holy Ghost, which cometh from the Father and the Son.

Use 1. Is there such a power, and excellent power, in the ordinance of God, when the Spirit of God accompanieth it? Then make this use of it, *for to depend on the ordinance of God with meekness and humility:* and take heed of Naaman's pride. Naaman was self-conceited. He being put in mind of washing himself in Jordan, what saith he? What reason is there in this? Is there not as good rivers in our country as the river Jordan? 2 Kings v. 1, *seq.* But if Naaman had not hearkened to his servant's counsel, he had gone home as leprous as he came. Saith he, the prophet, he biddeth thee do thus, and therefore do it, or else return a leper as thou camest; and then he hearkened to him. So many [are] of Naaman's conceitedness. Cannot I read a good book in my chamber? Cannot I have good lessons out of philosophy and morality? It is true; this is Naaman's mind; are not other rivers as good as Jordan? But God hath sanctified his word, and the dispensation of his word too. His word is holy, and the ordinance is holy, which holiness is in consideration distinct from the word. The very unfolding of the word hath a Spirit with it. God will not set up an ordinance in his church to no end. Therefore, if we will not stoop to it, as we be lepers by nature, so we may die as we are born, for anything I know. Therefore humbly depend on God's ordinances, and be thankful that God vouchsafeth to teach men by men. It is the most suitable teaching. We cannot endure the presence of an angel, nor an angel the presence of God. Therefore this is proportionable teaching, when God will teach man by man. If an angel were to administer it, the word would not be entertained for its own sake, but for the messenger's sake: but now God would have it regarded not for the vessel's sake, but for the treasure's sake. Whatsoever the vessel be, therefore, God will teach man by man. Therefore depend upon it. But if God hath not wrought this power and efficacy in our hearts, yet wait at the posts of wisdom, wait at the pool of Bethesda till the good hour come. Perhaps the good hour is not yet come, for the ordinance is the grand conduit that conveyeth all Spirit, and all grace, and all comfort in life [and] in death. And therefore, unless we will quarrel with our own comforts and salvation, and the kingdom of heaven, and life, do not despise 'the word of life,' the word of the kingdom,' 'the word of salvation,' 'the word of faith,' 'the word of reconciliation.' Despise that, and despise all these, because God is pleased to convey these things no otherwise ordinarily, where he hath established a church; ordinarily I say, extraordinary things we leave. And therefore God styleth his word with these titles, 'the gospel of reconciliation and peace' and the 'word of the kingdom,' to shew there is no way to come to grace, peace, and life, but by the word of grace, the word of peace, the word of reconciliation; and therefore be stirred up to attend upon it, to make the best use of it, even as we desire the good that is conveyed by it.

Use 2. Again, if the ordinance of God, in unfolding the truths of God, hath such a savour, and power, and relish in it, then *examine ourselves whether we have found such power and efficacy or no.* If not, then search what is the cause, what standeth between our souls and divine truth. And finding out the cause, be not more in love with our corruptions than with our souls. This word is able to save our souls, and therefore let us see whether there be stubbornness in our wills resisting the truth of God, withstanding it, rebelling against it. As the chiefest hindrance of divine truths is not so much the veil of ignorance in the glorious times of the gospel, as a kind of wilful stubbornness and pride, men will not stoop to God's ordinances, and when truths be revealed, men shake them off, as Stephen telleth them, 'You resisted the Holy Ghost,' Acts vii. 51; and as Christ telleth them, 'You would not come to me that you might have life,' John v. 40; and as he saith, 'I would have gathered you, as the hen gathereth her chickens under her wings, but ye would not,' Mat. xxiii. 37. We are in love with our corruptions more than with our souls; and therefore the word hath not that power, that efficacy, that excellency of power, that otherwise we should have experience of. And it is a pitiful thing indeed it hath not. We may justly take up lamentations over the times. What power hath the word, when it hath not power to make men leave fruitless sins? What fruit is in swearing? Declaring only frothy hearts and rebellious dispositions, that we get nothing, no other good by it, but only publishing our shame? God saith, 'the plague shall not depart from the house of swearers, and for oaths the land mourneth,' Zech. v. 3, 4; Jer. xxiii. 10. There is no good in the world by it. Every sin hath its *auctoramentum*,* but this hath no end at all in it. The word hath not power to make men leave superfluity, to leave an ugly fashion, that becometh them not, but disgraceth them, serving only to discover that they desire to fashion themselves to the worst deboist† persons.

Use 3. *If this power hath not virtue one way, it will have virtue another; if it draws not and quickens, it will have virtue to confound.* The threatenings of God against sins, that they are willing to live in, was made good, as Zechariah, i. 6, saith, 'Where be your fathers and the prophets?' They are dead and gone, 'but their words catch hold' of your fathers. They be gone; they threatened for these and these sins, and their threats remain. Moses is dead, but the threats extend to the people of the Jews, and stick upon them. The prophets and apostles are dead, but the threatenings of the sins of the times light upon the people, and they feel them now in hell; as Rev. vi. 2, it is said 'that Christ, who rideth on the white horse of the gospel,' and goeth to conquer and to conquering, he 'goeth with his bow, and woundeth as he goes,' either to conversion, to alter their wicked course of life, or to confusion. There is an arrow shot in every man that heareth, and that either maketh him better or worse.

Obj. But you will say, What efficacy is there in the word, when men leave not off their swearing and deboist† courses of life?

Ans. I answer, There is an efficacy on these very persons even before they come to hell, which doth as it were gape for them, unless they alter their ways. There is an efficacy in hardening their hearts for the present, for every sermon maketh them worse and worse; and is it not a terrible judgment to be hard-hearted? Son of man, 'harden this man's heart,' Isa. vi. 10. What! with preaching? That is the way to soften them; but if they stoop not to it, it shall harden them. Every sermon they hear striketh them more and more with hardness, till they have filled up the measure of their sins, and then God payeth them home with confusion in hell for ever. Is it not a judgment of God to sink deeper and deeper in sin? If you ask who is the most wretched man of all that liveth in the church? Surely those that will hear many things, and yet will go against them; that will set their wills against God's will, and set their authority against God's authority; that will live as they list, and live as they please; for every sin they commit is a step deeper to hell, and the more they have their wills, the more they shall be tormented against their wills.

* That is, 'wages, reward.'—G.

† That is, 'debauched.'—G.

No man so deeply tormented as they that will have their lusts most freely, for God will have his will first or last. And the deeper they fall into sin here, the deeper they shall be in hell hereafter. What is the punishment in hell? To suffer what they would not. Now, your wilful persons, of what rank soever, that despise the law of God and reason, though never so free and never so great, a wilful person is in the most dangerous condition; because he sinketh deeper and deeper in rebellious courses, and therefore his account will be heavier; and when conscience is awakened, it will charge sin on them with more terror than on other men. Because he would have his will, God will pay him home with suffering that that shall be clean contrary to his will. And therefore learn to stoop to God, submit to the ordinances of God; and labour that it may be effectual, and that we may find it effectual, since all is of God.

Use 4. *The power, and the efficacy, and the excellency of it; I join prayer together with the ordinance.* Lift up the heart to God, that God would accompany what we hear with his own Spirit, and accompany the receiving of the sacrament and every ordinance with his own Spirit, to make it effectual, for they be dead ordinances without it. As food to a dead man, or cordials poured into a dead man's mouth, they have no efficacy; and therefore desire God to afford his Spirit, to quicken us by the ordinance. And if we have spiritual life, that he would more and more increase it by his ordinance, and make our studies *oratoria*, places of prayer, as well as studies; because the virtue of all is of God. And think not to break through things with your own wit,* which is it that hath made all the heretics in the world. They will break through things with their own wit, and not submit to God's truth; and this makes profane men. They will not submit their profane wills to God's rule. Therefore know that thou canst not do it without the Spirit of God, joining prayer with the ordinance, for the Spirit.

I beseech you, take these things to heart. I cannot enlarge them. That that hath been spoken may be sufficient to stir us up to a care of the ordinances. Let me say this and no more at this time: It will bring an ill report upon all God's ordinances, if we are not careful to get good by them. We bring reproach upon them. How? God saith his word is mighty to salvation, and it is his strong word to salvation, and his arm, but we by hearing and growing no better, shew there is no such thing. Our lives deny it, and therefore the word will conclude it. Look upon many a Christian, he heareth the word, and converseth about it, but what power hath it in him? Surely, if there were any such power, it would appear in them that attend upon it. If there be such power in the ministry, why is their lives no better? And so the word is reproached to be a dead word, and the sacrament a dead ordinance. And therefore in honour of God, and the blessed things of God, I beseech you, labour to go to God by prayer, and attend on the means, and to find more virtue and power, and never give over till we find something in ourselves above the nature and course of other men. And then we shall honour the ordinances of God, and shall witness that they be powerful, that we have felt their power casting us down in ourselves and lifting us up in God, resisting of temptations, subduing our corruptions, enabling us to go through adversity and all conditions. And then we credit and adorn our profession, and grace religion, when we find the Spirit of God making these things effectual

* That is, 'wisdom.'—G.

to us, otherwise we bring reproach upon them, and bring discredit to them in the hearts of carnal men.

The holy apostle, as we have heard, after he had out of the fulness of his apprehension of the divine mysteries of the gospel set it out gloriously, cometh to avoid imputation of arrogancy, lest he should seem to advance his calling too far. The gospel is indeed a treasure, and the preaching of it is a treasure; the dispensation of it, being God's ordinance, is a treasure, because it hath a special virtue distinct. But we are but 'earthen vessels' though. The end why God would convey such excellent things as are in the gospel by such poor means, is, that the excellency of the power may be of God, and not of us.

We have spoken at large of the first part of the verse, wherein we shewed, first of all, that the gospel is a treasure in the dispensation of it, so largely, that I will not now stand to repeat anything then delivered. The ministers are 'vessels,' and 'earthen vessels.'

Now the end is, 'that the excellency of power may be of God, and not of us,' wherein we propounded to speak of these particulars.

1. That there is a power, and an excellency of power, in the gospel, and in the dispensation of it. In divine truths dispensed, there is a power, and excellency of power. This power takes place even of God. It is not of the instrument that conveyeth truths to us, exclusively set down, and not of us. He strikes off us, because proud men will be ready to touch upon God's prerogative, if he had not an exclusive with it. And therefore he saith, 'it is of God, and not of us.' Now, the end of all is, that it may appear to be of God, and not of us. It is so; but it appears not to be so, unless there were such a disproportion between the vessels and the treasure. And therefore God would have the vessels that carry it to be earthly, the treasure to be excellent, that as there is a great difference in the reality of the things themselves, so it may appear to be so in regard of man. *Non esse, et non apparere;* it is all one; for if it appear not to be so, man will not believe it is so. And yet because God will have it appear to be so, therefore is that disproportion between the vessel and the treasure.

Because the point is not perfected, we must add a little.

Now, the power is wrought by degrees; as in the 14th chapter of Revelation, ver. 2, where St John 'heard a voice from heaven, as the voice of many waters,' where heaven is taken for the church, because the church is from heaven, and begotten to heaven. Now, he heard a voice from heaven, 'as the voice of many waters, as the voice of great thunder; and I heard a voice of harpers, harping with their harps.'

1. The word in the dispensation of it is like 'the voice of many waters;' that is, it is confused, and raiseth a kind of wonder and astonishment, but the people know not why. Take an ignorant man that cometh to hear, and read the word and divine things, he is astonished at it, and filled with a kind of wonderment. So that it is as the noise of many waters to him, Mat. xxii. 22. You have the description of such persons, 'when they heard these words they marvelled, and left him, and went their ways.' Some will hear the word, and if there be any extraordinary parts, or extraordinary actions of a preacher, perhaps they will come and hear, and marvel, and leave him, and go their way. Many come to sermons, and hear, and marvel, and so away.

But the second effect that the word hath, 'it is as the voice of great thunder;' that is, where the word prevaileth a little more, it is as the voice of thunder. Now thunder astonisheth, and breedeth fear and terror. So they that wonder confusedly at first hearing, a while they hear as they heard it thunder; and therefore the thunder is called 'the Lord's voice,' Job xxxvii. 4, 5, because it breedeth fear and terror. So before the great work of conversion, the word, as thunder, terrifieth, and affrighteth, and casteth down.

But the word leaveth not the soul there. Therefore, saith he, 'I heard the voice of harpers harping with their harps;' that is, the sweet tune of the gospel. As the sound of the harp is delightful to the ear, so the sweet tune of the gospel breedeth joy and peace to the soul. After thunder cometh the voice of harpers harping with their harps. So the power of divine truths is first a kind of marvel, confused wonderment, but then it hath the power of thunder and astonishment, then it endeth in the sweet voice of harping, in peace, and joy, and comfort. The Epistle to the Hebrews, 4th chapter, maketh an excellent description of the power of the word in the 12th verse, 'The word is quick and powerful, sharper than a two-edged sword, piercing and dividing asunder the soul and the spirit, the joints and the marrow, a discerner of the thoughts of the heart.' When the word is let into the soul, it is a discerner. It hath power to discern what is flesh in the word, and what is spirit. And likewise of all actions that proceed from contrary principles, it hath power to tell when we do well, when ill; what will hold water, what not; what we may stand to, what not. And not only in actions, but in afflictions also; and therefore is the 'discerner of the thoughts and intents of the heart,' Heb. iv. 12; and thereupon rippeth up and anatomiseth the whole inward man when the Spirit of God accompanieth it.

Obj. Now, we will answer some cases and objections that may be made, and so proceed. *Why is it not so powerful in some*, say many, *as in others?* The apostle Paul telleth them, Heb. iv. 2.

Ans. 1. They do not '*mingle the word with faith.*' You know physic must have nature to work with it. Physic will do no good to a dead man. No. They do not 'mingle the word with faith,' and therefore they feel not the virtue of it. They lift up their own conceits against the word, and hear it, and know it, but yield not their hearts to believe and assent certainly to it, and therefore it worketh not. And,

Ans. 2. Then they *let it not into the heart and affections.* They give it room in the mouth to talk of it, but the word is never powerful till it hath its own seat and throne, till it getteth into the heart and affections, and alters the frame of the inward man. When it is not engrafted into the heart, it yieldeth not forth its virtue and power

Ans. 3. Again, *there is a great deal of opposition.* What is the hindrance of the power of the word? A foolish conceitedness and presumption. Men think they have enough already, and think they have a divinity point when they can talk of it. But, beloved, we know no more of religion than we love, and we love no more than we do. He that doth not, knoweth nothing as he ought to know. He may prate and talk for ostentation sake, and to satisfy conscience. But this conceit, that people have divinity when they can talk of it, it is a very destructive conceit that hindereth all the working of the word. Religion standeth not upon words, but it is a matter of power. Religion is not matter of fancy and imagination, faith is another thing.

You have many, especially great scholars, they think they have all they know, but they have nothing but what they love, and obey, and subject their hearts to. What they have more, it tendeth to damnation. 'Out of thine own mouth will I judge thee, thou faithless servant,' Luke xix. 22; thou knowest this, and thy courses are contrary. Therefore, take heed of this conceitedness, I beseech you, for it overthroweth all.

But I would not have such absent from the word; for the word is able to remove all the obstacles and hindrances between the heart and it. Physic will not do a dead man good, but this physic will give life to dead men; for the power of the word is such, that it hath a quickening power, and a raising power, and a directing power; and therefore, though there be never such mountains of oppositions between the heart and divine truths, as indeed they that be given to a profane course of life, there is much opposition between their hearts and divine truths.* . . . They that be practisers of any profession called to great employments, they should be so far from absenting themselves from the means of salvation, that they should offer themselves the more carefully and diligently, that whatsoever is between their hearts and divine truths may do them good. When all other things will fail, this may be removed; and therefore the main thing hindering from doing them good. The word is able to make way for itself, by removing the hindrances upon the word by a careful and continual attendance upon it. There is an excellent place in this Epistle, chap. x. ver. 4, 'The weapons of our warfare are not weak, but mighty through God for the pulling down of strongholds, and every thing that exalteth itself against the knowledge of God, to bring into captivity every thought to the obedience of Christ.' It is an excellent portion of Scripture. There be three things in a man which much hinder and indispose a man from taking good.

(1) There be λογισμοὺς, 'reasonings of flesh,' as, Is not reading as good as preaching? which men that have much wisdom in them think. Then,

(2.) There be ὑψώματα; that is, 'exaltations of the heart.' What! shall I stoop? Shall I be so base-minded as to regard what common persons do? I ever judged it more for my credit and reputation not to stoop than to yield up myself to be obedient to what they say. And when divine truths are propounded, seeming to be contrary to reason, though no truth be contrary to reason, but above it, as the great matters of predestination, and election, and free will, the pride of man's heart seeing no great reason for this, being above reason, it riseth, and will not yield, but the divine truths beat down these, ὑψώματα, λογισμοὺς. There is,

(3.) A word, that is, νοήματα, 'actions of the flesh against divine truths.' As when a man is exhorted to be liberal, it suggesteth, I shall want myself, and it is good to look to a man's self; and for suffering, it is good to sleep in a whole skin. Whatsoever the disputes or reasonings of flesh and blood there be, let a man attend upon the word, it will subject and subdue all in time, if a man belong to God; therefore it is powerfully said to make way for itself. For God will let himself and his Spirit into the heart in spite of corruption, and in spite of Satan. Never despair of a man that hath care of God's ordinances.

Obj. 2. But you will say, *How or by what means doth God make this word effectual?*

Ans. I answer, this excellency of power in the word and his truth worketh in the heart by the Spirit.

(1.) *By way of revelation.* It revealeth to us excellent things above

* *Sic.* The sentence unfinished. Cf. Vol. I. p. 38.—G.

nature, and better things than corrupt nature can apprehend in the world —Christ, and all the good we have by him; and that is the first thing— a revelation of divine truths.

(2.) Then again, by the Spirit, as all this is *offered to a soul* that will receive it. There is not only a discovery, but an offer.

(3.) There is not only these discoveries and offers, but divine truth is the *instrument that worketh faith* to apprehend and lay hold upon this. And therefore it is called the 'word of faith.' And when faith is wrought by the Spirit, after revelation, and after offer of divine truths, then that faith draweth out of Christ. Faith hath a drawing and sucking power out of the word, and Christ revealed in the word, of whatsoever is necessary for grace and comfort, that may be needful to bring to heaven; for the Spirit of God worketh faith, and by faith bringeth all other graces in, and maketh them effectual in the soul. Faith is the grace of union, that knitteth us to the principle of life, Christ.

And therefore God, upon revelation and offer of divine truths, first worketh faith, and by faith knitteth us to the fountain of life, Christ; and it is a wise grace, teaching the soul to fetch sovereign advantages from Christ, as in nature there is an instinct in every creature to fetch nourishment from the dam. So when God hath wrought faith in the soul, God putteth this supernatural divine instinct into the soul, to fetch whatsoever is needful, all comfortable graces out of Christ. And thus it becomes an effectual word, an excellency in a believing soul. 'It is the power of God to salvation to all them that believe,' Rom. i. 16. When we believe, God sheweth his power in the soul. God, by his almighty power, first worketh faith, and then faith layeth hold on that mighty power again. When God hath by the word wrought faith, we do apprehend the almighty power of God in Christ, and to make use of it on all occasions. And therefore it is called, Col. ii. 12, 'The faith of the operation of God.'

Obj. 3. And by resolving of this question we may answer another.

Quest. That is, *what degree of power is here meant, when he saith the excellent power that is of God?* Whether it is only a revealing of divine truths, or likewise in working upon the soul effectually? For you know that distinctly there is a moral kind of working which is by persuasion, and entreaty, and efficacious working, which is more than entreaty, which worketh as the sun worketh upon inferior things, which is called a virtual* working, and maketh an impression therein. Now whether doth the word by the Spirit only reveal, and offer divine truths, or have a work sometimes in the soul?

It is no nice† question, as it is made. And I will give you the truth of it.

Ans. The excellency of the power is not only in revealing, but in working. The word and the Spirit not only reveal, but work something in the soul, and in every part of the soul.

(1.) *In the understanding* there is not only a revealing of truth, but a light. In the understanding he giveth not only life but sense.

(2.) So *the will* not only apprehendeth what is good, and excellently good, but God's power goeth, together with the revealing of things, to the will, and putteth a relish into the will to relish that good, else natural corruption will will above what is good, without power wrought in the will to clear itself, and bend itself, and weigh itself towards the best things.

(3.) And so *for the affections;* good things are not only revealed to love

* That is, = energetic working.—G. † That is, = delicate or difficult.—G.

and joy, but the affections themselves are altered and changed. The corrupt natural affections have no proportion to supernatural objects, without an inward work, wrought in the heart, in the will and affections. So the power and efficacy of the word and Spirit is not only in presentation and offer, but in powerful working upon the soul, because there is no connaturalness, no proportion between a soul unturned, unchanged, and objects of a higher nature. Can an eye see things invisible? Can a natural soul apprehend and love things supernatural, above nature, before it be altered? It cannot. There is a vicious humour overspreadeth the soul, and therefore alters the taste of it, that we cannot naturally like nor approve the best things. And therefore the taste must first be altered. Take a sick man, if he have never so much skill, the palate is vitiated, and he cannot relish the wholesomest thing in the world, but answerable to the corruption of his palate. So let a man have never so much knowledge, if the power of the soul be not altered, he relisheth divine truths only according to his corrupt fancy. And therefore there must be wise and powerful workings upon the soul, that as divine truths are savoury in themselves, so they may be savoury to us. Therefore they speak very shallowly of the work of grace, that take it only to be matter of entreaty, and leave the soul to its own liberty. *Nolo hanc gratiam.* I will not this grace (saith one of the ancients), that leaveth the will to be flexible, and at liberty (*n*). It is a dangerous thing when a man hath no more grace but what is left to himself. One mischief will necessarily follow, that God hath not so much power as the devil hath. If he propounds any motion, we have a corrupt heart that yieldeth to the temptation, and betrayeth the heart, but if God's persuasions be only moral, and alter not the frame of the heart, he findeth nothing of his own goodness in us, only he findeth in us what is contrary to God's Spirit. And therefore the devil hath the advantage of God, if God should not work in us powerfully. For supernatural things have no friends at all in us, but opposition and enmity. Propound the sweet truths of the gospel to a proud natural man, he hath no more relish in them than in the white of an egg, Job vi. 6, till his heart be humbled and subdued, for we have no friends within us to hold correspondency with such truths. But let the devil offer a temptation to any natural man, he is iron to God, and wax to the devil. And therefore of necessity there must be more than a moral work, by effectual persuasion. I speak it to advance the power of the word, that we may know what degree of grace to beg. What is suitable to the apprehension of these things prayer will be for. If we conceive grace to be only a motion and persuasion, and no powerful work upon the heart, we will beg no more. No man was ever brought to heaven with such a grace, but it is an altering, changing, converting grace that bringeth us to heaven.

I will name one reason out of the text. It is more than revealing, offering, and persuading by reason, because that is not the excellent manner of work. God in the gospel works in the most excellent manner, but working by persuasion is not the most excellent manner of working; but working powerfully and really and effectually. Now the excellentest manner of working belongeth to the most excellent worker, who worketh powerfully in the heart, which is the most excellent manner of working.

Now, how prove you that?

Ans. Is not he that is able to do stronger than he that persuadeth to do?

Therefore the most excellent manner of work is to work inwardly and effectually, not only by entreaty and persuasion, which is a weak and shallow kind of work, in regard of an efficacious work in the soul. Now God, the most excellent worker, worketh in the most excellent manner, and therefore works not only by persuasion, but worketh powerfully in the inward man. God made the soul, and framed the soul, and knoweth how to work upon the soul, and how to work upon it with preserving the liberty and power of it untouched. And therefore as they say very well, he worketh *suaviter* and *fortiter: suaviter*, by entreaty, agreeable to the nature of man; and *fortiter*, powerfully (*o*).

There are two things that are the principles of action in men working by reason, working by strength. When there is power to do a thing, and reason why to do it, they work like men. If a man had never so much reason, and not strength, he worketh not. If he hath strength and not reason and grace to guide the action, the action is common, and there is no religion. But when a man worketh by power from reason it is like a man. So there be excellent and strong reasons in the word to dissuade from sin, make us in love with heaven and happiness, if we were believers; and without a power accompanieth the reason secretly and sweetly, and altereth the soul powerfully, all will do the soul no good; and therefore together with reason goeth a divine power to the soul. So God at one time worketh powerfully and sweetly by entreaty. He works suitably to the nature of man, and powerfully to overcome that nature.

Obj. 4. I come now to answer this—*How shall we know whether this virtue, and excellency of virtue, hath wrought on the soul by God and the Spirit of faith?*

To give you some evidences; and first, you may know easily that it hath wrought, but we cannot tell the manner in working, because we will answer a secret objection.

Quest. I feel not how God works upon my spirit by his Spirit.

Ans. It is true, *for the present you do not.* For instance, grace is wrought in the heart, as the sun works on inferior bodies. Influence cometh from heaven to it, but who can tell you how influence entered into his body? Who can in spring-time see the manner how he is cheered? He seeth he is cheered, but to say exactly the time and measure, that is unknown. It is a sweet and strong influence. We see there is a sweet influence in the working of things, but the very working is unperceivable; so the power of God's ordinances in the working is concealed, but presently after there is an alteration, as we know the spring is come when we see nature altered, and things flourishing and green, and a new face of things over there was in winter. So we know the Sun of righteousness hath shined on our souls in the ordinances and means of salvation, when there is a flourishingness and fruitfulness in our conversations. When our speeches and actions savour of the word and Spirit, we may know that the Sun of righteousness hath shined upon our souls, Ps. cx. 3. The church is compared to dew that falleth in the morning. 'The birth of thy womb is as the dew of the morning.' So the best translators have it (*p*). 'In the day of thy power;' that is, in the powerful work of thy ordinances, the word and sacraments. The birth of Christ, which is* the church begotten by the Spirit, is [as] the womb of the morning; that is, the dew of the morning which falleth from heaven, but insensibly and unperceivably. It hath an high cause to draw it up, and let it fall, and to put virtue into it, to make things fruitful, but

* Misprinted 'as' here, evidently a misplacing of that required a little onward. —G.

none perceiveth the falling of it. So grace is wrought in the heart, as dew falls from heaven; that is, we feel the power and virtue of it, but the manner how grace is wrought, and the church is begotten of God and Christ, is unperceivable. And therefore go to the fruits, where there is a power and excellency of power wrought, and a change is seen in life and conversation; for being a lion before, thou art a lamb, there is a triumphing and prevailing power over corruptions that they were enthralled to before, themselves are not themselves, and therefore judge by obedience.

Then there is a power and excellency of power in the soul, when we have turned by a natural power the nourishment into our constitutions; then we be strong, as Elias, that by strength of the nourishment sent from heaven walked forty days, 1 Kings xix. 8. So when we have received the sacraments, and heard as we should, we shall find more ability for duty, for fitness to die, more intercourse with God, more strength of faith against all temptations; and therefore if thou wouldst know what power and excellency of power is wrought in thy soul, examine it by thy strength derived thereby. If you find not strength to overcome temptations and resist corruptions, then you have not yet been good hearers, nor good readers, nor good receivers of the sacraments, as you should be. We know sheep and such creatures are judged of not by that they chew, but by their flesh and fleece, and so should a Christian by his life, his strength, what he is able to do.

And here we may take up just complaint, that many that have great knowledge of the gospel, and have been long professors of the truth, yet they fall before their spiritual enemies; as when Israel, falling before their enemies, complained, 'Lord what is it?' Josh. vii. 8. What is the reason that we fall before the enemy? So a man may complain, what is the reason a Christian should fall before his spiritual enemies? That every temptation should overturn him, every corruption and passion enslave him, why is he so enthralled to temptation? Certainly there hath not been that power and excellency of power in the soul that should be.

By these and the like circumstances, we may know whether we have felt this power and excellency of power or no.

There is, as we said before, a power in religion, if it be mingled with a believing heart; and till we find that power all will do us no good. Profession of religion and knowledge will be in the brain, therefore labour not to know but to feel divine truths. And when be they felt? When the virtue is felt. It is not enough *scire sed sentire*. It is not enough to know, but to feel. And when do we feel? When we find the virtue of the word in comforting, in raising and directing, in changing, in transforming.

We think we believe all things necessary, when we can say them and speak of them, but there is never an article of our creed, but being apprehended by faith, worketh mightily upon the soul in an excellent manner. As for example, 'I believe in God the Father Almighty,'* how shall I know I believe? If the Spirit of God witness to my spirit that God is my Father, and teacheth me to go to him as a Father in all my necessities, I know he is Almighty. When I am under strength of temptation and oppositions whatsoever, he is able to raise my soul, and after death to give it a better being than in this world; and I believe in him as the Father Almighty, when I will not distrust him. He is my Father, and will do me good. He is Almighty, and can do all for my good. So 'I believe in Christ, born of the Virgin Mary.' This a man believeth not till Christ be born in the heart and the image be stamped upon his soul, and a disposition suitable to

* Throughout under the several articles, cf. Pearson and John Smith.—G.

Christ; and so 'for the death of Christ.' The cross of Christ, it is a crucifying knowledge. I know Christ died for my sins. The faith of this crucifieth this corruption for which Christ was crucified, when I look upon my corrupt nature, with that odium and detestation that Christ had when he suffered for them. So that I feel not things with power and efficacy, till something be wrought by them. So I believe not Christ 'is risen again,' unless I find that power that raised him quicken my heart and raise me to heavenly-mindedness, to ascend with Christ, and sit in heaven with Christ. A man believeth not that Christ is in heaven unless he hath glorious thoughts. He doth but talk of them. He that believeth Christ his head is in heaven, Christ and he being all one, can he be much cast down with any trouble here, or be abased here when he believeth this? No. And therefore saith the apostle, 'If you be risen with Christ,' as you be, if you belong to Christ, and have the same Spirit that raised his body raising you, then 'seek the things above, and not the things beneath,' Col. iii. 1, and savour the things that be spiritual, and suitable to your condition. So a man cannot believe his 'sins be forgiven,' but he must love, he must have joy and peace: 'Being justified by faith, we have peace with God,' Rom. v. 1. He that findeth not peace in his conscience, how knoweth he that his sins are forgiven? 'Be of good comfort, thy sins are forgiven,' Mat. ix. 2. A man that knows his sins are forgiven, he is comforted, for his debt is paid, and all discharged. And so 'the resurrection of the body and life everlasting,' what is the power of it? It maketh him as willing to die as when he goeth to sleep, for when he goeth to bed he knoweth he shall rise again, and rise better and more refreshed. So a man that is to die he resolveth, I lay down my body, and shall rise again, as sure as I shall rise out of my bed, and more sure, for many die in their sleep. So if we believe 'the coming of Christ to judgment,' the virtue of it will shew itself in walking fruitfully and carefully. Christ must come again, and I must make account of all. And so 'life everlasting.' If a man believeth that, what courage will it infuse! There is never an article but if it be believed hath a spiritual infusion in it. Let a man believe life everlasting, he will not care to venture his life for religion and his country. What will he care to adventure a life [which] is nothing but vanity?

I do but touch these things, to shew that out of the grounds of religion there is a power in them, if they be apprehended and believed; and if they have not this power, we believe them not. We talk of them, but are not moulded to them; as the apostle's phrase is, 'We are not fashioned to them,' 2 Cor. iii. 18. So that we may try whether the word hath wrought mightily on us, by the power we find in us altering our natures.

Quest. 5. Well, *what course shall we take, that we may find this power of the ordinances and word, and an excellent power?*

Ans. (1.) *Remember all is of God, from God's Spirit.* The third person in the Trinity is next to us, and next in working. God the Father and Son work by the Spirit. For as it is in the body, there be the veins and arteries put together, the veins carry the blood, the arteries carry the spirits, the blood in the veins nourish the spirits in the arteries, the spirits in the arteries quicken and enliven the blood; [so] the word is as blood in the veins. For as blood spreads itself over all the body by the veins, and feedeth the several parts, so the word spreadeth itself over the whole man, over all the powers of man, over his understanding, will, and affection. It spreadeth itself over all the actions of man, for all must be done in virtue of some word. It spreadeth itself as blood spreadeth over the body, but together with the blood there must be spirits to quicken the blood; so there must be the Spirit with the word. The word is *vehiculum Spiritus*, the chariot which carrieth the Spirit. And therefore consider the concurrence of these two when ye come to God. They be coupled together as the veins and arteries; and when we have to do with divine truths, remember to beg for the Spirit, and therefore, Ps. cxix. 18, 'Open mine eyes, Lord, open mine eyes.' His eyes were opened, and yet 'Lord, reveal the wonders of thy law more.' So we must pray for a fresh, new revelation of truths to us. And are we quicker and better-sighted than he or Paul, that prayed so often for the Spirit of revelation, and that God would take off the veil of ignorance and unbelief from the heart?* There is a natural veil upon divine things, that we cannot see them in their truths and excellency. Therefore pray to God by the Spirit to take away this veil.

Ans. (2.) And if we would feel the power, and the excellency of the power, of the word, *enter into our own hearts, and see our own necessity every day, and see our own wants of God*, who doth shew his power in weakness, labour to see a necessity of divine power and divine truths, a necessity to do anything well, and that our callings are not sanctified unless we sanctify them in a morning by prayer, and direct them to ends above nature and above the world, and make them serviceable for the soul. See a necessity of grace and of the efficacy and power of the word, and necessity will enforce us out of ourselves to him, in whom is the fountain of all strength, that we may be 'strong in the power of his might,' Eph. vi. 10, 2 Tim. ii. 1. Beloved, times are coming to every one of us that will enforce us to seek for strength and for power. Can we undergo afflictions when they come without spiritual strength? We may carry them as civil† men, but great crosses may come above all morality and civility. Ahithophel had brains enough, but having no grace he sunk. Judas had much knowledge, but sunk under it. So though we have strong brains and great parts, we shall sink under them if we have not grace. A Christian must be more than a man, as grace raiseth a man above a man, makes him spiritual. By virtue of this power we must be more than men, else we shall meet with things which are above a man, fiery temptations and Satan's darts, and if we are not more than a man, woe be to us. Therefore labour to feel and see our own wants; present and propound beforehand all possibilities. What if our lives should be questioned? Sickness will come, death will come. What strength have I? What faith have I? What have I lived upon before, and what do I know? Do I believe all I know? As Joseph provided against hard times, Gen. xli. 48, times of spending will come, therefore lay up knowledge, and often examine if things be to us as to themselves. Divine truth is holy, full of majesty and power in itself. What is that to me if it be not so to me? It will do me no good, but help to damn me. Do I find that power and efficacy that is said to be in them? If not, never give over waiting on the means that God hath appointed for that purpose.

Beloved, it concerneth us nearly and very much, for if we do find the power of divine truths in our hearts, Oh happy men! If we find it hath wrought a change and alteration, it will make the weakest Christian stronger than all the gates of hell. Take a weak Christian that hath digested the word and mingled it with faith, a few divine truths digested and mingled with faith will stand out against the devil and all temptations, even at the hour of death, because they be divine truths, and God goeth with them; the truths being divine of themselves, and likewise divine power going with

* Cf. Eph. i. 17. 2 Cor. iii. 14.—G.

† That is, 'moral.'—G.

them, having the strength of God for every word. As a man is, the word of a man is. It is as powerful as himself, and the word of a noble man, the word of an honest man, is as the man is. Now consider what word it is, and what power is annexed to it. Labour to feel the power of these divine truths, and all hell let loose cannot overcome the weakest Christian, not a fool, not a novice, not a child in religion, much less a strong Christian. But the tongue of men and angels, if men will be drowsy, and lazy, and dead, will not make them affected with these things, but those that belong to God understand what these things mean.

We are speaking of the end of this dispensation of God, that he would have this blessed treasure of divine truths carried in 'earthen vessels,' that 'the excellency of the power may be of God and not of us.' Now in the end three things are considerable.

1. First, That there is a 'power' in the ordinances of God, and an 'excellency of power.'

2. That this excellent power of the ordinances of God 'is of God.' It is not of the 'earthen vessel.' No. It is not in the treasure itself. It is not in the gospel, distinct and abstracted from divine power accompanying it, but it is of God, exclusively set down, and not of us.

3. The intention why God would have this power, and excellent power, to be in earthen vessels and not of us. See how he demonstrateth it, that it may appear that the power is of God and not of us. There is excellent power, and it is of God. How doth it appear? Compare the meanness of the vessel with the excellency of the treasure, and it shall appear that all the good done by the ordinance is not by the vessel, but from the treasure, or rather from God himself, whose treasure it is.

That there is a power, and an excellent power, of God's ordinance, we have shewed at large.

We have shewed wherein this power consisteth, and how it is of God. All the power is of God, else the ordinance is dead; and indeed unless God's virtue go along with it, what can do the soul good? Afflictions make men worse. The law hath only a power to harden us. The law by the power of God killeth, but it quickeneth not. Let not the power of God go with the ministry of Christ, it doth no good.

How many sermons did Christ preach which did no good? 'He piped and they would not dance.' They would not 'mourn' when he preached matter of humiliation, when he preached matter of comfort 'they would not dance,' Mat. xi. 17, but, like froward children, they were untractable, and nothing would work upon them; and therefore without God and the work of the Spirit, not man, not an angel, not Christ himself, can work upon an obstinate stubborn soul.

I shewed that the excellency of this power must be of God and not of us. I propounded divers cases and questions, and answered some. I will briefly answer some now, as,

Quest. First, Not to speak of what I then delivered, *if there be no power in the ordinances, why do we exhort people and stir them up to believe and to repent, if all power be conveyed from God, as we proved the last day at large, and that they have no power at all in themselves?*

Ans. I answer, God's word in the ordinance *is an operating word, a working word,* as in the creation, 'Let there be light, and there was light,' Gen. i. 3. So in miracles, 'Lazarus, come forth,' John xi. 43. There went an almighty power with the word of Christ, and Lazarus comes out.

'Believe and repent.' There goeth out an almighty power with the ministerial word, and giveth power to believers. *Dum jubet juvat*, where God commandeth he helpeth. His word is clothed with an almighty power. And therefore though we exhort men to do so and so, we say not, they can do it themselves, but together with the speech there goeth a commanding power. The Spirit of God clotheth the word. *Loquitur Deus ad modum nostrum, agit ad modum suum*, God speaketh according to our measure, worketh according to his own. We are men, and are to do things by reason and understanding. God speaks to us by way of open reason, and shewing grounds of reason, because *loquitur ad modum nostrum*. But when he comes to give strength and power to reason, all moral power or reason will do no good without inward strength, and therefore *agit ad modum suum*, mightily, powerfully, and by way of persuasion and reason, and all to condescend to our manner, yet still all the while as a God.

And therefore it is a childish thing for them to infer that there is power in man, because God persuadeth and exhorts. God with these infuseth his power, he conveyeth power into the will and affection this way. Then he works powerfully when he seemeth to condescend thus far, and this exhortation is but to drive us out of ourselves to the rock of our strength, and to the spring of all comfort. It is but to drive us to Christ, and therefore wheresoever you have a commandment in one place, ye have a promise in another. If you are commanded to turn to God, to mortify lusts, we have a promise of assistance that we shall do these things. The commandments may make us go out of ourselves with humility, the promise makes us go to God with confidence in him. And therefore it is ignorance of God's divine dispensations to enforce any power and strength in us from those sweet exhortations that are commended to us in Scripture.

Quest. 2. Secondly, *If there be such power and efficacy in God's ordinances accompanied with the Spirit, as indeed there is, whence then cometh the resisting in men?* It sheweth there is more in man's malice than in God's ordinance. I answer thus,

Ans. That God intendeth to convert and put forth his strength that way. For those whom God intendeth to put forth his strength for, it tendeth to conversion. He joineth such a strength with the ordinances, as overcometh all rebellion and resistance in them that he doth convert, as Augustine saith well, *volentem hominem salvum facere*, when God will save a man, no stubbornness of his will shall withstand (*q*), else the will of man were stronger than God's. And it is a high point of comfort that the goodness of God is above the malice of man, that there is a greater power in the ordinances and efficacy, than there can be indisposition in man, whatsoever it is in the party.* For all things in the world, in the soul of man, which is the most rebellious, refractory, and stubborn thing, all things in the world are in obedience to the first worker. There is an aptness which is of purpose for this matter which we speak of. There is an active power in the creature, whereby it is ready to work, and this active power to do good we have none at all. There is a passive power, as in wax to receive impression. This we have not. We cannot so much as receive goodness. The reason is, because good things, so long as we be corrupted, be presented to us as folly. A wise man will never take that he apprehendeth [to be] folly. To a carnal wise man, the most excellent things in the world are presented as folly, and he will not subject† to the impression of divine truths when they be presented. And therefore there is neither active nor mere passive power.

* Cf. footnote, Vol. III. page 9.—G.

† That is, = submit.—G.

But there is *potentia obedientialis*, a power obediential. That is, in plain terms, there is such a subjection of the soul of man to God the first cause, that it yields to him when he worketh. He knoweth all the windings and turnings of it. He can deal as he pleaseth, preserving the liberty of it without prejudice of its liberty. For both things, and the manner of working things, are of God, and preserved by God. God he carrieth things so, as he preserveth *modum agendi*, the manner of working peculiar to things; so that all things are obedient to God's manner of working. For they cannot resist him: there is no question of that.

Obj. But we say, that as the Scripture speaks, *there is resistance in things*. Resistance is in them that belong not to God, or in them that belong to God, till he putteth forth an invisible strength to convert them. But if they resist, they may resist the work of God's Spirit. Then there is some excuse for them.

Ans. I answer, No. They may pretend the word is not powerful enough. the ordinance is not able enough; but let them leave secret things to God. There is no man converted, but his heart will tell him that God was before-hand with him. God enforceth goodness on men; they willingly resist it. God is then before-hand with them, and there is no man that withstandeth God's workings, but his heart will tell him that the fault is altogether in himself; for God is willing to yield more power to him than he is willing to receive, and that maketh him afraid of the means of salvation. If I go to such, and converse with such, they will advise me to alter my course. They will put conceits in me, disquiet my mind, vex me and torment me. I shall hear what crosseth my old ways, and I am resolved still to walk in my old courses, and so their hearts tell them they willingly betray their own souls. So that they cannot pretend the weakness of the understanding, but strength of corruption, which declineth the ordinance.

The two witnesses, Rev. xi. 10, 'tormented the world;' and so the ordinances, the truths of God, torment some kind of men, But to let such go, I speak to them that belong to God. Here is our comfort, that the ordinances of God are powerful, 'and mighty, but through God, to beat down all strongholds,' 2 Cor. x. 4, and therefore come and attend upon the means of salvation. Come; though you be lions, you may go out lambs! Come; though you be wolves, you may go out sheep! For the knowledge of God, accompanied with the Spirit of God, as Isa. xi. 6, may alter and change your natures, transforming you to be like to Christ, whose word it is. It is a transforming, converting word.

Where it doth not convert the heart and conscience of men, or tell them that God was willinger to convert them than they were willing to be converted, the fault is in themselves; but I will always hope well of them that carefully and diligently come within God's reach. The ministry of the gospel is said to be the power of God; and Isa. liii. 1, 'the arm of God.' 'To whom is the arm of God revealed?' that is, the power of God in the ordinance. Those that will come within the power and reach of God, never despair of them. They that will meekly subject* to God's dispensation, and not proudly despise the powerful working of God, that attend 'at the posts of wisdom,' Prov. viii. 34, if not at one time, yet at another, there is a blessed hour to come for the angel to stir their waters; for the Holy Ghost to stir the waters to heal their souls. Therefore I speak to all them that love their own souls, never to weary of God's ordinances. Though the means be weak, yet the glory of God, and power of his Spirit, will be more

* As *ante*.—G.

eminently apparent in the weakness of the means, as the apostle saith here, 'The excellency of the power is of God, and not of man.'

Now, to make some further use of this: *Is all the power of God?*

1. Therefore observe another thing, *we must not depend on the power of the ministry*, and the excellency of the minister his parts and gifts. Why? The power and excellency is of God. And we may say by experience, that men that think themselves converted by some excellent parts of a rare man, it is usually but a shallow repentance. And they that be hanged by the ears upon men of good parts, they seldom hold out. But where the soul is wrought upon by grounds from the word, and evidence from the Spirit in the teacher . . . .* But conversion wrought only by admiration of the parts of the teacher, it is with them as with them in the gospel: 'They marvelled at him, and stood astonished, but they left him, and went their ways,' Mat. xiii. 54. And therefore take heed of depending on men for the efficacy of the sacraments. Some are to blame that way. Unless they have such a preacher they will not receive it, as if the doing and efficacy of the sacrament depended on that, if they be placed in the office of the ministry and have a calling. Now look 'to the power of God, and the excellency of that power,' in his own ordinance by whomsoever. We will receive gold out of any hand, we will receive a pearl from a mean person. Do we regard the pardon itself, or the person that bringeth the pardon? No, we look to the pardon. If that be right, it is no matter who bringeth the pardon, who offers this treasure of life. Look to the excellency of the things themselves, and God, though in the course of means—we must add that,—God doth ordinarily convert by the best men, that can speak from the heart to the heart. He can kindle others best that is kindled in his own heart, begetting, being from a love in the teacher. They that are truly, sanctifiedly affected, they can beget others sooner than others. And therefore in the course and ways of means, God for the most part useth blessed and holy means for working of the great work of conversion for the most part.

Yet God tieth not himself to the excellency of means. Oftentimes the greatest men of all, God humbleth them, to do others good. As we see Isaiah, that great kingly prophet, saith he, 'We have laboured in vain,' Isa. xlix. 4, *seq.* I have laboured to subdue the people to God, but to no purpose. 'Son of man, go, harden the people's hearts.' So excellent a power, instead of converting, maketh them worse, and so it is, that the most excellent preacher, both for parts and likewise for graces, oftentimes doth harden and make them worse. God will have it so; it shall be the savour of death to some presumptuous proud persons, and not a savour of life, 2 Cor. ii. 16. And therefore we must not look altogether on the excellency of the persons that preach, nor to their meanness, but to the ordinance of God.

2. Give me leave farther to add this thing: God sheweth his power, and his excellent power, *by his own ordinance;* and therefore other courses are not sanctified for conversion, nor for spiritual good to the soul. This observe. There is a conceited superstitious generation of men, ill-bred for the most part, not for want of parts, but for superstitious breeding. They have great admiration of a bastardly means of good, what do I call them? Means they set up themselves, which God never sanctified. Oh, they will have crucifixes, and such and such helps. Who ever sanctified this? Every workman will work with his own tools and instruments. Did God ever sanctify crucifixes and the like to stir up devotion? What kind of

* As before, sentence unfinished. Cf. Vol. I. page 38.—G.

devotion is like to come to that, that God never blessed to that end? A bastardly devotion from a bastardly means. And usually people give to those kind of things higher measure of admiration than to good and sanctified means.

I never knew, nor ever shall know, a superstitious person to like of things sanctified of God, but in that proportion he grew bitter against that which is indeed sound. See what religion popery is, their study being to weaken that powerful instrument that God hath sanctified to convey all saving power by. How do they weaken it? By all the means they can. They labour to take away the strength of it. They lock it up in an unknown tongue, in Latin; and not only so, but in a corrupt, vicious translation, and lest it should do much good, they add Apocryphal writings with it—many of which indeed are holy books, but yet they equal their authority with the Scriptures. Nay, that they may weaken the strength and efficacy of the blessed word by which is wrought whatsoever is savingly good, they make traditions of equal authority with the word. They make the present determination of the present pope of equal power with the word, nay, above it; for the life and soul of words is the sense and meaning of them. The meaning is the form, and being, and life of speech; the words are but husks. The kernel and life of words, is the meaning of them. Now they take upon them to give the sense and meaning of the Scriptures. But they go about to judge that, which will one day judge them; to keep under the word, that will keep them under, and blast them, and consume them, as 2 Thes. ii. 8, 'Antichrist must be consumed with the breath of his mouth,' that is, with the ordinance of God. It is such a wind as he cannot endure; it will consume him. There is no means sanctified of God to consume antichrist, but the ordinance. There be other civil and apparent ways to weaken him, but that that shall 'consume' him indeed, as he 'is antichrist,' is the powerful ordinance of God. And therefore blame them not for being such enemies to that which is such an enemy to them, that is, the powerful preaching of the word. But we must not dwell upon these things, only I thought it necessary to put you in mind of it, that our hearts may be brought to think highly of that which God so esteemeth, even as we love our own souls.

Other truths may civilise, and other helps may be profitable; other books besides God's book may do us a great deal of good, and many holy treatises there are, in which the word is unfolded, and made familiar to us. The water in the spring, and water brought in a pipe, is the same water. So that the word in Scripture, and the word brought in preaching and holy treatises, is the same. But I speak of other truths we read of in human writers. God giveth a power to every truth, and there be inferior works of the Spirit. But this work of conversion, of setting the image of God upon us, is reserved especially for the ordinances of God. All the learning in the world will not set the image of God upon the soul, will not bring the soul out of darkness into the kingdom of Christ, but the powerful ordinance of God, and the powerful work of the Spirit accompanying it. It is not every work of the Spirit, but an almighty work. By embalming, a dead body may be preserved from putrefaction and annoyance a long time, but all the spices and embalmments in the world will not put life into a dead body. So the inferior works of the Spirit, by inferior means, may embalm the soul, that is, may make it civil, and it is very good conversing with civil men. You shall have them fair-conditioned men, and excellent things will break from them, but this is but embalming; the quickening of a dead soul, the putting of life into that, is reserved for the ordinance of God, and the power of the Spirit accompanying it. This is that the apostle speaks of, 'the excellency of the power of God.'

3. One thing give me leave to add more, That as God doth powerfully work by his ordinance in us, and in the church, so he doth powerfully work by his ordinance *on others*, by the church on others. To make it plain thus: There is an excellency of power in the word, in faith, in prayer, in fasting, in the sentence of the church; there is an excellent power in all these, not only on the soul, upon whom they work, but likewise on others. There is a power in the church and in the minister for to threaten; and God, to make good those threats to others, worketh on others. And there is a power in prayer, not only of grace to make us fit to pray, but a power by prayer, for God thereby to confound the enemies of the church. Therefore the phrase in the psalms, is, 'God send thee help out of Sion,' Ps. xx. 2, that is, out of the church, by church means; and 'God is terrible in his holy place,'* Ps. lxviii. 35. What is the meaning of that? The meaning is: in the church, where God is truly worshipped, where the ordinances are in purity and power, there God is terrible out of his holy place. If there come forth prayers against the enemies of the church, God saith Amen to them. Woe be to the enemies of the church, when the church falleth a-praying and fasting. Woe be to Haman, when Esther, Mordecai, and the rest fall to this duty. And woe to popery! If all Christians would join in prayer and fasting, antichrist had been brought upon his knees, and to nothing ere this time. There is a power in God's ordinances, let them be used as they should be, with faith and persuasion, that God will say Amen to them all, they will work. What! Let a man pray with confidence, that God will bless it, though not in the particular that he desireth, yet you shall see what wonders God will work by it.

No question, but the humiliation of God's people brought antichrist so much upon his knees, as he hath in Germany. God's people humbled themselves, and believed the threatenings against antichrist, and believed the promises of the church, and laboured to have faith suitable to God's promises, suitable to God's threatenings; and in that faith, as an exercise of it, pray to God, we shall see God make good all his ordinances. 'God will be terrible out of his holy place, and he will send help out of Sion.' Pray therefore for the church and against the enemies, and we shall quickly see an end of them. And therefore you have 2 Cor. x. 6, that speaking of the power of the ordinances of God, he saith in the 6th verse, 'God is in readiness to revenge all disobedience.'† There is a power in the ordinances of God to kill men, to send men to hell. You think the words of the ordinances are wind, but they are not; for as it is in Zech. i. 5, 6, 'the prophets be gone, and are dead, but their words are made good.' Whom we bind, God bindeth from heaven; whom we loose, God looseth from heaven. If we threaten the judgments of God, and punishment upon swearers, or profane persons, or despisers of the ordinances, do you think it doth them no harm? Beloved, they are struck, they be men under the sentence of damnation. They are not yet in hell, but the word hath damned them,

* Our version is, 'out of' his holy place: but this is not = *out*side of, but 'from *out*.' The Hebrew is מִמִּקְדָּשֶׁיךָ = *e, ex, sanctuariis tuis.*—G.

† Query—Is it not rather the Corinthians who are asked to be thus ready, not an affirmation that God *is* ready? The latter is true no doubt, but does not seem to be taught here.—G.

the ordinance hath damned them, they be struck men. There is a power in God's ordinances to be revenged on the disobedience of men, when men will live in sins, threatened and condemned by the ministers. They go up and down like glorious men, but they be condemned and under sentence. There is but a step between them and hell. And they shall know one day God will make good every one of his threats in his ministry against their profane courses, though they make slight of it. No! it shall not be made light off, when God cometh to execute it; when God shall come immediately from heaven, to execute the word he hath spoken mediately by the minister, as one day he will. What we speak mediately, he will immediately from heaven come to execute it. How will they shake off that, 'Go, ye cursed, into everlasting fire'? Mat. xxv. 41. You that have lived in sins against conscience, can you shake off that? God is now patient to them, if his patience can win them, but can they shake off God's immediate peremptory sentence from heaven? Oh no! And therefore I beseech you, labour to bring your souls to obedience of the ordinances of God, for it is mighty to take vengeance of all obstinate sinners. Therefore take heed of living in sin, condemned by the ordinance; for God will make good every word that he hath spoken.

The last thing I propounded in the words to shew us is, that God doth shew his power, and excellent power, by weak means, that it may appear by the disproportion that it is of God.

Doct. The point from hence is this, *that God is wonderful curious,* as we may with reverence speak; he is wonderful exact in this, that his glory may be advanced in all.* And therefore he would have this carriage of things, that heavenly treasures should be carried in earthen vessels; not gold, not silver, but earth, that the good done may not be attributed to the vessels, being so base, but to him. God's aims and our aims must concur. God aimeth at his own glory, and it is no pride in him, because there is none above him, whose glory he should seek. And therefore it is natural for God to do all for his own glory, as it is natural for him to be holy, because he is the first cause, and the last end, of all things. It is fit the first cause and last end of all things should have all the glory: 'Of him, and through him, are all things: therefore to him be all the glory,' Rom. xi. 36. It is God's prerogative. The grace is ours. He giveth grace to us, but the glory is his own, and his glory he will not part withal.

To make this clear. God takes all the course he doth in the government of the world, in the ministry and church, that it may appear that the glory is his in all things. Look to his providence in governing the world. Doth not he do great things sometimes without means, and sometimes with poor weak means? What be the blowing of rams' horns to the fall of 'the walls of Jericho'? Josh. vi. 20. Was it not that it might appear that the falling of the walls was from God? What was Gideon's 'pitchers with lamps' for the confounding of the Midianites? Judges vii. 19. What was a victory to an earthen pitcher? So what is the light of the gospel to an 'earthen vessel'? Doth the virtue come from these? No. God appointeth to us these means, that the glory and excellency of power may appear to be of him. The ministers are but Gideon's pitchers, with the light of the gospel in them. What was Shamgar's 'ox-goad' to the slaying of so many? Judges iii. 31; Samson's 'jaw-bone of an ass' to the slaying of so many Philistines? Judges xv. 15. It was to shew that the

* That is, 'careful.'—G.

glory was God's. What is the converting of so many souls by so mean fishermen, when ignorance overcame knowledge, folly overcame wisdom, weakness overcame strength? Fishermen and their consorts made the crown of the Roman empire stoop to them. The poor preachers of the gospel brought it to pass at length, that the great empire of Rome should subject* to the gospel; and why is all this but that the power may appear to be of God?

I might with this truth go through all ages, from the beginning of the world to the end, and shew how God hath done great things, sometimes by no means, sometimes by weak means, sometimes when means have been armed against him, in opposition of means. When others are opposite, then hath he got greatest glory. But it is so plain a truth, that I will not spend time to no purpose to declare the point; and therefore I will come more close, and bring the truth home to ourselves.

Now, because we are naturally forgetful of this, and so rob God of his glory, I will shew you divers courses that God taketh with his children to train them up to learn this hard lesson, to give all the glory to God, which naturally they love to finger themselves. For man is naturally a proud creature, and would have all things to himself. Therefore observe in five or six particulars what course God taketh to teach men this lesson, 'that the excellency of power may be of God, and not of us.'

Reason 1. First of all, what is the reason why God *deserts men, his dearest children, oftentimes, leaveth them to terrible plunges, maketh them apprehend he is their enemy, and that they be none of God's, leaving them in a state of darkness, that they see no light?* This is the state of God's dear children. The end of this is, that they may know they must needs go out of themselves if they will have any comfort: 'They are in darkness, and have no light; therefore let them trust in the name of God,' Isa. l. 10. If it were not for these desertions, to see nothing but darkness in themselves, they would not fly to the rock of strength, they would not retire to their rock of defence, they would not trust God. Why do men suffer the sentence of death, and are brought to death's door? No help, no physic will do them good. St Paul giveth the reason, that they may learn 'to trust in the living God,' 2 Cor. i. 9. What! Paul to learn this lesson? Yea, Paul had need to learn this lesson, to go out of himself, and give all the glory of all things to God. And therefore St Paul received 'sentence of death, that he might trust in the living God,' and perfectly go out of himself.

Reason 2. Again, what is the reason that sometimes the child of God *is foiled very foul in little temptations, and standeth in great ones?* Because indeed in these temptations he goeth on in his own strength, and in greater temptations he goeth out of himself and flieth to God. And therefore a good Christian sometimes is basely foiled in a little temptation, and standeth out like a man in a great one, because in the one he is confident of his own strength, in the other he is enforced to repair to God for assistance. That is the reason of it, to learn this doctrine, to give God the glory in all things.

Reason 3. Again, what is the reason that men *are better after a foil, after some base fall, than ever they were before*—as oftentimes God suffers them to fall into foul faults—what is the reason of this strange dispensation of God? To shew that they stood too much on their own bottoms. And why are they better after them? Because, seeing their own weakness and wilfulness, they are driven out of themselves. The sink of corruption was

* That is, 'submit.'—G.

opened to them. They saw they had rebellious hearts. There was depth of corruption which they discerned not before; and now after a fall, that they see the depth of corruption more than before, they grow more humble, more wary in time to come, having more experience of God's infinite mercy in pardoning, of his infinite power in raising; and so in some measure they learn that lesson, to give all the glory to God. God sometimes sanctifieth a gross fall to make them strong. Peter learned to stand by his fall; and Christians once falling by presuming too much upon their own strength, are made to stand stronger for time to come.

Reason 4. Again, what is the reason that sometimes *the church is foiled by weak enemies; and sometimes, when the church is very weak itself, it overcometh strong enemies*, as you have instances of both? It is that men may learn to know that God must be sought to in all things. When there be strong means, they place too much confidence in that strength; and when they offend God, though the means be never so strong, God curseth and blasteth all helps, as the prophet tells them: 'You shall fight against the Chaldeans, but God will curse you,' Jer. xxxvii. 9.* You that think you be strong men, you shall fight against them, but they shall prevail. You have not made your peace with God; and if so, let all the best means be gathered together, God will blast them all. To teach us that whatsoever means we have, we must seek to God. There is an excellent place for this, Jer. xxxvii. 9, *seq*. The Jews thought they were stout men, but they had offended God. Therefore in the ninth hour saith God to them, 'Thus saith the Lord, Deceive not yourselves, saying, The Chaldeans shall depart from us, we shall do well enough.' Saith he, 'Though you had smitten the whole number of the Chaldeans that fight against you, and there remain but wounded men amongst them, yet should they rob every man in his tent, and burn this city with fire.' Though you had smitten them so, yet God is your enemy. It is no matter what weak men they are, what strong means you have. You have broken peace with God. God hath decreed and determined your ruin, and therefore your city must be burned with fire. Never therefore trust to any means if you have offended God, for God can do great things with small means if we please him. Gideon's three hundred can overcome the Midianites, though they cover the earth as grasshoppers, Judg. vii. 6. And if God be offended, [though] the enemies be all wounded men, yet they shall rise and burn the city. And therefore if God be our enemy, trust not to our walls, nor to the sea, nor to our strength and courage of men. All is nothing if we have not God our friend. And therefore it is true that is usually spoken, that where God will defend a city and country, a cobweb may be the walls thereof; but where God will not defend a city or country, a wall is but a cobweb (*r*). Why is all this but that all power may be known to be of God—that we may resign ourselves to him, make our peace with him? If he be our friend, it matters not who is our enemy; if he be our enemy, it matters not who is our friend. 'If God be for us, who is against us?' Rom. viii. 31. It is sin within the city, and sin within the land, doth more hurt than all enemies without it; because it estrangeth and animates God against the place and country.

Reason 5. And what is the reason likewise—to add one more instance—*that he helpeth most in extremity, that he deferreth help till that time*, that in the mount he is seen, and not till he be in the mount, as the proverb is?

* An inference from the passage, or an interpretation, rather than a translation of it.—G.

Gen. xxii. 14. The reason is, that by this means he may mortify and subdue all confidence in the means, that there may be no spiritual adultery with the means. Then faith is stirred up, then prayer is set upon, then is more communion with God, the fountain of strength; and the more communion with God, the fountain of strength, the more strength; and the more communion with God, the fountain of power, the more power. In extremity we have more communion with God's strength and power. Therefore God withdraweth help oftentimes, to wean us from the creature, and to train us up to trust in him.

Use 1. Now to make use of what I have spoken. *Doth God take this course, to do great matters by weak means, that we should acknowledge the virtue of all to be from him? I beseech you, then, to learn this lesson.* Mark the Scriptures, how curiously careful holy men have been not to finger anything of God's. They feared sacrilege, spiritual theft, and lies; that is, to attribute that to them which belongeth not to them. And therefore Saint Paul, 1 Cor. xv. 10, 'I have laboured more than they all: yet not I, but the grace of God within me.' Not the grace of God and I together, as two horses draw a coach, but grace with me did all. I was subordinate, not co-ordinate, with grace, but I under grace. We do but act as we are acted, move as we are moved, and therefore you see how careful he is, and you see the phrases of Scripture, of holy men. 'I am not worthy to loose his shoe latchet,' saith John the Baptist, John i. 27. 'I am not worthy to be called an apostle,' saith Saint Paul, 1 Cor. xv. 9. 'I am not worthy thou shouldst enter into my house,' Mat. viii. 8. Papists stand upon merit of congruity, but the phrase of Scripture saith, 'I am unworthy;' 'Not unto us, not unto us be the praise, but unto thy name.' And therefore give God all the glory of anything that is done. If any good thing be wrought, if any good news be heard from beyond the seas, be sure to advance the instrument so that we rob not God of his glory.* And when God worketh in us anything that is gracious and beneficial, let God have all the glory. All cometh from him, therefore let all go to him again. You see in the Lord's prayer the connection of these two together; 'Thine is the power,' therefore 'thine is the glory,' Mat. vi. 13. The excellency of power is of God, both in governing the world and in governing the church, in subduing corruptions. If power be his, then let glory be his too, let them not be severed.

Use 2. Again, *let this teach us to resign up ourselves to God in the use of all good means, give ourselves to him, for he doth all.* Trust not in the means, rest not in confidence of wit† and parts, but depend upon him. It is a lesson easily understood, but not so easily practised. Therefore look to God. All things belong to God. Art thou of God? Ministerial teaching is not enough. There be two teachers concur to save souls: ministers and God. There are two to be preached to, the outward man and the inward. We speak to the outward man, God to the inward. Paul speaketh to Lydia's ear, but God openeth the heart, Acts xvi. 14. And we baptize with water, but Christ baptizeth 'with the Holy Ghost,' Luke iii. 16. And therefore in all the ordinances of God, see them administered by the outward man, but there is virtue from Christ and from God. He must baptize with the Holy Ghost and with fire. He must open the heart, unlock that, and teach that. If this were experimentally known and practised, we should have greater exercise of grace than there is in people's hearts, but

* In margin here, 'He relateth to the wars of the Swedes in Germany.'—G.
† That is, 'wisdom.'—G.

it is known as a notion, but not for matter of obedience and practice. The last thing we will speak of from the words is,

Use 3. That seeing all power and excellency is from God, then take heed we keep God our friend. Take heed we offend not this God, in whom is all power, our life, our strength. 'In him we live, move, and have our being,' Acts xvii. 28. Take heed we do not offend him. You know what the apostle saith, Phil. ii. 12, 'Make an end of your salvation in fear and trembling.' Why? 'It is God that giveth the will and the deed, and according to his good pleasure.' That is, God worketh all in matters of salvation. He giveth not power, if you will; but he giveth the will, he saveth us and converteth us, and maketh our will answerable to his will. He giveth the virtue τὸ θέλειν, and according to his good pleasure. As long as we submit to him he will work powerfully in us, and therefore 'make an end of your salvation with fear and trembling.' If we leave his Spirit, we be as air without light, presently dark, and as the earth without the sun. All things will decay and become dead, if the light and influence of heaven be withdrawn. Let God subtract the influence of grace, and we shall grow barren, and dead, and cold; and therefore fear him. No man is wise more than God maketh him wise upon every occasion, nor no man is stronger than on every occasion God strengthens him.

And, therefore, if at any time you have a distrusting heart to look to the creature, he withdraweth his strength, and then we are at a loss, and fall, and die; because we work not our own salvation. We are given to self-sufficiency and self-dependency, and therefore God oftentimes blasts our endeavours. 'Blessed is the man that feareth always,' Prov. xxviii. 14, not with a fear of distrust, but a fear of jealousy. Oh this fear of jealousy! We have false hearts, ready to trust in the creature, in wits, in friends. But all that be God's children must have this fear of jealousy, to make an end of salvation with fear and trembling, for God worketh both the will and the deed. He giveth a power according to his good pleasure, and can suspend it when he list.* So much shall serve for the unfolding of this verse, which I did specially intend; the other verses are but an application of this, 'We are troubled on every side, but not distressed,' &c.

VERSES 7–9.

That the excellency of the power may be of God, and not of us. We are troubled on every side, yet not distressed; we are perplexed, but not in despair; persecuted, yet not forsaken; cast down, but not destroyed.

I have spoken largely of the verse before, wherein you may remember that the apostle might take away all suspicion of arrogancy in taking too much upon himself, he saith, 'We carry treasures but in earthen vessels.' The end of which dispensation of God is, 'that the excellency of the power may be of God and not of man.' There we shewed there is a 'power,' and an 'excellent power' in the ordinance of God. And that this is of God, and exclusively, not of us. All which we have propounded at large.

We shewed, there is a blessed presence of God and of his power, and sweetness, and goodness, in all his ordinances. He distilleth and conveyeth whatsoever is in his Father's breast to us by his ordinance. He doth good to us by men like ourselves. As the devil conveyeth all his mischief by men unto men, so God conveyeth all his good by men to men. But they are but the conduits, for the virtue and excellency of the power is of God.

* That is, 'chooseth.'—G.

Things otherwise seeming alike differ in regard of virtue, as cold water differs from hot water. They differ not in colour but in virtue. It is the Spirit of God that accompanieth his ordinance, that giveth power, and virtue, and efficacy to it. For the ministers of the gospel are ministers, and no more nor no less, to be regarded as ministers and no farther. To regard them more is to make idols of them; to deny* them less is to deny them due right. This should stir up a wonderful care of diligence in all the ways and courses that God hath sanctified to convey grace by. They that be God's children love God's presence wheresoever they find it; and because God vouchsafeth his presence in his ordinance, therefore they regard it, and remember always to give the glory of all to God. For the power and excellency is of God, and not of us. 'Why gaze ye on us, as if we by our own power had cured the man?' Acts iii. 12. It is not from man, but from God.

Now to come to the 8th verse, 'We are troubled on every side, yet not distressed; we are perplexed,' &c.

The apostle's words have an elegant antithesis of things seeming contrary. 'We are perplexed, not in despair; persecuted, not forsaken; cast off, but not destroyed.' There is a kind of elegancy in the dispensation of God. And this serveth to the former argument to shew that we carry these treasures in 'earthen vessels.' That we should not despise the earthen vessels because they be weak, he sets down what befalls them in the world, and how God supports and giveth supply of comforts suitable to the distress. He grants 'we be troubled on every side, yet not distressed; perplexed, but not in despair.' Those that are to deal with enemies, and are to prevent objections, they must grant the worst that may be granted, that so they may make their apology† better. Saint Paul freely granteth all that can be objected by any that look on the outside of the professors and ministers of the gospel. I grant these fall out, and yet it must be granted God hath a special care likewise, as you shall see in the unfolding of the words, which we will particularly go over, and then jointly raise out of them some observations.

'We are troubled on every side,' The word signifieth pressed, *θλιβόμενοι*, but yet not oppressed. God suffers his children to be pressed. Afflictions, they are the wine-press of God, to press out of them all that is good, to the view and taste of others. They have liquor in them, but it is not tasted of, but by pressure. For the most part spices relish not, savour not, unless they be beaten. So it is with grapes unless they be pressed. The works the enemies of the church do to the children of God, is to press the ill that is in them, and to press out the ill that is in themselves. For at the same time they press out by trouble, and disgraceful usage, better men than themselves, at the same time they press out and make apparent their own malice and poison. So that afflictions are discoveries of their evil, and of good men's good. And it is helpful for the church, that there be both, that all men may be known, and the thoughts of men discovered; and that the graces of the good may be also manifested. And therefore he saith, 'We be troubled or pressed on every side.'

Indeed, *ἐν παντὶ* in the original signifieth 'in every place,' in every time, as here 'on every side,' for the children of God are on every side pressed. Sometimes from above, God seemeth to be their enemy; and

* Qu. 'regard'?—Ed.

† That is, = defence.—G.

sometimes from within, by the terror of conscience; and sometimes on the right hand vexed with their friends, and sometimes on the left hand vexed with their enemies; and sometimes round about them with the states and conditions of the times; sometimes from beneath, with Satan's molestations and vexations; something before them, fear of hell, damnation, and trouble to come; and something behind them, remembrance of former sins. So that they be pressed on every side, 'yet not distressed,' στενοχωρούμενοι, or oppressed, or altogether distressed, as the word signifieth, not altogether in desperate straits; when the body is in straits and pinched, that it cannot tell what way to turn, and the mind in strait doth not know whither to retire. But God's children are not in such straits. For though they be 'troubled on every side,' yet they are not straitened in spirit, they have large hearts; as David saith, Ps. cxviii. 5, and xviii. 19, 'Thou hast set my feet at large;' and Ps. cxix. and ver. 92, he declares how God had enlarged his heart. And so God enlargeth the paths of his children. Though they be afflicted, yet they be not so straitened but they find inward enlargements; enlargedness of prayer to God. They can vent their desires to God largely; before men they are bold to maintain God's cause. They find a large heart in regard of inward peace and comfort; and indeed there is never a child of God but he hath incomparably a larger heart than wicked men. All wicked men are all vainly-hearted, base-spirited persons, but the child of God hath a large heart; for the grace of God and sense of heavenly comforts enlarge the heart, and so he hath a more heroical spirit than any worldling hath. So that though they be in pressure, yet they be not overpressed. Wicked men have a prison in their own breasts. Take a wicked man that is not besotted: when he understandeth himself, though he be never so free, though above all men, though a commander of the world, yet he is imprisoned and straitened in his own heart; his conscience upbraids him with his sins, commands him to come before the tribunal-seat of God. In greatest liberty he is oftentimes in straits for abusing that liberty. But a child of God can in all afflictions lay open his soul before God. So much for that particular.

'Perplexed, yet not in despair.' The word is elegant in the original: ἀπορούμενοι, we are perplexed, but not in extremity. The word in the original signifieth want of counsel, what course to take, when a man is in such difficulty for want.* Want of things necessary, and then want of counsel to get them supplied, breedeth perplexity. Now, saith Paul, we want many things. And therefore among other troubles the apostle reckons hunger, thirst, fasting, 2 Cor. xi. 27. God's children are oftentimes in want, not only of outward things, but seemingly in want of counsel what course to take for a time. In regard of danger, what a difficulty was Abraham in when he was to offer his son Isaac, his eldest son, his only son, the son of the promise! Gen. xxii. 1–3; and Jacob when he parted with Benjamin, and thought he had lost Joseph, Gen. xliii. 13, 14. Exod. xiv. 10–12, *seq.*, Moses at the Red Sea; present to yourselves what straits he was in. The mountains were on either side, the Red Sea before them, the Egyptians behind them. In what strait was David when they were ready to stone him? 1 Sam. xxx. 6. Certainly exceedingly great. In what strait was Jonah in the belly of hell, the whale in the depth of the sea? Jonah i. 17. And so God's children are oftentimes not only in want

* In margin here, 'ἀπορεῖσθαι hærere et inops esse consilii.'—*Erasm*[*us*] *in loc.* —G.

of help, but in want of counsel. So they be almost at their wits' ends, not knowing what course to take.

'Yet we are not in despair,' ἀλλ' οὐκ ἐξαπορούμενοι. For God at the pinch of time cometh, and as it was in Abraham's case, in the mount, appeared. When the knife was ready to cut the throat of Isaac, then God sheweth himself. So Moses at the Red Sea, he was in wonderful straits perplexed. And he crieth to God. Why dost thou cry to me? saith God, though he said nothing, Exod. xiv. 15. God made way for him through the Red Sea. God makes his way where he findeth none. He can divide the Red Sea, and cause Jordan to fly back. When the ways be desperate, and the plunges extreme, then God makes way for his children. God is wonderful near to them in their extremities. He was nearer to Daniel than the teeth of the lion, Dan. vi. 16, *seq.*, and nearer Moses than the water was, when he was swimming in his basket, Exod. ii. 3. God is nearest in danger when it is nearest of all. When Jonah was in the whale's belly, he was in wonderful perplexity, Jonah ii. 1. It could not be otherwise; and yet at the same time God enlarged his heart that he did not despair. So that you see the words are true. Though God's children are perplexed, yet they be not in 'despair.' They have a God to go to at all times. At the worst they can send forth their sighs and groans, though they cannot speak; and those sighs and groans are great cries in God's ear. God knoweth the desires of their souls; God hath an ear in their very hearts, and knoweth the meaning of his own Spirit joining with their spirits. No man is in desperate condition that can pray, and though he cannot pray in words, yet prayer being matter of affection and desires to God, and any man being in such extremity may do that. There is no prayer but it fetcheth help from heaven. There is not a groan lost that is sent to heaven, and therefore 'though they be perplexed, yet not in despair.'

The church seemed to be in a perishing condition, and David saith, 'I am cast out of thy sight, yet thou heardest the voice of my prayer,' Ps. xxxi. 22; yea, a prayer joined with such expressions that I said, 'God hath forsaken me.' The spirit sighs and groans, and God regardeth such a prayer. And so, that howsoever in regard of the flesh we be in desperate conditions, yet the Spirit hath an eye to God, and moveth a sigh and tear to him, and at the same time fetcheth help from heaven. You see then the point is clear.

Verse 9. 'We are persecuted, but not forsaken.' διωκόμενοι. The Greek word signifieth to pursue. God sometimes personates an enemy, and seemeth to be against us, and that is a heavy case. It was Job's case: 'Thou writest bitter things against me,' Job xiii. 26. In divine temptations God seemeth to be our enemy. We are persecuted and pursued; sometimes by the arm of the Almighty, sometimes again by Satan, and by his instruments. When we have made by conversion to God escape from the world, the world sendeth hue and cry out after the saints, pursuing and labouring to bring them to their old conditions and labours, to trip them in their ways. The children of God have been from the beginning of the world so pursued, that they never leave pursuing them, till they have driven them to death, and even to hell itself. And this is the state of all God's children if once any will be righteous. 'Whosoever will live godly in Christ Jesus must suffer persecution.' He may be civil,* and no man will say black is his eye; but if he have power of religion, and labour

* That is, 'moral.'—G.

to express it in his conversation, he shall have persecution of the tongue or of the hand. Saint Austin saith well, Though we live well in times of peace, yet, *audi, audi mi frater*, begin to live as a Christian should live, and see if you be pursued; you shall find a Babylon in Jerusalem (*s*). And truly in times of peace a man will find enemies enough at home. For it is almost equally difficult to be truly righteous at all times. In the primitive church the doctrine of religion was opposed in applying the truth of doctrine. Now the power of practisers. At all times religion hath been so much persecuted, as may stand with salvation. The devil is content with profession. The thing may stand with lust and sin, but so much as is necessary to bring to heaven that hath been always under persecution in one kind or other. 'Though persecuted, yet not forsaken,' viz., of God. No. So far from being forsaken of God, that God is never nearer them than when trouble is nearest of all. 'Be not far off,' saith the psalmist, 'for trouble is nigh,' Ps. xxii. 11. Then there is most use of God's presence and comfort. In persecution usually the souls of God's people fly under the shadow of his wings, and being driven to him they find more support and succour than at other times. It was a good speech of the Landgrave of Hesse, Philip the First, that was of fame and note, to Charles the Fifth, when not only the Duke of Saxony, but he, was taken prisoners, and a great while continued so. How did you all the time demean yourselves? Said he, 'I found those divine comforts that I never felt before.* So that there is certain evidence of God's presence in persecution and standing out in a good cause, which God's children never felt before, as after. There is a hidden manna conveyed to them, which is appropriated to those times. So saith he, 'We be persecuted, but not forsaken;' nay, God is never nearer than at that time.

When there is a new moon, the space between the old and the new is *interlunium* (*t*), that it is as good as lost now, yet hath more light in itself than ever it had, for it is nearer the sun than ever, though it appears not to the world. And though the comforts of the soul appear not in afflictions, yet then God shineth more upon them than at any other time.

'Cast down, but not destroyed.' Cast down, by persecution prevailing. Persecution prevailing doth cast men down, and give them the worst in the eye of the world, but yet we are not destroyed. The children of God go masked, many thousands of them, to the sight of flesh and blood, and in appearance of flesh destroyed. But they be nothing less than destroyed. For to take it at the worst, though their meat is taken from them, yet they are not distressed.

(1.) For what is the worst the world can do? They take away their lives which they must leave ere long, and thereby they are made partakers of their wish, which every child of God hath, 'to depart and to be with Christ,' Phil. i. 23. Now when they drive them out of the world, they make them partakers of what they most desire, for they have more communion with God in heaven than ever they had before; they are in their seats and proper place.

(2.) Again, though in regard of some particulars the church may seem to be destroyed, some boughs are cut, yet the body remains, so in regard of the whole body they are not destroyed.

(3.) In regard of the 'inward man,' they are not destroyed. They take courage still, and comfort still, while they are in the world. When they go out of the world they have accomplishment of all desires. Put case God deliver them not, but give them up to death: he delivereth them in

* Cf. Vol. III. page 530, *et alibi.*—G.

not delivering them. For what is death but delivering them from all trouble? When he delivereth not in particular danger, he giveth them a general deliverance by death from all trouble whatsoever.

(4.) Again, there is a double deliverance. There is an inward secret deliverance, and an apparent open deliverance. Put case they be cast down, and not openly delivered, yet secretly they are delivered, that is, from fear and despair. The soul is set at liberty within. So that though they be cast down, yet not destroyed.

(5.) If they be destroyed to the appearance of the world, it is but seed sown. Saints are the seeds out of which grow many other. The blood of martyrs is the seed of the church.* As often as we are mowed and cast down, saith Tertullian, by your cruelty, it is but an allurement to our profession. So when they seem to be destroyed, they be but seed sown, and out of their ashes many rise out of them. How much are we beholding to the bloody times in this kingdom, for this after-glorious church!

(6.) 'Not destroyed' in this world, while they have any work to do. You may imprison them, fetter them, but God will work a miracle rather than his children shall be taken out of the world before they have done their work. The three young men in the furnace, the fire shall cease to burn rather than they shall before their hour cometh, Dan. iii. 27. In the gospel Christ was not hurt by them, for his hour is not yet come; they cannot hurt one hair of the head. 'They are afflicted, but not oppressed; they are persecuted, but not forsaken; cast down, but not destroyed.'

From all which we may raise some general truths, and make use of all that hath been spoken.

Doct. First of all we may from hence observe, *that troubles and afflictions of God's people in this world they are many, and they are great and growing.* They wax greater and greater till God's time be appointed. Here is distress, persecution, perplexity, casting down, they be many and manifoldly different in their kind. And then they be great, for here he reckons the greatest troubles than can befall, except death itself, which is usually included. And then there be degrees of them; to be afflicted is less than to be perplexed, and persecution added to perplexity. Then to persecution without is added the trouble following. And not only afflicted, perplexed, persecuted, but cast down.

That is no matter, *mille mali species, mille salutis erunt*, if a thousand ways of trouble, there will be a thousand ways of deliverance. God is never at a loss to help his children. Therefore God grant we are so. So, but we are not in distress, we despair not, we are not forsaken, we are not destroyed.

'We,' that is, Paul, and not only we as men, and we as Christians, but we as eminent men. For the troubles of God's children happen to them as men. Sometimes sickness, death, losses, crosses. Sometimes as Christians, as they be maligned and opposed by the wicked world. Sometimes in an eminent calling, as Pharaoh, that desired to slay the male children especially, that were strong and able to do service; they were objects of malice, Exod. i. 16. Now we are thus used not only as men and Christians, but as eminent men. So that it is the condition of the most eminent of all to be thus used. It pleaseth God to let his children endure many and manifold and great troubles. Now what is the reason of this? I might be large, but I will give a few.

Reason 1. Of necessity *there must be a conformity between the members*

* In margin here, '*Sanguis martyrum semen ecclesiæ.*' [Cf. Vol. iii. p. 530, note *m.*]

and the head. It behoved Christ to suffer, that he might enter into glory. And all we in our time must suffer, and so enter into glory. 'We are predestinate to conformity to our head,' Rom. viii. 29. We are not only predestinate to salvation, but to all between us and salvation. We are ordained to pass through such and such good actions, such and such turnings. There is no man but hath so many actions to perform, so many sufferings to endure, to which they be by God ordained.

Reason 2. And again, the best of God's children have something to be wrought out of them by a spirit of burning and affliction; the best need refining.

Reason 3. And again, grace needeth trials and exercise and increase. Now God sanctifieth all these, passing from 'vessel to vessel,' Jer. xlviii. 11. These transfusions [are] to work out what is evil, to try, exercise, and increase what is good.

Reason 4. And if there were no more but the malice of Satan and his cursed seed, the seed of the serpent, it is not possible to avoid the cross. And God, that his children may not love the world, hath made the world hate them. And it is safe for God's people to have the hatred of the worst people. Their hatred will do them more good than their love. Their hatred breeds a separation, and commands a separation in conclusion. For what shall we do with familiarity and acquaintance with them whose company we cannot enjoy in heaven? And therefore God will have his children exercised with the worst men; and then he desires to take them out of the world, and to set God up in his due place. God is God, and the Creator, when we be stript of all worldly comforts. Then vanity is vanity. God will not have us idolize anything below, and therefore suffers us to fall into extreme wants and dangers. Many other reasons there be, which I do give you but a taste of.

You see then the state of God's children in regard of the world. But what is it in regard of him? They be not forsaken, they be not utterly cast off. So they are patient in both; patient in regard of the trouble they meet with in the world, patient in regard of God's dealing with them. God forsakes them not so as to destroy them. He leaveth them not in a desperate condition, as he doth the wicked.

Doct. 2. Again, observe this, *that the life of God's children in this world is a mixed life,* woven of afflictions and of comforts, intermixed of both. It tastes of both the malice of the world and the goodness of God.

They oftentimes enjoy sickness. They be sometimes in dumps and sadness. Their life is woven of comfort and discomfort, and it is good for them in this world to be so, till they be in their proper place in heaven. And this is our comfort always, though troubles be many, and manifold, and great, and growing, and the last day worst, yet as the waters of afflictions grow, so do their comforts and the graces of the Spirit grow like waters of the sanctuary;* as troubles increase, so the waters of consolation increase. And it is better to be in trouble than to be kept from the trouble without the comfort. There is more sweetness in affliction than in freedom from it without the sweetness. If we look to the world, you see what we may look for. If we look to heaven, you may see what to expect thence.

Use. If this be so, that their condition is thus mixed, *it is good in our prayers to allege to God our ill condition, to argue extremity.* 'Help, Lord: for vain is the help of man,' Ps. lx. 11. 'Save, Lord: the water is entered into my soul,' Ps. lxix. 1. Help, Lord: if thou wilt not, none will; if thou

* Cf. Ezekiel xlvii. 1, *seq.*—G.

canst not, none can. God will be bound with these arguments. It was the speech of Philo, 'A man's help faileth, where God's begins' (*u*).

And it [is] a good argument to allege to God in matters of sin, 'Lord, pardon, Lord, forgive, for my sins are many and great,' Ps. xxv. 11. This is a good argument with God, for he is infinite in mercy; therefore allege it as a binding argument.

But if God himself seem to be our enemy, What course shall we take then? Sometimes God acts a part that is not his own, that he may shew afterward a greater mercy. In such times we must get the eye of faith, and break through the clouds between the soul and God's face, and see his fatherly countenance in Jesus Christ. Faith hath piercing eyes, and breaks through the clouds between God and us, and bindeth him with his own nature and promise, whatsoever part he acts. 'Lord, howsoever thou dealest, thy nature in Christ is gracious, merciful.' 'Thou hast made rich promises that thou wilt not fall from.' 'Forsake me not.' Bind him with his word, with his nature; he cannot deny his word, his nature, himself; allege them to him in Christ, and allege his own promise, and they will be effectual.

Use. Again, we see here *that it is a good art, and needful in times of trouble, to look to the good, as well as to the ill.* The apostle doth not only confess ingenuously all the ill that the enemies might object to weaken the reputation of the gospel, they are people cast down and despised. All this is true, but we are not forsaken, we are not in despair, not destroyed. This is a good art in every affliction. It is better to have our eyes on the good, than to have our eyes altogether upon the ill. God hath taken away one child, he might have taken many. God hath afflicted with sickness, but he might have taken away our wits. Therefore have not both eyes fixed upon the grief, for that is Satan's policy, to rob God of his glory, and our souls of comfort.

Use. Therefore learn a blessed skill from hence. When there is objected anything by Satan to disgrace the gospel or discourage it, reject* the objections of Satan with better. It is so, I confess; but [while] God seemeth to be displeased, and I am afflicted, God is yet a gracious God, hath left many comforts, his word, and promises, and therein I will trust: he hath given me his Spirit to support me. Thus return all the temptations of Satan, learn to be as witty† and ingenious to argue that, for the strengthening of our faith, which may drive us to the acknowledgment of God's goodness and mercy, as Satan is to do the contrary: Judges vi. 13, 'God be with thee, thou valiant man;' but if God be with us, 'why is it thus with us?' And so God's people look all to the grievance; why are we persecuted, and in distress, and want, and at our wits' end? Now, but consider the comfort as well as the discomfort; learn that heavenly wisdom from St Paul.

Let no man be discouraged, if he findeth himself sensible of the grief he lieth under. We be flesh, not spirit. God knoweth whereof we are made; and therefore he layeth not whole loads upon us, but in anger he remembers mercy. You see how he deals with the apostle Paul, and others in his case. Therefore, if we be sensible of trouble, God can help. No man more sensible of grief than Christ, *Christi dolor, dolor maximus*. For he had perfect wisdom to apprehend, and a sound body (*v*). St Paul speaks of these things as wonderfully sensible, but here is true patience, when we be sensible to the uttermost of the grievance, and yet withal are but sensible

* That is, 'cast back, retort.'—G.

† That is 'wise.'—G.

of the grievance. 'Why should I smite them any more?' Isa. i. 5, saith God to the prophet. It is not only sin, but judgment, to be given up to hard hearts, not to feel the condition. Well, St Paul was sensible of his condition.

Obj. Thou wilt object, What is this to us? We live in calm times, and enjoy health and prosperity, and know not what these things mean that Paul speaks of.

Ans. Beloved, the more we be beholding to God. But do we know to what times the Lord may call the best of us all? Therefore we must be prepared before hand. Comforts are not found in adversity that were not sought for in prosperity, as Austin saith (*w*). In times of peace, people should provide for war and defence; and so in times of peace let us think of these things. Our conditions may alter. Howsoever the state may continue, yet we that live under our vines and fig-trees, do we know how the Lord may exercise us? May not he exercise us with afflictions of mind and persecutions of body? May not he exercise us with trouble of conscience, and bring us into straits, which is a spiritual martyrdom too? In times of prosperity, God's children know better what to do and whom to depend on, because then he keeps them off from inward troubles. And therefore, seeing we know not how long in our personal condition we may be as we are, it is not amiss to think on these things.

And to direct us a little what to do now in times of peace and quietness.

(1.) *Labour to preserve our peace with God by all means*, that when changes come, as changes may come, and will come one way or other, we may say with the apostle, 'I am afflicted, but not forsaken.' If we make not God now our friend; if we shall now multiply sin and guilt, and run into God's books more and more, it will be a hell when trouble, and sickness, and persecution come. And therefore as we will have God our friend when we stand most in need of him, so let us labour to keep God our friend now at this time. The desperate course that many loose persons take: they run into an old course, they let the reins loose to licentiousness, let their tongue lie and swear, and deny nothing that they affect. 'Is there not times and months for these wild asses to be taken in? In their months you may take them.' There be months of trouble and months of sickness; and when their former courses have been nothing but a perpetual provoking of God, what comfort can these persons have? And therefore, as we desire to have God stand by us and help at every pinch, labour for peace with him now in time of prosperity.

(2.) *Let us be constant in his cause, in his religion*, that is so constant to us. And this constancy of the Spirit and the best things will be an evidence to us that we have found him constant in his love to us.

(3.) And that we may quiet ourselves the better, if such times come, *be careful, and treasure up promises for the time to come*, that we may allege them to God. Get good liquor into our hearts, that when times of pressing come, there may be good wine. If good knowledge be not gotten beforehand, what will afflictions press out but murmurings and despair, and something that was there before. Therefore treasure up now all we can; there is a spending time will come. Joseph's hard years may overtake us; we know not into what distress we may be brought. And because God is the best friend in extremity, be sure we offend not him for any creature, because let the creature do his worst, yet God will always be sure to be our friend. And if God be our friend, it matters not who is our enemy. I cannot press all that may be pressed out of this point.

(4.) Labour at all times *to maintain a good conceit of God and his goodness.* If Satan suggest he will cast us off, and that there is no hopes for us in our God, answer again, It is not so. Labour to have a spirit of faith to beat back all such temptations. You shall see strange temptations, and yet excellently answered. 'Yet God is good to Israel,' Ps. lxxiii. 1. When the child of God is low, yet he keeps good conceits of God, though things go strangely. I know not what to make of my condition and of the churches,* 'yet God is good.'

The reason is, when we be at worst, God can help us. And therefore come those comfortable exceptions in the Psalms. 'Great are the troubles of the righteous, *but* the Lord delivereth them out of all,' Ps. xxxiv. 19. 'They were afflicted sore, *but* not delivered to death,' Ps. cxviii. 18. So here mark the exceptions: we be in straits, persecuted and cast down, *but* yet delivered.

Thus labour for a good conceit of God. The like things you may observe out of these words of the apostle; and I beseech you, let us make use of them for the right knowledge of these things. Hence it is said, Rom. viii. 37, 'That in all these we are more than conquerors;' a strange speech, in affliction, pressures, casting down, 'we are more than conquerors.' And how cometh this? 'We are more than conquerors in him that loved us, in Jesus Christ;' more than conquerors, because we are overcome† when we seem to be overcome; because religion hath grown even by blood and suffering. St Austin saith, by straits and afflictions the church hath been delivered and spread abroad to the uttermost parts of the world (*x*).

'We are more than conquerors' in all these in a treble regard.

[1.] *Specially in regard of ourselves;* for the devil aimeth at separation between God and us. 'Now, what shall separate us?' saith the apostle, Rom. viii. 35.

The devil intends a divorcement; but when by a spirit of faith we draw near to God, and cleave fast to God, then the devil's policy is overthrown. The more the world driveth us from God, the faster we cleave to God; and then we be more than conquerors.

[2.] *In regard of spiritual courage.* The more God's Spirit is depressed, the higher it riseth. The enemy labours to quail the spirits of them that be good, but they cannot do it, for the Spirit of God is invincible. And the spirit of a Christian being supported by an higher Spirit than their own, 'I can do all things through Christ that strengthens me,' Philip. iv. 13. Therefore they are more than conquerors by the invincible Spirit of Christ.

[3.] And then they be more than conquerors *in regard of the cause.* The devil labours to drive men to the dislike of the cause and religion by suffering disgrace, but he cannot.

Use. Firstly. And therefore, I beseech you, let me conclude *with a point of encouragement,* considering it is spoken with a great deal of courage. 'We are afflicted, but not forsaken; cast down, but not destroyed;' let it encourage us *to take the cause of God in hand, and go through with it in spite of Satan and his instruments, and fear nothing that shall befall us.* Why should we fear the devil? Let no man think what the devil threats, but what God promises. Therefore fear nothing, for God will make it good; he will be never nearer than when we stand most in need of help. And therefore set upon God's cause with courage; and not only on the cause of religion, but cause of honesty and justice. The truth of God in any kind is dearer than our lives. The worst that can befall us is to be persecuted

* Qu. 'church's'?—ED.

† Qu. 'we overcome'?—ED.

and distressed. You shall have more comfort from heaven than discomfort from the world; and what do you lose then?

Therefore let us all support ourselves with this. There is more force in God's help from heaven to secure and support by an inward invincible strength, than there is in the world, or Satan the prince of the world, to cast us down; we have more for us than against us. When we be stripped of all, yet know, that God is the God of all; when he hath taken all, yet he leaveth himself. We have all at the fountain, all at the spring. Therefore let that be ground of resolution; 'If I perish, I perish,' saith the good woman, Esther iv. 16. But never depart from God, from religion, from justice, from the cause of the church; because I know God will be like himself; he cannot deny himself, but constantly deals with his church and children, as in former times. It cannot be otherwise with me, than Paul the great apostle of the church. If that befalls me that did befall Paul, as I am in Paul's distress, so I may look for Paul's support and comfort.

The apostle, to avoid the objection of the scandal of the cross, by which they were the less accepted in the hearts of many, sets down the state of the people of God in this world, take them at the worst. He speaks here of himself not only as a man (since the fall of our weak nature is subject to many calamities), but he speaks of himself as a Christian, opposing the sins of the world. And he grants what they may object. 'We are troubled on every side, but not in distress.' The apostles take advantage from the troubles they were in, to advance the love and mercy of God in those troubles. We lose nothing by them, for that which is gained in any trouble, is better than that that can be lost. 'We are troubled on every side, yet not distressed,' so as we know not what to do, when we are in such straits. Take a Christian at the worst, yet he hath freedom to the throne of grace by the spirit of prayer; and God looks upon him in the worst condition. The more strait his condition is, the more large his [supply of the] Spirit is; therefore though troubles increase, yet his comforts increase.

Secondly, 'We are persecuted with wants, and by reason of wants we know not what course to take,' so that we are oftentimes 'perplexed, but yet not in despair,' for God supplieth. This I unfolded before.

A Christian man hath some bottom, in his worst condition, to uphold him, but take a man out of the state of grace, and he hath no bottom to stand upon, but he sinks presently in any trouble of mind or conscience to hell, though never so strong in wit and parts. He cannot encounter with a divine temptation, he hath no power with him above himself. We see Ahithophel, that wise politician. He was a bad man; and what became of him? He hanged himself.* So Cain, Judas, and Saul. What saith Saul in his perplexity? 'The Philistines are upon me, trouble is upon me, and God hath forsaken me,' 1 Sam. xxviii. 15, a pitiful complaint; and this may be the complaint of all carnal men, 'The Philistines are upon me, trouble is upon me, and God hath forsaken me.' But the children of God, when they are perplexed, they do not despair. It is a pitiful case with those that shall desire the mountains to cover them, Rev. vi. 15. Your wicked persons that now outlook anybody, that despise every one but themselves, the time shall come when they shall desire the mountains to cover them, a pitiful strait that they cannot tell where to betake themselves, as Christ saith, Mat. xxiv. [throughout]. Oh, but the child of God in his worst he hath something to stay himself upon. Though he be in deep troubles, there is a help above him, a power of God to support him on the

* Cf. 2 Sam. xvii. 23.—G.

left hand and on the right. If there be a height and depth of troubles, there is a height and depth of mercy to support them.

Thirdly, 'Persecuted, but not forsaken.' Grant what is to be granted. 'We are persecuted.' How far? They will never leave us till they have taken us out of the world; and what hurt do they then? Drive us nearer to God. God owneth his children most when the world owneth them least, and there is a blessing pronounced upon all those that suffer for good causes. 'Blessed are you when men persecute you, for great is your reward in heaven,' Mat. v. 10. As he said, It is a kingly thing to suffer evil, &c. (*y*). I am sure it is a Christian's condition to do good and suffer evil.

In sufferings let us look to three things.

(1.) First, *To the cause*, considering that it be free from sin.

(2.) To look *to our carriage in the cause*, that we carry not ourselves tempestuously.

(3.) Look *to those that persecute*. Let them persecute; and though they do, you shall not be forsaken. Though a man may desert him that stands for him and his cause, yet when the children of God shall stand for God, he will not desert them in his cause; 'though persecuted, yet not forsaken.'

Fourthly, The fourth is, 'cast down, but not destroyed.' Persecution prevails sometimes to casting down, but 'yet we are not destroyed.' We are cast down, trodden down, insulted over, but not 'destroyed.' Beloved, you see the great persecution of the church. What a pitiful condition the church hath been brought unto within these late years: trodden down, 'yet not destroyed.' For they are partakers with Christ that is now in heaven, and they are assured of a blessed resurrection; and therefore not destroyed, when they seem to be destroyed in the eyes of the world. As he said before, they 'are earthen vessels.' So every man is but an 'earthen vessel,' but it is much that an earthen vessel should be cast down and yet not broken; they may be cast down, but not destroyed. For when the enemies have done the worst they can to destroy them, that destruction is no destruction, but salvation.

Again, 'We are cast down, but not destroyed.' We see here is a kind of eloquence of things as well as words. Here is a sweet harmony of things: 'they are afflicted, but not in despair; perplexed, but not distressed; persecuted, but not forsaken.' Every one of these are greater than the former. I shewed you God's children are troubled in this world, and their troubles grow more and more till they are scarce able to bear them, and then God giveth a gracious promise, 'that he will not suffer us to be tempted above our strength,' 1 Cor. x. 13. For God limits the time and the measure of all troubles in this world. He stands by and turneth the glass,* and limits the measure. 'Thus far shalt thou go, and no farther,' Job xxxviii. 11, as we may see in Job's case; and his promise is, 'that the rod of the wicked shall not rest upon the back of the righteous,' Ps. cxxv. 3. This is one comfort, that a Christian's times are not in the enemies' hands, but 'our times,' as David saith, 'are in thy hands,' Ps. xxxi. 15. Our times of coming into trouble, and our times of going out of trouble, are in the hands of God. As he made all things, in the first creation, in number, weight, and measure, so he rules and governeth all things in number, weight, and measure, especially his church. He will not put in a dram too much; he weigheth their strength, and weigheth their crosses, and exactly observeth

* The allusion is to the hour-glass used to mark time; and which, when the hour had expired, was 'turned.'—G.

what their strength is able to bear. For he is a most wise father; and that is our comfort, whatsoever falls upon us. If troubles grow upon us, comforts shall grow; if they grow great in number and measure, comforts shall grow great in number and measure too; for he is a God of comfort. He comforts in every trouble, as we see here, 'perplexed, cast down, persecuted,' yet God hath comfort for every one of these.

Last Obs. Again, here see *the comfortable condition of God's children in this world.* All their happiness is not reserved for heaven, but they are happy in affliction itself. In them there is comfort. There is support not only in heaven, but in the very time of affliction, as we may see it in Ps. xciv. 19: 'According to the multitude of my thoughts, thy comforts delighted my soul.' According to my distracted thoughts, thy comforts have refreshed my soul. There be present comforts in troubles that keep God's children from despair. St Paul nameth the lowest comforts that God's children have here. Though they are 'persecuted, yet they are not forsaken;' though they are 'cast down, yet they perish not.' He sheweth here, that if we regard not the great matters that we shall have in heaven, yet God dispenseth his comforts here now in the time of troubles. Here is matter of comfort, and not of despair. Miserable heathens, that had not the knowledge of God in Christ, what condition were they in? As one saith, 'I would pray, but my prayers are in vain' (*z*). They were in great misery. Wanting the knowledge of God in Christ, they fell into despair. So in the church: those that are not acquainted with God, in great troubles fall to despair; but you see the comfortable condition of a Christian, take him at the worst.

Ver. 10. It followeth, 'Always bearing in our bodies the dying of the Lord Jesus, that the life of Jesus may be made manifest in our bodies.' Here he addeth a comfort to those that suffered before, shewing the end of all that God intends. 'We bear in our bodies the dying of the Lord Jesus.' He calls all troubles by the name of dying. This is the first.

All the troubles God's children are exercised with here, are named with the name of dying.

(1.) *Because troubles are little deaths.* Death is not the last parting of soul and body, but every separation from comfort is a kind of death. Therefore he calls afflictions dyings, because they make way for greater deaths. He calls afflictions dyings, from the intent and purpose of the persecutors, for their intent is, if it were in their power, to kill.

(2.) Likewise it is called a dying, because *this is in the preparation of spirit that they are ready to die;* for no man is a true Christian but he labours to deny father and mother, and all comforts, and resigns himself to Christ. If I can serve him with mine honour, yea, with my life, he shall have it, so that I am ready to die upon all occasions, as you may see in the next verse. 'We are always delivered unto death for Jesus' sake,' that is, the enemies expose us to death, and if it were in their power they would kill us.

Quest. But why doth he call his troubles a dying 'of the Lord Jesus?'

Ans. [1.] There be some troubles that Christ suffered, which we cannot; as the curse of the law, and the wrath of God due to our sins. These Christ suffered alone. 'He trod the wine-press of God's wrath alone,' Isa. lxiii. 3. In these there is no partaking.

Ans. [2.] There is another dying, a dying in his mystical body, his church. He suffers affliction in every Christian. He was stoned when

Stephen was stoned, Acts vii. 59. Christ was beheaded when John Baptist was beheaded, and in prison when Paul was in prison. Christ suffered in all the martyrs, by reason of that union between him and his church. So that besides that, he suffers in every Christian, this is called 'the dying of the Lord Jesus.'

Ans. [3.] Because he measures out to every one their cup. Afflictions are called a cup, and therefore they are his, because they are measured out by him.

Ans. [4.] And then they are his dyings, because by them they are made like unto him. He suffered first; and then every Christian must express that suffering. As he suffered and entered into glory, so 'we must suffer with him, if we mean to reign with him,' 2 Tim. ii. 12.

Ans. [5.] And then again, they are called the dying of the Lord Jesus, because Christ hath a fellowship and communion with them in all their dyings. As a Christian hath communion with Christ when he dieth, we are 'crucified with him;' so Christ suffers with us. He is afflicted with us, reproached with us, as Moses, Heb. xi. 26, counted 'the rebukes of Christ' greater riches than all the treasures of Egypt. Christ enters into prison with us, 'Saul, Saul, why persecutest thou me?' Acts ix. 4. Christ takes upon him all the wrongs done to his children as done to himself. As it argueth madness in those that persecute, so a sweet comfort to them that do suffer, that they have Christ to suffer with them. The presence of Christ so sweetens everything, as he said, 'The presence of Christ made the gridiron sweet unto Lawrence' (*aa*). A beam of Christ's presence that is now in heaven scatters all troubles. The presence of Christ made Paul sing in prison, Acts xvi. 25. The presence of Christ sweetens all conditions and all places whatsoever, because our dyings are the dyings of Christ; Christ hath fellowship and communion with us in them.

Ans. [6.] Then again, they are the dyings of Christ, *because they divorce and wean us from the world.* Now we being separated from worldly comforts, are fitter for farther fellowship and communion with Christ, as you shall see afterward.

Thus we see some reasons why all the miseries of a Christian are called 'the dyings of our Lord Jesus.'

We see then there must be a dying of the outward man; first there must be little dyings, and then a consummation of all. And why? Because sin is so invested and so sunk into our natures, that without death it cannot be divorced. Afflictions are to make a divorce between sin and our nature, for 'no unclean thing can enter into heaven,' Rev. xxi. 27. As the Spirit did separate sin in the nature of Christ, so doth the Spirit of God purify the nature of every man by afflictions. Because grace needs help, therefore afflictions join as fire with grace, to make a more perfect separation between the soul and sin. Together with the sanctified spirit there is a spirit of burning. When the canker hath seized deeply on metals, it must pass through the fire before it can be purged; so the nature of corruption hath so eaten into our natures, that we need fire to purge it out.

'Flesh and blood,' saith the apostle, 'shall not enter into the kingdom of heaven,' 1 Cor. xv. 50. What is the meaning of that? That is, there be some remainders of corruption in it. Until this body be returned to dust, till the Lord make this body of ours new again, which is now so stained with sin, it shall never enter into heaven. Our blessed Saviour's body the third day, before he saw corruption, did rise again, because there was no sin in him, and therefore it was not necessary he should see corruption.

Now divers reasons there were why he should not see corruption. But all our bodies must be turned to dust, or changed, which shall have the force of a death, as 1 Cor. xv. 52: 'And therefore we bear in our bodies the dyings of the Lord Jesus.'

Use. This should sweeten all our afflictions, that we are dying with Christ, whereby Christ hath communion with us, and whereby we are fitted for communion with Christ; as put case we have sickness or trouble, &c. Christ took upon him flesh, but what? As it was in Adam unpassible?* Christ took upon him our passible nature, as subject to suffer cold, and hunger, and pain, of weariness, and it is fit our bodies should be conformable to the body of Christ, 'for we are predestinate to be conformed to Christ,' Rom. viii. 29, and therefore when we are put to pain in our callings, or troubled for good consciences, and thereby wear out our bodies, it is but as Christ's body was used. He took a body that he might suffer, and going about doing good, and be put to hardship. Therefore, if we be put to hardship, it is no more than our Lord Jesus Christ did. And therefore those that be so delicate that will take no pains, endure no sickness, the wind must not blow upon them, the sun must not shine upon them, they love no saving goodness, nothing of the Spirit of Christ, who out of love took our nature upon him, obnoxious to all pain and labour; though not infirmities of our particular persons, yet of our nature. He took upon him our miserable nature, our passible nature, and then he hath our nature in heaven. If ever we will be glorified with him in heaven, we must be content to take upon us his miserable† nature here, that our flesh may be used as his was, even to death if there were occasion. If we be humbled to death, happy is that mortification that brings us to conform with Christ, whatsoever it is. And therefore be not discouraged; let what will come, come on this body of ours.

Now if you ask me, who are the happy men in the world? Truly those that are most active in good, and suffer most for good, for they are the flesh of Christ. What did the flesh and nature of Christ? He did all the good he could, and suffered all the evil that the pride and malice of man's nature could possibly lay upon him. He therefore that doth most good, and suffers most ill, he cometh nearest to Christ, and carrieth about with him the 'marks of the Lord Jesus.'

To pass on in the words.

To what end is all this? 'That the life of Jesus may be manifested in our bodies.' What is the life of Jesus? You all know what life is. I will speak of it as a Divine especially.

(1.) You know that the life of Jesus is either the life *secret in himself;* and therefore he is called 'our life.' 'I am the way, the truth, and the life,' John xiv. 6, when 'Christ our life shall appear,' Col. iii. 4. Christ is life, as having life in himself as God. Or,

(2.) Else *the life of Jesus as mediator, and as God and man;* and so it is here meant. Life is first founded in the Godhead. He is the living God, and therefore wise and powerful, and all because he is living. But life as it is in God doth not comfort us a whit, but rather is a matter of terror, because we have no communion with God, considered absolutely, without a mediator. And therefore we must consider of life as derived to a middle person, a mediator, God-man. So that life is derived to us by Christ our

* That is, impassible = incapable of suffering.—G.

† That is, = misery-enduring nature, or passible nature, as above.—G.

brother, who hath taken our nature. Our Christ is derived to us in our nature. God alone doth not comfort us; mere man alone doth no good, John vi. 32, *seq.* The argument is profoundly followed by our Saviour. The flesh profiteth nothing. The human nature without the divine profiteth nothing. It is the Spirit that quickens. Look to the death of Christ. Consider Christ dying as man, he doth us no good at all if he had not been God. As God he could not have died, but the person of God dying in our nature makes his flesh bread indeed, and his blood drink indeed; that is, the soul may feed upon the satisfaction, the sacrifice of God-man, as full satisfaction to God's divine justice. So that the Spirit and the flesh, the divine and human nature, is the ground of all life.

[1.] First, *of the life of sentence*, whereby we are freely acquitted from sin; for there is life of sentence when a malefactor waiteth for death, and hath a life of sentence given him. So Christ is the fountain and author of this life of sentence, for that God in our nature died to satisfy God, and therefore we be acquitted. The guilt of our soul is taken away, and a life of sentence is conveyed to us.

[2.] The life of Jesus is as *the life of an head.* We have not only life through Christ, but life in Christ; and not only life through Christ as mediator, but life in Christ as an head, conveying the same Spirit that is in himself to every member. So that if you will have the fountain of life, here it is. God is the first living, he is life itself. God conveyeth life to the mediator, God-man. He restores life to us, the life of sentence, and hath likewise conveyed the life of sanctification to us. Sometimes ye read both of God and Christ mediator. 'The Father liveth, and I live; and because I live, you shall live also,' John xiv. 19. But to come nearer to ourselves.

(3.) The life that cometh from Jesus, *cometh first upon his own person, then by the second on us.* Christ exercised this life first upon himself in raising himself from the grave. Christ as God raised himself as man from the grave, and so he is called the Lord of life; he hath the key of hell and of the grave; Lord of life, Lord of death, because being dead he as Lord of life raised himself again.

Now after he had exercised this power in giving his body life again, so by the same power by which he raised his own dead body, by the same he raiseth every Christian's. So that every Christian is raised and quickened by the life of Jesus; that is, by the power by which Jesus quickened himself being dead in the grave; and that is St Paul's meaning, Phil. iii. 10, 'That we might find the power of his death, and the virtue of his resurrection.' There is virtue in Christ's resurrection. What is that? It is nothing but the quickening power whereby the body of Christ was raised out of the grave; and Paul desires to feel the power and virtue of that resurrection from the life of Jesus.

And therefore in particular, what is the virtue of Christ's resurrection, whereby Christ doth raise himself?

The virtue of it in us is, first of all, the same Spirit that raised his body out of the grave doth raise us out of any affliction, or quickens and strengthens us in it.

The argument is from the greater to the lesser. If Christ hath such an almighty power to quicken his own body when it is dead, hath not he power to quicken and strengthen a man in any poor and miserable condition in this world? Doubtless he hath; and therefore Paul desires the virtue of this in all his troubles and dying. And so the life of Jesus is manifested to a man in trouble, when he findeth divine power supporting him above nature in any trouble, or else bringing him out of that condition to a glorious one. Take a man in any uncomfortable condition of soul, perplexed, deserted, cast down by sense of sin: he may be raised to the divine power of Christ to comfort, and to stand stronger by his falls, grow better by his sins.

And because death is the consummation of all trouble, the life of Jesus is manifested there, when our bodies are in the grave, as Rom. viii. 11, 'If the Spirit, that raised Jesus from the grave, be in us,' the same shall raise up our bodies when they be turned to dust and rottenness.

So then, in a word, the life of Jesus is made manifest in us, when we find this life powerful in the midst of all our worst conditions, supporting us in our falls, and making us better and more comfortable afterward; and at length the spiritual life that raised him from the grave, shall raise up our bodies to be conformable to his glorious body now in heaven. St Paul was content to suffer the dyings of the Lord Jesus, that the life of Jesus might be made manifest in him; that is, the power of Jesus. To add another thing.

(4.) It is not only a manifestation of the divine power in our falls and raising us from the grave by the life of Jesus, but withal *he infuseth a life to every one;* he sanctifieth the soul and body, and worketh the same impression in others that is in him; that is, his life. When he is meek, we are framed to be meek; he obedient, we are framed to be obedient; he humbled, we are framed to be humbled; he is good and holy, we are framed to be answerable. This is the life of Jesus. And the more we bear in our bodies the life of the Lord Jesus, the more we are like to Jesus, and fashioned to him.

Therefore it may be well called his 'power,' and his 'inward grace;' because it cometh from him, and it makes us like to him altogether, and it tendeth to Jesus. It is from Christ, and maintained by Christ, and it carrieth the soul to Christ, makes us like to Christ; therefore it is called the life of Jesus.

We all know life is a sweet thing. We desire it above all, and fear the contrary, death, above all. Now blessed is that mortification, that dying, that makes us partakers of the life of Jesus. If life is sweet, what is this life of Jesus? Alas! what is a life to the life of Jesus; that is, to the divine power shewed in us, which was shewed in him.

Use. You see then that dying to Jesus Christ makes way for the life of Christ. If we will live with Christ, then we must die first. You know all life springs from death, so the life of Christ springeth from death; his own life that he liveth, any spiritual life, it was after his death. And so spiritual life in us cometh after dying. The papists will have a life of their own; others will have power in corrupt nature; but there is no resurrection without death before; there must be dying before there is a living.

If we will feel the life of Christ, we must be content to carry bodies dying to Christ. If we will have strength and power and joy, and the presence of Christ, then endure the dying of the Lord Jesus. Endure whatsoever he will please to exercise us withal. And if we carry his dyings, we shall be sure to be partakers of his life.

Use 2. I beseech you, consider *whether we be partakers of this life, strength, and power, and grace, and comfort.* And let us be content then with any condition in the world wherein we may have communion with Christ by anything, that we may be subject to Christ; to be poor that we may be rich with Christ; to die to all, that so we may live to Christ; to be nothing to all others, that so we may be all in all to Christ. By dying to Christ we lose perhaps health, but we gain it in strength; we may lose countenance and friend, we gain it in spiritual things. God takes nothing from his children, but he giveth better in a better kind. And happy is that parting that is recompensed in an higher kind; happy is that death that is made good by a better life; happy that self-denial that is made up in Christ; happy that discomfort that is made up with comfort in Christ; and therefore let us not be against any suffering, fear nothing that God may call us to in this world; no, although death itself. Life with Christ is better incomparably than anything we lose. Our life is but a dying life, take it at the best; die we must. Now if we die suffering afflictions, which are the passage to life, why then there is a benefit made of necessity. We owe to God a death by nature, and now we get an advantage by anything we suffer for Christ's sake. For we have a hundred fold for anything we suffer in this world. It is hard to persuade this reason to flesh and blood, but they that find experience in it once, as Christians do in sufferings, they find peace and comfort from the presence of Christ's Spirit in their souls; they know what a benefit it is to suffer for Christ's sake, though with loss of anything in this world. Would Saint Paul have wanted those whippings and imprisonments, or wanted his comforts of Christ's presence? Would the martyrs have wanted that sweet comfort they had for present life? Surely they had it offered, they might have entertained it if they would, but they would not. And if glimpses of glory, the little life derived to us now, supporteth under the troubles of the world, what is the 'exceeding weight of glory' reserved for us in another world? We can soon fathom and compass the things we suffer. We know what contempt meaneth, and poverty meaneth, but the life in this world passeth understanding. 'The peace of God passeth understanding,' Philip. iv. 7, and 'is joy unspeakable and glorious,' 1 Peter i. 8. Therefore if there be a measure and narrow measure of trouble in this world, and that there be inward peace and glory immeasurable, then we be gainers here, setting aside consideration of heaven.

Therefore, I beseech you, let us be willing to undergo anything God shall call us to; for,

(1.) *We shall find a divine energy of God's Spirit, which we never perhaps had before, nor ever shall have hereafter.* Therefore fear nothing God shall call us to. The comforts of God's Spirit, from the life of Christ manifested in the hearts of his children, are above the course of nature, for it is an high life. The life of Christ is above the life of reason or sense. Therefore suppose troubles lie in sense, the large peace and enlargement of spirit is above them all.

Now as the life of reason is above the life of sense, so the life of grace is above all conditions whatsoever. No inferior subordinate condition can prejudice the life of grace and comfort. Therefore if all tyrants in the world conspire to make a man miserable, they vex his outward life, but there is a life of Jesus, and they cannot hinder the influence of grace and comfort to the soul. They cannot hinder the inward peace of inward joy, they be comforts of an higher rank. And therefore if ever God calleth us to stand in a good cause, for justice, for religion, never go off: we shall have comforts of an higher rank.

(2.) Consider, the worst they can do is, *to take this life of ours, which we cannot keep long.* These things be easy to be known, for matter of understanding, but hard to practise upon occasion; therefore we ought to think of them beforehand, and to labour more and more, persuaded of the love of God in Christ. And to see the life of Christ quickening them to all holy actions and duty, this is a spiritual life. As Christ, when he rose, never dieth more, so he that hath this spiritual life hath an eternal life, he never dieth more. When Christ begins to quicken our souls by joining our spirits with his Spirit, that conjunction is everlasting. And it is nearer after death than before; when death separates the soul from the body, then cometh the conjunction of the soul to Christ. Therefore labour after the spiritual life that makes us happier and happier still. The longer we live the nearer we are to Christ, and when we die nearest of all. Labour to feel the power of Christ's Spirit quickening our spirit, putting life into them, vigour into them, beauty on them, strength into them by his Holy Spirit.

(3.) Again, *when the body is severed from the life of the soul, we see how deformed it is, how stiff and inactive it is; we cannot endure the sight of our dearest friend if life be gone.* If the life of Christ be severed from our souls, what carrion souls have we to God. There is no beauty on the soul, no strength to duty. But now if we enter upon the first degree of life here, and find the beginning of it in altering and changing our natures, we are sure to leave* farther degrees of it in our death, and the consummation of it at our resurrection; then body and soul shall enjoy the same life that Jesus doth now. But the scope of the apostle, which I desire you mainly to remember, is this, that you should fear nothing; nothing can befall us, though never so grievous to the outward man.

(4.) I add, *because we shall experimentally feel the life of Christ manifested to us.* It is that that makes a Christian. Experience is the life [of] a Christian. What is all knowledge of Christ without experience, but a bare knowledge, if the power that raised Christ's body raise not our souls? This is to know Christ to purpose, to know the virtue of Christ. We hear that Christ is powerful to quicken his own body. You hear that Christ is gracious, and good, and full of comfort; but what is this unless we feel it in ourselves? It is the experimental knowledge of Christ, and of the life of Christ, that doth us good, and makes us abound in all things. I suffer bonds, saith the apostle, for the gospel, but I am not ashamed, Rom. i. 16. Why? 'I know whom I have believed.' He felt the power of Christ in all his tribulations and afflictions. When we find by experience Christ is a quickening Spirit, hath quickened our souls to grace, comforts, peace, joy in our worst condition, then we know Christ to purpose, and then are fit to be carried through all afflictions of the world, and beyond all, and above all, to bear us through all things we meet with in the world between us and heaven. The life of Christ being a divine life, without a little experience of it, all is to no purpose. And a little of this beareth down all that stands between us and glory.

VERSE 10.

Always bearing about in our bodies the dying of the Lord Jesus, that the life also of Jesus might be made manifest in our bodies.

The apostle, as before we have heard, labours to vindicate the credit of the gospel, and the ministry of it, preventing† all objections that carnal men might make from the trouble that usually accompanieth both the preaching and profession of the blessed truths of God. And he setteth it

* Qu. 'have'?—Ed.

† That is, 'anticipating.'—G.

down by way of opposition and contrariety. He grants all that the adversary can say, and then sheweth on the contrary how God is present graciously in the midst of the troubles of his children. And this in five particulars.

1. 'We are troubled on every side, yet not distressed.'

2. 'Perplexed, yet not in despair.'

3. 'Persecuted, yet not forsaken.'

4. 'We are cast down, yet not destroyed altogether.' Every [one] of these is worse than [the] other. The waters of trouble do arise, but as the waters of trouble do arise, so comforts arise in every one, especially in the fifth, which is the worst of all.

5. 'Always bearing about in our bodies the dying of our Lord Jesus.' It is true, yet for all that 'the life of Jesus is made manifest in our bodies,' beside these unspeakable comforts that are preserved for religion in the world to come, God doth not desert his children nor his cause even in this. It is a happy condition when they be at the worst; so that the blessed apostle, though he had something in the flesh to discourage him that he had no better in him than nature, yet notwithstanding, he had something whereby he was encouraged, whereby he should be able to retort all upon any that should object anything in religion to his discouragement; a blessed art and skill which we should all learn, not to look altogether upon the grievances, but consider likewise what is in our condition wherein we may be comforted; nay, more comfort if we have spiritual eyes than grounds of discouragement. God is gracious; he never taketh anything from his children but he makes it up in a better kind.

We came the last day to the beginning of the 10th verse. 'We bear about in our bodies the dyings of the Lord Jesus'; the end of it is, 'that the life of Jesus may be made manifest in our bodies.'

God afflicts not any one of his children but he makes it up by a gracious and blessed recompence; and what he takes away he maketh up; and in what measure the outward man decayeth by mortification, in that measure, in a more excellent kind, he makes it up in the life of Jesus; and what is the decay of the life of nature, or the life of condition, that stands in riches, and pleasures, and honours, suitable to the growth in a life of a higher kind, the life of Jesus?

'We always bear in our bodies the dying of the Lord Jesus.'

The words are a yielding to that objection that might be made concerning the affliction of the outward man. It is true, 'we bear in our bodies the dying of the Lord Jesus.' We spake of that first part the last day.

That is, such afflictions whereby we are conformed to Christ, not only which Christ permits and suffers, and which are like to the dyings of Christ, and conformable to him, which is called the mortification of Christ and the dying of the Lord Jesus, but also such a dying wherein we have the Lord Jesus to be partners with us, and which is for his sake, and whereby we are framed to be like to him, and conformed to his image.

Obs. Whatsoever we suffer for Christ's sake, we have Christ a partner with us in it. Even as by virtue of communion with him we die with him and rise with him, so by virtue of communion with us he suffers with us and dieth with us. He was stoned in Stephen, he was beheaded in Paul, he was reproached in Moses. Christ suffers in all those that suffer for him. There is that near communion between Christ and his church. And therefore it is the mortification* of Christ, because he bears part with his children

* That is, 'dying.'—G.

in it, and likewise because we are framed thereby to be like unto him. For, beloved, not to say any more in this argument, there must be a great deal of alteration in the outward man before it will be like Christ. Our flesh and outward man is so tainted with original corruption, that there must be a great deal of change to fashion it to be like to the pure nature of Christ. Ye know the nature that Christ took upon him. It was an afflicted nature, but a human nature, before it was a glorious nature in heaven. And so likewise this nature of ours, this outward man, before it can be a glorious nature, must be a human nature, it must be an afflicted nature. For sin hath eaten so deeply into our natures, that there needs, as it were, a spirit of burning to consume and waste the corruption that is in us; and therefore it is called the mortification* of Jesus, because by it we are conformable to Jesus in our natures and dispositions, by little and little, till at length our bodies and souls be for ever conformable to him in the heavens, death being the accomplishing of mortification.

And then again, the mortification of Jesus is such a mortification whereby we are content our bodies should be like the body of Christ on earth, which is in all hardship, labour, affliction, weariness; and all God's people have such a spirit, all that come to heaven have such a spirit. They are not so dainty that their bodies should be better used than the body of Christ. Christ took upon him our flesh and our miserable condition, he took a nature subject to pain and labour. He took not our nature as in Adam, impassible, that could not suffer, but he took the weakness of our nature, and in our nature went about doing good, hungry, and thirsty and weary, and taking a great deal of pains; and shall any man that is a member of Christ be so dainty and delicate as not to be content to have his body like as Christ's body was? And therefore, the more that any man by Christ's Spirit is content, his body should take pains in any calling to do good, and the more he is content to suffer ill in doing good, the more he carrieth the mortification and dying of the Lord Jesus in him. And, beloved, so soon as ever a man is become a Christian, his life is no more his own; his health, his liberty is Christ's, not his own. Self-denial is the first lesson. There is a hatred, a not loving of anything in comparison of Christ, even of life itself, and whatsoever stands in the way; and therefore we must be content to be partakers of Christ's sufferings, that our bodies should be so used as Christ was; we must give up life and liberty and all to Christ; and that is 'the dying of the Lord Jesus.' This we shewed more largely upon the last day; but I will now specially insist on the end and use of all this, 'that the life of Jesus may be made manifest in our mortal flesh.'

You see there is nothing lost by the dying of the Lord Jesus. It is made up in a better kind, being for this end, 'that the life of Jesus may be made manifest in our bodies.' This is God's end, and this is Christ's end, and this is Paul's end. It is both the effect and issue that cometh of the dying of our bodies, and it is the end intended by Christ, who will use our bodies in his service, so that his life may be made manifest in us. St Paul's end is suitable to Christ's in bearing the afflictions of the outward man, that the life of Christ may be made manifest in him; for being once in Christ, Christ's aims and ends are our aims and ends; and therefore saith Paul, we are content to 'bear in our bodies the dyings of the Lord Jesus,' so this be the issue of it, 'that the life of Jesus may be made manifest.' Christ will have this end, and it is his end. He taketh away nothing but he makes it up in a better kind to the better man. It shall

* That is, 'dying.'—G.

be supplied by a life of the Spirit, which shall be perfected in a life of glory in heaven.

Now what is this life of Jesus?

There is a life of Jesus whereby he liveth himself, as God, and as mediator, God-man. There is a life of Jesus whereby Christ was upheld while he lived upon the earth; for that Spirit that quickened the dead body of Jesus in the grave, that Spirit carried Christ along in all his lifetime, freed him from all dangers till he had done his work. There was a Spirit of life in Jesus that upheld him, and strengthened him to do the great work he took in hand, till at length he did a greater work than all before, that is, raised up his dead body. So that beside the life of Jesus enjoyed in heaven, a glorious life, there was a life that Jesus led on earth, which was carried by the Spirit, and acted by the Spirit of God in all things he did as mediator, God-man. And there is a life that he hath now in heaven, which is either the life that he enjoyeth himself and as our head, which we shall be conformed to when we die; for we shall enjoy the same life in our proportion and measure that he doth in heaven, the glorious life which is the life of Christ our head; that is, that life of Christ which is now hid, as the apostle saith, 'our life is hid with Christ in God,' Col. iii. 3; or else the life of Jesus is that quickening power which comes from Christ unto us.

Not to speak of higher matters, how God is life, which be speculations, not to the present purpose, the life of Jesus here, it is not the life of Jesus as it is and was in himself, but the life of Jesus as it is conveyed to us. The life of Jesus is derived to every Christian.

Not to speak of the life of justification, which is a life of sentence, and not here principally intended, though it be the spring of all the rest, for we are dead in law, and we must be quickened by sentence. We are dead in our sins. Guilt is upon us, and the guilt must be removed in justification. We must live in law, and in sentence, and in absolution. God must forgive our sins for Christ's sake, and remove the guilt of all death, before we can have inward grace, which is the life of sanctification. Though it be not here meant, it is supposed, as that which leadeth to all the rest. But here is meant the life of grace in us which is from the work and function of the Spirit of Christ. The Spirit of Jesus is the Spirit of every Christian. As there is one soul in the head and all the members, so there is one Spirit in Christ and all the members, and one spiritual life in Christ and all the members. Now this Spirit of Christ conveyeth to us the Spirit of life, and Christ is the life of our life, the soul of our soul, the union with our spirits. For even as the body liveth by fellowship and communion with the soul—for what is life but the vigour of the soul in the body by reason of union?—so doth our souls and bodies live a spiritual life by union and fellowship with Christ, [which] is the vigour of the Spirit in our souls by virtue of Christ. And therefore that spiritual life by which we live here is the life of Christ, not only exemplary, because it is like Christ's life, but by way of efficiency. Christ is the head of it, and conveyeth it to us. There is no better comparison than to express it by the life of the body which hath communion from the soul. The soul hath a distinct life of its own. It hath a life when it is out of the body. It hath reason, it hath discourse, it wills, it understandeth, it joyeth, it delighteth, yet notwithstanding, distinct from the body. That is not a life that it liveth in the body that is severed.* The body's life is that that is communicated by conjunction and communion. So the life of Jesus [is] not the life that he liveth

* The meaning seems to be, that it is not the life of the soul apart from the body,

in himself, but in this place specially, the life that we have by communion and friendship with him.

And this life that we have, the life of Jesus, it admitteth of a double consideration.

First of all, it is that *habitual life as we may call it, that inward frame of divine nature which is in us Christians, which raiseth us above other men*, as other men by a rational life are raised above other creatures; that temper and composure of soul whereby they mind heavenly things, and have a supernatural end and aim in all things, have enlargements of understanding, enlargements of will and affections, larger souls than others. Narrow-spirited men they are that are carried only to the things of this life; and this is a constant life, by reason of the constant dwelling of the Spirit in us, as there is constant life in the body by the constant dwelling of the soul in it. And it is besides that, a perpetual influence of life from Christ, especially in dangerous and difficult times, as Saint Paul speaks of here. It is a power above nature conveyed to uphold and carry us along through all dangers till we come to heaven; so that it is a life first in us, and then the life of Christ drawing out the life in us to all kind of grace, and addeth a divine strength.

For, beloved, it is not that life that is in us doth all the great matters, but it is the life of Christ as it joineth with the life of grace, supporteth it, strengthens it, draweth it forth, increaseth it. For the life that is in us it is a created thing, it is a new creature, but a creature; but the life that maintaineth a Christian, that upholds him specially in the dangerous matter, ay, in the 'dyings of the Lord Jesus,' in great difficulty, that is not a thing created in us, but the life of Jesus as it hath influence from him, and is conveyed from him by a perpetual kind of derivation. For if troubles grow, then the quickening power must increase with them, and habitual grace in us must be raised, and strengthened, and quickened; and besides the graces formerly in us, there must be an addition of strength from the spring, still more and more. In natural life we do not only live in God, but move in God: 'In him we live, and move, and have our being,' Acts xvii. 28. So in regard of spiritual life, we not only live by Christ, but our motion and the prompting of our power being sanctified to any particular action, it is from the quickening power of Christ, which is a quickening Spirit quickening us. Sometimes this quickening power must be shewed in way of strength, when the trouble is great that the strength may be suitable; sometimes by way of comfort, when the discouragement is great; sometimes by way of joy and peace, when the discouragement is to assault us with the contrary. So that perpetually there must be quickening power in our lives from Christ our quickening head, besides the habitual, constant grace we carry about with us always. We know, in the body, if there be obstructions that hinder the spirits from the brain, whence motions come, there is an apoplexy or lethargy, causing a cessation of motion. So if there be ceasing of the quickening powers continually derived from Christ our head, there would be an apoplexy or lethargy in our spiritual life, and a kind of death. Therefore when we speak of the life of Christ, we must not understand the life that we lived; 'because I live, therefore you shall live also;' but to think of the habitual grace wrought in ourselves, whereby we are conformed to Christ, and to think of a quickening power that Christ sheweth continually, he being the Sun of this world. Though the things

but the life of the body through its union with the soul, that is the figure of the life of Jesus spoken of in the text.—Ed.

of this world, as plants and the like [grow], yet let the sun withdraw his vigour and efficacy, and they seem to die presently. The light of the air ceaseth when the sun ceaseth to shine. So besides that, in us habitually and continually, there must be influence of Christ into us answerable to the exigencies and occasions a Christian hath, either of peace, or joy, or comfort of some portion of spiritual life or other. Now this is called the life of Jesus, because it is radicated in him originally, as the 'second Adam.' We all derive it from him. The grace and quickening power we have continually, it is from him, the glory we look for is from him. He is the 'first-born' to whom we are predestinate to be conformed every way, in grace here, and glory hereafter; and therefore it is called the life of Jesus. That is specially herein meant. Both these lives, the inward frame of spiritual life and grace in us, and likewise a perpetual influence specially discovered and manifested then, when there is most need of it, in times of trouble, with the accomplishment of it in heaven. The life of Christ is manifested in his children here when they stand in most need of grace and comfort, and it is manifested continually to the day of judgment, when the life of Jesus shall indeed be manifested to the full, as it is manifested in him in heaven; for as Christ is glorious himself in heaven, so his mystical body shall be like himself too.

I need speak no more for the unfolding of the meaning of the words. The points considerable are these,

Obs. 1. *That Christ is the foundation of all spiritual life that is in us.* He is the 'second Adam' that conveyeth all that is spiritually good. As the first Adam conveyeth all that is spiritually ill, it was his office so to do, to convey life. 'Because I live, you shall live also,' John xiv. 19; and he saith, John x. 10, 'I am come that they might have life, and that they might have life abundant.' Christ came that we might have life, and that we might have abundance of life at the length. We have it by degrees here, but there is abundance of life preserved for us, such abundance as he enjoyeth himself in the heavens. So that Christ as the 'second Adam' conveyeth spiritual life to us, as the common root of all believers, as the 'first Adam' was the common root of all mankind, but more peculiarly by virtue of office as an head. As the head conveyeth spirit and life to all parts of the body, so doth Christ convey spiritual life to all his.

It is the end of his coming and incarnation, to procure life of sentence and reconciliation, which is the life of justification and freedom from condemnation, and the life of acceptation to life everlasting. He died that he might expiate* God, and get the lives of men by getting them to be acquitted from sin, and entitled to heaven; and thereupon he came to convey (as head unto all his members) life like his own, that the Spirit that is in him may quicken all his members. Therefore he hath taken upon him the sweet relation of an head, of a root, the Sun of righteousness, to shew that he is a powerful head, a powerful root, a powerful husband that can alter and change by virtue of the Spirit of God, that he hath in abundance, all that belong to him, and be knit to him; and therefore our spiritual life is in Christ.

He first exercised this life on his own body by quickening that. As he was mightily declared to be the Son of God, by raising his own body, Eph. i. 19, 20, so he will be mightily declared to be the head of all his, by raising the bodies of his children out of the grave, and by raising them out of troubles, which are partial deaths, little deaths. So that all spiritual life comes from Christ, from union and communion with Christ.

* That is, = to pacify by sacrifice, atonement.—G.

Use. Therefore we must labour *to have union and communion with Christ strengthened by all means;* by hearing, and by the sacraments, and by all means. For all our life is derived and fetched from Christ, as a 'second Adam,' who by virtue of his office deriveth life to all that be his. The more we know of Christ, the more experimentally we feel the power of Christ, the more we live.

Obs. 2. For the second point: As all life is from Christ, so (which is the main point of the text) *this life is most discovered in afflictions and evil times, in the dying of the outward man.*

Beloved, both the spiritual lives I speak of, both the inward frame of grace is made more manifest, and likewise the power of Christ in upholding a weak creature in such a condition; for all grace shineth most, and appears most in trouble; as obedience, courage, faith, love to God, love to others, love of the truth. I need not stand to particularise. And therefore the life of Christ is manifested in the decays of the outward man, whether by outward persecutions, or by sicknesses, and the like, that is the time of the discovery of grace; and likewise it is the time of the discovery of the power that Christ exercised and shewed, the divine power that God declared in raising his body, that is, the time wherein he sheweth that power in all his.

Reason 1. The reason is, *things are best known by opposition.* The decay of the outward man is a foil as it were to grace, to make it appear more clear and glorious, and the weakness of the outward man is a means to discover more the power of God's Spirit, and the power of the life of Christ in such a weak body; for a weak man, or a weak woman, or a weak child, to be able to stand up for the truth, here is divine power shewed, as the martyrs did not only* shew, but declare it gloriously. And for a sick body to believe, makes the soul glorious and comfortable. Here is divine power shewed more gloriously by reason of the opposition of the outward man.

Reason 2. And then again, in this time *the soul itself uniteth itself more unto God, and to divine things;* and therefore the life of Christ is more manifested, because there is a near union between Christ and the soul. For the soul gathers itself from the sphere, down to worldly things, as in times of prosperity, ease, and plenty, when the soul scatters and looseth † itself in the creature. Now there is a sweetening power in that which is inflictive, to make the soul gather itself to God, to the fountain of life; and so it is a means sanctified by the Spirit of God to procure union with the Spirit of Christ; and therefore the life of Christ is then more manifested in the flesh.

Reason 3. And then these things that befall the outward man, they are as it were *removentia prohibentia, they remove the hindrances of the life of Christians;* for what hinders the life of Christ from appearing in us, but that our affections are eaten up with the world and vanity, one way or other? For naturally we are not so vigorous in spirit when we have vigour in the outward man; and that which farthers the life, and strength, and comfort of the outward man, will diminish the strength of the inward. It should not be so. It should be that the more vigorous in the outward man, the more vigorous we should be in the inward; but it is not so. Now suffering takes away that, when these be embittered by the cross, by some suffering that is against the feeling and sense of the outward man. Hereupon cometh a better relish of divine things, other things being embittered

† Misprinted 'all.'—G. * Qu. 'loseth'?—Ed.

to the soul; and hereupon the soul, in times of any great pressure, doth hear with other ears, and doth see with other eyes heavenly things, and doth feel and judge after another manner than it did before. Take a man when he is under any thing that afflicts the outward man, for his body or condition, which are both called life, the life of body, and the life of condition, we shall fasten a few good things sooner on him than at another time. Speak ten times as much at another time, it shall have no passage, no entrance, but the state of all things without being made less delightful, his soul recovereth a spiritual taste, and relisheth heavenly company, and heavenly truths, as they be suggested by others or us. Experience sheweth this in David and other saints, and in every Christian; and therefore the blessed life of Christ, such a spiritual life as is in Christ, it is his most of all glorious and conspicuous, specially in times of afflictions and crosses.

Reason 4. And then another reason may be, that the point may be clear. *God doth delight, and Christ delighteth to shew himself most glorious at such times*, not only because his virtue and strength and power is most manifest then, but likewise out of tenderness to the condition of his children; for he sees they more need his presence, and they more need his immediate comforts. Then immediate comforts are specially desired of the soul. When outward comforts are taken away, there is a sweeter communion with Christ in any trouble than at other times. No communion in prosperity for the most part that is so sweet to a Christian as at that time, for the soul knoweth then it is most acceptable to the soul. The soul stands in need of it. Therefore comforts are immediate to the soul at this time, and immediate comforts that come from the fountain are pure. When the comforts derived from friends and outward helps be all taken away, there must be immediate comforts, or else the soul will sink. And now Christ, out of love to his children, comes forth to them and joineth with their spirits more than at other times; so that the sweetest communion any man hath with Christ is at the worst times. The martyrs verified it abundantly, for they never had the comforts before that then they had; for Christ came into the dungeon and supported them with strength above nature; and all this is from the sweet love and mercy of Christ, that applied himself to the necessity of his children. These and the like reasons that the life of grace, the life of comfort, and the life derived immediately from Christ, is the most apparent in afflictions.

I will not press the point any further.

Use of trial. To make use of what is spoken. If it is true that there is a spiritual life, another life, and this is most manifested in affliction; how then shall we know whether we have this life of Christ or no? for Christ conveyeth a spiritual life to all his.

We will speak of the evidence of them both, whether is there a gracious frame of life in us from Christ or no.

If the life of Christ be not in us, beloved, we are stark dead in regard of a better life; and it is woeful to be in a dead condition. And therefore it behoveth us a little to take heed that we have the life of Christ, and if we have it, we may know it familiarly. I do but name the heads. Because it is a word borrowed from the life of nature, you may know it from proportion to the life of nature. Where spiritual life is, there it is. As in the outward life you know there is sense and motion, appetite, and such like; so where the life of Jesus is, there be spiritual senses, eyes that see spiritual things, a taste that relishes spiritual things, a taste that can relish them above all other things, that can set the highest price upon the best things, that judgeth of things as they be. There is a spiritual taste and judgment suitable to the judgment of Christ. And so I might run through all the senses, if I would affect correspondency in this kind.*

And as there is spiritual sense, so there is sensibleness. A natural life makes us sensible of any injury, of any comfort. So where there is the life of Jesus, it makes us sensible of anything that is suitable to nature, or contrary to it. Where there is life there is sympathy and antipathy; sympathy, agreement with what is suitable to nature, and antipathy to what is contrary. So where there is the life of Jesus, there is a sympathy with all things that are Jesus his stamp† upon them, to spiritual things and spiritual persons, and an antipathy to the contrary.

And here is the ground why a godly man may be known by his hatred of sin, because it sheweth an antipathy; and antipathy sheweth the kinds of life. Sin is contrary to union and communion with Christ, for it is a dissolving and divorcing nature.

Now the soul that liveth by Christ, and knoweth sin to be of a divorcing and separating nature, to sever his soul from his head and life, and so to cause apoplexies and death itself, if it be not looked to in time, hereupon comes the soul to hate sin to the death, and to seek the death of sin by all means, because sin seeketh the death of the soul; for what is sin but a separation of the soul from Christ, and a joining to the creature? Therefore wheresoever there is grace, there is antipathy to sin, not only as bringing damnation with it, but as contrary to the life of Christ; as every creature hath an antipathy to its enemy, as we see in doves and eagles; the dove is the prey. The tamer and wild creatures have an antipathy in them by nature. So the soul that hath the life of Christ hath an antipathy to sin. So far as the life of Christ prevaileth in him it must be so, for every life labours to preserve its being. We are bid to be wise as serpents, that wind and turn themselves about, that cover their heads and will suffer all manglings so the head be safe, because the life is in the head; so the Christian that hath the life of grace will endure anything, so the life of grace be not hurt. There be sympathies and antipathies, an inward joining to that that preserveth, and an inward hatred to that that is destructive; and therefore they that live in sin against conscience, that divideth between God and them, I cannot see how they can think of spiritual life; for the soul liveth, and is swallowed up in base pleasures and in the creature. Now if they had spiritual life, it would preserve itself from breaches and all dangers.

Let us not deceive ourselves. Christ came not to free us from damnation only, but as an head, to infuse spiritual life into us, and to live in us by his Spirit. He came not only to purchase a life of glory for us, but likewise to live in us by his Spirit; and if he overcome for us, he will overcome in us; if he hath a life for us, he will have a life in us. The life of Jesus must be manifested in us. And therefore take heed of joining in affliction, to any sin; for it doth divorce the soul from God, and joins it to the creature. And so the soul becomes fading like the creature, and cometh to nothing; and indeed it is worse than nothing, to be for ever in hell. It comes to that degree in misery that it would otherwise have had in happiness.

* Cf. for a very full and ingenious exhibition of these and kindred 'analogies,' Thomas Adams' Soul's Sickness, Practical Works, Vol. I. page 471, *seq.*—G.

† Misprinted 'stamped.'—G.

Creatures have their instincts. There is a natural instinct in every creature to run to that that feeds it, as lambs and other creatures as soon as ever they are born run; they know whither to go to suck, becauso that is ordained by nature for its preservation. So there is an instinct in the soul to carry it to that that feedeth and maintains it. Bees go naturally to the flowers by an instinct; so the spiritual soul that hath the life of Christ runs to whatsoever may feed and maintain that life.

I beseech you, therefore, not to speak of the outward actions that are objected to hypocrites. Look therefore to the sympathy and antipathy of your souls and your instincts. Whither doth the bent of the soul lead you? Wherewith do you preserve the inward man? How is the soul taken up? And this will discover the frame of the soul more than anything else. Every creature that hath life, hath an element wherein it is preserved above another place, as the fish in the sea, the birds in the air. So the element of a Christian is holy, he is *piscis in avido*,* when he is in other courses and company. He walketh by the Spirit, he liveth by the Spirit, and he walks in the Spirit. He liveth in the Spirit as in his element. So that spiritual things and good company is his element. Till in heaven, indeed, he is never in his centre, in his proper place till he is in heaven. But in the mean time his element here is in heaven on earth; that is, spiritual actions wherein he walks and solaceth himself, as fish in the sea, wherein he draweth in the breath that is suitable to his disposition. Ill company or evil hearts will not suit with that spiritual life; and by these ordinary resemblances we may judge a little of the frame of our spirits, whether they be living souls or no.

But to go a little higher.

The life of Jesus, as it riseth from Jesus, from as high as heaven, so it leadeth to Jesus. It makes the soul to look to Jesus, to look to Christ. It subordinateth all things unto Christ. It takes all things in the way as furtherances for Christ, and considers of his hindrances as they hinder the main, and of furtherances as they further the main. It looks on all things below, as they further and do hinder the main. It is a life bred from heaven, and aims at heaven, and cares for no more of these things than can stand with a spiritual and eternal state. It considers of things, and reasoneth of things, how doth this help or hinder the main? And when it doth anything it fetcheth reasons for it from Christ, and from heaven, and from the main end. As a man that hath life of reason, that is adorned with policy and wisdom, it considers of things as they help his state; or if he be a man of narrow apprehension, as the sot with his particular good, and goeth no higher. So a man that hath the life of Christ, hath a larger soul than any of these, for he hath a larger end, and an higher end, because he hath a higher light to discover that end. Light is the first thing in life, and that discovers greater things than any other man can apprehend. His spirit is too narrow for them. And when by a supernatural light he apprehends a glorious condition in heaven, he makes that his aim. And as he hath large aims, so he hath large affections, and nothing below can satisfy him, because his soul is enlarged by the life of grace, and by the life of the Spirit to see better into things, and to have better aims. Therefore let every man look what his ordinary aims are, whether he rest in any thing below, whether he maketh things below serviceable to greater things. If he delight in inferior things, he hath but a common life. Many think their conditions good, because they attend religion, but there is false-

* Qu. '*arido*'?—G.

hood in that; for a man that hath not the life of grace, that makes the practice of religion serviceable to his base ends, he makes heavenly things serviceable to his ends; that is, out of self-love, because he would not be damned, or he would be so reputed, but he hath not the aim of spiritual actions: he doth not spiritual things from a spiritual life, but from self-love, from a false principle within. Now where the life of Jesus is, it resteth not in anything but in Jesus, and makes all things serviceable to that. The skill of referring things to the main end is one main property of spiritual life.

Firstly, For a man may do the same thing, and yet from divers principles: one from flesh and blood, and vain-glory, and base ends, and the other from higher considerations, as men and beasts. A man hath a higher life than the other creature hath. Both may refresh themselves, but a man doth it as a man, and directs that strength of his to human actions. If he be a Christian, he directs not only human actions, but refers human actions and all to serve God in his place. So that he works like a man, though for the actions they be the same. So the shallow creatures that be determined to one, and have not latitude of reason to look to many things. Thus you see there is great difference between men and men.

Secondly, Men may do the same things, *come to church, receive the sacrament.* The one may have base, low ends, the other higher ends; nay, higher ends in civil actions than another in spiritual actions. For he doth holy actions with a carnal end; and the other having spiritual life, by virtue of that life carrieth his calling in the duties of it in a spiritual manner. I beseech you, therefore, let us examine our life of Jesus by the carriage of our souls towards Jesus; he never suffers us to rest in subordinate things. I might be very large on this point, but I will name no more.

Consider what setteth you on work in all things you do. There be things we call *αὐτόματα*, 'things that be moved by art.' One would think they moved themselves; but they be moved by a weight, that is not seen presently, as in clocks and such like. In all frames of art that move, one would think it is from themselves, but there is no principle of life in them; an external thing, a weight without, sets all the wheels a going. But in living creatures that have principles of life within them, something within them guideth their life and sets them a-going. So a Christian and another man, he that hath the life of Christ, from the life within him, he is set on work with his actions. The other man moveth to the same thing, but he moveth from an extrane[ous] principle. There is something or other that swayeth his course and biasseth his actions, which is outward and not spiritual: either freedom from outward troubles, or to hold correspondency with others. I beseech you, look to our motives and to our aims in all our actions, for these will best distinguish.

But that is not the life mainly intended by the apostle, but the life that is with* him, flowing and having influence from Jesus, specially in hard conditions. 'The life of Jesus is manifested then.' That is, both the inward frame it sheweth itself then, and likewise the power that comes from Christ.

Now, how doth it appear that a man is upheld in every condition by a divine virtue, besides his inward frame of soul?

Beloved, when the state of spirit he is in is contrary to the outward condition and above it. When if a man looks to ordinary courses such a man

* Qu. 'within'?—Ed.

should sink; and when he doth not, and that from supernatural principles and strength, that argueth there is a power in him above nature and above his own. As for a man in restraint, to have his soul at liberty; for a man disgraced in the world, to have a bold spirit to God-ward; for a man weak in outward shew, to have strong courage, forcible courage, that all the enemies of truth cannot daunt; when a man is pining away, and is nothing but skin and bones, yet to have a heavenly soul that is in heaven before its time, and altogether in heavenly conversation; when the outward man is in great pain, and all confidence is to be cast away in regard of outward hopes, yet he is strong, and assures himself of a better condition afterward, and the very faith and hope, casting anchor in heaven, though they be not seen or felt, yet there is that power in spiritual things, laid hold on by faith, waited on by hope, that it supports a soul in such a condition; so that if it were not for these heavenly supports, by the Spirit of God, it would sink. If thou wouldst have the life of Jesus manifested, compare thy condition and thy strength. When a man can master all conditions, when a man can master imprisonment, disgrace, restraint, weakness, anything, from considerations above nature, and strength together with consideration; for the Spirit worketh not only by reason, but by an inward strength, it sheweth there is something in a man above nature, that there is in him a life of Jesus. When nothing shall stand between a man and heaven, neither fears of great ones, nor frowns, nor hopes of preferment; when nothing below can stand in a man's way to heaven, but he will break through all by an invincible courage, it argueth he hath a frame of spirit above his own. There is not only a frame of grace, but a spirit of strength, to carry him through all conditions whatsoever. As St Paul, 'I am able to do all things through Christ that strengthens me,' Philip. iv. 13. 'I have learned to want and to abound,' to do all things through Christ that strengthens me, that supplieth me with perpetual strength from above.

Beloved, in a Christian, especially in evil times, there is more than a man, there is more than a holy man, there is something that floweth from this head, Christ, that doth administer supplies of comfort, and of peace, and of joy, and of friends, whereby he is carried through all. By these and such like particularities, we may discern whether there be the life of Jesus manifested in us or no.

Use 2. Of exhortation. Beloved, let us labour by all means therefore *to have this spiritual life;* to have a frame, to have the divine nature stamped upon our nature, the frame of grace; and let us not rest on that, but labour for a perpetual and continual stream of life from Christ, the fountain and the spring.

I speak of this the rather, because there is a main defect in this, and the cause of many foils.* But our hearts be good, and we trust to the frame of life and grace that is in us, without looking to the supernatural spring and fountain of all grace out of ourselves; and we think to-morrow shall be as to-day, and by the same strength we do to-day, we shall stand against temptations to-morrow. Beloved, it will not be. There must be supplies not only of new strength, but also of greater strength, to new conflicts, to new oppositions, and new temptations. For as that strength will not carry a great burden that carrieth a little, they that carry burdens put forth greater strength to carry more than others. So in Christianity, when we meet with a strong temptation, we must not think to overcome it without setting upon

* That is, 'falls.'—G.

it with spiritual strength. Lord, I need divine strength, else I shall sink under this temptation; this cross is too heavy for me, and so not going about to oppose any extraordinary thing with strength of nature, for nature will do nothing in great matters. It will make us do things comely to the outward eye. Nor common grace will not make us able to set upon great matters, but we must have a supply from grace, from heaven. And therefore a Christian is a depending creature. None is so dependent or independent. Certainly none so independent on the creature as a Christian, especially when he carrieth Christ in his heart by faith; but then he is continually depending upon Christ the head, who is the treasure and spring of all spiritual life, to convey to us on all occasions. 'Without me you can do nothing,' John xv. 5, much less suffer without me. And therefore, I beseech you, let it be a rule for us in our ordinary course, when we set upon any duty, withstand any temptation, conflict with any corruption, when we are to enjoy any prosperity above the common model of grace, to enjoy it without surfeiting of pride, security, or the sins that accompany prosperity. Consider with ourselves, Have I a frame of grace enough to set upon this? No, I have not. Surely that must be, there must be a power from Christ, a perpetual drawing of strength from Christ to master this, to meet with this, to bring it under. As a Christian is lord of all conditions, of prosperity and adversity, but not by an ordinary frame of grace, but that together with a divine strength and power, which is here called the life of Jesus, specially manifested by dependency. So let the life of a Christian be continually dependent. Peter by his ordinary graces could say, 'Though all forsake thee, yet will not I,' Mark xiv. 31. But that he may see he stands by his own strength, he falls foully. And why do so many fall foully, but because they undertake things with their own strength, with former strength, and not with dependency, or a supply suitable to present necessity, and thereby they learn to stand by falling? God sanctifieth their slips and falls, to teach them better dependency for time to come.

I beseech you, therefore, let this be a direction how to guide our lives; and that we may depend on Christ for strength in all courses, take heed of offending him, and grieving his Spirit, [take heed] that he suspendeth not his divine power.[a] That strength obstructs this life, to call it home to himself, and then to leave us to our own principles, and then we fall presently. The life of a Christian is perpetually watchful, 'to work out faith with fear and trembling,' Philip. ii. 12. How? Not doubting of your salvation, but fear for offending Christ, 'for he giveth the will and the deed;' he giveth will to supply, and the deed to perform. And it is 'according to his good pleasure,' Philip. ii. 13. You stand upon your good behaviour. If you work not your salvation with a holy jealousy over your corruptions, and with a holy trembling, he may suffer you to fall. Therefore consider our dependency is not in ourselves. Now, since the fall, God will not trust us with our own strength, but will lay up all in Christ. Therefore take occasion to go to Christ, and that he may be our friend, and have his Spirit, as he doth all by his Spirit as the sun doth all by his beams; take heed of grieving the Spirit, and giving it occasion to suspend its influency of grace and influence of comfort. For it is another thing than it is taken, to be lively Christians. We should not only labour to have lives, but to be lively, to have the life of Christ manifested in us, and not only for crosses; in that time God preserveth great comforts; but labour in time of prosperity for the life of Jesus. There is little life of Jesus in times of peace.

Security deadeth the life of Jesus. Sins of plenty, and sins of long peace, stick upon us, that there is not that vigour, that liveliness of Jesus in us that ought to be.

Now our endeavour should be to labour after an increase of this inward frame, and together with increase of grace in us, increase of continual dependency by faith, which fetcheth all from Christ. And why should we labour for it? For the credit of Christian profession. What a glory is it to have a company of lively professors, in whom the life of Jesus is manifested, that are above all conditions, that are thralled with no condition, that can bring under all things, master their desires! 'The spiritual man judgeth all things,' 1 Cor. ii. 15, subdueth all things. He orders them so that he maketh them serviceable to his own ends. And what a glorious thing is it to be like a lion, bold in all conditions, to be afraid of nothing but of offending God! And then fear and tremble because God may suspend his Spirit. A wicked man may fear everything, but he feareth not God, which is to be feared above all. But a true Christian is a lord, a master above all other things, only he feareth to offend God, whereby this spiritual life may be obstructed. Now in regard it is such an excellent thing to be not only a living Christian but a lively Christian, and that it is for the honour of religion to be so, let us labour more and more for it, specially considering we know not with what dangers we may encounter, with what temptations and corruptions. Having now the life of Jesus, it will be manifested more and more till it end in glory. Is it not an excellent thing to have that in us, to have such a conquering principle in us, to have the Spirit of Christ in us, not only a frame of grace, but a Spirit enabling us, and acting us, and carrying us through all conditions?

Then this life of Jesus is a life that sets us in an order above all other lives. There is a great latitude of life from that plant, the powerful life* to God, which is life itself. What a gradation is there of life! There is life of sense, and life of reason, and the spirit. Now a Christian that hath the life of Jesus, which is a spiritual life here, and will end in a glorious life in heaven, sets him in a glorious rank above all lives under him; for it makes him one with Jesus. The Spirit of Christ acteth in him, loveth in him, joys in him, delights in him, carrieth him through actions, bears him through crosses. Even as the soul acts his body, so the life of Jesus acts him, and sets him in a higher rank. Indeed, a spiritual man is as much above another man, as another man above another creature.

What excellency is there, you will say, of a man that hath the life of Jesus in him? What excellency! Beloved, this life makes him eternal. All other excellencies are but 'grass, and the flower of grass,' as the apostle speaks, 'but the word of life, begotten by the word, endures for ever,' 1 Pet. i. 25. Spiritual life endures for ever. He that believeth in Christ endures for ever; for it is an everlasting life. All other things perish and fall. Put case they be the flower of grass. The flower perisheth before the grass. They be of shorter continuance. Wit, and greatness, and honour, and the like, they are of shorter continuance than life. Life is but grass, and all the ornaments of life are but flowers of the grass. These be fading things, and they must all end in death. All honours are determined in death. All excellencies lie in the dust. And we must rise up equally, all kings and subjects, great and small. But this life is a life that endures for ever, and therefore called an everlasting life. Then we live to purpose, and never till then, when we live the life of Jesus, when that is manifested

* Qu. 'of the plant, the flower'?—Ed.

in our souls, that is, *vita vitalis;* the other is, βίος ἄβιος, a life not worthy the name of life. The conditions of life, riches and nobility, which is a condition of life, all have their end; but this life of Jesus is begun in Christ, and ends in glory. And therefore it is worth labour to grow in it more and more, to have it more and more manifested in us above all conditions and life whatsoever.

I beseech you, let us not pass the time as careless, but labour to have something in us above nature, to have the life of Jesus to quicken our rational life, to sanctify all. The life of Jesus hinders us not of anything, but ennobles all other excellencies. A man that hath the life of Jesus may be as wise as he will, as learned as he will, he may be noble, this doth make him more noble, it doth dignify all. It is a diamond set in gold; it addeth excellency to all other excellencies. A Christian is truly noble. A man that hath the life of Jesus is truly rich, truly great, truly beautiful; he hath the image of Christ stamped upon the soul, and hath excellencies added to all other excellencies.

It is an unworthy thing that we should pass over this life, which is altogether to get into Christ, and to die before we begin to live. How many live a natural rational life, and live in an outward condition perhaps great in the world, and then all endeth in death; and they be out of the world before they come in. Here they come, here they live, and hence they go, and never do the work for which they came; which is, to get out of nature and to grow in grace; to get into the spirit of the life of Christ, who is the life of a Christian, the sun that quickens all. Instead of this, they go on from day to day, from year to year, and so die before they begin to live. And thousands do this in the bosom of the church.

This is a fearful condition. Therefore let this be the conclusion of this point.

Never rest till we find ourselves in a condition above nature, till we find ourselves in such a state that none can come to but a child of God. Let us enter into eternal life while we live. For none shall be transported into heaven that is not engrafted into Christ here. This is the entrance of heaven. Therefore begin the life here, get into the church here, else it shall never be obtained hereafter. Labour for more and more experiment,* that Christ is in us, that at the day of judgment Christ may know us, by his own stamp, and by his own life, that the life that raised him up out of the grave, may raise our bodies out of the dust. For this is our comfort we may have from the life of Jesus, efficacy to quicken us to duty. We shall find the life of Jesus to quicken us from troubles, and at the consummation of all, we shall find the Spirit that cometh from him powerfully able to raise our dead bodies. If the Spirit that raised up Christ from the dead be in us, it will raise up our bodies likewise. Indeed, I should never satisfy myself almost in this subject, but that the time is past, and you may in your own meditations work better upon that I have said, than I can by any strength of mine press at this present.

VERSE 11.

For we which live are always delivered to death for Jesus' sake, that the life also of Jesus might be made manifest in our mortal flesh.

The holy apostle, by a more than ordinary wisdom, by a spirit enlightened from heaven, doth not only take benefit from the weak estate he

* That is, 'experience.'—G.

was in with his fellows, but makes use likewise of such objections as were made against the profession of religion by such as looked on the outside. He grants to all that might be objected tending to the outward disparagement of religion, but then he retorteth all upon them, and makes a gracious and comfortable use of it. As you may see in these two verses: 'We bear in our body the dying of the Lord Jesus, but the life of Jesus is made manifest in our mortal bodies.' Of the tenth verse, we spake something largely the last day: 'Always bearing about the dying of the Lord Jesus, that,' &c.

We will now proceed to the next verse, which is but an illustration and exposition of the former. For what he said before, 'we bear in our bodies the dying of Christ,' here he saith, 'we are always delivered to death for Jesus' sake.' And where he saith there 'that the life of Jesus might be made manifest in our bodies,' here by way of exposition and illustration, 'that the life of Jesus might be made manifest in our mortal life.' So that it is but an illustration and exposition of the former verse.

'For we which live,' saith he; we apostles and ministers, and it is true of all Christians, we which live, while we live, are in some sense always delivered from* death for Jesus' sake.

Here is the circumstance of time, added to the condition they were in, and the aggravation of what they were delivered to. 'We are always delivered to death,' 'we are delivered to death, and always,' and 'for Jesus' sake.' These three things are a little considerable before we go further.

The condition is 'deliverance to death,' the circumstance 'always,' and 'for Jesus' sake.'

Obj. How could they die, being alive?

Ans. I answer, we are delivered to death, because God, by his permission, gave them over to Satan ruling in the children of obedience,† to molest, and threaten, and deliver them, to death, in regard of the designing of cruel men of them to death, on all advantages they could take against them. And likewise delivered to death in their preparation for death continually, for they could make no other account every day they rose but that they might die before they slept again. And in this respect, they and every Christian ought to be a dying man to be delivered to death.

God is ready to permit them to die when they may honour him. God is not prodigal of our lives. When our lives may save his truth, he will permit our lives into the mercy of merciless men, and they have bloody minds. Their malice is more than their power; their cruelty is more than their ability oftentimes, but their hearts are altogether bloody. And so a Christian is always prepared for the worst, as the apostle saith. For, beloved, as soon as ever a Christian becomes a Christian, the first lesson in religion is self-denial. And in what respect must he deny himself? In regard of goods or honour? Not only so, but in the grand matter of life itself. He must hate, that is, not love, father, mother, not life itself, if the question be for God's glory and the good of the church; if they come in competition with divine truths of the gospel. We must give up our lives for Christ and his church; we must have resigned minds. This we must do in preparation of spirit. God indeed calleth not always for it. There be more difficult times sometimes than other, and the times of the gospel be sweet times of rest; for in the Acts it is said the churches had rest, ix. 31; but we must be prepared for it. St Paul saith to the Corinthians,‡ that when they 'gave themselves to Christ,' they gave their

* Qu. 'to'?—Ed. † Qu. 'disobedience'?—Ed. ‡ The Macedonians.—G.

goods to Christ, 2 Cor. viii. 5. And when a Christian giveth himself to Christ, he giveth his goods and himself to Christ. It is no hard matter, when a man hath given himself to Christ, to part with any things else that serve only for necessary comforts and provision, and then he takes all back again when he hath his life. Lord, it is thy life; thou hast bought me and my life, I am thine; thou hast paid a dear price for me, and thine it shall be when thou callest for it. If thou wilt have my credit, my state, my liberty, thou shalt have it; if my life itself, thou shalt have it; of thee I have it, to thee I return it again, if it may be for thy glory and thy church's good. And this should be the disposition of every Christian, to count nothing his own so much as not to be ready to part with it when Christ calleth for it. Beloved, a Christian is a sacrifice, and the end of all the favours of Christ is, that from a free willing spirit 'he should offer himself a free willing sacrifice to God,' as the apostle speaks excellently, Rom. xii. 1. When he had spoken of all the favours of God in Christ, election, justification, sanctification, the comforts of his children in trouble, the end of all is, 'that we should offer ourselves as a willing, reasonable sacrifice to God' as the end of all. And therefore reservation in our spirits of anything that we will have limitations in: we profess religion, but with reservation of liberty, and not offend so and so, and not endanger their skin in hazard, or reputation, and life; it cannot stand with the truth of Christianity. No man is a true Christian that hath such reservation. He never knew what faith and implantation into Christ meant; he hath not entered into the first form of religion; he hath not learned to deny himself. 'Whoever will be a disciple of me, let him take up his cross,' Mat. xvi. 24. There be two hindrances of religion, one within, another without; within us ourselves, that we must deny; without us is the cross, and that we must take up; and he that doth both these, is fit to follow Christ. And none but those.

And therefore thou must be content, as the apostle saith, to be 'always delivered to death for Jesus' sake.' So is Christ himself our head. He was delivered to death, as I named before. God permitted them by little deaths to afflict him, and misuse him; at length God gave him up to death itself. They thought to have swallowed him up continually, and to have made an end of him; at length God gave him indeed. And he was himself a willing sacrifice, ready to die. So we must be as Christ was, ready to part with this life, as Christ did part with all for us; else we are not suitable members of so glorious and gracious a head. He gave himself for us, and shall not we give ourselves back again to him, specially when it is the only way to save ourselves? 'He that loseth life, shall get his life; and he that will spare his life, shall lose his life,' Mat. x. 39. It will prove so in the end. You will say these be good things, and true matters, but they be not for us in these times. The more we are to bless God, beloved. And yet we are delivered to death if we regard that sympathy that should be between us, and the mystical body of Christ. In France now and in Spain, and in many places of Germany, and Italy, Christ hath a church. And are not the poor souls there continually, as it were, delivered to death? Are they not always between the block and the hatchet, either killed or ready for death, continually as sheep to the slaughter? The persecutor makes no more bones of killing them, than a butcher makes conscience of killing a sheep, or a man to eat bread when he is hungry.

'They eat up my people, as they eat bread,' Ps. xiv. 4, and 'they think they do God good service,' John xvi. 2. This is the state of all countries beyond the seas, except ours; and shall not we have actions of sympathy? That member that sympathiseth not with the body is a dead member. And therefore we cannot make it good to ourselves, that we are living members of a living and glorious head, except we sympathise with them. So that in regard of the body of Christ now in Europe, under the cross a long time, and under tyranny of crosses, we may say we are delivered to death continually. And it may be our portion and lot, before we go out of the world, for anything we know, and for anything we discern. That is the truth of it.

But what speak I of delivering to death, when some nice* Christians will not endure a scorn, a frown, a reproach for Christ? They will not part with anything for Christ; how then will they part with their blood? Are those likely men to be 'delivered to death for Christ's sake,' if times should be, that will not yield up anything they have?

Now that we be enabled to do it, I will not trouble you with many directions. I will give but one. When a Christian cometh to be a Christian, let him think he is not a man for this life, farther than God will suffer him to live for the good of others, and to get assurance of interest in another world. He is estated in heaven, therefore let him be at a point for this present life. And now he hath given himself to Christ, his life is Christ's, and let him think his life is not his own. 'If I live, I live to Christ; if I die, I die to Christ,' Rom. xiv. 8, and be content that Christ should have what he hath bought so dearly, whensoever he will call for it. Be content with partial little deaths under them, for many of us die in times of peace, such partial deaths, as sickness, and infirmities. This life goes out many ways, sometimes by infirmities of body, sometimes by violence, at length by age. All partial deaths, we must learn to make use of them every day as we should, and in every of them some little part and glimpse of the light of Christ is manifested. And therefore labour every day to bear every day's cross comely, and as Christians should do; and the bearing of partial crosses will enable us to bear the grand crosses. The undergoing of little deaths will make us able to undergo the grand death, when the time cometh.

To go on: 'For we which live are always delivered to death for Christ's sake.' 'Always,' for anything we know. 'We die daily,' saith the apostle, 1 Cor xv. 31; in our expectation, and in our resignation of spirit; we die daily in the designs of malicious spirits. God and Christ may challenge our right in our life, when he will, in regard of that disposition of soul answerable to Christ's dispensation, which we are ignorant of, and answerable to the malice of wicked men, which we know not. When our humanity will vent itself, we are always 'delivered to death for Christ's sake.' It is not the life we are to make account of, not to reckon of. 'We are dead men,' as the apostle saith, Rom. viii. 10, 11. We are dead in sin, not only dead to sin, but in regard of the sentence of mortality pronounced on us, which I shall have occasion to touch when I come to 'mortal bodies.'

'Delivered to death for Jesus' sake.' Jesus' sake! What, will the enemies say so? No! it is for your heresy, schism, faction, unquiet spirit; it is that you be troublers of state, but by no means for Jesus' sake. But the course of the enemy is first of all to be liars, and then to be slanderers, to take away the good name of God's people, and then to take away their lives. They be serpents and dragons for cunning, and then to be lions to devour. That is their method, and the devil's method, when they cannot with colour

* That is, = delicate.—G.

execute their cruelty, but under lies and slanders. Therefore the course of [the] wicked is to devour them in their names, civilly* to devour them first; and then they have afterwards better colour to shew all the malice they can. And all that be led with cursed spirits at all times, their fashion is to disgrace them, that by it they may blemish them all they can, and then they shall be counted excellent men, for pursuing such men for such sins; they blast them, but in their reputation specially. Such as will take any leisure to examine things, may plainly see their malice against the life of Christ. And then they have glorious pretences to carry their malice, and cruelty which they list. But doth God interpret it so? No! He interprets it for Christ's sake; Christ interprets it for his own sake. They do for such and such ends, but Christ takes it as done for himself; his religion, his profession, for the cause of religion, and a good conscience. Whoever therefore do suffer for the discovery of a good conscience, if but in a civil matter, as John Baptist (it was not for a matter of religion), it is for God's sake, the truth of God, and justice of God; and we may suffer in way of justice, and rather than not stand out in a civil matter for Christ's sake. Therefore we count John among the martyrs. For religion, in the profession of it in word, or the profession of it in life, or in discharge of a good conscience, any way, that is for Christ's sake. Christ will take it so, and that is our comfort; and if he take it so, surely he will be partner with us, he will suffer with us; and if he suffers with us, surely we shall be well borne out, and he will glorify us hereafter. 'Blessed are ye when men persecute and revile you for my name's sake,' Mat. v. 11; so did their fathers the prophets before you. Whatsoever the world makes pretence to, their wisdom, folly, thinking to daub things as they may well enough with the world, yet God will take it out otherwise. It is for his sake. He will revenge it, as done against his children, and afterward crown them.

They that be enemies to God's people for religion, either in the profession or practice of it, as upbraiding them with their loose practice, and their false opinion, they are not so much enemies of men as of Christ. And if Christ were on the earth, they that persecute anything for Christ's sake will persecute him more. If Christ were on the earth he should find like entertainment, as amongst the Jews; for the wicked would devise this and that pretence to put him to death.

This is a terrible consideration to wicked men; he that hateth good in any degree, because it is good, hateth the best good most of all. And he that hateth good men as good men, will hate him that is the head of all good men, Christ himself. And they that be malicious against good men, and carry matters cunningly, they would do the same to Christ, and much more. He that hateth any thing as it is such a thing, he hates it most of all; and he that hateth goodness as goodness, hateth it most of all where it is to be had in the fountain.

What can such people therefore look for, that be enemies to God's people, and cause, and religion, as far as they dare, when they would use him as ill, if he were upon the face of the earth? For if they malign and hate them for Christ's sake, surely they would more malign and hate Christ if he were here. But I have not much occasion to press this point. I only open it, hoping there will not be much need of pressing it in this place; but you may use it to help your judgments, how malice is dangerous, and how it is interpreted by Christ himself, what colour soever the world sets upon it.

* That is, 'morally' = in their 'good name,' character.—G.

Now what is the event of this delivery to death? What is the issue and fruit of it in God's intendment? What is the event? Now God's intendment is, 'that the life of Jesus might be made manifest in our mortal flesh.'

The life of Jesus I spake of in the former verse, and some things lately. I will add some things, and so go on.

'The life of Jesus is manifested to our mortal flesh.' The life of Jesus is not only his glorious life, that he liveth in heaven himself, and that he liveth here on earth with a gracious person; but the life of Jesus is that quickening power that cometh from Christ our head, whereby he doth enliven and quicken all his members, and that with a double life.

First, A habitual and constant life, by reason of the constant dwelling of the Spirit in us.

And besides this, there is a *quickening power*, continually to act and draw forth this life of grace upon all occasions. But of this I have spoken largely heretofore.

I am willing to add something for the further clearing of this point, that you may better understand what the life of Jesus is.

Now, beloved, if we would know whether the life of Jesus be in us or no, I give you some evidences. And that I desire you specially at this time to take notice of is this: *Observe the beating of the pulse; that is, holy desires to heavenly things.* Where this life is, that is the lowest thing in this life of Jesus, that there be holy desires, which are the pulse. As, beating of the pulse is the liveliest life; where they beat there is hope of life; and then there is breath to take in fresh air, and to send out that that is taken in. So where there is grace there is breathing, receiving of new air, new strength from Christ, and sending out by contempt all that is naught. There is some little suitableness between the life of nature and the life of Jesus. And then there is spiritual sense, whereby we are able to feel, and taste, and see, and discern spiritual things in another manner than before; and answerable to spiritual sense there is spiritual motions to the things we are sensible of, and motion is always where senses are. For we have sense but to discover what is good or evil, and upon discovery of good or evil, power to move from what is evil to good; else senses were rather fit to torment us than anything. Therefore there is likewise a power to move in natural life. So in spiritual life, whereby we are enabled to taste and relish heavenly things, there is a power to move them, and carry the soul to them, and to remove from what is spiritually evil. And therefore together with the pulse, and breathing, and sense, and motion, usually there be sympathies and antipathies to what is suitable or contrary to their being. As spiritual life hath antipathy to sin, as the bane and the poison of it; and works it out by little and little, being like the poison of nature, that when poison enters it works against the poison as much as it can to cast it up; so where there is spiritual life, it works against the sinfulness of corrupt nature, and whatsoever is opposite to it, and works it out by little and little, as a counter-poison to it. For this spiritual life is opposite, and contrarious every way to sin. And therefore they that cherish corruption by occasion, company, and objects, which they should mortify, alas! where is the life of grace in them?

But to leave these things, though they help our understanding in the mystery I speak of: the thing I would have you specially to discern in the spiritual life of Jesus is, that it leadeth a man higher than all other lives. It sets a man in a higher rank of creatures. It makes a man a spiritual man, and it guideth his life by reason above nature, by reason above common course; for it is called 'the life of Jesus,' because it comes from Jesus, and as it comes from Jesus it leadeth to Jesus.

Now, therefore, a man may know he liveth the life of Jesus, that cometh from Christ, if he hath such a spirit as leads him to Christ, that leads him to honour Christ. Though not immediately in his person, yet Christ hath in the world his religion, his children, his ordinances, and by these he is carried to Christ, and findeth Christ. So he that hath the life of Christ in him, he will relish Christ in all these, and in all these will be carried to Christ, and will honour Christ in all these, and will be a friend of the church, a friend of religion, a friend of all God's ordinances, not only as finding a relish in them, but he hath a life from Christ, that teaches us to refer all to him. And he will venture his natural life to save his spiritual life, because it is his best life. There is no man that is a sound Christian, and in a right frame as a Christian, but will adventure anything of his inferior life to maintain his head. (As it is one point of the wisdom of the serpent to maintain his head) he will maintain his union and communion with Christ, religion, and the ordinances, whereby he preserveth his life, though with some prejudice of the outward life.

Life is taken oftentimes not only for the life that cometh from the union with soul and body, but from the condition together with that, as to be rich, and poor, and in credit. So many, not only to maintain their natural life, but their life of condition; that is, to maintain an honourable condition in the world, to be of high esteem; they make the life of Jesus only to serve their turns. If they can keep their natures continually, and grow in favour with men, they think the life of Jesus is a hidden and secret thing, as indeed it is, and they will not trouble themselves much about it. Oh, this is far from the disposition of a lively Christian that hath the life of Jesus, for he is ready to suffer in his natural life, in his condition of life whatsoever it be, rather than prejudice his best life, and he will consider and esteem of things, not so much as they further his natural condition in the world, or natural life, but how it stands with his spiritual life. Nothing against religion, nothing against grace, nothing against the Spirit. This is such a thing for his head, his religion; then he will consider things as they tend to that, though it be to the discredit of his person, though with loss of liberty, with peril of the decays of natural life, though with prejudice in worldly things whatsoever they be, rather than he will endanger his best life, the life of Jesus; and he will esteem of things suitable to that, that shall be his glory, the life of Jesus. But whatsoever is between him and Jesus shall be lightly esteemed. Those that be in a true Christian frame of soul are thus disposed to God; and there is good reason for it, for it is the best life of all, and it is that for which we have natural lives. Beloved, if we have not the life of Jesus, we had better have no life at all. As it was said of Judas, 'better we had never been born,' Mat. xxvi. 24; if we have not a new life besides what we have by nature we had better not be born at all. Therefore, let us not deceive ourselves, but labour to have something above nature.

I will not trouble you with farther evidence in the point, because I desire that what I have spoken may sink into your souls.

And to stir you up after this life of Jesus, this frame of grace, this quickening from our head Christ, it is that for which we live, it is that which our life is decreed unto. You know there be three degrees of life: a life in the womb, a life in this world, and a life in heaven; the first for the second, the second for the third. The life in the womb is for civil life among men. The child hath not eyes and ears for that place where it is, for in that strait place it hath no use of eyes, or ears, or tongue, or anything. All the sense it hath there, is not for that life, but for a civil life amongst men, where there is use of eyes, and sense, and tongue, and all the members it hath. So high are a man's designs and large, vast things, that nothing will satisfy. When a man understandeth, he desires more; his affection is large, nothing will satisfy desire. There is large expectation and love, that nothing here will satisfy, but fresh, fresh, still for desire. Hath God given them vast understanding, and this vast will, and vast affections for that which will not remain with them? They are for another life. The very frame of our soul sheweth it. As the frame of the infant in the womb sheweth that that frame is for the life in the world, so the life we live, in regard of the large capacity of our souls, is for another life in heaven.

Therefore, if we labour not for the life of Jesus to be begun here, which is called the life of grace, the beginning and infant of glory, we miss of our end. This life is for that life; we are not for this life. God ordained us not for this life. Therefore he will take this life away to advance it to a spiritual life. He takes liberty to take away our health and natural life, that he may advance our spiritual life, for he knoweth what is in this life is well lost, if it be gained in a better life, and it is for a better life. I beseech you, let us think seriously of these things.

What should I speak on the life of condition, that you may be moved to the excellent life of Jesus? There is a better condition together with it than any condition. For a natural life* takes a condition with a king. A Christian is a king, and a king over that that is terrible, a king over death, and hell, and the world, and above all. Take our natural life with the condition of a rich man; there is better riches in the life of Jesus. The riches of heaven are his. Take the natural life with any outward condition, and there is better in grace, better in religion. The life of Jesus hath better endowments accompanying it. Is it not better to have the image of God stamped upon the soul? What better honour? Name you what you will, is there not a better condition in the life of Jesus? So as the life itself being a spiritual and divine thing, for the divine nature is most excellent; so the endowments and appurtenances that accompany the life of grace, are incomparably above all the endowments and appurtenances that is of natural life. Take it in the life of kings, emperors, or what you will, they are nothing to the life of Jesus.

Now this life of Jesus is manifested most when we are delivered to death. Both the frame of grace, and the quickening power of grace, they are both more manifest when we are delivered to death; that is, in trouble, sickness, or any cross whatsoever, there is more discovery of the life of Jesus than at other times. I have touched some reasons of it heretofore: I shall give some now, because the apostle repeateth the thing, and we will not pass it over, because the apostle doubles a little upon it.

Reason 1. Beloved, if we speak of the inward frame of grace, *is not that most manifested when our outward man decayeth, and is afflicted?* It is. For everything is increased by the exercise of it. 'When we are delivered to death,' that is, prepared for sufferings, or do suffer, there is opportunity of exercising all the branches of spiritual life. We put forth the exercise of spiritual life. Then we pray more than at ordinary times. Then we exer-

* Qu. 'take'?—ED.

cise our faith and dependency upon God. Then we exercise our hope of life everlasting. Then we exercise our love to God, his church and people. Then we are advanced for exercising of all functions of spiritual life. Therefore the life of Jesus is most manifested in the dyings of Jesus.

Reason 2. Beloved, it is a clear point, *if we take it for the quickening power of Christ, together with the inward frame that is most in the dyings of Jesus.* When we suffer any thing for God, it is his honour to be most present with us, and graciously present with us, when we stand most in need of his presence. But we stand most in need of his gracious presence at these times; therefore he, out of the bowels of pity and compassion, is nearest to us. 'I will be with thee in fire and water,' Isa. xliii. 2. The Spirit of God enters into all conditions, into prisons, into dungeons, into every condition whatsoever. The quickening power of Christ is as much manifested in the outward condition as in any kind of way. As now for Christ to make a weak man, a weak woman, or a weak child, an old man, one being weak, another by sex, a third by age, when these three shall be able to stand out for God, for Christ in times of persecution: when these shall in times of peace and prosperity hold out the profession of religion, there must needs be a manifestation of a power above nature. By nature children are tender, by nature women are fearful, by nature old men are timorous, and fearful too. I say, the disproportion of the condition to the grace and power that is shewed, discovers the manifestation, that there is a quickening power more than ordinary. For the martyrs, when they were to seal the truth with their blood, to have a fire of love kindled in them, above the flames of fire, and the spiritual comforts kindled in them, here was manifestation of the life of Jesus, when they were delivered to death. Nay, a sick worn body; take it in times of peace, a good Christian that hath given himself to the study of mortification, and hath supplied the wants of affliction by mortification. . . .*

As that it is a gracious use of afflictions to supply the want of them by mortification, you shall see the life of Jesus in afflictions. A great deal of patience in a body tormented with sickness, a great deal of heavenly mindedness, when he is ready to go out of the world; a great deal of comfort in the midst of disgrace in a stout Christian; when the condition is one, and the strength another above it to master it, here is manifestation of power. Are the conditions so, that the manifestation of the life and quickening power of Jesus is most of all in such times when we stand most in need of it, times of suffering, times of sickness, hour of death?

Reason 3. Thirdly, Another main reason that the life of Jesus is more manifested then is, *because Christ reserveth his comforts for the fittest times.* Then is the fittest time for Christ to close with the soul, for then the soul stands most in need of grace. He is an head, and therefore wise, because an head. As all wisdom resteth in the head to guide the body, so all wisdom in Christ to guide his church. And he knoweth the fittest opportunity for the measure of grace and comfort. There is no comfort comparable to the comfort God's children find in the greatest abasement; for then they empty themselves, and therefore are most fit to be filled with the Spirit. Then God delighteth to have communion with them at all times. God draws them into the wilderness, and then speaks to their hearts, as the prophet saith, Hosea ii. 14: 'God will let the world know that he hath hidden manna for his children, which they know not, nor feel not.' And so God hath his hid manna, which he suffers them to taste more especially

* Sentence left unfinished—G.

when they be distressed in the outward man, and then is the life of Jesus most manifested to them.

Use. And therefore, beloved, I beseech you, fear not any thing in the world that may befall us; fear nothing that may befall us in our own quarrel. Shall we fear our advancement in a better kind? What we lose in nature, we gain in grace; what we lose in outward comforts, we gain in spiritual. It is made up in a better kind, and shall we be discouraged for any thing that befalls us in this world? Shall not we give Christ liberty to take what he will, so he make it up in a better kind? Shall not we suffer him to take our credit, our liberty, our life, so he make it up in the life of Jesus? What damage is it if we be delivered to little deaths, to partial deaths, that is, to vexation, to restraint of liberty, to fall into disgrace with the world, if we gain as much in spiritual life? That is well parted withal, and lost in this world, that is made up in spiritual things; for the spiritual things are eternal. They make us good, they commend us to God, they be proportionable to us, they add a worth and value in themselves to us: whatsoever, therefore, we part with for God's cause, if we find access and increase of inward grace, and peace, and comfort, are we losers by it? Doth not God make sweet recompence to his children, according to that general rule, 'All things work together for the best to them that love God'? Rom. viii. 29. Let us remember this, and lay it up against times of trial. And when we are sick, shall we fear sickness? Oh, if we had the Spirit of faith then, Lord, now I am delivering up to death, and cease to live; Oh, as the life of nature decays, let me find the life of Jesus; let me find some drop of that life which Jesus lived. For the life of Jesus makes us like Christ in some measure; that is, full of grace, full of peace; full of glory; the life of Jesus in heaven is glorious, a gracious life. Now when drops of it are dropped into a man in times of sickness or persecution, it will make a man forget all troubles whatsoever; as it is a saying in the Canticles, 'Thy love,' saith the spouse, 'is better than wine,' Cant. i. 2. Now what is wine? It will make a man forget his trouble. And so the love of Jesus, which is a principle of the life of Jesus, a distillation of the love of Jesus, is better than wine. It will make a man forget his disgrace, forget his afflictions, forget all, because it is a beam of such a sun, a drop of such an ocean. It is a supernatural, a commanding life, a life of a higher nature, above all things below, an independent life, which will be sufficient in heaven when we have neither meat, nor drink, nor conversation, nor converse with men; and if we have a little of this derived* to us in any troubles, it will carry us through all. Therefore labour to think of these things. You see what need we have to be one with Jesus, who is the spring and Lord of life, that hath received life, to convey it to us, as the 'second Adam.' Therefore we had need of sacraments, to confirm and strengthen our union with this head, from whom we have spiritual life. Therefore come with joy, and comfort, and courage to the sacrament; the end whereof is to increase union and communion with the fountain of life, Jesus; who gave his body to be broken, and his blood to be shed, that he might give life to us, that he might by satisfaction in his death give us life of sentence, that we might be acquitted at the bar of God's justice. 'He died, and is risen again; who shall lay any thing to the charge of God's people?' Rom. viii. 33. Therefore come to the sacrament, that we may grow in assurance of the life of sentence, in removing the guilt of sin, because Christ died for us. And we shall likewise have great increase of

* That is, 'communicated.'—G.

the inward frame of life and grace. For the more we are assured of forgiveness of sins, and acceptation to life everlasting, the more we live; as, where many things are forgiven, there is much love, Luke vii. 47. And the more we love, the more willing and cheerful we shall be; for all obedience springs from love. When we love we are ready for all duties. And therefore come with encouragement to increase our union and communion with Jesus Christ, now at this time.

VERSES 12, 13.

So then death worketh in us, but life in you. We having the same spirit of faith, according as it is written, I believe, therefore have I spoken. We all believe, and therefore we speak.

In the former part of the chapter we have heard how the apostle doth grant freely what might be objected to the disparagement of the ministry of the gospel, in regard of many particulars, and then he retorts, and makes use of all; as you may see in the several particulars.

We spake the last time of the eleventh verse, which is but the same with the tenth, only a more full expression and exposition of it, by some addition.

I observed divers things from thence.

That God's children must make account of the worst in the world; 'that the life of Jesus may be made manifest in our mortal flesh.' Here is the event of the troubles God's children meet withal in this world, and the intendment on God's part.

'Made manifest in our mortal flesh.' I did not speak anything of that, therefore I will add something.

'The life of Jesus is made manifest in our flesh,' though mortal, and subject to death; and mortal, not only because subject to death, but also subject to miseries, which are little deaths. For, beloved, we do not only die when our lives are ended, when the last day of our life is cut off; but all that makes way to that is death. All the petty miseries, that by little and little unloose the affections from earthly things, that unloose the soul from the body, all those partial things, they are little degrees of that separation which is in death. So that in our mortal body, that is, our body that is subject to death, and to that that makes way for death.

'Our mortal flesh.' Flesh is a diminishing word in Scripture, implying mortal and frail nature. This is a matter of use, rather than to be unfolded; the best of us all carry but mortal flesh. We carry our deaths, and our hearse about us; our life is dying and mortal. It is a matter rather to be thought of to make us wise indeed; as Ps. xlix. 3, 'I will speak of wisdom.' What wisdom is it that he speaks of? He speaks of mortality and of death common to all, that is wisdom indeed. And therefore, Ps. xc. 12, the holy man with order teacheth us 'to number our days, that we may apply our hearts to wisdom.' There be no wiser thoughts in this world than to judge aright of the condition of earthly things, and of our estate hereafter; for wisdom is in the judgment of things. When do we rightly judge of ourselves? When we judge this life to be a dying kind of life, and our estate to be a fading kind of condition. Mortal flesh it is; 'we are but earthen vessels.' 'Dust we are, and to dust we shall return again,' Gen. iii. 19.

Beloved, think of this. It is but mortal flesh we carry; and therefore do not stand too much in adorning of it, in feeding of it, in providing for the lusts of it. How many betray their souls, their better part, by studying to give contentment to their mortal flesh! This is not the life for mortal flesh. The time for that is the life to come, at the resurrection. Then when we shall have other flesh, we shall be all spiritual, even our bodies spiritual, not maintained with meat and drink, as now they are. That is the life of the body, a glorious life. Now it is a mortal life, that must end in dust and rottenness.

It is the vanity, especially of the younger sort, as if all their commendation were in setting out their bodies in apparel, and such things. It is a poor thing for a man, that hath a reasonable soul, to fetch his commendations from his flesh, from that which is worms' meat. Hath he nothing else to fetch his commendations from but what covereth his body? What is the flesh but the garment of the soul, and a rotten one? And what are other garments but a covering of that? And for a man to seek commendations, which should arise from parts and worth within, to be studying to provide for this mortal flesh, is a course unworthy of them that prove themselves to be Christians.

And therefore we must labour not to value ourselves by the body, nor by any worth we have in the outward man neither. If we have diseased bodies, or weak bodies, more mortal than others, not to be cast down, even the best are but mortal flesh; let us value ourselves by that which is to eternity, by the life of Jesus. Learn humility hence, not to be proud of mortal flesh, and sobriety. Many wise observations are from hence, but they are so easy, that the meanest of them, the Spirit accompanying them, may be sufficient to you that be of understanding. Therefore I will not speak of it now, being more largely spoken of in the latter part of the chapter. 'So death works in us, but life in you.' That is the conclusion of the former comparison of Paul's suffering with the presence of God supporting him in his sufferings; he concludeth them all with this, 'So then death works in us, but life in you.'

Some take this for an irony, or a sarcasm, as we call it, a bitter kind of speech.* You be free from the cross, and from death. But I take not that to be the meaning of the place, but rather this: we die daily, we carry the death of Jesus about us, but life works in you. You have the good of all our deaths, not only we ourselves, that be apostles, but you have life by our death, glory by our shame, happiness by our misery; you are gainers by it. And indeed so it is. Those that be the grandees † of the church, when they die, others live by them, as you shall see.

'So that death works in us.' How doth death work in us? Death works two ways at once.

It works in the outward man a decay. And then, by a command of a higher power, by God's Spirit, death works life, the contrary in us. Death works in us; that is, we are subject to death, and dying. It works in us a farther and farther disposition to death. And life is taken away continually by partial deaths, which fit us for the last death; death as a canker eateth out our life and natures. As he said before, death is not only the conclusion of our life, but it eateth into it continually. Every day taking away a piece of it, especially them that be under crosses, death by little and little worketh a separation of soul from the body. And then death works in us the life of Jesus, that is, not in itself—for it works nothing but dissolution, and turneth us to our dust out of which we were taken—but death works in us by the command of God, who can raise light out of darkness,

* Cf. Hodge, Stanley, Alford, and Wordsworth, *in loc.*—G.

† That is, 'leaders' as explained a little onward.—G.

and life out of death, and happiness out of misery. God, who hath all things in obedience to him, can raise contrary out of contrary. And therefore death works in us the life before spoken of, not of itself, but by the command of God himself, who extracteth out of death, and mortality, and misery we suffer, a farther degree of spiritual life. Beloved, it is a strange thing that death should work; but consider all things under heaven, even they work not in themselves, but under command and at obedience of the Supreme Worker, who is so excellent and powerful a worker, that he can raise contraries out of contrary, that cannot only raise from death, and make happy after misery, but make happy in misery, in life, in death, he is so powerful a worker.

Use. And of this make this use of it. *We are in covenant with a powerful God, that can make any condition work to our good.* He hath command over life, death, imprisonment, abasement whatsoever. He can raise out of them whatsoever is contrary, that no state shall be over-troublesome to us, that we shall not distaste of any condition. Shall we distaste of any conditions, when God can make that condition serve for our best good? Oh no.

Use 2. Comfort. And let this comfort us in the greatest misery. God works life in death. He giveth spiritual life, and makes it appear we are upheld by a divine power, another power than our own; therefore be not discouraged, and never despair.

But what benefit have they by it? Life works in you by our death; life works in him too. And the life of Jesus is manifested not only in him but them too. God bringeth his own children into great troubles for the good of others. They be the standard-bearers of the church, but he commands their lives to be manifested in their dyings, two or three ways.

(1.) The more he dies, the more death was wrought in him, the more the Spirit liveth in him, the more spiritual life was in him; that is, a divine power and strength of grace, to enable him in the inward man. And was not this for the church's good, being a public man, as he was? And therefore the church loseth nothing by the afflictions of their godly pastors. Oh your Christians, the more they be afflicted, the more free they be to comfort and instruct. Of all physicians the experienced physician is the best. And they be the best teachers, and do most good, that can speak from experience of the life of Christ manifested in them; in that regard life was theirs, by death working in him.

(2.) Then again, as death wrought in him, so life in them, that they might have good by his sufferings, and the presence of God's Spirit in his sufferings, to be less troubled with the cross. We see St Paul nevertheless hath his partial death, his abasement in the world, as an 'earthen vessel' despised of all; how straight he walks and comfortably he walks! how God is present with his Spirit! And surely if we suffer for a righteous cause, the same Spirit that was present with Paul shall be present with us. And thus by way of example life works in them, but death in him.

(3.) Life wrought in them, by death in him, that they might be in love more with religion, which is such as bringeth comfort and strength from heaven in the greatest sufferings for it. And that they might love the cause the better, God is present with the cause. If it were not God's cause, he would not accompany it with such increase of grace and comfort. Therefore, as death in Paul, so life in them; for they are more and more in love with religion. And so it was with the martyrs: when they saw it was such a cause, then they went cheerfully to suffer. They knew God had neither persons nor cause, that he was so present with all; and therefore they were encouraged themselves, because they saw others victoriously and triumphingly to suffer. So we see that we ought not to take scandal at the sufferings of any for a good cause. Their death is our life. If we be of the same body, we may take good by it. We should be so far from taking scandal at them that suffer for justice or religion, that we should honour them the more. 'I Paul, a prisoner,' Eph. iii. 1. Is that a weakening of himself? No. As a prevailing argument, [he] here mentioneth his bonds and sufferings. It is so far therefore from being a matter of offence as to make us not to be ready to taunt them, as proud flesh is ready to do; and therefore they have counted crosses and suffering, a contemptible thing, that we should honour it the more. And therefore take no offence at them that suffer in the cause of religion; their sufferings is for the good of others. For this we have a more clear place in the latter part of this chapter.

Obj. But have not all God's children their death, without dying to you? Are not all God's children partakers of the cross?

Ans. Beloved, sometimes it is thus with God's church and children, that God to favour them doth give them an exemption from any great cross till they be trained up, and get fortitude and strength; not that God loveth them more than he loveth others that he exerciseth; but it is clean contrary, for where he causeth to suffer for a good cause, it is a privilege. 'To you it is given, not only to believe, but also to suffer,' Philip. i. 29. He favours them more, and tenders them more. The rest have not that strength of grace, and therefore God cherisheth them; as when plants be young, we set them about with bushes against excursion of outward causes; but when they have taken root, those be taken away. So God besets his children with props and comforts till they have gotten root; but afterwards exposeth them to storms and wind, that they may take root deeper. Therefore let none think they be better because they be free. God is preparing and fitting them for that which is prepared for them.

'We having the Spirit, as it is written, I believe, therefore have I spoken; we also believe, therefore we speak.'

The holy apostle doth here, as an entrance into this discourse, fully set forth his condition under the cross, and the sufferings as a believer; that is, he was bold and confident, notwithstanding all sufferings, in hope of the resurrection, and glory to come. And he sets out his faith by comparing his faith with them in former times. 'We having the same Spirit of faith' that they had before, as Abraham, and David, and others, we are not alone, neither in sufferings nor in our comforts. We have the same combats and the same comforts, the same Spirit of comfort and grace, according 'as it is written, I believe, therefore I have spoken; we also believe, therefore do we speak.' He made David's case, Ps. cxvi. 10, parallel to his own. They were both in trouble and affliction, both confess to God in the midst of his congregation. Saint Paul had the same Spirit: 'we believe and speak,' as they believed and spake. I shall have the present life of Christ manifested in me. I know by experience that I shall be carried along by the life, and power, and Spirit of Christ, and afterward I look for a glorious resurrection, as is specified in the next verse.

'We having the same Spirit of faith,' not the same with you, and the rest of the members that now live. Now that I conceive is not so much his meaning,* as we having the same Spirit of faith with David, and them before Christ died, with all the professors of religion from the beginning of

* Cf. as *ante, in loc.*, and Webster and Wilkinson.—G.

the world to the end, the same Spirit with you. Now the same spirit with the church in former times, one Spirit runs through the veins of the church in all ages; having the same spirit of faith, he hath the same commanding act of faith. For there be two acts of faith: one we call *elicitus*, which is, the inward proper act of faith; and there is *actus imperationis*, whereby it commands the exercises of other graces. As I believe in the proper exercise of grace in itself, and I not only believe, but courageously confess; confession is not so much the proper act of faith, as it is commanded to be exercised by faith. Here is first the life of faith, and then the act and expression of faith with a parallel, David: as David believeth and speaks, so I believe and speak.

'We have the spirit of faith.' Faith is here the fundamental grace, the radical grace of all. We have faith, and a spirit of faith, and the same spirit of faith. So that faith is the radical grace, it being the grace that exercises all the rest. It is the grace of the new covenant, whereby we are knit to Christ: 'Whosever believeth shall not perish, but have everlasting life,' John iii. 15. It is the grace of union that knits us to the root, the foundation of lively Christianity. And therefore he mentions faith in the first place.

Think of faith as the first grace of the Spirit, that acteth and stirs up all other graces. It is the first, because it is the grace of union that knits us to Christ. It is the grace required in the covenant of grace. It is the grace that giveth God all the glory, therefore fit to be the grace of the covenant. And [it] takes all from man, emptieth a man of all, and giveth all the glory to God, and Christ, whose righteousness we lay hold upon by faith; being therefore the grace of the covenant, the grace of union, the grace of abasing man and glorifying God above all other graces, and the grace that acts and stirs up all other graces; and all other graces do increase, or decrease, as faith increaseth or decreaseth. Therefore 'having received the spirit of faith, we also believe,' &c. Therefore above all other graces labour for faith.

But now we have not only faith, but 'the same Spirit of faith,' which sheweth the original whence faith cometh. The spirit of faith is an excellent attribute to faith, to shew that faith as all other graces comes from the Spirit; and if all other graces come from the Spirit, then the grace of graces, faith especially. The Spirit is either the Holy Ghost himself, called the Spirit, partly passively, because the Holy Ghost is breathed from the Father and Son, and partly actively, because the Spirit doth *spirare*, breathe into us. All the life and comforts we have is from the Spirit. The Holy Ghost comes *a spirando*, not *a generando*. He doth breathe all grace and comfort into God's children, and therefore [is] called the Spirit. Now as the Holy Ghost infuseth all grace and comfort, he works first a gracious disposition in God's children, which is called the Spirit. The Holy Ghost is called not only the Spirit, but a gracious disposition and temper of our soul, whereby our spirits are made suitable to the Holy Ghost; for the Holy Ghost puts an impression upon every soul that comes to heaven, like itself, and sets a stamp of holiness upon it, and renews the image of Christ. Again, the Spirit is also called spirit, as to 'walk by the Spirit, and live by the Spirit;' that is, to live in an holy and gracious disposition wrought in us by the Holy Ghost. Now as in general a gracious frame of soul is called spirit, so every grace is called the grace of the Spirit; as the 'spirit of faith,' and the 'spirit of love,' and the 'spirit of a sound mind,' and the spirit of the 'fear of the Lord,' and the 'spirit of counsel,' because they issue immediately from the Spirit, and sanctification wrought in us by the Spirit of God. For the Spirit of God will infuse a divine nature into us, which we call the Spirit, being the seed of all grace. And then comes the spirit of all other graces. As in original sin there is the seed of all corruption, so in the Spirit the seed of regeneration is the seed of all grace, hope, and faith, and love, and whatsoever.

Now, as we say, though there be one general ocean, yet it hath several names according to the several coasts it washeth, and therefore called the British seas, the Irish seas, the Mediterrane* seas, the French seas. There is but one sea, yet [it] hath its terms according to the several coasts. So the Spirit is one Spirit, but as it begets several graces, so it hath several names. As it giveth faith, it is called the spirit of faith; as it enableth us to suffer, the spirit of assistance, or supportation. There be also animal spirits in the veins, and vital spirits in the liver and heart. So it is with the Spirit of God. It is the spirit of such a grace and such a grace as there is occasion to use it. So that the apostle terms the work of God's grace in the hearts of his children a spirit of faith; faith therefore is wrought by the Spirit of God, and that is the doctrine. The excellent grace of faith is from the Spirit. For it is called from the work of it, 'a spirit of faith.'

What need I prove it? For all things above† faith are above nature. The objects of faith are above nature, which are merely ‡ mysteries. There is no seed of faith in us at all. It is harder to believe than to fulfil the law; for there are seed of all commandments of the moral law, some impressions of it are yet left in our natures to serve God in some measure, to do justice. So that the moral men and pagans have been excellent in that kind. But to believe requires the revelation of the objects, which are supernatural things, above nature, contrary to carnal reason. Faith hath no friend at all in us. There is a cursed enmity of nature against every article of faith to call the foundation itself into question; and we are prone to believe our own lying hearts and Satan in time of temptation, rather than divine truths. To believe the favour of God to a sinner, the heart will not conceive of it, unless the Spirit of God sets down to the soul that it is so. To believe life everlasting and glory, they be things above nature. Unless they were revealed by the Spirit, who would have believed these things? And therefore it must be power divine that must raise the heart above itself. Nothing can work above its own sphere. Nature cannot rise higher than nature; a river cannot rise higher than the spring from whence it ariseth; nothing can do above its activity. Natural things cannot apprehend spiritual things. The acts of faith are above nature. For a soul, a guilty soul, a soul under the guilt of sin, to apprehend the favour and mercy of a just and holy God, unless there be a Spirit to raise the soul above all guilt, and to see more mercy in God than sin in itself, it must be a supernatural act to do this. To overcome the world, all temptations on the right hand of pleasure and profit, and on the left hand fear and danger, is above nature. But faith enableth a man to overcome the world. Therefore it must be the spirit of faith that enables him to overcome himself, the world, and the prince of the world and his temptations, where the object and the act is supernatural. Therefore surely we must have a spirit above our own. A man must be more than a man, he must be a spiritual man, that doth the things that faith enableth him to do. Therefore faith is wrought by the Spirit; for a man to be able to conquer God himself, by his word and promise, it must be by God. And this must be by a spirit of faith.

* That is, 'Mediterranean.'—G. † Qu. 'of'?—Ed. ‡ That is, = altogether.—G.

As our Saviour Christ overcome by the woman of Canaan, 'O woman, great is thy faith,' Mat. xv. 28. And then Satan especially joineth against this grace of faith, because it most opposeth him in all his temptations and methods. Moreover, we must have a Spirit of faith not only to work faith in us, but likewise in every act and exercise of faith; for though we have the grace of faith, we cannot act and raise ourselves upon occasion, as the object is present, and duties to be done by the Spirit. 'He giveth both the will and the deed,' Phil. ii. 13. And for all these reasons there is a necessity of the Spirit to work faith.

Therefore faith is a gift of the Spirit. 'To you it is given to believe,' Mat. xiii. 11. 'Faith is not of ourselves, but the gift of God,' Eph. ii. 8, and a rare, excellent, and peculiar gift it is. The point is plain, that this excellent grace of faith, whereby we go out of ourselves and fetch all without, it is from the Spirit of God, which indeed is first a Spirit of faith before it is a Spirit of love and patience. This is the first work of the Spirit; the first work of the Spirit is a spirit of faith, and then of love, and patience, and contentation with the condition, but first the spirit of faith.

Use 1. And if it be so that faith comes from the Spirit of God, and groweth not in ourselves, then we must learn *whither to go for it;* to pray, 'Lord, increase our faith,' Luke xvii. 5. If we want it, to expect it in the use of sanctified means, even to look for it from above. 'Every good and perfect gift cometh from the Father of lights,' James i. 17, and therefore this excellent gift of all gifts. And account it an excellent grace, and that will make us sue more for it. We must have a Spirit of faith, else all things are nothing, for that is a fundamental grace. Therefore look to the power of the Spirit of God for it, the Spirit being the agent of the Father and the Son here below. As it proceeds from the father and the Son, so it works from the Father and the Son; and by faith assures us of the love of the Father and the Son, for it knoweth what is in the breast of the Father and the Son.

Use 2. And then if God doth give this act of faith, this supernatural eye of faith, this supernatural hand of faith to lay hold, eyes to see, this supernatural hand of faith to lay hold, and stomach of faith to digest, *then it is not every one that hath it;* all have not faith. And therefore if we have faith, if we can go out of ourselves and rely on the promise, thank God for it; thank God for it more than for any grace or gift in the world. For, beloved, we are stubborn, alike dead, dark, rebellious alike by nature; and for us that be all of the same condition by nature to be raised to a supernatural condition, to have an eye and hand to see and reach to things above nature, and to make them our own, this is a peculiar grace; and therefore not unto us, but unto the Spirit of God, be all the glory and praise.

Use 3. And then *let us take heed that we do not rashly or hastily attempt any suffering or doing, without looking to the Spirit of God for a new exercise of faith, that now being to use faith, we may have the Spirit to raise up the habit, which otherwise will be a dormant and sleepy habit;* that as occasion is offered, so we may have fresh strength suitable to the fresh occasions. The same faith we had before will not serve for the present time, especially if there be increase of trouble. And if the actions to be performed be more difficult, according to the increase of trouble and hardness of business we are about, we must beg a greater measure of faith. So that indeed the life of a Christian is nothing but a dependency since the fall, under the covenant of grace. We are under guidance of the Spirit, not only to prop and strengthen us with habits, as we call them, but likewise on every occasion to raise and stir up our graces, and to persuade the soul to receive them. It is faith that stirs up all grace, and directs all grace, and holds every grace to its work, and, so long as it continueth, keepeth all other graces in exercise.

But more particularly, by the spirit of faith he meaneth the receipt of a powerful faith, because a spirit of faith; and a constant faith, because it is a spirit of faith; for the spirit is put to things that be strong and constant. And the Spirit is a strong worker, and it is the spirit of faith; and a free worker, because it is a spirit of faith that works more or less according as it seeth need. It is an holy grace, because it comes from the Holy Spirit; and therefore it is a grace indeed that makes us holy.

First, It is a spirit of faith, that is, a powerful work of faith. Now a spirit of faith doth overcome our unbelieving natures, a spirit works strongly, takes away actual resistance. Faith comes not by persuasion, but by a powerful waking strength; for if it came by persuasion, the devil would persuade to unbelief sooner than the Spirit should persuade to faith. For he hath more help for unbelief than there is for faith. We have in us more arguments against truth and against goodness than for it. And therefore if it were but a mere persuasion, and the soul not overpowered by the Holy Ghost to believe, it would never believe. So that it is not left indifferent to us to believe or not believe when God's Spirit comes. But the Spirit, as wind, is a powerful work[er], and because it takes away all prevailing resistances from the soul, and makes way for itself, bringing an heavenly light into the understanding, and a spiritual kind of reasoning, and an heavenly obedience into the will, bowing it to obedience of divine truths to yield to them, because by little and little it consumes corruption, it takes away prevailing corruption, and makes the soul believe, though there be roots of infidelity remaining.

The Spirit takes down the rebellion of nature so far that it shall not prevail. They never have the spirit of faith that think they can resist. When the Spirit comes it subjects all to its work. But I will not make a counterpoint of it. But, indeed, the spirit of faith takes away all resistances, which is to be observed, not only against divers heresies in this time, or opinions at least that tend that way, for they end in a little better than heresy; but likewise to think what an excellent grace it is, how much we are beholding to God for it, how to importune God for it, considering it is such a supernatural, holy, and powerful grace of the Spirit. And then it is a constant work. God's children do not only believe now and then, but they have a spirit of faith. Now spirit implieth a constant inclination, in the Scripture phrase, as a spirit of lying, of falsity, of envy, is an inclination that way; and a spirit of faith is a constant inclination wrought in the spirit to live by faith constantly, to depend upon God for all things, pardon of sins, life everlasting, provision and protection in this world.

Again, Because it is called the 'spirit of faith,' it sheweth that it is a free grace, and the grounds why some have more or less faith, it is free for measure and free for time. They that have faith have the spirit of faith. They have not faith at command. No. The Spirit bloweth where it listeth, more or less. If you ask why some have great, some less, faith? It is because God seeth it needful for them in afflictions to have a great measure of faith, them that are wretched in the world, that have pre-encountered great dangers and afflictions, it is necessary to have a great measure of faith, and God giveth it. For the Spirit is a wise Spirit, and giveth faith according to the exigencies of particular persons more or less, for it is a Spirit.

The things God works by his Spirit, in regard of the freeness of them, are called graces; they as they are wrought by the Spirit are called the graces of the Spirit. The graces of the Scriptures are not like the graces of the heathens in their ethics and morals, who call them *habits*,* but they have their names from their efficiency, the spirit of love, as they be from God's freeness; they are called the spirit of faith, as referring all to the work of God's Spirit, because as we are saved by grace, so we must be ready to give all glory to the work of the Spirit.

And therefore we should not be much discontent if we have not so great a measure as others have, but thankful for the least properties of faith, for the measure of it comes from the Holy Ghost, who is a free worker. The Holy Ghost is not a natural worker, as fire burneth with extremity of its strength, because it is a natural agent, but the Holy Ghost being a wise and free agent, works according to his good will and pleasure. And therefore take heed how we grieve the Spirit of God, which is a Spirit of faith; but as the apostle giveth wise counsel, 'Work out your salvation with fear and trembling,' Philip. ii. 12, because it is God that giveth the will and the deed of his good pleasure. If we esteem not the Spirit as we should, the Spirit may withdraw and suspend the sweet exercise of faith, though not wholly take it away, because it is a grace that proceeds from a free agent, the Holy Ghost.

And it is said likewise, we have the same spirit of faith, because the same Spirit of God works the same faith from Adam, the first believer, to the end of the world. Beloved, those before Christ, they were saved by Christ, as we read, Acts xv. 8, 9, 'When our hearts are purified, we are saved by faith as they were.' There is one Spirit breathed into all the children of God to the end of the world, the same Spirit is in the hidden members. What shall I say? The same Spirit with them, the same Spirit with Christ their head; one self-same Spirit is in Christ our head, and in all the members of Christ from the beginning to the end of the world. And as there is one Spirit, so one spirit of faith in regard of the object, the same things believed. For though faith be diverse, according to the diversity of belief, yet in regard of the things believed, and the cause of faith, the Spirit, they are all one: 'Jesus Christ, the same yesterday, and to-day, and for ever,' Heb. xiii. 8.

There is nothing we believe in the gospel, but they did believe before Christ. Our faith is Abraham's faith and David's faith. I will give an instance before Christ. Abraham believed in Christ, 'and saw his day and rejoiced,' John viii. 56. And the sacrament of circumcision was 'a seal of the righteousness of faith,' Rom. iv. 11, as our sacraments are seals of our faith. And likewise they gave all to the Spirit of God. 'Breathe thy law into our hearts.' And Moses giveth the reason why they heard and saw in the wilderness, and profited not. God gave them not an heart. All was given to the Spirit, as now, and life everlasting.

They believed as well as we do now. 'At thy right hand are pleasures for evermore,' Ps. xvi. 11. Christ was believed as well as now. He was Immanuel then, and with them as well as with us, though we have a farther measure of revelation. Christ is laid, Christ is a corner stone, 'and whosoever believeth on him shall not be ashamed,' 1 Peter ii. 6. There was the same covenant of grace. 'Whosoever believeth shall not perish, but have everlasting life,' as now, John iii. 15. And therefore believers are called 'the children of Abraham,' Gal. iii. 7, heaven, 'the bosom of

* Cf. note *vv*, p. 533, Vol. III.—G.

Abraham,' Luke xvi. 23. Women-believers are called 'the daughters of Abraham,' Luke xiii. 16, because there is one spirit of faith in believers from the beginning of the world to the end of it. Now the particulars are revealed more clearly, the canon is enlarged, the gospel is added to the precepts of the law, but notwithstanding, for fundamental points, they are the same from the beginning to the end of the church. The difference between them and us was in outward garments, in outward affections. As a man differs from a child in garments and outward habit, and yet is the same man, so the church of the Jews and our church are all one church, only differing in ceremonies and outward concernments, and yet still the same church. The difference is the accidental and outward; the essential main points are always the same. And therefore the grand point of faith, we believe, is not yesterday's faith, as the papists would make it, like the Gibeonites, that when they came but from hard by, came with mouldy bread and shoes, counterfeiting that they came from a far country.* So you shall have it in every papist's mouth, Ours is the ancient religion, the fathers' religion, when it was but of yesterday, and of all novelties; but we are true catholics, because we believe an universal truth, the same spirit of faith which they had in ages of the church before. We believe nothing but what Abraham, Moses, David, and the prophets believed. We are the catholics. We are not upstarts, and I prove it by this reason. There is nothing we believe but they believed; whatsoever we believe all the ancient fathers and patriarchs believed.

Now that faith is most catholic that all the patriarchs, prophets, and apostles believed, and that they themselves believe. They only add patcheries of their own, and therefore they have a new faith, but we the same. They believe the two sacraments, but they add their own. They believe the Scriptures, but they add traditions. They believe salvation from Christ, but they add works; believe we must call upon God, but they add saints to Christ in invocation and mediation. They have destructive additions of their own, which spoileth all in the conclusion. What they have we have; but their patcheries neither they nor we have; and therefore is not our faith more catholic, that holds the same things with the patriarchs and prophets, more than they that have only mere additions of their own?

That wherein they differ from us is not catholic in their own confession, for they have it not out of Scripture, nor catholic with us in regard of the divided church that they had. It was neither the faith of the ancients, patriarchs, nor prophets before Christ, nor of the ancient fathers since Christ; and therefore they are fain to fly to traditions and their own devices, and to make articles of their own, as Pius IV. made not many years since as many articles of his own as there be articles in the creed. For they say the present church is led by the Spirit of God infallibly, and according to the present state of the church things must be expounded. Therefore they be true catholics that hold with the ancient church, and them too, in such things as be true. And therefore we deserve the name of catholics, and they of neutralists. For is not that more catholic which is the same with ancient pariarchs, with ancient fathers since Christ, and the same with them, than that wherein they differ from us? Indeed, that wherein they differ from us is merely the act of a private spirit of the one, not as if they did only add and still retain truth, but they defile whatsoever passeth from them. For they do change some things, add some things,

* Cf. Joshua ix. 5.—G.

take away some things. They change the government of Christ into a tyranny, making the pope head, the sacrament of the Lord's supper into a sacrifice, and transgress every article of religion. They take away the cup in the sacrament, and then their additions are destructive additions. If they add, they overthrow all. As Paul saith to the Galatians, 'If ye be circumcised, Christ shall profit you nothing,' Gal. v. 2; and if you look to be saved by the law, you shall miss of salvation; and 'whosoever teacheth another doctrine different, is anathema, is accursed,' 1 Cor. xvi. 22. Their additions are destructive additions. If they were perfective, it were another matter, but they add something to faith which overthroweth faith, and something to Christ which takes away Christ. They do not hold to the head, but have another head than Christ, other mediators, and other rules of faith. They do not agree in the principles of faith. They agree that the word is the word; but then to take away the edge of it, they add something to weaken it: their own expositions, traditions, and applications. So that they have what we have, yet they change all points of religion; and the additions are against the foundation, and destructive. Not that but divers of them go to heaven, but it is not by their tenets. But they hold contradictions; and in the hour of death they cleave to the one, and forsake the other. Howsoever, for cavil sake, they hold merits and righteousness with obedience of Christ, yet they that belong to God amongst them, at time of death renounce that religion, and cleave only to Christ and obedience of Christ by justification to faith. But my meaning is not to take up time in these things, but only to breed a love of the religion we have, that hath a justification in the main tenets we hold from the enemy, from the ancient church, from the Christian church, having one spirit of faith. And to say truth, they have the old spirit, as in Revelations, the spirit of Egypt, for so is Rome called, and the spirit of Sodom, and, as it is for the most part called, the spirit of Babylon; for they have a cruel and bloody spirit; and the filthy spirit of the Sodomites, and the idolatrous spirit of Egypt, and the tyrannical city of Babylon: for they have the same spirit with them. But for ancient tenets of religion, we may safely say, that in the main points of religion we have the same spirit of faithful Abraham, the patriarchs, David, the prophets, apostles, and ancient fathers; therefore we may be bold.

There is one faith from the beginning of the world to the end of the world, the faith of the elect: 'faith once given,' as Jude calls it, ver. 3.

I cannot press this point, but make this use further of it. We have the Spirit of faith, and the same Spirit of faith with them that were before. Therefore let this comfort us, that if we truly believe, we are brought into communion and fellowship with the church that hath been and shall be to the end of the world, that is now in heaven; for we have all one Spirit. Though instead of faith they have vision, yet we have all one Spirit. Is it not a sweet thing to have communion with Abraham, Isaac, and Jacob, and all the prophets and apostles? And so we have, if we be true believers, by the same Spirit of faith. Perhaps we differ in the measure and degree, because the necessities of one are more than the necessities of another; as in organ pipes the same breath is in all the pipes, but some sound little and some have a greater sound, answerable to the making of them, yet one breath makes them all sound. So there is the same Spirit in all the church, but some have little, some great measure, according as their necessities and places in the church are; and therefore it is of great comfort, and it may teach us, as a comfort, that we have communion of saints in this church, that the Spirit is in all, so to love communion of saints. We have 'one faith, one spirit, one baptism,' Eph. iv. 5.

That wherein Christians agree is better advantageous to this purpose to enforce unity and peace than anything wherein they disagree, to make a rupture and fraction. Perhaps they may disagree in ceremonies, in opinion of this or that; but if there be one faith, one baptism, if there be unity in the main, shall other things of less concernment be of force to make a fraction in the church? Oh beloved, no! The church before Christ, and the church after Christ, for garments they did differ, for outward appurtenances. As a child and a man, it is the same person, yet he hath one apparel when young, another when a man; so the church when young had one kind of ceremony, when old another, yet at all times one Spirit. So one church may differ from another in this or that particular outward appendixes, but what is that to the spirit of faith? There is one Spirit of Christ in all; and is not that of greater force to knit together than other lesser matters to make a division? which should teach us more and more to study the unity of the Spirit. Were it not an excellent thing if all Christians in the world had the spirits to agree in the same things, and love the same things that shall be our life in heaven? And it were not heaven on earth if there were no agreement in the judgment and affections of Christians. Therefore study peace; and for other matters, they will follow. Let them not be of that concernment as to make any separation: Philip. ii. 1, 'If any consolation, if any peace, if any love,' &c., 'be of like mind one toward another.' Why, what is the cause they press union so much? Because our happiness is in it, and Christ in his excellency, to pray that 'Christ and all may be one,' John xvii. 11; because the same Spirit that knitteth to Christ knitteth to one another by love, and all grace and comforts are derived to Christians as knit to Christ by faith, and to others by love. If we be not knit to Christ, there is no derivation of grace from the head; where there is no derivation, there is decay of grace suitable. Therefore as we will grow in grace and comfort, there is more force in union than is thought of; and if it were serious[ly] thought of, in regard of our own benefit, we should labour to maintain it.

VERSE 13.

We having the same spirit of faith, according as it is written, I believed, and therefore have I spoken; we also believe, and therefore speak.

You have heard before at large how the apostle answers all discouragements, from God's gracious dealing with them.

Now, St Paul goeth forward with the words read to the end of the chapter, in setting down divers encouragements to help him to go on in his Christian course. One is in the verse I have read to you; 'We have the same spirit of faith, as it is written,' &c.

We must go through many afflictions, inward and outward, before we come to heaven. And therefore the apostle multiplies grounds of comfort, whereby he may be carried through all to the end of his race.

The first ground of comfort in these words is from the words, 'We have the same spirit of faith' that David and others had before, 'and therefore we speak;' therefore we are bold in our profession.

In these words we have already considered divers things. Of faith we shall have occasion to speak afterward.

Now whereas he comforts himself from the example of David: 'David believed and spake, and therefore I believe and speak.' We have a sweet pattern how to make use of the Scriptures; in reading of them, read ourselves in the Scriptures. The Scriptures are not only written for us, and written for them that lived in those times; but God, in his infinite wisdom and foresight, knew that whosoever* was in Scripture should be appliable to all times and states of the church: for though it was written at divers times, yet nothing shall fall out to the end of the world, but there is something in Scripture to rule it, else there would need multiplication of Scriptures to the end of the world. And therefore the Scriptures contain necessary truths, both for the times wherein they were written, and for all times to the end of the world. As the apostle argues, 'David believed, and spake,' therefore we may, because the case is alike. The church in regard of prerogatives of salvation, and in regard of many duties and promises, hath the like command and interest from the beginning of the world; as we say of *corpus homogeneum*, every part of an homogeneal body hath respect to the whole. Every drop of water is water; every spark of fire is fire; but every piece of an arm is not an arm, because it is heterogeneal. I speak of it, because in many prerogatives and promises there is the like reason of every member, and of one member and another; as David speaks and believes, and therefore we speak. 'Abraham believed, and it was imputed for righteousness,' Rom. iv. 22; let us believe, and it shall be imputed for righteousness. I believed, and found mercy: if we believe, we shall have mercy. Peter, after he denied his Master, found mercy; if we do the same, we shall find the same, because there is the same reason for the whole church, and every particular member. And, therefore, when we read the Scripture, we should read to take something out for ourselves. When we read any promise, this is mine; and any privileges, these belong to me; when we read a good example, this concerns me; as I said before, 'Whatsoever was before written was written for our learning, that through patience and learning of the Scripture we might have hope,' Rom. xv. 4.

There is not anything that befalls a Christian in his life, but there is a rule or pattern for it in Scripture. If we were skilful to bring the places and rules together, we should see a ground in Scripture for everything, both for all duties and all things to be believed. And there be not only rules in Scripture, but also rules quickening by example; for divinity is of practical knowledge, and therefore it is enlivened and interlaced with examples, as here he makes use of the example of David. God doth not write us laws, and leave them barely in our possession as commands; but God quickens and enlivens all the rules and promises with the practice of some of the blessed saints. None can read David's psalms but he shall read himself in them. He cannot undergo a trouble, but he shall find David under the same trouble; he shall not need a comfort, but he shall see David comforted with the same comfort; so that he is a pattern for them. It is a comfortable thing to read the Scriptures, because there we shall find whatsoever is useful for us. They that go into a garden that is beset with flowers, they cannot but receive a sweet spirit and breath from the flowers in the very walks; and so there is such a spirit in Scripture, that we cannot read the Scriptures with reverence but there is a sweet savour that springeth from them, which both delights and strengthens at once. No walk is so comfortable as the walk of Scripture; therefore, take our solace there, and we shall see the promises, and those enlivened with examples and patterns, and the Spirit of God bringing the like sweetness and the like strength into ourselves. Oh that we would be more in love

* Qu. 'whatsoever'?—Ed.

with reading of Scripture. We see the apostle Paul, as great a man as he was, encourageth himself and strengthens himself with the pattern of holy David: 'David believes and speaks, and I believe and speak.' So that you see how you may make benefit of the Scripture.

From hence you have a rule of enlargement of the Scripture to you, and a rule likewise of application, that when we read the Scriptures we may enlarge them, and apply them to ourselves in particular. And so much for that point, we have faith, the spirit of faith. 'And the same spirit of faith, according as it is written.'

The next thing observable is this, *that after the spirit of faith he names belief; and after belief, he names speaking;* whence observe the connection and knitting together of these things by God, the coherence that God hath made betwixt. First, there is the Father, Son, and Holy Ghost. The Spirit is the agent that works all in the church, it being Christ's vicar on earth, and that Spirit works a spirit of grace in us, in particular a spirit of faith. When the Holy Ghost hath framed our hearts to believe, then we believe; and when we believe, then we speak. So that these go together, the Spirit of God, begetting in us a spirit of faith, and an act of believing answerable to the frame proceeding from a spirit of faith; and then, because faith is the spring and foundation of all other graces, 'we believe, therefore we speak.'

First of all, the Spirit of God works a blessed frame in our hearts, here called the 'Spirit of God.'* The Holy Ghost doth not only work by a Christian as an instrument, but works in him as a subject. Our soul is altogether out of frame. The Holy Ghost, therefore, puts us in frame by a spirit of faith, infusing a spirit of knowledge into the understanding, a spirit of obedience into the will. He draweth the will and enlighteneth the understanding, and then we believe. All actions come from a fountain, and spring, and life, and frame within: the Holy Ghost worketh a holy frame, and then we act. We must not think of believing without a spirit of faith first, for that is to conceive of a river without a spring head, or a beam without a sun, or a branch without a root. And therefore, as faith cannot be without the Holy Ghost, so belief cannot be without the spirit of faith, which is only for the clear conceiving of the point. We shall make use of it afterwards.

First, a spirit of faith, and then we believe. So that the grace of faith cometh from the Spirit, but the act is ours, and comes immediately from us, which serveth to answer an idle objection against those that be all for grace. If we do all by the help of the Spirit, and we have no liberty, then the Holy Ghost believeth, and the Holy Ghost speaketh, and the Holy Ghost loveth, and not we. The objection is [not] idle against those that be all for free grace.

It is true, the grace is from the Spirit, but when the grace is received, the act is from ourselves, not only from ourselves, but immediately from ourselves. We cannot but confess it so.

For instance, a windy instrument is fit to sound, but it actually soundeth not till it be blown. So other instruments of hand are fit for music, but it makes not music till it be strucken by the hand. So we do not actually believe, but by an act of the Spirit; but yet the act of believing is our own. The wind in one instrument, and the hand on the other instrument, must make the sounds, and yet the instruments sound. And so, though we have the grace of faith, and faith is ours in believing, yet the very act

* Qu. 'faith'?—ED.

of believing cometh from the Holy Ghost, though not immediately. We speak, but the Spirit opens our mouth; and we believe, but the Holy Ghost inspires a spirit of faith; and we do, but as we are enabled to do; *acti agimus*, we move, but *moti movemus*. So that there is an action and passion in all the graces and exercises we do. We are first patients, and then agents; first the Spirit of God works on us, and then we work; not the Spirit immediately, but we by the Spirit.

So we see how these two are reconciled. We believe, we speak, we do good, and yet the Holy Ghost doth all. How? Thus; the Holy Ghost sets us in a holy frame, and then being in that frame, the Holy Ghost fits us to speak, to do, to work, to suffer, to do all that is to be done. We are the agents, and yet we do no further than as acted by a superior agent. As with the orbs, the inferior orbs move but as they are moved by an higher, except the highest of all: so all the subordinate agents under God, they are moved by God. For if the will were moved, and were not moved by God, then so many wills, so many gods, for there is nothing independent but God.

But to speak of the positive truth: all the frame of grace comes from the Spirit. We work, but by the Holy Ghost, as Ps. li. 15, 'Open my lips, my mouth shall shew forth thy praise.' Now David saith here, 'We believe, therefore speak;' we speak, but it is God that opens our mouth.

But I rather intend points of practice. For besides that proper act of faith to believe, there is a commanding act of faith, which stirs up the soul to do, for faith stirs up all other graces. The proper act is to believe, but by believing it stirs up and quickens all other graces of the soul. Therefore, Heb. xi., you see that all other graces are attributed to faith. By faith Enoch did walk with God, and by faith Noah prepared an ark, and by faith Moses was courageous and bold; and so you see all their excellent graces, they have their spring and stirring up from faith. So that having the same Spirit we not only believe but speak.

The next point observable hence is, *that a Christian knows he doth believe.* 'I believe, therefore I speak.' And a Christian knoweth his own faith, and by consequence he may know certainly his state in grace. It is not an idle, dormant, sleepy faith; but 'I believe, therefore I speak.' It makes them fix the eyes of their souls so much on their deserts and guilt, that they look all to that till they be surprised with horror, till God hath humbled them, though there be a striving of soul against despair, and striving for favour and mercy.

In these particular cases there may be faith without the knowledge of the act. But ordinarily the frame of a Christian is such, that he knoweth what he knows, and he doth know that he doth believe when he believeth; and thereupon he knoweth his state in grace. How else should he be thankful to God? how should he be pitiful? how should he be content and quiet in his condition? how should he be fruitful in his conversation? Beloved, the knowledge that we are in a good condition is a most fruitful knowledge. It is the best frame of the soul, when it hath grace, and knows it hath grace, and never hath a good frame till then. When we are in God's favour, and we know that we are in God's favour, it puts us in a holy disposition to God, to love him, to be thankful to him, and in a gracious disposition to him to be abundant in the work of the Lord. It works a sweet disposition in ourselves, begetting in us much patience, when we know we believe, and believing that we shall be saved, for salvation is the end of faith. Faith never endeth but in salvation.

And therefore it should be our main endeavour to believe, and then labour to know that we do believe, that Satan may not hide our evidences from us, and make us bear false witness against ourselves; and so when he cannot hinder our salvation, he hinders our comforts in the way to heaven, as it is his way, by casting a mist and cloud between our souls and God's favours. 'Therefore give all diligence to make our calling and election sure,' 2 Peter i. 10. The more we grow in assurance that we believe, and by believing our interest in Christ, the more we grow in grace, and in all comforts whatsoever. They pretend it is a way to bring to security. Indeed, of heavenly security it is. But who fears to displease God most? and who takes most care to please him? Is it not them that have sweet contentment in his favours? that be loath to displease him? And is it not their whole care to please him, and continue sweet communion with God? They speak against the nature of the things, and against experience. But how shall a Christian know that he doth believe? Will he think he doth not believe, when he cannot peremptorily conclude, I do believe? Though he cannot reflect upon himself strongly, yet he may reflect upon himself, especially by conference with them that can discern that he hath desires. There is afterwards in a Christian, Christian mourning, sighing, and groaning, and he will not deny but he desires to have faith, he mourns that he hath it not. Let them reflect on that, and bring the Scripture to that case. The Scripture speaks comfortably of desires, of parts, of the gracious desires; he that desires faith hath a measure of faith, if he desire it truly.

And therefore you say you have no faith. Your desires shew you have. You can reflect, and know you desire, mourn, hunger, and thirst, and would have grace. Now are the promises made to this desire? 'Blessed are they that hunger and thirst, blessed are they that mourn, blessed are the poor in spirit,' Mat. v. 6, *seq.*

Then again, there is a combat in them. They that have the main act of faith, they have strife between flesh and Spirit, between unbelief and faith. None will say but he striveth against unbelief, and endeavours against it. That very strife is an argument that there is a spirit of faith, an act of faith; and they may know that act of faith, if they will consider seriously. The very strife is a greater argument of comfort that they have faith, than the confidence of many carnal men that they have faith. For their confidence is a false argument; and then the others doubting, and striving against doubts and remainders of infidelity, is an argument of their having faith.

Again, they that have the least degree of faith, they look up to God, they never forsake God, they will die at his feet, and they will cast themselves down before his footstool, before his mercy; let him deal with me as he will, they resolve of that. And where this is, it argueth a spiritual act of faith. So that in some cases a man may have an act of faith, and yet not know it. And in some cases there may be a confidence of the presence of faith, when yet they have it not.

How shall I know false confidence? It is a large point, and I will name but two or three things.

(1.) *False confidence is groundless*, voluntarily taken up of themselves without the Scriptures, because they wish well to themselves; and out of self-love they think they have anything they want. If they go to the grounds of Scripture, they would rather despair, because there be many blasphemous, loose lives secure of goodness. Faith affirms he is not worthy to live that believeth not. If they did believe, they would believe their own damnation. They should believe there is nothing between them and hell, but a little uncertain life: for they live in the curse of God, and live in sin, damned by Scripture. And therefore their faith is not only a barren faith, but a presumptuous faith, and groundless.

(2.) And again, you may know false confidence, because as it is groundless, *so it is careless in the use of good means.* A confident spirit, out of self-love, will persuade itself all is well, and yet be bold in the use of means. And so it is fearless till trouble comes; and when trouble comes, then they sink. He is confident, before trouble of conscience or outward troubles seize upon him; but when any trouble comes, then they see all was but a spirit of presumption and carnal confidence; then they see there was never sound peace between God and them, never sound union between Christ and them. For it is the nature of false confidence to be confident before, and to sink into despair in times of trouble.

(3.) And again, false confidence, as it is groundless in the use of means, and spiritless in danger, *so it is fruitless.* It brings not forth fruit of faith, it is barren. And therefore let people that be careless of the exercise of love and other graces in their conversation boast of faith what they will, it is but a confidence; they think they believe when they do not believe.

(4.) In the next place, faith *is an exercising grace wheresoever it is.* 'I believe, therefore I speak.' It is a working grace wheresoever it is. He shews his faith by obedience and practice, so that the truth of faith is an active and working grace. And therein it differs from the confidence spoken of before. It works in heaven, it works with God, it layeth hold upon him, wrestles with him for a blessing, and overcometh him; it works on earth, and overcomes all on the right hand and left, all temptations of prosperity, presenting better things than the world can; it overcometh all temptations on the left hand, all fears and threatenings, and presents to the soul worse dangers than anything here. What can be threatened comparable to hell? and what can be promised comparable to a good conscience and heaven hereafter? It works stronger than hell and temptations. And it must needs be so, because it is a grace of union that knits us to Christ. It is the fountain of life. We cannot touch Christ without life, virtue comes from him upon every touch; his grace, his union, and being. So it draweth virtue from Christ. The spirit of faith is a spirit of power, a spirit of vigour. Faith infuseth vigour into the whole soul, silencing all objections that the heart can make; answers all temptations that the devil can make; triumphs over all that can be presented to it, and draweth it from God. It is powerful with God himself. I will not enter into commonplaces of faith, but only as it comes in my way shew that where belief is it will work, and the particular work of it is to 'speak.'

(5.) As it is a working grace, *so it is a bold grace.* 'I believe, therefore I speak.' If there be faith in the heart, it will express itself in the tongue. If the heart be a good treasure, it will vent that treasure. 'Out of the abundance of the heart the mouth will speak,' Mat. xii. 34. And therefore as there will be encouragement and strength and vigour, so there will be boldness in speaking to God. Faith is a grace that hath liberty with it. Where the Spirit is there is liberty, specially where the spirit of faith is; because faith sets the soul at liberty from fear of guilt and damnation, and persuades the soul of contentment with God in Jesus Christ.

(6.) Where the spirit of faith is, *there is boldness to the throne of grace;* and therefore because we believe we speak. We speak to God in prayer, because we believe we are reconciled to God in Jesus Christ. Wheresoever faith is there is prayer. Speaking to God in prayer is the prime expression of faith; as faith is the birth of a Christian, for it knits him to Christ the fountain of life. A child as soon as it is born crieth, and a new-born child as soon as it is born crieth to God. He hath a familiar kind of boldness to go with reverence to God, and say, 'Abba, Father.' As soon as ever Paul was converted, 'behold, he prayeth,' Acts ix. 11. He might speak prayers before, but he never prayed till then. A man never prayeth till he believeth; and when he believeth, he prays presently with the spirit of faith. Therefore it is a spirit of supplication; they go always together.

And the reason is, because as soon as ever a Christian is new born, he is sensible of the root and spring whence he hath all his strength and all he hopes for. It is in Christ. And therefore as by faith he is knit to Christ, so by faith he makes use of Christ. Faith is an emptying grace of itself, and emptying the soul, sendeth forth his ambassador, prayer, to fetch all help from heaven. Prayer is the messenger, the ambassador of faith, the flame of faith. Where faith is kindled within, it flames out in prayer. Prayer, you know, sheweth that there is nothing at home, for then we would not go abroad. Faith is a grace that goeth out of itself. It hath the greatest humility that can be, and is always seated in an humble soul, that despaireth of itself, and is emptied of itself; and therefore the first expression of faith out of itself must be to the fountain of help and fountain of strength and comfort together, and therefore sends forth prayer. Prayer and faith are all one, prayer being nothing but faith digested into words and conceptions. Faith prevails, so prayer prevails; and according to the measure of faith, so are the degrees of the spirit of prayer. And then again, our tongues being our 'glory,' Ps. xvi. 9, it hath a desire to glorify God, and that is in speaking, praising of God, and praying to God. And therefore those that do not pray, they have no faith. Little faith, little prayer; and great faith, great measure of prayer. And as faith groweth, so the spirit of prayer and supplication groweth. They increase and decrease in a proportion.

And therefore let us examine ourselves, if we believe, to pray; if we believe, to speak. A Christian is no still-born creature. He that is new-born, he is not still-born. He crieth to his Father for strength of grace. There is a spirit of boldness, together with the spirit of faith, whereby we can look God in the face reconciled in Jesus Christ. Now, looking upon God as a Father, we cannot but as to a Father repair to him in all our necessities. So you see the connection of these two, 'I believe, therefore I speak.'

And as it is true of prayer, so of praise, for that is also the language of the Spirit of God. God will have occasion, for our tongue is our glory; we glorify him in our whole man. The heart giveth him the glory of all his attributes; the speech giveth the glory of it to him. And therefore, Ps. lxiii. 5, 'When I am filled with marrow and fatness,' the inward comforts of grace, 'then shall I praise thee with joyful lips;' that is, then shall he sound forth the praises of God in his speech. He praiseth God not only for what is past, but he praises him for what is to come. 'I believe, therefore I speak.' For if a man by the spirit of faith apprehend the resurrection of the body and glory in the world to come, that Spirit, apprehending the excellency to come, will stir him up to praise God beforehand; as by a spirit of faith we take things in trust, as if present; we see heaven, and glory to come, as if present: 'For faith is the evidence of things not seen,' Heb. xi. 1. So it stirs up affections as if present. In heaven we shall praise God for ever, and therefore faith makes heaven and happiness as if present to the soul. It enlargeth the soul with thanks beforehand. Therefore when the apostles speak of the glorious condition to come, presently they break out into praises. As they believe, so they speak, as Peter prayeth, 'By the Father of our Lord Jesus Christ, that hath begotten us again to an inheritance immortal, undefiled, reserved for us in the heavens,' 1 Pet. i. 3, 4. He believeth heaven is kept for him, and he for heaven, and therefore he praiseth God for it. If we believe the blessed state to come, we will speak the praises of God before hand; and therefore it is the state of God's children in time to come, revealed now, that God may have present praise. Faith sets the soul in heaven in some sort, and as it setteth us in heaven where Christ is our head, so it setteth us into the employment of heaven; and what is that? To have a heart enlarged to praise God.

Likewise if we believe we will speak to men, not only to God in prayer, but of God to men, 'in the great congregation,' as the prophet speaks, Ps. xxii. 25; we will not be ashamed of God, but speak to him by prayer in all things, and of his truth; and speak for him too when religion is opposed, and his children disgraced. He that hath not a word to speak of God for the benefit of others by way of edification, that hath not the spirit of prudence to speak a word in season, nor a spirit of courage to speak for God, I will never believe he will speak to God as he should, I will never believe he doth believe. For he that believeth, he will speak to God in prayer, and praises, and of God, and for God. Beloved, in this world God puts his cause and his truth, and the state of God's people, into our hands, and counts himself beholding to us if we will stand for him, and trieth what we will do for him, whether help him in his church and people or no. He crieth, Who will be on his side, who? as Jehu said, 2 Kings ix. 32. Specially in times of opposition and lukewarm times, when there is a clouding of religion, men will be of all sides, and no side to serve their turn. Therefore 'Curse ye Meroz, for he helped not the Lord,' Judges v. 23. God thinks himself helped by us when we speak for a good cause, for a good person, for justice, for truth; and if we will not own the cause of God in doubtfuls, God will never own us. Doth God honour us so far as to put his cause into our hands, making himself beholding to us for his word? And shall not we speak a word for his church, his children, but rather join with backbiters, and slanderers, and secret papists? All slander her religion, her faith. What saith our Saviour Christ? Is not that an idle thing?* 'He that is ashamed of me before men, I will be ashamed of him before my Father which is in heaven,' Mat. x. 32, 33. They have the name of God in their foreheads. As the antichristian limbs carry his mark, so they that belong to Christ carry his mark; that is, they are bold for the Lord, known of their Master, to speak as to him, so for him, when occasion is offered. 'Wisdom will be justified of her children,' Mat. xi. 19, and therefore they that believe will justify wisdom, will justify the cause of religion. And they that do it not do not believe, for he that believeth will speak. Christ is called λόγος, the speech, the word, because as a word expresseth the mind, so Christ expresseth what is in the bosom and heart of God towards us. And as he hath truly expressed from God to us what is the Father's good pleasure to us, being the word, so every Christian must be the word to express what Christ hath done for him and for the church. And we must do this bodily,† sincerely, freely, and roundly, without ter-

* Qu. 'That is not an idle thing'?—G.

† That is = personally.—G. Qu. 'boldly'?—Ed.

giversation, equivocation, or delusion; we must be bold for a better Master. It is true out of the nature of the thing we cannot but speak. A convinced understanding and sanctified heart cannot but speak when an opportunity is offered. I wonder any should ever think to look the blessed Saviour in the face with comfort, and yet notwithstanding betray his cause, betray religion here. And therefore, I beseech you, consider the connection of these two together, 'I believe, therefore I speak.'

By this therefore I have spoken, you may learn what to judge of your natures. Those that are partial of both sides, and of neither, that count it a policy to conceal themselves, they think whatsoever shall fall out they will be sure to displease no party beforehand, that so they may have friends; and so, to redeem a peace to themselves, they betray religion and the cause of Christ. You may say, What wisdom is that? It is a wisdom of the flesh, and a plain discovery they have no faith at all, or at the least a very weak faith, no faith at all.

And therefore they are called Nicodemites; that is, such as keep religion to themselves; it is a false means.* For Nicodemus at first indeed[so] came for Christ, but after he defended him against the Scribes and Pharisees. And at his death, when all forsook him, then Nicodemus and Joseph appeared. So it was a growing faith. And therefore let no man that conceals religion pretend Nicodemus. If they mean to be in that condition they are in, if they will sleep in whole skins, then it argueth they have no faith at all; but if they are ashamed of it, and grow, and by falls learn to stand strongly, and find their weakness sanctified to get more strength, it is a good sign. But those that are neuters, and for all turns, you may say they have no faith. He is not worthy of a tongue that will not speak for Christ, that will not speak for the giver of speech. He is unworthy to speak that will not speak for him that hath enabled him to speak. You are more like the Samaritans, that would be of no certain religion. They would worship God, and they would worship the gods of their country likewise; they would be of the Jewish religion when the Jews flourished, and against the Jews when the Jews were down.† So that they would be of all religions and of no religion. And so you have some that have their religion to choose for all turns; so far as stands with outward conveniences they will appear, and when it doth not, they will betray it; *vespertiliones in fide*, as he calls them, bats, that will neither be amongst the birds or other creatures, but doubtful creatures, you cannot tell what to make of them (*bb*). So there will be always some doubtful persons that you cannot tell what to conceive of them in religion; but this you may make out, they do not believe, for if they did believe, they would speak.

And therefore let us be stirred up to speak in the cause of Christ as occasion serveth. There must be a spirit of discretion and wisdom when and how to speak, of which I have spoken at large heretofore out of Rom. x.‡ Only, I beseech you, if occasion be, be entreated to be as bold for Christ as others against Christ, as bold for religion as others against religion. I am sure we serve a better Master. It is a shame to hear papists, and popish spirits, and half atheists speak dangerously to the destruction of youth, that they may be saved in any religion if we believe in God and keep his commandments; and so run to some few generals, whenas the will in the mean time falls a-swelling and breaks the commandments. They bring all to a few heads, and shuffle off all with a generality

* Qu. 'name'?—G.

† Cf. note *eeee*, Vol. III. p. 536, 537.—G.

‡ These sermons are not extant.—G.

in any religion; if you live well you may be saved. Therefore let us be as bold and impudent* for Christ as his enemies shall be against him. And because we see that boldness in the cause of Christ comes from a spirit of faith, as all other graces come from faith, let us be stirred up to labour for faith above all other graces, that that may be planted in our hearts. And that it may be so, do but observe these directions.

First of all, consider *who it is that giveth us comfort and giveth us promises;* dwell much in the consideration of the loving faithful nature of God, and then consider former experiences, how God hath made good all things to us; consider what pure and glorious pledges and promises we have for time to come. Peace of conscience is pledge of the peace which is heaven; joy in the Holy Ghost, a pledge of the joy in heaven. And then consider the excellency of the things we are to believe. The objects of faith, the promises, are surpassing things, even surpassing admiration. Oh the excellent things laid up in another world! If we cannot express the first fruits, the earnest here, what shall we do with the fulness of happiness that we shall enjoy hereafter? A probability of excellent things will set men more to endeavour than a certainty of petty and base things.

Now that we have offered to us things above admiration, we may stand in wonderment at the love of God, that hath laid up things 'that eye hath not seen, nor ear heard, neither hath it entered into the heart of man to conceive,' 1 Cor. ii. 9. And shall not these things stir up the spirit of faith and endeavours suitable, whenas a probability of excellent things, though earthly, will stir up endeavours? Therefore, where there is no endeavour against earthly things, we do not believe a whit. The evil things we be forced from are so terrible, and the good things present to faith so excellent, that if they were but probable conjectures, they would be better than they were. Therefore many are so far from faith, that they have not conjectures there be such things, for infidelity reigneth in their hearts. If faith set up a kingdom in their hearts never so little, it would stir up boldness; and therefore consider of all the sweet natures of God reconciled, and approve but the excellency of the things, which if we have the apprehension of in weak measure, they will make us better than most of your common blasphemers, and swearers, and scorners of goodness. He inwardly laugheth and scorns at all parts of religion. Though for shame of men he comforteth himself something, yet notwithstanding, infidelity reigneth in his heart.

Second. Again, that faith may set up a regiment† in the soul, consider now *that this is the grace that infuseth vigour and strength into all our graces*; all are nothing without faith. Faith must fetch from Christ strength for patience and contentation. There is no other grace but hath his vigour from faith, as faith from the Spirit of God. Therefore pour water upon the root, water the root of all other graces, cherish faith. Oh, this consideration that all springeth and have their life and vigour from faith, and that now the government of the church, by the Spirit of God under covenant of grace, is to fetch all out of ourselves! We must have a supernatural eye, and a supernatural hand to reach to heaven and fetch treasure out of Christ, and spiritual virtue to draw out of Christ and his promises, and have all. Every time, every thing, every word, every action whatsoever, is out of ourselves, and cometh from a principle that is in Christ. And therefore, considering the excellency and necessity of grace, labour for it,

* That is, = bold, or without (false, cowardly) shame.—G.

† That is 'government.'—G.

and let it be more and more planted in us, that according to our apprehension of the excellency and necessity of it, and misery without it, we may earnestly endeavour after it.

VERSE 14.

Knowing that he which raised up the Lord Jesus shall raise up us also by Jesus, and shall be present with you.*

The apostle, in the former words, as we heard at large, sets down the afflicted and comfortable condition of God's people; and because our nature is very unfit as to do good, so to suffer evil, therefore he opens a further spring of comfort to the end of the chapter.

Among others, as you heard the last day, this in the 13th verse is one. 'We having the same spirit of faith, according as it is written, I believe, and therefore I have spoken.' Here is a double comfort in whatsoever we suffer. 'We have a spirit of faith,' which is a spirit of strength wrought by the power of God itself, and laying hold likewise upon divine power.

And another ground of comfort is, 'We have the same spirit of faith,' and faith stirs up not only to believe,—the proper act of it,—but it stirs up speaking both to God in prayer and of God in praises, and for God in times of opposition. These things were more enlarged. I pass on now, only I add this, that before we speak we must believe. Mark the method, 'I believe, therefore I speak.' A man cannot speak to God in prayer, in praises, or speak of God aright, but he must believe what he speaks. You know it is monstrous that there should be a birth without conception, that a man should speak of that he doth not know, or speak of that he doth not believe. And we must labour to know and believe things in their own light by the Spirit. We must have a spirit of faith before we speak of spiritual things. This is a careless neglect that sometimes people will speak of good things, but they will speak of them in an human spirit, others in a diabolical spirit, by way of scoffing or blaspheming, as some never speak of God but they blaspheme and swear, nor ever speak of religion but with scorn, as if not grave enough for them; or if they speak sadly, they speak of holy things with human spirits, not truly believing, as their hearts tell them, what they speak. Now the tongue must be the true messenger of the heart. The heart must indite, and the tongue write. And therefore we must endeavour by all means to have a spirit of faith, and labour with these false hearts of ours to believe, and then to speak. Our hearts else will give the tongue the lie. Thou speakest these things, but thou dost not believe them. And indeed a man may see by the manner of men's speaking of holy things that they believe not what they speak. As he said, 'If thou didst believe these things, wouldst thou speak so of them?' (*cc*). So if a man did believe divine things, would he speak so irreverently, so slightly of them as they do? And therefore we must labour to believe what we speak. If we speak to God or others of the state of grace, or the like, we must first have the Spirit of God; we must know the meaning of God, to speak of holy things in God's meanings. Were it not a bold part for a man to speak of another man's meaning, and never know his meaning? God discovers his meaning in the Scripture, and if we do not know his meaning; if we speak of certainty of salvation and of such matters, and of great spiritual things, and of knowing them by the Spirit of God, by his own

* Qu. '*present us*'?—Ed.

Spirit; we speak of the love of God, and care and providence of God, and know not by his Spirit that he is this to us. Indeed, it is presumption for us to speak anything of God, unless God discover it at first; to speak anything of our own condition in an intimate manner, as if we were so and so, when the Spirit of God doth not truly dictate so much to our souls. We see spiritual things with spiritual light, and we must speak of spiritual things with help of the Spirit, and must judge of spiritual things by the discovery of the Spirit, or else we had better say nothing all* than speak presumptuously. 'We believe, and then we speak.'

Obj. But you will say, Many divines speak excellent well for points of religion, and hold them, and yet their lives discover they have no faith. And therefore there may be a spirit without faith.

Ans. Beloved, mark what I said before. They may speak of religious things in a human manner, and see spiritual things with a common light, but they cannot see spiritual things in their proper light without the Spirit of God. And they cannot speak of spiritual things in a spiritual manner without the Spirit of God. We must first believe, and then speak. Therefore our labour should be in the ground-work, to get faith in the heart. And when faith is gotten into the heart, it will quickly overpower all fears and doubts and despairings, and all rebellion. It is a victorious and conquering grace. If we can get that, it will subdue the heart unto itself. And it will make us speak boldly, and speak of holy things, and to purpose; to speak to God and of God in divine things, and of God in oppositions. So we must speak likewise for the good of others, by way of edification. And we must speak to our own hearts in times of temptation, speak to Satan by his solicitations. When Satan and our hearts shall speak to us, and judge us to be thus and thus, Thou art thus, and thus God saith by his Spirit, for saith faith, thus he hath told me, 'I am thy salvation,' he saith in Scripture, Ps. xxxv. 3. 'If I believe, I shall not perish, but have everlasting life,' John iii. 15. And he saith in particular to me by his Spirit, 'Thy sins are forgiven thee,' Mat. ix. 2. Therefore care not what our doubtful hearts, or Satan joined with them, saith. God saith thus, and the spirit of faith saith thus; 'and as I believe, so I speak.' So that if there be a spirit of faith, we shall speak to our own hearts, 'Why art thou so disquiet, O my soul; and why art thou troubled in me? trust in God,' Ps. xlii. 5. Faith will quail† all the rising doubts of our own hearts and temptations of Satan. Satan saith thus and thus, but what saith God? what saith the spirit of faith in me? That saith thus. Alas! when our hearts shall rise against us, and Satan shall join with our accusing consciences and have not a spirit of faith to speak against our hearts, and against our hearts accusing us, guilt is a clamorous thing. Oh, the conscience and Satan makes great ado. When he getteth guilt he is an excellent rhetorician and orator, to set colours on things. If we have not something to still our clamorous consciences, and to quiet the accusation of conscience, what will become of us? And therefore labour so to believe that we may speak, not only to God, but for God and profitably to us; but in defence of ourselves, against our own unbelieving hearts and Satan's temptations.

What is the reason that poor souls yield themselves to despair, and so to a desperate conclusion of themselves oftentimes? Oh they labour not for the Spirit of God to believe first in their own hearts, and to have a word to answer Satan's temptations. And therefore, of all things, labour for the spirit of faith, that we may believe, and believing, may be able to

* Qu. 'at all'?—Ed.

† That is, quell—G

speak, to speak every way, to express ourselves for God, for ourselves, for the truth.

The next verse is, 'Knowing that he that raised up the Lord Jesus shall raise us up with Jesus, and present us with him.'

Here is farther grounds of comfort, that God will raise us up by Christ, and present us with him. Paul comforted himself with this, that God should raise him by Christ, and present him with the believing Corinthians. Now this hath a double meaning: first, that God should raise him out of troubles, which are a kind of deaths, as in the beginning of the chapter he calls the troubles he was in 'a great death;' and then, that God would raise him at length out of the grave, and present him and them at the day of judgment, as his crown before the Lord.

This was his comfort. Now, for aught I see, the apostle may mean both subordinately one to another; for God doth raise us out of trouble by Jesus, and present us one to another in this world for our comfort, and at length raise us out of the dust, and present us altogether, to be for ever together with the Lord. His comfort then is, that God will raise us up, and then he will present us with you. This is set down by the effect. 'God will do it; God that raised up Jesus will do it.' And the cause why God will do it is, because he hath raised up Jesus. First, God that hath raised up Jesus will by Jesus raise up us, and present us with you. So that here is the comfort and the ground of it. The comfort is double. God will raise us up, and then God will present us with you. The ground of it is this, why he will do it, because he hath raised up Christ. God is the author of it, and he that hath raised up Christ will raise up you. There is such a connection and blessed union between Christ and us, that the same power that raised up Jesus out of the grave will raise us up likewise.

So that here is a comfort above comfort; but yet 'knowing' is prefixed. 'Knowing that God will raise us up, because he hath raised up Jesus.' So that I may observe in the passage of it, *that all comfort cometh into the soul by knowledge*. God not only raiseth us up, and presents us one with another, by the same power that he hath raised up Jesus by, but we must know that it must be so, if we will have comfort. Whatsoever cometh into the soul to strengthen it cometh through knowledge. As from the heavens come light, and through light all influences, and whatsoever is sweet from heaven, to make things flourish, comes with light, so all things that come to the soul to make it comfortable and cheerful, comes with the light of knowledge. Indeed, all graces are nothing but knowledge digested, knowledge turned into affection and practice. What is anything but knowledge? any grace, but the performance of such a thing from such and such grounds? As we see in fruit, all that is in the fruit cometh from the juice that is [in] the root. And so the vigour and strength of everything is knowledge; I mean knowledge and a spirit of faith to believe what we know, to assent to it, and acknowledge it.

Light, you know, is very comfortable. Darkness is a state of fear. So ignorance is a state of doubting and fear. There is no good where ignorance is; but light and knowledge is a state of boldness. We believe, and speak, and are bold. Why? 'We know.'

And therefore the people that be careless of growing in knowledge, they be enemies of comfort and of grace. 'Grow in grace, and in the knowledge of our Lord Jesus Christ,' 2 Pet. iii. 18. The most knowing Christian is the most constant, courageous, comfortable, fruitful Christian, because together with divine light enlightening the soul, there goeth divine heat, enlarging the soul to every duty, and to all comforts whatsoever. So much for that.

We will speak a little of the comforts and places of the ground of the comfort. 'He will raise us up, and present us with you.' Troubles that be greater are called death, as in the first chapter of this epistle.* The Lord that delivered me from so great a death, and why? Specially for this end; because, as they be partial deaths, so likewise they agree with death. In this we despair of life and recovery. So when a trouble is great, as when a man is dead, the trouble is desperate. It is a death, there is no hope of recovery again. Now, saith Paul, though my troubles be great, yet notwithstanding God will raise me up, even out of death, and present me with you.

Quest. How knew Paul that God would do this?

Ans. It is like he knew it by a spirit of revelation, having nearer communion with God, as a more public person, than we have. But what is that to us? Can we say God will raise us up, and present us one to another, as Paul did? No, beloved, we cannot say so; but this we can say, God will raise me up out of this trouble, or if I die in it, God will raise me out of the grave. This is the happy condition of a Christian. He is sure, if he be in trouble, either to be raised for the good of the church, if he hath any service for him to do; else if I die, he will raise me up at the last day with all his people, to be for ever with him. If it be for the good of the church, and mine own good to live, I shall live still; if not, I shall be sure to be raised at the latter day; fall out what will fall out, all falleth out well for the children of God.

Now the holy apostle no question had reference to both. He had both in his view, raising out of trouble, and raising to eternal life; because he could never speak of any inferior deliverances but his mind would run on the future, and that did terminate all comforts. All comforts end in the resurrection. Usually when Paul maketh mention of an inferior thing, he mounteth higher, he mounts to the highest of all; he resteth not his thoughts till he hath thought of that, as in the end of this chapter he endeth in the resurrection, and endeth in comfort, speaking gloriously of it. So at this time no question but there was present all deliverances in this world, but especially eternal deliverance in the world to come. As 2 Tim. iv. 17, 'The Lord delivered me out of the mouth of the lion, and can and will deliver for the time to come, and present me to his heavenly kingdom,' that I am sure of.

So that it were a very heavenly course for Christians, if they think of anything that cometh from the love of God to them, to take hints from that, to take notice of the issue of all. All deliverances are terminated in their last deliverance out of the grave, and all blessings are terminated in the last blessing, life everlasting. And take every thing as a pawn, a pledge, a beginning of that, for the same love that giveth eternal comforts, giveth comforts in this world; and the same God that delivers out of the grave, delivers us out of troubles; and the same God that will bring us all to heaven, will bring friends together in this world, if it be for their good. And therefore if we will comfort ourselves solidly in any condition, extend our thoughts to the time to come. Was it David's comfort when he said, 'One thing have I desired of the Lord'? Ps. xxvii. 4. Was it his meaning to confine his thoughts on that only desire, and to dwell in the

* Cf. i. 9.—G.

church for ever? No; 'that I dwell in the house of the Lord for ever,' here while I live, and in heaven for ever when I am gone, Ps. xxiii. 6: 'Doubtless I shall dwell in the house of the Lord for ever;' here while I live, and for ever in heaven. Then they will be solid comforts. If the drops of comfort we have in holy things be carried on to the end of all, everlasting deliverance, by the resurrection, and eternal comforts in heaven, then they would be comforts indeed. It is a good disjunction when friends promise to meet again. Well, we shall meet either here or in heaven, and perhaps here and in heaven. The same God that will comfort us in heaven, if he seeth it good for us, he will comfort us here with the presence of one another.

'He will raise us up, and present us with you.' That is another of his comforts. But what comfort is that in this world, if he meaneth only the joy in the world to come? as I am persuaded it is that he mainly aims at, the other was but that that by meditation he raised his thoughts to. What comfort is it that friend shall be presented to friend, pastor to people, believers among friends!

There be divers kinds of communion, if absent, by letters, by real tokens, by message; but what are these to presence? Presence is the sweetest kind of communion that can be. Communion one with another in presence is in deed, in word, of communion in presence. And therefore God will deliver us from trouble, and present us with you; for in presence every thing speaks comfort. Without discourse the very presence of a friend comforts. There is a quick and living power in the very face of a friend. The eye comforts, the speech comforts, all comforts, and nothing but comforts if they be hearty friends in the Lord.

And therefore saith Paul, this shall be my comfort and your comfort, that I shall be delivered out of this death, and presented with you, for your good, for my own comfort. And no question this is a beginning of heaven in this world. If there be any heaven on earth, it is the communion of saints; it is when many join together in an holy affection, that have not only general likings of the same things, but have the same spirit acting and living in them all, one and the same Spirit of God stirring up approbation and dislike of the same thing, the same end for good causes. This is a special comfort, if there be any comfort in this world. And so Paul meaneth, when he saith, 'I shall be delivered, and presented to you.' And therefore we should take special care to improve communion by all means, considering it was so sweet a thing. *O qui congressus, et gloria quanta fuerunt!* when Paul was severed a great while. Paul came with abundance of blessings of God, and they came with abundance of desire to have heavenly discourse with St Paul.

Thus while we be in this world we must be exercised with these intermitting comforts. This is a life of separation; we shall enjoy a while, and then part, till we be in heaven, 'and then we shall be for ever with the Lord,' 1 Thess. iv. 18. 'Therefore comfort one another with these words.' What is the comfort? 'We shall be for ever with the Lord.' If it be such a comfort to enjoy communion one with another, what is it to enjoy communion for ever with the Lord in heaven? That is the meeting time, when body and soul shall meet, when Christ and all his members shall meet, when all the members of the church from the first to the last shall all meet. These three blessed meetings shall be, Christ and we, and we one with another, and body and soul. Then is the meeting, then is the presenting. But all other meetings together are comfortable, as they be tastes of the last and everlasting meeting that shall be revealed. This may comfort us in the parting of friends, in the loss of friends by death. There will be a time of meeting again. Our head will bring all the members together, as it is said of Christ, 'that he shall gather all to a head,' Eph. iv. 15: that being Christ's office, to gather all the children of God together, from whom they were fallen; to gather them to the angels in* whom they were in terms of difference; to gather them together, one to another in love, and gathering to themselves in peace. This is Christ's work. This gathering together to a head belongeth to Christ. And though we be not together now, yet in heaven we shall be.

Now the ground of this is, God that hath raised up Jesus, will by Jesus do this. He considers of God as serveth his purpose. It is an act of a Christian, of a discreet and wise soul, to single out of God those attributes and those actions that suit to his present distress or present condition; as if a man be in perplexity, think of him as a God strong and wise; if a man be in any trouble, think of him as a good and powerful God; if a man be wronged, think of him as a God of vengeance. Thou God of vengeance, shew thyself! And when we be in any trouble and cast down, and dead, as troubled by others' deaths, then can God raise Christ out of the grave, who is our head. And out of the love that he loveth both mystical Christ and natural Christ, the Lord is gracious to all for his sake. He that loveth Christ as his own natural son loveth Christ mystical, all that be Christ's, with the same love that he loved Christ. As Christ himself prayeth he will embrace all such with the same love he loved himself withal, John xvii. 24, so God is well pleased and rests in his love, not only in his natural Son, but all that be his; and therefore out of love to his own Son, as he hath raised up him and set him in heavenly places, he will raise up all them that be his, and are engrafted into him. He that raised up the Lord Jesus shall raise us up also. What is the consequence? Because he hath raised up Jesus, therefore by Jesus he will raise us out of trouble. The ground is, Christ is a public person, and so in heaven is a public person, a second Adam, and raised up as a second Adam; and therefore be raised up as [a] public person, and as a second Adam, and a root of all believers. He hath taken heaven in our place as our husband, and we sit in heavenly places with him; and therefore God that raised up him will raise us up also. 'If Christ be risen, we shall rise.' There is no question of it, as he proveth at large, 'because I live ye shall live also,' John xiv. 19. I cannot follow the point, but it is a point you are acquainted with all, being an article of faith. Therefore see the ground of this comfort. God will raise up us and bring us together, because he hath raised Jesus. He is the first-fruits of them that slept. Now all the harvest is blessed in the first-fruits. Our first-fruits is Christ now. And therefore we shall be here raised out of little deaths, and at the resurrection out of the great death, and be for ever with the Lord, which may teach us this comfortable observation; *to see all our comforts in Christ first;* to see all we look for from God, first in Christ and then in ourselves. If we look for love from God, see his love on Christ first: 'He loveth us because he loveth him first,' and he loveth us in him. If we look to resurrection, ascension, or glory, see it in Christ first. If we look for the performance of any promise, see that promise in Christ first, for all are made for his sake, and made good in him, to Christ first and then to us. If we want any grace, see it in Christ first, for he hath fulness of the Spirit for our sakes: 'And of his fulness we have received, and grace for grace,' John i. 16. So that in both

* Qu. 'with'?—Ed.

estates of humiliation and exaltation severally, see all first in Christ and then in ourselves. Look on Christ in state of humiliation, and see ourselves there. 'Christ was a curse for us,' died for us. All this is for us. And see all the evil that belongeth to us taken away by him in his state of humiliation. He humbled himself to death, and became a curse for us. And so in his state of exaltation in several degrees. See our resurrection in his resurrection, our ascension in his ascension, our sitting in heavenly places by his sitting in heavenly places. The ground is, the union I spake of before. And then God hath decreed that we shall be made conformable to his Son. 'We must be conformable to Christ our elder brother.' We are chosen to be conformable to him. And therefore whatsoever was in him, there will be a conformableness in us thereunto. And we must be content to go to heaven as Christ went. 'He first suffered and then entered into glory,' 1 Peter i. 10, 11, he rose again, but he died first. We must be content to go to heaven by that way that our blessed head and Saviour hath gone before us. And if we do so, surely that God that raised him will raise us up too.

I beseech you, therefore, when we are to consider of any comfort, see it in Christ first, not only as a pattern to whom we must be conformed, but see it in Christ as a cause, because Christ will raise us up. We shall not only be raised because he is raised, and ascend because he is ascended, but God will raise us up with Jesus. Between God and us cometh Jesus, for all that comes from God comes from Jesus. So all that cometh from us to God must go through the mediation of Jesus. 'He that raised up Jesus will by Jesus raise us up.' Christ is not only a pattern of conformity, but likewise a cause. And it is an improvement of the favour, that God doth us favour through such a one that standeth between him and us; that there should be so excellent a person as Christ to do all, to be a pattern of all, and cause of all. For can there be a better than he to raise us out of trouble here, and to heaven hereafter? Then he that is our own head, will he suffer his members to perish? And he that is so favourable with God, and one with God, that as a man layeth hold on us, and as God layeth hold on God, as a friend to him, being between both as a friend of both. As God, so we must trust him with all, with our rising again, with our ascension, with our glory in heaven. He is the Joseph between God and us. As he conveyed all favour to the patriarchs, from Egypt through Pharaoh,* so Christ is the high steward of all, that hath the dispensing of all his comforts by our sweet head, that is bone of our bone and flesh of our flesh, to make us for ever one with him. So that there is comfort in the deriving of comfort by so sweet, so loving, so gracious a head as Jesus is.

But you will say, Will Christ raise us out of trouble likewise? Yes, by the same power and virtue. For the virtue of Christ's resurrection reacheth farther than to raise us from death, for it extendeth itself to all abasements in the world. God raiseth us out of all abasements by the power that he raised up Christ, and by the power that Christ raised up himself. And therefore we should comfort ourselves in the distress of the church and personal distresses. And first for the church. God raised up Christ the head of the church after three days, and when they had rolled a stone upon the grave, and set a watch too, and when Christ had been a surety to bear the sins of all the elect of the world from the beginning to the end; Christ having a stone upon his grave, so much mould, and such a stone, and his

* Qu. 'As Pharaoh conveyed all favour to the patriarchs in Egypt through Joseph'?—Ed.

grave watched and sealed; and then having as a public person the sins of all the world, yet Christ rose up again for all this.

Beloved, Satan and his instruments labour to bury the church if they can, and to roll a stone on the church, that it should never rise up again. It was their plot of late,* and it is their purpose now, but that their power is a little broken. They would bury Christ and his church altogether, roll a stone on him, watch him that he should never rise again. This they do; and now in the third day he shall rise again. There may be a limited time of Jacob's sorrow, but there will be a day of deliverance. He that raised up the head of the church, after the time he had appointed he should lie there under the bondage and captivity of death, he will raise up the body of Christ. Our times are not in our hands, nor in the devil's time, nor in man's time, but in God's time. Men may oppose his time, and be against his time. 'They shall cast you into prison for ten days.' It is certain and sure, which may be a comfort to the church. The church beyond seas was lately under hatches, and the enemy had got her into the grave, and thought to have rolled the stone upon the church; but God, that raised up Jesus, hath raised up the church in some comfortable measure, which may put us in hope, that now there is time to set prayer on work.† It puts encouragement into our hands. That that God hath done, encourageth us to pray to God for the finishing of his own good work. We have not only faith and promises, but performances to encourage us. We see the stone is rolled off as it were. This is our comfort, and this is the church's comfort to the end of the world. She may be for a while under the grave, but God will send his angels, his messengers, one or another, to take away the stone, and raise up the church, as in the parable of the dry bones, Ezek. xxxvii. 1, *seq.* The church was 'as dry bones,' but 'the Spirit entered into them, and made them live.' So at length a spirit shall enter into the church, and it shall live. Babylon must fall; the church must rise. Christ will enlarge his church to the end [of] the world. Heaven hath said it, and hell cannot disannul what God hath concluded. He that raised up Jesus will raise up the church out of all its troubles. And for ourselves, in all deaths and all our desperate troubles, sink not under them. Make use of the articles of faith. They are of wonderful enlarged sweetness. The sweet article of the resurrection and life everlasting have influence into all our lives. Make use of that; God, that doth the greater, will not he do the less, if for our good? Will God raise my body out of the grave, and not out of this sickness? God that can raise me out of dust, cannot he raise me out of this trouble, and present me to my friends again? If for my good, he can do it.

And rise from inferior things to strengthen our faith, and the greatest things we have in faith for the time to come. Will God give me life everlasting, and not daily bread? Will God give heaven, and not provision to bring me thither? Will God raise me out of the dust, when it is scattered I know not where, and get all my dust together, and quicken that dust, and not quicken me out of this, if it be for my good and the good of others? If he have any service to do for me, he will do it. And therefore, I beseech you, beloved, let us labour to strengthen our faith in the way to heaven, by that which is to come. What made the apostles pass through thick and thin, break through all troubles between them and heaven, but [that] they thought God would deliver them? If he did not deliver them,

* In margin here, 'Gunpowder Plot.'—G.

† In margin here, 'By Gustavus Adolphus, king of Sweden.'—G.

he would deliver them to heaven, and present them to his heavenly kingdom. Having heaven in their eyes, time to come in heaven, resurrection in their eyes, and glorious times in their eyes, it will be of such force and influence into their hearts, that they shall go through all things between, and make this disjunction; either God will raise me out of this, or out of the grave, and present me to his heavenly kingdom. I beseech you, therefore, learn this, that in all our dejections we make use of that last and powerful work of God in raising from the dead. Raising comforteth for what is past. Our Saviour Christ, our best part, our head, is in heaven, and we shall all draw to him in time. Let us not lose the benefit of such a meditation, of such a ground as this. See all in Christ beforehand; all is done in Christ. Beloved, can we have a better pledge and pattern, than to see all we look for done in Christ beforehand? We look for the resurrection, Christ is raised; and ascension, Christ is ascended. We look for glory in heaven: Christ is glorified, Christ, and we in Christ; for when we think of Christ, we must think of ourselves in Christ. And therefore, when we hear the creed repeated, and the articles of religion, or anything of Christ, let us wrap up ourselves by the spirit of faith in Christ, see ourselves crucified in Christ, and dead in Christ, and raised in Christ, and set in heavenly places with Christ.

I but administer the heads to you, for your meditations to work upon. You see what excellent use the apostle maketh of his faith. It made him believe, speak confidently for the present. And therefore, with cheerfulness attend upon the blessed means of the word and sacrament, that God hath appointed to strengthen our union and communion with Christ. Christ is our life, and the nearer communion with him, the more life we have. And the sacrament is appointed for to seal to us this communion, to strengthen this near union, and receive* with the spring and fountain of life, Jesus Christ. And therefore, come with exceeding comfort; and the more our union with Christ, the more our comforts in life or death. All depends on that: as we see hope of resurrection, hope of deliverance, hope of glory, doth all depend upon that, union first in Christ, then in us, and in us because in Christ. Therefore, strengthen union with Christ, and strengthen all. For matter of the sacrament, you are acquainted with the doctrinal part of it, have this conceit of it. It is a high ordinance of God, which strengthens faith, which being strengthened, strengthens all the powers of soul.

VERSE 15.

For all things are for your sakes, that most plenteous grace, by the thanksgiving of many, may redound to the praise of God.

The holy apostle, as we heard, labours to arm himself and all others against all discouragements in religion, by comforts fetched from religion.

He bringeth in divers springs of comfort in this latter part of the chapter. 'I believe, and therefore I have spoken; as David believed, and therefore he spake.' It is no otherwise with us than with David and other saints before us, as we shewed at large.

The last day this comfort was handled, that God would raise him out of his trouble, and present him together with the Corinthians in his† life, and at the last in the world to come. And from this ground, 'Because God raised up Jesus.' 'Knowing that he which raised up the Lord Jesus,

* Qu. 'revive'?—ED.

† Qu. 'this'?—ED.

shall raise us up by Jesus, and shall present us with him.' Of this I have spoken at large already.

I beseech you, before I leave this point, learn this, that in all our dejections, we make use of that last and powerful work of God, in raising from the dead.

I now proceed to what followeth.

'For all things are for your sakes.' Here is a farther ground of comfort, both of present deliverance, as for their sakes.

The second ground is, 'All is for the glory of God.'

And the means of that glory, 'Because the grace aboundeth,' that these deliverances spring from, 'thanksgiving abound to the glory of God.' Why should we be discouraged in suffering, since God will be presented with us in sufferings, delivering us in time, considering it is for the church's good, and for the glory of God? And for the glory of God in this way, because it will minister matter of praise, not of one, but of many, out of which praise God will be glorified. This is the scope of the words.

The first ground of comfort is, 'All are for your sakes,' both our sufferings, and assistance, and presence of God in them, and deliverance out of them, all is for you, 2 Tim. ii. 10: 'We suffer for the elect's sake,' all is for your sake. Indeed, beloved, it is a large diffused consideration, for all is for the church's sake, the world itself. The standing of the world is for the church's sake. If God had gathered his elect, there would be an end of these sinful days. Another sinful generation, God would not suffer the world to stand for a company of wretches, that daily blaspheme his name, that pollute and defile their souls and bodies, that oppose his truth like rebels.

That the world continueth, it is for the elect's sake, that they may be gathered out [of] the world. The world is as it were reprieved, because many are to be born in the world; as lewd women are reprieved, being with child, for that's sake that is to be born. So the world continueth because there is a generation to come; the number of the elect is not yet accomplished.

Thus you see the very world, and the standing of the world, is for the church's sake. The world is elect; and so are things in the world, in heaven or earth, in some sort. They are for the church's sake. 'To us a child is born, to us a son is given,' Isa. ix. 6; for the church he died, for the church he rose again, for the church 'he appears in heaven and makes intercession,' as Rom. viii. 34. He sits at God's right hand making intercession for us. John xvii. 17, 19, 'I sanctify myself;' that is, I prepare myself as a sacrifice to suffer for them. 'I pray not for the world, but for them thou hast given me out of the world.' All that Christ did suffer, enjoy, and do in heaven, as our head, it is for the church's sake. That he giveth gifts to wicked men, that they continue, it is for the church's sake, that they may be instruments and servants of the church. In that sense they be redeemed by Christ as servants of the church. We see in nature that summer and winter serveth for vines, and fruitful trees, and plants, for the good corn. Cold weather and warm weather, they have the leaves to cover them. And every thing serveth to bring forth the fruit; all these circumstantial things. So whatsoever is circumstantial in the world, as kingdoms, states, government, they think to tumble in the world for their own ends, and to toss the world as they list. It is for a number of men unregarded, unknown, that pass here as unknown men, hidden men for the most part, it is for the church's sake that they continue, that they have any favours. They are beholden to the church for their lives, to the church for their standing, and for the gifts they have, though they think not so. God, the great God of heaven and earth, and Christ the great king of the church, in reference to his church, giveth gifts to men, magistrates, ministers, people, yea, even to them that be not good men, and all for the good of his church. So that 'all is for you,' word, sacraments, every thing.

I might make a large dispute here, but that I unfolded it at large out of that place in Corinthians, 'All is yours,'* which is the general. The church is yours, 'whether Paul, or Apollos, or Cephas, or things present, or things to come, or life, or death, or the world, all is yours, you are Christ's, and Christ is God's.'

And from this general truth the apostle deducts this, 'it is for your sake.' All things that we suffer, all things that are done to us is for your sake. If so be all things are for the church's sake, beloved, *we ought to join with God, as Paul doth here.* Christ hath passed as it were a deed of gift of all things to the church, to serve her turn, to bring the church to heaven. Shall not God's intent, and Christ's intent, be ours? Saith he, all that I do and suffer is for your sake. It is a happy thing when God's intentions and ends, and our ends, shall meet in one, beloved, voluntarily. And God will bring all men's ends to serve his against their wills. Oh but happy are we if we can make our ends meet with God's ends willingly and cheerfully.

Quest. What is the ground of this, 'that all things are for the church's sake'?

Reason 1. The ground of it is, *that covenant, wherein God passeth over himself as it were to the church*, 'I will be your God.' And Christ he is as it were not his own; he is the church's. Christ is the church's. Therefore all are the church's. All the three persons of the Trinity have their title of excellency from relation to the church. God a Father in regard of the church; Christ a redeemer in regard of the church; the Holy Ghost a comforter in regard of the church. So God the Father, Son, and Holy Ghost, they are in covenant with the church. And they are the church's, as it were making themselves the church's, out of that infinite bottomless love; being God, they have made themselves the church's.

Now if God himself be the church's, and in covenant with it, that the church may improve him, and whatsoever is in him, all his excellent attributes for their comfort and good, shall not all other things be the church's? If God himself be reconciled to the church, shall not all things else be reconciled? If God be in covenant, shall not every thing? 'The stones in the street be in covenant with him,' as Job saith, v. 23.

Reason 2. A second subordinate ground to this is, *the union with Christ the king of the church.* Now all things serve Christ, who is the king of heaven and earth; his kingdom reaches from heaven to the bottom of hell; he overruleth cursed devils and wicked spirits. Who is he whom the devils obey? saith God. Now if all things serve Christ, they serve his spouse, by reason of the union and spiritual commerce with Christ, to whom God hath dedicated and committed the rule and government of heaven and earth. All things are mine in heaven and earth, committed to me, saith Christ, when he ascended into heaven; and therefore as Christ is the great Lord of the world, so the church is the great queen and empress of the world. All things serve Christ the husband, and all things must serve the church his spouse. It must be so. God is in covenant with the church, and Christ is hers by union with the church. 'Touch

* Cf. 'A Christian's Portion,' *ante*, p. 6, *seq.*—G.

not mine anointed, and do my prophets no harm,' Ps. cv. 15. Withhold the hand of violence from them, they are mine. So Christ is head, king, and husband of the church, and will not suffer her to be wronged in his sight, but all things shall serve for the church's good.

Reason 3. Again, to come nearer and lower to us. *If you look to us, all is for the church's sake, the children of God too;* because God hath put a Spirit into his church to extract good out of all. 'All is for your sakes.' The Spirit of God shall teach you to see God seeking your good in all things. God puts it into the spirit of his children to seek the good of his church in all things. Paul had the Spirit of God to direct his aims, as none but the child of God hath right aims to seek God in all things, and his glory.

The church hath the Spirit of God to see God seeking their good in all things. 'This shall turn to my good,' saith Paul, 'through the supplies of the Spirit and your prayers,' Philip. i. 19. The church prayeth that all things may serve for his good; that God would sanctify all his crosses and afflictions; that God would bless magistrates, ministers, and all ordinances for their good; that, with the Spirit of God, and this action's* exercise of the Spirit of thanksgiving and prayer, all things are made for the church's good, because they have a spirit specially shewing itself in a spirit of prayer, to work good out of everything. Therefore the children of God pray that God would bless his sufferings and deliverances, and all things, not for his own good, but for the church's good. And the church itself and every good Christian labours to see God, seeking and deriving good to themselves out of everything; for the covenant of God, being friends of God; and they are near to Christ, and near to God in Christ. And they labour to see the love of God and the love of Christ in all things, that so the sweetness and communion of the love may be increased. God acquaints them with his secrets in everything, so much as may be for their eternal good; and with the secrets of his election, how he directeth and ordereth all things to their good. He never corrects but he instructs with it; he never afflicteth but they know the ground of it; and so by the Spirit of God are enabled to draw good out of everything. In prosperity they see God seeking their encouragement; in crosses they see God seeking their humility and repentance. So that on these and other grounds which I might name, all things are for the church's sake. Why do the children of God look for the good of the church?

The reason why Saint Paul as a minister sought the good of the church, was the relation between a master and a people, between an apostle and people, called and gathered by him; and in relation as a Christian, because fellow-members with them.

If I were to speak to ministers, I would speak of the relation between pastors and people, how they should seek the good one of another; but as a Christian, all is for your sake. No Christian but as soon as [he is] a Christian hath a public mind inspired into him to seek the good of others; he concurs with God willingly. As soon as ever he is a Christian, he learneth self-denial; he knows he hath given up himself and all to God, to the church, and he is become a servant to others for Christ's sake. As soon as ever a man begins to be a Christian he hath a spirit of love, and seeketh not his own good. As soon as ever a man becomes a Christian, he hath a spirit enlarged, he hath higher and farther aims, and large affections towards God and the church; his soul is large. All other men are straitened

* Qu. 'active'?—G.

in their affections, and strengthened in their aims. They have poor aims and ends of their own. And in their affections they be straitened; they cannot love, nor long after good things, yea, they be straitened to their own in all things. He is within his own circumference, within his own term; his *terminus reductivus* is himself. He reduceth all to himself, and seeks himself in all things. He thinks not that he doth sin, but he doth, for it is impossible any but a Christian should seek the good of others as they should; but as soon as [he is] a Christian, the Spirit of God maketh the heart public to seek the good of others. And the more Spirit of Christ, the more they seek the good of others; and they that be greatest in heaven are the greatest servants. Christ is greatest in heaven, and who was more made a servant? He became a curse to make us blessed: poor to make us rich. As he was the greatest servant that died for others, so they that be the greatest next to him have learned self-denial.

Not they that heap up great states, and are put into great places, but they that have public minds and public spirits, that seek the good of others, and abase themselves for the good of others, such as Paul is here, 'All is for you, and for your sake.'

I beseech you, therefore, make this use of it; *learn of so excellent an apostle as Saint Paul was, to have large affections and public aims and ends.* Labour to discern of your conditions and states by this, that you have the Spirit of Christ in you; because to do good to others you can deny yourselves. 'All things are for your sake.'

This should teach us likewise *to have honourable and high esteems of God's people.* Are they such whom Christ gave himself for, and made himself of no reputation and power for? Are they such as heaven and earth serve, and shall we despise them? Are they God's darlings, as dear to him as the apple of his eye? Are they the jewels, as the Scripture sets them out in such excellent terms? Are they his friends? are they his heirs and fellow-heirs with Christ? Are they such as the Holy Scriptures sets them down? Are 'all things for their sakes?' and shall not we have honourable esteems of them? Let this rectify our conceits of them, that they be not worthy to live in the world, when indeed the world is not worthy of them, 'All things are for your sake.' Suppose they have nothing in possession, yet in use and service all things serve them to bring them to heaven, and direct them for their good.

They are here as princes in a strange country, that must be honoured for their father's sake, and for their country's sake. They shall be great men when they come home; and therefore howsoever the world valueth and esteemeth them, when we see any price of grace and of the Spirit of God, think that these be yours, for the present all things be theirs. Oh but how great will they be? These shall be Christ's, not the world's; these shall sit and judge the world; they shall judge me, if I be not a Christian, ere long. Now, therefore, let me take heed how I despise one of Christ's little ones, how I debase such a one that is so great in God's esteem, for whose sake the world stands; and let this respect to them evidence to us that have another spirit than the world hath, that we know another Christ.

And again, *let it comfort God's people, who have some testimony that they are his, in their losses, in their crosses, in their misusage in the world.* Let them consider, are they so to God, are they so to Christ? Oh no! Let them labour therefore for a spirit of patience and courage to go through good reports, bad reports; good usage, bad usage; for the worst thing that befalls them hath a command to do them good. 'Do the young man no harm,' saith David of Absalom, 2 Sam. xviii. 5. And so all things have a command to do God's people no harm. Kings have a prohibition: 'Touch not mine anointed,' Ps. cv. 15. There is a prohibition given that no hurt shall be done. They may kill them, but not hurt them; imprison them, but not hurt them; they may wrong them, but not hurt them; that is, they cannot hinder their everlasting good, they cannot take away their Christ, their comfort, their peace, or touch them in their names; but oftentimes, against their wills, do them most good when they think to do them most harm. And therefore, I beseech you, labour for a spirit of comfort, considering all things are for our sakes, if we be Christ's.

I have been something long in the point, but it is comfortable and useful. I will now haste to that which followeth.

'All things are for your sakes, that the abundant grace, through the thanksgiving of many, may redound to the glory of God.'

The second ground of comfort is from the main end of all, *which is the glory of God*. Here is a sweet combination of the grace of God and the glory of God, 'that abundant grace, through the thanksgiving of many, might redound to the glory of God.' The links of this chain are these:—God suffers his children in this world to be exercised; in the exercise he giveth evidence of his presence, by grace and by comfort; and after all delivers them, giving them cause and matter of praise; and that praise is the praise not only of themselves, but of many. The praise of themselves and many, returneth to the glory of God. Here is grace breedeth praise, praise breedeth glory.

We will handle the words as they lie: 'that the abundant grace, through the thanksgiving of many, may redound to the glory of God.'

'The abundant grace.' What doth he mean by abundant grace? We shall know it a little by distinguishing a little the word of grace in the Scripture.

*Primitive** grace is *the free favour of God* in forgiving of sins, and access to life everlasting.

Secondly, The next grace that springs from that *is grace whereby we are sanctified*, usually called habitual† grace, whereby our natures have a stamp of Christ on them, and we are transformed into his image.

Thirdly, Grace *is the stirring of us up*, *exciting grace* stirring up that grace that is in us; and draws it forth to particular actions, of doing, and suffering, and resisting, and carrying ourselves as Christians should do. For besides the favour of God, and the fruit of that favour, which is of our nature, there must be spiritual stirring grace to act and stir up the grace which would otherwise lie sleeping in us; there must be new grace on all occasions. 'God must give the will and the deed,' Philip. ii. 13. God must stir us up to every good action, as I have shewed at large heretofore. A man cannot do the good he is enabled to do by an habitual grace, unless he have grace to stir him up to do. As he hath all graces in general to enable him, so he must have new graces for every new act; he must have constancy of spirit. And if the troubles be great, there be enlargements of grace; as if a man carries a greater burden, he must have more strength. But,

Fourthly, Grace is *any favour that cometh from the primitive grace and favour of God*. As we say of a great man, when he giveth a petty thing to an inferior person, This is such [a] man's grace.

Or grace is such a thing that springeth from his love and favour to

* That is, 'primarily.'—G. † That is, = grace as a 'habit.'—G.

us. So not only the favour of God that accepts to life everlasting, and that inward grace of God's Spirit, and that actual grace that stirs to every good action, but everything that comes from God is grace.

When God once enters into covenant with us, to become our God, to love us in Christ, whatsoever befalls us comes to us as a fruit of that love; for he being Lord of heaven and earth, and having all things at command, will not suffer the wind to blow upon his church, will not suffer the waves to beat upon it, but out of love, and for the good of the church; for otherwise his government and wisdom would be impeached. And,

Fifthly and lastly, By abundant grace is meant *the presence of God, the assistance of God unto Paul in suffering, and God's delivering him out of trouble*. These two things he specially means. God's presence in troubles, and delivering him out of them.

It is a grace of God that we have faith. It is a grace of God that we have strength to suffer for that faith. To endure anything is a special grace. 'To you it is given to suffer,' Philip. i. 29. It is a more special grace when we have not only grace to believe, and grace to suffer, but strength of faith. And therefore 'it is given, not only to believe, but to suffer.' It is grace to have special peace, and joy, and comfort in the midst of all spiritual contrary conditions. And therefore God's presence and comfort in the midst of his disconsolate estate was a grace; and not only the doctrine of suffering for Christ [is] a grace, but whatsoever comes from the presence of God is a grace likewise. And likewise his deliverance out is a grace. For as gold comes purer out of the furnace, so Paul comes richer in experience out of trouble; rich in faith, rich in love, rich in mortification; more heavenly-minded in the experience of God and his ways, and every way; and therefore it is an exceeding grace. And then [it is] a grace that God will bound and limit the malice of the devil and his instruments, that thus long they shall trouble them, and then set them at liberty. So that hereby we may plainly see, that all is done in favour of the church.

So it is a grace, that God hath put bounds and limits to the boundless malice of Satan and his instruments, to deliver the church, or any poor member of the church, as Paul was, at any time; and therefore they were to reckon all graces that they were to praise God for, both for his trouble and for his deliverance out of trouble, they being both graces.

Quest. But why doth he call it 'abundant grace?'

Ans. This St Paul doth out of his abundant humility, and out of his abundant love to God; out of his abundant measure of knowledge of the love of God towards him; for Paul's seeing and knowing were his own; want of worth in himself and his own weakness in himself, at the best, are nothing in themselves.* And St Paul, weighing and considering the mighty power and malice of the enemy, the devil and his instruments, that laboured to trouble him and oppose the gospel,—when Paul saw that opposition and his own weakness; when Paul saw likewise the evidence and demonstration of the excellency of God in being present with him in trouble, and delivering him out of trouble, saw the power, and goodness, and mercy of God, here was an abundant grace, here was a spring-tide of grace, as an overflowing, as he saith, 'My cup overfloweth,' Ps. xxiii. 5. I have not only for necessity, but something for abundance: 'My cup overfloweth, and thou

* Qu. 'for Paul seeing and knowing his own want of worth in himself, and his own weakness in himself, and that his own worth and his own strength, at the best, are nothing in themselves'?—Ed.

hast spread my table in the sight of mine enemies.' David considered the circumstances of God's bounty, for it was abundant. And Paul considering the great comforts that he had in the Lord, his great enemies and God's, and the malice of them against him and his God ; here was an abundant grace.

Beloved, let us learn from hence, first of all, *to see God in everything that befalls us :* in sufferings, deliverance, the dealing of others towards us. See the grace of God in it. There is, you know, in things in this world, the bulk and surplus, or body of things ; and then there is the spirit, and quintessence, and vigour of things : an extract, the vigour and quintessence of things. What are they ? They are next to nothing. Take out God's grace, God's mercy out of things, what are things ? what is the world ? Take away God's love, what is riches ? what is honour and worth ? Therefore, in every thing, see it as a grace, see it as derived from the primitive grace, from the favour and mercy of God in Jesus Christ. And then we cannot but be thankful, for we shall see the sweetness of grace. Every little gift, though by the hand of man, nay, every injury that is sanctified, he seeth it as a grace of God, looks to see God in it, his free love and grace among men. What is that that commends any thing to us that comes from another ? Not the thing, but the mind of the person that sends it ; not the bringer, but the sender. So when we have anything, look to God the sender. Look not to the thing, but to the love of God in the thing, which is the spirit, and quintessence, and vigour of the thing, the best thing. Nay, anything in the world is the love of God in it, derived to us through it. Let the grace of God be derived through losses, crosses, injuries ; they be sweet. 'It is given to suffer,' Philip. i. 29. Every one is not partaker of such a favour. See the grace and favour of God in health, and wealth, and strength, and riches, the life and quintessence of all, which commends all to a Christian soul. God deriveth and conveyeth his grace and love to men through this. This is a little drop of that great love that he beareth to me in Jesus Christ. This cometh from that love by which he intends heaven to me. And when God intends heaven and happiness, and to be with him for ever, everything that befalls us by the way hath something of that love, as it were dipped in that love. Whatsoever befalls us between this and heaven, if we be God's children, it hath a tincture of that love, to make him keep heaven for us. And therefore labour to see the grace and love of God in everything, see the language of Canaan, the language of the Spirit of God. That that puts the style upon grace, a free gift, an undeserved thing issuing from love, it implieth love and freeness and undeserving in the person that hath it. Therefore, conceive of every thing, we have it first from it ; is undeserved on my part, comes from love. This will make us use things as we should, to the glory of the Giver, and it will make us comfortable in all conditions, as grace. And labour, as the apostle doth here, to see them abundant graces, to raise the favours of God to an high esteem, as Paul doth here : 'It is abundant grace.' And that we may think the grace of God is great, considering to whom he hath denied it. Hath not he denied it to thousands ? Therefore we have abundant grace in us, with great opposition ; therefore an abundant grace. Consider the designs of the devil and devilish-minded men, who would have the church trampled under foot. Is it not above our worth ? Do we deserve so much ? Oh no ! Then it is 'abundant grace.' We that deserve nothing should be thankful for everything, as a beggar that deserveth nothing is thankful for every little gift. Labour thus to see a grace in everything, and labour to see an abundant grace.

The graces of God bestowed on St Paul raiseth up thankfulness of many, and that tendeth to the glory of God. Many had the prayers of St Paul,* for he had commended himself to their prayers: Rom. xv. 30, 'Strive with God for me by prayer;' and so the Philippians and others, 'I shall be delivered by your prayers,' Philem. ver. 22. It was usual with Paul to commend himself to the church and people of God; and having done so, he knew that of course they would praise God. As he desires them to pray for him, that God would be present with him in trouble, and deliver him out, so he knew they would praise God. And as many prayers for him, so many praises for him; and therefore, 'through the thanksgiving of many,' &c.

Beloved, here see that the blessing of God bestowed upon public persons, or upon the church, or public persons in the church, should stir up thanks, and many thanks of many persons. Many thanks were given for the grace of God shewed to St Paul.

Reason 1. I said before, that a Christian, when he becometh a true Christian, hath the Spirit of Christ in him, and hath learned self-denial. He can love others, especially public persons that be eminent in their standing for the good of the church, upon whom the good and honour of the church dependeth in a great measure. And therefore you see the Corinth[ian]s praise God for St Paul.

We should therefore labour for *to consider what favours God sheweth to his church, to any public person in the church, magistrates, ministers, or any notable Christian or friend; praise God for his benefits to others.* Thus, in the prophet David's time, the good people made a circle as it were; 'The righteous shall come about me,' and were glad and joyful, and gave praise for his sake, and this made him, Ps. lxvi. 16, say, 'Come hither, ye children, and I will teach you what the Lord hath done for my soul.' He inviteth them to come, and tells them what the Lord hath done for him, that they may praise God. 'The righteous shall hear it and be glad,' Ps. lxiv. 10. And therefore, in the communion of saints, the sweetest communion is the rejoicing and giving of thanks for the good that God doth to others, especially those that be eminent in the church.

Reason 2. Another reason that concerns ourselves is this: *Our good is laid up in the good and prosperity of others;* our good is in the communionship of the church and commonwealth; our private welfare in the public. As it is in the state, so especially in that heavenly commonwealth of the church, the communion of saints, the good of one dependeth on the good of the other. Why? Because God deriveth and conveyeth all good to man by man. It is his ordinance, he will have it so. And therefore, considering he deriveth good to men by men, therefore, when he sheweth any favour unto men, we ought to praise God for it, because God deriveth good by that man to us. A Christian is a public good, because he hath a public mind. When any favour he hath of God, he is sure the public shall be the better for it, he will be useful, he will be serviceable. As soon as ever a man is a Christian, he becomes as a tree of righteousness; and therefore, if you see favours bestowed upon any good man, thank God for it, especially if it be a Paul, a blessed instrument on whom the good of many dependeth.

Therefore, what shall we say of them that be led by the spirit of envy, that think they have the less the more others have, that have an ill eye? Oh, beloved, take away that cursed spirit of envy! That that I have is thine, and that that thou hast is mine; in religion, there is a kind of blessed community. The more thou hast the more I have. If thy envy

* Qu. 'St Paul had the prayers of many'?—G.

hinder thee not, and if envy be taken away, the more thou hast the more I have. Oh take heed of this cursed spirit, that hinders us from praising God for the good of others; as Paul doth here, that saith, God shall have praise, and many praises for his goodness shewed to me.

Now, he saith many praises, because many had prayed. When they receive the harvest of prayers, they are thankful. You know prayer is a sowing in God's bosom. Prayer is a seed. So many prayers, so many seeds sown in heaven. When the harvest comes, when they see the fruit and issue of their prayers, then they praise God.

If we will therefore praise God, learn this one thing, for *to observe what we pray for;* not to pray at random and never to observe whether God answers or no, that we may be able to render his tribute due to him. How he answers our prayers for the church, for the special instruments of the church's good, king, and state; how he answers our prayers for our particular friends; and then let him have the tribute that he requires of every one, which is only praise. There is a kind of friendship between God and us, by which we enter into covenant with him; and friendship is maintained by duty, by returning of whatsoever we receive. Now, when we pray to God, and have this blessing, and that blessing, and give nothing to God again, friendship will not be maintained without. When men are graves for benefits, to bury them, and return nothing again, this dissolveth the bonds of friendship among men, and it dissolveth also that bond with God, when they derive blessed benefits and return nothing back again. Thanks is nothing but a reflection to the favours wherein he hath shined on us first. It is his due, and an echo; therefore, give thanks for blessings to ourselves and others. And to that end, observe how he hears our prayers for ourselves and others.

But how doth the thanksgiving of many redound to the glory of God? Certainly it doth, 'that the thanksgiving of many may redound to the glory of God.' The more heart, the better music in God's ears, the better music and the louder music; the more the prayers are, the more are the praises, Prov. xiv. 28. The wise man saith, 'The glory of a king is in the multitude of his subjects,' and the glory of God is in the multitude of subjects, thankful subjects, that will return praise to him, give him the tribute he requires at our hands; the wages and service is to him the more the better. When a company can, as it were, levy an army, not only in prayers, to offer an holy violence to God, to get a blessing, but when it is gotten to join in company to praise God, Oh it is a blessed sound, a blessed noise in God's ears, when many do it.

Reason. The reason is this, *because there is more abundance of incense.* Prayers and praises be incense, and if the prayer of any one man be powerful with God, of one righteous man, what is the prayer of many righteous men? If the praise of one man be incense, what are the praises of many? 'If where two or three be gathered together, Christ is in the midst of them,' Mat. xviii. 20, what will he do where two or three thousand be gathered? will not he be much more in the midst of them? O beloved, company is excellent here, and therefore as you have it recited well in the psalms, stir up one another to praise the Lord, 'Praise the Lord, O my soul; and all that is within me, praise his holy name,' Ps. ciii. 1. But that is not enough, 'Praise the Lord all his angels, all the creatures.' The holy prophet, he puts a voice into hills, dragons, mountains, rivers, and every creature, that they may praise the Lord, Ps. cxlviii. 7.

But fearing he should not have heart and spirit enough to praise God enough, he stirs up 'sons of Levi, sons of Aaron, angels of heaven, to praise God.' So large was the heart of that blessed man, because he knew if the praises of one would be acceptable, what would the praises of many be? Why have we such narrow hearts? Indeed, God intends our good, God intendeth it, for to make us heavenly-minded, who would otherwise have been like moles in the earth, but in regard of God, that we may think of God, and praise God, and therefore, Ps. xcii., there is a psalm of the Sabbath, wherein is a high exaltation of God's works. And we have the sacrament. Why is it called *eucharist*, the Greek word,* but because it is a praising of God? We having the sacrament are to praise God for the good we have by his body broken, his blood shed; and therefore have cause of the greatest praise that ever was, for the greatest gift that ever was given, 'the Son of man.' It is God's end in Sabbaths, in sacraments, his end in all his favours and blessings both in this and a better life; and therefore let us stir up our hearts, and stir up others to praise God, that thanksgiving may abound by many. But I cannot finish this argument so necessary.

For some rules how to do it I will not go out of the text, because I have spoken of thanksgiving upon every occasion.

If we will praise God, *see that everything be a grace, be a grace and abundant grace*, answerable to the degrees of goodness. The abundant grace indeed is Jesus Christ, who is the gift of gifts, and cause of all gifts, and the good we have by him. The abundant mercy in God is, new birth in Christ. There is the abundant grace. But even in the things of this life, that we have sacraments, ministers, helps to heaven, is abundant grace. Beloved, whatsoever we have more than hell by nature, it is all grace; and when we be Christians, and delivered from fear of hell, whatsoever is overplus is a grace. If we were poor all our life, and miserable all our life, what were it? But when to our way to heaven God giveth double portions, mercy here, and abundant hereafter, here is 'abundant redundant grâce.' Therefore if we will be thankful, see grace and abundant love in everything. And consider the circumstances that increase the favours of God in Christ towards us, when we were unworthy, when we deserved the contrary. It came in opposition of the enemy; it came when we had much comfort in it, being stripped of all other comforts. See it come from the spring of God's favour, and see all the sweet circumstances of it, and that will make us thankful.

And then consider *it is all we can do or need to do*. It is just we should do it. God needeth not our thanks or praises, but it is justice on our part. Is it not just that we should return praise, 'that rivers should run into the sea, from whence they came?' that beams should reflect to the sun, from whence they came? An unthankful person is an unjust person. Therefore stir up others, that the thanksgiving may be by many.

But now ye see what cause he gave the church to be thankful. Beloved, if we have† the Spirit of God; and if we consider the churches abroad to whom is not only grace, but to us also, we being all the spouse of one husband, branches of one root, heirs of one inheritance, sheep of one flock and pasture, all as from one head; whatsoever God doth, and whatsoever favours he sheweth to our brethren beyond the seas, there is grace, and abundant grace shewed. And now there ought to be thanksgiving, and 'thanksgiving of many,' if there were many prayers, and for the church. Every one that hath the spirit of prayer, hath many prayers for the church

* That is, εὐχαριστία.—G.

† Misprinted 'had.'—G.

of God. And so much humiliation for the misery of the church, that, as the psalmist saith, 'lay among the pots,' Ps. lxviii. 13, as scullions do, all besmeared and all bedaubed with misery. But now God hath brought it from 'among the pots, and covered it with silver wings,' the wings of a dove, and begins to restore beauty and excellency to the church. As we were then ready to pour forth our prayers in the behalf of the church, now let us labour to have our hearts enlarged for his mercy to the church, that there may be thanksgiving, and thanksgiving of many. This is our duty, and all that have the Spirit of God will do it.

Thus the saints of God have done at all times. You see when the ark was brought into Jerusalem, how David forgot himself and kingly state, and danced before the ark, so far that Michal his wife scoffed at him, 2 Sam. vi. 14, *seq.* And so we should rejoice so, as if we had forgot ourselves, especially them that it nearly concerneth ; as it concerneth us all, indeed, as if we were in their case, we would desire others to rejoice in our behalfs. Prayers went 'out of Zion.' God blessed the church out of our Church of England ; our prayers did help them. An army of prayers is as good as an army of fighters. Now as an army of prayers went out of our Zion, so let an army of praises go out of our Zion : 'Praises wait for thee in Zion,' saith the psalmist, Ps. lxv. 1.

When there is matter of praise, make the best use of it. We have waited for matter of praise, we have waited for good news, and we have news. Now as God hath helped out of Zion, so let us help with our praises, for praises help as well as prayer. As in the story of Jehoshaphat, after they had praised God in solemn special manner, the victory came, 2 Chron. xx. 21. Now praises prevail more than prayers, for there is more self-denial in praises than in prayer. God hath more honour, and all his attributes to him, whereas self-love may move a man to pray. Therefore, I beseech you, as we have helped them with our prayers, so help them with our praises to God, for that will help them still farther and farther. When God sees he gaineth a return by our praises, we shall have matter of praise more and more, and still cause to pray that we have an heart to praise ; and praises shall be evermore a pleasing obligation to God. But a place of all places is, Rev. xix., where you see a voice in heaven crying to God to avenge the blood of his saints, on that man of sin, and that cursed seat there ; how all creatures in heaven and earth, they have their alleluiahs against these things. 'I heard a great voice and much people in heaven,' that is, the church, say, 'Alleluiahs ! Salvation, glory, and honour, and power, be given to the Lord our God,' much people. Here is many thanksgiving. When antichrist begins to fall, Babylon to fall, we that belong to the people of God, if we have part in heaven, or any portion in heaven, we will praise God, we will have our alleluiahs. And now because the work is beginning we should join with a choir of heaven, join with the people of God, join with angels, join with all God's people. 'Alleluia ! Salvation, glory, honour, and power, be to the Lord our God.' Why, what is the reason ? 'For true and righteous are his judgments ; he hath judged the great whore, which corrupted the earth with her abominations.' And again 'they cried, Alleluia. And her smoke rose up for ever and ever ;' and so 'the four and twenty elders fell down and worshipped God. Alleluia. Praise God all ye servants, ye that fear him, both small and great,' praise and glorify God, and let all, small and great, in heaven and earth, join in praises. If we had any wise consideration what God is working now in heaven, how he exalts himself, what excellent attributes he sheweth in delivering his church, of power, and justice, and mercy in destroying his enemies; if we have divine spirits, let us sing forth praises to God, expecting by God's blessing more matter to praise God, to sing alleluiahs as the church did there.

VERSES 16–18.

For which cause we faint not; but though our outward man perish, yet the inward man is renewed day by day. For our light affliction, which is but for a moment, worketh for us a far more exceeding weight of glory; while we look not at the things which are seen, but at the things which are not seen: for the things which are seen are temporal; but the things which are not seen are eternal.

A little to touch the two former verses, for they are a part of that heavenly comfort whereby the holy apostle raiseth up his spirit in the midst of all discouragements, multiplying comfort upon comfort, as trouble upon trouble.

Verse 16, 'But we do not faint; though our outward man perish, yet our inward man is renewed day by day.' 'We do not faint.' Indeed, if we look upon outward causes, there is great reason why we should faint. For if we look within, nature is weak, the suggestions of the flesh strong since the fall; and then we are usually beset with temptations of discouragements in our particular calling, thinking we could do anything better than that we are called unto. This is an heavy temptation. And if it were to do such a thing, or such a thing, it might more easily be done. And then hard usage from the ungrateful world; when a man doth any good he receiveth ill for it.

These are great grounds of fainting, but the apostle saith he faints not for all this, 'though our outward man perish.' He grants that the outward man, body and condition, strength and health, may grow more and more downward; but the inward man, the soul, is under the guidance of the Spirit of God, that is, renewed day by day. The outward man consumes continually, death and life work together, we die as soon as we live. As he that hath a lease, every day it is shorter and shorter, and while we live we die, and the more we live the more we die. Death is at the last moment, the candle is going out continually till it be spent. Nay, more, let a man use his body never so holily, let him endure many crosses, the outward man will perish; it must be so.

But where is the comfort? 'The inward man is renewed day by day.' The inward man is the sanctified soul. All the graces of God are renewed, they are upheld under a consuming condition of the outward man. This is the blessed condition of a true Christian, that when he groweth downward he groweth another way. He doth not wholly perish as a base wretch doth, but as he decayeth in one part he reneweth in another. God by his Spirit reneweth him. For as in the body the Spirit is that which giveth a life to what we do, so the Spirit of God giveth a vigour to the inward man day by day.

But when is this, that the inward man is renewed day by day? In the time of affliction, for then we grow most; for in time of prosperity, then we grow backward. Usually in time of prosperity, when all things are according to our will and desire, we go backwards; but when the outward man decayeth, the inward man is renewed day by day. We decay in prosperity, but we grow in adversity; as a body shoots out more after sickness than before. Why should we then be afraid of sickness and weakness of body, considering it is a time of growth of the inward man? Mark the gracious goodness of God. When he takes away strength, because we are not for this life, he makes it up, working strength and vigour in the inward man. We owe God a death. Since we must die, is it not better the decay be made up in the inward man? If we gain that which is gain to the soul, though with weakness and sickness to the outward man, it is well gained, because that is for eternity.

But this is a constant course with God. He is so good, he never takes away anything from his children, but he giveth it another away. Shall we then be discouraged when God takes strength, and he makes it up in the inward man? If anything be a ground of patience, this is. Whatsoever God doth to his children, there is love hid in the doing of it. If he give comfort, it is to encourage. Doth he follow us with crosses? It is that we may grow in the inward man. If we had hearts to follow God in his dealing, we should lose nothing but that he takes away.

Verse 17, 'For our light affliction, which is but for a moment, works a far more exceeding weight of glory.' Here is a ground of comfort to those that are in any crosses and afflictions. Whatsoever they suffer, it works glory, it works happiness; it is set out by glory. Now the Spirit of God sets out this estate of a Christian to come by way of comparison to anything that we suffer. Here are afflictions, here is glory; momentary afflictions, eternal glory; light afflictions, a weight of glory; and not only a weight, but a superlative, an exceeding weight of glory. So the Spirit of God meets with all discouragements here, for we can suffer nothing here, but we shall have better for it after. Grace is glory, but mixed with imperfection. What are those things we suffer here in this world, to glory, and eternal glory, and excessive glory? What cause have we to be discouraged for anything we suffer here?

But he saith afterwards, 'causeth unto us an eternal weight of glory.' That is more than to say glory follows afflictions; but there is a causal virtue in that we suffer, to work glory. We know the working by way of merit and desert, that is done by Christ; we have right to glory only by Christ. And it is sacrilege to attribute it to any creature, but when there is a working power fitting us. Now afflictions working by way of fitting us to that glory, whereto we have title by Christ, as soon as a man is a Christian, he hath title to heaven. But how doth God fit us for heaven? One way is by crosses and afflictions. He fits us for heaven, as the winter fitteth the ground for the spring, by killing the weeds, and mellowing the ground. So that whatsoever we suffer here, fits us for heaven, and that many ways.

(1.) *By weaning our hearts from the love of these things, upon which we are desperately set.* When we see what they are, we see they are vanity.

(2.) And then again, *they exercise and try our graces, and they increase a desire of heaven;* and we know the more hardly we are used here, the more we desire to be at home. And usually God reveals himself more sweetly and more comfortably in these hard times. We feel more of heaven in our worst times. Therefore they have fitting power.

Quest. How comes this to pass? Are crosses, losses, curses, and such things naturally?

Ans. God by his Spirit doth overpower and overrule these things, and there is a sanctified use of them, that helps them to work. 'All things work together for the best to them that love God,' Rom. viii. 28; that is, God's power so overruleth them, that it makes them advantageous to his children. And they by the grace of God's Spirit, draw a sanctified use out of everything. So that by the grace of God the worst things work an eternal weight of glory.

As God prepares heaven for us, so he prepares us for heaven: he prepares us by Christ, but by the cross and affliction. So you may see the truth of the point.

Use 1. *But what shall I speak of popish merits?* For in merits there must be a proportion to the things we suffer. We receive glory for ever, and suffer afflictions for a time; a weight of glory. This overthrows popish conceits.

Use 2. Beloved, are they not out of their wits, *that add vexation to God's children?* What is the worst they do? They work their good, they vex them; ay, but they work their happiness, as if a man would hurt a fish by casting him into the sea, or a bird into the air. And a Christian being vexed, it driveth him nearer to heaven. It is his best condition. Compare our secure estate with our afflicted condition, and see which is best. There is no man that is a Christian but will say, there is more in the cross than in prosperity; the one dulleth, but the other sharpeneth.

Use 3. *Be not discouraged, whatsoever befalls us in this world.* While Satan works our hurt, God is then working our good at the same time. When the outward man is wronged by the world, at the same time the inward man is set at liberty. So much for that.

But how cometh it to pass that these things we suffer, fit us for glory?

Verse 18. It is wrought by grace, enabling us to eye things that are not seen. And then we reason, 'because the things that are seen, are temporal, but the things that are not seen, are eternal,' 2 Cor. iv. 18.

To omit divers things, I hasten to other things.

But you see the things we suffer do work unto us an eternal weight of glory, as physic doth upon the body. That that we suffer doth no good unless we use those parts and graces that God hath given us. And therefore he saith, whilst our minds are occupied, and 'looking on things that are not seen,' God having made man a reasonable creature. And so in way to salvation he sanctifieth those principles he hath given him to bring him to heaven, by way of discourse and reason. And as a Christian is saved, so is he saved by something in his understanding. As we see in this world, man worketh by principles in him, so in the way of Christianity. Some things are hindrances to heaven and happiness, as conceitedness and self-sufficiency. Therefore the apostle saith these things 'work an eternal weight of glory,' not whether we think of them or no; but these things do so because God giveth a sanctified understanding, to see the difference of heavenly things from earthly, when we do not look upon things that are seen.

So much shall serve to give you a reason how to see the inward man groweth more and more, and we faint not; because we look upon things that are not seen.

That which I will speak of at this time is this.

That the best things in this world are not seen; the meanest things are those that are seen. The best things are to come; the meanest things are present. The best things are such as are eternal; the meanest things are temporal.

And when I have unfolded these, then I will shew you a wise and gracious use the sanctified soul makes of looking upon things that are not seen, and how his sight worketh, what use we are to make of it.

Doct. The observation is, *that a Christian is to look to the things not seen, for things seen are not the object of a Christian's eye.* The best things are not seen; the meanest things are such as are seen. I will not stand to unfold the negative part much, because I have spoken of that before.

But to speak especially, What are the things that are not seen?

Beloved, if you labour to be good Christians, you shall better feel them than I can tell you what they are; you shall better know them by experience than by discourse here.

(1.) *We cannot see God face to face.* We have not immediate communion with God here. We have it in the word and sacraments; but in heaven we shall see all things that are good. Here we may see God in everything; there we shall see everything in God. There we shall see health, and strength, and comfort in God.

(2.) The things not seen here *is Christ in our flesh.* The heavens are between us and him now. The sight of him is the happiness of a Christian, for the head and members to be together, husband and wife together. Ay, but here we are severed. Here is a spiritual communion; but that is not that that the soul looks for.

(3.) Neither have we *full communion of saints;* for here is a mixture of good and bad, and here the best have their imperfections. If here an holy joining together of two or three wise Christians be so sweet, what shall it be when we all meet together in heaven? Now we see not God, and Christ, and the blessed souls in heaven.

(4.) Here we see not *our perfect liberty.*

(5.) Here we see not *that eternal Sabbath we shall have there.*

(6.) Here we see not *that perfection of grace.*

(7.) Here we see not *that comfort we shall have there.* Here we have a taste and the beginning, but what is this to that there? Therefore let us think of what is not seen.

Obj. But why do we not see them here?

Reason 1. *You may as well ask me, Why is not heaven upon earth? God will have a difference between heaven and earth;* he will have us to walk by faith and not by sight. Heaven is a place for sight: if we will have happiness in sight, it is in heaven. But here we have hope, and faith, and some feeling of comfort; and therefore, considering our condition is by faith, therefore God preserveth matter of sight for another world.

Reason 2. Again, the best things are not seen, *because we have not proportionable parts.* Our parts are not fitted for that glory. Peter, James, and John, they were as it were drunken with this sight, so that Peter speaks he knows not what, Mat. ix. 33. And Moses, when he came from God, he was fain to cover his face, 2 Cor. iii. 13. If these glimpses were such as people could not endure them, how could we endure a full manifestation of glory, when Christ saith, 'No man can see God and live'? Exod. xxxiii. 20. Therefore let us be content to die to have this sight. Our understandings here are too shallow, our hearts too narrow, our imperfections too many: darkness cannot conceive of light. So no soul can see what is in heaven.

And so here we cannot tell what happiness there is, till we be there. That is the reason why the best things are not seen. And these are the proper objects of a Christian. For things seen are exposed to the outward man; they are not fitting for the soul. The soul will soon spend all the good that are in things seen. Take all the beauty, and all the riches, and all the honour that can be, and the soul will be quickly weary of it. The soul will draw out all the good. We see those that are in great place, within a little while grow weary of them.

But there is an everlasting spring of comfort and contentment in things not seen. They are larger than the soul. The more we see of them, the more we may see; the communion with God, joys in heaven, and such things. Alas! the soul is a very capacious thing, yet the joys in heaven are larger than it; therefore things seen are not the object of the soul.

Quest. But doth the soul never look upon things that are seen?

Ans. Yes; but if the soul look upon them, it looks also beyond them.

If it look upon them, it looks upon them as in a glass, to see farther. It looketh not upon them as clouds to stay our sight from the sun, or as placing contentment in them. For the soul taketh no rest here. The things seen 'are vanity and vexation of spirit,' Eccles. i. 14; 'unrighteous mammon,' Luke xvi. 11. We may and ought to look upon them as helps and comforts in our pilgrimage. If there be such comforts here, what is in heaven? Doth God convey such sweetness in outward things, that cast-aways have with us? What are those then that he hath reserved for his friends? And so by way of a gracious use we ought to look upon things seen; but to pitch upon them, and make them our bottom to stand upon, they are no fit objects for the soul. But is there no way to see things that are not seen?

Quest. But have we nothing of them here?

Ans. Yes; there is nothing seen but we have some little taste of it here. For full peace to come, we have peace of conscience here. For full joy to come, we have joy in the Holy Ghost here. For full communion of saints to come, we have some communion of saints here. If there be any heaven upon earth, it is in the meeting of two or three judicious, wise, gracious persons; and our employment here in hearing, praying, and conference with God is but a taste beforehand of that in heaven. So that God doth not reserve all for the time to come. But in regard of the full accomplishment he doth. But those that have not the first-fruits here shall never have heaven in the harvest. Those that have not the earnest here shall never have the bargain hereafter. But that which is the full satisfaction of the soul is for hereafter. Therefore, whatsoever sweet employment is here, it is not like to that the soul shall have hereafter. Therefore rest not in them, but rather let them set an edge upon us, to desire it more and more, till we have it fully in heaven.

Reason 3. Why these objects are things not seen. Things *that are not seen are eternal, things that are seen are temporal.* No man that hath an eternal soul, and knoweth it, will make that his object that is temporal. Therefore the soul must look upon things that are of equal excellency with it, and that is, things not seen. For things that are seen are temporal: riches are fading, honours are but blazing comets, pleasures are but worm-eaten vanities. So for the ill we suffer, it is but temporal; all determined in death. The grave makes an end of all things that are seen. This should be a comfort to us when we are under any sickness. It is a seen thing. This sickness I feel, and this I taste, it is but for a time. The thing I look at is that which is not seen, and which lasteth to eternity. So the good not seen is eternal in the cause of it. It is in Christ, who is for ever in the heavens; and God is for ever in the heavens: and Christ reconcileth the Father. And then the place is eternal. Heaven is eternal.

Now the influence from which all good comes being eternal, the soul being itself a spiritual, eternal substance, the influence of grace and comfort being eternal from God, and Christ, who is an head for ever and a husband for ever; and heaven being an inheritance immortal, undefiled, continuing for ever; and the soul being an everlasting substance, the joy and comforts of it are eternal. Whom God loveth, he loveth for ever; whom he makes happy, he makes happy for ever. 'He is life everlasting.' It is a kingdom 'that cannot be shaken,' Heb. xii. 27. 'It is an inheritance that fadeth not,' 1 Peter i. 4. It is not only everlasting, but everlastingly fresh. It is not only immortal, but it keeps its beauty still, eternal joy, eternal peace, eternal communion one with another in the heavens, everlasting Sabbath, everlasting triumph over all enemies. There is no end of this joy, no cessation of this comfort.

I come now to the wise improvement that the soul makes of beholding the things that are not seen, because they be eternal, and neglecteth the sight of things that be present and temporal. You see the wise use the blessed apostle maketh of it. For he bringeth it as a reason why he faints not, but is renewed day by day in the inward man. You wonder why I faint not, and why day by day I grow fresher and fresher, and still fitter and fitter for heaven; and that all things I endure here fit me for heaven. All is because I have an eye to things that are not seen, not regarding things that be present. So that if we will find a difference of the things, we may easily understand, some things be fading, and some things eternal. If we will get comfort in this, that our portion is not only in fading things, we must have grace to consider of it, and not to look on the other overmuch.

To give trial, whether we look at the things that be seen or no.

(1.) If we look to things not seen, because they be eternal, *this is a sight that ravisheth the soul*, that lifteth the soul above itself. Things above be so exceeding above things below, that it makes the soul almost forget itself; it worketh an high esteem of heaven, of heavenly things. For as it is said of knowledge, it hath no enemy but the ignorant, so there is no enemy of grace but they that feel it not from conscience.* All that see it have a high admiration of it, which appeareth by the mean esteem of all things else. When the sun riseth, the stars hide themselves. And when these comforts rise in the soul, upon the apprehension of the glory in the glass of the word and promise, and a little feeling here, all earthly comforts are gone. When Moses saw God that was invisible, what cares he to look for Pharaoh? Heb. xi. 27. And when Micaiah had seen God sitting on the throne, what cares he for Ahab? 1 Kings xxii. 14. We have seen the Lord, and what have we to do with base idols? Not anything in the world must be co-rival with God. What have I to do with pride, with riches, with honour? I have seen God, I have seen heaven. When the patriarchs had with the eye of faith seen the excellency of the world to come, what cared they for banishment or death? When Paul had seen Christ, all things else were 'dung and dross,' Philip. iii. 8. Therefore your great admirers, that admire worldly things, it is a sign they never saw better. They that doat upon worldly things, it is an argument of spiritual folly.

(2.) Again, the consideration of things spiritual, *it is a purifying sight*, a purging sight, that makes the soul fit for the object. A man cannot with the eye of faith apprehend things to come, nor by hope wait for them, but that hope will be effectual to purify the soul. They that have any faith, any hope of good to come, they will prepare their souls suitable to that

* That is, 'consciousness.'—Ed.

condition, 1 John iii. 3. And therefore where the apprehension of these things hath not a purging power in some degree, it is but a conceit. We do not so see them as that we be convinced that they are so excellent as they be.

(3.) Again, this is a sight that *doth marvellously affect.* Love comes of sight. Sight is the most affecting sense. That which moveth the affection most is sight. Feeling is but dull. And therefore if we have the eagle's eye, a sharp-sighted faith, to see things which are not to be seen with the eye of reason and flesh, then certainly this sight will quicken and affect a man greatly; move to joy and move to delight, move to the love of God and heavenly things. A man cannot see any excellency but his heart embraceth it; as the patriarchs, Heb. xi. 2, *seq.*, saw the promises afar off, and their hearts did join with them; they did embrace them, grasping as it were the things they saw in the arms of their affections. In what measure that I apprehend and see things, in that measure the heart lets in the things to embrace them and close with them. Therefore where no love is there is no sight. And the reason why affections are so flat and dead is, because they do not exercise this sight of faith. Let us examine ourselves by these things, whether we have spiritual sight of the things we see. Do they affect us? Do they quicken us? And do they put into our hearts holiness? Do they raise our hearts to a holy admiration? If so, certainly we have seen them.

I will give you a familiar comparison. The nearer the object is to any man, the more glorious it seemeth; the farther off anything is, the less it seemeth. The stars are bigger than the world, and yet appear to us little.

Now, ask our souls how great things are in comparison of former times. Are heavenly things greater? And for earthly pomp and state, have they less esteemed them than in former times? It is a sign we are nearer heaven, and heaven nearer us. When we can look upon earthly things in a distance, it is a sign we are removed from them, and drawn nearer to the best things. And then the best things seem to be great to us, when we conceive of them in their own magnitude.

Quest. But how shall we come to look on things not seen, and things eternal, according to their own worth?

Ans. (1.) First of all, *labour every day more and more to be purged and purified,* and then we shall have delight to look upon that which is proportionable. The holier a man is, the more delight he hath in holy and heavenly objects, and laboureth to grow in grace more and more. The more we see, the more gracious we are; the more gracious we are, the more desire we shall have to behold with the eye of faith these excellencies.

There is no apprehension without light. We cannot see light without light; we cannot see heavenly things without heavenly faculties. And therefore labour for something within gracious, which may have correspondency and harmony with what is in heaven, else contraries will not apprehend contraries. But heaven and a sanctified soul have some proportion and co-naturalness; and therefore never rest till we have something like that which is in heaven, though not in degree, yet in quality.

Ans. (2.) Again, labour *to get the eye of the soul clear; that the dust of the world may not be in it.* Satan's policy is to cast pleasure and profit into the eye of the soul; and then corruption raiseth a foggy mist in the soul, that we should have natural love to present things. And present things raise a cloud in the soul, and that cloud doth interpose itself between heaven and us. Labour therefore for mortification more and more.

That the eye may be clear, consider seriously they be temporal things;

shorter than the soul, meaner than the soul, not fit for it. We shall outlive them all. And when base affections rise in the soul to cast a mist thereupon, consider what a foolish thing it is for us to doat upon things meaner than ourselves. Why should such affections intercept this heavenly sight from us?

The dignity of the soul is an excellent substance. The whole world is not worth a soul. The soul is between heaven and earth, and all earthly things are meaner than itself. Shall the soul marry itself and join itself with things baser than itself? Doth it not then debase itself? And therefore keep the eye of the soul clear from impediments within and without; labour to have true judgment of things in their own nature.

Ans. (3.) And then let us *dwell often in the consideration of things to come; have serious considerations of it, and every day redeem some time to think we cannot live here for ever.* We have an immortal soul, that must be immortal in misery or immortal in happiness. If we be not good, heaven will not take us, and nothing but hell will receive us. And these things may quicken us. I have an immortal soul, I must not stay long, I must give account; and how shall I appear?

Get these and the like considerations every day. We live as we see; and considering life is guided by inward notions and apprehensions of soul, labour to have apprehensions of soul, that may guide the life as it should be. Labour to see what is reserved in the heavens; consider how we be assured for it; what ground we have; what assurance we have if we should die presently, for we have not the certainty of a minute. These be wakening considerations. And these will be a means that we should look on things not seen. And when we do take liberty to think upon these things, dwell upon them till the heart be warmed. The sun doth not heat without some staying. Those beams that are broken, they do not gather themselves to heat by reflection. So let the soul stay a while in consideration of these things. Our soul is unstable naturally; and therefore labour by grace to settle the soul till the affections be warm, till the resolutions be pitched; for then we shall see to purpose when we resolve to take this course, else we see not to purpose. And therefore because we know not in morning what will befall us before night, never rest till we be set in heaven by faith. And consider the condition there, so far forth as shall be effectual to guide our lives suitable to what we see. This were a wise course indeed, to guide our courses suitable to eternity, and to fetch reasons for a holy and good life from eternity, and not from pleasing this body and that body. I will do this, because I shall get riches, because I shall satisfy my flesh, and raise myself. Are these reasons for a Christian to work by? Let a Christian work like a Christian, having his reason raised by faith higher than himself, to consider of things as they are in themselves, and as they shall be hereafter. This is temporal, my soul is eternal; and I will fetch my reasons of my course from eternity. What if I should have all the world and die, what will the satisfying of the carnal desires of others do me good? And therefore I will sway my actions by rule that shall hold to eternity. Is not a man wise that doth thus? and is any man wise that doth not thus? He is wise that guideth his life to the last end, how he shall be happy hereafter, how he shall avoid torments for ever. He that is wise to get preferment, to undermine others, to flatter and insinuate, to give contentment against conscience to the carnal humours of others; is he a wise man that is penny wise and pound foolish? He is wise in a particular, he is wise in a little.

But what is this particular wisdom, when in the general scope of his life he is foolish, not considering what is good for him as a Christian? None is wise but a Christian. Every man else is a mad man, or a fool. What are all other things but straw and baubles to eternity? Therefore regard the things that be beyond the soul, and more excellent than the soul.

I beseech you, take this course. It will make us wise and diligent in our place and calling; for we should eye what is to eternity, notwithstanding all discouragements. Many have fainted and given over, because they be unthankful persons, and they grow cold in doing good. What is the reason? They look not to eternity. It is good sometimes to meet with ill usage from unthankful persons, for God will make amends, though we deserve well of ungrateful persons. And sometimes again I will do them good, and let the glory alone to God. It is good to meet with ill usage in the world; for there is sufficient amends made in the world to come. Wilt thou have all thy wages here? And therefore do as St Paul did, get into heaven in our thoughts by faith, and meditation how it will be with us ere long; and that will set us in such a frame of conversation as shall fit us for Christ, and only that. It will keep us in a growing condition, in a fruitful condition, in a constant courageous condition.

And when we do not so we fall into discouragements. The cause of sin, is it not some present temporal thing we doat upon? So sin is nothing but placing that affection on that which is temporal, which should be on that which is eternal.

Now when doth a man sin, but when he lets go his object? As long as a man keeps his eye on heaven he is well enough; but when he looks to discouragements, to the arm of flesh, then he is discouraged. But when is he not discouraged? When he hath heaven in his eye, and God in his eye, and spiritual things in his eye. And now in this pitch he is neither sinful nor discouraged; and then he is as well as he can wish in this world. Therefore labour with Paul to have the eyes of your souls exercised about these spiritual things. Look on things that be not seen, because they be eternal; and be not carried away with outward things, nor dazzled with them, because they be temporal.

NOTES.

(*a*) P. 309.—'Luther was wont to say, If he were to choose his calling, he would dig with his hands rather than be a minister.' In the midst of his superabounding labours, even the stout heart of the great Reformer was sometimes like to give way under the 'care of all the churches,' when he sighed for the lowly toil of the miner; as appears from various of his 'Table Talk' sayings, though I have not been able to trace the exact words ascribed to him by Sibbes. Cf. note *uu*, Vol. III. page 533.

(*b*) P. 309.—'The disposition both of speakers and hearers, saith Chrysostom, makes this work difficult,' &c. (De Sacerd., lib. v.) Such is the reference in the margin. The whole fifth book of the *De Sacerdote*, is on the difficulties of the ministerial work, from the relation in which the preacher stands to the people; the dangers of popularity, and the discouragements of unpopularity. The summing up is as follows:—

'Ει μὲν ὄυν τίς ἐστιν ἀνθρώπων τοιουτος, ὡς δύνασθαι τὸ δυσθήρατον τοῦτο καὶ ἀκαταγώνιστον καὶ ἀνήμερον θηρίον, τὴν τῶν πολλῶν δόξαν καταπατεῖν, καὶ τὰς πολλὰς αὐτῆς ἐκτεμειν κεφαλὰς, μᾶλλον δὲ μηδε φῦναι τὴν ἀρχὴν συγχωρεῖν, δυνήσεται εὐκόλως, καὶ τὰς πολλὰς ταυτας ἀποκρόυεσθαι προσβολὰς, και ἐυδίου τινὸς ἀπο-

λαύειν λιμένος. Ταυτῆς δὲ οὐκ ἀπηλλαγμένος, πολεμόν τινα πολυειδῆ, καὶ θόρυβον συνεχῆ, καὶ ἀθυμίας, καὶ τῶν λοιπῶν παθῶν τὸν ὄχλον κατασκευάζει τῆς ἑαυτοῦ ψυχῆς.

(*c*) P. 309.—'Alas! how many think the work is done when the glass is out.' The allusion is to the hour-glass placed by the side of the pulpit to mark the lapse of time. A rare portrait of the notorious Hugh Peters represents him reversing an hour-glass, with the legend, 'One glass more.' For many interesting and curious *memorabilia* concerning hour-glasses in churches, cf. *Notes and Queries*. In illustration of the lamentation of Sibbes, I quote the following from Philip Goodwin's 'Evangelical Communicant':—'It is reported of a good man, that coming home from a public lecture, and being asked by one whether the sermon were ended, made this answer, fetching a deep sigh: "Ah! it is said, but not done." And to speak truth, the sermon cannot be said to be *done* till it be *practised*. But herein the Lord be merciful to most of us. We are apt to think that when a sacrament-day is over, all the sacrament duties are over too; when the discourse from the pulpit is finished, the sermon is finished; as if when the ordinance were at an end, there were an end of the ordinance, and of us with the ordinance also. Audire est obedire. *Isidore*.'

(*d*) P. 309.—'God would have the very snuffers in the tabernacle *pure gold*.' (See Exodus xxxvii. 23.) For a very effective enlargement of this thought, cf. 'The Golden Snuffers: or Christian Reprovers and Reformers characterised, cautioned, and encouraged. By Daniel Burgess.' 12mo. 1697.

(*e*) P. 315.—'You know there was a primitive light; *lux primogenita*, as Basil calls it.' The reference is as follows:—'Lux primogenita. Τοῦ πρωτογόνου φωτὸς ἐκείνου.' Basil in Hexaëm, Hom. ii. § 8, tom. i. p. 20. Ben. Ed. Milton translates this phrase in his invocation to Light at beginning of Book III. of Paradise Lost.

> 'Hail, holy Light, offspring of heaven first born,
> Or of the Eternal co-eternal beam,
> May I express thee unblam'd? since God is light,
> And never but in unapproached light,
> Dwelt from eternity, dwelt then in thee,
> Bright effluence of bright essence uncreate.'

(*f*) P. 316.—'Therefore Ambrose calleth it, *Lux prima gratia mundi*.' See Ambrose Hexaëm, lib. i. c. ix.

(*g*) P. 323.—'Therefore Saint Ambrose saith well, *Christus umbra in Lege, imago in Evangelio, veritas in cœlo*' This will be found in Ambrose, *in Psalm* xxxviii. § 25. For 'in cœlo' he has 'in cœlestibus.'

(*h*) P. 331.—'He is the first-fruits of God's predestination, as Austin observeth.' See Exposit. Epist. ad Rom. Inchoat lib. i., 'Ergo ille tanquam Filius Dei unigenitus, etiam primogenitus ex mortuis predestinatus est, ex resurrectione mortuorum.'

(*i*) P. 341.—'As Lactantius saith well, "All morality without piety is as a goodly statue without a head." See *Div. Inst.* lib. vi. c. ix. 'Omnis enim justitia ejus similis erit humano corpori caput non habenti.'

(*j*) P. 355.—'As candles that have thieves in them.' That is, little bits of the wick that have got into the body of the candle, causing sputtering and waste. In nearly every country, the oddest superstitions are linked with such 'thieves;' *e. g.*, a large one that has melted a considerable portion, was in Scotland called a 'shroud,' and foretokened death.

(*k*) P. 361.—'The fishermen cast their great nets into the great world, as Austin saith, and got in whole nations.' The following is the passage:—'Acceperunt (Apostoli) ab eo retia verbi Dei, miserunt in mundum tanquam in mare profundum, ceperunt quantam multitudinem Christianorum cernimus et miramur.' *Serm. de temp.*, c. xviii. Fer. 4 Paschæ, Serm. i.

(*l*) P. 367.—'It [the sword of the Spirit, = the Bible]. is no leaden dagger, as the papists blasphemously term it.' A commonplace of the popish controversy.

(*m*) P. 368.—'It is difficult as for a camel, so for a cable too.' The word Κάμιλον, which signifies a cable-rope to which sailors attach the ship's anchor, is supposed by many to be the proper reading in Mat. xix. 24, and to have been changed by an error of transcription into Κάμηλος, a camel. Sibbes refers to both readings. For erudite and elaborate annotation upon the passage with special reference to Κάμιλον and Κάμηλος, consult Nicolaides' Evangelical and Exegetical Commentary upon Select portions of the New Testament, founded on the writings of Nicephoros Theotoces, vol. i. pp. 181–186, London, 1860.

(*n*) P. 379.—'*Nolo hanc gratiam.* I will not this grace (saith one of the ancients), that leaveth the will to be flexible, and at liberty.' Augustine has this sentiment in every variety of expression in his great Controversies with the Donatists.

(*o*) P. 380.—'Therefore, as they say very well, he worketh *suaviter et fortiter*; *suaviter*, by entreaty, agreeable to the nature of man; and *fortiter*, powerfully.' Sibbes probably has reference to the Latin proverbial saying—'Suaviter in modo, fortiter in re.'

(*p*) P. 380.—'The birth of thy womb is as the dew of the morning.' So the best translators have it. For the different renderings as well as interpretations of this obscure verse consult Dr Joseph Addison Alexander on the Psalms *in loc.* Sibbes's seems rather an exegesis of the words than a translation.

(*q*) P. 385.—'As Augustine saith well, *Volentem hominem salvum facere*, when God will save a man, no stubbornness of his will shall withstand,' &c. The often-repeated adoring acknowledgment of this illustrious father in reverting to his own conversion after obstinate resistance. Cf. 'The Confessions' throughout.

(*r*) P. 392.—'And therefore it is true that is usually spoken, that where God will defend a city and country, a cobweb may be the walls thereof; but where God will not defend a city or country, a wall is but a cobweb.' The allusion here is to an incident in the history of St Felix of Nola. The legend runs, that this saint, being hotly pursued at the close of the Decian persecution, took refuge behind a ruinous old wall, the aperture through which he passed being almost immediately covered with a large spider's web. His enemies not imagining that any person could have entered a spot which was so closely covered by a tender fabric which ordinarily requires much time for its completion, missed their prey; and the saint, reflecting upon the mode of his escape from his blood-thirsty pursuers, observed, that 'with Christ's presence a spider's web becomes a wall; if he be absent, a wall is no better than a spider's web. *Præsente Christo, aranea fit murus: absente Christo, murus fit aranea.* The circumstances are recorded by Paulinus (A. D. 398) in a poem, *De Sancto Felice Martyre, Natalis* V., of which the following lines refer to the event already mentioned:—

'Et capiendus erat, quia nullius obice claustri,
Ille repellendis locus obsistebat iniquis.
Nam foribus nullis in publica rostra patebat
Semiruti paries malefidus fragmine muri.
Sed divina manus Sese sanctum inter et hostes
Opposuit, miroque locum munimine sepsit;
Non strue saxorum, neque ferratis data valvis
Claustra, per humanas quibus atria claudimus artes
Rudere sed subito concrevit sordidus agger,
Jussaque nutantes intendit aranea telas,
Et sinibus tremulis in totum struxit apertum,
Desertæque dedit faciem sordere ruinæ.
Quæ simul occurrit minitantibus, obstupuerunt,
Defixoque gradu, simul et dixere vicissim:
Nonne furor tentare aditus, aut credere quemquam
Hac intrasse hominem, minimi qua signa dedissent
Vermiculi? Modicæ rumpunt hæc retia muscæ,
Nos penetrasse virum per clausa putamus inepti,
Et tenerum tanto non ruptum corpore textum?'

The saint is then introduced as saying,—

'Vana salus hominum, virtus mea non mihi virtus,
Si caream virtute Dei. Quo vasta gigantum
Robora? quo Pharii regis? ubi magna Hierichus?
Omnibus exitio sua gloria, qua tumuerunt,
Cassa fuit. Neque vero suis virtutibus ista,
Sed magis infirmis divina potentia fregit.
Ille gigas pueri funda pastoris obivit,
Ut canis: illam urbem sonitus solvere tubarum;

Littorea jacuit Rex ille superbus arena,
Divitias regni pendens in funere nudo
Sic ubi Christus adest nobis, et aranea muro est
At cui Christus abest, et murus aranea fiet.'

The last couplet may be thus imitated,—

'With Christ, a cobweb is a wall to thee;
Without Him, walls shall but as cobwebs be.

It may be worth mentioning, that like preservation by a spider's web occurs in the life of more than one mediæval saint; and a very similar story respecting a pigeon plays a part in the history of Mahomet.

(*s*) P. 398 —'Saint Austin saith well, Though we live well in times of peace, yet *audi, audi, mi frater*, begin to live as a Christian should live, and see if you be not pursued; you shall find a Babylon in Jerusalem.' Probably the following is the reference:—'Incipiat ergo pie vivere in Christo et probet quod dicitur, incipit desiderare pennas elongare, fugere et manere in deserto.' Enarrat. in Ps. liv. The *thought* occurs several times in his *De Civitate Dei.*

(*t*) P. 398.—'A new moon . . . is *interlunium.*' Milton has grandly Anglicised the word in his famous reference to the moon retiring to her 'vacant *interlunar* cave.' *Sam. Agon.*, ver 89.

(*u*) P. 401.—'It was the speech of Philo, "A man's help faileth where God's begins."' This is represented by our apophthegm, 'Man's extremity is God's opportunity.'

(*v*) P. 401.—'*Christi dolor, dolor maximus.*' Cf. note *u*, Vol. III. page 531.

(*w*) P. 402.—'Comforts are not found in adversity, that were not sought for in prosperity, as Austin saith.' A *thought* which is probably a reminiscence from *De Civitate Dei*, lib. i. *et alibi.*

(*x*) P. 403.—'Saint Austin saith, by straits and afflictions the church hath been delivered, and spread abroad to the utmost parts of the world.' Cf. Augustine under Acts viii. 1, in his Sermons.

(*y*) P. 405.—'As he said, It is a kingly thing to suffer evil,' &c. Antisthenes being told that Plato spoke ill of him, replied, 'It is a royal privilege to do well, and to be evil spoken of.' See Diogenes Laertius *sub voce.* But perhaps Sibbes's reference is to the following sentence from Chrysostom on the words of Paul: Obsecro vos ego vinctus, &c. 'Magna dignitas et multa, regno, consulatu, universisque major, pro Christo ligari.'

(*z*) P. 406.—'Miserable heathens, that had not the knowledge of God in Christ, what condition were they in? As one saith, "I would pray, but my prayers are in vain."' A sentiment that pervades the classics, and barbs the sarcasms of Lucretius.

(*aa*) P. 407.—'The presence of Christ so sweetens everything, as he said, "The presence of Christ made the gridiron sweet unto Laurence."' The *thought* is found in Augustine in S. Laur. Serm. ii. 'Has flammas fidei calore non sentit, et dum Christi precepta cogitat, frigidum est illi omne quod patitur.' Again, 'Dum Christi ardet desiderio, persecutoris pœnam non sentit. Divinus Salvatoris ardor materialem tyranni restinxit ardorem.' (*Ibid.* Serm. i.)

(*bb*) P. 455.—'*Vespertiliones in fide*, as *he* calls them; bats that will neither be amongst the birds or other creatures,' &c. This term is not unfrequent in the vocabulary of abuse of the fathers in their controversies; *e. g.*, Augustine, and also Luther.

(*cc*) P. 457.—'As he said, If thou didst believe these things, wouldst thou speak so of them?' The context seems to have reference to want of interest in the things spoken of, revealed by the listless mode of speaking of them. The *thought*, but not the specific wording, occurs in *Quintilian.* G.

THE CHURCH'S RICHES.

THE CHURCH'S RICHES.

NOTE.

'The Church's Riches' forms one of a collection of four treatises entitled 'Light from Heaven' (4to 1638). Each treatise is independent: and it has been deemed proper to detach the 'Church's Riches,' in order that it may take its place in the Sermons from the Epistles to the Corinthians. The general title-page of the volume and the separate title-page of the 'Church's Riches' will be found below. [* and †] As the 'Church's Riches' is our first contribution from 'Light from Heaven,' the 'Epistle Dedicatory' and 'Address to the Reader,' of the whole volume, is prefixed to it. G.

* LIGHT
FROM
HEAVEN

Discovering

The { Fountaine Opened.
Angels Acclamations.
Churches Riches.
Rich Povertie. }

In foure Treatises.

BY

The late Learned and Reverend Divine,
RICH. SIBS,
Doctor in Divinitie, Master of Katherine Hall
in Cambridge, and sometimes Preacher
at Grayes-Inne.
Published according to the Authors owne
appointment, subscribed with his hand;
to prevent imperfect copies.

Amos 3. 7.
Surely the Lord God will doe nothing, but he revealeth
his secrets to his servants the Prophets.

London,
Printed by E. Purslow for N. Bourne, at the Royall
Exchange, and R. Hartford at the gilt Bible in
Queenes-head Alley in Pater-Noster-Row.
1638.

† THE
CHVRCHES
RICHES
BY
CHRISTS POVERTY

By
The late Learned and Reverend Divine.
RICHARD SIBBS,
Dr. in Divinity, Master of *Katherine*-Hall in
Cambridge, and sometimes Preacher at
GRAIES-INNE.

Luke 9. 58.
The Sonne of man hath not where to lay his head
EPHES. 2. 7.
*That in the ages to come he might shew the exceeding riches
of his grace, &c.*

LONDON,
Printed by *R. Badger* for *N. Bourne* at the Royall
Exchange, and *R. Harford* at the gilt *Bible* in
Queenes-head Alley in *Pater Noster Row.*
1638.

TO THE RIGHT HONOURABLE

ROBERT, EARL OF WARWICK,*

AND TO THE RIGHT HONOURABLE

THE LADY SUSANNA, COUNTESS OF WARWICK,

HIS PIOUS CONSORT.

Right Honourable,

There are two things common to man, whose nature is capable of honour: one is, an appetite of honour; the other, a mistaking himself about the matter or way of honour. Ambition stirs up the one, and ignorance causeth the other; that swells, this poisons the heart of man. The first humour did so far transport some ancients, that they placed very felicity in honour, and made strange and unnatural adventures for the same. The second, as an evil, made them to make that to be honour which is not; and deny that to be honour which is honour indeed. It is no honour to be wicked; nor yet a way to honour with God or good men; and yet some men do 'glory in their shame,' Phil. iii. 19, accounting baseness itself to be their honour.

It is the highest honour, and indeed, nothing so truly ennobleth, to be truly gracious and godly; and yet, with multitudes of men, religion and godliness are thought stains and blemishes of honour, ignobling greatness itself, which they shun as the greatest shame. The Scriptures make godliness the formal and intrinsecal cause and root of honour. Nay, it is and was the opinion of the most moderate philosophers, that virtue is the proper basis of honour; and that it doth belong to virtue as a debt; and so much as virtuous, so much honourable; and though it did not make, yet it did dress a moral happiness. The honour of being virtuous is great to all; most unto personages whose blood runs noble, and places are eminent. The world eyeth such most, and are willing to see if they will shine; and

* Robert Rich, second Earl of Warwick, and his excellent Countess, were 'fast friends' (Clarendon's words) of the Puritans. Clarendon, Neal, and indeed all the histories of the period, shew the important part the Earl played among his contemporaries. His death in 1658 is one of the events enumerated by Clarendon as having darkened the 'latter days' of Cromwell. Besides the Peerages, consult Ross's Historical account of the Earls of Warwick, published by Hearne in 1729.—G.

ready to commend if they will be forward. When great ones are but in the common way of honouring God, which is merely formal and verbal, this is pleasing, and many times winning name and fame unto themselves. But when they are found upon the special way of honouring God, which is radical and vital, the heart being inwardly affected with the love and purpose, and the life full of the courses and discourses of godliness, this makes nobility itself glorious, and eminently to shine. And certain it is, that such shall have from God the honour of secret acceptation, special protection, external publication, and of eternal glorification, they being all heirs under blessing.

This honour, in all eminency, I wish unto your honours, by how much the more God hath already advanced and enlarged your names and families, not only in many outward, but also in many choice and spiritual respects. For your further help herein, I make myself bold to present you with certain sermons, heretofore preached by Dr Sibbes, a man whose piety and parts made him honourable living and dead. For me to commend the author unto your honour, were to make the world to judge him either a stranger unto you, or a man that had not ingratiated himself with you whilst he lived near unto you. I well knew that he had an honourable opinion of you both, and of yours; and that maketh me not blush to pass these his own labours under your noble patronages. I know his works do and will sufficiently praise him; and you that knew and loved him so well, shall, in vouchsafing to read over these ensuing sermons, find his spirit in them, and in a manner hear him, although dead, yet speaking unto you, Heb. xi. 4. Look upon the work with acceptance for the father's sake, and let the world know that he was a man so deservedly respected of you, that his learned labours shall profit you; and you by them may be quickened in all the passages of your life, to honour that God who hath so much honoured you, which is the hearty desire of

Your honour's to be commanded,

JOHN SEDEWICK.*

* This is John Sedgwick, B.D., though curiously enough misspelled here 'Sedewick,' a younger brother of the more celebrated Obadiah Sedgwick. Against none of the Puritans has Anthony a-Wood written more bitterly or slanderously. He died in 1643. Thomas Case preached his funeral sermon. Consult Brook's 'Puritans,' ii. pp. 485–486, and Wood and Newcourt. His 'Bearing and Burden of the Spirit' (1639, 18mo), and his 'Eye of Faith' (1640, 18mo), breathe much of the spirit of Sibbes.—G.

TO THE READER.

The highest points of Christian religion, and such as are most above the reach of human wisdom, are those that lie below, in the foundation; and therefore are they called the 'mysteries of the kingdom of heaven,' Mat. xiii. 11; and the 'deep things of God,' 1 Cor. ii. 10. And the knowledge of these things is termed an ascending into heaven, John iii. 13; a knowledge of such things 'as eye hath not seen, nor ear heard, nor would ever have entered into the heart of man,' had they not been revealed to us by him that came down from heaven, even the Son of man that is in heaven. That blessed apostle St Paul, that was rapt up into the third heaven, did yet chiefly desire to study and teach these principles of the doctrine of Christ. 'I determined not to know anything among you, save Jesus Christ, and him crucified,' 1 Cor. ii. 2. Yea, and after all his study and teaching, was not ashamed to confess of himself that he was not yet perfect in the knowledge of Christ, nor had attained so much as might be attained, but was still therefore looking upward, and pressing forward to that which was before, Phil. iii. 12, 13. And indeed what David acknowledged, concerning his searching the Scriptures in general, that though he had proceeded further in the discovery of divine truths than those that went before him (Ps. cxix. 99), 'I have more understanding than all my teachers, for thy 'testimonies are my meditation;' yet he was still to seek of that which might be known; ver. 96, 'I have seen an end of all perfection, but thy commandment is exceeding broad.' Even as those great discoverers of the new-found lands in America, at their return, were wont to confess that there was still a *plus ultra*, more might be descried than was yet seen, that may we say concerning those glorious things revealed unto us in the gospel concerning Christ. Proceed we as far as we can in the study of them; that, we know, will be nothing, to that which is still to be learned; for the riches of Christ herein discovered are indeed unsearchable, Eph. iii. 8.

It is no disparagement therefore at all, either to those that are the chief masters of the assemblies, Eccles. xii. 11, to teach, or those that are of the highest form * in Christ's school, to learn, yea, and that again and again, 'the first principles of the oracles of God,' Heb. v. 12. Sure I am, however others puffed up with an opinion of their own worth may be otherwise minded, the reverend and learned author of these ensuing treatises was of this judgment, who, though he were a wise master-builder, yet according to the grace that was given unto him (which was indeed like that of Elisha in regard of the other prophets, 2 Kings ii. 9, the elder brother's privilege,

* That is, 'seat,' a scholastic or educational term.—G.

a double portion), he was still taking all occasions to lay well the foundation, and that in one of the most eminent authorities for learning and piety that are in the kingdom.

They that were his constant hearers know this well. They that were not, may see it by these his sermons now published, reduced, as was deemed most fit, into four several treatises; wherein, as the season required, he still took the opportunity of instructing his hearers in this great mystery of our religion, the incarnation of the Son of God, one of the chief fundamentals of our faith; one of the chief of those wonders in the mercy-seat, which the cherubins gaze at, which the angels desire to pry into, 1 Peter i. 12. And, indeed, by reason he spake at several times, and by occasion of so many several texts of Scripture concerning this subject, there is scarce any one of those incomparable benefits which accrue to us thereby; nor any of those holy impressions which the meditation hereof ought to work in our hearts, which is not in some place or other sweetly unfolded. In the first treatise * the mystery itself is indeed chiefly opened, and is therefore called, 'The Fountain Unsealed;' the rest, as in so many streams, convey to us that water of life which is issued from thence, teaching us how to improve the knowledge hereof to the glory of God, and the spiritual enriching of our own souls. The noted humility of the author I now the less wonder at, finding how often his thoughts dwelt on the humiliation of Christ. If we that now read them be not changed into the same image from glory to glory, it will be our own fault. This take from me; the treatises following are published by copies of his sermons which himself approved and appointed, and that by subscribing his own hand, purposely to prevent imperfect copies. Embrace them, therefore, as truly his; and the Lord so raise up thy heart in the careful perusal hereof, that 'thy profiting may be seen of all,' 1 Tim. iv. 15.

Thine in the Lord Jesus,

A. Jackson. †

London, Woodstreet, April 18. 1638.

* This, with the other two, will duly appear in their respective places.—G.
† Cf. Vol. II. p. 442.—G.

THE CHURCH'S RICHES BY CHRIST'S POVERTY.

For ye know the grace of our Lord Jesus Christ, that, though he was rich, yet he became poor for your sakes, that ye through his poverty might be rich.— 2 Cor. VIII. 9.

The nature of man is very backward to do good; our hearts being like to green wood that hath but a little fire under it, that must be continually blown up: so those sparks of grace that are in us must be stirred up. Therefore the apostle being to stir up these Corinthians to beneficence, and bounty towards the poor, he labours to enforce it by many reasons, in this and the next chapter. Man being an understanding creature, God would have what we do in matters of religion to proceed from principles, becoming men and Christians. Therefore he sets us upon duties from reasons. And because examples together with reasons are very forcible, therefore the apostle, after many forcible reasons to be liberal to the saints, he joins examples: first, of the Macedonians that were a poorer people, 2 Cor. viii. 2; then the Corinthians, to whom the apostle now wrote. But because people are not so comfortably led by the example of equals and inferiors (they think it a kind of upbraiding of them, accounting themselves as good or better than they); therefore the apostle leaves exhorting them from the example of the Macedonians that were poorer, and propounds an example beyond all exception, the example of Christ himself. He stirs them up to bounty and goodness, by the example of him who is goodness itself. 'You know the grace of our Lord Jesus Christ, who, though he were rich, he became poor,' &c. As if he should have said, if the example of the poor Macedonians will not move you to give bountifully, yet let the example of our Saviour; he was rich, yet he became poor to enrich you; therefore you must not think much to bestow somewhat on his poor members.

Examples have a very great force in moving, especially if they be examples of great persons, and those that love us, and we them, and that are near us. The example of Christ, it is the example of a great person, and one that loves us, and whom we ought to love again; therefore the apostle propounds that.

He might have alleged the precept of Christ. There are many commands that Christ gives of bounty and liberality to the poor: 'Be merciful, as your heavenly Father is merciful,' Luke vi. 36; and 'give freely, looking for nothing again,' vi. 35; and 'the poor ye shall have always with you,' Mat. xxvi. 11. But because example hath a more alluring power, it moves more freely (precepts have a more compelling* force); therefore herein he follows the stream of our disposition, which rather desires to be easily drawn than to be forced and pressed; he brings not the precept but the example of Christ: 'For you know the grace of our Lord Jesus Christ,' &c.

The points considerable in the words are, first of all, that

Doct. 1. *Christ was rich.*

There is no question to be made of this truth, 'Christ was rich,' because he was the second person in Trinity, the Son of God, the heir of heaven and earth, rich every way. When he was poor, he was God then. Though he covered his Godhead with the veil of humanity, with our base and beggarly nature that he took upon him, he was alway rich. But especially this hath reference to what he was before he took our nature: he was rich, because he was God; and indeed God only is rich to purpose, independently and eternally rich. Riches imply, among other things, plenty; and plenty of precious and good things, and propriety.† They must be good things that are our own. Christ had plenty of excellent things, and they were his own. He was not only rich in treasure, as he saith, 'Gold is mine, and silver is mine,' Hag. ii. 8, but heaven and earth, that contains all treasures, are his. 'The earth is the Lord's, and the fulness thereof,' Ps. xxiv. 1; and it is he that made the heavens. He that made heaven and earth must needs be rich; nay, if there were need, he can make a thousand heavens and earths. He is not only mighty, but almighty; not only sufficient, but all-sufficient. He can do what may be done; he can do what he hath done, and more than he hath done, and more than we can conceive; he can remove all difficulties that hinder him; he is rich in power and wisdom every way. The point is very large, but it is not so pertinent to the text to shew what he was in himself, but what he was for our sakes; therefore I will be shorter in it.

Hence then you see that Christ was, before he was exhibited.‡ He did good before he appeared. He was rich before he took our nature upon him. He was God before he was man. [I say this] against the cursed heresy of Arius (*a*), which I will not now rake up again. But undoubtedly you see here a good ground of that grand article of our faith—Christ was God before he took our nature. He came; therefore he was before he came. He was sent; therefore he was before he was sent. He was God, before he was God 'manifest in the flesh.' In Philip. ii. 6, it is largely and excellently set down: 'Let the same mind be in you that was in Christ Jesus: who, being in the form of God, thought it not robbery to be equal with God; but he was made of no reputation; he took upon him the form of a servant, and was made in the likeness of man: he was found in the fashion of man; he humbled himself, and became obedient to death, even to the death of the cross; therefore God hath highly exalted him, and given him a name above all names.' It is a large comment and explication upon this text, 'he was God; he thought it no robbery to be equal with God.'

The devils, which were angels before they fell, would be gods by usurpation and robbery. They were not content in the place they were in, but they would be gods, independent, of themselves. It was robbery for them to do it; therefore from that high place of excellency they were thrown

* That is, = commanding.—G. † That is, 'property.'—G.

‡ That is, 'manifested.' Cf. 1 John i. 2.—G.

down to the lowest hell; of angels they became devils. But Christ was God, not by usurpation and robbery against God's will, but he was God by nature. He was rich by nature. He thought it no robbery, no disparagement, nor usurpation to be equal with God; he did God no wrong in it. Therefore when he became man, he was not cast into these inferior parts of the world, to punish him, as if he had been an usurper; but it was a voluntary taking of our nature on him, 'being rich, he *became* poor,' and 'being in the form of God, he *made himself* of no reputation.' If he had usurped his divinity, his abasement had been violent, against his will. You see then that Christ was rich, as God.

Therefore, before he took our nature upon him, he was mediator from the beginning; he was 'yesterday, to-day, and to-morrow, and the same for ever,' Heb. xiii. 8, as the apostle saith; 'he was, and is, and is to come,' Rev. i. 8; he was the 'Lamb slain from the beginning of the world,' Rev. v. 12. For howsoever he took our nature upon him, and paid the debt, yet he undertook the payment before the beginning of the world. A man may let a prisoner loose now, upon the promise to pay the debt a year after; so Christ undertook to take our nature and to pay our debt in the fulness of time. By virtue, therefore, of his future incarnation, he was an effectual mediator from the beginning of the world: as we have now the fruit of his mediation though his death be past. The act is past, but the fruit remains. So that he was a mediator before he came in the flesh, because he undertook to his Father to discharge the office.

Quest. But Christ being God, was it needful that he should become poor? Might not an angel, or some other creature, have served for the work?

Ans. No. God being rich must become poor, or else he had not been able to bring us back again to God. It is an act of divine power to bring us back again to God; and he that shall settle us in a firmer state than we had in Adam, must be God. To stablish us stronger, and to convey grace to us, to make our state firm, only God can do it. There are some things in the mediation of Christ that belongs to ministry, and some things to authority. Those that belong to ministry, are to be a servant, and to die; and that he must be man for. But there are some things that belong to authority and power, as to bring us back to God, to convey his Spirit, to preserve us from Satan our great enemy. For these works of authority it was requisite he should be God. In a word,

1. *The greatness of the ill we were in required it.* Who could deliver us from the bondage of Satan but God? He must be stronger than the 'strong man,' that must drive him out. Who could know our spiritual wants, the terrors of our conscience, and heal and comfort them, but God by his Spirit? Who could free us from the wrath of the great God, but he that was equal with God?

2. And then in regard *of the great good we have by him.* To restore us to friendship with God, and to preserve us in that state; to convey all necessary grace here, and to bring us to glory after,—it was necessary he should be God. Therefore he was rich, and became poor. It is rather to be admired than expressed, the infinite comfort that springs hence; that he hath* undertaken to reconcile us, to make our peace, to bring us to heaven, is God the second person in Trinity.

All the three persons had a hand in this work. God the Father sent him, and the Holy Ghost sanctified that mass that his body was made of,

* Qu. 'that he that hath'?—Ed.

but he himself wore the body. The Father gives his Son in marriage; the Son married our nature; and the Holy Ghost brings them together. He sanctified our nature, and fitted it for Christ to take. So though all three persons had a work in it, yet God the second person of rich became poor. And indeed who was fitter to bring us to the love of God, than he that was his beloved Son? Who was fitter to restore us to the image of God, than he that was the image of God himself? and to make us wise, than he that was the Wisdom of God himself? There was infinite wisdom in this. I will not be larger in that point—Christ was rich.

The next thing I observe is this, that

Doct. 2. *Christ became poor.*

The poverty of Christ reacheth from his incarnation to his resurrection. All the state of his humiliation, it goes under the name of his poverty. The resurrection was the first step or degree of his exaltation. He wrought our salvation in the state of humiliation, but he applies it in the state of exaltation.

1. *The incarnation of Christ it was an exaltation to* our nature*, to be united to God, to the second person in Trinity. It was a humiliation of God, for the divine nature to stoop so low as to be vailed under our poor nature. So that God could stoop no lower than to become man, and man could be advanced no higher than to be united to God; so that in regard of God, the very taking upon him of our nature, it was the first degree and passage of his humiliation.

2. But when did he take upon him our nature? *He took it upon him after it was fallen;* when it was passible,† obnoxious to suffering; not as it was in innocency, free from all misery and calamity, but when it was at the worst. And,

3. He not only took our nature, but our condition. 'He took upon him the form *of a servant*,' Phil. ii. 7. He was not only a servant in regard of God, but in regard of us; for he came into the world not to be 'ministered unto,' but to 'minister.' He took upon him our nature wheu it was most beggarly, and with our nature he took our base condition. Nay, that is not all.

4. He took upon him *our miseries;* all that are natural, not personal. He took not the leprosy and the gout, &c., but he took all the infirmities that are common to the nature of man, as hunger, and thirst, and weariness; he was sensible of grief.

5. He took upon him likewise *our sins*, so far as there is anything penal in sin in respect of punishment. You know there is two things in guilt; there is the demerit and desert of it; and there is an obligation to punishment. Now the obligation to punishment he took upon him, though the merit‡ and desert he took not: 'He became sin,' Phil. ii. 8; that is, by sin, he became bound to the punishment for sin. He took not the demerit; for in respect of himself he deserved no such death as he underwent. To clear this a little further. He took upon him our nature, that he might become sin for us; he took upon him the guilt as far as guilt is an obligation to punishment. The son of a traitor, he loseth his father's lands, not by any communion of fault, but by communion of nature, because he is part of his father. So Christ took the communion of our nature, that he might take the communion of our punishment, not of our fault; as the son is no traitor, but because he is part of his father that was a traitor, by his

* That is, = 'of.'—G.

† That is, 'capable of suffering.'—G.

‡ That is, = blame.—G.

nearness and communion with his father he is wrapped in the same punishment.

In a city that is obnoxious to the king's displeasure, perhaps there are some that are not guilty of the offence that the body of the city is, yet being all citizens, they are all punished by reason of their communion; so in this respect Christ became poor; he took upon him our nature, and by communion with that nature, he took upon him whatsoever was penal, that belonged to sin, though he took not, nor could take, the demerit of sin.

'He was made sin for us.' We cannot have a greater argument of Christ's poverty than to be made sin for us. Sin is the poorest thing in the world, and the cause of all beggary and poverty and misery He was made under the law, and so became a curse for us; he was made sin, a sacrifice for our sin. In particular, he was born of a poor virgin, and instead of a better place, he was laid in an inn, and in the basest place in the inn, in the manger. As soon as he was born, his birth was revealed to poor shepherds, not to emperors and kings; not to Cæsar at Rome. Then presently after his birth he was banished together with his mother into Egypt, Mat. ii. 19. When he came home again, he was fain to be beholding to a poor woman for a cup of water when he was thirsty, John iv. 7, *seq*. Again, when he was to pay tribute, he had not wherewith to pay it, but was fain, as it were, to be beholding to a fish for it, Mat. xvii. 27. And though he made heaven and earth, yet he had no habitation of his own. 'The foxes had holes, and the birds of the air had nests, but the Son of man had not where to lay his head,' Mat. viii. 20. When he was to ride in pomp to Jerusalem, he had not a beast of his son;* he was fain to send for and ride upon another man's ass. All his life was a state of poverty.

He was poor in death especially, for when life is gone all is gone. 'He gave himself to death for us.' In death he was poor every way. They stripped him of all his clothes; he had not so much as a garment to cover him. He was poor and destitute in regard of friends. They all forsook him when he had need of them most of all, as he foretold that they all should leave him, John xvi. 32. And as he was thus poor in respect of his body and condition, so he was poor in soul in some respects; and indeed the greatest poverty was there. For the greatest riches that Christ esteemed, it was the blessed communion that he had with his Father, which was sweeter to him than all things in heaven and earth. When his Father hid his face from him, that he felt his displeasure, becoming our surety, in the garden before his death, the sense of God's displeasure against sin affected him so deeply that he sweat water and blood, Luke xxii. 44. He was so poor, wanting the comfort of his Father's love, that an angel, his own creature, was fain to come and comfort him, Luke xxii. 43. And at his death, when he hung upon the cross, besides the want of all earthly comforts, wanting the sense of their sweet love that he always enjoyed before, it made him cry out, 'My God, my God, why hast thou forsaken me?' Mark xv. 34; not that indeed God had forsaken him in regard of protection and support, or in regard of love and favour, but in regard of solace and comfort that he felt before, in regard of the sense of divine justice being then upon him that stood surety for sin. When he was dead he had no tomb of his own to lie in; he was fain to lie in another man's tomb, Mat. xxvii. 60; and then he was held under the captivity of the grave three days. So that, from his birth to his death, there is nothing but a race of poverty.

And which adds to this abasement of Christ, it was from an excellent

* Qu. 'own'?—Ed.

condition to so low a state; as we say it is a miserable thing for a man to have been happy; it makes him more sensible of his misery than in other men. For Christ, who was alway in the presence and favour of heaven, to come into the virgin's womb; for him to stand in need of the necessities of this life; for life to die; for riches to become poor; for the glory of heaven and earth to be abased; for the Lord of all to become a servant to his own servants—it must needs be a great abasement to him that was so highly advanced to become so poor.

But though Christ became thus poor, yet he ceased not then to be rich, but that his riches was veiled with our flesh. The sun, though he be kept from our sight by clouds, he is the sun still, and hath his own proper lustre still. He is as glorious in himself as ever he was, though he be not so to us. So Christ veiled his divinity under our human nature and under our misery; he became man and a curse; therefore though he were 'the Son* of righteousness,' glorious in himself, yet to appearance he was otherwise, 'he became poor.'

The papist would have him a beggar. Bellarmine, to countenance begging friars, would have Christ to be so (*b*). It is a disgraceful false conceit. If we divide his life before he was thirty years old that he was invested into his office, he lived with his parents in that calling and submitted to them; he was no beggar. Afterward he lived by ministering the word of God, and this was not *eleemosynary*, but honour. It is not charity that is given to governors, especially ministers. It is not alms to receive temporal things for spiritual, but it is due. Besides, he had somewhat of his own. He had a bag, and Judas was good enough to carry it, John xii. 6. He gave to the poor; therefore he was not a beggar. For he that came to fulfil the law would not break the law. The law forbids beggars. It was one of Moses's laws, 'There shall not be a beggar among you,' Deut. xv. 4.† So much briefly for that, 'Christ was rich, and became poor.'

The next point is, the parties for whom this was.

Doct. 3. *For your sakes.*

Why doth not the apostle say 'for our sakes,' and so take himself in the number. He applies it to serve the argument in hand, being to stir up the Corinthians to bounty. He tells them 'Christ was poor for their sakes;' that they might be assured of their salvation by Christ, that his example might be more effectual. The example of those whom we have interest in is effectual; therefore he saith, 'for your sakes he became poor.' This should teach us, when we speak of Christ, to labour for a spirit of application, to appropriate Christ unto ourselves, or else his example will not move us.

As without application we can have no good by him, so we can have no comfort by his example. It is not prevalent, unless we can say as the apostle to the Corinthians here, 'for your sakes.'

Again, 'for *your* sakes, not for himself.' He became not poor to make himself richer; he did not merit for himself. What need he? For by virtue of the union of the human nature with the Godhead, heaven was due to him at the first moment, as soon as he was born. What should hinder him? Had he any sin of his own? No. There was nothing to keep him from heaven, and all the joy that could be, in respect of himself. But he had our salvation to work; he had many things to do and suffer, and therefore of his infinite goodness he was content that that glory that was due to him should be stayed. He became a servant to appease his Father's wrath for us, and procure heaven for us; for us men, for us

* Qu. 'Sun'?—Ed. † See marginal reading in authorised version.—Ed.

sinners, as it is in the ancient creed, and as the prophet saith, 'To us a child is born, to us a Son is given,' Isa. ix. 6. For us he was born; for us he was given; for us he lived; for us he died; for us he is now in heaven; for us he humbled himself to death, even to the death of the cross, to a cursed death,' Philip. ii. 8. Therefore when we hear of Christ's poverty, let us think, this is for me, not for himself; and this will increase our love and our thankfulness to him.

Again, it was for us, for mankind, not for angels. For when they fell they continue in that lapsed state for ever. This advanceth God's love to us more than to those noble creatures the angels, who remain in their cursed condition to all eternity.

The end of Christ's becoming poor.

'That we through his poverty might be made rich.'

Quest. How are we made rich by the poverty and abasement of Christ?

Ans. By the merit of it, and by efficacy flowing from Christ; for by the merit of Christ's poverty there issued satisfaction to divine justice, and the obtaining of the favour of God, not only for the pardon of our sins, but favour and grace to be entitled to life everlasting. And then by efficacy; we are enriched by the power of his Spirit, who altereth and changeth our natures, and makes them like to the divine nature.

Quest. But more particularly, what be the riches that we have by the poverty of Christ?

Ans. (1.) First, *Our debt must be paid before we could be enriched.* We are indebted for our souls and bodies. We did owe more than we were worth. We were under Satan's kingdom. Therefore Christ discharged our debt. There is a double debt that he discharged, the debt of obedience and the debt of punishment. Christ satisfied both. For the debt of obedience, he fulfilled the law perfectly and exactly for us; and for the debt of punishment, he suffered death for us, and satisfied divine justice. So by his poverty we are made rich, by way of satisfaction for our debts.

(2.) And not only we are made rich by Christ paying our debts, *but he invests us into all his own riches.* He makes us rich, partly by imputation, partly by infusion.

[1.] By *imputation;* his righteousness and obedience is ours. His discharge for our debts is imputed to us, and likewise his righteousness for the attaining of heaven. He having satisfied for our sins, God is reconciled to us; and thereupon we are justified and freed from all our sins, because they are punished in Christ. For the justice of God cannot punish one sin twice. So we come to be reconciled because we are justified; and we are justified from our sins, because Christ, as a surety, hath discharged the full debt.

And hence it is that we are freed from all that is truly ill; from the wrath of God and eternal damnation; and freedom from the greatest ill hath respect of the greatest good. For what had we been had we lain under that cursed condition? But God's works are complete. He works like a God. Therefore we are not only freed from evil in justification, but entitled to heaven and life everlasting.

[2.] And then he makes rich *by infusion of his Holy Spirit,* by working all needful graces of sanctification in us. For by the virtue of Christ's death the Spirit is obtained, and by the Spirit our natures are changed. So we have the riches of holiness from Christ, the graces of love, of contentment, of patience, and courage, &c. 'Of his fulness we receive grace for grace,' John i. 16; grace answerable to the grace that is in him. The same Spirit that sanctified his human nature and knit it to his divine, it sanctifieth his members, and makes them rich in grace and sanctification, which is the best riches.

[3.] Then again, we are rich *in prerogatives.* '*We are the sons of God by adoption.* 'What love,' saith the apostle, 'hath the Father shewed, that we should be called the sons of God,' 1 John iii. 1. And this we have by the poverty of Christ. Whatsoever Christ is by nature, we are by grace. He is the Son of God by nature, we are his sons by grace; and being sons, we are heirs, heirs of heaven, and heirs of the world as much as shall serve for our good. All things are ours by virtue of our adoption, because we are Christ's, and Christ is God's. There is a world of riches in this, to be the sons of God.

And what a prerogative is this, *that we have liberty and boldness to the throne of grace,* as it is Eph. iii. 12; that we have boldness to appear before God, to call him Father, to open our necessities, to fetch all things needful, to have the ear of the King of heaven and earth, to be favourites in the court of heaven! Every Christian may now go boldly to God, because the matter of distance, our sins, which make a separation between God and us, they are taken away, and the mercy of God runs amain to us, our nature in Christ standing pure and holy before God.

And then we have this grand prerogative, that all *things shall turn to the best to us,* Rom. viii. 28. What a privilege is this, that there should be a blessing in the worst things! that the worst things to a child of God should be better than the best things to others! that the want and poverty of a Christian should be better than the riches of the world, because there is riches hid in his worst condition! Moses esteemed the rebuke of Christ greater riches than the treasures of Egypt, Heb. xi. 26. A cross, or the want of any blessing sanctified, is better than the thing enjoyed that hath not God's blessing with it. A Christian is so rich, that he is blessed in his very afflictions and sufferings. It is a greater prerogative to have ill turned to our good than not to have the ill at all. It is an argument of greater power and of greater goodness, that God should turn the greatest ills, the greatest wrongs and discomforts, to the greatest good, as he doth to his children, for by them he draws them nearer to himself. Hereupon the apostle saith, 'All things are yours, things present and things to come,' &c., 1 Cor. iii. 22; reductively they are ours: God turns them to our good. He extracts good to us by them. All good things are ours in a direct course; and other things, by an overruling power, are deduced to our good contrary to the nature of the things themselves. What! did I say all things are ours? Yea, God himself is ours; and he hath all things, that hath Him that hath all things. Now, in Christ, God himself is become ours; 'All things are yours, you are Christ's, and Christ is God's,' Rom. v. 2. 'We rejoice in God as ours.' If God be ours, his all-sufficiency is ours; his power is ours, his wisdom, all is ours for our comfort.

[4.] Again, *for glory, the riches of heaven,* which are especially here meant; for however the riches of heaven be kept for the time to come, yet faith makes them present. When by faith we look upon the promises, we see ourselves in heaven, not only in Christ our head, but in our own persons, because we are as sure to be there as if we were there already. But for the joys of heaven, they are unutterable. The apostle calls them, Eph. iii. 8, 'unsearchable riches.' 'Eye hath not seen, nor ear hath heard, or hath entered into the heart of man to conceive, the things that God hath prepared for them that love him.' There shall be fulness of glory in soul and body; both shall be conformable to Christ. 'At the right hand of God there is fulness of joy, and pleasures for evermore,' Ps. xvi. 11.

Nay, the first fruits, the earnest, the beginnings of heaven here are unsearchable to human reason, the riches of Christ's righteousness imputed to us, the glorious riches of his Spirit in inward peace of conscience 'and joy in the Holy Ghost.' The comfort and enlargement of heart in all conditions, 'it is peace that passeth understanding,' and 'joy unspeakable and glorious.' It is not only unsearchable to human reason, but Christians themselves, that have the Spirit of God in them, cannot search the depth of them, because we have the Spirit but in measure. We see then what excellent riches we have by the poverty of Christ.

Quest. Was there no other way to make us rich but by Christ's becoming poor?

Ans. God in his infinite wisdom ordained this way. He thought it best. We may rest in that. But besides, to stay our minds the better, we were to be restored by a way contrary to that we fell.

(1.) *We fell by pride, we must be restored by humility.* We would be like God; God to expiate it must become like us, and take our nature, and suffer in it.

(2.) Then again, God would restore us by a way *suitable to his own excellency every way*, wherein no attribute of his might be a loser. He would bring us to riches and friendship with him by a way of satisfaction to his justice, that we may see his justice shine in our salvation (though indeed grace and mercy triumph most of all, yet notwithstanding) justice must be fully contented. There was no other way wherein we could magnify so much the unsearchable and infinite wisdom of God (that the angels themselves 'pry into,' 1 Peter i. 12), whereby justice and mercy, seeming contrary attributes in God, are reconciled in Christ. By infinite wisdom, justice and mercy meet together and kiss one another. Justice being satisfied, wisdom is exalted. But what set wisdom on work to devise this way to satisfy justice? The grace, and love, and mercy of God. It could not have been done any other way; for before we could be made rich, God must be satisfied. Reconciliation supposeth satisfaction, and there could be no satisfaction but by blood; and there could be no equal satisfaction but by the blood of such a person as was God. Therefore Christ must become poor to make us rich, because there must be full satisfaction to divine justice, and all his precious poverty before his death. His incarnation, his want, his being a servant, &c., all was part of his general humiliation. But it was but to prepare him for his last work, the upshot of all, his death, which was the work of satisfaction.

(3.) Again, all the inherent part of our riches infused into our nature, *it comes by the Spirit of God.* Now the Spirit of God had not been sent, if God had not been satisfied and appeased first, because the Holy Ghost is the gift of the Father and the Son. He comes from both. Therefore there must be satisfaction and reconciliation before the Holy Ghost could be given, which enricheth our nature immediately. The immediate cause of sending the Holy Ghost, it is Christ's coming in our nature. Now, if God had not been satisfied in his justice, he would never have given the Holy Ghost, which is the greatest gift next to Christ. Therefore 'Christ became poor to make us rich,' that we might have the Holy Ghost shed in our hearts.

(4.) Now all these riches that we have by Christ, it supposeth *union with him by faith*, as the riches of the wife supposeth marriage. Union is the ground of all the comfort we have by Christ. Our communion springs from union with him, which is begun in effectual calling. As soon as we are taken out of old Adam and engrafted into him, all becomes ours. Christ procures the Spirit, the Spirit works faith, faith knits us to Christ, and by this union we have communion of all the favours of this life and the life to come. Therefore, I say, all is grounded upon union by the grace of faith. Christ married our nature that we might be married to him by his Spirit; and until there be a union, there is no derivation of grace and comfort. The head only hath influence to the members that are knit unto it. Therefore Christ took our nature, that he might not only be a head of eminency, as he is to angels, but a head of influence. Now, there must be a knitting of the members to the head before any spirits can be derived from the head to the members. Therefore the apostle saith that Christ is our riches. But it is as he is in us, 'To whom God would make known what is the riches of this mystery among the Gentiles; Christ in you, the hope of glory,' Col. i. 27. Christ is all to us, but it is as he is in us and we in him. We must be in him as the branches in the vine, and he in us as the vine in the branches. So Christ is 'the hope of glory,' as he is in us. We must labour therefore by faith to be made one with Christ, before we can think of these things with comfort.

And when by faith we are made one with Christ, then there is a spiritual communion of all things. Now, upon our union with Christ, it is good to think what ill Christ hath taken upon him for me; and then to think myself freed from it, because Christ that took it on him hath freed himself from it. Whatsoever he is freed from, I am freed from it. It can no more hurt me than it can hurt him now in heaven. Therefore, when I think of sin, and hell, and damnation, and wrath, I see myself freed from it in Christ. 'He became poor' to take this away from me. My sins were laid on him, and he is justified and acquitted from them all, and from death and the wrath of God that he underwent; and I am acquitted in him by virtue of my union with him; and the devil can no more prejudice the salvation of a believer, than he can pull Christ out of heaven.

And as we see ourselves freed from all ill in Christ, so for all good: see it in him first, and conveyed by him to us. Whatsoever he hath, I shall have. He is risen and ascended; I shall therefore rise and ascend, and sit at the right hand of God for ever with him: 'We shall be for ever with the Lord.' Let us see our riches in him. He is rich first as the head or first fruits, and then we as the lump afterwards. The first fruits were sanctified, and then the lump. The first fruits are glorious, and then the rest after. Whatsoever we look for in ourselves, see it in him first; and then the consideration of a Christian condition is a comfortable consideration. Take a Christian in all conditions whatsoever. If he be poor, Christ was poor for him, that his poverty might not be a curse to him. If he be poor, Christ was rich to make him rich in the best riches, and to take the sting out of poverty, and to turn it to his good. If he be abased, Christ was abased for him to sanctify his abasement. Let us labour to see the curse taken away in everything, and not only so, but to see a blessing in all, being made ours; and then it will be a comfortable consideration.

Obj. But it may be objected, We see no such thing; we see Christians are as poor as others.

Ans. The best riches of a Christian are unseen. They are unknown men; as we say of a rich man that makes no show of his riches, he is an unknown man. It is said of Christ, 'All the riches of wisdom are hid in

Christ,' Col. ii. 3. That that is hidden is not seen. So the riches of a Christian they are hidden. As Christ was rich when he was upon earth; he was rich in his Father's love and in all graces, but it was a hidden riches; they took him to be a poor ordinary man. So a Christian he is a hidden man; his riches are hid; he hath an excellent life, but it is a hidden life. 'Our life is hid with Christ in God,' Col. iii. 3. It is not obvious to the eye of the world, nor to himself ofttimes in the time of desertion and temptation.

Obj. But you will say, For outward things we see Christians are poor now, as there were poor Christians in St Paul's time.

Ans. It is no great matter. The riches we have especially by Christ are spiritual, in grace here and glory hereafter. He came to redeem our souls here from sin and misery; and he will hereafter come to redeem our bodies and invest them into the glory that we have title to now by him.

Yet also for outward things a Christian is rich. Though they be not the main, yet they are the *viaticum*, provision in his journey; and he shall have enough to bring him to heaven. 'Fear not, little flock, it is your Father's will to give you a kingdom,' Luke xii. 32. Surely if he will give them a kingdom, they shall not want daily bread; upon seeking the kingdom of God, these things shall be cast in unto them.

Again, put case a Christian be poor, he is rich in Christ, and he bears the purse. What if a child have no money in his purse, his father provides all necessaries for him. He is rich as long as his father is rich. And can we be poor as long as Christ is rich, being so near us, being our head? We shall want nothing that is needful; and when it is not needful and for our good, we were better be without it.

Again, he must needs be rich whose poverty and crosses are made riches to him. God never takes away or withholds outward blessings from his children, but he makes it up in better, in inward. They gain by all their losses, and grow rich by their wants. For how many are there in the world that had not been so rich in grace, if they had had abundance of earthly things? So that though they be poor in the world, they are rich to God, rich in grace, 'rich in faith,' as St James saith, James ii. 5. The greatest grievances and ills in the world turn to a Christian's [benefit]: sickness and shame and death. The Spirit of God is like the stone that men talk so of, that turns all into gold. It teacheth us to make a spiritual use, and to extract comfort out of everything. The worst things we can suffer in the world, 'All things are ours,' as I said before, even Satan himself. The Spirit of God helps us to make good use of his temptations, to cleave faster to the fountain of good.

Again, though a Christian be poor, yet he hath rich promises; and faith puts those promises in suit, and presseth God with them. If a man have bonds and obligations of a rich man, he thinks himself as rich as those bonds amount to. There is no Christian but hath a rich faith, and rich promises from God; and when he stirs up his faith, he can put those promises in suit (if it be not his own fault) in all his necessities. Therefore a Christian cannot be so poor as to be miserable. I know flesh and blood measureth riches after another manner. But is not he richer that hath a fountain than he that hath but a cistern? A man that is not a Christian, though he be never so rich, he hath but a cistern; his riches are but few; they are soon searched. But a Christian, though he be poor, his riches are unsearchable. Another man, though he be a monarch, his riches may be reckoned and cast up; it is but a cistern, and such riches as he cannot carry with him. But a Christian hath a fountain; a mine that is unsearchable, in the rich promises of God.

Again, a Christian, though he be never so poor, yet he hath a rich pawn.* Saith St Paul, 'If he spared not his own Son, but gave him to death for us all, how shall he not with him give us all things?' Rom. viii. 32. If he have given us such a pawn as Christ, who is riches itself, shall he not with him give us all other things? We have a pawn that is a thousand times better than that we need. We want poor outward things, but we have Christ himself for a pawn.

Lastly, Sometimes God sees that poverty and want in this world is part of our riches, that it is good for us; and what is good for me is my riches. If poverty be good for me, I will be poor that I may be humble; humility is better than riches. If I be in any want, if I have contentment, it is better than riches. If I fall into trouble, he will give me patience, that is better than friends. A man may have outward things, and be naught.† But he that wants outward comfort, and hath supply in his soul, is it not better? Therefore take a Christian in any condition, he is a rich man; and this riches we have by the poverty of Christ. 'He became poor, that we through his poverty might be made rich.'

Use 1. We see here then that a Christian's estate *is carried under contraries*, as Christ was. 'He was rich, and became poor.' He carried his riches under poverty. He was glorious, but his glory was covered under shame and disgrace. So it is with a Christian. He goes for a poor man in the world, but he is rich; he dies, but yet he lives; he is disgraced in the world, but yet he is glorious. As Christ came from heaven in a way of contraries, so we must be content to go to heaven in a seeming contrary way. Take no scandal‡ therefore at the seeming poverty and disgrace and want of a Christian. Christ himself seemed to be otherwise to the world than he was. When he was poor, he was rich; and sometimes he discovered his riches. There were beams brake forth even in his basest estate. When he died, there was nothing stronger than Christ's seeming weakness. In his lowest abasement he discovered the greatest power of his Godhead. For he satisfied the justice of God; he overcame death and his Father's wrath; he triumphed over Satan; he trod on his head (what hath Satan to do with us when God's justice is satisfied?); so that his hidden glory was discovered sometimes. So there is that appears in the children of God that others may see them to be rich, if they did not close their eyes. But we must be content to pass to heaven as Christ our head did, as concealed men.

Use 2. Again, here is matter *not only for us men, but for the angels of heaven to admire and wonder* at this depth of goodness and mercy in Christ; that he would become poor to make us rich by his poverty. See the exaltation of his love in this. Saith St Bernard well, 'O love, that art so sweet, why becamest thou so bitter to thyself?' (*c*). Whence flowed Christ's love and mercy, that was so sweet in itself, that it should be only sour and bitter to him from whence it had its rise and spring? His love, that is so sweet to us, it became bitter to him; he endured and did that that we should have done and suffered. There be some men that will do kindnesses, so that themselves may not be the worse, so that they may not be the poorer, that they may not be disgraced, or adventure the displeasure of others. But Christ hath done all this great kindness for us by

* That is, 'pledge.'—G.

† That is, 'naughty' = wicked.—G.

‡ That is, offence.—G.

being poor for us; by taking our nature, our poverty, our misery. He doth us good in such a way as that he parted with heaven itself for a time, and with that sweet communion that he had with his Father, the dearest thing to him in the world. He parted with it for our sakes, that made him cry out, 'My God, my God, why hast thou forsaken me?' Mark xv. 34. Hereupon he made us rich in a way that cost him something.

And let us be thankful to him in a way that may cost us something; let us be content to be abased for him; to do anything for him. He descended from heaven to the grave, as low as he could for us; let us descend from our conceited greatness for him. Can we lose so much for him as he hath done for us? What are our bodies and souls in comparison of God? It was God that became poor for us. We cannot part with so much for him as he did for us. And then we are gainers by him if we part with all the world, whatsoever we do for him. 'I will be yet more vile for the Lord,' saith David, 2 Sam. vi. 22. He became vile for us; he became a sinner, and 'of no reputation;' and shall not we be vile and empty for him? Certainly we shall. If we have the Spirit of Christ in us, it will work a conformity. If he had stood upon terms and disdained the virgin's womb, and to become poor for us, where had our salvation been? And if we stand upon terms when we are to suffer for him or to stand for his cause, where will our comfort be? Surely it is a sign that we have no right by the poverty of Christ, unless we be content to part with our Isaac, with the best things we have, when he calls for it.

Use. 3. Again, hath the poverty of Christ made us rich; *what will his riches do?* Could he save us when he was at the lowest, when he was on the cross, and satisfied divine justice by his death; what can he do for us now he is in heaven, and hath triumphed over all his enemies? What can we look for now by his riches, that have so much by his poverty? Therefore we may reason with the apostle, Rom. v. 10, 'If, when we were enemies, we were reconciled to God by the death of his Son, how much more, being reconciled, shall we be saved by his life?' It is a strong argument, not only as it hath respect to us (because there is more likelihood that any good should be done for us now when we are reconciled to God, than before when we were enemies); but also as it hath respect to Christ; since he that stuck not to reconcile us to God by his death, cannot be unwilling to save us by his life; and he that was able to redeem us by dying for us, is more clearly and evidently powerful to save us, now he lives and reigns triumphantly in heaven. For is not he able to preserve us, to protect us, and invest us into the glory that he hath purchased for us? He that did so much for us in the time of his abasement, will he not preserve the riches he hath gotten for us? Is he not in heaven in majesty, to apply all that he hath gotten? Is he not our intercessor at the right hand of God, to appear before God for us to make all good? Certainly he will preserve that which he hath procured by his death.

It is a disabling of Christ to think of falling away from grace. He is able to maintain us in that glorious condition that he hath advanced us to; especially considering that he is now in heaven, and hath laid aside the form of a servant; all his humiliation, except our human nature. That for ever he hath united to his person; but all other things of his abasement he hath laid them aside; he is able perfectly, not only to save us, as by his death, but to apply all that he hath gotten, and preserve us to life everlasting. We are kept by the power of God, to that glory that Christ hath purchased by his death. Therefore why should we fear for the time to come, falling from grace, or the want of that that is good? Is not Christ able to maintain that that he hath gotten? Let us raise our hearts with this consideration, what Christ can do now in glory, when his poverty could do this much.

Use 4. Again, *let us despise no man for his poverty;* for Christ was poor to make us rich. And as those that despise Christ, and esteem him not, but 'hid their faces from him,' because he grew up 'as a root out of a dry ground, because there was no beauty in him,' Isa. liii. 2; that is, because of his poverty, because he was a carpenter's son; they despised by this means the Lord of glory; so those that despised his poor members afterward that 'wandered up and down in sheepskins and goatskins; being destitute and afflicted,' Heb. xi. 38, they despised God's jewels, his choice favourites, 'of whom the world was not worthy.' Let not the brother of low degree be cast down because he is poor, nor let the brother of high degree be lifted up because he is rich; for if riches had been the best thing, Christ would have been outwardly rich. But Christ was poor, to shew us what are the best riches; and that the riches of this world are but things by the by: 'Seek the kingdom of God, and all other things shall be cast on you,' Mat. vi. 33, by way of addition and supplement. The true riches of a Christian are spiritual. Christ did not become poor to make us rich in this world, to make us kings and emperors, and great men here, but to make us rich spiritually, and to have such a moiety of earthly things as may serve as a *viaticum* to bring us to heaven. The main riches of a Christian are spiritual and eternal in grace and glory. In popery they live as if Christ came to make them lords of the world; to usurp jurisdiction over kings and princes. Christ came to make us rich in another manner. St Peter saith, 'Silver and gold have I none,' Acts iii. 6, but his successors cannot say so. Christ came not as a servant to make us lords here, much less to set us at liberty to live after the flesh, and to do what we list. No; the end of Christ's coming was to take away sin, 'to destroy the works of the devil,' 1 John iii. 8. The common course at this time, and devilish practice of many, overturns the end of Christ's coming, as if he came not to destroy, but to let loose the works of the devil; to let us loose to all licentiousness. He came to bring us to God, and not to give us liberty in courses to run further from God. But that by the way. Christ, as I said, came not to make us rich in the things of this life; for do but consider a little of outward riches, what be they?

(1.) *They are not our own*, as Christ saith, Luke xvi. 1, *seq.*, 'We are but stewards,' and we must give a strict account ere long how we have used them.

(2.) And as they are not our own, *so they are not true riches*, because they make not us rich. We usually call a poor man a poor soul. A poor soul may be a rich Christian, and a rich man may have a poor soul, naked and empty of spiritual riches. These are not true riches, because *they make not a man better*. They may be a snare to him, and make him worse, and puff him up; as every grain of riches hath a vermin of pride and ambition in it. 'Charge rich men that they be not high-minded,' Rom. xi. 20. They may make a man worse; they cannot make him better. Can that be true riches that makes a man poorer, that hath not a gracious heart? Surely no. These riches ofttimes are for the hurt of the owners. Men are filled as sponges, and then squeezed again. Are these true riches that expose a man to danger? True riches are such as not only we may do good by, but they make us good. Grace makes us better; it commends us to God. All the riches in the world do not commend us to God. It is said of Antiochus, a great monarch, he was a vile and base person, because he was a wicked man.* There is no earthly thing can commend a man to God, if he be naught,† if he have a rotten profane heart.

(3.) Again, they are not true riches, because *a man outlives them*. Death screws him out of all; death comes and examines him when he goes out of the world, and will suffer him to carry nothing with him. If a man come to another man's table, and think to carry away his plate, or anything else, he will be stayed at the gate, and have it taken from him. Nothing we brought into this world, and with nothing we must go out; and are they true riches that determine in this life?

(4.) Then again, these riches, *they are not proportionable to the soul of man*. When the soul of man hath the image of Christ on it, nothing will satisfy it but spiritual things. There is nothing in the world will satisfy a gracious soul but grace and glory. It is only grace and the spiritual things by Christ that are the true riches, that make us good, and continue us good, and continue with us. We carry them to heaven with us. Therefore, as the apostle saith, we should desire the 'best things,' 1 Cor. xii. 31; labour for the best portion, that shall never be taken from us. When we have many things in this world set before us, shall we make a base choice? as the Gadarenes, to save their hogs, they would lose Christ, Luke viii. 37. Shall we make choice of poor things, and leave grace and Christ? No. Since we have judgment to make a difference, let us make a wise choice. Judgment is seen in choice of different things; for though these things be good, yet they are inferior goods; and we lose not these things by labouring for grace and the best things. The best way to have these things is to labour for the best things. Solomon desired wisdom, and he had riches too. 'Let us seek the kingdom of God, and these things' (as far as they be needful) shall be 'cast on us,' Mat. vi. 33. These are the truths of God. Therefore let us be ashamed that we discover our ignorance by making a base choice, and let us labour to choose the best things. Christ became poor to make us rich in the best things, to make us rich in grace, in joy, in peace, and comfort, &c.

Therefore let us esteem ourselves and others highly from hence, and let us not judge by appearance. When Christ was put to death, how did the world judge him? A miserable man, a sinner, because they judged by appearance. So it is the lot of God's children. Though they be never so rich, yet those that look upon their outward condition, that judge by appearance, because they are outwardly poor, they think they have no riches at all. 'But judge not by appearance,' as Christ saith, John vii. 24. The life that we have is hidden, our happiness and riches are hidden with God. Yet those that we have now are worth all the world. Is not a little peace of conscience, and joy in the Holy Ghost, and assurance that God is ours, worth all worldly things? The least measure of grace and comfort is worth all, and yet what we have here is nothing to that we shall have in heaven.

We may be ashamed, the best of us all, that we live not answerable to our estate. We are ofttimes poorer in grace than we need to be. Having such a fountain so near us, to perish for thirst; to be at a feast, and to perish for hunger; to be at a mine, and to come away beggars: it is a sign we want spiritual senses; it is a sign of infidelity, that we are not

* The whole race of the Antiochi seem to have been wicked; but Sibbes's reference is probably to Antiochus II., surnamed the Great—G.

† That is, 'naughty,' = wicked.—G.

capable of our spiritual wants. That we should profess ourselves to be Christians, to be members of Christ, and yet have no grace, no spiritual ornaments, no garments to hang on our souls; it is a sign there is no union because there is no communion. We draw nothing from Christ, we are Christians without Christ, we have no anointing from Christ. Let us take heed that we be not titular Christians, to have only the name of Christians. Let us labour to be Christians indeed. And for that end consider what was the end why Christ became poor? To 'make us rich.' Why should we frustrate his end?

Therefore let us search what riches we have from Christ; whether our debts be paid; whether our sins be forgiven. We may know we have our sins forgiven if we have sanctifying grace. God never pays our debts but he gives us a stock of grace. Let us examine therefore what riches we have. Some Christians are rich, but they are deceived in their own condition. They think they are poor and beggarly, and have nothing, when they are rich. What is it that deceives them? Sometimes it is because they have not so much as others; therefore they think they have nothing, not considering the degrees in Christianity.

Or because they have not so much as they would have. As a covetous man, he always looks forward, he is never satisfied; so a Christian, out of a spiritual covetousness, by looking to that he wants, forgets that he hath.

Sometimes a Christian in case of temptations and desertion, conscience may suggest his wants altogether. God will humble him this way. Though it may be an error in conscience, yet I would there were more of this kind. Such people are to be encouraged, as in Rev. ii. 13, 'Thou sayest thou art poor' (and the world thinks so), 'but thou art rich.' So there are many that are poor in their own conceits, that think they have nothing, but indeed they are rich; and they discover their interest in the true riches by their desire, and hungering, and thirsting after grace; by their care to please God in all things, to approve themselves to God, to do nothing against conscience; by their care in using the means of salvation, and their walking circumspectly. A man may see and discover their riches in their carriage. And if there be the least degree of grace, it is great riches in regard of inferior things, though it be little in regard of that we shall have in heaven. Let us search what we have, that we may walk thankfully and comfortably. We see worldly men, how they set themselves out in a little riches, and swell in their own conceits. A Christian hath that that is infinitely better, and shall he alway droop and be cast down? If he be a sound Christian that hath any goodness in him, let him walk a comfortable and cheerful life answerable to his riches. We account them base-minded men, that being very rich, yet they live as if they had nothing. So Christians are to blame, that having great riches in Christ, they live as uncomfortably as if they had none. What is the reason, Christ being so rich, that Christians have no more grace? Sometimes it is because they search not their own estates for good as well as bad. And then they do not empty themselves enough that Christ may fill them. They are not thankful enough for that they have, for thankfulness is the way to get more.

Quest. How shall we carry ourselves that we may improve Christ's riches; to be made rich in grace by him?

Ans. 1. First, Let us labour *for the emptying grace of humility*, which will empty the soul and make it of a large capacity to contain a great measure of grace. God 'fills the hungry with good things,' Luke i. 53; he 'resists the proud, but he gives grace to the humble,' James iv. 6. Let us labour to see our wants and necessities, and the vanity of all earthly things, and then we shall be fit to receive grace.

2. And then labour *to see the excellency of the grace we want*, and that will stretch and enlarge our desires. And withal see the necessity of grace. We must have faith, hope, and love. We cannot live as Christians else. We must have contentation.* We shall live miserably else. We cannot be like Christ without grace.

3. And withal know that *Christ is rich for us.* He hath not only abundance of the Spirit, but redundance, to overflow to us his members. As the head hath redundance of spirits, and senses for the use of the whole body; it sees, and feels, and smells, for the use of the whole body; whatsoever Christ hath, he hath for us. Let us labour to know our riches as we are Christians, as we grow in other things, so to be acquainted with that we have in Christ's.† As children that are heirs to great things, at the first they are ignorant of what they have, but as they grow in years so they grow in further knowledge of that that belongs to them; and they grow in spirit answerable and suitable to that they shall have. Let grace agree with nature in this, let us desire to know our riches in Jesus Christ.

4. And not only know that they are ours, *but use ours to our own good and benefit upon all occasions.* If we offend God, as every day we do, make use of our riches in Christ for the pardon of our sins. He is full of favour, he is our High Priest, he makes intercession for us. If we want knowledge he is a Prophet to teach us by his Spirit. If we find our natures defiled, and want power over our corruptions, he is a King to guide and lead us, in the midst of all our enemies, to heaven. If we find our consciences troubled, consider what peace we have in Christ. If we want outward things, let us consider we are under age. Great persons enjoy not their inheritances when they are under years. If God dispense outward things to us, it is for our good. If he send poverty and disgrace, it is for our good, to fit us for a better state. God in his infinite wisdom knows better what is good for us than we do for ourselves. In the want of anything let us believe that Christ is given as a public treasure to the church. Thus we may improve the grace and riches we have in Christ.

5. Again, let us labour *to make a good use of every favour we enjoy; of our liberties and recreations.* We have all by the poverty of Christ. Therefore let us use them in a sober manner, not as the fashion is, to cast off all care of Christ; to pour out ourselves to all licentiousness. Let us consider, this liberty and refreshing that I have, it is from the blood of Christ; as David's worthies, when they brake through with the danger of their lives to get him water, 'Oh,' saith he, 'I will not drink it, it is the blood of these men,' 2 Sam. xxiii. 15, *seq.* So whatsoever liberties and good things I have, I have it by the poverty of Christ, by the blood of Christ; and shall I misuse it?

And certainly it will make us *esteem more highly of our spiritual privileges than of outward*, considering they cost Christ so dear. He became poor to set us up when we were utterly bankrupt. He stripped himself of all, to make us rich. Shall we not therefore esteem and use these things well? And when we are tempted to sin, this will be a great means to restrain us; I am freed from sin by the blood of Christ; shall I make him poor again by committing sin? Shall I wrong him now he is in heaven? The Jews despited him on earth in the form of a servant; but our sins are of a higher nature, of a deeper double dye; we sin against Christ in heaven in glory.

* That is, 'contentment.'—G.

† Qu. 'Christ'?—Ed.

When we are tempted to sin, this consideration will make us ashamed to sin: Since Christ hath bought our liberty from sin at such a rate, shall we make light of sin that cost him his dear blood, and the sense of his Father's wrath? that made him cry out, 'My God, my God, why hast thou forsaken me?' It is impossible that any man should pour out himself to sin that hath this consideration. Christ became poor, that we through his poverty might be made rich.

The next thing is *the ground or spring from whence all this comes;* it is from grace. 'You know the grace of our Lord Jesus Christ.' It was his mere grace. There was nothing that could compel him. God the Father could not compel him, because he was equal with his Father; being God, there was an equality of essence.

And then, what was there in us that should move him to abase himself so low? Was there any worth in us? No. We were dead. Was there any strength in us? No. We were dead in sins. Was any goodness in us? No. We were Christ's enemies. Was there any desire in us? No. We were opposite to all goodness in ourselves; there was no desire in us to be better than we were. If God should have let us alone to our own desires, we were posting to hell. It is the greatest misery in the world, next to hell itself, to be given up to our own desires. A man were better to be given up to the devil than to his own desires. He may torment him, and perhaps bring him to repentance; but to be given up to his own desires, leads to hell. It is merely of grace, grace. It was the grace of God the Father that gave his Son; and it was grace that the Son gave himself.

What is grace? It is a principle from whence all good comes from God to us. As God loves us men, and not angels, it is *philanthropia*;* as God's affection is beneficial to our nature, so it is love; as it is to persons in misery, so it is mercy; as it is free, without any worth in us procuring it, so it is grace. It is the same affection; only it differs outwardly in regard of the object. Hence we see that Christ must be considered as a joint cause of our salvation with the Father. 'It is the grace of our Lord Jesus Christ.' You see here he became poor to make us rich. Indeed, he was sent and anointed and sealed, and had authority of his Father; yet notwithstanding his joint grace and consent went with it. Therefore he was a principal, as Chrysostom speaks, with a principal (*d*). He differs nothing at all from his Father, but in order of persons; first the Father and then the Son, both being jointly God, and both joint causes of the salvation of mankind. The Father chose us to salvation; the Son paid the price for us; and the Holy Ghost applies it and sanctifies our natures. God the Father loved the world, and gave his Son. Christ loved the world, and gave himself: 'He loved me, and gave himself for me,' saith St Paul, Gal. ii. 20. Therefore we should think of the sweet consent of the Trinity, in their love to mankind. So the Father loved us, that he gave his Son; so the Son loved us, that he gave himself; so the Holy Ghost loves us, that he conveys all grace to us, and dwells in us, and assures us of God's love.

We must not think of Christ as an underling in the work of salvation. He is a principal, in the work, from his Father. The grace of our Lord Jesus Christ it is the cause of all. It was the cause why he was man. It is the cause of all grace that is in us. That that is the cause of the cause, is the cause of the thing caused. The grace of Christ is the cause of all in us; because it was the cause of Christ's suffering from whence we have grace. Grace was the cause that Christ was man, and that he suffered;

* That is, φιλανθρωπία.—G.

therefore it is the cause of grace in us. Christ was a gift; the Father gave him, and he gave himself. 'If thou hadst known the gift of God,' saith Christ to the woman of Samaria, John iv. 10. Oh it is the greatest gift that ever was!

Therefore when we think of any one of the persons in the Trinity, we must not exclude the rest, but include all, which is a comfortable consideration; because there is a sweet union of all the three persons in the great work of salvation. As Christ saith, 'I in the Father, and the Father in me,' John xvii. 21: not in essence alone—he is God, and I am God—but I am in the Father, and he in me. I consent with the Father, and the Father with me. We both agree in the great work of salvation.

Therefore we should return the glory of all the good we have to God the Father, and to Christ; and as it is in Rev. v. 12, 'Worthy is the Lamb, because he hath redeemed us.' When we think of the good we have by Christ, 'Worthy is the Lamb, because he shed his blood for us.' 'The Lamb of God, that takes away the sins of the world,' he is worthy of all praise and honour. We should honour the Father, and honour the Son, and the Holy Spirit that applies the good we have by Christ to us. When we glorify God, let us glorify Christ too, 'who together with the Father is to be glorified,' because it was his grace to give himself; he made himself poor for us. We cannot honour the Father more than by honouring the Son; for God the Father will be seen in his Son, as the apostle saith, 'In Christ we behold the glory of God,' Eph. iii. 21. Therefore what he saith of Christ here tends to the glory of the Father.

Christ not only as God is gracious, and was willing to the work of salvation, but as the meritorious cause of the grace of his Father; for grace should not have been derived to us from the Father, unless first it had been seated on Christ in our nature, and in him derived to us.

The work of salvation, as it is from Christ, so it is from the grace of Christ; therefore it was free and voluntary. What so free as grace? Therefore Christ's abasement and poverty, it was merely* voluntary. If it had not been voluntary, it had not been meritorious and satisfactory. It was a free-will offering; it was of grace, not forced and commanded without his own consent. It was merely of grace, for our good and salvation; that we might have the more comfort. It was a free-will offering. He seemed as man to decline death, to shew the truth of his manhood; but when again he considered wherefore his Father sent him, 'Not my will, but thine be done,' Mat. xxvi. 42; and with joy, 'With a desire have I desired to eat my last passover with you; and I have a baptism, and how am I pained till I be baptized with it!' Luke xxii. 15. However, to shew the truth of his manhood, he feared death; yet, when he considered what he was sent for, it was with a resignation on the divine nature. So it was a free-will offering, and a sacrifice 'of a sweet smell to God the Father,' Philip. iv. 18.

Therefore when we think of Christ, let us think of nothing but grace; or when we think of heaven or of any blessing by Christ, all comes under the notion of grace, because all comes from mere favour. There are four descents of grace:—

[1.] *First, Grace as it is in God and Christ in their own breasts;* the favour of God resting in his own bosom.

[2.] And then this grace and favour *shewed in grace;* that is, in habitual grace; in bestowing grace upon our nature, to sweeten and sanctify it, to fit it for communion with God.

* That is, 'altogether.'—G.

[3.] And then *actual grace;* the movings of the Spirit to every good work; to every action of grace.

[4.] And then *every gift of God, every blessing is a grace;* because it riseth from grace. As we say of the gifts of a great person, this is his grace or favour; so every good thing we have is a grace. It is the favour of God in Christ that sweeteneth all. Let us labour to see grace in all, especially the fundamental grace, the favour of God and of Christ, the cause of all. And let us see any grace in us as from that grace, and every good act we do, a grace, from mere favour; and every blessing we have is a grace, if our hearts be good: as the apostle calls the Macedonians' benevolence a grace, 2 Cor. viii. 2. Everything that is good is a grace. 'Therefore, not unto us, not unto us, but unto thy name be the glory,' Ps. cxv. 1, both of thy favour and of all that comes from it; all that we have is sweet, because it issues from grace. The favour in the thing is better than the thing itself. As we say of gifts, we care not for the gift, but for the love of him that gave it; so the good things that we have are not so sweet as the favour of him that gives it, when we deserve not so much as daily bread, but that also is of grace. The source and spring of all that is in us, is free grace in the breast of God and Christ.

In the controversy between us and the papists, when we say we are justified by grace, we must not understand it of inherent grace, whereby our natures are sanctified, and that but in part; but it is meant of the free grace and mercy of God in Christ, and the free grace of Christ in his own breast. Let us take heed that we build not our justification and salvation upon a false title. The title is the grace of Christ, and of God the Father.

Now the grace we have in Christ in the breast of God is, either the good will of God, whereby he is disposed to give Christ, and to do all good to us . . .* There is no cause of that at all. Christ as God joins with the Father in that grace, which is *amor benevolentiæ*, the grace of good will. Christ as mediator is the effect of that grace. But then there is the grace of complacency, whereby God delights in us. This is bestowed upon the creature in effectual calling. Then God shews the grace of delighting in us, engrafting us into Christ by faith; for though before all worlds God had a purpose to do good to us, yet that is concealed till we believe. As water that runs under ground, it is hid a long time till it break out suddenly; and then we discover that there was a stream run under ground, as Arethusa, and other rivers (*e*); so it is with the favour of God from eternity: it runs under ground. Till we be called we see not Christ's good will to us; but when we believe and become one with Christ, God looks upon us with the love of complacency; with the same love wherewith he loves Christ; because we are in Christ, as it is in John xvii. 23, 'I in them, and they in me.' God loves the head and members with the same love. Christ as God was freely disposed to choose men; but Christ as mediator continues this favour and mercy of God, when we are grafted into him, to shine on us continually. It is this second that we must labour for as a fruit of the first. Let us labour not only to know that there was an eternal love of God to some that are his; but labour by faith in Christ, to know that he shines upon us in Christ; and all other graces within us, and all other gifts, are from this first grace. Therefore they have the name. Why do we call faith, hope, and love graces, but because they issue from the mercy and favour and love of God in Christ? And, as I said before, why do we

* Sentence unfinished.—G.

call any benefit we have a grace? Because it comes from grace. All good things have the term of grace on them, to shew the spring from whence they come.

I will not enter into dispute with points of popery, that stinks now in the nostrils of every man that hath but the use of ordinary reason, it is so full of folly and blasphemy. I rather speak of positive truths, to see God's grace and favour, and bless God for it in every thing we have.

Doth all that we have in Christ come from grace, the grace in us, and comforts and outward things merely from grace? Then esteem them more from the spring from whence they come than for themselves. The necessaries of this life, food and raiment, they are but mean things in themselves; but if we consider what spring they come from—from the blood of Christ that hath purchased them, and from the grace and love of Christ—grace will add value to them. Grace will make all sweet that we have; when we can say, I have this from the grace of God, as Jacob said, 'These are the children that God hath given me of his bounty and grace,' Gen. xxxiii. 5. This is the provision, the help and comfort that I have from the grace of Christ; for the same grace that gives heaven gives necessaries and daily bread. Let us look on every thing, and put the respect of grace upon every thing. It is grace that we meet with afflictions whereby we are corrected. God might have let us go on in the hardness of our hearts. Look upon every thing as a fruit of God's grace and favour. What is the reason that we are no more thankful for common benefits? Because we look not on them as issuing from grace. Take away grace, the free favour of God, extract this quintessence, take the love of God out of things—what are they? Let a man be rich, if he have it not from the love and mercy of God, what will all be in time but snares? Let a man be great in the world, if it be not from the grace of God, what is it? As God saith, 'I will curse you in your blessings,' Deut. xxviii. 17. Without grace we are cursed in those things that else are blessings. Take grace from Adam in paradise, and Adam is afraid in paradise, and hides his head. Take the favour of the king from Haman, and nothing will do him good. Take the favour of the king from Absalom, and all other liberties that he had are nothing worth, when he must not go to the court, 2 Sam. xiv. 24, *seq*. So take the grace and favour of God away that sweetens all, they will prove snares, and we shall find by experience that God will curse us in all our blessings. Let us labour therefore to have a sensible feeling of this free grace and mercy of God in Christ.

And, to add this further, the grace of Christ, it is a fruitful grace, it is a rich grace, as the apostle saith here. 'You know the grace of our Lord Jesus Christ, who became poor to make us rich by his poverty.' The favour of God and Christ, it is no empty favour. It is not like the winter sun, that casts a goodly countenance when it shines, but gives little comfort and heat. Many men give sweet and comfortable words, but there is nothing follows, it is but a barren favour. It is not so with God's favour, to give only a shining countenance but no warmth. No; saith the apostle, 'You know the grace of our Lord Jesus Christ, who, though he were rich, he became poor.' It was a grace that made him empty himself of himself, to make us full; it made him poor to make us rich; he abased himself to make us glorious. As is the man, so is his strength, saith the proverb: so, as is the person, such is the favour and good-will we expect from him. Now Christ being so potent a person, being God and man, his grace must needs be wondrous rich, suitable to his greatness. If God will free a man, he will free him from all miseries; if he advance a man, he will advance him to heaven; if he will punish a man, he will punish him to hell; his wrath shall seize on him for ever; what he doth, he will do like a God. The grace of Christ, it is a powerful rich grace.

Therefore let us examine ourselves, am I in the favour of God and of Christ? If I be, surely it is a rich favour, it tends to the best riches; he became poor to make me rich. Where is my faith, my love, my hope, my contentation, my patience and victory over temptations and lusts? Is it a dead favour? Am I in the favour of Christ, and find no fruits of it? Certainly it is but an illusion: therefore as yet I am not in the compass of Christ's favour. Therefore I must wait in the use of means, and humbling myself; 'he gives grace to the humble,' James iv. 6. And with a sense of our spiritual poverty, let us pray to God to shine on us in Christ, that we may find the fruit of his love enriching us with grace. Oh that my faith, and hope, and grace, were more! Oh let this evidence that I am in thy favour [be revealed] by the fruits of it, that I may find those riches that thou hast procured by thy poverty. And let us not rest till we find the fruits of this grace, though not alway in the comfort, yet in the strength and ability, that we may perform, in some measure, what is required. Though we have not much of the comfort that we desire, yet if we have strength we have that that is better. It is better to have grace than comfort here. God reserves that for another world. But let us always look for one of them, either sensible peace and joy; or if not that, yet strength against our corruptions, and ability to do God service in some measure; to do something above nature. Holy desires, and ability, and strength, they come not from nature, but from the favour of Christ. Therefore having these, I know I am in the love of Christ. These are favours that he bestows only upon his own. Favours of the left hand he gives to castaways; but his special favours, the riches of grace, he gives only to his children. Therefore let us labour to find somewhat wrought in our natures, that may evidence to us that we are in this rich favour of God.

Lastly, This grace of Christ being free, that we neither desired it nor deserved it, why may not Manasseh take hope as well as David, if he submit himself, though he were so horrible a sinner as he was? Why may not Paul, a persecutor, find mercy as well as Timothy, that was brought up to goodness from his youth? It is free. Therefore let no man despair that hath been a wicked liver in former time. The best stand in need of grace, and it is of grace that they are what they are; as St Paul saith, 'By grace I am that I am,' 1 Cor. xv. 10; and the worst, if they come in and submit themselves, and take Christ for their Lord, and submit to his government, and will be ruled by his word and Spirit, and not continue to live in rebellious courses, they may partake of this grace.

But again, let none presume. For though it be free grace, yet we must confess our sins and forsake them, or else we shall find no grace. We must be poor in spirit, and sensible of our misery; for God enricheth those that are empty and poor, 'the rich he sends empty away,' Luke i. 53. We must sue to God for grace by the Spirit of grace, and take heed that we turn not these offers of grace to occasions of wantonness, and so divide Christ; to take out of Christ what we list, and leave what we list. We must know that Christ, as he is our Jesus to save us, so he is our Lord; as he saith here, the *Lord Jesus Christ*. We must submit to him for the time to come, and then we shall find experience of his sweet grace.

The next thing I observe briefly is, that

Doct. 5. *This grace must be known.*

Saith the apostle here, 'You *know* the grace of our Lord Jesus Christ.' A man may know his riches, he may know his interest in Christ. The apostle useth it here as an argument to persuade them to good works. That that is used as an argument must be known before the thing can be persuaded. A thing cannot be made light by that which is darker than itself. But the apostle here useth this as an argument, 'You know the grace of our Lord Jesus Christ,' so that these truths are taken for granted, that all grace comes by the poverty of Christ. And then, that we may know ourselves to be interested in it, that Christ's poverty was for us. A man that is a true Christian may know his share and interest in the grace of Christ, or else how should he be persuaded by this as an argument if he know it not? Or how shall he be comfortable except he know that he hath interest in Christ? It may be known out of the Scriptures, as a history, that Christ is gracious for matter of fact. The devils know it as well as we; and Judas knew it. But he speaks here of a knowledge with interest. You know it by experience; 'the Spirit witnesseth to your spirits' so much, that Christ gave himself for you. I know the grace of Christ as mine, as belonging to me, as if there were no man in the world besides. And as this knowledge is with interest, so it stirs up to do.* All other knowledge but knowledge with interest may stand with desperation; and what good will it do to know in general that Christ came to save sinners, and yet go to hell for all that? It is the knowledge that applies Christ in particular that saves a man; that knowledge that determines the general to my own person. Therefore we must labour for this. Christ was poor for me; 'he loved me and gave himself *for me*,' Gal. ii. 20. The love and free grace of Christ, it may and it ought to be known. 'We ought to give all diligence to make our calling and election sure,' 2 Peter i. 10. It may be known, but it cannot be known without a great deal of diligence and self-denial. This knowledge is a super-added grace. It is one thing to be a sound Christian, and another thing to know it. A man cannot know it by reflection, but he must first be good in exercise; he must find grace working, he must give all diligence to make his calling and election sure *to him*. It may be sure in itself, but it cannot be sure to him without diligence. Therefore those that know their estate in grace, they are fruitful, growing, careful, watchful Christians.

It is no wonder that in these secure times, if we ask many whether they know themselves to be in the state of grace upon sound grounds, they wish well, and they have many doubtings. There are many that have the seeds and the work of grace in them, but the times are so secure, that they know it not. Usually it is made known to us in the worst times, either in the time of affliction, and temptation, and trial, or after, when we have 'fought the good fight,' 1 Tim. vi. 12, and overcome our corruptions. 'To him that overcometh will I give of the hidden manna,' Rev. ii. 17; that is, he shall have a sweet sense of Christ to be manna, to be bread of life to him, to him that conflicts and gets the victory over his corruptions. The reason why many feel not that sweet comfort from the 'grace of our Lord Jesus Christ,' it is because either they do not conflict with their base corruptions, or if they do strive, they get but a little ground of them.

And let us take heed of that cold and injurious conceit,† as if it were a thing not to be known whether we belong to Christ or no. What! Do

* The word here is 'due.' Qu. 'do' or 'duty'?—G.

† That is, 'conception,' idea, = opinion.—G.

we think that Christ would come in the flesh and become poor, nay, become a curse for us, and that he is now in heaven for us, and all that we should doubt whether we be in his love or no, and that we should not labour to find our portion in that love? What a wrong is this to the grace of Christ. Is not all his dealing towards us that we might be joyful in ourselves, and thankful and fruitful to him; and how can this be without some knowledge that our state is good? How can we live well and die comfortably without it? Therefore let us make it the main scope and aim of our endeavour. Oh, the happiness of that Christian that is good, and knows himself to be so! What in this world can fall very uncomfortably to such a man? Nothing in the world can take down his courage much; whereas another man that doubts of this can never be comfortable in any condition: he cannot be joyful and thankful in prosperity; he cannot be comfortable in adversity, for he knows not from what ground this comes, whether it be in love to him or no.

You see from hence, likewise, that grace is no enemy to good works, neither the freedom of God's favour, being without any merit on our part; nor the knowledge and assurance of salvation. It is no enemy to diligence and to good works; nay, it is the foundation of them. The apostle doth not use it here as an argument to neglect good works. No. He stirs them up by it. If anything in the world will work upon a heart that hath any ingenuity,* it is the love, and favour, and grace of God. 'The love of Christ constraineth,' 2 Cor. v. 14. The love of Christ, as known, it melts the heart. The knowledge of the grace of Christ, it is very effectual to stir us up, as to all duties, so especially to the duty of bounty and mercy; for experience of grace it will make us gracious, and kind, and loving, and sweet to others. Those that have felt mercy will be ready to shew mercy. Those that have felt grace and love, they will be ready to reflect, and shew that to others that they have felt themselves. Those that are hard-hearted and barren in their lives and conversations, it is a sign that the Sun of righteousness never yet shined on them. There is a power in grace, and grace known, to assimilate the soul to be like unto Christ; it hath a force to stir us up to that that is good, Titus ii. 11, 12. The apostle enforceth self-denial, a hard lesson; and holiness to God, justice to others, and sobriety to ourselves. What is the argument he useth? 'The grace of God hath appeared.' The grace of God hath shined, as the word signifieth.† He means Christ appeared, but he saith, 'The grace of God hath appeared;' when Christ appeared, grace appeared. Christ is nothing but pure grace clothed with our nature. What doth this appearing of grace teach us? 'To deny all ungodliness and worldly lusts, and to live holily, and righteously, and soberly,' &c. Holily and religiously in regard of God; justly in regard of men, and not only justly, but bountifully, for bounty is justice. It is justice to give to the poor. 'Withhold not good from the owners.' They have right to that we have. Grace, when it appears in any soul, it is a teacher; it teacheth to deny all that is naught,‡ and it teacheth to practise all that is good. It teacheth to live holily and righteously in this present evil world. Many men like the text thus far, 'The grace of God bringeth salvation.' Oh it is a sweet text! Ay, but what follows? What doth that grace teach thee? It teacheth to deny ungodliness and worldly lusts; it doth not teach men to follow and set themselves upon the works of the devil, but to live soberly and justly and

* That is, 'ingenuousness.'—G.

† That is, φαίνω.—G.

‡ That is, 'naughty' = wicked.—G.

righteously in this present evil world. It is said of the woman in the gospel, 'She loved much, because much was forgiven her,' Luke vii. 47. What made that blessed woman so enlarged in her affection and love to Christ? She had experience of the pardon of many sins, and having felt the love of Christ, she loved him again. And what is the reason that those that are converted from dangerous courses of life, do often prove the most fruitful Christians? Because they have felt most love and mercy. Who was more zealous than the blessed apostle St Paul? Oh, he found rich and abundant love! How large is he in setting forth the mercy of God: 'Oh the height, and breadth, and depth!' Rom. xi. 33. Nothing contents him, no expressions, when he speaks of God's mercy; because he had been a wicked man, and found mercy. Let no man be discouraged, if he have been never so sinful, if he come in. The more need he hath of mercy, the more abundant God is, as the apostle saith here, 'You know the grace of our Lord Jesus Christ.' And those that have felt most grace will be most wrought on, to shew the fruits of that grace in all good works, in duties towards God and men.

And if we find not our hearts wrought on, by the consideration of the grace of Christ apprehended and known to this end, 'we turn the grace of God into wantonness,' Jude iv. It is a sign of an ill condition. The Scripture speaks nothing but discomfort to such that take occasion from the free grace and infinite and boundless mercy of God, to be loose and careless in their lives and conversations; that think it is a time of liberty, and we may do what we list. Though the tongues of men say not so, nor they dare not for shame, yet their lives speak it. Would men else live in swearing, and other debauched carriage, that is offensive to God and men? Do they know that there is a God, a Christ, and mercy? Doth mercy and grace teach them that lessou? No. It teacheth us to deny such base lives and lusts, and to live holily, and soberly, and justly in this world. Therefore such men are atheists. Either they must not believe the Scriptures, or else exclude themselves from interest in mercy; for as yet they are not in the state of grace, in whom the consideration of mercy and grace doth not work better effects than these.

The gospel hath as strong encouragements, and stronger, to be good and gracious, than the law. Grace enforceth strictness of life more sweetly and strongly than the law. The law saith, 'We must not take the name of God in vain,' Exod. xx. 7; and we must be subject to our superiors, and to live chastely, &c., under a curse. Doth not the grace of God teach this as well as the law, and from a higher ground? It teacheth the same thing by arguments taken from love and grace. A man perisheth by the law in such sins, but then there is a pardon offered, if men will come under the government of Christ, and lead new lives. But if men refuse, there is a super-added guilt. Not only justice condemns such wretches, but mercy itself; because they refuse mercy upon these terms rather than they will leave their sinful courses. Mercy and justice both meet to condemn such persons. Let us take heed therefore of abusing the mercy and love of God. For then we quite overthrow God's end in the gospel. For why doth he convey all to us by love and mercy and grace, but that it may work the same disposition again in us to him? Or else we overturn the end of the gospel. Let us take heed of this, as ever we will find interest in this grace, without which we are the miserablest wretches that live. It were better for us that we had never heard of Christ and the gospel, than to live in sins against conscience, under the manifestation and publication of grace.

Doct. 6. Now, together with the grace of Christ, the apostle *brings the example of Christ, that both may stir them up to the duties of mercy and bounty and fruitfulness.* Indeed, the grace of Christ makes his example more sweet. Men willingly look upon examples.

The examples of great and excellent persons; the example of loving and bountiful persons; the example of such as are loving and bountiful to us in particular; the example of such as we have interest in, that are near and dear to us, and we to them—these four things commend examples. Now is there any greater or more excellent person than Christ? Is there any fuller of love and mercy and grace than he, that hath made himself poor to make us rich? And all of us, if we be Christians indeed, we have interest in this. Our hearts and consciences by the Spirit of God have some persuasion of this. And then again he is dear and near unto us. He is our head and husband; he is 'all in all unto us,' 1 Cor. xv. 28. Therefore the example of Christ joined with his grace, it is a wondrous forcible example.

Quest. How shall we make this example of Christ profitable to us?

Ans. (1.) First of all, let us look often *into the grace of Christ;* the grace and free mercy of God in giving Christ. Consider how God hath laid forth all his riches in Christ, and consider how miserable we had been without Christ, even next unto devils in misery. A man is the most miserable creature under heaven if he have not interest in Christ; he is a lost creature. Let us dwell upon the meditation and consideration of this till we feel our hearts warmed. If one pass through the sunshine, it doth not much heat; but if the sun beat upon a thing, there will be a reflection of heat. So let us stay upon this consideration of the infinite love and mercy of Christ to us wretches, and this warming the heart, it will transform us to the likeness of Christ; as the apostle saith, 2 Cor. iii. 18, 'We all as in [a] mirror beholding the glory of God' (he means the glory of God's mercy in Christ), 'we are transformed and changed from glory to glory,' from one degree of grace to another. The serious consideration of the love and mercy of God in Christ, it is a wondrous sweet thing, and it hath a transforming power with it. And that is the reason why the gospel converts men, and not the law. The law never converts a man; but, together with the Spirit, it will cast him down. But the gospel, which is the promulgation of grace and mercy to penitent sinners, that confess their sins and forsake them, and come under a new government of grace, the publishing of this hath the Spirit of grace with it to work conversion. Therefore it is called the ministry of the Spirit; because the Spirit goes with the doctrine of grace, to change us and make us gracious, to persuade us that God loves us, and to stir us up to perform all duties in that sweet affection that God requires in the gospel, the affection of love. Therefore if we be or ever were converted, it is this way. Our hearts are wrought on by the consideration of the love and mercy of God in Christ; so that love begets love, and mercy begets a sweetness in us to God again. In the nature of the thing it cannot be otherwise, when the soul stands convinced of the sweet mercy of God in Christ, and of the sweet love of Christ, who being God became man, to take our nature, and suffer the punishment that was due to us, and is now in heaven appearing and making intercession for us, it cannot be but the soul will be stirred up to a desire of conformity to this blessed Saviour. Therefore let us let go all disputings of election, concerning God's decree, and let us do our duty, and depend upon God in the use of means. Let us labour to see the love of God in Christ, and that will put all questions out of question (though in some cases we must labour to know how to vindicate the truth, but when it comes to our own particular), lay other things aside, let us do our duty in the use of means, and think of the end of the gospel, of the end of Christ's incarnation and death, namely, to reveal the bowels of God's mercy to sinners; and then we shall find the intendment of all working upon us, that God had an eternal purpose to save us.

(2.) Again, if we would make good use of the example of Christ, *we must converse with those that have the Spirit of Christ in them*, as Christ is in every good Christian, and see what lovely things the Spirit of Christ discovers in them. That will have a transforming power likewise. And certainly next to the meditation of Christ, and the excellencies that are in him, I know no way more effectual than holy communion with those that are led with the Spirit of Christ, when we see the sweet fruit of it in others. It hath been a means sanctified to do a great deal of good to many; and those that delight not in it, they never knew what the likeness of Christ meant; for those that desire to be like to Christ, they love the shining of Christ in any. In these careless times, all companies are alike one with another. Indeed, when men's callings thrust them upon it, they must be allowed to converse with all men; but in familiar and intimate society, those that do not make choice of those that find some work of grace on their hearts by the Spirit of God, they may well doubt of their condition; for grace it will make us love the like. As we see creatures of the same kind, they love and company one with another; doves with doves, and lambs with lambs; so it must be with the children of God, or else we do not know what the communion of saints means, which indeed is a thing little understood in the world. These times of security are times of confusion. Affliction will make us know one another better.

(3.) Again, if we would make use of the example of Christ, *let us put cases sometimes to ourselves, what Christ would do or not do in such a case.* I profess myself to be a member of Christ, to be one with him, and he one with me. Would Christ be cruel if he were on earth? would he swear, and look scornfully upon others? would he undermine others, and cover all with a pretence of justice? Oh no! It is the devil's work to do so. If we be not members of Christ, woe unto us! And if we be, do such courses suit with such a nearness to Christ? Either let us be religious to purpose, or else disclaim all; for it is better a great deal never to own religion, than to own it and to live graceless lives under the profession of Christ.

Now to stir us up to express Christ in our lives and conversations let us consider, the more like we are to Christ, the more he delights in us; for every one delights in those that are like them. And what a sweet state is it for God and Christ to delight in us. God the Father will delight in us because we are like the Son of his delight. Whom doth God delight most in? In his own blessed Son. And who come nearest in his delight to his Son? Those that express him in their lives and conversations.

The more like we are to Christ, the more like we shall be one to another. As if there be one statue, or picture, or effigies, that is set for the first sample, the nearer the rest come to that, the more like they are one to another; so I say, the nearer Christians come to the first pattern of goodness, Christ himself, who is God's master-piece as it were, that which he glories in, the more we come to be like one another, and love and joy one in another. What is the sweet communion that we shall have one with another for ever in heaven? Is it not that the Spirit shall be all in all in every one, and each shall look upon another as perfect in grace and love, and so shall solace and delight themselves, first in God and Christ, and then in one another, admiring and reverencing the graces and sweetness one of another. This is the very joy of heaven itself, and it is the heaven upon earth, when we can joy and solace ourselves one in another as we are good. Now the nearer we come to Christ, who is the image of God, the more we shall attain this. Therefore let us labour that Christ may be all in all in us; that as the soul doth act the body, so the Spirit of Christ may act us, that Christ may speak in us, and think in us, and love in us by his Spirit; that he may dwell in us, and joy, and hate in us by his Spirit; that we may put off ourselves, and our carnal affections, and the spirit of the world, and that we may 'put on' Christ, and be clothed with him, that we may say with St Paul, 'I live not, but Christ lives in me' by his Spirit. Whence was Paul stirred up to that? Oh, saith he, 'Christ loved me, and gave himself for me,' Gal. ii. 20. The grace of Christ stirred him up, 'Christ loved me, and gave himself for me,' and by his Spirit he witnesseth to my soul that he did so. Therefore the life that I live is by the Spirit of Christ; Christ lives in me.

But to come to the particular duty whereunto the grace and example of Christ should stir us up to be like him; that is, in kindness, and mercy, and bounty, to the poor saints; for that is the scope of the apostle here, in this and the next chapter. 'You know the grace of our Lord Jesus Christ, who, though he was rich, he became poor,' &c. Wherefore doth the apostle bring all this? To move them to the duty of bounty and liberality. This duty it is legal* from the example of Christ; it is a thing that hath much equity in it; and it is enough to a Christian heart, that hath the love of God, to put him in mind of the grace of God to him. You need not beat upon him, or press him further than thus, 'You know the grace of our Lord Jesus.' Remember you are a Christian. You have felt the experience of God's love in Christ. Every man will judge of the equity, that we should therefore be gracious and kind and loving to others, in imitation of Christ; because he hath been so to us. Wherein stands the equity?

First, It may appear in this, if we consider in how near a relation those that need our help are to us, and likewise to Christ?

First, What is their relation to us? Not only that they are our flesh, for so are all men; but they are heirs of the same salvation, bought with the death of the same Christ; such as Christ feeds with his own body and blood; such as he clothes with his own righteousness. They are fellow-members with us, fellow-heirs of heaven, and members of Christ; such as he died for, to redeem with the price of his own blood. There is an undeniable equity, if we consider their condition, their relation to Christ, and to us.

Second. Again, there is a marvellous binding equity, *to see the grace of God to us in particular.* Christ became poor, to make us rich in grace here, and in glory hereafter. And shall not I out of my riches give somewhat to the poor? Is it not equal? Christ from heaven came in my nature and flesh to visit me; as it is in the song of Zacharias, 'The day-spring from on high hath visited us,' Luke i. 78; and shall not I visit Christ in his members? He came from heaven to earth to take notice of my wants and miseries, to do and suffer that that I should have done and suffered. He feeds me with his body and blood, that is, with his satisfaction to divine justice by his death; and shall not I feed his poor members? Christ clothes me with his righteousness, and shall not I clothe Christ in

* That is, incumbent or enforced.—Ed.

his poor members? In the consideration of these things the Spirit of God will be effectual to stir us up to this marvellous neglected duty, of kindness and mercy to those that stand in need.

And because Christ is our pattern herein, let us labour to imitate Christ in the manner of relieving, and shewing kindness, and communicating to others, that we may do it as Christ hath done.

How is that?

First, Christ prevented* us when we never desired him; so we should prevent others. Sometimes the modesty of those that want is such that they will not lay open their wants. We should see it and prevent it. He gives too late ofttimes that gives to a man that asks him. Therefore herein let us imitate Christ, to consider of the miseries of others. He looked on and considered the miseries of mankind, and it drew him from heaven to the virgin's womb; from thence to the cross, to the grave, even as low as hell, in his preventing love and mercy. Therefore, when we see any need, especially if there be any worth in them in any kind, let us not stay till it be wrested from us by entreaty, for it is dearly bought ofttimes that comes that way.; but prevent them in mercy, as Christ hath done to us.

Secondly, What Christ did for us, he did *marvellous cheerfully and readily*. O what a desire he had to eat his last passover, a little before he was crucified! 'With a desire have I desired to eat this passover with you,' Luke xxii. 15. He was cheerful in it; he had a great desire to do us good; and, as he saith, John iv. 32, when his disciples put him in mind of eating, when he had not eat in a long time before, saith he, 'It is meat and drink to me to do the will of my Father.' So whatsoever we do to others, we should do it cheerfully and readily, as he did.

Third, Again, whatsoever Christ did for us, he did it *out of love, and grace, and mercy; he did it inwardly from his very bowels:* so when we do anything for others, we should not only do the deed, but do it from an inward principle of love and mercy. Therefore the Scripture phrase is, pour 'out thy bowels;' and saith St John, if a man see his brother in need, and pretend he loves God, and yet relieves him not, 'how is there bowels in such a man?' 1 John iii. 17; and so in Micah vi. 8, 'He hath shewed thee, O man, what is good, to love mercy;' not only to be merciful, to do works of mercy, but to love it; to do what we do out of love and affection; and 'pour out thy heart to thy flesh,' as it is in Isaiah,† to give the heart and affection when we do anything; or else we may give with the hand and deny with the heart. A man may give a thing so untowardly that one may see it comes against his heart and will. Therefore let us labour to do that we do with our whole man, especially from our heart, and affection, and bowels. It is said of Christ in the Gospel, when he saw the people in misery, his bowels yearned within him; the works of grace and mercy in Christ, they came from his bowels first. Let us work our hearts to pity, and love, and mercy first, that it may come from the soul as well as from the outward man.

Fourth, Again, Christ *gave that that was his own*, his own body, his own life, for his sheep; and his own endeavour, whatsoever he gave, was his own. So if we will be kind to others, we must do it of our own; we must not do good with that that we have gotten from others by unjust means. For the 'sacrifice of the wicked,' in this kind, 'is an abomination to the Lord,' Isa. i. 13. Let us have interest in that we give. Christ gave his own life, and God gave his own Son for us.

* That is, 'anticipated.'—G.

† Isa. lviii. 7, 10.—Ed.

Fifth, And as Christ gave his own self, so he gave himself *in life and death for us*;* he did not reserve all for his death; but for us he was born, for us he lived, for us he died; he deferred not all till his death. Christ did us wondrous good by his death; and men may do much good when they die. But let us endeavour to be like Christ in both; to do good while we live, and do good when we die likewise. The common speech is, the gifts of dying men are dying, dead gifts. It is a speech tending to the disparagement of gifts in that kind, because they are not so acceptable as the gifts of living men in many respects; notwithstanding, let not men be discouraged from doing good even when they die. Indeed, it is most comfortable to do it while they live, because,

(1.) It is an evidence then *that they have a spirit of faith*, to depend upon the promise of God. It is no exercise of faith, to give when a man can keep it no longer.

(2.) Again, he that doth good while he liveth, he *hath the prayers of others*; he is under the blessing of the poor; and that is a sweet thing. Suppose the poor be barbarous base people, that they bless not a man with their words, yet their 'sides bless him.'† Now those that defer all till they die, they want this comfort; they are not under the blessing of the poor. The rule of our religion is, that we have no good‡ by the prayers of others. I will not discuss that point now. But undoubtedly it is a sweet comfort that we have of that we do while we live, by the blessing and prayers of the poor, to whom we do good.

(3.) Then again, in civil respects, it is our own, and *we are sure it is well bestowed*. When we are dead, the propriety is gone from us. It comes into the possession of another man, and we know not how he will dispose of it. Perhaps he may die before thee that needs thy help; or thou mayest die; or thou mayest not have the same mind. Therefore while thou hast a heart and opportunity to do good, forget not to do it presently. We have need to be urged in these cold dead times, to labour that the grace of Christ may be effectual in our hearts, to do all the good we can, in our life time, as Christ did.

Sixth, And let us labour to do it as he did, *constantly*, that we may 'never be *weary of well-doing*,' Gal. vi. 9. 'In the morning sow thy seed, and in the evening let not thy hand rest,' Eccles. xi. 6. It is comfort enough that it is called *seed*. Who grieves to cast his seed into the ground? He knows he shall have a plentiful return. So all that we give, it is seed. We see it not for the present. No more we do the seed that is sown. But 'cast thy bread upon the water, and after many days thou shalt find it,' Eccles. xi. 1. Though we see not this seed for the present, yet we shall have a plentiful harvest. Only labour to do it with discretion. For men do not sow upon the stones, nor upon the fallow ground; they do not scatert their seed in any place. Sowing is a regular thing. Men cast seed into ground that is prepared. Therefore there must be spiritual discretion, the wisdom of a steward in this kind: Ps. cxii. 5, 'The just man doth all things with wisdom and discretion.'

Quest. But must we not be liberal, and kind, and bountiful to all?

Ans. Yes, in case of necessity. Then we are to look to man's nature, because he is a partaker of our nature. And he is such an one as may be a member of Christ, and one for whom Christ died. For aught we know, he now bears the image of Christ; and he may come to the obedience of

* In the margin here, 'seasonably.'—G.

† Cf. Job xxxi. 20.—G.

‡ Qu. 'that we have good'?—G.

Christ; and our kindness may be effectual to bring him to goodness. Therefore, as we, if we be in need, do not stand upon it, but receive kindness from wicked men, so when wicked men are in need, we must not stand upon it, but give to wicked men. We must do as we would be done by, in such cases, in necessity.

But our kindness must be most to those that are nearest God, to those of the family 'and household of faith,' Gal. vi. 10. To those that God loves most we must be most kind; to whom God hath dispensed the greatest things, we should not deny the less.

Indeed, it is a hard matter to give wisely in these times, and not to abuse the sweet affection and grace of pity (it is an affection in all, but it is a grace in them that are good), because there are so many wretched people that live without God, without church, without commonwealth, without marriage, without baptism, like beasts. If anything be an object of pity, certainly this is, that there are so many that carry God's image on them, that are God's creatures, and for aught we know, such as Christ died for, that they should be suffered to live irregular, debauched, and base lives, scandalous to the church and state. And without question, if things be not better looked into, these will be instruments of much mischief by God's just judgment; because there be good laws that are not executed. The best mercy to such, is to see them set on work and to give them correction. But then for such as are beginning the world, that are poor, and cannot set up, and those that have the church of God in their families, that are ready to fall, and a little relief would keep them, that they fall not into inordinate courses, it is mercy to set them up and maintain them; and also by upholding those that are in the ministry. There are many ways in the church and state. A wise man can never want objects of mercy and charity: as Christ saith, 'The poor you shall have alway with you,' Mat. xxvi. 11; but, as I said, we must labour for a spirit of wisdom to do good as we should, and not to feed drones, instead of bees.

The Spirit of God is frequent in pressing this point; but this argument in the text, it may melt any man's heart, and take away all objections, 'The grace of our Lord Jesus Christ.'

If a man object, he that I should give to is an unworthy person; do but think how worthy we were of the favour of Christ to us? And then again, consider if there be any goodness in them, we give it to Christ in them, as Salvianus saith well *(f)*, Christ doth hide himself under the person of the poor. The poor man reacheth out his hand indeed, but Christ receives that that we give, and they are Christ's exchangers; for they take from us, and Christ rewards us with grace and increase of our substance here, and with glory hereafter. They receive it instead of Christ, and Christ begs in the person of the poor, in all jointly, and in every one particularly. Think of the grace of Christ to us, and then think Christ comes to me in the person of this or that poor man, and it will stir us up to this duty.

Obj. But some will say, If Christ were on earth himself, I should be ready to do it to him.

Ans. Certainly thou wouldst not. You know the place, Mat. xxv. 45: 'Inasmuch as you have not relieved these, you have denied it to me,' saith Christ. Let us not deceive ourselves; for even as we would do to Christ if he were on earth, we will do to his poor members; he hath made them his receivers.

Obj. But I shall want myself: I have a family and children.

Ans. It is the best way to provide for thy children, Ps. cxii. 3. God provides for the posterity of the righteous bounteous man. A man is not the poorer for discreet mercy. It is seed, as I said before. A poor man labours to have his seed sown, because it returns plentifully. Let us be sober, and abate of our superfluous expenses. Pride is an expender. And superfluous lusts, let us cut off from them, that we may have somewhat for seed. Let us labour in an honest calling, that we may have somewhat to give. Oh, it is a blessed thing to give! It is a thing that must be gotten by use. Our souls must be exercised to it. And when we have gotten it, learn an art of giving; we must exercise faith in it. And when we come to die, it will make us die wondrous sweetly; for when a man hath depended by faith and trust upon God's promise, that 'he that gives to the poor lends to the Lord,' Prov. xix. 17, and other like promises; I have exercised liberality, and now I come to give up my soul to God, I believe that God will make good the promise of life everlasting; I have believed his other promises before, and though I have cast my seed into the ground, that I saw it not, yet I have found that God hath blessed me the better in a way that I know not; and now I depend upon the same gracious God, in the promise of life everlasting. We should labour to do this, that we may die with comfort. What is it that troubles many when they come to die? Oh, they have not wrought out their 'salvation with fear and trembling,' Philip. ii. 12. They have neglected this duty and that duty; they have been careless in the works of mercy, &c. The time will come that that which we have given will comfort us more than that we have; we shall alway have that which we give, for that goes in bank: many prayers are made for us. We have the comfort of it here and when we die. What we leave, we know not what becomes of it.

Therefore let us labour to be discreetly large and bountiful, as we desire to die with comfort; as we would make it good that we know 'the grace of our Lord Jesus Christ,' with interest in it; and as we would make it good to our souls that the example of Christ is a thing that hath any efficacy with us; or else we shew that we have no interest in the grace of Christ; and then how miserable are we! We shall wish ere long that we had part in this grace and love of Christ; that he would speak comfortably to us at the latter day, 'Come, ye blessed of my Father, inherit a kingdom,' Mat. xxv. 34. Our life is short and uncertain; as we shall desire it then, so labour to be assured of it now; and let us be stirred up from this 'grace of our Lord Jesus Christ, who, though he were rich, became poor for our sakes, that we through his poverty might be made rich.'

NOTES.

(*a*) P. 496.—'Against the cursed heresy of Arius.' For a brief but excellent memoir of this famous heresiarch, see Dr Smith's Dictionary of Greek and Roman Biography and Mythology, *sub voce* by Dr Schmitz.

(*b*) P. 500.—'The papists would have him a beggar. Bellarmine, to countenance begging friars, would have Christ to be so.' This is a *commonplace* of papists, found in Bellarmine and all Romanist writers, in their advocacy of that 'voluntary humility' which Paul denounces (Col. ii. 18).

(*c*) P. 506.—'Saith St Bernard well, "O love that art so sweet, why becamest thou so bitter to thyself!"' One of the many pathetic exclamations of this father, repeatedly met with, in varying phraseology, in his letters. Cf. recent Memoir by Morison.

(*d*) P. 512.—'Therefore he was a principal, as Chrysostom speaks, with a principal.' This Chrysostom expresses at large in his Homilies on Genesis—'Let us make man;' and in his treatise on Christ's prayers as not inconsistent with his equality with the Father. The following sentences are from the latter of these treatises:—*ὅταν γαρ κολάζειν δέῃ, καὶ ὅταν τιμᾷν, καὶ ὅταν ἁμαρτήματα ἀφιέναι, καὶ ὅταν νομοθετεῖν, καὶ ὅταν τι τῶν πολλῷ μειζόνων δέῃ ποιεῖν, ὀυδαμου τὸν πατέρα καλουντα ἀυτὸν εὑρήσεις, ὀυδὲ εὐχόμενον, ἀλλὰ μετ' αὐθεντίας ἅπαντα πράττοντα. Chrys. De Christi precibus, contra Anomœos.*, lib. x.

(*e*) P. 514.—'Under ground, as Arethusa and other rivers. The reference is to the well (or river) of Arethusa, in the island of Ortygia, near Syracuse. Cf. Dictionary as in Note *a*, *sub voce*, and under Alpheius.

(*f*) P. 525.—'We give it to Christ in them, as Salvianus saith well; Christ doth hide himself under the person of the poor.' For the *thought*, cf. his *Adversus Avaritiam, frœsertim Clericorum et Sacerdotum*, and also incidentally his *De vero Judicio et Providentia Dei*. These treatises were translated into English, and published in 1700. 8vo. G.

END OF VOL. IV.

THE WORKS OF
RICHARD SIBBES

THE WORKS OF
RICHARD SIBBES

VOLUME 5

Expositions and Treatises from Portions of Several of the Epistles of St Paul

Edited by

Alexander B. Grosart

THE BANNER OF TRUTH TRUST

THE BANNER OF TRUTH TRUST

Head Office
3 Murrayfield Road
Edinburgh, EH12 6EL
UK

North America Office
610 Alexander Spring Road
Carlisle, PA 17015
USA

banneroftruth.org

The Complete Works of Richard Sibbes
first published in 7 volumes 1862-64
This reprint of volume 5 first published by
the Banner of Truth Trust 1977
Reprinted 1978, 2001, 2023

*

ISBN
Print: 978 0 85151 246 4

*

Printed in the USA by
Versa Press Inc.,
East Peoria, IL.

PREFATORY NOTE.

The present volume contains the whole of Sibbes's remaining Expositions and Treatises based upon portions of the Epistles of St Paul. The single sermons, from Pauline texts, not already included, will be given in Volume VII., along with those from other passages of Scripture, all of which it is proposed to place together therein.

A. B. G.

CONTENTS.

THE CHRISTIAN WORK.

THE CHRISTIAN WORK.

NOTE.

'The Christian Work' forms a portion of a considerable quarto, published in 1639. The *general* title-page is given below.* The 'Exposition' of chap. iii. follows this, and the other pieces specified therein will appear in their proper places. The 'Epistles Dedicatory and Prefatory' of the entire volume are herewith prefixed.

G.

AN
EXPOSITION
OF THE
THIRD CHAPTER
OF THE EPISTLE OF
St. *Paul* to the PHILIPPIANS :

Also {
Two Sermons of Christian watchfulnesse.
The first upon Luke 12. 37.
The second upon Revel. 16. 15.
An Exposition of part of the second Chapter of the Epistle to the *Philipp.*
A Sermon upon Mal. 4. 2. 3.
}

By the late Reverend Divine *Richard Sibbes*, D. D. Master of *Katherine* Hall in *Cambridge*, and sometimes Preacher at *Grayes-Inne.*

1 TIM. 4. 8.

But godlinesse is profitable, having promise of the life that now is, and of that which is to come.

LONDON,
Printed by *T. Cotes* for *Peter Cole*,* and are to be sold at the Glove & Lyon in *Corne-hill*, neare the *Royall Exchange*, 1639.

* For curious notices of Cole, see the Bibliographical List of the editions of Sibbes' different works in the 7th volume.—G.

TO THE RIGHT HONOURABLE

SIR MAURICE ABBOT KNIGHT,

NOW LORD MAYOR OF THE HONOURABLE CITY OF LONDON.*

RIGHT HONOURABLE—My respects unto you, being your honour's engaged many ways, have put me upon a design or project for you; the God of heaven graciously prosper it in my hand! The tenor of it is briefly this: to increase your honour, and to ease the burden of that laborious government which now lieth upon your shoulder.

To mention your name before the glorious labour of so great and worthy an agent in the factorage of heaven as the author of this piece was, and to make you a protector of them, cannot, I conceive, in sober interpretation but be conceived to add honour unto him that hath, and cause him to have more abundantly. Blessed is the wing that is spread over any of the things of Jesus Christ, to shelter them.

Again, to put into your hand, and from your hand into your heart, the remembrance of that God that will gloriously recompense your faithfulness in that great trust committed to you, cannot but (by the blessing of him to whom blessings belongeth) be a cordial means to strengthen your heart in the pang of government, and cause you to travail and bring forth with more ease. There is no labour, nor travail, nor sorrow, nor difficulty, nor danger, nor death, that hath any evil or bitterness in it when heaven is before us, and the truth and faithfulness of the living God embracing us.

If I have miscarried in point of good manners or otherwise in this dedication, your honour shall do but justice to charge your own courtesy and respects always shewed unto me (at least in part) with the blame of it. Had not there been the tempter, doubtless in this case I had not been the transgressor. The God of peace prosper the government of this great city in your hand, and make it a glorious rise and advantage unto you of your greater glory in the heavens. And your Honour may assure yourself that so it shall come to pass, unless that God that heareth prayer shall reject the prayer of,

Your honour to command in the Lord,

J. G.†

* Sir Maurice Abbot was the fifth son of Sir Maurice Abbot of Guildford, Surrey, grandfather of Abbot of Farnham. His more famous brothers were George, Archbishop of Canterbury, and Robert, Master of Baliol College, Oxford, and subsequently Bishop of Salisbury. Sir Maurice was Lord Mayor of London 1639, Drapers' Company; Sheriff, 1627. Family epitaphs still remain on a plate of brass on the south wall of the church of Guildford. Cf. Manning and Bray's History of Surrey, *sub voce;* also Guildhall MSS.—G.

† These initials here, and at close of the Epistle to the Reader, in all probability represent John Goodwin, the renowned champion of Arminianism. It were superfluous to annotate such a name. He died, it is believed, in 1665. Cf. Jackson's 'Life,' one vol. 8vo, 1822.—G.

TO THE READER.

Good Reader, to discourse the worth or commendations of the author (especially the pens of others having done sacrifice unto him in that kind), I judge it but an impertinency, and make no question, but that if I should exchange thoughts or judgments with thee herein, I should have but mine own again. The book itself, judiciously interpreted, is a volume of his commendation; and those, though from his own mouth, without any touch or tincture of vanity or self-affectation. The best sight of a man is to hear him speak—*loquere, ut videam*—the tongue being a voluntary and pleasant rack to the heart, to make it confess its treasure, whether it be good or evil. The diligence and care of those that have interposed for the preserving of what came from him in this way from perishing, have made the Christian world debtors unto them; and great pity it had been, that what he spake in public should have died in secret, and not be made seven times more public than speaking could do. The sparks of such fires as he kindled would have been ill quenched till the world had been further served with the light and heat of them.

It is true, heaps of books is one of the oppressions of the world, and the invention of the press hath been the exaltation of weakness and vanity amongst men, as well as of learning and knowledge. Yet know I no way better to retain the oppressed in this kind, than for men of worth and grown judgments and learning to appear in books also among the multitude. The time was when there were, as the apostle speaketh, 'gods many and lords many in the world,' 1 Cor. viii. 5; when the world was pestered with devils of all sorts, instead of gods; but the only means of discharging the world of them, was the setting forth and preaching of the one true God and Lord Jesus Christ. So the furnishing the world with such books, as are books indeed, that breathe spirit and life, and are strong of heaven, speaking with authority and power to the consciences of men, is the only way to affamish the multitude of idol* books, and to have them desolate without a reader. It is, questionless, with men in respect of books, as it is in respect of men themselves (and indeed how there should be any difference between men and books I know not, the book being but the mind of a man, and the mind of a man being the man himself). *Homo homini Deus, homo homini lupus.*† There are men that are gods to men, and there are men that are wolves to men; and the more men-wolves there are in the world, the more men-gods there had need to be; otherwise the darkness would overcome the light, and make the earth as the shadow of

* Qu. 'idle,' = useless.—G. Rather 'idol,' in the sense of unreal, false.—Ed.

† In margin here, 'Animus cujusque is est quisque.'—G.

death. So there are books that are laden with divine and true treasure; that will recompense the reader, his labour and pains sevenfold into his bosom; that will open his mouth and enlarge his heart to bless God, that hath given gifts unto men. Again, there are books also that will deal cruelly and deceitfully with men, consuming their precious time and opportunities; taking their money for that which is not bread. Now the more dreamers of dreams there are, there had need be the more that see visions. The weak, hungry, loose, and empty discourses the world is overlaid and encumbered withal, the more need it hath, by way of a counter recompence, of a full provision of solid and masculine writings, that may make men men, and not always children in understanding.

But I must remember that prefacing authors with long epistles is no employment of any sovereign necessity. Therefore I will no longer separate between thee and that which I desire to recommend unto thee more than anything of mine own. The blessing of Him that giveth the increase be upon the labour of him that planted and watered much in the courts of the house of his God; that though he be dead, he may yet speak to the edification of thine and of many souls.

Thine with a single heart and multiplied affections in the Lord,

I. G.*

DIRECTIONS TO THE READER.

CHRISTIAN READER, thou mayest please to take notice that this book is divided into two parts: the first whereof is upon the whole third chapter of the Epistle to the Philippians, and contains 256 pages; and because it is entire, and upon the whole third chapter, we have therefore put it first. The second part is upon some certain verses only of the second chapter to the Philippians, and some other texts of Scripture, and contains 204 pages.

Now, for the ready finding out of any principal or material things in the whole book, we have to the book annexed this alphabetical index; for the understanding whereof take thou notice, that the first *p* signifies the *part*, and the second *p* the *page* of that *part*, as for example: There being nothing observed in A, we begin with B, where first thou seest, *Christians must be blameless*, p. 92; that is, part the second, page 92 of the second part; then *how Saint Paul was blameless, when he was without the law*, p. 1, p. 67, 68; that is, part the first, page 67, 68 of the first part.†

* See note to Dedication.—G.

† As wishing to give all the Prefaces, &c., this prefatory note by Goodwin to 'The Table' is here inserted; but 'The Table' itself will be incorporated with the general Index.—G.

THE CHRISTIAN WORK.

Wherefore, my beloved, as ye have always obeyed, not as in my presence only, but now much more in my absence, work out your salvation with fear and trembling.—PHIL. II. 12.

THE first word, 'wherefore,' carries our minds back to things formerly delivered. Before, the apostle had taught them out of the example of Christ that they should not mind their own things: 'He went about doing good,' and humbled himself. Now when God is humble, how shall any man be proud? Having therefore such an example as Christ, without all exception, as he hath done do you, be obedient, &c. In the words consider,

First, The duty, 'work.'

Secondly, Directions to the right manner of performing this duty.

Thirdly, The motives to this duty.

The manner of performance of this work: *First*, it must be in sincerity; *secondly*, in obedience; *thirdly*, it must be earnestly and thoroughly; *fourthly*, it must be constant; *fifthly*, it must be ever tending to assure to us our salvation; *sixthly*, it must be in fear, or holy jealousy. The motives to this duty: *First*, Christ, he was obedient, follow him; *secondly*, 'my beloved,' that is, as you shew or deserve my care of you and diligence to do you good, obey; *thirdly*, you have done it heretofore: it is no new thing I require; it is not impossible; you have done it already; *fourthly*, if you do, it shall not be in vain. It tends to the assurance of salvation here, and to the accomplishment thereof hereafter, therefore 'work.'

1. '*Work.*' The estate of a Christian is a working estate, not idle. Christianity is not a verbal profession, nor speculative. 'If ye know these things, blessed are ye if ye do them,' saith Christ, John xiii. 17. Observe, he placeth the word 'blessed' in the midst, to unite those two which the world so ordinarily divides. I mean knowledge and practice. If words would go for excellent payment, many there are that would be admirable Christians; but we must know that a Christian's estate is accomplished by works; and that not only outwardly but inwardly, and by all manner of works: works of preparation; works of propriety;* and these inward, or outward and all, is in our general or particular calling.

Works of preparation are those that prepare men to believe; as hear-

* That is, 'appropriation.'—ED.

ing, reading, meditating; for these make not a Christian, but by these a Christian is prepared to be wrought on by God's Spirit. In these a Christian must be still working, and from these he ought to proceed to works of propriety: as belief in God, hope more strongly; love more ardently; pray fervently; do works of charity cheerfully—the three first duties being inward, the two last outward. And these concern our general callings as we are Christians, and then in our particular callings, to love, to reverence one another; seek the good of others, and to be bountiful to others. A Christian he must work in all these.

Use. The use of all this is, *to cause in us a right conceit of religion.* Many are good talkers, use fair words, are excellent in discourse; and these pass for current Christians. Nay, many there are that come not to this degree of speaking well. No; cannot endure to hear others speak well, but endeavour to turn their speech to other matters. Yet these go for good Christians, and think they shall be saved as well as the best, when, alas! they never came one step to salvation. Thus for the work. Now,

2. To the manner. He said before, 'As you have heretofore obeyed, even so work now,' shewing the first thing:

(1.) *That all our works must be done in obedience.* Whatsoever we do, it must be done in obedience to God. Many are damned for misdoing their good works, because they did them not in obedience to God. To this end it is expedient,

First, That we should know what God's will is: Rom. xii. 2, 'That you may prove what is that good, that acceptable and perfect will of God,' saith the apostle; and in the Ephesians v. 10, 'Proving what is acceptable to the Lord.' And therefore an ignorant man is a rebellious man. When he knows not God's will, how can he do his will?

Secondly, This obedience must be *to all God's laws,* for partial obedience is no obedience. For he is a lord, and not a servant, that will cull and pick out his obedience. 'Then shall I not be confounded,' saith David, 'when I have respect to all thy commandments,' Ps. cxix. 6. It is the devil's sophistry to put men in heart with the consideration of some few good duties that they have done; when, alas! if a fowl or bird be catched by one wing or leg, it is as sure as if a man had her whole body in his hand. The devil hath a man as sure in one sin unrepented as in many; and therefore the apostle limits not this obedience, but lays it down indefinitely.

(2.) The second thing in the manner is, *that this working must be in sincerity.* 'Whether I am present to see you or not, obey God: he sees you.' A Christian must do all things sincerely, as in the presence of God. The Pharisees did many good works, but it was to be seen of men. Therefore Christ saith, 'they have their reward already,' Mat. vi. 2. I will pay them no wages; they did it not to please me. Many are this way faulty. They do nothing but for applause: pray in public for fashion sake, never in private; whenas Christ saith, 'Enter into thy chamber, and when thou hast shut the door, pray to thy Father in secret,' Mat. vi. 6. Many can talk well and discourse well; but for inward graces they never look nor regard: and it is this that upholds many Christians. They see religion is respected of those of whom they desire to be had in some esteem, but God sees thy hypocrisy, and thou hast thy reward.

Joash was a good king so long as Jehoiada lived.* Many seem to be good, so long as those in authority are good; but if they die once, all good goes away with them. But a good Christian is ever good; and in all

* Cf. 2 Chron. xxiv. 2.—Ed.

places, occasions, companies, he will be like himself. Thus much of the second thing in the manner. Now for the third.

(3.) He says, 'Work out.' The word signifies, with toil to labour. So in the 6th of St John's gospel, 'Labour not for the meat that perisheth.' It is a good saying, no perfunctory thing can please God. To this end as Seneca says (*a*), of performing of duties natural; so in religious duties there is required, first, a right judgment of the nature of the things we do; secondly, an affection to do it; and thirdly, that affection must be proportionable to the worth of the things we do, else what do we; yea, as good not do it at all. And therefore the Scripture to every part of God's worship adds words of intention: 'Take heed how you hear,' Mark iv. 24; 'so run,' 1 Cor. ix. 24; 'pray fervently in spirit,' Rom. xii. 11; 'give cheerfully,' 2 Cor. ix. 7; 'repent throughly,' Acts xvii. 30. So that our affection must be proportionable to the thing we are about, serious in good. A thorough serious prayer is worth a thousand perfunctory; and one doctrine well digested and applied, worth all the rest, be they never so many, if they be done slightly; and the rather are we to look to this duty, for that the devil is busy in such duties to withdraw thy mind, and to steal away the seed sown. The poor husbandman lost three parts of his seed. Many feel such flashes of comfort while they hear the word, as they could wish they might be dissolved at that present; but being gone, pleasures, profits, and such like, take away and choke the seed sown. Many there are that will play or recreate themselves with all their might; but when they come to pray, instead of all their sinful life, think the saying of 'Lord, have mercy upon me,' or 'I am a sinner,' or such like, make even all accounts between God and their consciences. Those that are and will be Christians indeed, they see what they ought to do, and how they are to perform duties. They shall find themselves to be no losers, but gainers at the end; for by performing of things in this manner they shall strengthen the assurance of their salvation to themselves more and more. For God punisheth such slighting of duties justly, with slight assurance, and with many doubtings of salvation and of their secure estate. Well, the next thing to be considered in the manner of working is;—

(4.) Fourthly, *It must be constant*, not like the morning dew, or Lot's wife that looked back. For religion is a living and trade. It must be maintained with continuance in labour, and working in a constant course of goodness 'all the days of our life,' saith Zacharias' song, Luke i. 75. 'Father,' saith Christ, 'I have finished the work thou gavest me,' John xvii. 4. He never left till all was finished. 'It is finished,' saith Christ on the cross, John xix. 30; and the apostle, 'I have fought a good fight, I have finished my course,' 2 Tim. iv. 7, and then he speaks of 'a crown of righteousness,' 2 Tim. iv. 8. The want of this makes many die in extreme grief. They wish they had done such and such things, when it is too late. To this end we must come with a resolution not to be scared from performance of duties, and therefore to furnish ourselves with patience. For we must meet with many discouragements from without and within. Brethren, saith the apostle, 'you have need of patience,' Heb. x. 36. For 'you shall reap if you faint not,' Gal. vi. 9. And then consider that all promises of a crown are made to such as are sincere. 'To him that overcometh,' saith John, 'I will give,' &c., Rev. iii. 21. 'He that endures to the end shall be saved,' saith Christ, Mat. x. 22. Many decay in their first love, and God justly suffers them to fall into many gross sins, and he vomits up such as are grown cold.

(5.) The fifth thing in the manner is, that it must *tend to salvation.* We must go on in a constant course of goodness till we come, and that we may come, to the end of our faith. Let this end, viz., salvation, make you work in the duties of grace. For salvation is begun here; and the state of grace here is called salvation, even as well as the state hereafter.

The doctrine is, *that all which we do here ought to tend to the assurance of salvation.*

We say in nature that all conclusions are to be reduced to their principles. So is Christianity. All is to be referred to our salvation as to a main principle; those things that tend directly to salvation to be done in the first place, and most especially. And then other works, they must tend the same way, for all works that are good, do either express holiness, or increase it in us; and thereby they increase our own salvation, as in our ordinary callings, if we perform them in obedience to God constantly, it expresses the gifts and graces of God's Spirit in us. Do we sanctify them by prayer? Do we refer all the good to the good of those amongst whom we live, especially to the good of the faithful? This strengthens the assurance of our salvation, and tells us that God's Spirit is in us. The poorest servant in his drudgery, he serves God if he does it as in the presence of God, Col. iii. 24. The poor woman, in bearing and bringing up of children, shall be saved; that is, notwithstanding that sentence, 'that in sorrow and pains she should conceive,' yet her salvation is no whit hindered thereby, but rather furthered. So that it is grace that elevates earthly works, and makes them heavenly.

But take this caution withal, that we more highly esteem our Christian calling than our ordinary vocations and duties; and to that end we ought to redeem some time from our ordinary callings to meditate, and to examine ourselves, and to pray. And this to be done daily, for Christ saith, 'Labour not for the meat that perisheth,' in comparison of that meat which lasteth for ever. Especially on that day which God hath chosen to his own use, I mean the 'Lord's day.' Mingle not thine own callings with holy duties on such days, unless it be in case of mercy, and that also of great necessity. God made this day for his own glory, and for our good, knowing how earthly-minded else we would be, unless some time were allotted wholly to vindicate our minds from these earthly things. Take heed, therefore, how we be bold * on this day especially.

'Your own.' Here is contained another direction in this Christian work. In our works and doings we must begin with ourselves, contrary to the custom of many, who are in their own duties negligent, but lord-like in overseeing of other men's works. We are to know, true zeal and practice begins at home.

'Work out your own.' Whatsoever others do, look you to yourselves. So did Joshua: 'Let the people do what they will, I and my house will serve the Lord,' Josh. xxiv. 15. So that a Christian ought to resolve with himself concerning his own carriage; he that is wise is wise for himself. Better it is that you alone should work out your own salvation, than go to hell with others for company.

'Your own.' Every one hath a cup that he in particular must taste of, and every one a particular work to do. Though all go one way that are saved, yet some go by more sufferings than others. Some hath harder tasks set them to perform than others. Some must live in some callings, and therein 'work out their own salvation,' others in others. Eph. ii. 10, 'Every one is created to good works which God prepares for him.'

* Cf. Eph. iii. 12; Heb. iv. 16.—G. Qu. 'cold'?—Ed.

For the sixth direction, contained in 'fear,' &c., the time is too short to speak of; and therefore I come,

3. To the *motives*.

(1.) The first is taken from the *example of Christ*, comprehended in the word 'Wherefore.' Christ, he did as he would have us to do; he did all in obedience to God; he came to do his will; he was sincere, cared not for the world. What he did, he did thoroughly; he healed all; did all good; did all things well; and he finished his course. Now we must imitate Christ in all these; never give over till we may say with comfort at our deaths, 'All is finished.' This must needs move us, if we consider what an honour it is for us to be like him and to follow him; and then it will be gainful to us. He got honour by it—was exalted; so shall we therefore be like him. And then he is a pattern without all exception. We cannot offend so long as we propound him for our example. It is a foolish opinion therefore that men may be too religious. Can any go beyond Christ, nay, or come near him?

(2.) The second motive is taken *from the apostle's love*, 'my beloved.' Shew that you will answer my care and love to you. Whence observe,

That it ought to be a motive to Christians to take good courses, that they may thereby comfort those that have care of their good. The apostle, Heb. xiii. 17, bids the Hebrews, 'that they obey them that are their guides.' Why? 'That they may give account with joy, and not with grief, for it is unprofitable for them.' But to leave this personal manner of speech. Christians ought to seek good courses, to give content to the souls of those Christians with whom they live; for they make it a matter of joy to see one grow in religious behaviour, and contrarily are grieved when they see it decay in any.

(3.) The third motive is drawn *from the possibility of it;* as if he should have said, You have already begun; you know what it is I require; it is no new thing, nor is it impossible; do but work out that which you have begun. He that hath set one step into religion is half way. It was a great commendation in the church of Thyatira, that their last works were more than the first, Rev. ii. 19. We should labour to grow on still, from one degree to another, even as the sun 'shines more and more to the perfect day,' Prov. iv. 18; and therefore it is a Christian course to compare ourselves with ourselves daily, and if we find a decay in ourselves, rest not contented till thou findest thyself amended. We pity men when they decay in outward things; but of all decays, the decay of goodness is the most lamentable; and therefore as you have obeyed, so obey still.

'Now much more in my absence.' These words I take not to be so meant, as if the apostle had spoken of what they already had done, but rather what he would have them to do, as if he should have said, 'I know now that I am absent, you shall want no allurements nor temptations to draw you away; and I know now I am gone grievous wolves shall enter in, not sparing the flock,' as it is in Acts xx. 29, 'therefore now be much more careful, and watch.' Hence therefore observe, the want of means that formerly men had is no sufficient plea to excuse decay in grace in any man. 'Redeem the time.' Why? Not because goodness increases amongst all sorts, but 'because the days are evil,' Eph. v. 16. The world would have reasoned clean contrary. Because the days are evil, be thou also evil, follow the fashion. Religion teaches us to reason otherwise. Because you have not the helps you formerly enjoyed, double your diligence; God will graciously supply you. If you be not wanting to yourselves, he will never depart from you though I am gone. He was a sanctuary to the Jews in Babylon when they wanted the sanctuary; and yet then were they in greatest glory. And it is remarkable, men have been still most glorious for religion in want of outward means.

(4.) The fourth motive is laid down *in the end.* It is to our salvation; which as it carries the form of a direction, so as it is an end it hath a power to move us to it. Considering we are not yet perfect, go on till you come to perfection. It is an encouragement to us to begin, and when we have begun, it doth encourage us to go on forward. See this in Titus ii. 11: 'The grace of God teacheth us to deny ungodliness and worldly lusts, and to live soberly,' &c., and encourageth us on, looking for the glorious appearing of Christ. We are sons; shall we be rebellious? We look for salvation; shall we not then work it out? Yes. Moses chose rather to suffer afflictions with the children of God than to enjoy the pleasures of sin for a season. Why? 'He had respect to the recompence of reward,' Heb. xi. 26. We have an evidence here [that] we shall be saved hereafter; and this makes us strive to ascertain it more and more to us. And indeed, he that carries his salvation in his eye, needs no better encouragement. What made them, in Heb. xi. 38, to wander about and to forsake all? They looked for another city, whose builder was God. Thus it is in ordinary affairs. What seasons war but the hope of peace? the troubles and the tempests on the sea, but the hope of the haven? the labour and cost in sowing, but the expectation of harvest? Shall not we much more endure a little labour here, for endless happiness assured to us hereafter? This is much forgotten. What makes persons so dull in good duties? They either know not, or forget this reward; for he that sets his mind on it cannot be cold or dull. But here's the pity! Men labour, sweat, take pains and travail, spare no cost; and all this to go to hell, to heap up wrath against the day of wrath. The devil has more servants in his barren and fruitless service than God gets with all his promises and good things that he liberally gives. Besides, I add one or two directions more.

First, *Labour to get a platform of wholesome words.* If we would work, we must have an idea of the thing we work in our head. We must labour to get a form of practice and doctrine out of the word of God, and to carry it still about with us.

Then *cast thyself into that mould thou hast thus framed*, Rom. vi. 17. Be moulded in that form of doctrine; believe what he will have us to believe; love that which he will have us to love. And having this frame in thy mind, in what estate soever thou art, whether single or married, governing or governed, thou shalt have still with thee a platform of duties, fitting for the carriage of thyself; and there will be no duty thou hearest taught but thou wilt be able to draw it to thine own practice. The want of this makes most men unfruitful, heaping up thereby damnation unto themselves.

Lastly, *Observe the good motions of God's Spirit in thee;* further them to the most advantage; turn them to present practice; lose nor delay them not; for the devil will steal thee away from them.

Now when we come to another part of the manner of a Christian's work, it must be done 'in fear and trembling,' Not to stand on the divers kinds of fear; in general, it is an affection planted by God in our natures, whereby we, foreseeing dangers which may hinder our being or wellbeing, are afraid of them. This is incident to our natures, and it was also in Christ. And were it not for this, men would be prodigal of their lives, and would rush into desperate dangers. There is a carnal fear, as when we fear the creatures of whom we are lords; and this proceeds from a carnal distrust in God. But in this place is meant a spiritual fear, which may be branched into three divers kinds. First, a fear of reverence, which is a fear mixed with love; when we fear one or stand in awe of him for his greatness, yet love him for his goodness to us; and thus a Christian fears God. Secondly, hence proceeds the second kind of fear, which is a fear of watchfulness; and thirdly, a fear of jealousy, lest we should offend against God; and this arises from the consideration of our weakness and the falseness of our hearts. So that he here saying, 'Work out your salvation with fear,' bids them that they proceed on in their course with reverence, watchfulness, and jealousy. As for the word 'trembling,' it is none other but an effect or symptom of the passion of fear, arising from excess of fear in regard of fearful objects. For then the spirits retiring in to comfort the heart, leave the outward parts destitute, so as they tremble. And on the contrary, in objects of delight and comfort, they come outward, to the outmost parts as it were, to meet with such pleasing objects as are presented to the sense. It being thus in nature, it is also in us spiritually; for we beholding the majesty and power of God, and considering our own baseness and infirmities, are drawn to a kind of fear, which, if it be somewhat more than ordinary, it produces a spiritual trembling. Having thus opened the words, we will come to some doctrine; and first, in general observe,

Doct. God requires all duties that are done to him to be done with affection. The careless Christian thinks the deed done to be sufficient to please God. No; verily he requires work, but it must be done with affection. The affection must first be obedient, and then the outward man. 'Thou shalt love the Lord thy God with all thy heart, soul, and strength, and thy neighbour as thyself,' Lev. xix. 18. 'My son, give me thy heart,' saith Solomon, Prov. xxiii. 26. I might infer this doctrine to shew how many are faulty this way, but I come to this particular affection of fear. *All things that are done must be done in the fear of God;* and this must we do before our calling and after our calling: before our calling to work ourselves into our salvation, and in our calling to work out our own salvation. Before our conversion fear is necessary for us. God uses it to bring us to Christ. Legal fear is always or most commonly before evangelical. It is as the needle that draws faith after it as the thread. Such is God's goodness to us, that lest we should fall into hell ere we are aware, he hath left us objects of terror and threatening judgments, to keep us from hell; and all to provoke fear in us that we may be saved. There is a spirit of bondage before the spirit of adoption: Rom. viii. 15, 'Ye have not received the spirit of bondage again to fear, but you have received the Spirit of adoption,' implying that once they had received the spirit of bondage. For verily, first men see their miserable estate by nature, and this convincing their consciences, comes to stir up fear in them, which drives them to the rock of salvation, Christ Jesus. I speak this the rather, for that it is evident many never yet came to this spirit of fear. They live in a course of known gross sins, between whom and damnation is but a step. They know they are abominable sinners, yet fear not hell. How can men think well of such? They never yet came to the spirit of bondage to fear. Tell them of hell, they tush at it scornfully, being herein more brutish than an ass. Lay burdens on him, he will bear them patiently; but press him never so much to go into the fire, you cannot make him come near to it; whenas wicked men, they cannot be kept from running into hell with all violence. They are worse than the devil, James ii. 19. They neither tremble nor believe, but live contemptuously and presumptuously in their courses. Well, let such look to it. What they do now they shall do it hereafter, when there will be no comfort left for them, though they seek it with tears.

Thus have I shewn that before conversion fear is necessary. I add, moreover, that men after conversion, believers, they ought to have fear of reverence; wherein we will speak somewhat of fear in general; then of the manner of it; and lastly, of the motives thereto. For the fear that here is spoken of observe that,

First, *It must be general* at all times, in all actions. Job said, 'I feared all my works,' Job iii. 25, and indeed in this estate we must continually fear till we be in heaven. And as it belongs to all works and times, so to all Christians, nay, and to them most of all, for that the devil is set against you. And your actions, if they be ill, are the most scandalous; and by them is God most of all dishonoured. And therefore the more grace a man hath he will fear the more. Even as a rich man, the more riches he hath the more care he taketh, lest they should be stolen from him.

Secondly, *This fear must be serious.* It must work a kind of trembling, by reason of the dangers that we meet withal, which are like to be many and great.

Thirdly, *This fear must be total*, in the whole man. For that the image of God is in the body, even as in the soul, and as in other affections a proud man is known by his proud eye and careless carriage, even so the countenance will be wray whether the heart be humble, loving, careful, and the like. It is an idle speech that many have, they will say their heart is good. Let such know, where grace is, it works a change, and that thoroughly in body and soul. David therefore joins prostration with calling on the Lord: Ps. xcv. 6, 'Let us fall down;' and in other places, casting up of the eye, and extending of the hands.*

Means to this duty; observe,

[1.] First, We must *consider God's love to us.* It is the first and main thing in reverence. This will breed fearfulness in us; for the more assured we are, the more fearful will we be of offending.

[2.] Secondly, *Set before your eyes the other attributes of God, as his justice.* What though it be true, he revenges not the sin of his children, so as it were better for him that he had not offended, for he will not suffer sin to dwell in his children.

[3.] Thirdly, Add *the examples of those that have felt his justice*, especially of the best servants of God. Moses, for a few words, never entered the land of promise. David, for a proud conceit in numbering the people, lost seventy thousand men of the pestilence. The Corinthians, for unworthy receiving of the Lord's supper, many of them died. And if it be thus with his dearest children, have not we cause to fear? Yes, assuredly. God will be honoured in all those that come near him.

Obj. It will be said that there are no examples of late of God's justice in this kind, as to strike with sudden death.

Ans. I answer, true. But God strikes with hardness of heart, which is far more worse. And God doth strike men with temporal judgments, although they think not of it, even for those sins they think not of. And if it were not thus, let such men know there is a judgment to come, and that God is the same God now that he was ever, a powerful, just, and all-

* Cf. Ps. cxlv. 15 and Ps. xxviii. 2; lxiii. 4.—G.

seeing God. And it will make them, if they belong to God, to set themselves in the presence of God even in their most secret closets. This is, notwithstanding, forgotten everywhere. And many sins are committed which sinners would be loath that a child should see, yet are they not afraid of God, that sees them and sets them down in a book. Well then, a Christian after conversion ought to fear with a fear of reverence.

It follows, in the second and third place, a Christian must have a fear of jealousy and watchfulness, and thus 'work out his salvation.' For by this means we keep ourselves from displeasing God, it being a carefulness wrought in us by the Spirit of God, causing us to take heed how we offend God in any thing. For a Christian, knowing the falseness of his own heart, is jealous thereof, there being a spiritual marriage between Christ and us, lest it should offend. And this is the ground of this spirit of jealousy, and therefore none deceives another, but he also deceives himself; for his corrupt heart is as a traitor in his own bosom. Another ground is Satan, that ever joins with our corruptions; for so long as there is a false heart there will be a fawning devil. Now this should make us to examine ourselves, and to fear our hearts, and to 'try our thoughts,' Ps. cxxxix. 23, before they come out into word or action.* For sin is like Elijah his cloud, at the first small, but afterward covers the whole heaven. See it in David. One eye-glance! What a world of sins followed. And therefore we must take heed of beginnings. And then look that thou drawest not the guilt of other men's sins on thyself. Take heed of 'scandal.'† See how Jeroboam is branded; ever mention being made of him, 'Jeroboam that made Israel to sin,' 1 Kings xiv. 16. Then again, labour to set thy corruptions in thine eye continually, and to stir up our hearts to hate them. For they trouble us more than the devil, although most men study to gratify their enemy, and how to satisfy the lusts of the flesh. And who are their enemies but such as tell them and bid them beware of their enemies? Now to the reason.

VERSE 13.

For it is God that worketh in you to will and to do according to his good pleasure.

It is as much as if he should say, because God works, therefore work you, lest he should take both the power of working from you and also the act. For he gives both 'to will and to do,' not only the power to will and to do, but the very act of willing and doing; and this he doth out of his free grace and pleasure. In the opening of which words, observe with me these things. *First*, that a Christian hath a power in him to will and to do good; *secondly*, that God works this in him; *thirdly*, this work is a powerful work; *fourthly*, it is an inward work; *fifthly*, this work is entire; *sixthly*, observe how this work is a ground of fear and trembling.

1. For the first, *that a Christian hath a will and power to do good*, this is necessary. For in all estates, whether a man be good or bad, his will is the chief; and therefore, in conversion of any one, the will and judgment is first wrought upon and converted. And therefore this may be noted to

* Consult Dr Faithful Teate's searching and quaint treatise 'Right Thoughts the Righteous Man's Evidence: a Discourse proving our estate, God-ward, to be as our Thoughts are. Directing how to *try* them and ourselves by them,' &c. 12mo, 1669.—G.

† That is, of being a 'stumbling-block.—G.

shew us our estates, whether we be good or not. If we be good, we will that which is good, and choose the better part; for those that choose the worst ever are opposite to the best. Their estate is naught, let them boast what they will. The Christian therefore ever hath a will to do, though many times he doth not what he will, being sometimes (for secret causes best known to God) kept by him from performing their wills. David would have built a temple, and Abraham would have sacrificed Isaac. Other times hindered by corruptions. The will, or to will, saith Paul, is present, but not the deed, Rom. vii. 18; and Christ saith, 'The spirit is ready, but the flesh is weak,' Mat. xxvi. 41. If we do therefore any good, the deed is God's. If we will it, the will is God's. And then we please God when we will that which God wills, and not when we do that which God wills not.

2. Secondly, *This power that we have, we have it not from ourselves, but God gives it to us.* Some things are done for us which were neither wrought by us nor in us; and thus Christ's death was wrought. Some things wrought in us, not by us, as our first work of conversion. Other things are wrought both in us and by us, and these are all good works after conversion. This will whereof we speak is wrought in us by God, as we be his temples, and the deed is wrought by us as instruments of God's working in us. Thought is not so much as will, it being but a way to it. Yet can we not think a good thought without the Spirit of God working in us. For we have no life at all, but are 'dead in sins and trespasses,' much less can we have any motion to that which is good for ourselves.

Quest. But it will be demanded, how can the work be done by God, and yet we work the same work?

Ans. I answer, in every work that is done, there is God's power and man's joined together. But how? So far as we think or will, it is from us, but to think or will that which is good, that is from God. We work not as horses draw together and equally. We are not co-ordinate, but subordinate. We work as understanding creatures. But God guides our understanding to this or that as he pleases. We hear, but God he bores the ear first. Lydia believed, but God opened her heart, and framed it to believe, Acts xvi. 14. We think, but God gives us to think well.

3. In the next place we are to shew, *that this work of God in us is a powerful work.* It determines our will. God deals not *per omnipotentiam* to constrain our wills to this or that which is contrary to the will, but he gives us to will that which he wills. Now when God intends that man shall do anything, he gives him a will to do it; and in this respect his work is powerful in us. Magnify therefore this power, that preserves us in the midst of temptation, even as it preserved the three children in the fire from burning, Dan. iii. 27; that makes earth to be in heaven; and labour to find experience of this power in thee, the want of the sense whereof brings much want of inward comfort of God's Spirit.

4. In the next place, note *that this work is inward within us, not without us.* He uses exhortations, monitions, allurements, but he puts power to these to prevail: *Fortiter pro te, suaviter pro me, Domine,* saith the Father (*b.*) For God may work *fortiter*, strongly, and yet liberty be preserved too, as it is evident in the angels. For freedom consists not in doing this or that *ad libitum* as we say; but then are we free and at liberty, when we do anything out of a sound judgment. The angels see good reason why they should depend on God, and man seeing that happiness only lies in the enjoyment of the favour of God, do voluntarily depend on him. God there-

fore enters into the heart, changes the stony heart into a heart of flesh, takes away all rebellious dispositions of our heart, and makes them pliable to his will.

5. Come we in the next place to consider *the perfection and entireness of this work.* God, he is 'Alpha and Omega, the author and finisher of our faith,' Heb. xii. 2, and the beginning and perfection of every good thing is from him. *Omne bonum, a summo Bono;* and therefore he is the cause of the not doing of that which is not done; he is *causa quiescendo*, as well as *agendo*. For why is a thing not, but because he gives it not a being? So that all the ill which we will not, is of him. We should therefore be as thankful to him for any sin he keeps us from, as for any good that he causes us to perform; for there is not any sin that another hath committed, but if God had pleased I might have committed. This is an excellent point to teach us humility. Note therefore hence,

Doct. That perseverance is from God. He gives to will and to do. 'He that hath begun will finish the good work,' saith the apostle in the first of this epistle, and the sixth verse. It is not in our strength to hold out; for after we are once changed, God gives grace sufficient to restrain us and to hold us up. God deals not with us as the husbandman does, sows the ground and leaves it. No. God watches and weeds us, and continues his labour upon us, till he brings us to the end of his promise. If he uphold us not, we are ready to return to our first principles again.

Use. This enforces a particular and resolute dependence on God, in full assurance that what he hath promised, he will perform. He will put his fear into our hearts, so as we shall not depart from him.

Doct. And this is done freely of his own good pleasure; and thus he doth all things. Not of necessity; he is not forced to this or that, either by any foreign power, or internal; he is not bound to this or that, as fire burns necessarily: as the school saith, *necessitate naturæ*. Indeed, he is good necessarily, for it is his nature; but in his acts he is free from all manner of compulsion, for none can compel him, neither is he drawn to this or that by any merit in us, for we merit nothing but destruction. It was his own will that he made any creature at all; that he ranked them into angels and men; that he passed by the angels, and redeemed man; to give means of salvation to some and not to others; to make the means effectual to some and not to others; that some are called sooner, some later; some have more strength, some less; to some more comfort, some less; and to those that have more, to give more at some time and less at other times, as is his free will. What meritorious disposition can there be in a dead person, as the apostle saith we are? Oh, but it will be objected that one grace deserves another; and God giving us, for example, the Spirit of prayer, we deserve the thing we prayed for. I answer, nothing less. God indeed uses this order, but hereby do we not deserve anything. God says, 'Ask, and it shall be given,' Mat. vii. 7. But how? Not by desert in praying; but he hath established this order, that men shall ask before we have.

Uses. (1.) Hence have *we a ground of thankfulness to God.*

(2.) Secondly, *take not offence though thou seest thou hast less grace than others have.* All are not strong; some are babes; and it is God's will it should be so, even as there are divers degrees in ages. If thou beest in any esteem with Christ, thank God for that thou art. I speak the rather, being* many are vexed because they are not so holy and pure as such are

* = 'because.'—G.

to whom God hath given a large portion of the grace of his Spirit. No. God gives according to his good pleasure.

(3.) *Despair not therefore.* If thou wantest grace, go to God for more. He gives according to his own good pleasure. Many complain they are sinners, dead, dull, indisposed. Go to God. He gives sharpness of wit to the dull, but according to his good pleasure. More hurt and hindrance comes ordinarily from the abundance of God's gifts of this sort than good. For it may be God sees thou wilt be hereby lifted up and extolled, as Paul was; and therefore for thy good he withholds it from thee. Vex not thyself therefore for the want of that which, if thou hadst it, would turn to thine own bane.

Take heed how thou insultest over others, that as yet are not wrought upon. It may be their hour is not yet come; and therefore use thou all means to do good to such as stand in need. God appoints times and seasons, when and what means he will bless. Thou mayest be the instrument to convert thy brother.

And above all take heed of self-conceit. God gives thee all, and if it be not of or from thyself, why shouldst thou boast, or be lifted up? Be therefore content, and repose thyself on God. What though perchance thou wantest outward means and worldly riches? Pass* not for them. Thank God that he hath wrought a spiritual change in thee. He hath given thee the main. I am sure thou wouldst not change thy estate for all the riches in the world, nor pomp and pride thereof. And if thou findest a decay of the sense of God's love and favour towards thee, seek it of him, but with submission. What if thou findest an ebb of goodness in thee? and that it is not with thee now as formerly it hath been, that thou art more easily overcome with temptation, and that thou canst not wrestle as once thou couldst against thy corruptions? Know, God he gives his power to work and fight, as his pleasure is. God by suffering thee thus to be foiled, tells thee that the work is not thine own, but his, and that he gives and bestows increase as he pleases. Take notice therefore of these things. Thus far have we spoken of the words simply considered.

Now, let us come to them, as they have relation one to another, and particularly of the force of the reason. 'God gives the will and deed, according to his own good pleasure:' therefore fear, and take heed how thou neglectest the means. Fear exaltation of spirit, and trust not on outward means. David, that holy man, he had a touch of this: Ps. xxx. 6, 'I said in my prosperity, I shall not be moved.' Fear how thou vowest anything in thine own strength in time to come; for in that St James gives a good instruction, 'You ought to say, If the Lord will,' iv. 15. Submit thyself to him, for he gives the power 'to will and to do, according to his own good pleasure.'

Doct. It ought therefore [to] be an encouragement to a Christian to work, when he considers that *God works the will and the deed, according to his good pleasure.* That God is willing to give 'the will and the deed' in obedience to his ordinance, will make a Christian confident in every good work; and therefore, to that end, he must learn to know God's will, as favourites in court they learn to know what will please the prince, and accordingly they fashion their behaviour. And when we know his will, then come boldly to him for to desire strength in doing his will. For he hath made us gracious promises, 'to take away our stony hearts, and to give us hearts of flesh,' Ezek. xi. 19, and 'to lay no more on us than we are able to bear,' 1 Cor.

* That is, 'pause.'—G.

x. 13. Let us repair to him for the accomplishment of these promises and others. Take heed how we distrust his promises. It made the Israelites travel forty years, till all the generation of them perished, and entered not into that good land. God hath promised us, not an earthly inheritance, but an heavenly, and victory over our sins. Let us then set on this conquest boldly and with courage, for God hath made himself our debtor by his promise, and he is faithful that hath promised: where, by the way, observe the difference between our estate in the 'first,' from this present estate of ours in the 'second Adam.' The first Adam had no such promise to continue in that estate of integrity. But we have. We are assured. We are united to Christ more surely than he was to his estate in paradise. Magnify, therefore, this condition of thine. And in the fourth place, labour to know aright the nature of the covenant of grace; for it is a part of his covenant with us, that what he enjoins us he will enable us to perform. 'If we believe, we shall be saved,' saith the covenant. Well, God, he gives us to believe, he bids us to repent, he gives us power to repent. The commandments which are given us concerning faith and repentance, and the like graces here, they shew the order that God uses in saving man. 'To you,' saith Christ, 'it is given to know and believe,' Mat. xiii. 11. This ought, therefore, to comfort us, seeing this covenant of grace is, not only a covenant which requires duties of our parts, but also it is a testament wherein these graces are given us in way of legacies. If we knew the privileges that in this covenant do belong unto us, it should surely make us bold. God promises the will and deed, that we may apply these things unto ourselves; which if we do, we may go about our works with resolution, that they shall be prosperous to us: our labour shall not be in vain in the Lord. In reverence, therefore, use all means. Trust not on the means, but use them in reverence and in fear; and hereby thou shalt avoid many corrections, which otherwise thy sins will draw on thee, For the difference in the performance of duties makes the difference of Christians. Some are more careless in their performances than others. Is it not just with God to punish such, by letting them fall into many gross sins? See this in David and Peter. They trusted to themselves, and called not on God for his gracious direction in temptation. Mark their sins. Observe what comfort they lost. And surely those that are watchful Christians are ever careful of their rules; and God to such gives what he requires of them. He sends us not to seek straw ourselves as Pharaoh, Exod. v. 7; but he provides it to us.

Obj. But it will be objected that, by this doctrine of trusting and relying on God, men will grow idle. God will work his will in us though we sleep, say they.

Ans. But to answer them. First, such men as these will be ashamed to argue thus in outward and worldly businesses. For example, in husbandry, God hath promised every good thing to us; therefore, let me sit still: the corn will grow, though I sow not nor till the ground. Would not such an one be thought mad, that should reason thus? Because we know that as God hath appointed every end, so he hath ordained order and means, whereby such things shall be effected. Thus is it in grace. He gives 'the will and the deed,' but he prescribes prayer and other ordinances, as the means attaining to this will, for we have it not of ourselves. And therefore he bids us hear, read and meditate, watch, and such like, and depend on God for a blessing in the use of the means he appoints us. Do that which is required of you. God will do that [that] belongs to him. He will give 'the will and deed.' Christ he knew that the Father loved him and would honour him, but yet he prays, 'Father, glorify thy Son,' John xvii. 1. So in sickness, to whom God purposes and decrees health, he shall do well. But how? Without means? No. They must use advice of physicians, as one of God's ordinances. Thus is it with our souls. We are all naturally sick and dead. God hath predestinated some to live. But how? 'Faith comes by hearing,' Rom. x. 17. He must be conversant still in the use of means appointed to that end. But the comfortless and weak soul will say, 'Alas! I use means, yet feel I no grace; I am not the better.' To such I say, 'It may be thou art not so instant and urgent in the use of the means as thou mayest and should be.' And secondly, thou must not measure thyself by thy will; for a Christian's will is ever beyond his ability, tending still to that perfection which they cannot come to in this world. Rich men that are covetous think themselves poor, and still desire more. 'I know thy tribulation and thy poverty, but thou art rich,' saith the Spirit to the church of Smyrna, Rev. ii. 9; and therefore discourage not thyself. God is faithful. Use the means, and depend not on the means; but depend on God in the use of the means, else thou shalt find but little comfort. And if thou findest thy affections any whit enlarged to good duties, and lifted up, and cheered in the performance of them, and art glad that thou art not so conversant in sinning as formerly thou wert, but that thou makest a conscience of thy ways, thank God and give him the glory, and abase and humble thyself. David was much conversant in this. 'Blessed be the Lord, that hath kept me from shedding of blood,' saith he to Abigail, 1 Sam. xxv. 32, 33, *seq.* And his psalms are full of praises and thanksgiving. And if thou hast any good motions in thine heart, practise them with all speed, and strengthen them.

VERSE 14.

Do all things without murmurings and disputings.

This verse contains a new precept of Christian modesty, enforced by removing of contraries. 'Murmuring' is well known among us, it is so ordinarily practised of us. It arises from discontent against God or one another, breaking into words, works, disputings; whereby one endeavours to defend that with reasons which in the heat of his affections passed from him, lest he should be thought inconsiderate and rash. But to come to the particulars, consider with me, *first*, the kinds of it; *secondly*, the causes of it; and *thirdly*, the cure and remedies of it. *For the kinds of it*, it is either against God or against man.

First, Against God. Man since the fall quarrels with his Maker. Whenas heaven and earth must be judged by him, man thinks this unequal, and therefore he first *murmureth against God's counsels and decrees.* God he appoints some to this, others to that. This is unequal, saith the proud man; all of us are alike, saith he; I am as good a man as another. 'Who art thou that contendest with God?' Rom. ix. 20. Remember thou art clay, and God is the potter; he hath power to make one vessel to honour, another to dishonour, Rom. ix. 21. God's decrees are divine and above thy reach. If that men could apprehend them by reason, then they were not divine. Lay thy hand therefore on thy heart, and cry, 'O the depth of the counsels and wisdom of God,' Rom. xi. 33. Shall not we give him leave to do what he will, whenas he is the just Judge of all the world? Can he do any wrong?

Second, It is usual with natural men to murmur *against God's providence, in doing better to some others than unto themselves*. They think themselves much wronged when they see some others rich and have all, whereas they themselves are poor; and this sin is many times found in the children of God, in David, Job, Habakkuk, 'Why do the wicked prosper?' They found fault with the wicked's prosperity, till they went into the sanctuary of the Lord. There they found the end of such men, Ps. lxxiii. 17. Therefore judge not of any but by his end. Think not all things run round, because thou seest no reason thereof, for God's wisdom is unsearchable. Observe the sweet end, issue, and event of all things. Princes they have *arcana imperii*. Shall not we suffer God to enjoy such privileges? Can we endure that our servant should know all our counsels and minds? Let us therefore yield to God liberty in that which belongs to him; yield glory, who disposes all things sweetly.

A *third* thing which men often murmur at is *God's ordinance in magistracy and ministry*. Such men, they think God is not wise enough, but they will teach him whom he shall advance to high place, and whom not; and thus they despise not only the magistracy, but God himself. 'They have not cast thee off, but me,' saith God to Samuel concerning the people, 1 Sam. viii. 7; and indeed what are they but lawless and wild persons, that cannot away with order? They will have none to overrule them; or, if they be content for shame to admit thereof, yet *nolumus hunc regnare*, Christ must not rule over them, nor this nor that man. But know, whosoever thou art, that all power is from God, and he will defend his own ordinance against all such as malign it. Ministers are not free from murmurers. How many have we that think it tedious to attend on God at public service! how many that think and are not ashamed to say they can profit more in their private studies! and that this observation of the Lord's day causeth them to lose a whole year in seven!* Ay, but consider, God justly curses thy calling whenas thou makest them a stay† to good duties. It is also thus in families; wife murmurs against husband, and husband against wife, blaming themselves in that they matched with such, whenas they think they might have done better with others. No. Thou couldst not have done better. God he hath decreed this, and his decrees are not to be blamed. Servants also are troubled with this disease. They murmur against their masters, and learn to dispute with them; and therefore St Paul wills servants to count their masters worthy of all honour, that the word of God be not blasphemed, Tit. ii. 5. And that they do not contend in 'answering again,' verse 9. It is also much in children against parents, and likewise parents against children; so that this sin reigneth over all estates and degrees. Take notice therefore hereof, that thou beest not overtaken in it.

Causes of murmuring.

1. The first cause of murmuring is *ignorance of God's particular providence;* his excellency and thy baseness. Job when he came to see the glory and power of God, then said, 'I abhor myself, I will dispute no more,' Job xlii. 6. If we did likewise consider of his majesty, power, wisdom, and goodness, would we contend with our Maker? Consider this in thine own cause, will any of us endure a murmuring servant? shall we think it is reason in us, and that God must notwithstanding suffer with patience our murmurings and disputations with his sacred Majesty, who is justice itself, and is not bound to render account of his actions to any.

* In margin here, 'Men murmur against men.'—G. † That is, = 'hindrance.'—G.

2. The second cause of murmuring in us is *self-love.* Man thinks himself worthy of all honour, never considering his weakness and infirmities. Moses was very meek; he gave no cause to Dathan and Abiram, and the rest, to provoke them to murmur. God yet having set them in some place in the congregation, they were so lifted up with desire of honour as they were too good to be governed, Numb. xvi. 3. Thus is it with every one of us. We willingly puff up ourselves in our own conceits of self-sufficiency, and hence arises discontentedness, when we think God is not so good to us as our merits do deserve. We look on those good things that God hath given us, we think not of our infirmities. Hence it is we are never thankful for that we have, but desirous of that which we have not. Hence also arises unfruitfulness, for such look for greatness, but never or seldom to do good with that they have, whether power, or riches, or such like.

Cures for this.

The cures of this disease consists partly in meditation, and partly in practice. *First, labour to have a right understanding and knowledge of God's justice without all exception. Secondly,* that *he is infinitely good, disposing all for the benefit and good of his own children. Thirdly,* labour to *know and observe his particular providence to these baser creatures,* as that the hair falls not without his providence, and that he regards the sparrows, Mat. x. 29. These will make us practise these things. First, in justifying God in whatsoever is done and decreed, as David, Ps. cxix. 137, 'Just art thou, O Lord, and holy, and righteous are thy judgments.' This was Eli his practice, 1 Sam. iii. 18: 'It is the Lord,' said he. And Hezekiah, 'the word of the Lord is good,' 2 Kings xx. 19; and in the 39th Psalm, David held his tongue, ver. 1.* The reason he renders, 'It is thou, Lord, who art good, and dost all for good.' Therefore learn a holy silence as David leads us, 62d Psalm ver. 1: 'My soul waiteth on God with silence,' for so is the signification of the word (*c*). Thus did Aaron: though his sons were destroyed, 'yet he held his peace,' Lev. x. 3. And when thou findest any discontented thoughts to arise in thine heart, check thyself in the beginning, Ps. lxxiii. 22: 'So foolish and like a beast am I,' saith David; and 'why art thou disquieted, O my soul? and why art thou troubled within me'? Ps. xlii. 5. And examine ourselves: Is it fit that God should answer me? is he not wiser than I? 'What am I?' Am I not wicked, dead, dull? Have not I infinitely displeased him? Let me judge myself, that he may not enter into judgment with me. What though God hath not heard my prayers! I have not hearkened to him when he called me; he may justly neglect me, I have neglected him. Yet hath he been wonderfully good to me; I have received much good from him, and no evil; he hath often spared and doth now spare me; his corrections are gentle and loving, above that we deserve. In his judgments his mercies are great: 'It is his mercy that I am not consumed,' Lam. iii. 22. Propound to thyself the example of Christ. He suffered more than we do, when there was no ill found in him. What says he? 'Not my will, but thine be done,' Luke xxii. 42. Indeed, we may wish afflictions to be removed as grievances, but joining them with the will of God, then our will must give place to his. Resign thyself into his hands. It is God that will have it thus with me; and therefore take and bear with meekness. And as Paul did, also pray that the will of the Lord may be done. Let his wisdom be thine, his will thine. And why? It will be so; it shall be so;

* Cf. the pungent and admirable treatise of John Brinsley 'ΓΛΩΣΣΟ-ΧΑΛΙ'-ΝΩΣΙΣ; or, a Bridle for the Tongue,' &c., 1664, 12mo, *not* to be confounded with his 'Stand-Still; or, Bridle for the Times,' 1647.—G.

subject thyself therefore to it. Though we behave ourselves as stubborn horses, he will tame us and overrule us well enough; he is too mighty for us. Our stubbornness is the ground of all our crosses and afflictions; for if we will not easily be brought in, God, that out of his mercy chose us, will bring us in to yield. For he will have his will in us, or of us. He will glorify his justice upon us, if his mercies will not work. Lastly, consider the greatness of this sin, to whet us on to the duty enjoined. Though we seem to murmur only against men, we murmur against God; for what saith he to Moses?* 'They have not cast off thee, but they have cast off me,' 1 Sam. viii. 7. God takes part with those in authority, as Moses was. For there is no contempt of man, but comes from a contempt of God. The breaches of the second table do spring from the breaches of the first. Observe also, this sin hath ever been grievously punished, it being a sin that pulls God out of his throne, and makes men dare to teach God how to rule. It robs God of his worship, fear, trust, reverence; for it proceeds from the want of them; and lastly, it brings with it great unthankfulness, making men forget all God's goodness bestowed on them.

'Disputing or reasoning.'

It issues from murmuring. For when we are come to that pass that we murmur, lest men should think us rash in doing it without cause, we then endeavour to defend ourselves with reason; and indeed there is nothing that a carnal man does, but he will have reason for it; and he will have the world see that he doth not anything without reason. He will dispute with God by questioning whether this or that duty is necessary, and against civil authority by questioning the lawfulness or necessity of such duties as he is enjoined. This is a great sin. In divine truths, disputing is partly about probables, and therefore it is excellent to find out of probables the truth; but in divine truths, to dispute or make question, is little less than blasphemy. And it is observable that in those times when there was most disputing, as among the schoolmen and the like, about religion and divinity, there was least divinity practised, and very few good men. For the heart of man was then taken up in the consideration of this or that quiddity; and quite neglected the practice of those truths that were known.

Quest. But it will be asked, is all disputing evil?

Ans. No. The Turk will have none about the Alkoran, and the pope he will not have men dispute about anything that concerns him. The devil and his instruments they ever run into extremes. Either men must call in question all the grounds of divinity, or else receive upon trust whatsoever is delivered to us. No. We must know in doubtful things, this is good and required to find out certainty. The end of motion is rest, and the end of questions and doubts tends to truth. Yet have we many spend all their life in this or that question or doubt, and edify little or nothing. Like those physicians are they who contend and question about the goodness or badness of this or that meat, when a strong labouring man eats it, and finds as good nourishment out of it as out of any other. While men dispute and talk about this or that doctrine, a sound downright Christian receives it, digests it, and is nourished thereby, while the others do even starve themselves. Let therefore God alone with his secret will. *Homo sum*, said Salvian, *secreta Dei non intelligo* (*d*). God does what is done, be thou content. In human authority also we ought not to dispute, for the subject hath no calling to know the mysteries of state. It may be a sin to command, and yet a virtue to obey. It is thy duty to obey, not to question.

* Samuel.—G.

But if in thine understanding it be plainly evil which is commanded, obey not.* Job did thus, and Job would hear his servant speak, Job xix. 16. But if it be uncertain to thee and doubtful, certain it is thou must obey. Obedience must be without syllogisms. The servant ought to obey, the master must question.

VERSE 15.

'*That we may be blameless, and harmless, the sons of God without rebuke, in the midst of a crooked and perverse nation, among whom you shine as lights in the world.*'

This verse contains a reason, drawn from the end, why we should do all things without murmuring or disputing. The reason is threefold.

First, that you may be blameless. *Secondly*, harmless. *Thirdly*, that you may be the sons of God.

'Blameless.' This word, if it be taken generally, is a thing that none can attain to. God cannot be without blame, for wicked men will quarrel with him, be he never so good. Christ could not live without blame, though he went about doing good continually, Heb. xii. 3. It is said he endured the cross and despised the shame ; nay, the best men are subject to most shame. Stop wicked men in their lewd courses, they† are thought presently to be enemies. And the wicked take that for a wrong, whenas they receive so much good from others that they cannot requite it. But the proper signification of the word is in effect thus much, that they should so behave themselves, as they should not give any just occasion of offence, either to their own consciences, or that of other men. Walk towards God without all manner of profanation or irreligious course, and let your gesture towards men be just, that your conscience may clear you of all fraud or guile ; and let your carriage toward your own self be free from all abuse of your person, by gluttony, drunkenness, and the like. In a word, be holy, righteous, and sober.

'Harmless.' The word signifies simple, without all mixture or composition ; or else void of hurt, without horn, as the word imports (*e*).

The doctrine is, *that it is the property of Christians to do no harm.* The reason is, because our nature now is changed from that it was ; for by nature we are to one another lions and wolves, as Heb. xi. 33. Now therefore our nature being changed, our actions also become changed. The gospel makes us tame. The Spirit of Christ in all our members is as Christ himself. His miracles were for good, and they were beneficial to men. He did all things well. Those therefore that are led by this Spirit of his do no harm, so far as they are Christ's.

Use. For use note this as a main difference between the Christian and another man. For all other people are harmful creatures. The four monarchies were as so many beasts, because to the poor church of God they were as so many beasts, cruel and devouring. Nay, the civillest man of all, to his neighbours he seems to be harmless, but towards the church none so fierce as they.

On the contrary, Christians are meek as doves. The wicked are as ravenous birds, like eagles' feathers ;‡ self-love turns all to its own end.

* Cf. above sentiments with those referred to by Bishop Patrick, note *g*, Vol. I. page 290, *seq.*—G.

† Qu. 'you'?—Ed.

‡ Qu. 'feathered eagles.' Cf. Ezek. xxxix. 17, and Ps. lxxviii. 27.—G.

Among the beasts, the Christian is as a lamb, innocent, fruitful; a common good. 'When he is exalted the land rejoices,' Prov. xi. 11. Contrarily the wicked are termed lions and bears, and the like. Among the plants wicked men are as briars: a man must be fenced that deals with them, 2 Sam. xxiii. 7; the godly as lilies, sweet, not fenced with pricks. Among earthly creatures the godly are as the worm; the wicked, a generation of vipers and serpents. They will do no right, take no wrong, but a word and a blow; a word and presently to suit, right Esaüs and Ishmaels. Nay, they glory in it. Oh, say they, he is a shrewd man. Hence comes duels, combats, and the like. Men now are come to that pass, they will not put up a word. Nay, those that are innocent, and will pass by injuries, tush! they are fools. But know, thus to be foolish is to be wise, to be Christian like; and such fools as these are shall find comfort on their deathbeds, when those wise men shall wish they had been such fools.

Such fools as these are, I mean the innocent, shall have God for their help and shelter, for want whereof these worldly wise men come often to ill ends, and to be made fearful examples. The Psalms are full of encouragements herein: Ps. xviii. 2, 'The Lord is my rock and fortress,' said David; and so in Ps. xxv. 8, 9, 10, &c. Wicked men have horns, but God is a hammer to break the horns of the wicked. The innocent person, and he that is harmless, brings peace to the land, and a blessing to the place where he lives. Here prayers and intercessions are as the chariots of Israel and the horsemen thereof. Let those things be noted to provoke us unto this duty.

'Sons of God.'

This is the third ground whereby we are incited, to be without murmuring and disputing, that you may be 'the sons of God;' that is, that by this you may appear to your own comfort to be the sons of God, or that herein you may be as the sons of God, in shewing yourselves harmless and blameless, which may testify it to yourselves and others.

Doct. Therefore Christians that are harmless and blameless indeed, are the sons of God. The ground of this is the love of God, who freely gave his own Son to take our nature upon him, and to die to save us from the sting of death; he became the Son of man to make us the sons of God without rebuke. And as God gave him to us, so by faith doth he give us to him; and by this God gives us power to be his sons, John i. 12. Our nature is hereby changed; for whom he makes sons he sanctifies them and makes them new, and thus become we his sons. God hath adopted us, not as natural men, for this or that respect, to an earthly inheritance, but God freely adopts us to an heavenly inheritance that fadeth not; neither doth God adopt us as men do men *in solamen orbitatis*,* for God hath a Son in whom he is pleased; neither again can men's adoption make their adopted sons to be good; but when God adopts us, he makes us as he would have us to be, like himself. Fourthly, other adopted sons, many of them are not sharers together of the inheritance to one allotted; but we are made heirs and fellow-heirs with Christ himself. This love of God was such as the apostle could not express in any fit terms; therefore he saith, 'Behold what love hath the Father shewed us!' 1 John iii. 1. David thought it not to be a small thing to be the son-in-law of an earthly prince, 1 Sam. xviii. 23; behold, we are sons of the King of kings. By nature we are sons of the devil, and rebels. Now, that God should freely, out of his own free love, set his love on us, passing over angels and other men, and not sparing his own Son, have we not hence cause to cry, 'Behold what love!' and

* That is, for the solacing of childlessness.—G.

'Oh the depth of that love!' Earthly fathers adopt sons because they die, but God is eternal; he never dies; his Son is everlasting. Consider this as a point of comfort, for this relation is everlasting; he never leaveth us nor forsakes us. Servants are cast out, but the Son abideth for ever; servants know not the counsels of their masters, but sons they know the whole will of God. Consider this as a ground of protection in all dangers, and of provision of all good. 'I have a father,' saith the prodigal; 'what need I die for hunger? I will go to him,' Luke xv. 17. In a word, the word *Father* is an epitome of the whole gospel. All the promises therein contained are sealed up by and in this one word, God is our Father. Can we go to our Father for pardon of sin and not obtain it? By Christ's death and satisfaction he is become our Father; and therefore Christ is Christ after his resurrection. Can we then want any good thing? How can we think he will deny us his Spirit, or that inheritance in heaven, which as a Father he hath promised! How then, or at what shall we be dismayed and discomforted? What can trouble us? Mark what is promised in Ps. ciii. 2, *seq.* All good that may any way concern thy soul or body. Dost thou fear thy corruptions? The Spirit tells thee that God is thy Father; there can be no condemnation to thee, Rom. viii. 1. Dost thou fear want? Surely he that hath given thee Christ, his own Son, how shall he not with him give thee all things, Rom. viii. 32. Thou shalt want nothing for thy good. Thou mayest fall into sin, but God is still thy Father. This relation is everlasting. He will not forsake thee. From hence thou mayest have an argument against all suggestions. This brings with it comfort; but to whom? It must be to such as are sons, not to the traitorous and rebellious. It hath been treason for any man to term himself the son of a king, not being indeed so, yea, though the king were dead; and is it not high treason for a presumptuous traitor to come into the presence chamber of the great God, and with an impudent face to style God his Father? Verily God's answer will be to such, 'You are of your father the devil: his works ye do,' John viii. 44.

1. Those that are God's sons* *he renews to do his will and commandments.* 1 Pet. i. 16: 'Be ye holy,' saith he, 'for I am holy.' But when men hate goodness and good men, nay, and persecute them, defame them, murder them, John viii. 44, they are of the devil. They are murderers and liars; and that religion that teacheth them is devilish.

2. Again, If God be thy Father, *thou wilt have a spirit of prayer.* We are no sooner born but we begin to cry, as Paul did at his first conversion, Acts ix. 11. Every child of God, in respect of his measure of grace, he will do his endeavour to sigh and sob out his grief to God: and as the grace increases, so will this duty be more perfect, till at length he comes to provoke† God, by his promise to urge and bind him by reasons to hear him. Those, therefore, that pass day after day, never finding time for the performance of this duty, they have not God's Spirit; for by it we have access to God, Eph. ii. 18; Eph. iii. 12; and there is no child but will use this privilege; and those that use it not may well suspect they are not children.

3. Thirdly, If thou be the child of God, and hast his Holy Spirit in thee, thou shalt have, whensoever thou standest in need, *a sweet consolation;* for that ever reveals to thee what thou art, and comforts thee in all distress. For, Rom. v. 1, 'being justified by faith, thou hast peace with God.'

* In margin here, 'Signs of God's sons.'—G.

† That is, etymologically, to 'call forth,' = to appeal to.—G.

What cross soever troubles the child of God, this will ever comfort him: Well! I am the child of God; I am assured God is reconciled to me; I have my confidence in him, that when he sees fit I shall be eased; in the mean time I am assured I shall not be overcome. This is that which no natural man can have; he cannot rejoice in affliction.

4. Fourthly, If thou beest the son of God, thou art not *overmuch careful for the things that concern this life*. Thou usest the means that God hath ordained, and thou trustest God with the issue and event of all. It is the property of orphans to care much for their living, and for the things of this world; not for those that have such a father as God, that provides for all his children liberally; and men in thus doing shew themselves orphans, or bastards, and not sons.

Quest. But some will ask, Is it not possible to be the son of God, and yet ignorant thereof?

Ans. I answer, Yes. For the child at the first knows not his father; but by little and little he comes to know him as he grows in years. So is it with the child of God. At the first he only cries and bewails his miserable estate; but as they grow up, out of the word they learn to see their estates that is laid up for them, and to know their Father that hath been so good to them, and to call upon him as their Father for anything that they want. They know that the Scripture gives it as a note of one that is born of God, that 'he sins not'; that is, that not with delight and continuance in sin, but that his new nature stirs him up to repent, and to beg pardon and to strive against it, so as at length he comes to grow so perfect as no temptation shall overthrow him, though it may foil* him. But he always considers his estate when any temptation comes: Shall I, that am a prince, a son and heir to God, do thus, and offend against him?

'Without rebuke.'

This is comprehended in the former words, and therefore I speak the less thereof. The words are not to be taken in a strict legal sense, but in an evangelical sense, implying that we should walk so as we may be free from rebuke of the best, from gross sins, from common infirmities and personal corruptions. Whether it be rashness, anger, worldliness, intractableness, the child of God must labour to free himself of them. He ought to endeavour to attain to perfection, though we cannot attain to it in this world; and we ought to pray as the apostle, Eph. iii. 18, 'to know the length, breadth, depth, and height, and to know the love of Christ, that passeth knowledge;' and thus doing we shall dignify this estate of ours.

'In the midst of a crooked and perverse nation.'

The word 'crooked,' or 'perverse,' is a borrowed word from timber,† whose excellency is to be right and straight; and if it be not, must be squared by the rule. Here it is applied to the disposition and nature of men, who naturally are of a crooked condition, especially those that are in the bosom of the church. They are so crooked as they cannot be squared aright by means; and so it is with those that are right, they are very right.

Doct. The doctrine then is, *that wicked men are all perverse and crooked*, Deut. xxxii. 5.

Reason. The reason hereof is, since the fall of Adam we are under sin and Satan. Sin is nothing but crookedness. We lying in sin are therefore crooked inwardly and outwardly, in will and in judgment. Even in the church, men *perversely judge* of a Christian's life, and of preaching. So

* That is, sometimes get the better of him.—G.

† That is, σκολός, on which cf. Bishop Ellicott *in loc.*, with his references.—G.

that till we be converted, our wisdom is enmity to God. But *the will especially is perverse.* Men they *will* die. 'Why will ye die, O house of Israel?' Jer. xxvii. 13. 'How often would I have gathered you,' saith Christ, 'and you would not!' Mat. xxiii. 37. Endeavour to bring men to rules: they will not; they will perish. Bring them to make conscience of private prayer, good company: away with it, they will not yield. Our *affections are also perverse.* Do not most men love their bane? Ill company, bad courses, swearing and blaspheming. Men will die rather than they will leave their courses. *Men are also naturally perverse in opposition to means.* God commands, promises, sends mercies and judgments, but who regards? They will go on in their ways; nay, as in Deut. xxix. 19, 'they will bless themselves in them.' This is the nature of most men in the visible church, more perverse than the Jews.

'Signs hereof.'

1. The first sign of this perverse estate is, *bring thyself to the rules of God's truth; if thou do it unwillingly, and art brought to it by violence, if you shun the word and the means of salvation, if you shun good company, it is a sign you are crooked;* nay, so crooked, as you desire to be crooked still.

2. But be it so that thou canst be content to apply thyself to the rule, then *whether do you tremble to apply the rules to your lusts and corruptions?* You have many are so set on their sins as they will justify sin by the word, and wrest the meaning thereof to their own lusts. This is a sure infallible sign of a perverse estate.

Cure hereof.

1. *Bring thyself to God's ordinance,* where thou shalt know thine own crookedness and the danger of it.

2. But especially do this *when thou art young;* for those that are settled in their dregs are not to be dealt withal. It is good therefore to do as nurses do, strengthen ourselves when we are young and pliable.

3. Thirdly, *Keep good company, and such as by their life will discover to thyself thy corruptions and perverse estate;* and thus when thou findest it,

4. *Consider what a miserable estate thou art in.* We amongst us account it a great eyesore to see a body that should be straight to be crooked. Oh that we had eyes to see this spiritual crooked estate we are in! Oh what fear and grief would possess us! How would we labour to free ourselves of it, and to straighten ourselves every day, lest we should be found unfit for God's building, and good for nothing but to burn! With such as walk perversely God will deal perversely, Lev. xxvi. 28. It may be he will seem to sleep for a while, but at the hour of death it will shew that he looked for better courses at thy hands.

5. Pray with the psalmist, Ps. cxix. 5, 'Oh that my ways were so direct, that I might keep thy statutes!' Observe again, that the godly here live in the midst of lions and wolves; those that are of a froward and perverse heart. For those that live under the means of grace, and will not be wrought upon, they are much worse for it. There is more innocence in a Turk than in some that profess better. And those that profess most, if they be hypocrites, of all other make the most bitter opposition against the truth.

The reasons hereof are: *First, God hereby shews his power,* in that he can and doth preserve his children among lions from the wrath of the lion. Christ he must rule, but it is in the midst of his enemies; and therefore his church must be in the midst of his enemies, for he is king of his church.

2. Again, in regard of the wicked, *it justifies their just condemnation.* They cannot say but that they had the means, as well of the gospel as the examples of those that were good. Thus did Noah justly condemn the old world, and Lot Sodom.

3. Furthermore, those that are not desperately wicked, but of whom we may conceive some hope, *surely they by living with the godly* may be won; as when they see religion in others bringing forth good works, they see religion is no impossible thing, for they see men troubled with the like infirmities that they are that practise it; and they see it is sweet, because it makes men tractable and loving.

4. Moreover, in regard of the godly, God suffers them to be amongst the wicked, *for it refines them.* Envy and malice are quick-sighted. God's children know they live in the midst of envy, therefore they are wary. Lot lived more uprightly in Sodom than when he was out of it. Wickedness binds in religion, and makes it more forcible, even as by an *antiperistasis*;* it unites it and strengthens it. It makes the godly to be more careful, to be unblameable, and to watch to keep themselves from doing hurt, and from taking hurt; for wicked men are watchful to take advantage of any ill example in the weak Christian, and to follow it. But, on the contrary, the weak Christian is overcome, and carried away with the streams of vice, and therefore are the more watchful.

'Directions for life.'

1. *Remember thy calling*—that you are sons of God; and forget not your profession, and fetch reasons from your callings. You are God's children; you are called with a holy calling. Shall I do thus, and offend against my Father? and shall I disgrace that holy calling, and scandalise it? Shall I give cause to make the enemy to blaspheme?

2. Again, *Observe the persons with whom thou conversest.* Are they malicious and envious?

3. Beware how thou *give them offence;* especially watch thy natural corruptions and weaknesses. Take heed of secret ill thoughts.

4. *Carry the example of David about with thee;* see in him what his thoughts wrought. That which thou tremblest to do, tremble to think on; for God justly leaves such in great sins that solace themselves in ill thoughts.

5. Again, *Look to duties of the second table.* These sins are great sores in the eyes of our enemies.

6. *Use a loving, pitiful carriage towards them that are without.* Though they be never so wicked, give them their due, and consider the goodness thou hast was given thee. Therefore be not puffed up in thine own conceit, but fear continually.

'Among whom you shine as lights in the world.'

These words contain another reason why the children of God ought to be unreprovable. For, saith the apostle, 'you are lights.' All God's children are lights, but so as there is an order of them. God is the ground of all light; he is the Father of lights. Christ he is the Sun of righteousness. These are the grand lights. The word of God is also a light and a lantern to light us in the dark ways of this world. From hence light is derived to the saints, who receive it from Christ by the word and Spirit. You being therefore thus enlightened, you are to converse amongst men as lights, saith the apostle. For the better understanding thereof, consider in what things God's children resemble light; and,

* That is from *αντι* and *περίστᾰσις*.—G.

1. First, We know this creature of light *is an excellent creature*, shewing the excellency of all other creatures; and it is a beautiful creature. Thus is the word, and children of God. By it all the world is discovered to be as Egypt, and the church to be as the land of Goshen.* And this is beautiful in the eyes of God, who loves that which is like himself. He is light indeed, and nothing but light is lovely to him. He loves those sparks which our natural corruption hath left unto us; and therefore much more the light of his own Spirit which he places in us.

2. Secondly, *Light is pure, and admits of no contagion*, though it be in the most contagious places of all. So is the word: it is pure, and makes us pure and sincere, and that we should not be defiled with the lusts and corruptions of this world wherein we converse.

3. Thirdly, *Light makes us to discern of differences*.. It shews itself, and discovers other things. Thus doth the word shew itself where it is, and the man that hath it doth discern of things that differ. He judges of the wicked, and censures their lewd courses. The child of God is above all wicked men, and themselves are justly judged of none; for the wicked men cannot judge of those that are lights, no more than a blind man of colours, for they are blind by nature. The world would indeed censure them, when indeed they cannot discern themselves, when contrarily he discerns himself and knows his infirmities and his slidings.

4. Again, *Light is a heavenly quality*. So is the word of God, holy, pure, transforming godly men to its own likeness, to be heavenly. His bread is from heaven; his affections, desires, thoughts, endeavours are heavenly. His way is upward. He is heavenly-minded; while he is on earth he is in heaven.

5. Moreover, *Light is a most comfortable thing in darkness*, expelling terrors and discomforts. Thus is a Christian that is enlightened by the word. Terrors are in the word, but the word comforts the heart of a Christian. It makes him able to judge of his way and estate; to know he is the Son of God; that all the promises are his; that heaven is his; that he hath God's mark. Contrarily, the wicked have no light at all; for while they live here their life here is as a death, full of discomfort; they having no comfort in anything, save a little glimpse of false joy in the creatures; which when they leave them they are in the more terror,—all their comfort being in this, that they see not that miserable estate before they fall into it and feel it.

6. Furthermore, *Light makes a thing full of evidence*. All the world cannot persuade a man contrary to that they see. Thus the word so discovers to us our estates in grace, and so surely as all the world can never shake the foundation of our faith. 'Though he kills me,' saith Job, 'I will trust in him,' Job xiii. 15. But for the wicked, their life is full of staggering, full of doubtings; and hence is it that the children of God are counted by God holy, pure, comely, fair and dear, because they live with a resolution. The papists, they will tell us that the word is obscure; let them tell us the light is obscure, for we may as well believe one as the other.

7. But to proceed: *Light is a quality of surest motion*. It spreads suddenly. Thus do the children of God. They communicate to others. They shine, spreading forth the grace, first of all to those that are next them, as children and friends, then to such as are further off. Those that have

* Cf. Exodus x. 23.—G.

not this nature, that do not desire to do good to others, they are not children of the light; for it is the nature of all good to communicate.

8. *Light*, we know, *hath a secret influence wheresoever it is.* Thus also is the grace of God in his children. It is ever operative and working. What light soever they receive from the Sun of righteousness, they diffuse it and spread it to others, like the moon; and therefore he adds further:

'As lights in the world.'

We that are 'lights in this world,' we are, it is true, in a dampish place, yet must we shine, though but dimly. Therefore ministers, let them look both to their doctrine and life, for they are great lights, or at the least should be so, and they will be noted. We know when the sun or moon are eclipsed. We all observe it as a wonder. And thus will it be with such lights as ministers should be. Men continually eye them. If they be eclipsed, it will be wondered at and observed of all. Let therefore not only ministers but others also look to themselves, that they take heed of those things that will eclipse them. We know whence the eclipse in nature of these heavenly bodies do come; from the interposition of dark, gross, earthly bodies. Thus it is with God's children. Their cares, griefs, and studies in this world being ever more carnal than is meet, they eclipse us and make us dark, keeping us from the presence of that light which should enlighten us. But especially, and above the rest, self-love, that blinds us and eclipses all other lights from us.

9. Again, *Heavenly lights are perpetual.* Even as *stellæ cadentes*, so is it with the wicked man. Though he seems to shine fairly, yet because the causes of this light in him are earthly, no marvel if after the force of them be spent they suddenly vanish. But the godly man's light is of another substance and nature. It is heavenly, and is ever like himself. It may indeed be obscured, but never wholly eclipsed. Either worldly sorrow or joy doth for a time sometimes darken them, and may be so obscured as neither the world, no, nor themselves can discern their estates for their own comfort; yet for all this will they at length recover their former brightness and glory again. Saint Paul, he saith, a Christian life is concealed and hid with Christ in God, Col. iii. 3; but yet when he shall appear, then shall we also appear.

Use. The use of all this is to try us whether we be lights. Surely if we be, we will have no communion with those that work the works of darkness. So saith Saint John, 1 John i. 5–7. Again, if we be lights we shall wonder at our glorious estate we are in; we shall think all our life before we came into this estate to be dark; yea, though formerly we were civilly disposed. And especially shall we wonder at that which we have in future expectation and hope, reserved to us in heaven. A carnal man wonders still at worldly matters, as stately buildings and the like; a Christian thinks all base in respect of the immense love of God freely set upon him.

Directions how to attain to be lights.

1. First, If we desire to be lights, *communicate thyself with the chiefest light*, as the stars are ever in the presence of the sun, and from his light they receive theirs. Be sure thou placest thyself in God's eye continually.

2. Secondly, *Use the means*, use the glass of God's word. Thou shalt not only see thy estate therein, but by it thou shalt be transformed into God's image, 2 Cor. iii. 18. Other glasses have no such power like this mirror of the gospel. It makes us like God, because it hath the Spirit of God ever accompanying with it, whence it is the word of light. Those therefore that are out of the sunshine of the gospel, no marvel if they be

dark. The moon, so far as it is averse from the sun, is ever dark. So is a Christian. So far as he is turned from Christ, so far he is dark. Let thine eyes therefore be ever towards him in the use of the means, the word, prayer, and the sacraments, and such like.

3. Again, *In thy conversation have no correspondency with the world*, for what fellowship is there between light and darkness? How foully do they therefore deceive themselves that will be wise. They will be protestant or papist, zealous or profane, according as their company are. God will turn such worldly wisdom into mere folly, who will be ashamed of such when he shall come in his kingdom. It is a comely thing to be Christians with Christians. Light with light augments the light, even as the multitude of stars joined in the heaven make the *galaxia*.* A company of Christians meeting in one make a glorious light indeed, and such a lustre as will dazzle the eyes of the wicked world. Be stirred up therefore to use good company.

4. *And follow the example of those that be lights*, and the directions thou findest in the word, and thou shalt shine as the sun in the kingdom of God. It is true the wicked they will labour to cover this light with clouds of disgrace and detraction, and thus they reward God for his goodness, but they have their lesson. There is no surer sign of a wicked man than when they endeavour to deprave these lights and to obscure them. And yet this practice is very usual, when they see especially any new light risen up, they deride and scoff at that man or woman; they hate him for his light. Like Cain are they, that hated his brother for his goodness; and herein are not only imitators of Cain, but they shew themselves to be of their father the devil, for his works they do. Well, as we desire not to be of this sort, let us see that we use the means. Go and be where the word of light is, where it shines; for those that live without it live in darkness. Set not thy carnal reason against God's wisdom. He bids thee do this. And as thou desirest the peace of Zion,

5. *Pray for this light that it may grow more and more unto the perfect day thereof.*

6. And *labour to see the contrary estate of such as are in darkness*, where the king of fear ruleth, and where is nothing but terror.

7. *And entreat God that he would open thy dull eyes, that the glorious light of the gospel may shine therein.* So doth the apostle, Eph. i. 18; and thus shalt thou at the length come to shine here in this world, without which thou shalt not shine in the world to come. The light of nature and reason cannot bring thee to the light of glory.

8. And when thou art converted, '*strengthen thy brethren*,' Luke xxii. 32; labour to bring others into this marvellous light. 'He that gains a soul shall shine as the stars,' Dan. xii. 3. But will some men say, May we converse then or live among wicked men? Yes, verily; for the Holy Spirit saith that we must 'shine *in the world*.' Christ did not pray that God would take his disciples out of the world, but that he would keep them in the world from evil, John xvii. 15. But that which is forbidden is familiar conversation and amity with them; otherwise we may live with them so as by example to gain them. And herein the Christian reasoneth contrary to the world; for the world saith, Do this. Why? Because it is the custom, and most men use it. Nay, saith the Christian, we must live so as we ought to endeavour to make others, which are wicked, like ourselves. We must gain others by our good example. We must 'redeem

* That is, = the milky way.—G.

the time, because the days are evil,' Eph. v. 16. Because others are perverse, be thou good. Noah was not as the old world, nor Lot as Sodom. We as they ought to be preachers of righteousness; and if we cannot bring others to the light of the truth, yet to grieve and pity their estates. And as David bewailed, 'Woe is me, that I am constrained to dwell in Mesech,' &c., Ps. cxx. 5, and yet to comfort ourselves in this, that it will not be always thus with us. The time will come that we shall be freed from them, and we shall have communion with the Trinity and with all the saints. In the mean time shine here; swear not with them; be not dissolute with them, but be constant in going against the stream. Call to mind thy calling, that thou art the son of God. Thou art to be a light to those that are in darkness. Reason not for thy corruptions, but ever against them. I am a Christian; shall I hate him that I profess to follow? I am a son of God; shall company make me perverse? I am a light; shall I cease to shine? No, Lord; while I am here give me grace that I may grow more and more fit for that light and glorious estate that thou hast in keeping for me against that great day of accounts.

VERSE 16.

Holding forth the word of life.

That which is of light is life, saith John, i. 4: 'The life was the light of men;' and therefore he saith we should be as lights, 'holding forth the word of life.' It is not enough for us to shine to ourselves, but we ought to shine to others in speech and conversation. By 'the word of life' here especially is meant the gospel; for the law is a killing letter. We being in our corrupt estate, the law pronounces us dead as concerning ourselves. Then comes the gospel, that sends us out of ourselves to Christ; and in him it pronounces life to such as come to him; and it describes to us the way that leads to life, and the degrees of life, as redemption, grace, and glory, 2 Tim. i. 10. It again begins this life in us, and works faith in us, whereby we lay hold on life; and therefore it is also called the word of faith. It is called the word of the kingdom; for it offers the kingdom to us. It is also called the word of reconciliation; for that it tells us where it is to be had, and works it in us. It is therefore the word of life; and those that believe it not, are dead in law, for the sentence is already passed upon such. He is already condemned as dead men. He wants sense, motion, and comeliness. For *sense*, he cannot relish any goodness, either in hearing or seeing it. He is blinded, and he stops his ear at the voice of the charmer; and this makes him wonder how others are affected with any good thing. For *motion*, he cannot set one step onward to salvation. And for that *comeliness*, we all by nature are more loathsome than the dead carcase. Abraham could not endure the sight of his own wife when she was dead, though living she was so dear to him, Gen. xxiii. 4. Thus are we by nature altogether rotten and polluted; speech, fine discourse, favour, and all other outward good parts, they can put no comeliness upon us. They are but on us as flowers stuck upon a dead carcase. All men know that it is rotten and stinking, and void of all comeliness notwithstanding them. This then must teach us to regard more this word of life, and to pity them that have it not; and how to judge of such that withhold this word of life from them that live in darkness, as the papists do. Surely there is no cruelty like this cruelty, to starve men's souls. Observe we therefore from hence, he that refuseth God's ordinance he refuseth life.

What shall we then think of those private devotions, wherewith many men put off God's ordinance, thinking that they can get as much good in their warm chamber by reading of books, as in the public congregation by hearing God's word taught? These are fools, setting their foolish inventions against God's wisdom, as though they could tell God better means to beget and strengthen faith, than he himself can appoint. Oh, but men will say, it hinders us from our callings; in seven years we lose a year. But dost thou not live by this word? Shalt thou do well to be ashamed of that, and lightly esteem of that word that brings with it life and glory? But why is this word no more esteemed? Surely men deceive themselves with self-conceit. They think themselves good, when they are stark naught; and that they are alive, whenas like to the Laodiceans they are dead in sin and iniquity, Rev. ii. 16, *seq.*

(1.) The reason hereof is, *they want the Spirit to convince them.* For the Spirit convinces us of death. Where this Spirit is not, none will seek for life; for they know not that they are dead by nature; they believe not God's law that should convince them. No marvel then if they affect not a change.

(2.) A second reason is, *for that such men as these are carried by sense.* They see they want no outward content, and for other things they think God will be merciful; they think God loves them, for that he gives them worldly riches. There is another sort of men, and these are brought to despair; how is it that these, seeing their misery, do not esteem of this word aright, and come to it as to the word of life? I answer, they consider not of this word aright; they think their sins so many as that the word cannot enlighten their darkness. To such I say, they are most fit for this word of life; for Christ bids such come to him as are 'weary and heavy laden' with their sins, and he hath promised release, Mat. xi. 28. And he saith he came 'to bind up the broken in heart and the bruised in spirit,' Isa. lxi. 1; and therefore, let such be encouraged by these and such like gracious invitations and promises to come to the word, and with attention to search into the depth of these promises made to them. But thus much of this, that the word is a word of life. Now we come to the next, that Christians must 'hold forth this word of light or life.' And this is done in speech and action, profession and confession, when they are called thereto. For every Christian is a light that must shine. What use is there of light under a bushel? Many are of contrary judgment. They think it wisdom to be close in their profession; in company of papists, to be popish; of religious, to be religiously disposed. Surely this wisdom is carnal and devilish. What use is there of such light? They are like false lanthorns, which are commonly called thieves' lanthorns. They carry their light to themselves; none is benefited thereby; they are fit for works of darkness. Of such, Christ hath already said, 'He will hereafter be ashamed,' Mark viii. 38. Others there are inwardly one thing, outwardly another, contrary to the Christian's duty, which is to hold forth the light that he hath. And this do they, whenas in all passages of their life they are turned into the word, and cast into the mould thereof; then it teaches us to pray, to be patient, to joy, yea, in the midst of afflictions, and to do good even to those that hate us. And if we, according as we are taught, do these things, then do we hold forth this word of life, and it will be an exceeding great comfort to us in life, in death, in all estates. It will assure us that we are transformed into the image of this word, and the holding forth of this word in our lives thus, will cause a far louder report in the ears of God than all the verbal profession we can make.

In temptation, if we find ourselves even at despair, by considering the curse of the law, due to us for our sins, if in this estate we can apply the gospel so to us, as thereby we find comfort out of it, and such as upholds us, surely this is a great sure sign that we are transformed; and by this we hold forth the power of the word, and thereby the light thereof. In the hour of death, when the devil is most busy to shake our faith, we notwithstanding are not daunted, but ground our faith on the word, and can comfortably apply that speech of St Paul, 'There is no condemnation to those that are in Christ.' We hereby do set forth the power, comfort, and truth of the word. Contrarily, those that are impatient in trouble, and puzzled with every temptation, swallowed up with fear, and shew no assurance of faith in them, notwithstanding the great means they have had, these live as though there were no word. Nay, they do in a manner slander the word in their lives, making show as if the word had no power, comfort, or strength at all in it. For our parts, let us not leave till we have digested all the promises and comfortable assurances the gospel doth everywhere lay out to us. Hereby we shall shew ourselves far above all other men, and in all estates we shall be the same, not moved at all. Let us be therefore thankful for this word of life, and joyful in it, and treasure it up against the evil day, setting our minds ever upon it; let it be as a paradise to us, where the tree of life is placed. Christ in the word is as the tree of life. He that tasteth of this tree shall never die. By the 'first Adam' we come to eat of the tree of knowledge of good and evil, by woeful experience, by the which we all died, but by the second Adam we come to eat of the tree of life, by which we live perpetually.

NOTES.

(*a*) P. 8.—'No perfunctory thing can please God. To this end, as Seneca says, of performing of duties natural, so in religious duties there is required: first, a right judgment of the nature of the thing we do; secondly, an affection to do it,' &c. This is a commonplace of the Stoic philosophy; and while I have not been able to trace the words, the *sentiment* is frequent in the Letters of Seneca, as well as in those of Cicero.

(*b*) P. 15.—' "Fortiter pro te, suaviter pro me, Domine," saith the father.' A variation or adaptation by Augustine of the apophthegm, 'Fortiter in re, suaviter in modo.'

(*c*) P. 21.—' "My soul waiteth on God with silence," for so is the signification of the word.' The literal rendering is, 'Only to God (is) my soul silent;' one of the standard proof-texts with the Quakers, in support of their 'silent' meetings.

(*d*) P. 22.—'Homo sum, said Salvian, secreta Dei non intelligo.' This is one of various of the reverential sayings of this priest of Marseilles, who is usually classed with the Fathers. It occurs in the most thoughtful of his books, his *De Providentia Dei*, which, from its frequent citation by the Puritans, must have been a favourite with them. Cf. lib. i., near beginning.

(*e*) P. 23.—'Harmless.' The word signifies without all mixture or composition; or else void of hurt, without harm, as the word imports. The word is 'αμεμπτοι, on which cf. Bishop Ellicott, who gives valuable references on its derivation and lexical meaning.

G.

OF THE PROVIDENCE OF GOD.*

But I trust in the Lord that I myself also shall come shortly.—Phil. II. 24.

In the former verses the apostle Paul shews his care and love that he bore to the Philippians, in that he would not leave them destitute of a guide and director; and therefore he sends Timothy, whom he commends, to shew his love the more; and for his greater commendations, he shews the wickedness of the contrary sort, that thereby Timothy his sincerity may the better appear; 'others seek their own, but Timothy as a son hath served me.' He lays down the causes of this his sincerity. He first had learned the Scriptures of a child; then he had a gracious grandmother and mother. It is an excellent comfortable thing whenas children can say, 'I am the son of thy servant and thy handmaid,' Ps. lxxxvi. 16. And a third cause or help was his conversing with him. He drew in the sweet spirit of the blessed apostle. God, he derives† good to men by good society. They are therefore enemies to themselves that regard not good, choice company; for it makes of good excellent, and of those that are not yet good, if they belong to God, it makes them good.

In this verse he shews a further degree of his care of the Philippians. There are‡ divers ways to come to the knowledge of men's estate: as first by report; secondly, by messengers; thirdly, by letter. St Paul had used all these; but his care was such as all these would not content him. He must see them himself, which is indeed the surest means and way of all.

In these words, therefore, consider the manner of the delivery of this speech, 'I trust in the Lord.' Then the matter, which contains a purpose of his coming. Then the ground, his trust in God. Here, first of all, mark the language of Canaan; and the heavenly dialect,

1. *To express future purposes with a reservation of, and resignation to, God's will and guidance.* '*I trust in God,*' saith the apostle; for the hearts of men, yea of kings, are in God's hand, to turn and wind them as the rivers of waters, Prov. xxi. 1. This shews Christ to be God, for he is the object of trust. Observe in the second place,

2. *God's providence extends to every particular thing.* He guides our incomings and our outgoings; he disposes of our journeys; nay, his providence extends to the smallest things, to the sparrows and to the hair of our heads; he governs every particular passage of our lives.

* 'Of the Providence of God' immediately follows 'The Christian Work,' without separate title-page, in the 4to of 1639. Cf. note, page 2.—G.

† That is, 'communicates.'—G.

‡ Misprinted 'is.'—G.

Use 1. This should teach us to set upon our affairs *with looking up to heaven for permission, power, and sufferance;* and this St James enforces by reproving the contrary. 'Go to,' saith he in his fourth chapter, and ver. 13th, and adds the instruction thereupon; 'for that ye ought to say, if the Lord will, we shall live and do this or that.' Let us therefore in all our affairs be holy, and not bind or limit our holiness only to coming to church; but seeing at all times and in all places we are Christians, and ever in the presence of God, let us place ourselves still in his eye, and do nothing but that we would be willing God shall see; and labour to behold him in every good thing we have, and give him thanks in all the good we enjoy.

Use 2. And secondly, it ought to give us warning, that *we ought not to set upon anything, wherein we cannot expect God's guidance;* and so consequently cannot trust on him for a blessing upon what we do. For if we do, we must look to meet the Lord standing in our way, as Balaam did, in opposing our lewd and wicked intentions.

Use 3. And thirdly, it ought to teach us *to take nothing but that for which we may give God the thanks and praise;* as contrarily many do, who may thank the devil for what they have gotten, and yet make God implicitly the giver of their most unjust exactions.

VERSE 25.

Yet I supposed it necessary to send to you Epaphroditus.

Paul thought it not enough to plant the seeds of the word amongst them, but he would be viewing it and watering. 'I purpose shortly to see you,' saith he; but because I am now in prison I cannot come myself, but I purpose presently to send you Epaphroditus, and afterwards Timothy; and this he thought necessary—for well he knew that the residence of the pastor is necessary to the flock of the Lord, in some sort. But to stand upon this doctrine is not my purpose. The next thing I come to is, the commendations of Epaphroditus, which is divers; out of which generally thus much we learn, that it is our duty *to give them commendations that are praiseworthy,* even to this end that thereby we might raise a good opinion of them, especially of the ministers of the gospel; for hereby is the gospel itself glorified by us. And indeed it is a great sign that the spirit of the devil rests in that man, that doth detract and disparage the good children of God. For it comes hereby that the gospel of God is also blamed, and neglected. For the commendation of the minister is a preparative, and makes way for the word.

My brother.

The word in this place signifies one of the same office. As judges call one another 'brother,' so doth St Paul call Epaphroditus 'brother,' in regard of his office and spiritual function; and hereby he shews his love to him; for 'brother' is a name of love and friendship. Secondly, it shews his care of Epaphroditus; for one brother will care for another, unless they be of a Cainish nature. Thirdly, it is a name of equality, for brothers are equal. And hereby the apostle shews his humility, who being an apostle and pillar of the church, descended so low as to call one of inferior rank and calling, 'brother.' He had another spirit before his conversion; he persecutes the church of God. But afterward those that he formerly persecutes are now his 'brethren.' Now he thinks he is a debtor to all, both Jew and Grecian, Rom. i. 14. The proud man thinks all are debtors to him, that all do owe him respect and reverence; and indeed it is the spirit of the devil that 'lifteth up.' Antichrist is his eldest son indeed, who lifteth himself up against, and above all that is called God. Contrarily Christ humbles himself to the death to call us brothers. Shall we then disdain to live together in terms of equality and love? Is there not infinite difference between Christ and us? Was there not in him such a glory as passeth our apprehension? and what had we, or what have we, that we should lift ourselves up after this fashion? If we will strive to be above and outgo others, let it be in humility. Go each before others, in giving honour to others above ourselves. Observe, therefore, grace takes advantage of all bonds to increase love; bonds of office as well as of nature. Men of the same profession emulate and envy one another. Thus it is naturally, but let religion teach us better, and take away this natural poison from us.

Fellow-labourer.

The apostle commends him yet further. He calls Epaphroditus his 'fellow labourer,' in regard of the pains he endured; and 'fellow soldier,' in regard of the perils and dangers he jointly did undergo with the apostle. The doctrine that hence arises is, that *ministers are fellow-labourers.* They are not, or should not be, fellow-loiterers, as many are. No. The Scriptures compares them to the most painful and laborious professions; to husbandmen, whose labour is circular, every year renewing as the year doth renew. Such is the ministers' labour, converting and strengthening others. It is a great labour to break the shell of the word; to lay open the right interpretation thereof; to divide it aright; to convert a soul; to preserve it from the devil. It is as the peril of women in travail; 'My little children, of whom I travail in birth till Christ be formed in you,' saith Paul our apostle in Gal. iv. 19. Idle people are therefore unjust esteemers and judgers of the pains of ministers, they knowing it is out of their proper element.

Use. If ministers then be labourers, you to whom we preach are God's orchard; you must submit yourselves to be wrought on. If we be builders, you must be lively stones of this building. You must suffer yourselves to be squared, and cut, and made fit for this building while you are here. At the building and finishing of the material temple there was no noise of hammers, or such instruments; all were fitted in the mountain. Thus* must we expect to be fitted here while we live; for in that beautiful temple in heaven, there is no fashioning or fitting, either by crosses to hammer us, or by any other means. We must here be conformable to his death, that we may also be conformed to the similitude of his resurrection hereafter. If ministers be husbandmen, you must be 'ground,' and such as may bring forth fruit to perfection, else all our labour and pains that we take with you will be to no other end than to make you to be near cursing, Heb. vi. 7. And know, it is not sufficient that you bring not forth evil fruit; but every tree that bringeth not forth good fruit, must be hewed down and cast into the fire, Mat. iii. 10. Remember Christ cursed the fig-tree for unfruitfulness; and with what curse? Even unfruitfulness. Thus will God do with us. If he finds us unfruitful, he will take away his Spirit, and we shall be unfruitful still; and this† by woeful experience we see daily, with many that come indeed within the sound of the word every day, but mend not one jot; nay, they become every day worse. May not God complain, as he did of Judah in the parable of the vineyard, Isa. v. 5,

* Misprinted 'this.'—G. † Misprinted 'thus.'—G.

that he hath hedged us and fenced us about with government, and authority, and good laws, and hath taken out of us the stones and thorns of popery, and profaneness; and yet we bring forth wild grapes. And might he not break down the wall; and that justly, and suffer us to be devoured. Surely yes; and yet must needs we acknowledge him to be just. But it follows, the apostle calls Epaphroditus here his,

Fellow-labourer. It is observable here, concerning God's goodness, that he suffers not his faithful labourers to be alone. Christ sends them out by 'two and two,' before his face, Mark vi. 7; and this he doth that they might be a mutual aid, strengthening and comforting one another. Thus did Christ in old time, and thus he doth also in later times. He sent Augustine and Jerome, Luther and Melancthon; where, by the way also, observe God's wisdom in sending men of diversity of gifts: Jerome, severe and powerful; Augustine, meek and gentle; Luther, hot and fiery; Melancthon, of a soft and mild spirit; one to temper the other's over forwardness, and thereby to prevail with some that liked not of the strictness of the other. And by this means God sent teachers suitable to the natures and fitting the several humours of men, among whom some desire to hear the 'sons of consolation,' others the 'sons of thunder.'

Fellow-soldier.

Every man's life is a warfare, but most of all and above all, the minister is continually in war and strife. They are soldiers, leaders; they carry the standard, but they of all others are in the most danger, they stand in the brunt of the battle. The reason hereof is: the devil, having malice against the whole church in general, specially aimeth at them that pull men out of his service into the church, even as beasts do rage against such as take their young away from them. It is the minister that treads on the serpent's head: no marvel, then, if the devil endeavoureth to bite them by the heel. Thus dealt he with Christ, when he first set upon his office of mediator; and thus did he with Moses and Paul, in the main plots contrived against them. Such as those are great eyesores to him, and this is it that makes them soldiers and captains. But how? I answer, even as Paul, 1 Cor. x. 4. So the ministers do fight against the strongholds of corruption within us, against natural reason, corrupt affections, proud conceits; they fight against these imaginations, and in them, against the devil himself, who doth* use these instruments to bring his purposes to pass. In ministers, therefore, it is required principally knowledge in the stratagems of the devil, in especial manner in those amongst whom they should converse; by observing the corruptions of the times, places, and the corrupt customs, and also the general corruptions of callings. He, therefore, that would be a good soldier, had need be continually resident in his charge; for the devil having gotten hold once, he seeks to sing them asleep with 'Soul, thou hast much goods,' &c., Luke xii. 19. This is dangerous. The minister had need look to it; for men do soothe themselves up in pleasure, thinking that religion may well stand with the love of the world. The watchman must tell them plainly, 'You cannot serve God and mammon.' If these false conceits, this false divinity that is in us, were once removed, we should easily resist the devil. Our enemies are within us, and therefore what saith Christ? 'The prince of this world cometh, and hath found nothing in me,' John xiv. 30, and therefore he got nothing. 'Be not deceived,' saith St Paul; thereby shewing that their

* Misprinted 'doe.'—G.

offence did arise of a false conceit and an error in judgment. If then the ministers be soldiers under Jesus Christ our general,

Use 1. *Then all by nature are in an opposite kingdom.* We have natural lusts in us against every commandment, and there is no act of faith in us, but we have false conclusions in us to fight against them. We are by nature not only void of all goodness, but we have a nature opposite to all goodness.

Use 2. The second use is for instruction. If we would be brought and redeemed out of this estate, *let us not hold forth against the ministry of the gospel.* Some will have such carnal conceits, that do what we can, they will not see; they are wilfully blind. Such as these are by the ministry of the gospel hastened to hell. Their course is made more swift, their fall more desperate. Let it not be with us so; but let us come with yielding hearts to the word, not resisting the Spirit. God will not always strive with us, but will give us up to our own courses, to live and die under the dominion of the devil, and so will glorify himself in our confusion. For the word is as the man on the white horse which is spoken of in the Revelation, it goes forth conquering, it condemns men already, Rev. xix. 11. It is like Jonathan's bow, it never returns empty from the blood of the slain,* 2 Sam. i. 22. Christ he continues to preach to us here by his Spirit, as he did to those in the time of Noah, 1 Pet. iii. 19. If we will not hear, we shall into prison, as they are now without redemption, for blood shall be upon our own heads.

Use 3. In the third place, if ministers be soldiers for us, *let us help them by our prayers.* 'Curse Meroz,' saith the angel of the Lord. Why? 'Because they came not to help the Lord,' Judges v. 23. If those are cursed with a bitter curse, that came not to help them that fight for the Lord, what curse remaineth to them that fight against them, and deprave them that fight for the Lord?

Use 4. Lastly, Seeing we are here in a working estate, nay, in a warring estate, it should make us *more willing, nay, to desire, to be dissolved, and to be with Christ,* where all assaults and trials shall cease, all tears shall be wiped away. And therefore, if we see afflictions, be not terrified, for God will give thee strength here and hereafter. Thou shalt be recompensed in the resurrection of the just.

But your messenger, and he that ministered to my wants.

The word in the original that is translated 'messenger,' signifieth an apostle,† and it may be taken, either for a messenger sent by them to the apostle Paul, or for a messenger sent by the apostle Paul to them. However, it is an honourable office to be an ambassador to the church of God, or to be a messenger from the church of God; and therefore the Philippians sent him that was most dear to them to the apostle Paul, out of the love they bare to him; and Paul again would not keep him long from them, because he loved them. It is a happy contention, when men contend who shall express most love and affection toward each other. This Epaphroditus brought refreshing to the apostle, being then in durance, from the Philippians. Whence observe,

Doct. 1. That *the child of God is subject to wants here whiles he lives.* Thus it is with them at all times. Thus is it with us. Sometimes we want this thing, sometimes that; but [he] gives them what they most want. Thus was it with Christ. He wants water, and was constrained to beg it

* Also of Saul.—G.

† That is, ἀπόστολος and λειτουργος.—G.

of a poor silly woman, John iv. 7, *seq.* And if it was thus with Christ, we must not look for better. And therefore, let us be comforted against it; for, as it followeth in the next place,

Doct. 2. *The children of God shall be satisfied.* Rather than Elias shall perish for hunger, the ravens shall feed him, 1 Kings xvii. 4.* If rich Dives will not have mercy on such, the brutish dogs shall, Luke xvi. 21. For Paul, God provides one Epaphroditus, or Onesiphorus, 2 Tim. i. 16–18. In Acts xvi. 25, Paul's trials were many; but see, those places which of themselves were places of horror become† so comfortable as in them he sings psalms; and those persons that were his tormentors, become his great friends and comforters in his adversities. So that assuredly, one way or other, God will provide for his children, especially for his ministers. And therefore Christ bids his apostles, that when they went to preach, they should not carry anything with them; for well he knew that those that were converted would not suffer them to lack anything that was necessary. It must encourage us to our work. God, he will give us wages, even for the performance of our ordinary duties of our callings, if we do them in obedience to his laws. And indeed, if we could live by faith as we should, we would not care for anything, for God hath promised liberally, and if we could believe, he would not be less than his word, who doth suffer his children to want some few outward things, but it is for their good. And to such God ever gives patience to suffer, and to expect and wait the time of God's visitation.

VERSE 26.

For he longed after you all.

Epaphroditus, he longed after all the Philippians; yea, there was none but he had a regard of; yea, of the meanest, whom he knew to be as dear in Christ's acceptation as the greatest. For the soul and salvation of the meanest cost him as dear as the salvation of the greatest. Again, the weakest are soonest discontented and most subject thereunto, who therefore ordinarily are soonest brought to complain. It is a ground therefore for the ministers so to behave themselves, that they also have a respect unto all the meanest even as the greatest.

And was full of heaviness.

It grieved Epaphroditus to think that they mourned for his sickness. Grief returns by reflection on the party loved. Observe then the wicked nature of men that make music in the sorrow of others. Surely they have a poisonous heart within them; and it ought to reprove those that regard not to grieve those by whom they were brought into the world. Surely if such had the principles of nature within them, such a slavish condition of serving their own unbridled lusts could never settle on them.

Because that ye had heard that he had been sick. For indeed he was sick, &c.

Observe here how one wave follows another. After Epaphroditus had endured a long and dangerous voyage, he meets with a long and dangerous sickness. It is the nature of us. Let us not dream of any immunity. *God's children are subject to sicknesses while they live.* Daily experience proves it; for they have bodies that have the seeds of sickness in them.

* 'And it shall be, that thou shalt drink of the brook, and I have commanded the ravens to feed thee there.'—G.

† Misprinted 'becomes.'—G.

Their heaven is not here; for they are not clean from corruption, which bringeth death and sickness, by which also God intends good to the body. For if such recover, their bodies are purged from many bad humours; if they do not recover it, God by little and little unties the marriage knot between the soul and the body, and so death comes more easy. And thus also grace is strengthened in the soul; as the outward man is weakened, so is the inward man renewed, 2 Cor. iv. 16. For by sickness we are put in mind to make even our accounts with God, and by it he also makes pleasures of the world to be bitter unto us, that we may the more willingly part with them; even as nurses use to anoint the pap with some bitter thing to make the child refuse the pap. Observe in the second place, that God often suffers his *children to come to extremities, yea, even to death itself, and into desperate estates.* Thus did he suffer Hezekiah, Job, Jonas, David, Daniel, and the 'three children' to run into the jaws of death. Thus suffered he also his disciples to be overwhelmed with water ere he would seem to take notice of it.* Nay, thus suffered he his only Son Christ upon the cross while he said, 'My God, my God, why hast thou forsaken me?' and by this means it comes to pass that when all natural and ordinary means fail them, their trust is not placed on the means, but on some more durable and constant help, upon God's own good will and power. For else our nature is such as soon we should idolise the means, and set them in the place of God, if means should continually recover us. And this offence was Asa † guilty of in his sickness; he trusted not the Lord, but physicians. God is jealous of our affections. And hence lest Paul should be lifted up, he gave him over to some base temptation, which he calls 'the messenger of Satan.' In the second place, God suffers his children to fall into extremities, to the end that we having experience of God's helping hand in them, we might come to rely more confidently on him in all adversities. He suffers us to receive the sentence of death in us, to the end that we should not trust in ourselves, but in God, 2 Cor. i. 9. For God is never nearer than in extremities. His power is seen in man's weakness. In the third place, God suffers us to fall into extremities that he might try what is in us, and that he might exercise the graces in us. And commonly it is seen, those that rely upon means in such extremities make themselves executioners of themselves. Thus did Saul, Ahithophel, and Judas; for while they trust on the means, they failing them, what marvel if they seeing no remedy run into despair, whenas God's children go to their own Father, exercising their faith, hope, prayers, and all Christian graces and duties. And therefore afflictions are called trials, because they try our graces. For if it were not for them, we should not know what faith, patience, hope, or grace were. Fourthly, hence it comes that the communion between God and us might be more sincere; for whenas nothing is between God and us to rely on, then do we come more sensibly and experimentally to taste, see, and feel God more to our comfort; for where ordinary helps fail, God's help begins.

The use of all this is, That we should not be dismayed, though we be in the most forlorn estate; for in extremity God is most near us, and then shall our graces be strengthened, and we shall have experience of God's favour strengthening us. And in the second place, when thou seest any in great afflictions, pronounce not thy sentence rashly on him, for even then he may be nearest God: Ps. xli. 1, 'Blessed,' saith the prophet, 'is he that considereth the poor aright: the Lord will deliver him in the time of

* Cf. Mat. xiv. 25.—G. † Misprinted Ahaz. Cf. 2 Chron. xvi. 12.—G.

trouble.' The papists, indeed, are unmerciful in this kind. See what he is by his diseases and sicknesses, say they of Calvin, who, as Beza writes of him, was much afflicted that way (*a*). But see even in Epaphroditus, of whom Paul said none was minded like to him, yet he in a good cause was afflicted, and came to great extremities. Seeing then we cannot avoid sickness nor death, but we must all come to it, let us consider briefly how to fit ourselves for it beforehand, that it comes not suddenly, and takes us before we are aware thereof. And herein let us consider what we are to do before sickness, and what in sickness.

(1.) *Before sickness labour to make God thy friend, who is Lord of life and death.* Is there any hope that a prisoner which abuses the judge continually till he be on the ladder shall have pardon? How can he imagine that a man that all his lifetime followed his own wilful courses of sin, and persecuted, by scandalising and slandering good men; that continually blasphemed God and abused him in his word; how can this man think to command comfort in sickness? How can he think God will be pleased with him? No. All such repentance in sickness may justly be suspected to be hypocritical, that it is made rather for fear of punishment than loathing of sin; and therefore God often leaves such men to despair, and that justly. See what he saith, Prov. i. 25, 'Because I have called, and ye refused; I have stretched out my hand, and no man regarded; I will laugh at your calamity, and mock when your fear cometh,' and so forth to the end of the chapter. It is just with God, seeing when he called you would not answer, that when you call he should not answer. Be wise therefore to foresee the time to come.

(2.) In the second place, if thou wilt be sick to thy comfort, *disease not thy soul beforehand.* Those that will avoid sickness, they will abstain from such meats and other things as may increase their malady. Let it be thus in our soul sickness; find what thou art sick of, and take heed of hunting after such temptations and occasions as may inflame thy soul. Those that are profane swearers and loose livers they think they shall never hear of their wickedness; they think it will be forgotten and borne withal, whenas, even while they are thus wretched, they distemper both their souls and their own bodies also. Thus do they eat their own bane. Take away the strength and power of sickness. Take heed of sin beforehand. For it is the sin that thou now committest that breeds sickness. And he that tempts thee now to sin, when sickness comes will tempt thee to despair of pardon.

(3.) Thirdly, *Wean thine affections from the earth;* for else when any cross comes, we shall not be able to endure. The saying is true, *qui nimis amat, nimis dolet.* In what proportion a man loves this world too much in the enjoyment of it, in that proportion he grieves too much at his departure from it. It is an easy matter for one to die that hath died in heart and affection before. And to help this, consider the uncertainty and vanity of these things, and how unable they will be to help thee when thou shalt stand most in need of help. Men when they are well, they consider not what these things will do, but they consider what they cannot do. Friends in adversity are true friends. Alas, when thou art sick, what will thy friends or thy riches do! Yea, what can they do for thy recovery!

(4.) In the fourth place, *make up thy accounts daily,* that when sickness and weakness comes we have not our greatest and most laborious work to do. It is an atheistical folly to put off all till sickness, whenas they know not but God may call them by sudden death, or if he warns them by sickness, God may suffer their understanding and senses to be so troubled as they shall neither be able to conceive or judge. Now, what madness is it to put off our hardest works to our weakest estate. There is no day but the best of us gather soil, especially those that have much dealing in the world. We had need to wash ourselves daily, and pray to God that he would cleanse us.

(5.) Fifthly, *While thou art in health, lay a foundation and ground of comfort for sickness;* and still be doing of something that may further thine account, and testify of the reconciliation between God and thee. It is strange to see how many account of death; send for a minister, be absolved, and take the communion, and say, 'Lord, have mercy on me;' and we presently conclude he is assuredly saved. 'Tis true, these are good if well used; but if there be not a foundation laid, these are but miserable comforters. A good death is ever laid in a good life. Absolution to such as these that so lightly esteem of their estate is no other than as a seal to a blank. It is true, we ought to deny absolution to none as will say they repent; but know this, you may be hypocrites, notwithstanding our absolution. We spend all our wits and powers to get unto us a little worldly pelf; and shall we think to go to heaven, and to be carried thither, through pleasures and ease? No. He that made thee without thee will not save thee without thee. This is one reason why we condemn popery; and though we in show hate it, yet are we popish in our conceits. It is the good that in our health we do that comforts us in our sickness; for considering how it hath pleased God not only to put into our minds but into our wills to do this or that good—Such a good man have I raised; such a poor man have I relieved—we think of it as an evidence of God's Spirit in us. Contrarily, when we think how brave our apparel hath been, how gallant our company, what pleasing plays and spectacles we have seen, what can this comfort us? Nay, will it not discomfort us to consider we have spent our means and time unprofitably; we have delighted in worldly delights? How shall I account with that just Judge for my time and means ill spent? Doth not this argue want of grace, want of God's Spirit? Be wise therefore with Joseph against times of famine, of sickness, of death; prepare such cordials as may strengthen thee. Now,

2. In the next place consider we how we are to behave ourselves in sickness.

(1.) First, therefore, know and consider that as Job saith, 'Sickness comes not from the dust,' Job v. 6; but *consider thy ways, especially thy antecedent course of life, which of late thou hast passed over next before thy sickness.* For God corrects not for sin in general so much as for some one sin that rules. If it appears not, pray to God to help thee in this thy search: and when thou hast found out the Jonah, the Achan that thus troubleth thee, 'then judge thyself and justify God,' Josh. vii. 19.

(2.) '*Judge yourselves, that ye be not judged of the Lord,*' 1 Cor. xi. 31; lay thyself open by confession; renew thy repentance, and confess thyself thoroughly, and spare not thyself. It is cruelty to be merciful to thyself in this thing. And justify God; say with the holy prophet, 'Just art thou, O Lord, and righteous are thy judgments,' Ps. cxix. 75; and thus by meeting with God we do allay our sickness. For God uses it no other than as a messenger to call us to meet with him, who else would never look after him; and when the messenger hath his answer, he is gone. When we repent and amend, the sickness departs, unless it be sent for a better end, to call us out of this miserable world, to perfect his promises to us. When therefore God summons thee, do not as the common course is, send first for the bodily physician, and when thou art past natural care,* then for the divine; but contrarily let the divine begin, Ps. xxxii. 3, *seq.* Until David had confessed his sin, 'his bones waxed old with roaring, and his moisture was turned to the drought of summer.' But when he confessed his sins, 'Thou forgavest the iniquity of my sin;' for indeed the sickness of the body begins from the iniquity of the soul. Begin with it; look to heal it, and comfort in thy bodily estate will follow; and it is just with God to suffer those that trust so to the physician to continue in hope of health, till they be past recovery, and then to send them to their own places, as it was said of Judas, without thinking of their soul's good. Thus, when thou hast found out thy disease, and laid it open to God,

(3.) In the next place, *look for evidences of comfort; desire God to witness to thy soul his peace with her;* and upon every warning of sickness, look for thy evidence afresh. This will strengthen thee as it did Job. Whatsoever discomforts he saw, 'yet I know my Redeemer liveth, and that I shall see him,' Job xix. 25. And thou thus going to God, if thou lookest on the earth, thou wilt count all as dross and dung, as Paul did, Philip. iii. 8. All worldly matters will be despised in thine eyes.

(4.) In the fourth place, *labour for love.* Consider how the world is with us. We know not what will become of us. Begin with justice, in giving every man his own, and then with bounty; then forgive. We cannot go to heaven with anger. Thus did Christ, 'Father, forgive them,' Luke xxiii. 34; and Stephen, 'Lord, lay not this sin to their charge,' Acts vii. 60. Be far from revenge. If thou lookest to come where Christ is, do as he did. This is hard to fleshly minds, but it must be done. Thou must first deny thyself before thou canst be saved.

(5.) In the next place, *labour for patience;* but such as must be ruled by reason, and not blockish. To this end consider, first, *whence the sickness is.* It is from *God who is powerful.* [Consider] that we shall get nothing by striving or murmuring; that we cannot resist him so but he will have his will fulfilled upon us; and therefore let us humble ourselves under the mighty hand of God. Then also, consider *it comes from God, who is thy Father,* and therefore loveth thee. What then though the cup be bitter? Shall I not drink of the cup which my father giveth me to drink of? Know also, that all the circumstances of thy sickness are ordered by him, the degree and time are limited by him, he knows what is needful and fitting, he is Lord of life and death, resign thyself therefore to him; and then hath God his end he looks for, viz., that his children should cast themselves on his mercy. In the next place, *remember that thou deservest much worse,* and that he shews thee favour in this gentle correction. Remember what Christ hath done for thee, what he hath suffered, what he hath delivered thee from, and what these things are in comparison of those that thou justly deservest.

Consider also what will be the fruit and end of all these thy troubles and griefs, even the quiet fruits of righteousness; all shall be for our good. Is it for thy good rather to drink of a bitter potion than sickness? what though it be bitter? It is for my health; God is working my good. Though I feel it not now, hereafter I shall in his good time. And thus shall we justify God, as David did, and behold him as in Christ a most loving Father who was an angry judge, and being turned, all are turned. Corrections they are now, which were before punishments, and they are become trials of graces.

* Qu. 'cure'?—Ed.

(6.) In the last place, *let us being sick be ever heavenly-minded*, thinking on nothing but that which may administer to us spiritual comfort. If we have not this, look not to come thither. It is not fit our minds should be on these earthly things, whenas our souls are going or should be going to heaven. It is God's just judgment to suffer men's minds, being ready to depart the world, to be taken up with the world, and as they have lived, so to die. If we would have a pattern of dying well, look on Christ; before his death, when he was troubled, he will have his disciples with him. So when we are vexed with any temptation or trial, use such company as may bring spiritual comfort to thee, and thereby to strengthen thee. As Christ left his 'peace behind him,' John xiv. 27, let us study also how to preserve peace after our departure. As Christ did all the good he could so long as he lived, so should we, that our sickness may be fruitful of comfort. As Christ studied how to do all his work, thus should we endeavour to do what we have to do, that with a clear conscience we may say as Christ did, 'Father, I have done the work thou gavest me to do,' John xvii. 4. Christ had care of his disciples and friends before he died: of his mother, 'Woman, behold this son,' saith he, &c., John xix. 26. 'I go away, but I will send you the Comforter,' John xv. 26. We also ought to be careful for the well-leaving of them whom God hath committed to our care to provide for. Christ was not vindictive; 'Father, forgive them,' saith he, Luke xxiii. 34. So we, specially when we die in peace, forgive all the world, yea, our enemies, for so also did Stephen. Lastly, Christ commends his soul to God: 'Father, into thy hands I commend my spirit,' saith he, Luke xxiii. 46; dying, he dies in faith and obedience. Thus also ought we to imitate him; die in faith, be sure of God that he is thy Father, and obediently submit thy soul into his hands when thou diest. Thus when we die we shall die with comfort, and we shall count it exceeding joy when we fall into any trouble or adversity whatsoever.

But the Lord.

Doct. Observe this comfortable exception: *God brings his children low, but he raises them up again*, if it be for their good: Ps. cxviii. 17, 'I will not die, but live, and declare the works of the Lord.' Nay, then especially, when they are past all worldly means of recovery; and as it is in sickness, thus also is it in other troubles; and this God doth.

Reason 1. First, *To glorify his power the more.*

2. Secondly, *That his enemies might not triumph still in overcoming us.*

3. Thirdly, That we being thus delivered, *might consecrate our lives and breath to him anew*, as having received them from him, even by a new gift.

Use 1. The use hereof is, If God helps us above and against means, *we ought to hope above, yea, against hope*, believe in the greatest extremities; 'though he kill us, yet trust in him.' God is not tied to Galen's rules.* He can work above physical means, as he shewed in the cure of Hezekiah. Especially in soul troubles let not our faith fail us, for he hath absolutely promised his helping hand in them.

Had mercy on him.

Observe the language of the Holy Ghost, shewing the recovery of Epaphroditus, by the ground and cause of it, 'God had mercy on him.'

Doct. Observe, therefore, *God's mercy is the spring of all God's dealing with us.* Both his benefits and his corrections of us all comes from his

* That is, to the use of ordinary means; *e. g.* Galen, a physician.—G.

mercy; all his ways are mercy and truth. We are sick, well; we live, we die; all comes from his mercy. Seeing, therefore, all comes from his mercy, yea, our greatest extremities, because he might have dealt worse with us,

Use 1. *Let us look that we wilfully neglect not or cast away mercy*, in what estate soever we are.

Doct. In the next place observe, *God's mercy extends to this temporal life.* We think his mercy is only for things that belong to life everlasting. No. The same love and mercy that gives us heaven, it is the same that gives us our daily bread; and therefore the same faith we must have to God for the things of this life that we have on him for the other life in heaven. And thus did the saints, as we may see in Heb. xi. 4, *seq.*

Use 2. This should direct us *not to rest in deliverance, but to look to the ground of it, the mercy of God*, and endeavour to taste the love and mercy of God in his gifts, for all his gifts are less than his mercy. This will cause us to have more comfort in our daily bread than the wicked have in all their abundance.

Use 3. Thirdly, We should learn from hence, *in giving, to give thy soul and affection;* let thy brother have thy heart with thy gifts, and thus shalt thou imitate thy heavenly Father.

Use 4. Lastly, If the very recovery from sickness comes from God's free love and mercy, *what can we look for by merit?* If health for Epaphroditus his body came from the free mercy of God, how can we expect for to merit the salvation of our souls. No. It must be from God's free grace and mercy in Jesus Christ.

And not on him only, but on me also.

As if he had said, It may be for him it had been good to have been taken away, and to have remained with Christ, but God had mercy on me in sparing him.

Obj. But it may be objected, *How can it be the mercy of God that spared him, whenas God had rather shewed his mercy in taking him away from the evil to come*, and in placing him with himself in glory? and Paul, he desired 'to be dissolved and to be with Christ,' and said it was far better for him so to be.

Ans. I answer, life, and especially health, is God's mercy, for without it life is no life. But why, and how?

1. Because *by it we recover our spiritual comfort and assurance of heaven*, Ps. xxxix. 13. To this end David prayed, 'Spare me a little, that I may recover my strength.'

2. Secondly, *In regard of others' health*, life is a blessing. Thus, Hezekiah desired it, that he might get assurance of his salvation, and praise the Lord, Isa. xxxviii. 22.

3. Thirdly, Life is to be desired as a blessing from God, *in regard of the church, that we might do good;* for after death we are receivers only, and not doers. All the good we convey to others, we must do it while we live here. Therefore it is not unlawful to desire to live to see thy children brought up in the fear of God, and yet let that be with a resignation to God's will and purpose. We see Christ, that had contrary desires, who came to perform his Father's will and to die willingly, yet he said, 'Let this cup pass from me,' Mat. xxvi. 39; for the soul is to be carried to desire as the objects are offered. If thou beest well, rejoice in it, and count it as God's blessing. If thou beest sick, patiently submit thyself to God's will, and count it as

his merciful dealing with thee. Indeed, as we look on death being an enemy to our nature, and a destroyer thereof, we desire it not. Yet, considering it as God's decree and will, say still, 'Thy will be done, O Lord, and not mine.' Paul, he considered for himself it was better to die, but looking to the Philippians, 'nevertheless, to abide in the flesh is better for you,' Phil. i. 24. Learn from hence the sweet estate of God's children; whether he lives or dies, all is mercy; and this they have by being assured they have their part in the covenant of grace. Labour therefore to find an interest therein for thyself. Observe, in the next place, *God does good to us by others, as here he conveys good to Paul by Epaphroditus his life.* Let us therefore praise him for parents, friends, benefactors; for by them God hath mercy on us. God uses man for the good of man, that he might knit the communion of saints together more straightly.* No doubt but the apostle Paul had begged Epaphroditus his life from God, and he here acknowledges it as a great mercy of God. Thus ought we to acknowledge God's mercy on us, by taking mercy on others for our sakes.

VERSE 27.

Lest I should have sorrow on sorrow.

Our blessed apostle had sorrowed much for the sickness of Epaphroditus; if he had died, he had had wave on wave. Observe, *God's children have not sorrow on sorrow.* We have matter of sorrow while we are here, as our corruptions, and the troubles of the church. These minister unto us matter of grief while we are here in this vale of tears. Let us not therefore be delicate nor dainty. We must sow in tears here, if we would reap hereafter in joy. We must shed tears, if we would hereafter have them wiped away. Yet is the sorrow of a Christian mingled ever with joy to support them. The Lord he weighs and measures the distresses of his children. The rod of the wicked shall not rest upon the godly man's back, Ps. cxxv. 3. And this mingled estate must be till we come into heaven, where all tears shall be wiped away.

Obj. But it will be objected, *David had sorrow upon sorrow: one depth calls another, saith he,* Ps. xlii. 7.

Ans. I answer, *It is true there may be divers occasions of grief, but God doth so temper them as he giveth joy upon joy, grace upon grace, and comfort upon comfort;* faith upon faith, patience upon patience; and it is much better to have access of comfort in extremities than to want extremities and occasions of sorrow, by reason of the good we receive by such trials. And there is no distress but we may gather ground of comfort to ourselves in them. Art thou sick? Bless God that he hath left thee the use of reason and thy wits. Hast thou lost friends, and hath not God taken all away? He leaves thee some, nay, he leaves his Spirit to accompany thee. Paul was in prison, it is true, but did he want comfort? No. God will raise us up with one hand as he casts us down with the other; it is his 'mercy we are not consumed,' Lam. iii. 22. But the wicked they shall have sorrow on sorrow. He lets them ruffle a while here, but at length their judgments come suddenly and unavoidably. He hath no mercy for them if he once begins. Thus did he add judgment to judgment on Pharaoh till he was consumed; and therefore upon little griefs they run into desperate courses, as Cain, Ahithophel. God suffers the wicked to add sin to sin, and so doth he add sorrow to sorrow. Lay up this for our comfort against

* Qu. 'straitly'?—Ed.

the ill time. God will not suffer us to be tempted above measure. He will either abate our trouble or enlarge our grace, so as it shall not overwhelm us. Note this example of God as one for us to imitate and to follow. When we see any one afflicted, let us not vex them the more by adding sorrow to sorrow. David he complains of a kind of men that were of the nature of the devil, going over where the wall is lowest, like ill humours that resort all to ill affected places. No. God's children have pitiful and compassionate hearts. Examine therefore thy spirit, whether thou canst weep with them that weep; for as the Spirit of God helps us in misery, so do those that are led by his Spirit. It is the custom, and hath been, of God's children, to comfort those in misery. Thus did Job's friends, although they erred in the performance thereof.

VERSE 28.

I sent him therefore more carefully.

In this verse St Paul sets forth the end of sending Epaphroditus, viz., that they might have the more joy, and he the less sorrow. But it will be said, Paul had use of Epaphroditus himself; he was in prison; he had none to comfort him. But it is no wonder for him, that could set light by his own soul for God's people, to part with a friend for the comfort of his people; and this ought we also to respect, namely, the comforts of God's people above all. Thus did this apostle. He was content to forbear the joys of heaven for the good of the Philippians, in the first chapter. The children of God are of excellent spirits. They can overcome and deny themselves.

That when you see him again you may rejoice.
The Philippians hereby had a double cause of joy. First, sight of their pastor whom they loved. Seeing friends is more comfortable than all ways of hearing from them; and the joys of heaven are commended to us by the beatifical vision we hear of these joys here. But when we see them, then is our joy accomplished. The second cause of joy was in this, that now they should see Epaphroditus, as given them anew and sent from God; whose love, mercy, goodness, and power is more clearly seen in delivering men from danger than in preserving of men from falling into danger. It is more honour to God, and more comfort to men. For the Philippians received him as a token of God's love to them, and as an effect of their prayers. Let us take notice of the enlargement of God's love to us in delivering and enlarging any of our friends to us free from afflictions.

And I may be the less sorrowful.
The apostle was, and we must be sorrowful in this world; but sometimes more, sometimes less. For a Christian's estate is ever full of ebbs and floods. But of this I spake formerly.

VERSE 29.

Receive him therefore in the Lord with all gladness.

Our apostle first entreats them generally 'to receive him;' then he shews the manner, 'in the Lord with gladness;' thence he grounds a general, 'make much of such.' But it may be urged—the apostle might have spared this exhortation, for no doubt but the Philippians being glad to see him would receive him. It is true; but this is not all: they must receive him *in the Lord,*' as a man of God; as a man sent you from God; as a messenger of Christ; and receive him with a holy affection.

Doct. A Christian must do all things in the Lord: marry in the Lord; love in the Lord; salute in the Lord. All matters, both of necessity and courtesy, must be in the Lord. A Christian must 'live in the Lord,' and he must 'die in the Lord.'

Reason. The reason is, for that a Christian in all looks to God. Whatsoever befalls him he receives, whatsoever he does, he does in the Lord, looking only to him, and depending on him. Carnal men contrarily do all things carnally: marries, loves, salutes carnally; he lives carnally, dies carnally. But the Christian's life is ever to die and behold Christ in all things; in all estates; in all his thoughts, words, and deeds; in life, in death. Let this acquaint us with the manner of a Christian's life and estate, and with the language of the Holy Ghost.

And hold such in reputation.

Others read it, 'make much of such' (*b*). The sense is the same with the former. 'Esteem of such as they are;' esteem of such ministers that are faithful as he is; of such Christians as he is; such excellent Christians as he. So as the words have a double reference, as to both his general and particular calling. For his particular calling of the ministry, see how he is formerly commended; that he was painful* and careful, and neglected his own life. Ministers, if they be such, they must be had in repute and esteem. If they be not of the best sort, surely they are of the worst. Angels and good men, none better than the good; none worse than them if they turn. But especially ministers, if they be not good, they are unsavoury as salt;† neither good for the ground, nor yet for the dunghill.

Reason. The reason of this is, for by such as these are God conveys greatest good to men. He builds by them, he plants by them. They are watchmen, husbandmen, they are God's labourers; nay, they are his angels, discovering to the church the secrets of God's counsel. They are as Job saith, but as 'one among a thousand.' Such surely as these are worthy of all respects.

Obj. But it will be objected, *they are ever opposite to us, they cross men.*

Ans. Even then when they are most opposite they are to be esteemed the more, for they are 'the light of the world.' Their office is to discover the works of darkness. They are husbandmen to break up the fallow grounds of our hearts; and it is our part to embrace them in doing their duties. For it is a note of a wicked man to count such as these troublers. It was Ahab's speech to Elijah, 1 Kings xviii. 17. God's children loves them and reverences them when they are most sharp; for they know that they themselves do want such reproofs to check their corruptions; they wish their corruptions might be ripped up thoroughly. This is impossible that carnal men should allow of this. They have beloved sins. When they are met with they are touched to the quick, no marvel therefore if they repine. A true Christian will acknowledge and esteem the meanest part of them blessed and beautiful. The carnal man may esteem ministers indeed, but such as cry 'Peace, peace, when there is no peace,' Jer. vi. 14; and surely such a prophet is a fit prophet for such a people. But let the true Christian love and reverence those that are the messengers of peace, and esteem of them by so much the more, by how much their degree in

* That is, 'painstaking.'—G.

† Qu. 'they are as unsavoury salt'? Cf. Mat. v. 13.—G.

grace is the greater; for there will be an affection suitable to the proportion of grace they have.

And to this end observe with me some motives to incite us to this duty; and first, 1. *It is the character of the child of God*, and a sign we are translated from death to life, if we love and reverence the brethren. If we be brethren as we profess ourselves, we are led with the same spirit; and therefore we ought to love those most especial that are means of begetting the grace of the Spirit in us. It is a part of grace to desire grace. Now there is no desire of grace but there must be a love of it; and therefore if we will prove ourselves to be marked with the mark of God in our foreheads, and that we are his children, let us get this character for a witness to us.

2. The second motive in regard of God,—the former was in regard of ourselves,—*those that God esteems most we ought to make most account of.* God spared not his own Son for their sake. The saints are precious in the eyes of the Lord. And in the second place, Christ he esteems of them above his own blood; he gave himself for them freely. Thirdly, the angels they esteem of them. Christ says, Offend them not, for the angels in heaven behold the face of God continually, Mat. xviii. 10. Fourthly, the ministers esteem them. 'I suffer all for the elect's sake,' says Paul. The Spirit of God esteems them; they are his temples to dwell in, 2 Tim. ii. 10.

3. In regard of themselves they are to be esteemed, *they are lively.* They have the 'new creature' in them; they have God's Spirit ever in them. All created excellency is as 'the flower of grass.' It withers suddenly. But they have that which continues for ever, grace and the Spirit of God. They have the image of God seated in them. They have the word and the promises made sure to them. They are free-born; free from hell, death, wrath. They are of disposition free; they can want and they can abound. They are rich in the best riches, strong in the greatest strength. They overcome the devil, the world; they overcome and conquer death, who is the king of fears.

4. In the next place, in regard *of the good we reap by them* they are to be esteemed. God blesses us by them. They are the pillars of this tottering world. In regard of a few of God's elect not yet brought in, this world continues yet; but if the number be accomplished once, God will no longer withhold his coming. Lot's presence in Sodom stayed God's wrath; he could do nothing till he was gone. So Noah in the old world, Joseph in Egypt, Moses among the Israelites, they stopped the passage of God's wrath; and therefore Job, xxii. 30, saith, 'He shall deliver the island of the innocent.' They are 'the chariots and horsemen of Israel;' their prayers are our protectors. And thus mayest thou try thyself and thy estate; for dost thou despise those that are good, thou art ranked amongst vile persons. Look 2 Tim. iii. 3, and such as are signs of the last times, wherein corruption shall abound. Many things are much set by, but where are those that have their delight set on the excellent of the earth? A wicked man, I deny not, may esteem some one that is good, but it shall not be for that they are good, but it may be for some by-respects of profit or pleasure that they shall reap thereby. They will commend stars that be within their own horizon; praise martyrs being dead, whom, if alive, likely it is they would be the first persecutors of them; for thirty pieces of silver, a little gain, sell even Christ himself, and make shipwreck of their faith. Yet the time will shortly come when these despised shall be had in greatest honour,

and those that scorn them now would be glad to keep them company, and ever be with them.

Quest. But it will be asked, Where are these men you speak of? how is it they are not respected?

Ans. I answer, They are not known, 'the world knows them not;'—*First*, Because it knows not their Father; for if it esteemed him, it would esteem also of them; and therefore, *Secondly*, they are 'strangers and pilgrims,' although excellent in themselves. *Thirdly*, 'Their life is hid with Christ,' Col. iii. 3. They are eclipsed and disgraced. Disgraces, scandals, miseries, and their own infirmities, these make the children of God to be unknown; yet those that know them will even in their infirmities see many things worth observation and practice. Contrarily in wicked men what is to be respected? Shall we think of them the better for their degree, state, comeliness, riches, or the like? Surely these end in death, whenas all respects are taken away; but goodness is more accomplished in death, it shall never be at an end; and therefore to be the rather respected and esteemed, and men also as they are good. Wicked men may be also esteemed, but not otherwise than as they are marked with the image of God, as they are in place of magistracy and government; and so *they* are not esteemed, but *their images* they carry about with them of superiority. And therefore among these of the like kind those are to be most esteemed that are most good, and this is, as I said before, a note of a good man; for what saith David, Ps. xv. 4? 'He shall enter into the tabernacle of God, in whose eyes a vile person is contemned; but he honoureth them that fear the Lord.' To this end begin with thyself. How dost thou value thyself? Dost thou do it carnally? How then canst thou esteem aright of others? Be therefore of Theodosius his mind, 'value thyself according to thy measure in grace and assurance of salvation' (*c*). What though the world think basely of thee! So did it of those saints, Heb. xi. 38. They thought them unworthy to live. But remember God is not ashamed to be called our God and Father. Heaven is ours, Christ, grace, and glory are all ours. Thus by esteeming thyself aright thou shalt begin to reverence that in others which thou so much accountest of in thyself; and we all together shall find what God esteems most of, and of whom, when we shall be together crowned with joys unspeakable, which are hidden from the eyes of the world. It appears not to them what we shall be, the glory being such and so great as they, judging carnally, cannot conceive thereof.

VERSE 30.

Because for the work of Christ he was nigh to death.

This work of Christ especially aims at works of mercy to Paul while he was in prison, and for these he is said to be nigh to death. By his long and tedious journey he took a sickness, and thereby was nigh to death. And these are called 'the works of Christ;' partly because all good works are from Christ—for he commands them, he allows them, he did them—and partly also because in the doing of them our aim is at Christ's honour. *So then the excellency of good works consists not in doing those which are good in their own nature, but in well doing of them.* All our particular actions must be done with having an eye on and a respect to Christ. What if therefore thou doest any good thing with an eye on credit or a good name, nay, if of mere pity, without respect of Christ's command, example, and obedience thereunto; all that thou doest in this manner cannot merit the name of a good work, or a work of Christ. For Christ saith, that which you do to any of his little ones you do to him. And do you think that he will take it done to him, when he seeth in thy heart that thou regardest by-respects, and never intendest him in the thing thou doest? No. You did it for commendation, to get popular applause, or for your own profit, or the like. Let it not be with us in this manner. Let us do all things commanded in the second table, as in obedience of the first, to glorify God. Let us do good works thoroughly, though they cost us labour, cost, and danger; also pray zealously, give cheerfully. 'Cursed is he that doth the work of the Lord negligently,' Jer. xlviii. 10. Give freely therefore to every one in whom Christ comes a-begging to thee. 'This is pure religion before God and undefiled, to visit the fatherless and widows,' James i. 27; but see that you keep yourselves 'unspotted of the world.' And these things done as they ought to be, will comfort us on our deathbed, and be an assurance to our consciences of our faith, and will strengthen us when all other works, done for any self-respect, shall be so far from comforting us, as they shall weaken and discomfort us, and bear witness to our guilty consciences of our hypocrisy. But to proceed. It may seem St Paul was ill advised of his work of Epaphroditus, that he called it a work of Christ, when it had like to have cost him his life. Yet ought it not to seem strange, for by this very pattern we learn *not to avoid or fly from the doing of any work of Christ; no, though by doing of it we incur danger of our lives.* For the best good must take the chief and first place with us; and by how much the soul is more excellent than the body, by so much is the good of the soul to be preferred before the good of the body. He that hates not father, mother, yea, his own life, in respect of God's glory, cannot be the disciple of Christ. God would have us exercise our judgments in these things beforehand, that we may go about all such things with a holy and zealous resolution. Hence we may gather grounds to answer divers doubts.

1*st Quest.* As, first, *whether in time of persecution we ought to lose our lives or deny the truth?*

Ans. To this I answer, out of the example of Epaphroditus, affirmatively, that we ought rather to lose our lives than deny the truth; for God's truth is better than our lives. It was commendable in Priscilla and Aquila that they laid down their necks for Paul's life, Rom. xvi. 3, 4; much more is the truth of God's word to be esteemed above man's life. And they are counted wise that have that esteem; as the martyrs, whose estate is accounted a blessed estate.

2*d Quest.* Furthermore, it will be asked, *Whether a minister ought to leave his congregation in the time of pestilence, or not?*

Ans. I answer, upon the same ground, he ought not; for he is not, in regard of the work of God, to esteem his own life. But so as he is not bound to a particular visitation of every one whom it hath pleased God to visit with sickness, neither ought the sick party to require this at the hands of the pastor; but rather to reserve him to the general good of all of them, and the rather to spare him. Thus did Beza. And in the law the leprous person was to go about and to cry 'Unclean, unclean,' to the end that others might not unawares be polluted by him. And therefore every one ought to be a good husband for himself, to lay up with himself grounds of comfort against such a time as it may please God to afflict him in any such manner. Another question may hence be answered.

3*d Quest. Whether a man may equivocate to save his own life?*

Ans. I answer: If a man be lawfully called to answer for himself, he must know that he ought to tell the truth, and not to be ashamed thereof; for why do men live but to live honestly, and to keep a good conscience? And it is more necessary that truth should flourish and be cleared than that thou shouldst live. Those that now are ashamed to confess the truth, the God of truth will be ashamed of them hereafter. And therefore a fourth question may arise.

4th Quest. Whether a man may break prison to save himself?

Ans. I answer: Thou oughtest not to do anything that may endanger another man to save thine own life; and therefore mayest not, by breaking of prison, endanger the jailor's life to save thyself. And the reasons are, *for that it shames the truth and equity of thy cause;* and therefore when the prison doors were open Paul would not fly, Acts xvi. 28, *seq.* Peter did it indeed, he came out of prison; but it was an extraordinary and miraculous deliverance by the command of the angel, Acts xii. 11. Secondly, *it is a contempt of magistracy and law;* for every man is to be governed by and to submit himself to the law.

5th Quest. Again, some have doubted *whether a minister, being called to a place of unwholesome air, whether he may leave it.*

Ans. I answer: Let them consider before they go whether they shall be able to endure or not; but if they be once called, and are there, let them look to the salvation of God's people, and provide for themselves as they may. We see Epaphroditus neglects his own life for the service of God.

6th Quest. A sixth question or doubt may hence be resolved, *Whether, in case of persecution, a minister may fly.*

Ans. I answer: We may fly for our own safeties; and a minister may, if there be those left that being good shepherds will stand for the flock, that it be not scattered. Yet if God gives thee a spirit of courage to hold out, consult thou with God by earnest prayer for the direction of his Holy Spirit, and he will assuredly direct thee; for if out of thine own confidence thou shouldst stand out, and afterward give back, it would weaken and discourage others, who else it may be would stand out. Yet if thou beest once taken, whether thou art a minister or not, thou art under the law, thou must obey.

7th Quest. And in the seventh place, *we may and ought to be ready to lay down our lives for the commonwealth,* for common good is to be preferred before private good. The hand doth endanger itself for the good of the head, and therefore a private man may venture himself to save a public person; and from hence is grounded the lawfulness of a Christian war.

Quest. But it will be asked, How shall we come to this resolution, to lay down our lives for the truth?

Ans. I answer: First, *thou must labour to have thy judgment enlightened,* discern of the order of good things; and this only a Christian can get to account of his life but slightly in comparison, knowing that it is 'but a vapour that soon vanisheth,' James iv. 14, and that the peace of conscience will never leave a man till it hath brought him to eternity. He knows also the terrors of conscience are above all terrors, and that it will never leave him. He knows the world cannot be worth a soul, that nothing can redeem it being once lost; and these things being truly learned, we shall be ready to deny father, mother, yea, our very life, if they once oppose Christ; and thus shall we beforehand get a resolution by daily considering these things, and a mind truly prepared for all trials. And to that end put cases with thyself. Now, what thou wouldst do or suffer rather than be drawn to offend God, if the time of trial were now to come. If thy heart doth tell thee that thou canst forego all, and countest them as nought in respect of Christ, surely God he accepts of this thy resolution. If thou canst not find this in thee, know for a certainty thy faith is but weak. And therefore consider with thyself, that if thou come to this, to lose all for Christ, thou shalt be no loser. The peace of conscience is above all good that can be desired; and [consider] that thy life is not thine own, for both it, our estate, friends, are all of God's gift to us, who may take them when he will. But if they be lost for God's service, thou shalt be no loser. It cannot stand with God's justice to suffer it. Let this bring shame upon many that will do nothing for the church, lose no credit amongst the wicked men, part with no jot of their goods, take no pains nor labour. We see it that martyrs they will spend their blood. Esther counted not her life dear unto her: 'If I perish, I perish,' iv. 16. And yet these are loath to venture displeasure of some inferior, mean person. How can such ever think to get assurance of salvation? In this case those that thus love their lives do hate them, and that which they fear shall fall suddenly on them; as it was with those that, starting aside for fear, and denying their profession, thinking to save themselves from the fire, they fell into a worse fire, the hell of a guilty conscience, which cannot be quenched, nor they made insensible thereof.

NOTES.

(*a*) P. 42.—'See what he is by his diseases and sicknesses, say they of Calvin, who, as Beza writes of him, was much afflicted that way.' Beza speaks very touchingly of the last illness of the great Reformer, who, as another has observed, seemed to forget in his over-studiousness that he had a body as well as a soul to care for.

(*b*) P. 49.—'"And hold such in reputation." Others read it, "make much of such."' The original is *καὶ τοὺς τοιούτους ἐντίμους ἔχετε* = 'and such, *e.g.*, as Epaphroditus, hold in honour.'

(*c*) P. 51.—'Be therefore of Theodosius his mind, value thyself according to thy measure in grace and assurance of salvation.' Many similar sayings are put into the mouth of this famous Emperor by the Puritans; but it seems impossible to trace their authorities. Consult Long's exhaustive Memoir, *sub voce*, in Dr Smith's Dictionary of Greek and Roman Biography and Mythology. G.

EXPOSITION OF PHILIPPIANS CHAPTER III.

EXPOSITION OF PHILIPPIANS CHAPTER III.

NOTE.

For title-page, &c., see Note prefixed to 'The Christian Work,' *ante*, page 2. This concludes Sibbes's Expositions *proper*. G.

AN EXPOSITION

OF

THE THIRD CHAPTER OF THE EPISTLE OF ST PAUL TO THE PHILIPPIANS.

Finally, my brethren, rejoice in the Lord.—PHILIP. III. 1.

THIS chapter contains a general exhortation to several duties. In this verse you have the manner of doing them—all must be done in rejoicing. From thence he proceeds to back other particular exhortations, with reasons and examples of himself, which we will speak of particularly when we come at them. Now in this verse I will speak first of the compellation, 'brethren;' then of the exhortation, 'rejoice;' and lastly, of the limitation, 'in the Lord.'

1. The appellation, 'brethren.' By this loving compellation he labours to enter into their hearts and affections; well knowing that exhortations are of the more force, being directed to those that are persuaded of the good affection of the speaker. If exhortation comes from the pride of a man, the pride of a man in the hearers will beat it back, and give entertainment thereunto.

But why are Christians brethren?

First, They have the same beginning of life from the same Father: as also they have the same common brother, that is, Christ. They have the same womb, the church; the same food, the word of God. They have the same promises; they are all heirs, all born to an inheritance.

Furthermore, the word *brother* is a word of equality and of dignity: of *equality*—though in personal callings one is superior to other, yet this takes not away the common brotherhood. This should fill up the valleys of men's hearts dejected here, in regard of their mean estates; as also pull down the mountains of the proud hearts of men, lifted up through these outward things. Kings must not lift up themselves in disdain of others, because all these personal respects end in death; we carry them not to heaven. And in those respects that we agree in here, as in grace and goodness, we shall continue united for ever. And yet must we honour such as are in eminency, and acknowledge them as men worthy of all respect, and give them dignity according to their places.

But further, this is a name of *dignity*. It argues that we are not basely born, that we are sons of God and heirs of heaven. Christ after his resurrection, the first term he gives his disciples, 'Tell my brethren,' saith he, 'I go to my Father and their Father.'

This word is also a word of *love;* and therewith the apostle insinuates the affections of the Philippians. Examine therefore thy affections towards the sons of God. If we love and respect them as our own brethren, good is our estate; if we hate them, our estate cannot be good.

And in the second place, Let not this word be appropriated to some, and not to others, which are notwithstanding of the same number. For one brother cannot make another no brother; for it is one and the same Father that makes brethren. So long therefore as thou seest anything of Christ in any, break not off thy affection, and disdain not the name of brother to such; for where the Spirit is, it works in us a resemblance of God; and where it stamps his image, it makes them brethren.

2. Exhortation, 'rejoice.' It is not only an affection, but a duty that we are enjoined. Wherein first observe,

(1.) *It is a Christian's duty to rejoice.* It is commanded here. Ministers are enjoined to speak comfort to such, Isa. xl. 1, 'Comfort ye, comfort ye, my people;' and Christ came to 'bind up the broken in heart,' Isa. lxi. 1, and the ministers sent to shew men their unrighteousness, Job xxxiii. 23. The spirit that is in such is the spirit of joy; and therefore joy is reckoned as a fruit of the spirit, Gal. v. 22.

And why should not Christians rejoice? They are free from the spiritual Egypt, from greatest miseries. Nay, why should not we sing as the Israelites did after their deliverance? Our enemies and deliverance is far greater than theirs. And we have the greatest prerogatives. We have here an assured hope of eternal perfect happiness hereafter; we have 'peace with God,' Rom. v. 1. We have free access in all our wants to the throne of grace; and we have a God ready to hear all our prayers, and to help us. We have many gifts already received. Christ is already given us. We are in a state of regeneration. And for the time to come, we have promises from God, the God of truth, that nothing shall separate us from Christ. Surely these are great causes of joy in us; and having such things as these, we dishonour them, the giver of them, and ourselves and our profession, if we rejoice not in them.

(2.) In the second place observe, that *it belongs only to Christians to rejoice.* Others have neither cause of joy, nor commandment to rejoice. The ministers and prophets are bidden to bid such howl and lament, to shew them their miserable estate.* And indeed what ground can a condemned person have of joy? For the wicked, till they have remission of sins, they are in a damned estate; and though they will snatch this to themselves and say that they are sure to be saved, yet is salvation not their portion. They joy indeed, but it is in sin; in seeing or doing evil to others. Or if sometimes they joy in the gospel (for a wicked man may do so), it is but a forced joy, and much like hot waters to a cold fit of an ague. It brings heat and expulses cold for the present, but it burns them after. So this joy seems to comfort them now, but when trial comes it fails him, and makes him more disconsolate to see himself thus beguiled. Fitter it were for such to be first humbled and brought to the sight of their estate, than to administer comfort to them. To speak peace where none belongs is to undo men. It is the broken that must be healed, and the weary that must come to Christ.

* Cf. Jer. xxv. 34.—G.

(3.) *Limitation.* In the third place, observe the *limitation* of this joy: it must be 'in the Lord;' that is, in Christ, who in the New Testament is often called Lord. And he is our Lord: first, by *gift;* God hath given us all to Christ. Secondly, by *conquest;* he hath gotten victory of Satan. And thirdly, by *marriage;* and therefore we may well call him Lord, and rejoice in him, because he is our Lord; for by him we come to conquer all our enemies; by him we have peace, Rom. v. 1. He makes us kings and priests, and brings us to heaven.

Now, for the practice of this duty of rejoicing in the Lord, that we may be encouraged, let us consider how it is a means not only of adherence to God, but also of obedience to his laws.

[1.] *Adherence to God.* Joy, if it be found,* knits us firm to God, so as we rest contented in him as our only and sufficient joy, seeking for no other joy in any other thing. To us Christ is made 'all in all' that we should solace ourselves in his fulness, which if we truly do, we will count all other things as despised, assuring ourselves they cannot minister or add any jot of sound comfort at all; and therefore will not endure any thought of mixture of other things with Christ, thereby to make him more sufficient and complete for our joys to rest on.

[2.] *Obedience to his laws:* for joy stirs up cheerfulnsss to every duty, and makes all duties acceptable to God and man. For the want hereof many are dead and dull in good duties; and where a large portion of this joy is, it will remove all lets and delays to duty. It doth not only enable us to, but in, duty. Cain no doubt came cheerfully to a good duty, to sacrifice; but for want of this cheerful and joyful spirit, what was his behaviour in the performance thereof? 'His countenance was cast down,' Gen. iv. 6. This God espies suddenly, and so he doth in all our dull performances. For he looks things should be done cheerfully, and reason too, for he hath left us a treasure of excellent promises to encourage us. We see it in men. They love when a thing is done cheerfully; they know it betokens love in the party that doth it: and can we then think it strange that God requires it? Again, if we can fashion ourselves to this duty, God hath promised to increase our joy more abundantly. And he performed it to Hezekiah, 2 Chron. xxix. 36. He will give delight as a reward to him that delighteth in his work. And therefore we ought to labour to bring ourselves to this duty; to the obtaining of which observe these directions.

Means to get joy. First, Consider that joy *comes from faith.* For it is the sense of our reconciliation with Christ that makes us rejoice, Rom. v. 2, and 1 Pet. i. 6. Now, therefore, whatsoever strengthens faith, strengthens also our joy; and contrarily what weakens the one, must of necessity weaken the other.

Furthermore, joy *comes from peace.* Whatsoever, therefore, disturbs our peace, must needs disturb our joy. Therefore Satan, to despoil us of our joy, he spoils our faith through our sins; and by them he weakens our hope and our comfort. What is to be done then? Surely repair to the fountain of health, the well of joy, the word of God, Isa. xii. 3. And from thence must we draw all our comfort. Use, therefore, the ordinances of God, but use them in the Lord, in obedience to his commandment, and expect the issue with patience. Many there are that use the means, but take no joy at all in them. Why? They do it not as in obedience to God's command, but they rest in the deed done, and they think God is

* Qu. 'sound'?—Ed.

bound to give them joy. God justly denies such that which they presume of.

In the *second* place: *Pray that your joy may be full.* See this in most of David's psalms. At the first he complains for the want of God's presence, of God's wrath and anger, but comes off with a large portion of comfort. 'Depart from me, ye wicked, for the Lord hath heard my prayer,' Ps. vi. 8. In the use of all means, therefore, join prayer: pray for faith, for hope, and such graces as may bring joy. Though at first thou findest thyself to be cold, to have little or no comfort at all, yet give not over; thou shalt at length find plenty thereof. Remember the woman of Canaan: at the first despised and called dog, but what did her constancy gain? A gracious answer, 'O woman, great is thy faith: be it to thee as thou desirest,' Mat. xv. 28.

In the *third* place: *Remember former times,* as David did, Ps. lxxvii. 6. He was so oppressed, his 'sore ran in the night, and ceased not,' as he saith. But then, 'I remembered the days of old,' &c. Consider thou also in thy deepest affliction, times were once when thou hadst the clear and comfortable light of God's Spirit present with thee. He will not leave thee, his nature is unchangeable, &c.

In the *fourth* place: *Have society with the saints,* and keep company with those that are good. And as the two disciples' hearts did burn when they talked with Christ, so verily thou shalt find this heat of comfort by little and little to increase. For God blesses the communion of saints, and such as are discerning Christians can tell us more, and opportunely bring things to mind which thou thyself rememberest not, and can inform our judgments when they are blinded with grief and melancholy. Use, therefore, the company of the good, when thou findest doubts arise, and make thy griefs known to some wise and judicious Christian. For the devil is too strong for any one alone. He will prevail against thee. Thou wilt be too weak to wrestle with him hand to hand. It is no wonder, therefore, that melancholy persons are so destitute of comfort.

Quest. It will be asked, May we not rejoice in friends' society, deliverance from dangers, and the like good things of this world?

Ans. I answer, Yes; and yet joy in the Lord also; for whenas whatsoever we have, we receive it as a token of God's particular love to us in Christ, who both gives us our daily bread and the word of life; comforts both heavenly and earthly; these outward things then, I say, do strengthen the faith of a Christian, and thereby our joy is strengthened. Wherefore we may thus joy in them, nay, it is our duty to do it. The wicked they indeed receive them, but only as from God's care of the general good of the world, or the race of mankind; and therefore can take no joy truly from them as the child of God doth: who in the right use of them, first rejoiceth that he is the child of God, and is reconciled to him in Christ: that Christ is his; and then that he having the field, hath also the pearl, Mat. xiii. 45, *seq.* All blessings belonging to this life and a better are in Christ made his, and he so rejoices in them, as he refers the comfort and strength that he receiveth from them to the honour of God. God's children receiving good things from him, are threatened for not rejoicing in them, Deut. xxviii. 47. In the 45th verse he saith, 'The curses shall be upon thee, for that thou servest not the Lord thy God with joyfulness and gladness of heart, for the abundance of all things.' And it is expressly commanded, Deut. xxvi. 11, 'Thou shalt rejoice in every good thing which the Lord thy God hath given thee, and thine house.'

Quest. But it may be questioned, *Why, if this be true, are God's children so disconsolate?* none are so much troubled in conscience as they? I answer,

1. Their sorrow proceeds *not from their good estate,* in that they are Christians, *but from the want of the perfections to make them absolute Christians indeed.*

2. They either do *not know themselves, or if they do, because they glorify not God, nor adorn their profession,* God justly suffers his joy to be hid, by hiding the comfortable presence of his Spirit.

3. God's children's joy, though it be great, *yet is not discerned of the world.* It is a hidden joy. The feast is kept in the conscience. It is not seen of the world, which discerns all things carnally. Carnal joy is always outward, and easy to express.

4. While God's children live here, they have *ever a mixture of the two affections of joy and grief,* to temper one another; for fulness of joy is only in heaven. This life will not endure perfect joy; but ever when there is cause given of joy, we have something to humble us, and to keep us from being exalted above measure. As Paul had some base temptation, which he calls the 'prick of the flesh,' who therefore bids us to fear and tremble, that we lose not the sense of God's Spirit by the prevailing of our corruptions.

Obj. But it will be objected, that the Christian is fuller of sorrow than joy. To which I answer,

Ans. It arises either from ignorance of the grounds of comfort, or from want of application of them. When a man is a young Christian, newly begun, he knows not nor understands what grounds he hath of joy. They are as children, that know not their inheritance at the first, nor their father's love; especially if he correct them, they think he loves them not. Even those that are grown Christians fail too often in this, either by misapplying the grounds, and misjudging of their estate; or sometimes through the distemper of their body, through melancholy. These judge of grace by the measure, when they should judge by the truth of it, be it never so little. For it is not the measure that is the evidence of the child of God, but truth of grace. For there are degrees of grace: in some more, in some less, and in one more in one time than in another. Take, therefore, a Christian in his right estate, one that is a grown Christian, whom neither melancholy nor temptation doth trouble; take him, I say, as he should be, he doth rejoice more soundly, with true joy and hearty, than any one can, being an ungodly man, be he never so merry. However, this we may be sure of, a Christian hath the greatest cause to rejoice, and, as I said before, he ought to stir it up in him by all means. And therefore, however indisposed he be thereto, he ought to search what good things God hath wrought in him. If he doth not know his estate, he cannot praise God as he should. He must meditate also of the vanity of all worldly things. They vanish, and they that put their trust in them ever failed of any true joy. It never comes to the heart of a man. They are not deep enough to comfort men that meet with afflictions. They only touch the fancy, as the fancy of a beast may be delighted.

Let him also *compare all discomforts that can come, with this joy in the Lord,* and he shall find that it countervails a world of sorrow. This has no end; they are momentary, they last but for a night. This is in the Lord, in whom is fulness of joy. This made the saints of God so resolute, that they set light by all afflictions whatsoever; and therefore, in their greatest afflictions they have the sweetest joy and greatest comforts. And let him also consider, that by this he avoids the reproach of religion, and shews the force and efficacy thereof to be such as is formerly declared.

And let him *take heed of the hindrances of this joy.* As first of all, of sin committed and not repented. Let him repent betimes, else it keeps a man dead, and dull, and backward. So long as this Achan is unfound, it will keep him in discomfort, 1 Chron. ii. 7. Let him take heed of secret purposes, either to sin or to favour himself in any one sin, how small soever, for time to come. This will rob him utterly of comfort, for joy cannot lodge in such a heart. 'If I regard iniquity in my heart, the Lord will not hear me,' saith David, Ps. lxvi. 18.

Furthermore, Let him *take heed of negligence in good duties.* For it is not enough to do them, but he ought to stir up the graces of God in him to do them thoroughly; and he must strive against his corruptions. For Christians have never so much joy, as when they have laboured with their endeavours to overcome their imperfections in good actions.

Lastly, Let him take heed *of casting himself into dull or dead acquaintance.* It is true we cannot avoid conversing with them, but we must have no secret and inward acquaintance but with the best. A companion of fools shall be beaten, and the wise with the wise will learn wisdom. We are all travellers to heaven; let us therefore choose such company as may, as it were, be a chariot to carry us thither, with their good example and discourses. And with the prophet David, think it a great grief when we have not such society as may do us good. 'Woe is me, that I am constrained to dwell in the tents of Meshech,' Ps. cxx. 5. And therefore, if heretofore any of us have been faulty, let us take warning of this hereafter.

VERSE 1.

To write the same things to you, to me indeed is not grievous, but for you it is safe.

Although the apostle had formerly bidden them to rejoice, in the former chapter, 18th and 28th verses, yet notwithstanding he bids them 'rejoice' again, saying that it is safe for them to hear the same things often, and it is not grievous to him to write the same things twice. Besides, he doth also bid them to beware of such as may hinder their joy, as dogs and those of the concision, preventing* thereby secret objections which they might make against repeating the same things. Whence we may in general observe,

Doct. 1. *The wisdom of the word and Spirit of God, to know secret objections* that might be made, *and to prevent them;* turning away thereby whatsoever might hinder the force of the word.

Doct. 2. And in the second place, it teaches us that *it is the duty of those* that mean to prevail by instruction, *to know the secret dispositions of those they deal withal.* For when their minds are not quieted or cleared from doubts and hindrances, they are not fit to entertain any good counsel at all.

Doct. 3. And thirdly (for I cannot stand on these things), it shews *our dispositions by nature, to count repetition of the same things to be tedious and irksome.* For since the fall of man, we wander in our thoughts, affections, and intentions; and it is a part of our loss, to lose our constancy and settled disposition. Wherefore, we find it noted of the Israelites, that they were weary of one kind of food, although it is called 'angels' food,' Numb. xi. 6.

Doct. 4. In the fourth place (which I intend more to stand upon), observe

* That is, 'anticipating.'—G.

with me, that *dwelling on the same things is necessary, even for the best Christians.* And the reasons are,

Reason 1. First, *Because truth is supernatural, and our minds are carnal; and that which must change these our minds must be assiduous,* or else our minds will sink into their first estate. We are naturally changeable, and therefore had need to have the truth, as at the first to change us, even so to be continually presented to our souls, to keep us perpetually in this spiritual change. And a

Reason 2. Second reason may be, *because we often regard not the truth at the first, second, or third time urged and taught unto us.* Wherefore, Job xxxiii. 14, it is said, 'God speaketh once or twice, yet man perceives not.' Therefore, if the caution and point be necessary, the reception must needs be necessary also.

Reason 3. In the third place, *there is such a breadth and depth in the points delivered out of the word of God, that although we hear often the same thing, yet we never come to understand the full extent of them.* Our souls are narrow. We cannot at the first so soundly and deeply consider of them, neither can we understand so many particulars as otherwise we should; for in every Christian truth there is milk for children and strong meat, which requires digestion and likewise repetition.

Reason 4. A fourth reason may be, *because our corruptions daily increase and grow upon us, and variety of occasion and worldly business being natural to us, and therefore more delightful, are too powerful, and do thrust out the consideration of divine truths, which are commonly against the hair.* And we cannot have variety of two things in our minds at the same time in strength. Whence it comes to pass that the better is ever more subject to be thrust out, and therefore had need to be hammered in with often repetition and insisting upon again and again.

Reason 5. A fifth reason may be, Because *we work as well as understand, weakly or strongly.* When we work well, we must have things present strongly in the understanding; as when we tell men of God's justice, omnipresence, of the day of judgment, of death, and the like. The lively and present remembrance of these things keeps the mind of man so in frame as it cannot will any evil, no more than a lewd person will offend in the presence of the judge. And this lively remembrance of things is wrought chiefly by repetition and often enforcing the same things, and it makes the mind to be wholly taken up therewith. And therefore it is a good way, when we would do any good action well, to be taken up with reading or hearing of good, by way of preparation thereunto. And the want of the presence of good things in our mind lays us open and makes us fit for all companies and occasions of sin.

Reason 6. In the next and last place, *our memories are very weak to remember and to retain anything that is good.* Since the fall they are broken, and good things sink through them as water through a sieve, and therefore hath great need of remembrancers. And after this manner hath God dealt with man, as in the promise of the blessed seed. How often is it reiterated and typified; and to Abraham it is renewed seven times.* So God to David often renewed his promise concerning the kingdom, as also the promise concerning the deliverance of the people of Israel from captivity in Isaiah is often repeated. This also did Christ, the great doctor † of his church, in his parables. In one chapter [he] argueth one principal matter

* Cf. Genesis xii. 1–3; xii. 7; xiii. 14–16; xv. 18; xvii. 8; xxiv. 7; xxv. 8.—G.
† That is, teacher.—G.

with four parables one after another,* although with some variety, teaching ministers thereby to do the like to avoid tediousness. Repetition in Scripture serves to divers ends; sometimes for the stronger averring of the certainty thereof. Wherefore it was that Pharaoh's dream was doubled. Sometime for emphasis sake, as Christ did often, 'Amen, amen,' and 'in dying thou shalt die,' (*a*) and the like phrases. But the main end is, to stir up us and our affections, and to keep them in life and action when they are stirred up. Therefore, 2 Peter i. 12, because they knew they could not be over sure of salvation, nor grow too much in grace, he says, 'So long as he lives he will put them in mind of such things.'

Use 1. Let it not therefore *be grievous to ministers to do what is for the safety of God's children.* They must do it till they see practice come to perfection, and they must cast and cast again. Peter he cast often and got nothing, yet at Christ's word he cast again. So must ministers. God that blesseth not every cast, may bless the last cast to the catching of many; and therefore a minister had need of a fatherlike affection to his hearers, as St Paul had, 1 Thes. ii. 11.

Use. 2. A second use may be for ourselves: if we hear the same things repeated, *hear them as an impression* which may carry force, and work upon our hearts more strongly than before. And know that God may work on us by one means at one time which he did not at another; as a dart pierces deeper being cast by one than by another. And therefore let us not be weary of attendance on God's ordinances, for our corruptions daily increase as our age doth. Our minding of things is but slight, and our memory very brittle. And we must know that the word teaches doing and practising, as well as knowing. And therefore to conceive a necessity of a continual ministry to perfect a church as well as to begin it. The sacraments are necessary; receive them often. The primitive church had them every Lord's day (*b*). Till we come to the holy land of that heavenly Canaan, let us submit ourselves to this manna. It is angels' food, and they desire to look into these mysteries, 1 Peter i. 12. And therefore take heed of fulness or loathing; for when we come to that pass that we must have *novum* or *nihil*, God takes away this manna thus loathed. Thus did he with the Greek churches, Rev. i. and ii. They gave themselves not to the plain, sincere truth, but man's inventions, whereby God gave them over to strange opinions. And indeed it is a rule: none absents himself from God's word, but he is given over, and that justly, to believe toys;† to attribute all praise and delight to this or that idle author, which it may be is heathenish or popish. The Greek churches, affecting novelties, were justly given over to Mahomet. But to a true Christian heart there cannot be more delight than in the experimental knowledge of Christ's death and office, of perseverance in grace. There are standing dishes in this Christian banquet. It is a sign God means to plague that person or nation that is delighted in such ill sauces. He will make them come out of our nostrils. We shall have our fill of them, and never hunger after the sincere milk of the word.

VERSE 2.

Beware of dogs.

Doct. 1. In this general exhortation, consider first the persons to whom

* Viz. in Matthew xiii. the parables of the sower, of the tares, of the mustard seed, and of the leaven.—G.

† That is, 'trifles.'—G.

it is directed, to all the Philippians; not only to the pastor, but even to the common Christians. 'They must beware of false teachers.' Is it so? Then surely they ought to take notice of them, and to know them; and therefore they ought to have rules to discern them by. Christ's sheep they discern between a wolf and a shepherd, John x. 4, 5. His sheep discern an heretic or false teacher from those that are true shepherds in the main points of Christian religion. And therefore, 1 John iv. 1, he bids all in general 'to try the spirits;' and the apostle, 1 Thes. v. 21, bids them 'prove all things, and hold fast the good.' If they were then all of them bound to try and prove, they were no doubt bound to know the rules by which they were to try, which rules are only laid down in the word of God.

Quest. But some popish heart may ask, How common people should know the word to be the word of God?

Ans. For answer, I would ask such an one, how they know the pope's canons, or any book of his constitutions, to be the pope's? They will say, their teachers brings them in the pope's name, and they believe their teachers. So say we: we believe our teachers and ministers, who tell us this is the word of God.

Obj. But they object and say, that we make every one a judge.

Ans. I answer, there is a threefold manner of judging. First, a judging whereby we discern of anything; and this every Christian must have, so as it cannot be any plea to him at the day of judgment, to say, my teacher did mislead me. No. Both the leader and he that is led, if they be blind, shall fall into the ditch, Mat. xv. 14. Then there is a second kind of judging, which is by way of direction. This is required principally in the pastor, to direct his flock. And there is a third kind: that is, of jurisdiction. This belongs to the church and the magistrate; yet every one must have a judgment to discern the good from the bad. For he that knows not his master's will shall be beaten.

In the second place, not only the young ordinary Christians, but even the best settled Christians had need to beware also. The Philippians were a church established in the truth. Eve was seduced, being in her innocent estate. But I need not stand on this at this time. I proceed to the duty, which is to '*beware*.' Which word signifies: first, to discern of, then to avoid. And because those that are aware of evil, by nature will avoid it; therefore 'beware' here, intends both discerning and avoiding of evil. For the church of God in this world is ever subject to danger. And God suffers it to be so: first, to try who be true, and who false; and secondly, to try them that are good, and to be as an evidence to them of their own estates, so as where such trial and danger is, it is true, *ingeniosum est esse Christianum.*

But concerning the words 'dogs, concision, evil workers,' they all signify the same thing; and he repeats the word 'beware' thrice, to shew the necessity thereof. Take heed of them that urge works of the law with doctrines of faith, especially of pastors. Nay, take heed of these, for so the word in the original is, 'these dogs' (*c*). By 'concision,' he means those that urged circumcision, when it was out of date, and when it was dangerous to be admitted of. But observe the term the Holy Ghost calls these 'dogs,' a strange term, and such an one as I should not have dared to have given them, had not the Holy Spirit led the way thereunto. And therefore since it is so, let us not be more modest than he is; but boldly affirm that *wicked men are dogs.* Now, wicked men are either without the church or within. Without the church, all are dogs: Mat. xv. 26, 'It is not meet to take the children's bread and to cast it to dogs.' Of this number are all Turks and Jews, who were *filii*, children, but are *canes*, dogs. We were *canes*, but now through God's mercy are come to be *filii*. All, therefore, that are without the church are dogs. But there are also dogs within the church; and therefore the Philippians were bidden beware of them, which St Paul needed not to have done if they had not been troubled with them. And those dogs he describes, in that they join works of the law and Christ together, in matter of salvation. These are in St Paul's esteem dogs. And the reason hereof may be grounded on God's esteem, on their behaviour towards other men, and in regard of themselves. For God's esteem, we may see it in Isa. lxvi. 3; he detests them as dogs. For their behaviour towards men, whom they go about to seduce, they fawn on them, and use all manner of enticing, flattering, and false alluring words, Rom. xvi. 18. See the picture of a Jesuited papist, a pleasing, humane, fawning nature. They creep into houses; and when these dogs cannot prevail by flattery, then they snarl and bark against them, by false calumnies, and slanders, and railings, and bitter scoffs, and the like; and this they do when they cannot bite. But having gotten power in their hand, they persecute with fire and sword, and the most exquisite torments that they can devise. In regard of themselves also they are dogs, rotten in nature, corrupt in life, filthy in their own courts, devouring their own vomit; and God justly punishing them, by suffering of them to heap up wrath in store, 2 Peter. ii. 22, and to return with the sow that was washed to wallow in the mire of corrupt courses. Hence we may observe and see, what a man is now brought to by sin. He that would be like to God is justly compared to the beasts that perish. Now all by nature are no better than dogs, who are all for their bellies, for present contentments, an envious and currish disposition against any that shall endeavour to cross them in their unlawful lusts; and that rule of reason which should overrule him and amend him, he so abuses it, as thereby he is made more like a devil than a dog.* Would we be then changed? Let us attend on that word, that is able of lions to make lambs. It can cleanse us throughout, John xv. 3. It sanctifies and alters us. Moral precepts may restrain and alter outward practices. The word that alters the condition and nature of men, it is the word of him that works all with his Spirit. And therefore take heed of them, and deal not more with them than thou must needs. They will fawn; they will not be dogged at the first: but till religion altereth him, assuredly he hath a currish nature. But to proceed. He saith not only, 'beware of dogs' in general, but beware of these dogs of the concision. And these also ought we to beware of, for there is a perpetual litter of them. Though those that the apostle spake of are gone, yet the same spirit is now-a-days in many. Fawners they are and flatterers, yet do they bark at Protestants; and of this sort are our Jesuited papists and seminaries. Our fathers were troubled with them. Let these take heed; for were these men dogs that press circumcision with Christ? and shall not such be also, that press merits with Christ, saints with Christ, and equal traditions with the word of God? The dogs in St Paul's time had some excuse. Circumcision they urged, but it was first founded by God. But these men out of their own brain endeavour to establish fancies; and where they cannot prevail by conference, they by scattering of books seek to accomplish their intents. Magistrates therefore in their place ought to look to them; and every private person look to their own salvation. We ought also to take heed of neuters, such as are or

* Qu. 'god'?—Ed.

would be mediators, and will be of every religion, or rather of none; who jumble religions, mixing truth and falsehood, light and darkness together. But he that made distinction between the 'seed of the woman' and the 'seed of the serpent,' made also eternal distinction between religion and irreligion. Though Judas thought he might keep fair quarter with the Pharisees and his Master, yet his fawning kiss could not keep him, but desperation overtook him. So these neuters: let them fawn never so much, let them halt between two opinions never so long, they shall at length know that they have betrayed their religion; and desperation shall at length assuredly overtake them, as it overtook Spira (*d*). Take heed of them. There hath been a continual brood of them. In the emperors' time the Jews had some liberty granted to them, because their ceremonies carried a show of a reverend antiquity. The Christians they were *ludibrium humani generis*;* there were even then, as St Paul found, such Christians as, finding they were scorned, because they would be scorned of neither, took part with neither. †

Quest. But some will say, What a great matter do you make of this! Is it not policy and wisdom for us thus to avoid reproach, and to get the good will of all?

Ans. Remember what Christ says, 'He that denies me before men, I will deny him before my Father,' Mat. x. 33. True, say they, 'I yet may inwardly be sound in my heart; I may honour Christ, though outwardly I may please others.' What place is left for profession? 'With the mouth man confesses to salvation,' Rom. x. 10; and such as are ashamed to confess Christ before men, Christ may justly deny to acknowledge them in that fearful day of judgment. For shall we try all things to be sure of our temporal estate, and shall not we much more seek to assure our spiritual and eternal estate unto us? God forbid.

In the next place, let us not be discouraged or hindered in a good course. Though these dogs bark never so much, yet they are but like the dogs who bark against the moon. Though we meet with many changes, let us keep our course still constantly, without turning aside. For thou must look to be barked at beforehand. Thou art or shouldst be a stranger to this world, and then assuredly the dogs will take notice of thee. And comfort thyself, thou shalt be admitted into thine own country, when these dogs shall be kept out, as it is in the last of the Revelations, Rev. xxii. 15. And though we cannot have too harsh a conceit of them in regard of their estate, yet are we to respect the image of God they carry about with them, and to esteem of them as of such as may become lambs. And thus did St Paul respect and reverence Agrippa. Yet see how sharp he is, not to those that are heathen, but to those that, making a profession of Christianity, did add circumcision to Christ, wherein we may observe his zeal for Christ's honour.

Beware of evil workers.

Beware of such as in general were bad; and in this particular especially they were 'evil workers,' thereby seducing men from Christ. Seducers therefore are evil workers, and magistrates ought to look to them. They are the keepers of the two tables, and are to look to the souls of men as well as to their bodies. Let also private members look to themselves, lest they be seduced by them. Neither is it likely that these were only seducers by false doctrine, but were also ill men and wicked livers; for God justly

* That is, 'the derision of the human race.'—G. † Qu. 'either'?—Ed.

gives such up to wickedness in life that are seduced in judgment. And thus dealt he with the scribes and Pharisees: 'Do not after their works,' saith Christ, Mat. xxiii. 3. Some think if they so live as none can lay any gross sin to their charge, they are good enough. It is no matter what the heart is, how ignorant, how dark; God will bear with them. Alas! poor ignorant men, is not the understanding God's, as well as the outward parts? 'Thou shalt love the Lord thy God with all thy mind,' Mat. xxii. 37. The understanding is *sponsa veritatis*.* And know God looks to purity of judgment. He cannot endure his children should be ignorant; for it is a dishonour to God for his children to conceit of things, in religion especially, otherwise than is fitting, yea, otherwise than they are.

Beware of the concision.

That is, as I formerly said, circumcision, called here by the name of concision, because it tended to cut and make a division and sect in the church, with a natural and proper elegance, not affected, describing and naming it by the effect. It is God's use to call things from the event and effect of them. 'Why will you perish?' Jer. xxvii. 13. That is, Why will you do those things that will lead you to destruction? The end of them is death; and those that neglect wisdom hate themselves. As it was also said to the Jews that neglected the gospel, 'They judged themselves unworthy of salvation,' Acts xiii. 46; because in effect they hated themselves and deprived themselves of salvation. Circumcision formerly had been an honourable ceremony, serving for a partition between Jew and Gentile, and for a seal of the covenant of grace. But the ceremony was to cease, it not having a continual promise. It was to last till Christ came, and when he died, it and all other died also. St Paul, and Christ, and Timothy, were circumcised. But after the time came that Christ had broken down the partition wall by his suffering, they did not only die, but were also deadly to all such as would maintain the observancy of them. The use of them was prejudicial to Christ's honour, and therefore Paul bids us 'beware of them.' And now-a-days this instruction by proportion is of good use. For are there not those that teach concision, and that urge merits, as the papists do? Take heed of them. They say we are the concision; we have cut ourselves from the true mother church of Rome.

I answer, We have suffered a concision; we have made none. And again, we acknowledge we have separated from these Romans, not from those that were in Paul's time. It is they that have made a concision, and cut themselves from the mother church. But to pass from these: we have a concision among us, and that in a contrary extreme, that think every ceremony and thing that suits not with their opinion to be antichristian and concision; not considering that there be many things urged as fitting for order, being no parts of God's worship. Yet even for these things they make a concision, cutting themselves off from our church, and unchurching us. It is dangerous for such; for when the member is cut from the body, it must necessarily die; and how can we receive grace from Christ as our head, but by union of ourselves to the body, whereof Christ is the head.

It must be our duty to beware of all manner of seducers; and to this end let us,

Remedy 1. First, *Get fundamental truths into our heart; affect and love truth:* for want hereof the eastern churches were given up to Mahomet; and antichrist ruled over many in these western churches, because they

* That is, 'spouse of the truth.'—G.

loved not the truth, 2 Thes. ii. 10. For none are seduced that are not cold in love.

Remedy 2. Secondly, *Let us labour to practise that we know, and God will give us a fuller measure of knowledge*, whereby we shall learn to find and know seducers. John vii. 17, 'If any man will do his will, he shall know.'

Remedy 3. Thirdly, *Pray to God for wisdom to discern of schisms, and heresies, and ill-disposed persons.* God hath promised us anything that is necessary for our strengthening, and bringing us to heaven. God will not deny us so necessary an aid as this is.

Remedy 4. Fourthly, Let us look that we keep in us an holy fear and reverence of God: Ps. xxv. 12, 'What man is he that feareth the Lord? him shall he teach in the way he shall choose.' And those things are we duly to observe, the rather because we shall ever find seducers. It will ever be a hard matter for men to find the way to heaven. And though the doctrine and profession of religion be not ever in all places opposed, yet shall we ever find the practisers thereof maligned; as it is in these days, where none are accounted of to be protestants that are not loose libertines. And thus instead of concision from religion, they join that with it which is quite contrary to the power thereof. Beware also of such, for their courses of life are as pernicious as fundamental errors; for none shall be saved for his knowledge.

VERSE 3.

For we are the circumcision.

In these words, and those that follow, our apostle describes who are truly circumcised. 'We are the true Israel, the circumcised sons of Abraham, who are members of Christ.' The Philippians they were not circumcised outwardly, yet were they truly circumcised, they had the truth of it; even as they that were under the cloud and in the sea were said 'to be truly baptized in the cloud and in the sea,' 1 Cor. x. 2. The sacraments therefore, before and after Christ, were in substance all one. As the church was one and the same, they may be said to be baptized as we, and we circumcised as they. The difference was only in the outward ceremony and show, which the church being then young had need of. It is the same religion clothed diversely. Bellarmine saith that their government was carnal, and the promises to them were carnal, but it is carnally spoken of him (*e*), Heb. xi. 2. The fathers before Christ had respect to the recompence of reward; and in ver. 35 they 'accepted not deliverance that they might obtain a better resurrection.' Are these carnal promises? The anabaptists they press rebaptizing, not considering that the same covenant was before Christ and after, in substance; so as every true Christian is spiritually circumcised, being once regenerate. Before, indeed, he is uncircumcised, and a spiritual leprosy overspreads all his frame of body and mind, which must be washed, pared, and cut off. We must part with uncircumcised hearts, ears, and lips; that is, such ears as do delight themselves to hear corrupt lewd discourse; such a tongue and lips as delight to utter and let out words savouring of a rotten and uncircumcised heart; such eyes as do delight themselves in the beholding of lustful and sinful objects, whereby the heart is kindled into vain desires. I say, a Christian must circumcise himself, his heart, and those parts that are uncircumcised, before he can ever think to go to heaven, whither nothing that is corrupt or unclean entereth. Religion therefore is no easy thing, circumcision is painful and bloody. Mortification is very hard. Corruption it must be cut off though the blood follow, else it will kill thee at length. Wherefore we are also to labour for circumcised hearts to understand God's truth, his will, and commandments. Cut off all extravagant desires, which* by little and little take away comfort and communion with God. It is no mercy therefore to spare them. Circumcise thy eyes; pray with David, 'Turn away mine eyes from regarding vanity,' Ps. cxix. 37. Stop thy ears at the charming of such objects as may infect thy soul. We can never enjoy that beatifical vision hereafter, if we wean not ourselves from the liking of these things. And though we cannot, while we are in this house of clay, come to that perfection we should, yet endeavour to it earnestly, and God will accept our very endeavours, and will further them; yea, we shall get the victory at length. If sin begins to fall it shall surely fall; the house of David in us shall grow stronger, and the house of Saul shall daily be weakened. The means to this duty are,

1. First, *Know thy sin, and thy particular sin*, by thy checks of conscience and by the checks we receive from our enemies, who shall spy what they can in us thereby to scandalise us. As also observe what thy thoughts work most upon, what is the main thing that generally takes up your cogitations.

2. When thou hast found out thy sin, *make it as odious as thou canst*. For circumcision implies a thing that is odious and superfluous. Now all sins that be cherished in us may well be odious to us, for that it hinders us from all good and clothes us with all evil, and makes all outward things evil to us; which* otherwise are no further ill than as they strengthen our corruptions. It hinders us from all good duties. Pride of heart and corruption do dog us. This made Paul cry, not of temporal bonds, but of the bonds of sin and of death. 'Who shall deliver me, wretched man that I am?' saith he, Rom. vii. 23, 24.

3. Thirdly, Having found out thy sins, and the abominableness of them, *complain of them to God*, as Hezekiah did of the blasphemous letter that Sennacherib wrote, *and challenge the fruit of God's promise*. For he that bids us circumcise, Deut. x. 16, promised that he himself will do it, Deut. xxx. 6. Faith in the promises is an effectual means to attain to them. Men come with doubtings. They see a great deal of corruption. They think their labour is vain. They cannot be relieved against them. They are deceived. Touch but thou the hem of Christ's garment. Fly to God in his name, and thou shalt find this 'issue' of sin, though not wholly dried up, yet much abated. And here is the excellency of faith that assures us of all the promises concerning sanctification here, as concerning glory hereafter.

Which worship God.

The apostle places circumcision before worship; for unless there be a cutting off, we cannot bring our corruption to perform duties of God's worship aright.

The words contain a description of a Christian by his proper act, *worship*; and by the proper object thereof, *God*; and by his most proper part, *in spirit*. And the word 'worship' is taken for the inward worship of God, commanded in the first commandment; also comprehending our fear, love of God, and joy in him, issuing from the knowledge of the true God. All our obedience issuing herefrom is worship of God, including our duties to

* Misprinted 'who.'—G. * Here also misprinted 'who.'—G.

man, in obedience and relation to God's commandment. The ground of this obedience and worship is the relation between God and the reasonable creature, being the image of God. Now this image being lost in the fall of our first parents, we must worship him not only as *our creator and maker*, but *as 'reconciled to us in Christ,'* as he hath made us anew.

Secondly, We are to worship him *as the well-spring of all grace, goodness, excellency, and greatness.*

Thirdly, *As he doth communicate all unto us.* He is ours. Christ is ours. All is ours. This should carry our souls to love him, be his as he is ours; especially to be his in spirit, by which is meant the reasonable soul, understanding, will, and affections. And, secondly, with sanctified understanding, sanctified will, and sanctified affections. Thirdly, With all our strength, spirit, life, and cheerful readiness. Wherefore God is the proper object of spiritual worship. Trust on him, love him, joy in him, invoke and pray to him and to him only; not to the Virgin Mary, saints, or images, as the papists do: Mat. iv. 10, 'Him only shalt thou serve,' as Christ saith, because our commandment is only from him and extends only to him. The promises are only from him. He only is present in all places; he only supplies our wants; and he only knows what our wants are and how to help. Saints are not present in all places. They cannot hear many at once; nay, they cannot hear our prayers unless they be present. They are finite creatures, they have no infinite properties. Christ he bids us, invites us, to come to him, he hath promised to hear us and to ease us.

And further, God knows the secret wants, which the saints cannot know. We ourselves know them not. And therefore are we to go only to God in all our necessities, because it is most gainful for us to go to him that can help us; nay, we owe him this honour by going to him, to acknowledge his omnipresence, his willingness and ability to do good.

In spirit.

The apostle in these words shews the manner of true worship, by the most proper and fit part of a Christian; to wit, his spirit; that is, a soul truly sanctified, lively, and cheerfully, with a willing and ready mind, fitly disposed, contrary to outward, false, and hypocritical worship.

1. And the reason is, 'Because God is a Spirit, and therefore must be worshipped in spirit,' John iv. 24.

2. Secondly, *It is the best part of a man;* and God who challenges all, and that justly, looks especially that he hath the best part.

3. Thirdly, The *spirit hath a being of itself,* and praiseth, loveth and rejoiceth in God when it is out of the body; and the body is stirred up to this duty only by the spirit, being of itself senseless as a block; and outward worship without inward is but the carcase of worship. The prayer of a wicked man is abominable, because he regards inquity in his heart, Ps. lxvi. 18. And this spirit of ours, without the Spirit of God, cannot worship him; and therefore every one that is not changed makes God an idol.

Use. This may *deprive all such of comfort as care not for this spiritual worship,* thinking they have done enough if they have mumbled a few idle words over. God accepts it no more than if they had sacrificed a dog's head, as he saith, Isa. lxvi. 3. And verily, what other is popery, but a body without a soul, when they worship in blind sacrifices, in a strange language? Is this a spiritual worship, when they neither know what they do nor say? Let us shew that we are not of their number. Come we with love, and with the intension* of all our affections; and this will sway the whole man, body and soul; and so shall we worship him in truth, and not in hypocrisy, as many do, that bring their idols with them. Their minds are on their pleasures and riches, though their body be present before God. And it hath ever been an error in the world, this limiting and tying God's worship to outward worship of the body, with a kind of ceremonious gesture; and it is very much liked for such like reasons as these are.

First, *The outward gesture:* as holding up hands, bending the knee, casting up the eyes, they are things that may easily be done.

Secondly, *They make a glorious show in the eyes of the world.* It is a commendable and good quality to be religious, especially if they be observed so to be.

Thirdly, *It is beneficial to men,* whenas hereby they are known to be no atheists, and therefore not that way incapable of preferment or the like.

Fourthly, *Outward worship satisfies conscience a little.* Men know they must worship God, and go to church, that these are means to save men, and they think that in doing so they stop the cries of their consciences. Alas! alas! these sleepy, blinded consciences of theirs will at length awake, and will accuse them, for the outward ceremonious hypocritical worship of him that requires the Spirit to worship him with.

Obj. But some men say, How shall we know whether we serve God in spirit or no?

Ans. I answer, Observe these properties.

First, *Whether thou lamentest thy defects in the best actions thou dost,* and are not puffed up with conceit of the sufficiency of thy performances. Paul found this in him; for although he lived, being a Pharisee, as concerning the law unrebukable, yet when he was converted he saw much corruption which before he knew not, and laments and bewails it, Rom. vii. 23, 24.

Secondly, Examine thyself, *whether thou makest conscience of private closet duties.* Of prayer in thy study when none sees thee. Of thy very thoughts. Dost thou serve God with thy affections and thy very soul? Dost thou weep in secret for sins, yea, for thy secret sins? Dost not thou do good duties to be seen of men, as the Pharisees did? Contrariwise, wilt thou omit no place nor time, but always and in all places thou wilt worship God? This must be done; for God is always and for ever God; and he is in all places, in private as well as public; and therefore a Christian's heart must be the *sanctum sanctorum,*† where God must remain present continually. And therefore he makes conscience of, and is humbled for, the least sins, yea, those that the world esteems not of, and counts them as niceties; and that in as great a measure as ordinarily men are for the greatest sins they commit.

Thirdly, *Canst thou endure the search of thyself* and thy infirmities by all means? By thyself, by others, by the word, by private friends? Nay, canst thou desire this search, that thou mayest know thy sin more and more, for this end, that thou mayest truly hate it with a more perfect hatred? Canst thou truly appeal to God, as Peter did to Christ, 'Thou knowest that I love and prefer thee above all'? John xxi. 15. It is a sure sign of thy sincerity which the world cannot have; and therefore when they see their sins laid open, they spurn at the ordinances, and spite the minister and their true friends, that put them in mind of their faults, accounting them

* That is, 'stretch,' = earnestness.—G. † That is, 'holy of holies.'—G.

as their only enemies. Surely they shall never be able to endure the search of God hereafter; and the last day when he shall lay them open, they shall be overcome with shame.

A fourth sign is, *That at the hour of thy death this spiritual worshipping of God will give thee content, when nothing else can.* Thou mayest say with comfort, as Hezekiah did, 'Lord, remember how I have walked before thee in sincerity,' Isa. xxxviii. 2, 3. When downright affliction comes, outward verbal profession vanisheth, with all the comforts thereof; then perisheth the hope of the hypocrite. Two things upheld Job in comfort, in his great extremity. He was first assured that his Redeemer lived; and secondly, he knew his innocency in those things that his friends charged him with. And such times will fall on us all, either at the time of death or before, when nothing but innocency and sincerity shall be able to uphold us.

Labour therefore for sincerity and spiritual worship. 'Worship God in spirit,' but let it be done outwardly also. But first, bring thy heart and intention to what thou dost, and that will stir up the outward man to its duty. And for the performance hereof follow these directions.

First, *Learn to know God aright.* For worship is answerable to knowledge; for how can we reverence God aright, when we know neither his goodness nor his greatness? How can we trust on God when we see not his truth in the performance of his promises, in the Scriptures, and in our own experience? Those that do not these know not God. For as the heart affects according to knowledge, so also it is true in divinity; as we know his justice we shall fear; as we know his mercy we shall love him, as we know his truth we shall trust on him. Ps. ix. 10, 'They that know thy name shall trust in thee;' and in other places of the said psalm, the Lord is known in the judgment he executeth, ver. 16.

Secondly, *Know God to be the first mover and cause of all.* Men ordinarily fear the creature, attributing that to it which belongs to the Creator. But God he is the giver of all, and Christians look on the secondary means as to* the first author and ground of all the rest. They behold the magistrate as in God, fear them no otherwise but in the Lord. Atheists they will not stick at any sin whatsoever, to get the love of those that may bring them any worldly commodity. A Christian, he pleases and seeks the love of him that can make enemies friends when he lists, and when it is for our good. He knows 'in him we live, move, and have our being.'

Thirdly, *Make much of spiritual means.* God he works by means, by his word; attend to it. It works love, fear, joy, and reverence in us; and therefore no marvel if those that neglect those means are not acquainted with these graces of God's Spirit.

Fourthly, *Lift up thy heart to Christ, the quickening Spirit*, 1 Cor. xv. 36, *seq.* Our hearts naturally are dead; Christ is our life. When thou art most especially called to love, to fear, to humility, pray to him to move thee, and yield thyself to him, and then shalt thou pray in spirit; as it is said in Jude 20, 'Hear in spirit, do all in spirit;' do outward works of thy calling in spirit; for a true worshipper will out of spiritual grounds do all outward works of his particular calling, as well as the works of his general Christian vocation. Let us therefore do all things from our hearts to God and to our neighbour, else will not God accept of our works. It is the Jew inwardly who shall have praise of God. The want of this sincerity

* Qu. 'from the secondary means to'?—G.

hath extinguished the light of many a glorious professor, and thereby hath brought a great scandal upon the true worshippers of God in spirit.

And rejoice in Christ.

The word 'rejoice' implies a boasting or glorying of the heart, manifesting itself in outward countenance and gesture, as also in speech. It also implies a resting on and contenting in the thing we glory in, proceeding from an assurance that we glory in a thing worthy of glory, for they are fools that delight in baubles. Observe hence, therefore,

Doct. 1 That *those that will worship Christ aright must glory in him.* For the worship of Christ is a thing that requires encouragement, and nothing can work this encouragement like the glorying in Christ. And therefore Paul, in the first part of his epistle to the Romans, having shewed that God had elected them freely, and had begun the work of sanctification in their hearts, he comes in the 12th chapter, ver. 1, 'I beseech you,' saith he, 'present yourselves as a holy, living, and acceptable sacrifice to God.' And in Titus ii. 11, 'The grace of God teacheth,' by encouraging us 'to deny ungodliness, and to walk unblameably, soberly, righteously, and godly in this present world.' And therefore, whensoever we grow dull or dead, think of the great benefits that we have by Christ, and it will quicken us and all our performances.

Doct. 2. In the next place observe, *That Christ is the matter and subject of true glory and rejoicing, and only Christ,* for they well go together, a full and large affection with a full and large object. Boasting is a full affection, the object is every way as full.

Reason 1. First, *As he is God and man.* He is God full of all things; he is man full of all grace and void of all sin. He is Christ anointed to perform all his offices; he is a prophet all-sufficient in all wisdom. In him are the treasures of wisdom. He teaches us not only how to do, but he teaches the very deed. He is our high priest. He is the sacrifice, the altar, and the priest, and he is our eternal priest in heaven and on earth: on earth as suffering for us, in heaven as mediating for our peace. 'Who shall condemn us? It is Christ that died, yea rather, that is risen again, who is even at the right hand of God, who also maketh intercession for us,' Rom. viii. 34. He is also our King. He is King of all, King of kings, and Lord of lords; a king for ever and at all times, subduing all rebellions within us, and all enemies without us; and he is all these so as none is like him, and therefore is worthy of our glory.

Reason 2. Secondly, *Christ is communicative in all these.* He is prophet, priest, king, for us; he is God-man; he is Christ for us. He sought not his own. It was his communicative goodness that drew him from heaven to take our nature.

Reason 3. Thirdly, *He is present and ready to do all good for us;* he is present with us to the end of the world; nay,

Reason 4. Fourthly, *We are his members.* He is in us. We are his wife; nay, we are him. 'Saul, why persecutest thou me?' Acts ix. 4. 1 Cor. xii. 12, *seq.*, 'We are all one body with Christ.'

Reason 5. Fifthly, *We are even whiles we are here glorified with Christ.* He is our husband. If he be honoured, we his spouse also are advanced. If he be our king, we are his queen. If the head be crowned, the body is honoured; and,

Reason 6. Sixthly, *All this is from God, and freely comes from him.* Christ is anointed by the Spirit and sent from the Father. 1 Cor. i. 30,

'He is made of God wisdom, righteousness, sanctification and redemption to us.' And John vi. 44, 'No man can come to me, except the Father who hath sent me draw him;' and it is further said that God 'sealed him,' John vi. 27. So that we may rejoice in Christ, because that thereby we come to joy in God, for he reconciles us to God who called him to this office, which was witnessed at his baptism, whenas the whole Trinity bare witness thereof.

Quest. But it may be questioned, What! may we not joy in any other thing else but in Christ?

Ans. I answer, There may be two causes of our joy. One principal, the other less principal. We must only rejoice in Christ as the main and principal cause of our happiness. But we may rejoice in creatures so far forth as they are testimonies of Christ's love, and in peace of conscience as coming from Christ, and in the word of God as it is the gospel of the revelation of Christ to us.

Use 1. For use. We may observe this doctrine as *a ground of the necessity of particular faith.* For none can boast, but the boasting must arise from a particular faith, which only is the true ground of every man's particular assurance.

Use 2. Secondly, Let it serve *as a direction to every Christian that will rejoice; let him go out of himself and rejoice in Christ,* his king, his priest, and his prophet. Let him observe what he hath done for him, and what he will do for him, and thereby see himself perfectly happy; and,

Use 3. In the third place, *Let us first boast that we have Christ, and then in his benefits and blessings that follow him.* First, rejoice that we have the field, then rejoice in the pearl. And therefore the apostle says not rejoice in *faith* or in *obedience*, but 'in Christ,' who being once mine, how shall I not have all things with him?

Use 4. *Those that are burdened with sorrow for their sin, let them consider.* Why do they grieve? Do their sins trouble them? Christ he came to die for sin, he is their high priest, he came to save sinners. Doth the devil accuse them? Let them know Christ chose them, he pleads for them. Who can lay anything to their charge? Christ he is dead, risen; nay, he is ascended into heaven. Are they troubled with crosses? That is the best time to rejoice in Christ. 'We joy in tribulation,' Rom. v. 3. When nothing comforts us, then hath Christ sweetest communion with our hearts. St Stephen, when the stones flew about him, and Paul in the dungeon, had the most sweet consolation and comfortable presence of God's Spirit that upheld them. Nay, in death we may glory most of all. It lets us into that state, into that sweet society with our Saviour and the saints, the very hope whereof doth now sustain us and cause us to glory here, as in Rom. v. 2. And death now is but a drone,* the sting is gone, all enemies are conquered.

Use 5. In the fifth place, *See wherein the glory of a man, of a nation, of a kingdom consists.* It is in Christ, and that which exhibits Christ. What made the Jews rejoice? Mark the prerogatives they had, Rom. ix. 3, 4: adoption, covenant, promises, and Christ. What made the house of Judah so famous? and Mary so bless herself? 'All generations shall call me blessed,' Luke i. 48: Christ, that vouchsafed to proceed out of her loins and from that stock. 'Abraham rejoiced to see Christ's day,' John viii. 56, though he saw it afar off by the eye of faith. And what should we glory in above the Jews, above other nations, but in this? The veil is taken away: Christ shines, and we have the gospel in its purity. This the apostle looks

* That is, a 'drone,' or stingless bee.—G.

for in the Corinthians, 2 Cor. ii. 3, 'Having confidence that my joy is the joy of you all.' Now, what was Paul's joy? 'God forbid,' saith he, 'that I should rejoice, but in the cross of Christ,' Gal. vi. 14. Let us not, therefore, rejoice in peace or plenty, fortified places, or the like. No. If we had not Christ to rejoice in, we were no better than Turks. 'Happy is the people whose God is the Lord,' Ps. cxlvi. 5; for in him shall we have fulness of joy and comfort. Make use of this in time of temptation. When the devil would rob us of our joy, fly to Christ: oppose him against all; oppose the 'second Adam' against the first: he came to do whatever the other did undo. Learn to see the subtlety of the devil and thine own heart; and fill thy heart with the Scriptures and with meditations of the promises, and they will cause our love to be so fervent, as all our service of God will seem to be easy to us; as the time that Jacob served seemed nothing, for the love he bare to Rachel, Gen. xxix. 20.

But how shall we know whether we rejoice in Christ or not?

Ans. I answer, By these signs:

1. First, *When we glory, see the ground whence it arises, whether from God reconciled to us or not.* If otherwise, remember that of Jer. ix. 23: 'Let not the wise man glory in his wisdom, nor the strong man in his strength;' all such rejoicing is evil; 'but let him that glorieth glory in this, that he understandeth and knoweth me, that I am the Lord.'

2. Secondly, *If we glory in the Lord, it will stir us up to thanks.* What we joy in we will praise. If we joy in Christ, we shall, like the spouse in Canticles, ever be setting forth the praises of our beloved. Thus did Paul, Eph. i. 3, and Peter, 1 Pet. i. 3; and therefore, where deadness and dulness is, it shews no true Christian joy.

3. Thirdly, *Our glorying will be seen in duty.* Delight ever implies the intention to do any good work, and diligence.

4. Fourthly, *If we glory in Christ aright, we shall not endure any addition to Christ;* and therefore, we shall abhor that popish tenent* which puts so many additions to Christ in the meritorious work of our salvation. A true rejoicer in Christ sees such all-sufficiency in Christ's merits and work, that he abhors purgatory and such trash; and so much the more, by how much his glorying in Christ is the more fervent and sincere. Christ is our husband, we are his spouse; if we cleave to any other than to Christ, we are adulterers. No; let him kiss us with the kisses of his mouth, and none but he, Cant. i. 2.

5. Fifthly, *This joy, where it is, it will breed content in all estates.* Paul could want and abound, and so can a true rejoicer: in Christ he hath all. He cares not for earthly wants, so he wants no heavenly comfort. If he be poor, he is rich in heaven; nay, what he most complains of, are good for him: life or death, all is one with him. Christ is his, and in him all things.

Quest. But it may be said, There are many Christians are not in this happy condition.

Ans. I answer, It is their own fault, to yield to the devil's policy; and their own weakness, that will not labour to break through these clouds, and challenge the promises.

And have no confidence in the flesh.

These words are in truth included in the former, for he that glories in Christ 'will have no confidence in the flesh.' But the apostle notes this as a plain demonstration and evidence of the glorying in Christ. For by

* That is, 'tenet.'—G.

the copulative enjoining of them, it is all one as if he had said, What a man trusts to he glories in, and what he glories in he trusts to, and is confident of. If in wit his glorying be, he trusts to it, though it be to his ruin, as it fell out with Ahithophel, 2 Sam. xvii. 23. If in eloquence of speech, he trusts to it, and it brings shame, as it did to Herod, Acts xii. 23. If in honour, he trusts to it, and brings himself to dishonour, as Haman did, Esther vii. 10.

By 'flesh' is meant outward things, as prerogatives, privileges, actions of a man's own doing, and particularly, he aims at circumcision, which he calls 'outward, and that of the flesh,' Rom. ii. 28. So as the observation that we may gather is, *that confidence in Christ takes away confidence in outward things.* The reason is, if Christ be fully all-sufficient, what need is there of any outward thing to put confidence in? For these are two opposite things, and one overthrows the other.

Doct. The second instruction is, *that naturally men have confidence in outward things;* for having not hearts filled with grace, they relish not Christ, but fly to ceremonious outward actions as their refuge. Nay, in the church, till we be converted, we naturally fly to outward fleshly confidence. We have the word taught to us; we come to hear it twice on the Lord's day. Alas! what is this, if thou be not transformed, and inwardly and outwardly conformed in obedience! Hast thou the sacraments? dost thou uncover thy head, or bow the knee? These are good, and they seem fair; but where is the heart? how is that prepared? hast thou an earnest desire to leave off thy course of sinning, and dost thou resolve hereafter to amend thy life? Oh, here is the hard spiritual work! So, in outward fasting and abstinence, it is an easy matter. The Pharisees did it often. But this is the fast that God hath commanded, to loose the bands of wickedness, to fast from sin, Isa. lviii. 6. The suffering of the flesh, if it be separated from spiritual use, and alms, they profit nothing, 1 Cor. xiii. 3. All Paul's prerogatives, which were many, 2 Cor. 11th and 12th chapters, yet they were in his account but 'dross and dung,' in comparison of Christ. Most men are like Ephraim, Hosea x. 11, as heifers, who serve to tread out corn and to plough. Ephraim loved to tread corn, where he might eat his bellyful; for by the law of Moses, the mouth of the ox that treadeth out the corn was not to be muzzled. Men they are delighted in the performance of slight duties; but to put their neck under the yoke, to plough, it is a hard work; who can bear it?

Obj. But some will say, Oh, what! do you condemn outward duties and use of them?

Ans. I answer, We may consider religious duties two ways. First, as they are outward means to salvation, for so they are. Secondly, as they are expressions of inward truth; and so out of a sincere, entire affection we bear to them, and out of a desire to be wrought upon by them, we do them. Thus they are commended that use them. But let them want but an inch of this, all is abominable, all is 'flesh.' The Jews they boasted in the name of 'holy people,' in their law, 'in the temple,' in the 'Holy Land;' yet for all these, saith God, you shall go into captivity. Against such Christ preached: 'Woe to you, Scribes and Pharisees! you tithe mint, but let pass justice and judgment,' Mat. xxiii. 23. And Paul, 'Be not high-minded, but fear,' Rom. xi. 20. And the reasons why men are taken up with this fleshly confidence are,

Reason 1. First, *Outward things are easy,* and men cannot bend themselves to perform the hard matters of the law.

Reason 2. Secondly, *They are glorious*, and men desire to be observed.

Reason 3. Thirdly, Men have *a foolish conceit* that God is delighted with the outward act, when the inward sincerity is wanting.

Reason 4. Fourthly, Men *want knowledge of themselves*, want the inward change, want sense of their own unworthiness and Christ's worthiness.

Reason 5. Fifthly, *God followeth such with prosperity* in this world. Thereby they think God is well pleased with them, till the hour of death come, and then they find all but froth.

Quest. How shall we know whether our confidence is fleshly or not?

Ans. I answer, Where this fleshly confidence is, there is bitterness of spirit against sincerity. The Pharisees, the doctors of the law, sat in Moses' chair, yet who more opposed Christ than they? Mat. xxiii. 2. Nay, they wholly and only in their whole course sought to persecute him, and made it their trade.

2. Secondly, Where this fleshly confidence is, there is also a secret blessing of ourselves in our performance of good duties, without humiliation for our defects. Hypocrites think that God is beholden to them, and therefore do bless themselves in the deed done.

In the fourth verse he comes to an argument, taken from himself, against those of the concision.

VERSE 4.

Though I might also have confidence in the flesh. If any other man thinketh that he hath whereof he might trust in the flesh, I more.

As if he had said, If any other man may glory in the flesh, then may I much more. But I do not think that I have cause sufficient to glory in the flesh; therefore have not they, or may not they, glory in the flesh. And the reason or ground of this proposition is taken from his many prerogatives he had, which he comes to in the 5th and 6th verses following.

First. Circumcision was the first prerogative before conversion; and it was not before the eighth day, to the end that the child might gather some strength to bear and endure the ceremony, for it was of itself grievous, and a bloody ceremony; wherefore it was that Moses his wife called him a bloody husband, Exod. iv. 25. And this ceremony was not to be respited above eight days, that the parents might not be delayed in their comfort. Whence we may gather, that dying before baptism is no necessary impediment to the salvation of the child, for the same covenant is annexed to circumcision that is to baptism; and the papists, that hold that the death of children before baptism hindereth the salvation of the infant, may as well hold that all the children that died before the eighth day, being the day of circumcision, were damned. Secondly, Observe this, that children, though infants, may, nay, must, be baptized, if it may be with conveniency; for children were circumcised, nay, they were enjoined circumcision, on the eighth day. Now, seeing the covenant is the same, and given to children, now as then, why may not the seal thereof be now given in their infancy as then?

VERSE 5.

Of the stock of Israel.

Jacob had his name changed of his wrestling with the angel, and prevailed. St Paul says he was of that stock of Israel that prevailed with God.

Of the tribe of Benjamin.

There were two tribes of especial credit, Judah and Benjamin. They were kingly tribes. Benjamin was honoured with the first king, Saul the son of Kish, who though he were a castaway, yet it is a matter of great joy in the flesh to have great men, personages and learned men, of their lineage.

An Hebrew of the Hebrews.

More ancient than an Israelite, for Abraham was an Hebrew before Jacob was an Israelite. And he was an Hebrew born, no proselyte or converted Jew.

As touching the law, a Pharisee.

Before Christ's time there were divers sects among the Jews, as Pharisees, Scribes, Herodians, and Essæi.* But the Pharisees were the greatest sect of all; and as the word signifies, so they did separate themselves as better than other Jews whatsoever. And St Paul lays down this as one especial carnal thing, wherein he might glory. He was no common Jew, but a zealous Jew. So as thence we may observe, that there is a fire and zeal that is not kindled by heaven; but, as St James saith of the tongue, 'is set on fire of hell,' iii. 6, out of ignorance. Blind zeal therefore is a ground of destruction. We are therefore to take heed; for unless our zeal have an eye, nothing is more tempestuous and troublesome than that man is whom it possesses.

VERSE 6.

Concerning zeal, persecuting the church.

Where zeal is, if it be meant in the largest sense, it is very hot against all opposites. It hath the name from fire, separating *heterogenies*, and gathering things *homogeneal*. Our apostle was none of those drowsy professors that would be content to mingle religions, so as where there is no opposition there is no zeal. And therefore those that would reconcile religions, false and true, they have not a spark of zeal, but are key-cold. Again, Paul well joins persecution and a Pharisee together, for there was never hypocrite but he was a persecutor. For he, making and grounding his profession on pride and a desire to be counted holy, when a downright person esteems him not, but by his integrity, puts the other's outward profession out of countenance, presently he falleth a persecuting, especially if his hypocrisy brings any profit or gain, as it was with Demetrius in the Acts, xix. 24, 38; and as it is now with the Romish Church, whose chief end is profit, as appears by their purgatory, indulgences, pardons, dispensations, and the like. You shall have as much mass as you will, and as little preaching. We may observe further, that carnal zeal is persecuting zeal, and the persecuting church is the false church. Christ's flock never persecutes wolves. It will not indeed endure to be near them, but it is not cruel against them. The papists indeed they speak much of their mildness and meekness, but what is the reason? Their hands are bound. *Solve leonem et senties leonem*, loose the lion and then you shall find he is a lion.

* That is, Essenes. Cf. Westcott's excellent paper in Dr Smith's Dictionary of the Bible, *sub voce*.—G.

Touching the righteousness which is in the law, blameless.

This was a great prerogative.

Obj. But how can he be said to be blameless as concerning the law, when he was without the law? Rom. vii. 9.

I answer, It is true he was without the law in respect of the inward man, in respect of sanctified knowledge, love, and fear; but in regard of his outward course of life, no man could blame him. Let this be observed by carnal civil men; they may be blameless as concerning outward conversation, and yet without the law.

Quest. But if he was blameless as concerning the law, how could he blame himself so as he did? Rom. vii. 15.

Ans. I answer, St Paul then had a new esteem and judgment; he had a new light which shewed him much corruption, where before he saw none. This meets with weak Christians, that think themselves unconverted and castaways, because they see a great deal of sin in them. Paul was without blame; now 'miserable man, who shall deliver me?' Rom. vii. 24. Christians therefore are to be comforted; and to know that they are not the worse because they see themselves sinful daily more and more, but that they are better, as to whom God does daily bestow the light of his Holy Spirit, to make them see more clearly into their estates. We know that we see only the motes where the sun shineth; yet cannot we deny but all the air is as full as that part which the sun enlighteneth.

∴ Let not such therefore be discouraged, but let them know where there is any opposition, there is spirit as well as flesh; and that at length the spirit will have the victory.

VERSE 7.

But what things were gain to me, those I count loss for Christ.

1. *Those things and privileges that formerly he counted gain, now he counts them loss.*

2. *It is good therefore to teach by example;* as St Paul does here enforce rules by his own experience and example.

It is also expedient sometimes to speak of prerogatives and privileges that a man hath in himself; and it is not universal that we must not speak of anything that might concern our own praise. For we may do it as St Paul does here, to beat down the pride of others that are vain-glorious; or we may, as Paul does, lift up ourselves to abase and beat down ourselves the lower.

3. In the third place, *when God vouchsafes his children any outward privileges, he doth it for the good and help of others,* though we see it not at the first. Paul had these privileges, that he might beat down the pride of the Jews more powerfully. And Solomon had all abundance of wisdom, riches, and the like. Why? But only that he might without control judge of all, as of 'vanity and vexation of spirit;' and make it to be believed more firmly. For had an ordinary man said it, men would have thought it easy for him to say so; but if he had tried them, he would have been otherwise minded. In these later times, our best teachers were at the first papists, and of the more zealous sort; as Bucer (*f*) and Luther (*g*), being also learned men; as also Peter Martyr (*h*) and Zanchius (*i*), was brought up in Italy, and all this, that they seeing once their blindness, might be the more able to confound them, as being not a whit inferior to them in any outward respect whatsoever, when they were of their belief.

4. In the fourth place, *God* (having to deal with men of a desperate condition) *suffers great and famous men to be in ignorance, nay, to be persecutors, that after their conversion they might comfort weak Christians;* and therefore let them comfort themselves. Do they find that their sins are many and great? Paul was a Pharisee, a persecuting Pharisee, and continued so a long while. Nay, after his conversion, he complains of a body of sin, and yet found mercy; and therefore do not despair.

But to proceed. We see what St Paul was, and what now he is, how his judgment is quite contrary to that it was; for where grace is, it makes men opposite to themselves; and therefore this re-creation is called a new creature: Paul quite contrary to Saul, and yet both one person. Out of which we may gather,

First, *That a man before conversion hath ever that which is his gain;* for we are prone to think too highly of natural things, and our esteem shall be grounded upon probabilities, rather than we will lose our esteem of them. For we know this outward gain is easily gotten, the duties are easily performed, fair outwardly; and will procure praise from men, which is all we naturally look for.

Secondly, Observe hence *that that which we before conversion thought gain, is indeed loss and unprofitable, nay, it is dangerous;* for things may in use be good, but in abuse dangerous. Riches are good in use, but in abuse 'mammon' and 'thorns,' as Christ terms them. Circumcision and sacrifices and baptism in themselves were good, and many things are still good; yet when we trust in them, and neglect inward graces, sacrifice is no more acceptable than a dog's head, Isa. lxvi. 3. Good works are in their proper nature good; yet if we rely on them, they stop the way to Christ. So as it is our wicked and abusing affections that hath brought an ill report on the good creatures of God, so as to us they are dross and dung, nay, loss. These terms doth the Holy Spirit give to alienate our affections from these earthly things; an outward, civil, and conformable life [those things which] are, by our high esteem of them, stops,* staying many from heaven; for while they tell themselves they live honestly and justly, doing no wrong, they suppose themselves to be very saints, and look no further. But every true Christian knows his infirmity, and the more he is enlightened, the more he sees his darkness; he knows these things cannot be gain to him.

For, first, *he knows they are meaner than the soul.* These are earthly, the soul is from heaven; these are outward, the soul is spiritual, and therefore is only satisfied with spiritual and heavenly comforts.

Secondly, *A Christian sees these things are fading, arising of nothing, and tending to nothing; contrarily, he knows his soul is eternal,* and requires comforts that may last with it for ever. For those that joy in these outward things, when they leave him or he leave them, as of necessity he must, it is true they vanish to nothing; but he cannot, but must continue comfortless for ever, and undergo the just wrath of God. Furthermore, a Christian doth not only know these things to be no gain, but he also knows them to be loss. For that is loss which a man finds by experience to be loss, when his understanding is awakened. But all things outward, whatever they be, whether that a man is a Christian by profession, or that he is a preacher, who hath good utterance and is embraced of the people and approved of, or what privilege else soever, when the conscience is awakened they breed more horror, at the hour of death, when we are to give an account of

* That is, 'hindrances.'—G.

them, and they set us further off from Christ. A profane person is nearer conversion than a proud Pharisee; as Christ saith, 'The publican and harlots go before you into the kingdom of God,' Mat xxi. 31. The reason is, because they that are thus outwardly affected sing peace to their souls; whenas the profane man hath no starting-holes of excuse, his vileness being more manifest.

Secondly, *God detests such boasters more than those that are outwardly profane*, and therefore Christ inveighs against such ever, 'Woe to you pharisees, hypocrites,' Mat. xxiii. 13, and often threatens such with the punishment that is provided for hypocrites, as if those were the men which his soul abhorred, and for which only hell was prepared.

But how shall we be qualified, that outward things may not be hinderers of us?

First, Look to the foundation of all conversion; consider *the nature of God and his law*. By them we shall see a further degree of holiness than the best of us can attain to. The excellency of God's nature is such as God's children have been ashamed to be in his presence. As Job when God spake 'abhorred himself,' Job xlii. 6. Peter when he saw the power of Christ said, 'Depart from me, Lord, for I am a sinful man,' Luke v. 8. We are, therefore, to think often of the presence of God, before whom ere long we must all appear.

Secondly, *Bring thyself to the spiritual meaning of the law*, as Paul did, Rom. vii. See into thy thoughts, and behold the uncleanness of thy heart.

Thirdly, *Converse with those that are better than thyself, and compare thyself with them*. Not as the Pharisees, who compared themselves with the publicans; and herein are many deceived, and by undervaluing others they overvalue themselves. For things compared with less they seem somewhat, but with bigger seem nothing. It ought not to be so with us. Let us compare ourselves to that rule that we live by, and to such examples as we are to follow. Compare we ourselves with Christ, our righteousness with his, and then shall we see our wants.

Fourthly, *Practise that which Christ so much beats on*; that is, *self-denial*. Hate father, mother, world, nay, thyself, or never think to come to Christ. They will be loss to thee unless thou account them loss. The young rich man's wealth made him a loser. The love of the praise of men kept the Pharisees that they could not believe. Whosoever nourisheth any lust, it will rule him and his affections, that he shall make it his gain, be it never so vile in itself. But St Paul, being guided by another spirit, casts away all; and so must we. If we will not lose Christ and suffer shipwreck, cast away these commodities that load us and hinder us in our course. Neither is it meant here of an actual casting away of our goods, thereby to establish the foolish vow of poverty. But herein is meant a judicious discerning of the true worth of these things in comparison of Christ, and from thence a preparation, and a resolved mind to part with all that may hinder us from the enjoyment of peace of conscience and the love of Christ. For a man may have a weaned soul in the midst of abundance; and he may live in the world, though not to the world, which is a duty easily spoken of, yet not easily performed; neither was it easily wrought in our apostle, who, being a persecutor of the church, was powerfully altered and changed from heaven. And thus doth God deal with his children, whom he doth first cast down and afflict, that they may find by experience that these outward things can stand us in no stead. It may be he suffers them to fall into some grievous scandalous sin, that they might see the 'body of sin' that lies in them, and seeing no good nor help in themselves, their desires are stirred up to the embracing of some better thing wherein they may find comfort. Then doth God reveal Christ to us, to whom he will have us to fly, and say, 'Lord, what wilt thou have me to do?' So as this power of changing ourselves is not in ourselves, but it is an almighty power.

If we think, therefore, that we are self-lovers, go to God, present thyself in the means, and then our eyes shall be opened to see and discern good and evil. For God hath promised to annex his Spirit to the use of the means, if that we in obedience submit ourselves to them.

VERSE 8.

Yea doubtless, and I count all things but loss.

The words contain a kind of correction, as if in few words he had said, All things whatsoever I formerly boasted in, nay, my very privileges, I count them not only 'dung,' but I do count them to be 'loss' to me; nay, I have suffered the loss of them all in comparison and for Christ my Lord. Yea, I desire to express the earnest intension * of my affections by my desire to win him, to know him, to be found in him, and to be conformable to his death.

In general observe,

1. *The apostle's resolution and zeal,* his assured certainty, his large heart being not able to express his affection, but by many words, viz., his love of Christ and hate of all outward things whatsoever. Therefore *we also in main fundamental points must be resolute,* carrying a full sail. As in the truth of the thing there is a certainty, so in us there must be an assured persuasion thereof. For even from these uncertain irresolute hearts comes apostasy. Men being not grounded are carried about with every 'wind of doctrine,' and hence also comes different measures of grace in Christians. Some say with Paul, 'doubtless;' others are of doubting hearts. But the end of the word is 'to settle us,' Eph. iv. 13. And though it be never so true, yet if we [do] not believe it: though the foundation be sure, yet if we [do] not build on it, the truth and force of it is not good unto us.

2. In the second place, from the apostle's example, *we are to learn in fundamental truths to be zealous.* The apostle speaking of anything that seeks competition with Christ for value, how doth he vilify it, that he hath not words sufficient to press his fervent hatred thereof? For zeal is such an affection as causes a constant hatred against anything that opposes that which we entirely love, even such a hatred as will cause us not to endure to hear of it. And God therefore promiseth Ephraim he shall so abhor idols, as he shall not have to do with them, Hosea xiv. 8.† And indeed a jealous God and a zealous heart do well agree. When we have to do with any one that opposes God in his truth, we are not to be cold, but to be zealously affected.

3. In the third place, *we are to learn to be large hearted in expressing our affection we bear to the truth;* and therefore we are to be ashamed of our shortness of breath in speaking or meditating of God's honour and glory and his truth. But particularly from our apostle's esteem we may learn *that God's children have sanctified and regenerate thoughts and esteems.* For with new souls, they have new eyes, new senses, new affections and judgments; what they saw before to be gain, they see now to be loss. Beasts

* That is, intentness, warmth.—G.

† Cf. 'The Returning Backslider' on the passage in Vol. II.—G.

we know conceive not of men's matters, neither do weak simple men of State matters. That which weak silly men admire, the apostle scorns and condemns. Moses accounted of the afflictions with the children of God more than of the pleasure of Egypt. We may observe this as a mark to know our estates by, What is high in thy esteem ? Is honour, riches, pleasure, or the like ? Thou are not yet thoroughly sanctified ; for if thou wert, thou wouldst have a sanctified judgment.

But some may say, did Paul esteem all things to be loss, yea, his good works ?

1. I answer, *Good works in their own nature are good: but weighing them with Christ, as Paul did, they are also dross and dung.*

2. Secondly, It teaches us, that *we are not righteous, or justified, by any works ceremonial or moral, either before or after our conversion.* The papists allege works as meritorious ; we contrarily do disclaim them. As to that purpose : ay, say they, you mean ceremonial works ; we say no, we mean also moral. For Paul was unblameable as concerning the works of the law, and yet counts them dung. Oh, say they, St Paul meaned those works before his conversion, and not those after his conversion. I answer, Yes ; all things in respect of Christ. I do now account them dross and loss. To prove them the fuller : *If nothing after conversion be perfect, then cannot they entitle us to heaven*, but all our best works in state of regeneration are imperfect. To prove this, see the examples of David, a man after God's own heart, Ps. cxliii. 2 : 'None righteous in thy sight, and who can say his heart is clean ?' and Isa. lxiv. 6 : 'We are all as an unclean thing, and all our righteousness as filthy rags.'

Oh, but Bellarmine says (*j*), the prophet speaks this in the person of the wicked. I hope he will not put the prophet into that number ; for he saith, 'we,' and 'our ;' and 'our righteousness,' not our ill deeds ; and 'all our righteousness.' Nay, of himself in particular, Isaiah saith as much in Isa. vi. 5. And besides, the wicked do not use to pray, as the whole chapter is to that end. And Daniel also includes himself in his confession, Dan. ix. 20. And to prove this by reason : we know that weak and corrupt principles must needs produce imperfect effects. Now the principles of all our motions are evilly affected ; our understandings, memories, affections, all are corrupt and weak. Corruptions make combats in all parts of the soul and body : in whatsoever therefore we do, there is flesh and spirit ; and their own authors agree hereunto : as Ferus (*k*), and *Catharen*, a cardinal of their own, says there is *donata justitia*, and *inhærens* (*l*). When the question is what we must lean to, it must be only on Christ and his righteousness, wherewith from him we are endowed. And a pope of theirs, Adrian the Fourth (*m*), saith that all our righteousness is as the reed of Egypt, which will not only fail us if we rest on it, but will pierce our sides. St Cyprian saith also, that he is either *superbus* or *stultus*, that says or thinks he is perfect (*n*). And good reason, for that which shines in the eyes of man, in God's esteem is base. 'In thy sight shall no flesh be justified,' Rom. iii. 20. Now there are divers degrees of judgments. In God's judgment none shall be justified ; nor in judgment of law, for in many things we offend all : and for the judgment of the world, what is it if it clear us ? Can that acquit us, if God and the law condemns us ? and for the judgment of our own consciences, if they be cleared they will condemn us. Yea, the papists are not satisfied in their own consciences for this point. For if there may be a perfect fulfilling of the law in this life, by a man's own inherent righteousness, why do they teach the doctrine of *doubting* as necessary to salvation? But however they may brabble* in schools to maintain this their assertion, yet when death comes, they must fly those shifts, and lay hold only on God's love (*o*).

Some will say, What are the graces of God's Spirit? Are the sacrifices, the sweet odours, and ornaments of the spouse, are these dung?

I answer, *Things admit of one esteem simply considered, and of another comparatively.* Stars in the day are not seen, yet in the night are great lights. So works in regard of Christ's works are not visible, are nothing, but in themselves are good.

Secondly, *I say there are two courts: one of justification, another of sanctification.* In the court of justification merits are nothing worth, insufficient; but in the court of sanctification, as they are ensigns of a sanctified course, so they are jewels and ornaments.

Obj. But the ignorant papist objects against us, saying that we discourage men from good works, because we do so basely esteem of them.

Ans. I answer, A sick man cannot eat meat, but it breeds humours that strengthens the disease. Shall he therefore forbear all manner of meats? No. For meat strengthens nature, and makes it able to overcome the power of the disease. So by reason of our corruption we have within us, we halt in every good work we put our hand to. Shall we not therefore work at all? Yes. For notwithstanding our weakness, though we merit not any good, yet God, he overlooks the illness of our works, and accepts and rewards the good that is in them, giving us comfort and assurance of our justification, by the sanctified fruits, which, though imperfect, yet are true. To conclude: seeing we cannot have Christ, putting any confidence in outward things, *let us labour to get an esteem of the weakness and imperfections that are in them, as also in our persons and actions*, that we may hunger after Christ. To this end, daily renew we our repentance and examination of our hearts; and when we do any good, examine what weakness, want of zeal, want of affection or attention hath possessed us in our performances (of praying, hearing, reading the word, and the like), and want of watchfulness in our courses; and then shall we be of St Paul's mind, all will be naught. *And take heed of spiritual pride and conceit of any good in us;* for it hinders spiritual comfort from us. Let us meditate of the greatness of God's love to us, and the infinite reward; and it will make us ashamed of our weak requittance of God's love to us. Consider the multitude of our sins before the time we were called; and consider of our proneness to spiritual pride; let us by all means abase ourselves. For those that God loves, he will have them vile in their own esteem: for it is his method, first, to beat down, then to raise up. And therefore John, he comes thundering, 'Hypocrites, generation of vipers!' Mat. iii. 7. Then comes Christ, 'Blessed are the poor, those that hunger and thirst after righteousness,' Mat. v. 6; as if only they were blessed that feel their wants. We must disdain any other titles to any good, but only in God's mercy, and accordingly give the glory of all to him. Thus did the church militant, 'Not unto us, not unto us, Lord, but to thy name,' Ps. cxv. 1; and thus do the church triumphant, Rev. vii. 12, 'Honour, glory, and power be to the Lamb.' Those that do not thus are no members of the church.

Last of all, *Let us take heed of extenuating sin.* The papists tell us of divers sins that are venial. Such are surreptitious thoughts, taking of pins, stealing of points,† and the like; these they call venial. But we must

* That is, = argue, quarrel.—G.

† That is, = laces or latchets, small things.—G.

know (to admit that sin, as a sin, to be venial, is a contradiction, though God do pardon it; for that is out of his free mercy), these surreptitious stealing motions, that unawares do creep into us, though the Papists do make them of small account, God may punish with his fierce indignation. Moses his anger kept him out of Canaan. Adam his apple cast him out of paradise. Every sin is a breach of the law. The least sin soils us. We must give account of idle words. And the wages of any sin, though never so small, is death, Rom. vi. 23.

For the excellency of the knowledge of Christ Jesus.

That is, either all things are loss to me, that hinder me from the knowledge of Christ Jesus; or, all things are loss in comparison of Christ Jesus. Wherefore, *before we can know Christ as we ought, we must know all other things to be loss*; for when we learn to know Christ aright, we then cast those things out of our affections, which would else keep Christ out of our heart. Wherefore it is no wonder that great scholars should be erroneous in many points of religion; for look to their lives, and we shall see them envious and ambitious; they maintain idols in their hearts, they account not those things loss which must be loss, or else they must account Christ loss. Secondly, *This knowledge of Christ is an excellent knowledge, better than the Jews', who had all their knowledge shadowed out in ceremonies;* but this is unvailed, and therefore Christ said, 'Blessed are the eyes that see those things that you see,' Luke x. 23. And as the estate of the church grows more excellent now than before Christ's coming, and shall be most excellent hereafter in heaven, even so our knowledge doth, and shall grow in its excellent perfection. It is better also than human arts and sciences; not in regard of the author, for all knowledge is from God; but,

First, *In regard of the manner of revealing thereof;* for whereas we come to the other by the light of nature and reason, this is inspired into us by the Spirit.

Secondly, *In regard of the matter of this knowledge*, which is far beyond the other, for this teaches the natures and person of Christ, God and man in one person, which may swallow up the thoughts of man. 'Great is the mystery of godliness,' 1 Tim. iii. 16. In the next place, it teaches us his offices, that he is a king to rule over us and deliver us; a priest to make us acceptable to God; a prophet to teach and instruct us. And thirdly, it teaches us the benefit of his offices; exercising them in his state of humiliation and exaltation. Fourthly, it teaches us to know our duties, to entertain him, rest on him, glory in him only, and that all other things are loss in comparison of him.

Thirdly, This knowledge is better than other knowledge, *in the effects it hath*, it being a transforming knowledge, 2 Cor iii. 18. It makes glorious, happy, full of comfort, carrying the Spirit with it, which changes us into his similitude, and therefore it is called the 'word of the Spirit.'

Fourthly, In the fourth place, it is better than other knowledge, *in regard of the depth of the knowledge;* and therefore called 'The manifold wisdom of God,' Eph. iii. 10. That a virgin is a mother; God is become man: this is far above natural reach; and therefore Christ may well be called 'Wonderful,' Isa. ix. 6, who being God should be also man, die, rise, and ascend far above all power.

Fifthly, *This knowledge is a sweet knowledge*, and therefore excellent. It tells us who were miserable and lost; it tells us also of redemption, of a kingdom, of a Saviour. 'How sweet are thy testimonies to my mouth,

Ps. cxix. 103. And if the promises here be so sweet to us, what shall then the accomplishment of them be to us hereafter!

Sixthly, This knowledge, furthermore, is excellent *in regard of the continuance thereof.* The knowledge of other things dies with the things; the world must perish, and what use is there then of our skill in the nature thereof? Only this knowledge abideth for ever, working grace, love, heavenly-mindedness, and brings us to glory.

In the seventh place, *This knowledge of Christ teacheth us to know God aright;* his justice in punishing sin, his wisdom and mercy in reconciling us to him, and in willing that Christ should become man and die for us. Neither could we know these things, but by knowing Christ, who is the engraved image of his father.

Eighth, Furthermore, *it teaches us to know ourselves,* our filthiness, our ignorance, in esteeming triflingly of sins, counting them venial. But great surely must the sore be, that necessarily requires such a salve and such a physician as Christ, and his blood to be shed for the curing thereof.

Ninth, In the next place, *this knowledge is altogether sufficient in itself,* without all other knowledge; and none without this to make a man wise to salvation, both of soul and body; and all men without this are but fools.

Use 1. For use hereof. *This improves the shallow conceit men have of divinity;* that the knowledge is but shallow; that every man may know it, and that any man may soon have enough thereof. But, alas! St Paul had a large heart, and had more insight into the deep mysteries of this knowledge than such, however they boast; and yet he desires more, and could not pierce the depth thereof; for none ever could do it but Christ Jesus only. Nay, the very angels they desire to pry and look into, and to know more of these deep mysteries, 1 Peter i. 12. It is therefore no shallow knowledge.

Use 2. In the second place, *This ought to put us in mind to put apart times, to meditate of the excellency of this knowledge;* and to this end we are to empty ourselves of whatsoever fills us. Especially, we are to empty us of sin, and of care for the world and the vanities thereof, and the knowledge of them; because both it and they shall all perish; make no excuses of venturing displeasure, or suffering discommodity; true love pretends no delays, nor will endure them. 'Behold, Lord, half of my goods I do give to the poor, and I do restore to every man his own,' said Zaccheus, Luke xix. 8.

Use 3. In the next place, *We must call upon God to open our eyes,* that we may see and know his nature, his offices, his benefits, and our duties; to know more distinctly, effectually, and settledly; to see the wonders of his law; that we may be even ravished, when we behold his fulness.

Use 4. We, in the fourth place, *are to frequent places where we shall have a fuller knowledge of Christ;* such places where the commerce is between Christ and the church. In Cant. v. 1, Christ had more love to his church, and wooed her by his gracious promises. She, in the second to the eighth verse, being drowsy, pretends excuses. Hereupon Christ goes away, but leaves a gracious scent of his quickening Spirit, enough to stir her up to seek after her well-beloved that was gone, who, asking after her well-beloved, those whom she inquired of, inquired of her who he was? and upon her description of him, are enamoured with him, and stirred up to seek him also (where by the way mark the benefit of conference), Cant. vi. 1, and are told that he is gone into his garden to the beds of spices; that is, into the congregation and assembly of his saints. If we will know Christ therefore, we must go into these gardens, where he is ever present, and there will he teach us.*

* Cf. on the passage in Vol. II., in 'Bowels Opened.'—G.

Use 5. And then *shall we be stirred up to magnify God's goodness and mercy, that hath reserved us to these times of knowledge*, and this marvellous light, wherein we are more blessed than John, who was the greatest of those born of women. We see more than he saw, Christ our Saviour, already ascended to be our eternal high priest.

My Lord.

This is the end of all our knowledge, to know Christ to be our Lord, for else the devils knew Christ. 'Paul I know, and Christ I know,' said he to those conjurors, but he could not know Christ to be his Lord. 'My Lord.' Not only for his title that he hath in me, but 'my Lord,' for the title I have in him. 'My beloved is mine, and I am his,' Cant. ii. 16. Mine he is, for he made himself mine, by redeeming me and paying the price for me. My head, from whom I receive force and vigour; my husband, my head of eminency. Briefly, 'my Lord,' making me his and stirring up in me a love and desire to make him mine, and to rest upon him by faith. *In the covenant of grace therefore, there is a mutual consent between God and us.* He is ours; we are his by faith to trust on him, and by love to embrace him, which stirs up the whole man to obedience. We may not think that this proceeded from a spiritual pride in the apostle, as though he thought himself the only darling of Christ. No. They are the words of a particular faith and love in the apostle; not excluding others from the like; for every Christian must labour for this faith, that we may know Christ to be our Jesus, our Saviour, which we shall be assured of; for if he makes us his, he will make us to love him, and to say from our hearts, 'my Lord,' and my head. His love of us is the cause of our love to him. We love him because he loved us first. His knowledge is the cause of ours; he chose us, and therefore we choose him; and if he loved me when I hated him, surely now I love him, he must needs love me. Again, we shall know that we are Christ's; for *then there will be a likeness of Christ wrought in our hearts.* For that Spirit that stirs us up to own Christ, doth ever work the image of Christ in our souls; as a seal it imprints on our soul the image of Christ, in all graces, of love, meekness, heavenly-mindedness, and goodness. If we be the spouse of Christ, we shall represent and shew forth his glory, 'for the woman is the glory of the man,' 1 Cor. xi. 7. Else whate'er we boast, we are therein but hypocrites. We must forsake all in regard of Christ.

For whom I have suffered the loss of all things.

Here St Paul confirms his resolution and judgment of the value of Christ above all other things; first, he said he accounted him gain, and all other things loss. Lest men should think these were but brags, he infers* he had suffered the loss of all for him, and therefore did so highly esteem of him; and then it was he was for Christ's sake stripped of all. He was in want, hungry, naked, went in danger of his death often, nay, he willingly suffered the loss of his privileges. He was an apostle, yet not worthy of the name, as he says; and for his care in his office, though he were very diligent, yet by it did he not look to merit. He suffered the loss of all willingly. He wrought this on his heart, to lose all for Christ; which is the duty that a Christian must learn, not to be only patient, but willingly to lose, to part with all. And therefore we are bidden to examine ourselves, to judge and condemn ourselves. And though the Lord hath not called us

* That is, 'he gives this inference,' = shews.—G.

to the loss of all, yet win thus much of thy mind, as to be prepared for to lose all when we shall be called thereunto, and that in regard thereof, we may say we have parted with all; for in that we part with them in our affections, God beholds it and takes notice thereof, and likes it, and looks for it; and therefore he bids us leave all and follow him; and if we forsake not all, honour, credit, yea, our lives, we cannot be his disciples.

And do count them but dung.

Shewing his loathing of them, and that he could not endure the thought of them, but did abhor it as dogs' vomit, or dogs' meat, accounting it fit meat for none but such dogs as he spake before of. If therefore we love Christ, there will be a detestation of those things that cross the power of Christ's merits, in the same degree that we love Christ, and we will express our degree of love of him, by expressing the degree of hatred we bear to other things in comparison of him.

Quest. But why doth the apostle so often inculcate these words?

Ans. To shew the expression of the largeness of his own heart; and thereby to work an impression thereof in the hearts of the Philippians.

2. Secondly, *To shew the power of the Spirit,* that where it once leads, it leads further and further to a higher degree of love of Christ; that the longer he is loved, the greater will love grow and more fervent, so as the spirit constrains the person where it rules, that he cannot but speak, Acts iv. 20.

3. Thirdly, *To shew the excellency of the subject.* He dwells upon it, that we should think highly of it. Also,

4. Fourthly, *To shew the necessity thereof;* without which we cannot look for salvation.

5. Fifthly, *To shew the difficulty of coming to this esteem of Christ;* and to subdue our proud imaginations of our own selves, which, however, it will prove a hard and difficult matter.

6. Lastly, *In regard of the Philippians, he knew it would be a difficult matter for them, and therefore he sought out fit words to express the nature of the subject and the truth of his esteem.* Thus did the wise man, Eccles. xii. 10, 11, who knew that the words of the wise man are as goads. It is our duty to take notice hereof therefore, and to learn in what respect these outward things are good, and to rank them in their right places.

That I may win Christ.

To win Christ, in this place, is to get a more near communion with Christ; a fuller assurance of him, and a larger portion in him. For St Paul had Christ already; and that made him desire a fuller enjoyment of him. Though his heart was not large enough to entertain all Christ, yet he desired to be satisfied with his fulness.

1. First, then, it is here to be granted that *Christ is gain,* else why should the apostle desire to win him? He is gain, I say, both in himself considered, and having respect to us. *In himself considered;* for no jewel is comparable to God-man, to a Mediator. He was enriched with all graces that the manhood was capable of. But much more in regard of us; for, first, he is our 'ransom' from the wrath of God. Now we know a ransom must be a gainful thing, and of no small price that must satisfy God's wrath.

2. Secondly, He is not only our ransom, but *our purchase;* purchasing God's favour and heaven to us.

3. Thirdly, *He is our treasure ;* for all things for this present life, as also for a better; in him are the treasures of heavenly wisdom; and of his fulness we all receive grace for grace. He is our comfort in trouble, and direction in all our perplexities.

4. Fourthly, He is of that precious virtue, *as he turns all to gold ;* all things are sanctified to us, death, grave, crosses, all which, though we be not freed from, yet he turns them all to work our good.

5. Fifthly, *By him we are made heirs,* and have title to all things. He is our Lord; and he that hath given Christ to us, how shall he not with him give us all things, Rom. viii. 32, so as in all our wants we may boldly come to the throne of grace.

6. Sixthly, *We by Christ gain such offices as he himself had.* We are kings; we are priests; we are over the greatest of our enemies. No more thralls to lust, or to the world. We may freely offer sacrifice for ourselves and others, in the name of this our high priest.

7. Seventhly, *We have communion with all that are good*—the angels, the saints, the ministers. They are all ours to defend and pray for us. Had the young rich man this spirit of St Paul, he would have thought it the best bargain that ever he made, though he had parted with all, if he had gotten Christ.

Obj. But it may be said, True, Christ is gain; but what hope is there for us to attain hereunto? It may be as paradise in itself, yet kept from us by a flaming sword.

Ans. 1. I answer, No. *This gain may be gotten;* which is the thing I propound to speak of. Christ is a treasure in a field. If any one will seek, he may find. We had a Saviour before we were born. He was elected thereunto, and we to gain heaven through him; and he was manifested in the flesh in the fulness of time to encourage us. And Christ our gain calls us to buy 'without money,' and invites us that are laden with sin to come to him, Isa. lv. 1; 2 Cor. v. 20. To this end he appoints men to lay open his riches to allure us.

2. Secondly, *We have the Spirit, by which we lay hold on this gain.* If we depend on God by prayer for his Spirit, and when we have gotten but a little portion of this gain, it makes our gains increase. To this end he gives us the word and sacraments; and this condemns those that live in the field where this pearl is, and have the ministry to shew them it; and yet they do neglect this so great a jewel. And this ought to stir us up to magnify God's goodness to us, who hath recovered us, that were the lost sons of a lost father, and keeps us from returning back into our former natural estate.

3. Thirdly, This gain *is not to be gotten but at a price.* It must be gotten by parting with all outward things, so far as to make them gain to us.

Quest. Ah, but is God thus hard to us, that he will not allow us the enjoyment of the comforts of this life, but we must for them lose Christ?

Ans. I answer, God denies us not our worldly comforts; for Paul had them. But when they come in competition with Christ, for excellency and superiority in esteem, as also when thou art called forth for the confession of the truth, then be at a point to count all, yea, thy life, dross and dung. We must therefore resolve and forecast the worst; and leave not till thou workest this mind within thee, to endure the worst rather than lose peace of conscience.

And therefore we may well conclude from hence, *that confidence in Christ and in outward things cannot stand together.* We cannot love God and mammon; and therefore, if we part not with the world, look to part with Christ, which we may note against the politicians of our times, that think themselves the only wise men. In their esteem Paul was but a weak man, and knew not how to esteem things. They can trust in God, they hope, and yet provide against the worst. The time will come when they will find they have been made fools indeed; when God will say he knows them not, and their riches shall take their wings and leave them without hope of comfort.

And *therefore let us acquaint ourselves with Christ's value, with the vanity of outward things*, and meditate hereon; and at length thou shalt find the same mind in thee that was in St Paul.

In the last place, we may hence observe *who they be that have not gained Christ;* for are there not many that will not part with a sin, no, though it be a sin that brings no profit or pleasure at all with it, as swearing and blaspheming God's name? Nay, are there not those that, Judas-like, sell Christ for thirty pieces of money, nay, it may be for less? A goodly price to set heaven, happiness, and their own souls at! Let any man tell them hereof, they will swear you do them open wrong, and be ready to cut your throat for saying so. How far are these from true grace!

4. The fourth and last general observation is, that when we *have parted with all, we are to know that we are gainers.* For Christ in Mark x. 30 saith—whose promises are yea and amen—that he shall have a hundredfold in this life; that is, so much content as shall be worth an hundredfold. For when a man's conscience can tell him, These and these things I parted with, only to obtain peace of conscience, that peace of conscience shall give him more content than the whole world can bring to him. And what can a man desire above content and comfort? It is all we seek for here, which if we have not, all is nothing.

5. Fifthly,* He that hath Christ can be no loser; *for in him all things are eminently and fundamentally;* for he is Lord of all, and what I lose for his sake, if it be good for me, he hath said I shall have it.

Hence we may see therefore *the wisest man and the noblest spirit.* Who is the wisest man? He that makes the best choice. It is judgment makes a man; not he that hath confused notions swimming in his brain. Now a Christian considers things, lays them together, judges of them duly; he therefore is the wise man. The wicked man he is a fool. He parts with an invaluable pearl for his present delight in a few idle, vain, childish baubles and toys. Who is also the most truly noble-minded? An advised true Christian. He is able to set at nought that for which the world forget God, heaven, soul, and all for. He can despise the pleasures of a court and of a country. His eye is on his soul, on heaven, on the innumerable company of angels, on that presence where is fulness of joy. A wicked man routs † in the dirt of this world. 'See what manner of stones and building are here,' Mark xiii. 1. That is their delight, to admire the stage of this world. But had they known this gift of God, this peace of conscience, and the comfort thereof, they would look after another city and foundation, whose builder only is God.

Quest. But how shall we know whether we have made this choice or not?

Ans. I answer, By these signs:

First, If a man accounts of anything, *his eye and mind will be on it.* If we account Christ as our gain, our hearts will be set on him continually; if he be our treasure, our hearts will be on him.

* Misprinted 'Secondly.'—G.

† That is, 'digs.'—G.

Secondly, If we have made choice of him, *our hearts will joy in him above all things;* as he that found the jewel went away rejoicing. 'Shew me the light of thy countenance; for therein do I delight,' saith David. Where true belief is, there is joy. Zaccheus, the jailor, and the eunuch, after they were converted, they rejoiced. This makes a covetous man not regard at all what men say of him, for he hath that which they would be glad of. So ought it to be with us; let us be taunted, mocked, flouted at, if we have chosen Christ, all is one. We have other things to comfort us, and our eyes will be upon them.

The *third* note is, *If we can part with anything for Christ*, and endure any hard measure, for the sense and assurance we have in Christ Jesus. Many are so far herefrom as they will not part with the least earthly pleasure for Christ. Such as these, though they say they have peace of conscience, they lie; for they can have no more peace of conscience than they have love to Christ; nor more love than they have an esteem of him above all things.

Fourthly, He that hath made this choice must part *with all things whatever he loves, yea, his dearest affections and lusts;* for a bird catched, though but by a wing, yet is she as surely the fowler's as if her whole body were bound; so if we favour or like and embrace but one sin, though we think not thereof, there is a flood of sin comes in at that gate. He that is guilty of one sin is guilty of all.

Quest. But the weak Christian will object, Are we not, yea, the best of us, troubled with our personal secret infirmities? What shall then become of us?

Ans. I answer, 'Fear not.' For it is true, though the best child of God be thus troubled, yet he pleads against it, he hates it, he undermines it, and strives against it; and thus opposing it, it is not accounted to him by God. But if he forsakes all sin in heart but one, the devil will suffer it and endure it well enough, for he knows he is sure enough.

The *fifth* note is, *That such an one can be content to be at some cost, yea, loss and pains, for the word, for the field wherein this pearl is hid.* He that is not of this mind cares not for the word. It is not that men can speak well and commend it; for many will do so, yet afterward make a mock of it, especially being in some company. But he that esteems it once will ever esteem it, and in all company will extol it. Herod, a very reprobate, may seem well affected where there is no temptation, or while the word is preached. Can this be a plea to God at the last day, who searcheth and knows thy heart? Many dream they have this when indeed they have nought but the shell. How few can say in truth, I have denied this or that commodity, and refused my profit for Christ's sake! Those that have done this, let them know they have a most rich gain, and the best gain of all others. They have a universal gain, that will comfort at all times. Riches and honours cannot cure the troubled mind; neither can they deliver in the day of wrath.

Then, in the *next* place, let them know they have an everlasting gain, that will comfort us for ever and ever. In the *last* place, *such as have won Christ, they have such a gain as makes them that have him truly rich, and noble, and good.* Other riches without grace do corrupt us. The image of God is the true and intrinsecal worth. Let this encourage us to labour to get Christ, to attend the means that lay his riches open; and thereby shall our love be so stirred up, and our judgment so sanctified, as we shall be of St Paul's mind, to account all other things loss in regard of him; and therefore it is no wonder that those that have not the benefit of the means want this esteem.

VERSE 9.

And be found in him.

Some read the words actively, that I may find Christ; but the phrase in the original varying from the former, therefore it is better translated as we have it, passively (*p*). But when is it that St Paul desireth to be found in Christ? Ever, no doubt, but especially at the hour of death and day of judgment.

The phrase implies, first, that there is an estate in Christ; secondly, an abiding in it; and thirdly, to be found abiding in him. For the handling whereof, we will first explain the phrase; secondly, we will shew what doctrines it doth clear; then we will come to some instructions arising therefrom. The phrase, 'to be in Christ,' is taken from plants which are grafted into stocks, or from the branches, which are said to be in the tree. Thus are we in the vine. It is Christ's own comparison. And of this union with Christ there are three degrees.

First, We are in Christ and in God, first loving us; and so we were in him before we were. He chose us from all eternity.

Secondly, When Christ died, then we were in him as a public person.

Thirdly, We are said most properly to be in him now when we believe in him; and thus principally is the sense understood in this place. And thus we are in Christ, not as the manhood is in Christ, but mystically; not as friends in one another by love, but by faith we are engrafted; as truly as the branches are in the vine, so are we one.

Obj. But Christ is in heaven, we are on earth; how can we be united to him that is so far distant from us?

Ans. I answer, If a tree did reach to heaven, and have its root in the earth, doth this hinder that the branches and the root are not united? In no wise. So Christ he is in heaven, and we on earth, yet are we united to him by his Spirit, and receiving influence from him of all grace and goodness.

Now let us see what doctrines are cleared hereby: first, it clears the point of *justification by Christ*. For if the question be, How we are saved by Christ's righteousness? I answer, Christ and we are both one. Doth not the eye see for the body? Are not the riches of the husband and wife all one? Yes. And even also whatsoever Christ hath is ours; he is our husband; he is our head. In the second place, it clears the *matter of the sacrament*. The papists would have the bread transubstantiated into the body of Christ, that it may be united to us. I answer, how is the foot in the head? Is it not by spiritual vigour passing to and fro through the body, but chiefly in the head. It is not therefore necessary that there should be any corporal union. Nay, Christ comforted his disciples more by his Spirit when he departed from them than he did by his corporal presence. We say also, that the mystical body of Christ is invisible, because the Spirit whereby we are made one is invisible.

This should comfort us at all times and in all estates. Before we were in Christ we were in an estate of horror, in an estate of damnation. Now to be reduced to Christ (what comfort is it to be one of a politic body? It is but for life. Or to be in any man's favour? It is but at will); this is a most excellent, glorious, and eternal being; that man's nature should be so highly advanced as to be united to the Godhead. Yea, our persons are mystically united to Christ. Secondly, *in all crosses or losses.* What though we lose other states, here is a state cannot be shaken. Thirdly, *in the hour of death we are in Christ;* and blessed are they that die in the Lord. Death, that separates the soul from the body, cannot separate either from Christ. Fourthly, *after death.* Can it go hard with me that am in Christ, that am his spouse? I am in him in whom is fulness of comfort. Fifthly, *in all wants here* I have him to supply all. He will give what is necessary. If we should have fulness of grace here we should not desire to be in heaven hereafter. Sixthly, in persecution all my hurt redounds to him: 'Saul, Saul, why persecutest thou me?' Acts ix. 4. That which thou dost to my members thou dost to me?

In the fourth place, Let us consider *how this being in Christ is a ground of doing of all duty.* I say therefore it will direct us in duties to God, towards men, and to ourselves.

First, In duties towards God, *how thankful ought we to be to him,* for taking us to himself, for being Immanuel, God with us, so that we are become bone of his bone. What need we now saints or angels to intercede for us? Who should Christ hear above his own flesh? For duties towards men, this ought to stir us to duties of peace and unity. Shall we be so unnatural as to fall out with the members of our own body? *Non est concors cum Christo ubi est discors cum Christiano.*

Secondly, It ought *to stir us up to duties of respect to each other,* considering they are members of Christ as we are, and shall so be found in him ere long.

Thirdly, This should *stir us up to charity to the poor members of Christ.* They being his members are fellow-members; and in loving them and doing them good, we shew our love to Christ himself.

And in the *last* place, Towards *ourselves, we are to carry ourselves with more respect,* and not to prostitute ourselves to every base pleasure. Consider in whom am I, and to what I am redeemed, and with what price? Shall I make my body the member of an harlot, who am the member of Christ? This pride and high esteem of ourselves above base pleasures and lusts, this is commendable; and therefore the apostle had good reason thus to account of these earthly things to be 'dross and dung.' In the second place, this will teach us *to see our residence in Christ, and growth in him;* for if we be in Christ, we will have an especial eye to our conversation, that we be not feet of iron and clay under a golden head, as many base licentious drunkards and filthy persons esteem of themselves. Will Christ own such members as these, think we? No. Those that are in Christ, Christ will be in them, discovering himself by ruling in them. His house is holy. If we be of his house, we will not desire, grieve, nor affect,* but by the sway of his Spirit.

In the last place, *How shall we come to be found in Christ?*

Ans. I answer, we must first come where he is. We shall find him in the temple, teaching and strengthening our faith and love; and so in our judgments and affections we shall be in him. Secondly, we must separate ourselves from the contrary to Christ, as a loyal wife will from all doubtful acquaintance. We must depart from antichrist, our own corruptions and lusts, and daily we must labour to get ground of them.

And from the words this we may learn: first, that *a Christian is con-*

* That is, 'love.'—G.

tinually under Christ's wing till he be in heaven, else how could the apostle desire to be found in him at the day of judgment?

Secondly, We learn *that there is such a time when God will, as it were with a candle, search men out, and lay them open as they are*. This is not thought upon. Men now shuffle it off, I shall be saved as well as any other, and this and that good company I am acquainted withal. Trust not, I say, to good acquaintance. There is a time of separation, when thou shalt be found out as thou art in thine own colours.

Thirdly, Hence we learn *that the foundation of future happiness must be laid now*. Before we can be with Christ in the kingdom of glory we must be his members in the kingdom of grace. Dost thou live therefore a corrupt and carnal life here? Never think to be found in him hereafter. And therefore let the uncertainty of this life be a spur to thee, to watch over thy ways, so as thou be such at this and all other times as you would be willing to be found at that day. Many boast hereof, but their lives savour nothing hereof, but are knit altogether to their lusts or to antichrist. Woe to such. They shall go on the left hand. But such as Christ finds in him it must needs go well with them. Christ will not judge them for whom he died, but shall set them on his right hand for evermore.

Not having mine own righteousness, which is of the law.

In these words, and those following, the apostle lays down summarily his desire, first, negatively in these words, he desired 'not to be found in Christ trusting to his own righteousness;' implying a difference and distinction between his righteousness by the law and that by Christ. The righteousness 'by the law' he disclaims as any way meritorious, and that as well habitual, wrought by God in him, or actual righteousness, consisting in the outward works that he did. And that with good reason; for, first, man's righteousness *is but finite*, and therefore unfit to work or deserve infinitely, and impossible to deserve heaven and the joys thereof. Secondly, This righteousness *is imperfect, and stained* as a 'menstruous cloth,' and unable to quiet or satisfy our own consciences, much less God who is greater than our own consciences. And therefore the saints prayed, 'Enter not into judgment with thy servants, Lord, for in thy sight shall no flesh be justified.' But the papists answer, the work of God is perfect; but our righteousness is the work of God, and therefore perfect. We say that the works of God are within us or without us. The works of God without us are perfect, but those that are within us are imperfect, still savouring of our pollution and corruption, by reason that the old man in us perverteth all that is good in us, and therefore *partus sequitur ventrem*.* Secondly, It is true that the works of God within us are so far perfect as tend to the end he works them for in us, but our righteousness was never ordained of God to that end as to save us by them, and therefore they cannot accomplish that end; but God works this righteousness in us to convince us of our own weakness, and to be a testimony of the presence of his Spirit in us. Paul therefore says not, I will not have mine own righteousness; but, 'I desire not to be found in my righteousness,' so as to merit salvation thereby.

But that which is through the faith of Christ, the righteousness which is of God by faith: that I may know him and the power of his resurrection.

That is, that righteousness which is in Christ, but laid hold on of me

* That is, 'the birth takes of the womb.' Cf. Ps. xli. 5.—G.

and apprehended by faith; and all that righteousness that he had, both active and passive obedience as Mediator, but especially his passive. For he was born, lived, and died for us; and this is that which St Paul desired to be 'found in,' and this is that which we must trust to.

But how can this righteousness, performed wholly by him, be mine?

I answer, By faith it is made ours; for if Christ be ours, all his righteousness must consequently be made ours.

But how can this righteousness performed by Christ be sufficient for us?

I answer, *First*, Because God ordained it to that purpose: 1 Cor. i. 30, 'Christ by God is made to us wisdom, righteousness, sanctification, and redemption;' and to this end God the Father sealed him,' John vi. 27.

Secondly, I say, Christ is a 'second Adam,' and a public person, and became ours, we then being in his loins; so the righteousness of Christ is made ours, we being born in Christ by faith and found in him. He being our head, we have a spiritual life descending upon us; he being our husband, all his goods are ours also. This point is the soul of the church, and the golden key which opens heaven for us. If we join any other thing to it, it opens hell to us, as God will reveal at that great day. It is true the papists do acknowledge now that their good works are not of themselves but from God; but thus did the Pharisee, 'he thanked God that he was not as other men, nor as the publican,' Luke xviii. 11. But the poor publican, disclaiming all such goodness, went away justified rather than the other. Let it be our wisdom therefore to rely only on Christ, whose obedience and righteousness is so all-sufficient as nothing may be added thereto, and say with the apostle, 'Not I, but the grace of God in me,' 1 Cor. xv. 10.

VERSE 10.

And the fellowship of his sufferings.

The apostle having shewed his desire of Christ's righteousness, now comes to shew his desire also of having communion with Christ in his sufferings; shewing that whosoever brags of justification, he must shew it in his sanctification. He must shew that he hath his part in the fellowship of his sufferings, if he meaneth to shew he hath his part in the power of his resurrection. Water is not alone, but water and blood must go together. Now Christ's sufferings are either for us as Mediator, or with us as being our head, and we his members. As Mediator he suffered death, which was only for our good. We can have no trust in our death as to deserve anything thereby as he did; for by his death he appeased God's wrath, and got his favour to us which we lost, and by it he sanctifies our sufferings and pulls out the sting of all our afflictions; as it is with the unicorn, who having put his horn into the water, discharges all poison thereout, so as the beasts may freely drink without hurt (*q*). So it is with us: we may suffer and endure afflictions without hurt, seeing Christ hath purged them of all poisonous nature that was in them.

But there are other sufferings that we and Christ suffer jointly, he as our head suffering with us his members; for as if the foot be grieved the head is grieved, so the Christian's sufferings are called Christ's sufferings, and a Christian must look to suffer if he be a lively member of the body of Christ. Yet is not every suffering of affliction Christ's suffering, for a man may suffer justly for his deserts. Notwithstanding even then, when a man suffers for his faults, after repentance Christ may be said to suffer with him; and therefore the fathers called the death of the repentant thief a martyrdom. For in all our sufferings Christ is in us, teaching and helping us to bear them with patience, and as a sanctifier of all of them to a blessed end, and as one that frames us to bear all of them, even as he himself did.

Use 1. This ought to teach us *to conceive aright of the estate of a Christian*, that he is not alone when he seems to be alone. Christ leaves them not in misery. No. For in misery he is most near and present. It is therefore a good estate, though misery in itself be not desirable, for Christ desired to die and not to die, and so we in several respects may do. For if we regard death as a destroyer of nature, so is it not to be desired; but considering it as the will of God my Father, so are we to desire it and yield ourselves to it. And accordingly we desire not afflictions for their proper natural good, yet in regard they are a means to prepare and fit us for heaven, we say with David, 'It is good for us to be afflicted,' Ps. cxix .67.

Use 2. In the second place, this will teach us *that we are not to fear anything that we shall suffer*, because there are more with us than against us. Joseph in the dungeon, Israel in Egypt, Daniel among the lions, the three children in the fire, Paul in prison, feared not danger; for what cared they so long as they knew God was with them; and therefore they rejoiced. If we have Christ we have all, if we want Christ we want all.

Use 3. Thirdly, This may serve *to daunt Christ's enemies*. They cannot hurt the least of his little ones but they hurt him. 'Saul, why persecutest thou me?'

Use 4. Fourthly, This should teach us *to take part with God's children*. What though they suffer affliction. Moses chose the better part, that did choose to be with the afflicted people of God before the court of Pharaoh. Wicked men may bite and kick, but they can do no hurt, *lingua malorum est lima bonorum*.

Being made conformable to his death.

This conformity here meant is not in regard of the end, that as Christ died for sin so should we, but in the manner of suffering. As he did suffer and die, so must we suffer and desire death. Secondly, As he died patiently and meekly, so must we suffer patiently and meekly. Thirdly, As he had, so must we have, sweet comforts to sustain and support us; and fourthly, As he had, so must we endeavour to obtain the same issue of our affliction; that is, eternal glory. Briefly, We are to be conformable to Christ in grace, in suffering, and in glory. All these are inevitably linked together, and our head having led us an example, we are to follow. Every Christian must therefore die to sin, as Christ died for sin.

But how shall we know whether we die to sin or not?

A dead man does no harm, hath no power; contrarily, are we strong to commit sin, and do we earnestly intend* it? Surely we are not mortified. Secondly, Dead men's senses are not delighted with fair and sinful objects. If we be dead with Christ, let the sinful objects be never so delightful, they will not move us or affect us one whit; nay, they will be distasteful to us. Most are of a contrary mind. Offer them good discourse and occasions, they cannot away with them; offer any fleshly pleasure: like tinder, they are soon set on fire. Such as these, as they have no heart to suffer for

* That is, = follow after it, 'stretch toward it.'—G.

righteousness, so if for vain glory they would, neither would God honour them so much as to suffer them. For grounds of this doctrine.

First, It is *honourable to be like Christ our captain*, our head, our husband.

Secondly, It is *not proportionable for the head to be crowned with thorns, and the members to be clad delicately;* that the natural son, in whom there is no blemish, should suffer, and the adopted sons, who are the causes of all offence, should go free. It is equity, that we having taken Christ for our husband, he should be accompanied by us in sickness and in health, in dishonour as in honour.

Thirdly, *It is long ago decreed of God, aud predestinated*, and therefore cannot be avoided. Rom. viii. 7, 9, 'Whom he did foreknow, them he predestinated to be conformed to the image of his Son.'

Fourthly, *It is equal*, that if he were conformed to us, we should be conformable to him. Now he was conformed to us, in that he suffered that which we should have suffered, and did that for us which we were to do and could not. He having drunk deep of the cup prepared for us, let us therefore, at the least, taste of it. Yea, let us suffer anything with an undaunted courage when we are called thereto for Christ. He will come with comforts, he is not empty, he will make us like him, he will prepare us hereby for glory. Fear not, therefore. God will turn all thy troubles to thy good. And thus we do fill up the measures of the afflictions of Christ in our flesh, Col. i. 24. And are made partakers of Christ's sufferings, 1 Peter. iv. 13. We have the like exhortations hereunto, 1 Peter ii. 21; 1 Peter iii. 14–18. Thus did Paul, 2 Cor. iv. 10, he carried the dying of Christ about with him. Let no Christian therefore promise to himself immunity from crosses. He that will be a Christian must be conformable to Christ, and he that will be like to him in glory, he must be like to him in drinking the cup he drank of while he was here in the flesh.

VERSE 11.

If by any means I might attain to the resurrection of the dead.

By 'resurrection of the dead,' he means the glorious estate after this life, whereas* the resurrection is but the beginning; and the words sound as much in effect as if the apostle had said, I know I shall be happy at length, but between this time and that, I know I shall meet with troubles, with many crosses; yet let the way be never so difficult, I pass† not by any means to come to such an excellent end as the resurrection of the dead is; in which words we will,

First, Consider *that there is a happy estate reserved hereafter*, which begins with the resurrection of the body, whereby we are far more happy than the angels that fell, and also more happy than we were in our first estate in Adam, which we lost; and therefore our hearts should be enlarged with thanks to God, that respects us above the angels, whom he hath left without hope of recovery.

2. In the next place, consider that *the beginning of our blessed estate hereafter is at the resurrection*, which is called the day of restoring of all things, and a time of refreshing, Acts iii. 19. It is a day when all good shall be perfected, and all evil shall cease; all grief of mind, all trouble of body, and death itself, shall be swallowed up into victory.

Quest. But why are we not happy before our resurrection?

Ans. I answer, because our bodies and souls are partakers of misery and

* Qu. 'whereof'?—ED.

† That is, 'value.'—G.

sin here, and therefore cannot partake of fulness of happiness before they be united together again. God will have us to stay while all his family of blessed saints shall meet together, as well us that are now alive as our seed and posterity after us.

3. In the third place observe, that the apostle makes resurrection of the dead the last thing; *establishing thereby an order*, that there must be means to the resurrection, and then the resurrection itself. 'Ought not Christ to suffer these things, and so to enter into his glory?' Luke xxiv. 26. And if we suffer with him, we shall also reign with him, 2 Tim. ii. 12. The second resurrection must begin with the first. We are sons and saints hereafter, but so we must also be here; only a difference there will be in degree of holiness. This resurrection doth not follow every manner of life, although men ordinarily expect a crown without crosses, and never look for justification and sanctification, but think they shall be in heaven at an instant without them. But we must suffer with Christ in mount Calvary, before we come with him to the mount Olivet.

4. In the fourth place, we may likewise note, that *it is hard to come to heaven*, because of this order established by God: not in comparison of the end—for that surmounteth in excellency the hardness of the means,—but in respect of the means; some by fair death, with many crosses in their life; some not by many outward crosses, yet have store of inward troubles of the mind, by reason of their inward corruption that doth trouble them; others by violent deaths and by martyrdom. The ways are so many, and the means so diverse, as there is no certainty which way we shall pass. As St Paul knew not the means, so he cared not what the means were; for he was content to go thither by any means. Let the cup of affliction be never so bitter, the glory ensuing will sweeten all.

1. Away, therefore, with all idle and secure thoughts *of sparing ourselves.* 'Pity thyself,' said Peter to Christ; but was answered sharply, 'Get thee behind me, Satan,' Mat. xvi. 23.* No; the way is very hard. We must come to health by physic. The end is so amiable, as it will sweeten all sour means; and therefore it is good for us to be afflicted. Crosses bring at length the sweetest comforts. Deny we ourselves, therefore, in Christ's cause; know nobody; look upon God and Christ's promises, and promise we ourselves no more than God promises. It is beyond our knowledge what God will do with us. He promises no immunity from crosses.

Nay, the saints and the apostles chose crosses and afflictions, rather than the pleasures of sin, who were wise, and had trial of both kinds; and yet accounts these momentary afflictions not worthy of comparison with the glory that shall be revealed. They were but light, 2 Cor. iv. 17; Rom. viii. 18. And if we would truly believe this, it would be easy for us to be resolved, as St Paul was, to come to heaven by all assurances, and to come to all manner of assurances, by any means; for no worldly thing can bring content like these heavenly assurances of the presence of the light of God's love, which the children of God will by no means lose.

2. Secondly, *In all crosses let us not look into the state we are in, so much as that we are going into.* We are going to a palace: let us not be dejected in the consideration of the narrowness of the way that leadeth thereto. God will not suffer this fiery trial to consume anything but dross; and therefore, let us with Christ suffer the cross, and despise the shame, Heb. xii. 2.

3. Thirdly, *Labour for a right esteem of the things of this world.* They are but momentary and fading; yea, our lives they are given to us by God.

* Cf. Note *g*, Vol. II. page 194.—G.

What if we part with them? If it be for his cause, he will bring us to a better life which shall not be taken away from us, and this life we must part with ere long. And thus we ought to work on ourselves, by often meditating of them, as the saints have done.

4. In the fourth place, *We are to labour to strengthen three graces in us especially: faith,* to assure us that we are the children of God, and that we have heaven, and all things belonging thereto, laid up for us; and we are to labour to see more and more into the value of them. And then we are to strengthen our *hope,* which makes us cheerfully to undergo and do anything for God's cause, through our expectation of that which faith believes. Lastly, let us cherish our *love of Christ.* This made St Paul desire to be dissolved, and to be with Christ, which was best of all, Philip. i. 23.* And this love comes from faith and hope; and these together will breed a largeness of heart that cares for no worldly thing, and will be daunted with no affliction or crosses whatever.

But how far are we herefrom? Did St Paul part with life? It pertains not to us. No; not to leave a new-fangled fashion, nor an oath whereby we tear God's name daily. Alas, where is faith? What corruption is here overcome? Which of us will ever be of Paul or David's mind, to become vile or base for God's cause?† Where is he that will endure a scoff or scorn for religion? Let us beg of God this large spirit and large affections. The children of heaven have a free spirit, basely esteeming all worldly things. Zaccheus, when he is called, cares not for his goods, nor Paul for his privileges. The Stoics commend this resolution in men, to be willing and ready to die. Alas! crosses and afflictions Paul esteemed not, so as he might attain to the resurrection of the dead. These are the things that the Stoics feared most; and it was the fear of these made them so willing and ready to die, together with a base servitude to pride. But a Christian heart is more noble. It not only fears not these, but it contemns them. Yea, cares not for life without afflictions, but with joy can undergo all manner of torments.

Let us therefore take heed how we quiet ourselves in our earthly dwellings here, supposing our estate to be happy. Surely it is the main ground of apostasy. We shall never come to see the price of religion, nor the excellency of a peaceable conscience, nor the vanity of these things, so long as we bless ourselves in them. And contrarily, *let us exercise our graces in the daily trials we meet with here.* Doth favour of great men, doth pleasure, profit, or honour, cross and oppose thy conscience? Let the peace thereof be preferred above all evermore, else shalt thou never come to Paul's holy resolution. And dream not of a vain, empty faith. Thou hast no more than thou dost practise. It is not 'Lord, Lord,' that will prevail at the day of judgment; but Christ will be ashamed of them at the day of judgment, that made no more account of him while they lived, than to prefer every vain, idle, wanton delight and pleasure before his honour.

VERSE 12.

Not as though I had already attained, either were already perfect.

It is a correction of the apostle. He formerly spake of his desire, choice, and esteem of Christ's death and resurrection, and the force thereof he found in him. Now, lest secret, insinuating, proud conceits might arise, either in himself or in them, concerning his holiness, he crosses them with

* The original is, 'πολλῷ γὰρ μᾶλλον κρεῖσσον' = 'for it is very far better.'—G.
† Cf. 2 Sam. vi. 22; Mat. v. 11, 12; Acts v. 41, 42; Heb. xii. 2; 1 Pet. iv. 14.—G.

a 'not as,' shewing that the best estate of God's children in this world is imperfect. There is ever something to do or suffer; some lust to conquer, or some grace to strengthen.

There is no absolute perfection but only in God himself; yet in Christians there is a kind of derivative spiritual perfection, which consisteth chiefly in the parts. A Christian hath this perfection. He hath all grace in some measure. We have no other perfection; no, not so much as *perfectio viæ*, though the papists say they have it. Indeed, we are so far from it, that never could Christian keep the rules of nature, much less can we attain to the perfection of obedience to the law, for by it we are all cursed. Nay, in Christ none attains to evangelical perfection of grace, so as thereby we can be justified, as by a work of our own; for our righteousness is but in part; and this *perfectio viæ*, which they boast of so much, differs not from their *perfectio finis*, no more than love to a man raised by good report of him differeth from love caused by the good I find in him, by personal communicating with him; and this is only in degrees in nature. They are the same love.

But why or how is it that there is no perfection of grace in this life?

Because *there is and ever shall be in us, during this life, a perpetual combat between the flesh and spirit*, so as one weakens and hinders the other. Paul at the best found a law in his members warring against the law of his mind, Rom. vii. 23; the flesh continually lusting against the spirit, Gal. v. 24, hindering us from doing good, or in doing good, or in doing thereof, from doing it in a right manner.

Obj. 1. But the papists object, Love is the fulfilling of the law. We may love; *ergo*, we may fulfil the law, and consequently be perfect.

I answer, Love in the abstract being perfect, is the fulfilling of the law, but in this or that subject it is not perfect. Paul's love, nor Peter's love, was not the fulfilling of the law.

Obj. 2. They urge further, All God's works are perfect; *ergo*, the grace that is in us.

It is true God's works are perfect, but in their times when they are finished; grace at length shall be perfect in us.

Secondly, All God's works without us are perfect, as justification and glorification they are perfect. For we are perfectly justified even now; but his works within us, such as are his sanctifying graces, are not perfected till our time of glorification. For he suffers the old Adam to be within us, for divers reasons, so long as we live in this earthly tabernacle.

For use hereof, *observe this as a ground for justification by faith.* Paul, Rom. v. 9, proves that even now he was justified, and in this place he denies and disclaims absolute perfection, and therefore could not be justified by it; and therefore must needs be justified by faith. If it were his case it is much more ours, who come not to that measure of the fulness of grace that he attained to.

Secondly, This may serve *to comfort Christians that find themselves burdened with divers wants*, with dulness and frowardness of spirit, and with manifold corruptions, and are induced thereby to call in question their Christian estate. Let them look upon a better pattern than themselves. They may be grown Christians, and yet complain with Paul of corruptions. Nay, the most strong Christians see most deeply and clearly into their corruptions, and find most opposition. There is in all men by nature a spring of popery. They would fain deserve heaven by a perfect and holy life, without blot; and God, to humble them, suffers corruptions to check them and to keep them under, who else would be lifted up through good conceit and esteem ot themselves.

Thirdly, It may serve as a caution to many who, being *reproved justly for their faults, What! say they, we are not angels;* you have your own imperfections as well as I. And stir them up to any good duty, they are presently so good, as those that are better than they are too precise and too nice. St Paul contrarily rests in no degree of goodness, but strives on to perfection; and it is the devil's sophistry to turn that to a plea for negligence, which should stir us up to be more diligent, watchful, and careful.

But I follow after, if that I may apprehend that for which I also am apprehended of Christ Jesus.

The word that is translated 'I follow after,' signifies properly to labour with earnest intention of the heart and affections; and the lesson that we may hence learn is, *that the life of a Christian is a laborious and painful life.* For in what proportion the things we labour for are more excellent than these worldly things, so much greater our desire and labour should be in the obtaining of them than in the obtaining this world's goods. And to this end the Scripture ever enforceth this duty with words suitable to work: 'Labour for the meat that perisheth not,' John vi. 27; 'Strive to enter in at the strait gate,' Luke xiii. 24; 'Give all diligence to make your calling and election sure,' 2 Pet. i. 10.

Those that will take no pains, it is a sure sign they find no sweetness in the thing; and therefore in such there can be no true goodness. And hence we may observe a difference between the desires of men. Some are effectual, some ineffectual. Those that are ineffectual commonly desire and delight in the thing they desire, but will none of the means: 'Let me die the death of the righteous,' says the wicked man, Num. xxiii. 10. Glory and happiness is excellent, but the gate is narrow, the way is tedious and full of troubles: he will none of that. We will laugh at one that shall wish his work and journey were done, whenas he will sit down and never go about it. Why should we not much more laugh at such sluggards, that wish daily, Oh that they might be saved! whenas they do not only not further, but hinder their salvation. But where true desire of grace is, there will be joined thereto an endeavour, with jealousy over our corruptions, with grief and shame for them, and for our backwardness and want of goodness; for else hell itself is full of good wishes and desires. If we mean to be better, we must use all means, undertake all pains, and travail with vehemency; even as those that pursue gains with delight, they follow through thick and thin, especially if the gain be in the eye; and those that go for company, they are soon tired. And thus did Paul. He went through fire and water, through all manner of dangers, good and ill report. His gain is still in his eye. He looks not after the way, if by any means he may attain his desired mark.

But how shall we come to this grace?

I answer, *Get first faith;* for by it the weak are made strong, Heb. xi. 35, *seq.* Get assurance that heaven is thine; and God hath promised thee grace sufficient, and this is Paul's argument: 'Be ye constant and unmoveable, always abounding in the work of the Lord, knowing your labour shall not be in vain.' Where hope of reward is in the use of the means, it will stir us up to a constant use of the means, 1 Cor. xv. 58. Secondly, *Get a fervent love:* for it is a strong affection. If lust so prevail with us, as we will omit no means to accomplish it, then a love in itself is much more powerful, nothing being too hard for it. It hath an enlarging, knitting, and communicating power. It makes a man bestow all, and rejoice more in doing good by much than in receiving. It is a grace comprehends a number under it; and therefore Christ comprehended all the law under the love of God and our neighbour. Thirdly, *Cut off all superfluities.* Men think they are happy when they have much to do, when indeed they were happy if they had less to do than they have. Satan he does as Cyrus did with the waters of Babylon; he diverts and separates our affections that he might pass over (*r*). As nurses, they hurt themselves and the children too when they keep over many; so do men hurt themselves with over much business. The Lord hath not made us all for the world, but hath reserved one day in seven for his service. For shame let us shew we have some respect of religion and goodness; seeing God requires but one in seven, let us not be so unjust as to deny him his service on that day.

Use. Well, let those that profess themselves of another world, by all means pursue it. In nature every thing tends to his centre and place; heavy things go downward, light things ascend upward. In handicrafts and arts every one looks after excellency. Shall it be thus with them? Shall mediocrity in other arts merit dispraise, and is it only praiseworthy in religion? The wicked they labour for hell, venturing loss of credit, strength, and estate; and is there not better gain in goodness? Have we such rich promises, and do we esteem of them no more? Are not the afflictions we shall meet with many and great, and do we think to undergo them with ordinary grace, gotten without labour and watchfulness? But let us go on to the next words:

'That I may apprehend.' Whence we may observe, *that the main scope of a Christian is to apprehend Christ:* here by revelation, that we may apprehend him hereafter by vision. Many there are that may follow good things and use good means, yet wanting these apprehending graces of faith and love (which makes us have communion with Christ), they perish notwithstanding. Human knowledge is commendable, yet is it no other than as a scaffold in this building. It helps, but the building once done, it is for little use. Apprehend we, therefore, him by knowledge of his truth, rely on him by faith, and embrace him by love; and then if we be chased by him, we may, as Joab, lay hold on the horns of the altar Christ Jesus, and there live and die, 1 Kings i. 50. And as we have daily breaches, even so get more and more hold on him, and this will make us desire with Simeon, 'Lord, let me now depart in peace, for mine eyes have seen thy salvation,' Luke ii. 29. Let us, therefore, daily learn to see our own foulness, and go to him the rock of our refuge.

Obj. Oh, but some will say, Christ is in heaven, and we on earth, we cannot go to him when we please.

Ans. I answer, Yes; for the arms of faith are large. It takes hold of things past and to come. No height is out of the reach thereof. And, besides, Christ he is present with us. He is in his word, in the sacraments, in the communion of saints. 'Where two or three are gathered together in my name, I will be in the midst of them,' Mat. xviii. 20. It is his own promise.

'For which I am apprehended of Christ.' Christ he apprehends us, and that in several degrees.

First, *As he is God.* In his eternal love we had a being before we had any being here. God conceived us in his eternal affection, and embraced us. Secondly, Christ apprehends us *in his effectual calling of us.* Paul he was posting another way when Christ called him, 'Saul, Saul.' Others he calls from their mother's womb; some by afflictions and powerful crosses, as he did the jailor; others by more gentle means, as Lydia. Thirdly, There is an apprehending *in all our actions, courses, and estates,* directing us continually in them, never leaving us. None can pluck us out of his hands. He is stronger than our corruptions. He will not let us go till he hath drawn us up to heaven, and placed us with himself. For the use of this doctrine more shall be said in the next doctrine, which is taken from the order.

Doct. Christ he first apprehends us when we apprehend him. He apprehends us that we may apprehend him, and because he hath apprehended us, therefore is it that we apprehend him. For 'in him it is that we live, and move, and have our being,' Acts xvii. 28; and therefore much more our best being. He it is that gives us the will and the deed; to us it is given by him to believe and suffer with him.

Use 1. For use hereof it would teach us *in all our actions to beg ability and strength of him,* and get a persuasion that his Spirit doth apprehend us in love; and that he will direct us and remove all impediments, and stand by us in all our crosses, that we are able to do nothing but by reflection from him; that though we are naturally dead and dull, yet he will quicken us by shining on our hearts with the sunshine of his grace.

Use 2. Secondly, *Give him the praise of all the good thou doest, for the deed is his.* Those that do not, do apprehend and are apprehended of themselves; and therefore it may serve as a mark to discern of our estate, whither do we run? and what do we apprehend in our trouble? Is it Christ who is our present help in time of trouble? Then there is a blessed change in us. But do we seek to our own devices, to our own policies and inventions? Surely we have not apprehended Christ as we ought to do; and therefore we are to stir up the graces in us, and beg increase of grace from him that is the fountain of all grace.

Use 3. In the next place, it should *comfort us, by the consideration of the certainty of our estate, without falling away, if we hold fast unto the end.* If it were ourselves that did apprehend us we could not long continue, but it being Christ that holdeth us, our comfort is he will not forsake us. It is the mother that holds the child. The child cannot lay hold on the mother, but is subject to falling every hour. Christ he holding us, hath promised to love us to the end, and to put his fear in our hearts, that we shall not fall or depart from him. This being daily considered will greatly comfort a weak Christian. Christ may seem to let him fall, by suffering him to fall into some great sin, but it is only to humble him, and to teach him not to trust to his own strength, which will soon fail him, but upon his mercy and grace. And therefore,

Use 4. In the next place, it teacheth us *to hold fast unto him, and rely on him, and to pray to him that he would hold us fast,* and then we fall not from God, but to God. He hath delivered us, and will deliver us and keep us to his heavenly kingdom. If we fall into sin, let us repent and go to God. There is mercy in Israel concerning this, and with him is plenteous redemption. His right hand is under us ever to hold us up, that we cannot fall so deeply but he will lift us up again.

Use 5. In the next place, *this may be a comfort to us in all our troubles and afflictions of this life.* Are troubles near? God is not far off, Ps. xxii. 11, *seq.*, and Ps. cxviii. 5, *seq.*, but full of comforts for such. We have an invisible wall about us, the wall of angels; and God fights for us. There is more with us than against us. God will not suffer us to be tried above that we are able to bear. Let us therefore pray, Forsake me not, Lord, lest I forsake thee. If we pray to him he will be found of us. Paul prayed for this. Christ also, that knew he was apprehended, yet prayed all night; and this are we to do; he hath promised to hear us. And therefore let us go in faith and assurance to him, in all our troubles.

VERSE 13.

Brethren, I count not myself to have apprehended.

The holy apostle dwells upon the point, that he might press it the more; and it is good to press matter of weight. The apostle shewing that conceit of perfection to be dangerous, again tells the Philippians, that he had not that which they boasted of. This pride of ourselves, and conceit, is a sin that climbs up to heaven, and enters on God's prerogative, and a sin that God doth directly set himself against. Of this compellation, 'brethren,' I have formerly spoken.

I might also touch that doctrine, that *the kingdom of heaven is not perfected in us here, but that it grows by degrees.* It is at the first as a grain of mustard seed. There are babes in Christianity, and old men grown Christians. And the ground hereof may be partly in the subject, partly in the object.

In regard of the subject, for that graces are imperfect in us, the more the soul hath, the more it desires.

In regard of the object, for that Christ is so full, that we are not able to receive all his fulness, so as there is imperfection in us, and superabundant perfection in him. Paul had a large affection, yet came far short. This possibility of the soul to receive more will be in us, till we be in heaven, where we shall be full; and therefore while we are here, we pray still, 'Thy will be done on earth as it is in heaven,' and 'Thy kingdom come,' more and more. It is a strange conceit, therefore, for any to think he may be too good; yet do these daily, or should do, pray for more and more perfection here on earth, although they say they know not what. And another reason why we apprehend Christ not so fully here as we shall do hereafter, is, because the manner of making Christ known to us is by revelation, 1 Cor. xiii. 12, *seq.* We behold him here but as it were in a glass; in the glass of his word and sacraments, which cannot represent him to our understanding so clearly, as hereafter we shall behold him in the beatifical vision.

Take heed therefore of a self-conceit of perfection. When we begin to be unwilling to grow better, we begin to wax worse. There is no stay in Christianity. It is the sight of our imperfection that makes us strive to perfection, and the more we see into our misery, the more earnestly we strive on to be freed from it.

But this one thing I do, forgetting those things which are behind, and reaching forth to those things that are before.

See what is the apostle's *unum necessarium,* to grow more and more to the fulness of the knowledge of Christ. All other things he counts as 'dung and loss.' So as we may hence observe, *that the Spirit of God in a Christian heart, subjects all things to one Christ.*

'One thing have I desired of the Lord,' said David, Ps. xxvii. 4; make this therefore a rule to difference our estates by. What is the thing we intend chiefly? Is it riches, or pleasures, or honours? This one thing will be the utter overthrow of all religion in us. Christ will be supreme, or he will not be. 'He that loves father or mother more than me, is not worthy of me,' saith Christ of himself, Mat. x. 37. There is none so wicked but would be religious, till religion comes to cross that one thing, their darling sin. And thus have they base limitations, which must needs prejudice their growth in religion; for where religion is, it will cross their base affections and lusts.

Therefore, whosoever we are that intend to be true Christians indeed, resolve first to prefer the peace of conscience and the fruit of religion above all; and resolve to abhor all things that will cross this one thing of St Paul.

VERSE 14.

I press towards the mark.

Behold an excellent description of a Christian course, borrowed from the exercise of running a race, being a manlike and commendable exercise, fitting men and enabling them for war. The very heathen herein condemns us, whose ordinary chief exercises, what are they but good company, as we call them, continual lying at taverns, to the impoverishing of our estates and weakening our bodies? The kind I condemn not, but the excess is such, as the heathen would be ashamed of; for which they shall even rise up in judgment against us, and condemn us.

But from the simile, we may gather thus much, *that Christianity is a race*. The beginning of this race is at the beginning of our conversion. It should begin at our baptism. The first thing we should know ought to be God. The race is the performance of good duties, concerning our general calling, and concerning our particular. For the length of our races, some are longer, some shorter, but the end of every man's race is the end of his life. Some men's ways are plainer, some rougher. The prize is fulness of joy. The lookers on are heaven, earth, and hell. God is the instituter of this race, and the rewarder. The helpers are Christ, good angels, and the church, which helps by prayer. The hinderers are the devil and his instruments, who hinder us by slanders, persecutions, and the like. For ground of this race in us, we are to know that man is created with understanding, directing him to do things to a good end and scope. Other creatures are carried to their end, as the shaft out of a bow, only man foreseeing his end, apprehends means thereto. His end is to receive reconciliation and union with God, to which he aims by doing some things, suffering others, and resisting others.

And this race is also ordered by laws; for every runner is not crowned. There is a running ill that shall never procure the prize. The laws hereof concern either preparation, or the action itself. For preparation,

1*st Direct.* First we are to know, that *there is a dieting requisite*. As those that ran in a race had a care hereof, to use such diet as did strengthen, not cloy, and such apparel as might cover them, not clog them; so ought it to be in our spiritual race, we must cast aside all heavy loads, every weight and sin which doth so easily beset us, as it is Heb. xii. 1. If God cast on us any place or riches, let us use them for a good end, but not make them our end; and therefore with them take up daily examination of ourselves, how we behave ourselves towards these worldly things. It were a madness in a runner, in his race, to take up a burden, and not to think it will be a sore trouble to him; and why do we not think thus in our spiritual race? Cast we off therefore original corruption, and the corruption of our place, time, and calling, which in time will grow unsupportable to us. Let us desire no more than God gives; and what afflictions God sends us, let us take, assuring ourselves they are for our good.

2d *Direct.* A second law is, *to consider the ways that we are to run in*, what dangers we are like to meet with. Forecast and resolve against the worst, and withal promise we ourselves God's assured protection in our worst estate. The want of this is the seminary and ground of all apostasy; when men promise to themselves in Christianity such things as God never promised. Christ therefore promiseth and sheweth the worst first. But the devil, to deceive us, keeps the worst out of our eyes, and shews a sort of vain delights and pleasures. But the sting of them, through his subtilty and craft, he suffers us to feel before we see it.

3d *Direct.* A third law is, that *we enter the race betimes.* It is the devil's trick to put off the care of this, telling us we need not yet enter; we are but young, and have many years to live, as they did that hindered the building of the temple. But consider we the uncertainty of life, that we may die suddenly, and that it is just with God to take us away after that manner, if we neglect ourselves and him. And we must know also we shall lose no pleasure nor delight, but we shall find such sweet delights in those ways as we shall with St Augustine be grieved that we enjoyed them no sooner.* And besides, those that begin betimes get a great advantage of others, and through continual custom come at length to a habit of religion.

In the next place, we are to take heed of hindrances of us in our preparation; as,

1*st Hindrance.* First of all, *hope of long life*, whereby we are besotted, thinking life and death is in our command, that we shall have time enough, and need not so soon enter upon good duties.

2*d Hindrance.* Secondly, *A conceit that when we have once given up our names to Christ, that presently we bid adieu to all delight, mirth, and pleasure;* when, alas! we are far deceived. God denies not pleasure to us, but will give us whatsoever is good for us. We shall delight and rejoice, but with a joy spiritual; and we shall see nothing in this world that may any way deserve our delight therein.

3*d Hindrance.* A third hindrance *is a despair of ever going through this race.* This settles upon some, strangely making them cast away all care, and desperately trust to Christ's mercy. This made Cyprian to complain of his corruptions, saying they were bred and brought up with him; and therefore feared they would hardly give place to grace, being but a stranger (*s*). While men consider how great and powerful their corruption is, they with the Israelites despair of ever entering into the land of Canaan—these sons of Anak do so terrify them.

But consider we withal that God is above all our corruptions; that he can make of a lion a lamb; and that if we will trust upon him, in his time he will help us, and we shall overcome these giant-like corruptions. Christ he hath conquered them already; and though while we live we cannot wholly overcome them, yet David's house shall grow stronger and stronger, and Saul's house weaker, 2 Sam. iii. 1. We shall have grace sufficient for us. God will sweeten religion to us, that we shall delight therein; and Christ will not lead us into temptation till he hath fitted us to it by his grace, and then we shall rejoice, as the apostles did, Acts v. 41, that we are accounted worthy to suffer.

* The reference is to Augustine's pathetic plaint, elsewhere quoted by Sibbes, 'Too long, Lord, have I wanted thy goodness.'—G.

Contrary to this humour, some think it so easy a matter to run this race, as they think they cannot be out of it or tired therein, whenas indeed they never yet set foot therein. Let such look to themselves if they be in this race, they shall find it no easy matter.

But thus much concerning rules or laws for preparation to this race. Now there are laws to be observed of those that are in the race; as,

Direct. 1. First, They *must resolve to hold on, without discontinuance of their course of good duties;* for some, by omitting good duties now and then upon slight occasions, do come, through God's just sufferance, to leave them off and never take them up again; and thereby, while they are not getting ground by continuing their course, they do lose thereby. Even as watermen rowing against the stream, if they do not row, but rest never so little, the stream carries them back again, and they cannot recover themselves but with great difficulty; so it is in this Christian race. A little interruption of duty causes thrice so much pains to recover our former estate. Therefore we are to take up a holy resolution not to be interrupted in good duties.

2. The next law is, *that we must look to gain ground still, to grow from grace to grace.* It is the apostle's aim still to grow better than himself. Contrary to this many forsake their first love. They think themselves wise, but are fools, such as the Lord will spew out of his mouth, as he threatens the Church of Laodicea, Rev. iii. 16. And indeed the most men at the best are but civil; and do but provide for their own ease, and can endure any mixture of religion or company; and the ground of this coldness is a self-conceit, whereby men think well of themselves and their estate. Paul, he was of another spirit, ever pressing forward.

3. A third law is, *that we do things with all our might;* that we run this race with all our earnest endeavour. There is no bodily exercise that profiteth, but it must be with putting forth of our strength. So our Christian actions should shew even outwardly, that we do things as if we intended thereby to honour God indeed; and to this end we are to depend on God by prayer, that he would give us strength and minds to put forth our strength for gaining most honour to his Majesty, and this will bring great assurance and comfort to us in time of need.

4. A fourth rule is, that *we are to run this race with a cheerful and speedy course.* A dead performance of duties is no part of our race. Yea, as many go to hell by ill performance of good duties, as by committing sins that are scandalously evil; for this resting in the work done is the cause of hardness of heart, and thereby of despair; and at the best never brings any sound comfort at all to us. And therefore we are enjoined to do good duties, and to do them in a good manner. 'Let a man examine himself, and so let him eat of this bread, and drink of this cup,' 1 Cor. xi. 28; and 'so run that you may obtain,' 1 Cor. ix. 24. It is no lingering. We know not how long we shall live, how soon we shall die; and therefore let us make haste to do our work before God takes away time from us, by taking us out of the world. And those especially are to look to this, that have lived long in their own courses, and are but lately reclaimed. They are much behind, and had need make haste. The journey is long, their time but short. And to this end look we not what we have done, and how far we have gone, but look what remains to be done, and know we have done nothing till we have done all.

Quest. But it will be asked, What! may we not think of duties that are past?

Ans. I answer, We may think of them by way of defence, and to give

God the glory, and also to encourage us on, but not to rest or solace ourselves on them till we have done all.

Quest. But men may say, What, is there no pause? is there no Sabbath?

Ans. I answer, Yes, when we are dead. 'Blessed are the dead in the Lord,' Rev. xiv. 13. It is they that *rest from their labours.* Heaven is a sufficient reward for all the pains we can any way take here. Besides, the comforts that we have here are many, which none knows but them that enjoy them. And God hath promised the continual assistance of his blessed Spirit, that shall encourage us and lead us into all truth. Alas! what comfort have we of all that we have done, if we continue not, but sit down and take up our rests here? What good got they that came out of Egypt and died in the wilderness, it may be even in the border of the land of promise, yet never saw it? It will assuredly fall out with us as it did with them, if we harbour any infidelity in our hearts. We shall be cast out, that we shall never see this good land, the spiritual Canaan.

In the next place, take we heed of such hindrances as may make us either slack or intermit this race of ours.

1. As first, *We must take heed of idle scruples and temptations.* These are no other than as dust cast in the eyes of the runners, and as stones that gall their feet. Interpret them to be the subtleties of the devil, and therefore shake them off, and intend* thy duty thou art about, and pray for wisdom to discern aright of things. Regard not the golden apples of the profits and pleasures of this life, that lie in thy way to divert thy steps,† and sweep off evermore the dirt of these worldly cares, which we gather in our race, and by little and little grow to clog us.

2. In the second place, *Beware of sins against conscience.* They take away joy, and make our hearts dead. There are many that seeing divers of their sins before them, concerning which they find no peace in themselves, are soon out of breath, and quite out of heart, and so by little and little run into despair, and without hope ever to attain the prize.

3. Thirdly, *Take we heed of ill and dull company,* that are cold in religion, that cannot away with good religious duties. For as it is in our ordinary travels, good company makes time and way pass away speedily and with comfort; so it is in this race, good and gracious company by exhortation and example do wonderfully encourage us; and ill company contrarily do dishearten us, dissuade us and clog us, and draw us back from every good duty we take in hand. But many men's conceits are, they need not all this ado; they are well enough, though they be not thus holy; all cannot come to the high pitch of mortification. Surely there is hardly any beginning of grace in such who allow themselves in a dead course; for where the love of God is, it will constrain men to shew their thankful and loving hearts to him, in walking before the Lord with all their might.

4. In the fourth place, *Take heed how we suffer our minds to wander in this race.* Let us not look at the lookers on. The world and the devil and wicked men, pass not for their censures. We may assure ourselves before we enter this race we shall have no applause from them. Let a slow dull jade come by, like dogs, they let him pass, none regards; but if another comes by apace, every man runs barking and slandering and backbiting after him; and if they can they will bite

* That is, = attend, be earnest in.—G.

† The allusion is to the legend of Atalanta, who being set to run in a race with her suitors, threw golden apples on the course, which they stopping to pick up, were conquered.—G.

too. Shall a man care for such as these? No. We must resolve beforehand to have the world, the devil, and all the enemies he can make to be against us. Let us, therefore, set our eyes only on him that has our reward in his hand, that observes us and is ready to crown us; and let us beg courage and strength from him, and spiritual wisdom how we should perform every action; with what intention or remission of heart and affection; how to sanctify his name in the performance of the duties of our callings; how to make every action, yea, our recreations, a furtherance in this our Christian race.

Secondly, *Let us daily search and try our hearts and ways.* See how we profit or go back, how we grow like or unlike Christ; particularly, examine we how the pomp of the world seems to us, whether base or contemptible? If so, then the further we are run in this Christian race. For as in objects of sight, the further we are from them the less they seem to us, and the nearer we are to them they appear the greater, so it is in the object of our minds. Doth heaven appear full and beautiful to us? It is a sign we are near to it, and we are come a good way in our race. But contrarily, if it be mean and of no esteem or account, it is far from us; we are at the most but coming towards it.

Secondly, *Examine what doth take up daily the powers of our souls and affections.* Do we delight in the best things, and with Mary choose 'the better part,' which shall not be taken away from us? Luke x. 42. Or contrarily, are our delights here below, and our rest set up here? Then we have our reward here, and the prize is not prepared for us, but God will spew us out for our coldness. And, therefore, if we find coldness creeping on us, let us take heed of it. It is a dangerous estate. God cannot endure it. For while we allow of good things, but shew not intension of spirit in the performance of them, we do even judge them, and tell the world they be things not worthy of our pains and endeavours. Let us, therefore, not allow of this coldness, though it be in us, but strive against it. Meditate of such things as may inflame us, and pray against it.

For the prize of the high calling of God in Christ Jesus.

'I press forth.' It is a word of vehemency, signifying to set forth his utmost bent and endeavour, both of the inward man and of the outward (*t*); and all is to heaven. So as a Christian's aim is always to Jerusalem, his looks is that way; his tongue speaks the language thereof; his carriage will tell he seeks another city, Heb. xi. 14. But for these words, observe there is first a 'prize.' Secondly, 'it is a prize of a calling.' Thirdly, this calling is 'high.' Fourthly, this calling we have here in part.

Concerning this word 'prize,' it is a metaphor taken from the reward of victory gotten in some exercise. *God hereby brings heaven down to us.* Because we cannot go to it, he insinuates into our affections by pleasing things, and teaches faith by sense.

Use 1. And therefore, we must *not rest in these borrowed words*, but ever know that the thing that is described goes beyond the description by any earthly similitude.

Doct. From the thing observe that *God hath reserved a happy estate for such Christians as are elected to run in this race*, that are fitted to it, and that are preserved to it.

Use 2. And this should teach us *to magnify God's goodness;* that whereas by nature death with his pale horse and hell should follow us, now the course is altered. A holy life in God's commandments is given to us here, and then glory shall be heaped upon us. God hath begotten us to a lively hope, but hath passed by the angels, and left them without hope of recovery.

Doct. Secondly, observe *this happy prize is to be given after running.* God keeps this order to exercise his graces in us, that we might be a means to gain others, and that we might value happiness the more. If we did not suffer here, we could not taste heaven so sweetly; after labour sleep and rest is sweet. And it is fitting that we should be followers of Christ, to fill up the measure of his sufferings. He did first run, and then was crowned. And this order we must keep if we mean ever to be with him.

Use. And *let us be comforted herein, though the race be long and painful, yet there is an end.* It will not continue for ever, and with the end there comes a prize. The world runs in a mass here and there; they have their reward, and their happiness will end soon; but a Christian's happiness will never end.

Doct. In the next place observe, that *it is expedient and useful to have an eye to this prize.* It made Paul, and it will make us run cheerfully; and God tells us of it, to the end we may fix the eyes of our minds upon it, Col. iii. 23. Whatsoever we do, do it heartily, as to the Lord, knowing of the Lord we shall receive the reward of the inheritance.

Quest. But some may say, If it be an inheritance to us, how is it then propounded as a prize to us?

Ans. I answer, It is both a reward and an inheritance. It is an inheritance because it is given to adopted sons. It is a reward *after* labour, not *for* labour; so as running is the way to a crown, not the cause of it.

Quest. But the papists say, we have it by faith. Why then is it a prize or reward? Why or how can it be a prize or reward, and yet ours by belief?

Ans. I answer, Encouragement and this prize are not given to works, as works, but as works by faith; for by it we run and overcome all trials and troubles. Reward is due to perseverance, but perseverance cannot be without faith.

But for the matter in hand, I say it is expedient to look to the prize, that we be not carried away with temptations on the right hand or on the left; and therefore let us not look on them. Moses's eye was so fixed on this prize, as he set light by all the pleasures of his life, Heb. xi. 25, 26. The eye of faith in a Christian is stronger than that of sense, yet let us take these cautions: *First,* that we know ourselves sons, and that we come to this prize by inheritance. And *secondly,* that we love not God so much for his goodness to us, as for that goodness which is in him. For a Christian aims first at God's glory, then at his own good. And so he loves God for being goodness itself, then for being good to him. And yet a Christian in order comes first to see God's goodness to him, and therefore loves him; and then he arises higher to the love of God, even for that he is goodness, and henceforth admires and adores his fulness, for else to love God because God loves us is mercenary.

Use 1. *We are therefore to think of this happy estate;* and as children, though at first we know not what belongs to inheritances and rewards, yet the elder we grow in Christianity, the more let us search into these things, and see what is laid up for us. It is an invaluable prize that will free us from all evil, of company, of enemies, of Satan's annoyances, of hindrances, of sin, from all occasions without us and inclinations within us, from sickness of body and troubles of mind. It is a Sabbath after six days' work. It is beyond all earthly crowns, The runners here envy not one another, nay, they help and further one another, and are glad of one another's forwardness. All are heirs, all happy, all shall be crowned, and with an incorruptible crown, an inheritance that fadeth not, but is undefiled; and such an one as is kept for us, 1 Pet. i 4. It is not like the crowns of leaves that soon fade. No. We shall ever be in the presence of the Son* of righteousness, where we shall have a continual spring.

Use 2. But to proceed in the next place: *This is a prize of calling.* We must be called to it. Who can take a calling on him, unless God calls him? And who can be enabled but those that he enables? This calling of his is the beginning of his golden chain of salvation. He calls us from a cursed estate to a happy communion; from death and bondage under the devil, to be kings and princes. And this is done by outward means, and inward work of the Spirit. This calling is a powerful calling, enabling them to come that are called.

And hereby we may try whether we have any title to heaven or not.

Sign 1. For, first, if we be effectually called, *it supposeth we are chosen, called, and singled out from others of the world;* and therefore all swearers, and those that are given to drunkenness and profaneness, they are not called nor singled; they remain as they were. For this singling out is the first part of the execution of God's decree of election. And whom God calls, he qualifies. Princes they may call men to places, but they cannot qualify them. But God, when he calls Saul to be a king, he gives him a king's heart; so if we be called to this heavenly kingdom, we shall have holy and kingly hearts and minds given us.

Sign 2. Secondly, *Men's tongues will shew what calling they are of, in their discourse.* A Christian will remember he is a Christian, and will walk worthy of his calling; and with Nehemiah he will reason, 'Shall such a man as I do thus?' Neh. vi. 11; speak thus? think such vile sinful thoughts? And those that are not of this carriage shew no great religion in them. And just it is with God to give such over to a great measure in sin.

Sign 3. Thirdly, *This calling is to glory;* and therefore he that is called, he will think of heaven, and magnify and admire God's goodness to him. What thing is man, Lord, that thou shouldst be mindful of him? and therefore those that admire the pomp and glory of this world, it is a sign their calling is worldly, and that they are called by the world.

Sign 4. Fourthly, If a man be called by God, he shall find *a spiritual answering within himself to God's call.* If God say, 'Thou art my son,' the heart answereth, 'Thou art my God.' 'Behold I come quickly,' saith Christ; 'Even so come, Lord Jesus,' saith the Christian heart. And therefore a rebellious disposition shews that God's Spirit is not there.

Thirdly, This calling of ours *is a high calling.* It is from heaven to heaven. It is from a heavenly spirit, by spiritual means, to Christ in heaven, to saints, to spiritual employments and privileges.

Use 1. Hence, therefore, we may learn *who are the greatest men.* Sensual men think those in outward place the greatest men of all other. Alas! they are nothing to a prince of heaven. He is a spouse to Christ; shall judge all the world, and triumph over Satan. All other callings end in the dust with our bodies. Kings shall rise as peasants, and it may be in a worse estate than many of the meanest. There is no difference in death. All other callings are by men, from men to men, to earthly purposes. Let us make, therefore, a difference, and know whence our calling is, that we may be thankful; and whither it is, that we may be joyful.

* Qu. 'Sun'?—Ed.

Use 2. We may also, in the next place, hence gather, *who are of the highest spirits*. It is a Christian, and only he. He overlooks all these base things. His way, his mind, is ever upwards; and with Paul, he thinks all 'dross and dung' that is here. It is the disposition of the world to mind high matters. Here in religion are the true aspiring thoughts; as if men will be covetous of honour, here is the right honour, and these are the honourable persons. 'Who honour me, I will honour,' saith God. Only a Christian is partaker of his desire; other men desire high matters. God knows to what end, but they leave them in the dust. But when a Christian dies, he is then partaker of his desires in fulness.

Quest. But it will be questioned, Does a Christian ever know he is called?

Ans. I answer, Sometimes a Christian staggers a little, either being not an experienced Christian, or through sight of corruptions and temptations. But setting these aside, a Christian knows his calling, and will live by his rules. For it is not only a calling, but it works a disposition. And, therefore, if we find it not, attend we on the means of the gospel, which is called the kingdom of heaven, and it will bring us into a good estate, and shew us our estate also, which being once made known to us, we may assure ourselves it will remain with us for ever; which also may be gathered from this, that it is a high calling. For nothing can break any one link of that chain made by God, and demonstrated in the 8th of the Romans.

But to proceed. This is the calling *of God;* for by nature we are dead, and it can be none but God that revives the dead. God, together with the voice of his ministers, sends his quickening Spirit; giving ears to hear, and understandings to understand.

Again, We are not only dead, *but in thraldom under the devil.* It must needs be one that is stronger than this strong man, that must dispossess us of him. This calling is God's calling in Christ, and that is first as *our head.* God looks on us as we are in him; and he elects us as in Christ. For from eternity he appointed so many to be members of Christ, as he meant to save. We are called and justified in Christ. He must be ours before his obedience be ours. We are sanctified in Christ. We must be in him as branches in the vine, partaking in the quickening sap and juice of his grace; and when we are glorified, we must be glorified as being of his members. Then we are called by Christ, who is the author of this holy calling; and, lastly, we are called through Christ as *our mediator.* And thus chiefly is it meant here, not through works, as the papists will have it. No. Christ is the author and *finisher of our faith,* Heb. xii. 2. In him are we crowned, as the body is said to be crowned when the head is. Let us therefore cherish this communion with Christ by all means, for thereby we shall communicate with him of his fulness.

VERSE 15.

Let us therefore, as many as be perfect, be thus minded.

St Paul he proceeds to others. If any of you be perfect as I am, be you also thus minded as I am. Perfection in this place is not meant of that perfection we shall have hereafter, or should have now, or legal perfection; but he is said to be perfect, that is, in his growing estate, increasing more in grace, righteousness, and sincerity; or it may be meant of perfection in regard of degrees, comparatively, whereby one out-goes another that is but a novice in religion. Such are those that can rule their affections, and can live in a settled course of holiness, called in Heb. v. 14 men of 'full age.' For there are children in religion, new entered into Christ's school. Then those that are come to 'full age' surely are exercised to discern good and evil. And then those that are come to their full pitch in heaven, between whom and the former there is no more comparison than is between the sun and a star for light. So as in regard of the saints in heaven, the best here are imperfect; yet in regard of the beginners, they may be said to be perfect. However, we may safely gather this,

Doct. That in Christianity there are degrees of holiness; divers grounds, some bring thirtyfold, some sixty.

Let this comfort those that discomfort themselves in regard of their imperfections. Grace must be at the first as a grain of mustard seed, and therefore let such with patience attend the means, and trust God for the issue.

Doct. Secondly, We may observe, that *there is a kind of perfection attainable in this life*, which we ought to strive to. The reason is, that in all things God hath ordained a set pitch, beyond which they cannot come, and to which they all tend; and as it is in nature, so in grace. Though he hath appointed to every one his several portion and measure of grace here, yet a pitch he also hath set to all, which we are to aim at, to grow better still, though in this life we cannot attain to it; and the reason is, because we know not how God will exercise us. He doth exercise all his children, but some with greater trials than others. Besides, we have a perfect God and a perfect word, that is able to make the man of God perfect to every good work. And these are not given to us for nought; and therefore it is a shame for a Christian to sit down at any degree upon pretence of imperfection. We see plants in nature desire growth, that they may be able to stand in and withstand storms. And where this spiritual nature is, and this new creature, there will be endeavour to increase in strength, to undergo and overcome all temptations and hindrances whatsoever.

And to know whether we have this perfection or not.

1*st Sign.* There *will ever be a base esteem of these outward earthly privileges and honours;* nay, of the good endowments of our minds, counting them loss in comparison of Christ; and this will work a sure settled hope in Christ evermore.

2*d Sign.* Again, *There will be a perfection of holiness;* a neglect of things past, and an earnest endeavour to things before, 'to press to the prize.'

3*d Sign.* Thirdly, *A perfect Christian desires the coming of Christ;* but the weak one ever cries, 'Let me, O Lord, recover myself before I go from hence.' He has not that assurance of his good estate that a well-grown Christian hath.

4*th Sign.* Fourthly, A perfect Christian *hath sweet communion with Christ, and can go to God with boldness,* without fear of judgment or terror of his presence. Whereas the weakest are driven to God by fear, others by hope, this man comes to God, being moved by a sweet disposition of love.

5*th Sign.* Fifthly, *A strong Christian is not moved with any change either of prosperity or adversity.* Weak brains are soon overturned with strong waters, so weak Christians are soon drunken with prosperity. But a strong Christian, in any prosperity, is pliable and fit for anything. David in the midst of all his royalty saw a greater blessedness than honour and riches: 'Blessed is the man to whom the Lord imputeth not sin, and in whose lips is no guile,' Ps. xxxii. 2. In adversity also a sound Christian will not shrink, knowing God cannot be changed, though his estate may alter; and therefore he 'can want as well as abound,' growing stronger in patience as in other Christian graces. But it is contrary with the weak Christian, for every cross strikes at his heart, and at the foundation of his faith, making him presently doubt of God's love and favour to him.

6th Sign. Sixthly, *A grown Christian he is experienced to find out Satan's devices and plots,* and can put a difference between the motions of the flesh and the spirit, and therefore knows what corruption to weaken and what grace to strengthen; whenas a new beginner, for want of practice and experience, sees not these things; and therefore, ere he is aware, runs into many offences, and looks for no remedy.

7th Sign. Seventhly, *A well-grounded Christian can withstand the bitter blasts and oppositions of this world;* nothing could move Paul, nor separate him from the love of God; but a weak Christian either is blown away, or at least shaken, with every blast; as it is in young trees newly planted.

8th Sign. Eighthly, *A grounded Christian bears with the infirmities he sees in others.* He pities them, and helps them if he can; but judges not of them as those that are weak, who for the most part are captious. 'You that are spiritual must restore,' saith the apostle, 'those that are weak, with the spirit of meekness,' Gal. vi. 1. So as it is the weak ones that are scandalised, and as they are soon offended, so do they soon give occasion of offence to others by their ill example. But the grown Christian endeavours to live free from offence; in the least things he is watchful against Satan's wiles.

9th Sign. Ninthly, *A perfect man doth most of all others see into his particular wants,* and looks hence after a further degree of grace; and therefore the apostle bids such as are perfect to forget things past, not to look on those that are before,* but to see what is yet before to be attained unto, and to press forward thereunto.

10th Sign. Tenthly, *A strong Christian is of ability and endeavour still to beget other Christians.* It is the property of a grown creature to beget its like. A weak Christian hath enough to do to look to himself.

There may be many more signs named, but these will suffice. Let us come to the means whereby we may grow to this strength and perfection.

1. And first of all, *we must know there must be an order.* We are to grow in fundamental graces in the first place; for we water not the leaves, but the root, of our plants; and the graces that are the foundation of all works being gotten and diligently cherished, the works, which are but as leaves, will soon put forth. The main fundamental grace of all is faith, which we are principally to look after.

First, *In getting assurance of our salvation.* To this end walk holily. For many live in sins against conscience, and so can have no assurance of the pardon of their sins; and how dead and blockish are they! David, though a man after God's own heart, yet losing the comfortable assurance (by his sinning against conscience) of the pardon of sin, thought God's Holy Spirit had quite forsaken him; therefore he prays, 'Take not thy Holy Spirit from me,' Ps. li. 11. Therefore labour for assurance of pardon of sin; for where the soul is wounded with the guilt of sin, it cannot enlarge itself in love, but is possessed with a fearful expectation of judgment. But when the soul is assured of the pardon of its sins, it breeds love to Christ;

* Qu. 'behind'?—ED.

and there it is said of Mary,* 'She loved much, for many sins were forgiven her,' Luke vii. 47.

In the next place, we are to labour for faith in the promises of the forgiveness of sin, and God's goodness to us; that 'he will give grace and glory, and that we shall want nothing,' Ps. lxxxiv. 11. This will put courage into us.

And as we are to labour for faith, so *also for love;* which is cherished by meditation of God's mercies and his love to us; and this will set us on fire in all good works. And so much of this grace as we have in us, with so much strength and intension of spirit shall we endeavour to please God in all things; and this argument the apostle used to stir up the Corinthians, 1 Cor. vii. 1, 'Having these promises, let us cleanse ourselves from all filthiness, perfecting holiness in the fear of God.'

2. In the next place, *whatsoever we do, let us labour to do it with the best advantage,* labouring to practise and exercise as much grace, and as many as we can; as in giving, give in zeal to God's honour, in love, in mercy towards our brother that is in need, and in regard of justice we owe it to him. God hath commanded us to give him, and he will reward it; for we lend to the Lord when we give to the poor, Prov. xix. 17. If we are to abstain from any evil, we are to abstain from it with a perfect hatred thereof, and consider how it will offend. It will break peace of conscience and dishonour religion, scandalise those that are weak, dishonour God, and bring shame to ourselves; yea, we must remember that the talents that God gives us do increase in the use of them. The more we strive to do things exactly, the more perfection we shall attain to, in the use of performances.

3. Thirdly, *Let us not neglect little things either in good or ill.* Omit no occasion of doing good, and take heed of the least beginnings of ill; abstain from all occasions and appearance of evil, for though in comparison they seem small, they are of great consequence.

4. Fourthly, *We must keep our affections to holy exercises and means;* for God works by means. Neglect none, for so much perfection thou losest thereby, and consider what means will fit our disposition when we are indisposed. Are we dull in prayer? Then read. If that will not be endured, then use the communion of saints; and still remember that we be not wearied with prayer, for God sends not his away empty. And that these things may be the more effectual, observe some motives to stir us up.

And to this end, consider,

1. *The privilege of a perfect Christian.* 'He is as mount Sion, which cannot be moved,' Ps. xlvi. 5. If we tell him of death, it is his heart's desire. Tell him of afflictions: he is resolute; he looks for them; he knows he lives God's child, and so he shall die; when a weak professor fears afflictions, fears ill tidings, fears death, and when it comes, seeks for comfort and hardly finds it.

2. Secondly, A perfect Christian is *a beautiful example, and makes others in love with religion.* He is thoroughly exercised and practised. The weakling is scandalous, makes men offended at religion; soon takes offence, soon stumbles, and gets many knocks so as his life is bitter.

3. Thirdly, The *perfect man honours God, and gets him much glory* by hearing, reading, praying, and such duties. Now as parents love those children best that are most like unto them, so those whom the Lord finds like unto him, he will make them more near to him in likeness.

* There does not seem to be sufficient reason for the belief that the woman spoken of in this passage was Mary Magdalene.—Ed

4. Fourthly, The *perfecter a man is, the more near communion he hath with Christ;* and hath the greater fruit of Christ's love, and findeth peace of conscience and joy in the Holy Spirit; to such as these, Christ hath promised to come and sup, and feast and refresh with his graces. For even to this end Christ came, to make us holy and pure, that he might present us to himself a glorious church, Eph. v. 26, 27; and therefore that Christ may attain to his end in us, let us endeavour unto perfection.

5. Fifthly, *Our estate hereafter should move us hereunto.* We look for 'a new heaven and a new earth,' 2 Peter iii. 13, and we desire to be ever with the Lord in that heaven wherein dwelleth righteousness; and therefore we ought to be diligent that we may be found in him in peace, without spot and blameless. It is the apostle Peter's argument, 2 Peter iii. 13, 14; and therefore 'as many of us as be perfect, let us be thus minded,' that we cannot go far enough; we must strive still on to perfection.

And if in anything ye be otherwise minded, God shall reveal even this unto you.

St Paul aims at the comfort of those that are weak, implying that every Christian stood not in this pitch of disposition with the apostle; and yet they were not to be discouraged. God will reveal the same mind to them also in his time.

1. In which words we may observe, *first, that some Christians see not so far as others, neither at some times so well as at other times;* but are like the man in the gospel; they see at the first men walk like trees, and after see things more plainly. 'The way of the righteous shineth more and more unto the perfect day, as the light doth,' saith the wise man. Prov. iv. 18. And as the church grew to knowledge by degrees, so do we; for we first know things in general. At the first, Peter knew not that the Gentiles should be called, Acts x. And the disciples were at the first weak and subject to many infirmities, and therefore we must *take heed of judging and censuring others, and also that we discourage not ourselves,* by reason of our weakness. God will in his time strengthen us, and it may be call them. *Secondly, Observe it is God reveals this unto such.* It is God that must take away the veil first, the veil *of the thing,* opening our understandings by reading and hearing; and thus the thing itself is made fit to be known. Then he opens the veil *of the heart* and affections, to embrace and love the things. It is God that opened the heart of Lydia, Acts xvi. 14. Let us therefore bear with the ignorant. Though God's time is not yet come, it may hereafter.

2. Secondly, *Ministers, when they come to preach, must pray that God would take away the veil from the people's ears and hearts; and people when they come, let them pray that God would open their hearts,* and not come in the strength of their own wit, knowing that God openeth and shutteth: none can open or shut till he doth it.

3. In the third place, we may observe *that God in mercy will do this for us.* He will open our hearts. He will reveal, though not every particular truth, yet all necessary truths, according to our estates. Some stand in need of more than others: as ministers ought to have more than people; and governors are to have a larger spirit than other inferiors: yet all shall have sufficient.

Therefore for our necessities let us go to God. He hath promised to lead us; and with David pray, 'Lord, open thou mine eyes, that I may see the wonders of thy law,' Ps. cxix. 18. He hath promised to anoint our eyes with eye-salve; and it is his office to guide us; he is our prophet to instruct us.

4. In the next place, *observe that if any man belong to God, he must at one time or other be thus minded as Paul was:* to hate all things as vain; to strive on to perfection; to make conscience of the least offences; yea, of idle thoughts and words; of loose, wanton behaviour; to know he is not perfect enough, vigilant enough; to look how far he is short of that pitch of perfection he ought to attain unto; not to content himself that he hath outgone others. These things they shall know either here, in time of trial and temptation, or at the hour of death, when no man ever repented of his goodness or forwardness in religion, nor of his care or constancy in good courses.

And therefore let us be stirred up to be of the same mind now; and if any man shall think with himself, because God will reveal this, therefore he will neglect means, and stay till God inspires this mind into him, let such take heed: if they love goodness, they will set about it presently; but if they quench the good motions of God's Spirit, God will take his Spirit from such. Beg that God would now change thee, for thou art not master of thy thoughts. If we now put off God till we die, it is just with God to suffer us to forget ourselves. Let us be well affected for the present; and though we see not so clearly as we should do, let us attend the means; and though we cannot grow in religion, yet let us not think it a shame, but allow and uphold such courses, else is our estate desperate.

Observe further this speech, *as it is a discovery of a moderate spirit in the apostle.* There are some graces that seem in show to cross one another, as zeal and moderation, but they do not. For zeal, when it meets with a fit subject for moderation, can be moderate. Paul condemns not, but hopes; and it is an example for our imitation. Love bears all and hopes all. While God suffers, why should not we suffer? Christ's Spirit will not break the bruised reed, in whomsoever it is. God hath a time for such as we condemn, even as he had a time for us, and therefore we must *use all means*, waiting if at any time God will give us repentance, 2 Tim. ii. 25. Ministers must not be harsh with weak Christians. It is God's work to bow affections, and not man's. And secondly, when we have used all the means we can, *we must depend on God's providence;* and therefore we are to fetch grounds of toleration and patience towards others from God's love and wisdom, who reveals the seed sometimes long after.

The papists they check us for want of means to reduce men into unity, and to compound controversies. They brag of the pope's power this way; but it is but a brag. For why do they not conclude their own?

They are far more happy than the church was in Christ's time: he says, 'Offences must come,' Mat. xviii. 7. Paul sees there 'must be errors,' 1 Cor. xi. 19. He could not compose all. God must reveal it in his time.

But how do they compose differences? By excommunication, imprisonment, and death; and this by the censure of an ignorant man perhaps, which is brutish and unfit for the church of God. For our part we want no means; but the effect or success we must leave to God. We are not to force men tyrannically to our opinions in lesser matters, but leave them to God's time of revelation.

And lastly, As this hope of revelation is promised, *so are we to expect it and wait for it;* 'for to him that hath, more shall be given,' Mark iv. 24. And therefore let them that have beginnings of grace be comforted to walk on; and for those that are not entered, let them not be discouraged. God will reveal. But upon what condition it follows.

VERSE 16.

Nevertheless, whereto we have already attained, let us walk by the same rule.

The word 'nevertheless,' some read it 'only' (*u*), as if it were a condition. But it implies both a precept and a condition, shewing that those that look for revelation of further knowledge and goodness they must walk according to that measure of knowledge they have. The word 'rule' implies in general the Scripture, more particularly a company of sound truths concerning faith, love, and hope. There is a great Bible, which is the whole word of God. The little Bible is the grounds of religion; and these are not only to be understood in the book, but comprehended and invested in our understanding and affections; and according to these we must walk. Truth is no guide to us, being only in the book, but as it is seated in the heart.

Doct. But let us come to some observations. First, we may learn that God out of his goodness *hath left to his church a rule of faith and manners.* There is a rule whereby men must walk, otherwise should we be in a labyrinth of errors continually, having no other light but this torchlight of nature to guide us in this thick darkness wherein we are by nature.

The properties of this rule are divers. First, *It is a fixed and unchangeable rule;* and therefore we must bring all to it, not it to all.

Secondly, This rule *is a perspicuous and clear rule.* 'Thy word is a lantern to my steps, and a light to my paths.'

Thirdly, *This rule is homogeneal.* All things therein are spiritual, all holy, all pure; and therefore, when the question is about religion, we must have recourse thereto as the only absolute complete rule. And therefore we must know this rule and then be led by it; for the word 'rule' implies that there must be a thing to be ruled, else what needs rule, or to what use should it serve? An instrument is in vain without use. It is true, many men make religion and Scripture but a mere object of discourse. But their example ought to be no rule to us. If we look to be saved, it must be by walking according to this rule; and therefore a Christian life is no licentious life. Though he be freed from the law, yet must he serve God day and night. Therefore it is that the Christian prospers not nor thrives in this world, because he will not lie, nor swear, nor have a broad conscience, as the children of this world have, that take all occasion and scope to be rich. But a Christian lives by rule. He hath little, and it is blessed to him; for he looks at riches and profits of another kind.

In the second place, we *may observe that a Christian walketh by this rule.* He thinks it not sufficient to take a step, but keeps a right course stedfastly onward.

But how may this be done? may some men say.

1. I answer: Let us use the means; as first, *let us treasure up the word in our consciences.* Let us get the rule within us; get the articles of faith and assurance of the promises, and let this be betimes while we are young. It is the ordinary cry, The Scriptures are heard,* they cannot understand them. But what is the reason? They are bred up in earthly businesses, and are stuffed with them so as they find no place for the word; and it is a miracle to see men thus brought up to live by this rule.

2. Secondly, When we have once treasured up the knowledge of these things, *we must learn to apply them upon several occasions;* for where no

* Qu. 'hard'?—Ed.

practice is, there knowledge is idle, and makes us worthy of more stripes. Many have general truths in their minds, but coming to apply them, they find a great want. David knew adultery was a sin, and Peter knew it was dangerous for a man to rely on himself, yet how foully did they fall.

3. Thirdly, *Let us compare our experience with our rule.* We shall find there is nothing therein but is fulfilled; that there is no suffering but for some sin or other; and that besides heaven hereafter, God rewards particular obedience here with paricular rewards; and particular sin with particular corrections. We shall know that his judgments are not scarecrows. The work of the wicked is accursed, but it shall go well with the righteous; and by this means we shall be encouraged to good and scared from bad courses.

4. Fourthly, *Be inquisitive and watchful over our particular steps.* Take and hear admonitions and instructions, and be inquisitive after them. Those that are otherwise minded, no marvel if they, like libertines, spurn against all instruction and advice, and accordingly feel the smart of their ways before they see it.

5. Fifthly, *Get a wonderful jealousy over our hearts.* We often offend in thoughts and desires, which God, the searcher of the heart, looks into; and we must therefore be jealous of idle thoughts and words, not only of others, for so a hypocrite may be.

Obj. But loose persons will say, Oh, this is an unpleasant course; we must bid all joy farewell when we come to this.

Ans. I answer, No. The ways of wisdom are ways of comfort and pleasure. God approves of them, and our consciences will tell us so, and thereby will fit us for life or death, and will so settle us, that no estate shall be unwelcome to us; and, as Ps. l. 23, 'To such as order their conversation aright God will shew his salvation;' and, as in the text foregoing, 'God will reveal himself more and more,' so as if we be faithful and conscionable in little, we shall have greater matters revealed to us; and contrarily, if we be unfaithful and careless, God will take from us the key of knowledge, and the use thereof, and will give us up to foul vices, even sins against nature, as he punished the Gentiles, and to believe lies, as Paul says, 2 Thess. ii. 11. And will answer us as he did the idolaters, even according to their multitude of idols, Ezek. xiv. 4. So as would we have favour in our sins, and teachers that shall bolster us up in them, and not cross our vain courses? God will let us have our heart's desire, but we must know that this is an inevitable way to a desperate estate; and therefore marvel not so much at the loose liver because of his good breeding, for as they desire the ill, so they have, and are justly punished therewith.

Let us mind the same thing.

Observe here, that we are not only to walk suitable to others, but we must mind the same thing that others of our profession do. So as this is a direction to concord, shewing that a *Christian is a member of Christ as his head, and of the mystical body the church.* Faith ties him to Christ, love ties him to the body, so as he must walk with Christ and also with the body. He must look to himself first, and then to the body. The ground of this union is laid down here to be first an union of mind and affection, and this must be in good, or else we are brethren in evil. It is no marvel the world complains of want of love, when there is no agreement in the rule of our love, when there is no agreement in the objects of our love. It is not riotous fellowship, but fellowship in the gospel that unites us. Let us mind this same thing, and then we shall affect one another; and because our knowledge doth not extend to every particular alike, let us agree in the main points, and let not less things break us off one from another. If we did walk according to our measure of knowledge in those things wherein we agree between us and the Lutherans, [there] would not be that bitterness of spirit that there is; all censures and distempers would cease. And it is a fault in many Christians, though bred up well in knowledge, yet being of a harsh spirit and nature, while he walks not according to the same rule, and minds not the same things in the main as he should do, he grows to be bitter. As for those that would be sincere, they must endeavour to be united in one, as they have one God, one faith, one baptism; for a Christian loves not to go to heaven alone. And when he is there, he knows he shall be one with Christ and one with the holy saints, and therefore will endeavour to be in perfect unity here. Considering there is no good he hath but he enjoys it as being a member of the body of Christ, he knows it is a horrible thing that members of the same body should fall out one with another; and therefore what shall separate or divide us? Shall infirmities? Alas! we are all sick of this disease, *veniam petimus damusque*. Are they too hot? We are too cold. Why should we not stoop and yield? Christ he stooped from heaven to us. Shall errors? Why, the time will come God will reveal himself more fully. Shall sin? We know what the apostle saith, Gal. vi. 1: 'Those that are spiritual must restore such with the spirit of meekness.' We must not cut off members for every sore. Shall injuries? It is the honour of a man to pass by such. Do we look Christ should forgive us when we will not forgive others? Consider it is the practice of all holy men. Paul 'became all things to all men, if by any means he might win some,' 1 Cor. ix. 20, *seq.* Peter received reproof of him, yet fell not out with him. Some there are of such a perverse spirit, as if they see in any one any infirmity, presently they break into these or the like words, 'I will not be of that man's profession,' thus forsaking all the good in the holy profession because of some weakness in the professors.

If they will needs be separating, let them separate from the world, from scandalous, careless, riotous persons, else Satan rules in division. He knows he is best able to deal with them that are alone, and therefore draws Eve from Adam, and one Christian from another, and so quickly overcomes them. If in company one fall, another may help him up; if he be cold, another may warm him by exhortation and example.

Consider, therefore, *who are best minded, and mind the best things with them.* If we find we have attained to a greater degree in grace than others, endeavour to bring them to us. The communion of saints is an article of our faith. Every one believes it, but few knows what it means; and therefore no marvel they desire it not.

VERSE 17.

Brethren, be followers together of me.

These words contain another exhortation, with a friendly compellation, which I pass over, having heretofore had often occasion to speak of it. The exhortation is to imitation of the apostle, 'follow me.' And because I cannot ever be with you, therefore follow those among you that walk as I do.

Whence we learn, *that together with the rules of religion we must propound*

God's graces in us, as examples for others to imitate; and this arises not from pride, but from confidence of truth and holiness in our own hearts and conversations; and religion maketh this a virtue and duty, without which it were boasting; and so it doth many things, of themselves not seemly, very fitting. David's dance was in worldly esteem counted but folly, yet having respect to God's glory is commendable. And therefore we must not be captious when we see such things in others, that men ordinarily count indiscretion. But mark their ground, and by it esteem of them, and accordingly follow such. 'Be ye followers of me,' saith St Paul; that is, observe what my doctrine is, and what I do and acknowledge, follow and imitate me. The apostle's doctrine consists chiefly of three heads; whereof the first, concerning our natural condition, as Rom. 1st, 2d, 3d chapters, and Eph. ii. And the second, concerning our remedy by Christ Jesus, God and man, being king, priest, and prophet, as in the Hebrews. And the third, the manner how Christ is become ours by imputation, and is laid hold on by faith, which is given to us by God, who being unchangeable and true, we persevere in this rule and course of obedience, by the mercies of God, though with many combatings and strivings, even to fulness of glory. The apostle's example see in part in this chapter, in holiness of life and death to sin, and esteem of the goods of this world as base. In the Acts see his pains in the ministry, his calling, his heavenly and holy mind in the next verse.

And therefore, let us read these often, and consider them. They are an excellent glass, that will transform us into an holy form and fashion. Many things there are in him that are extraordinary and not imitable. He wrought in another calling for his living. He was an apostle, had extraordinary gifts by revelation, and indeed not so much by study as the ministers of the gospel now, to whom God gives gifts, but in the faithful and painful* use of the means; and therefore are they not bound to imitate the apostle in this thing as in other things which he did as an apostle?

But to proceed to particulars. Imitation implies four things:

First, *A doing that which another doth.*

Second, *A doing it in the same manner.*

Third, *A doing thereof grounded upon the same affections*, not as in a stage play, where he that acteth the person of a king is often a varlet. But it implies such an imitation as is in a child, that endeavoureth to be like the father in disposition as well of mind as of body.

Fourth, It implies *a doing, studio imitandi*, with an earnest desire to be like him. For he that doth that which God commands, and not as expressing his desire of imitation, he is no follower; and therefore in all our actions we ought to desire to be like God, and endeavour to express in action what we desire; and to this end we are to search for examples and patterns in the Scripture, for those that are more excellent. For the most excellent in all kinds are the best rules for others; and because in many things we offend all, let us follow the examples of men no further than they follow Christ, 1 Cor. xi. 1. And it was one end of Christ's incarnation, that he might be an example unto us. 'As I, your Lord and Master, have washed your feet, so ye ought to wash one another's feet,' John xiii. 14; 'and learn of me, for I am meek,' Mat. xi. 29.

Hence we may gather the ground why we have not only rules in Scripture to live by, but also examples. For, first, they shew that *the things commanded are possible to be done.* Then they shew us the *way and means*

* That is, 'painstaking.'—G.

more plainly, how to do them. Thirdly, they shew *how graceful and acceptable they are when they are done*. So as the Scriptures are not penned altogether in a commanding fashion, but have mingled sweet alluring examples. For there are four ways of teaching: rule, reason, similitudes, and examples. The two former enjoins, but works not on the affections. Similitudes are but slight; only examples conforms us in a most sweet alluring manner.

Use 1. And therefore we ought to be exemplary, as *to follow others, and especially those that are above others*. They should be burning and shining lights, as stars giving light to passengers in the darkness of this world. To this end observe some means. And,

Direct. 1. *First, Reverence not only the eye of God but of weak Christians, maxima debetur puero reverentia* (*v*). We are to be awful of our carriage, that we may give no ill example to them; and to this end we are to know that we should give account for those sins that we either cause or suffer others to fall into if we may hinder them. Give therefore no offence or scandal to the little ones.

Direct. 2. *Labour to deny ourselves in liberties*, especially when we are in the presence of such as will take scandal; and to this end labour for the grace of love, which will cause us to endure much, and put up many things which we count injuries.

Direct. 3. Thirdly, *In our carriage we are so to demean ourselves that we value, esteem, and respect those with whom we converse;* for else our actions being visible to others, they will seem to be done out of a self-respect, and so will not affect or work on them. Grace will teach us to honour the meanest, as those that may be dearly beloved of God, who also may excel us in many excellent qualities, and in some kind of grace may also go beyond us.

Use 2. Secondly, *If we be bound to give good example, then woe to the world for offences*. What shall become of those who wonnd and vex continually the hearts of those with whom they converse? Many are in hell, *propter alienum peccatum*. In the eyes of God, who knows the heart and intentions, sin is committed before it be acted, and therefore it is all one whether thou committest it or not. But it is not thus before men; for when it is committed it turns to scandal, and opens the enemies' mouths, and grieves the Spirit of God in his children. The prophets complain hereof; and we may observe God correct his children most to keep them from scandalising others, and that others may beware of scandal. So David's sin was pardoned, yet because he gave scandal the child died.

Use 3. Thirdly, *As we must give good example, so we must endeavour to take good from others' example;* and to this end,

1. First, *We must eye them*, and pry into their actions; for this end hath God left us a continual succession of examples.

2. Secondly, We must eye them *not to observe their weaknesses, to uncover their shame;* for this is a poisonous disposition, proceeding even from the devil. Neither are we to observe them, thereby to take liberty to the flesh from their ill example; but we are to eye them as we view glasses, to deck and adorn ourselves by them, and to compose ourselves in a good course.

3. Thirdly, In imitation *we are to observe the best, and the best of the best*, and not to compare ourselves with those that are inferior to us. For he that thinks himself good by comparison, he is not good, as a runner will not conclude he runs swiftly, because he hath outrun a lame man. And therefore St Paul says elsewhere, 'Brethren, follow me as I follow Christ,' 1 Cor. iv. 16, propounding to himself the most excellent pattern of all,

Christ Jesus. Contrariwise he blames the Corinthians because they measured themselves by themselves, 2 Cor. x. 12.

4. Fourthly, *We must learn truths before we practise*, for the best have their blemishes. So that we must learn to know how to avoid them. The papists urge us with the succession and universality of their church. No, say we, it is the doctrine that must try the church, whether it be true or false, for men are *mensura mensurata*. It is the doctrine is *mensura mensurans*, the measure measuring, whereby our actions ought to be squared and framed aright. The papists urge us with an implicit faith. Alas! what example, what imitation can there be, when they know not what to imitate? They know not what the church believes, and yet they must believe as the church believeth.

5. Fifthly, *We must labour to have soft hearts*, sanctified with grace and mollified, for a stony hard heart will receive no impression; and to this end are we to use the means, to embrace the word, to receive the sacraments, and to pray that God would open our eyes and soften our stony hearts.

6. Sixthly, *We are to look to every one that hath any good thing worthy of imitation*, as those that delight in gardens, where they hear of any choice flowers, they will have a slip for their own garden. Thus it should be with us; where we see any flower of any grace, get that and place it in our own gardens. In every Christian there is something imitable, and something that may further us; and therefore this apostle longed to see the Romans, that he might be comforted by their faith, Rom. i. 12. It is with the church as with the firmament, ever some are rising and some are setting. Let us look to the stars of our time, and walk by their light. It is not enough that we can commend the martyrs, for that is ordinary, as it was with the Jews in Mat. xxiii. 29. Though they builded the sepulchres of the prophets, if they had been alive together with them, they would have persecuted them; and therefore Christ saith, 'They killed the prophets.' And the ground of it is because it is a dishonour to God not to take notice of his goodness and glorious graces in others; and therefore if the stars do praise him, surely these stars must much more set forth his glory, that being of themselves sinful wretched men, by his power are made glorious lights for others to walk by.

7. And in the seventh place, In things whereof *there is no certain rule to direct us, we ought to imitate the example and custom of the most holy and sober sort*. As in apparel much question is, what sort, what fashion is most to be imitated, let the most sober and moderate of thine own rank be guide unto thee. It is singularity to differ from such, with a desire to be noted, and it savours of pride; and such shall be condemned by their examples, even as Noah condemned the old world.

Use. For use of all this, learn hence what is the best succession. That is the best and surest note of succession which is both in doctrine and example. Local succession is nothing. They are the children of Abraham that do the works of Abraham. They are Jews which are Jews inwardly in the spirit. The papists they cry out against us we have no succession, but it is they have no succession. Their doctrine everywhere crosses the doctrine of the ancient Church of Rome. Their practice is without precedent. What precedent have they for rebellion, for their equivocation, and the like? They follow, indeed, but as corruption doth generation.

VERSE 18.

For many walk, of whom I have told you often.

These words contain a reason of Paul's exhortation; and from the connection we may observe, *that where truth is, error is.* Where wheat is there are tares. Walk as I do, for there are many with whom ye converse that walk as enemies to the cross of Christ. Our enemies tell us, because of our errors we are not the true church. They may better conclude contrarily, that because we have some few errors, therefore there is a true church amongst us. Where truth is there will be opposers, and therefore we are not to be scandalised hereat. The skill and courage of a Christian is seen most where truth is in danger, as the goodness of a pilot is seen specially in a tempest.

The papists will not have the word read in the vulgar tongue. Why? Because they say many errors will thence arise, while the common people understand it not. They may as well argue, because there is much deceit, therefore I will not buy nor sell. St Paul was of another mind. He would preach at Ephesus, 'for a great door and effectual was opened,' though he knew there were 'many adversaries,' 1 Cor. xvi. 9.

In the next place, observe he saith, 'many there were,' meaning of the better and more eminent sort, that is, of teachers. A pitiful thing, that in the golden times of the church the chief leaders of the church should be misled; and therefore we are not to wonder that we should find it thus, and therefore we must not be scandalised by the multitude. One Micaiah is better than four hundred false prophets; and therefore we must not number the followers, but weigh them aright (*w*).

To proceed. He saith there are 'many.' He nameth none in particular, yet no doubt but noted scandalous persons may and ought to be particularly named, that others may take notice and heed of them; yet this must be warily done. The apostle curses the coppersmith, but only names Demas. Those that are weak must be gently touched; those that are obstinate and scandalous must be plainly made known; and this draweth some of our writers particularly to lay open the vices and falsehoods of those that are obdurate, and therefore we must not take scandal thereat, it arising from a zealous care of God's church, not of malice.

In the next place, he saith he told them 'often.' The apostle was affectionately bent for their good, and therefore to write the same things often to them it was not grievous to him, seeing to them it was false.* For the nature of man is very dull in conceiving of things that belong to salvation, and their memories are but brittle. If therefore we do often inculcate and lay open the danger of that whorish religion long since condemned, it must be well taken in these times, especially wherein men are so secure, daring to venture on anything, yea, to go to their masses, upon pretence of their strength, that they can come away without being defiled.

And now tell you weeping.

As if he should have said, if nothing else will make you beware, yet let my tears move, my tears proceeding from grief and compassion of the miserable estate of such teachers, and of such as are led by them.

Affections therefore are lawful, yea, necessary in God's children. All actions in God's worship are esteemed according to the affections that they are done with. We are as we love, not as we know. What is the life of

* Qu. 'safe'?—ED.

a Christian but the performance of things with courage, delight, and joy? And therefore the strongest Christians have strongest affections. For religion doth not harden the heart, but mollifies it; and regeneration doth not take affections away, but restores them sanctified and pure.

But to come particularly to the matter here. He is compassionate, and so compassionate as his natural constitution will admit; he expresseth this with tears, which ariseth from grief for something within ourselves, or by reason of sympathy with others for some danger that they are in, or like to fall into.

Reason 1. The reasons hereof are, *because they are led by the Spirit of Christ*, who was all made of compassion; for he wept for his friends, for Lazarus, and for his enemies. 'O Jerusalem, Jerusalem, how often would I have gathered you, and you would not.' He was tender in bearing the infirmities of his weak disciples and of weak women. His compassion was such as drew him to the lowest degree of humiliation to free us from danger.

Reason 2. Secondly, *The saints have clear sanctified judgments to apprehend true causes of remorse.* They know what danger is, as Paul saw here that the sheep were in danger of wolves, and saw the danger so much the greater by how much they saw not the danger they were in.

Reason 3. Thirdly, *The saints have their hearts broken with sense and feeling of Christ's compassion in their hearts, and so are mollified, expressing it outwardly towards their brethren;* contrarily, the wicked never felt any remorse or pity of Christ in them, and therefore know not what compassion means, so as their mercies are cruelties. Use this as a note whereby we may discern of our Christian estate; for surely where there is no compassion there can be no excellent estate.

Again, From the apostle's object of compassion and weeping observe, *that spiritual evil and danger is the most proper object of Christian compassion.* Paul he pities not himself because of his fetters he was in, but it was the bonds of sin made him cry, 'O wretched man that I am, who shall deliver me from the body of this death?' Rom. vii. 24. And good reason, for these spiritual evils of error in judgment, hardness of heart, security, seared conscience, and the like, they lead us the assured way to damnation, as it is said in the words following, 'whose end is damnation.' Contrarily, outward crosses being sanctified to us, they bring us to heaven, as it is 1 Cor. xi. 32, 'We are chastened of the Lord, that we should not be condemned with the world.' For those crosses are occasions of good affections, purging the heart from deadness and fleshly trust, they draw us to God; and therefore spiritual danger is the proper object of pity. It is otherwise with us. We lament Christian bloodshed. But how many souls are carried into error daily, turned to popery, and no remorse, no pity! There is great need thereof both in the magistrate and the minister, that they should be moved to provide remedies against such mischiefs.

And let us be far from *envying such as are in ill courses;* let their outward pomp be never so great, rather lament their misery. Alas! poor souls, how are they hurried, nay, do willingly run to destruction, while they are blinded with those idle shows of vanity.

But much more *miserable is their estate that draw on others to mischief*, that are brethren in evil. What other end can they look for but to be as tares bound up and cast into the depth of hell, being guilty of as many men's deaths as they are of ill examples in their past life?

But for ourselves, *let not our souls come into their secrets; let us mourn at the lewdness of some, and the danger of all.* And to this end let us consider duly the afflictions of Joseph, taking heed of sensualities, which, as

Hosea saith, taketh away the heart, Hosea iv. 11. Moses saw the misery of his brethren, and pitied them; so should we consider of the danger of popery, of schism, and rebellion: and this will break our hearts, and cause us, with Jeremiah, to mourn in secret for the sins of the times, Jer. xiii. 17.

They are the enemies of the cross of Christ.

In these and the following words is a description of these inordinate walkers which the apostle speaketh of. They are described by their disposition: first, outwardly, 'that they are enemies to Christ's death.' Then inwardly, 'Their belly is their God, they glory in their shame, and they mind earthly things.' Then by their end, which is 'damnation.' They are pointed out and described to us, to the end we might take notice of them. By the cross is not meant the sign of the cross, as the papists fondly imagine, but Christ's death on the cross, whereby was made satisfaction and redemption and reconciliation.

1. The enemies of this cross are, first, such as added hereto the ceremonial obedience to the law and their own satisfactory * works.

2. Secondly, Such as are carnal, denying the power of Christ's crucifying in not crucifying their affections.

3. Thirdly, Such as could not endure or suffer for the testimony of Christ's crucifying; and therefore to avoid persecution, they pressed circumcision with Christ, and so were enemies to his cross, Gal. vi. 12. Such were the enemies thereof then, and such have we now of the papists; let them brag never so much of their esteem and reverence they give to the sign thereof. While they seem to kiss it, they betray it Judas-like. For while they teach merits, satisfaction in purgatory, indulgences, and the like, they make the cross of Christ of none effect, which is only and wholly sufficient in itself.

And whereas they say they do add, they take nothing from the sufficiency of Christ:—

I answer, Circumcision was added here by those, who are notwithstanding condemned. For as to join poison with wholesome meat takes away the nourishment of the meat, so if we be circumcised, Christ shall profit us nothing; and grace is no grace where there is merit, Rom. xi. 6. Again, consider the equity thereof in natural reason. Can it be thought likely that God should become man, to do anything which lies in the power of man to patch up and make good, or else it is insufficient? Shall finite corrupt man be able to make an infinite work perfect. No. God will not give his glory to another; and will he part with his glory in this great work, which propounds his glory as the main end thereof? Eph. i. 6, 12.

4. Fourthly, There are another sort of enemies, *such as cast not themselves on the merits of Christ's cross,* those whose consciences were never convict of sin. Abundance there are who glory in their proud presumptuous swaggering courses, shewing that they are either blind or stark mad. They wilfully run to perdition, they will not hear nor be controlled. Others that see their forepast life how wicked it hath been, they are so far from casting themselves on Christ's merits, as they despair and grow more and more obstinate therein, even to their own destruction; either by not seeing the merits of Christ, or through want of confidence on them, though they see his righteousness to be above their sins. And some are so detestably wicked, as because they see no salve for them, they run desperately into a custom of sin, and continue therein to their death. As we would desire to avoid this fearful estate and condition, so let us take heed of custom of

* That is, 'satisfying.'—G.

sinning, for that will make us senseless, and will move God to give us over. And therefore let us take heed that we receive not the grace of God in vain, it being so freely proffered to us. And to this end, know that so far as we suffer our lusts to overrule us, and we not crucify them, so far we are enemies, Gal. v. 4. For while we know and consider Christ as crucified for our sins, it will make us, if we have any grace, think of sin as of a thing that deserves to be crucified, and hate that that caused the death of our dear Saviour; for they were the cruel tormentors of Christ. And if we embrace Christ, we shall have the same affection to sin that Christ had; for Christ will not lodge but in a heart humbled for sin. And the estate of those men is miserable, that are so far from crucifying lusts, as they thrust themselves upon all occasions of temptation and sin, and esteem them as their only enemies, that tell them of their unchristian courses. Surely, however they may daub for a time, yet their outward profession will never administer sound comfort to them, but they shall find bitterness at their latter end.

5. There are yet another sort of enemies, namely, *such as will endure nothing for Christ;* who notwithstanding bore his cross, and bids us take up our cross of reproach for religion. Some will endure any pain, travail, danger, and watchings, for riches or ambition, but dare not speak a word, or appear in Christ's cause. Are not these enemies? Shall Christ out of his love come from heaven to the basest abasement for us, and shall not we endure for a while here, seeing it is also for our own good, and we are gainers thereby, and considering that Christ called us to suffer. For while we live here, and embrace true religion, there will ever be a cross and shame in the world, accompanying the profession thereof, if it be sincere.

Preachers therefore that preach not Christ plainly and boldly, and hearers that come to the hearing of the word rather for rhetorical flourishes, witty sentences fit only for discourse sake, even thus far they are enemies. For if Christ be not preached mainly and chiefly to this end, to amend the lives of men, to win souls to Christ; and if men, coming to hear, come not even for this end mainly, to be bettered in their salvation, to be strengthened in grace; they shall be damned as enemies for this, that the means of salvation they profane and despise.

And therefore let *us abase ourselves for our sins, and magnify God's goodness* in affording means of salvation. Labour also to shew how we profit by suffering for the gospel, and count it an honour, and 'rejoice that we are worthy to suffer' for Christ, Acts v. 41, labour to overcome the world and our lusts, and to honour Christ even in his meanest children. If the love of Christ will not constrain us, no motives will draw us.

VERSE 19.

Whose end is destruction.

The word signifies a reward, and is translated and taken often for an end,* because reward is given at the end of the work; and thus is salvation called a reward for goodness, because it is given at the end of a holy life. The other word signifies damnation or destruction, which implies all things tending to or accompanying the punishment of a wicked life. And the connection of these words with the former may be thus framed. He that is an enemy to the cause of life is an enemy to life, but those that are enemies to the cross of Christ are enemies to the cause of life and to that

* The original is τέλος.—G.

which saves them; and therefore they must needs be destroyed. This made the apostle judge of them thus, and withal he saw they were void of grace, and were incorrigible. And from hence we may infer,

That *we may in some sort judge of the spiritual estate of men, even while they are alive.* For as astronomers can judge of eclipses, and statesmen of the continuance or danger of the State, and physicians of the event of diseases, by the course of natural causes, so in religion there are predictions on good grounds, what will follow of ill courses tending to damnation.

But more particularly, there is a threefold judgment.

1. First, *One by faith*, which concerning ourselves brings certainty; and so we are able to judge of ourselves.

2. Secondly, There is a judgment *by fruits*, comparing men's disposition and state with their fruits; and so we say, if men walk riotously, we can infer, Surely he is in no good estate. 'By their fruits shall you know them,' saith Christ,' Mat. vii. 16.

3. Thirdly, *There is a particular revelation of God's Spirit.* This the prophets and apostles had, but now we have no such rule. Yet by the fruits and course of men, it is an easy matter to judge what the end of those men will be, following those courses; for God's word is the same now that it was then. Indeed, when we judge men in things indifferent, this is rash, and condemned by the apostle, Rom. xiv. 3.

For use hereof, *let us learn to judge ourselves*, and know if we break wilfully the known rules of salvation, we are in a fearful estate. And we should also submit to the judgment of God's ministers while we are here, and amend; for else look assuredly for the sentence of death hereafter from God himself, when there will be no revoking thereof. For though punishment may be deferred a while, yet assuredly it shall not go well with the wicked at the last, Eccl. viii. 13.

In the next place observe, *There is an end to every way*, for it is taken for granted that they have an end; and surely we will not, nor cannot, be always as we are. We are labourers, and there is a time of payment of our wages. And therefore, we should look whither our ways do tend. There will be an end of this life, but damnation shall be without end. We should also *be inquisitive to see if we be out of this way*, that we may be reformed; for these worldly pleasures must end in eternal vengeance, and this life is but a way to that end.

And in the third place, *Learn to be patient.* When we see the wicked run on in a broad highway, what though they be admired here and lifted up! They are but condemned persons; and therefore, envy them not, seeing we would be loath, upon serious deliberation, to change estates with them. Observe we further from these words, *that God will judge eternally, not only for gross, scandalous sins in the course of our life, but even for errors in judgment.* For we must judge aright, as well as affect aright, and God hath no service from corrupt judgments. Those that join man's merits with Christ's merits, they cannot rely on God alone, neither can they rejoice in Christ. Christ hath but half of them. Therefore, let us keep the virginity of our judgments; prostitute them not to lies, but reserve them chaste and pure to Christ.

And secondly, *Take we heed how we converse with such as are of corrupt judgments.* They are God's and Christ's enemies, and will labour to bring us into their ways; and then, assuredly let us look for their end. It is reason, that those with whom we converse here, we should converse withal hereafter.

Whose god is their belly.

These words do partly shew the inward disposition of these men. By 'belly,' in this place, he means in general all contentments and worldly pleasures, whereof these teachers being satisfied, they lived at large and at ease.

Quest. But how may they be said to make their belly their God?

Ans. 1. I answer, We may be said to make anything our God, first, *when we count it one*, as some of the papists have esteemed of the pope, as of an essence between man and God; and some emperors have required themselves to be so esteemed, and adored as a deity (*x*).

2. Secondly, When *we give such affections to it as are only due and proper to God*, as to trust in it, to repose content in it, to joy in it; and so is that sentence true, *amor tuus, Deus tuus* (*y*).

3. Thirdly, When *we use actions of invocation and adoration thereto;* and thus the papists make saints their god, attributing such power in working to them, as is only proper to God.

4. Fourthly, *When we bestow all labour to give satisfaction thereunto.* For explication, these men gave the intension of their most inward affections, to procure content to their lusts. All their labour was to this end, and so quieted themselves in the enjoyment of them. And as they made their 'belly their god,' so their belly acted the part of a god, in giving them laws, bidding them to do, project, devise this or that; undermine such, and grounding them in this first fundamental law, 'Thou canst not live long, neither wilt thou live well; therefore, while thou livest, live for thy pleasure, take thy ease;' and from thence, enjoins them to use all means thereto: take all acquaintance, undermine all that cross thee; and all to this end, that thou mayest have thy ease.

As it was then, so now is it with the papists, their successors. All the differences in religion between them and us, are by them grounded on the belly. That is the monarchy of the pope, and worldly pomp, and masses invented for idle priests, Latin prayers, little or no preaching; only that the people being ignorant, they might more easily command them. If their errors were not invested in gain, we should soon accord* their worship, especially the manner thereof, only to delight the sense.

And among ourselves, many are not wanting that make profession of religion, but deny the power thereof. So long as religion and outward content do meet, and when religion brings preferment, all will be religious, for they live by no rules but those that their lusts prescribes: morning and evening taking care for the flesh, how to be rich, how to live at ease; and for this will sell their birthright in happiness, refusing the word, refusing good company, yea, heaven itself. And this justly comes as a judgment for man's first rebellion. When men will not serve God as they should, they are justly given over to the service of those that are no gods.

Quest. But it may be asked, May we not seek to content our flesh?

Ans. I answer, We may respect our bodies; and there is a due honour that belongs to the outward man, but we must so seek for them, as in the first place and principally we seek the kingdom of heaven, and its righteousness; and then God hath promised to cast these things upon us, Mat. vi. 33. But when we break order and measure, being first and principally careful for our lusts, the devil knowing our haunts, offers baits fitting for your humours, and we, like filthy swine, devour our own destruction.

* That is, = 'we should soon agree that their worship is only,' &c.—G.

And therefore, to avoid this, *let us set the fear of God and damnation before our eyes;* and if we use not these things moderately and soberly, let that in Rom. viii. 13 be as a flaming sword to keep us from the way of destruction. 'If we live according to the lusts of the flesh, we shall die;' and therefore, 'as strangers and pilgrims, let us abstain from fleshly lusts, which fight against the soul;' against our comfort here, and our happy estate hereafter.

Secondly, *Let us avoid the company of condemned persons,* but look on them with a kind of horror and detestation of them; and pass not for their wicked censures, 'Their end is damnation, and their belly is their god.'

But because the best are drawn away by these pleasures, let us observe some directions.

And first, Let us see the reasons why we are thus inveigled with them.

Reason 1. First, These earthly contentments *are present to our sense.* The other only are present to faith, which the carnal man looks not after, neither cares for.

2. Secondly, *We nusle* up ourselves in an opinion of the necessity of these things,* seeing the present use of them; and we see no present use of those better things.

3. Thirdly, These *things are bred up with us, and we are acquainted with them from our infancy,* and so they plead prescription; and when we are thus taken up before, religion comes after, and very hard it must needs be, to keep our minds lifted up; and yet is it most necessary to be; for lusts do drown men in perdition, 1 Tim. vi. 9.

1. But for helps in this estate of ours, observe first, with due consideration, *the nature, dignity, and excellency of the soul;* that it is a spirit of an excellent beauty, adorned with understanding and judgment, not made to cast off the crown, submitting itself to the rule of every base lust, which indeed is the only happiness of the beasts; nay, if happiness consists in pleasing the senses, beasts are more happy than we, for they have neither shame without, nor conscience within, to disquiet them in the enjoyment of their pleasures.

And know also that this body of ours, being of that excellent temper, is a fabric which was not made only to be a strainer for meat to pass through. The quality of the brain in man, the structure of the eye, do testify man was made for divine meditation, to contemplate of the works of God, which it doth behold with the eye as through a glass.

2. Secondly, *We must know, by giving our affections to these things, we are made like the things we affect;* for the soul is placed in the midst, as it were, between heaven and earth, and as it affects the one or the other, so is it fashioned. If we love the flesh we are flesh; if we follow the Spirit, we are transformed to its likeness.

3. Thirdly, *Consider that God is better than the worshipper,* else is he mad that will worship it. But the belly is baser than ourselves. Reason teacheth us the pleasures of this life end in death, when our souls must still continue after all. Now to seek such pleasures as cannot continue with us is madness, as appears even by the light of reason; and therefore are of more power with natural men than pure religious truths. But for those that are called, the Scripture puts them in mind of the last day of judgment, and tells them that they are made for heaven; and such are therefore to set their minds on things which are above, where Christ sitteth on the right hand of God, Col. iii. 1; and when they begin to grow

* That is, = nurse = confirm—G.

worldly, and to follow their belly, it calls them back with a 'but know for all this, God will bring thee to judgment;' which, duly pondered, cannot but be as a hook in our jaws to bring us back to a more diligent watch over our ways.

And whose glory is in their shame.

A second part of the inward disposition, shewing that they glory in that which brought shame to them; for circumcision was a ceremony given to the church when it was but in the infancy; and for them that were born in the strength of the church, being well grown, to glory in such beggarly rudiments was shameful. In the words, first consider the affection; second, the object or end, for the word implies both. And in the first consider the sin, then the cure.

The sin that is reproved in them is 'vain-glory;' that is, glorying in a thing not to be gloried in; and it is grounded upon pride, which is a desire of excellency in vain things; and it is for the most part in vain injudicious men, who ordinarily do glory in things that tend to shame. These Philippians saw that Paul was now committed. The doctrine he taught they thought was not good enough; they would be wiser than he, and of deeper reach.

And thus even within the pale of the church, what a scandal is it that men should glory in a graceless grace of swearing, filling up rotten discourse with new devised oaths! And others glory in their foolish conceited gallant apparel; which was for no other end but principally to cover shame. Is not this to glory in shame? And much more those, that blaming, as it were, God for making them no fairer, will mend the workmanship of God by painting. These, while they seek to keep outward blemishes from the eyes of men, do discover to the whole world that they have a spotted rotten heart within them.

And, indeed, it is too common for men ill bred up, to think admirably of themselves, when all their courses are mere vanity. He is the only man of account that cannot put up a cross word without blood. Is not this to glory in shame, whenas it is the glory of a man to pass by an offence, and they are the best men that can overcome themselves? And as helpers on of this vain boasting, we have a generation of ignorant unsettled understandings, that admire at such shameless boasters, and so are causes of strengthening such in their vain-glory. Such are flatterers of great men. Let them remember what is denounced against such. Woe be to them that call evil good and good evil.

In the next place, *Shame is not only the object of vain-glory, but the end.* They that are vain-glorious shall be brought to shame at length. Thus it is said of Babylon in Isaiah, and mystical Babylon in the Revelations: 'Though she say, I sit as a queen, and shall see no mourning, yet shall her plagues come in one day, death, and destruction, and mourning,' Isa. xlvii. 9, and li. 19; Rev. xviii. 8.

For God hath knit vain-glory and shame, a punishment proportionable and fitting to the sin, and striking the offender most near, even to the heart. And thus did God meet with Ahithophel, Absalom, and Haman. They sought vain-glory, and their ends were shameful; and such shall be the end of all such as boast that they can do mischief like Doeg, Ps. lii., title, *et seq.* And the righteous shall see, and fear, and laugh at them.

For use to ourselves, therefore, *let us take heed of sin.* For by nature the best of us are subject to it. We are all inclinable either to glory in such things as we should not, or to receive glory from such things as we ought not; or else to glory after an inordinate manner. And in that measure we glory amiss, in that measure we consult shame to ourselves. Glory we may, but it must be well grounded, and in a right manner.

And to the attaining thereto we must first *labour for a sound knowledge of God, and for a sound dependence upon him in all things, and also labour for to see our own estate, and our many wants;* for wanting this knowledge, men glory in merits while they live. But when they die they grow ashamed of their courses and blind judgment. For while they live they judge of themselves by their own conceit of themselves, which is grounded either by comparing of themselves with those that are worse than themselves, as the Pharisee, that thanked God he was not as the publican, Luke xviii. 11; or else upon the conceit that shallow persons have of them.

1. But these are not rules for us to follow. *Look rather what says the humbled conscience;* what says God's word and his justice; and take example of the apostles and holy men of God, that gloried in the Lord reconciled to us in Christ, 'who is made to us wisdom, sanctification, and redemption,' 1 Cor. i. 30. 'Rejoice that our names are written in heaven,' Luke x. 20. Rejoice that we understand and know God to be just and merciful, Jer. ix. 23, 24. Glory in the testimony of a good conscience, that we are true Christians, though but weak, 2 Cor. i. 12.

2. Secondly, *We should be content with the judgment and approbation of God, and hearken to the admonitions of his ministers*, and care not for the censures of the world.

3. Thirdly, *Take we heed of the first beginnings and motions of sin;* at the first they are ever modest. The worst man that ever was, was not shameless in sin at the beginning, but giving way to sin by little, loses all shame, and causes at last corruption in judgment, and justifying a man's self in wicked courses. Pleasures, riches, and such things, they are like a vizard, only an outside of beauty; or like one that vaunted himself, he can act the person of a king, but is in himself a bond slave. They act their parts here on this worldly stage for an hour, and leave all their followers in eternal bondage for ever. Therefore let us not be ashamed for Christ's cause; but stand out, labour for sincerity now, and we shall have glory hereafter, which as the light shall increase, whenas 'the candle of the wicked shall be put out,' Prov. xxiv. 20.

Who mind earthly things.

To 'mind,' in this place is taken largely, to think upon, remember, desire, joy, and to have all the soul exercised. 'Earthly things;' that is, lusts of the flesh, lusts of the eyes, pride of life, pleasures, and profits, and honours, which are therefore called 'earthly,' because they are conversant about earthly things, and because they make their followers 'earthly minded;' and lastly, they are called earthly, in opposition to those that are heavenly. And thus in particular, those that mind honour are ambitious; those that mind riches are covetous; if pleasure, then they are voluptuous, and all of them are earthly. For as the ocean is but one, and yet divers parts thereof have several names, so worldliness is but one sin, yet having many kinds it hath also divers names.

1. The observation that hence we may gather is, *that the earthly disposition and mind is the temper of that man who is in the estate of damnation;* for the mind of such do shew a dead soul, estranged from the life of God: 'To

be carnally-minded is death,' saith the apostle, Rom. viii. 6. For a man lives as he minds and loves.

2. Secondly, Earthly disposition is opposite to God; so Rom. viii. 7, 'The carnal mind is enmity against God.'

Observe we further, the apostle describes not these by any notorious gross scandalous sin, but by the inward disposition of the heart; for outward actions are only effects and rivers flowing from the spring of corruption in our hearts.

Whence we may note, *that God looks to the inward frame of the soul in men;* and therefore though in the eyes of men a man may be without spot, yet is his corruption that is within, open and manifest to the all-seeing eye of God.

And therefore from hence we are *to be stirred up to humble ourselves before God, by examining our hearts,* and laying open our most secret corruptions.

2. And secondly, This ought *to comfort us,* that though in our daily practice we often fall, yet God in his goodness looks at the inward frame of the soul, and accepts of it.

3. Thirdly, This *justly lays open the folly of men's censures.* If a man break not out into open outrageous sins, they esteem and commend such for good men, though it may be his soul is full stuffed with atheism, revenge, and all manner of villany.

4. Fourthly, This should teach us *to condemn ourselves, even for sinful thoughts;* for know, though thou livest without danger of man's law, thou mayest have a rebellious mind opposite to the divine law of God, by which thou shalt be judged.

Yet seeing for this present life we stand in need of earthly things, and are not to cast off all care of them, let us hearken to some directions in the use of them. For riches and other necessaries, God sends them unto us to be as means to sweeten our pilgrimage here.

Rules. 1. In using them, take heed *they do not possess and take up our whole heart, immoderately labouring after them, and before any spiritual grace.* This the apostle blames in these men. He saw they made religion to be subordinate, and to give place to their worldly lusts, and that as he cared not, if by any means he could attain to the resurrection of the dead; so they contrarily cared not, if by any means, through any cross or loss whatsoever, they could attain to riches, honour, or the like; yea, if religion stood in their way, though it were with the loss of religion and a good conscience.

2. Secondly, We must take heed that we use *these earthly things so as to draw good out of them,* and to employ them to good. Labour we to see God in pleasure, in riches, and in our abundance, knowing and esteeming of them as a beam of the bright sunshine of God's favour to us, and thus to be lifted up to admire and praise his goodness.

3. Thirdly, *Make them instruments of mercy and bounty.* It is an excellent way to further our accounts. So receive the good as we avoid the snare. The way is not to hide our talents in a napkin, to enter into a monastery, to live idle; but to occupy, use, and employ them in the service of God and of our neighbours.

4. To conclude, *Let us so use them as they be helpers of us to a better life, not hinderers;* for we are in an estate between two, in a warring and conflicting estate, even as a piece of iron between two loadstones, and know not which way to lean; and yet may offend in the excess of either side.

And therefore let us observe some signs, whereby we may know whether we be right or not.

Signs. 1. And first of all, this affection of love, being the primary and principal part, is known by other affections. *If therefore our love be set on the world, we shall grieve and vex ourselves for worldly losses, and fret and be chafed when we are crossed in them;* and this made Ahab so lumpish, as nothing could comfort him but Naboth's vineyard.

2. Secondly, Let us *observe whither our labours and endeavours are carried*, what we talk of most, what think we or meditate we on, first and last, morning and evening. If we observe our carriage, it will discover our mind.

Such *are also opposite to any religious good course.* He that is rich bitterly opposeth goodness; and therefore it is that Christ said, 'Ye cannot serve God and Mammon,' Mat. vi. 24; and concludeth, 'It is harder for a rich man to get into heaven, than for a camel to pass through a needle's eye,' Mat. xix. 24.*

But to cure this sore, *let us fetch arguments from the nature of the soul of man, and the nature of these things;* and consider the incongruity between the soul, a pure heavenly spiritual essence, and base earthly corrupt things. Dust was made meat for the serpent by a curse, and not for man.

And remember, *the God of truth hath threatened vengeance against his dearest children that do not mortify their carnal lusts.* Abhor we therefore the first thoughts of this sin, and divert our souls to higher thoughts; and be humbled, shaming ourselves for debasing our souls in that manner, else will God take us in hand. For he will not suffer his children to surfeit on the world, but will bring them back, that they shall see and know 'all is but vanity and vexation of spirit.'

VERSE 20.

For our conversation is in heaven.

The word translated here 'for' in the former translation is 'but' (*z*); and so it depends on the foregoing words, 'some walk as enemies to the cross of Christ,' &c. '*But* our conversation is in heaven.' If it be as it is here translated, 'for,' then doth it follow the 17th verse: 'mark them that walk, as ye have us for an example. For our conversation is in heaven,' shewing the reason why he was so confident in propounding his example to be imitated. Which way it be taken, it is not much material, only from the opposition between those examples he speaks of immediately going before, and is propounded in this verse.

Note *That in the church there are always men of divers dispositions.* Some ever go within the current into *Mare Mortuum*,† and others ever against the stream, like the stars that are carried with a secret motion of their own, notwithstanding that in this world they seem to be carried by the violent motion of the common course of men.

1. And this was first *in God's eternal decree*, that there should be perpetual enmity between the seed of the woman and of the serpent.

2. Secondly, *There is a difference in calling;* some only outwardly, some inwardly by his Spirit: 'Many are called, but few are chosen,' Mat. xx. 16.

3. Thirdly, *They differ in their rulers;* one are governed by the devil, and led captive to do his will, others by God.

* Cf. note in Vol. IV. p. 368.—G.

† That is, the Dead Sea.—G.

4. Fourthly, *In regard of their conversation;* some are heavenly minded, others are altogether earthly.

5. Fifthly, *Their ends are different;* the way of the one is upwards to heaven, the way of the other is downward, tending to the gates of death, even to hell.

But to come to the words. The apostle saith not '*my* conversation,' but '*our* conversation;' implying that those that mean not to be of the number of those that have their end in damnation, they must be of the number of those of a holy conversation. The word in the original signifies most properly a freedom, or a burghership.† So as from the metaphor we may gather thus much.

Doct. That heaven is a city, and all true Christians are citizens and inhabitants of this city; for as it is in the city of this world, so may it be said comparatively of this city and the inhabitants.

First, *It is under a governor*, who is the Lord Christ.

Secondly, It is governed *by law*, which is God's law.

Thirdly, It hath *a storehouse of all good things*, as of food, and of other of the like sort, which is heaven, for it hath bread of life; it hath rich and plenteous treasure.

Fourthly, It hath *liberties*. They are free from Satan's tyranny, free from the law's curse and condemning power; and are all kings, and shall all reign. They shall be free from all weakness, from ill company, from temptation. The Lamb shall be all in all. 'Glorious things are spoken of thee, thou city of God,' Ps. lxxxvii. 3.

Fifthly, *They speak one language*, the language of Canaan. The language of the beast they abhor.

And lastly, *Their carriage is alike.* Grave like citizens of heaven, their faces are still as they were going to Jerusalem, their continuing and abiding city; for while they are in this life, they are still as it were in the suburbs.

Hence we may gather divers grounds, that while we live in this world, a Christian is but a pilgrim and stranger. First, *Heaven is his home, and this life is but a way, and he a passenger.* And thus David accounted of himself, though a king, yet but a stranger, both himself and his fathers; and therefore, as a passenger, he provides for his journey, he stands not for ill usage, cares not to look after delights in the way, but uses them as advantageous to his journey.

And secondly, *He is inquisitive after the way*, fearing he should go amiss; and furnisheth himself with cordials, to cheer him and strengthen him in his journey. He inquires after the guide of God's Spirit, to be as the pillar of fire to guide him in the darkness of this world.

Thirdly, *He is well provided of weapons* against such enemies as he shall meet with in the way. He hath the shield of faith, and the sword of the Spirit, which is the word of God.

2. The second ground that arises hence is, that *a Christian's endeavours are of a high nature.* His look is high, his soul and mind are ever upward, casting all burdens of earthly cares and delights from him, that he may freely mount up in the presence of his Maker.

3. Thirdly, This carriage of a Christian *is not by fits, but it is his trade*, his conversation and course of life. In all things he looks to heaven. His course is by rule and by law. Whatsoever he does he does as in obedience to God chiefly, with all his power, as approving himself to God, in whose

* The original is πολίτευμα.—G.

sight he ever sets himself. Briefly, he doth all things as a citizen of heaven.

4. Fourthly, We may also ground hence, that a Christian *may have his conversation in heaven, even while he is here alive;* for he is born anew, having received the life of grace. God requires not impossibilities, but always gives ability to the discharge of that which he enjoins.

Quest. But in particular, how may a Christian be said to be in heaven, or to have his conversation in heaven?

Ans. (1.) I answer, A Christian may be said to be in heaven; first, *as in his head Christ Jesus,* who is in heaven already, being gone to prepare a place for us.

(2.) Secondly, *He is there by faith,* which makes things absent as present; and so it is that 'Abraham saw Christ's day and was glad;' and therefore is faith called, 'The evidence of things not seen,' Heb. xi. 1.

(3.) Thirdly, A Christian is in heaven *by his hopes.*

(4.) Fourthly, He is there *by his desires. Animus est ubi amat* (*aa*).

(5.) Fifthly, A Christian is in heaven, *whenas his meditations are there;* when his thoughts are thereon continually busied, as St Paul was, when in admiration of those joys he crieth out, 'O the depth both of the riches and wisdom of God!' Rom. xi. 33.

(6). Sixthly, He is there, *when by continual prayers to God, he hath an inward admittance to the throne of grace,* where he may freely open his heart to his God; and therefore it is that those that are Christians indeed are often in this duty.

5. Hence we may gather, that *the glorious estate in heaven is of the same kind with this life of grace, only differing in degrees of happiness;* both estates are free: there only a freedom of glory, here a freedom of grace. Both are estates of redemption. There we are redeemed from sin and death and the devil, here we are only redeemed from the power of them; there have we the full harvest, here we have the first fruits; here we are heirs by faith, there by full possession; to all of us Christ is all in all, only there he rules immediately, here he rules by means, by his deputies. There they have communion with the saints, here we also have communion, though we live amongst the wicked. There they praise God continually, here we endeavour it continually. There they have communion with the beatifical vision, here we have communion with the ordinances which will bring us to it.

And, therefore, *let such as intend to be saints hereafter be saints here,* and live by the laws that are given us from heaven, and that they live by in heaven; for the kingdom is in such sort one and the same. The kingdom of grace, the preaching of the word, is called 'the kingdom of heaven,' as well as the kingdom of glory; and men do think in vain ever to enter into glory, without coming in at the gates of grace, as appeareth out of the apostle's argument, 2 Peter i. 10, 11, 'Give diligence to make your calling and election sure, for so an entrance shall be ministered unto you abundantly, into the everlasting kingdom of our Lord and Saviour Jesus Christ.'

And to this end, amongst many other, observe with me these following directions.

1*st Direct.* First, For a preparation, *hear the word of God;* for by this we are in heaven in part already. For where the word is preached, there is the presence of the blessed Trinity, and the holy angels bringing down heaven itself to us, teaching us in the laws of that kingdom. *Use reading also;* for even thereby we talk with the saints who wrote those things for our instruction, and that Spirit that guided them in writing will also guide thee in reading. Receive the sacraments often, for these ordinances are the heavenly manna to us, and strengthen us in our way to the spiritual Canaan.

2d Direct. Secondly, *Rejoice in often communicating with the saints.* These earth moles that are delighted in *cœno*, not in *cœlo*,* all company is alike to them; but a Christian will here converse with such as he shall be with hereafter, and the saints have found much help this way. Even Saul, in the company of prophets, became a prophet; and the most earthly man that is amongst good men, in good discourse, will suit himself to them; and indeed good discourse is of much avail this way, if it be frequent as it should be. I enforce it not as a duty to be done at all times, but it should be oftener than it is.

3d Direct. Thirdly, *Use such means as are of force to subdue the hindrances of this disposition.* Such as are lusts of youth, which ought to be tamed by fasts, and such watchfulness that may make us at the length wise; for so far as we overcome our lusts, so far we have our conversation in heaven; and therefore we must often in private watch, and in private pray; as the Scripture saith, we must watch unto prayer.

4th Direct. Fourthly, *Use much meditation.* Be ever setting our minds something to this end, that our affections may be wrought upon, to forsake the world with detestation, and to love and embrace heaven; and for this duty we ought to redeem some time continually. Thus principally Enoch walked with God; and David, though a king, meditated in God's law day and night.

5th Direct. And from this duty, *let us be brought to a holy use of soliloquies;* checking and shaming ourselves for following these pleasures, for unthankfulness and want of cheerfulness, as David, 'Why art thou cast down O my soul, why art thou so disquieted?' Ps. xlii. 5. By these recollections a Christian is indeed himself, and for the present even seated in heaven.

6th Direct. In the last place, besides ejaculations, *use daily a set prayer;* for thereby we ascend into heaven, and are fitted thereby to be more and more heavenly. It is the trade of citizens that make them rich. This is our trade, to trade by prayer with that heavenly city, where our treasure is, and by it we shall grow daily in riches. Thus is our soul strengthened and our affections stirred up to converse with God, and thus come we to set our faith in heaven, together with our love, where our Father is, where angels and saints, our city and eternal happiness, is. Thus is our hope strengthened, which carries us through all afflictions undauntedly, and so is a heaven to us before heaven; and thus are our desires in heaven, to be at rest, to be with Christ, which is best of all.

Obj. But some will say, We cannot always intend† such things as these, we have our callings, and are busied about earthly matters and cares.

Ans. 1. I answer: True it is, yet in the use of these things, we may be heavenly minded; for God in mercy appoints us callings, to busy our minds about, which else would be delving in the idle pleasures of sin: only he requires, that we in the first place 'seek for heaven.' We shall not continue here, but we are travelling still; and therefore it is good for us ever to redeem some time for heaven, that we may come with more speed to our journey's end.

2. Secondly, As a help to us, *he hath left us his Sabbaths*, in pity to our

* That is, with the *filth* of earth, not with *heaven.*—G.

† That is, 'attend.'—G.

souls, which else would altogether be rooting in the earth. Let us have a care of the well spending of them; for by this we pay homage to heaven, and are put in mind thereof.

3. Thirdly, *Every day redeem some time for meditation* of the vanity of this world. Hereby will our untunable souls be still set in tune; and for our callings, every day sanctify them by prayer, and then all is clean.

4. Fourthly, *Go about them as in obedience to God*, knowing that God hath placed us in these callings, and he looks for service in employing those talents bestowed on us, and in our serving one another. And let us endeavour *to shew what our religion is, in avoiding the corruptions of our callings.* Labour also to see God in everything, *in crossing us, in encouraging and assisting us;* and this will stir us up accordingly to pray continually, and in all things to give thanks; and it will make us fear always, for the same care and love of God that brings us to heaven, doth guide us in our particular actions and callings. And in other matters use ourselves so as we by these things raise our minds on high, for there is a double use of the creatures. First, temporal, and from thence a spiritual use is raised. Thus did Christ. By considering water he was raised to think of spiritual regeneration and washing; and thus we should do, labour to see God in his creatures, and thus shall we help our souls by our bodies. God will have it thus, and therefore setteth down heavenly things in earthly comparisons.

7th Direct. Lastly, *We must endeavour to make a spiritual use of all things as God doth.* Doth God send crosses on us? Then before they leave us beg a blessing, that they may work his intended effect in bettering us. Doth God bless us with prosperity? Pray that God would sanctify it to encourage us on to good duties, so as in all estates we may have our conversation in heaven. Let no man therefore make pretence that he is poor, that he hath no time for this. No. Grace works matter out of everything. Poor Paul, nay, Paul a prisoner, see how he is busied; and the truth is, that worldly prosperity is the greatest enemy to a heavenly mind that can be.

Obj. But the weak Christian will complain *that he cannot find this in him*, but he is still carried away with worldly matters. Though he strive against it never so much, yet the world goes away with him.

Ans. To such I answer, Strength of grace this way is not in every Christian, neither is it at the first. Paul had his distractions, Rom. vii. from ver. 15 to ver. 24, yet must our labours and endeavours be that way. The sin that is in us cannot hurt us if we strive against it. God suffers his children to see their weakness, as he did deal with Solomon, to humble us and make us learn his lesson, that all 'is vanity and vexation of spirit.' Let not such therefore be discouraged, but cheerfully go on in a good course, wherein the *more we labour and strive, the more we beautify religion*, and credit our city, and draw on others to be fellow-citizens with us.

And thus shall we free ourselves from terrors of conscience, and from the snares of the devil, even as birds when they soar aloft need fear no snares. Thus *also shall we get a portion here*, for it is the promise of the God of truth, that if we first seek the kingdom of heaven, all these things shall be cast upon us. Thus also shall we be sure of God's gracious and faithful protection, who hath said he will keep us in our ways.

And lastly, Thus shall we end our days with comfort. Woe be to him that dies not to the world before he goes hence. But to him that hath his soul in heaven, even while it is in his body, this life is but a pilgrimage, and death is advantage.

From whence we also look for the Saviour, the Lord Jesus Christ.

These words lay down such an estate of a Christian, as is both a cause and a sign of heavenly conversation; and in them we may consider, first, That Christ is in heaven. Secondly, That there is a second coming of Christ. Thirdly, That Christians expect it. Fourthly, That this expectation is a cause of heavenly carriage.

For the first, *that Christ is in heaven*, we have the Scripture to warrant it, but the text is pregnant herein. We look for him from heaven, *ergo* he is in heaven.

And therefore it is a gross conceit of the papists, that dream that his body is everywhere *in* the bread, or *with* the bread, as the Lutherans would have it. The Scripture determines that the heavens must contain him; that he sitteth now on the right hand of God; that he shall hereafter come to judge, and therefore he is not now here; nay, because he is not here he sent us the Comforter, the Spirit, that shall lead us into all truth, as he himself expressly saith, John xvi. 13.

Secondly, Hence we may observe, *that there is another coming of Christ, which yet is not fulfilled.* There is a twofold coming of Christ, one whereby he comes in the flesh. This was his first coming. The second coming is in triumph, when he shall perfect our salvation. This appeareth by the desires of the creature, Rom. viii. 37, *seq.* Secondly, By the faithful desires of his children, which cannot be in vain. Thirdly, To this end he took our flesh to draw us after him. Fourthly, To this end he left his Spirit with us to testify it. Lastly, He hath left us his promises and prophecies thereof, witnessed by the angels: Acts i. 11, 'This Jesus shall so come, even as you have seen him go into heaven.'

Thirdly, *That Christians do expect this coming of Christ* is evident out of the words, 'from whence we look for the Saviour,' saith the text. The word 'look' signifies an earnest expectation, implying faith, hope, and patience.* Faith is a ground of hope, supposing the promises which are grounded on an almighty God of truth. Now patience comes from hope, so as the word implies thus much. We hope, we believe, we patiently wait for the second coming of Christ. This is the disposition of every sound Christian, and it begins with the beginning of our new birth; for so, 1 Peter i. 3, it is said, 'We are begotten to a lively hope;' and Titus ii. 13, 'The grace of God once appearing, teacheth to look for the blessed hope.'

Reason 1. For as in nature *the seed desires growth, everything desires perfection,* so much more in grace. Where once it is settled it continually desireth a more perfect estate, until the coming of Christ, when it cometh to the top and pitch thereof.

Reason 2. Secondly, *There is such a relation betwixt Christ and us, we being contracted to him here, as there is a continual longing for the consummation of this marriage;* even as the time between the contract and the marriage is a continual longing.

Reason 3. Thirdly, Our estate here *is a warring and laborious estate, and a painful service,* and therefore what marvel if a sabbath, a peaceable, victorious, and triumphant estate, be sweet and to be desired?

Use. Hence we may learn that the estate of the children of God here *is imperfect,* for they are under hope of a better estate. Before Christ's time they expected the first coming of Christ. So it is said of Abraham, that he longed to see Christ's day. Now after Christ's first coming, we look

* The original is, *ἐξ οὗ καὶ σωτῆρα ἀπεκδεχόμεθα* Κύριον Ἰησοῦν Χριστόν, on which cf. Bishop Ellicott, with his references.—G.

after his second coming, when we shall be perfected; and thus the souls in heaven are in expectation of a further happiness.

Use 2. And this *is the reason of the contrarieties of estate that are in a Christian.* He rejoices because he is under hope, but he sorrows because he hath not already obtained the thing he hopeth for. He rejoiceth because of his assurance, but sorroweth because of the crosses he daily meets with; rejoiceth in the communion of saints, but 'woe is me that I dwell in Mesech,' Psa. cxx. 5. We are kings, but over rebels; prophets, but have much ignorance, for we see but in part; priests, but are daily polluted with the soil of this world, and therefore do stand in need of continual washing.

Use 3. Thirdly, *This expectation is not only a work of ours, but a grace wrought in us by Christ,* by virtue of the covenant: for God fits us with graces that have reference to our future happiness; and it arises from love and patience, grounded upon assurance of an end and glorious issue. Christ knew we were to meet with enemies, and therefore gives us hope as an helmet and an anchor to keep us from shipwreck; for he is a saviour as well in saving us here from despair, as hereafter from hell.

Use 4. This, lastly, may serve *for a trial of our estates:* for many that think themselves to be good Christians, think with Peter 'it is good being here,' Mat. xvii. 4; it is good for them to be in this world. They fear the coming of Christ. The very thought thereof destroys all their mirth. It is to them like the handwriting on the wall to Belshazzar. The child of God is of another disposition. He is begotten to this hope: his desire is accordingly; his endeavour and labour is by any means to attain to the resurrection of the dead, Philip. iii. 11.

Obj. But it will be said, *that it is often seen that good Christians do not always desire the coming of Christ.*

Ans. To which I answer, It is true; but it is caused by their careless carriage. And yet, ever there is a spirit in them, to endeavour to do something that may prepare for his coming. But a strong Christian hath ever this desire; and if he be a mortified and growing Christian, he never wants this hope, and comfort, and earnest longing: and therefore his prayer ever is, 'Come, Lord Jesus.'

Fourthly, We may observe out of the words, where this hope is, and this expectation, it *stirs up and quickens the soul to a holy conversation.* It is propounded here as a ground of the apostle's holy conversation.

For *it stirs us up to be pure,* even as he is pure, as it is 1 John iii. 3. For we are a holy spouse, and there will shortly come the marriage-day; and fitting it is that we prepare ourselves fitting for such a husband. Thus it was with the concubines of Ahasuerus. Though a temporal and earthly king, yet the custom was, they should be twelve months before they came to the king, Esther ii.; and much more should it be our duty, evermore to be prepared to come into the presence of our eternal, heavenly King, to meet with the bridegroom; because we know not how soon it may be that he will come, and send his angels for us to appear before him in glory, to call us to the wedding.

Secondly, This hope will stir us up *to do all good duties, and to right performance of good duties;* to do all things sincerely, as in the presence of God our judge. And therefore, not only the duty of preaching is urged upon Timothy, but the manner, 2 Tim. iv. 2, who is charged by the Lord Jesus Christ, who shall judge all at his appearing, that he should 'preach the word: be instant in season, out of season, reprove, rebuke, exhort, with all long-sufferance.' And the apostle Peter having declared the second coming of Christ, thence infers, 'What manner of men ought we to be in all godly conversation,' 2 Pet. iii. 11. And indeed, meditation of the principles of religion will inform us well in the manner of our duties, as in the nature of them; and thus shall we be fruitful in particulars, according as our meditations are directed, though the principal matters and objects of our meditation are but few.

Thirdly, This hope and expectation will stir us up *to pray for the consummation and bringing to pass the performance of all those promises which are to be performed before the coming of Christ*, as that the gospel should be preached in all places; that the conversion of the Jews might be hastened, and the downfall of antichrist might speedily come to pass. And this hope will also encourage us and put us forward, that in our several callings and standings, we should help on the performance of them as much as is in our power to perform, by helping on the building of the church and the enlargement of Christ's kingdom, and the confusion of his enemies.

Lastly, This hope will *work in us a sweet and comfortable carriage in all estates and conditions, carrying us through all impediments with courage.* For 'yet a little while, and he that shall come will come, and will not tarry,' Heb. x. 37, and he will come full handed. 'My reward is with me,' saith Christ; and lest we should think it long before he comes, he told us long ago that those were the latter days, and that the ends of the world were then come upon them. Do men, then, molest us, persecute, and vex us? Let us be comforted. He comes that will tread all our enemies under our feet. Do we find that we have but short spirits, that our graces are but weak? Let us not dishearten ourselves. He that keeps heaven for us will give us necessary graces to bring us thither. If we want, go to the God of faith and love. He hath promised to give us his Spirit, to make all grace abound in us, never to leave us nor forsake us till he hath perfected his work, in setting us with him in glory.

But to proceed to the object of this expectation, it is Christ who is described unto us by the Saviour, whom he calls also Jesus, which signifies a Saviour; and this he doth to impress it the deeper into his affections.

Quest. But some may say, Christ hath saved us already. What need is there, therefore, of his second coming?

Ans. I answer, It is to perfect our salvation. For redemption of our bodies and glorious liberty are reserved to his second coming. We look not that he should die any more, but appear as a Lord of glory in glory, without humiliation for sin, having already gotten victory of it.

Doct. The observation is, *that Christ is a Saviour, and the Saviour by way of excellency.* He saves all that are of his mystical body from all evil, and preserves them to all good. He saves their bodies and their souls now from the power of all evil, and hereafter he will free them from all evil. He is the everlasting Saviour. While we live here his blood runs continually. This is the 'fountain opened for the house of Judah for sin and uncleanness,' Zech. xiii. 1. In it are we cleansed from the guilt and damnation of sin. What would we have more? 'We are kept by faith to salvation,' 1 Peter i. 5. Let this raise up our souls. Are we swallowed up with the sense of any misery? Let us know that we trust a Saviour that is every way absolute, that invites those that are sick with sin to come unto him; and 'how can we escape, if we neglect so great salvation?' Heb. ii. 3. Away, therefore, with all popish conceits of meriting by our works. All glory must be given only to his mercy; all that he did for us was to the glory of his grace, Eph. i. 6.

Lastly, This should *comfort us when we think of the last day*, to think withal, that he shall be our judge that is our Saviour, and therefore should cast away all terror from us, knowing that our head will not destroy his members, but that he our husband being a great king, will also crown us his spouse with a glorious crown. Therefore, when we see the foregoing signs come to pass, 'let us lift up our heads, knowing our redemption draweth near,' Luke xxi. 28.

To go on, in the next place: Christ is not only our Saviour, 'but he is our Lord,' wherein we may see the apostle's Christian wisdom. He useth such titles as may most of all strengthen his faith and affection of the present meditation, which being a point of the resurrection, a thing seeming contrary to reason, to flesh and blood, he strengthens himself in this consideration, that he 'is the Lord,' who hath all power and authority committed to him, Mat. xxviii. 18.

Secondly, He is Lord *by title of redemption*, so as we are no more our own, but his; for he hath bought us with a price.

Thirdly, He is Lord *of the world, and of the devil by conquest*, Heb. ii. 14.

Fourthly, He is Lord over *his church by marriage*. He is our husband, governing his church with sweetness and love.

He is also the Lord by way *of excellency above others*, depending on no creature. He is 'Lord of lords.'

Secondly, He is Lord *of body and soul and conscience*, punishing with terrors here and damnation hereafter.

Thirdly, He is Lord *eternal*. He endures for ever, and cannot die.

Fourthly, He is such a Lord *as cannot abuse his authority*. He cannot tyrannise. His grace and virtue are of equal extent with his power.

Fifthly, He is *a holy Lord*. Holy, holy, holy, Lord God of Sabaoth, that is, Lord of hosts, Rev. iv. 8.

In all these he is far above any earthly man, yea, above all creatures. And therefore it is a sweet estate to be under government and rule. *They then that are lords here on earth must consider, though they rule and are above others, yet they are under the Lord.* Thus did Joseph. Therefore they must rule, 'but in the Lord.' It is his will that must rule their wills.

Secondly, This should *comfort Christians*, that they have such a Lord as is Lord of angels, at whom the devils tremble; whom storms, winds, seas, sickness, death, and all creatures do obey. Yet we cannot challenge this comfort, but upon condition of our obedience. The apostle joins Lord and Saviour together, to shew that he is a Saviour only to those that take him for their Lord to govern and rule them. As he is our priest, he must also be our king. He comes by water to purge and wash us, as well as by blood to suffer for us. The wicked; they will not have this man rule over them, but they shall not say nay. God will be a Lord over them, ruling by his power; with a rod of iron he will bruise them in pieces, none shall deliver them. If we will avoid this miserable estate, let us make him Lord in us. Thus shall we crown him, and then he will crown us with himself.

VERSE 21.

Who shall change our vile body.

The words are plain, and shall need no exposition; therefore we will briefly come to the doctrines.

Doct. 1. And first, We may observe hence *that our bodies are base;* and thus are the bodies not only of wicked profane men, but of the servants and dearest children of God; all are vile. And that in these respects.

First, In life our *original is base*. We are dust, and to dust we must return, Gen. iii. 19; and our continuance is full of change, subject to diversity of estates, sickness, health, pain, ease, hunger, fulness. And base we are, because we are upheld by inferior creatures. We enter into the world by one way, but go out by divers deaths; some violent, some more natural, and by divers sicknesses loathsome to the eyes, to the nostrils, and especially when we are nearest our end, whenas our countenance is pale, our members tremble, all our beauty is gone. But after we are departed, so loathsome is this our carcase, it must be had out of sight; yea, though it be the body of the patriarch Abraham,* Gen. xxiii. 4. For as the body of man is the best temper, so the corruption thereof is the most vile. The best countenances of the greatest personages are the most ugly, ghastly objects of all others, by so much the more, by how much they were the more excellent; so much the greater is their change. And yet are we not to conceive of this body so as though there were no glory belonging to it; for, first, it is God's workmanship, therefore excellent, and so excellent as the heathen man Galen, being stricken into admiration at the admirable frame thereof, breaks out into a hymn in praise of the Maker (*bb*). And David could not express it, but says, 'I am wonderfuily made,' Ps. cxxxix. 14. God made this his last work, as an epitome of all the rest.

Secondly, *We are told that we owe glory to our bodies;* and therefore we are bidden that we should not wrong our bodies; and the Scripture speaks infamously of self-murderers, as of Judas, Saul, Ahithophel. They are branded with a note of shame and reproach. And God, to shew the respect we owe to our bodies, hath provided to every sense pleasing recreations, as flowers for the smell, light for the eyes, music for the ear; to be brief, he made all things for the bodily use of man.

Thirdly, *These bodies of ours are members of Christ*, redeemed and sanctified temples of the Holy Ghost, as well as of our souls. And therefore we must take heed, when we read of the base terms that are given to the body, that we do not mistake. For it is true in regard it keeps the soul from heaven, it is the grave of the soul; but indeed it is the house, the temple and instrument of the soul. But being misused, it proves an untoward dark house, an unwieldy instrument.

We are to take heed, therefore, of the error of those who afflict it by writing and declaiming against it, or by whipping of it, when, alas! it is the sin of the soul, the unruly lusts and affections, that are the causes of all rebellions in us; and if the body doth rebel, as often it doth come to pass since the fall, this proceeds from the corruption of the soul yielding to the body aid to serve the lusts; and God hath appointed a religious abstinence as a means to tame such lusts and weaken them, which it were to be wished were used oftener than it is.

Quest. But it will be said, Are the bodies of Christians base, for whom Christ shed his most precious blood?

Ans. I answer, While we live here, we are in no better condition than others, as concerning our bodies. Hezekiah is sick; Lazarus hath his sores; David and Job troubled with loathsome diseases; and thus it is fitting it should fare with us.

For, first, *Christ laid us this example.* He took our base, ragged nature on him. He hungered and thirsted, was pained, and death had a little

* Qu. 'Sarah'?—Ed.

power over him. And shall we desire a better estate than our master, our head, had? or do we ever think to partake with him in happiness, that will not partake with him in his mean estate? The decree of God is, that to dust we must, as all the rest of our fellow-saints and servants shall.

Secondly, Hereby God *doth exercise our faith and hope;* causing us to look and expect a better resurrection; and by this means are our desires edged to a better life, for else would we set up our rest here, and make this our paradise.

Thirdly, As yet there *is sin in us;* from the danger whereof, though we be delivered, yet there is a corruption that remaineth behind in us; and by this he will teach us the contagion of sin, and teach us to see how the devil hath deceived us, by the effects thereof bringing pain, torment, and loathsomeness.

Fourthly, It shews *God's wisdom in vanquishing sin by death,* which is the child of sin; for by it shall we be purged from sin, from corruption both of body and mind, and thus is our base estate made a way to our excellent estate hereafter.

We must therefore moderate our affections to the best things of this life. Health is changeable, and will not continue. Beauty is a flower of a stalk. The flower quickly fades away and perisheth. The stalk that is more base continues longest. Flesh is grass, either cut down by violent death; or if by age, the longer it lives the baser it is, and increases continually therein till death, whenas it is most base.

It is therefore foolish for any to swell because of beauty or strength, which at the best are but curious* excellencies of a base body; and far more sottish are they that think to resist old age and God's decree, by trimming up and painting a withered stock. This is not the way to conquer vileness. But if we will be rid thereof, labour for the meat that perisheth not, John vi. 27 But that which maketh us endure to everlasting life is, with Mary, to choose the 'better part, that shall not be taken away.' 'Meat for the belly, and the belly for meat: but God shall destroy both the one and the other,' 1 Cor. vi. 13.

And let this be as a cooler, to quench the base wildfire of love; and consider what is it we so affect.† It is but beautiful dust, a painted sepulchre, a body that after death will be vileness itself, that while it breathes it is full of rottenness, the matter of worms, supported it may be by a carrion soul, that whether it willeth or nilleth‡ must leave it and go into a far worse place.

And contrarily, in the last place, it should teach us *to be at a point,§ cheerfully to honour God by sacrificing ourselves to him when he calls for us.* Count it no shame with David to be vile in the eyes of men for God's cause. If the worst could be imagined, which cannot be, we had as good perish with usage as with rust. But this is the only way to be glorious, to avoid vileness, even to sacrifice our bodies and all in a good cause. What though the world esteem vilely of us, as good for nothing but the shambles, Rom. viii. 36; shall we fear them? No. Fear him that can destroy both body and soul. It is better to go to heaven without a limb, than to go to hell with a sound healthful body. Therefore when temptations of the world do begin to provoke thee, say to thy flesh with Bernard, Stay thy time; the time is not yet to be happy (*cc*).

And therefore, to conclude, *our soul is but a stranger here; we must enter-*

* That is, 'nice.'—G.
† That is, 'choose,' 'love.'—G.
‡ That is, = willeth not.—Ed.
§ That is, = a resolution.—G.

tain it well into this house of our body. It is but a guest, use it not basely. It is no ill guest. It gives us sight, taste, speech, motion. When it goes away, our body is but a dumb, dull, base lump of earth. Nay, when it is gone, whilst the body is in the ground, the soul having a most vehement and earnest desire to be knit to it again, puts God continually in mind of raising it up at the last day of the general resurrection, and of glorifying it in a holy, eternal, and happy estate.

2. Secondly, Out of the words we may observe, *that these vile bodies of ours shall be changed.* This we receive as an article of our faith; and yet were it believed truly as it ought, it would work a strange alteration in the minds and manners of men, contrary to that they are now; and howsoever it is not embraced, yet it remains a grounded truth, that these bodies of ours, sown in corruption, shall rise incorruptible, 1 Cor. i. 15. It was foretold in way of consequence in paradise; for the head of the serpent could not be broken but by conquering death, which is the last enemy. It was figured out unto us in Aaron's dead sear rod that budded, and Jonah's deliverance out of the belly of the fish, where he had been three days and three nights. It was believed of all the fathers, Heb. xii. 1, *seq.* And for security before the flood Enoch, and after the flood Elias, were taken up in their bodies.

And besides, it is not contrary to reason. I do not say that reason can reach unto it. For Christ he is alive still. The dust whereof we are made, and whither we go is preserved. It is not annihilated. And why cannot Christ raise a body out of the dust, as at the first make it out of dust. Why should he not be as able to quicken dust now as at the first? and especially, seeing the soul is reserved in heaven to this end, till the day of his second coming.

Nay, it is not contrary to the course of nature. We see every year summer comes out of winter, day out of night, youth out of infancy, man's age out of youth. And the apostle in the Corinthians, 'Thou fool, the corn is not quickened except it die,' 1 Cor. xv. 36. Nay, we see what strange changes are daily wrought by art; and shall we think God's almighty power cannot work far more strange effects?

Use. The use therefore is to instruct us if we believe that Christ shall change these vile bodies, *then sure the same bodies shall rise that died; for change is of qualities, it abolisheth not substances.* And therefore Job's confidence herein is remarkable, Job xix. 26, 'Whom I shall see for myself, and mine eyes shall behold,' speaking of Christ; so is it, 1 Cor. xv. 53, 'This corruptible must put on incorruption, and this mortal must put on immortality,' and the ancient creeds had, *credo resurrectionem carnis hujus.*

Secondly, *It is very unequal that one body should honour or defile itself, and another body should be honoured or damned.* It is comfortable therefore to us that love our bodies and honour them, that they shall rise again and we shall enjoy them for ever.

Thirdly, *Christ our surety he raised the same body that was crucified:* and therefore the same bodies here that fulfil the measure of the sufferings of Christ here, shall partake of his fulness in glory.

Use 2. A second use is *for comfort.* Is this a life of changes? Let it not daunt us, but know they are all to end in glory, and they all tend to bring us thither. We ever change for the better, and the last change of all is the best of all. And therefore let us endure these changes with a light heart.

Use 3. In the third place, Who is the author of this change in us? The text saith that 'Christ shall change us.' John vi. 39 and 40, 'I will raise them up at the last day,' saith Christ, of those that know him and believe on him. He is furthermore our head. Now we know the body must be conformable to the head. If it be crowned the body is crowned; and therefore, Rom. viii. 11, the apostle saith, that if the Spirit dwell in us that did dwell in him, the Spirit that raised him up will raise us up also.

Thirdly, *Christ is a whole Saviour.* He therefore will raise up our bodies as well [as] our souls; for he is the Saviour of both. He hath delivered both from hell; he will raise up both to heaven.

Fourthly, *He is the second Adam.* As we did bear the image of the first Adam in corruption, so must we bear the image of the second Adam in glory.

Fifthly, *He is the seed of the woman,* that must break the serpent's head; and therefore he must work this change.

Sixthly, *Christ changed his own body,* being burdened with all our sins; and therefore, as an exemplary cause, shall much more raise us up. For sin being once overcome, which is the sting of death, what can keep us in the grave?

Use 1. Let *this strengthen our faith* in the consideration that we have such a strong Saviour, that nothing shall be able to separate us from his love, nor to take us out of his hand.

Use 2. Secondly, *Make it a ground how to direct us how to honour our bodies;* not making them instruments of sin against him, but so to use them, that we may with comfort and joy expect and desire his coming to change these vile bodies.

Use 3. Thirdly, Let us labour *to assure ourselves of our parts in this change, in this resurrection.* This we shall know if we *find Christ's Spirit in us.* The same Spirit that raised up him, if it be in us, will raise us up also, Rom. viii. 11. For the first resurrection is an argument of the second; and he that finds his understanding enlightened, his will pliable, his affections set upon right objects, will easily believe the second resurrection of his body. Secondly, *If we hope for this change,* and so hope that we are stirred up thereby to fit ourselves for it, to cleanse ourselves. Thirdly, *If we grow in grace,* 2 Pet. iii. 18, it is a sign that we have an entrance into Christ's kingdom; for God doth ever honour growth, with assurance of a blessed estate.

Use 4. Fourthly, *This should comfort us in time of death,* considering we lose nothing but baseness, and our bodies are but sown in the earth; and this *depositum* which God committeth to the fire, air, earth, and the water, they must render up again pure and changed by Christ. And, therefore, it was a foolish conceit of the heathen to burn the martyrs' bodies, and to cast their ashes into the water, thereby to put them out of hope of their resurrection, not knowing God is as able to raise them out of fire and water as out of earth.

Use 5. Fifthly, This ought *to administer comfort to us at the death and departure of our friends out of this life,* knowing that they are not lost; that the earth is but a house and a hiding-place for them to sleep in; and that at length God will not forget to raise them up with the residue of his saints. He will change them, and make them like his glorious body; and this was the use made by the apostle, 1 Thes. iv. 18.

Use 6. And lastly, *Pray to God to teach us to number our days,* so as we may apply our hearts to wisdom, Deut. xxxii. 29.* But when is the time

* Qu. 'Ps. xc. 12'?—G.

of this blessed change? It is not laid down, only it is implied by the word 'shall,' that the time is to come. But out of all question it is meant at the last day, and not before.

First, Because *all are to be gathered together*, even those that were buried four thousand years agone, must stay till the number be fulfilled; and it will make for God's glory that we should all meet together to attend on him, with multitudes of angels, so as they cannot be perfected without or before us, and we shall not prevent those that are asleep, 1 Thes. iv. 15.

Secondly, It is *for the comfort of Christians that are weak*, that the martyrs and constant professors of Christ should be pledges of their rising, who continually cry, 'How long, Lord?' Rev. vi. 9.

Thirdly, *God wills that things should now be carried as in a cloud*, and that the last day should be a day of revelation; which could not be, if before there should be this change.

For *use*. This must teach us to *desire that day, and pray for the hastening thereof;* till when, the souls in heaven are not perfectly happy. For all must be brought in before they can be made perfect. And therefore they desire and hope for, and pray for, to be united to those bodies again, that they lived withal, and so dearly loved.

But who are these that shall be thus changed? The text saith, 'our bodies;' that is, our bodies that have had 'our conversation in heaven.' And, therefore, those that have had no part in the first resurrection, they shall have no part in the second. The baker and butler of Pharaoh all shall arise and be lifted out of prison, but some to the resurrection of life, and others to the resurrection of condemnation. But to proceed.

That we may be fashioned like unto his glorious body.

So that Christ shall be the exemplary cause, as well as the efficient cause of our resurrection. For he is our head and our husband; and it is reason we should be suitable to him, and be ruled by him. He came not to make himself like us, but us like him. He first must be a king, blessed and anointed, and a Son. The head makes us like to him, kings, blessed and glorious. Enoch and Elias, though before his real incarnation, yet they ascended by virtue of his resurrection, and so shall we. They are glorious like to him; so shall we in his good time and pleasure.

Quest. But how?

Ans. I answer, In these particulars:

First, As he is *immortal*, never to die again, so shall we. We shall be freed from all sin; and so, consequently, from all mortality.

Secondly, We shall be *incorruptible*. We shall have no corruption within us or without us, as it is, 1 Cor. xv. 53. We shall be embalmed with the Spirit, that shall cause us to remain for ever incorruptible.

Thirdly, We shall be *unchangeable;* always the same, without sickness of body, or indisposedness of mind.

Then, in the *fourth* place, we shall be in *perfect strength*. Here we contract to ourselves weakness by every little thing, as alteration of air, study, and the like; there the body shall be enabled to every thing. But here we are weak, unfit, and soon weary of any duty, soon tired in prayer, weary in hearing, so as even Moses his arms must be supported, Exod. xvii. 12.

Fifthly, We shall have *beauty and comeliness*, the most lovely complexion and proportion of parts. There shall be no dregs in our body: all shall be spent by death; far better than after physic, which notwithstanding brings the body into a quiet repose. All wants shall be supplied. What is misplaced shall be reduced into right order. And therefore, what though we lose limbs for Christ's sake, he will not be indebted to us; none shall go thither maimed.

Obj. But some will say, Christ himself retained wounds after his resurrection, and therefore much more shall we be imperfect.

Ans. I answer, This was a voluntary dispensation. He suffered them to appear for the faith of Thomas, not of necessity.

Sixthly, These bodies of ours *shall be spiritual,* as it is 1 Cor. xv. 53, *seq.* A natural body is upheld by natural means, as meat, drink, physic, but then shall there be no need of such things. Christ shall be all in all to us. And again, our body shall obey the spirit. Now the body keeps the spirit in slavery, but then shall it readily yield to every motion of the spirit. The *ubiquitaries** when they speak of the spirituality of Christ's body, they would have it in all places. But they may as well conclude, because we shall have spiritual bodies, therefore our bodies also shall be in all places like to Christ's body. The ground of the glory of these bodies shall be the beatifical vision, and our union with Christ. If our beholding him here in his ordinances be of such a power as to transform us from glory to glory, 2 Cor. iii. 18, what a change shall be wrought in us when we shall see him as he is! And if his first coming had that power to make all things new, 2 Cor. v. 17, much more when he cometh the second time in glory shall he make all things new and glorious.

Use 1. This therefore, in the first place, *should encourage us* in all causes of dismay and trouble, rather than we will offend God to lose our bodies, knowing that we give them to God, and shall receive them again with advantage.

Use 2. Secondly, Labour we *to make our bodies instruments of his honour,* that honours us; and let us honour our bodies wherein are the seeds of immortality, and glory in so using them as that they be carried to the grave with honour.

Use 3. Let us also *honour the bodies of the deceased saints of God, and the places of their sepulture,* as cabinets wherein the precious dust of the holy saints are laid up in keeping.

Use 4. And let us not be like them *without faith, that think the bodies are lost for ever that are cast into the grave;* like children seeing the silver cast into the furnace, think it utterly cast away, till they see it come out again a pure vessel.

Use 5. And when we die, *let us not trouble our minds with the discomfortable thoughts of worms, rottenness, darkness, and the like;* but with the eye of faith let us look beyond these, on the haven whither we are going. This made Job, though covered all over with ulcers, to say with a cheerful heart, 'My Redeemer liveth, though after my skin worms consume this flesh,' Job xix. 26.

Use 6. If *we want limbs to our bodies, to comfort ourselves,* the resurrection will restore all things.

Use 7. Furthermore, *Let us serve here with our best endeavours.* It is but a while, and it shall not be in vain. Is it not better thus to do and partake of this blessed change, than to spare this vile body, and pamper it by sacrificing all, or to employ all our time in the serving and pleasing others; and to that end not to care to prostitute ourselves to all manner of

* Those who argue for transubstantiation, or consubstantiation, generally maintain the *ubiquity* of Christ's body.—G.

filthiness? What shall we get by these courses? but at the resurrection of the just, when we should lift up our heads because our redemption draweth nigh, then shall we be overcome with shame, grief, terror, and horror of conscience. But happy are we therefore, if in a good course we can so resign up ourselves, so as to be resolute with Esther, 'If I perish, I perish,' Esther iv. 16; 'if I live, I live to Christ; if I die, I die to him,' Philip. i. 21. What I have committed to him he will keep. I am assured thereof; and therefore I will not offend him for any pleasure or profit whatsoever. These resolutions had the patriarchs and God's saints, and these made them die with comfort.

According to the working whereby he is able even to subdue all things to himself.

The word that is translated 'working,' may and doth signify power; and so it was translated heretofore, and is to be [so] meant* (*dd*). But the words being plain, we will come to some observations.

Doct. 1. And first of all observe, *That Christ hath a power able to subdue all things to himself;* and this he hath by virtue of his office of mediatorship, and this in respect of God to reconcile and appease him. Secondly, In respect of opposite powers to overcome all of them. Thirdly, In respect of the persons to be saved, that he might free them from all ill, and raise them to all happiness; and these things requires a power that must be above all created powers. For God could not be appeased but by an infinite price, the blood of one that is God. And we could not be defended from sin and hell—whose power is the greatest of all finite power—but by a power beyond it; and such a power as must regenerate and renew us, notwithstanding the opposite power of the devil, and our corruptions within us, which is a greater work than the work of our creation. And all this he hath done. 'He hath subdued him that had the power of death, the devil,' Heb. ii. 14. He hath subdued diseases and winds with a word, and with a word he smote his enemies to the ground. He hath subdued all ill of the body and mind, forgiving sins, opening our hearts, subduing our corruptions, and death hath yielded to his power. 'O death, I will be thy death.'

Doct. 2. In the next place, as Christ hath this power, *so he will use this power for the good of his saints*; and this he will do because *whatever Christ is, he is for the good of his church.* He is powerful, merciful, and loving for his church's sake. And secondly, *Because our bodies do require it.* For it must be an infinite power that makes the body of dust. And therefore though Christ was the Son of God, declared from the beginning, yet it was said he was mightily declared to be the Son of God by his resurrection from the dead, Rom. i. 4. For from a privation to a habit† there can be no regression by a natural course; and therefore for our bodies to return from dust, must be by a supernatural infinite power of one that is God. *Let those that are enemies to Christ his members consider this.* Against whom do ye strive? even against the Almighty, who in his humiliation was able with a word to strike his enemies to the ground; and now being in glory, how fearful and terrible should his power be to such? who should learn betimes to kiss the Son, before they perish in the midway, Ps. ii. 12. And for his children, *let them comfort themselves that are under the government* of so powerful a majesty; for he will bruise all their enemies under them. Nay, they are already all conquered. And let them consider of all his

* That is, 'understood.'—G.

† That is, 'a having.'—Ed.

promises, and apply them to his power. It is a powerful Saviour that said, 'Come to me, all you that are heavy laden, I will raise you up,' Mat. xi. 28. It is he that is able to subdue all things to himself, that promises, 'My grace shall be sufficient for you,' 2 Cor. xii. 9. He is a prophet, to instruct fully; a priest, to satisfy God's wrath to the utmost; a king, to subdue all their corruptions. Thirdly, *Let this encourage us to set ourselves against our corruptions.* Some there are that having a little strove with their lusts, and finding that they have not gotten any sensible ground against them, they as out of hope and heart sit down with this opinion, 'as good never a whit as not the better,'* and so yield up the bucklers. What a distrustful incredulous estate is this! Is not he God that hath promised? Is he not truth itself? Hath he said, and shall it not come to pass? Fear not these Anakims nor Canaanites. Depend on God in the use of the means, and let him alone with the performance of his promises. Fourthly, *Despair of none, though never so weak,* so long as they use the means; for Christ hath created all by his word, he will raise us up by his word, and will change us by his word; and by this word he is able to change others though never so obstinate. For so long as they are under the word and means, they are under the arms of an almighty power; and therefore, if any be in our power, or if we wish well to any, we should persuade them to prize the word and to use the means. In the next place, *this is a ground of trial of our estates.* Would we know whether we are of the number of those that shall be raised up hereafter and changed? Then examine whether we have found this power changing us, and bringing us to grace here; for, Eph. i. 19, 20, the same power worketh in us to believe, that raised up Christ. Do we then find our understandings enlightened, our wills conformable to his will? Do we find the strongholds of sin in us rased, and new spirits, new thoughts, new desires in us? Oh, these are blessed evidences of Christ's almighty power in us, that will raise us up at the last day.

By this means also *we may try our profession.* Do we come by faith and religion, with pleasure and ease? Alas! this is no sign of any powerful strong work in us. It is easy to go to church to hear the word or read it, to receive the sacraments. Contrarily, if we find an inward change, that our hearts are so altered as we can overrule our members contrary to our lusts, and contrary to occasions, then 'stronger is he that ruleth in us than he that ruleth in the world,' 1 John iv. 4. It is easy to resist a temptation where none is. The mighty power of Christ is seen, when, being environed with temptations, we are enabled to resist. I pray, saith Christ, that thou should[st] keep them from evil in the world, and not that thou shouldst take them out of the world, John xvii. 15. If we be under crosses, if this Spirit and power of Christ be in us, it will enable us to bear all patiently, it will keep us from murmuring and fretting. It will also convince us of our natural estate, so as we shall see evident necessity of God's almighty power to change us. This made the apostle Paul and the jailor to look about them for help. 'Lord, what wouldst thou have me to do?' And thus it will make us never to give God rest, nor Christ respite, till that power that shall raise up our bodies do raise up also our souls, and he shine in us by his Spirit that did bring light out of darkness, and fashion us as in his wisdom shall be most meet.

In the next place, the consideration of God's almighty power should teach us not *to be dejected or cast down at the reports of the afflicted state*

* That is, as good have no success if we are not to have complete success.—Ed.

of the church abroad. It should bring us rather to God, to rely upon his goodness and power, for God is ever God almighty, and the same merciful God that ever he was; and therefore, we should pray for the church the more instantly, that God would give them beauty instead of ashes. We should urge him with his promise of building up and defending of his church, and destroying of antichrist; and let us make the resurrection of the body a ground to strengthen us in the belief thereof, as the return of the children of Israel from Babylon was sealed by the resurrection of the dry bones, Ezek. xxxvii. 1, *seq.;* as also the apostle, from the resurrection of the dead, gathereth that God by that power hath and will deliver him, 2 Cor. i. 9, 10.

Furthermore, *when we are oppressed with any extremity, though never so great, by continual meditation of his promises, we should strengthen ourselves, and apply them to our present estate and condition,* knowing that he that raised us out of dust will not suffer us to be buried in misery, but will with the trial give us a gracious issue at the last, by raising up our bodies at the last day by his almighty power, which made also the patriarch Abraham to hope above hope. What though our helps be few? It is no matter what the instrument is, so as Christ is the chief worker.

In the next place, *This should encourage us to stand out stedfast in a good cause for the truth.* Do not think with ourselves, Alas! I am but one, and a weak, silly man: what can I do against a multitude? Let not such thoughts discourage thee. Think of Luther, a poor monk, who alone set himself against the whole world, and wrought that effect that we have all cause at this day to honour the memory of him. It is not thou, but God in thee, that is able to confound all thine enemies; and therefore, with Moses, behold him that is invisible.

Yet further, This should be observed by a Christian, as a ground of his perseverance to the end; for when we know we are Christians, what can bereave us of our blessings? what can make our faith fail? It is God's power that will keep us to salvation, and he that believeth shall have life, and shall not come into condemnation, John vi. 39, 40, 44, 47, and many other places; and Christ, by his almighty power, sways all our life to our building up to salvation; and therefore in contraries we should believe contraries, that death will work life, misery happiness, corruption incorruption, and this vileness glory; for it is God's order to work by contraries, that his power might the more appear.

And at the hour of death, then behold him that is thus able and all-sufficient; that shall presently glorify our soul, and at length will raise up our body also, and unite it to our soul, to partake with it in glory and happiness; that will then quit us of all sin, corruption, death, change. All our enemies shall be trodden under our foot, and all this by his almighty power, whereby he is able to do far above that we are able to think; and therefore let us, with a holy admiration thereof, say with the apostle, Eph. iii. 20, 21, 'To him be glory for evermore. Amen.'

NOTES.

(*a*) P. 64.—'Doubled. . . . Sometime for emphasis sake, as Christ did often, "Amen, amen," and "in dying thou shalt die."' The 'Amen, amen' (ἀμὴν, ἀμὴν) is rendered by 'Verily, verily,' throughout the Gospel of John in our English

Bible. Cf. i. 51, iii. 3, 5, 11, and frequently. 'Dying thou shalt die' is the more literal translation of Gen. ii. 17.

(*b*) P. 64.—' The sacraments. . . . The primitive church had them every Lord's day.' This has been matter of controversy in all sections of the church. It fills a large space in ecclesiastical histories. The annotated editions of the Apostolical Fathers, in the original and translations, furnish the most satisfactory materials for a decision. Cf. also among others, Blunt's 'History of the Christian Church during the First Three Centuries' (2d ed., 8vo., 1857); and on the *heretical* side, Dr Lamson's 'Church of the First Three Centuries' (Boston, 1860, 8vo).

(*c*) P. 65.—' Nay, take heed of these, for so the word in the original is, "these dogs."' The original is τοὺς κύνας, which is rather '*the* dogs,' = those designated. Cf. Bishop Ellicott *in loc.*, and for much quaint lore and vehement denunciation of 'false teachers,' Airay's Lectures *in loc.* (4to., 1618).

(*d*) P. 67.—' Spira.' Cf. note *qq*, Vol. III. p. 533.

(*e*) P. 69.—' Bellarmine saith that their government was carnal, . . . but it is carnally spoken of him.' The reference is to the Mosaic ritual and service, which Bellarmine empties of their spiritual significance.

(*f*) P. 80.—' Bucer.' Martin Bucer, born 1491, died 1551, an eminent Reformer.

(*g*) P. 80.—' Luther.' Born 1483, died 1546. Cf. note *uu*, Vol. III. p. 533.

(*h*) P. 80.—' Peter Martyr.' That is, Peter Vermilius Martyr, a celebrated divine. He was born at Florence 1500, died 1562. Having been a professor of divinity at Oxford, his works were early translated in England, and seem to have been very popular. His name is prominent in English *ecclesiastical* history.

(*i*) P. 80.—' Zanchius.' This is Jerome Zanchius, a famous Reformer, born 1516, died 1590. He must not be confounded with Basil Zanchius, a contemporary.

(*j*) P. 84.—' Oh, but Bellarmine says, the prophet speaks this in the person of the wicked'—*i.e.*, in Isa. vi. 5. Cf. Bellarmine *in loc.*

(*k*) P. 84.—' Their own authors agree hereunto: as Ferus.' By Ferus is intended Vincent Ferre, a Dominican, who died 1682. His Commentary on the Sum of Theology of Aquinas fills several huge folios.

(*l*) P. 84.—' Catharen, a cardinal of their own, says there is *donata justitia*, and *inhærens*.' Ambrose Catharinus was born at Sienna 1487, died 1553. The distinction referred to by Sibbes is found in his 'Speculum Hæreticorum et Liber de Peccato Originali et Liber de Perfecta Justificatione a Fide et Operibus,' 1541. This remarkable book, as well as his less known 'Disceptationes de Certitudine de Prædestinatione,' &c., contains many not merely Protestant-like, but evangelical, opinions.

(*m*) P. 84.—' A pope of theirs, Adrian the Fourth, saith that all our righteousness is as the reed of Egypt, which will not only fail us if we rest on it, but will pierce our sides.' This renowned pontiff was an Englishman, born near St Alban's. His own name was Nicholas Brakespeare. He was pope from 1154 to 1159. It is a pity that Sibbes has given us no clue to his authority for the sentiment.

(*n*) P. 84.—' St Cyprian saith also, that he is either *superbus* or *stultus*, that says or thinks he is perfect.' Repeatedly. Cf. Indices *sub vocibus.*

(*o*) P. 85.—' However they may brabble in schools to maintain this their assertion, yet when death comes, they must fly those shifts, and lay hold only on God's love.' Cf. note *w*, Vol III. p. 531.

(*p.*) P. 93.—' Some read the words actively.' The original is εὑρεθῶ ἐν αὐτῷ, = 'be found in him;' but cf. Dean Alford *in loc.*

(*q*) P. 96.—' As it is with the unicorn, who, having put his horn into the water, &c.' This and similar singular illustrations recur over and over in the Puritan and Church writings equally, being accepted apparently as a *stock* metaphor. Probably they are to be traced to the quaint translations of Pliny's 'Natural History,' whose infinite wonders commended the old folio to our forefathers. On the 'Unicorn,' consult Dr Bostock's and Riley's Pliny, ii. 279, 281, and relative notes.

(*r*) P. 103.—' As Cyrus did with the waters of Babylon.' Cf. note *a*, Vol. II. p. 248.

(*s*) P. 107.—This made Cyprian to complain of his corruptions, saying they were bred and brought up with him; and therefore feared they would hardly give place to grace, being but a stranger.' A reminiscence, apparently, of a sentiment in one of his Letters.

(*t*) P. 110.—' "I press forth." It is a word of vehemency, &c.' The original is κατὰ σκόπον διώκω, on which cf. Bishop Ellicot *in loc.* and on ver. 12.

(*u*) P. 119.—' The word "nevertheless," some read it "only."' πλήν is the adversative preposition here, on which consult the very able Treatise of Professor Harrison on 'The Greek Prepositions' (Philadelphia, 1858, 8vo).

(*v*) P. 123.—'Maxima debetur puero reverentia.' This trite quotation is from the 14th Satyre of Juvenal. The whole passage reads thus:—

Nil dictu fœdum visuve hæc limina tangat
Intra quæ puer est. Procul hinc, procul inde puellæ
Lenonum, et cantus pernoctantis parasiti.
Maxima debetur puero reverentia. Si quid
Turpe paras, ne tu pueri contempseris annos;
Sed peccaturo obsistat tibi filius infans.

(*w*) P. 125.—'Therefore we must not number the followers, but weigh them aright.' The saying, which has since been so frequently in the mouths of politicians, 'Votes are to be weighed, not numbered,' seems thus to have originated with Sibbes.

(*x*) P. 130—'Some emperors have required themselves to be so esteemed and adored as a deity'—*e. g.*, Alexander the Great and the Cæsars.

(*y*) P. 130.—'Amor tuus Deus tuus.' Cf. note *aa.*

(*z*) P. 135.—'The word translated here "for," in the former translation is "but."' 'But' is the translation by Wickliffe (1380), Tyndale (1534), Cranmer (1539), Geneva version (1557), Rheims (1582), and, as stated by Sibbes, 'for' first occurs in the authorised translation of 1611. Bishop Ellicott adheres to the 'for,' laying the emphasis on the 'our.' The conjunction is *γαρ*.

(*aa*) P. 136.—'Animus est ubi amat.' Another way of expressing the sentiment of note *y*. Both sentiments common to the proverbs of all languages. Probably Sibbes's reference is to a saying of Augustine, which in full runs, *Anima magis est ubi amat quam ubi animat.*

(*bb*) P. 144—'As the heathen man Galen, being stricken into admiration at the admirable frame thereof, breaks into a hymn in praise of the Maker.' Galen styles a portion of his great work, Περι χρειας των μοριων, a hymn to the Creator; calling it, 'Ιερὸν λόγον, ὃν ἐγὼ τοῦ δημιουργήσαντος ἥμας ὕμνον ἀληθινὸν συντίθημι· καὶ νομίζω τοῦτ' εἶναι τὴν ὄντως ἐνσέβείαν, ὀυχὶ εἰ ταύρων ἑκατόμβας ἀυτοῦ παμπόλλας καταθύσαιμί', &c. (Lib. iii. cap. x.). Also, at the close of the whole work, he describes it as an ἐπωδος, such as the priests sing at the altars of the gods.

(*cc*) P. 145.—'Say to thy flesh with Bernard, "Stay thy time."' A very frequent saying with this father. For many extraordinary quotations shewing how Bernard would have the 'flesh' denied, and how caustic he could be against the luxuries of his age, see the recent 'Life' by Morison (1863).

(*dd*) P. 150.—'The word that is translated "working," may and doth signify "power."' The original is *κατὰ τὴν ἐνέργειαν*, on which cf. Calvin *in loc.* for admirable exegesis. G.

THE REDEMPTION OF BODIES.

THE REDEMPTION OF BODIES.

NOTE.

'The Redemption of Bodies' forms one of a volume of sermons called 'Evangelical Sacrifices,' published in 1640, 4to. It is given here as being related to the preceding 'Expositions' of portions of Philippians. The separate title-page will be found below;* and as this is our first contribution from 'Evangelical Sacrifices,' the general title-page is also given here,† and the epistles dedicatory and prefatory of the entire volume, for after reference. G.

* THE
REDEMPTION
OF
BODYES.
In one Funerall Sermon upon
PHIL. 3. 21.
BY
The late Learned and Reverend Divine,
RICH. SIBBS:
Doctor in Divinity, M^r of KATHERINE Hall
in *Cambridge*, and sometimes Preacher
to the Honourable Society of
GRAYES-INNE.
1 COR. 15. 44.
It is sowne a naturall Body, it is raised a spirituall body.
LONDON,
Printed by *E. Purslow*, for *N. Bourne*, at the Royall Exchange, and *R. Harford* at the gilt Bible in Queenes head Alley, in Pater-Noster-Row. 1639.

† EVANGELICALL
SACRIFICES.
In xix. Sermons.

1. *Thankfull commemorations for Gods mercy in our great deliverance from the Papists powder plot.*
2. *The successefull seeker.*
3. *Faith Triumphant.*
4. *Speciall preparations to fit us for our latter end in foure Funerall Sermons.*
5. *The faithfull Covenanter.*
6. *The demand of a good Conscience.*
7. *The sword of the wicked.*

BY
The late Learned and Reverend Divine,
RICH. SIBBS.
Doctor in Divinity, M^r of KATHERINE Hall in *Cambridge*, and sometimes Preacher to the Honourable Society of GRAYES-INNE.
The third Tome.
Published and perused by *D. Sibbs* owne appointment, subscribed with his hand to prevent imperfect Copies after his decease.

ROMANS 12. 1.
I beseech you brethren, by the mercies of God, that yee present your bodies a living sacrifice, holy, acceptable unto God, which is your reasonable service.

LONDON,
Printed by *T. B.* for *N. Bourne*, at the Royall Exchange, and *R. Harford*, at the guilt Bible in Queenes-head Alley, in Pater-noster-Row. 1640.

TO THE RIGHT HONOURABLE

EDWARD VISCOUNT MANDEVILE,

AND HIS

LADY ANNE, HIS PIOUS CONSORT,

INCREASE OF GRACE.*

Right Honourable,

A pious Christian, whilst upon earth, takes his time to do his task. He is or would be all in grace and all to duty, well knowing that 'the time is short,' 1 Cor. vii. 29, the work great, the wages sure; and that the best improvement of parts and talents will bring in the Master the greatest advantage, and himself the present and most lasting comforts. This is the fruit of a well-led life, to advance God in glory and a Christian in comfort. Such as serve God in fulfilling his will, must to heaven carry their graces with them, enter into their Master's joy, &c.; if they be eminent in profession or public in place, leave behind them their example or some other monument to the world of their fidelity in their places. Happy such servants that can thus employ their times and improve their talents. This was the endeavour of that shining and burning lamp Dr Sibbs, the author of this work, which I now make bold to present unto your honours. Such holy and useful truths were delivered by him in his lifetime, that the judicious conceive may prove very profitable unto the church being published after his death. I conceive thus of the man, what he did in his ministry in public, or in his conference in private, it was done aptly, pithily, and profitably; his art was to hide his art, *est celare artem, &c.*, to say much in few words. He did not desire to cloud his matter from his hearers, or to walk so long about any one text till errors were vented, or his auditors tired. You shall find him to be himself, and one constant to his own principles, all along the treatise. Here you have no new errors broached, or old truths deserted, but opened, maintained, and honoured, the glory of teachers, expectation of hearers, and recompence

* Cf. note, Vol II. page 3.—G.

of readers. Having found this to be your honour's honour, and let it still be, to content yourselves with humble knowledge, cordial respect, and vital expressions of received truths; that you are not in number with those that change their judgments, and I fear their religion, as they do their friends and fashions, being constant in inconstancy; and that with you it is not truths for persons, but persons for truth;* I doubt not the admittance of these sermons unto your respect and patronage. My only request is, that as the author did honour you, so these labours of his, now made public, may be as so many divine beams, holy breathings, and celestial droppings, to raise up your spirits to hate the dominion of the beast, to help forward the ruin of mystical Jericho and all other unprosperous buildings and builders; that you may become successful seekers, gaining faith triumphant, to acquaint you with the hidden life; that at length you may obtain the redemption of your bodies, knowing that Balaam's wish is not enough, unless the faithful Covenanter take you into covenant with himself: this alone yielding to you the demand of a good conscience, which shall be your defence against the sword of reproach.† These I leave with you, and you with God, and rest

Your honour's at command,

JOHN SEDGWICK.‡

* Non ex personis probamus fidem, sed ex fide personas.—*Tertullian Apolog.*

† Cf. note, Vol. IV. page 492.—G.

‡ It will be noticed that Sedgwick ingeniously brings together here all the subjects of the several sermons in the volume. Cf. title-page, *ante*, 156.—G.

TO THE READER.

So precious the remembrance should be of God's thoughts of mercy to us-ward, when he delivered us from that hellish plot of the Gunpowder Treason, that if there were nothing else to commend this treatise to us, the first sermons here presented to us, which were preached upon that occasion, may justly procure it a ready and hearty welcome.

When God works such wonders for a church and people as that was, it is not enough to praise God for the present, and to rejoice greatly in the great salvation he hath wrought for them; yea, the more a people are in such a case affected for the present, the more inexcusable they must needs be if afterward they slight and disregard it, and that because their former joy proves they were thoroughly convinced of the greatness of the mercy, and so discovers their following ingratitude to be the more abominable; whence it was that when Jonathan put his father Saul in mind how David killed Goliah, and thereby had wrought a great deliverance for them (to the end he might no longer seek his ruin, that had been the means of so much good to God's people); withal he wished him to consider that he himself stood by, an eye-witness of that noble exploit of David's, and was then mightily affected with joy when he saw that formidable giant fall under his hand: 'Thou sawest it,' saith he, 'and didst rejoice,' 1 Samuel xix. 5, intimating how inexcusable it would be if he should forget that deliverance, concerning which himself had been so wondrously affected when it was done.

As therefore we have great cause to bewail the general decay of men's thankfulness for this great deliverance; at the first discovery of that cursed plot, 'Our mouths were filled with laughter, and our tongue with singing,' Ps. cxxvi. 2, all the land over, and every man could say, 'The Lord hath done great things for us, whereof we are glad,' as Ps. cxxvi. 2, 3; and yet now scarce one amongst many is affected with it, as in former times; so have we also great cause to bless God for the holy alarms of God's watchmen, whereby they have endeavoured to stir up those that are fallen from their first joy; and so amongst the rest for these of Reverend Dr Sibbes, the author of them, wherein he hath so feelingly set forth the misery of that antichristian bondage, from which we were delivered in that deliverance, that methinks he that reads them with due care must needs find his heart rousing up itself, as Deborah did: 'Awake, awake, Deborah; awake, awake, utter a song,' Judges v. 12.

As for the other sermons, which, in this third tome, be styled Evangelical Sacrifices, which are published together with these, you shall find them no less profitable than these, though in divers other respects. The most of them tend to fit Christians for their latter end, a work of greatest importance, and do so sweetly set before our eyes that recompence of reward reserved for us in heaven, that I hope many of that brood of travellers, 'the generation of those that seek God's face' and favour here on earth, shall find them a great help to the 'finishing of their course with joy,' and others shall be wakened that are too ready to slumber and forget whither they are going, 'to strive to enter in at the strait gate,' Luke xiii. 24, and not to content themselves with a lazy Balaam's wish; which, reader, let us seek from Him who only gives the blessing, to whose grace I commend thee, resting still

Thine in the hearty desire of thy spiritual welfare,

ARTHUR JACKSON.*

* Cf. Note Vol. II. page 442.—G.

*** The other sermons of 'Evangelical Sacrifices' will be found in their proper places in the present and subsequent volumes. Meantime, with reference to those commemorative of the 'Gunpowder Plot,' and Jackson's remarks thereupon, *supra*, the following calm words from a recently published and very masterly 'History' of the period may be acceptable:—'On their reassembling (1606), the attention of the House was necessarily directed to the danger from which they had escaped. A Bill was eagerly passed, by which the 5th of November was ordered to be kept as a day of thanksgiving for ever. [3 Jac. I. cap. 1.] That Act continued in force for more than two centuries and a half, and was only repealed when the service which was originally the outpouring of thankful hearts had long become an empty form.' [History of England from the Accession of James I. to the Disgrace of Chief Justice Coke, 1603–1616. By Samuel Rawson Gardiner. (2 vols. 8vo, 1863.) Vol. I. chap. v. p. 271.]—G.

THE REDEMPTION OF BODIES.

Who shall change our vile body, that it may be fashioned like unto his glorious body, according to the working whereby he is able to subdue all things to himself.—PHILIP. III. 21.

THE apostle was now in prison, yet he had a spirit of glory resting upon him; for he speaks as if he were entered into heaven, as if he were there before his time; and therefore in chapter i., ver. 23, saith he, 'I desire to be dissolved, and to be with Christ, which is best of all.' And 'I account all but dung in comparison of Christ,' as he saith in this chapter, ver. 8. And here in the former verse, 'Our conversation is in heaven; from whence we look for the Saviour, Jesus Christ: who shall change our vile bodies,' &c. God reserves abundance of comforts to the fittest times, as we see here in St Paul in this place. Now he brings in his own example to good purpose, as opposite to false Christians and false teachers, that he had mentioned before. 'There are many walk, of whom I have told you oft, &c. They are enemies to the cross of Christ: that mind earthly things,' &c., ver. 18. But saith he, 'Our conversation is in heaven.' He regards not which way they went. He took an opposite course to the world, and swims against the stream. As we see the stars, they have a motion of their own, opposite to the motion that they are carried with. So St Paul had a motion of his own, opposite to the course of the world. 'Their end is damnation,' but 'our conversation is in heaven.' A Christian hath his conversation in heaven. While he is on earth, he rules his life by the laws of heaven.* There are alway in the visible church some that walk contrary ways, who make 'their belly their god, whose end is damnation.' There were some that were Christians, nay, and teachers of Christians many of them, yet he saith, 'Their end is damnation, their god is their belly.' Carnal Christians say, We have all received the sacrament, &c. Alas! we may all partake of this common privilege, and yet our end may be damnation. St Paul looked on them with a spirit of compassion, 'I tell you weeping.' So it may be with us in our Goshen here. There may be a spirit of castaways in many; and in the abundance of means there may be many dead souls. But St Paul regards not what their course was, for saith he, 'Our conversation is in heaven.'

* We have here, long anticipated, the title of the racy and suggestive book of Rev. William Arnot of Glasgow, 'Laws from Heaven for Life on Earth' (2 vols., 1857-58).—G.

'From whence we look for the Saviour,' &c.

That shews why his conversation was in heaven, because his Saviour was in heaven; and therefore his hope was in heaven: 'Where the treasure is, the heart will be,' Mat. vi. 21. Having entered into this blessed discourse, he goes on still: 'Who shall change our vile bodies, and fashion them like his glorious body.' He brings it in by way of answering an objection. If our conversation be in heaven, why are our bodies yet subject to such afflictions and baseness in this world? It is true they are; but the time shall come that Christ shall change these vile bodies of ours, and 'fashion them like to his glorious body.' Ay, but this requires a great deal of power and strength, and we see not how it may be. Therefore, saith he, he shall do it by 'that almighty power whereby he is able to subdue all things to himself.' Therefore he shall subdue death, the last enemy. He will not do it perhaps according to thy fancy and conceit, but 'according to the working whereby he is able to subdue all things to himself.' We must not regard our weak conceits in great matters, but God's power. 'Ye err,' saith Christ to the Pharisees, 'not knowing the Scriptures, nor the power of God.'

St Paul then in these words, and in the verse before, sets down three reasons why his course is opposite to the course of wicked men in his time.

1. First, *My city is in heaven, and my conversation is answerable.* I take a contrary course, for I am a citizen of another city.

2. And then another reason is, *his hope and expectation of a Saviour from heaven*, the Lord Jesus. Hope, and faith, which is the ground of hope, carry up the soul where the thing hoped for is. 'Our conversation is in heaven: we hope for a Saviour from thence.'

3. The third reason is, *from the condition of the body.* However it was now for the present, 'he shall change our vile body, that it may be like his glorious body.'

'Who shall change our vile body.'

You see here the apostle, having set himself upon a holy and heavenly meditation, he could not satisfy himself, but goes from point to point, setting down his present holy conversation, grounded upon his future hope of a blessed state to come. 'Christ shall change our vile body.' Our bodies are vile, and *our* bodies. Here is the point then, that

The best men's bodies in this world are vile.

Vile in regard *of the matter whence they are taken*, the earth, from the dust. The fairest body is but well-coloured dust; base and vile from the beginning, from the womb; base in the whole life, base in death; most base after death. They are base, I say, in the beginning.

But especially, *base in our life.* Our bodies are *base in regard of labour.* 'Man is born to labour'—in this world—'as the sparks fly upward,' Job v. 7. God would humble the body of every man with labour; or else those that have not the labour of men here shall have the labour of devils hereafter. The best body of the best saints are condemned to labour.

Vile likewise in regard *of sickness and diseases*, which grow out of the body; so that be it kept never so warm and tenderly, yet as the worms grow out of the very wood, and consumes the wood that breeds it, so diseases grow out of and come from the body. There is a fight and conflict between moisture and heat, till the one prey upon the other and consume it. In regard of sickness therefore they are vile bodies.

In regard likewise *of disposing the soul the worst way;* for take all tempers of the body, they incline the soul to some sin or other, to some ill disposition or other. *Choler* inclines it to intemperate anger, *melancholy* to distrust and darkness of spirit. The *sanguine* inclines it to liberty and looseness, &c., *phlegm* to deadness and dulness of spirit. So our base bodies make the soul dull. It becomes an unfit instrument, whereby the soul cannot work as it would; an unfit house. The body is ofttimes a dark house; sometimes a house that drops in with moist diseases; a house that lets in water, and so consumes it to rottenness. Sometimes it is a house fired by hot diseases. It is thus indisposed, and therefore a vile body.

A vile body likewise, that when it is thus indisposed, *there is no comfort in the earth that can comfort it;* for all the foundation of comfort in this world is the health of this poor body. A kingdom, nay, all the kingdoms in the world, will not comfort a man if his body be not in tune; and, alas, how soon is this body out of tune! An instrument that hath many strings is soon subject to be out of tune,* and there are many strings in the body. How many turnings, how many instruments, doth the soul use! If any be out of tune, the music is hindered. It becomes an unfit instrument. In this regard it is a vile body.

In regard likewise *of the necessities of nature,* this body is vile in this world. I speak not of what comes from the body, in which respect it is base and vile. But how many things doth this vile body stand in need of! Man, in that respect, is the basest creature in the world. He is beholden to the worms; he is beholden to nature to feed him in health, and in sickness the body needs patching up and piecing by this creature and by that. So it is a vile body in regard of the necessities of it, in health, in sickness, in youth, in age. It is vile in life. I need not stand on this.

It is more *vile in death.* In the hour of death, then it is base and vile indeed. Can we endure the sight of our dearest friends? How noisome is their presence after death! And the most exquisite temper† is the most vile and noisome of all. Those that are most delicately fed, and most beautifully faced, are most offensive; and this is the condition of all. That head that wore a crown, those hands that swayed a sceptre, those brains and that understanding that ruled many kingdoms, all are subject to death, yea, and to baseness after death, as well as those that are poorer. And then they are vile bodies, because they are subject to all manner of deaths. The bodies of God's saints have been cast out to the fowls of the air. The poor martyrs, how many ways have they tasted of death! These bodies are subject to all manner of deaths, to variety of deaths; therefore they are vile bodies.

And then they are vile *after death.* As we were taken out of dust at the first, so we return to dust again; and if these bodies be not transformed to be like the glorious body of Christ, they are most vile of all. The spirit of despair, the spirit of anger, that is in reprobate persons, how doth it disfigure their faces! One may see their shame, their grief, their despair in their very looks. So their bodies are most vile and dishonourable. But I speak of God's children. I say here in this world, in regard that they come of parents that are miserable and sinful, 'Man that is born of a woman hath but a short time to live, and is full of misery,' Job. xiv. 1; man that is born of a woman, of a weak, miserable, sinful woman. In

* "Strange that an harp of thousand strings
Should keep in tune so long."—*Cowper.*—G.

† That is, 'attempered' body.—G.

this respect it is a vile body. And in all passages of our life, in respect of labour, and pain, and sicknesses, and diseases, and likewise for indisposing the soul, that it is an instrument to ill. And in death itself more vile than in life; and after death most of all vile. So you see they are vile bodies every way. To make some use of this.

Use 1. If this be so, considering what the condition of our body is here, *let this abate the pride of the greatest*. Let them consider, when they look upon their gay apparel, what doth these garments hide? When great magistrates and others have their purple on, let them consider, what doth this glorious garment cover? Nothing but dust; a vile body. Why should we be proud then of our bodies, or of any ornament of our body, seeing it is a vile body?

Use 2. Again, If our bodies be vile and base, *why should we spend the strength of our souls in searching to satisfy the lusts of so vile a body*, and so make our souls nothing else almost but stewards to prowl how to content, how to clothe, and how to feed this body? As it is the study of many idle vain persons, almost all the day long, to give contentment to the craving lusts of this vile body; they make even an idol of this poor base piece of flesh, and sacrifice the best of their thoughts, and the best of their studies and endeavours and labours, to the contentment of it. Certainly this is forgotten which the apostle saith here, 'It is a vile and base body.'

Use 3. Again, Is our body a vile body, a base body, as we have it here? Then *let us not make it more vile by intemperate courses, as wicked persons do*. They dishonour their bodies. They are vile indeed, make the best of them we can, and they will end in dust; but we ought not sinfully to make them more vile and base, as many wretched persons do by their loose and licentious courses of life.

Use 4. Again, If our bodies be vile, base bodies, while we live here, *let us not offend God for anything to gratify our vile bodies*. Let us do as Joseph did, when his mistress tempted him; he left his garment behind him rather. So when we are tempted to any sin, let us rather leave our garments behind us, let us leave our bodies. They are but vile bodies, let us be stripped of them, rather than offend God. It is pitiful to consider how this vile body, as vile as it is, and shall be in death, how it tyranniseth over the poor soul, and how men wound their souls for their bodies. How many are there that justify errors that they condemn in their hearts, to live a lazy, idle, a full, a plentiful life. And how many do condemn those things, those courses, and those truths, to please others, and to live a large and idle life —which they justify in their very souls—and all to please the flesh? It is but a bad counsellor, a bad solicitor I say, it tyranniseth over the poor soul. Let us not offend God or conscience, to break the peace of it for anything, to gratify this vile flesh. This I thought good to touch concerning that.

'Who shall change our vile bodies.'

'Change.' The action that Christ shall exercise about them is 'change.' Christ will 'change' our vile bodies. They are vile now. They shall not be always so; but Christ will 'change' our vile bodies. He will not give us other bodies for them, but he will change them in regard of quality. For even as the great world was the same after the flood as it was before the flood, and shall be when it is consumed by fire, it shall be a new world for quality, but the same for substance; so this body of ours, it shall be the same after the resurrection for substance that it is now. It shall be altered for quality, it shall not be changed for substance. Therefore he shall 'change,' he shall not abolish our vile bodies. This is the action that our blessed Saviour will exercise upon these vile bodies ; they shall be changed. Man is the most changeable creature in the world, for soul and for body too.

Take him in his soul, how many states is he in? There is first the state of nature in perfection ; and then the state of corruption in original sin ; and then the state of grace in the new creature ; and then the state of glory. So likewise he is changeable in his body. He was first taken out of the dust. Out of the dust God made this glorious creature of man's body. He is a painful creature, in labour, in sickness ; and then from strength he is changed to old age ; and from thence to death, and dust ; and from dust then he is changed again to a more glorious estate than ever he was in. The body is made like the glorious body of Christ. He is changeable in soul and in body.

But this is our comfort, we shall change for the best. All the changes of our body serve for the last change ; after which, there shall never be any more change. When they are changed once to be glorious, they shall be for ever glorious. A blessed change, a blessed estate of a Christian ; all his changes tend to a state that shall never change. For after these bodies are once changed from base to be glorious, they shall be for ever glorious.

'Who.' The person that shall change them is Christ: '*who* shall change our vile bodies.' In the person, we may consider the object and the action. Christ shall change our vile bodies. He that made us will make us again. He that is the image of God will refine us. He will renew us in body and soul to be like God, to be like himself; and he that changeth our souls in this world, will change our bodies in the world to come. His first coming was to change our souls, to deliver them from the bondage of Satan. His second coming shall be to deliver our bodies from the bondage of corruption, that is, the day of 'the redemption of our bodies,' as the apostle calls it, Rom. viii. 23. So it is he that shall change. But of this I shall speak more afterward.

What is the pattern according to which this body shall be changed, by this author of it, Christ Jesus? His own body. 'He shall change our vile bodies,

'That it may be made like, or fashioned like, his glorious body.'

He is both the cause and the pattern ; the efficient and the exemplary cause. He is the pattern. Our bodies shall be like his glorious body, even as our souls are like Christ's soul. For this is certain. We are renewed in grace, not to the image of the first Adam, but to the image of the second Adam. We are conformed in soul to the image of Christ in holiness and righteousness. So likewise in the body, we shall be conformable to the body of Christ, 'the second Adam.' As we bare the image of the first Adam in our first creation, so we must bear the image of the second in our restoration, at the day of the resurrection. The glorious body of Christ is the pattern of this transmutation and change.

But we must understand this, as I said, in regard of quality, and not in regard of equality: our body shall be like his glorious body, not equal to his glorious body. There must be a reservation therefore of difference in heaven, between the head and the members, the husband and the spouse. Our bodies shall be like his glorious body, not equal to it. To our capacity we shall have full satisfaction and contentment for body and soul too ; and they shall have security to be in that estate for ever. Therefore, though there be a difference of glory, yet that difference is no prejudice to the glory we shall have. We shall have that that is fit for us. 'Our body shall be made like unto his glorious body.' Christ is our pattern.

Whence we see this point of divinity clear to us, that

Whatsoever is in us, both for soul and body (but here we speak of the body), whatsoever excellency is in us, it is at the second hand.

It is first in our head, first in Christ, and then in us. He is first the Son of God by nature. We are the sons of God by adoption. He is the predestinated Son of God to save us, to be our head. We are predestinate to be his members. He is the Son of God's love ; we are beloved in him. He is full of grace : 'Of his fulness we receive grace for grace,' John i. 16. He rose and we shall rise, because he rose first. He ascended into heaven ; by virtue of his ascension we shall ascend into heaven too. He sits at the right hand of God in glory, and by virtue of his sitting we sit there together with him in heavenly places. Whatsoever is graciously or gloriously good that is in us, it is first in our blessed and glorious Saviour.

Therefore *let us look to him, and be thankful to God for him.* When we thank God for ourselves, let us thank God first for giving Christ, who is the pattern to whom we are conformed. Let us give thanks for him, as St Peter doth, 'Blessed be God, the Father of our Lord Jesus Christ,' 1 Peter i. 3. If he had not been his Father, he had not been ours. We cannot stand before God of ourselves, but in one that is perfect in himself, God-man. Therefore when we bless God for grace and glory that belongs to us, let us bless him for giving Christ, that in him we are happy. He conforms us in grace here and in glory hereafter, in body and soul, to our glorious Saviour.

And as it is a ground of thankfulness to God for Christ, so it yields us *a rule for meditation.* When we would think of anything in ourselves, let us go to our head, to Christ, in whom we have all we have and that we hope to have. 'Of his fulness we receive, not only grace for grace,' but glory for glory. Of all the glory he hath, we have answerable to him ; and surely it is a transforming meditation to think of Christ's glory, and to see ourselves in him ; to think of grace in Christ, and of our interest in grace in him. We must not think of him as an abstracted head severed from us, but think of his glory, and our glory in him and by him. He is glorious, and we shall be glorious likewise.

Again, You see here that howsoever our bodies are vile for the present, yet they shall not be so for ever. They shall be 'glorious bodies,' like to Christ's body. The point then is that,

As Christ is the pattern of the glory of our body, so our body undoubtedly shall be glorious as his body is.

This vile body shall be glorious, even like Christ's glorious body. I need not stand to prove it. I proved it before. What should this afford us? Then let us use them to a glorious end ; let us not use these base bodies to base purposes. Let every member of this vile body, while we live here, be a weapon of a sanctified soul ; a weapon of righteousness ready to do good. Let us put honour upon these bodies that shall be thus honoured ; let us use them for honourable purposes. Let us lift up our eyes to heaven ; let us reach forth our hands to good works. Let our feet that have carried us to ill heretofore, carry us to the service of God ; for these very vile bodies shall be glorious bodies. The very same eyes that have been lift up to God in prayer ; those very hands that now are instruments of good works ; those very knees that are humbled to God in prayer ; and those feet that have carried us to holy exercises ; and those spirits that are wasted and spent in holy meditation: even these, this vile body that is thus holily used, shall be a glorious body. Therefore let us use it answerably.

And labour to lay it down with honour in the dust, to leave it with a good report to the world, considering it shall be so glorious afterward. Do those think of this that use their bodies for base purposes? whose eyes are full of adultery, whose hands are full of rapine, whose feet carry them to base places where they defile themselves, whose bodies every member is a weapon and instrument of sinning against God? How can these dare to think of that glorious day, wherein our vile bodies shall be made like the glorious body of Christ? Can they hope that those hands and those feet of that body shall be made glorious that have been defiled, that have been instruments to make others likewise sin? Can such a body look for glory? Let us not deceive ourselves. This vile body indeed shall be a glorious body. Ay, but it must be used accordingly, unless we have a presumptuous hope.

This body shall be glorious; this very vile body, 'this corruptible shall put on incorruption,' the same body, as the apostle saith, 1 Cor. xv. 54. I believe the resurrection of this body, as we say in the creed. St Paul pointed to his own body: this body, 'this mortal shall put on immortality.'

If this body shall be glorious, how base soever it be in this world, then again *let us honour poor Christians*, though we see them vile and base, and honour aged Christians and deformed. Alas! look not on them as they are, but as they shall be; as they are in the decree of Christ, and as they shall be ere long by the power of Christ. He will make them like his glorious body. Let us not despise weak or old or deformed persons. These vile bodies shall be glorious. Those that died in martyrdom, whose bodies were cast into the fire and cast to wild beasts, &c., they shall be glorious bodies. The Emperor Constantine would kiss the very holes of the eyes of those that had their eyes pulled out, that had been martyred (*a*); so even our vile bodies, when they are used in the service of God in suffering, they shall be glorious bodies. Let us honour our bodies, or theirs that suffer for Christ. St Paul made it his plea, and a ground of his confidence, because his body was vile for Christ. 'I Paul, a prisoner of Jesus Christ, and I bear in my body the marks of the Lord Jesus, the dying of Christ, that the life of Christ might be made manifest,' 2 Cor. iv. 10, and Gal. vi. 17. He carried Christ's marks in his body, making this an argument of respect, that he was a prisoner. So when any are abased for Christ's sake, let us think these are such as shall have glorious bodies, however they are esteemed of the world. But to enlarge the point a little further. These bodies shall be made like the body of Christ.

Quest. Wherein shall this glory of our bodies consist?

Ans. Especially in these six endowments. Our bodies be now vile *and perhaps imperfect*. They want a member, a sense, or a limb. Our bodies then shall be perfect, even as Christ's body is. Those martyrs that have been dismembered shall then have perfect bodies. Let us not be afraid to lose a limb or a joint for Christ or a good cause. If our bodies be made vile for Christ, they shall be made perfect afterward.

Then again, our bodies then shall be *beautiful*. Adam in his innocency had such a beauty in his body that the very creatures reverenced him. He was awful to the very creatures. So the body of our blessed Saviour, now in heaven, is wondrous beautiful; and so shall our bodies be, how deformed soever they be now. Let us not stand, therefore, upon any present deformity of our bodies now with years, or sickness, or other means. They shall not always be so. We shall have beautiful bodies.

Nay more than so, the third endowment is, we shall have *glorious bodies.* As we see Christ in the mount when he was transfigured, and Moses and Elias were with him, his body was glorious. They could hardly behold him. And Christ, in Rev. i. 16, he appears 'as the sun in his full strength.' His body is wondrous glorious now in heaven, and so he is represented there. If the very representation of him while he was upon earth was so glorious in the mount, what is it in heaven? St Paul could not endure the light that shined to him, Acts ix. 3, *seq.* So shall our bodies be like the glorious body of Christ.

What a glorious time will it be when the glorious body of Christ shall appear, and all the saints shall appear in glory! what a reflection of beauty and glory will there be, one shining upon another, when Christ shall come 'to be glorious in his saints!' Oh, the glory of the body of God's children, it shall put down all created glory. All the glory of the sun and moon, and all the glory of these inferior bodies, are nothing to the glory of the body of a Christian that doth abase his body here for Christ and the church's sake. You see, then, these bodies shall be perfect, and beautiful, and glorious bodies in regard of the lustre of them.

And likewise, in the fourth place, they shall be *immortal bodies*—bodies that shall never die, unchangeable bodies. There shall be no alteration, no death, no sickness. 'All tears shall be wiped from our eyes,' Rev. vii. 17. They shall be immortal bodies, that shall never die; as St Peter saith, 'We shall have an inheritance undefiled, immortal,' &c., 1 Peter i. 4. This is clear: therefore I will not stand in the enlarging of it.

In the next place, Our bodies shall be *powerful and vigorous.* Now they are weak, as St Paul saith, 1 Cor. xv. 43. Our bodies are 'sown in weakness,' but then they shall be able to ascend and descend. They shall be strong, even as the body of Christ. We shall have strong bodies; as all imperfections, so all weakness shall be taken away.

In the sixth place, They shall be *spiritual* bodies; that is, they shall not stand in need of meat, and drink, and sleep, and refreshings as now they do, but Christ will be all in all to them. He will be instead of meat, and drink, and clothes. Yea, and instead of the ordinances that we stand in need of here, the word and sacraments, he will be all in all. And our bodies shall be spiritual in another regard, because they shall be subject to the spirit. Whereas now, our very spirits are flesh, because the flesh rules and tyranniseth over them, so our souls follow our bodies. The soul of a carnal man is flesh, but then our flesh, our bodies, shall be spiritual. Not that they shall be turned into spirits, that is not the meaning, but spiritual bodies, obedient and obsequious to the very guidance of the soul, to a sanctified and glorious soul. These shall be the endowments of our bodies. They shall be perfect bodies; beautiful, glorious, shining bodies; immortal, unchangeable bodies; powerful, strong, and vigorous bodies, ready to move from place to place; and spiritual bodies. They shall stand in need of no other help, and they shall be obedient altogether to the spirit. You see now how these vile bodies draw away our souls. Then all imperfections shall be taken away. We shall have purged bodies and purged souls. Thus you see wherein the glory of the body shall consist.

Let us therefore often seriously think of these things; and let me renew my former exhortation: let us be content to make our bodies here vile for

Christ's sake, that they may be thus glorious. Let us abase them in labour and pains in our calling; in suffering, we do no more than he did for us first. Was not his body first vile and then glorious? And do we think that our bodies must not be vile before they be glorious? Not only vile whether we will or no, but we must willingly make them vile. We must be willing to be disgraced for Christ's sake, to carry his death about us, to 'die daily' in the resolution of our souls. How was he abased before he was glorious! He took on him our bodies at the worst, not in the perfection as it was created, but he took the body of man now fallen. Again, what pains did he take in this body! And how was he disgraced in this body! That sacred face was spit upon; those blessed hands and feet were nailed to the cross; that blessed head, that is reverenced of the angels, it was crowned with thorns. How was his body every way, in all the parts of it, abased and made vile for us! He neglected his refreshings for us: it was 'meat and drink' to him to do good. If he became vile for us, if he abased his body for us, certainly we should be ashamed if we be not content that our bodies should be made vile for him, that afterwards they may be made like his glorious body. Away with these nice Christians that are afraid of the wind blowing on them or the sun shining upon them, that are afraid to do anything or to suffer anything, and so in sparing their bodies destroy both body and soul. Consider, whoever thou art, this is not a life for thy body. This present life is a life for the soul. We come now to have the image of God in our souls in this life especially, and to have in our souls the life of grace here, but the life and happiness of our body is for this second coming of Christ, the glory of the body. This life is not a time for the body. Do what we can, it will be a vile body: cherish it, set it out how thou canst, those painted sepulchres that would out-face age and out-face death, and by colours and complexions, &c., hide those furrows that age makes in the face, they are but vile; and age and death will be too good for them; to dust they will. Why should we regard our bodies? This life is not for them though we be dainty of them. Let us use this body here so as it may be glorious in the world to come. We should suffer our souls to rule our bodies, and to do all here, that both body and soul may be glorious after. For indeed all that the body hath here it is beholding to the soul for. Why, therefore, should it not be an instrument for the soul in holy things? Doth not the soul quicken it? Hath it not its beauty from the soul? When the soul is gone out of the body, where is the life? Where is the beauty? Where is anything? The body is a loathsome carcase. Now, therefore, while the soul is in this body, look to the soul especially, that when the soul shall go to heaven, the soul be mindful of, and speak a good word for, the body, as Pharaoh's butler did for Joseph; that the soul there may think of the body, that it may think of the pains, of the suffering; as the soul doth, it hath an appetite in heaven, a desire to be joined again to the body which it useth to labour in, to pray to God in, which it used to fast in, which it used as an instrument to good actions. Let us use it so here that the soul may desire to meet it again, that Christ at that day may bring body and soul together to be glorious for ever.

'That it may be fashioned like unto his glorious body.'

We see here, then, that the best is to come. The best change, after which there shall be no change, is to come. The weakest is the first, and the second is better. The second Adam is better than the first; and the second life shall be better than the first. Our bodies, as they shall be glorious, shall be better than they were in the first creation. They shall be glorious bodies, like unto Christ's. Oh, the comfort of a Christian! There is nothing that is behind, nothing to come, but it is for the better. There shall be a change, but it shall be a change for the better. A Christian is a person full of hope. He is under a glorious hope, under a hope of glory of soul and body. He is alway under hope, the 'hope of glory.' Therefore 'he joys under this hope,' Rom. v. 2.

'That it may be fashioned like unto his glorious body.'

Quest. But how shall any Christian know that his body shall be like to the glorious body of Christ?

Ans. 1. I answer, He may know it from this: The change of a Christian *begins in his soul.* Christ begins the change of our souls to be like his: full of love and obedience to God; full of pity and compassion to men; full of industry to do good. Our souls will be like Christ's soul. First look to thy soul, what stamp that bears. Is there the image of Christ on thy soul? Certainly he that hath transformed this soul to be gracious, he will transform the body to be glorious, like his glorious body. Look to thy soul then. If thou art the child of God by adoption, if thou hast the spirit of adoption and grace, and findest peace of conscience and joy in the Holy Ghost, thou mayest know thou shalt have the adoption of thy body. Thou hast the first adoption in thy soul; thou art the child of God: know that thou shalt have the second adoption, spoken of Rom. viii. 23, 'We wait for the adoption of our bodies.' If thou partake of 'the first resurrection,' that thy soul is raised from sin, thou shalt partake of the second resurrection at the day of judgment.

For Christ is a perfect Saviour. He saves not only the soul, but the body. Though he begin with the soul, he ends with the body. He took our bodies as well as our souls; and he will glorify our bodies as well as our souls. And if we find the work of grace a 'spirit of glory' in our souls, undoubtedly we may know that our bodies shall be glorious.

Ans. 2. Again, Thou mayest know that thou shalt partake of this glorious estate, that thy body shall be like the glorious body of Christ, *by the use that this body is put to.* How dost thou use this vile body for the time thou livest now? Dost thou use it to the base services of sin? Dost thou beat thy brain, and thy breast, and thy spirits? Dost thou take up thy time and all to provide for the flesh? Whither doth thy feet carry thee? What dost thou meddle with in the world? Are all thy members weapons of an unsanctified soul to offend God, and to 'fight against thy soul?' 1 Pet. ii. 11; to cherish lusts that fight against thy soul and against thy Maker and Redeemer? Then know this, that thou hast no hope of glory: 'He that hath this hope purgeth himself, and is pure as he is pure,' 1 John iii. 3. This hope, where it is found, it is a purging, a cleansing hope; and all the members of the body will be used to a sanctified purpose. A man will not sacrilegiously use those members that are dedicated to Christ; that are temples of the Holy Ghost; that are fellow-heirs, as St Peter saith, concerning the wife and the husband, 1 Pet. iii. 7. The body is a fellow-heir with the soul, of glory. He will not use it to the base services of sin. He that shall have a glorious body will esteem so of it here. What! shall I use the temple of the Holy Ghost? That that is a fellow-heir of heaven with my soul! that is the spouse of Christ, a member of Christ, as well as my soul! Shall I use it to these and these base services? It cannot be. If a man have the new nature in him, he cannot. It will not suffer him to sin in this manner. He cannot prostitute his body to base services.

Those that do so, how can they hope that their bodies should be glorious, like unto Christ's?

St Paul gives three evidences in one place, to know our interest in this glory of our bodies, in 2 Cor. v. 1. Saith he, 'We know that when this earthly house or tabernacle shall be dissolved, we have a building,' &c. We know we have a glorious building, a double building, heaven and our bodies. We have two glorious houses. Heaven and these bodies shall be a glorious house. But how do we know this?

Saith he, in the second verse, 'We groan earnestly, desiring to be clothed upon.' There is a wondrous desire after this clothing, Rom. viii. 23: 'The creature groaneth, much more we that have the first fruits of the Spirit.' There will be a sighing for this glory, a waiting for the blessed coming of Christ; for Christ to redeem soul and body perfectly. That is the first sign, a desire and groaning earnestly.

In the fourth verse there is another evidence, 'He that hath wrought us for the same things is God.' He that hath wrought us for the blessed estate to come is God. So, whosoever hopes for a house in heaven, when this tabernacle is dissolved, he is 'wrought' for it, that is, he is a new creature for it. God hath wrought his soul and body for it. God fits our souls here to possess a glorious body after; and he will fit the body for a glorious soul. So both shall be glorious; a glorious soul and a glorious body. He hath 'wrought us' for the same. If a man therefore find the beginning of the new creature, that it is begun to be wrought in him, he may know that he shall partake of this glory of the body, because he is 'wrought' for it.

The third is, 'Who hath also given us the earnest of the Spirit.' Whosoever finds in them the Spirit of God, sanctifying their souls and bodies, stirring them up to holy duties, guiding, and leading, and moving them to holy actions, they may, from the sanctifying Spirit that is an earnest to them, know what shall become of their bodies: 'He hath given us the earnest of the Spirit.'

To confirm this, there is an excellent place in Rom. viii. 10, 'If any man have not the Spirit of Christ, he is none of his.' 'If Christ be in you, the body is dead,' &c. It is a vile body: it is as good as dead; it hath the sentence of death already. It is dead, in regard it is sentenced to death for sin, as a malefactor that hath his sentence. 'But the Spirit is life in regard of righteousness.' What then? If the sanctifying Spirit of Christ dwell in you, 'he that raised Jesus from the dead shall also quicken your mortal bodies.' The same Spirit that sanctifies these souls of ours, and quickens them to holy duties, the same Spirit shall raise our bodies. As the same Spirit that sanctified the blessed mass of the body of Christ that he carried, and raised his body, the same Spirit that sanctifies our souls shall raise our bodies. The Spirit of God, when he hath begun to sanctify us, he never leaves us. He goes along in all changes, in life, in death, to the grave, as God said to Jacob, 'I will be with thee there,' Gen. xxxii. 28, *seq.* The Spirit of God he will mould our dead bodies, and make them like the glorious body of Christ. The Spirit of God never leaves our souls or bodies. Therefore, if we find the earnest of the Spirit, if we find the work of the Spirit, or the comfort of the Spirit, which is the term the Scripture gives, 'joy in the Holy Ghost, and peace of conscience,' together with the Spirit sanctifying us, especially in the time of trouble, when God sees his children have most need, they have the earnest of the Spirit, the beginnings of grace and joy, the beginnings of heaven upon earth. By this they may know, as the first fruit is, so likewise is the harvest; as the earnest is, even so is the bargain; as we have it now in our souls, so we shall also have it in our bodies and souls hereafter. These three grounds St Paul hath, why his hope of heaven was a good hope. We groan for it, and we are wrought for it, we are fitted for it. There is no man can hope to be glorious in his body, but his soul must be fitted for it. It must be a fit jewel for so glorious a casket, a fit inhabitant for so glorious a temple as the body shall be. The body shall be fitted for the soul, and the soul for the body: they are 'wrought' for it. And then he hath given us 'the earnest of the Spirit.' What need I quote further evidences, the Scripture being thus pregnant?

I beseech you, often consider your desires, whether you be content to live here alway or no, to satisfy the vile lusts of your body; or whether you desire 'to be dissolved and to be with Christ,' when you have done the work that God sent you for into the world. If we be content to abase ourselves for God here, who hath provided so much glory for us hereafter, and when the time comes, we can desire to be dissolved and to be with Christ, it is a good sign,—if we have the beginnings of the new creature, 'ye are wrought for it'—that our souls are fitted for a glorious body. We have 'the earnest of the Spirit,' the same Spirit that sanctifieth our souls, and that quickens our souls with joy and peace, the same Spirit shall raise our bodies. Comfort yourselves, you that are Christians, though you be weak, with this, that if you have but the earnest of the Spirit, undoubtedly you shall have a glorious house, instead of this tabernacle of dust.

Christ 'will change these vile bodies, that they shall be fashioned like his glorious body.' I beseech you, therefore, oft think of this; think of the time to come, comfort yourselves with things to come. In 1 Thes. iv. 18, St Paul would have us talk one to another often of this. This should be the matter of our conference: not only the state of the church, and our own estate here, but how it shall be with us when we are gone hence; how it shall be with us world without end hereafter. We should confer and speak, and oft meditate and think of these things.

What can be grievous,—what can be over-burdensome to that soul that knows it hath the pledge and earnest of glory hereafter? How doth it quicken the soul to any endeavour, when once we know that howsoever we abase ourselves here, yet we shall have glorious bodies hereafter! It will quicken us to any endeavour, to anything for Christ. Therefore let us oft think of our estate to come: let us set our thoughts forward to the time to come; let faith make the times to come present, and that will make us heavenly-minded. What made St Paul converse as if he were in heaven? Faith made the estate to come present; and hope, which is grounded on faith, it looks to Christ's coming to change our vile bodies. So faith and hope they make the soul look upward, they make it heavenly-minded.

Our souls are dull, and our bodies are dull in this world, but as iron, if it be touched with a loadstone, up it will; so if we get faith and hope to look forward, what shall be done to us for the time to come! The Spirit of faith and hope, if it touch the soul, will carry our dull bodies and our dead souls upward.

Therefore let us cherish our faith and hope by often meditation of the blessed estate to come, and think of these two things, of the excellent estate of our bodies and souls then. For if our bodies shall then be glorious like the body of Christ, our souls much more; the inhabitant, which is the special part, the soul shall be much more glorious. Let us think oft of this glory as it is described in the word. It transcends our thoughts. We cannot think high enough of it, and our interest and assurance of it. And daily search ourselves, whether our hope be good or no, that we have found evidence that our title is good to glory. Let us examine ourselves by those signs I named before. Where are our desires? What work hath the Spirit of God in us? How do we use these bodies of ours? As we use them now, we must look they shall be used hereafter. Let our tongues be our glory now, and they shall be glorious tongues afterward to praise God in heaven. Their bodies that have been glorious here shall be glorious in heaven. We may read our estate to come by what we are here. Those that carry themselves basely, and filthily, and dishonourably here, we may know what will become of them hereafter. Let us oft think of the estate to come, and of our interest in it; and both these together, the excellency of the estate, and our interest in it, without deceiving of our souls, what life will it put into all our carriage! What will be grievous to us in this world when our souls are thus settled? Oh, let us spend a few days fruitfully and painfully here amongst men, and do all the good we can; and use these bodies of ours to all the happy and blessed services we can! Why? We shall have glory more than we can imagine.

Let it comfort us in the hour of death, what death soever we die, or are designed to. Now you know the sickness is abroad; and alas! those bodies especially are vile bodies that are under the visitation: so that their dearest friends dare not come near them. Yet let this comfort us. They are vile bodies for a time. Put case we die the death that may hinder the comforts of this life. Those that die in much honour and pomp, and have their bodies embalmed, do all what they can with the body, it will come to dust and rottenness. It will be vile in death, or after death, at one time or other; and those that die never so vile and violent a death for God's sake, those that die of this base death, that they are deprived of much comfort, yet let it comfort them, Christ will transform their vile bodies to be glorious.

They talk much of the philosopher's stone, that it will change metals into gold. Here is the true stone that will change our vile bodies to be glorious. Let us die never so base or violent a death. Let us comfort ourselves in our own death, if it be thus with us, and in the death of our friends; these vile bodies, when they are most vile in death, they shall be made like the glorious body of Christ. Let us oft think of these things.

NOTE.

(*a*) P. 167. 'The Emperor Constantine would kiss the very holes of the eyes of those that had their eyes pulled out, that had been martyred.' Cf. Memoir of Constantine, with valuable references, in Dr Smith's Dictionary of Biography and Mythology, *sub voce*. G.

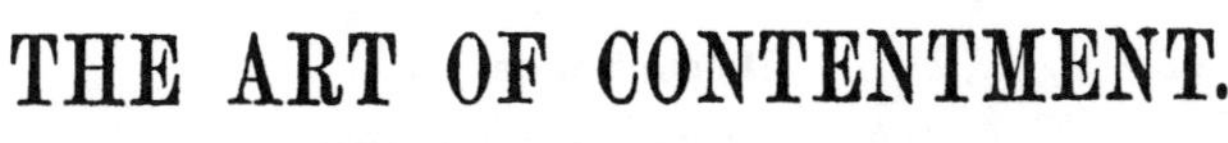

THE ART OF CONTENTMENT.

THE ART OF CONTENTMENT.

NOTE.

'The Art of Contentment' forms the last of the sermons of the 'Saint's Cordials, published in 1637 and 1658. It had previously been No. 1 of the first edition, 1629. The text of 1637 is followed in our reprint. In Vol. IV. pp. 75–111 will be found a specimen of the 'various readings' of the editions of 1637 and 1658 on a comparison with that of 1629. These may suffice. The result of a minute collation shews that the edition of 1637 presents a careful revision and enlargement of the *anonymous*, and, I suspect, *surreptitious* edition of 1629. Instead therefore of encumbering our margins, and distracting the reader with these corrections and improvements of the first edition, it has been deemed better to make the edition of 1637 our text in the remainder, leaving it to those curious in such matters to compare the other two therewith, in the way 'Judgment's Reason' in Vol. IV. is exhibited. *The edition of* 1637, *let it be understood, represents Sibbes's own version of his sermons*, either from fuller 'Notes,' or from a revision of that of 1629.

For the general title-page of the three editions of 'The Saint's Cordials,' see Vol. IV. p. 60. The separate title-page of 'The Art of Contentment' will be found below.* It may be proper to state, that the text of 'The Art of Contentment' now given is less full than in the first edition, the explanation being that the suppressed passages had been appropriated in other sermons in the interval. G.

* THE ART OF
CONTENTMENT.
In one Sermon.

Wherein is shewed.

- That this Art of Contentment is a Mysterie.
- That Gods Children are carried, and know how to behave themselves in variety of Conditions.
- How this hard Lesson is learned.
- What Infirmities are.
- The right use of them.
- That Christianity is a busie trade.
- The way how one is said to doe all things.
- What it is to doe things Evangelically.
- When a Christian can doe all things.
- Why he failes when he failes.
- Where his strength is.
- Lastly, The skill to fetch strength from Christ.

2 Sam. 15. 25, 26.

Then the King said unto Zadok, Carry the Arke of God back againe into the Citie: If I shall find favour in the eyes of the Lord, he will bring me again, and shew me both it and the Tabernacle thereof.

But if he thus say, I have no delight in thee, Behold, here am I, let him doe to me as seemeth good in his eyes.

LONDON,

Printed for R. Dawlman, at the brazen Serpent in *Pauls* Churchyard. 1637.†

† The imprint of the first edition, 1629, is, 'London, Printed for Robert Dolman in Pauls Church-yard at the signe of the Brazen Serpent. 1629,' and of the third, 1658, 'London, Printed for Henry Cripps at his Shop in Pope's-head Alley. 1658.' The former has the woodcut described in note, Vol. IV. p. 60.—G.

THE ART OF CONTENTMENT.

I have learned, in what estate soever I am, to be content. I know how to be abased, and how to abound: everywhere, in all things, I am instructed both to be full and to be hungry, both to abound and to suffer need. I can do all things through Christ that strengtheneth me.—PHILIP. IV. 11, 12, 13.

THE words are the blessed apostle's concerning himself, expressing the glorious power of the Spirit of God in a strong and grown Christian, and are to wipe away the imputation of worldliness in the apostle, serving herein also for a pattern to all God's children, that they may learn by his example that as they must be careful to avoid all blemishes and imputations, so especially that of worldliness, as being most contrary to the profession of a Christian, who hath an 'high calling,' and whose 'hope is in heaven,' Philip. iii. 14.

The Philippians had sent Paul some relief; and lest they should think that he expected great matters, he tells them that he had 'learned to be content in what estate soever he was.'

It is not amiss sometimes for God's children to speak of themselves, as Paul here as to other good ends so also to avoid false imputations in the way of just apology,* and likewise to be exemplary to weaker Christians. Is not the doctrine of contentment and the power of grace in all estates better learned by this blessed example of Paul, when he speaks thus of himself, 'I have learned, in what estate soever I am, to be content: to want, and to abound,' &c., than if he had weakly said, Be content with your present condition? The Scriptures be intended for practice; and therefore it is that there are so many examples in them, to shew the power of God's Spirit. This is the end of Paul's speaking so of himself, 'I have learned,' &c.

To come to the words. First, In general he sets down *the power of God's Spirit in him* in regard of that blessed grace of contentment. 'I have learned, in what estate I am, therewith to be content.'

And then he doth *parcel out this general into particular conditions in this same state,* 'I know how to be abased, and how to abound.'

And then he *wraps up all in general again,* 'I can do all things,' &c.

But lest this should seem to be somewhat vain-glorious, 'I can do all

* That is, 'defence.'—G.

things,' as if he were omnipotent (in some sense, indeed, a Christian is omnipotent), therefore he adds, 'I can do all things,' but with a blessed correction, 'through Christ that strengtheneth me.'

'I have learned,' saith he, 'I am instructed.' It is very significant in the original, viz., I am consecrated to this knowledge of contentment in all estates (*a*). It is a learning not of great persons, or of learned persons, but of holy persons. It is a mystical knowledge. There is a mystery in it. For as all religion is a mystery,—'great is the mystery of godliness,'—not only the speculative part, but likewise the practical part of it, so every part of religion is a mystery, repentance a mystery, faith a mystery, and this practical part of contentment in all conditions is a great mystery. And therefore St Paul saith he is instructed in it, as a consecrated person, having in him the Spirit of God. All the degrees in this world cannot teach this lesson that Paul had learned, 'to be contented.' He learned it in no school of the world, not at the feet of Gamaliel; he learned it of Christ, and by blessed experiences in afflictions. Some graces are reserved for some estates. He had learned patience and contentment in variety of estates. He had it not by nature, for he saith, 'I have learned.' It is a mystical thing, not so easily attained unto as the world is fondly* persuaded. Your ordinary Christian thinks that religion is nothing, that it is easily learned; whereas there is no point in religion but is a mystery. There is no Christian but he finds it to be so when he sets himself heartily to go through any religious work; as to humble himself, to repent, to go out of himself, and to cast himself upon the mercy of God in Christ. Oh, will he then say, it is a mystery. There is a difficulty in this work that I never thought of till I came to it. And so to be content with our condition, whatsoever the case be, to bring our hearts low, it is a mystery. Nature never teacheth this. It is learned in the school of Christ, and not without many stripes. We must be proficients a good while before we can learn to any purpose this one lesson of contentment in any condition. But the last verse is that which I will now dwell on, wherein we may see three things observable.

First, *That God carries his children in this world through variety of conditions*. They sometimes want, and sometimes abound. Their condition is sometimes more comfortable than at others. That is the first point.

2. The second is, *That in this variety of conditions, as they know what it is to want and to abound, so in all variety of conditions they know how to carry themselves.*

Thirdly, *They know in all variety of conditions how to avoid the sins incident to that condition*. As there are graces belonging to every state, so there are sins incident to every condition. And the child of God hath learned to practise the one, and to avoid the other.

1. First, *God's children know what it is to want, and to abound by experience*. God leads them through variety of conditions, Their estate is not always one and the same.

Quest. What is the reason of this dispensation in God thus to rule his children, to bring them to heaven by variety of conditions?

Sol. Among many other reasons this is one, *that their graces may be tried*. Every grace that brings a Christian to heaven must be a tried grace. He must try his patience, his contentment, his humility. How shall these graces be tried but in variety of estates and conditions? And secondly, How should we have experience of the goodness of God but in variety of estates?

* That is, 'foolishly.'—G.

When we find the stable, certain, constant love of God in variety of conditions, that howsoever our conditions ebb and flow, be up and down, like the spring weather, sometimes fair and sometimes foul, yet notwithstanding the love of God is constant always, and we have never so sure experience of it as in the variety of conditions that befall us; then we know that in God there is 'no shadow of changing,' howsoever the changes of our life be. Is it not a point worth our learning, to know the truth of our grace, and to know the constancy of God's love, with whom we are in a gracious covenant? And then again, we learn much wisdom how to manage our life hereby, even in the intercourse of our changes, to be now rich, now poor, now high, now low in estate. Wisdom is gotten by experience in variety of estates. He that is carried on in one condition, he hath no wisdom to judge of another's estate, or to carry himself to a Christian in another condition, because he was never abased himself. He looks very big at him. He knows not how to tender* another, that hath not been in another's condition. And therefore to furnish us, that we may carry ourselves as Christians, meekly, lovingly, and tenderly to others, God will have us go to heaven in variety, not in one uniform condition in regard of outward things.

Use. Learn hence *not to quarel with God's government;* for though he alters our conditions, yet he never alters his love. A Christian is unmoveable in regard of the favour of God to him, and in regard of sanctifying grace. In all moveable conditions he hath a fixed condition. Therefore let us not find fault with God's dispensation, but let him do as he pleases. So he bring us to heaven, it is no matter what way, how rugged it be, so he bring us thither.

2. The second general thing is this, *That in this variety of conditions, God's children know how to carry themselves.* As they know what it is to want and to abound, so they know how to abound and be abased as they should do. For there is no condition but a Christian may pick good matter out of it. As a good artsman will make a good piece of work of an ill piece of matter sometimes, to shew his skill, so a Christian can frame matter that is good out of any condition; he knows how to want, and how to abound, and that with the expression of graces too. He can practise the graces that ought and may be practised in all conditions. For instance, he can abound; that is, with expressing the graces that should be in abundance, which is, thankfulness to God; he hath, in abundance, a spirit of thankfulness; he hath a spirit to be a faithful steward in abundance; a spirit to honour God with his abundance. He hath a spirit to be humble in abundance, knowing all is as 'grass and the flower of the field.' He can be humble, he can stoop under the mighty hand of God, he can have experience in the abasement of the vanity of worldly favour, and worldly greatness. He learns what it is, and so he can learn patience, and all other graces that are to be practised in a mean estate. It were too long to name particulars; a Christian can do this. Grace is above all conditions. It can manage and rule all estates of life. It makes them serviceable to its own ends. A gracious man is not dejected over much with abasement; he is not lifted up over much with abundance, but he carries himself in a uniform manner, becoming a Christian in all conditions.

3. The third general thing is, *He can want and he can abound, without tainting himself over much with the sins of those conditions.* For instance, he

* That is, 'touch,' = make tender, move, or qu. 'care for'? = regard. Cf. Richardson, *sub voce.*—G.

can abound without pride, though it be a hard matter. Abundance works upon the soul of a man. He had need to have a strong brain that digests abundance; it is a wild untamed thing. And we see by experience in God's children how hard a matter it is for them to manage abundance. We see how it wrought upon Solomon and David. They were better in adversity, 1 Kings, xi. 1, 2 Sam. xi. 2; and yet notwitstanding the child of God hath grace even to overcome the sins that are incident to abundance. He hath grace to be lowly-minded in a great estate; not to trust to uncertain riches; he knows by the Spirit of God what they are, and that he hath an inheritance of better things in another world, which teacheth him to set a light esteem upon all things below.

And so for dejection; the sin that we are subject to fall into in want, is putting forth our hands to evil means, to shift.* God's child can learn to want without tainting his conscience with ill courses, and then he can want without impatience, without too much dejection of spirit; as if all were lost; whenas, indeed, a Christian in a manner is rich all alike. For God is his portion, and howsoever a beam may be took away, the sun is his; take away a stream, the spring is his; in the poorest estate, God all-sufficient is his still; and so in a manner a Christian is rich all alike. God never takes away himself, Gen. xvii. 1. He knows this, and therefore he can want, he can be abased as long as he hath the spring of all. Though a cistern be took away, he cares not, he can want and abound without murmuring, without dejection of spirit. Whereas those that have not been brought np in Christ's school, nor trained up in variety of conditions, are able to do nothing. If they abound, they are proud; if they be cast down, they murmur and fret, and are dejected, as if there were no Providence to rule the world, as if they were fatherless children. This is the excellency of a Christian, that as he knows what it is to abound by experience, so he knows how to abound with the practice of the graces, and how to want with the avoiding of the snares that usually are in that condition.

Obj. But hath a Christian learned this at the first?

Ans. No; he learns it not very easily, nor very soon. *Self-denial is the first lesson in Christ's school:* to have no wit of our own further than Christ's wisdom; to have no will of our own further than his commandment guides us; and he that hath learned self-denial, he is in a great way to learn this blessed lesson of contentment in any condition whatsoever. So that every Christian hath some degree of that, as he can deny himself. But there are many things to be learned before we can come to carry ourselves wisely in any condition.

For besides self-denial, we must learn *the doctrine of the covenant of grace*, that God in Christ is become a Father to us, and carries a fatherly mind to us. In what condition soever we are, he is a father still, and intends us well, and will provide for us in the hardest condition. Having took the relation of a father upon him, do you think that he will fail in the carriage of a father towards us? He is pitiful to us, he respects us in the basest condition. He that knows God to be his father, cast him into what condition you will, knows he hath a good portion.

And then we must know *the doctrine of the providence of this Father*, that all shall work together for the best to those that love him, Rom. viii. 28, want and abundance, prosperity and afflictions, whatsoever. God by his overruling power will bring all things to this blessed issue, to help forward the eternal good of his child. A man must know this, and divers the like

* That is, = to resort to expedients.—G.

things that are to be known, before he can learn this blessed lesson of contentment. There is a venom and a vanity in everything without grace, wherewith we are tainted; but when grace comes, it takes out the sting of all ill, and then we find a good in the worst. There is a vanity in the best things, and there is a good in the worst. Grace picks out the good out of the worst; as God turns all to good, so grace finds good in every condition. The Spirit of God sanctifies a Christian to all conditions, and sanctifies every condition to him. Now, I beseech you, think of this that I have said, which I wish without further enlargement may add to your care, and desire to be in the happy condition of Christians. What a blessed thing is it to be in the covenant of grace, to have God to be our father, to be in Christ, that let our condition outwardly be what it will be, we shall have grace to carry ourselves in it, God will go along with us by his Holy Spirit! What a blessed thing is it, in all the uncertainties of the world, to have a certain rule to go by, as a Christian hath, which carries him along in all the uncertainties in this world! None but a Christian hath this. 'I have learned,' saith Paul. When did he learn it? Not before he was a Christian. This I could desire to press, but that I have other things to speak of, to make us in love with religion, with the state of Christians, that is thus above all conditions whatsoever, and can rule all other conditions. A Christian is not at the mercy of the world; his contentment is not a dependent contentment. You may cast him into prison, you may impoverish him, you may labour to debase and disgrace him; but can you take away his comfort? Can you take away his grace? Can you take away the love of God? No; God will rather increase all upon him. For the best things of a Christian are not at the mercy of the world, nor at the mercy of his several conditions. Prosperity and adversity, these are out of him. He hath a state depending upon the good will and pleasure of his Father, that loves him better than he loves himself, and out of love will work good out of the worst condition that can befall him. So I hasten to that which follows.

4. Having spoken in particular, then he comes to the general, wherein he wraps up all: 'I can do all things, but in Christ that strengthens me.' Here is,

1. First of all, *The blessed apostle's ability*, 'I can do all things.'

2. And then here is, secondly, *the spring of his ability, whence he hath it:* 'I can do all things, but in Christ that strengthens me.'

In the apostle's ability you have,

1. *His strength itself.* 2. *The enlargement of it.*

'I am able.' And what to do? A few things? No; 'all things.' The point of doctrine offered is this, that *a Christian man is an able man.* Whosoever hath the Spirit of Christ is an able man, and his ability is a large ability; he is able to do all things. Take doing in a transcendent sense, not only to do, but take it to resist ill, to resist temptation, to suffer affliction, to enjoy prosperity, to break off sinful courses, and to take a new course, to practise all duties; for so the apostle means 'I can do,' that is, I can carry myself in all conditions, I can express all graces, I can resist all temptations, I can suffer all afflictions, I can do all this. What is the reason a Christian is so able?

1. Because, first of all, *he hath a stronger and abler spirit than his own.* The Spirit of God is a spirit of strength, 2 Tim. i. 8. It is the Spirit of power, which is the soul of his soul, and the life of his life. Now the strength of a man is in his spirit. The stronger spirit makes the abler man,

and the Spirit of God being the strongest of spirits, indeed the strength of spirits, it makes a Christian in whom it dwells the ablest man.

2. And then again, *A Christian is a new creature;* therefore he is furnished with abilities fit for the new creature. When Adam was created he was endued with all graces fit for an entire state. As when God made heaven he made stars to beautify heaven; when he made the earth, he made trees and flowers; so, when he made man, he furnished him with graces, and fitted him for that estate. Now after the fall, when God brings a man in Christ to be a new creature, he hath abilities to furnish him for that new condition.

3. And then again, *Every particular grace of the new creature is a grace of strength.* As the Spirit is a strong Spirit, so the spirit of love is as strong as death, it hath a 'constraining power,' 2 Cor. v. 14. The Spirit of God is so strong in his children, that are truly his, that it makes them even with willingness to lay down their lives, that is dearest to them in this world. Here is a sweet kind of tyranny in the affection of love, that will carry a man through thick and thin, through all, and that with pleasure, willingly and comfortably too; as the apostles were glad to suffer anything for Christ's sake, their hearts were so enlarged with a spirit of love. The spirit of faith it is a strong and mighty spirit, an able spirit. It conquers God himself, as Jacob wrestled with the wrestlings of God, and by the strength of God overcame God, Hosea xii. 3, 4. And the woman of Canaan overcame Christ by the strength she had from Christ, Mat. xv. 28. In the sense of God's displeasure it will believe God's favour in Christ, and is able to break through the thickest clouds of discomfort whatsoever, and to see the loving face of God. In a base condition it can struggle with God, saying with Job, 'Though he kill me, yet will I trust in him,' Job xiii. 15. It is a strong grace. Faith prevails with almighty God. It prevails in all inferior conditions whatsoever. You see the fruit and strength of all graces is attributed to faith, Heb. xi. 33. By faith they overcame, by faith they were strong, and did this and that; insinuating that faith is not only a strong grace in itself, but it gives vigour and strength to all graces. And so we see love, 1 Cor. xiii. 4, it is not only a strong grace, but the office of other graces is attributed unto it. It suffers long, which is the office of patience. What should I speak of other graces, these radical and fundamental graces being of such force? Now every Christian in some measure hath a spirit of faith and a spirit of love, and these are very strong, to carry him through all estates and conditions; and that with such glory and lustre that every one may wonder at the condition of a Christian. Even in the worst estate he hath a spirit not of the world but above the world. This faith overcomes the world; and he that is in them, the Spirit of God, is stronger than he that is in the world, 1 John iv. 4.

To proceed to a further demonstration of a Christian man's ability, which is intimated unto us in his very name. What is the name of a Christian? 'Anointed.' The Spirit of God is compared to oil. What is the virtue of oil? It is to make nimble, for the Spirit of God makes Christians nimble; and oil it makes strong. The wrestlers were wont to be anointed beforehand with oil; so the Spirit of God makes Christians strong. The virtue of oil anointing is to be above. Jumble it together with other liquors, it is a regal liquor, it will have the pre-eminence, and be above. So grace, although it be mingled with corruption, the Spirit of grace and faith at last will apear, the Spirit of God will be above all, at length it will work itself clear. In all temptations, a Christian as a Christian is an able man. If he be answerable to his own name, if he be not an hypocrite, he hath an ability in him, he can do more than the world.

Use 1. First of all then, learn here, *that religion is not a matter of word, nor stands upon words*, as wood consists of trees. To speak thus and thus, it may come from parts, from memory, and wit; but religion is a matter of power, it makes a man able. It made Paul, what! To speak only? No; his learning made him able to *do* all things. It is a matter of practice, and there is nothing so speculative in religion but it tends to practice. Religion is an art, not of great men, not of mighty men, but of holy men. It is an art and trade. A trade is not learned by words, but by experience; and a man hath learned a trade, not when he can talk of it, but when he can work according to his trade. So we see Paul shews his learning he speaks of before, by his ability. The point of the Trinity it is a speculative point, and it tends to practice. First, to be a foundation of our worship, that we worship one God in three persons. And then it tends to shew the unity among Christians, that God will work among Christians at length, that they shall be all one in some sort, as the Father, Son, and Holy Ghost are one: which, though it be a point of high and deep speculation, yet it tends to practice. Now if the sublime and high points do, what point is there in religion but it tends to practice? And therefore let us not please ourselves that we have deep understandings, but let us shew our understandings by our practice. As the sheep shews how he thrives in his pasture by his wool and fleece, so shew how thou profitest in religion, by being enabled with the power of grace, that carries thee through all conditions, to avoid the sins and to express the graces in such conditions. So much grace as thou hast to carry thyself thus, so much ability thou hast, and so much religion.

Use 2. If a Christian be an able man, I beseech you, *let it serve to try ourselves by this scantling* that I have spoken of.* Is Christianity a point of strength and ability? Let us try the truth of our estate then. Thou wouldst be a Christian; what canst thou do then? What sin canst thou resist? What canst thou bear? What holy duty canst thou do? How canst thou enjoy the good blessings that God sends thee, without defiling of thyself with those blessings, that thou art not proud of the riches nor of the honour thou hast? Grace manageth all conditions. Thus, if thou be a Christian, answer thy name; if not, thou art a hypocrite yet. For a Christian in some measure is able 'to do all things, through Christ that strengtheneth him.' I beseech you, let us not deceive ourselves. The best of us all may mourn for our want in this kind. Our consciences tell us that we might have done a great deal more than we have; that God would have enabled us if we had not been false-hearted, and betrayed ourselves, and been negligent in the use of the means, to have done a great deal more than we do. What a shame is it for Christians, that indeed have some truth of grace in them, that they cannot be a little abased in the world, but they are *à la mort*.† Why, where is the power of grace? They cannot be lift up in their condition a little, but they will scant know their brother of low degree. Where is religion now? What hast thou better in thee than a worldling hath? Nay, a heathen man, out of principles of morality, would learn to conform his carriage, outwardly at the least, better than thou. Let us learn therefore to shame ourselves when we find any murmuring and rising of corrupt nature in any condition whatsoever, and know that this

* Cf. note *a*, Vol. I. page 117.—G.

† That is, 'deadened' = dead-afraid.—G.

becomes not a Christian. This is it which the apostle presseth so oft, that we should carry ourselves as becometh Christians. Oh, doth this become a Christian? A Christian should be able to do all things through Christ that strengtheneth him. What a shame is it for a professor of religion to be as worldly, as distracted with cares, as passionate, if he be a little touched, as a man that professeth no religion at all? Where is the power, where is the glory and credit of religion here? I beseech you, let us be ashamed, and know that our profession requireth that we should be able.

Use 3. Again, *This answers the common objection of carnal men.* They ward off all reproofs with this. Tell them of their faults, why it is my infirmity, it is my weakness. Is it so? Art thou a Christian or no? If thou be a Christian, thou labourest for strength against thy weakness; thou dost not make a plea for it. There is weakness indeed in the best; but that is the matter of their humiliation, and the object of their mortification. It is not their plea for idleness, to give themselves to sinful courses. Men therefore make a false plea of infirmities and weaknesses. There is no infirmity in a carnal man that hath not the Spirit of Christ. He is dead. There is no weakness in a dead person. In regard of civil carriages there may be weakness in such a man. He may be passionate, he may be froward, unbeseeming a man that is civil; but that is not in the rank we speak of. None can have infirmities but a Christian that hath the life of grace in him in sincerity and truth. And therefore if thou discover that thou hast not the truth of grace, never say it is thy infirmity. To shew what infirmities be, I rank them to three heads.

1. In the first rank of infirmities are *the imperfection of good actions*, which are either distractions and deadness in prayer and hearing; or invincible infirmities, of which as an ancient father saith well, 'Lord, deliver me from my miserable necessities' (*b*). A man may be in such a state sometimes in regard of the temper of the body, it being out of tune, that he cannot pray as he would do. 'The spirit is willing, but the flesh is weak,' saith our Saviour, Mat. xxvi. 41. It was almost an invincible necessity in the apostles then. Again, we might resist, and we might be more cheerful than we are ofttimes. But sometimes there may be such distemper in the body, that may almost of necessity unfit us for the duty. This we call the infirmity of a Christian, because he is ashamed of it, and grieved for it.

2. Again, Infirmities are *those indeliberate passions that carry us sometimes to actions that we should not do*, being carried with a tempest of passion, when we understand not ourselves well.

3. And lastly, It is an infirmity *when we are hindered from doing that which we should do, upon passion, upon surprisal of some great fear and terror*, that we are not so bold as we should be to stand out in a cause on the sudden, as Peter was surprised with a spirit of fear that he should lose his life, Mat. xxvi. 70. It was no presumption in him, it was an infirmity in the blessed apostle for that time. These then be the signs of infirmities: to have invincible imperfections, or distraction and deadness, accompanying our good actions; to be carried in the heat and tempest of passion to that which afterwards we are ashamed of and repent for; or to be hindered from that we should do by some prevailing passion.

But otherwise infirmities are not, when we live in them, when we make a custom of them. *Customary sins are not sins of infirmity*, but the sins that we fall into, that we are overtaken with, on the sudden. Only in some cases a man may live in a sin of infirmity, when the ground of the infirmity is rooted within him, and he hath not yet purged out the root. As for instance, a man by temper prone to anger may live long in that infirmity, being many times inordinately pettish and peevish, because he carries about him the root, temper of the body, and inclination that way. Now he that lives in such an infirmity repents daily, and gets ground of it; he is still hewing at the root, and at length, at the last stroke it falls, and he gets the victory over it.

Again, A sin of infirmity *is not a sin that we plead for.* A man is ashamed of his infirmities; he is grieved for them. Now when a man pleads for them, and makes them a shelter and cover-shade to go on in sinful courses, they are not infirmities. Therefore whosoever pleads for sins discovers a false heart; his sins are enormities, not infirmities. A Christian gets the better of infirmities. After he falls, he riseth stronger and stronger still. But when a man grows worse and worse, and is habituated in an evil course, it is not an infirmity, because he grows not out of it. Let us not deceive ourselves with this plea, to say, It is my weakness. A Christian should be ashamed to plead this; he should be able to do all things. Well, you see then this point is clear, that a Christian is an able man, he hath a strength above nature in him, notwithstanding all his infirmities. This will appear more in the second branch, in the generality, he is able to do 'all things.'

To come to that, therefore, there are many things required of a Christian. Christianity is a busy trade. If we look up to God, what a world of things are required in a Christian to carry himself as he should do! A spirit of faith, a spirit of love, a spirit of joy, and delight in him above all. And if we look to men, there are duties for a Christian to his superiors, a spirit of subjection. And duties to equals, to carry a spirit of love; and to inferiors a spirit of pity and bounty. If we look to Satan, we have many duties, to resist him and to watch against the tempter. If we look to the world, it is full of snares. There must be a great deal of spiritual watchfulness, that we be not surprised. If we look to ourselves, there are required many duties, to carry our vessels in honour, and to walk within the compass of the Holy Ghost, to preserve the peace of our consciences, to walk answerable to our worth, as being the sons of God and co-heirs with Christ. The state of a Christian is no idle condition. Sometimes a Christian is in this state, sometimes in that; and then he must have these graces, and anon use other graces; he must have a suit of all graces, fit for all conditions. Now answerable to the variety of all the duties that are required of him, he must have ability; and therefore the apostle saith, 'I can do all things through Christ.'

5. So then the point of doctrine is this, *that the trial of a sincere Christian's estate is universality of obedience.* Universality of carriage in all conditions is the trial of Christian sincerity. He must dispense with himself in no sin, and he must be a vessel prepared for every good work, 'a vessel of glory,' as the apostle speaks, 2 Tim. ii. 21. He must baulk no service that God calls him to. What is the reason of this?

The reason is, *because a Christian hath the sanctifying Spirit, and the sanctifying Spirit hath the seeds of all graces in it;* so that where it is, there is the subduing of all sin in the root. And then all graces are answerable to the commandments of God in all duties, and to the avoiding of all sins. And therefore James saith pregnantly to this purpose, he that 'offends in one is guilty of all,' ii. 10.

Use 1. Let us take heed *we plead not immunity and freedom from some things,* and think that the good we do in some kind may excuse the bad we do in others. You have some that will take liberty in an unclean conversation, because they are bountiful and liberal; and they will take liberty to be oppressive in their callings, because they attend upon the means of salvation. Oh no! take heed of that carriage that is against the profession of religion. There must be an universal disposition to all graces and to all duties, though they be never so contrary and cross to corrupt nature. The devil knows well where to have some men, for he sees they mind some sin, and are careless in the practice of other duties; and therefore, in the hour of temptation, the devil will surprise such men, and it will be a ground of despair if they take not heed. Put the case a man will say this, I can part with all things else, Oh, but I cannot die: I can be content to be imprisoned, but I cannot endure to be disgraced. Let a man dispense and favour himself but in one thing, and when the time comes he will be discovered to be but an hypocrite. Then Satan will work upon that, and there he will be shaken in his condition. By reason that he did not learn self-denial perfectly, he hath not grace disposing him to the practice of all Christian duties. He hath not learned to know God in covenant, to supply his wants of honour, credit, wife and children, and all that he is to part withal for Christ's sake. Now he that hath not learned this in resolution, though God do not yet call him to it, by entering into his own soul, and asking himself what he can part with, and what he can resist for Christ's sake, 'What can I endure? what can I suffer?' If his heart do not tell him, I can part with all, I will rather endure death itself, rather endure shame, or any thing, than break the peace of a good conscience, and grieve the Spirit of God. If he cannot answer his soul thus, surely I can speak little comfort to that man. For we see a Christian must be able to do all things; that is, to resist all ill, to practise all duty, to break off all sinful courses.

Quest. But some will object, May not a Christian be subject to some especial sin?

Ans. Yes, he may. God, for especial purposes sometimes, will have men of eminent graces to be subject to notable infirmities. But what, do they plead for them? No; but as by temper, or by former custom, or as they find themselves more inclined one way than another, so they gather strength especially against their especial sin. And in the beginning of conversion, there is a blow given to the reigning sin that was before; and as when Goliah was slain, and all the rest fled, 1 Sam. xvii. 51, so grace strikes at the Goliah. In conversion, there is a main stroke given unto sin. Perhaps somewhat remains still, that grace will be hewing at, and therefore grace may stand with an especial sin that a man is inclined to. But this he labours to get all strength against, as other, so strength of direction. You shall find a Christian when he is subject to any infirmity, he will speak more learnedly, and more judiciously, with greater detestation against that sin that he is most prone unto than against any other. He labours to make up the breach where the wall is weakest. So a man may be a good man, and be subject to an infirmity, but then he gathers more strength against it.

Use 2. Well, you see then a Christian is able to do all things through Christ that strengthens him. I beseech you, let us often enter into ourselves, and make *an use of trial*, also of that which hath been spoken, what we can do, what we can part with, what we can resist. Let us never think ourselves to be in such an estate as is fit to be, to comfort ourselves, till we can in truth and sincerity of heart renounce all whatsoever. Yet notwithstanding, this must be understood evangelically, 'I can do all things.' What! legally, without a flaw? No; 'I can do all things' so far forth, as shall shew that I am a true Christian, and not an hypocrite; so far as shall be beautiful in the eye of others, to allure them to the embracing of religion; so far as shall make base spirits to envy to see my even carriage, and to see the power of religion; so far as shall put the world to silence for reproaching; so far as I shall enjoy assurance of the truth of grace; so far as Satan shall not get his will in every sin. Our obedience is evangelical, and not legal.

Quest. Now, what is it to do all things evangelically? To clear that point.

Ans. To do all things evangelically is, first of all, for a man to know that he is in the same state of grace, and that he hath his sins pardoned, and that he is accepted in Christ to life and salvation. That is the ground of all evangelical obedience. He must know that he is in the covenant of grace; that he hath the forgiveness of sins, and a right to life everlasting in Christ. And then comes obedience answerable to that condition; that is, a desire to obey God in all things: a grief that he cannot do it so well as he would; a prayer that he might do it so; and an endeavour together with prayer that he may do so, and some strength likewise with endeavour. For a Christian, as I said before, he hath the Spirit of God, not only to set him to an endeavour, but to give him some strength. So there is a desire, and purpose, and prayer, and grief of heart, and endeavour, and likewise some strength in evangelical obedience.

A Christian then in the gospel can do all things when he hath his sins forgiven, and is accepted in Christ, when he can endeavour to do all, and desire to do all, and in some measure practise all duties in truth. For the gospel requires truth and not perfection. That is the perfection that brings us to heaven in Christ our Saviour. We have title to heaven; in him is the ground, because forgiveness of sins is in him. Now a Christian's life is but to walk worthy of this, and to fit himself for that glorious condition that he hath title unto by Christ, to walk sincerely before God. Sincerity is the perfection of Christians. Let not Satan therefore abuse us. We do all things, when we endeavour to do all things, and purpose to do all things, and are grieved when we cannot do better. For mark, this goes with evangelical obedience always. God pardons that which is ill, for he is a Father. He hath bound himself to pardon, 'I will pity you as a father pitieth his child,' Ps. ciii. 13. From the very relation he hath took upon him, we may be assured he will pity and pardon us, and then he will accept of that which is good, because it is the work of his own Spirit, and will reward it. This in the covenant of grace he will do. A Christian can do all then; and wherein he fails, God will pardon him. What is good, God will accept and reward; and what is sick and weak in him, God will heal, till he have made him up in Christ.

Thus we see in what sense this is to be understood, a Christian can do all things through Christ. For as it is said of gold, the best gold you have hath allowance of such grains, so take the best Christian, you must have some allowance. Some imperfection cleaves to him. He cannot do all perfectly. For then what need the covenant of grace? He can do all things so as he flies to the mercy of God in Christ for life everlasting. He can do all things required of a Christian in the covenant of grace in regard of sincerity. These things must be well and soundly understood, and then we can take no offence at the doctrine.

Quest. What is the cause that a Christian fails then when he doth fail?

Ans. 1. A Christian fails, *when he doth not understand the promises of the new covenant of grace*, that God hath given not only promises of the pardon of sin, but of all kind of graces, a promise of the Spirit in general. He will give his Spirit to those that ask it, and a promise of every other particular grace: that he will write his law in our hearts, and he will teach us to love one another, and he will put his fear into our hearts. We have not a grace but either there is a promise of it generally, or specially. Now when a Christian forgets this, he fails for want of understanding the privileges and promises.

Ans. 2. Again, he fails *for want of wisdom to plant himself in such helps, whereby he might be able to do all things;* for it is the folly sometimes of Christians to be rash in venturing upon occasions; and then he hath no more strength than Samson had when he adventured. He loseth his strength when he ventureth rashly. But if a Christian be wise to keep out of temptation, and to keep himself in good company and acquaintance, using holy means and helps to godliness, wherein the Spirit works, a wise Christian may perform all.

Ans. 3. Again, *for want of resolution.* A Christian goes not out always with his spiritual armour, as he should. He goes not out with a purpose to please God in all things, and to avoid all sins; but his armour is loose about him. If a Christian would resolve, in the power of God, to break through all difficulties, and to do all duties, God would second him. 'Arise, and be doing, and the Lord will be with thee,' 1 Chron. xxii. 16. Let a Christian go on constantly in a good way, and he shall find experience of God's helping of him. Without manly resolutions, a Christian fails.

Quest. What is the reason that a Christian many times stands in strong and great duties, and is foiled in little duties?

Ans. Because he is watchful in the one, and careless in the other. Indeed, it is want of will. If we would have strength, and would carry ourselves manfully, we might have grace to carry ourselves even to the glory of our profession and to the credit of it. But we willingly favour corruption, and are not willing to put it out of ourselves to the utmost; whereupon we want much comfort that Christians should enjoy; and hereupon come many breaches in our life. In a word, if a Christian were careful, there is no duty, but he might perform it in some measure. He may go wondrous high upwards, always with this exception, that he never look to be justified by it. For God hath not established the covenant so. That is done by Christ. Again, if he be careless, he may sink wondrous low. There is no sin but the sin against the Holy Ghost, but he may fall into it in some manner.

I hasten to the last point. 'I can do all things,' but how? with what strength? 'Through Christ that strengtheneth me.'

This is to salve up an objection which might be made against the blessed apostle, 'I can do all things.' Here is a proud word. Oh no; 'it is in Christ that strengthens me.' St Paul was wondrous cautious and careful to avoid spiritual pride, or the least touch of it, as it is 1 Cor. xv. 10. 'Not I,' saith he. He checks himself presently: 'I laboured more than they all; not I, but grace within me.' Of all other sins, take heed of spiritual pride, check it presently. 'I can do all.' Oh but, lest proud thoughts should arise, 'it is in Christ that strengtheneth me.' My strength is out of myself. As the heads of those rivers, that ran through paradise, and that watered the city of God, they were out of paradise, so the head and spring of those streams that water the church of God, and particular Christians, they are out of themselves, they are in Christ. It is otherwise with us than it was in the 'first Adam.' He had strength, and had no promise to stand. He had power to stand, if he would. But a Christian's strength is out of himself, in the 'second Adam,' Christ. And it is well that it is in the keeping of so strong a Saviour, for we should forfeit it as Adam did, if it were in our own hands. It is derived to us, as much as he thinks good; but the spring is in him. And we have not only a will, but the promise and ability to do good; we do all through Christ.

6. So the point of doctrine is this, *that the original of a Christian's strength is in Christ.* God is the original of all strength. But God himself hath no intercourse of the new covenant with man out of the second person. All our comfort, and all our grace, it comes through Christ, who having taken our nature upon him, and having satisfied God, is fit to derive all grace and comfort to us. For he is near us, he is of our nature, and God in him is well pleased so as we may now go boldly to Christ; we are bone of his bone and flesh of his flesh. God himself out of Christ is 'a consuming fire.' Now, in Christ God favours man; he is gracious and lovely to us, and we to him; because Christ his beloved Son hath took our nature upon him, and now in our nature he is in heaven. So Christ the mediator is the fountain of all strength; he is the spiritual Joseph that had laid up store for all Egypt, and all that came. He is the high steward of his church, the second in the kingdom of heaven; he is the Joseph, he dispenseth all riches and treasures; all are in him for the church's sake. In him we do all things. As we can do all things for him as a mediator that died for us and procured favour for us, so we can do all things in him as an head to whom we are united. For there must be union before there can be communion. As in marriage there must be a uniting before there be a communion of estates and conditions, so before we can do anything for Christ we must be in Christ. We have all as through Christ, as in Christ. Thence comes communion with Christ's Spirit. So then it is Christ by his Spirit, for he doth all by his Spirit: 'The Lord is that Spirit,' 2 Cor. iii. 17. Christ doth all in the church by his Spirit. Now, the Spirit is the union of Christ, he strengthens all; all our strength is by Christ's Spirit. Now, this Spirit of God first sanctifies Christ, the human nature of Christ, before he sanctifieth us. We have all grace and power and strength at the second hand. It comes not from Christ as God immediately. And grace comes not from the Holy Ghost immediately to us; but the Holy Ghost first sanctifies Christ his human nature and then he sanctifies us, and we out of Christ's fulness receive grace for grace. The same Spirit that sanctified his nature in the womb of the virgin, and that sanctified his holy nature that now he hath in heaven with him, the same Spirit is sent from him to sanctify every member of the church. All is in the head, John i. 16. As first the ointment was poured on Aaron's head, and from thence it ran down to the skirts of his garments, Ps. cxxxiii. 2, so all grace is poured upon the head of Christ first, and then from him upon the skirts, even upon the meanest Christian, as answerable to their portion; and to those things that God means to call them to, they have grace to carry them. You see then how to conceive of this, how we have all in Christ, that is, by the Spirit of Christ, and how it comes by the Spirit.

Use 1. First of all, then, you see here how these two agree: a Christian, when he is a Christian, hath freedom of will and power. He hath power and free will. As far as he is freed by the Spirit of Christ, so far he is free. For, 2 Cor. iii. 17, 'where the Spirit of the Lord is, there is liberty.' So, John viii. 36, Christ says, 'If the Son shall make you free, then you shall be free indeed.' 'He can do all things,' therefore he is free. But it is in Christ; therefore his freedom is from him. We speak, but it is Christ's Spirit that openeth our mouth. We believe, but it is Christ by his Spirit that opens our hearts to believe. We are mighty, but it is in God. We are able to do great matters, but it is in Christ that strengtheneth us. We are strong, but it is in the Lord; as it is written, 'Be strong in the Lord, and in the power of his might,' Eph. vi. 10. The understanding is ours, the affections are ours, the will is ours; but the sanctifying of all this, and the carriage of all these supernaturally above themselves, to do them spiritually, that is not ours, but it is Christ's. So we see what is ours, and what is not ours. We are able to do; but the strength, and the grace, and ability is from Christ. A wind instrument sounds, but the man makes it sound by his breath. We are like wind instruments. Indeed, we sound, but no further than we are blown upon; and we yield music, but no further than we are touched by the Spirit of God. We are light, but as the air is, as it is enlightened by the sun; and therefore we must understand these points, that God may have glory, and that we may know what is ours.

And then again we see here, *that we have in Christ not only a general ability, that we are able, but we have the very act itself, the deed itself.* He strengtheneth us. There is a spiritual life and a spiritual power and will, and then the act and deed itself. Now, we have not only from Christ the life of grace at the first, and then a spiritual power answerable to that again, whereby our powers are renewed, so as we are able to do something in our will, but we have the deed itself. The doing is from Christ; he strengtheneth us for the present. Now, you have some that teach loosely this point, that we have general universal grace, whereby we are enabled, if we will, to believe, and to do this thing, if we will. But I say that is not all; but we have the will and the deed itself from Christ by his Spirit, and in every holy action Christ helps us to do these things in very deed.

First, *He moves the soul to the action, and applies the soul to the thing.* By the Spirit he doth this. For though we have power, we could not exercise it but by the Spirit, in this or that particular act.

Second, Again, *he works a preserving of the grace in that act.* God preserves his own work against temptation, and against impediments; for there is no act but it is opposed. The devil is in every good work, either at the beginning to hinder it, or at the end to defile it, one way or other. Now, God preserves his own work by his Spirit. First, He moves us to do, and then he preserves us in doing, and arms us against the impediments of good works. Then he determines the good work, and limits it, how far we shall do well, thus far, and thus far; the degrees come from Christ. For sometimes he doth it by his glorious power, as Paul saith, Eph. i. 19. Sometimes we are strengthened to do more, and sometimes less, as he will. Not only the act itself, and the application of the soul, and the preserving of grace in every act, we sink else, but the degree that we do sometimes better, it comes from Christ now strengthening of us more, and now less, as he sees good.

Know, by the way, that *he is a voluntary head.* Though he be an head of influence that flows into every member, yet he is a voluntary head, according to his own good pleasure, and the exigents of his members.

Sometimes we have need of more grace, and then it flows into us from him accordingly. Sometimes we have need to know our weakness, and then he leaves us to ourselves, that we may know that without him we cannot stand; that we may know the necessity of his guidance to heaven, in the sense of our imperfections; that we might see our weakness and corruptions, that we had thought we had not had in us: as Moses was tempted to murmur, a meek man, Num. xi. 21, *seq.*, and David to cruelty, a mild man, 2 Sam. xi. 15, that thought they had not had those corruptions in them. God leaves Christians sometimes to themselves, that they may know that they are not strong by their own spirit. So the degrees are from Christ, sometimes more and sometimes less. Sometimes we are in desertion, that we may know the manner of Christ's governing us till we come to heaven.

Use 1. Well, I beseech you, let us know that out of Christ there is no grace. A civil man doth nothing in religion well. There cannot be a beam without the sun; there cannot be a river without a spring; there cannot be a good work without the spring of good works, Christ. Therefore, we should fetch all from him, since there is no grace out of him at all.

Use 2. Again, let us be sure, in all particular actions, to be poor in spirit. When we have any temptation to resist, any trouble to bear, or any duty to do, let us empty ourselves. No grace is stronger than humility. No man is weaker than a proud man. For a proud man rests on nothing, and an humble man that empties himself, he stands upon the Rock. We should therefore make use of the strength of Christ, that hath not only abundance for himself, but an abundance for us, an overflowing for every Christian for his good. Let us empty ourselves, as the prophet saith to the widow, Bring 'empty vessels' now, and we shall have oil enough, 2 Kings iv. 3. There is enough in Christ; but first we must empty ourselves by humility, and then there is fulness in him. 'Of his fulness we receive grace for grace,' John i. 16. His fulness is like the fulness of the clouds that is ready to drop, and like the fulness of breasts, that are ready to yield what they have. He is willing. It is our fault, and baseness, and pride, that hinders us. Let us as much as we can empty ourselves of ourselves, and stir up the spirit of faith. Go to Christ. So much faith as we carry, so much grace we bring from him. If we do but touch him by faith, the issue of our corruptions will be dried up in some measure, and we shall have a spring of graces in us answerable to the graces in him, Mat. ix. 20.

I beseech you, therefore, let us labour for these two graces, especially since all is out of us in the covenant of grace; not only salvation is out of us, but grace that brings us to heaven is out of us, to empty ourselves in humility, and by faith to go to Christ. The one grace makes us go out of ourselves, the other carries us to Christ and to the promises of Christ. Learn to do this in every action, for we may be foiled in every particular action for want of humility and faith. We must not trust to any grace or any ability in us, but trust to our spring, go to Christ when we have anything to do.

Quest. What is the reason that Christians fail?

Ans. They think, I had grace yesterday, and before, and hereupon they go not for supply of new strength to Christ. Know that in every act, in every temptation, in every particular suffering, we need a particular new strength, and a greater strength than we had before, if the temptation be greater, if the work be greater. As it is with a porter, he cannot carry a new burden that is heavier than he did before, without a new strength, without more strength than he had before, so a Christian cannot bear a new affliction without new strength, without more strength. Therefore consider what the nature of the business is that we are to do, and the strength of the temptation that we are to encounter with, and answerably go to Christ for a measure greater than we had before. He never upbraids us nor casts us in the teeth, as James saith, chap. i. 5 (*c*). There is an art, a skill of fetching strength from Christ to do all things, if we would learn it. As there is a skill to be a Christian, it is a trade, so there is a skill to fetch the strength that he hath from his spring, from Christ. Now, that skill in a word is this:

1. First, *To know our own want, and to know the necessity of grace, and the excellency of the state of holiness*, that of all conditions it is the best, and of all conditions a sinful estate is the worst. This will make us go out of ourselves to Christ. Well, how shall we fetch strength from Christ then?

2. *Consider wherefore Christ hath the treasures of all in him*, and go to him for particular graces we want whatsoever. When we know the excellency and necessity of it before, then make use of the virtue of his death and resurrection. Thus, are we tempted to any sin? Make use of the death of Christ, of his great love in giving himself, and then of the holiness of God in giving Christ to die for sin, he hates sin so; and then,

3. *Consider of the fruit of his death* that was to free and deliver us from sin. When we think of these things, Did God and Christ so love me? Is it the holiness of God, and the holiness of Christ, that God became man to die for me, and shall I go and trifle, and be tempted to sin, and offend so holy and so gracious a God, that hates sin so infinitely?

These be strong reasons fetched from Christ. We have from him both the reasons why we should do good and why we should not do evil, and we have the strength. There are two things requisite for a man to do a thing as a man. The reason why he should do it, and strength to perform it, both these are from Christ.

As from ill we are stopped by the consideration of Christ's death, so when we are moved to grace, consider the virtue of Christ's resurrection. Why is Christ now in heaven in our nature? Is it not to fill his church with his Spirit? Why doth he make intercession in heaven? Is it not that we should not be discouraged notwithstanding our daily infirmities? Shall we not make use of it? He is glorious for us, not for himself, but for his mystical body. As he hath made his natural body glorious, so he will make his mystical body glorious by little and little. He being, therefore, in heaven making intercession, go to him in the want of grace. And so for infirmities. The Spirit of God raised him at the lowest, and shall not the Spirit of God raise me from this and that. Yes, the Spirit of God will raise me from the baseness and misery of sin to be better and better. The same Spirit will enable me that raised his body. And so fetch virtue and strength from Christ, make use of Christ for every turn. Oh that we could learn these things! Then we should be able to go through all conditions: we should be able to live, able to die. I beseech you, therefore, consider what hath been spoken. Let us study Christ every day more and more, not for redemption and reconciliation only, though that in the first place, but study Christ to be all in all to us, to be our sanctification to fit us for heaven. Study the promises in Christ, lose no privilege. God would not have left them in his word but for our good. Take heed of base despair; Oh, I shall never overcome this sin and that. What! shut the people out of Canaan? Base despair lost them earthly Canaan, Numb. xiv. 22, *seq.* So take heed it shut not you out of heavenly Canaan. I shall not be able to get the victory over sin, and I shall not be able to suffer. No. Why are the promises? and why is Christ in heaven? Shall we, by despair and by base infidelity, lose Christ, and the promises, and all that is put into our hands, and betray our souls basely to Satan? I beseech you, consider of the necessity of these things. We know not what times God may call us to ere long. Despair not beforehand. Let fall what will, get into Christ, to be in him in an happy and eternal condition. We shall have strength from him to carry ourselves in all estates. Come what will, he will stand by us; he will not fail us nor forsake us. When did Paul speak these glorious words? In prison. 'I can do all things through Christ,' &c. Did the Spirit of God leave Paul in prison? Was it not better for Paul to have grace than to be freed from the thing? Wicked men may be freed from trouble, only a Christian hath grace to carry himself well in trouble. Come what will, if we be in Christ, either we shall be freed from troubles, or we shall have grace to bear them. Either we shall have that we want, or we shall have contentment without it. Is it not better to have grace without the thing? Is it not better to have a glorious Spirit of glory resting on us? Did not the Spirit of glory rest on Paul? Could not God have freed Paul from prison? Yes. But where had been then the demonstration of a contented spirit, of an heavenly mind? Where had been this example of a Christian bearing the cross comfortably? Paul lost nothing. Here you see how many stars shine in the night of his affliction, what a lustre he had in the dark state of imprisonment. Shall we then be afraid of any condition? No. Get the Spirit of God; get understanding of Christ, and the promises and privileges by him, and then let God cast us into what condition he will, we shall be safe and well.

NOTES.

(*a*) P. 178.—'I have learned. . . . . It is very significant in the original.' The original is μεμύημαι, = I have been fully taught, I have been initiated. The Vulgate is closer than our version, 'institutus sum.' The Bishop of Gloucester (Ellicott) has an interesting note on this ἅπ. λεγόμ. of the New Testament *in loc.* (ver. 12).

(*b*) P. 184.—'Lord, deliver me from my miserable necessities.' The saying is that well known one of Augustine, 'A necessitatibus meis libera me Domine.' Cf. note *a*, Vol. IV. p. 304.

(*c*) P. 192.—'"He never casts in the teeth," as James saith.' The verb is ὀνειδίζω, which the authorised version in Mat. xxvii. 44, renders precisely as Sibbes does here. G.

THE POWER OF CHRIST'S RESURRECTION.

THE POWER OF CHRIST'S RESURRECTION.

NOTE.

'The Power of Christ's Resurrection' forms the second of two sermons issued in a tiny volume in 1638 (18mo). The former has already appeared. See Vol. II. pp, 200–208. The general title-page will be found at page 198; the separate one is given below.* In footnote at page 198, read Cotes, not Coates. The present sermon takes its place naturally here along with the others from the Epistle to the Colossians. G.

* THE SECOND
SERMON.
THE POWER
OF CHRIST'S
RESURRECTION:
OR,
A SERMON UPON
COLOS. 3. 1.
Preached by that Faithfull and
Reverend Divine, *Richard Sibbes*,
D. D. and sometimes Preacher to
the Honorable Societie.
of *Grayes-Inne;*
And Master of *Katherine* Hall in
Cambridge.

EPHES. 2. 4, 5, 6.
*According as he hath chosen us in him,
before the foundation of the world,
that wee should be holy, &c.*

THE POWER OF CHRIST'S RESURRECTION.

If ye be risen with Christ, seek those things which are above, where Christ sitteth at the right hand of God.—Col. III. 1.

This verse hath dependence on the second chapter, and the twelfth and thirteenth verses of that chapter, where the apostle tells the Colossians that 'they were risen with Christ from the dead by faith, and quickened by his Spirit;' and thereupon follows this inference: 'If therefore ye be risen with Christ,' shew it by seeking after those things which are in heaven, and are heavenly.

The apostle hath much ado to root out those dangerous conceits, which false teachers had settled in the hearts of the Colossians, touching some legal ceremonies, as 'touch not, taste not, handle not.' These dead things he tells them have no more use now; and therefore, 'if you be risen with Christ, seek those things that are above.' These ceremonies were indeed appointed by God at the first, but now they are ended and brought to their grave; and therefore no more to be revived, because they were not only dead, but deadly. *Non solum mortuæ sed mortiferæ.*

Now the apostle finding their hearts tainted with this false doctrine, having first sought to purge it out of their hearts, he then begins to season them with heavenly doctrine; and he begins with general instructions, and so proceeds to particular callings, as of husbands and wives, and children and servants. Now because the well managing of the particular duties of these particular callings depends on a good general; therefore he begins first to season their hearts with grace, knowing that it is so much the easier to be good in their particular callings, when they are first good in their general. But if not good in general, then never good in the particular. If a good man, then a good husband, a good father, a good master, fit for any good service; but if not a good man, then good for nothing. So a woman, if a good woman, then a good wife, or good in any calling. So for children and servants, if good in the general, then good in every particular.

These words contain a ground, and an inference upon the ground: 'If you be risen with Christ.' There is the ground. 'Then seek the things that are above.' There is the inference. From the ground observe two things: first, that Christ is risen himself; secondly, that we shall rise.

Doct. 1. For the *first*, It is an article of our faith;* and the Holy Ghost

* In margin here, *Fiducia Christiana.*—G.

hath taken a great deal of pains to prove it. It is the confidence of Christians.* It is the main freehold that we have, for we hold all by the resurrection of Christ. Therefore we had sixteen apparitions of Christ to make it firm and evident. It was impossible that he should be held of the bonds of death, Acts ii. 24. Impossible, first, as he was invested with these three offices, a king, a priest, and a prophet. Impossible, first, as he was a king; for how then could he have triumphed over his enemies? Secondly, impossible as he was a priest; for if he had not risen, how could he have made daily intercession for his people? Thirdly, impossible as he was a prophet; for else how could he have instructed his people?

Use. Now as Christ rose the third day—manifesting thereby that he was dead—to his greater glory, so is it with his members. Never nearer help than when they are at the worst. Then that it may appear to be God's work, he will raise them apparently,† that he may be glorified. So likewise when we are in any distress in the world, void of the help of man, then comes God in and raiseth us up, whether in our credit, estate, &c., as he will do our bodies at the last day. Let us therefore have patience for a while.

Doct. 2. Secondly, *As Christ is risen, so shall we rise.* He is the meritorious cause of our resurrection, he hath deserved that we should rise; he is the worker of it. By that same power whereby he rose again, by the same will he raise us up at the last day. He is every way the cause; and which is something more, we are risen with him. He was a public person. Upon the cross he stood in the place of all the world, and all their sins committed, or foreseen to be committed, lay upon him. 'He bare the iniquity of us all,' Isa. liii. 6; and then he freed himself, and so us, by his resurrection. First, freeing himself of his suretyship; and we are freed in him; and he rising, we also rise with him. This resurrection is twofold, spiritual and corporal: spiritual, when we take life from Christ; and being quickened by him, then we begin to rise with him when we believe that Christ is dead for our sins. Christ is then crucified to thee, when thou beginnest to believe in him.

Use 1. And every true Christian may draw from hence water of life *to comfort him in all distresses;* for Christ hath conquered all our spiritual enemies; and his resurrection is an evidence of his conquest. For if he had not conquered he could not have risen; and therefore when he rose again he bade his disciples not to fear, Mat. xxviii. 10. Fear not death, for I have overcome death; and witnessed the same by my resurrection. Fear not sin, for I have satisfied for it. Fear not the devil: I by my resurrection have bruised his head; nor the world, for I have overcome it. He hath trode upon the necks of all our spiritual enemies, and conquered them all. Fear not, for if once you be risen with Christ, you are begotten to a lively hope. Where spiritual resurrection is, there is hope of life, as the apostle doth soundly reason, 1 Peter i. 3. A ground of precious comfort to every true Christian.

Use 2. Now in that we are raised by the same power to a spiritual life, whereby Christ rose from the grave, it teacheth us how *to conceive of the work of the new birth, of the image of God, of the new creature.* The work of grace in a Christian is not a slight work, a word and away, as many think; but it is a powerful work, as appears in that there are more hindrances to keep a man dead in sin from rising out of it, than there was to

* In margin here, Tertullian, *de resurrect.*, cap. i.—G.

† That is, 'openly,' 'visibly.'—G.

keep Christ from rising out of the grave. Yet in his resurrection did the power of God mightily appear, as Eph. i. 19, 20. As Christ was killed and had a stone rolled on his tomb, so he that is dead in sin hath the stone of custom rolled upon him, which is as great a work of God's power to remove as it was to raise Christ. Wherefore let those that find a change in their hearts break forth into hearty thanksgiving unto God for his inestimable favour, especially for this powerful work, more powerful than the making of the whole world, because there are many oppositions.

Use 3. Consider this aright, partly *for thanksgiving*, if you have been wrought upon, and partly *for prayer* if you are not, seeking unto God in the use of the means, who only is able to work this change in you.

To cut off many things, we shall now speak of the inference: 'If you be risen,' and risen 'with Christ' by his power, 'then seek those things which are above.' The reason depends thus. They that are risen have a new life, for every resurrection notes a new life; if spiritual, then a spiritual life; if bodily, then a glorious life, Rom. vi. 5, *seq.* Life is suitable to our resurrection. You are risen with Christ from the death of sin. Therefore manifest your resurrection by actions proportionable and suitable to your estate. From hence we note this doctrine,

Doct. 3. *That every life and state requireth answerable actions.* 'If you be risen with Christ,' and so have a spiritual life as you profess yourselves, then carry yourselves answerably, and 'seek those things that are above,' that may maintain that life of yours. This is the apostle's reasoning in this place. This is so in nature. It is so in corrupt nature. It is so in grace, and shall be so in glory.

For the *first*, Those creatures that are in the water, they delight in it, because it is their proper element, and they cannot live out of it; *secondly*, it is so in corrupt nature. He that is covetous, the very conceit that he hath of his riches doth as it were feed him; and he cannot live without them. For he that lives a carnal, brutish life, he dieth if he be taken from it. He is like a fish upon dry ground. *Tanquam piscis in arido.* Take him out of his element and he cannot live. It is so in grace, and shall be so in glory. When the body is risen unto glory, there is a forsaking of all communion with sinful men here, and we have communion with God and Christ. Christ shall be all in all unto us, Col. iii. 11. Then that which all creatures supply to us here, Christ supplieth to us there. Then our songs are holy and our actions holy, fitting such a glorious estate. Now heaven is begun here, or else never begun. Grace is therefore called heaven, because heaven is begun here. Glory must begin in grace.

Use 1. So then a Christian that is risen with Christ, *must have nothing to do with carnal men, no further than he is thrust upon them, or that he may convert them.* They must not accompany with men of a contrary spirit; seeking by all means to express the love of piety. Thus should the life of a Christian be suitable to his state that he is in and called unto.

Use 2. If we should try all by this rule, *how few then would be found to be risen with Christ.* How few delight in heavenly company, in heavenly actions! as to praise God, or to commune or partake with God in prayer. This is a death to most men to have such company, or to exercise themselves in such actions.

Explan. 1. The apostle saith here, 'we must seek those things which are above with Christ.' Seeking implieth, first, *want;* for a man will never seek for that which he hath; secondly, it implieth *a valuation and esteem of the excellency of the thing* that is sought for; thirdly, it implieth *hope to get it*, else none would seek it, but leave it as a thing desperate; fourthly, it doth imply *means and use of means* to attain to that we want, esteem of, and hope to attain; lastly, he that wants a thing which he doth highly esteem and hopes to attain in the use of the means, will by all means *avoid all contraries that may hinder him from attaining thereunto.*

2. Now consider what this thing is that we must seek for. Briefly this is here meant, viz., Christ Jesus the joy of our hearts, in whom are hid all the treasures of knowledge and wisdom, Col. ii. 3, together with all those things which are above, or whatsoever tends thereunto. And indeed all the excellency which we have or can hope for, is from above. Our full happiness and glorious inheritance is kept for us in the heavens. All our privileges are from above. Our kingdom is in heaven; qualification for this happy estate is from above. Our holiness and heavenly-mindedness is from above, fulness of grace is from above, and all graces to lead us to that perfection are from above. Power to enable us to any holy duty is from above; yea, the means, as the ordinances, the word and the sacraments, are from above. Here then is the sense of the words, seek for a nearer communion with Christ, for a further assurance of heaven, for a further qualification for heaven, that you may be more and more in heaven while you are here, by enjoying through faith your heavenly privileges, prerogatives, and excellencies. Seek for further actions of holiness; for fulness of grace; for grace to bring you to the fruition of all from above. Therefore attend upon the word of God, upon the sacraments, upon holy conference, where Christ will be present in a special manner; and by holy actions seek for glory in the use of the means. Reach not for things above your reach. That is arrogancy. But seek for heavenly things, such as before named.

We see from hence this further to be observed:

Doct. 4. *That heavenly duties have their spring from the articles and grounds of religion.* 'Seek those things which are above.' Why? Because you are risen with Christ.

The ground of our faith is the cause of holy duties. Whosoever is corrupt in faith, is corrupt in obedience in that degree. Evil opinions breed an evil life, and a sound understanding breeds an holy life.

Use. Understand therefore *the main grounds of religion*; and labour to digest them, to see the truth of them; and labour with God by prayer that he would write them in your hearts by his Holy Spirit.

Again, in that the apostle willeth them to seek heavenly graces: and that because they are risen with Christ, note further this inference.

Doct. 5. *That as a Christian ought to be heavenly-minded, to seek heavenly graces, so he must do it for this reason, viz., because he is in an estate fitting for it.*

Use. Therefore let none say, *he cannot for outward troubles or business*, unless thou wilt deny thyself to be a Christian at the same time. He that will be a Christian must pretend no impossibilities herein. Art thou risen with Christ? Then thou hast power to seek those things that are above, to be heavenly minded. A Christian or no Christian! God doth not as Pharaoh, bid us do our work, and we must gather straw ourselves; but he bids us do, and quickens us by his Spirit, and enables us to do. He fits us for such actions; he gives us power to do them.

Doct. 6. Again, *So far as a Christian is raised by Christ, so far he cannot but seek those things that are above.* We need not teach a bird to fly, for it will learn it of itself; it is natural to her. So a Christian cannot but do the things answerable to his nature. He is of a new nature, and therefore cannot but be heavenly minded. He cannot profane the Lord's day; he cannot swear; he cannot lie; he cannot blaspheme; he cannot delight in carnal courses. He cannot do these things, so far as he is a Christian. In the hour of temptation he is not himself. It is in this sense that the apostle saith, 'He that is born of God sinneth not,' 1 John iii. 9. So far as he is born again he cannot sin; he can do no evil.

Again, as a Christian may do it, and ought to do it, and cannot but do it;—

Doct. 7. So I add further, *he glories in it.* To be heavenly-minded, and exercised in spiritual duties, is his happiness and his joy. He is never so well, never so much himself, as when he is most possessed with heavenly-mindedness, and most frequent or exercised in spiritual duties. So far forth as he is a Christian, and enlarged with the Spirit of Christ, so far forth he glories in holy actions, in heavenly-mindedness.

Use. Is this in all true Christians? *What then may we think of the most part in the world, that profess religion but from the teeth outward?* They are not risen with Christ, as the ambitious man, the covetous man, the voluptuous man. They savour not the things that are above. They have no new nature; for if they had, it would lead them higher than these things. Those that live in defilements of the flesh, shew that they have no new natures; for if they had, they should get strength against them, at least they would have a continual conflict and wrestling in themselves to overcome them.

For trial of thy estate, see what power is there of the Spirit of God in thee to make thee heavenly-minded: to joy in things that are above, more than in all the world besides. If thou find this power in thee, then thou art a Christian indeed. Thou canst then speak by experience what is the work of the Spirit; and thou knowest well what is the virtue of the resurrection of Christ. Then thou canst say with St Paul that thou art still striving to find the virtue of Christ more and more in thee, to make thee more fully assured of thy part in Christ, and to find the power of his Spirit subduing corruption in thee more and more, Phil. iii. 9 and 10. Let us therefore labour for this power. This is to 'seek the things that are above.' Labour to find a want of them, that we have not so much of them as we have need of. Labour then to know the excellency of them: esteeming of them to be more excellent than all other things. When all other things leave us, then they will comfort us. Labour also to see an hope to grow in them. Thou hast hope to attain unto them, because the same Spirit is promised thee that raised up Christ from the dead. Use then all sanctified means for the attaining of these spiritual good things. Use heavenly means for heavenly things. Attend upon the ordinances of God, labour with him in prayer, that he would make us such as he may delight in, fit us for that estate that he hath provided for us. Labour to increase in all holy actions; take heed of all contrary courses, of worldly-mindedness, of the pleasures of the world, that they draw not away thy heart from an earnest seeking of heavenly things as we should be. We are all seekers. We are a generation of seekers. As the psalmist saith, we are seeking while we are here; our possessing is hereafter, Ps. xxiv. 6.

Labour, therefore, to see the want of heavenly graces, and to esteem of them aright; and to see hope to attain them, and hope to increase them; and use the means, and avoid all contrary courses. So shall you find the virtue of Christ's resurrection raising you up more and more to seek after heaven and heavenly things, 'those things that are above.'

THE HIDDEN LIFE.

THE HIDDEN LIFE.

NOTE.

'The Hidden Life' is another selection of Two Sermons from 'Evangelical Sacrifices' (4to, 1640). Its separate title-page is given below.*—G.

* THE
HIDDEN
LIFE.

In two Funerall Sermons upon
COL. 3. 3, 4.

BY
The late Learned and Reverend Divine,
RICH. SIBBS:

Doctor in Divinity, Mr. of KATHERINE Hall
in *Cambridge*, and sometimes Preacher
to the Honourable Society of
GRAYES-INNE.

1 JOHN 3. 2.
Beloved, now yee are the Sonnes of God, and it doth not appeare what wee shall be.

LONDON,
Printed by *E. Purslow*, for *N. Bourne*, at the Royall Exchange, and *R. Harford* at the gilt
Bible in Queenes head Alley, in Pater-Noster-Row. 1639.

THE HIDDEN LIFE.

For ye are dead, your life is hid with Christ in God. When Christ, who is our life, shall appear, then shall ye also appear with him in glory.—Col. III. 3, 4.

The dependence of these words, in a word, is this. The apostle, after he had laid the grounds of some doctrines, he doth frame the building of a holy life and conversation. It is in vain to believe well unless a man work accordingly. He that lives against his faith shall be damned, as he that believes against it. Thereupon in this chapter he comes to raise their affections to be heavenly-minded, and stirs them up to subdue whatsoever is contrary to heavenly-mindedness. And because it is a duty of great moment to be heavenly-minded, and to subdue base affections, he inserts weighty reasons between. 'If ye be risen with Christ, seek those things that are above.' And among other reasons there is this, 'Ye are dead, and your life is hid with Christ in God.' And thereupon he forceth seeking of the things that are above, and the mortifying of earthly members. For the duties of Christianity are to be applied two ways; to be heavenly affected, and to subdue that which is contrary; to be heavenly-minded, and to mortify our earthly members. Now how shall we do both? 'For ye are dead, and your life is hid with Christ in God,' &c.

You see the first proposition, 'Ye are dead.' With whom? 'With Christ, in God.'

A Christian is dead many ways. He is dead *to the law, to the moral law*. He looks not to have comfort and salvation by it, by the law; he is dead to the law, and so flies to Christ.

A Christian is dead also *to the ceremonial law*. Now, in the glorious lustre of the gospel, what have we to do with those poor elements that were for children? A ceremonious disposition is opposite to the glory and lustre of the gospel, as the apostle speaks in the former chapter.

He is dead likewise *to sin*. Having communion with Christ, when he died for sin, he is dead to sin. He that hath communion in the death of Christ, hath the same affection to sin that Christ had. Christ hated it infinitely when he suffered for it; so every Christian thinks that Christ died for my sins, and by union with Christ he hath the same affection to it, he is 'dead' to it.

And because this is but an inchoation and beginning, a Christian is not perfectly dead to sin. He stands in need of afflictions, and in regard of *afflictions* he is dead. They must help the work of mortification. And because no affiiction can sufficiently work mortification but death itself, which is the accomplishment of mortification, we are dead in respect *of death itself*, which is the accomplishment of all. Though we live here for a time, we are dead in regard of the sentence that is passed on us, as we say a man is dead when the sentence is passed on him. In that respect we are dead men, for our life is but a dead life. Besides the sentence that is passed upon us, death seizeth upon us in the time of our life, in sicknesses, &c. And so they prepare us to death. Thus, and many other ways, we are dead.

The second proposition is, 'Our life is hid with Christ in God.'

We are dead, and yet we have a life. A Christian is a strange person. He is both dead and alive, he is miserable and glorious. He consists of contraries. He is dead in regard of corruption and miseries, and such like, but he is alive in regard of his better part, and he grows two ways at once. It is a strange thing that a Christian doth. He grows downwards and upwards at the same time; for as he dies in sin and misery, and natural death approaching, so he lives the life of grace, and grows more and more till he end in glory.

This life is said to be a hidden life, 'It is *hid* with Christ in God.'

The life of a Christian, which is his glorious spiritual life, it is hid. Among other respects,

1. It is hid *to the world, to worldly men*, because a Christian is an unknown man to them. Because they know not the Father that begets, therefore they know not them that are begotten, as St John saith, 1 John iii. 1. They know not the advancement of a Christian: he is raised into a higher rank than they. Therefore, as a beast knows not the things of a man, no more doth a carnal man, in any excellency, know the things of the Spirit, 'for they are spiritually discerned, 1 Cor. ii. 14. Therefore it is a hidden life in the eyes of the world. A worldly man sees not this life in regard of the excellency. He passeth scorns and contempts of it, of folly and the like. A Christian, in respect of his happy life, is a stranger here, and therefore he is willing to pass through the world, and to be used as a stranger.

2. It is a hidden life likewise ofttimes, not only to worldlings, but in regard *of the children of God themselves;* because by reason of some infirmities that are in the best of God's children, they are apt to judge amiss, harshly and rashly one of another. Likewise by reason of those calamities that are common to all men alike. They are afflicted as others, and have sicknesses, and are contemned more than others; and by reason of this the children of God often censure those that have the beginnings of spiritual life in them. It is hid from them.

It is hid likewise from themselves, for often God's children know not themselves, in temptation, in their nonage, in the beginning of their conversion, in the time of desertion, and spiritual slumber and sleep, grace seems to be dead in them, and then they know not that they have this spiritual life. Especially if this desertion be joined with outward abasement, they call their estate into question, as in Ps. lxxiii. 2, *seq.*, and in divers places of Scripture. God's children ofttimes, by reason of their inquisition and search, they raise clouds, whereby they conceal from their own eyes their own life. Partly through distemper of body, and partly by distemper of spirit, there are clouds raised between them and their happiness, that they cannot see their spiritual life.

But especially it is hid in regard *of common infirmities*, wanting gifts that others have, that have not a dram of grace sometimes, that live to please men, and look altogether to the outside. They do that many times to please men better than a Christian.

Sometimes God himself hides himself out of wisdom and mercy to us, when he sees that we carry not ourselves so reverently as we should. And this reason may be sufficient of God's dispensation. God will have it so, partly for the further hardening of wicked persons, and for trial. For if all were laid open in this excellent estate of a Christian, who should try their patience? Who would not be a Christian for the comfort, and for the sense and feeling? Oh, but this is not so. A Christian hath a life, but it is a hidden life. Therefore God will try whether men will live by faith or sense, whether they will have their ways now or no, or whether they will depend upon that glorious life that God will reveal in time to come, and to exercise and strengthen faith. God will have it so that this life shall be now hid, that we may live by the promises, though we have no feeling at all; that we may persuade ourselves in the greatest desertions and extremities, yet I have a hidden life in Christ. Though I have little influence and manifestation of it in me, yet I have a glorious life in my head; and I live now by faith till I come to live by sight. This is one reason.

We should not therefore take offence. We must not judge of Christians by outward show and appearance, as Christ saith, 'We should not judge of ourselves by outward appearance,' John vii. 24, nor of the church. The whore of Babylon hath more painting and setting out, in all glorious shows —it being an outside religion—than the true spouse of Christ, whose glory and beauty is within. Doth it follow therefore that she is the true church? Oh no; for the beauty of the wife of Christ it is a hidden beauty, 'She is glorious within,' Ps. xlv. 13. A stranger doth not meddle with the joy of the church. Christians have a name indeed, and 'a stone that none know but them that have it,' Rev. ii. 17. It is 'hidden manna.' We must not judge of the church, or of Christians, by outward appearance; we shall be deceived in that. Our life is hid with Christ, the spring of all spiritual life. The life of a Christian is a secret life. It is a peculiar life. It is a safe life. It is secret because it is hid. As I said, God's children are secret ones. They are not known to the world, nor to themselves ofttimes.

But ordinarily faith in them breaks through the cloud, and unmasks God himself; and sees God's fatherly face, though he hide himself. They have a promise to lay hold upon; and they acknowledge him to be their Father, and wrestle with him. It is a secret life, but it is not so secret, but that faith sees into it. It pierceth the veil and sees a glorious life there. Faith will see God's glorious countenance. Faith makes it a glorious life though it be secret. Therefore let us not judge ourselves nor others by appearance.

And it is also *a sure life*. 'It is hid with Christ in God.' Mark on what grounds it is sure.

First, it is hid *in heaven*. No enemy can come there. The devil comes not there since he first lost it and was cast out. It is safe in regard of the place. It is hid in heaven.

And it is safe, because it is hid *in Christ*, who purchased it with his blood; who hath trampled upon all opposite powers, over death, and hell itself. It is hid in heaven and in him who hath overcome all opposite power. Therefore it is a safe life.

And it is hid with Christ *in God*. Christ is in the bosom of God, Christ mediator. 'It is hid with Christ in God.' He is the storehouse of this life. It is hid with him. If any can rob God, then they may rob our life from us; for it is hid with Christ in God. It is a sure life therefore.

Obj. Oh, but we may lose it, though it be sure in respect of God.

Ans. Nay, saith St Peter, 'We are begotten again to an inheritance, immortal, and reserved for us in heaven, and we are kept by the power of God to salvation,' 1 Peter i. 4. It is kept for us, and we are kept to it. God hath prepared it for us, and prepared us for it. So it is a most sure life, especially because Christ lives for ever, with whom it is. 'It is hid with Christ in God.'

It is likewise *a peculiar life;* only to God's people. For they only have union and communion with Christ; and therefore he saith here, 'your life is hid with Christ in God.'

It is likewise a glorious life; for it is hid with Christ, who is the glory of God; and he saith in the next verse, 'When Christ, who is our life, shall appear, we shall appear with him in glory.' It is a glorious life. But of that I shall speak in the next verse.

We see then that our life is hid in Christ; and what kind of life this is.

It is a secret, sure, peculiar, glorious life. Alas! we are ready to judge of ourselves by the present, and not to think it a glorious life. But he saith, it is hidden for us. 'Light is sown for the righteous,' Ps. xcvii. 11. It doth not appear for the present. A garden hath seeds sown and herbs, but in the winter there is no difference between it and a common field; but when the sun shines and appears, then the herbs appear in their lustre. So it is with a Christian. There is light and immortality and happiness sown for him. When Christ, the 'Sun of righteousness' shall appear, 'then we shall appear with him in glory,' 1 John iii. 2.

As we may say of all things below, they have a hidden life: the plants and the flowers in the winter, they live by the root; and when the sun appears, then they also appear with the sun in glory. So it is with the righteous: they have a hidden life. It is hid now in the root, in their head, in this life. When Christ the Sun of righteousness shall appear; when the spring comes; when the resurrection comes: then we shall appear with him in glory. And so I come to speak of that verse.

'When Christ, who is our life, shall appear, then shall ye appear also with him in glory.'

Our life is now hid. Our happiness is veiled over. There are many things between us and our life. But shall it always be so? Oh no! 'When Christ, who is our life, shall appear, we shall appear also with him in glory.' He meets with a secret objection. The parts here to be stood on are these.

1. First, *Christ he is our life*. He shall appear in glory as our life. This is taken for granted, it is a supposed truth, 'when Christ, who is our life, *shall appear*.' It is taken for granted that he shall appear in glory.

2. The next thing is, *that we shall appear likewise with Christ*. Christ shall appear, and we.

3. And then *the consequence:* how these depend upon one another. Because Christ appears in glory, therefore we, 'when Christ, who is our life, shall appear.'

The apostle cannot mention Christ, without an addition of comfort; and the Christian soul loves Christ. It sees such matter of comfort, and such righteousness in him, that it cannot think of Christ without a comfortable addition of Lord, Saviour, life, hope, glory, &c. Christ carries with him all comforts. He is food, the bread of life, the water of life, all that is good to the soul. Therefore the apostle gives this sweet addition 'Christ *our life*.'

How is Christ our life?

He is every way the cause of the life of grace and of glory. And not only so, the cause, but the root and spring in whom it is. We have it from Christ and in Christ. We have it in Christ as a root, and from Christ as a working cause, and by Christ as a mediator. For Christ procured life at God's hands, by his sacrifice and death. We have it in Christ as a head, from him as a cause, together with both the other persons; and through him as mediator, who by his death made way to life, appeasing the wrath of God. So we are reconciled and pardoned by the death of Christ.

Christ is not only our life so, but as the matter of our life that we feed on. When he hath wrought spiritual life in us, then the soul lives by faith in Christ still, and feeds upon him. He is our life because we feed on him. For as food nourisheth the body, so the soul, being every day set on by fresh temptations, and afflictions, and troubles, and fresh discomforts, the soul of necessity is forced to look to Christ every day; and to feed upon Christ; to feed upon his blood afresh, which runs continually. For he is a mediator for ever; and he is in heaven to make good that he hath done by his death; and we look upon him every day and feed on him; and so he maintains the life he hath begun. Christ is our life thus.

More particularly—for memory's sake—Christ, when by faith we have union with him once—as we can have no communion without union with him—when we are one with him once by faith, we have life from Christ, *the life of reconciliation in law*, opposite to our death in law and in sentence. For by nature we are all dead and damned as soon as we are born, for our own sins and the sins of our first parents. We are dead in sentence. Now by Christ there is a reversion* of this sentence. Christ by his obedience and suffering hath satisfied his Father. So by our union with Christ we are alive in sentence. We are absolved in God's court of justice; for he will not punish sin twice.

And then after the life *of justification*, being justified by faith, we have the life *of sanctification and holiness*. For God out of his love, when he hath pardoned our sin, he gives his Spirit as the best fruit of his love; and we having our consciences absolved and acquitted by the Spirit of God, through the obedience of Christ, we love God. God so loveth us when he is appeased by Christ, that the bar being taken away, our sins being pardoned, and the sluice of mercy open, there is way made for another life, the life of sanctification by the Spirit. Upon pardon of our sins he gives the Spirit; and we feeling that love, have love wrought in us to him again, and that love stirs up every Christian to obedience.

In the next place, After he hath acquitted us by his all-sufficient satisfaction, being God and man, and hath given us his Spirit, there is another life, the life of comfort, which is the life of our life, in *peace of conscience and joy unspeakable and glorious*. This life issues from the former. For when we find our conscience appeased, that God saith to our souls he is 'their salvation,' Ps. xxxv. 3, and find a newness wrought in our nature by the Spirit of God, and some strength to obey him, then we begin to have a sweet

* That is, 'reversal.'—G.

peace, as the children of God find in themselves, and joy unspeakable and glorious.

This is the life of this life. Having union with Christ and his righteousness and Spirit, we have this peace, which is the way to glory and the beginning of it. For besides that Christ is our life in glory afterwards, in this life he is our life. Answerable to our servile fear, as we are dead in law, we have a life in justification. As we are dead in nature, so we have a life in sanctification. We are dead in despair, and run into terrors of conscience ; so we have a life in joy and peace.

But all those in this life are imperfect, because there is only an union of grace here, till we come to the union of glory in heaven ; and then at the day of judgment there will be a *perfect justifying of us*. We shall not only be acquitted in our conscience, as we are now, but we shall be acquitted before angels and devils and men, and Christ will acknowledge us. These are they for whom I died. These are they for whom I made intercession in heaven. We shall be acquitted there, and there we shall be acknowledged.

And then the life of sanctification, that is now in part, shall then be perfect, and likewise the peace that now 'passeth understanding' shall then be full ; and our joy shall be full by Christ who is our life.

So then we see we have in Christ, 'the second Adam,' whatsoever we lost in the first root. Whence did we draw sin and misery ? By union with the first Adam we have damnation, we have the wrath of God, we have corruption opposite to sanctification, we have terrors and horror of conscience. By the second Adam, and union with him, we have a spring of life and peace, and all that we lost in Adam ; and more than all we lost, he being God-man. The sin of the first Adam was the sin of a man ; the obedience of the second Adam was the obedience of God-man, which raiseth us to life everlasting, Rom. v. 16, *seq*. So that there is more comfort in the life we have by Christ than there is discomfort in our death by Adam.

We see then hence that in all our deadness and dulness and want of grace, there is a spring in our nature. God hath given Christ, God-man, that there should be a treasure in him for all the church, that we may fetch supply out of our nature. He is fit to be our life, for our nature in him is united to the Godhead ; therefore Christ is a fit fountain to derive* grace to believers, because man's nature in him is advanced; by being united to the second person he is God-man, able to derive all grace and comfort and righteousness whatsoever. Shall the first Adam derive unrighteousness, discomfort, and misery, that was a man ? and shall not Christ, God-man, derive righteousness and comfort and joy and peace, and whatsoever is good ? Undoubtedly he shall. Therefore in all want of grace, in all temptations and assaults, let us go to the fountain, to the fulness of grace, to the fulness of God's love in Christ. Christ, God-man, is our life. As when we are cold we come to the fire, so when we are dull-hearted let us come to this quickening Spirit.

And to this end let us be stirred up to use those means wherein Christ will be effectual, whereby, as by veins, the blood of this spiritual life is conveyed, as the word and sacraments, the communion of saints and all sanctified means, whereby the life of grace and comfort may be conveyed to us. Let us never be out of such ways and courses as whereby Christ derives this life of grace ; and let us take heed of those that are contrary.

Quest. But how shall I know, saith a weak soul,—that finds little comfort

* That is, 'communicate.'—G.

and peace, and little sanctification; and is besieged with troubles and is doubtful, and knows not whether his sins be forgiven or no, how shall I know,—whether Christ be my life or no?

Ans. I answer that the life of Christ is but now *begun in us*, and it is very little at the first. There is nothing less than grace at the beginning. The life of Christ is conveyed to us from Christ voluntarily, not by necessity. 'He gives the will and the deed according to his pleasure,' Philip. ii. 13. Therefore we must know that we have more or less comfort, and more or less grace as he pleaseth. He brings all to heaven in all ages that have the true life of grace, though he make a difference, and give to some more and to some less; because he is a head that flows into his members, not out of nature, but out of his own pleasure.

2. And a Christian soul that hath union with Christ, that hath a being and station in him, *may know it*. There are always some pulses from this heart. As we know there is some life by the beating of the pulses, so Christ's dwelling in the heart is known by these pulses. There will be striving against corruption, and complaining of it. Nature and corruption will not complain against corruption; corruption will not strive against corruption. There will be sighing and groaning, which is seconded with a constant endeavour to grow better. It is not a flash. These pulses beating in the soul of a true Christian shew that there is the life of grace in him, that Christ dwells in his heart. And this ofttimes doth more appear in the greatest temptations. Take a Christian at the worst, his heart sighs to God to recover him; he is sick, and yet he hopes in Christ. Christ in the greatest desertion is his life, who was also our pattern when he was at the lowest: 'My God, my God.' So a Christian at the lowest, he hath a spirit of prayer. Though it may be he cannot pray distinctly, yet he can sigh and groan; and God hears the sighs of his own Spirit always. Therefore when these pulses beat in him, in the greatest temptations he may know that Christ lives in him.

Sometimes Christ, in respect of this life, in this world reserves himself to the chief occasion, as some great affliction of the outward man. In 2 Cor. iv. 10, we see there when the body of Saint Paul was afflicted, when it was abased by many afflictions, 'the life of Christ was most manifest in him.' God reserves to poor Christians, that now live in peace and quiet, the greatest feelings and manifestations of Christ's living in them, till some great cross, till the hour of death, till a time of need. The life of Christ is most manifest in the time of abasement.

By the way, therefore, let us not avoid crosses for Christ's sake. Avoid not any abasement, though it be imprisonment or death. The more our outward man is abased, if it be for Christ's sake, the more this life of Christ, this blessed life, this peace that 'passeth understanding,' and this 'joy in the Holy Ghost' is increased. We shall feel our absolution and justification the more. This life of Christ is most manifested when we honour him most by suffering for him. Therefore let us avoid no cross for him.

'Christ, who is our life, *shall appear*.' There are two appearings, we know, of Christ; his first appearing and his second appearing. His first appearing was to work our salvation; his second shall be to accomplish and finish what he hath begun to work. His first appearing was to redeem our souls from death, and his second shall redeem our bodies from the corruption of the grave. So his second appearing shall be to accomplish all the good that he came to do and to work by his first. As verily, therefore, as Christ is come in his first appearing, so verily and certainly he shall appear the second time. And as it was the description of holy men before his first coming to wait for him, 'to wait for the consolation of Israel,' Luke ii. 25, so Christians now. Those blessed souls that have the report of this, they wait for the coming of Christ.

There were all kind of witnesses then of his first coming: angels, men, women, shepherds, the devils themselves. The Trinity from heaven witnessed of him. So for his second coming there are witnesses. Christ himself saith he will come. The angels say, 'This Jesus that ye see go up shall come again,' Acts i. 11. It is an article of our faith that he shall come. The Spirit of God in every Christian saith 'Come,' and that is not in vain. The desires of the Spirit of God must be fulfilled. Therefore he shall come. And the Spirit of God stirs up our spirits to say 'Come.' There are all kind of proofs and arguments for it. It is an article of our faith. It is laid here for a ground, and therefore I will not enlarge myself in it, but come to the next point. Christ will appear, and

'We shall also appear with him in glory.'

We shall appear, and appear with him, and appear in glory with him. Christ himself his glory is in some sort hid now. For though he be king of the church, yet we see what enemies are in the church; and Satan ruffles* in the church a great while, and the nearer he is to his end the more he rageth. So that Christ's glory seems to be hid. But Christ then shall appear, and his church shall appear with him in glory.

Quest. Why shall we appear with Christ and be glorious with him?

Ans. I answer, This is clear, partly because *it is Christ's will*; in John xvii., 'Father, I will that where I am they may be also.' It is Christ's last testament that we should be where he is and be glorious with him, and Christ's will must be fulfilled.

Again, Consider *what we are to Christ*, how near we are brought to him, and then this will be clear, that when Christ shall appear in glory, we must appear with him. For Christ is our husband, and we are his spouse. When Christ comes to be glorious, therefore, his spouse must be glorious. Now is but the time of contract, the time of the marriage solemnity shall be at the appearing of Christ. Therefore, 'when he shall appear, we shall appear with him in glory.' Christ, in his own person, distinct from his church, is now glorious as a head; but Christ mystical is not glorious, Christ mystical suffers. There are many members that are not yet called. Some are abased, and some are not brought to the fold. And Christ hath a care of his mystical body, as of his natural body; and as that is glorious in heaven, so he will bring all his members to be one glorious body. He gave his natural body to redeem his mystical body. Therefore, as he is glorious in that in heaven, so he will be glorious in his mystical body in every believing soul at the last, when he 'shall come to be glorified in his saints,' as the apostle saith, 2 Thess. i. 10. He is glorious in himself now, then he will be glorious in his spouse.

And then *from the ground of predestination:* Rom. viii. 29, 30, 'We are predestinate to be conformed to Christ, that he might be the first-born of many brethren.' Now, Christ being glorious, and we being predestinate before the world was to be like unto Christ; first, in abasement, to be abased for him that was abased for us, to suffer for him that suffered for us, and to be conformed to him in grace, there must be a time to be conformed to him in glory. From the ground of election there must be a state of glory. Our glory must be revealed when Christ shall come and appear.

* This is, = makes a stir, or puts on state.—G.

I will press no more reasons that we must be glorious at the second coming of Christ as well as himself.

Quest. Wherein stands this glory?

Ans. To clear this point a little—I will not be long in it,—because, indeed, this glory is such as 'eye hath not seen, nor ear heard, nor hath it entered into the heart of man,' 1 Cor. ii. 9. The apostles speak not much of it. They speak of it in negative terms, by denying imperfections. 'It is an inheritance incorruptible, immortal,' &c., 1 Peter i. 4. And when it is resembled to earthly things, it is compared to a banquet, to a marriage, &c. But this glory it shall be in body, in soul, in the whole man.

In soul there shall be the knowledge of those mysteries of salvation that now we are ignorant of. Now we are in the grammar-school, but that shall be as the university. Then we shall know things more clearly. We shall see God face to face, and then our souls shall be raised to be capable of more knowledge and grace. Now the vessel of our soul is not capable to know that that we shall then; they are not capable, as they shall be in heaven. St Paul himself was not capable; therefore when he was taken up into the third heavens, lest he should be proud of his revelations, he was fain to be abased. We are not capable, we cannot know the glory of heaven in a full measure now; but then, God shall enlarge the heart and sanctify it, that we shall have strong spirits, and holy understandings and affections to understand holy things; we shall know God face to face. There shall be a proportion between the glorious things in heaven and our soul; there shall be a heavenly soul for a heavenly place, whereas yet it is not so.

I forbear to shew the particulars of the glory of the body. The apostle Paul sets it down: 1 Cor. xv. 44, 'It shall be a spiritual body.' It shall be guided by the Spirit; and the body, it shall not then need meats and drinks, but God 'shall be all in all.' Now, our life at the best is fed and clothed by the creatures; then, all shall be taken out of God himself. God himself shall be all in all. The presence of God, and of Christ our Saviour, shall supply all that we have now other ways. Now comfort is conveyed from this creature and from that; but whatsoever comfort we have now dropped by the creatures we shall then have all in him, and in fulness, and for evermore. So we shall be glorious in soul and body.

And in our whole man the image of God and Christ shall be perfectly restored. We shall be like Christ, reserving the difference between the head and the members; reserving the difference of a natural Son and of sons adopted. He shall be more glorious than we. We shall be glorious as much as we are capable of. In all fulness of joy, and grace, and dominion over the creature, in freedom from ill and readiness to good, we shall be glorious sons of God. I need not to be long in unfolding these things.

Quest. When shall this be?

Ans. 'When he shall appear,' saith the apostle, 'we shall also appear with him in glory.' It is carried indefinitely, to stop curiosity. There is no time set down; but '*when* he shall appear,' &c. In a word, when all the elect shall be gathered together. It is not meet that our bodies and souls should be glorified till all God's people be gathered together. As in a family they do not sit down till all the servants be come in, and then they sit down together, so in this great family of God, the saints in heaven and earth, there shall not be perfect glory till all be gathered and saved. And then what a blessed time will that be, when every one shall be glorious himself, and shall put down the sun in glory in his body and soul, and when there shall be such a world of them so glorious.

If every star be beautiful, how beautiful are all in their lustre! When so many saints shall be gathered together, they shall be far more glorious than the sun in his majesty; and this glory is reserved till all be gathered together. God said of the creatures severally they were good, but when he looked on them together they were exceeding good. So the several souls of Christians are glorious, but at the day of judgment, when all shall be gathered together, there shall be an exceeding glory. It is reserved, I say, for the gathering together of the saints; when Christ, who is the head, shall have gathered all by his word and ministry out of this sinful world—which are scattered here and there—then they shall come to perfect glory. Then there shall be perfect union between the body and soul; then there shall be a perfect union between us and all that are dead together; then there shall be a perfect union between us and Christ; then we shall have the perfect fruition of God, of angels, of all the blessed company in heaven. Oh what a blessed time will this be! and this shall be at the glorious appearing of Christ.

Christ shall appear in glory himself, as verily as he appeared in his first coming; and we shall appear with him in glory.

Why should we doubt of it? Is not that which is greater done already? Hath not God himself become man? Hath not God died, and God been abased in his first coming? Is not that more wonder than that a man should become like God in his second coming? Whether is greater, for God to become man, or for men to be raised out of their graves and become glorious? Certainly this is the lesser. Why should we doubt of it? Let us raise our hearts with this, that as verily as he came in abasement to work our salvation, so verily he shall come and raise us to glory; and this is a lesser work than the former.

But to come nearer, to make some further use of this, surely these are main points, and should be oft thought on. Oh that the hearts of Christians were exercised with them! Could we be dead either for grace or comfort, if we did oft think of this with application? Let us oft warm ourselves with these things; let us bring ourselves to the light; let us think of the blessed times to come: could we be unfruitful? This made Saint Paul adjure Timothy and the Thessalonians: 'I beseech you, by the coming of our Lord Jesus Christ,' &c., 2 Tim. iv. 1, 2 Thes. ii. 1. I shall need no greater argument to press you, than as verily as Christ shall come in glory, and as you shall be gathered to him, so hear what I say. So Saint Paul chargeth Timothy: 1 Tim. vi. 13, 'I charge thee before Christ, who at his coming, &c., keep this commandment.' This will move a man's conscience, and carry him to duty, if nothing else will. Let us think seriously, Christ will come with thousands of his angels in glory and majesty, and all shall be glory then, there shall be nothing but glory: glorious in his company, glorious in himself, glorious in his enemies; he shall trample them under his feet by a glorious confusion; there shall be nothing but glory in heaven and earth then. And we shall come to the same glory. The spouse shall partake of the glory of her husband. Let us think of this, it will quicken and inspire all our courses with a spiritual kind of light to all actions; it will enliven and quicken them.

And it will put a kind of manner upon all our actions that they shall be acceptable to God. For how should we perform all that comes from us? All should be done in sincerity, and constantly, and abundantly, and cheerfully, readily, and willingly; for God requires these qualifications in what we do. Now, what stirs us up to do all in this manner, acceptably to God, but this consideration?

What stirs us up to do things sincerely to Christ? He will appear in glory; therefore let us do things that may stand with his judgment. It is no matter what the reprobates of the world judge; let us do things so as we may stand before Christ at that day. A Christian studies to arraign himself before Christ, that he may do that that may approve him to him that shall be his judge ere long.

And so *let us hold out;* we shall receive a reward. What will make us constant but this? What makes a man sow his seed, that he scarcely can spare, but the hope of a harvest? What makes a man run, but the victory and the crown? So what makes a man work, but the hope of reward? Be constant, 'for in him ye shall receive the reward if ye faint not,' Gal. vi. 9.

And so for *abounding in good works,* 'your labour is not in vain in the Lord,' 1 Cor. xv. 58. What made Saint Paul press the abounding in good works? 'Finally, my brethren, be stedfast and unmoveable, alway abounding in the work of the Lord.' Why? 'for your labour is not in vain in the Lord.' Your bodies shall rise again ere long in glory; when Christ shall appear you shall appear, and be glorious with him. 'Therefore abound in the work of the Lord,' 1 Cor. xv. 58; 'sow to the Spirit,' Gal. vi. 8, and you shall reap glory. 'They that sow sparingly shall reap sparingly,' 2 Cor. ix. 6. What makes men abound in works of mercy and love, but this appearing of Christ? If their love be perfect, they have comfort in this appearing, and if they abound in mercy, Christ will appear in mercy to them.

And so *for cheerfulness.* That God also requires in every action. What enlargeth the heart of a man in God's work? What puts fire into his affections but this, that Christ will come and appear in glory ere long? That he will come and crown every good work; that we shall not lose a good word that hath been spoken in a good cause; not the least good action; not a cup of cold water; but all shall stand on our reckoning 'at that day when Christ shall come to be glorious in his saints.' This makes us do things sincerely, constantly, abundantly, and cheerfully.

I beseech you, consider from what ground these things come; for these are principles that should be grounds of faith. They are pregnant, and spread themselves through the whole course of a Christian's life, and therefore are worthy to be thought often on.

Again, Why doth God reveal these things beforehands, that we shall appear in glory in our body and soul, in our whole man? As it shews us our duty and the manner of it, so *it is a ground of comfort* in all estates. A Christian may think, Now my life is a hidden, secret life. I pass under censures. It is thus in the world, and thus with me. Well, there will a time come, the time of resurrection, that will make amends for all—for this sickness of body and disquiet of mind, and all annoyance and adversity; and it is revealed beforehand for our comfort that there shall be such a time, that we may make use of it, that we may ground our patience upon it. When Saint Paul exhorts to patience, saith he, 'The Lord is at hand,' Phil. iv. 5; and Saint James saith, 'The Judge standeth at the door,' chap. v. 9. Let us be patient in infamies and sufferings; it will be otherwise ere long, Christ is at hand.

Again, *That we might continually be breathing out thankfulness to God.*

Our whole life should be spent in thankfulness to God. Even as the angels in heaven that stand in the presence of God, and the blessed spirits in heaven, they spend that vigour that is in them, they spend all that is in them in praising God, in thanks and laud to God, and sing, 'Glory, glory;' so beforehand knowing that ere long we shall appear with Christ, and appear in glory, let us thank him beforehand. As Saint Peter saith, 'Blessed be God, that hath begotten us again to an inheritance, immortal, undefiled, &c., reserved in heaven for us,' 1 Peter i. 3. Let us bless God beforehand, as if we were in heaven already. Certainly if we hope to be with those that shall sit in heavenly places in heaven to praise God, we will begin it on earth; for the life of heaven is begun on earth. We are kings now; we are priests now; we are conquerors now; we are new creatures now. We must praise God, and begin the employment of heaven now; for what they do perfectly, that we begin to do. In heaven we know there is no ill company; we will abstain from it now. There is no defilement of sin; we will conform ourselves to that estate we hope for. There is nothing but praising of God; as much as may be we will warm our hearts with the meditation of what God hath done, what he doth, and what he hath reserved for the time to come, with that we have in hope. The best things of a Christian especially, are in hope; for that which we have by Christ principally is not in this world; therefore considering that the best things that Christ died for are in hope, 'let us rejoice in hope,' and in rejoicing have our hearts enlarged with praising of God for that we hope for.

And be comforted in all the changes of this life, all the changes for the time to come, and in death itself, which is the last change. Are not all degrees to make way for that glorious appearing with Christ? for the soul at death goes to heaven, and the body shall come after. Why should we be loath to die, when death is nothing but a change from misery to happiness? a change from the danger of sinning, to an impossibility of sinning; from a vale of misery to a place of happiness; from men to God; from sinful persons that trouble our peace and quiet to better company in heaven; from actions that are sinful to actions altogether free from sin. It is a glorious and blessed change every way. We shall have better company, better place, better employment, all glorious then, till the time come that all the elect be gathered together, and then body and soul shall be 'for ever with the Lord,' 1 Thess. iv. 17. Why then should we fear changes, when all changes shall end in that that is better? Is a labouring man loath to have his hire, or a weary man loath to have rest? Is a king loath to be crowned? Is a party contracted loath to have the marriage consummate? Why should we be loath to die? We should be ashamed of ourselves, that we have been so long in the school of Christ, and yet have not learned to unloose our affections from earth to better things; that we stand in fear of death, that makes way to the glory of the soul now, and the eternal glory of body and soul after.

In a word, we are exhorted, in the beginning of the chapter, to have our minds in heaven, where Christ is; and we are exhorted, after the text, to mortify our earthly members; two necessary duties, to have our conversation in heaven, before we be there, and to mortify our earthly members; to die in our affections to earthly things, before we die indeed. Would we have strength put into our souls to perform both these? Let us oft meditate of the things that are between these verses. Let us consider that we are dead, so we should be more lively to God. Consider that our life is hid with Christ; that Christ shall appear ere long and we with him in glory.

We should raise our thoughts to be with Christ, and draw our souls up to heavenly things; for the more our affections are upwards, the less they will be below. Our affections are finite. The more we spend them on heavenly things, the less they will run on earthly. As a man in a trance, his thoughts are taken up with one matter, that he is dead to other things, so the soul which is taken up with the glory to come, and with Christ, it is dead to earthly things; only it takes them for necessary use, as having use of them in our travail; but it useth the world as if it used it not. And this issues from this principle, that we shall ere long appear with Christ in glory. There is no man but will drown himself too much with the things of the world, that hath not this to raise up his soul, 'I shall appear ere long with Christ in glory,' and then these things will be consumed.

The last point is, *how these depend one upon another*, that because Christ shall appear in glory, therefore we.

I will touch it a little, because it is a point of faith that helps our judgment a little. It is a ground of divinity, that whatsoever is in us that are members, it is in our head first; for God is first, and then Christ mediator, and then we. Whatsoever is good in us, or shall be to us, it is in Christ first. He is justified from our sins, for he was our surety from sin. He was abased for them first; therefore he shall appear then without sin to glory. Our sin was but imputed to Christ; he became our surety for sin and he must be abased; therefore we cannot be glorious here, because of our corruptions. Christ was surety for our sins in his first coming. Now his resurrection shewed that he had satisfied for our sins. The second time he shall appear in glory. Why are we justified from our sins? Because Christ, our surety, was acquitted.

We ascend gloriously to heaven. Where is the ground of it? He ascended first, and we ascend for him and in him.

We sit in heavenly places. Why? Because he is in heaven beforehand; as the husband takes up a place for his wife. Why doth she go into the country and take it up after? Because her husband hath gone before and taken it. Our ascension riseth from his, and our sitting at the right hand of God from his.

And so at the day of judgment, our being glorious, it comes from his. He then shall appear in glory, as the head and husband of his church, and shall shine upon all his members. He, as the sun, shall cast a lustre and beauty and glory upon all that are his; and then they shall reflect that glory they have from him upon him again, and he upon them again. So he shall be glorious in them and they in him; but the ground of all is, he is first in glory. He shall appear in glory, and then we in him.

I speak this the rather, because I would have humble consciences to make use of it in times of desertion, when God seems to be a God that hides himself, when they find no life nor comfort. Yet if they have but grace to believe, they may comfort themselves in this. Well, I have it but from Christ, and he is perfect in glory. He is ascended, and I shall ascend and rise, and be glorious, because he is so. Put case now I feel no such matter. It is no matter. I live by faith in Christ, that hath all in fulness; and what he hath done for me, he will do in me, if I believe in him.

Let a troubled soul comfort itself with this. It is as impossible that he should be damned that believes in Christ, as that Christ should be damned, because he, believing in Christ, is one with him, and as verily as Christ is in heaven, he shall be there; for Christ rose for all his. The little finger lives the same life as the hand or the foot doth. So a weak Christian that hath little grace, he lives by the same faith in Christ that is in glory, as well as they that are stronger. Let us strive and fight, with this encouragement, as St Paul saith, 'fight the good fight of faith,' 1 Tim. vi. 12. Oh, but shall we be always fighting and striving? No, saith he; lay hold of eternal life, and then we may well fight against doubts and despair. Let us therefore labour to fight, so that we may lay hold on eternal life, which Christ keeps for us, and keeps us for it; and ere long we shall partake of that we hope for.

THE SPIRITUAL JUBILEE.

NOTE.

'The Spiritual Jubilee' is designated in the title-page '*two* sermons.' Probably only the substance of them is given. There is no division between them. They form No. 6 of the 'Beams of Divine Light' (4to, 1639). The separate title-page will be found below,* and also the general title-page of the volume from which the 'Spiritual Jubilee' is taken.† The Epistles Dedicatory and To the Reader of 'The Beams of Light' are herewith prefixed. G.

* THE
SPIRITVALL
IUBILE.
In two Sermons.
By
The late learned and reverend Divine,
RICH. SIBBS:
Doctor in Divinitie, M^r^ of *Katherine Hall*
in *Cambridge*, and sometimes Preacher
at GRAYES-INNE.

JOHN 8. 36.
If the Sonne therefore shall make you free, yee shall be free indeed.

GAL. 5. 1.
Stand fast therefore in the liberty, wherewith Christ hath made us free.

LONDON,
Printed by *E. P.* for *Nicholas Bourne*, and *Rapha Harford*, and are to be sold at the South entrance of the Royall Exchange, and in Queens head Alley, in *Pater-Noster-Row*, at the gilt Bible. 1638.

† BEAMES
OF DIVINE
LIGHT,
Breaking forth from severall places
of holy Scripture, as they were
learnedly opened,
In XXI. Sermons.
The III. first being the fore-going Sermons
to that Treatise called *The Bruised-Reed*,‡
Preached on the precedent words.
By the late Reverend and Iudicious Divine,
RICHARD SIBS,
D.D.Mr. of *Katharine Hall* in *Camb:* and sometimes
Preacher at GRAYES INNE.
Published according to the Doctor his owne
appointment subscribed with his hand;
to prevent imperfect Coppies.

ESAY. 60. 3.
The Gentiles shall come to thy light, and Kings to the brightnesse of thy rising.

PSALM. 84. 11.
For the Lord God is a Sun and shield, the Lord will give grace and glory; and no good thing will he withhold from them that walke uprightly.

LONDON
Printed by *G. M.* for *N. Bourne*, at the Royal Exchange, and *R Harford*, at the guilt Bible in Queenes-head Alley in *Pater-Noster-Row.*
MDCXXXIX.

‡ See Vol. I. page 42.—G.

TO THE RIGHT HONOURABLE

JOHN LORD ROBERTS, BARON OF TRURO;*

AND TO THE RIGHT HONOURABLE

THE LADY LUCIE,* HIS PIOUS CONSORT,

GRACE AND PEACE FROM JESUS CHRIST.

RIGHT HONOURABLE AND TRULY NOBLE,

It was not so much the nobility of your blood, as that of grace given unto you from the divine hand, which did so much interest you in the love and esteem of that worthy servant of Christ the author of this work; in whom 'Urim and Thummim' met, whose whole course being a real and vital sermon, sweetly consonant to the tenor of his teaching, made him amiable living, and honourable dead, in the opinion of as many as well knew him. This was the thing, I suppose, which wrought unto him from you, as well as from many others of your noble stock and rank, more than an ordinary esteem; and this is that which maketh me in nothing to doubt but that his labours made public under your names shall be very welcome unto you. The work is answering unto the man, and therefore worthy you and your acceptance; only this is the disadvantage, that though these sermons had his own tongue to preach them, yet they want his own pen to commend them unto your honours. I well know that the expressions of holy truths from a gracious heart, by lively voice, do breed deeper impressions in thirsting and reverent hearers, than any publishing of them in dead letters can do; yet this we find in experience, that holy and necessary truths, this way coming abroad into the churches of God, do get the advantage to continue longer, and to become a more general good. They may stir up the affections, and set onwards in the course of holiness where the comforts are sure, and the honours honouring everlasting.

In these ensuing sermons you have variety, the mother of delight; and such notable descriptions of the person, offices, love, and life of Christ, that by them you may not only be settled in divine assurances to your further

* For notices of these well-known patrons of the Puritan clergy, consult any of the Peerages.—G.

comforts, but also directed and encouraged, both in your inward and outward conversation, to follow the example of Christ, the most blessed and unerring example unto all Christians. This champion I beseech you both to follow unto your lives' end. Make it your work to set up Christ, and his religion, both in your hearts and in your houses. Acknowledge none but Christ in matter of salvation; and none to Christ in point of affection. Let Christ be Christ with you, and then if Christ,—and if not Christ nothing can be worth anything—he will make you worthy indeed, he will prove unto you in life and death a sun, a shield, even a full and an answerable good. With this Christ I leave you, and with you these ensuing sermons, to be read and observed for your spiritual furtherances in the enjoyment of eternal life by Jesus Christ, desiring the great God of heaven and earth to look upon both you and yours in much grace and mercy; giving unto you all the comfort and crown of religion here on earth, and hereafter in heaven. I rest,

Your honours' to be commanded,

JOHN SEDGWICK.*

* Cf. Vol. IV. p. 492.—G.

TO THE READER.

Christian Reader—The word of God is given us as a most precious treasure, and that not for ourselves only, but for our children after us, and therefore is called Israel's inheritance: Deut. xxxiii. 4, 'Moses commanded us a law, even the inheritance of the congregation of Jacob.' All the wealth in the world is but as dirt and trash in comparison of the word to the people of God. 'Thy testimonies have I taken as an heritage for ever: for they are the rejoicing of mine heart,' saith David, Ps. cxix. 111. And therefore as they rejoice in their own enjoying of it, so they do what they may to assure it to their children when they are dead, that it may be entailed upon them and their posterity after them; yea, so they do also with the knowledge of divine truths which they have found in the word; which is not indeed found out by men all at one time, but by degrees, as gold is found in mines, as men come to search farther and farther, and dig deeper and deeper for it. It was not, they know, imparted to them for their own use only, but for the benefit of others. 'The manifestation of the Spirit is given to profit withal,' 1 Cor. xii. 7; and therefore as it comes to them from heaven they hand it to others, that so it may be continued in the church, 'the ground and pillar of truth,' 1 Tim. iii. 15, for the good of those that shall live in future times.

This was, I hope, the chief aim of those that have published these sermons of that worthy light of our church, Dr Sibs. And surely we have great cause in this regard thankfully to acknowledge their care and pains, who both took them so exactly from his mouth as he delivered them, and then kept them so charily as τὴν καλὴν παρακαταθήκην, 'a precious thing committed to their trust,' 2 Tim. i. 14, and have now published them for the common good of all that will make use of them. For by this means what was delivered to a few may now build up many to farther degrees of knowledge and grace, even all the land over, and they that never saw his face may be made sharers in those his labours, which only a few were so happy as to hear.

Being myself one amongst others that have found the advantage hereof, I was not so hardly won as otherwise I should have been, to commend these 'Beams of Divine Light' to the respect of others. Divers truths of greatest consequence are exactly handled in the several sermons here presented to you, as concerning the misery of our natural estate, and the bliss and happiness of those that are quickened by Christ; concerning the necessity of the word, our spiritual food, and the zealous violence of the faithful in pressing after it; concerning the divers both joys and sorrows, complaints and triumphs of God's children here, when they are black though comely, Cant. i. 5 ; and concerning their happiness in death, and glory after it, and many other, whereof these few are only a taste.

The study of the Scriptures made the author a man of God, 'perfect, thoroughly furnished unto all good works ;' and as became a faithful steward of the manifold grace of God, he endeavoured 'to teach the whole counsel of God,' and to store men with the knowledge of God's will, 'in all wisdom and spiritual understanding.' I desire that both thou and I, and all God's people, may so read these his labours, that it may further our growing in grace, and in the knowledge of our Lord Jesus Christ, to whose grace I commend thee, being

Thine in him,

ARTHUR JACKSON.*

Wood Street, November 6. 1638.

* For notice of Jackson, see Vol. II. p. 442.—G.

THE SPIRITUAL JUBILEE.

For the law of the Spirit of life in Christ Jesus hath made me free from the law of sin and of death.—Rom. VIII. 2.

There be four things especially that trouble the peace of a Christian, and indeed of any man, in this world.

The first is, *sin, with the guilt of it*, binding them over to the wrath of God, and the expectation of misery, a heavy bondage.

The second is, besides the guilt of sin, *the remainders of corruption*, with the conflict that accompanies them while we live in this world; and that conflict must needs be tedious.

The third is, *the miseries of this life* that accompany alway both the guilt and remainders of sin in this world. We are condemned to a great deal of trouble here, and this doth much exercise and perplex God's children. And then the shutting up of all, *death and damnation*.

The thought of these things doth much disquiet and disturb the peace of a Christian's soul.

Now, in this Epistle we have comfort against all these. First, for *the guilt of sin*, that binds us over to eternal judgment and the wrath of God; we are freed by the obedience of Christ, the second Adam, as is excellently shewed in the fifth chapter.

And for the *remainders of corruption* that we conflict with in this world, we are assisted against that by the Spirit of Christ. For as by the obedience of Christ we are freed from the guilt, so by the Spirit of Christ we are helped and assisted against the remainders of our corruptions.

For the third, *the miseries of this life*, we have victory in Christ: 'In him we are more than conquerors,' as you have it in this chapter, Rom. viii. 37. They can do us no harm. 'Nothing can separate us from the love of God in Christ Jesus.' We have many singular comforts in this chapter against all the troubles that can befall us, and this is one that triumphs over all: 'All things shall work for the best to them that love God.' What should I speak of hurt from anything that befalls us, when all shall work for the best, by the over-ruling of him that commands all? ver. 28.

And for death itself: 'Neither life nor death shall be able to separate us from the love of God.' And for damnation which accompanies death: 'It is God that justifieth, who shall condemn?' There is opposite comforts in God's book, nay, in this epistle and in this chapter, against all that may any way trouble our peace. 'There is no condemnation to them that are in Christ Jesus,' saith the apostle; and then he goes on after to shew how, by the help of the Spirit, 'all things work for the best,' &c. In this very verse likewise, you have this comfort set down, of our freedom by Christ from any thing that may hurt us. 'For the law of the Spirit of life in Christ Jesus hath made me free from the law of sin and of death.'

The words are dependent, as we see in the particle 'for;' '*for* the law of the Spirit of life,' &c. They depend upon the first verse thus; as a reason why, however there be sin in God's children, yet there is no damnation to them. 'There is no condemnation to those that are in Christ Jesus.' He proves it thus. Those that are free from the law of sin and of death, which brings in condemnation, those undoubtedly are free from damnation. But those that are in Christ Jesus, they are freed from the law of sin and of death; therefore there is no condemnation to such. But how shall we know that we are in Christ Jesus? Those that have the Spirit, and are led by the Spirit of Christ, they are in Christ. 'The law of the Spirit of life in Christ Jesus hath freed me from the law of sin and of death.' So I say, the words are especially a reason of the former, 'There is no condemnation to them that are in Christ Jesus;' because by the 'Spirit of Christ they are freed from the law of sin, and of death;' and by consequent, they are freed from damnation; for what brings in damnation but sin?

In the words, then, there is an opposition. There is law against law. 'The law of the Spirit of life in Christ,' and 'the law of sin and of death.' Now, where there are contrary laws, if there be contrary lords, as there must be, new lords will have new laws; especially if they be lords by conquest, they will alter the very fundamental laws that were before; as you know the old conquerors have done in this kingdom. Here is law against law, and lord against lord; Christ against sin and death. Here is a Lord by conquest over all other lords and laws. Therefore, here must needs be an alteration of laws upon it; the very fundamental laws must be altered. But to come more particularly to the words,

'For the law of the Spirit of life in Christ Jesus hath freed me from the law of sin and of death.'

The words are much vexed by expositors (*a*). I will rather speak my own judgment of them, and reconcile them, than dash one man's judgment against another; for that tends not to edification. 'The law of the Spirit of life,' &c. The meaning of the words is plain, if we compare it with other Scriptures.

'The law.' It is nothing but a commanding power; for so the word written the law, in the apostle's meaning, is but a power forcing and commanding. So the 'law of the Spirit of life' is the commanding and forcing power of the 'Spirit of life in Christ Jesus;' and so the 'law of sin,' it is either the tyrannical command and forcing power of sin, or else the condemning for sin afterwards, as we shall see hereafter. For we shall unfold the words better in the particulars.

First, then, here we have set down what estate we are in by nature: 'We are under the law *of sin and of death*.'

And then, here is our freedom and deliverance from that: '*We are made free* from the law of sin and of death.'

And then the author of it, Christ Jesus: 'The law of the Spirit of life *in Christ Jesus* hath freed me from the law of sin and of death.'

In the words, and those that go a little before, there are these three main fundamental points of religion:

The misery and bondage of man.

The deliverance of man.

And his duty.

Here you have his *misery*. He is under 'sin and death.'

Here is his *deliverance*. He is 'free from this by Christ.'

And for his *duty;* you have it in the last verse of the former chapter, speaking of his deliverance. 'Oh wretched man that I am, who shall deliver me from the body of this death?' Then it follows, 'Thanks be to God through Jesus Christ our Lord.' Thankfulness is due, not verbal thankfulness only. Indeed, the whole life of a Christian, after his deliverance, is a real thanksgiving. But that is not in my text.

To speak, therefore, of our estate by nature, and of our deliverance; our estate is, that we are under the law of sin and death.

'We are under the law of sin.'

Obs. We are *under sin*. What sin? We are under a threefold sin.

1. We are under the *first sin* of our *first father;* for as Levi paid tithes in Abraham to Melchisedec, so we all sinned in the loins of Adam our first parent; and the guilt of that first sin lies upon us.

2. Secondly, There is another sin that is derived and springs from that first sin; which is the *deprivation of the image of God*, the pravation of our nature. We call it original sin, whereby we are stripped of that good we had in our first creation, and have the contrary image, the image of Satan stamped upon us. So we are under the first sin, the guilt of it; and we are under the sin of nature, which we call original sin, because it is derived to us even from our birth and first original we had in Adam.

3. And then we are under *actual sins*, which are so many bonds to tie us fast under sin. We are dead by nature; but we are dead and rotten by actual sins. We superadd to the guilt of our sin by our daily conversation. We are blind by nature; but we are blinded indeed much more by our custom of life. Every sin doth, as it were, tie us faster to damnation, and keeps us faster under the bondage of sin. Every new sin takes away some part of the light of the understanding, and takes away some freedom of the will. It darkens the judgment more and more, and enthralls the will and affections; and binds a man more and more to the just sentence of God, that, as it is Prov. v. 22, 'the sinner is tied with the bonds of his own sins.' He is under the chains of an habituated wicked course of life, as well as of the sin of nature, which is the spring of all.

This is the miserable state of man; and these chains of his sins reserve him to further chains. Even as the devil is reserved in chains; that is, in terrors of his conscience, which as chains bind him till he be in hell, the place he is destinated to; so we being in the chains and bondage, vexed with our sins, we are at the same time in the chains of terrors of conscience, the beginnings of hell, and reserved to chains of damnation and death world without end. It is another manner of matter, our estate by nature, than it is usually taken for. If men had but a little supernatural light, to see what condition they are in, till they get out into Christ Jesus, they would not continue a minute in that cursed estate.

And we have deserved to be cast into this estate by reason that we left our subordination and dependence upon God, which, being creatures, we should have had. Therefore we turning from God to the creature, God punisheth our rebellion to him with rebellion in ourselves; because we withdrew our subjection from him, that therefore there should be in us a withdrawing of the subjection of sin and of the whole soul to God. So this captivity to and giving up to sin in us, it is penal and sinful; but as it comes from God, it is merely* judicial. Therefore we have it oft in the New Testament, in Rom. i. 21 and 2 Thes. ii. 10. The Gentiles, because they would not entertain the truth that they might have had by the light of nature, 'God gave them up to their sins.' And then the Christians after the apostles' times, they set slight by the good word of God, the gospel. Therefore 'God gave them up to believe lies.' It was sin in them; but as God gave them up, it was justice. So this captivity and giving men up to their own lusts, it is justice; as it comes from God, it is a horrible judgment. It is worse than to be given up to the devil himself; for by being given up to our lusts we increase our damnation. To be given up to be tormented of the devil, it is not such a mischief as this spiritual captivity under sin. We are guilty ourselves of our own thraldom. And this will increase both the shame and the punishment. The shame, that a man shall say in hell afterward, 'I have brought myself hither, I had means enough, prohibitions enough; I had sometimes chastisements of God, sometimes motions of his Spirit, sometimes one help from God, sometimes another; yet notwithstanding I brake through all oppositions that God set between me and the execution of my lusts, and to hell-ward I would, and hither I have brought myself.' So that indeed the greatest part of hell-torments, the shame of them especially, it will be that men have brought themselves by their own wits and carnal lusts thither. And indeed all the wit a carnal man hath, that is not sanctified by God's Spirit, it is to work himself to misery, to be a drudge to his lusts; that sets all the parts he hath on work, not how he may serve God and be happy in another world, but how he may prowl and provide for his own carnal lusts. This is the estate of all men by nature. They are under sin, under the power of sin. The blind judgment leads the blind affections, and both 'fall into the ditch,' into hell, Luke vi. 39.

1. The fearfulness and odiousness of this condition, to be in prison and thraldom and bondage to all kind of sin, natural and actual, it will appear further by this, that being in subjection to our base lusts, by consequence we are *under the bondage of Satan;* for he hath power over death by sin, because he draws us to sin, and then accuseth us and torments us for sin. By sin we come to be under his bondage. So that we are under the fearful captivity of the devil while we are under the captivity of sin; for all the power that he hath over us it is by sin. He is but God's executioner for sin. First, God gives him power to draw us to sin, to punish one sin with another; and then he suffers him to accuse and to torment us afterward. What a fearful bondage is this, that being under sin we are under Satan! We are servants to our enemy, as God threatened his people that they should serve their enemies. But this is a greater judgment, to be slaves to this enemy. This is the condition of every sinner. To be a slave to a man's enemy, it is a judgment of judgments; yet notwithstanding this is the case of every man by nature; he is a servant to his enemy, to Satan and his own lusts. He is a right Ham, a 'servant of servants;' for Satan useth him as the Philistines did Samson: he puts out his eyes; he puts out his judgment, his wits; he besots him; and so he goes blind in Satan's blind work and business: he is in a maze all his life long, till at length he sink into hell. So this is the aggravation of a man's estate by nature, he

* That is, 'altogether.'—G.

is a slave to his enemy. You know blessed Zacharias saith, Luke i. 74, 75, 'That, being delivered out of the hands of our enemies, we might serve him without fear, in righteousness and holiness, all the days of our life.' There is no wicked man, but he is acted by the devil. Oh that we would consider of it! We think we are led only by our own lusts and sins, as men; but until a man be in Christ, 'he is ruled by the command of the prince of the air,' Eph. ii. 2, and in 2 Tim. ii. 26, 'he is ruled by Satan, according to his will.' Even as a bird in a snare, it may move up and down, but it is still in the snare, and he that hath it there cares not: he knows he hath it safe, and he goes about to catch other birds; so when we are in our lusts and follow them, the devil hath us in his snare: he is secure of us, and goes about getting more and more still. The devil acts, and moves, and leads all carnal men.

But how chanceth it that they do not know and perceive it?

It is because he goeth with the stream of their own corruptions. Indeed, we must make some limitation of this. In some cases the devil doth not move carnal men. They are better than the devil would have them be for the good of the commonwealth and state; but yet take them as they stand in relation to religion, they may be devilish, secret, bitter, dark enemies to that. Though they may have strong heads for the good of the state, yet it is not from any intrinsecal good in themselves; but God useth them and makes them do that. For the devil would have all naught;* he is an enemy to the very swine; therefore much more to the good of a state. Therefore there are many politic civil† virtues, as we see in Ahithophel and Judas, which no question is more than the devil would have. He would not have civil men so good; he would not have them do that they do for the common good ofttimes. Yet the devil will be sure to be at one end of the good they do, to taint them, that their aim shall not be good. It shall not be to the glory of God; it shall not be in reference to salvation.

And so, as the good is temporal, they have a reward suitable to their desire; they care for no more. For they believe not heaven but in a general notion. It may be there is such things, it may be not. Therefore the good they do is some little petty obedience. And what do they desire? To be well esteemed and respected; to be venerable, and to have honourable opinions in the hearts of men, that men may stoop in their conceits to them as men of respect. This they deserve indeed, and this they have; God gives them that they would have. But as Christ tells the Pharisees, who did excellent good things, but it was to be 'seen of men,' he tells them 'they had their reward,' Mat. vi. 2. They had all they looked for, for they were atheists; they looked not for heaven. So a man may say of all that are out of the state of grace: though they do more than the devil would have them, and for divers degrees of what they do they are not subject to the devil, yet he taints their actions one way or other in the end; he joins himself in the action first or last; he hath a hand in all their actions. So that, notwithstanding there be many good things, yet this hinders not a whit but that they may be under the power of the devil; for it is but in reference to civil government and state, which is but for a time. 'The fashion of this world passeth away,' 1 Cor. vii. 31. Here will be no magistrates to govern nor no people to be governed ere long.

I speak it, because many men are ready to propound such and such, to imitate them in their courses; and to say, I will be no more religious than he; when, perhaps, all may be but formality and common graces for this

* That is, 'naughty,' = wicked.—G. † That is, 'moral.'—G.

world. God will honour some so much, to be instruments for common good here; but what is that to eternal salvation? He may be a slave to his lusts, and an enemy to the power of grace, for all that. Therefore, unless we see men wrought upon thoroughly, to be of the mind of Christ, to have the Spirit of Christ, to judge of things as Christ judgeth, to judge the service of God and doing his will to be the best things, and to 'go about doing good,' Acts x. 38, and that with reference and obedience to God, all is nothing else. A man may be under the bondage of his corruptions, and so by them to Satan.

Again, When we are under our lusts and sins, it is about earthly things; *we are in slavery to that which is worse than ourselves.* Sin is the vilest thing in the world, and the things whereabout sin is occupied are the profits and pleasures and trifles of this world—mean petty things. It is a base slavery to consider whom we serve.

3. And to consider what it is that is in bondage, *the immortal soul of man*, that had the image of God stamped upon it; and in the soul of man, the most excellent part, the will, that is most free, yet being under sin, it is most bound. Our will was given us to cleave to God and the best things; to make choice of the best things, and to cleave to them undivided in life and death, and for ever; and so by cleaving to things better than ourselves, to advance ourselves to a higher condition. For when the soul of man that is under better things, that is under God and Christ, and doth cleave to God and Christ in his affections, and to the things of a better life, these be things bettering a man's condition, even raising the soul from its own present estate to a glorious condition; for we are as we affect.* Our wills and our affections do transform us. Therefore wicked men are called the world, because they love it; and holy men are called heavenly, because they are carried in their affections and wills to heavenly things. Our affections and wills do denominate us, they give us the name; nay, that is too little, they do give us the reality, the state. When God so alters and changes our dispositions, that out of a sanctified judgment we make a right choice of things, and then cleave to them in our wills and affections constantly, this raiseth our nature to be higher than itself: 'He that cleaveth to the Lord is one spirit,' as the apostle saith, Acts x. 38.† Indeed, our affections transform us anew. As it is with the fire, it transforms cold and gross bodies to be all fiery; so God and heavenly things work upon our hearts, they transform us to be like themselves.

Now, for this inward soul of man, which is so excellent a thing, fitted by God to cleave to better things, for communion with himself and everlasting happiness, for this to be a drudge to base pleasures and profits, to the windy empty things of this world, to vain titles and such like empty things, and to place its happiness in these things, it is a pitiful degeneration that so excellent a thing as the immortal soul of man, that shall never die, should join with those things that shall make him miserable, that it shall be better for a man that he had never been; as it is said of Judas, 'It had been better for that man that he had never been born,' Mat. xxvi. 24.

4. In the next place, consider that *that follows this thraldom and baseness to our lusts.* There is a double fruit of it. (1.) The one is *uncertain.* I mean, for our yielding to our base affections, what get we? 'The pleasures of sin for a season,' Heb. xi. 25; a little pleasure or profit, perhaps not that neither; but if we have it, it is a fading commodity, that goes

* That is, 'choose,' 'love.'—G. † Qu. 1 Cor. vi. 17?—Ed.

away quickly. When they are gotten, what are they? Vanity. They promise more before we get them than they perform when we have them. But then (2.) There is another wages, that God in justice hath appointed for it, that is, *damnation:* 'The wages of sin is death,' Rom. vi. 23. It cries for wages. When we are under sin we can look for nothing but death, and therefore he joins them together here: 'the law of sin and of death,' an expectation of eternal misery. This a man hath that is wedded to himself, that hath not learned the first lesson in the gospel, to deny himself. He is a wretched slave to the devil in his best part and power; his lusts imprison his will and affections; his wit, that should devise how he should be happy for eternity, it is only a drudge to his base lusts. There are a company of men that are the shame and blemish of the gospel, that set their wits a-work only how to devise to satisfy their base lusts; and then the issue and conclusion of all this is eternal misery; and in the meantime, the expectation of misery in terrors of conscience. This is the estate of every man till he be translated by the Spirit of God to a better condition in Christ, that he spends out his time in a base and miserable thraldom, worse than the thraldom of the Israelites in Egypt or in Babylon.

5. And it is so much the more fearful, because *men are insensible of it,* like bedlams, that make nothing of their chains, that laugh in their chains. A frantic man, when he is bound in chains, he laughs, when they that are about him weep at his misery. So you have men frolicking in sin. They will swear at liberty, and besot themselves at liberty, and corrupt their consciences, even for base trifles. They think they are in no bondage, and they do all wondrous cheerfully and well; whenas indeed the more cheerfully and readily any man performs the base service of sin, the more he is in bondage. Freedom is opposite to bondage. Notwithstanding, such is the nature of sin, that the more freely we do it the more we are bound; because the more freedom we have, the more we are entangled. We run into guilt upon guilt, till after guilt comes execution, an eternal separation from the presence of God, and an adjudging to eternal torments for ever.

So that it is a false judgment that the world hath. They think great men happy men. Why? They do as they list. Ay, they may do so, and ofttimes they take the liberty to do so. They will be under no laws. They are so far from obeying the law of God, that they are loath to be hampered with the laws of the state, or with any laws, but they will be above all. A miserable condition! Why? The more will a man hath in evil, the more miserable; for the more freely and with less opposition he tangleth himself. Let his place be never so great, the deeper he sinks in rebellion, and the deeper he sinks into guilt upon guilt; which will all come to a reckoning at the hour of death and day of judgment. So the men that we admire and envy most—out of simpleness and want of judgment—they are the most miserable creatures in the world, if they be out of Christ and have not grace. For they have nature let loose in them without restraint; and nature being under the captivity of sin, becomes out of measure sinful in such. The less a man is curbed either from laws above him or the law within him to check him, the more wretched man he is. For the deeper he goes in rebellion and sin, the deeper his torment shall be afterward.

Great persons have a great privilege. What is that? They shall be greatly tormented. That is all the privilege that I know if they be naught.* Those that shake off all bonds, any earthly privilege and pre-

* That is, 'naughty,' = wicked.—G.

rogative is so far from exempting them from misery, that it makes them more miserable; for unless they have grace to use those things that might be an advantage to better things, they sink deeper and deeper into sin, and so into terrors of conscience first or last; and, by consequence, to damnation. Oh it is a fearful condition to be the greatest monarch in the world and not to be in Christ, and under the law of 'the Spirit of life in Christ'! They are the objects of pity above all kind of men to truly judicious souls, that know out of God's truth, and by the light of the Spirit, what is to be judged of the state of men. You see then what kind of misery it is that natural men are under, being under the law of sin.

6. To declare it a little further, for men will hardly think it is such a bondage to be under sin. Therefore, I beseech you, do but consider *how sin tyranniseth where it gets strength*. See it in some instances. The covetous worldly man that is under the law of that lust, he hath the law of other lusts, but that is predominant—see how it tyranniseth. It takes away his rest; the use of God's blessings; the good things he hath given him to enjoy. It makes him in thrall to the creature. We see it in carnal pleasure. Amnon, when he lusted after his sister Tamar, it took away his rest, 2 Sam. xiii. 2, *seq.* And how doth this base affection tyrannise in some men? It makes them forget their bodies so, that they overthrow their health and hasten death temporal. It hurts the natural man. It makes them forget their credit; it makes them forget their souls; it makes them stink, by living in that carnal noisome sin. The judicious heathen were sensible of it, by the strength of natural judgment; yet sin where it is in any strength uncurbed, it so tyranniseth, that it makes men forget both health and life and credit and estate in this world, that they come to nothing. What should I speak of forgetting life eternal and damnation? They have no faith to believe that. But such is the tyranny of sin, that it makes them forget things sensible; that by experience, after they see how dearly they have bought their base pleasures, with the loss of credit, and health, and comfort; with the loss of the estate that God hath trusted them withal in this world.

Take a man that is under the base law of ambition, a proud person. See how it tyranniseth over him. It makes him forget blood and kindred, all the bonds of nature. He will kill his brethren to make his way; as you know in our own stories, such tyrants. If there were not stories enow in this kind, daily experience shews it. Where the law of ambition and pride reigns, it makes the heart wherein this tyrant sets up his throne, to forget all bonds whatsoever, of nature and justice. You know whose speech it was, 'If the law must be violated, it must be for a kingdom' (*b*). But men will do it for far less. We see what men will do for a base place to command others in this world, when they are conscious of their own ill courses, and commanding corruptions; and all to give way to the base affection of ambition. A touch is enough of these things, for experience witnesseth and goes along with me. All men that are not in Christ, they have some predominant sin; either some base sin, or some more refined sin and lust, that keeps them from Christ and salvation; and this tyranniseth over them.

And this is the nature of this tyrant sin. It hath such possession of a man till he be got out of it and be in Christ, that it takes away the sight of itself. It hinders the knowledge of itself; it puts out a man's eyes. For that whereby a man should judge of corruption, it is corrupt itself. 'The wisdom of a man is death, it is enmity to God,' Rom. viii. 7. The wit that he hath that should discern of his base courses, it tangles him more and more to his own lusts ; so that wit and wisdom, the highest part of the soul, it is imprisoned by base affections ; and that power that should discern corruption, it is set on work to satisfy corruption. What is the wit of a man that is not in Christ occupied about all his lifetime ? It is nothing but a drudge and a slave, to devise means to satisfy his base lusts. Take a worldly man : he is exceeding witty to contrive worldly plots and business, though he be a dunce and a sot in matters that are spiritual. In his own tract and course, he hath a shrewd wit. Why ? Because his lusts to the world, they whet his wit. So we see the best thing in man now is enthralled to sin, his very wisdom itself; therefore it is enmity to God.

Every man hath some Herodias,* some sin or other that he is in bondage to, till he be in Christ. He cannot in a like measure be given and enthralled to all sins. It is unnecessary; because one sin serveth another. Many sins serve one great one. Corruption doth not run in all streams in one equality: but it runs amain one way unchecked and uncontrolled and unmortified, in all men that are not in Christ, and subdues the soul to itself, that it can devise and plot for nothing, but to satisfy that base lust. This is the state of man by nature.

Obj. But some will say, it is not our state and condition. We are baptized, and receive the sacrament, and hear sermons, and read good books ; and therefore we are not under sin.

Ans. But saith the apostle, 'His servants ye are to whom ye obey,' Rom. vi. 16. You may know the state of your service and subjection, by the course of your life. And as Christ saith to the Jews, John viii. 33, they bragged that they were free. Alas ! proud people ! They were neither free for soul nor state ; for they were under the Romans. They thought they were free because they were 'Abraham's children.' Were they not in captivity to the Egyptians, and under the Babylonians, and in present captivity under the Romans ? Yet they forget themselves out of pride. 'If the Son make you free, ye are free indeed,' John viii. 36 ; but because they were in a sinful course, they were slaves of sin. So it is no matter what privileges men are under, that they receive the sacrament, and are baptized, and live in the church, &c. 'His servants ye are, whom ye obey.' If there be prevailing lusts that set up their throne and tyrannise in our hearts, and set our wits on work, to devise how to satisfy them more than to please God, it is no matter what privileges we have. It is no matter whose livery we wear, but whom we serve. We may wear God's livery, that shall be pulled over our heads afterward and we be uncased ; that it shall appear that we are the devil's servants under the profession of Christ.

There is no man that is not in Christ, that denies his corrupt nature anything. If revenge bid him take revenge, he will if he can ; if he do not, it is no thanks to him, but to the laws. If any sin rise in the heart, all the parts of the body, and powers of the soul, are ready weapons to this tyrant to keep a man in slavery. As if anger and wrath keep a man in bondage, you shall have it in his countenance ; his hand will be ready to execute it ; his feet will be ready to carry him to revenge. If it be a proud heart that a man is kept under, you shall have it in his looks and expressions outward. If it be the base affection of lust, you shall have adultery in the eye ; an unchaste and uncircumcised ear and filthy rotten language. Men you see upon all occasions are ready to execute the com-

* Cf. Mat. xiv. 3.—G.

mands of these tyrannical lusts, in some kind or other. Therefore never talk of thy freedom, when lusts are raised up within thee, either ascending from thine own corruption, or cast in by Satan, and so joining with thy heart. Presently thy tongue will speak wickedly, and thine eyes, and looks, and countenance, shew that there is a naughty heart within ; and the whole man is ready to execute it, further than a man is curbed by law, or respect to his reputation or the like, which is no thanks to him. Yet a man cannot act the part of a civil man so well, but the corruption of his vile heart will betray itself in his looks or language. One time or other this tyrant will break forth. Therefore let us look to our hearts and courses ; for if we be not in Christ, we are under the 'law of sin.'

'And of death.'

We are not only under the law of sin, but also 'of death.' Now, 1, there is a death in this world, the separation of the soul from the body. But that is not so much meant here. For when we are in Christ we are not free from this death. But there is, 2, a worse death, which is a separation of the soul from the favour and love of God, and from the sanctifying and comforting Spirit of God. When the Spirit of God doth not comfort and sanctify the soul, it is a death. For as the soul is the life of the body, the body hath but a communicated life from the union it hath with the soul. The soul hath a life of its own, when it is out of the body, but the body hath its life from the soul. So it is with the soul.*

1. *When there is an estrangement of the soul from the Spirit of God and Christ*, sanctifying, and comforting and cheering it, then there *is a death of the soul.* The soul can no more act anything that is savingly and holily good, than the body can be without the soul. And as the body without the soul is a noisome odious carcase, offensive in the eyes of its dearest friends, so the soul without the Spirit of Christ quickening and seasoning it, and putting a comeliness and beauty upon it, it is odious. All the clothes and flowers you put upon a dead body cannot make it but a stinking carcase ; so all the moral virtues, and all the honours in this world put upon a man out of Christ, it makes him not a spiritual living soul ; he is but a loathsome carrion, a dead carcase, in the sight of God, and of all that have the Spirit of God. For he is under death. He is stark and stiff, unable to stir or move to any duty whatsoever. He hath no sense nor motion. Though such men live a common natural civil life, and walk up and down, yet they are dead men to God and to a better life. The world is full of dead men, that are dead while they are alive, as St Paul speaks of the 'widow that lives in pleasures,' 1 Tim. v. 6. A fearful estate, if we had spiritual eyes to see it and think of it.

2. But then after the death of the soul in this world, there is another degree of spiritual death ; which is, *when the soul leaves the body.* Then the soul dies. For then it goes to hell. It is severed for ever from the comfortable and gracious presence of God, and likewise it wants the comforts it had in this world.

3. And the third degree of it is, when body and soul shall be joined together ; then there is an eternal separation of both from the presence of God, *and an adjudging of them to eternal torments in hell.* This is the state of all men that are not in Christ. They are dead in soul while they live ; dead after the separation of the soul and body, and after to be adjudged to eternal damnation, world without end. Life is a sweet thing, and we know death it is terrible. When we would set out our hatefulness to anything,

* In margin here, 'In this world.'—G.

we use to say, 'I hate it as death.' Do we love life, and do we hate death? We should labour then to be out of that condition that we are all in by nature, wherein we are under sin and death, in regard of spiritual life, I mean; for, for civil life, and government, and policy, men may have life and vigour enough, that are hypocrites. But I speak of a better life, an eternal life, that is not subject to death.

Now, mark the joining of both these together. We are under sin and death by nature. Where a man is under sin he is under death; for as the apostle saith, Rom. v. 12, 'Sin entered into the world, and by sin death.' They were neither of both God's creatures, neither sin nor death. But sin entered into the world by Satan, and death by sin. 'Oh, ye shall not die,' saith Satan. He was a liar alway from the beginning. So now he saith to men, you shall not die; you may do this and do well enough. But he is a liar and a murderer. When he solicits to sin he is a murderer. Let us take heed of solicitations to sin, from our own nature or from Satan. Mark how God hath linked sin and death, 'The wages of sin is death,' Rom. vi. 23. When we are tempted to sin, we think, I shall have this credit, or profit, or contentment, or preferment, and advancement in the world. Ay, but that that you get by sin, it is not so great as you look for, when you have it, if you get it at all. But afterwards comes death, the beginnings of eternal death, terrors of conscience, universally follow, if a man be himself, if he be not besotted. The more a man is a man, and enjoys the liberty of his judgment to judge of things, the more he sees the misery that is due after sin, with a fearful expectation of worse things to come. Sin and death are an adamantine chain and link that none can sever. Who shall separate that which God in his justice hath put together? If sin go before, death will follow. If the conception go before, the birth will follow after; if the smoke go before, the fire will follow. There is not a more constant order in nature than this in God's appointment: first sin, and then death and damnation after.

Use. Therefore when we are tempted to sin let us reason with ourselves, 'There is death in the pot,' 2 Kings iv. 40. Let us discern death in it. It will follow. And if a man after repent of it, it will be more sharp repentance and grievous than the sin was pleasant; that a man shall have little joy of his sin, if he do repent. If he do not repent, what a fearful estate is a man in, after he hath sinned! Sin and death go together. No human power can sever them; for take the greatest monarch in the world, when he hath sinned, conscience is above him as great as he is, for conscience is next under God. It awes and terrifies him, and keeps his sleep from him; as we see of late in our bloody neighbour country, after that great massacre, he could not sleep without music and the like.* All that they have and enjoy in the world, all their greatness, it will not satisfy and stop the mouth of conscience; but when they sin, they feel the wrath of God arresting, and they are as it were shut up in prison, under the terrors of an accusing conscience, till they come to eternal imprisonment in the chains of hell and damnation. This is the estate of the greatest man in the world that is not in Christ. They are not so happy as we think they are. They are imprisoned in their own hearts, though they walk at never so much liberty abroad, and do what they list; for sin and death goes together, and before eternal death comes, the expectation and terrors of it seize on them for the present. So that whatsoever our first birth be, though it be noble and great, yet by it we are bond-slaves under sin and

* Cf. Vol. I. p. 149.—G.

death, unless our second birth, our new birth, make amends for sin, for the baseness of our first birth. This prerogative, our spiritual nobleness, is such an estate wherein we are not born, but are born again to it, 'to an inheritance immortal,' &c., 1 Peter i. 4. But by nature we are all bondmen, though we be born never so nobly. Therefore let us never brag of our birth, as the Jews did, that they were the children of Abraham. No, saith Christ, you are of your father the devil, John viii. 44. Let none stand upon the gentry and nobility of their birth, unless they be taken out of the condition they are in by nature, to be in a better condition in Christ; for we see all men naturally are under the law of sin and death.

These things are slighted, because we enjoy 'the pleasures of sin for a season,' Heb. xi. 25. Men think to be enthralled to sin, it is pleasant thraldom, they are golden fetters; for I shall have the pleasures of sin all my lifetime, &c.; and for death, I will set a Roman spirit against death. Saith a Roman, What! is it such a matter to die? It is nothing to die (*c*). They set a good face on the matter. And this is the conceit of many men till they come to it. But, alas! to be enthralled to death, it is another matter, for behind death there is a gulf. A man may break the hedge well enough with a strong resolution to die; it is nothing to die if there were an end. But there is a gulf, there is damnation and destruction behind; there is eternal torment behind; to be adjudged from the presence of God for ever: to be separated from all good and all comfort, and to have society with the devil and his angels in hell, and that for ever and for ever. Thou mayest, perhaps, make slight of the service of sin, because thou hast the present baits to delight thee, but thou shouldst regard death. Thou mayest neglect death, but then regard eternal death. This word 'eternal' it is a heavy word, 'eternal' separation from all good; and eternal communion with the devil and his angels; and for the wrath of God to seize on thy soul eternally, world without end. Methinks men should not set light by that. Therefore considering that this is our estate by nature,—we are all slaves to sin and death,—let us labour to get out of this cursed estate by all means, which is by

'The law of the Spirit of life in Christ Jesus.'

Now, I come to speak of our freedom: 'The law of the Spirit of life in Christ Jesus hath *freed me* from the law of sin and death.' This is good news indeed, to hear of freedom: good news to the Israelites to hear of freedom out of Egypt, and for the Jews to hear of Cyrus's proclamation for their freedom out of Babylon. Freedom out of bondage is a sweet message. Here we have such a message of spiritual freedom, from other manner of enemies than those were. The year of jubilee, it was a comfortable year to servants that were kept in and were much vexed with their bondage. When the year of jubilee came they were all freed. Therefore there was great expectation of the year of jubilee. Here we have a spiritual jubilee: a manumission and freedom from the bondage we are in by nature. 'The Spirit of life in Christ makes *us free* from the law of sin and death.' There is life in Christ, opposite to death in us. There is a Spirit of life in Christ and a law of the Spirit of life in Christ, opposite to the law of sin and of death in us. So that this is our happiness while we live here (Oh, it is the blessedness of men to make use of it while they have time and space and grace to repent, and to cleave to Christ), that whatsoever ill we are under by nature, we may have full supply in Christ for all the breaches that came by the first Adam. There came the wrath of God, the corruption of our nature, terrors of conscience, death and damnation. All these followed the sin and breach of the first Adam. All these are made up in the second. He hath freed us from all the ill we received from the first Adam, and that we have added ourselves; for we make ourselves worse than we come from Adam by our voluntary and daily transgressions. But we are freed from all by the 'law of the Spirit of life in Christ Jesus.'

How comes this freedom?

1. There can no freedom be *without satisfaction to divine justice.* For why are we under sin? God gives us up to sin. Why are we under death? God gives us up to death. Why are we under Satan's government? He is God's executioner, God's serjeant. He gives us up to him here because we offend him. Why are we under damnation and wrath? Because God is offended. All our slavery comes originally from God. However it be sinful in regard of Satan that keeps us, yet the power whereby he keeps us is good, for he doth it from God. His will is always naught, but his power is always lawful. Therefore the power whereby the devil keeps us, if we look up to God under whom the power is, it is a lawful power; for God hath a hand in giving us up to sin: it is a judicial giving up, and then by lusts and sin, to Satan and death and damnation. So if we speak of freedom, we must not begin with the executioner: the wrath of God must be satisfied. God must be one with us, so as his justice must have contentment. Satisfaction must be with the glory of his justice, as well as of his mercy. His attributes must have full content. One must not be destroyed to satisfy another. He must so be merciful in freeing us as that content must be given to his justice, that it complain not of any loss. Now, reconciliation alway supposeth satisfaction. It is founded upon it.

2. And satisfaction for sin, it must be in *that nature that hath sinned.* Now man of himself could not satisfy divine justice, being a finite person; therefore God the second person became man, that in our nature he might satisfy God's wrath for us, and so free us by giving payment to his divine justice. The death of Christ, God-man, is the price of our liberty and freedom.

But why doth the apostle speak here of 'a law of the Spirit of life in Christ' which frees us? But here is no mention of satisfaction by death.

Oh, but death is the foundation of all, as we shall see afterwards. To unfold the point, therefore, because it is a special point, and the words need unfolding.

Here it is said there is life in Christ.

'A Spirit of life,' and a law of the Spirit of life in Christ.

1. There is life *in Christ,* not only as God, for so indeed he is life. God his life is himself; for life is the being of a thing, and the actions and moving and vigour and operations of a thing answerable to that being. So the life of God is his being: 'As I live, saith the Lord;' that is, 'As I am God, I will not the death of a sinner,' Ezek. xviii. 32. Now, Christ hath life in him as God, as the Father hath. But that is not especially here meant.

2. There is life in Christ as *God-man,* as mediator. Now, this life is that life which is originally from the Godhead. Indeed, it is but the Godhead's quickening and giving life to the manhood in Christ; the Spirit quickening and sanctifying the manhood. And we have no comfort by the life of God, as it is in God's life alone severed; for, alas! what communion have we with God without a mediator? But our comfort is this, that God, who is the fountain of life, he became man, and having satisfied God's justice, he conveys life to us. He is our head; he hath life in himself as

God, to impart spiritual life to all his members; so there is life in Christ as mediator.

And there is a Spirit of life. That life it is a working life, for spirit is an emphatical word. Spirit added to a thing increased the thing. Again, he saith, '*The law* of the Spirit of life.' Law is a commanding thing. To shew that the life in Christ is a commanding life, it countermands all opposite lives whatsoever, of sin and death; and this law is a countermand to all other laws. 'The law of the Spirit of life' frees us from all other laws. So here is life, the Spirit of life, and the law of the Spirit of life—all words of strong signification.

But for the clear understanding of this sweet and comfortable point, first, consider how the law of the Spirit of life is in Christ, what it doth in him, and then how it is derivatively in us.

First of all, We must know this for a ground, whatsoever is done to us *is done to Christ first;* and whatsoever we have, Christ hath it first. Therefore life is first in Christ, and then in us; resurrection first in Christ, and then in us; sonship first in Christ, and then in us; justification from our sins first in Christ—he is freed from our sins—and then in us; ascension first in Christ, and then in us; glory in heaven first in Christ, and then in us. We have nothing in us, but it is derived from Christ. Therefore, this being laid as a ground, we must consider how the Spirit of life works in Christ, what it doth in Christ, and then what it doth as it is in us; for whatsoever Christ hath, it is not only for himself, but for us.

What doth it in Christ?

1. The Spirit of life in Christ, first of all, it did *quicken and sanctify his human nature.* That nature that Christ pleased to take upon him it stopped sin, it made a stop of original sin, in sanctifying that blessed mass out of which his body was made. For the foundation of his obedience actual, that it was so holy, it was hence that his nature was purified by the Holy Ghost in the womb of the virgin. The foundation that his death and sufferings was satisfactory and acceptable, it was that his holy nature was sanctified by the Spirit of God. So the first work of the Spirit of life in the Son of God, it was to sanctify and quicken that blessed mass that he took upon him.

2. And the Spirit of life that quickened and sanctified our nature in Christ did likewise *ennoble our nature;* for even as a base woman is ennobled when she is taken in marriage with a great man,—she hath his dignity accounted hers—so our nature, by the Spirit being sanctified, is knit into the union of person with Christ, that our nature and the second person make one Christ. So our nature by the Spirit is ennobled by this union. And

3. Also *enriched it with all grace* that our nature is capable of; for the nature of Christ had this double prerogative above ours: first of all, that blessed mass of flesh, it was knit to be one person with God; and then, that nature was enriched and ennobled with all graces above ours. And this the Spirit of life did to Christ himself, to his human nature that he took upon him, that he might be a public person. For God, the second person, took not upon him any man's particular person, of Peter, or Paul, or John, for then there should have been distinct persons, one person should have died, and another rise; but he took our nature into his person. So that the same person that did die was God, though he died in our nature, that he might be a public person. So we must consider Christ sanctifying our nature, that he might fit and sanctify all our persons.

But did the Spirit of life do nothing else but sanctify and enrich the human nature of Christ with grace?

4. Yes. For the Spirit of life in Christ did sanctify him *for his sacrifice*, as he saith, John xvii. 19, in that blessed prayer, 'I sanctify myself for them.' It prepared him for his death, and made him a fit sacrifice. When he entered upon his calling, he had more of the Spirit: the Spirit of life, as it were, was increased. For it is no heresy to think, that the gifts of Christ, for the manifestation of them, were increased. For in every state he was in, he was perfect; and when he set upon his office, and was baptized, he was fuller of the Holy Ghost: as it were, there was a fuller manifestation than before, when he did not set upon his office openly.

5. In his death, what did the Spirit of life then? *It supported him in his very death;* for there was an union of the Spirit. When there was a separation of his soul and body, there was not a separation of the union. That which gave dignity, and strength, and value, and worth to his death, it was the Spirit. Though there was a suspending of the comfort a while, yet there was no separation of the union. But I speak no more of that, being not especially meant here.

6. But especially *in his resurrection* (which we are now to think of by reason of the day, and it is not amiss to take all occasions), especially then, the Spirit of life that had sanctified Christ, and quickened him, and enriched his nature, and supported him, and done all, that Spirit of life quickened the dead body of Christ. 'And he was mightily declared to be the Son of God by the Spirit of sanctification, by his resurrection from the dead,' Rom. i. 4. The Spirit of life raised him from the dead, and put an end to all that misery that he had undergone before for our sakes. For until his resurrection, there was, as it were, some conflict with some enemies of Christ, either with Satan, or the world, or with death itself. He lay under death three days. Until Christ's body was raised, our enemies were not overcome. God's wrath was not fully satisfied. It was not declared to be satisfied at least. For he being our surety, till he came out of the grave, we could not know that our sins were satisfied for. But now, when the Spirit of life in Christ comes, and quickens that body of his in the grave, and so doth justify us, as it is, Rom. iv. 25, 'He died for our sins, and rose again for our justification:' that is, by the Spirit of life in Christ quickening his dead body, he declared that we are fully discharged from our sins, because he was fully discharged from our sins; being our surety, he shewed by his resurrection that he was fully discharged from all that he took upon him. When a man comes out of prison that is a surety, his very coming out of prison shews that he hath a full discharge of all the debt he undertook to pay. So the Spirit of life, raising Christ's body the third day, manifestly declared that the debt he took on him was fully discharged. And so as he died for sin, to satisfy God's justice for them, so he rose again for our justification, to shew that he had a full discharge for all.

Now, since the Spirit of life in Christ Jesus hath quickened his body, the soul may make a bold demand to God, as it is in 1 Pet. iii. 16. It may make that demand, Rom. viii. 33, 'Who shall lay anything to the charge of God's elect? It is Christ that died, nay rather, that is risen again,' and ascended into heaven, and makes intercession for us. 'Who shall lay anything to the charge of God's people? it is God that justifieth, who shall condemn?' Our sins? Christ hath taken our sins upon him, and satisfied divine justice for them; and by the Spirit of life hath quickened that dead body of his, that was surety for us himself. We may well say, 'Who shall lay anything to our charge?' He that is our surety is dead. Dead? Nay, risen again; nay, ascended, and sits at the right hand of God. Therefore now the conscience of any Christian may make that interrogation and bold demand there. It may stand out any that dares to oppose the peace of his conscience, now that he may say, Who is it? It is God-man that died. It is Christ that died in our nature, and hath raised that nature of ours again, and is at the right hand of God. Who shall lay anything to our charge? The Spirit of life in Christ, quickening him, hath quickened us together with him; so that now we may boldly demand we are freed from our sins, because our Surety is freed from all.

All this was for our good. What Christ did, it was not for himself, but for us. And in his birth, and life, and death, and resurrection, we must consider him as a public person, and so go along with all that he did as a public person. Whatsoever may be terrible to us, we must look upon it first in Christ. If we look upon the corruption and defilement in our nature, look upon the pure nature of Christ. His nature was sanctified in his birth, and he is a public person: therefore this is for me; and though I be defiled in my own nature, and carry the remainders of corruption about me, yet the Spirit of life in Christ sanctified his nature, and there is more sanctity in him than there can be sin in me. When we look upon our sins, let us not so much look upon them in our consciences, as in our surety, Christ. When we look upon death, look not upon it in ourselves, in its own visage, but as it is in Christ, undergone and conquered: for the power of the Spirit of life in Christ overcame death, in himself first, and for us, and will overcome in us in time. When the wrath of God is on our consciences, look not upon it as it is in ourselves, but as undergone by Christ, and as Christ, by the Spirit of life now in him, is raised up, not from death alone, but from all terrors. 'My God, my God, why hast thou forsaken me?' See Christ, by the Spirit of life, quickened from all; not only bare natural death, but from all enemies thou needest to fear. From the law: it is nailed to his cross; he now triumphs over it; and from sin: he was a sacrifice for it; and from the wrath of God: he hath satisfied it, or else he had not come out of his grave. So whatsoever is terrible, look on it in Christ first, and see a full discharge of all that may affright thy conscience, and trouble thy peace any way. See him in his death, dying for every man that will believe. Consider him in his resurrection as a public person, not rising himself alone, but for all us. Therefore in 1 Pet. i. 3, there is an exeellent place, 'Blessed be God, the Father of our Lord Jesus Christ, who hath begotten us again to a lively hope by the resurrection of Jesus Christ, to an inheritance immortal, undefiled,' &c.; and so go along with him to his ascension, and see ourselves 'sitting with him in heavenly places,' as St Paul speaks, Eph. ii. 6. Oh this is a sweet meditation of Christ! to see ourselves in him, in all the passages of his birth, and life, and death, and resurrection, and ascension to glory in heaven; for all that he did was as a public person, as the second Adam. But now, before the Spirit of life in Christ come to free me, I and Christ must be one; there must be a union between me and Christ; I must be a member of Christ mystical. For as Christ quickened his own body, every joint when it was dead, because it was his body, so he quickens his mystical body, every member of it. But I must be a member first; I must not be myself severed from Christ. Therefore, the law of the Spirit of life which is in Christ, the first thing it doth (next to impetration* and obtaining of happiness), it works application:

* That is, = procuring by prayer, entreaty, or request.—G.

for these two go together, impetration and application. Christ by his death obtained all good, and by his resurrection he declared it; but there must be an application to me. Now this Spirit of life which is in Christ, which quickened him and raised him up, and all for my good, must apply this to me.

The grace of application it is faith. Therefore this must be wrought in the next place. How doth the law of the Spirit of life free me? Because first it freed Christ, therefore me. But that is not enough, except there be application. Therefore the law of the Spirit of life works faith in me, to knit me to Christ, to make me believe, that all that he hath done is mine; and the same power that raised Christ from the dead, works the power of faith and application. For we must not think that it is an easy thing for a carnal man to believe, to go out of himself, that it is salvation enough to have salvation, by the obedience of another man. No. Both in the Ephesians and Colossians, in divers places, it is St Paul's phrase, that the same power 'that raised Christ from the dead,' must raise our hearts, and work faith in them.* For as the good things that faith lays hold on are wondrous good things, even above admiration almost; that poor flesh and blood, a piece of earth, should be an heir of heaven, a member of Christ; that it should be above angels in dignity: as the things are super-excellent things, even above admiration in a manner, so the grace that believes these things, it is a strange and excellent, and admirable grace, that is faith. Therefore faith must be wrought by the law of the Spirit of Christ; by the ministry of the gospel. This is the grace of application, when a man goes out of himself; when he sees himself first in bondage to his corruptions, to Satan, and to death; and then sees the excellent way that God hath wrought in Christ to bring him out of that cursed estate; then he hath by the Spirit faith wrought in him. And indeed the same power and Spirit that quickened Christ from the dead, must quicken our hearts to believe in Christ. It is a miracle to bring the heart of man to believe. We think it an easy matter to believe. Indeed, it is an easy matter to presume, to have a conceit, but for the soul in the time of temptation, and in the hour of death, for the guilty soul to go out of itself, and cast itself upon the mercy of God, who is justly offended, and to believe that the obedience of Christ is mine, as verily as if I had obeyed myself, here must be a strong sanctified judgment and a mighty power to raise the soul, to cast itself so upon God's mercy in Christ. So that besides the obtaining salvation by Christ, there must be a grace to apply it; and this faith doth.

Faith is said to do that that Christ doth, because faith lays hold upon Christ. What faith doth, Christ doth; and what Christ doth, faith doth. Therefore it hath the same actions applied and given to it that Christ hath. Faith is said to save us. You know it is Christ that saves us. But faith lays hold on Christ that saves us. Faith purgeth the heart, and overcomes the world. Christ by his Spirit doth all this. Because faith wrought by the Spirit is such a grace as lays hold on the power of Christ, it goes out of itself to Christ, therefore what Christ doth, faith is said to do. So then the law of the Spirit of life in Christ not only freed Christ himself by his resurrection, but likewise by the same power whereby he raised himself, he raiseth our hearts to believe what he hath done, both in his state of humiliation and exaltation, and makes all that Christ did ours.

The Spirit of life in Christ Jesus, working faith in us, and by faith other

* Cf. Ephesians ii. 6, and Colossians ii. 12.--G.

graces, doth free us from the law of sin and death. Christ doth it, and faith doth it, and grace, which issues from faith, doth it subordinately. Christ doth it by way of merit; and by his Spirit working faith in us, to lay hold upon whatsoever Christ hath done or suffered, as if we had done it ourselves. So it frees us from the law of sin and death, because it lays hold of the freedom wrought by Christ for us. But besides, and next to faith, there is a Spirit of sanctification, by which we are free from the commanding law of sin and death. But to clear all this, consider there is a freedom in this life, and in the life to come from sin and from death.

I. A freedom in this life, in calling, in justification, in sanctification; and in the life to come a freedom of glory.

1. There is a freedom *in effectual calling*, by the ministry of the gospel. The gospel being preached and unfolded, faith is wrought, whereby we know what Christ hath done for us; and we see a better condition in Christ than we are in by nature. Seeing by the Spirit of God the cursed estate we are in, we are convinced of sin in ourselves, and of the good that is in Christ; and hereupon we are called out of the thraldom we are in by nature, by the Spirit of Christ and the word of God, unfolding what our condition is; for man by nature having self-love in him, and that self-love being turned the right way, he begins to think, Ay, doth the word of God say I am a slave to sin and damnation? The word of God can judge better than myself; and then the Spirit of God sets it on with conviction, that undoubtedly this is true. And together with the cursed kingdom and slavery that I am under, there is discovered a better estate in Christ; for the gospel tells us what we are in Christ; freed from hell and death, and heirs of heaven. Oh the happy estate of a Christian to be in Christ! The gospel, with the Spirit discovering this, a man is called out of the cursed estate he is in by nature to the fellowship of Christ by faith, which is wrought in this calling. So that now he comes to be a member of Christ by faith. So that whatsoever Christ hath, or is, or hath done or suffered, it is mine by reason of this union with him by faith, which is the grace of union that knits us to Christ, and the first grace of application. So there is the first degree of liberty and freedom wrought by the Spirit of God, together with the gospel in effectual calling.

2. The second is *in justification*. That faith and belief in Christ that was wrought in effectual calling, it frees me from the guilt of my sins. For when the gospel, in effectual calling, discovers that Christ is such a one, and that there is such an estate in Christ, and there is faith wrought in me, then that faith lays hold upon the obedience of Christ to be mine. For Christ in the gospel offers his obedience to be mine, as if I had done it in mine own person. Whatsoever Christ did or suffered is mine; for he is made of God to be 'wisdom, righteousness, sanctification, and redemption,' 1 Cor. i. 30, to be all in all. The gospel sets him forth to be so. Now faith laying hold of Christ, to be made of God all in all, obedience, righteousness, &c., whatsoever is needful, hereupon this faith justifies me; hereupon I come to be free from the guilt of my sins, because my sins were laid upon Christ. Christ's death was the death of a surety. It was as if I had died myself, and more firm. Thus I come to be free in justification; for what my surety hath done I have done.

3. Again, There is a freedom *in sanctification;* that is, when a man believes that Christ is his, and that his sufferings are his, then the same Spirit that discovers this to be mine, it works a change and alteration in my nature,

and frees me from the dominion of sin. The obedience of Christ frees me from the condemnation of sin, and the Spirit of sanctification frees me from the dominion of sin. This is the freedom of sanctification, which faith lays hold on. 'Whosoever hath not the Spirit of Christ is none of his,' Rom. viii. 9. Christ as a head derives* to me the Holy Spirit to sanctify my nature; and 'of his fulness we receive grace for grace,' John i. 16. So the Spirit of sanctification in Christ frees me from the dominion of sin and death.

It is said here, that by Christ we have spiritual liberty and freedom, not from sin and death, but from *the law* of sin and of death. It is one thing to be freed from sin and death, and another thing to be freed from the *law* of them; for we are not indeed freed from sin and death, but from the law of sin and death, that is, from the condemning power of sin; that though sin be in us yet it doth not condemn us; and though we die, yet the sting is pulled out. Death is but a passage to a better life. So I say in justification, we are freed from the condemning power of sin; and in sanctification, from the commanding power of sin. When we are knit once to Christ, we have the obedience of Christ, ours in justification; and the holiness of Christ is derived to us, as from the head to the members in sanctification; and so we are freed from the law of sin. To understand this a little better, the same Spirit that sanctified the natural body, the human nature of Christ, whereby he 'became bone of our bone, and flesh of our flesh,' Eph. v. 30: the same Spirit doth sanctify the mystical body of Christ, that it may be 'bone of his bone, and flesh of his flesh.' For before we come to heaven, Christ must not only 'be bone of our bone,' &c., that is, in his incarnation, but we must be 'bone of his bone,' &c.; that is, we must have natures like Christ, not only flesh and blood—for so a reprobate hath flesh and blood, as Christ hath—but we must have his Spirit altering and changing our nature: that instead of a proud, disobedient, rebellious nature, now it must be a holy and humble and meek nature, together with human frailty, for that we carry about with us. Then the Spirit of life derived from Christ makes us 'bone of his bone.' For indeed, in his human nature being 'bone of our bone and flesh of our flesh,' he made us 'bone of his bone and flesh of his flesh.' He became man that we might partake of the divine nature, being partakers of the divine Spirit. So that now the Spirit of life in Christ, when we are knit to him, is a Spirit of sanctification, altering our natures and working in our hearts a disposition like Christ's: that we judge as Christ judgeth, and choose as Christ chooseth, and aim at God's glory as Christ did; for there is 'the same mind in us that was in Christ,' Philip. ii. 5—in our proportion, growing still more and more to conformity with Christ, till we be in heaven, till 'Christ be all in all,' 1 Cor. xv. 28, when he will change our nature to be holy as his own.

II. Besides this liberty from sin and death in this life, there is a glorious liberty and freedom that we have by the Spirit of Christ when we are dead; for then the Spirit of life that raised Christ's dead body will raise our bodies; and that Spirit of Christ that raiseth his body and raiseth our souls in this world from sin to believe in him, will raise our dead bodies. The same virtue and power that works in Christ works in his members. This is called 'the glorious liberty of the sons of God.' Then we shall be freed indeed, not only from the law of sin, but from sin itself; and not only from the law of death, but death itself; and we 'shall live for ever with

* That is, 'communicates.'—G.

the Lord,' 1 Thess. iv. 17. Christ then 'shall be all in all by his Spirit.' Christ will never leave us till he have brought us to that glorious freedom. We are freed already from sin and death. He hath 'set us in heavenly places together with himself' now, Eph. i. 3. In faith we are there already: but then we shall be indeed. Thus you see how we come to have the law of the Spirit of life in Christ, to free us from the law of sin and death, and all the passages of it.

Use. You see here that there is law against law—the law of the Spirit of life in Christ against the law of sin and death. I beseech you, consider that God hath appointed law to countermand law; the Spirit of Christ to overcome sin in us, not only in justification but in sanctification. Oh let us therefore comfortably think there is a law above this law. I have now cold, dead, base affections; but if I have the Spirit of Christ, he can quicken and enliven me. He will not only pardon my sin, but by the law of his Spirit direct, guide, and command me a contrary way to my lusts. And this is an art of spiritual prudence in heavenly things, whensoever we are beset with dangers, to set greater than that against it. The devil is an angel; but we have a guard of angels about us. The devil is a serpent; but we have a brazen serpent that cures all the stings of that serpent. We have principalities and powers against, but we have greater principalities and powers for us: the law of life against the law of sin and death. We have a law of our lusts tyrannizing over us and enthralling us. It is true. But then there is a law of the Spirit of life in Christ Jesus, to overcome and subdue that law of our lusts, if so be that we use the prerogatives we have, if we use faith and go to God and Christ, in whom are all the treasures of grace. He is the treasury of the church: 'Of his fulness we receive grace for grace,' John i. 16. Are we troubled with any corruptions? Go to the Spirit of liberty in Christ, and desire him to set us at liberty from the bondage and thraldom of our corruptions. And remember what Christ hath done for us, and where he is now, in heaven. Let us raise our thoughts that we may see ourselves in heaven already; that we may be ashamed to defile our bodies and souls with the base drudgery of sin and Satan, that are sanctified in part in this world, and shall be glorified in heaven. Certainly faith would raise our souls so. We betray ourselves, when, being once in the state of grace, we are enthralled basely to any sin. 'For sin shall not have dominion over you, because you are under grace,' saith the apostle, Rom. vi. 14. Being under grace, if we do but use our reasoning and use faith and exercise the grace we have given us, we cannot be in thrall to corruptions. We shall have remainders to trouble us, but not to rule, and reign, and domineer. For sin never bears sway, but when we betray ourselves, and either believe not what Christ hath done for us, or else exercise not our faith. A Christian is never overtaken basely, but when he neglects his privileges and prerogatives, and doth not stir up the grace of God in him.

Learn this then, when we are troubled with anything, set law against law: set the law of the Spirit of life in Christ against all oppositions whatsoever; and let the temptation lie where it will.

1. Let it lie in justification, *as when we are tempted by Satan to despair for sins, for great sins.* Oh, but then consider, the law of the Spirit of life *in Christ* hath 'freed me from the law of sin and of death.' Christ was made sin, to free me from sin. Consider that Christ was God-man. He satisfied divine justice. 'The blood of Christ cleanseth us from all sin,' 1 John i. 7, 'though they be as red as crimson,' Isa. i. 18. Thus set

Christ against our sins in justification, when the guilt of them troubles our souls.

2. And so likewise, *when we are set on by base lusts*, set against them the power of Christ in sanctification. What am I now? A member of Christ; one that professeth myself to be an heir of heaven. There is a Spirit of life in Christ my head. There is a law of the Spirit of life in Christ; that is, there is a commanding power in his Spirit; and that Spirit of his is not only in the head, but in the members. If I go to him for grace, I may have grace, answerable to the grace that is in him, grace that will strengthen me with his power. 'Be strong in the Lord, and in the power of his might,' Eph. vi. 10, and in 'Christ I can do all things,' Philip. iv. 13, by his Spirit, though in myself I can do nothing.

3. And *so in deadness and desolation of spirit*, when the soul is cast down with discomfort, let us think with ourselves, the Spirit of life in Christ is a quickening Spirit. If I can believe in Christ, he hath freed me from the guilt of sin; and he hath by his Spirit given me some little enlargement from the dominion of my corruptions: why should I be cast down? I am an heir of heaven. Ere long Satan shall 'be trodden under my feet,' Luke x. 19. Ere long I shall be free from the spiritual combat and conflict with sin, that I am now encountered with. Therefore I will comfort myself; I will not be cast down overmuch.

4. *In the hour of death*, let us make use of this freedom of the Spirit of life in Christ Jesus from the law of sin and death. When the time comes that there must be a separation of soul and body, Oh let us think with our ourselves: Now I must die, yet Christ hath died; and I must die in conformity to my head; and here is my comfort—'The law of the Spirit of life hath freed me from the law of death.' It hath freed me from spiritual and eternal death. So that now through Christ death is become friendly to me. Death now is not the death of me, but death will be the death of my misery, the death of my sins; it will be the death of my corruptions. Death now will be the death of all that before troubled me. But death will be my birthday in regard of happiness. 'Better is the day of death than the day of birth,' Eccles. vii. 1. When a man comes into this life he comes into misery; but when he dies, he goes out of misery and comes to happiness. So that, indeed, we never live till we die; we never live eternally and happily till then. For then we are freed from all misery and sin. 'Blessed are they that die in the Lord; they rest from their labours,' Rev. xiv. 13. They rest from their labours of toil and misery; they rest from the labours of sin, from all labours whatsoever. 'Blessed are they that die in the Lord,' and of all times then blessed, more blessed than before. They rest from their labours, and then begins their happiness that shall never end. So you see what comfort a Christian's soul sprinkled with the blood of Christ may have, if it go to God in Christ, and beg of Christ to be set at liberty from all enemies, to serve God in holiness and righteousness.

I speak too meanly when I say, the law of the Spirit of life hath freed us from sin and death. This is not all. The Spirit of life not only frees us from ill, but advanceth us to the contrary good in every thing wherein this freedom is. For we are not only called out of misery, but to a kingdom. We are not only freed from sin, but entitled to heaven in justification; and in sanctification we are not only freed from corruption, but enabled by the Holy Spirit of liberty to run the ways of God's commandments, and make them voluntary; to serve God cheerfully, 'zealous of good works,' Titus

ii. 14. We are not only freed from the command and condemnation of sin, and the rigour of the law, but we have contrary dispositions, ready and willing, and voluntary dispositions, wrought by the Spirit of Christ, to every thing that is good. And so we are not only free from death and misery (for so things without life are, they suffer no misery), but we are partakers of everlasting life and glory, the liberty of glory. God's benefits are complete; that is, not only privative, freeing us from ill, but positive, implying all good; because God will shew himself a God: he will do good things as a God, fully. For the law of the Spirit of life not only frees us from the law of sin and of death, but 'writes the law of God in our hearts.' He not only frees us from the law of death, but advanceth us to everlasting life, to the glorious life we have in heaven, 'to live for ever with the Lord,' 1 Thes. iv. 17. Oh happy condition of a Christian, if we could know our happiness!

Let us often meditate deeply of Christ, and of ourselves in him; let us see all our ill in him, and all our good in him: see death overcome, and sin overcome by his death, he being 'made a curse for us,' Gal. iii. 13: see the law overcome, he being 'made under the law for us,' Gal. iv. 4, 5. When the wrath of God vexeth and terrifieth us, see it upon him. 'He sweat water and blood in the garden,' Luke xxii. 44. It made him cry out, 'My God, my God, why hast thou forsaken me?' Mark xv. 34. See all that may trouble us in him, as our surety. And all the good we hope for, see it in Christ first. Whatsoever he hath in his natural body, it is for his mystical body; for he gave his natural body for his mystical. God in the world, to humble us, exerciseth us with troubles and calamities, as he did Christ. We must be conformable to our head. But consider, the poison and sting of all ills we need to fear is swallowed up and taken away by Christ. And, as I said, let us see all our good in him. We are sons in him, raised in him, blessed in him, 'set in heavenly places with him,' Eph. i. 3, and shall be fellow-heirs and kings with him; for we are his members, his spouse. The wife shall enjoy the same condition as the husband; whatsoever he hath she shall have. What a comfortable estate is this! We can fear no ill, nor want no good. Whatsoever he hath, it is for us. He was born for us. He died for us. He is gone to heaven for us; for us and our good. He did and suffered all these things. We cannot exercise our thoughts too much in these meditations.

The Lord's supper is a sacrament of union and communion. Hence it hath its name; and by receiving the sacrament, our communion and union with Christ is strengthened. What a comfort then is it to think, if I have fellowship with Christ it is sealed by the sacrament! When I take the bread and wine, at the same time I have communion with the body and blood of Christ shed for my sins; and as Christ himself was freed from my sins imputed to him, and by his resurrection declared that he was freed, so surely shall I be freed from my sins. So that this communion, taking the bread and wine, it seals to us our communion and fellowship with Christ, and thereupon our freedom from sin and from the law, and sets us in a blessed and happy estate. We should labour therefore by all means to strengthen our union and communion with Christ; and amongst the rest, reverently and carefully attend upon this blessed ordinance of God, for the body of Christ broken doth quicken us, because it is the body of the Son of God. 'My flesh is meat indeed, and my blood is drink indeed,' John vi. 55. And he calls his body broken 'the bread of life.' Why? Because it was the body of the Son of God, 'who is life,' John vi. 35. All life comes from God. Now, Christ taking our nature upon him, his death is a quickening death, and by reason of the union with the divine nature, now it is the body of God broken and the blood of God shed for us. There is our comfort; and he was declared to be so by his resurrection, that declared that he was God, and that he was freed from our sins. Powerful must that Saviour needs be that was so strong in his very death, when his very body was broken and his blood let out. Then he did work the foundation of all comfort, for then he satisfied the wrath of God. Christ was strongest when he was weakest. The resurrection was but a declaration of the worth of that he had done. Now, in the sacrament we have communion with Christ dying, especially as his body is broken and his blood shed, for that is the foundation of all comfort by his resurrection. And because the Spirit of life was in Christ, and did quicken his body while he was alive, and was a Spirit of life even when he died, and gave worth and excellency to his death, therefore, when we take the communion, we ought not to meditate merely of the death of Christ, as his blood was shed and his body broken, but of the death of such a person as had the Spirit of life in him, as was God and man. And so set the excellency of his person against all temptations whatsoever. Set the excellency of Christ so abased, his body broken and his blood shed, against all temptations. If it be the greatest, the wrath of God upon the conscience, yet when conscience thinks this, God, the party offended, gave his own Son to be incarnate, and the Spirit of life in him did quicken man's nature, and in that nature did die for satisfaction, now God will be satisfied by the death of such a surety as his own Son. So that the excellency of the person having the seal of God upon him, 'For him hath God the Father sealed,' John vi. 27, doth wondrously satisfy conscience in all temptations whatsoever. What need a man fear death, and damnation, and the miseries of this life, and Satan? What are all? If God be appeased and reconciled in Christ, then a man hath comfort, and may think of all other enemies as conquered enemies. Now, we cannot think of the death of Christ, who was a 'quickening Spirit,' but we must think of the death of an excellent person, that gave worth to his death, to be a satisfactory death for us. Therefore let us receive the communion with comfort, that as verily as Christ is mine, so his quickening Spirit is communicated to me, and whatsoever he hath is mine. If I have the field, I have the pearl in it; his obedience, his victory over death, his sonship, is mine; his sitting in heaven is for me; he sits there to rule me while I am on earth, and to take me up to himself when I am dead. All is for me. When we have communion with Christ we have communion with all. Therefore 'the Spirit of life in Christ Jesus,' when I am one with him, it quickens me, and 'frees me from the law of sin and death.'

NOTES.

(*a*) P. 226.—'The words are much vexed by expositors.' For a full exhibition of the 'vexing' of previous expositors, consult Willet's Hexapla, that is, 'A Sixfold Commentarie upon the most Divine Epistle of the holy Apostle St Paul to the Romans,' (folio, 1611); also Elton and Thomas Wilson of Canterbury, *in loc.* Of modern commentators, Hodge, and *practically*, Haldane.

(*b*) P. 232.—'You know whose speech it was, "If the land must be violated, it must be for a kingdom."' This is another of Sibbes's tacit allusions to Shakspeare, who puts into the mouth of Edward, in Third Part of King Henry VI. (Act i., Scene 2) the sentiment here noticed :—

'For a kingdom, any oath may be broken ;
I'd break a thousand oaths to reign one year.'

(*c*) P. 236.—'Saith a Roman, What! is it such a matter to die? It is nothing to die,' &c. A *sentiment* of Stoicism. What follows reminds us of the immortal soliloquy in Hamlet, of Sibbes's greatest contemporary, 'To be, or not to be,' &c.

G.

THE PRIVILEGES OF THE FAITHFUL.

THE PRIVILEGES OF THE FAITHFUL.

NOTE.

'The Privileges of the Faithful' forms the second half of the little volume entitled 'Yea and Amen. For the title-page and relative note, see Vol. IV. page 114.

G.

THE PRIVILEGES OF THE FAITHFUL.

Also we know that all things work together for the best to them that love God, even to them that are called of his purpose.—Rom. VIII. 28.

There are three things especially that trouble the life of a Christian, or at least should trouble the same.

1. The first whereof is *sin*, with the guilt and punishment thereof.

2. The second is the *corruption of nature*, which still abides in him, even after his vocation and conversion to Christ.

3. The third is, the *miseries and crosses of this life*, which do follow and ensue both upon sin and the evil thereof, as also by reason of that corruption of nature still remaining in him, after his recovered estate in grace.

For the first, the guilt of sin, which doth bind men over to death and damnation, that is forgiven to all believers in Christ Jesus, the 'second Adam.'

The second, which is the corruption of nature, which cleaves so fast to us, that is daily mortified and crucified in the saints by the word and Spirit of God.

For the third, which is the grievous crosses and afflictions, which do accompany and follow the guilt of sin and the corruption of nature still remaining ln God's children; however they are not taken away, yet they are made to have an excellent issue, 'for all things work together for the best unto them that love God.' So that these words of the apostle do afford us,

1. *A ground of patience.*

2. *A ground of comfort.*

In the former part of this chapter, the apostle had told us, 'that we know not how to pray as we ought, but that the Spirit itself doth teach us how to pray, and makes requests for us with sighs that cannot be expressed.' And therefore however our corruptions and miseries in this life are not quite taken away, yet the evil of those evils is removed, God teaching and directing us by his Spirit to seek, by prayer unto him, for grace to profit by them. And this is the coherence of these words with the former.

The parts here to be handled may be these.

1. *An excellent prerogative:* 'All things work together for the best.'

2. Secondly, *The persons to whom this prerogative belongs:* 'To them that love God,' and 'whom he doth call.'

3. Thirdly, *The main cause of this blessed prerogative.*

Those that 'love God' have this privilege belonging to them, because they are 'effectually called' by his word, 'according to his purpose.' We know, saith the apostle, 'that all things work together for the best to these.' He doth not say, 'we hope,' or 'we conjecture,' but 'we know it assuredly.'

We have the Scriptures of God for it. David saith, that 'it was good for him that he was afflicted,' Ps. cxix. 67, for thereby he had learned to reform his ways; he knew by observation that all things would tend to his future happiness. For he had seen in the example of Job, that notwithstanding his sore afflictions, yet he had a blessed issue out of all. He knew this many ways. He knew it by faith, as also by experience, that every thing should further the saints' well-being.

We know, that is, we only know it, who are 'led and taught of God,' and none but we can be assured hereof, which excludes the wicked, who shall never know any such thing. But what is it that Paul is confident of here? Namely, 'that all things work together for the best to them that love God.'

And this may serve to be a prevention of a question, which weak Christians might move in their troubles, and say, 'Never was any more afflicted than I am.' Why, saith the apostle, be it so. Yet, nevertheless, *all things whatsoever*, all thy crosses, vexations, and trials, 'shall work together' and join issue. Though they be averse one to the other, and opposite to the good of God's children, as Herod and Pilate were, yet all things thus contrary notwithstanding shall work for the best unto them. There is,

1. *A good of quality.*
2. *A good of estate.*

Quest. Now therefore what kind of good is this the apostle meaneth?

Ans. He doth not here mean the natural or civil good estate of them that love God, but their spiritual condition in grace, and their glorious estate for the life to come; for the furthering whereof, whatsoever befalls them in this life shall help forward still.

And thus much for the words themselves.

Doct. The first point to be spoken of is, *the excellent privilege of God's children*, 'that all things shall work together for the best;' both good and evil shall turn to their happiness. The reason stands thus: 'All things shall work together for the best to them that *love God*.' Therefore all afflictions, crosses, and vexations whatsoever, that betide such persons, shall work together for their good; and for this cause all God's servants must learn patiently to bear, and cheerfully to undergo poverty or riches, honour or dishonour, in this world.

That all good things do work for the best to God's servants, is most apparent by daily proof and experience.

1. To begin with the first chief good of all, which is *God the Father, who is goodness itself, and unspeakably comfortable to all his.* Do not all God's attributes conduce to our eternal welfare? Is he not set forth in Scripture under the sweet name of a 'Father,' of a 'Shield and Buckler,' of a 'Tower of defence,' of an 'all-sufficient and almighty God,' 'just, wise, provident, merciful,' full of boundless compassion, and all to support his poor creatures from failing before him?

As he is our 'Father,' he is careful of us above the care of earthly parents to their children; as he is a 'Shield,' so he shelters us from all wrongs; as he is 'God almighty and all-sufficient,' so his power and bounty serve to sustain us in this world, and reserve us for ever safe in the world to come. His 'wisdom' makes us wise to prevent the politic plots of the devil or wicked men; his justice and providence, they serve to defend us in our right, to provide for us in all our wants, and prevent the evils of the ungodly intended against us; his power is ours, to keep us; his providence, to dispose all things for our advantage. Everything in God shall co-work to provide and foresee all good for us, and mercifully to impart and bestow whatsoever is behoveful upon us. So that God being our Father, we have right and title to his love, mercy, power, justice, truth, faithfulness, providence, wisdom, and all-sufficiency: all which 'shall ever work together for the best to them that love his appearing.'

2. So for *Jesus Christ, the eternal Son of God.* All his glorious titles and attributes serve likewise for the everlasting comfort of his poor saints on earth. He is called the 'husband of his church,' to cherish and maintain the same. His love unto his church is far above the love of any husband to his wife. He is called the 'Saviour of the world,' because he 'so loved the world, that he gave his life for it,' Gal. ii. 20, and hath promised, 'that whosoever believeth on him shall not perish,' 2 Peter iii. 9. He is called the 'Fountain of life,' the 'Well of life,' the 'Water of life,' the 'Bread of life,' the 'Way, the Truth and the Life,' because that in him is our life, and by him we are fed and nourished to eternal life. Here in him we obtain the life of grace, and in the world to come shall for ever enjoy the life of glory.

3. So likewise for the *Holy Ghost.* What heavenly attributes are ascribed to him in the Scriptures! He is called 'the Comforter' of God's servants; the 'Sealer of the redemption of God's children in their hearts. He teacheth the elect to call God Father; he 'beareth witness with their spirits that they are the sons and daughters of God;' he teacheth them 'to pray as they ought;' 'he fills them with peace that passeth all understanding,' and refreshes their spirits with such unspeakable joy as eye hath not seen, nor ear heard the like.* He that is instructed by the Spirit knoweth the things of God, which a natural man is ignorant of. The Holy Ghost doth call to remembrance the doctrine of God taught unto his servants, and writes the same in their hearts;† so that the operations of the blessed Spirit are all appropriated to them that 'love God,' and they alone have their right in them. The direction, comfort, teaching, and guiding of the Spirit of God do serve entirely and peculiarly to order and work all things together for the best to the godly.

4. Yea, the angels themselves are called 'messengers and ministering spirits,' appointed by God to attend and wait upon his servants. 'He gives his angels charge over these, to serve them in all their ways, and to pitch their tents round about them,' Ps. xxxiv. 7. Whensoever God pleaseth to call any of his out of this world, the angels are a safe conduct, to carry their souls into 'Abraham's bosom.' And at the 'last judgment,' the Lord shall send forth his angels 'to gather his elect,' Mat. xxiv. 31, from one end of the world to the other, that they may fully enjoy that which they have long waited for, even eternal bliss and glory.

5. Under the angels *all other creatures are likewise made serviceable for his people's good.* Princes in authority are called in Scripture 'nursing fathers

* It has not been thought necessary to encumber and confuse the text with specific references to these and like fragmentary citations of familiar titles and designations from Holy Scripture.—G.

† Cf. John xiv. 26, Jer. xxxi. 33.—G

and nursing mothers' unto the church of Christ, Isa. xlix. 23, the end of all magistracy being that we might live religiously and peaceably in all the ways of God.

6. *Ministers also are styled in the word by the names of* 'watchmen and seedsmen,' and 'spiritual fathers,' to beget men again to the kingdom of heaven. They are called 'God's husbandmen,' to manure and till his ground. They are called 'God's lights,' and 'the salt of the earth,' both to enlighten the church with the light of the glorious gospel whereof they are ministers, and to season them with such savoury and sweet instructions as may make them wise to salvation: this being the very end of all God's giving gifts to men, that they might build up the church of Christ here below.

7. So also *the word of God* is called the 'savour of life, and 'the power of God unto salvation.' It is 'the seed of God,' which being sown in the hearts of God's children, springeth up in them to everlasting happiness. God's word is a 'light and a lantern' to guide and direct us in all his ways.* It is the sword of the Spirit, to arm us against sin and to maintain us in grace.

8. *The sacraments likewise are the seals of life and pledges of our salvation in Christ;* and excommunication, though it be rough, and the extremest censure of the church (and therefore ought to be undertaken upon weighty grounds), yet the end of it is, to save the souls of God's people, and to make them by repentance turn unto him.

9. *So all outward gifts*, as beauty, strength, riches, and honours, these are given by God to serve for the good of his children. As the beauty of Esther was an instrument of her preferment, whereby she became a preservation to God's children, and an overthrow of her and their enemies: [and as] Joseph's outward honours and wealth were made by God's disposing hand a means of the preservation and nourishment of the Israelites, in the time of their great extremity and famine; the like may be said of learning and other natural acquirements, all which do often tend to general and public advantages.

10. Yea, *the outward gifts of God, which are bestowed upon reprobates, are still for the good of his;* for they who had skill and knowledge to build Noah's ark, though they themselves were not saved therein, yet were they the means of Noah's preservation;† and so it many times falleth out, that men of excellent parts and great abilities without grace, though themselves are not profited thereby, yet God so useth them as their gifts much conduce to further and build up the church of Christ.

11. Even *outward favour of princes* oft tend to God's servants' good. 'A just man,' as the heathens could say, 'is a common benefit.' And so a true Christian, whatsoever good he hath, it is communicable to all the faithful; and therefore St Paul saith of himself that 'he was a debtor to all men, both Jews and Gentiles,' Rom. i. 14; and that he 'became all things to all men, that he might win some,' 1 Cor. ix. 22.

But here the main question will be, and the difficulty arises, how all ill things can work together for the best to God's children. I shall therefore demonstrate,

1. The truth of this, *how it can be so*.
2. The reasons *why it is so*.

* Cf. 2 Cor. ii. 16, Rom. i. 16, Luke viii. 11, Ps. cxix. 105.—G.

† This thought has been enlarged upon very effectively, in a popular American tract entitled 'Noah's Carpenters.'—G.

3. Observe a *caution*, that it be not abused.

4. Let us see the *sweet and comfortable use* of this doctrine.

That this may the better appear, we must know that all evil things are either—

1. *Spiritual evil things.*
2. *Outward evil things.*

And for spiritual evil things, they are either, first, sin; secondly, that which hath a reference to sin, as being evils following after sin.

1. *The first sin of all*, which hath gone over whole mankind, and is spread abroad in every one of us, this by God's mercy and our repentance proves to all believers a transcendent good; for the fall and sin of the first Adam caused the birth and death of the 'second Adam,' Christ Jesus; who, notwithstanding he was God, took upon him the nature of man, and hath made us by his coming far more happy than if we had never fallen. Neither would God have suffered Adam to have fallen but for his own further glory, in the manifestation of his justice and mercy, and for the greater felicity of his servants in Christ their mediator.

2. The next spiritual evil is the *corruption of nature* remaining in all mankind; howsoever broken and subdued in the Lord's dear ones. This worketh for the best to them after this manner.

(1.) First, *It serveth to make us see and know we are kept by God;* how that we are not the keepers of our own selves, 'but are kept by his power through faith unto salvation,' 1 Pet. i. 5. For were it not that God upholds and sustains us, our corruptions would soon overturn us; but the sight of corruption being sanctified to the soul, causeth us to ground our comfort out of ourselves in Christ, and no whit to rely on anything that is in us.

(2.) Our corruptions are also good *to abase the pride of our natures, and let us see the naughtiness of our spirits, that we may be humbled before God.*

(3.) And it is good we should have something within us *to make us weary of the world;* else, when we have run out our race, we be unwilling to depart hence. Now our bondage to this natural corruption serves exceedingly to make us mourn for our sinful disposition, and hunger after our God, to be joined with him; as we see in St Paul's example, Rom. vii. 24, where, finding the rebellion of his nature and the strife that was in him, the flesh lusting against the spirit and the spirit against the flesh, he cries out, saying, 'O wretched man that I am! who shall deliver me from this body of death?' and seeketh to God in Christ for mercy straight.

(4.) Sometimes God suffers corruption to break out of us, *that we may know ourselves the better:* and because corruption is weakened, not only by smothering, but many times by having a vent, whereupon grace stirs up in the soul a fresh hatred and revenge against it, and lets us see a necessity of having whole Christ, not only to pardon sin, but to purge and cleanse our defiled natures. But yet that which is ill itself must not be done for the good that comes by it by accident; this must be a comfort after our surprisals, not an encouragement before.

(5.) It is our great consolation *that our nature is perfect in Christ*, who hath taken our nature upon him, and satisfied divine justice, not only for the sin of our lives, but for the sin of our natures, who will finish his own work in us, and never give over till by his Spirit he hath made our natures holy and pure as his own; till he hath taken away, not only the reign, but the very life and being of sin out of our hearts. To which end he leaves his Spirit and truth in the church to the end of the world, that the seed of the Spirit may subdue the seed of the serpent in us, and that the Spirit may be a never-failing spring of all holy thoughts, desires, and endeavours in us, and dry up the contrary issue and spring of corrupt nature.

(6.) Lastly, It is good that corruption should still remain in us, *that the glory of God may the more appear, whenas Satan, that great and strong enemy of mankind, shall be foiled and overturned by a weak and poor Christian, who is full of corruptions;* and that through the strength of faith, though mixed with much distrust. For a Christian in the state of sin and corruption to overcome the great adversary of mankind, what a wonderment is it! It tendeth much to the shame and dishonour of that 'fiery dragon,' that weak and sinful man should be his conqueror. Oh how it confounds him, to think that 'a grain of mustard seed,' Mat. xiii. 31, should be stronger than the gates of hell; that it should be able to 'remove mountains of oppositions and temptations cast up by Satan and our rebellious hearts between God and us. Abimelech could not endure that it should be said 'a woman had slain him,' Judges ix. 53; and it must needs be a torment to Satan that a weak child, a decrepit old man, should by a spirit of faith put him to flight.

3. A third kind of spiritual ill of sin are *the things that issue out of this cursed stock;* and those are either inward or outward. For inward sins, they are either errors or doubtings, or pride or wrath, or such like.

1. And first, *for doubtings* of the truth. This makes God's servants often more resolute to seek and search out the same, and to stand afterwards more firm and courageous for it. For if we doubted not of things, we should not afterwards be put out of doubt, nor seek to be better grounded and instructed in them. The Corinthians doubted once of the resurrection, but were ever after better resolved in that doctrine, the benefit whereof hath much redounded to the church's good ever since. Thomas had the like wavering disposition, but this doubting more manifested the truth. Luther being a monk at the first, and not fully grounded in the doctrine of the gospel, did therefore suspect himself the more, and wished all men after him to read his writings warily (*a*). The doctrine of the Trinity hath formerly been much doubted of, and therefore hath been with the greater pains and study of worthy men then living in the church more evidently proved. And when the Pelagians grew into heresies, they were by St Augustine gainsaid, and very strongly withstood. So the doctrine of the Church of Rome, being branched into divers erroneous opinions, and broached to the great hurt and prejudice of Christians, hath occasioned the truth of God against them to be the more excellently cleared and made known. For when religion is oppugned, it is time then 'to hold fast,' as the apostle St Jude saith, 'with both hands the word, and to fight for the faith' (*b*), that so we may know both what to hold, and upon what ground we oppose heresy.

2. Now for *inward sins*, as anger, covetousness, distrust, and such like, these often prove advantageous to the saints. Their corruptions are a means of their humiliation. Paul and Barnabas having a breach between them, were so exasperated that they forsook each other's company, by which means it came to pass that the church was more instructed than before.* And hence we may see what the best men are in themselves. If Luther had had no infirmities, how would men have attributed to him above measure? As we see, they were ready to sacrifice to Paul and Barnabas; which shews us that even the distempers and weaknesses of God's servants are disposed by divine providence to their eternal welfare.

* Cf. Acts xv. 39 with 2 Tim. iv. 11.—G.

3. Yea, God often suffereth his children to fall into some *outward gross sins*, that by means thereof they might be humbled and abased, and in the end be cured of that provoking sin of being proud in spirit.

4. *The falling of God's children doth much deject them, and bring them upon their knees with shame.* It makes them gentle and meek in the reprehension of their brethren; for having slipped out of the way themselves, and being by repentance recovered, they learn to 'restore others with the spirit of meekness,' as the apostle speaks, Gal. vi. 1. A man humbled by experience of sin in himself will soon relent at the fall of others. Those oftentimes prove the most excellent instruments in the church who have formerly been overtaken with some gross sin, by means whereof they have ever after been much abased in their own eyes.

We see David, Paul, and Peter fell grievously, but being afterwards raised again and finding comfort themselves, they were a great means of strengthening others; for he which teacheth out of his own experience and feeling, is the fittest and best teacher of all. So it was with Jonah: when by casting him into the sea God had humbled him, he was fit to preach repentance to Nineveh. This is a most certain truth, that never any of God's elect fell grievously, but he was the better all the days of his life for his fall. David having been thoroughly humbled for sin, when Shimei his subject cursed him to his face, how patiently did he bear the same, 2 Sam. xvi. 13, *seq.* So Peter having denied his Master, and afterwards recovering himself again, we see how zealous he was for his Lord Christ, and suffered death for him.

5. Furthermore, not only the sins of God's children, which they themselves commit, do work for their best, *but also the sins of others of the saints with whom they converse and live*, do much tend to their good and welfare. Do not the falls of David, Peter, Manasseh, and Paul comfort the distressed and despairing souls of such as languish and are ready to faint under the burden of their sins? And do not the registry of their sins in Scripture give hope to us that God will be merciful to our sins also? We may not think it is God's will to set upon perpetual record the sins of his servants for their shame, disgrace, and punishment, but for our comfort, who live and remain to the end of the world. And the faults of the saints have two excellent uses, whereof the one is for comfort, the other for instruction.

Use 1. The use in regard of comfort is this. *God hath shewed mercy to David, Paul, Peter, and others, sinning grievously against him, and repenting of the same.* Therefore if I also shall sin and truly repent as they did, surely God is where he was, as full of mercy and readiness to forgive now as ever.

Use 2. The second use for instruction is this: *If such excellent and eminent saints by sin have fallen grievously, how then much more are we poor weak souls subject to fall if we neglect watchfulness over ourselves!* If a weak Christian, oft assaulted with temptations, should not see the falls and slips of God's worthier servants, he would be in a wonderful desperation, and cry out of himself, saying, Alas! what shall I do; never was any so assaulted and tempted, so cast down and overcome in temptations as I am; and therefore my case is more fearful and worse than ever was any. But when he considereth the grievous falls of God's special servants, how they have stepped aside foully and yet obtained mercy, by their examples he beginneth to be revived and receive inward comfort, whereby it is evident that all sins whatsoever of God's elect, as vile and as loathsome as they are, do by

God's providence and our own serious repentance turn to their good, and the good of those with whom they live.

4. The next spiritual evil is that which followeth after sin committed, viz., *God's desertion* or forsaking of us, when he seems to hide his favour from men after they have sinned against him. When God manifests himself as an enemy to his people, this grieves them more than anything else in the world beside. We see David, how he calls upon God not to 'rebuke him in his wrath, nor forsake him in his displeasure,' Ps. vi. 1, where he sheweth how grievously he was afflicted with the anger of the Almighty.

But albeit that God doth seem sometimes to forsake his servants, it is not for their confusion, but for their consolation; for by this means they come to be poor in spirit, and wonderfully emptied of themselves. And it is very observable that when such as are thoroughly wounded and afflicted inwardly come to recover strength and peace again, they often prove the most comfortable Christians of all others, walking with more care to avoid offence all their lives after.

Christ Jesus himself, though he never sinned, but only stood as a surety in our room to pay the ransom of our debts, seemed to be forsaken of God his Father; and because he was thus humbled, therefore he was after most highly exalted above all, both in heaven and in earth. So Job seemed to be forsaken, and doth grievously bemoan his miseries; but this was not because he had sinned against God more grievously than others had done, but for the trial of his faith and patience, to give him experience of God's love to him in the cross, that he might cleave the closer to his Maker all his time after.

5. Another evil arising from the guiltiness of sin is *anguish of mind* and *a wounded spirit*, 'which,' saith Solomon, 'who can bear?' Prov. xviii. 14. But for all this, grief for sin is an happy grief, yea, a grief never to be grieved for. This wound in spirit breedeth afterwards a sound spirit. Repentance is good, and faith in Christ is good. But what doth prepare us to these happy graces? Is it not a wounded spirit? Who would ever repent of his sins, and lay hold on Christ for remission of the same, if he were not pricked and pierced in the sense thereof. Christ professeth himself to be a physician, but to whom? 'To the lost sheep of Israel,' Mat. xv. 24. He promiseth ease and refreshment, but to whom? 'To them that are weary, and laden with the burden of their sins.' 'The Spirit of the Lord was upon him, that he might preach the gospel to the poor,' Isa. lxi. 2, and 'he was sent to heal the broken hearted, that he might preach deliverance to the captives, and recovering of sight to the blind, and set at liberty them that are bruised,' Luke iv. 18.

6. Again, Divers Christians do walk very heavily and uncomfortably, by *reason of inward tentations, and blasphemous imaginations*, which oft are suggested and enter into their minds; but these sins which so vex the souls of poor Christians, are a means of their humiliation, causing them to sue more earnestly to God for pardon. And these sinful corruptions do further serve for a testimony to themselves, that they are not under the power of Satan, but live in the kingdom of grace; for if they were captived to the devil, and under his government, then would he never molest and vex them, but suffer them quietly to live and die in their sins; but because they are from under his rule and jurisdiction, therefore he perplexeth and troubleth them all he can. By which it is evident, that all sins, by God's mercy and our repentance, 'do work together for the best unto us.'

7. Yea, the circumstances of sin, *as continuance therein*, which much

aggravates the sin; when such a one truly repents and is restored to Christ, it maketh him more zealous and watchful ever after; as we see in Paul, and the thief on the cross, who finding favour, acknowledgeth his worthiness of punishment, reprehendeth his fellow on the cross, and justifieth Christ to have done all things well; and so giving glory unto God, and crying for mercy, receiveth a comfortable promise of an heavenly kingdom, Luke xxiii. 43. All things are possible to God. We can never be so ill as he is powerful and good; God can bring contrary out of contrary. He hath promised to pour clean water upon us, Ezek. xxxvi. 25, which faith sues out, and remembers that Christ hath taken upon him to purge his spouse, and make her fit for himself.

8. Further, *the very relapses and backslidings* of God's servants into sin do not argue no repentance, but a weak repentance; and therefore when they are again rebuked and turned from sin, their relapses do make them set upon the service of God more strongly, and run more constantly in his ways. Where true grace is, sin loses strength by every new fall; for hence issues deeper humility, stronger hatred of evil, fresh indignation against ourselves, more experience of the deceitfulness of our hearts, and renewed resolutions till sin be brought under. Adam lost all by once sinning, but we are under a better covenant, a covenant of mercy, and are encouraged to go to God every day for the sins of that day.

For it is not with God as it is with men, who being offended will scarce be reconciled, but God offended still offereth mercy. He is not only ready to receive us when we return, but persuades and entreats us to come unto him; yea, after backsliding and false dealing with him, wherein he allows no mercy to be shewed by man, yet he will take liberty to shew mercy himself, as in Jeremiah, 'If a man have an adulterous wife, and shall put her away, and she become another man's, he will not receive her any more to him.' But saith the Lord, 'Thou hast played the harlot with many lovers, yet turn again unto me,' Jer. iii. 1; 'for I am merciful, and my wrath shall not fall upon you: I will not always keep mine anger,' ver. 12. 'Though your sins be as crimson, they shall be white as snow, and though they be red like scarlet, they shall be as white as wool,' Isa. i. 18; 'if ye will turn to me, and wash ye, and make ye clean, and cease to do evil, and learn to do well,' ver. 16, 17. So Rev. ii. 4, Christ speaking to the church of Ephesus, saith, 'She hath fallen from her first love;' but saith he, 'Remember from whence thou art fallen, and repent, and do thy first works, and I will receive thee to favour;' by which we see that the relapses of God's elect, as they do not finally hinder mercy from their souls, so notwithstanding the same, they are still encouraged to return to God, to renew their covenant by faith and repentance, and cleave more strongly to him.

8. As for *outward evils*, they are, first, evils of *estate*, as want and poverty, which oft falls out to be the portion of God's children, yet are they not any whit the worse hereby, but rather the better in their inner man; for the less they have in this world, the greater and larger happiness shall they partake of in another world. What they lose one way is supplied another. Whatsoever comfort we have in goods or friends below. it is all conveyed from God above, who still remains, though these be taken away. The saints see, that if to preserve the dearest thing in the world, they break with God, he can make it a dead contentment and a torment to them; whereas, if we care to preserve communion with God, we shall be sure to find in him, whatsoever we deny for him, honour, riches, pleasures,

friends, all; so much the sweeter, by how much we have them more immediately from the spring-head. Our riches, and friends, and life itself, may soon depart. But God never loseth his right in us, nor we our interest in him. Every thing beneath teaches us, by the vanity and vexation we find in them, that our happiness is not there; they send us to God; they may make us worse, but better they cannot. Our nature is above them, and ordained for a greater good. They can but go along with us for a while, and their end swallows up all the comfort of their beginning.

Besides, none have that experience of God's goodness and faithfulness, as those that are in want and misery. God in his wisdom foreseeing what is best for his servants, knows that the more worldly wealth they do abound in, the less their estimation would be of heavenly things. He sees how apt the poor creature is to be carried away with present comfort, and to have his love drawn to the world from better contentments. The poorer they are in worldly riches, the more they seek to be rich in grace, in knowledge, faith, and repentance, which heavenly treasures incomparably surmount the most transcendent excellency which the creature can yield.

9. As for the evil of losing *a good name*, a thing oft befalling the children of God, to be slandered and evil spoken of, they upon every small disgrace take occasion to enter into themselves and try whether they be guilty of such hard imputations as are flung upon them.

And if upon a serious consideration he find himself disgraced for good things, he wears it as a crown and as a garland upon his head, 'rejoicing that he is accounted worthy to suffer for the Lord Jesus,' Acts v. 41, esteeming 'the rebukes of Christ greater treasure than the riches of Egypt,' Heb. xi. 26. A true believer resigns his good name, and all that he hath, to God. He is assured that no man can take away that from him which God will give him and keep for him. It is not in man's power to make others conceive what they please of us.

10. For the evils *of body*, such as sickness and diseases of all sorts, which daily attend our houses of clay, God by means hereof acquaints his children with their frail condition, and shews them what a little time they have to provide for eternity, thereby driving them to search their evidences, and to make all straight betwixt him and them. Outward weaknesses are oft a means to restrain men from inward evils. God usually sanctifies the pains and griefs of his servants to make them better. The time of sickness is a time of purging from that defilement we gathered in our health. We should not be cast down so much for any bodily distemper, as for sin, that procures and envenoms the same. That is a good sickness which tends to the health of the soul. Naaman, the Assyrian, if he had not had a leprosy in his body, had continued a leper, both in body and soul, all his days: his outward grievances made him inwardly sound. The very heathen could say, that we are then best in soul when we are weakest in body (*c*), for then we are most in heavenly resolutions and seeking after God. Yea, then it appears what good proficients we have been in time of health. Oh how happy were our conditions, if we were as good when we are well and in health, as we usually are when we are sick and ill.

11. *Even death itself*, which is the end of all, though it be fearful and irksome to nature, yet it is to God's servants a bed of down, easing them of all their miseries, and putting them in possession of an heavenly kingdom; therefore saith Solomon, 'The day of death is better than the day of birth,' Eccles. vii. 1. God will be the God of his, not only unto death, but in death. Death is the death of itself, and not of us. It is a disarmed

and conquered enemy to all the faithful; for which cause St Paul desired to be dissolved and to be with Christ, which is best of all, Philip. i. 23. Death, albeit it seems terrible and dreadful, yet the sting thereof being taken away by the death of Christ, it brings everlasting joy along with it, and is only as a groom* porter to let us in to a stately palace. Whither tend all the troubles we meet with in this world, but only to fit us for a better condition hereafter, and to assure the soul that when earth can hold it no longer, heaven shall.

12. Yea, *when friends forsake us, and are false unto us*, 'God is a sure help in time of need,' Ps. xxxvii. 39. He is our refuge from one generation to another. Do we not see that in the decay of worldly comforts, God then manifests himself most comfortably to his people? Doth he not style himself 'the comforter of the comfortless, and the help of them that are in distress;' and do not 'with him the fatherless find mercy?' Ps. x. 14. If men were more fatherless, they would find more mercy at God's hands. As Christ makes us all to him, so should we make him 'all in all' to ourselves. If all comforts in the world were dead, we have them still in the living Lord. How many friends have we in him alone, who, rather than we shall want friends, can make our enemies our friends? Thus it appears that all miseries are a trial of us to God and to the world, what we are. They are a cure of sin past, and a preparation to endure further crosses. They have many excellent uses and ends, and all for the best to God's servants.

It is good we should be exercised with present crosses, to put us in mind of the evils we have done long ago, that so we may repent of them. Joseph's brethren, being afflicted and imprisoned, called to mind how hardly they had dealt with their brother long before, Gen. xlii. 21. It should be our wisdom, while we remain here, to consider our warfaring† condition; how we are daily environed with enemies, and therefore ought to stand continually upon our guard against Satan and the powers of darkness, and as pilgrims and strangers go on in our journey to heaven: not starting at the barking of every dog, nor entangling ourselves in worldly things, whereby we should be stopped in our way.

It is for our best, not to be condemned with the world. Afflictions serve for this very end, to make us more prize God, and deny the creature with all its excellencies. Are our crosses great here? Let us not be daunted, but bear them patiently: our comfort shall be the greater afterwards. It is not only good for us that we should have crosses, but that they should be continued upon us, that we may the better know ourselves. If all were well with a man wounded, and the sore clean healed, the plaster would fall off itself. So, were we thoroughly cured of our spiritual wants, and in a continual resistance of every evil way, these afflictions, which are the plasters of our souls, would soon cease and leave us.

13. Furthermore, *Satan himself and all his instruments, when they most set themselves against God's people, and seek their overthrow, then are they working their chief good.* The devil, when he thought to make an end of Christ by putting him to death, even then, by that very thing, was vanquished himself, and the church of God fully ransomed from hell and damnation. God suffers many heretics to be in the world; but why? Not that the truth should be held in darkness; but that it might thereby be more manifested and known. It is Satan's continual trade, to seek his rest in our disquiet. When he sees men will to heaven, and that they have good title to it, then he follows them with all temptations and discomforts

* Qu. 'grim'?—G. † Qu. 'wayfaring'?—Ed.

that he can. He cannot endure that a creature of meaner rank than himself should enjoy a happiness beyond him; but our comfort is, that Christ was tempted, that he might succour all poor souls in the like case. We are kept by 'his power, through faith unto salvation,' 1 Pet. i. 5.

Now, the causes why all things do work together for the best to them that love God are these, viz.:—

1. It is God's *decree.*
2. It is God's *manner of working.*
3. It is God's *blessed covenant.*
4. It is the *foundation of the covenant of Christ Jesus.*

1. *God's decree and purpose is,* of bringing all his elect unto eternal salvation; and therefore all things in heaven and earth must conduce to bring his servants unto glory. The reason is this, God is infinitely wise and infinitely strong, provident, and good; therefore by his infinite wisdom, power, providence, and mercy he turneth all things to the best for his. Whatsoever is in heaven, earth, or hell, is ordered by God, neither is there anything without him; therefore nothing can hinder his decree. Satan himself, with all his instruments, yea, the worst of creatures, all must serve God's purpose, contrary to their natures, for the good of his children. The prophet saith, 'God hath commanded salvation, and he hath commanded deliverance to Jacob,' Ps. xliv. 4. When God hath determined to save any man, all things must needs serve him that overrules all things. As it was said of Christ when he stilled the seas, 'Who is this, that the very wind and seas obey him?' Mat. viii. 27. God commanded the whale to serve at his beck to save Jonah, and it obeyed. All creatures in the earth are at his disposing, and serve to accomplish his pleasure.

2. The second cause why all works together for the best to believers, *is the manner of God working in things,* which is by contraries. He bringeth light out of darkness, glory out of shame, and life out of death. We fell by pride to hell and destruction, and must be restored by humiliation to life and salvation. Christ humbled himself, being God, to become man for us, and by his death restored us to life. When our sins had brought us to greatest extremities, even then were we nearest to eternal happiness. Therefore saith the apostle, 'When we are weak, then are we strong in the Lord,' 2 Cor. xii. 10. When we are abased, then are we readiest to be exalted; when we are poor, then are we most rich; and when we are dead, then do we live. For God worketh all by contraries. He lets men see his greatness and his goodness, that so they may admire his works and give more glory to him. He worketh without means, and above means, and against means. Out of misery he bringeth happiness, and by hell bringeth men to heaven; which, as it manifesteth God's glory to his creatures, so it serveth for the confusion of man's pride, that he may discern he is nothing in himself, but is all that he is in the Lord.

3. The third cause why all things work for the best to them that fear God is, *God's covenant with his church:* when once this gracious covenant is made, that 'he will be their God, and they shall be his people,' Lev. xxvi. 12; that he will 'be their Father and protector,' must not all things then needs serve for their good? Whenas God tells Abraham, 'I am thy God, all-sufficient; only walk before me, and be thou perfect,' Gen. xvii. 1, doth not this engage him to set his power and mercy, his wisdom and providence, all on work for the happy estate of Abraham? When once God by his promise is become our God, there is a covenant betwixt us and the creatures; yea, and the stones in the street, that nothing shall wrong

us, but all conduce to our good. The angels are ours; their service is for our protection, safety, and welfare. Heaven and earth is ours, and all things in them for our behoof. Christ himself, and together with him, all things else are become ours; in him we are heirs of all. What a wondrous comfort is this, that God hath put himself over to be ours; whom to enjoy is to possess all things, and to want is misery inexpressible. Had we all the world without God, it would prove a curse and no blessing to us; whereas if we have nothing and enjoy God, we have happiness itself for our portion. If we have no better portion here than these things, we are like to have hell for our portion hereafter. Let God be in any condition, though never so ill, yet it is comfortable. He is goodness itself. And, indeed, nothing is so much a Christian's as God is *his;* because by his being ours in covenant, all other things become *ours*, and therefore they cannot but co-operate for our good.

'When thou art in the fire and water, I am with thee,' saith God, Isa. xliii. 2. And 'Thou art my buckler, my glory, and shield; therefore I will not be afraid though ten thousand of people shall beset me round about,' saith David, Ps. xci. 7; for 'salvation belongeth unto the Lord.' And if God be on our side, who can be against us? 'If God justify us, who shall condemn us?' Rom. viii. 34. Can anything hurt us when he is become our loving Father? Neither 'death, nor life, nor things present, nor things to come, nor principalities, nor powers, nor anything whatsoever, can separate us from his love toward us,' ver. 35.

4. A fourth ground why all things fall out for the best to the saints is, *the foundation of this covenant of God with his church*, which is *Christ Jesus*, who by his blood hath purchased our peace. He being God became man, and is the sole author of all our comfort. Without Christ God is 'a consuming fire,' Heb. xii. 29; but in him, a most 'loving Father,' and 'ever well pleased.' God promiseth in Christ his Son 'to marry his people unto himself for ever; yea,' saith he, 'I will marry thee unto me in righteousness, and in judgment, and in mercy, and everlasting compassion,' Isa. lxii. 5, and liv. 8. Now upon this blessed contract made in Christ to his church, what followeth? 'In that day,' saith the Lord, 'I will hear the heavens, and they shall hear the earth: and the earth shall hear the corn, and the wine, and the oil; and they shall hear Israel: and I will have mercy upon her that was not pitied; and I will say unto them which were not my people, Thou art my people; and they shall say, Thou art my God,' Hosea ii. 22, 23. Where we see what is the reason of all their happiness; even this, that God will marry them to himself. So that this marriage worketh all our bliss; our conjunction with Christ, and reconciliation through his death, is the cause of all our comfort; in him we have the adoption of sons. Hence it is that we are at peace with God, and have freedom from all harms. Christ in his greatest reproach and deepest humiliation had his greatest triumph and exaltation. In his death on the cross he vanquished death, and entered into eternal life. When Christ came into the world, and took upon him our nature, even then the greatest monarch in the world, Augustus Cæsar, was at his command; whom he so ordered as that by his causing all the world to be taxed, Christ was manifested to be born at 'Bethlehem in Jewry,' Luke ii. 1.

How cometh it to pass that death, which is fearful in itself, cannot hurt us? The reason is, 'Death is swallowed up in victory' by his death, 1 Cor. xv. 54. It is Christ that sanctifieth all crosses, afflictions, and disgraces to the saints' advantage. The evil of them all is taken away by him, and turned to his people's good. How cometh it to pass that the law cannot hurt us, which pronounceth a curse against every one that abideth not in all things written therein, to do them? The reason is, 'Christ was made a curse for us; he was made under the law, that he might redeem us who were under the law,' Gal. iii. 13; and thus is Christ a meritorious and deserving cause of procuring all good to us, and removing all ill from us.

He doth not only overcome evil *for* us, but also overcometh evil *in* us, and gives us his Spirit, which unites us to himself; whereby we have ground to expect good out of every ill, as knowing that whatsoever Christ wrought for the good of mankind, he did it for us in particular.

In outward favours grace makes us acknowledge all the blessings we have to be the free gifts of God, and invites us to return the glory to him.

God's servants take all occasions and opportunities of doing good, by those gifts and abilities wherewith they are endowed. When Esther was advanced to great honour, Mordecai told her that God had conferred that dignity upon her for his people's welfare, that she might be a means of their safety. Whereas, on the contrary, a proud heart, destitute of the Spirit of Christ, ascribes all to itself, waxeth more haughty, and grows worse and worse the more good he enjoys.

A gracious soul, upon the sight of the evil of sin in itself, is more deeply humbled before God, and with St Paul crieth out of his wretchedness, Rom. vii. 24. A heavenly-minded man being smitten for his wickedness, laboureth for subjection under the hand of the Almighty, and saith, 'I will patiently abide and endure thy correction, because thou, Lord, hast done it,' Ps. lii. 9. When the gracious man is held under the cross, and suffereth bitter things, he saith, 'It is good for me that I am afflicted, for thereby I am taught to know thee,' Ps. cxix. 67. In all troubles that befall him, he professeth that 'it is good for him to cleave unto God.' And the less outward wealth he hath, the more he seeks for inward grace, making a holy use of all things.

Upon these instructions hence delivered, let us take a view of ourselves, and try whether we in our afflictions are such as cleave to God, and are drawn nearer to him thereby. Call to mind the crosses wherewith God hath exercised thee, and the blessings which at any time he hath bestowed upon thee, and see how in both thou hast been bettered; see what profitable use thou hast made thereof for thy soul's comfort.

Let us see how we have followed the providence of God in his dealing with us; for if we have an interest in his goodness, then will we be careful, as God turns all things for our good, so to follow the same, together with him, for the good of our souls.

Obj. Now, because things do not *always* conduce to the good of God's children, as outward peace and prosperity oftentimes make them worse, therefore some may object, how can this be true which here the apostle saith, 'that all things do work together for the best to them that love God?'

Ans. 1. The answer hereunto is, *That for the most part the children of God do take the good of the blessings which God bestows on them, and avoid the snares of evil which accompany the same.* Job saith, 'The things I feared are come upon me.' By which we see, that Job in the midst of all his prosperity did fear and was jealous over himself, Job iii. 25.

2. But a more plainer answer of the objection is, *That if the good things of God, as peace, plenty, and prosperity, do fall out at the first to their ill, yet, nevertheless, they shall prove in the end a great gain unto them;* for whereas

by occasion of these they formerly fell (having too high an estimation of the creature, and overprizing the same), they see *now* more into their nature, and learn to contemn them.

3. Again, *The outward good things of this life shew the weakness of God's servants, and serve to try what is in them;* and therefore we read of Hezekiah, that God left him 'to try what was in him,' 2 Chron. xxxii. 31. The outward treasure which he had was a means to make known to himself and others the pride and vanity of his mind; the plenty and prosperity of the saints are greater triers of them than adversities and wants. For many that have comfortably gone through a low condition have yet foully failed in a full estate, their corruptions breaking forth to the view of others. Prosperity teaches men themselves. It tries their spirits, and lays them open to the world. Therefore it seemeth good to God to strip his servants of these outward things. They can acknowledge with patience his righteous dealing, knowing that man's happiness consists not in abundance of these things, but that the blessing of God is riches enough.

Obj. But some may object, and say, I have been long afflicted, and have had many crosses upon me, and little good do I find by them; I am never the better, but rather the worse for all.

Ans. This may be true thou sayest, but stay a little and consider the event. Howsoever, by reason of the bitterness and continuance of the cross, hitherto thou findest little good thereby, yet know that God is all this while but in hammering and working of thy unruly heart, thy good will follow afterwards. We see by experience, that sick persons, while they are in physic, are made sicker and sicker, but after that hath done working, then the party* is far better than before. It is a folly to think that we should have physic and health both at once. It is impossible that a man should sow and reap both together. We must of necessity endure the working of God's physic. If trouble be lengthened, lengthen thy patience. When the sick humour is carried away and purged, then we shall enjoy desired health. God promiseth forgiveness of sin, but thou findest the burden of it daily on thee. Cheer up thyself; when the morning is darkest then comes day; after a fight victory will appear. God's time is best; therefore wait cheerfully.

Ofttimes God's servants under his cross are so sore wrought upon that they have hardly leisure of making a good use of the same, being distracted and dejected for the present, so as that they burst out rather into further evil than before. But afterwards, when their afflictions are thoroughly digested, then they begin to find the fruit of patience, humiliation, and obedience, and are better for the same ever after; therefore wait contentedly God's leisure; thou shalt surely find a sweet calm after the storm is over. Though we find little benefit by afflictions for the present, yet let us not conclude all is naught with us; for temptations being bitter, will not suffer men in them to lift up their hearts straight. After the extremity and vexation thereof is laid, then ensueth the 'quiet fruit of righteousness,' Heb. xii. 11.

Obj. 1. But if all things, yea, sin itself, shall turn to the best to those that love God, what need we then care for the committing of sin?

Ans. The apostle St Paul was in his days troubled with the like question. Therefore, observe with what detestation he answers, saying, 'God forbid, the damnation of such men is just,' Rom. iii. 8. But to answer more fully and plainly for the satisfaction of weak Christians.

* Cf. Note, Vol. III. page 9.—G.

2. True it is, that all things, even the sins of God's servants, shall by God's mercy turn to their good; yet, nevertheless, the rule of God's word must ever be regarded, which is this, 'we may not do evil that good may come thereof.' That which is evil in itself must not be done, no, though for the doing thereof we might gain the greatest good, or avoid the greatest evil whatsoever; as if it were to win a world, we might not tell a lie, because it is a breach of God's law; Christ saith to the devil, 'It is written, Thou shalt not tempt the Lord thy God,' Mat. iv. 7. We may not therefore by sin tempt God, so to set his goodness in working good out of our wickedness.

If, therefore, upon this ground of doctrine (that all things shall turn to the good of God's children, yea, even their sins themselves), any of us shall commit wickedness, and displease his Majesty, to try what mercy and wisdom is in him, to draw good out of our evil; this is a provoking of God's goodness, and those who thus do, turn the truth of God's word into poison, and make even that their destruction which should build them up in grace and holiness.

If we sin through weakness and frailty of our flesh, and through strength of temptation, upon repentance we may find grace; but if presuming that God will turn all things to our good, we break his law, what else do we but first of all make God the cause of our evil; and secondly, vex and scandal* the saints on earth; thirdly, we sad† the blessed angels in heaven; and, fourthly, rejoice the devils and damned spirits in hell, putting darts and deadly weapons into their hands to work our ruin and overthrow; nay, fifthly, we grieve the good Spirit of God, who continually putteth us in mind of better things, if we would hearken to him, and by whom we are sealed up unto the day of redemption; sixthly, we slacken grace in our hearts, and whereas we should grow forward in virtue and holiness, we weaken the power of godliness exceedingly in us; seventhly, all willing sins do abate our affiance in God, and the feeling of his favour towards us; yea, oftentimes by so sinning, many of his dear children have walked heavily without spiritual joy all the days of their lives; for howsoever in regard the Lord hath elected us, we shall never finally fall away and perish, yet we may want the sweet sense of his favour, and remain afflicted in spirit all our life long. And then we shall know that the grief and trouble which we here undergo to avoid sin and subdue it, will be nothing so much as the mischief and sorrow that sin once committed and yielded to will bring on the soul.

Yea, there is no child of God but by experience shall one day feel that howsoever God by his wisdom and mercy can turn every sin to our good, yet it will prove bitter as wormwood in the end; the pleasure will never answer the smart and vexation that attends it. The contrition and breaking of thy heart for thy sins committed, if thou be God's, will more disquiet and trouble thee than possibly it can be a trouble to resist and forsake sin.

Nay, oftentimes God doth punish the very want of reverence in his servants to him, as also their slackness and unfitnesss in good duties, so as they may easily discern he is offended with them for the same. As we may see by the example of the Corinthians, who coming unpreparedly to the Lord's supper, for this very cause were so punished, 'that some of them were sick, and some weak, and some were struck by death,' 1 Cor. xi. 30.

David's numbering of the people, and Hezekiah's shewing of his treasures

* That is, scandalise.—G. † That is, sadden.—G.

to the princes of Babel, howsoever by some they may be thought small sins, yet God scourged them for the same very sharply. And it is good that God's servants should a little know what it is to offend their Maker, for if they will be so negligent and careless in walking with him, it is fit they should reap the fruit of their own devices. It causeth much relapsing and backsliding from God, when men have never truly smarted for their sin. Having had knocks in our own ways, it establisheth us in God's ways. For we love to wander from ourselves, and bite* strangers at home, till God by one cross or other brings us to himself, and then we think of returning to him. Nay, it is better for them a thousand-fold, that God should so school them, than that they should be let alone, and so go on without controlment from sin to sin till they come to desperation.

Howsoever therefore that God can and will turn the sins of his servants to the best advantage, yet better it were for them they had never sinned at all. Do we not think that David wished he had never fallen into that sin of adultery? And would not Peter have been glad that he had never denied his Master? The sin of David cost him many a cry for pardon: 'Mercy, Lord, mercy;' 'against thee have I sinned, forgive me this heinous crime;' and it cost Peter many a bitter salt tear, too, howsoever both David and Peter, after their recovery by repentance, were the better for it to their dying day.

As for all such as persist in sin, that God may turn all things to their best, let them know that all things shall work together for their bane and utter destruction for ever, which I now come to shew.

1. First of all, *God himself and his blessed angels* are at enmity with them. And therefore,

2. *All the creatures, both in heaven and earth, are against them.* In Pharaoh's ten plagues we see the creatures were all ready to execute the pleasure of the Almighty against him. And the 'bears out of the forest' were armed by God to devour those scoffing children, 2 Kings ii. 24. This is one part of the burden under which the creatures of God do groan, that they serve God against wicked men, and are his armies to punish the rebellious world.

3. *Even the good gifts of God are turned to the bane of the wicked.* Absalom's glory, his goodly long locks, were his halter to hang him up by. Ahithophel's wit† and policy brought him to that fearful end of being his own hangman. Haman's honour, what good did it to him, but only brought him to greater shame? His greatness made him swell in pride, and his pride had a sudden fall. What became of Herod's high mind in taking to himself the glory of God? which when foolish people ascribed it to him, was he not presently smitten, so as the 'worms consumed him,' Acts xii. 23, and he died a loathsome death? What became of Dives his riches? Did not his abuse thereof plunge him deeper into hell? Wicked men, though they abound in this world, yet not being in covenant with God, they have nothing with a blessing. The wicked are but as traitors before God; and oft it is seen that great traitors, who are by the prince kept in prison, are nourished very liberally until their time of execution come. So it is with all graceless persons. However for the present they have great allowances, yet as traitors, in the conclusion, they shall have an hard account to make unto God for all those things they have sinfully enjoyed. And not only so, but they abuse the very truth of God, as shall appear in divers particulars.

* Qu. 'bide'?—Ed.

† That is, 'wisdom.'—G.

(1.) First, *For the comfortable doctrine of justification by faith alone:* they pervert the same to their own destruction, saying, We are justified by faith only, what need we then care for doing of good works? Alas! they profit us nothing to our salvation. Therefore it is to no end to strive to do good.

(2.) Again, For the doctrine *of Christian liberty.* God having given us lawful recreations and plentiful use of his creatures, they turn all into licentiousness; and instead of moderate refreshment, they make a daily occupation of sports and games; instead of a lawful use of the creatures, they run into all excess of riot, in meat, drink, apparel, buildings, and delights.

(3.) And for the doctrine *of morality*, how do wicked men abuse it, saying, 'Let us eat, drink, and be merry, for to-morrow we shall die,' Luke xv. 23. That which should put them in mind of spending of their time well, increaseth their sin.

(4.) Whereas *the longsuffering of God should lead men to repentance, the wicked by means of God's patience run more securely on in sin,* 'treasuring up to themselves wrath against the day of wrath, and the declaration of God's just judgment,' Rom. ii. 5, which one day shall cease* upon them. 'Because he doth not speedily execute his displeasure,' Eccles. viii. 11, therefore they grow worse and worse, those never considering the lamentable condition that sin brings them into; which did they thoroughly weigh, they would give the whole world if they were possessors of it, to have their spirits at freedom from this bondage and fear. God will take a course that his grace shall not be turned into wantonness. First or last, thou shalt find, whoever thou art, at what rate thou buyest the pleasure of sin. Those that have enjoyed long the sweet of sin may expect the bitterest sorrow and heart-breaking for it.

Nay, the greater good things they have, the greater evil they receive thereby by abuse of the same.

5. *The more they are illuminated by the word, their hearts become more rebellious against it;* and the greater authority, wealth, and health they enjoy, the more mischief they do with them. Those heavenly doctrines which should build up a good heart unto holiness, do they abuse to bring their souls deeper into wickedness; shewing themselves like to their father the devil, whose children they indeed are. God hath said, 'He would give his angels charge over thee,' Ps. xci. 11, which is a most comfortable place to a good heart. But how doth Satan abuse this to Christ? That he should fling himself headlong from the pinnacle of the temple; and as the devil, so every wicked man, by all his instructions of the word, takes occasion to tempt God the more; turning both grace itself, and the doctrine of grace, into wantonness.

Are there not many that hear the word and know God's mind, who yet profit nothing to amendment of life? Were it not better for these never to enjoy such means of heavenly wisdom, than now having the light still to live in darkness. Their knowledge only makes their damnation the greater if they continue in sin. What a lamentable condition is that man in, whose knowledge is only sufficient to damn his own soul! But let us see further how all evil things work together for the worst to ungodly persons.

(1.) And to begin with spiritual ill things, as *heresies and errors.* They serve but to ensnare the wicked; for instead of making them cautelous† and diligent to search out the truth, they are carried away 'with every wind of doctrine.'

* Qu. 'come'?—Ed.

† That is, 'cautious.'—G.

So for the ill of *good men*, their falls and sins. The wicked of the world reap no benefit thereby, but encourage and hearten themselves the more in a sinful way, rejoicing thereat and making it their daily talk; neither do their own daily sinnings any whit better them, but are as so many punishments of their former transgressions: God in his justice suffering them still to run on to the fulfilling of the measure of their iniquities.

(2.) And for *outward evils in this life*, those that do turn to a good man's happiness fall out continually to their destruction. Pharaoh's ten plagues, which might have humbled his soul, made him but worse and worse. Therefore saith God, 'Why should I smite you any more?' for even since I punished you 'ye revolted still,' Isa. i. 5. The wicked are like to the smith's anvil, which by often beating is made harder and harder. So the more they are corrected, the stubborner and stiffer in sin they grow. Their crosses are laid upon them from an angry God, and are forerunners of his eternal wrath, which shall seize upon their souls in hell, where the more they are tormented the more they shall blaspheme, and the more they shall blaspheme the more they shall be tormented without cessation.

Causes. The cause of all this evil upon the wicked is, *first*, *God's infinite justice*, which will not be unsatisfied; *secondly*, *their own vile hearts*, which, like a sick man having an ill stomach, digests nothing, but turns all to poison. Therefore saith the apostle, 'To the unclean all things are unclean,' Titus i. 15. As poisonsome plants put into a fertile place do envenom the ground whereinto they are removed; so the same crosses that turn unto a good man's welfare prove a bad man's ruin, by reason of the corruption within him. *Another* cause is, the *devil's malicious working* by it. He makes wicked men abuse all their parts, both inward and outward, to God's dishonour and their own confusion, endeavouring to conform them to himself. None hath greater knowledge and understanding in the word of God than the devil. Yet he turns all his knowledge unto the sin against the Holy Ghost. But yet the devil cannot force men to wickedness. It is their own sinful hearts which betray them into his hands.

Use 1. Whence we learn *that all wicked men, in the midst of their happiness, are most unhappy*, because they turn the sweetest blessings into bitter poison; for all the gifts of God, without his special gift of using them well, are turned into a curse; as Balaam had good parts, but they not being sanctified proved his bane.

Use 2. We see further, *that outward prosperity is no mark of the true church.* Abundance of temporal blessings is no sign that we are in God's favour; neither are learning and knowledge evidences of spiritual grace. For the devil hath greater understanding and parts than any man. Howbeit, sight of sin preserves us from falling into it; and such as shut their eyes against the light, plunge themselves into the deeper misery.

Obs. 1. Now to proceed to further instructions. Do all things work together for the best to God's servants? Then hence we may learn *the certainty of the salvation of God's elect.* I take my reason from the text itself after this manner. That which nothing can hinder, that is certain; but the salvation of God's children cannot be hindered; therefore the salvation of God's children is most certain. If anything do or can hinder the saints' recovery or perseverance, it is sin; but to such as are united unto Christ by faith, sin is so far from hindering their happiness, that by God's overruling providence it turns to their best good.

Obs. 2. The second thing which we may ground here for the information of our judgment is this: *That as we know the providence of God is the cause* *why all things work together for the best to his children, so we should eye this very particular providence in all that we enjoy, turning the same to our good.* There is a working hand of God in everything towards us, as we may see in the examples of Job, Joseph, and David, with other of his servants, whose present sorrow and humiliation was but a means of their future glory and exaltation. There is nothing so bad, but he can draw good out of it when any evil is intended. God either puts bars and lets* to the execution of it against us; or else limiteth and boundeth the same, both in regard of time and measure. The God of spirits hath an influence into the spirits of all men, and knows how to take them off from doing us harm. All the strength of the creature rests in the great Creator of all things, who if he denies concourse,† the arm of their power soon withereth. It cannot but bring strong consolation to the soul, to know that in all variety of changes, and intercourse of good and bad things, our loving God hath a disposing hand. So as all blessings and crosses, all ordinances and graces, nay, our very falls, yea, Satan himself, with all his instruments, being over-mastered and ruled by God, have this injunction upon them, to further God's good intendment to us, and in no wise hurt us, which should move us to see his disposing hand in all that befalls us. We owe God this respect, to observe his providence in the particular passages of our lives; considering he is our Sovereign, and his will is the rule, and we are to be accountable to him as our Judge. We should question our hearts for questioning his care in the least kind. So long as God sits at the stern and rules all, we may be sure no evil shall betide us that he can hinder (*d*).

Obs. 3. Thirdly, Hence we may learn, *that there is not two, but one sovereign Head over the whole world*, which is plainly proved by this text of Scripture. For '*all* things work together for the best to them that love *God*:' and things which in themselves are contraries agree together to procure their good. Therefore all things whatsoever are overruled by the sole power of the Almighty. The devil himself, although he be called 'the god of this world,' yet he is at Christ's beck, and could not enter into a few swine without leave first obtained. He raiseth up hideous storms and tempests against the saints, but perisheth himself in the waves at last. Persecutions and perils may follow us, but they are all limited in the doing of hurt, which plainly demonstrates that there is but one main worker and wise disposer of all things.

Obs. 4. Further, Hence observe, *that there is nothing in the world that to God's servants is absolutely evil; because nothing is so ill but some good may be raised out of it;* not as it is an evil, but as it is governed and mastered by a supreme cause. Sin is of all evils the greatest; and yet sinful actions may produce gracious effects, through God's ordering and guiding the same.

Obs. 5. Again observe, *that a child of God is truly happy in the midst of all misery.* To prove this, I reason thus. In what estate soever the child of God is, it shall turn to his good; therefore no affliction can make him truly miserable. The proof of this the apostle sets down in his own example: 'He was poor, yet made many rich; he sorrowed, yet always rejoiced; he had nothing, yet possessed all things; he was chastened, and yet not killed,' 2 Cor. vi. 10. God's children, although to the world they may seem to be miserable, yet having communion and fellowship with him, they are always happy. The very worst day of God's child is better than the very best day of the wicked. The worst day of St Paul was better to him than the best day of Nero was to him; for the wicked, in the midst of

* That is, 'hindrances.'—G. † That is, 'concurrence.'—G.

their happiness, are accursed; whereas the godly, in the midst of their miseries, are blessed.

This doctrine is a ground of understanding divers other places of Scripture, as Ps. xci. 3, the Lord promiseth that he will 'deliver his from the snare of the hunter, and from the noisome pestilence;' and yet ofttimes his dear servants are in the hands of the wicked, and taken away by the stroke of his judgments, this truth nevertheless remaining firm, that 'all worketh together for their best.' So God teacheth us in his word that he doth make a league between his servants and the creatures. But all such expressions of his love we must bring to this text, and then they are true, else they may seem to be false. 'The plague shall not come near thy dwelling-place,' Ps. xci. 10, but only so far forth as it is for thy benefit. The good prophet was torn in pieces by a lion, 1 Kings xiii. 24; and sundry holy men have received hurt by wild beasts, whose eternal welfare were furthered thereby. Therefore this phrase of Scripture, that 'the creatures are in league,' is to be understood, not that they have put off their hostile nature, but that they have the same issue as those that are at peace with us.

Here likewise is a direction for us *how to pray for earthly blessings*, and the removal of temporal judgments. Oftentimes worldly honours and riches are snares unto God's children, and temporal chastisements, which we so earnestly pray against, work much good unto us. And therefore it falleth out that when we pray against temporal calamities, we pray against our own good.

Being therefore afflicted, we should desire not absolutely that God would remove our troubles, but that he would work his own good pleasure upon us thereby. Our prayers for temporal blessings and removal of temporal crosses must always be conditional; for what good will it be for us to come out of the fire worse than we were when we went into it? If, therefore, God in his wisdom see it good for us to have affliction, we should not desire him absolutely to remove the same till it have done us good. And then, 'Lord, deal with us as seems best in thine own eyes.'

As for such as affect* neither God nor goodness, let them know that if all things work for the best to the saints, then they may forbear their successless endeavours which they daily enterprise against them. In going about to hurt the godly they do them most good, for God will benefit them by their malice. Their wicked practices shall not only be made frustrate, but dangerous to themselves. After the chastisement of his servants for their good, God will cast the rod into the fire. Men may know whether they are 'vessels of mercy' or no by the use they are put to. The basest of people are fit enough to be executioners. It is a miserable wisdom when men are wise to work their own ruin. Do not many spin a fine thread and weave a fair web, when by their turnings and devices they turn themselves into hell? Whatever we get by sin for the present, it will one day prove the heaviest business that ever we undertook.

God is the only monarch of the world, and makes all things and persons whatsoever serviceable to his own end and his church's good. He is higher than the highest. Satan with all his instruments are but slaves to the Almighty, executioners of his will. Can we think that God's children, who are so near and dear to him, shall always be trampled upon by the powers of darkness. No, certainly. He is interessed† in all their quarrels, and takes their injuries as done to himself. When we can be more subtile than the devil, or more strong than God, we may think to thrive against them. He

* That is, 'choose,' 'love.'—G. † That is, 'interested.'—G.

is a 'wall of fire' round about his church, not only to defend and preserve it, but to consume all the adversaries thereof. God doth great matters for his servants; he rebukes kings and princes, and ruinates empires for their sakes. For the bringing home back again of the Jews, he translated the Babylonish empire to the Persians; and therefore the wicked must take heed of attempting anything against God's church: because the harm thereof will redound upon their own heads. God delights to take the oppressed party's'* part, and serves himself of all his enemies for his people's good. They practise against the righteous, and he 'laughs them to scorn.' Wicked men cannot do God's children a greater pleasure than to oppose them; for by this means they help exceedingly to advance them.

Satan and all his instruments, what get they by their cruelty to the saints? They do but increase their own torment, and do them the more good. But this is both against their knowledge and wills. Therefore if they be loath to do them any good, let them take heed how they attempt any evil against them.

Use 1. And here let all such be admonished *how they provoke God's children to cry in their prayers against them.* For it is better for the wicked that they had all the creatures in heaven and earth against them than the poor saints; for a few of these will more prejudice them than all the world besides.

Come we now to the grounds of practice hence to be observed.

Use 2. Again, Doth God order all 'for the best' to them that love him?

Let us not then *except against any evil that shall befall us;* for this our present cross shall turn to our future comfort. It is the saints' happiness, that their best is in working still, till they be complete in heaven. But the wicked and men of the world, their worst is always in contriving. Their life is bad, their death is worse; and after death it is worst of all with them. God himself, and all under him, work continually for the good of his children. Their best is last. Their light groweth on clearer and clearer 'as the light, until the noonday,' Prov. iv. 18. But the worldly grow worser and worser every moment. To them that fear God, sin and sorrow, their very worst, is by God's mercies best for them; whereas all the best of the wicked by abuse turns to their worst.

Use 3. Observe here the excellency of the saints' comfort, above all other comforts whatsoever. The nature of it is this: it must be stronger than the grievance of which it is a cordial. And the reason of spiritual comfort must be more forcible than any carnal reason can be to undermine it. Now what stronger consolation can a man have than to be assured that all things, without exception, shall work together for his good? But this is not all. What a sweet refreshment is it when the soul can say, God will either stop me from falling into sin, outwardly by afflictions; or else subdue my corruptions inwardly by his Spirit, that I shall not be overthrown by them. He will never suffer me to rot in my sins, but when I do fall, will raise me up again. It bears up a Christian's heart, that rather than we shall continue in an evil way, God will send some Nathan or other to rouse us out of our security.

Therefore to all thy comforts add this, that God will not only save thee at last, but turn all things to the best whilst thou art here. This is the highest strain of consolation. It is far stronger to refresh and quicken us than any grievance can be to afflict us. It maketh evil things, in comparison, to seem good; as, 'Moses counted the rebukes of Christ greater

* Cf. Note, Vol. III. page 9.—G.

riches than the treasures of Egypt,' Heb. ix. 26. He made more choice of 'affliction' than he did of the world's glory. If God be with us, who can be against us. If he be our shepherd, we are sure to lack nothing. There is such a force of comfort in salvation, that we will rather choose outward evils than to enjoy outward good things. Moses, by faith, seeing that outward affliction and shame were knit to salvation, chose these, and refused dignity and ease.

How ought this to stay the soul under all its heavy pressures! Why should not I be patient in sickness, in poverty, in disgraces; or why should I despair at the hour of death? Am I not under the hand of my God, working my good out of every evil? It is the subtilty of our arch-enemy to drive us to a stand, that we may doubt of our conditions, and say with Gideon, '*If* the Lord be with me, and that I am his child, why is it thus with me?' Judges vi. 13. How is it that all this sorrow and misery hath befallen me, and lieth so heavy upon my soul? But our comfort here is, that God who turneth all things to our best is stronger than Satan.

Use 4. Again, *Considering all things conduce unto our goods, though in appearance never so opposite*, this comfort ariseth, that if God do so work this or that, then I must believe against belief; I must stand firm against contraries, my faith must answer his manner of working, and believe that God can bring me to honour by shame, and to heaven by hell-gates. For if it be his course of dealing, first to cast down and then to lift up, by disgrace to bring his servants to glory, then in all my extremities I must rest upon God, who is never nearer unto his, to succour them, than when he seems to be furthest off. When he means to give victory he suffers us to be foiled first, and when he intends to justify a poor sinner he will condemn him first. Let us therefore hope against hope, and desire God in our distresses to open our eyes that we may see our consolations.

Hagar had a well by her when she was ready to perish for thirst, and yet she saw it not; and Elisha's man had angels to defend him when the Aramites* compassed him about, but perceived not the same. So 'the angel of the Lord continually pitcheth his tent about the godly,' though they are not aware of it; yea, God is then nearest to us when we are in most straits. Cordials are kept for faintings. When Christ went to cast the devil out of a child, he then most raged and tare him. So likewise Satan and wicked men most rage when they are nearest to their end and destruction. In thy greatest danger, never rest on thy friends, but on the Lord, who never standeth nearer and firmer to us than when we are most perplexed and know not what to do. A distressed soul seeth oft no comfort in outward things, and therefore retireth unto God, in whom it finds whatsoever may make it happy. 'Our strength may fail, and our heart may fail,' Ps. xxiv., but God is our portion for ever. When we are weak, then we are strong; and when we are most cast down in ourselves, we are nearest to God's helping hand. This carriage of the Almighty ought to establish our faith.

In all cases of extremity we should have a double eye: one to look upon our grievances and troubles, and another to look upon the issue and event of them. Why do men in time of dangerous sickness take bitter physic, which is almost death unto them? Why do they then undergo such things as they loathe at other times? Is it not because they rest upon the skill of the physician? And shall we then in our distresses distrust God for our souls, when we will trust a weak and mortal man with our

* That is, the Syrians. Cf. 2 Kings vi. 17.—G.

bodies? If conceit be so strong in earthly things, as indeed it is, then faith is much stronger, when it grounds itself upon the truth of the word. When God exercises us with poverty or other afflictions, this should teach us submission to his providence in any condition, saying, Lord, do with me what thou wilt, only let this poor soul be precious in thine eyes! Thou hast promised that howsoever these afflictions lie heavy upon me, yet in the end, all shall turn out to my good; therefore dispose of thy servant at thine own pleasure; I resign all to thee!

Here is the rejoicing of a Christian, which makes him cheerfully pass through any affliction; he knows that good is intended in all that befalls him. With what alacrity did Joseph say unto his brethren, 'Ye sold me hither, but God hath turned it to the best, that I should preserve and nourish you all, and save much people alive, who otherwise were like to have perished with famine,' Gen. xlv. 5. This made Job so patiently to say, 'The Lord giveth, and the Lord taketh; blessed be the name of the Lord,' Job i. 21.

This is the ground of all true contentation.* I have learned, saith St Paul, 'in all estates to be content: to be rich and to be poor, to abound and to be in want,' Philip. iv. 11; and why so? Whatsoever his estate and condition was, God turned it to the best. Shall any man dare to mislike of God's allowance? Doth not he know better what is good for us than we can possibly imagine what is good for ourselves?

This likewise should teach us not to take offence at the reproach and disgrace which is cast upon God's children; for 'mark the righteous,' saith David, 'and behold the upright: the end of that man is peace,' Ps. xxxvii. 37. The issue of their trouble is ever quietness. Take not one piece of a Christian man's life by itself, but take it altogether, and then thou shalt see the truth of this doctrine. To see Joseph in the dungeon and in his irons, we haply may be offended, and call God's providence in question; but beholding him in his honour and advancement, we cannot but conclude him a happy man. So if we look on Job sitting with sores on the dunghill, there is matter of offence; but to see him restored again, and blessed with a greater estate than he had before, this is matter of praising God. If we consider of Christ abased, and hanging upon a cross, so there will be scandal;† but look on him exalted to glory, far above all dignities and powers, and then the scandal is soon taken away. Let us therefore lay one thing to another when we eye God's people, and we shall see a blessing under their greatest curse. Those things which are contrived by man's wit‡ may argue great folly if one part be not annexed to the other. Therefore look to the whole work towards his servants, and then thou shalt never be offended at their condition.

Use 5. This also is a ground of *Christian boldness in holy courses*, when a man is fully resolved, that come what will come, God will turn all to his good. It encourages him cheerfully to go through any difficulty. What is the reason of the fearfulness and dastardness of most men, but only this, that if we do this or that duty, or abstain not from this or that good action, then this cross and this dipleasure by such and such a person will be brought upon me. The wise man saith, that 'the fear of man bringeth a snare, but he that trusteth in the Lord shall be exalted,' Prov. xxix. 25. Let us not, regarding the fear of man, neglect our duty to God, for he can turn the hearts of the kings on the earth to seek the welfare of his poorest creature,

* That is, 'contentment.'—G.
† That is 'offence.'—G.
‡ That is, 'wisdom.'—G.

and make thy very enemies to be thy friends. He that for sinister ends will offend his Maker, may well be excluded to the 'gods whom they have served,' Judges x. 14. Go to the great men, whose persons you have obeyed for advantage, to your riches, to your pleasures, which you have loved more than God or goodness: you would not lose a base custom, a superfluity for me; therefore I will not own you now. Such men are more impudent than the devil himself, that will claim acquaintance with God at last, when they have carried themselves as his enemies all their days. God wants not means to maintain his, without being beholden to the devil. He hath all help hid in himself, and will then shew it when it shall make most for his own glory. He deserves not to live under the protection of a king, that will displease him for fear of a subject. The three children in Daniel said, 'Know, O king, that our God can deliver us out of thy hands; but if he will not, yet, nevertheless, we will not fall down and worship thine image,' Dan. iii. 5, *seq.* 'The righteous are bold as a lion,' saith the wise man, Prov. xxviii. 1; 'the Lord is his strong tower,' Ps. lxi. 3. What need we fear any creature, when we have him on our side who hath both men and devils at his back?*

Use 6. And if God turn all things whatsoever to our good, *should not we through the whole carriage of our lives chiefly aim at his honour?* God writes our names in his book, he numbers our hairs, and bottles up our tears.† He hath a special care of us. Every good deed we do he writeth down to eternity; yea, if we give but 'a cup of cold water in his name,' Mat. x. 42, he taketh notice of it; and shall not we then take special occasion to magnify him in all things? We pray daily, 'Hallowed be thy name,' therefore ought accordingly to observe God's dealing with us. How is it possible that we should give him the glory of his mercies, if we never observe them?

A wicked man considers, This makes for my advantage and this for my profit, this tends to my ease and wealth, &c.; studying how to make friends, and please persons in place above him, not respecting God's honour and glory in the least kind; whereas the sincere Christian looks on all things as they tend to his best happiness, and therefore forecast thus, If I do this or that good, then I shall grow in grace and wisdom and knowledge; but if I neglect it, and be careless of well doing, I shall hurt and wound my soul, and break the peace of my conscience. By this company and good acquaintance I shall be furthered in holiness, become wiser and better in heavenly understanding; if I fall, they may raise me up, and help maintain a gracious frame within me. Where true holiness is, the soul is sensible of all advantages and disadvantages of good. An indifferency for any company or employment shews a dead heart.

This is a main difference to distinguish a child of God from a profane wretch that only lives to himself. His heart is taken up wholly with the world and matters below, whereas the godly are all for thriving in grace and increase of godliness. The wicked man considers of things as they serve to satisfy his lust; and if we have better thoughts at any time, it is but for a start. But a godly man's aims are always holy, and the strength of his soul is put forth that way. He values himself as he stands in relation to God and a better life; and esteems all other things more or less as they further or hinder his spiritual growth, and bring peace and ‡ sorrow at the last unto him.

2. But I hasten to the second part of the text, *the persons to whom this*

* Qu. 'beck'?—Ed. † Cf. Ps. lvi. 8.—G. ‡ Qu. 'or'?—Ed.

privilege belongs; that is, 'to them that love God.' And why to them that love God? Because the apostle speaketh of afflictions; and we know that the grace which is most conversant in the saints' sufferings is patience, which floweth from love.

Also, for that of all other graces is the first and sweetest. It is the first; for whom we love we are sorry to offend; and hate whatsoever is contrary to that we affect.* We rejoice in that we love, and grieve in the absence thereof.

It is the commanding affection of all others, and setteth the whole man sweetly a-work to attain its desire. Love makes us forward and zealous Christians. All the inward worship of God is in the affections; as, Thou shalt rejoice in no God but me, and fear no God but me. All the commandments of God are brought by Christ to this duty.

Again, Love hath a special part in this privilege of bringing all things to work for our good. For when we love God, we will make the best use of everything which we suffer or do, if we love God and eye his glory therein. Love makes any burden easy. It makes us studious of pleasing the party loved; as we say in the proverb, 'Love me, and do with me what you will.' Love is full of inventions. It studies complacency, and sets the soul a-work to honour God in all things.

In that the apostle saith, 'to them that love God,' and not to the children or servants of God, we may observe, *that Christianity is not a bare title, but it requireth some qualification.* Therefore the Scriptures, when they describe a saint on earth, do not usually say, 'the child of God,' but they set him forth by some holy affections or actions wrought in him; as such as love God, or fear God, and 'walk in his ways;' hereby shewing that religion is not a matter of compliment, but a real and holy endeavour to please the Lord; and although the Scriptures do name but some one particular affection, yet it is all one as if they had named all; for where one is in truth, there all follows.

Again, In that the apostle here ascribes privileges to those only that are thus qualified, we must take heed in applying the promises of God and these sweet consolations, that we be such persons to whom of right they do belong; 'for all things work for the best,' not to every one, but to such as 'love God.' We must not therefore preach comfort to all, but must first labour to make men capable of it. To this end,

1. First, We will shew the nature of this love.

2. Secondly, The exercises of it, and directions unto it.

3. Thirdly, Some incitements to this holy affection.

1. The ground of love is a considering of God *as our own God* in the covenant of grace, and an acknowledging of ourselves to be his peculiar children in Christ Jesus; when we can say as the spouse in the Canticles, 'I am my beloved's, and my beloved is mine,' ii. 16. This is a loving of God, not as the God of nature only, but as ours peculiar by grace. This union of love, which knits us to Christ, implieth another union by faith first, which is a cleaving to God as *my* God, and to Christ as *my* Christ; whence issues a second conjunction or cleaving to him in love, as my Saviour, my husband, and my head.

To come to the nature of this grace, and then to the working of it. The nature of love is seen in four things:

1. In admiring of some secret good in the thing beloved, which stirs up the soul to make out for it.

* That is, 'love,' 'choose.'—G.

2. In a studiousness of the contentation* of the person beloved.

3. In a desire of union and fellowship with the person we affect.†

4. In a resting and solacing of ourselves in the thing we love.

By these let us examine ourselves whether we have the true love of God or no. For it concerns us much to have this grace. It will distinguish us from all others, who fear him not.

1. First, Our love to Christ cometh

(1.) *From the high esteem of the good things we see in him.* But how shall we know whether that we have this admiring of the good things we see in God and in his word and children? We shall know it by our choice; and our choice follows our judgment. Would we know whether our judgment be good? See what do we choose, especially when things of the world and God come together. And here we want not examples to guide us. The question was, Whether that Moses should still choose to live in Pharaoh's court and be accounted his son-in-law, or else depart and suffer adversity with God's children. Now Moses, by sound judgment, had an high esteem of the excellency and privileges of the saints; and therefore chose rather to endure afflictions 'than to enjoy the pleasures of sin for a season,' Heb. xi. 25. Let us then see whether we can be contented to part with our preferment or pleasure for God or no. And whether we do esteem the rebukes of Christ greater riches than the treasures of the world: whether we can lay down our lives and liberties at Christ's feet, and gladly want all, so we may enjoy him. If it be so with us, our estate is good.

(2.) Again, Let us see whether *We have a right prizing of the good things in God.* Do we delight to speak much and often of Christ and the benefits we receive by him? How was St Paul's heart enlarged, and his tongue full of heavenly eloquence, in setting forth the 'unspeakable mercies of God,' which we have by Christ Jesus our Lord. If 'God be on our side, who can be against us?' saith he; 'What shall separate us from the love of Christ;' 'shall tribulation, shall anguish and affliction? I am persuaded that neither death, nor life, nor any other thing can do it,' Rom. viii. 38.

(3.) Another sign to know whether we have a secret admiration of the good things we see in God is this, *if we do undervalue all things else for Christ.* Worldly men are ever admiring of the things below, accounting such men happy and blessed that abound most therein. Therefore there is nothing that doth more truly try a man than this. The soul that sees a vanity in the things beneath, and can rejoice in God only as his true riches, is in a good condition. Where there is a true judgment of God and religion, the soul of that man will never stoop to the creature; the soul so rejoiceth in God, as that it will not yield itself to any other. Adam and Eve, in their innocency, were both naked and were not ashamed. One reason might be, because their thoughts were taken up with higher matters. In heaven we shall not be ashamed of things we now are ashamed of. A Christian soul is so ravished with the enjoying of God, that it mindeth almost nothing but him.

2. The second branch in love is a desire to do all things, (1.) *to the content of the party‡ beloved.* Our love to God will frame us to the obedience of his will. Obedience is the proof of love: 'If ye love me,' saith Christ, 'keep my commandments,' John xv. 10. If we love God, we will pray for the enlarging of his kingdom. Where love is kindled in any heart, there

* That is, 'contentment.'—G.

† That is, 'love.'—G.

‡ Cf. foot note in Vol. III. page 9.—G.

is a care to be approved of him whom we so love. This makes our obedience general to all God's commandments, in all places and all things whatsoever. It makes us give our inwards to God, serving him with the soul and spirit.

Those therefore that nourish unclean hearts within them, and think it enough to abstain from the outward act of evil, love not the Lord sincerely. The devil himself will do outward things as readily as you; he will confess Christ to be the Son of God, and say, 'Why art thou come to torment me before my time?' Matt. viii. 29. So that if thou dost outwardly only confess God, what dost thou more than the devil? In outward duties, without sincerity, there is no love. You will pray; the devil will do as much. The devil hath a bad end in good actions. So there are many that come to church, and make show of religion, to cloak their evil courses. But such poor wretches, however they are pleased with shadows, are little better than Satan himself.

(2.) Again, If we be desirous to content him whom we love, *then will we suffer anything for his sake*. Therefore the apostles went away 'rejoicing, and accounted it their glory that they were esteemed worthy to suffer hardship for Christ,' Acts v. 41. And David, for 'dancing before the ark,' being by Michal mocked, saith, 'I will yet be more vile for my God,' 2 Sam. vi. 22. He cared not for any reproach that could happen to him in a good way. Yea, this will make us 'zealous in his truth.' He that hath no zeal hath no love. If our hearts rise not when God is dishonoured, what love have we to him? Is God's glory and the church's welfare dear to us? It is a sign we love him. But can we see those things go backward and have no zeal, nor be anything affected therewith, surely then we have no love.

3. Again, if we have a true love to God, then

(1.) *Have we a desire of union and communion with him.* We will be much in meditating of him, in speaking to him and conferring with him. Those therefore that go on from day to day, without private speeches with God, or solacing of their souls in him, what affection have they to him? Love is communicative; and what desire of communion can that soul have that lives a stranger to his Maker? Can we say we love one with whom we never confer or speak to any purpose?

(2.) Again, If we love a man, *we will advise with him, especially in matters of moment.* So if we love God we will take counsel of him in his word, for the guidance of our lives and stablishing our consciences. If we advise not with God, it is a sign that we either think he doth not regard us, or else that we count him not worthy to be counselled by.

(3.) Another sign is, to examine what *desire we have to be dissolved, and to be with Christ.* Do we love his appearing to judgment? and are we now fit for his coming? Surely then it is a plain sign that our love is fixed and set upon him; so much as we do fail of this desire, so much we fail in love to Christ. What was the reason that the people under the law were so much afraid at the appearing of an angel unto them? Was it not this, that they were not fitted and prepared for God? A man may be a good Christian, and yet not at all times willing to die; for as eyes that are sore cannot always endure the light, so a soul galled with sin desires not to hear of the day of judgment: yet ought we to thirst after it.

(4.) Another sign of this grace is *our eager and hungry desire after God*, when with David we can say, 'O God, my heart panteth after thee, as the hart panteth after the brooks of waters,' Ps. xlii. 1, when a soul is never at rest till he enjoys his Maker, but cries out still, 'O when shall I appear in his presence!' it is a good sign, ver. 2.

4. The last branch or property is, *resting and quieting ourselves in the love of God above all things whatsoever*, saying with David, 'Whom have I in heaven or in earth besides thee? or what do I esteem in comparison of thee?' Ps. lxxiii. 25; let me enjoy but 'the light of thy countenance, and it suffices me,' Ps. iv. 6. Demand therefore of thine own heart, what the things are that trouble thee most? and what is the cause of thy sorrow and disquietments? whether it be for losses or crosses outwardly, or for want of God's love and the sense and feeling of his favour inwardly? They which grieve chiefly for outward evils are most carried in their affections that ways; but if in the confluence of all worldly blessings, we can grieve for our spiritual wants, it is a comfortable evidence. When a man reckons not his happiness to stand in the possession of the creature, but in the fruition of the Creator, and desires his favour above anything, it is a gracious sign.

David had an abundance, yea, he had a kingdom, yet nothing would satisfy him but the mercies of God. And when he was in want, what course did he take, but 'still comforted himself in the Lord his God,' Ps. li. 1, *seq.* That which a man sorroweth most for when he wanteth it, that he rejoiceth most in when he hath it. Can we in our crosses rejoice that God is ours? This is an excellent sign, and plainly discovers, that we place our contentation* more in him than in anything else. Can we delight more in the solace of his favour than in outward prosperity? It is a heavenly testimony of a renewed condition. When David was in his greatest distresses, what desires had he then most in him? Why, he longed after the house of God. When the people were ready to stone him, wherein did he trust, but in 'the Lord his strong tower'? Ps. lxi. 3.

In the last place, Would we know whether we can rest in God or no? Let us

(1.) *Examine ourselves then what endeavours we make every day to cleanse our souls from sin*, that so God may take pleasure in us, and we again may delight in him.

(2.) *Let us see how we restrain our affections from running riot after the world and sinful pleasures.* And

(3.) *How we set our joy upon God, and frame ourselves to do his will.* I beseech you, let us deal faithfully with our own souls in this particular. And if we find

(4.) That our hearts tell us, as Peter's told him, 'Lord, thou knowest that I love thee,' John xvi. 30; I desire, O Lord, to please thee above all things; I have set mine heart upon thee, and I joy in thee and in thy love more than in all things else in the world; if thus, I say, we can in the integrity of our spirits appeal to God, who only knows and searches our ways, and say, 'Truly, Lord, thou knowest that I love thee,' it is a certain and infallible sign unto us that we are his, and all things shall work for the best unto us.

But take we heed how we deceive ourselves in these things. By love we are Christians; therefore labour for sincerity of affection. A reprobate or a castaway may go far in these four signs of love. He may admire and wonder at the good things of God; but he doth it not from anything within him, but from the outward beholding of them. He can admire and talk of them, but yet such men are without any relish or sweet taste of the thing they speak of. So likewise an hypocrite may desire to please God

* That is, 'contentment.'—G.

in many things, but not in all things; as we see in Herod, he heard John Baptist willingly, and obeyed in some things, but not in all. He could not be crossed in his beloved sin which abode in him; that must not be touched. Then farewell God, and farewell Christ and all.

So a castaway may desire to be in heaven, as being a place good for him; and he may have some little 'taste of those joys above,' as is mentioned in the Hebrews, vi. 4, 5; but he hath no relish of them from the love of God, but only from the love of himself. And his desire is not such as will draw him on to the use of means for spiritual growth and progress thereunto, as we see in Balaam; he had a desire 'to die the death of the righteous,' Num. xxiii. 10, but this could not make him leave his covetous disposition, and find a contentment in God alone.

A reprobate may be content with religion and with God's ways, so long as peace doth accompany the same (as now in this our country, Christ cometh amongst us with plenty and prosperity, therefore Christ is a good Christ), but if the gospel and religion should be professed with persecution and danger and disgrace, it would soon appear where men's contentments were. There is a resting not in the truth, because it is truth, but in regard of the good things which follow it. If we desire to approve ourselves to God, let us examine ourselves about this affection, and every branch of it. The deceit is both common and deadly; and the profession of religion in many Christians is not for religion itself, but for by-ends and sinister respects. To which end consider further these particulars.

Where there is true love, *there will be a desire of union to the beloved object;* so where the love of God is, there will be a desire of the accomplishment of the marriage between God and the soul. 'He that loves a harlot,' saith the wise man, 'is one with her,' 1 Cor. vi. 16. So he that affects* the Lord, desires to be one with him; therefore men have their names from what they love. If they love the world, they are called 'worldlings;' if they love Christ, they are called Christians. How canst thou say that thou lovest the Lord, and dost not desire his presence in his ordinances? Can we say we love such a man, when we care not for his company? God observes not so much what we do, as from what affection our duties proceed.

Again, If we love, *there will be a desire to give content to the party beloved.* This appears even in carnal self-love; for take a man that loves himself, he makes himself his utmost aim and end in all his actions. But when once God hath plucked this fleshly love out of our souls, then our affections will be carried to Christ only. This made the prophet David say, 'I love the Lord dearly,' Ps. xviii. 1. 'He is my rock, my fortress, my deliverer,' Ps. lxxi. 3. A Christian hath his contentment in God alone; he finds an all-sufficiency in the Almighty, and therefore makes him his resting-place. In all his troubles he will make God his deliverer, and find more true comfort in him than in all the things of the world besides. Therefore, if God should take all other things from us, yet if he leave us himself, a Christian is well contented, because he knows his best being is in God.

Quest. But how shall I know whether I do esteem rightly of God or no?

Ans. If we highly esteem any thing, whether it be of this or a better life, we will be often speaking of them. It is a sign men undervalue heavenly truths when they discourse little about them. They much set light by God that have him not in all their thoughts.

Again, What we esteem of, *we will choose above other things.* It appears

* That is, 'loves.'—G.

we have a precious esteem of God when we choose him, and him alone, for our portion; as David, when he said, 'One thing have I desired of the Lord, that I may dwell in his courts for ever,' Ps. xxvii. 4. Where God is truly loved, there will be a fall of all earthly things in that man's estimation. So he may gain Christ, he counts all else but dross and dung.

Lastly, If thou lovest God, *thou wilt be afraid to offend him, and careful to please him in all things.* God delights not in a proud and haughty spirit, but in an humble and meek soul. These then should be thy delight. God is wonderful well pleased with faith; for it is that which binds him to perform his promise; therefore seek it earnestly. Whatsoever God approves, a Christian should take pleasure in. Every grace is an ornament to a Christian; and God delights to see his own graces in us. Isaac, before he took Rebekah to wife, sent her jewels to adorn her; so Christ sends rich jewels to his children, even the graces of his Holy Spirit, to make us love him, and fit us the more for him. Those that live in sins against conscience, think we that these love God? No, certainly. If they did, they would love that which he loves, and hate that which he hates. What a pitiful thing is it to see men glorying in that which is their shame; in swearing and profaneness, and yet for all this say they love God! Is it possible that the love of God and the love of sin should ever stand together?

Proceed we now to some reasons and directions for the attaining of this grace.

1. And first, *Let us not rest in an inferior degree of this affection, but rise up therein, and labour that it may have full assent.* There are degrees of assent, as when we love God because we love ourselves. A natural man may do so, but this is not enough; for if we love God for ourselves, we make ourselves our god. Where the heart is truly set upon God, it delights in him only for himself, and takes comfort in no condition further than he sees God in it. He never affected Christ in truth that is more taken with the benefits and privileges that come by him than with the excellency of his person. What friend will be content that a man should only love him because he doth him good? We must love ourselves and all other things in and for God. Moses and Paul rejoiced to honour the Lord, though themselves were accursed and deprived of happiness; and if we could so love Christ as not to desire heaven itself if Christ were not there, this were truly to affect* him; for indeed if Christ were not there, heaven should not be heaven unto us. We must love our happiness no further than we can have with it God's leave and liking.

2. Again, We shall know our love to God, whether it be sincere or no, *by our abstaining from sin.* If we avoid evil for fear of punishment or hope of reward only, our love is unsound; but when we so love God that we will not do anything contrary to his Spirit, it is a special sign. Such a man, if there were no hell to punish him, nor place of bliss to receive him, yet would not break with God upon any terms.

For the means to attain this love, we must, in the first place, *labour for an humble and empty soul.* 'Blessed are the poor in spirit,' saith Christ, for such only apprehend their misery without Christ and their need of him, which occasions an holy rejoicing in the Lord, and unfeigned love to him. What is the reason that some are so ravished with the favours of the Almighty? Is it not for that they were so formerly stung with the sight and feeling of their sins? The more loving Christian ever the more humble

* That is, 'choose,' 'love.'—G.

Christian. Mark it when you will, and you shall find this disposition manifest in every true convert. They are daily humbling themselves for the least offence.

A second direction is, to *taste of the love of God in Christ.* When the beams of his favour once shine into our hearts, we cannot but reflect upon him again. 'We love him,' saith the apostle, 'because he loved us first,' 1 John iv. 10. Mary therefore 'loved much,' because she had the experience of God's love 'in forgiving her many sins,' Luke vii. 47. When a broken humble soul truly savoureth the goodness of the Lord, it cannot but be inflamed with desire after him. A Christian, after he hath had a taste of the love of God, hath another manner of judgment of justification than before. 'Taste and see,' saith David, 'how good and gracious the Lord is,' Ps. xxxiv. 8. A man that relishes the sweetness of a thing can better judge of it than he which never tasted it.

A third direction is, to *see what motives and reasons we have from the love of God in Christ to exercise our understandings this way.* We know heat cometh from light, and there is a sympathy between the brain and the heart. The brain must make a report to the heart before that can be inflamed with affection; therefore seriously search into the grounds of thy affection.

(1.) The first ground is, *goodness in God.* God is goodness itself, in whom all goodness is involved. If, therefore, we love other things for the goodness which we see in them, why do we not love God, in whom is all goodness? All other things are but sparks of that fire, and drops of that sea. Seest thou any good in the creature; remember there is much more in the Creator. Leave, therefore, the streams, and go to the well-head of comfort.

(2) Another reason of love is *our affinity with God our Father and friend*, who is unto us in all degrees of nearness, both our head and our husband. Were not the Son ours, what fellowship could we have with the Father? Having such a Mediator with God, that is 'bcne of our bone, and flesh of our flesh,' why should we fear to go unto him? He hath taken upon him these comfortable relations of shepherd and brother, to possess us of his acquaintance with our infirmities and readiness to relieve us. For shall others by his grace fulfil what he calls them unto, and not he that out of his love, hath taken upon him these relations, so thoroughly founded upon his Father's assignment and his own voluntary undertaking? How doth the tender mother sympathise in the anguish of her child, notwithstanding all its froward averseness? And shall we think there is more bowels in ourselves than in God? Can there be more sweetness in the stream than in the spring? If the well of consolation be always open, and the fountain of living water be never shut up, let us teach our hearts to suck and draw comfort from these rivers of refreshing. What a shame is it that men should hunger at such a feast!

Consider, likewise, the benefits which we have bestowed upon us, and the end why God vouchsafes us so much favour.

Benefits win love even from brute creatures. Therefore we are worse than beasts, if we love not God for his benefits. 'The ox knows his owner, and the ass his master's crib,' Isa. i. 3. What are we indeed but an heap of God's benefits? All our faculties of soul and body are the blessings of God. Whatsoever we have or hope to have is from him. Our breath, life, and being subsists in God, who hath promised that 'heaven and earth, men and devils, crosses and blessings, sin and death,' all shall be turned by his over-ruling power to our good.

(3) Consider *what now we are, and what a happy condition God hath made us capable of hereafter.* Is it a small matter that we should be regarded above the angels that fell? and that he who knew no sin should be made sin for us, nay, become a curse to free us from the curse? It was strange that the 'three children,' being cast into the hot fiery furnace, should not burn. So likewise it is a wonder that Christians, being in the midst of the flame of God's love, should be so cold and dead-hearted. It is not only the guilt of sin that we are freed from, but the unsupportable vengeance of the Almighty due for the same. And is this a small matter?

(4.) If we regard *the manner of bestowing his benefits*, it will much advance God's goodness towards us, and raise up our spirits to love him again. Doth not he love us first of all, and prevent* us with his favours? Is not his love full and overflowing, so as he never leaves us until he make an end? Where he freeth a man from danger, he settleth him in a good estate, never ceasing till he possess him of glory; as it is 2 Tim. iv. 17, 'The Lord hath freed me out of the mouth of the lion, and he will preserve me to his everlasting kingdom.' He delivers us from spiritual evil, and gives us spiritual good. The meditation of these things will warm our hearts.

(5.) The next means is, to *join fear with our love to God.* Whom we love thoroughly, we will do nothing that shall displease. The fear of God, whom we love, will cause us to make conscience of the least sin against him; for there is no sin, be it never so little, but it will weaken our affection to goodness. When we venture upon anything against conscience, is there not a decay of our love to God and of our sense of his favour towards us? Surely sin is the only make-bait in our souls, and weakener of all our comforts. Those, therefore, are the lovingest souls towards God that are most conscientious in their ways. Careless Christians have not that feeling of God's love which humble fruitful Christians have, neither do they live or die with that comfort as these do.

We are the spouse of Christ, and he is jealous of our love. Our betrothed husband cannot abide that we should set our affections upon strangers. Take heed, therefore, of adulterous and false affections. The more we love earthly things, the less we shall esteem of heavenly; and as our affection towards the creature increaseth, so our heat towards Christ abateth.

(6.) The next direction to stir up our love to God is, *to exercise the same daily.* For true love is not an abstractive † affection, but an affection in practice; and we know everything doth increase by exercise. Exercise it, therefore, in fighting against the love of the world and all self-love; for as there are contrary commands, so there are contrary desires in a Christian. As there is the old man and the new man, the flesh and the spirit, so there are contrary affections, one setting itself against another in him.

When we see a poor Christian, the love of God will say unto us, Now shew thy love unto Christ in succouring one of his members. No, saith flesh and blood, charity begins at home; thou mayest want, thyself, another day.

In doing good likewise we should say, Here is now an occasion offered me of honouring God, and I will embrace it. Oh but, saith self-love, there is time enough hereafter; hereby you may run into poverty and disgrace; be not too forward. Therefore there must be a perpetual denial of ourselves against our whole thwart ‡ nature. Those that are Christians know experimentally what belongs to these things. But take a carnal man or woman, and they are led altogether by their sensual lusts as brute beasts. What-

* That is, 'anticipate.'—G.

‡ That is, 'abstract' = theoretic?—G.

† That is, 'thwarted' or 'twisted' = evil.—G.

soever ease and self-love wills, that sways their hearts any ways. And indeed the most sincere Christian hath the motions of these carnal and wordly respects; but his love unto God constrains him to deny all, and listen to what Christ whispereth in his heart.

Consider we a little what may stir us up to exercise ourselves herein. Love, it is the light of our life; love we must, something; and he lives not that loves not. Seeing then we cannot but love, and that the misplacing of our affection is the cause of all sin and misery, what can we do better than attend to directions how to love as we should?

To come therefore to the four things before mentioned, being the branches of love. First, *We must admire God above all things*. And can we admire anything with wisdom but God alone? It is commonly said that we cannot be wise and love together, for that this affection is blind, except it be in God. Again, Is there anything more comfortable than that we give content to God? Is any service comparable to the service of a prince? We must serve the Lord only, and others in and for him, or else all we do is naught. All other services are bondage; this a perfect freedom. Again, Is there anything more worthy our souls than to be united to God? Can we have a greater happiness than to be made one with Christ? By loving a thing we come to be like to it. Is there anything that may or ought to challenge our love but Christ? Is it not a base thing to unite our souls, which are the best things under heaven, to earthly contentments, than which we shall one day find nothing to be worse? The love of God planted in our hearts maketh Christ and us one. As a pearl in a ring makes the ring more precious and valuable, so the soul united unto Christ cometh to be more gracious and heavenly. The more excellent the soul is, the more loving it will be to God. The holiest saints have ever burned with most affection to Christ, as Moses and Paul. Can anything satisfy us more than God? Know we not that all things here shall perish? Therefore when we place our love and joy in the world, do we not lose them too? We shall leave behind us the things of this life; our sins only we carry away, which cleave fast unto us and stain our consciences world without end. What might more content us than the love of God, which will endure for ever and accompany us to heaven, when all other loves perish?

Consider that every thing thou dost without love is dead and empty. Love is the life of all actions; as we say of a gift, the love of the giver is better than the gift itself; not only our performance is nothing without love, but we ourselves are nothing without it. Every acceptable service we do must proceed from this heavenly flame: 'Though we speak with the tongues of men and angels, and have not love, we are like to a sounding brass and tinkling cymbal,' 1 Cor. xiii. 1. Have we not much to do and suffer in this life? And what is it that makes us constant in duty, and carries us through so many oppositions as we meet withal—is it not love? Doth not love sweeten our hearts, and take away every difficulty in our way to heaven? Whilst we live here, we must of necessity suffer ill things and go on in well-doing; neither of which can be performed without love. This rules our whole lives. Beg therefore of God to quicken thee in all cheerful and willing obedience: pray that the Sun of righteousness would enlighten thy heart. We cannot serve God without God, nor have any holy affection, except by his Spirit he work the same in us.

NOTES.

(*a*) P. 256.—'Luther . . . wished all men after him to read his writings warily.' One of many of the great Reformer's modest self-estimates, found in his Table-Talk. Cf. note *uu*, Vol. III. page 533.

(*b*) P. 256.—'As the apostle St Jude saith, "with both hands the word."' The verb is ἐπαγωνίζομαι, upon which Bengel says, '*Officium duplex pugnare strenue pro fide, contra hostes; et ædificare se ipsum in fide,*' ver. 20. Curiously enough he gives as a reference, Neh. iv. 17 (by a misprint handed down through all the editions of the *Gnomon* ver. 16), which embodies Sibbes's thought, though it is difficult to see where he finds it in the *word.*

(*c*) P. 260.—'The very heathen could say, that we are then best in soul when we are weakest in body, for then we are most in heavenly resolutions and seeking after God.' Is this another form of the apophthegm, 'Man's extremity is God's opportunity'?

(*d*) P. 270.—'So long as God sits at the stern and rules all, we may be sure no evil shall betide us that he can hinder.' Cf. John Newton's beautiful letter to Mr Bean. Having been himself formerly a 'seaman,' he often employs nautical phraseology with great effect.

G.

THE CHRISTIAN'S END.

THE CHRISTIAN'S END.

NOTE.

'The Christian's End' was published in 1639, in a thin volume, with a finely engraved portait of Sibbes prefixed. The impression must have been very limited, as it is among the least frequently occurring of his books, and brings a high price. The title-page is given below.* G.

* THE
CHRISTIANS
END.
OR,
The sweet Soveraignty of CHRIST,
over his members in life and death.
Wherein is contained the whole scope of the
godly MANS life, with divers Rules, Mo-
tives and Incouragements, to live and
die to IESUS CHRIST.
Being the substance of five SERMONS preached
to the Honorable Society of *Grayes* Inne, by
that Learned and faithfull Minister of *Gods
Word*, RICHARD SIBBES, D.D.
and sometimes Preacher to that
Honorable Societie.
1. COR. 6. 20.
Yee are bought with a price, &c.
HEB. 11. 4.
He being dead, yet speaketh.
LONDON,
Printed by *Thomas Harper*, for *Lawrence Chapman*, and
are to be sold at his shop at Chancery lane end
next Holborne, 1639.

THE CHRISTIAN'S END.

THE FIRST SERMON.

None of us liveth to himself, and none of us dieth to himself. For whether we live, we live unto the Lord; and whether we die, we die unto the Lord: whether we live therefore, or die, we are the Lord's.—ROM. XIV. 7, 8.

THE scope of the chapter in the former part of it, is to discover to the Romans, and in them to us all, how to carry ourselves to others in matters of indifferency. As there is difference of things in the world—some good, some ill, and some of a middle nature—so there are different affections in men. About these things of a middle nature some are strong, and they are prone to despise the weaker, for they know their liberty; some more weak, and they are prone to censure and complain of them that be strong, as all weakness is full of impatience. Thus it was with the Romans. The strong despised the weaker, as ignorant; the weaker censured, and in their hearts condemned, the strong, as too adventurous.

The apostle sheweth here an excellent peaceable spirit, hating contention as an evil thing in a church. In a family, when children fall together by the ears, the father taketh up the quarrel, by beating them both. So in a church, while people fall a-contending and breaking the bonds of love, God taketh them in hand. And therefore the apostle taketh them off from this danger by* despising one another, and presseth it by a reason in the fourth verse, drawn,

First, *From their relations.* 'Who art thou that judgest another man's servant?'

Secondly, *From their aims.* They do it both out of religious respects. 'He that eateth, eateth to the Lord; he that eateth not, eateth not to the Lord; he that regardeth not a day, regardeth it not to the Lord; he that doth it, doth it to the Lord.' And therefore if both have a religious respect, censure may be forborne.

There is that force in a good aim, that in some actions of an indifferent nature they may be done, or not be done; and God may bear with both, though he allow not of either's carelessness in searching out the truth. Till the time of growth, God beareth with them, so their aims be gracious, their fault being simple ignorance, not malicious pertinancy.† When St Paul saw the hypocritical aims of the Galatians in things of indifferent natures, he

* Qu. 'of'?—ED. † That is, 'pertinaciousness.'—G.

would not yield a whit to them. But the defect of the Romans was in their knowledge, not in their wills; they did it with respect to the Lord. And therefore as in Acts xiii. 18, God is said ἐτροποφόρειν (an excellent word), to bear with their manners in the wilderness, dispensing with many things, as putting away of wives, &c.; not that he liked that course, but he would set up a meek kind of government, not taking advantage to cast them off. So he dealt with the Romans. Now, shall God be merciful and indulgent, and man severe?

1. In the text you have a general reason why they that did it, or did it not, did or did it not 'to the Lord.' 'For none liveth to himself, or dieth to himself; but whether we live or die, we are the Lord's.'

2. In this reason here is, first, a general negative: 'None of us liveth to himself, none of us dieth to himself'—a figurative speech and rhetorical expression, beginning and ending alike. Secondly, There is a general affirmative; when he hath taken them off from themselves, he assigneth them to a true Lord: 'Whether we live, we live to the Lord; whether we die, we die to the Lord.' And this is set down with a disjunction: we neither live to ourselves, nor die to ourselves.

3. And, thirdly, a general ground that wrappeth up all: 'Whether we live or die, we are the Lord's.' And therefore in reason we should live to him and die to him.

4. Fourthly, There is the ground of all, in that that followeth: 'For to this end Christ died and rose again, that he might be Lord of life and death.' So here is reason upon reason, and ground upon ground.

Conclusion. The sum of all is, we cannot certainly conclude of life or death. For we live but for a while; and when we have acted our part upon the stage we die, and go to another world. Of life and death we can make no reckoning. As soon as we begin to live, we begin to die. For some part of our life is taken away daily; as it is with a sum, the more you take away, the less remaineth. But certain it is, living and dying, 'we are the Lord's.' We ought therefore to have a conjunctive consideration. I now live, yet that is not my comfort; but sure I am, 'whether I live or die, I am the Lord's.'

He riseth from a general to a particular, which may teach us this point of wisdom.

First, *That to have good general truths is an excellent point of wisdom, for they have affluence* into all particulars.* A comprehension of principles is the ground of prudence for direction in particular cases. There is no art but hath some general maxims, as in law, in physic, and in the mathematics, there be canons or principles, call them what you will, that have influence into all particulars. So religion hath general rules, which should be deposited in memory at all times; that on all occasions we may see how particulars spring from and agree to the generals. Therefore we should labour to treasure up in our memory good principles, for men work in all things according to their principles. If they have good principles, or general truths, they work answerably. And the reason of any error in a Christian's life is from false principles.

Men of a bad conscience, whose *synteresis* (being the part of the soul that preserveth principles) is corrupt, they think they do God good service in killing of men, from an abominable principle, John xvi. 2. As in popery, which is grounded upon false principles, making men's traditions a rule of faith.

* That is, 'flowing to' = adaptation or application.—G.

Therefore it is good to have general true grounds. Mark how the Scripture is frequent this way. What an excellent general rule is that of Christ. 'Seek the kingdom of God and his righteousness, and all other things shall be *cast upon you*,' Mat. vi. 33. Carry that along, and what a light doth it give into all our actions. What need we by indirect courses seek to be great in the world, if we take Christ's method?

Again, Our Saviour Christ in his ordinary speech delivered it as a general rule, 'It is better to give than to receive,' Acts xx. 35, which containeth a direction to men to be public and liberal. St Paul's ordinary course was so: 'Knowing therefore the terror of the Lord, we persuade men,' &c., 2 Cor. v. 11. What an influence hath this into our conversations, 'That I must do, as I must give account at the day of judgment.' And so what use made he of the glorious state to come, in that house 'and building of God not made with hands, not seen, but apprehended only by faith,' 2 Cor. v. 1. It enabled him to do and suffer all things that became a Christian to do and suffer. If a man have that principle and mindeth it, 'that all things work together for the best to them that love God,' Rom. viii. 28, what can discourage him? He knoweth in the issue all shall be for the best, and God will not fail him nor forsake him in his way, 'but giveth his angels charge over him,' Ps. xci. 11. So Christ's direction. One thing is necessary, how may it rectify* us when we trouble ourselves about many impertinences? If these generalists† were always present upon solicitations to sin or discomfort, 'It shall go well with the righteous, and it shall not go well with the wicked; if we take good courses it shall be well, if ill courses sin will be bitter:' it would be a marvellous help and advantage in all particulars of our lives.

The second general observation is this, *that as we must get good principles laid* up in store upon all occasion, so *we must specially have gracious aims.* Men are as their aims are. Noble spirits have noble aims (*a*). Christians are of an higher rank than ordinary men, and therefore they have higher aims. Religion giveth command to all other particulars, and prescribeth to them a general end. It taketh a man off from a false end, and pitcheth him upon a true end. It taketh him from himself, the great idol that man naturally setteth up above God and above Christ, and above heaven and happiness, and telleth him that the true end of all is to live to Christ; and that on good grounds, 'for we are his,' and his by good title: 'he died for us, that he might be Lord both of quick and dead,' Acts x. 42. As in state policy, those that are governors in a state they prescribe ends of trades, and reduce them to a serviceableness of state—if they find anything hurtful, they look to it as it stands in reference to the common good—so religion considereth of all particulars as they have reference to Christ and the main end, taking us off from false ends, and prescribing the last and best end, and directing all particulars to that end. But we shall see this better in the unfolding of the words.

The first thing he begins in the general is, to take us off from false ends: 'None of us liveth to himself.'

(1.) First, To live to ourselves is not altogether to be taken in a civil sense. A man liveth to himself *when he liveth privately or retiredly: Benè vixit, qui benè latuit* (*b*). So a man may do in some things, especially in times of persecution; but this ordinarily is not good. A man is a creature for communion; and God hath fitted him for communion by speech and

* That is, = 'put us right.'—G.

† Qu. 'generals,' or 'generalities'?—G.

other endowments, that there may be preserved a communion of saints. But because a retired life is sometimes good, it is not here mainly aimed at.

(2.) Again, secondly, we live to ourselves *when we mind ourselves altogether, and not one another;* when we have more respect to ourselves, than to God or to our Christian brother. And this is even contrary to nature. We see in nature, that a particular nature will in some cases yield to a general, and thwart itself. The fire is a light body, and in the natural motion of it mounteth upward; yet this body will go downwards to preserve whole the universal nature from a vacuum, from emptiness, that the fulness and solidity in nature may not be disturbed. And we see heavy bodies go upward for the same end. As a man will venture the hand to save his head, and to save his body, so it should be in society and government; particular men should venture themselves for the prince or state, for the head or for the body.

(3.) But in a more large and religious sense. To live to a man's self is *to make himself his last end,* his *terminus reductivus,* to reduce all to himself, and make religion and everything serviceable to himself. When a man will serve himself of God for base ends, because his service will advance him; as the Shechemites were circumcised for Dinah, Gen xxxiv. 1, *seq.*

And to die to ourselves is much like it.

(1.) A man dieth to himself, *when he regardeth himself in death, and is regarded much of nobody else.* Persons that have an absolute being of themselves, that have no kindred, not much acquaintance, or have been little fruitful in their lives, die to themselves in a civil sense; that is, no man mourneth for them, saying, 'Ah, my brother,' 1 Kings xiii. 30. They were of little use in their lives, and so little missed in their deaths.

And usually they that live thus to themselves, they die to themselves, little regarded, little lamented. Only this oftentimes, they do most good when they die; as we say of swine, 'They are never good till dead.'

(2.) But this is meant in a theological higher sense. No Christian 'dieth to himself;' that is, *dieth unregarded of God and of good men.* As he liveth not to himself but to Christ, so he dieth not to himself: 'Precious to the Lord is the death of all his saints,' Ps. cxvi. 15. He is not *despotos,** without lord and master; but 'whether he liveth or dieth, he is the Lord's.' So much for the negative part, which we see may be taken both actively and passively.

But this clause will be better understood by adding the other. 'Whether we live, we live to the Lord; or whether we die, we die to the Lord.'

Quest. What is it to live to the Lord?

Ans. First, *To acknowledge the Lord in all our ways to be our Lord, to whom we owe ourselves.*

And secondly, Thereupon *to resign ourselves to the Lord in our whole carriage,* so as to obey him, to give up ourselves to be disposed of him, and directed by him as he pleaseth.

And then, thirdly, *to refer all things to his glory as our last end, and to endeavour that God and Christ may be known and magnified in the world.* When we labour to practise what we pray for, according to that first petition, Hallowed be thy name, his religion and truth, and whatsoever else is God's, may be advanced, set high, published, and enlarged; that he may be known and worshipped; that he may be to us what he is in himself, the great God, 'Lord of quick and dead.' So by our giving respect to him suitable to our knowledge of him.

* Qu. '*adespotos*'?—Ed.

Fourthly and lastly, He that liveth to the Lord *comforteth himself in this, that the Lord taketh notice of him in everything.* For it is a phrase importing a direction to a duty; and likewise to confirm and comfort us in this, that we do our duty. We do not serve a dead master, but one that taketh notice of us 'living and dying.'

(1.) So 'to die to the Lord' is *to acknowledge Christ* 'to be the Lord of life' and the 'Lord of death,' of death as well as of life. 'He hath the keys of hell and of death,' Rev. i. 18, and the disposing of both. Therefore we must resign up ourselves to him in death.

(2.) And then study *to honour him by death in any kind*, yea, by martyrdom, if he shall call us to seal the truth of religion with blood.

(3.) And then *to acknowledge him to be owner of us, and one that will receive us dying*, as he took notice of us living. And so the words are a privilege as well as a duty. As it is sealed up in the last words, 'whether we live or die, we are the Lord's.' Thus I have unfolded the text.

He first premiseth the general negative: 'No man liveth to himself, no man dieth to himself.' You must apply this to Christians only, that are true professors and members of Christ. For other men, that are not in Christ, and have not the Spirit of Christ, 'they live to themselves, and die to themselves,' and aim at themselves in all things; and therefore they are not the Lord's. Therefore it is a fearful condition to live and die to ourselves.

Yet you have some kind of men, not only in their particular persons, but in their callings, are all for themselves. But why should I call it calling; for there is no calling but it is for public good. As an usurer, for whose good is he? Let all sink or swim, what careth he? So times hold, and months and years continue, he will have his returns. And such are they that live in a course of oppression, that live by the ruin and spoil of others.

But there is a more subtle living to a man's self, as all men do that have not the Spirit of Christ; they live within that circle, self. The devil keepeth them that they go not out of it; so that self doth run through all their actions, their civil actions, yea, their religious actions, which are all tainted with self-respects.

Ever since the fall it is so. Man withdraweth himself from God's government, and setteth up himself instead of God, and thought to have a secured happiness from God, in eating the forbidden fruit, and therefore would not depend upon God to be happy. He saw another way to be like God. God hath highest place in our heart by order of creation, and according to the degrees of excellency in things should our esteem of them be, 'everything being beautiful in his place,' Eccles. iii. 11. But where God is put down,—as he is in all men till they be in Christ,—something self-love sets up in the heart above God. Hence cometh the necessity of this method of taking us off from ourselves before we can live to Christ; because self-love is an impediment and block in the way between us and Christ, heaven and happiness. And therefore Christ begins the gospel with self-denial: 'Whosoever will be my disciple, let him take up his cross and follow me,' Mat. xvi. 24.

Now there be four degrees of self.

There is, 1. Natural self. 2. Civil self. 3. Sinful self. 4. Religious self.

(1.) First, *Natural self* is the state we are in as men.

(2.) Secondly, *Civil*, as we are poor, or rich, or honourable, according to our several places in the commonwealth.

(3.) Thirdly, *Sinful self* is, as we are carried to sinful lusts and the creature.

(4.) Fourthly, *Religious self* is our condition in Christ, when we are engrafted into him and made new creatures.

'Now we must not live to ourselves.'

1. First, Not to our *natural self*. We must not live only to live. For as all other creatures are to serve us, so we are to serve something else that is better. For that that is not of itself, cannot be for itself. Now we have not beings from ourselves, but from God. He giveth us beings, and a being in that rank of creatures wherein we are. Therefore our natural self must be to a higher end. A man is not the end of things. There is another end than he, and that is God, who is of himself, and hath made all other things for himself, and therefore riches, and honours, and the like.

2. We should not live to our *civil self*. Nature teacheth us that, having spirits, we are not for anything meaner than ourselves. We do not live here to be rich, to be great, to command others; for these things do not answer the soul of man.

[1.] First, *Nothing that hath an end can be a chief end*. That that hath *finem consummatum* cannot be *finis consummans*. That that hath an end consuming itself, cannot be an end perfecting* itself. We have a journey beyond all things, and that cannot be our end that leaveth us in the way. Riches and honour are determined† in death. Let our preferments be never so great, though to the monarchy of the whole world, yet we have a being beyond them. They have consumptions in themselves.

[2.] And then they be *inferior*. No truth in them can fill up the understanding; no good in them can fill up the will. But the understanding can pierce through them. And the will, in relishing and tasting the good of them, can look on them as cast commodities. It can quickly suck out all the sweet that is in them. Therefore they cannot be a man's end, because he hath larger parts than they can fill.

[3.] That that must be a man's end *must be larger than the soul;* and that wherein he can rest, it must be some universal good, fit for all turns and purposes. Now there is nothing in the world that hath more than a particular service, for men's particular service, for men's particular ends. Honour can do something, but not all things. Riches cannot command health, they cannot cure a fit of an ague; they be for a particular good only. They can command many things, but not all things. Men consider what they can do, and therefore desire them. But they consider not what they cannot do, and therefore they rest in them. That which is a man's last end must be a satisfying, general, universal good, an immortal good, of equal continuance with him, as nothing in the world is.

[4.] It must be such a good *as he cannot offend or be defiled withal*, such as he cannot misuse. And what is there in the world, but Christ and the best things, but a man is prone to defile himself in? Knowledge is the best thing, but that worketh like leaven, it swells: as the apostle saith, 'Knowledge puffeth up,' 1 Cor. viii. 1. Therefore we must live to no worldly thing.

3. And much less must we live to *sinful self*. Some things are to be denied in way of competition and in opposition, but some things are to be denied absolutely. Absolutely a man must not own, or live to a base lust, pride, or sensuality. He oweth nothing to these but mortification. 'We

* Qu. 'perfect in'?—Ed.

† That is, 'ended.'—G.

are not debtors to the flesh,' saith the apostle, Rom. viii. 12. Therefore when a proud vindictive motion ariseth, say, I owe no suit or service to the flesh. What should these do in a heart dedicated to God, consecrated to Christ? I am not mine own, much less Satan's, or lusts'; which be objects of mortification, but no way worthy of my service. Absolute denial is required here.

Of other things, a denial is required only as they stand in competition with Christ. In that case a man must sacrifice Isaac, not only his sinful self, but natural self also, his life and bodily liberty, the dearest thing in the world, and whatsoever is sweet, for Christ.

He having taken us off from ourselves, assigneth us to a true Lord. 'We live to the Lord, and die to the Lord.' It had not been enough to say, 'We ought not to live to ourselves, or die to ourselves,' if he had not told whom we must live to, and die to. For naturally man will never leave anything, though but an apparent good, till he knoweth something better. A man will not part with a bad master till he hath a better service. Therefore he sheweth where to bestow ourselves; namely, upon Christ, who hath care of us both in life and death.

4. This is to be laid down for a ground; *had we not a better being in Christ than in ourselves, he would never take us from ourselves, for God never biddeth us to our loss.* We have a better condition in Christ than we can have in the world. It is our gain and advantage to live and die to Christ; though it be to the loss of natural self, of civil self, and whatsoever else, yet it is our advantage. It is *mercatorium*, not a loss, but a trading. We have a better for worse. No man ever parted with anything for religion, or a public good, but God made it up in a better kind. Though God should not make it up in this world, in the same kind, yet in religion there be all things better than in the world. If we lose honour here, we have honour from God. If we lose riches, we have them made up in grace here, in glory hereafter. If we lose liberty, we have it in the enlargement of a good conscience. If we lose friends, we get a God for a friend, who can make our enemies friends. If we lose life, we are put into possession of eternal life, and therefore we need not stand at the bargain. We have a better being in Christ than in ourselves. Water is not lost when it emptieth itself into the sea, for there it is in its proper element. A Christian is not lost when he loseth himself in his God, in his Saviour; for in him he hath a better being than in himself. He is brought nearer the fountain: 'I desire to depart and to be with Christ, which is the best of all,' saith the apostle, Philip. i. 23. Religion is a most excellent condition; for as he 'that saveth his life shall lose it, so he that loseth his life shall save it,' Mat. x. 39.

All our comforts have a better being in Christ than in ourselves; and therefore we should labour to have communion with him, and to strengthen our faith in Christ, and be in love with our happy condition in him, which yieldeth comfort in life and death. And all by virtue of the death of Christ, and the resurrection of Christ. As he saith afterward, 'Christ both died and rose again, that he might be Lord both of the dead and of the living.'

The resurrection of Christ is the consummation of all. 'If Christ had not risen again,' where had our comfort been? But the very thought of it, that we are engrafted in one who hath not only purchased us by his death—'for we are the price of his blood;' but to make it clear that it is so, is now in heaven as our head, having overcome death, and intending to bring all his body where he is, as it was his will 'that where he is, we should be also,' John xvii. 24—is a glorious thought. The glory of Christian religion is in the resurrection of Christ; and to consider that we that are creeping here on earth shall be members of him that is glorious in heaven, 'Lord of heaven and earth,' who not only 'died for us, but is risen again,' and will make us all, both in body and soul, conformable to his glorious self, as the apostle saith to the Philippians, Philip. iii. 10, cannot but infuse life and vigour into all our actions, estates, and conditions, be they never so mean, and have a wonderful influence into the whole life of a Christian.

THE SECOND SERMON.

None of us liveth to himself, and none of us dieth to himself. For whether we live, we live unto the Lord; and whether we die, we die unto the Lord: whether we live therefore, or die, we are the Lord's.—Rom. XIV. 7, 8.

1. First, The general scope of the apostle is, to take us off from our false ends: 'None of us liveth to himself,' &c.

2. Secondly, To assign us to the true object, to whom we ought to dedicate ourselves, that is, 'to the Lord.'

3. Thirdly, The ground of all, 'Whether we live or die, we are the Lord's.'

4. And then, fourthly, the spring of all: 'Christ both died and rose again, that he might be Lord both of quick and dead.'

There is a concatenation and knitting together of divine truths, they following one another by a necessity of consequence. As from the body of the sun, there is a natural issue of beams; and as in plants derivation* from the root into the branch; so there is from Christ into all truths. Grant him to be the second Adam, and grant him Lord of the living and of the dead, and it will follow, we ought to live to him. If we grant we ought to live to Christ, then we must grant we ought not to live to ourselves. For we ought to live to Christ. Why to Christ? Because he is Lord both of life and death. Why is he Lord? Because he hath purchased it by his blood. How do we know he hath purchased it by his death satisfactorily? Because he is risen again, and sitteth at the right hand of God to make all good for us. Things are best to us when they are digested and made our own by the presence of good principles. But here is the mischief: Sin is ready, and good principles are not engraffed into us; but if divine truths were as near as corruption is, then we could withstand and repel all temptations.

As travellers have the end of their journey in their thoughts habitually, though not actually—for every step they take is in virtue of their end—so we should consider that we are all travellers in the way to heaven, and every step of our life should be to that end.

The ignorance of this maketh the life of most men to be but a digression from the main, as if they were brought into the world only to satisfy base lusts, and to seek themselves, to serve Satan and sin, the professed enemies of God, which are not only digressions, but motives† to hell and eternal destruction. What a pitiful thing is it, that creatures should come

* That is, 'communication.'—G.

† That is, 'motions.'—G.

into the world and live, some twenty, some forty, some more* years, and go out of the world again, not knowing wherefore they lived.

Good reason it is we should live to Christ, acknowledge him in all our ways, live answerable to our knowledge, resign up ourselves to his government, and seek his glory in all things; that we may make Christ known in the world; that all that see us may see Christ in us, and perceive our love to him 'that hath called us out of darkness into his marvellous light.' 1 Peter ii. 9.

And also to acknowledge him to be Lord of our life; and in death to resign ourselves to him 'as a faithful Creator;' knowing that he taketh care of us in life and death.

1. For we are not our own: 'We are bought with a price,' as the apostle saith, 1 Cor. vi. 20.

2. Again, Ourselves are our greatest enemies. There is no such flatterer as the bosom flatterer. That enemy self, that we have in our bosoms, betrayeth us to Satan, else all the devils in hell could not hurt us. Self is our own enemy and God's enemy. Nay, enemy is too easy, too good a word: the best thing in us is enmity itself against God.

3. By woful experiment† we find that which hath brought all the misery that the world ever felt hath been self-will. Men will be turned upside down, rather than their wills shall be crossed. But doth not this provoke God? Shall a piece of earth strive against him? and will not he break it to powder? Surely God will set us a mark to shoot at, and will triumph and get himself victory and glory over those creatures that will have their wills. Hell is fit for such. God will be sure to have his will of them. When the creature shall set his will against God's will, when an earthen pot shall set itself against a mace of brass, which will have the worst, think you?

4. If we live to ourselves, we lie open to Satan. But, on the contrary part, a man that liveth to God is fit for any gracious motions, whatsoever they be. He is fit for God and a blessed communion of saints.

5. Man is a reasonable creature, made for God, And if you grant there is a God, you must grant that man is to do service to that God. God is the creditor and man the debtor, and of necessity there must be an obligation.

Now, to shew the nature of this living to Christ.

(1.) First, *It imports a vital operation*, an exercise that proceeds from life. Now, as natural life springeth from union of the body with the soul, so the union of the soul with Christ bringeth into the soul true principles of an holy and spiritual life. For Christ and the soul cannot touch one another, but presently he infuseth a living principle. All artificial motions proceed from something without. And such are the self-seeking Christians that do only act a part in religion; but those that truly live to God and Christ, they have an inward instinct that inclines them to holiness.

(2.) Secondly, *There is entireness in a Christian course*, so that he liveth to none but Christ. Life is not only taken for the space of his being in the world, but for the improving of all the furtherances of our life to Christ. As to bestow ourselves upon him, in all the civil relations we have in the world, by being obedient to him and to others in him and for him; and in whatsoever callings we are, not only in our natural life, but also in our civil life, to go on in a constant tenor all the whole course of our lives aiming at Christ; not to set ourselves in our callings to get riches—for

* Spelled 'moe,' as in Spenser.—G.

† That is, 'experience.'—G.

those shall be cast in by the way—God alloweth us riches, but not to be our ends, but that we may serve him and honour him. There is no time to sin, but a time for everything else.

(3.) Thirdly, In our living to Christ there must be *evenness and uniformity*. We must not live to Christ for a fit, but constantly; not to do now and then a good action, but to make it our course, our trade, to live to Christ entirely, constantly, uniformly.

(4.) Fourthly, And then living to the Lord implieth, *that all Christians' counsel and advice is how to live to Christ*. Heaven is always before him, because his way is to God and to Christ. Other men will rage and swell, though they know well enough they are out of the way, when they be put in mind of it. But a gracious man is glad to have any Scripture opened that may give him more light, either by a discovery of a sin or duty, because he now knoweth an enemy and friend, which before he knew not, and hath learned a duty which before he was ignorant of; for it is his scope and endeavour to set himself in the way of living to Christ.

(5.) Fifthly, He that liveth to Christ hath likewise this quality, *he is not carried on his course by false winds;* he doth not sail by a false compass. Though the world encourageth or discourageth him, all is one, he regardeth it not. His care is wholly taken up in the service of his God. And with Joshua, think the world what it will, 'he and his house will serve the Lord,' Josh. xxiv. 15; and with holy David will resolve to be yet 'more vile for God's glory,' 2 Sam. vi. 22. And though he getteth disgrace in the world, he regardeth it not, but is willing to suffer it, so that his God may be honoured, knowing he shall not be a loser by the bargain.

Other men, if so be they are disgraced, they are so shallow in religion, that they are quickly taken off, because the truth hath no root in them, like the bad and naughty* ground. And not only so, but they will speak contrary to the truths in their consciences; but, alas! one day they shall know that God accounteth them as his enemies.

(6.) Sixthly, Again, a true Christian *will live to the church of Christ*. For we are members of Christ. We ought to labour for the advancement of the truth of his religion, the kingdom of Christ; and to be of the same spirit with good Nehemiah, 'that all may be well with us, when the church of God prospereth,' ii. 20, and groweth up in the world, getting victory over all her enemies.

Now carnal men live not at all to Christ; they care not whether religion sinketh or swimmeth. Tell them of heavenly matters, Tush, they are not for them. But God doth hate such persons; for as they regard not to serve God, or to own Christ in their lives, so he will not own them at their deaths. As in prosperity they are not on his side, neither will own his part, which one day will prove the best, so in times of trouble they cannot expect or look for any favour or mercy from him.

And to add one thing more, though it must be our chief aim to look to Christ, yet God allows us to look also to our own salvation, how to be saved and happy in another world. God hath joined these two together, as one chief end and good. The one, that he might be glorified; the other, that we might be happy: and both these are attained by honouring and serving him. And this is no self-love; for we cannot seek our salvation but in honouring God and yielding† the means that he hath sanctified for us, which is to cast ourselves on him for our salvation in his way. Thus

* Cf. Mat. xiii. 3, *seq.*, 'Naughty' = worthlesss.—G.

† Qu. 'yielding to'?—Ed.

our happiness and God's chief end agree together. As when there be two lines about a centre, one drawn within the other, a third line cannot be drawn from the utmost line to the centre without cutting the line within, because it is included within the other, so our salvation and happiness is within the glory of God, and we live to Christ, not only in serving him, but in seeking our own souls; and what a sweetness is this in God, that in seeking our own good we should glorify him.

This likewise teacheth us to live to Christ in a way of humility and self-denial. God will not deny to teach the humble and lowly soul his ways. And thus a gracious man is fit for all the counsels of God, as a carnal heart is fit for all the services of the devil. Therefore let us dedicate ourselves and services to God, for happy are they that can lose themselves in God, and be swallowed up in the love of Christ. Certainly, there is never better finding of ourselves, than when we are thus lost. And therefore I beseech you, whatsoever our corruptions have been heretofore; let us now know it is heavenly wisdom to seek Christ's glory in the use of the blessed means sanctified for that end.

Surely we have all been baptized; and what is our baptism, but the renouncing of the world, the flesh, and the devil? Our life is for nothing but to live unto God. And having entered into covenant in baptism in the name of the Father, Son, and Holy Ghost, that we intend seriously to lead a new life, we must not trifle with God; he will not be dallied with. It is not only sufficient that we have spent our precious time amiss, but more than sufficient. For time will come, if we belong to Christ, in which we shall lament for spending our time in the pursuit of our own vanities.

For if we live according to our own lusts, we are but rebels under God's livery; we are but traitors fighting under his banner. And how can we give account at the day of judgment of our lives, that have been nothing else but a constant service for Christ's enemies under the colour of religion? This would* seriously be thought upon.

Therefore, as we know a great deal, and are beholding to God for living in times and places where there is abundance of the truth revealed, so we ought to make it our life and course to honour him, to be vigorous in his service, and to stir up the grace of God in us; to awaken ourselves and to live to Christ, and to put this *quære* to our souls, Whom do I serve? myself or Christ? him or his enemies?

Out of the text you may see that a Christian will learn how to carry himself, not only to himself, but to Christ. His carriage to himself is to live as a Christian exercised in his duty and calling. His carriage to Christ is to live to him and die to him. And for this end he taketh this course, to search out himself what is unsound and corrupt in him; and when he hath found himself, then he abhorreth himself, and judgeth himself. And having found out corruption in his heart, he not only loatheth it, but crucifieth it; and this is the course that a Christian taketh with himself in the searching and discovery of his sins.

And this being done, he setteth up Christ in the place of self, which ruleth in all men till they be Christians indeed, either by way of admission or covenant. But when grace hath once taken place in the heart, then the soul begins to live to Christ, and that conscionably,† entirely, and uniformly; consulting with all things how to help and further that life. Other men consult how they may keep their honours and reputations in the world. But a Christian having other aims, deviseth not only ways to

* Qu. 'should'?—G.

† That is, 'conscientiously.'—G.

live to Christ, but how to be better more and more, how to get into Christ, and how to grow up in him, knowing that by living to Christ here he shall live with him for ever hereafter. This is the course of a true Christian, that looketh to have benefit by Christ.

THE THIRD SERMON.

None of us liveth to himself, and none of us dieth to himself. For whether we live, we live unto the Lord; and whether we die, we die unto the Lord: whether we live therefore, or die, we are the Lord's.—Rom. XIV. 7, 8.

We have heard from the apostle's general negative, that self must be removed out of the way, before we can live or die to Christ. Self, indeed, will come in everything till the Spirit of Christ be all in all in us. It is like Esau, that came first out of the womb. It will appear first in all consultations. And therefore it is the method of our blessed Saviour; 'Whosoever will be my disciple, let him deny himself, and take up my cross,' Mat. xvi. 24. And it will be easy so to do when we have denied ourselves.

From the apostle's general affirmative, we have shewed that to live to the Lord is to acknowledge ourselves to be his, and him to be ours; and answerably to do him service, to resign up ourselves to him, to seek his glory, and honour, and credit in all things, and to be well persuaded that he will stick to us. So that it is a comfort as well as a duty.

To die to the Lord is to be willing to give up ourselves to him when the time cometh, and to submit to him for the manner of our death, whether he will call us home to himself by a quiet or troublesome death, by a bloody or dry death, with confidence that he will receive our souls.

That we may be directed to pitch upon a right end, we may know by the principles of nature a man is not for himself; and from the order that God hath placed him in, all things below are for him, but he is for something above himself. He is not of himself, and therefore not to himself. God only is of himself, by himself, and to himself. Everything under God is of God, and by God, and therefore to God. As Saint Augustine saith, 'Thou hast made us for thee, and our hearts rest not till we come to thee;'* as the rivers never rest till they discharge themselves into the ocean.

And being not his own end, it is his wisdom and understanding to look principally to that which is his last and best and main end, which is God, and union and communion with God in Christ, who is God in our nature, God-man, the best of all, and therefore it is fit he should be the last. He communicateth all good to them that be his, and preserveth all the good he communicateth. He is for ever with them, and cannot fail to do them good, as long as he fails not to be good. He is the original cause, and the communicating cause, and the maintaining cause of all good.

Now it is the nature of the utmost and furthest end to stir up to every action leading to that end; for every deliberate rational action that is done with advertisement and observation, and is not an action of fancy or common nature, must fall under the consideration of an end, or else we cannot give account for it, as we must for every word, desire, and thought.

* Cf. note *h*, Vol. I. p. 294.—G.

Now the end stirreth us up to all means leading to that end, either immediately as they are the services of God properly, or else remotely. As things that help reason and furtherances thereunto, as the apostle willeth 'that whether we eat or drink, or whatsoever we do,' 1 Cor. x. 31, all should be done to the glory of God, because these maintain us in health and strength, and that health and strength enable us to God's service. And in this sense every action a Christian doth is a service of God; for the end doth advance it and raise it above itself, and make it spiritual: as recreation to cheer him to diligence in his calling, the serving of his brother, and the like. Some actions are holy in the stuff and matter of them, others are such for the end to which they are directed. For the meanest action becomes holy, if an holy end be put upon it.

And therefore the actions of the second table are the service of God as well as the first, as they do all agree in the end. No man violateth a magistrate in the second table, but he wrongeth God in the first. No man stealeth, or committeth adultery, or disgraceth his neighbour by false witness, which is prohibited in the second, but it is for want of fear of God commanded in the first.

Duties of the second rightly performed are in virtue of the commandments of the first, when they are done not only from human and lower grounds, as things good in themselves, but also because God and Christ have commanded them; and that is included in the general words of 'living to the Lord;' for to live is comprehensive, and includeth all our actions, from the beginning to the end and closing up of our days. Whatsoever actions fall within the term of life ought to be referred to God as the last end.

1. The reason is, Christ *hath redeemed our persons, and our times, and all that we are, or have, or can do;* all our ability, our whole *posse*, is Christ's, and not our own. I must be filled up with actions suitable to Christ, therefore if I could do a thousand times more than I do, it were all due to him. Myself, my time, my advantages, my calling, and all, are his.

2. Again, As the end stirs up to actions of all kinds, so *it prescribeth a measure to those actions, to do them, so far as shall be advantageous to that end.* As he that hath a race to run will measure his diet suitable to that end, so he that hath an aim 'to live to Christ' will use all things here as may serve that turn. He will use the world as if he used it not, will buy as if he possessed not, will marry as if he married not. Not that he will be slight or superficial in these things; but he will do them no further than may be advantageous to the enjoying of Christ here, as comfortably as he can, and for ever hereafter.

Indeed, no man can set measures to his desire of happiness, that being a vast ocean; his main end cannot be desired too much. For as it is his good and happiness, it is larger than himself, yea, his thoughts and desires are too short to reach it. But though a man desires not health too much, yet he may desire too much physic. The measure must be in our pursuit of inferior things, because therein we are apt to exceed. And that advantage a Christian hath in setting a right end. He will not be drowned in the world, nor live to recreations, but to a farther aim, and which prescribes a measure and duration to all things else.

3. The end likewise *maketh everything that tendeth to the end lovely.* It maketh the cross lovely, for by it we grow better, and get more in large communion with Christ. Welcome is poverty, or disgrace, or whatsoever

that maketh a man live more to Christ, and die to himself. Men call for physic, though in itself distasteful, as it is in order to health; an end which we desire without end. So it is the disposition of a gracious soul, if Christ bestow himself on him, communicate his gracious Spirit, peace of conscience, joy in the Holy Ghost, increase of the image of God. Let God lay upon us what he will, yet it will appear lovely.

4. It prescribeth likewise *a right order to every duty*. For as the end sets one thing above another, so a wise man that looketh to his best end will do the main work first, and other things in the second place, according to our Saviour's counsel, 'Seek first the kingdom of God and his righteousness, and all other things shall be cast upon you,' Mat. vi. 33. Some indeed love to be all in by-works, and in the mean time neglect and slight the main. But our care should be so to use the world that we may not lose Christ, or communion with him in better things; so to look to things temporal, as that we lose not things eternal. For as things are in themselves, so they should be to us. Now as some thing is better than another, so we should conceive of them, and affect them as better than another, and labour to do them before another, as deserving the first place. And that is the reason the saints have so prized and entertained communion with God and Christ. 'One thing I desire,' saith the prophet; that is, 'to dwell in the house of the Lord for ever,' Ps. xxvii. 4. And 'one thing is necessary,' saith Christ, Luke x. 41. Other things be necessary in their order, but to have communion with God is the main thing necessary.

Use. Let us therefore often *consider of the end of our life in this world*, and take shame to ourselves that we have let so much water run besides* the mill, that we have let so much precious time, and strength, and dear advantages be lost. Too much strength hath been spent in the service of sin and our base lusts, which we can give no account of. How many scandalous blasphemous words are many guilty of, which help only to advantage their destruction, if God be not merciful.

Now a little to shew the guise of the world, and the difference of it from the actions of God's children, for these words employ† a restraint to God's people as well as an extension.

Obj. The Christian's whole life is only to Christ; but what is the life of a man out of Christ?

Ans. His first aims being corrupt, 'God is not in all his thoughts,' as the psalmist speaks, Ps. x. 4, neither to have communion with him here in grace, nor in glory hereafter. Therefore whatsoever good he doth, a false end poisoneth it. If a man, misunderstanding of a thing, be from a false principle, he misunderstands it grossly. As, if an house be built upon a weak foundation, such is all the fabric, though otherwise never so costly; if the principles be naught, the conclusions drawn from thence must needs be naught also. As in physic, if the first concoction be naught, the second can never be good. So if a man's ends are naught, if he seek himself, or doth things only from foreign motives, out of terror of conscience, or for vain glory, or to be seen of men, his corrupt aim spoileth all his actions; yea, he reduceth religion to himself, because he will enjoy his pleasures the better. He will act some part of religion, lest conscience should bark and clamour against him. This self will moderate religion, and restrain it to such a measure as may stand with his lusts and sinful customs.

If he loveth others, it is in order to himself, because he hath use of them,

* That is, 'beside' = past.—G. † Qu. 'imply'?—Ed.

as they comply with him in wicked courses, and so help to bear him out the better.

And if any man stands in the ways of his ends of honour or riches, he removeth them by disgrace, though it amounteth to slandering; as undermining and rising by others' ruins, because self, his idol and main end, must not be crossed. He desireth to be somebody in the flesh. All things must be measured by that, yea, religion, and acquaintance, and all; and whatsoever stands in the way, it crieth down with them, but however it killeth them in the esteem of others, that they themselves might be thought something; and thus all is turned clean contrary upside down.

But a gracious man's end and aim is to get out of himself and his corrupt nature, and to order all his actions in reference to that, and all his acquaintance and communion with others as may help his communion with God. And whatsoever is an impediment to that he laboureth to remove.

But to give you some directions how to live, not to ourselves, but to live and die to the Lord.

First, We must have a spiritual life from him, for life is but the issue of life.

We must live by faith, from union with Christ by faith, and then live to Christ.

And again, we must do it constantly and uniformly. No part of our lives must be alienated from Christ; all must be done in order to him; even our recreations must have some good aims in them.

Motives. Now do but consider we are his. We are not our own, but his, and therefore we ought to live to him, bringing in all our strength, all our advantages, our callings. That we may do service to him in our places, we are redeemed even from ourselves. A world of people think they be redeemed to live as they list. But because God is merciful, and Christ a Saviour, may you therefore live like libertines? No. You are redeemed *from* yourselves, not *to* yourselves.

And to former rules delivered let me add, that this living to Christ (though naturally we count it bondage, because it is the acknowledging of a superior) is the most perfect liberty, *Deo servire, est regnare* (*c*). For he that serveth that which is better and larger than himself, that hath more good and ability than himself, he doth advance himself by his service, and freeth himself from the service of all inferiors. For the more dependent any man is on Christ in his service and in expectation of reward from him, the more independent is he upon the world. And indeed who is free in his thoughts and desires from base engagements to the creature, but he that sets up Christ highest in his soul, and suffers him to prescribe rules to him in his life? Which is freer in the world than they that have hearts freed from overmuch love of earthly things, overmuch fear of earthly things, overmuch delight in earthly things? He useth them as helps to the main, but is not engaged or enthralled to any. *Quanto subjectior, tanto liberior.* The more subject the more free, is St Augustine's rule (*d*). And it is undoubtedly so. You shall find by experience that the soul is never at a more gracious liberty, than when Christ is all in all. We see it in the example of Zaccheus. When once he believed in Christ, presently, 'Half my goods I give to the poor,' Luke xix. 8. St Paul, that was all for the world and vain-glory, can say now, 'My life is not dear to me, so I may finish my course with joy,' Acts xx. 24. 'In comparison of Christ, all is dung,' Philip. iii. 8. When Moses had seen God that was invisible, he was freed from all base dependence on the favour of Pharaoh; nay, he esteemed the reproaches of Christ better than all the riches of Egypt,' Heb. xi. 28. And that makes men's stomachs inwardly to rise against Christians, because they be not men to serve times and turns. They will not prostitute their consciences and religion for any man's pleasure; whereas other men, though naturally never so stout and strong in parts, yet having base aims, and hearts fastened to the world, will debase their very natures, and when their end cometh in competition with honesty, they love it more than goodness. As Christ telleth the Pharisees, 'You cannot believe, that seek honour one of another,' John v. 44.

This is it that maketh a Christian better than his neighbour, because he hath a better aim. All other men have narrow spirits, whose hearts are not filled with the enlarging spirit of grace and of Christ. But the course of the children of God is a course contrary to the stream of the world. Let others take what course they will, it matters not; they will look to themselves. It is good for them to draw near to God, and to be guided by his Spirit. A Christian seeks communion with him that is all in all, with an infinite good, with God in Christ, and Christ God-man, and happiness. Another man is straitened in his affections to some particular good, that is meaner than himself, which maketh him a base-spirited man. He that enlargeth his heart to seek out a condition that is larger and better than himself, is both wise and happy. One would require no more to Christianity, but to have sanctified judgments, that God is God, and Christ is Christ, and the word is the word, and rules that cannot be denied are true, unless he will be an atheistical beast below himself. And therefore Lactantius saith well, 'Religion is the true wisdom' (*e*). Let a man be judicious, and he must needs be a Christian; the necessity and excellency of it standing upon such undeniable grounds.

Obj. Oh but I shall lose my reputation, saith the doubtful heart of man, and be counted a fool. I shall lose my friends and contentment, if I come to be religious and serious indeed.

Ans. These be idle objections, as if they were not in this kind better in religion than in the world: as if God did bid us to our loss, as if Christ bid us follow him to our disadvantage. Surely no! He is Lord of heaven and earth, and can recompense us in this world. But what is all pleasure here to the pleasure of a good conscience? What is friendship here to communion with God, and friendship with Christ, and the protection of angels? What are riches to him that is the fountain of all riches? Did not Moses know what he did, when he forsook Pharaoh's court? or Paul, when he said, 'to be with Christ is best of all?' Philip. i. 23. Did not Abraham know what he did, when he left his father's house and followed God, though to the giving up of Isaac, whom he knew God could raise up again, he being all-sufficient? Heb. xi. 19. Perhaps I lose a friend, or petty pleasure, or contentment, but that was but a particular good, serving for a particular turn only. But instead thereof I have God, that is all-sufficient for all turns, that is near to me, and never nearer than when I deny anything for his sake. A man hath never more of God than when he denieth himself most for God; for in what measure we empty ourselves of love to any creature, in that measure God fills the soul with contentments of an higher kind. We have within that particular good, which we parted with; and we have peace and grace, which is incomparably above it. Think of that, and it will be an infinite encouragement to live to Christ.

And therefore take these rules. Seek the end in the means? I can have Christ my end, my riches, pleasures, friends. It is well. But if I cannot have my end with these things, away with them! When they be gone, the end will remain. Christ will continue, though they leave us. We may enjoy anything here, if the main end can be enjoyed with them. If not, let us be willingly stripped of all, for we shall be stripped of them by death. God hath enough. He hath all things at command; and hath wisdom enough a thousand ways to provide, that we shall not be losers by him, no, not in this life.

Consider then what it is to give ourselves to the Lord. When we give ourselves, we give all things else with ourselves. 'They gave themselves to the Lord,' 2 Cor. viii. 5, and then they would easily part with their goods, as the apostle saith.

But we will never give ourselves to the Lord, till we consider what he hath done for us. He hath given himself wholly for us; left heaven for us; denied himself for us; made himself of no reputation for us; became a worm and no man, a curse for us. And in way of requital we should answer him, with giving ourselves and all we have to him. This is to be a Christian to purpose. Christ hath given himself to me, and therefore I will give my goods, myself, my life to Christ, that is, in affection and preparation of spirit, though not in action. And in action too, when he calleth for them. I am not mine own; he hath myself. And *fructus sequitur fundum*. He shall have whatsoever is mine. If he call me to suffer losses, crosses, disgrace, or death itself, welcome all. I am his: and therefore whatsoever is mine is his. And it is no more than he hath done for me. He went so low, that he could not be lower, and be God. He hath advanced my nature as high as my nature could be advanced, by union with his person; and he will advance my person to heaven. And therefore the martyrs were willing to part with their lives. They 'loved not their lives to death,' as Christ's phrase is. 'He that loveth his life shall lose his life,' Mat. x. 39. 'My life is not dear to me,' saith St Paul, Acts xx. 24, so ready was he to resign all for Christ.

Reason. The reason is, which I desire may not be forgotten, we have a better being in God than in ourselves. If we lose our natural life, we have in him a better life. If we lose our riches, we have them in heavenly treasures. The water is not lost that runneth into the sea; it is in the ocean still, its better receptacle.

It was St Paul's desire 'to be dissolved and to be with Christ, which is best of all,' Philip. i. 23. But if he will have me to serve the church here and enjoy my life longer, his will be done. So he liveth to the Lord, and dieth to the Lord; and whatsoever cometh, he is *in utrumque paratus* (*f*): whether he liveth or dieth, he is the Lord's.

THE FOURTH SERMON.

For none of us liveth to himself, and no man dieth to himself. For whether we live, we live unto the Lord; and whether we die, we die unto the Lord: whether we live therefore, or die, we are the Lord's.—Rom. XIV. 7, 8.

In these words the apostle taketh us off from ourselves, and assigneth us to a true end. As the first thing that grace doth, is to set God and Christ in his own place, the heart; so, in the second place, it begets a regard of ourselves, such as may stand with the love of Christ. For till Christ hath a place in the heart, by our coming to some degrees of self-denial, self hindereth us in all our whole course, both of believing and doing. For we have naturally contrary principles to all articles of faith, and contrary motions to all the commands of God. It hinders us in our duties to God, to others, to ourselves. And therefore to what I formerly said, I may add this consideration,

Doct. That it is no easy thing to be a Christian. If we were required to renounce anything else, we might obtain it of ourselves, sooner than deny ourselves; for what is nearer to ourselves than ourselves? 'Thousand rivers of oil, the first fruits of the body, would be given for the sin of the soul,' Micah vi. 7. That outward mortification, so much magnified in popery, is nothing to the renouncing of a lust. But if we would be Christians to purpose, we must be stripped of ourselves; as they say of the serpent, he must part with the old slough. We must have an higher principle than ourselves before we can do it. A Christian is above himself, and better than himself, and stronger than himself, because he hath a better self than himself. And by virtue of that better self, which is grace in his heart, he is able to bring under all his other self, not only his sinful self, but his natural self; neither his life nor anything is dear unto him, in comparison of Christ.

Therefore we must not have conceits of religion as easy. Indeed, if we had sanctified judgments, and hearts set at liberty, it were an easy thing. If we had judgments to see, that we are never more ourselves, than when we are not ourselves; that we have a better being in Christ than in ourselves; that ourselves are our worst enemies—if the judgment were thus possessed, and the will and affections made answerable to this judgment, it were easy to deny ourselves. But self hinders the knowledge of itself all it can. *Peccatum impedit sui cognitionem:* sin naturally hinders the knowledge of its own foulness. That which should discern sin is clouded, and that which should hate sin is engaged to sin. So that under the use of means we must labour to know our condition, and the foulness and danger of that condition. And that is the excellency of God's ordinances and divine truths, that by them we come to know ourselves. But I will not enlarge myself in that.

What it is to live and die to the Lord we have declared. That it is to make Christ his chief aim and end, and do all in virtue of that end. Then is a Christian in his right temper, when God's end, Christ's end, and his end have the same centre—a qualification very excellent.

That that makes God delight in his children so much is, that they have the same end, the same God, the same Spirit with Christ. It is so excellent to prefix a right end to all our actions, that it spiritualiseth common actions. As St Paul saith of servants, 'They serve the Lord in serving their masters,' Eph. vi. 5. Whatsoever the stuff of our actions be, yet in that aim and spirit in which they be done, they may be services of the Lord.

Now life implieth the whole course of our actions. All our actions should be to the Lord immediately and directly, or mediately and reductively, as they are quickened by the Spirit of God. And that is the excellency of a Christian. He considers of everything as it helpeth his last end; as on the other side, a base worldling considers religion, and all things else, as they suit to his worldly aims. But to speak of the next point.

'Whether we live or die, we are the Lord's.'

Inference. This is the inference drawn from the former two generals, negative and affirmative. 'None of us liveth to ourselves, or dieth to ourselves.' And from thence it is inferred, 'whether we live or die, we are the Lord's.'

And as it is an inference raised from the former, so we may consider it as a cause why we must 'live to the Lord, and die to the Lord: for whether we live or die, we are the Lord's.'

The words are a certain bottom and foundation for a Christian's comfort in the uncertainty of his condition here, being between life and death. Sure he is of death, as of life; but when to die, and how long to live, he is uncertain. But be that as it will be, this is certain, 'living and dying, he is the Lord's.'

So that, take the whole condition of a Christian, take him in all estate of life or death, which two divide the whole condition of man, for all men may be ranked into these two orders of 'quick and dead;' I say, consider a Christian in either of them, Christ is Lord of both. Take him in a condition of life, while he liveth 'he is the Lord's.' When he giveth up his breath, 'he is the Lord's.' So that, come of him what will in this uncertain condition, this is certain and sure, 'he is the Lord's.'

Now a Lord is he that hath *dominum* in rem et personam* (*g*), right to persons and things, and the disposing of them *pro arbitrio*, as it pleaseth himself; and so Christ 'is Lord both of life and death.'

1. First, In general, *as he is Lord of all creatures by creation*, God having given 'all power into his hands, both in heaven and earth,' Mat. xxviii. 18.

2. Secondly, *In a more particular manner and right.* He is Lord of all those that be his by a peculiar gift from all eternity. God hath given us to Christ in his eternal electing love. 'Thine they were, and thou gavest them me,' saith Christ, John xvii. 6.

3. Thirdly, And then we are Christ's *by his own purchase.* We are the price of his blood. 'We are bought with a price,' 1 Cor. vi. 20, 'not of gold or silver, but with his precious blood,' 1 Peter i. 18; by that price God's justice is satisfied. God so gave us to Christ, that he gave him to redeem and shed his blood for us, that his justice might be no loser.

4. Fourthly, *We are his by conquest.* For he being so excellent a person as God-man, hath rescued us from all our enemies, sin, Satan, death, hell, and whatsoever else. What have they to do with us, when God's justice is once satisfied?

5. Fifthly, Those that are true believers are his in regard *of a peculiar interest between him and them.* They give themselves over to him by a contract of marriage and covenant, and therefore he is Lord of them, by their yielding of themselves to him as a Lord. They take him for a Lord, as well as for a Saviour, and that is the foundation of the spiritual marriage and the covenant of grace on both sides. Christ giveth himself to us, and we by the Spirit of Christ have grace to give ourselves back again to him.

By our own voluntary contract, we have given up ourselves to him in our effectual calling, which is our answer to God's call, when he calleth on us to believe, to take him; and the soul answers, 'Lord, I believe, and accept thee.' This by St Peter is termed the answer of a good conscience, 1 Peter iii. 16, and is, when we can say, I am thine, thou art mine, and I yield myself to thee, to be disposed of by thee. No Christian can claim Christ his Lord, but this contract hath passed between his soul and Christ.

* Qu. '*dominium*'?—Ed.

So that if you look to God the Father, we are Christ's by *donation;* if you regard Christ himself, we are his by *purchase*; if we regard the enemies we have, we are Christ's by *conquest;* if we regard ourselves, we are his by *voluntary acceptance of the covenant of grace*, and by contract passed between him and us; yea, and Christ is so our Lord, as that he is our *husband;* our Lord, as our *king;* our Lord, as our *head.* We owe to him a subjection, as subjects; a subjection, as his *spouse;* a subjection, as his *disciples*, to be taught by him our Lord and Master.

Now the term of *Lord* is usually given to Christ, rather than to God the Father, both in the New Testament and the Old too.

And if there were no other reason for it, it is enough that God so styleth him.

But, secondly, God in the second person hath done those things that make him our Lord, more than the Father or Holy Ghost. For he in the second person hath taken our nature, and died and rose again for us; and hath conquered all our enemies. He hath in the second person made us his spouse, his members, and in all degrees of nearness to him. And because God in the second person hath done all, therefore in the second person he is more termed Lord than God the Father or the Holy Ghost. And therefore, Acts ii. 36, God the Father 'hath made him Lord and Christ.'

This is a point of wonderful comfort, and not only a comfort, but a direction how to carry ourselves. It is not only a point of dignity and prerogative, but a duty.

1. First, It is a grand comfort 'we are the Lord's,' and the Lord's in a peculiar manner, as before. The devil is the Lord's, the earth is the Lord's; all is the Lord's. But we are the Lord's by eternal donation, by purchase, by conquest, by voluntary yielding to him. And therefore it is a most excellent condition.

Quest. What is the Lord?

Ans. If we be Christ's, we have him for Lord; that is, Lord of life, Lord of glory, Lord of grace; that is, Lord of lords, King of kings. He is an independent Lord. None is above him, the Father and he agreeing together; if you know one, you know both. He is an absolute Lord, a free Lord; he hath no dependence at all upon any creature whatsoever. An eternal Lord; we have an eternal being in him; for we are when we are dead. And therefore the apostle divideth it: 'Whether we live or die, we are the Lord's.' We have a substance* when we be dead, and a Lord of equal continuance with ourselves, a king for ever. Therefore it is a point of wonderful comfort.

Obj. But you will say, Freedom is a sweet thing, especially freedom from government, so as to have no lord to control us; therefore how can this be so excellent estate, to have Christ our Lord?

Ans. 1. Beloved, *we are creatures.* We are neither of ourselves, nor by ourselves, nor for ourselves.

2. Besides, *we have enemies greater than ourselves, the powers of hell;* and therefore, if we had not a better above us, what would become of us, but to be totally subjected under the power of enemies? It is the happiness of the inferior, to be in full subjection to the superior. It is the happiness of beasts to be under man, that they may keep from destruction. It is the happiness of the weak, to have tutors and governors. It is the perfection of inferiors, to yield a gracious subjection to that that is better than themselves.

* Qu. 'subsistence' = being? But cf. page 320, last line.—G.

For everything is perfected by being subject to that which is better; and therefore we, especially in our lapsed condition, seeing we are our own greatest enemies.

2. *God in love will not trust us with ourselves since the fall, but will have our happiness to be dependent and subject to another*—to a God in our nature, an excellent Lord; and therefore an excellent Lord, because, what I spake before, Christ hath all the authority in heaven and earth committed to him, not only over us, but over our enemies, that they shall not do us harm. And, indeed, he cannot be Lord of the church, but he must be Lord of all creatures in heaven and earth, that no creature may prejudice his church. He hath universal authority over all things, and all for the church's cause.

4. And then *he hath all the good qualities of a Lord;* not only authority, but wisdom and strength and power and bounty and goodness, and whatsoever may make him a gracious Lord. And therefore it is our perfection to be in subjection to this Lord.

To set forth a little the excellency of this Lord.

He hath the sweetness of all superiors whatsoever; as he hath taken the name of all superiority that is sweet and lovely, so he hath the affections of all, and eminently more than all. He is a Lord, as a husband; he loveth more than any husband can do. He is a Lord, as a king; he can do more for us than any king. 'He hath all power in heaven, and earth, and hell, over the devils themselves.' 'All knees bow to him, of things in heaven and in earth, and under the earth,' Philip. ii. 10. And he is Lord as an head. Whatsoever superiority is near and dear, that he is to his church.

He requires service. Ay, but he is such a Lord as enableth us to serve him, 'helpeth our infirmities by his Spirit,' Rom. viii. 29. Without him we can do nothing, but in him we can do all.

And as he enableth us to perform service, so doth he reward every service, every good thought; nothing is lost that is done for Christ's sake, not a cup of cold water. He giveth strength to perform, accepteth it as a work of his Spirit, and then rewardeth it. He is so a Lord, as he standeth for his; so a Lord, as he appeareth for us now in heaven, against all accusations of Satan. Who shall lay anything to the charge of God's people? For Christ maketh intercession for them. He stood for his disciples here on earth, and upon any occasion was ready to defend them; and he is as ready in heaven to stand for his subjects and servants, and will answer all accusations of a malicious world against his church and children, 'and will bring forth their righteousness to light, as the noonday,' Ps. xxxvii. 6. He standeth for their credit, and engageth himself for the defence and protection of his Mount Zion, his church.

And to add one thing more out of the text concerning the excellency of this Lord: he is an unchangeable Lord. His love is as himself, and his care as himself, eternal; 'for whether we live or die, we are his.' What other people that are under a government can say so? For all their governors' love and care endeth in death. In the mean time their minds are variable, their affections may die before themselves; as how many have been cast off in their old days! But God will not do so. 'Forsake me not in my grey heirs,' saith David, Ps. lxxi. 18. He is our Lord while we live, and he leaveth us not when we leave to live, but is our God to death, in death, and after death, and for ever. It is a relation that holds for eternity, as our Saviour Christ saith of Abraham, Isaac, and Jacob. He is the God of Abraham. Abraham is dead; Isaac and Jacob rotten in their graves. Ay, but their souls are in heaven; and because he is their whole God, their bodies shall be raised again and united with their souls, and be for ever with the Lord.

In all the vicissitude and intercourse of things in this world, we need something to stick to; and this the Christian hath to stick to, that never faileth. He is the Lord's, and the Lord is his; he is Christ's, and Christ is his. Christ hath a love that is as himself, unchangeable. 'Whom the Lord loveth, he loveth to the end,' John xiii. 1. The promises made in Christ are as Christ—the promises of grace here, and glory hereafter certain. As his nature and love is unchangeable, so the fruit of his love in his gracious promises is always certain. They are the everlasting portion of the church.

The good things promised are everlasting likewise. We may build upon them. We cannot build on riches here, or life here, but we may build on eternal life, eternal glory and happiness.

So that, cast a Christian into what condition you will, he hath God and Christ in covenant with him, and the love of Christ, and all the gracious promises and the things promised. And these do not vary. Life varieth: we may live now, die to-morrow; but whether we live or die, these four things mentioned are certainly ours.

A Christian cannot say of anything here, that it will be his long. His estate is his now, and many ways there are to take it away; his friends are his now, but their friendship may decline; anything in the world may be so ours to-day, as not ours to-morrow. And therefore, were it not that in this variety of conditions we had something that is afterward, where were our comfort? We may outlive all comfort here, but we cannot outlive our happiness in Christ: 'for whether we live or die, we are the Lord's.'

To speak of this a little, as it yieldeth comfort in death. 'We are the Lord's,' not only while we live, but when we die. Why? Because we have a being in Christ when we die. Christ is a living root; because I live, you shall live also.' This Lord is the 'Lord of life;' and therefore whosoever is one with the Lord of life, he can indeed never die. Death is only a change of a natural gracious life here, to a glorious life in another world; from the church warfaring here, to the church triumphant in heaven.

It is not properly death, for misery dieth, death itself dieth; we do not die. Death overthroweth itself, but a Christian's life is hid with Christ; and when he dieth he dieth to live, and is found in Christ at the day of judgment, and shall be for ever with Christ. Therefore it is no great matter what kind of death a Christian dieth, because he dieth in the Lord. 'Blessed are they that die in the Lord,' Rev. xiv. 13. He saith not, them that die a fair death. A wretch, an opposer, an hypocrite may do so, and go to hell. But blessed are they that die in the Lord, because Christ is their Lord in death; and so saith the apostle, Heb. xi. 13, 'All these died in faith.' He saith not, they all died a fair death, for they did not, but many of them died a bloody death; yet they 'all died *in faith*,' and so they died in the Lord.

And therefore when we read in the histories of the church that some were torn in pieces with wild beasts, that 'they gave the bodies of the saints to the fowls of heaven,' as David hath it, Ps. lxxix. 2, which may discourage some to be Christians, let us not think that any matter; 'they died in faith.' And as the psalmist saith, 'precious to the Lord is the death of all his saints,' Ps. cxvi. 15; for he taketh notice of them in their lives, not only in their lives, but the hairs of their head, they being all numbered. He taketh notice of the tears that fall from their eyes, and will not he take notice of their blood? He taketh notice of their persons, their hairs, their tears, and will he part with their lives for nothing? No. He will be paid for the lives of his children. When he parts with them, his enemies shall be sure to pay for it. He will be avenged on them for it, as the blood of Naboth was on Ahab. So he will be revenged on all the persecutors of his church, and take a strict account of every drop of blood that hath been shed, for their persons are precious. God taketh special notice of them. They are his members, his spouse, and near unto him.

And then he will not have them die till they have done their work. He taketh special notice of them all their life. And when they have done what they came for, as Christ saith of himself, 'I have done the work thou gavest me to do,' John xvii. 4, then he sendeth for them home. They die not at adventure, but under the care of one that knoweth them well both in life and death.

And therefore it is that God so revenged the persecutors of his church, for the blood of his saints, from the blood of Abel unto this day.

And as the 'death of his saints are precious,' so are all things that the saints have. Their credit is precious, their goods are precious. God taketh notice of everything they part with for his sake. As he and all his is ours—himself, his happiness, his Spirit, his privileges—so when we are his, all ours are his. He taketh care of our lives, of our deaths, of our credits, of our riches, of our estates. We part with nothing for him but he considers it, and will reward it abundantly.

'He that dieth in the Lord is a blessed man;' so saith the Spirit, Rev. xiv. 13. The flesh will not say so, but rather will infer who would be so religious, for such venture their lives, and are counted as the offscouring of the world. The devil will teach this lesson, and the world. As they have lived in the flesh, and will sell all to be somebody in the world, though they go to hell when they have done. But, saith the Spirit, blessed are they who not only die for the Lord as martyrs, but that die in the Lord; whether to seal the truth of God with their blood, or otherwise, they die happily; and so this is a ground of special comfort.

And as it is a ground of special comfort, so it is a ground of direction. 'Whether we live or die, we are the Lord's.' Therefore it may be a foundation of living to the Lord. If we be the Lord's, surely we ought to live to him. If we be his, all our endeavours, whatsoever is ours, are his. *Fructus* and *fundus*, go together, the fruit and the soil; and therefore if we be the Lord's in life and death, we must not live to ourselves as our own, but give ourselves to him, and not to anything else; we are not our own, nor man's, but the Lord's. And therefore we ought not to yield up ourselves to our self-wills, self-wit, self-love, to be at our own disposing, and to live as we list. We are redeemed from ourselves, yea, from all our vain conversations.

Some think Christ died, and therefore they may be vain, especially at the solemn time of Christ's nativity. The devil hath so prevailed with the world, and will till there be a new face of the church; they never honour the devil more than when they seem to honour Christ. For, say they, Christ came to set us at liberty. Did he so? But it was to deliver us from wickedness; yea, from vain conversations, and not to purchase us liberty to live as we list.* 'Our tongues are our own,' say they in the psalms, Ps. xii. 4. Ay, but Christ saith, they are not your own, they are his. And if they be not Christ's, they are the devil's. Our thoughts are not our own, but all should be dedicated to Christ. Therefore we should be content that Christ should set up a regiment† in our souls, that he may rule our thoughts, desires, our language, and members, that they may be all 'weapons of righteousness,' Rom. vi. 13.

We have nothing our own, much less sin, from which we are redeemed. And not only from gross sins, but from such conversations as are vain in themselves, and will be vain to thee.

And when we are redeemed from sin, and from vain conversations, we are redeemed from ourselves, from the world, from the devil; whom now hath a man to serve? None but this Lord. We have renounced all other in baptism, and we are revolters and rebels, and renounce our covenant in baptism, if we renounce not the world and the lusts of it in our lives.

Ourselves we must not serve. For we are redeemed from ourselves, and not only from our carnal selves, but natural selves. Christ is Lord of our natures. And a Christian ought to say, Lord, of thee I had this body; of thee I had this life of mine, these goods of mine, this credit of mine, this reputation and place in the world. As I had all from thee, so I return all to thee again.

And as we are not our own, we must not be other men's. 'We are not servants of men,' as the apostle saith, Rom. viii. 12, *seq*.‡ We must not take upon trust the opinions that others would put upon us, or what we list ourselves in religion. We must not have men's persons in admiration, for advantage. We must not idolise any creature, for as we are not our own, so we are not any other's, but we are the Lord's.

The happiness of a Christian is to be independent on the creatures. He may use them as subordinate helps, but he is to depend only on this Lord, what to believe, what to speak; and not to take up this or that opinion to please this or that man, thereby to rise to greatness.

It is a base thing to say, I believe as my parents believe. Are you your parents'? Your parents are the servants of this great Lord, whose you are, and to whom it is your duty to yield yourselves.

Use 1. And therefore, in solicitation to any sin, make that use of it, that the holy apostle doth in that gross sin that reigns so much in the world, and brings many to hell, defilement of body. Saith he, 'Our bodies are bought with a price,' 1 Cor. vi. 20. 'And shall I take the members of Christ, and make them members of an harlot?' 1 Cor. vi. 15. So when we are tempted by corruption, and Satan joining with it, reason thus: Shall I defile this body of mine? My body is not mine, it is the Lord's; my members are not mine, they be dedicated and consecrated to him. What should such base abominable thoughts do in a heart consecrated to Christ? I am his, my thoughts his; my desires should be his.

Let those that be given to swearing, and blaspheming, and idle talk, consider that their tongues are not their own; and yet for whom do they employ their tongues as an instrument, but for Satan?

Use 2. So when we come to die, make use of it, not only for comfort, but for duty. 'We are Christ's,' and therefore if he doth call us by any kind of death, if he sends for us by a bloody death, go to Christ that way, because he is Lord, and disposeth of whatsoever befalleth us, and determineth

* That is, 'choose.'—G.

† That is, 'government.'—G.

‡ Qu. 'Gal. i. 10'?—Ed.

by what death we shall glorify him. Be of Saint Paul's resolution, to 'glorify God both living and dying,' Phil. iii. 13, *seq*. He knew God should be glorified by his death as well as by his life. So we may glorify Christ by any death, be content to yield ourselves any kind of way to him.

There be two virtues we ought specially to exercise in the hour of death: assurance of faith that we are Christ's, and a resignation to his will, that in faith and in obedience we may commit ourselves to him, as to a faithful Creator and Redeemer. This is our duty.

And it is no easy matter to do this. Many bequeath themselves to God, but, alas! they have alienated themselves before to the world. They have given their bodies to wine, to women, as the Scripture phrase is, Rev. xiv. 4. Or they have given their spirits to the world. As we use to say in our common speech of some men, they are given to the world. But when they have given their strength to the flesh before, and do at time of death bequeath their spirits to the Lord, will he own them? Alas! they are alienated before, and so put out of their own disposing. And therefore ordinarily, unless the Lord work a miracle, it is impossible to die in the Lord, if a man have not lived to the Lord before; which may teach us to give ourselves really to him in our lifetime, that our lives being a service to Christ, we may comfortably die to him, and have our souls to dispose of.

The like subjection must be shewed in all conditions whatsoever. If God will have me to honour him in a mean calling, I am not mine own, I am his; my life, and all my condition of life, are only to him. My calling, my estate, it may be, is low, that my pride may be humbled. But God hath set me in my calling; he will have me to honour him in it. In the meanest calling, a man shall have enough to give an account of;* and therefore there is no reason to be ashamed of our calling. I am the Lord's, in my life, in all the passages of it; in my calling, in all the troubles of it, I am to look for support and protection and provision and direction from God. I am here by his appointment. And therefore he that hath set me in this place will provide for me, protect me, guide me by his Spirit what to do in my place. And so it is a ground for contentation in all conditions.

You see, then, there is great reason why we should not live to ourselves, but to the Lord; that we should not die to ourselves, but to the Lord. For it is a great comfort, and a special duty; and therefore, in a word, we cannot have a more comfortable experiment in all divine truths than this, that God in Christ hath passed over himself to be ours, and we have passed over ourselves to him, if we have grace to do it. And then to plead and improve it when it is done, there is not a comfort of greater comprehension; and therefore the apostle dwelleth on the point, 'No man liveth to himself, no man dieth to himself; but we live to the Lord, and die to the Lord.' To what end is all this, but that we should settle it as a bottom and ground of comfort and contentment and happiness, that we are not our own, but the Lord's?

Think, therefore, of this one thing, that we are his, that hath a command in heaven and earth, to whom all knees bow with subjection; his that is Lord of lords, and King of kings, that is Lord *paramount;* who will not suffer anything to befall his church, or any particular Christian, that shall not be for their good, for he hath all power in heaven and earth for that purpose, and for ever. What a comfort is it in life and death, in the midst of oppositions here, or from the powers of hell, that we have a Lord that is commander

* Cf. note *i*, Vol. I. page 294.—G.

of all, 'Lord of life or death.' He 'hath the keys of hell and death.' Himself hath conquered all, and he will conquer all in us by little and little. What happiness is it, I say, to be under such a Lord!

THE FIFTH SERMON.

For none of us liveth to himself, and no man dieth to himself. For whether we live, we live unto the Lord; and whether we die, we die unto the Lord: whether we live therefore, or die, we are the Lord's.—Rom. XIV. 7, 8.

There is nothing more available to the living of a Christian's life than to have the eye of the soul on his main end and scope. And then to be furnished with some maxims and principles to direct our lives to that scope. Where the parts are most noble and large, there the aim and scope is most excellent. Now a true Christian, being raised above others, hath an end and scope above other men; and that indeed maketh him a Christian in good earnest, when God by his Spirit discovers an higher excellency than the world can afford, and setteth our hearts towards it.

Now the apostle setteth down the scope of our whole condition, both of life and death. First, negatively, 'No man liveth to himself;' 'no man dieth to himself.'

Then, affirmatively, 'We live to the Lord, and die to the Lord.'

And he giveth the ground of both: 'Whether we live or die, we are the Lord's.'

If we live to the Lord, we shall have a being after life. A Christian is, when he is not; when he is not here, he hath a being in heaven; and suitably to his several conditions he hath a Lord to own him in all. Now he liveth, yet cannot build on life, nor anything below, because life is short and uncertain. But this he may build on: 'Whether he liveth or dieth, he is the Lord's.'

Now Christ is said in Scripture to be Lord oftener than God, because God in the second person hath appeared in our nature, overcome all our enemies, hath triumphed, and is now in heaven in our nature; and because *Lord* is a word of authority and sovereignty. And God hath made him governor of quick and dead.

He is a Lord in regard of God the Father, by donation. God hath given the elect to him before all worlds.

He is Lord in regard of himself, by conquest over the enemies of our salvation.

And then by ransom. He hath paid a price to divine justice for us. For though God gave Christ to us from all eternity, and us to Christ, yet on these terms, that he should ransom us. God will not have his justice a loser; therefore Christ must pay a price to divine justice. Such was his mercy, and the glory of his mercy, to find out such a way to satisfy justice, that God should die.

No attribute of God must be a loser; he must have the honour of all his attributes; and therefore of his justice. And here is the glory of his wisdom, in contriving a way that mercy may triumph and justice may be satisfied.

And then he is Lord by our voluntary submission to him; for we set a crown upon his head when we subject ourselves to him.

He is our Lord in all estates, 'living or dying;' at all times, without limitation; in all conditions, whether it be a life of prosperity or adversity, let us die by what manner of death soever.

And so I shewed we are the Lord's in a double sense: in regard of our carriage to him, and in regard of his care over us; both must be included. We are not the Lord's only for that he taketh care of us, and without our service; nor that we do him service without his care of us; but he is so our Lord, that we have grace to acknowledge him, and he hath grace, and love, and mercy to protect and acknowledge us both in life and death.

It is no prejudice to a Christian's estate that he is another's. It is the happiness of the weak to be under a stronger; of those that be deficient, to be under fulness. Now there is all-sufficiency in Christ. Therefore to be under him is our happiness.

Give me leave to illustrate this. Everything is beautiful in its own place. Things that are highest, it is fit they should be highest; things that are lowest, it is fit they should be lowest. If the head were not in its own place, there would be deformity in the body. And so it is fit Christ should be our Lord, being God-man and the glory of our nature. And it is our happiness, our beauty and comeliness, our safety and perfection, to be under Christ, and to be only under him. He is only* larger than the soul; he is of equal continuance with the soul; he is only suitable to the soul, being a Spirit, he only is eternal; and therefore being every way so abundantly satisfactory to the soul, it is the happiness of the soul to have him for its Lord, especially considering what a Lord he is—a Lord independent; Lord of lords, that hath all other lords at command; a bountiful and gracious Lord.

And we are not only the Lord's while we live, but when we come to die. Therefore we should be willing to die when our time cometh, yea, to die any kind of death, because he is Lord of 'quick and dead.' We should be like David and Moses, who were very fruitful towards their ends. And as we are not ashamed to live to so good a Lord, so we should not be afraid to die to him, as one said of himself (*h*).

This word *Lord* implieth, *there be some duties owing by us*. We are the Lord's in our souls, in our bodies, in our conditions; and therefore we should wholly give up ourselves to him, and entertain no thoughts to dishonour him; give way to no risings, no desires which become not the subjects and servants of the Lord; believe nothing that we take up of ourselves, keep the chastity of our faith and understanding, not to believe lies and untruths; but submit our very understandings and faith to God. We must not be servants of men, in our judgments or souls, no *mancipium alienæ libidinis*, as the philosopher saith (*i*). But consider what Christ hath revealed, and let us submit to that.

And therefore it is a grand error in the Church of Rome, who would have people to believe as the church believeth, which is, πρῶτον ψεῦδος, *primum mendacium*, the first lie, that leadeth them into all those errors; to believe Christ and Scripture no further than the church discovers them. And so they overturn all. For they believe God because men say so. It is a dangerous error that runneth into practice. If the church say treason must be done, we must be traitors. It is no matter what the Scripture saith. The pope he is the head of the church, and he can dispense with what he pleaseth. But 'my sheep,' saith Christ, 'hear my voice,' John x. 4. And it is our duty to hear what the Lord of our faith saith, which

* That is, 'he only is.'—G.

is only Christ. If he be our Lord, then let our wills be brought into subjection to his will; nothing is more out of order than this will of ours. If that were once subject to Christ, all controversy between God and us were taken away. All the strife is, whether we shall have our wills or he his will. The spouse hath no will of her own, but it is resigned to her husband. So must we submit our wills to Christ's desire.

And then again, *we ought not in anything to regard the humours of men.* Christ is Lord of our affections. We must hate what he will have us hate, and love what he loveth; our whole souls must be conformable to Christ.

And our bodies are wholly his too, and therefore we must be content that our bodies should be used as they used his body. He gave his body for us; he took our nature; and in that nature went about doing good, suffering hardship. He was hungry and thirsty; he was crucified in our nature, suffered in our nature; and so should we be content our natures should be used as he would have them, to take much pains in doing good; to suffer hunger, thirst, restraint, yea, death itself for Christ, because we are Christ's! It is no more than he did for us. He being our Lord, was abased for us in his blessed body and flesh; and therefore shall not we suffer for him?

So our conditions are his. Suffer him therefore to cut us out a portion, to allot us any condition.

The word implieth more particularly an *application to ourselves.* 'We are the Lord's, and the Lord is ours.'

And likewise *a renunciation and severing from all others.* 'We are the Lord's, and none else;' the Lord's, and none but the Lord's; if we are anybody's else, it is in the Lord and for the Lord.

Here is likewise *resignation.* 'We are the Lord's,' and therefore we will give up ourselves to him, with a resting in him, and high estimation of him, and glorying in our condition through him.

And then here is an improvement of this implied: We are the Lord's; therefore we ought to improve it on our part, by serving him; and on his part by believing that he will have care of us.

We are the Lord's, first, by particular application, which is wrought by degrees.

First, God by his Spirit revealeth himself to be ours, not fully, but by letting in so much light into the soul as may carry the soul to him, and make us yield to him, trust in him, and cast ourselves upon him; and by doing so we grow into further acquaintance with him, and he honours our faith with a further sense and assurance that he is ours, and we are his.

There is a great deal of distance and breadth between the first act of faith, by which we cast ourselves on Christ, and a confident persuasion that Christ is ours and we are his. That is a fruit of faith; and there needeth a great deal of growth before we come to that.

And therefore if you ask, What doth the soul first to make Christ his own? It is this, *In the use of means,* wherewith God pleaseth to be effectual, *a light is by the Spirit let into the soul, whereby the heart is persuaded that he hath a good meaning towards it,* that he is a gracious Lord, and will forgive the sins of all that rely upon him. And with the acknowledging of these truths, together with the offer of mercy in Christ, there is so much sweetness let into the soul as carrieth the soul back again to Christ to rest upon him. For unless Christ begin in some degree to make love to the soul, and giveth a taste of his sweetness, we cannot rely upon him nor love him, not only because we are creatures, and he is first and must begin to us, but because it is the nature of a guilty soul, when it is under terror and awakened, to forecast such doubts, that till Christ letteth in some glimpse of his love, the soul dare not look Christ in the face.

Now in the unfolding of these divine truths of the gospel, some intimations are given 'that Christ is mine, and I am Christ's,' which afterward becometh the claim of an experienced Christian. This therefore directeth what course they shall take to get Christ that want him. They must attend upon the blessed means of salvation, and then consider how far forth they may lay claim to Christ.

For, first, all that live in the church are Christ's in some degree. God hath prevented* men with his love in admitting them to the visible church, and there is an obligation on them to think well of Christ for that, because he had care of them before they had care of themselves, by vouchsafing them the seal of baptism, and making them members of the visible church.

Secondly, Unless they labour, being come to years of discretion, to feel a further assurance that Christ is theirs, they disannul and deny their baptism; and therefore it is good for such souls as are touched with sight of sin to gather upon Christ, and to wind about all helps they can to work on Christ, as the vine gathereth on the tree it windeth about. I am born in the church, I have been baptized, lived in times of the gospel, have opportunities to hear the blessed truths, and therefore I will have good conceits of Christ that he meaneth well to my soul.

Indeed, a company of wretches that rest in their baptism, being profane swearers, vile persons, abusers of their calling or anything, can say, Are not we baptized? and do not we come to church? But they forget that this is an obligation on them to be good, and no excuse for them to be evil. It tieth thee to renounce that thou livest in, else thou deniest thy baptism.

We must know, beloved, that Christ loved us, not as we love a goodly pillar or other curious piece of art that cannot love us again, but the intercourse between God and man is mutual. If he say he is ours, we say again, I am thine, Lord, and give myself to thee; and the claim is mutual. He claimeth us for his, and we claim him for ours; for he deals with reasonable creatures, that can enter into covenant with him as friends. We must therefore give up all to God. If God be God, let us own him. And as we cannot serve Christ and sin, we cannot serve Christ and antichrist; we cannot comply with Christ and his enemies. Those that have the mark of the beast absolutely cannot be Christ's, nor have communion with him, but are enemies to Christ, though under pretence of religion. But where a man is truly Christ's, he is none but Christ's; Satan is content with any part, but Christ must have the whole heart.

God's children have something in them that usurpeth, some corruption in them which is not absolutely removed, but it is but a rebel, and they have an enemy's mind to it; all that is contrary to Christ is renounced; whereas in them that be carnal sin is as a lord, but in God's children it is as a thief. He is there, yet they own him not, but get strength against him. He ruleth not there but as a tyrant. There is a renunciation of lordship and dominion of sin. Though they have inclinations to this and that sin, yet they have no liking to that liking, no inclinations as spiritual to that inclination as carnal, but make it an object of mortification. They renounce all other lords; when all other men, that have not the Spirit of Christ, are under the dominion of some reigning lusts.

And as it implieth a possession, so likewise an estimation; as God esteemeth us, so we esteem him above all. And therefore God calleth his

* That is, 'gone before' = 'anticipated.'—G.

church his portion, his jewel; and we call Christ our portion, our treasure, our pearl, our all. St Paul counts 'all dung and dross in comparison of the excellent knowledge of Christ,' Phil. iii. 8. And all that belongeth to Christ he esteemeth. And therefore the church glorieth that God is their God, and makes claim to him as St Paul, 'I live by the faith of the Son of God, who loved me, and gave himself for me,' Gal. ii. 20. And as Thomas, 'My Lord, and my God,' John xx. 28. This is the best evidence of a true Christian, whose estate is no way known better than by his estimation. 'Whom have I in heaven but thee, or in earth in comparison of thee?' saith David, Ps. lxxiii. 25.

It implieth likewise *a duty of resignation to Christ in life and death*, because we are not our own, and therefore are in all things to be at his disposing, to be led what way he pleaseth, and to pursue his directions, though to the crossing of our corrupt nature, to be content to go to heaven as he will lead us, by fair ways or foul ways, by fair death or bloody death, 'if by any means we may attain to the resurrection of the dead,' as St Paul saith it, Philip. iii. 11.

Besides this, we must have a care to implead this and to improve it, as the apostle doth here, 'Whether we live or die, we are the Lord's.' He will have care of us, and therefore we ought to serve him.

It is a special after-part to be able to make it good to God in all troubles and conditions whatsoever: 'I am thine, Lord, save me; I am thine, Lord, teach me; I am thine, Lord, protect me.'

Avouch and make it good against the temptations of Satan, urging thee to distrust, I am not mine own, I am God's and Christ's; and therefore if thou hast anything to say to me, go to him that hath paid my debt. Thus plead the goodness and graciousness of God.

Plead it against temptation to sin. I am not mine own, 'I am bought with a price,' 1 Cor. vi. 28. My body is not for uncleanness, but for the Lord.

Plead it against our own consciences in times of desertion; search narrowly what we have of Christ's in us, and do not cavil against ourselves too much in times of temptation. If we have but desires of the soul to God, lose not anything that is good; if I renounce my interest in Christ, I am where the devil would have me; then he can do anything with us. And therefore plead it against our own distasteful* hearts in times of darkness. I give myself to him, and my desires are to him; my faith is little, but yet something; my love is little, but yet I love the Lord. 'I believe, help my unbelief,' Mark ix. 24. We must take notice of anything Christ hath wrought in our spirits, that we may implead our interest on all occasions; for if we yield to despairing hearts in times of temptations, we are gone. Therefore say with Job, 'If thou kill me, I will trust thee,' Job xiii. 15. Lie at Christ's feet; if thou wilt damn me, so it is, I will lie here, and wait here. For if I have not present audience, I shall have it. God waiteth to do them good that wait for him. He will try our spirits, whether we will take a seeming repulse; therefore we must, as the woman of Samaria,† grow on Christ, and catch at his words, Mat. xv.; and as the servants of Benhadad, who retorted on Ahab presently, 'Thy servant Benhadad,' 1 Kings xx. 33.

And as we must implead our interest, so we must improve it in the whole course of our life, and in all conditions whatsoever. If we have any loss or crosses, yet the soul can say, Christ is mine, and I am Christ's. Though a man taking a journey lose things of less value, yet if he hath a pearl left him, he is content, for he hath that that will make him a man.

* Qu. 'distrustful'?—G.

† Qu. 'Canaan'?—Ed.

And therefore be not much disconsolate for any crosses. They cannot take away my Christ, my promises, the comforts of the Spirit. I have a Christ, and in him all that shall be for my good.

Improve it in all opposition of flesh and blood, hell and the instruments of hell, Satan and wicked men. They are mine enemies; but if Christ be my friend, it matters not. Christ can make our enemies our friends.

And all things are ours if we be Christ's. We have a general charter. Things to come are ours, life ours, death ours; and therefore if we be Christ's, make use of him.

As it is baseness of spirit to rest in anything in the world but Christ, so it is baseness of spirit for us that are Christ's to be dejected for anything in the world. We have the treasure, we have the mine. We have the sun; what if we lose a beam? We have a spring; what if the stream be dried up? If Christ giveth us himself, it is no matter what we lose. But we are sure of him, 'for in life and death we are the Lord's.'

And therefore let us hence answer all objections. Oh that we should have such grounds of comfort and stability, and yet make no more use of them! If these things were fresh in our thoughts, nothing would discourage us.

Quest. If you ask, How shall we know in particular that it is so indeed that we are Christ's?

Ans. 1. I answer, If we have given ourselves to him by a contract of our own, if we be married to him. You know marriage must have consent of both parties. Those that give not themselves up to Christ to be his, they are not his. They that live under the power of any sin against conscience, as their Lord, that love anything better than Christ, and will not part with it for Christ's sake, Christ is not theirs, for they be engaged another way.

Ans. 2. Again, If we live to Christ, we are sure we are his; if we do not live to Christ we are not his. If Christ be ours, as the life which we live is his, so our course of living will be to him. We shall direct all our courses to him, making him our last end; and therefore, if we will know whether we be Christ's, what is the scope of our lives? what is our aim? If so be that Christ may be glorified by me, I am content to part with anything, with life itself, I may know that I am Christ's. 'He that will not deny all, that hateth not father and mother for my sake, is not worthy of me,' Mat. x. 37. Self-denial, and hatred of all things in comparison of Christ, argueth an interest in him. Therefore it is a great deal of grace, and the soul is much subdued before it can say, 'I am Christ's, and Christ is mine.'

For when sin and other withdrawings from Christ are to be deserted, first, there is much ado in the understanding.

Have I reason to do this? Well, if my judgment say it is good, yet my will saith it is better to have my will than to yield to God, though I hazard the ruin of myself. Oh this is a fatal, naughty disposition, and a sign of ruin; yet the reputed happiness of many men consisteth in their chief misery.

Again, Good things first coming to the judgment are there repulsed. But if they come to the will, there they be more opposed. And then the affections make a stir and bustle, love and hatred, and engagements to worldly things, and all to hinder our claim and interest to Christ. But he must be set up in place of self-love, before he can say, 'Christ is mine, and I am Christ's,' and that is an hard matter. Therefore let us consider what our aim and scope is.

In a word, if we be Christ's, undoubtedly we will side with Christ. 'Who is on my side? who?' saith Jehu, 2 Kings ix. 32. In ill and doubtful times Christ's calls are for a party, and calleth out, Where is my party? who standeth for me? who owneth Christ and his truth and doctrine and good ways, honesty, and religion? Who is on my side? saith Christ. Why, I am for the Lord, as in the prophet Isaiah, saith the soul that can own Christ. Ay, Christ will own us, we shall own him; if we be ashamed of him, he will be ashamed of us at the day of judgment.

They that for hope of preferment and to be somebody in the world can cross their own consciences, and Christ in their consciences, by doing that which by his Spirit he telleth them is naught;* are they Christ's when they set up self as an idol above Christ, and side with the world and the flesh against Christ?

Again, He that can say in truth of heart Christ is his, and he is Christ's, he will solace himself, delight himself, and live upon this comfort. It is a rich claim, and there will be spiritual wisdom where there is this interest to implead and improve it. It is not given to lie dormant, but grace is given with it to improve it, and live upon it. All that is Christ's will please him that hath Christ. His truth is sweet to him; the Lord's day, the Lord's work, the Lord's servants, the Lord's ordinances, whatsoever hath the stamp of the Lord, it is sweet to him, because he is the Lord's, and the Lord is his.

This is contrary to the disposition of that generation that can cunningly despise persons and causes, if they see anything in them opposite to their own base courses and lusts.

But above all, where Christ is any man's in truth, the Spirit of Christ is in that man's heart, a witnessing Spirit and a sanctifying Spirit. The Spirit will witness an interest, and fit and sanctify the soul, as a gracious vessel for Christ's service here, and for glory hereafter. And though the Spirit witness not so loud that he is Christ's, yet he may know by the work of the Spirit that Christ is his; for the Spirit frameth him to a connatural disposition to Christ, and all that is Christ's. They love his ways and government. A gracious man would not be under another government than Christ's, if he were to choose. He hath made his choice indeed; but if he were to choose he would have Christ's government, because he findeth a sweetness in it, and a suitableness to the dignity of it. A man never findeth himself more himself than when he is most gracious.

Carnal men, though they submit to outward means, yet they cast away the bond of Christ, they cannot endure the yoke; but they that are Christ's have a connatural disposition to the government of Christ. And they complain to Christ of other lords, 'Other lords rule me,' Isa. xxvi. 13. This lust reigns in me: Lord, subdue it; claim thine own interest; let nothing rule in me but thy Spirit. I am weary of my inclinations to this and that lust. And so there is a conflict ever maintained.

To stir us up, in a word, to labour to be more under the government of Christ, and to get assurance of it, let us consider, if we be not Christ's, whose are we? There is but two kingdoms. If Christ rules us not, the devil and the world must rule us.

And what kind of subjection is it to be subject to our own lusts? to a damned world and to Satan? Is it not to be ruled by our enemies, and base enemies? Our lusts are baser than the devil himself. For the devil is a substance, and ruleth by them. Now who would be willing to serve

* That is, 'naughty' = wicked.—G.

an enemy? nay, to be a servant of servants, to be under these tyrannical enemies, restless enemies, that do encroach upon us more and more? and all the fruits we have by their service is shame and grief at the best; and shall we serve those that will pay no better wages? Yet this is the condition of all that have not Christ for their Lord. They serve some base lust, and Satan, a tyrannical lord, that instead of better rewards, punisheth them with eternal destruction; so that they serve him with the price of their own souls.

I beseech you, seriously consider of it, and put this *quære* to your souls; I have lived in such and such a sin, but what is the fruit of it? The best is shame. If I am not ashamed here, it will end in eternal shame. So that it is a sweet thing to be under the government of Christ. It is *utile dominium*, a dominion for our good.

And lest we should be discouraged, take heed of all temptations that withdraw us from the love of Christ's government, because our nature is opposite to this yoke. If they seize upon us, we shall be great losers by them in our reputation, and in much of that comfort which otherwise we might have gotten.

Beloved, you should lose nothing by Christ. What we lose for his sake, we shall gain in peace of conscience, in grace, and in this world too, if he seeth it good. No man ever lost by the service of Christ. Let a man lay beginning and end together, and tell me if he hath gotten anything by serving his lusts; for God payeth him home here, in much terror of conscience, and crosses, and losses at the end, besides hell hereafter, though at first he enjoy some seeming comfort.

And therefore lay it as a principle, that God's service is the best and and most profitable service.

Obj. Ay, but it appeareth to the view of the world that they that stick close to Christ, and will disclaim all for a good conscience, fall into this and that misery.

Ans. 1. First, The reason is, *because they be not good enough*. It may be they be negligent in the service of Christ; and therefore God will purge them, and make them better, and will try their graces, that they may know themselves the better.

2. Secondly, One main end is, indeed, Christ will suffer his to be exercised with this and that affliction, *that he may have glory in his servants*; that the world may see he hath some that are content to lose something for his sake; that will part with anything, and break with any man that they may please the Lord.

3. Thirdly, If we serve Christ, *he will speak to our consciences that it is not in vain to serve him*, howsoever things fall out in the world. I confess there is a mystery in Christ's government, which we must take notice of. We can give no reason why his enemies should so reign, and his church be put under hatches. Only in general we know, that all this, in conclusion, shall serve for the church's good. 'And all shall work for the best to them that love God,' Rom. viii. 28. God is all this while a-working the church's good and the enemies' ruin, though we see not the mystery of Christ's kingdom.

I beseech you, labour to make a good use of this; get under Christ's government, and when flesh and blood shall put up a petition, or suggest anything, give it a *non placet*, deny the petition; say, I am Christ's, and I owe nothing to any but to Christ; therefore not to sin or myself. All my debt is to the Spirit, and to Christ. Therefore I will 'sow to the Spirit, not to the flesh,' Gal vi. 8. 'I am bought with a price,' 1 Cor. vi. 20; my liberty cost Christ dear, therefore I will die honourably, rather than prostitute myself to any base courses. Thus we should have high thoughts of ourselves. And upon all temptations suggested to us, make use of this consideration, that we are not our own, but Christ's.

NOTES.

(*a*) P. 291.—'Men are as their aims are. Noble spirits have noble aims.' Again we are reminded that Sibbes was a contemporary of Shakespeare. This instantly recalls Vincentis's exquisite words :—

. . . . 'Spirits are not finely touch'd
But to fine issues.'—(*Measure for Measure*, I. 1).

Cf. note *b*, page 247, and note *c*, Vol. IV. page 58. With reference to the former, it may here be added that the 'little Latin' of Shakespeare probably sufficed to make him acquainted with Cicero, de Offic. lib. iii. c. 21, where the same sentiment occurs. Perhaps this is Sibbes's reminiscence.

(*b*) P. 291.—'Benè vixit, qui benè latuit.' A proverbial memorial of the Lord's frequent 'hiding' and retiring of himself. Cf. John viii. 59, from which and parallel passages the Fathers and Puritans are never weary in inculcating the above lesson. This apophthegm was used very touchingly by the saintly Philip Henry under the shadows of his 'Ejection' from Worthenbury. In his straits some of his friends urged him to revive his acquaintance and interest at Court, which it was thought he might easily do. It was even reported that the Duke of York, a playmate of his boyhood, had inquired after him. But he heeded not the rumour, nor could he be induced in any way to ask for royal favours, remarking, 'My friends do not know so well as I the strength of temptation, and my own inability to deal with it. *Qui bene latuit, bene vixit.* Lord, lead me not into temptation. Cf. the well-known 'Life,' and an interesting paper entitled 'The Family of the Henrys,' in *Evangelical Magazine*, April and May 1863.

(*c*) P. 303.—'Deo servire, est regnare.' This is one of the watchwords of the Schoolmen.

(*d*) P. 303.—'Quanto subjectior, tanto liberior.' This is only the saying of note *c* in another form.

(*e*) P.304 .—'Therefore Lactantius saith well, "Religion is the true wisdom."' Cf. his *De Vera Sapientia*, throughout; and is also found incidentally in his *De Falsa Sapientia.*

(*f*) P. 305.—'Whatsoever cometh, he is *in utrumque paratus*.' The legend of the Johnstone arms (Scotland). 'Nunquam non paratus' is another form of this saying.

(*g*) P. 315.—'Not afraid to die to him, as one said of himself.' One of the blessed commonplaces of the Martyrs, *e.g.*, Polycarp, Ignatius.

(*h*) P. 315.—'We must not be servants of men . . . no *mancipium alienæ libidinis*.' *The* philosopher is Aristotle. G.

CHRIST'S EXALTATION PURCHASED BY HUMILIATION.

CHRIST'S EXALTATION PURCHASED BY HUMILIATION.

NOTE.

The title-page of the original and only edition of 'Christ's Exaltation purchased by Humiliation' is given below.* The T. G. and P. N. represent, as in his other volumes, Dr Thomas Goodwin and Philip Nye, both whose names have been already annotated (cf. Vol. II. p. 3). The volume is a thin 18mo. It is among the rarer of Sibbes's lesser pieces.

G.

* CHRISTS
EXALTATION
PVRCHAST BY
HVMILIATION.

Wherein you may see
Mercy and *Misery* meete
together.
Very Usefull

I. For Instructing the Ignorant.
II. For Comforting the Weake.
III. For Confirming the Strong.

By *R. Sibbs* D.D. and Preacher of
Grayes-Inne, London.
Published by *T. G.* and *P. N.*

1 Cor. 15. 45.
The first man Adam was made a Living Soule, the last Adam was made a Quickning Spirit.

LONDON
Printed by *Tho. Cotes*, and are to be sold by
Iohn Bartlet at his shop, at the Signe of the guilt
Cup, neere S. *Austins* gate. 1639.

CHRIST'S EXALTATION PURCHASED BY HUMILIATION.

For, for this end Christ both died, and rose, and revived, that he might be Lord both of the dead and of the living.—Rom. XIV. 9.

The dependence of these words upon the former I take to be this: The scope of the apostle in this chapter is to stay the rigid censures of others concerning weaker Christians, especially about matters of indifferency, or at the least of a less nature. In the 6th verse, saith he, 'He that regards not a day, regards it not, to the Lord he that eats, eats to the Lord; and he that eats not to the Lord, he eats not, and gives God thanks,' &c. His reason is this: they that in eating or in not eating do it with a religious respect to the Lord; if they eat, it is to the Lord; if they eat not, it is to the Lord; that is, in obedience to the Lord. They are to be borne withal, because they do it with religious respects. Though perhaps there may be a little error in the matter, yet there be some things of such indifferency that they [do] not give denomination to the action, if it be to the Lord. Howsoever the action be not altogether to be excused, yet the person is to be excused, and is not to be hardly censured. Therefore considering that they* do it, and they that do it not, do it to the Lord, be not hasty in your censures.

Quest. How doth he prove that these holy Christians did eat or not eat to the Lord?

Ans. From this, because they were the Lord's. They that are the Lord's, they live to him, and die to him; and therefore they do particular actions to him. 'No man,' ver. 7, 'lives to himself, nor no man dieth to himself,' which includes all particular actions. 'Whether we live, we live to the Lord; or whether we die, we die to the Lord; whether we live therefore, or die, we are the Lord's.' He proves therefore that they do eat or not eat to the Lord, if they be good Christians, because they are the Lord's.

Those that are the Lord's live to the Lord, and do all particular actions to the Lord. Such must not be harshly censured, because they are the servants of the Lord.

Quest. In the third place, How doth he prove that they are the Lord's that live and die to him?

* Qu. 'they that'?—Ed.

Ans. He proves it from the main ground in the text: 'For, for this end Christ both died, and rose, and revived, that he might be Lord both of the dead and of the living.' So you see the dependence of the reason, they eat or eat not to the Lord. Why? 'Because they are the Lord's.'

But how is it they are the Lord's? It is the end of the three actions of Christ here. 'Christ died, and rose again, and revived, for this end, that he might be the Lord of the dead and of the living.' So you see the connection of these words with the former.

In the words you have *argumentum et argumenti ratio*, the argument, and the reasoning from the argument; the ground, and the inference from the ground. The ground is: 'Christ died, and rose again, and revived.' What is the inference from that? 'That he might be Lord of the dead and of the living.'

In the words therefore we will consider the argument itself, and the ground itself, and then the inference.

'For, for this end Christ both died, and rose, and revived.'

There are three branches of the ground.

Christ died, rose, revived.

Of the inference we will speak afterwards, and shew how these grounds enforce that inference, that he should be 'Lord both of the dead and of the living.'

'Christ died.'

1. First of all, you must know *that Christ died here as a public person*, or else the inference were not good. Christ took upon him the person of no man, but the nature; for this end, that he might be a public person. If Christ had taken the person of any body, there had been two persons of Christ. He had died in one person and not in another. Now having the nature that is common to all men, and not the person of Peter or James, &c., when he died the person died in that nature wherein he might die; so when it is said, 'Christ died,' we must consider Christ as a public person, not taking the particular person of any man, but the general nature of man into union with the second person. Christ died as a public person.

2. Secondly, Christ died as the '*second Adam*.' The spring of all misery and death was from the 'first Adam,' but the 'second Adam' was a quickening Spirit, 1 Cor. xv. 45. He died as a public person, and the 'second Adam.'

We must know, moreover, that he died as the great High Priest of the church, offering to God the Father a sacrifice that made him Lord over all, as we shall see after. He died as a priest, as indeed he that was foresignified by all the sacrifices and priests. He was both priest and sacrifice: Heb. ix. 14, 'By the eternal Spirit, the Godhead, he offered himself to his Father.'

3. Again, He died a *voluntary death*, for else he had not died in obedience. His death was violent in regard of them that forced it, but it was voluntary in regard of them that he offered himself for, as a sweet sacrifice to his Father. That voluntariness made his death a sweet sacrifice; for whatsoever the Father did to him, he joined with the Father in it. The Father gave him; he gave himself. The Father appointed him to be so and so; and he joined with the Father in all things. 'No man takes away my life from me,' saith he himself, John x. 18. It was a voluntary death in regard of his freedom; nay, he thirsted after it, as you have it in the Gospel. He longed after it, upon high considerations, howsoever in a lower consideration, as it was a tormenting thing and a bitter cup, he had a desire that it might pass; but it was upon lower respects. Upon higher respects, the

will of his Father and the salvation of mankind, he thirsted to drink of that cup.*

A man may will and nill the same thing upon presenting different objects and respects, and reasons. That which a man may decline, as we say, in this respect, looking to a particular end, that a man may desire, looking to a higher end; because man is framed so to yield to the stronger reason alway. Thereupon that is no objection, 'he seemed sometime a little unwilling.' It was looking upon something presented to him that made him in that respect unwilling; but looking upon other respects he gave himself willingly; the Father and he joined together.

And therefore by the way, when they talk of the active and passive obedience, there was action in all his passion; chiefly in his passion there was action; for if it had been mere suffering without voluntary obedience, what obedience had that been? A beast may so suffer, but against his will; but his voluntary obedience was the chief in all his passion. 'He humbled himself to the death of the cross,' as it is Phil. ii. 8.

4. Yet further, as he died voluntary, *so he died as our surety*. Therefore he died a 'cursed death' due to us. 'He was made a curse for us,' Gal. iii. 13, that he might remove the curse from us. These and such like conclusions must be observed in this, that the apostle saith, 'To this end Christ died,' because we shall have use of them afterwards.

Here we might stay and admire,† that life should die! that glory should become shame for us! and that he that is the author of all blessing should become a curse! Indeed, it is a great mystery that Christ, being God, should stoop so low that he could join together the infinite majesty of God, and that low degree of abasement, that he might condescend unto. *Domine quo descendis*, &c.: Lord, how far goest thou? (*a*) He could not go lower and be God. God, to shew his love to us, shewed himself God in this, that he could be God and go so low as to die; and not only to die, but to die a shameful and cursed death for us. But I pass to the particulars.

'For this end Christ both died and rose,' &c.

1. *He rose again;* and indeed it was impossible but he should rise again, because he is the Lord of life. Now the Lord of life, and life itself, could not long die. It was but by dispensation that he died, viz., to work our salvation. But he could not be detained any longer by the sorrows of death. He died therefore, and rose. He rose, even as he died. He rose a public person, and as a 'second Adam,' to give and infuse spiritual life into all his branches. He rose as our surety in our room. He rose in spite of the Jews, that laboured to keep him down all they could. By the way, this shews that he will rise in his church, and in his children, in his religion, and in his cause. Let the world and all the devils in hell lay a stone upon Christ, upon his cause, and church, and children; they will rise again, even as his blessed body did, in spite of all the watchfulness of the Jews.

2. Again, As he rose, so *he rose with many;* not alone, to shew, as I said before, that he rose as a public person. Another man riseth as himself; the rest rise not with him as caused by his rising. But Christ rose as a public person. Therefore many rose with him, Mat. xxvii. 53. The graves were opened to shew that he rose as a public person, as our surety, as a spiritual head, and as the 'second Adam,' who could infuse life into others (*b*). What became of those bodies that rose with him after? The

* Cf. Luke xxii. 15 with Mat. xxiii. 39, *seq.*—G. † That is, 'wonder.'—G.

Scripture saith nothing of it; nor what became of Moses's body. They rose to do God a service and Christ an honour, which when they had done they were content to be disposed of by God again, and, it is likely, to return from whence they came. For if the head of the church himself was content to come from heaven into the virgin's womb, and from thence to the cross, and from thence to the grave, and to be abased for us, those that have the Spirit of Christ, those blessed souls in heaven, might well be content for a time to be abased, to take bodies, to do a service for their Lord and Master, who was content to forego heaven thirty-four years, and the glory due to him.

Therefore by the way, if God will use us, though we be never so great, for a particular service to the church, shall we stand upon it, when the blessed saints in heaven, those blessed souls, were content to come and take bodies for a time, to do God service, and then to sleep again?

3. Again, *He rose on that day which was ever after, and well may still be, called the Lord's day;* for a new world began with his rising, therefore a new Sabbath. Saint John saith, 'I was in the Spirit upon the Lord's day,' Rev. i. 10. If a man be ever in the Spirit, it is upon the Lord's day, when the Lord of the day doth honour his people, giving them to enjoy his ordinances, and joining effectually with them, maketh them full of the Spirit, and raiseth up our dead hearts after him.

'And revived.'

Why is this added to rising again? 'He revived.'

1. *To shew that he rose never to die again,* and that indeed he never meant to lay aside that body again, as once he had, to die for us. Consonant hereunto is that Rev. i. 18, 'Behold, I was dead and am alive, and I live for evermore; I have the keys of death and of hell.' He lives for evermore, as Heb. vii. 25, 'He sits for evermore at the right hand of God, there making intercession for us.' He dies no more.

2. Again, This 'revived' is added *to shew the kind of his life,* differing from that life he lived before. That life he lived before he died, was supported with meat and drink and refreshings, even as our poor lives are. It was a life subject to death that he died in, but after his resurrection, except it were for a particular dispensation, to confirm the faith of his disciples, he needed no more to eat or drink or sleep, or any natural supports and helps; for he was enlivened immediately by the Spirit of God which flowed into him. He was full of the Spirit, and that did supply all other things whatsoever. Even as in heaven, 'God shall be all in all,' 1 Cor. xv. 28; that is, he shall be so immediately to us, to supply all, as we shall neither eat nor drink nor sleep, nor have magistrates nor ministers; but the Spirit of God will be all in all; so it was with this life of our blessed Saviour when he revived. The Spirit supplied the absence of all other supports whatsoever that he used before he died. And indeed our Saviour Christ came to bestow that life upon us that he lived after his resurrection; not this natural life of ours, that needs meat and drink and refreshings. This is not that life that Christ specially aimed at when he came to die, but that spiritual and eternal life that he lived after the resurrection; a life not subject to death; a spiritual life, not needing any created support whatsoever.

You see the grounds; the inference from these grounds follow in these words, 'that he might be Lord both of the dead and of the living.' The ground hath three branches: death, resurrection, and reviving. How all these do flow and give strength to this inference, I will touch in the particulars. First, then, Christ died '*that he might be Lord of the dead and of the living*,'

Christ died, 1 Peter i. 18, to offer himself a sacrifice, to redeem us by his precious blood. 'We are not redeemed with gold or silver, but with the blood of Christ.' He could not be our Lord till he had bought us. Now his death was the price of our redemption; I say 'redemption,' not 'emption.' A thing may be bought that was never sold away before. Now we were sold to Satan, and under a contrary government. Now Christ satisfying divine justice redeems us. He buys us again. We had subjected ourselves to the devil, and put ourselves under his regiment,* till we were ransomed by Christ. Now Christ shall have no right to us till the price be paid to divine justice; for mercy must have justice satisfied; the attributes of God must not fight one against another. Christ, therefore, is Lord of us, because by death he gave full content to divine justice. So that now, notwithstanding justice, yet we are Christ's, and are saved. Nay, now the justice of God helps us. The most terrible attribute, justice, is a ground of comfort, for it stands not with justice to have the same debt paid twice. For God is just and faithful, saith the apostle, 1 John i. 9. So then you see there is a ground from death why we are the Lord's. We are Christ's because we cost him dear. He hath paid a price for us that is worth more than the whole world. Now God shewed his love in nothing more than in this, that he parted with that that is next himself, the greatest, his Son, who being God, yet died, in that nature that could die, to redeem us, and hereupon becometh Lord.

2. Secondly, He rose again, therefore 'he is Lord of the quick and the dead.'

(1.) First, Because *his rising again was a manifestation that his death was a full satisfaction to divine justice*, or else our sins should have kept him in the grave still, he being our surety. But our surety being out of prison, it is a sign he hath fully discharged all our debt, and the price is paid. If the surety and the creditor be agreed, we know the debt is paid.

(2.) Secondly, In that he rose again, he is Lord, because *in rising again he entered into the possession and exercise of that Lordship that he had purchased*. The right is one thing, and the use and possession of the right is another. Christ was Lord of us before he died. He was Lord of us when he died. But he did not enter into possession of his Lordship till he rose again. Therefore he saith, 'All power is given to me, both in heaven and earth,' Mat. xxviii. 18, when he was ready to go up to heaven, to shew that by his resurrection the right he had by death was manifest.

(3.) Lastly, Because his rising again *shewed that the Father was fully pacified*. He obtained the gift of the Spirit, which next Christ himself is the greatest gift. God gave his Son first, and then the Spirit that comes from the Father and the Son. The Spirit was not given till his resurrection and ascension, as it is John vi.; vii. 39. Why? Because till all enemies were fully subdued by his death, and witnessed to be subdued by his resurrection, the Spirit could not be so fully given, the Spirit being a declaration of the good will of God that sent it. Now when the enemies of Christ were triumphed over, and God had shewed by the raising of his Son again, that he was fully satisfied, then the Spirit comes as the Son† of God's favour, which Spirit doth enable us to be subject to Christ, and makes us come under Christ's kingdom, which is a spiritual government. Wherefore because he obtained the Spirit for his members upon his resurrection,

* That is, 'government.'—G. † Qu. 'sun'?—Ed.

thereupon is the inference good. He rose again, therefore he is Lord 'of the quick and of the dead.'

3. Thirdly, He *revived;* therefore he is Lord of the quick and of the dead. Reviving and taking such a life as is not subject to death any more, he is now in heaven to make good that he purchased on earth. He revived, I say, to be a king, priest, and prophet at the right hand of God for ever: there to rule his church, and to overrule all the enemies of it till he hath subdued all; till he hath 'gathered all the elect,' Mat. xxiv. 31, and brought his church out of the world, and made 'his enemies his footstool,' Ps. cx. 1. You see then the ground is good, and the inference is good. 'Christ died, and rose, and revived,' that he might be Lord of the quick and dead.' I come now to the thing proved.

'That he might be Lord both of the dead and of the living.'

Christ is Lord both of the dead and of the living. For the better clearing of the point, let us see what is lordship.

'Lordship' properly is *jus in rem et personas*. It is a right, and where it is full, it is a right with possession either in things or persons.

But what manner of 'lordship' is this?

1. Christ is an *universal Lord of and over all*, over all the world; both over all the dead, and all the living; but more especially, and in a peculiar manner, he is Lord of his church, even as a husband is lord over his wife, which is a lordship with sweetness. So Christ's government is with unspeakable, with unconceivable sweetness. He is Lord as the Elder Brother, as the first begotten is over the rest; for he is the 'first begotten among the dead,' Rev. i. 5. This likewise is a sweet government. It is indeed a lordship of a king over his subjects, as his lordship is a branch of his kingly office; but it is such a lordship as is for the good of his subjects. It is not a derived* happiness. They enjoy the head and the subjects. Christ accounts himself happy in his church, which is his fulness. The church is 'the fulness of him that filleth all things,' Eph. i. 23. And more especially is the church most happy in this government. It is such a lordship as is, indeed, altogether for the good of the subjects. 'To us a child is born, to us a Son is given,' Isa. ix. 6. He died, and rose, and revived, and all is for us. A Christian may say of Christ that he is *totus in meos usus expensus*, as one well said (*c*). He is all mine; he is all expended for my use and profit. It is such a lordship as makes all his subjects kings. Therefore it is said, Rev. i. 5, 'He loved us, and gave himself for us;' to purge his church, as it is Eph. v. 26, and likewise to 'make us kings and priests.' Where note, Christ hath a notable attendance upon him. He is served with none but kings. All God's children are kings. Even the meanest servant that is anywhere in the world, in spiritual respects is a king. What a Lord and King is this, that makes all his servants kings! You see, therefore, as Christ is an universal Lord, so also he is a peculiar Lord over his church.

2. Again, He is an *independent Lord;* only his Father joins with him in all. He is subordinate to his Father as Mediator, but he is independent in respect of all human authority whatsoever. All human authority is derived from him. 'By me princes reign,' &c., Prov. viii. 15. His government in regard of all those governments is altogether independent. Therefore he is called 'the Lord of lords,' and 'King of kings.' He is Lord Paramount, as we say, over all; and they all are or should be dependent upon him.

* That is, = 'communicated.'—G.

3. And likewise he is a Lord *of the whole man*, body and soul; he is a spiritual Lord. He commands not the body only, but the soul. He sits in the throne of conscience especially, and there he subdues the conscience and the soul to him. There he prescribes laws to the conscience and pacifies the conscience, and stablisheth conscience and settles it against all fears and terrors whatsoever. He is Lord of body and soul, especially of the soul. He bows the neck of the inward man, and brings it wholly to be subject to him. He lays his command upon the very soul itself.

4. And he is *an eternal Lord*. You see here he is Lord of the 'quick and of the dead;' all other lords have nothing to do with men when they are dead. They can do them no more harm. They have some power, indeed, over their dead bodies, but, alas! * that is senseless (*d*). Their government ends in death, because they are lords over the outward man only. But Christ's lordship is when we are gone hence, and then more especially. For then we are more immediately with him. We are nearer the fountain when our souls are gone to him that gave them. 'I desire,' saith St Paul, 'to be dissolved, and to be with Christ, which is best of all,' Philip. i. 23; especially then he is Lord, when we are gone hence.

5. In a word, he is an *excellent Lord*, for he hath all things that a lord should have. A lord should have three things: authority, suitable virtues and abilities, power and strength answerable to all. Now the Lord Christ hath all these. And, first, he hath *authority*, for God the Father gave him power over all. He purchased it, and his Father gave it him. 'He gave him the heathen for his possession,' Ps. ii. 8; and 'All power is given to me in heaven and earth,' Mat. xxviii. 18; and he hath full authority, as it is John xvii. 2, 'Thou hast given me power over all flesh.' He hath then authority. Secondly, he hath all *graces and virtues* fit for a lord and governor. He hath righteousness, wisdom, bounty, affections, &c. We need not make doubt of it; for he is the spring of all these in others. 'His sceptre is a sceptre of righteousness,' Ps. xlv. 6. Thirdly, he hath *strength* answerable to his authority; for he is a Lord that is God. Sometimes among men authority wants power or other qualifications; but in Christ is all, the utmost and greatest fulness of all. These things premised, let us make some use of all.

But, first, let us see why it is said, 'He is Lord both of the dead and of the living,' prefixing the dead before the living? To shew, I conceive, that Christ is Lord of those that were dead before, as well as of those that are alive now. Christ is the Lord of all from the beginning of the world, from Adam to the last man that shall stand upon the face of the earth; therefore he is Lord of those that were dead before, as well as of those that are alive now, and that shall die after. 'He is Lord of the dead, and of the living.' Now for use, first, where he saith,

'For this end.'

Use 1. It is a point wondrous pregnant, and full of very comfortable use: first, shewing *that the grounds of a Christian's faith and comfort are very strong*, as you see how the Holy Ghost dwells upon the argument. 'For this end,' saith he, Christ died and rose again and revived, that he might be Lord of the quick and of the dead.'

God doth all to ends, it being a point of wisdom to prefix an end, and work to it. If God hath an end and providence in the hairs that fall from our heads, hath he not a far greater in disposing of things for the good of

* One of the many examples of Sibbes's peculiar use of this interjection. Cf. page 334, line 5 from top.—G.

the church? His Son is given to death, and raised agian. It is for the greatest end in the world, being the greatest work. The greatest work hath the greatest end. Such was this end, the lordship of the church: 'For this end,' saith he, 'Christ died, and rose again, that he might be Lord of the dead, and of the living,' which is his church.

And is this Christ's end, to be Lord of the living and of the dead? *We must have it then our end too, to serve Christ, to live and die to him;* for being under him, our ends must be answerable to his, as we shall see after.

'For this end.'

Use 2. Again, where it is said he died, and rose, and revived, 'that he might be Lord of the dead and of the living'—It is a profitable course—I speak it only in general—when we think of the abasement of Christ, *to think of the end why. So of his exaltation: it is good to keep these together to avoid scandal* that might arise in our minds from either, thought of by itself,* that God should stoop so low. Lest the thoughts of Christ dying and stooping so low should offend us, it is good also to think of the end, that 'he might be Lord of quick and dead;' and if that dazzle thee again, to think of our Saviour now in glory, full of majesty in heaven, and how shalt thou have access to so glorious majesty. Oh come down again, and think of God incarnate, God going up and down in our flesh, of God dying, dying a cursed death, and rising again. Thus in your meditations interweave these thoughts, to avoid scandal. Think of his glory; and that you may not be amazed at the glory, so as to be deterred from going boldly to him, think of bone of our bone and flesh of our flesh, God dying in your nature. Join these two together. 'For this end the Son of God died, and rose, and revived, that he might be Lord both of the dead and of the living.'

Use 3. Again, You see here in general *that the grand principal points of religion have an influence into all the particulars;* and there is a homogeneal deduction, as we call it, of divine truths one from another. All depend one upon another, and all divinity; for howsoever divine truth be contrary to carnal reason sometimes, yet there is strong reason in all divine truth. For one is the cause of another, and one depends upon another, as here, 'Christ died, and rose, and revived.' One follows another. What from all this? 'To be Lord of quick and dead.' How then proves he that he is Lord of all? Because he died, and rose, and revived. One riseth from another. So that, though carnal reason be one thing and all divinity be another, yet there is reason and deduction issuing of one thing from another in divinity, most wisely and holily; and it is a part of wisdom to observe how conclusions rise from principles, as branches and buds do from roots. Indeed, if we would enter into serious considerations of the grounds of religion, how they give life, and rise unto their particulars, they would have an influence into the whole course of our life, as perhaps we shall see in the particulars more clearly.

'For this end,' &c.

Use 4. Again, in general, when he saith Christ is 'Lord of the quick and of the dead,' we see hence *the truth of the catholic church, from the first man living to the end of the church, under one head Christ.* Christ is the Saviour of those that were before the law, under the law, under the gospel. Christ was the Saviour of all. He is the Saviour of the dead as well as of the living. All come under one head, which hath no further use than to inform us in that one point of doctrine, to shew that Christ is 'yesterday' as well as 'to-day,' to-morrow, 'and for ever,' Heb. xiii. 8. All that were

* That is, 'offence.'—G.

saved before, that are saved now, and shall be for ever, are saved by Christ. 'There is no other name under heaven whereby we can be saved,' Acts iv. 12. 'He is Lord of the dead and of the living.' Now, therefore, to come more particularly, 'Christ is Lord both of the dead and of the living.' What a Lord [is] we heard before.

This is a point of wondrous comfort, and likewise a point informing us of our duty; and withal shewing us that Christ will work that duty in us, because he is a Lord not only that should rule over us, that we should be subject to him, but to make us subject to him. It is a point of wondrous comfort and of duty, and of this issue, that we under the covenant of grace shall be enabled to perform that duty to our Lord.

And then it is a point of wondrous security in life, in death, as, alas! sometime one thing amazeth us, sometime another; sometime we are willing to die—Elias was afraid to live; sometimes we are afraid of death, as we are all naturally. Why, come life or death, come what will come, we are under a Lord that is Lord of 'the dead and of the living.' So it is a point of wondrous security and quiet to a Christian in all passages. He sometimes lives and sometimes dies, but his salvation is not at that hazard to be off and on, but 'whether he live or die,' he is sure to be saved, for he is under the Lord of the living and the dead.

But to speak a little of the first. It is intended for comfort, as well as direction to duty, and to be subject, to submit to the Lord. It is a comfort that we have a Lord that rules us for our good while we are living, and when we are dead, and for ever; and indeed we cannot have a greater comfort, beloved, than this, that 'we are not our own, but that we are bought with a price,' 1 Cor. vi. 20, that we are under Christ. Why, what a comfort is this, will you say. *Homo non est natus*, &c. (*e*), as the natural man said, a man is not born to subjection but to honour and government. What comfort is this to be under Christ, to be under a governor!

Ans. Oh beloved, know that it is the greatest comfort; as the rule is, everything is perfect if it be weak, by that whereby it is subject to a higher. The vine is perfect by leaning to the elm. It would lie on the ground else, and be spoiled. The perfection of the weak creature the sheep is to have a shepherd. The perfection of a weak nature is to have a rule for their good. The perfection of the ship is the pilot. It would dash on every rock, and be tossed with every wave else. And so it is our perfection, that we are under a Lord, such a Lord as this is, *cui servire regnare est*, &c. (*f*), to whom to serve is to reign; for all his servants are so many kings. It is our perfection to be subject to him, therefore it is a wondrous comfort that Christ is become 'Lord of the living and of the dead.' I beseech you, therefore, think of it in your meditations. All the Scripture aims at this end to comfort. Whatsoever is written, is written for our comfort; and this is a principle of divinity among the rest, that a Christian is not his own man now, but he is under Christ. And this is a comfort both in life and death at all times. As the psalmist saith, 'My times are in thy hands, Lord,' Ps. xxxi. 15. He saith not, 'my time,' but 'my times are in thy hand;' so we may say our times are in Christ's hands; our time of being born, our time of living and dying; and when we are dead, our time of rising again. Our time, the whole current of our time, is in thy hands, not in the devil's hands, not in our enemies' hands, beloved, for they would make short work with us then; but our times are in our Lord's hands. Christ is the Lord of our times, the Lord of our life and death; and when we are dead, he is a Lord for ever; for he lives for ever, and therefore he is or ever a Lord. Beloved, we do not die at the devotion* and good pleasure of any man whatsoever. They cannot stir so much as a hair from our head, without the will of this Lord. All the devils in hell cannot stir a hair of our head, I say, nor all men that are acted by the spirit of the devil. They may threaten punishment, but, alas! they can do no more than this Lord of lords will give them leave. Therefore it is a point of wondrous comfort.

Obj. Oh but will a poor soul say, Christ indeed is Lord of the living and of the dead, but I find a great deal of corruption in me, &c., and I am a sinner.

Ans. Why, he is Lord over thee. He hath a sweet lordship over thee, as well as a commanding lordship. He is not only a king, but a husband, as it is Eph. v. 26, 27, 'He gave himself to purge his church,' and to make his church fit by little and little. Thou hast sin and corruption, but thou hast a merciful husband that will bear with the weaker vessel. Doth he command others to do that; and will he not practise that that he enjoins others? Undoubtedly he will; and therefore it is a comfort, it is a sweet government and subjection, as of the husband over the wife. Christ purgeth and cleanseth his church; he doth not cast it away.

For I beseech you, consider, he that died for his church and children, when they were enemies, will he cast them away now they are poor friends, and desire to please him? as Saint Paul divinely reasoneth, Rom. v. 10, 'Much more shall we be saved by his life.' If he saved us by death, much more now by his life, being in heaven. Consider he rose and lives for ever; therefore will he cast us away for some imperfections, that died for us when we were enemies? He that will not 'quench the smoking flax, nor break the bruised reed,' Mat. xii. 20, will he cast away his poor children that strive against their corruptions? He will not, nay, he hath promised where he hath begun a good work, he will finish it to the day of the Lord, Phil. i. 6, Though it go but slowly forward, yet that beginning is a pledge of proceeding. God will never remove his hand from his own work till he have brought it to perfection. Therefore let any soul comfort itself that will come under this Lord. In a word, what greater comfort can we have than this, that he is such a Lord over us, as is Lord over all other things in the world besides? For he could not be Lord of his church, except he were Lord over hell, and all power were subject to him. Now being so he is such a Lord of the church as can restrain the power of all creatures whatsoever; because else they might annoy the church and affront him in his government by opposition, if he were not Lord of all things else, as well as of the Church. But this is the comfort of a Christian; he is under a Lord that is Lord of all the enemies of the church; and he is so Lord over them till by little and little he make them his footstool. That that is begun in this world shall be consummate hereafter by that lordship; nay, he will make all the enterprises of the very enemies of his church whatsoever serviceable to his poor church; for as the apostle saith, 'All things are yours, because ye are Christ's,' 1 Cor. iii. 23. He is such a Lord as that besides himself being onrs, he makes all the world ours, yea, the devil is ours; for in spite of him, whatsoever he doth, it is ordained to the salvation of the church. The church's enemies are the servants of the church, the involuntary servants; for they weaken† the church and scour it. God raiseth them up for the exercise of the church; and when he hath done, you know what course he takes with them. So then he is Lord, not only over all, but he overrules their actions for the good of the church,

* That is, 'option.'—G. † Qu. 'waken'?—Ed.

whatsoever they are; and he makes all the endeavours and plots of the enemy for the church's good; all is yours, life and death. Though it be death by tyrants, all kind of death whatsoever, it is yours. What a comfort is this, that we are under such a Lord as this.

Especially, what a comfort is this at the hour of death, when Christ, that ruled us all our lifetime before, will take then the government and possession of that jewel that he hath bought with such a price, our precious souls; that when we must part with friends, and part with this sweet body, that the soul so much loved, and with the world and all things in the world, then Christ will own [us] for his when the world will own us no longer. Therefore methinks Christians should be at a point, for life or death. He never goes out of the dominion of Christ; nay, he is nearer Christ; he is more Christ's. If there be any comparison to be made when he is dead than when he is alive, 'Blessed are those that died in the Lord.'

To apply this a little to the present occasion.* Here in this sacrament we are to have communion with the Lord, of his death and resurrection. For what is the sacrament but a representation of his body broken, and of his blood poured out for us, that he might be Lord over us? The more communion and fellowship you have with Christ, the more assurance you shall have that you are his, which is indeed the grand comfort of all, that we are Christ's, that Christ is ours; for then heaven and earth is ours, all is ours. Now God hath ordained these sacraments for this end. The word is the sceptre of his kingdom whereby he rules. The sacrament is the seal of the word. Therefore all good subjects, that submit themselves to the kingdom of Christ, must submit themselves to this sweet ordinance of Christ, that he hath ordained for our good, the word and the sacraments. Thereby we shall find the effectual working of his Spirit in us, subjecting the whole inward man to his gracious government. But having spoken of this subject at large heretofore, I only desire you to raise up your thoughts to consider whom you have to deal with; with him that is Lord of the quick and of the dead. We have to deal with the mighty Monarch of heaven and earth, Christ. Therefore come, as with faith, because he hath ordained these things to strengthen faith; so come with reverence, knowing with whom we are to feast and to deal. Consider of these things; and then I hope that God will vouchsafe a blessing answerable to the intendment† of his ordinance.

THE SECOND SERMON.

For to this end Christ both died, and rose, and revived, that he might be the Lord both of the dead and of the living.—Rom. XIV. 9.

I shewed the dependence in the forenoon; a Christian, by the Spirit of God in him, he hath a blessed aim at all times. Howsoever he may fail in particulars, yet his aim is right.

This doubt rose from difference of aims, whether he should please God or man. His doubt rose in pleasing of God, what might please him most; and because he sees not always what might please him, therefore he carries this honesty, that whatsoever he doth he will do it to the Lord, and whatsoever he doth not he will not do it to the Lord. His aim is for good at all times.

* That is, celebration of the sacrament.—G. † That is, 'intention' = 'design.'—G.

Now this is proved from the general disposition of Christians. They live and die to the Lord. Therefore their particular actions must be to the Lord. If their whole life and death be to the Lord, their actions must be to him.

Now he proves their whole life and death are to the Lord, because they are the Lord's. How doth he prove that they are the Lord's—that is, Jesus Christ's? Because the text saith here, 'For this end Christ both died, and revived, that he might be Lord both of the dead and of the living.'

And surely he is Lord. He will not miss of his end. God never misseth of his end, because he can remove all impediments between him and his end. Now it being Christ's end to be Lord of the quick and of the dead, he is Lord. If he be Lord, then those that are under him, and led by his Spirit, aim both in life and death to glorify him in all things. This in a word be spoken, for the inference of the words.

'To this end Christ both died, and rose, and revived.'

Here you have a ground and an inference; an argument and a reasoning from it.

The argument or ground is, '*Christ died, and rose, and revived.*'

That that riseth thence is, '*That he might be Lord both of the dead and of the living.*'

In the ground itself I told you how Christ died as a public person, as the 'second Adam,' &c.; and now here you are to take notice likewise that he rose again as a public person, as the 'second Adam,' &c.

And likewise he revived, not to die again, as in his first life. When he began to live, he began to die; but when he revived he did not die again. He lives for ever to make intercession for us in heaven. Christ never dies again, Rom. vi. 8, *seq.* He rose to a life that shall never end; for the divine nature doth flow into his human nature, and doth immediately inspire such a spiritual life into it, as it lives for ever, by virtue of the Spirit of Christ actuating, and stirring, and moving him, as his natural life did here, when he was upon the earth.

'Christ died, and rose, and revived.'

To what end is all this? What is grounded hence? That Christ therefore is Lord of quick and dead? This is inferred from all three.

'Christ died,' that he might reconcile us to God by his death, satisfying justice; and so justice being fully satisfied, he might have his end in being Lord of his church. He had a mind to marry us, but he could not till he had rescued us. Therefore to rescue us out of divine justice, and from the tyranny of Satan, God's jailor, he made satisfaction to divine justice. As for Satan he brought us out of his kingdom by strong hand; and so doth continually by the power of his Spirit. Now hereupon it must needs be that he must be Lord of that he paid so dear a price for.

And then he rose again for this end, that he 'might be Lord,' because, howsoever he had a title to be Lord of the church,—by the union of the human nature with the divine, he was Lord alway,—yet in regard of the exercise of his lordship, it was deferred till his glorious resurrection and ascension. Then that that lay hid before, Christ's divine power, majesty, and lordship, that appeared and manifested itself, as it is Rom. i. 4, 'He was mightily declared to be the Son of God by the resurrection from the dead.' He was the Son of God before; but then it was a kind of begetting, because it was then manifest. Things are said in Scripture and divinity to be when they are apparent to be. So this day of the resurrection Christ was begotten; because it was apparent then by raising himself from the dead, that he was the only-begotten Son of God. Now that made way for his lordship; for after his resurrection God gave him power over all things in heaven and earth; and then upon the resurrection he had the Spirit in more abundance, having conquered all enemies between God and us. Therefore he was fit to be Lord by that, because he could give the Spirit to them over whom be meant to rule.

But then in his own person, he rising, triumphed over all opposite enemies whatsoever; over death the last enemy, and over Satan, sin, and the law, having cancelled all. Surely [since] he hath overruled all for himself, he will overrule all for his church and people; and therefore he rose again to be 'Lord of quick and dead;' and he may well be, because he is Lord of 'quick and dead' in his own person. He is Lord over all in his own person, and therefore he is Lord over the church, and all the enemies of the church. So far as the enemies seized upon his person, so far he overcame them all. He hath as much care of his mystical person the church, as he had on* his own body; and more too, for he gave that for the other.

And then he revived to be Lord over all; that is, he lives for ever to make good what he hath gotten by his death. He will not lose the price of his own blood. He is in heaven to appear before God, and sits at the right hand of God, and rules there till he have made his enemies his footstool, till he draw his church home to heaven, to himself. 'He lives for ever,' as the apostle saith, 'to make intercession,' Heb. vii. 25. Hereupon it must needs be that by living for ever he is fitly qualified to be Lord over all the 'quick.' Now I proceed.

'That he might be Lord both of quick and dead.'

Christ is Lord both of the dead and of the living. You see upon what ground he is Lord of all, as well as of his church. He is an eternal Lord over the dead and the living. He is a transcendent Lord, above all other lords whatsoever; and he is independent. He is not obnoxious† to any. All have power from him; and in some sort indeed Christ hath redeemed even all other creatures. They are Christ's. And in some sort even proud wicked men, that live in the church, that have perhaps some parts (which are the occasion of their damnation, because of and by them, they are proud and insolent), they are redeemed by Christ, thus far to be serviceable to his church, to use their parts to his own ends. They go a great way in salvation, that so by their parts they may be fit to do service to the church. So he is Lord not only over the church, but of others for the service of the church.

Now this point, that Christ is Lord of the dead and of the living, it yields many comfortable uses. I spake of some things in general, and then we came to some particulars, as,

1. First, Seeing Christ is Lord of the quick and of the dead, *we may comfort ourselves under the sovereignty of Christ.* To be Solomon's servant was accounted a great happiness. Those that did observe the government of Solomon did think so, as the Queen of Sheba, 1 Kings x. 8. Alas! what shall we think of those that are under Christ, who 'is greater than Solomon,' Mat. xii. 42, a most great, a most wise, a most loving, a most gracious and powerful Lord over all. Therefore it is a most comfortable condition, here in this life, to add a little to that point, however it be service. It is against the nature of man to serve a man, yet not to serve a more noble; to serve God is to reign.

Besides, while we live here, such is our disposition, such is the weakness

* Qu. 'of'?—G. † That is, 'subject to.'—G.

of base sinners, that they must be ruled by another; and indeed our happiness and security consists in being ruled by another higher than ourselves. We are not fit to be our own governors. St Paul saith to the Galatians, 'an heir in his non-age differeth little from a servant,' Gal. iv. 1. So it is with Christians. Till they be in heaven they differ little from servants; and therefore they must be under tutors and government.

And as it is a comfortable, so it is an honourable condition; for Christ's servants are so many kings. Christ is served of none but kings, and such kings as do not rule over slaves, but such kings as in Christ rule over the greatest and terriblest enemies of all. A Christian can think with comfort and encouragement upon those enemies that make the greatest tyrants of the world to quake; he can think of death, of sin, of damnation, of judgment, of the law: of all these things Christ's kingdom is another manner of kingdom than the kingdom of the world. They are poor kingdoms; their monarch's head must lie as low as the basest subject they have. They know not how soon, and perhaps have a more terrible account to give than any other under them. It is not so in Christ's kingdom.

Therefore those Christians that are afraid of death, they forget their dignity; they forget him on whom they depend, for Christ is Lord 'both of the quick and *of the dead*.' If so be Christ be their Lord when they die, what need they fear to die? And therefore let us comfort ourselves when God calls for us. He is our Lord as well when we die as while we live, and more too; for then our souls have more immediate communion with him. Can there be more comfort than this, that we have a Lord ever that died for us, that rose for us, and lives for ever, and doth immortalise his subjects too? Join these together, an ever-living Lord and ever-living subjects, co-existent, I mean, for the time to come. We indeed have a beginning—Christ hath none as God—but we have an eternal state to be for ever, and an eternal Lord to rule us for ever, and to make us happy for ever. What comfort is more than this, that howsoever there be variety of conditions in this world, we live, we die, we are in prosperity, we are in misery; yet here is no variety in the state of salvation. Christ is not a Lord to-day and none to-morrow; but 'yesterday, to-day, and the same for ever,' Heb. xiii. 8.

2. Again, As it is a point of comfort, *so it is also of duty*. If Christ be our Lord in life and death, our duty is to look to him in life and death, to live and die to him. For our aim must answer his aim, if we ever intend to come to heaven; for we are understanding creatures, and have a communion with him in a poor measure. Therefore what he will make his end must be our end. His end was that whether we live or die he might rule over us. Our end should be, in life and death to be ruled by him.

How shall we live to Christ?

We live to Christ—this is a ground of all other duties that follow—when we know and acknowledge Christ hath a full interest in us, by being our head, by being our husband, by being our king, our elder brother. He hath all the sweet interest to us that any relation can inright* (*g*) him to; for all other relations among men are but shadows of that grand relation. There only is the reality of things. He is a true head, a true king, a true elder brother, a true husband to his church. All ours are but poor representations of those glorious things. Then know and acknowledge so much. That is the ground of all living to him.

Upon knowing and acknowledging issues all other obedience in our life to Christ. Those that thus acknowledge Christ, they must be directed by

* That is, = entitle by right. Leighton uses 'inrighted.' Cf. Note *g*.—G.

his will, and not their own. As a servant as far as he is a servant, and a wife so far as she is a wife, they have no will of their own, so he that lives to Christ and acknowledgeth him to be a Lord, he must have no will of his own, but he must live according to the will of Christ, as you have it excellently set down, 1 Peter iv. 1, 2, 'Christ suffered for us in the flesh. Let us arm ourselves therefore with the same mind; for he that suffered in the flesh hath ceased from sin, that he should no longer live the rest of his time in the flesh, to the lusts of men, but to the will of God.' It is a comment upon this place, 'Christ died, and rose, and revived, that he might be Lord of the quick and of the dead;' that is, that we might live according to his will, and not after our own. Do you think our Saviour Christ would so far deny himself to leave heaven, to take upon himself our base nature, and be so far abased in it, to let us live as we list? Oh no; we must live the rest of our days, not according to the lusts of men, or our own lusts, but according to the will of God; and therefore as the apostle admonisheth, Rom. xii. 2, we must search 'what is the acceptable will of God in all things.' What is the end of our hearing sermons, of our reading, and all the pains we take in the means of salvation? Not only to know what God will do to us, but what he will have of us. He will have the directing of our lives; and therefore if we live to Christ, we must labour to know his good pleasure to us; what he means to do for us and so his good pleasure with us; what he will have us do again by way of thankfulness. Christ squared his life immediately according to his Father's will. 'It is written in the volume of thy book, that I should do thy will, O God,' Ps. xl. 7. So all that are Christ's must have the same spirit, to direct all their lives according to his will. Now the most grand things of his will—for his will is in the Scriptures—are that we repent. He commands all to repent. His will is that we believe in him. His will is our sanctification, as it is 1 Thes. iv. 23. His will is that we suffer, and in suffering submit ourselves to him; and the Scriptures is express in many other particulars, but these especially are named, to shew something wherein we must direct ourselves according to his will. But, not to insist upon particulars, in all things we must labour to direct our lives *according to his will.*

Secondly, That we may live to God, we must aim *at the glory of Christ in all things*, and at the credit of religion, not at our own credit. If Christ be Lord of the quick and dead, while we live we must not seek our own glory but his. The contrary to this the apostle complains of: 'All seek their own,' saith he, 'and not the things that are of the Lord Jesus Christ,' Phil. ii. 21. We must consider what is for the credit of religion and the honour of Christ; and not what is for our own advantage. Is it not good reason that we should seek the glory of him that is Lord over us? Naturally proud man is led with a spirit of self-love; and he seeks himself in all things, even in his religion. So far as it stands with his own lusts he will be religious, and no further. So long as God's will is not contrary to his, he will do God service; but if it cross his will once, then he will give God leave to seek him a servant.

Thus man makes himself an idol; he sets up himself in the room of God; he doth all things, as from himself, so for himself; nor indeed can he do otherwise, till he put off himself wholly, and deny himself—a man cannot go beyond himself but by grace, that raiseth a man above himself. It makes him have an eye to some excellency, out of himself, conformity whereto and interest whereinto will make him happy.

Now that we may aim at Christ in all things, it is good to call ourselves to account for our aims. Wherefore we live and wherefore we have, are, or do anything, either in grace or nature, it is or should be, not only that we may be saved ourselves, but that Christ in all may be glorified. We need not sever these; for Christ joins them both together; and he that seeks his own salvation seeks the glory of God, because God will be glorified in saving us. The end hath a main influence into all actions; and as it differenceth man from other creatures, that though he do the same action as a beast, he eats and drinks and sleeps, all for another end, for an end beyond himself, because he is a reasonable creature, whereas other creatures rest in themselves. So it differenceth between natural men and Christians; they differ in their aims, not in their actions. Both do the same thing. One doth it for base ends of his own; keeps within the circle of those ends. The other having a light discovering excellencies better than the world can afford, and having another spiritual life above, he is thereby directed to further aims in all; yea, even in his civil actions.

Saint Paul gives a rule, that 'whether we eat or drink, or whatsoever we do, we should do all to the glory of God,' 1 Cor. x. 31. Though the action be common and civil, not tending directly to the glory of God, as eating, &c., yet our aim should be in it, at Christ and at God, that the body thereby being refreshed may be fit to serve God.

And indeed there is not the commonest action of this life, but we may shew that we have a good end in it, and therein glorify God. Therefore in Scripture it is put as a kind of limitation: 'Obey in the Lord,' 'marry in the Lord,' do all things in the Lord; that is, in Christ. He shews that we should do all such things, intimating that as we must go about such enterprises with invocation of the name of the Lord, &c., so chiefly we should do them so far, and no farther, as they may stand with the favour and glory of Christ. In subordinate things, the rule of subordinate things is to do them so far as they may help to the main end. Now the service of all other is subordinate to the service of Christ, and all other bonds are serviceable to the main bond in marriage, or whatsoever may not prejudice the bond of marriage in the Lord; marry not rich, nor honourable, but in the Lord. All things must have their limitation to be done in the Lord; that is, so far as they may stand with pleasing the Lord. Thus we see what it is to live to the Lord with his good pleasure and likening.*

Now an assistant help—of living to the Lord—is a perpetual self-denial of our own wisdom, will, and affections in all things, else we shall live to ourselves, and to the Lord we shall never attain.

But you will say this is a hard saying. True. But consider this one thing, that we are the greatest enemies to ourselves of all; and we carry in ourselves a cursed enmity to all that is divine and supernatural. Naturally we are trained up to our own will, therefore we cannot endure the yoke of Christ without supernatural strength.

Again, Divine things *perpetually cross the liking of the soul;* whereupon there is an antipathy between us and Christ, and divine things. Therefore there must be self-denial of necessity. Now the knowledge of this will be a good means to enable us to the duty.

Another help to this, of living to Christ, is *to complain of ourselves to Christ,* as Saint Paul, Rom. vii. 24, 'O wretched man that I am, who shall deliver me?' &c.; to inform against our rebellions, that we live too much to the flesh and too little to the Spirit, too much to ourselves and too little to Christ, by reason of that principle of flesh and blood, and to

* Qu. 'liking'?—Ed.

desire him to captivate all,* and bring all in subjection by his Spirit. This is alway a sign of a man led by the Spirit, that it directs him to Christ. The Spirit, as it comes from Christ, and the Father, so it directs to Christ, to the pleasing of the Father, and of Christ in all things.

Here I might take just occasion to reprove a company of men that live under the gospel, that will be saved by Christ forsooth, but will not have Christ a Lord to rule over them. They will be ruled by rules of state, or rules of flesh and blood, and their own lusts, by the rules of hell sometime, so that they may have their own aims, their own ambition satisfied, and raise themselves to their own pitch; a disposition cursed, and opposite to that religion which they profess. For our life should be a living to Christ, and under Christ a living to the church and state. But say they, 'Let us break their bonds, and cast their cords from us,' Ps. ii. 3. What! do they think we will be awed with a company of poor preachers? Away with them! We will have our own wills; let us break their bonds in sunder. Christ sits in heaven, and laughs them all to scorn, Ps. ii. 4. They shall know at length he will be no Saviour where he is no Lord. If he may not rule them by his Spirit and holy directions while they live, he will not own them when they die. For you see the text joins both here, 'he died,' and 'he is Lord.' When he died there came water and blood out of his side, to shew that he came not only to shed his blood, to die, and to satisfy divine justice, but by water to cleanse us, and to fit us to be subject to his government. Therefore those that take him as a priest to die, and will not have him as a Lord, they rent† his offices. I do but touch these now.

We see what it is to live to Christ. Let us see what it is to die to the Lord?

(1.) 'To die to the Lord' is *to know and acknowledge that Christ hath power over us when we die; thereupon to submit ourselves to him*, and not to murmur and fret, when he comes to call for our life and soul, as if we were unwilling to part with them.

(2.) Then again, to die to Christ, is *when upon any good occasion he calls for our lives in standing for a good cawse—for the church or state—to be ready to lay it down.* There is not the least tittle of truth, but that it is better than a man's life. A man may not only die, in case of martyrdom, but in case of justice and truth, and so he must be willing to die if he will die to Christ.

(3.) Again, We die to the Lord *when we carry ourselves so when death comes, as we may express some graces to glorify God, even in our very death*; when we study to do all the good we can, that we may die fruitfully; out of this consideration, my time is short, I will labour to be sowing to the Spirit as much as I can, not to die like fools, but wisely, knowing that there is no further opportunity. Here is the time of seed; hereafter will be the time of reaping. Therefore there is no Christian that is master of himself at the hour of death, if some disease disable him not, but he studies how to shew himself as fruitful as he can at that time; as you see our Saviour when he was to die, what long chapters there are, three together, of his demeanour, how he strengthened his disciples, what an excellent prayer he made to God. See Moses, how he carried himself at his death, what excellent admonitions he gives; and good Jacob, what an excellent will he made; and St Peter, knowing he must put off his earthly taber-

* That is, = 'subdue.'—G.

† That is, 'rend,' = divide.—G.

nacle, 2 Peter i. 14, he labours to put them in mind 'to glorify God,' as Saint Paul saith, 1 Cor. vi. 20.

A Christian ought to end his days in faith and obedience; in faith that God will take his soul, when he commits it to him, and he shall reign for ever in heaven. In obedience thereupon, because he believes, he dies in faith, he will die in obedience. I even offer myself to thee, because I believe thou wilt care for me when I am gone hence; for thou art the Lord of life and death, and thou art the Lord of me when I live, and when I am dead.

Well, as it implies duty, so it implies a gracious effect, that we shall be enabled to this duty. He indeed in himself is a Lord. We ought to acknowledge him so, nay, we shall have the Spirit if we be his, to cause us to acknowledge him. You have a notable place, 2 Cor. v. 15, to this purpose, 'The love of Christ constrains us, because we thus judge, if one died for all, then we are all dead.' If he died to redeem us from death, to what end did he die? He died for all, that 'they might not live to themselves, but to him that died, and rose again,' 2 Cor. v. 15. It is nothing but this in the text, 'we should live to him.' Now this, that we should live to him, it is not an aim of ours only, but an effect that he works in us. He died 'that we might live to him.' For he died and rose that he might obtain the Spirit. By this Spirit he enableth us to live and die to God: as you have it, Rom. viii. 8, at large proved. Those that are Christ's have the Spirit of Christ, and are led with it.

Beloved, it is a part of the new covenant, that whatsoever our duty is, we shall have ability to perform it by the Spirit of Christ; for all the gracious promises of the gospel are not only promises upon condition, and so a covenant, but likewise the covenant of grace is a testament and a will (a will is made without conditions; a covenant with conditions), that as he hath made a covenant what he would have us to do, so his testament is, that we shall have grace to do so; he will put his Spirit into us, and circumcise our hearts, or else, beloved, there would be no more strength of the covenant of grace than there was of that of nature in Adam. Why did Adam fall? He had not the Spirit to uphold him, nor had he the promise of it to keep him that he should not fall. Therefore the covenant of works was frustrate. But now the covenant of grace is this, that whatsoever God requires he will give his Spirit to enable us to do it, that the covenant may not be frustrate. If God should not make good our part as well as his, we should not be saved. Therefore, now in the covenant of grace we may boldly go to God and Christ; and allege unto him, when any duty is pressed upon us, and when we are about to perform any duty, and find want of strength, 'Lord, thou knowest I have no strength of myself, I am a barren wilderness; but thou hast entered into a covenant of grace with me, which covenant now is a testament, a free will, that thou wilt give what thou requirest, Lord, in the use of means that thou hast ordained; in attending upon thee, and looking up to thee, I desire that thou wouldst give me strength to submit to thee, to live and die to thee, to direct my course as I should.' This should be the course of a Christian, and not to set upon things in his own strength; but when duty is discovered, look to the promise of grace and of the Spirit, and put them into suit, and allege them to Christ in the use of sanctified means, as reading, hearing, holy conference, and the like; and he will enable us to do that that is our duty.

Therefore a man may know who is indeed under Christ's government by this, for he that is actually under Christ's government and acknowledgeth him to be his Lord, he hath ability to live and die to him in some comfortable measure; to deny himself, to go out of himself, to live and to die to the glory of God. The Spirit of God hath given him this victory and triumph over his own heart.

Last of all, if this be so, here *see the wondrous secure state of a Christian.* Beloved, that as Christ is his Lord both in life and death, and it is his duty to subject himself, so Christ will give him grace so to direct his life. Therefore let us do our duty, attend upon the means, and lift up our hearts to God; let God and Christ alone with all the rest, let Christ alone with ruling us and with enabling us to be ruled by him. He is Lord not only over us, but in us by his Spirit. But the Spirit 'breatheth where it listeth,' John iii. 8. There must be waiting upon God in his ordinances, till we find ability to holy duties; and those that have so much patience to honour God and Christ so far as to attend in the use of good means till the good hour come, till the Spirit come to subject their spirits to duty, no doubt but God intends well to them. But those that are so short-spirited that if they find not ability to deny themselves and to live to God, and to break off their course of sin, but give over in a kind of base despair, it is just with God to leave them to themselves, that they shall even live and die to themselves; that is, they shall live without respect to Christ, and die without respect to Christ at all, as if there were no Christ to take care for them.

Now out of this branch of holy security, upon the care and power and lordship that Christ hath over us for the time to come, it riseth that a Christian *may be assured of his salvation, of his perseverance, because Christ is Lord of all.* He is Lord of his heart. He is Lord not only of the things without us, but of our spirits within us, and he will enable us to subject ourselves to him, 'that neither things present, nor things to come, or anything, shall ever be able to separate us from the love of God in Christ,' Rom. viii. 39; not only from God's love to us, but from our love to God.

Beloved, let this encourage us to come under the government of Christ. There is no security or safety but in his government. We are sure of nothing in this world, but we are sure of this, that Christ, if he be our Lord, is our Lord for ever, and that nothing in the world shall ever be able to separate us from him.

I will close with this. You see Christ is ours, whether 'we live or die.' He is 'Lord of quick and dead.' Let us labour to live to him, that he may rule over us while we live, else when we come to die, though we never so much—perhaps out of principles of self-love—desire him to be ours, it is to no purpose. While we live, therefore, let us submit to his government, and if we live to him we shall easily die to him. If we do not inure ourselves by daily self-denying and practising of the duties of obedience to live to him, how shall we come to die to him? Our life may be snatched from us against our wills; we may die with a kind of fretting and indignation that we can live no longer, that we can enjoy our pleasures no longer. But to die meekly and quietly, as to a Lord, submitting ourselves to him that is the Lord of life and death, a man can never do it that hath not lived to the Lord. Therefore I beseech you every day be acquainted with the actions of living to the Lord. Whatsoever you do to men, do it as to the Lord, in the Lord's strength to please him, and as it may stand with his favour and no further. And especially take the advantage of your younger years to root out lusts that will grow to that head else, that God in his judgment, giving you up to yourselves—after long rebellion—you shall never be able to deny yourselves to live to Christ, and, when death comes, to die to Christ; therefore let us inure ourselves to deny ourselves in the practice of every holy duty, as to the Lord betimes, that so we may get the upper hand of our flesh in these holy performances, that they may be easy and sweet to us, as indeed the yoke of Christ is after it is worn a while. The subjection of Christ is the sweetest subjection in the world. It breeds the greatest peace and joy and love and contentment to the soul, and which is more than all, a blessed hope for the time to come. He that is* life is inured to holy duties, and hath overcome the rebellions of his base flesh; when he comes to die he can say with Simeon, 'Lord, now let thy servant depart in peace,' Luke ii. 29; that is, Thou Lord of life, now thou wilt have me die, I am even content to die, to resign myself to thee. Who can say so but he that makes Christ his Lord all his lifetime? Then when death comes he is content to yield unto him as a Lord, else it will be just in the hour of death for Christ to say, as it is Judges x. 14, 'Do you come to me and commend yourselves to me? go to the lords you have served.' You have served the humours of such a one, you have alienated your souls to such a one, you have given your souls to sin and to such men as are instruments of the devil, you have denied your honesty, your faith, your religion; go to him, go to the gods you have served, they are your lords; I am not your Lord, I was not all your lifetime. Though these speeches be not uttered, the effect of them will; the soul will conclude I have served mine own lusts and the humours of others all my lifetime, how can I look that the Lord should take my soul? Therefore let it be our daily practice to live to the Lord, to have the chief aim of our life in our eye to direct our actions so as they may be serviceable to the main, else not to perform them.

Herein consists the main happiness of a Christian, that whether he lives or dies he is not his own, but he is his, that can dispose of him better than ever he could of himself; for if we had the disposing of ourselves, as Adam had, what would become of his?† What became of Adam when he was master of himself? He lost himself and all. The 'second Adam' hath bought us with his blood and life, to rule us for ever. Will he then suffer us to be disposed of by ourselves? No. Whether 'we live or die, we are his,' if we yield ourselves sweetly to his government, in life and death.

THE THIRD SERMON.

For to this end Christ both died, and rose, and revived, that he might be the Lord both of the dead and of the living.—Rom. XIV. 9.

In these words, as you heard heretofore at large, the apostle labours to stay the thoughts and affections of men concerning the things of indifferency, that they should not be hasty to censure another's servant, who stands or falls to his own master, as you have it in verse 4.

The reason is, because whatsoever they do they do it to the Lord. 'He that regards a day, regards it to the Lord; he that regards not a day, regards it not to the Lord.' Some things are of that nature that the right aim puts a qualification upon the actions. A good end cannot qualify many actions, but some actions are of that nature that a good end doth not altogether

* Qu. 'in'?—Ed.

† Qu. 'us'?—Ed.

justify it, but it frees the person from some censure; he doth it to God. Some upon some conceit may abstain from a thing for religious ends, and are not to be censured; some again perform it, and are not to be censured, because they do it to the Lord; that is, out of religious respects.

How doth he prove that they do it to the Lord? He proves it more generally, ver. 7, 'None of us live to ourselves, nor none of us die to ourselves,' which I spake of before.

Then he proves that we are the Lord's, because it was the end of Christ's dying and rising and reviving, 'that he might be the Lord both of the dead and of the living; and if he be the Lord, then we ought to live to this 'Lord of the quick and dead.'

We see Saint Paul here makes use of a general truth, of a grand principle, that we are the Lord's, and therefore live to him and die to him, and do particular actions to him, or not do them to him, to shew that we should have in mind information on sound general truths, that are the ground of all particular practice, as we shall see after.

'For to this end Christ both died, rose, and revived,' &c.

The words they are Christ's universal government of the dead and of the living, inferred from the end of his death, reviving and rising again, a comfortable inference from a strong ground.

We considered the particulars, Christ's death, rising and reviving.

Christ *died* as a 'second Adam,' as a public person, in whom dying all died. When other men die particular men die; when Paul was dead, Paul died and there was an end, only there was an exemplary good in his death. But there is more than an exemplary good in the death of Christ. Christ died alone and singular in this respect; because in him dying all died that were his, that the Father gave him to die for. For they go parallel, God's gift and Christ's death. He did all by commission, and he would not transgress his commission, and he died a violent and cursed death, because otherwise he could not have saved us that were under a curse. So as a 'second Adam' *he rose*, and as a public person. Therefore we see in the resurrection of Christ many rose. It is like enough they died again. It was for a particular dispensation, to shew that Christ rose as a public person; and it is not strange to think so that to honour God they should be content to live a while, when Christ himself that was God was content to be man, and to be abased to death. That grand mystery makes all other things credible. He rose, therefore, as a public person, to give life to all that he died for.

So he *revived*. That is more than to rise again, never again to lay down his life, as you have it excellently set down among other places, Rev. i. 18, 'I am he that liveth and was dead, and behold I live for evermore, Amen;' and he seals it too, 'I have the keys of hell and of death;' that is, the dominion of hell and death; for indeed Christ is life itself, and life cannot die. As God he could not die, and therefore he took upon him that nature, wherein he might die for us; and now having done that dispensation, that office, there is a perpetual influence of life from the fountain of life, his Godhead, to his humanity. So he never dies any more. Then here follows the scope and end of all,

'That he might be Lord of the dead and of the living.'

The three offices of Christ, they have this order in regard of manifestation. First, he was a prophet to instruct and teach his in himself, and likewise by his ministry. And then a priest to die for those that are his, to make intercession now for ever in heaven. And then a king. First, a prophet, then a priest, and then a king. He was all at once. The very union invested him in all these, but in regard of manifestation he was first a prophet to instruct us of the end of his coming into the world; and then a priest to do that grand office that we have most comfort by; and then a king to rule us. He could not be otherwise, for if he had manifested himself a King and a Lord in his glory, where had been his abasement? If they had known him to be the Lord of glory, they would never have crucified him. Only some sparkles of his Godhead and lordship and kingdom and royalty over all flesh break out in his miracles; yea, in his greatest abasement there were some sparkles, I say. Even when he lay in the manger, kings came to adore him. When he paid tribute, he had it out of a fish by a command, by majesty. When he was on the cross he converted the good thief. So somewhat brake out of him that he was a person more than ordinary, but that was for special ends. Ordinarily he went on in a course of abasement, and all that he might perform the great work of redemption. Therefore he made a stop of his glory and kingly office, that he might not manifest himself in that relation and office; that he might do the office of a priest to die for us. Therefore you have it here in the due order. Christ died and rose again, as the high priest of his church, 'that he might be Lord of the dead and of the living.' He was so before, but he was not manifest before. Therefore he is said to be manifest to God by the resurrection, Rom. i. 4. He was God from eternity, but he was born then: 'This day have I begotten thee,' Ps. ii. 7. It is spoken of the resurrection. So you see here Christ's offices, the state and condition of his humiliation and of his exaltation, and the use and end of all, 'that he might be Lord of the dead and of the living.'

And if we be anything offended with that abasement, that God should die, look to his rising and reviving and lordship over all, both quick and dead; and if we be dazzled with his glory, look back again to God in our flesh, and God in our flesh abased, even to the death of the cross. Oh, it is a sweet meditation, beloved, to think that our flesh is now in heaven, at the right hand of God; and that flesh that was born of the virgin, that was laid in the manger, that went up and down doing good, that was made a curse for us and humbled to death, and lay under the bondage of death three days; that this flesh is now glorious in heaven, that this person is Lord over the living and the dead. It is an excellent book to study this. Beloved, study Christ in the state of humiliation and exaltation.

'That he might be Lord of the dead,' &c.

How is Christ Lord? He is Lord of the dead, those that died before he was born, and of the living, those that are since. He is 'yesterday,' that is, to those that were before he was; and 'to-day,' that is, when he was; and 'to-morrow' and 'for ever the same.' Therefore he saith of the dead and of the living; of the dead, that is, in reference to former times Christ; is the 'Lamb of God slain from the beginning of the world,' Rev. xiii. 8.

By what title is he Lord?

By a title, beloved, not as God, but by a title of conquest as a redeemer, for he died that he might be Lord. We are a 'bloody spouse' to Christ. We are the price of his blood. He died that he might be Lord. He must win us before he could have us. Thereupon dying and purchasing us, now he is Lord of his church and children by marriage. Before he could marry us he must be born in our nature, for the husband and wife must be of one nature; and being in bondage to a contrary king, to Satan, he must redeem and purchase us out of Satan's hands. So he is a Lord by conquest; and then he is a Lord in a nearer relation, he is a Lord as a husband, 'He is Lord both of the dead and of the living.'

But the point is sweetest in the use of it; only know for a ground that 'Christ is Lord of the dead and of the living,' as mediator, God-man, not as God, but as God-man, God in our nature; and hereupon we have divers sweet comforts, as for example,

First of all, *it shews what we may expect from Christ*, what Christ will do to us, and what we ought to return to him again. For relations are bonds, especially when they are so founded as this of Christ's is, to be Lord over us both in life and death. It is founded upon redemption and upon our spiritual marriage. Relations are bonds, and therefore they tie on his part to shew what we may expect from him. He is 'Lord of the living and of the dead.' We may expect on his part all that a gracious Lord should do to provide for his church and children. We may expect that from him that we can from none else, that he should not only be Lord over us, *but that he should make us subject, that he should flow into us by his Holy Spirit.* For here is the prerogative of Christ, that he is such a head as quickeneth dead members. He is such a husband as makes his spouse beautiful. He puts glory upon her; no other husband can do it. Moses married a black woman, but he could not alter her hue, much less her disposition. It is not in the power of any man. A king cannot alter his subjects; but he is such a King as alters the nature of his subjects. He makes them subject, he takes them out of a contrary kingdom, as being not born his subjects, but 'born anew by the Spirit.' He doth all provision, protection, the changing of our natures, the beginning of a good work; and where this Lord begins a good work he finisheth it to his own day. For, beloved, know this for a ground, that now in the second covenant we are not left, as Adam was, in the hands of our own free will to stand or fall, but now in the second covenant that is founded upon Christ's death and satisfaction for us, Christ gives grace. He gives his Holy Spirit to bring us within the compass, and performs both our part and his too. He makes good his own to be a gracious Saviour to us; and he performs our part too, or else the second covenant, the covenant of grace, should be frustrate as the first was, if it were left to our freedom. Therefore that is that that we may expect from this lordship of Christ, the performance of the covenant of grace in 'writing his law in our hearts,' Jer. xxxi. 33. Other kings give laws and write them in tables, but they cannot write them in the hearts of their subjects. But he is such a lawgiver as writes his own will in the heart; he teacheth the very heart obedience. We are taught of God 'to love one another.' 'I will write my law in their bowels, and in their inward parts;' that is, they shall not only know what they should do, but they shall know the doing, the affecting,* and performing of the things. They shall be able to do the things. So Christ is a Lord over us, not only teaching us what we should do, and enjoining us in a kind of superiority, this is your duty, and not this; but enabling us to do that that he commands. He gives us the very doing, the affections and loving. He teacheth our hearts to love. I say this we may expect from him in the use of means, and subjecting to his ordinances; which is a wondrous prerogative to those who will submit to his law.

We may expect again from this Lord *advancement*. He is such a Lord as makes all his subjects kings. The meanest man that is a subject to Christ, that hath the Spirit of Christ, is a king. Now he is a king over

* That is, loving, choosing.—G.

that that all others are slaves to, that are not Christians. They rule over others, but they are in thraldom to their own lusts. But he is a spiritual king, a king over hell and death, and those things that the very greatest of men are afraid of, as who fears death most and hell most? Those that deserve it most, by reason of their great place, sink most in sin and rebellion against God, and contract more guilt than other men. That that they are afraid of, a true Christian as a Christian is most triumphant over. He is a king over those things, for every subject of this Prince is a king.

Christ's manner of government is hid now. There is more reality in this than can be expressed; therefore wonder not. In a word, Christ as our Lord binds himself to bring us to glory, never to leave us till he hath brought us to that place that he is in himself. 'Father, I will that where I am they be also,' John xvii. 24; and he purgeth his church, Eph. v. 27, 'that he may make it a glorious church.' He takes upon him not only to die, to redeem us from hell and damnation, and to set us in a state of favour with his Father, but to go on in a course of fitting us till he have brought us to the glorious condition that he is in. It lies upon him to do it. Therefore let us do our duty, as we shall see after; and let him alone with that that belongs to him.

For ourselves, beloved, this is our honour, that we are under such a King, such a Lord, both living and dying. It was the honour of those who lived in Solomon's time, that they were under such a wise king and prince. The queen of Sheba judged it so, 1 Kings x. 8. But what an honour is it to a Christian now, that he is under such a blessed prince as Christ is. It is a great honour to be the spouse of such a husband, to be the subject of such a King, to be members of such a head. And therefore we should oft think of it, to put honourable thoughts into us; and I know no greater way to keep us from sin, from base courses, than to have our thoughts strained to this high point, to think of the dignity of a Christian, what a condition he is now brought into in Christ, and what he shall be brought unto ere long. This should make him honourable to himself, to make him in a holy state, to think himself too good to defile his soul or body, that is so dearly bought and so highly advanced: 'Shall such a man as I flee?' saith Nehemiah, Neh. vi. 11. Oh look to that. Shall such a man as I flee? It is the honour, beloved, of a Christian, that he is Christ's, living and dying.

Obj. But you will say an honour. It is an honour to be free; the subject is bound, *non sumus nati*, &c., as the heathen man said; we are not born to slavery, but to honour and liberty,* and it is an appetite ingrafted in man, to desire freedom above all things.

Ans. It is true, *in regno nati sumus Deo*, &c., we are born in a kingdom, and to serve Christ is to reign (*h*); for where there is a subordination it is a prerogative to be under a better; as for the body, being baser than the soul, it is for the good of it to be under the soul, because it is more excellent. It hath life and wisdom. The body is a loathsome dead thing of itself. The sheep being a weak, simple creature, shiftless,† to be guided by a shepherd, who is of a superior nature, and wise to defend it. It is its security and safety for the vine, that is a weak plant of itself, to have support. It is for the good of it. For man that is in a subordination to a higher nature, to God, for him to be under the government of Christ, God-man, of God in our nature, it is a great honour; as they could say in the schools, everything hath its perfection, by being subject to a superior,

* Cf. note *e*.—G.

† That is, = 'without expedients.'—G.

except the highest of all, which is not subordinate, but independent (*i*). Whatsoever is dependent hath its perfection by dependence; therefore it is an honour that we be under Christ, the greatest honour in the world; especially if we consider what manner of government Christ's is. It is a rational government, agreeable to our principles; for he guides us as a prophet. He is not only a king, but a prophet to teach us. He saith, not, you shall do this; he stands not upon terms of will; no. He is a prophet to teach us what we should obey. He convinceth us, and then useth us, that we would not be but under such a government; and then when he rules our will he doth it sweetly. He draws it with the cords of a man, as the prophet speaks, Hosea xi. 4; that is, by allurements, he brings us to heaven by way of love and enticements. What greater rewards can there be thought of than those that Christ leads us by, and draws us to subjection by? And therefore he works upon our will sweetly, by persuading us by allurements in that kind.

In a word, he is such a king as is a husband. Would you have a milder government than that of a husband, which though it be not a parity, yet it comes as near as can be. Such a government is Christ's. As he is a king, so he is a husband. He knows how to bear the infirmities of his church. He that bids the husband to favour the wife as the 'weaker vessel,' doth not he practise his own principles? Will not he favour his own spouse as the 'weaker vessel,' think you, that hath promised not 'to quench the smoking flax, and break the bruised reed'? Undoubtedly he will. Therefore it is an honour to be under the government of Christ, so rationally and sweetly he draws us with the cords of a man. It is the government of a husband, and of a wise husband. I do but give a taste. You may enlarge them in your own meditations.

And as it is our honour, so it is our security and safety to be under him. Why? Because when we come sweetly under Christ's government, we need fear nothing. He that fears Christ, all things fear him. Since Christ hath taken our nature upon him, the devil himself is afraid of man's nature. He trembles to think God hath appeared in our nature. Now he is afraid of a Christian [since] God hath taken this nature. Then he is such a king as we may be secure under him, as a universal King over all things, that he may be King over his church; for he hath all power in heaven and earth: Mat. xxviii. 18, 'All power is given to me in heaven and earth,' and all for the government of his church. It is our security to be under him that governs all things for the good of the church. He saith, John xvii. 2, 'Thou hast given me power over all flesh.' Christ hath all power given to him in relation to his church; therefore he hath power over the devil, over hell, and over all wicked men; and all monarchs and opposite power is subject to him, that they shall serve the church. When they do scourge the church, they are but Christ's rod; they are but instrumental to Christ; they do but his work; therefore it is a great security, and we need to fear none if we be under Christ.

3. Again, To go on: as it is our honour and security, *so it is a spring of our duty*. Christ is our Lord. He is Lord of all. Therefore it teacheth us our duty every way.

Our duty one to another—to those that are not Christians—to Christ himself.

It teacheth us in all standings how to carry ourselves. To give a taste of this, the apostle presseth it oft, that Christ is our Lord, and will be our judge.

Therefore *for others we ought not to be hasty in judging or censuring.* We ought to love them, because we have all one Lord. This must force love. 'We have all one Lord, one baptism,' &c., Eph. iv. 5. We are many in our severals; but we are all one under this bond, being all under one Lord.

2. Then again, it teacheth us how *to carry ourselves to men* otherwise affected; not to be servants to the humours of men. Christ rules over us, both living and dying; therefore be not the servants of men, but according to the Scripture's limitation, 'marry in the Lord,' 'obey in the Lord,' 'walk in the Lord,' do all in the Lord; that is, so far as it may stand in the will and pleasure of him that is the Lord of lords. For when the authority of any superior doth countermand against the will of this Lord, it ceaseth to bind. When they command anything in subordination that may stand with the pleasure of the Lord, then the authority is divine. We obey Christ in obeying them. As Christ said to his own mother, when she commanded things that she had no authority to do, he calls her mother no longer, but 'woman,' she stretching then beyond her compass, John ii. 4.

3. Again, To go on: this should teach us, in that Christ is the Lord of the living and of the dead, *to account ourselves not our own.* It should teach us perfect self-denial in matters of religion, especially not to be overwhelmed of our own conceits in the great mysteries that Saint Paul cries out of, 'Oh the depth,' Rom. xi. 33. You have many that quarrel with those things, and would bring them to reason. They will go no further in religion than they can see reason; whereas one saith, I believe, because it is impossible, and too far above reason; therefore I the rather believe it *(j)*. It is ofttimes good to stand at a stay in God, as if we were at a *nonplus*, to admire* at him in the mysteries of Christ's governing the church, why he suffers some part of the church, that perhaps is better than other parts, that are quiet and exempt from the cross, to be exercised with afflictions, and others not, not to scandal† at this, and to be over-busy in searching out the reason of this. Christ is our Lord, and he is infinite in wisdom; and it is his prerogative to do such things, as he is not liable to give a reason of to us. So God 'will have mercy upon whom he will have mercy,' Rom. ix. 18. In great mysteries remember the sovereignty of this our Lord. He is 'Lord of quick and dead.' Let this stop our judgments, and teach us to deny ourselves when we cannot give a reason of them; in a holy admiration, say with Saint Paul, 'Oh the depth.'

And so for our *will*. He is Lord of the quick and dead. We say of a wife she hath no will; and a servant is not a distinct person, as it were, in law, he is another's. We are Christ's servants, his subjects, and his spouse; and when we begin to be Christ's we have lost our own wills, we resign them up to Christ. Thy will shall be mine in all things. If thou wilt have me do this, I will do it; if thou wilt have me suffer, I will suffer; if thou wilt honour thyself with my goods and with my life, thou shalt have them. Of thee I had this body, this soul, this state, this reputation; I have whatsoever I have from thee; it is maintained by thee. Thou art mine, and I am thine; therefore I give up all to thee back again. It is a ground of perfect resignation, that Christ is Lord of the quick and of the dead. Therefore stand not upon terms with Christ. When he calls for anything, in case of suffering and sealing the truth, let him have it. It is not lost. We have a better foundation in him than we have in ourselves. When we give anything to him, life, or state, or credit, or whatsoever, we have a better life, a better state and condition in him; because all is more emi-

* That is, 'wonder.'—G. † That is, 'stumble.'—G.

nently in him, the primitive fountain, than in the derivation and beams from him. When we lose anything it is but a beam from the sun, and whatsoever we lose in particulars we have in the whole, in the fountain again, in Christ. Therefore faith would help all this. In case of suffering and trial, what! is the cause good or no? Then I will resign myself and all that I have and am to Christ. He is Lord both of the quick and of the dead.

We must know, beloved, that we are redeemed from ourselves; and therefore make this use of it when we are tempted by any sin: Christ is my Lord; I am redeemed from my base lusts. What have I to do with this anger? what have I to do with this ambition? I am no debtor to the flesh. I am under Christ. I am under grace. He hath redeemed me from my vain conversation. I owe it nothing but mortification and denial. Therefore, in all solicitations of corruption, learn this lesson, fetch arguments hence. Christ hath done great matters for me. He lived and died, and lives for ever, that is Lord of me living and dying. There is no greater slave than he that is a slave to his own flesh and to his own lusts. Therefore when we are stirred to anything by our base nature, which must die, or else we shall never live eternally, we must kill it more and more daily; and death is the sum and accomplishment of mortification. When we are stirred to anything, go to Christ and complain to him. Blessed Saviour, thou didst die, and rise, and revive, that thou mightst be Lord of the living and of the dead. I beseech thee, claim thine own interest in me. Bring all into captivity to thine own Spirit. What hath this base affection to do with me? What have I to do with it? I am freed from it; I am redeemed from myself. What have I to do with myself but deny all? I am thine altogether; therefore take thine own interest in me, possess me, fill me with thy Spirit, be all in all in me; let pride and ambition and such things have no footing in me. It is good pouring out the soul to God to that purpose: to complain to Christ when it is thus with us, because it is his office to rule us. Now, Lord Jesus, do thine office. Thy office is to be king; to rule in me. Other lords would fain rule in me. Pride, and lust, and base covetousness would fain rule, as the prophet saith, Isa. xxvi. 13; but what hath other lords to do with me? Thou art my Lord, and hast right to me living and dying.

It is a point of wondrous comfort likewise to us in all afflictions whatsoever, especially such as concern the state of the church. We are now in ill times, if we look about us. However, God continues better to us than we deserve. We are as the three young men in the fiery furnace, untouched, when all is in a combustion round about us. Where is Christ's ruling now, when his poor church is thus used and trampled upon in France, in the Palatinate, in Bohemia, and the Princes of Germany (*k*).

Beloved, it is our faults. Perhaps we waken not Christ as the disciples; they awaked Christ when there was a mighty storm, and moved him to rebuke the winds and the waves, and there followed a calm; so should we. Christ loves to be awaked by our prayers; and if the church would join in forces, one church with another, altogether they might work wonders. Let us offer a holy violence to Christ by prayer and the use of holy means. He is Lord still of the church; and take things at the worst as they are, he is but carrying things to his own ends. Beloved, if we consider things aright, it can hardly be otherwise with the church than it is. If we consider the former security, and dulness, and want of prizing the great things of Christ, the ministry of the word, and the sacraments, we live under the gospel in such deadness and such sins as a Turk would scarce commit. We are no more affected with it than a Jew or a Turk that hath not the means. Will Christ endure this, that we should come to be careless whether we have the gospel, the blessed truth of God, or no, and grow sinful, and have less conscience than a Turk or a Jew? Will Christ continue his blessed prerogatives and privileges to such? Therefore, if we do but look to the ordinary dispositions of most men, a man would think it impossible but that judgment should come. Will there be a reformation of these men without a spirit of fire, without some purging flame?

Then again, Christ is humbling his church for the advancement of it, and suffers the enemies to triumph for their further abasement. He is compassing a blessed work. There is a great wheel a-going, but we do not see the issue of things. All this great wheel the Lord rules, and governs, and moves. You shall see at length what it will drive to. We see in a clock there are many wheels, one contrary to another, but all helps the clock to strike, all join in that; so there is a stroke, there is somewhat that will come out of all these troubles that seem contrary one to another, some up and some down; but all these wheels will help to bring out some stroke, some glorious thing, that posterity perhaps may see that is now a-working. Therefore let none take scandal.* Christ 'rules now in the midst of his enemies,' Ps. cx. 2. We must not catch at pieces of Christ's workmanship; as in a poem, we judge not by a piece, but look to the catastrophe, we look to the upshot and closure of all. Though all was in a combustion, there we see all things brought to an excellent and wise issue. Therefore, I beseech you, suspend your judgments a while, and then you shall see with a spirit of faith all the enemies overthrown, even as if we did see it with our eyes of sense; and in the mean time, persuade ourselves that Christ is about a blessed work, as he is king of our church.

One question the papists move upon such texts as this, that I will assoyle† briefly, because it may trouble some, though it be of no great moment. It is said here that Christ died, and rose again, and revived, that he might be Lord of the dead and of the living. Hence, not only papists, but some others move this question, which I will give a little light unto.

Whether Christ by his dying and abasement did merit anything for himself, because it is said here he did this that he might be Lord of the dead, &c.

He abased himself to the death of the cross. 'Therefore God gave him a name above all names,' Phil. ii. 9.

The papists they fall upon Calvin that saith he did not, and that makes me the rather to touch it. Calvin, as he was a very holy man, so out of his holiness he avoided curious questions as much as he might, therefore gives an excellent answer. Saith he, whether he did or no, 'It is curious‡ to search, it is rash to define' (*l*). For satisfaction, take these grounds, and all is well.

1. First of all, that Christ is perfectly glorious now in heaven, both body and soul. There is no question of that; and that he came to this glory, both of body and soul, and the manifestation of it, after his abasement by his humiliation; first, he must die and suffer, and then enter into glory.

2. Again, remember this for a ground that Christ as man merited not

* That is, = make it a stumbling-block.—G.

† That is, = clear up.—G.

‡ That is, = uselessly curious.

the grace of union or unction, for how could he merit before he was? Could Christ merit to be united to the second person, that was the greatest grace that ever was? No; nor the grace of unction, habitual grace in Christ, whereby the human nature was filled with all grace. It was upon unction. Presently they follow one another. There was no meriting of that thing, because from the beginning of his incarnation it was by union of his nature. These things being thought upon, for other things they are not material; only it is best and safest to think that he did not for himself merit anything. For if so be all glory was due to him by virtue of union, which he had by grace and by virtue of unction, if he had died presently; he might have gone to heaven presently indeed, without dying, if there had not been a dispensation laid upon him to die for us; and therefore by virtue of union and unction that was free, heaven was due to him presently, and all that glory that he had afterward.

Why was there a stop of that glory? that his body being united to the divine nature, was not presently glorified, as now it is in heaven, so that he lived in abasement, and died a most cursed death?

Beloved, all this was for us; and then after the dispensation was finished for us, after God's justice was satisfied for us, there was no more stop or stay of his glory. But then his divine nature did flow into his human nature; and then his human nature became glorious, so glorious as it was capable of what he did for us. Therefore it is good to think of the love of Christ, that he considered us and not himself in that his abasement, as the Scripture runs in that strain: 'To us a Son is given, for us a child is born,' Isa. ix. 6. He died for us. He gave himself for us. He rose for us. He ascended for us. He sits at the right hand of God for us. Himself indeed hath glory, but together with us. And therefore when we think of the glory of Christ, think of us in him. When we see him born, think he was born for me; when we see him die, think we die with him; when we see him buried, think ourselves buried with him. So in the state of exaltation, when we see him rise, and sit at the right hand of God, think he is there to prepare a place for me. Whatsoever he hath, or whatsoever he did, he regards us in all; therefore it somewhat obscures the glory and the love of Christ to us, to conceive that he had a self-respect in these things, when he saith in the text, 'For this end Christ died, and rose, and revived, that he might be Lord of quick and dead.' I beseech you, consider whose goods he respects in this lordship. Is it not a profitable lordship for us? Is it not for our good that he is our Lord in life and in death? and not only our Lord, but the Lord of Satan, of death, and of all our enemies. He is Lord over all, saith the apostle, 'God over all, blessed for ever,' Rom. ix. 5. Therefore he is Lord over sin, over death, over hell, over all that we need to fear. It is for us. Therefore our good is intended. Though there be a redundance of glory in Christ, in all these things, yet think he respects our good. The best meditation of Christ is to think all is for us.

Beloved, is it not a great mercy that he should stop the issue and the beams of glory, that should otherwise have come upon his human nature, that he should be content to be in the shape of a servant, and be eclipsed in regard of manifestation, and abase himself to the death of the cross, and all for our redemption, when he might have gone to glory another way? But as one of the ancients saith well, 'If he had gone to heaven another way, he might have come thither himself, but he could not have helped us that way; therefore he would go to heaven by way of abasement and concealment, and stopping that of his glory that he might help us and pay the price to God for us and reconcile us' (*m*). I beseech you, let us see his love to us in all this. Enough for that question, which I would not have mentioned, but that it hath a special use and comfort, and may be an incentive to kindle love to Christ regarding us in his birth and life and death, in his resurrection, in his ascension, in his glory, in all.

To draw to a conclusion therefore; Christ is our Lord both in life and death. It is for ever. Oh beloved, therefore I beseech thee, let us project for his glory for ever as much as we can. He is our Lord. When we are dead, he is Lord of our souls, of our happiness. We are nearer him then than we are now. He that is my Lord both living and dying and for ever, shall I not labour that when I am dead there may be a church here? that when I am dead posterity may serve him, and be subject to him? Shall he for ever be Lord for my good, and shall not I as much as lieth in me, lay a foundation for ever in his service, that when I can serve him no longer myself, then posterity may serve him?

It was a cursed wish of a pagan emperor, When I am dead, let heaven and earth be mingled if they will (*n*). But a Christian thinks, Christ is mine, and for my good both living and dying; nay, I have more good by him when I am dead than alive; therefore I will labour that he may have glory in his church by me and mine, and all my counsels and projects shall be that it may be for ever and ever, world without end. Therefore they desire that God may be served and glorified in the church for ever, as he is their Lord living and dying.

And let it be our comfort in the hour of death—that may be nearer us than we are aware of—that he is not only Lord of the living, but of those that are dead. He hath the keys both 'of hell and death;' that is, he hath the government of death; and therefore shall I be afraid to commit my soul to Christ? What a ground is this comfortably to yield our souls to Christ! Lord, take the soul that thou diedst to purchase, that thou didst rise again to justify, that thou dost live now in heaven to make intercession for, that thou hast given thy Holy Spirit in some measure to sanctify; take this soul to thee! It is thy soul as much and more than mine; I am not mine own, nor my soul is not my own. 'Into thy hands I commend even *thy* spirit; for thou hast redeemed me, O Lord of truth,' Acts vii. 59. Thou hast redeemed this soul of mine, therefore now take this soul, that thou by thy Spirit hast wrought in some poor measure to desire to please thee: that soul that thou hast sprinkled with thy own blood; take that soul, for thou art Lord both living and dying. And what a comfort is it, when death shall close up our eyes, that we can look forward and see then ourselves nearer Christ; for then we go to Christ our husband, as Paul saith, 'I desire to be dissolved, and to be with Christ, which is best of all,' Philip. i. 23. When a Christian thinks at death, Now I am changing for the better; Christ will not leave me at the hour of death, neither dying nor living, but will watch over my dust. My dead body is a member of Christ. Death may separate body and soul, but it cannot separate soul or body from him; therefore take no thought for body or soul. For my soul I know he will receive it; and my body, as a good *depositum*, is laid up in the dust. He watches over all the dust and ashes and everything, and will make the earth faithful in giving up that *depositum*. He is Lord of me dying as well as living. Shall I be afraid to die, when in death I commend my soul to such a sweet Lord, and go to my husband and to my king?

And that is the end of the sacrament, for the word and sacrament are parts of the regiment * of Christ whereby he rules his church. He rules his church outwardly by the word and sacraments, and inwardly by his Spirit. His Holy Spirit makes good his own good means; and therefore as the subjects of Christ, I beseech you let us come to the ordinance of Christ. He is such a Lord as doth great things by despised means, bread and wine, poor means. But consider what a mighty Lord useth them for our soul's good; and it is his glory to magnify himself by base and weak means. He goes contrary to the course of the world, that stands all upon outward excellency; therefore let no man stumble at the meanness of the means, but consider what great things he works by the foolishness of preaching, and the meanness of his ordinance, the sacraments. He beats down strongholds. He builds us up in Christ to salvation. He communicates himself and all his benefits to us. Therefore, I beseech you, come with faith; come with this persuasion, Christ will bless his own ordinance; and come with comfort. Christ communicates himself to us. The nearer we come to the fountain, the more we draw. And come with preparation; know with whom we have to deal, with him that is 'Lord of quick and dead.' Come with reverence. But these things I have oft upon this occason stood upon. So much for this text.

NOTES.

(*a*) P. 327.—'Domine quo descendis, &c. Lord, how far goest thou? He could not go lower and be God.' Qu. One of the many adoring sayings of Bernard?

(*b*) P. 327.—'Christ rose. . . . Therefore many rose with him. . . . And as the "second Adam," who could infuse life into others.' The Fathers and Schoolmen supply many singular disquisitions upon the topic here enunciated by Sibbes, more subtle than profitable. Mrs Clive has finely described the *uniqueness* of the Lord's resurrection:—

'One place alone had ceased to hold its prey;
  A form had pressed it and was there no more;
The garments of the grave beside it lay,
  Where once they wrapped Him on the rocky floor.
He only with returning footsteps broke
  Th' eternal calm wherewith the tomb was bound;
Among the sleeping dead, alone he woke,
  And blessed with outstretched hands the hosts around.'

IX. Poems by V.

(*c*) P. 330.—'A Christian may say of Christ, that he is *totus in meos usus expensus*, as one well said. He is all mine; he is all expended for my use and profit.' This saying I have failed to trace.

(*d*) P. 331.—'They have some power indeed over their bodies, but, alas! that is senseless.' Two generations were scarcely gone after Sibbes's death until the miserable vengeance on the 'bodies' of Cromwell and Bradshaw, and other of the illustrious Commonwealth heroes and worthies, furnished a memorable example of such impotent 'power' as he here describes. Cf. also note *m*, Vol. II. p. 434.

(*e*) P. 333.—'*Homo non est natus*, &c., as the natural man said, "A man is not born to subjection, but to honour and government."' Seneca has the *sentiment*, and likewise Juvenal, and later Philo.

(*f*) P. 333.—'Such a Lord as this is *cui servire regnare est, &c.*, to whom to serve is to reign.' Cf. notes *c* and *d*, p. 322.

(*g*) P. 338.—'Inright.' See footnote on page 338. The following is Leighton's use of the word:—'If he be righteousness in himself and holy, and victor over his enemies, and set free from wrath and death; then are we too in him, for he is ours, and so ours that we become what he is, are *inrighted* to all he hath, and endowed with all his goods.' (Ten Sermons. Ser. 5.)

* That is, 'government.'—G.

(*h*) P. 348.—'It is true, *in regno nati sumus Deo, &c.* We are born in a kingdom, &c. Cf. note *e*.

(*i*) P. 349.—'As they could say in the Schools, every thing hath its perfection by being subject to a superior, except the Highest of all, which is not subordinate, but independent.' One of the commonplaces of the Schoolmen.

(*j*) P. 350.—'Whereas one saith, "I believe because it is impossible."' The famous paradox of Descartes, 'I believe because it is impossible,' is here anticipated. The philosopher was a contemporary of Sibbes, but his philosophical treatises were not published until years after his death. From whom had *he* got it?

(*k*) P. 351.—'Now . . . when his poor church is thus used and trampled upon in France, in the Palatinate, in Bohemia, and the princes of Germany.' Our Memoir of Sibbes shews the deep interest Sibbes took in the 'Troubles' of the Protestant Continental Churches.

(*l*) P. 352.—'Calvin. . . . Saith he, whether he did or no, it is curious to search, it is rash to define.' Cf. Calvin *in loc.*, who invariably shews the same reticence and reverence in dealing with the 'secret things' of God.

(*m*) P. 354.—'But as one of the ancients saith well, "If he had gone to heaven another way, he might have come thither himself, but he could not have helped us that way,"' &c. Qu. Bernard?

(*n*) P. 354.—'It was a cursed wish of a Pagan emperor "When I am dead, let heaven and earth be mingled if they will."' One of many wild sayings ascribed to Nero.

G.

THE LIFE OF FAITH.

THE LIFE OF FAITH.

NOTE.

'The Life of Faith forms Nos. 27 and 28 and (with 'Salvation Applied' as its sequel) 29 in the edition of 'The Saint's Cordials' published in 1629. In the editions of 1637 and 1658, the three Sermons form Nos. 17, 18, and 19. The text followed in that of 1637, on which see note page 176 *ante*. The separate title-page of 'The Life of Faith' will be found below,* and that of 'Salvation Applied,' the third of the Sermons composing it, in its place. G.

* THE LIFE
OF FAITH.

In three SERMONS.

WHEREIN IS SHEWED,
What this Life of Faith is: Why
Faith has so much attributed unto it: And
how to live this glorious Life in all the severall
passages of our Pilgrimage.

BY R. S. D. D.

[Woodcut here as before. Cf. Vol. IV. page 60.]

LONDON,
Printed for R. DAVVLMAN, at the brazen Serpent in
Pauls Churchyard. 1637.

THE LIFE OF FAITH.

SERMON I.

And the life which I now live in the flesh I live by the faith of the Son of God, who loved me, and gave himself for me.—GAL. II. 20.

THEY are the words of a man pursued by the law unto Christ, proceeding from the Spirit of Christ; the nature whereof is, to apply generals to particulars. So St Paul here, 'The life which I now live in the flesh, I live by the faith of the Son of God.' He sees he is dead by the law; therefore he seeks for a better husband. The law finds him dead, and leaves him dead. Thus pursued by the tenor of the law, he flies to Christ, and says, 'I am crucified with Christ,' nevertheless I live. How? 'Yet not I, but Christ liveth in me.'

There be three ranks of men in the world, under which all men may be comprehended.

1. The estate of nature.
2. The estate of men under the spirit of bondage.
3. The estate of grace under the gospel.

This is the speech of one of the third rank, of a man awaked by the spirit of bondage, who hath attained to a clear and evident sight of his misery, and of the excellent remedies, of a man who hath attained to a new frame and temper of soul. It is the speech of a person in the state of grace, who now aspires to a more noble and excellent life. In the words we may consider divers things.

1. That there is another manner of life than the ordinary life of nature.

2. That it is a better and more excellent life than that he formerly lived; as if he had said, Now, since I have seen the misery of my former natural estate, and the excellency of a spiritual life by faith in the Son of God, I esteem my former life to have been wretched, not worthy of the name of life, compared with that which I live now, as being founded in a better root than the 'first Adam.'

3. The spring of this life is the Son of God. God is life naturally, and we have life no otherwise than from him who quickeneth all things.

4. The conveyance of this spiritual life is by faith. Water springs not without a conduit to carry and spread it. The sun warms not without beams, and the liver conveys not blood without veins. So faith is that vessel which conveys this spiritual life, that conduit wherein all spiritual

graces run, for the framing and working of spiritual life, conveying all, to pitch upon those excellencies of the Son of God.

5. The object and root of this spiritual life is, faith in the Son of God, loving him, and giving himself for him.

So there is a life besides the natural life, and the root of it is Christ, who is our life. Life is the best thing in the world, most esteemed of us; as the devil said concerning Job, 'Skin for skin, and all that a man hath will he give for his life,' Job. ii. 4. Life is the foundation of all comforts; life is the vigour proceeding from soul and body. So the spiritual life is nothing else but that excellent vigour, and strong connected strength of the soul and body renewed, grounded on supernatural reasons, which makes it follow the directions of the word, over-master the flesh, and so by degrees be transformed into the image of Christ, consisting in holiness and righteousness.

Doct. The first point then is, *that there is a better life than a natural life*, because there is somewhat in a man which aspires and looks to a better estate. A child in the mother's womb hath life and senses in that dark place, but it is not contented therewith, but is restless as in a prison, tumbles and turns up and down; for this life that it hath is not to dwell there, but a beginning-life to fit it to live in the more open and spacious world, whither it must shortly be sent forth. So in this dark life of ours there is a divine instinct, power, and faculty in men, that nothing here can suffice; which shews, that there is a place to satiate the will and the understanding, and fill the affections; that there is a condition which shall make a man fully happy. That there must be a better life, which is this spiritual life; for this life which we live in the flesh is a thing of nothing. Our little life we live here, wherefore is it? To live a while, to eat and drink and enjoy our pleasures, and then fall down and die like a beast? Oh no, but to make a beginning for a better life. If this life be such a blessing, what is then that most excellent spiritual life we speak of? It holds out beyond all. By this spiritual life, when one is most sick, you shall see him most lively and spiritual. When sense, and spirit, and sight, and all fail, yet by reasons drawn from spiritual life he comforts himself in Christ, the glory to come, and what he hath done for him. So the apostle shews the aim of a Christian is to be in sufferings of this life for the increase of a better, 2 Cor. iv. 10, saith he, 'Always bearing about in our body the dying of the Lord Jesus, that the life also of Jesus might be made manifest in our body.' When the body is weakest, the spirit is strongest. Take a man who hath not this spirit and hope, he is *à la mort** at the apprehension of death, because he hath no faith, no knowledge, no quickening life, no sense or taste of more excellent things; he knows not whether there be a Holy Ghost or not: or if he be convinced in conscience, yet he is taken up with horrors, and fears condemnation at hand for evermore. Oh what are we without this life? Otherwise an heathen or an infidel were as happy as we.

A Christian furnished with this spiritual life can see Christ and glory, beyond all the things of this life; he can look backwards, make use of all things past, see the vanity of things so admired of others; he can taste things nature doth not relish; he hath strength of reasons beyond all the apprehensions of reason; he is a man of a strong working. This should stir us up above all things to get this spiritual life in us, lest, like St Paul's living dead widow, we be dead whilst we be alive, 1 Tim. v. 6. Therefore,

* That is, 'deadly afraid.'—G.

unless we will be dead creatures, labour we must for a spiritual life, for there is another death which follows the first death. We not only lose God and Christ, life and glory, eternal life, communion with saints and angels, but also we come to eternal torments with the devil and his angels. Therefore above all things go we to Christ, that we may live in his sight.

What is the reason we seek not more for this spiritual life? Because, when the conscience is not awakened, we think there is no such thing: like Judas, walking on in the state of nature, in drunkenness, voluptuousness, covetousness, and the like, until we perish suddenly. If the conscience be awakened, oh then it is easy to work upon such a one who sees his misery and desires the remedy. It was easy to persuade Jacob to send for corn into Egypt, when a famine was in the land of Canaan. It is easy to persuade men hungry and thirsty to eat and drink; easy to persuade a laden, weary man to lay down his burden and rest. So it is with us. If the conscience be awakened to have a sense of sin, and that intolerable wrath and eternal punishment due thereunto, we should and would long for this spiritual life.

I beseech you, let us believe there is such a life. Look 1 Pet. i. 3. There he blesses God, 'who hath begotten us again unto a lively hope by the resurrection of Jesus Christ from the dead.' None can go to heaven but they who are begotten again here. The main help is the use of the means. This is that pool of Bethesda, at which if we lie the angel of the covenant will put us in to be healed. Never rest then till this life be gotten in us. When we find such an antipathy betwixt our spirits and sin as is between poison and them, then there is a beginning of the work. So we should hate sinful persons, whose conversations hinder the progress and increase of our spiritual life. Those who venture on all occasions, no wonder they do fall in sinful courses. What is all their care and endeavour but to draw one into sin? They care for their lusts, and never think of any more. A Christian will care most for the nourishing of his best life, knowing that good and bad company do, the one quicken, the other dead him.

Christ is called life, the bread of life, tree of life, and he gives us living water to refresh our souls, not that he is so essentially bread, or a tree, but by the efficacy of his working in us. For God is life in himself. Therefore he swears by it: 'As I live, saith the Lord, I desire not the death of a sinner,' Ezek. xxxiii. 11. We consider not here of life so high, though this life must be derived from him principally. It is so naturally. The Son is the fountain of life, because he is God, who is radically, fundamentally, and essentially life.

But before Christ be fitted to be life for us, he must be man first, as John vi. 55, 'For my flesh is meat indeed, and my blood is drink indeed.' And the reason why he so quickens is, because he is also God, being that bread which came down from heaven, of which 'whoso eateth shall live for ever.' Now this great work of our salvation being of necessity to be performed by an infinite person as God, who could not die, he therefore took upon him a mortal nature, to open a current to mercy and justice. Therefore his flesh is meat indeed; but the flesh profiteth nothing without the Spirit which quickens; for there must be a Spirit to seal up all this unto us. As without shedding of blood no forgiveness of sins, so without the Spirit sealing these things unto our souls, we can have no comfort of them. When we speak of spiritual life, he it is that we live for; by him, and in him, and through him we live. Therefore, 1 Cor. xv. 45, 'the last Adam is called a quickening Spirit,' because by that Spirit he quickened himself, and quickens us now to live the life of grace, and shall hereafter quicken our dead bodies at the resurrection. So he is called 'the Sun of righteousness,' for light and heat, because, as the sun lightens and warms, so he is the light of the world, as John speaks, 'lighting everything which cometh into the world,' John i. 9, warming also and cherishing the mass of things, and therefore is called light and life.

Thus have we seen briefly there is another life than the life of nature; that this is a most excellent life; and that the root and spring of it is the Son of God. Now the way of conveyance of this life is 'by faith.' A fountain is not sufficient to send forth water abroad; there must be pipes to convey it for use. So from the heart and liver there must be arteries and veins for the maintenance of life and conveyance of blood through all the body. Christ is the heart and liver of all spiritual life; but there must be a conveyance to bring it to us, and this is faith. But why is faith the grace to convey life to us?

(1.) *Because we are saved now out of ourselves by another.* Therefore that grace which brings us to this great good must lead us out of ourselves. This faith doth, which is the hand of the soul, to lay hold of all the graces, excellencies, and high perfections of Christ.

(2.) *Because faith gives all the glory to the party* on whom it relies on and trusts*, as Rom. iii. 26. Paul shews why works were excluded; and such a righteousness was brought in, saith he, that he might be just, and the justifier of him which believeth; and then he adds, 'Where is boasting then? It is excluded. By what law? Of works? Nay, but by the law of faith.' If by love it had come, or humility, patience, or anything in us, some boasting might have been; but this looks another way, lays hold upon another's riches. Faith acknowledgeth nothing to be at home; therefore it goes to another to fetch it, which else it would not do.

(3.) *Because we must be brought back again to God by a contrary way than that we were lost by;* for the same way we could never have recovered. The serpent, we know, shaked Eve's faith in believing the threatening. Whilst they kept the word and feared the commandment, they kept their life; but, losing this awful respect, they lost communion with the fountain of love. So we fell by infidelity, and must return again by faith in the righteousness of another.

By this time we are come to the main thing intended, *how we live by the faith of the Son of God.* We shall not haply reach the depth of so profound a mystery; only I will endeavour to give you some few heads, wherein faith principally exerciseth her powers and functions.

1. The life of faith is exercised in our effectual calling.
2. In the state of justification, whence comes reconciliation.
3. In a vigorous life, arising on the comfort of our justification.
4. In our sanctification; in those supplies faith finds out to make up the imperfection thereof.
5. The life of faith in glorification.
6. We live by faith in all the several passages of this life, as we shall see when we come to them.

Thus we live continually by the faith of the Son of God, and so we must live till we come to heaven.

1. *We live the life of faith in our effectual calling.* The Spirit works it, the Spirit is God's hand. This makes, that our eyes are bent upwards to

* Cf. footnote Vol. III. p. 9.—G.

see a better life, to see a calling, to live holily and righteously in all things, to see what a rich means is provided to reconcile God and man, to satisfy justice, and so to draw us in a new way and course of life, to rely on God, and look unto him in all our actions. Then the grace of union is given. God's Spirit works our hearts by this faith, to have first union, and then communion with God. Thus the soul being seasoned, and seeing the excellency and necessity of another new life, touches Christ, and begins to live the life of faith in effectual calling; for at first we are dead and unlovely creatures, estranged from grace and gracious actions, until, in this estate, Christ is discovered by the Spirit, and faith to unite us to him.

2. Secondly, *We live the life of faith in justification.* This is a life of sentence that the soul lives by, peace being spoken unto it by the pardon of sin; for God by his Spirit doth report so much to the soul, giving us assurance that Christ our surety and peace-maker is raised up again. So Eph. ii. 5, it is said, 'Even when we were dead in sins, he hath quickened us together with Christ, and raised us together, and made us sit in heavenly places with him.' And why? Because our Surety hath paid our debt. We say of a man condemned, he is a dead man till he have a pardon, which when he hath obtained, we turn our speech, and say, he lives. So in justification: being united unto Christ, and believing our pardon, we are said to live. Our sins lie on him as our surety; for then, as our husband in charge, he doth pay all our debts. Thus by virtue of our marriage to Christ, he discharges all our debts, and goeth away with them; even as the scapegoat in the wilderness went quite away with all the sins and iniquities of the people, never to return again. Look we therefore to our sins, the curse and wrath due unto them, and all as laid on him. Look at whatsoever is good in him, that is for us; whatsoever is evil in us, look in him for it, to have it taken away, pardoned, and not imputed.

As we sin daily, so Zech. xiii. 1, 'There is a fountain daily running, to wash away sin and uncleanness.' Therefore for our daily sinning, we must continually run and bathe our souls in this blood, apply the comforts of his sufferings, intercession, and obedience unto us. St John teaches us thus much; saith he, 'If any man sin, we have an advocate with the Father, Jesus Christ the righteous, and he is the propitiation for our sins; and not for ours only, but also for the sins of the whole world,' 1 John ii. 1. If we sin daily, he justifies the sinner daily: he came to save sinners: therefore, when sin stirs us up to run from God, we should run to him. Faith says, 'There is no condemnation to them that are in Christ Jesus,' Rom. viii. 1. Why? My sin was condemned in Christ, and a condemned person hath no voice. Christ came to destroy sin, and condemned sin in the flesh. Our sins were crucified with him, and are now all condemned sins, if we will go unto Christ, who hath borne all our iniquities, as the prophet Isaiah excellently shews.* Therefore St Paul triumphantly demands the question, 'Who shall lay any thing to the charge of God's elect? It is God that justifieth, who is he that condemneth?' Why? 'It is Christ that died, yea rather, that is risen again, who is even at the right hand of God, who also maketh intercession for us. Who shall then separate us from the love of Christ?' Rom. viii. 33, 34. So in our daily sins you see we have use of these things, to have, upon our confession, a daily pardon of course taken out every day. Thus God would not have us sink. So long as there is matter of guilt in us, God will have a way to cleanse our souls, and renew our comforts. Every day we run into new debts, and

* Isa. liii. 5.—G.

every day in the Lord's Prayer we are taught to ask pardon, and to run unto God, to have the book crossed out with his blood. Every day a Christian must eye the brazen serpent, I mean the Lord Jesus, signified thereby; he must sprinkle his heart with the blood of Christ, that the destroying angel may pass by him in the day of wrath, as the Israelites then did. This is it to live by faith; every day to sue out our pardon; to look unto our advocate and surety, who hath paid our debts, and cancelled that obligation against us, contrary to us, as the apostle speaks, daily to wash in that ever-running fountain. 'Christ is a priest for ever, after the order of Melchisedec,' Ps. cx. 4. Though the act be past, he remains the same still. What puts down our courage, strikes us with terror and fear, but our sins? Oh, but why is this brazen serpent lifted, but thus to wash away our daily frailties and failings, so as whosoever believeth in him should not perish, but have everlasting life? John iii. 14, 15.

So justification is not only a sentence of pardon, but it is also, as Rom. v. 15, a title to life everlasting: 'For if by one man's offence death reigned by one, much more they which receive the abundance of grace, and of the gift of righteousness, shall reign in life by Jesus Christ.' Where God pardons, he advances. So if Satan shall come to shake my title, to shake this faith, assure him that Christ came to save sinners. If he object, thy title is naught and stained, being thou hast so many sins and corruptions about thy mortal body, answer him, What serves my faith for but for my comfort, to shew me that my title is in Christ? my strength and ground of comfort is in him, not in myself. See one parallel example, how David lived this life of faith in justification: 'If thou, O Lord, shouldst mark iniquities, who shall stand?' Ps. cxxx. 3. There he pronounces death on himself ere he be acquitted, and so must we in the like case. But then comes the appeal: 'But mercy is with thee, that thou mayest be feared.' Enlarge it yourself. If a man be not sound in this point, all he does is nothing. This is all in all. Our sanctification without this is nothing. This is the ground of all. Be careful of this, to look to Christ's obedience, life, death, and sufferings, and those comforts flowing from our interest therein.

But to direct you a little further ere we leave this sweet point.

First, *Look back every day unto the passages thereof.* See how we have passed along, see what sins have escaped thee; then come at night to God, confess and be sorry for all, resolve against all, crave strength against all. Oh it is a fearful state to sleep in sin; better sleep in a house full of adders and venomous beasts. See also and watch every morning; corruption doth cleave to all our best actions; we pass no day so, but we have cause to say, Lord forgive us our sins. By this course we shall keep our souls free, being ready for death. We shall by our particular reckoning, every day clearing the score, be ready for our great general pardon, and when trouble comes, have only that to encounter with. I beseech you, therefore, put this in practice. Be sure with the day to clear the sins of that day; so shall ye live a comfortable life, and be fit for all estates, for life, for death, for sickness, trouble, or whatsoever, all our business lying in heaven then.

Obj. If it be thus, we need not care how we sin: it is but every day to sue out a new pardon.

Ans. Oh beware; ere our pardon be sealed, there must be confession, sorrow for sin, resolution with full purpose to do so no more; there must be arraigning, condemning, and judging of ourselves for it, because whatsoever we would not have God to do, we must do it ourselves. Our time in getting this *quietus est* sealed, is for the most part according to our sin. He that hath such a resolution to sin every day, because sin is every day pardoned, he may go long enough without pardon, at least comfort of his pardon. For though pardon of sins be pronounced, yet God hath the keeping of joy in his own hand. As David had his sin pardoned,—by the judgment of faith he knew thus much—yet Ps. li. 8, how doth he pray for joy, and that God would heal the bones which he had broken! He roared all the day, and still felt a pain like the breaking of bones. The joy of the Spirit had left him. This he cries to have restored. Thus though sin may be pardoned, yet the more we sin, the more hardly we shall repent, the longer we shall want joy; or, it may be, go all our lifetime mourning without comfort in such a case. Now let us see *how it may be known that we live the life of faith in justification.*

Trial 1. First, *By trying how it comes in the soul;* as Rom. vii. 4, saith the apostle, 'Wherefore, my brethren, we also are become dead to the law by the body of Christ; that ye should be married to another, even to him who is raised from the dead, that we should bring forth fruit unto God.' After a man is dead by the law, and apprehends himself slain, then he comes to live this life of faith. Christ quickens none but the dead. Why do not the papists attain to this grace of justification? They never see themselves wholly dead, but join some life to the natural estate of man. Therefore Christ quickens them not. Such only are quickened by him who find themselves dead in the law. Then they come to have a holy despair, and to see that life and comfort is out of themselves in another. Justification springs from a holy despair, and receiving life, after we have seen ourselves dead.

Trial 2. Secondly, Where this life of faith is, *there is a wonderful high valuing and prizing of Christ,* his righteousness, merits, obedience, and wisdom of God in that way of forgiveness of our sins by this God-man, the wonderful mediator; as Philip. iii. 8. Paul accounts all things 'but loss and dung for the excellency of the knowledge of Christ Jesus our Lord,' being contented to suffer the loss of all things to win Christ. It is the precious pearl to sell all for. Paul accounts all our own righteousness as nothing in regard of this. There must be a high estimation of the riches of Christ's obedience and sufferings: for where there is not this high estimation of it, they are rotten in the point of justification. But you see how Paul sets at nought and vilifies all things in regard thereof; so Rom. iv. 16. Abraham is brought in to be justified by grace, to the end the promise might be sure to all the seed. And Ps. xxxii. 2, he is pronounced to be the blessed man, 'unto whom the Lord imputeth not iniquity, and whose sin is covered.'

Trial 3. Thirdly, *When we have a zeal against all contrary doctrine,* as St Paul shews to the Galatians, who would have joined works to faith: 'Christ is become of none effect unto you; whosoever of you are justified by the law, you are fallen from grace,' Gal. v. 4. And in the third chapter he says, 'O foolish Galatians, who hath bewitched you, that you should not obey the truth, before whose eyes Jesus Christ hath been evidently set forth crucified among you?' 'This only would I learn of you, received ye the Spirit by the works of the law, or by the hearing of faith?' Gal. iii. 1, 2. A man sound in the point of justification hath a hatred to popery, and all such doctrine which impairs the riches of the grace of Christ. Death is in the Romish religion. Why are some of them then saved? Not because they die in that religion, but because they reverse their judgment in this point of justification.* So you see there is a hatred, a zeal in such, as St Paul had against contrary doctrines.

Trial 4. Fourthly, *There is peace and joy settled in the heart:* as Rom. v. 1, 2, 'Therefore being justified by faith, we have peace with God through our Lord Jesus Christ: by whom also we have access by faith into this grace wherein we stand, and rejoice in the hope of the glory of God.'

Quest. To add one thing more ere I leave this point, In the case of relapse, what shall we do then? Are we not cut off? Must we not have a new incision?

Ans. I answer, Every man who falls does not fall on all-four, fall away quite. There be degrees of falling; as in a sick man, though ill, he is not by and by dead. Some life and strength remains, which works out towards health again. There is so much grace and life in justification left, as to recover him again. But as in other cases, so in relapses also, a man must live by faith. We see, 2 Cor. v. 20, even such as were in the state of grace, are entreated to be reconciled. Though we fall, we must not therefore fall off, but stir up grace, and recover ourselves again. So Isa. lv. 7, there it is said, 'Let the wicked forsake his way, and the unrighteous his thoughts: and let him return unto the Lord, and he will have mercy upon him, and to our God, for he will abundantly pardon.' And then he adds the reason, 'For my thoughts are not your thoughts, neither are your ways my ways, saith the Lord. For as the heavens are higher than the earth, so are my ways higher than your ways, and my thoughts than your thoughts.' So Jer. iii. 1, 'They say, If a man put away his wife, and she go from him, and become another man's, shall he return unto her again? Shall not the land be greatly polluted? But thou hast played the harlot with many lovers; yet return again to me, saith the Lord.' Thus we must live by faith, for all our slips and falls, yet not to let go our hold, but still run to the horns of this altar, still fly to this city of refuge, and so we shall be safe.

Quest. But what is the reason that many who are justified yet find not daily comfort?

Ans. Perhaps they daub up† themselves, and do not search the bottom of their corruption: as Ps. xxxii. 3, David, when he kept close his sin, his bones waxed old through his roaring all the day long, and God's hand was heavy upon him day and night. Then he shews how he found comfort: 'I acknowledged my sin unto thee, and mine iniquity have I not hid. I said I will confess my transgressions unto thee; and thou forgavest the iniquity of my sin.' So it may be in this case. We come not off with God freely, we do not ransack our sins, we search not all the corners. Sin is a marvellous subtle thing. Again, thereby many times God will humble us for a former sin, and keep off comfort, until we be more humbled, and stand in awe of sin.

3. Thirdly, *Hence springs a vigorous life.* A life of cheerfulness, when a man hath his pardon sued out, then comes life and joy, strength of holy actions well rooted and grounded. Who should joy, if a triumphant righteous person should not? Who have cause to rejoice more than kings? By justification we are made kings and priests, are lifted above all sins and lusts, world and devil; have a right and title to heaven. Shall a carnal man joy in his titles and privileges, and shall not we much more, being

* Cf. Note *w*, Vol. III. p. 531.—G. † Cf. Ezek. xiii. 11, 12, and xxii. 28.—G.

sons of God by adoption, and heirs of all things? So Rom. v. 1: 'Being justified by faith, we have peace with God, and joy in tribulation.' Being once justified, the sting of all troubles is taken away. God is ours. We joy in God. This is all in all. The blood of Abel, that cries for vengeance; but the Spirit of God in this estate tells me, that the blood of Christ speaks better things, mercy, mercy; in his blood is always comfort, though we be weak and unskilful to apply it. The washing in this blood should make a Christian walk on cheerfully in the comforts of the Holy Ghost. But I hasten to the next, which is,

4. Fourthly, *The life of faith in sanctification.* This springs from these grounds:

(1.) First, Faith lays hold on Christ, as God offers him. How is this? See 1 Cor. i. 30: 'But of him are ye in Christ Jesus, who of God is made unto us wisdom, and righteousness, and sanctification, and redemption.' God gives Christ, not for justification only, but sanctification also: and thus faith must apprehend him.

(2.) Faith receives him as whole Christ in all his offices; not as a priest to save only, but as a king to rule; as a wife receives her husband, to be governed and ruled by him.

(3.) Again, Christ came not only to take away the guilt of sin, but the dominion of sin. He came, as John speaks, to destroy the whole work of the devil; as it is said, Eph. v. 25, 26, 'He gave himself for his church, that he might sanctify and cleanse it with the washing of water by the word, that he might present it to himself a glorious church, not having spot or wrinkle, or any such thing, but that it should be holy and without blemish.' Christ doth purge his church, not only from the guilt of sin, but also from the meddling and polluting of itself in the world with filthy things. So Rom. viii. 3, the apostle shews, that 'God sending his own Son in the likeness of sinful flesh, and for sin, condemned sin in the flesh: that the righteousness of the law might be fulfilled in us, who walk not after the flesh, but after the Spirit.' He came as well by water as by blood. Therefore faith puts him on, not only by justification, but also in sanctification. To clear this.

[1.] Upon justification of necessity comes sanctification. For what is the stop of God's mercy? His anger for sin committed; in which case he denies his Spirit. But with reconciliation there comes also the Spirit: as Ephes. i. 13, saith the apostle, 'In whom also, after that ye believed, ye were sealed with that Holy Spirit of promise.' Now the Spirit once given, is the seed of all graces. Whosoever is justified, hath the Spirit of Christ: Rom. viii. 9, 'And if any man hath not the Spirit of Christ, he is none of his.'

[2.] Again, having the Spirit of Christ, faith fetches all strength from Christ. Samson's strength was in his locks; a Christian's strength is in Christ. This the devil knows well, and therefore labours especially to weaken faith, and draw us from our strength. Christ says, 'Without me ye can do nothing,' John xv. 5; and St Paul affirms, that he 'can do all things through Christ who strengthened him,' Philip. iv. 13. The Spirit gives strength.

[3.] Again, as by Christ and his Spirit we have strength, so by his Spirit we have strong convincing reasons to work with strength from reason. Why doth a Christian carry himself in a holy just carriage answering his profession? Oh, saith he, I have great reason; Christ hath loved me, and given himself for me; and should not I give myself to him, deny my lusts, and live to him? For, indeed, the foundation of all Christian obedience is laid by faith in Christ. So when a man looks to heaven, he hath a reason to abstain from all lets and hindrances of his safe and comfortable passage; to magnify the riches of Christ's love, which hath provided for him such an inheritance, and to live accordingly. So when he looks to the pardon of sins past, he sees reason to hate them more and more, to strive against them in time to come, and to love Christ the more, who hath pardoned them. And when he looks to God's free love in Christ, he sees reason to be inflamed with divine love, to admire the riches of that grace, and to be thankful.

[4.] Again, Christian affections are as the wind, to carry us on in a holy life. Thus strength, and reason, and affections, these make a man work. First, love sets us awork: 'we love him,' saith the apostle, 'because he loved us first,' 1 John iv. 19. We have his love first shed abroad in our hearts, inflaming the affections, and kindling the heat of divine love; and then we send back a reflex of love unto him. God cares for nothing but faith which works by love. This love is a most operative affection stirred up by faith. Indeed, all our Christian graces are set a-work by faith in Christ.

Thus you see faith apprehending Christ, as God offers him; and these things which I have mentioned following, we come to live the life of faith in sanctification: an example whereof see in that woman, who because many sins were forgiven her, loved much. Love is bountiful. All obedience comes from love. Love is the keeping of the law. This affection is stirred up by faith, yea, by Christ, for by him we have the promise of the Spirit, whence all graces come, and promises of the new covenant, to have fleshly hearts given, and his Spirit put in us. All promises of justification and sanctification are derived from Christ. They are in him, made for him, and effected for his sake; for he is 'yea and amen,' the centre and ground of all the promises. Now being brought by faith to live in justification, we must of necessity also live by faith in sanctification. There be two parts of a holy life: 1. *In mortification, dying to sin;* 2. *In vivification, living to righteousness.*

For the first, What does it to a man in this case? Why, he looks what brought Christ to suffer so much; my sin. So this affection stirs up the same passion in him, in a sort, which was in Christ, and makes him hate sin with a perfect hatred, as in Zechariah it is said, 'They should look upon him whom they have pierced, and mourn for him as one mourneth for his only son, and shall be in bitterness for him, as one that is in bitterness for his first born,' Zech. xii. 10. Secondly, It looks on the love of Christ, that made him give himself for us. This makes us to hate sin, and provokes us to live unto him who hath done so much for us. These two things in the death of Christ stir up hatred to sin.

Then again, in vivification, the same Spirit which quickened him doth also quicken us: as Col. iii. 1, 'If ye then be risen with Christ, seek those things which are above, where Christ sitteth at the right hand of God: set your affections on things above, not on things on the earth.' So that the same Spirit which is in Christ, being sent into us, quickens us also to have mounting and heavenly thoughts. As the foot and little finger, though distant, live and stir by the same life and spirits diffused through the whole body, so the same Spirit quickens every Christian this way. As also by imparting strength, he imparts reasons from the resurrection of Christ to make us heavenly-minded, so when the soul dies one way, it lives another way. For Christ having by the Spirit discovered a better state, and life to come, of eternity, immortality, tranquillity, and glory; then a Christian dies to all worldly things, and hath the affections taken up that way.

Thus we see every day so to lead our lives, as we not only live the life of faith in justification, but also of sanctification; how out of Christ's fulness to fetch grace for grace. Therefore in all our wants go to him still. He is not only a sacrifice satisfactory for our sins, but he is a storehouse also and treasure of all good things. He is made unto us sanctification, therefore beg we favour from him, and endowments of grace conformable to his grace. And again, when we lack fulness, let us not despair, but fetch the large vessel of faith, and we shall have a share of the large graces which are in Christ, according to the largeness of our faith.

Quest. What is the reason that so few find strength and comfort in Christianity?

Ans. They set upon getting of grace, and killing corruptions by their own strength, and so are ever wanting; but if a man depend upon God, he shall have fulness out of Christ. God hath sanctified his nature for this purpose, that out of his fulness we might have grace for grace. And so again, every day go to God, and plead for strength against sin, power to lead a holy life, and imputation of Christ's righteousness, to supply the defects of our sanctification. St Paul says, 'I can do all things through Christ that strengthens me,' Philip. iv. 13. It is a magnificent speech, and a great matter to have a man ready to suffer all things, and overcome all things. This will make us work wonderfully, if we have this strength supplied. See an instance, Luke xvii. 3, 4. Our Saviour tells his disciples, that they must forgive their brother seven times, and seven times, as often as he confesses his fault. They thought this a wonderful hard duty, for nothing is so sweet to a man as revenge, for he would willingly be his own carver in all things, and do things in his own strength. The disciples upon this fall a-praying, 'Lord, increase our faith;' as though they had said, We had need of faith to believe the pardon of so many sins, and to enable us to forgive so often. And so I say of the subduing of sin, we had need of faith to have so many sins subdued; yet faith will do it.

Now in this great work, 1. Go to God, and beg his Spirit, and repent of all manner of sin; 2. Then beg faith. This will set all other graces a-work. It is like the blood and spirits which run all the body over. So in our spiritual life, this faith must run along in all graces, and set them a-working, yea, it sets God and all his attributes a-work. It runs to Christ, and prays, Lord, increase my faith, that can bear nothing as I should, resist nothing, believe nothing, and trust nothing. This indeed must be all our strength, to see nothing in ourselves, but all in Christ.

Since Adam's fall, it was appointed that Christ must keep all our joy, our strength, and ability, yea, to be our life. God will not since that time trust us with it, for we would quickly lose all again. It is Christ's office. He hath these endowments, as man, given him, to furnish us with all things fitting to a spiritual life. Faith will fetch all from God in Christ, who is made the mediator of the New Testament, to convey all these things unto us. Yet further, let us see *some trials to discern whether we live this life of faith in sanctification.*

Trial 1. If it be thus with us, *There will be a putting of ourselves upon Christ's government in all duties.* Faith will do all that Christ commands, depending upon him for strength; and who so depends upon Christ for strength in one duty, will depend upon him for strength in another. There is a harmony betwixt the soul of a Christian and the command of obedience. He hearkens to the precepts of duty, as well as to the promises of forgiveness of sins. Where this universal obedience is not, here is not the life of faith in sanctification; for faith here takes not exception at one duty more than another, but looks for all the strength of performance from Christ, who for this cause is stored with all fulness, that it may drop down upon all his members.

Trial 2. Again, *There will be a wonderful care not to grieve the Spirit*, in such a one. As if he should say, I must depend upon the Spirit for help and assistance to do all, to guide me in my whole course, and shall I grieve and leave off the Spirit? Shall I carry myself so as to make him leave me? He must lead, instruct, comfort me, and assure me of my happiness; shall I then quench the Spirit? Therefore, I say, there will be a giving way to it, and a resolution settled, that this guiding in sanctification is the best guidance of all. A believing heart does tremble at any thing which hinders the Spirit's working. It sets not a step forward in anything without direction of the word and Spirit.

Trial 3. *There will be courage to set upon any duty, to encounter and resist any sin;* upon this ground, as he should say, have not I a storehouse of strength to go to? Is not he full of grace and goodness? Are not all his works wrought for us? Have not I exceeding many, great, rich and precious promises of help? Is not he the truth itself? Is there not then supply enough in Christ to help me out in all things? It were Pharaoh-like to set us to work without strength and ability to go through with our work. There is light and heat in the sun to direct and cherish, much more in Christ their Maker. It is grace that leads us through all. We are justified freely through his grace, and by his grace we have continual strength supplied to enable us in all things. It is grace, grace! A sanctified liver by faith will therefore cheerfully set upon every duty.

Trial 4. Again, in this case, *all is lively in a man.* As we see a lively fountain, the water whereof will sparkle and leap, so there will be living joys, speeches, delights, exhortations, sensible of good and evil. He will trust God, rely on his word and promise, because Christ cannot touch the soul, but we must be lively. As the man who no sooner touched Elisha's bones, but he stood up and revived, 2 Kings xiii. 21, so a touch of Christ quickens and makes vigorous. As Christ's promise is, John iv. 14, 'Whosoever drinketh of the water that I shall give him shall never thirst; but the water that I shall give him shall be in him a well of water springing up unto everlasting life.'

Let *the use of all* be this, *Upon this discovery remember to go to Christ for succour, and labour to live plentifully and abundantly in him this life of faith.*

Obj. But, may some say, how should I go on to finish this great work of grace? It is a mighty thing to attain to, so many sins to overcome, so many temptations to buckle with, so many right hands and eyes to cut off and pull out.

Ans. I answer, Faith teaches us to fetch all from Christ, to beg his Spirit to help us in the course of sanctification, that by his might we may prevail; and so in all mastering sins beg strength of Christ, and then set upon the walls of Jericho, and they shall fall before you.

How shall this be done?

As they did; they believed the promise, that compassing it seven times it should fall to the ground. So we, having so much and so many promises for the subduing of sin in us, let us set upon them, look up unto Christ, believe the promise; and our walls of sin shall fall so far before us, as they shall neither hinder our comfort nor our salvation. Eclipse it they may for a little while, but the sun will shine again, break through and dispel all those clouds and mists.

Let us set upon all Goliahs, therefore, by the word and Spirit, and withal set our will against them, that we heartily desire and endeavour to be rid of such lets and incumbrances, and we shall in the end find a notable victory over them; and so in all troubles and vexations, as Luke xvii. 3, 4, *seq.*, with the disciples beg of God the increase of faith. This will help us out in all storms and tempests; help faith and help all. This will set heaven and earth a-working for our good. We see, Heb. xi., that all is attributed to faith. Why? Many other things concurred in those excellent actions for doing of them; but all is attributed to faith, because faith is that great wheel which set all the rest a-working, and stirs up all, as, 1 Cor. xiii. 4, *seq.*, it is said of love, that it does all: for the same reason, because in those things there mentioned it stirs up all the rest. So in any grace which is wanting in us, go to Christ and say, Lord, I lack wisdom, counsel, strength, understanding, prudence in thy holy fear. The fulness of these are in thee; Lord, it is for thy glory to help thy poor servant, and bestow some measure of these upon me to do thy own work with. Lo! Lord, I lay myself down to thee to work by me. I have an angry spirit, full of tossings and turmoilings, but thou art the Prince of peace, abounding in meekness. Oh bestow on me such a meek and peaceable spirit, as, learning of thee, I may be meek and lowly in heart. I instance but in a few things; enlarge them yourselves. In all things let us, with confession of our wants, have an eye unto his fulness, and then we shall find the more of his abundance, when we set not upon these duties in our own strength only.

Two things are opposite to this life of faith.

(1.) *Despair.* This cuts the pillars of hope. Against this divers, as Luther for one, have been tempted to despair, but yet setting on the work, have overcome.* So the Israelites were afraid, upon the evil report of the spies of Canaan; but when they went on, they overcame and beat down all their enemies. So we say, Oh, I shall never overcome such a sin, or such a corruption, or do such a duty. This is not true, go on, look to Christ, join his strength with thy endeavour, be out of love with it, resolve thoroughly, set upon it strongly, and down it shall before thee.

(2.) The second is *presumption;* for this know, that in his own strength shall no man be strong. In St Paul's speech, 'By grace I am that I am,' 1 Cor. xv. 10. So again, saith he, 'In him'—to wit, in Christ—'we live, and move, and have our being,' Acts xvii. 28. If we do presume, it is just with Christ to forsake us, as he did Peter. Take heed also of spiritual self-sufficiency, lest we rest on ourselves, and go not to Christ. Our moving to all good duty is by him. It is but a word for him to help us, either in things tending to a spiritual or a natural life. Therefore, for conclusion of all, leave him not. In thy emptiness go to his fulness. If thy cistern be dry, turn the cock of thy faith, and his fountain will fill it again. Take him still along with thee, and thou canst not choose but live this life of faith in sanctification.

* Cf. footnote, Vol. I. page 126.—G.

THE LIFE OF FAITH.

SERMON II.

And the life which I now live in the flesh I live by the faith of the Son of God, who loved me, and gave himself for me.—Gal. II. 20.

We see here our blessed apostle doth exemplify himself a man living another life than the life of nature, from higher reasons, grounds, and principles: 'I live,' saith he, 'by the faith of the Son of God.' First, he considers of another life than that which is rational, correcting the error of the same; for as reason corrects sense, so faith doth reason. This makes a man a new creature. The spring of this life is Christ. The means of conveyance is faith. It is meet now we should fetch all out of* ourselves; for since Adam lost what he had, it is dangerous to trust ourselves with it any more. Therefore Christ keeps it for us, and makes it ours by conveyance of his Spirit, making us all children of grace. Faith is wrought in us by the Spirit of God, and then it works, as Augustine says, *acti agimus*. Thus by effectual calling being once knit unto Christ, it is consecrated, as that by which we live. Christ is conceived in our souls by faith. As he was conceived in the Virgin's womb by her yielding to the promise, so we, closing with the promise, faith is wrought, and then Christ comes to live in the heart, as, believing the promise, he came thereafter to live in her womb. In the last sermon we propounded many things touching the life of faith, how it lives in effectual calling, in justification and sanctification, in glorification, and in the several grand passages of this life, one of which remains yet to be unfolded, as, *the life of faith in glorification*.

Quest. 1. But how? Vision is for glory; what hath faith to do with this, which is of things unseen?

Ans. 1. I answer, we live by faith in glorification thus, because faith lays hold on the promise, and we have the promises of glory set down in the word, and with the promise we have the first-fruits of the Spirit, and having the earnest and first-fruits, God will surely give the harvest. We have the Spirit, and thence faith reasons, God will make good his promise, he will not take back his earnest. Thus faith gathers great matters, believes all, and so lives comfortably in expectation of fruition.

Ans. 2. Again, faith lives by the life of glorification in Christ the head. There is but one life of Christ and his members, and one Spirit, one with

* That is, 'from without.'—Ed.

him in union in the first degree of life. His glory is our glory. As in justification our debts are made his, so his glory is made ours, as it is John xvii. 1, *seq.*, and he is gone to prepare a place for us, to bring us where he is. 'The glory which thou gavest me,' saith Christ, 'I have given unto them;' yea, 'and in him also we sit in heavenly places,' Eph. i. 3. So in regard of Christ to whom we are knit, we live the life of glory.

Ans. 3. Thirdly, by reason of the nature of faith, as Heb. xi. 1, which is to make things absent have a certain being. Now faith being wrought by an almighty power, raising us above ourselves to fasten and lay hold on so many mysteries, so it makes an almighty working in the soul, makes things afar off to come evident. Thus it presents glory to us, as though it were present, and we in some sort live by it.

How to know whether or not we live the life of faith in glorification.

1. This, where it is in faith, *makes a Christian glorious, puts him in a spirit that is glorious in all estates.* There is no grace in him, but it is set a-fire by this faith of glory to come. When faith looks back on things, it hath strength, but when it looks on glory, all graces and virtues are set a-work.

1. *Hope is set on work by faith,* and keeps the soul, as an anchor, stedfast against all assaults.

2. *Hope doth stir up patience;* for, saith the apostle, 'what we hope for, we wait patiently for it.' Thus patience is exercised in two ways. (1.) In suffering of grievances. (2.) In the expectation of time.* So faith doth thus put life in patience, reasoning;—Why? What! it will not be long; these afflictions will not endure ever; I myself shall away ere long; glory will come at last for ever and ever; therefore I will bear all patiently.

3. Again, *it sets courage and magnanimity a-work,* as Heb. xi. What made all the patriarchs so stout to hold out and endure so many miseries, but that they had an eye to the glory to come? What made Abraham forget his father's house, going he knew not whither, but that he looked for a city which hath foundations, whose builder and maker is God, and therefore he was a stranger at home? The like we have of Moses, who forsook Pharaoh's court, because he saw him who is invisible. Yea, and of Christ himself it is said, that for the glory which was set before him, he despised the shame, endured the cross, being now set at the right hand of the Father in glory and majesty, Heb. xii. 2. So 2 Cor. iv. 16, saith Paul, 'For this cause we faint not, but though our outward man perish, yet the inward man is renewed day by day;' and the reason is, 'For our light afflictions, which are but for a moment, work for us a far more exceeding and eternal weight of glory, while we look not at the things which are seen, but at the things which are not seen,' &c. He who thus hopes, does not want a comfortable life. And therefore upon this ground it is the apostle's concluding exhortation, 1 Cor. xv. 58, 'Therefore, my beloved brethren, be ye stedfast, unmoveable, always abounding in the work of the Lord, forasmuch as you know that your labour is not in vain in the Lord.' This makes a man zealous and fruitful, so it makes a man sincere, as 2 Cor. v. 9, 'Wherefore we labour (saith he), that whether absent or present we may be accepted of him.' The ground whereof is, 'For we must all appear before the judgment-seat of Christ, that every man may receive the things done in his body.' In this case our comfort is in all things to be sincere in working.

Now there is an order of things. Whosoever lives the life of faith in these grand passages, that soul lives the life of faith also in all other pas-

* Qu. 'them.'—G.

sages of our life; and these grand passages will run in the lesser courses of our life. To touch one: when a man is in extremity of both outward and inward affliction, then faith lays hold on this general, that God is wonderful in working, and that his ways and thoughts are not like our thoughts and ways. In all several cases faith makes use of all things God hath done or promised; as,

1. *Of a man in the state of grace, God in desertion appearing his enemy.*

(1.) In this case faith at first conquered God, and obtained a blessing *by wrestling*, as Jacob did. Faith therefore knows the same way again, to go to those precious promises God hath made, of returning again, not to forsake and be angry for ever, not to plough all the day to sow, as Isa. xxviii. 24, speaks. Faith knows that God works by contraries. It knows God takes away the sense of his love, not in anger, but to stir up the conscience and sense of sin, that we may lament and mourn for it the more, and so receive a surer report of the forgiveness of it. Faith does know that his name is wonderful. He raises things past hope. When a man is in despair touching himself, and all things in himself, and of all comforts, then he is nearest home, as Paul said excellently: 'But we had the sentence of death in ourselves, that we should not trust in ourselves, but in God which raiseth the dead,' 2 Cor. i. 9. So faith looks at God working with Christ the Son of his love, how roughly he dealt, yet lovingly, with him; for Christ is a pattern as well as a cause of good unto us. Christ in the case of his forsaking went unto God, saying, 'My God, my God, why hast thou forsaken me?' Mark xv. 34. Faith sets God's promise against his present working; as though it should say, 'Though thou killest me, yet will I trust in thee,' Job. xiii. 15; for all this thy love is the same; thou art merciful and gracious, and wilt not be angry for ever. Faith, as I may say, pulls off God's mask, sees through the dark cloud, that God appears an enemy for a time, that he may return again with the more abundance of comfort afterwards. Faith knows, as Paul speaks, that it is God that comforts the abject, raises the dead, will be seen in the mount, making our extremity his opportunity.

So faith reasons, Is it so, indeed? and is he wonderful in working? Doth he thus and thus work by contraries? Then I will answer his working the same way; I will believe one contrary in another, I will expect the sun will shine again, though now it be under a cloud. The like I may say of any other extremity, as in the raising of our dead bodies. Faith, as it is in Ezekiel, sees a spirit quickening and putting life in dry bones, assuring us thereby that he can as easily raise up the dead as deliver us out of any extremity. Saint Paul's argument is to trust in God, who raiseth the dead, [that he] can do all things, work wonderful changes in our greatest miseries. As for the church now in misery, there is a promise that Babylon shall be cast into the sea as a millstone, Rev. xviii. 21. Now faith believes the promises of glory, how that God will outwork all human policy, and catch the crafty in their own nets; that as certainly as day comes after night, so assuredly all God's promises shall be made good, as David resolves, Ps. cxxx. 6, 'My soul waiteth for the Lord more than they that watch for the morning: I say, more than they that watch for the morning. Let Israel hope in the Lord: for with the Lord there is mercy, and with him is plenteous redemption.'

So in any cloud get faith, and it will break through all impediments. Believe the former grand passages of calling, justification, and sanctification, and then we will trust God for the rest. Then is faith most glorious.

When it works alone, then it works most strongly. Then also God delights to shew himself most effectually; for when all other means fail, and faith works it out alone in wrestling, then he hath all the glory, and then all is well; and therefore we must do in this case as the prophet advises, 'Let him who sits in darkness and hath no light, trust in his name,' Isa. l. 10.

Faith does raise men up, and set them upon a rock, so sure as nothing can take away their comfort and joy in God; because Christ's name is wonderful, who then works in desperate cases when it is seasonable. A mighty God delights to work mightily, in mighty plunges. Then faith plies the suit hard: Help, Lord, or none can. Our Saviour, you see, slept in the ship until a mighty tempest rose, and then he rebuked the winds and the seas; so he seems to sleep now in the church. Why? That we may wake and stir him up by our prayers. When the Israelites' tale of brick was doubled, and the people greatly perplexed, then Moses came fitly to promise deliverance. So when the afflictions of Christians are doubled, then they are commonly most humbled. They pray hard, search, believe, and apply the promises, and then deliverance comes. Therefore in all exigents set we faith a-work, for this stirs up prayer, and prayer stirs up God, and God stirs up all the creatures. Blame we not, therefore, any trouble so much as to cry out, Oh I am undone! what shall become of me now! No, find fault with an unbelieving heart. It is not the trouble, but our weak faith which makes us to sink in these waves. Beg then of God, in great trouble, great faith to go through. Cry, Lord, increase my faith, for then the trouble is small when the faith is great.

(2.) Secondly, *In daily afflictions*. Whatsoever we suffer by them, labour to take away the sting of sin by living the life of faith in justification, as David Did, Ps. xxxii. 5; confess we our sins to God, beg to have the sting of them taken away, and hereupon we shall find him to forgive our iniquity, as in David. So in all our weaknesses and imperfections of sanctification, go to Christ for more grace, and say, Lord, though I be poor and empty of goodness, and of that which thy exact holiness requires, yet Christ hath abundance of fulness to supply my wants. Oh let me receive some grace for grace out of his fulness, and accept what he hath done for me in his pure and perfect obedience; good Lord, impute it to me, for thou hast made him to be for us wisdom, righteousness, sanctification, and redemption. And so for glorification; in all afflictions set we glory before our eyes, as Paul did, remembering that 'our light and short afflictions, which are but for a moment, cause unto us a far more excellent and eternal weight of glory, not being worthy of that glory which shall be revealed,' 2 Cor. iv 17. So in any affliction, we have still use of the life of faith in glorification. All these must be used in our afflictions, living the life of faith in all.

(3.) Thirdly, *In sickness of body*. Trust to Jesus, he is as powerful and as willing to help us now as he was to help others in the days of his flesh. All things are possible to us if we believe. It is but a word for him to rebuke all storms and tempests whatsoever. Let us not do like Asa, trust only in the physician or in subordinate means, but know that all physic is but dead means without him, 2 Chron. xvi. 12 Therefore with the means run to Christ, that he may work with them, and know that virtue and strength comes from him to bless or curse all sort of means.

(4.) Fourthly, *So for disgraces*. Commit we our credits to him as our lives—he cares for both—remembering what Peter speaks, 'If ye be reproached for the name of Christ, happy are ye; for the Spirit of glory and of God resteth upon you: on their part he is evil spoken of, but on your part he is glorified,' 1 Peter iv. 14. He means such a Spirit shall rest on us, which shall make us glorious. So Heb. xii. 2, 'We are therefore in sufferings pointed unto Jesus, the author and finisher of our faith, who for the glory which was set before him, endured the cross, despising the shame, and is set down at the right hand of the throne of God.' This suffering hinders our happiness; look to him, he is now set in glory, so shall we be. It is not in man's power to alter men's conceits. God hath this in his power, when he will heap honour, or pour disgrace upon any man. Therefore let us look up and desire no more good name than God will afford us. If dogs bark, no matter; at length God will clear our name, and our righteousness shall break forth as the noonday. Thus much the church assures herself of, Micah vii. 8, 'Rejoice not against me, O mine enemy: though I fall, I shall rise again.' As though she should say, God's servants are never finally forsaken. A time will come when God will do me good for all this, when I am humbled and have made a right use of it. That we may do this, think God in Christ hath given me the pardon of sin; what matter then of all other things which cannot hurt me, and shall all work together for my good? David, we know, Ps. vi. 8, began to complain grievously in this kind; but afterwards, ver. 8, when the Lord had spoken peace to his soul in the life of faith in justification and sanctification, then he says, 'Depart from me all ye workers of iniquity, for the Lord hath heard the voice of my weeping.' Then he despises the shame.

(5.) Fifthly, *In our particular places and graces.* Thus must we here live by faith also; for a Christian knows that he stands as in a circle set there by Christ to work. Therefore faith concludes, Here look I for understanding, wisdom, success, blessing, and ability to go through-stitch (*a*) with the business I am set about. He that set me here will enable me, and if I have ill sucess, then I will go to Christ, and I shall speed well with his assistance, as Peter did, who, though he had toiled all night and catched nothing, yet at length, at Christ's command, casting forth his net, catched abundantly, Luke v. 5. So there may be many who take much care and toil for heaven, to subdue and overcome corruptions, and yet catch nothing; find no answerable success. Oh let them go to Christ, and trust him as Peter did, and they shall overcome so at length, as all shall be well. So if magistrates, ministers, and people would trust God for strength more than they do, things would be better than they are with them, as we see the instance in Moses, who being commanded to go to Pharaoh, complained for want of utterance. But what saith God to him? 'Who hath made man's mouth? or who maketh the dumb, or deaf, or the seeing, or the blind? have not I the Lord?' Exod. iv. 11. Therefore in all such wants, faith goes unto him for it. The like, we read, was Christ's encouragement to his disciples, Luke xxi. 15, 'Settle it therefore in your hearts, not to meditate before what you shall answer, for I will give thee a mouth and wisdom, which all your adversaries shall not be able to gainsay nor resist.' This was made good also in the bypast troubles of the church, when poor silly women put to silence with their answers great learned men.

Now faith sees what Moses did, Heb. xi. 24. It looks up to Christ, to him who is invisible. It is with faith in this case, as it was with Micaiah, 1 Kings xxii. 19, when he had seen the Lord sitting on his throne, and all the host of heaven standing by him on his right hand. Then Ahab, a king on earth, was nothing unto him when he had seen the King of heaven in his glory. So we by faith seeing Christ, heaven and glory over our head, caring for his church, standing at the right hand of God, by assistance of his Spirit, this will put invincible courage in us.

(6.) Sixthly, *For provision and protection.* Faith goes to Christ, hangs and depends upon him for all these things. Faith knows that it hath encouragements, promises, and examples enough to strengthen our dependence on him, as to name one: Luke xii. 32, 'Fear not, little flock, for it is your Father's will to give you a kingdom.' Hence the believing soul argues from the lesser to the greater. What! will God deny me daily bread, that will give me heaven, and raise me up to life everlasting? and so it cites and revolves the promises often, that a little which the righteous hath is better than the abundance of the wicked; for he adds no sorrow with it; that a little with love is better than a stalled ox with contention, Prov. xv. 17. Yea, and in this case by faith we know that the saints, in extremity, shall be extraordinarily provided for. Sometimes he will bless a little, as the seven loaves and five fishes multiplied suddenly to feed five thousand people. They were in great want before, and were suddenly supplied. So it shall be with us. Sometimes we know the woman's oil increased; the ravens also in distress shall feed Elias; Lazarus shall have the dogs to lick his sores. In the use of the means we need not fear, and wanting means God will create means when all doth fail; for then faith lives best, knowing that God commands all means, and can suddenly do what he will.

And so for protection and preservation, faith knows that Christ will be our shield and protector, therefore it relies upon him. 'Fear not,' saith God to Abraham, 'for I am God, all-sufficient, thy buckler and thy exceeding rich reward,' Gen. xv. 1. Hence the saints have so esteemed him in all ages their rock, fortress, strong tower, salvation, helper, deliverer, refuge, and the like; and Christ tells his disciples, that he is with them even unto the end of the world, Mat. xxviii. 20. He rules his by his kingly office for the good of his church. Thus much we know he made good, both in Egypt and in the wilderness, bringing his people safely into Canaan, through all those dangers they were in; providing also for the women, persecuted by the dragon, a place of refuge in the wilderness, where she was safely kept, Rev. xii. 6.

(7.) Seventhly, *And for our children.*

Obj. Oh, say some, I could be content with a little, but I have many children.

Sol. Here faith sets in, and answers, But are they not also Christ's children, and must not he provide for his own? Do therefore what thou canst, and for the rest despair not, but cast this burden upon him, who hath commanded thee in nothing to be careful, but in all things to make thy suits and supplications known with prayer and thanksgiving. In this case faith in a dying parent follows Christ's example, John xvii. 6, 11: 'Thine they were, and thou gavest them me; and they have kept thy word. Holy Father, keep through thine own name those whom thou hast given me: that they may be one, as we are.' So a dying father may say, Lord, thine they were, thou gavest them me; I have done what I can for them. Thou, Lord, art the first, best, and last Father, the world* and the fulness thereof. Now, therefore, holy Father, keep them in thy name, for thou art the refuge of the poor and needy, and thy time is to help when all other help is at a stand. Why, consider, is not he the Father of the fatherless? Then let us leave them to him with that resolution and confidence of the prophet

* Qu. 'thine are the world'?—Ed.

David, 'When my father and mother forsake me, the Lord will take me up,' Ps. xxvii. 10. Not that he means fathers and mothers use to do so, but though they should, or even when they forsake us by death, yet God doth wonderfully save and protect their posterity. Then learn to exercise thy faith. Though thou leave them little, yet trust in God, and know that he who rests under the shadow of the Almighty, as the psalmist speaks, shall be safe, Ps. xci. 1. He who provided for them in the womb, and prepared breasts for them ere they came into the world; he who put so tender affection in women: know that he will also have care, and be more compassionate over thy children after thee. Let faith then settle thy heart on these grounds. In the womb they were nourished and bred thou knowest not how. Oh, saith David, 'I am fearfully and wonderfully made,' Ps. cxxxix. 14. And after thy death they shall be nourished, thou knowest not how. For this cause many are punished in their generations, because they would not trust to God, but did use ill means to perpetuate their houses, as covetousness, worldly policy, and the like.

(8.) Eighthly, *In prosperity.*

What use is there in this, of the life of faith? Oh yes, very much; for,

[1.] First, What makes prosperity sweet, but because by faith one knows that his sins are pardoned? What comfort, I pray you, hath a prisoner in the Tower of his life, though he abound in all outward plenty of gold and silver, so long as his pardon is not sealed? This sweetens prosperity, the life of faith in justification, that all my sins are nailed with Christ upon the cross, that the handwriting against me is cancelled and done away. Thus one comes to be of the first-born, 'whose names are written in heaven,' Heb. xii. 23, and to joy that he hath a double portion, being exempt from many fears, crosses, and miseries others are vexed with. Who are better Christians than they that know they enjoy all good things with God's favour and blessing? Here faith hath a continual work, to see God's love in all, and so to be abundantly thankful, according unto that we have received.

[2.] Secondly, The life of faith orders our prosperity. How? Not to abuse those good blessings bestowed on us, not to be puffed up by them, not to disdain, but to relieve others by them. Faith causes us to think of them as they are set forth in the word. It causes that we delight not too much in them, shews us better and more lasting riches, friends, and the like. It makes us take Saint Paul's counsel, 1 Cor. vii. 29, to rejoice and do all things as though we did them not, and to use the world as though we nsed it not, because the fashion of this world passeth away; and therefore it makes men, as Paul speaks in another place, not trust in uncertain riches, but in the living God who can do all things. In sum, it causeth us manage all the things of this world, so as thereby not to have our hearts drawn away from the chief good.

So again, in all the comforts of this life, it makes a man eat and drink and sleep, and do all in Christ, looking up into him in all his actions, living by faith, and joying that now he hath a title and a right to all the creatures. He being clean, now to him all things are clean, because he is now in Christ, who is pure, without spot, and Lord of all; for to the unclean all things are unclean. It cost Christ dear to purchase our liberty to the creatures. Therefore finding and joining in this freedom, we live the life of faith in prosperity; whilst it eyes God in all the passages of this estate, sets him in the first place, receives all, and joys in all as coming from the love and graciousness of so good a God; returning in humility the strength and glory of all unto him; supplying also the necessities of his members.

(9.) Ninthly, *In God's ordinances*. In the preaching of the word and in the sacraments, faith makes us live this life of faith, not to be captious how this comes that God hath appointed this means, especially, unto the end of the world to teach men by. It makes us lay aside by-conceits to think, why it is enough for me, his will shall be the rule and square of all my thoughts and actions. He hath sanctified and made effectual this ordinance to this purpose; therefore I believe he will bless his own means, which though to the world it seems to be the foolishness of preaching, yet it shall be effectual to my salvation and the rest of his church. He made the world by his mighty word, he repaired the decayed world thereby, and by it he will also call for and raise up all the dead at the last day. Therefore I will rest upon his ordinance without further dispute.

And so for the sacraments. What is a little water to the washing away of sin? Oh, but the blood of Christ, this is the cleanser, this washes away our sins. His ordinances make it powerful and effectual to that end he hath appointed it, for the believing soul. So the bread and wine in the Lord's Supper seem weak and feeble things; ay, but they are ordained to strengthen and increase faith. Here the Christian soul believes God can so strengthen faith by his Spirit, working in us a nearer communion with Christ and hatred of sin thereby, blessing his own ordinances, so that, as meat and drink refreshes, sustains and feeds this mortal body, so shall his ordinances by his blessing be effectual for the refreshing, fortifying, and nourishing of our souls to life and endless immortality. Again,

(10.) Tenthly, So in our combats. Of necessity we must fight the good fight of faith many ways. First, if any trouble assault a believer, he hath recourse to the life of faith in justification and sanctification. As he conquered God at first, in repenting, praying, and wrestling for forgiveness of sins, and applying the promises, so now he knows how to conquer any evil that befalls him. As it was said to Jacob, 'Thou hast, as prince, had power with God and with men, and hast prevailed;' so a Christian, having in his first new-birth-pangs conquered God, and prevailed, now by the same assistance and skill he can conquer all things also. Secondly, A Christian fights this good fight by living the life of faith in glorification. Saint Paul says, 'Fight the good fight of faith, lay hold of eternal life,' 1 Tim. vi. 12; insinuating that the way to live this life of faith is to lay hold of eternal life, having serious and constant meditations of the glory to come. Canaan, we know, was given to the Israelites, divided and given by Jacob, ere his death, long before they came there. Who would not fight then for such an inheritance? Now there were serpents, giants, strong and many enemies by the way; so they fought against all, and overcame all. Even so betwixt us and heaven there be many enemies to overcome: the flesh, the world, the devil, and all those numberless number of events which by their malice and our frailty we are tempted unto. But here faith must lay hold of eternal life, answer all objections with this, All these shall not make me lose eternity, there is no comparison betwixt heaven and earth; false pleasures here, and true substantial joys to come. This, saith the Scripture, is our victory which overcometh the world, even our faith, 1 John v. 4. Why? Because faith makes Christ's victory ours. Christ overcame sin, hell, death, the world, and all; and Christ himself being ours, we have all made effectual for us, which we have done and suffered. So Christ overcomes in us by his Spirit, as the apostle hath it, 1 John iv. 4,

'Stronger is he that is in you than he that is in the world.' So that a weak Christian hath a strong Spirit in him, which no power can prevail against, though he hath some foils.

Quest. But how doth faith fight against the world by the life of glory?

Sol. The world offers and presents petty base things before us. Faith keeps off, and opposes the glory to come, preferring that before all; as Moses did, who because he saw him who is invisible, refused to be called the son of Pharaoh's daughter, esteeming the rebukes of Christ before all the treasures of Egypt; because this glory presented better things unto him than this world hath, Heb. xi. 24, *seq.* And if, on the left hand, the world threaten troubles, afflictions, persecutions and the like, for well doing, and not running into sinful courses with others, then faith remembers, as it is Rom. viii. 18, that 'all the sufferings of this present world are not worthy to be compared with the glory which shall be revealed in us.' We see then that the life of faith of that glory to come, helps us in all temptations to fight the good fight against all enemies whatsoever. He who hath a crown before him, it will make him run through the pikes or anything to attain it; so faith, having glory, immortality, and the joys of heaven before it, overlooks and despises all oppositions, and sees all things subdued to Christ, as though all were past; whereupon it gathers assurance that it shall triumph over all in him.

(11.) Eleventhly, *So we persevere unto the end,*

Fighting and living this life of faith; that is, a Christian makes it his daily and continual life. This is a ground of perseverance. A Christian then lives in a sort the life of Christ, as it is said, Rom. vi. 9, 'Christ being raised from the dead dieth no more, death hath no more dominion over him.' So such a one once living by faith, dies no more. There is a perpetual supply of spiritual strength imparted unto him from Christ the head, whereby he lives by faith in all the passages of this life. Rom. viii. 35, 'What shall separate us from the love of God in Christ?' Nothing can. It is a never-failing river, entertained unto death, that whosoever drinks thereof shall never thirst again; for Christ's promise is, 'Whosoever liveth and believeth in me shall never die,' for after faith ends, then comes the life of vision, so that all our life the life is the same, we continue so living even until death, and then faith leaves us to the fruition of the thing believed. But doth faith leave us when we come to die? Oh no!

(12.) Twelfthly, *We die by faith also.*

For a Christian knows that he is in heaven already. As he lives by faith, so he dies in faith also. Faith makes him, like Stephen, resign his soul to God with comfort. He knows that Christ will receive that soul, which he hath purchased by his blood. He dies by faith, because he sees death conquered in Christ before him, and because he looks beyond death, and over-eyes all things that are betwixt him and glory, having the Spirit of Christ in him, which makes him bold and fearless, as David says, 'I will not fear though I walk in the valley of the shadow of death, because thou art with me,' Ps. xxiii. 4. This blessed faith in the Son of God makes us do all things, suffer all things cheerfully and comfortably. Faith makes absent comforts present to us. It eyes such sweet contentment in God's presence, that all difficulties below seem as nothing. It knows whom it hath trusted, and what is laid up for it. A believer sees invisible things. Oh the glorious things that the faithful soul beholds! He sees the angels ready to carry him from a house of clay to a heavenly paradise; from the company of sinful men here in misery, to the sweet society of saints in perfect bliss, which he himself now enjoys the first-fruits and earnest of, and longs to be fully possessed with.

Obj. But how can this be, when neither eye hath seen, nor ear heard what God hath prepared for his?

Ans. Indeed, to carnal sense these things are undiscernible; but to a renewed soul, the Spirit that God hath given them discovers the eminency thereof above all earthly contentments whatsoever. We see they are compared to a kingdom, to a feast, to a crown, familiar resemblances, that so the meanest capacity might conceive and be taken with them. What more desirous* than a kingdom for honour! what glory is there in a rich diadem! and what sweet refreshings are there in a feast! Yet, alas! these are all but shadows; the reality is heaven itself. Talk not then of riches, but of thriving in grace, which will make you rich indeed. What good will the riches of the world do us at the last day? They take them wings and fly away. If we have not the true riches, we may die in want for all these, as Dives did. Know this, that if there be anything good in earthly kingdoms, there is much more in this spiritual kingdom.

Again, the children of God know these heavenly things by their taste. They have the first-fruits of them even in this life; and if the communion of saints here be so delectable, how much more will it be in heaven! God's children have a taste of that eternal Sabbath in heaven, by keeping a holy Sabbath to God here on earth; they have a taste of that eternal rest and peace which they shall enjoy hereafter, by the peace of conscience which they have here; and that heavenly joy which doth flow into the soul now, is but a taste of that eternal joy which we shall have our fill of one day.

God is so far in love with his children that he keeps not all their comforts for another world, but gives them a taste of the sweetness here. But what are all refreshments below to that which we shall have above in God's presence? As John saith, 'We are the sons of God, but we know not what we shall be,' 1 John iii. 2. Only this we know, that when Christ our head appears, all his members shall be like to him. Our life may well be said to be hid with Christ in God, because flesh and blood discerns not the things prepared for those that love him. We lead a hidden life. We cannot see God face to face, or know him so perfectly here as one day we shall do. All that we have now is a taste of the good things to come, and but a taste.

The life which we now live is a life of faith, and we are to walk by faith, not by sight. Therefore, if God did give us all here, what need have we of faith? It were no commendation for a Christian to abstain from the sinful courses of the world, if he did see the glory that he shall have present before him. But God will manifest to the world that he hath a people whose comforts are higher and greater than the world affords, who live by faith and not by sight.

God doth not reveal to us now all that we shall have hereafter, because we are not capable of such delicates, we cannot digest them; as Peter and John, they could not see Christ's glory in his transfiguration, but they must be spiritually drunk with it: 'Master, it is good being here: let us build tabernacles.' Oh but saith the Holy Ghost, 'They knew not what they said,' Mark ix. 5. So likewise St Paul, when he was caught up into the third heaven, and heard unspeakable words, he could not digest them, they did so ravish him; therefore God gave him 'a prick in the flesh,' that he might not be exalted above measure, 2 Cor. xii. 7. Are we stronger than

* That is, 'desirable.'—Ed.

Peter and Paul, to bear these revelations from above? Is it not goodness in God to reserve them till such time as we are able better to relish them? Moses, desiring to see the face of God, had this answer, 'No man can see my face and live,' Exodus xxiii. 20. So he that would conceive aright of the joys of heaven must die first.

Though we cannot see or understand these spiritual excellencies, yet let us often think of them. The life of a true Christian is taken up with the consideration of those things which he shall hereafter have in heaven. There is no grace in a Christian, but it is set a-work this way. What is faith without this? The chief work of faith is about things not seen. It makes absent comforts to be in a manner present; and so overcomes the world by seeing these things above the world. How is patience strengthened, but by the consideration of future relief? If there were not better times hereafter for the godly, they were of all creatures most miserable; but the thought of that makes them wait with patience. What makes men so tender in conscience, and so fearful to sin, but the eyeing of him who is invisible?

And have we such glorious comforts in another world? Let this cheer up our hearts with joy against all contempts and slighting here below. The world knows not God, nor us, neither doth it not know what things are prepared for us; and shall we care for their abuse and scorn? What though we walk up and down here unknown, our condition shall one day be manifested with glory in the sight of all, and then we shall esteem of things below as they are. The consideration of this should raise up the spirit of every Christian. What makes us do things that are excellent, but our believing an excellency in such ways and courses? He that sees an excellency in God, you may turn that man loose to any temptation; for if Satan tempts him to any sin, he thus considers with himself, Shall I lose the sweet contentments of heaven for a base lust? Shall I lose my peace of conscience, and joy in the Holy Ghost, for the satisfying of my unruly corruptions? Consider what we lose in the committing of any sin. The profit and pleasure that a man gets in following the world, alas! what is it to the precious comforts which we lose? Who would be beholden to Satan for anything? Is it not a disparagement to go from God, as if there were not sufficient in him to quiet the soul? Hath not God enough, but we must be beholden to the devil our enemy?

Oh, then, let us admire the love of God to his poor creature, in preparing such great things for him. Let us say with David, 'Lord, what is man, that thou art so mindful of him? or the son of man, that thou so regardest him?' Ps. viii. 4. How wonderful is thy mercy in having such high thoughts towards lost sinners? 'Blessed be the God and Father of our Lord Jesus Christ, that hath thought us meet to be partakers of an inheritance, immortal and invisible, reserved in the heavens for us,' 1 Pet. i. 4. A sound Christian begins his life in heaven here upon earth: he praises and glorifies God by a holy and fruitful conversation. This is our best way of blessing God. Praise in the heart will soon break forth in the tongue.

The apostle, when he speaks of the state of God's children, calls it a 'heavenly kingdom,' a 'glorious inheritance,' a 'wonderful light,' a never-fading condition. He is not able to express their happiness, it is every way so full. 'So God loved the world.' *So*, as I cannot utter it. 'Behold what manner of love the Father hath shewed, that we should be called the sons of God,' 1 John iii. 1. It is so free and so rich love, that I am not able to declare it. Envy not, then, the wicked in their pleasure and bravery. Alas! they are but for a term of life; pity thou rather to see them delight in such sinful vanities. Shall a Christian envy any in their pleasures here, when he himself is in such a state of admiration? He should be so far from grudging and repining at the prosperity of others, that he should solace himself cheerfully with his future hopes. The thoughts of his good to come should revive him more than any want or discouragement should deject him. What though we have not our comforts in possession? We are sure of them; God reserves us for them, and them for us. We are like little children, that think not of the portions that their parents have left them till they come to age. Many weak Christians think not of their Father's portion, they mind not those unspeakable joys laid up for them in their minority; but as they grow in grace, so they will have more knowledge of it, and longings after it.

If it be a great matter to come out of a dark prison, to see the light of the sun, what will it be to come out of this dark world, into the glorious light of heaven? A natural man knows not this, but when once we come to see that light that we shall have in glory, then we will admire it, and cry out with the apostle, 'Oh the exceeding love of God in Jesus Christ!' Indeed, those things that came by the gospel cause wonderment, that God should love flesh and blood so as to prepare such excellent things for them.

But we must know, God doth qualify all those here that he prepares happiness for hereafter. The reason is, because no unclean thing shall enter into heaven. We must not think to come out of the mire and dirt, and enter into heaven presently. No. There must be a suitableness wrought in us for such a condition. Those that will not live holily here, have no dwelling in that holy place. If thy heart can tell thee that thou hadst rather have this honour, and that pleasure, than grace in thy soul, the word of God doth as plainly tell thee, that the excellencies of heaven are none of thy portion. A swine loves the puddles rather than the sweet fountain; so wicked men delight in the world more than in heaven, which plainly shews they shall never come thither. Nothing will comfort us at last but a true change of heart. If thou beest not a new creature, thou shalt have no part in the New Jerusalem: therefore let us not feed ourselves with vain hopes. There is none of us but desires heaven; but why dost thou desire it? Is it because it is set forth to be a kingdom, an excellent place of joy and rest? Is it for this only? Assure thyself, then, thou wilt never come there. Thou must desire to have heaven, because of the divine nature, because it is a holy place, and near to God, if thou wouldst possess it indeed; and 'if thou hast this hope in thee, thou wilt purge thyself, as he is pure,' 1 John iii. 3.

If we would have faith ready to die by, we must exercise it well in living by it, and then it will no more fail us than the good things we lay hold on by it, until it hath brought us into heaven, where that office of it is laid aside. Here is the prerogative of a true Christian above an hypocrite, and a worldling; whenas they trust, and things they trust in fails them, then a true believer's trust stands him in greatest stead.

For use of all. See then how faith is the life of our life, and the soul of our lives, because by this we are knit to Christ Jesus, the life and food of our souls. Let us then make use of it; house and entrench ourselves in him, as it is Ps. xc. 1, 'Make him our dwelling-place in all generations.' He is our buckler; our enemies must break through Christ ere they come at us; all is ours in him, and in his strength and might we shall overcome all adverse powers whatsoever. You see then that this is no idle, but a mighty working grace. It works in heaven, and earth, and hell. It works against Satan, it works by love to God, makes us love him and work to him, and makes us industrious to work for others. Faith is the root of the tree, love the branches. Thus faith works mightily and strongly; it is a quickening and an active grace. Those therefore who find it not active, no marvel they want the comfort of it; they must strive to stir it up, and set it a-work to live by it. Those who find they have it, let them improve it to a better use than many do, to swear by it. This shames us in troubles to be unarmed. Where is our shield of faith, when every little poor dart strikes our armour through? This shews we have but a paper shield. We ought therefore to bewail our unbelief, and labour for this grace, which is so active and useful, so much the rather, because it is most miserable to be in a storm without a shelter. This will help us in all miseries whatsoever, and make us conquerors over all in him who hath loved us. Oh the excellent use of the life of faith! It looks back, and makes use of all God's works, promises, wonders, threatenings, and judgments; and gathers strength, wisdom, courage, instruction from all. It looks and sees all things past, as it were a-working, doing, promising, threatening in present, and is answerably affected; when by strength of fancy it presents the ideas of things past, to work upon us the more, as present, and so is overawed from sinning against God. Sometimes it sees all this world a-fire, and therefore for worldly things and enticements it puts them over so much the more lightly, as perishing things condemned to be burnt. So it is the best prospective in the world; it presents to itself things afar off, as present and at hand, and makes them excellent, great and glorious to the sight afar off. Therefore above all things study we to live this life of faith—Oh it is worth all our pains—and shun infidelity as that which only makes us miserable, causing the guilt of sin to lie on us, and shutting us up under the wrath of God; yea, it seals us up to the day of wrath, turns all our actions to be sinful in God's sight, and is cause of that great condemnation John speaks of; whereas by the contrary, the believing soul lives a comfortable life, is admitted into the glorious liberty of the sons of God, hath a shelter to keep off all storms and tempests whatsoever, and comes by this life of faith to be assured of his part and portion in the love, merits, obedience, sufferings, death, resurrection, ascension, and intercession of the Son of God; in sum, to be assured of its salvation in particular, as Saint Paul was, 'who loved me, and gave himself for me.' But thus much shall suffice for this time. I shall prosecute things more fully in the next.

NOTE.

(*a*) P. 376.—'Through-stitch.' To go through-stitch is = to go through or accomplish completely. 'Now wee are in, wee must goe *through-stitch*.'—Tragedy of *Hoffman*, 1631, sig. F. iii. '*Passe-par-tout*, a resolute fellow, one who goes *through-stitch* with every thing he undertakes, one whose courses no danger can stop, no difficulty stay.'—*Cotgrave*. 'To go through-stitch with the work, *opus peragera*.'—*Coles*. Sibbes adds another example to these illustrations from Halliwell's Dictionary of Archaisms and Provincialisms (2 vols. 4to, 1852). G.

SALVATION APPLIED.

SALVATION APPLIED.

'Salvation Applied' forms the third of the 'three Sermons' which compose 'The Life of Faith.' See page 358. The separate title-page is given below.* G.

* SALVATION
APPLYED.

In one SERMON.

WHEREIN IS SHEWED,

The more speciall and peculiar worke of Faith, in apprehending Christ as our *owne*; the grounds thereof are shewed, with meanes to attaine it, and most of all the knotty objections against particular assurance of Gods love answered.

[Woodcut as before. Cf. Vol. IV. page 60.]

HEB. 10. 22.

Let us draw neare with a true heart, in full assurance of faith, having our hearts sprinkled from an evill conscience, and our bodies washed with pure water.

LONDON,
Printed for R. DAVVLMAN, at the brazen Serpent in *Pauls* Churchyard. 1637.

SALVATION APPLIED.

And the life which I now live in the flesh I live by the faith of the Son of God, who hath loved me, and gave himself for me.—Gal. II. 20.

We have already, out of the words immediately going before, spoken of spiritual life, and of the excellency of it; and, in the third place, of the manner of conveyance, which is by faith; and, fourthly, the spring and fountain of this spiritual life, which is the Son of God, described here by his love and the fruit of it: 'He loved me;' and, as a fruit of that love, 'he gave himself for me.' Now, to come in the last place to the apostle's particular application, which he expresseth in this word 'me:' 'Who loved *me*, and gave himself for *me*;' wherein these points offer themselves to our consideration:

First, That God loves some with a peculiar and with a special love: 'Who loved *me*, and gave himself for *me*.'

Secondly, That faith answers God and Christ's particular love by a particular application: 'Who loved *me*.'

Thirdly, That this particular faith in God's particular love is the ground of assurance, which springs from this particular faith.

Fourthly, That this assurance which proceeds from our particular faith in God's particular love, is the spring of all spiritual life, which sets the whole soul a-working. For what is the ground of my living by faith in all the passages of my life, but the apprehension of his love, who loved me, and gave himself for me; and can I then do less than give myself to him? Now to unfold these in order.

1. *That Christ loves some with a special, superabundant, and peculiar love;* for Christ, when he suffered upon the cross, looked with a particular eye of his love upon all that should believe in him; as now in heaven he hath carried our names upon his breast. As the high priest had on his breastplate written the names of the twelve tribes in precious stones, Exodus xxviii. 21, 30; so Christ, our high priest, hath the names of all his children in his heart, to present them always to God by his intercession, so as when he now appears before God, the church with him appears before God in his heart. The Father sees the church in the heart and breast of Christ. Now as this, I say, is true in heaven, so upon the cross the church was in the breast of Christ. There was but a certain number for whom Christ savingly laid down his life, John xvii. 9. Paul was in the breast of Christ when he

shed his blood: 'Who loved me, and gave himself for me.' So that then Christ loves some with a peculiar, special, and superabundant love. Here then the question is concerning,

1. General love. 2. General gift.

Quest. Whether Christ loved all, and gave himself for all, because here the apostle saith, 'He loved me, and gave himself for me'?

Ans. 1. I answer briefly, first, that Christ's loving and giving himself was parallel in even lines with God's love and gift, John vi. 37, 39; for Christ gives himself for none but those which God hath first given him. Christ had his commission, and he came to do his Father's will, not his own, John vi. 38, and will save all whom his Father hath given unto him; as it is John xvii. 6, 'Thine they were, thou gavest them me.' Those that the Father gives in election, Christ redeems, and by redemption saves; for redemption, in regard of efficacy, is no larger than God's election. Therefore he joins, 'Christ loved me, and gave himself for me.' His love is only to those whom God gave him, for he looks upon all he died for as they were in his Father's love. There are a company in the world whom God hates: 'Esau have I hated,' Rom. ix. 13. Here love and gift go both together. He gives himself for no more than he loves, and he loves no more than God loves.

Ans. 2. Again, whomsoever Christ did love and give himself for to death, there be other fruits which accompany this. They who have interest in Christ's redemption, they have the spirit of application. Where there is obtaining by Christ anything of God, there, I say, is grace to apply it by his Spirit; and many things go with it. For them that he died for, as the apostle shews, Rom. viii. 11, 'for them he rose again, and for them he sits at the right hand of God.' These go together: 'For if he spared not his own Son, but gave him to death for us all, how shall he not with him also freely give us all things?' Rom. viii. 32. Where God gives Christ, he gives the spirit of application with him, Mat. xvii. 13, 2 Thess. iii. 2. But we see that the greatest part of the world have not faith; for it is the faith of the elect, which worldlings not having, nor the grace of application, therefore they have not the favour of God obtained by Christ. So it is written, Rom. v. 10, 'For if, when we were enemies, we were reconciled to God by the death of his Son, much more, being reconciled, we shall be saved by his life.' These go together. Now the greatest part are not saved by his life, therefore they are not reconciled by his death.

Other places do clear this truth, as Heb. ix. 14, where is shewed, that where Christ hath offered up himself for any, there is also a purging of the conscience from dead works to serve the living God. But the most are not purged, therefore they have no interest in Christ's death.

A strong reason is further shewed hereof by Christ, John xvii. 9, where he avouches plainly, and makes a main difference between two sorts of people, saying, 'I pray for them: I pray not for the world, but for them which thou hast given me, for they are thine.'

Obj. But here some may object, Christ's death is of larger extent than his intercession.

Ans. To cut off this objection, Christ says after in the same chapter, ver. 17, 'And for their sakes I sanctify myself, that they also may be sanctified through the truth.' That is, I prepare and sanctify myself to be a sacrifice as a priest; I prepare myself to be a holy sacrifice for such; therefore Christ sanctified himself for them, not for the world. Under the law there was a brasen altar for sacrifice, and the golden altar for incense, which golden altar for incense was effectual for no more than the brazen altar was for sacrifice. And Christ offered himself a sacrifice for all those that he makes intercession for. The point is clear. I will not answer all the objections might be brought, only encounter with some of the main ones, which are brought by the papists against this truth. Saint Paul's meaning, therefore, is not that he loved me with that love wherewith he loved all mankind. The apostle means a more special love, 'He loved me so as he gave himself for me;' that is, with a more special love than he bears to all mankind. This is a point that tends to God's honour and man's comfort; for God hath the more praise and thanks from his elect, and those that are redeemed by the peculiarness of it, which the more it is, the more they acknowledge themselves bound unto God and Christ. These are they that are elected, these are they for whom the Scriptures are, for whom the world stands and Christ came, Ps. cxvi. 1. They love God and single him out, and the more they do so, God doth single them out to delight in. Peculiarity enhanceth and raiseth favours to higher degrees than otherwise. The fewer that are taken out of the world from the refuse of mankind, the more their hearts are inflamed to love God again. God, as the psalmist says, hath not dealt so with every nation, Ps. cxlvii. 20. When will a man be most thankful to God and give him glory, but when he can say, Thou hast not dealt so with the rest of the world; what is in me more than in the rest of mankind? I differ nothing from them but in thy peculiar love. Hereupon comes the heart to be knit in love unto Christ again. But against this it will be objected,

Obj. Why doth Christ by the ministry persuade all in the church for to believe in Christ, and for to believe forgiveness of sins, if Christ did not die for them all?

Ans. I answer, that in the church he calls all, that he may cull out his own. The minister speaks promiscuously both to the elect and those that are not, because God will not rob his own children of the benefit, though they are mingled with others to whom the blessed things do not belong; as it is with the rain, it rains as well upon the rocks of the sea, and upon the barren heath as upon the good ground. Why, for any good to the rocks? No, but because, together with it, it rains upon the fruitful ground, which hath the benefit of the rain. So God rains the showers of his ordinances upon all, but the benefit thereof is only to his ground, not to the reprobates. The sun shines upon all, but who hath the comfort of that shining? Those who have eyes to see it only and use it, not the blind. But to them that believe not, they have another use. They have this benefit by Christ's death, that there is mercy offered them, and some gifts of the Spirit. God offers and stirs up good motions in them, but they rebel against them. There be many degrees and means of faith. They use not all the means they ought, neither take all the degrees, therefore they are without all excuse, because he gives more grace, not only the means, but he is ready to give more grace than they are willing to entertain. So it is their rebellion, which is the cause of their damnation. They are said to resist the Holy Ghost, such reprobates in the church, to quench the Spirit, Acts vii. 51, which implies the Holy Ghost is ready to work more in them than they are willing to entertain. Is it not so by experience? There is a company of profane persons, that, out of the abundance of their wicked hearts, and the poison of their breeding, will not vouchsafe to hear at all; others that do come, though for some bye and carnal ends. Happily the Holy Ghost, in hearing, beats upon their consciences and awakes them. But what say their rebellious hearts? Shall I stoop to leave such and such courses that are pleasurable and gainful? Hereupon they resist the work of the Holy Ghost in the ministry, when their hearts tell them there is a readiness in the Holy Ghost, and that he is sent from Christ and the Father to work more effectually in them than they are willing to be wrought upon, and therefore it is they are damned. 'Thy perdition,' saith the prophet, 'is of thyself, O Israel!' Hosea xiii. 9. Their own consciences will tell them thus much. So it is no matter what cavils they raise of Christ's intention and God's election. Look thou, man, to thine own heart. Doth not thy own heart tell thee thou art a rebel, and livest in profane wicked courses, in neglect of holy duties? Thou carriest thine own sentence and cause of damnation in thy breast. I appeal to the worst, who live in sins against conscience. Here is the ground of thy damnation. There be many ascents and degrees to saving faith. Thou withstandest the beginnings and the motions of the Spirit. If they come in and work upon thy heart any estrangement from sin, thy proud heart begins to rebel, and will not yield. It is the only true obedience which lays itself at the foot of Christ, and is willing to be led and persuaded in anything so far as frailty will permit, and allows itself in no evil course. This is that which brings sound comfort, which they not doing, therefore are without all excuse.

Obj. If this were not so, they might object another day, Christ did not die for me, therefore why should I be damned for not believing?

Ans. Their consciences therefore will tell them, that they used not all means to believe, neither took the degrees of faith; for God's Spirit doth work after a kind in wicked men, as in the three bad grounds, the word was effectual in divers degrees; but when it comes to the upshot, they hated not their sins, were worldly minded; or, the plough had not made furrows deep enough to humble them, to value mercy and Christ above all things, and to hate sin above all. This is enough to justify their condemnation. Howsoever Christ is offered, and there is a command to believe, yet their hearts tell them they do not all they might. They must know that God's secret purpose in electing some, and redeeming some, and leaving others, it is hid from the world, as his secret will, that is not the rule of our obedience, but God's revealed will and commandment. Therefore men must look unto what God commands. If their conscience tell them that they yield not that obedience which they ought and might, but rather resist the motions of God's Spirit, hereupon comes their damnation to be just. They are commanded to believe. What! Not to believe remission of their sins; for know,

1. There is the act of faith; and 2. The fruit of faith.

Now a wicked man is not first commanded to believe the forgiveness of his sin, but in this order, in obedience to subordinate duty before. He is commanded to believe that he shall have benefit by Christ, by yielding obedience of faith to Christ. The act is one thing, and the fruit is another. Every one is bound to believe and cast himself upon Christ for salvation, but not bound to believe the fruit, unless they have the act.

Obj. But it will be objected, we are not bound to have the first act of faith to believe; if we should, it were in vain, we should believe a lie.

Ans. I say no. The gospel runs, whosoever believes in Christ shall have the fruits of the death of Christ, shall have everlasting life. Thus whosoever believes and casts himself upon Christ, doth the act, shall have the fruit. Away with idle questions; What? Doth the fruit of Christ's death belong to me? Did he die for me? Go thou to the act; if thou hast grace to cast thyself upon Christ, and to assent when he offers and invites thee, it is well. Yield the act of faith, and leave questioning of that, which is then put out of question. Reason not this, whether God hath elected, or Christ hath died for thee. This is the secret will of God. But the commandment is, to believe in Christ. This binds. Therefore, yield to Christ when thou art called and bidden to cast thyself upon him; then thou shalt find, to thy soul's comfort, the fruit of his death.

Caution. Let no man excuse himself by quarrelling against Christ, for not giving himself for all. There is no man condemned, but for not yielding obedience in the act of faith, and doing all that his heart tells him he might, but is unwilling to do. It is for rebellion he perishes: as when a malefactor is condemned, who hath a book given him to read, which he refuses to do. His not reading is the cause of his execution and death, as well as his ill deeds which he hath done: his refusing pardon, that he will not read, with the other. Both are causes of his death, because he doth not read, and because he is a malefactor (*a*). So in this case, when a man will not yield the act of faith, though his other sins will damn him, yet, if he would believe and take the mercy offered, his other sins would not damn him. If men would or could believe, no other sins would hurt them; but because they do not, their other sins shall be laid to their charge, and their rebellion, that they will not believe, and take the benefit of God's offer. They refuse mercy, because mercy cannot be had without conditions of obedience; as Christ reproves the Jews, John iii. 19, 'And this is the condemnation, that light is come into the world, and men loved darkness rather than light, because their deeds were evil.' This is the condemnation, with a witness, the great and main cause of condemnation: they would have heaven, if they might have it with their lusts; but they will not yield to the act of faith, to take Christ as he is offered unto them, upon his own terms, to be ruled by him, for better and for worse. This they will none of, which is that which damns them. They would single out of Christ what they list.

When Christ sent the seventy disciples forth to preach and heal the sick, notwithstanding they were to be refused of many, as it is Luke x. 11, yet they were taught by our Saviour, as to wipe off the dust of their feet against them, so also to convince them in this, that the kingdom of heaven was come near unto them. In vain, therefore, do wicked men and our adversaries cavil against God's justice in this, which every man's conscience shall accuse himself at last to be guilty of, and clear God of; in that they would none of wisdom's counsel, shutting their eyes against all instructions, refusing to be reformed. This I thought good to add, to avoid the snarling of wicked, carnal, profane persons.

2. The second point is, *that true faith doth answer this particular love and gift of Christ, by applying it to itself.* True faith is an applying faith. There is a spirit of application in true faith; for God in the Scriptures offers Christ, and Christ offers himself in the ministry to all that believe. Hereupon comes faith to make Christ our own. It doth appropriate Christ to itself in particular. Christ is a garment, faith puts him on; Christ is a foundation, faith builds upon him; Christ is a root, faith plants us in him; Christ is our husband, faith yields consent, and consent makes the match. So then there is a particular truth that strikes the stroke betwixt Christ and us: 'He loved me, and gave himself for me.' The nature of faith is to make generals become particulars, to restrain generals into particulars;

for there is a particular cause, which must have a particular restraint. Christ's love is propounded to all in general. Before it do me good I must have a particular restraining faith for to make it my own. Now the papists are enemies to this particular faith, it being opposite to their opinions and authors, save some of the honester that incline to us. They say, that we ought to believe with a catholic general faith, that there is remission of sins for the church, but not 'for me;' for where, say they, is your name set down in Scripture? They are against this special faith, because they know it is the ground of assurance, unto which they are enemies; this assurance also being an enemy to all their fooleries, forgeries, and courses they take to have assurance.

We must know more clearly, that there is a particular faith required of us. A Christian ought to say, 'Christ loved me.' Neither is this by any special revelation; for God's Spirit doth witness ordinarily, first or last, so much to all that are his, except in some cases. Now that you may know this particular faith is aimed at by God in the Scripture, look what is the end of the ministry and of the sacraments. Are not we ambassadors from God to men, to unfold Christ's love in particular unto them: if they believe, then to tell them, that they may be assured of salvation? Doth not the apostle, Rom. x. 9, speak in particular, that, 'if thou shalt confess with thy mouth the Lord Jesus, and shalt believe in thine heart that God hath raised him from the dead, thou shalt be saved.' This is spoken to every man in particular.

And for the sacraments, what kind of faith doth baptism seal, when water is sprinkled upon the child? Doth it seal a general washing away of guilt? No; but a particular washing away of the guilt and filth of the sins of the party* baptized. Wherefore are the sacraments added to the word, but to strengthen faith in particular? Therefore every one in particular is sprinkled, to shew the particular washing of our souls by the blood of Christ. What is the reason that the sacrament of the Lord's Supper is added to the word, but that every one may be persuaded that it is his duty to cast himself upon Christ, and to eat Christ, and to believe his own particular salvation? It overthroweth the main end of the sacraments, to hold a confused faith in general. Therefore seeing it is the main end of the word and ministry, let us labour for this particular faith, that we may say in special, 'Christ loved me, and gave himself for me.' Nay, 'for me,' if there had been no other men in the world but I. And the rather labour for this, because it is that which distinguisheth us from counterfeit Christians and believers. For wherein is the main difference? It is in appropriation. True faith doth appropriate Christ unto itself, makes Christ a man's own, it being the nature of saving faith to draw the general into particulars, which is meant by eating Christ, drinking his blood, and putting on Christ; all which enforce particular acts of faith. But against this it will be said,

Obj. St Paul had a special revelation, without which no man ought to believe thus much.

Ans. I answer, he had no special revelation, for, Rom. viii. 38, he enlargeth the comfort unto all: 'For I am persuaded that neither death, nor life, nor angels, nor principalities, nor powers, nor things present, nor things to come, shall separate us from the love of God, which is in Christ Jesus our Lord.' It is idle to speak of a special revelation, unless we call it so, as it is hid from the world; so every Christian hath a special revela-

* Cf. footnote, Vol. III. p. 9.—G.

tion from the Spirit. For the Spirit, which knows the 'secret things' of God, and which knows his heart, testifies to him that he is a child of God, and so he hath a special revelation; but not if we distinguish one Christian from another. Every true Christian hath this revelation, because they have the spirit of revelation, for which the apostle prays, Eph. i. 17. 'For if we have not the Spirit of Christ, we are none of his,' Rom. viii. 9. Thus we have seen that God loves some with a peculiar and a special love; and secondly, that they have a special faith to make this love their own.

3. The third point is, *that assurance doth spring from this particular faith;* so that a Christian man may be assured of the love of Christ. But here divers questions and cases must be answered and explained to clear the point, else our speech shall not be answerable to the experience of God's people, or the truth itself. First, we must know that there is a double act of faith in the believing soul,

1. An act of faith, trusting and relying; and 2. An act of assurance upon that act of relying.

For it is one thing to believe and cast myself upon Christ for pardon of sins, and another thing upon that act to feel assurance and pardon. The one looks to the word more principally; the other is founded upon experience, together with the word. We ought to labour for both, for affiance and consent in the will, to cast ourselves upon Christ for salvation; and then upon believing we ought to find and feel this assurance. But these many times are severed, and sometimes the first is without the second. The first brings us into the state of grace. A man may be in the state of grace, by giving consent to Christ and relying on him for mercy, and yet want assurance of pardon and reconciliation in the second place.

This falls out ofttimes, especially in the new birth, that in those strugglings when little grace strives with corruption, there the Spirit of God is exercised in the act, in yielding the obedience of faith, to cast itself upon the arm of Christ, into the bosom of Christ, and upon God's mercy. As for any feeling, it doth not so much stand upon it at first, as it doth regard the act; after which assurance it comes for a reward, as God sees it good.

Then again, it often falls out in the time of temptation, that the first act of affiance, it is without the act of persuasion or feeling, which requires more experience, when a Christian, in the time of temptation, hath rather experience of corruption and the wrath of God, having no experience of the contrary; yet he yields the first act of affiance with a particular faith, casting himself upon the mercy of Christ and upon his death, for the comfort of redemption.

Quest. But here a question must be asked, What is the reason that, where the first act of faith is, to cast itself upon the mercy of Christ in the promises, that yet there is not the sense of pardon and reconciliation, nor that full persuasion: why is this many times suspended?

Ans. 1. I answer, many causes there be of it. To name some:

(1.) *First, In some the distemper of the body helps the distemper of the soul;* I mean a melancholy temper, which is a constitution subject to distrust, fears, and temptations. As some tempers, that are of a bold spirit, are subject to presumption, the devil suiting himself to their temper; so where there is this melancholy abounding, which is prone to fear and distrust, the devil mingling his suggestions with their constitution, causes that those tempers are inclined to fear, where there is no cause of fear. They are careful enough to do their duties abundantly, as God doth discover his will unto them; they cast themselves upon God's mercy, and renounce themselves; humble souls, only, out of distrust, helped by Satan applying himself to their distemper, they are kept in darkness.

(2.) And also it is, many times, *from a judgment not rightly persuaded:* as when they think they have no faith, because they have it not in so great a measure. And when they are not rightly conceited of the covenant of grace, which requires truth for perfection, and not measure. For Christ will not quench the smoking flax. He despiseth not the day of small things, but cherisheth it. 'Thou hast a little strength,' saith he to the church of Philadelphia, 'and hast kept my word,' Rev. iii. 8; yet they think, out of a spiritual covetousness, that they have none, because they have not so much as they would, and as stronger Christians have. They misconceit the covenant of grace, where truth goes for perfection. Sincerity is our perfection, which is known by a strife against the contrary, and by a desire of growth in the use of all means. There is not so much as truth where there is not this; where the least is, there is this strife against the contrary, and a desire of growth in a further measure by the use of means.

(3.) Also, they are held perhaps without this persuasion and assurance of the pardon of their sin, because perhaps *they are taken up with other cares.* They do not value this so much as they should do; whereas this is another manner of gift than the most take it for. God vouchsafes not this sweet heaven upon earth, the sense of his love in Christ to any, but it is sought for long, and valued highly, that afterwards we may be thankful for it.

(4.) Again, Perhaps *they are negligent in holy communion with those that are better than themselves;* casting themselves into dead and dark company that want life, who bring them into the same temper with themselves. Many other causes may be reckoned why these acts are severed, that men, casting themselves in the spirit of obedience upon Christ, have not that assurance of the pardon and forgiveness of their sins. Hence we may give an answer to another question.

Quest. Why do some Christians feel more comfort than others do, who have the same means of grace?

Ans. 1. I answer, Because God stirs up in some an higher esteem of it than others; they have more spiritual poverty.

2. Again, There is difference in the ages of Christians; some have had longer experience in the ways of God than others.

3. Again, Men differ in their temper. Some are of a more cheerful temper. Therefore there is a clearer manifestation which helps the work a little, the disposition of the outward man.

4. Again, Men differ in their worldly temper. Men, for want of Christian prudence, cast themselves too much upon the employments of the world, that they suffer the strength of their soul to be carried so one way, that they have no time to gather assurance of salvation. Howsoever, for the main they are conscionable,* yet many such are so worn out with the world, as they differ in heavenly-mindedness and want of care of this, so they differ in assurance and want of God's love.

5. Again, As God hath a purpose to employ men, as he hath great and many things for some men to do, so he suffers them to have a greater measure of assurance and pardon of sin, because he intends they shall go through a great deal of business. Those who he intends shall not go through such employments, he vouchsafes not unto them them that portion of assurance; for these are distinct gifts of the Spirit, to give the spirit of

* That is, 'conscientious.'—G.

faith, to cast ourselves upon Christ, and to give the spirit of assurance. Howsoever the Spirit doth both, as 2 Cor. ii. 14, *seq.*, it teacheth us those good things that we have of God; yet sometimes the Spirit doth not so teach us the good things of God, as it enables to do the works of the Spirit, because God hath divers employments for Christians.

Quest. Another question which some may move is, Why oftentimes it comes to pass that Christians of greater parts want assurance, and sometimes die without it, when many times a weaker Christian of meaner parts has it? Men of ordinary rank do many times die with more assurance than their great teachers. What is the reason it falls out that poor Christians of mean knowledge and gifts have a heaven upon earth, and enjoy a great deal of comfort when they end their days, men of greater parts dying more concealed?

Ans. I answer, Many reasons may be given. Christians are prone too much to value gifts; and those that have are much prone to be proud of them, and to think that grace and gifts go together, when these are often severed. Men of excellent gifts have many times no grace at all; and are given them for the good of others, not for themselves, being proud and barren all their days, not having any feeling of that they can largely talk of with glory to others; because they value these things, and neglect grace, humility, faith, and broken spirits, which things God values more than all gifts. Therefore you have men far above other[s] in gifts and glory of the world, which want this assurance.

Quest. But put the case they be good Christians, yet often they grow proud, and puffed up with great gifts, for the apostle says, 'Knowledge puffs up,' 1 Cor. viii. 1.

Ans. Again, When there is a great deal of good parts in knowledge, there is oftentimes great inquisition made after things which should not be looked after, and many impertinences, wanting knowledge and experience in that which they should more look after.

Then again, men of greater gifts may out of some error look for comfort too much in sanctification, and in the covenant of works, more than in faith. A poor Christian, perhaps out of right judgment, when he stands in need of comfort, may seek it in faith, in justification, casting himself upon Christ, when another man, thinking to find his comfort more in graces and gifts than in casting himself upon Christ in justification, he may justly be deprived of that comfort; whereas we honour God most, whatsoever our graces are, in casting ourselves upon Christ, and ending our days in mercy, making our appeal to mercy; whereas the graces of sanctification and excellent parts are excellent for the good of others, but if we place too much affiance in them, it is just with God we should oftentimes go mourning to our graves. Therefore we must set them in a right place, take them as signs and evidences of our comfort, but not forget to rely rightly on our free justification, and the fruits thereof, as the foundation of comfort, which made Saint Paul, Phil. iii. 8, count all things 'but dung and dross in comparison of the righteousness of Christ.'

Then again, God doth it to shew his freedom, that to whom he pleaseth he will give more assurance, to shew that he is a free giver. Our salvation is according to his good pleasure, so is the feeling of it; some shall have more, some less. God will sometimes manifest his comforts and feeling more to weak Christians than others, as a father or mother shews the greatest love to the weakest child. God knows that strong Christians have other things to support them with than feelings; they can go back, as holy

David doth, to former experiences, and rely upon the word and promise strongly; so he suffers them to support themselves with stronger things than present feelings. Those who are weakest, he vouchsafeth unto them the sweet feeling of his love, as parents dandle and study most to please the sickest and weak children. But we should leave this to God, who gives us what measure he will, and at what time he will. Some he thinks good to keep a long time from feeling this assurance, to humble them for being too bold with sin; and some, likewise, he will keep longer from this assurance, perhaps all the days of their life, because they have been too confident heretofore in touching and meddling with petty sins, which, as pitch and fire, hath burned and defiled them too much; in the mean time supporting them with sufficient grounds of a happy estate, notwithstanding their infirmities; they may be as good Christians after a fall as ever, though perhaps never attain unto that feeling and sense which formerly they enjoyed; for though they have not feeling, yet they may have strong faith, as Christ upon the cross had strong assurance without feeling, when he said, 'My God, my God, why hast thou forsaken me?' Thus we see that assurance may be obtained.

Quest. Now we come to a more principal question, How we may know whether we have the act or no, the first act to yield the obedience of faith, for that is the main. Perhaps a Christian may die in the rage of a fever, or in child-birth, and never have strong assurance. Many go to heaven that never have it.

Ans. 1. But for the first, a man may know in his right temper that he performs the act of faith in affiance, by the reflect act of his soul, if it be not hindered, let him return upon himself; as, how do I know I understand a thing when I do conceive it? Why, by a faculty the soul hath to know it understands. So, how doth a soul know that it believes, but by a reflect act of the soul, whereby it knows it believes when it doth believe, especially when the soul is in a right temper? If a natural soul knows it understands when it understands, and loves when it loves, so doth the soul by the Spirit know that it believes when it doth believe. If, as I said, the soul be not distempered, it is the nature of the conscience to bear witness of the act of itself; and usually God's Spirit, together with the conscience, doth discover it, Rom. viii. 16.

2. But the safest course is to go to the fruit. Know thou hast the act of faith by the fruit. To name one now, because in the next point I shall have occasion to speak more of it. The fruit of this act is seen especially in the greatest temptation; for if a man have a spirit of prayer, then to go to God, and have boldness in extremity, certainly he believes; for faith is the cause of prayer, prayer is the breath and flame of faith. Where there is the spirit of prayer, there is always the spirit of faith; where there is boldness to go to God, there certainly is the Spirit, whereby we may be assured that we have the spirit of adoption, howsoever we find not so evident witness that we are the sons of God. Yet if we have liberty and boldness to go to God in extremity, it is a sign there is the spirit of faith; as we may see in David, Ps. xxxi. 22, 'For I said in my haste, I am cut off from before thine eyes: nevertheless thou heardest the voice of my supplication when I cried unto thee.' He said he was cut off, yet he cried unto God when he was in temptation. Though his flesh yielded, and said he was cut off from God, and that he was not the child of God, yet there was a better principle within him to pray, 'nevertheless I cried unto thee.' So saith Job, 'Though he kill me, yet will I trust in him,' Job xiii. 15.

Job wanted this assurance and feeling, yet notwithstanding, see the act of his faith, 'Though he kill me, I will trust in him.' When in extremity we can trust God, and go boldly to the throne of grace, and not sink in despair, it is a sign that we are in the state of grace, and yield the act of faith. Though we find not that sweet feeling, at length God will be merciful to us; so that after we have yielded the obedience of faith, we shall find the assurance.

Quest. But at what time specially?

Ans. 1. First, Especially when a man hath yielded the act of faith, and cast himself upon God, and a long time lived by faith, then God will seal this believing with the spirit of adoption. When we believe specially against a temptation of distrust, then we usually have the sealing of the Spirit.

Then again, when we have striven with any corruption a long time, God, as a reward of our holding out, will crown our faith and our obedience with a sweet sense of his love. After that Job had strove a long time, at length concluding, 'Though he kill me, yet will I trust in him,' God manifested himself in mercy unto him. The woman of Canaan, after she had striven and wrestled with Christ, at last gets a gracious answer; so when we can subdue our corruptions, and perform holy duties in some strength of grace, in reward of our diligence and care, we have some comfortable revelation of the Spirit, and taste of the life to come more than ordinary, God crowning our diligence with the sweet sense of his love.

And also, when he hath some great employment for us, to encourage us the more, he will give us the more evidence and manifestation of his love, more ravishment; as the disciples which were with Christ in the mount, they did see his glory there, because they were to see him abased afterwards. Those that God means to honour and use in any great employment, oftentimes before he gives them the full assurance of his love.

Again, sometimes in the midst of sufferings, to reward our faithfulness, as Paul in the dungeon was so filled with joy as to sing at midnight; to encourage us, that whatsoever our threatenings and torments shall be in our sufferings for the name of Christ, yet if we yield obedience to God, our comfort shall be more than our discomfort, as St Paul had the spirit of glory, which raised him above his abasement. Thus we see when they are severed, and when God pleases for to vouchsafe the manifestation together with the act.

Now I come to the fourth and last point, indeed the chief of all, *that this particular faith in obedience to Christ, with assurance of his particular love, is that which carries us along all our life of faith unto the day of death.* 'I live,' saith he, 'this life of faith in the Son of God.' Why, what makes him to do so? Oh I have good cause to love Christ and to depend upon him. Why? 'He hath loved me, and given himself for me;' and I feel so much to my soul's comfort, therefore I will wholly depend upon him, in life, in death, and for ever. And indeed particular special faith, if it be joined with some assurance, it is the ground of living by faith. No man can live a holy life by faith, but first he must know that God loves him and Christ loves him. Holy actions spring from love, and are directed by love to the right end, which only love moveth us to intend. How can any spirit aim at his glory whom he loves not first? Can any soul, not knowing whether Christ loves it or not, intend Christ's glory as it should do?

Quest. I beseech you, if we speak of doing or suffering, thankfulness or cheerfulness, especially at the hour of death, whence come all these?

Ans. Come they not from some taste of God's love? When do we love, but when many sins are forgiven? And when are we willing to suffer anything for Christ's sake, but when we know that he hath suffered so great things for us? We count it a glory to suffer anything for Christ, when we know he hath loved us and given himself for us.

Quest. Again, for thankfulness, how can a man be thankful for that he hath no knowledge of? What makes a man thankful for the great work of redemption in Christ, but a particular faith?

Ans. This made St Paul and the rest of the apostles so often to break out, 'Blessed be the God and Father of our Lord Jesus Christ.' He breaks out into thanksgiving that he, together with other Christians, had the Spirit, which doth persuade them of God and Christ's particular love. Then again, for thankfulness for ordinary blessings, how can a man thank God for any ordinary blessing, if he be not assured that it comes from the love of God in Christ? When he is persuaded of this, then he can give thanks, both for the principal and other lesser favours,

Obj. He may think else, What is all this to me? I am but fatted against the day of slaughter. It is good for me to take my pleasure whilst I may enjoy these things, to think I am but as a traitor, who hath the liberty of the prison. This smothers our thankfulness.

Ans. It is the believing soul that is thankful for mercies, and also cheerful in duties. Whence come Christians to be a voluntary people, zealous of good works? as Tit. ii. 11, the apostle sets zeal betwixt faith and works, looking both ways, saying, 'The grace of God, which bringeth salvation unto all men, hath appeared,' by the first coming of Christ, and giving him to death, 'teaching us to deny ungodliness and worldly lusts.' Here faith looks backwards. Then, looking forward, says he, 'Looking for, and waiting for the appearance of the blessed God and our Saviour Jesus Christ, who hath redeemed us, that we might be a peculiar people, zealous of good works.'

Quest. Whence comes a zeal to good works, but when we look to the grace that hath brought salvation and redemption from our sins, and to the glorious coming of Christ?

Ans. When faith looks both these ways, it is set a-fire, it makes us zealous, as Heb. ix. 14. When the heart is sprinkled with the blood of Christ in the forgiveness of sins, then we serve the living God, and are a voluntary and a cheerful people when our hearts are enlarged with assurance.

Quest. Further, what makes a man ashamed of his evil life? What breeds those affections of repentance, grief, and shame mentioned Ezek. xxxvi. 31, 32, 'Then shall ye be ashamed,' &c.?

Ans. When God had once pardoned their sins, and given them many favours, then shall ye be ashamed that ye have served me thus and thus, and grieve that ye have departed from me. So that then do Christians come to have those two penal affections of shame and grief, the two ingredients to true repentance. Why? 'Christ hath loved me, and given himself for me.' As if one should say, Hath he done so? Was my sins the cause of his death, and did his love move him? I am ashamed that I have offended so gracious and so sweet a Saviour. It makes a man weep over Christ. It was my sins which caused his death and torments. This particular faith fills the soul with all divine graces, and it follows Christ, and sees that he did all for us. Then a man sees that Christ was born for him: 'To us a child is born, and to us a son is given,' Isa. ix. 6. It follows Christ in his whole life, and so all that he did was for me. His death, 'He died for me;' his sweating in the garden was for me, my sins caused it. So I see his love, and the foulness of my sins. He was thrust through the side for me, and cried upon the cross, 'My God, my God, why hast thou forsaken me?' My sins had an active power there. He rose again for me, he is now in heaven for me, as carrying me in his breast. The sight and consideration of this draws the soul again unto Christ in repentance for sins, and in all holy duties whatsoever. This is the reason why those Christians that have been pulled out of the fire, and converted oftentimes by a violent conversion, are the most fruitful and loving Christians, as St Paul and others; because they know Christ hath forgiven them a mighty debt, a thousand talents; the more which debt appears to be, the more they know they are bound to God, and to sacrifice and give up themselves to Jesus Christ, that hath discharged so great a debt for them.

When they consider his wonderful love to such as they are, they are inflamed with love again; as in the gospel, the woman who had many sins forgiven her, therefore she loved much. The prodigal young unthrift in the gospel, for whom the fat calf was provided, no question he could not satisfy himself in expressions. God sometimes provides fat calves, great measures of comfort, even for prodigals, and they of all shew most love, they cannot tell how to satisfy him by any painstaking. 'The love of Christ,' saith Paul, 'constrains me, a holy violence moves me, who was a persecutor and a blasphemer,' 2 Cor. v. 14. So the sense of the love of Christ in pardoning of sins will constrain one to a holy violence in the performing of all duties. Why, if any base ends come into a man's mind, in that, is a Christian to regard himself, to seek his own ease, honour, pleasure? No; this consideration, if he have any assurance of the pardon of his sins, will move him to the contrary. Christ died for me; shall I not live to Christ, live to him that gave himself for me? Seek his honour that abased himself for me? So that it quells all base ends, the consideration of Christ's particular love.

So it stirs us up to be at cost for Christ and for his church, at any cost, to sacrifice our Isaacs. He loved me, and gave himself for me; is anything then I can give satisfactory? He gave himself for me, therefore I will give myself for him. This will make a man prodigal, even of his blood, for Christ's sake. When a man is moved to be discontented with his estate, and to doubt of God's providence in particular things, this will help, Christ hath loved me, and given himself for me. Will he not give me all necessaries who hath given himself? So that this stirs up to all duties, cuts the sinews of all spiritual sins, of distrust in God's providence, and all base ends. It stirs me up in particular practice of holy life to go to him for all graces. I have himself, therefore he will give me his Spirit and grace. I have the field, therefore I shall have the pearl.* He hath given me himself, he will give me therefore all that he hath; his Spirit, graces, and privileges, all shall be mine.

Thereupon it is used in all Paul's epistles as a compelling argument, as elect, and by the mercies of God do this; moving them to all spiritual duties from the love of God in Christ. And, dearly beloved, you are dearly beloved; the love that Christ bears you cost him dear indeed; it is a strong enforcement. Saint Peter's argument to this effect is very strong: 'You are not bought with silver and gold, but with the precious blood of Jesus Christ are we redeemed from our vain conversation,' 1 Peter i. 18. You

* 'Treasure,' *not* 'pearl,' a repeated slip of Sibbes's.—G.

see, then, I give you but a taste of it, what strong motives here are to live a holy life, and all fetched from particular assurance; because Christ loved me, and gave himself for me. Hereupon, by the way, we may have a strong argument against the papists, who hold we cannot have particular assurance, for that which is brought as an argument to stir up to holy duties must be known of us. The arguments in this case which serve to persuade must be known. We do not persuade another to a duty by those arguments he is ignorant of. Here he speaks to Christians, as taking it for granted that they knew they were elected of God, and dearly beloved in Christ. That which is an argument stirring up to duty must be known better than the duty, because therefore this is an argument that stirs us up to all kind of duties whatsoever; therefore we may be assured. But here a question may be asked,

Quest. Doth not a holy life and holy actions sometimes proceed from a soul not fully assured? Then what shall we think of those good works that proceed from a Christian without strong assurance? If all obedience in doing and suffering, that is pleasing, comes from faith and assurance, then what shall we think of such works as proceed not from it? If you ask many a good Christian, what assurance have you that Christ hath given himself for you? they will perhaps stagger at it; for a humble broken-hearted Christian is subject to speak worse of himself than there is cause, though he be diligent in good works. What shall we think of such works then, when therewith they are not assured of Christ's love in particular?

Ans. I answer, There can no holy life proceed but from faith; from the first act of it. There must be that; but sometimes we know not our faith, because the reflect act is hindered; we know not we believe when we believe. There may holy duties proceed from a man when he knows not his grace and estate: in which time let him but examine himself, why doth he duties, whether out of love to God or no? Yes. Can he endure God to be evil spoken of? No. Will he allow himself in any known sin? No. In this case, though he dares not say he is assured, yet the things he doth are from some love and desire of glorifying God. Christians do not know their estates often in such cases. They do work from a secret persuasion of God's love, though they know it not. He hath that he thinks he hath not, he works from that he thinks he doth not work from. He works from love to God, when he thinks he doth not, because he thinks he hath not so much as he would have: he works from grace, when he thinks he hath none. A child lives when it knows not that it doth live; a child when it draws nourishment from the mother's breast, doth not know it lives itself, but the lookers on do, because they see the actions of life: so a Christian doth not know that he lives the live of grace, when the lookers on do, because they see spiritual hunger in him, and attending upon the means. Now he himself doth not see it, because of some spiritual covetousness, temptation, or desertion which is upon him. Yet that is a true and gracious action, which issues from a soul that discovers faith, however itself cannot be assured of its estate, there being for the time a suspension of it, through ignorance or other causes; but certainly in such there is faith in the first act of obedience, and some assurance, where there are actions of spiritual life, though they have not that they covet to have.

The best way is to labour for both, for assurance and for the act itself; for howsoever those who have the act only perform good obedience, yet it is not so large, so thorough, so cheerful as it would otherwise be. We ought to desire both that God would give us a spirit of faith, and discover himself unto us, that our sins are pardoned, and that we are accepted to life, to give us strong assurance, that so we may be more plentiful in the work of the Lord. There is no Christian who hath a good heart but he will labour for the second as well as the first; he will labour to make his calling and election sure by all means, that God may have more glory, and smell a more sweet sacrifice from him, and that he may have more comfort in this world. Howsoever without assurance much good may be done, yet not so much as when there is full assurance, for then the soul is carried amain* in obedience to God; doing and suffering is nothing then.

Use 1. Now for the uses of this, seeing that the persuasion of Christ's love to us in special is the spring of all holy life, this serves, in the first place, *to free this doctrine of assurance from scandal.* Assurance then is not the ground of presumption or security. These spring not from a particular faith, for a holy life, the clean contrary, springs from it. None can live a holy life but by a particular faith; and whosoever in particular doth believe the forgiveness of his own sins, will live a holy life, and not put himself into former bondage. It is a sign he is not that person for whom Christ gave himself, that doth enthrall himself into his former courses, unless he repent. We see those of the Israelites who had a mind to go back again into Egypt, did all perish in the wilderness; and those in Babylon's captivity who would not come out when they were called, did perish. It is pity they should ever be delivered that are in love with bondage. Those that will serve and be slaves still, it is pity but their ears should be bored to perpetual servitude. Some will live in their sins, and yet think that Christ died for them. No; whom Christ loves in particular, he gives them grace to lead a holy life, and to be freed from the bondage of their former corruptions. Those that are not redeemed from their vain conversation, are not redeemed from hell and damnation, unless God give repentance. Those both go together. Therefore let it be also a rule of trying and discerning, whether we truly believe that Christ loved us, and gave himself for us, by our care to live to him, and to give ourselves to him back again by a holy life. Wheresoever the one is, there is the other. This is that which may stop the mouths of many, and will shame them at the day of judgment, notwithstanding all their boasting that God is merciful, and Christ died for them. Oh!—their hearts will tell them,—but I have not cared to have the fruit of Christ's death in the governing of his Spirit; I would not have him my king; my conscience tells me I would not have Christ upon those terms: he offered himself to rule me; the minister told me of the danger, but I have preferred some base lust or other, such and such a course, before Christ; I hated to be reformed, I flattered myself with hope of mercy on no ground at all; therefore I never had any benefit by him.

Use 2. To make another use: *if particular faith and assurance be the ground of a holy life, let us labour for it by all means;* and let those that are in the state of grace, let them come to this fire if they will be kindled: if they find themselves dull to holy duties, let them come to this fire. Are we dead spiritually? Are we not so enlarged as we should be? Why, come and consider of the infinite love of God in giving his Son for thee, and the sweet love of Christ in giving himself for thee; and dwell in the meditation of this love. Do not let thy heart go off the consideration of Christ's sweet love, in stooping so low, not only in becoming man, but so low as hardly ever creature was, and all in love. Should not this kindle love in us again? So much the more dearer he should be unto us, the more base

* That is, 'all at once,'—a sea term. Cf. Halliwell, *sub voce.*—G.

he was for us. When we have warmed our frozen hearts with the consideration of his particular love towards us, then we add fire to holy duties. Iron, when it is warm, is fit for any impression ; so our cold hearts, though stiff of themselves, being warmed and fired by the love of Christ, are fit to receive any impression, and to do and to suffer any thing.

When we find ourselves backward to suffer anything for Christ, consider that Christ gave himself; or, if we be not thankful and fruitful enough, consider what was the end of Christ's giving himself, that we should serve him in holiness and righteousness all the days of our lives without fear; and being freed from the fear of death, damnation, and slavish fear, that we should serve him cheerfully in the spirit of adoption and love. I beseech you, in all indispositions of soul, let us make use of this, to come unto Jesus Christ. Experience teacheth any one when they are fittest for suffering, doing of any duty, to resist a sinful temptation to discontent or murmuring, even when they enjoy the assurance of Christ's love, and can read their own evidence that they are God's children, and the members of Christ. Then they are fit for anything. Therefore we should, as the apostle Peter exhorts us, 'give all diligence to make our calling and election sure,' 2 Pet. i. 10. It is a thing which requires all diligence. And the reason why we have it no more, is because we do not give all diligence to attain it. It requires our utmost endeavour, being of the greatest consequence, by which God hath most honour, and we most comfort, because it makes us most fruitful in our conversation.

Obj. But you will say, what then shall we say unto those who cannot say in particular that Christ loved them and gave himself for them? What course shall they take who have not this particular assurance and faith? What grounds have they to come to Christ if they be willing?

Ans. I answer, Those that have it not should labour to have it by all means whatsoever.

Obj. But what ground have I, who have been a wretched sinner, an unworthy wretch, what ground have I for to meddle with Christ, and to believe that he loved me, and gave himself for me?

Sol. 1. Consider, even the vilest that can hear me have the gospel offered unto them. Again, consider that Christ took thy nature, and how many inducements are there in this, for thee to take degrees of this particular faith, to come to it, that thou mayest be in this estate, to glorify God and to enjoy comfort.

Sol. 2. Hath not Christ taken thy nature, not the nature of angels? Oughtest not thou to think that he loves mankind, and why not thee, if thou wilt come in and cast thyself upon him? He is Jesus, a Saviour; and Christ, anointed of God; and Immanuel, to reconcile God and man together.

Sol. 3. Besides, thou sayest thou art a sinner. Why, but alas! * what are thy sins? Is not his righteousness above them? His righteousness is the righteousness of God-man, of a mediator that is God, therefore far above thy sins. Considering then the excellency of his person, believe that the blood of Christ is able to purge thee from all.

Sol. 4. For a further ground for this particular faith, we may think of this inviting of all those who are unworthy: 'Whosoever will, let him come and drink of this water of life freely,' Rev. xxi. 17; yea, those that think themselves farthest off he bids them come: 'Come, all that are weary and heavy laden,' &c., Mat. xi. 28. If thou findest sin a burden, then Christ invites thee, and sends his minister to beseech thee to be reconciled.

* Another example of Sibbes's peculiar use of 'alas!'—G.

Those that stand at the staff's end, he desires them to lay aside their weapons and come in.

Sol. 5. If that will not do, he lays his charge and command upon you to believe. If you will not believe, you add this sin unto all the rest. This is his commandment, that you should believe, or else you are rebels to his commandment. Nay, he counts it a sin worse than the sin of Sodom and Gomorrah, a crying sin, not to come in when the gospel is proclaimed. Therefore never pretend your sins are great and many, but because of his offer, invitation, and command, it being without all restraint of person, sin, and time; even now, whatsoever thou hast been and art, seeing at whatsoever time a sinner repenteth there is no restraint of any sin but the sin against the Holy Ghost; if thou therefore come not in and cast thyself upon Christ, to be ruled by him hereafter, thou hast nothing at all to pretend. It is not the greatness of thy sins, but thy willingness to be still in thy sins, which hinders thee, for the greater thy sins have been, the greater will his glory be in forgiving: 'Where sin abounded, there,' saith the apostle, 'grace superabounded so much the more,' Rom. v. 20. Is it not for the honour of the physician or surgeon, to cure great diseases and sore wounds? A mighty God and Saviour loves to do mighty things: 'He loved me, and gave himself for me.' Did Paul find mercy? Who then should despair when such find mercy? He had sinned against the first table by blasphemies, and against the second by oppression and persecution. Who shall despair then when such as he and Manasseh shall find mercy? Therefore in any case come in, and the greater glory Christ shall have by thy coming. Do not flatter thyself with this, as if thy sins and unworthiness were such as God cannot shew mercy to such a wretch as thou art, or at least will not. No, no; deceive not thyself. Examine thine own false heart, and thou shalt find thou art in love with thy sins and wilt not leave them; and this will be alleged at the day of judgment against thee by thine own conscience, that thou wast more in love with thy sins than with the mercies of God in Christ, and therefore didst willingly remain in thy infidelity. This is the true cause, indeed, of thy backwardness, and not the greatness of thy sins. You see then that there is ground sufficient for any sinner to come in and labour for this particular assurance.

Obj. But put the case, I be not one that Christ redeemed, and God elected.

Sol. Away with disputing, and fall to obey. Put this question out of question, by believing and obeying. Come in and stoop unto Christ, and then it will appear that thou art one that Christ died for; for he gives himself for all that believe in him. Do thou thy duty, bring thou thy heart to rest upon Christ, and to be ruled by him, and then thou wilt put this question out of question, that thou art one of God's elect. The devil holds many in a state of darkness by this delusion.

Obj. If I knew that I were elected, or that Christ died for me, then I could believe.

'Secret things belong unto God, revealed things to us,' saith Moses. Thy duty is, when thou art sought for, invited, entreated, and commanded to be reconciled, then to come in and yield obedience, and in yielding thereof, thou shalt find the fruit of Christ's redemption, that thou art one for whom he gave himself. Thus much is for those who want this particular assurance.

Well then, to draw to an end, for those that pretend they have a particular faith and assurance of salvation, by this they shall know it. These things will follow.

1. *Then thou hast a care to live by faith in the Son of God daily*, and in all estates and conditions; and where this faith and assurance is, it is with care and conscience of duty always. Herein it is distinguished from a false conceit. Where there is no conscience of duty, there is no assurance of particular faith. This particular hath its ground from the general, from the word of God. The word saith that Christ gave himself for all believers; now I know I do believe: he loves all those that love him; and I know I love him, therefore I am beloved of him. Thus true faith goes to the conditions of the word. Those that live in courses contrary to the word have not this faith. 'Be not deceived,' saith the Scripture: 'neither whoremonger, adulterer, nor unclean person, shall inherit the kingdom of God,' 1 Cor. vi. 9. But I am such a one, saith a wicked man, and yet I think to enter into heaven, and that God will be merciful. No; in this case he will not be merciful, because one thus concludes wrongly, by a diabolical persuasion, contrary to the word.

2. Again, *This is with conflict*. You may know particular application where it is, to be good, because it is with conflict against temptations. A man never enjoys his own assurance of Christ's particular love, but with a great deal of conflict. There are two grounds that faith lays:

(1.) That general truth, that whosoever casts himself upon Christ shall be saved.

(2.) The particular application hereof—but I cast myself upon Christ, therefore I shall be saved.

This particular application, which is the work of faith, is mightily assaulted, more than the general. The devil is content that a man should believe the former, but he troubles us in the application, 'but I believe.' He hinders, what he may, the reflect act, that we may not say, I know I believe. Thus, wheresoever the sense of Christ's love is, there is a mighty conflict before it comes. The devil labours by all means to hinder application, for he knows that particular faith brings Christ home, which is all in all. But false Christians go on in a smooth course, are not thus assaulted from day to day. They hope well, not considering that whilst the strong man keeps the hold, all things are in peace; whereas there is no Christian but he finds his particular faith strongly assaulted, more than his general: which is the reason why these two equal truths are not equally believed, because Satan doth hinder the application, the minor part assuming more than the general. Those who have no conflict may fear they have no faith at all, God in wrath and justice suffering them to go on in a smooth uninterrupted state. But all who have experience know what this spiritual conflict with an unbelieving heart means, when it comes to application.

3. Again, a man may know his faith to be true *by his willingness to search himself, and to be searched by others*. He that hath a true sound faith, and particular assurance from thence, is willing oftentimes to search his heart. He would be better and better, labouring to examine himself and to be examined of others. Those who are willing to go on in a still smooth course, because they will not break the peace of their own deluding false hearts, rather thinking all well than to put themselves to the trial, we may know this is but presumption. Where there is true application there is always willingness to search our own evidence; nay, a Christian will be willing, when he cannot find his own evidence, to have the help of other Christians to read his evidence for him, and to tell him of his estate, and is inquisitive, especially when he meets with the skilful in those things.

4. Again, This particular faith *it is with a high prizing and admiration of*

the love of God in Christ, 'who loved me, and gave himself for me.' It is a sign that he hath no interest in this love, that prizes and values other things above it. If one had any assurance of this, he would value it above all other things in the world. He knows that howsoever Christ gives other things, riches, kingdoms, and honours to castaways, that yet Christ gives himself to none but his dear children. Therefore when he knows that he hath interest in Christ, he values him above all things in the world; will part with all rather than with his interest in him, when others go on with a general conceit that Christ died for them and loves them, or howsoever, that yet come what will, they will go on in their pleasures and profits, though their hearts tell them there is something higher in their souls than Christ and his love. You see then that we may all come in who will. There is ground enough to draw them on, if they be not false to their own comfort, and how we may try whether we be assured or not.

Exhortation. I beseech you, therefore, as we desire to do anything that may please God, labour for particular faith and assurance. Would we have our whole course of life to stink before God? I tell you, without this faith it is not possible to please God. Would we have all our life to pass fruitfully, and nothing to run upon our account when we are to die? Oh pray that the Lord would increase our faith; above all, labour for particular faith and assurance, for there is nothing Satan opposes us more in. It is a happy estate, a heaven upon earth. If Satan doth oppose it most, and it be the greatest happiness we can enjoy, it is worth the labouring after.

Let especially those that have ground and cause to be assured, humble broken-hearted Christians, let them by all means not yield to Satan, so much as to obscure the beauty of a Christian life, and to weaken the good things in others; who see them so mopish and cast down as though Christianity were a life of perpetual sorrow, and not rather of perpetual rejoicing, Ps. xxxii. 10, 11. Our blessed Saviour indeed shews that mourners are blessed, but it is chiefly because it tends and ends in joy. There is a command to 'rejoice evermore,' but nowhere is it written, 'mourn continually.' Every one, therefore, ought to express by all means this assurance in the beauty of a holy life. Therefore those who make conscience of holy duties and of their ways, let them not yield to temptations of this kind. If we be in such darkness, let us not trust unto our own judgment, but let us trust the judgment of others. Oftentimes others know more by us than we by ourselves. We ought to yield much to the discerning of Christians in this kind. It is an easy matter when all things go well with us, in a right current, having some feeling, then to have comfort and to be fruitful; but when we are in our dumps, and in the hour of temptation, then it is not so easy. When a tree bears a great deal of fruit, and abounds with leaves, it is an easy matter to say, This is a fruitful tree; but when in winter the sap falls to the root, is covered with snow and frost, the leaves shaken off, and the root that is unseen lies hid, then it requires some judgment and former experience to say, This tree hath life, and is fruitful, though now there appears none. So a Christian may be in such an estate, that he requires the judgment of some others to look upon him. When in such a case, he must go to former times, for God's love is constant, always like himself.

And go to the secret working of grace; when outwardly there appears little, go to the pulses. As, if we would know whether a man who is in a swound hath life and breath, we go to feel the pulses, to see if there be any breath remaining; so in a case of desertion, or seeming deadness of spirit, try which way goes the soul in the desires of it. Is there not a desire to please God? Are there not groans and endeavours with those desires? Are not those desires restless, and thy soul unsatisfied? Thou dost not content thyself with a little faith, but thou desirest more and more, and thou art ashamed, because thou hast so little. This is the pulses beating, and the breathings of a living soul. Yield not to Satan, who tells thee there is no ground for thee to be assured of thy estate. Where we find these evidences of a living soul, we ought to believe there is true life there; which I speak to those, who, without cause, are carried to doubt of their estates.

Obj. And do not tie Christ to thy conditions: If I had feeling and joy, I could believe, and be cheerful; if God would send a messenger from heaven, an interpreter, one of a thousand unto me, or if I had those supernatural suavities that some others have found, and those joys; or were not corruption so busy with me, and I so prone to be overtaken by them.

Sol. But I say unto thee, know this for thy comfort, that whilst thou art clothed with flesh, two fountains will have two streams; that which is born of the flesh will be flesh, and which is born of the Spirit will be spirit still. Inform thy judgment, mistake not, neither say thou wilt not be comforted unless thou find such a thorough mortification of thy corruption, as admits no strong combustion.

Quest. Shall St Paul, that chosen vessel, have cause to cry out, 'O wretched man that I am, who shall deliver me from the body of this death?' Rom. vii. 24, and canst thou think to be freed from them?

Ans. No; deceive not thyself. Thy comfort stands in this, with St Paul, not to allow the evil that thou doest; that sin shall not have dominion over thee, as the apostle speaks, thou not being under the law, but under grace; for saith he in another place, 'The flesh lusteth against the Spirit, and the Spirit against the flesh: and these two are contrary, so that ye cannot do the things which ye would,' Gal. v. 17. Comfort thyself rather from this self-combat, and thence even gather thy assurance, that now sin and thou are not one lump; that a heavenly light hath discovered this thy darkness unto thee; only be sure, sin hath no quiet possession in thee. Complain of thyself, and of thy corruptions, unto thy Christ as fast as they come; lay the burden upon the strongest, and then fear not the issue: that which thou allowest not of, complainest of, and repentest of, shall not, cannot undo thee, but the Spirit at last shall have a final victory. So much for thy corruptions.

And for thy joy and feeling: tie not thy Saviour to thy conditions and qualifications; look to thy desires, thy constant walk, not thy straying fits and thine infirmities; remember that this is Christian perfection, not to live in any gross sin, nor allow of any smaller sin; and for thy imperfections, look up unto that infinite fulness of thy Saviour, and storehouse of all grace, whence we receive grace for grace: 'who is made unto us of God the Father, wisdom, righteousness, sanctification, and redemption,' 1 Cor. i. 30. And then, whatsoever thy emptiness be, a part of his riches being fetched and applied by the hand of faith, will make thee up complete with the best. And know, that as in the state of innocency under the first Adam, his comfort came from within himself upon his obedience or disobedience, so now under the second Adam, the true and substantial ground of thy comfort is without thyself, in thy justification, and application of his all-sufficient merits and righteousness to thy trembling soul.

Walk on therefore in the obedience of faith, having a respect unto all

God's commandments, and then assure thyself the promise is so, thou shalt not be ashamed. Labour as much as thou canst for an higher measure of sanctification and mortification, for this will assure and confirm thy justification the more it is; but with these cautions.

Caution 1. *Be not discouraged at thy small measure whatsoever, if in truth, so as to fly off from applying the riches of thy Saviour and sweet husband unto thee;* in whom, whatsoever thy poverty be, if married to him, thou art complete and rich with the best; for the weaker thou art, thou hast so much the more need of a stronger helper to uphold and sustain thee: it being the law of marriage for the wife to be endowed with all the husband's riches, who is to pay her debts, whatsoever she be, being once married unto him.

Caution 2. Again, *Whatsoever pitch of sanctification or mortification thou obtainest, rest not in that, but on the all-sufficiency of thy blessed Lord Jesus,* who is thine, and so with him all his obedience, righteousness, and merits of his life, death, and resurrection; for there is nothing so exact in thee, but in the time of tentation the devil will find a hole in it, and so make his advantage thereof for thy discouragement; whereas it is clear, 'the prince of this world being come,' as our Saviour says, 'found nothing in him,' John xiv. 30.

Caution 3. And for the remainder, *in those eclipses which damp thy spirit in this thy pilgrimage, by desertion, afflictions, or howsoever, know that precious faith, that it may shine the more, must be tried.* Make then a virtue of necessity, buckle thyself to this business of most importance; strive to obey whatsoever thou feelest; in sense of thy misery believe thy happiness in Christ; in sense of God's anger believe his love, and that he will not be angry for ever. Faith, where it is, is of a victorious nature. Therefore, as in contraries thou wouldst have an evidence of any goodness in thee, in contraries strive against contraries. When thou feelest nothing but matter of discouragement, know the commandment is to believe, and thy duty is to obey. No service can be performed comfortably without some persuasion. Strive then to get all the arguments thou canst of a good estate; and when thou thyself art not able get others to read thy evidences for thee, believe the judgments of others who can tell thee, that these things found in thee come not from a corrupt and false heart.

And withal, *pray for the spirit of revelation,* as St Paul doth, Eph. ii. 17. Pray that God would vouchsafe thee his Spirit, to discover unto thee that love he bears thee, and the riches thou hast in Christ; to shew thee the height, and breadth, and depth, and length, with all the dimensions of his love in Christ more and more; that so the more we grow in the sense and feeling of his love to us, the more we may be inflamed to love him again; for we cannot love him unless we find him loving us first. So beg of him to give us the spirit of revelation. And attend upon the means that doth beget faith, which is especially the word, which is called the word of faith, and look to the examples of others, how God hath brought them from a wicked course of life into a sweet state of grace. Take benefit likewise by the example of those we live with. Use all means to take notice of Christ's particular love. It is the main thing we should labour after in this world. Can we know how long we have to live in this world? What will make us die willingly, but when we know that Christ will have a care of our souls? What made David to commend his soul into God's hands, but this, 'Thou hast redeemed me, O Lord God of truth?' Ps. xxxi. 5. What will make us die in the faith cheerfully? Why, Lord, thou hast redeemed my soul; when at the hour of death we can commend our soul to Christ, Take my soul, blessed Saviour: thou hast redeemed me, thou hast loved me, and given thyself for me; look upon that soul in mercy that thou hast sprinkled with thine own blood. Strive we then for this particular faith, without which we cannot resign up our souls comfortably unto Christ at the last.

NOTE.

(*a*) P. 391.—'It is for rebellion he perishes: as when a malefactor is condemned, who hath a book,' &c. The allusion here, which is a not unfrequent one in Sibbes and his contemporaries, is to what used to be called 'the benefit of clergy,' by which a convicted felon saved himself from capital punishment on being able to read a verse or two from the Psalms on being found guilty. It was restricted originally to the clergy—hence the designation—but was afterwards extended to any person who could read. There was a certain rough justice in its original limitation, in so far as pardon was disallowed to a 'clergyman' unable to read. But altogether it was a strange statute, and more strange than even its original enactment was its vitality—having only been abolished in the year 1827. A reference is made to it by Sir Walter Scott, in his 'Lay of the Last Minstrel,' canto i. v. 24:—

'Letter nor line know I never a one,
Were't my neck-verse at Hairibee.'

G.

A FOUNTAIN SEALED.

A FOUNTAIN SEALED.

NOTE.

'A Fountain Sealed' was originally published in a small volume (12mo) in 1637. Its title-page is given below.* A second edition was issued in the same year, and a third in 1638. The last has a beautiful miniature portrait of Sibbes introduced into an engraved title by Marshall.

G.

* A

FOUNTAIN SEALED:

OR,

The *duty* of the sealed to the
Spirit, and the *worke* of the Spirit
in Sealing.

Wherein

Many things are handled about the
Holy Spirit, and grieving of it:
As also
Of assurance and sealing what it is, the
priviledges and degrees of it, with the
signes to discerne, and meanes to preserve it.

Being

The substance of divers Sermons preached at *Grayes Inne.*

By that Reverend Divine,
RICHARD SIBBES,
D.D. and sometimes Preacher to that
Honourable Society.

LONDON,
Printed by *Thomas Harper*, for *Lawrence Chapman*, and are to be sold at
his shop at Chancery lane end, in
Holborne, 1637.

TO THE TRULY NOBLE AND MUCH HONOURED LADY,

THE LADY ELIZABETH BROOKE,

WIFE TO SIR ROBERT BROOKE.*

MADAM,—Besides that deserved interest your ladyship held in the affections and esteem of this worthy man, more than any friend alive, which might entitle you to all that may call him author, this small piece of his acknowledgeth a more special propriety† unto your ladyship. For though his tongue was as the 'pen of a ready writer' in the hand of Christ who guided him, yet your ladyship's hand and pen was in this his scribe and amanuensis whilst he dictated a first draft of it in private, with intention for the public. In which labour both of humility and love your ladyship did that honour unto him which Baruch—though great and noble—did but receive in the like, transcribing the words of Jeremiah from his mouth, Jer. xxxvi. 4. Wherein yet your ladyship did indeed but write the story of your own life, which hath been long exactly framed to the rules herein prescribed. We therefore that are entrusted in the publishing of it, deem it but an act of justice in us to return it thus to your ladyship, unto whom it owes even its first birth; that so wherever this little treatise shall come, there also this that you have done may be told and recorded for a memorial of you. And we could not but esteem it also an addition of honour to the work, that no less than a lady's hand, so pious and so much honoured, brought it forth into the world; although in itself it deserveth as much as any other this blessed womb did bear. The Lord, in way of recompence, write all the holy contents of it yet more fully and abundantly in your ladyship's heart, and all the lineaments of the image of Jesus Christ, and seal up all unto you by his blessed Spirit, with joy and peace, to the day of redemption!

Madam, we are, your ladyship's devoted,

THO. GOODWIN.‡
PHILIP NYE.‡

* Cf. Vol. I. p. cxix; also, besides the Baronetages, Hanbury, and nearly every History of Puritanism.—G.

† That is, 'proprietorship.'—G.

‡ Cf. Vol. II. p. 3.—G.

A FOUNTAIN SEALED.

And grieve not the Holy Spirit of God, whereby we are sealed unto the day of redemption.—EPH. IV. 30.

WHETHER the words be a command ensuing from authority, or counsel from wisdom, or a caveat from God's care of our souls, it is not material, considering both counsel and caveats of the great God have both force of a command, with some mixture of the sweetness of love. The apostle, as his manner is, from the largeness of his spirit, riseth from a particular dissuasive from corrupt communication in the verse before, to this general advice of not grieving God's Spirit by sin, especially against conscience enlightened. And this dissuasive from evil is enforced from a dangerous effect of grieving the Spirit of God; and the danger of grieving ariseth from this, that it is the Spirit of God, and God himself, whom we grieve, and a holy Spirit: holy in himself, and holy as the cause of all holiness in us; and he that, after he hath wrought holiness in us, sealeth and confirmeth us in that act of grace, until the day of our glorious redemption. So that the grounds of not grieving are from the greatness and goodness of the person whom we grieve, and from the greatness and constancy of the benefits we have by him. To speak something of the person: the Holy Spirit is called a Spirit, not only by nature, as being a spiritual essence, but in regard of his person and office; he is both breathed from the Father and the Son, as proceeding from them both; and by office, breatheth into all that God hath given Christ to redeem and him to sanctify. He is so the Spirit of God in proceeding from God, as that he is God, which whoso denieth deny their own baptism; being as well baptized into the name of the Holy Ghost as into the Father and the Son. And no less a person than God is needful to assure our souls of God's love, and to change our nature, being in an opposite frame. Who can reveal to us the mind of God but the Spirit of God? And herein we may see the joint forwardness both of the Father and Son and Holy Ghost: when both Father and Son join in willingness to send so great a person to apply unto us, and to assure us of that great good the Father hath decreed, and the Son performed for us.

That attribute the Spirit delights in is that of holiness, which our corrupt nature least delights in and most opposeth.* Holiness is the glory

* In margin here, 'Holiness not only an attribute in God, but the excellency of all his attributes. He is holy in mercy, in justice, in goodness, &c.'—G.

and crown of all other excellency, without which they are neither good in themselves, nor comfortable to us. It implies a freedom from all impurity, and a perfect hatred of it; an absolute perfection of all that is excellent. What is it then to grieve such an Holy Spirit, before whom the heavens themselves are impure, and not only the devils tremble, but the angels cover their faces? What shall we think then of them which do not only neglect, but despise, yea, oppose this holiness, and endure anything else? What is hated in the world with keen and perfect hatred but holiness, 'without which yet we shall never see God,' Heb. xii. 14, nor enter into that pure place into which we all profess a desire to enter? There was planted in man by nature a desire of holiness, and a desire of happiness. The desire of happiness is left still in us, but for holiness, which is the perfection of the image of God in us, is both lost, and the desire of it extinguished; and that men might the better drive it out of the world under a form and show of it, they oppose the truth of it, and that with the greater success, because under that great colour the devil and his vicar carry all their devilish policies under a show of holiness. We see in popery, everything is holy with them but that which should be holy, the truth of God and the expression of it. The Man of Sin himself must have no worse title than 'His Holiness.' A show of devised holiness pleaseth man's nature well enough, as being glorious for appearance, and useful for ends. But the truth of it being cross to the whole corrupt nature of man, will never be entertained until nature be new moulded by his Holy Spirit in the use of holy means, sanctified by himself for that end. It is this that makes a man a saint, and civil virtues to be graces; which raiseth things that are otherwise common to an higher degree of excellency. This is that to a Christian which reason is to a man. It gives him a being and a beauty different from all other. It makes every action we do in obedience to God a service, and puts a religious respect upon all our actions, directing them to the highest end.

Now that which the apostle dissuades from is from grieving so holy a Spirit. These truths are presupposed.

First, That the Holy Ghost is not in us personally as the second person is in Christ man, for then the Holy Ghost and we should make one person; nor is the Holy Ghost in us essentially only, for so he is in all creatures; nor yet is in us only by stirring up holy motions, but he is in us mystically, and as temples dedicated to himself. Christ's human nature is the first temple wherein the Spirit dwells, and then we become temples by union with him. The difference betwixt his being in Christ and us, is, that the Spirit dwells in Christ in a fuller measure, by reason that as a head he is to convey spirit into all his members. Secondly, the Spirit is in Christ entirely without anything to oppose. The Spirit always finds something in us that is not his own, but ready to cross him. Thirdly, the Spirit is in us derivatively from Christ. As a fountain we receive grace at second hand, answerable to grace in him. The Holy Ghost was in Adam before his fall immediately, but now he is in Christ first, and then for Christ in us, as members of that body whereof Christ is the head. And it is well for us that he dwells first in Christ, and then in us. For from this it is that his communion with us is inseparable, as it is from Christ himself, with whom the Spirit makes us one. The Holy Spirit dwells in those that are Christ's after another manner than in others in whom he is in, in some sort by common gifts, but in his own he is in them as holy, and as making them holy; as the soul is in the whole body in regard of divers operations, but in the head only as it understandeth, and from thence ruleth the whole body. So the Holy Ghost is in his in regard of more noble operations, and his person is together with his working, though not personally. And though the whole man be the temple of the Holy Ghost, yet the soul especially; and in the soul the very spirit of our minds, as most suitable to him, being a Spirit. Whence the apostle wishes 'the grace of Christ to be with our spirits,' 2 Tim. iv. 22. The best of spirits delight most in the best of us, which is our spirits. In the temple the further they went all was more holy, till they came to the holy of holies. So in a Christian the most inward part, the spirit, is, as it were, the 'holy of holies,' where incense is offered to God continually.* What a mercy is this, that he that hath the heaven of heavens to dwell in will make a dungeon to be a temple, a prison to be a paradise, yea, an hell to be an heaven. Next to the love of Christ in taking our nature and dwelling in it, we may wonder at the love of the Holy Ghost, that will take up his residence in such defiled souls.

2. The second thing presupposed is, *that the Holy Spirit being in us, after he hath prepared us for an house for himself to dwell in, and to take up his rest and delight in, he doth also become unto us a counsellor in all our doubts; a comforter in all our distresses; a solicitor to all duty; a guide in the whole course of our life, until we dwell with him for ever in heaven*, unto which his dwelling here in us doth tend. He goeth before us as Christ did in the 'pillar of the cloud and fire' before the Israelites into Canaan, being a defence by day, and a direction by night. When we sin, what do we else but grieve this guide?

3. The third ground is, that we, the best of us, *are prone to grieve this Holy Spirit.* What use were there else of this caveat? We carry too good a proof of this in our own hearts. We have that which is enmity to the Spirit within us, sin; and an adversary to the Spirit and us, Satan. These joining together and having intelligence, and having correspondency one with another, stir us up to that which grieves this good Spirit.

4. The fourth thing presupposed is, *that we may and ought, by Christian care and circumspection, so to walk in an even and pleasing course, that we shall not grievously offend the Spirit, or grieve our own spirits.* We may avoid many lashes and blows, and many an heavy day which we may thank ourselves for. And God delighteth in the prosperity of his children, and would have us walk in the comforts of the Holy Ghost; and is grieved when we grieve him: that then he must grieve us to prevent worse grief. The due and proper act of a Christian in this life is to please Christ, and to be comfortable in himself, and so to be fitted for all services.

These things premised, it is easy to conceive the equity of the apostle's dissuasive from grieving the Holy Spirit. For the better unfolding of which, we will unfold these four points. *First,* What it is to grieve the Spirit? *Secondly,* is Wherein we specially grieve the Spirit? *Thirdly,* How we may know when we have grieved the Spirit? *Fourthly,* What course we should take to prevent this grief?

1. For the first: *The Holy Ghost cannot properly be grieved in his own person, because grief implies a defect of happiness in suffering that we wish removed.* It implies a defect in foresight, to prevent that which may grieve. It implies passion, which is soon raised up and soon laid down. God is not subject to change, It implies some want of power to remove that which we feel to be a grievance. And therefore it is not beseeming the majesty

* In margin here, 'The Holy Ghost dwells not in us as in ordinary houses, but as temples. The Holy Spirit makes all holy, wherever he comes.'—G.

of the Spirit thus to be grieved. We must therefore conceive of it as befitting the majesty of God, removing in our thoughts all imperfections. *First*, then, we are said to grieve God *when we do that which is apt of itself to grieve;* as we are said to destroy our weak brother when we do that which he taking offence at, is apt to mislead him and so to destroy him. *Secondly*, We grieve the Spirit *when we do that whereupon the Spirit doth that which grieved persons do;* that is, retireth and sheweth dislike and returns grief again. *Thirdly*, Though the passion of grief be not in the Holy Ghost, *yet there is in his holy nature a pure displeasance and hatred of sin, with such a degree of abomination, as though it tend not to the destruction of the offender, yet to sharp correction;* so that grief is eminently in the hatred of God in such a manner as becomes him. *Fourthly*, We may conceive of the Spirit *as he is in himself in heaven, and as he dwells and works in us;* as we may conceive of God the Father, as hidden in himself and as revealed in his Son and in his word; and as we may conceive of Christ as the second person and as incarnate. So likewise of the Holy Ghost as in himself and as in us. God, in the person of his Son, and his Son as man and as minister of circumcision, was grieved at the rebellion and destruction of his own people. The Holy Spirit as in us grieveth with us, witnesseth with us, rejoiceth in us and with us; and the Spirit in himself and as he worketh in us hath the same name; as the gifts and graces and the comforts of the Spirit are called the Spirit; even as the beams of the sun shining on the earth are called the sun, and when we let them in or shut them out, we are said to let in or shut out the sun. We may grieve the Spirit, when we grieve him as working grace and offering comfort to us. The graces of the Spirit have the name of the Spirit whence they come, as the Spirit of love and wisdom. Again, our own spirits, so far as sanctified, are said to be the Spirit of God. So the Spirit of God, not in itself, but in Noah, did strive with the old world, 1 Pet. iii. 19. And so we grieve the Spirit, when we grieve our own or other men's spirits, so far as they are sanctified by the Spirit.

Now the Spirit, as in us, worketh in us according to the principles of man's nature, as understanding and free creatures, and preserveth the free manner of working proper to man; and doth not always put forth an absolute prerogative power, but dealeth with us by way of gentle and sweet motions and persuasions, and leaveth it in our freedom to embrace or refuse these inferior works of the Spirit. And our hearts tell us it is in our power to entertain or reject the motions, which, when we do in our own apprehension, we churlishly offend the Spirit, as willing to draw us to better ways; and we cannot otherwise judge of this but as grieving. God in his dealing with men puts his cause into our hands, that by our prayers and otherwise we may help or hinder him against the mighty. And Christ puts himself into our hands in his ministers and in the poor, counts himself regarded or neglected in them. So the Holy Spirit puts, as it were, his delight and contentment in our power, and counts when we entertain his motions of grace or comfort we entertain him, and when we refuse them we grieve him. And the Holy Ghost will have us interpret our refusing of his motion to be a refusing of him; and not only a refusing of him, but of the Son, and of the Father, whose Spirit he is. Oh, if we did but consider how high the slighting of a gracious motion reaches, even to the slighting of God himself, it would move us to give more regard unto them. As we use these motions, so would we use the Spirit himself if he were in our power. They are not only the ambassadors, but the royal offspring of the Spirit in us; and when we offer violence to them, we kill as much as in us lieth the royal seed of the Spirit.

Obj. It may be objected, when we do anything amiss, we intend not the grieving of the Spirit.

Ans. It is true, unless we were devils incarnate, we will not purposely and directly grieve the Spirit; but when we sin, we will the grieving of him in the cause. No man hates his own soul, or is in love with death; yet men will willingly do that which, if they hated their own souls, and loved death, they could not do worse. 'Why will you perish, you house of Israel?' Jer. xxvii. 13, saith God. They intend no such matter as perishing. God's meaning is, why will you go on in such destructive courses as will end in perishing. If we could hate hell in the cause of it and way to it, as we hate it in itself, we would never come there.

2. For the second point, *wherein we especially grieve the Spirit;* grief ariseth either from antipathy and contrariety, or from disunion of things naturally joined together. In greater persons especially, grief ariseth from any indignity offered from neglect or disrespect, and most of all from unkindness after favour shewed. Thus the Holy Ghost is grieved by us. What more contrary to holiness than sin, which is the thing, and the only thing that God abominates, yea, in the devil himself. But, then, add to the contrariety in sin the aggravations from unkindness, and this makes it more sinful. What greater indignity can we offer to the Holy Spirit than to prefer base dust before his motions leading us to holiness and happiness? What greater unkindness, yea, treachery, to leave directions of a friend to follow the counsel of an enemy,; such as when they know God's will, yet will consent with flesh and blood, like Balaam, who was swayed by his profit against a clear discovery of God's will. We cannot but make the Spirit of God in us in some sort ashamed to think of our folly in 'leaving the fountain, and digging cisterns, Jer. ii. 13; in leaving a true guide, and following the pirate. Men are grieved especially when they are disrespected in their place and office. It is the office of the Spirit to enlighten, to soften, to quicken, and to sanctify. When we give content to Satan, it puts the Holy Ghost out of office. The office of the Holy Ghost is likewise to be a comforter. It cannot therefore but grieve the Holy Spirit, when 'the consolations of the Almighty' are either forgotten, or 'seem nothing' unto us in the pettishness of our spirits; when, with Rachel, 'we will not be comforted,' who, instead of wrestling with God by prayer, wrangle with him by cavilling objections. They take pleasure to move objections, instead of a holy submission to higher reasons that might raise them to comfort, and take Satan's part against the Holy Spirit and their own spirit, and against arguments that are ministered by those that are more skilful in the ways of salvation than themselves. How little beholding is the Holy Spirit to such, who please themselves in a spirit of opposition; and yet so sweet is this Holy Spirit that after long patience, he overcomes many of these with his goodness, and makes them at length with shame lay their hands upon their mouths and be silent. Yet that is one reason they stick so long in temptations, and are kept so long under 'the spirit of bondage.' Those likewise cannot but grieve the Comforter, that leave his comforts and seek for other comforters; that think there is not comfort enough in religion, but will bow down to the world; such as linger after the liberties of the flesh, after 'stolen waters,' as if God kept house not good enough for them. It is a great disparagement to prefer husks before the provision of our Father's [house], and to die—like fish out of their proper element—if we want

carnal comforts. But above all, they grieve the Spirit most that have had deepest acquaintance with the Spirit, and have received greatest favours from the Spirit. When the Holy Ghost comes in love, and we have given way to him to enlighten our understandings; and when in our affections we have tasted of the good things of God, that the promises are sweet, and the gospel is good; when we have given such way to the Spirit, then to use him unkindly, this grieves the Spirit. Where the Holy Ghost hath not only set up a light, but given a taste of heavenly things, and yet we, upon false allurements, will grow to a distaste, it cannot but grieve the Spirit. And this makes the sin 'against the Holy Ghost' so desperate, because there hath been a strong conviction and illumination. Therefore, of all sins, the sins of professors of religion grieve the Spirit most; and of all professors, those that have most means of knowledge, because their obligations are deeper, and their engagements greater. The deeper the affection hath entered, the greater the grief must needs be in unloosing. The offence of friends grieves more than the injuries of enemies. And therefore the sins that offend God most are committed within the church. Where is the greatest sin of all, the sin against the Holy Ghost, committed, but within the church, and where there is the greatest light and the greatest means? Sins against knowledge grieve most, especially if there be a malicious opposing, for there can be nothing to excuse it. The malice of the will maketh the sin of the deeper die, and it is contrary to the Spirit, as it is a Spirit of goodness; and hence is it that presumptuous sins so much grieve the Spirit; for by such sins we abuse the sweetest attribute of God's Spirit, his goodness, and be therefore evil because he is good, and turn his grace into wantonness, the sin of this age. Sins against knowledge are either such as are

(1.) *Directly against knowledge*, as when we will not understand what we should do, because we will not do what we understand. Such put out the candle that they may sin with the more freedom. This kind of ignorance doth not free from sin, but increaseth it. Some men will not hear the word, nor read good books, lest their consciences should be awaked (*a*). This affected* ignorance increaseth the voluntariness. Again, *when we maintain untruths for any advantage, knowing them to be untruths*, as many learned papists cannot but do. What a great indignity is it to the Spirit of God to 'sell the truth,' which we should 'buy,' yea, with the loss of our lives, and to prefer the pleasing of a base man, or some gain to ourselves, before a glorious beam of God!

(2.) Other sins, if we know them to be sins, are sins against knowledge, not so directly, *but collaterally*. Yet this will be the chief aggravation, when our consciences are once awaked, not so much that we have sinned, as that we have sinned against the light; when the will hath nothing to plead for itself. It would, because it would, though it knew the contrary. Involuntariness takes away something of the heinousness of sin. When there is ignorance, perturbation, or passion, there is less sin and less grieving of the Spirit. But when there are none of these, but a man will sin because he will, accounting it a kind of sovereignty to have his will, this will prove the most miserable condition. For not to have the will regulated by him that is the chiefest good, is the greatest perverseness, and will end in desperation.

Quest. Why are voluntary sins so great, and so much grieve the Spirit of God?

* That is, = 'chosen.'—G.

Ans. When there is passion there is some colour for sin, as profit, pleasure, fear to displease, &c. When there is ignorance, there is a want of that that might help the understanding; but when there are none of these, and a man willingly sins, he is more directly carried against the command and will of God. There is nothing puts him on. Yet he accounts it so small a matter that he will do it without any provocation, out of a slight esteem of the good pleasure and will of God.

As common swearers, can they plead ignorance? They know the commandment, 'God will not hold them guiltless that take his name in vain,' Exod. xx. 7. Can they plead perturbation? They do it oft in a bravery, when they are not urged. There is no engagement in that sin of profit or pleasure, but a voluntary superfluity of pride. They would have you to know that they are men that care not for God himself; let God and his ministers take it as they will. Though I have no pleasure or profit by it, yet I will have my liberty. The heart that hath been thus wicked will hardly admit of comfort when it stands in need of it.

We are not said to be ill, because we know ill, but because we will and consent to ill. It is the will that makes up the bargain; sin were not sin else. God hath given us the custody of our own souls, and as long as we keep the keys faithfully, and betray not our souls to Satan, so long we possess our own souls and our comforts. But when he suggests, Do this, or speak this, and we consent, he takes full and free possession of us, as much as in us lies; and God in judgment saith 'amen' to it. God saith, Take him, Satan. Since he will not have my Spirit to rule him, it is fit he should have a worse. The more willingness, the more sinfulness, and the less defence; and God's justice cannot better be satisfied than by punishing them most against their wills, who sinned most with their will. The clearer the light is, and the more advantages it hath, the more we sin.

In this respect it is that sins against the second table grieve more than sins against the first, because here the conscience is more awakened. These be sins against a multiplied light, against the light of nature, light of the word and Spirit; and such sins are contrary to human society. They dissolve those bonds that nature, even by the common relics it hath left, studies to maintain. Though corrupt nature hath no good in it, for we deserved to be like devils, yet God intending to have civil society, out of which he usually gathers his church, preserveth in man's nature an hatred of sins that overthrow society. Such sins, therefore, being committed against more light, wound more; as in case of murder, notorious perjury, theft, &c.

Therefore God oft gives up men, upon breach of the first table, to breaches of the second, that so they may come to more grief and shame, as being the breakers of both tables. Men never fall into the breach of the second table, but upon breach of the first. No man despiseth man's law, but he despiseth God's law first. No man breaks the law of nature, but he despiseth the God of nature. Profane atheistical persons, that glory in the breach of the third commandment by swearing, God meets with them by giving them over to gross abominable sins of the second table; which vexeth them more, though they should not, than sins against the first table; exposing them, besides inward grief, to open shame. Then God opens conscience to tell them, not only that they are to blame for their gross sins, but for the root of them, atheism, profaneness, looseness, which are sins against the first table. This is an aggravation of sins against knowledge, when our knowledge hath been holpen and strengthened by education, by example of others running into our eyes, which is a more familiar teaching than that of rule, and strengthened also by observation and experience of ourselves, and the former strength we have had, against the sin we now commit; and sweetness we have found in the resisting of it. None are worse than those that have been good and are naught,* and might be good, and will be naught, when there is more deliberation and foreknowledge of the dangerous issue, and this also joined with the warning of others. As Reuben said unto the rest of his brethren, 'Spake I not unto you,' &c.,† so may God's Spirit and conscience say to men, Did not I acquaint you with the danger of sin? You are now in misery and terrors of conscience, but did you not slight former admonitions, and helps, and means? Conscience is an inferior light of the Spirit: to do things against conscience is to do them against the Spirit. God spake to me, and I heeded him not. How doth God speak? When conscience speaks, and saith, This is good, this is bad, then God speaks. Conscience hath somewhat divine in it. It is a petty god. It speaks from God. Especially when the Spirit joins with conscience, then God speaks indeed; then there is light upon light.

Upon divers respects some sin may grieve more or less than another. As the Holy Ghost is a Spirit, so spiritual sins grieve most—as pride, envy—imprinting upon the soul as it were a character of the contrary ill spirit. Carnal sins, whereby the soul is drowned in delight of the body, may more grieve the Spirit in another respect; as defiling his temple, and as taking away so much of the soul. Love and delight carry the soul with them; and the more deeply such sins enter into the creature, besides the defilement, the less strength it hath to spiritual duties. Grace is seated in the powers of nature. Now carnal sins disable nature, and so sets us in a greater distance from grace, as taking away the heart, Hos. iv. 11. Hereupon the apostle sets being 'filled with wine,' contrary to being 'filled with the Spirit,' Eph. v. 18. And hence it is the apostle forbids, in the former words, 'unclean communication.' The Holy Spirit is a Spirit of truth, hates hypocrites, being *painted* sepulchres; but as a spirit of purity hates foul livers, and foul-mouthed speakers, as '*open*' sepulchres. They cannot therefore but much grieve the Spirit, that feed corrupt lusts, and study to give contentment, and pay tribute to the flesh, to which they owe no service and are no debtors, and by sowing to the flesh, from which we can reap nothing but corruption, Gal. vi. 8. When our thoughts are exercised to content the outward man, to contrive for the things of the world only, this is to pay tribute of the strength and vigour of our affections to the utter enemy of God's Spirit, and our own souls. When our thoughts run deeply into earthly things, we become one with them.

Who will think himself well entertained into an house, when there shall be entertainment given to his greatest enemy with him, and shall see more regard had, and better countenance shewed, to his enemy than to him? When the motions of corrupt nature are more regarded than the motions of the Spirit? The 'wisdom' of the Spirit, 'which is from above, *is first pure*,' James iii. 17, and maketh us so, and raiseth the soul upward to things above. Christians indeed have their failings; but if a true Christian examine himself, his heart will say, that every day he intends the glory of God, and the good of the state he lives in. He hath a larger heart than a base worldling, that keeps within the sphere of himself, spending all his thoughts there, and consults only with flesh and blood, with profit

* That is, 'naughty' = wicked.—G. † Cf. Gen. xxxvii. 22, and xlii. 22.—G.

and pleasure, to hear what they say. Such baseness cannot but grieve the Spirit, as contrary to our hopes and heavenly calling, which are glorious.

It is a dangerous grieving of the Spirit, when, instead of drawing ourselves to the Spirit, *we will labour to draw the Spirit to us*, and study the Scriptures to countenance us in some corrupt course, and labour to make God of our mind, that we may go on with the greater liberty; when men get to themselves teachers after their own lusts, as many do, especially if they be in place—Ahab shall not want his four hundred false prophets;—when men cut the rule and standard to fit themselves, and not fit themselves to it (*b*). You have some that are resolved what to do, and yet will be asking counsel; and if they have an answer to their minds then they rest; if not, then their answer is, This is your judgment, but others are of a contrary opinion. And thus they labour to make the Spirit of God in his ministers to serve their turn. So did the Jews in Jeremiah's time, Jer. xlii. 2, *seq.*

Some will father those sinful affections that arise from the flesh, and are strengthened by Satan, upon the Holy Spirit, counting wrath that is kindled from hell to be fire of holy zeal coming from heaven. Thus the enemies of religion think they do God service in their massacres.* Such are those that wickedly oppose the ways of God, and yet are ready to say, 'Glory be to the Lord.' Such men study holiness in the show, that they may overthrow it in the power, and will countenance an ill course by religion.

Such also are faulty who lay the blame of an uncomfortable life upon religion; when men are therefore uncomfortable, because they are not religious enough. 'The ways of wisdom are the ways of pleasure,' Prov. iii. 17.

In these times, being the second spring of the gospel, we must take heed of sins *against the gospel*. Benefits, the greater they are, being neglected or abused, bring the greater judgment. The office of the Holy Spirit is, by the ministry, to lay open the riches of Christ, and the glory of God's grace in him. By neglecting so great salvation, and by thinking this favour of God to be a common favour, we sin against both Father, Son, and Holy Ghost; and in that they desire most to be glorified. Such therefore as say to the clouds, 'Drop not,' and to the winds, 'Blow not,' and to the prophets, 'Prophesy not;' that study to keep out the light and sin against it, as discovering them, and awakening them, and hindering them from taking that solace in carnal courses of the world; as opening the eyes of others to know them further than they would be known, and so to lose that respect they would have in the hearts of men: this cannot but grieve the Spirit of God, and move him to take away that truth that we are so far from thinking a blessing, that we are weary of it, and fret against it.

The office of the Spirit is to set out Christ, and the favour and mercy of God in Christ. *When we slight Christ in the gospel, the ordinance and organ of working good in us, the Holy Ghost is slighted and grieved.* Bad is our condition by nature; and what a deal of misery do we add to this bad condition! Are we not all the children of wrath? And have we not since we were born added sin unto sin? Do we not grow in sin as we do in years? Is not God just? and hell terrible? Now God out of infinite mercy having provided a way to free us from the danger of sin; and not

* *E.g.* of Bartholomew, of the Waldenses, of the Huguenots.—G.

only so, but to advance us to life everlasting; and that we should not be ignorant of that he hath done for us, he hath set up an ordinance wherein the Holy Ghost discovers his love. When we slight this, and account it but an ordinary favour, nay, rather a burden, and think the opening of divine mysteries things that may be spared, that there is too much preaching; and what needs all this ado?—this grieves the Spirit, whose office is to lay open 'the unsearchable riches of Christ,' Eph. iii. 8, the infinite and glorious mercy and goodness of God in Christ, wherein God hath set himself in all his attributes to triumph and be glorified. We grieve all the sacred Trinity. God the Father is grieved to see his mercy slighted; God the Son to see his blood accounted common; and God the Holy Ghost, whose office it is to discover these things. This is the common sin of the times and kingdom, which threateneth judgment more than anything else. When the gospel, the blessed truth of salvation, is published, 'the axe is laid to the root of the tree,' Mat. iii. 10, the instrument of destruction; if men slight the mercies of God, entertain not Christ, walk not worthy of the gospel, they shall feel the stroke of his sharp anger. The blood-red horse followeth the white horse, Rev. vi. 4. The white horse is the publishing of the gospel. When God sets himself to glorify himself, in mercy, in the greatest benefits, and we account them nothing, or but common favours, God removes the candlestick; the red horse of blood and destruction follows. And indeed what man will endure his greatest favours and kindnesses to be slighted?

Now a degree in grieving the Spirit this way is, when men will not be thoroughly convinced of their own sinful condition, and of the infinite love and mercy of God in Christ, in the pardoning of them. If God by his Spirit in the ministry, or in a particular reproof, come to men and discover their natural condition, and tell them they are worse than they take themselves to be, they will oppose it and study revenge, as St Paul saith: 'Am I become your enemy, because I tell you the truth?' Gal. iv. 16. This must needs grieve the Spirit.

Again, The Holy Spirit is grieved *when ye have a corrupt judgment of things*, not weighing them in the right balance, nor value them according to their worth. When we esteem any knowledge rather than divine knowledge, any truths but truths that concern Christ, when men look upon grace as contemptible, and prefer other things above it; make a tush at holiness—Give us, say they, gifts and parts—alas, what are all gifts and parts without a gracious heart? Have not the devils greater parts than any man? Are they not called *dæmones*, from the largeness of their understanding? (*c*) If parts and gifts were best, the devils were better than we.—What an indignity is this to the Holy Spirit, to think it better to be accounted witty and politic, than to be holy and gracious!

Again, *Those sins wherein there is plotting aud contriving exceedingly grieve the Spirit*, because they are done in cold blood. David deeply wounded his conscience, and grieved the Spirit, in plotting the death of Uriah, which was the diminution of the credit of David, that the Scripture saith, he was good in all things, except in the matter of Uriah, 1 Kings xv. 5. Why? Because therein he grieved the Spirit most, in plotting and contriving the cruel murder of so good a man. How can they think they have the Spirit of God, that plot and undermine men's estates, to have their wills in unjust courses? or if they have the Spirit, can this be without grieving it? for the Spirit will perpetually suggest the contrary.

Again, We grieve the Holy Spirit *when we commit such sins as we might avoid*, such sins as we have some helps against and least provocation unto. It is a general rule, *Quanto major facilitas*, &c. (*d*). The more the facility of not sinning, the greater the sin. Therefore, when we are tempted to sin, consider what conscience saith: I have been an hearer of the word; what hath the Spirit of God revealed and discovered unto me? He hath shewed that this is a sin. Whom do I grieve by the commission of it? The Spirit of God, and wound my own conscience. And then consider, will that that I sin for countervail this? Do I not buy my sin too dear? Sins are dearly bought with the grieving of the Spirit of God. Therefore, wisely think beforehand what sin will cost.

Men grieve the Spirit *by cavilling against the truth*. The heathen man could say, It is an ill custom to be cavilling against religion, whether in good earnest or in jest (*e*). Yet we have a sect, a generation of men, that are of all religions, of no religion; men of a contradictory spirit, that always take the opposite part, that cavil at the truth to shew their parts. This is too ordinary among the wits of the world.

This grieves the Holy Spirit also, *when men take the office of the Spirit from him; that is, when we will do things in our own strength and by our own light*, as if we were gods to ourselves. Man naturally affects a kind of divinity. It was the fault of Adam. And till God drive him out of himself by his Spirit, and by afflictions, he sets much by his own parts and wit, and thereupon neglects prayer and dependence on God, as if the Spirit had nothing to do with his regiment.* When men set upon actions in the strength of natural parts, perhaps they may go on in their course as civil† men, but never as Christians, to have comfort of their actions, because they will be guides and gods to themselves. If a man belong to God, God will cross him in such ways wherein he refuseth to honour God and to give him his due place. He shall miscarry, when, perhaps, other men shall have success, though it be to harden them to destruction. This is a subtle way by which Satan abuseth men. The life of a Christian is dependent on an higher principle than himself, to rule and guide him.

Another way whereby we commonly grieve the Spirit of God is, *when the mind is troubled with a multitude of business;* when the soul is like a mill, where one cannot hear another, the noise is such as takes away all intercourse. It diminisheth of our respect to the Holy Spirit when we give way to a multitude of business; for multitude of business begets multitudes of passions and distractions; that when God's Spirit dictates the best things that tend to our comfort and peace, we have no time to heed what the Spirit adviseth. Therefore we should so moderate our occasions and affairs, that we may be always ready for good suggestions. If a man will be lost, let him lose himself in Christ and in the things of heaven; for if we be drowned in the world, it will breed discomfort.

Lastly, *Omission or slight performance of duties* grieve the Spirit. The Spirit, as he comes from the Father and the Son, from God, so he is great in himself, being God: 'Offer this to thy king,' saith Malachi, i. 8, when he saw them come negligently and carelessly to the worship of God. When people hear drowsily, and receive the sacrament unpreparedly, this grieves the Spirit, because it comes from irreverence and disrespect. And the reason why so many are dead-hearted, is because they make no conscience of omissions, of drowsiness, of negligent cold performances. Such Christians, what do they differ from carnal men in duties, for they will hear, pray, receive sacraments. He is the best Christian that is the most reve-

* That is, 'government.'—G. † That is, 'moral.'—G.

rent Christian, the most careful Christian, most jealous over his own heart. Usually those are the richest in grace. Even amongst good men, those that are most careful and watchful over themselves, they go away enriched with the greatest blessing. Therefore let us hear, and *so* hear; let us receive, and receive 'thus:' '*So* let us eat of this bread,' &c., 1 Cor. xi. 28. The Scripture fixeth a reverent respect before duty, suitable to the majesty of the great God whose business we are about.

Besides grieving God's Spirit in ourselves, *there is an heavy guilt lies upon us for grieving the Spirit in others*, which is done many ways.

First, By neglecting the grace of God in them, or despising them for some infirmities which love should cover. Contempt is a thing which the nature of man is more impatient of than of any injury. Those that are given this way to wrong others are punished with the common hatred of all.

We likewise grieve the spirit of others *by sharp censures*, and the greater our authority is, the deeper is the grief a censure inflicteth. Many weak spirits cannot enjoy quiet, while they are exercised with such sharpness. They think themselves excommunicated out of the hearts of those in whose good liking they desire to dwell.

Again, Those that are *above others* grieve the spirits of those under them *by unjust commands;* as when masters press their servants to that which their conscience cannot digest, and so make them sin, and offer violence to that tender part.

Again, We grieve the spirit of others, when those that *are inferior* shew themselves untractable to those above them in magistracy or ministry, when they make them spend their strength in vain. Thus the Spirit of God in Noah strove with the old world, 1 Pet. iii. 19. Our duty is, therefore, to walk wisely in regard of others; and if it be a duty to please men in all things lawful in the way of humanity, much more ought we to please Christians in those things wherein we do not displease God, as being joined in communion with them in the same spirit. Yet here we must remember that it is one thing to cross the humour and offend the pride of another; and another to grieve the Spirit in him. No cures can be wrought without grief in that kind; and if we grieve not their spirits when such humours prevail in them, we shall grieve our own for neglect of duty.

And in the last place, this causeth another grief, *when those that are good watch not over their ways.* The Spirit is grieved for the reproaches of religion that come from the wicked; for what say they? Doth religion and the Spirit teach you this? Thus Christians make the name of God to be ill spoken of; and this grieves the Spirit, and will grieve them if they belong to God. Oh, wretch that I am, that I should open the mouths of others, and grieve the Spirit of God, not only in myself, but in others, because he is grieved by me!

Scandalous courses; either by unreasonable use of our liberty, without respect to the weakness of others, or by actions that are in themselves evil or of ill report. By such actions we grieve the spirit of others. An ill example always either grieveth or infecteth. The spirit of Lot was grieved for the unclean conversation of the Sodomites, which no question hastened their ruin, 2 Peter ii. 7.

How shall we know when we grieve the Spirit? We may know that by the sins before mentioned as the cause of grief. Again, the Spirit will bring report of its own grief. We may know when we have offended a friend, when he leaves our company; so we may know we have discontented the Spirit by spiritual desertions, both in respect of assistance in the performance of duties, and resisting temptations, and bearing afflictions; as also in respect of comfort, as when we find a strangeness and dulness of disposition, unless it be from some natural distemper of body, we may fear all is not well.

When we find a proneness to divert* to other comforts, and to hold correspondency with carnal persons, and delight not as formerly in the communion of saints, but find an indifferency for any acquaintance; when we drive hardly, and our wheels fall off;† when conscience will not let us omit good duties, and yet we want the oil of the Spirit to make us strong and nimble in the performance of them, whereupon they come not off with that acceptance to God or our own spirits: these indispositions shew we have not used the Spirit well, whom otherwise we should find a Spirit of strength, a Spirit of comfort, a quickening Spirit.

The issues of grieving the Spirit will prove very dangerous, for the Spirit may justly *leave us to our own spirits and deceitful hearts*, which, as they are arch-flatterers, so will prove arch-traitors to us, and so let in a worse guest into our souls. The ill spirit is always ready presently to take possession, who, by joining with the stream of our corruptions, may please us for a time, but will destroy us for ever.

When we grieve the good Spirit of God, and cause him to leave us, our soul is left as a hell; for what is hell but the absence of God in his favour and mercy?

Again, We cannot grieve the Spirit of God in doing anything against it *but it will grieve us again*, and, being a Spirit, may fill our spirits with that grief that may make our conditions a kind of hell upon earth. Few reprobates feel those terrors here that the godly oft do by their bold adventures; for besides the terrors of the natural conscience, they have the Spirit to set them on, and that Spirit which had so well deserved of them before, which cannot but increase the horror and shame. In hell itself this will be the bitterest torment, to think of refusing mercy, mercy pressed and offered with all love. A careless spirit oft proves 'a wounded spirit,' and that, 'who can bear?' Prov. xviii. 14, until he that woundeth healeth again, by giving grace to afflict ourselves, and wait his good time to take pity of us. That which we say of conscience is true. It is our best friend, and our worst enemy. If a man's conscience be his friend, it will make all friendly to him (*f*). It will make God his friend, affliction his friend; nothing can sit at the heart to grieve him. But if a man's conscience turn his enemy, there need no other enemies be sought out. He hath enow in his own heart, his own tormenting conscience tearing itself. This may be as truly said of the Spirit of God, who is above conscience. If we make him not our best friend, we are sure to have him our worst enemy, that sets all other enemies upon us. Displeasure is as the person is. 'It is a fearful thing to fall into the hands of the living God,' Heb. x. 31. 'Who knows the power of his wrath?' Ps. xc. 11. It is a powerful wrath. No creature hath power over the spirit immediately, but this Spirit of spirits, who can fill the soul, the whole soul, and every corner of it. Being adequate to the soul, as large as the soul and larger, he can fill it with wrath that shall burn to hell; and who shall take off the wrath of God when the Spirit of God sets it on once?

Quest. Whence is it that we grieve the Spirit?

Ans. Because there is a cursed principle in us, always active, which is not perfectly subdued in this life. Death is the accomplishment of morti-

* That is, 'turn aside.'—G

† Cf. Exodus xiv. 25.—G.

fication; but while we are here, this corruption in us will alway be working. 'The flesh lusteth against the Spirit,' Gal. v. 17. The flesh is an active busy thing. It bestirs itself. Now, when contraries are so near as the flesh and Spirit, in the same soul, they must needs thwart and grieve one another continually.

Quest. It may be demanded how far forth a child of God may grieve the Spirit, and yet remain the child of God?

Ans. In answer to this know, *that we must not judge of sin by the matter in which, but by the spirit from which, sin is committed.* There is no sin so gross but the saints of God may fall into it; but yet the child of God is hindered by a contrary law of the Spirit from yielding full consent before, or taking full delight in a sin, or allowing or persisting after. And though, in regard of ingratitude, the sin of a godly man admits of a greater aggravation than the sin of others, yet setting that aside, the sin itself of a godly man is less, for his temptations be stronger, and Satan's malice more eager against him, and his resistance of sin greater, all which doth abate the heinousness of the guilt. The more resistance from within argues a stronger party from within in the godly; the force of sin is broken from within. Take a godly man at the worst, there is some work of the Spirit in him, that in some measure is answerable to the counsels and motions of the Spirit without him. The Holy Spirit hath some hold in him, by which he doth recover him. A wicked man proceeds from grieving to quenching, and from quenching to resisting. The Spirit hath no party, no side in him; and therefore, when the Spirit is gone, farewell. They are glad that then they can follow their pleasures and sins without check.

Sometimes God leads his children to heaven through some foul way, by which he lets them see what need they have of washing by the blood and Spirit of Christ, which otherwise perhaps they would not so much value, when they grieve the Spirit, and the Spirit thereupon grieves them, and that grief proves medicinal. The grief which sin breeds, consumes the sin that bred it. We are in covenant with so wise and powerful a God, that overrules even sin itself to serve his purpose in bringing his to heaven. They have that in them whereby they hate the sin they do, and love the goodness they do not; whereas others hate the good in some respects they do, and love the ill which they dare not commit. Howsoever they are drawn into sin, yet they will never break the conjugal bond betwixt Christ and their souls, so far as that sin should reign in them as a commanding lord, they will not forsake their oath of allegiance to serve willingly a contrary king. They may presume sometimes upon Christ, thinking they have a balm ready to cure the wound again,—as some, to shew the virtue of their oils, do make wounds in themselves,—the deceitfulness of sin seducing them. But God ever chastiseth this boldness, and taketh such a course with them, that it ends in taking the greater shame to themselves, and by so much as they have been more presumptuous. The loss of comfort, and the sense of sorrow they feel, makes them say *from experience*, that there is nothing gotten by sin, and that it proves bitterness in the end.

Again, Though they are kept from sins, in some sense, presumptuous, *yet they are always kept from that 'great offence.'* Though they may commit *a* sin against the Holy Ghost, yet they can never commit *the* sin against the Holy Spirit, because this is a sin of malice after strong conviction; expressed in words dipped in malice by 'a tongue set on fire by hell,' James iii. 6, and in actions coming from an opposite spirit, and tending to opposition, and to bitter persecution, if their malice be not greater than their power. And it ends always in impenitency, by reason they despise that grace, and cast away that potion whereby they should recover. Their pride will not stoop to God's way.

Thirdly, *After such fearful relapses, darkness in the understanding and rebellion in the will increaseth*, sin grows stronger, and they weaker and weaker to resist.

Fourthly, *Satan being once cast out by some degree of illumination and reformation, brings 'seven devils after, worse than himself,'* Mat. xii. 45. When they see their former courses stand not with their lusts and hopes, they take a contrary course, and so fall to bitterness in the end.

There is a double miscarriage about this sin.

(1.) *Some are too headlong in their censures of others;* whereas the greater the sin is, the greater caution should be in fastening it upon any, especially whose spirits we are not thoroughly acquainted withal, considering so many things must meet in this sin.

(2.) The second miscarriage is, *in an ungrounded censure of ourselves.* There be three things that fear frees us from the danger of. First, Fear lest the time of our conversion be past, because we have so often grieved the Spirit; whereas if their time were past they would be given up to a careless security. A second is, fear of some judgment, which God stirs up in the heart to prevent the judgment that we may not feel that we fear; because fear stirs up care, and care stirs up diligence to avoid what we fear. A third is, fear lest we have committed the sin against the Holy Ghost, which shews we have not committed that sin. It is never committed but without fear and with delight. In these cases we need fear them least that fear themselves most.

The fourth point is, What course we should take to prevent this grieving of the Spirit.

1. *Let us give up the government of our souls to the Spirit of God.* It is for our safety so to do, as being wiser than ourselves, who are unable to direct our own way. It is our liberty to be under a wisdom and goodness larger than our own. Let the Spirit think in us, desire in us, pray in us, live in us, do all in us; labour ever to be in such a frame as we may be fit for the Spirit to work upon; as Nazianzen saith of himself, 'Lord, I am an instrument for thee to touch' (*g*). A musical instrument, though in tune, soundeth nothing unless it be touched. Let us lay ourselves open to the Spirit's touch. Thus Saint Paul lived not, but Christ lived in him, Gal. ii. 20. This requires a great deal of self-denial, to put ourselves thus upon the guidance of the Spirit. But if we knew what enemies we are to ourselves, it would be no such hard matter.

2. Secondly, *Study to walk perfectly in obeying the Spirit in all things;* which requires much circumspection in knowing and regarding our ways; and then we shall find the Spirit ready to close with us, and tell us, 'This is the way, walk in it,' Isa. xxx. 21. And upon obedience we shall find the Spirit encouraging us by a secret intimation, that this or that is well done. Thus Paul was said to be 'bound in Spirit,' Acts xx. 22. The Spirit so put him on, that he could not withstand the motions, until the execution of it. We must take especial heed of slighting any motion, as being the Spirit's messenger. They are God's ambassadors, sent to make way for God into our hearts; therefore give them entertainment. Many men, rather than they will be troubled with holy motions, stifle them in the birth, as harlots, that to avoid the pain of child-birth, kill their fruit in the womb. Let us take heed of murdering these births of the Spirit. But

seeing Satan will oft interrupt good motions by good motions, that he may hinder both,

Quest. How shall we know from whence the motions come?

Ans. 1. *When two good motions arise, seeming diverse, the Spirit of God carries strong to one—and that is from God—more than to the other.* Good motions are either raised up in us, or sent unto us by the Spirit. Both these, if they be raised by the Spirit, will carry us to God. They will rise as high as the spring is whence they come. What ariseth from ourselves endeth in ourselves.

2. Those motions that the Spirit stirs up from within *come from sanctified judgment and estimation of what they are moved to.* Other motions are hasty, and gone before they have their errand. Holy motions are constant (as strengthened from constant grace within), till they see the issue of what they are moved to. Other motions are like lightning, and sudden flashes, that leave the soul more dark and amazed than before. Holy motions are answerable to the duties of our calling. Other motions oft lead us out of the compass of our calling.

3. The Spirit moveth in the godly: *first, by a dwelling in them, and working in them gracious abilities; and then draws forth those abilities to good actions.* But the Spirit dwelleth not in others, nor produceth any sanctified abilities in them, but only moveth them sometimes to good actions, without changing of them.

4. The Holy Spirit's motions *are seasonable.* Other motions oft press upon us to disturb an holy duty. The breath of the Spirit in us is suitable to the Spirit's breathing in the Scriptures; the same Spirit doth not breathe contrary motions.

5. Motions of the Spirit, when they come in favour, *carry their own evidence with them, as light doth.* The motions of the Spirit are sweet and mild, and lead us gently on. They are not ordinarily violent raptures, removing the soul from itself, but leave in the soul a judgment of them, and of other things.

6. Again, The Spirit moveth us so to duties of religion *as agree with civil honesty and charity to our neighbours.** Those therefore know not what spirit they are of, who, under a pretence of zeal, will be uncivil and cruel, shewing they are not led by that Spirit that appeared in the shape of a dove. Both tables in this are one, that they come from one Spirit; and 'the second is like the first,' and requires love. And because all graces and duties come from the same Spirit, therefore one duty never crosses another; but the wisdom of the Spirit moves to all holy duties in their several and suitable places.

7. Motions, for the matter good, yet may be carnal in *regard of self-confidence from whence they come.*† That which Peter resolved upon was good, but confidence in himself marred it. Those motions which the Spirit stirs up are carried along in relying upon assisting grace. So much for that question.

3. Again, If we would not grieve the Spirit, *let us take heed of being wanting to the Spirit's direction.* The flesh here will make a forward objection, 'We can do no more than we can.'

Ans. The Spirit is always beforehand with us, preventing‡ us with some knowledge and some ability, which if we join with the Spirit in putting forth, the Spirit is ready to concur with us, and lead us further. And our

* In margin here, 'Orderly.'—G.

† In margin here, 'Dependent on God.'—G.

‡ That is, 'anticipating.'—G.

conscience will tell us so much, that if we do otherwise it is not for want of present assistance or privity, that the Spirit will deny us strength if we put ourselves upon it. Our own hearts, though deceitful, will tell us that we do what we do out of willingness, preferring some seeming good before the motion of the Spirit. Herein we carry in our conscience that which will quit God and condemn ourselves. There is not the worst man, whose heart runs away from God, but God follows him a great while with sweet motions, though such be the invincible stubbornness of the heart, that it will not yield. This will take away all excuse, as Saint Austin argues well (*h*). If I had known, saith a wicked man, I would not have done thus. Saith he, the pride of thy heart suggests that. Hadst thou not motions and admonitions that told thee the danger of it? If the Spirit, even in the worst actions, concur so far as they are actions and motions, may we not think that he is much more ready to concur with holy motions stirred up first by himself? If the Spirit be willing to concur in natural actions, much more in spiritual, whereunto itself is the first mover. The Spirit leaves not us till we leave the Spirit.

4. When the Spirit suggests good motions, *turn them presently into holy resolutions.** Is this my duty, and that which tends to my comfort? Certainly I will do it. Let not these motions die in us. How many holy motions are kindled in hearing the word, and receiving the sacraments, &c., which die as soon as they are kindled for want of resolution! Therefore let us not give over till these motions be turned into purposes, and those good purposes ripened to holy actions, that they be not nipped in the blossom, but may bring forth perfect fruit. Let us labour to improve these talents to the end for which they are sent. Are they motions of comfort? Let us use them for comfort. Are they motions tending to duty? Let us make conscience to do our duty: let not our despairing hearts cross the Spirit in his comforts, nor stand out stubbornly as enemies against our duty, for that is to cross God, and to nip his motions in the bud.

5. Let the Spirit *have full scope, both in the ordinances, and in the motions stirred up by the ordinances.* This is the way to make the ordinances and the times glorious, but the liberties of the gospel are contrary to the liberties of the flesh. It turneth all things upside down, and men out of themselves. Hence is it that there is nothing so much opposed by the spirit of the world, as the purity and power of the gospel, which is a sufficient prejudice of an ill condition that all such men are in. But there is another spirit in gracious men. They are the children of light, and love it. If we would not grieve the Spirit, we must be willing to bring ourselves under all advantages of the Spirit's working; as conversing with those that are spiritual, and especially attending on those ordinances wherein the Spirit breatheth; wherein we may meet the Spirit. The walks of God's Spirit are, in the means of salvation, hearing the word preached, and holy communion one with another. The word and Spirit go together. Therefore if we will have the comforts of the Spirit, we must attend upon the word. Men grieve the Spirit by neglecting the word, and holy conference, &c. It is with the word and Spirit as with the veins and arteries. The veins have arteries, that as the veins carry the blood, the arteries carry the spirits to quicken the blood. The word is dead without the Spirit, and therefore attend on the word. And then wait on the Spirit to quicken the word, that both word and Spirit may guide us to life everlasting. Motions of this kind come from the Spirit; as it is said of old Simeon, that

* In margin here, 'Cherish holy motions.'—G.

he came by the motion of the Spirit into the temple, Luke ii. 27. John was 'in the Spirit on the Lord's day,' Rev. i. 10. Our manna falls most then. Christ's Spirit and word dwell together in the heart. Therefore the apostle useth the dwelling of Christ in us and the word indefinitely.* Faith wrought by the word lays hold upon Christ, and brings him into the soul, and keeps him there. It is a blessed thing when the Spirit in the ordinance and the Spirit in our hearts meet together. This is the way to feed and cherish the Spirit in us, and to put oil as it were into our lamp; because the Spirit, as it is in us, is thus nourished, even as the fire, though in its own element, feedeth upon nothing; yet with us here below it is maintained with fuel, otherwise dieth and goeth out. Take heed of slighting any help of faith that God affords us, as wicked Ahaz, Isa. vii. 3, *seq.* God offered him, for the strengthening of his faith, a sign from heaven, or from earth, or any other creature. Oh no! he would not tempt God. He seemed a pious man; he would not tempt God; but what saith the prophet? 'Is it little for you to despise me? but you will grieve God;' insinuating, that when we despise those helps God hath given, we grieve the Spirit of God. Those that neglect the word and sacrament, what do they despise? A poor minister? and neglect bread and wine? No. They despise God himself, who knows better than ourselves what need we have of these helps.

6. Again, *When we find the Spirit not assisting and comforting as in former times, it is fit to search the cause,* which we shall find some slighting of holy motions, or the means of breeding of them; or yielding to some corruption which we are more especially addicted unto, or some sin unrepented of, which we take no notice of. It is good, therefore, to search our souls to the bottom. There may be some hidden corruption lying in the soul, which may undermine our grace and comfort; there may be a privy thief that robs us of all. And besides beloved and secret sins, it is good to bethink ourselves of old sins, which perhaps hitherto we have but outwardly thought of; and God is willing by some deadness and trouble of spirit, to mind us of renewing of sorrow for them. For want of strict accounting with ourselves, God calls us to these arrearages and back-reckonings, as we see in Joseph's brethren, Gen. l. 15. If we find not that sweetness of communion with the Spirit that formerly we enjoyed, bethink ourselves when and wherein we lost it, that we may meet the Spirit again in these ways wherein we found him before we lost him, and take heed of those courses, in the entrance of which we found the Spirit leaving us.

7. Again, *Take heed of little sins,* which we count lesser sins perhaps than God doth. We weigh sin in our own balance, and not in his, whereas no sin is to be accounted little; for if it were once set upon the conscience, and the wrath opened due unto it, it would take all comfort from us. And therefore we must judge of sin as the Spirit doth, if we would not grieve the Spirit. As the communion of the Spirit is of all the sweetest, so the preserving of it requires most exact watchfulness and thorough understanding of ourselves. Take heed of the beginning of sin. When any lust ariseth, pray it down presently; say nay to it; let it have no consent; be presently humbled; otherwise we are endangered by yielding to grieve, by grieving to resist, by resisting to quench, by quenching, maliciously to oppose the Spirit. Sin hath no bounds but those which the Spirit puts, whom therefore we should not grieve. And let us look to the head and spring of sins, whereby we grieve the Spirit of God; not to the sin so

* Qu. 'indifferently'?—Ed.

much as to the root. We are angry with ourselves for being passionate, but what is the cause of passion? It comes from pride. Jonah was a passionate man; in that measure that he was passionate he was proud. He was loath to be shamed when he had said, 'Nineveh shall be destroyed,' Jonah iv. 11. He thought upon the sparing of them he should be discredited; and he preferred his credit before the destruction of a populous city. So there is much depraving and detraction in the world; and thereupon brawls and breaches. What is the cause? A spirit of envy, and ofttimes a spirit of pride. So men run into the danger of others by wronging them. What is the cause? Worldliness, base earthly-mindedness. Men think not of the root of sin, but dwell upon the act done. We should be led from the remote streams to the spring and source of all, and bewail that especially.

This care will be helped by spiritual wisdom, whereby we may discern both wherein we have grieved the Spirit, and wherein for the time to come we may. We cannot maintain friendship in perfect and sweet terms with any whose dispositions we know not; what will please or displease them. Therefore we should study the nature and delight of the Spirit, and wherein we are prone both to forget ourselves and the Spirit. We esteem not much the friendship of those who are so much friends to themselves, as they pass* not much whether friends be contented or discontented. The Spirit dwells most largely in that heart that hath emptied itself of itself. The Israelites felt not the sweetness of the manna till they had spent their flesh-pots and other provision of Egypt. The nature of God's Spirit is holy; as it is holy, so [it] delighteth only in holy temples. Those, therefore, that set up any 'idol of jealousy' in their souls against God, that do not 'preserve their vessels in holiness,' cannot think of any communion with the Spirit. The Spirit is jealous of our affections, and will have nothing set up in the heart above God. Though the Spirit stoops to dwell in us, yet we must not forget the respect due to so great a superior, but reverently entertain whatever comes from him. Reverence and obedience is the carriage due to a superior, and where the distance is not kept a breach will follow. We should reverence ourselves for the Spirit's sake, and think ourselves too good for any base lust to lodge in. The heart that the Spirit hath taken for itself should turn off all the contrary motions with abomination. What should pride and envy and passion do in an heart consecrated to the Spirit of meekness and holiness?

Upon any breach we must look by renewing repentance and faith in Christ, to renew our peace with God, before we can expect the grace and comfort of the Spirit. For as the Spirit cometh from the Father and the Son, and is procured by the death and satisfaction of the Son to the Father, without which we could never have expected the gift of the Spirit, so still we must have an eye to this satisfaction by Christ, and reconciliation through it, before we can recover communion with the Spirit, as being the best fruit of the love of God reconciled through Christ. We see David in the 51st Psalm first importunes God for mercy again and again, and then 'for the Spirit,' and for 'the joy of salvation.'

And take heed that nothing come in nor go out of our souls that may grieve the Spirit of God. Some things come in to us that grieve the Spirit, the corruptions we receive from others. Some things come out of our hearts that grieves God's Spirit, as corrupt thoughts and speeches. That indeed is the scope of this place, 'Let no corrupt communication come out

* That is, = consider.—G.

of your mouths,' &c., and then follows, 'And grieve not the Holy Spirit of God.' And after again he saith, 'Let all bitterness, and wrath, and clamour be laid aside,' insinuating that one way of grieving the Spirit is by ill and corrupt language. We can never talk with company that is not spiritual, but they will either vex and grieve us, or taint and defile us, unless it be in such exigencies of our calling as requires our converse with them. But I speak of a voluntary choice of such as favour not good things. Many men, to please their own carnal spirits, and the carnal spirits of others, they vent that that is against conscience, and against that that is higher than conscience, a more divine principle, the Holy Spirit of God; loose carnal speakers are people void of the power of religion.

Obj. Let no man say, Here is ado, indeed! duty upon duty. This will make our life troublesome.

Ans. The life of a Christian is an honourable, a comfortable, sweet life. Indeed, it requires the most care and watchfulness of any life in the world, being the best life. It is begun here, and accomplished in an everlasting life in heaven. Nothing in this world, neither our estates nor our favour with great persons, can be preserved without watchfulness; and shall we think to preserve the chief happiness of our souls without it, having so many enemies without and within, that labour to draw us into a cursed condition?

Therefore, to stir us up to the practice of these duties, that we may give contentment to so sweet a guest, consider what reason we have to regard the Spirit and his motions, from the good we have by them.

The Holy Spirit of God is our guide. Who will displease his guide, a sweet comfortable guide, that leads us through the wilderness of this world? As the cloud before the Israelites by day, and the pillar of fire by night, so he conducts us to the heavenly Canaan. If we grieve our guide, we cause him to leave us to ourselves. The Israelites would not go a step further than God by his angel went before them. It is in vain for us to make toward heaven without our blessed guide. We cannot do, nor speak, nor think anything that is holy and good without him. Whatsoever is holy and pious, it grows not in our garden, in our nature, but it is planted by the Spirit.

There is nothing in the world so great and sweet a friend that will do us so much good as the Spirit, if we give him entertainment. Indeed, he must rule. He will have the keys delivered to him; we must submit to his government. And when he is in the heart, he will subdue by little and little all high thoughts, rebellious risings, and despairing fears. This shall be our happiness in heaven, when we shall be wholly spiritual, that 'God shall be all in all.' We shall be perfectly obedient to the Spirit in our understandings, wills, and affections. The Spirit will then dwell largely in us, and will make the room where he dwelleth sweet and lightsome and free, subduing whatsoever is contrary, and bring fulness of peace and joy and comfort. And in the mean time, in what condition soever we are, we shall have suitable help from the Spirit. We are partly flesh and partly spirit. God is not all in all; the flesh hath a part in us. We are often in afflictions and under clouds. Let us therefore prize our fellowship with the Spirit. For are we in darkness? He is a Spirit of light. Are we in deadness of spirit? He is a Spirit of life. Are we in a disconsolate estate? He is a Spirit of consolation. Are we in perplexity, and know not what to do? He is a Spirit of wisdom. Are we troubled with corruptions? He is a sanctifying, a subduing, a mortifying Spirit. In what condition soever we are, he will never leave us till he hath raised us from the grave, and taken full possession of body and soul in heaven. He will prove a comforter when neither friends, nor riches, nor any thing in the world can comfort us. How careful should we be to give contentment to this sweet Spirit of God!

No Christian is so happy as the watchful Christian that is careful of his duty, and to preserve his communion with the Holy Spirit of God; for by entertaining him, he is sure to have communion with the Father and the Son. It is the happiest condition in the world, when the soul is the temple of the Holy Spirit; when the heart is as the 'holy of holies,' where there be prayers and praises offered to God. The soul is as it were an holy ark; the memory like the pot of manna preserving heavenly truths. It is an heavenly condition. A man prospers to heavenward when the Spirit of God is with him. You know Obed-Edom, when the ark was in his house, all thrived with him, 2 Sam. vi. 12; so while the Spirit and his motions are entertained by us we shall be happy in life, happy in death, happy to eternity. For it it is he

'By which you are sealed to the day of redemption.'

The apostle sealeth this grave admonition by an argument taken from the Spirit's sealing of them 'to the day of redemption.'

We are all by nature in bondage to sin and corruption. We are all redeemed from sin by the first coming of Christ, and are to be redeemed from corruption by the second.

There is a day appointed for this glorious work. In the mean time, God would have us assured of it aforehand. This assurance is by 'sealing.' And this sealing is 'by the Spirit.' None else need do it, no meaner person can do it.

And what respect is due to the Spirit for doing so gracious a work? That we grieve him not; and not only so, but that we endeavour so to please him, as he may with delight go on with this blessed work that it hath pleased him to take upon him.

As the duty is spiritual, so the arguments that enforce it are spiritual; and the argument here is fetched from that which hath a most constraining force; love expressed in the sweetest fruit of it, and the stability of it, 'sealing,' and 'sealing to the day of redemption,' as if the apostle should reason thus: God the Father hath ordained you to salvation by the redemption of Christ his Son; and that you might have the comfort of it in the way to it against all discouragements you may meet with, the Holy Ghost hath assured you of it, and set his seal upon you as those that are set apart for so great salvation; that the sense of this love might breed love in you again, and love breed a care out of ingenuity,* not to offend so gracious a Spirit.

The Holy Spirit by which you are sealed.

The Holy Ghost delighteth to speak in our own language. We cannot rise to him, therefore he stoopeth to us.

This 'sealing' is either sealing of persons, or of good things intended to the persons. Sealing is not only a witnessing to us, but a work upon us and in us, carrying the image of him that sealeth us; whereby we are not only assured of the good promised to us, but fitted for the receiving of it. God prepareth no good for any but whom he prepares and fits for that good. There is not only an outward authorising of the great grants we

* That is, 'ingenuousness.'—G.

have by promise, oath, and sacrament, but an inward by the Spirit persuading of our interest in them, and working that which doth authorise us to lay claim unto them, after the use of a seal, both in confirmation and representation, and resemblance of him that sealed.

The persons sealed are, first, Christ, and then those that are given to Christ.

I. Christ is sealed,*

1. *By the Father*. Christ was ordained by him to be a saviour in our nature, predestinate to be the head of the church. Wherefore he often saith he came to do his Father's will: 'Him hath the Father sealed,' John vi. 27, anointing him, calling him, setting him forth, sanctifying him by the Spirit, and every way fitting him with all grace to be a saviour.

2. He was sealed *by the fulness of the Godhead dwelling in flesh*, abased and exalted for us; so as his flesh is the flesh of the Son of God, and his blood the 'blood of God,' Acts xx. 28.

3. Sealed *by a testimony from heaven of all three persons:* by the Father, 'This is my well-beloved Son;' by the Holy Spirit descending like a dove; by himself to his human nature dwelling in all fulness in it. Christ is sealed by miracles done upon him and by him; by his baptizing and installing into his office, and by giving himself up to shed his blood for sin, by which blood the covenant is established and sealed.

4. *In being justified in the Spirit*, being raised from the dead, and 'declared thereby to be the Son of God mightily with power,' Rom. i. 4; and then advanced to the right hand of God, that through him our faith and trust might be in God, 2 Peter iii. 14; and appearing there for ever for us, sheweth not only his ability and willingness to save us, but that it is done already. We may see all whatever we can look for to ourselves performed in our head to our comfort.

II. As Christ was sealed and fitted for us, *so we are sealed and fitted for Christ.*† There is a privy seal in predestination. This is known only to God himself: 'The Lord knoweth who are his,' 2 Tim. ii. 19. And this knowledge of God of us is carried secret, as a river under ground, until his calling of and separating us from the rest of men, when first by his Spirit he convinceth us of what we are in ourselves, and of our cursed condition, and thereby layeth us low by sorrow and humiliation for sin as the greatest evil. And then a pardon is more to us than a crown; then we will wait for mercy and continue so, and beg for mercy, and that upon Christ's own condition, by denying and renouncing anything of our own; then Christ is Christ unto us. Indeed, after this, it pleaseth Christ by his Spirit to open 'a door of hope,' and give some hints of mercy; and to let in some beams of love, and withal to raise up the soul by a spirit of faith, to close with particular mercy opened and offered by the Spirit, whereby the soul sealeth to the truth of the promise: John iii. 33, 'He that believeth hath set to his seal that God is true.' It is strange that God should stoop so low as to receive, as it were, confirmation by our belief, but thus God condescends in the phrase of Scripture, as we are said to help God: 'Curse ye Meroz, because they came not to help the Lord,' &c., Judges v. 23. God stoops to be helped by us, and to have his truth, and power, and goodness ratified and confirmed by us. When we believe the promise of God in Christ—though it be by the help of the Spirit—we seal God's truth. And then God honoureth that sealing of ours by the sealing of his Spirit: 'After you believed you were sealed,'

* In margin here, 'The sealing of Christ.'—G.

† In margin here, 'Christians are sealed.'—G.

saith the apostle, Eph. i. 13; that is, the gracious love of Christ was further confirmed to them. God honours no grace so much as faith. Why? Because it honours God most of all others. It gives God the honour of his mercy, and goodness, and wisdom, and power, and of his truth, especially he that believe sin God by believing, seals that God is true; and God honours that soul again by sealing it to the day of redemption. God hath promised, 'Those that honour me, I will honour,' John xii. 26; therefore, 'He that believeth hath the witness in himself,' 1 John v. 10. That grace promised belongeth to him, for he carries in his heart the counterpane* of the promises, he that confesseth and believeth shall have mercy. I believe, saith the soul, therefore the promise belongs to me. My faith, answering God's love in the promise, witnesseth so much to me. The Spirit not only revealeth Christ and the promises in general, but in attending upon the ordinances, by an heavenly light, the Spirit discovers to us our interest in particular, and saith to the soul, God is thy salvation, and enableth the soul to say, I am God's. 'I am my beloved's, and my beloved is mine,' Cant. ii. 16. 'Christ loved me, and gave himself for me,' Gal. ii. 20. Whence came this voice of Saint Paul? It was the still voice of the Spirit of God, that, together with the general truth in the gospel, discovered in particular Christ's love to him. It is not a general faith that will bring to heaven, but there is a special work of the Spirit, in the use of means, discovering and sealing the good will of God to us, that he intends good unto us; and thereupon our hearts are persuaded to believe in God, and to love God as our God, and Christ as our Christ.

This is excellently set down in the sweet communion of marriage. The Spirit is the *paranymphos*,† the procurer of the marriage, between Christ and the soul. Now it is not sufficient to know that God and Christ bear good will to all believers (though that be the ground and general foundation of all, and a great preparative to the special sealing of the Spirit); but then the Spirit comes and saith, Christ hath a special good will to me, and stirs up in me a liking to him again, to take him upon his own conditions, with conflict of corruptions, with the scorns of the world, &c. Whereupon the mutual marriage is made up between Christ and us. This work is the 'sealing of the Spirit.'

Many are the privileges of a Christian from this his sealing, as the use of a seal in man's affairs is manifold.

1. Seals serve *for confirmation and allowance*. To that purpose measures are sealed. God is said to seal instruction, Job xxxiii. 16. Confirmation is either by giving strength, or by the authority of such as are able to make good what they promise, and also willing; which they shew by putting to their seal, which hath as much strength to confirm him to whom the promise is made, as he hath will and power to make it good that hath engaged himself. Amongst men there is the writing, and the seal to the writing. When the seal is added to the writing there is a perfect ratification. So there are abundance of gracious promises in the Scriptures. Now when the Spirit comes and seals them to the soul, then they are sure to us; the Spirit puts the seal to the promises.

2. The use of it likewise is *for distinction* from others that carry not that mark. So the sealing of the Spirit distinguisheth a Christian from all other men. There is a distinction between men, in God's eternal purpose, but that concerns not us to meddle with, further than to know it in general.

* That is, 'counterpart,' = pattern or copy.—G.

† That is, the Greek παρανυμφιος = brideman.—G.

God 'knoweth who are his,' 2 Tim. ii. 19, and who are not his; but in time the Holy Spirit distinguisheth and ranks men as they were distinguished before all worlds, and as they shall be at the day of judgment. The beginning of that distinction that shall be afterward is in this life.

A seal maketh the impression of an image; the prince's image useth to be in his seal. So is God's image in his, which destroyeth the old image and print that was in us before. Holy and good men by this work of the Spirit are distinguished,

(1.) From *civil* men by the work of holiness*, which mere civil men have not at all, but despise.

(2.) And, secondly, *from seeing † good men by the depth of that work.* The Spirit of God works a new nature in them, whereby they are distinguished. Now nature in every creature is carried to one thing more than to another. There is a distinct propension‡ in a good man to God, to grace and goodness; his aims and bent are distinct; and thereupon he hath a greater enlargement of heart suitable to his great aims. He looks above the world and worldly men. They are narrow, low, base-spirited men, the best of them.

(3.) Again, Things by nature *work from within.* Herein painted hypocrites are distinguished from a true substantial Christian. He works from a principle within. Another man is moved as the *automata*, things of motion, clocks, and the like engines of wit,§ that move from a weight without that poiseth them. If they do any good it is from somewhat without that swayeth their aims and ends, and not from an inward principle. Nature works from an inward principle; light things go upward and heavy things downward, naturally; artificial things are forced. Thus good men are distinguished from those that are seemingly holy; there is a new nature wrought in them.

(4.) Again, *Nature is constant.* What is done naturally is done constantly. Heavy bodies go always downward, and light bodies upward. Every creature works according to his nature. An holy man is exercised in holiness constantly, because he doth it from an inward principle, from a work and stamp within. Different things may seem the same; as wild herbs may have the colour and form of those that are planted in the garden, but there is difference in the virtue of them. The seeming graces and actions of an hypocrite, they have no virtue in them; as there are some drugs without virtue, dead things. But there is a distinguishing virtue in the faith of a Christian, whereby he overcomes the world and his lusts; whereby he doth all duties, prays and hears, and is fruitful in his conversation. In all his graces there is a comforting, strengthening virtue. True gold hath the virtue to comfort and strengthen the heat‖ that alchymy gold hath not (*i*). True grace hath a working, comforting virtue. Another man's formal artificial actions have no virtue in them; neither is it intended, they being only put on to serve a turn. Two men may do the same things, and yet there be a grand difference: the one doing them from the seal of the Spirit, from a deeper die and stamp of the Spirit; the other if from the Spirit, yet it is but from a common work at the best. Some dyes cannot bear the weather, but alter colour presently; but there are others that, having something that give a deeper tincture, will hold. The graces of a true Christian hold out in all kinds of weathers, in winter and summer, prosperity and adversity, when superficial counterfeit holiness will give out. Thus we see the seal of the Spirit serves for distinction.

* That is, 'moral.'—G.

† Qu. 'seeming'?—Ed.

‡ That is, 'tendency toward.'—G.

§ That is, 'skill.'—G.

‖ Qu. 'heart'?—Ed.

3. The use of a seal is likewise *for appropriation.* Merchants use to seal their wares they would not have others have any right unto.

A Christian is God's in a more peculiar manner than others. There is not only a witness of the Spirit that God is his; but the Spirit works in him an assent to take God again. There is a mutual appropriation: 'I am my beloved's, and my beloved is mine,' Cant. ii. 16. When the soul can say, 'Thou art my God,' it is not frustrate, because God saith before, 'I am thy salvation,' Ps. xxxv. 3. Where the Spirit seals, God appropriates. 'God chooseth the righteous man to himself,' Ps. iv. 3. And we may know this appropriation by appropriating God again: 'Whom have I in heaven but thee? and what have I in earth in comparison of thee?' Ps. lxxiii. 25. There is no action that God works upon the soul, but there is a reflect action by the Spirit to God again. If God choose and love us, we choose and love him again. God appropriates us first. We are his and we are Christ's. We are God's, because he hath given Christ for us. We are Christ's, because he hath given himself for us. We are, as the apostle saith, a people of acquisition, 'a people purchased,' Acts xx. 28—purchased at a dear rate by the blood of Christ. Those that are Christ's, the Spirit appropriates them. This appropriation is by sealing.

4. Again, We use to set our seal only upon that we have *some estimation of.* 'Set me as a seal,' saith the church in the Canticles, 'upon thy right hand,' viii. 6; have me in thy eye and mind as a special thing thou valuest.

The witness and work of the Spirit shews God's estimation of us. The Scripture is abundant in setting forth the great price that God sets on his children. They are his children, his spouse, his friends, his portion, his treasure, his coin. He sets his mark, his likeness on them. They are things hallowed and consecrated. They are first fruits. 'Israel is a holy thing,' Jer. ii. 3. Their titles shew the esteem that God hath of them. He values them more than all the world besides, which are as chaff and dross: 'The righteous man is more excellent than his neighbour,' Prov. xii. 26. As there is a difference of excellency between precious stones and other common stones, between fruitful and barren trees, so there is amongst men. And in this regard, God sets a higher esteem upon some; and thence it is that they have those honourable and glorious titles in Scripture, of 'sons,' 'heirs,' 'kings,' and 'co-heirs with Christ;' when others are termed 'dross and dung,' and thorns,' and have all the base terms that may be.

Now this estimation, by 'sealing,' is known to us by the grace God works in us. Common gifts and privileges and favours of the world are no seal of God's estimation. If God should give a man kingdoms and great monarchies, it seals not God's love to him at all; but when God makes a man a spiritual king to rule over his base lusts, this is a seal of God's valuing him above other men. Therefore we should learn how to value others and ourselves, not by common things that castaways may have, but by the stamp of God set on us by the Spirit, which is an argument that God intends to lay us up as coin for another treasury, for heaven. It is the common grand error of the times to be led with false evidences. Many think God loves them, because he spares them and follows them with long patience, and makes them thrive in the world. Alas! are these fruits of God's special love? What grace hath he wrought in thy heart by his Spirit? 'He gives his Spirit to them that pray,' Luke xi. 13; insinuating that next the gift of his Son, the greatest gift is the Spirit, to fashion and fit us to be members of his Son. This is an argument of God's love and esteem.

5. Seals likewise are used *for secrecy*, as in letters, &c. So this seal of the Spirit is a secret work. God knoweth who are his. They are only known to him and to their own hearts: 'The white stone is only known to him that hath it, and the hidden manna,' Rev. ii. 17. None so infallibly can know the state in grace, as those that have the gracious work themselves. Holy men in some degree are known one to another, to make the communion of saints the sweeter. There is a great deal of spiritual likeness in Christians; 'face answereth to face,' Prov. xxvii. 19, that one hath strong confidence of the salvation of another. But the undoubted certainty of a man's estate is known only to God and his own soul; nay, sometimes it is hidden from a man's self. There are so many infirmities and abasements and troubles in the world, that this life is called a 'hidden life' in Scripture: 'Our life is hid with Christ in God,' Col. iii. 3. It is unknown to the saints themselves sometimes, and the world alway: 'They neither know him that begets, nor them that are begotten,' 1 John v. 1.

6. Hence, likewise, the use of a seal is to shew that things should be kept *inviolable*. Hereupon the church is as a 'sealed fountain,' Cant. iv. 12. Sealing shews a care of preservation from common annoyance. Hereupon likewise it is that sealing is the securing of persons or things sealed from hurt. No man will violate a letter, because it is sealed. The tomb where Christ was buried was sealed, and the prison doors upon Daniel, that none might meddle with them. So the Spirit of God, by this work of sealing, secures God's children; as the blood sprinkled upon the posts of the doors of the Israelites secured them from the destroying angel. In Ezek. ix. 4, there was a mark set upon those that were to be preserved that secured them; and in Rev. vii. 3, the 'sealed ones' must not be hurt. So where this seal of the Spirit is, it is an argument that God means to preserve such a one from eternal destruction, and from prevailing dangers in this world. They are God's sealed ones. No man can hurt them without wrong to God himself. 'Touch not mine anointed, and do my prophets no harm,' Ps. cv. 15. And likewise from devouring sins and dangerous apostasy. A man that is truly sealed by the Spirit of God he never becomes a member of antichrist, a stigmatised papist—for antichrist hath his seal too—he is kept from soul-murdering errors; he hath this security upon him by the work and witness of God's Spirit. Whatsoever the use is, or can be, of a seal in man's affairs, that God will have us make use of in his heavenly intercourse betwixt him and us.

Whereby you are sealed.

Now there are divers degrees of the Spirit's sealing.

1. *Faith*; 'He that believes hath the witness in himself,' 1 John v. 10. He carries in his heart the counterpane* of all the promises. This grace is first planted in the heart, and answereth to God's love and purpose towards us of giving eternal life. The seal and first discovery of election is manifested to us in our believing. Acts xiii. 48, 'As many as were ordained to eternal life believed.' This believing is also a seal to us, in that it is of those gifts that 'accompany salvation,' Heb. vi. 9, of which God never repents him by calling back again. It is a 'seed that abideth for ever.'

2. The work *of sanctifying grace upon the heart is a seal.* Whom the Spirit sanctifieth he saveth. 'The Lord knoweth who are his,' 2 Tim. ii. 19. But how shall we know it? By this seal: 'Let every one that nameth the name of the Lord depart from iniquity,' not only in heart and

* Cf. footnote, page 434.—G.

affection, but in conversation, and that shall be a seal of his sonship to him. None are children of God by adoption, but those that are children also by regeneration; none are heirs of heaven but they are new born to it. 'Blessed be God, the Father of our Lord Jesus Christ, who hath begotten us anew to an inheritance immortal,' &c., 1 Peter i. 4. This seal of sanctification leaves upon the soul the likeness of Jesus Christ, even grace for grace.

But because in time of desertion and temptation we are in a mist, and cannot read our own faith and our own graces, it pleaseth Christ after some trial and exercise to shine upon his own graces in the heart, whereby we may know we believe and know we love; until which time, the heart sees nothing that is good, and seems to be nothing but all objections and doubtings. We may be sometimes in such a state as Paul and his company was in the ship, Acts xxvii. 20, when 'they saw neither sun nor stars many days together;' almost past all hope. So a Christian may for many days together see neither sun nor star; neither light in God's countenance nor light in his own heart; no grace issuing from God; no grace carrying the soul to God; though even at that time God darts some beam through those clouds upon the soul. The soul again, by a spirit of faith, sees some light through those thickest clouds, enough to keep the soul from utter despair, though not to settle it in peace.

In this dark condition, if they do as St Paul and his company did, cast anchor even in the dark night of temptation, and pray still for day, God will appear, and all shall clear up; we shall see light without and light within; the day-star will arise in their hearts.

Though by reflecting upon our souls we are able to discern a spirit of faith, God may hide himself from the soul in regard of comfort. Nay, a Christian may know himself to be in the state of grace, and yet be in an afflicted condition. As in Job's case, he knew his Redeemer lived, and he resolved to trust in him, 'even though he killed him,' Job xiii. 15; he knew he was no hypocrite; he knew his graces were true; and for all the imputations of his friends, they could not dispute him out of his sincerity: 'You shall not take my uprightness from me,' Job xxvii. 6. Yet for the present he saw no light from heaven till it pleased God to reveal himself in special favour to him. There is always peace and joy in believing; yet not in that degree which gives the soul content, until by honouring God in believing, and waiting still his good time, he honoureth us with further sense of his favour, and poureth forth his Spirit to us, manifesting his special love towards us; and this is a further degree of sealing of us, confirming us more strongly than before.

The reason why we can neither have grace to believe, nor know we believe, nor when we know we believe enjoy comfort without a fresh new act of the Spirit, is because the whole carriage of a soul to heaven is above nature. Where the Spirit makes a stand, we stand and can go no further. We cannot conclude from right grounds without some help of the Spirit; some doubts, some fears will hinder the application to ourselves, even as those that live in some damnable sin cannot but grant that those that live in such a sin shall never inherit heaven; and their conscience tells them they live in such a sin, yet self-love blinds them so, that they will not conclude against themselves that they shall be damned; so true believers cannot conclude for themselves without divine light and help.

It pleaseth God thus to keep every degree and act of sealing in his own hand, to keep us in a perpetual dependence upon him, and to awe us that we should not grieve the Spirit of grace, and cause him to suspend either act of grace or comfort.

Joy and strong comfort come from a superadded seal of the Spirit. The works of the Spirit are of a double kind: either *in* us, by imprinting sanctifying grace; or *upon* us, by shining upon our souls in sweet feelings of joy. What the Spirit worketh in us is more constant, as a new nature which is always like itself and worketh uniformly; but comfort and joy are of the nature of such privileges as God vouchsafeth at one time and not at another, to some and not to others.

This degree of sealing in regard of joy hath its degrees likewise; sometimes it is so clear and strong, that the soul questioneth not its state in grace ever after, but passeth on in a triumphant manner to that glory it looks for. Sometimes after this sealing there may be interrupting of comfortable communion so far as to question our condition; yet this calling into question comes not from the Spirit, which, where it once witnesseth for us, never witnesseth against us, but it is a fruit of the flesh not fully subdued, it is a sin itself, and usually a fruit of some former sin. For howsoever we should not doubt after a former witness of the Spirit, yet there will be so much weakening of sense of our assurance, as there is yielding to any lust. The knowledge of our estate in grace and comfort thereupon, though it may be weakened by neglect of our watchfulness, yet still it hath the force of an argument to assure us when the Spirit pleaseth to direct us to make use of it, because God's love varies not as our feelings doth; and a fit doth not alter a state. The child in the womb stirs not always, yet it lives; and that may be gathered from the former stirrings.

This degree of sealing by way of witness and comfort, is appropriated to the Holy Spirit. Every person in the blessed Trinity hath their several work. The Father chooseth us and passeth a decree upon the whole groundwork of our salvation. The Son executeth it to the full. The Spirit applieth it, and witnesseth our interest in it by leading our souls to lay hold upon him, and by raising up our souls in the assurance of it, and by breeding and cherishing sweet communion with Father and Son, who both of them seal us likewise by the Spirit. This joy and comfort is so appropriated to the Spirit, as it carrieth the very name of the Spirit, and is one of the three witnesses on earth, that witnesseth not only Christ to be a Saviour, but our Saviour, 1 John v. 7. The three witnesses on earth are, the 'Spirit, water, and blood.'* For the better conceiving of which place, we must know that the great work of Christ's redemption and justification was typified in the Old Testament by blood; and the great work of our sanctification typified by their washing. To answer which types, when Christ's side was pierced, there came forth both blood and water, shewing that Christ came not only by blood to justify us, but by water to sanctify us. Hereupon blood and water have the power to be witnesses. The blood of Christ being sprinkled on the heart by the Spirit, doth pacify the conscience in assuring it that God is pacified by blood, as 'being offered by the eternal Spirit,' Heb. ix. 14. This quieting power sheweth that it was the blood of God, and shed for me in particular.

The witness of water is from the power the Spirit hath to cleanse our nature, which no creature can do, but the Spirit of God. Change of nature is peculiar to the Author of nature. If we feel, therefore, our natures altered, and of unclean become holy, in some measure we may know we are the children of God, as being begotten by the Spirit of Christ, conforming

* Cf note *dddd*, Vol. IV. page 536.—G.

us to his own holiness. Our spirit as sanctified can witness to us that we are Christ's,

But oft it falls out, that our own spirits, though sanctified, cannot stand against a subtle temptation strongly enforced. God superadds his own Spirit. Guilt often prevails over the testimony of blood; that of water, by reason of stirring corruptions, runneth troubled. Therefore the third, the immediate testimony of the Spirit, is necessary to witness the Father's love to us, to us in particular, saying, 'I am thy salvation,' Ps. xxxv. 3, 'thy sins are pardoned,' Mat. ix. 2. And this testimony the word echoeth unto, and the heart is stirred up and comforted with joy inexpressible. So that both our spirits and consciences, and the Spirit of Christ joining in one, strongly witness our condition in grace, that we are the sons of God.

In this threefold testimony, the order is this: blood begets water; satisfaction by blood procures the Spirit from God, as a witness of God's love; and by feeling the power of blood and water, we come to have the Spirit witnessing and sealing our adoption unto us, to establish us in the state of grace against storms of temptation to the contrary. The Spirit persuadeth to look unto blood, convinceth the heart of the efficacy of it, and then quieteth the soul, which giveth itself up to Christ wholly and to whole Christ; and thence feels his heart established against carnal reason, so as he can and doth oppose Christ's blood to all the guilt that doth arise. And this witness of the Spirit comforting the soul is the most familiar, and affects most.

If we feel it not, as oft we do not, then rise upward from want of this joy of spirit to water, and see what work we find of the Spirit in cleansing our souls; and if we find these waters not to run so clearly as to discern our condition in them, then go to the witness of blood, and let us bathe our souls in it, and then we shall find peace in free grace procured by blood; for ofttimes a Christian is driven to that pass, that nothing can comfort him, within or without him, in heaven or earth, but the free and infinite mercy of God in the blood of Christ, whereon the soul relieth when it feels no comfort, nor joy of the Spirit, nor sees no work of sanctification. Then it must rest on the satisfaction wrought by the blood of Christ, when the soul can go to God and say, 'If we confess our sins, thou art just to forgive them; and the blood of Christ shall cleanse us from all sin,' 1 John i. 9. Therefore, though I feel not inward peace, nor the work of the Spirit, yet I will cast myself upon thy mercy in Christ. Hereupon we shall in God's time come to have the witness of water and the Spirit more evidently made clear unto us.

The Spirit it is that witnesses with blood, and witnesses with water, and by water, whatsoever of Christ's is applied unto us by the Spirit. But, besides witnessing with these witnesses, the Spirit hath a distinct witness by way of enlarging the soul; which [is] joy in the apprehension of God's fatherly love and Christ's setting the soul at liberty. The Spirit doth not always witness unto us our condition by force of argument from sanctification, but sometimes immediately by way of presence; as the sight of a friend comforts without help of discourse. The very joy from sight prevents the use of discourse.

This testimony of the Spirit containeth in it the force of all, word, promise, oath, seal, &c. This is greater than the promise, as a seal is more than our hand, and as an oath is more than a man's bare word. The same that is said of God's oath in comparison with his bare promise, may be said of this sealing in comparison of other testimonies. That as God was willing more abundantly to clear to the heirs of promise their salvation, he added an oath, Heb. vi. 18; so for the same end he added this his Spirit as a seal to the promise, and to the other testimonies. Our own graces indeed, if we were watchful enough, would satisfy us. The fountain is open as to Hagar, but she seeth it not, &c., Gen. xxi. 17, *seq.* Howsoever the Spirit, if that cometh, it subdueth all doubts.

As God in his oath and swearing joineth none to himself, but sweareth by himself, so in this witness he taketh in no other testimony to confirm it, but witnesseth by himself. And hence ariseth 'joy unspeakable and glorious,' 1 Pet. i. 8, and 'peace which passeth all understanding,' Philip. iv. 7; for it is an extract of heaven when we see our being in the state of grace, not in the effect only, but as in the breast and bosom of God.

Quest. But how shall we know this witness from an enthusiastical fancy and illusion?

Ans. This witness of the Spirit is known from the strong conviction it bringeth with it, which weigheth and overpowers the soul to give credit unto it. But there be, you will say, strong illusions. True. Bring them therefore to some rules of discerning. Bring all your joy, and peace, and confidence to the word. They go both together. As a pair of indentures, one answers another. In Christ's transfiguration upon the mount, Moses and Elias appeared together with Christ. In whatsoever transfiguration and ravishment we cannot find Moses and Elias and Christ to meet—that is, if what we find in us be not agreeable to the Scriptures—we may well suspect it as an illusion.

That you may know the voice of the Spirit of God from the carnal confidence of our own spirits, inquire,

1. What went before.
2. What accompanieth it.
3. What followeth after this ravishing joy.

1. *The word must go before it*, in being assented unto by faith, and submitted unto by answerable obedience: 'In whom, after you believed' the word of promise, 'you were sealed.' So that if there be not,

(1.) First, *A believing of the word of promise*, there is no sealing: 'The God of peace give you joy in believing,' 1 Thes. v. 23. There must be a believing, a 'walking according to rule,' Gal. vi. 16, or else no joy nor peace will be unto us. If we cannot bring the word and our hearts together, it is not God's, but Satan's sealing, a groundless presumption, and it will end in despair. As Christ came by water and blood, so doth this testimony; it cometh after the other two. First, the heart is carried to blood, and from thence hath quiet; then followeth water, and our nature is washed and changed; and then cometh this of the Spirit. Though it be not grounded on their testimony, but is above theirs, yet they go before. Where we thus find the work, we may know it to be right by the order of it.

(2.) It cometh after *deep humiliation and abasement*. Though we know ourselves to be the children of God in some such measure, as we would not change our condition for all the world, yet we would have more evidence; we would have further manifestation of God's countenance towards us; we are not satisfied, but wait. After we have long fasted, and our hearts melted and softened, then God poureth water upon the dry wilderness, and then it comes to pass, through his goodness and mercy, that he comforts and satisfies the desires of the hungry soul. God will not suffer the spirit of his children to fail.

(3.) Likewise, *after self-denial in that which is pleasing to us*. It is made up with inward comfort. If this self-denial be from a desire of nearer communion with God, God will not fail them in that they desire. There are wretches in the world that will deny their sinful nature nothing. If they have a disposition to pride, they will be proud; if they have a lust to be rich, to live in pleasures, to follow the vanities of the times, they will do so; they will not say nay to corrupt nature in any thing. Will God vouchsafe to give any true joy or comfort of spirit to such ones? No. Those that let loose their natures without a check shall never taste of this hidden manna. But when we deny ourselves, deny to hear or see that which may feed corruption, when we deny to take delight in that, that we might if we would go the course of the world, there is a proportionable measure of joy and peace and comfort in a higher kind made good to the soul. God is so good, we shall lose nothing for parting with anything for his sake.

(4.) It is usually found, *after conflict and victory*, as a reward. 'To him that overcometh, will I give to eat of the hidden manna,' Rev. ii. 17. God's children, after strong conflict with some temptation or inward corruption, especially that which accompanieth their disposition and temper, when they have so conflicted as that at last they get the better, they find by experience sweet enlargement of spirit. To strive against them is a sign of grace, but to get victory over them, even to subdue our enemies under us that rise up against us, this bringeth true peace and joy.

(5.) *After we have put forth our spiritual strength in holy duties*, God crowns our endeavours with increase of comfort. A Christian that takes pains with his heart, and will not serve God with that which cost him nothing, enjoys that which the spiritual sluggard wishes for, and goes without. God is so just that those men which have striven to live according to the principles of nature, have found a contentment proportionable to their endeavours; some degree of pleasure attends every good action, as a reward before a reward.

2. Besides these things that go before this joy and testimony, there are, secondly, *some things that do accompany it, if it be right*, as,

(1.) This spiritual comfort *enlargeth our hearts to a desire after an high prizing the ordinances*, so far is it from taking us off from a dependence upon them. In the word and other means it found comfort from God, therefore it delights to be meeting God still in his own ways. The eye of the soul is strengthened to see further into truths, and is enabled more spiritually to understand the things it knew before, as in many of the same truths that wise men understand, they understood them when they were young as when they were old, but then more clearly. So all truths are more clearly known by this. The Spirit by which we are sealed is the Spirit of illumination, not that it reveals any thing different from the word, but giveth a more large understanding and inward knowledge of the same truths as were known before.

(2.) A liberty and boldness with God, for 'where the Spirit is, there is a gracious liberty;' that is, further enlargements from the law, guilt of sin, and the fear of the wrath of God, that we can come with some boldness to his throne and to him as our Father; a freedom to open our souls in prayer before him. This stands not so much in multitude of words, or forms of expressions, but a son-like boldness in our approaches in prayer. The hypocrite, especially in extremity, cannot pray; his conscience stops his mouth. But where the Spirit sealeth, it giveth this liberty, freely to open and spread our case before him and call upon him, yea, under the evidence of some displeasure.

(3.) There doth likewise ordinarily accompany this sealing of the Spirit, *Satan's malice and opposition*; who, being cast from heaven himself, envies this heaven upon earth in a creature of meaner rank by creation than himself. We must not think to enjoy pure joy here without molestation. If there be danger of exalting above measure, we must look for some messenger of Satan.

3. After this witness it *leaves the soul more humble;* none more abased in themselves than those that have nearest communion with God, as we see in the angels that stand before God and cover their faces, so Isa. vi. 2, *seq.* Job, after God had manifested himself unto him, abhorred himself in dust and ashes, Job xlii. 6. It brings with it a greater desire of sanctification and heavenly-mindedness. As Elias ascended up into heaven, his cloak fell by degrees from him; the higher our spirits are raised, the more we put off affections to earthly things.

(2.) Again, The end of this further manifestation of the Spirit being encouragement to duty, or suffering in a good cause, *the soul by this witness of the Spirit finds increase of spiritual mettle.* It finds itself steeled against opposition. Whilst this wind filleth their sails, they are carried on amain,* and are frighted with nothing that stands in their way. See how the believers triumph upon the Spirit's witnessing to their spirits that they are the sons of God, Rom. viii. 16-33, &c.

God usually reserveth such comforts for the worst times: 'Give wine to those that be of heavy heart,' Prov. xxxi. 6. The sense of this love of Christ is better than wine. This refreshing Paul had in the dungeon, and he sung at midnight. After this witnessing, therefore, look for some piece of service to do, or trial to undergo.

Much must be left to God's fatherly wisdom in this, who knows whom to cheer up, and when and in what degree, and to what purpose and service; and remember always that these enlargements of spirit are as occasional refreshings in the way, not daily food to live upon. We maintain our life by faith, not by sight or feeling. Feasting is not for every day, except that feast of a good conscience, which is continual; but I speak of grand days and high feasts. These are disposed as God seeth cause.

(3.) Where this sealing of the Spirit is, there followeth also upon it *a lifting up of the head in thinking of our latter end.* It makes one think of the times to come with joy, as the Holy Ghost here mentioneth the day of redemption, as a motive to them to take heed that they did not grieve the Spirit; intimating they should think of the day of redemption with a great deal of joy and comfort. The saints are described in Scripture to be those that 'look for the appearing of Christ,' 2 Pet. iii. 12. They are Christ's, and in him their reckonings and accounts are even. And therefore with delight they can often think and meditate upon the blessed times that are to come.

There be divers degrees of sealing, arising from divers degrees of revelation. God first reveals his good will in his promises to all believers. This is the privilege of the church, especially in these latter times. Then by his Spirit reveals those saving truths to those that are his, by a divine light. So that by argument drawn from the power they feel from truths, in searching secrets, in casting down, in raising up, in staying the soul, they can seal to them that they are divine.

The same Spirit that reveals the power of the word to me, reveals in particular mine own interest in all those truths upon hearing them.

* Cf. footnote on page 401.—G.

Whereupon they are written in my heart, as if they had been made in particular to me: the comfortable truths in the word are transcribed into my heart answerable to the word; as that God in Christ is mine, forgiveness mine, grace mine: whereupon adoption in Christ is sealed; which God still sealeth further to my soul by increase of comfort, as he seeth cause for encouragement. The same Spirit that manifesteth in me the word I hear and read to be the truth of God, from the power and efficacy of it: the same Spirit teacheth to apply it, and in applying of it sealeth me.

Therefore we ought to desire to be sealed by the Spirit, in regard of an holy impression; and then that the Holy Spirit would shine upon his own graces, so as we may clearly see what is wrought in us above nature; and because this is furthered by revealing his love in Christ in adoption to us, we must desire of God to vouchsafe the Spirit of revelation, to reveal the mysteries of his truth unto us, and our portion in them in particular, and so our adoption; and in the mean time to wait and attend his good pleasure in the use of all good means. Thus we waiting, God will so far reveal himself in love to us, as shall assure us of his love, and stir up love again; and the same Spirit that is a Spirit of revelation will be a Spirit of sanctification, and so adoption. Dignity, and fitting qualities suitable to dignity, go both together.

In that grand inquiry about our condition, there is a great miscarriage when men will begin with the first work of the Father in election, then pass to redemption by Christ: I am God's, and Christ hath redeemed me; and never think of the action of the third person in sanctification, which is the nearest action upon the soul, as the third person himself is nearest unto us; and so fetch their first rise where they should set up their last rest. Whereas we should begin our inquiry in the work of the third person, which is next unto us; and then upon good grounds we may know our redemption and election.

The Holy Spirit is both a Spirit of revelation and of sanctification together, as hath been said; for together with opening the love of the Father and the Son, he fitteth us by grace for communication with them.

People out of self-love will have conceits of the Father's and Son's love severed from the work of the Spirit upon their hearts, which will prove a dangerous illusion. Although the whole work of grace by the Spirit arise from the Father's and Son's love, witnessed by the Spirit, yet the proof of the Father's love to us in particular, ariseth from some knowledge of the work of the Spirit; the error is not in thinking of the Father's and Son's love, but in a strengthening themselves by a pleasing powerless thought of it against the work of grace by the Spirit, which their corruption withstands. So they will carve out of the work of the Trinity what they think agreeable to their lusts, whereas otherwise, if their heart were upright, they would for this very end think of God's love and Christ's, to quicken them to duty and to arm them against corruption.

To the day of redemption.

1. There is a double redemption: redemption of the soul by the first coming of Christ to shed his blood for us; redemption of our bodies from corruption by his second coming. We have not the perfect consummation and accomplishment of that which Christ wrought in his first coming till his second coming. Then there shall be a total redemption of our souls, and bodies, and conditions. There is a double redemption, as there is a double coming of Christ, the first and the second; the one to redeem our

souls from sin and Satan, and to give us title to heaven; the other to redeem our bodies from corruption, when Christ shall come 'to be glorious in his saints,' 2 Thes. i. 10. As likewise there is a double resurrection, the first and the second, and a double regeneration, of soul and body.

In sickness and weakness of body, or when age hath overtaken us that we cannot live long here, and the horror of the grave, the house of darkness, is presented to us; Oh let us think there will be a redemption of our bodies as well as of our souls! Christ will redeem our bodies from corruption, as he came to work the redemption of our souls from sin and death; and he that will redeem our bodies out of the grave, he will redeem his church out of misery. He will call the Jews; he that will do the greater will do the inferior. When we hear of this, let us think with comfort of all the promises that are yet unperformed.

2. Secondly, Full redemption is not yet. What need I bring Scripture to prove it. It is a point that every man's experience teacheth. Alas! let our bodies speak: we are not free from sickness and diseases; nay, what is our life but a going to corruption? The sentence is passed upon us, 'earth returneth to earth,' Gen. iii. 19. Till death we are going to death; so besides sickness and weakness here, we must die, and after death be subject to corruption. The apostle in this respect calleth our body 'a vile body,'* Philip. iii. 21. As for our souls, though they be freed from the guilt and damnation of sin, yet there are remainders of corruption that breed fear and terror; and though they be freed from the rule of Satan, yet not from his molestation and vexations by temptations. In a word, our whole state and condition in this world is a state and condition of misery; we are followed with many afflictions, so that there is not yet perfect redemption, whether we look to body, soul, or state; the body being subject to diseases, the soul to infirmities, the state to misery.

But there is a 'day' appointed for it.

By a 'day' we are not to understand the time measured by the course of the sun in twenty-four hours, but in the Scripture meaning, a day is a set time of mercy or judgment. As there was a solemn day, 'the fulness of time,' Gal. iv. 4, for the working of the first redemption, so there is a solemn time set for the second redemption, when all the children of God shall be gathered; those that lie in the dust shall be raised and for ever glorified. It is the day of all days; that day that by way of excellency is called '*that* day,'† in the Scriptures, and 'the day of the Lord,' Mat. xii. 8—the day that we should think of every day, especially in sickness, and trouble, and crosses, and molestations, from the wicked world, and in sense of the remainders of corruption. There is a day of redemption to come that will make amends for all. The frequent thoughts of that day would comfort us, and keep us from shrinking in any affliction and trouble; it would move us to a carriage and conversation answerable to our hopes, and also it would help to fit us, it would infuse a desire of qualification to be prepared for that great day.

But how little of our time is spent in thoughts this way! If we could oft think of the day of redemption, our lives would be otherwise, both in regard of gracious as also of comfortable carriage. Should we be disconsolate at every loss and cross, at sicknesses and the thought of death, when we shall be turned into our first principle, the earth, if we did think of the day of redemption, when all shall be restored again, all the decays of nature,

* Cf. *ante*, pp. 61, *seq.*, on the phrase.—G.

† Cf. Mat. vii. 22; xxiv. 36; 1 Thes. v. 4, *et alibi*.—G.

and the image of God be perfectly stamped? The thought of this would make us go willingly to our graves, knowing that all this is but a preparation for the great 'day of redemption.' The first day of redemption, when Christ came to redeem our souls, and to give us title to heaven, it was in the expectation of all good people before Christ. They are said 'to wait for the consolation of Israel,' Luke ii. 25. That was the character to know those blessed people by. And what should be the distinguishing character of gracious souls now, but to be such as wait for the coming of Christ? How oft in the epistles of St Paul is it? 'There is a crown of righteousness for me, and for all that wait for the appearing of Christ,' 2 Tim. iv. 8.

There was a year of jubilee among the Jews every fifty years. Then all that were in bondage were set at liberty. So at this blessed jubilee, this glorious day of redemption, all that are in bondage of death and under corruption shall be set at everlasting liberty. No question but the poor servants that were vexed with hard masters, they thought of the jubilee; and those that had their possessions took away, they thought of the jubilee, the day of recovering all. So let us oft think of this everlasting jubilee, when we shall recover all that we lost, for ever to keep it, and never to lose it again as we did in the first creation. Let us oft think of this day. It will infuse vigour and strength into all our conversation. Indeed, to the ungodly, it is not a day of redemption, but a 'day of judgment,' and the 'revelation of the just wrath of God,' when their sins shall be laid open, and receive a sentence answerable.

Alas! there is such a deal of atheism in the world—and the seeds of it in the best, unless it be wrought out daily—that we forget the God of vengeance and the day of vengeance. Would men go on in sins against conscience if they thought of this last day? It is impossible. Such courses come from this abominable root of atheism and unbelief; for had they but a slight faith, it would be effectual to alter their course in some measure. Therefore the Scripture gives them the name of fools, though they would be thought to be the only wise men. 'The fool hath said in his heart, There is no God,' Ps. xiv. 1. And what follows? 'Corrupt are they, and abominable.' The cause of all is, the fool hath said in his heart. He will needs force it upon his heart that there is no God, hell, nor heaven, nor judgment. Thence come abominable courses.

Grieve not the Holy Spirit of God, whereby ye are sealed unto the day of redemption.

From the consideration of all that hath been formerly spoken of, the sealing of the Spirit to the day of redemption, there ariseth these four conclusions:

First, That we may attain unto a knowledge that we are in that state of grace.

Secondly, That upon knowledge of our state in grace for the present, we may be assured of our future full redemption.

Thirdly, That this assured knowledge is wrought by the Spirit.

Fourthly, That the consideration of this assurance wrought by the Spirit is an effectual argument to dissuade from grieving the Spirit.

1. For the first, *we may know we are in the state of grace,* first, because the apostle would not have used an argument moving not to grieve the Spirit from a thing unknown or guessed at. It is an ill manner of reasoning to argue from a thing unknown.

2. Again, Sealing of us by the Spirit *is not in regard of God, but our-*

selves. God knoweth who are his, but we know not that we are his but by sealing.

3. *The scope of the Scriptures indited by the Spirit is for comfort.* The apostle saith so directly; and what comfort is in an uncertain condition, wherein a man knows not but he may be a reprobate? Wherefore came our Saviour into the world and took our nature upon him? Why became he a curse for us? Why hath he carried our nature into heaven, and there appears for us till he hath brought us home to himself, but that he would have us out of all doubt of his love after once by faith we have received him? Whence proceeded those commandments to believe, those checks of unbelievers, the commendation of them that did believe, those upbraidings of doubting, as springing from unbelief? To what use are the sacraments, but to seal unto us the benefits of Christ, if upon all this we should still doubt of God's love, especially when, besides the sealing of the promises to us, we are sealed ourselves by the Spirit of promise?

Obj. This is true if we know we do believe.

Ans. It is the office of the Spirit, as to work faith and other graces, so to reveal them to us. Every grace of God is a light of itself coming from the Father of lights; and it is the property of light not only to discover other things, but itself too; and it is the office of the Spirit to give further light to this light, by shining upon his own grace in us. An excellent place for this is 1 Cor. ii. 12, 'We have received the Spirit that is of God, that we might know the things that are freely given to us of God.' 'In the mouth of two or three witnesses shall every thing be confirmed.' One witness is, 'the spirit of man,' which knows 'the things that are in man,' 1 Cor. ii. 11; the other witness is 'the Spirit of God, witnessing to our spirits that we are the children of God,' Rom. viii. 14. Here is light added to light, witness added to witness, the greater witness of the Spirit to the less of our spirits. The apostle joins them both together: 'My conscience bears me witness through the Holy Ghost,' Rom. ix. 1.

Obj. Man's heart is deceitful.

Ans. But the Spirit of God in man's heart is not deceitful. It is too holy to deceive, and too wise to be deceived in this point of assurance. We plough with the Spirit's heifer, or else we could not find out this riddle, Judges xiv. 18. Where there is an object to be seen, and an eye to see, and light to discover the object to the eye, sight must needs follow. In a true believer, after he is enlightened, as there is grace to be seen, and an eye of faith to see, so there is a light of the Spirit discovering that grace to that inward sight. In the bottom of a clear river, a clear eyesight may see anything. Where nothing is, nothing can be seen. It is an evidence that the patrons of doubtings have little grace in them, and much boldness in making themselves a measure for others. Those that are base-born know their mothers better than their fathers. The Church of Rome is all for the mother, but the babes of Christ know their father. The remainder of corruption will indeed be still breeding doubts, but it is the office of the Spirit of faith to quell them as they arise. We are too ready in time of temptation to doubt. We need not help the tempter by holding it a duty to doubt. This is to light a candle before the devil, as we use to speak.

Quest. May not there be doubtings where there is true faith? May not a true believer be without assurance?

Ans. There be three ranks of Christians: First, Some that are yet under the spirit of bondage, that like little children do all for fear. Secondly, Those that are under the spirit of adoption, and do many things well, but yet are not altogether free from fear. These are like those children that are moved with reverence to obey their parents, and yet find their commands somewhat irksome unto them. The third are such as, by the love of God shed into their hearts by the Spirit of adoption, are carried with large spirits to obey their Father; and herein like unto those children that not only obey, but take a delight in it, upon a judgment that both obedience and the thing wherein they obey is good. This we ought to labour for. But we find many Christians in the second rank. Many truly believe in Christ by some light let into their hearts by the Spirit of adoption, who are not yet fully assured of the love of Christ. There is the act of faith and the fruit of faith. The act of faith is to cast ourselves upon God's mercy in Christ; the fruit of faith is in believing to be assured of this. We must know that faith is one thing, assurance another. They may have faith, and yet want a double assurance : first, assurance of their faith, being not able to judge at all times of their own act; likewise, secondly, assurance of their state in grace, as in time of desertion and temptation. A soul at such a time casts itself upon Christ, as knowing comfort is there to be had, though he be not sure of it for himself; and this the soul doth out of obedience, though not out of feeling, as the poor man in the gospel, 'Lord, I believe: help my unbelief,' Mark ix. 24. The soul oftentimes out of the deep, cries, and in the dark, trusts in God; and this is the bold adventure of faith, the first object whereof is Christ held out in a promise; and not assurance, which springeth from the first act when it pleaseth God to shine upon the soul; and is a reward of glorifying God's mercy in Christ by casting the soul upon his truth and goodness. Assurance is God's seal, faith is our seal. When we set to our seal by believing, he sets to his seal, assuring us of our condition. We yield first the consent and the assent of faith; and then God puts his seal to the contract. There must be a good title before a confirmation, a planting before a rooting and establishing, the bargain before the earnest. Some would have faith to be an overpowering light of the soul, whereby undoubtedly they believe themselves to be Christ,* and Christ to be theirs; which stumbleth many a weak yet true Christian; for this is rather the fruit of a strong faith than the act of a weak, which struggleth with doubting until it hath gotten the upper hand. True it is, there must be so much light let into the soul as the soul may rely upon Christ; and this light must be discovered by the Spirit; and such a light as shews a special love of Christ to the soul. And again, it is true that we are not to take up our rest in the light until the heart be further subdued; as many are too hasty to conclude of a good condition upon uncertain signs, before they have attained unto fuller assurance; but yet we must not deny faith where this strong assurance is wanting, so far as to conclude against ourselves, if there be desires putting on, to endeavour with conflict against the rising of unbelief, with a high prizing of the favour of God in Christ, so as to value it above all things. Degrees do not vary the kind; weakness may stand with truth, but where truth is there will be an incessant desire of future sealing.

2. The second conclusion: *We may, upon the knowledge of our present estate in grace, be assured for the time to come*, for this sealing is to the 'day of redemption;' that is, till we be put into full possession of what we now believe; and besides, sealing is for securing for the time to come; and our Saviour's promise is, that though he departed from them, yet the Comforter should abide with them for ever, John xiv. 16. And why are

* Qu. 'Christ's'?—Ed.

we certain of the favour of God to our comfort for the present, but that we doubt not of it for the time to come?

Faith and love, and these graces, they never fail finally; therefore when the Scripture speaks of faith, it speaks of salvation by it for the present; as if a man should be in heaven presently so soon as he believed. 'We are saved by faith,' say the Scriptures, Eph. ii. 8. We are not yet saved, but the meaning is, we are set by faith into a state of salvation. Being put into Christ by faith, we 'are risen with Christ, and sit in heavenly places with him,' Eph. i. 3. Faith makes the things to come present; and faith believes that 'neither things present, nor things to come, shall be able to separate us from the love of God in Christ,' Rom. viii. 39. So that our assurance is not only for the present, but for the time to come. We are sealed 'to the day of redemption,' and who can reverse God's seal, or God's act or deed? Grace is the earnest-penny of glory.* God hath made a covenant, and given earnest. He will not lose it. The earnest is never taken away, but filled up. If we be assured of grace for the present, we may be sure it shall be made up full in glory hereafter. If the Spirit of Christ be in us, the same Spirit that raised Christ from the dead will raise us up likewise, and not leave us until we be in full redemption: 'We shall awake filled with his image,' Rom. viii. 11, *seq.*, and Ps. xvii. 15.

No opposition shall prevail. God hath set us a seal on his right hand to keep us; ay, and on his breast (as the high priest had the twelve tribes) to love us, and on his shoulder to support us. The marked and sealed ones in Ezek. ix. 4, and Rev. vii. 2, were secured from all destruction. If we be in Christ our rock, temptations and oppositions are but as waves; they may dash upon us, but they break themselves.

Quest. Why then do we pray for the forgiveness of sins?

Ans. We pray for a clear evidence of what we have; secondly, as the end is ordained, so the means must be used. God doth and will pardon sin; and therefore we must pray for pardon, as a means ordained. Thirdly, Prayer doth not prejudice the certainty of a thing. Christ prayeth for that he was most sure of: John xvii. 24, 'I pray for them which thou hast given me, for they are thine.'

Pregnant for the proof of this point is that of Peter: 'We are begotten again to a lively hope,' a hope of that life which maketh lively, 1 Peter i. 3–5. Oh but we are weak! True, but 'we are kept by the power of God.' An inheritance is not only kept for us, but we are kept for it.

Obj. But Satan is strong, and his malice is more than his strength.

Ans. True. But we are kept as by a garrison. We have a guard about us.

Obj. All this is true while faith holdeth out, but that may fail.

Ans. No. We are kept by the power of God 'through faith.' God keepeth our faith, and us by faith.

Obj. But the time is long between us and salvation, and many dangers may fall out.

Ans. Be it so that the time is long, yet we are 'kept *unto salvation*,' even until the 'day of redemption;' for the Spirit, by virtue of the covenant, puts the fear of God into our hearts, that we shall never depart from him. God doth not promise what we shall do of ourselves, but what he will do in us and by us. Thus the Holy Ghost putteth a shield into our hands to ward off all objections; and helps us to subdue the reasonings that are apt to

* Cf. footnote, Vol. III. page 476.—G.

rise within us against this blessed hope. So that this happy condition is not only sure to us, but God hath assured us of it. God's gracious indulgence is such, he sees here we go through a wilderness and are molested every way; therefore he would have us assured of a blessed condition to come. So good is God, he doth not only find out a glorious way of redemption by the blood of his Son God-man, but he acquaints us with it in the days of our pilgrimage, partly that we may glorify him, that he may have the praise beforehand of what good he intends us; for assurance of that blessed condition will stir up our spirits to bless God. What the thing itself would work, faith works the same in some measure. Therefore Saint Peter, 1 Pet. i. 3, 4, 'Blessed be God,' saith he, 'who hath begotten us again to a lively hope of an inheritance immortal, undefiled, that fadeth not away, reserved in the heavens.' Why doth he bless God before we have it? Because we are as sure of it as if we had it. What is revealed beforehand is praised for beforehand. God would have us assured, that he may have glory.

Partly to comfort us: for faith is effectual to work that comfort that the thing present would do in some measure. What comfort would the soul have if it should see heaven open and itself entering into it, if redemption were at hand? The same faith works in some measure. What is more sure than the thing itself? What more comfortable than faith in it?

When the Israelites were in the wilderness, going to Canaan, they had many promises that they should come to Canaan, and many extraordinary helps to lead them thither—the pillar, and cloud, and angel; and God, out of indulgence condescending to their weakness, gave them some grapes of Canaan. He put it into the mind of the spies to bring of the fruits. So God gives us some work of his blessed Spirit, whereby he would have us assured and sealed to the day of redemption.

3. The third conclusion is this, that *the Spirit doth seal us*. This cannot be otherwise; for who can establish us in the love of God, but he that knows the mind of God towards us? and who knows the mind of God but the Spirit of God?

Then am I sealed, when I do not only believe, but by a reflecting act of the soul know I do believe; and this reflection, though it be by reason, yet it is by reason enabled by the Spirit. Our spirits by the Spirit only, can discern of spiritual acts. It is not for us to know things above nature; without a cause, above nature. None can know the meaning of our broken desires, so as to help us in our infirmities, but that Spirit that stirred up those desires. Again, none knows the grievances of our spirits, but our own spirits and the Spirit of God, who knows all the turnings and corners of the soul.

Who can mortify those strong corruptions that would hinder us in the way to heaven, but the Spirit clothing our spirit with power from above? Who purifieth the conscience, but he that is above conscience? Who can raise our spirits above all temptations and troubles, but that Spirit of power that is above all?

The strength and vigour of any creature is from the spirits; and the strength of the spirits of all flesh is from this Spirit, whose office is to put spirit into our spirit.

As God redeemed us with his blood, so God must apply this blood, that conscience may be quieted. He only can subdue the rebellion of our spirits, and soften our hearts, and make them fit for sealing. The Spirit only can so report the mercy of God to our souls, as to persuade and work our hearts to this assurance, otherwise we would never yield. For partly the greatness of the state is such that none but God can assure; and partly the misgiving and unbelief of our heart is such that none but God can subdue it. The thing being so great, and our deservings so little, being unworthy of the things of this life, much more of that eternal happiness, this cannot be done without the high and glorious Spirit of God.

How earnest and desirous then is both the Father and the Son to save us, that pleased to send such an orator and ambassador as is equal with themselves to persuade us, to assure us, to fit us for salvation! And how gracious is the Spirit that will vouchsafe to have such communion with such poor sinful spirits as ours! And should not this work upon our hearts a care not to grieve the Holy Spirit? And so we come to the fourth conclusion.

4. The fourth conclusion is, that *the sealing of the Spirit unto salvation should be a strong prevailing argument not to grieve the Spirit;* that is, not to sin, for sin only grieves the Spirit. 'The grace of God,' saith Paul to Titus, 'that bringeth salvation,' Tit. ii. 11, 12. Christ appeared; and what is Christ but grace? Christ appeared, and the free favour of God in Christ, whereby we are assured of salvation, 'which teacheth us'—what to do?—'to deny all ungodliness and worldly lusts, and to live soberly, righteously, and godly in this present world.' Even the consideration of the benefits of Christ that are past, such as came with Christ's first coming; but that is not all: ver. 13, 'Looking for that blessed hope, and the glorious appearing of the great God and our Saviour Jesus Christ.' The second coming of Christ enforceth likewise the same care of holiness: 'Our conversation is in heaven,' Philip. iii. 20, and not as theirs, spoken of in the former verse, whose end is damnation, whose belly is their god, who mind earthly things. No. We mind heavenly things. And these heavenly desires, from whence sprung they but from the certain 'expectation of our Saviour, the Lord Jesus Christ, who shall change our vile bodies?' &c., Philip. iii. 21; that is, shall redeem us fully, even our bodies as well as our souls.

1. It is an argument of force *whether we be not yet sealed, or be sealed.* If not sealed, then grieve not him whose only office is to seal, entertain his motions, give way to him, that he may have scope and liberty of working. Set no reasons against his reasons. Hearken to no counsel against his counsel. Stand not out his persuasions any longer, but yield up your spirits to him, lest he put a period to his patience. He is long-suffering, but not always-suffering. If he give us up to our own spirits, we shall only be witty* to work out our own damnation. We are not given up to our own spirits but after many repulses of this Holy Spirit; and at length, what now will not serve for an argument to persuade us shall be used hereafter as an argument to torment us. The Spirit will help our spirits to repeat and recall all the motions to our own good that we formerly put back. We should think, when conscience speaks in us, God speaks; and when the Spirit moves us, it is God that moves us; and that all excuse will be cut off: answer will be, Did not I tell you of this by conscience, my deputy? Did not I move you to this good by mine own Spirit? Take heed of keeping out any light; for light, where it doth not come in and soften, hardens; none so hard-hearted as those upon whom the light hath shined. There is more to be hoped from a man that hath only a natural conscience, than from him whose heart and spirit hath been long beaten

* That is, 'skilful or ingenious.'—G.

on; there is more to be hoped from a heathen Pilate than a proud Pharisee. Those that will not be sealed to their salvation, it is just with God that they should be sealed up to their destruction. The soul without the Spirit is darkness and confusion, full of self-accusing and self-tormenting thoughts. If we let the Spirit come in, it will scatter all and settle the soul in a sweet quiet.

2. *For those that have been sealed by the Spirit, and yet not so fully as to silence all doubts about their estate:* those should, out of that beginning of comfort which they feel, study to be pliable to the Spirit for further increase. The Spirit sealeth by degrees. As our care of pleasing the Spirit increaseth, so our comfort increaseth: our light will increase as the morning light unto the perfect day. Yielding to the Spirit in one holy motion will cause him to lead us to another, and so on forwards until we be more deeply acquainted with the whole counsel of God concerning our salvation. Otherwise, if we give way to any contrary lust, darkness will grow upon our spirits unawares, and we shall be left in an unsettled condition, as those that travel in the twilight, that cannot perfectly find out their way. We shall be on and off, not daring to yield wholly to our lusts, because of a work of grace begun; nor yield wholly to the Spirit, because we have let some unruly affection get too much strength in us; and so our spirits are without comfort, and our profession without glory.

We shall lie open to Satan if he be let loose to winnow our faith; for if our state come to be questioned we have nothing to allege but the truth of our graces, and if we have not used the Spirit well we shall not have power to allege them, nor to look upon any grace wrought in us, but upon those lusts and sins whereby we have grieved the Spirit; they will be set in order before us, and so stare us in the face, that we cannot but fix our thoughts upon them. And Satan will not lose such an advantage, but will tempt us to call the work of grace in question, which though it be a true work, yet, for want of light of the Spirit to discern it, we cannot see it to our comfort; whereas, if the Spirit would witness unto us the truth of our state and the sincerity of our graces, we should be able to hold our own, and those temptations will vanish.

3. *For those that the Holy Spirit hath set a clearer and stronger stamp upon,* that do not question their condition, they of all others should not grieve the Spirit.

(1.) A Spirit of *ingenuity** will hinder them, and stir up a shame in them to requite so ill such a friend. Nothing so ingenuous as grace. What is commendable in nature is in greater perfection in grace. How doth the conscience of unkindness to a friend that hath deserved well of us trouble our spirits, that we know not with what face to look upon him? And will not unkindness to the Spirit make us ashamed to lift up our face to heaven?

(2.) Benefits are bonds, and the greater favour the stronger obligation. Now what greater favour is there than for the Spirit to renew us according to the image of God our glorious Saviour, who carried the image of Satan before? And by this to appropriate us unto God, to be laid up in his treasure, as carrying his stamp; and by this to be separated from the vile condition of the world, although we carry in us the seeds of the same corruption that the worst doth, differing nothing from them but in God's free grace and the fruits of it; for God to esteem so of us, that have no worthiness of our own, but altogether persons not worthy to be loved, as to make

* That is, 'ingenuousness.'—G.

our unworthiness a foil to set out the freeness of his love in making us worthy, whom he found not so; for the Spirit by sealing of us to secure us in the midst of all spiritual dangers, and to hide us as his secret ones, that that evil one should not touch us to hurt us: these, as they are favours of an high nature, the more care they require to walk worthy of them. We cannot but forget ourselves, before we yield to anything against that dignity the Spirit hath sealed us to.

(3.) *Nature, helped with ordinary education, moveth every man to carry himself answerable to his condition:* a magistrate as a magistrate, a subject as a subject, a child as a child; and we think it disgraceful to do otherwise. And shall that which is disgraceful to nature not be much more disgraceful to nature renewed and advanced by the Spirit? And indeed, as we should not, so we cannot grieve the Spirit so far forth as we are renewed, 1 John iii. 9. Our new nature will not suffer us to dissemble, to be worldly, to be carnal, as the world is. We cannot but study holiness, we cannot but be for God and his truth, we cannot but express what we are and whose we are.

It is impossible a man should care for heaven, that doth not care for the beginnings of heaven. He cannot be said to care for full redemption and glory, that doth not care for the Spirit of grace. Fulness of grace is the best thing in glory. Other things, as peace and joy and the like, they are but the shinings forth of this fulness of grace in glory.

Again, When the Spirit assureth us of God's love in the greatest fruits of it, as it doth when it assureth this redemption, that love kindles love again, and love constrains us by a sweet necessity to yield cheerful and willing obedience in all things. There is nothing more active and fuller of invention than love, and there is nothing that love studies more than how to please. There is nothing that it fears more than to discontent. It is a neat* affection, and will endure nothing offensive, either to itself or the spirit of such as we love; and this love the Spirit teaches the heart, and love teaches us not only our duty, but to do it in a loving and acceptable manner. It carries out the whole stream of the soul with it, and rules all whilst it rules, and will not suffer the soul to divert to by-things, much less to contrary.

Again, These graces that are conversant about that condition which the Spirit assureth us of, as faith and hope, are purging and purifying graces, working a suitableness in the soul to the things believed and hoped for; and the excellency of the things believed and hoped for have such a working upon the soul that it will not suffer the soul to defile itself. Our hopes on high will lead us to ways on high. Therefore whilst these graces are exercised about these objects, the soul cannot but be in a pleasing frame.

It hath been an old cavil, that certainty of salvation breeds security and looseness of life. And what is there that an ill-disposed soul cannot suck poison out of? A man may as truly say the sea burns, or the fire cools. There is nothing quickens a soul more to cheerful obedience than assurance of God's love, and that our 'labour should not be in vain in the Lord,' 1 Cor. xv. 58. This is the Scripture's logic and rhetoric, to enforce and persuade [to] a holy life, from knowledge of our present estate in grace. 'I beseech you by the mercies of God,' saith St Paul, Rom. xii. 1. What mercies? Such as he had spoken of before,—justification, sanctification, assurance, that all shall work together for good, that nothing shall be able to separate us from the love of God in Christ. All duties tend to assurance, or spring from assurance.

* That is, = pure. Cf. Vol. II. page 80, *et alibi.*—G.

God's intendment* is to bring us to heaven by a way of love and cheerfulness, as all his ways towards us in our salvation are in love. And this is the scope of the covenant of grace, and for this end he sends the Spirit of adoption into our hearts, that we may have a child-like liberty with God in all our addresses to him. When he offers himself to us as a Father, it is fit we should offer ourselves to him as children; nature teaches a child, the more he desires his father's love, the more he fears to displease him. And he is judged to be graceless that will therefore venture to offend his father, because he knows he neither can or will disinherit him. Certain it is, the more surely we know God hath begotten us to so glorious an inheritance, the more it will work upon our bowels, to take all to heart that may any way touch him. This wrought upon David. When the prophet told him God hath done this and this for thee, and 'would have done more if that had been too little,' 2 Sam. xii. 8, it melted him presently into an humble confession. Those that have felt the power of the Spirit of adoption on their hearts, will both by a divine instinct, as also by strength of reason, be carried to all those courses wherein they shall approve themselves to their Father. Instinct of nature strengthened with grounds will move strongly.

To conclude this discourse, let Christians therefore be careful to preserve and cherish the work of assurance and sealing in them.

Means. 1. What God doth for us, *he doth by grace in us*. He will preserve us that we shall not fall from him by putting the grace of fear into us, Jer. xxxii. 40. He will keep us, but by what means? 'The peace of God, which passeth all understanding, shall guard our hearts,' Phil. iv. 7. God maketh our calling and election sure in us, by stirring our hearts up to be diligently exercised in adding one grace unto another, and in growing in every grace, as 2 Pet. i. 5. Therefore we must attend upon all spiritual means of growth and quickening: so shall you have a further 'entrance into the kingdom of Jesus Christ, 2 Pet. i. 11; that is, you shall have more evident knowledge of your entrance into the kingdom of grace here, and likewise into the kingdom of glory hereafter. Those that do not so shall have no comfort either from the time past, for they shall forget that they were purged from their sins; or from thoughts of the time to come, for they shall 'not be able to see things far off.'

2. *If assurance be in a lesser degree, yet yield not to temptations and carnal reasonings*. If our evidences be not so fair, yet we will not part with our inheritance. Coins, as old as groats, that have little of the stamp left, yet are current. We lose our comfort many times, because we yield so easily, because we have not such a strong and clear seal of salvation as we would. To be borne down that we have none at all, is a great weakness. Exercise, therefore, the little faith thou hast, in striving against such objections, and it will be a means to preserve the seal of the Spirit.

3. *Because this sealing is gradual, we should pray*, as Paul, Eph. i. 17, *for a spirit of revelation*, that we may be more sealed. The Ephesians were sealed, for whom Paul prays, and so the Colossians; yet [he prays] that God would reveal to their spirits more their excellent condition. There are '*riches* of assurance,' Col. ii. 2. The apostle would have them to labour not only for assurance, but for the riches of it. That will bring rich comfort, and joy and peace. Times of temptations and trial may come, and such as, if we have not strong assurance, we may be sorely troubled and call all in question. This may be the sad condition of God's own children; and

* That is, 'intention.'—G.

from this, that in times of peace they contented themselves with a lesser degree of this assurance and sealing.

4. Lastly, *Be watchful over your own hearts and ways*, that according to what you have now learned you grieve not the Spirit, 'for by it you are sealed;' intimating, that if [in] anything we withstand and grieve the Spirit, we shall in so doing prejudice ourselves, and suffer in the comfort and evidence of our sealing.

NOTES.

(*a*) P. 417.—'Some men will not hear the word, nor read good books, lest their consciences should be awaked.' We have an example of this in relation to Sibbes himself, in Giles Firmin's 'Real Christian' (4to, 1670). He is illustrating the enmity of the carnal heart to holiness, and goes on to say, 'For others, I know they like it not. And what is the matter? Alas! this would spoil all the sport. Should we once have sin, guilt, and our misery discovered, we must never see merry day after; and that which we fear must follow, our lovers and we must part; and that we find a hard thing, yea, impossible, to bid farewell to those lusts, companions, and ways, which have brought us in so much pleasure and profit in our days." Then he adds, 'These or such like were the thoughts of him *who would not hear Dr Sibbes, for fear he should convert him*, he said," (page 56). Many neglected anecdotes of this sort will be found scattered up and down in Firmin's quaint treatise, which is a *medley* of vividly-put truth, odd yet vigorous thinking, and chatty *memorabilia*, each turning up in the most unexpected corners.

(*b*) P. 420.—'When men cut the rule and standard to fit themselves, and not fit themselves to it.' We have herein a far-back anticipation of Archbishop Whateley's well-known apophthegm, 'It is one thing to wish Scripture to be on our side, and another to wish to be on the side of Scripture;' which indeed is met with under various forms elsewhere.

(*c*) P. 421—'Have not the devils greater parts than any men? Are they not called *dæmones*, from the largeness of their understanding?' The Greek is δαίμων, and the well-known passage in the *Cratylus* of Plato (xxiii) illustrates the text: 'On this account, therefore, it appears to me (Socrates), more than other, he calls them *dæmons*, because they were *prudent* and *learned* (δαημονες).' Cf. Richardson *sub voce*, to whom I am indebted for above reference.

(*d*) P. 421.—'*Quanto major facilitas*, &c.: the more the facility of not sinning, the greater the sin.' One of the familiar distinctions found in nearly all the Fathers—*e. g.*, Augustine and Bernard.

(*e*) P. 422.—'The heathen man could say, It is an ill custom to be cavilling against religion, whether in good earnest or in jest.' Seneca, often.

(*f*) P. 424.—'If a man's conscience be his friend, it will make all friendly to him.' On conscience, cf. notes *gg*, *hh*, *ii*, Vol. III. page 532. Henry Stubbes has enlarged the thought of the present reference in his searching and precious little volume entitled, 'Conscience the best Friend upon Earth; or, the Happy Effects of Keeping a good Conscience' (1677); *not* to be confounded with his namesake and contemporary, the mendacious opponent of the Puritans.

(*g*) P. 426.—'As Nazianzen saith of himself, "Lord, I am an instrument for thee to touch."' The passage is, at the commencement of Orat. viii. *Ad patrem suum*, as follows:—"Ογανον ειμι θεῖον, ὄργανον λογικὸν ὄργανον καλῶ τεχνιτῇ, τῷ πνεύματι, ἁρμαζόμενον και κρουόμενον· John de la Mark has beautifully expanded this idea in his vindication of the inspiration of the Holy Scriptures.

(*h*) P. 428.—'This will take away the excuse, as St Austin argues well. If I had known, saith a wicked man, I would not have done this. Saith he, the pride of thy heart suggests that. Hadst thou not motions and admonitions?' &c. Augustine has this idea in his 'Confessions,' with reference to himself and his long delays in turning to the Lord.

(*i*) P. 435.—'True gold hath the virtue to comfort and strengthen the heat that alchymy gold hath not.' Cf, note *r**, Vol. III. p. 530. The allusion above is to the extraordinary '*pill of gold*,' which was a regular prescription in the days of Sibbes and long after. Richard Baxter in his 'Life' gives a description—grotesque in its seriousness—of the terrible ordeal he passed through after having swallowed a very large one. G.

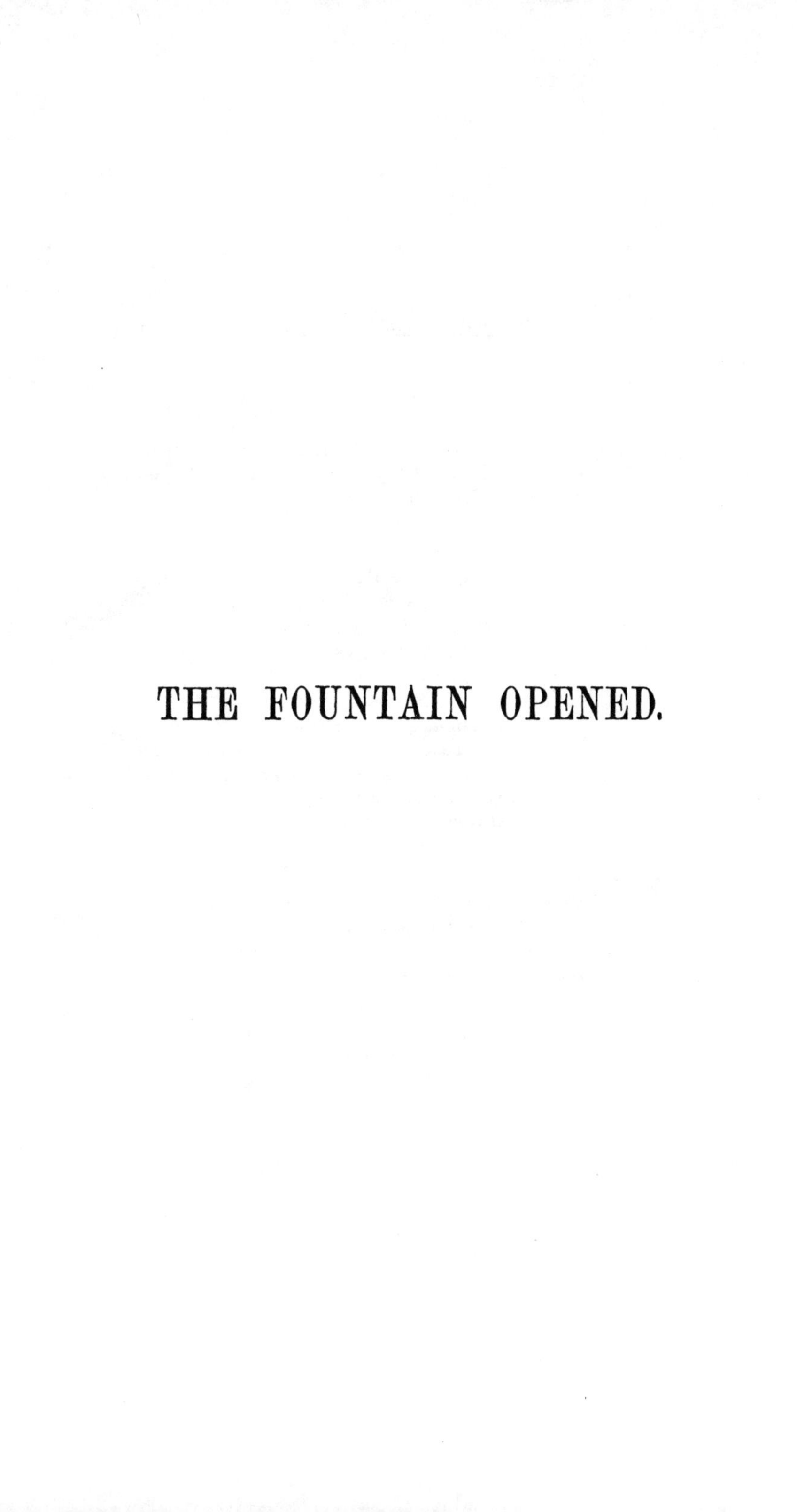

THE FOUNTAIN OPENED.

THE FOUNTAIN OPENED.

NOTE.

'The Fountain Opened' forms one of the four treatises which compose the volume entitled 'Light from Heaven.' (Cf. Vol. IV. p. 490.) Its separate title-page is given below.* It naturally follows 'A Fountain Sealed.' G.

* THE
FOVNTAINE
OPENED:
OR,
THE MYSTERIE
OF GODLINESSE
REVEALED.
BY
The late learned & reverend Divine
RICH. SIBS,
Doctor in Divinitie, Master of *Katherine Hall* in *Cambridge*, and sometimes Preacher at GRAYES-INNE.

JOEL 3. 18.
And a Fountaine shall come forth of the House of the Lord, and shall water the valley of Shittim.

EPHES. 3. 3.
He hath made knowne the Mysterie unto me, which in other ages was not made known unto the sonnes of men.

LONDON,
Printed by *E. Purslow* for *N. Bourne*, at the Royall Exchange, and *R Harford*, at the gilt Bible in Queenes-head Alley, in *Pater-noster-Row.*
1638.

THE FOUNTAIN OPENED;

OR,

THE MYSTERY OF GODLINESS REVEALED.

And, without controversy, great is the mystery of godliness: God manifested in the flesh, justified in the Spirit, seen of angels, preached unto the Gentiles, believed on in the world, received up to glory.—1 TIM. III. 16.

THERE are two things that God values more than all the world besides—the church and the truth. The church, that is the 'pillar and ground of truth,' as it is in the former verse. The truth of religion, that is the seed of the church. Now the blessed apostle St Paul being to furnish his scholar Timothy to the ministerial office, he doth it from two grounds especially: from the dignity of the church, which he was to instruct and converse in; and from the excellency of the mysteries of the gospel, that excellent soul-saving truth. Hereupon he doth seriously exhort Timothy to take heed how he conversed in the church of God, in teaching the truth of God. The church of God, it is 'the house of God,' a company of people that God cares for more than for all mankind besides, for whom the world stands, for whom all things are. 'It is the church of the living God, the pillar and ground of truth.' And for the truth of God, that must be taught in this church, that is so excellent a thing, that we see the blessed apostle here useth great words, high styles, lofty expressions concerning it. As the matter is high and great, so the holy apostle hath expressions suitable; a full heart breeds full expressions. As no man went beyond St Paul, in the deep conceit of his own unworthiness and of his state by nature, so there was no man reached higher in large and rich thoughts and expressions of the excellency of Christ, and the good things we have by him; as we see here, setting forth the excellency of the ministerial calling, being to deal with God's truth towards God's people, he sets forth evangelical truth gloriously here. 'Without controversy, great is the mystery of godliness: God manifested in the flesh,' &c.

In these words, then, there is a preface; and then, a particular explication. There is a fountain or spring, and the streams issuing from it, the root and the branches. There is, as it were, a porch to this great house. Great buildings have fair entrances; so this glorious description of the mysteries of the gospel, it hath a fair porch and entry to it. 'Without controversy, great is the mystery of godliness.'

Then the fabric itself is parcelled out in six particulars:—

God manifested in the flesh.
Justified in the Spirit.
Seen of angels.
Preached unto the Gentiles.
Believed on in the world.
Received up to glory.

First, *For the preface*, whereby he makes way to raise up the spirit of Timothy, and in him us, unto a reverent and holy attending to the blessed mysteries that follow.

'Without controversy, great is the mystery of godliness.'

In this preface, there is first *the thing itself*, 'godliness.'

Then the *description of it*, it is a 'mystery.'

And *the adjunct*, it is a '*great* mystery.'

And then the *seal of it*, it is a great mystery 'without all controversy;' by the confession of all, as the word ὁμολογουμένως signifies. There are none that ever felt the power of godliness, but they have confessed it to be a 'great mystery.'

Godliness is a 'mystery,' and a 'great mystery;' and it is so under the seal of public confession. To observe somewhat from each of these.

'Godliness.'

1. Godliness is either the principles of Christian religion, or the inward disposition of the soul towards them, the inward holy affection of the soul. The word implieth both: for godliness is not only the naked principles of religion, but likewise the Christian affection, the inward bent of the soul, suitable to divine principles. There must be a godly disposition, carrying us to godly truths. That godliness includes the truths themselves, I need go no further than the connection. In the last words of the former verse, the church is 'the pillar and ground of truth;' and then it follows, 'without controversy, great is the mystery'—he doth not say of truth, but—'of godliness;' instead of *truth* he saith *godliness*.

The same word implies the truths themselves, and the affection and disposition of the soul toward them. '*Truths*,' to shew them that both must alway go together. Wheresoever Christian truth is known as it should be, there is a supernatural light. It is not only a godly truth in itself, but it is embraced with godly affections. These blessed truths of the gospel, they require and breed a godly disposition; the end of them is godliness; they frame the soul to godliness. Thus we see the truths themselves are godliness, carrying us to God and holiness. That I need not much stand on. But that there must be an affection answerable, and that this truth breeds this, is a little to be considered. Why is religion itself called faith, and the grace in the soul also called faith? To shew that faith, that is, the truth revealed (as we say the 'apostles' faith'), it breeds faith, and must be apprehended by faith. Therefore one word includes both the object, the thing believed, and likewise the disposition of the soul to that object. So here 'godliness' is the thing itself, the principles of religion; and likewise the disposition of the soul that those truths work, where they are entertained as they should be. Hence follows these other truths briefly.

1. First of all, *That no truth breeds godliness and piety of life but divine truths;* for that is called 'godliness,' because it breeds godliness. All the devices of men in the world cannot breed godliness. All is superstition, and not godliness, that is not bred by a divine truth.

2. Again, hence, in that divine truth is called godliness, it shews us, *if we would be godly we must be so from reasons of Christianity;* not, as I said,

by framing devices of our own, as graceless foolish men do; as we see in popery, it is full of ceremonies of their own devising. But if we will be godly, it must be by reasons and motives from divine truth. That breeds godliness. It is but a bastard godliness, a bastard religion, that is from a good intention, without a good ground. Therefore the word implies both the tenet, the doctrine, and the frame of soul answerable to that doctrine. Good principles, without an impression of it on the soul, is nothing. It will but help us to be damned; and godliness, without a frame of doctrine, is nothing but superstition. Godliness in doctrine frames the soul to godliness in conversation. There are many that, out of a natural superstition (which is alway accompanied with a poisonful malicious disposition against the truth of God), they will have devices of their own; and those they will force with all their power. But if we will be godly, it must be from reasons fetched from divine truth.

3. Again, hence we may fetch a rule of discerning *when we are godly.* What makes a true Christian? When he nakedly believes the grounds of divine truth, the articles of the faith, when he can patter* them over—doth that make a true Christian? No. But when these truths breed and work 'godliness.' For religion is a truth 'according to godliness,' not according to speculation only, and notion. Wheresoever these fundamental truths are embraced, there is godliness with them; a man cannot embrace religion in truth, but he must be godly. A man knows no more of Christ and divine things, than he values and esteems and affects,† and brings the whole inward man into a frame, to be like the things. If these things work not godliness, a man hath but a human knowledge of divine things; if they carry not the soul to trust in God, to hope in God, to fear God, to embrace him, to obey him, that man is not yet a true Christian; for Christianity is not a naked knowledge of the truth, but godliness.

Religious evangelical truth is 'wisdom;' and wisdom is a knowledge of things directing to practice. A man is a wise man, when he knows so as to practise what he knows. The gospel is a divine wisdom, teaching practice as well as knowledge. It works godliness, or else a man hath but a human knowledge of divine things. Therefore, he that is godly, he believes aright and practiseth aright. He that believes ill can never live well, for he hath no foundation. He makes an idol of some conceit he hath, besides the word; and he that lives ill, though he believe well, shall be damned too. Therefore a Christian hath godly principles out of the gospel, and a godly carriage suitable to those principles. And indeed, there is a force in the principles of godliness, from God's love in Christ, to stir up to godliness. The soul that apprehends God's truth aright cannot but be godly. Can a man know God's love in Christ incarnate, and Christ's suffering for us, and his sitting at the right hand of God for us, the infinite love of God in Christ, and not be carried in affection back to God again, in love and joy and true affiance, and whatsoever makes up the respect of godliness? It cannot be. Therefore it is not a cold, naked apprehension, but a spiritual knowledge, when the soul is stirred up to a suitable disposition and carriage, that makes godliness. Now this godliness is

'A mystery.'

What is a mystery?

The word signifies a hidden thing. It comes of *muein*,‡ which is, to shut

* That is, 'mutter,' from the formal 'muttering' of their Latin prayers by the papists, *e g.*, the *pater*noster.—G.

† That is, 'loves.'—G.

‡ The verb is μυέω.—G.

or stop the mouth from divulging. As they had their mysteries among the heathen, in their temples, which they must not discover, therefore there was an image before the temple with his finger before his mouth, shewing that they must be silent in the discovery of hidden mysteries. Indeed, the mysteries of the heathens were so shameful, that they did well to forbid the discovery of them. But I speak only to unfold the nature of the word, which is to shut, or keep secret.

1. A mystery *is a secret*, not only for the present, but that it was a secret, though it be now revealed; for the gospel is now discovered. It is called a mystery, not so much that it is secret, but that it was so before it was revealed.

2. In the second place, that is called a mystery in the Scripture which, howsoever it be clear for the manifestation of it, *yet the reasons of it are hid*. As the conversion of the Gentiles, that there should be such a thing, why God should be so merciful to them, it is called a mystery. So the calling of the Jews, it is called a mystery, though the thing be revealed. Yet that God should be so wondrous merciful to them, that is a mystery. When there is any great reason that we cannot search into the depth of the thing, though the thing itself be discovered, that is a mystery; as the conversion both of Jews and Gentiles.

3. In the third place, a mystery in Scripture is taken for that *that is a truth hid, and is conveyed by some outward thing*. Marriage is a mystery; because it conveys the hidden spiritual marriage between Christ and his church. The sacraments are mysteries, because in the one, under bread and wine, there is conveyed to us the benefits of Christ's body broken and his blood shed; and in the other, under water, a visible outward thing, there is signified the blood of Christ.

In a word—to cut off that which is not pertinent—mystery in Scripture is either the general body of religion, or the particular branches of it. The general body of religion is called a mystery in this place. The whole Christian religion is nothing but a continued mystery, a continuation of mysteries, a chaining together of mystery upon mystery.

And then the particular branches are called mysteries, as I said before. The conversion of the Jews, and likewise of the Gentiles, before it was accomplished, it was a mystery. So the union between Christ and the church is a great mystery, Eph. v. 25; but the whole gospel is here meant, as Christ saith, Mark iv. 11, 'The mysteries of the kingdom of God,' that is, the description of the gospel. What is the gospel? The mystery of God's kingdom, of Christ's kingdom—a mystery discovering how Christ reigns in his church, and a mystery of bringing us to that heavenly kingdom. So, then, the whole evangelical truth is a mystery.

For these reasons:

1. First of all, *Because it was hid* and concealed from all men, till God brought it out of his own bosom: first to Adam in paradise, after the fall; and still more clearly afterwards to the Jews; and in Christ's time more fully to Jews and Gentiles. It was hid in the breast of God. It was not a thing framed by angels or men. After man was fallen to that cursed state, this plot, of saving man by Christ, came not into the head of any creature, to satisfy justice by infinite mercy; to send Christ to die, that justice might be no loser. It could come from no other breast but God's. It must be a divine heavenly wisdom. Therefore it was a plot devised by the blessed Trinity, the Father, Son, and Holy Ghost. It was hid in the secret closet of God's breast. Christ brought it out of the bosom

of his Father. 'No man hath seen God at any time; Christ the only begotten Son, in the bosom of the Father,' John i. 18, he discovers the Father, and his meaning to mankind. Who ever could have thought of such a depth of mercy unto fallen man, when God promised the blessed seed, Gen. iii. 15, if God himself had not discovered it? Therefore this reconciling of justice and mercy, it is a mystery of heavenly wisdom that the creature could never think of, as it is excellently set down, 1 Cor. ii., through the whole chapter.

2. Again, It is a mystery; because when it was revealed, *it was revealed but to few.* It was revealed at the first but to the Jews: 'God is known in Jewry,' &c., Ps. xlviii. 3. It was wrapped in ceremonies and types, and in general promises, to them. It was quite hid from most part of the world.

3. Again, When Christ came, and was discovered to the Gentiles, yet it is a mystery even in the church, *to carnal men, that hear the gospel, and yet do not understand it,* that have the veil over their hearts. It is 'hid to them that perish,' 2 Cor. iv. 3, though it be never so open of itself to those that believe.

4. In the fourth place, It is a mystery, because though we *see some part and parcel of it, yet we see not the whole gospel.* We see not all, nor wholly. 'We see but in part, and know but in part,' 1 Cor. xiii. 9. So it is a mystery in regard of the full accomplishment.

5. Yea, and in the next place, it is a mystery, in regard of what we do not know, *but shall hereafter know.* How do we know divine truths now? In the mirror of the word and sacraments. We know not Christ by sight. That manner of knowledge is reserved for heaven. So here we know as it were in a kind of mystery. We see divine things wrapped up in the mirror of the word, and the mysteries of the sacraments. Indeed, this comparatively to the Jewish church is to 'see the face of God in Christ,' 2 Cor. iv. 6—a clear sight, but compared to that we shall have, it is to see in a glass, or mirror. If we look back, it is a clear sight; if we look forward, it is a sight as it were in a mystery. Even that little that we do know, we do not know it as we shall know it in heaven.

Quest. But is the doctrine of the gospel itself only a mystery?

Ans. No. All the graces are mysteries, every grace. Let a man once know it, and he shall find that there is a mystery in faith; that the earthly soul of man should be carried above itself, to believe supernatural truths, and to depend upon that he sees not, to sway the life by reasons spiritual; that the heart of man should believe; that a man in trouble should carry himself quietly and patiently, from supernatural supports and grounds, it is a mystery. That a man should be as a rock in the midst of a storm, to stand unmoveable, it is a mystery. That the carriage of the soul should be turned universally another way; that the judgment and affections should be turned backward, as it were; that he that was proud before should now be humble; that he that was ambitious before should now despise the vain world; that he that was given to his lusts and vanities before should now, on the contrary, be serious and heavenly-minded: here is a mystery indeed when all is turned backward. Therefore we see how Nicodemus, as wise as he was, it was a riddle to him when our blessed Saviour spake to him of the new birth, that a man should be wholly changed and new-moulded; that a man should be the same and not the same; the same man for soul and body, yet not the same in regard of a supernatural life and being put into him, carrying him another way, leading him in another manner, by other rules and respects, as much different from other men as a man differs from a beast. A strange mystery, that raiseth a man above other men, as much as another man is above other creatures. For a man to be content with his condition, in all changes and varieties, when he is cast and tossed up and down in the world, to have a mind unmoveable, it is a mystery. Therefore St Paul saith, Philip. iv. 11, 12, 'I have entered into religion,' as it were, 'I have consecrated myself.' The word is wondrous significant. 'I have learned this mystery, to be content.' It is a mystery for a man to be tossed up and down, and yet to have a contented mind. 'I can want, and I can abound; I can do all through Christ that strengtheneth me.' Why? I have consecrated myself to Christ and religion, and from them I have learned this point, to be content. Therefore in the text here,—as we shall see afterwards,—not only divine truths are a mystery—'great is the mystery of godliness'—but he insists on particular graces, 'preached to the Gentiles, believed on in the world:' these are mysteries.

In Christ, all is mysteries: two natures, God and man, in one person; mortal and immortal; greatness and baseness; infiniteness and finiteness, in one person.

The church itself is a mystical thing. For under baseness, under the scorn of the world, what is hid? A glorious people. The state of the church in this world, it is like a tree that is weather-beaten. The leaves and fruit are gone, but there is life in the root. So, what is the church? A company of men that are in the world without glory, without comeliness and beauty; yet notwithstanding, they have life in the root, a hidden life: 'Our life is hid with Christ, in God,' Col. iii. 3. The church hath a life, but it is a hidden mystical life, a life under death. They seem to die to the world, but they are alive. This is excellently and theoretically followed by St Paul: 'As dying, and yet we live; as poor, yet making many rich,' 2 Cor. vi. 9. A strange kind of people; poor and rich, living and dying, glorious and base. Yet this is the state of the church here in this world. They are an excellent people, but they are veiled under infirmities of their own, and the disgraces and persecutions of the world. So we see both the doctrine itself, and the graces, and the head of the church, and the church itself, are nothing but mysteries.

Use 1. Is it so that religion is a mystery? Then, first of all, *do not wonder that it is not known in the world:* and that it is not only not known, but persecuted and hated. Alas! it is a hidden thing. Men know not the excellency of it. As great men's sons in a foreign country, they find not entertainment answerable to their worth, but as they are apprehended to be by strangers: so these divine truths they find little acceptance in the world, because they are mysteries; not only mysteries in the tenet, but in the practice. Therefore the practice finds such opposition in the world: 'Father, forgive them,' saith our blessed Saviour, 'they know not what they do,' Luke xxiii. 34. The world knows not what they do, when they hate and persecute religion and religious persons. The church is a mystical thing, and religion is a mystery. It is hid from them. Shall we be moved with the disgraceful speeches of carnal men? They speak they know not what. The thing they speak against is a mystery. Therefore what should we regard the speeches of the world, or follow the example of the world, in embracing religion? Religion is a mystery. Let the world be never so great, it is not the knowledge of great men, or of rich men, it is the knowledge of godly men; it is a 'mystery of godliness.' Shall we follow the example of the world in religion when it is a mystery, and a mystery 'of godliness,' that only godly men know and embrace? Look not, therefore, to the greatness of place, or parts, &c. It is a mystery.

Use 2. Again, If it be a mystery, then it should *teach us to carry ourselves suitable to it.* Nature taught even the heathens to carry themselves reverently in their mysteries; *Procul este profani,* Away, begone all profane (*a*). Let us carry ourselves therefore reverently toward the truth of God, towards all truths, though they be never so contrary to our reason. They are mysteries altogether above nature. There are some seeds of the law in nature, but there are no seeds in nature of the gospel. Therefore we should come to it with a great deal of reverence. St Paul teacheth us an excellent lesson, Rom. xi. 33. When he entered into a depth that he could not fathom, doth he cavil at it? No. 'Oh the depth! Oh the depth!' So in all the truths of God, when we cannot comprehend them, let us with silence reverence them, and say with him, 'Oh the depth!' Divine things are mysteries; the sacraments are mysteries. Let us carry ourselves towards them with reverence. What is the reason that there is one word in the Greek (*b*) and in other languages to signify both common and profane? Because those that come with common affections and common carriage to holy things, they profane them; because as the things are great, so they require a suitable carriage, not a common carriage. We profane the sacrament if we take the bread and wine as a common feast; as St Paul saith, 'You discern not the Lord's body,' 1 Cor. xi. 29. We profane mysteries when we discern not. Beasts and beast-like men discern not the relation of things; that these outward elements have reference to great matters, to the body and blood of Christ. They do not discern them from common bread and wine, though they be used to raise up our souls to the bread of life.

So likewise when we come to the word of God, and 'look not to our feet,' Eccles. v. 1, but come to the church as if we went to a play or some common place, without prayer, without preparation; when we come with common affections, this is to come profanely. Here we come to mysteries, to high things, to great matters. Therefore when we come to converse with God we must not come with common affections; we must carry ourselves holily, in holy business, or else we offer to God 'strange fire,' Num. xxvi. 61. 'God was in this place,' saith Jacob, 'and I was not aware of it,' Gen. xxviii. 17. So when we come to hear the word, when we go to pray, when we receive the sacrament, God is here, and mysteries are here, and we are not aware of it. It is a shame for us not to labour to bring suitable dispositions. It is a matter of that consequent, life or death depends upon it. You know what St Paul saith, 1 Cor. xi. 30, 'For this very cause some are sick, and some weak, and some sleep,' some die. Why? For coming with common affection, for 'not discerning the Lord's body,' for not examining ourselves, for not having answerable dispositions to the greatness of the mysteries we go about. Let us not think it enough to come to the sacrament, and then let the reins loose to all kind of vanity. The very heathens would be ashamed of that. It is the bane and blemish of religion, and such a thing for which we may fear that God will give whole Christendom a purge, I mean, for our excess.

There is a lawful use of feasting* and comely recreations; but to come with unjustifiable vanities, that are not fit at any time, when we should honour God for the greatest gift that ever was, for the incarnation of his Son; to be more profanely disposed then, and to give ourselves to more

* In margin here, 'Application to the Feast of Christ's Nativity.'—G.

loose courses than at other times, how can it but provoke the justice of God, especially it being common? Amongst other things we may justly look for the vengeance of God for this, not only upon this or that place, for it is the fault of Christendom. Shall we carry ourselves thus profanely at these times, when we should walk in a holy disposition? Is this the way to be thankful to God? Let us labour to entertain and embrace these mysteries of the gospel as we should, with a suitable carriage to them; for the gospel will no longer tarry than it hath suitable love and affections to the greatness of the thing. The gospel may leave us, we know not how soon, and go to people that are as barbarous as we were before the gospel came to us. The Romans thought they had victory tied to them, but we have not these mysteries of the gospel tied to us. If we labour not for an answerable carriage, as God hath removed the gospel from the Eastern churches of Asia, that are under the tyranny of the Turks now, so he may, and we know not how soon, take away these blessed and glorious mysteries. Let us reverence these mysteries and bless God for them, and labour to express our thankfulness in our lives and conversations, that God may delight to continue with us, and continue his blessed truth among us. Do but conceive in your own selves what equity is it, that truths should be obtruded to men that care not for them; that live under the mysteries of the gospel with as much liberty to the flesh as if they had never heard of it; that their lives are not better than pagans, perhaps worse. When these things grow general, will God continue these mysteries to us, when there is such a disproportion of affection and carriage? Judge of these things. God should deal justly with us if he should leave us to the darkness of Gentilism, and popery, and confusion, and carry the gospel further west still, to a people that never heard of it, where it should have better entertainment than it hath had of us. I beseech you, let us labour to carry ourselves answerable to this blessed and great mystery, if we would have it continued longer among us.

Use 3. Again, Are these things mysteries, great mysteries? *Let us bless God, that hath revealed them to us*, for the glorious gospel. Oh, how doth St Paul, in every epistle, stir up people to be thankful for revealing these mysteries? What cause have the Gentiles, that were 'in the shadow of death' before, to be thankful to God? What kind of nation were we in Julius Cæsar's time? As barbarous as the West Indians. The cannibals were as good as we (*c*). We that were so before, not only to be civilized by the gospel, but to have the means of salvation discovered, what cause have we to be enlarged to thankfulness? And shall we shew our thankfulness in provoking his majesty? There is nothing in the world that is a ground of that thankfulness, as the glorious gospel, that brings such glorious things as it doth. Men are thankful to men for teaching and discovering the mysteries of their trades, and shall God discover the great mysteries of the gospel of Christ, and shall not we be thankful? Are there not thousands that 'sit in darkness?' Is. xlii. 7. The Romish Church, is it not under the 'mystery of iniquity?' 2 Thes. ii. 7. And that we should have the glorious mysteries of the gospel revealed to us; that the veil should be taken off, and we should see 'the face of God in Christ,' 2 Cor. iv. 6; what a matter of thankfulness is it to all gracious hearts that ever felt comfort by it!

Use 4. Again, It is a mystery. Therefore it should teach us likewise *not to set upon the knowledge of it with any wits or parts of our own*, to think to search into it merely by strength of wit and study of books, and all human helps that can be. It is a mystery, and it must be unveiled by God himself, by his Spirit. If we set upon this mystery only with wits and parts of our own, then what our wits cannot pierce into, we will judge it not to be true, as if our wits were the measure of divine truth; so much as we conceive is true, and so much as we cannot conceive is not true. What a pride is this in flesh, in worms of the earth, that will make their own apprehensions and conceits of things the measure of divine truth, as heretics heretofore have done? It was the fault of the schoolmen in later times. They would come with their logic only and strong wits, and such learning as those dark times afforded, to speak of grace, of the gospel, of justification. They spake of it, and distinguished in a mere metaphysical and carnal manner. Therefore they brought only human learning. They were furnished with Plato and other natural learning, and with these they thought to break through all the mysteries in religion. We must not struggle with the difficulties of religion with natural parts.

It is a mystery. Now therefore it must have a double veil took off: a veil from the thing, and the veil from our eyes. It is a mystery in regard of the things themselves, and in regard of us. It is not sufficient that the things be lightsome that are now revealed by the gospel, but there must be that taken from our hearts that hinders our sight. The sun is a most glorious creature, the most visible object of the world. What is that to a blind man that hath scales on his eyes? So divine truth is glorious. It is light in itself, but there are scales on the eyes of the soul. There is a film that must be taken off, there is a veil over the heart, as St Paul saith of the Jews; therefore they could not see the scope of Moses directing all to Christ. Naturally there is a veil over men's hearts, and that is the reason, that though they have never so many parts, and the things be light in themselves, yet they cannot see. Therefore I say the veil must be taken both from the things and from our hearts; that light being shed into lightsome hearts, both may close together.

Use 5. Again, Being a mystery, *it cannot be raised out of the principles of nature, it cannot be raised from reasons.*

Quest. But hath reason no use, then, in the gospel?

Ans. Yes. Sanctified reason hath, to draw sanctified conclusions from sanctified principles. Thus far reason is of use in these mysteries, to shew that they are not opposite to reason. They are above reason, but they are not contrary to it, even as the light of the sun it is above the light of a candle, but it is not contrary to it. The same thing may be both the object of faith and of reason. The immortality of the soul, it is a matter of faith, and it is well proved by the heathen by the light of reason. And it is a delightful thing to the soul in things that reason can conceive of to have a double light, for the more light the more comfort; to have both the light of nature, and the light of grace and of God's Spirit.

That which reason should do here is to stoop to faith in things that are altogether above reason, as to conceive Christ in the womb of a virgin, the joining of two natures in one, the trinity of persons in one divine nature, and such like. Here it is the greatest reason to yield reason to faith. Faith is the reason of reasons in these things, and the greatest reason is to yield to God that hath revealed them. Is not here the greatest reason in the world, to believe him that is truth itself? He hath said it, therefore reason itself saith, it is the greatest reason to yield to God, who is truth itself. Therefore faith stands with the greatest reason that can be. For things have a greater being in God's word than in themselves, and faith is above reason. Therefore it is the reason of reasons to believe when we have things revealed in the word. That is one use of reason in mysteries, to stop the mouths of gainsayers by reason, to shew that it is no unreasonable thing to believe.

Use 6. Again, Seeing it is a mystery, *let no man despair.* It is not the pregnancy of the scholar here that carries it away. It is the excellency of the teacher. If God's Spirit be the teacher, it is no matter how dull the scholar is. It is a mystery. Pride in great parts is a greater hindrance than simplicity in meaner parts. Therefore Christ, in Mat. xi. 25, he glorifies God that he had revealed 'these things to the simple,' and concealed them from the proud. Let no man despair, for the statutes of God 'give understanding to the simple,' Ps. xix. 7, as the psalmist saith. God is such an excellent mighty teacher, that where he finds no wit he can cause wit.* He hath a privilege above other teachers. He doth not only teach the thing, but he gives wit and understanding. It is a mystery. Therefore as none should be so proud as to think to break thorough it with wit and parts, so let none despair, considering that God can raise shallow and weak wits to apprehend this great mystery.

Use 7. It is a mystery, therefore *take heed of slighting of divine truths.* The empty shallow heads of the world make great matters of trifles, and stand amazed at baubles and vanities, and think it a grace to slight divine things. This great mystery of godliness they despise. That which the angels themselves stand in wonderment at and are students in, that the wits of the world they slight and despise, or dally withal, as if it were a matter not worth reckoning. But I leave such to reformation, or to God's just judgment, that hath given them up to such extremity of madness and folly. Let us labour to set a high price on the mysteries of godliness.

Quest. How shall we come to know this mystery as we should, and to carry ourselves answerable?

Ans. We must desire God to open our eyes, that as the light hath shined, as the apostle saith, Titus ii. 11, 'the grace of God hath shined;' as there is a lightsomeness in the mysteries, so there may be in our eye. There is a double light required to all things in nature,—the lightsomeness in the *medium*, and in the sight; so here, though the mysteries be now revealed by preaching and books and other helps, yet to see this mystery and make a right use of it, there is required a spiritual light to join with this outward light. And hence comes a necessity of depending upon God's Spirit in conversing in this mystery. There must be an using of all helps and means, or else we tempt God. We must read and hear, and, above all, we must pray, as you see David in Ps. cxix. 18, 'Open mine eyes, Lord, that I may see wonders in thy law.' There are wonders in thy law, but my eyes must be opened to see them. He had sight before, but he desires still a further and clearer sight; and as the poor man in the gospel that cried after Christ, when he was asked, 'What wouldst thou have? Lord, that mine eyes might be opened,' Mat. xx. 33, so should every one of us,—considering it is such a ravishing mystery,—cry after God and Christ, 'Lord, that my eyes might be opened, that I may see wonders in thy law;' that I may see the wonders in thy gospel, 'the unsearchable riches of Christ,' Eph. iii. 8. Therefore it is that St Paul, in Eph. i. 17 and Eph. iii. 8, he prays for 'the Spirit of revelation,' that God would vouchsafe that Spirit to take away the veil of ignorance and unbelief from our souls that we may see; and as it is Eph. iii. 18, 'that we may comprehend the height, and

* That is, 'wisdom.'—G.

breadth, and length, and depth,' and all the dimensions of God's love in Christ. This must be done by the Spirit of God, for as St Paul divinely reasons in 1 Cor. ii. 11, 'Who knows the things of God, but the Spirit of God?' Therefore we must plough with God's heifer. If we would know the things of the Spirit, we must have the same Spirit.

Now the Spirit doth not only teach the truths of the gospel, but the application of those truths, that they are ours. This truth of the gospel is mine, the sacrament seals it to me. The preaching of the word takes away the veil from the things, and the Spirit takes away the veil from our souls. It is the office of the Spirit to take the veil off the heart, and to lighten our understandings; and likewise to be a Spirit of application to us in particular. It is to no purpose to know that these things are mysteries, unless they be for us and for our good, that we know Christ is ours, and that God is reconciled to us. Therefore, saith the apostle, 'he hath given us the Spirit, to know the things that are given us of God' in particular, Rom. v. 5. So the Spirit doth not only bring a blessed light to the Scriptures and shew us the meaning in general, but it is a Spirit of application, to bring home those gracious promises to every one in particular, to tell us the things that are given us of God; not only the things that are given to the church, but to us in particular. For the Spirit of God will tell us what is in the breast of God, his secret good-will to the church; he loves the church and he loves thee, saith the Spirit: therefore he is called an 'earnest' and a 'seal' in our hearts, because he discovers not only the truth at large, but he discovers the truth of God's affection in all the privileges of the gospel,—that they belong to us. What a blessed discovery is this, that not only reveals divine truths to us, but reveals them so to us, that we have our share and interest in them!

1. Therefore, whensoever we take the Book of God into our hands, when we come to hear the word, *beg of God the Spirit:* 'My house,' saith God, 'shall be called the house of prayer,' Isa. lvi. 7; not only the house of hearing of divine truths, but the house of prayer. In the use of means, we must look up to God and Christ. It is impudency and presumption to come to these things without lifting up our souls to God. Therefore there is so little profit under these glorious mysteries, because there is so little prayer and lifting up the heart to God. We should go to Christ, that 'opens, and no man shuts; and shuts, and no man opens,' Rev. iii. 7. He hath the key of David. Go to him, therefore, that he would both open the mysteries and open our hearts, that they may close with them.

In Rev. v. 4, St John wept when the book with 'seven seals' could not be opened. He wept that the prophecy was so obscure, that it could not be understood; but then Christ takes the book and opens it. So when we cannot understand divine mysteries, let us groan and sigh to Christ. He can open the book with seven seals, and he lays open all the mysteries as far forth as it concerns us to know. God's children grieve when things are not discovered to them.

There is a contrary disposition in God's people to carnal papists. They vex, that mysteries should be discovered. God's people grieve that they are not discovered enough. They make a perverse use of this. Divine truths are mysteries; therefore they may not be published to people. Nay, divine truths are mysteries; therefore they must be unfolded. Hence comes the necessity of the ministry; for if the gospel be a mystery, that is, a hidden kind of knowledge, then there must be some to reveal it. God hath therefore stablished an office in the church, with which he joins his own sacred Spirit, that both ordinance and Spirit joining together, the veil may be taken off: 'How can they understand without a teacher?' Rom. x. 14. And 'to us is committed the dispensation to preach the unsearchable riches of Christ,' saith St Paul, Eph. iii. 6–8. Therefore there is this ordinance to unfold these depths as much as may serve for us. Profane people, they think they know enough, they need not be taught; as if this were a shallow mystery, or none at all. It argues a profane and naughty heart, not to attend upon all sanctified means; all is little enough. And sometimes God will not grant his Spirit in one means, because he will make us go to another, and from that to another, and run thorough all. He denies his Spirit of purpose in hearing, because he will have us to read; and denies it in that, because he will have us confer and practise the communion of saints; and all little enough to apprehend this glorious, excellent mystery. A man may know a profane heart, therefore, by despising the improvement of any means of knowledge. It is a mystery. Therefore God's people desire to have it taught.

2. Again, If we would understand these mysteries, *let us labour for humble spirits;* for the Spirit works that disposition in the first place: 'The humble, God will teach,' Ps. xxv. 9; the humble, that will depend upon his teaching. Now this kind of humility here required, it is a denial of our own wits,* though they be never so capacious for the things of the world. We must be content 'to become fools, that we may be wise,' 1 Cor. iv. 10. We must deny our own understandings, and be content to have no more understanding in divine things than we can carry out of God's book, than we can be taught by God's word and ordinances. This humility we must bring if we will understand this mystery.

3. And bring withal *a serious desire to know, with a purpose to be moulded to what we know; to be delivered to the obedience of what we know*; for then God will discover it to us. Wisdom is easy to him that will. Together with prayer and humility, let us but bring a purpose and desire to be taught, and we shall find divine wisdom easy to him that will. None ever miscarry in the church but those that have false hearts. They have not humble and sincere hearts, willing to be taught. For if they have that, then God, that hath given this sincerity and will, this resolution, that they will use the means and they will be taught, he will suit it with teachers. God usually suits men with teachers fit for their dispositions. Let a man have a naughty† heart, and he shall find flatterers to build him up in all violent and naughty courses. God in judgment will give him teachers that shall suit his disposition. But if he be a child of God, and have a sincere heart to know the truth, he shall meet with some that shall be as sincere again to tell him the truth. Therefore we should less pity men when we see them run into errors. God sees that they have naughty dispositions; indeed, if they be silly fools, God will have mercy on them, if they be sincere, though they be in error; but if we see men that may know the truth, and yet run into errors, know that such a man hath a poisonous heart, a malicious bent of heart against the truth, or else God would not give him up to such and such things as he is carried with. There is much in that man's disposition that is carried away with false teachers; I mean, where light is discovered. But where God gives a willing mind, there he opens his meaning. Wisdom is easy to him that will understand.

4. And *take heed of passion and prejudice*, of carnal affections that stir up passion; for they will make the soul that it cannot see mysteries that are

* That is, 'understanding.'—G. † That is, 'wicked.'—G.

plain in themselves. As we are strong in any passion, so we judge; and the heart, when it is given up to passion, it transforms the truth to its own self, as it were. Even as where there is a suffusion of the eye, as in the jaundice, or the like, it apprehends colours like itself; so when the taste is vitiated, it tastes things, not as they are in themselves, but as itself is. So the corrupt heart transforms this sacred mystery to its own self, and oft-times forceth Scripture to defend its own sin, and the corrupt state it is in. It will believe what it list. What it loves, it will force itself to believe,—although it be contrary to divine mysteries,—when the heart is deeply engaged in any passion or affection. Let us labour therefore to come with purged hearts (it is the exhortation of the apostles James and Peter*) to receive these mysteries: they will lodge only in clean hearts. Let us labour to see God and Christ with a clear eye, free from passion, and covetousness, and vainglory. We see a notable example of this in the scribes. When they were not led with passion, and covetousness, and envy against Christ, how right they could judge of the gospel, and the unfolding of the prophecies to the wise men. They could tell aright that he should be born in Bethlehem. But when Christ came among them, and opposed their lazy, proud kind of life, that kept people in awe with their ceremonies, &c., then they sinned against the Holy Ghost, and against their own light, and maliced† Christ, and brought him to his end. So it is with men. When their minds be clear, before they be overcast with passion, and strong affections to the world, they judge clearly of divine things; but when those passions prevail with them, they are opposite to that truth that before they saw, in God's just judgment, such is the antipathy and emulation of the heart against this sacred mystery. The heart of itself is an unfit vessel for these holy mysteries; let us desire God to purge and to cleanse them. It is said of the Pharisees in the gospel, that when Christ spake great matters they scoffed at him. But what saith the text? Luke xvi. 14, 'They were covetous.' Let a covetous proud man come to hear the word: he cares not to hear these mysteries. His heart is so engaged to the world, he scorns and laughs at all. And men are unsettled. Sometimes they will grant truths, sometimes they will not, as their passions lead them. As we see in them towards St Paul, Acts xxii. 11, before he discovered himself to be a Pharisee, 'This man is not worthy to live.' But when he discovered himself on their side, 'I am a Pharisee, and the son of a Pharisee,' Acts xxiii. 6. Oh how finely do they mince the matter! 'Perhaps an angel hath revealed it to him,' &c., ver. 9. He was an honest man then. So men either judge or not judge, as their passions and affections carry them. Therefore it is of great consequence to come with clean hearts and minds to the mysteries of God.

There is besides this mystery, a mystery of iniquity, that St Paul speaks of, 2 Thes. ii. 7. There is the mystery of antichrist, as well as the mystery of Christ.

Quest. And why is that called a mystery?

Ans. Because there is mischief, and error, and wickedness conveyed under seeming truth, and goodness, and virtue; even as in this, grace and goodness is conveyed to the world under a show of baseness and meanness. Therefore in Rev. xvii. 5, it is said, the beast hath 'mystery' in her forehead. Indeed, there is the 'mystery of iniquity' in popery. It was literally performed in Julius the Second; for in his papal crown there was written '*Mysterium*,' &c., till at last it was blotted out, and instead thereof

* Cf. 2 Peter iii. 1, and James iii. 17.—G. † That is, = 'maligned.'—G.

was written, '*Julius secundus papa*' (*d*). They began to smell it might be found out. This is recorded by those that saw it. It is a mystery indeed, but a 'mystery of iniquity.' But more particularly;—

Quest. How a mystery of iniquity?

Ans. Because, under the name of Christ and of Christian religion, he is antichrist, opposite to Christ. He is both opposite—the word signifieth antichrist—and *emulus*, one that would be like Christ, a vice-Christ. He is such an opposite as yet he would be his vicar. Under colour of religion he overthrows all religion; and while he would be head of the catholic church, he is head of the catholic apostasy.

These God will have in the church together—the mystery of godliness and ungodliness, of Christ and antichrist. Why? That the one may be a foil to the other. And how shall men magnify, and relish, and highly esteem this mystery I speak of, except they look by way of opposition to the mystery of antichrist, and see how contrary those courses are? Alas! the reason why they so oppose as they do the gospel, and the purity of it, is, because they are contrary mysteries. That must be maintained by ignorance. The gospel, that is a mystery, that must be revealed; and God hath ordained that it should be revealed more and more. Therefore those that would second popery, that are friends of that, they are enemies to the gospel, and to the publishers of it; they cannot carry their conveyance handsomely.* All popish spirits are enemies to the mystery of godliness, because where this is, it blows upon the 'mystery of iniquity;' as indeed the overthrowing of error is the discovering of it; for none would willingiy be cozened. Popery must be discovered with the breath of Christ; that is, with a mystery which is too sharp a breath for his mystery to feel. Therefore blame them not, that they are so bitter opposites to the publishing of divine truths; the one mystery consumes the other. As Moses' rod devoured all the other rods, so truth eats up all opposite errors whatsoever. See but in experience. Wheresoever truth is planted—the gospel and ordinances, and religion of God—how Satan 'falls down like lightning,' and antichrist falls, Luke x. 18. But this by the way, to give a lustre to the other. There are many other mysteries besides the mystery of iniquity in popery. Every trade hath its mystery; and there are mysteries and secrets of state. But this is the mystery of all mysteries, that we should give ourselves most of all to understand. Therefore it is said to be a 'Great mystery.'

1. *That is the adjunct.* It is a 'great mystery.' And here I might be endless; for it is not only great as a mystery—that is, there is much of it concealed—but it is a great and excellent mystery, if we regard whence it came, from the bosom of God, from the wisdom of God. If we regard all that had any hand in it—God the Father, Son, and Holy Ghost, the angels attending upon the church; the apostles, the penmen; preachers and ministers, the publishers of it—it is a 'great mystery.'

2. If we regard *the end of it*, to bring together God and man—man that was fallen, to bring him back again to God, to bring him from the depth of misery to the height of all happiness; a 'great mystery' in this respect.

3. Again, It is 'great,' *for the manifold wisdom that God discovered in the publishing of it, by certain degrees:* first, in types, then after he came to truths; first, in promises, and then performances. First, the Jews were the church of God; and then comes in the Gentiles: a sweet, manifold,

* That is, = becomingly, suitably.—G.

and deep wisdom. It was a great mystery in the manner of conveying of it from time to time, from the beginning of the world.

4. Again, It is a great mystery, *for that it works.* For it is such a mystery as is not only a discovery of secrets, but it transforms those that know it and believe it. We are transformed by it to the likeness of Christ, of whom it is a mystery; to be as he is, full of grace. It hath a transforming, changing power. It gives spiritual sight to the blind, and spiritual ears to the deaf, and spiritual life to the dead. Whatsoever Christ did in the days of his flesh to the outward man, that he doth by his Spirit to the inward man, even by the publication of this mystery; wonders are wrought by it daily.

5. If we consider *any part of it:* Christ, or his church, or anything, it is a mystery, and a 'great mystery.' It must needs be great, that the very angels desire to pry into, 1 Pet. i. 12.

6. *If we regard those that could not pry into it;* as it is 1 Cor. ii. 6, 8, that the wise men of the world understood nothing of it: 'Where is the philosopher?' &c. There are no parts in the world that could ever enter into this. It is above the sharpest wit, the deepest judgment, the reachingest head. They are all nothing here. It is a 'great mystery.' It is a depth above all depths of natural parts whatsoever. It is a wondrous depth. It hath all dimensions, 'the depth and height of the love of God in Christ,' and the 'unsearchable riches of Christ,' saith the apostle Paul.*

7. Again, it is a great mystery, because *it makes us great.* It makes times great, and the persons great that live in those times. What made John Baptist greater than all the prophets and others in those times? Because he saw Christ come in the flesh. What made those after John Baptist greater than he? They saw Christ ascend gloriously; that John Baptist did not. So persons and times are more or less glorious, as they have greater or less manifestation of this mystery. Great is that mystery itself that makes all things great; that makes times and persons great. What made the times of Christ so great? 'Happy are the eyes that see that that your eyes see, and the ears that hear that that your ears hear,' Mat. xiii. 16. Why? Because the Messiah was come. What made the second temple greater than the first? The first, which was Solomon's temple, was more magnificent than the other. Oh it was because Christ came in the time of the second temple and taught there. So it is the manifestation of Christ's truth that makes times and places glorious. Will he not make the soul glorious then where he is? Certainly he doth. What makes these times glorious? But that we have unthankful, dark hearts, or else we would acknowledge they are blessed times that all of us have lived in under the gospel. What makes them so glorious? The glorious gospel that shines in these times out of Egyptian darkness of popery. Little thankful are we for it, and that threateneth a removal of the gospel; for, being *great* things, and disesteemed, and undervalued—men living under the gospel as bad as under paganism—will God continue these great things among us, to be thus vilified and disesteemed?

Let us take heed therefore *that we set a higher price on religion.* It is a mystery, and a great mystery; therefore it must have great esteem. It brings great comfort and great privileges. It is the 'word of the kingdom.' It is a 'glorious gospel;' not only because it promiseth glory, but it makes the soul glorious, more excellent than other persons. Let us raise a greater esteem in our hearts of this excellent truth. It is a 'great mystery.'

* Cf. Eph. iii. 18, and iii. 8.—G.

8. Again, It is a great mystery, *if compared to all other mysteries.* Creation was a great mystery, for all things to be made out of nothing, order out of confusion; for God to make man a glorious creature of the dust of the earth, it was a great matter. But what is this in comparison for God to be made man? It was a great and wondrous thing for Israel to be delivered out of Egypt and Babylon; but what are those to the deliverance out of hell and damnation by the gospel? What are the mysteries of nature, the miracles of nature, the loadstone, &c., to these supernatural mysteries? There are mysteries in the providence of God, in governing the world, mysteries of Satan, mysteries of iniquity, that deceive the world. 'The wise men of the world all wonder at the beast,' Rev. xiii. 3, a great mystery. But what are all mysteries, either of nature or hell, to this 'great mystery'? I might be endless in the point.

Use 1. First of all, learn hence from blessed St Paul *how to be affected when we speak and think of the glorious truth of God;* that we should work upon our hearts, to have large thoughts and large expressions of it. St Paul thought it not sufficient to call it a mystery, but a great mystery. He doth not only call it 'riches,' but unsearchable riches.' So when he speaks of the fruits of the gospel, what strange words the Scripture hath: 'Peace of conscience that passeth understanding,' Philip. iv. 7; and, 'joy unspeakable and glorious,' 1 Peter i. 8; 'we are brought out of darkness into marvellous light,' 1 Peter ii. 9; as if all things were full of wonder in the gospel, both the thing and the fruits of it. Surely all that have the same spirit, and have their eyes open to see in any measure these excellent mysteries, they are in some measure so disposed as the blessed apostle was; that is, they have full hearts, and answerable to that, they have full expressions. Out of the riches and treasure of the heart the mouth will speak. Therefore let us be ashamed of the deadness, and dulness, and narrowness of our hearts, when we are to conceive or speak of these things, and labour to have full expressions of them.

(1.) And that we may the better do this, let us labour *to have as deep conceits in our understandings as we can of that mystery of sinfulness that is in us, and that mystery of misery.* It is not to be conceived the cursed state we are in by nature. It is not to be conceived what a depth of corruption is in this heart of ours, and how it issues out in sinful thoughts, and speeches, and actions every day. Indeed, there is a height, and breadth, and depth of corruption in man's heart; and there is a height, and breadth, and depth of the misery of man. For as it is said of this blessed estate, 'neither eye hath seen, nor ear hath heard, nor hath entered into the heart of man to conceive the things that God hath prepared for those that love him,' Isa. lxiv. 4. So indeed, neither eye hath seen, nor ear hath heard, nor hath entered into the heart of man to conceive the misery that men are in by nature; only there are some flashes of conscience, to give a little taste in this world, of that misery that men in the state of nature fall into, when they go hence. Therefore the more clear knowledge we have of the mystery of corruption—how prone our hearts are to deceive us—and of the great misery we are in by nature, the more we shall wonder at the boundless and bottomless goodness of God in the mystery of our salvation. The one will sharpen the appetite of the other. And, indeed, we ought to have views of these two every day, to look to the state we are brought out of if we believe. If we be not yet in the state of grace, consider but what we are, how little there is between us and eternal destruction, that we are ready to drop into hell irrecoverably; and withal, consider again the infinite love of God in Jesus. These be things fit to take up our thoughts.

(2.) Again, If we would have large and sensible thoughts and apprehensions of these things, such as the blessed apostle, *let us set some time apart to meditate of these things, till the heart be warmed;* let us labour to fasten our thoughts, as much as we can, on them every day; to consider the excellency of this mystery of religion in itself, and the fruit of it in this world and in the world to come. It is a good employment; for from thence we shall wonder at nothing in the world besides. What is the reason that men are taken up with admiration of petty mysteries, of poor things? Because their thoughts were never raised up to higher considerations. A wise man will wonder at nothing, because he knows greater things than those objects presented to him, he hath seen greater measures than those; so it is with a wise Christian. Do you think he will stand wondering at great and rich men, at great places and honours, and such things? Indeed, he knows how to give that respect that is due. Alas!* he hath had greater matters in the eye of his soul, and hath what is great in this world to him, to whom the world itself is not great. What is great in this world to him to whom Christ is great; to whom heaven and the mysteries of religion are great? All things else are little to him to whom these things are great. Christ took up his disciples, when they said, 'O, Master, what kind of stones are here?' Here are 'goodly stones and buildings' indeed. 'Oh,' saith Christ, 'are these the things you wonder at? I tell you, that not one stone shall be left upon another,' Mat. xxiv. 2. So it is the nature of shallow men to wonder at the things of this world, to be taken with empty vain things. Are these the things we wonder at? If we would wonder, let us come to religion. There we have him 'whose name is Wonderful,' Isa. ix. 6. Christ's name is Wonderful, because all is wonderful in Christ. He is wonderful in his person, in his offices, in the managing of them; to bring us to life by death, to glory by shame. He is wonderful in his government of his church, to govern by afflictions, by conforming us to himself, to bring us to glory; to perfect his work in abasement; to bring it low that he may raise it after. There are wonders every way in Christ, not only in himself, but in all his courses. There is 'peace that passeth understanding,' joy unspeakable and glorious. Religion will teach us what to admire† at. We see those that are under antichrist, under the mystery of iniquity, it is said, Rev. xvii. 8, 'They wonder at the beast.' Oh what a goodly order they have among them, one under another! What a wise fabric it is! What a linking together of things! All is wonderful. Indeed, it is fit for them to wonder at, that have not seen these wondrous mysteries of the gospel; but those that have spiritual eye-salve to enlighten the eye of their souls, to see these blessed mysteries how great they are, they will be far from wondering at any earthly thing, much less at the mystery of antichrist. It is a 'great mystery,' therefore,

Use 2. Let us bring great endeavours to learn it, and great respect towards it, and great love to God for it. Let every thing in us be answerable to this 'great mystery,' which is a 'great mystery.'

'Without controversy.'

It is so under the broad seal of public confession, as the word ὁμολογουμένως in the general signifies; by the confession of all, it is 'great.' It is

* Another example of Sibbes's peculiar use of 'Alas!'—G.

† That is, 'wonder at.'—G.

a confessed truth, that the 'mystery of godliness is great.' As if the apostle had said, I need not give you greater confirmation; it is, without question or controversy, a great mystery.

Obj. What is more opposed than the mystery of godliness?

Ans. We must therefore take St Paul's meaning in a right sense. It is therefore 'a great mystery,' because it is controverted by so many great wits.* Were it altogether obvious and open, they would never controvert it. Upon these two reasons it is without controversy.

(1.) First, *In itself*, it is not to be doubted of. It is a great grounded truth, as lightsome and clear as if the gospel were written with a sunbeam, as one saith (*e*). There is nothing clearer and more out of controversy than sacred evangelical truths.

(2.) And as they are clear and lightsome in themselves, so they are apprehended *of all God's people*. However it be controverted by others, yet they are not considerable. All that are the children of the church, that have their eyes open, they confess it to be so, and wonder at it as a 'great mystery.' They without all doubt and controversy embrace it. Things are not so clear in the gospel that all that are sinful and rebellious may see whether they will or no. For then it were no great matter to have faith; it were no great matter to be a Christian; and then men could not be rebellious, because things would be so clear. Things are not so clear in the gospel that they take away all rebellion; and that it is not a grace to see that they are clear; to those that are disposed and have sanctified souls, they are 'without controversy;' and things are said to be in Scripture as they are to those that are holily disposed. The immortality of the soul, it is clear by reason from nature, yet notwithstanding, ill-disposed souls will not be convinced of the soul's immortality, but live and die like atheists in that particular. The reason is clear; but it is not clear to a lumpish, ill-disposed, perverse soul. Therefore God doth carry the manifestation of evangelical truths especially, that they may be clear to those whose eyes are open, and not to others: not because they are not clear to them if their eyes were open, but because they oppose them, and raise up rebellion and stubbornness of heart against them. It is an undeniable argument to prove the Scripture to be the word of God, to a well-disposed soul, but come to another, and he will never leave cavilling. Yet a man may say, 'without controversy,' it is the word of God, because it is so to a sanctified soul. Other persons are not considerable in divine things. Therefore the apostle speaks of them, as they are to God's people, 'without controversy.' Hence then, we may know who is a true Christian; he that brings a firm assent to evangelical truths, that they are 'great without controversy.'

Quest. But is there no staggering, is there no *formido contrarii?*† Is there no fear that it may be otherwise?

Ans. Yes. But in faith, as far as it is faith, there is no doubting, no contrariety; for staggering and wavering is contrary to the nature of faith and believing. But because there are two contrary principles always in a believer, therefore there is doubting in a believer, and wavering. Therefore we are exhorted to grow more and more; and the end of the ministry is not only to lay the foundation of a believer at the first, but to build them up, that they be not carried away with every vain doctrine. It is a truth, confessed to be true; for divine truths are conveyed in an history, in the

* That is, 'wise men,' *i.e.*, in self-estimate.—G.

† That is, 'no fear of the contrary.'—G.

history of the gospel; and what ground have we to call them in question, more than the story of Thucydides, or the story of Livy, or such like? We take them, because they are the histories of such times. So the mystery of the gospel is 'without controversy,' because it is a mystery in a history. In this respect a man is more unreasonable that denies it, than he that denies Livy's book to be Livy's, or Tacitus to be Tacitus. No man calls these into question. Why should we question this that is the 'mystery of godliness,' set down in the history of Christ, of his birth, his life, and death? &c. But not to press that further.

Use 1. I will only make that use of it that a great scholar in his time once did upon the point, a noble earl of Mirandula *(f)*. If there be no calling these things into question, if they have been confirmed by so many miracles, as they have been in a strict sense, why then, How is it *that men live as if they made no question of the falsehood of them?* What kind of men are those that live as if it were 'without controversy,' that Christian truths had no truth at all in them? Men live so carelessly and profanely, and slight and scorn these great mysteries, as if they made no question but they are false (*g*). The lives of men shew that they believe not this. That it is out of the question true: to give an instance or two. If a man were to go through a storm for some great matter, if he did believe he should have some great preferment, would he not adventure? Certainly he would. Those, therefore, that will not venture anything for this excellent treasure, this unsearchable treasure, for his interest in the gospel, do they believe it? He that will not part with a penny for the gaining of a thousand pounds, doth he believe that he shall have so much? Certainly he doth not. There is such a disproportion between that that he parts with, and that that is promised, that if he did believe it, his heart would yield and assent to it, he would redeem it with the loss of such a petty thing; much more in this case, having such an excellent treasure propounded. Those, therefore, that will deny themselves no lust, that will part with nothing for Christ's sake, do they believe these things that the apostle saith are 'without controversy'? Certainly they do not; for there is a less disproportion in the things I named before, than between any earthly thing and the great good things we have discovered here in the mysteries of salvation. Therefore, we may see by this, *there is little faith in the world.*

Use 2. Again, in that he saith, 'Without controversy,' or confessedly, 'great is the mystery of godliness:' here we may know then, *what truths are to be entertained as catholic universal truths*, those that without question are received. Then, if the question be, which is the catholic truth—popery, or our religion—I say, not popery, but our religion. I prove it from hence. That which 'without controversy,' all churches have held from the apostles' time (yea, and the adversaries and opposites of the church), that is catholic. But it hath been in all times, and in all churches, even among the adversaries held, the positive points of our religion, that the Scripture is the word of God; that it is to be read; that Christ is the mediator; that Christ hath reconciled God and man, &c.,—all the positive parts of our religion have been confessed, 'without controversy,' ever since the apostles' times, of all writers; and are still, even among the papists themselves, for they hold all the positive points that we do: they hold the reading of the Scripture, but not in the mother tongue; they hold that the Scripture is the word of God, but not alone, but traditions also; that Christ is mediator, but not alone. So they add their part, but they hold the positive parts that we hold. Therefore I ground that from the text:

that which 'without controversy' hath been held in all times and ages of the church, and 'without controversy' held by ourselves and the adversaries, it is more catholic and general than those things wherein they dissent from us, that were neither held from the apostles' times (for they were the inventions of popes, one after another; their fooleries, wherein they differ from us, they are late inventions, and we hold them not), they are less catholic than that that they and we and all Christians hold ever since the apostles' times. But to come to a use of practice.

Use 3. Therefore when we have the truths of religion discovered to us by the ministry, or by reading, &c., when they are conveyed to our knowledge by any sanctified means, *let us propound these queries to our own souls*, Are these things so or no? Yes. Do I believe them to be so or no? Yes. If I do believe them, then consider what the affection and inward disposition is; whether it be suitable to such things, and so work upon our hearts that our knowledge may be affective knowledge, a knowledge with a taste, that sinks even to the very affections, that pierceth through the whole soul; that the affections may yield, as well as the understanding; and let us never cease till there be a correspondence between the affection and the truth. Are they true? Believe them. Are they good? Embrace them. Let us never rest till our hearts embrace them, as our understanding conceives them. And let us think there is a defect in our apprehensions, that we call them into question, if the affections embrace them not; for alway, answerable to the weight and the depth of the apprehension of the truth, is the affection stirred up, and the will stirred up to embrace it. A man knows no more in religion than he loves and embraceth with the affections of his soul.

The affections are planted for this end upon the report of that which is good to them, to embrace it, to join with it. Therefore let us never think our state good, till we find our hearts warmed with the goodness of divine supernatural truths. 'Oh! how do I love thy law!' saith David, Ps. cxix. 97. He wonders at his own affections. Let us labour to have great affections, answerable to the things; and never leave till we can love them and joy and delight in them, as the greatest things; and with blessed St Paul, account 'all as dung and dross, in comparison of them,' Philip. iii. 8. That knowledge is only saving knowledge that works the heart to a love, to a joy and delight, that works the whole man to practice and obedience; that is only spiritual knowledge. All other knowledge serves for nothing but to minister God matter of justifying our damnation; that our damnation will be just; that knowing these things, we do not work our hearts to love them, but we rest in the naked barren knowledge of them. It is a pitiful thing, to know things no further and no deeper, than to minister matter of our just damnation. Now all that have not a transforming knowledge, that have not a spiritual knowledge, they are in this state. Therefore we should labour to see spiritual things, in a spiritual light; for where spiritual light is, there is alway spiritual heat; where spiritual evidence is in the understanding, there is spiritual embracing in the affections. Evidence brings quickness. Supernatural light and supernatural life, they go together. Let us labour, therefore, that our apprehension of these great mysteries may be supernatural and spiritual; and then as the judgment apprehends them 'without controversy' to be true, the affections will be present, to close with them. So much for the preface, 'without controversy, great is the mystery of godliness.' Now we come to the particulars of this great mystery,

'God manifested in the flesh.'

This, and the other branches that follow, they are all spoken of Christ. Indeed, the 'mystery of godliness' is nothing but Christ, and that which Christ did. Christ was 'manifested in the flesh, justified in the Spirit, seen of angels, preached to the Gentiles, believed on in the world, received up in glory.' So that from the general we may observe this, that

Christ is the scope of the Scripture.

Christ is the pearl of that ring; Christ is the main, the centre wherein all those lines end. Take away Christ, what remains? Therefore in the whole Scriptures, let us see that we have an eye to Christ; all is nothing but Christ. The mystery of religion is Christ 'manifested in the flesh, justified in the Spirit,' &c., all is but Christ.

And that is the reason the Jews understand not the Scriptures better, because they seek not Christ there. Take away Christ, take away all out of the Scriptures, they are but empty things. Therefore, when we read them, think of somewhat that they may lead us to Christ, as all the Scriptures lead, one way or other, to Christ, as I might shew in particular, but I only name it in general.

He begins here with this, 'God manifested in the flesh;' not God taken essentially, but taken personally. God, in the second person, was manifested. All actions are of persons. The second person was incarnate. The three persons are all God; yet they were not all incarnate, because it was a personal action of the second person.

Quest. And why in that person?

Ans. 1. Because he was the image of God. And none but the image of God could restore us to that image. He was the Son of God, and none but the natural Son could make us sons. He is the 'wisdom' of the Father, to make us wise, and he is the 'first beloved' to make us beloved. Such reasons are given by the school-men, and not disagreeable to Scripture. For, indeed, it is appropriate to the second Person, the great work of the incarnation, 'God in the flesh.' Therefore they usually compare the incarnation of Christ to a garment made by three virgins, sisters; and one of them wears it. So all the three persons had a hand in the garment of Christ's flesh. The Father had a work in it, and the Holy Ghost sanctified it, yet he only wore it. Therefore the second person is 'God manifest in the flesh.'

By 'flesh,' here, is meant human nature; the property of human nature, both body and soul. And by 'flesh' also, is usually understood the infirmities and weakness of man, the miserable condition of man. So 'God manifest in *the flesh*,' that is, in our nature and the properties of it, he put that on; and not only so, but our infirmities, and weaknesses, our miseries, and which is more, he took our flesh when it was tainted with treason, our base nature after it was fallen, which was a wondrous fruit of love. As if one should wear a man's colours or livery after he is proclaimed traitor; it is a great grace to such a man. For Christ to wear our garment when we were proclaimed traitors, after we were fallen, it was a wondrous dignation.* And he took not only our nature, but our flesh. He was 'God manifest in *the flesh*,' that is, in the infirmities of our nature. He took our whole nature, a human body and human soul. And he took our nature upon him when it was at the worst; not in innocency, but with all the infirmities that are natural infirmities, not personal. Therefore he came to be so that he might be pitiful.

* That is, 'doing honour.'—G.

Quest. You will say, How can he be pitiful? There are many infirmities that he took not upon him; he took not upon him all infirmities.

Ans. I answer, by proportion to those that he took, he knew how to be pitiful to those he took not. He is infinitely wise. He knows how to make the proportion. It is often set down, in Heb. ii. 18 and Heb. iv. 15, as one end of his taking our nature upon him, that he might be a pitiful and merciful redeemer.

Obj. But some will say, Indeed, he took my nature and the general infirmities, as weariness, and hunger, and the like; but I am sick and troubled in mind and conscience.

Ans. Though he felt not all particular grievances, yet notwithstanding, having taken our nature upon him, that he might be pitiful and merciful, according to the proportion that he felt himself, he knows how to pity us in our sicknesses, and losses, and crosses, every way. And for the chief, the trouble of mind, alas! he knew it in that great desertion, when he cried out, 'My God, my God, why hast thou forsaken me!' So we may comfort ourselves that we have a merciful, and pitiful, and gracious Saviour, 'God in the flesh.' He hath taken our flesh upon him for that purpose, that he might have experimental knowledge of our infirmities and weaknesses, and from that he might be the more sweet, and kind, and gentle to us. He was not sick himself; but by experience of labour, and thirst, and the like, he knew what it was to be sick by that he felt. He knew not what it was to sin and to be troubled for sin, because he felt it not in himself; but being our surety for sin, and feeling the wrath of God for it, he had experience to be compassionate from this. He was weary, to pity those that are weary; he was hungry, to pity them that are hungry; he was poor, to pity those that are so; he was misused and reproached, to pity those that are in the like condition. You can name nothing, but he can out of his own experience be merciful and pitiful unto.

In that God, the second person, appeared in our nature, in our weak and tainted disgraced nature after the fall; from hence comes,

1. First of all, *the enriching of our nature with all graces in Christ*, as it is in Col. ii. 3, 'All the treasures of wisdom and knowledge are in him,' in our nature. In Christ there is abundance of riches. Our nature in him is highly enriched. Hence comes again,

2. *The ennobling of our nature.* In that God appeared in our nature it is much ennobled. When our nature is engraffed into a higher stock, a mean graff or syens,* into so glorious a stock as Christ, it is a high dignity. That now our flesh is married to the second person, it is a wondrous advancement of our nature, even above the angel call, 'He took not the nature of angels,' Heb. ii. 16. It was a great exaltation to our nature, that God should take it into the unity of his person, for the human nature of Christ had no subsistence but in the second person. And this doth not any way debase the human nature of Christ, that it had no subsistence but in the Godhead. Peter, and James, and John, &c., had a subsistence of their own, but Christ had no subsistence but in the second person. And yet, I say, it did no way demean the human nature of Christ, because it was advanced to a higher stock, where it hath a glorious subsistence and being.

3. In the third place, hence comes *the enabling of our nature to the work of salvation that was wrought in our nature.* It came from hence, 'God was in the flesh.' From whence was the human nature enabled to suffer?

* That is, 'scion' = graft.—G.

Whence was it upheld in suffering, that it did not sink under the wrath of God? 'God was in the flesh.' God upheld our nature. So that both the riches, and dignity, and the ableness of our nature to be saving and meritorious, all came from this, that God was in our nature.

4. And hence comes this likewise, that *whatsoever Christ did in our nature, God did it,* for God appeared in our nature. He took not upon him the person of any man, but the nature. And therefore our flesh and the second person being but one person, all that was done was done by the person that was God, though not as God. Therefore when he died, God died; when he was crucified, God was crucified. If he had been two persons, he had died in one person, and the other had not died. Now, being but one person, though two natures, whatsoever was done in the [one] nature, the person did it according to the other nature. He could not die as God. Therefore, because in love he would die, and be a sacrifice, he would take upon him such a nature wherein he might be a sacrifice. This is a great dignity, that our nature is taken into the unity of the person of the Son of God. Therefore hence it comes, I say, that whatsoever was done in our nature God did it.

5. Hence comes also *the union between Christ and us.* Whence is it that we are 'sons of God?' Because he was the 'Son of man,' 'God in our flesh.' There are three unions: the union of natures, God to become man; the union of grace, that we are one with Christ; and the union of glory. The first is for the second, and the second for the third; God became man, that man might be one with God; God was 'manifested in the flesh,' that we might be united to him; and being brought again to God the Father, we might come again to a glorious union. By this, that God was 'manifest in the flesh,' it is that he was married first to our nature, that we by union might be married to him. We had never had union with God unless God had united our flesh to him, and in that flesh had satisfied God. All that Christ did, saith Peter, it was to 'bring us back again to God,' 1 Peter iii. 18.

6. Hence likewise comes *the sympathy between Christ and us;* for Christ is said to suffer with us. 'Saul, Saul, why persecutest thou me?' Acts ix. 4. He is said to be imprisoned in us; and we are said to ascend gloriously with him, because he took upon him our nature. So if he be honoured, we are honoured; if we be despised, he is despised. There is a mutual affection and sympathy between Christ and us.

7. Hence likewise comes *the efficacy of what Christ did,* that the dying of one man should be sufficient for the whole world. It was, that 'God was in the flesh.'

The apostle may well call this, 'God manifest in the flesh,' a 'mystery,' and place it in the first rank For God to be included in the womb of a virgin; for happiness itself to become a curse; for him that hath the riches of all men to become poor for our sake; for him that ever enjoyed his Father's presence, to want the beams of it for a time, that he might satisfy his Father's justice, and undergo his wrath for our sins—here is a matter of wonderment indeed!

Use 1. *And shall we think that so great a mystery as this was for small purpose?* that the great God should take upon him a piece of earth? that he should become a poor and weak man? the immortal God to take upon him our flesh and to die? that he whom heaven and earth cannot comprehend should be enclosed in the womb of a virgin? for him to be so abased as there was never any abasement like unto Christ's, because of the greatness of his person? If angels had done so; alas!* they were inferior creatures; they were servants to God; but for the Son of God to take our nature when it was so low, for so excellent a person to be abased so low! There was none ever suffered that, that 'God in our flesh' suffered. For as communion with his Father was sweeter to him than to all men besides, so for him to want communion with his Father upon the cross, when he cried, 'My God, my God, why hast thou forsaken me?' it was the greatest abasement to him, being the most sensible of it.† Therefore there was no suffering like that of Christ's. And shall we think so great a matter was for small purpose, for little sins or for few sins only? Oh no. It was to give a foundation to our faith in all extremity of temptations; to stay our conscience in the guilt of great and crying sins. Oh despair not, despair not! This great mystery the apostle speaks of, for the great God to become man, it was for great sins; that where 'sin hath abounded, grace might superabound,' Rom. v. 20. God intended in this to set down the accusing conscience, to quiet and still it. God is offended, it is true; but 'God manifest in the flesh' hath made reconciliation and satisfaction. He was a sacrifice for sin, and God will answer God. God the Son will answer the displeasure of God the Father, because he is appointed to this office by him. He is 'set forth,' as it is Rom. iii. 25, 'to be the propitiation.' Therefore in all risings of conscience in the time of trouble, in the hour of death, let us remember this great mystery, 'God manifest in the flesh.' God's purpose in this was to triumph, as it were, over all the clamours of conscience whatsoever, over all things that Satan and the power of hell can object. Let Satan object what he will, here is a shield put into the hand of faith to beat back all his fiery darts.

God in the covenant of grace, which is founded in Christ, in God in our nature, doth intend to be gracious to sinners. It is a greater mystery than that of the creation. For God there did good to a good man; he made Adam good, and continued him good while he stood; but after the fall, God intended to raise up the doubting, unbelieving soul against the greatest ills of sin and despair, and against all objections for sin whatsoever; from the greatness of sin either natural or actual. It is the glory of God in the gospel to glorify his mercy and goodness in prevailing and triumphing over the greatest ills that can be. Now he is good to sinners, and to great sinners; so that if there be faith wrought by the Spirit of God, raising up our souls to lay hold of this 'God manifest in the flesh,' let us not be discouraged with any sin. Our sins are but the sins of men; but 'God manifest in the flesh' was made a sacrifice for our sins, and hath given a price answerable. What temptation will not vanish as a cloud before the wind when we see God's love in sending his Son, and Christ's love in taking our nature on him, to reconcile us by the sacrifice of his blood? Therefore let us treasure up this comfort. It is a spring of comfort, a well of consolation, as the Scripture speaks; therefore let us suck comfort out of this breast of consolation.

We may turn over things now, in the time of peace, with ease; but in time of temptation, when the soul is touched with guilt, and Satan plies us with temptations, the soul will have no rest but in an infinite ground of comfort. The soul is prone naturally to misgive, and to forecast the worst, and to conceive hardly of God in the time of temptation, as an enemy, and Satan is then busy about nothing so much as that we should have hard conceits of God, and to make us forget the main end of the great work of

* Cf. page 475, line 16.—G.

† Cf. note *u*, Vol. III. page 531.—G.

our redemption; which is, to undermine our unbelief by all means, by setting before the soul such grounds as the most unbelieving heart in the world, if it did consider of, would fasten and lay itself upon. Therefore let us labour to cherish, at such times especially, large thoughts of the infinite goodness and mercy of God, and of the love of Christ condescending so low as to be manifest in the flesh for our sakes.

It is a point of wondrous comfort, that now in Christ Jesus, God becoming man, we can in him break through the justice of God. For, as I said, when conscience is awaked, there are other manner of conceits of God than when it is sleepy and drowsy. A sleepy Christian hath a slight conceit of God, as if he as little thought of his sins as he doth himself. Oh but when conscience is awaked, and when we are drawn from the pleasures of sin, and they from us, and conscience hath nothing to do but to look upon God and upon the time to come, which is eternity, then if there be not somewhat for conscience to oppose that is equal to the justice of God, if there be not somewhat about us to clothe us and arm us, to pass through the justice, what will become of us? Therefore it is a fruitful consideration, that God was 'manifest in our flesh,' and that, to give satisfaction to God, that so conscience might have full satisfaction.

This teacheth us what we should do when we find any trouble rise in our conscience for sins and unworthiness. Cast ourselves upon 'God in our flesh,' God that became 'flesh' for us and died for us: let us stay ourselves there. I am unworthy! a lump of sin! There is nothing in me that is good. Oh but I have all in Christ. He is righteousness for me. He hath abundance for me. His fulness is for me. Therefore you have it, Col. ii. 9, 'The fulness of the Godhead dwells in him bodily.' To what purpose is this fulness in him? He shews in the words following, 'In him we are complete,' ver. 10. Suppose in ourselves we be sinners and weak, that we are as ill as sin or the devil can make us in the time of temptation, yet 'in him we are complete.' And for this end 'the fulness of the Godhead dwells in him bodily.' Therefore, in all doubts in regard of sin and unworthiness, let us labour for faith (for faith is a grace that carries us out of ourselves, and plants and fixeth us in Christ), let us consider of ourselves in him, and consider of whatsoever is in him, it is for us. It is no matter what we are ourselves; in him we are in a glorious condition.

And oppose him to the wrath of God and the temptations of Satan; for all will fall before this 'God manifest in the flesh.' He is God, therefore he can subdue all; he is man, and therefore he will love us. 'I know whom I have believed,' 2 Tim. i. 12—him that is merciful, because he is man, and he hath taken my nature; and him that can subdue all enemies, because he is God, God in the flesh: a fit bottom and foundation for faith to rely upon. Let us have recourse to this therefore in all temptations whatsoever. We cannot glorify God and Christ more than to go out of ourselves and fix our comfort here.

By this we have communion with the Father, Son, and Holy Ghost. This incarnation of Christ, it brings us into fellowship with the blessed Trinity; and it teacheth us what conceits we should have of God, to have loving thoughts of him. Whence is that that we can call God Father? From this, 'God manifest in the flesh.' The second person, to take away enmity, was 'manifest in the flesh.' Hence it is that I can call God Father, that I can boldly go to God, that I can conceive of God as gracious and lovely. And whence is it that our persons are become lovely to God?

From this, that God hath taken our nature upon him. Our nature is become lovely to him, and his is sweet and fatherly to us.

This should help us against Satan's transforming of God and Christ to us in the time of trouble. He presents him as a terrible judge. Indeed, so he is to sinners that will go on in sin. His wrath shall 'smoke against such,' Deut. xxix. 20. There is no comfort to them in Scripture. But to repentant sinners all is comfort: 'Come unto me, ye that are weary and heavy laden,' Mat. xi. 28; and, 'Christ came to seek and to save that which was lost,' Mat. xviii. 11; and, he came 'to save sinners,' as St Paul saith, 1 Tim. i. 15. Let us conceive of God now as lovely, as a father; and of Christ as a sweet saviour, made 'flesh' for this purpose. He is God and man, because he came to be a mediator between God and man; a friend to both, being to deal with both. Therefore we should thus conceive of Christ: as a great and mighty God, the ruler of the world, as Isaiah describes him, Isa. ix. 6, and conceive of him likewise as a meek, humble man—the one, to stablish our faith, that we be not shaken, having such a great God to rely upon; and the other, to stablish our faith in his good will, 'God in *our flesh*.' God, a name of power; 'God in our *flesh*' implieth mercy and love, pity and compassion.

Therefore, let not Satan abuse our imaginations, if we have a mind to turn to God; for, as I said, there is no comfort to them that go on in their sins. God will wound the 'hairy scalp of them that go on in iniquity,' Ps. lxviii. 21; and, 'they treasure up wrath against the day of wrath,' Rom. ii. 5. There is nothing but discomfort to such: 'The wrath of God abides upon them,' John iii. 36. They are in danger of damnation every minute of their lives. There is but a step between them and hell. But for such as intend to turn to God, God meets them half-way. We see the prodigal did but entertain a purpose to come to his father, and his father meets him. 'God in our flesh' hath made God peaceable to us. If we go to Christ, and lay hold on him for the forgiveness of our sins, God in him is become a loving, gracious, sweet Father to us. Let us frame our conceits of God as the Scripture doth. When sorrow for sin possesseth our souls, take heed of going away from God, that took our nature for this very purpose, that we may boldly go to him.

Oh what boldness have we now to go to 'God in our flesh.' To think of God absolutely, without God in the flesh, he is 'a consuming fire,' Heb. xii. 29, every way terrible; but to think of God in our nature, we may securely go to him: 'He is bone of our bone, and flesh of our flesh,' Gen. ii. 23. We may securely go to God our brother, to him that is of one nature with us, and now having our nature in heaven. Think of God born of a virgin, of God lying in the cradle, sucking the breast! Think of God going up and down teaching and doing all good! Think of God sweating for thee, hanging on the cross, shedding his blood, lying in the grave, raising himself again, and now in heaven 'sitting at the right hand of God,' our intercessor! Eph. i. 20. Conceive of God in this 'flesh' of ours, lovely to us; and now our nature must needs be lovely to him. The nature of God must needs be lovely to us, since he hath joined our poor beggarly flesh to the unity of the second person. Let us thus think of 'God manifest in the flesh.' To think of God alone, it swallows up our thoughts; but to think of God in Christ, of God 'manifest in the flesh,' it is a comfortable consideration. To see the sun alone in itself, in the glory and lustre of it, it is impossible, without hurting of the eye; but to see the sun in water, as we do in an eclipse, &c., we may do it. So we cannot conceive of God alone absolutely; but to conceive of 'God in our flesh' is to look upon the sun as it were in the water, or upon the ground. God in himself is so glorious that we could never see him, as he tells Moses, Exodus xxxiii. 20, 'None can ever see God and live;' that is, God nakedly or absolutely. Oh but 'God manifest in our flesh' we may see; and it shall be our happiness in heaven to see him there, to see 'God in our flesh face to face,' Exodus xxxiii. 11.

We cannot too often meditate of these things. It is the life and soul of a Christian. It is the marrow of the gospel. It is the wonder of wonders. We need not wonder at anything after this. It is no wonder that our bodies shall rise again; that mortal man should become afterwards immortal in heaven, since the immortal God hath taken man's nature and died in it. All the articles of our faith and all miracles yield to this grand thing, 'God manifest in the flesh.' Believe this, and believe all other. Therefore, let us often have these sweet cherishing conceits of God in our flesh, that it may strengthen, and feed, and nourish our faith, especially in the time of temptation.

Use 2. Again, From this, that God was 'manifest in our flesh,' let us take heed *that we defile not this flesh of ours, this nature of ours.* What! Is this 'flesh' of mine taken into unity with the second person? Is this 'flesh' of mine now in heaven, 'sitting at the right hand of God?' And shall I defile this flesh of mine that I profess to be a member of Christ? 'Shall I make it the member of an harlot?' 1 Cor. vi. 15. Shall I abuse it, as intemperate persons do? Let us honour our nature, which Christ hath so honoured; and let us take a holy kind of state upon us, to think ourselves too good, since God hath so advanced our nature, to abase it to the service of sin.

Use 3. Likewise, it should teach us *to stoop to any service of Christ or our brethren.* What! Did the love of God draw him into the womb of the virgin? Did it draw him to take my nature and flesh on him? And shall I think much to be serviceable to my poor brethren, for whom God was made flesh, and not only so, but was crucified? Such thoughts will take down such proud conceits as enter into our hearts when we are about any work of charity for the members of Christ. Shall I have base conceits of any man, whose flesh Christ hath taken? Especially, when I see any goodness in him, let me abase myself to any work of charity.

Take heed of pride. God himself emptied himself, and wilt thou be full of pride? He became of 'no reputation,' Philip. ii. 7, and wilt thou stand upon terms of credit? He 'took upon him the form of a servant,' and wilt thou be altogether a lord and king in thy affections, and not serve thy brethren? Did Christ do this that thou shouldst be a proud person? He came to expiate thy pride. Away with thy proud conceits! If thou be too proud to follow and imitate humble men, yet think not thyself too good to imitate an humble God. There is no spirit more opposite to the spirit of a Christian than a spirit swelling and lift up, that thinks itself too good to be abased in the service of others, that carries itself loftily. A proud spirit is most opposite to the spirit of God, that became man to expiate this pride of ours, and to work out salvation in this flesh of ours. Of all sins let us take heed of this diabolical satanical sin; let us be abased for Christ that was abased for us; and as he left his heaven—to do us good he left heaven itself—so let us. If we have a conceited heaven and happiness in ourselves, leave it, and become base and low, to do any good we can. Shall he stoop and bend to us from heaven to earth, and conceal his majesty, not to be known to be as he was; and shall not we stoop one to another to do good, and come down from our conceited excellency?

Use 4. Here we have a good ground likewise *not to envy the blessed angels their greatness;* nay, here we have that wherein we are above the angels themselves; for 'he took not upon him the nature of angels,' Heb. ii. 16, but he was 'God manifest in our flesh.' Christ married our nature to himself out of his love, that he might marry us to himself by his Spirit; and now, by our union with Christ, we be nearer him than the very angels are. The angels are not the spouse of Christ, but now, by reason of his taking our nature, we are kin to Christ: 'He is bone of our bone, and flesh of our flesh,' Eph. v. 30, and we are 'bone of his bone, and flesh of his flesh.' We are the body, Christ is the head. We are nearer to Christ than the very angels. No wonder, then, if those blessed spirits daily pry into this great mystery, 1 Peter i. 12.

5. Lastly, *Let us labour that Christ may be manifested in our particular flesh, in our persons.* As he was God manifest in the flesh in regard of that blessed mass he took upon him, so we would every one labour to have God 'manifest in *our* flesh.'

Quest. How is that?

Ans. We must have Christ as it were born in us, 'formed in us,' as the apostle speaks, Col. i. 27. Certainly the same Spirit that sanctified Christ doth sanctify every member of Christ; and Christ is in some sort begotten, and conceived, and 'manifested' in every one that is a Christian. We must labour that Christ may be 'manifest' in our understandings, in our affections, that he may be manifest to us, and conceived, as it were, in us; as St Paul's phrase is, 'That the life of Christ may be made manifest in our mortal flesh,' 2 Cor. iv. 11. The life and spirit of Christ must be 'manifest' in every true Christian, and their 'flesh' must be sanctified by the same Spirit that Christ's flesh was sanctified withal. As Christ's flesh was first sanctified, and then abased, and then glorious, so the flesh of every Christian must be content to be abased, as the flesh of Christ was, to serve Christ, to be conformable to Christ in our abased flesh. And let us not make too much of this flesh of ours, that shall turn to rottenness ere long. It must be gracious sanctified flesh, as Christ's was, and then glorious flesh. Christ must be manifest in our flesh, as he was in his own, that when a man sees a Christian, he may see Christ manifest in him.

Obj. But how shall I come to have Christ manifest in my flesh? My heart is not fit to conceive Christ in. There is nothing in it but deadness, and darkness, and dulness, and rebellion?

Ans. Even as the virgin Mary, she conceived Christ when she yielded her assent. When the angel spake to her, what saith she presently? 'Be it as thou hast said,' Luke i. 38; let it even be so. She yielded her assent to the promise, that she should conceive a son. So when the promises are uttered to us of the forgiveness of sins, of salvation by Christ, as soon as ever we have a spirit of faith to yield our assent, let it be so, Lord, as thou hast promised; thou hast promised forgiveness of sins: let it be so; thou hast promised favour in Christ: let it be so. As soon as the heart is brought to yield to the gracious promise, then Christ is conceived in the heart. Even as Christ was conceived in the womb of the virgin when she yielded her assent to believe the promise, so Christ is in every man's heart, to sanctify it, to rule it, to comfort it, as soon as this consent is wrought. We should labour, therefore, to bring our hearts to this. So much for this. Because it is of great consequence, and the leading mystery to all that follows, I have been somewhat the longer in unfolding these words, 'God manifest in the flesh.'

'Justified in the Spirit.'

These words are added, to answer an objection that may rise from the former. He was 'God manifest in the flesh.' He veiled himself. He could not have suffered else. When he took upon him to be the mediator, he must do it in abased flesh. If Christ, being God, had not abased himself, he should never have been put to death. Satan and his instruments would never have meddled with him. Therefore God being veiled in the flesh, being clouded with our flesh and infirmities, thereupon the world had a misconceit of him. He was not generally thought to be what he was indeed. He appeared to be nothing but a poor man, a debased, dejected man; a persecuted, slandered, disgraced man in the world. He was thought to be a trespasser.

It is no matter what he appeared, when he was veiled with our flesh; he was '*justified* in the Spirit,' to be the true Messiah; to be God as well as man.

'Justified.'

It implies two things in the phrase of Scripture: a freedom and clearing from false conceits and imputations, and declared to be truly what he was; to be otherwise than he was thought to be of the wicked world. When a man is cleared from that that is laid to his charge, he is 'justified.' When a man is declared to be that he is, then he is said to be justified in the sense of the Scriptures. 'Wisdom is justified of her children,' Mat. xi. 19, that is, cleared from the imputations that are laid upon religion, to be mopish and foolish. 'Wisdom is justified;' that is, cleared and declared to be an excellent thing of all her children. So Christ was 'justified.' He was cleared, not to be as they took him; and declared himself to be as he 'manifested' himself, a more excellent person, the Son of God, the true Messiah and Saviour of the world.

'In the Spirit.'

That is, in his Godhead: that did shew itself in his life and death, in his resurrection and ascension. The beams of his Godhead did sparkle out. Though he were 'God in the flesh,' yet he remained God still, and was 'justified' to be so 'in the Spirit,' that is, in his divine power, which is called the Spirit; because the spirit of anything is the quintessence and strength of it. God hath the name of Spirit, from his purity and power and vigour. So God is a Spirit; that is, God is pure, opposite to gross things, earth, and flesh; and God is powerful and strong. 'The horses of the Egyptians are flesh, and not spirit,' Isa. xxxi. 3, that is, they are weak. A spirit is strong; so much spirit, so much strength. So, by the purity and strength of the divine nature, Christ discovered himself to be true God as well as true man.

The word *Spirit* is taken in three senses especially in the gospel.

1. It is taken *for the whole nature of God*. 'God is a Spirit,' saith Christ to the woman of Samaria, John iv. 23. The very nature of God is a Spirit; that is, active and subtile, opposite to meanness and weakness.

2. Then again, Spirit is taken more particularly *for the divine nature of Christ*, as it is Rom. i. 4: 'Of the seed of David, according to the flesh,' but 'declared mightily to be the Son of God with power, according to the Spirit of sanctification,' or holiness, 'by the resurrection from the dead.' The opposition shews that *Spirit* is taken there for the divine nature of Christ. He had spoken in the verse before concerning his human nature.

He was made 'of the seed of David, according to the flesh;' and it follows, 'declared to be the Son of God, according to the Spirit of holiness, by the resurrection from the dead.' And so likewise in 1 Pet. iii. 18: 'He was put to death in the flesh, but quickened in the Spirit.' He was put to death in his human nature, but quickened and raised as he was God.

3. The Spirit is taken likewise *for the third person in the Trinity*, the Holy Ghost, the Holy Spirit. And indeed, whatsoever God the Father or God the Son doth graciously to man, it is done by the Spirit. For, as the Holy Spirit is in the order of the persons, so he is in the order of working. The Father works from himself; the Son works from the Father; the Holy Spirit from them both. The Holy Spirit proceeds from the Father and the Son, as a common principle. Therefore, sometimes the Father is said to raise Christ's body by his Spirit. Christ is said to do things by the Spirit. Here, in this place, it is especially to be understood of Christ's divine nature, not excluding the Holy Ghost. For as the Holy Ghost, in the incarnation, sanctified his 'flesh,' the second person took flesh, but the third person sanctified it. So in the resurrection of Christ, [it was] the second person that raised itself up, but yet it was by the Holy Ghost too. So when there is mention here of Christ 'justified by the Spirit,' that is, by his Godhead and by the Holy Ghost, which he alway used, not as an instrument—for the Holy Ghost is a common principle with himself, one with himself, of equal dignity, only differing in the order of persons; whatsoever Christ did, he did with the Spirit. That must not be excluded. Christ was as well 'justified in the Spirit,' as God, as 'manifest' in our nature to be man.

And this was in the time of his abasement. In the greatest extremity of abasement, there was somewhat that came from Christ, to 'justify' him that he was the Son of God, the true Messiah. There is no part of his abasement but some beams of his Godhead did break forth in it.

He was made flesh, but he took upon him the 'flesh' of a virgin. Could that be otherwise than by the Spirit, to be born of a virgin, she remaining a virgin? When he was born, he was laid in a manger. Indeed, there was God in the low estate of the flesh. Ay, but the 'wise men worshipped him,' and the 'star' directed them, Mat. ii. 11. There he was 'justified in the Spirit.' He was tossed when he was asleep in the ship, but he commanded the winds and the waves, Mat. xiv. 24, *seq*. He wanted money to pay tribute, as he was abased; but to fetch it out of a fish, there he was justified, Mat. xvii. 27. The one was an argument of his poverty and meanness, but the other was an argument that he was another manner of person than the world took him for, that he had all the creatures at his command. He was apprehended as a malefactor, but he struck them all down with his word, 'Whom seek ye?' John xviii. 4.

Come to the greatest abasement of all; when he was on the cross, he hung between two thieves. Ay, but he converted the one of them. When the thief had so much discouragement to see his Saviour hang on the cross, yet he shewed such power in that abasement, that the very thief could see him to be a king, and was converted by his Spirit. He did hang upon the cross; but, at the same time, there was an eclipse. The whole world was darkened (*h*), the earth trembled, the rocks brake, the centurion 'justified' him, 'Doubtless, this was the Son of God,' Mat. xxiii. 47. He was sold for thirty pence (*i*), but he that was sold for thirty pieces did redeem the whole world by his blood.

Nay, at the lowest degree of abasement of all, when he struggled with the wrath of God, and was beset with devils, then he triumphed. When he was visibly overcome, then invisibly he overcame. He was an invisible conqueror when he was visibly subdued. For, did he not on the cross satisfy the wrath of God, and by enduring the wrath of God free us from it and from Satan, God's jailor, and reconcile us by his blood? The chief works of all were wrought in his chief abasement. At length he died and was buried; ay, but he that died rose again gloriously. Therefore he was 'mightily declared to be the Son of God by raising himself from the dead.' That was the greatest abasement when he lay in the grave; and especially then he was 'justified' by his resurrection from the dead and his ascension, in his state of glorification especially. So, if we go from Christ's birth to his lowest degree of abasement, there was alway some manifestation of his justification by the Spirit.

He was 'justified' in a double regard.

1. *In regard of God*, he was justified and cleared from our sins that he took upon him. He 'bore our sins upon the tree,' and bore them away, that they should never appear again to our discomfort. He was made 'a curse for us.' How came Christ to be cleared of our sins that lay upon him? When by the Spirit, by his divine nature, he raised himself from the dead. So he was 'justified' from that that God laid upon him, for he was our surety. Now the Spirit raising him from the dead, shewed that the debt was fully discharged, because our surety was out of prison. All things are first in Christ and then in us. He was acquitted and justified from our sins, and then we.

2. And then he was justified by the Spirit *from all imputations of men, from the misconceits that the world had of him*. They thought him to be a mere man, or a sinful man. No. He was more than a mere man; nay, more than a holy man; he was God-man. Whence were his miracles? Were they not from his divine power? He overcame the devil in his temptations. Who can overcome the devil, but he that is the Son of God? He cast out devils, and dispossessed them with his word. All the enemies of Christ that ever were, at length he conquered them, and so 'declared himself mightily to be,' as he was, 'the Son of God.' He healed the outward man and the inward man by his divine power; he caused the spiritual as well as the bodily eyes to see, the dead to live, and the lame to go, &c. Whatsoever he did in the body he did in the soul likewise. In those excellent miracles he was 'justified,' and declared to be the Son of God,' especially in his resurrection and ascension, and daily converting of souls by his ministry; all being done by his Spirit, which is his vicar in the world, ruling his church and subduing his enemies. So that he was every way 'justified in the Spirit' to be God, to be the true Messiah prophesied of and promised to the church. Therefore he was 'justified' in his truth, that all the promises were true of him; and in his faithfulness, that he was faithful in performing the promises he made. He was 'justified' in his goodness and mercy, and all those attributes; he was 'justified in the Spirit.'

Obj. But you will say, it seems he was not 'justified in the Spirit.' There are many heretics that think not Christ to be God; that take not Christ to be so glorious as he is.

Ans. I answer: When we speak of the justifying of Christ, it is meant to those that have eyes to see him, to those that shut not their eyes. He was 'justified' to be so great as he was to those 'whose eyes the god of the world had not blinded,' 2 Cor. iv. 4; to all that were his; as it is excellently set down, John i. 14, 'The Word was made flesh, and dwelt among us; and we beheld his glory, as the glory of the only begotten Son of the Father, full of grace and truth.' We 'beheld his glory.' *We* did; others did not take notice: but they were those 'whose eyes the god of the world hath blinded,' the malicious Scribes and Pharisees, that sinned against the Holy Ghost, and would never acknowledge Christ; and ignorant people, that had not faith nor the Spirit of God. He was justified by the Spirit of God, to all that had spiritual eyes to see and take notice of his course; as St John saith in one of his epistles, 'What we have seen and heard, and our hands have handled, the Word of life, that we declare to you,' 1 John i. 1. So that he was 'God manifest in the flesh,' and he shewed himself to be the 'Word of life' to those that were his apostles and disciples, and those that were converted by him. As we see St Peter, when he had felt his divine power upon his heart by his preaching, 'Lord,' saith he, 'thou hast the words of eternal life; whither shall we go?' John vi. 68. He felt the Spirit in his preaching. And so another time, St Peter, in Matt. xvi. 16, he confessed him to be 'the Son of the living God.' You see to whom he was 'justified' and declared to be the true Messiah, to be God as well as man by his Spirit.

The reason why he justified himself to be so, 1. It was *the more to strengthen our faith.* All his miracles were but so many sparkles of his divine nature, so many expressions of his divine power. And after he was raised from the dead, at his ascension and sending of the Holy Ghost, he shewed his divine power more gloriously; and all to strengthen the faith of the elect; and, 2. *To stop the mouths of all impudent rebellious persons.* For, considering that he wrought such miracles, that he raised men from the dead, and raised himself; considering that he called the Gentiles, and converted the world, by the ministry of weak men, he shewed that he was more than a man. Well! to make some use of this, that Christ was

'Justified in the Spirit.' Then first of all,

Use 1. *Christ will at length justify himself.* This is a ground of faith. However he be now as a sign set up that many speak against and contradict, yet the time will come when he will gloriously justify himself to all the world. Now some shut their eyes willingly, and the opposites of Christ seem to flourish; yet Christ will be 'justified by his Spirit' to all his elect in every age, especially in the resurrection. For 'when he shall come and appear to be glorious in his saints,' 2 Thes. i. 10, it will appear who he is indeed. Now he suffers many to tread upon his church, and he suffers many heretics to deny him, sometimes in one nature, sometimes in another, and so to offend against him. But the time will come that he will trample all his enemies under his feet; he will be 'justified by his Spirit.' That is our comfort. There are many schismatics and heretics and persecutors, but Christ will be 'justified' at length. 'The kingdoms of the earth will be the Lord Jesus Christ's,' Rev. xi. 15. Are they not now so? They are. But truly they appear not to be so. But at length they will appear to be so. At the conversion of the Jews and the confusion of antichrist, then it will appear more and more that he is King of the world indeed. Now, as it were, his offices are darkened: his kingly office is darkened and his prophetical office is darkened; but at length it will appear that he is King of the church, and all kingdoms will be Christ's. There are glorious times coming, especially the glorious day of the resurrection. Christ at length will be cleared, he will be justified. The sun at length will scatter all the clouds. In the morning they gather about the sun, as if they would cover it. Oh, but the sun breaks through all, and gloriously appears at length. So Christ will scatter all clouds, and gloriously appear to be that which the word sets him forth to be.

Again, As Christ will justify himself, *so he will justify his church and children, first or last*, by his Spirit. His children are now accounted the offscouring of the world. They are trampled and trod upon, they are the objects of scorn and hatred, and who accounted so base? Will Christ endure this? No. He that 'justified' himself; that is, that declared himself, and will more and more declare himself to be as he is; will he not 'justify' his church, his mystical body, to be as they are indeed? Certainly it shall appear to the world that he will justify them, to be kings and priests, to be heirs, to be glorious, to be so near and dear to him as the Scripture sets them forth to be. Whatsoever the Scripture hath spoken of the saints and children of God, the time will come that all this shall be 'justified' and made good by that Spirit of Christ, whereby he made good whatsoever he hath said of himself.

Therefore in our eclipses and disgraces let us all comfort ourselves in this. Let the world esteem us for the present as the refuse of the world, as persons not worthy to be acquainted with, not worthy to be regarded; we shall be 'justified' and cleared and glorified, especially at that day 'when Christ shall come to be glorious in his saints.' There is a hidden life of the church and every Christian; they have a life in Christ, but that 'life is hid in Christ,' in heaven, Col. iii. 3. As the flowers in winter they have a life, but it is hidden in the root. 'When Christ shall appear,' as blessed St Paul and St John say, then it 'shall appear who we are.' Then our 'glorious life,' that now is in our Head, 'shall appear;' then we shall be 'justified to be so glorious,' as the Scripture sets us forth to be. The church shall be glorious within and without, too, at that day. Therefore let us comfort ourselves. This hidden life, though it appear not now, yet we shall be justified. And hence we may answer some objections likewise.

Obj. Some may say, How doth it appear that Christ is King of the church? We see how the church is trampled on at this day. Where is the life and glory of the church? What! his spouse, and thus used! What! his turtle, and thus polluted and plucked by the birds of prey!

Ans. I answer, Look with other spectacles, with the eye of faith, and then you shall see a spring in the winter of the church. However she be now abased and eclipsed, yet she shall be 'justified;' and it will appear that Christ regards his church and people and children more than all the world besides, only there must be a conformity.

It was fit there should be a time of Christ's abasement; how should he have suffered else? The world would never have crucified God. They could not have done it. Therefore he was abased; he veiled his Godhead under his manhood, under a base condition, so he passed through 'suffering to glory.' So it must be in the body of Christ. It must pass through the veil of infirmities, of weakness, affliction, and disgrace. How else should it be conformable to Christ? If Christ had 'justified' himself at all times in his humiliation, he could not have suffered; if we should be justified now and appear to all the world who we are, who would persecute us? how could we be conformable to Christ? Therefore let us quietly and meekly a-while endure these things, that are nothing but to conform us to our Head, knowing this, that as he was 'justified' by little and little, till he was perfectly 'justified' when he was raised from the dead, so we shall be perfectly 'justified' and freed from all imputations at the last day, when by the same Spirit that raised him we shall be raised up too.

Nay, in this world, when it is for his glory and for our good, he will bring our righteousness to light as the noonday, Ps. xxxvii. 6; he will free us from the imputations that the world lays on us; he will have a care of our credit. For as Christ was 'mightily declared to be the Son of God' in a fit time, so shall we when we are fit. Then the world shall see that we are not the men that profane, bitter, malicious persons, led with the spirit of the devil, charged us to be.

Let us take no scandal at the present afflictions of the church. Christ will justify his mystical body by his glorious power in good time. Antichrist shall not alway ruffle* in the world. Christ will be justified to be the King and Ruler of the world. 'All power is committed to him,' Mat. xxviii. 18. But we see it now. Antichrist rages in the world, and the church seems to be under hatches.† So it is with particular Christians. Those that belong to God, and indeed are truly such as they profess themselves to be—though with much weakness—we see in what respect and esteem they are had. 'Let us comfort ourselves, beloved.' Christ justified himself by his Spirit, and will he not justify his poor church, and free it from the tyranny of antichrist? Will he not advance those that are trodden on now and made as the dirt in the street, that 'they shall shine as the sun?' Daniel xii. 3. Therefore when you hear of the dejected state of the churches abroad, be not dismayed. Consider there is a glorious King that rules the world, and he will make it appear ere long. He will justify himself and his church, for he suffers in his church. He is wise. He sees cause to do this. He is working his own work. He corrects and rules and purgeth his church in the furnace of affliction. But be sure the time will come that he will bring the cause of religion to light, and he will shew what side he owns; he will justify his truth, and tread Satan and all his members under feet. This frame of things will not hold long. As verily as Christ is in heaven, as verily as he is 'justified' in his own person by his Spirit, by his divine power, so he will justify his mystical body. And as he hath conquered in his own person, so he will by his Spirit conquer for his church.

Use 2. And as he will overcome for his church, so he will overcome in his church; 'stronger is he that is' in the church, 'in you, than he that is in the world,' 1 John iv. 4; and God's children will be triumphant. Though they may be discouraged in respect of the present carriage of things, yet the Spirit that is in them, above the world, will gather strength by little and little, and it will appear at length, notwithstanding present discouragements. Undoubtedly the best things will have a true lustre and glory at length, however they seem to be carried for the present. You see as Christ hath 'justified' himself to be the true Messiah, and as he hath justified himself, so he will justify all his. There is the same reason for both.

For our further instruction and comfort, let us consider, that in regard of God likewise, we shall be 'justified' from our sins in our consciences here and at the day of judgment, before angels and devils and men. As Christ was 'justified' from our sins himself, and he will justify every one of us by his Spirit, his Spirit shall witness to our souls that we are justified; and likewise his Spirit shall declare it at the day of judgment; it shall be openly declared that we are so indeed. There is a double degree of justification: one in our conscience now, another at the day of judgment. Then it shall appear that we have believed in Christ, and are cleansed from

* That is, 'swagger or bully.'—G. † That is, = restraint or concealment.—G.

our sins. When we shall stand on the right hand of Christ, as all that cleave to Christ by faith [will do], then it shall appear that by him we are 'justified' from all our sins whatsoever.

Use 3. Again, Christ was 'justified in the Spirit.' Then hence we may learn *our duty*; *we ought all of us to justify Christ.* To whom is Christ justified by the Spirit? Only to his own church and children; not to the reprobate world. We may know, that we are members of Christ, if we be of the number of those that justify Christ.

Quest. How do we justify Christ?

Ans. (1.) We justify Christ when, from an inward work of the Spirit, we feel and acknowledge him to be such an one as he is: *Christ is God.* Now, when we rely upon him as our rock, in all temptations, we justify Christ to be so; when we 'kiss the Son' with the kisses of faith, of subjection, of obedience, of reverence and love; this is to justify Christ to be the Son of God, as it is Ps. ii. 12, 'Kiss the Son, lest he be angry.' Those that in temptation are to seek for their comfort, they do not justify Christ; they do not live as if he were a Saviour, not as if he were a God. In temptations to despair, they justify not Christ.

(2.) Those that have Christ *illuminating their understandings*, to conceive the mysteries of religion, they justify Christ *to be the prophet of his church;* because they feel him enlightening their understandings.

(3.) Those that find their consciences pacified, by the obedience and sacrifice of Christ, they justify him *to be their priest;* for they can oppose the blood of Christ sprinkled on their hearts, to all the temptations of Satan, and to the risings of their own doubting conscience. Their hearts being sprinkled with the blood of Christ, they can go to God, and the blood of Christ speaks for them 'peace;' it pleads 'mercy, mercy.' Thus we justify Christ as a priest, when we rest in his sacrifice, and do not, with papists, run to other sacrifices. This is not to justify Christ. To justify Christ, God-man, is to make him a perfect mediator of intercession and redemption, to make him all in all. They do not justify Christ, that think God was made man to patch up a salvation; that he must do a part and we must merit the rest. Oh no! Take heed of that; account all our obedience, and all that is from us, as 'menstruous cloths,' Isa. xxx. 22, not able to stand with the justice of God.

(4.) In a word, we justify and declare and make good that *he is our king*, and put a kingly crown upon his head, when we suffer him to rule us and to subdue our spirits and our rebellions; when we cherish no contrary motions to his Spirit; when we rest in his word and not traditions, but stoop to the sceptre of Christ's word. This is to justify him as a king. Thus we should labour to justify and declare to the world the excellency and power of Christ in our hearts, that we may make religion lovely, and make it be entertained in the world; because we shew it to be an excellent powerful thing. Let us examine our hearts, whether we thus justify Christ or no; that by our carriage towards him, we make it good that he is such an one as the Scripture sets him forth to be.

In particular, we justify him, that 'he rose from the dead,' when we believe that we are freed from our sins, our surety being out of prison. We justify him as 'ascended into heaven,' when we have heavenly affections, and when we consider him as a public person gone to heaven in our name. We justify him as 'sitting at the right hand of God,' when we 'mind the things that are above,' Col. iii. 1, and not that are here below; or else we deny these things, we believe them not, we justify them not, when our conversations are not answerable to the things we believe. If we be the children of wisdom, undoubtedly we shall justify wisdom. If we be the members of Christ, we shall justify our head. If we be his spouse, we shall justify our husband. Let us examine ourselves that we do in this kind, and never think our state good till we can justify Christ.

In the next place, for our direction; as Christ justified himself by his Spirit, by his divine power, so let us know that it is our duty to justify ourselves, to justify our profession, justify all divine truth. Let us make it good that we are the sons of God, that we are Christians indeed; not only to have the name, but the anointing of Christ; that we may clear our religion from false imputations; or else, instead of justifying our profession, we justify the slanders that are against it. The world is ready to say none are worse than Christians; and their religion is all but words and shews and forms. Shall we justify these slanders? No. Let us, by the Spirit of God, justify our religion; let us shew that religion is a powerful thing; and so indeed it is. For divine truth, when it is embraced and known, it alters and changeth the manners and dispositions; it makes of lions lambs; it makes our natures mild and tractable and sweet: it raiseth a man from earth to heaven. Let us justify this our religion and profession against all gainsayers whatsoever. 'Wisdom is justified of all her children.' Let us justify our religion and profession, by maintaining it and standing for it, and express in our lives and conversations the power of it.

Quest. How shall this be?

Ans. The text saith, 'by the Spirit.' For as Christ 'justified' himself, that is, declared himself to be as he was 'by his Spirit,' so every Christian hath the 'Spirit of Christ, or else he is none of his,' Rom. viii. 9; and by this Spirit of Christ he is able to justify his profession; not only to justify Christ to be the true head, &c., but all things he doth must be done by the Spirit, or not at all. For as Christ, when he became man and was in the world, he did all by the direction of the Spirit. 'He was led into the wilderness by the Spirit,' he 'taught by the Spirit.' The Spirit that sanctified him in the womb guided him in all his life. So a Christian is guided by the Spirit. God doth all to him by the Spirit. He is comforted, and directed, and strengthened by the Spirit; and he again doth all to God by the Spirit. He prays in the Spirit, and sighs and groans to God in the Spirit. He walks in the Spirit. He doth all by the Spirit. Therefore by the Spirit let us justify and declare ourselves what we are; that there is somewhat in us above nature; that we have love above carnal men, and patience and meekness above the ability and capacity of other men. We justify our profession when we do somewhat more than nature, or when we do common ordinary things in a spiritual holy manner. Religion is not a matter of form, but of spirit. Let us not shew our religion only by word, but by the fruits of the Spirit; by love, and mercy, and meekness, and zeal, when occasion serves. The whole life of a Christian, as far as he is a Christian, it gives evidence that he is a Christian. The whole life of a carnal formal man evidences that he is not a Christian, because he hath nothing in him above other men; as our Saviour Christ saith, 'What peculiar thing do ye,' to distinguish yourselves from other men? Mat. v. 47. So let us ask ourselves. We profess ourselves to be the children of God, the heirs of heaven, 'What peculiar thing do we?' How do we justify ourselves? A true Christian can answer, I can justify it by the Spirit; I find I do things from other principles, and motives, and inducements, than the world doth, who only respect terms of civility and aims of the world, or to content the clamour of conscience. But, I find, I do things out of assurance that I am the child of God, and in obedience to him. Let us see what peculiar thing we do.

Alas! I cannot but lament the poor profession of many. How do they 'justify' their profession? How do they make good that they have the Spirit of God raising them above other men, when they live no better than pagans, nay, not so well, under the profession of the gospel and religion? Would pagans live as many men do? Did they not keep their words better? Were they so loose in their lives and conversations, and so licentious? Would they swear by their gods idly? Most of our ordinary people are worse than pagans. Where is the 'justifying' of religion? If Turks and heathens should see them they would say, You talk of religion, but where is the power of it? If you had the power of it you would express it more in your fidelity, and honesty, and mercy, and love, and sobriety. The kingdom of God, that is, the manifestation of the government of Christ, 'it is not in word but in power.' Therefore let us labour to 'justify' that we are subjects of that kingdom, by the power of it.

Mere civil* persons, the apostle saith of them, 2 Tim. iii. 5, they are such as 'have a form of godliness, but deny the power of it.' All that rabblement that he names there, they have 'a form.' A form is easy, but the power of it is not so easy. Therefore, let us justify our religion by our conversation. Let us justify the ordinances of God, the preaching and hearing of the word of God, by reverence in hearing it as the word of God, and labour to express it in our lives and conversations, or else we think it nothing but the speech of man. Let us 'justify' the sacrament to be the seal of God, by coming reverently to it, and by finding our faith strengthened by it. So labour to 'justify' every ordinance of God, from some sweet comforts that we feel by them; and then we shew that we are true members of Christ, that we are like Christ, who 'justified himself in the Spirit.'

Beloved, it is a great power that must make a true Christian, no less than the 'power of the Spirit, that raised Christ from the dead;' as it is Eph. i. 20, St Paul prays that they might 'feel the power that raised Christ from the dead.' It is no less power for Christ to shine in our dark hearts, than to 'make light to shine out of darkness.'

Now, what power is in the lives of most men? The 'power that raised Christ from the dead'? Certainly no. What power is there in hearing the word, when many are so full of profaneness that they altogether neglect it? What power is there now and then to speak a good word, or now and then to do a slight action? Is this the 'power that raised Christ from the dead,' when by the strength of nature men can do it? There must be somewhat above nature, to justify a sound, spiritual Christian. We must have something to shew that we have our spirits raised up by the Spirit of Christ, to justify our profession in all estates. In prosperity, to shew that we have a spirit above prosperity, that we are not proud of it. Then in adversity, then we justify that we are Christians, by a spirit that is above adversity; that we do not sink under it, as a mere natural man would do, when we have learned St Paul's lesson, 'in all estates to be content,' Philip. iv. 11. In temptation we justify our Christian profession by arming ourselves with a spirit of faith, to beat back the 'fiery darts of Satan,' Eph. vi. 16. When all things seem contrary, let us cast ourselves, by a spirit of faith, upon Christ. That argues a powerful work of the Spirit, when we can, in contraries, believe contraries.

* That is, 'moral.'—G.

Thus let us shew that we are Christians; that we have somewhat in us above nature; that when the course of nature seems to be contrary, yet we can look with the eye of faith through all discouragements and clouds, and can see God reconciled in Christ. That will justify us to be sound Christians. Therefore let us labour, not only for slight outward performances, that are easy for any to do, but by an inward frame of soul, and by a carriage and conversation becoming our profession, that we may 'walk worthy of our profession,' fruitfully and watchfully, carefully and soberly, as becometh Christians every way. So much for that: I proceed to the next words,

'Seen of angels.'

The word is not altogether so fitly translated, for it is more pregnant than it is here rendered, 'He was seen.' It is true. But he was seen with admiration and wonderment of angels. He was seen, as such an object presented to them should be seen, and seen with wonderment. It implies the consequence of sight. Sight stirs up affection. It stirs up the whole soul. Therefore it is put for all the rest (*j*).

1. They saw him with *wonderment*. For was it not a wonder that God should stoop so low, as to be shut up in the straits of a virgin's womb? that Christ should humble himself so low, to be 'God in our flesh? Was not here exceeding wondrous love and mercy to mankind, to wretched man, having passed by the glorious angels that were fallen? And exceeding wisdom in God, in satisfying his justice, that he might shew mercy? It was matter of admiration to the angels, to see the great God stoop so low, to be clothed in such a poor nature as man's, that is meaner than their own. This doubtless is the meaning of the Holy Ghost: they saw it with admiration.

(2.) And because he was their head, as the second person, and they were creatures *to attend upon Christ*, their sight and wonderment must tend *to some practice* suitable to their condition. Therefore they so see and wondered at him, as that they attended upon Christ in all the passages of his humiliation and exaltation—in his life, in his death, in his resurrection and ascension.

(3.) They saw him so as they were *witnesses of him to men*. They gave testimony and witness of him. So that it is a full word, in the intention of the Holy Ghost. Indeed, not only the angels, but all gave witness of him, from the highest heavens to hell itself; all witnessed Christ to be the true Messiah.

In his baptism there was tho Trinity; the Father in a 'voice from heaven,' the Holy Ghost in the shape 'of a dove.' He had the witness of angels, of men of all ranks, Jews and Gentiles, men and women; yea, the devils themselves ofttimes confessed him in the gospel. He was witnessed of all ranks. They saw him, and gave evidence and testimony of him that he was the true Messiah.

He was seen of angels. To declare this a little more particularly.

The angels knew of Christ's coming in the flesh before it was, for what the church knew the angels knew in some measure. When God made the promise of the promised seed, the angels knew of it. And in Daniel the angel speaks of the seventy weeks; therefore before his incarnation they knew of him. But now they saw him with wonderment in our flesh, now they had an experimental knowledge of him; for the angels, besides their natural and supernatural knowledge, they have an experimental knowledge, that is daily increased in them, in the church. They see somewhat to admiration continually in the church, in the head, and in the members. They knew of the incarnation of Christ before. You know the angel brought the news of it beforehand to the virgin Mary. The angels attended upon Christ from his very infancy. The angels ministered to him in his temptation, Mat. iv. 11. Before his death they comforted him in the garden, Luke xxii. 43. He was made 'lower than the angels,' in some sort, as it is in Ps. viii. 5; for they came to 'comfort him.' He was so low that he had the comforting of angels. Then they saw when he was buried; they 'rolled away the stone,' Mat. xxviii. 2.

By the way in general, it is the angels' office to remove impediments that hinder us from Christ. A Christian shall have angels to remove the stones, the hindrances that are between heaven and him, rather than they shall be any impediment to his salvation.

Then when he rose there were angels, one at the head and another at the feet; and they told Mary that he was risen. And then at his ascension the angels told the disciples that Christ should come again. You have the story of it at large in the Gospel, how from the annunciation of his conception to his ascension they saw him, and attended on him, and witnessed of him.

As soon as ever he was born, when they appeared to the shepherds, what a glorious hymn they sang! 'Glory to God on high, peace on earth, good will to men,' Luke ii. 14. How joyful were they of the incarnation of Christ, and the great work of redemption wrought thereby!

And, as I said, they did not only see these things, but they wondered at the love and mercy and wisdom of God in the Head and members of the church; as we see in divers places, in 1 Pet. i. 12, 'We preach the gospel, which things the angels desire to look into.' The very angels desire to pry and look with admiration into the wondrous things of the gospel. So in Eph. iii. 10, 'To the intent that unto principalities and powers in heavenly places might be made known by the church the manifold wisdom of God.' There is somewhat done by Christ, by his incarnation and resurrection and government of his church, that the very angels look into, and wonder at the 'manifold wisdom of God' in governing his church; his wisdom in electing them, and after in restoring mankind. And in his manner of dispensation to the Jews, first by ceremonies, and then after by the body itself, Christ 'in the flesh.' There is such a world of wonders in the government of the church, such 'manifold wisdom,' that the very angels themselves look upon this with admiration and wonder, and with great delight.

Use 1. Shall angels see and wonder at these things? at the love and mercy and wisdom of God in governing his church, in joining together things irreconcilable to man's comprehension, infinite justice with infinite mercy in Christ, that God's wrath and justice should be satisfied in Christ, and thereby infinite mercy shewed to us? Here are things for angels to wonder at. Shall they wonder at it, and joy and delight in it, and shall we slight those things that are the wonderment of angels? There are a company of profane spirits—I would there were not too many among us—that will scarce vouchsafe to look into these things, that have scarcely the book of God in their houses. They can wonder at a story, or a poem, or some frothy device; at base things, not worthy to be reckoned of. But as for the great mysteries of salvation, that great work of the Trinity, about the salvation of mankind, they tush at them, they slight them; they never talk seriously of these things, except it be as it were with a graceless grace of slighting and scorn. They account it a disparagement to be serious in these things. They make no mysteries of that which the glorious creatures the angels themselves look upon and pry into, even with admiration. But it is not to be conceived of, the profaneness and poison that is in man's nature against divine truths, as I shall shew afterwards, how it slights the means of its own salvation, and stands wondering at baubles and trifles; and so men waste away their precious time in admiration of that which is nothing but 'vanity of vanities,' whereas we should take up our time in studying these transcendent things that go beyond the capacity of the very angels. Yet these things we dally and trifle withal.

Use 2. Again, from hence, that Christ was seen and attended on and admired by angels, *there is a great deal of comfort issueth to us*. It is the ground of all the attendance and comfort that we have from the angels. For this is a rule in divinity, that there is the same reason of the head and of the members; both head and members are one. Therefore what comfort and attendance Christ had, who is the head, the church, which is the body, hath the same, only with some difference. They attended upon him as the head, they attend upon us as the members. They attended upon him immediately for himself, they attend upon us for his sake; for whatsoever we have of God, we have it at the second hand. We receive 'grace for grace' of Christ. We receive attendance of angels, for the attendance they yielded to Christ first; they attend upon us, by his direction and commission and charge from him. So we have a derivative comfort from the attendance of angels upon Christ. But surely, whatsoever they did to him they do to us, because there is the same respect to head and members. Therefore the devil did not mistake, he was right in that, when he alleged out of the Psalm: 'He shall give his angels charge over thee, that thou dash not thy foot against a stone,' Ps. xci. 11. He was right in that, applying it to Christ. For however it be true to Christians, yet it is true to Christ too; it is true to the members, as well as the head; and to the head, as to the members. For 'he that sanctifieth, and they that are sanctified, are all one;' as the apostle saith, 'one Christ,' Heb. ii. 11.

Now the care of angels concerning Christ and his church, it was shadowed out in Exod. xxv. 17, *seq*., and xxvi. 31. There the mercy-seat, which covered the ark wherein the law was, upon the mercy-seat there were two cherubins counter-viewing one another, and both pried* to the mercy-seat. They shadowed out the angels that look on the mercy-seat, Christ; for he is the mercy-seat that covers the law and the curse, in whom God was merciful to us. There they look upon that with a kind of wonderment and attendance,† which St Peter alludes unto in that place, 'into which mysteries the very angels pry,' 1 Pet. i. 12. And so in the veil of the tabernacle, the veil had round about it pictures of cherubins, Exod. xxvi. 31. What did that shadow out unto us? The multitude of cherubins and seraphins and angels that attend upon Christ and his church. So he was 'seen' and attended on by 'angels;' and it belongs to all that are his, as you have it, Heb. i. 7, 'They are ministering spirits, for the good of the heirs of salvation.' They that serve the king serve the queen too. Christ is the King of his church, and the church is the greatest queen in the world. They attend upon her; nay, Christ hath made us, with himself, kings. Now, what a king is that that hath a guard of angels! As they guarded and attended upon Christ, so they guard and attend all that are his; as you

* That is, 'looked into.'—G.

† Qu. 'attention'?—G.

have it excellently in Dan. vii. 10, 'There are thousand thousands of angels about the throne continually.' All this is for our comfort, because we are one mystical body with him.

You have in Jacob's ladder a notable representation of this. Jacob's ladder, it reached from earth to heaven; and that pointed to Christ himself, who is 'Immanuel,' God and man, who brought God and man together. He was a mediator between both, and a friend to both. He was that ladder that touched heaven and earth, and joined both together. Now it is said, the angels ascended and descended upon that ladder; so the angels descending upon us, is, because they ascend and descend upon Jacob's ladder first; that is, upon Christ. 'All things are yours,' saith the apostle. What be those? God is ours, the Spirit is ours, heaven is ours, the earth is ours; afflictions, life, death, Paul, Apollos, the angels themselves, all is ours. Why? 'Ye are Christ's.' That is the ground. So it is a spring of comfort to consider that Christ was 'seen' and admired and attended by angels. They are ours, because we are Christ's. Let us consider what a comfort it is, to have the attendance of these blessed spirits for Christ's sake.

And hence *we have the ground of the perpetuity of it*, that they will for ever be attendants to us; because their love and respect to us is founded upon their love and respect to Christ. When favour to another is grounded upon a sound foundation; when the favour that a king or a great person bears to one is founded on the love of his own son; he loves the other because he loves his son whom the other loves; so it is perpetual and sound, because he will ever love his son. The angels will for ever love and honour and attend us. Why? For what ground have they respect to us at all? It is in Christ, whose members and spouse we are. So long as the church hath any relation to Christ, so long the angels shall respect the church; but the church hath relation to Christ for ever. Therefore, the respect that the blessed angels have to Christ and to the church, it is for ever and for ever.

Well, let us think of this, so as to make use of it; that now in Christ we have the attendance of angels. We do not see them, as in former time, before Christ's incarnation. It is true; because now, since Christ is come 'in the flesh,' the government of Christ is spiritual; and we are not supported with those glorious manifestations, but they are about us in an invisible manner. We have Elisha's guard about us continually, but we see them not.* There were more apparitions† in the infancy of the church, because the dispensation of Christ to the church was according to the weak state of the church. But now Christ is come 'in the flesh,' and 'received up in glory,' and there is more abundance of spirit. We should be more spiritual and heavenly-minded, and not look for outward apparitions of angels; but be content that we have a guard of them about us, as every Christian doth. 'Despise not,' saith Christ, 'these little ones.' They are about Christians, and about little ones, little in years, and little in esteem; 'for their angels,' &c., Matt. xviii. 10. It is a strange thing. They are God's angels, but they are theirs for their service. 'Their angels behold the face of your heavenly Father.' So that Christ's angels are our angels; they are angels even of children, of little ones. Nay, let a man be never so poor, even as Lazarus, he shall have the attendance of angels, in life and death. There is no Christian of low degree, of the lowest degree, that shall think himself neglected of God; for the very angels attend him, as

* Cf. 2 Kings vi. 17.—G.

† That is, 'appearances.'—G.

we see in Lazarus. There is a general commission for the least, the little ones.

Likewise, *it may comfort us in all our extremities whatsoever, in all our desertions.* The time may come, beloved, that we may be deserted of the world, and deserted of our friends; we may be in such straits as we may have nobody in the world near us. Oh! but if a man be a true Christian, he hath God and angels about him alway. A Christian is a king; he is never without his guard, that invisible guard of angels. What! if a man have nobody by him when he dies, but God and his good angels, to carry his soul to heaven, is he neglected? Every Christian, if he hath none else with him, he hath God, the whole Trinity, and the guard of angels, to help and comfort him, and to convey his soul to the place of happiness. Therefore, let us never despair, let us never be disconsolate; whatsoever our condition be, we shall have God and good angels with us in all our straits and extremities. Go through all the passages of our life, we see how ready we are to fall into dangers. In our infancy, in our tender years, we are committed to their custody: after, in our dangers, they pitch their tents about us; as it is, Ps. xxxiv. 7, 'The angels of the Lord pitch their tents about those that fear the Lord.' In our conversion they rejoice. 'There is joy in heaven at the conversion of a sinner,' Luke xv. 10. At the hour of death, as we see in Lazarus, they are ready to convey our souls to the place of happiness. Lazarus's soul 'was carried by angels into Abraham's bosom,' Luke xvi. 22. At the resurrection they shall gather our dead bodies together. It is the office of the angels. In heaven they shall 'praise and glorify God,' together with us for ever; for 'Christ shall come with a multitude of heavenly angels,' at the day of judgment: 'when he shall come to be glorified in his saints,' 2 Thess. i. 10. Then we shall for ever 'glorify God,' saints and angels together, in heaven. Therefore, in Heb. xii. 22, it is said, 'We are come to the innumerable multitude of angels.' What is the meaning of that? That is, now in the New Testament, by our communion with Christ, we have association with the 'blessed angels, innumerable company of angels,' saith the Holy Ghost there. We have association with them even from our infancy, till we be in glory. Indeed, they are as nurses: 'They shall carry thee, that thou dash not thy foot against a stone,' as it is in Ps. xci. 11. They keep us from many inconveniences.

Obj. But you will say, God's children fall into inconveniences; how then are they attended by angels?

Ans. I answer: First of all, God's angels preserve those that are his, from many inconveniences that they know not of. And certainly we have devils about us continually, and there is a conflict betwixt good angels and devils about us continually. And when we do fall into any inconvenience, it is because we are not in our way. If we go out of our way, they have not the 'charge over us;' they are to keep us '*in* our ways.' And if they keep us not from 'dashing our foot against a stone,' if they keep us not from ill, yet they keep us in ill, and deliver us out of ill at length; for they deliver us not only from evil, that we fall not into it, but they keep us in ill, and deliver us out of ill, nay, and by ill. If we suffer in the custody of angels any inconvenience, it is that we may be tried by it, that we may be exercised and bettered by it. There is nothing that falls out to God's children in the world, but they gain by it, whatsoever it is. This, therefore, doth not prejudice the attendance of angels.

Therefore let us comfort ourselves in all conditions for ourselves and for the state. Put case it be brought to a very small number, that the enemies were thousands more than we, many thousands and millions; yet, if we be in the covenant of grace, and in good terms with God, we have 'more for us than against us,' we shall have angels fight for us. You know Elisha's servant, when he saw a multitude of enemies, his eyes were opened to see a company of angels; and saith the prophet, 'There are more for us than against us,' 2 Kings vi. 17, *seq.* So let us be to the eye of the world never so few and never so weak; let us but have Elisha's eye, the eye of faith, and we shall have his guard about us alway and about the commonwealth. This should comfort us.

But then we must learn this duty, *not to grieve these good spirits.* As it is wondrous humility, that they will stoop to be servants to us, that are of a weaker, baser nature than they, so it is wondrous patience, that they will continue still to guard us, notwithstanding we do that that grieves those good spirits: one motive to keep us in the way of obedience, that we do not grieve those blessed spirits that are our guard and attendance. Let us consider when we are alone—it would keep us from many sins—no eye of man seeth; ay, but God seeth, and conscience within seeth, and angels without are witnesses: they grieve at it, and the devils about us rejoice at it. These meditations, when we are solicited to sin, would withdraw our minds and take up our hearts, if we had a spirit of faith to believe these things.

Let us learn to make this use likewise, *to magnify God, that hath thus honoured us;* not only to take our nature upon him, to be 'manifest in the flesh,' but also to give us his own attendance, his own guard, a guard of angels. Indeed, we are in Christ above angels, advanced higher than angels. What cause have we to praise God! How are we advanced above them? We are the spouse of Christ, and so are not angels. They are under Christ as a head of government and a head of influence. They have strength and confirmation from Christ. He is not a head of redemption, but of confirmation to them. St Paul calls them 'elect angels' that stand. They stand by Christ, they have good by him. But they are not the spouse of Christ. We are the spouse and members of Christ. He hath honoured our nature more than the angelical: he did not take upon him the nature of angels, but of men; and as he hath advanced us above angels, so his dispensation is, that those glorious creatures should be our attendants for our good; and they distaste not this attendance.

And this is that we should know, what care God hath over us, and what love he bears us; that he hath honoured us so much that creatures of a more excellent rank than we are, even the angels, should be serviceable to us in Christ. And all is, that we should be full of thankfulness.

Obj. But you will say, What need the guard or attendance of angels to Christ or to us, to head or members, considering that God is able to guard us with his almighty power?

Ans. It is true. The creatures that God hath ordained in their several ranks, they are not for any defect in God, to supply his want of power, but further to enlarge and demonstrate his goodness. He is the 'Lord of hosts,' therefore he will have hosts of creatures, one under another, and all serviceable to his end. His end is, to bring a company to salvation, to a supernatural end, to happiness in the world to come; and he being Lord of all, he makes all to serve for that end. He could do it of himself; but, having ordained such ranks of creatures, he makes all to serve for that end, for the manifestation of his power and of his goodness, not for any defect of strength in himself. He could do all by himself. He could have been content with his own happiness, and never have made a world; but he made the world to shew his goodness and love and respect to mankind. So he will have angels attend us, though he watch over us by his own providence. This takes not away any care of his, but he shews his care in the attendance of angels and other creatures. He useth them to convey his care and love to us.

Obj. But you will say, How can the angels help our souls any kind of way? They may help our outward man, or the state where we live; but what good do they to the inward man?

Ans. I answer, The inward man is especially subject to the Spirit of Christ. It is God that bows the neck of the inward man. But yet notwithstanding, if the devils can suggest sin, angels are as strong as devils, and stronger and wiser too. They are wiser than the devil is malicious, and stronger than the devil is powerful. Whatsoever they can do in evil, the good angels can in good. Therefore no question, but they suggest many thoughts that are good They are not only a guard about us, but they are tutors to teach and instruct us; they minister good thoughts, and stir up good motions and suggestions. They work not upon the heart of man immediately, to alter and change it—that is proper to God—but by stirring up motions, and by way of suggestion; as the devils do in ill, so they in good. Therefore it is said, they 'comforted' our blessed Saviour; which I suppose was more than by their presence. So they comfort God's children, by presenting to their thoughts (we know not how, the manner is mystical; it is not for us to search into that) good motions, by stirring up to good. Only the altering and changing of our dispositions, that is proper to the Holy Spirit of God.

Let us often think of this, what a glorious head we have, for whose sake the angels attend upon us in all estates whatsoever, even till we come to heaven.

And this should stir us up to labour to be made one with Christ. All the good we have any way is by the interest we have in Christ first. He holds it *in capite*. If we have not a being in our head Christ, we can challenge nothing in the world, no attendance of angels; for the angels are at variance with us out of Christ. We see presently after the fall, the cherubin was set with his sword drawn to keep the entrance of paradise, from whence Adam was shut, to shew that presently upon the fall there was a variance, and a mighty distance between the angels and us. But now the angels no longer shut paradise; no, they accompany us in the wilderness of this world, to the heavenly Canaan, to paradise. They go up and down Jacob's ladder. They attend upon Christ; and for his sake they are ministering spirits for the comfort of the elect. So that all things are reconciled now in Christ, both in heaven and earth, angels and men. It should stir us up to get interest in Christ, so that we may have interest in all these excellent things that first belong to Christ, and then to us. Whatsoever is excellent in heaven or earth belongs to the king of all, which is Christ, and to the queen of all, the church; and the time will come that there will be no excellency but Christ and his church. All whatsoever is in the world is nothing. It will end in hell and desperation; all other excellencies whatsoever.

This should teach us likewise *to carry ourselves answerable to our condition, to take a holy state upon us*. We should think ourselves too good to abase ourselves to sin, to be slaves to men, to flesh and blood—be they what they will be—to the corruptions and humours of any man, since we have angels to attend upon us. We are kings, and have a kingly guard. It should move us to take a holy state upon us. It should force a carriage suitable to kings, that have so glorious attendance. Undoubtedly, if we had a spiritual eye of faith to believe and to know this, answerable to the things themselves and their excellency, it would work a more glorious disposition in Christians than there is, to carry ourselves as if we were in heaven before our time. Oh that we had clear eyes, answerable to the excellency of the privileges that belong to us.

Again, It should teach us *not to despise the meanest Christians*, seeing angels despise not to attend on them. Shall we disdain to relieve them, that the angels do not disdain to comfort? To comfort and relieve one another, it is the work of an angel. Shall any man think himself too good to help any poor Christian? Oh the pride of man's nature! when the more glorious nature of the angels disdain not to be our servants, and not only to great and noble men, but to little ones, even to Lazarus. What a devilish quality is envy and pride, that stirs us up to disdain to be useful one to another, especially to those that are inferiors! We know it was the speech of wicked Cain, 'Am I my brother's keeper?' Gen. iv. 9. Shall I stoop to him? Flesh and blood begins to take state upon it. Alas! if angels had taken state upon them, where had this attendance been? The devils that kept not their first standing, being proud spirits, they disdained the calling they had; the good angels humble themselves. God himself, as it is Ps. cxiii. 6, disdains not to look on things below. When the great God became man, shall we wonder that angels should attend upon the nature that God hath so honoured? What a devilish sin, then, is envy, and pride, and disdain! Let these considerations move us to be out of love with this disposition. The angels joy at the conversion of others. Shall that be our heart-smart and grief that is the joy of angels? Shall we despise the work of regeneration and the image of God in another? Shall it be the joy of angels, and shall it be our sorrow, the welfare and thriving of others spiritually or outwardly? Shall we, out of disdain and envy, think ourselves too good to do anything when it is the delight of angels?

The angels are described with wings to fly, in Isa. vi. 2, *seq*, to shew their delight in their attendance; and wings to cover their faces and their feet, to shew their adoration and reverence of God. The nearer they come to God, the more reverence. So there is no Christian, but like the angels, the nearer he comes to God, the more he abaseth himself and adores God; as Job, when he came nearer to God than he was before, 'I abhor myself,' saith he, 'in dust and ashes,' when God came to talk with him, Job xlii. 6. The angels, the nearer they come to God, the more reverence they shew; the more they cover their faces in his presence. And with the other wings they fly and do their duty, to shew their expedition in their service to Christ and his church. They do readily what they do. Let us imitate the angels in this.

The angels have a double office: a superior office and an inferior. The superior office they have is to attend upon God, to serve God and Christ, to minister to our head. The inferior office is, to attend his church, and to conflict with the evil angels that are about us continually.

It is good for us to know our prerogatives, our privilege, and our strength; not to make us proud, but to stir us up to thankfulness, and to a holy carriage answerable. It is a point not much thought on by the best of us all. We forget it, and betray our own comfort. Satan abuseth us to make us forget the dignity and strength that we have. Hereby we dishonour God and wrong ourselves, and wrong the holy angels, for want of faith and consideration of these things. A Christian is a more excellent creature than he thinks of. It is necessary ofttimes to think what a great degree God hath raised us to in Jesus Christ, that we have this glorious attendance about us wherever we are. Oh it would move us, as I said, to comfort and to a reverent carriage! and, indeed, when we carry ourselves otherwise, it is for want of minding and believing these things. I have spoken something the more of it, because we are subject to neglect this blessed truth. Therefore, for the time to come, let us take occasion to meditate oftener of this spring of comfort than formerly we have done.

'Preached to the Gentiles.'

Christ, our blessed Saviour, being the king of his church, it was not sufficient that he was 'manifested in the flesh,' and 'justified in the Spirit;' that is, declared by his divine power to be God; but he must have his nobles to acknowledge this too. Kings in their inaugurations not only make good their own title what they can themselves, but they would have others to acknowledge it. Therefore it is said Christ was seen of angels, those noble and glorious creatures.

But not only the greatest of the kingdom, but likewise the meaner subjects, must know their king. There must be a proclamation to them to know who is to rule over them. Therefore, Christ being a general catholic king, there must be a publication and proclamation of Christ all the world over. He must be 'preached to the Gentiles.' But yet that is not enough. Upon proclamation, there must be homage of all those he is proclaimed a king to. Therefore it follows, 'Believed on in the world;' that is, the world must stoop, and submit, and give homage to Christ as the Saviour of the world, as the Mediator of mankind. Thus we see how these things follow one upon another. To come to the words,

'Preached to the Gentiles, believed on in the world.'

These follow one another by a necessary order, for 'preaching' goes before faith. Faith is the issue and fruit of preaching. Christ is first 'preached to the Gentiles,' and then 'believed on in the world.' The points considerable are these:

First, *That there must be a dispensation of salvation wrought by Christ unto others.* It is not sufficient that salvation was wrought by Christ 'manifest in the flesh, justified in the Spirit,' but this salvation and redemption wrought, it must be published and dispensed to others. Therefore he saith 'preached to the Gentiles.'

And then *this publication and 'preaching,' it must be of Christ.* Christ must be published to the Gentiles. All is in Christ that is necessary to be published.

Then *the persons to whom.* 'To the Gentiles,' that is, to all. The church is enlarged since the coming of Christ; the pales and bounds of the church are enlarged.

And then *the fruit of this.* Christ being thus dispensed to the Gentiles, the world 'believes.' All preaching is for 'the obedience of faith,' as St Paul saith,' Rom. i. 5, and Rom. xvi. 19, 'That the obedience of the faith may be yielded to Christ;' 'preaching to the Gentiles' is, that he may be believed on in the world.'

First of all, *There must be a dispensation of Christ.*

See the equity of this, even from things among men. It is not sufficient that physic be provided; but there must be an application of it. It is not sufficient that there is a treasure; but there must be a digging of it out. It is not sufficient that there be a candle or light; but there must be a holding out of the light for the good and use of others. It was not sufficient that there was a 'brazen serpent,' but the brazen serpent must be 'lifted up,' that the people might see it. It is not sufficient that there is a standard, but the standard must be set up. It is not sufficient that there be a foundation, but there must be a building upon the foundation. It is not sufficient that there be a garment, but there must be a putting of it on. It is not sufficient that there be a box of ointment, but the box must be opened, that the whole house may be filled with the smell. It is not sufficient that there be tapestry, and glorious hangings, but there must be an unfolding of them. Therefore there must be a dispensation of the mysteries of Christ; for, though Christ be physic, he must be applied; though Christ be a garment, he must be put on; though he be a foundation, we must build on him, or else we have no good by him; though he in his truth be a treasure, yet he must be digged up in the ministry; though he be a light, he must be held forth; though he be food, there must be an application. Of necessity therefore there must be a dispensation of the gospel, as well as redemption wrought by Christ; 'preached to the Gentiles.'

To unfold the point a little, seeing the necessity of it, to shew

What it is to preach.

What it is *to preach Christ.* And,

What it is to preach Christ *to the Gentiles.*

1. *To preach* is to open the mystery of Christ, to open whatsoever is in Christ; to break open the box that the savour may be perceived of all. To open Christ's natures and person what it is; to open the offices of Christ: first, he was a prophet to teach, wherefore he came into the world; then he was a priest, offering the sacrifice of himself; and then after he had offered his sacrifice as a priest, then he was a king. He was more publicly and gloriously known to be a king, to rule. After he had gained a people by his priesthood and offering, then he was to be a king to govern them. But his prophetical office is before the rest. He was all at the same time, but I speak in regard of manifestation. Now 'to preach Christ' is to lay open these things.

And likewise the states wherein he executed his office. First, the state of humiliation. Christ was first abased, and then glorified. The flesh he took upon him was first sanctified and then abased, and then he made it glorious flesh. He could not work our salvation but in a state of abasement; he could not apply it to us but in a state of exaltation and glory. To open the merits of Christ, what he hath wrought to his Father for us; to open his efficacy, as the spiritual Head of his church; what wonders he works in his children, by altering and raising of them, by fitting and preparing them for heaven: likewise to open all the promises in Christ, they are but Christ dished and parcelled out. 'All the promises in Christ are yea and amen,' 2 Cor. i. 20. They are made for Christ's sake, and performed for Christ's sake; they are all but Christ severed into so many particular gracious blessings. 'To preach Christ' is to lay open all this, which is the inheritance of God's people.

But it is not sufficient to preach Christ, to lay open all this in the view of others; but in the opening of them, there must be application of them to the use of God's people, that they may see their interest in them; and there must be an alluring of them, for to preach is to woo. The preachers are *paranymphi*,* the friends of the bridegroom, that are to procure the marriage between Christ and his church; therefore, they are not only to lay open the riches of the husband, Christ, but likewise to entreat for a marriage, and to use all the gifts and parts that God hath given them, to bring Christ and his church together.

And because people are in a contrary state to Christ, 'to preach Christ,' is even to begin with the law, to discover to people their estate by nature. A man can never preach the gospel that makes not way for the gospel, by shewing and convincing people what they are out of Christ. Who will marry with Christ, but those that know their own beggary and misery out of Christ? That he must be had of necessity, or else they die in debts eternally; he must be had, or else they are eternally miserable. Now, when people are convinced of this, then they make out of themselves to Christ. This therefore must be done, because it is in order, that which makes way to the preaching of Christ; for 'the full stomach despiseth an honeycomb,' Prov. xxvii. 7. Who cares for balm that is not sick? Who cares for Christ, that sees not the necessity of Christ? Therefore we see John Baptist came before Christ, to make way for Christ, to level the mountains, to cast down whatsoever exalts itself in man. He that is to preach must discern what mountains there be between men's hearts and Christ; and he must labour to discover themselves to themselves, and lay flat all the pride of men in the dust; for 'the word of God is forcible to pull down strongholds and imaginations and to bring all into subjection to Christ,' 2 Cor. x. 4. And indeed, though a man should not preach the law, yet by way of implication, all these things are wrapped in the gospel. What need a Saviour, unless we were lost? What need Christ to be wisdom to us, if we were not fools in ourselves? What need Christ be sanctification to us, if we were not defiled in ourselves? What need he be redemption, if we were not lost and sold in ourselves to Satan, and under his bondage? Therefore all is to make way for Christ, not only to open the mysteries of Christ, but in the opening and application to let us see the necessity of Christ. In a word, being to bring Christ and the church together, our aim must be, to persuade people to come out of their estate they are in, to come and take Christ. Whatsoever makes for this, that course we must use, though it be with never so much abasing of ourselves. Therefore the gospel is promulgated in a sweet manner. 'I beseech you, brethren, by the mercies of God,' &c. The law comes with 'Cursed, cursed;' but now in the gospel Christ is preached with sweet alluring. 'I beseech you, brethren,' and 'We as ambassadors beseech you, as if Christ by us did beseech you,' &c., 2 Cor. v. 20. This is the manner of the dispensation in the gospel, even to beg of people that they would be good to their own souls. Christ, as it were, became a beggar himself, and the great God of heaven and earth begs our love, that we would so care for our own souls that we would be reconciled unto him. It was fitter, indeed, that we should beg of him. It was fit we should seek to be reconciled to him, but God so stoops in the dispensation and ministry of the gospel, that he becomes a beggar and suitor to us to be good to our souls. As if he had offended us, he desires us to be reconciled. The wrong is done on our part, yet he so far transcends the doubtings of man's nature, that he would have nothing to cause man's heart to misgive, no doubts or scruples to arise. He himself becomes a beseecher of reconciliation, as if he were the party that had

* That is, παρανυμφιοι = Bridemen.—G.

offended. This is the manner of the publication of the gospel. I do but touch things, to shew what it is to preach Christ.

Use. Seeing then of necessity there must be a dispensation together with the gospel, *let us labour to magnify this dispensation of preaching*, that, together with redemption and the good things we have by Christ, we have also the standard set up and the brazen serpent lifted up by preaching 'the unsearchable riches of Christ' unfolded to us. It is a blessed condition. Let us magnify this ordinance, without disparaging other means, of reading, &c. This preaching is that whereby God dispenseth salvation and grace ordinarily.

And God in wisdom sees it the fittest way to dispense his grace to men by men. Why?

(1.) *To try our obedience to the truth itself*. He would have men regard the things spoken, not for the person that speaks them, but for the excellency of the things. If some glorious creatures, as the angels, should preach to us, we should regard the excelleney of the preachers more than the truth itself; we should believe the truth for the messengers' sake.

(2.) And then *God would knit man to man by bonds of love*. Now there is a relation between pastor and people by this ordinance of God.

(3.) And then *it is more suitable to our condition*. We could not hear God speak, or any more excellent creatures. God magnifies his power the more in blessing these weak means.

(4.) And *it is more proportionable to our weakness* to have men that speak out of experience from themselves that preach the gospel, that they have felt the comfort of themselves. It works the more upon us. Therefore, those that first preached the gospel, they were such as had felt the sweetness of it themselves first. St Paul, a great sinner out of the church, and St Peter in the church, he fell, after he was in the state of grace; that these great apostles might shew to all people that there is no ground of despair, if we humble ourselves. If they be sins out of the church, if they be sins against the first table, as Paul he was 'a blasphemer;' or against the second, he was 'a persecutor;' yet he found mercy notwithstanding, and for this end he found mercy, he saith, that he 'might teach the mercy of God to others, that he might be an example of the mercy of God to others, 1 Tim. i. 16. And so, if we relapse and fall, let none despair. Peter, a great teacher in the church, an apostle, see how foully he fell! Now, when men subject to the 'same infirmities' shall discover the mercy of God out of the book of God, it works the more upon us.

It is good for us to have a right esteem of the ordinances of God, because the profane heart of man doth think it a needless matter.

Quest. Some are ready to say, Cannot I as well read privately at home?

Ans. Yes. But the use of private exercises, with contempt of the public, they have a curse upon them instead of a blessing. It is with such men as with those that gathered manna when they should not; it stank. Hath God set up an ordinance for nothing, for us to despise? Is not he wiser to know what is good for us better than we do for ourselves? God accompanies his ordinance with the presence of his blessed Spirit. The truth read at home hath an efficacy, but the truth unfolded hath more efficacy. As we say of milk warmed, it is fitter for nourishment, and the rain from heaven hath a fatness with it, and a special influence more than other standing waters; so there is not that life and operation and blessing that accompanies other means that doth preaching, being the ordinary means where it may be had.

Obj. Ay, but this ordinance of God, 'preaching,' it is only for the laying the foundation of a church; it is not for a church when it is built. Then other helps, as prayer and the like, without this, may suffice.

Ans. Those that have such conceits, they make themselves wiser than the Spirit of God; in St Paul, we see in Eph. iv. 8, *seq*. Christ, 'when he ascended on high, he led captivity captive, he gave gifts to men, some apostles, some prophets, some evangelists, for the edifying and building up of the church.' So that this ordinance it is necessary for building up still, and for the knitting of the members of Christ together still. Therefore, that is a vain excuse.

Obj. Oh, but what need much, less would serve the turn.

Ans. Thus people grow to contemn and despise this heavenly manna. But those that are acquainted with their own infirmities, they think it a happiness to have plenty; for naturally we are dull, we are forgetful, we are unmindful. Though we know, we do not remember; and though we remember, yet we do not mind things. We are naturally weak, and therefore we need all spiritual supports and helps that may be, to keep the vessel of our souls in perpetual good case. The more we hear and know, the fitter we are for doing and suffering; our souls are fitter for communion with God for all passages, both of life and death. Therefore we cannot have too much care this way.

Oh let us therefore choose Mary's part, 'the better part,' that will never depart from us; and take heed of profane conceits in this kind. It is to the prejudice of our souls. We must know, that whensoever God sets up an ordinance, he accompanies it with a special blessing. And we are not so much to consider men in it, but consider the ordinance, which is his; and being his, there is a special blessing goes with the dispensation of the word, by the ministry.

Obj. Others object, they know it well enough; and therefore they need not to be taught.

Ans. The word of God preached, it is not altogether to teach us, but, the Spirit going with it, to work grace, necessary to 'strengthen us in the inward man,' 2 Cor. iv. 16. And those that say they know it enough, deceive themselves. They know it not. Religion is a mystery, and can it be learned at the first? There is no mystery but it requires many years to learn. If it be but a handicraft, men are six or seven years learning it. And is religion, and the mysteries and depths of it, learned so soon, think we? There is a mystery in every grace, in repentance, in faith, in patience, that no man knows, but those that have the graces [and] what belongs to those graces. Religion consists not in some parts and abilities to speak and conceive of these things; and yet that is hardly learned, being contrary to our nature, having no seeds of these things. Even the outside of religion, that is the preparative to the inward; there is somewhat to do to bring our hearts to these things. But, then, religion itself is a deep mystery; it requires a great deal of learning.

Let us therefore set a price upon God's ordinance. There must be this dispensation. Christ must be 'preached.' Preaching is the chariot that carries Christ up and down the world. Christ doth not profit but as he is preached. For supernatural benefits, if they be not discovered, they are lost; as we say of jewels, if they be not discovered, what is the glory of them? Therefore there must be a discovery by preaching, which is the ordinance of God for that end. Whereupon God stirred up the apostles before, that were the main converters of the world. They had some prerogatives above all other preachers. They had an immediate calling, extraordinary gifts, and a general commission. In them was established a ministry to the end of the world. 'Christ, when he ascended on high and led captivity captive'—he would give no mean gift then, when he was to ascend triumphantly to heaven—the greatest gift he could give was, 'some to be prophets, some apostles, some teachers, for the building up of the body of Christ, till we all meet a perfect man in Christ.' 'I will send them pastors according to my own heart,' saith God, Jer. iii. 15. It is a gift of all gifts, the ordinance of preaching. God esteems it so, Christ esteems it so, and so should we esteem it.

And to add this further, to clear it from whatsoever may rise up in any man's mind, *do but consider in experience, where God sets up his ordinance, how many souls are converted.* Some are savingly cast down and then raised up again. Their lives are reformed. They walk in the light, they know whither they go. They can give an account of what they hold. The state of those that live under the ordinance of God is incomparably more lightsome, and comfortable, and glorious, than those that are in the dark, that want it. If we had no other argument, experience is a good argument. Where doth popery and profaneness reign most? In those places where this ordinance of God is not set up; for popery cannot endure the breath of the gospel. Thus we see the necessity and benefit of preaching.

But then, in the next place, this preaching *it must be of Christ;* Christ must be 'preached.'

Quest. But must nothing be preached but Christ?

Ans. I answer, Nothing but Christ, or that that tends to Christ. If we preach threatenings, it is to cast men down, that we may build them up. If a physician purge, it is that he may give cordials. Whatsoever is done in preaching to humble men, it is to raise them up again in Christ; all makes way for Christ. When men are dejected by the law, we must not leave them there, but raise them up again. Whatever we preach, it is reductive to Christ, that men may walk worthy of Christ. When men have been taught Christ, they must be taught to 'walk worthy of Christ, and of their calling,' Col. i. 10, that they may carry themselves fruitfully, and holily, and constantly, every way suitable for so glorious a profession as the profession of Christian religion is. The foundation of all these duties must be from Christ. The graces for these duties must be fetched from Christ; and the reasons and motives of a Christian's conversation must be from Christ, and from the state that Christ hath advanced us unto. The prevailing reasons of an holy life are fetched from Christ. 'The grace of God hath appeared'—saith St Paul, 'it hath shined gloriously'—'teaching us to deny all ungodliness and worldly lusts, and to live soberly, and righteously, and holily, in this present evil world,' Titus ii. 12. So that Christ is the main object of preaching. This made St Paul, when he was among the Corinthians, to profess no knowledge of anything but of 'Christ, and him crucified;' to esteem and value nothing else. He had arts and tongues and parts. He was a man excellently qualified, but he made show of nothing in his preaching, and in his value and esteem, but of Christ, and the good things we have by Christ.

Now Christ must be preached wholly and only. We must not take anything from Christ, nor join anything to Christ. The Galatians did but believe the necessity of ceremonies with Christ; and the apostle tells them, 'Ye are fallen from Christ,' Gal. v. 4. It is a destructive addition, to add anything to Christ. Away with other satisfaction. The satisfaction of

Christ is enough. Away with merits. The merits of Christ are all-sufficient. Away with merit of works in matter of salvation. Christ's righteousness is that that we must labour to be found in, and 'not in our own,' Philip. iii. 9. All is but 'dung and dross,' Philip. iii. 8, in comparison of the excellent righteousness we have in Jesus Christ. You must hear, and we must preach all Christ and only Christ. St Paul saith, he was 'jealous with a holy jealousy' over those he 'taught.' Why? 'Lest Satan should beguile them, and draw them from Christ,' to any other thing, 2 Cor. xi. 2. Why is the Church of Rome so erroneous, but because she leaves Christ and cleaves to other things? Therefore we must labour to keep chaste souls to Christ, and those that are true preachers, and ambassadors, and messengers, they must be 'jealous with a holy jealousy' over the people of God, that they look to nothing but Christ.

Christ must be preached; but to whom? 'To the Gentiles.'

Here lies the mystery, that Christ, who was 'manifest in the flesh, justified in the Spirit,' &c., should be 'preached to the Gentiles.' What were the Gentiles? Before Christ's time they were 'dogs,' in our Saviour Christ's censure. 'Shall I give the children's bread to dogs?' Mat. xv. 27. Before Christ's time they 'sat in darkness, and in the shadow of death,' Ps. cvii. 10. Before Christ's time they were 'the halt and the lame,' that he, the great feast-maker, sent to bid come in, Luke xiv. 21. They were 'aliens from the commonwealth of Israel,' without Christ, 'without God in the world,' Eph. ii. 12; without God because they were without Christ. It is not to be imagined in what misery the poor Gentiles were before the coming of Christ, except some few proselytes that joined themselves to the Jewish Church, for the Gentiles worshipped devils. What were all their gods but devils? They were under the kingdom of Satan when the gospel came to be preached among them. They were 'translated' out of the kingdom of Satan, into the blessed and glorious kingdom of Christ, Col. i. 13. Yet we see here, notwithstanding, they were such kind of people; the mystery of the gospel is preached to these, 'to the Gentiles.'

It was such a mystery as St Peter himself, although he were acquainted with it ofttimes by Christ, and he might read of it in the prophets, yet, notwithstanding, he was to be put in mind of it, Acts x. 13. When he was to go to Cornelius he saw a vision full of beasts, and a voice saying, 'Kill and eat,' and indeed, the 'Gentiles' were little better than beasts. They were esteemed so before they had the gospel, and the preaching of it to them. You see it was a mystery to St Peter himself.

Obj. But why did God suffer the Gentiles to 'walk in their own ways?' as the apostle saith, Acts xiv. 16. Why did he neglect and overlook the Gentiles, and suffer them to go on 'in their own ways,' so many thousand years before Christ came? Were they not God's creatures as well as the Jews?

I answer, This is a mystery, that God should suffer those witty* people, that were of excellent parts, to go on 'in their own ways.' But there was matter enough in themselves. We need not call God to our bar to answer for himself. They were malicious against the light they knew. They imprisoned the light of nature that they had, as it is Rom. i. 21. They were unfaithful in that they had. Therefore, besides that it is a mystery, God may well be excused. Do but look to the judgment that some of the heathens had of divine things, what reprobate and malicious judgments they had, how basely they esteemed of the Jews. The Jewish nation, saith Tully, shew how God regards them, in that she hath been overcome

* That is, 'wise.'—G.

so oft, by Nebuchadnezzar and Pompey, &c.* What a reasoning was this. And that proud historian Tacitus, how scornfully doth he speak of Christians (*k*). It is not to be imagined the pride that was in the heathens against the Jewish religion, especially the Christian religion, how they scorned and persecuted it, in the beginning of it. So you see, in the best of the heathen men there was matter and ground of God's just condemning of them; therefore we need not quarrel with God against that.

Obj. But here is another mystery, Why the Gentiles, being all alike naught,† God should leave the better of the Gentiles, and reveal Christ to the worst. Were not Socrates, and Plato, and such like, more goodly moralists than the Corinths and Ephesians? What kind of people were the Corinthians? A proud people, 'fornicators, idolaters;' as the apostle saith, 'such were some of you,' Eph. v. 8, and 1 Cor. vi. 11. Here is a mystery.

Ans. It is God's sovereignty. We must let God do what he will. 'He will be merciful to whom he will be merciful,' and 'he will neglect whom he will.' Saith Austin, 'We must be very reverent in these matters;' it is most safe to commit all to God, and usurp no judgment here (*l*). It is a mystery; yet there is some satisfying reason may be given why the Gentiles were called, when Christ came in the flesh, and not before; besides many prophecies foretold that it should be so, and some reason may be given why it was so.

Because they were to be incorporate to the Jews, to be 'fellow-citizens' with the church of the Jews. They were to be of God's household, as it is excellently and largely set down in Eph. ii. 19. Now Christ coming took down the 'partition-wall.' Christ is the centre in whom they meet, in whom they are one. Therefore they met one with another when Christ came, because he is the Saviour of both. He is the 'corner-stone' whereupon both are built. So that now they are 'fellow-citizens' since Christ came.

And you see in the genealogy of Christ, he came both of Jews and Gentiles, as we see in Ruth. Divers of our Saviour's ancestors, they were Gentiles as well as Jews, to shew that he that came of both, he came to be the Saviour of both. But it is the safest, as I said before, in these queries, to rest in the wise, unsearchable dispensation of God, and rather be thankful that God hath reserved us to these times and places of knowledge, than to ask why our forefathers did not know Christ. We enjoy a double spring of the gospel, and the benefits of it. First, we were delivered from heathenism. What kind of people were we in Julius Cæsar's time? Barbarous people.‡ And after, when popery came in, God delivered us from that; there was a second spring. Yet how few give God praise, that hath had mercy on us Gentiles, that hath delivered us from Gentilism, and from the darkness of popery. But we grow weary of religion, as they did of manna, Numb. xi. 6.

Let us therefore make good use of it, that God hath been merciful to us Gentiles in these later times. And let us that are born in the precincts of the church help our faith in the time of temptation this way. Certainly God means well to my soul. I might have been born before, in times of ignorance and places of ignorance, and never have heard of Christ; but I have been baptized and admitted into the church: and by that there is an obligation. Before I understood myself, I was bound to believe in Christ. God was so careful of my soul when I understood nothing, that there should

* Cf. Note in Vol. I. page 303.—G.

† That is, 'wicked.'—G.

‡ Cf. note *c*, page 539.—G.

be a bond for me to believe in Christ. If God had not meant well to my soul, I should not have lived so much as to hear of the gospel. Thus we should gather upon God, as the woman of Canaan did upon our Saviour Christ, and fight against all distrust and unbelief, and all temptations of Satan, that present God as though he cared not for us. There cannot be too much art and skill to help our faith this way.

Again, the Gentiles have now interest in Christ since the coming of Christ, and not before. It is a mystery. It were not a mystery, if the Gentiles had had an interest in Christ, and been within the pale of the church before.

There are several degrees of the dispensation of salvation. There is, first, the ordaining of salvation. That was before all worlds. And then the promise of salvation. That was when Adam fell. Then there is the procuring of salvation promised. That was by Christ, when he came in the flesh. Then there is the promulgation and enlarging of salvation to all people. This was after Christ was come in the flesh. Then there is the perfect consummation of salvation in heaven. Now the execution of the promise, and the performance of all good concerning salvation, it was reserved to Christ's coming in the flesh; and the enlargement of the promise to all nations was not till then. I do but touch this, to shew that God hath had a special care of this latter age of the world. Some account the first age of the world to be a golden age, the next silver, and then an iron age. But indeed we may invert the order. We live in the golden age, the last ages, when Christ was 'manifested.' What is the glory of times and places? The 'manifestation of Christ.' The more Christ is laid open with his 'unsearchable riches,' the more God glorifies those times and places; and that is the golden age where the gospel is preached.

Therefore, we cannot be too much thankful for that wondrous favour which we have enjoyed so long time together, under the glorious sunshine of the gospel.

Hence we have a ground likewise of enlarging the gospel to all people, because the Gentiles now have interest in Christ; that merchants, and those that give themselves to navigation, they may with good success carry the gospel to all people. There are none shut out now, since Christ, in this last age of the world; and certainly there is great hope of those Western people. We see the gospel hath imitated the course of the sun. The Sun of righteousness hath shined like the sun in the firmament. The sun begins east, and goes to the west; so the gospel. It began in the eastern parts. It hath left them; they are under the Turkish barbarous tyranny at this time. The gospel is now come to the western parts of the world.* For Christ will take an holy state upon him, and will not abide long where he is disesteemed, where the gospel is under-valued, and blended with that which is prejudicial to the sincerity† of it; when there is little care had what men believe. The state of the gospel and truth is such, that if it be mingled overmuch with heterogeneal stuff, it overthrows it; and Christ will not endure this indignity. Therefore, let us take heed that we keep Christ and his truth with us exactly; and let us take heed of sinning against the gospel, if we would have it stay with us, especially of sins immediately against the gospel, as for instance,

1. Take heed *of joining superstition and popish trash with it*, or the like, that will eat out the very heart of the gospel, and sets up man in the place of Christ.

* Cf. note *i*, Vol. I. p. 101.—G.

† That is, 'purity.'—G.

2. Again, Take heed *of decaying in our first love.* We see God threateneth the church of Ephesus, for not cherishing and maintaining her first love; that he would remove not only the gospel, but the 'candlestick,' the church itself. For security in abundance and plenty, and decay in her first love, God threateneth that he will scatter the candlestick, the church itself, into foreign places.

3. Again, A sin against the gospel *is unfruitfulness under it.* When men shall have the blessed influence of the gospel, the soul-saving truth, the good word to be long among them, and to be as barren under it as if they were pagans; for the gospel to have no more power over our souls than if we had no gospel at all; that there is no difference between us and heathens in regard of our conversations; to go no further then they, nay, not so far in honesty, and justice, and sobriety: let us take heed of these and the like sins against the gospel. And I say, it should be a ground of labouring the conversion of those that be savages, be they never so barbarous, to labour to gain them to Christ. There are indeed some hindrances. There be Jannes and Jambres among them, instruments of the devil, to keep them in blindness and ignorance, and then custom that they are bred in,—which prevails most with the sorriest people,—for ignorant people that have their wits determined to one way they are so strong in it, as they are not to be untaught; as it is hard to teach a beast, because he is taught to go one way, for want of variety of conceptions, being void of reason. Now, people by nature are little better than beasts. Therefore they are so fixed and determined in that way they are brought up in, and are so settled by the devil and those priests among them, and by the tyranny of those that have come among them, the Spaniards, &c., that hath hindered their conversion much, yet, take them as bad as they can be, God hath a time for them. What were we of this nation sixteen hundred years agone? There is a fulness of the Gentiles to come in; and certainly it is not yet come fully. For it is probable, nay, more than probable, that there are some people that never had the gospel; and the fulness of the Gentiles must come in before the other mystery of the calling of the Jews. I speak it to encourage those that have interest that way, not to take violent courses with them. There is nothing so voluntary as faith. It must be wrought by persuasions, not by violence; and there is a ground of encouragement hence, that since the coming of Christ there is a liberty for all nations to come in. Christ must be 'preached to the Gentiles.'

To conclude this point. Let us consider that we are those Gentiles that have enjoyed this preaching of Christ; and it is the glory of our nation. It is not our strength, or riches, or any ornament above others, that sets us forth, so much as this, that we have the gospel 'preached' among us, that these blessed streams run so plentifully everywhere among us. Let us labour to value this inestimable benefit. Where the gospel is not 'preached,' there the places are salt-pits, despicable places, whatsoever they are else, as it is in Ezekiel.* They are under the kingdom of Satan. It is the glory of a nation to have the truth among them. 'The glory of Israel' was gone when the ark was taken, 1 Sam. iv. 21. The religion and truth we enjoy it is our ark; our glory is gone if we part with that. Therefore, whatsoever God takes from us, let us desire that he would still continue the gospel of truth, that he would still vouchsafe to dwell among us, and not leave us. What were all things in the world besides, if we had not the blessed truth of God? We must leave all ere long. Therefore let

* Query, Zeph. ii. 9? But cf. also Ezek. xlvii. 11.—G.

us labour to have the eyes of our understanding enlightened, to conceive aright of the difference of things, and to value ourselves by this, that Christ is 'manifested' to us; and thereby we have interest in Christ, more than by any interest and part and portion in the world besides. For then Christ will delight to be with us still, when we make much of him, and esteem, and prize, and value him.

'Believed on in the world.'

After 'preached to the Gentiles,' he joins 'believed on in the world,' to shew that faith 'comes by hearing.' Indeed, 'preaching' is the ordinance of God, sanctified for the begetting of faith, for the opening of the understanding, for the drawing of the will and affections to Christ. Faith is the marriage of the soul to Christ. Now in marriage there must not be a mistake and error in the person, for then it is a kind of nullity. Now that the person to whom we are to be married by faith may be known to us, there is an ordinance of preaching set up, to lay open our own beggary and necessity, what we are without him; and to open the riches of our husband, the nobility, and privileges, and whatsoever is glorious in Christ, that the church may know what a kind of husband she is like to have. In Rom. x. 14, *seq.*, you have the *scala cœli*, the ladder of heaven, as a good old martyr called it; and we must not presume to alter the staves of that ladder (*m*). 'How can they call upon him in whom they have not believed? and how shall they believe without a preacher? and how shall they preach unless they be sent?' Here is preaching, and believing, and then prayer. There are some that are bitter against this ordinance of preaching, and advance another excellent ordinance of prayer, to the disparagement of this: if they would join them both together, it were well. You see what the apostle saith: 'How shall they call upon him in whom they have not believed? and how shall they believe without a preacher?' without this ordinance of preaching? shewing that we cannot have the spirit of prayer without faith, nor faith without preaching. And the wise man saith, 'He that turns his ear from hearing the law' (under what pretence soever), 'his prayer shall be abominable,' Prov. xxviii. 9. The prayers of such men that would cry down this ordinance, how are they like to be accepted? They are abominable. We see here the apostle sets them down in this degree, hearing, and believing, and prayer; and here in this place preaching goes before believing.

Therefore the gospel unfolded is called 'the word of faith,' because it begets faith. God by it works faith; and it is called the 'ministry of reconciliation,' 2 Cor. v. 18, because God by it publisheth reconciliation. As preaching goes before believing, so it is the blessed instrument, by reason of the Spirit accompanying of it, to work faith. In the ministry of the gospel there is not only an unfolding of the excellent things of Christ, but there is grace given by the Spirit to believe. And herein this publication and proclamation differs from all other publications in the world. Men may publish and proclaim what they would have, but they cannot give hearts to believe it. But in the blessed promulgation and publishing of divine truths, there is the Spirit of God accompanying it, to work what it publisheth. It opens the riches of Christ, and offers Christ; and Christ is given to the heart with it. It publisheth what is to be believed and known, and it alters our courses. Together with it there goes a power—the Spirit clothing the ordinance of preaching—to do all. Therefore it is called 'the ministry of the Spirit,' 2 Cor. iii. 8. Why? Because what is published in the preaching of the word, to those that belong to God, it hath the Spirit to convey it to the souls of God's people. Therefore he saith here, first preached and then believed.

Therefore, those that are enemies to this ordinance of God, they are enemies of the faith of God's people, and by consequent, enemies of the salvation of God's people. But the more the proud and haughty atheistical heart of man riseth against it, the more we should think there is some divine thing in it. It must needs be excellent, because the proud heart of man stomachs* it so much. We see here it is the means to work faith. Therefore, as we esteem faith and all the good we have by it, let us be stirred up highly to prize and esteem of this ordinance of God. So much for the coherence or connection, 'preached to the Gentiles,' and then

'Believed on in the world.'

For the words themselves, we see here, first, that Christ, as he must be unfolded in preaching, so he must be 'believed on.'

Because the dispensation ministerial is not enough, unless there be an applying grace in the heart; and that is a spirit of faith, whose property is, to make peculiar that that is offered. There is a virtue of application in this grace of faith. Where there is a giving there must be a receiving, or else the gift is ineffectual. Christ is the garment of the soul. He is the foundation and food, &c. As I said before, he is our husband. We must give our consent. 'Believing' is a spiritual marriage. In marriage there must be a consent. This consent is faith. That makes up the bond between Christ and the believing soul. Therefore of necessity there must be faith; all else, without believing in Christ, is nothing. Faith is the means of making Christ our own, and no other thing whatsoever.

The papists have ridiculous means, that they understand not themselves, nor anybody else. They make the sacrifice of the Mass a means to apply Christ, and other courses; but the ministerial means to apply to Christ is the preaching of the gospel, and faith that is wrought by the ministry of the gospel; and there is no other way of application, by the Mass, or any such thing. Christ without faith doth us no good; in Heb. iv. 2, 'The word that they heard did not profit them, because it was not mingled with faith.' The word of God, the gospel, it is the 'power of God to salvation;' but it is to all that 'believe,' 1 Peter i. 5. Whatsoever good Christ doth to us, he doth it by faith. It is a rule in divinity, and it is to purpose in the deciding some controversies, that a spiritual benefit, not known and applied, is a nullity; because God intends all, whatsoever we have, to be opened to us and applied, that he might have the glory, and we the comfort. We see the excellency and necessary use of this grace of faith.

How is Christ to be believed on?

1. *We must rest upon no other thing, either in ourselves or out of ourselves, but Christ only.* In popery they have many other things to rest on, and their faith being corrupt, all their obedience likewise is corrupt that springs from it. They dishonour Christ to join anything in the world with him. The apostle is wondrous zealous in this, to have nothing joined with Christ; as in Gal. v. 2, 'If ye be circumcised, Christ shall profit you nothing;' only Christ must be believed on in matter of salvation.

2. *And whole Christ must be received.* 'Believing' is nothing but a taking or receiving of Christ as a Lord and as a Saviour; as a priest, to redeem us by his blood; and Christ as a king, to govern us. We must take whole Christ.

We see what manner of faith is in most men, that snatch out of Christ

* That is, = resents, dislikes.—G.

what they list, to serve their own turn. As he died for their sins, so they are glad of him; but as he is a lord and king to rule and govern them, so they will have none of him, but 'turn the grace of God into wantonness,' Jude 4. But Christ, as we must rest and rely on him only, so we must receive him and believe on him wholly.

Now faith looks upon Christ as the main object of it, as it justifieth. The same faith it looks upon the whole word of God as a divine truth revealed; but for the main work of it, it looks upon Christ. Christ is the jewel that this ring of faith doth enclose; and as the ring hath the value from the jewel, so hath faith from Christ. In the main point of justification and comfort, faith lays hold upon Christ for mercy; for the distressed afflicted soul it looks first of all to comfort, and peace, and reconciliation; therefore it looks first to him that wrought it—that is, Christ. Now, the same faith that doth this, it believes all divine truths, the threatenings, and precepts, &c. Faith chooseth not its object to believe what it lists, but it carries the soul to all divine truths revealed. But when we speak of justifying faith, then Christ, and the promises, and the mercy of God in Christ, is the first thing that the soul looks unto.

Christ is the first object of faith, before any benefit or gift that we have from him; first, we must receive Christ before we have any grace, or favour, or strength, from him. And a sanctified soul looks first to Christ, to the love of Christ, to the person of Christ, and then to his goods and riches. As one that is married, she regards first the person of her husband, and then looks to the enjoyment of his goods, and inheritance, and nobilities, or else it is no better than a harlot's love. So faith looks to the person first. It knits us to Christ, to be in love with, and to embrace Christ, and then it looks to all the good things we have by him. For he never comes alone. There is a world of good things in him: all that tends to grace and glory. Yet it is the person of Christ that the soul of a Christian principally looks to. Other divine truths are the object of faith to direct and sway our lives; yet, notwithstanding, they are not the object of faith; when we look for comfort, for forgiveness of sins, and reconciliation with God, then it looks to Christ especially.

Therefore we that are ministers of the gospel of Christ should especially look to unfold the riches of Christ; and those that are God's people should especially desire to have Christ unfolded, and the riches of God's love in Christ. The soul that ever found the sting of sin, the conscience that ever was awakened to feel the wrath of God, it accounts nothing so sweet as evangelical truths, those things that concern his Husband and Saviour. A carnal man loves to hear moral points wittily spoken of, as delightful to his ear; but the soul that understands itself, what it is by nature, that ever felt in any degree the wrath of God for sin, of all points, it desires most to hear of Christ and him crucified. Therefore we may judge ourselves by our ears, of what tempers our souls are; for 'the ear tastes of speeches as the mouth doth meat,' as Job saith, Job xii. 11.

'Believed on in the world.'

By 'world,' especially here in this place, is meant the world taken out of the world, the world of elect. There is a world in the world, as one saith well in unfolding this point; as we see, man is called a little world in the great world (*n*). Christ was preached to the world of wicked men, that by preaching, a world might be taken out of the world, which is the world of believers. Hence we may clear our judgments in that point, that when Christ is said to redeem the world, it must not be understood generally of all mankind. We see here, the world is said to believe in Christ. Did all mankind believe in Christ? was there not a world of unbelievers?

We see here Christ 'believed on in the world'—the world that was opposite, that were enemies, that were under Satan. Who shall despair, then? Therefore, let us conceive well of Christ. Why was he 'manifest in the flesh?' and why is there an ordinance of preaching? Wherefore is all this, but that he would have us believe, be our sins what they will? Put the case that there were a world of sin in one man, that one man were a world of naughtiness; as in some sense, St James saith, 'there is a world of wickedness in the tongue,' James iii. 6. If in the tongue, much more in the heart, which is the sink of wickedness. But put the case, there were a world of wickedness in one man, what is this to the satisfaction of 'God manifest in the flesh,' and to the infinite love of God, now pacified in Christ, looking upon us in the face of his beloved Son? You see here Christ is 'believed on in the world.' Do but consider what is meant by the world in Scripture, how it is set down to be in an opposite state to Christ, and look to the particular state of the Gentiles, that are said to be the world. What wretched people were the Corinthians before they believed, and the Ephesians, and the rest!

Let no man therefore despair; nor, as I said before, let us not despair of the conversion of those that are savages in other parts. How bad soever they be, they are of the world, and if the gospel be preached to them, Christ will be 'believed on in the world.' Christ's almighty power goeth with his own ordinance to make it effectual. Since the coming of Christ, the world lies before Christ, as beloved of him, some in all nations. The gospel is like the sea: what it loseth in one place it gaineth in another. So the truth of God, if it lose in one part—if it be not respected—it gets in another, till it have gone over the whole world.

And when the fulness of the Gentiles is come in, then comes the conversion of the Jews. Why may we not expect it? They were the people of God. We see Christ 'believed on in the world.' We may therefore expect that they shall also be called, there being many of them, and keeping their nation distinct from others.

Now, I shall shew how this is a mystery. 'Great is the mystery of godliness, Christ believed on in the world.' This is a great mystery to join these together: 'the world' and 'believing.' It is almost as great a mystery as to join God and man together; a virgin and a mother; to bring an unbelieving rebellious heart, such as is in the world, and believing together. It is a great mystery in divers considerations.

1. First, *If we consider what the world was*, an opposite and enemy to Christ; and under his enemy, being slaves to Satan, being idolaters, in love with their own inventions, which men naturally doat on; here was the wonder of God's love and mercy, that he should vouchsafe it to such wretches. We may see by St Paul's epistles what kind of people they were before they embraced the gospel. Here was God's wondrous dignation,* that God should shine upon them that 'sat in darkness, and in the shadow of death,' that were abused by Satan at his will. That the world, that is, all sorts of the world, from the highest to the lowest, should at length stoop to the cross of Christ; that the emperors should lay their crowns at Christ's feet, as Constantine and others—Christ at length subdued the Roman empire itself to the faith; that the philosophers of the world, that

* That is, 'deigning, or condescension.'—G.

were witty* and learned, should at length come to embrace the gospel—for divers of the fathers were philosophers before (*o*); that men of great place, of great parts, and learning, and education, and breeding, should deny all, and cast all prostrate at the feet of Christ; for these to be overcome by plain preaching; for meanness to overcome mightiness; for ignorance to overcome knowledge; yet, notwithstanding, these great and wise men of the world were overcome by the gospel.

It was a mystery that the world should believe. If we consider, besides their greatness and wisdom, the inward malicious disposition of the world, being in the strong man's possession, for these men to believe the gospel, surely it must needs be a great mystery.

2. Again, if we consider the parties† *that carried the gospel*, whereby the world was subdued—a company of weak men, unlearned men, none of the deepest for knowledge, only they had the Holy Ghost to teach and instruct, to strengthen and fortify them,—which the world took no notice of,—men of mean condition, of mean esteem, and few in number: and these men they came not with weapons, or outward defence, but merely with the word, and with sufferings. Their weapons were nothing but patience, and preaching, offering the word of Christ to them, and suffering indignities; as St Austin saith, 'The world was not overcome by fighting, but by suffering' (*p*). So the lambs overcame the lions, the doves overcame the birds of prey, the sheep overcame the wolves. 'I send you,' saith Christ, 'as sheep among wolves;' and how? By nothing but by carrying a message, and suffering constantly and undauntedly for going with their message; for they had cruel bloody laws made against them, that were executed to the utmost; yet by these means they overcame by preaching, and sealing the truth that they taught by suffering—a strange kind of conquest. The Turks conquer to their religion, but it is by violent means; it is a religion of blood. But here, as I said, meanness overcame greatness, ignorance overcame learning, simplicity overcame pride, baseness overcame glory; a mystery in this respect.

3. Again, If we consider *the truth that they taught*, being contrary to the nature of man, contrary to his affections; to enforce self-denial to men that naturally are full of self-love, that make an idol of their wit and will; for them to come to be taught to be fools, in respect of wit, and to resign up their wills to the will of another—for these men to believe things that are above belief to carnal men, as St Austin observes, it was the wonder of the world (*q*). What a kind of doctrine was this, to win such entertainment in the world as it did! Yet it did make men deny themselves, deny their wits, their wills, their goods, their lives. Therefore in this respect it was a great mystery that Christ should be 'believed on in the world.'

4. Again, If we consider another circumstance, it adds to the mystery; that is, *the suddenness of the conquest*. The world was conquered to the faith and obedience of Christ. In a short time after Christ, one man, St Paul, spread the gospel almost all the world over; he conquered almost all the world; he spread the savour of the gospel like lightning, suddenly and strongly, because there was an almighty power and Spirit accompanying the glorious gospel; and thereupon it came to be thus effectual with the world.

5. Again, It is a wonder *in respect of Christ*, whom the world 'believed on.' What was Christ? Indeed, he was the Son of God, but he appeared in abased flesh, in the form of a 'servant.' He was crucified. And for the proud world to believe in a crucified Saviour, it was a mystery.

* That is, 'wise.'—G.

† Cf. Vol. III. page 9, footnote.—G.

6. Lastly, It is a great mystery, especially *in respect of faith itself*, faith being so contrary to the nature of man. For the heart of man, where faith is wrought, to go out of itself, and to embrace a beginning, and principle, and rising of life from another; to seek justification and salvation by the righteousness and obedience of another; for the proud heart of man to stoop to this, to acknowledge no righteousness of its own to stand before the tribunal of God, but to have all derived from Jesus Christ; to fetch forgiveness of sins out of the death of another; to wrap itself in the righteousness and obedience of Christ, given of God for it: the heart of man, without a supernatural work of the Spirit to subdue it, will never yield to this, because proud flesh and blood will alway have somewhat in itself to doat upon, and to set it out before God; and when it finds nothing in itself, then it despairs. For the heart of man thus to go out of itself, and rely only upon the righteousness of Christ, not having its own righteousness, this is the greatest mystery. Especially for a guilty soul, that hath its eyes opened to discern of its own estate; for a conscience awakened to trust in God, being a holy God, a just God: for these two to meet together, God, and a doubting, galled, misgiving conscience, forecasting the worst; for such a conscience to find peace by this act of faith casting itself upon Christ, this is more than can be done by any power of nature.

There is somewhat in nature for all legal obedience. Man naturally hath some seeds, to love his parents, to hate murder, and the like; but to go out of himself, and cast himself upon God's love and mercy in Christ, there is no seeds of this in nature, but all against faith in Christ. Ofttimes when a man is cast down, all in the world seems to make against him; and then for a man to have his heart raised up by an almighty power to 'believe,' certainly this must be a mystery. I say, when all makes against him; his conscience makes against him, and the judgment of God against him, and Satan's temptations against him—all the frame of things present seems to be against him—God himself ofttimes seems to be against him, to be an offended God, justly offended with his sins. For the soul in this case to cast itself upon God in Christ, there must needs be a hidden and excellent deep work on the soul. This is the greatest mystery. The greatest difficulty is in this branch, considering how contrary to the heart of man faith is.

Let us take heed of shallow conceits of faith, as if it were an easy common universal grace to 'believe.' No, beloved! It is a supernatural powerful work. Saint Paul sets it out divinely and largely in Eph. i. 18. He calls it the 'mighty power of God.' It requires not only a power, but an almighty power, to raise the heart of man to believe. For even as the work of redemption by Christ is a greater work in itself than the work of creation, so also the work of conversion.

1. Though they be all one to an infinite power, yet the thing itself *is* more difficult, *to make the heart of man to believe, than to make a world of nothing;* for when God made the world there was nothing to oppose. There he had to do with simply nothing. But when God comes to make the heart believe, he finds opposition and rebellion. He finds man against himself. He finds the heart and conscience against itself. He finds opposition from Satan, that helps man's distrustful heart. Then all meet together, afflictions, the sense of God's anger and man's guilty conscience. Now to make such a man believe, is more than to create a world.

2. And as God shewed more power, so he shewed *more mercy in the work of redemption than in the creation.* In the creation there he did good to a good man; Adam was created good, and he should, had he stood, have

continued in a good condition. But in the work of redemption God doth good to evil men. God transcends in his love, because the glory of his mercy reigns in the work of redemption; so that the power, and wisdom, and mercy being greater in the work of redemption, it requires a more supernatural power in the soul to apprehend this than any other truth. As the work in redemption is more glorious, so the divine grace and virtue in the soul, that makes use of this, which is faith, it must be more excellent than all other graces whatsoever. And as it must be God that must save and redeem us, so it must be God that must persuade the heart of this. As Christ, who is God, must perform the work of redemption, so it must be God the Holy Ghost that must persuade the heart, that God loves it so much, and raise the heart to apprehend it, and make use of it; no less power will do it. Let us, I say, have great conceits of this excellent grace of faith. 'All men have not faith,' 2 Thes. iii. 2. It is a rare grace, a rare jewel. When Christ comes, 'shall he find faith in the world?' Luke xviii. 8. Certainly it is a mystery for a man to believe in Christ, for a natural man to be brought to rely upon Christ. 'To you it is given to believe,' saith the apostle, Mat. xiii. 11.* He might well say, it is 'given.' It is no ordinary gift neither. Therefore let us pray with the disciples, 'Lord, increase our faith,' Luke xvii. 5; and with the poor man in the gospel, 'Lord, I believe, help my unbelief,' Mat. ix. 24.

The next thing I shall touch shall be this, *that faith is put here for all graces*. Here, in these six clauses of this 'great mystery of godliness,' there is only this one that is within us. 'God manifest in the flesh, justified in the Spirit, seen of angels, preached to the Gentiles, received up in glory'—these are all without us. But this one, 'believed on in the world,' that is only within us, and it is set down instead of all, and indeed so it is; for it draws all other graces after it. It enlivens and quickens the soul. It is the spring of spiritual life in us. It is the first grace of all. There are some degrees of the Spirit perhaps before it; but all graces have their quickening from faith. It infuseth supernatural vigour into all the parts and powers of the soul, and into all graces whatsoever. Where Christ is 'believed on in the world,' all follows, love and patience, and courage and fortitude whatsoever; as we see in Heb. xi. 2, 'By faith they had a good report.' They had a good report for patience and for courage, and other good works; but all these came from faith. Therefore, 'by faith they had a good report.' Therefore the acting of all other graces, it comes from faith. By faith, 'Enoch walked with God;' by faith, Noah and Moses did so and so, signifying that faith is the ground of all. Faith it fetcheth spiritual life from Christ for all, whatsoever is good; it knits us to the spring of life, Christ; it is the grace of union. Even as Satan, by unbelief, did infuse all his poison at the first; for by making our first parents stagger in the word of God came sin; so by faith all obedience comes; all have their rising and beginning from faith.

As it draws spiritual life from Christ, so the encouragements are by faith, to all other graces whatsoever, for patience and love, &c. Faith must set before them the object and the reasons from the glory to come, from the love of God in Christ. When faith propounds all this, then it stirs and quickens all graces. Faith yields strong reasons and discourse, to stir us up to whatsoever is necessary. Why do I hope for the glory to come? I believe it first. Why do I love God? I believe he is my Father, in

* Rather Phil. i. 29.—Ed.

Christ. All have strength from love, and that from faith: unless I believe that God loves me in Christ, I cannot love him; unless I love him, I can express no virtue for him, no patience, no good work. So it puts life into all; therefore it is here put for all, 'believed on in the world.' It should stir us up to make much of this faith; above all graces to desire it.

And being a mystery, and so excellent a grace, we have need to discern whether we have it or no. Therefore I will touch a few evidences, some of them out of the text.

1. First, If you believe, *it comes usually after preaching*. We see here, 'preached to the Gentiles,' and then 'believed on in the world.' Whence came thy faith? If not by the ordinance of God, thou mayest expect it to be a bastard faith; it hath not a right beginning; especially if it be joined with contempt of God's ordinance, it is no faith, but a presumptuous conceit. Preaching and believing here go one after another. Therefore examine how thy faith was wrought in thy heart.

2. Again, as I said, faith being a mystery in regard of such a world of opposition between the heart of man and Christ, Satan helping the unbelieving heart, here must needs be *a strife and conflict with faith*. Therefore those men that never had conflict with their own unbelieving heart, that never had conflict with Satan's temptations, they never had faith; for it is a mystery to have faith. It is with opposition and conflict. No grace hath the like conflict and opposition from Satan; for Satan aims, in all sins, to shake our faith and affiance in God's love. As God aims at the strengthening of faith above all, so the devil hates it above all, and in all temptations whatsoever he aims to shake our faith at the last. Therefore there must needs be opposition to ourselves and our own doubting nature, and to Satan's temptations, and to the course of things, that sometimes are clean opposite to a man. For a sinner to believe the forgiveness of sins; for a miserable man to believe glory in the world to come; for a dying man to believe life eternal; for a man tumbled into the grave to believe that he shall rise from the dead: if there be no conflict with these things, so opposite to faith, there is no faith.

3. Then again, in the third place, *it is the spring of all obedience*. The apostle calls it the obedience of faith, Rom. i. 5. All preaching is for the obedience of faith. Obedience of faith brings obedience of life and conversation. Examine thyself, therefore, by the course of thy obedience, by that that comes from faith. See what it works in thy soul, in thy life and conversation. And here I might be very large; for where faith is,

(1.) First of all, after it hath been a means to justify, to lay hold upon the all-sufficient righteousness of Christ, to stand between God and us, to clothe and cover our souls, then *it pacifieth the conscience*. 'Being justified by faith, we have peace with God, through Jesus Christ our Lord,' Rom. v. 1. Faith hath a quieting power. It quiets the soul, because it propounds to the soul a sufficient satisfaction in God-man. It propounds to the soul Christ sealed by God the Father. Having done all that is necessary to salvation, it sets down the soul: for he was God, and therefore able; and man, and therefore willing to save. Faith sets Christ as wooing us first; in his ministers inviting us, alluring us, commanding us, removing objections from our unworthiness. 'Come unto me, all ye that are weary and heavy laden,' Mat. xi. 28; and objections from our want of any goodness: 'Come and buy without money,' Isa. lv. 1, the all-sufficiency of Christ. Hereupon faith comes to quiet the soul, in the sweet course that Christ takes to bring the soul to him, being so able and willing, and shewing his willingness by all means that may procure love, that the soul may rest without doubting. Saith the soul, Surely Christ intends well to me, being so able, 'God in the flesh,' and setting up an ordinance, a ministry, whereby he invites me, and allures me, and commands me; and then also I have examples before me, of wicked men that have been converted: hereupon the soul comes to be at rest. Faith hath a quieting power.

(2.) And then again, there is presently *an alteration of the course:* Jordan goes backward; there is a turning of a man wholly; for faith is a turning of the soul clean another way. It turns the soul from the world to God and Christ, from the present evil world to a better world. We see as soon as Zaccheus believed, his thoughts were altered, his esteem of the things of this life was altered; 'half my goods I give to the poor,' Luke xix. 8. We see in the Acts of the Apostles, as soon as they believed, they burned their books, Acts xix. 19. As soon as a man believes in Christ, down goes the esteem of the world, and all worldly things whatsoever, because he sees a higher excellency in Christ. The poor jailer, when he had misused the apostles, as soon as he believed, we see how he neglects all, and makes a feast for them presently.

(3.) As soon as faith enters into the soul, *there is a mean and base esteem of all things, and a high esteem of Christ.* 'All is dung, in comparison of Christ,' Philip. iii. 8. There is a change of the soul, and an esteem that goes before that change. We work as we esteem. As soon as we believe, we esteem Christ, and the things of a better life, above all other things; and thereupon goes the whole soul, and the bent of it, that way, though with some conflict. We see in the epistles of St Paul, before those men believed in Christ, the Ephesians, the Colossians, the Romans, &c., what wicked people they were before, and how they were changed, as soon as they believed; then they were saints.

(4.) Again, Where this faith is, *it is a triumphing, a conquering grace, a prevailing grace.* It overcomes the world and whatsoever is opposite, for it sets before the soul greater things than the world can. The world presents terrors. What are these 'to the glory that shall be revealed?' The world sets out pleasures to allure us, and profits, and favours, and this and that; but what are all these to the favour of God in Christ? what are they to heaven? What can the world set before the soul of a believer that is not beneath? Faith can raise the soul above all worldly things. It subdues the natural doubts and loves, the fears of troubles and cares for the world, and all the affections that were before ruling in the soul. Faith coming into the soul subdues all to itself, and makes them all serviceable. Thus it prevails, if not at the first, yet in the continuance of time. It prevails by little and little in the hearts of all believers. It is a victorious grace, as we see in Moses and Abraham, &c., how it prevailed against all obstacles whatsoever. How many discouragements had blessed Abraham to leave his father's house, and to go he knew not where, and after to sacrifice his son! Yet faith overcame all. So Moses to leave the court, and to cleave to a despised people, what a work of faith was there! Faith is victorious. Therefore when people are drawn away with anything, that the looks of any man scares them, that the very noise of danger affrights them; when the hope of any rising will make them warp to do anything, when the hope of any gain will make them crack their conscience; where is the triumph of faith? As I said before, there is a prevailing power in faith, because faith sets before the soul that which is incomparably better and incomparably worse. What is all that man can do in comparison of hell and damnation? Conscience saith, If you do this, ye shall die. And on the other side, what is all the world can give, in comparison of heaven, which faith presents to the eye of the believer?

(5.) Again, Where this believing is, it is a working grace; *it works by love*. By the love to God it desires the communion and fellowship of that it desires, and it works by love to other believers. It works towards Satan hatred, toward wicked men strangeness in conversation. It is a working grace. It works by love, to all good, to God and God's people, and to ourselves. It makes us have too high esteem of ourselves to be stained with the base services of sin. It works every way; and indeed it must needs be so, when faith sets before the soul the love of God in Christ: Hath God loved me so, to redeem me from such misery by such a course as this, 'God manifest in the flesh,' to advance me to such happiness, being, such as I was before, a sinner? Oh the thought of this will constrain us, as the phrase of the apostle is, 'The love of Christ constraineth me,' 2 Cor. v. 14; and then the soul will be active and earnest in anything that may be for the honour of Christ. Hath Christ thought nothing too dear for me, not his own blood, for the salvation of my soul is the price of his blood? He came down from heaven, he was 'God manifest in the flesh,' on purpose, in love to my soul; and shall I think anything too dear for him? And hereupon faith works and stirs up love, and when it is stirred up by it, it is acted by it; it useth the love of God in all the performance of worship to God, and in doing all good to our brethren and to ourselves, to carry ourselves as we should every way.

We see the woman in the Gospel, Luke vii. 47, when she had much forgiven her, 'she loved much.' All duties come from love. What need I speak of particular branches? Christ brings all to love. He includes all duties in that one, in love, because they come from love, and have love to carry them, and to mingle itself with them; and love comes from faith. 'Faith working by love' evidenceth that we believe, Gal. v. 6. Where there is no love there is no faith. Therefore let us labour to have this affection of love kindled. If we would have love kindled, we must stir it up by faith. You see then that this believing is the leading grace.

Let us labour by all means therefore to water this root. When we would have trees flourish and thrive, we pour water to the roots of them. Now, the radical grace in a Christian's soul is this believing, this trusting in God reconciled in Christ, this relying upon Christ; a convincing persuasion that God and Christ are mine. This is the radical grace of all other. Let us water and cherish this by all means whatsoever.

And to this end, let us labour to increase in knowledge. 'I know whom I have believed,' saith the apostle, 2 Tim. i. 12, for all grace comes into the soul by the light of knowledge. Whatsoever is good is conveyed by light into the heart. Faith especially is the bent of the will to Christ, receiving him; but this comes by a supernatural light, discovering Christ. Therefore let us desire to hear much of Christ, of his privileges and promises. The more of Christ we know, the more we shall believe, and say with the apostle, 'I know whom I have believed,' 2 Tim. i. 12.

It is a fond* and wicked tenet† of the papists, to say that ignorance is the mother of devotion (*r*); and Bellarmine's tenet is, that 'faith is better defined by ignorance than by anything else' (*s*)—a fond and unlearned conceit. For howsoever the reason and depth of the things of faith cannot

* That is, 'foolish.'—G. † Spelled 'tenent.'—G.

be searched, yet we may know the things that are revealed in the Scriptures. The more I know the things that are revealed concerning Christ, and know that they are God's truths, the more I know, the more I shall believe. Faith of necessity requires knowledge; therefore knowledge is put for all other graces. 'This is eternal life, to know thee, and whom thou hast sent,' John xvii. 3, because it is an ingredient in all graces. It is a main ingredient in faith. The more we know, the more we shall believe. 'They that know thy name will trust in thee,' Ps. ix. 10. Is it not so in men's matters? The more we know a man to be able and loving and faithful of his word, the more we shall trust him. Is it not so in divine things? The more we know of Christ and of his riches and truth, the more experimental knowledge we have of him, that we find him to be so, the more we shall trust him. Therefore, by the knowledge that is gotten by the means, let us labour for an experimental knowledge, that so we may trust and believe in him more and more. Let us look to the passages of our lives in former times, how gracious God hath been towards us, and take in trust the time to come, that he will be so to the end. 'He is the author and finisher of our faith,' Heb. xii. 2. And let us search into the depth of our own wants and weaknesses; and this will force us to grow in faith more and more. This will be a means to increase our faith. The more we see of our own nothingness and inability, without Christ, that we are nothing, nay, that we are miserable without him, the more we shall cleave to him and cast ourselves upon him. Those that have the deepest apprehensions of their own wants and weakness, usually they have the deepest apprehensions of Christ, and grow more and more rooted in him. The searching of our own corruptions every day is a notable means to grow in faith, to consider what we are, if it were not for God's mercy in Christ; and this will make us to make out of ourselves to Christ, it will make us fly to the city of refuge. Joab, when he was pursued, he fled to the horns of the altar, 1 Kings ii. 28. When conscience pursues us, it will make us fly to the horns of the altar, to the city of refuge. A search into our own conscience and ways will force us to live by faith and to exercise faith every day in Christ Jesus.

And this is to feed on Christ daily, to fly to Christ, when we are stung with sin, and hunger, in the want of grace and strength, to fly to him for supply; and so to keep and increase faith by this excellent means. Christ is all in all to those that hope to be saved by him. Christ is the ground of our life and comfort, and our happiness. Therefore we should make out to him upon all occasions, to cleave to him in life and death. We cannot press this point of faith too much. Why are Christians called believers? Because believing is all. If we can prove the truth of our faith and belief, we prove all. If we be faulty in that, all is rotten. 'Whatsoever is without faith is sin,' Rom. xiv. 23. All men's natural morality and civility, it is, as it were, but copper graces; but counterfeits. They are but for the outward appearance, and not in truth. They are not enlivened and quickened by faith in Christ. But I leave this, and come to the last clause,

'Received up in glory.'

This is the last branch of this divine 'mystery of godliness,' but it is none of the least. Christ 'ascended,' if we respect himself; he was 'received,' if we look to his Father;' himself 'ascended,' his Father 'received' him. The Scripture hath both words: ἀνέβη, he 'ascended up,' that is, for himself; ἀνελήφθη, he was 'received up,' that is, he was assumpted.*

* 'Assumpt' means to 'lift or take up.' Cf. Richardson *sub voce*.—G.

There is no difficulty in the words. He 'ascended up' as well as he was 'received up,' positively as well as passively. In his death, he was not only crucified by others, and delivered by his Father, but he gave himself to death; so he was not only 'received up in glory,' but he 'ascended up into glory.' This shews the exaltation of Christ. The apostle begins with 'God manifest in the flesh.' There is the descent; a great mystery, for the great God to descend into the womb of a virgin, to descend to the 'lowest part of the earth,' Ps. lxxxvi. 13; and then he ends with this, received up in glory.' The ascent is from whence the descent was. Christ ascended, and was 'received' as high as the place was whence he came down. 'God manifest in the flesh,' that is the beginning of all; 'received up in glory,' that is the consummation and shutting up of all. It implies all—his exaltation, his resurrection, his ascension, his 'sitting at the right hand of God,' and his coming to 'judge the quick and the dead;' especially is meant his glory after his resurrection, his ascension and 'sitting at the right hand of God;' yet supposing his resurrection,

'Received up to glory.'

'Glory' implies three things. It is an exemption from that which is opposite, and a conquering over the contrary base condition. It implies some great eminency and excellency as the foundation of it, and then a manifestation of that excellency; and it implies victory over all opposition. Though there be excellency, if there be not a manifestation of that excellency, it is not 'glory.' Christ was inwardly glorious, while he was on earth in the state of abasement. He had true glory, as he was God and man; but there was not a manifestation of it, and therefore it is not properly called 'glory.' There was not a victory, and subduing of all that was contrary to his glory; for he was abased, and suffered in the garden, and died. But where these three are,—an exemption and freedom from all baseness, and all that may diminish reckoning and estimation, and when there is a foundation of true excellency, and likewise a shining, a declaring and breaking forth of that excellency,—there is glory. But Christ, after he was 'manifest in the flesh,' and had done the work here that he had to do, he was 'received up to glory;' that is, all baseness was laid aside. His glory appearing, all abasement did vanish; he was victorious over that; for, in his resurrection, that was the first degree of his glory. You know, the cloths that he was bound with were left in the grave, the stone was removed. All things that might hinder his glory, that might abase him in body, in soul, or condition, they were removed. There was an excellency in all that was not before, in regard of manifestation. For his body, it was now impassible, an immortal, spiritual body. It could suffer no longer. It was not fed with meat and drink, as in the time of his abasement. It was a body so agile and so nimble, that he could move even as he would himself. So there was a glory put upon his body above the sun. There was a glory upon the soul. All that might hinder that, was subdued; for there was no sorrow, no fear, nor grief, as there was in his soul before he was glorified. So both in body and soul, he was more glorious.

And then for his whole condition, that was glorious. He was abased no longer, for now he was taken into the highest place of all, above the heavens; and as his place is most eminent, so his government is most eminent. For he is taken up there 'above all principalities and powers,' as it is Eph. i. 20, and 'is gloriously set down at the right hand of God,' 1 Peter iii. 22. All being subject to him, he hath the domination and government of all. So that whatsoever might shadow and cloud him, all ills, either in body, in soul, or condition, all was removed, and he was glorious in all.

For excellency, the foundation of glory, that was always with him in his very abasement, but now it was 'manifested.' He was 'mightily declared to be the Son of God, by raising himself from the dead,' Rom. i. 4. He was declared to be glorious in all those things wherein he could be glorious. As no person can be glorious but either it must be in body or soul or condition, he was glorious in all; for he was 'received up' into the place of 'glory,' to heaven, to the assembly of glory, to the presence of his Father and the blessed saints and angels, and no question but there was a glorious welcome. If the angels came so cheerfully to proclaim his incarnation when he was born, and sang, 'Glory be to God on high, on earth peace, and good will towards men,' Luke ii. 14, what kind of triumph do you think was made by all the blessed company in heaven when he was entertained thither after his abasement? It is beyond our conceits to imagine.

It will not be altogether unuseful to speak of the circumstances of Christ's being 'taken up to glory.'

1. *Whence* was he taken? He was taken 'up to glory,' from mount Olivet, where he used to pray, and where he sweat water and blood, where he was humbled. From the place of humiliation was his ascension to glory, shewing unto us that the place ofttimes where we pray, where we are afflicted, our sick-beds, nay, the places of our abasement, the very prisons, they may be as mount Olivet to us, from whence God will take us to glory. Let no man, therefore, fear any abasement; it may prove as mount Olivet to him in this respect.

2. And *when* was he taken 'up to glory?' Not before he had finished his work, as he saith, John xvii. 4, 'I have finished the work thou gavest me to do.' Then he was taken up, when he had done all, when he had accomplished our salvation; and after his abasement, not before. So our taking 'up to glory,' it must be when we have done our 'work,' when we have finished our 'course,' when we have run our 'race,' when we have 'fought the good fight.' And also after our abasement. We must first 'suffer' with Christ, before we can be 'glorified' with him. Again, if we speak of the first degree of Christ's glory, his resurrection: he was taken 'up to glory' when he was at the lowest that could be, when he was in the grave. So God's church and children, at the lowest they are nearest to glory. We use to say, Things when they are at the worst are nearest mending. So is the state and condition of the church of God, and every particular Christian. When he is lowest he is nearest rising, as we shall see afterwards.

3. *The witnesses* of this were the angels. They proclaimed his incarnation with joy; and without doubt they were much more joyful at his ascending up to glory. It was in the presence of the angels. So likewise, when he shall come to manifest his glory at the day of judgment, there will be 'innumerable thousands of angels.' Those glorious creatures were witnesses of his glory, and no question but they yielded their joyful attendance and service, that were so willing to attend him at his birth and coming into the world.

4. He was *carried up in the clouds*, in which also he shall come again at the last day.

But before he was taken up 'to glory' he was forty days on earth, to give evidence to his apostles and disciples of his resurrection, and to instruct and furnish them in things concerning their callings; afterwards he was taken 'up to glory.' And in all that time of his abode on earth, after his first degree of glory, his resurrection, he was never seen of sinful eye for anything we see in Scripture—I mean of those that were scorners of him, that despised him. The Scribes and Pharisees and carnal people did not see him. They had no commerce ot all with him after his resurrection. They that despised him in his abasement had no comfort by his exaltation.

But that which I will chiefly press in this clause shall be to shew, that, as this is a mystery, so how it is a 'mystery of godliness' to stir us up to godliness; for, as I said before, divine truths and principles they are called 'godliness,' because, where they are embraced, they work godliness, the soul is transformed into them. Where these truths are 'engrafted in the soul,' as St Peter saith, they turn the soul into their own nature. Therefore I will shew how this mystery, Christ 'received up to glory,' breeds a frame of godliness in the heart.

That it is a mystery it will easily appear. For was it a 'great mystery' that God should take our nature upon him, to be abased in it? Surely it must needs be a mystery that God will be glorified in our nature. Was our nature advanced in his incarnation? Much more was it glorified in his exaltation, when he carried it to heaven with him. Here was the mystery of the exaltation of our nature. God was as much abased as he could be, being born and dying for us. Our human nature was as much advanced as it could be, when God raised it up to heaven. God could be no more abased, remaining God; and man's nature can be no more advanced, remaining the true nature of man. This is a 'great mystery,' the advancement of our nature in Christ, that was made 'lower than the angels;' he was 'a worm, and no man.' Now our nature in Christ is advanced above the angels. Now this nature of ours in Christ, it is next to the nature of God in dignity; here is a mystery.

Among many other respects it is a mystery for the greatness of it. We see after his ascension, when he appeared to Paul in glory, a glimpse of it struck Paul down; he could not endure it. Nay, before he suffered, a very shadow of his glory, it amazed Peter and James and John; they could not bear it; they forgot themselves: 'Let us build,' say they, 'three tabernacles,' &c. If a little discovery of his glory on earth wrought these effects, what great glory is it then that he hath in heaven! Certainly it is beyond all expression.

In this glorious condition that Christ is received into, he fulfils all his offices in a most comfortable manner. He is a glorious prophet, to send his Spirit now to teach and open the heart. He is a glorious priest, to appear before God in the holy of holies, in heaven for us, for ever; and he is a king there for ever. From thence he rules his church and subdues his enemies. So that though he accomplished and fulfilled those blessed offices that were appointed him in the state of humiliation on earth, as it became that state to suffer for us, yet it was necessary that he should enter into glory, to manifest that he was a king, priest, and prophet; for he was not manifested who he was, indeed, to our comfort, till he was 'received up in glory.' We had not the Spirit, the Holy Ghost, sent from above till he ascended; as it is in John vii. 39, 'The Holy Ghost was not given, because Christ was not ascended,' to apply and to help us make use of Christ and all his benefits and riches. So that in regard of the manifestation of Christ's offices, and of application of all the good we have by it, it is by Christ 'received up in glory.' To come to some application.

1. First of all, we must lay this for a ground and foundation of what

follows, *that Christ ascended as a public person.* He must not be considered as a particular person, alone by himself, but as the 'second Adam.' As he took the nature of man in his incarnation, so he ascended into heaven in it, as a public person. As the first Adam was, in whom we all sinned, and all came to misery and baseness, and died, so Christ must be considered as the 'second Adam,' as in other things, so in his ascension to glory.

2. In the second place, we must know that *there is a wondrous nearness between Christ and us now;* for before we can think of any comfort by the 'glory of Christ,' we must be one with him by faith, for he is the saviour of his body. Therefore we must be in him, we must be his members, we must be his spouse; and being so once, we are one with Christ. There is no relation in the world that is able to express the nearness between Christ and us sufficiently; and therefore, when we speak of Christ ascending into glory, we must needs think of ourselves, and of our glory and advancement. He was taken up to glory in onr nature, not only for himself but for all his. As the husband of the church, he is gone before, to take up heaven for his wife. As a husband takes up land in another country for his spouse, though she be not there, Christ hath taken up heaven for us: 'I go before to prepare a place for you,' John xiv. 3. So likewise he is in heaven as a glorious head, ministering virtue, and comfort, and strength to all his. All our power and strength, it comes from Christ now, as our head in heaven.

3. Again, *There is a causality, the force of a cause in this;* because Christ, therefore we. Here is not only a priority of order, but a cause likewise; and there is great reason. Was there the force of a cause in Adam, that was but mere man, to convey sin and misery, and the displeasure of God to all that are born and descend of him? and is there not the force of a cause in the 'second Adam,' to convey grace and glory to his, he being God and man? Therefore, whatsoever is good, it is first in Christ and then in us. Christ first rose, therefore we shall rise; he ascended into glory, therefore we shall be afterward in glory.

4. And then we must consider Christ not only as an efficient cause, *but as a pattern and example* how we shall be 'glorified.' He is not only the efficient of all glory within and without, but he is the exemplary cause; for all is first in him and then in us. He was first abased, and so must we; and then he was glorified, and so shall we. We must be conformable to his abasement, and then to his glory. 'He is the first-fruits of them that sleep,' 1 Cor. xv. 20; he being the first-fruits, we succeed. These things being premised as grounds, I come to make some use of this comfortable point.

Use 1. Christ is received up in glory; therefore, first of all, for our information, *we must not seek him in a wafer-cake, we must not look for him in the sacrament bodily: how can he be there when he is* 'received up in glory'? Therefore when we come to the sacrament, let us consider we have now to deal with Christ who is in heaven. Cannot Christ shew his virtue to comfort and strengthen us, but we must have his body in the communion to touch our bodies? The foot hath influence from the head, yet the head is distant from it in place. The utmost branches have life and sap from the root, yet they are remote in respect of place. A king spreads his influence over his whole kingdom, though it be never so large, yet he is but in one place, in respect of his person. Doth the sun in the heavens come down to the earth to make the spring, and to make all fruitful? Cannot he send beams and influence from thence to cherish the earth? Must Christ come down in his body to us, or else he can do us no good? Must there be a corporeal descent, or else we can receive no influence from him? There may be a derivation of virtue from Christ though his person be in heaven; where he shall remain till the last day, when he shall come to be 'glorious in his saints.' The sun doth more good being in heaven, than he could do if he were on the earth. If the sun were lower, what would become of the earth? But being so remote, and so far above, he hath opportunity to shine over the greatest part of the earth at once; being greater than the earth, he shineth over more than half the earth at once. Christ being in heaven, as the 'Sun of righteousness,' he shines more gloriously over all; and we have more comfort, and benefit, and influence from Christ, now in heaven, than we could if he were on earth. Must we needs make him bodily present everywhere, as the papists do, and other heterodox strange conceited men in Germany?* What need we do thus when there may be influence from Christ, now in heaven, to us on earth,—as we see in other things,—without confusion of his divine properties to his body, or making his body as his Godhead is? Therefore seek him not bodily anywhere but in heaven. Those opinions overthrow three articles of our faith at once: 'He ascended into heaven;' 'He sitteth at the right hand of God;' and, 'He shall come to judge the quick and the dead.' And where is his body in the mean time? in the sacrament? No. He is 'received up in glory.' Therefore we must have our thoughts in heaven when we are about that business. We must 'lift up our hearts,' as it is in our liturgy, which is taken out of the ancient liturgy, 'We lift them up unto the Lord.' We must have holy thoughts raised up to Christ in heaven.

Use 2. Again, Is Christ 'received up to glory'? Here is *singular comfort*, considering what I said before, that he is ascended as a public person, in our behalf, in our nature, for our good. Therefore, when we think of Christ in heaven, think of our husband in heaven, think of ourselves in heaven: 'We are set together in heavenly places with Christ,' as the apostle saith, Eph. i. 20. We have a glorious life, but it is hid with Christ, in heaven. When Christ himself shall be revealed, our life shall be revealed. Though we creep upon the earth as worms, yet notwithstanding we have communion and fellowship with Christ, who is joined with us in the same mystical body; who is now 'at the right hand of God' in heaven; and he that hath glorified his natural body in heaven, that he took upon him, he will glorify his mystical body; for he took flesh and blood, his natural body, for the glory of his mystical body, that he might bring his church to glory. Therefore, we ought as verily to believe that he will take his mystical body, and every particular member of it, to heaven, as he hath taken his natural body, and hath set it there in glory.

It is a comfort, *in the hour of death*, that we yield up our souls to Christ, who is gone before to provide a place for us. This was one end of his taking up to heaven, to provide a place for us. Therefore, when we die, we have not a place to seek. Our house is provided beforehand. Christ was taken up to glory to provide glory for us. Even as paradise was provided for Adam before he was made, so we have a heavenly paradise provided for us. We had a place in heaven before we were born. What a comfort is this at the hour of death, and at the death of our friends, that they are gone to Christ and to glory! We were shut out of the first paradise by the first Adam. Our comfort is, that now the heavenly paradise

* The reference is evidently to the Lutheran doctrine of consubstantiation.—Ed.

in Christ is open: 'This day shalt thou be with me in paradise,' saith Christ to the good thief, Luke xxiii. 43. There was an angel to keep paradise when Adam was shut out; but there is none to keep us out of heaven; nay, the angels are ready to convey our souls to heaven, as they did Lazarus, and as they accompanied Christ in his ascension to heaven, so they do the souls of his children.

Likewise, *In our sins and infirmities.* When we have to deal with God the Father, whom we have offended with our sins, let us fetch comfort from hence. Christ is ascended into heaven, to appear before his Father as a mediator for us; and, therefore, God turns away his wrath from us. We have a friend, a favourite in the court of heaven, the Son of God himself, at his Father's 'right hand:' he makes intercession for us. As Jonathan appeared in Saul's court to speak a good word and to plead for David, so our Jonathan, Jesus Christ, but with far better success, appears in the court of heaven for us, continuing our peace with God in our daily breaches, perfuming our prayers. And there is no danger of his death, for 'he is a priest for ever at the right hand of God,' to make intercession for us; his very presenting himself in heaven speaks for us. As if he should say, These persons that ask in my name, they are such persons as I was born for; such as I obeyed for; such as I died for; such as I was sent into the world to work the great work of redemption for; for he wrought our redemption in his abased estate; but he applies it as he is exalted. Application is as necessary as merit. We have no good by the work of redemption, without application: and for that end he appears in heaven for us and pleads for us. For even as there is speech attributed to Abel's blood—it cried, 'Vengeance, vengeance!'—so Christ appearing now in heaven for us, his blood cries, 'Mercy, mercy! These are those I shed my blood for; Mercy, Lord!' The very appearing of him that shed his blood, it cries for mercy at the throne of mercy, which is therefore a throne of mercy because he is there. He shed his blood to satisfy justice, to make way for mercy.

In the law, the high priest, after he had offered a sacrifice of blood, he was to go into the 'holy of holies;' so Christ, after he had offered himself for a sacrifice, he went into the 'holy of holies,' into heaven, to appear before God. And as the high priest, when he went into the holy of holies, he had the names of the twelve tribes on his breast, to shew that he appeared before God for them all, so Christ being gone into the 'holy of holies,' into heaven, he hath all our names upon his breast; that is, in his heart the name of every particular believer, to the end of the world; to present them before God. Therefore, when we have to deal with God, think of Christ, now glorious in heaven, appearing for us; God can deny him nothing, nor deny us anything that we ask in his name; we have his promise for it.

It is a ground likewise of contentment *in all conditions, whatsoever our wants be.* What if we want comfort, houses, &c., on earth, when we have heaven provided for us, and glory provided for us; when we are already so glorious in our Head? Shall not any condition content a man in this world, that hath such a glorious condition in the eye of faith to enter into? We should not so much as look up to heaven without comfort: Yonder is my Saviour, yonder is a house provided for me. We should think and look upon heaven as our own place, whither Christ is gone before, and keeps a room for us. Here we may want comforts, we may be thrust out of house and home, out of our habitation and country and all; but all the world, and all the devils in hell, they cannot thrust us out of heaven, nor dissolve and break the communion that is between Christ and us. They cannot take away either grace or glory from us. Therefore we should be content with any condition in this world. Christ is ascended into heaven, to keep a blessed condition for us.

Likewise, when we think *of the troubles of this world*, of the enemies we have here, think of Christ taken 'up to glory,' and think of Christ's order. First, he suffered, and then he entered into glory. So we must be content to suffer first, and then be glorious. We are predestinate to be conformable to Christ. Wherein stands our conformity? It is in abasement first, and then in glory. Christ entered into glory in this order, and shall we think to come to heaven in another order than Christ did? Shall we wish for a severed condition from him? If we be in Christ, all that we suffer in this world, they are sufferings of conformity to make us suitable to our Head, and to fit us for glory. And our greatest abasements, what are they to the abasement of Christ? None was ever so low, and there is none so high. As he was the lowest in abasement, so he is the highest in glory. When he was at the lowest, in the grave, not only dead, but under the kingdom and command of death, then he rose gloriously and ascended. Our lowest abasements are forerunners of our advancement and glory. This assumption of Christ to glory should help us in this respect.

In all disconsolations there is a world of comfort hence. We must not think of Christ, as if his honours had changed his manners, as it is among men; that now he is become stately, that he doth not regard his poor church. No such matter; he regards his poor church now he is in heaven as much as he ever did. The members here cannot suffer anything but the Head in heaven is sensible of it; as it is Acts ix. 4, 'Saul, Saul, why persecutest thou me?' The foot is trod upon, and the tongue complains. Our blessed Saviour is not like Pharaoh's unkind butler, that forgat Joseph when himself was out of prison. Christ being advanced to honour now, forgets us not here. No; he is as good Joseph, that was sent into Egypt to provide for all his family beforehand. So this our Joseph, the great steward of heaven and earth, he is gone to provide for us all, against we come to heaven. He forgets us not: 'He disdains not to look on things below,' Ps. cxiii. 6; he considers every poor Christian. He is as merciful now as he was when he was upon earth; as you have it largely proved Heb. iv. 7, 'He was man for this end, that he might be a merciful high priest;' and he is so in heaven, and pities all our infirmities. It is not here 'Out of sight, out of mind,' for, as I said, he hath us in his breast; ay, and he is with us, by his Spirit, to the end of the world. He is taken up to heaven by his body; but his Spirit, which is his general vicar, is here with us to the end of the world: 'I will send you the Comforter, and he shall abide alway with you,' John xiv. 26. And it is better for us to have the Comforter here, without his bodily presence, than to have his bodily presence without the abundance of his Spirit; as it was better with the disciples when he was taken up to heaven, and was present by his Spirit, than it was before. We lose nothing therefore by the ascension of Christ. It was for us. He was given for us, born for us. He lived for us, he died for us, he rose and ascended to heaven for our good: 'It is good for you that I go,' John xiv. 28. It was to provide a place for us, and to send the Comforter. All was for our good, whatsoever he did, in his abasement and exaltation.

Again, This administereth comfort in regard *of the afflictions of the church*. When the church is under any abasement, at the lowest, it hath a glorious head in heaven; and what! doth he sit there and do nothing? No. He sits 'at the right hand of God,' and rules his church, even in the midst of his enemies. If he do give the chain to them, it is for special ends. His people stand in need of all that they endure, and he measures it even to a drachm, whatsoever his church suffers; for they are his members, and he is sensible of their sufferings. He is 'a high priest that is touched with our infirmities,' Heb. iv. 15. Therefore nothing can befall his church without his government. He lets loose the enemies thus far, and then he restrains them, and subdues and conquers them, making them his 'footstool.' The enemies seem to domineer now, and trample on the church; but ere long they shall become the church's 'footstool.' Christ will govern his church till all his enemies 'be under his feet.' He is ascended into heaven for this purpose; and he is fitting his church by these afflictions, for greater grace in this world, and for eternal glory in the world to come.

Therefore, let us not take scandal* at the present sight of things. We stand amazed to see the state of Europe at this time; but for our comfort let us consider that Christ is taken 'up to glory,' and he sits in heaven and rules his church, and will guide all these wars to a good and gracious end. He sits at the stern. The ship may be tossed where Christ sleeps, but it cannot be drowned. The house that is built upon a rock, it may be blown upon, it shall never be overthrown. The bush wherein the fire is, it may burn, but it shall never be consumed. The church, wherein Christ rules and governs, it may be tossed, it shall never be overcome and subdued. Nay, by all these things that the church suffers, Christ rules, and exerciseth his church's graces, and mortifies his church's corruptions. It is necessary there should be some change. Standing waters breed frogs, and other base creatures; so it is with Christians. If there be not some exercise by afflictions, what kind of vices grow? As we see in these times of peace, what kind of lives most men live, that we may take up an admiration† that God should be so merciful to continue his truth to a company of proud base carnal persons, that lead lives, under the gospel, no better than if they were in paganism. Therefore we cannot look for any good, without further abasement. And certainly, if troubles come, we should many of us be better than we are now: afflictions would be so far from doing us harm, that they would refine us. We shall lose nothing, but that that doth us hurt; that, that we may well spare; that, that hinders our joy and comfort.

But, I say, let us comfort ourselves in respect of the present state of the church. Christ rules in the midst of his enemies, in the midst of crosses and persecutions, not to free us alway from them; but he rules in turning them to good, in strengthening and exercising our graces; and he rules in the midst of his church at this time by turning his enemies' cruelty to the good of the elect. As he ruled in the Israelites when he suffered Pharaoh to go on in the hardness of his heart, but he had a time for Pharaoh's ruin; so Christ hath a time for the persecutions of the church, as he had for all the ten persecuting emperors, that came to base and fearful ends. 'Was there ever any man fierce against God and prospered?' saith Job, chap. ix. 4. Was there ever any that set themselves against the church of God and prospered? No, no. It is with the church as it was with Christ; to have looked on Christ hanging and bleeding on the cross, to have seen him grovelling on the ground in the garden, men would be ready to take offence. What! he the Saviour of the world? But stay and see him in the text,

* That is, 'be offended.'—G. † That is, 'wonder.'—G.

assumed to glory, and then there would be no offence taken at Christ. So it is in the church. You see the church suffers persecutions, but lay one thing with another. See the church in heaven with the Head of the church. See the church advanced. See it in glory ere long. See it refined and fitted by sufferings, to come better out of afflictions than it went in, and then none will take scandal at the afflictions of the church, as they ought not at the abasement of Christ. For though he was 'God manifest' in weak 'flesh,' yet we see he 'ascended up in glory.'

There is a comfortable speech, Jer. xxx. 7, 'It is even the time of Jacob's trouble; but he shall be delivered out of it.' So we may say, this is the time of the church's trouble, but the church shall be delivered out of it. The enemies have their time to afflict and trample upon the church; but Christ hath his time to trample on them. Let us wait and expect with comfort better times. The kingdoms of the world will be known to be the Lord Jesus Christ's. There will be a further subjection to Christ's kingdom than ever there was since the first times, when the fulness of the Gentiles and the conversion of the Jews shall be. Let us comfort ourselves with the times to come. Christ is in glory, and he will bring his church to further glory even in this world, besides eternal glory at the latter day. 'Rejoice not over me, O mine enemy: for though I be fallen, yet shall I rise,' Micah vii. 8. Let not the enemies of the church insult* over much; though the church be fallen, yet she shall rise again 'after three days,' saith the prophet, Mat. xxvii. 63.† Christ, though he were abased as low as possible he could be, yet after three days he arose; so the church shall rise out of her troubles after three days; that is, after a certain time that we know not; but the exact time is only in the hands of Christ. But certainly there are glorious times of the church coming.

Consider the wonderful love of Christ, that would *suspend his glory so long*. The glory of heaven was due to him upon his incarnation, by virtue of the union of his human nature with the divine; for that nature that was united to the Godhead, it must needs have right to glory by that very union. What should hinder, when it was so near to God as to be one person, to be taken into the union of the person? Oh but where had our salvation been then, if Christ had entered into glory upon his incarnation, if he had not shed his blood, if he had not been abased to the death of the cross? Therefore the schoolmen speak well (*t*), he enjoyed the presence of God *affectione justitiæ*, with the affection of justice and all virtues; that is, he was as gracious from the beginning, from his incarnation, for matter of grace and love of all that is good; yet not *affectione accommoda*. There was a nearness to God in pleasure, and joy, and comfort. This he denied himself till he was assumpted to glory after his resurrection; and this he did in love to us, that he might suffer and be abased, to work out our salvation. That redundance of glory that should have been upon his person presently upon the union, it was stayed till his resurrection, that he might accomplish and fulfil our salvation. What a mercy and love was this! So it is with the church. It is glorious as it hath union with Christ. Is not the church a glorious thing, that is joined to Christ, that is 'Lord of lords, and King of kings,' the ruler of heaven and earth? What is the reason the church is so abased then?

If the church were not abased, it could not be conformed to Christ. Christ, that he might work our salvation, he must be abased, and have suspension and stopping of the glory due to him, till the resurrection. Of

* That is, 'triumph, boast.'—G.

† Qu. 'Rev. xi. 11'?—Ed.

necessity, we must be conformed to Christ as far as we may; and, that we may be conformed to him in abasement and suffering, there must be a stop of our glory, till we be dead and turned to dust, until we rise again, until Christ come to be 'glorious in his saints,' 2 Thes. i. 10. If Christ, as I formerly said, had shewed all his glory in his abasement, he could never have suffered. The devil himself would have done him no harm. There had been no pretence. The Pharisees would never have persecuted him and hated him, if they had seen him to have been such a person as he was; but he veiled his glory that he might suffer. If the world did but see the thousandth part of the glory that of due belongs to Christians, would they revile them, and disgrace, and malign, and trample on them? Certainly they would not. This is discovered in Scripture; but the world, to discover their atheism, that they believe not the word of God, take no notice of it. And that the children of God may be conformed to their head, and that way may be made to the malice of wicked men, to trample upon them, they go in the shape of miserable men.

Therefore let us not be discouraged for any abasement. We have a glorious life hid with Christ, which shall be revealed one day; in the mean time, in the midst of abasement, let us believe glory. And let me add this to the rest:

As the same body wherein Christ was spit upon, and mangled, and crucified, in the same body he rose again, and in the same body ascended into heaven, so it shall be with us. The same body that suffers anything for Christ, the same body that dies, the same body shall rise, and be assumed to glory.

Hence likewise we have a ground of patience in all our sufferings from another reason, not from the order *but from the certainty of glory*. Shall we not patiently suffer, considering the glory that we shall certainly have? 'If we suffer with him we shall be glorified with him,' Rom. viii. 17. Who will not be patient awhile, that hath such glory in his eye? Therefore let us look upon the glory of Christ in all our sufferings whatsoever. What made Moses and all the saints in all times to be so patient? They had an eye this way. What made Stephen not only patient but glorious? 'His face shone as the face of an angel,' Acts vi. 15. He looked on Jesus Christ, and saw him 'sitting at the right hand of God.' What made the martyrs not only patient but triumphant in all their sufferings? They had an eye of faith to see Christ sitting in glory, and to see themselves in heaven 'glorious in Christ;' and not only to see themselves 'glorious in Christ,' but in themselves afterwards. We are not only glorious in our Head, but we shall be ourselves where he is, 'taken up in glory.'

And let it stir us up likewise not to be ashamed of religion, and *to stand out in good causes for Christ and the church*. 'He is not ashamed to be called our brother,' Heb. ii. 11. No; not after his resurrection. 'Go tell my brethren, I ascend to my Father and your Father,' John xx. 17. He was not ashamed of it when he began to be in the state of glory. He is not ashamed of our nature now, to take it up into heaven. He is not ashamed to own us here, and at the day of judgment to set us at his right hand. And shall we now, for fear of men, for fear of shame, for any base earthly respect, be ashamed of our glorious Head? Do we believe that we have a Head that is glorious in heaven, 'sitting at the right hand of God,' that ere long will come to 'judge the quick and the dead;' and shall we be ashamed to hold out the profession of religion for a scorn, for a word, for a frown? Where is the 'Spirit of glory,' the spirit that should be in

Christians that hope to be glorious? 'He that is ashamed of me here,' saith Christ, 'I will be ashamed of him at that great day.' How can we think that Christ will own us, when we will not own religion here? When we are ashamed to stand for him, shall we think to stand at his right hand? All base carnal atheistical spirits, that are afraid of disgrace, of displeasure, of loss, of anything but of him they should be afraid of; let them know there is no comfort for them in Christ's exaltation; for if they had any communion with Christ, he would infuse another manner of spirit into them. Let us therefore stand for Christ. We have a glorious head, a glorious hope, a glorious inheritance.

And let us go on *with encouragement in good duties*, with a spirit of faith; for wherefore is Christ in heaven but to rule his church by his Spirit; 'to lead captivity captive, and to give gifts to men,' Eph. iv. 8. Let us therefore go on with confidence, that Christ from heaven will give us his Spirit to subdue our corruptions. He is in heaven to rule his church; and what is his kingdom but the subduing of our spirits by his Spirit, to be more humble, and more holy and gracious every way? Let us not think that our corruptions will be too hard for us, but go on in a spirit of faith; that Christ that died for us as a priest, he will rule us as a king; and if we be true to our own souls, we shall have strength to sustain us. He sits in heaven to rule us by his gracious Spirit. Let us not despair. Though we carry this and that corruption about us, we shall by little and little overcome all. He will 'lead captivity captive,' and overcome all in us, as he did in his own person. He that overcame for us will overcome in us, if there be a spirit of faith to depend upon him.

Again, This mystery is a 'mystery of *godliness*.' It tendeth to and enforceth godliness and holiness of life. Christ 'received up to glory.' You see then our flesh is in heaven. Christ hath taken into heaven the pledge of our flesh, and given us the pledge of his Spirit. It was a dignifying of our nature that God should be manifest in our flesh. That that was an abasing to him, as God, was an honour to our nature. The incarnation of Christ it was the beginning of his abasement in regard of his Godhead, for the Godhead to be clouded under flesh; but it was a dignifying of the human nature that it should be grafted into the second person. And is it not a greater honour to our nature that now in Christ it is gone to heaven, and is there above angels? Our nature in Christ rules over all the world. And wherefore is all this? As it is for wondrous comfort, so for instruction, to carry ourselves answerable to our dignity. What! hath God taken our nature upon him to the unity of the second person, and exalted and honoured and enriched it? Is he likewise gone to heaven in our nature, and is there above all principalities and powers? All the angels in heaven attend upon him. And shall we debase and dishonour our nature that is so exalted? Let it work upon us, to carry ourselves in a holy kind of state. Shall we defile ourselves with sinful courses, and make ourselves baser than the earth we tread on, worse than any creature? for a man without grace is next to the devil in misery, if God be not merciful to him. If God have thus honoured our nature above all created excellency whatsoever, shall not this stir us up to a correspondent carriage? It is oft pressed by the apostle that we 'walk worthy of our calling,' Eph. iv. 1. And, indeed, let us oft consider to what great matters we are called; for the life of heaven it must be begun upon earth. 'Whosoever hath this hope,' to be glorious with Christ in heaven, 'it purgeth him,' 1 John iii. 3. It frames him to be like the state he hopes for, and he that hath not a care to suit and fit his carriage and disposition to the state he believes, it is an empty hope; he deludes himself. Whosoever shall be glorious with Christ in heaven, is also glorious now. There is a Spirit of glory resting upon them, that is, grace; grace makes them glorious. Those that have not a Spirit of glory, that is, a Spirit of grace, to fashion and conform them, in some measure to be like Christ, by little and little, they have no right nor interest in the state of glory that shall be revealed after.

Is Christ taken up to glory, and for us as well as for himself? 'What manner of men ought we to be in holy conversation,' 2 Peter iii. 11. We should 'keep ourselves unspotted of the wicked world,' James i. 27. Shall we think to have communion and fellowship with Christ in glory, when we make 'the members of Christ the members of an harlot?' 1 Cor. vi. 15; when we make our tongues instruments of blaspheming God and Christ; as a company of vile wretches, that will come to the ordinances of God, and yet have not overcome their atheistical nature so much, as to leave their swearing and filthy courses? Do we think to have communion with Christ in glory, and not get the victory over these base courses? Do we profess ourselves to be Christians, and live like pagans? Hath God such need of people to fill heaven with, that he will have such unclean persons? Shall we have such base thoughts of heaven? No, beloved. These things must be left, if ever, upon good ground, we will entertain thoughts of fellowship in this glory. There is 'a new heaven and a new earth,' 2 Peter iii. 13, for the new creature, and only for such. Let us not delude ourselves. There must be a correspondence between the head and the members, not only in glory, but in grace; and the conformity in grace is before the conformity in glory. Will God overturn his method and order for our sakes? No, no; all that come to heaven, he 'guides them by his Spirit' here, in grace, and then he brings them to glory.' He gives 'grace and glory, and no good thing shall be wanting to them that lead a godly life,' Ps. lxxxiv. 11; but first grace and then glory.

Therefore let not the devil abuse us, nor our own false hearts, to pretend a share in this glory, when we find no change in ourselves, when we find not so much strength as to get the victory over the base and vile corruptions of the world. The apostle from this ground infers mortification of our 'earthly members:' 'You are risen with Christ,' 'Your life is hid with Christ in God,' and 'we are dead with Christ.'* Therefore we ought to mortify our sinful lusts. For the soul being finite, it cannot be carried up to these things that are of a spiritual, holy, and divine consideration; but it must die in its love, and affection, and care to earthly things and sinful courses. Therefore let us never think that we believe these things indeed, unless we find a disposition, by grace, to kill and subdue all things that are contrary to this condition. Though somewhat there will be in us to humble us, or else why are the precepts of mortification given to them that were saints already, but that there is somewhat will draw us down to abase us? But this is no comfort to him that is not the child of God, that lives in filthy courses, that he might easily command himself in. Let him abandon the name of a Christian. He hath no interest to the comfort of this, that Christ is 'received up to glory.'

Again, The mystery of Christ's glory it tends to godliness in this respect, *to stir us up to heavenly-mindedness*. The apostle doth divinely force this in the fore-named place, Col. iii. 1, 'If ye be risen with Christ, seek the things that are above.' From our communion with Christ, rising and

* Cf. Col. ii. 12, iii. 3, and ii. 20.—G.

ascending into heaven, and sitting there in glory, he forceth heavenly-mindedness, that our thoughts should be where his glory is, where our Head and husband is; and certainly there is nothing in the world more strong to enforce an heavenly mind than this, to consider where we are, in our Head. Christ, our head and husband, is taken up into glory. There is our inheritance; there are a great many of our fellow-brethren; there is our country; there is our happiness. We are for heaven, and not for this world. This is but a passage to that glory that Christ hath taken up for us; and therefore why should we have our minds grovelling here upon the earth? Certainly if we have interest in Christ, who is in glory 'at the right hand of God,' it is impossible but our souls will be raised to heaven in our affections before we be there in our bodies. All that are Christians, they are in heaven in their spirit and conversation beforehand. Our heavy, dull, earthly souls being touched by his Spirit, they will ascend up. The iron when it is touched with the loadstone, though it be an heavy body, it ascends up to the loadstone, it follows it. The sun it draws up vapours, that are heavy bodies of themselves. Christ as the loadstone being in heaven, he hath an attractive force to draw us up. There is not the earthliest disposition in the world, if our hearts were as heavy as iron, if we have communion with Christ, and have our hearts once touched by his Spirit, he will draw us up, though of ourselves we be heavy and lumpish. This meditation, that Christ our head is in glory, and that we are in heaven in him, and that our happiness is there, it will purge and refine us from our earthliness, and draw up our iron, heavy, cold hearts.

It is an argument of a great deal of atheism and infidelity in our hearts, as indeed our base nature is prone to sink down, and to be carried away with present things, that professing to believe that Christ is risen and ascended into heaven, and that he is there for us, yet that we should be plodding and plotting altogether for the earth, as if there were no other heaven, as if there were no other happiness but that which is to be found below. There is nothing here that can satisfy the capacious nature of man. Therefore we should not rest in anything here, considering the great things that are reserved for us, where Christ is in glory. Therefore when we find our souls falling down of themselves, or drawn downward to base cares and earthly contentments, by anything here below, let us labour to raise up ourselves with such meditations. I know not any more fruitful, than to consider the glory to come, and the certainty of it. Christ is taken into glory, not for himself only, but for all his; for 'where I am,' saith he, 'it is my will that they be there also,' John xvii. 24. Christ should lose his prayer if we should not follow him to heaven. It is not only his prayer but his will, and he is in heaven to make good his will. The wills of men may be frustrate, because they are dead; but he lives to make good his own will, and his will is, that we be where he is. Now, if a man believe this, can he be base and earthly-minded? Certainly no. 'Where our treasure is, our hearts will be there also,' Mat. vi. 21, by the rule of Christ; 'Where the body is, the eagles will resort,' Mat. xxiv. 28. If we did make these things our treasure, we would mount above earthly things. There is nothing in the world would be sufficient for us, if we had that esteem of Christ, and the glory where Christ is, as we should and might have.

And it is not only meditation of these things that will cause us to be heavenly-minded; but Christ, as a head of influence in heaven, conveys spiritual life to draw us up. 'When I am ascended, I will draw all men after me,' John xii. 32. There is a virtue from Christ that doth it. There is a necessity of the cause and consequence, as well as strength of reason and equity. There is an influence issuing from Christ our head, to make us so indeed. Therefore, those that are otherwise, they may thank themselves. The best of us, indeed, have cause to be abased, that we betray our comfort, and the means that we have of raising up our dead and dull hearts, for want of meditation. Let us but keep this faith in exercise, that Christ is in heaven in glory, and we in him are in heaven, as verily as if we were there in our persons, as we shall be ere long, and then let us be uncomfortable, and base, and earthly-minded, if we can.

To conclude all. As the soul of man is first sinful and then sanctified; first humble and then raised; so our meditations of Christ must be in this order: first, think of Christ as abased and crucified, for the first comfort that the soul hath is in Christ 'manifested in the flesh,' before it come to 'received up into glory.' Therefore, if we would have comfortable thoughts of this, 'Christ received up in glory,' think of him first 'manifest in the flesh.' Let us have recourse in our thoughts to Christ in the womb of the virgin; to Christ born and lying in the manger; going up and down doing good; hungering and thirsting; suffering in the garden; sweating water and blood; nailed on the cross; crying to his Father, 'My God, my God, why hast thou forsaken me?' finishing all upon the cross; lying three days in the grave; have recourse to Christ thus abased, and all for us, to expiate our sin; he obeyed God to satisfy for our disobedience. Oh! here will be comfortable thoughts for a wounded soul, pierced with the sense of sin, assaulted by Satan; to think thus of Christ abased for our sins, and then to think of him 'taken up into glory.'

In the sacrament, our thoughts must especially have recourse, in the first place, to Christ's body broken, and his blood shed, as the bread is broken and the wine poured out; that we have benefit by Christ's abasement and suffering, by satisfying his Father's wrath, and reconciling us to God. Then think of Christ in heaven, appearing there for us, keeping that happiness that he hath purchased by his death for us, and applying the benefit of his death to our souls by his Spirit, which he is able to shed more abundantly, being in that high and holy place, heaven; for the Spirit was not given in that abundance, before Christ was ascended to glory, as it hath been since. In this manner and order, we shall have comfortable thoughts of Christ. To think of his glory, in the first place, it would dazzle our eyes, it would terrify us, being sinners, to think of his glory, being now ascended; but when we think of him as descended first, as he saith, 'Who is he that ascended, but he that descended first into the lower parts of the earth?' Eph. iv. 9. So, who is this that is taken 'up in glory?' Is it not he that was 'manifest in our flesh' before? This will be comfortable. Therefore let us first begin with Christ's abasement, and then we shall have comfortable thoughts of his exaltation.

These points are very useful, being the main grounds of religion; having an influence into our lives and conversation above all others. Other points have their life and vigour and quickening from these grand mysteries, which are the food of the soul. Therefore let us oft feed our thoughts with these things, of Christ's abasement and glory, considering him in both as a public person, 'the second Adam,' and our surety; and then see ourselves in him, and labour to have virtue from him, fitting us in body and soul for such a condition. The very serious meditation of these things, will put a glory upon our souls; and the believing of them will transform us 'from glory to glory,' 2 Cor. ix. 18.

NOTES.

(*a*) P. 465.—'*Procul este profani,*' &c. The reference is probably to the famous 'Procul o, procul este, profani' of Virgil (Æn. vi. 258). Of course the thought is contained in the word 'profanus' itself, pro-fanum = *before* or *outside* of the temple —not sacred or dedicated to a divinity.

(*b*) P. 465.—'What is the reason that there is one word in the Greek and in other languages to signify both common and profane?' Query βέβηλος? = accessible, open to all, and hence *common*. But while what is profane is common, it is not true that what is common must be profane.

(*c*) P. 466.—'What kind of nation were we in Julius Cæsar's time?' &c. Cæsar's famous description contained in lib. v. *De Bell. Gall.* is too long for insertion here.

(*d*) P. 472.—'It was literally performed in Julius the Second; for in his papal crown there was written "*Mysterium,*" &c., till at last it was blotted out, and instead thereof was written, "*Julius secundus Papa.*"' Scaliger on the authority of an informant of the Duke of Montmorency, whilst at Rome, affirms this. So again, Francis Le Moyne and Brocardus, on ocular evidence, saying that Julius III. removed it. Consult Daubuz, Vitringa, Bishop Newton, earlier, and Elliott's *Horæ Apocalypticæ* on Rev. xvii. 5.

(*e*) P. 476.—'As lightsome and clear as if the gospel were written with a sunbeam, as one saith.' A common saying since Sibbes's day; but it seems to be impossible to trace it to its original author.

(*f*) P. 477.—'I will only make that use of it that a great scholar in his time once did upon the point, a noble earl of Mirandula.' This is John Picus of Mirandula, a pre-eminent scholar in his age. Died 1494. His Works have been repeatedly published in collective editions.

(*g*) P. 477.—'Men live . . . as if they made no question but they are false.' It is striking to find Bishop Butler, a century later, taking up the same lamentation in nearly the same words; *e.g.*, 'It is come, I know not how, to be taken for granted by many persons, that Christianity is not so much as a subject of inquiry, but that it is now at length discovered to be fictitious, and, accordingly, they treat it as if, in the present age, this were an agreed point among all people of discernment,' (Preface to 'The Analogy').

(*h*) P. 488.—'The whole world was darkened.' This remains matter of debate. The original in Mat. xxvii. 45, is τὴν γῆν *the* Land, = *The* Holy Land?

(*i*) P. 488.—'He was sold for thirty pence.' *Query?* The 'price' can hardly be thus definitely fixed. Cf. Mat. xxvii. 9, and Jer. xviii. 1, 2; xxxii. 6, 12.

(*j*) P. 496.—'The word is not altogether so fitly translated.' The original is ὤφθη = viewed with wonder. Cf. 1 Pet. i. 12.

(*k*) P. 511.—'That proud historian Tacitus, how scornfully doth he speak of Christians.' The famous 'quatuor millia libertini generis ea *superstitione infecta*' (Annals, ii. 85), and the like phrases, warrant Sibbes's reference. Cf. also Annals, xii. 23; xv. 44; Hist. i. 10; ii. 4; ii. 79; v. 1, 2, *et alibi.*

(*l*) P. 511.—'Saith Austin, "We must be very reverent in these matters [election, &c.]; it is most safe to commit all to God, and usurp no judgment here."' This Father, like Calvin, abounds in modest statements concerning the becoming attitude toward the 'secret things' of God.

(*m*) P. 514.—'In Rom. x. 14, *seq.* you have the *Scala Cœli,* as a good old martyr called it.' I have failed to trace this saying, but *Scala Cœli* is a trite designation of this and other portions of Scripture. The sermons on the Lord's Prayer by Bishop Andrewes were originally published (1611, 12mo), under the title of 'Scala Cœli.'

(*n*) P.516 .—'There is a world in the world, as one saith well in unfolding this point,' ['believed on in the world']. Cf. Pearson and John Smith *in loc.*

(*o*) P. 518.—'Divers of the Fathers were philosophers before.' It will be remembered how Augustine in his 'Confessions' self-accusingly expatiates upon this. The observation holds equally of Athanasius, Bernard, and other Fathers, Greek and Latin; but most particularly of Justin Martyr,—a providential arrangement, as it enabled them the more effectively to combat 'the philosophers' with their own weapons.

(*p*) P. 518.—'St Austin saith, "The world was not overcome by fighting, but by suffering."' One of many of Augustine's plaints in his 'worry' under his numerous controversies with the Donatists.

(*q*) P. 518.—' St Austin observes, " It was the wonder of the world." ' A common saying in the *De Civitate Dei.*

(*r*) P. 523.—' Ignorance is the mother of devotion.' It would be difficult to award this apophthegm to its original author.

(*s*) P. 523.—' Bellarmine's tenet, " that faith is better defined by ignorance than by anything else." ' See the *sentiment* under *Fides*, in any of the editions of the Works of this eminent cardinal.

(*t*) P. 533.—' Therefore the schoolmen speak well, he enjoyed the presence of God *affectione justitiæ*, . . . yet not *affectione accommoda.* The distinction has the ring of Aquinas.

G.

END OF VOL. V.

EDINBURGH:
PRINTED BY JOHN GREIG AND SON.

THE WORKS OF
RICHARD SIBBES

THE WORKS OF
RICHARD SIBBES

VOLUME 6

Edited by
Alexander B. Grosart

THE BANNER OF TRUTH TRUST

THE BANNER OF TRUTH TRUST

Head Office
3 Murrayfield Road
Edinburgh, EH12 6EL
UK

North America Office
610 Alexander Spring Road
Carlisle, PA 17015
USA

banneroftruth.org

The Complete Works of Richard Sibbes
first published in 7 volumes 1862-64
This reprint of volume 6 first published by
the Banner of Truth Trust 1983
Reprinted 2001, 2023

*

ISBN
Print: 978 0 85151 372 0

*

Printed in the USA by
Versa Press Inc.,
East Peoria, IL.

CONTENTS.

THE FAITHFUL COVENANTER.

THE FAITHFUL COVENANTER.

NOTE.

'The Faithful Covenanter' forms a portion of the miscellaneous sermons of 'Evangelical Sacrifices' (4to, 1640) Its separate title-page is given below.* For general title-page, see Vol. V. page 156. G.

*THE
FAITHFUL
COVENANTER.
In two Sermons upon GEN.
17. 7.
BY
The late Learned and Reverend Divine,
RICH. SIBBS:
Doctor in Divinity, Mr of KATHERINE Hall
in *Cambridge*, and sometimes Preacher
to the Honourable Society of
GRAYES-INNE.

NEHE. 1. 5.

O Lord God of heaven, the great and terrible God, that keepeth Covenant and mercy for them that Love him.

LONDON,
Printed by *E. Purslow*, for *N. Bourne*, at the Royall Exchange, and *R. Harford* at the gilt
Bible in Queenes head Alley, in Pater-Noster-Row. 1639.

THE FAITHFUL COVENANTER.

I will establish my covenant between me and thee, and thy seed after thee, in their generations, for an everlasting covenant, to be a God to thee, and to thy seed after thee.—Gen. XVII. 7.

God having framed man an understanding creature, hath made him fit to have communion and intercourse with himself; because he can by his understanding discern that there is a better good out of himself, in communion and fellowship with which, happiness consists. Other creatures—wanting understanding to discern a better good out of than in themselves, their life being their good—desire only the continuance of their own being, without society and fellowship with others. But man, having the knowledge of God, the Creator of heaven and earth, but especially of God the Redeemer, providing for him a second being better than his first, understandeth that his best and chiefest good dependeth more in him than in himself; and because his happiness standeth in acquaintance and fellowship with this God, which is the chief good, he desireth a communion with him, that he may partake of his good.

This communion and fellowship of man with God, was first founded on a covenant of works made with Adam in paradise. If he did obey, and did not eat of the forbidden fruit, he should have life both for himself and his posterity; the which covenant, because God would not have forgotten, he afterward renewed in the delivery of the ten commandments, requiring from man obedience to them in his own person, exactly, at all times, perpetually: promising life on the obedience, and threatening death and cursing if he continued not in everything the law required to do. But this fellowship being placed in man's own freedom, and having so weak a foundation, he lost both himself and it, so that now by the first covenant of works, Adam and all his posterity are under a curse; for we cannot fulfil the law that requireth personal obedience, perfect obedience, and exact obedience. He that 'continueth not in all is cursed,' Gal. iii. 10. The law then findeth us dead and killeth us. It findeth us dead before, and not only leaves us dead still, but makes us more dead.

Now after this fall, man's happiness was to recover again his communion and fellowship with God; and therefore we must have a new covenant before we can have life and comfort. God must enter into new conditions with us before we can have any communion with him.

God therefore, loving man, doth after the breach of the first agreement and covenant, when Adam had lost himself by his sin, and was in a most miserable plight as ever creature was in the world, falling from so great a happiness into wondrous misery; he raised him up and comforted him by establishing a second, a new and better covenant, laying the foundation of it in the blessed seed of the woman, Christ the Messiah, who is the ground of this new covenant, and so of our communion and fellowship with God, without whom there can be no intercourse between God and us in love. And because this covenant was almost forgotten, therefore now in Abraham's time God renewed it to Abraham in this place: 'I will be thy God, and the God of thy seed after thee,' &c.

There are four periods of time of renewing this covenant: first, from Adam to Abraham; and in those first times of the world, those that were under the covenant were called the 'sons and daughters of God,' 'the children of the promise,' and the covenant of grace was called a promise of the blessed seed.

Secondly, From Abraham to Moses; and then it was called a covenant, and they the children of the covenant. 'I will establish my covenant.' A covenant is more than a promise, and a more solemn thing, because there be ceremonies.

The third period of renewing the covenant of grace was from Moses to Christ; and then it was more clear, whenas to the covenant made with Abraham, who was sealed with the sacrament of circumcision, the sacrament of the paschal lamb was added, and all the sacrifices Levitical; and then it was called a testament. That differeth a little from a covenant; for a testament is established by blood, it is established by death. So was that; but it was only with the blood and death of cattle sacrificed as a type.

But now, to* Christ's time to the end of the world, the covenant of grace is most clear of all; and it is now usually called the New Testament, being established by the death of Christ himself; and it differs from a covenant in these respects:

First, *A testament indeed is a covenant, and something more.* It is a covenant sealed by death. The testator must die before it can be of force. So all the good that is conveyed to us by the testament it is by the death of the testator, Christ. God's covenant with us now, is such a covenant as is a testament, sealed with the death of the testator, Christ; for 'without blood there is no redemption,' Heb. ix. 22; without the death of Christ there could be no satisfaction, and without satisfaction there could be no peace with God.

Secondly, A testament *bequeatheth good things merely of love.* It giveth gifts freely. A covenant requireth something to be done. In a testament, there is nothing but receiving the legacies given. In covenants, ofttimes it is for the mutual good one of another, but a testament is merely for their good for whom the testament is made, to whom the legacies are bequeathed; for when they are dead, what can they receive from them? God's covenant now is such a testament, sealed with the death of Christ, made out of love merely for our good; for what can God receive of us? All is legacies from him; and though he requireth conditions, requireth faith and obedience, yet he himself fulfilleth what he asketh, giveth what he requireth, giveth it as a legacy, as we shall see afterward.

Thus you see that the communion and fellowship of man with God, must

* Qu. 'from'?—Ed.

either be by a covenant of works or by a covenant of grace. And we must distinguish exactly between these two covenants and the periods of them.

When the covenant of works was disannulled by our sins, because we could not fulfil the law exactly and perpetually, God will have a new covenant. If we believe in Christ, we shall have everlasting life. Now, if we stick to the one, we must renounce the other. If it be of faith, it is not of works; and if it be of works, it is not of faith. This was excellently signified by Joshua and Moses. Joshua bringeth the people to Canaan, and not Moses. Moses doth not bring any to heaven. It must be Joshua, the type of the true Jesus, that must bring them through Jordan to Canaan. This was typified also in the ark. There was the law, the covenant of works in the ark, but the propitiatory, the mercy-seat, was above the ark, above the law, and from thence God made all his answers; to signify to us that we can have nothing to do with the law without the propitiatory. Christ is the propitiatory, the mercy-seat. In Christ God heareth us. He makes all his answers in the propitiatory, Christ. Therefore when the question is our salvation, how we have title to heaven, not by the merit of works, for then we reverse the covenant of grace; but our title is merely by God's mercy in Christ apprehended by faith. The evidence indeed to prove our faith to be a true faith, is from works, but the title we have is only by Christ, only by grace. Here we must appeal from Sinai to Sion; from the law to the gospel; from Moses to Christ. We must fly with Joab to the horns of the altar, 1 Kings ii. 28. That must be our refuge. Fly to Christ in the covenant of grace, and we shall not be pulled from thence, as Joab was from the altar. There let us live and die.

Remember, I say, that the covenant of grace is distinct in the whole kind from the covenant of works; yet this, they are both in the church, and both taught, one subordinate to the other; as thus, the covenant of works is taught to shew us our failing, that seeing our own disability to perform what the law requireth, we may be forced to the new covenant of grace. And therefore, saith Paul, 'By the law I am dead to the law,' Gal. ii. 19. It is an excellent speech, 'By the law I am dead to the law;' by the covenant of works I am dead to the covenant of works. That is, by the law's exacting of me exact and perpetual obedience in thought, word, and deed, I come to see that I cannot fulfil it, and therefore am dead to the law; that is, I look for no salvation, for no title to heaven by that; and therefore he saith, 'The law was added for transgression.' Why was the law added to the promise of salvation by Christ made here to Abraham? Why was the covenant of works added in the wilderness afterwards? It was for transgression, to increase the sense of transgression, that we by the law might see what we should do, and what we have not done, and that we are by that come under a curse, and so might fly to the promise of grace in Christ. I have stood the longer in the clearing of this, because it is a main point.

But to come to that which I specially intend. The words, as I said before, contain the renewing of this blessed and gracious agreement between God and man to Abraham, the father of the faithful.

'I will establish my covenant between me and thee, and thy seed after thee, in their generations, for an everlasting covenant, to be thy God, and the God of thy seed after thee.'

The words, you see, contain a covenant; and here are all things—all the articles and circumstances that agree to any covenant whatsoever.

Here are the parties, both that make the covenant and that are covenanted with.

Here is the substance of the covenant, and the qualities of the covenant, and the condition of the covenant.

The party making the covenant is God, 'I will be *thy God*.'

God is the party covenanting. God indeed is both the party covenanting and the substance of the covenant: 'I will be a God to thee.' They fall both together in one. It is a most sweet sign of God's great love, that he will stoop so low as to make a covenant with us, to be our God; to be himself all in all to us. For consider but both these parties: God and we; the Creator and the creature; the immortal God and mortal man; the glorious God and 'dust and ashes;' the holy God and sinful man; the great King of heaven and earth, and rebels and traitors as we are. For him to condescend so low as to make a covenant with us, to enter into terms and articles of agreement with us, it is a wondrous sign of his gracious mercy and love. What can we but hope for from so gracious a God? But I shall have occasion to touch that afterward.

The parties covenanted with, are Abraham and his seed—his seed by promise.

The substance of the covenant is, 'I will be a God to thee and to thy seed after thee.'

The qualities of the covenant are, first, it is a *sure* covenant: 'I will *establish* my covenant.'

Secondly, It is an *everlasting* covenant: 'I will establish my covenant for an *everlasting* covenant.'

Thirdly, It is a *peculiar* covenant: 'I will establish my covenant between me and *thee and thy seed;* that is, only between me and thee, and thy seed; not with the refuse of the world, but only with thy seed by promise; only believers, whether Jews or Gentiles.

Fourthly, It is a most *free* covenant. It was made to Abraham, whom God called out of Ur of the Chaldees, out of an idolatrous nation, out of an idolatrous family; even as it was at the first most freely made to Adam in paradise, when he was in a most desperate estate. When he was as low as hell in a manner, ready to sink into despair, then the 'seed of the woman' was promised. So here it was freely made to good Abraham: First, the love of God was free to him when he called him, being an idolater; and then it was freely renewed afterward, when he was good, as we shall see anon.

And lastly, It is a covenant *consisting most of spiritual things.* It is a spiritual covenant. I mean especially, promising spiritual favours, although the other things, as appendices of the main, are likewise meant. For after that the covenant was made to Abraham and his posterity, they endured many afflictions. After the promise was renewed to Jacob, we know he fled from his brother Esau, to whom the covenant of grace was not made, and yet of Esau presently came duke such a one, and duke such a one, Gen. xxxvi. 15, *seq.;* and poor Jacob was fain to fly for his life in regard of the promise. So that I say it must be specially of spiritual blessings.

These are the qualities of the covenant. It is a sure, an everlasting, a peculiar, and a most free covenant, aiming specially at spiritual things.

And then, lastly, you have the condition of the covenant; and that, though it is not expressed, yet it is implied. 'I will be thy God, and the God of thy seed.' Therefore thou shalt take me for thy God, carry thyself to me as to thy God, &c. It is usual in other places of Scripture, where mention is made of this covenant, to imply the condition required on our parts. Sometimes both the covenant and condition are mentioned together, as in Zech. xiii. 9, 'I will say,' saith God, 'It is my people; and they shall say, The Lord is my God.' The one springeth from the other. When God is a God to any, he makes the heart to answer, Thou shalt be my God, and I will be thine always. This is the condition on our part that we make with God in this covenant, to take him for our God, to be his people, and his peculiar ones.

'I will be thy God, and the God of thy seed.'

Though these words, 'I will be a God to thee, and to thy seed,' be the last words of the text, yet being the substance of the covenant, I think it shall be best to speak of that before I speak of the qualities of the covenant or anything else.

'I will be thy God.'

This is the covenant in the Messiah; but first, what is it to be a God?

I answer, To be a God, take it in the general, *is to give being to the creature that had no being of itself, and to protect and preserve the creature in its being:* in a word, to be a creator; for providence is the perpetuity and continuance of creation. This is to be a God. The office of God, as God, is a most glorious function. To be a king is a great matter, but to be a God, to give being to the creature, to support it when it hath a being, to do all that God should do, this is a most glorious work. But this is but creation. This is not intended especially here, for thus he is the God of all his works. Thus by creation and preservation he is the God of all the men in the world out of the church.

What is then to be thy God? 'I will be thy God.'

I answer, To be a God in a more peculiar manner, is to be a God in covenant; that is, not only to be a God to preserve and continue this being of ours in a civil life, but it is to be a God in a higher relation to us; to be a God in a reference to an eternal, supernatural estate in heaven; to be a God here in grace, and hereafter in glory; and thus God is a God in a gracious covenant, only by Jesus Christ, and to those that believe in him. 'I will be thy God;' that is, 'I will be thy God in Christ,' to give thee a better being than this world can afford; to free thee from the cursed estate thou art in by nature; to deliver thee from all ill, spiritually and eternally; especially to bestow on thee all good, spiritually and eternally; especially as we have it in the words of the covenant, Gen. xv. 1, 'I will be thy shield and thy exceeding great reward;' a shield to keep off all ill, and a reward for all good. So in Ps. lxxxiv. 9, 'God will be a sun and a shield,' &c.: a sun for all sweet comfort and good, and a shield in regard of defence from ill; a sun and a shield till we come to the possession of eternal happiness. This is to be a God in a peculiar manner, to give all things necessary for grace and life too—for this life and for a better; to do all things requisite to bring us to heaven and happiness through Christ, 'in whom all the promises are yea and amen,' 2 Cor. i. 20; to be all in all; to direct the protections and provisions of this life, of our estate here, to a supernatural happiness hereafter, to a state beyond nature. For God directs the favours of this life, so that he takes them away or he giveth them, as he seeth them advantageous, or hindrances to a better estate. So is God a God to those that are in covenant with him. To do all this, and to do all this in opposition of all enemies whatsoever; to do all this in weakness and in the impotency of the creature; to do all this when all second causes are contrary, as it were, to bring a man to heaven in spite of the devil and of our own corruptions, or all oppositions whatsoever—this is to be a God indeed.

But why doth he say only, 'I will be thy God'? Why doth he not say,

I will give thee grace and protection, I will give thee heaven and life everlasting?

Because all is one, for all things in the world are in this one promise, 'I will be thy God.' See the wisdom of heaven, how much he speaks in how little. There cannot be more spoken than thus, 'I will be thy God.' For in saying, 'I will be thy God,' he implies that whatsoever he is, or hath, or can do, shall be thine too. 'I will be thy God;' that is, my wisdom shall be thine, to watch over thee, to find out ways to do thee good; my power shall be thine, to keep thee from danger, to defend and rescue thee from all enemies, and to subdue them by degrees unto thee; my providence shall be thine, to turn all things to thy good; my mercy shall be thine, to forgive thy sins; my love shall be thine, to bestow on thee all necessary comforts. There is no phrase in the Scripture that hath so much in so little as this here, 'I will be thy God,' if we could unfold and lay open this excellent promise. All other particular promises in the covenant of grace are members of this. What is the reason, as Saint Paul saith, 'all things are yours?' '*Because* you are Christ's, and Christ is God's,' 1 Cor. iii. 23. God is the God of Christ, and our God. We are in covenant with the God of Christ. Christ is the heir of all, and we are members of Christ. God who is the God of all things is ours. It is a wondrous comprehensive promise.

'I will be thy God, and the God of thy seed.'

The substance of the covenant then is, that God will be a God to us. The point to be observed is this, *that God graciously in the blessed seed, the Messiah, Christ Jesus, he takes upon him to be a God to all those that are in covenant with him;* that is, to be all-sufficient, to bring us to happiness—all-sufficient in this world and in the world to come, to be our portion, to be all in all.

This is the first and fundamental promise of all other. Indeed, it is the life and soul of all the promises, and it is the life and soul of all comfort whatsoever. For all other relations spoken of God tend to this, that he is 'our God.' This is before to be a Father, before to be anything. God first is a God, and then a Father, and then all in all to us. As he is first the God of Christ, and then the Father of Christ; as you have it usually in the beginnings of the epistles, 'God the Father of our Lord Jesus Christ;' first the God, and then the Father. To be a God, then, is the fundamental and principal favour. From thence cometh our election; his choosing of us to eternal salvation before all time; his protection and preservation of us in time unto heaven.

I shall not need to speak more of this, having unfolded it before.

But you will say, How shall we know that this covenant belongeth to us? that we are such as we may say, God is our God?

I answer, first—to lay this for a ground—you must know that to be a God is a relation. Whosoever God is a God to, he persuadeth them by his Spirit that he is a God to. The same Spirit that persuadeth them that there is a God, that Spirit telleth them that God is their God, and works a qualification and disposition in them, as that they may know that they are in covenant with such a gracious God. The Spirit as it revealeth to them the love of God, and that he is theirs, so the Spirit enableth them to claim him for their God, to give up themselves to him as to their God.

And the Spirit doth this, because friends cannot be in covenant and confederate without there be a likeness or an agreement. There must be more words then, on* to a covenant. Though God's grace do all, yet we must give our consent; and therefore the covenant is expressed under the title

* Qu. 'than one'?—Ed.

of marriage. In marriage there must be a consent of both parties. In reconciliation between a king and subjects, that are fallen out, when they are rebels, there must be an accepting of the pardon, and a promise of new subjection. So then if God be our God, there will be grace given to take him for our God; to give him homage as a king; to give him our consent as to our spouse. 'Thou shalt be my God, and I will cleave to thee, as to my lord and husband.' 'Can two walk together,' saith the prophet, 'and not be friends?' Amos iii. 3. There can be no friendship with God, except there be somewhat wrought in us by his Spirit, to make us fit for friendship, that we may look on him as an object of love and delight. If we look on him as an object of hatred, what terms of friendship can there be? Now, that we may look on him as an object of love, fit for converse with him, he must make us such by consent and yielding to him, by framing the inward man to his likeness, that so there may a peace be maintained with him. You see the ground of it, of necessity it must be so.

Well, to come to the trials. But let me first add this to the former: *whomsoever God is a God to, it is known specially by spiritual and eternal favours.* A man cannot know certainly that God is his God by outward and common things that castaways may have; for a castaway may have Ishmael's blessing and Esau's portion, blessings of the left hand, common graces. To know undoubtedly, therefore, that God is our God, must be by peculiar matters; for those whose God God is are a peculiar people, a holy nation, severed from others. First of all, then, know what the Spirit of God saith to thy soul; for they that are God's have his Spirit, to reveal to their spirits the secret and hidden love of God. But if the voice of the Spirit be silent in regard of testimony, go to the work of the Spirit; but go to the peculiar work of the Spirit. For though the Spirit may be silent in regard of his testimony, yet there are some works or other of the Spirit in a man, whereby he may know that God is his God; as the Spirit of God works in some sort a proportion in him unto God, and none can know better what God is to him than by searching of his own heart, what he is back again to God; for as God saith to him by his Spirit, Thou art mine, so they say to God, Thou art mine. Let us then come to the trial by our carrying ourselves to God. Can we say with David, 'Whom have I in heaven but thee?' or 'What is there in earth in comparison of thee?' Ps. lxxiii. 25. When the conscience can tell us that we make God our treasure and our portion above all earthly things, then we make him our God. A Christian singleth out God above all things in the world for his happiness. Lord, thou art mine! Whatsoever wealth is mine, or riches mine, or friends mine—I stand not upon that, but thou art mine. A rich man runneth to his wealth, and makes flesh his arm. He runneth to friends, to bear him out in ill causes; but a true Christian that hath God for his God, he may know it by this, he singleth out God for his portion, runs to him in all extremities. Lord, thou art mine. This is a sign that God hath said to his soul first, 'I am thy salvation,' Ps. xxxv. 3. How can the soul appropriate God to himself? How can he say, as Thomas did, 'My Lord and my God,' John xx. 28, except the Lord have spoken peace to the soul before, and have said, 'I am thy salvation'? It is a sign we have made God our God, when we prize him and value him above all the world; and when, with St Paul, Phil. iii. 8, we count all things 'dung and dross, in comparison of Jesus Christ our Lord.' What we will do most for, that is our god. If we will do most for God, he is our God. If we do most for pleasures, they are our god. If we do most for riches, break our rests and crack our consciences for them, that is our god. In a word, whatsoever we value highest, that is our god.

Examine what affections we have to God: for it is affection that makes a Christian. Single out some few that we are most offending in. As, first, for *fear*, it may shame us all. Indeed, a Christian upon his best resolution is better. But the ordinary carriage of men is, they fear men more than God; they fear everything more than him that they should fear above all. For instance, is the retired carriage of men to God such as their carriage is to the eye of the world? Will not they do that in secret ofttimes that they will not do openly? In secret they will commit this or that sin, and think, Who seeth? There are secret abominations in the closet of their hearts. They will not fear to do that in the eye of God, that they fear to do in the eye of a child of six years old, that is of any discretion. Is this to make God our God, when we fear the eye of a silly mortal creature more than the eye of God, that is ten thousand times brighter than the sun, that is our judge? Is God our God the whiles? Undoubtedly, when God is made our God, there is an awe of the eye of heaven upon a man in all places. Therefore this is the condition of the covenant, 'Walk before me,' or 'Walk as in my sight,' 1 Sam. ii. 30. How do we walk before God as in his sight, when there is such a great deal of difference in our carriage secretly, and before the eyes of men? when we labour more to approve our carriage to men, than we make conscience of our spirits to God? This may shame us. Even the best of us who are in covenant with God, and have made God our God, we have cause to be abased for this: and surely one of the best ways to make God's children abased and humbled, is to compare the different proportion of their carriage; how they carry themselves to men whom they respect, and to outward things in the world, and how they carry themselves to God. If God be our God, there will be an universal fear and care to please God in all times and in all places, because he is everywhere; darkness and light are all one to him.

Try yourselves therefore by this affection. *If we make God our God, we will fear him above all;* for there being such a distance between God and us—he the mighty God, and we creatures whose breath is in our nostrils—there can no other way be a covenant of peace betwixt us, but with much reverence. Therefore all Christians are reverent creatures; they do all in fear; they pass 'the whole time of the conversation here in fear,' 1 Peter iii. 2; they 'make an end of their salvation with fear and trembling,' Philip. ii. 12; they enjoy their liberties in fear. St Jude makes mention of a number of wretched people in his time, that ate without fear, ver. 12. You may know a man that hath not this grace of God in his heart, by his unreverent carriage. He never thinks of the presence and all-seeing eye of God. A Christian that hath God to his God, knows that wheresoever he is, he is in the eye of heaven. Therefore he is jealous, even of his own most secret corruptions. He knows that they are lawless of themselves; and therefore he always sets himself in the presence of God. He is full of reverence, full of fear, even in the enjoying of his Christian liberties.

So likewise for the affection *of love*. If God be thy God, thou hast grace given thee to love him above all things. With whom God is graciously reconciled, he giveth them his Spirit to be reconciled back again to him. He loveth us, and we love him again; for we are by nature enemies to God, as he is to us. There is no wicked man in the world can love God; indeed, as God is a God that promiseth salvation, he loveth him—he would fain have that, and therefore would fain be in his favour—but he cannot love God as he is in all respects; but he hateth him, and he hateth his children. He trifleth with his name by oaths and blasphemy, and the like. He scorneth God. He wisheth that there were no God. Can this man say that God is his God, when he doth not carry himself back again to him in his affection as his God? No such matter. He is God's enemy, and God is his enemy. So if God be our God, if he have set his love upon us, we cannot but love him again. If he be reconciled to us, we are reconciled to him. This is a sure sign that God is our God, if we love him above all.

Now, that may be known *if we be zealous when God is dishonoured any way;* for whatsoever we make our god, we will not endure to have touched. If a man make his lust his god, if that be touched, he is all in a chafe. When that which a man loveth is touched, experience shews it, he is presently all on a fire. And here the best Christians have cause to be abased. Hath God their love, when they can hear him disgraced, and his name abused, without being greatly moved, and yet notwithstanding, in the mean time, will not endure their own credit to be touched, but they are, as I said, all on a fire? Where there is no zeal, there is no love. Certainly when we can hear God's children misused, and religion endangered, and profession scoffed at, &c., and yet not be affected, nor cannot take God's cause to heart, this is great fault in our love.

And so for *joy* and delight: we make God our God when we joy in him above all things in the world; when we make him our boast all the day long, as it is Ps. xliv. 8; when we make him our glory, as he is called our glory in Jer. ii. 11, 'They changed their glory.' God is our glory if he be our God. We count it our chiefest glory that we are his, and that he is ours. Whatsoever our estates be, we glory in God, and not in ourselves. A Christian when he would joy and glory, he goeth out of himself to God, he is his joy. But do not men joy in the creature, and delight in it ofttimes more than in God? It is a great shame for us, and that for which even the best of us all may be abased, to consider what a deal of delight and comfort we take in the creature more than in God. We see Jonah, a good man, when his gourd was taken from him, that God raised up to be a shelter for him—a poor simple defence it was; and yet we see how pettish the good man was. All the comfort he had could not keep him from anger and fretting when the gourd was gone; and yet God was his God. So many men, whereas they should joy in God above all things, yet if God take outward comforts from them, they are as if there were no God in heaven, no comfort there; as if there were no providence to rule the world; as if they had no Father in covenant with them. I say this is a great shame for us.

Again, If God be our God, *we will trust in him,* rely and depend upon him above all things; for whatsoever our trust is most in, that is our god. Now if our conscience tell us that we trust most in God, more than in wealth or friends, and will not, to displease God, please any man, it is a sign that we have made God our God, because we trust in him. And surely, if we would examine ourselves, the best of us all, it would bring us on our knees, and make our faces be confounded, to consider what a deal of atheism there is in our heart (though we are not altogether atheists, yet what a deal there is), that must be mortified and subdued. For if an honest man, and that we know is faithful, should say to us, I will be yours; I will take upon me to provide for you, to defend you, to protect you, to stand by you against all adversaries; we believe and hope that he will do it. But do we so to God? Hath he our trust and affiance? Alas, no! so far forth, I mean, as we are not subdued to God. A Christian, indeed, in some measure is enabled to make God his trust and confidence, but there remains abundance of atheism even in the best of us. If God be our God, why do we not trust in him, depend upon him for all things; depend upon him for protection and deliverance from all ill, spiritual ill specially, from sin, Satan, hell, and wrath; depend upon him for all good, the good of grace specially, for the change of our nature and the forgiveness of our sins, for spiritual privileges, adoption and sonship, for the inheritance of heaven, &c. It is a sign, I say, that God is our God when we trust in him above all the world, and trust other things only from him and for him. I will trust man, but man may deceive me. I will not trust him therefore with an absolute confidence. No. That were to make a god of him. What is the reason that God confoundeth proud men at last? David shews the reason. 'This man he took not the Lord for his God.' When men will, in contempt of religion, set up themselves and somewhat else to rely on, besides God, God at the last brings it to pass, that the world shall note them out, This man trusted in his greatness; he trusted in his policy, in his wit, in his friends; this man took not the Lord for his God.

Again, If we make God our God, *we may know it by our obedience*, especially by the obedience of the inward man. When the inward man is vowed to God, when a man yieldeth inward obedience to God, it is a sign that God is his God. When a man can arraign his thoughts and desires before God, and when lusts rise in his heart contrary to the Spirit, he checks them presently. This becometh not those that are God's; it beseemeth not those that walk after God, that have God's Spirit for their leader. Therefore he is ashamed presently of base tentations.* A Christian can perform the first and last commandments, which are the most spiritual commandments. He can make God his God in his affections. His affections are placed upon him alone, as I have shewed before. He can yield up all his inward affections of fear and love and joy, and such like, unto God, which is the sum of the first commandment; and he can be content not to have his lusts rage and range, suppresses his very thoughts and desires, will not suffer anything to rise in his heart unchecked and uncontrolled, which is the sum of the tenth commandment. I mean, he can do it in some measure. And there is a inward passive obedience too. It is God, as David and other saints said. 'It is the Lord, let him do what seemeth him good in his own eyes,' Ps. cxix. 68. I am God's, and he shall dispose of me. The soul that knoweth God to be his God hath an inward obedience of contentation with his estate. God is my portion, and it is large enough. The earth is his, and the fulness thereof, Ps. xxiv. 1. Therefore I will be content to be at his disposing, whether it be more or less; and if any murmuring arise in his heart, against God in respect of his estate or otherwise, he presently suppresseth it, as being contrary to the blessed government that a Christian is under, that should resign his whole soul unto God.

Thus by our affections, by the trial of them, we may know whether God be our God, if we give him the affections of the heart, which religion most stands in; when we make the whole inward man stoop, and bow, and bend unto him; when we make him our king, and give him the supremacy; when we set the crown upon his head; when he hath our fear, our joy and delight, our love, our trust; I mean, when he hath the supreme of all, for we may love man, as God deriveth† good to us by him, and so for the rest.

* That is, 'temptations.'—G.

‡ That is, 'communicateth.'—G.

But God must be supreme. Others must be loved and feared, &c., in him and for him, but he chiefly, when we depend upon him for all deliverance out of ill and for all good, and shew our dependence on him by our subjection to him in all his ways, by our yielding to him obedience answerable to all this ; and especially when we shall shew it by performing inward worship to him, when we walk before him perfectly and sincerely, as it is in the beginning of this chapter, 'I am God all-sufficient : walk before me and be perfect.' By this we may know that God is our God. I need not enlarge it. The practice of the first commandment will teach us what is our God. Whatsoever we give the supremacy of the inward man to, whatsoever we love most, whatsoever we trust most, whatsoever we fear most, whatsoever we joy and delight most, whatsoever we obey most—that is our god. 'I am the Lord thy God,' in the first commandment. There is the ground. What follows? 'Thou shalt have no other gods but me ;' that is, thou shalt love nothing in the world, nor fear nothing, nor trust in nothing, nor joy in nothing more than me, no, nor with me ; but all things else thou shalt trust them and fear them, &c., in me and for me. Otherwise what is our love is our god, what is our trust is our god, what is our greatest fear is our god. If we fear man, fear him to do ill, man is our god ; if we love the creature, or sin, that is our god ; if we crack our consciences for wealth, the covetous man's wealth is his god ; if we crack our consciences for pleasures, or for our bellies, our pleasures and our bellies and our lusts are our god. We make not God our God except we give him the supremacy of the inward man.

But to proceed, and to come to some few familiar signs more that will try us, though these may try us, in the intercourse that is between God and us.

Whosoever hath God for their God, *they have the Spirit of supplication and prayer*, to cry unto God, to run unto him, especially in extremity. All God's children have the Spirit of adoption to cry, 'Abba, Father!' They have the Spirit to give them boldness to God, when otherwise their nature, and likewise trouble joining with nature and tentations, would make them run from God ; yet the Spirit of God in them makes them bold to go to God in Jesus Christ. God's children, that are in covenant with him, can at all times pray to God. If they cannot pray, they can 'chatter' and sigh to God. There is somewhat they can do. There is a Spirit in them that groaneth and sigheth, as Rom. viii. 26, and God heareth the voice of his own Spirit. They are cries in his ears. 'My groans and sighs are not hid from thee,' saith the Psalmist, Ps. xxxviii. 9. The Spirit of supplication will shew God to be our God, because if he were not ours, we could not be bold to go to him, in the time of extremity especially. This sign you have in Zech. xiii. ver. 9, 'They shall call upon my name, and I will hear them ; they shall be my people, and I will be their God.' Invocation and prayer is a sign that God is our God, when we go to God presently in all our wants and necessities by prayer. Pharaoh and reprobate spirits say to Moses, 'Pray you for me,' Numb. xxi. 7 ; but as for a spirit of supplication in themselves, they have not. They may speak of prayer, but they cannot pray. Whosoever is God's, he can cry to God. A child, we know the first voice is uttered as soon as it is born, it cries ; so God's new-born children they can cry unto God. Paul in Acts ix. ver. 11, you shall find him praying as soon as ever he was converted ; and certainly those that use not to pray morning and evening, and upon all occasions, that acquaint not themselves with God, God is not their God. If he were their

God, they would seek to him, and be acquainted with him. The Spirit will teach them to go unto God as to a Father.

Again, We may know that God is our God by this, *by our separating from all others, in ourselves and out of ourselves*. There is a separation in ourselves, for there is the first separation. God, whose God he is, he giveth them his Spirit, and that like fire severeth the dross, and gathereth the fold together. And as heat in the body, that severeth good nourishment and separateth that which doth not nourish the body, so where the Spirit of God is, he works a separation between the flesh and the spirit. The Spirit will know what is spiritual, and will discern what is in us that is fleshly, and will join to spiritual things, and the Spirit will be one as it were. There will be a sweet agreement in the word, in the sacraments, in good company, in holy meditation and the like, and a separation from the flesh. A Christian knows that he is redeemed from himself, as far as he is naught.* We are redeemed from ourselves and our own base nature, as well as from hell and damnation. Therefore there is first a separation in ourselves from ourselves. It begins there. We have nothing to do with our corruptions. We will not own them.

And where this sweet covenant is, that God is our God, as there is a separation from ourselves and our corruptions, so there is a separation from all that joineth with our corruption; a separation in affection from delighting in all that is not God, from all such occasions and company as strengtheneth our corruption. A Christian knows what he hath of God's in him, and what he hath of Satan, and that he must weaken. Therefore he severeth himself from that which strengtheneth the one and weakeneth the other. This trial is expressed in 2 Cor. vi. 17, 18, 'Come out from amongst them, separate yourselves, and I will be your God, and you shall be my people.' He speaks for direction, especially in our society and acquaintance, for that is the thing he aimeth at. How shall we know that God will be our God? We must separate ourselves, and touch no unclean thing, nothing that will help rebellion. Therefore those that have an indifferent disposition to all companies, and can solace themselves in any society, though never so corrupt, that bear themselves plausible to all, and would be thought well of all, and so will venture upon all occasions, it is an ill sign that they are carnal people. When in the nearest league in friendship or amity, or in intimate familiarity, they will join with any,—all are alike,—it is a sign they have not God for their God. For then they would have common enemies and common friends with God; common enemies with God. Whom God hated they would hate. As God in covenant blesseth them that bless us, and curseth them that curse us, so they that are in covenant and friendship with God will hate with a perfect hatred whatsoever it is that hateth God; they will have nothing to do in intimate familiarity further than their callings press upon them; they will give them their due in humanity and courtesy, but no more. Their love and delight will be in God and those that are his, that represent him, that have his Spirit and image. How oft is this 'I am the Lord your God' repeated by Moses as a ground of separation from idolatry? It is expressed almost everywhere; and indeed, if the Lord be our God, there is ground enough of separation from all that is not God. It cannot be otherwise.

Another sign and evidence that God is our God is victory over our base corruptions in some measure. This you have in Rev. xxi. 7: 'He that overcometh shall inherit all things; I will be his God, and he shall be my

* That is, 'naughty' = wicked.—G.

son.' How shall I know that God is my God, and that I am his son? If by the power of his Spirit I am able to overcome and conquer in some comfortable measure base tentations and my base corruptions and lusts; when I lie not as a beast or as a carnal man under sin, but God hath given me in some measure spiritual strength over sin.

Undoubtedly these and such like works of the Spirit, together with the testimony of the Spirit, will be wheresoever God is our God.

In a word, to name no more trials but this, whosoever God is a God to, *there will be a transforming unto God, a transforming unto Christ*, in whom God is our God. For we must know that we are renewed according to the image of the 'second Adam.' Our comfort is by God revealed in Christ. If God be our God in Christ, we will be like to God; and that will be known that we are like to God, if we be like to God in the flesh, God incarnate. For we are predestinated to be like God incarnate. God, first he is Christ's God before he is ours; and as Christ carried himself to God, so if we be God's, we must carry ourselves like Christ, be transformed unto him. How did Christ carry himself to God? God was his God. '*My* God, *my* God,' saith Christ upon the cross. Now the gospel sheweth that he obeyed his Father in all things, in doing and suffering: 'Not my will, but thy will be done,' Luke xxii. 42. You know how full of mercy and compassion he was; how he prayed all night sometimes. Though he knew God would bestow things on him without prayer, yet he would pray in order to God's appointment. You know how full of goodness he was, going about continually doing good, Acts x. 38; and that in obedience and conscience to God's command. In a word, look how Christ made God his God, and carried himself to God. So must we; for we are predestinated to be transformed to the image of the 'second Adam,' Christ. Especially observe one thing—I touched it before—whom we run to and trust to in extremity, is our god. Christ in extremity, when he felt the anger and endured the wrath of God, being a surety for our sins, yet 'My God, my God' still. So if we make God our God, chiefly in the greatest extremity, in the time of desertion, as Christ did, it is a good sign. I do but touch these things. The point, you see, is large. I only give you matter of meditation. You may enlarge them yourselves in your own thoughts. These I think sufficient trials, whereby you may know whether God be your God.

Having now thus unfolded these terms, let us see what we may draw from thence for our use and comfort.

1. First, then, if by these trials we find that God be not, or have not been, our God, alas! *let us never rest till we make it good that God is our God.* For what if we have all things, if we have not God with all things? All other things are but streams; God is the fountain. If we have not the spring, what will become of us at last? Ahithophel had much wit and policy, but he had not God for his God. Ahab had power and strength, but he had not God for his God. Saul had a kingdom, but he had not God for his God. Herod had eloquence, but he had not God for his God. Judas was an apostle, a great professor, but he had not God for his God. What became of all these? Wit* they had, strength they had, honour they had, friends they had, but they had not God; and therefore a miserable end they made. What miserable creatures are all such, when they shall say, Friends have forsaken me, wealth hath forsaken me, and health hath forsaken me; terrors lay hold upon me, the wrath of God hath over-

* That is, 'wisdom.'—G.

taken me. But they cannot say, God is my God. Oh, such are in a miserable case, in a fearful estate indeed. Nay, suppose they have all these, suppose they could say they have a world of riches, they have inheritances, they have friends, &c., yet if they cannot say, God is my God, all is vanity. The whole man is this, to have God to be our God. This is the whole man, to fear God and keep his commandment, Eccles. xii. 13. If a man have all the world, and have not God for his God, all is but vanity and vexation of spirit. Never rest therefore till we can prove ourselves to be in the covenant of grace, till we can say, God is my God.

But, secondly, when we have found God to be our God, *then make this use of it, a use of resolution.* Is God my God? then I will resolve to please him, though all creatures be against me. This was their resolution in Micah iv. 5, 'Every nation walketh in the name of his god, but we will walk in the name of the Lord our God for ever and ever.' Resolve with Joshua and others to please God, whosoever saith the contrary; to walk after the commandments of God, whatsoever others do or say. In all discouragements from men or devils, let us set this as a buckler, God is my God. Arm ourselves with resolution against all fears and threatenings of men, of men of terror, against the arm of flesh. They say they will do this and this; ay, but God is my God. All that they do they must do in his strength. Arm ourselves with this against the power and gates of hell. Fear not the devil. If we fear man or devil more than God, fear them so as to do anything to displease God, we make them god. If our conscience rightly tells us that what is to be done by us is the will and command of God, and that herein I serve God, we need not fear any opposer; but oppose this as an armour of proof against all creatures, against all discouragements whatsoever. And certainly experience telleth us, and approveth it to be true, that nothing can dismay a man that doth things in conscience to God, and knows God will bear him out in it, though not from danger in this world; and yet for the most part he doth that too. Those that are the stoutest men for God are oftentimes most safe, always freed from inward dejection. Yet God disposeth of it so as that he that keeps a good conscience shall always be a king, and rule over the world; and therein he performs his promise. Whatever discouragements he endureth outwardly, yet no discouragement can cast down that soul that looks to God. In his conscience he knows that he takes God to be his, that he serveth him, and that it shall go well with him at last, that God will be all-sufficient to him; and this raiseth him above all, makes him rule and reign over his enemies, and be a terror to those that do him hurt.

3. Again, If God be our God, *then let this stop all base and covetous desires after earthly things.* If God be our portion, why should we grapple too much after the world then? What need we crack our consciences and break our peace for the muck of the world? Is not God our portion? Is he not rich enough? Is not he Lord of heaven and earth? Hath not he promised that he will not fail us nor forsake us? 'I am thy exceeding great reward,' saith God to Abraham. Is not this enough? What doth Satan for us when he getteth us to crack our consciences by gripleness* after earthly things? He promiseth, thou shalt have this and that, but I will take God from thee, as he did Adam in paradise. Thou shall have an apple, but thou shalt lose thy God. All his solicitations to base and earthly courses tend to nothing else but to take God from us. Now, when

* That is, 'gripingness,' = greed, rapacity.—G.

God is our God, and he hath promised to be our portion, let it be sufficient for us; let us not, for the displeasing of him, take any condition from Satan or the world upon any terms.

4. Again, If so be we know this for a truth, that God is our God, then let it be a use of exhortation *to stir us up to keep, and maintain, and cherish acquaintance and familiarity with him;* as it is in Job xxii. 21, 'Acquaint thyself with God.' If we be acquainted with him now, he will be acquainted with us in time of sorrow, in the hour of death; therefore cherish acquaintance with him. Wheresoever we may meet with God, be there much; be much in hearing, in receiving the sacrament, in praying to him and making our suits known to him in all our necessities; be much in the society of saints, God hath promised to be there. Therefore cherish the society of all that are good. What a friendly course doth God take with us! He seeks for our acquaintance, and therefore giveth us his ordinances, the word and sacraments; sendeth his messengers, the good motions of his Spirit, to our hearts, to leave the world and vanities of it; to make us out of love with bad courses, and join with him in friendship and familiarity. Oh let us make use of these blessed means, check not these good motions, but yield unto them and obey them, grieve them not! The Spirit is sent to make God and us friends, who were enemies. Grieve not the Spirit, entertain his motions, that we may be acquainted with God. But do we do so? Truly no. Indeed, if God will be our God to save us, and let us live in our swearing and lying and deceiving, and in other base courses, we would be content with him upon these terms; but to be our God, so that we must serve him, and love him, and fear him, and joy in him above all, and have nothing in the world without his favour, then let him take his favour to himself, we will have none of it. Though men speak it not with their mouths to the world, yet the inward speech of their hearts is to this purpose. If we must be the people of God upon these terms, to renounce our pleasures and profits, let him be a God to whom he will for us! If he will save us, then welcome his favour, we will be glad of his acquaintance; otherwise we will have none of it. What is the speech of the world but this? These men, when they shall at the day of judgment claim acquaintance with God, and say, 'Lord, Lord, open to us,' 'we have known thee in the streets,' &c., what will God say? 'Depart from me, you workers of iniquity, I know you not,' Mat. xxv. 41. You were acquainted with me indeed outwardly in the ministry of my word, but you kept not an inward and spiritual familiarity with me in my ordinances; you used not the society of the saints, you entertained not the motions of my Spirit, which I sent to you, to leave your ill courses; I know you not. This shall be the answer to such wretched persons.

5. Lastly, If by these comfortable signs we find God to be our God, *then here is a spring of comfort opened to a Christian.* If God be mine, then all that he hath is mine; he is my Father; he is my husband; he is my rock; his goodness, his wisdom, his providence, his mercy, whatsoever he hath is mine. If we had any man in the world that had all wisdom in him, and all the strength of the world, and all goodness, and all love in him, and all this for us, what an excellent creature were this! God hath all this, and a Christian that hath God for his God hath all this and much more; for whatsoever is in the Creator* is much more in him. Hereupon cometh all those styles and sweet names that God hath taken upon him in the Scripture, because he would have us to know, that all comforts are

* Qu. 'creature'?—Ed.

together in him. The names of all the creatures that are comfortable, God hath been pleased to take upon him, to shew us what a God he is. He is water to refresh us, a sun to comfort us, a shield to keep evil from us, a rock to support us, chambers to cover us in the time of danger, and such like; and in every creature God hath left footsteps and beams of himself, that man, being an understanding creature, might find out God in them. In water there is a beam of his refreshing power; in the sun, a beam of his cherishing power, and the like; and when we receive comfort from the creature, which hath but a drop, a beam of his goodness, we should consider how good God himself is. If this be so comfortable, what is God that is my God! Here we use the creatures to refresh us, and God deriveth his goodness usually to us by them. What will he be to us in heaven, when he will be all in all; and whatsoever comfort God hath, Christ hath; because God and Christ join together for our good. For God is in Christ 'reconciling the world to himself,' 2 Cor. v. 19; and if God be ours, Christ is ours; and if God and Christ be ours, all things are ours, because all things are God's. Angels are ours, cherubins are ours, because God is ours. It is a point of wondrous comfort. A poor Christian, when he hath nothing to trust to, he may perhaps say sometime, that he hath no friend in the world, and he hath many enemies. Ay, but he hath a God to go to. If he have not the beam, yet he hath the sun; if he have not the stream, yet he hath the fountain; if he have not particular benefits that others have, yet he hath better. Whatsoever portion he have in the world, he hath a rich portion, for God is his portion. 'God is my portion,' saith the church in the 3d of Lamentations, ver. 21, 'therefore will I hope in him.' The poor church had nothing else in the world to comfort it, for it was in captivity, in the midst of enemies, had no wealth, nor friends, nor anything; yea, but God is my portion, saith my soul, and therefore God being mine, in him I have friends, and wealth, and pleasure, and all whatsoever; and so hath every Christian soul, and never more than when the creature and the comfort of it is taken away. He never finds God more his God than when he is deprived of those means that usually derive comfort to him, for then God immediately cometh to the soul and comforteth it; and the disposition of a true Christian is, at those times, to take advantage by grace to get nearer to God, to cling faster to him, to solace himself more in him as his portion. What a spring of comfort is here arising to a Christian in all estates! If God be his God, then he may claim him upon all occasions and at all times, as the saints in the Scripture have done. David, Jehosaphat, and all the saints, what do they allege in their prayers to God? 'Thou art our God,' 'we are thy people,' 'the sheep of thy pasture,' 'the vine that thy right hand hath planted,' 'the Lord is my shepherd,' &c. What made the disciples, when they were ready to be drowned, to cry out, 'Master, save us,' but because they knew that they were servants in covenant, that he was their Master. We should use this as a plea to God in all the calamities of the church. We are thine, thou art ours! Doubtless thou art our God, saith the church, though Abraham have forgotten, and Israel be ignorant of us, Isa. lxiii. 16. It is a point of spiritual wisdom, when we know we are in covenant with God, to improve it as an argument to persuade God to help us in any strait. 'I am thine: Lord, save me,' saith David, Ps. cxix. 94. Thou art my God; Lord, look to me, protect me, direct me, ease me, receive my soul. This is a plea that obtaineth anything of God in all extremities whatsoever.

'I will establish my covenant between me and thee, and thy seed after thee,' &c.

I come now to the qualities of this covenant; and before I speak in particular of them, I beseech you observe one thing (which I will but touch, to make an entrance to that which follows), from the manner of setting down the covenant; it is not here set down as it is in other places of Scripture: 'I will be thy God, and thou shalt be my people;' but here is only the first part, the main of the covenant of grace recited, 'I will be thy God.' Why doth he not say, too, Thou shalt take me for thy God? Because where the first is, he ever works the second; our part depends upon his. All our grace that we have to answer the covenant, is by reflection from God. He chooseth us, and then we choose him. He knoweth us, and therefore we come to know him. He loveth us first, and then we love him. He singleth us out to be a peculiar people, and we single out him above all things to be our portion. 'Whom have I in heaven but thee?' Ps. lxiii. 25.

It is therefore—to come to the first quality—called *a free covenant.* It cometh from God merely of grace. It is of grace that he would enter into any terms of agreement with us. It is of grace that he would send Christ to die to be the foundation of the covenant. It is of grace that he giveth us hearts to take him for our God, to depend upon him, to love him, to serve him, &c. All is of grace, and all cometh from him.

So you see that it is a free covenant. That is the first quality.

Again, secondly, it is *a sure, a certain covenant.* I will establish my covenant. But in whom is it established? how cometh it to be sure? It is established in Christ, the mediator of the covenant, in the Messiah; for 'in thy seed shall all the nations of the earth be blessed,' Gen. xii. 3. That is the fundamental promise. All other promises, the promise of the land of Canaan, the promise of the multiplying his seed as the stars of heaven, they were all but accessary. This is the grand promise: in thy seed, in Christ, shall all the nations of the earth be blessed. So it is *a sure covenant,* because it is established in the Messiah, Christ, God-man. And Christ being God and man, is fit to be the foundation of the covenant between God and man, for he is a friend to both parties. As man he will do all that is helpful for man; and as God, he will do nothing that may derogate from God; and so being God, and being God and man, he brings God and man together comfortably and sweetly, and keepeth them together in a sure and firm agreement. For first of all, he takes away the cause of division that was between God and us, because by his sacrifice and obedience he did satisfy God's wrath; and that being satisfied, God and us are at peace and friendship; for God till then, though he be a fountain of goodness, yet he was a fountain sealed. The fountain was stopped by sin; but when there is a satisfaction made by Christ, and we believing on him, the satisfaction of Christ is made ours. It is a sure covenant, because it is established in Christ the blessed seed.

And as it is a sure covenant, so, thirdly, it is an *everlasting covenant.* 'I will make an everlasting covenant with thee.' So it is set down here.

Everlasting in these respects. For when we are in Christ, and made one with him by faith, he having satisfied God's wrath for us, and made him peaceable, then God is become our father, and he is an everlasting father. His love to us in Christ is like himself, immutable. For even as Christ, when he took upon him our nature, he made an everlasting covenant with our nature, married our nature to himself for ever, and never layeth aside his human nature, so he will never lay aside his mystical body, his church. As Christ is God-man for ever, so mystical Christ, the church, is his body for ever. As Christ will not lose his natural, so he will not lose his mystical body. 'I will marry thee to myself for ever,' saith God in the prophet. So then it is everlasting in respect of God, he being immutable. 'I am God,' saith he, 'and I change not,' Mal. iii. 6; and Christ, the foundation of the covenant, is everlasting.

And then again it is everlasting in regard of us; because if we be not wanting to ourselves, we shall be for evermore, in grace here and in glory for ever. The fruits of grace in us—that is, the work of the Spirit—it is everlasting; for howsoever the graces we have be but the first-fruits of the Spirit, yet our inward man grows more and more, till grace end in glory, till the first-fruits end in a harvest, till the foundation be accomplished in the building; God never takes away his hand from his own work.

Everlasting also in regard of the body of Christians. God makes a covenant with one, and when they are gone, with others. Always God will have some in covenant with him. He will have some, to be a God to, when we are gone, so long as the world continueth.

So that we see it is in every respect an everlasting covenant. God is everlasting, Christ is everlasting, the graces of the Spirit are everlasting. When we are dead, he will be a God unto us, as it is said, 'I am the God of Abraham, of Isaac, and of Jacob,' their God when they were dead. He is the God of our dust, of our dead bodies. He will raise them up, for they are bodies in covenant with him. I am the God of whole Abraham, and not of a piece; therefore his body shall rise again. It is an everlasting covenant. That is the third quality.

Lastly, It is *a peculiar covenant.* 'I will be *thy* God, and the God of *thy* seed. All are not the children of Abraham, but they that are of the faith of Abraham. God is in covenant only with those that answer him, that take him for their God, that are a peculiar people. It is not glorying in the flesh; but there must be somewhat wrought that is peculiar before we can be assured we are of Abraham's seed, and in covenant with God.

And we may know that we are God's peculiar by some peculiar thing that we can do. What peculiar thing canst thou do? To speak a little of that by the way. Thou lovest and art kind; but, saith Christ, what peculiar thing canst thou do? A heathen man may be kind and loving, but canst thou overcome revenge? Canst thou spare and do good to thine enemies? Canst thou trust in God when all means fail? What is the power of the Spirit in thee? Doth it triumph in thee over thy natural corruption? Canst thou do as Abraham did? He left all at God's command; canst thou do that if need should be? Canst thou leave children, and wife, and life, and all at God's command? Canst thou sacrifice Isaac as he did? Canst thou more trust in the promise of God than in the dearest thing in the world, yea, than in thy own feeling of grace? Whatsoever is not God, canst thou be content to be without? Canst thou rely upon God when he appeared* to be an angry God? Abraham knew that there was more comfort in the promise than in Isaac. If thou have comfort in the promise more than in anything else, then thou art one of Abraham's seed, thou hast sacrificed thy Isaac. Never talk of Abraham else; never think that thy portion is great in God, be what thou wilt by profession, if there be no particular thing in thee which is not in a natural man. If thou art covetous, as gripple† for the world, as very a drudge in thy calling, as licentious in thy course as carnal men are, thou art none of

* Qu. 'appeareth'?—Ed.

† That is, 'greedy, rapacious.'—G.

God's peculiar ones, thou art none of Abraham's seed. God's people have somewhat peculiar that the world hath not. It is a peculiar covenant.

Thus you see the qualities of this covenant. It is a free covenant; a sure covenant, established in the blessed seed, the Messiah; it is an everlasting covenant; and it is a peculiar covenant.

To make some use of this, in a word.

Here, then, you see *is another spring of blessed comfort opened to a Christian.* If he findeth God, though his assurance be little, to be his God in regard of peculiar favours, let him remember it is an everlasting favour. His love is everlasting. The foundation is everlasting; the graces of the Spirit are an everlasting spring, always issuing from Christ our head. Grace is never drawn dry in him. God is our God to death, in death, and for ever. All things in the world will fail us: friends will fail us; all comforts will fail us; life will fail us ere long; but this is an everlasting covenant, which will not fail.

It is a point of comfort in the loss of friends, in the loss of estate in this world. If I lose friends, yet I cannot lose God; if he be mine, he is mine for ever; a friend now, and a friend ever; my portion now, and my portion for ever. Whatsoever God takes away, he never takes away himself; and in him I have all that is taken away. All the comfort that he doth still derive* to me by friends, he resumeth to himself. It is not perished with the party.† He can immediately, by himself, convey whatsoever comfort was derived to me by others. He is God all-sufficient; that is, put the case all the world were taken away; not only friends, but the sun, the light, the earth, food and raiment, all, as it shall be at the day of judgment; if all be taken away, yet I have him; yet I have him that made all, that supporteth all. Cannot he do all in a more excellent manner? Is not he all-sufficient, though I lose all things else? It is a point of wondrous comfort. God knew it well enough. Therefore he laboureth to establish the heart of the father of the faithful, good Abraham, here, with this instead of all, 'I am God all-sufficient, and I will be thy God.'

Again, If this be so, that God will be a God to us for ever, let us comfort ourselves hence *in all the unfaithful dealings of men.* They are friends to-day and enemies to-morrow; but God is my God; and whom he loveth he loveth to the end, John xiii. 1. An ingenuous spirit certainly esteemeth it the greatest cross in the world; and if anything will whet a man to heaven, this is one, that those whom he trusteth will prove false, and at length deceive him. Man is but man; in the balance he is lighter than vanity; but he that is in covenant with God, his promise, and love, and faithfulness never faileth. A Christian in all the breaches of this world hath this comfort, that he hath a sure God to trust to. He that hath not God to trust to, and is unfaithfully dealt withal in the world, what a wretched man is he! This was David's comfort. When he was beset with calamities and miseries, all took from him, and the people were ready to stone him, he trusted in the Lord his God. I come to the extent of it.

'To thee and to thy seed after thee.'

Why doth he make the covenant with his seed as well as with himself?

I answer, *We apprehend favours and curses more in our seed ofttimes than in ourselves;* and it will humble a man to see calamities on his posterity, more than on himself; and a man more rejoiceth to see the flourishing of his seed than of himself. It is said that Josiah did die in peace, though he died a bloody death, because he saw not the ruin of his house and

* That is, 'communicate.'—G.

† Cf. Vol. III. page 9.—G.

family, which was worse than death. God saw how Abraham apprehended and valued seed, when he said, 'What wilt thou give me, since I am childless?' Gen. xv. 2. Therefore God, intending a comfortable enlargement of the covenant of grace to Abraham, extends it to his seed: 'I will be the God of thy seed.' It is a great blessing for God to be the God of our seed. It is alluded to by St Peter in the New Testament, 'The promise is made to you and to your children,' Acts ii. 39.

But what if they have not baptism, the seal of the covenant?

That doth not prejudice their salvation. God hath appointed the sacraments to be seals for us, not for himself. He himself keepeth his covenant, whether we have the seal or no, so long as we neglect it not. Therefore we must not think if a child die before the sacrament of baptism, that God will not keep his covenant. They have the sanctity, the holiness of the covenant. You know what David said of his child, 'I shall go to it, but it shall not return to me;' and yet it died before it was circumcised. You know they were forty years in the wilderness, and were not circumcised. Therefore the sacrament is not of absolute necessity to salvation. So he is the God of our children from the conception and birth.

But how can God be the God of our children, when they are born in corruption, children of wrath? Can they be the children of wrath and the children of God both at one time?

I answer, Yes; both at one time. For even as in civil matters, in our city here, a man may be a freeman of the city, and yet be born lame or leprous, or with some contagious disease—this hindereth not his freedom—so the children of a believing father and mother may be freemen of the city of God, and in the covenant of grace, and yet be tainted with original sin, that overspreadeth the powers of the soul notwithstanding.

Whence we see a ground of baptizing infants, because they are in the covenant. To whom the covenant belongs, the seal of it belongs; but to infants the covenant belongs; therefore the seal of it, baptism, belongeth to them. If circumcision belonged to them, then baptism doth; but circumcision belonged to them, for the eighth day they were circumcised; therefore baptism belongeth to them.

Anabaptistical spirits would not have children baptized if they believe not. Why then were the children of the Jews circumcised? They were circumcised because they were in covenant; and is not the covenant of grace enlarged? Wherein doth the new covenant differ from the old, but, among many other things, in the enlargement of it? There is now a new people, the Gentiles, in covenant, that were not before, new priests, new sacrifices, new sacraments. All is new in the covenant of grace. If all be enlarged in the covenant, why should we deny the seal of the covenant to them in the new that had it in the old, even children? It is senseless. The Scripture, to meet with such, applieth baptism to them and circumcision to us, to shew that in the covenant of grace they are all one in effect: 1 Cor. x. 2, 'All they were baptized under the cloud;' and St Paul saith, Col. ii. 11, 'We are circumcised with circumcision without hands.' We are circumcised, and they were baptized; to shew, I say, that all are one in Christ. Christ is all one, 'yesterday, to-day, and the same for ever,' Heb. xiii. 8: 'yesterday,' to them that were under the law; 'and to-day,' to us under the gospel; and 'for ever' to posterity. And therefore, if children had interest in Christ then, so they have now. This is clear and undeniable: God is the God of our children.

This should be an encouragement to parents to be good, if not for love of themselves and their own souls, yet for their children and posterity's sake, that God may do good to their children for them. They cannot deserve worse of their children than to be naught* themselves.

How many examples are there in Scripture that God plagued and punished the children for the fathers' sins! Though in the main matter he will not do it sometimes, because he is gracious and good; he will be good to the children, though their parents be naught,* as Joshua and Caleb came into Canaan, though their parents were rebels, and died in the wilderness. Yet it is a discomfortable thing. When parents are naught,* they may look that God should punish their sin in their children.

There is a great deal of care taken by carnal parents here in the city (and everywhere too, but in the city especially) by covetousness, a reigning sin; they will not make God their God, but the wedge of gold to be their god. They labour to make their children great. If they can leave them rich men, great men in a parish, to bear office, to come to honour, that is their main endeavour; for this they drudge, and neglect heaven and happiness. But, alas! what is this? Thou mayest leave them much goods, and the vengeance of God with them; thou mayest leave them much wealth, and it may be a snare to them. It were better thou hadst left them nothing.

Look into the state of the city. Those that are best able in the city, do they not rise of nothing? And they that have been the greatest labourers for these outward things, that they may call their lands after their own names, Ps. xlix 11, God hath blown upon them, and all hath come to nought in a short time, because they have not made God their portion. Of all things, parents should labour to leave them God for their God, to leave them in covenant with him; lay up prayers in heaven for them, lay the foundation there; sow prayers there, that they may be effectual for them when you are gone.

And this likewise should be a comfort to poor Christians, that have not much to leave their children. I can leave my child nothing, but I shall leave him in covenant with God; for God is my God, and always hath been, and ever will be; he will be the God of my seed. I shall leave him God's blessing; and a little well gotten goods that the righteous hath is better than a great deal ill gotten. God addeth no sorrow with that. There is no 'fearful expectation' another day, as there is of that which is ill gotten; when the father and child shall meet in hell, and curse one another; when the son shall say to the father, You ensnared yourself to make me happy, and that turned to my ruin. This shall make wicked wretches curse one another one day. A poor Christian that cannot say he hath riches to leave his children, yet he can say, God is my God, and I am sure he will be their God; though I have but little to leave them else, I shall leave them God's blessing. Good parents may hope for a blessing upon their children, because God is their God, and the God of their seed.

For the sacrament, a word.

The sacrament is a seal of this covenant, that God is our God in Christ, and we are his people. God to his word addeth seals, to help our faith. What a good God is this! how willing is he to have us believe him! One would think that a word from him, a promise, were enough; but to his promise he addeth a covenant. One would think a covenant were enough, but to that he addeth seals, and to them an oath too: 'I have sworn to David my servant,' Ps. lxxxix. 3. Thus he stoops to all condi-

* That is, 'naughty,' = wicked.—G.

tions of men; he condescendeth so far to use all these means that he may secure us. You know that a promise secures us, if it be from one that is an honest man. We say that we are sure to have it because of his promise; but when we have his covenant, then we are assured more, because there is somewhat drawn. Now, we have God's covenant and his seal, the sacrament; and then his oath. If we will take him for our God, and renounce our wicked courses, we shall lose nothing by it; we shall part with nothing for God but we shall have it supplied in him. If we lose honour, wealth, or pleasure, we shall have it abundantly in him.

What do we hear in the sacrament? Do we come only to receive his love to us? No; we make a covenant with God in the sacrament that he shall be our God, and we promise by his grace to lead new lives henceforth. We have made a covenant with God at first in baptism, now we renew it in taking the sacrament; and it is fit, for if he renew his covenant oft to us in love to be ours, we should renew ours oft with him, to take him to be our God. Seven times in Genesis he renewed his covenant to Abraham, because he would have him trust what he said.* Then we should seven times, that is, oft, come to the sacrament, and renew our covenant with him, to take him for our God; and remember what it is to sin after the receiving the sacrament. Sins against conscience break off a covenant renewed. Sin hath an aggravation now. You that mean to receive, if you sin willingly after, it were better you had not received. What makes adultery worse than fornication? Saith Malachi, 'It was the wife of thy covenant,' ii. 14. Adultery breaks the covenant of marriage. It is worse than fornication, where there is not a covenant. So you have made a covenant with God in your baptism, and now you come to renew it. If you sin now, it is an aggravation of the sin. It is adultery, it is disloyalty against God.

Remember, therefore, that we do not only take here God's kindness sealed in the sacrament, but we re-promise back again to lead new lives. All must resolve by his grace to obey him henceforward, and to take him for our God. The way, therefore, will be to put this into the condition of your promise now, and prayer after. Lord, I have promised this; but thou knowest I cannot perform the promise I have made, and the condition thou requirest, of myself. But in the covenant of grace, thou hast said that thou wilt make good the condition. Thou hast promised to give the 'Spirit to them that ask him,' Luke xi. 13; thou hast promised to 'circumcise my heart,' Col. ii. 11; thou hast promised to 'teach me,' Ps. xxxii. 8; thou hast promised to delight over me for good; thou hast promised to 'wash me with clean water,' Ezek. xxxvi. 25; thou hast promised to put thy fear in my heart,' Jer. xxxii. 40; thou hast promised 'to write thy law in the affections,' Jer. xxxi. 33. I would fear thee, and love thee, and trust in thee, and delight in thee; thou knowest I cannot fulfil the conditions. Thou art able and willing; thou art as able to make me do these things as to command me to do them.

Thus we should desire God to give the grace that he requires in the use of the means; for that must not be neglected. We must attend upon the ordinances; use the parts that are given us; and in that, 'to him that hath shall be given,' Mat. xiii. 12. Thou shalt not need any necessary good to bring thee to heaven, if thou wilt claim the promise of the covenant in the use of means. We shall want degrees perhaps; but in the covenant of grace, it is not degrees that brings us to heaven, but truth.

* Cf. Vol. V. p. 63.—G.

Now, in our renewing the covenant with God, let us not despair of his performance; let not that hinder us from coming to the sacrament, but come cheerfully, and know that he that hath made the covenant with thee to be thy God, and to give thee all particular grace, in the use of all good means, will perform it. He will perform it if we come in sincerity of heart. If we come to 'daub'* with God, and after to follow our sinful courses, this is to mock God. This made David take it to heart so much, that 'his familiar friend, that ate at his table, lift up his heel against me,' Ps. xli. 9. May not God complain of us, that we come to the communion, to his table, with false, Judas hearts, and afterwards betray him? He may say, My familiar friends they came and ate with me, yet they have lift up the heel against me; they are rebellious; they will leave no sin that before they were enthralled to. So, instead of a blessing, we bring a curse upon us, a just reward of our disloyalty. Oh remember that it is a great aggravation of sin after the sacrament.

I speak not this to discourage any, but to encourage us rather. If we come with sincere hearts, and with resolution to please God, we may look for all the promises from God. All that he hath promised he is ready to perform, if we in faith can allege the promise, 'Lord, remember thy promise, wherein thou hast caused thy servant to put his trust!' Ps. cxix. 49.

* Cf. Ezek. xiii. 10–14, and xxii. 28.—G.

JOSIAH'S REFORMATION.

JOSIAH'S REFORMATION.

NOTE.

'Josiah's Reformation' forms Nos. 8, 9, 10, 11 of the first edition of 'The Saint's Cordials'—1629; and in the second and third—1637 and 1658—Nos. 1, 2, 3, and 4. Cf. Notes, Vol. IV. page 60, and Vol. V. page 176. For account of a manuscript copy of these delightful sermons, in my possession, see Bibliographical List of Editions in Volume VII. The title-page of 'Josiah's Reformation,' in the edition of 1637, which is our text, is given below.* G.

* JOSIAHS
REFORMATION.
Laid open in foure SERMONS.

viz.
1. THE TENDER HEART.
2. THE ART OF SELFE-HUMBLING.
3. THE ART OF MOURNING
4. THE SAINTS REFRESHING.

VVHEREIN IS SHEVVED THE
TVRNINGS AND WINDINGS OF THE
Soule in this great worke of Reformation: and how the stout heart may so be brought low, as to be made humble, melting, and compassionately mournfull: even to the comfort of a sweet Assurance.

[Wood-cut here, as described, Vol. IV. p. 60. See also Memoir, p. cxxiv.]

By R. SIBBS D. D. Master of *Katherine Hall* in Cambridge, and preacher of *Grayes Inn* London.

The second Edition.

ESAY 57. 15.

For thus saith the high and lofty One, that inhabiteth Eternity, whose Name is Holy; I dwell in the high and holy Place: with him also that is of a contrite and humble spirit, to revive the spirit of the humble, and to revive the heart of the contrite ones.

LONDON,
Printed for R. DAVVLMAN, at the brazen Serpent in
Pauls Churchyard. 1637.

THE TENDER HEART.

SERMON I.

And as for the king of Judah, who sent you to inquire of the Lord, so shall ye say unto him, Thus saith the Lord God of Israel concerning the words which thou hast heard, Because thine heart was tender, &c.—2 Chron. XXXIV. 26.

These words are a part of the message which the prophetess Huldah sent to good King Josiah; for as the message was concerning him and his people, so his answer from her is exact, both for himself and them. That part which concerned his people is set down in the three foregoing verses; that which belongs unto himself is contained in the words now read unto you, 'But to the king of Judah,' &c. The preface to her message we see strengthened with authority from God, 'Thus saith the Lord God of Israel;' which words carry in them the greater force and power from the majesty of the author. For if words spoken from a king carry authority, how much more then the word of the Lord of hosts, the King of kings? Here is her wisdom, therefore, that she lays aside her own authority, and speaks in the name of the Lord.

We see that waters of the same colour have not the same nature and effect, for hot waters are of the same colour with plain ordinary waters, yet more effectual; so the words of a man coming from a man may seem at first to be the same with others, yet notwithstanding, the words of God coming from the Spirit of God, carry a more wonderful excellency in them even to the hearts of kings. They bind kings, though they labour to shake them off. They are arrows to pierce their hearts; if not to save them, yet to damn them. Therefore she speaks to the king, 'Thus saith the Lord God of Israel concerning the words which thou hast heard,' &c.

Here we read of Josiah, that he was a man of an upright heart, and one who did that which was right in the sight of the Lord; and answerably we find the Lord to deal with him. For he, desirous to know the issue of a fearful judgment threatened against him and his people, sendeth to Huldah, a prophetess of the Lord, to be certified therein; whereupon he receiveth a full and perfect answer of the Lord's determination, both touching himself and his people, that they being forewarned might be forearmed; and by their timely conversion to the Lord, might procure the aversion* of so

* That is, 'turning away.'—G.

heavy wrath. He in uprightness sends to inquire, and the Lord returns him a full and upright answer. Whence we may learn,

Doct. 1. *That God doth graciously fit prophets for persons, and his word, to a people that are upright in their hearts.* Where there is a true desire to know the will of God, there God will give men sincere prophets that shall answer them exactly; not according to their own lusts, but for their good. Josiah was an holy man, who, out of a gracious disposition, desirous to be informed from God what should become of him and his people, sends to the prophetess Huldah. It was God's mercy that he should have a Huldah, a Jeremiah, to send to; and it was God's mercy that they should deal faithfully with him. This is God's mercy to those that are true-hearted. He will give them teachers suitable to their desires; but those that are false-hearted shall have suitable teachers, who shall instruct them according to their lusts. If they be like Ahab, they shall have four hundred false prophets to teach falsehood, to please their lusts, 1 Kings xxii. 6; but if they be Davids, they shall have Nathans. If they be Josiahs, they shall have Huldahs and Jeremiahs. Indeed, Herod may have a John Baptist, Mark vi. 27; but what will he do with him in the end when he doth come to cross him in his sin? Then off goes his head.

Use. This should teach us *to labour for sincerity, to have our hearts upright towards God;* and then he will send us men of a direct and right spirit, that shall teach us according to his own heart. But if we be false-hearted, God will give us teachers that shall teach us, not according to his will, but to please our own. We shall light upon belly-gods and epicures, and shall fall into the hands of priests and Jesuits. Where such are, there are the judgments of God upon the people, because they do not desire to know the will of God in truth. We see, Ezek. xiv. 3, 4, the people desired to have a stumblingblock for their iniquity. They were naught,* and would have idols. Therefore they desired stumblingblocks. They would have false prophets, that so they might go to hell with some authority. Well, saith God, they shall have stumblingblocks: for thus saith the Lord God of Israel, 'To every man that setteth up his idols in his heart, and putteth the stumblingblock of his iniquity before his face, and cometh to the prophet to inquire; I the Lord will answer him that cometh, according to the multitude of his idols; according to his own false heart, and not according to good.' What brought the greatest judgment upon the world, next to hell itself, I mean antichrist—the terriblest judgment of all, that hath drawn so many souls to hell—but the wickedness of the place and people, and his own ambition? The sins of the people gave life to him. They could not endure the word of God or plain dealing; they thought it a simple thing. They must have more sacrifices, more ceremonies, and a more glorious government. They would not be content with Christ's government which he left them, but were weary of this. Therefore he being gone to heaven, they must have a pope to go before them and lead them to hell. Therefore let men never excuse those sins, for certainly God saw a great deal of evil in them, and therefore gave them up to the judgment of antichrist. But let us magnify God's mercies that hath not so given us up. Thus we see how graciously God deals with a true-hearted king: he sends him a true answer of his message.

Ver. 27, 'Because thine heart was tender,' &c.

Now here comes a comfortable message to good Josiah, that he should

* That is, 'naughty,' wicked.—G.

be taken away and not see the miseries that should befall his people; the cause whereof is here set down, 'Because thy heart was tender, and thou didst humble thyself before God;' which cause is double.

1. *Inward.* 2. *Outward.*

1. The inward is the tenderness of his heart and humbling of himself. 2. And then the outward expression of it is set down in a double act:

(1.) Rending of clothes. (2.) Weeping.

'Because thou hast rent thy clothes, and wept before me.' After which comes the promise, 'I have also heard thee,' saith the Lord; 'behold, I will gather thee to thy fathers, and thou shalt be put in thy grave in peace, and thine eyes shall not see all the evil which I will bring upon this place, and upon the inhabitants of the same.'

I will first remove one doubt, before I come to the tenderness of Josiah's heart.

Quest. What! may some say, Is there anything in man that can cause God to do do him good?

Ans. No. One thing is the cause of another, but all come from the first cause. So tenderness of heart may be some cause of removal of judgment; but God is the cause of both, for they all come from the first cause, which is God. So that these words do rather contain an order than a cause. For God hath set down this order in things, that where there is a broken heart there shall be a freedom from judgment; not that tenderness of heart deserves anything at God's hand, as the papists gather, but because God hath decreed it so, that where tenderness of heart is, there mercy shall follow; as here there was a tender heart in Josiah, therefore mercy did follow. God's promises are made conditionally; not that the condition on our part deserves anything at God's hand, but when God hath given the condition, he gives the thing promised. So that this is an order which God hath set down, that where there is grace, mercy shall follow. For where God intends to do any good, he first works in them a gracious disposition: after which he looks upon his own work as upon a lovely object, and so doth give them other blessings. God crowns grace with grace.

By 'heart' is not meant the inward material and fleshy part of the body; but that spiritual part, the soul and affections thereof. In that it is said to be 'tender' or melting, it is a borrowed and metaphorical phrase. Now in a 'tender heart' these three properties concur:

1. *It is sensible.* 2. *It is pliable.* 3. *It is yielding.*

1. First, A tender heart is always *a sensible* heart.* It hath life, and therefore sense. There is no living creature but hath life, and sense to preserve that life. So a tender heart is sensible of any grievance; for tenderness doth presuppose life, because nothing that hath not life is tender. Some senses are not altogether necessary for the being of a living creature, as hearing and seeing; but sensibleness is needful to the being of every living creature. It is a sign of life in a Christian when he is sensible of inconveniences. Therefore God hath planted such affections in man, as may preserve the life of man, as fear and love. Fear is that which makes a man avoid many dangers. Therefore God hath given us fear to cause us make our peace with him in time, that we may be freed from inconveniences; yea, from that greatest of inconveniences, hell fire.

2, 3. Again, A tender heart *is pliable and yielding.* Now that is said to be yielding and pliable, which yields to the touch of anything that is put to it, and doth not stand out, as a stone that rebounds back when it is

* That is, 'sensitive.'—G.

thrown against a wall. So that is said to be tender which hath life, and sense, and is pliable, as wax is yielding and pliable to the disposition of him that works it, and is apt to receive any impression that is applied to it. In a tender heart there is no resistance, but it yields presently to every truth, and hath a pliableness and a fitness to receive any impression, and to execute any performance; a fit temper indeed for a heart wrought on by the Spirit. God must first make us fit, and then use us to work. As a wheel must first be made round, and then turned round, so the heart must be first altered, and then used in a renewed way. A tender heart, so soon as the word is spoken, yields to it. It quakes at threatenings, obeys precepts, melts at promises, and the promises sweeten the heart. In all duties concerning God, and all offices of love to men, a tender heart is thus qualified. But hardness of heart is quite opposite. For, as things dead and insensible, it will not yield to the touch, but returns back whatsoever is cast upon it. Such a heart may be broken in pieces, but it will not receive any impression; as a stone may be broken, but will not be pliable, but rebound back again. A hard heart is indeed like wax to the devil, but like a stone to God or goodness. It is not yielding, but resists and repels all that is good; and therefore compared in the Scripture to the adamant stone. Sometimes it is called a frozen heart, because it is unpliable to anything. You may break it in pieces, but it is unframeable for any service, for any impression; it will not be wrought upon. But on the contrary, a melting and tender heart is sensible, yielding, and fit for any service both to God and man. Thus we see plainly what a tender heart is. The point from hence is,

Doct. 2. *That it is a supernatural disposition of a true child of God to have a tender, soft, and a melting heart.* I say that a disposition of a true child of God, and the frame of soul of such an one, to be tender, apprehensive, and serviceable, is a supernatural disposition; and of necessity it must be so, because naturally the heart is of another temper—a stony heart. All by nature have stony hearts in respect of spiritual goodness. There may be a tenderness in regard of natural things; but in regard of grace, the heart is stony, and beats back all that is put to it. Say what you will to a hard heart, it will never yield. A hammer will do no good to a stone. It may break it in pieces, but not draw it to any form. So to a stony heart, all the threatenings in the world will do no good. You may break it in pieces, but never work upon it. It must be the almighty power of God. There is nothing in the world so hard as the heart of man. The very creatures will yield obedience to God; as flies, and lice, to destroy Pharaoh; but Pharaoh himself was so hard-hearted, that after ten plagues he was ten times the more hardened, Exod. x. 28. Therefore, if a man have not a melting heart, he is diverted from his proper object; because God hath placed affections in us, to be raised presently upon suitable objects. When any object is offered in the word of God, if our hearts were not corrupted, we would have correspondent affections. At judgments we would tremble, at the word of threatenings quake, at promises we would with faith believe, and at mercies be comforted; at directions we would be pliable and yielding. But by nature our hearts are hard. God may threaten, and promise, and direct, and yet we insensible all the while. Well, all Josiahs, and all that are gracious, of necessity must have soft hearts. Therefore I will shew you,

1. *How a tender heart is wrought.*
2. *How it may be preserved and maintained.*

3. *How it may be discerned from the contrary.*

1. First, A tender heart is made tender *by him that made it.* For no creature in the world can soften and turn the heart, only God must alter and change it; for we are all by nature earthly, dead, and hard. Hence is it that God doth make that gracious promise, Ezek. xi. 19, 'I will give them one heart, and put a new spirit within their bowels; and I will take away the stony hearts out of their bodies, and give them a heart of flesh;' that is, a living, sensible heart.

Quest. But doth God immediately make the heart tender, and change it, without any help by means?

Sol. 1. I answer, Means do not make the heart tender, but God through the use of means softens it by his word. God's word is a hammer to break, and as fire to melt the hardened heart, Jer. xxiii. 9. And thus it works, first, when God doth shew to the heart our cursed estate, and opens to the same the true dangers of the soul, which it is in by nature and custom of sin, and sets before it the terrors of the last day and present danger of judgment. When the Spirit of God, by the word, doth convince the soul to be in a damned estate, dead, born under wrath, and an heir of damnation; that by nature God frowns, and hell is ready to swallow us up; when the soul is thus convinced, then the heart begins to be astonished, and cries out, 'Men and brethren, what shall I do?' Acts ii. 37. When the word is thus preached with particular application, it doth good. For a man may hear the word of God generally, and yet have no broken heart. But when a Peter comes and saith, 'You have crucified the Lord of life;' and when a Nathan comes to David, and saith, 'Thou art the man,' then comes the heart to be broken and confounded.

But it is not enough to have the heart broken; for a pot may be broken in pieces, and yet be good for nothing; so may a heart be, through terrors, and sense of judgment, and yet not be like wax, pliable. Therefore it must be melting;* for which cause, when God by his judgments hath cast down the heart, then comes the Spirit of God, revealing the comfort of the word; then the gracious mercy of God in Christ is manifested, that 'there is mercy with God, that he may be feared,' Ps. cxxx. 4. This being laid open to the quick, to a dejected soul, hence it comes to be melted and tender; for the apprehension of judgment is only a preparing work, which doth break the heart, and prepare it for tenderness.

Sol. 2. Again, Tenderness of heart is wrought by an apprehension of tenderness and love in Christ. A soft heart is made soft by the blood of Christ. Many say, that an adamant cannot be melted with fire, but by blood. I cannot tell whether this be true or no; but I am sure nothing will melt the hard heart of man but the blood of Christ, the passion of our blessed Saviour. When a man considers of the love that God hath shewed him in sending of his Son, and doing such great things as he hath done, in giving of Christ to satisfy his justice, in setting us free from hell, Satan and death: the consideration of this, with the persuasion that we have interest in the same, melts the heart, and makes it become tender. And this must needs be so, because that with the preaching of the gospel unto broken-hearted sinners cast down, there always goes the Spirit of God, which works an application of the gospel.

Christ is the first gift to the Church. When God hath given Christ, then comes the Spirit, and works in the heart a gracious acceptance of mercy offered. The Spirit works an assurance of the love and mercy of

* Qu. 'melted'?—Ed.

God. Now love and mercy felt, work upon the tender heart a reflective love to God again. What, hath the great God of heaven and earth sent Christ into the world for me? humbled himself to the death of the cross for me? and hath he let angels alone, and left many thousands in the world, to choose me? and hath he sent his ministers to reveal unto me this assurance of the love and mercy of God? This consideration cannot but work love to God again; for love is a kind of fire which melts the heart. So that when our souls are persuaded that God loves us from everlasting, then we reflect our love to him again; and then our heart says to God, 'Speak, Lord; what wilt thou have me to do?' The soul is pliable for doing, for suffering, for anything God will have it. Then, 'Speak, Lord, for thy servant heareth,' 1 Sam. iii. 9.

And when the heart is thus wrought upon, and made tender by the Spirit, then afterward in the proceeding of our lives, many things will work tenderness: as the works of God, his judgments, the word and sacraments, when they are made effectual by the Spirit of God, work tenderness. The promises of God also make the heart tender, as Rom. xii. 1, 'I beseech you, brethren, by the mercies of God, offer up your souls and bodies a living sacrifice, holy and acceptable unto God.' There is no such like argument to persuade men to tenderness of heart, as to propound the love and mercy of God. And so the fear of any judgment will work tenderness. This made Josiah's heart to melt, but yet this did not work first upon him; for he having a tender heart before, and being sure of God's love, when he heard the judgment that should come upon his people, out of love to God and to his people, his heart melted, not so much for fear of judgment, but to think that God should be provoked by the sins of his people.

And thus we have seen how tenderness of heart is wrought. Now I come to shew,

2. *Second, The means how we may preserve this tenderness of heart*, because it is a disposition of God's children. How then shall we preserve ourselves in such a perpetual temper? The way to preserve a tender heart is,

1. First, *To be under the means whereby God's Spirit will work;* for it is he by his Spirit that works upon the heart, and doth preserve tenderness in us; and he will work only by his own means. All the devices in the world will not work upon the heart. Therefore let us be under the means that may preserve tenderness, and hear what God's word says of our estate by nature, of the wrath and justice of God, and of the judgment that will shortly come upon all the world. This made Paul to cry, though he knew that he was the child of God, and free from the law. 'Therefore,' saith he, 'knowing the terror of the law, we admonish you.'

2. And then, *go into the house of mourning, and present before yourselves the miserable and forlorn estate of the church of God abroad.* It was this that broke Nehemiah's heart. When he heard that the Jews were in great affliction and reproach, that the wall of the city was broken down, and the gates thereof burnt with fire, he sat down and wept, and mourned certain days, fasted and prayed before the God of heaven, Neh. i. 4. This made this good man Nehemiah to mourn, so that all the princes of the court could not comfort him. This also made Moses's heart to melt, when he looked on his brethren's affliction in Egypt. So we might keep our hearts tender if we did but set before our eyes the pitiful estate of God's church abroad, and that we may come to be in such an estate ourselves ere long.

3. And if thou wilt preserve tenderness of heart, *labour for a legal and evangelical faith.* We must believe that all the threatenings of God's

vengeance against the wicked shall come to pass. Faith doth make these things present before our eyes; for it is the nature of faith to set things absent as present before us. What makes the malefactor to tremble and be cast down, but when he sees that he is ready for to die, is going to the place of execution, and sees death look him in the face? So faith setting the day of judgment before our eyes, will make us to tremble. Therefore Paul doth so often adjure Timothy by the coming of the Lord Jesus to judgment, 2 Tim. iv. 1; and Enoch set the day of judgment before him, at the beginning of the world, as we may see in Jude 14. He had a faith, that set things to come as present, and made him to walk with God. So if we had an evangelical faith to believe the goodness of God, pardon from him, and everlasting life, this would preserve tenderness of heart.

4. Again, *Good company will preserve tenderness of heart, sorting ourselves with those that are tender-hearted.* For the soul will reason thus: Doth such a one make conscience of swearing, profaning the Sabbath? and doth he mourn for the miseries of the church? Then what a hard piece of dead flesh am I, that have nothing in me!

5. Again, If thou wouldst preserve tenderness of heart, by all means *take heed of the least sin against conscience*, for the least sin in this kind makes way for hardness of heart. Sins that are committed against conscience do darken the understanding, dead the affection, and take away life; so that one hath not the least strength to withstand the least temptation. And so it comes to pass by God's judgment; for when men will live in sins against conscience, he takes away his Spirit, and gives up the heart from one degree of hardness to another. For the heart at first being tender, will endure nothing, but the least sin will trouble it. As water, when it begins to freeze, will not endure anything, no not so much as the weight of a pin upon it, but after a while will bear the weight of a cart; even so at the beginning, the heart being tender, trembles at the least sin, and will not bear with any one; but when it once gives way to sins against conscience, it becomes so frozen that it can endure any sin, and so becomes more and more hard. Men are so obdurate, having once made a breach in their own hearts by sins against conscience, that they can endure to commit any sin; and therefore God gives them up from one degree of hardness to another. What will not men do whom God hath given up to hardness of heart?

6. Again, If thou wilt preserve tenderness of heart, *take heed of spiritual drunkenness;* that is, that thou be not drunk with an immoderate use of the creatures; of setting thy love too much upon outward things. For what saith the prophet? 'Wine and women take away the heart,' Hosea iv. 11; that is, the immoderate use of any earthly thing takes away spiritual sense; for the more sensible the soul is of outward things, the less it is of spiritual. For as the outward takes away the inward heat, so the love of one thing abates the love of another. The setting of too much love upon earthly things, takes away the sense of better things, and hardens the heart. When the heart is filled with the pleasures and profits of this life, it is not sensible of any judgment that hangs over the head; as in the old world, 'they ate and drank, they married and gave in marriage, they bought and sold, while the flood came upon them and swept all away,' Mat. xxiv. 37. When a man sets his love upon the creature, the very strength of his soul is lost. Therefore in the Scripture, God joins prayer and fasting both together, Mat. xvii. 21; that when he would have our hearts raised up to heaven, we should have all use of earthly things taken away. Therefore

when we are to go about spiritual duties, we must cut ourselves short in the use of the creatures. Talk of religion to a carnal man, whose senses are lost with love of earthly things, he hath no ear for that; his sense is quite lost, he hath no relish or savour of anything that is good. Talk to a covetous man, that hath his soul set upon the things of this life, he hath no relish of anything else; his heart is already so hardened to get honour and wealth, though it be to the ruin of others, that he cares not how hard it become. Therefore we are bidden to take heed that our hearts be not overcome with drunkenness and the cares of this life, for these will make a man to be insensible of spiritual things, Luke xxi. 34.

7. Again, If thou wilt preserve tenderness of heart, *take heed of hypocrisy;* for it causeth swelling, and pride makes the heart to contemn others that be not like unto us. They bless themselves that they live thus and thus, they think themselves better than any other; and if they hear the minister reprove them for sin, they will shift it off, and say, Oh, this belongeth not to me, but to such a carnal man, and to such a wicked person; as the Scribes and Pharisees, who were vile hypocrites, yet they were the cause of all mischief, and more hard-hearted than Pilate, an heathen man; for he would have delivered Christ, but they would not, Luke xxiii. 14, *seq.* So, take a Romish hypocrite, that can proudly compliment it at every word with enticing speech, yet you shall find him more hard hearted than Turk or Jew; for full of cruelty and blood is the 'whore of Babylon.' Therefore, if thou wilt have tenderness of heart, take heed of hypocrisy.

8. Again, Above all things, *take heed of great sins*, which will harden the heart; for little sins do many times not dead the heart, but stir up the conscience; but great sins do stond* and dull a man; as a prick of a pin will make a man to start, but a heavy blow maketh a man for to be dead for the present. Therefore take heed of great sins. Thus it was with David. He sinned in numbering of the people, and for this his heart smote him; but when he came to the great and devouring sin of Uriah and Bathsheba, this was a great blow that struck him and laid him for dead, till Nathan came and revived him, 2 Sam. xii. 1. For when men fall into great sins, their hearts are so hardened, that they go on from sin to sin. Let us therefore be watchful over our own hearts, to preserve tenderness. The eye being a tender part, and soonest hurt, how watchful is man by nature over that, that it take no hurt. So the heart, being a tender thing, let us preserve it by all watchfulness to keep blows from off it. It is a terrible thing to keep a wound of some great sin upon the conscience, for it makes a way for a new breach; because when the conscience once begins to be hardened with some great sin, then there is no stop, but we run on to commit sin with all greediness.

9. Lastly, If thou wilt preserve tenderness of heart, *consider the miserable estate of hardness of heart.* Such an one that hath an hard heart is next to hell itself, to the estate of a damned spirit, a most terrible estate. A hard heart is neither melted with promises nor broken with threatenings. He hath no bowels of pity to men or love to God. He forgets all judgment for things past, and looks for none to come. When the soul is in this case, it is fit for nothing but for sin and the devil, whereas a tender-hearted man is fit for all good. Let God threaten: he trembles and quakes; let God promise: his heart melts and rejoiceth, and makes him even to break forth into thanksgiving; let God command: he will perform all; he is fit for any good thing to God and man. But when a man's heart is hardened

* That is, 'stun,' = harden.—G.

by hypocrisy, covetousness, or custom in sin, he hath no pity, no compassion: let God command, threaten, or promise, yet the heart is never a whit moved. This is a terrible estate of soul.

Now, to speak a little to young men that are like to this holy man Josiah. Surely his tenderness had some advantage from his years. Let those that are young by all means labour to keep tenderness of heart; for if young persons be good, there is a sweet communion between God and them, before the heart be pestered with the cares of the world. God delights much in the prayers of young men, because they come not from so polluted a soul, hardened with the practices of this world. Let such, therefore, as are young, take advantage of it, to repent in time of their sins, and let them not put it off unto their old days. While we are young, let us not neglect natural tenderness; although we cannot bring ourselves under the compass of God's kingdom by it, yet shall we get our hearts the sooner to be tender. In our youth, therefore, let us not neglect this good opportunity, as good Josiah did not when he was but young. Therefore let us repent of every sin betimes, and acquaint ourselves with those that are good; as it is said, Heb. iii. 13, 'Let us provoke one another daily, while it is called to-day, lest any of you be hardened through the deceitfulness of sin.' Let us use all means to keep our hearts tender. Oh, it is a blessed estate! We are fit to live when our hearts are tender; fit to die, fit to receive anything from God, fit for duties of honesty to men, for any service to God. But when we have lost sense and feeling, it must be the almighty power of God that must recover us again, and not one amongst an hundred comes to good. Therefore labour to preserve a tender, soft, and melting heart.

Now, ere I proceed, give me leave to answer some cases of conscience, as,

Quest. 1. First, Whether the children of God may be subject to this hardness of heart, opposed to this tenderness?

Quest. 2. Secondly, Whether a Christian may be more sensible of outward things than of spiritual, as the love of God, or his own sin, and the like?

Sol. 1. To the first I answer, *that the child of God may be hard-hearted.* He may have some degrees of hardness of heart in him. For a Christian is a compounded creature; he hath not only body and soul, but flesh and spirit. He is but in part renewed; and therefore, having in him both flesh and spirit, he is subject to hardness of heart; and it is clear that it may be so. Examples shew that God's children are not always alike sensible of the wrath of God and of his mercy. They do not yield so to his commands as they should. But what is the reason that God doth suffer his children to fall into this hardness of heart? There is something in us that makes him give us up unto it, for we are no longer soft than he works upon us.

Quest. But what doth move him to leave us in this disposition?

Sol. I answer, he doth it for correction of former negligences, for sins of omission; especially when they neglect some means of grace whereby their hearts might be kept tender: it is for want of stirring up of God's grace in them; for want of an high esteem of grace bestowed upon them; want of care of their company, for not associating themselves with such as are tender-hearted; and from hence it comes that God suffers his children to fall into hardness of heart.

Quest. But now, from hence ariseth another question: How may a man know his heart from the heart of a reprobate, seeing that God's children may have hardness of heart?

Ans. I answer, that the heart of a man that is a very reprobate is totally, wholly, and finally hardened, and it is joined with security and insensibleness; it is joined with obstinacy, and with contempt of the means. But the child of God hath not total and final hardness of heart, but hath a sensibleness of it, he feeleth and seeth it. Total hardness doth feel nothing, but a Christian that hath hardness of heart, doth feel that he hath it; as a man that hath the stone in his bladder, feels and knows that he hath a stone. A hard-hearted man feels nothing, but he that hath but only hardness of heart doth feel: for there is difference between hardness of heart and a hard heart; for the child of God may have hardness of heart, but not a hard heart. Now, I say a child of God that hath hardness of heart is sensible of his hardness, and performs the actions of a sensible soul: he useth some good means for the softening of it, for the sense thereof is grievous to him above all other crosses; and whiles he is under it, he thinks that all is not with him as it should be: therefore he complains of it above all other afflictions, which makes him cry to God, as we may see, Isa. lxiii. 17, 'Why hast thou hardened our hearts from thy fear?'

Obj. But some may demand how God doth harden.

Sol. I answer, the cause is first from our own selves; but he hardens four ways:

First, *Privatively*, by withholding and withdrawing his melting and softening power. For as the sun causeth darkness by withdrawing his light and warming power, so God withdrawing that melting power whereby we should be softened, it cannot be but that we must needs be hardened.

2. Secondly, *Negatively*, by denying of grace; by taking away from us his graces, which are not natural in us. Thus God doth to those whom he doth absolutely harden; he takes away that which they have, and so they become worse than they of themselves were by nature. When men walk unworthy of the gospel, God takes away very rational life from them, and gives them up to hardness of heart, that they run on in such courses, as that they are their own enemies, and bring upon themselves ruin.

3. Thirdly, And as God hardens by privation and negation, so, in the third place, he hardens *by tradition*:* by giving us up to the devil, to be vexed by his troubles, to harden us. It is a fearful judgment. When we take a course to grieve the Spirit of God, the Spirit will take a course to grieve us: he will give us up to Satan, to blind and to harden us. So that though God doth not work, as the author, effectually in this hardening, yet as a just judge he doth, by giving us up to Satan and the natural lusts of our own hearts, which are worse than all the devils in hell.

4. Fourthly and lastly, He doth harden *objectively*, by propounding good objects, which, meeting with a wicked heart, make it more hard, as, Isa. vi. 10, it is said, 'Harden these people's hearts.' How? By preaching of the word. A good object, if it lights upon a bad soul, hardens the heart; for they that are not bettered by religion, under the means, are so much the worse by their use. So we see God cannot be impeached with the hardening of our hearts, because all the cause is from ourselves; for whether he hardens by privation, negation, tradition, or by propounding good objects, it is all from ourselves; and likewise we have seen that God's children may have hardness of heart in some measure, but yet it differs from a reprobate, because they see and feel it, grieve for it, and complain of it to God.

Quest. The second question is, *But whether may a child of God be more*

* That is, 'giving up.' Cf. 1 Tim. i. 20 for the *word*.—G.

sensible of outward joys or crosses, than of spiritual things? for this makes many think they have not tender hearts, because they are more sensible of outward things than of spiritual.

Ans. I answer, *It is not always alike with them;* for God's children are still complaining of something: of their carelessness in good duties, of their want of strength against corruption. They go mourning when they have made God to bring them down upon their knees for their hardness of heart; but there is an intercourse, in the children of God, between the flesh and the spirit. They are partly flesh and partly spirit. Therefore many times, for a while, when the flesh prevails, there may be a sudden joy and a sudden sorrow, which may be greater than spiritual joy or spiritual sorrow; but yet it is not continual. But spiritual sorrow, grief for sin, though it be not so vehement as, for the sudden, outward sorrow is, yet it is more constant. Grief for sin is continual; whereas outward sorrow is but upon a sudden, though it seem to be more violent.

2. And again, *in regard of their valuing and prizing of earthly things*, there may be a sudden sorrow: for a child of God may, upon a sudden, overprize outward things, and esteem them at too high a rate; but yet after that, valuing things by good advice, they prize spiritual things far beyond outward; and therefore their sorrow and joy is more for spiritual things, because it is constant. This I speak, not to cherish any neglect in any Christian, but for comfort to such as are troubled for it; therefore let such know, that God will not 'break the bruised reed, nor quench the smoking flax.' If they have but a desire, and by conscionable* use of means, do shew their desire to be true, they shall have it at last, for Christ doth continue to make intercession for us; and if there were no weakness in us, what need Christ continue to make peace for us? for peace is made for those that fall out. Therefore, if there were no falling out between God and us, what need Christ to continue to make intercession for us? For these reasons, we see a child of God, for the present, may be more sensible of outward things than of spiritual.

Quest. But here another question may be asked, How shall we know that we have sensibleness and pliableness, or not?

Ans. I answer, Easily, by applying of the soul unto objects, as 1, to God; 2, to his word; 3, to his works; 4, to man.

We may try our tenderness and pliableness of heart these four ways:

1. *To God.* As it is tender from God, so it is tender for God; for the three persons of the Trinity. He that hath a tender heart cannot endure to dishonour God himself, or to hear others dishonour him, either by his own sins or by others.' He cannot endure to hear God's name blasphemed. So that they have a tender heart who when they see Christ in his religion to be wronged, cannot choose but be affected with it. So again, a man hath a tender heart when he yields to the motions of the Holy Ghost. When the Spirit moves, and he yields, this shews there is a tender heart. But a hard heart beats back all, and as a stone to the hammer, will not yield to any motion of God's Spirit.

2. Now, in the second place, to come downward, a tender heart is sensible in regard *of the word of God;* as, first, at the threatenings a true tender heart will tremble, as Isa. lxvi. 2, 'To him will I look, even to him that is of a contrite and broken spirit, and trembleth at my words.' A man that hath a tender heart will tremble at the signs of the anger of God: 'Shall the lion roar, and the beasts of the forest not be afraid?'

* That is, 'conscientious.'—G.

Amos iii. 4. Yes, they will stand still and tremble at the roaring of the lion; but much more will a tender heart tremble when God roars, and threatens vengeance. A tender heart will tremble when it hears of the terrors of the Lord at the day of judgment, as Paul did: 'Now knowing the terrors of the Lord, we persuade men,' 2 Cor. v. 11. It forced him to be faithful in his office. This use the apostle Peter would have us make of it: 2 Pet. iii. 11, 'That seeing all these things must be dissolved, what manner of persons ought we to be in holy conversation and godliness?' And so for the promises in the word. The heart is tender when the word of God doth rejoice a man above all things. How can the heart but melt at God's promises, for they are the sweetest things that can be. Therefore when a tender heart hears God's promises, it makes him to melt and be sensible of them. Again, a tender heart will be pliable to any direction in the word. To God's call it will answer, 'Here I am;' Lord, what wilt thou have me to do? As Isaiah, when he had once a tender heart, then 'Send me, Lord,' Isa. vi. 8. So David to God's command, 'Seek ye my face,' answers, 'Thy face, Lord, will I seek,' Ps. xxvii. 8. There is a gracious echo of the soul to God in whatsoever he saith in his word. And thus a true, tender heart doth yield to the word of God, and is fit to run on any errand.

3. Thirdly, By applying it *to the works of God;* for a tender heart quakes when it doth see the judgment of God abroad upon others. It hastens to make his peace with God, and to meet him by repentance. So again, a tender heart rejoiceth at the mercy of God, for it doth see something in it better than the thing itself; and that is the love of God, from which it doth proceed.

4. Fourthly, A man may know his heart to be tender and sensible, in regard *of the estate of others, whether they be good or bad.* If they be wicked, he hath a tender heart for them; as David, Ps. cxix. 136, 'Mine eyes gush out with rivers of water, because men keep not thy law.' So Paul saith, 'There are many that walk inordinately, of whom I have told you before, and now tell you weeping,' &c., Phil. iii. 18. So Christ was sensible of the misery of Jerusalem, wept for it, and a little while after, shed his own blood for it, Mat. xxiii. 37. Thus had he a tender heart. But when Christ looked to God's decree, he saith, 'Father, I thank thee, Lord of heaven and earth, that thou hast hid these things from the wise and noble, and hast revealed them unto babes,' Mat. xi. 25. And so likewise for those that are good, in giving and forgiving; in giving, they give not only the thing, but they give their hearts and affections with it; and so in forgiving, they apprehend Christ's love in forgiving them; therefore they forgive others. So for works, will God have a tender heart to do anything, it will do it. If he will have it mourn, it will mourn; if to rejoice, it will rejoice; it is fit for every good work. By these marks we may know whether we have tender hearts or no.

But to apply this; how is this affection of Josiah in the hearts of men in these days? How many have melting hearts when they hear God blasphemed, and the religion of Christ wronged? How few are there that yield to the motions of the Spirit! We may take up a wonderful complaint of the hardness of men's hearts in these days, who never tremble at the word of God. Neither his promises, nor threatenings, nor commands will melt their hearts; but this is certain, that they which are not better under religion, by the means of grace, are much the worse. And how sensible are we of the church's miseries? For a tender heart is sensible of the miseries of the church, as being members of the same body, whereof Christ is the head. But men now-a-days are so far from melting hearts, that they want natural affection, as Paul foretells of such in the latter times, 1 Tim. iv. 1. They have less bowels of pity in them, when they hear how it goes with the church abroad, than very pagans and heathens. This shews they have no tender hearts, that they are not knit to Christ by faith, who is the head; nor to the church, the body, in love. How is thy heart affected to men when they commit any sin against God, as idolaters, swearers, drunkards, liars, and the like? Is it mercy to let these go on in their sins towards hell? No, this is cruelty; but mercy is to be shewed unto them, in restraining men from their wicked courses. Therefore do not think thou shewest mercy unto them by letting them alone in sin, but exhort and instruct them. Coldness and deadness is a spiritual disease in these days. But surely they that have the Spirit of God warming their hearts, are sensible of their own good and ill, and of the good and ill of the time. Well, if you will know you have a tender heart, look to God, look to his word, to his works, to yourselves, and others; and so you shall know whether you have tender hearts or not.

Quest. But here may be another question asked, How shall men recover themselves, when they are subject to this hardness, deadness, and insensibleness? If after examination a man find himself to be thus, how shall he recover himself out of this estate. I answer,

Ans. 1. First, As when things are cold we bring them to the fire to heat and melt, so *bring we our cold hearts to the fire of the love of Christ*; consider we of our sins against Christ, and of Christ's love towards us; dwell upon this meditation. Think what great love Christ hath shewed unto us, and how little we have deserved, and this will make our hearts to melt, and be as pliable as wax before the sun.

2. Secondly, If thou wilt have this tender and melting heart, then *use the means*; be always under the sunshine of the gospel. Be under God's sunshine, that he may melt thy heart; be constant in good means; and help one another. 'We must provoke one another daily, lest any be hardened through the deceitfulness of sin,' Heb. iii. 13. Physicians love not to give physic to themselves. So a man is not always fit to help himself when he is not right; but good company is fit to do it. 'Did not our hearts burn within us while he talked with us?' said the two disciples, holding communion each with other at Emmaus, Luke xxiv. 32. For then Christ comes and makes a third, joins with them, and so makes their hearts burn within them. So Christ saith, 'Where two or three are met together in his name, he is in the midst of them,' Mat. xviii. 20. Now they were under the promise, therefore he affords his presence. Where two hold communion together, there Christ will make a third. Therefore let us use the help of others, seeing David could not recover himself, being a prophet, but he must have a Nathan to help him, 2 Sam. xii. 7. Therefore if we would recover ourselves from hard and insensible hearts, let us use the help one of another.

3. Thirdly, *We must with boldness and reverence challenge the covenant of grace;* for this is the covenant that God hath made with us, to give us tender hearts, hearts of flesh, as Ezek. xi. 19, 'I will give them one heart, and put a new spirit within their bowels; I will take away the stony hearts out of their bodies, and I will give them a heart of flesh. Now seeing this is a covenant God hath made, to give us fleshly hearts and to take away our stony, let us challenge him with his promise, and go to him by prayer. Entreat him to give thee a fleshly heart; go to him, wait his time, for that

is the best time. Therefore wait though he do not hear at first. These are the means to bring tenderness of heart.

Now, that ye may be stirred up to this duty, namely, to get a soft and tender heart, mark here,

1. First, *What an excellent thing a tender heart is.* God hath promised to dwell in such an heart, and is it an excellent thing to have God dwell in our hearts, as he hath promised, Isa. lvii. 15, 'For thus saith he that is high and excellent, he that inhabiteth eternity, whose name is the Holy One: I will dwell in the high and holy place, and with him also that is of a contrite and humble spirit, to revive the spirit of the humble, and to give life to them that are of a contrite heart?' So Isa. lxvi. 2, 'To him will I look, even to him that is poor and contrite in spirit, and doth tremble at my words.' Now God having promised to dwell where there is a soft heart, and no hardness, no rocks to keep him out; can God come into a heart without a blessing? Can he be separated from goodness, which is goodness itself? When the heart therefore is pliable and thus tender, there is an immediate communion between the soul and God; and can that heart be miserable that hath communion with God? Surely no.

2. Secondly, Consider *that this doth fit a man for the end for which he was created.* A man is never fit for that end for which he was made, but when he hath a tender heart; and what are we redeemed for, but that we should serve God? And who is fit to be put in the service of God but he that hath begged a tender heart of God?

3. Thirdly, To stir you up to labour for this, consider *that a tender heart is fit for any blessedness.* It is capable of any beatitude. What makes a man blessed in anything but a tender heart? This will make a man to hear the word, to read, to shew mercies to others. 'Blessed are the poor in spirit,' saith Christ, 'for theirs is the kingdom of heaven.' A tender heart is blessed, because that only heareth God's word, and doth it; and it is always a merciful heart, and therefore blessed.

4. Again, Consider *the wretched estate of a heart contrary, that is not tender, and will not yield.* Oh what a wonderful hardness would the heart of man grow to, if we do not follow it with means to soften it! What a fearful thing was it to see what strange things fell out at Christ's death, what darkness there was, what thunders and lightnings. The veil of the Temple rent, the sun was turned into darkness, the graves opened, and the dead did rise, yet notwithstanding none of these would make the hypocritical Pharisees to tremble, but they mocked at it, although it made a very heathen man confess it the work of God, Mat. xxvii. 45-54. For a ceremonial hypocrite is more hard than a Turk, Jew, or Pagan. All the judgments of God upon Pharaoh were not so great as hardness of heart. The papists, after they have been at their superstitious devotion, are fittest for powder-plots and treasons, because their hearts are so much more hardened. What fearful things may a man come to, if he give way to hardness of heart! He may come to an estate like the devil, yea, worse than Judas, for he had some sensibleness of his sin; he confessed he had sinned in betraying the innocent blood. But many of these hypocrites have no sensibleness at all, which is a fearful thing. Eli's children hearkened not to the voice of their father, because that the Lord had a purpose to destroy them, 1 Sam. ii. 25. So it is in this case a shrewd sign that God will destroy those that are so insensible that nothing will work upon them. But these hypocrites shall be sensible one day, when they shall wish they were as insensible as in their lifetime they were. But it will be an unfruitful repentance to repent

in hell; for there a man shall get no benefit by his repentance, seeing there they cannot shake off the execution of God's judgment, as they shake off the threatenings of his judgments here. Well, to this fearful end, before it be long, must every one that hath a hard heart come, unless they repent. Therefore let every one be persuaded to labour for a tender, pliable, yielding, and sensible heart here, else we shall have it hereafter against our wills, when it will do us no good; for then hypocrites shall be sensible against their wills, though they would not be sensible in this life.

And thus I have done with the first inward cause in Josiah that moved God so to respect him, namely, tenderness of heart.

THE ART OF SELF-HUMBLING.

SERMON II.

Because thine heart was tender, and thou didst humble thyself before God, when thou heardest his words against this place, and against the inhabitants thereof, and humbledst thyself before me, and didst rend thy clothes, and weep before me, &c.—2 Chron. XXXIV. 27.

Of tenderness of heart, the first inward cause in Josiah, which moved God to pity him, so as he should not be an eye-witness of the fearful calamities to come upon his land and people, is largely spoken in the former sermon; wherein is also shewed how it is wrought, preserved, discerned, recovered when it is lost; what encouragements we have to seek and labour for it, with some other things which I will not here repeat, but fall directly upon that which follows, 'And thou didst humble thyself before God.' In which words we have set down the second inward cause in Josiah, that moved God to shew mercy unto him; the humbling of himself. 'And thou didst humble thyself before God.' Tenderness of heart and humbling a man's self go both together; for things that are hard will not yield nor bow. A great iron bar will not bow, a hard stony heart will not yield. Now, therefore, humbling of ourselves, the making of us as low as the ground itself, is added unto tenderness; for the soul being once tender and melting, is fit to be humbled, yea, cares not how low it be abased, so mercy may follow. For the better unfolding of the words, we will consider,

1. *The person that did humble himself:* 'Josiah,' a king, a great man.

2. *Humiliation itself, and the qualities of it:* 'and humbledst thyself before God,' which argued the sincerity of it.

3. *The occasion of it:* 'when thou heardest the words against this place, and against the inhabitants thereof.'

4. *The outward expression of it, in weeping and rending his clothes;* which we will handle in their place.

1. First, for the *person*, 'Thou didst humble thyself,' Josiah a king, who was tenderly brought up, and highly advanced; a thing which makes the work so much the more commendable; whence we learn,

Doct. 1. *That it is a disposition not unbefitting kings to humble themselves before God.* For howsoever they are gods downward, to those that are under them, yet if they look upward, what are kings? The greater light hides the lesser. What are all the inhabitants of the earth in his sight, but as a drop of a bucket, as dust upon the balance, of no moment! Isa. xl. 15. 'I have said you are gods, but you shall die like men,' Ps. lxxxii. 6, 7. For howsoever the saints of God differ from other men in regard of their use, and the inscription God hath set upon them, yet they are of the same stuff, dust, as others are. And so kings, though in civil respects they differ from other men, yet are they of the same metal, and shall end in death, all their glory must lie in the dust.

Therefore it is not unbefitting kings to humble themselves before God, seeing they have to deal with him who is a 'consuming fire,' Heb. xii. 29, before whom the very angels cover their faces. I say it is no shame for the greatest monarch of the earth to abase himself when he hath to do with God; yea, kings, of all other persons, ought most to humble themselves, to shew their thankfulness to God, who hath raised them from their brethren to be heads of his people. And considering the endowments which kings usually have, they are bound to humble themselves, as also in regard of the authority and power which God hath put into their hands, saying, 'By me kings reign,' Prov. viii. 15. But usually we see, from the beginning of the world, that kings forget God. Where there is not grace above nature, there kings will not stoop to Christ; but so far as it agrees with their pleasure and will, so far shall Christ be served, and no farther.

But yet God hath always raised up some nursing fathers and mothers, —as he hath done to us, for which we ought to bless God,—who have and do make conscience of this mentioned duty, so well beseeming Christian princes, as in sundry other respects, so also in this, that therein they might be exemplary to the people. For no doubt but Josiah did this also, that his people might not think it a shame for them to humble themselves before God, whenas he their king, tender in years, and subject to no earthly man, did before them, in his own person, prostrate himself in the humblest manner before the great God of heaven and earth.

As that ointment poured upon Aaron's head fell from his head to the skirts, and so spread itself to the rest of the parts, even to his feet, Ps. cxxxiii. 2, so a good example in a king descends down to the lowest subjects, as the rain from the mountains into the valleys. Therefore a king should first begin to humble himself. Kings are called fathers to their subjects, because they should bear a loving and holy affection to their people, that when anything troubles the subjects, they should be affected with it. Governors are not to have a distinct good from their subjects, but the welfare of the subjects should be the glory of their head. Therefore Josiah took the judgments threatened as his own: howsoever his estate was nothing unto theirs.

It is said moreover, 'Thou didst humble thyself.' He was both the agent and the patient, the worker and the object of his work: it came from him, and ended in him. Humiliation is a reflected action: Josiah humbled himself. And certainly this is that true humiliation, the humbling of ourselves; for it is no thanks for a man to be humbled by God, as Pharaoh was; for God can humble and pull down the proudest that do oppose his church. God by this gets himself glory. But here is the glory of a Christian, that he hath got grace from God to humble himself; which humbling is, from our own judgment, and upon discerning of good grounds, to bring our affections to stoop unto God; to humble ourselves. Many are humbled that are not humble; many are cast down that have proud hearts still, as Pharaoh had. It is said, 'Thou humbledst thyself.' Then we learn,

Doct. 2. *That the actions of grace are reflected actions.* They begin from a man's self, and end in a man's self; yet we must not exclude the Spirit of God; for he doth not say, thou from thyself didst humble thyself, but 'thou didst humble thyself.' We have grace from God to humble ourselves. So that the Spirit of God doth work upon us as upon fit subjects, in which grace doth work. Though such works be the works of God, yet they are said to be ours, because God doth work them in us and by us. We are said to humble ourselves, because we are temples wherein he works, seeing he useth the parts of our soul, as the understanding, the will, and the affections, in the work. Therefore it is foolish for the papists to say, good works be our own, as from ourselves. No; good works, say we, are ours, as effects of the Spirit in us. But for the further expression of this humbling of ourselves before God, we will consider,

1. The kinds and degrees of it.
2. Some directions how we may humble ourselves.
3. The motives to move us to it.
4. The notes whereby it may be known.

1. First, for the *nature and kinds of it;* we must know that humiliation is either

(1.) *Inward, in the mind* first of all, and then in the *affections;* or,

(2.) *Outward, in expression of words*, and likewise in *carriage*.

(1.) To begin with the first *inward humiliation in the mind*, in regard of judgment and knowledge, is, *when our understandings are convinced, that we are as we are;* when we are not high-minded, but when we judge meanly and basely of ourselves, both in regard of our beginning and dependency upon God, having all from him, both life, motion, and being; and also in regard of our end, what we shall be ere long. All glory shall end in the dust, all honour in the grave, and all riches in poverty. And withal, true humiliation is also in regard of spiritual respects, when we judge aright how base and vile we are in regard of our natural corruption, that we are by nature not only guilty of Adam's sin, but that we have, besides that, wrapt ourselves in a thousand more guilts by our sinful course of life, and that we have nothing of our own, no, not power to do the least good thing. When we look upon any vile person, we may see our own image. So that if God had not been gracious unto us, we should have been as bad as they. In a word, inward conviction of our natural frailty and misery, in regard of the filthy and foul stain of sin in our nature and actions, and of the many guilts of spiritual and temporal plagues in this life and that which is to come, is that inward humiliation in the judgment or understanding.

Again, Inward humiliation, besides spiritual conviction, is *when there are affections of humiliation.* And what be those? Shame, sorrow, fear, and such like penal afflictive affections. For, upon a right conviction of the understanding, the soul comes to be stricken with shame that we are in such a case as we are; especially when we consider God's goodness to us, and our dealing with him. This will breed shame and abasement, as it did in Daniel. Shame and sorrow ever follow sin, first or last, as the apostle demands, Rom. vi. 21, 'What fruit had ye then in those things whereof ye are now ashamed?' After conviction of judgment there is always shame; and likewise there is sorrow and grief. For God hath made the inward faculties of the soul so, that upon the apprehension of the understanding, the heart comes to be stricken through with grief, which works upon our souls. Therefore we are said in Scripture to afflict ourselves; that is, when we set ourselves upon meditation of our deserts. Hereupon we cannot but be affected inwardly, for these sorrows are so many daggers to pierce through the heart.

The third penal affection is, *fear and trembling before God's judgments and his threatenings*, a fear of the majesty of God, whom we have offended, which is able to send us to hell if his mercies were not beyond our deserts. But his mercy it is, that we are not consumed. A fear of this great God is a part of this inward humiliation. So we see what inward humiliation is: first, a conviction of the judgment; and then it proceeds to inward afflictive affections, as grief, shame, fear, which, when upon good ground and fit objects, they are wrought in us by the Holy Ghost, they are parts of inward humiliation. But as for the wicked, they drown themselves in their profaneness, because they would not be ashamed, nor fear, nor grieve for them. But this makes way for terrible shame, sorrow, and fear afterwards; for those that will not shame, grieve, and fear here, shall be ashamed before God and his angels at the day of judgment, and shall be tormented in hell for ever.

2. Secondly, His *outward humiliation* is expressed and manifested in words, in outward behaviour and carriage. The words which he used are not here set down; but certainly Josiah did speak words when he humbled himself. It was not a dumb show, but done with his outward expression and his inward affection. This is evident by those words of the text, 'I have heard thee also,' saith the Lord. Without doubt, therefore, he did speak something. But because true sorrow cannot speak distinctly,—for a broken soul can speak but broken words,—therefore his words are not here set down, but yet God heard them well enough. And indeed, so it is sometimes, that the grief for the affliction may be stronger than the faculty of speech, so that a man cannot speak for grief. As a heathen man, by light of nature, did weep and grieve for his friends, but when his child came to be killed before him, he stood like a stone, because his sorrow was so great that it exceeded all expression. So humiliation may so exceed that it cannot be expressed in words; as David himself, when he was told of his sins by Nathan, did not express all his sorrow, but saith, 'I have sinned;' yet afterwards, he makes the 51st Psalm, a composed speech for supply, a fit pattern for an humble and broken soul. So doubtless there was outward expression of words in Josiah, although they be not here set down. This speech, which is a part of humiliation, is called a confession of our sins to God; with it should be joined hatred and grief afflictive, as also a deprecation and desire that God would remove the judgment which we have deserved by our sins; and likewise a justification of God, in what he hath laid or may lay upon us. Lord, thou art righteous and just in all thy judgments; shame and confusion belongeth unto me; my sins have deserved that thou shouldest pour down thy vengeance upon me; it is thy great mercy that I am not consumed. The good thief upon the cross justified God, saying, 'We are here justly for our deserts; but this man doth suffer wrongfully,' Luke xxiii. 41. Justification and self-condemnation go with humiliation. This is the outward expression in words. Now the outward humiliation in respect of his carriage, is here directly set down in two acts:

1. Rending of clothes. And 2. Weeping.

But of these I shall speak afterwards when I come at them. Thus we have seen the degrees and kinds of humiliation.

Seeing it is such a necessary qualification, for humiliation is a fundamental grace that gives strength to all other graces; seeing, I say, it is such a necessary temper of a holy gracious man to be humble; how may we come to humble ourselves as we should do? I answer, Let us take these directions:

1. First, *Get poor spirits*, that is, spirits to see the wants in ourselves and in the creature; the emptiness of all earthly things without God's favour; the insufficiency of ourselves and of the creature at the day of judgment; for what the wise man saith of riches may be truly said of all other things under the sun: they avail not in the day of wrath, but righteousness delivereth from death, Prov. xi. 4.

Josiah was not poor in respect of the world, for he was a king; but he was 'poor in spirit,' because he saw an emptiness in himself. He knew his kindgom could not shield him from God's judgment, if he were once angry.

(1.) Let us consider *our original*. From whence came we? From the earth, from nothing. Whither go we? To the earth, to nothing. And in respect of spiritual things, we have nothing. We are not able to do anything of ourselves, no, not so much as to think a good thought.

(2.) Likewise, consider we *the guilt of our sins*. What do we deserve? Hell and damnation, to have our portion with hypocrites in that 'lake that burneth with fire and brimstone.'

(3.) Let us have before our eyes the picture of old Adam, our sinful nature: how we are drawn away by every object; how ready to be proud of anything; how unable to resist the least sin; how ready to be cast down under every affliction; that we cannot rejoice in any blessing; that we have no strength of ourselves to perform any good or suffer ill; in a word, how that we carry a nature about us indisposed to good, and prone to all evil. This consideration humbled Paul, and made him to cry out, when no other afflictions could move him, 'O miserable man that I am, who shall deliver me from this body of death?' Rom. vii. 24. By this means we come to be poor in spirit.

2. If we would have humble spirits, let us *bring ourselves into the presence of the great God:* set ourselves in his presence, and consider of his attributes, his works of justice abroad in the world, and open* ourselves in particular.

Consider his wisdom, holiness, power, and strength, with our own. It will make us abhor ourselves, and repent in dust and ashes. Let us bring ourselves into God's presence, be under the means, under his word, that there we may see ourselves ripped up, and see what we are. As Job, when he brought himself into God's presence, said, 'I abhor myself, and repent in dust and ashes,' Job xlii. 6. Job thought himself somebody before; but when God comes to examine him, and upon examination found that he could not give a reason of the creature, much less of the Lord's, afflicting his children, then he saith, 'I abhor myself.' So Abraham, the more he talked with God, the more he did see himself but dust and ashes. This is the language of the holy men in Scripture, when they have to deal or think of God. 'I am not worthy,' says John Baptist, John i. 27. So Paul: 'I am not worthy to be called an apostle,' 1 Cor. xv. 9. So the centurion: 'I am not worthy thou shouldst come into my house,' Mat. viii. 8. 'I am less than the least of thy blessings,' saith Jacob, Gen. xxxii. 10. Thus let us come into the presence of God, under the means of his word, and then we shall see our own vileness, which will work humiliation; for, as the apostle saith, when a poor simple man doth come, and hears the pro-

* Qu. 'upon'?—Ed.

phecy, that is, the word of God, with application unto himself, laying open his particular sins, doubtless he will say, God is in you, 1 Cor. xiv. 24, 25.

3. That we may humble ourselves, *let us be content to hear of our sins and baseness by others.* Let us be content that others should acquaint us with anything that may humble us. Proud men are the devil's pipes, and flatterers the musicians to blow these pipes. Therefore it is, that though men have nothing of their own, yet they love to give heed to flatterers, to blow their bladder full, which do rob them of themselves; whereas a true, wise man, will be content to hear of anything that may humble him before God.

4. And withal, that we may humble ourselves, *look to the time to come, what we shall be ere long,* earth and dust; and at the day of judgment we must be stripped of all. What should puff us up in this world? All our glory shall end in shame, all magnificency in confusion, all riches in poverty. It is a strange thing that the devil should raise men to be proud of that which they have not of their own, but of such things which they have borrowed and begged; as for men to be proud of themselves in regard of their parents. So, many there are who think the better of themselves for their apparel, when yet they are clothed with nothing of their own, and so are proud of the very creature. But thus the devil hath besotted our nature, to make us glory in that which should abase us, and to think the better of ourselves, for that which is none of our own. Nay, many in the church of God, are so far from humbling themselves, that they come to manifest their pride, to shew themselves, to see and to be seen. Thus the devil besots many thousand silly creatures, that come in vainglory into the house of God; that whereas they should humble themselves before him, they are puffed up with a base empty pride, even before God. Therefore let us take notice of our wonderful proneness to have a conceit of ourselves; for if a man have a new fashion, or some new thing, which nobody else knows besides himself, how wonderful conceited will he be of himself! Let us take notice, I say, of our proneness to this sin of pride; for the best are prone to it. Consider, it is a wonderful hateful sin, a sin of sins, that God most hates. It was this sin that made him thrust Adam out of paradise. It was this sin which made him thrust the evil angels out of heaven, who shall never come there again. Yea, it is a sin that God cures with other sins, so far he hateth it; as Paul, being subject to be proud through the abundance of revelations, was cured of it by a prick in the flesh: being exercised with some dangerous, noisome, and strange cure. Indeed, it is profitable for some men to fall, that so by their humiliation for infirmities, they may be cured of this great, this sacrilegious sin.* And why is it called a sacrilegious sin? Because it robs God of his glory. For God hath said, 'My glory I will not give to another,' Isa. xlii. 8. Is not the grace, goodness, and mercy of God sufficient for us, but we must enter into his prerogatives, and exalt ourselves? We are both idols and idol-worshippers, when we think highly of ourselves, for we make ourselves idols. Now God hates idolatry; but pride is a sacrilege, therefore God hates pride.

5. If we would humble ourselves, *let us set before us the example of our blessed Saviour;* for we must be conformable to him, by whom we hope to be saved. He left heaven, took our base nature, and humbled himself to the death of the cross, yea, to the washing of his disciples' feet, and among the rest, washed Judas's feet, and so suffered himself to be killed as a traitor, Philip. ii. 5–7; and all this to satisfy the wrath of God for us, and

* Cf. Augustine in references and quotations of note *y*, Vol. III. p. 531.—G.

that he might be a pattern for us to be like-minded. Therefore, if we would humble ourselves by pattern, here is a pattern without all exception. Let us be transformed into the likeness of him; yea, the more we think of him, the more we shall be humbled. For it is impossible for a man to dwell upon this meditation of Christ in humility, and with faith to apply it to himself, that he is his particular Saviour, but this faith will abase the heart, and bring it to be like Christ in all spiritual representation. A heart that believeth in Christ will be humbled like Christ. It will be turned from all fleshly conceit of excellency, to be like him. Is it possible, if a man consider he is to be saved by an abased and humble Saviour, that was pliable to every base service, that had not a house to hide himself; I say, is it possible that he which considers of this, should ever be willingly or wilfully proud? Do we hope to be saved by Christ, and will we not be like him? When we were firebrands of hell, he humbled himself to the death of the cross, left heaven and happiness a-while, and took our shame, to be a pattern to us. We know that Christ was brought into the world by a humble virgin. So the heart wherein he dwells must be an humble heart. If we have true faith in Christ, it will cast us down, and make us to be humbled. For it is impossible that a man should have faith to challenge any part in Christ, except he be conformed to the image of Christ in humility. Therefore let us take counsel of Christ: 'Learn of me, for I am humble and meek; and so you shall find rest to your souls,' Mat. xi. 29.

Lastly, That we may humble ourselves, *let us work upon our own souls by reasoning, discoursing, and speaking to our own hearts.* For the soul hath a faculty to work upon itself. Now this, being a reflected action, to humble ourselves, it must be done by some inward action; and what is that? To discourse thus: If so be a prince should but frown upon me when I have offended his law, in what case should I be! Yet, when the great God of heaven threatens, what an atheistical unbelieving heart have I, that can be moved at the threatenings of a mortal man, that is but dust and ashes, and yet cannot be moved with the threatenings of the great God! Consider also, if a man had been so kind and bountiful to me, if I should reward his kindness with unkindness, I should have been ashamed, and have covered my face with shame; and yet how unkind have I been unto God, that hath been so kind to me, and yet I never a whit ashamed! If a friend should have come to me, and I have given him no entertainment, what a shame were this! But yet how often hath the Holy Ghost knocked at the door of my heart, and suggested many holy motions into me of mortification, repentance, and newness of life, yet notwithstanding I have given him the repulse, opposed the outward means of grace, and have thought myself unworthy of it; what a shame is this!

Thus, if we compare our carriage in earthly things with our carriage in heavenly, this will be a means to work upon our hearts, inwardly to humble ourselves. Thus was David abased; for when Nathan came and told him of a rich man, who having many sheep, spared his own and took away a poor man's, which was all that he had; when David considered that he had so dealt with Uriah, he was dejected and ashamed of his own courses. Let us labour to work our hearts to humility, into true sorrow, shame, true fear, that so we may have God to pity and respect us, who only doth regard a humble soul. Thus we have seen some directions how we may come to humble ourselves.

Further, There is an order, method, and agreement in these reflected actions, when we turn the edge of our own souls upon ourselves and examine ourselves; for the way that leads to rest is by the examination of ourselves. We must examine ourselves strictly, and then bring ourselves before God, judge and condemn ourselves; for humiliation is a kind of execution. Examination leads to all the rest. So, then, this is the order of our actions; there is examination of ourselves strictly before God, then indicting ourselves, after that comes judging of ourselves.

Oh that we could be brought to these inward reflected actions, to examine indict, judge, and condemn ourselves, that so we might spare God a labour, and so all things might go well with us!

3. Now I come to the third thing I propounded, *the motives to move us to get this humiliation.*

(1.) First, *Let us consider of the gracious promises that are made to this disposition of humbling ourselves;* as Isa. lvii. 15, 'For thus saith he that is holy and excellent, he that inhabiteth eternity, whose name is the Holy One; I dwell in the high and holy place, with him also that is of an humble and contrite spirit, to revive the spirit of the humble, and to give life to them that are of a contrite heart.' So there is a promise that God will give grace to the humble. An example of mercy in this kind we have in Manasseh, who, though a very wicked man, yet because he humbled himself, obtained mercy. Peter humbled himself, and David humbled himself, and both found mercy. And so likewise Josiah; yea, and in James iv. 10, we are bid to 'humble ourselves under the mighty hand of God, and he will exalt us in due time.' There is the promise. Yea, every branch of humiliation hath a promise. As confession of sins, if we confess and forsake our sins, we shall have mercy and find pardon. So those that judge themselves shall not be judged.

A humble heart is a vessel of all graces. It is a grace itself, and a vessel of grace. It doth better the soul and make it holy, for the soul is never fitter for God than when it is humbled. It is a fundamental grace that gives strength to all other graces. So much humility, so much grace. For according to the measure of humiliation is the measure of other grace, because a humble heart hath in it a spiritual emptiness. Humility emptieth the heart for God to fill it. If the heart be emptied of temporal things, then it must needs be filled with spiritual things; for nature abhorreth emptiness; grace much more. When the heart is made low, there is a spiritual emptiness, and what fills this up but the Spirit of God? In that measure we empty ourselves, in that measure we are filled with the fulness of God. When a man is humbled, he is fit for all good; but when he is proud, he is fit for all ill, and beats back all good. God hath but two heavens to dwell in; the heaven of heavens, and the heart of a poor humble man. The proud swelling heart, that is full of ambition, high conceits, and self-dependence, will not endure to have God to enter; but he dwells largely and easily in the heart of an humble man. If we will dwell in heaven hereafter, let us humble ourselves now. The rich in themselves are sent 'empty away;' the humble soul is a rich soul, rich in God; and therefore God regards the lowly and resists the proud. As all the water that is upon the hills runs into the valleys, so all grace goes to the humble. 'The mountains of Gilboa are accursed,' 2 Sam. i. 21. So there is a curse upon pride, because it will not yield to God.

(2.) Again, *All outward actions benefit other men; but this inward action of humbling a man's self makes the soul itself good.*

(3.) *An humble soul is a secure and safe soul;* for a man that is not high, but of a low stature, needs not to fear falling. A humble soul is a safe soul;—safe in regard of outward troubles; for when we have humbled ourselves, God needs not follow us with any other judgment: safe, in regard of inward vexation or any trouble by God; for when the soul hath brought itself low, and laid itself level as the ground, then God ceaseth to afflict it. Will the ploughman plough when he hath broken up the ground enough? or doth he delight in breaking up the ground? See what Isaiah saith to this purpose in chap. xxviii. 28. When God seeth that a man hath abased himself, he will not follow with any other judgment; such a one may say to God, Lord, I have kept court in mine own conscience already, I have humbled and judged myself, therefore do not thou judge me; I am ready to do whatsoever thou wilt, and to suffer what thou wilt have me. I have deserved worse a thousand times, but, Lord, remember I am but dust and ashes. Thus God spares his labour when the soul hath humbled itself. But if we do not do this ourselves, God will take us in hand; for God will have but one God. Now if we will be gods, to exalt ourselves, he must take us in hand to humble us, either first or last. And is it not better for us to humble ourselves than for God to give us up to the merciless rage and fury of men, for them to humble us, or to fall into the hands of God, who is a 'consuming fire'? For when we accuse and judge ourselves, we prevent much shame and sorrow. What is the reason God hath given us up to shame and crosses in this world, but because we have not humbled ourselves? What is the reason many are damned in hell? Because God hath given them reason, judgment, and affections, but they have not used them for themselves, to examine their ways, whether they were in the state of condemnation or salvation. They never used their affections and judgment to this end, therefore God was forced to take them in hand. Well saith Austin, all men must be humbled one way or other; either we must humble ourselves or God will;* if we will do this ourselves, the apostle promiseth, we shall not be judged of the Lord, 1 Cor. xi. 31. But we do not these things as we should, because it is a secret action. We love to do things that the world may take notice of, but this inward humiliation can only be seen by God, and by our own consciences. Let these motives therefore stir us up to humble ourselves, for humbled we must be by one way or other. How many judgments might be avoided by humbling ourselves! How many scandals might be prevented if we would judge ourselves! What is the reason so many Christians fall into scandalous sins, whereby, provoking God's anger, they fall into the hands of their enemies, but because they spare themselves, and think this humbling themselves a troublesome action. Therefore to spare themselves, they run on. Because they would not work this upon themselves, they grow to be in a desperate state at last. Wherefore upon any occasion be humble, let us prepare ourselves to meet the Lord our God. When we hear but any noise of the judgments of God, we should humble ourselves, as good Josiah did; when he did but hear of the threatenings against his land, it made him humble himself.

Quest. But here it may be demanded, considering that wicked men do oftentimes humble themselves, being convinced in their consciences, and thereupon ashamed,

4. *How may we know holy from hypocritical humiliation?* which is the last thing I propounded concerning humiliation, namely, the notes and marks whereby we may know true humiliation from false, which are these.

Ans. 1. First, *Holy humiliation is voluntary;* for it is a reflected action,

* In 'Confessions' repeatedly.—G.

which comes from a man's self. It ends where it begins. Therefore Josiah is said to humble himself. But, on the contrary, the humiliation of other men is against their will. False humiliation is not voluntary, but by force it is extorted from them. God is fain to break, crush, and deal hardly with them, which they grieve and murmur at. But the children of God have the Spirit of God, which is a free Spirit, that sets their hearts at liberty. For God's Spirit is a working Spirit, that works upon their hearts, and hereby they willingly humble themselves, whereas the wicked, wanting this Spirit of God, cannot humble themselves willingly, but are cast down against their wills. For God can pluck down the proudest. He can break Pharaoh's courage, who, though he was humbled, yet he did not humble himself. A man may be humbled, and yet not humble. But the children of God are to humble themselves, not that the grace whereby we humble ourselves is from ourselves; but we are said to humble ourselves, when God doth rule the parts he hath given us, when he sets our wits and understanding on work to see our misery, and then our will and affection to work upon these. Thus we are said to humble ourselves when God works in us. An hypocrite God may humble and work by him. He may work by graceless persons, but he doth not work in them. But God's children have God's Spirit in them, not only working in* them his own works, as he doth by hypocrites and sinful persons, but his Spirit works in them. So that here is the main difference between true humiliation and that which is counterfeit. The one is voluntary, being a reflected action, to work upon and to humble ourselves; but the other is a forced humiliation.

2. Again, *True humiliation is ever joined with reformation.* Humble thyself and walk with thy God, saith the prophet: Micah vi. 8, 'He hath shewed thee, O man, what he doth require of thee, to humble thyself, and walk with thy God.' Now the humiliation of wicked men is never joined with reformation. There is no walking with God. Josiah reformed himself and his people to outward obedience, as much as he could, but he had not their hearts at command.

3. Again, *Sin must appear bitter to the soul,* else we shall never be truly humbled for it. There is in every renewed soul a secret hatred and loathing of evil, which manifests the soundness both of true humiliation and reformation, and is expressed in three things.

(1.) In a serious purpose and resolution not to offend God in the least kind. The drunkard must purpose to leave his drunkenness, and the swearer resolve between God and his own heart, to forsake his base courses, and cry mightily herein for help from above.

(2.) Secondly, There must be a constant endeavour to avoid the occasions and allurements of sin. Thus Job made a covenant with his eyes, that 'he would not look upon a maid,' Job xxxi. 1; and thus every unclean and filthy person should make a covenant with themselves against the sins which they are most addicted unto. When they came to serve God, in Hosea, then 'away with idols,' Hosea. xiv 8. So must we, when we look heavenward, cast from us all our sins whatsoever.

(3.) Thirdly, There must be a hatred and loathing of sin in our confessions. We must confess it with all the circumstances, the time when, and place where. We must aggravate our offences, as David did: 'Against thee have I sinned, and done this evil in thy sight;' Ps. li. 4; and as the apostle: 'I was a blasphemer, I was a persecutor,' I was thus and thus. He did

* Qu. 'by'?—Ed.

not extenuate his sin, and say, the rulers commanded me so to do; but, 'I persecuted the church' out of the wickedness of mine own heart. A true Christian will not hide his sins, but lay them open, the more to abase himself before God. This aggravating of our sins will make them more vile unto us, and us more humble in the sight of them. True reformation of life is ever joined with an indignation of all sin, there is such a contrariety in the nature of a child of God against all evil.

[1.]* We should therefore first *hate sin universally;* not one sin, but every kind of sin, and that most of all which most rules in us, and which is most prevalent in our own hearts. A sincere Christian hates sin in himself most. We must not hate that in another which we cherish in ourselves.

[2.] We should *hate sin the more, the nearer it comes to us*, in our children and friends, or any other way. It was David's fault to let Absalom his son go unreproved in his wicked practices, and Eli for not correcting his sons. We see what came of it, even their utter overthrow.

[3.] He that truly hates sin *will not think much to be admonished and reproved when he errs.* A man that hath a bad plant in his ground, that will eat out the heart of it, will not hate another that shall discover such an evil to him; so if any one shall reprove thee for this or that sin, and thou hate him for it, it is a sign corruption is sweet to thee.

Only this caution must be remembered, reproof must not be given with a proud spirit, but in a loving, mild manner, with desire of doing good. There is a great deal of self-love in some men, who, instead of hating sin in themselves and others, approve and countenance it, especially in great men, flattering them in their base humours, and fearing lest by telling them the truth they should be esteemed their enemies.

[4.] Our hatred of sin may be discerned *by our willingness to talk of it.* He that hates a snake, or toad, will flee from it; so a man that truly abhors sin, will not endure to come near the occasions of it. What shall we say then of those that prostitute themselves to all sinful delights? As hatred of sin is in our affection, so it will appear in our actions. Those that love to see sin acted did never as yet truly loathe it.

It is a sign that we do not hate sin when we take not to heart the sins of our land. 'Woe is me that I am constrained to dwell in the tents of Kedar,' saith David; 'mine eyes gush out with tears because men keep not thy law,' Ps. cxx. 5. Lot's soul was vexed at the unclean conversation of the wicked, 2 Peter ii. 7. But, alas! how do we come short of this! The greatest number are so far from mourning for the abominations of the land, that they rather set themselves against God in a most disobedient manner, and press others to sin against him. Are magistrates of David's mind, to labour to cut off all workers of iniquity from the land? Indeed, for small trifling things they will do a man justice, but where is the tenderness of God's glory? Where are those that seek to reform idolatry, Sabbath-breaking, and profaneness amongst us? Pity it is to see how many do hold the stirrup to the devil, by giving occasions and encouragements to others to commit evil. Do we hate sin, when we are like tinder, ready to receive the least motion to it, as our fashion-mongers, who transform themselves into every effeminate unbeseeming guise? Shall we say that these men hate sin, which, when they are reproved for it, labour to defend it or excuse it, counting their pride but comeliness, their miserable covetousness but thirst,† and drunkenness only good fellowship?

* In margin here, 'Signs of a true hatred of sin.'—G. † Qu. 'thrift'?—Ed.

To strengthen our indignation against sin the better, consider,

1. *The ugliness thereof*, how opposite and distasteful it is to the Almighty, as appears in Sodom and in the old world. It is that for which God himself hates his own creature, and for which he will say to the wicked at the day of judgment, 'Go, ye cursed, into everlasting fire,' Mat. xxv. 41. Sin is the cause of all those diseases and crosses that befall the sons of men. It hath its rise from the devil, who is the father of it, and whose lusts we do whensoever we offend God.

There is not the least sin but it is committed against an infinite majesty, yea, against a good God, to whom we owe ourselves and all that we have, who waits when you will turn to him and live for ever; but if you despise his goodness, and continue still to provoke the eyes of his glory, is a terrible and revengeful* God, and ready every moment to destroy both body and soul in hell.

Sin is the bane of all comfort. That which we love more than our souls undoes us. It embitters every comfort, and makes that we cannot perform duties with spiritual life. Our very prayers are abominable to God so long as we live in known sin. What makes the hour of death and the day of judgment terrible but this?

2. Again, *Grow in the love of God*. The more we delight in him, the more we shall hate whatsoever is contrary to him. In that proportion that we affect God and his truth we will abhor every evil way, for these go together. Ye that love the Lord, hate the thing that is ill. The nearer we draw to him, the farther we are separated from everything below.

3. And to strengthen our indignation against sin, we should *drive our affections another way, and set them upon the right object*. A Christian should consider, Wherefore did God give me this affection of love? Was it to set it on this or that lust, or any sinful course? Or hath he given me this affection of hatred that I should envy my brethren, and condemn the good way? No, surely. I ought to improve every faculty of my soul to the glory of the giver, by loving that which he loves, and hating that which he hates. God's truth, his ways, and children, are objects worthy our love, and Satan with his deeds of darkness the fittest subjects of our indignation and hatred.

4. Fourthly, *True humiliation proceeds from faith*, and is in the faithful not only when judgment is upon them, but before the judgment comes, which they foreseeing by faith, do humble themselves. True humiliation quakes at the threatenings, for the very frowns of a father will terrify a dutiful child. As Josiah, when he did but hear of the threatenings against the land, he humbled himself in dust and ashes. 'He rent his clothes.' So true humiliation doth quake at the foresight of judgment, but the wicked never humble themselves but when the judgment is upon them. Carnal people are like men that, hearing thunder-claps afar off, are never a whit moved; but when it is present over their heads, then they tremble. So hypocrites care not for judgments afar off; as now when the church of God is in misery abroad we bless ourselves, and think all is well. It is no thanks for a man to be humbled when the judgment is upon him, for so Pharaoh was, who yet, when the judgment was off, then he goes to his old bias again.

Let us try our humiliation by these signs, whether we can willingly humble ourselves privately before God, and call ourselves to a reckoning; whether we add reformation of life to outward humiliation, when our heart

* That is, = 'avenging.'—G.

doth tell us that we live in such and such sins; whether our hearts tremble at the threatenings, when we hear of judgments public or private. What is the ground that may deceive themselves? They say, if any judgment come upon them, then they will repent, and cry to God for mercy; and why should I deny myself of my pleasures of sin before? Oh, this is but a forced humiliation, not from love to God, but love to thyself. It is not free, therefore thou mayest go to hell with it. Others defer off their repentance till it be too late. When they have any sickness upon them they will cry to God for mercy. This is but Ahab's and Pharaoh's humiliation. It is not out of any love to God, but merely forced. It is too late to do it when God hath seized upon us by any judgment. Do it when he doth threaten, and now he hath seized upon the parts of the church abroad already; therefore now meet thy God by repentance.

5. A fifth difference between true humiliation and false is, that *with true humiliation is joined hope*, to raise up our souls with some comfort, else it is a desperation, not a humiliation. The devils do chafe, vex, and fret themselves, in regard of their desperate estate, because they have no hope. If there be no hope, it is impossible there should be true and sound humiliation; but true humiliation doth carry us to God, that what we have taken out of ourselves by humiliation, we may recover it in God. Therefore humility is such a grace, that though it make us nothing in ourselves, yet doth it carry us to God, who is all in all. Humiliation works between God and ourselves, and makes the heart leave itself, to plant and pitch itself upon God, and looks for comfort and assurance from him. And where there is not this there is no true humiliation. There is nothing more profitable in the world than humility, because, though it seem to have nothing, yet it carrieth the soul to him that fills all in all. Hence it is, that there is an abasing of ourselves for anything that we have done amiss, from love to God and love to his people, but yet it is joined with hope. We know God to be a gracious God unto us, and therefore we humble ourselves, and are grieved for offending of him.

6. A sixth difference between true humiliation and false is this, *That hypocrites are sorrowful for the judgment that is upon them; but not for that which is the cause of the judgment*, which is sin; but the child of God, he is humbled for sin, which is the cause of all judgments. As good Josiah, when he heard read out of Deuteronomy the curses threatened for sin, and comparing the sins of his people with the sins against which the curses were threatened, he humbled himself for his sin and the sins of his people. For God's children know, if there were no iniquity in them, there should no adversity hurt them; and therefore they run to the cause, and are humbled for that. Whereas the wicked, they humble themselves only because of the smart and trouble which they do endure.

7. The last difference between true humiliation and false is this, *that true humiliation is a thorough humiliation.* Therefore it is twice repeated in this verse, 'thou didst humble thyself before God;' when thou heardest the words against this place, and against the inhabitants thereof, 'and humbledst thyself before me.' It is twice repeated in this verse, and afterward expressed by 'rending of clothes,' and 'tears.' It was thorough humiliation. For he dwelt upon the humbling of his own soul. So that the children of God thoroughly humble themselves, but the hypocrite, when he doth humble himself, it is not thoroughly. They count it a light matter. As soon as the judgment is off, they have forgotten their humiliation, as Pharaoh did. Many will heave a few sighs, and hang down the head like

a bulrush for a time; but it is, like Ephraim's morning dew, quickly gone. They have no sound and thorough humiliation. It is but a mere offer of humiliation. Whereas the children of God, when they begin, they never cease working upon their own hearts with meditation, until they have brought their heart to a blessed temper, as we see in David, Ezra, Nehemiah, and Daniel, how they did humble themselves.

But why do God's children take pains in humbling themselves?

Partly because it must be done to purpose, else God will not accept it; and partly because there is a great deal of hardness and pride in the best, and much ado before a man can be brought for to humble himself. Therefore we must labour for this. We see what ado there was before Job could be brought to humble himself. Yet Job must be humbled before there comes 'one of a thousand' to comfort him, as Job xxxiii. 23. If a man be once thoroughly and truly humbled, he shall soon have comfort. By these marks we may know true humiliation from an humiliation counterfeit.

Quest. But here may arise another question, How may we know when we are humbled enough, or when we are grieved enough?

Ans. To this I answer, 1. That *there is not the same measure of humiliation required in all.* For those whom God did pick out for some great work, he doth more humble them than others, as he did Moses and Paul before he wrought the great work of converting the Gentiles. So David, before he came to be king, was a long time humbled.

2. Again, *There are others that have been greater sinners, and more openly wicked in their courses than others,* and in them a greater measure of humiliation is required.

3. Again, *There are others that are more tenderly brought up from childhood,* who have often renewed their repentance. These need not to be humbled so much as others; for humiliation should be proportionable unto the sinful estate of the soul; which because it differs in divers men, in like manner their humiliation ought to differ. But to answer the question more directly, we are said to be humbled enough,

1. First, *When we have wrought our souls to a hearty grief that we have offended God,* when we have a perfect and inward hatred of all sin, and when thou dost shew the truth of thy grief by leaving off thy sinful courses. So that, dost thou hate and leave thy sinful course? Then thou art sufficiently humbled. Go away with peace and comfort, thy sins are forgiven thee. Therefore it is not a slight humiliation that will serve the turn, but our hearts must be wrought unto a perfect hatred and leaving of all sins; for if this be not, we are not sufficiently humbled as yet. And when we find ourselves to hate and leave sin in some measure, then fasten our souls by faith, as much as may be, upon the mercy of God in Jesus Christ. For the soul hath two eyes, the one to look upon itself and our vileness, to humble us the more; the other, to fasten upon the mercy of God in Christ, to raise up our souls. For if the whole soul were fastened upon its own misery and vileness, then there could not be that humiliation which ought to be, neither could we serve God with such cheerfulness; therefore we must have our souls raised up to God's mercy. Now let us labour for the first, because the devil is so main an enemy unto it; for he knows well enough, that so much as we are humble and go out of ourselves to God, and rest upon him, so much we stand impregnable against his temptations, that he cannot prevail against us; and so much as we do not trust in God, but upon the creature, so much must we lie open to his snares.

Therefore all his temptations tend to draw us to trust in the creature, to have a conceit of ourselves, and to draw our hearts from relying upon God. His first plot is always to make us rest in ourselves. Therefore let us labour to go out of ourselves, to see a vanity in ourselves, and a happiness in God, that so going out of ourselves, and relying upon God and his mercies, we may stand safe against Satan's temptations.

Use. This should teach us *to take heed of such affections as tend directly contrary to humiliation;* for how can it be but that those should be proud, that hold the doctrine of the Church of Rome, as, first, that we have no original sin in us, but it is taken away by baptism; that we are able to fulfil the law fully in this life. This is presumptuous. Whereas Paul cries out after baptism, 'O wretched man that I am, who shall deliver me from this body of death!' Rom. vii. 24. Nay, they can do more, namely, works of supererogation, whereby they merit heaven. How do these blow up the heart of man, and make it swell with pride! This must needs make men very proud, to think that a man can merit by works. With such blasphemous opinions they have infected the world, and led captive millions of souls into hell. Therefore let this be a rule of discerning true religion; for surely that is true religion which doth make us go out of ourselves; that takes away all from ourselves and gives all the glory to God; which makes us to plead for salvation by the mercy of God through the merits of Christ. But our religion doth teach us thus. Therefore it is the true religion, and will yield us sound comfort at the last. Thus much for inward humiliation, the humbling of ourselves, as Josiah did.

THE ART OF MOURNING.

SERMON III.

But because thine heart was tender, and thou didst humble thyself before God, when thou heardest his words against this place, and against the inhabitants thereof, and humbledst thyself before me, and didst rend thy clothes, and weep before me; I have even heard thee also, saith the Lord.—2 Chron. XXXIV. 27.

As the waters issuing from the sanctuary, mentioned by the prophet Ezekiel, grew deeper and deeper; first to the ancles, then to the knees, and after to the loins, until it came to an overflowing river, so hath it fared with us in handling of this text; wherein, from tenderness of heart, we have waded deeper and deeper through the mysteries of humiliation in the inward man, until at length from thence we are broken forth to the outward expressions of Josiah's inward humiliation, his 'rending of his clothes,' and overflowing floods of 'tears;' which sprung partly from his apprehension of ruin at hand, to come upon God's sanctuary, and partly from the sorrow and sense of sin in himself and the people, as causes of his fear.

But to come to the text now read in your hearing, 'And didst rend thy clothes, and weep before me,' here we have set down the outward expression of Josiah's inward humiliation.

For true humiliation shews itself as well outwardly as inwardly. Now, the outward expression of his inward affection is set down in two things:

1. By rending of his clothes; 2. By his weeping.

No doubt but he did express his sorrow as well by words as by these gestures, although they be not here set down with the other; for he might for the time be surprised with so great a measure of sorrow and grief, as could not be expressed presently at that instant, or we may conceive that for the time he was so thoroughly humbled, that he could not speak orderly. Wherefore God did regard and look more to his affections and tears than to his words, for he rent his clothes and wept before God. As it is written of the poor publican, that he could not say much, and looked down with his eyes, saying, 'Lord, be merciful to me a sinner,' Luke xviii. 13; and as it was with the poor woman in the gospel who came to Christ weeping, and washed his feet with her tears, yet she said nothing, Luke vii. 38; and as when Christ, upon the cock's third crowing, looked upon Peter, we find not what he said, but that he went out and wept bitterly, Luke xxii. 61, 62; so here, we may imagine Josiah's affection was too full of sorrow to speak distinctly and composedly; for from a troubled soul can proceed nothing but troubled words; from a broken heart comes broken language. But howsoever, likely it is that Josiah did speak somewhat; for God saith, 'I have even also heard thee.' But to leave this and come to the outward expressions here set down, let us learn somewhat from his rending of his clothes and weeping.

'Rending of clothes' was a thing frequently used in old times, as we see in the Scriptures; and it was a visible representation of the inward sorrow of the heart. Job rent his clothes, Job i. 20; his friends rent their clothes, Job ii. 12; Paul and Barnabas rent theirs, Acts xiv. 14; the high priest rent his clothes, being to accuse Christ, Mark xiv. 63; and Hezekiah rent his clothes when he heard the words of Rabshakeh, Isa. xxxvii. 1. Nay, this was a common action, and frequently used among the heathen also; for they likewise, upon any disastrous accident, were used to rend their clothes; as we read of a heathen king, that having his city invaded round about with enemies, rent his clothes.* So that it hath been the custom both of God's church and also of heathen, to rend their clothes. But what is the ground or reason of this? The reason of such their rending of clothes was, because that in their sorrow they thought themselves unworthy to wear any. They forgat all the comforts of this life; as holy Josiah forgets his estate, his throne, his royal majesty, and crown. He looks up to the great God, and considers duly whom he stood under, and the miserable estate of the people, over whom he was governor; and thereupon he rends his clothes, shewing hereby that he was unworthy of those ornaments wherewith he was covered. We know that clothes have divers uses; as,

1. First, For *necessity*, to cover our nakedness, and to preserve from the injuries of the weather.

2. Secondly, Clothes are given for *distinction of sexes and degrees:* to know the great man from the mean, the woman from the man.

3. And lastly, *They serve for ornaments* to honour our vile flesh, which is so base that it must fetch ornaments from base creatures. Now, so far as they served for ornaments, he rent his clothes, as thinking himself unworthy of any garments; for he being in grief doth rend his clothes, thinking with himself, why should I stand upon clothes and outward things to cover me? God is angry. Till he be appeased I will take no pleasure in any earthly thing. Therefore, apprehending tho wrath of God, he rent his clothes. Well, this is but an outward expression, and therefore it must proceed from inward truth. This rending of clothes was a national ceremony, which seeing we have not used amongst us, we must rend our hearts with grief. For the rending of clothes shews the rending of the heart before, without which there is no acceptance with God; for the rending of the clothes without the rending of the heart is but hypocrisy; as Joel ii. 13, he says, 'Rend your hearts, and not your garments, ye hypocrites.' So that outward expressions of sorrow are no further good, than when they come from inward grief and affection. Now, when both these are joined together it is a comely thing; for wherein stands comeliness but when all the parts of our body do agree in proportion, when one limb is not bigger than another? So it is uncomely and an hypocritical thing for a man to have all outward

* Query, Is this an allusion to the Sultan—the 'raging Turk' of the Puritans—in his anguish at the siege of Scodra? Cf. among others Trapp on Ezra ix. 3.—G.

expression and yet to have no inward grief. This is but acting of humiliation, when we hang down the head like a bulrush, and the heart is not sound. But outward expressions are good when the heart is grieved to purpose; when they proceed from inward humiliation.

Quest. And why ought this to be?

Ans. Because both body and soul have a part in the action of sin. Therefore it is needful that they should be joined in humiliation for sin. There is no sin of the body but the soul hath part in it, nor any sin in the soul but the body hath part in it. Therefore both body and soul should be humbled together. Labour then to have outward expressions and shows of sorrow come from a true sorrowful heart. There be two things in the religious actions of men.

1. There is the outward action or expression.
2. There is the inward, which gives life to the other.

The outward is easy, and subject to hypocrisy. It is an easy matter to rend clothes and to force tears, but it is a hard matter to afflict the soul. The heart of man taketh the easiest ways, and lets the hardest alone, thinking to please God with that. But God will not be served so; for he must have the inward affections, or else he doth abhor the outward actions. Therefore let us as well labour for humble hearts as humble gestures. We must rend our hearts and not our clothes, when we come into the presence of God. We must labour, as to shew humility, so to have humility, that so we be not like hypocrites, who make show of a great deal of devotion in carriage, but yet have none in heart; a great deal of outward humiliation, whenas they have none within.

The papists are wicked and erroneous in all their devotions, especially in the point of justification, and in other points of the worship of God; for is it not a superstitious error, to think to please God with outward observations, when they do not come from inward truth? Their religion is all an outside, consisting merely of outward performances. But true devotion, the Scripture teacheth, cometh from a heart judicially understanding the case of its own self; considering what a great God it hath to deal withal, a God full of glory and majesty. Doth God love blind sacrifices? No. Devotion must come from the heart, and spread itself from thence into the countenance and carriage. For then it is true, when the outward expression doth shew the inward disposition.

Use. This *reproves the negligence of people in these times.* Where is their inward humiliation? Nay, where is their outward humiliation? In popery, there is an acting of humiliation. They whip themselves in their bodies, and other such outward fooleries and gestures they have in their hypocritical devotions. Thus do they in some sort humble themselves. But how few are there amongst us that humble themselves in apprehension of their own misery, who yet, if they look to their own persons, have cause enough! Yea, and how few are there that are humbled for the miseries of the church abroad! Where shall we find a mourning soul?

Well, seeing it is not a custom amongst us to rend our clothes, yet let us make conscience of being proud in apparel; for it is a wicked and a fearful thing when men will regard some wicked and foolish fashion, and set more by it than by God's favour, threatenings, and judgments abroad. Many there are that, instead of rending their clothes, come into God's house to shew their bravery; to see and to be seen. Where they should most of all humble themselves, there they come to shew their pride, even before God. Whereas they should come to hear the voice of the great God of heaven, and stand in his presence, who is a 'consuming fire.' Before whom the very angels cover their faces and the earth trembles, they, contrariwise, come to outface and provoke him with their pride. We see Josiah, though he were a king, he rent his clothes, forgot all his bravery, and considers himself not so much a king over the people, over whom God had set him, as a subject to God. Wherefore, though, as I said, the custom of rending of clothes be not used in our church, yet let us ever make conscience of rending our hearts, and so to make our peace with God, as this good king did. It follows;—

'And weptest before me.'

In which words is set down *the second outward expression of Josiah's inward humiliation*, which is 'weeping.' This came nearer to him than rending of clothes, for it touched his body. Hence, in a word, observe,

Doct. 1. *That the body and soul must join together in the action of humiliation*, for the soul and body go together in the acting of sin, therefore they must go together in humiliation. As they were both made by God, and redeemed by Christ, so they sin and practise good together. Now I will shew three ways wherein the soul and body have communion one with another, whereby it may appear how reasonable and fitting a thing it is they should be both humbled together.

1. First, The soul and body have communion together *by way of impression or information*; for sensible things have an impression upon the senses, and so come into the soul; for nothing comes into it but through the senses of the body; because, though the soul may imagine golden mountains, and things that it never saw, yet the working of the soul depends upon the body, for the body informs it of all outward objects. As the body is beholding to the soul for the ruling and guiding of it, so the soul is beholding to the body for many things; as now in the very sacrament, God helps the soul with the senses; Christ, as it were, in the sacrament enters through the senses more lively than in the preaching of the word, for there he enters in by the ears, but in the sacrament he is seen, tasted, handled, felt. So that the soul and body have communion together by way of information.

2. Secondly, The soul and body have communion together *by way of temptation;* for the soul standing in need of many outward things which are pleasing and delightful, and having sympathy with the body, it is led away by the body. Outward objects are pleasing to the senses of carnal men. Now these passing through the senses into the soul, it is led away, and so they become a dangerous temptation.

3. Thirdly, The soul and the body have communion together, both in sinful and in good actions, *by way of subjection or execution;* for God hath made the body, with the parts thereof, to be the instruments and weapons of the soul. The body is a house wherein the soul is kept. It is a shop for the soul. Now the soul useth the body, with the members thereof, as instruments or weapons, either to honour God or dishonour him. The wicked fight against God with all the members of their body, with their eyes, tongue, feet, hands. Now the body having thus a part in sin, as well as the soul, therefore it is necessary that the body and soul should join together in humiliation.

Caution. Here we must take heed of a notable sleight of the devil in popery. The papists think the body only in fault for sin, and therefore they humble and afflict their bodies for it, while they puff up their soul with pride, a conceit of merit and satisfaction. They are falsely humble and truly proud, while they afflict the body and omit the soul. They are falsely humbled, because they humble their body only; but truly proud, because they think by afflicting and humbling their bodies to merit. But let us take heed of this gross error, and remember to let both soul and body join in the work.

Doct. 2. The second thing here to be noted is, that *when God will afflict or humble a man, it is not a kingdom that will save him.* As Josiah, though he were a monarch,—for he was an absolute monarch,—yet if God threaten, his kingdom can do him no good. If God will abase men, whether they be his children or enemies, it is not a kingdom can protect them. When God shewed Belshazzar the handwriting upon the wall, he could take no comfort in anything, Dan. v. 5; yea, his dear children, if he shew but tokens of his displeasure against them, though they be kings, as Josiah was, yet he can humble them. If God roar, it is not their greatness can keep them; if not now, yet he will make them to tremble hereafter.

Doct. 3. The third thing here that we learn from the example of Josiah, being a king, is, *That tears and mourning for sin, when it comes from inward grief, is a temper well befitting any man.* It is a carriage befitting a king. It is not unbeseeming any, of what sex or degree soever. It is no womanish or base thing. When one hath to deal with God, he must forget his estate and take the best way to meet with God. This is evident by many instances, for David, though a man of war, yet when he had to deal with God he watered his couch with his tears, Ps. vi. 6. So Hezekiah, though a great king, yet he humbled himself, Isa. xxxviii. 1, *seq.* Nay, our blessed Saviour himself did it 'with strong cries and tears,' Heb. v. 7, when he had to deal with God.

Use. This serves *for the justification of this holy abasement and humbling of ourselves.* When we have to deal with God, then all abasement is little enough. 'I will be yet more vile than thus,' saith holy David, 2 Sam. vi. 22. So let us say when we have to deal with God; I will be yet more vile, and so cast ourselves down before the Lord. All expression of devotion is little enough, so it be without hypocrisy. Yet I pray give me leave once again to give warning unto you concerning outward actions, for most have conceived wrong of devotion and humiliation. They think that devotion is only in outward actions; as in outward act to hear a little, to read, confer, or pray a little, whereas in truth these outward acts do only make up the body of devotion, which, without the soul, namely, the inward religious affection, looking unto God, is no better than a dead carrion. Our outward expression must come from the apprehension of the goodness, mercy, and justice of God, before whom the very angels veil their faces. It is not outward devotion that will serve the turn, as to come to the church with this bare conceit and forethought; I will go pray, and kneel, and express all outward carriage, in the meantime neglecting to stir up the soul to worship God with these or like thoughts; I will go to the place where God is, where his truth is, where his angels are, to hear that word whereby I shall be judged at the last day. Therefore let all holy actions come from within first, and thence to the outward man. Let us work upon our hearts a consideration of the goodness, justice, majesty, and mercy of God, and then let there be an expression in body, such as may bring men off from their sins; for else there is a spirit of superstition that will draw men far from God in seeming services, conceiving that God will accept of outward and formal expressions only. Well, we see that weeping and mourning for sins is a carriage not unbeseeming for a king. Therefore it is a desperate madness not to humble ourselves and be abased, now we have to deal with God. Your desperate atheists of the world will not tremble at threatenings, nor humble themselves till death comes, which humbles them and makes them tremble; whereas, on the contrary, that soul which, feeling the wrath of God, humbles itself betimes, and trembles at threatenings, that soul, I say,—when the great judgment of death comes, and appearance before God,—looks death in the face with comfort; whereas your desperate atheists, that can now scorn God, swear at every word, and blaspheme God to his face; let God but shew his displeasure, they tremble and quake upon any noise of fear. Therefore when we have to deal with God, it is wisdom, and the ground of all courage, to humble and abase ourselves with fear, as Josiah did although he were a king.

'And thou didst weep before me.'

His tender heart did melt itself into tears. In the first clause of the verse you have his tender heart set down, and here we have *the melting of the tender heart*. There we have the cloud, here we have the shower. Therefore I will speak something of the original of tears. We know that tears are strained from the inward parts, through the eyes; for the understanding first conceiveth cause of grief upon the heart, after which the heart sends up matter of grief to the brain, and the brain being of a cold nature, doth distil it down into tears; so that if the grief be sharp and piercing, there will follow tears after from most. But to come to the particulars; we see the provoking cause of tears, from without, in Josiah, was the danger of his kingdom, hearing the judgment of God threatened against his country and place. Whence, for the instruction of magistrates, I will enforce this point.

Doct. 4. *That it concerns magistrates above all others, to take to heart any danger whatsoever, that is upon their people;* for as kings are set above all other people in place, so they should be above them in goodness and grace. They ought, above all others, to take to heart any judgment, either upon them already, or feared; as good Josiah did, whom, while he looked not so much to himself and his own good, as to that state whereof he was king, the very threatenings of judgment against it, made to express his grief with tears. The bond that knits the king to the people, and the people to the king, requires this; for kings are heads, and shepherds over the people. Now the shepherd watcheth over his flock; the head is quickly sensible of any hurt of the body; all the senses are provident for the body. So it should be with all great persons in authority. They should cherish the good estate of the subjects as their own; for they are committed to their care. And even as the head doth care for the body, and forecast for it, so those that are in authority should forecast for any good to the body of the commonwealth. An excellent example of this we have in holy David; who, when there was a judgment coming upon his people, Lord, saith he, let the judgment come upon me and my father's house; what have these sheep done?' 2 Sam. xxiv. 17. And surely such magistrates as are tenderly affected with the case of those under them, shall lose nothing by it; for the people likewise will carry a tender affection towards them again. As we see, when the people went to fight against Absalom, they would not let David go with them, but they said to him, 'Thou art worth ten thousand of us,' 2 Sam. xviii. 3; that is, they had rather that ten thousand of them should die in the battle, than that David should have any hurt come to him; so he lost nothing for his love and affection towards the people, for they shewed the like love to him in his distress. So likewise when Josiah was dead, the people wept largely for him (for with him perished all the glory of that flourishing kingdom), as we may read in the story, 2 Chron. xxxv. 24, 25, compared with Zech. xii. 11. They mourned for him with an exceeding great mourning, in Hadadrimmon, in the valley of Megiddo. So that there is no love lost between the magistrate and the people; for if the magistrate be tenderly affected to them, the people will likewise weep for him again, and lament his case in his distress. But now to come to a more general instruction, we will leave speaking of Josiah as king, and take him into consideration as an holy man, and make him a pattern unto us all, of whatsoever civil condition we be; and so we learn this point,

Doct. 5. That *it is the duty of every Christian to take to heart the threatenings of God against the place and people where he doth live;* to take to heart the afflictions and miseries of the church and commonwealth, the grievances of others as well as his own. The mourning and weeping of Josiah was for the estate of the church, when he heard the judgment threatened against the place and inhabitants thereof. There be tears of compassion for ourselves and for others. There were both of them in Josiah; for no doubt but he wept for himself and his own sins, and over and above his own had special tears of compassion for his people. Thus then it becomes a Christian that will have the reward of Josiah, to abase his heart as he did for the estate of the church. Good Nehemiah took to heart the grief of his country. The joy of his own preferment did not so much glad him, as the grief for his nation the Jews cast him down. What joy can a true heart have, now the church of God is in affliction? We are all of one house. When one part of the house is a-fire, the other part had need to look to itself. There were many things wrought upon the heart of Josiah, which caused him to weep; so there are many causes should move us, as the seeing of the sins that are committed in the land ought to make us grieve, and to express our grief one way or other. And the love of Christ, were it in us, would make us mourn; as when we hear God blasphemed, and his name dishonoured, and when we see the people bent to idolatry; how can this but break even a heart of stone, nay, a gracious heart will mourn and weep for the judgment of God upon wicked men, considering them as men, and as the creatures of God. Thus Christ wept for the wicked Jews in Jerusalem, though they were his enemies: 'O Jerusalem, Jerusalem,' &c., Luke xix. 41; and so good Jeremiah, though he were ill used, and exceedingly abused by the people, yet he saith, 'Oh that my head were water, and mine eyes a fountain of tears, that I might weep day and night for them,' Jer. ix. 1. Though they had wronged, persecuted, and counted him a contentious fellow, only because he taught the truth of God; yet such was the affection of tender-hearted Jeremiah, that he desired that he might weep day and night for them. But continual weeping must have a lasting spring affording continual issues of tears, which Jeremiah not finding in himself (such is the dryness of every man's heart, that it is soon emptied of tears), and thereupon fearing he should not weep enough, he doth earnestly desire it, and if hearty wishes may obtain, he would have it to be supplied with a plentiful measure of tears in his lamentation for the ensuing calamity of his people: 'O that mine head were a well of water, and mine eyes a fountain of tears, that I might weep day and night for the slain of the daughter of my people!'

Quest. But why did not Jeremiah rather pray that they had a fountain of tears to weep for themselves?

Ans. Because he, knowing the hardness of their hearts, thought it to no end to entreat them to weep for themselves. Their hearts were harder than the nether millstone. They never desired it, yet he weeps for them. Thus we see how godly men have been formerly affected, and [that] it is our duty even to weep and mourn for the very wicked. We have matter enough of lamentation and weepings at this day, if we look abroad; and at home, if we look to judgments felt and feared, we have cause to weep, before the decree come out against us. Therefore we should meet God beforehand. It is no thank for a man to be humbled when the judgment is come upon him; but when we can weep before the judgment is come, it is a sign of faith. Happy were we if faith could make us do that which sense makes wicked men to do. If the believing of the judgment before it come would make us seek unto God, Oh how God would love such a one! This should teach us every one to mourn; and indeed a Christian soul cannot but do it, and that for divers reasons.

1. First, *Because of that sympathy between the Head and the members.* A Christian hath the spirit of Christ, who takes to heart the miseries of the church. Now, can that spirit of Christ be in any, and he not affected as Christ in heaven is affected? Surely no.

2. Again, It must needs be so *in regard of the communion which is between the members of the body.* We are all a part of one mystical body, whereof Christ is the head. What member can he be of this body that doth not take to heart the miseries of the other members? There is want of life where there is no sense of misery.

3. Thirdly, Where there is true grace there will be weeping and mourning for the church, in regard of *the insolency of the church's enemies* and their blasphemous speeches. Where is now their God? their religion? What is now become of their Reformation? What child can hear the reproach and dishonour of God his Father without bowels of compassion?

4. Again, A gracious man will weep in regard of *the danger of not mourning;* for by not mourning we have a kind of guilt lying upon us, for we make the sins and miseries of the church our own, as Paul tells the Corinthians, reproving them for not mourning, 1 Cor. v. 2. Therefore as we are a part of the body, so we must have a part of the shame and grief. Again, God hath promised to mark and single out all those that mourn for the sins of the time; therefore, on the contrary, those that do not mourn are in a dangerous estate, Ezek. ix. 4.

5. Again, We must add *reformation unto lamentation*, else the whole church and commonwealth is in danger. If Achan be not sought out and punished, the whole state is in danger, and lies open to the wrath of God.

For these reasons we ought to take to heart the sins and miseries of the times; for the Spirit of God is in every Christian, that will not suffer him otherwise to be, than to weep and mourn for his own sins, and for the sins and miseries of others.

Use 1. If this be so, what will become of those that take not to heart nor mourn for the miseries of the church? that judge not aright of the poor, but censure the judgment of the afflicted, add affliction to the afflicted and misery to the miserable? What shall we say to those that are so far from helping God, that they help the enemies of God, and are grieved at the heart to hear any cause of comfort on the church's part? whose hearts it doth joy to hear of any overthrow on the church's side? Such false hearts there are, and many that are glad of the sins of others, thinking thereby to hide their own wicked courses. These men are far from mourning. Let our souls also be far from entering into their secrets.

Use 2. If this be so, that holy men ought to take to heart and weep for the judgments of the commonwealth, both felt and feared, and also for the judgment of God upon the churches abroad, then

Quest. How may we get this weeping and mourning for others? I answer,

Ans. 1. First, *Remove the impediments that hinder;* as, first, a hard and stony heart, which is opposite to tenderness. Josiah had a melting heart, and therefore it was soon dissolved into tears. Our hearts are worse than brass or stone, for workmen can work upon them; but nothing will work upon the hard heart of man. All the judgments in the world will not work upon it; for all the Israelites saw the judgments of God in Egypt, and all his mercies and blessings unto them in the wilderness, yet it would not work upon them, because they had hard hearts. Therefore let us get a good spring of tears, that is, a soft and tender heart, and let us beg it of God, for it is his promise to give us tender hearts; and then there will be an easy expression of it in the outward man.

2. The second, *Let us beware of the love of earthly things, and get a heart truly loving towards God;* for love is compared to fire; and fire, among many other properties it hath, melts the gold, and makes it pliable. Heat is the organ of the soul, whereby it doth anything, and the instrument of nature. So spiritual heat, a warm soul, warmed with the love of God and of our Christian brethren, will make the heart pliable, and melt into tears. Therefore get a loving heart, filled with love to God and Christian brethren, that we may mortify self-love, which dries up the soul. There can be no melting in such a self-loved soul. Let us therefore labour for spiritual love, to cross and subdue carnal self-love. It is this blessed heat that must send forth this heavenly water of tears; it is the spirit of love that must yield this distillation from the broken heart; this works all heavenly affection in us. Therefore Christ compriseth all the commandments under love. And indeed that is all.

3. Thirdly, If we would have our souls fit to grieve, *let us be content to see as much as we can, with our own eyes, the miseries of others.* The best way to weep is to enter into the house of mourning, and set before our eyes the afflictions of others. The very sight of misery is a means to make the soul weep. And let us be willing to hear that which we cannot see; as Nehemiah was content to hear, nay, to inquire, concerning the church abroad; and when he heard that it was not well with them, it made him weep. Every man will cry, What news? But where is the man, when he hears of the news beyond the seas, that sends up sighs to God? prayer, that he would take pity upon his church? It is a good way to use our senses, to help our souls to grieve.

4. Again, *Let us read [of] the estate of God's church*, what it hath been from the beginning of the world; what miseries God's children have endured in former ages by reason of war and the like, that so we may work grief upon our own hearts. We have always matter of grief while we are in this world; if we look abroad, we shall find matter of mourning. And surely we should labour to mourn if we desire to be blessed. For 'blessed are they that mourn: they shall be comforted,' Mat. v. 4.

5. Fifthly, That we may get this weeping and mourning, *let us work this tender affection upon our own hearts.* The soul hath a facutly to work upon

itself. Therefore let us shame ourselves for our own deadness, dryness, and spiritual barrenness this way, that we can yield no sighs, no tears for God, for his church and glory. Let us reason thus with our souls: If I should lose my wife, or child, or my estate, this naughty heart of mine would weep and be grieved; but now there is greater cause of mourning for myself and the church of God, and yet I cannot grieve. Augustine saith he could weep for her that killed herself out of love to him, but he could not weep for his own want of love to God.* We have many that will weep for the loss of friends, wealth, and such like things, but let them lose God's favour, be in such an estate there is but one step between them and hell, they are never grieved nor moved at it. Therefore, seeing they do not weep for themselves, let us weep for them. Can we weep when we see a man hurt in his body, and ought we not much more for the danger of his soul? Therefore let us work this sorrow upon our hearts. Now, we are to receive the sacrament, which is a feast, and therefore must be eaten cheerfully. The passover was a banquet, and therefore to be eaten with joy, but withal it was used to be eaten with sour herbs. So must it be in this blessed banquet which God hath provided for our souls. There must be sorrow as well as joy. It is a mixed action, and therefore it must be eaten with sour herbs, presenting to the eyes of our mind the object of the old Adam; thinking upon the vileness of our nature, that have such filthy speeches, disobedient actions, such rebellious thoughts in us. Great need have I of the mercy and favour of God to look upon such a defiled soul as I am. And also, having in the eyes of our soul Christ crucified, look upon Christ, which is crucified in the sacrament, sacramentally. What was that which broke the body of Christ? Was it not sin? That sin which I so often cherish, this pride, this envy, unbelief, and hypocrisy, this covetousness of mind was that which put Christ into such torment. It was not the nails, but my sins. The sacrament must work upon our hearts so as to work grief in us. We must weep as the people did for Josiah, according as God hath promised we should do. It is said, Zech. xii. 10, 'They shall look on him whom they have pierced by their sins, and weep and mourn for him as one that mourneth for his only son.' So then, the sacrament is not only a matter of joy and thanks, but a matter of sorrow. Therefore, if we would joy in the sacrament, let us first be humbled for sin, and then joy in it afterwards.

Obj. But here it might be objected, Are we not bid for to rejoice always? and always to be thankful? 1 Thes. v. 16. Then how can these agree? for weeping and mourning are contrary to thanksgiving and joy.

Ans. To this I answer, that the estate of a Christian in this life is a mixed estate, both inward and outward; his outward estate and the inward disposition of the soul is mixed. Therefore, having this mixed estate, our carriage must [be] answerable; as we have always cause of mourning and rejoicing both from that in us and from without us, therefore a Christian ought to rejoice always, and in some measure to mourn always. As, for example,

A Christian hath cause of mourning within him when he looks upon his sinful nature and the sins which he doth daily commit, yet notwithstanding, at the same time, there is cause of joy, and great reason to bless God, when he considers that God hath pardoned his sins in Christ. Thus the apostle did, Rom. vii. 24; when he looked upon himself and his own vileness, he cries out, 'O wretched man that I am, who shall deliver me from this

* Augustine on the death of his mother Monica.—G.

body of death!' yet for all this, at the same time he rejoiceth and blesseth God: 'I thank God through Jesus Christ my Lord, who hath freed me from the law of sin and of death.' Thus, you see, we have always in respect of ourselves both cause of joy and mourning, therefore we must do both. So have we in like manner continual causes both of joy and sorrow from without us, if we look to the church of God: of joy, in regard there is a God in heaven who hath an eye to his church, who pitieth it and tendereth* it as the apple of his eye; that takes to heart the afflictions of it; that will be glorious in the midst of the troubles of his people, by upholding, comforting, and turning all to the best for them;—of sorrow also, in respect of the miseries under which the church of God doth groan, of which we are bound to take notice, and so to weep with them that weep, Isa. xxii. 12; Amos vi. 6; Rom. xii. 15. You see the rare mixture of joy and sorrow in a Christian, whereby he is made capable of this great privilege, as neither to be swallowed up of grief, because that his sorrow proceeds from a heart where there is cause of joy, nor to lose himself in excessive joy, because he always sees in himself cause of sorrow. Now, as it is to be seen in other mixtures that there is not at all times an equal quantity or portion of each particular thing to be mingled, but now more of the one, and at another time more of the other, according as the cause doth vary, so is it in this mixture of joy and sorrow for ourselves and for others; sometimes joy must abound with the causes of it, and sometimes sorrow with its causes doth superabound. It will be worth our inquiry, therefore, to know when to joy most, and when to weep most, which we shall know by God's call in outward occasions, and by the spirit of discretion within us, which will guide us. For God hath given his children a spirit of discretion, that will teach them when to joy and when to weep most. As God calls to mourning now in these times that the church of God is in misery, as he calls for sighs for the afflictions of Joseph, so the spirit of discretion within us doth tell us what to do.

Quest. Yet here may be a question, How shall we know when to cease and leave off mourning? for the soul is a finite thing, and cannot dwell upon one action always, because it hath many things to do; and therefore it cannot always mourn nor always rejoice.

Ans. To this I answer, that we have mourned enough, and discharged our duty sufficiently therein, when we have overcome our hearts, and brought them to a temper of mourning, and have complained before God, spread the ill of the times before him, and entreated pity from him, having poured out ourselves in prayer, though short, yet effectual. When we have this done, then we have discharged our duty in mourning, and may turn to other occasions as God doth require of us; for when we have mourned and wept, then we must look upon causes of rejoicing and thanksgiving. We must always remember so to mourn and weep that yet notwithstanding, looking upon God's blessing upon us both in kingdom, state, and our own particular persons, we may be excited to thankfulness; for we must not always be sullen, looking upon the evil, but casting our eyes upon the good things we do enjoy, we must provoke ourselves to be thankful. Even as men that have their eyes dazzled will look upon some green colour to recover their sight again, so when we have wrought upon our souls and brought them to mourn, then to help and raise them up, we ought to look upon causes of joy and thankfulness. We have cause of thankfulness when we consider that many churches in France and other places are invaded by enemies,

* That is, 'guardeth.'—G.

oppressed with cruelty, and deprived of liberty, while yet we enjoy the liberty and free passage of the gospel, being freed from the destruction of war and pestilence, which devoureth so many that it makes the land to mourn. He continueth to us liberty to hear the word, and gives us many blessings which others have not. Nay, we have cause to bless God for freeing us from that terriblest judgment of all judgments,—which makes both church and commonwealth to mourn,—because he doth not suffer us to fall into the hands of man, but takes us into his own hand to correct. It is God's infinite mercy that he doth not humble us by our enemies, but takes us into his own hand. Therefore let us not provoke him, lest he give us up to the hands of our merciless enemies, which is a terrible judgment. We had better an hundred times meet him by repentance, and cast ourselves into his hands, for then we have only to deal with a merciful God; but when we are to deal with merciless men that scorn the gospel, then we have both God and them to deal with, which doubles our affection.

Therefore let us mourn, seeing we have cause, for ourselves and the estates of others; but yet let us be thankful, for if we would be more thankful for God's benefits, we should have them longer continued. For, as prayer begs blessings, so thanksgiving continues them. As the best way to obtain good things is prayer and mourning, so the best way to preserve them is thanksgiving and rejoicing. So, then, we have plainly seen that Christians should not always be dumpish and look sourly, but they must as well rejoice and be thankful, as mourn and weep.

Quest. 1. But here, ere I proceed, I must answer some cases of conscience. As, first, What shall we say to those souls that cannot weep for the sins and miseries of the church, and therefore complain for the want of it?

Secondly, What shall we say to that soul that can weep, but more for outward than for spiritual things?

Sol. 1. To the first I answer briefly, that we must not speak friar-like of tears, and never know from whence they come. But when we speak of weeping, we must always understand that tears are no further good than when they spring from sorrow and love within, than when they proceed from inward hatred to sin, and from fear and love to the church of God. If this be in a man, the matter is not much for tears. There may be weeping without true sorrow, as there was in Esau for the blessing, Gen. xxvii. 38; and so the Jews, they could weep and howl upon their beds when there was a famine, yet there was no sound sorrow in them.

And, on the contrary, there may be true sorrow without weeping, yea, and such may it be that there can be no weeping, because their sorrow may be so great that it is rather an astonishment than a weeping. In a fresh wound in the body, at the first there is not such pain felt nor the blood seen, because the part is astonied only; so the soul for a time may be in such an astonishment and grief that there may be no expression of tears. Again, the soul doth follow the temperature of the body. Some are of a more easy constitution to shed tears than others, so that there may be more grief where there are fewest tears.

But to come to the question more directly, we ought to think our estates not so good as they should be, if we cannot at one time or other weep for the sins and miseries of the church. If we can shed tears for outward things at one time or other, and cannot weep for spiritual, it is a bad sign; for certainly, one time or other ordinarily God's children express their sorrow for their sins, and the estate of the church, by tears. They either have tears for spiritual respects, or else they mourn that they cannot mourn, grieve that they cannot grieve, and desire that they might mourn and that they could weep. They wish with Jeremiah that their head were a fountain of tears, they wish they might have their bodies to answer the intent of their soul, that so they might largely express outwardly their inward grief. As Jeremiah feared he should not have tears enough, therefore wished that his head were a fountain of tears, so they desire, Oh that I could mourn, and that I could weep!

Sol. 2. But what shall we say to those that can weep for other things? Shall they be condemned for hypocrites?

1. I answer, No; for a torrent may run faster for the present than a continual current; so on the sudden there may be tears and grief for outward things, but yet grief for sin is more because of the continuance thereof. For sin is a continual cause of sorrow. Whereas sorrow for outward things is but on a sudden, as it was in David when he cried, 'Oh my son Absalom, my son Absalom!' 2 Sam. xviii. 33. What ado is here on the sudden for Absalom! but yet he wept for his sins more, because that was a continual grief. So in a Christian, there may be some sudden passion, when he may seem to weep and grieve most for outward things, but yet his grief for sin and the misery of the church is more, because it is a continual grief.

2. Again, Spiritual grief comes from spiritual causes. Tears for sin, and for the church of God, do issue merely from spiritual grounds; whereas in natural grief for outward things, we have both the Spirit and nature that make us grieve. Now when both these meet together, they carry the soul strongly, as in a stream. So that there must needs be more tears and grief for outward things. As when the windows of heaven were opened from above, and the foundations below were broken up, there must needs follow a great flood, Gen. vii. 11; so when we have the Spirit from above, and our nature below, there must of necessity be a great grief for outward things. But yet in these cases, a little of spiritual sorrow is better than a great deal of natural, for spiritual grief fats the soul. As the river Nile runs through Egypt, and fats the land, so this heavenly water of tears and grief fattens the soul, and makes it fit for all holy services. They are both good, but one less than the other. Natural grief is allowable, which if a man have not, he is in a reprobate sense; for the apostle reckons this up as a great sin, that in the latter days men should be without natural affection. So then we see, that for this reason also there may be a great store of grief and tears for outward things.

3. Again, Let them that grieve that they cannot more grieve, know and comfort themselves, that they have the Spirit of God within them, which is an everlasting spring that will in time overcome all carnal and worldly respects whatsoever, and make the heart in a fit temper of weeping and grieving for spiritual respects.

Use. Well, if this be thus, what shall we think of the jovial people of the world, who are so far from this sorrow, that—when a man shall come and ask them when they wept for their sins, when they did ever mourn and send up sighs to God for their swearing, lying, profanation of God's Sabbath, for the wrong they have done to others, or for any of their sins—the time was never yet wherein they ever shed a tear for sin, or had a sigh, groan, or mourning for sin? In what estate are we born in? All children of wrath, and heirs of damnation. But when got you out of this state? You have ever lived in jollity. Therefore as yet you are as you were born, a child of wrath. Do ye think to reap, and never sow? to reap in joy, and never sow in tears? God puts all his children's tears in a bottle; but thou sparest God a labour, because thou never weepest. There are a company that engross all jollity and mirth, as if they had no cause to weep, whose language yet when any man hears, and observes their courses and living in gross sins, he may quickly judge that they of all others have most cause to weep, though there be none more free from mourning, and though they seem to be the only men of the world. But I say to such, go weep, howl, and lament for your sins; for your peace is not yet made with God. Therefore never rest till thou hast got an assurance from heaven that thy sins are forgiven thee. Many people are angry because ministers tell them of this, but surely we must be damned if we do not.

Therefore, as any would hope for comfort, and have God to wipe away their tears from them in another world, let them work upon their hearts here, to shed tears for their own sins first, and then for the sins of the time; for their own first, I say, for a man must first be good in himself before he can be good to others; and then let their grief extend to their brethren even beyond the seas, to the forlorn estate of the church there.

Now the last thing that is noted in Josiah's weeping, is the sincerity of it. 'Thou hast wept *before me*;' that is, sincerely, before God. He sinned before him, and is humbled before him. There is nothing hid from his sight, not only open sins, but he knows the very thoughts of our hearts: therefore let us weep before him without hypocrisy. No matter whether the world see it or no; but let us weep before God, as the prophet saith, Jer. xiii. 17, 'My soul shall weep in secret for you, and mine eyes shall weep, and drop down tears in the night season.' Let us weep in secret before God; for this is without hypocrisy. Now follows the issue of his weeping and humbling of himself.

'I have even heard thee also,' saith the Lord.

In which words is set down *God's gracious acceptation of Josiah's humiliation;* which was not without his special observation. 'For I have even heard thee,' saith the Lord: so that it seems Josiah did utter some words of grief, because God saith, 'I have *heard it.* And we may the rather think so, because usually God's children do in their prayers add words unto their tears, as David and good Hezekiah did. Howsoever then his prayer was not a distinct prayer of a composed tenor of speech; yet it was a prayer, because that with these tears he did send up sighs, and groans, and uttered broken words from a broken heart. There was such a language in his heart that God did understand, for God understands the language of his own Spirit in the hearts of his children. The Spirit knows what we mean, as Rom. viii. 26, 27. God hath an ear to hear our desires, our sighs and groans; for tears have the weight of a voice, they speak for us. Where there is true grief, many times there cannot come a composed tenor of speech; for a broken heart expresseth itself more in sighs, groans, and tears, than in words. Though we do not utter distinct words in a form of prayer, yet he hears our sighs and groans: his ears are open to the cries of his children. So we learn from hence, for our comfort against all Satan's temptations,

Doct. 6. *That God takes a particular notice, and understands the prayers we make unto him:* he hears the groans of his children. So David saith, 'My groaning is not hid from thee,' Ps. xxxviii. 9. So the prophet says, Ps. clxv. 18, 19, 'He will fulfil the desire of them that hear* him; he will also

* Qu. 'fear?'—Ed.

hear their cry, and will save them;' yea, he knows our thoughts long before. This must needs be so.

Reason 1. First, Because he is gracious and merciful; he is a God hearing prayers.

2. Because of the relations which in his love he hath taken upon himself, to be a Father. So that when a man shall, by the Spirit of adoption, call God Father, there is such a deal of eloquence and rhetoric in this very word, it works so upon the bowels of God, that he cannot choose but hear. Even as a child, when he speaks to his father, and calls him by this name, this word father doth so work upon him that he cannot but hear. So it is with God; when he hears us call him Father, he cannot but hear us.

3. Because of his nature and love, which is above the love of an earthly father. Though a mother should forget, and not hear her child, yet the Lord will hear us.

And likewise this is his promise: 'Call upon me in the day of trouble, and I will hear thee, and thou shalt glorify me,' Ps. l. 15.

4. Again, God cannot basely esteem of our prayers, because they are the motions of his own Spirit. Oh, but they are broken prayers. It is true; but the Spirit understands them and makes intercession for us, with sighs and groans that cannot be expressed; and none can understand them but the Spirit, Rom. viii. 26, 27.

6. Again, God cannot but hear our prayers, because they are offered up in the name of a mediator. They are perfumed with the incense and sacrifice of his Son. Therefore he cannot but hear them.

7. Again, God must needs hear our prayers, because they are made according to his will. When we pray for ourselves, and for the church of God, it is according to God's will. So then, if we consider these respects, God cannot but hear our prayers.

Obj. But some will object, God doth not hear me: I have prayed a long while, and yet he hath not given me an answer.

Ans. 1. I answer, God doth always hear, though he seemeth not to hear sometimes, to increase our importunity. Christ heard the woman of Canaan at first; but yet, to increase her importunity, he gave her the repulse and denial, and with the same, inward strength to wrestle with him.

Ans. 2. Again, God seems not to hear, because he delights in the music of his children's prayers. Oh how he loves to hear the voice of his children! As a father to hear the language of his child, though it be none of the best; so it is sweet music in God's ears to hear the prayers of his children. He will have prayers to be cries. Therefore he defers to hear; but in deferring he doth not defer, for he increaseth our strength, as in Jacob's wrestling, that we might cry after him, wrestle with him, and offer violence unto him again.

Ans. 3. And sometimes, indeed, he will not hear us, because, it may be, there is some secret Achan in the camp, or some Jonah in the ship; some sin, I mean, in the heart unrepented of; for in this case we may come before God again and again, and he not hear us. This is the reason why God hears not many Christians, because they have not made a thorough inquisition into their own estates, found out their sins, and humbled themselves for it. Thus we see for what reasons God defers to hear our prayers.

Use 1. If this be so, that God doth hear us, let us make this use, to be plentiful in prayers, and lay up a great store of them in the bosom of God, for this is that will do us the most good. He hears every one in due time. We do never lose a sigh, a tear, or anything that is good, which proceeds from his own Spirit, but he will answer abundantly in his own time. For he that gives a desire, and prepares our heart to pray, and gives us a Mediator by whom to offer them up, will doubtless accept of them in his own Son, and will answer them. The time will come when he will accept of nothing else, and we shall have no other thing to offer up. What a comfort will it then be, that we have in former times, and can now call upon God! The day is coming when goods will do us no good, but prayers will. What a comfort then is it to a Christian, that he hath a God to go to, that hears his prayers! Let all the world join together against a Christian, take away all things else and cast him into a dungeon, yet they cannot take away his God from him. What a happiness is it to pray! We can never be miserable so long as we have the Spirit of prayer. Though we were in a dungeon with Jeremiah, or in the whale's belly with Jonah, yea, though in hell, yet there we might have cause of comfort.

Let us therefore be ashamed of our barrenness in this duty, and observe whether God hear our prayers, or else how can we be thankful? There be many that pray, because their consciences do force them to some devotion, and therefore they slubber over a few prayers that their consciences may not smite them, but they never observe the issue of their prayers, whether God hears them or not; whereas God is a God hearing prayers, and the child of God doth esteem of nothing but that which he hath from God, as a fruit of prayer, and therefore accordingly he doth return thanks. God will have his children beg all of him. As some fathers will give nothing to their children, but they will have them first ask it of them, so God will give us nothing but what we pray for. And though he doth exceed to give us more than we ask, yet he looks that we should return thanks in some measure proportionable to the benefit received. Therefore let us observe how God hears our prayers, that so we may be suitably thankful. This will strengthen our faith in evil times when we can thus plead with God. Hear, Lord! Heretofore I came before thee, though weakly, yet with a broken heart, and thou didst hear me then. Thou art still a God hearing prayer, therefore, Lord, look upon my estate now and help me. Seeing, then, God hears our prayers, let us think of this glorious privilege, that we have liberty to go to the throne of grace in all our wants. The whole world is not worth this one privilege. We cannot command the prince's ear at all times; but we have a God always to go to, that will hear us. What a wretched folly is it therefore of those that, by their sins, bring themselves into such a condition that they cannot have God to hear them.

Quest. But how shall we make such prayers as God will hear?

Ans. I answer first of all, Would we be in such an estate that we may enjoy this blessed privilege, to have God's ear ready to hear?

1. First, Then hear him. If we will have God to hear us, then let us hear God, as Josiah did. When he heard the word read, his heart melted. For 'he that turneth away his ears from hearing the law, even his prayers shall be abominable,' saith God, Prov. xxviii. 9.

And is it not good reason, think we, for God not to hear us, when we will not hear him? Prov. i. 24, 25, 'Because I have called, and you have refused; when you are in misery, and shall out of self-love cry to me to be delivered, then I will refuse to hear you,' saith the Lord. Therefore let all profane persons, that will not hear God, know a time will come, that though they cry and roar, yet he will not hear them.

2. Secondly, If we will have God hear our prayers, they must proceed from a broken heart. Prayers be the sacrifice of a broken spirit. Josiah

had a tender and a broken heart, and therefore God could not despise his prayers. So David pleads with God: Ps. li. 17, 'The sacrifice of God is a broken and a contrite spirit.' So holy Bernard saith, 'I have led a life unbefitting me; but yet my comfort is, that a broken heart and a contrite spirit, Lord, thou wilt not despise.'* God will hear the prayers and tears of relenting hearts.

3. Thirdly, To strengthen our prayers we must add to them the wings of love, faith, hope, and earnestness, as Josiah did here. Out of love to his country his prayers were joined with weeping, and he wrestled with tears. Oh! the prayers that have tears with them cannot go without a blessing.

4. Lastly, If we would have God to hear us, let us have such a resolution and purpose of reformation as Josiah had; for his prayers were joined with a purpose of reformation, which he afterwards performed in so strict a manner, that there was never such a reformation among all the kings of Judah as he made. To this purpose David saith, 'If I regard wickedness in my heart, God will not hear my prayer,' Ps. lxvi. 18. If we have but a resolution to live in any sinful course, let us make as many prayers as we will, God will not respect them. God regarded good Josiah, because he had no purpose to live in any sin against him.

If we come with a traitorous mind unto God, with our sins in our arms, we must look for no acceptation from him. When a man comes to a king to put up a petition unto him, and comes with a dagger in his hand to stab him, will the king accept of this man's petition? So, do we think that God will hear our prayers when we bring a dagger in our hand, to stab him with our sins? If we will not leave swearing, lying, pride, covetousness, and the like, if we have not covenanted with our own hearts, but still go on in sin, we shall never go away with a blessing. Josiah reformed himself; therefore God saith, 'I have also heard thee.' Thus if our prayers issue from a heart rightly affected, as good Josiah's was, then we shall speed as he did; for God did not only hear his prayer, but see how he rewards him with an excellent blessing; to be taken home to heaven from the troubles of this life: which we shall in the next place speak of.

* In his Letters very often.—G.

THE SAINT'S REFRESHING.

SERMON IV.

Behold, I will gather thee to thy fathers, and thou shalt be gathered to thy grave in peace, neither shall thine eyes see all the evil that I will bring upon this place, and upon the inhabitants of the same. So they brought the king word again.—2 CHRON. XXXIV. 28.

IT is for the most part the privilege of a Christian, that his last days are his best; and 'though weeping be in the evening, yet joy comes in the morning,' Ps. xxx. 5; though he do begin in darkness, yet he ends in light. Whereas, on the contrary, the wicked begin in jollity and light, but end in darkness; yea, such a darkness as is 'utter darkness,' Mat. viii. 12—by Peter called the 'blackness of darkness,' 2 Pet. ii. 17—the preparations whereunto are, God's outward judgments in this life inflicted upon the impenitent and rebellious, wherein God many times puts a sensible, visible difference betwixt the godly and the wicked; as betwixt Lot and the Sodommites, Noah and the adulterous world, Moses and the Israelites with him, from Korah, Dathan, and his company, the Egyptians and the Israelites at the Red Sea; and in this text, betwixt this good king and his people. He must not see all the evil that God was to bring upon his wicked and rebellious subjects. Oh the happiness of holiness, which is sure to speed well in all storms whatsoever; because on all the glory there is a defence, as Isaiah speaks, Isa. iv. 5. Light is sown for the righteous, Ps. xcvii. 11; and whatsoever his troubles be, yet his last end shall be blessed. 'Let me die,' saith Balaam, 'the death of the righteous, and let my last end be like his,' Num. xxiii. 10. Such honour have all his saints, such honour had this good king Josiah; being removed from hence that he might not see the evil to come. Though he were taken from earth, yet it was for his good, that he might be gathered into heaven, and make a royal exchange.

The words contain *a promise of a reward, and great favour unto good king Josiah*, that he should die, and be gathered unto his fathers; and that which is more, the manner considered, that he should 'die in peace;' the ground whereof is shewed unto him: 'Because thine eyes shall not see all the evil that I will bring upon this place, and upon the inhabitants of the same.' God's promises are of three sorts. First, Such as he made upon condition of legal obedience: 'Do this and thou shalt live.' Secondly, When we are humbled upon sight of our sins, then he propounds another way, and promises that if we believe in Jesus Christ our surety, who hath made satisfaction for us, then we shall live. This is the grand promise of all, the promise of life everlasting, and pardon of sin. Thirdly, There are promises of encouragement unto us, when we are in the state of grace. As a father, who means to make his son an heir, doth give him many promises of encouragement, so God deals with his children, when they are in the covenant of grace.

There are, I say, promises of particular rewards to encourage them, as they are sure of the main and great reward, namely, everlasting life. Therefore Josiah being an heir of heaven, God did propound a promise of encouragement unto him, by way of favour, to shew that his good works were not unregarded. In general here,

Doct. 1. First, We may observe *God's gracious dealing with his children*, that he takes notice of every good thing they do, and doth reward them for it, yea, in this life. There is not a sigh but God hears it, not a tear but he hath a bottle for it. Most men spare God a labour in this kind. He promiseth 'to wipe away all tears from our eyes,' Rev. xxi. 4, but they will shed none. Yet the least tear shed, and word spoken in a good cause, goes not without a reward from God; not so much as a cup of cold water, but he rewards. Which must needs be so:

Because God looks upon the good things we do, being his own works in us, as upon lovely objects, with a love unto them; for though Josiah had said nothing, yet his deep humiliation itself, was as it were a prayer, that cried strongly in the ears of God, that he could not but reward it. So that partly because God looks upon us as lovely objects, he loving the work of his own Spirit, and partly because they cry unto God, as it were, and pluck down a blessing from heaven, they cannot go unrewarded.

Use. This is matter of comfort, that God will not only reward us with heaven, but will also recompense every good thing we do, even in this world; yea, such is his bounty, he rewards hypocrites. Because he will not be beholding to them for any good thing they do, nor have them die unrewarded, he recompenseth them with some outward favours, which is all they desire. Ahab did but act counterfeit humiliation, and he was rewarded for it, 1 Kings xxi. 27–29. So the Scribes and Pharisees did many good things, and had that they looked for. They looked not for heaven, but for the praise of men. This they had, as Christ tells them, 'Verily, I say unto you, you have your reward,' Mat. vi. 5. God will be beholding to none; but whosoever do anything that is good, they shall have some reward, whether they be good or bad. If the conscience of a man did judge well, he might come to God with boldness, not to brag of good works, but out of an humble heart saying, 'Remember me, O Lord, as I have dealt with thee.' So good Hezekiah did: 'Remember, Lord, how I have walked before thee in truth,' Isa. xxxviii. 3. When we labour in all our actions to please God, we may with boldness approach to the throne of grace, and say with Peter, Remember, Lord, 'Thou knowest that I love thee,' John xxi. 15. If there were no other reward but this, that we have a privilege to go to God with boldness, our conscience not accusing us, it were enough. What a shame is it, then, that we should be so barren in good works, seeing our labour shall not be unrewarded of the Lord! Oh then let us take counsel of the apostle: 'Finally, my brethren, be ye stedfast and unmoveable, abounding in the work of the Lord, knowing that your labour is not in vain in the Lord,' 1 Cor. xv. 58. He hath a reward for every cup of cold water, for every tear. Every good deed we do hath the force of a prayer to beg a blessing; yea, our very tears speak loud to God, although we say nothing. But to come to particulars.

'Behold, I will gather thee to thy fathers,' &c.

Here we see this word *behold*, a word serving to stir up attention, set before the promise, which was formerly set before a threatening, 'Behold, I will bring evil upon this place,' &c. Behold is as necessary before promises as threatenings. For the soul is ready to behold that which is evil, and by nature is prone to dejection, and to cast down itself. Therefore there need be a 'behold' put before the promise, to raise up the dejected soul of Josiah or others, and all little enough. Christians should have two eyes, one to look upon the ill, the other upon the good, and the grace of God that is in them, that so we may be thankful. But they for the most part look only upon the ill that is in them, and so God wants his glory and we our comfort.

'Behold, I will gather thee to thy fathers, and thou shalt be gathered to thy grave in peace.'

Doct. 2. Mark here the language of Canaan, *how the Spirit of God in common matters doth raise up the soul to think highly of them.*

Therefore it is that the Holy Ghost sweetens death with a phrase of 'gathering.' Instead of saying, Thou shalt die, he saith, 'Thou shalt be gathered.' How many phrases have we in Scripture that have comfort wrapped in them, as there is in this phrase, 'Thou shalt be gathered to thy grave in peace.' I will not speak how many ways peace is taken in Scripture. 'Thou shalt die in peace;' that is, thou shalt die quietly, honourably, and peaceably. And thou shalt not see the misery that I will bring upon the state and kingdom. Thou shalt be gathered to thy fathers, which is meant to Abraham, Isaac, and Jacob, and to all the faithful patriarchs.

Doct. 3. Only observe, it is a very sweet word, and imports unto us, *that death is nothing but a gathering*, and presupposeth that God's children are all scattered in this world amongst wicked men, in a forlorn place, where they are used untowardly, as pilgrims use to be in a strange land. Therefore we had need be gathered, and it is a comfort to be gathered. But from whence shall he be gathered? He shall be gathered from a wicked, confused world; and to whom shall he go? To his Father. His soul shall go to their souls, his body shall be laid in the grave with theirs. As if he had said, Thou shalt leave some company, but go to better; thou shalt leave a kingly estate, but thou shalt go to a better kingdom.

Doct. 4. *The changes of God's children are for the better.* Death to them is but a gathering. This gathering doth shew the preciousness of the thing gathered; for God doth not use to gather things of no value. Josiah was a pearl worth the gathering. He was one of high esteem, very precious. So every Christian is dearly bought, with the blood of Christ. Therefore God will not suffer him to perish, but will gather him before the evil days come. As men use to gather jewels before fire comes into their houses; or as husbandmen will be sure to gather their corn, before they will let the beasts come into the field; so saith God to him, I will be sure to gather thee before I bring destruction upon the land. We are all by nature lost in Adam, and scattered from God, therefore we must be gathered again in Christ. For all gathering that is good is in him; for he is the head of all union that is good. And this is to be wrought by the ordinances of God, by the means of the ministry, which is appointed unto that end, to gather us, as Mat. xxiii. 37, Christ speaks to Jerusalem, 'How often would I have gathered you together, as a hen gathereth her chickens under her wings, but you would not.' Christ would have gathered them unto himself, by his word, but they refused.

All the gathering of a Christian in this life is a gathering to Christ by faith, and to the communion of saints by love, 1 Thes. iv. 17; and the more he doth grow in grace, the more near communion he hath with Christ. Then after this gathering by grace, there comes by death a gathering to Christ in glory. For the soul goes for ever and ever to be with the Lord. After this comes a higher degree of gathering at the day of judgment, when there shall be a great meeting of all saints, and the soul and body shall be reunited together, to remain for ever with the Lord. Let us then think of this, that whatsoever befalls us in the world, we shall be sure to be gathered, for death is but a gathering. For from whence goes Josiah? From a sinful world, a sinful estate, a wretched people, unto his fathers, who are all good, nay, to God his Father. We are all here as Daniel in the lion's den, as sheep among wolves; but at death we shall be gathered to our fathers. It is a gathering to a better place, to heaven; and to better persons, to fathers, where we shall be for ever praising the Lord, never offending him, loving and pleasing one another. Here Christians displease one another, and cannot be gathered together in love and affection, but there they shall be gathered in unity of love for ever.

Use. This serves, first of all, *to comfort us in departure of friends*, to render their souls up with comfort into the hands of God. We know they are not lost, but sent before us. We shall be gathered to them, they cannot come to us. Therefore why should we grieve? They are gathered in quietness and rest to their fathers. This should also make us render our souls to God, as into the hands of a faithful Creator and Redeemer. From whence go we? From a sinful world and place of tears, to a place of happiness above expression. Why should we be afraid of death? It is but a gathering to our fathers. What a comfort is it to us in this world, that we shall go to a place where all is good, where we shall be perfectly renewed, made in the image of God, and shall have nothing defaced? Let this raise up our dead and drowsy souls. Thus we shall be one day gathered. The wicked shall be gathered together, but a woeful gathering is it. They shall be gathered like a bundle of tares, to be thrown into hell, there for ever to burn. They are dross and chaff, never gathered to Christ by faith, nor to the body of the church by love; and therefore they are as dross and chaff, which the wind scatters here, and shall for ever be scattered hereafter, Ps. i. 4. They are, as Cain, vagabonds in regard of the life of grace here; and therefore shall be for ever scattered from the life of glory hereafter. They shall be gathered to those whom they delighted in, and kept company with, whilst they were in this world. They loved to keep company with the wicked here, therefore they shall be gathered to them in hell hereafter. This is sure, thou shalt live in heaven or hell afterwards, with those whom thou livedst with here. Dost thou live only delighted in evil company now? It is pity thou shouldst be severed from them hereafter. If thou be gathered to them in love and affection here, thou shalt be gathered to them in hell and destruction hereafter. It is a comfortable evidence to those that delight in good company, that they shall be with them in heaven for ever. 'Hereby we know that we are translated from death to life, because we love the brethren,' 1 John iii. 14. And on the contrary, those that are brethren in evil here, may read in their own wicked courses and conversation what will become of them hereafter. They are all tares, and shall be gathered together in a bundle, and cast into hell fire for ever.

'And thou shalt be gathered to thy grave in peace.'

Here is a reward, not only to die, but to die in peace. Josiah goes the way of all flesh; he must die though he be a king. This statute binds all. All are liable to death. 'And thou shalt be gathered, or put in thy grave in peace.' This doth declare that he should be buried; the ground whereof is out of Gen. iii. 19, 'Dust thou art, and to dust thou shalt return.' From earth we came, and to earth we shall return. The earth we carry and the earth we tread on shall both meet together. In that God doth here promise it to Josiah as a blessing, we may hence learn,

Doct 5. *That burial is a comely and honourable thing*, and that we ought to have respect unto it, partly because the body of a dead Christian is a precious thing. They are temples of the Holy Ghost, members of Christ, and therefore ought to have the honour of burial. Partly because it shews our love and affection to the party buried, for it is the last kindness we can do unto them. Again, we ought to have respect to burial, to shew our hope of the resurrection, that though the body be cast into the earth, yet it shall rise; though it be sown in dishonour, yet it shall rise in honour. So we see that for these reasons burial is honourable. Therefore it is said of the faithful in Scripture, that they were buried, to shew how honourable a thing it is; and indeed it is an honour, specially for fathers, to be buried by their friends and children, and carried by them into their graves. For to be buried like a beast is a judgment to wicked men.

Quest. But what then shall we say to all those that are not thus buried, whose bodies are given to be torn by wild beasts, or burnt to ashes, or flung into rivers, as antichrist useth to deal with many saints?

Ans. I answer, that in this case faith must raise itself above difficulty; for though it be a favour and blessing of God, to have Christian burial after we are dead, yet Christians must be content to go without this blessing sometimes, when God calls them to the contrary, as when we cannot have it upon good terms, with peace of conscience, or with God's love. In this case a burial in regard of God's favour is not worth the naming. Therefore let all Christians be content to put their bodies, life and all, to hazard; not only to be willing to want burial when we are dead, but to sacrifice our lives and whatsoever else for God, as many saints have been martyred, and their bodies burnt to ashes. Yet God will gather together the ashes of the dead bodies of his children; for 'right precious in the sight of the Lord is the death of his saints,' Ps. cxvi. 15. And is it not better to want this with God's favour, than to have the most honourable burial in the world on evil terms? For what saith the Spirit of God? 'Happy and blessed are they which die in the Lord,' Rev. xiv. 13; not happy are they that die in pomp, and are buried in state, but happy are they that die in the Lord. Therefore when we may not have it, although it be a comely thing, yet if we have God and Christ, we have all that is good. Therefore it is no matter what becomes of our bodies after we are dead; for though we be flung into the sea, burnt to ashes, yet both sea and earth must give up all the dead, as it is Rev. xx. 13. Therefore as for our bodies, let us be willing that God may have them, who gave them; and if he will have us to sacrifice our lives for him, let us do it willingly.

'And thou shalt be gathered to thy grave in peace.'

Obj. How is this ? for we read, in the succeeding chapter of Josiah, that he died a violent death; he was slain by the hands of his enemies. Is this to die in peace ?

Sol. I answer, the next words do expound it. He died in peace, 'because his eyes should not see the evil that God would bring upon the land afterwards;' as if he had said, Thou shalt not see the ruin of the church and commonwealth. So, though Josiah were slain by idolaters, by Pharaoh and his chariots, yet he died in peace comparatively with a worse state of life. For though he died a bloody death by the hands of his enemies, yet he died in peace, because he was prevented by death from seeing that which was worse than death. For God may reserve a man in this life to worse miseries than death itself.

From hence we learn this instruction,

Doct. 6. *That death may be less miserable than the ill which a man may live to see in this life; or, that the miseries of this life may be such as that death may be much better than life, and far rather to be chosen.* We may fall into such miseries whilst we do live, that we may desire death, they being greater than it. The reason hereof is, because that a sudden death, in some respects, is better than a lingering one. One death is better than many deaths, for how many deaths did Josiah escape by this one death! It would have been a death to him if he had lived to see the ruin of the commonwealth, the church of God, and his own sons carried into captivity, to have seen them slain, their eyes plucked out, the temple of God plucked down, and idolatry set up.

We ought then to be careful how to avoid a cursed and miserable estate after death. All the care of wicked men is to avoid death. But they may fall into such an estate in this life that they may wish death, as an heathen emperor once did, who complaining said, 'I have none will do me so much favour as to kill me.'* All the desire of atheists is, that they may live. Thou base atheist, thou mayest fall into such an estate as is worse than death, and if that be so terrible, what will that† estate be after death ? An atheist in this life desires life, Oh that I might not die! But in hell thou wilt desire, Oh that I might die! The time will come that thou shalt desire that which thou canst not abide to hear of now. What desperate folly is it therefore to redeem life with base conditions; not to give it for the gospel when we are called to it. In this case, that base life which we so stand upon, will cost us the loss of our soul for ever in hell, when we shall desire to die.

'Behold, I will gather thee to thy fathers, and thou shalt be put in thy grave in peace.' The Lord saith, he 'will gather.' So we see,

Doct. 7. *Our times are in God's hand*; as David saith, 'My time is in thy hand,' Ps. xxxi. 15. Our times of coming into the world, continuing in it, and going out of it, are in God's hand. Therefore he saith, 'Thou shalt be put in thy grave in peace.' God hath power of death. Our going and coming is from God; he is the Lord of life and death.

Use. This is a comfort unto us while we live in this world, that whilst we live we are not in our own hands, we shall not die in our own time; neither is it in our enemies' hands, but in God's hand. He hath appointed a certain time of our being here in this world. This should tie us to obedience, and to die in hope and faith; because when we die we are but gathered to our fathers, to better company and place than we leave behind us.

* Qu. 'Nero'?—G. † Qu. 'thine'?—Ed.

Again we see here *that men may outlive their own happiness*, that at last life may be a judgment unto them, because they may see that which is worse than death. How many parents live to see the ruin of their own families! the undoing of their children by their own miscarriage! We see God takes away Josiah, because he will not have him live, as it were, beyond his happiness. We see how tenderly affected God is for the good of his children. He pities them when they are in misery, knows what they are able to bear, and will lay no more upon them than he gives them strength to endure. God knew that Josiah was tender-hearted, and melted at the very threatenings, which if he could not endure to hear against his country, could he ever have endured to have seen the miseries upon his people and country? Surely no. Therefore God will rather gather him to his fathers.

Now this is a wonderful comfort, that many times God will not let us see too great matter of grief. Let us then imitate God, and deal so one with another as God deals with us—the husband with the wife, and the wife with the husband, and the like. Let us not acquaint them with such things as may make them more grieve than is fitting, or they are able to bear. God would not have Josiah to see the misery he brought upon his country, because he knew that he was tenderly disposed, that a little grief would soon overcome him. So let us beware of causing any to grieve, or to let them know things which they are not able to bear.

Again, Seeing this is a grief to a kind and loving father, yea, worse than death, to see the ruin of his child, this should teach all those that are young, to take care that they give no occasion of offence to those that are over them, for to grieve; which will be worse than death unto them. It would have been worse than a death unto Josiah to have seen the ruin of his children. So for those children which have been cherished by their parents in their nonage, it will be worse than death to them in their age to see their children lewd and come to ruin, whereby they bring so much sooner the grey head of their father to the grave in sorrow. These offend against the sixth commandment, which saith, 'Thou shalt not kill.' Let us then rather revive and comfort the heart of those that have been good unto us, and not kill them, or do that which is worse than death unto them.

'Neither shall thy eyes see the misery I will bring upon this people.'

Doct. 8. Here we learn again *that it is the sight of misery which works the deepest impression.* It is not the hearing of a thing, but the sight of it, which affecteth most deeply; as in the sacrament, the seeing of the bread broken, and the wine poured out, works a deep impression; and because God knew Josiah's heart would break at the sight of the misery, therefore he tells him, 'Thine eyes shall not see the evil that I will bring upon this place.' The sight is a most working sense, to make the deepest impression upon the soul. What shall be our great joy and happiness in heaven, but that we shall see God for evermore? Sight is a blessing upon earth, both the eyes of the body wherewith we see, and the eyes of the soul—that is, faith—which makes us see afar off, till in heaven we shall see him face to face. So that sight makes us both happy and miserable.

Use 1. *How wretched, then, is the estate of them that shall see themselves,* with their own wicked eyes, *sent to hell, with the creature they delighted in.* That which the eyes see, the heart feels. There are many atheists, whose whole care is to preserve life. They would live, although they live the life of a dog. But the time will come, that thou wilt more earnestly desire death than life. Thy eyes shall see, and thy body feel, and thy conscience too, that which is worse than a thousand deaths. Thou shalt then die a living death. The worm of thy conscience shall gnaw thee for ever, and shalt see and feel the tormenting fire which shall never be quenched. That which the wicked nourish now to follow their humour, never caring to please God, the day will be when they shall desire to avoid it; and that which they labour to avoid most now, the time will come when they shall most desire it. Death is the king of fears. It is terrible. But then look beyond death: what is behind that? Thou shalt see at the heels of it hell and eternal damnation.

Use 2. This should teach us also how *to understand the promise of long life.* It is a promise and a favour of God to be desired. It is a prayer with condition, if God see it good; else God may give us long life, to see and feel a world of misery. Therefore such promises are to be desired conditionally: if God see it good for us.

Doct. 9. Again, The Holy Ghost saith here, 'Thy eyes shall not see the evil I will bring upon this place.' Hence we learn, *that those which be dead in the Lord, are freed from seeing of any evil or misery.* The godly shall see no misery after death. If this be so, then they do not go into purgatory after death, as the papists hold. The Holy Ghost saith, Josiah is taken away from seeing any evil to come. Then sure they do not fall into such misery after death, which is worse than death. True, say the papists, such excellent men as Josiah do go to heaven immediately. Ay, but the Holy Ghost saith by Isaiah, lvii. 1, that 'the righteous are taken away from the evil to come.' It is spoken of the whole generation of righteous men. Therefore it is a sottish thing for them to hold that any of them shall see purgatory, when God saith the righteous are taken away from seeing any evil to come.

Doct. 10. And as it is against them in this, so *here is another conclusion against popery, that takes away their invocation of saints:* for the righteous go to heaven, and cannot see or know our wants and miseries; yea, they are taken away, because they should not see the miserable estate that befalls their posterity. Then if they do not know our wants, how can they hear and help us when we pray, seeing it is a part of their happiness not to understand our miseries? For if Josiah, from heaven, could have seen the desolation and misery that befell his country afterwards, it would have wrought upon him. But Josiah was taken away, that he should not see it. Therefore, why should men spend that blessed incense and sacrifice of prayer, unto those that cannot hear? But put case, they could hear some; yet can they hear all that pray unto them? A finite creature hath but a finite act and limited power. How can one saint give a distinct answer and help to perhaps a thousand prayers, as the virgin Mary hath many thousand prayers offered her? How can she distinctly know, and give a distinct answer to every prayer?

'Thou shalt be put in thy grave in peace, neither shall thy eyes see all the evil that I will bring upon this place.' *Let us learn here a mystery of divine providence in his death;* for there is a mystery of providence, not only in great matters, as election and predestination, but in ordering of the common things of the world. How many excellent mysteries are here wrapt together in this death of Josiah! As, first, it is said that he died in peace, whereas he died a violent death, and was slain by the hands of his enemies. His death was both a mercy and a correction: a correction for his error in being so hasty in going to war with Pharaoh, king of Egypt; and yet it was a mercy, because it prevented him from seeing the evil to come, and so likewise brought him sooner to heaven. It is a strange thing to see how the wisdom of heaven can mingle crosses and favours, corrections and mercies together; that the same thing should be both a mercy to Josiah to be taken away, and yet a correction also for his error, in going to fight against Necho, king of Egypt, as we see 2 Chron. xxxv. 23. We may have mercies and afflictions upon us at the same time, as God, by the same death, corrected Josiah's folly, and rewarded his humility.

Mark here again another mystery, *in the carriage of divine providence:* how he brings his promises to pass strangely above the reach of man; as here, he having promised Josiah that he should die in peace, one would have thought that Josiah should have died in pomp and state. No. Thou shalt die in peace, although thou be slain by the hand of thy enemies; thou shalt come to heaven, although it be by a strange way. Thus God brings his children to heaven by strange ways, yea, by contrary ways, [by] afflictions and persecutions. Paul knew he should come to Rome, although it were by a strange way; though he suffered shipwreck, and was in great danger, as we may see Acts xxvii. 2, *seq.* God hath strange ways to bring his counsels to pass, which he doth so strangely, as we may see his own hand in it.

Again, Here we may see another mystery in divine providence, concerning the death of Josiah, *in that he was taken away being a young man*, but thirty-nine years old, who was the flower of his kingdom, and one upon whom the flourishing estate of such a kingdom did depend. Now, for such a gracious prince to be taken away in such a time, and at such an age, when he might have done much good, a man would hardly believe this mystery in divine providence. But 'our times are in God's hand,' Ps. xxxi. 15. His time is better than ours. And therefore he, seeing the sins of the people to be so great, that he could not bear with them longer,—for it was the sins of the people that deprived them of Josiah. It was not the king of Egypt who was the cause of his death, but the sins of the land—those caused God to make this way, to take away their gracious king.

Use. Here we may admire the wisdom of God, who doth not give an account unto us of his doings, why he suffers some to live, and takes away others; why he suffers the wicked to live, and takes away his own. We can give little reason for it, because it is a mystery; but God best knoweth the time when to reap his own corn.

'Neither shall thy eyes see all the evil I will bring upon this place, and upon the inhabitants of the land.'

Doct. 11. Here the Holy Ghost doth insinuate unto us that whilst Josiah was alive, God would not bring this judgment upon the land, but after his death, then it should come upon them. So here we learn this comfortable point of instruction, *that the lives of God's children do keep back judgment and evil from the place where they live, and their death is a forerunner of judgment.* Their life keeps back ill, and their death plucks down ill. While thou art alive, I will bring no evil upon this place, but when thou art gone, then I will bring it down, saith God. The reasons of this are,

Reason 1. Because *gracious men do make the times and the places good where they live.* It is a world of good that is done by their example and help. While they live the times are the better for them.

Reason 2. And again, *they keep back ill, because gracious men do bind God by their prayers.* They force, as it were, a necessity upon God, that he must let the world alone. They bind his hands, that he will do nothing while they are in it; as to Lot in Sodom, 'I can do nothing while* thou art gone, saith the angel,' Gen. xix. 22. They stand in the gap, and keep God from pouring down the vials of his wrath. But when they are gone, there is nothing to hinder or stop the current of divine justice, but that it must needs have his course. As when men have gathered their corn into their barns, then let their beasts, or whatsoever else go into the field, they care not; and as when the jewels are taken out of a rotten house, though the fire then seize upon it, men regard not. So when God's jewels are gathered to himself, then woe to the wicked world, for then God will break forth in wrath upon them. Woe to the old world when Noah goes into the ark, for then follows the flood. Woe to Sodom when Lot goes out of it, for then it is sure to be burned. Luther prayed that God would not bring war upon the people in Germany all his time, but when he died, the whole land was overspread with war. So, before the destructiou of Jerusalem, God did gather the Christians to a little city called Pella, near Jerusalem, then came Titus and Vespasian and ruinated the city of Jerusalem.† So there are many gracious parents that die, after whose death comes some miserable end to their wicked children, but not before. God takes away the parents out of the world, that they might not see the ruin of their children. So then we see that it is clear, that good men keep back judgment from the places where they live.

What should we learn from hence?

Use 1. This should teach us *to make much of such men as truly fear God*, seeing it is for their sakes that God doth spare us. They carry the blessing of God with them wheresoever they go. As Laban's house was blessed for Jacob's sake, Gen. xxx. 27, and Potiphar's for Joseph's sake, Gen. xxxix. 23, so the wicked are spared and fare the better for the saints who live among them. But what is the common course of wicked men? To hate such with a deadly hatred above all others, because their lives and speeches do discover the wickedness of theirs, and because they tell them the truth, and reprove them.

Therefore it was that Ahab could not endure the sight of Micaiah, that holy prophet, who without flattery spake downright truth, 1 Kings xxii. 8, *seq.* So it is now beyond seas and elsewhere. They labour to root out all the good men. But what will they get by it? Surely it will be a thousand times worse with them than it is; for if they were out, then woe to the land presently.

Use 2. This should also teach us *to pray to God to bless those that are good.* Is it not good for us to uphold those pillars whereby we stand? What madness is it for a man to labour to pull down the pillar whereby he is holden alive? As Samson, pulling down the pillars of the house, brought death upon himself, so godly men, the pillars of this tottering world, which uphold the places whereby they live, being once shaken, all the whole state falls. Therefore let us not be enemies to our own good, to hate the godly; for it is for their sakes the Lord shews mercy to us, and refrains to pour out his judgment upon the wicked world. And when the best gathering of all gatherings shall come, that the elect of God shall be gathered together, then comes the misery of all miseries to the wicked. So we see this point is clear, that the godly, while they are alive, keep back ill and bring much good. For doth God continue the world for wicked men? Surely no. For what glory and honour hath God from such wicked

* That is, 'until.'—Ed.

† Cf. Note *cccc*, Vol. III. p. 536.—G.

wretches? Do they not swear, lie, live filthily, and abuse his members? Is it for these that God doth continue the world? Surely no; but for the godly's sake are judgments deferred, and the world is continued.

Use 3. If this be thus, *well may we lament the death of those that are good.* For when they are gone, our safety is gone. 'They are the chariots and horsemen of Israel,' 2 Kings ii. 12. Therefore well may we bewail their loss. Well might Jeremiah lament for the death of Josiah, for together with the breath of Josiah the life of that state breathed out; together with him, the flourishing condition of Jerusalem died, and lay buried with him as it were in the same grave.

See here again how God correcteth too much resting on the arm of flesh. They blessed themselves under Josiah, as if no evil should come near them; as appears, Lament. iv. 20, 'The breath of our nostrils, the anointed of the Lord, was taken in their pits, of whom we said, Under his shadow we shall live.' There is no greater wrong to ourselves, and to others on whom we rest so much, than to secure ourselves so much on them as to neglect serious turning to God.

'Neither shall thy eyes see all the evil I will bring upon this place.'

This is the ground why he should die in peace, 'Because he shall not see all the evil I will bring upon this place.' Here we see that the judgment which God threatened to bring upon the church and commonwealth is set down by this word 'evil.' 'Thine eyes shall not see all the evil I will bring upon this place.' But who sends this evil. It is an evil brought by God. Thou shalt not see the evil 'I will bring,' &c. It was not God that brought it properly, but Nebuchadnezzar, who carried his sons into captivity. Howsoever, God had a hand in it. 'For is there any evil in the city and God hath not done it?' saith the prophet, Amos iii. 6. But we must distinguish between evil. There is,

1. The evil of sin; and 2. The evil of punishment.

First, The evil of sin; and this God doth not bring, for it is hateful unto him. Then the evil of punishment, which is twofold:

(1.) Either that which comes immediately from God, as famine, pestilence, or the like; in which punishments we are to deal with God alone.

(2.) Or else, the evil that comes from God, but by men, which he useth as instruments to punish us, and this is by war and cruel usage.

Now thus Josiah is taken away from this greatest evil we can suffer in this life; to have God correct us by the hands of men. For when we have to deal with God, the labour is easier to prevail with him, as David did, 2 Sam. xxiv. 14. But when we have to deal with merciless men, then we have to deal with the poisoned malice of men, besides God's anger. Now the evil that comes from God is chiefly,

The ill which seizeth upon the soul after death; or else, the evil which seizeth upon the whole man, both soul and body, both in this and after this life.

Thus God is said to bring evil, not the evil of sin, but the evil of punishment.

Doct. 12. Hence we learn, that *the evils which we suffer, they are from the evil of sin.* It is sin that makes God to bring evil upon the creature. If we look upward to God, there is no evil in the world, for in that consideration all things are good so far as he hath a hand in them. Therefore, whatsoever the creature suffers, it comes from the meritorious evil, the evil of sin. It comes from God, but through the evil of sin provoking him.

Quest. If any man ask, How can God, which is good, bring that which is evil?

Sol. I answer, We must know that the evil of punishment is the good of justice. All the evil that he doth is good, as it comes from him in his justice punishing, because it doth good to them that are punished, either to cause them return, or if they will not, to shew the glory of his justice in condemning them. It is the good of justice, and it is not always in God only permitting or suffering such a thing for to be done; but it is in him as an act, having a hand in it. Therefore God saith, 'Ashur is the rod of my wrath;'* so that in all punishments God hath a hand, whether it be upon the body or soul.

Use. This serves for direction unto us, *To begin where we should begin;* in all our afflictions to go to heaven and make our peace with God, and not go to secondary causes. For all evil of punishment comes from him. Let us, if we fear evil, make our peace with God by repentance and new obedience; and then he will overrule all secondary causes so as to help us. Go not in this case to the jailor, or to the executioner, but go to the judge. Let us make our peace in heaven first, and then there will be soon a command for our ease. Yea, Christ can command the wind and sea to be still, the devil himself to be quiet, if our peace be made with him.

Therefore let us learn this lesson, and not fret against the instrument whereby God useth to correct us. David had learned thus much when Shimei railed upon him: 'It is God that hath bid him, therefore let him alone,' 2 Sam. xvi. 11. So holy Job saith, 'It is God that gives, and God that takes away,' Job i. 21. He doth not only say, God gives, but God takes away. Oh but it was the Chaldeans that took it away. Ay, but it is no matter for that, God gave them leave. Therefore let us carry ourselves patiently in all troubles, submitting ourselves under the mighty hand of God, from whom we have all evil of punishment.

Obj. Again, Here we have another mystery of divine providence. For it may be objected. What! will God bring evil upon his own church and people? upon the temple and place where his name is called upon, and that by idolaters. Where is divine justice now?

Sol. I answer. Hold thy peace, take not the balance out of God's hand. He knows what is better for us† than we ourselves. We must not call God to our bar, for we shall all appear before his. God useth servants and slaves to correct his sons; worse men than his people to correct his people. It is his course so to do, when they of his own sin against him. For evil men many times make evil men good, when they are used as instruments to correct them; as here God useth wicked men to make his children good. So God makes a rod of Ashur, to make his evil children better. He useth slaves to correct his sons, because it is too base a service for the angels or good men to do. Therefore he useth the devil and his instruments to do it. Wherefore let us not call into question God's providence; for when he will punish his people, he can hiss for a worse people; for Egypt, or Ashur, or the like. So if he will punish England, he can hiss again for the Danes, or Normans, to punish his own people. Let us not boast we are God's people and they idolaters. No; God can hiss for a baser people to punish his own servants. It is the will of God so to dispose, and the will of God is *summa justitia*, the height of justice. God will have it so. Let us make our peace with him, and not demand why he doth thus and thus.

* That is, 'Assyria.' Cf. Isa. x. 5.—G.

† Qu. 'what is good for us, better'?—Ed.

'And so they brought the king word again.' I will but touch this in a word, and so make an end.

Here we see that the messengers deal faithfully with Josiah. They brought the direct message which the prophetess did bid them, which was good for himself, but doleful for his estate. He was a gracious man, and God gave him gracious servants.

Doct. 13. *For God will give good men faithful servants*, that shall deal faithfully with them. As for the wicked, God will give them such servants that shall humour them to their own ruin. If they have a heart not desirous to hear the truth, if they be Ahabs, they shall have four hundred false prophets to lead them in a course to their own ruin. But Josiah had an upright heart, desiring to know the truth. Therefore God gave him a faithful prophetess to deal truly with him, and faithful messengers to bring the true answer.

'Then the king sent and gathered together all the elders of Judah and Jerusalem. And the king went up into the house of the Lord, and all the men of Judah, and the inhabitants of Jerusalem, and the priests, and the Levites, and all the people great and small,' &c.

Which words shew what good king Josiah did upon the receipt of this message. As soon as ever he heard it, he did not suffer it to cool upon him. But when his spirit was stirred up, he did as a gracious king should do, he sent and gathered all the elders of Judah, and the inhabitants of Jerusalem, both great and small, and they went up to the house of the Lord, and there read in their ears all the words of the book of the covenant which was found in the house of the Lord.

Here, first, we see that Josiah gathered, as it were, a parliament and a council; as also, in both Josiah and the people, we may behold an excellent and sweet harmony of state, when all, both king and priests, Levites and people, did meet amiably together. This was an excellent time, when there was such an harmony between king and people, that he no sooner commands but they obeyed him.

But more particularly we learn,

Doct. 14. *That the care of the commonwealth and of the church is a duty belonging to the king*, that the reformation both of church and commonwealth belongs unto the prince. There is a generation which think that the king must only take care for the commonwealth. But they have also power to look to religion. We see Josiah doth it, he is the keeper of both. Josiah hath a care of religion, and it doth become his place. He is a head, and it is befitting his relation. He is a father, not only to look to the temporal state, but to the church.

The Donatists in Augustine's time did ask, What had the emperor to do with the church? But it was answered that the emperor could not rule the commonwealth except he govern the church, for the church is a commonwealth. So that we see, as a chief right, the ordering of the matters of religion belongs to the care of the prince. But there are two things in religion: first, intrinsecal, within the church, as to preach, administer the sacraments, and ordain ministers. These he ought not to do. But for those things that are without it, these belong unto him. If any of those that are placed in church or commonwealth, do not their duty, it is fitting for him to correct. He ought to set all a-going without, and to remove abuses, but not to meddle with the things within the church aforesaid, as to execute the same, but to oversee and govern their execution, and those persons whose proper office it is to execute them.

This observe against the usurpation of the pope, and see the supremacy of king Josiah, that he is supreme over all; not only over temporal persons, but over evangelical persons. For there was an high priest at that time and the Levites, but none were above king Josiah.

Quest. Ay, but this was under the law, say the papists.

Sol. 1. I answer, that this is a rule in divinity, that the gospel doth not take away or dissolve the laws of nature and reason. Therefore if the supremacy belonged to the prince then, surely now much more. Therefore saith one, We give respect to the emperor as next to God; to God in the first place, and then to the emperor.* The ministers have power over the prince for to direct him and give him counsel, but yet they are not above him. A physician doth give directions for his patient. Is he therefore above him? So a builder giveth direction for the building of the king's house. Is this any supremacy? So the minister may give direction and counsel to the prince; but hath he therefore any superiority above the prince? Surely no.

Sol. 2. In the second place, here we see who it is that called this parliament. It was king Josiah. He was the first mover in calling of this council, for he was the head; and had it not been a strange thing to have seen the foot move before the head? The head must first give direction before any of the members can move. Therefore it is only in the authority of the king to gather a council, and none must gather a public assembly without authority from the king.

The calling of assemblies belongs to the prince. If it be a general council, then it must be by the emperor; if it be a national council, then by the king or prince of that nation; if provincial, then first from the king or princes, as first movers of it, and so to others. As the heavens, and these celestial bodies over the earth, first move, and then all other afterward, so kings ought first to move, and then all to follow.

Use 1. If this be so, we see how the pope wrongfully takes this right of calling councils to himself, which properly belongs to the emperor; for we know that for a thousand years after Christ the emperor called councils, if any were. But of late years the pope, encroaching upon the emperor, hath usurped this right of calling them, whenas you see no assemblies ought to be gathered without the authority of the prince.

Though fasting be an excellent thing, yet public fasting must not be without the consent of the king. Let Christians have as much private fasting as they will, thereby to humble themselves, but public fasts must not be without the consent of the king; for great matters are to be done by great motions. Here is a great matter of gathering a council. Therefore the head and body and all join together. As it is when the body is to do some great thing, all the members of the body stir together to do it, so it is with the commonwealth. When great matters are in hand, all must be joined together, as here king, priests, Levites, and all the people, both great and small, joined together for to prevent the judgment threatened.

But what must we do if things be amiss? I answer, Take the right course; that is, go to God by prayer, and entreat him who hath the hearts of kings in his hands, to incline and stir up the hearts of princes for to reform abuses. Well, but what did the king do when he had gathered all the elders and inhabitants of Judah and Jerusalem into the house of the Lord? They went up thither to fast, and pray, and read the book of the law.

* Tertullian. Cf. Apology, c. xxxiii. to xxxvi.—G.

Reformation makes all outward things fall into a good rule, but they are to be called only by the authority of the prince, and when a fit time and occasion requires.

The papists brag much of the Council of Trent; but if ever there was a conspiracy against Christ, it was in that council; for the parties that had most offended, and were most accused, and should have been judged, were the judges; and the Holy Ghost, which should have been in the council, and should have been their judge, him they excluded, and received a foul spirit of antichrist sent unto them, in a cap-case* from Rome, whence they had all their counsel. Was not this a goodly council?

Again, In that Josiah gathered a council in time of public disorder and public danger, here we learn that it is not only lawful, but many times necessary, to gather assemblies and councils for reformation of abuses, both in church and commonwealth, which otherwise cannot be abolished. So councils are good to make canons, rules, and to prevent heresy; yea, much good may be done by gathering of them, if they meet to a good end, for the good of the church, and the glory of God; for God who is willing and able to perform the good will be strongly amongst them. For if Christ by his Spirit hath promised to be in that assembly, 'where two or three are gathered together' upon good grounds, and to good ends, how much more will he be, when two or three hundreds are so gathered together? But this must be done by the consent of authority, otherwise it would be an impeachment to government. So much briefly for this text, and for this time.

* That is, a small case or travelling-box. Cf. Nares and Halliwell *sub voce*.—G.

*** The frequent allusions in the preceding sermons, and throughout, to wars and accompanying evils abroad, receive interpretation from 'The Thirty Years' War,' which, beginning in 1618 and ending in 1648, was thus contemporary with the whole of Sibbes's public life.—G.

THE SPIRITUAL FAVOURITE AT THE THRONE OF GRACE.

THE SPIRITUAL FAVOURITE AT THE THRONE OF GRACE.

NOTE.

'The Spiritual Favourite' forms a small volume (18mo). The title-page is given below.* Prefixed is a portrait of Sibbes, differing from the usual miniature one. He holds a book in his hand; and underneath, in engraved letters, is this inscription, 'The reverend, faithfull, and profitable Minister of Gods word, Richard Sibbes, D:D: master of Katherine Hall, in Cambridge, and preacher of Grayes Inne, London.' *The copy from which our reprint is taken is believed to be unique.* I had searched for it in all the 'public' libraries of the kingdom, and advertised through innumerable channels, but utterly in vain; nor could I hear of any one who had so much as seen it, when, through the spontaneous kindness of W. E. Whitehouse, Esq., Birmingham, I was unexpectedly put in possession of it. It becomes me thus publicly and cordially to acknowledge my obligation to Mr Whitehouse. G.

* THE
SPIRITVALL
FAVORITE
AT THE THRONE
OF GRACE.

By the late learned, and reverend Divine RICHARD SIBBS Doctor in Divinity.

Published by the Authors owne appointment, subscribed with his hand; to prevent unperfect Copies.

Proverbs 29. 26.
Many seeke the Rulers favour, but every man's judgement commeth from the Lord.

LONDON,
Printed by *Thomas Paine*, for *Ralph Mabb*. 1640.

THE SPIRITUAL FAVOURITE AT THE THRONE OF GRACE.

O Lord, I beseech thee, let now thine ear be attentive to the prayer of thy servant, and to the prayer of thy servants, who desire to fear thy name; and prosper, I pray thee, thy servant this day, and grant him mercy in the sight of this man.—NEH. I. 11.

IN the ninth verse the holy man minds God of his promise made to his people, that if they should 'turn unto him, and keep his commandments, and do them, though they were cast out to the utmost parts of heaven, yet he would gather them thence,' &c., ver. 9. I will touch a little on them, [on the] two verses, and then come to that I mean to dwell on, from the words read.

'If you turn unto me, and keep my commandments.' There is no promise of mercy but to those that turn. The Scripture is peremptory in denial of mercy to such as go on in their sins. Heaven could not brook* the angels themselves, having sinned; and neither such, nor such 'shall enter into the kingdom of heaven.' Yet how many are there that bless themselves that it shall go well with them, though they cast off all God's yokes and divine bonds, that might bow them to better courses, as if words were but wind; when we see here God made his word good against his own dear people, 'If ye sin, I will scatter you to the farthest parts of the world,' ver. 8. We see in the former verse, ver. 7, a proud, presumptuous sinful disposition may slight God, and the messengers of the word and all, now when we come to threaten; but when God comes to execute, will he shake it off then? Will swearers and blasphemers and filthy persons shake off the execution as they can the threatenings? God saith, none that are such shall enter into heaven, 'but his wrath shall smoke against them, and shall be as a fire that shall burn to hell,' against such persons as 'bless themselves' in wicked courses, Deut. xxix. 20; and when God comes to the execution, they desire 'the mountains to fall upon them,' Rev. vi. 16. There are none more presumptuous against the threatenings, and none more base and fearful when it comes to execution. As we see in presumptuous and profane Belshazzar, that was quaffing in 'the bowls of the temple,' and scorning religion and God, when there comes a handwriting on the wall, 'his knees knock together and his joints tremble,' Dan. v. 6. So

* That is, = 'suffer, endure.'—G.

let there be any evidence of execution, and we see all the tyrants in the book of God, and that have been in the world, that have trifled at religion, of all men they are most disconsolate and fearful, as we see in Belshazzar and others.

I beseech you therefore take heed. God will seal all his threatenings with executions in due time, as he did to his own people. What is the reason we should promise ourselves more immunity than they had?

'If ye turn and keep my commandments, and do them.' Here are three conditions. 'Though you were cast to the utmost parts of the world, I will gather you thence,'

'If you turn.' The holy man Nehemiah puts God in mind of his promise, and his argument is from the like, and indeed from the less to the greater. Because God would rather of both, perform his promises than his threatenings, because mercy is his own proper work. Now, as he had been just in punishing his people, so he would be merciful in restoring of them again; therefore he saith, 'Return and keep my commandments and do them, and though ye were scattered to the utmost parts of the earth, yet I will gather you thence.' And he did gather them thence upon their repentance; he did perform his promise at length.

Beloved, the full accomplishment of this yet remains; for this people to this day, since the death of Christ, since they drew the guilt of that sacred blood on them, they are scattered about the earth to every nation, and have not a foot of land of their own, but are the scorn and hissing of nations. Notwithstanding, this promise will be performed. Upon their repentance, God will bring them again. As St Paul calls it a kind of a resurrection, the conversion of the Jews, so it is true of us all. Though we were scattered as dust, as we shall be in the grave ere long turned to dust, God will gather the ashes; he will gather all those parts of ours. Even as his power gathereth his people together, so his power at length will gather us all. We have his promise for the one as well as the other.

Therefore let us comfort ourselves with the performance of this promise, for the performance of the grand promise of the resurrection. Indeed, the grand promise of the resurrection is the ground of the performance of all other promises. As you have it in Ezekiel, concerning the dry bones: saith God, 'I will clothe these dead bones with flesh and skin,' &c., 'therefore I will restore you again,' Ezek. xxxvii. 1, *seq.* God that will restore our dust and bring our bodies together, that were scattered here and there, he will restore us out of our sickness and trouble, if it stand with his glory and our good.

Now, after the argument that he useth to persuade God from his word of threatening and promise, he comes to the argument from their relation.

'These are thy servants.'

Though sinful servants, yet they are thy servants. 'These are thy people.' Thou hast no other people in the world but these, and 'thou art their God.' He pleads from former favours. 'Thou hast redeemed them by thy great power and strong hand.'

It is a good argument to plead with God for former favours: because 'there is no shadow of change in him,' James i. 17; he is always like himself; he is never drawn dry. And it is a great honour to go to him for new favours upon former, because he hath an infinite supply. We may draw so much from men as they have not afterwards to make good, but we cannot honour God more than to go to him with a large faith, to fetch large favours from him. The more he gives, the more he can give, and the more he is willing to give. 'To him that hath shall be given,' Mat. xiii. 12. We cannot honour God more than to go to him upon former favours and with enlarged desires. 'Thou hast redeemed us, and been gracious to us before,' Ps. cvii. 2.

We may much more take this argument in our mouths, and press the majesty of God. 'Thou hast redeemed us,' not out of Egypt or Babylon, the land of the north, but 'with the blood of thy Son,' from hell and damnation; and therefore thou canst redeem us from this petty misery, from these enemies. We may allege that grand favour to all other petty redemptions, whatsoever they are. He that hath given us Christ, that 'hath not spared his own Son, but gave him to death for us all, how shall he not with him give us all things else? Rom. viii. 32. He that hath been so large and bountiful as to give us his own Son, that gift to admiration*—'*So* God loved the world,' John iii. 16—how cannot we plead with him for all other favours whatsoever, whether they concern the life of grace or glory, or our present condition while we live in this world? We may plead it much more I say, 'Thou hast redeemed us.' But these things I will not press further now.

In the eleventh verse he comes to press it still, and repeats that which he had said before, 'Lord, I beseech thee, let thine ear be attentive to the prayer of thy servant, and of thy servants that desire to fear thy name.'

'Let thine ear be attentive to the prayer of thy servants.' It is a prayer; and thou art 'a God hearing prayer.' They be thy servants, and thou regardest thy servants. Here are but a few petitions in this large request: 'remember,' 'be attentive,' and 'give me favour.' The most of the prayer is spent in a preparative considering the attributes of God, and in confession and strong reasons from the word, of promises and threatenings, and from their relation; and then he makes good the relation, 'We are thy servants, because we desire to fear thy name.'

To shew that indeed:

It is an excellent skill and art in prayer, to have strong arguments.

Then the suit comes off easily, as in Ps. xc. It is a prayer of Moses, the man of God; and yet the least part of the psalm is prayer: 'Teach us to number our days,' &c., ver. 12. That is all the petition. Though the petition be short, yet it is efficacious, when the heart is warmed and strengthened with strong reasons before; when the heart is elevated and raised with the consideration of the majesty and the truth of God; and when the heart is strengthened with strong convincing reasons, that God will hear when we press him with his word; I say, when the heart is thus raised and warmed, all the petitions come easily off.

Therefore, it is an excellent thing, beloved, to study the Scriptures, and to study all the arguments whereby holy men have prevailed with God in Scripture; and to see in what case those arguments were used. They are of use and force to prevail with God.

It is a pitiful thing now, for Christians under the glorious light of the gospel, to come to God only with bare, naked petitions (if they come from a true heart, they have their force that God should regard them), and have not reasons to press God out of his own word. They cannot bind God with his own promise, nor with arguments that he hath been bound with before. Let a child but cry to the father or mother, there is relief pre-

* That is, 'wonder.'—G.

sently for the very cry (*a*). But if it be not one that is a child, but is of grown years, the father looks for arguments that are moving to press him with. So here, Nehemiah he presseth God with moving and strong arguments, and he repeats and forceth them. He doth not only allege them, but enforceth them: 'O Lord, I beseech thee, let thine ear be attent to the prayer of thy servant, and of thy servants that desire to fear thy name.'

He desireth God to be 'attentive.' He presseth God; and indeed he doth it to warm his own heart, for when we have humbled our heart low enough, and broken it with the consideration of our own unworthiness, and then warmed it with the consideration of God's goodness, and strengthened it with the consideration of God's promise and truth, then we are sure of a gracious success.

'Let thine ear be attent to the prayer of thy servant, and of thy servants.'

How did they know that they were thine?

Because there was no other people in the world that knew God but they. And he knew that the saints, wherever they were, had a spirit of prayer, and would remember the case of the church. Therefore he saith, remember 'my prayer and the prayer of thy servants.' For if 'the prayer of one righteous man prevaileth much,' James. v. 16, much more the prayer of many. If there had been but ten righteous in Sodom, Sodom had been preserved. Now this he allegeth to God, 'remember the prayer of thy servant,' of mine, and the prayer of thy servants. As Tertullian, an ancient father, saith very well, 'When men join together, they offer a holy kind of violence to God' (*b*). Prayer is a kind of wrestling and contending with God, a striving with him. 'Let me alone,' saith God to Moses, Exod. xxxii. 10. It is a binding of him with arguments and promises of his own, and it is so forcible, that he desires, as it were, to be let alone. Now, if the prayer of one be a wrestling, and striving, and forcing of him, as it were, against his will, that he said, 'Let me alone,' as if he could do nothing except he gave over praying, what are the prayers of many, when there is a multitude of them?

Therefore we may look for a comfortable issue of our prayers and humiliation that is performed at this time.* The desires of so many Christian souls touched with the Spirit of God, and with the case of the church, which God doth tender,† cannot be ineffectual. It must needs draw plenty of blessings from heaven. I will not enter into the commonplace of prayer, having spoken of it upon another occasion; but surely you see the holy man Nehemiah stood so much upon it, that he hoped to speed, because he and others prayed: holy Daniel, and others with him. It was such a gracious messenger to send to heaven for help and for all good, that Daniel, though it cost him his life, that he should be cast into the lion's den, he would not omit it for his life. Take away prayer, and take away the life and breath of the soul. Take away breath and the man dies; as soon as the soul of a Christian begins to live he prays (*c*). As soon as Paul was converted, 'Behold he prayeth,' Acts ix. 10. A child, as soon as he is born, he cries, and a Christian will not lose his prayer for his life, as we see in holy Daniel. For what is all the comfort that he hath, but that that is derived from God? and God will be sued unto for all the favours he bestows. Whatsoever is from his favour, it comes as a fruit of prayer for the most part. Though he go beyond our desires many times, yet ordinarily, what we have if we be his children, we have it as a fruit of prayer. Therefore,

* A 'National Humiliation' by royal proclamation'—G.

† That is, = 'care for,' regard.—G.

I beseech you, let us be stirred up to this duty, as we see Nehemiah here: 'Remember the prayer of thy servant,' &c.

And when we pray to God, let us press him, as we see here, 'Be attentive,' verse 6, and here again, 'be attentive.' He presseth upon God. It is no sinful tautology to come again and again. God loves to hear the same song again and again. This music is not tedious but pleasing to him. And this pressing is for us to warm our hearts; perhaps one petition will not warm them, and when they are warmed by a second, let us labour to warm them more and more, and never give over till we have thoroughly warmed our hearts. 'Be attentive, be attentive to my prayer;' and if mine will not prevail, be attentive to the prayers of others; let the prayers of all prevail—'the prayer of thy servant, and of thy servants.'

But how doth he make it good, they are thy servants?

'They desire to fear thy name.'

Empty relations have no comforts in them: to profess one's self a servant, and not to make it good that he is a servant. We must make good the relation we stand in to God, before we can claim interest in the favour of God by our relation. Servants, and Christians, and professors—here are glorious titles; but if they be empty titles, if we cannot make them good when we come to God with them,—we cannot say we have any interest in God from empty titles,—it is rather an aggravation of our sin.

God will be honoured in all those that come near him, either in their obedience, or in their confusion. Therefore here the holy man did not think it enough to say, 'Thy servant, and thy servants, but who desire to fear thy name.'

He goes to make it good that he was the servant of God, not from any outward thing, but from his inward disposition, 'the fear of God,' which I will not now stand to speak largely of. God requires the heart; and religion is most in managing and tuning the affections, for they are the wind that carries the soul to every duty. A man is like the dead sea without affections. Religion is most in them. The devil hath brain enough, he knows enough, more than any of us all. But then he hates God. He hath no love to God, nor no fear of God, but only a slavish fear. He hath not this reverential fear, childlike fear. Therefore let us make it good that we are the servants of God, especially by our affections, and chiefly by this of fear, which is put for all the worship of God. It is put instead of those conditions spoken of verse the 9th, 'If you turn to me, and keep my commandments, and do them,' then I will make good my promise. Now, saith he, taking up the same strength of argument, 'We desire to fear thy name.' As if he should have said, we turn to thee and obey thy commandments, and desire to do them. It is all one. 'We desire to fear thy name,' for those that fear God will turn to him; and to desire to obey his commandments and to do them, it is all one as to do them. If a man should do them, and not from the fear of God, all were nothing but a carcase of obedience. I will not stand longer on that.

How doth he make it good that he feared the name of God?

He makes it good from this, that he had good desires. '*We desire* to fear thy name.' We desire it for the present, and for the time to come; whence we will observe two or three things shortly, as may be useful to us. First of all, out of this, that this desire to fear the name of God is brought as an argument to prevail in prayer, we may observe that,

Those that will prevail with God in prayer, must look to the bent of their souls for the time to come, and for the present.

'Regard thy servants that desire to fear thy name.' For to come to God without such a frame of soul as this, to desire to please God in all things for the present, and for the time to come, it is to come as God's enemy; and will God regard his enemies? When one comes with a purpose to live in any sin, without a desire for the time to come, to regard all God's commandments, he comes as God's enemy, he comes as it were with his dagg* to shoot at God, he comes with his weapon. Who will regard the petition of a man that comes to wound him at the same time? When a man comes to God with a purpose to sin, he comes to wound God at the same time, as an enemy, and is he like to speed? For what are our sins, but that that makes us enemies to God? They are opposite to him as can be, they make us hateful to God. Therefore we must be able to say with good Nehemiah, when we come to God, to make it good that we are servants indeed, '*We desire* to fear thy name.' As Jeremiah tells them, Jer. vii. 10, 'Will you steal, and oppress, and commit adultery, and yet stand before me?' Will you do this and this villany, and stand before me? 'What hast thou to do,' saith God, Ps. l. 16, *seq.*, 'to take my name into thy mouth, and hatest to be reformed?' If we hate to be reformed, and do not desire to serve God for the time to come, what have we to do to take his name into our mouths, especially in the holy exercise of prayer? Ps. lxvi. 18, 'If I regard iniquity in my heart, the Lord will not hear my prayer.' If a man do but regard to live in iniquity for the time to come, the Lord will not hear his prayer. Therefore, if we will be able to prevail with God in our petitions, we must say with holy Nehemiah, 'We desire for the time to come to fear thy name.' I beseech you, let us remember it.

And then, to omit other things, 'we desire to fear thy name,' we see that

Religion especially is in holy desires.

The greatest part of Christianity is to desire to be a sound Christian with all his heart. Religion is more in the affections of the soul than in the effects and operations. It is more in the resolutions and purpose of the soul, than in any effects we can yield to God. There is much desire in all our performances. Therefore saith the holy man here, 'We desire to fear thy holy name.'

Why are desires such trials of the truth of grace?

Because they are the immediate issues of the soul. Desires and thoughts, and such like, they are produced immediately from the soul, without any help of the body, or without any outward manifestation. They shew the temper and frame of the soul. Thereupon God judgeth a man by his desires; and that which he desires, if it be a true desire, he shall have and be partaker of. The godly man desires to serve God all the days of his life, and for ever he shall do it. A wicked man desires to offend God if he might live everlastingly. God looks upon him as his desire is. He shall not alway sin here; but because he hath an infinite desire of sin, he shall be punished in hell eternally. God looks upon him as he desires. God values men by their desires.

But how are the truth of these desires known?

I will name a few signs. The truth of those desires may be tried thus:

1. *If they be constant desires and not flashes;* for then they come from a

* That is, = pistol. Cf. Halliwell's Dictionary of Archaisms and Provincialisms, *sub voce*, 2 vols. 4to, 1852.—G.

new nature. Nature is strong and firm. Art is for a turn to serve a turn. When men personate a thing, they do it not long. Creatures that are forced to do so and so, they return to their own nature quickly; but when a man doth a thing naturally, he doth it constantly. So, constant desires argue a sanctified frame of soul and a new creature. They argue that the image of God is stamped upon the soul. Thereupon we may know that they are holy desires, that they spring from a holy soul, if they be constant, if they be perpetual desires, and not as a torrent that is vented for the present on a sudden, and then comes to nothing after. They are constant.

2. And likewise, *if these desires be hearty, strong desires;* and not only strong, but *growing desires*—desire upon desire, desire fed with desire still, never satisfied till they be satisfied. Strong and growing desires argue the truth of desires; as indeed a child of God hath never grace enough, never faith enough, never love enough, or comfort enough, till he come to heaven. They are growing desires more and more. The Spirit of God, that is the spring in him, springs up still further and further, till it spring to everlasting life, till it end in heaven, where all desires shall be accomplished, and all promises performed, and all imperfections removed. Till then they are growing desires still. '*We desire* to fear thy name,' and to please thee in all things.

3. Again, True desires, *they are not only of the favour of God, but of graces for the altering of our nature*; as Nehemiah here, he desires not the favour of God so much as he desires to fear God's name. Now when desire is of graces, it is a holy desire. You have not the worst men but would desire, with Balaam, 'to die the death of the righteous,' &c., Numb. xxiii. 10, that they might enjoy the portion of God's people. But to desire grace, that is opposite to corrupt nature as fire and water, this is an argument of a holy principle of grace in us, whence this desire springs, when we desire that that is a counter poison to corrupt nature, that hath an antipathy to corruption. Therefore, when a man from the bottom of his heart can desire, Oh that I could serve God better! that I had more liberty to serve him! that I had a heart more enlarged, more mortified, more weaned from the world! Oh that I could fear God more! And of all graces, if it be a true desire, it is of such graces as may curb us of our sinful delights, and restrain us of our carnal liberty, and knit us near to God, and make us more heavenly-minded. The desire of these graces shew a true temper of soul indeed.

4. True desire *is carried to grace as well as glory, and the desire of heaven itself.* A true spirit that is touched with grace, with the Spirit of God, it desireth not heaven itself so much for the glory, and peace, and abundance of all contentments, as it desires it, that it is a place where it shall be freed from sin, and where the heart shall be enlarged to love God, to serve God, and to cleave to God for ever, and as it is a condition wherein he shall have the image and resemblance of Jesus Christ perfectly upon his soul. Therefore we pray, 'Thy kingdom come;' that is, we desire that thou wouldst rule more and more largely in our souls, and subdue all opposite power in us, and bring into captivity all our desires and affections; and let 'Thy kingdom come' more and more. 'Let thy will be done by us,' and in us more and more, 'in earth as it is in heaven.' Here is a sweet prayer now serving to the first petition, the hallowing of God's name, when we desire more to honour God, and to that purpose that he may rule in us more and make us better. These desires argue an excellent frame of soul; as we see in Nehemiah, 'our desire is to fear thy name.'

5. True desires are likewise *to the means of salvation*, and to the means of salvation as they convey grace, as sincere milk; as you have it, 1 Pet. ii. 2, 'As new-born babes, desire the sincere milk of the word.' Where a man hath holy desires of any grace, and hath them in truth, he will desire those means whereby those graces may most effectually be wrought in his heart. Therefore he will hear the word as the word of God. He comes not to hear the word because of the eloquence of the man that delivers it, that mingles it with his own parts. He comes not to hear it as the tongue of man; but he sees God in it. It is the powerful word of God, because there goes the efficacy of the Spirit with it to work the graces he desires.

Therefore a man may know by his taste of divine truth whether he desire grace. He that desires grace desires the means that may convey grace, and especially so far as they convey grace, 'As new-born babes, desire the sincere milk of the word.' You cannot still a child with anything but milk. He desires no blending or mixing, but only milk. So a true Christian desires divine truths most, because the Spirit of God is effectual by them to work grace and comfort in him. I will not enlarge myself in the point.

Use. The comfortable observation hence is this, *that weak Christians that find a debility, and faintness, and feebleness in their performances*, hence they may comfort themselves by their desire to fear God, and to worship God, and to serve him, if their desires be true. Therefore, in Isaiah xxvi. 8, the church allegeth it to God, 'In the way of thy judgments have we sought thee,' &c. 'The desire of our souls is towards thy name.' They bring it as a prevailing argument to God. So when we come to God, 'The desire of our souls is toward thy name.' Lord, our endeavours are weak and feeble, but 'the desire of our souls is to thy name,' and 'thou wilt not quench the smoking flax,' Mat. xii. 20. Therefore we come to thee with these weak and poor desires that we have. 'The Lord will fulfil the desires of them that fear him,' Ps. cxlv. 19, if they be but desires, if they be true, and growing, and constant desires, and desires of grace as well as of happiness, as I shewed before.

The reason why God accepts them is partly because *they spring from his own Spirit.* These desires they are the breathings of the Spirit. For even as it is in places where fountains and springs are digged up, they are known and discovered by vapours; the vapours shew that there is some water there, some spring, if it were digged up. So these desires, these breathings to God for grace and comfort, these spiritual breathings, they shew that there is a spring within and Spirit within, whence these vapours and desires come. Therefore they are accepted of God, because they spring from his own Spirit.

And because *they are pointed to heavenward, to shew that a man is turned*; for it is put here instead of turning, 'Turn ye to me, saith the Lord,' ver. 9; and he answereth here instead of turning, 'My desire is to fear thy name,' because, when the desire is altered, then the frame of the soul is altered, a man is turned another way. The desire is the weight of the soul. What carries the soul but desire? Now, when the soul is carried another way than before, it argues an alteration of the frame; therefore it pleaseth God to accept of them.

I beseech you, let us often enter into our own souls, and examine what our desires are, which way the bent of our souls is; what cause we would have to flourish and prevail in the world, Christ's or antichrist's; for God esteems us by the frame of our desires. 'Who *desire* to fear thy name.',

'And prosper, I pray thee, thy servant this day.'

Now he comes to his petition, 'Prosper, I pray thee, thy servant this day.' He doth not capitulate* with God for particular matters much—for he knew he had to deal with an all-wise God,—but he commends his petition in general, 'Prosper, I pray thee, thy servant,' &c. He was to attend the king, and he was in his attendance to mind the state of the church, for the re-edifying the walls and gates of Jerusalem. Now saith he in general, 'Prosper thy servant.' He leaves it to God how and in what manner, being to deal, as I said, with an infinite wise God; only he prays in general, 'Prosper thy servant this day.'

He comes again with his relation of 'servant,' to teach us alway when we come to God to look in what relation we stand to him, whether we be true servants or no, what work we do for him, in what reference we do what we do; whether we do it to please him as servants or no. I said something of the relation of servant before. I will add a little here, because he repeats it four or five times in this short prayer.

In all our services we should look to God; for our aim in our works shew what they are, whether they come from servants or no. As the stamp upon a token makes it, if there be a good stamp on it; it is not the matter that makes it current. A stamp on silver makes it current as well as gold, though the metal of gold be better. So when things are done, because God commands them, to please God, as a service to him, this makes it good that we are servants indeed, that the relation is good. When we go about the service of the church or country, or place we live in, to think I do God service here, and do it as a service to God, who will be honoured and served in our service to others, herein I am a good servant. Though the matter of my service be a common, base, and mean matter, yet it hath a stamp upon it. It is God's will. God hath placed and planted me here, and he will be served of me in this condition at this time, though the matter of it be an ordinary thing. I know it may help the good of the church. It hath reference to the will of God and the good of the church. Thus if we do what we do with an eye to God in the place where he hath set us, that we do it as to him, we are God's servants, whatsoever the work is.

And let us remember oft to think of it, to bring it in our prayers. 'Master,' say they when they were ready to be drowned, 'dost thou not care that we perish?' Mark iv. 38. They put him in mind of the relation they were in to him. So when we can put God in mind of our relation—'Father, we are thy children;' 'Lord, we are thy servants'—it will strengthen our faith and hope of all good. Will a master suffer his servant to miscarry in his service? Surely God will never turn away true-hearted servants that have served him a long time. It puts us in mind of our duty, and serves to strengthen our faith; for as it is a word of service on our part, so it is a promising word of all good from God. Doth he expect that masters should be good to their servants because they have a Master in heaven? and will not the great Master of heaven be good to his servants? You see how he follows the relation.

'Prosper thy servant this day.'

What is included in this word '*prosper?*'

It includes not only success, which is the main upshot of all, but all that tends to good success. 'Prosper thy servant this day;' that is, direct thy

* That is, = 'make terms.'—G.

servant this day how to do and to carry himself. And likewise assist thy servant. When thou shalt direct him, assist him by thy strength, direct him by thy wisdom, prosper him with thy grace, give him good success in all. It includes direction, and assistance, and good success. In that he saith, 'prosper thy servant,' it includes these things.

First of all, that in ourselves *there is neither direction, nor wisdom, nor ability enough for success.* We have not power in ourselves to bring things to a comfortable issue. So it enforceth self-denial, which is a good disposition when we come to God in prayer.

2. And then again, *to attribute to God all,* both wisdom, and strength, and goodness, and all. Here is a giving to God the glory of all, when he saith, 'Prosper thy servant this day.'

3. Then in the third place, here is *a dependence upon God;* not only acknowledging these things to be in God, but it implies a dependence upon God for these: 'Prosper me, Lord.' I cannot prosper myself, and thou who art the Creator hast wisdom, and strength, and goodness enough. Therefore I depend upon thee, upon thy wisdom for direction, and upon thy strength for assistance. I depend upon thy goodness and all for a blessed issue. Here is dependence.

4. Again, in the fourth place, here is *a recommendation of all by prayer;* a recommendation of his inward dependence upon God for all. Now, Lord, 'prosper thy servant.'

So that when we come to God for any prosperity and good success, let us remember that we bring self-denial, and an acknowledgment of all excellency to be in God, to guide, and direct, and assist, and bless us. And remember to depend upon him, to cast ourselves on him, to bring our souls to close with the strong, and wise, and gracious God, that God and our souls may close together. And then commend all by prayer 'to cast ourselves and our affairs, and to roll ourselves,' as the Scripture saith, and all upon God, Ps. lv. 22; and then we shall do as the holy man Nehemiah did here, we shall desire to good purpose that God would 'prosper us.' Indeed, 'it is not in man to guide and direct his own way,' Jer. x. 23. We are dark creatures, and we have not wisdom enough. And we are weak creatures. We have no strength. We are nothing in our own strength. And for success, alas! a thousand things may hinder us from it. For success is nothing but the application of all things to a fit issue, and foreseeing all things that may hinder, and a removing of them. Now who can do this but God?

One main circumstance that besiegeth and besets a business may hinder an excellent business. Who can see all things that beset a business? all circumstances that stand about a business? Who can see all circumstances of time, and place, and persons, that are hindrances or furtherances? It must be an infinite wisdom that must forsee them; man cannot see them. And when men do see them, are there not sudden passions that come up in men, that rob them of the use of their knowledge? that though they know them before, yet some sudden passion of fear or anger may hinder the knowledge of a man, that he is in a mist when he comes to particulars. When he comes to apply the knowledge that he had before, he knows not what to do. So that unless God in a particular business give success, who is infinitely wise and powerful to remove all hindrances, there will be no success.

As it is in the frame of the body, it stands upon many joints; and if any be out of tune, the whole body is sick. And as it is in a clock, all the wheels must be kept clean and in order, so it is in the frame of a business. There must all the wheels be set a-going; if one be hindered, there is a stop in all. It is so with us in the affairs of this world. When we deal with kings and states, if all the wheels be not kept as they should, there will be no success or prosperity. Nehemiah knew this well enough; 'prosper thou therefore.'

He meant not to be idle when he said this, 'prosper thou;' for he after joined his own diligence and waited. Therefore join that. If we would have our prayers to God and our dependence upon him effectual for prosperity and success, be careful to use the means as he did. He stands before the king, and observed how he carried himself, to see what words would come from the king, and then he meant after to put in execution whatsoever God should discover.

Use. It should teach us to make this use of it, when we deal in any matter, *to go to God to prosper it, and give success, and direction, and assistance, and a blessed issue*. For God, that we may alway depend upon him, he keeps one part in heaven still. When he gives us all likelihood of things upon earth, yet he reserves still the blessing till the thing be done. Till there be a consummation of the business, he keeps some part in heaven. Because he would have us sue to him, and be beholding to him, he will have us go up to heaven. Therefore, when we have daily bread, we must pray for daily bread, because the blessing comes from him. Our bread may choke us else. We may die with it in our mouths, as the Israelites did. But when we have things, we must depend on him for a blessing; all is to no purpose else.

Let us learn by this a direction to piety and holy walking with God; in all things to pray to God for a blessing. And to that purpose we must be in such a condition of spirit as we may desire God to prosper us; that is, we must not be under the guilt of sin when we come to God to prosper us. And we must be humble. God will not prosper a business till we be humble. As in the case of the Benjamites, when they came, they were denied the first, second, and third time. Till they prayed and fasted, and were thoroughly humbled, they had their suit denied, Judges xx. 36, *seq.* If the cause be never so good, till we be humbled, God will not prosper it, because we are not in frame for the blessing; if we had it, we would be proud. God in preventing* mercy and care, will grant nothing till we be humbled. Therefore let us see that we be humble, and see that the matter be good that we beg God to bless and prosper us in, or else we make a horrible idol of God. We make (with reverence be it spoken) a devil of God. Do we think that God will give strength to an ill business? This is to make him a factor for mischief, for the devil's work. We must not come with such 'strange fire' before God, to transform God to the contrary to that he is; but come with humble affections, with repentant souls for our former sins. And let the thing itself be good, that we may come without tempting of him; let the cause be such that we may desire God's assistance, without tempting of him, as we do when it is good and when we come disposed. Then come with a purpose to refer all to his service. Lord, if thou wilt bless me in this business, the strength and encouragement I have by it, I will refer it to thy further service. Let me have this token of love from thee, that I have a good aim in all, and then I am sure to speed well.

'Prosper now thy servant.'

* That is, 'anticipating.'—G.

It is an excellent point, if I had time to stand on it. I beseech you, let it have some impression upon your hearts.

What is the reason that God blasts and brings to nothing, many excellent endeavours and projects? Men set upon the business of God, and of their callings, in confidence of their wit* and pride of their own parts. They carry things in the pride and strength of their parts. Men come as gods to a business, as if they had no dependence upon him for wisdom, or direction, or strength. They carry things in a carnal manner, in a human manner, with human spirits. Therefore they never find either success, or not good success. Let us therefore commend all to God: 'Prosper thy servant.' Before he went about the business, holy Nehemiah he sowed prayers in God's bosom, and watered the seed with mourning; as it is in this chapter, he mourned and prayed. When this business was sown with prayers, and watered with tears, how could he but hope for good success! He mourned and prayed to God, 'Hear thy servant.'

Now when we deal with things in a holy manner, we may, without tempting God, trust him. That which is set upon in carnal confidence and pride, it ends in shame; when men think to conceive things in wit, ay, and in faction and human affections, God will not be glorified this way. God will be glorified by humble dependent creatures, that when they have done the business, will ascribe all to him. 'Not unto us, but to thy name give the praise,' Ps. cxv. 1. The direction and assistance and blessing was thine. Saith God in Isa. l., towards the end, ver. 11, 'Go to now, ye that kindle a fire, walk in the light of your own fire: but be sure you shall end in sorrow.' You will kindle a fire of your own devices, and walk in the light of your fire; you will have projects of your own, and be your own carvers: but be sure you shall lie down in darkness and discomfort, you shall lie down in sorrow.

A proud unbroken heart accounts these poor courses. It is but a course of weak and poor spirits to pray and fast, and humble themselves to God, and to fear God. Alas! what are these? These are weak courses. I hope we have stronger parts and means to carry things. So they have a kingdom in their brain. What is the issue of these vain men, when God discovers all their courses to be vain at length, to be wind, and come to nothing? 'Prosper now thy servant,' saith he.

Let us learn this lesson likewise. If we come to God in a particular business, that we are not so confident in, to be pleasing to God, yet in general to submit ourselves, 'Lord, prosper thy servant;' go before thy servant; let me deal in nothing against thy will; direct me what is for thy glory; and not to prescribe or limit God. 'Prosper thy servant this day.'

'And grant him mercy in the sight of this man.'

He comes more particularly to this request, 'Grant me mercy in the sight of this man.' We see that

A king is a great organ or instrument to convey good things from God, the King of kings, to men.

Therefore he prays that God would give him favour in the sight of the king. For a king is the first wheel that moves all other wheels, and as it were the sun of the commonwealth, or the first mover that moves all inferior orbs. Therefore in heavenly wisdom he desires God to give him favour with him; for if he had that, the king could turn all the inferior orbs to his pleasure. Indeed, it were a point worthy enlarging, but that

* That is, 'wisdom.'—G.

it is not so seasonable for this time, the time being already spent. You see what great good God conveys by kings and princes. And when God means to do good to a church or state, he raiseth up 'nursing fathers and nursing mothers,' Isa. xlix. 23. He will raise up both kings and subordinate Nehemiahs, excellent men, when he hath excellent things to do.

But the main thing here intended, which I will but touch, is, that considering they stand in such a subordination to God as to be instruments to convey so much good or so much ill as they may, as it is said of Jeroboam, they either cause others to sin or to worship God, therefore we should do as good Nehemiah: he prays that he might find favour in his sight.

A wise and holy prayer! He begins at the head; he goes to the spring of all good. Prayer is the messenger or ambassador of the soul. Being the ambassador of the soul, it goes to the highest, to the King of kings first; to the Lord of lords first. It goes to the highest mover of all, and then desires him to move the next immediate subordinate mover, that is, the king, that he may move other orbs under him, that things may be carried by a gracious sweet course to a blessed issue. Therefore the observation hence is this, *that when we have to do anything with great men, with kings, &c., however, begin with the King of kings*, and do all in heaven before we do it in earth; for heaven makes the laws that earth is governed by. Let earth conclude what it will, there will be conclusions in heaven that will overthrow all their conclusions. Therefore in our prayers we should begin with God, and desire him with earnest and fervent entreaties that he would set all a-going, that he would set in frame these inferior causes. And when we have gotten what we would in heaven, it is easy to get in earth. Let us win what we desire in heaven at God's hands, and then what an easy thing is it to work with princes and other governors in state when we have gotten God once! Hath not he 'the hearts of kings in his hand as the rivers of water,' Prov. xxi. 1, to turn this way or that there way? As a skilful man derives water by this channel or by that, as he opens a vent for the water, so God opens a way to vent the deliberations and determinations of kings and princes, to run this way or that, to this good or that, as he pleaseth. Therefore considering that there is an absolute dependence of all inferior things from God, when we have to do with kings or great men, let us always begin with prayer.

As Jacob, when he was to deal with Esau, he falls down and prays first; and when he had gotten of God by prayer, God, that makes 'even of enemies friends,' he turned Esau's heart of an enemy to be a friend. And God put into Jacob's heart a wise course to effect this, as to offer a present, and to give him titles, 'My lord Esau,' &c., Gen. xxxiii. 4. God, when he will effect a thing amongst men, and hear the prayers that are made to him for the favour of men, he will put into their hearts such ways whereby they shall prevail with men, as Jacob did with Esau. So Esther, before she goes to Ahasuerus, she got* in heaven first by prayer. When she had obtained of God by prayer, how placable and sweet was Ahasuerus to her! So we see in other places of Scripture, when holy men have been to deal with men, they began with God.

I beseech you therefore learn this point of Christian wisdom. If you would speed well,—as we all desire to speed well in our business,—especially those that have public employments, [this must be the course] that they would pray to God, that hath the hearts of kings and princes in his government and guidance, that he would make them favourable; and not to

* Spelled 'gate,' *i. e.*, gat.—G.

think to carry things in a violent course, for then God doth not usually give that good success; but to carry things in a religious course to the King of heaven, and then to know in what terms to stand in all inferior things as may stand with the will of God in heaven.

If so be there be a dependence of all inferiors to God, then we must not offend God, and go against conscience, for any, because he is 'King of kings, and Lord of lords.' He doth not set up authority against himself, to disarm and disable himself. He never went to set up gods under him, to make him a cypher; that he should make them gods, and God a man, or nobody, to alter all the frame of things. He never meant to set up any ordinance to nullify and make himself nobody. Therefore, I say, we ought to pray to God for kings, that so in our obedience we may be sure to do nothing against conscience for any creature. We must do all things that possible can be, that may procure the favour, and ingratiate us, because it is in vain to pray unless we use all possible means to win their favour; but if it cannot be upon good terms, then 'whether to obey God or man, judge ye,' Acts v. 29. And as the three young men, 'we take no thought to answer in this matter; our God can defend us if he will,' Daniel iii. 16. And as Esther said, 'If I perish, I perish,' Esther iv. 16. When things are clear, we are to be resolute, yet reserving due respect to God's ordinance and to his lieutenant upon earth; I say, always reserving due respect, and using means to win favour, and also to use prayer.

Holy Nehemiah, he prays here; and together with that, he attends upon the king. As good Jacob observed Esau, so all good means must be used, or else God will not bless our proceedings.

Remember that all inferior governors whatsoever, they are subordinate and dependent, and therefore they must be regulated by a superior. They are limited, they are dependent, they are derivative. They are dependent upon God; they are derived from him. Therefore, as the apostle saith that 'servants must obey their masters in the Lord,' Eph. vi. 5, so we must obey and do all 'in the Lord.' That limitation must be always added; but reserving that, it is a good thing to pray that there may be favour from the king, because it is of much consequence to bring business to a good issue. And with prayer, there must be a using means to get favour, always with this liberty, to do it so far as we can with preserving a good conscience.

As they have a distinction among civilians, there is a parting with a thing *cumulativè* and *privativè*: *cumulativè*, that is, when we part with a thing so as that we reserve the propriety;* *privativè*, when we give away the propriety and all. Now, so God parts with nothing below, as to strip himself; but *cumulativè*, he derives† authority to others, but reserves the propriety to himself. Therefore we must obey them in him, and with this limitation, as it may stand with his favour.

To draw to a conclusion in a word. You see here that any good Christian may be a good statesman in one good sense. What is that? A good Christian hath credit in heaven, and he hath a spirit of prayer, and his prayer can set God on work; and God can set the king on work; and he can set his subjects on work. Now, he that can prevail with God to prevail with the gods upon earth here, surely such a man is a profitable man in the state. And you know, God he can alter all matters, and mould all things: it is but a word of his mouth. And what God can do, prayer can do; for prayer binds God, because it is the prayer of faith; and faith, as it

* That is, property, 'possession.'—G. † That is, 'communicates,' bestows.—G.

were, overcomes God. Now, prayer is the flame of faith, the vent* of faith; and faith is a victorious, triumphant grace with God himself. If it be any, it is Christians that can prevail with God for a blessing upon a state. Then certainly there is no good Christian but is of excellent service in the state. Though in particular perhaps he hath not policy, and wisdom, and government, yet he hath God's ear to hear him, and he can pray to God that God would make the king and other subordinate magistrates favourable.

You see what great good a good man may do in a state. 'The innocent man delivers the land,' as it is in Job xxii. 30. And the 'poor wise man delivers the city,' as it is in Eccles. ix. 15. A few holy, gracious men, that have grace and credit in heaven above, they may move God to set all things in a blessed frame below. And surely if this holy means were used, things would be better than they are; and till this be used, we can never look for the good success and issue of things that otherwise we may hope for.

Divers things might be spoken of the doctrinal part. I will give you but a word of it. *That God hath our hearts in his government, more than we ourselves.* I speak it to inform our judgment in a point of doctrine, whether God foresee and determine of things below upon foresight, which way they shall go; or whether he foreordain that they shall go this way, because he directs them thus: that is to make God, God indeed. He determines that these things shall be, because he determines, in the series and order of causes, to bring things to pass, and to guide kings, and princes, and magistrates, and all, this way. Again, whether God hath set all men at liberty, in matters of grace especially, that they may apply grace at their liberty, which way they will; and in foresight, which way they will apply their liberty, to determine thus or thus of them. This is to make every man's will a god, and to divest God of his honour, as if God could foresee the inclination of the creature, without foresight that he meant to incline it this way or that way.

Can God foresee any entity, any thing that hath a being in nature or grace, without foresight to direct it this way or that way? He cannot. This is to make him no God. We see God hath the hearts of kings in his power, and that is the ground of prayer for grace to them. Why should we pray for them, if they could apply their own will which way they would? Why should we give thanks for that we have liberty to do this way or that way? It stops devotion, and petition, and thanksgiving, to say that the creature hath liberty to apply itself, and God, seeing it would apply itself thus, determined so. Oh no. We must go to God. He hath set down an order and course of means; and in the use of those means, desire him to guide us by his good Spirit, to enlighten our understandings, to guide our wills and affections by his Holy Spirit, because our hearts are in his government more than our own. If it were needful to prove it, I could prove it at large. If there had been such a liberty, good Nehemiah would never have made this prayer. But God doth strangely put thoughts and guide all, even of himself, as we may see excellently in the story of Esther. I will give you but that example and instance. What a strange thing was it that Ahasuerus could not sleep; and when he could not sleep, to call for the book, and then that he should read of Mordecai, and thereupon to advance Mordecai. All this tended to the good of the church: it was a strange thing. And so in other things. It is a strange thing that God should put little thoughts and desires into great persons, and then follow

* That is, 'outlet,' = utterance.—G.

it with this circumstance and that; and so bring things to pass. All this is from God. Except we hold this, that God rules all without, and especially the hearts of men, where it is his especial prerogative to set up his throne, we shall never pray heartily or give thanks. And if we do pray and give thanks, he will put thoughts into governors' minds, strange thoughts and resolutions for the good of the church, that we could never have thought of, nor could come otherwise, but from the great God of heaven and earth. We shall see a strange providence concur to the good of all. But I must leave the enlargement of these things to your own thoughts and meditations.*

* Here is added, 'Imprimatur. Thomas Wykes. August 24. 1639.'—G.

NOTES.

(*a*) P. 96.—'Let a child but cry to the father or mother, there is relief presently for the very cry.' Tennyson has finely put this :—

> 'What am I?
> An infant crying in the night,
> An infant crying for the light,
> And with no language but a cry.'—*In Memoriam*, liii.

(*b*) P. 96.—'As Tertullian saith, . . . "When men join together, they offer a holy kind of violence to God."' In his 'Apology' the *sentiment* is found, *e.g.*, c. xxxix.: 'We are a body united in the profession of religion, in the same rites of worship, and in the bond of a common hope. We meet in one place, *and form an assembly, that we may, as it were, come before God in one united body, and so address him in prayer. This is a violence which is well-pleasing to God.*' Cf. Temple Chevallier's excellent edition of the post-apostolical Letters and Apologies (8vo, 2d ed., 1851), *in loc.*

(*c*) P. 96.—'Take away prayer, and take away the life and *breath of the soul.* Take away breath, and the man dies; as soon as the soul of a Christian begins to live, he prays.' This recalls the beautiful hymn of James Montgomery—

> 'Prayer is the Christian's vital breath,
> The Christian's native air,' &c.

G.

THE SUCCESSFUL SEEKER.

THE SUCCESSFUL SEEKER.

NOTE.

'The Successful Seeker' appeared originally in 'Evangelical Sacrifices' (4to., 1640). Its separate title-page is given below.* For general title-page of the volume, see Vol. V. page 156. G.

* THE
SVCCESSEFVLL
SEEKER.
In tvvo Sermons, on
PSALME 27. 8.

BY

The late Learned and Reverend Divine,
RICH. SIBBS.
Doctor in Divinity, Mr. of KATHERINE Hall
in *Cambridge*, and sometimes Preacher
to the Honourable Society of
GRAYES-INNE.

1 CHRON. 16. 11.
Seeke yee the Lord, and his strength: seeke his face continually.

LONDON,
Printed by *T. B.* for *N. Bourne*, at the Royall Exchange,
and *R. Harford*, at the guilt Bible in Queenes-head
Alley in Pater-noster-Row. 1639.

THE SUCCESSFUL SEEKER.

When thou saidst, Seek ye my face; my heart said unto thee, Thy face, Lord, will I seek.—Ps. XXVII. 8.

In the former verse, David begins a prayer to God, 'Hear, O Lord; have mercy upon me, and answer me.' This verse is a ground of that prayer, 'Seek ye my face,' saith God. The heart answers again, 'Thy face, Lord, will I seek;' therefore I am encouraged to prày to thee. In the words are contained,

God's command and David's obedience.

'Seek my face; thy face, Lord, will I seek.' God's warrant and David's work answerable, the voice and the echo: the voice, 'Seek my face;' the rebound back again of a gracious heart, 'Thy face, Lord, will I seek.'

'When thou saidst.' It is not in the original. It only makes way to the sense. Passionate speeches are usually abrupt: 'Seek my face;' 'thy face, Lord, will I seek.' The first thing that I will observe from the encouragement is, that,

Obs. God shews himself to his understanding creature.

God begins you see, 'Seek my face.' He must open his meaning and shew himself first. God comes out of that hidden light that he dwells in, and discovers himself and his will to his creature, especially in the word. It is our happiness now, that we know the mind and meaning of God.

What is the ground of this? What need God stoop thus?

There is the same ground for it as that there is a God. These things go in an undivided knot, God: the reasonable, understanding creature; and religion, that ties that creature to God; a discovery of* God what that religion shall be.

For in the intercourse between God and man, man can do nothing except he hath his warrant from God. It is extreme arrogance for man to devise a worship of God. Do we think that God will suffer the creature to serve him as he pleaseth? No. That were to make the creature, which is the servant, to be the master. It belongs to the master or lord to appoint the service. What master or lord will be served according to the liberty and wisdom and will of his servant? And shall the great God of heaven and earth be worshipped and depended upon as man pleaseth, or from any encouragement from himself? Shall not he design his own worship? He that singles out his own work makes himself master in that.

* That is, = '*by* God.'—G.

Therefore God begins with this command, 'Seek my face;' and then the heart answereth, 'Thy face, Lord, will I seek.' God must first discover his mind, of necessity, to the creature.

Scriptures might be forced hence to shew the duty owing from the creature, man, to God. For the creature must have a ground for what he doth. It must not be will-worship, *infringit*, &c. It is a rule, it weakens the respect of obedience that is done without a cause. Though a man doth a good deed, yet what reason, what ground have ye for this? And that we may do things upon ground, God must discover himself; therefore he saith, 'Seek my face.'

It may be objected that everything proclaims this, to seek God. Though God had not spoken, nor his word, every creature hath a voice to say, 'Seek God.' All his benefits have that voice to say, 'Seek God.' Whence have we them? If the creature could speak, it would say, I serve thy turn that thou mayest serve God, that made thee and me. As the prophet saith, the rod and chastisement hath a voice. 'Hear the rod, and him that smiteth,' Micah vi. 9. Everything hath a voice. We know God's nature somewhat in the creature, that he is a powerful, a wise, a just God. We see it by the works of creation and providence; but if we should know his nature, and not his will towards us—his commanding will, what he will have us do; and his promising will, what he will do for us—except we have a ground for this from God, the knowledge of his nature is but a confused knowledge; it serves but to make us inexcusable, as in Rom. i. 19, *seq.*, it is proved at large. It is too confused to be the ground of obedience, unless the will of God be discovered before; therefore we must know the mind of God.

And that is the excellency of the church of God above all other people and companies of men, that we have the mind and will of God; what he requires of us by way of duty to him, and what he will do to us as a liberal and rich God. These two things, which are the main, are discovered; what we look for from God, and the duty we owe back again to God, these are distinctly opened in the word. You see here God begins with David, 'Seek ye my face.'

Indeed, God is a God of order. In this subordination of God and the creature, it is fit that God should begin. It is God's part to command, and ours to obey. This point might be enlarged, but it is a point that doth but make way to that that follows, therefore I will not dwell upon it.

Again, in this first part, God's command or warrant, 'Seek ye my face,' you see here,

Obs. 2. *God is willing to be known.* He is willing to open and discover himself; God delights not to hide himself. God stands not upon state, as some emperors do that think their presence diminisheth respect. God is no such God, but he may be searched into. Man, if any weakness be discovered, we can soon search into the depth of his excellency; but with God it is clean otherwise. The more we know of him, the more we shall admire him. None admire him more than the blessed angels, that see most of him, and the blessed spirits that have communion with him. Therefore he hides not himself, nay, he desires to be known; and all those that have his Spirit desire to make him known. Those that suppress the knowledge of God in his will, what he performs for men and what he requires of them, they are enemies to God and of God's people. They suppress the opening of God, clean contrary to God's meaning: 'Seek my face;' I desire to be made known, and lay open myself to you.

Therefore we may observe by the way, that when we are in any dark condition, that a Christian finds not the beams of God shining on him, let him not lay the blame upon God, as if God were a God that delighted to hide himself. Oh no; it is not his delight. He loves not strangeness to his poor creature. It is not a point of his policy. He is too great to affect * such poor things. No; the fault is altogether in us. We walk not worthy of such a presence; we want humility and preparation. If there be any darkness in the creature, that he finds God doth not so shine on him as in former times, undoubtedly the cause is in himself; for God saith, 'Seek my face.' He desires to open himself. But it is a point that I will not be large in.

We see hence likewise, that

Obs. 3. *God's goodness is a communicative, spreading goodness.*

That is peculiar to God and to those that are led with the Spirit of God, that are like him; they have a communicative, diffusive goodness that loves to spread itself. 'Seek ye my face.' I am good in myself, but I desire to shine on you, to impart my goodness to you.

If God had not a communicative, spreading goodness, he would never have created the world. The Father, Son, and Holy Ghost were happy in themselves, and enjoyed one another before the world was. But that God delights to communicate and spread his goodness, there had never been a creation nor a redemption. God useth his creatures, not for defect of power, that he can do nothing without them, but for the spreading of his goodness; and thereupon comes all the subordination of one creature to another, and all to him.

Oh that we had hearts to make way for such a goodness as God would cast into us, if we were as we should be. God's goodness is a spreading, imparting goodness. It is a common distinction. There is the goodness of the fountain and the goodness of the vessel, that is our goodness, because we contain somewhat in us that is good. The goodness of the creature, that is but the channel or the cistern; but the goodness of God is another manner of goodness, the goodness of the fountain. The fountain begs not from the river; the sun borrows not light from the candle; God begs not goodness from the creature. Ours is a borrowed goodness, but his is a communicative goodness: 'Seek my face,' that I may impart my goodness. The sun delights to spread his beams and his influence in inferior things, to make all things fruitful. Such a goodness is in God as is in a fountain, or in the breast that loves to ease itself of milk.

I note it, that we may conceive aright of God, that is more willing to bestow good than we are to ask it. He is so willing to bestow it, that he becomes a suitor to us, 'Seek ye my face.' He seeks to us to seek him. It is strange that heaven should seek to earth, and yet so it is.

Quest. Whence comes this in God, the attribute of goodness, the spreading goodness in his nature, that he desires to impart and communicate himself?

Ans. There is no envy in God. He hath none above him, and therefore he labours to make all good. There is a mystery in it; but if some be not good, the fault is in themselves. As it is a prerogative in him to make some more and some less good, so there is a fault in them; that I am no better, it is my own fault. The prerogative belongs to God. We must not search into that. But every man may say, I might have been better and more enlarged; I did not seek his face, that he might take occasion to

* That is, 'choose' = love.—G.

enlarge himself towards me. Would we be like our heavenly Father? Let us labour to have large affections, to have a spreading goodness.

Two things make us very like God, that much concern this point: to do things freely of ourselves, and to do them far. To communicate goodness, and to communicate it far to many. The greater the fire is, the further it burns; the greater the love is, the further it extends and communicates itself. There are none more like God than those that communicate what good they have to others, and communicate it as far and remote as they can to extend it to many. Our Saviour Christ, you see what a world were beholding to him; heaven and earth were beholding to him. And the nearer a man comes to Christ, the more there is a kind of self-denial, to do good to others. Saint Paul had a great measure of Christ in him. He was content to be bestowed for the good of the church; the care of all did lie upon him, 2 Cor. xi. 28. A public mind is God's mind; a public mind is a mind that loves to do good freely and largely to others. Therefore God saith, 'Seek my face,' that I may have better opportunity to empty my goodness to you. 'Seek my face;' that is, seek my presence. The face is the glass of the soul, wherein we see the mind of a man. 'Seek my face;' that is, seek my mind, seek my presence, as we shall see afterward. I will speak no more of that point, God's warrant or command, but go on.

'My heart said unto thee, Thy face, Lord, will I seek.'

Here is the work and obedience, 'My heart said unto thee,' &c. David's heart was set in a good and sanctified frame by God; it was between God and his obedience. The heart is between God and our obedience, as it were an ambassador. It understands from God what God would have done, and then it lays a command upon the whole man. The heart and conscience of man is partly divine, partly human. It hath some divinity in it, especially if the man be a holy man. God speaks, and the heart speaks. God speaks to the heart, and the heart speaks to us. And ofttimes when we hear conscience speaking to us, we neglect it; and as St Augustine said of himself, 'God spake often to me, and I was ignorant of it' (*a*). When there is no command in the word that the heart directly thinks of (as indeed many profane careless men scarce have a Bible in their houses), God speaks to them thus; conscience speaks to them some broken command, that they learn against their wills. They heed it not, but David did not so. God said, 'Seek ye my face;' his heart answers, 'Thy face, Lord, will I seek.'

The heart looks upward to God, and then to itself. 'My heart said.' It said to thee, and then to itself. First, his heart said to God, Lord, I have encouragement from thee. Thou hast commanded that I should seek thy face. So his heart looked to God, and then it speaks to itself, 'Thy face, Lord, will I seek.' It looks first to God, and then to all things that come from itself.'

'My heart said.' It said of that point, concerning the thing thou saidst, 'Seek my face.'

'My heart said *to thee*.' David saw God in all his commandments: 'Thou saidst to me, Seek my face; my heart said to thee.' I know the command is from thee; I have to deal with thee in the command and encouragement, and in the warrant. I look not to the words, but to thee; the authority and strength of them comes from thee.

'My heart said to thee, Thy face, Lord, will I seek.'

Between the answer of David and God's command and warrant, the heart comes to think seriously upon the command, and then to enjoin the duty. This is to be considered, because there is no knitting of these two together but by the heart, the serious consideration of the heart. When God saith, 'Seek my face,' he answers, 'I will seek thy face.' How comes this return? The soul considers the ground of the return before the return. A man, when he doth anything, he doth it from the principles of a man. A holy man, when he doth a thing, he doth it from the principle of a holy man; and what is the principles and foundation of the practice of a holy man? A sanctified understanding to tell him what God hath said, and what he hath promised, and wherein God hath discovered himself.

Well, when the heart knows that once, the heart hath enough from heavenward, it hath enough from heaven. God hath said and promised it. Then the heart, by a work it hath of itself, speaks to itself, and to the whole man, to seek God. The heart will not stoop without reason, the heart of an understanding man; but when it sees the command first, 'Seek my face,' then it answers, 'Thy face, Lord, will I seek.' So that this command of God, and this encouragement and warrant from God, 'Seek ye my face,' it was in David's heart, it was written, and set, and grafted in his heart; and then his heart being awed with the command of God, God hath said thus, the heart goes again to God; thou hast said thus, Lord, 'thy face will I seek.'

See the depth of David's speech, when he saith, 'Lord, thy face will I seek.' It came from his heart root, not only from the heart, but from the heart, grounded upon the command and encouragement of God. 'Seek my face.' There is the ground; the heart digesting this thoroughly, this is God's command; I understand it, and understand it from God; I see the authority from whence it comes. Therefore I will stir up myself, 'Thy face, Lord, will I seek.' I shall have occasion to speak somewhat of it afterwards, in the next thing, his obedience. Therefore I go on.

'Thy face, Jehovah, will I seek.'

Here is his return again to God, that he will seek the face of God. I will seek thy face in all my necessities. Then will I seek to thee; and in all thine ordinances I will seek to thee, whereinsoever thy presence is discovered. Thy presence is in all places, especially in thine ordinances; thy presence is in all times, especially in the time of trouble and need. In all times of need I will seek to thee; in all exigences I will seek unto thee; and in all thine ordinances wherein I may find thee. I know I may meet with thee there; thou givest thy people meetings in thine ordinances. It is thy walk; therefore thy face, Lord, will I seek, where I may be sure to meet thee, in thine own way and ordinances. So much for the meaning.

'Thy face, Lord, will I seek.'

Here is, first of all, an application, and obedience from application. They be words of particular application. 'Thy face will I seek.' God had given him a ground, 'Seek ye my face.' His heart makes the application, 'Thy face I will seek,' applying the general encouragement to himself in particular. So that you may observe hence that,

Obs. The ground of all obedience, of all holy intercourse with God, is a spirit of application.

Applying the truths of God, though generally spoken, to ourselves in particular. It is spoken here in the plural number, 'Seek ye my face;' but the general implies the particular, as London is in England. 'Seek ye my face,' all ye that are the people of God. But I am one of them: what though I be not named? That tenet in popery is against sense. When a man is condemned by the law, is his name in the law? It is against such a fact; he is a malefactor: and so the particular is included in the general, 'Seek ye my face.' David knew that; reason taught him that, and not religion.

1. Now the ground of application of divine truths to ourselves in particular is this, *that the truth of God* (setting aside some circumstantial things that arise sometimes to particular persons, that sometimes limit the command to one person, or the promise to one person, cut off those distinctions), *all comfortable truths agree to God's people in all ages, while there is a church in the world.* All truths are eternal truths, die not as men do. David is dead, and Moses is dead; but this truth is not dead, 'Seek ye my face.' Paul is gone, and Peter is gone. We are the Davids and the Moseses, and the Peters, and the Pauls now. Those truths that were good to them are good to us. Whatsoever was written before was written for our comfort, Rom. xv. 4. There is an eternal truth, that runs through all ages of the church, that hath an everlasting comfort. God hath framed the Scriptures not to be limited to the times wherein they were written, as the papists idly speak, Bellarmine and others (*b*); as if they were occasional things; that the Scriptures were written by such and such men, and concerning only those times. But the Scriptures were written for all times, and it concerns all times to apply all truths to themselves, setting aside those circumstances that are applied to particular men, which are easy to discern. In Heb. xiii. 5 that that was said to Joshua, Josh. i. 5, the apostle applies it to the church in his time, and to all: 'Be not afraid; I will not fail thee nor forsake thee.' It is a general truth. 'And Abraham believed God, and it was imputed to him for righteousness,' that whosoever believes as Abraham is a son of Abraham, Rom. iv. 5. These truths are universal, and concern every one, as well as any. And so many other places of Scripture. 'The promise of the blessed seed,' the believing of it runs from the beginning of the world, in all ages to the coming of Christ. All other promises were but an enlargement of that, that was the mother promise. That is the ground of application, that the general truths agree to all the churches. The truth of God is the portion of every child of God. He may claim every promise, and ought to follow the direction of every command.

The reason is, because all the church of God are heirs alike—heirs of the promise, children of Abraham, heirs of salvation. They have interest in Christ alike, 'in whom all the promises are yea and amen;' in whom all the promises have their making and their performance. And by reason that there is an indifferent equality, in regard of the main things, of all the children of God, they have interest alike in all the benefits by Christ: in all truths, in all substantial duties to God, and all favours from God. That is the ground of the equity of application.

2. But if you will have the ground *of the necessity of it*, nature will shew that. For the truths are food. If food be not taken, what good doth it do without application? The word of God is a sword: what will a sword do if it hangs up in a man's chamber? or if it be not used when the enemy approacheth? The application of the sword of the Spirit gives the virtue to it. It is to no purpose else. Divine truths are physic. If it be not applied, what use is there of physic?

There is a necessity, if we will obey God, of a spirit of application. There is nothing that will do good but by application, neither in nature nor in grace. There must be a virtual* application at least. The heavens

* That is, = in efficacy, energy.—G.

work upon the earth. There is no application bodily, the heavens are too high. But there is a virtual application; there comes light in, and influence to these inferior bodies. Therefore we say the sun is in the house, and in the place we are in, though there be only his influence there. But there must be application of divine truth to the soul. It must be brought near the soul before the soul can move. There is a necessity of application from a principle of nature to make it our own.

Now as in nature there is a power in the soul to work out of the food that that is good for every member, which we call a digestive power and faculty, that applies and assimilates the meat and nourishment we take to every part; there be *fibræ*, sucking veins, that suck out of the meat strength for this and that purpose; so there is in the soul of every Christian and holy man: there is a spiritual sucking; there is a drawing digestive spirit, that digests and draws out nourishment out of the book of God, that is fit for him; that he can say, This is mine, this is for me. I want comfort and strength and direction, here it is. I want light, here it is. I am weak, here is supply for it. So there is a digestive power by the Spirit of God in every Christian, to suck and to draw out of the word that that is fit for all purposes and turns; and he can apply the word upon every occasion: as, if it be a command, he obeys it; if it be a threatening, he trembles at it; if it be comfort, he rests in it; if it be a direction, he follows it likewise. He applies it answerable to the nature of the word, whatsoever it is. His heart is moulded answerable to the word, by reason of the Spirit of application.

3. As there is a ground of the application of the word, and a necessity of it, *so there is a principle of application;* that is, the Spirit of God in the hearts of the children of God, teaching their spirits to draw wholesome truths fitting to themselves; and none but the children of God can do it, that have the Spirit of God. They cannot apply the word of God aright. False application of the word of God is the cause of all mischief sometimes, when those that apply the law should apply the gospel; and on the contrary, when those that should apply the law, sinful, secure persons, apply the gospel. Many times poor distressed persons, that comfort belongs to—'Oh comfort my people,' Isa. xl. 1—they apply the law that belongs not to them. In that case false application is the ground of mischief. Therefore the Spirit of God is the principle of application of divine truths, according to the exigence and estate of God's people.

Use. Therefore *we should be stirred up to beg the spirit of application, to maintain our communion and intercourse with God,* that we may apply every thing duly and truly to ourselves and our own souls. All is to no purpose else, if we do not apply it, if it be not brought home to our souls and digested throughly in our hearts. We must say, This is from God, and this belongs to me; when we hear truths unfolded, to say of ourselves, This concerns me, and say not, This is a good portion and a good truth for such a one and such a one, but, Every one take out his own portion, this is for me. God saith, 'Seek my face; thy face, Lord, will I seek,' with a spirit of application.

If we do not—as indeed it is the fault of the times to hear the word of God loosely—we care not so much to hear the word of God, as to hear the gifts of men. We desire to hear fine things, to increase notions. We delight in them, and to hear some empty creature, to fasten upon a story or some phrases by the by. Alas! you come here to hear duties and comforts, if you be good, and sentences against you, if you be naught. We speak God's threatenings to you that will wound you to hell, except you pull them out by repentance. It is another manner of matter to hear than it is took for. 'Take heed how you hear,' saith Christ, Luke viii. 18. So we had need, for the word that we hear now shall judge us at the latter day. Thereupon we should labour for a spirit of application, to make a right use of it as we should.

Therefore those humble souls that are cast down in the sight and sense of their sins, they must apply the sweet and blessed comforts of the gospel, such as are contrite in spirit: 'Blessed are the poor in spirit; blessed are they that hunger and thirst after righteousness. Come unto me, all ye that are weary and heavy laden,' &c., Mat. xi. 28. Those on the other side, that go on in a course of sin, and will not be reclaimed, let them consider what Moses saith, Deut. xxix. 20, 'If a man go on and bless himself, my wrath shall smoke against such a man, and burn to hell.' I will not remove my wrath from him, till by little and little I take my good Spirit from him, and let him go with some temporal comforts, and then bring him to hell. 'I will curse him in his blessings.' He shall have blessings, but he shall be cursed in all that he doth; and all things shall be in wrath and anger that shall burn to hell. Such like places, let such men apply to themselves. There is no comfort at all to men that live in sin wittingly and willingly. 'If I regard iniquity in my heart, God will not hear my prayer,' Ps. lxvi. 18. If a man despise the ordinance of God, hearing and good means, 'his prayer shall be abominable:' 'He that will not hear the law, his prayer is abominable,' Prov. xxviii. 9. The applying of these things would make men bethink themselves, and turn to God, when he considers what part of the word belongs to him, and makes a right application.

If we make not a right application of God's truths, this mischief will come of it.

(1.) *We dishonour God and his bounty.* Hath God been so bountiful, as to give us so many instructions and such promises? and shall not we make them our own? What is the end of the ministry but to spread before us the unsearchable riches of Christ? They are yours, if you will take them. When you have not a spirit of application, and are not in case to take them, they are lost: God's bounty is discredited.

(2.) *The devil rejoiceth when he seeth what excellent things are laid open in the church of God, in the ministry, what sweet promises and comforts, but here is nobody to take them and lay hold on them;* like a table that is richly furnished, and there is nobody comes and takes it. It makes the devil sport, it rejoiceth the enemy of mankind when we lose so great advantage, that we will not apply those blessed truths and make them our own. There is no greater delight to Satan, than for us to refuse those dainties that God hath provided for us. What can rejoice an enemy more, than to see courtesies refused? He sees that all the Scripture is for comfort to poor distressed souls; and when they refuse their comforts and set light by them, as they tell Job, 'Settest thou light by the consolations of the Almighty?' Job. xv. 11, then Satan, the enemy of mankind, and especially the enemy of our comfort, since he hath lost all comfort and all hope of it himself, he rejoiceth to see us in this condition comfortless. Therefore let us lay claim to the promises by a spirit of application.

(3.) Again, *We are injurious to ourselves, we rob our own souls.* The want of this makes Christians be discouraged and droop as they do. When they are cast down, all comfortable truths belong to them, yet they put them off: This is not for me and those in my case. When God saith he will come and dwell with a humble heart, This is not for me. This spirit of peevishness and forwardness* is that that keeps them long from that comfort that they might enjoy. What! to be in the midst of comforts and to starve; for a man to be at a feast and to starve, because he hath not a spirit to digest and to take that that is fit for him!

We detest, and deservedly, those misers that, in the midst of all their abundance, will not spend sixpence upon themselves. What a spirit of baseness is this, in the midst of spiritual contentments and refreshings, when God offers to feed our souls with the fat things of his house, to say, Oh no! this belongs not to me; and cherish a peevish froward spirit that puts all away. Why do we not labour to be in such a condition that we may be cherished? and that we may have satisfaction? to be truly hungry and poor in spirit, that we may be filled and satisfied, and not to go on thus stubbornly? There is a proud kind of modesty. Oh, this belongs not to me; I am unworthy. If we will hearken to our own misgiving hearts in the time of temptation, we shall never answer God and say, 'Lord, thy face will I seek.' Therefore let us labour for a spirit of supplication.† I will not enforce that point further.

Now from this spirit of application, from this general 'Seek ye my face,' comes obedience; for it is a speech of obedience.

'Thy face, Lord, will I seek.'

I will seek *by thy strength and grace;* for when God utters a general command to his children, there goes with that command a secret virtue, whereby they are enabled to seek him. There came a hidden virtue with this 'Seek my face,' when David's spirit was raised by God to think of it. Together with the thought of this 'Seek my face,' there was a virtue enabling his soul to return back to God, to say, 'Lord, thy face will I seek.' So though David said, 'I will seek thy face,' yet there was a spiritual virtue that enabled him. God must find us before we can seek him. He must not only give the command to seek his face, but together with the command, there goes a work of the Spirit to the children of God, that enableth them to seek him.

In the covenant of grace, God doth his part and ours too. Our part is to seek God, to please him and walk before him. They are all one; I need not be curious in particulars. Now this was not a speech of self-confidence, but a speech of the Spirit of God, that went with the command to him.

This is a great encouragement, by the way, to hear good things, and to come to the congregation. We hear many great things, high duties, but we are not able to perform them. It is true, but the gospel is the ministry of the Spirit; and together with the duty there goes the Spirit to enable us to the duty. 'Stand up and walk,' saith Peter to the poor lame man, and there went an enabling virtue to raise him, Acts iii. 6. 'Arise,' saith Christ to Lazarus, and there went a divine virtue to make him rise, John xi. 43; and here, 'Seek my face,' there went a divine virtue to make him seek, which those that contemn the ordinances of God want, because they will not attend upon the ordinances. So much for that.

Now I come to his obedience.

'Thy face, Lord, will I seek.'

This obedience ariseth from application, and his obedience hath these qualifications:

1. *It was present.* As soon as he heard God's will, as soon as his heart did think of the word, he puts not off. The Spirit of God and the works

* Qu. 'frowardness'?—Ed.

† Qu. 'application'?—Ed.

of it, are not slow in the children of God ; but when they hear their duty, there is a spirit presently, 'Thy face will I seek,' before the heart grow cold again.

2. Again, This return and answer, as it was present, so likewise *it was a pliable obedience :* 'Thy face will I seek.' It is a speech of a ready, cheerful, pliable heart. Where the Spirit of God works, it makes not only present and quick, but cheerful and pliable. For the Spirit of God is like fire, that softens the hardness of the heart, that naturally is like iron, and makes it pliable. God's people are a voluntary people, as it is Ps. cx. 3 ; a people of devotion, of readiness of will, and cheerfulness ; a free-hearted people, a people set at large. They are led with a royal spirit, a spirit above their own ; and that makes that easy and pleasant to them, that otherwise is difficult and impossible to nature.

When Isaiah's lips were touched with a coal from the altar—that is, he had somewhat from the Spirit of God to encourage nature—then 'Here I am, Lord ; send me,' Isa. vi. 8. He detracted* the business before, and put it off as much as he could. The Spirit of God makes pliable, as we see in the Acts. They cared not for suffering whips or anything, because they were made pliable to God's service ; they accounted it an honour to suffer anything for God's sake, Acts v. 41. The obedience that is good is pliable and cheerful.

God would have things in the church done by such people. The very building of the tabernacle was done by such voluntary people, that brought in as God moved their hearts. Oh, beloved, a Christian knows what it is to have a royal spirit, a free spirit. David knew it. When he had lost it by his sin, he prayed that he might have a free spirit, a cheerful spirit, in the service of God, and in his particular calling, for sin darkens and straitens the soul. 'Thy face will I seek.' His heart was weary and pliable now, as God would have it.

So should our hearts be ; and they will be so, if we have the Spirit of God, ready and cheerful. God hath none to fight his battles against Satan and the kingdom of darkness, but voluntaries. All God's people are voluntaries. They are not pressed soldiers ; I mean, not against their wills, in that sense. Indeed, they have press-money in baptism, to fight against the world, the flesh, and the devil ; but they are not pressed, they are voluntaries. They know they serve a good general, that will pay them abundantly ; therefore they labour to be voluntary. It is a good saying, There is no virtue in men that do things against their wills ; for that is virtue and grace that comes from a man from his own principles, from cheerfulness : 'God loveth a cheerful giver.' I might enlarge this, but I do but take it as it may strengthen the point. Our obedience to God, it must be pliable, and cheerful, and voluntary.

3. Again, Obedience, if it be true, *it is perfect and sincere*, looking to God : 'Thy face, Lord, will I seek.' We must eye God in it, and God's commandment, and not have a double eye. We must not look to our own selves. It must be perfect obedience ; that is, opposite to that which is hypocritical. That is the best perfection. For the perfection of degrees is not to be attained here, but this perfection of soundness is to be laboured for ; as we see here it was a sound obedience : 'Thy face, Lord, will I seek.' I will not seek thy favours and blessings so much as thy face. It was perfect obedience, as perfection is opposed to unsoundness.

4. It was likewise a *professed obedience before all the world, in spite of*

* That is, 'drew back from,' = delayed.—G.

Satan: 'Thy face will I seek.' Let the devil and the world do what they can; let others do as they will; but as Joshua saith, 'If you will worship other gods,' if you will fall away, do; 'but I and my house will serve the Lord.' What if his house will not serve the Lord? If my house will not serve the Lord, I will. So we should all be of Joshua's mind, 'I and my house will serve the Lord,' Josh. xxiv. 15, let the world go which way it will. In blessed St Paul's time, Oh, saith he, 'There are many of whom I have told you often, and now tell you weeping, who are enemies to the cross of Christ, whose end is damnation, who mind earthly things,' Philip. iii. 18. What doth Paul in the mean time? Oh, but 'our conversation is in heaven.' We swim a contrary way. We care not to let the world know it. Our conversation is another way. So our obedience must not only be present, and pliable, and perfect, but a professed obedience: that is, to break through all the oppositions of the devil and the world; with an invincible resolution to break through all difficulties, and scandals, and examples of great persons, and of this and that, if we will go to God, and say truly, 'Lord, thy face will I seek.' Let other men seek what they will: let them seek the face and favour of others; 'Thy face will I seek.' Thou shalt be instead of all to me, as indeed he is.

5. Again, As it is a professed, so it is a continued, *a perpetual obedience.* He is resolved for the time to come. 'Thy face will I seek:' not only now, and then turn my back upon thee afterwards; but I will seek thy face, till I see thee in heaven. I see thy face in thine ordinances, in the word, in thy people; where two or three be gathered, thou art among them, Mat. xviii. 20. I will see thy face as I may, till I see it in heaven. So here is a perpetual resolution: 'Thy face I will seek.'

6. Lastly, There is one thing more in this *obedience and answer to God's command,* that his answer to God is an answerable answer; that is, the answer and obedience is suitable to the command. God's command was, 'Seek my face.' His answer is, 'Thy face, Lord, will I seek.' So the point is, that

Obs. Our obedience to God must be proportionable to that that is commanded.

It must not be this or that devised by men. When the Lord's eye is on you in this place, and gives you a charge to do thus, the obedience must be suitable. When he saith, 'Seek my face,' we must obey: 'Thy face, Lord, will we seek.' Therefore it may, in some poor sense, be compared to an echo. We return obedience in the same kind. The Spirit of God teacheth the children of God to do so, to answer God in all the things he doth. I know not a better evidence of a child of God, than this answering spirit. How shall I know that God loves me? I love him again; therefore I know he hath loved me first. It is an undoubted argument. How shall I know that God hath chosen me? I choose him: 'Whom have I in heaven but thee? and what is there in earth in comparison of thee?' Ps. lxxiii. 25. It is an undoubted argument: Shall I be able to single out God, to be instead of all to me? and hath not he chosen me first? Can there be anything in the current, that is not in the spring before? It is impossible. I know God; I look on him as my father: certainly he hath shined on me first. I have said to him, 'Thou art my God;' certainly he hath said before, 'Thou art my servant.' If I say to him, 'Thou art my God,' certainly he hath said before, 'I am thy salvation.' He hath begun. For this is the order: God begins. He saith, 'Seek my face;' then if we have grace to return answerable obedience to God, 'Thy face, Lord, will I seek.' When thou biddest me, Lord, I will love thee, I will choose thee, and delight in thee; thou shalt be my God. If we have this returning spirit back again, we cannot have a better argument that God loves us, than by answering God's course.

This is that that St Peter hath in 1 Peter iii. 21. That that doth all in baptism, it is not 'the washing of the filth of the body,' but the ἐπερώτημα, 'the answer,' or the demand 'of a good conscience;' but 'answer' is better. The answer of a good conscience cleanseth in baptism. What is that?

In baptism, dost thou believe, saith the minister, in God the Father Almighty? I do believe. That was the answer. Dost thou believe in God the Son? I do believe. Dost thou believe the forgiveness of sins, the resurrection of the body, and the life everlasting? I do believe. Dost thou renounce the devil and his works? I renounce them. That is the answer of a good conscience. Where that is from the heart, there God hath spoken to that heart before, and there is obedience to purpose. 'Thy face will I seek.' It is that that brings comfort, not the washing of the water. It is not the eating of the bread, and drinking the wine, and hearing the word of God: when there is not the answer of a good conscience, when we say we believe, and we will do this, to do it indeed, Lord, 'I will believe;' I will go out of the church with a purpose to practise what I hear. Here is the answer of a good conscience, when we mingle what we hear with faith, and labour to practise it, or else it will do no good.

Our obedience must be suitable and answerable, as I said before: if it be a direction, to follow it; if it be a command, to obey it; if it be a threatening, to fear it; if it be a comfort, a promise, to rest upon it. Let there be a suitableness of obedience to the word thereafter as the word is. Let us have a spiritual desire to these things, to imitate the holy man of God, as we desire to share in his comforts.

I will follow this point of the answerableness of obedience a little further, and then come to the particular of seeking.

Let our obedience be every way answerable first. Let the heart think what God saith, what God commands and promiseth; let the heart take the word of God the second time and ruminate on it, and go over it again. Let us look into the word, and see what is commanded, and what is promised, and then let the heart go over it again. And then upon that allege it to God.

(1.) *Put case a man be in trouble*, Lord, thou hast commanded, 'Call upon me in the day of trouble, and I will hear thee,' Ps. l. 15. Let the heart think of it and go over that encouragement. It is rather an encouragement than a command. Though indeed God lay a command on us to be good to our own souls, it is a duty to love ourselves. Therefore he commands us to go to him, to seek his face, as though we wronged him by disobedience, when we injure ourselves by our peevishness, as indeed we do. God loves us better than we love ourselves. Let us think of the command and invitation; thou hast commanded me, Lord, and encouraged me to come; I am now in trouble, experience teacheth me. I come to thee. Thou hast said, 'He that sitteth in darkness, and seeth no light, let him trust in the name of the Lord,' Isa. l. 10. I am in darkness, and see no light now, I trust in thy name. Let the heart think of the promise, and then allege it to God, and come with an obedient answer, and cast itself upon him, and trust in him.

(2.) *We are in want, perhaps*, and see no issue, no supply. Think of God's gracious promise, 'I will not fail thee, nor forsake thee,' Heb. xiii. 5. I come to thee and claim this promise; I am in covenant with thee, &c.

(3.) *So we should take the promise.* Thou hast said, 'At what time soever a sinner comes to thee with a repentant heart, thou wilt forgive his iniquities; and though his sins were as scarlet, thou wilt make them as snow, and white as wool,' Isa. i. 18. My soul thinks of that command, and I come to thee.

Thou hast bid all that are weary and heavy laden in soul, that are troubled in conscience with the sense of their sins, to come unto thee. My heart thinks of thy command and invitation, I come to thee; I am weary and heavy laden. First, let us think of the encouragement, that is our warrant, and then yield present obedience. And then what will be the issue? What will spring from it when the heart and obedience join with the command, that there is a meeting, that they concentrate the heart and obedience? God bids the heart obey. The heart saith, I do obey. When these meet, the issue must be exceeding comfortable. It cannot be otherwise, when the obedient heart meets God in his command, in his promise.

In all perplexity of business, 'commit thy way to the Lord, and he shall establish thy thoughts,' Prov. iii. 6, and other places. Lord, I commit my ways to thee; establish my thoughts and designs agreeable to thy will, because thou hast bid me commit my ways to thee.

In the hour of death, let us commend ourselves to God, 'as to a gracious and merciful Creator,' 1 Pet. iv. 19. Lord, I commend to thee my soul, who art the Creator of my soul and the Redeemer of it. Here is an obedience answerable. What can be the issue of it but comfort?

Therefore let us learn by the example of this blessed man, that when he had but a hint from God, 'Seek ye my face,' answers, 'Thy face, Lord, will I seek.'

Faith will see light at a little crevice. When it sees an encouragement once, a command, it will soon answer: and when it sees a promise, half a promise, it will welcome it. It is an obedient thing, 'the obedience of faith,' Rom. xvi. 26. It believes, and upon believing, it goes to God. As the servants of the king of Assyria, they catch the word presently, 'Thy servant Benhadad,' 1 Kings xx. 32; so faith, it catcheth the word.

To put God in mind, it is an excellent thing with the prophet, whosoever penned the 119th Psalm, whether David, or some other, 'Remember thy promise, wherein thou hast caused thy servant to trust,' ver. 49. As it is Neh. i. 8, 'Remember, Lord.' He puts God in mind of his promise; and so it is good often to put God in mind. Lord, thou hast made such and such promises. I know thou canst not deny thyself. If thou shouldst deny thy word, thou must deny thyself. Thy word is thyself. 'Remember thy promise, wherein thou hast caused thy servant to trust.' If I be deceived, thou hast deceived me, for thou hast given me this promise and this command. This is an excellent way to deal with God, as it were, to wrestle with him. 'By thy promise thou hast quickened me,' Ps. cxix. 50. When I was dull and dead-hearted, then I thought on such and such a promise. I allege that promise, and apply it by a spirit of faith, and that quickened me.

And indeed, as I said, God hath made us fit to answer him, and we should study in all things to return unto him by his Spirit. Whatsoever God doth, the heart should return back again—love for love, knowledge for knowledge, seeking for seeking, choosing for choosing. He begins with us, he chooseth us, he loves us, he seeks us; and we, if ever we intend to be friends with God, and to entertain a holy communion, as all that shall be saved must do, we should labour to have our hearts to return to God, what we find from God first. 'Thy face, Lord, will I seek.' To come more particularly to this seeking, which is the particular of the obedience and of the application.

'Thy face, Lord, will I seek.'

Seeking implies that our happiness is out of ourselves. It implies that there is somewhat in ourselves, in the application to which there must be some happiness. Therefore we go out of ourselves to seek. It is a motion, and it is out of an apprehension of some want; a man seeks out of some want, or out of some loss, or out of some duty. Either he hath loss, and therefore he seeks; or else he wants, and therefore he seeks; or else he owes respect and duty, and therefore he seeks. It is somewhat without a man that moves his seeking.

God need not seek the creature; he hath all fulness in himself. Indeed, his love makes him seek for our love, to be reconciled to him. But the creature, because his happiness is out of himself in communion with God, the fountain of all good, he must seek.

Christians must be seekers.

This is the generation of seekers, Ps. xxiv. 6. All mankind, if ever they will come to heaven, they must be a generation of seekers. Heaven is a generation of finders, of possessors, of enjoyers, seekers of God. But here we are a generation of seekers. We want somewhat that we must seek. When we are at best, we want the accomplishment of our happiness. It is a state of seeking here, because it is a state of want; we want something alway.

But to come more particularly to this seeking the face of God, or the presence of God.

The presence of God, and the face of God, where is it to be sought for?

(1.) Know that first for a ground: *The presence of God it is everywhere.* But that is not the thing here purposed.

(2.) There is a face and presence of God *in everything, in every creature.* Therefore every creature hath the name of God; sometimes a rock: because God is strong, so a rock is strong. So likewise a shield; as a shield defends, so God defends us. There is some resemblance of God in the creature. Therefore God hath the name of the creature. But that is not here meant.

(3.) The presence of God meant here is, that presence that he shews *in the time of need, and in his ordinances.* He shews a presence in need and necessity, that is a gracious presence to his children, a gracious face. As in want of direction, he shews his presence of light to direct them; in weakness he shews his strength; in trouble and perplexity he will shew his gracious and comfortable presence to comfort them. In perplexity he shews his presence to set the heart at large, answerable to the necessity. So in need God is present with his children, to direct them, to comfort them, to strengthen them, if they need that.

(4.) And *in the issue of all business* there is a presence of God to give a blessing; for there is a presence must be even to the end of things. When we have all we would have, yet God must give a blessing. So you see there is a presence of God answerable to the necessity of man, as it hath reference to this place.

'Thy face will I seek,' to direct me by thy heavenly light when I know not what to do, as Jehoshaphat said, 'We know not what to do, but our eyes are towards thee,' 2 Chron. xx. 12. And so in weakness, when we have no strength of our own, then go to God, to seek the face of God, that he would be present with us. So when we are comfortless, go to God that comforts the abject, 'the God of all comfort;' go to him, for his presence, for help. And when we are troubled in our hearts about success, what will become of such and such a business; go to God, that gives success and issue to all. Thus we see a presence of God answerable to every necessity of man.

(5.) There is a gracious presence of God likewise *in his ordinances.* That is the chief presence, next to heaven, the presence in God's ordinances; that is, in the unfolding of the word, in the administration of the sacraments, in the communion of saints. Indeed, in the ordinances God is graciously present. 'Where two or three are gathered together, I will be in the midst of them,' Mat. xviii. 20. Therefore in Rev. i. 12, *seq.*, it is said, 'that Christ walks in the midst of the seven golden candlesticks;' that is, in the midst of the church. There is a gracious presence of Christ in the midst of the candlesticks. He takes his walk there. Christ hath a special presence in his church in the ordinances; and that David aims at here too, not only, I will seek thy face in trouble and necessity, when I need anything from thee, but 'Thy face will I seek in all thine ordinances,' to enable me for the other. For it is in vain for a man to think to seek God in his necessity and exigence, if he seek not God in his ordinances, and do not joy in them. So you see where the face and presence of God is to be sought; in necessities of all kinds, and in the ordinances.

Now, in our seeking the presence or face of God, there is four or five things that I will touch the heads of.

[1.] First of all, seeking implies *observance.* Seek my face; that is, observe me, respect me as a God. 'Thy face I will seek,' I will be a follower of thee; as in English an 'observer' is a follower, a creature. It is a proud word; as if man could make a man of nothing. And indeed they are creatures in that kind, they are raised of nothing. To seek a man is to observe him. There is a notable place for it, Prov. xxix. 26, 'Many seek the ruler's favour.' In the Greek translation, the Septuagint, the word is, to observe and respect a man, which is translated seeking (*c*). Many observe the ruler; but every man's judgment cometh from the Lord. You see those that think to rise by the favour of such or such a man, they will be his followers, as I said, and observe him; they study men; as those that rise by favour that way, they study not books so much as men, what may delight such a man, what he respects. Surely they will serve him at every turn. A base atheist makes a man his god. That he may rise, he will deny God and the motions of conscience, and honesty, and all to observe the face of a great man whom he hopes to rise by. But a true Christian observes the great God. The greatest preferment comes from him. So it signifies to 'observe.'

In Ps. lxii. 11, there you shall see the ground of observation is, that power belongs to God. 'I have heard once, nay, twice.' He heard it twice by the meditation of it, by going over it in his heart again. I have heard once, nay, twice; that is, I thought again and again on it; that is, hearing of it oft. We may hear a truth a hundred times, that is, by meditating of it. 'I have heard once, nay, twice, that power belongs to God;' that is, riches and power to advance a man. Atheistical men think all belongs to the creature, but power belongs to God. That is one thing that is meant by seeking, diligent observing of God, and respect to him and his will and commandments in all things.

If so be that a person of great place should say, Observe me, and I will prefer you, I hope men would be ready enough, they need no more words. Here is the atheism of our hearts. God saith, I will do all good for you. The greatest preferment is to be the child of God here, and the heir of heaven after. What preferment is there to that of Christianity! And he saith, Seek my face, observe me, respect me, let the eye of your souls be to me, as it is in the Psalm, 'As the eyes of a maid are toward the hand of her mistress,' Ps. cxxiii. 2. The obedience of a servant is toward the eye of the commander, so the obedience of a Christian is toward the eye of God, to see what God commands. We should be more serviceable to God. It is an argument of the atheism of our hearts, to take more encouragement from a mortal man that can raise us and do us a pleasure, than from God himself. But to let that go, that is the first branch, 'Seek my face,' that is, observe me.

[2.] Then seek my face; that is, *depend upon me*. To seek God's face, is to depend upon him for all. It argues dependence. For him that we observe, we observe him for something. We depend upon him to be our raiser and maker. So seek my face, seek my countenance and favour; depend upon me, and it shall be sufficient for you.

[3.] Then, in the third place, 'Seek my face;' that is, *seek my favour and grace*. Favour appears and shines in the face. 'Seek my face,' observe me, depend on me; for what? For my favour. What is that? It is all. If we have the grace of God, we have all. For the grace of God is in every thing that is good to us. If we have the graces to salvation, they come of free grace: every good gift is the grace of God. Children are the grace of God. So, if we have the grace of God, we have all for our good. We have all in the spring of good, which is the grace and favour of God. As men, if they be graced from a great person, they study not this and that particular thing. They think, I have his favour, and that favour of his is ready for all exigences. And therefore, in way of compliment, they say, I seek not this or that, but your favour.

The favour of God, it is a storehouse, and spring, and fountain, better than life itself; as the psalmist saith, 'The loving-kindness of the Lord is better than life,' Ps. lxiii. 3. When life fails, the favour of God never fails. Life will fail, and all earthly comforts; but the favour of God is better than life itself; it is everlasting and eternal. In Psalm iv. 7, you see how worldly, atheistical men rejoice when their corn and wine and oil increase. And 'who will shew us any good?' who? It is no matter who; any good, any hope of preferment, it is no matter what way; and it is no matter what, any good; and let them but shew it and we will work it out, we have wit enough. Oh, saith he, but your wit I stand not upon, nor your courses; but, 'Lord, let thy face shine upon me, lift up the light of thy countenance,' and that shall be instead of all honours and preferments. So in seeking we must observe God, and depend upon him; and for what? For his favour especially; for the face and favour of God. Let me have a good look from thee, O Lord; let me have thy favour and love. For other things I leave them to thy wisdom, thou art wise enough; only let thy face shine on me.

Oh this favour and face of God, it is a sweet thing, this presence of God! What is heaven but the presence of God there? Let God be present in a dungeon, it will be a paradise; let God be absent, paradise it is as a hell or dungeon, as it was to Adam; after he had sinned, he ran to hide himself. What is hell but the want of God's presence? God's face and favour is not there. What makes hell in the heart of a man? God is not there, but leaves the heart to its own darkness and confusion. Oh therefore, the face and favour of God, seek that especially!

[4.] Again, To seek the face of God *is to pray to him, to put this in execution in prayer.* Everywhere in Scripture it is all one to pray and to seek God's face. It is called the spirit of prayer; which because I have spoken of at large out of another scripture, I will now say nothing of it.*

[5.] Likewise, in the next place, to seek the face of God *is to attend upon the presence of God, wheresoever he reveals himself;* to attend upon the word and ordinances is to 'seek the face of God.' It is said that Cain went from the face of God when he went from the worship of God in his father's house; he went out from God, Gen. iv. 16. Where God is worshipped, there God is present; and when we leave the place where God is worshipped, we leave God's presence. God is more especially present there, therefore seeking the face of God is to attend upon God's ordinance: 'I will seek thy face;' that is, wheresoever there is any presence of thee I will seek thee.

Christ when he was lost, he was found in the temple. That hath a literal sense, but it is true in a spiritual sense. If we lose Christ, and have not comfort from Christ, we shall find him in the temple. The sweetest presence of his Spirit is there. His body is in heaven, and his Spirit is his vicar in the world. If we want comfort and direction from Christ, we shall meet him in the temple. There he gives us sweet meetings by his Spirit; there we have the comfort, and direction, and spiritual strength that we wanted before we came. There is the best meeting. As in the Canticles, Christ goes into the 'garden of spices.' He goes among his children, that are as a watered garden, and as so many plants of righteousness and beds of spices. He delights to be there. Christ is in the communion of saints in the ordinances, therefore 'thy face will I seek,' especially in the tabernacle, and temple after; especially in the church and communion of saints, there thy face will I seek. Thus we see the unfolding of this promise of a gracious, obedient, respective heart: 'Thy face will I seek.' I will add no more, but come to the use of it.

Use. And in the first place, by way of direction, that we may seek the face of God—that is, observe him, and depend upon him, and enjoy his favour, and meet with him in his ordinances—we must first get

The knowledge of God [and of] ourselves.

1. *Get the knowledge of God,* for they that know him will seek to him. They that know his riches, his power, his sufficiency, in a word, his all-sufficiency for all things, they will seek to him. And they that know themselves, that know their wants, their inability to supply those wants, and know the greatness of those wants, and that they must be supplied, they will out of themselves. They that have nothing at home will seek abroad. The knowledge of these two therefore, of the great God, the all-sufficient God; and of ourselves, the insufficiency of ourselves every way, either for direction, or for protection, or for comfort in distress, or for strength in duty to go through business, or for issue when we are about anything; 'they that know that the way of man is not in man,' as Jeremiah saith, x. 23, they would certainly out of themselves. Therefore let us grow in the knowledge of God and of ourselves, of our own wants and necessities.

And especially know God now in Christ. For there is enmity between the nature of God and the nature of man, of sinful man; but that Christ

* Cf. the General Index under 'Prayer.'—G.

hath taken our nature now and made it lovely to God, and God lovely to us. Christ Immanuel, God and man, 'God with us,' hath made God and us friends. Therefore now we must go to God in that Immanuel, in Christ, that ladder that joins heaven and earth together. See God's face shining in Christ, his gracious face, and this will encourage us to go to God together with our wants. Go not to absolute God, a God without a mediator; for then God is 'a consuming fire,' Heb. xii. 29.

2. In the next place, when we go to God, and seek to God, be sure *to seek his favour and grace in the first place.* If we want any particular thing, protection or direction or comfort in distress, go not for that in the first place, but let us see in what terms God and we are; let us be sure that reconciliation and peace be made. For if we seek to God in our particular wants, and have not made our peace before, but have sought to other gods, to men, and to our shifts,* God may say, You seek to me! Go to the gods you have served, to the great men you have served, to the riches you have trusted unto, go to your shifts.* Therefore, first, make peace and reconciliation with God before you seek other things. If a man have offended a great person, he doth not go and seek particular favours, till first he have made peace and taken up the quarrel. Let us take up the quarrel between God and us, by repentance and a promise of new obedience; get reconciliation that way, and then seek for particular favours after.

For what if God give you particular favours, if they be not from his grace and favour, what will they do us good? What will all that a reprobate wretch hath do him good? What will his favours, his riches, and honours and preferments do him good when he dies, when he shall conflict with the anger of God? when he shall see hell before him and see heaven shut? He seeth he hath all, from a general providence and as a reward for his care in this world. God answereth him with a civil enlargement for his civil obedience, but he hath his reward. Heaven he hath not, he cared not for it. What will all do without the love of God in Christ? Therefore I beseech you, let us first seek the favour and mercy of God in Christ.

And then for particular things go to him as the exigence is; for in God there is a supply for all turns, and that is the ground of seeking; for our seeking it must be a wise seeking. Now it were not wise, unless there were a supply in God for every want, whatsoever it is. If the creature could do anything without God, we should upon good ground make that God. If anything could raise us without God, I mean, to comfort, we might seek to them, and make them God upon good reason; but what can they do? In anger, God may let a man enjoy favours, as the fruits of his displeasure, but what can they do without him? They can do nothing. Therefore it must be the supreme cause, the highest cause, the great wheel that turns every little inferior wheel in the world. They turn with the great wheel of divine providence and goodness; therefore go to him as the first cause.

3. Again, In seeking the favour of God, we must search our consciences, *to come with pure and clean hearts to God to seek him.* If we regard 'iniquity in our hearts, God will not hear our prayers,' Ps. lxvi. 18. We come to God with a purpose to offend him. If we come not with a purpose to leave our sins, why do we come? God will not regard our prayers. We must come with pure consciences to God, as it is excellently set down, Ps. xxiv. 3, 'Who shall ascend into thy hill, O Lord? who shall stand in thy holy place? He that hath clean hands and a pure heart.' And then he saith after,

* That is, 'expedients.'—G.

'This is the generation of them that seek him,' those that have clean hands and a pure heart. Thou hast foul hands; thou art a briber, a corrupter; thou hast an impure heart; thou art a filthy creature; thou hast lived in such and such sins; cleanse thy hands and thy heart. 'This is the generation of them that seek him.' If a man seek the pure and holy God with an unclean heart and unclean hands; if he be corrupt in his hands and in his heart, that is the fountain, he may seek God long enough before he find him, and if he see God, it is in anger.

4. Again, If we would seek the face and favour of God, *let us study the word hard.* Study the promises, as I said before, bind him with his own word. Thou hast said thus, I allege thy own word. Jacob, when he wrestled with God, Gen. xxxii. 24, then he saw God; he called the place Peniel, that is, the face of God, because of seeing God. Upon wrestling, when the heart by faith wrestleth with God by the promise—'Lord thou hast done this; though I feel no comfort, yet I will rest upon thee'—that place will be Peniel; the face of God will be there, God will shew himself.

And let the extremity be what it will, seek God in extremity; allege the word of God in extremity. What word have you for extremity? 'In the mountain God will be seen,' Gen. xxii. 14. His face will be seen in the mount; that is, when there is no other help whatsoever. 'God is a present help in trouble,' Ps. xlvi. 5. He is the 'God that comforteth the abject,' 2 Cor. vii. 6, that none else can comfort; 'and he that is in darkness, and sees no light, let him trust in the name of the Lord,' Isa. l. 10. And 'though I were in the valley of the shadow of death,' if the Lord be with me, 'I will trust in him,' Ps. xxiii. 4. 'And though thou kill me, yet will I trust in thee,' saith Job, Job xiii. 15. In extremity seek God then, and find out words and promises then, as the Scriptures is large in that kind; for then there is most need of seeking God. Lord, if thou help not now, none can help.

And this is the difference between a true child of God and another. In the time of extremity, Saul seeks to the witch; but David seeks to God, as here, 'Lord, thy face will I seek.' Many things upbraided David, no question, with his sin and the affliction he was in. Thou seek God! Thou hast offended him, and now thou endurest some sign of his displeasure. A heavy case, beloved, sometimes, especially in the time of extremity. Then conscience saith, I am in extremity, and withal God follows me with such and such sins. A guilty conscience meets me in my prayers to God and upbraids me, Thou hast done so and so; that if there be not faith, and a word of God to lay hold on in extremity, what will become of the poor soul? It is swallowed up. No question David was now in pangs, and many things offered to thrust him off, and he might say, 'I have many things to discourage me,' yet 'thy face, Lord, will I seek,' for deliverance out of trouble and for pardon of sin. Set the promise of God and the pardon of sin above all extremity whatsoever. God is the God of all and above all, he is 'the God of comfort.' If comforts be wanting, he can make them anew. In the want of means, and when means are against us, let us seek to God. Jonah in the whale's belly, that was a creature that might have consumed him with heat, 'when he was in the belly of hell, he called unto God,' Jonah ii. 2. If a man be as low as hell, if he have a command to come, and a promise, it will fetch him thence. Therefore allege the promises and the word.

What a miserable taking are they in, that in extremity have no acquaintance with God's word—with the promises or good examples—that have stored up nothing! Alas! they are in the midst of a storm naked; in the midst of war and opposition disarmed; they lie open to all assaults. Therefore, as you love your own souls, gather grounds of comfort, treasure up promises and holy truths, that in extremity you may say with David, upon good ground, Lord, thou hast said thus and thus; and in this extremity I come to thee. 'Thy face, Lord, will I seek.' Break through all fears and discouragements whatsoever; allege the command of God, and the promise of God, and the encouragements of God. My discouraged heart saith thus, and Satan saith thus; but, Lord, thou sayest thus, 'Seek my face.' Shall not I believe and obey God more than the devil or mine own lying false heart? Therefore, except we will betray our souls to temptations, and betray the comforts that we have, let us seek God in all extremities.

I desire you to remember these directions, and be encouraged to seek to God. Join the seeking in extremity, with the seeking him in his ordinances. If we do not seek him in his ordinances, in the time of peace, let us never think he will be so familiar with us in the time of trouble. If we be not acquainted with him in his ordinances in prosperity, in extremity he will be far off. Therefore 'seek the face of God' now, in all his ordinances. That is the way to have provision of strength against all other extremities whatsoever. It is a great comfort in extremity to one that hath sought God in his ordinances before. Foolish atheistical men seek not the wisdom of God in his ordinances. God cries to them and they regard it not. But then they cry to God, and God will not answer them, but 'laugh at their destruction,' Ps. xxxvii. 13. And as it is in Zechariah, you cry, 'and I will not hear, because I cried and ye would not hear,' vii. 11. When God speaks and we regard it not, we shall cry and he will not regard it. Therefore, as we desire his presence in the evil day, let us labour to hear him now. Let us search his will, what he requires of us, and what he will do for us, and labour to be armed with obedience against the time of distress.

And *let us seek him betimes*. Now presently seek the favour of God, you that are young. 'In the morning early will I seek thee,' Ps. lxiii. 1. In the morning of your years, in the morning of the day, it is good to seek God, before the heart be possessed with other business, that he may bless all our affairs. Seek his face, that his blessing, and direction, and strength may be upon all. Let us set upon things in his wisdom and strength, and hope on his blessing.

And in the morning of your years, early, put not off. For here is the mischief. If we seek not God early, betimes, the heart will be hardened, and will grow worse; to-morrow we shall be more unfit than to-day. Then those that seek in their sickness, and at the hour of death, that is self-love. It is grace to seek God for himself, out of old acquaintance and love. But to seek him in sickness only, and to neglect his ordinances, it is merely self-love. As a malefactor that carries himself ill in prison, and then seeks the judge's face at the bar; when God arraigns a man at the bar, then to seek him, it comes from self-love. But that obedience we owe to God is to seek him out of a new nature, out of love of God's goodness and grace. When we seek him in extremity, not out of the love of grace, but to escape the danger of hell and damnation, such seeking seldom proves good. Many make a great show of repentance and turning to God, many of those prove false. He that is good in affliction only is never good. Therefore put not off seeking God's face, by prayer and the use of all good means.

Many men first settle their estates, and then send for a physician, and the divine last of all, when they are sick. Oh but seek God first, and above all things in the world, or else we have adulterous, idolatrous hearts, to make the face of man our idol, or health our idol. We should seek God's face above all.

The Scripture sets him out sweetly to us. Therefore one way to encourage us to seek to God, is to present to our souls God, under those sweet terms. He is a rock in the midst of the waves; he is a habitation in the midst of a storm: 'Thou art our habitation,' Ps. lxxi. 3. He is called a hiding-place, he hath the shadow of his wings to cover us; let us fly under the shadow of his wings. He is presented sweetly to us in Christ. Therefore let us have recourse to him upon all occasions; and now, now that we may be familiar with him, that we may be acquainted with him now, in the days of our youth, and he will know us in age and sickness. If we be not acquainted with him now, he will not acquaint himself with us then. Therefore seek his face now, and above all things seek it.

And can we have more encouragement? There was never any that sought the face of God that went away sorry. It is said of some good emperors, that never any man went sorry out of their presence; either they had the grant of their suits or good words (*d*). God sends none sorry away. There are none that come into the presence of God but they are the better for it. They go away more cheerful and more satisfied. Their consciences are quieted when they pour out their souls to God. There is 'the peace of God which passeth understanding, preserves their soul,' as it is Philip. iv. 7. 'In nothing be careful: but let there be thanksgiving for favours received, and let your requests be made known to him; and the peace of God shall preserve your hearts and minds,' Philip. iv. 6. You shall not despair and be over much cast down, peace will preserve you.

And if we do not seek the face of God now, when we may enjoy his presence, we shall never see his face in glory hereafter. We must now be acquainted with him, or else we shall not when we would. Therefore, as we may enjoy the presence of God in his ordinances, so in all our affairs let us seek his face and blessing. Let us have what we have, and do what we do, in his blessing and assistance, and not in the strength of wit and shifts.* Let us do what we do by divine strength, and in confidence of his blessing. That that we do by his strength we may expect his blessing on; we cannot do so by our shifts. Let us inure ourselves in these courses, and we shall find much peace; and by long acquaintance with God we shall be able to commit our souls to him; we shall be able to look him in the face at the hour of death. He that looks God in the face often in prayer, and seeking him, may look death in the face. These things may be made effectual if your hearts be prepared, as the Scripture phrase is.

And because I mentioned preparing: that is a word in Scripture that is set before seeking. Rehoboam did not thrive, he did not 'prepare his heart to seek God,' 2 Chron. xii. 14. Jehoshaphat was blessed of God, 'he prepared his heart to seek the Lord,' 2 Chron. xx. 3. Therefore let us come prepared to seek God, prepare our hearts to seek him. Think, When I go to the congregation, I go to seek God's face; therefore come in humility and subjection. And in all the courses of our lives, let all of us prepare, and set our hearts in frame to seek God in all things; and let us set upon nothing that we cannot depend on him for assistance, and look to

* That is, 'expedients.'—G.

him for a blessing. And when we cannot enjoy his favour and blessing in anything, we were as good be without it as have it.

This is the way to have our wills in all things. Christ, the truth itself, hath left us this one sweet promise, 'Seek ye first the kingdom of God,' Matt. vi. 33. He speaks there of seeking our own good. What is the best thing we should seek for? 'Seek ye first the kingdom of God,' of grace, and of glory; the favour of God, and the fruit of his favour, grace. Seek those best things in the first place. What then? It is the way to have all things else, as far as they are for our good. But we would have more. We think if we seek to God, and depend upon God's divine principles and rules, it is a way to beggary and disgrace. Oh no. It is the way to have our own desire in all things, as far as it is for our good. Let us seek first the kingdom of God, that God may rule and reign in us, and we shall reign in the kingdom of God. For other things, God will bring it to pass I know not how, they shall be cast upon us. He that is full for heaven and happiness, God will make him full for the world, and successful, as much as he sees fit to bring him to heaven. If God see anything that would hinder him, he must leave that to his wisdom.

Therefore let us labour to be able from truth of heart to return to the commandment and promise of God, this sweet and gracious answer of the holy man David, when God saith generally or particularly, 'Seek my face,' 'Thy face, Lord, will I seek.'

NOTES.

(*a*) P. 114.—'As Saint Augustine said of himself, "God spake often to me, and I was ignorant of it."' A frequent self-accusation in the 'Confessions.' Cf. note *f*, Vol. II. page 194.

(*b*) P. 116.—'God hath framed the Scriptures not to be limited to the times wherein they were written, as the papists idly speak, Bellarmine and others.' A commonplace of the popish controversy. Cf. *nnn*, Vol. III. page 535.

(*c*) P. 125.—'"Many seek the ruler's favour." In the Greek translation, the Septuagint, the word is to "observe" and respect a man, which is translated "seeking."' The LXX rendering is *πολλοὶ θεραπεύουσι*, *i.e.*, θεραπεύω = to wait upon, to minister unto, to serve.

(*d*) P. 131.—'It is said of some good emperors, that never any man went sorry out of their presence; either they had the grant of their suits or good words.' This is said of various of the Cæsars: *e.g.*, Julius Cæsar, Antoninus, and later, of Constantine. G.

A RESCUE FROM DEATH, WITH A RETURN OF PRAISE.

A RESCUE FROM DEATH, WITH A RETURN OF PRAISE.

NOTE.

For the full title-page of the book of which 'A Rescue from Death' forms the second moiety, see Note to the Treatise composing the former, entitled 'Lydia's Conversion,' in the second division of the present volume. G.

A RESCUE FROM DEATH, WITH A RETURN OF PRAISE.

Fools, because of their transgressions, and because of their iniquities, are afflicted, &c.—Ps. CVII. 17, &c.

This Psalm containeth some passages concerning God's particular, sweet providence; not only to the church, but to other men; for he that created all things, even the meanest creature, must have a providence over all things; his providence must extend itself as large as his creation. For what is providence but a continuance of creation: a preservation of those things in being that God hath given to have a being. The prophet here of purpose opposeth the profane conceits of them that think God sits in heaven, and lets things go on earth, as if he cared not for them. It was the fault of the best philosophers to ascribe too much to second causes. The psalmist here shews that God hath a most particular providence in everything. First, he sets it down in general, and then he brancheth it out into particulars, especially four, wherein he specifieth God's providence.

The first instance is of those that 'wander in the wilderness hungry and thirsty;' ver. 4, 'They cry, and God regards them.'

The second is in ver. 10, 'They that sit in darkness and in the shadow of death, bound in iron, they cry, and the Lord heareth them.'

The third is in the words of the text, 'Fools for their transgressions are afflicted; their soul abhorreth all manner of meat.' He instanceth in sickness, the most ordinary affliction, and shews that God hath a most particular providence even in that.

The fourth is in ver. 23, 'Those that go down into the sea, they see' experiments* of God's particular providence.

Since the fall, the life of a man is subject to a wondrous many inconveniences, which we have brought on us by our sins. Now in this variety it is a comfortable thing to know God's care of us in our wanderings and imprisonments, in our sickness, &c. But to omit the other three, and to come to that that is proper to the place, that is, the instance of God's providence in sickness.

'Fools, because of their transgressions, and because of their iniquities, are afflicted,' &c.

* That is, 'have experience of.'—G.

In these words you have,

First, The cause of this visitation, and of all the grievance he speaks of: 'transgression and iniquity.'

And then the kind of this visitation: 'sickness.'

And the extremity, in two branches: 'Their soul abhorreth all manner of meat;' and secondly, 'They draw near to the gates of death.'

And then the carriage of the affected* and sick parties: '*They cry unto the Lord* in their distress.'

And the remedy, of the universal and great physician: 'He saves them out of their distress.'

And the manner of this remedy: 'He sent his word and healed them;' his operative and commanding word, so as it works with his command.

Lastly, the fee that this high commander asks for; all the tribute or reward that he expects is praise and thanksgiving. 'Oh that men would therefore praise the Lord for his goodness, and his wondrous works for the children of men,' &c.

So you see this Scripture contains several passages between God and man, in misery and in deliverance. In *misery*:—God afflicts man for his sin. The passage of man to God is, 'He cries to God.' God's passage back again is his 'deliverance,' and then his return back again must be 'thanksgiving.' So here is a double visitation, in justice God correcting sin; and then a visitation in mercy, upon their crying and praying, God restores them; and then man's duty, 'thanksgiving.' But to proceed in order.

'Fools, because of their transgressions,' &c.

Here you have first the quality of the persons set down.

'Fools.'

We must understand by 'fools,' wicked fools; not such fools as are to be begged, as we say; that are defective in their naturals,† but the 'wise fools' of the world. They are the chief of fools. However in the courts of men they be not found fools, yet they are fools in God's esteem, who is wisdom itself. Those that think themselves wise, that are conceitedly wise, they are these fools here.

In the phrase of Scripture and the language of the Holy Ghost, every sinner is a 'fool.' It were a disgraceful term if any man should give it; but let no man stumble at it. It comes from the wise God that knows what wisdom is, and what is folly. If a fool shall call a man 'fool,' he doth not regard it; but if a wise man, especially the 'God of wisdom,' call a man 'fool,' he hath reason to regard it. Who can judge better of wisdom than God, who is 'only wise'?

Why are wicked men fools? and God's children, so far as they yield to their lusts?

In divers respects.

1. First, *For lack of discerning in all the carriage and passages of their lives.* You know a fool is such a one as cannot discern the difference of things, that is defective in his judgment. Discerning and judgment, that especially tries a fool, when he cannot discern between pearls and pebbles, between jewels and ordinary base things. So wicked men are defective in their judgments. They cannot discern aright between spiritual and heavenly things, and other things. All your worldly fools, he hunts after and placeth his happiness in things meaner than himself; he takes shadows for substances.

2. A fool *is led with his humour and his lust*, even as the beast. So there

* Qu. 'afflicted'?—G.

† That is, (natural) 'reason.'—G.

is no wicked man that shakes off the fear of God, 'which is true wisdom,' Prov. i. 7, but he is led with his humour, and passion, and affection to some earthly thing. Now a man can never be wise and passionate, unless in one case, when the good is so exceeding that no passion can be answerable; as in zeal in divine matters. That will excuse all exorbitant carriage otherwise. When David 'danced before the ark,' a man would think it had been a foolish matter, except it had been a divine business, 2 Sam. vi. 14. When the matter is wondrous great, that it deserves any pitch of affection, then a man may be eager and wise; but for the things of this life, for a man to disquiet himself and others, to hunt after a 'vain shadow,' as the psalmist saith, after riches and honour, and to neglect the main end of a man's life, it is extreme folly. A man that is passionate in this respect cannot be wise. All fools are passionate, and wicked men have their affections set deeply on somewhat else besides God. Because passion presents things in a false glass, as when a man sees the sun through a cloud he seems bigger. When men look on things in* the judgment of the Scripture, and the Spirit of God, and right reason, but through affection, things appear to them otherwise than they are, and themselves afterwards see themselves fools. Take a worldling on his deathbed, or in hell. He sees himself a fool then. When his drunkenness is past; when he is come to himself and is sober, he sees that he hath catched, all his lifetime, after shadows. Wicked men that are carried with their lusts to earthly things, they cannot be wise. Therefore the 'rich man' in the gospel, is called a 'fool,' Luke xii. 20; and in Jer xvii. 11, he speaks of a man that 'labours all his lifetime, and in the end is a fool.' Is not he a fool that will carry a burden, and load himself in his journey more than he needs? And is not he a spiritual fool that 'loads himself with thick clay,' as the prophet calls it, Hab. ii. 6, and makes his pilgrimage more cumbersome than he needs? Is not he a 'fool' that lays the heaviest weight on the weakest? that puts off the heaviest burden of repentance to the time of sickness, and trouble, and death, when all his troubles meet in a centre, as it were, and he hath enough to do to conflict with his sickness?

3. Again, He is a 'fool' that will play with edge tools, *that makes a sport of sin.* He is a 'fool' that provokes his betters; that shoots up arrows and casts up stones, that shall fall on his own head. He that darts out oaths and blasphemies against God, that shall return back upon his own pate, Ps. vii. 16. Many such fools there are. 'God will not hold them guiltless,' Exod. xx. 7.

4. He is a 'fool' that knows not, *or forgets his end.* Every wicked man forgets the end wherefore he lives in the world. He comes here into the world, and lives, and is turned out of the world again, and never considers the work that he hath to do here,' but is carried like a 'fool,' with affections and passions to earthly things, as if he had been born only for them. A wise man hath an end prefixed in all that he doth, and he works to that end. Now there is no man but a sound sanctified Christian, that hath a right end, and that works to that end. Other men pretend they have an end, and they would serve God, &c.

They pretend heaven, but they work to the earthward; like moles, they dig in the earth. They work not to the end they pretend to fix to themselves. All men, how witty soever they are otherwise, in worldly respects, they are but 'fools.' As we say of owls, they can see, but it is by night: so wicked men are witty, but it is in works of darkness. They are wise 'in

* Qu. 'not in'?—Ed.

their own generation,' among men like themselves. But this is not the life wherein folly and wisdom can be discerned so well. It will appear at the hour of death, and the day of judgment. Then those will be found wise that are wise for eternity; that have provided how it shall go with them when all earthly things shall fail them; and those will be 'fools' that have only a particular wit for the particular passages of this life; to contrive particular ends and neglect the main. They are penny wise and pound foolish. Ahithophel, a witty wiseman, his 'counsel was an oracle, yet he was not wise to prevent his own destruction, 2 Sam. xvi. 23.

5. He is a madman, a 'fool,' *that hurts and wounds himself.* None else will do so. Wicked carnal men, they wound, and hurt, and stab their own consciences. Oh, if any man should do them but the thousandth part of the harm that they do themselves every day, they would not endure it. They gall and load their consciences with many sins, and they do it to themselves. Therefore it is a deserved title that is given them. God meets with the pride of men in this term of folly. For a wicked man, above all things, is careful to avoid this imputation of 'fool.' Account him what you will, so you account him a shrewd man withal, that can overreach others, that he is crafty and wise, he glories in the reputation of wisdom, though God account him a fool, and he shall be found so afterward; and to abate the pride of men, he brings a disgraceful term over their wit and learning, and calls them fools.

Use 1. This should *abase any man that is not a right and sound Christian,* that the 'God of wisdom,' and the Scripture—that is, God's word—esteems of all wicked men, be what they will, to be 'fools,' and that in their own judgments, if they be not atheists, if they will grant the principles they pretend to believe.

Let this, therefore, be an aggravation in your thoughts when you are tempted to commit any sin. Oh, besides that it is a transgression and rebellion against God's commandment, it is 'folly in Israel,' and this will be 'bitterness in the end.'

Use 2. Is he not a 'fool' that will do that in an instant, *that he may repent many years after?* Is he not a foolish man, in matter of diet, that will take that that he shall complain of a long time after? None will be so foolish in outward things. So when we are tempted to sin, think, Is it not folly to do this, when the time will come that I shall wish it undone again, with the loss of a world if I had it to give?

Use 3. And beg of God the *wisdom of the Holy Ghost,* to judge aright of things, the 'eye-salve of the Spirit of God, to discern of things that differ,' Rev. iii. 18; to judge spiritual riches to be best, and spiritual nobility and excellency to be best; and to judge of sinful courses to be base, however otherwise painful.* Let us labour for grace. 'The fear of the Lord is the beginning of wisdom,' Prov. i. 7. Those that do not fear the Lord, they have no wisdom.

Use 4. And pass not† *for the vain censures of wicked men.* Thou art hindered from the practice of religious duties, and from a conscionable‡ course of life. Why? Perhaps thou shalt be accounted a fool. By whom? By those that are fools indeed, in the judgment of him who is wisdom indeed, God himself. Who would care to be accounted a fool of a fool? We see the Scripture judgeth wicked men here to be 'fools.'

We must not extend it only to wicked men, but even likewise God's children, when they yield to their corruptions and passions, they are foolish

* Qu. 'gainful'?—Ed.

† That is, 'heed not.'—G.

‡ That is, 'conscientious.'—G.

for the time: in Ps. xxxviii. 5, 'My wounds stink and are corrupt, because of my foolishness;' and in Ps. lxxiii. 22, 'So foolish was I and ignorant,' &c.

Therefore, when any base thought of God's providence comes in our mind, or any temptation to sin, let us think it 'folly;' and when we are overtaken with any sin, let us befool ourselves, and judge it, as God doth, to be foolishness. This is the ground and foundation of repentance. So much for the quality of the persons here described, 'fools.'

I come to the cause.

'Because of their transgressions, and because of their iniquities.'

Transgression especially hath reference to rebellion against God and his ordinances in the first table. *Iniquity* hath reference to the breach of the second table, against men; and both these have their rise from folly. For want of wisdom causeth rebellion against God, and iniquity against men. All breaches of God's will come from spiritual folly.

Why doth he begin with transgressions against the first table, and then iniquities, the breach of the second?

Because all breaches of the second table issue from the breach of the first. A man is never unjust to his neighbours, that doth not rebel against God's will in the first table; and the foundation of obedience and duty to man, it riseth from man's obedience to God. Therefore the second table is like the first: that is, our love to our neighbour is like to our love of God; not only like it, but it springs from it. For all comes from the love of God. Therefore the first command of the first table runs through all the commandments. 'Thou shalt honour God;' and honour man, *because* we honour God. A man never denies obedience to his superior, to the magistrate, &c., but he denies it to God first; a man never wrongs man, but he disobeys God first. Therefore, the apostles lay the duties of the second table in the Scriptures upon the first. St Paul always begins his epistles with the duties to God and religion, and when he hath discharged that, he comes to parents, and masters, and children, and servants, and such particular duties; because the spring of our duty to man is our duty to God, and the first justice is the justice of religion to God. When we are not just to give God his due, thereupon come all breaches in our civil conversation and commerce with men. For want of the fear of God, men do this: as Joseph said, 'How shall I do this, and offend God?' Gen. xxxix. 9; and Abraham, he had a conceit they would abuse his wife, 'Surely the fear of God is not here,' Gen. xx. 13. Therefore he thought they would not be afraid to do anything. He that fears not God, if opportunity serve, he will not be afraid to violate the second table. He that fears God, he will reason, 'How shall I do this,' to wrong another in his name and reputation, or in his estate, and sin against God? For I cannot sin against man, but I must first sin against God. That is the reason he sets it down thus, transgressions *and* iniquities.

See an unhappy succession of sin, that where there is transgression there will be iniquity; when a man yields to lust once, presently he breaks upon God's due, and then upon man's. One sin draws on another. As we see David giving way to one sin, it brought another; so the giving way to transgression, neglecting the word of God and duties of religion, presently another follows, neglect of duty to men.

Use. Take heed of the beginnings of sin. There are degrees in Satan's school from ill to worse, till we come to worst of all; and there is no staying. It is like the descent down a steep hill. Let us stop in the beginning by any means. As we would avoid iniquity, let us take heed of transgression.

'Are afflicted.'

He means, especially, that affliction of sickness, as appears by the words following.

Doct. Sin is the cause of all sickness.

'Fools, for their transgressions and iniquities, are afflicted.' For God's quarrel is especially against the soul, and to the body because of the soul. I will not dwell on this point, having spoken of it at large on another text, 1 Cor. xi. 31.*

Use 1. The use that I will make of it now, shall be, first of all, if sin be the cause of all sickness, *let us justify God and condemn ourselves:* complain of ourselves, and not of God. 'Wherefore doth the living man complain,' Lam. iii. 39, and murmur and fret? Man suffereth for his sin. Justify God, and judge ourselves. 'I will bear the wrath of the Lord, because I have sinned against him,' Micah vii. 9. Judge ourselves, and we shall not be judged,' 1 Cor. xi. 31.

2. Then again, is sin the cause of sickness? *It should teach us patience.* 'I held my tongue, because thou, Lord, didst it,' Ps. xxxix. 2. Shall not a man be patient in that he hath procured by his own evil and sin?

3. And *search ourselves;* for usually it is for some particular sin, which conscience will tell a man of; and sometimes the kind of the punishment will tell a man. For sins of the body, God punisheth in the body. He pays men home in their own coin. 'What measure a man measureth to others shall be measured to him again,' Mat. vii. 2. If a man have been cruel to others, God will stir up those that shall be so to him; therefore we should labour to part with our particular transgressions and iniquities. It is a general truth for all ills whatsoever, as well as this of sickness. Therefore we should first of all go to God by confession of sin. It is a preposterous course that the athestical careless world takes; where the physician ends, there the divine begins; when they know not what to do. If diseases come from sin, then make use of the divine first, to certify the conscience, and to acquaint a man with his own mercy. First, to search them, and let them see the guilt of their sins, and then to speak comfort to them, and to set accounts straight between God and them, as in Ps. xxxii. 4—an excellent place—David 'roared; his moisture was turned into the drought of summer.' What course doth he take? He doth not run to the physician presently, but goes to God. 'Then said I.' It was an inward resolution and speech of the mind. Then I concluded with myself, 'I will confess my sin to God, and thou forgavest my iniquities and sins,' Ps. xxxii. 5. So body and soul were healed at once. Divinity herein transcends all other arts; not only corrupt nature and corrupt courses, but all other. For the physician he looks to the cause of the sickness out of a man or in a man; out of a man, and then especially in contagious sickness, he looks to the influence of the heavens. In such a year, such conjunctions and such eclipses have been; he looks to the infection of the air, to subordinate causes, to contagious company, and to diet, &c. (*a*). And then in a man, to the distemper of the humours and of the spirits. When the instrument of nature is out of tune, it is the cause of sickness. But the divine, and every Christian,—that should be a divine in this respect,—goes higher, and sees all the discord between God and us. There is not

* Cf. Sibbes's 'Glance of Heaven,' in Vol. IV.—G.

that sweet harmony there; and so all the jars in second causes come from God as the cause inflicting: from sin, as the cause demeriting. The divine considers those two alway. The physician looks to the inward distemper and the outward contagion; and this is well, and may be done without sin. But men must join this too, to look into conscience, and look up to God, together with looking for help to the physician, because we have especially to deal with God.

I would this were considered, that we might carry ourselves more Christian-like under any affliction whatsoever. What is the reason that people murmur, and struggle, and strive, 'as a bull in a net,' as the prophet speaks, Isa. li. 20, when God hampers them in some judgment? They look to the second causes, and never look to clear the conscience of sin, nor never look to God, when indeed the ground of all is God offended by sin.

'Fools for their transgressions are afflicted.'

We by our sins put a rod into God's hand—'a rod for the fool's back,' as Solomon saith, Prov. xxvi. 3; and when we will be fools, we must needs endure the scourge and rod in one kind or other. Those that will sin must look for a rod. It is the best reward of wicked and vain fools, that 'make a jest of sin,' Prov. xiv. 9—as the wise man saith, 'They cast firebrands, and say, Am I not in jest?' Prov. xxvi. 18—that rail and scorn at good things; that swear and carry themselves in a loose, ridiculous, scandalous fashion, as if God did not eye their carriage; and yet 'Am I not in jest?' Well, it is no jesting matter. Sin is like a secret poison; perhaps it doth not work presently. As there are some kind of subtile poisons made in these days,—wherein the devil hath whetted men's wits,—that will work perhaps a year after, so sin, if it be once committed, perhaps it doth not kill presently, but 'there is death in the pot,' 2 Kings iv. 40. Thou art a child of death as soon as ever thou hast committed sin; as Salvian saith well, 'Thou perishest before thou perish' (*b*). The sentence is upon thee. Thou art a dead man. God, to wait for thy repentance, prolongs thy days; but as soon as thou hast sinned without repentance, thou art a 'child of death.' And as poison, that works secretly a while, yet in time it appears; so at last 'the fruit of sin will be death.' Sin and death came in together. Take heed of all sin; it is no dallying matter.

'Their soul abhors all manner of meat.'

This is one branch of the extremity of the sickness, the loathing of meat; for God hath put a correspondency between food that is necessary for man and man's relish. For man being in this world to be supported, the natural moisture being to be supplied and repaired by nourishment, as it is spent by the natural heat which feeds upon it; therefore God hath put a sweetness into meat, that man might delight to do that which is necessary; for who would care for meat if it were not necessary? Therefore, being necessary, God hath put delightful tastes in meats, to draw men to the use of them, to preserve their being for the serving of him. Now when these things savour not, when the relish of a man is distempered that he cannot judge aright of meats, when the palate is vitiated, there must needs follow sickness. For a man cannot do that that should maintain his strength; he cannot feed on the creature; therefore the psalmist setting down the extremity of sickness, he saith, 'Their soul abhorreth all manner of meat.' This the great physician of heaven and earth sets down as a symptom of a sick state, when one cannot relish and digest meat. Experience seals this truth, and proves it to be true.

You see, then, the happiness of epicures, how unstable and vain it is, whose chief good is in the creature! God by sickness can make them disrelish all 'manner of meat;' and where is the *summum bonum* then of all your belly-gods, your sensual persons?

Again, In that he saith, 'Their soul abhorreth all manner of meat,' it should teach us to bless God not only for meat, but for stomachs to eat. It is a blessing common, and therefore forgotten. It is a double blessing when God provides daily for our outward man, and then gives a stomach to relish his goodness in the creature. Sometimes a poor man wants meat, and hath a stomach; sometimes a rich man wants a stomach, when he hath meat. They that have both have cause to bless God, because it is a judgment when God takes away the appetite, that men 'abhor and loathe all manner of meat.'

Therefore, if we would maintain thankfulness to God, labour to thank God for common blessings. What if God should take away a man's stomach? We see his state here: he is 'at the gates of death.' Therefore thank God that he maintains us with comforts in our pilgrimage; and withal, that he gives us strength to take the comfort of the creature.

We see here again one rule how to converse with them that are sick. Blessed is he that understands the estate of the afflicted and sick, not to take it ill to see them wayward. It comes not from the mind, but from the distemper of the body. As we bear with children, so we must bear with men in those distempers, if they have food and yet loathe it. You see how it is with men in that case, 'their soul abhorreth all manner of meat.' It should teach us to sympathise with those that are sick, if we see them in these distempers.

The next branch of the extremity is,

'They draw near the gates of death.'

Death is a great commander, a great tyrant; and hath gates to sit in, as judges and magistrates used to 'sit in the gates.'* There are things implied in this phrase.

1. First, 'They draw near to the gates of death;' that is, they were '*near to death;*' as he that draws near the gates of a city is near the city, because the gates enter into the city.

2. Secondly, Gates are applied to death *for authority*. They were almost in death's jurisdiction. Death is a great tyrant. He rules over all the men in the world, over kings and potentates, and over mean men; and the greatest men fear death most. He is 'the king of fears,' as Job calls him, Job xviii. 14; ay, and the fear of kings. Yet death that is thus feared in this life by wicked men, at the day of judgment, of all things in the world they shall desire death most; according to that in the Apocalypse, 'they shall desire death, and it shall not come to them,' Rev. ix. 6. They shall subsist to eternal misery. That that men are most afraid of in this life, that they shall wish most to come to them in the world to come—Oh that I might die! what a pitiful state are wicked men in!—Therefore it is called the 'gate of death.' It rules and overrules all mankind. Therefore it is said 'to reign,' Rom. v. 21. Death and sin came in together. Sin was the gate that let in death, and ever since death reigned, and will, till Christ perfectly triumph over it, who is the King of that

* Cf. Gen. xix. 1; 2 Sam. iii. 27; Job xxxi. 21; Ps. lxix. 12.—G.

lord and commander, and hath 'the key of hell and death,' Rev. i. 18. To wicked men, I say, he is a tyrant, and hath a gate; and when they go through the 'gate of death,' they go to a worse, to a lower place, to hell. It is the trap-door to hell.

3. Thirdly, By the 'gate of death' is meant not only the authority, but *the power of death;* as in the gospel, 'the gates of hell shall not prevail against it,' Mat. xvi. 18: that is, the power and strength of hell. So here it implies the strength of death, which is very great, for it subdues all. It is the executioner of God's justice.

Use. If death hath such a jurisdiction, and power, and strength, let us labour *to disarm it beforehand.* It is in our power to make death stingless, and toothless, and harmless; nay, we may make it advantageous, for the 'gate of death' may become the gate of happiness. Let us labour to have our part and portion in Christ, who hath the 'key of hell and death,' who hath overcome and conquered this tyrant: 'O death, where is thy sting? O grave, where is thy victory?' 'Thanks be unto God, who hath given us victory, through Jesus Christ our Lord,' 1 Cor. xv. 55, 57, that now we need not fear death; that though death have a gate, yet it is a gate to let us into heaven, as it is a door to let the wicked into hell. So much for that.

In the next place, we come to their carriage in their extremity.

'They cried to God in their trouble.'

This is the carriage of man in extreme ills, if he have any fear of God in him, to pray; and then prayers are cries. They are darted out of the heart, as it were, to heaven. It is said, 'Christ made strong cries,' Heb. v. 7. In extremity, prayers are 'cries.' Hence I observe briefly these things.

Doct. That God suffers men to fall into extreme ills, even to the gates of death; that there is but a step between them and death.

Why?

Reason 1. *To wean them perfectly from the world.* To make them more thankful when they recover; for what is the reason that men are so slight in thanksgiving? Usually the reason is, they did not conceive that they were in such extreme danger as they were.

2. Likewise he suffers men to fall into extreme sickness *that he may have all the glory,* for it was his doing. There was no second cause to help here, for their soul 'abhorred all manner of meat, and they were even at the gates of death.' Now, when all second causes fail, then God is exalted. Therefore he suffers men to fall into extremity. The greater the malady, the more is the glory of the physician.

The second thing is this, as God brings his children into extremity, so *God's children in extremity they cry to him.*

Extremity of afflictions doth force prayers: 'In their affliction they will seek me early.' When all second causes fail, then we go to God. Nature therefore is against atheism. As one observes, that naturally men run to God in extremity (*c*)—'Lord, succour me'—so, especially in the church, in extremity, God's people cry to God; and as afflictions, so particularly this of sickness of body drives men to God. God should not hear of us many times, unless he should come near us by afflictions, and deep afflictions. 'Out of the deep have I cried,' Ps. cxxx. 1. God brings us to the deep, and then we cry. Our nature is so naught,* that God should not hear of

* That is, 'naughty' = wicked.—G.

us, as I said, unless he send some messenger after us, some affliction to bring us home, as Absalom dealt by Joab when he 'fired his corn.' In the gospel, Christ had never heard of many people, had it not been for some infirmity. But blessed are those sicknesses and infirmities that occasion us to go to God, that makes us cry to God. It was the speech of a heathen, 'We are best when we are weakest' (*d*). Why? As he saith very well, 'Who is ambitious, voluptuous, or covetous for the world when he is sick, when he sees the vanity of these things?'

This should make us submit more meekly unto God, when we are under his hand, when we are his prisoners by sickness, when he casts us on our sick beds, because God is working our good, he is drawing us nearer to him.

'Then they cried to him.'

So we see, then, that *prayer it is a remedy in a remediless estate*, when there is no other remedy; and this is one difference between a child of God and another. In extremity, a carnal man that hath not grace, he hath not a spirit of prayer to go to God; but a child of God he cries to God. He had acquaintance with God in the time of health. Therefore he goes boldly to God as a father in the time of extremity. God's children can answer God's dealing; for as he brings his children to extremity, when there is no second cause to help, so they answer him by faith. In extremity, when there is nothing to trust unto, they trust him; when there is no physic in the world that can charm the disease, they have a spirit of faith to answer God's dealing in the greatest misery, as Job saith, 'Though he kill me, yet will I trust in him,' Job xiii. 15.

For God is not tied to second causes, and therefore if he have 'delight in us,' and if he have any service for us to do, he can recover us from the 'gates of death,' nay, from death itself; as we see Christ in the gospel raised from the dead—and at the resurrection he will raise us from death—much more can he raise us from the 'gates of death,' when we are 'near death.'

Therefore, considering that prayer is a remedy in all maladies, in a remediless estate, let us labour to have a spirit of prayer, and to be in such a state as we may pray.

What state is that?

1. First, *Take heed of being in league with any sin.* 'If I regard iniquity in my heart, God will not hear my prayer,' Ps. lxvi. 18; nay, he will not hear others' prayers for us. Oh what a pitiful state is it when God will not hear us nor others for us. 'Pray not for this people,' saith God to Jeremiah, 'and if Noah, Daniel, and Job stood before me, they should but deliver their own souls,' Ezek. xiv. 14. If a man be in a peremptory course of sin, and will not be reclaimed, but is like the 'deaf adder, that will not be charmed,' Ps. lviii. 4, God will not hear prayers for him. Will God hear a rebel when he comes to him for mercy, and is in a course opposite to God's will? As if a traitor should come to sue for pardon with a dagger in his hand, which were to increase the treason; so when a man comes to God and cries to him, and yet purposeth to live in sin, and his conscience tells him that he offers violence to God by his sins, and lives in rebellious courses, God will not hear his prayers.

2. Again, If we would be in such a state as God may accept us when we come to him, *let us hear God when he cries to us*. He cries to us in the ministry of the word: 'Wisdom hath lift up her voice,' Prov. i. 20; and this is God's course. He will hear us when we hear him. 'He that turns

his ear from hearing of the law, his prayer shall be abominable,' Prov. xxviii. 9. Those that do not attend upon God's ordinances, that will have a kind of devotion private to themselves, and avoid the public ordinance, that fear perhaps they shall hear somewhat that would awaken their conscience, and they would not 'be tormented before their time,' Mat. viii. 29, let them consider—it is a terrible speech of Solomon—'He that turns his ear from hearing the law, his prayer shall be abominable.' Let us take heed. It is a fearful thing to be in such an estate, that neither our own prayers nor others, shall be regarded for us; and let any man judge, if we will not hear God speak to us, is it fit that he should hear us speaking to him?

And before I leave the point, let me press it a little further. At this time we have cause to bless God for the deliverance of the city.* Oh, but let all that have the spirit of prayer, that have any familiarity with God, improve all their interest in heaven at this time. Do we not conceive what danger we are in? what enemies we have provoked? What if we be free from the sickness, are we not in danger of worse matters than the sickness? 'Is it not worse to fall into the hands of our enemies?' 2 Sam. xxiv. 14. Have we not great, provoked, cruel, idolatrous enemies? Therefore let us jointly now, all cry to God, and importune him, that he would be good to the State; that as he hath given us a pledge of his favour in delivering us from the plague, so he would not be weary of doing good unto us, but that he would still make it a token of further favours and deliverances hereafter; that as he delivered us in former times, in '88,† and magnified his mercy to us, so now he would not expose us to the cruelty of idolatrous enemies, 'whose mercies are cruel,' Prov. xii. 10. Let us stir up ourselves. Security and carelessness alway foreruns one destruction or other.

Prayer will do a great deal more good now, than when trouble hath overtaken us; for now it is a sign it comes from a religious seeking of God, then it comes from self-love. There is a great deal of difference when a malefactor seeks to the judge before the time of the assizes, and when he seeks to him at the present time; for then it is merely out of self-respect, and not respect to him. If we seek to God now, he will single and mark out those that mourn for the sins of the time, and pour out their spirits to him in prayer, that he would still dwell and continue the means of salvation amongst us; when God, I say, 'comes to gather his jewels,' Mal. iii. 17, he will single and call out them as peculiar to himself.

Therefore let us in all our prayers put in the church. Things do more than speak. They cry to us to cry to God earnestly. Put case we be not in trouble ourselves, our prayers will be the more acceptable. Before trouble come, it is the only way to prevent it, as it is the only way to rescue us when we are in trouble.

I come now to the remedy.

'He saved them out of their distress.'

God is a physician, good at all manner of sicknesses. It is no matter what the disease be, if God be the physician. Though they be as these 'at the gates of death,' he can fetch them back. Herein God differs from all other physicians.

First of all, he is a general physician. He can heal a land, a whole kingdom, of sickness, of pestilence, and as it is in 2 Chron. vii. 14.

* The plague of 1625–6.—G.

† That is, 1588, from the Armada.—G.

Then he is a physician of body and soul, of both parts. And then he is not tied to means.

Other physicians can cure, but they must have means. Other physicians cannot cure all manner of diseases, nor in all places, but God can cure all. 'He saved them out of their distress.'

Other physicians cannot be alway present, but God is so to every one of his patients. He is a compassionate, tender, present physician.

Use. Which should encourage us in any extremity, especially in sickness of body, *to have recourse to God*, and never to despair though we be brought never so low. He that can raise the dead bodies can raise us out of any sickness. Therefore let us use the means; and when there is no means, trust God, for he can work beyond means and without means.

'They cried to the Lord, and he saved them out of their distress.' It was the fruit of their prayers.

Doct. There was never any prayer from the beginning of the world made to God successlessly.

What, should I speak of prayer! Our very breathings are known to God, when we cannot speak, our sighs; as it is Ps. xxxviii. 9, 'My groans and sighs are not hid from thee.' God hath a 'bottle for our tears,' Ps. lvi. 8, and preserves our sighs and groans. There is nothing that is spiritual in us but God regards, as in Rom. viii. 26, 'We know not what to ask, but the Spirit of God stirreth up in us sighs and groans that cannot be expressed.' And God hears the voice of the sighs of his own Spirit.

Let us also be exhorted from this issue to 'cry unto the Lord;' for there was never any man did sow prayers in the breast and bosom of God, but he received the fruit of it. He is a God 'hearing prayer.' He will not lose his attribute. Nay, further, mark, the instances in this psalm are not made only of men in the church, but likewise of men out of the church, of men that have not the true religion. They pray to God, as creatures to the Creator; and though God have not their souls, yet he will not be beholding to any man for duties. If Ahab do but hypocritically fast, Ahab shall have outward deliverance for his outward humiliation; and these men mentioned in the text, if they call to God but as creatures, and not to idols, God will regard them in outward things, and deliver them. God will not be in any man's debt for any service to him, though it be outward.

And do we think that he that regards 'dogs' out of the church, will neglect his children in the church? He that regards heathen men when they pray to him in their extremity, and delivers them to shew his overflowing bounty and goodness, will he not regard his own children, that have the spirit of adoption, of supplication, and prayer; that put up their suits and supplications in the mediation and sweet name of Christ? Will he not regard the name and intercession of his Son and of his Spirit, the Holy Ghost, stirring up prayers in them, and the state of his children, being his by adoption, since he regards the very heathen?

Nay, more than so, 'God hears the very young ravens,' Job xxxviii. 41, and spreads a table for every living thing; and will not suffer them to die for hunger, but provides for them, because they are his creatures. And will he not for his children, those that he hath taken to be so near him, to be heirs of heaven and happiness? Let us, I say, be encouraged to cry unto the Lord upon all occasions. If God be so good as to deliver sinful men,—that have nothing in them but the principles of nature,—when they fly to God in prayer, as the author and preserver of nature, much more will he hear his own children. 'He will give his Spirit to them that ask him' Luke xi. 13.

Obj. But here may an objection be made, I have cried long! I am hoarse with crying! I have waited a long time! I have been a long time sick, or annoyed with some particular trouble! and God seems, as it were, to stop his ears, to harden his heart against me, to shut up his bowels of compassion and pity, therefore I were as good give over as continue still crying and not be heard.

Ans. I answer, there is no one duty almost, more pressed in Scripture than 'waiting and watching to prayer.' Wait still. Hath not God waited thy leisure long enough, and wilt not thou wait on him?

A patient, when he feels his body distempered by physic, Oh, he cries out, partly for the physic, and partly for the sickness, that trouble him both together, and make civil war in his body, yet notwithstanding the physician wisely lets it work. He shall have no cordial, nor nothing to hinder it; he lets it go on till the physic have wrought well, and carried away the malignant matter, that he may be the better for it, and [in] that, he is a loving and tender physician. Yet so God, when we are in trouble, it is as physic. We cry, but God he turns the glass* as the physicians do. Nay, this time shall be expired. It shall work so long. Till thy pride be taken away, thou shalt be humbled thoroughly; till thou be weaned from thy former wicked pleasures; till thou be prepared to receive further blessings. Therefore they cry and cry, and God defers to hear the 'voice of his children.' In the mean time he loves to hear the 'cry of his children,' and their prayer is as 'sweet incense;' yet he defers still. But all is for the patient's good. Be not weary of waiting. It is a great mercy that he makes thee able to continue crying, that thou hast the Spirit of prayer; that thou canst pour out thy soul to God. It is a great mercy, and so account of it.

Perhaps thou hast not cast out thy Jonah, thy Achan; that there is some particular sin unrepented of; and thou criest and criest, but thy sin cries louder. Thy pride or thy oppression cries, thy wicked course cries. Thou criest unto God, and there is another thing cries in thee, that cries vengeance as thou doest for mercy. Therefore search out thy Achan; cast out thy beloved sin; see 'if thou regard iniquity in thy heart,' if thou regard any pleasing, or profitable, or gainful sin; and never think that God will hear thee till that be out, for it will outcry thy prayers.

The next thing is the manner of God's cure.

'He sent his word and healed them.'

What word?

His secret command, his will.

Let such a thing be, as in the creation, 'Let there be light,' &c. Besides his word written, there is his word creating, and preserving things created; and so here, restoring them that were sick, 'He sent his word and healed them;' and so at the resurrection, his word, his voice shall raise our bodies again. It is a strange manner of cure for God to cure by his word, by his command. It shews that God hath an universal command of all things in the world, in heaven and earth, over devils, and over sicknesses; as it is said in the gospel, 'He rebuked the sicknesses,' Mat. xvii. 18. He can rebuke the agues, the plague, and the pestilence, and they shall be gone by his word, as the centurion said, 'I am a man that have servants under me: and I say to one, Come, and he cometh; and to another, Go, and he

* That is, 'hour or time-glass.'—G.

goeth,' Mat. viii. 8, *seq.;* so thou hast all things under thee, thou art God; and if thou say to a disease, 'Come, it cometh;' and if thou say, 'Go, it goeth.' God 'sent his word of command and healed them.' It is but 'a word of God' to heal, but 'a word of God' to strike. He is the 'Lord of hosts.' 'If he do but hiss,' as the prophet saith, 'for the fly of Egypt,' Isa. vii. 18, if he do but call for an enemy, they come at his word; as we see in Pharaoh's plagues, the flies and frogs, all things, obey his word.

There is a secret obedience in all things to God, when his will is that they shall do this or that. Why doth the sea keep his bounds, whenas the nature and position of the sea is to be above the earth? It is the command of God, that hath said, Let it be there, and 'hither shall thy proud waves go, and no further,' Job xxxviii. 11. I might give many instances how God doth all by his word. The devils are at his word; the whales; the sea, when Christ rebukes it, obeys.

Use. It should teach us not to displease this God, that can strike us in the midst of our sins even with a word. Let us fear this God. Put case we had no enemy in the world: God can arm a man's humours against him. He can raise the spirit and soul against itself, and make it fight against itself by desperate thoughts. He needed not foreign forces for Ahithophel and Saul, he could arm their own souls against themselves. And when he will take down the greatest giant in the world, he needs not foreign forces. It is but working of a disease, but giving way to a humour, but inflaming the spirits, and the soul 'shall abhor all manner of meat.'

Again, He gives a command, a rebuke, *and they are gone presently.* Therefore let us not offend this great God, that is commander of heaven and earth; let us labour to please him, and it is no matter who else we displease. For he hath all things at his command, even the 'hearts of kings as the rivers of water,' Prov. xxi. 1. When Esau sought for Jacob to hurt him, there was a secret command God set upon him to love him. Therefore we should fear him, and all other things shall fear us. We need fear nothing, so we have a care to fear God, further than in God and for God. But not so to fear them, as to do evil for them and offend the great God, that can with a word command sickness to come, or bid it begone.

Again, In that God, when all second causes fail, can 'heal by his word,' therefore *let us never be discouraged from praying.* Though we see a hurly-burly and tumult in the church, though we see all Europe in combustion, and the church driven into a narrow corner, let us not give over prayer. For Christ, that with a word commanded 'the waves to be still,' and 'the devils to be gone,' and *they* presently obeyed him, he can still the waves of the church; he can put a 'hook into the nostrils' of his enemies, and draw them which way he please; he can still all with 'his word.' Therefore, howsoever things seem to run contrary and opposite to our desires, yet let us not give over. He that sees no ground of hope in carnal fleshly reason, let him despair of nothing. Despair shuts the gate and door of mercy and hope, as it were. You see here, when all means fail, when they were 'at the very gates' and entry of death, God fetcheth them back again. How? With physic? No. He is not tied to physic. There is difference between God and between nature and art. Nature and art can do nothing without means; but the God of nature and art can do it with his word. How made he this heaven and earth, this glorious fabric? With his word, 'Let there be light, and there was light,' &c., Gen. i. 3. And how shall he restore all again? With his mighty commanding word. How doth he preserve things? By his word. How are things multiplied? By his word, 'Increase and multiply,' a word of blessing. He doth all things with his word.

So he can confound his enemies with a word. Nay, Christ in his greatest abasement, when they came with staves and arms to take him, 'Whom seek ye?' saith he. That word 'struck down all the officers of the Scribes and Pharisees; they fell flat on the ground,' John xviii. 4, *seq.* Could he in his humiliation, before his great abasement on the cross, strike down his enemies with his word? What shall he do at the day of judgment, when all flesh shall appear before him? And what can he do now at the right hand of God in heaven? Let us never despair, what state soever we be in, in our own persons, or in respect of the church or commonwealth. Let us yet pray, yet solicit God, and wrestle with him; for we see here, when they were at the 'gates of death,' he fetcheth them again with 'his word.' He can fetch things again when they are at destruction, as it were. When man's wit is at a loss, that he knoweth not what course to take, God with a word can turn all things again.

'Oh that men would therefore praise the Lord for his goodness, and for his wonderful works to the children of men! Let them sacrifice the sacrifice of thanksgiving, and declare his works with rejoicing.'

You see that God, the great physician, he is good at all diseases. He is never set at anything, for he can create helps and remedies, of nothing. If there be none in nature, he can create peace to the soul. In the midst of trouble of conscience, God can make things out of nothing, nay, out of contraries. You see here what this great physician hath done. He fetched them 'from the gates of death, when their soul abhorred all manner of meat;' and what doth he require for all this great cure? Surely the text tells us he looks for nothing but praise.

'Oh that men would therefore praise the Lord for his goodness,' &c.

In which words you have these circumstances considerable, together with the substance of the duty:

First, The persons who must praise God: 'Oh that men would praise the Lord.'

And then the duty they are to perform: 'to praise God,' to 'sacrifice to God,' to 'declare his works'—one main duty expressed by three terms.

The third is for what they should praise him: 'for his goodness.' It is the spring of all, for all particular actions do come from his nature. His nature is goodness itself, and indeed all other attributes are founded on goodness. Why is he gracious, and merciful, and long-suffering? Because he is good. This is the primitive attribute.

And then another thing for which we must praise him: 'for his wondrous works for the children of men.'

Fourthly, The manner how this should be done: 'with rejoicing and singing,' as the word signifies (*e*), 'declare his works with rejoicing.' For as all holy actions must be done joyfully and cheerfully, so especially praise: 'God loveth a cheerful giver,' 2 Cor. ix 7, much more a cheerful thanksgiver, for cheerfulness is the very nature of thanksgiving. It is a dead sacrifice, of thanksgiving, it is a dead sacrifice else. These are the many things considerable in these words,

First of all, of the persons.

'Oh that men would praise the Lord.'

The blessed psalmist, whosoever he were, directed by the Spirit of God, he would have all men to praise God; not only those that participate and have interest in the favour, but the beholders also of the goodness of God to others. For here he that was not interested in these favours for his own particular, yet he praiseth God for the blessings to others; and he wisheth that God might have praise from them.

For we are all of one society, of one family, we are all brethren; therefore we must praise God for his blessings and benefits on others: and not only for ourselves, but we must wish that all would do so; and specially we must 'praise God' for ourselves, when we have part of the benefit. For shall others 'praise God' for us, and shall not we for ourselves? Shall the churches of God abroad 'praise God' for his great deliverance of this city—as there is no church in the world that hears of it but is thankful for it—and shall not we for ourselves? Shall the angels in heaven 'praise God,' and sing for the redemption of the church by the blood of Christ, 'Glory to God on high, peace on earth, good will to men?' Luke ii. 13, 14; and shall not we, that have interest in the work of redemption? for Christ is not a mediator of redemption to angels. He hath relation to them in another respect. Yet they out of love to God and the church, and a desire to glorify God, they 'praise God' for this; and shall not we much more for ourselves? We must praise God ourselves, and desire that all would do so, as he saith here, 'Oh that men would praise the Lord,' &c.; and in some other psalms he stirs up all the creatures, 'hail, and snow, and wind,' and all to praise God.

How can these 'praise God'?

They do it by our mouths, by giving us occasion to praise him. And they 'praise him' in themselves; for as the creature groaneth, Rom. viii. 23, that none knows but God and itself; they groan for the corruption and abuse that they are subject unto, and God knows those groans. So the creature hath a kind of voice likewise in praising of God. They declare in their nature the goodness of God, and minister occasion to us to praise God. Therefore the psalmist being desirous that God might be praised for his 'goodness and mercy,' he stirs up every creature, Ps. ciii. 20, *seq.*, even the very angels, insinuating that it is a work fit for angels.

The children of God have such a love and zeal to the glory of God, that they are not content only to praise God themselves, but they stir up all. They need not to wish angels to do it, but only to shew their desire. Oh the blessed disposition of those that love God in Christ!

What shall we think then of those wretched persons that grieve that the 'word of God should run and have free passage, and be glorious,' 2 Thes. iii. 1, and that there should be a free use of the sacraments and the blessed means of salvation? They envy the glory of God, and the salvation of people's souls. What shall we say to those that desire to hear God dishonoured, that perhaps swear and blaspheme, themselves, or if they do not, yet they are not touched in their hearts for the dishonour of God by others? This is far from the disposition of a Christian. He desires that all creatures may trumpet out the praise of God, from the highest angel to the lowest creature, from the sun and stars to the meanest shrub; only devilish-spirited carnal men take delight to blaspheme God, that can strike them with his word and send them to their own place, to hell, without repentance, and can hear him dishonoured without any touch of spirit. A child of God desires God to be glorified from his very heart-root, and is grieved when God is dishonoured any kind of way. So much briefly for the first.

Now what is the duty this holy man wishes?

'That men would praise God. And sacrifice the sacrifice of thanksgiving, and declare his works.'

Out of the largeness of his heart he expresseth the same thing in many words, therefore I shall not need to make any scruple in particularising of them, because there is not so much heed to be given in the expressions of a large heart as to be punctual in everything.

First, He begins with praise.

'Oh that men would therefore praise the Lord,' &c.

It is a duty, as I said before, fit for angels. Fit! Nay, it is performed by them. For it is all the work they do. It is the only work that was religious, that Adam did in paradise, and that we shall do in heaven with God. Therefore we are never more in heaven than when we take all occasions of blessing and 'praising God.' We are never in a more happy estate.

It is a duty therefore we should aim at, and the rather, because it is the fruit and end of all other duties whatsoever. What is the end of all the good we do, but to shew our thankfulness to God? The end of our fruitfulness in our place? That others may take occasion to glorify God. What is the end of our hearing? To get knowledge and grace, that we may be the better able to praise God in our mouths and in our lives. What is the end of receiving the sacrament? Nay, what is the duty itself? A thanksgiving. What is the end of prayer? To beg graces and strength that so we may carry ourselves in our places as is fit; that so we may not want those things without which we cannot so well glorify God. So the end of all is to glorify God.

It is the end that God intended in all. He framed all things to his own praise in the creation. Why hath God given man reason here upon the stage of the world? To behold the creatures, Rom. i. 19, 20, that seeing in the creature 'the wisdom of God in ordering things,' 'the goodness of God' in the use of things, and the 'power of God' in the greatness of things, the huge, vast heaven and earth, he might take occasion to glorify and magnify this God, to think highly of him, to exalt him in our thoughts; that his creatures, heaven and earth, be so beautiful and excellent, what excellency is in God himself!

And as the end of creation, so in redemption, all is for his glory and praise. In Eph. i. 6, how sweetly doth Saint Paul set forth the end of it: 'To the glory of his rich mercy and grace.' To be merciful to sinners; to give his own Son; for God to become man, not for man in that estate as Adam was in innocency, but for sinners; for God to triumph over sin by his infinite mercy: here is the glory of his grace shining in the gospel. All is for the glory and praise of God there.

And for particular deliverances, in Ps. l. 15, 'Call upon me in the day of trouble: I will deliver thee, and thou shalt glorify me.' His deliverances of us in the passages of our life is, that we may glorify him, by taking notice in imminent dangers of some of his attributes, when there is no means of deliverance, of his power and goodness, &c. In Rev. iv. 10, the elders are brought in praising God for the work of creation; and then in the fifth, ver. 12, for 'redemption,' 'Thou art worthy, for thou hast redeemed us.' So indeed the work of creation, redemption, and the particular passages of God's providence, and protection, and preservation, they are matter of praise in heaven and earth among God's people.

Now to name a few helps and means to perform this duty the better.

If we would stir up ourselves to praise God, *let us consider our own unworthiness.* As in prayer there must be a humble heart—for a man will not seek abroad if he have somewhat at home: poverty of spirit and humility of heart makes a man pray—so it is the humble soul that 'praiseth God,' that sees no desert in itself. This is one way to help us to 'praise God,' to see nothing in ourselves why God should so regard us, as 'to give us our lives for a prey,' Jer. xxi. 9, to set his love on us, and to follow us with good; nay, we have deserved the contrary, that God should leave us and expose us to misery, rather than to watch over us by his providence. What is in us? 'It is he that hath made us, and not we ourselves,' Ps. c. 3; and he made us again when we were sinners, when we were worse than nought. Therefore, to humble us, we must consider our own unworthiness. He that knows himself unworthy of any favour, he will be thankful even for the least, as we see in Jacob, 'I am less than the least of all thy favours,' Gen. xxxii. 10. Therefore he was thankful for the least. So we see here in the text. These men are stirred up to 'praise God.' They saw no other help, no worthiness in themselves. They were at the gates of death, in a desperate estate; 'Oh that such men would praise God.' Indeed, such men are fittest to 'praise God,' that can ascribe help to nothing but to God, to no second causes.

Therefore, in the next place, as a branch of the former, if we would praise God, *dwell not on the second causes.* If God use second causes in any favour he bestows on us, either in keeping us from any ill, or bestowing any good, consider it as a means that God might dispense with; that he might use if he would, or not use. See God in the second causes; rise from them to him. Art thou healed by physic? Use physic as a means, but see God in it. But if God hath cured thee without physic, without ordinary means, then see him more immediately doing good to thee without the help of second causes. That is one way to help us to praise God, to see him in every favour and deliverance. For what could second causes do, if he should not give a blessing? Especially praise him when he hath immediately* done it, as he can. Did not he make light before there was a sun? He is not tied to give light by the sun; and he made waters before he made the clouds. He is not tied to the clouds. Therefore especially 'praise God' when we have deliverance we know not how, without means, immediately from the goodness and strength of God.

Again, If we would 'praise God' for any favour, *consider the necessity and use of the favour we pray for,* as these men here; they were at death's door, and 'loathed all manner of meat.' Alas! they had died if God had not helped them. If thou wouldst bless God, consider what a miserable state thou shouldst be in if thou hadst not that favour to praise God for. If thou be to bless God for thy senses, put case thou shouldst want thy sight, what a miserable case thou shouldst be in! So for any of the senses that a man wants, whereby he should glorify God, and take the comfort of the creature, put case a man should want his taste, as these men here—'their soul abhorred all manner of meat'—alas! what a miserable case is it to want a relish and taste of the comfort that God hath put into the creatures; put case we should want the meanest benefit we enjoy, how uncomfortable would our lives be!

This spark of reason that God hath given us, that we have understanding

* That is, 'without means.'—G.

to conceive things, which is the engine whereby we do all things as men, and are capable of the grace of God, what a miserable thing were it if God should take away our wits, or suspend the use of them?

But especially in matters of grace, if God had not sent Christ to redeem the world, what a cursed condition had we lain in, next to devils?

Again, If we would praise God, *let us every day keep a diary of his favours and blessings:* what good he doth us privately, what positive blessings he bestows upon us, and what dangers he frees us from, and continues and renews his mercy every day; and publicly what benefit we have by the state we live in. Oh what a happy state is it that we live in peace, that we enjoy such laws, 'that every man may sit under his own vine, and under his own fig-tree,' Micah iv. 4, and enjoy the comforts of life, when all the world about us are and have been in combustion! We should keep a register of God's blessings. Oh that we could learn to have such exact lives! It would breed a world of comfort, and we should have a less account to make when we die.

Every day labour to be humbled for our sins, specially such as break the peace of our consciences, and never give our bodies rest till our hearts have rest in the favour of God; and together with matter of humiliation, daily observe how God bestows new favours, or else continues the old; that notwithstanding our provocation and forgetfulness of him, he strives with us by his goodness. This is a blessed duty that we should labour to perform.

And then when we have done this, let us rouse up all that we are, and all that we have within us, to praise God. Ps. ciii. 1, 'My soul, praise the Lord, and all that is within me praise his holy name.' What have we within us to praise God? Let us praise God with our understanding, to conceive and have a right judgment of God's favours, of the worthiness of them and our own unworthiness, and then a sanctified memory. 'Forget not all his benefits,' Ps. ciii. 2. Forgetfulness is the grave of God's blessings. It buries all. And then there is in us the affection of joy and love to God to taste him largely, and then all within us will be large in the praising of God. And our tongue likewise, though that be not within us, it is called our 'glory,' Ps. xvi. 9 and Ps. lvii. 8; let us make it our glory in this, to trumpet out God's praise upon all occasions. All that is within us, and all that we are, or have, or can do, let it be all to the glory and 'praise of God.'

To draw to a conclusion, with some general application of all that hath been spoken, and then in particular to the present occasion.

You know how God hath dealt of late with this city,* and with ourselves indeed; for we are all of one body politic, and however God visited them, yet it was our sins also that provoked him. We brought sticks to the common fire. A physician lets the arm blood, but the whole body is distempered. God let the city blood, but the whole kingdom was in a distemper. So that it was for our sins as well as theirs. We all brought, I say, something to the common flame, and God afflicted us even in them. God hath now stayed the sickness almost as miraculously as he sent it. It was a wonder that so many should be swept away in so short a time. It is almost as great a wonder that God should stay it so soon. And what may we impute it unto? Surely as it is in the text. 'They cried unto the Lord.' God put it into the hearts of the governors of the State to appoint humiliation and 'crying to God,' and therefore since God hath

* In margin here, 'In the great visitation, 1625.'—G.

been so merciful upon our humiliation, it is religiously and worthily done of the State, that there should be a time to 'bless God.'

Again, God did it with a word, with a command. It was both in the inflicting and delivery, as it were, without means; for what could the physician do in staying the plague? Alas, all the skill in the world is at a loss in these kinds of sicknesses! It comes with God's command. It is God's arrow more especially than other sicknesses. God sent it by his command, first to humble us for our sin; and now he hath stayed it with a word of command, that from above five thousand a week it is come to three persons. 'God hath sent his word and healed us.'

It was a pitiful state we were in before; for indeed it was not only a sickness upon the city, but a civil sickness. The whole state was distempered; for as there is sickness in the body when there is obstruction, when there is not a passage for the spirits and the blood from the liver, and from the heart, and from the head, these obstructions cause weakness, and faintings, and consumption. So was there not an obstruction in the State of late? Were not the veins of the kingdom stopped? Was not civil commerce stayed? The affliction of this great city, it was as the affliction of the head, or of the heart, or of the liver. If the main vital part be sick, the whole is sick; so the whole kingdom, not only by way of sympathy, but it was civilly sick, in regard that all trading and intercourse was stopped; it was a heavy visitation. And we have much cause to bless God that now the 'ways of this Sion' of ours 'mourn not;' that there is free commerce and intercourse as before; that we can meet thus peaceably and quietly at God's ordinances, and about our ordinary callings. Those that have an apprehension of the thing, cannot choose but break out in thanksgiving to God in divers respects.

1. First of all, have not we matter to praise God that he *would correct us at all?* He might have suffered us to have gone on and been 'damned with the wicked world;' as it is 1 Cor. xi. 32, 'We are therefore chastened of the Lord, that we should not be damned with the world.' It is his mercy that he would take us into his hands as children, that he would visit us at all.

2. Another ground of thanksgiving is this, that since he would correct us, he *would use this kind of correction*, that he would take us into his own hands. Might he not have suffered a furious, bloody, dark-spirited, devilish-spirited enemy to have invaded us? to have fallen into the hard hands of men acted with devilish malice? David thought this a favour, even that God would single him out to punish him with the plague of pestilence, that he might not 'fall before his enemies,' 2 Sam. xxiv. 14. The mercies of God are wondrous great when we 'fall into his hands.' He is a 'merciful God.' He hath tender bowels full of pity and compassion. But the very mercies of wicked idolaters 'are cruel.' There was a mercy, therefore, in that, that God would take us into his own hands.

3. In the third place, We see when he had taken us into his own hands, how he hath *stopped the raging of the pestilence*, and hath inhibited the destroying angel even in a wondrous manner; that the plague, when it was so raging, that it should come to decrease upon a sudden. God was wondrous in this work. Is not here matter of praise?

4. Then again, It is a mercy to us all here that he should 'give us our lives for a prey;' as God saith in Jeremiah to Baruch, 'Wheresoever thou goest, thou shalt have thy life for a prey,' Jer. xxi. 9. Might not God's arrow have followed us wheresoever we went?

Whither can a man go from this arrow, but that God being everywhere, might smite him with the pestilence? Now, in that he hath watched over us, and kept us from this noisome contagious sickness, and hath brought us altogether here quietly and freely, that so there may be intercourse between man and man in trading and other calling, this is the fourth ground of 'praising of God.'

5. And that *it did not rage in other parts*. In former time God scattered the pestilence more over the kingdom. It is a great matter to bless God for. I beseech you, let us say with the same spirit as this holy man here, 'Oh that men, therefore, would praise the Lord for his goodness, and for the wonders that he doth for the children of men!'—for his goodness, that he would rather correct us here than damn us; for his goodness, that he would not give us up to our enemies; for his goodness, that he stayed the infection so suddenly, and that he stayed the spreading of it further; for his goodness unto us in particular, that he hath kept us all safe.

What shall we do now but consecrate and dedicate these lives of ours; for he gives us our lives more than once, at the beginning. There is never a one here but can say by experience, God hath given me my life at such a time and such a time. Let us give these lives again to God, labour to reform our former courses, and enter into a new covenant with God. This is one part of thanksgiving, to renew our covenant with God, to please him better; and indeed, in every thanksgiving that should be one ingredient. Now, Lord, I intend and resolve to please thee better. Whatsoever my faults have formerly been, I resolve by thy grace and assistance to break them off. Without this, all the other is but a dead performance.

Now, briefly, by way of analogy and proportion, to raise some meditations from that that hath been delivered concerning the body, to the soul; for God is the physician both to soul and body.

If God with his word can heal our bodies, as the psalmist saith here, much more can he with his word heal our soul. There are many that their bodies are well, thanks be to God, but how is it with their souls? Here you have some symptoms to know their spiritual state; and oh that people were apprehensive of it! Have you not many that their 'soul loatheth all manner of meat,' and they 'draw near the gates of death?' Their souls are in a desperate state. They are deeply sick. How shall we know it? Their soul 'abhorreth all manner of wholesome meat.' How many are there that relish poets and history, any trifle that doth but feed their vain fancy, and yet cannot relish the blessed truth and ordinances of God? Where is spiritual life when this spiritual sense is gone, when men cannot relish holy things? If they relish the ordinance of God, it is not the spiritual part of it, so far as the Spirit toucheth the conscience, but something that, it may be, is suitable to their conceit, expressions, or phrases, or the like. But it is a symptom and sign of a fearful declining state when men do not relish the spiritual ordinances of God, which should be, as it were, 'their appointed food;' when they do not 'delight to acquaint themselves with God,' in hearing of the word, and reading, and the like. Let such, therefore, as delight not in spiritual things, know that their souls lie gasping; they are at the 'gates' of spiritual death. All is not well. There is some fearful obstruction upon the soul that takes away the appetite. The soul runs into the world over much. They cloy themselves with the world. When men cannot relish heavenly things, they are ate up with the delight and joy of other things, pleasures, and profits.

Let them search the cause, and labour for purging, sharp, things that may procure an appetite.

Let them judge themselves, and see what is the matter, that they do not delight more in heavenly things; let them purge themselves by confession to God, and consideration of their sins, and labour to recover their appetite. For it is almost a desperate estate, 'they are at the gates of death.'

Especially now when we come to the communion. What do we here, if we cannot relish the food of our souls? Let us examine if we desire to taste the love of God, and to be acquainted with God here. If not, what shall we do in these spiritual distempers?

Desire of God, cry to God, that he would forgive our sins and heal our souls by his Holy Spirit, that he would make us more spiritual, to relish heavenly things better than we have done before, that as the things that are heavenly are better in their kind than other things are, so they may be better to our taste.

A man may know the judgment of his state when he answereth not the difference of things. What the difference is between the food of life and ordinary food; what the difference is between the comforts of the Holy Ghost and other comforts; between the riches and pelf of the world and the riches of the Spirit; the graces of God, that will cause a man to live and die with comfort; the true riches, that make the soul rich to eternity: there is no comparison. Beg of God this spiritual relish to discern 'of things that differ,' Heb. v. 14, that we may recover our appetite. God by his word and Spirit can do it, not only the word written, but the inward spiritual word written in our hearts. Desire God to join his Spirit with his word and sacraments, and that will recover our taste and make us spiritual. that we shall relish him that is both the feast-maker and the feast itself. He is both the meat and the provider of the banquet.

For whence is it that all other things are sweet to us? deliverance from trouble and sickness? Because it is a pledge of our spiritual deliverance in Christ. The deliverance from hell and damnation, what comfort can a man have that knows not his state in grace, in the enjoying of his health, when he shall think he is but as a 'sheep kept for the slaughter?' He knows not whether he be in the favour of God or no.

Therefore let us come and renew our faith in the forgiveness of our sins through the blood of Christ, of whom we are made partakers in the sacrament. For if we believe our deliverance from hell and damnation by the body of Christ broken and his blood shed, then everything will be sweet. When we know God loves us to life everlasting, then everything in the way to life everlasting, even daily bread, will be sweet, because the same love that gives heaven gives daily food, and the same love that redeems us from hell, redeems us from sickness. Therefore let us labour to strengthen our faith in the main, that we may be thankful for the less. And as we enter into new covenant with God, so labour to keep it; in Lev. xxvi. 14, *seq.*, everything avengeth the breaking of God's covenant. When we make covenant to serve him better for the time to come, and yet break it, God is forced to send his messenger. He sends sickness to avenge his covenant. Considering that he hath lately so avenged it, let it make us so much the more circumspect in our carriage. So much for this time and text.

Imprimatur.
Thomas Wykes.

May 11
1638.

NOTES.

(*a*) P. 140.—'In such a year, such conjunctions and such eclipses,' &c. One of various allusions to astrology, a faith in which Sibbes shared with the most illustrious of his contemporaries, *e. g.*, Bacon, Sir Thomas Browne, &c.

(*b*) P. 141.—'As Salvian saith well, "Thou perishest before thou perish."' Cf. note *d*, Vol. V. page 34.

(*c*) P. 143.—'As one observes, that naturally men run to God in extremity.' Many curious and striking illustrations of this will be found in the old Puritan 'Commentaries' on the Book of Jonah, chap. i. verses 5, 6, and parallel passages. It is an observation common to Cicero, and all writers on 'Natural Religion.'

(*d*) P. 144.—'It was the speech of a heathen,' &c. A variation of the proverb, 'Man's extremity is God's opportunity.'

(*e*) P. 149.—'"With rejoicing and singing," as the word signifies.' Cf. Dr Joseph Addison Alexander *in loc.*, who, with Sibbes, supplies 'joyful' before 'singing.' G.

THE SAINT'S COMFORTS.

THE SAINT'S COMFORTS.

NOTE.

'The Saint's Comforts' forms a moiety of a small volume (18mo) published in 1638. The general title-page of the volume is given below.* It will be observed that Sibbes's name does not appear thereon, but on the other sermons it does. Probably the name was withheld from the 'Comforts,' as being from 'Notes' without Sibbes's sanction. Next to 'The Spiritual Favourite,' this volume is the rarest of his books. I have been able to trace only another copy besides my own, viz., that in the Bodleian. I have to acknowledge the kindness of the Rev. Henry Creswell of Canterbury in procuring 'The Saint's Comforts' for me. The other sermons will be found in their place in Vol. VII. G.

* THE
SAINTS
COMFORTS.

Being the substance of diverse Sermons Preached on, *Psal.* 130. the beginning.

The *Saints Happinesse,* on *Psal.* 73. 28.

The *Rich Pearle;* on *Math.* 13. 45, 46.

The *Successe* of the *Gospell,* on, *Luk.* 7. 34, 35.

Maries Choyce, on *Luk.* 10. 38, 39, 40.

By a Reverend Divine now with God.

Printed at *London* by *Tho. Cotes,* and are to be sold by *Peter Cole,* at the signe of the Glove in *Corne-hil* neere the *Exchange.* 1638.

On reverse—

Imprimatur,
Tho. Wykes. Octob. 5. 1637.

THE SAINT'S COMFORTS:

AN EXPOSITION UPON PSALM CXXX.

Out of the depths have I cried unto thee, O God.—Ver. 1.

This psalm is a pithy psalm, and therefore is called a psalm of degrees. Other reasons the Jews give of this title, but they agree not. Some will have it that these psalms were sung upon the fifteen stairs that went up to the temple. Some call them thus, for that they say they were sung with an extraordinary high voice. But in these difficulties, *Melius est dubitare de occultis, quam litigare de incertis.* All historical truths are not necessary to be known, for Christ did many things that were not written, John xx. 30.

The author is not named. However, we may assure ourselves the Spirit of God indited it, setting down, first, the state of the writer, ver. 1; secondly, his carriage in that estate: 'He prayed, being in depths,' ver. 2; thirdly, the ground of his prayer, which was God's mercy, ver. 3; his own faith, hope, and patience; his waiting, is simply laid down, ver. 5, and comparatively, ver. 6; and fourthly, an application to the whole church, ver. 7, from his own experience of God's mercy and sufficiency.

Out of the first part, concerning the state of the writer of this psalm, let us observe these particulars, following in their order: first, *that the children of God do fall into depths;* that is, into extremity of misery and affliction, which are called 'depths;' because as waters and depths, so these, do swallow up and drown the soul, and because they do compass about the soul, burying it in great, terrible, continuing deep dangers; and these depths of a Christian are either outward or inward. *The outward troubles* and depths are those of the body. These God's children are afflicted with, as Jonah was when he was in the bottom of the sea, Joseph in prison, and Paul in the dungeon; and these are like the man of God to the Shunamite, 1 Kings xvii. 18, they do but call our sins to remembrance. *But the inward spiritual* troubles are the great depths; that is, trouble of mind for sin that lies upon us, causing us to doubt of our estate, to feel God's wrath, to fear rejection and excluding from God's presence. This is the soul of sorrow; other outward sorrows being but the carcase of sorrow. 'The spirit of a man will bear his infirmities; but a wounded spirit who can bear?' Prov. xviii. 14. In such an estate, in regard of the extremity of the burden of the sins of the whole world laid on him, was our head, Christ Jesus, making him sweat 'drops of blood,' Luke xxii. 44; and when he was on the cross, when he cried with strong cries and tears, 'My God, my God, why hast thou forsaken me?' Mark xv. 34. *But why is this thus*, that the Prince* of our salvation should be in such a depth of misery? I answer, because it was requisite that salvation should be repaired by the contrary means to that whereby it was lost. It was lost by lifting up. Adam would be like a god; and Christ he regained us by abasing himself. The Son of God must become man, and a man of sorrows; and as the head was, so the members have been and must be, Rom. viii. 29, 'for we are predestinated to be like the image of his Son,' and so to pledge him in the same cup wherein he drank deep to us. In this plight we find David often, though a man after God's own heart, Ps. vi. 2, 3, Ps. lxxxviii. 2, &c., Ps. xl. 12; and Jonah, a prophet, Jonah ii. 2, &c.; and Hezekiah, Isa. xxxviii. 13; and Job especially, Job vi. 4. But why is this thus, seeing our head, Christ Jesus, hath suffered for us? I answer, we must suffer,

Reason 1. First, *That we may know what Christ suffered for us by our own experience*, without which we should but lightly esteem of our redemption, not knowing how to value Christ's sufferings sufficiently, which is a horrible sin, Heb. ii. 3.

Reason 2. Secondly, *By our sufferings we know what a bitter thing sin is*, Jer. ii. 19, as by the ill consequents thereof: for without the taste of God's wrath, we find nothing but sweetness and pleasure in sin; and therefore, we have so much sense of God's wrath as to humble us, but shews not the extremity of the depth of sin, lest we should sink down into despair.

Reason 3. Thirdly, *By our afflictions and depths, we manifest God's power and glory* the more in our deliverance: for the greater the trouble is, the greater is the deliverance; as the greater the cure is, the greater credit the physician gets.

Reason 4. Fourthly, *Many times, by less evils, it is God's manner to cure greater;* and thus he suffers us to feel wrath, to cure us of security, which is as a grave to the soul; as also to cure spiritual pride, that robs us of grace, dealing with us as he did with the Israelites. He would not cast out all the nations from before them, but left some that might be employed in hunting and destroying the wild beasts, which might else multiply against the children of Israel. And thus God dealt with Paul, gave him to be vexed by a base temptation, lest he should be lifted up with spiritual pride, through the abundance of revelations, 2 Cor. xii. 7.

Reason 5. Fifthly, *These depths are left to us, to make us more desirous of heaven;* else great men, that are compassed about with earthly comforts, alas, with what zeal could they pray, 'Thy kingdom come,' &c.? No; with Peter they would rather say, 'Master, it is good for us to be here,' Mark ix. 5; and therefore, it is God's usual dealing with great men, to suffer them to fall into spiritual desertions, to smoke them out of the world, whether they will or not.

Reason 6. Sixthly, *God works by these afflictions in us a more gentleness of spirit, making us meek and pitiful towards those that are in depths*, which was one cause of Christ's afflictions: he suffered, that he might help and comfort others. He suffered Peter to stumble, that when he was converted, he should 'strengthen his brethren,' Luke xxii. 32.

Use 1. Hence therefore we learn *not to pass a rash censure on ourselves or others that are in such depths* as this holy man was in; for the afflicted soul no sooner tastes of this bitter fruit, but presently breaks out into complaints.

* Misprinted 'point.'—G.

'Never was any thus afflicted as I,' thinking it unpossible that there should be greater crosses, than it feels; when indeed the draught that Christ our head did drink to us, was far beyond the apprehension of mortal man, and therefore much more beyond his power to undergo. Let us beware how we censure others that are afflicted, for God's ends are hid. It may be God sends afflictions to manifest some excellent graces which lie in him, unknown both to the world and himself; and so he set Job as a flag of defiance against the devil, bidding him do his worst. He should find him upright, and a just man; and therefore we should rather take notice of affliction as a sign of some excellent grace with which God hath furnished such; for God will not call out any of his to suffering, but he will get himself honour thereby.

Use 2. In the second place, *note this doctrine against the profane persons that tush at religion*, and make a mock at the dejected condition of those that are good, because they seem despised, afflicted, and forsaken. They, alas! are ignorant of God's ways and works. It were much safer for them to consider their own ways, and to reason, if God deals thus with his dearest ones, with the 'green trees,' what shall become of those that are his enemies, that are 'dry trees?' If such troubles arise to the godly, even from God's love to them, what shall defend the wicked when the vials of God's wrath shall be poured down upon them, when they shall 'call to the rocks and mountains to hide, cover, and defend them?' Rev. vi. 16. If the 'righteous hardly be saved, where shall the ungodly appear?' 1 Peter iv. 18. And to conclude, know that the afflictions of the children of God are far better than the pleasures of sin.

Doct. 2. In the second place, observe we, though Christians fall into depths, *yet God upholds them that they sink not down into them without recovery*. Thus it was with our Head. Though he on the sudden apprehended not the presence of God, so as he thought himself forsaken, yet he could even at the worst say, 'My God.' Thus also Jonah, ii. 4, 'I said I was cast out of thy sight; yet will I look towards thy holy temple.' So Ps. xxxi. 22, and Ps. cxviii. 5 and 6 verses.

Reason 1. *For the Spirit of God is in them*, and where it is, it is stronger than hell, yea though the grace be but as a grain of mustard seed.

Reason 2. Again, As there are depths of misery in a Christian, *so in God there are depths of love and of wisdom.*

Reason 3. Thirdly, *Faith, where it is, unites the soul to Christ, and to God through him*, and draws down divine power—to lay hold on the almighty power of God by true and fervent prayer,—at whose rebuke the waters of affliction flee away, Ps. lxxvii. 16; and so the stronger the faith is, the stronger is the delivery, for it is of a mighty power, enabling us to wrestle with God, as Jacob did. Thus when we lay hold on God, and God on us, what can drown us?

Reason 4. Fourthly, *It is the nature of God's working to be by contraries:* in his works of creation, making all things of nothing; in his works of providence, he saves by little means from greatest dangers. That he might bring us to heaven, he suffers us to go down even into hell, to see our worst estate, to humble us; and it may therefore be a cause why many men lie long in afflictions, even because they come not low enough to see their sins and need of help. In glorifying our mortal bodies, he first brings them to the grave, that they may rot and corrupt, and so be refined and moulded anew.

Use 1. *This should teach us a note of difference* between those that are

God's children and those that are not. Those that are his, when they are in danger, go to him. They have ever that hold by faith, as to say, 'Yet God is good to Israel,' Jer. xxxi. 1. Others seek to escape by desperate undoing of themselves, as Saul, and Judas, and Ahithophel, for all his strong natural parts; and indeed such are in most danger of such courses of all other; for God will tread on such for their pride. Contrarily he mingles comforts, in the worst estate that his children are in, with griefs, one to humble them, the other to support them from despair; and so he sets them on a rock that is higher than they.

Use 2. Secondly, *It should teach us in all extremities how to carry ourselves.* We should take heed of the stream of grief, striving against it, as we desire a note of our good estate; take heed how we think that God forsakes us. It is an imputation unbefitting him that never forsakes his. Take heed of judging ourselves by sense. Is meat sour because one that is sick doth not relish it? No. The fault is in his indisposition. So in such desertions, be sure thou retainest thy anchor of hope, though contrary to hope; and therefore in the next place,

Use 3. *We should answer God's dealing by our dealing.* He works by contraries; we should judge by contraries. Therefore, if we be in misery, hope and wait for glory, in death look for life, in sense of sin assure thyself of pardon, for God's nature and promises are unchangeable; and when God will forgive, he lets us see our troubles; and therefore with resolute Job say, 'Though he kills me, I will yet trust in him,' Job xiii. 15. But to come particularly, I will set down cures of such depths as may arise from several causes; and these depths are either imaginary or real. Christians sometimes think themselves to be in depths when indeed they are not, but it is only imaginary, raised it may be *from a melancholy distemperature of the spirits*, which also distempers the reasonable working of the mind; raising as false and feigned conceits of their souls as it doth in many of their bodies; and yet these conceits have real effects, as in Jacob, who sorrowed as truly for Joseph as if he were dead indeed. Therefore for the avoiding hereof be not alone; a friend and good company are made for such times. For the devil sets on men in such case most when they are alone, and the strongest are then too weak for him; and believe not thine own fancy, but rather believe those that can discern us better than we ourselves can. We know how men have been deceived thus, and therefore when we are advised thus by friends, and counselled, let us suspect that it is a motion of the devil or a fancy of thine own that thus troubles thee.

There is another depth that is imaginary, arising *from mistaking of rules*, concluding because they have not so much grace as others, have not so much subduing and prevailing power over sin, therefore they have no grace at all, they are damned hypocrites and the like. Little do they think that perfection is not attainable here, but is reserved to the blessedness of that other life hereafter. Little do they look to the imperfections of the best saints of God, and the great depths that they have been in; and indeed they know not what the covenant of grace requires, nor perfect fulfilling of the law by our own persons, for that was the end of the law. But the covenant of grace requires sincerity with growth; and this is the only perfection which we can look for here.

Another depth also there is, which ariseth *from the taking of the motions of the devil for those of his own corrupt nature.* The baseness and unreasonableness of them makes them think they cannot be God's children, and have such detestable motions within them. Let such know *that such shall be cast upon Satan's score.* And it is a sign rather that such are none of the children of the devil, who, if they were, would suffer them to rest in quiet without vexing them.

Again, some men fall into another depth, which ariseth *from an apprehension of God forsaking them.* To such I give this advice, that they *judge not of themselves by their distemper,* for a sinful conscience puts a veil sometimes between God and us, hiding his favour; which nevertheless may be as great to us then as at any other time, and it may be intended by God to drive us to him by scourging us from our wicked ways and sins, which formerly we lived in. By faith therefore pull off the vizor from the face of God; judge not according to present appearance, but by God's nature and his promises, who hath said he will be with us for ever, that no temptations shall be above measure, 1 Cor. x. 13; judge by his nature who is unchangeable; and thus did the Canaanitish woman see Christ's loving nature under his frowning look, who doth as Joseph, hide his love and person from his brethren out of a increasement of love, not out of any ill intent. Again, in such a case let us be sure *we trust others that are our friends rather than ourselves.* I mean in time of temptation, whenas others can better discern of our health by our spiritual pulses than we ourselves, who then are blinded; and in such cases there is the trial of faith and love.

There is another sort of depths, and these are *before conversion*; and thus was Paul troubled, 'Lord, what shall I do?' and thus was Manasseh. *Let such consider the commandment,* to humble them and cast themselves on Christ and his promises, considering the end of Christ's coming was to save and seek such as are lost.

Use 4. And if any one shall find himself already escaped such depths as are formerly mentioned, *let him take comfort to himself,* as being thereby evidently proved to be the child of God; for that is utterly impossible, that nature should overcome such difficulties, and to that end let him reason after this sort, God's children go to him in depths. I go only to him in depths, therefore I am God's child; for to have the spirit of prayer to go to God in time of trouble, it is a work of the Spirit; a natural man hath it not, Job xxvii. 9, 10.

Use 5. Hence therefore, in the next place, note *a sure sign of the true religion, namely, to be able to support men in danger and in spiritual troubles.* This is verified in ours, as the subtile Jesuit will acknowledge, while they hold that reposing ourselves merely on mercy and favour in Christ, and not on man's good works, is the safest way. Why, therefore, they live by their uncomfortable rules; and when they die, fly for succour to these, which in their lifetime they despise.*

Use 6. Moreover, let this be a *ground to encourage us never to give over God's cause.* He hath said he will not leave us though we be in depth of our sins, if we belong to him, and therefore much less will he leave us in that work which he himself sets us about. He was with Daniel among the lions, with Moses in the bulrushes, with the 'three children' in the fire, with his church through 'fire and water.'

Use 7. Lastly, Let us therefore *be sure to keep God our friend,* that he may own us; else when we cry he will not hear us, Prov. i. 28. Acquaint we ourselves with him, as it is in Job xxii. 21, in prosperity, and he will be our refuge, &c.

Doct. 3. In the third place, observe we that *afflictions stir up devotions;* for prayers in time of afflictions are cries. *Oratio sine malis est avis sine alis;*

* Cf. note *w*, Vol. III. page 531.—G.

for what allays worldly joy, and embitters it, but affliction? Now we know that it is the worldly afflictions* that quenches our zeal and makes us cold. Affliction is a purgation opening the soul, causing it to relish and to affect† spiritually, and to see the wants and necessity of supply, and so procures longing and earnest hungering, Hosea v. 15. 'In their affliction they will seek me early,' and therefore, Ps. cvii. 6, it is said they *cried* to the Lord in their trouble. Now crying supposes want and sense of misery and ardency. Thus were Christ's cries called 'strong cries;' and indeed weak afflictions many times makes men rather pettish and froward, as Jonah, than ardent in feeling relief; and therefore,

Use 1. *Let us interpret God's dealings with a sanctified judgment.* He is a wise physician, and knows when strong or gentle physic is most requisite. Sometimes God by great afflictions doth manifest great graces, but so as notwithstanding they may be mingled with a deal of corruption; and it is God's use that hereby his graces may be increased, and the corruption allayed, to bring down the greatest cedars, and to eclipse the greatest lights.

Use 2. Secondly, *Let us oppose desperations by all means, by prayer, by crying;* and if we cannot speak, by sighing; if not so, yet by gesture, especially at the time of death, for God knows the heart. For then it stands upon eternal comfort. And therefore let us do anything to shew our faith fails not. We must know that every one shall meet with these enemies, that would cause us to despair if they could, for this life is a warring and striving life. We shall have enemies without and within us that will fight against us.

Doct 4. In the next place, *observe by the example of this holy man, that prayers are to be made only to God,* who knows our wants, supports us and binds us up; and it is only Christ that doth this. None can love us more than he that gave himself for us. He is our eye whereby we see, our mouth whereby we speak, our arms whereby we lay hold on God; and therefore it is an intolerable unthankfulness to leave this 'fountain opened for sin and for uncleanness, and to dig to ourselves cisterns that will hold no water,' Jer. ii. 13; to leave Christ, and run to saints and angels, and the like, &c.

Ver. 2. 'Lord, hear my voice; let thine ears be attentive to the voice of my supplications.'

Mark here his constancy and instancy in prayer by his ingemination;‡ and this he doth not to work upon God, as if he were hard to be entreated to mercy, but to waken up his own heart, and to entreat of God a more inward and clear communion, communicating increase of grace; so as God's children are not satisfied with small portions of grace. And this did Daniel, Dan. ix. 18, 19. O Lord, hear, forgive, hearken, do, defer not! His ardency shews into what an exigent he was brought; and indeed the Lord regards lukewarm prayers no more than lukewarm persons, so as he will spue them out. Prayers must be like incense. It must be fired with zeal.

Quest. But some will ask, How shall we come to make our prayers fervent?

Ans. I answer, *consider of our wants, and our necessity of supply, of our misery in our want, of our hope to prevail by prayer;* and these will edge our affections in prayer. Consider also how these times, and the estate of

* Qu. 'affections'?—ED.

† That is, 'choose.'—G.

‡ That is, 'repetition.'—G.

the church do sympathy with thy particular depths. The church abroad is in great depths; and if we will have proof that we are fellow-members, that we are children of that mother, let us labour for a fellow-feeling of their miseries, and make them our own; and to that end in our prayers allege the depths and pray, 'Help thou, Lord, for vain is man's help,' Ps. lx. 11. For extremity itself is a good argument to a father to help his children. Allege also the insolency of the enemies. 'Why should the heathen say, Where is our God?' Ps. lxxix. 10. There is no church but useth more helps of humiliation than we do, which foretells a great judgment; for God cannot endure this lukewarmness. Therefore call upon God with fervency, else will he cast us into such extremities as shall force fire into us. He that is poor doth naturally speak supplications.

Direct. 2. Secondly, *Look that we always be in such an estate as God may hear us.* If we be not within the covenant with God, our prayers shall turn to sin.

Direct. 3. Thirdly, *Take heed of wilful neglect of God's word.* He that turneth his ears from hearing the law, his prayer shall be abominable, Prov. xxviii. 9. Some cry down preaching and cry up prayer, making opposition between duties where none is. Dost thou think God will hear thee, and thou wilt not hear him? Prov. i. 28.

Direct. 4. Fourthly, *Take heed of double dealing with God.* This is hateful to God, and therefore David, till he dealt plainly with himself by condemning himself, his prayers were but roaring as a beast taken in a snare and [that] cannot get out, roars for pain and despite, Ps. xxxii. 3.

Direct. 5. *Take heed,* in the next place, *of allowance of any sin, though never so little;* and though it be only entertained in heart, the Lord will not hear our prayers, Ps. lxvi. 18. For shall we think that God cares for our prayers when we make covenant with his enemies?

Direct. 6. *Take heed also of unmercifulness and cruelty.* God would not hear the Israelites. Their hands were full of blood, Isa. i. 15. God will rather have no sacrifice than no charity. Let us take heed of these things, and let us come boldly to the throne of grace while he holds out his sceptre to us.

But against this a man may object and say, that he is a wicked wretch, and his prayers shall but increase sin.

To such I answer, let them offer their prayers in obedience to God's commandments, who commands them to pray, and he will respect the very 'groans' of his Spirit within. Elias was a man subject to the like infirmities; yet God heard his prayer, James v. 17. Where God's Spirit stirreth up, man's spirit is stirred up; and where Christ joins to offer the prayers to his Father as in his own name, why should we vilify that which God highly esteemeth? Let God have his sacrifice. He knows how to accept of that which is good, and to pardon that which is amiss. He will second his beginnings, and will enlarge the heart more and more. Though in the beginning, prayer may be dull and untoward, it shall end in fulness, and therefore let these spiritual depths be so far off from hindering us from prayer, as that rather it should encourage us to pray. For it may be one end why the Lord suffers us to fall into depths, to the end that we may be stirred up to come to him; that thus we may glorify him, and he glorify his mercy in hearing our prayers and granting our requests. For sure it is, he that hath not a heart to pray when he is in depths, shall never come out of them; and let such as do come to him know, that however God is not present to sense, but rather seemeth to hide himself, yet he is most near to such as, with Mary, cannot see him for their tears and griefs, if with her in humility they seek after him.

Ver. 3. 'If thou, Lord, should mark iniquities, O Lord, who shall stand?'

These words are a removal of hindrances of prayer, following God with an humble confession of that which is evil, which is ever better than a proud boasting of that which is good; and thus preventing* a secret objection, which God and a guilty conscience may make, that he was a guilty wretch. To which he answers by way of confession, 'Truth, Lord! yet if thou shouldst mark iniquities, none could abide it. Whence in general we may observe,

Doct. 1. *That sin hinders and discourages the soul from prayer;* for the conscience will object, and the soul will upbraid us, telling us we are sinners. God, he is holy, and how can we think he will hear us then, where there is no faith? The soul must needs sink. This estate was David's, Ps. li. 14, 15. Sin and a guilty conscience had almost sealed up his lips; and thus was the publican, who durst not lift up his eyes to heaven; and thus will our estate be, especially if we yield to sins against conscience; like Adam, we shall run from the presence of God to hide ourselves, though our former estate and conversation with God were never so inward and familiar. Therefore let us look to our souls as we desire to appear with comfort before the throne of grace, for consciousness of the remainder of sin hinders boldness in prayer in the best.

Doct. 2. In the second place, *the way to get out of misery is first to get discharged from sin;* for sin is the beginning and cause of all misery. Therefore the sons of Jacob, when they were handled roughly by Joseph, presently the thought of selling Joseph into Egypt came into their minds, as the cause of all their trouble, though the fact was many years before; and the widow, when her son died, presently called to mind her sin: 'O thou man of God, why comest thou to call my sin to remembrance, and to slay my son?' 1 Kings xvii. 18. If therefore we will remove the misery, let us remove sin first. Thus David began with desiring pardon, Ps. cxliii. 2, then prayer for deliverance, for misery follows sin, even as the shadow doth follow the body.

Doct. 3. Thirdly, We may observe from the general, *that the way to purge and take away sin is by confession;* thereby clearing God and laying load on ourselves. The way to cover our sin is to uncover it by confession. The way for God to spare us is, not to spare ourselves. And this God requires, not for himself, as if he were not able to be merciful but by this means, but to the end that 'we may glorify him,' as Joshua said to Achan, 'My son, give glory to God,' Josh. vii. 19. Secondly, God will have it a way to mercy, because *he hath so decreed it;* and in the third place, that thereby *there may be wrought in our souls a greater shame for sin.* And this confession must be serious, thorough, humble, with grief, shame, and hatred. Every 'Lord, have mercy,' is not enough, for many deceive themselves this way, misapplying the promises, that Christ will not 'break the bruised reed,' that he looks at the desire. Alas! these belong to such as are not lazy, that are plain dealers with themselves, that will not spare themselves; that by reading, hearing, meditation, conference, and all other duties, will not give over till they have found out the bottom of their iniquity hidden in their heart. And let only such apply them, and not those to whom they do not belong. Thus much in general. Now, to come to

* That is, 'anticipating.'—G.

some particulars; and first, let us observe out of this interrogation, having the force of a strong affirmation,

Doct. 4. *That the best men in the estate of grace are sinners;* some may be *sine crimine*, but not *sine peccato;* for in every man there are two principles: one of good, another of evil, the old man and the new. In all there is a 'combat between flesh and spirit.' Christ is not a mediator for such as are already perfect; for mediation needs not be, where all is friendly. And therefore there must be some enmity that must make God's children stand in need of the perpetual intercession of Christ, who is a high priest for ever. And the servants of God have acknowledged thus much, Ps. cxliii. 1, 'Answer me in thy righteousness,' not mine. I will not have a quarrel with thee; thou art righteous, I am sinful. I may be just in mine own eyes, but in thy sight no man shall be justified. We acknowledge thus much in our daily prayers, while we still pray 'Forgive us our trespasses.' Though we profit every day never so much, yet, like leaking ships, we gather that which will drown our souls at length if we repent not; for as it is Isa. lxiv. 6, 'Our best performances are as filthy rags.' Isa. vi. 5, 'I am a man of polluted lips.' Dan. ix. 20, 'While I confessed *my own sins*.' The papists themselves imply so much, for else why teach they the doctrine of doubting? If we be perfect, it is a sin to doubt of salvation, for thereby we deny God to be just. If they be perfect, what need they force the doctrine of penance, or of going to saints to be their mediator? And when they are upon the rack of conscience, the best of them will renounce then their dreams of perfection. From this observation, therefore, we learn, that *no man can perfectly fulfil the law;* and secondly, that *there can be no justification by works*. Only, that that must make us just must be perfect. Our best works are imperfect.

Doct. 5. In the next place, we may observe that *community of offenders is no ground of lessening or diminishing of sin*. A formal Christian, it is his trick to wrap himself up in general confessions. We are all sinners; and if God should deal with us as we deserve, we were damned; but come to reckon with him for his particular sins, then he is all in a chafe. He cannot be a saint, and the like speeches, tending to the defence of his course. The psalmist is not of this nature. He argues otherwise: neither Adam nor Abraham could stand, how much less shall I, poor worm! David, he aggravates his sin while he tells us that he was conceived and born in sin. But men now-a-days, contrarily, 'You must bear with me; it is my natural disposition; I cannot do otherwise.' Yet do I not deny but to the dejected sinner this may be used as a comfort; for while they see the mass of corruption within them, they presently conceive worse of their estate and condition, as if none were so ill, or in as ill a case as they. Such should be stayed by considering it is the general estate of all men, only the difference is, some see their sins more than others do; and thus Solomon useth it, 2 Chron. vi. 36, 'If any man sinneth against thee, as there is no man that sinneth not;' and God himself useth it as an argument to move him to mercy. 'The imaginations of man's heart are evil continually, therefore my Spirit shall not always strive with flesh,' Gen. vi. 3.

Doct. 6. In the next place, observe that *God opens the heart and eyes of his children to see and feel what sin is*, and keeps their eyes open, and their consciences continually tender. The wicked are blind in most heinous crimes of all. David he complains of this, that his sin was ever before him, Ps. li. 3. And God threatens this, Ps. l. 21, 'I will set them before thee;' and the reasons hereof are,

Reason 1. First, *To make our judgments conformable to his in hatred of sin;* for we being his children, it is fit we should be of his image, and like to him.

Reason 2. Secondly, *To make us apprehend mercy the more dearly,* and thereby glorify him in it the more.

Reason 3. Thirdly, Because *he would have us beg of him to cover our sins* from his eyes, that it may be covered from our eyes; for the best cannot shake off the sense of sin, be it ever so burthensome. But God keeps it in our minds to humble us the more thoroughly.

Reason 4. Again, *God's children have a new life which is sensible of the least thing that is contrary to itself;* and those that are in most perfect life are most perfect in the sense of sin, though never so small, though but motions. Where the sun shines most clear, then motes are most easily seen; and therefore the best Christians do complain most of corruptions, for they see more than others do. Hence, therefore, we may know our estate, whether we are still-born or have life. If we have life, we have light, and can see and discern between good and evil. Some are still-born, yet think they live. Thus are many, thinking themselves unblameable in conversation, yet in heart full of pride; and like the Pharisees, count well of themselves, nothing knowing what belongs to the Christian warfare. *Others are more bold,* and their very lives bewray they think not of sin, but are bold in their courses, proud in speech and carriage, contemptuous of others and the means of salvation, contented with a little, and think anything enough. But the worst of all are those *that think indeed of sin, but it is to defend it* and maintain it by translation* and recrimination. They will be sure to repay double, to those that tell them of their courses in friendly manner.

Quest. But how shall we come to be sensible of sin?

Direct. 1. First, *Let us have the picture of the law in our hearts,* seeing all ill and the degrees thereof; also learn us to desire† to avoid sin, so to endeavour to flee all occasions thereof, though never so small; and to take up all occasions of doing good; and doing good spiritually from judgment, affection, faith; and consider the extent of the law, reaching to the least thought.

Direct. 2. Secondly, *Bring ourselves continually into the presence of God.* Human frailty appears in nothing more, than when it is brought to the light; opposites being compared illustrate one another. Consider therefore in whose presence we are, what we are, what God is, what we have done, what he commandeth; and then, with Job, we shall abhor ourselves in dust and ashes, though formerly we defended ourselves, Job xlii. 6.

Direct. 3. And *because God is invisible, bring ourselves to that which is divine; hear we the word often unfolded,* and we shall, with the unbeliever, 1 Cor. xiv. 24, 'be convinced, and falling down shall confess God's power with it.'

Direct. 4. Furthermore, *Let us converse with those that are better than ourselves;* for the image and likeness of God is seen in his children. It is the custom of many men to converse with the worst company, that they may appear to be the best; and thus do they increase an overweening self-conceit in themselves.

Direct. 5. Let us also *use to go to places visited with God's corrections;* for seeing misery, the conscience retires to itself, considering of the ways of sin, and how the devil pays those that serve him. And this use we ought to make of objects of misery, to see God's correcting hand, else do

* That is, 'transference.'—G. † Qu. 'learn, as to desire . . . so'? &c.—Ed.

we provoke God, Isa. i. 3–5, 'who curseth such;' Jer. v. 3, and branding them with the brand of king Ahaz, 'this is Ahaz.' And while we delight ourselves with pleasing worldly objects, our eyes shut against sin, but corrections and punishments makes them see and discern. All Christ's admonitions could not make Judas see his sin of covetousness, which the weight of a burdened conscience afterward so wrought, as could not be pacified. Let us look therefore on the afflictions of other men, of our own persons and estates, and know the least crosses comes not without a just cause.

Direct. 6. Lastly, *Let us pray to God to give us tender hearts;* not to deliver us up to a hard impenetrable heart, and to spiritual judgments, but to keep us continually sensible of our sins and least infirmities.

Doct. 7. In the next place, out of the manner of delivery of this speech, we may gather thus much, that *sin once truly felt is ever unsupportable,* none can stand under it. There are three impotencies in sinners: first, they cannot see sin: Ps. xix. 12, 'Who can understand his errors.' Secondly, when the Lord causes them to see their sins, they cannot justify themselves; and then, in the third place, they cannot bear the burden of them; for death, the wages thereof, none can bear or endure; nay, God himself cannot endure sin, Amos ii. 13—nay, the wounded conscience, which is but a part of the wages thereof in this life, none can endure—but is 'pressed under them as a cart loaden with sheaves.' Christ he could not endure them, but had such sense of them as if he had been quite forsaken: 'My God, my God, why hast thou forsaken me?' And angels could not bear the burden, but were thrown down to hell thereby, and so angels of light became angels of infernal darkness. Adam could not endure it, till Christ raised him up by the promise of the blessed seed; and therefore much less can we since the fall, as it appears in Cain, Saul, Ahithophel, Judas. The earth could not bear Korah and his company, and neither would it bear us if we had our due. Sin is a debt we cannot answer: Job ix. 3, 'We cannot answer one of a thousand.'

Use 1. This therefore *confutes the papists, who say that Christ hath endured the great punishments; but there are other lighter punishments, which we also must undergo, as purgatory* and the like; to whom we say the wages of the least sin is death. That which the angels could not satisfy for, how shall we weak creatures.

Use 2. Secondly, *This may put a just defence into the mouths of careful Christians.* Let others term them by what names of scorn they list, such have good ground for what they do. They know what sin is, and have felt the sting thereof; and what they do, they do it in love to their souls. As for them that scorn, they know there is more cause to pity them than envy their estate. Though they can outswagger and outface sin now, which none could undergo heretofore, and though they can with a grace and authority, as they think, censure those that are careful, and themselves swear and profane the holy name of God, shewing thereby a heart full of unbelief and of unreverence,—which is more odious than the sin of swearing,—yet there is a time coming, when God will set their sins in order before them, in such manner that they shall melt away in the sense of the multitude and greatness of them, without hope of relief; when they shall see nothing but vengeance and death before their eyes, and without all manner of hope they shall die.

Quest. But how comes it to pass, will some say, that many nevertheless seem to bear their sins well enough, and live and die without tears?

Ans. I answer, The estate of such may be dangerous, for Christ is not sweet till sin be bitter. But God is infinite in wisdom, not presently burdening every sinner, nor comforting those that shall desire it. For then who would not be good, and who would be ill? And if evermore comforts were present, what need were there of faith? And therefore, this is most especially true at the day of judgment, when the wicked shall be blown away as chaff, Ps. i. 4–6; when there will be a guilty conscience, watching devils, and an angry God. Where shall the wicked then appear? And there must be a hell hereafter, that men may then feel what now they will not believe.

Use of direction. Wherefore *let us learn to submit ourselves to the correcting hand of God*, saying, 'It is thy mercy we are not consumed,' Lam. iii. 22; considering that this light affliction is nothing to that we deserve, or that Christ suffered for us, or that the damned suffer in hell, or to that joy we have laid up for us in heaven; and therefore as it is in Micah vii. 9, 'Let us bear the indignation of the Lord, because we have sinned against him.'

Secondly, *Let us justify God.* We have deserved affliction. He hath dealt justly with us: Neh. ix. 31, *seq.*, 'Righteousness belongeth to him, but to us shame and confusion of face,' Dan. ix. 7.

Thirdly, *Let us moderate our censure* of those that are dejected and out of heart, through sense of sin: Prov. xviii. 19, 'A wounded spirit, who can bear?' Impute it not therefore to melancholy, or despair and madness, or as Eli unadvisedly did, to drunkenness, when he reprehended Hannah, 1 Sam. i. 14; for can we think it strange, when God sees sin in his children, that he causes them to see it, and that when they see it they should shew it in their outward gestures? No; it is no light burden, that a man may run away with.

Ver. 4. 'But there is forgiveness with thee.'

This verse contains a blessed appeal. God hath a court of justice, and a tribunal of mercy. If God should examine in justice what we have done, we could not stand: 'but there is mercy or forgiveness with the Lord,' Therefore it is an appeal from the throne of justice to the mercy-seat; and yet this is not so properly an appeal but it admits of limitations. For, first, *appeals are used in aid of those that are innocent.* Now we by nature are all unclean. Again, *appeals are grounded for the most part upon discovery of insufficiency*, or of violent indirect courses in the managing of the cause. This can no ways be attributed to God, who is not rigorous nor insufficient, or swayed by indirect means; for he accepts the person of none. Again, *an appeal is from an inferior court to a higher.* But here it is not so, for we appeal from God to God; from God armed with justice, examining by law, to God a father armed with love, looking upon us in the comfortable promises of the gospel; from Sinai to Sion, from Moses to Christ. And in this appeal, as in others, the former sentence of the law, whereby we are 'cursed,' is utterly disannulled, so as 'no condemnation is to those that are in Christ,' Rom. viii. 1. But this belongs to such (as it is in other appeals) *who must see themselves condemned, before* they can have the benefit of this appeal. There is no flying to mercy unless we find ourselves in need. But to come to some observations. In the first place, we may see by this example *that the soul of a Christian apprehends God according to its estate*, to comfort itself, and therefore beholds him as a forgiving God. And therefore tho children of God, when they are at the lowest, they recover themselves with something they find in God's nature and promise, and to that end have a spirit of faith to trust and rely upon God; and those that have it not, sink lower and lower.

Doct. 1. Here we may observe, that the *Christian soul, once stung with sin, flies to the free mercy of God for ease.* Let a sinner be in Haman's estate, tell him of all pleasures, whatever they be, he cares not; nothing but pardon delights his soul. David, a king, a prophet, a man after God's own heart, Acts xiii. 22, beloved of his people, wonderfully graced, yet being troubled with his sin, could not stand. He respects not his outward privileges, prerogatives, majesty, and the like. No; he is the blessed man to whom God imputes no sin, Ps. xxxii. 1. And this is the reason why so much is attributed still to *the blood of Christ, everywhere, in the Scripture;* because the soul once pricked, finds no ease nor cure but in it principally, yet not excluding the other merits and obedience of Christ. And David, when he would raise up his soul to praise God, describes him to be a God 'forgiving sin and healing infirmities,' Ps. ciii. 3; and therefore we should, when our consciences are burdened, go as Joab did and catch hold on the horns of the altar, to the mercy of God. There live and there die. And though the conflict be never so great, we shall at length find that, as Jacob, we shall be children of *Israel,* and such as shall prevail with God, and that for our depth of misery, he hath a depth also of mercy; and this mercy will appear either in preserving us from sin, before we are fallen into it, or rescuing us from it if once we be fallen into it.

Quest. But how comes it, may some say, that God forgives? Doth he it without satisfactions?

Ans. I answer, No.

Quest. How then is it done, seeing he hath decreed that without blood shall be no remission? Heb. ix. 22.

Ans. I answer, This is done in Christ.

Quest. But why is he not mentioned here, nor in the Old Testament neither?

Ans. I answer, He was laid down to us in the Old Testament, in types and promises; for what other was the paschal lamb but 'the Lamb of God taking away the sins of the world,' by sprinkling our hearts with his blood? He was the priest that, before he could open an entrance into the holy of holies for us, must first shed blood and offer sacrifice. What signified the ark with the law covered within it, the mercy-seat upon it, and over them two cherubins covering one another, but Christ our ark covering the curses of the law, in whom is the ground of all mercy? 'which things the angels desire to pry into,' 1 Pet. i. 12, as into the pattern of God's deep wisdom. And whenas any prayed in the temple they looked towards the mercy-seat, what meaneth it other than that, whenever we do pray to God, we should behold Christ, through whom God appears to be merciful and gracious? What signified the temple, towards which they looked when they prayed, 2 Chron. vi. 38, Dan. vi. 10, but that we in our prayers should evermore have reference to our temple Christ Jesus? And being thus assured, we may safely pass the flaming fire of God's justice. If there were any other to be trusted besides Christ, there would be no peace of conscience. The sinner would argue, I am a creature, my sin is infinite; no creature can satisfy, they are not infinite; angels cannot stand; it must be an infinite majesty that must satisfy, and it must be with blood. Now, Christ by his blood hath obtained eternal redemption for us, and therefore none but Christ, none but Christ! He is God-man, making

God and man at one. It is his nature, and it is his office. So as God is just as well as merciful; for as it is Rom. iii. 24th and 25th verses, 'God the Father hath proposed or set forth Christ' in types and figures 'to be a propitiation,' alluding to the mercy-seat, 'to declare his righteousness and justice, that he may be just in punishing sin,' that is in Christ; 'and a justifier of the sinner that believes in Christ Jesus,' because he accepted of Christ's satisfaction, so as his mercy devised a remedy to satisfy his justice. Thus much in general; now to come to particulars. First, take it exclusively, and we may observe,

Doct. 1. *That only God can release a guilty conscience;* only he can speak peace to a soul in distress. Ministers indeed have keys to open and shut heaven; but they use them only ministerially, as they find persons disposed, but Christ independently. Now, then, whenas man assumes this prerogative to himself, as the popes were wont to do, giving indulgences, it is no other than to set them in the place of God. 'I, even I, forgive sin,' saith God, Jer. xxxi. 34. None can quiet the conscience but one that is above the conscience, which is God, who is only* the party offended; though there be also an offence against men. *This ought to comfort us, that we have to do with a forgiving God,* Neh. ix. 31. There is none like to him, to whom it is natural to remit and forgive sin. It is his name: Exod. xxxiv. 6, 'Forgiving iniquities, transgressions, and sins,' all manner of sins; sins against knowledge and against conscience; with him is plentiful forgiveness.

Doct. 2. Secondly, Observe *that as God only forgives sin, so he ever forgives sin.* It is always his nature, as the fire always burns; as he is Jehovah, he is merciful. John i. 29, Christ he is 'the Lamb of God,' that doth take away the sins of the world. It is a perpetual act; as we say the sun doth shine, the spring doth run. He is, Zech. xiii. 1, that 'fountain that is opened for sin and uncleanness.' Mercy is his nature, and forgiveness is an effect of his mercy.

Obj. Therefore it is no satisfying objection that the distressed soul will be ready to make, that God was merciful to David and Peter, but how can he be to me, miserable sinner? For God, as he forgave Peter, Paul, David, so he forgives now. He is a fountain of mercy never drawn dry. He is unchangeable; and therefore we are not consumed, Mal. iii. 6; and Christ is the same 'yesterday, and to-day, and for ever.' The consideration of this should be as a perpetual picture in our hearts.

Doct. 3. Thirdly, Hence we may gather, that *God's mercy is free, and from himself.* Though in us is sin and iniquity, yet in thee is mercy; and therefore God saith, I do not this for your sakes, but for mine own sake, Ezek. xxxvi. 22. Yet must not this be understood so as if it were freely and only from God the Father, excluding Christ. But therefore it is, in that we shall stand in need of no satisfactory merits of our own. Away therefore with popish doctrines of satisfactions by our own works. The holy man saith not, with thee is justice to take my works as satisfaction for my sin. No; though this holy man were a gracious man, yet mercy is all his plea. And if the question be, how the sinner stands free from punishment and entitled to all good, it is from forgiveness, which is from God's mercy, grounded on Christ's satisfaction. All is laid upon him, Isa. liii. 5. He was wounded for our transgressions; he bore our sorrows; he was made sin for us, that knew no sin, 2 Cor. v. 21. The nature of man will hardly stoop to this divine truth. But the Spirit teacheth us to rely

* That is, 'alone is.'—G.

on the free forgiveness of God in Christ; and therefore Christ and his apostles bid such 'believe on the Lord Jesus Christ, and thou shalt be saved.' We may think this an easy lesson. But hereafter, when God shall open our sins and lay them upon our consciences, they will then tell us fearful things. There is no hope! thou must be damned! Against such times lay up grounds of comfort; and let this text be a haven to resort to. It is true, 'if thou markest what is done amiss, who can stand? but there is mercy with thee that thou be feared.'

Doct. 4. Fourthly, We may from hence observe, that *the best Christian and most gracious man alive needs forgiveness of his sins;* for where the conscience is enlightened it will discover what corruption it finds, and so the necessity of being delivered. So 1 John ii. 1, 'If any man sin, we have an advocate;' that is, such as I am, have need of an advocate; and one reason may be, because indeed such see in their sins much more ingratitude than others, for they sin against the knowledge of God's love to their souls in forgiving former sins; and then to fall into sin again, it is as broken bones, Ps. li. 8. And the apostle, 2 Cor. v. 20, speaking to the believing Corinthians, 'I beseech you to be reconciled to God;' for Christ was made sin for us; for you, and for me. Even we sin daily, and stand in need of reconciliation. We must daily pray, 'Forgive us our sins,' yea, the best of the disciples must do it. If we come not with this petition, 'our sins are written with a pen of iron, and with the claw of an adamant,' Job xix. 24.*

Doct. 5. Fifthly, *This mercy and forgiveness is general to all that cast themselves on his free mercy.* It is Satan's subtilty to persuade us at the first, that sin is nothing; but when it is committed and cannot be recalled, then he tells us it is greater than can be pardoned. No. The gospel is the power of God to salvation to all that do believe. Let none despair. It is a greater sin than the former. *Deus non est desperantium pater, sed judex.* God's pardon is general, to all persons, that repent of all sin, whereby he frees them from all evil. He pardons all persons: Manasses the sorcerer, Cornelius, Zaccheus, persecuting Paul. The parable of the lost sheep, the lost groat, the prodigal son, testifies it. God offers it freely, 'Why will you die, O house of Israel'? Jer. xxvii. 13. He complains when it is neglected: 'O Jerusalem, Jerusalem, how oft would I have gathered you together.'! Mat. xxiii. 37. 'He threatens' because men will not hear, and 'he pardons all sins.' There is no disease above the skill of this Physician. He healeth all thy sins and all thy infirmities, Ps. ciii. 1-3. Yea, if it were possible that the sinner against the Holy Ghost could repent, there were hope in Israel concerning this! He hath pardon for sin long lived in. 'At what time soever a sinner repenteth, he will blot out his wickedness,' 2 Chron. xx. 9. What though they be never so enormous? God's thoughts are not as ours, Isa. lv. 8. Conscience may be overcharged with sin. We may play the harlot with many lovers; yet return to me, saith the Lord, Jer. iii. 1. He that bids Peter forgive seventy-seven times,† shall not he have plenteous redemption? What proportion is there between the sin of a creature, and the mercy of an infinite Majesty? He frees from all ill, from all punishment. His forgiveness is perfect. Though we be as red as crimson with sin, he will make us white as snow, Isa. i. 18. He removes our sins from his presence as 'far as the east is from the west,' Ps. ciii. 12.

Quest. But some will say, Why corrects he then his children?

* Cf. A. B. Davidson's 'Commentary' *in loc.*, and also Caryl.—G.

† Rather seventy seven-times; that is, seventy times seven times.—G.

Ans. I answer, not from revenging justice, for he is our Father; and what he does, it comes from love, and is mingled with love and moderated with love to our strength, and are turned by love to our good. When he follows us with prosperity, he is our alluring Father; and when he corrects us, he is our correcting, not punishing, Father, Heb. xii. from 3d to the 12th. Yet let not this be sinisterly taken. It is spoken only to the humble heart, that is broken with sin, which is the sixth general observation*; there must be first sight of sin, then sense of misery, then confession of sin and begging pardon*, or else none is granted. For God bestows pardon so as may be most for his glory and our comfort. What glory can he reap by pardoning those that will sin, 'because grace may abound,' Rom. vi. 1, and so 'will turn the grace of God into wantonness'? Jude 4. And what comfort can we have of the pardon of our sins till we see our sins, and feel what it is to want pardon? Sight of sin and mercy are inseparable. Sometimes the sense of pardon is delayed, to make us hunger after it; sometimes it follows suddenly after sight of sin, as it did to Matthew and Zaccheus, Mat. xi. 28. But one must go before the other: first, must the wind of the sight of God's anger come breaking and rending the rocky hard hearts that are within us; then comes the soft still voice speaking peace to the humble soul. The reasons may be, first, *to set an edge on our prayers* for forgiveness, else who would care for it. Secondly, *to make us highly to esteem forgiveness of sin.* The promises are sweet to the dejected soul, as a pardon is to the condemned person. Thirdly, *that God might have the more glory and thanks.* When we find the bitterness of sin, as it is Jer. ii. 19, to be sweetened by God's mercy, then 'My soul, praise thou the Lord; and all that is within me, praise his holy name.' He forgives all my sin, and heals all my infirmities, Ps. ciii. 1, 2, 3. And, lastly, *because our sins unrepented keep good from us, and us from the fountain of all good*, and must be removed before there can be any way for mercy.

This therefore justifies those ministers that in these days of the gospel do enforce the law; and people must not be offended thereat, but suffer their consciences to be laid open, that the word may come close and home to them; and secondly, they must use the means, to come to a sense and feeling of their sin. To which end let *us make sin as odious and dangerous in our eyes as we can.* It is odious to God. To us it is poison and leprosy though we cherish it, and hate ministers and friends for touching it. It is abomination to God. It thrusts him out of our hearts, and puts in the devil, God's arch enemy. It causes us to prefer base pleasure, fading profits, before the favour and mercy and love of God. Must not this needs be hateful to God? But then how much more intolerable are those sins that bring neither profit nor pleasure, but causes us to thrust out God, even because we will? But this is not all, for as it is abominable to God, *so it is dangerous to us*; for whence comes judgments? Whence is it that the wrath of God is revealed from heaven? Rom. i. 18. Whence is sickness, disgrace, troubles? All these are the fruits of sin. Nothing makes us miserable but sin. Take a man when he lies a-dying. Ask him what troubles him? Oh! he cries out of sin, of the wrath of God. He feels not sickness, even as the gout is not felt by one that hath a fit of the stone upon him. Let us think of this in time; let us shame the devil, shame ourselves. But is this all? No. Judas saw his sin and confessed, yet was he never the better. He wanted that which should make his repentance perfect. He wanted faith to lay hold on pardon. A poor man is fit for treasure, but unless he lay hold on treasure, he shall never be rich.

Therefore faith and repentance are ever joined in the gospel. Repent and believe the gospel, as was said to the jailor. So Christ saith, 'Come to me,' Mat. xi. 28. Christ came to satisfy for all sin, to cure all diseases, but they must first come to him, and say, 'Lord, if thou wilt thou canst make me clean,' Mat. viii. 2; and to such as these I may say, as they said to the blind man, 'Be of comfort, for Christ calls thee,' Mark x. 49.

'That thou mayest be feared.'

Fear in this place is taken for the spiritual worship of God, arising from a reverential fear mingled with love. 'Fear God and keep his commandments,' Eccles. xii. 13, is the whole duty of man. So that these words being considered with the former, brings this observation to our consideration.

Doct. That God's goodness, forgiveness, grace, and mercy, is a means to stir up his children to all duties; and therefore we are commanded to do all things in fear: to 'work out our salvation with fear,' Philip. ii. 12, eat and drink with fear; and in Jude 12, the wicked are branded with this, 'that they eat without fear.' So as whatever we do, we must do it in fear, shewing the reverence of God continually, and jealousy over ourselves, lest we should stop the light of God's countenance from us.

Quest. But it will be said, How is it then said 'that we should serve him without fear,' 1 Cor. xvi. 10, being redeemed from our enemies?

Ans. I answer, There is a twofold fear: one a slavish fear, whereof that place is meant. We should serve him without fear of damnation, of punishment, and of judgment. But the fear that we speak of here is a fear of reverence and love, that stirs us up to worship him.

Quest. But how doth it stir to duty? may some say.

Ans. I answer, first, it *stirs up faith in our hearts.* Hope of forgiveness will cause us to cast ourselves into their arms whom we have offended. Where no hope of mercy is, there follows nothing but fear, causing us to fly away; even as we see proclamation of pardon to rebels causes them to come in, but the contrary makes them run away. Again, *sense of forgiveness works more love.* David's murder, Paul's persecution, Peter's denial, caused abundance of love. Where many sins are forgiven, there will be much love, Luke vii. 47; and where much love is, there will be obedience to all God's commandments, for 'love is the fulfilling of the law,' Rom. xiii. 10. Contrarily, desperation is the ground of all sin. This is the ground of all hate. The devils they hate God. Because they know there is no remedy left for them, therefore they cannot endure the remembrance of him. Contrariwise, as it is Ps. lxv. 2, 'Unto thee shall all flesh come.' Why? 'For thou hearest prayer.' Again, *fear and forgiveness are joined in the new covenant.* 'I will put my fear in thy heart, and thou shalt not depart from me,' Jer. xxxii. 40; and Christ, to all his, is both king, priest, and prophet. He comes to all by water as well as blood. He is become righteousness, wisdom, and holiness, 1 Cor. i. 30. Again, *a Christian he will, by reason, enforce this on himself,* as Paul did, 2 Cor. v. 15. Christ died for us; therefore must we live to him, and not to ourselves.

Use 1. This therefore should cause us *to take heed of all thoughts of despair.* Let it be enough that we have broken the law; let us not pull a greater sin on us by denying the gospel, the mercies and truths of God. Let us by any means take heed, for Satan will join with guilty consciences, speaking with cursed Cain, 'My sin is greater than can be pardoned,' Gen. iv. 13. No article of our creed is so much opposed by him, as that of the forgiveness of sin by Christ's merits, which is the very life and soul of a church. All the former articles of the creed are perfected in this, and all the following articles are effects hereof.

Use 2. Secondly, This doctrine *furnishes an answer to the papists*, who lay scandals* on the doctrine of free justification by the merits of Christ, without our own works; saying that we nourish thereby carelessness in a Christian life, whenas the Scripture, and the Spirit of God in the hearts of those that are truly regenerate, do reason quite contrary. 'There is mercy with thee, that thou mayest be feared;' not that we may live as we list, for whom God forgives, he first truly humbles; whom he washes, he gives hearts to keep themselves clean; so as with the burnt child, they dread the fire ever after. No; it is themselves that overthrow good works, while they ground them on false grounds. For either they do them to satisfy God's wrath, which is slavish, or to merit by them, which is a token of a hireling; and most of their works are such, as if God should ask them, 'Who required them at their hands?' Isa. i. 12, they could never be able to answer. They, while they talk of good works, in the mean time overthrow faith and love, which should be the ground of a good work. What can they do more than a Cain or a Judas, or the wickedest man alive.

Secondly, *We may hence gather a ground of discerning our estate*, whereby we shall know whether God's mercy and forgiveness belong to us or not; for it is impossible, where there is no inward worship of God in the heart, where there is no fear and jealousy of sin, where there is no conscience of swearing, blaspheming, and such abominations, that ever such yet had any true taste of God's mercy and forgiveness. Let them not take comfort by the example of the thief on the cross, that cried for mercy and had it; for there is a time of grace, and there are some sinners, as those that flatter themselves in a course of sin, thinking to repent when they will, against which the wrath of God will smoke, Deut. xxix. 20. Therefore let not such soothe up themselves. Those that have their sins forgiven do fear God. Such fear not God, and therefore their sins are not forgiven. Many shall say in that day, 'Lord, Lord,' to whom Christ will profess, 'he never knew them,' Mat. vii. 23; and therefore let us never assure ourselves of forgiveness, farther than we find in us a hatred of sin. For a man to live in a course of known sin, it stops the current of God's mercy; who will wound the 'hairy scalp of such as despise the patience and long-suffering of God,' Rom. ii. 4. While we have time, therefore, and are young, before lusts settle themselves in us, serve the Lord with fear; deny him not the service due to him. If we do, it is just with God to take us away suddenly, or to deliver us over to an impenetrable hard heart; and when we die, that God should take away from us our senses, or to give over our consciences to such a horror and trembling fear, as shall not suffer us to come so near as to have any hope of mercy, but die in despair. Let us pray, therefore, against a careless heart, and say to him, Lord, thou camest to redeem and set me free from the works of the devil! Lord, deliver me from the power of sin and of my own corruption. For we may assure ourselves, he that never discerned this hatred of sin in him, never asked pardon from his heart; and he that never asks it shall never have it.

Use. Let us in the next place learn thereby *to go the right way, to work assurance of forgiveness:* first, *learn to see our misery;* then, *get persuasion that there is a remedy;* then, *get knowledge thereof;* and then *beg it*. It is a preposterous course that many men take. They will change their ill courses, but without confession or acknowledgment of sin; and therefore they turn

* That is, 'take offence at.'—G.

indeed, but it is from one sin to another: from being dissolute they will become covetous, and so change to the worse; for they change not from right grounds; not from love to God and hatred of sin, but ever from the love of one reigning sin to another. For all such, and all other, that either find* their sin, or think not of it, this Scripture is of excellent use; and we may speak of it as St Paul, 2 Tim. iii. 16, speaks of all the Scripture, 'It is profitable for doctrine,' teaching us what we are by nature since the fall; wherein we may have remedy of our misery; how and in what manner to attain the remedy. It is profitable for 'reproof' of the doctrine of justification by works; and it is profitable for 'correction' of our lives, teaching us to avoid despair, and yet withal to avoid security. It is profitable for 'comfort' to all those that are dejected by sin, by considering the mercy of God in Christ, which is more and greater than sin in us, if we have faith to lay hold on it; so that we may say with St Augustine, *Ego admisi, unde tu damnare potes me, sed non amisisti unde tu salvare potes me.*

Ver. 5. 'I wait for the Lord, yea, my soul waiteth.

These words do shew the estate and disposition of the holy man after his prayer. Though he had formerly sense of mercy and pardon, yet he waits for more full and sweet apprehension thereof. In them we may observe, first, *though God be exceeding gracious, yet there is matter of waiting,* so long as we live here on earth, for he gives not all the fulness of his blessing at once. Though he may give taste of pardon of sin in present, yet not presently deliverance out of danger. 'The light of the righteous shineth more and more unto the perfect day,' Prov. iv. 18. There is no day that is perfected in an instant; and the reasons hereof may be,

Reason 1. First, *To force us to search our souls,* whether we be fit for blessing; whether we be thoroughly humbled, and have thoroughly repented or not. Thus dealt he with Jonas, and thus with the children of Israel for Achan's cause.

Reason 2. Secondly, It may be a means *to stir us up to more earnestness in seeking:* to make us like the woman of Canaan, more earnest the more she was repelled.

Reason 3. Thirdly, He gives us occasion of waiting, *to shew the truth and soundness of his graces in us;* otherwise should we have no means to try how the grace in us would serve us in time of need.

Reason 4. Fourthly, Hereby God *doth endear those favours that we want, that it may come the more welcome to us, and we be the more thankful for it.* Thus God dealt with this holy man; and thus doth he with his church. For while we live here we are always children of hope; not miserable, because we have a sweet taste of what we hope for, and not perfectly happy, because we want fulness. Before Christ they hoped for his coming in the flesh; since Christ, we look for his 'second coming in glory;' in grace we look for glory; and when our souls are in glory, they look for the redemption of the bodies, and for the day of restoring of all things. 'How long, Lord, how long?' Rev. vi. 10. Else would this life be heaven to us; and we should not desire or pray, 'Lord, let thy kingdom come.'

Use. And for use, *This should whet in us our desires and prayers for our heavenly estate;* and not make our heaven here on earth, but desire earnestly the full harvest, by considering how excellent the first-fruits of glory in this life are; and with the creature, Rom. viii. 19, 'wait, and expect,

* Qu. 'hide'?—Ed.

and long, and groan for the time of the dissolution of all things ;' and make this a note *to discern of our estate ;* for it is a certain infallible token of a good frame of spirit in us, if we can long for that better life in the fulness, that we have here ; that we can desire to be with Christ. Furthermore, note this *as a difference between the estates of the wicked and the godly.* The wicked must look for worse and worse continually. His best is here, and while he hath this world ; but the godly, their worst is here, their best is to come.

THE CHURCH'S COMPLAINT AND CONFIDENCE.

THE CHURCH'S COMPLAINT AND CONFIDENCE.

NOTE.

'The Church's Complaint' forms a portion of 'The Beams of Divine Light' (4to, 1639). Its separate title-page will be found below.* For general title-page, see Vol. V. page 220. G.

*THE
CHVRCHES
Complaint and
Confidence.
In three Sermons,
By the late Reverend and Learned
Divine RICHARD SIBS,
Doctor in Divinity, Master of Katherine Hall in
Cambridge, and sometimes Preacher at
Grayes-Inne.

LAM. 1. 20.

Behold O Lord for I am in distresse, my bowells are troubled, mine heart is turned within me, for I have grievously rebelled, abroad the sword bereaveth, at home there is as death.

LONDON,
Printed by *G. M.* for *Nicholas Bourne* and *Rapha Harford*, 1639.

THE CHURCH'S COMPLAINT AND CONFIDENCE.

But we are all as an unclean thing, and all our righteousness are as filthy rags; and we all do fade as a leaf; and our iniquities, like the wind, have taken us away. And there is none that calleth upon thy name, that stirreth up himself to take hold of thee: for thou hast hid thy face from us, and hast consumed us, because of our iniquities. But now, O Lord, thou art our Father: we are the clay, and thou our potter; and we are all the work of thine hands.—ISAIAH LXIV. 6–8.

THE words are part of a blessed form of prayer prescribed to the church long before they were in captivity. It begins at the 15th verse of the former chapter, 'Look down from heaven; behold from the habitation of thy holiness,' &c. The blessed prophet Isaiah was carried with the wings of prophetical spirit over many years, and sees the time to come, the time of the captivity; and God by his Spirit doth direct them a prayer, and this is part of the form. For God in mercy to his people, as he foresaw before what would become of them, so he vouchsafes them comfort beforehand, and likewise he prescribes a form of prayer beforehand. It is very useful to use forms. The 102d Psalm, it is a form of pouring out the soul to God when any man is in misery, as you see in the preface. But that by the way. These verses are a part of a form prescribed for the pouring forth an afflicted soul; 'We are all as an unclean thing, and all our righteousness,' &c. The words they are,

First, An humble confession of sin.

And first, of the sins of their nature, of their persons themselves, 'We are all as an unclean thing.'

And then, of the sins of actions: 'all our righteousness is as filthy rags.'

And then, in the third place, a confession of the sin of non-proficiency, of obduration, and senselessness, that notwithstanding the corrections of God, they were little the better: 'There is none that calleth upon thy name, or that stirs up himself to take hold of thee.'

In the second place, there is an humble complaint of the miserable estate they were in by their sins: 'We all fade as a leaf; our iniquities, like the wind, have taken us away: thou hast hid thy face from us, and consumed us, because of our iniquities.' The complaint is set forth in these four clauses.

And then an humble supplication and deprecation to God, in ver. 8, and so forward. 'Now, Lord, thou art our Father: we are the clay, thou art the potter; we are all the work of thy hands,' &c. These be the parcels of this portion of Scripture.

'But we are all as an unclean thing,' &c.

Here is, first, *an humble confession.* And first, observe in general what afflictions will do, especially afflictions sanctified. That which all the prophetical sermons could not do, that which all the threatenings could not do, affliction now doth. Now when they were in captivity and base estate, they fall a humbling themselves. So the prodigal, nothing could humble him but afflictions. 'By the waters of Babylon we sat down and wept,' Ps. cxxxvii. 1. All the denunciations of judgments before they came to the waters of Babylon could not make them weep. One affliction will do more than twenty sermons. When God teacheth and chastiseth too, when together with teaching there is correction, then it is effectual. And this is the reason of God's course; why, when nothing else will do, he humbles his people with afflictions, because he cannot otherwise teach them.

Affliction withdraws that which is the fuel of sin; for what doth our sinful disposition feed on? Upon pleasures, and vanities,. upon the honours of this life, and riches, &c. Now when affliction either takes these things away, or embitters them if we have them, then that which sin carried us to, and that we fed our own base earthly lusts with, being gone, when a man is stripped of these, he begins to know himself what he is, he was drunk before. I deem a man in prosperity little better than drunk. He knows neither God, nor himself, nor the world. He knows it not to be as a vain world. He knows not himself to be vanity, to be an empty creature, except he consist* in God, and make his peace with him. He knows not God to be such a holy God, and such an angry God for sin. But when affliction comes, and withdraws and strips him of those things that made him fierce against God, then he begins to know God, and to tremble at the judgments of God when he begins to smart. He begins to know himself to be a madman, and a fool, and a sot. He did not know himself before in his jollity. And then he knows the world indeed as a vain world. Blessed be that affliction that makes us know a gracious and good God, and the creature to be a vain creature, and ourselves out of the favour of God to be nothing. You see what afflictions will do.

God doth use to break men, as men use to break horses. They ride them over hedge and ditch, and over ploughed lands, uneven grounds, and gall them with the spur and with the bit, and all to make them tractable; and then afterward they ride them gently and meekly, and rather so than otherwise. So God is fain to carry his children over ploughed lands; he is fain to break them in their wickedness, to bring their ways upon their heads; he is fain to gall them, and humble them every kind of way, that they may carry him, that he may bring their spirits under him, that he may lead them in the ways that lead to their own comfort.

Use. Let us never murmur, therefore, at God's hand, but willingly yield at the first. What doth a stubborn horse get, but the spur and stripes? And what doth a man get, that stands out when God comes to humble him by affliction, and intends his good? Nothing but more stripes. To come to the parts.

'We are all as an unclean thing,' &c.

* That is, = stand.—G.

Here, first, you see there is an humble confession. I will not enlarge myself in the point of humiliation, but speak a little, because this is the day of humiliation: the occasion is for humiliation. All this is to bring us low, to humble us, to make us know ourselves. Without humiliation, Christ will never be sweet unto us, and the benefit of health, &c., will never be precious to us. I mean by humiliation, when God humbles us, and we humble ourselves; when we join with God. When God's humbling of us and our humbling of ourselves go together, then mercy is sweet, and favour and protection is sweet, when God pours his judgments on others, and spares us.

Now humiliation, it is either real (or inward), or verbal.

Real humiliation indeed, that is, our humbling ourselves by fasting, especially when it is joined with reformation of our wicked ways, or else it is a mockery of God, as it is in Isa. lviii., 'to hang down the head for a while,' and in the mean time to have a hard heart, to shut up our bowels to our brethren; but that is a real kind of humiliation, when we think ourselves unworthy of the creatures, of meat or drink, of any refreshing, for this humiliation of fasting is a kind of profession, though we speak not so, that we are unworthy of these things. But all is nothing, without inward humiliation of the soul. Verbal humiliation is in words, as we shall see after in confession; and it must come from inward humiliation of spirit.

Use. Therefore, considering it is here the first disposition of God's people, let us labour to work upon ourselves those considerations that may make us humble. I will name a few.

1. First, *To bring ourselves to the glass of the law.* Examine ourselves how short we have been of every commandment.

2. But especially bring ourselves *to the gospel.* We hope to be saved by Christ; and have we mourned for our sins 'as one mourneth for his first-born'? Zech. xii. 10. Our sins have wounded Christ. Have we preferred Christ, in our thoughts, above all the things in the world? Have they all been dung to us? Have we had that blessed esteem of the gracious promises of the gospel, and the prerogatives therein set forth, that they have been so precious to us, that we have undervalued all to them, as St Paul did? A base esteem of the gospel is a great sin: 'How shall we escape, if we neglect so great salvation?' Heb. ii. 3. Put case we be not enemies to the ministry and to holiness of life, expressed in the gospel, as many cursed creatures are; yet a base esteem and undervaluing in our thoughts is a thing punishable. 'How shall we escape, if we *neglect* so great salvation?' Have we walked worthy of the dignity we are called to by the gospel? Have we carried ourselves so in spiritual things, as to rule our base lusts? Have we been careful of private prayer, to offer ourselves to God as priests? Are we not pressed in St Paul's epistles, 'to carry ourselves worthy of our profession?' Eph. iv. 1; and have we done so? Let us bring our carriage, and see how proportionable it is to God's advancing of us in these glorious times of the gospel, and this will bring us on our knees.

We are ashamed of a little unkindness to men. But when we consider how unkind we have been to God, that thought not his dear Son, and heaven and happiness, too much for us; besides other favours, that he protects, and clothes, and feeds us every day, and yet we have not been answerable: these considerations would humble us, proportionable to our carriage to men. Can we be ashamed to offer an unkindness to men, and are we not ashamed, cannot we be abashed with this, that we have carried ourselves so towards God? It comes from atheism and infidelity of heart, that either we believe not these things to be good, or else that we have not our part and portion in them. Could we ever be so dead and dull-hearted else?

3. Again, That we may be humbled, *let us call to mind*, now in this day of humiliation, *our special sins*. We may soon know them. Our consciences and our enemies will upbraid us for them, and we are loath to hear of them above all, either by the ministry or by our friends. We wish, above all, that the preacher would not speak of them, and fret if he do; and our hearts run upon them above all. So let us search our false hearts, which way they run; and now, in the day of our abasement, let us think what would lie heaviest on our conscience, if God should take us now with sickness or sudden death. Let us think with ourselves, What is the sin that would afflict me most? that would stagger me most? that would shake my faith most? whether it be filthiness, or profaneness, or swearing, or injustice; and whether have I made satisfaction or no? Let me examine, if God should strike me with his arrow now, what sin would rob me of my comfort, and make me afraid to yield my soul to God? Now think of it. This is the way to be humbled. You may now bring yourselves to consider of that that at other times you will not give yourselves leisure to do. What are days of fasting for, but to give ourselves leisure, that we may not think of meat, and drink, and business? These days should be days of rest, that we may think of that which concerns our souls. Take the advantage when thou restest from thinking of other business. Think with thine own soul, what will lie heaviest upon thy soul. This is required to humiliation. This real humiliation that is outward, it is a protestation of the inward; and verbal humiliation is but an expression of what we do inwardly.

There are two things wondrous necessary, before the soul can be in the right frame it should be in.

First, The soul *must apprehend deeply what distance it hath from God, what alienates it from God, before it can be wise;* and it must be estranged from that before ever it can come to couple and join with God. When the soul apprehends what separates it from God, and conceives as it should do of that, then it will be the readier to apprehend God; and then all duties will come off easily. Therefore let us first of all work upon our own souls to be humbled, and by all the helps that can be.

4. And to help it, consider now at this time *how uncertain our life is.* We know not who may be stricken next. And consider what the dangerous issue is, if we humble not ourselves here before God humble us in our graves. Let us help humiliation by all that may be; for where this is, all will follow easily. A man will go out of himself to God when he is abased in himself, and sees no comfort in heaven or earth but in God; that there is nothing to be stuck to in the world, but all is vanity, and he may be stripped of life and of all these comforts ere long. When a man is abased, faith and obedience will come off easily. What is the reason that Christ is not relished more, and that many fall off? They were never deeply humbled. According to the depth of humiliation is the growth of holiness of life and the height of faith. All graces rise higher as the soul is more deeply humbled. The more we descend deeply in digging and rending up our hearts, the more the word of God sinks into the 'good ground' that suffers the plough to rend it up and to cut off the weeds. The more deeply we are humbled, the more the fruits of God's word appear in our hearts and lives, the more fruitful is our conversation. All

comes indeed upon the truth of our humiliation; and when that is not deep and true, all the rest is shallow and counterfeit. There[fore] we should work it upon our own hearts.

5. And labour *to be humble and low in all the powers of our souls;* to have humble judgments, to think of ourselves as God thinks of us. God thinks of us as sinners; God and Christ think of us that we are such as must deny all in us before we be fit for heaven. Let us judge of ourselves as he that must be our judge doth and will judge of us ere long. Labour to have low judgments of ourselves; what we are in ourselves, empty of all good, defiled with all ill.

And this will breed poverty of spirit in our judgments. Then let us labour for humility in our affections; to bring ourselves more to God; to stoop to him in fear and reverence; and humility in our obedience and conversation to God and to men every way. Let humility spread itself over all the parts and powers of the soul and body, and over our whole lives. I cannot stand further upon that.

Now, here is verbal humiliation, that is, by confession, expressing our humiliation by our words; as the people of God do here by confession, laying open our sins that God may cover them. What we hide God will never cure; therefore we should take heed that now we are to deal with God, we lay open the bottom of our souls to him; let not the iron be in the wound. You know a chirurgeon can heal nothing if the iron or poisoned arrow stick there. If there be corruption in the stomach, it must up. If it be ill-gotten goods, it will not digest, up it must all to God. For men, except there be scruples that a man cannot free his conscience, there is no necessity, though great conveniency; but between God and thy soul open all by confession, and give not over till thou hast brought pardon to thy heart of that sin thou hast confessed. Every slight confession is not enough, but it must be a resolved, downright confession, without guile of spirit, as it is in Ps. xxxii. 4. This is the course that David takes there. Until he dealt roundly with his soul, without guile, 'his moisture was as the drought of summer.' He was in some dangerous disease that could not be cured. And do we look to be preserved from falling into sickness? or if we be sick, to be cured? We must begin the cure in our souls; lay open the wound to God: 'I said, I will confess my sin, and thou forgavest me.' He begins with confession. So all persons that either fear or are under any judgment, let them begin with laying open their souls to God. When the soul is healed, he will heal the body presently after, for he lays sickness upon the body for the soul; and when the wound is healed, the plaster will fall off of itself. Therefore let us lay open our sins by confession, and shame our souls all that we can.

This is the way to give glory to God. Let us join both together, our own ease and glory to God. When we have laid open our souls to God, and laid as much against ourselves as the devil could do that way—for let us think what the devil would lay to our charge at the hour of death and the day of judgment, he would lay hard to our charge this and that—let us accuse ourselves as he would, and as he will ere long. The more we accuse and judge ourselves, and set up a tribunal in our hearts, certainly there will follow an incredible ease. Jonah was cast into the sea, and there was ease in the ship; Achan was stoned, and the plague was stayed. Out with Jonah, out with Achan, and there will follow ease and quiet in the soul presently; conscience will receive wonderful ease. It must needs be so, for when God is honoured conscience is purified. God is honoured by confession of sin every way. It honours his omniscience; that he is all-seeing, that he sees our sins and searcheth the hearts. Our secrets are not hid from him. It honours his power. What makes us confess our sins, but that we are afraid of his power, lest he should execute it? And what makes us confess our sins, but that we know there is 'mercy with him that he may be feared,' Ps. cxxx. 4, and that there is pardon for sin? We would not confess our sins else. With men it is confess and have execution, but with God confess and have mercy. It is his own protestation. We should never lay open our sins but for mercy. So it honours God; and when he is honoured, he honours the soul with inward peace and tranquillity. We can never have peace in our souls till we have dealt roundly with our sins, and favour them not a whit; till we have ripened our confession to be a thorough confession. What is the difference between a Christian and another man? Another person slubbers over his sins; God is merciful, &c.; and he thinks if he come to the congregation, and follow the minister, it will serve the turn. But a Christian knows that religion is another manner of matter, another kind of work than so. He must deal thoroughly and seriously, and lay open his sin as the chief enemy in the world, and labour to raise all the hatred he can against it, and make it the object of his bitter displeasure, as being that that hath done him more hurt than all the world besides; and so he confesseth it with all the aggravations of hatred and envy that he can.

But to come more particularly to the confession here spoken of: 'We all are as an unclean thing,' &c.

'We all.'

We see here holy men themselves confess their sins, and rank themselves among sinners in their confessions. So we learn hence this,

That we in our confessions (in our fastings especially) ought to rank ourselves among the rest of sinners, and not to exempt ourselves from other sinners. Perhaps we are not guilty of some sins that they have been guilty of. God hath been merciful to us and kept us in obedience in some things. But, alas! there is none of us all but we have had a hand in the sins of the times. The best of all conditions are guilty of them. Therefore we have cause to rank ourselves among others, as he saith here, 'We are all as an unclean thing;' and as Daniel, he makes a confession of the sins of all, 'we are all of us guilty.'

How are we all guilty?

(1.) We are all guilty in this respect, *we receive some taint and soil from the times we live in.* Either our zeal is weakened; we do not grieve so much for the sins of the times; and who is not guilty in this respect? We do not grieve and lament as we should; as St Paul tells the Corinthians, they should have been sorry and humbled, 1 Cor. v. 6. They were guilty of the sin of the incestuous person, because they were not humbled for it. We are thus far guilty at least, the best of us, that we do not sorrow for the common sins. Alas! how many sins are there that everybody may see in the times in all ranks! In pastors, what unfaithfulness, and in governors and in places of justice; what crying of the poor and men oppressed; and in all ranks of people we see a general security; we see filthiness and hear oaths, 'for which the land mourns,' as Jeremiah saith, Jer. xxiii. 10. These and such like sins provoke God and solicit the vengeance of God; and will have no nay till they have pulled down vengeance. Who hath been so much humbled for these sins as he ought? Perhaps ourselves are not personally guilty of them. But are they not our sins, so far as we are not abased for them, and oppose them, and repress them as we should in our places and standings, whether we be ministers or magistrates? Thus far we are guilty all. Therefore the prophet might well say, '*We all* are as an unclean thing,' &c.

(2.) Then again, *there is great sympathy in the hearts of good men.* They are full of pity and compassion; and therefore they join themselves with others, partly knowing that they are guilty in some degree with others, and partly because they are members of the same body politic and ecclesiastical. They live in the same church and commonwealth. Therefore all join their confession together. 'We all are as an unclean thing,' &c.

Use. Let us make this use of it, *every one of us to be humbled.* Do not every one of us bring sticks to the common fire? Do we not add something to the common judgment? If there be two malefactors that have committed a trespass, one of them is taken and used in his kind; he is executed. Will it not grieve the other? He will think, was it not my case? I was a wretched sinner as well as he. If there be divers traitors, and the king is merciful to one, and the other he executes, will it not grieve him that is spared, if he have any bowels of good nature, besides goodness in other kinds? Will he not think, it was my own case? There was no difference between me and them, only the mercy of the king? So the best of us may think, have I not a corrupt nature, and for the sins of the times, am not I soiled with them? Others have been stricken; might not the same arrow have stricken me? Certainly this consideration, that we bring something to the public sins, it will make us humbled for the public, as the church here confesseth, 'We are all as an unclean thing,' &c.

To come to the particulars of the confession.

'We are all as *an unclean thing.*'

Here is a confession of their persons. Their persons were tainted. We are all a tainted seed and generation in nature. What the wickedest is wholly, the best are in part. Therefore it is no error that we should say so and so of ourselves in our confessions; as Saint Paul saith of himself, 'I am sold under sin,' Rom. vii. 14. One would wonder that he should confess so. Alas! blessed man, he felt that in part that others in the state of nature are wholly. So we are all filthy. The best, as far as they are not renewed, are as other men are.

'Unclean.'

It is a comparison taken from the leprosy, or some other contagious disease. Those that were tainted of them were separated from the congregation seven days, or some set time. So it is with sin, especially the sins of this people. They had sinned grievously, and were severed from their land; not seven days, but seventy years, the leprosy and filthiness of their sins and lives was such.

Indeed, sin, especially the sin of nature, it is a leprosy, contagious, pestilential; and as a leprosy it spreads over all the parts and powers of body and soul. Take a man that is not changed; he hath a leprous eye, full of adultery; he hath a leprous, uncircumcised ear. Ask him how he judgeth of discourses and sermons. He relisheth nothing but that which is frothy and vain. Plain, substantial, solid discourses, either in hearing or reading, will not down with him. He hath a leprous judgment. His eyes, and ears, and tongue are defiled and corrupt. He is vile and abominable in his speeches. He is uncircumcised in all. All are unclean. All his powers are defiled by nature.

All the washings in the law did signify this, the corruption and defilement of our natures, which needs another washing which they typified, a washing by the blood and Spirit of Christ. 'Christ came by water and blood,' 1 John v. 6, both in justification and sanctification. 'There is a fountain opened for Judah and Jerusalem to wash in,' Zech. xiii. 1. All those washings shewed a defilement spiritually, that needed a spiritual washing. This sin is a leprous, contagious sin; therefore by nature we may all cry as the leper, 'Unclean, unclean.' The best of us may take up that complaint as far as we are not renewed. A leprous man defiled the things that he touched. So it is with sin, till it be forgiven; we defile everything. A proud man, especially when he is set out in his bravery, he thinks himself a jolly man, a brave creature. Alas! he is a filthy creature; not only in himself, but in everything he puts his hand unto. He taints and defiles everything, even civil actions. He sins in eating and drinking; not that they in the substance of them are sins, but he stains everything; for he forgets God in them; he forgets himself exceedingly; and he returns not thanks to God. So in moral, civil actions, much more in religious. He defiles himself in everything. He is defiled to all things, and all things are defiled to him. This is our state by nature, 'We are all as an unclean thing.'

Use. This should enforce *a necessity of cleansing ourselves in the blood of Christ*; that is, in the death of Christ, who hath satisfied the justice of God. Our natures are so foul in regard of the guilt and stain, that the blood of God-man, that is, the satisfactory * death of God-man, was necessary to breed reconciliation and atonement between God and us. 'And the blood of Christ, which by the eternal Spirit offered himself, must purge our consciences,' &c., Heb. ix. 14. Our consciences will not otherwise be pacified and cleansed in regard of guilt, but will clamour and cry still, much less will God be appeased. Neither God nor conscience will be pacified, but by the blood of him who by the eternal Spirit offered up himself; and then it will in regard of the guilt and stain, then God and conscience will both be appeased. Therefore in Zech. xiii. 1, 'There is a fountain opened for Judah and Jerusalem to wash in.' And 'The blood of Christ cleanseth us from all sin,' 1 John i. 7. Blood is of a defiling nature; but the blood of Christ cleanseth because it is a satisfactory blood. He died, and was a sacrifice as a public person for us all.

Then again, considering that we are all defiled, besides this cleansing from the guilt of sin, let us get our natures cleansed by the Spirit of Christ more and more. We are all defiled.

Use. And *take heed of those that are defiled; take heed of sinners*. Who would willingly lie with a leprous person? Yet notwithstanding, for matter of marriage and intimate society there is a little† conscience made; men converse with leprous company, they join in the most intimate society with those that are leprous in their judgments. The life of nature we know, and are careful to avoid what may impair it; but it is a sign we have not the life of grace begun in us, because we do not value it. If we had, we would be more careful to preserve it, and to take heed of contagious company. Who would go to the pest-house, or to one that hath 'Lord, have mercy upon us' on the door? (*a*) None but a madman. He might do so. And surely those that join with swearers and drunkards and filthy persons, and go to filthy places and houses (as many do, the more shame for them), they think they have no souls nor no account to make, they go to these places and infect themselves. It is a sign they have no life of grace; all

* That is, = satisfaction-giving.—G.

† Qu. 'little'?—Ed.

companies are alike to them. Is this strength of grace? No. They have no life of grace, they have nothing to lose; for if they had the life of grace, they would preserve it better.

Sin is a filthy thing, more filthy than the leprosy, nay, than the plague itself; for the plague or leprosy makes but the body loathsome, but the sin that we cherish and are loath to hear of makes the soul loathsome. The one makes unfit for the company of men; but the other, sin and corruption and lusts, unfit us for the kingdom of God, for heaven, for life or death. Therefore it is worse. The leprosy of the body makes a man not a whit odious to God; but the leprosy of the soul makes us hateful to him. We may have more intimate communion with God in the plague than out of the plague, because God supplies the want of outward comforts; but in sin we can have no comfortable communion and society with God. Therefore this plague of the soul is many ways worse than the pestilence. But we want faith. God hath not opened our eyes to see that that we shall see and know ere long, and it is happy if we consider it in time.

To conclude this point concerning the corruption of nature. Take David's course, Ps. li. 1, *seq.* When sinful actions come from us, or unsavoury words, or beastly thoughts, or unchaste and noisome desires that grieve the Spirit of God, let us go to the fountain. Alas! my nature is leprous as far as it is not purged. 'I was conceived in sin, my mother brought me forth in iniquity.' The more we take occasion every day to see and observe the corruption of our nature, the less it is, and we cannot better take occasion than upon every actual sin to run to the fountain, the filthy puddle from whence all comes, and be more humble for that than for particular sins. It is a mistake in men; they are ashamed of an action of injustice, &c., but they should go to their nature and think I have a false, unclean nature, whereby I am ready to commit a thousand such if God should let me alone. I have the spawn of all sin as far as the Spirit hath not subdued it. It is a defect of judgment to be more humbled for particular sins. Nature is more tainted than any action. That sowing, breeding sin, as the apostle saith, it is worse than the action, it breeds the rest. So much for that. They confess here, 'We are all as an unclean thing' in ourselves.

But what comes from us?

That that aggravates to the utmost a sinful state.

'All our righteousness is as filthy rags.'

He doth not say we have filthy actions, but our best actions are stained; and not one, but all. Mark how strong the place is, 'we all,' the people of God. He includes all, as Daniel saith, 'I confess my sins, and the sins of my people.' And there is no man in the church but he might have this confession in his mouth, 'we,' the people of God, and 'all we;' in all our actions, 'all our righteousness,' &c. So all the actions of all the righteous, the best actions of the best men, and all the best actions of the best men are defiled and stained. It is as great an aggravation as may be.

Some would have it to intend the legal righteousness, yet notwithstanding it is true of all. And when we now humble ourselves, it is good to think of all. So we may say, 'All our righteousness.' Whatsoever comes from us it is stained and defiled. As for their legal performances, there is no question of them; for, alas! they trusted too much to them. In Isaiah i. and Isaiah last, they thought God was beholding to them for them: 'Away with them, away with your new moons,' &c. They were abominable to God as 'the cutting off a dog's neck,' as it is Isaiah the last, Isa lxvi. 3. So all their righteousness, their ceremonial performances, were abominable.

But I say we may raise it higher. It is not only true of them, but in greater matters, in our best moral performances, they are all as tainted rags.

Obj. How can this be? It is strange it should be so. The papists cry out here that we discourage men from good works. If all our righteousness be as filthy rags, why should we perform good works?

Ans. Put case a man be sick, all the meat he eats it strengthens his sickness, shall he therefore not eat at all? Yes. He must eat somewhat. There is nature in him to strengthen as well as his disease. Thy best performances are stained; wilt thou do none therefore? Yes. Though they be stained, yet there is some goodness in them. Thou mayest honour God, and do good to others. Besides the ill there is good. There is gold in the ore. There is some good in every good action. Nay, there is so much good as that God pardons the ill, and accepts the good. So though our good actions be ill, yet for their kind, and matter, and stuff, they are good, they are commanded of God. For their original and spring they are wrought by the Spirit of God; for the person, the workman, it is one in the state of grace; and for acceptance God rewards them. But it is another thing when we come before God to humble ourselves. Then we must see what stains and sins are in them. There is no good action so good, but there are wants and weaknesses, and stains and blemishes in it as it comes from us. The Spirit of God indeed is effectual to stir us up to good actions; but we hinder the work of the Holy Ghost, and do not do them so thoroughly as we should. Therefore, besides our wants and weaknesses, there is a tainture of them. Either we have false aims, they are not so direct, or our resolutions are not so strong. False aims creep in for a while, though we do not allow them; and then there are some coolers of our devotion. Our love is cold, our hatred of sin is not so strong, our prayers are not so fervent, our actions are not so carried without interruption, but are hindered with many by-thoughts. Who cannot complain of these things? Who is not brought upon his knees for the weakness of his best actions? Nay, I say more, a Christian is more humbled for the imperfections and stains of his best actions, than a civil* carnal person is for his outward enormities; for he turns over all his outward delinquencies, and makes the matter but a trick of youth; when a poor Christian is abased for his dulness, and deadness, and coldness, for false aims that creep into his actions, for interruptions in his duties, that his thoughts will not suffer him to serve God with that intention† that he would, but puts him off with motions and suggestions and temptations in his best performances; this abaseth him more than outward gross sins doth a carnal person. When we deal with God, 'our righteousness it is as menstruous cloths,' Isa. xxx. 22.

Know this for a ground, that there is a double principle in a Christian in all things that he doth. There is flesh and spirit; and these two issue out in whatsoever comes from him. In his good words, there is flesh as well as spirit; in his thoughts and desires; in his prayer, his prayer itself stands in contraries. So everything that comes from him it is tainted with that that is contrary. The flesh opposeth and hinders the work of the Spirit, and so it stains our good works. Therefore contraries are true of a Christian, which seem strange to another man. A Christian at the same time is deformed and well-favoured. 'He is black and comely.' 'I am

* That is, 'merely moral.'—G. † That is, 'intentness.'—Ed.

black but yet well-favoured,' saith the spouse, Cant. i. 5; black in regard of sin, but well-favoured in regard of the Spirit of God and the acceptation of Christ. He is a saint and a sinner: a sinner in respect that sin hath spread over all parts, and a saint in respect of Christ's acceptance. 'My love and my dove.' Christ makes love to his church as if she had no defilement; but he looks on her better part; he looks on her as she is in his love, and as he means to bring her after. But the church looking upon herself as she is in herself, she is much abased. The ground of it is the imperfection of sanctification in this world. The best of our works are 'as menstruous cloths.' When we think of the corruption of the best things as they come from us, when we come to humble ourselves before God, we must down with proud styles and pharisaical thoughts, although there be somewhat that is good. Yet let us think of all the ill that may abase us.

There is a season for every thing, when we are tempted to be overcome by Satan. Then think of the good, as Job when he was tempted. 'I have done this and this; you cannot take away mine innocency,' Job xxxiii. 9. In false temptations from the world and Satan, then stand upon our innocency. But when we humble ourselves before God—'Alas! I am dust and ashes,' 'I abhor myself,' as Job and Abraham said, Gen. xviii. 27, Job xlii. 6—lay all proud apprehensions of ourselves aside; and all good works, especially in one kind, in matter of justification, 'all is dung in comparison of Christ,' Philip. iii. 8. All must be sold for the pearl, the righteousness of Christ. There is no reckoning must be had of good works by way of merit in justification and our title to heaven. What gives us title to heaven and frees us from hell? The death of Christ, the obedience and satisfaction of Christ. God by it hath redeemed us perfectly without anything in ourselves, and accepts us to life everlasting only by the righteousness of Christ. Therefore it is called God's righteousness, because it was done by Christ, it was wrought by God. Our righteousness is as 'a menstruous cloth.' It is spotted and stained and defiled. It will not do the deed. It will not satisfy conscience, much less the exact piercing judgment of God. That is the righteousness that must stay our souls in life and death, and we must oppose it to all temptations, as a satisfying thing that will set down conscience to be quiet. It must be righteousness of God-man; nothing else will do it. 'All our righteousness is as filthy rags.' That is the confession of their sinful actions.

The next thing he confesseth is senselessness. 'There is none that calls upon thy name, that stirreth up himself to take hold of thee.' There be other words between concerning the complaint of their miserable estate; but I will handle them that concern their sins first.

'There is none that calls upon thy name.'

In a word, he means that none worshipped him; because prayer is put for the whole worship of God, as indeed it may well be put for the whole, for it exerciseth all the graces of the Spirit. What one grace is not set on work in prayer? It is put for all the inward worship of God. If it be faith, prayer is the flame of faith. When there is faith in the heart there will be prayer in the mouth. The knowledge of God: prayer is grounded upon a promise. So it comes from that part of spiritual worship. Hope: hope makes a man pray. No man would pour out his supplications but to him that he hath hope in. And for love: God's love and mercy draws us into his presence; and joy and delight in the presence of God draws us to pray. We give God the honour of all his attributes in prayer; of his truth, of his goodness, of his mercy, of his presence everywhere, &c. So it sets all graces on work, and gives God the honour of all. It is the worship of God every way; for though it be an outward verbal worship of itself, yet it expresseth the worship of God inward. It gives God the honour of all.

Therefore, those that pray not, what kind of persons are they? Wretched persons. The sickness is now among us. If a man should ask now, What family is likeliest to have the vengeance of God on it?—though I speak not to censure those that have it, but I speak in God's ordinary course—surely those that do not exercise the duty of prayer. 'Pour out thy wrath upon those that call not upon thy name,' Ps. lxxix. 6. Those families that call not upon God humbly morning and evening, or that person that doth not morning and evening reverently call upon God, they are fit objects for the vengeance of God, for the plague or the like. 'Pour out thy wrath upon the families and persons that call not upon thy name,' insinuating that the Lord will spare us if we do call upon his name and humble ourselves. If thou wilt needs pour out thy vengeance, let it be on them that have not grace humbly to call upon thy name. Let us make conscience of this duty, except we will prove atheists, and lie open to all the vengeance of God.

'There is none that stirreth up himself to take hold of thee.'

He represents God to us as a great person, that would bestow some benefits, and is ready to turn away himself; yet none lays hold of him or desires him to stay. So, saith he, there is none that lays hold on God, to keep him that he should not go away. Therefore, when he saith, 'None calls upon thy name, or stirs up himself to take hold of thee,' he means there are none that pray earnestly. Incense was to be burnt, or else it cast no sweet smell. Our prayers must have fire and zeal in them. Our prayers must be cries that must pierce heaven. 'Out of the deep have I cried unto thee, Lord,' Ps. cxxx. 1. We must stir up ourselves; we must waken ourselves to waken God. Indeed, before we can waken God we must waken ourselves.

'There is none stirreth up himself *to take hold of thee.*'

Insinuating that if we would lay hold of God he will be stayed. To speak a little more particularly of this. God is so gracious that he will be stayed even by prayer. The way to stay God in his judgments, and to lay hold of him and keep him among us, it is prayer. Let us take notice now of the hand of God upon us; what is the means to stop his hand, that he come not among us with his public judgments? It is prayer. The way to stop God, and the angel that hath his sword now drawn over our heads, it is prayer. God so condescends that he will be stopped by prayer; as we see in Exod. xxxii. 10. He saith to Moses, 'Let me alone.' Moses prayed, and alleged arguments to God that he should not confound his people. 'Let me alone,' saith he, insinuating that prayer binds God's hands. So powerful is prayer, that it binds the Almighty. It makes the Omnipotent in some sort impotent. He cannot do that he would, he cannot execute his wrath; prayer binds him. When a company of Christians lay hold on him by prayer, he cannot do that he threateneth. The only way to lay hold of God is by prayer. In Ezek. xiii. 5, there is a complaint that 'none stood in the gap,' insinuating that if any had stood in the gap when the vengeance of God was coming abroad, they might have prevented the wrath. The way to stand in the gap and to keep God is to pray, and to pray heartily.

Now that God may be held by our prayers, they must be strong prayers. Every prayer will not hold God. They must be strong prayers that must bind such a Sampson that hath his strength. Therefore there must be a stirring up of ourselves. He saith here, 'There is none that stirreth up himself to take hold of thee.' So it is the duty of Christians to stir up themselves in these times.

Quest. How shall we stir up ourselves?

Ans. 1. First, *By considering the danger we are in.* Danger felt or feared, it will make a man lay hold. When a child feels the smart of the rod, he lays hold upon his father or his mother's hand. Strike no more! When the children of God feel the smart of his judgments, then they cry, 'Oh no more!' The cry of the child prevails with the mother, though it cannot speak ofttimes. So when in the sense of sin and misery we cry to God, we move his bowels with crying. There is no question but the serious apprehension of danger felt doth awaken the soul and stir it up. It is so also in danger feared. A danger feared, with belief, will work as if it were present; for a man that hath a spirit of faith to see that unless God be appeased with good courses, he will punish, as surely as if the judgment were upon him. Faith makes things present, both good and ill; and it makes a man sensible of things that are not yet upon him. This is the difference between a Christian and another man. Another man 'puts the evil day far off from him;' but a believing Christian, by a spirit of faith, sees God, except he be turned away by hearty and humble repentance, ready to seize upon him; and so he walks humbly in all his courses. So that danger felt or feared by a spirit of faith awakens and stirs up the soul to lay hold on God.

Therefore in spiritual dangers we should especially waken our souls to see in what need we stand of Christ and the pardoning mercy of God in Christ, that we may waken him and give him no rest till we find peace in our consciences.

2. Then again, that that we may stir up ourselves withal, is *meditation of the necessity and excellency of grace, and of the good things we beg.* The serious consideration of that will make us stir up ourselves to lay hold on God, and give him no rest till we have it. When a man thinks the 'loving-kindness of God is better than life,' Ps. lxiii. 3, and if I have not that, my life is nothing to me. It is not only better than corn and wine and oil, but than life itself. Pardon of sin, and a heart to do good, is better than life itself, than anything in the world. If one should offer such a man this, a heart patiently to bear ill, and large to do good, and strength against temptations, he would rather have this gracious disposition than anything in the world; he had rather have the pardon of sin with the sense of God's favour than anything in the world. This will stir up a man, as we see in David, Ps. li. 1, *seq.*, 'Mercy, mercy;' it binds God and lays hold on him, together with pardoning mercy, to have a heart enlarged with spiritual joy. There is nothing spiritual, but it is so excellent, that if we had the eyes of our spirits awakened to see them, we would bind God and lay hold of him. He should not go further till he had shined on us.

3. Therefore *let us offer violence to God this way; never give him rest till we obtain.* You see when the two disciples were going to Emmaus, Christ made as though he would have gone further, but they 'compelled' him, Luke xxiv. 29. Now there is a semblance as if God threatened war, and would take away the gospel. There are dangers toward. When God makes such a semblance, let us lay hold on him; let him go no further.

Lord, night approacheth and affliction approacheth. Lord, stay; thou shalt go no further. Let us stop God with importunity. The consideration of danger, and the necessity and excellency of the things we beg, will make us lay hold on God.

There is an hypocrisy among men, among a company of formalists, that are the bane of the times, that God will spue out. They are as ill as a profane person in his nostrils. They think that all devotion is in prostrating themselves, which is good, and more than profane men will do, and yield a dead sacrifice to God. They will come and hear, and yield the outward act in outward humiliation. Is this to rouse thyself? Outward things are never current but when they express outwardly the inward truth. Therefore take another course, man; God cares not for the dead, empty carcase thou bringest him. Work upon thine own heart by meditation of the danger thou art in, and of the excellency of the things thou art to beg, and meditate of the majesty of God whom thou appearest before, of his goodness and truth, &c. Affect thy heart deeply with these apprehensions; let these serious thoughts draw outward expressions of humiliation. And then it is excellent when the outward expression follows the inward impression; when there is somewhat inward that shews itself outward; when we stir up ourselves, and not to think that all devotion consists in a comely, outward carriage—which is commendable of itself—but because men usually rest in it, it is prejudicial to their soul's good. We must offer a reasonable sacrifice to God; we must love him in our hearts; we must work upon our hearts and carry ourselves so in our inward man, as that we may stir up our whole man and awaken our souls: 'Praise the Lord, O my soul, and all that is within me, praise his holy name,' Ps. ciii. 1. We should stir up ourselves by speaking to our own souls, that we may waken and take hold of God.

4. This again will help it, *A man should never come to pray, but he should have an answer before he hath done, either at that time or another.* Never give over till thou hast an answer. This will make us stir up ourselves indeed. How do you know a prayer from a formal lip-labour? A man that prays conscionably* marks what he doth, and expects a return, as a man that soweth his seed. He that doth a thing with hope of issue will do it throughly. Therefore never pray to perform an empty duty to God; but mark what you pray for, if it be forgiveness of sins, or for grace, or protection, &c., and do it with that earnestness that you may hope for an issue answerable; and this going about it will make us do it to purpose. Do we think to serve God with the deed done? God hath appointed prayer for our good, and to convey blessings to us. Let us pray so as we may expect a blessing by it. Now that prayer that expects a blessing to be conveyed, it will be a prayer to purpose. It will make a man stir up himself.

'There is none that stirreth up himself to take hold of thee.'

The complaint of this holy man of God may be taken up at this time of many of us now. How few are those that rouse and stir up themselves, but put off God with an empty compliment! Nay, in these times of danger, have ye not a company of idle persons that will not vouchsafe to hear the word, nor to come and humble themselves, but walk and talk offensively, as if they would dare God; or if they come here, they come not with a resolution to hear the issue of their prayers, to rouse up themselves 'to lay hold on God.' Because, as there is a great deal of atheism in regard of God, so there is much dead flesh in regard of men. Who is so pitiful of

* That is, 'conscientiously.'—G.

our brethren round about as he ought? We had need to stir up ourselves. The danger is present. We are beset round about, yet who is stirred up to earnest prayer? We want bowels of compassion. Those that have hearts compassionate, it is a sign that God intends good to them. But of the most we may take up this complaint, we are dead-hearted in regard of our sins against God, and in regard of the contagion among us. A man may see it by men's discourses. There is inquiry how the sickness spreads? how many dies? But men do not labour with God to make their accounts even with him; nor we are not compassionate to men: for that would be a means to stir and to rouse us up 'to lay hold of God,' to stay his hand out of love and pity and compassion to our brethren which are our flesh, though it should never seize on us. I say, I fear this complaint is too justly on many of us. I beseech you, let us labour to amend it as we tender* our own salvation—perhaps that we do not regard so much, we shall ere long, but then—as we tender the health of our bodies, which we prefer before our souls, let us humble ourselves more than ordinary now.

Some devils are not driven out but by prayer and fasting, Mat. xvii. 21. So some judgments, they will not away without prayer and fasting; not only public, but private fasting and prayer. Sometimes there must be more than ordinary humiliation for some sins; for some kind of temptations there must be prayer and fasting; for some maladies prayer and fasting, and more than ordinary stirring and rousing up of ourselves to lay hold upon God. God will not be held with ordinary humiliation. That will not do it; but there must be a resolution against, and a hatred of all sin, and to please God in all things. We must do it with extraordinary humiliation now, because the judgment is extraordinary. There is ordinary humiliation and extraordinary: as there are ordinary feasts and extraordinary, so there is ordinary humiliation for daily trespasses; but in extraordinary judgments, extraordinary fasting and humiliation. As there is ordinary washing daily, but there is washing and scouring at good times. God calls for extraordinary humiliation now; not only prayers, but stirring and rousing up of ourselves. We should apprehend the danger as seizing on ourselves. This night it may seize upon us, for aught we know. It should affect us and make us stir up ourselves. This is the way to hold God by prayer; and if we hold him, he will hold the destroying angel. He hath all creatures at his command. Thus you see how we should confess the sins of our persons, the sins of our good actions, our want of calling upon God. 'There is none that calls upon thy name, that stirs up himself to take hold of thee.' Thus far proceed the branches of their sinful disposition in those times.

Now he complains likewise of the judgments of God.

'We all fade as a leaf; our iniquities, as the wind, have taken us away. Thou hast hid thy face, and we are consumed because of our iniquities.'

The complaint hath these four branches; a little of each.

'We all fade as a leaf.'

Wicked men are 'as leaves;' and worse, they are 'as chaff.' Godly men, because they have a consistence, and are rooted in Christ, and set in a good soil, they are 'trees of righteousness.' But godly men in the state of their nature, and in regard of this life, they are as leaves. Wicked men are as leaves every way, and as 'chaff which the wind bloweth away,' as we shall see afterwards.

* That is, = 'care for.'—G.

'We all fade as a leaf.'

1. He means, first, in regard *of ceremonial performances that were without vigour aud spirit of true devotion.* There was no spirit in their legal performances. They were dead empty things. Therefore when judgment came they were as leaves. So an idle careless hearer, when judgment comes, all is as leaves. When conscience nips him, as his atheistical heart will do ere long, then he is as a leaf, all fades away. The Jews, when they were in trouble, all their legal performances faded, they were all as a leaf.

2. So it is true in regard *of mortality,* the vanity of health and strength. We all as a leaf fade away when God's judgments come to nip us. Men are as leaves; as the leaves now in autumn fall, and there is a new generation in the spring; and then they fall away, and a new generation comes again; so it is with men: some are blown off, and some come on again. 'We all fade as a leaf.' Not to be large in the point, at this time we are all as leaves. In this city now, there is a kind of wind that nips a world of men, many hundreds in the head.* It is an autumn wind that nips the leaves. Our autumn wind with us is before the time—a kind of autumn wind in the spring, in summer, that nips the leaves and takes away the vigour of health.

3. And so, as I said, *for all idle performances, that have not a foundation in substantial piety,* they are all as leaves. When trouble of conscience comes, they are as Adam's fig-leaves. When God comes to search and examine, they all fall off, both in respect of our performances and in respect of our lives. We are all as leaves when God comes in judgment. This is one part of the complaint. 'We are all as leaves.' The like we have of Moses, the man of God, Ps. xc. 6. When God blows upon us with the wind of his displeasure, we fall off as leaves.

Then another expression is,

'Our iniquities, as the wind, have taken us away.'

As chaff, or things that have no solidity in them, are blown away with a puff of wind, so it is with a man if he be not a Christian, set into and gathered unto Christ. By the fall we all fell from God, and were scattered from him. Sin blew the angels out of heaven. It blew Adam out of paradise; and now Christ, the 'second Adam,' gathers us to him again by his word and Spirit, and so we have a solid and eternal being in him. But out of Christ, our iniquities, as a wind, and God's judgments, blow us all away first or last. Wicked men settle on their dregs a great while, but when God's judgment comes, it blows them in this world to this part and that part ofttimes, when it pleaseth him to exercise his outward judgments. But if he do not blow them away here, he will give them a blast that shall send them to hell, their centre. Out of Christ there is no solidity, no consistence or being for any man. Therefore, when God's judgment comes, it blows them away in this world, and at the hour of death sends them to hell. This is the state of all. 'Our iniquities, like the wind, take us away.' He means here, they were blown out of Jewry to Babylon. It was a strong blast that blew them out of their own country.

May not we say, 'Our iniquities have blown us away?' What hath blown us from our callings and employments? Is it not the pestilence? And what brings that? Is it not our iniquities? So that we may all complain of this, 'Our iniquities have blown us away.'

We see here he lays the blame upon their iniquities. Did not the Babylonians carry them away? Alas! they were but God's instruments.

* Qu. 'day'?—Ed.

God was displeased by their sins; his wrath blew them away. So you may see here the child of God in all judgments looks to his sins. He justifies God. He murmurs not, and says this and that. No. But, it was my sins: 'We have sinned against the Lord,' Lam. v. 16; Micah vii. 9, 'I will bear the wrath of the Lord, because I have sinned against him;' and Lam. iii. 39, 'Man suffers for his sins;' and every one of us may say, 'It is our iniquities have taken us away.' A gracious heart justifies God and condemns itself. The children of God may complain sometimes of God's hand, but they will never censure God's hand. They justify God alway, though they may complain of the bitterness of his hand. Here they complain of the bitterness of the judgment. They were blown into another country, into captivity. They do not complain of God. God will have us complain; but as he will have us complain, so we must justify him and condemn ourselves; just are thy judgments.

An hypocrite thinks God is beholding to him for his outward performances, and when judgments befall him, he frets and censures God. Either he thinks there is no God, or he frets and fumes against God: he is discontented. But a Christian justifies God, and condemns himself. 'Our iniquities have blown us away.' Our sins keep good things from us.

Use. Therefore, let us now lay the blame where it is. Search out our sins, personal and particular, and complain of them. They have a hand in this plague. God is no tyrant. He delights not to confound his creatures; but sin makes him out of love with his creatures, the workmanship of his own hands. It is our sins. Therefore, let us lament the sins of the times. So far we may without hypocrisy, and ought to take to heart, and mourn for the sins of the times that we hear by others and see ourselves, and mourn for our own hearts that we cannot mourn. We must mourn for the sins of the times, as Daniel and Nehemiah, and all the blessed men of God have done. It is not the plague that hurts us. That is but God's messenger. Sin doth us more harm than all the devils in hell and all the plagues in the world. It is not outward evils we need to fear. Let us fear sin, and lay hold on God. He is the Lord of hosts. He hath all the creatures at his command. Let us get sin away, that doth all the mischief. It is that that makes bate between God and us, and then God makes a controversy between us and the creatures. It is our sins.

And that is the reason of the necessity of humiliation for our sins, because sin breeds a separation between God and us, and between the creatures and us. When God is offended, the creatures are infected. Let us see our sins; by them we infect the air: by our vain speeches, and oaths, and our filthiness. Our sins infect the air, and that breeds infection in our bodies. Our sins cry. They have a voice to cry to God, if our prayers do not outcry them. Therefore, let us cry to God to hear the cry of our prayers, and not of our sins. How many voices have crying sins! There is the voice of the people oppressed, the voice of filthiness, &c. Sins clamour in God's ears. They clamour for wages due, 'and the wages of sin is death,' Rom. vi. 23. Sin cries, though it says nothing in words. It cries in God's ears, and it will not rest till he hath poured out his vengeance. The filthiness and oaths, and atheism and profaneness, the suffering of the dishonour of his name: these sins of the times are those that pull miseries upon us. 'Our iniquities have taken us away as the wind.' So much for that.

'For thou hast hid thy face from us, and we are consumed because of our iniquities.'

Sin makes God hide his face from us, and then 'we are consumed, because of our iniquities.' 'We melt away in the hands of our iniquities,' as the word is (b). Indeed, sin is a cruel tyrant. When God leaves us in the hand of our sins, he leaves us in a cruel hand. Christ came to redeem us from our sins. Our sins are they that torment us. It is very significant in the original.

'We are melted.' We melt away as wax before the fire, as snow before the sun, 'because of our iniquities,' when God gives up men to be handled as their own sins will handle them. Nations melt before the hands of sin, and kings, and kingdoms, and all. Let God give up men to delight in sin, kingdoms or persons, they melt and moulder away in the hand of their sins.

But to speak a little more of the next words.

'Thou hast hid thy face from us.'

That is, thou hast hid thy comfort from us. God hath a double face: a face that shines on our souls in peace, and joy, and comfort, when he saith to the soul, 'I am thy salvation,' Ps. xxxv. 3; and his face that shines on the outward estate, that keeps misery, and sickness, and danger from us, and bestows good things on us. And God takes away his face from us in regard of the inward man, when he gives us no peace, but leaves us to spiritual desertion. In regard of the outward man, God hides his face when he gives us up to pestilence, and war, and sickness, and miseries in this life: when he gives us up to outward desertion.

Sometimes God shines on wicked men in outward things, but he hides his face for peace of conscience; and sometimes God's children have his face shining on their conscience, but he hides his face in respect of outward things. Sometimes he shines in neither of both: as at this time he neither shined on these blessed men in outward favours, for they were in captivity, nor in the sense of his love and favour, for they were in desolation, and eclipsed every way.

The face of God, it is as the sun to the creatures. When the sun hides his face, what is there but darkness and night? What makes the night, but the absence of the sun? What makes winter, but the absence of the sun, when he grows low, and cannot heat the earth? So what makes winter in the soul, deadness, and darkness, and dulness in God's service? The absence of the face of God; God shines not on the soul. What makes night in the soul, when the soul is benighted with ignorance, that it cannot see itself, nor see the judgments of God? God shines not. 'The Sun of righteousness' shines not on that soul.

God is the Sun of the creature. He gives life to the creature. What will become of the creature, when God neither shines outwardly nor inwardly on it? As at the day of judgment, he shall take away outward comforts;—there shall be no outward shining;—and all inward comforts, they shall have no hope: he shall altogether hide his face. When God, the Fountain of all good, shall hide his face altogether from the creature, that is hell. The place where God shines not outwardly with comforts, nor inwardly, nor there shall be no hope of neither, but a place of horror and despair, that is hell, as the hell of this life is when God shines not on our souls.

Now, these holy men they complain, yet they pray: 'Thou hast hid thy face,' Ps. lxxxix. 46. Here is the conflict of faith, that sees God hide his face, and yet will follow God. It sees God ready to turn away himself, and yet it will lay hold of him, and have a glance of him. It will wrestle with him, and not let him go without a blessing. So there be degrees of God's hiding of his face. Though God seem to hide his face, and to withdraw outward comforts, and perhaps in some to withdraw his favour from their hearts inwardly. What shall they do? Droop? No. Wrestle with God as Jacob. See through the cloud that is between God and thy soul. Break thorough by faith; and with Job say, 'Though he kill me, yet will I trust in him,' Job. xiii. 15. Let us stir up ourselves 'to lay hold on God' when he seems to turn away his face; and imitate good Jacob, never give over seeking the face of God.

How shall we seek the face of God?

1. *By prayer;* for that brings us to the face of God, though he seem to hide his face, as Jeremiah complains, Jer. xiv. 8, 'Why art thou as a stranger?' And yet he prays. Seek him by prayer.

2. Seek him *in his ordinances.* Hear the word of God. 'Thy face, Lord, will I seek,' Ps. xxvii. 8. God invites you to seek his face now by fasting and humiliation. Seek his face in this ordinance. Here is the blessed Trinity, 'Father, Son, and Holy Ghost.' Though outwardly God hide his face in some regards, yet when he offers outward liberties refuse them not. He offers his face to us now in Christ. Seek, by prayer and other means, holy communion with him still; and never leave seeking till you have got a glance of him; and stir up yourselves to lay hold on him, that he would shew his loving countenance upon you.

Those that turn their backs on God's ordinances, and in rebellion to his commandments, live in sins against conscience—can they wonder that he hides his face from them, when they turn their backs on him? Rebellious persons, that will not yield meekly to God's ordinances, and submit to his commandments, do they wonder that God takes good things from them? When we sin we turn our backs upon God and our face to the devil, and the world, and pleasures. When men turn their faces to sin, to pleasures and vanity, and their backs on God, do they wonder that he suffers them to melt and pine away? Let us do as the flowers do, the marigold, &c. They turn themselves to the sun. Let our souls do so. Let us turn ourselves to God in meditation and prayers, striving and wrestling with him. Look to him, eye him in his ordinances and promises; and have communion with him all the ways we can. Let our souls open and shut with him. When he hides his face, let us droop, as the flowers do till the sun come again. When the waters fall, the flowers droop and hold down their heads. When the sun riseth the next morning, up they go again, as if there had been never a shower. So when we have not daily comfort of spirit in peace of conscience, let us never rest seeking God's face in his ordinances and by prayer, and that will cheer a drooping soul, as the sunbeams do the flagging flowers. Then you may know that God's face shines upon you in some measure, when he gives you means and gives you hearts to use those means, and comfort in your consciences, that whether you live or die you are God's. This is a beam of that sunshine on the soul when God vouchsafes joy and comfort. A little of this will banish all fears. If you have one glimpse of his countenance, you shall not need to fear the plague, or war, or death. If he shine on you, one glance will take away all fear. Paul, when he was in the stocks, one beam of God's countenance made him sing at midnight, Acts xvi. 25. 'Let thy countenance shine on us, and we shall be safe,' Ps. lxxx. 3, let what will become of us outwardly. If God shine not on us for outward favours, if he shine on our souls and release them from fears and guilt, and speak peace to them, and say unto them, 'he is their salvation,' Ps. xxxv. 3, and as he saith in the gospel, 'Thy sins are forgiven thee,' all will be well whatsoever shall become of us.

'Let us seek the Lord while he may be found,' Isa. lv. 6. Hold him before he go; let him not depart. Attend upon the means; never miss good means of seeking his face till we have got a sweet answer from heaven that he is our God.

Now follows the supplication.

'But now, O Lord, thou art our Father,' &c.

Here is a prayer which is a kind of holding God by the relation of a Father. This is one way of stirring up our souls, to consider the relation of a father. It stirs up bowels when a child is beaten by his father, 'O stay, father, spare.' It works upon the bowels. There is a world of rhetoric in this one word 'Father.' Why, Lord, thou art my Father. Shall I be destroyed? Let us lay hold on God by this relation that he puts upon himself; and he will not lay it aside, though we be unworthy to be sons. He doth not say, Thou art our Father, and we are thy sons; because he thought they were unworthy, as the prodigal saith, 'I am unworthy to be called thy son,' Luke xv. 19; but instead of saying we are thy sons, he saith, 'We are the clay, thou art the potter.' Yet he is a Father continually; and though in Christ you cannot call him Father, yet you may by creation and initiation, being brought up in the church. Go to him with the encouragements you have, and cast yourselves upon him. There is a bond for you by creation; and there is his command. He bids you call him Father. He is a Father by creation. Look not upon this or that sin, but go to him and call him Father, as you may call him. Say, Thou art my Father, thou hast given me a being in the church. Wrestle with him as you may, though as sound Christians you cannot call him Father. Be weary of your courses. Are you willing to come under God's hands, to be sons? You are sons by creation already. Offer thyself to be of his family for the time to come, and God will give a sweet report to thy soul. Stand not out at the stave's end. 'Thou art our Father, Lord.' If you have a purpose to live in sin, the devil is your father, and not God. 'You are of your father the devil,' John viii. 44; but if we be willing to submit, we may say, 'Doubtless thou art our Father,' Isa. lxiii. 16.

'We are the clay, thou art the potter.'

Here is a resignation of themselves to God in this term, 'thou art the potter, we are the clay.' Indeed, we are but earthen vessels, the best of us, in regard of the bodily life we have; and we are at the liberty of God to dispose of as he pleaseth. So, before he comes to put forth this prayer to God, he useth this resignation of themselves into the hand of God: we are as clay in thy hands, Lord, 'dispose of us as thou wilt.' Let us remember this when we come to pray to God. Use all means of abasement that can be. Lay aside all terms other than abasing terms. 'We are the clay,' Isa. lxiv. 8; and as Job saith, 'I abhor myself in dust and ashes,' Job xlii. 6. So the saints have done in all times. 'I am not worthy to be called thy son,' Luke xv. 19; and 'I am less than the least of thy mercies,' Gen. xxxii. 10. Let us lay aside proud and lofty terms, and 'cast down our crowns' at the foot of Christ, as the saints in Rev. iv. 10, cast down all our excellencies. Let us have no thought of outward excellencies—of beauty, or strength, or riches, or high dignity. When we come to God, we must come with low thoughts to the high God. Can the creature be too low in his presence?

And then come with resignation. 'We are the clay, thou art the potter.' Do with us as thou wilt. If thou dash us in pieces as a potter's vessel, thou mayest do it. That is the way to escape. That is well committed, that is committed into God's hand. Some men shift by their wits, and will not trust God with their health and strength. They 'be double-minded,' as St James saith, i. 8. They will have two strings to their bow; if lawful means will not serve, unlawful shall. No. But we 'must commit ourselves to God as to a faithful creator,' 1 Pet. iv. 19; and then see what he will do. Then it stands with his honour. 'He will look to the lowly.' 'I am the clay, thou art the potter.' Here I am; do as thou wilt. As David saith, it is a blessed estate thus to resign ourselves into God's hands. If the devil and reprobates could be brought to this, they should never come there where they are in terrors of conscience. Let us labour to practise this duty: Lord, I commit to thy hands my body and soul. I cast myself into thy bosom; do with me as thou wilt. Some that have stood out at the stave's end with temptations many years, have gotten comfort by this resignation. 'We are the clay, thou art the potter.' Thou mayest mould and break us as thou wilt. The way now to escape the plague is not altogether to use tricks of wit and policy (though lawful means must be used), but labour to get into Christ, and resign ourselves into God's hands absolutely, and say thus, 'We are the clay,' &c. Lord, thou mayest dash us if thou wilt, as thou doest many hundreds weekly. Thou mayest dash us in that fashion if thou wilt. Only we may have a desire that God would make our lives and health precious to him, that we may serve him as if we were now in heaven, and that we may have grace to make good use of all. But if God have determined and decreed to take us away, let us resign ourselves into his hands. It is no matter though the body be 'sown in dishonour, they shall be raised in honour,' 1 Cor. xv. 43. 'We are the clay, he is the potter,' let him do what he will with our carcases and bodies, so he be merciful to our souls. These vessels of clay, when they are turned to earth, they shall be renewed of better stuff, like the glorious body of Christ. Then our souls and bodies shall be glorious by him that took a piece of flesh and clay for us. Oh the humility of Christ! We wonder that the soul should animate a piece of clay, so excellent a thing as the soul is; much more may we wonder that the Son of God should take a piece of flesh and clay upon him; to take our nature of base earth, to make us eternally glorious as himself. Let it comfort us, though God dash our clay as a potter. Yet Christ, that took our clay to the unity of his person, our nature being engrafted into him, he will make our bodies eternal and everlasting as his own glorious body. Let us resign ourselves into God's hands, as the church here, 'Thou art the potter, and we are the clay,' and then we shall never miscarry.

NOTES.

(*a*) P. 190.—'Who would go to the pest-house, or to one that hath "Lord, have mercy upon us," on the door?' The allusion is to the marks placed upon the 'pest-houses,' and the dwellings of those sick during the plague in London—a visitation very often and very solemnly referred to by Sibbes, who twice witnessed its devastation—viz., in 1603–4, and the subsequent one of 1624–5. Having died in 1635, he did not pass through the 'Pestilence' of 1636.

(*b*) P. 200.—'"We melt away," . . . as the word is.' Dr Joseph Addison Alexander renders the phrase, 'For thou hast hid thy face from us, and hast *melted us*, because of (or by means of) our iniquities.' It will generally be found that Sibbes's critical remarks harmonise with the results of the highest modern scholarship. Cf. Note *c*, Vol. I. page 31. G.

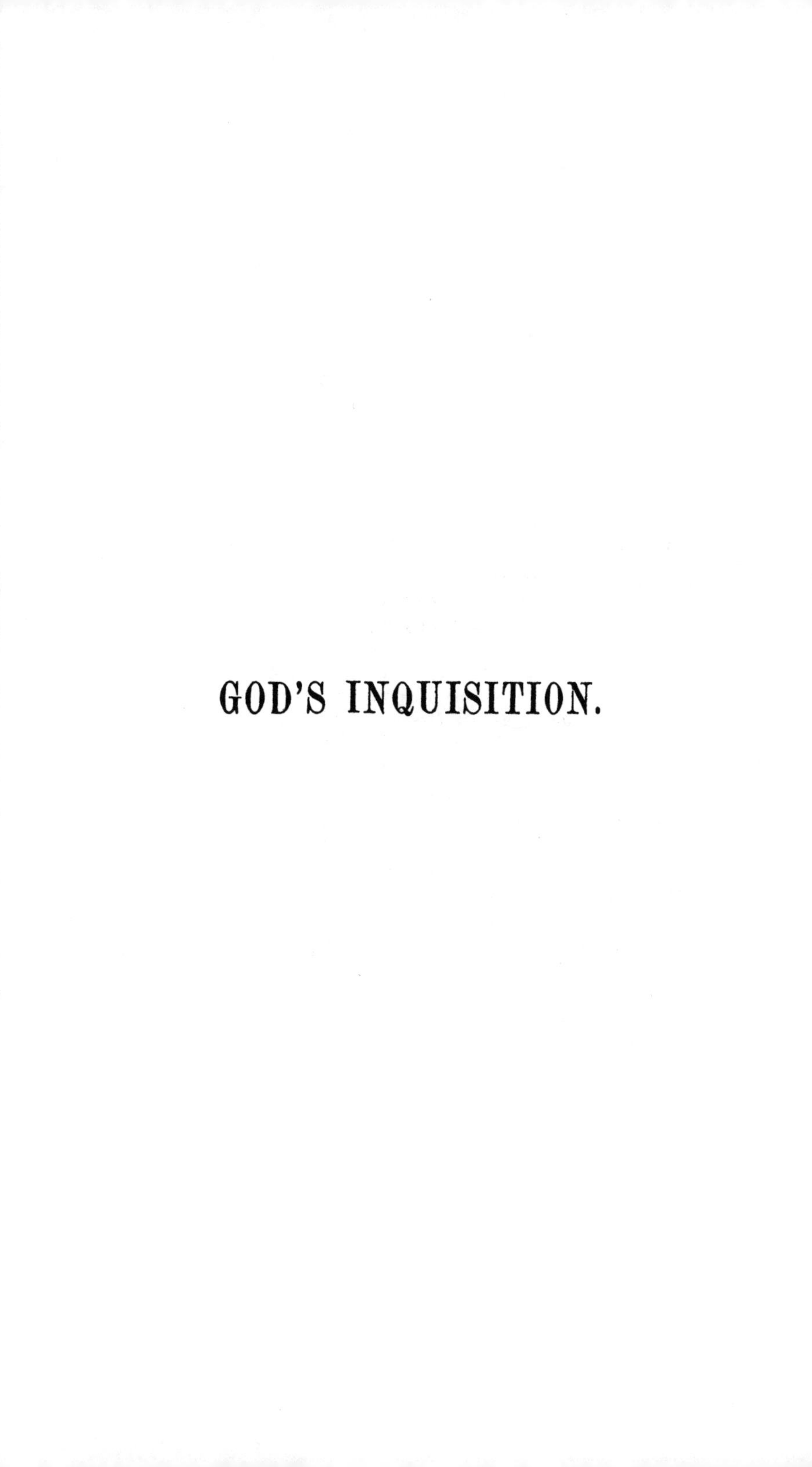

GOD'S INQUISITION.

GOD'S INQUISITION.

NOTE.

'God's Inquisition' forms part of the 'Beams of Divine Light' (4to, 1639). The separate title-page is below.* For general title of the volume, see Vol. V. page 220.

G.

GOD'S
INQVISITION,
In two Sermons
By the late Reverend and Learned
Divine Richard Sibs,
Doctor in Divinity, Master of Katherine Hall in
Cambridge, and sometimes Preacher at
Grayes Inne.

Gen. 18. 21.

I will goe downe now and see whether they have done altogether according to the cry of it, which is come unto me; and if not, I will know.

Psal. 14. 3.

They are all gone aside, they are altogether become filthy, there is none that doth good no not one.

[A wood-cut here of an angel, surrounded with a glory, leaning upon a cross; his right hand holding an open Bible, and his feet trampling upon the usual skeleton-representation of death.]

LONDON.
Printed by *G. M.* for *Nicholas Bourne* and *Rapha Harford.*
MDCXXXIX.

GOD'S INQUISITION.

I hearkened and heard, but they spake not aright: no man repented him of his wickedness, saying, What have I done? every one turned to his course, as the horse rusheth into the battle. Yea, the stork in the heavens knoweth her appointed times; and the turtle, and the crane, and the swallow, observe the time of their coming; but my people know not the judgment of the Lord.—JER. VIII. 6, 7.

UPON the sins of people it hath been alway God's course to send his prophets to warn them beforehand, and afterwards, upon that, to observe how they profit by that warning; and thereupon he takes occasion to proceed answerably. God usually exerciseth a great deal of patience ere he strikes. He made the world in six days, but he is six thousand years in destroying it.

In this verse, after the holy prophet had menaced the judgment of God upon them, there is set down what use they made of it. Alas! 'They spake not aright: no man repented him of his wickedness, saying, What have I done?' And lest they should object, How do you know this? He saith here it is upon inquisition, 'I hearkened and heard.' So the words contain *God's inquisition or inquiry*, and then God's evidence upon that inquiry, together with a complaint. His inquiry, 'I hearkened and heard.' For we must apply these words to God. There is the same phrase, Mal. iii. 16, 'The Lord hearkened, and heard; and a book of remembrance was written before him;' so here, 'I hearkened and heard.' Here is the inquiry.

Then, secondly, the evidence upon the inquiry, 'they spake not aright.'

And, thirdly, the complaint upon that evidence set down.

1. First, Positively, 'They repented not of their wickedness,' which is amplified, 1. From the generality of this their impenitency, '*No man* repented him;' and 2. From the cause of it: want of consideration. They did not say, 'What have I done?' If they had called themselves to account concerning what they had done, certainly they would have repented.

2. Comparatively, 'They turned to their course, as the horse rusheth into the battle.'

3. Lastly, Superlatively, preferring the skill of the poor storks and cranes, and the turtle and swallow, before the judgment of his senseless and stupid

people: 'The stork in the heavens knoweth her appointed time; and the turtle, the crane, and the swallow; but my people know not the judgment of the Lord.' This is the sum of the words.

1. First, Of God's inquiry, 'I hearkened and heard.' Ere Sodom was destroyed, the Lord came down to see whether there was just cause or no, Gen. xviii. 21. God is most just. He will see cause for his judgments. He hath no delight in punishing. When he judgeth, it is not out of his sovereignty, but out of his justice. He doth it not as a sovereign Lord, but as a just judge. Now, a judge must do all upon inquisition and evidence; therefore saith he, 'I hearkened and heard:' where, by the way, the gods of the earth, to whom he hath communicated his name, should learn hence, not to be rash in their judgments, but to have sound evidence before they pass sentence. 'I hearkened and heard.' To 'hearken' is more than to hear: to apply one's self with some affection to hear a thing.

God is all ear, as he is all eye. He hath an ear everywhere. He hath an ear in our hearts. He hears what we think, what we desire. He sees all the secret corners of our hearts. Therefore, when he saith here, 'I hearkened and heard,' it is by way of condescending to our capacity.

We may learn hence, briefly, *that God hath an ear and an eye to our carriage and dispositions, to our speeches and courses.* If we had one alway at our backs that would inform such a man and such a man what we say, one that should book our words, and after lay them to our charge, it would make us careful of our words. Now, though we be never so much alone, there are two always that hear us. God hearkens and hears, and God's deputy in us, conscience, 'hearkens and hears.' God books it, and conscience books it. As God hath a book wherein he wrote us before all worlds, and the book of his providence for our bones, and all things that concern us, so he hath a book for our works and words. Mal. iii. 16, 'They that feared the Lord spake often one to another; and the Lord hearkened, and heard it; and a book of remembrance was written before him,' &c. So here, 'I hearkened and heard.' God and conscience note and observe everything.

This doth impose upon us the duty of careful and reverent walking with God. Would we speak carelessly or ill of any man if he heard us? When we slight a man, we say we care not if he heard us himself. But shall we slight God so? Shall we swear, and lie, and blaspheme, and say we care not though God hear us, that will lay everything to our charge, not only words but thoughts. 'We shall give an account for every idle word, and for every idle thought,' Mat. xii. 36, and shall we not regard it? It is from the horrible profaneness of the poisonful, rebellious heart of man, that men do not consider these things. 'God hearkens and hears.' He is at our studies; he is at our windows; he hears us in our chambers, when we are in company, when we meet together, when we take liberty to censure and detract, when we swear and revile. What if men hear not! yet conscience hears, and God hears. And when God shall lay open the book of conscience, and lay before a man all his naughty* speeches and wicked works, what will become of him then for not making use of this principle, that 'God hearkens and hears'? God sees now with what minds and affections we come about this business, whether it be formally to put off God, to make it a cover for our sinful courses after, as if God were beholding to us for what we do now, and therefore might the better bear

* That is, 'wicked.'—G.

with us, though we make bold with him hereafter. He not only hears what we say, but sees our minds and purposes, nay, he 'knows our thoughts long before they are.' This is the cause why godly men have alway walked so carefully and circumspectly. They knew that God's eye and ear was over them; as Enoch and Noah, it is said in this regard that they 'walked with God,' Gen. v. 24, vi. 9; and Joseph when he was tempted, 'Shall I do this,' saith he, 'and sin against God?' Gen. xxxix. 9; and shall not God see if I do this? 'Doth not he see my ways and count all my steps,' saith Job, Job. xiv. 16. So again, What makes wicked men so loose? The prophet tells, Ps. xciv. 7, they say, 'The Lord shall not see, neither shall the God of Jacob regard it.' Or as it is, Job xxii. 12, &c., 'Is not God in the height of heaven? How doth God know? can he judge through the dark cloud? Thick clouds are a covering to him, that he sees not; and he walketh not in the circuit of the heavens.' Tush! he regardeth not; he is immured and shut up there. But to such atheists we see what the prophet answers, Ps. lxiv. 8, &c. Ye brutish, foolish people, shall he that makes others hear not hear himself? 'He that planted the ear,' he that is all ear, 'shall not he hear?' As it makes good men walk holily and reverently, to consider of this, that God is present, and present as an observer and a judge, so the want of taking this to heart makes wicked and carnal persons do as they do. So much briefly for these words, 'I hearkened and heard.'

'No man spake aright.'

But what evidence doth he give upon this inquisition? 'They spake not aright,' which is amplified from the generality of this sin. 'No man spake aright.' The meaning is especially that 'they spake not aright concerning the judgments of God threatened.' When God had threatened judgments, he hearkened and heard what use they made of them, but 'they spake not aright.'

Quest. In how many respects do we not speak aright in regard of the judgments of God?

Ans. 1. First, *In regard of God*, men speak not aright when they do not see him in the judgment, but look to the creature, to the second causes; as now in the time of the plague, to look to the air and weather, and this and that, which is a good providence, and to forget him that is the chief; to kill dogs and cats, and to let sin alone; to cry out, Oh what air there is this year! and what weather it is! to talk of the second causes altogether, and to forget God: this is to talk amiss of God's judgments threatened, in regard of God.

2. Again, We talk amiss *in regard of others*, when we begin to slight them in our thoughts and speeches. Oh they were careless people; they adventured into company, and it was the carelessness of the magistrates; they were not well looked to; they were unmerciful persons, &c. Is it not God's hand? Put case there might be some oversight; art thou secure from God's arrow? He that struck them, may he not strike thee? This is to talk amiss of the judgment of God in regard of others; when we think that God hath singled them out as sinners above the rest; as the disciples thought of the Galileans, 'whose blood Pilate mingled with their sacrifice,' Luke xiii. 1. No, no, saith he; 'think not they were greater sinners than the rest;' do not add your bitter censure of the judgment of God on them, and make it heavier (there is a woe to such persons as add afflictions to the afflicted, Prov. xx. 22, Phil. i. 16): 'Except ye repent, ye shall all

likewise perish.' Is not the ripest corn cut first? God ofttimes takes those away that are fittest for him, and leaves others to the cruelty of men. Therefore by this rash judgment there may be great wrong to men, and to wrong men in our censures, it is to talk amiss of God's judgments in regard of others.

3. Again, We talk amiss of God's judgments in regard of ourselves.

(1.) *When we murmur and fret any way against God*, and do not submit ourselves under his mighty hand as we should.

(2.) Again, We sin against the judgments of God abroad, when we take liberty *to inquire of the judgments of God abroad, and never make use of them*; as now to be asking what number die of the plague weekly, and our hearts tremble not at it, we lift not up our hearts to God, 'God be merciful to us,' 'Lord forgive our sins,' 'What will become of us?' We had need to make our accounts even. This is to talk amiss of God's judgments. It is a vein that men have naturally, to inquire after news of all sorts, be it the sharpest and bitterest that may be; though it be the destruction, and ruin, and death of other men; whatsoever it be they desire to hear it, if news. In the mean time there is no care to make use of it, which is directly that for which these men here are said to have talked amiss, 'No man spake aright.' Why? 'No man repented him of his wickedness,' &c., as we shall see afterwards. We should talk of the judgments of God to be bettered by them. We should 'learn righteousness when the judgments of God are abroad,' Isa. xxvi. 9, and the arrows that wound others we should make warning arrows to ourselves. Now when we triflingly only inquire of these things, and are not moved ourselves, we talk amiss of God's judgments.

Use. Let us labour to talk *of the judgments of God*, when they are abroad, as we should. In regard of God, to raise our hearts above all second causes, to see him in it. It is the hand of God, as the Scripture calls the plague, whatsoever the second causes are, whether it be the air, and the devil mingling himself ofttimes to corrupt the air, all is by God's permission and providence. We should look to the first wheel that leads the rest and sets them going. We should see God in all, and therefore speak reverently of him. And in regard of our brethren, to speak charitably of them, and think, it is the goodness of God that he hath not stricken us as he hath them. And when we speak of ourselves, when the judgments of God are on us, let us humble ourselves and justify God. We may complain, but it must be of ourselves and of our sins, that have brought judgments upon us, of our want of making use of the judgment of God upon others or upon ourselves. Lesser judgments would not serve turn; therefore God is fain to follow us with greater. Let us alway justify God and complain of ourselves, and then in regard of ourselves we 'speak aright' of the judgments of God. Let us never speak of the judgments of God but with affections fit for judgments, with awful affections. 'Shall the lion roar, and shall not the beasts of the forest tremble?' Hos. xi. 10. Shall we hear God roar in his judgments, 'and hear the trumpet blown,' and not be affected? We see here how God complains, that when 'he hearkened and heard, they spake not aright.' Let us therefore make conscience of all our words. We shall, if not now, yet at the day of judgment, 'give account for every idle word,' Mat. xii. 36, for every cruel word, as it is in the prophecy of Enoch, cited in the Epistle of Jude. But especially let us take heed of our words when we speak of God's judgments; for it is the not speaking aright of them that is here especially meant. 'I hearkened and heard, but they spake not aright.' So much for the evidence. Come we now to the next clause, God's complaint upon this evidence.

'No man repented him of his wickedness.'

They did not repent of their wickedness, and the fault was general: '*No man* repented.' The first yields this instruction,

Doct. That it is a state much offending God, not to repent when his judgments are threatened.

God will not suffer it long unpunished, to be impenitent when his judgments are abroad and threatened, much more when they have already seized* upon our brethren. For that is the end of all his judgments, to draw us near to him, to draw us out of the world, and out of our sinful courses. When therefore we answer not, God must take another course. What is the plague and other judgments but so many messengers sent to every one of us to knock? And our answer must be, 'Lord, I will repent of my evil ways,' 'I will turn from my evil courses and turn to thee.' If we give this answer, God will take away his judgments, or sanctify them, and that is better; but when there is no answer, the messenger will not be gone; God will add plagues upon plagues till we give our answer, till we repent and turn from our wicked ways.

Now that we may do this, we must be convinced thoroughly that the courses we live in are unprofitable, dangerous, hateful courses, and that the contrary state is better. For repentance is an after-wit,† and man being a reasonable creature, will turn‡ from his way except he see great reason why. Therefore there must be sound conviction that 'it is a bitter thing to offend God,' Jer. ii. 19. We must indeed be convinced by the Spirit of God; and the Spirit of God usually takes the benefit of affliction, affliction together with instruction. Instruction without affliction will do little good. Stripes and the word must go together, else we will not give God the hearing as we should. Therefore that we may be soundly convinced of our sins, we should desire God, especially in the hour of affliction, to help our souls by his Spirit, that we may be convinced that our courses are naught, that they are courses dishonourable to God and dangerous to ourselves; that sin defiles our souls; that it hinders our communion with God, which is the sweetest thing in the world; that sin puts a sting into all our troubles; that sin makes us afraid of that that should be comfortable to us, of death and judgment, and God's presence; that sin grieves the good Spirit of God, that would take up his lodging in us; that it quencheth the motions of the Spirit, that are sent as sweet messengers to us, to allure and comfort us; that sin grieves the good Spirit of God in others; that it grieves the good angels that are about us; that it gratifies none but the devil, the enemy of our salvation; that it defiles and stains our souls, wherein the image of God should shine; that it doth us more harm than all the things in the world besides—indeed, nothing hurts us but sin, because nothing but sin separates us from God; that it shuts heaven and opens hell, and so makes us afraid of death, lest death should open the gate to let us into hell; in a word, that it hinders all good, and is the cause of all ill. Let us consider of this, and work it on our hearts.

And consider withal our former courses, rip up our lives from our childhood, consider the sins of our youth, together with our present sins, that so we may the better stir up and awaken our consciences. Let us consider

* Spelled 'ceazed.'—G.

† That is, 'after-thought.'—G.

‡ Qu. 'will not turn'?—Ed.

whether we are now in a state wherein we could be content that God should send his judgments upon us. Consider how we have been scandalous* to others, how we have drawn others to sin, that the guilt of other men's sins will lie upon us. It may be we have repented, but have they? Consider the repetition of our sins, if we have not committed them again and again, and other circumstances that may aggravate them. Let us labour to work these things on our hearts, and desire the Spirit of God to convince our souls of the foulness and dangerousness of sin. When we sin against conscience, what do we but set the devil in the place of God? We make ourselves wiser than God. We leave God's ways, as if we could find better and more profitable and more gainful courses than his. Sound conviction of this will move us to repentance.

And let us be stirred up to repent presently. Doth not God now warn you? Is it not dangerous living one hour in a state that we would not die in? May not God justly strike us on the sudden? Do but purpose to live in sin one quarter of an hour; may we not be taken away in that quarter? Is not repentance the gift of God, and are not gifts given according to the good pleasure of the giver? Wait therefore for the gales of grace, and take them when they are offered. Grace is not like the tide, that ebbs and flows, that we know when it will come again when we see it go. No. God gives the gales of grace according to his good pleasure; therefore take the advantage of the present motions of the blessed Spirit.

The longer we live in any sin unrepented of, the more our hearts will be hardened; the more Satan takes advantage against us, the more hardly he is driven out of his old possession, the more just it may be with God to give us up from one sin to another. The understanding will be more dark upon every repetition of sin, and conscience will be more dulled and deaded. Those that are young, therefore, let them take the advantage of the youth, and strength, and freshness of their years to serve God. That which is blasted in the bud, what fruit may we look for from it afterwards? Alas! when we see the younger sort given to blaspheme and swear, to looseness and licentiousness, what old age may we look for there? Again, what welcome shall we expect, when we have sacrificed the best of our strength and the marrow of our years to our lusts, to bring our old age to God? Can this be any other than self-love? Such late repentance is seldom sound. It comes, I say, from self-love, and not from any change of heart. As in the humility of wretched persons, a little before the judge comes, though they have carried themselves as rebels before, yet then they will humble themselves, not out of any hatred to their courses, but out of fear of the judge. So it may be now thou art arraigned by God's judgments; thou forsakest thy sinful courses, not out of the hatred of thy sins—for if thou couldst thou wouldst sin eternally, and that is the reason sinners are punished eternally, because they would sin everlastingly—but thou seest thou art in danger to be pulled away by God's judgments. It is not out of love to grace, it is not from any change of nature that thou desirest to be a new creature, that thou admirest grace to be the best state, but it is to avoid danger; not that thou carest for the face of God, to be reconciled to him, but to avoid the present judgment.

And what a staggering will this be to conscience, when a man shall defer his repentance till God's judgments seize upon him! We see it is false for the most part, because such persons that are then humbled, when they recover they are as bad or worse than ever they were. Therefore an

* That is, 'stumblingblocks.'—G.

ancient saith well, 'He that is good only under the cross is never good' (a). It comes not from any change that God works, but merely from self-love. Therefore presently let us repent of those ways that God convinceth our conscience to be evil ways; God may strike us suddenly. Those that forget God, and care not for him now, it may be just with God to make them forget themselves, to strike them with frenzy, to take away the use of their memories then; and when sickness comes we shall have enough to do to conflict with sickness, we shall have enough to do to answer the doubts of conscience. Oh, it would upbraid them! We shall think it a hard matter then to have favour from God, whose worship we have despised, the motions of whose Spirit we have neglected and resisted. Conscience, after long hardening in sin, will hardly admit of comfort. It is a harder matter than it is taken for. Therefore, even to-day, presently, you that are young, now in the days of your youth, now in the spring of your years, repent you of your sins before old age comes, which indeed, as Solomon describes it, 'is an ill time' to repent in, Eccles. xii. 1. Alas! then a man can hardly perform civil duties; as we see in Barzillai, he complains that in his old age he could not take the comfort of the creatures, 2 Sam. xix. 32, *seq*. Therefore put not off this duty till then. And all, both young and old, now when the judgments of God are abroad in the world, take the advantage; return to God, renew your covenants, make your peace now. Now this danger doth warm our hearts a little, let us strike the iron now while it is hot; let us take the advantage of the Spirit now awakening us with this danger. Our hearts are so false and so dull, we have need to take all advantages of withdrawing ourselves from our sinful courses.

And to encourage us to do it, let us consider, if we do this, and do it in time, we shall have the sweetness of the love of God shed abroad in our hearts.

You will say, We shall lose the sweetness of sin; ay, but

1. *You shall have a most sweet communion with God*. One day of a repentant sinner, that is reconciled to God, is more comfortable than a thousand years of another man that is in continual fear of death and judgment. Oh, the sweet life of a Christian that hath made his peace with God! He is fit for all conditions: for life, for death, for everything. Now by this we shall have this grace and favour of God. The Lord will say unto us by his Spirit, 'I am your salvation,' Ps. xxxv. 3. And besides, you shall have his grace renewing and altering and changing you, framing you to a better course of life. And he will be so far from misliking any for their former sins, that he will give them cause to love him the more, as we see Luke vii. 47, 'She loved much, because she had much forgiven her.' Christ, we see, upbraided not any of his followers with their former sins. He regarded not what they had been formerly: Zaccheus the extortioner, Mary Magdalene, Matthew the publican, Peter that denied him. We never hear that he upbraided any of them. He doth not only vouchsafe mercy to Peter repenting, but advanceth him to his former office apostolical. So sweet a God have we to deal with! Let this encourage us.

2. Again, It is the way *to prevent God's judgments*, as we see in Nineveh and others. Put case we repent not: we cannot go safe in the city nor anywhere, but God may meet with us, and strike us with his arrow. The only way to prevent his judgments is to meet him speedily by repentance. This is the way, not only to turn away the wrath of God concerning eternal damnation, but outward judgments, as we see Joel ii. 12, *seq*., and many other places.

3. Then again, should we be stricken, if we have made our peace with God,

if we have repented, *all shall be welcome, all shall be turned to our good.* We know the sting is pulled out. If the sting of death be pulled out, if the malignity and poison of any sickness, be it the plague or whatsoever, be pulled out, why should we fear it? It comes in love, and shall be turned to our good; and in the mean time God sweetens it. Here is a grand difference between the children of God and others. If the judgment of God light upon a repentant person, it comes from favour and love, to correct him for his former sins. It is turned to good, and in the mean time it is sweetened with love, and mixed with comfort, and moderated, as it is Isa. xxvii. 7, 'Hath he afflicted thee as I afflicted others?' No. He moderates his judgments to his children; and not only moderates them, but sweetens them with comfort. If God do correct a repentant person, he is no loser by it, nay, he is a gainer. 'It is good for me that I have been afflicted,' Ps. cxix. 67. Oh the blessed estate of that person that repents and turns from his evil ways! But if a man do not repent, but live still in sin, what a state is he in! *God cares not for his prayers.* 'If I regard iniquity in my heart, God will not hear my prayers,' Ps. lxvi. 18. And what a state is a man in, when his prayers, that should beg for blessings, and avoid judgments, and procure deliverance, are not heard, 'but shall be turned into sin!' When God, that is 'a God hearing prayer,' shall not regard his prayer, what a case is this! Yet if we regard iniquity in our hearts, if we repent not of our sins, God will not regard our prayers.

Then, besides that, *there is a noise of fear in the unrepentant person's heart.* Wheresoever he goes, he is afraid of the plague, afraid of sickness, afraid of death, afraid of everybody. He knows he hath his heaven here: he hath not the sting of evils pulled out, therefore he is afraid he shall go from the terrors of conscience to the torments of hell. His conscience speaks terrible things to him. What a cursed state is this? How can he look with comfort any way? If he look to heaven, God is ready to pour the vials of his wrath, to execute his vengeance on him. If he look to the earth, he knows not how soon he shall be laid there, or that the earth may swallow him up. If he think of death, it strikes terror to him. Everything is uncomfortable to an unrepentant sinner. Let all this stir us up to this duty of repentance. It is the end why God sends his judgments. First, he warns us by his word. And if we neglect that, he sends judgments, and they seize on us. That is a second warning. And if lesser judgments will not warn us, then he sends greater, and all to make us repent. If we repent, we give the judgments their answer, and he will either remove them or sanctify them. So much for that. A word of the generality.

'No man.'

'No man repented of his evil ways.' We see, then,

Doct. That generality is no plea.

'We must not follow a multitude to do evil,' Exod. xxiii. 2. We must not follow the stream, to do as the world doth. Will any man reason thus? Now there die so many weekly of the plague. It is no matter whither I go. I will go now into any place, without any respect to my company, &c. Will he not reason, on the contrary, Therefore I will take heed, I will carry preservatives about me, and look to my company? Self-love will teach a man to reason so. The infection is great, therefore I will take the more heed. And will not spiritual wisdom teach us, the more spreading and infectious sin is, the more heed to take? 'When all flesh had corrupted their way, then came the flood,' Gen. vi. 12. Generality of sin makes way for sweeping judgments that takes all away. Therefore we have more reason to tremble when the infection of sin hath seized upon all, when 'no man repents of his wickedness.' A man should resolve, Surely I will come out of such company, as we see Lot departed out of Sodom, and David in his time 'was as a pelican in the wilderness,' Ps. cii. 6. I will rather go to heaven alone, than go to hell and be damned with a multitude. Multitude is no plea to a wise man. Shall we think it a means to increase danger in worldly things? and shall we think it a plea in spiritual things? It hath been the commendation of God's children, that they have striven against the stream and been good in evil times. 'Redeem the time, because the days are evil,' saith the apostle, Eph. v. 16. A carnal Christian saith, Do as the rest do; but saith David, 'Mine eyes gush out with rivers of waters, because men keep not thy law,' Ps. cxix. 136. Do not fear that you shall pass unrespected if you be careful to look to yourselves this way. If there be but one Lot in Sodom, one Noah and his family in the old world, he shall be looked to as a jewel among much dross. God will single him out as a man doth his jewels, when the rubbish is burnt. God will have a special care to gather his jewels. When a man makes conscience of his ways in ill times and ill company, God regards him the more for witnessing to his truth and standing for and owning his cause in ill times. It shews sincerity and strength of grace, when a man is not tainted with the common corruptions. 'No man repented.'

What was the cause of all this, that they were thus unrepentant, and that generally 'no man said,'

'What have I done?'

They did not say in their hearts and tongues, 'What have I done?' They were inconsiderate, they did not examine, and search, and try their ways. Here we see,

First, That a man can return upon himself; he can search and try his own ways, and cite, and arrest, and arraign himself, 'What have I done?' This is a prerogative that God hath given to the understanding creature. The reasonable soul, it can reflect upon itself, which is an act of judgment. The brute creatures look forward to present objects; they are carried to present things, and cannot reflect. But man hath judgment to know what he hath done and spoken, to sit upon his own doings, to judge of his own actions. God hath erected a tribunal in every man; he hath set up conscience for a register, and witness, and judge, &c. There are all the parts of judicial proceeding in the soul of man. This shews the dignity of man; and considering that God hath set up a throne and seat of judgment in the heart, we should labour to exercise this judgment.

Secondly, God having given man this excellent prerogative to cite himself and to judge his own courses, *when man doth not this, it is the cause of all mischief, of all sin and misery.* Alas! the vile heart of man is prone to think, it may be God hath decreed my damnation, and he might make me better if he would. But why dost thou speak thus? O wicked man, the fault is in thyself, because thou dost not what thou mightst do. Hath not God set up a judgment-seat in thy heart, to deliberate of thine own courses, whether thou dost well or ill? And thy own conscience, if thou be not an atheist and besotted, tells thee thou dost ill, and accuseth thee for it. An ordinary swearer, that by atheistical acquaintance and poisonful breeding is accustomed to that sin, if he did consider, What good shall I get by this? by provoking God, who hath threatened that I shall not go guiltless, and that 'I shall give an account for every idle word,' much more of every idle oath? the consideration of this would make him judge and condemn himself, and repent and amend his ways.

Thirdly. The exercising of this judgment, *it makes a man's life lightsome.* He knows who he is and whither he goes. It makes him able to answer for what he doth at the judgment-seat of God. It makes him do what he doth in confidence, it perfects the soul every way.

Fourthly, Again, Whatsoever we do without this consideration, *it is not put upon our account for comfort.* When we do things upon judgment, it is with examination whether it be according to the rule or no. Our service of God is especially in our affections, when we joy, and fear, and delight aright. Now how can a man do this without consideration? For the affections, wheresoever they are ordinate and good, they are raised up by judgment. They are never good but when they are regular and according to judgment. When judgment raiseth up the affections, and we see cause why we should delight in God, and love him and fear him more than anything in the world, they are then an effectual part of divine worship; but else they are flat, and dead, and dull, if we waken them not with consideration. The heart follows the judgment. The brain and the heart sympathise, when we see cause and reason to love, and fear, and worship God. We must 'love God with all our mind,' that is, with our best understanding. We must see reason why we do so.

Therefore let us labour to use our understanding more this way. Is our understanding and judgment given us to plot for the world, to be judicious for the things of this life only? No; but to be wise for the main end, to glorify God, to save our souls, to get out of the corruption of nature, to maintain our communion with God every day more and more. The end of our living in the world is to begin heaven upon earth; so to live here as that we may live for ever in heaven. Whatsoever is done in order to this end is good; but nothing can be done to this end but upon due consideration. Let us improve our judgments for that end. They are principally given us, not for particular ends, to get this or that man's favour, to get wealth, &c., but to use all as they may serve the main. We know not how short a time we shall enjoy these things; and further than they serve for the main, we shall have no comfort of them ere long. Our projects should be to gain glory to God, and to bring ourselves and others to heaven. There is excellent use of this consideration. This way it is one main way to repentance. We see here, 'No man repenteth,' because 'no man said, What have I done?'

Now if we would practise this duty, we must labour to avoid the hindrances. The main hindrances of this consideration are,

(1.) *The rage of lusts,* that will not give the judgment leave to consider of a man's ways; but they are impetuous, commanding, and tyrannous, carrying men, as we shall see in the next clause, 'as the horse rusheth into the battle.' We see many carried to hell that never enjoyed themselves, but are alway under some base pleasure. When the devil hath filled them with one pleasure, then they project for another, and never take time to say, 'What have I done?' Oh the tyranny of original corruption! If we had in our eye the vile picture of our nature, that carries us to things present, to profits and pleasures, and gives us not liberty and leisure to bethink ourselves, would we do as we do? Alas! we see some men so haunted with their lusts that they cannot be alone, they cannot sleep; and when they are awake they must have music, as that king when he massacred a world of men, he could not be quiet a whit, conscience raged so.* When men follow their pleasures, they rob them of themselves. Therefore they are said in Scripture to be madmen, and fools without wit. They are so taken up with the rage of their lusts that they have not liberty to enjoy themselves, they have no time for consideration.

(2.) And then another hindrance is *too much business*, when men are distracted with the things of this life. They are overloaded with cares, with Martha's part, and so neglect Mary's part. This makes men toil and droil† for the world, and never consider where they are nor whither they go, how it shall be with them when they go hence, how the case stands with them before God, whether they be gotten out of the cursed state of nature that we are all born in. They never think of this, but all the marrow and strength of their souls is eaten out with the world. Those that in their youth followed their lusts, when they come to years are taken up with the world, and slight religion. Their minds are employed how to get the favour of this man and that, and so have not leisure to consider what will become of their souls. Therefore too much distraction with the things of the world is joined with drunkenness: 'Be not overcome with the cares of this life, with surfeiting and drunkenness,' saith Christ, Luke xxi. 34.

(3.) Then, *it is a secret and hard action;* because it is to work upon a man's self. It is an easy matter to talk of others, to consider other men's ways. You shall have men's tongues ready to speak of other men; they do so and so. And thus they feed themselves with talking of other men, and in the mean time neglect the consideration of their own state. And again, it is a plausible thing. He that talks of other men's faults gives an intimation that he is innocent, and he had need be so. It is easy and plausible. Men glory in it. It feeds corrupt nature to talk of other men's faults, but to come home to a man's self, that is a hard thing. It is without ostentation or applause. The world doth not applaud a man for speaking of his own faults. Men are not given to retired actions. They care not for them, unless they have sound hearts; and this being a retired action, that hath no glory nor credit with it, men are loath to come to it.

(4.) Then, again, it is not only hard and secret, but this returning upon a man's self, *it presents to a man a spectacle that is unwelcome.* If a man consider his own ways, it will present to him a terible object. Therefore as the elephant troubles the waters, that he may not see his own visage, so men trouble their souls, that they may not see what they are. They shall see such a deal of malice and self-love, and fear and distrust, that they would not have others in the world to see for anything. But it is good to see it; for repentance and consideration it is physic, it is sharp but wholesome. It is better to have the physic a day than to have the sickness and disease all the year. So this consideration and repentance, though it be sharp, yet take it down, for it will prevent God's eternal judgment; as the apostle saith, 'If we would judge and condemn ourselves, we should not be condemned with the world,' 1 Cor. xi. 31. What an excellent thing is this, that we may keep sessions in our own souls, and so need not be called to God's assizes! Men are called to that, because they slubber over and neglect this. Men will not keep this sessions in their own hearts—which they might do not only quarterly, but daily—and thereby they make work for God. Is it not better now to unrip our consciences by consideration and repentance, than to have all ripped up then, when the devil shall stand

* Cf. note, Vol. I. page 149.—G.

† That is, 'drudge.'—G.

by to accuse us, who will say, This was done by my instigation; and it is so; and our own consciences shall take part with the devil, and accuse us also? It will be little for our ease to make God our judge. We might save the labour by putting conscience to its office now, to examine our ways every day, especially now, when God calls for it by his judgments. Repentance is the covenant of the gospel, and repentance depends upon this consideration. So much for that. 'No man repented him of his wickedness, saying, What have I done?' But did they stay here? No; it follows,

'Every one turns to his course, as the horse rusheth into the battle.'

Every one hath his course, his way, whether good or evil. The course of a wicked man it is a smooth way perhaps, but it is a going from God; it leads from him. And where doth it end? for every way hath its end. It is a going from God to hell. There all the courses of wicked men end. Examine, then, where thy course begins, and where it ends; from what thou walkest, and to what; whither thy course aims; consider where thy speeches and actions are like to end. The specification and denomination of our ways to be good or evil is especially from the end. The wicked they take their courses, smooth wide courses, the broad beaten way, where they may have elbow-room enough, though it end in hell and destruction. But the wicked and their ways are both hated of God. Otherwise it is with God's children. They may sometimes step into ill ways, but they have not an ill course; and God doth not judge a man by a step, but by his course and way. Therefore consider what is the tenor of thy life. Is thy way good? Oh, it is an excellent thing to be in a good way! for a man every day to repent of his sins, to make his peace with God, to practise the duties of Christianity in his general calling, and in his particular calling to call upon God for a blessing. Such a man's way is good; it hath a good end. Perhaps he may step out of his way by the temptations of Satan, but that is not his course. The best man in the world for a passion on the sudden may step into an ill way; as David, when he determined to kill Nabal, but it was not David's way. Therefore we see how soon he was put off with a little counsel, and how thankful he was: 'Blessed be the Lord, and blessed be thou, and blessed be thy counsel,' &c., 1 Sam. xxv. 32. His way and course was another way. And so on the other side the wickedest man in the world may set a step in a good way for a fit, a very Saul may be amongst the prophets, and speak excellently and divinely; but all this while he is out of his way. His way is a course of wickedness, to which therefore he will soon betake himself again; as it is here said of these men, 'They turned to their own courses.'

'As the horse rusheth into the battle.'

Here it is comparatively set down. If you would see how the 'horse rusheth into the battle,' it is lively and divinely expressed, Job xxxix. 19, by God himself: 'Hast thou given the horse strength? hast thou clothed his neck with thunder? Canst thou make him afraid as a grasshopper? the glory of his nostrils is terrible. He paweth in the valley, and rejoiceth in his strength; he goeth on to meet the armed men. He mocketh at fear, and is not affrighted; neither turneth he back from the sword. The quiver rattleth against him, the glittering spear and the shield. He swalloweth the ground with fierceness and rage; neither believeth he that it is the sound of the trumpet. He saith among the trumpets, Ha, ha! and he smelleth the battle afar off, the thunder of the captains, and the shouting.' There you have an excellent description of this creature's fierceness—the wit of man hath not such expressions—and how 'he rusheth into the battle.' God, to abase wicked men, compares them here to the horse; not for that which is good in him, but for their violence in ill courses. They rush into them 'as the horse rusheth into the battle.' Now, the horse rusheth into the battle, (1.) *eagerly*, as you see him described in the place of Job; and (2.) *desperately*, he will not be pulled away by any means; and then (3.) *dangerously*, for he rusheth upon the pikes, and ofttimes falls down suddenly dead. He regards not the pikes, nor guns, nor nothing, but rusheth on the danger. Herein wicked men are like unto the horse, going on in their course eagerly, desperately, dangerously.

1. *They go on eagerly.* It is meat and drink unto them: 'they cannot sleep until they have done wickedness.' They plot and study it; it is their delight. They are not in their element but when they are talking wickedly and corruptly, or deceiving, or satisfying their desires, the ambition and lusts of their corrupt nature. They can no more live out of these courses than the fish can live out of the water. Therefore they go eagerly upon them.

2. And as they go eagerly, so *desperately and irreclaimably too;* nothing will restrain them, no thorns nor troubles that can lie in their way. Though God hedge in their ways with thorns, they break through all, Hosea ii. 6. Even as Balaam, he would go on though there were a sword drawn before him, he was more brutish and unreasonable than his poor beast; the very sword of the angel could not move that covetous wretch to go back. So it is with every wicked man, he goes on desperately, nothing will keep him back and reclaim him. Though God take many courses to do it, by his ministers, magistrates, by the motions of his Spirit, by his judgments threatened, by judgments executed upon others, and upon themselves sometimes, yet they are so eager upon their sins, all this will not beat them off. They love their sins better than their souls; nor is it only open riotous persons that thus rush into sins, but civil* rebellious persons also, that bless themselves in their ways, and it may be live as irreligiously as the other. Take a covetous or an ambitious man: he sacrificeth all to get such a place, &c. Such a man mocks Christ, as the Pharisees mocked him, notwithstanding all his good sermons and miracles. He goes on desperately, nothing will hold him. He breaks through all bars and oppositions. He cracks his conscience, grieves the good motions of the Spirit, despiseth good counsel, and will venture upon the outward breach of laws sometimes, rather than he will be defeated of his designs.

3. And as they go eagerly and desperately, so *dangerously too;* for is it not dangerous to provoke God? to rush upon the pikes? to run against thorns? 'Do you provoke me to jealousy,' saith God, 'and not yourselves to destruction'? 1 Cor. x. 22. No. They go both together. If you provoke me to anger, it will be to your own ruin. In Lev. xxvi. 23, 'God will walk stubbornly to them as they have done to him; and he will be froward with the froward,' Ps. xviii. 26. Those that are rebellious sinners, whom no bonds will hold, no counsel, that break all laws, as the man possessed with the devil brake his chains, the time will come that when God executes his wrath he will be too good for them, the devil will be too good for them, hell will be too good for them, conscience will tear them in pieces, and the judgment of God will seize on them. The way of wicked men is a wretched, a desperate, and dangerous course. Thou art

* That is, 'moral.'—G.

stubborn against God, and he is so against thee. He will do to thee as thou doest to him. Who are we? 'Are we stronger than God'? 1 Cor. x. 23. Careless, atheistical persons think they are. Tush! they can wind out well enough: but they will find it otherwise. 'Do we provoke the Lord to jealousy? Are we stronger than he'? saith the apostle. Let us lay this to heart.

We see here again how sin hath clean defaced the image of God in man. 'Man being in honour,' he would become like God. He was weary of his subordination. He would be absolute; and because he would be like God, God made him like the beast; and it is worse to be like the beast than to be a beast. For the beast in his own condition follows the instinct of nature; but to be like a beast, is for a man to unman himself, to degrade himself to a baser condition than God made him in; and when a man doth this, he is either in malice like the devil, or in licentiousness as the beast is. He is alway like the devil or a beast till he be a new creature. And that our nature is come to this, we are beholding to our own yielding to Satan and his counsel. We 'rush as the horse into the battle.' Therefore let us beware of this. 'Be ye not as the horse and mule,' &c., saith David, Ps. xxxii. 9. Who would not labour to be in a better condition? to be a new creature, to be changed by the powerful ordinances and Spirit of God? So much for that briefly. Come we now to the last clause.

'Yea, the stork in the heavens knoweth her appointed times; and the turtle and the crane and the swallow observe the time of their coming; but my people know not the judgment of the Lord.'

Here is another expression comparative, or rather superlative. He compares them to the stork and turtle, the crane and swallow; and prefers these poor creatures, in wisdom and providence, as going before men. 'But my people know not the judgment of the Lord.' There needs no great explication of the words. Judgment is directive or corrective.

The directive is the law of God; setting down God's judicious* course. This you shall do, or if you do not this you shall be punished. When we obey not God's directive course, we meet with his corrective; for judgment is the stablishing of judgment. Judgment of correction is the stablishing of judgment of direction. God's laws must be performed. They are not scare-crows. If we avoid the one, we shall run into the other. If we do not meet him in the judgment of his directive law, we must be met with in his law corrective—if we be good men—or destructive if we be bad men. Now here, I take it, he means especially the judgment of correction, the time of visitation. It was a dangerous time, as it is now among us. They were already under several heavy judgments, as famine, &c. We see in the next verse, 'there was no vines, no grapes,' &c., all failed. And besides, a far heavier judgment was ready to come upon them. They were ready to be carried into Babylon, 'and they knew not the judgment of the Lord.'

'They knew not;' that is, they did not make use of it; for in divinity, things are not known when they are not affected.† God knoweth all things, but when he doth not affect and delight in us, he is said 'not to know us.' So we are said not to know, when we do not affect and make use of things. 'They know not the judgment of the Lord.' They were not ignorant. He had told them of vengeance; he had told them that they should be carried into captivity; but they made not that use they should of it. Therefore they

* That is, 'judicial.'—G. † That is, 'chosen,' = attended to.—G.

are said not to know it. So the old world. It is said they did not know of the flood. Certainly Noah had told them of it. But when they made not a right use of it, but went on brutishly, they knew it not. It is all one not to know it at all, and not to make use of it. Wicked men think they know God, and they know religion well enough ; ay, but what use do they make of it in their particular course ? That which we do not use we do not know in religion. If ill be discovered, and be not avoided by thee, thou art a brutish, senseless creature. Thou dost not know it, and so thou shalt be dealt with. 'They know not the judgment of the Lord ;' that is, they will not know it ; it was affected ignorance. The words being thus unfolded, here, first, we see,

That God confounds the proud dispositions of wicked men by poor, silly creatures—the crane, the turtle, the swallow, and the like.

What their wisdom is we see by experience. In winter, to fly from hard and cold parts to those where there is a spring. They are here in the moderate season ; and when the summer is gone, they go to a more moderate air, where they may live better. For the life is the chief good of such poor creatures, and their happiness being determined in their life, they labour to keep that. They have an instinct put in them by God to preserve their being by removing from place to place, and to use that that may keep life.

Now, man is made for a better life ; and there be dangers concerning the soul in another world, yet he is not so wise for his soul and his best being as the poor creatures are to preserve their being by the instinct of nature. When sharp weather comes they avoid it, and go where a better season is, and a better temper of the air ; but man, when God's judgments are threatened and sent on him, and God would have him part with his sinful courses, and is ready to fire him, and to force him out of them, yet he is not so careful as the creatures. He will rather perish and die, and rot in his sins, and settle upon his dregs, than alter his course. So he is more sottish than the silly creatures. He will not go into a better estate, to the heat, to the sunbeams to warm him. He will not seek for the favour of God, to be cherished with the assurance of his love, as the poor creature goeth to the sun to warm it till it be over hot for it. Man should know what is good and what is evil. The new creature doth so. For with the change of nature there is a divine wisdom put into the soul of a Christian, that teacheth him what is good and what is evil ; that he may be careful to avoid the evil ; that he may discern of things that differ ; that he may say, This is good for my soul, and all the world shall not scoff me out of that that I know to be good. With their profane jesting, they shall not drive me from that is good ; and for courses that are ill, they shall not draw me with all their allurements. I know what belongs to the good of my soul better than so. It should be thus with Christians, to be wise for their spiritual being, as the poor creatures, the stork, and the crane, and the turtle, are to preserve their poor life here with as much comfort as they can.

God takes out of the book of nature things useful, to insert them into his divine book ; because now no man shall be ashamed to learn of the creatures. Now, since the fall, man must learn of the poor creatures, and such a dunce is man, it is well for him if he can learn of the ant, and crane, and turtle ; and therefore doth God take lessons out of the book of nature, and put them into his book, to teach us to furnish ourselves with divine mysteries and instructions from the creatures. And indeed a gracious heart will make use of everything, and have his thoughts raised with them. As the prophet Jeremiah here, he shames them by the example of the creatures. But of this by the way.

The thing most material, with which I will end, is this:

Doct. That God, after long patience, hath judgments to come on people; and it should be the part of people to know when the judgment is coming.

There is a season when God will forbear no longer in this world. 'They know not the judgment of the Lord.' The meaning is not, in hell, though that may come in: that is implied in all; but 'they know not the judgment of the Lord,' that is, they know not the judgments that are coming. When judgments are coming, God opens the hearts and understandings of his people to know them; as there is an instinct in the creatures to know when there will be hard weather.

Quest. But how shall we know when a judgment is near hand?

Ans. 1. *By comparing the sins with the judgments.* If there be such sins that such judgments are threatened for, then as the thread followeth the needle, and the shadow the body, so those judgments follow such and such courses. For God hath knit and linked these together. All the power in the world and hell cannot unlink them, sin and judgment; judgment either correcting us to amendment, or confounding us to perdition. God, therefore, having threatened in the Scriptures such judgments to such sins; if we live in such and such sins, we may look for such judgments. Thus a wise man, by laying things together, the sins with the judgments, though he cannot tell the particular, yet he may know that some heavy judgment is at hand.

2. Again, There is a nearer way to know a judgment, *when it hath seized on us in part already.* He that is not brutish and sottish, and drunk with cares and sensuality, must needs know a judgment when it is already inflicted, when part of the house is on fire. We see judgment hath seized now on the places where we live, and therefore we cannot be ignorant of it.

3. Again, We may know it *by the example of others.* God keeps his old walks. Therefore it is said, 'As it was in the days of Noah, so shall it be when the Son of man comes: they were eating, and drinking, and marrying, and knew not till the flood came and took them away,' Mat. xxiv. 38, 39. God will be like himself, if sinners be like themselves. He will not change, if they change not; but will deal alike with them in his judgments, as he hath dealt with others. What ground have we to hope for immunity more than others? We may rather expect it less, because we have their examples; and so they wanted those examples to teach them which we have. In Jer. vii. 12, saith God, 'Consider, look to Shiloh, and see what I did there: so will I do to you.' So likewise the judgments on Jerusalem are a fearful spectacle for us. These and other examples may help us to judge of our condition in regard of approaching judgments.

4. Again, *General security is a great sign of some judgment coming.* In the days of Noah, there was a general sensual security. Notwithstanding the prophet foretold them of the deluge, they were eating, &c., and knew not till the flood came and took them away. So likewise, if we eat, and drink, and marry, and build, and be negligent and careless of making our peace with God, especially when warning is given us, it is a sign that some judgment, either personal on ourselves, or generally on the place we live in, will come upon us. There is never more cause of fear, than when there is least fear. The reason is, want of fear springs from infidelity, for faith stirs up fearfulness and care to please God: 'By faith Noah, moved with

fear,' or reverence, 'builded the ark,' Heb. xi. 7. It proceeds from infidelity, not to be afraid when there is cause. Again, where there is no fear, there is no care. So the root of the want of fear is infidelity, and the spring that comes from it is carelessness, which always goes before destruction. When men care not what becomes of them: if God be pleased, so it is; if judgment come, so it is; the care* is taken. 'When men thus say, Peace, peace, then cometh destruction.' It is a terrible thing for a state or a city, or a particular person, to be careless; for the life of a Christian it is a watching, as well as a warring, condition. He must be alway on his guard. Therefore he must not be careless, 'and say, Peace, when God speaks no peace.'

5. Again, We may know that some judgment is coming, *by the universality and generality of sin, when it spreads over all.* When there is a general infection of sin, we may well fear the infection of the air. Sin hath infected the souls of men; therefore no wonder if God, in the plague, have a hand in infecting their bodies. We see here, before the prophet threatened this destruction, there was a generality of sin. In the 10th verse of this chapter, he cries out against the covetousness and false dealing of the priests and prophets, and men of all estates. And so also chapter v. ver. 4, 'The poor they were naught:' they were poor in grace and goodness, as well as in condition. Then saith he, 'I will see if there be any goodness in the great ones: I will get me to the great men.' Ver. 5, &c., 'They have known the way of the Lord, and the judgment of their God; but they have broken the yoke, and burst the bonds.' When poor and rich, great and small, when all are sottish and brutish, 'when all flesh had corrupted their ways,' Gen. vi. 12, as it was before the flood, then judgment must needs come. Surely generality of sin makes way for generality of judgment. As the deluge of sin made way for the deluge of water, so the overflow of sin will make way for a flood of fire. God will one day purge the world with fire.

But now for particular sins, whereby we may know when judgment is coming. These they are:

(1.) First, Injustice and formality in religion. When men are generally unjust, destruction is near; and indeed, how can a Christian soul look upon men's courses abroad in these regards, 'but he shall weep in secret,' Lam. i. 16? Is there not a general injustice? Will not men get any cause, so they have a good purse? Is not innocency trodden down ofttimes?

2. And so for religion. It is generally neglected. Indifferency and formality they are the sins of the times. Here is a sweet progress. In Queen Elizabeth's time, we began with zeal and earnestness; but now we begin to stagger whether religion is the better. We will join and put them together, that God hath put an eternal difference between, 'light and darkness.' Is this our progress after so much teaching, to put off God with formality, and deny the power?

(3.) Again, Another particular sin foreshewing judgment, is *persecution of religion and religious men.* When God is worshipped with conscience as he should be, what imputations are laid on it! I need not speak. The world knows well enough. Can God endure this, when conscience of his service shall go under the brand of opposition? God is much beholding to the times, when there is nothing so heartily hated as that. There are many things loathsome, as deboishness,† &c. But what is so eagerly and heartily hated as the power of godliness? That which they have been known to do

* Qu. 'no care'?—Ed.

† That is, 'debauchery.'—G.

for conscience, hath been matter of reproach and ruin almost to many men. If a man will not prostitute his conscience to a creature, to make an idol of him, to set him highest, if he will not be buxom, and crack his conscience for a creature, he is scarce thought fit to live in the world. Will God suffer this, if these things be not amended? If anything be good in religion, the more the better, the more exact Christian the better. Exactness in other things is best. Is to be best in the best naught, when to be best in that which is not so good carries away the commendations? In 1 Thess. ii. 16, 'The wrath of God is come on them to the utmost; God they hate and they are contrary to all men.' This is a forerunner of destruction, the spiteful opposing of goodness. God will not endure it long.

(4.) And so when men will *go on incorrigibly in sin*, as these here, 'they rush as the horse into the battle;' when they will not be reclaimed, it is a forerunner of destruction. Alas! the ministers of God strive with men, 'but they break off the cords,' Ps. ii. 3, and cry, Tush! they are silly men; shall we yield to them? We know what is for our gain, and profit, and credit in the world better than so. Let us look to that, and not be hampered in these religious bonds. No; we are wiser than so. Thus when men are incorrigible, and account the wisdom of God stark folly, it is a sign of destruction. There is an excellent place for this, Ezek. xxiv. 12–14, 'She hath wearied herself with lies, and her great scum went not out of her: she would not have her filthiness taken from her. In her filthiness is lewdness; because I would have purged thee,' with the word and the preaching of judgments, 'and thou wouldst not be purged; therefore thou shalt not be purged till thou die, until I cause my fury to rest upon thee. I the Lord have spoken it: it shall come to pass, I will do it.' When God goes about to purge us by his word, and we will not amend our ways, we will not stoop, but 'strengthen an iron sinew, and a whore's forehead,' Jer. iii. 3. We will not be purged, nay, saith God, thou shalt not be purged till I purge thee out of the world to hell, till my fury rest on thee. I the Lord have spoken it, it shall come to pass, Isa. xlvi. 11. There is another notable place, Prov. xxix. 1, 'He that is a man of reproof,' that is, a man that is sermon-proof, that is often reproved and yet carries himself impudently and hardens his heart, and stiffens his neck, 'he shall suddenly be destroyed.' He doth not mean but that he had warning enough; but because after long warning he hardens his neck, he shall suddenly be destroyed, when he looks not for it, 'and that without remedy.' There is the same phrase in 2 Chron. xxxvi. 16, 'There was no remedy,' when they did not regard God's ministers, that directed them the way to heaven, but would live in rebellion against the means of salvation. Then saith God, 'there was no remedy.' God sent his messengers betimes, and had compassion on his people. He would not have had them perish. 'They trifled with him and mocked his messengers,' accounted them weak men. They despised his word, and misused his prophets; and then the Lord's wrath rose against his people, and 'there was no remedy.' So when people are as those here in the text, that 'they rush as the horse into the battle,' that they are sermon-proof, that when every sermon they hear, as the hammer on the smith's anvil, makes them harder and harder, as Moses speaking to Pharaoh increased the hardness of his heart, it is a sign of destruction.

Now whether it be so or no, I leave it to your particular consciences. We that are ministers tell you of your filthiness, of your profaning the name of God, and contempt of God's word. Whether have we gained upon you or no? Who hath left an oath? Who hath left his wicked courses and entered into a nearer communion with God for all our teaching? Blessed is that man. It is a sign God will not destroy him. It is a sign that in the general visitation God will regard that man. But, alas! we may almost complain with Jeremiah in his prophecy, Jer. v. 1, where he runs up and down to seek a man. Alas! they are very few. They are thick sown, but come thin up, that obey the ordinance of God. It is some comfort that men will submit to the ordinance, that they will come to hear. Some good may be learned. It is better than to keep out of the compass of God's law, as those men do that pretend they can read sermons at home, and so will teach God a course to bring men to heaven. There is hope of men when they submit to God's ordinance. But, I beseech you, how are you affected now for the present? How do you come now into the presence of God, if you will not amend and resolve to enter into a new course? He that is often reproved and will not come in, 'judgment will come suddenly on him without all remedy.' And it is good it should be without remedy; because it is without excuse. You cannot plead, and say that there were not prophets among you. If the heathens were hardened and given up to destruction,—'the wrath of God is revealed from heaven against them,' Rom i. 18, because they lived in a course of rebellion against the light of nature;—shall you, that have the light of nature, and the word of God, and the motions of his Spirit too, think to live in rebellion and not be accountable for it? It shall be easier for them that never heard of the word of God. Where God hath magnified his mercy, he will exalt judgment. Those that are lift up to heaven in privileges, shall be cast down to hell. 'Woe unto thee, Capernaum,' &c., Mat. xi. 21. The more in privileges, the more in judgment if they be abused.

(5.) Again, Another particular sin whereby we may discern a judgment coming is, *unfruitfulness under the means;* as the fig-tree, when it was digged and dunged, and yet was unfruitful, then it was near a curse. In Heb. vi. 3, the ground that is tilled and manured, and hath the rain falling on it, it is then 'near unto cursing' if it bring not forth. Perhaps a heathen, a pagan, if he were under the means, would be fruitful; therefore there might be hope of him. But those that are under the means, under the sunshine of the gospel, under the influence of it, the Spirit working on their hearts; and yet they live in the sin of unfruitfulness, it makes way for judgment. 'The axe is laid to the root,' Mat. iii. 10. When men are taught, then the instrument of vengeance is laid to the root, and down they go if they bring not forth good fruit.

Sins of omission, when that all hath been taught, are sufficient to bring a man to judgment. At the last judgment, 'you have not visited me in prison, you have not relieved the poor,' &c., will be evidence enough to cast a man into hell, Mat. xxv. 43. And the like may be said of the omission of other duties. When a man is called to place, when he hath opportunity to do good, 'he hath a price in his hand, and yet hath no heart to lay it out to his power.' God hath made him a steward, and yet he is unfruitful, and labours to undermine and ruin the state of others. What can such a man look for but the judgment of God to light on him first or last? If not present judgment on his body, yet to be given up to hardness of heart, and so to hell, which is worst of all.

(6.) Nay more, *decay in our first love* is a forerunner of judgment, when we love not God as we were wont. In Rev. ii. 5, 'I will take away thy candlestick, because thou hast left thy first love.' Is there not such a plenty and depth in good things, especially of the gospel, whereby our sins are pardoned, and grace is given? Is there not that sweetness in them whereby to gain our love more and more? Is there not a necessity to renew our peace? Why should we decay in our love? The things of the gospel are so excellent and so necessary, that when God sees them undervalued, it is a forerunner of judgment. Let us take heed of decay in our affections. When there is no zeal for the truth, it is an ill sign.

It is a good sign for the present that God hath some blessing for us, that now in our public meetings there is regard to religion; and that, in the first place, there is some zeal for the cause of God against those that would wrong the cause of religion. We have some cause to hope in respect of that. And let every one labour to stir up the Spirit of God, and study how he may do and receive good, and be fruitful and warm in his affections, considering what excellent blessings we enjoy in the gospel. What is the glory of the kingdom we live in above popery? Our religion that we have, the sunshine of the gospel. Now the riches of Christ are unfolded; we have the key of heaven, heaven opened; what glorious times are these! The glory of the times is the manifestation of the gospel; and shall we grow in the decay of our love? Is there not cause to grow in love to the gospel, when God hath taken it from others and hath given it to us? Now, idolatry is where true religion was; and the mass is said where God was religiously worshipped in other places and countries. Shall God so deal with us, and shall we not be in love with that truth? Since we have had the truth, what peace and plenty have we had! And if ever we lose it, it will go with other things. If God takes away the truth, away goes our peace and prosperity. He will not take it away alone. It came not alone, and he will not take it away alone. Doubtless it must needs make way for judgment, when our love to so precious a jewel as the gospel shall begin to die and decay, when we shall begin to slight and disregard it. And so for any particular man that hath had good things in him. If they now begin to decay, it is an ill sign, that God is fitting him for judgment.

Well, but what shall we do when judgments are coming? We see judgments are like to come, nay, are in part come. The plague of pestilence hath seized on us already; and then war is threatened, and that by enemies that have been foiled before. Foiled enemies are dangerous enemies, if they be proud. Now we have proud enemies that have been foiled, and idolatrous withal, and what mercy can we look for from them? God fought against them for us from heaven in some measure, and they being cruel provoked enemies, are the less likely to shew any mercy.* God is indeed so merciful to us yet, that he hath taken us into his own hands, rather than to give us up to the malice and fury of idolatrous enemies. But yet those that can lay things together, and consider the times, they shall see there is more cause of fear than is taken to heart.

Well, and in this case, what shall we do?

1. First, In the interim between the threatening and the execution. There are some judgments in the cloud, and the storm seems to hang over us, and the sword of the pestilence is drawn over our heads by the destroying angel, though he hath not yet stricken us in our particular. Now in the time between the threatening and the execution; *oh improve it, make use of this little time; get into covenant with God; hide yourselves in the providence and promises of God; make your peace, defer it no longer.*

2. And secondly, *Mourn for the sins of the time*, that when any judg-

* Spain.—G.

ment shall come, you may be marked with those that mourn. Take heed of the errors and sins of the times, lest, when a judgment comes, you be swept away in the general judgments. But let us rather have our part with those that mourn, that God may give us our lives for a prey.

3. And thirdly, *Be watchful.* Practise that duty, We have the plague to put us in mind of it, besides the threatening of dangers by enemies abroad. If we will not watch now and stand upon our guard, when will we? Let us be watchful to do all the good we can, to be fruitful, to be good stewards, to have large hearts. The time may come that we may be stripped of all, and we know not how soon. Having but a little time, let us do good in it; study all opportunities in these times; rouse up our sluggish souls. Fear, it is a waking affection. Jacob, when his brother Esau was ready to seize on him, 'he could not sleep that night.' We know not how soon the hand and arrow of God may strike us, besides other judgments. Let us shake off security, and do everything we do sincerely to God. We may come to God to make our account, we know not how soon. Let us do everything as in his presence, and to him. In our particular callings, let us be conscionable,* and careful, and fruitful. Let us do all in our places to God, and not to the world, or to our own particular gain, but do it as those that must give account ere long to God. Now, God threateneth us to come and give our account; who can be secure he shall have life for a week, or for one day? We cannot. 'Our times are in God's hands,' Ps. xxxi. 15. We came into the world in his time, and we must go out in his time. But now we have less cause to hope for long life. This is to make a right use of the judgment of God, to be watchful in this kind.

And withal, let us be good husbands now in the interim. Between the threatening and the execution of the judgment, let us store up comforts from the promises of God, and store up the comforts of a good life. We shall have more comfort of the means we have bestowed wisely than of that we shall leave behind us. Thus if we do, come what will, we are prepared. Many holy and heavenly men have been visited with pestilential sickness. Hezekiah was a king, and his was a pestilential sickness; and many holy divines of late, and other Christians, have been swept away by the sickness —Junius, and other rare men of excellent use in the church (*b*). Therefore let us labour to get into the favour of God; make use of our renewing our covenant for the time to come. That is one end of fasting now, to renew our covenants, to remake them for the time to come. And then come what will, and welcome, life or death; for there is a blessing hid in the most loathsome sickness and death. If we come to heaven, it is no matter by what way, though the body 'be sown in dishonour.' We may die of a noisome disease, that we cannot have our friends near us, yet 'the body shall rise again in honour,' 1 Cor. xv. 43. What matter, saith St Paul, 'if by any means I may come to the resurrection of the dead;' by fair death or foul death, it is no matter. And if so be that God makes not good his promise of particular protection of our bodies from contagion, &c., it is no matter. We have a general promise 'that he will be our God.' 'He is the God of Abraham,' the God of the dead as well as of the living, Mat. xxii. 32. He is a God that is everlasting in the covenant of grace, in life and death, and for ever. If we be entered into the covenant of grace, it holds for ever. And when all other promises fail, and all things in the world fail, stick to the main promise of forgiveness of sins, 'and life everlasting.'

* That is, 'conscientious.'—G.

When all things in the world will fail, we must leave them shortly, wealth and whatsoever, what a comfort is in that grand promise that God will forgive us our sins, and give us life everlasting for Christ! Therefore, when all things else are gone, let us wrap ourselves in the gracious promises of Christ, and then we shall live and die with comfort.

NOTES.

(*a*) P. 213.—'Therefore an ancient saith, "He that is good only under the cross is never good."' Qu. Bernard?

(*b*) P. 227.—'Junius.' The allusion to the 'plague' shews that Sibbes speaks of Francis Du Jou or Junius of Leyden, an eminent theologian who was swept off by the plague there in 1602. He is sometimes confounded with a contemporary Baldwinus Junius, and sometimes with his own son and namesake. There are others of the same name more or less distinguished. G.

THE RICH POVERTY.

THE RICH POVERTY.

NOTE.

'Rich Poverty' forms the last of the four treatises included in 'Light from Heaven' (4to, 1638). The title-page is given below.* For general title-page see Vol. IV. p. 490. G.

* THE
RICH POVERTY:
OR THE
POORE MANS
RICHES.

By the late Learned and Reverend Divine,
RICHARD SIBBS,
D[r]. in Divinity, Master of *Katharine* Hall in
Cambridge, and sometimes Preacher at
GRAIES-INNE.

Matth. 5. 3. *Blessed are the poore in spirit.*
Iames 2. 5. *Hath not God chosen the poore of this world, rich in faith?*

LONDON,
Printed by *R. Badger* for *N. Bourne* at the Royall
Exchange, and *R. Harford* at the gilt *Bible* in
Queenes-head Alley in *Pater-Noster Row.*
1638.

THE RICH POVERTY;

OR,

THE POOR MAN'S RICHES.

I will also leave in the midst of thee an afflicted and poor people, and they shall trust in the name of the Lord.—ZEPH. III. 12.

BEFORE the captivity in Babylon, God sent prophets to his people, as Jeremiah; and among the rest Zephaniah likewise, who lived in the time of Josiah, to forewarn and forearm them against worse times. And as the contents of all other prophecies are for the most part these three, so of this: they are either such expressions and prophecies as set forth the sins of the people; or, secondly, the judgments of God; or, thirdly, comfort to the remnant, to God's people. So these be the parts of this prophecy: a laying open of the sins of the time, under so good a prince as Josiah was; and likewise the judgments of God denounced; and then in this third chapter especially, here is comfort set down for the good people that then lived. The comfort begins at the ninth verse.

This particular verse is a branch of the comfort, that however God dealt with the world, he would be sure to have a care of his own: 'I will leave in the midst of thee an afflicted and poor people, and they shall trust in the name of the Lord.' The whole Scripture is for consolation and comfort. When God 'pulls down,' it is that he may build up; when he purgeth, it is that he may cure and heal. He is 'the father of comfort,' 2 Cor. i. 3. Whatsoever he doth, it is for comfort. Therefore he hath a special care in his prophets and ministers and ambassadors, that those that belong to him may be raised up with comfort, and not be over-much dejected and cast down. But to come to the words.

'I will also leave in the midst of thee,' &c.

In the words these three general heads:

First, God's dealings with his poor church when he comes to visit the world: 'I will leave in the midst of thee.'

Secondly, Their condition and disposition: they are 'an afflicted and poor people.'

Thirdly, Their practice and carriage towards God: 'They shall trust in the name of the Lord.'

From the first, God's dealing with his people in the worst times, we may observe, first, that

Obs. 1. *There is a difference of the people*, both in regard of providence in this world, and in regard of that love that tends to the world to come. For God hath a more special care, as we shall see afterwards, of some, than he hath of others; and he loves some to eternal life, and not others: 'I will leave in the midst of thee an afflicted and poor people,' refusing others. God will leave some. He will purge away others; as he saith in the verse before, 'I will take away out of the midst of thee them that rejoice in thy pride; and thou shalt no more be haughty because of my holy mountain.' He will take away them, 'but I will leave in the midst of thee,' &c. There is a difference. All are not alike, as the proverb is, as white lines upon a white stone, that we cannot see a difference. It is not alike with all men, for we see a difference in this world; but not much here, because God's government is veiled. It will appear at the last day; and whatsoever appears at the last day, it had a ground before. There is a difference in regard of grace and inward qualification, and in regard of the care of God. Even as there is a difference in the creatures; there be precious stones and common stones; and in plants, there be fruitful trees and barren trees; and as there is a difference likewise in the living creatures, so among men there is a difference.

The next thing is, that

Obs. 2. *God will have some in the worst times.* He will have some in all times, that are his, a remnant, as he saith here, 'The remnant of Israel shall do no iniquity;' and as in the text, 'I will leave in the midst of thee an afflicted and poor people,' &c. God will have alway some that are his in the world.

Reason 1. *For it is an article of our faith*, 'We believe the holy catholic church.' There must not be an article of faith and no object to believe. If there be faith to believe a thing, there must be somewhat to be believed. If I believe that at all times there shall be an 'holy catholic church,' there must be such a church in the world, that is the object of my belief, or else there were no foundation for that article of faith. Therefore there must always be a church to the end of the world; sometimes more, sometimes fewer, even as the discovery of Christ is. From whence comes the abundance of the Spirit? The Spirit follows the manifestation of the knowledge of Christ, who is the head of the church. Then is the church most glorious, when the riches of Christ are more gloriously discovered. Those times wherein there is most discovery of Christ, and the mercy and love of God in him, there are more 'elect' of God in those times than in other. There will be alway a church in the world. That is the object of our belief. What is the meaning of it? I believe that in all times to the end of the world there will be a company of people spread over the world, gathered out of the rest of mankind, whom Christ hath knit to himself by faith, and themselves together in a holy spirit of love, of which company I believe myself to be one; therefore there must be such a company, or else there would be faith without an object of faith, which were a great absurdity in divinity and reason too.

Reason 2. Then again, *The world should not stand, were it not for a company in the world that are his.* For what are others? A company of swearers and blasphemers, profane persons, belly-gods, ambitious bubbles, that care for nothing but the vanities of the world. What glory hath God by them? What tribute do they give to God? What credit to religion? They are the shame of the times. They are such as pull God's vengeance upon the times and places they live in. Such is the ill disposition and poisonful nature of men, if they have not the Spirit of God, that God would not endure the world to stand a moment, unless there were some to withhold his wrath, to be objects of his love, and to stay his hand; and when they are all gathered, there shall be an end of this wretched and sinful world. Some there must be while the world endures, and for their sakes God continues the world. Those that keep God's wrath from the world are those that are his; and till all those be gathered the world shall stand. There shall alway be some.

Use 1. It is a point not altogether fruitless. It yields some comfort to know, that when we are taken hence, others shall stand up when we are gone. The church shall not die with us. Is not that a comfort, when a Christian yields his soul to God, to think: yet God will have a church and people, if not amongst us, yet in some other part of the world. He will have some that shall glorify him in this world, that shall adorn and beautify religion, and shall for ever be glorified with him in heaven, till he have made an end of these sinful days. It is some comfort, I say, that goodness shall live after us, that the gospel shall continue after us. There shall be a posterity to the end of the world, that shall stand for the truth and cause of God. The world was not, nor ever shall be so bad, but God hath had, and will have, a party in the world that shall stand for him, and he for them. Now the children of God, as they know God hath a purpose to glorify them world without end; so they have a desire that God may be glorified world without end; and from this desire comes joy, when they think that there will be a people on earth to glorify God still when they are taken hence: for it is a disposition wrought from God's peculiar love, to wish that God may ever have his praise here in the world, while it is a world, and for ever in the world to come. Therefore it is a comfort to them to think that God will always have a church.

But these are but a few, called by Isaiah a remnant: 'a remnant according to election,' as it is, Rom. xi. 5. A handful in comparison of the world, yet they are a world in respect of themselves; for they are a world taken out of the world. But compared with the rest of mankind, they are but as a 'few grapes after the vintage, as the gleanings after the harvest, one of a city, and two of a tribe,' Jer. iii. 14. The prophets, every one of them have special phrases to set out the fewness of those that God hath a special care of. He calls them in the next verse the 'remnant of Israel.' God will have some continually; but those are but a few that are his. His flock is but 'a little flock.'

It is a point not mainly aimed at here; but it is very useful.

Use 2.* Is there but a few, but a remnant in all times? *Am I one of those?* What have I to evidence to me that I am of that little flock that is Christ's? What have I in me to evidence that God hath set his stamp upon me to be his? that I shall not go the broad way to destruction? This should force such *quæres* to our souls. When we hear of the few that shall be saved, we should make that use that Christ makes of that curious† question of the fewness of them that should be saved. 'Oh strive to enter in at the strait gate,' Luke xiii. 24. Stand not on many or few. Make this use of it. Strive to enter in at the strait gate. Take up and practise the duties of religion, that are contrary to the corruption of nature, and contrary to the times. Avoid the sins and courses of the times, and then

* In margin here, 'To examine if we be of those few.'—G.

† That is, = 'vainly inquisitive.'—G.

we shall know and evidence to ourselves that we are of that few number. Somewhat must be done to shew that we are not of those that go the broad way. We hear that there are few that go the other way; and indeed it will make a man look about him, the very consideration that there are but few that shall be saved.

Use 3. And it will make a man wondrous thankful. 'Who am I, and what is my father's house?' 2 Sam. vii. 18. What is there in me? What could God see in me to single me out of the rest, out of a great number that go the broad way to destruction, to set his love upon me? It will inflame the heart with thankfulness to God. It will not make a man proud to despise others. That is pharisaical. But it will inflame the heart to be thankful in a peculiar manner to God, and to single out God in a peculiar manner to be our God, as he hath singled us out to be his. For always he works somewhat in us, like to that he works for us. Those that God hath singled out to be his, he will give them grace to single out him again. God shall be my God, religion shall be my care, and that that God respects shall be that that I will respect. Since God so respects me, shall not I love and respect all that God respects? And shall I not grieve when anything goes amiss with that that God hath a care of? Certainly it will work this disposition, when we come to perceive, by grounded evidence, that we are of that few company, of that remnant here spoken of, that God will leave alway to trust in his name.

Obs. In the next place, though they be few, yet *God hath a special care of them*. Why? There is good reason; for they are his in a peculiar manner. A governor of an house, he cares for all his cattle, but he cares for his children more. A man hath some care for all the lumber and trash in his house; he sees them useful at some time or other, but he cares more for his jewels. If fire come, he will be sure to carry away his jewels, whatsoever become of the lumber. God's children are his after a peculiar manner. Therefore he hath an answerable peculiar care of them in all times. And indeed when they are once his, as he makes them have a peculiar care of him, so he looks upon them as such as he hath wrought upon to be good, and to witness for him; that have a care to stand for him and his honour, to own him and the cause of religion; he will have a care of them. Not that they have this of themselves to win his love, but he works in them a care to witness for him; he works in them a care to stand for him and his glory in all times; and therefore he will be sure to stand for them in the worst times. He will not be beholding to any man. What we have, we have it from him; and then he crowns his own graces after. He will have a special care of those that are his.

This might be instanced from the beginning of the world, from the infancy of the church to this present time. When he would consume the old world, Noah must come into the ark. And Lot must come forth of Sodom when it was to be destroyed; the angel could do nothing else, Gen. xix. 22. So he had a care for Jeremiah and Baruk, he gave them their lives for a prey. He will have a care of his own in the worst times, for they are sealed; he hath set his seal upon them. Those things that are sealed we have a special care of; now in Rev. vii. 8, there are a number that are sealed, sealed inwardly by the Spirit of God, they are marked out for God; they are a marked, sealed number, all those that God will have a special care of. As in Ezek. ix. 4, those that were marked in the forehead, they were looked unto and cared for before the destruction came. So in Mal. iii. 17, God had jewels that he saith he would gather. When he brings a general destruction, he will be sure to gather his jewels; his first care is of them. 'A book of remembrance was written for them.' He hath a book of providence to write their names in. He hath their limbs, all the parts of them written; not a hair of them can miscarry: their tears, their steps, their days are numbered. 'My times are in thy hands,' saith David, Ps, xxxi. 15. All things are numbered exactly of those that belong to God. He hath a care of them and all theirs to a hair; as our Saviour Christ saith, they shall not lose so much as a hair of their heads. God hath an exact care of his remnant at all times.

Obj. But you will say, Sometimes it falls out otherwise.

Ans. Indeed, so it doth, for sometimes God's children are taken away in common judgments, perhaps for too much correspondency with the sins of the times; therefore they are wrapped in the destruction of the times. But yet there is a main difference between them. Jonathan and Saul died by the sword, both of them; Josiah and others died in the field. But there is a main difference. Jonathan was a good man; Saul, for aught the Scripture saith of him, we have no ground to judge charitably of him, but leave him to his judge. But sure it is in general, though the same things befall good and bad outwardly, yet there is a difference between Lazarus and Dives when they die. Dives goes to his place, and Lazarus to heaven. But for the most part this is true: in regard of the body of the church (though, some few members, God hath hidden ways to bring them to heaven and happiness; but for the body of his church and dear children), 'he will give them their lives for a prey,' Jer. xxi. 9. He will have a special care of them and be a sanctuary to them. Nay, so far he will do it, that the world shall know that he hath a special care of them in the world; as it is in the psalm, the heathen shall say, 'God hath done great things for them,' Ps. cxxvi. 2. Men that have no religion shall say, Certainly God doth great things for these men. Though he suffer them to be carried captive and to be in affliction, yet in that very affliction shall be the glory of the church, in that very bondage and abasement. Was the church ever more glorious than in Babylon, when Daniel was there, and the 'three young men' were put into the fire? The glory of the church ofttimes is in outward abasement. The world shall see that God hath a special care of them more than of others. God so magnifies himself, and is so marvellous to his church and children, to do good to them sometimes, to the envy of the enemies, and admiration of all the world that take notice of them, as at the return from the captivity; and the like shall be at the conversion of the Jews.

Use. The use of it may be, *to comfort us against evil times, against the time to come.* 'Let us cast our care upon God; he will care for us,' 1 Pet. v. 7. He will be with us and stand by us; he will never forsake us in the worst times. Nay, his fashion is to deal with his children as becometh his infinite wisdom, that they shall find most comfort and sweetest communion with him in the hardest times. Therefore let us fear nothing that shall befall us with slavish fear, let us fear nothing whatsoever in this world, as long as we are in covenant with God, come what will. It is a great honour to God to trust him with all for the time to come. Let us do our duty, and not be afraid of this or that, as long, I say, as we have God in covenant with us, who is all-sufficient. What should we be afraid of? 'Can a mother forget her child?' saith the prophet; 'If she should, yet will I not forget thee; thou art written on the palms of my hands,' Isa. xlix. 16. Those things that are in the palms of our hands we have ever in our eye. God hath us in his eye. He sets his children before him alway. How can he forget them? How can Christ forget his church? He carries them in his breast, as the high priest had the names of the twelve tribes on his breast in twelve precious stones, when he went into the holy of holies. Christ carries our names in his heart; how can he forget us then? Let kingdoms dash one against another, and let the world tumble upon heaps; let there be what confusion of states there will, God certainly will have a care of his jewels. 'I will leave,' in spite of all the world, 'in the midst of thee, an afflicted and poor people,' &c.

Quest. You will say, When is this performed?

Ans. 'In that day,' saith he in the verse before my text. You must know it is the Scripture's fashion, when it saith, 'In that day,' to take it indefinitely, not to tie it to a certain day; though there is a certain day wherein there shall be an accomplishment of all prophecies and a performance of all promises, that is, at the last day. In the mean time, there is a gradual performance of promises, and the accomplishment of them is in several knots and points of time, so much as shall give content to God's children, yet always leading to a further and further performance. As, for example, God shewed mercy to these Israelites when they were in captivity. He brought them home again. They were a poor and afflicted people, and were much bettered by their abasement. There was a degree of performance then. And then there was a degree of performance in Christ's time, when he joined the Gentiles to them, and both made one church. There will be a more glorious performance at the conversion of the Jews, when God shall make his people 'trust in the name of the Lord,' and the Gentiles shall come in and join with them, and they with the Gentiles. But that which follows in the verse after, ver. 13, 'The remnant shall do none iniquity, nor speak lies; a deceitful tongue shall not be found in their mouth,' these things shall have their time, when the people shall be more thoroughly purged than ever they were; and certainly these glorious portions of Scripture cannot have performance but in such days as are to come. But the accomplishment of all shall be at the day of judgment. Indeed, in the mean time, as I say, there is a comfortable performance, leaving us in expectation of further and further still; because, while we live here, we are in a life of hope and expectation, and always we are under somewhat unperformed. So much for that.

I come now to the state and condition of these people:

'An afflicted and poor people.'

This is their state and condition, wherein is implied also their disposition. Their state is, they are 'an afflicted and poor people.' So it is answerable to the original, 'an afflicted and impoverished people,' a weakened people. However, God hath a special care of his church in this world. Yet it is with exception of some crosses and afflictions, 'You shall have an hundredfold,' saith Christ, 'in this life;' but 'with tribulations and afflictions;' *that* must come in. But yet, notwithstanding, here is a blessing in this: for howsoever he leave them 'an afflicted and poor people,' yet he leaves them a people; and though they be a people afflicted and poor, yet they are a people that are rich in God. They shall 'trust in the name of the Lord;' of which I shall speak afterward. In that he calls them 'an afflicted and poor people,' hence we see, in the first place, that,

Doct. The state of God's church and children in this world, for the most part, is to be afflicted and poor in their outward condition.

I say, for the most part, we must not make it a general rule. It is a point rather to comfort us when it is so, than that it is alway so with the church. For howsoever they are always in some respects afflicted, they have alway something to abase them; yet the times of the church are sometimes more glorious in the eyes of the world. They have the upper hand of the world sometimes. And sometimes again the children of God. they walk in the abundance of the comforts of the Holy Ghost, and increase and multiply, as it is in Acts ix. 31. When Saul was converted to be Paul, 'the church increased and grew, and went on in the fear of the Lord, and the comforts of the Holy Ghost.' There be good days and times for the church sometimes; but for the most part in this world, God's church and children are under some cloud. I will not enter into the common-place of it, but only touch it in a word or two.

Reason 1. God will have it so, *because it is fit the body should be conformable to the head.* You know our blessed Saviour, when he wrought our salvation, he wrought it in a state of abasement, and we 'in working out that salvation,' in going to that salvation that he hath wrought for us, we must go to it, for the most part, in a state of abasement in one kind or other; for we are chosen to be conformable to our head, and we are as well chosen to our portion in afflictions as to grace and glory. God hath set us apart to bear such a share and portion of troubles in this world, to suffer as well as to do. 'From my youth up,' saith the church, 'they have afflicted me; the ploughers have ploughed upon my back and make long furrows,' Ps. cxxix. 3; that is, from the infancy of the church, in all the growth of it, this hath been the state of the church, for the most part, to be afflicted and poor.

Reason 2. And indeed, if we look to ourselves, *by reason of the remainder of our corruptions*, it is needful it should be so. God in wisdom sees it fit it should be so, that we should be afflicted and poor, because he sees that we can hardly digest any flourishing condition in this world. It is as strong waters to a weak stomach. However strong waters intoxicate them not, to make them drunk, yet they weaken the brain. So, however a good condition in the world doth not altogether besot men, yet it weakens them without a great measure of faith, and makes them forget God, and the condition of worldly things, how empty and vain they are; and forget themselves and their own mortality; and forget others, what respect is due to them, as if the world were made only for them to toss and tumble in at their pleasure, to have all at their will, as if other men were scarce* men to them. You see when men are trusted with great matters, they deal with other men as if they were not men, as if all were made for their pleasure. This is the nature of man in great eminency. It sets up its own desire for a 'god,' as if all other were beasts, and base, and nothing. It is a pitiful thing to consider what our nature is in this kind. Nay, take the best. Hezekiah, in his prosperity, he would needs shew his treasures to the king of Babylon, a fair booty for him. You know what it cost him afterward. Naturally we are prone to outward carnal excellency, too, too much. God knows it well enough. David would be numbering the people, that he might be conceited what a goodly number he had to fight against his enemies. God punished him you see in that kind. He took away that people that he made his confidence. God deals thus with his children in this world, because he sees a disposition in them that cannot digest, and manage,

* That is, 'scarcely' *not* = rare.—G.

and overcome prosperity. They cannot command it as they should do, but are slaves to their own lusts, though they have a good measure of grace. We are prone to surfeit of the things of this life, and God is forced; as it is in Ps. cxix. 75, 'of very faithfulness thou hast corrected me.' God, of very faithfulness, because he will be true to our souls and save them, he is forced to diet us and to keep us short of the things of this life; to take away matter of pride and matter of conceitedness in carnal excellencies; to make us know ourselves, and him, and the world, what it is; the vanity of the world and worldly things. You see, then, God hath some cause to do it.

Use. And *we may justify God when he any way abaseth us in this world.* He knows what he hath to do with us: let us leave that to him, so he save our souls, and sanctify them, and delight in us to heaven and happiness. If his pleasure be to diet us in this world, in regard of riches and greatness, that he do not answer our desires, but keep us under hatches, let us leave it to his will. He knows what to do with us, as the physician knows better what concerns the sick than the sick doth. Therefore, let us take in good part the wise dispensation of God.

But why doth he join 'afflicted and poor' together? Because poverty is affliction, and because affliction goes with poverty? Poverty brings affliction. It brings abasement with it, and it is an affliction itself. For the poor man is trod on at all hands. Men go over the hedge where it is lowest. It is an affliction, and it goes with affliction. Therefore the apostle St Paul, Philip. iv. 12, he joins them together: 'I have learned to want and to be abased.' Why? Because a man that is in want in the world is usually abased. Every man scorns him that is in want. They look haughty and high over a man that hath any use of them. So that affliction and poverty usually go together.

Those that God doth abase in this kind, let them consider that it is no otherwise with them than it hath been with God's people before. And let them labour for true riches: take advantage from their outward estate to be rich in a better way.

In the next place, we may observe hence, that

Doct. God sanctifies outward affliction and poverty, to help inward poverty of spirit.

Poverty in outward condition helps poverty in the inward disposition. In their state and condition is implied their disposition: poor for condition, and likewise in inward disposition, for that is implied here. The prophet doth not mean he will leave poor people that shall only be poor, for we see a world of poor and proud. A man, as he goes along in the streets, shall hear a company of poor that are the greatest rebels in the world against God; that blaspheme and swear, that rail against magistrates and governors. They are the most unbroken people in the world, the poorest and beggarliest, the refuse of mankind. As they are in condition, so they are in disposition. The Scripture speaks here of God's poor, not of the devil's poor, such as are poor every way, outwardly and inwardly, and have their poverty as a just punishment of their wicked lives, and continue in that wicked life, having it not sanctified to them to make them desire better riches. Doth God esteem such poor? No. But such poor and afflicted as, together with the meanness of their outward condition, have it sanctified to them; so as they grow to be low and poor in their own esteem of themselves, they grow to inward poverty of spirit, and so to seek to God, to seek for better riches, 'to be rich in faith,' as the Scripture speaks, James ii. 5;

especially such, and only such, are here meant. So then, mark the point here, that

God sanctifies affliction and poverty for the inward good of the souls of his children.

Reason 1. This is the reason of it: outward poverty and affliction takes away the fuel that feeds pride, that is an opposite to spiritual poverty and humility, and sight of our wants. That which pride feeds upon, it is some outward thing, some outward excellency, that the flesh takes occasion by to swell, to over-ween itself, and to overlook all others. Now, when the fuel is taken away, the fire goes out. When the fodder and nourishment is taken away, those wanton steeds, you know, that grew fierce with pampering, they grow more tractable. So it is with the nature of man. Take away that that makes him fierce, and then, when his fierce and high conceits are taken away, he will be tame. Take away that that feeds his carnal disposition, and he grows tractable and gentle. Thus then, affliction and poverty, outward in our condition, it helps to inward poverty of spirit and disposition; for it takes away that which inflames the fancy of a carnal man. A carnal man thinks himself as great and as good as he hath possessions of the things of this life; and the devil enlargeth his conceit more upon the imagination, to think these things to be a great deal greater than they are. We come afterward, by experience, to see them nothing but vanity. But this is in man without grace: we are prone, as I said, to surfeit of them. They are too strong for us to digest and overcome; and therefore God takes them away, that he may help the inward disposition of our souls.

Afflictions and poverty sanctified, they have a power to bring us to God, and to keep us in and to recover us when we are fallen. They bring us in, as we see in Manasseh and in the prodigal son. Affliction and poverty they brought him to know himself. They brought him home. He was not himself before. They brought him to inward poverty. When he could not be satisfied so much as with husks abroad, it was time for him to look home again. So when we are in the state of grace, it keeps and pales us in: 'God hedgeth us in with thorns,' Hosea ii. 6, that we may not run out. And then, if we fall, it recovers us, and fetcheth us in again, by embittering sinful courses to us. We see, then, affliction and poverty is sanctified to God's children, to work an inward sight of their spiritual wants.

Use 1. Take notice, hence, *of the poison and sinfulness of our corrupt nature*, that defiles itself in the blessings of God; so that God cannot otherwise fit us for grace, but by stripping of us of those things that are good in themselves. This should abase us very much, considering that those things that should be rises to us, to raise us up to God, that should be glasses to see the love of God in, our nature useth them as clouds to keep God from us, and to fasten and fix upon the things themselves; so that there is no other remedy, but God must strip us naked of them. This consideration should humble us.

Use 2. And let us make this use of it: let us know, *when any abasement is sanctified to us, it comes from God's love.* If we find any affliction make us inwardly more humble and tractable, and more pliable, certainly it comes from love, and is directed to our good; and therefore it is in love, because it is directed to our good. For it is well taken away in earthly things, that is supplied in heavenly and spiritual. What if God takes away such outward honours, and respects, and riches, if God make it up in graces that are eternal, that make us truly and inwardly good, which all the outward things in the world cannot do! All the empires in the world cannot make a man an honest man. They may make him worse; they may be snares to make him forget God and himself; they may be a means of his damnation, without wondrous care. What if God take away a great deal of these things, and make them up in favours of a higher kind! Therefore, if we find God sanctify any outward abasement for the inward good of our souls, let us bless him for it, and take it in good part as an evidence of his love; for God thus deals with his children. He sanctifies their outward abasements for their inward good, to draw them nearer to himself.

Use 3. Therefore, those that are weak in their condition, for a man may be poor in regard of his condition, though not inwardly poor, those that are broken in their condition outwardly, they may know whether it be in love or no, *if they find this condition sanctified to a better disposition.* For as all things in general work to the best 'to them that love God,' Rom. viii. 28, so this is one: especial affliction and poverty work for good to them that love God. God sanctifies it to them for that end.

Therefore we should examine when we are under any cross, see how it works upon us, whether by it we are humbled or no, whether we join with God or no; for those that belong to God have the grace of the Spirit to join with him in the work. When he afflicts them, they labour to afflict themselves; when he goes to humble them outwardly, they humble themselves; when he goes about to make them poor, to wean them from the love of the world, they wean themselves and join with God. As we see the physician by his art and skill, when he sees nature working away, then he will help nature till the cure be wrought; so God gives his Spirit to those that are his, to work with him. When God goes about to take them down, they will take down themselves too, and so they grow inwardly better, together with their outward abasement.

Those therefore that swell, and storm, and murmur, and rage, what do they get but more stripes! They get not out of trouble by it, but if they belong to God, they get stripes upon stripes. What doth the horse get at last by shaking off his rider that is skilful? More spurring and more strokes. So when men are under God's hand, afflicted any way, and labour not to make a good use of it, but will pull the rod out of God's hand and swell and pine, if they belong to God they get more stripes. Therefore let us kiss the rod, and the hand that holds it. God is about a good work, let him alone; desire him rather to sanctify the visitation and abasement than remove it. A gracious heart desires rather the sanctification than the removal.

Use 3. Again, Hence we learn not to '*despise the brother of low degree*,' James i. 9, nor we should 'not have the faith of Christ in respect of persons,' James ii. 9. We should not take scandal at the church, that it is usually in a mean condition in this world, for the church is alway rich in another kind of riches. The church is rich in reversion. It hath heaven and happiness, and the church is rich in bills and promises. The church is rich in an apparent pledge, that is worth all the world besides; that is, Christ. 'If he have given us his Son, will he not with him give us all things else?' Rom. viii. 32. The church is rich in this world indeed, 'for all things are yours, and you are Christ's,' 1 Cor. iii. 23. Christ carries riches for the church, and dispenseth them to the church as occasion serves. Indeed, Christ's riches are the church's riches. The church cannot be poor if Christ be rich. It is only a medicinal poverty. It is God's dispensation to fit them for better riches. As a wise physician he purgeth a foul body, till he bring it almost to skin and bone; but why? That having made it poor, there may be a spring of better blood and spirits.

Let us take no offence therefore at God's dispensation, either towards others or ourselves, if we find him by his Holy Spirit sanctifying that outward condition to a holy inward bent and disposition of soul to God-ward. It is a happy affliction and póverty and abasement, whatsoever it be that draws us nearer to God, in whom we have more supply than we can want in the world. God never takes away anything from his children in this world, but he gives them more in better things. That is always his course. 'The poor receive the gospel,' Mat. xi. 5. The gospel is preached to them, and they receive it; those that by their outward abasements are brought to a sight of their spiritual wants, and thereupon to hunger after Christ.

Again, In that this outward poverty helps to inward poverty of the soul, outward afflictions help the inward disposition; hence we see likewise this truth that

Obs. Providence is serviceable to predestination and election.

God in election hath a purpose to call us out of the world, to save our souls. Providence, that is a general government of all things in the world. Election is in order to salvation; he hath chosen us to a supernatural end, and fits us for it by calling and sanctification. Now how doth providence serve the decree of election? Thus; whom God purposeth to save, to bring to an end above nature, he directs providence, so that all things shall serve for that end; therefore he encourageth them with outward things, or takes outward things from them in his providence, as may serve his purpose in election to save their souls. He hath a purpose to save them, therefore providence works all things for their good, Rom. viii. 28. All things, by the overruling providence of God, are serviceable to a higher degree of love that God bears to his children, to serve his purpose to bring them to heaven. Thereupon comes the dispensation of riches or poverty, honour or abasement. He takes liberty for outward things concerning this life, to give or take them as they may serve the spiritual and best good of his children.

Use. Therefore God's children, when they see God intends their good in taking away the things of this life, in letting them blood, as it were, for their health, *they should bless God as well for taking as for giving*, as Job did, Job i. 21. And there is as great mercy and love hid in taking away blessings as in conveying of them. 'I will leave an afflicted and poor people.' In the original it is poor and mild and gentle (*a*). Poverty of estate, and poverty of spirit, the disposition of soul, come almost in one word, and indeed in God's children they are joined together. For he sanctifies all dispensations and carriages of himself towards them. When God hath a purpose to save a man, everything shall help him homeward. And it is not a better outward argument to know a man's state in grace, than to see how the carriage of things serve God's purpose to do good to his soul, when we ourselves are bettered in our inward man by whatsoever befalls us. God complains of the Jews; they were as 'reprobate silver,' Jer. vi. 30, because he had melted them, and they were never a whit the better; they were like dross consumed in the melting. God's children are as gold refined. Those that find themselves refined and bettered, it is an evidence that they are God's; because there is a providence serving their spiritual good, directing all things to that end.

But from their condition, we come to the disposition implied, inward and spiritual poverty.

1. Now this poverty *is not a mere want of grace*. To be poor in spirit is not to be poor of that spirit, or to be of a poor spirit. To be of a poor spirit is to have no goodness, no worth at all, but to be of a dejected, base mind. God's children are not so. There are none more courageous than they, when they are called to it. It is not this poverty of spirit to have no goodness at all. But to be 'poor in spirit,' is a state and disposition of soul, that hath some goodness, wherein they see a want of farther goodness. They have so much goodness and worth, as to see an unworthiness in themselves, and a greater worthiness out of themselves. They are sensible of their own want, and see they have no means of supply in themselves; and they see an all-sufficiency out of themselves, in God, in Christ; they see a necessity of dependence for supply out of themselves, in their whole condition till they come to heaven. In a word, this poverty is a sight of our own nothingness in ourselves, and besides that, our own inability, and a sight of sufficiency out of ourselves, and a desire of it; and likewise a hope of supply from thence, which hope carries us to endeavour and to waiting till we have supply.

2. This will better appear, if we distinguish of this poverty in spirit by the two degrees of it. There is a poverty of spirit *before we are in the state of grace*, before we are in Christ; and a poverty *after*.

The poverty before we are in the state of grace, is, when God by his Spirit, together with his word and work of correction, doth open the eyes of our souls to see what we are by nature, what we are in ourselves. It is a work of God's convincing Spirit, to give us a true view into our own condition, and with the sight to work a sense; and from a sight and sense and thorough conviction, comes a wondrous abasement, and a desire to be otherwise than we are. There is some hope in spiritual poverty in God's children before their conversion, which stirs them up to look upon Christ, and to the mercy of God in Christ; and this stirs them up to beg, and to use all means; and at length God is gracious and answers all the desires of their souls. This is before they were in grace; for before a Christian is a sound Christian, he must be driven out of himself. Naturally we are prone to cleave to something, either out of ourselves or in ourselves, and we must be fired out by a sight and sense of the misery we are in.

We see God hath taken this course alway in Scripture. This course he took with Adam. He cites him, arraigns him, condemns him. He lets him see what a miserable creature he was; as no man on earth was ever so miserable, till he felt the sweetness of the promised seed. He that had been in so great happiness as he was, to have his conscience so galled as his was afterward, to feel such misery for the present as he did, he must needs be very miserable, as indeed he was the most miserable man that ever was since his time. It is the greatest unhappiness for a man to have been happy; for his former happiness makes his present unhappiness more sensible.* When God had prepared him thoroughly, then he raised him up with the promised seed. God deals as he dealt with Elijah; first, he casts him down with earthquakes and storms, and then he comes in a stiller voice. It is for that end that John Baptist comes before Christ, to level all, to cast down the 'mountains and fill up the valleys;' Luke iii. 5, for all must be laid flat to Christ. We must lay ourselves at his feet, and be content to be disposed of by him, before we know what belongs to being in Christ. There must be poverty of spirit antecedent therefore. We see this lively set out in the prodigal son, that while he had anything in the world to content him, he never looks homeward; but when he saw such an

* This idea is largely dwelt upon in Pascal's 'Thoughts.'—ED.

emptiness in all things he met with, that he could not be satisfied with husks, then he began to think of going home, and that there was some hope he had a father that would receive him. I will be short in this, because the other is mainly intended.

If we would know and discern by some evidences whether we have been poor in spirit, in this preparative poverty or no,

1. Let us consider *what we have judged of our condition by nature;* whether ever we have been convinced of the ill condition we are in; for if there be not conviction of sin, there will not be conviction of righteousness, as you have it, John xvi. 8. There are three works of the Spirit, 'to convince of sin, of righteousness, and of judgment,' of spiritual government. The Spirit, before it convinceth us that we have the righteousness of Christ, and convinceth us of the necessity of government and holy life in Christ, which is called there judgment, he convinceth of sin, which is an antecedent work. Let us examine ourselves whether the Spirit have had such a work or no.

2. Where this conviction and poverty is, a man *sees an emptiness and vanity in all things in the world whatsoever, but in Christ.*

3. And *there is a desire of the grace and favour of God above all things.* Ask a poor man what he would have; he would have that that may supply his poverty and want. Ask a man that is spiritually poor before he be in Christ; what would you have? Oh, mercy and pardon. Offer him anything else in the world, it contents him not. But that will content him, the sense and persuasion of God's love and mercy in Christ Jesus.

4. Where this poverty of spirit is, there will be a wondrous earnestness after pardon and mercy, and after grace. To be in another condition a man will labour, even as for life. If you come to a poor man that labours for his living, and ask him, Why do you labour so? he will wonder at your idle question. I may starve else, he will say. A man that is spiritually poor, and sees what a state he is in, he labours in the use of means to have an inward sense of God's love, to find some beginnings of the new creature, to find a change, to be otherwise than he is; he sees he must perish else. There is a prizing and estimation in him of mercy and pardon above all things in the world, and a making after it.

5. It is alway joined likewise *with a wondrous abasing of himself.* He thinks himself not worth the ground he goes on, till God hath mercy on him in Jesus Christ. This is not so sensible in those that are brought up in the church, or that have religious thoughts put into them continually in both kinds; both concerning their own estate by nature, and withal concerning grace and mercy in Christ. Therefore grace is instilled into them by little and little, and the change is not so sensible. But where the conversion is anything sudden, from an ill course of life to a better, God works such a poverty of spirit before he bring a man to Christ. In Mat. v. 3, it is the beginning of all happiness, the blessedness that leads to the rest, 'Blessed are the poor in spirit, for theirs is the kingdom of heaven.' And indeed, those that are poor in spirit are blessed, though they have not yet the sense of God's love so much as they desire; for this draws on all the rest, as I shall shew afterwards. To be poor in spirit therefore, is to see that we have no good in ourselves; that we are beggars and bankrupts, and have no means to pay or satisfy; and this stirs up desire and the use of means, and all the qualifications that follow there, 'hungering and thirsting after righteousness, mourning, and meekness.' For this will follow. A man that is poor in spirit, say what you will to him, he is so tractable and meek, let God do what he will with him so he give him grace; if he will cast him

down, so be it. 'What shall we do to be saved?' Acts xvi. 30, implying a pliableness to take any course; he is willing to do or to suffer anything.

And indeed there must be such a poverty of spirit, before we can believe in Christ, whereby we may be convinced of our debts and of our unability to pay those debts, and our misery; that we are in danger to be cast into eternal bondage for them.

1. There must be this *before;* for else,

(1.) *We will never repair to Christ nor God's mercy in him.* 'The full stomach despiseth an honey comb,' Prov. xxvii. 7. We will not relish Christ, nor value him as we should.

(2.) Then again, without this, *we will not be thankful to God as we should be.* Who is thankful to God but he that sees before what need he stands in of mercy and of every drop of the blood of Christ?

(3.) And then *we will not be fruitful;* for who is so fruitful a Christian as he that is thankful? And this depends upon the other. A Christian that was never truly cast down and laid low by the spirit of bondage, he is a barren Christian. The other having tasted of the love of God in Christ, the very 'love of Christ constrains him,' 2 Cor. v. 14, and he studies to be 'abundant in the work of the Lord,' 1 Cor. xv. 58, as St Paul saith, and every way to 'shew forth the virtues of him that hath called him out of darkness into marvellous light,' 1 Peter ii. 9.

(4.) Again, this is the ground, when men are not sufficiently humbled before, *that they fall away dangerously.* It is the ground of apostasy, because they did not feel the smart of sin. He that hath smarted for his estate before, and knows what it is to be in such a condition, he will be loath ever to come into the prison again. Therefore the ground of careful walking is a sense of our unworthiness and misery. The more we are convinced of this, the more careful and watchful we will be, that we never come into that cursed condition again.

(5.) And indeed it is an error in the foundation which is not mended in the fabric, as we say, when there is an error in poverty of spirit at the first, when the work of humiliation is not kindly wrought; hence is the defect *in all the whole carriage of a Christian.* The foundation of God's building lies low; he digs deep. God lays his foundation ofttimes as low as hell itself in a manner; he brings his children to see that that he means they shall never feel, to see his wrath against sin, that so he may build upon this foundation. For Christianity it is an excellent frame; it is a frame for eternity, a building for ever. Therefore it must have a sure foundation, which must be laid in humiliation and poverty of spirit. An error in the first digestion is not amended in the second; if that be not good, the rest are naught. If there be not sound humiliation, nothing will be sound afterward. Therefore we should desire that God by his Spirit would help us more and more to know what we are in ourselves, that we may get to be what we are in Christ.

2. But there is a continual frame and disposition of soul, which is a poverty in spirit *that accompanies God's children all the days of their life* till they be in heaven, till they enjoy that riches that is laid up there for them; and that is especially here meant. And indeed it is an ingredient into all the passages of salvation.

(1.) *For in justification there must be a poverty of spirit,* to make us see that there is no righteousness in ourselves, or that can come from us, that is able to stand against the law and against the justice of God; all is defiled and spotted and unanswerable. And upon this poverty and apprehension of what is defective in ourselves, comes an admiration of that righteousness of God in Christ—for it is of God's devising, and of God's approving, and of God's working, Christ being God and man—to force us every day to renew our right in the righteousness of Christ, and to be 'found in him.' There is such a poverty of spirit as to account all 'loss, and dross,' Phil. iii. 8, and nothing; to be willing to part with all to be found in Christ, 'not having our own righteousness, but that which is of God in Christ,' as Paul divinely speaks, ver. 9. So it is necessary in that main passage, of justification, to be 'poor in spirit;' that is, to see a defect in our own righteousness, to stand opposite to God's justice, who is 'a consuming fire.' It is requisite in regard of our daily living by faith in justification.

(2.) In the whole course *of sanctification* there must of necessity be poverty of spirit; that is, a sense that we have no sanctifying grace of ourselves, but we must fetch it from the fulness of Christ, whose fulness is for us: 'of his fulness we receive grace for grace,' John i. 16.

The ground of this is, that now in the covenant of grace all is of grace, both in justification and sanctification; all is of grace, nothing but grace. God hath set himself to get the glory of his free grace and mercy now in Jesus Christ. Therefore as our salvation is wrought out of us altogether by our surety, the 'second Adam,' Christ; so our righteousness is altogether out of ourselves, whereby we appear righteous before God. It is his, and given to us by marriage; being one with him, his righteousness is ours. And likewise in him we have the principle of all grace. He is the principle of our life, the root and foundation of spiritual life and sanctification: 'Without me you can do nothing,' John xv. 5. So that in Christ we have all that concerns our spiritual life in sanctification and justification, because it is a state of grace. Adam had it in himself. Though God at the first clothed him with his image, yet notwithstanding he had not such a necessity as we have to go to Christ for all; but now in the 'second Adam,' Christ, we must fetch grace for everything from him. Therefore there must be poverty in regard of our knowledge—we have no spiritual knowledge of ourselves—and poverty in regard of our affections. We have no joy, no peace, no comfort of ourselves, no delight in good things, nor no strength to them; we have all from Christ. 'By grace,' saith the apostle, 'I am what I am,' 1 Cor. xv. 10; as if grace had given him his being, his form, as we say. Indeed, so it doth; grace gives a Christian his form and being, his work and his working, for all working is from the inward being and form of things. By grace we are what we are in justification, and work what we work in sanctification. It is by what we have freely from Christ. Therefore in that respect there must be poverty of spirit.

Nay, I say more; in every action when we are in the state of grace, and have had the beginnings of the new creature in us, there needs poverty of spirit, in regard of our own inability to perform every action. For even as it is in our form—the life and soul, there is need of it in every moving and stirring—so there is a need of the spirit of grace, which is as the form and life and being of a Christian, to every holy action. 'In him we live, and move, and have our being,' saith the apostle, Acts xvii. 28. 'In him,' that is, in 'God reconciled to Christ,' we have not only our being, that is, our form, but in him we 'live and move' to every particular act. We are no wiser in particular things than God makes us on the sudden; the wisest man will be a fool if God leave him to his own wit. We are no stronger in every particular act that needs strength than God supplies us with spiritual strength. We are no holier than God by his Spirit shines on us, and raises our souls in particular actions. So that it is not only necessary that we have grace at the first to make us Christians, but we must have a perpetual regiment* of the Spirit, from whence we must have an influence to every particular act. Though we have grace, yet we cannot bring forth that grace to act without new grace. Even as trees, though they be fitted to bear fruit, as the vine, &c., yet without the influence of the heavens they cannot put forth that fitness in fruits; so though we be fitted by the Spirit of God, yet we cannot put it forth to particular acts when occasion serves, without the influence of Heaven to promote and further that grace; and applying our spirits to every holy action by removing the impediments that would hinder it, adding new supply and strength to help grace. If the temptations be too strong, as sometimes they are, former grace will not serve, without a new supply of strength. As he that may carry a lesser burden cannot carry a greater without new strength, so in every temptation there is required more strength than the former; and in every new action there is required not only a continuance of grace, but a fresh supply of stronger grace.

And for want of this, the best of God's saints have fallen foully. Though they have had grace in them, yet, notwithstanding, the Spirit had left them to themselves in regard of new supply, because they have been conceited; they have not been poor enough in spirit. As Peter, he was conceited of his own strength: 'Though all men forsake thee, yet I will not,' Mat. xxvi. 33. This conceit moved God in mercy, as well as in justice, to leave him to himself, that by his fall he might learn to stand another time, and not trust his own strength. The best of us all, I say, when there is anything to be done, we had need of a fresh influence of grace, and a fresh light to shine upon us.

It should force perpetual poverty of spirit, to see the want that is in ourselves, and the supply that is out of ourselves, and to make use of that by going out of ourselves, and making towards him in whom is all our supply. In all our communion we have with God, which is the happiness of our estates, this frame and disposition of soul, to be poor in spirit, it is necessary in every act. Even in our very prayers for grace, we are so void of it, that we want ability to call for what we want. We must have that from the Spirit, not only grace, but that disposition of soul which carries us to God. A spirit fitting us to pray, that must be also given us; we know not what to call for. We of ourselves are so poor, that we not only want grace and ability to action, but we have not ability to ask; but God's Spirit must dictate our prayers, and give us motions, and make us sensible of our wants, and must enable our faith to cherish those graces, and make us go out of ourselves even in our very prayers. What a state is this, then! Had we not need to be 'poor in spirit' all our lifetime, that have not so much as ability to go out of ourselves for supply from another, but that must come from Christ too? As St Augustine, who was a great advancer of the grace of God, and an abaser of man; he had indeed St Paul's spirit, saith he, 'We should boast and glory of nothing, because nothing is ours' (*b*). We have need of this poverty of spirit in the whole tenure of our Christian life.

Again, in the actions of this life, how pitifully do we miscarry, because we think we have wit† and strength enough, and set upon things in our own wit and strength, we speed and have success answerable. Where the

* That is, 'government.'—G. † That is, 'wisdom.—G.

beginning is confidence, the end is shame, of any business even of this life. What is the reason that ofttimes the great and weighty business of this life have not answerable success? Many times it falls out so; as one said of general councils, they seldom were successful, because men came with confidence and wit for victory rather than truth.* Certainly there is less success in great matters, because men come with self-confidence. Therefore it is a good sign that God means to bless great businesses, when he puts it into the hearts of those that are agents in them to seek him in the affairs of this life. We must be poor in spirit to see that the carriage and success comes from him.

Well, so it is in suffering likewise. We cannot suffer the least cross of ourselves but with murmuring and repining, without strength from him. When Moses came to the 'waters of strife,' Moses' spirit was discovered. He could not endure the harshness and rebellion of the people, Num. xx. 13. A Christian comes sometimes to such opposition that his spirit is moved, and he discovers much corruption. It is so with the best men. Even Moses, a meek man, when he had such temptations and provocations, it moved him. We must labour to get a greater spirit than our own, to have the Spirit of God to work this spiritual poverty in us.

This poverty of spirit, as we call it, is *spirituale vacuum*, spiritual emptiness. You know in philosophy there is nothing empty in the world, but it is filled either with air or some kind of body, and to avoid the enemy of nature, emptiness, things will change their seat; heavy things will go upward, and things that are above will come below to avoid emptiness; that is contrary to nature, there being a fulness of things with one body or other. So, I say, spiritual poverty, it is an emptying of the soul, which of force alway bring better things in. Wheresoever this emptying of the soul is, this making of ourselves poor, it is upon good ground by this course. It is always such a *vacuum* and emptiness of one thing that brings in another better. The soul can never be altogether empty. When wind and vain stuff is out, then comes better things in, which St Paul calls 'the fulness of God.' He prays and wishes that they might 'be filled with the fulness of God,' Col. ii. 9. Then comes fulness of knowledge and understanding, and fulness of affection, and fulness of contentment, and complacency in the will; and all the soul hath an answerable fulness to the proportion of the emptying itself of itself.

In the next place, let us come to discover this disposition of poverty of spirit where it is, and then shew some helps to it.

1. First, To discover where this blessed frame of soul is. Surely those that are thus poor in spirit they are *full of prayer*. 'The poor man speaks supplications,' as the wise man saith, Prov. xviii. 23; that is his dialect. The poor man is much in prayer. He that is 'poor in spirit' is much in supplication; for prayers, they are the ambassadors of the poor soul to God to supply it with the riches of his grace. Therefore where there is no prayer there is no sense of poverty, but there is a Laodicean temper, as if they were rich enough. You have a company of men, they say they cannot pray privately, their spirits are barren. They intimate much pride of spirit, for if a man be sensible of his wants you need not supply him with words. If a poor tenant came to a landlord, and find he hath a hard bargain, let him alone for telling his tale; I warrant you he will lay open the state of his wife and children, and the ill year he hath had; he will be eloquent enough. Take any man that is sensible of his wants, and you

* Vol. III. p. 436.—G.

shall not need to dictate words to him. There is no man that hath a humble and broken heart, though he be never so illiterate, but he will have a large heart to God in this kind.

2. Again, there is a care *of using all means*. Where poverty is, there will be a making out of ourselves unto places where God bestows any riches. They that are poor, and have no victuals at home, they will go to market rather than they will starve; and those that find in themselves want of grace and comfort, surely they will go out of themselves: they will go to God's market, they will attend upon the means. He that is like to be arrested for debt, and hath nothing at home, it is time for him to seek abroad for supply. So, when a man is poor spiritually, ready to be snared and catched in everything for want of spiritual grace, he will labour for strength in the use of all means. Therefore those that are of a Laodicean stamp, that think there is too much preaching, and too much hearing, and too much reading, and what need all this ado? alas! they were never humbled; they were never sensible of their state by nature; nor are not yet in the state of grace. For the soul of a true Christian is alway in the state of spiritual poverty, as that it relisheth spiritual means and is not fed with husks. A soul that is spiritually poor will discern in the use of means, this is flourishing; this is for the ear; this is conceits; alas! it comes for food for supply. A poor soul that finds the want of grace, and strength, and comfort, it judgeth of the means by what it finds. There will be a use of all means, and likewise some ability to taste where there is true poverty of spirit.

3. Again, Where this inward poverty of spirit is, it will make God's children *wondrous thankful, and thankful for a little grace*. A poor man that is sensible of his poverty will be more thankful for a penny, than another man for a pound that hath money of his own. A soul that sees the want of grace, and withal sees the excellency of grace, is thankful to God that he will work anything in such a poor defiled soul as he is; that he will work any good motions, any good affections, any degree of faith, that he will give him any assurance of salvation. Oh he thinks what a good God is this! He breaks out with the apostles, Peter and Paul, that had both been sinners themselves and found grace; oh they were much in thankfulness! 'Blessed be God the Father of our Lord Jesus Christ,' &c.* A thankful soul is a poor soul, and a poor soul is alway a thankful soul. He that is poor he knows he hath little and deserves little; therefore knowing that he deserves nothing, he is thankful for and content with anything. A humble man is alway thankful, and that is the reason that God may have his glory from him. He is forced sometimes to humble and abase him. He should have no sacrifice from him else. A proud man, a conceited man, so doats upon his own worth; he forgets the giver, he makes himself an idol to him. Therefore such, they are usurpers of what they have, they enter upon God's blessings, not considering from whom they have them, nor for what end they have them. They deny God his tribute of thankfulness because they are proud. But a man that is poor in spirit, he enters upon all by title of gift, and receives all from God in the form of a poor man. Therefore whatsoever he hath he returns thanks for it again. An unthankful soul, therefore, is a proud soul. A thankful soul is an humble abased soul alway; and the more humble and empty the soul is, the more thankful it is for every degree of grace and comfort.

4. Again, A soul that is thus disposed, that is poor in spirit, it is willing

* Cf. Eph. i. 3, and 1 Peter i. 3.—G.

to resign itself to Christ's government, with self-denial of anything it is able to do of itself. It is ready to say, 'Lord, I have neither wit* of mine own to govern myself, nor any strength and ability of mine own; therefore I put myself upon thy government, I desire to follow thy light and to go on in thy strength.' There is alway a resignation to Christ's government, and that in fear and trembling; for whom we resign ourselves unto, surely we will have a care not to displease them. A dependent life is alway an awful† life; for when a man hath resigned himself to the government of another, and knows he must depend upon him, he will have a care not to displease such an one; for he thinks, if I displease him he will withdraw his maintenance and countenance from me, and then what am I? So the soul that thinks it hath all from God, and from the Spirit of Christ, it resigns itself to the Spirit of Christ, and withal it is wondrous fearful not to grieve and displease the Spirit. For he thinks with himself, my life is but a dependent life, my graces are but dependent; let God but withdraw the beams of his Spirit and I sink; let him withdraw his comfort and his strength, what am I? Nothing but darkness, and deadness, and confusion. Those therefore that give not themselves up to Christ's government, but are governed by rules of policy, by the example of others, and have base dependence upon others, they know not what spiritual poverty is. They see there is a sufficiency in themselves to rule and govern themselves, as if Christ's wisdom were not sufficient. They are not so disposed as the apostle requires; they 'work not out their salvation with fear and trembling, because God gives the will and the deed,' Philip. ii. 12. The meaning is this, we should work out our salvation with a holy fear and trembling, a jealous fear, a son-like fear, lest we displease God. Why? 'He gives both the will and the deed,' Philip. ii. 13. He gives both the will to do good; and when he hath done that, he gives the ability of the deed itself. We cannot do anything, therefore we had need to walk in an awful condition, and not displease him in anything, lest he withdraw the assistance of his Spirit and leave us to ourselves; and then we shall fall, to his dishonour, to the discredit of religion, to the wasting of our own comfort, and the advantage of Satan. This is the temper of a man that is poor in spirit. He gives himself up to Christ's government, and depends upon it; and thereupon he is wondrous fearful to displease him in anything.

There are a company that know not what belong to this, that hope to be saved by Christ, and yet they will grieve the Spirit; they will venture into any place, upon any sight, into any company: but if ever they had been acquainted with the government of Christ's Spirit, they would know what it was to grieve the Spirit, and the Spirit would grieve them too. It is a sign they have not the Spirit of God, because he doth not check them when they have done. Therefore your adventurous careless persons, that are indifferent for all things, for all companies and places, that do not watch over themselves, and over their words and carriages, they have not this poverty of spirit. For then they would know what it were to displease God in anything, to walk and to speak loosely, because hereby they grieve the Spirit; and would presently find either want in grace or comfort. There is not one of many that are acquainted with the nature of this spiritual communion with God, and therefore they do not enjoy the happiness that those do, who are thus qualified, that are 'poor in spirit.'

5. Again, A man that is poor in spirit *is very tractable*, as it is in Isaiah: 'A child shall lead them.' 'The lamb and the lion shall feed together,'

* That is, 'wisdom.'—G.

† That is, 'a life full of awe.'—G.

&c., 'and a child shall lead them,' Isa. xi. 6; that is, such an one, you shall lead him with any counsel, let the person be never so mean; having smarted for his sins, and his own counsel and ways, 'a child shall lead him,' that is, any man shall lead and move him to that which is good, he stands not upon terms.

6. And alway he that is poor in spirit, he is no *upbraider of other men's wants*. He is more sensible of his own than that he sees in other men. He is not prone to upbraid and object against them their wants and conditions, he is so taken up with the sense of his own.

7. And lastly, He that is poor in spirit *is humbled in himself for spiritual wants;* not so much for outward things, but because he hath not a large heart to God, because he finds impatience, because he finds not that heavenly-mindedness and strength to go through the duties that God requires, that his flesh is so backward; these things abase him and bring him on his knees, and not so much outward things; and answerably he looks for spiritual supply. When a man is humble and poor in spirit he is not abased with any outward thing, that that he would have is mercy and grace. The apostle, when he would pray for all happiness to the churches, he prays for grace, mercy, and peace; for as they are more sensible of their spiritual wants, so they are carried in their desires after that that may give them satisfaction that way.

Use. Let us labour *to bring our souls to this blessed temper, to be poor in spirit;* the happy temper that our Saviour began his preaching withal. The first thing that he falls upon is, 'Blessed are the poor in spirit, for theirs is the kingdom of heaven,' Mat. v. 3. But before I come to any directions for the getting this spiritual poverty, we must know and premise this caution, that we must not be so 'poor in spirit,' as to deny the work of grace in our hearts. It is one thing to be 'poor in spirit,' and to see our wants; and it is another thing to be unthankful and unkind; to deny the work of grace, and so to gratify Satan. We must not give false witness against ourselves, and so deny the work of God's Spirit in us. It is not poverty, but darkness of spirit. We are not acquainted with that grace that God hath enriched us with. Therefore where the soul is in a right temper, there is a double eye, one to see the defects and the stains of those graces we have; to see what we are wanting in of what we should be, and to see how our graces are stained, and that there is a mingling of our corruptions with them. The viewing with the one eye, that we have any grace, that should make us cheerful, and thankful, and comfortably go on, considering that there are some beginnings that God will perfect; for he never repents of his beginnings. And then a sight of the want, and of the stains of those graces that we mingle our corruptions with them; that works again this poverty of spirit to go on still out of ourselves, to desire grace, to purge and cleanse ourselves more and more. Therefore, I beseech you, let us remember that, that we do not unthankfully deny the work of grace, and think that to be poverty of spirit, as some do out of covetousness, because they have not that they would have, they think they have nothing at all; that is a spiritual covetousness. But let us be wise to discern what God hath wrought in our hearts, what he hath done for and in our souls. A holy man, you shall have him much in mourning and complaining, but it is of himself, not of God, as if God were wanting to him. You shall have a holy man in a perpetual kind of despair, but it is in himself; he hopes in God still. Remember this caution, that as we complain, so let us be sure it be of ourselves; alway justify God in his mercy; and if we despair, let us despair of ourselves, that we can do nothing of ourselves. But be sure to maintain, all we can, the hope of God's rich mercy in Christ.

Now, having premised this caution, the way to come to spiritual poverty among many others is: first, to bring ourselves *into the presence of God*, to the presence of greater lights than our own. Men that think themselves somebody when they are alone; yet when they consider God sees them, whose eyes are a thousand times brighter than the sun, then they learn to abhor themselves in 'dust and ashes,' as we see Job did when God talked with him, when he saw God, Job xlii. 6; and Abraham when he talked with God, he accounts himself dust and ashes, Gen. xviii. 27. Let us bring ourselves into the presence of God; consider his holiness, his justice. And withal let us bring ourselves to greater lights than our own; that is, oft come into the company of those that have greater grace than ourselves. The stars give no light when the sun is up. The stars are somebody in the night, but they are nothing in the day. And those that are conceited of their own excellencies, when they come into the presence and company, and converse with those that are better than themselves, their spirits fall down, they are abased. It is a good course therefore not to love alway to be best in the company, as is some men's vanity, because they will be conceited of their own worth, but to present ourselves before God in his ordinances, and present ourselves in communion and fellowship with others that are greater and richer in grace than ourselves, and so we may see our own wants. This is one direction to get spiritual poverty.

2. Again, That we may come to be poor in spirit, let us consider what we are, *that we are creatures*. The term whence creation begins is just nothing. It is so in the creatures in the world. God made all of nothing, and is it not so in the new creature much more? Therefore if I will be anything in myself as of myself, surely I must look to no creature of God's making. For grace is God's creature. Therefore it must rise of nothing; there must be a sight of our own nothingness. Indeed a Christian in himself is nothing now in the state of grace. Whatsoever he is for grace or glory, it is out of himself. He hath nothing in himself as of himself; all that he hath he hath from Christ. He is poor in himself, but he hath riches enough in Christ, if he sees his own poverty. He is a sinner in himself, but he hath righteousness enough in Christ, if he sees his sins. Let us know that this is a qualification to interest us in the good that is in Christ. We renew our right in Christ no otherwise than we renew the sense of our own poverty and want. Would we see all in Christ, that we have riches, and wisdom, and happiness, and favour, and life, and all in him? With the same spiritual eye of the soul, let us see that we have nothing in ourselves; for I can no otherwise renew that right and interest I have in Christ, but by renewing this sight. We altogether shine in the beams of our husband. The consideration of this will be a means to work our care and endeavour towards it; that we are creatures, 'new creatures;' and therefore we must rise of nothing in ourselves, and we must be maintained and supported by the new Adam, 'the second Adam,' and have fresh grace from him continually. 'We move and live in him,' as I said before.

3. Again, That we may be poor in spirit, help ourselves *with presenting to ourselves abasing, emptying considerations*. What be they? Among the rest reflect our minds back to what we were before God shewed mercy upon

us; how unprofitably we spent our days; what a deal of good we left undone that we might have done. For the present, consider the imperfections that hang upon us, whereby we even defile the best performances that come from us. Let us have in the eye of our soul presented our special corruptions for the present. For the time to come let us present to our souls what will become of us ere long; that for outward things, that nature is prone to be highly conceited of, they shall lie in the dust. These bodies of ours must lie low in the dust; all other things must be taken from us, and we from them, we know not how soon. Let us oft think and consider of the vanity of all things, what will all things be ere long. They must all come to nothing, The fire will consume all that is glorious in the world. There will be no excellency but the excellency of Christ, and his church and children; and think of the day of judgment. What will stand for current then? Think of the time of our dissolution, how we shall appear before Christ; what we have in us that will give us confidence at that day and time, to look upon him with comfort; that those thoughts of the time to come, of death, and judgment, and eternity may not be frightful to us. The consideration of these things will make us to look about us, and make us indeed 'poor in spirit.'

Especially let us consider what our profession requires of us; not by the law, let that go; but what in the covenant of grace we should be, and are not, it will shame the best of us. Alas! how much good might we have done that we have not! How have we failed in bringing honour and credit to our profession! How barren have we been in good works! How unwatchful over our thoughts and speeches, whereby we have stained our religion and our consciences, and grieved the Spirit of God. Let us consider how short we are of that we might have been; and this will bring inward shame and confusion of spirit, from whence this temper of poverty of spirit comes. Consider of these things, and enlarge them in your own meditations. There is not a more fruitful spending of our thoughts, next to the consideration of Christ, and the riches we have in him, than to consider what we are in ourselves; that we may be in a perpetual disposition of soul, fit to receive the good that is to be had in Christ.

Two graces are the main graces that must go along with us all the days of our lives; this grace to go out of ourselves; and another grace to go to another that is better than ourselves, in whom lies our happiness. That we may go out of ourselves and the creature, and all that is in the creature, poverty of spirit is necessary, to see that there is not that in ourselves that will yield a foundation of comfort, and poverty of spirit sees that there is not that that we possess in the creature that will stand out. The creature, that is a particular good, for a particular case, to supply a particular want, and but for a time, it is fading and outward; but the comfort we must have it must be spiritual and universal, to give contentment to the soul. The consideration of these things will force us to go out of ourselves; this poverty of spirit, that we have not enough to make us happy. The heathen men, by the use of discretion and knowledge, had so much to see that there is nothing in the world to make man happy; the negative part they knew well enough. But there must be another grace to carry us to a positive happiness where that lies, and that is the grace of trust that follows. 'I will leave in the midst of thee an afflicted and poor people,' that shall be disposed and prepared by their outward poverty to inward spiritual poverty; to go out of themselves to Christ, to trust in him.

'And they shall trust in the name of the Lord.'

This is the carriage of these poor and afflicted people. 'They shall trust in the name of the Lord.'

God hath no delight in afflicting his children; he joys and delights in the prosperity of his children. It is our sinful nature that forceth him to afflict us, that he may wean us from the world, because we are prone to surfeit upon things here below. All that God doth is that we may trust in him, which we would never do unless he did afflict us, and make us 'poor in spirit;' but when we are afflicted and poor in spirit, and have nothing at home, we will make out abroad, as people in necessity will do. Supply must be had, either at home or from without; and when the soul is beaten and driven out of itself, which requires much ado, then we are fit for this blessed act here spoken of, to 'trust in the name of the Lord.' And the one is an evidence of the other. How shall we know that we are sufficiently humbled and made poor in spirit? When we trust in the name of the Lord.

In the unfolding of these words, take these for grounds; which I will but name.

First, That naturally every man will have a trust, in himself, or out of himself.

Secondly, That God is the trust of the poor man; what he wants in himself he hath in God. God is the rock or the castle to which he retires. He hath supply in him.

The third is, that

Obs. God is trusted as he is known. They shall 'trust in the name of the Lord.' For God can be no otherwise trusted than he hath made his will known. It is presumptuous boldness to challenge anything of God that we have not a promise for; or to attribute that to him that he is not. God is therefore trusted as he hath made himself by some name known to us. He hath made himself known by his attributes, by his nature and essence, Jehovah; and by his word, and the promises in his word. For his word is one of the best and sweetest names whereby he hath made himself known. The name of God is glorious in all the world, in the creation; and every creature hath a tongue to shew forth the power, and wisdom, and goodness of God. But what is this to us, if we know not the will of God toward us? There is the name of God discovered; what he is in himself; something of his power and wisdom, &c. But what he is to us, gracious, and merciful, and sweet; that we must gather out of the discovery of his own breast. He must come out of that 'light that none can attain unto,' 1 Tim. vi. 16, and discover himself as he hath done in his word; and by this name of God, his word, we come to make use of his other names. The next thing I will speak of is the improvement of God when he is known, to trust in him, to pitch our trust and confidence upon him. 'They shall trust in the name of the Lord.'

Obs. For there must be an application of the soul to God. We must lay our souls upon God. Though he be a rock, yet we must lay our souls upon him; and though he be a foundation, yet we must build upon him and his truth revealed. There is an adequate comfort in God and in the Scriptures, and superabundant too to all our necessities whatsoever. It transcends them all. There is more in the spring than we want ourselves. Yet notstanding there must be grace in the soul to repair to God. There must be an hand, an empty beggar's hand, such as faith is, to reach that help that God yields. There must be a wing to fly to our tower. The wing of the soul is this trust and faith; and when these two meet, faith or trust, and God, what a sweet meeting is there! For emptiness and fulness, poverty and riches, weakness and strength, to meet together, these will grasp sweetly; for the excellency and all-sufficiency of the one, and the necessity of the other meeting together, breeds a sweet correspondency. We must 'trust,' therefore, in the name of the Lord. That is the way to improve whatsoever is in God for our good.

Faith, the nature of it is, after it hath applied itself to the grounds of comfort, to draw virtue and strength from God. Of itself it is the most beggarly grace of all. Love is a rich grace, but yet notwithstanding in the covenant of grace, wherein grace and mercy must have the glory, God hath established such a grace to rule there as ascribes all out of itself, and is an empty grace of itself, to make use of the riches that is out of itself; therefore God hath made choice of this trusting instead of all other graces, as indeed leading to all other graces whatsoever. God brings us home by a contrary way to that we fell from him. How did we fall from God at the first, that was our rock, our defence, and trust? We fell from him by distrust, by having him in a jealousy, as if he aimed more at himself than at our goods. So the devil persuaded our first parents. The next way, therefore, to come back again to God, it must be to have a good conceit of God, not to have him in jealousy, but to be convinced in our souls that he loves us better than we can love ourselves, in spite of the devil and all his temptations. So to trust God is to rely upon him in life and death. Therefore God hath appointed this grace, as he saith here, 'They shall trust in the name of the Lord.'

Now, because we all pretend we trust in the name of the Lord, we will first examine our trust. Let us try our trust a little, that we may see whether it be true trust or no. And then upon that we will give some directions how to come to this blessed condition, to trust 'in the name of the Lord.'

For the first: I do not take trust here for the first faith, which is the grace of union to receive Christ; but for the exercise of faith afterwards in a Christian's life. So we speak of it as a fruit rather that comes from faith. And we may know our trust in the name of the Lord, being now conceived as a gracious Father in Christ, clothed with the relation of a father: for so we must trust him, not God absolutely, for there is no comfort in an absolute God, distinct from his relations; but when we apprehend him in relation as a sweet Father in Christ, in that name, then the nature of God is lovely to us, between whom and us there was an infinite distance before. Now Christ being Immanuel, God with us, has brought God and us together in terms of league. Now our nature is lovely to God in Christ, because it is taken to the unity of his person; and God's nature is lovely to us, having made himself a Father in Christ his beloved Son. Therefore, when we speak of God, our thoughts must run upon God as thus conceived, as clothing himself with a sweet term of Father, our God in covenant, we must so apprehend him.

1. Now one evidence of this trust in this our God, is a care to please him in all things. When we depend upon any men, *we have a care to please them.* A tenant that fears to be thrust out, will strive to please his landlord. We that hold all upon this tenure, upon faith and trust in God, we should fear to displease him.

2. And there will be likewise *an use of all means to serve God's providence and care of us,* if we trust in him; or else it is a tempting and not a

trusting. There are no men more careful of the use of means than those that are surest of a good issue and conclusion; for the one stirs up diligence in the other. Assurance of the end stirs up diligence in the means. For the soul of a believing Christian knows that God hath decreed both; both fall under the same decree: when God purposed to do such a thing, he purposed to do it by such and such means. Trust, therefore, is with diligence in the use of all means that God hath ordained. He that trusts a physician's skill, will be very careful to observe what was prescribed, and will omit nothing. It is but presumption; it is not trust where there is not a care in the use of means, as we see many pretend to trust in God and sever the means from the end; they are regardless of the means of salvation.

3. Again, Those that trust in God, *they are quiet when they have used the means*. Faith hath a quieting power. It hath a power to still the soul and to take up the quarrels, and murmuring, and grudgings that are there, and to set the soul down quiet; because it proposeth to the soul greater grounds of comfort, than the soul can see any cause of discomfort. The soul being reasonable, yields to the strength of the reason. Now, when faith propounds grand comforts against all discouragements whatsoever, that overcomes them, that is greater in the way of comfort than other things in the way of discouragement, the soul is quiet. It hopes comfort will be had. The soul is silent and at rest. We see in Ps. xlii. 11, when there was a mutiny in David's soul, by reason of the perplexed state he was in, he falls a-chiding downright with his soul, 'Why art thou disquieted, O my soul! and why art thou troubled?' v. 11. But how doth he take up the contention? 'Trust in God, he is thy God.' So that wheresoever there is faith, there is a quiet soul first or last. There will be stirring at the first; the waters of the soul will not be quiet presently. As in a pair of balances there will be a little stirring when the weight is put in till there will be poise; so in the soul there will be some stirring and moving; it comes not to a quiet consistence till there be some victory of faith with some conflict, till at length it rest and stay the soul. For this power faith has to quiet the soul, because it bottoms the soul so strongly. There is reason for it; it sets the soul upon God, and upon his promises. 'Therefore he that trusts in God is as mount Sion,' Ps. cxxv. 1. You may stir him sometime and move him, but you cannot remove him. The soul is quiet, because it is pitched upon a quiet object.

Therefore, where there is cherishing of disturbance in the soul, and cherishing of doubts, there is no faith, or very little faith; because it is the property of faith to silence the soul and to make quiet where it comes. This is one evidence and sign of true faith. And this is discerned especially in times of great trouble; for then the soul of the righteous is not disquieted, as you have it in Ps. cxii. 7, 8, 'His heart is fixed, therefore he is not afraid of ill tidings.'

4. And therefore this evidence to the rest, that faith as it hath a quieting power, *so it hath a power to free the soul from all base fears*, from *the tyranny of base fear*. There will some fear arise. We carry flesh about us, and flesh will alway be full of objections and trouble our peace; but, notwithstanding, it will free the soul—this trusting in God—from the tyranny and dominion of base fears. If any news or tidings be of any great hard matter, I beseech you, who hath his soul best composed at that time? A sound Christian, that hath made his peace with God, that hath his trust in God, that knows what it is to make use of God, to repair to him. But for

another man, in the time of extremity and trouble, he runs hither and thither, he hath not a tower to go unto, he hath no place of refuge to repair to. Therefore he is worse than the poor silly creatures. There is not a creature but hath a retiring place. The poor conies have the rocks to go unto, and the birds have their nests, and every creature, when night or danger approacheth, they have their hiding places. Only a wicked, careless man that hath not acquainted himself with God, when troubles come, he hath no hiding, nor no abiding place, but lies open to the storm of God's displeasure. Therefore he is surprised with fears and cares, and pulled in pieces with distractions. He is as a meteor that hangs in the clouds; he cannot tell which way to fall. But a Christian is not such a meteor, he falls square which way soever he falls, cast him which way you will. For his soul is fixed, he hath laid his soul upon his God. We see the difference in this between Saul and David. When David was in trouble, 'he trusted in the Lord his God,' when he was ready to be stoned. What doth Saul when he was in trouble? He goes to the witch; and from thence to the sword's point.*

5. Again, Where there is this excellent grace of trusting in God, and the soul is calmed by the Spirit of God, to rely upon God in covenant as a Father in Christ, *it will rely upon God without means and when all things seem contrary.* So the Spirit of God will difference a Christian from a natural man, that will go so far as his brain can reach. If he can see how things can be compassed, he will trust God, as if God had not a larger comprehension than he. Where he sees no way or means to contrive a deliverance, nor no means to satisfy his desire, there the soul of a natural man sinks and falls down: a politician will go as far as reason can carry him. But a Christian, when he sees no means, he knows God can make means. Now, when all things are opposite, if he hath a word of God, he will trust God, even against the present state and face of things, as Job saith, 'Though he kill me, yet will I trust in him,' Job xiii. 15. Therefore in the sense of sin, because there is a promise to sinners that, if they confess their sins, God will pardon them; he will believe the forgiveness of sins, though he feel the guilt of sin. And in misery he will believe an evasion,† and escape, and that God will support him in it, because God hath so promised. And in 'darkness, when he sees no light,' as it is Isa. l. 10; in such a state 'he will trust in God.' As a child in the dark clasps about his father, so a child of God in darkness when he sees no light, he will clasp about his God, and break thorough the clouds that are between God and his soul; as indeed faith hath a piercing eye. It pulls off the vizor of God's face. Though he seem angry, yet he will believe he is in covenant and he is a Father. Therefore though God shew himself in his dealing as offended, yet he argues God may be offended with me, but he cannot hate me; there is hope. Faith, where it is in any strength, it will believe in contraries. In death, when a man is turned to rottenness and dust, faith apprehends life and resurrection, and glory to come. It will trust in God's means, or no means, if it hath a promise.

6. Again, He that trusts in God truly *will trust him for all things, and at all times.* For all things; for faith never chooseth and singleth out its object, to believe this and not that, for all comes from the same God. Therefore he that trusts God for one thing, will trust him for all things. If I will trust a man for many pounds, surely I will trust him for a shilling.

* Cf. Ps. xiii. 15, xxvi. 1, with 1 Sam. xxviii. 9, *seq.*, and xxxi. 4.—G.

† That is, ='a way out.' Cf. 1 Cor. x. 13.—G.

He that pretends he will trust God—God will save me, God is merciful—and yet notwithstanding will not trust him for common things, it is an abusive delusion and flattering of his own soul in vain. There is no such trust in him, because he that trusts God for the main will trust him for the less. Therefore true trust is for all things. He that trusts God for forgiveness of sins, which is the main, and hath wrestled with God for the forgiveness of sins, and found peace with God there, he will easily wrestle in other baser and less temptations. As God saith to Jacob, 'Thou art Israel, thou hast prevailed with God, and shalt prevail over men,' Gen. xxxii. 28, so a true Christian, that in the grand point of forgiveness of sins, when his conscience is surprised with the fear of God's wrath, hath gotten assurance of the pardon of his sins, when he is to set upon other lesser temptations, he overcomes them easily.

1. Therefore a Christian will trust God, as for forgiveness of sins and life everlasting, so *with his good name*. Oh, will some say, you will be reported of thus and thus. He cares not. He knows the cause is just. He will trust his good name with God, 'who will bring a man's righteousness forth clear as the noonday,' as David speaks, Ps. xxxvii. 6. He that will not trust God with his good name is of a base spirit, and fear of disgrace keeps many men from many just actions.

2. He that truly trusts God, will trust him *with the righting of his cause*. He will not pull God's office out of his hands. He will not revenge himself, but he will trust God. God certainly will right me first or last. He will only use the legal means, and that quietly. But a man that is not acquainted with the Spirit of God is presently moved with revenge, and hath not learned to overcome himself in this conflict. A man hath gone indeed very far in religion, that can conquer himself in this conflict, that can trust his cause with God when he is wronged and overcome by might, &c. So our Saviour Christ committed his cause to him 'that was able to judge righteously,' 1 Peter ii. 23. Every true Christian hath the spirit of Christ. He, 'when he was reviled, retorted not again, but committed the cause to him that was able to judge righteously.' Shall I be able to commit my soul to God in the hour of death? and shall I not, in case of revenge, be able to commit my case to God, when I have done that that peaceably I may do? I may suspect that I am but yet an hypocrite; I have not true trust in God.

3. Again, He that hath learned truly to trust God for the grand main matters, he will trust him likewise *with his posterity, with his children, without using indirect means to make them rich*, as if they could not be blessed unless they have such a portion put into their hand when we die; as if God had not stock enough for them, 'for the earth is the Lord's, and the fulness thereof,' Ps. xxiv. 1. And he is the 'God of the faithful, and of their seed,' Gen. xvii. 19. Is he so? Then let us labour to leave our children in covenant, leave them in a gracious frame and state of soul, that they may be God's children; and then we leave them rich, for we leave them 'God all-sufficient' to be their portion. Therefore those that pretend, I do this but for my posterity and children, when they are unjust and unconscionable* in their getting, they make this defence for their unbelief. If they had true faith, as they trust God with their souls, as they pretend at least, so they would with their children and posterity.

4. Again, He that trusts God truly, will trust God *with his gifts, with the distribution of his alms, with parting with that he hath for the present*, when he sees it like seed cast upon the water. When seed is cast upon the

* That is, 'unconscientious.'—G.

water, we are likely never to see it again. Oh, but saith the wise man, 'cast thy bread upon the water, and thou shall see it after a certain time.' He that hath learned to trust God will believe this. Though he cast away his bounty, yet he hath cast it upon God and Christ, that will return it again; he knows he doth but lend to the Lord. Therefore those that think their bounty and alms and good deeds to be lost, because they see not a present return, a present crop of that seed, they have not a spirit of trust in God; for he that hath will endeavour to be 'rich in good works;' nay, he will account it a special favour, a greater favour, to have a heart to do good, than to have means. A reprobate may have means, abundance to do good; but only a child of God hath a heart to do good, and when he hath gotten a large and gracious heart to do good, it pleaseth him. Then he sees he hath an evidence that he is the child of God. He knows he shall not lose a cup of cold water, not the least thing that he doth in the name of Christ. The apprehension of this should make us more fruitful, and 'abound in the work of the Lord,' 1 Cor. xv. 58. It is for want of trust and faith that we are so barren as we are in good works.

5. Again, He that will trust God with the greatest matters, will trust God *with his ways for direction*. He will not trust his own wit and wisdom, but God. God shall be wise for him. He will follow God's directions, and whatsoever is contrary to God's direction he will not do. He will acknowledge God in all his ways. Prov. iii. 5, 'Acknowledge God in all thy ways,' acknowledge him to be thy guide, thy defender, thy light, to direct thee; acknowledge him to be able and willing to give thee success; acknowledge God in all thy ways and consultations; and when we have especially any great matters in hand, oh, I beseech you, let us learn to acknowledge God. What is it to acknowledge him? To go to him for direction and protection in doing our duty, that we seek to him for strength and for success; this is to acknowledge God in our ways. What makes men so unfortunate and successless in their consultations? Because they are so faithless; they do not acknowledge God in their ways, but trust too much to seeming things and appearance of things; they are carried too much with that. Though things seem to go never so well, yet let nothing make us give over to acknowledge God; nay, when things are never so ill, let us acknowledge God, for God can set all straight and at rights again. Alas! what a small matter is it for him that rules heaven and earth, and turns this great wheel of all things, to turn the lesser wheels to order lesser businesses, and bring them to a happy issue and conclusion! It is but a little matter with his command, seeing he rules all things. It is but trusting in him and praying to him, and then using the means with dependence upon him. Let us therefore acknowledge God this way, by committing our ways and affairs to him. We need knowledge and strength, and a comfortable issue for all that is necessary in our affairs; let us acknowledge God, and fetch all these from him.

6. Well, the last thing that we have any use of trusting God withal is, *when we are dying, to trust our souls, to commit them to God, and yield them up to him*, our *depositum*, to lay it with him. He that hath inured himself to trust God all his life, and to live by faith, he will be able at length with some comfort to die by faith. He that hath trusted God all his life with all things that God hath trusted him, he can easily trust God with his soul; and he that hath not inured himself to trust God in this life, undoubtedly he will never trust God with his soul when he dies. It is but a forced trust.

Thus you see in all the passages of our lives we must learn to trust God, and to make use of God, for God is so abundant that he is never drawn dry. He joys when he is made use of. It is an honour to him. Let us try ourselves by that I have said, whether we truly trust God or no. Let us not deceive our own souls, but labour to trust God for all things. Let it be our daily practice in the use of means. Look to the course that he prescribes us, and then look up to him for strength and blessing and success. This ought to be the life of a Christian, *Oculus ad cœlum*, as they say of the governor of a ship. He hath his hand to the stern, and his eye to the pole-star, to be directed by that. So the life of a Christian. He must have his hand to the stern, he must be doing that that God prescribes him, and he must have his eye to the star, to be guided in his course by God's direction. He that hath not this knows not what it is to trust in God.

How shall we bring our souls to this so necessary a duty? Indeed, it is a very hard matter. We know what it is to live by our wits, by our wealth, by our lands; but what it is to live by faith in depending upon God, few souls are acquainted with that.

Therefore, in the first place, *learn to know God*. You see here, we must trust in his name. We know men by their names. God and his name are all one. His name is himself, and himself is his name. Therefore, let us learn to know God as he hath discovered himself: know him in his works, but especially *in his word;* know him by that work, as he hath discovered himself in his word. Let us know his promises, and have them in store for all assays* whatsoever; promises for grace and for direction in this world. God will not 'fail us, nor forsake us,' John xiv. 18. He will be in all extremities with us, 'in the fire and in the water,' Isa. xliii. 2; and the promises of issue, 'All things shall work for good to them that love God,' Rom. viii. 28; and the promise of his Spirit, 'He will give his Holy Spirit to them that ask him,' Luke xi. 13. Besides particular promises, a world of them in Scripture, let us know God in these promises; they are our inheritance, our portion. And if we should go to God, and not be acquainted with these, he will ask us upon what ground? How shall we be able to go to God? But when we have his promise, we may say boldly with the psalmist, 'Lord, remember thy promise, wherein thou hast caused thy servant to trust.' We may put God in remembrance: not that he forgets, but he will have us mindful of what he promiseth, and put him in mind. And it is an evidence to our souls that he will grant any thing, when we have faith to put him in mind of his promise: 'Lord, remember thy promise, wherein thou hast caused thy servant to trust.' Lord, thou canst not deny thy word, and thy truth, and thyself, and thy promise, and thy name by which thou hast made thyself known. Thus we should know God in his word; as it is Ps. ix. 10, 'They that know thy name will trust in thee, O Lord.' We never trust a man till we know him; and those that are not good, we say they are better known than trusted; but the more we know God, the more we shall trust him.

And know him *in his special attributes that the word sets him out in*, besides the promises, that we may know that he is able to make good all these promises; and then we shall trust him. What are those attributes? He hath made himself known to be all-sufficient. What a world of comfort is in that. He saith to Abraham, 'I am God all-sufficient: walk before me, and be perfect,' Gen. xvii. 1. Take thou no thought for any other thing: 'I am God all-sufficient.' There is in him whatsoever may be for an object of trust. He is all-sufficient. He hath power. 'Our trust is in the name

* That is, 'essays,' endeavours, = undertakings.'—G.

of the Lord, that made heaven and earth,' Ps. cxv. 15. There is a consideration to strengthen faith : there is power enough. We believe in a God that made heaven and earth ; and there is will to help us, he is our God ; and there is skill to help us : as St Peter saith, 'He knows how to deliver,' 2 Pet. ii. 9. It is his practice. He hath used it from the beginning of the church, and will to the end. He knows how to deliver them, to protect and stand by them ; he hath power, and will, and skill to do it. And then again, he is everywhere. He is such a castle, and tower, and defence. We have him near us in all times : he is 'a present help in trouble,' as it is Ps. xlvi. 1. What an object of trust is here, if we had but faith to make use of it. Let us therefore know God in his word, in his attributes, and this will be a means to strengthen trust ; as it is Ps. xxxvi. 7, 'How sweet is thy goodness ; therefore shall the sons of men trust under the shadow of thy wings.' Why come we under the shadow of God's wing ? Because his goodness is sweet : he is a fit object for trust. The things of this world, the more we know them, the less we trust them, for they are but vain. But there is such infiniteness in God, that the more we know him, the more we shall trust him. Therefore, let us grow in the knowledge of God's word and truth.

And add *experimental knowledge.* It helps trust marvellously : the experience of others, and our own experience. When we see God hath helped his church in all times, especially when they have sought him by fasting and prayer : 'Our fathers trusted in thee, and were not confounded,' Ps. xxii. 4, 5. Therefore, if we trust in thee, we shall not be confounded. So for our own experience : 'Thou hast been my God from my mother's womb ; I have depended upon thee from my mother's breast : forsake me not in mine old years, in my grey hairs, when my strength faileth me,' Ps. lxxi. 18. Thus we may gather upon God from former experience, that God will not now forsake us, because we have had experience of his kindness in former times. He hath been my God from my childhood ; therefore he will be now. This is a good argument, because God is as he was ; he is the same, he is never drawn dry : 'Where he loves, he loves to the end,' John xiii. 1. Where he begins, he will end. Therefore, this should strengthen our faith, to gather experience from former things. Thus David allegeth the lion and the bear ; and so St Paul, 'He hath delivered me, therefore he will deliver me,' 2 Tim. iii. 11. It is ordinary with the saints of God.

Again, If we would trust in God, labour every day to be acquainted with God *in daily prayer, in hearing, and reading, and meditation.* We trust friends with whom we are much acquainted ; and those that are not acquainted with God, in that communion which belongs to Christians, that do not often talk with God by prayer and meditation, when they go to God in extremity, what will God say to them ? Upon what acquaintance ? You are strangers to me, and I will be a stranger to you ; and 'Wisdom itself will laugh at their destruction,' Prov. i. 26, when they will force acquaintance upon God when they have use of him, and never care for him in the time of peace. Therefore, if we would trust God, and go to God boldly, as who is there here now that will not have need of him ? We have need of him continually, but sometimes more than others. Therefore, I say, let us be acquainted with him, that we may after trust him. Those that have not the care to be acquainted with God, either they have not the heart to go to God, or if they have, they have but a cold answer. But indeed, for the most part, they have no heart to go to God, for their hearts misgive them, and tell them they have been careless of God, they have neglected God. Therefore, God will not regard them: 'Go to the gods ye have trusted,' as it is Judges x. 14. Answerable to our care, beloved, in the time of peace, will our comfort be when we are in trouble. Therefore I beseech you, let us remember this, as one means to strengthen our trust, our daily acquaintance with God; and acquaint ourselves so with him, as to keep him our friend, not to offend him, for if we offend him, we shall not trust him. A galled conscience is afraid of God, as a sore eye is of light. A comfortable conscience* is from a conscience to please God. 'This is our boldness and confidence,' saith Paul, that we have laboured to 'keep a good conscience,' that we may have him our friend, 2 Cor. i. 15, Heb. xiii. 18.

Again, Let us labour *to exercise our trust upon all occasions;* for things that are exercised are the brighter and the stronger. Let us inure ourselves to trust in God for all things, and to trust him with all things; with our bodies, with our souls, with our estates, with our children, with our ways, with our good name, with our credit and reputation, with all; as I said before in the signs of trust. Faith it grows in the exercise, as we see Ps. lxii., a psalm expressing David's trust in God, and the conflict with his soul in trusting. He begins, 'Yet my soul waits upon the Lord,' &c.; and in verse 2d, 'I shall not be greatly moved,' saith he; but when he had gone on, and exercised his faith still, then he saith in verse 6th, 'He is my rock, and my Saviour, and defence; I shall not be moved.' He that at the beginning saith, 'I shall not greatly be moved,' afterward, working upon his heart and soul, and exercising his faith, saith, 'I shall not be moved; he is my rock, my Saviour and defence.' Faith it is the engine by which we do all, by which we prevail with God and overcome the world, and all the snares on the right hand and on the left; it is that whereby we do all. Therefore we had need to keep it in exercise, and inure it, that we may have it to manage and use upon all occasions. It is not enough to have faith in us, but we must live by it. It must not only live in us, but we must live by it. This is another way to strengthen this faith, and assurance, and trusting in God.

The next is to practise that I spake of in the forenoon, to grow 'poor in spirit,' 'for they shall trust in the name of the Lord.' Let us labour more and more to see our own wants. A Christian should have a double eye: one to look to himself and to his own wants, to be abased; another eye to God's promise, to God's nature, to trust in God; and thus we should pass our days. The more we can empty ourselves, the more we shall be filled with God. We see here in the text the way to trust in God, to be 'poor in spirit.' The reason is in nature. Whosoever is not poor in himself, and sees a necessity, he will never go out of himself, for he hath some other supply. Therefore, if we would learn to trust in God, we must learn to empty ourselves of all self-confidence, by observing our weakness and wants; by taking notice, not so much of our graces, as of our wants. When Moses came from the mount, his face shone; he knew not of it. All the world about him knew it besides himself, but he observed it not, saith the Scripture, Exod. xxxiv. 29. So when a Christian considers not, especially in temptations to pride, what he hath, but what he wants—how little good he hath done, how many evil thoughts and actions have passed from him, how short he is in fruitfulness and thankfulness to God—this is the way to trust in God, for then we will keep close to God when we do see our own weakness.

* Qu. 'confidence'?—Ed.

And let us labour *to have a spirit of sanctification*, to have our souls more and more renewed to trust in God, or else all other courses are nothing; for when it comes to particulars, if the soul be not sanctified there is no correspondency and harmony between it and God. How can an unsanctified soul close with a holy God? Therefore we must labour to be good and to do good; as the apostle Peter saith, 'to commit our souls to God in doing good,' 1 Pet. iv. 19. Let us labour to be good, to get grace, and then there will be a harmony, a connaturalness between a holy God and a holy soul; and then we shall trust and rely upon him easily. Where there is not grace in the heart subduing corruptions, when it comes to particulars, whether to trust in God or man, then the soul will rebel, and scorn as it were trusting in God. It will go to wits, to friends, to favours, and other helps.

Let a man be never such a scholar, of never so great parts, when he comes to any shift, if he have not grace in him, he will disdain out of pride of spirit, as every man naturally is deeply proud, to rely upon conscience, and upon the truth and promises of the word, and upon such terms. These be weak things. No; he will stir hell rather, and earth, and all means. He accounts it greatness that he can do so. It is only the holy man that will cleave fast to God, and to his truth and word, for he relisheth it. The Spirit that penned the Scriptures and the promises, it rules in his heart, and therefore he relisheth them. Oh these promises are sweet! And as he can trust the promises, so he can trust God; because, as I said before, he is acquainted with them. Where there is not a gracious heart, there will never be a believing, trusting heart.

There is in God infiniteness of ways of supply, let us labour therefore *for a prudent heart*, to learn the skill of fetching out of God for all necessities. As our want is, so let us fetch supply from some attribute of God, and some promise answerable. This is the wisdom of the saints of God. Are we in extremity? Then with Jehoshaphat say, 'We know not, Lord, what to do: but our eyes are toward thee,' 2 Chron. xx. 12. Are we perplexed that we want wisdom? Then go to God, who is infinitely wise. Consider him so, for he is fit for the soul; nay, he exceeds all the maladies and wants of the soul. There is not only abundance in God, but redundance and overflowing abundance. Therefore there wants but skill to make use of what is in him for our turn. Are we wronged? Go to God, that 'judgeth righteously,' Jer. xi. 20; consider him in that relation, as a God 'to whom vengeance belongeth,' Ps. xciv. 1. Are we overpowered? Go to God, 'that made heaven and earth,' to the Almighty God, Ps. cxv. 15. Are we troubled with the sense of sin? Go to God, that is 'the Father of all mercy, and God of all comfort,' Rom. xv. 5. Are we cast down, and no man regards us? Go to God, that styles himself 'the comforter of the abject,' 2 Cor. vii. 6. This is the skill that faith learns, not only in gross to think of God, but to think of God answerable to all occasions; as indeed there is somewhat in God to satisfy the soul in all extremities whatsoever. I beseech you, let us learn to do this. What a happy condition is he in that hath learned to inure his soul to trust in God for the removal of all ill, and for the obtaining of all good! He is sure of all. 'For God is a sun and a shield;' a sun for all that is good, and a shield to defend us from all ill. He is so to all that trust in him. He is a 'buckler, and an exceeding great reward,' Ps. xviii. 30. He is a buckler to award* and shield ill from us, and an exceeding great reward for all

* That is, = 'ward off.'—G.

that is good. Therefore in how happy a condition is the soul that is acquainted with this blessed exercise of trusting and believing in God! It is a state wherein we shall be kept from all ill—I mean from the ill of ills: not from the ill of sense, but from the ill of ills, and from the poison of all ill. Whatsoever ill we endure, there shall be comfort mixed with it; and it is better to have it than the comfort. What a comfort is this! 'They that trust in the Lord shall want nothing that is good. He that trusts in the Lord is as a tree planted by the river side,' Jer. xvii. 7, 8. He shall alway have his leaf flourishing and bear fruit, because he is at the well-head. He that hath the spring can never want water, and he that is in the sun can never want light. He that is at the great feast can never want provision. He that hath learned to trust in God, and can improve what is in him, what can he want? Oh it is the scarceness of our faith that we want comfort! As our faith is, so is our comfort; and if we could bring a thousand times larger faith to grasp the promises, we should carry away larger comfort and strength.

NOTES.

(*a*) P. 241.—'In the original it is poor, and mild, and gentle.' Cf. Dr Henderson *in loc.*

(*b*) P. 246.—'As St Augustine . . . . saith, "We should boast and glory of nothing, because nothing is ours."' A frequent acknowledgment in the 'Confessions,' with varying phraseology. G.

SPIRITUAL MOURNING.

SPIRITUAL MOURNING.

NOTE.

'Spiritual mourning' forms Nos. 14 and 15 of the Saint's Cordials in first edition, 1629. It was withdrawn from the after-editions along with others, to give room for another series which had been published in the intervals. The title-page will be found below.* Cf. notes Vol. IV. page 76, and V. page 176. G.

* SPIRITVAL
MOVRNING:

In Two Sermons.

Wherein is laid open,

Who are spirituall mourners, and what it is to mourne spiritually.
That all godly mourning is attended with comfort.
How spirituall mourning is known and discerned from other mournings.
Together with the meanes to attaine it, and the tryall thereof, in sundry instances, &c.

[Wood-cut here, as described in Vol. IV. p. 60.]

Vprightnes Hath Boldnes.

LONDON,

Printed in the yeare 1629.

SPIRITUAL MOURNING

THE FIRST SERMON.

Blessed are they that mourn, for they shall be comforted.—Mat. V. 4.

We have spoken of spiritual poverty the last day, when we shewed you that it is a grace especially in the understanding.* We must now come to the affections. And first, our Saviour begins with mourning, which follows immediately from poverty of spirit. Mourning is a wringing or pinching of the soul upon the apprehension of some evil present, whether it be privative or positive, as we speak; that is, when a man finds that absent that he desires, and that present which he abhors, then the soul shrinks and contracts itself, and is pinched and wringed; and this is that we call mourning. Now this always comes to pass in poverty. Such as the poverty is, such is the mourning; and therefore our blessed Saviour's order is very good in joining mourning to that poverty of which we have spoken. Thus much for the order.

Now for the words. There are, you see, two things in this verse.

1. A point. 2. A proof.

Our Saviour's point shall be our point of doctrine at this time, because we would not speak one thing twice. Therefore we will lay down the point in our Saviour's own words, and that is this, *that spiritual mourners are blessed men*. He is an happy man that is a good mourner. He that can mourn for his sins, he is in an happy case. That is the point.

Now in the prosecution of this, we must first expound it; secondly, prove it; and then apply it to you, as our Saviour doth to his hearers, Luke vi. 21, 'Blessed are ye that mourn.'

1. For the first, I may expound the point and the text both under one. You see the proposition what it is, *every good mourner is in an happy condition*. Here let us consider a little the terms to explicate them. Who is the party in speech? 'Blessed is the mourner,' saith Christ in Matthew; 'Blessed,' saith he in Luke vi. 21, 'are the weepers.' Both these, mourning and weeping, they are fruits of the same tree and root. The root is sorrow and sadness, opposite to joy; the bud mourning, opposite to mirth;

* The reference is probably to 'Rich Poverty,' from Zephaniah iii. 12, in the present volume.—G.

the blossoms weeping, opposite to laughter. The matter then is this, that they that are spiritual mourners are happy men; that is, those men that have not only cause and matter of sorrow and mourning, for so all have, but have also a heart to mourn. There is in them a disposition of mourning, they can do it, they will do it occasionally, they do perform it inwardly, they bleed, which is termed mourning outwardly, they demonstrate it, as our Saviour instanceth in weeping. These be the parties here spoken of that are mourners. Now what is the thing that is affirmed of them? that is, blessedness and happiness; the mourners are blessed and happy. As mourning is in [it]self, it is not simply good, but because it makes way for happiness. To call mourning happiness simply, were to speak a contradiction, to term misery felicity, and to make felicity misery. But he that mourns aright, is happy in a sense, he is in a happy estate and condition. A mournful state is a happy estate; happy, because this mourning is an argument of some happiness and goodness for the present, and a pledge of more for the future. It makes way for comfort and future happiness, and therefore he is happy.

Obj. You see the proposition now, how it is mournful men are happy men. But now for the quantity and extent of this proposition. Is this, will some men say, universally true? Are all men that mourn blessed men?

Ans. Nothing less. There is a carnal mourning, when a man mourns for the presence of goodness, and for the absence of sin, because he is restrained and cannot be so bad as he would be. There is a natural mourning, when a man mourns upon natural motives, when natural losses and crosses are upon him. There is a spiritual mourning, when a man mourns in a spiritual manner, for spiritual things, upon spiritual motives, as afterwards we shall shew; when he mourns, because good things that are spiritually good are so far from him, and spiritual ills are so near to him. This is the mourner that Christ here speaks of, and this is the mourning that hath the blessing. Other mourning may occasion this through God's blessing, and may give some overture to this mourning, but the blessing belongs to the spiritual mourner and the spiritual mourning. Mourning must be expounded as poverty. Every poor man is not a blessed man, except his outward poverty bring him to spiritual poverty. So every mourner and every weeper is not therein blessed, except his outward losses, and crosses, and occasions, be an occasion through God's blessing and a means to bring him to spiritual sorrow and mourning. Thus now you see then the meaning of the proposition; it is thus much, that he that mourns spiritually and holily, why he is in an happy estate and condition. This is the meaning of the point.

2. Now let us proceed to the second thing, the proving of it. For proof we need go no further than our Saviour's own testimony; yet we have besides his testimony some proofs and some reasons to give. For his testimony: 'Blessed,' saith our Saviour's own mouth, 'are they that mourn;' and Luke vi. 21, 'Blessed are they that weep.' This weeping and this mourning must be understood of spiritual weeping and spiritual mourning, as we told you, and then the testimony is very clear, every man that so mourns is an happy man. Our Saviour doth not only speak this, but prove it, 1. By an argument drawn from the contrary: Luke vi. 25, 'Woe be to you that laugh now.' These carnal mirth-mongers are in a miserable estate, and therefore spiritual mourners are in an happy estate. 2. He confirms and backs this by a reason here in the text: 'Blessed are

the mourners, *for* they shall be comforted.' This reason will not hold in all kind of mourning and all kind of comfort. It is no good argument to say, Blessed is the man that is in pain, for he shall be refreshed and relieved; blessed is the man that is hungry, for he shall be fed and have his wants supplied. But yet this argument holds good, 'Blessed are they that mourn, *for* they shall be comforted;' namely, with God's comforts, with the comforts of the Spirit, with the comforts of the word, the comforts of heaven. The comforts of God are beyond all the miseries and sorrows that a man can endure in this life; and though he do mourn and weep for them, yet notwithstanding, the comforts, the wages, will so far exceed all his sorrows that he is happy in this. He cannot buy spiritual comforts too dear, he cannot have them upon hard terms possibly. Though they cost him never so many tears, never so much grief, and sorrow, and heart-breaking, yet if he have them, he is happy in having them upon what rate soever.

Yea, further, spiritual mourning carries comfort with it, besides the harvest of comfort that abides the mourner afterwards. There are first-fruits of comfort here to be reaped, so it is that the more a man mourns spiritually, the more he rejoiceth; the more his sorrow is, the more his comfort is. His heart is never so light, so cheerful, and so comfortable, as when he can pour forth himself with some sighs, groans, and tears, before God. So that then our Saviour clears the point, that they are happy men that mourn in an holy manner. Howsoever mourning be not comfort, and misery be not happiness, yet notwithstanding, affliction and mourning may argue an happy estate and blessed condition, and that in these respects following, which we shall name to you, which shall serve for reasons of the point.

1. First, He that mourns spiritually *hath a good judgment*, and therefore is happy. Spiritual affection it argues a spiritual judgment and understanding. For the affections they work according as they receive information. A creature that is led by fancy, hath brutish affections; a man that is guided with matter of reason hath rational affections, as we term them; but a man that hath his mind enlightened and sanctified hath holy affections. So that holy mourning and holy affections argues a sound mind, a holy, settled, and spiritual judgment, and that is an happiness.

2. Secondly, It argues *a good heart too*.

(1.) First, *A tender and soft heart*. For a stone cannot mourn, only the fleshy heart it is that can bleed. He that then can mourn spiritually, he hath an evidence to his heart, that his heart is soft, that he hath a tender heart, and that is a blessing, and makes a man a blessed man.

(2.) As his heart is tender, so also *it is sound*. It is a healthful soul and an healthful temper, as I may speak, that he hath. For mourning proceeds out of love and hatred; out of agreement, if it be a spiritual mourning, with that which is good, and out of a contrariety and opposition between us and that which is bad. So that he that can mourn after goodness, and mourn for sin and badness, if it be spiritual mourning, this man shews he hath a good heart, his heart agrees with that which is good, his heart disagrees, and stands in opposition, and hath an antipathy to that which is bad. And this is a right constitution and temper of soul, that makes a man happy. There is one reason then why he that mourns spiritually may well be deemed an happy man, because he hath a sound judgment, and because he hath a sound and a soft heart too.

2. Secondly, As he is happy in the cause, so he will be happy *in the effect too of his godly mourning*. For godly sorrow and mourning brings

forth blessed fruits and effects; the apostle in 2 Cor. vii. 10, *seq.*, delivers divers of them, as there you see.

(1.) First, this is one thing in spiritual mourning; *it secures and excludes a man from carnal and hellish mourning;* yea, this orders him and saves him harmless from all other griefs. A gracious mourning, it moderates natural grief, and expels and drives out carnal and hellish grief and sorrow, like good physic, that heals and strengthens nature, and expels that poison that is hurtful to nature. The more a man can mourn for his sins, the less he will mourn for other matters; the more heavy sin lies upon his soul, the more lightly he can bear other losses and crosses, whatsoever they be. So that this mourning prevents a great deal of unprofitable mourning. When a man bleeds unseasonably and unsatiably, the way to divert it is to open a vein and to let him blood elsewhere, and so you save the man. When a man pours forth himself unseasonably and unprofitably in needless tears, griefs, and cares, the only way is to turn his tears into a right channel, to make him mourn for that which is mournful, and to set him to weep for that which deserves tears. If he weep in an holy and spiritual manner, he shall be secured and preserved from poisonful and hurtful tears.

(2.) Secondly, This is another happy effect of godly mourning, that spiritual and godly mourning *alway doth a man good and never any hurt.* Worldly sorrow, saith the apostle, causeth death. It hurts the soul, it hurts the life, it hurts the body of a man; but spiritual sorrow, on the other side, causeth life. The more a man dies this way, the more he lives; the more he weeps, the more he laughs; and the more he can weep over Jesus Christ, the more lightsome and gladsome his heart is, and the more comfortably he spends his time. This brings him joy, this brings him peace, this brings him evidence of God's love, this brings assurance of pardon, and so this makes way for life, and doth a man no hurt at all.

(3.) Thirdly, This spiritual and godly sorrow and mourning *is a sorrow never to be repented of*, as the apostle there implies. All other sorrow a man must unsorrow again. When a man hath wept and blubbered, and spent a great deal of time in passionate tears, in cursed tears, in froward tears, in revengeful stomachful tears, he must blot out these tears with new tears; he must unweep this weeping, and undo his mourning because he hath thus mourned; he hath reason to repent for his sorrow. But when a man sets himself apart to weep over Christ, and sees his sins for the dishonour that is offered to God's name, and that his mourning is holy and spiritual mourning, he shall never have cause to repent of this time that is so spent, although he have spent many days and hours in that action.

(4.) Last of all, spiritual mourning *works repentance*, saith the apostle: that is to say, it works reformation and amendment; it sets a man further from his sin, and brings him nearer to God, and nearer to goodness; it works in himself partly, and in regard of others partly, those fruits that the apostle there mentions in the Corinthians. Saith he, what striving, what diligence and speed did you make, namely, to find out and to censure the incestuous person; and then this sorrow will make a man nimble to find out sin, to reform and redress abuses in himself, in his house, and his place in what he can. In the second place, it gives a man defence and apology to speak for himself, and to say, Though I live amongst a polluted people of uncircumcised hearts, yet I join not with them in their sins, I mourn for them, I censure them, I blame them, as the Corinthians did the incestuous person. And for himself, he is able to hold up his head with comfort, and to say, It is true I have corruptions, but here is my apology, I bewail them. It is true I have thus and thus sinned, but here is my defence, I am sorry. I found place for sin, I find place for sorrow also, I confess it, I bewail it, I repent of my sin. Thus he clears himself.

(5.) Further, Spiritual sorrow, *it works indignation against sin in himself and in others;* a zeal against all impediments in himself and in others, the desire to God's ministers and word; that revenge that the apostle speaks of there, and that fear of hazarding one's self into the like occasions of sin for the time to come. In short, the fruits and effects of godly sorrow are exceeding blessed, exceeding many, and therefore in this sense, in this respect, he that mourns spiritually is an happy man.

3. Thirdly, He is happy *in regard of the event and issue of his mourning, because all shall end well with him, and all his tears shall one day be wiped away, and joy and gladness shall come in place;* yea, he is happy in this, that spiritual mourning it is always accompanied with joy: that is an happy estate that tends to happiness. Things are termed from the term in their motion. That is an happy estate that is attended with comfort, that ends in comfort, and shall be swallowed up of it at the last. Now this is the state of the spiritual mourner; while he doth mourn he hath comfort, and comfort because he can mourn. This doth a Christian heart more good than all the good of this world, when he can get himself apart and shed tears for his sins, and bewail the miseries and the sins of the time, and take to heart the dishonour of God's name. This, I say, doth more refresh and glad his soul than any outward comfort in the world. There is a laughter which Solomon speaks of, that makes a man sad, a carnal laughter; the heart is sad whilst the face laughs. So I may say the contrary, as there is joined sadness in some laughter, so there is laughter in some sadness. Carnal laughter makes a man sad while he laughs; but spiritual mourning, it makes a man merry when he mourns; the more he mourns, the more merry he is. Again, as for the present his mourning is attended with comfort, so in the end it shall end in comfort. There is a sorrow that shall end in darkness, that wastes a man as fire and heat wastes a candle, and so goes out of itself and vanisheth into smoke, into nothing. There is a sorrow and grief that ends in a greater sorrow, and that empties itself into eternal misery, but this spiritual sorrow shall have an end. For there shall be an end of our sorrow. If it be holy sorrow, we shall not ever mourn, but the tears shall one day be wiped from all our eyes, it shall have an end, and an happy end too. For all our sorrow shall end in joy. For our garments of ashes we shall have garments of light and gladness, and 'everlasting joy shall be upon our heads,' Isa. xxxv. 10. So then, whether we respect the cause of our mourning, or the fruits and effects of it, whether we respect the close and event of it, it is clear that every man that can mourn spiritually is in that respect in a very happy and blessed estate and condition. We have given you now the point. You hear what our Saviour speaks is but reason, though he seem to speak a paradox to flesh and blood when he saith, every spiritual mourner is an happy man. Now then, my brethren, let us apply the point a little.

Use 1. If it be an happy man that mourns aright, we have reason, first, *to bewail our unhappiness*; unhappy time and unhappy men may we well say, touching ourselves, that vary so much from the mind and prescription of our blessed Saviour. 'Blessed,' saith our Saviour Christ, 'are they that mourn, for they shall be comforted.' 'Woe to you,' saith he, 'that now laugh.' We, on the other side, say, Woe to them that here mourn; happy are they that can here laugh and be merry. And as we vary in our judgment from our Saviour, so much more we vary in our practice from his direction and counsel. The Lord, when he gives direction that will bring joy and comfort, he bids us humble ourselves, cast down ourselves, afflict ourselves, &c., James iv. 10. God saith, 'Humble yourselves that you may be exalted.' We on the other side say, Exalt ourselves, and we shall not be humbled. God saith, Throw down yourselves; we say, Secure ourselves. God saith, Afflict yourselves, and then you shall have comfort. The Lord saith, Let your laughter be turned into mourning, that so you may laugh. We on the other say, Let our mourning be turned into laughter, that so we may not mourn. And therefore when any grief, natural or spiritual, begins to breed or to grow on us, presently we betake ourselves to company, to sports and exercises, that may drown the noise of conscience, that may put out of our minds motives to spiritual grief and sorrow, and that may provoke us to carnal, or at the best to natural mirth and rejoicing. Thus we vary from Christ's directions quite in our practice; nay more, vary further from the practice of the saints of God. We vary from the very time and season in which we live. For behold, it is a time of darkness and blackness; it is the year of God's visitation, as the prophet speaks; it is the time of Jacob's trouble, as Jeremiah speaks. For howsoever we have peace at home, the church hath war abroad; howsoever we have health, yet the pestilence rageth abroad. Though we have plenty, there is poverty and misery abroad in the bowels of the church in other nations. Now then, when the time calls for mourning, and weeping, and lamentation, we vary quite, and are like to them in the prophecy of Isaiah. 'In that day,' saith God, Isa. xxii. 12, *seq.*, 'did I call for mourning and sackcloth: and behold here is slaying of oxen, and killing of sheep, and making merry, and provoking ourselves to all kind of jollity and security.' Further, we vary from the practice of God's children in like cases. They gave themselves to spiritual mourning upon due occasion. We read of Nehemiah, when he heard that the church was distressed and afflicted abroad, though he lived in credit, and in honour, and in safety himself at the court, yet he betakes himself to God in private, and there he fasts, and prays, and mourns, and there he sues to the Lord to be merciful unto Jerusalem. We read of good honest Uriah, he refused to go to his house and to refresh himself with meat and drink, upon this reason, because the ark of God and the captain of the host lay in the field in tents. This was the affection and the mind of God's servants of old: they wept with those that wept, and they mourned in the mourning and lamentation of the church. But now, my brethren, we forget the afflictions of Joseph abroad. And, as it is said of them in Amos, 'We drink wine in bowls, we stretch ourselves on our beds,' vi. 7; we give ourselves to music and mirth, and we take not to heart the distresses of the church. So likewise for the sins of the time, we see what the saints did of old. Ezra, chap. ix. 10, when he heard of the sins that were committed among the people—the holy seed had mingled themselves with the cursed nations, whom the Lord had cursed—he betakes himself to prayer, and to mourning, and fasting; and there assembled to him many well affected men, and they trembled before the Lord, they cast down themselves, and wept in a solemn manner.

Thus the saints of God did for the sins of their time. But now, my brethren, what do we? We look on other men, and wonder that rulers and magistrates and public persons do no more. But what do we ourselves in private? My brethren, do we lay to heart our own sins, the sins of our kindred and acquaintance, of our families, the sins of our neighbours, of our towns, of our places where we dwell and have our abode? Had David lived in these days, he would have washed our streets with rivers of tears, as he speaks of himself, Ps. cxix. 136, to have seen such pride, such impiety; to hear such oaths and blasphemies so frequent and so rife amongst us. We, on the other side, my brethren, see, nay, we act and commit, gross sins; we hear, nay, we utter, cursed speeches and blasphemies and oaths, and commit abominable sins, and yet there are not rivers of tears, nay, not a tear almost shed amongst us. This is that we are to complain of now, that we do what we can to put off mourning, and to bereave ourselves of true comfort; and this dryness and emptiness of tears, were it only of temper of body, and not from distemper of soul, the matter were more sufferable and more pardonable. But what shall we say for ourselves, when we have tears at command for every trifle, for every bauble, and have not tears for sin and for the dishonour of God? If a friend cross us, we can weep; if an unkind word be uttered, we sob and grow sullen; if a loss or a cross befall us, we can pour out ourselves in carnal weeping and lamentation: but for the sins of our souls, for the sins of our friends, for the sins of our nation, for the unkindness that we offer to God, for the contempt that is cast upon his name, we cannot shed a tear; and were it now that we were ashamed of these things, the matter were less. But, alas! we take not to heart that we have not hearts to mourn, and we labour not so much as to grieve because we cannot grieve. In our carnal natural grief, we stand and plead, we think we have reason to mourn: I have lost such a friend and such a friend. We think we have cause to bewail our estate in regard of such outward misery as befalls us. But we see no cause, no reason to weep over Christ for the sins we have committed against God.

We think many times carnal sorrow, which in truth is but poison, will do us good, a great deal of ease; and when men have crossed us, and disappointed us, or dealt unkindly with us, we think we will go and weep it out; and when we have cried and blubbered a while, we think that we give ease to our souls, and content to our hearts. But when we come to spiritual mourning, which only is comfortable mourning, we think that undoes us. Many a man thinks he forfeits all his joy, all his peace, all his liberty, all his happiness, and he shall never see a merry day again in this world if he gives way to mourning for sin, to sound repentance, to works of humiliation, and examination of his own heart and ways. And hence it is that we do what we can to hold possession against the Spirit in sorrow and mourning. Oh misery! Oh unhappiness of ours! When we take things in this manner, when we take poison for cordial, and cordials to be no better than poison, no marvel though we have no more comfort of our tears and of our mourning; for certainly our mourning for the most part is not a blessed mourning. We mourn not for sin, but for sorrow; we mourn not for corruption, but for crosses: not because we have dealt unkindly with God, but because men deal unkindly with us. This is not a blessed mourning, and therefore it is that we find no comfort in it.

Use 2. Well, in the next place, we have another use, *to take Christ's direction for comfort.* Who would, who can be without it? Life is death without comfort. Every man's aim is to lead a comfortable life. Mark the way that Christ chalks out: 'Blessed are they that mourn, for they shall be comforted.' Do you believe Christ's word? Do you believe that he knows what he saith? Can you rest in Christ's testimony and in his promise? Then, if ever you will have comfort in your hearts, or in your lives, or in your ends, begin here, begin with spiritual mourning. Now that this you may do, we must,

1. First shew you how spiritual mourning differs, and is discerned from other mourning.

2. How it is gotten.

3. How it is exercised.

1. For the first of this: Spiritual mourning *is known by the objects*. Such as the object is, such is the faculty. Spiritual mourning hath spiritual objects, either materially or formally, as they speak in schools. This spiritual mourning is busied about spiritual goods and spiritual ills. Spiritual good, either the chief or universal good, which is God; or subordinately good, as grace and comfort, the ordinance and worship of God. Spiritual ills, whether they be simply ill, as sin and impiety; or painfully ill, yet with relation to sin, as a fruit of sin, and as a pledge of God's wrath and displeasure against it. We will instance in this first.

For, first, if a man would know whether his sorrow be spiritual sorrow or no, let him see how he mourns for the absence of spiritual good things, how he mourns for the absence of God, the chief good. That is spiritual sorrow, when a man mourns because he hath lost God in his graces, in his communion, and in his comforts. This was a proof of David's sorrow that it was spiritual, because, as the Scripture speaks elsewhere, he lamented after the Lord, and mourned after God. 'My soul,' saith he, 'thirsteth after the living God,' Ps. xlii. 2. He hungered after God, he was pained, and pinched at his soul when he could not see God, and enjoy God as formerly he did. This was the reason of that idolater, Judges xviii. 24, *seq.*, when his idols were taken from him, he cried after them: when a rude fellow asked him what he ailed, 'What ail I?' saith he; 'you have stolen away my gods, and taken away my ephod, and do you ask what I ail? what more have you left me?' What he speaks of his false gods, a true Christian heart may conclude much more of the true God. If the true God be departed from him,—stolen he cannot be;—but if he be departed from him, that he have driven away God in Christ by his sinful and rude behaviour, that God hides his face, that he communicates not himself in his comforts and graces as formerly he hath done, this goes to his heart, this punisheth him, and grieves him more than any thing in the world. And so for inferior goods, a man that mourns spiritually, he mourns because he sees the want of good things, the want of faith, the want of grace, he finds a spiritual want, the absence of things spiritually good. A man that mourns spiritually, he mourns because the means of grace is taken from him, because he sees not his teachers, as the prophet saith, because there is no vision; there is none to say, How long? as it is in Haggai i. 4: 'How long shall the house of God lie waste? the ways of Zion are unfrequented: the Sabbaths of the Lord are despised.' He mourns because he is kept away from the house of God, where he used to taste of the fat things of God's house, and where he used to see him in his beauty and in his glory.

So this is spiritual mourning, when a man mourns because God in his love and in his comforts leaves him, and his countenance shines not upon him; because the word of God and the grace of God spreads not, that it stirs not sensibly within him, as formerly it hath done. And so likewise for ills. A man that mourns spiritually, he mourns for spiritual ills, to find so much corruption, so much pride, so much hypocrisy, so much self-love, so much worldliness, so much naughtiness in his own heart. This is his grief, as it was Paul's. He cries, O tired, 'O wretched man that I am, who shall deliver me from this body of death?' Rom. vii. 24. He weeps, and takes on more for the corruption of his nature, for the sins in himself, and in the people of God, than for persecution and disgrace, than for losses and crosses that befall him. So when a man mourns for sin, that he takes to heart the sins of his family, the sins of the state and of the church that he lives in, this is spiritual mourning. And so also when a man mourns for outward things spiritually, say he be poor, say he be afflicted, say he be famished, say he be persecuted, he turns all his griefs to godly grief; he apprehends God's displeasure. In these he apprehends and sees sin: in these he considers his crosses, in the cause, and in the root of them, in sin; and so he mourns for sin and the cause. This is spiritual mourning. Now when a man thus mourneth for the absence of spiritual good things, and for the presence of spiritual ills that lie upon him and others, then he is said to mourn spiritually, and so he is a blessed man. This is all we can stay to say for the point.

Quest. Now, in the next place, how shall a man do to get this spiritual mourning?

Ans. First, He must labour *to have an heart capable of grief and sorrow that is spiritual*, a tender and soft heart. He must see that he have a disposition to holy mourning, able and inclinable so to do, when just opportunity and occasion is offered. Now how shall a man get this tender heart? Why surely he must go to God in his means and ordinances, who hath promised, as you heard, in the covenant, to take 'the stone out of our hearts, and to give us soft and fleshy hearts.' This a man must do for it. Withal he must be ready in the next place, when God hath given him a tender heart, to stir up the graces of the Spirit that are in him, to raise up his affections and his sorrow, and to provoke himself to mourn and to lament upon due occasion. Thus that he may do, he must,

1. First, Consider of a method that he must use; and then,
2. Of motives to stir him up thereunto.

1. For method. (1.) First, He must *have respect to the time*, that he do not let his heart lie fallow too long. Jer. iv. 3, it is said, 'Plough up your fallow ground.' Ground, if it lie long unploughed, it will require much pains to rear it and fetch it up, but if it be oft done, it will be the easier. So it is with the heart of man; he must not let his heart be fallow too long, but take it into task ever and anon, and labour to keep the flesh tender, and raw, and fresh, as we may say; and then upon every occasion it will be ready to bleed and to pour forth itself. To this end a man should every day be exercised in the duty of a godly mourning, every night reckon for the passage of that day, and say with thyself, What sin have I committed? What have I done? What have I said? What have I seen this day? What have I heard this day, that might be matter of humiliation and grief to me? And so work this upon the heart, that it may be turned to tears of godly sorrow.

(2.) Secondly, For the time, *a man must be sure to take God's time.* When God calls on him, when God gives them the heart, and is ready to close and to join with him, then take the advantage, set upon godly mourning, when the Lord hath ransacked thy heart, when the Lord hath dealt with thee in the ministry of his word, when he hath applied himself to thy soul and conscience, and detected thy corruption, and shewed thee thy sin, and hath wounded thy heart in public with afflictions, in private with terrors and fears. So when the nature of grief is stirred by the occasion of the word, then take the advantage of this, seize upon this for the king's use; set upon sorrow whilst it is there, turn it into the right stream, into the right channel; turn it for sin, weep for sin, and not for outward losses and crosses. Thus much for the time.

2. Secondly, There is another thing to be done *for the order*, and that is this, that a man must be sure *to give over carnal mirth and carnal mourning*, if he will mourn spiritually. His carnal laughter must be turned into mourning, as James speaks, iv. 9; and his carnal mirth must be turned into spiritual mourning too, or else he will never come to spiritual mourning. But we cannot stand upon that. We will only touch the motives, because the time is run out, and so conclude for this time. Consider well what are the motives to set us to work to mourn, and to mourn spiritually.

The motives are many. He that will mourn must look to these. There is one rule generally for mourning, and that is this: He that will mourn spiritually, he must apply himself to God's means and motives only. There be that tell us of a course of getting of sackcloth and haircloth, and I know not what, to work godly mourning. This makes men superstitious, and not humble. He that is an holy mourner, he will follow God's directions, he will work upon his motives and reasons, and no other; and therefore he mourns, because God bids him so mourn, for the Scripture bids us look upon Christ, not as he is in pictures, but in the word, presented upon the cross, and to weep, and to mourn, and to bleed out our souls there for our sins committed against him, and so to look upon him whom we have pierced, and to weep for him, as it is Zech. xii. 10. That is in general.

Now, in particular, consider these motives.

1. It is needful for us to mourn.
2. It is seasonable for us to mourn.
3. It is profitable. And,
4. It is comfortable.

Of these we should have said something more largely if the time and strength had given leave, but seeing both fail, we will only touch them now, and leave them till we can further prosecute them.

1. First, *It is needful to mourn in a spiritual manner.* Whosoever hath sin must mourn. Let him take his time and place, whether he will do it in this life or in that which is to come. Sin must have sorrow, that is a ruled case; and he that will not willingly mourn, shall, will he or nill he, in another place. And therefore, my brethren, we see there is a necessity laid upon us in regard of our sins. It is needful also in regard of others, to draw them to it by our example and practice. I know not how it comes to pass, but we are all fallen into a wondrous sleepy age, a time of security. Men bless themselves in their courses. They secure themselves in a formal, ordinary kind of religion and profession, with an ordinary stint of holy duties, when there is no powerful, hearty, sanctifying actions done in secret for our own sins, and the sins of the times. Why, sith* that all men sleep, let us be wakeful, and since others have need of provoking to this duty, let Christian men lead them the way. Let their faces, and apparel, and entertainment, and all their carriage and behaviour, speak mourning and lamentation to other men. Secondly, As it is needful in regard of others, so also it is needful *in regard of ourselves too;* for who doth not find in himself a wondrous proneness to sin, and aptness to take infection from others? Who finds not in himself a readiness to close with others in their

* That is, 'since.'—G.

sins? The way to preserve us is to mourn. That will preserve us from the infection now, and from judgment hereafter. How was Lot preserved in Sodom? By hearing and seeing they vexed his righteous soul, &c. While Lot mourned for their sin, he was free from sin; while he mourned for their impiety, he was free from the judgment. Because he did not partake of their wickedness, therefore he was not plagued with the wicked. If then we would not be infected by sin, if we would not be wrapped up in the common calamities and judgments, this course we had need to take, we must fall to mourning for our own sins and for their sins.

2. Secondly, As it is needful, so also it *is very seasonable*. The very time tends that way, as it were; the season is the time of weeping; the church of God weeps abroad. It is the time, as I told you, of Jacob's trouble. Oh the sighs, oh the tears, oh the griefs and sorrows that cover and overwhelm the people of God in other nations, and other places! The prophet David could say, his right hand should forget to play, rather than he would forget Jerusalem, Ps. cxxxvii. 5; but I know not how, what for play, and for sport, and for ease, and feasting, and one thing or other, we forget Jerusalem, we forget the misery of the church in other places. Well, now they pray, and call upon us, as far as Prague, as far as Heidelberg, as far as France, that we would take notice of their afflictions, and of their miseries; at the least, that we would comfort them so far as to mourn for them.* As it is seasonable in regard of the afflictions of the church, so in respect of provoking of others of this nation. For sin is now grown to a fulness, to a ripeness. Oh the oaths that are sworn in one day, in one city, and in one town! Oh the lies that are uttered in one fair, in one market daily! Oh the sins that are committed by high and low of all degrees within the compass of twenty-four hours! Who is able to reckon them? And the sins that are committed with an high hand against the knowledge, and against the light of the gospel, and against the express letter of the law, the word of God, should not these things cause us to mourn? They would cause a David to weep rivers of tears, and shall not we weep at all?

3. Thirdly, As it is seasonable, so *it is profitable;* for godly mourning it never hurts, it alway helps. Carnal sorrow leaves a man worse than it finds him. It makes him more sick, and more weak, than it finds him. Spiritual sorrow leaves him better. He that can pour forth his heart before God, he that can go charged and loaden to heaven, with his heart full of fear and full of grief and full of sorrow, as ever it can hold, that man shall return back again loaden with joy, and peace, and comfort. Thou shalt never in thy life go before the Lord in sorrow and grief, and there spend but one quarter of an hour in tears, and prayer, and lamenting before the Lord, but thou shalt find thy heart somewhat lightened, somewhat eased and refreshed in so doing. Well then, since it is profitable for us, let us do it. As it is profitable for the soul, so it is for the body. This is the only means that is left to save ourselves. In Ezek. ix. 2, you know one was sent, with a pen and inkhorn, to mark out the mourners, that they might be saved in the common plague and judgment; and that God might be gracious and merciful to them. It is the only thing that is now left us. We must betake ourselves to prayer, and tears, and to lamentation, if we would not have judgments to fall upon us. This is profitable for the whole state, if there be some righteous men. If there had been but ten of these mourners in five cities of the plague,† they had been upheld all for their sakes. The

* Cf. Memoir, Vol. I. pp. lvii.-lix.—G.

† Qu. 'plain'?—Ed.

righteous man upholds the land and nation; they do beat back the judgments; and therefore, for the common good, let us mourn.

4. Lastly, *It is very comfortable.* It doth wondrously refresh a man. It is that that kills a Christian man, when he remembers many times the comforts he hath had heretofore when his heart was enlarged; and if he could pour forth himself, and weep as once he could have done before the Lord, he would part with all the world for an heart so tender, and so soft, and so enlarged. There is no comfort to this in a Christian, he prizeth it above all other comforts in this world. Then he thinks himself in a safe estate, in the best case, in a comfortable estate and condition, when he can mourn best, when he can weep and sorrow for his sins, and weep over Christ.

Well, my brethren, let us consider these things, and now apply them to ourselves, and say, O my heart, thou hast need to mourn, it is time for thee to mourn! O my soul, it is profitable for thee to mourn! O my soul, it is comfortable for thee to mourn! If thou desire thine own profit, thine own ease, thine own comfort and safety, if thou desire life and salvation, betake thyself to this course; gather thyself from company; go alone, and set before thee thy sins thou hast committed, how bad thou hast been to God, how good he hath been to thee, what a kind Father he hath been, and what a froward child thou hast been. Lay these together till thou hast provoked thyself to some sorrow and tears. Thus if we could do, we should find comfort more than worldlings find in laughter, and in their merriment and sports; we should find more comfort this way than we shall in cold and comfortless weeping for crosses, and lamenting for afflictions; but, for that and other uses of the point, I am enforced, whether I will or no, to defer till next time.

SPIRITUAL MOURNING.

THE SECOND SERMON.

Blessed are they that mourn, for they shall be comforted.—Mat. V. 4.

The lesson here is thus much, they that mourn in an holy manner, they are in an happy case. The proof of this doctrine is this, 'they shall be comforted.' We heard the last day, he is an happy man that can mourn in an holy manner; he is happy in his judgment. A holy affection argues an holy understanding. He is happy in his heart and inward temper, for holy mourning comes from a kind of spiritual softness and tenderness. He is happy in the effect of his mourning. Holy mourning will keep out carnal and worldly sorrow. It is a sorrow that a man needs never to sorrow for again; it is such a sorrow that tends to life and salvation. Worldly sorrow tends to death. He is happy in the issue of his mourning, for mourning makes way for rejoicing. He that now weeps shall one day laugh. Nay, for the present, the more he mourns in an holy manner, the more solid and substantial is his present comfort.

It is our folly and misery both, therefore, that we so utterly mistake the matter. We give way to a sorrow that will hurt us, and keep possession against that which will do us good. We see reason, as we imagine, why we should grieve in a passionate manner; we can see no reason why we should mourn in a spiritual manner. It is our unhappiness we can find time and leisure for the taking in of poison, that tends to death; we can find no place fit, no time, no opportunity for the receiving of a preservative that will bound and keep the heart against all poison. Of this point we have already said something too. What remains to be spoken of it in further uses we will gather in anon, and touch upon it in the prosecution of a new point if we can.

We pass therefore from the doctrine here delivered, 'Blessed are the mourners,' and come to the reason of it, 'for they shall be comforted.' Let us join these together, and see how they do depend. The point will be thus much—

Doct. 1. *That spiritual mourning it ends in spiritual mirth.* He that can mourn spiritually and holily, he shall undoubtedly and certainly be comforted. Holy tears, they are the seeds of holy joy. You see our ground in the text for this point. For the clearing of it further, let us know that we have good security for it.

1. The promise of God; and then, 2. The experience of God's people.

The best proofs that may be. First, the Lord undertakes in his promise two things touching our comforts:

1. That all our godly sorrow shall end in true comfort. The next is,

2. That all our godly mournings are attended and accompanied with comfort for the present.

1. For the first of these, *you know the promise*, sorrow and weeping shall fly away, and joy and gladness shall come in place, Isa. xxxv., last verse, which place will refer you to many more. God hath made a succession of these things, as of day and night. His children's day begins in the night and in darkness, and ends in the day. After sorrow comes comfort; after they have mourned in a holy manner their sorrow shall be taken from them, and gladness shall come in the stead, Isa. lxi. 3. The Lord Jesus is appointed of his Father to give beauty for ashes, the garment of gladness for the garment of sackcloth and mourning. God hath promised it shall be so; God hath appointed Christ, and fitted him, and enabled him to this word, that so it may be. Not to insist on this, our mourning shall not only end in comfort, but it carries comfort along with it for the present. God hath undertaken it shall be so, speaking of the afflictions that should come upon the state: 'And my servants shall be full, but he,' the wicked and hypocrite, 'shall be hungry: my servants shall rejoice, but he shall mourn: my servants shall sing for gladness of heart, but you shall howl for heaviness of heart,' Isa. lxv. 13. Lo, when afflictions come upon a state, such afflictions as make the wicked cry and howl, then God in judgment remembers mercy for his. They shall have matter of joy and triumph even then. So in Isaiah lx., the beginning, he tells them, calling on his church, 'Arise,' saith he, 'and shine; put on brightness and glory; the Lord shall be a light unto thee in darkness.' When the church is enclosed with darkness, nothing but misery and affliction round about her, then the Lord shall shine* light, that is, he shall give comfort to his church. All their mourning and sorrow, their outward afflictions, shall cause them inwardly to mourn in spirit. God will take off the garment of mourning, and put on the garment of gladness in his due time. In the mean time, he will be a light to them in the midst of darkness. Thus God undertakes, this is the promise. Now, God promiseth nothing but what he purposeth, and God purposeth and promiseth no more than he will perform. Hath he said it, and shall he not do it? It shall certainly come to pass. All the counsels of God shall stand; every word of God is pure. All the promises of God are 'yea and amen.' They are certainly made good to the hearts and consciences of all God's people through Christ. Since therefore God hath said it, it shall be thus; sith Christ hath said, 'Mourn, and you shall be comforted,' we may build upon it that so it shall be.

2. To this promise of God let us add *the experience of God's people.* We will speak of the church in the bulk, and the particular members of the church they have all found this true, they have reported it by their own experience, and passed their word for God that it shall be thus with God's people. Thus the church is brought speaking in Micah vii. 8, 'Rejoice not against me, O mine enemy: though I be fallen, yet shall I rise;' comfort will come at the last. Nay, while I sit in darkness, the Lord for the present will be a light and comfort to me. Thus you know again what the

* Qu. 'send'?—G.

church speaks, Ps. cxxvi. 6, from their own experience, 'They that sow in tears shall reap in joy.' There is a seed that doth fail sometimes and disappoint our hopes, but this seed it never fails, it falls upon good ground, it will take root. If the seed-time be wet, the harvest will be dry. 'They that sow in tears shall reap in joy;' and in another, Ps. xcv., the latter end, 'light is sown to the righteous,' and he expounds what he means by light, joy to the upright in heart. So that though this seed lie covered for a time, yet notwithstanding there is light sown for the righteous, and they shall be sure to have it. Thus the church speaks and gives her word for God. So likewise you may see it in particular Christians. David always found this; Ps. xciv. 19 saith he, 'In the multitude of the thoughts of my heart, thy comforts did glad my soul:' when I was perplexed in my thoughts, my thoughts were tossed and tumbled up and down in mine own meditations, seeking here and there for comfort. Even then in this distress, and distraction, thy comforts, thy double comforts, as the word implies,* these comforts did refresh and glad this soul. So likewise Saint Paul, in 2 Cor. i. 4, he tells us that God did comfort him in all his tribulations; and as his sorrows did abound, so his consolations did overtop and superabound. And hence we may say, as it were, of the saints of God, that which they extracted from their own experience and particular case, that God comforts the abject, those that are cast down, as Paul saith, 2 Cor. vii. 6, and that of David, Ps. xxx. 5, 'Heaviness may continue for a night, but joy comes to the righteous in the morning.' We see then that if we look to the experience of God's people, they from their own experience give testimony to this truth, and give us to understand that true spiritual mourning shall end in true spiritual joy and comfort. If all this suffice not, let us consider of these reasons, and then we shall see that it is but reason that we should do so.

1. The first reason is drawn *from the nature of sorrow and mourning.* Sorrow is a kind of an imperfect thing, as it were. It is not made for itself, but for an higher and for a further end, to do service to something else, as it fares with all those that we call the declining affections. Hatred is servant to love; fear doth service to confidence; so likewise doth sorrow to joy. For God hath not appointed sorrow for sorrow's sake, but to make way for joy and true comfort. The physician doth not make a man sick for sickness sake, but for health's sake.

Many men's lives have been hazarded by carnal joy, as well as by worldly sorrow. And they that know anything in stories, they know many a man hath been taken away, his life hath leaped out of his mouth, as it were, by reason of extraordinary laughter and carnal joy. But now, the joy of a Christian man, a spiritual joy, it is *a safe joy.* It hurts no man, but doth a man good; it settles a man's mind, it strengthens his thoughts, it perfects his wits and understanding. It makes him to have *a sound judgment;* it makes for the health of his body; it makes for the preservation of his life; it doth a man good every way. There is no provocation in it, there is no danger in it. Thirdly, as a Christian's joy is best in that respect, that it is the safest, so in this, that it *is the surest joy.* For this joy is an everlasting joy. The rejoicing of the wicked it is for a season, it lasts not long; but the joy of the righteous, it is a constant joy in the root, and in the cause and in the matter of it. It shall never be taken from him. Indeed, everlastingness stands at the end of both kinds of joy.

The wicked hath a joy, and there comes something after it that is ever-

* The word being תַּנְחוּמֶיךָ, *consolationes tuæ* in the plural.—G.

lasting; but that is everlasting shame, everlasting pain and anguish. The righteous he hath some joy here, and there is something that is everlasting that follows at the end of that; but that is everlasting glory, everlasting joy. It is swallowed up of eternity. Further, the joy of the righteous is a *more rational joy* than the joy of the wicked: that is but brutish, as it were. A righteous man rejoiceth in matters that are worthy of his joy, those things that he hath reason to be glad of. He rejoiceth that his name is written in heaven; he rejoiceth that Christ hath taken upon him his nature; that the Spirit of God the Comforter dwells in him in the graces of the Spirit, &c. But now the wicked man, his is an unreasonable joy; he rejoiceth where he hath no matter nor cause of joy. You see many times madmen sing, and dance, and leap, and shout, and take on. Will you term this joy? Alas! this proceeds from distemper; not that they have cause to be merry, but it is from distemper that they so rejoice, if you term it mirth. That which Solomon saith you may say of the laughter of the wicked, 'it is madness.' He laughs, and he can give no reason for it; he rejoiceth for that which he hath no reason to rejoice in; he rejoiceth in the creature, he rejoiceth in himself, in his own wit, in his own worth, in his own strength. He rejoiceth many times in his shame, in his torment, in those things that tend to his utter ruin and destruction. The righteous, then, hath the start of the wicked for matter of comfort and joy. He hath a more solid, a more safe and sure joy, a more sweet joy, a more reasonable joy a great deal than the other hath. As he is beyond him in his joy,—

So, in the next place, he is beyond him in his sorrow too. Our life must have comfort and sorrow. It is compounded of sweet and sour. As the year is compounded of winter and summer, and the day of day and night, so every man's life is made up of these two. He hath some fair and some foul days, some joy and some sorrow. Now as the righteous is beyond the wicked in his joy and comfort, so he is beyond him in his sorrow. First, his sorrow is far better; it is a more gainful, a more comfortable sorrow than others' is. They are beyond the sorrows of the wicked in all the causes and in all the circumstances of them.

(1.) First, The sorrow of the righteous it proceeds *from a better spring and fountain* than the sorrow of the wicked. The sorrow of the godly, it comes from a sound mind, from a pure heart, from an inside that is purified from hypocrisy, from self-love, from private respects. Whereas, on the other side, the sorrow of the wicked comes from distemper of brain, from an utter mistake. He takes that to be matter of sorrow, which is no matter of grief; he takes that to be matter of great grief that deserveth but a few tears, &c. Again, his sorrow comes from distemper of heart, from pride, from passion, from cursedness of heart and spirit, that he cannot stoop. It proceeds not from love to God or to mankind, but out of self-love, and from the miry puddle and filthy spring of pride and passion and error, &c.

(2.) Secondly, The sorrow of the righteous, as it hath a better spring, so it *is busied and taken up about better objects, about better matters.* A wicked man howls and cries, and takes on many times for a trifle, for a bauble; yea, many times, because he is disappointed and crossed in his lusts, in his base sins. The child of God finds himself somewhat else to do than to weep and to cry, and take on for trifles and vanities. He looks up to God, and is sorry he hath displeased him. He turns his tears into the right channel, and sets them upon his sin. He weeps for spiritual losses and crosses, for public miseries and calamities, and he takes to heart such things as are worthy of a man's sorrow, and such as will perfect the affections, as every affection is perfected from the goodness of the object about which he works.

(3.) Thirdly, The sorrow of the righteous is better than the sorrow of the wicked in regard *of the manner of their mourning.* For the mourning of the righteous is a composed kind of sorrow. He mourns in silence; he weeps to the Lord; he carries it with judgment and discretion. His sorrow is a moderated sorrow; he holds it within banks and bounds. Whereas the sorrow of the wicked is a tempestuous, a boisterous, a furious kind of mourning and lamenting. He knows no mean. It is without hope. He observes no decorum. He forgets himself what he is, what he saith, what he doth almost. His mourning is little better than frenzy or madness.

(4.) Last of all, they differ much *in the end and upshot of their mourning.* Godly sorrow, it doth a man good. It humbles him, as we said. It drives him from all purpose, from all practice of sin; it makes him resolute against sin. On the other side, it draws him into the presence of God; it brings him before the Lord in the ordinance of prayer, in the ordinance of fasting and humiliation. This is his sorrow, and therefore it shall end well; whereas, on the other side, the sorrow of the wicked, it is a kind of vexing, tormenting sorrow, a painful sorrow, a despairing sorrow; a sorrow that drives a man from God, and is mingled many times with much murmuring, sometimes with cursing, sometimes with oaths and blasphemies. This sorrow of the wicked, it hath not so good an issue. There is great difference when a woman breeds a disease, and when she breeds a child. When a woman breeds a disease, there is no good comes of that: there is much pain, and no ease follows; there is much sickness, and no comfort in the close. But when she breeds a child, though there be much pain, yet it quits the cost when the child is born: 'She forgets her pain, because a child is born into the world,' John xvi. 21. So it is in the state of the godly and the wicked. The wicked are ever in travail, as we read in Job, viii. 22; he is always travailing with fear and with grief, with passion, discontent, and horror, &c., but then he never brings forth any fruit; and this travail, it never ends in comfortable birth. But it is contrary with the godly. He travails with pain, and with sorrow, and with fears; and some tears, and sighs, and groans he hath for the present; but in the end there is a deliverance. He is delivered of his fears, and of his pain, and his sorrows; and then comes joy and peace, and all his tears are wiped away; and then his sorrows are forgotten, and joy comes, and takes possession. So that the joy of the godly it is far better than the wicked's joy; and the sorrow that falls upon the good and the bad is far different. Both must needs sorrow in this vale of misery. But the sorrow of the godly, it is an hopeful sorrow, it is an healing sorrow, it is a comfortable sorrow, it is a fruitful sorrow; whereas the sorrow of the wicked is full of despair and vexation, and the further he wades in, the more danger he is in of drowning. Still, the righteous begins in the night, but ends in the day: saith David, 'Heaviness may continue for a night, but joy cometh in the morning,' Ps. xxx. 5. The wicked sets forth in the morning, but then there comes darkness at night; he begins merrily and happily, but then the issue is most miserable.

Well then, to shut up this first reason, for information—upon which we have stood the longer, because carnal judgment will not credit this point,—it is clear, the righteous man in prosperity is better than the wicked, and in adversity better. Whence he hath occasion to rejoice.

A surgeon doth not lance and sear men because he would put them to pain, but because he would give them ease. The Lord of heaven delights not in wounding and grieving of his children; but therefore he calls them to sorrow, that so they might come to comfort. Sorrow, then, never comes to its full end that it was made for; it obtains not its perfection, till such time as it convey a man to joy. And therefore, since it is appointed and ordained to this end by God, it is certain it shall arrive at joy, and obtain it in the end; for God doth nothing in vain, he will bring all to perfection.

2. The second reason may be drawn *from the nature of this spiritual comfort and joy that we speak of.* For spiritual joy is very strong: 'The joy of the Lord is your strength,' as he saith, Neh. viii. 10. A strong thing is spiritual joy, and therefore it will overmatch, and overcome, and drink up, as it were, all our sorrows and fears in due time, as the sun overcomes the darkness of the night, and the fogginess of the mist in the morning. Indeed, natural joy may be overmatched with natural grief, at the least with some grief, because we are more sensible of grief than we are of those comforts: they more infect the sense. And because natural grief weakens nature, therefore it is not able to make resistance; and therefore we say many times, natural grief overmatcheth natural comforts; much more will carnal grief, and other grief, overcome carnal joy, because these are weaker than natural, having less root in nature, and less subsistence in that way. But it is not so with spiritual joy and comfort, for these now have their root in God, and come from his strength; and therefore these will bear down before them all sorrow, all heart-breaking, all grievance whatsoever in due time. This is a joy that cannot be taken from us. It is a joy invincible, it is a joy impregnable. No sorrow, no affliction on the outside, no grief on the inside, can strip a man of spiritual joy and comfort, if it be in any strength. So then there be two reasons why we should think that all our spiritual mourning will end in joy and comfort: for joy will swallow it up at the last, it will be too hard for it; and because, again, mourning is made but for joy. Therefore, when joy comes in place, that must give place.

3. A third reason may be drawn *from the cause of our spiritual mourning and spiritual joy;* for these are fruits that grow both from the same root. Spiritual joy and spiritual mourning, they come from the same fountain, from the same Spirit. The same Spirit it causeth us to weep over him whom we have pierced, and it causeth us also to rejoice in the Lord whom we have pierced: 'The fruit of the Spirit is joy,' saith the apostle, Gal. v. 22. The same Spirit manageth and guideth both the one and the other. Carnal passions and affections they oppose one another, they fight one with another, because they are carried on headlong, without any guide or order at all. But spiritual affections they are subordinate and subservient one to another; the one labours to further and to advance another. Thus the more a man joys, the more he grieves; and the more he grieves, the more he joys. Joy melts the heart, and gives it a kindly thaw; grief, on the other side, it easeth the heart, and makes it cheerful and lightsome.

4. Lastly, a reason may be drawn *from the effects of godly mourning.* If they be considered, it will be cleared, that he that mourns spiritually shall end in comfort at the last; for this spiritual mourning, what will it do? First, it takes off the power and strength of corruption. It weakens sin, it pricks the bladder of pride, and lets out our corruption. Spiritual mourning it takes down a man, it humbles him; and an humble heart is always a cheerful heart, so far as it is humbled. Spiritual mourning, again, makes way for prayer. For spiritual mourning sends a man to God. It

causeth him to utter himself in petition, in confession, and complaints to his Father; to pour out himself to the bosom of his God in speeches, in sighs, and tears, in lamenting one way or other. All this tends to comfort. The more a man prays, the more he hath comfort. 'Pray,' saith Christ, 'that your joy may be full,' John xvi. 24. If a man will have fulness of joy, he must be frequent in prayer. Now, the more a man mourns spiritually, the more he prays; and therefore the more he is filled with true joy. Again, this spiritual mourning, it is a wondrous help of faith. It is an hopeful mourning; it helps a man's faith in the promises touching remission of sins. He weeps for it; he sues out his pardon in Christ's name. It helps his faith in the promises of our Saviour: 'Blessed are they that mourn, for they shall be comforted.' If they 'sow in tears, they shall reap in joy,' &c. Now, the more a man's faith and hope is furthered, the more his joy is furthered. Still, the apostle speaks that they should rejoice in believing. The more a man believes and reposeth himself upon the promises, the precious promises of the word, the more his heart is joyed and comforted still. Now, the more he mourns, the more reason he hath to believe that that furthers his faith; and therefore it advanceth his joy and comfort.

Let us look, then, upon the reasons that hath been given, and the case is clear enough. Whosoever he be that mourns in an holy manner, that man shall certainly, first or last, be comforted. This mourning tends to comfort. It is made to draw it on. His joy will overtop his sorrow, and overcome all at last. Joy and mourning go together. They are branches of the same root, and therefore the more we do the one, the more we have the other. This godly mourning it makes way for prayer, it makes way for faith; and therefore it makes way for comfort and consolation. This point then being thus cleared, let us a little make some use of it to ourselves. The use is threefold.

Use 1. First, Here is one use *of information touching others*. Since those men are certain to have comfort in the end that mourn holily, here we may learn to determine now that grand question that hath been so long controverted, namely, who is the happiest man in the world? And for the deciding of this question, we must not go with it to Solon, to Plato, or to the philosophers, but come to a judge, the Lord Jesus. And what saith he to the point? Blessed and happy, saith he, are they that mourn. His reason is, 'for they shall be comforted.' So that here, then, is the trial of a man's state that is blessed. The signs of a blessed estate are these two in this verse. The first is, if so be he mourn well; the second, if he speed well for his comfort. So that that man, then, that hath the best sorrow and the best joy, that man then is the happiest man. Now the Christian man is this man. He hath the advantage of all other men, in his joy and in his sorrow; and therefore he is the only happy man in this world. First, for his joy, happy is he, saith Christ, 'he shall be comforted' with those comforts that a man cannot buy too dear, though he shed many tears for them, though he spend many nights in sighing and mourning and lamenting. Though it cost him much he cannot over-rate it, he cannot over-prize it. This comfort cannot be bought at too high a rate. Now what is this comfort? What is the Christian's joy better than another man's joy? In many respects,

(1.) First, This joy is a *more solid joy than the joy of the wicked*. The wicked man rejoiceth in face, but not in heart; the wicked's joy is but a blaze, it is but a flash; his rejoicing is like the crackling of thorns under a pot, that the Holy Ghost tells us makes a blaze and is gone in an instant.

This joy is rather in show than in substance. His joy is not rooted in himself. It is not bottomed upon any sure foundation, but it is rooted out of himself, in the creature. A wicked man hath no matter of comfort within himself, but his comforts they hang upon outward things. His comfort sometimes lies in the bottom of a pot; sometimes it lies in the bottom of a dish; sometimes in the heels of an horse; sometimes in the wings of a bird; sometimes in some base lust, or in some such filthy sin. Here lies the comfort of a wicked man; but now the comfort of the godly is not so. The joy of the righteous, it is a massy and a substantial joy. His afflictions indeed are light and momentany, but then his joy is everlasting, as I shall shew anon. It is a joy that hath substance in it. The joy of the wicked, at the best, it is but a little glazed, it is but gilt over, but it is naught within; but the joy of the righteous it is a golden joy, it is beaten gold, it is massy and substantial and precious. As we said before, the root of his joy he hath it in himself, he hath matter of comfort in himself. There is faith and grace, there is truth. Nay, it is not rooted in himself only, but the root of it is in heaven, in his head, in Christ. He pitcheth his joy upon God, and therefore his joy is such a joy, as will hold out in the wetting, and will bear him through all pressures, all burdens, and all discouragements whatsoever.

(2.) Secondly, The joy of the righteous, as it is a more solid, so it is *a more safe joy* than the joy of the wicked. A carnal joy is many times prejudicial to a man in his safety, therefore we may safely conclude, the godliest man is the happiest man. He is in the best estate and condition, that gives most way to godly sorrow, and that gives least way to carnal sorrow. That is one use.

Use 2. Now the next use is to the godly. First, a word *of exhortation*, and then a word *of consolation*. A word of exhortation to God's people. That since all their sorrow shall end in comfort, and is attended with comfort, that therefore God's people should lay open themselves and give way to godly sorrow as much as possibly they can. Stop up, my brethren, all the passages, dam them up if you can, that make way for worldly sorrow and for carnal grief, for this will come but too fast upon you; but, on the other side, pluck up the floodgates, and open all the passages, and give all the way to spiritual mourning and to godly tears. Do this even for your own sakes. Conceive that it is your happiness to mourn in an holy manner, since your Saviour tells you, that they are happy and blessed that do so mourn. Conceive that your comfort lies in your godly sorrow, as our Saviour saith; 'blessed' are they in this, namely, in this respect, because 'they shall be comforted for their mourning.' Believe it, brethren, one day, one hour spent in godly mourning, a few tears shed over Jesus Christ, and over a man's sin, when he is in health, when he is in peace, when he hath no outward cause to move him to tears and sorrow, it will more satisfy the soul, and more quiet the conscience, and more relieve and refresh the heart, than all the mirth, and all the delights, and all the treasures, and all the comforts of this world will do. Why, then, if you would be comforted, mourn; if you would laugh, weep; if you would have cheerful hearts and lightsome spirits, if you would live comfortably and die comfortably, give way to this mourning, so it be spiritual mourning, as much as you can.

Ay, but what is spiritual mourning? We spake somewhat of it the last day. Thus, in short, because I see the time will much prevent us.

(1.) First, *Labour to mourn after spiritual things and spiritual persons.* That is spiritual mourning when it hath spiritual objects. First, for persons.

Is it so, that the Lord withdraws himself from thee in his comforts, that thy soul doth not feel them, doth not find them, as sometimes thou had done? Lament after the Lord, weep and cry after him, and say, O unhappy man, where have I lost my peace? How have I behaved myself, that my Father will not speak to me! that he will not look to me! And as you see a little child that hath lost the mother, it follows crying, My mother is gone, I know not what to do, so let God's children do in this case, weep and take to heart this loss of losses, when thy rude, and unkind, and unholy behaviour hath alienated and estranged thy Father from thee, that he will not look on thee.

(2.) Again, Is it so, that the Lord withdraws himself *in his ordinances, that we hear not the voice of his word*, that we see not our signs? 'There is not a prophet among us to tell us how long,' Ps. lxxiv. 9; let us then set ourselves *to mourn*, as the church in that psalm. 'Lord, we see not our signs.' Lo, how a man may be free from his misery, whatsoever befalls.

(3.) Is it so, again, that in our mourning, we see the church of God, *those sorrowful-spirited men, that they are distressed and afflicted?* Let us weep for these too. Is the church of God carried into captivity? Let us cry out with the prophet of the Lord, 'My belly, my belly, I cannot be quiet; give me way to weep! Oh that I could shed rivers of tears! Oh that my head were a fountain of waters, that I could weep day and night for the daughter of my people!' &c., as in Jeremiah everywhere.

(4.) Is it so, that the church of God *is foiled at any time by the adversaries?* Let us take on, as Joshua did, 'rend your garments, and cast down ourselves before the Lord, and say, What shall we say, when Israel shall turn their backs and fly before their enemies?' Joshua vii. 8. Is it so, that the host of the living God is reproached and railed on by the Rabshakehs of this world? Take the matter to heart, as Hezekiah did. He goes before the Lord, and rends his clothes, and spreads the blasphemies before him. 'Lord,' saith he, 'it is a day of darkness, and blackness: the children are come to the birth, and there is no strength to bring forth,' Isa. xxxvii. 3.

(5.) In short, is the church of God *in heaviness and lamentation?* Are the armies of God in the field in danger and distress? Let every man, that takes himself to be a member of the church, and a member of Christ, take the business to heart, and weep with them that weep, and lament with them that mourn. Let your mirth and your peace, which is carnal, in these days, be turned into mourning and lamenting, bear a part with the church of God, with that Uriah say, 'Shall I eat and drink, and solace, when the ark of God, and the camp, and the captain of the host lies in distress, and misery in the camp?' 2 Sam. xi. 11. So for spiritual matters. Is it so, that we hear that sin reigns everywhere? that we hear blasphemies, that we see pride and oppression, that we are eye-witnesses, or others report to us the horrible injustice, the monstrous filthiness, the unsufferable ills that cry mightily to heaven against our dwelling and against our nation? Let us here give way to mourning, and say with the prophet, Oh that I could weep! 'Oh that my head were a fountain of tears!' and with David, 'I shed rivers of tears, because men kept not thy law,' Ps. cxix. 136. Thus, my brethren, let us labour to be much in spiritual mourning, to mourn for the loss and for the absence of holy things, and to mourn for the presence and confluence of sinful persons and sinful things, to mourn for the sins of our land, for the sins of the church abroad, for the sins of our neighbours; mourn for the sins of our towns, mourn for the sins of our own families, mourn for the sins of our yoke-fellows, mourn for the sins of our children, mourn for our own sins. Oh happy is that man that can pour forth himself in godly tears. The more he mourns thus, the more he shall be comforted.

2. Secondly, Your mourning will be spiritual mourning, in case *you draw your tears from a good fountain:* that they come from a good rise, a good spring. When a man's zeal is for the zeal of God's glory, out of love, and mercy, and compassion to men's souls, out of a desire of men's salvation, of his own, and others'; and when he mourns out of hatred of ill, and of sin, and mourns for the love of grace and goodness, this is a spiritual mourning. Mourn now, and work upon these motives, and not upon private motives and respects; but let our sorrow come out of hatred of sin, and out of love to goodness, out of zeal to God's name, out of love, mercy, and compassion to men's souls. And this is holy and spiritual mourning.

3. Thirdly, Your mourning will be spiritual, in case *it have spiritual effects.* Let us look to those. Holy mourning, it sets a man further from sin. Holy mourning, it draws a man nearer to God. It makes him pray, as it is said of them, Judges ii. 4, 5, they wept; and the place bare the name of weepers: 'Bochim,' 'they wept' and offered sacrifice. Prayer and tears go together. Sacrifice and sorrow go together. Now when our mourning is such mourning that it makes us not sit in a corner in a sullen manner, but makes us bestir ourselves in praying and running to the Lord, it makes us wrestle with God, as Jacob did, in tears and sorrow, this is holy and spiritual mourning. This is the mourning that we describe to you from the objects, from the causes of it, and from the effects of it. This mourning is an healing mourning. It is a sweetening mourning. It is a comfortable mourning. It is a hopeful mourning. It will do a man much good. Therefore give way to this to the utmost of your power, as I said before. Let every man say to himself, I must mourn, I may mourn, and I will mourn.

(1.) First, I *must*, because God bids me, because the time calls for it. Therefore I must. Because my own need requires it, therefore I must weep. I find I am dead, and drowsy, and sluggish; and carelessness and sleepiness will creep upon me except I stir up myself to mourn. And then, as I must, so

(2.) I *may*. David, and Paul, and Jeremiah could weep upon spiritual occasions. So may we in case we will go to the same means, to the same God. Our nature is capable of godly sorrow. We see in them who was their Father, even God, who gave them a tender heart. He can give it us. You know the Spirit of God is a spirit of weeping. It is a Spirit of supplication. It will make us to look to him whom we have pierced, and to weep, &c., as it is Zech. xii. 10. Now Christ hath promised that he that asks for this Spirit shall have it.

Let us go to the Lord, and say, It is possible that we should have so fit and tender hearts to shed tears for our own sins and the sins of others, as David and others before us have done. It is possible for me so to do if I go to God and ask such a heart. God hath promised that he will give his Spirit if we call for it; and therefore let us call and desire the Lord to smite our rocky hearts, as Moses smote the rock, that he would cause water to gush out of thee as he did out of the rock.

(3.) Thirdly, As we may, so *let us resolve that we will do it.* Let us come to resolve. Well, I see the time calls for it; I see my brethren and myself have need of it, I will do it, I will set upon it; I will take a time when I will cast up all my reckonings between God and myself; I will take a time to unweep my former carnal sorrow; I will take some time from my carnal laughter for this. Take the time now, defer it not; now it is a fit time. You use to cast up your shops at this time of the year, then come and reckon how your estate stands, my brethren; cast up your shop with God; rifle your souls and see how matters stand between God and you; see whether you go backwards or forwards. Mourn there, and bewail your sins that you have committed against God, and the sins of the time; and one day spent in this manner between God and thy soul will do thee more good than all the feastings and merriments, and all the sports that you meet withal this time. That is for the second use.

Use 3. Now there followeth a third. Here is a word *of comfort to those that mourn*—comfort in regard of the whole church, and comfort in regard of the particular members of the church. For the whole church; here is comfort for the people of God in affliction. It is the time of Jacob's trouble, saith Jeremiah, but he shall come out, Jer. xxx. 7. He hath a time of trouble, but he shall be delivered, he shall have a time of comfort; he is weak, but then his Redeemer is strong. Jacob hath strong friends and strong means. All that is in heaven is for Jacob, for the church, I mean; all the saints in earth pray, and these prayers are not in vain. There will come comfort out of them at the last. Fear not, then, O worm Jacob, saith the prophet, fear not; though thou be as a worm, be not afraid, Isa. xli. 14.

Obj. Oh, but Jacob's grief is more than his fear.

Ans. Why should the people of God grieve? Do they grieve because the enemies insult? Let them answer the enemies in the words of the church: 'Rejoice not against me, O mine enemies: for though I be fallen, yet shall I rise again; and while I sit in darkness, God shall be a light to me.' Do they grieve because they are in darkness, and are encompassed with many sorrows and distresses? Hear what the Lord saith, Isa. lx. 1, 'Arise, and shine; put on glory; I will cause light to shine in darkness.' And saith another place, 'O thou tossed and afflicted with tempest, I will make thee walls of carbuncles,' Isa. liv. 11. They were before of ordinary stone, now they shall be made of precious stones; the Lord will make the conclusion of his children an happy conclusion. Mark the righteous, the end of his life is peace; and so the end of every particular temptation, of every particular affliction, is peace. All shall end well with him. It shall be well on his side.

Here, then, is comfort for the church. The church of God is afflicted, but she shall be comforted. She is despised, but she shall be honourable and magnified, and her enemies shall lick the dust of her feet. The church of God is opposed and put hard to it. But her Redeemer is mighty, and her hoofs are made of brass, and her feet of iron, to trample to dust and powder all the enemies that rise up against her. She is in the everlasting arms, as Moses speaks of the almighty God there, Deut. xxxiii. 27. She finds rest there; she finds peace and comfort. In the greatest miseries, this is comfort for the church. The Lord will comfort her and her mourners too: Isa. lvii. 18, 'He will comfort Sion and her mourners.' All Sion, the church of God, shall be comforted; all the friends of the church that mourn in her mourning, and that take to heart her sorrows and desolation, they shall be comforted too. All that mourn with her shall be comforted. This is comfort for the church in general. Now, for every Christian, for every member in particular, here is comfort.

Are we, my brethren, such as do mourn, and mourn spiritually? Do we mourn for the breach of God's Sabbath? for the contempt of his word? for the abuse of his sacraments? for the contempt of his name? Do we mourn for the church that is under captivity, under the sword? Do we mourn that Christians be under temptations, under misery, under afflictions? Do we mourn because the work of grace goes on no better in the hearts of God's people and in our own hearts? Do we mourn for our sins, and for the sins of our brethren? especially those that profess religion, is this the matter of our sorrow, my brethren? Here is comfort, you shall be comforted; the Lord hath passed his word that it shall be so. All these tears are registered and put into the bottle of God. He keeps them as a precious water, and there is not a tear shall be forgotten. All this is seed sown. If we sow in tears, we shall reap in joy. Harvest follows seed-time, so joy follows tears. It shall be so. 'There is light sown for the righteous,' Ps. xcvii. 11. It may be under the clods, it may be buried for a time, it may seem lost, but it will sprout at the last, and there will come a crop out of it. Well, here is comfort. All the sorrows of the godly, all his griefs, all his sighs, all his wants, all his heart-breaks, if all these turn to spiritual mourning, they shall all turn to his advantage and comfort in the end. Nay, his sorrow for the present hath comfort along with it, and the more he sorrows, the more he rejoiceth, and the more true comfort he hath still. The more a man can weep over Christ, the more bitterly he can weep, the more sweet Christ will relish to him. The more grief and sorrow he brings to the word and to the ordinances of God, the more true sweetness he finds in the word and carries from the word. And the more he can bewail himself before the Lord in his wants, in his bankruptness in grace, the more he is advanced, and enlarged to comfort and joy by the Lord. But for the wicked, woe to him; for 'in laughter his heart is sad,' saith the text; he laughs in the face, but his heart mourns. On the other side, happy is the spiritual mourner; in his mourning, his heart laughs, as it were. He hath matter of joy in sorrow, as the wicked hath matter of mourning in mirth. Woe be to the wicked, for all his joy shall end in sorrow; the end of that mirth is sadness in spirit, saith Solomon; but happy is the holy mourner. All his tears shall be wiped away, all his sorrows, all his griefs, all his fears shall end in comfort and consolation at the last.

Obj. Oh, but how shall I know that my mourning is spiritual mourning? I suspect it much this way. And why? First of all, my sorrow begins in the flesh; I never mourned, I never went to God in prayer and fasting, or any exercise of religion, till God tamed me and took me down with crosses and afflictions; then when he laid load on me, I went to it, and not before.

Sol. Well, my brethren, thus it may be: Thy sorrow may begin in the flesh; but, if it end in the Spirit, all is well. It may be a Christian's sorrow was first occasioned by crosses, by worldly sorrow, and worldly respects; but if he improve his sorrow, and turn it to holy sorrow, if he turn the stream into the right channel, if he set his grief, his indignations, his tears upon sin, all shall end well at the last, though the beginning were not so good.

Obj. Ay, but, will some say, my sorrow is more for outward things than for spiritual matters. I grieve when I am sick, but it is for pain more than for sin. I mourn when I am poor, but it is because I am poor in purse, because I am poor in state, rather than in regard of my spiritual wants; and so for other matters too.

Ans. My brethren, this is easily granted. There is no floor here, but there is chaff as well as wheat with it. There is no precious mine here so rich, but there is some dross as well as good gold, as well as good metal. So it is with a Christian. There is a mixture of flesh and spirit. They run both in the same channel, and they run within the veins of the same soul and spirit, as it were; the question is not, therefore, whether there be any fleshy sorrow, any carnal sorrow, grief, and mourning; but whether there be any holy and spiritual sorrow. How much there is of the one is not the point, but whether there be any of the other. And if it be so, it is spiritual sorrow, that thou canst shed some tears, vent some sighs and groans to God in spiritual respects, for spiritual losses, for spiritual evils. Here is matter of comfort, there is so much spiritual comfort, so much spiritual joy belongs to thee.

Obj. But how shall I know that my mourning is spiritual mourning, when I cannot mourn for sin? I have abundance of tears for losses, and for crosses, and unkindnesses; but I am dry, and barren, and tearless, when it comes to matter of sin and offence, and trespass against God. Is this well, that a man should have tears at command for outward losses and crosses, and not shed a tear in prayer, and in repentance for sin?

Ans. No, my brethren, it is not well; but how shall we do to amend this? Surely, even go to God and confess how it is; complain of thyself, and desire him to amend it; and, if we condemn ourselves, God is ready to receive us.

Obj. Ay, but the children of God are more plentiful in tears for sin than for outward things.

Ans. Ay, in what sense? Not in regard of the bulk, but in regard of the worth, in regard of the value of their tears. One tear spent for sin is worth rivers of tears for outward matters. In the regard of the price and excellency, it is more, because God accepts of a man's endeavour and desire in this kind, and he looks what his desire, and intention, and endeavour is. They are more also in regard of our esteem, that we would gladly weep more for sin than for other matters. Otherwise, the children of God are more plentiful many times in tears for the loss of children, as David was for Absalom; or for some cross that befalls them, as at Ziklag he wept so much that he could weep no more, than for sin against God, and yet they would weep most for that. They think that a matter of greatest sorrow, and they desire to be more plentiful in tears for it, and then God accepts it, according to that a man would do, and not according to that which he cannot do, and which he hath not.

Obj. Further, it will be said, How shall I know my sorrow to be spiritual sorrow? I answer in a word:

Ans. 1. First, Look to the object, *that it be universal.* So in spiritual things, he that is spiritually sorry he mourns for the want of goodness wheresoever he seeth it, be it in himself or in other men, nay, be it in his enemies. David saith, Ps. cxix. 53, sorrow seized on him, 'because his adversaries kept not the law of God.' Spiritual mourning, it makes a man sorry for painful evils that fall upon his brethren as well as himself; and on himself as well as them. Do we mourn for other men's faults as well as for our own? Do we mourn that our enemies do overshoot themselves, and that they disgrace themselves, as well, though not so much, as if our friends had done it? If our sorrow be universal, then it is spiritual.

Ans. 2. Secondly, Our sorrow will be spiritual and holy, *if it be accompanied with prayer;* for holy mourning makes way for prayer. Sometimes a man is so surprised and overwhelmed, as David saith, that he is not able to speak a word, notwithstanding there may be a mental real prayer. His eyes may be towards heaven, he may sigh, and groan, and lament, and bemoan his own estate, that he cannot speak and pour forth himself in prayer to God as he would do, and as he should do. Now, if our sorrow be such sorrow, that it sends us to God, that it brings us on our knees, that it makes us either speak or chatter, as Hezekiah did, it makes a man mourn, groan, as the dove doth, as he saith of himself; if it be such sorrow as this, it is spiritual sorrow. You know that it is said of Jacob, Hos. xii. 4, that he wrestled with the angel with tears, and sued to him with supplication. Tears and supplication went together. He begged apace, and cried apace; he hanged on him, and would not let him go without a blessing.

Ans. 3. Again, It is spiritual sorrow, *when it is accompanied with thankfulness.* A carnal man, when he is pinched and twinged, and knows not which way to turn himself, he will be glad to cry, when he sees there is no other refuge in the world, but either he must cry or sink. But a man that is a spiritual mourner, he will be thankful as well as prayerful. This is a comfortable kind of mourning. There is hope in it, there is sweetness and comfort in it; and that man that can so mourn, he blesseth God that he can mourn, that God hath given him time and leisure, that he may set himself apart to provoke himself to mourn. He blesseth God that God hath given him a word that can work upon him, that God hath given him friends to deal faithfully, that God hath applied this word to his heart, that it hath wounded him and made him bleed; he is thankful for the mercy, and thinks it a great promotion, when he can shed tears, when his heart yields under the stroke of the word of God, and of the hand of God that is upon him. Nay, he is thankful whatsoever it costs him. The child of God, when he sees his heart is enlarged to weep over Christ for his sins, he cares not how dear he pays for this sorrow, for this mourning, though he lose some of his estate, some of his credit with men; though he lose some of his wealth, some of his comforts, some of his friends; yet, notwithstanding, if he can weep and mourn, he thinks he hath a good bargain, a good purchase. Though God afflict him, though he pain him, though he cross him and cast him down, yet if he see that his heart can weep for his sin, that he can lament after the Lord, and can take to heart his corruptions, this man can rejoice in this estate, he can bless God's name, that hath given him an heart to mourn spiritually, though he pay dear for it in regard of outward losses and outward smart.

Now, then, if you have such a mourning as this, that you do mourn for spiritual things; and you so mourn that your mourning fit you for prayer, that it make way for praise and thanksgiving; then take comfort in your mourning, and know that it will end well. After night will come a day; after darkness there will come light; after seed-time there shall be an harvest, you shall have a crop. The more you mourn, the more you shall rejoice. Blessed are they that mourn for themselves and for others. Blessed are they, they shall be comforted. They are comforted, and they will be more comforted afterwards. So saith the mouth that cannot lie. It is the speech of Christ himself. Thus we have done with the point, and can no further proceed at this time.

VIOLENCE VICTORIOUS.

VIOLENCE VICTORIOUS.

NOTE.

'Violence Victorious' appeared originally in 'The Beams of Divine Light' (4to, 1639). The separate title-page will be found below.* For general title, see Vol. V. page 220. G.

*VIOLENCE
VICTORIOVS:
In two Sermons,

By the late Reverend and Learned
Divine RICHARD SIBS,

Doctor in Divinity, Master of Katherine Hall in
Cambridge, and sometimes Preacher at
Grayes-Inne.

GEN. 32. 26.
I will not let thee goe except thou blesse mee.

1 COR. 15. 57.
Thankes be unto God which giveth us the victory through Iesus Christ our Lord.

LONDON,
Printed by *G. M.* for *Nicholas Bourne* and *Rapha Harford*,
1639.

VIOLENCE VICTORIOUS.

From the days of John Baptist until now the kingdom of heaven suffereth violence, and the violent take it by force.—MAT. XI. 12.

JOHN BAPTIST and our blessed Saviour gave mutual testimonies one of another. He witnessed of Christ before he came, and our Saviour Christ gives witness of him here. The occasion of this you have in the second verse. John being in prison, sends two of his disciples to Christ, to know whether he were the Christ or no; not that John did doubt, but to confirm his disciples. Christ returns a real and a verbal answer. 'Tell John,' saith he, 'what ye have seen and heard,' &c.; and then he closeth up all, 'Blessed is he that is not offended with me.' Upon this occasion Christ enters into a commendation of blessed St John Baptist, even unto a comparative commendation, 'Amongst them that were born of women there had not yet risen a greater than John the Baptist;' not so much in eminency of grace, though that may have a truth, as in regard of the dispensation of his ministry, John living in more glorious times. For the excellency of the church is from Christ. He doth ennoble and advance times, and places, and persons. Bethlehem, a little city, yet not a little city in regard that Christ was born there; and saith Christ, 'Happy are the eyes that see that which your eyes see,' Luke x. 23. Everything is advanced by Christ. So John Baptist, in regard of his office, being the immediate forerunner of Christ, was greater than all that were before him; yet he saith, 'The least in the kingdom of heaven is greater than he;' not in grace, but in prerogative, in regard of the revelation and manifestation of more things. For John Baptist died before he saw the death, and resurrection, and ascension of Christ accomplished, before he was glorified. Therefore in regard of these prerogatives, the least in the kingdom of heaven, that is, in the church of the New Testament, is greater than he. It is a rule that the least of the greater is greater than the greatest of the less. John was greater than the greatest of them that were before him, but lesser than the least of those that were after him.

Then Christ commends John from the efficacy of his ministry: 'From the days of John Baptist until now the kingdom of heaven suffereth violence, and the violent take it by force.' So you see how the words depend upon the former. For the points we are to consider in them.

First, Here *you have the state of the church in the New Testament.* It is a kingdom, and the kingdom of heaven; together with the quality of the means whereby it comes to be a kingdom, the means of grace, the gospel. The gospel and the people that are wrought on by the gospel in the New Testament, they are both called the 'kingdom of heaven.'

Then, secondly, here is set down *the affection of those people that seek this kingdom at that time, and so forward to the end of the world.* The disposition of the persons is, 'They are violent.'

The third is, *the issue or success of this eagerness and violence.* Though the manner be violent, yet the success is good. 'The violent take it by force.'

The fourth is, *the date or time when it begins, and how long it continues.* It bears date from the preaching of Saint John Baptist to the end of the world. 'Until now;' that is, to the end of the world. As it was said, 'till now,' in the evangelist's time, so posterity may say, 'Until now,' from the first coming of Christ till his second coming. While there is a gospel preached, which is the ministry of the Spirit, the Spirit will be working; and there are such glorious things in the gospel, that there will be violence offered. So while there is a people to be gathered, and a gospel to be preached to gather them, and a Spirit that works by that gospel, there will be violence in the church offered to the means of salvation.

Doct. 1. First, *The state of the church, together with the means, the gospel preached, it is called the kingdom of heaven.*

Besides others, there are three main significations of these words, 'The kingdom of heaven.'

First, The famous, leading, proper signification is the state and place where God himself and his people are most glorious, 'the kingdom *of heaven.*' All the other significations end in that. But, secondly, because all that shall come into that glorious kingdom, they must be kings here first, in the state of the kingdom of grace, which consists 'in righteousness, peace, and joy in the Holy Ghost,' Gal. v. 22, in the graces and comforts of the Spirit, therefore the state of grace comes to have the name too of 'the kingdom of heaven.' And thirdly, Because grace in this world cannot be attained without an order, and means, and dispensations from God, hereupon the dispensation of the means whereby we come to have grace is also called 'the kingdom.' The unfolding the mysteries of salvation in the gospel is called the kingdom of God. As Christ saith, 'The kingdom of God shall be taken from you;' that is, the preaching of the gospel; therefore 'the gospel' is called 'the gospel of the kingdom,' and 'the word of the kingdom,' because by this word we come to have grace, and by grace, glory. There is no glory without grace, and no grace without the word. One makes way for another. The preaching of the gospel doth cause a church, which is the kingdom of Christ, wherein he rules by the sceptre of his word; by which word Christ and all his riches, and glory, and prerogatives are unfolded; and thereby grace is wrought, and grace leads to glory. This connection and subordination is to be observed,

1. First, *For the conviction of those who do not indeed belong to the kingdom of heaven.* Every man is ready to talk of the kingdom of heaven, and the glory there; ay, but there is a subordination of grace, and of the means of grace. How standest thou affected to the means of salvation, to the 'word of the kingdom,' the 'word of life,' the 'word of reconciliation'? for it hath the name from all the excellencies to which it brings us; to shew that as we value life, a kingdom, reconciliation, and all that is good, so we must value this gospel, or else it is a presumptuous confidence. If the

privileges of grace and glory belong to us, we must come to them by these steps. Those that regard not the gospel and means of salvation, they have nothing to do with grace nor glory. They are hereby convinced of arrogant folly.

2. Again, It is a ground *to comfort weak Christians that regard the means of salvation, and yet fear their falling away*. Be of good comfort whosoever thou art. God hath knit and linked these together; all the power of earth and hell cannot break one link of this chain. Conscionable* attending upon the means, and grace, and glory, will go together. Therefore hold on, attend upon the means of salvation, and wait with comfort. The gospel of the kingdom will bring thee to grace; and grace, though it be but a little measure, will bring thee to glory. Where God hath begun a good work he will finish it; he will second one benefit with another; diligent attending on the means with grace, and grace with glory.

In Scripture, works have their denomination from that they aim at, as the apostle saith, 'Ye have crucified the old man,' Rom. vi. 6, and 'ye are crucified with Christ,' Gal. ii. 20, because ye are in doing it, and ye shall do it perfectly. So we are saints, because we shall be so. We are kings now, because we are in part so, and we shall be so fully hereafter. So grace is called the kingdom of heaven, because it is the undoubted way to the kingdom of heaven and glory. God would help our faith by the very title; for we are not elected to the beginnings only of glory, but to the perfection, as it is excellently set down Eph. i. 6, 'We are elected to glory by means and beginnings.' Therefore undoubtedly we may hope for the accomplishment when we see the beginnings.

Quest. Why is the state of grace, and the means of grace, and glory itself, called 'the kingdom of heaven'?

Ans. Because they are all of and from heaven. The one is in heaven the kingdom of glory, and the other the kingdom of the word here; and truth and grace which are by it are from heaven. The truth we have and grace from that truth come from heaven; yea, and Christ, the author of all, is from heaven, and they all lead to heaven.

Which should teach us with what minds to converse in the hearing and reading of these things with heavenly affections. And it shews likewise why worldlings and base people are no more affected with the things of the gospel, because it is 'the kingdom of heaven.' If it were of the world, we should have it sought with eagerness enough, though it were a less matter than a kingdom; but it is a 'kingdom of heaven' remote from flesh and blood. There must be a new Spirit to work a new sight and a new taste, to work a change in the heart of man, and then he shall know the things of 'the kingdom of heaven.' He must come out of the world that will see this kingdom, as in Rev. xviii. 4, 'Come out of Babylon.' A man must come out of antichrist's kingdom to see the baseness of it. He cannot see it in the midst of it. So we must come out of the world if we would see the glorious kingdom of Christ. It is a heavenly kingdom. Therefore the greatest potentates of the world must abase themselves. There is no greatness in the world can help them to this heavenly kingdom.

Quest. But why should the gospel and the state of the church in the New Testament be called the kingdom of heaven, and receive the date *now?* was it not the kingdom of heaven before?

Ans. I answer, It is the manner of the Scripture to give titles to things from the glorious manifestation of them. Things are said to be when they

* That is, 'conscientious.'—G.

are gloriously manifested. The mystery of Christ is said to be revealed now in the time of the gospel. It was known before to Adam and Abraham and the rest. But now there was a more apparent glorious manifestation of it. Therefore now the manifestation of Christ, and the good things by him, they are called 'a kingdom.' Before it was kept enclosed in the pale of the Jewish church, it was veiled under types, it was hid in promises that were dark and obscure. But when Christ came, all was taken off and Christ was unveiled. It is said in the gospel, 'The Holy Ghost was not given yet, because Jesus was not yet glorified,' John vii. 39. The Holy Ghost was given before, but not so fully and plentifully. So there was a state of heaven before men were saved, before the coming of Christ; but it was not called 'the kingdom of heaven.' It was not a state of liberty and freedom from the bondage of ceremonies, &c.

And there is reason that there should be violence offered to this state, and means, and grace wrought by it. It is a kingdom. It is no great wonder that a kingdom should suffer violence, especially such a kingdom as 'the kingdom of heaven.' What is in a kingdom?

There is, first of all, *freedom from slavery and danger*. A kingdom is an independent state. There is none above it. He that is a king is free, independent, and supreme.

Then again, a kingdom *is a full state*. There is abundance and plenty of people and good things in a kingdom.

Again, In a kingdom there *is glory and excellency*—where is it to be had else?—all the glory, and sufficiency, and contentment that earth can afford.

Now in that the state of the church by reason of the glorious gospel is called a kingdom.

First, *It is a free state*, as indeed the 'word doth make us free' from former bondage. In particular, the gospel of Christ it frees us from Jewish bondage, and from all kind of bondage spiritual. 'If the Son make you free, ye are free indeed,' John viii. 36. A Christian is above all. He is over sin, and Satan, and the law. He is free, and supreme, and independent. All are under him. A Christian, as a Christian, he is under none but Christ, under no creature. 'The spiritual man judgeth all things, yet he himself is judged of no man,' 1 Cor. ii. 15. I speak not of civil differences; but as a Christian is a member of Christ, and a citizen of the kingdom of heaven, he hath a kind of independent state. His conscience is only subject to God and Christ. But all earthly things he commands, they are under him.

And *second*, The state of a Christian is *a full state*. God is his, Christ is his, 'all things are his,' 1 Cor iii. 21, so much as shall serve to bring him to heaven. That which is truly good is directly his, and indirectly all other things are made his by Christ, who hath the authority, and power, and strength of a king to command all things to work together for his good, Rom. viii. 28. Death, and sin, and all that befalls him, are thus his. And then he hath a spirit of contentment in the want of good, and of patience in the suffering of ill, that he 'can do all things,' as St Paul saith, 'through Christ that strengtheneth him,' Phil. iv. 13. What he wants in outward things he can fetch supply from the promises of the gospel, he can fetch supply from Christ, and from the state to come; and what he wants in other things he hath in grace, which is better.

Third, It is a state likewise *of glory and excellency*. But it is a spiritual glory, and therefore it consists together with outward baseness and meanness. It is a glorious state to be the 'Son of God,' to be 'heirs of heaven,' heirs of all things in Christ; by the Spirit of Christ in him he rules over all. How glorious is the Spirit of God in a Christian in the time of temptation and affliction, when he hath a Spirit ruling in him that is stronger than the world and all oppositions whatsoever? 1 John iv. 4. The state of a Christian is glorious even in this world in the beginnings of it. What then is the glory that is to be revealed on the sons of God 'in the day of revelation?' Rom. ii. 5. It cannot enter into our thoughts, it is above our expression, nay, it is above our imagination and conceit. Thus you see there is great cause why 'the kingdom of heaven should suffer violence.' When crowns and kingdoms are laid open to people with hope of getting them, especially such an one as 'the kingdom of heaven is,' it is no wonder if there be 'violence' offered to get them.

The next thing is the affection of those that seek after this kingdom. It is violent.

'The kingdom of heaven suffereth violence.'

How doth the 'kingdom of heaven,' the gospel and means of grace, 'suffer violence.'

1. First, *Because when these good things were revealed by John Baptist, and then by Christ, and after by the disciples and apostles, many thronged into the church, which is the gate of* 'the kingdom of heaven.' *They all pressed to be of the church, to hear the word of God.* They hung, as it were, upon the word of Christ, upon his mouth. They pressed so, that 'they trod one upon another,' Luke xii. 1; and it is said they all came out to hear John Baptist: 'Jerusalem, and all Judea, and all the region round about Jordan,' Matt. iii. 5. So that in regard of the multitude there was violence.

2. And then in regard *of their affections*, their zeal to the good things of the gospel was eager and earnest. To be citizens of a kingdom, to partake of the means of salvation, to come to grace and so to glory, it made them wondrous violent.

3. In regard likewise *of the persons*, 'the kingdom of heaven suffered violence,' the persons being such as might be judged to have no right unto it. Alas! for poor wretched sinful men and women, that had been notorious sinners, to come to receive a kingdom, to become kings, this was strange! What had sinners to do with grace? This doctrine was not heard of in the law, that there should be hope for such wretched persons as these. If such might be admitted, surely there must needs be great violence.

Then again, they were poor and mean people. 'The poor receive the gospel,' Luke vii. 22. For beggars to become kings; poor men that were advantaged by their outward abasement to come to spiritual poverty!

4. Again, they *were Gentiles*, 'aliens from the commonwealth of Israel, and strangers from the covenant of promise,' Eph. ii. 12, heathen people. 'The Jews were the children of the kingdom,' Mat. viii. 12, the Gentiles were foreigners and strangers. Now for these to come in, and 'the children of the kingdom' to be shut out, it must needs suppose violence. Where there is no apparent right, there is force. Now what right had the Gentiles, that were little better than dogs? Could they have anything to do with the kingdom? Ay, saith Christ, they take it by violence; and the Jews, and the proud scribes and Pharisees that seem to be the apparent 'children of the kingdom,' shall at length be shut out. 'They that were first,' in outward prerogatives, 'shall be last; and they that were last,' the Gentiles, sinners, mean people, that take the advantage of their baseness and sinfulness, to see their unworthiness, and to magnify the grace of God in Christ, 'shall be first,' Mat. xx. 16. In these respects the kingdom of

heaven is said to suffer violence.' People will to heaven, whatever come of it; when these good things are discovered they will have no nay. Hence, we may learn this,

Doct. That it is the disposition of those that are the true members of the church of God to be eager and violent.

Those that intend to enter into the kingdom, they must throng and strive to enter; and when they are in, they must keep the fort, and keep it with violence.

There is indeed a violence of iniquity and injustice; and so the people of God, of all others, ought not to be a violent people. 'Do violence to no man,' saith the Baptist to the soldiers, Luke iii. 14. Violence rather debars out of the kingdom of heaven than is any qualification for it. But this is another manner of violence which our Saviour here speaks of, necessary for all that desire to enter into the kingdom of heaven; and that for these reasons:

I. First, *Betwixt us and the blessed state we aim at there is much opposition;* and therefore there must be violence. The state of the church here, the state of grace and the enjoyment of the means of grace, it is a state of opposition. Good persons and good things they are opposed in the world. Christ rules in this world, 'in the midst of his enemies.' He must have enemies therefore to rule in the midst of; he must be opposed; and where there is opposition between us and the good things that we must of necessity have, we must break through the opposition, which cannot be done without violence. Now the means and graces of salvation they are opposed every way, within us and without us.

(1.) They are opposed from *within us;* and that is the worst opposition. For Satan hath a party within us that holds correspondency with him, our own traitorous flesh. In all the degrees of salvation there is violence. Hence, in effectual calling, when we are called out of the kingdom of Satan, he is not willing to let us go; he will keep us there still; and when we come to have our sins forgiven in justification, there is opposition; proud flesh and blood will not yield to the righteousness of the gospel; it will not rest in Christ; it will seek somewhat in itself. In sanctification there is opposition between 'the flesh and the Spirit.' Every good work we do it is gotten out of the fire, as it were, it is gotten by violence. In every good action, whether it be to get grace, or to give thanks to God, how many carnal reasonings are there! If a man be to give to others, the flesh suggests, I may want myself. If he be to reform abuses in others, he is ready to think, others will have somewhat to say to me; and I shall be offensive to such and such men. And then the affection of earthly things chains us to the things below, and self-love prompts a man to sleep in a whole skin. We love our wealth, and peace, and favour with men. So that a man cannot come to the state of grace without breaking through these; and hereupon comes the necessity of violence, from the opposition from within us. We must offer violence to ourselves, to our own reason, to our own wills and affections. 'You have not yet resisted unto blood,' saith the apostle, Heb. xii. 4. We do not resist by killing others, but we ourselves resist to death, when, rather than we will miss heaven and happiness, and rather than we will not stand for the truth, we will suffer death.

(2.) Again, There is opposition *from the world:* on the right hand, by the snares and delights of the world, to quench the delight in the good things of the Spirit; and on the left hand, by fears, and terrors, and scandals, to scare us from doing what we ought to do.

(3.) And then there is opposition *from Satan*, in every good action. He besets us in prayer with distracted thoughts; and in every duty, for he knows they tend to the ruin of him and of his kingdom. There is no good action but it is opposed from within us and without us. The means of salvation, and the attending on them, they are not without slander and disgrace in the world. God will have this violence therefore, because there is opposition to the means, to the attendance on them, to grace, to every good action, to everything that is spiritually good.

Nay, sometimes God himself becomes a personated enemy;* in spiritual desertions he seems to forsake and leave us; and not only to forsake us, but to be an enemy, 'to write bitter things against us,' Job xiii. 26; and that is a heavy temptation.

II. Again, God will have this violence and striving, *as a character of difference, to shew who are bastard professors and who are not;* who will go to the price of Christianity, and who will not. If men will go to heaven they must be violent, they must be at the cost and charges, sometimes to venture life itself, and whatsoever is dear and precious in the world. A man must be so violent, that he must go through all, even death itself, though it be a bloody death, to Christ. This discards all lukewarm, carnal professors, who shake off this violence. In all estates of the church, it is almost equally difficult to be a sound Christian; for God requires this violence even in the most peaceable times. Now, the truth and religion are countenanced by the laws, yet the power of it is by many much opposed. Therefore he now that in spite of reproach, in spite of slander, will bear the scorns cast upon the gospel, that will 'go with Christ without the gate, bearing his reproach,' Heb. xiii. 13, such a man may be said to be thus violent. It is an easy thing to have so much Christianity as will stand with our commodity or with pleasure, &c.; but to have so much as will bring us to heaven, I say, it is equally hard in all times of the church, it requires violence to carry us through these lesser oppositions.

III. Again, God will have us get these things with violence, *that we may set a greater price on them when we have them.* When we have things that are gotten by violence, that are gotten hardly, Oh we value them much! Heaven is heaven then. Things that are hardly gotten and hardly kept are highly prized.

IV. Again, *The excellency of the thing enforceth violence.* It is fit that excellent things should have answerable affections. Now, it being a kingdom, and the kingdom of heaven, what affection is answerable but a violent, strong affection?

V. Again, Together with the excellency, *the necessity requires it;* for the kingdom of heaven it is a place of refuge as well as a kingdom to enrich us. There were cities of refuge among the Jews. When a man was followed by the avenger of blood, he would run as fast as he could to the city of refuge, and there he was safe. So when a guilty conscience pursues us, when there is a noise of fear in the heart, when God's judgments awaken us and hell is open, when a man apprehends his estate and is convinced what a one he is and what he deserves, of necessity he will fly to the city of refuge; and where is that but in the 'kingdom of heaven,' in the church? Happy is he that can but get in at the gate of this kingdom, there is no doubt of his going in further. But there must be a striving 'to enter in at the gate,' Luke xiii. 24. And then there he shall be hid in his sanctuary; as the pursued doves get into their nests, and the conies

* That is, one who performs the part of an enemy.—Ed.

hide them in the rock, when they get that over their heads then they are safe. So a Christian, when he is pursued with conscience and with the temptations of Satan, he flies to his sanctuary. Do you wonder that a guilty man should flee to his sanctuary, and the pursued creatures to their hold and refuge? In this respect 'the kingdom of heaven suffereth violence.'

Herein it is compared to some great, rich city, that hath some great treasure and riches in it; and it must be besieged and beleagured a long time, and those that can enter into it they are made for ever. Or it is like the entrance or gate of a city where there is striving and thronging, and where besides enemies are, that if men strive not they are cut, and mangled, and killed. So it is in the state of this kingdom. When a man's eyes be opened, he sees the devil and hell behind him, and either he must enter or be damned; and being entered, it makes him rich and advanceth him for ever. So he is strongly moved to offer violence on both sides. If he look behind him there is the kingdom of Satan, darkness and misery and damnation; for as Pharaoh pursued the Israelites when they were gone out of his kingdom, so the devil pursues a man when he is broken out of his dominion: and then before him there is the kingdom of happiness and glory. The fear of that that follows them, and the hope of that that is set before them, both make them strive to enter into the gate of that city.

Use. What should this teach us?

First, *Let it be a rule of trial to know and judge of our estate, whether we be entered into this gate of heaven or no*. Our lives are very short, very uncertain; let us consider if we be in the way to heaven. What striving, what struggling, what violence have we ever offered? There are a company that regard not the means of salvation at all, either in private or public. Some come to the word and hear, but they do not hear it as the word of God, to be ruled by it, but as a discourse to delight themselves for the time; to have matter to speak of and to censure, not with a spirit of obedience to be guided by it as the sceptre of the kingdom. What 'violence' is this, now and then to hear a sermon, now and then to read a chapter, now and then to utter a yawning prayer between sleeping and waking, perhaps when thou knowest not what thyself sayest? How then wouldst thou have God to regard it? What violence is in the lives of most Christians? what strength to enforce good actions? How do they improve the means of salvation? Many means are wholly neglected. Some perhaps they use, that may stand with their convenience, now and then; whereas there must be an universal care of all the means. There cannot one be neglected without the loss of grace, and there must be attendance on them with violence. There is none of the means can profit us without rousing and stirring up our spirits. We cannot hear nor pray without drawing up and raising up our souls. The flesh will stop the comfortable performance of any action else, and Satan will kill them in the very birth if he can.

To search a little deeper, *do but compare your courses toward these good things of heaven with your courses towards the world*. If there be hope of preferment, the doors of great men are sure to suffer violence with favourites. The courts of justice suffer violence to have our right in earthly things. The stages and such places are thronged, and suffer violence. If a man could but overlook the courses of men abroad in the city, he should see one violent for his pleasures, running to the house of the harlot 'as a fool to the stocks,' Prov. vii. 22; another to the exchange, to increase his estate; another to the place of justice, to detract his neighbour, or to get his own right, perhaps neglecting his title to heaven in the mean time; another to the court, to get favour to rise to some place of preferment. These places suffer violence. But what violence doth the poor gospel endure? Alas! it is slighted; and men will regard that when they can spare time, &c. It is not regarded according to the worth and value of it. If ever we look to have good by the gospel, our dispositions must be violent, in some proportion answerable to the excellency of it.

Alas! we may justly turn the complaint on ourselves, that whilst we spend our strength in violence about the base and mean things of this life, the kingdom of heaven it offereth violence to us, and yet we will none of it. How doth God beseech us in the ministry! 'We beseech you to be reconciled,' 2 Cor. v. 20; and 'Why will ye die, O house of Israel?' Ezek. xviii. 31. As if the gospel and grace were commodities that God were weary of, he comes and puts them upon us whether we will or no, and yet we refuse them. We are so far from offering violence to the gospel and to grace, that God offers violence to us, as if we should do him a favour to receive the gospel, and to do good to our own souls; and yet the vile, proud, base heart of man will not regard and receive these heavenly things. How will it justify God's sentence at the day of judgment, when he shall allege there was a discovery of such things unto you, and instead of violence in seeking them, you slighted and neglected them? Nay, there is a worse sort of men than these, those that oppose the 'kingdom of heaven' in the means of it, in the persons of it; what kind of men are these, think you?

Again, We see here *that there is a blessed violence that may stand with judgment*. A man cannot be violent and wise in the things of this world, because the things are mean; and eagerness is above the proportion of them. A man cannot be violent after honour or riches, and be as he should be. These are things that he must leave behind him, and they are worse than himself. Much less after filthy pleasures can a man be violent and wise; a man 'must become a fool in this respect,' as the Scripture saith, 1 Cor. iii. 18. But in respect of heavenly things, a man may be violent and wise; for there is such a degree of excellency in the things that no violence can be too much. Men talk of being too strict and too holy. Can there be too much of that which we can never have enough of in this world? I speak it the rather to confound the base judgment that the world hath of a holy disposition, which is carried with a sweet, eager violence to these things. They are thought to be frantic, to be out of their wits, as they thought St Paul was; but he answers, 'If we be out of our wits, beside ourselves, it is to God,' 2 Cor. v. 13. Christ himself was sometimes laid hands on, as if he had been out of himself, John x. 20; and as Festus told blessed St Paul, 'that much learning had made him mad,' Acts xxvi. 24, when he saw him eager in the cause of Christ, so many, when they see a man earnest in the matters of God, they think surely these men have lost their discretion. No; it is the highest discretion in the world to be eager and violent for things that are invaluable; and if men be not eager for these, they are fools. They know not how to prize things. The most judicious men here are most violent. So that it be violence that hath eyes in its head, violence guided with judgment, from the knowledge of the excellency of the good things of the gospel, I speak of such a violence as that.

Away, then, with base reproaches! Let us not be affrighted with the ill reports of idle brains and rotten hearts of people, that know not the things that belong to the 'kingdom of heaven.' Alas! they know not what they say; they are to be pitied, and not censured. Is there anything that a man should be earnest for if not for these things? Were our souls made to pursue things that are earthly and base, worse than ourselves? Were our wits made only to plod in our temporal, and to neglect our heavenly, calling? If anything may challenge the best of our endeavours, the marrow of our labours, the utmost of our spirits and wits, certainly it is these: grace and glory, that will stand by us when all things will fail us. Therefore let not your own hearts besot you, nor the vain speeches of others affright you. It will be acknowledged by every one ere long that there is nothing worth a man's eagerness but these things. The worldling is violent and eager; he troubleth himself and his house about 'a vain shadow,' Eccles. vi. 12, for pleasures and profit, &c.; and what comes of all his violence? He is turned naked into his grave, and thence into hell; and there is an end of all the violence about all other things besides these.

We see then the disposition of true professors, *they are violent in respect of heavenly things. Those therefore that are not earnest in the cause of religion, when the state of things requires it, they have no religion in them, they are not in the state of grace.* We must be earnest, first of all, against our own sins. Violence must begin there, to subdue all to the Spirit of Christ, to suffer nothing else to rule there; and after that, violence to maintain the cause of Christ. 'To contend earnestly for the faith once delivered to the saints,' Jude 3; to contend with both hands; not to suffer it to be wrested from us or to be betrayed; and if it be opposed, to vindicate it. We must be violent both to propagate the truth of God, and, in case of opposition, to vindicate it. 'He that is not with me,' saith Christ, 'is against me,' Mat. xii. 30. If a man be not with Christ, he is against him. It may seem a strange speech, but Christ cannot abide lukewarm neuters. He cannot abide *nullifidians*.* He cannot endure cold persons. His stomach cannot brook them. 'He will cast them up,' as he saith Rev. iii. 15, 16, 'I would thou wert hot or cold.' A man had better be nothing in religion than be lukewarm. The reason is, if a man will have good by any religion, he must be in earnest in it: 'If Baal be God, stand for him, if you would have good by him: if the Lord be God, stand for him,' 1 Kings xviii. 21. Be earnest in his cause. If popery be good, then stand for that, if you hope for good by it; and if our religion be good, then stand for that, if you hope for good by it. There is no good received by religion if we be not earnest for it. Religion is not a matter to be dallied in.

Therefore they are bitter, sour, profane, scoffing atheists, that trifle with religion, as if it were no great matter what it be. They will be earnest in all things else; earnest to scrape riches, to satisfy their base lusts. But for religion, it is no matter what it be; it is a thing not worthy the seeking after; the old religion or the new, or both or none. These are persons to be taken heed of, breeding a temper opposite to religion more than any other. Christ can least brook† them. There is great reason for it. Who can brook any favour to be neglected and slighted? Especially for these excellent things to be undervalued and slighted, it cannot be that God can endure it. There will be a faction in the world while the world stands—Christ and Antichrist, good and evil, light and darkness. But a man cannot be of both; he must shew himself of one side or other in case of opposition. Therefore the temper of the true professor is to be earnest

* That is, persons of no faith.—Ed. † That is, 'bear,' 'endure,' 'suffer.'—G.

in case of opposition of religion, and in case of opportunity to advance his religion. In civil conversation, and dealing with men that are subject to infirmities, he must be gentle and meek: 'the Spirit of God descended in the shape of a dove' upon Christ, as well as in 'fiery tongues' upon the apostles, Mat. iii. 16, Acts ii. 3. But in the cause of Christ, in the cause of religion, he must be fiery and fervent. No man more mild in his own cause than Moses—he was a meek man, Exod. xxxii. 19—but when occasion served, when God was offended, down he throws the tables of stone. He forgat himself, though he were the meekest man in the world otherwise in his own matters. So, I say, the Spirit is both meek and gentle as a dove, and earnest, and zealous, and hot as fire. In Acts ii. 2, the Spirit of God comes down as a 'mighty wind.' The wind is a powerful thing, if it be in a man's body. There is no torment like to windy sickness, as their complaints witness well enough that feel them. And if a little wind be enclosed in the earth, it shakes the whole vast body of the earth. The Spirit is like wind: it makes men bold; it fills them with a great deal of eagerness in the cause of God. Again, the Spirit appeared to the apostles in the likeness of fire. It inflamed their zeal, and made them fervent, that were cold before; as we see in Peter, the voice of a damsel terrified and affrighted him, Mat. xxvi. 69, 70; but when the Spirit came upon him, it so fired him that he accounted it his glory, Acts v. 41, 'to suffer anything for the cause of Christ.' Therefore, those that hope for anything by religion, let them labour to be for that religion in good earnest. They shall find God in good earnest with them also.

Again, Hence we see *that religion takes not away the earnestness of the affections*. It doth direct them to better things; it changeth them in regard of the object. It takes not away anything in us, but turns the stream another way. Violence requires the height and strength of the affections. Religion taketh them not away, but turns them that way that they should go. If a stream run violently one way, if it be derived* by skill and cunning another way, it will run as fast that way when it is turned as it did before. So it is with the heart of man. Religion takes nothing away that is good, but lifts it up; it elevateth and advanceth it to better objects. There are riches, and honours, and pleasures when a man is in Christ, but they are in a higher kind. Therefore they draw affections, and greater affections than other things. But these affections are purified, they run in a better, in a clearer channel. Whereas before they ran amain to earthly, dirty things below, the same affections, of love, of desire, and zeal, do remain still. He that was violent before is as violent still, only the stream is turned. For example, take St Paul for an instance. He was as earnest when he was a Christian as before. He was never more eager after the shedding of the blood of Christians, and breathing out slaughter against them, as he was afterwards in breathing after the salvation of God's people and a desire to enlarge the gospel. Zaccheus was never so covetous of the world before, as he was covetous of heaven when he became a Christian. I say religion takes not away anything, only it turns the stream. But it is a miracle for the stream to be turned. It was God that turned Jordan. So it is a greater work than man can do to turn the streams of man's affections, that run amain to earthly things, to make them run upward. It is only God's work. This is the excellency of religion. It ennobles our nature. That which is natural it makes it heavenly and spiritual; that a man shall be as earnest for God and good things as ever he was before after the things of this life. So much for that point.

* That is, = 'conveyed.'—G.

The third thing is the success.

'The violent take it by force.'

The earnestness of affection and violence, it is successful. 'They *take it*.' The good things of God, they are here compared to a fort, or to a well-fenced and well-armed city, strengthened with bulwarks and munition, that is a long time besieged, and at length is taken; for this clause, 'The violent take it by force,' it doth as well shew the issue of the violent ones striving for the kingdom of heaven, to wit, that they do at length take it, as the manner how it is taken, namely, by force.

Doct. The violent, and only the violent, and all the violent, do at length certainly obtain what they strive for, the kingdom of heaven.

Why?

1. *Because it is promised to the violent.* 'Knock, and it shall be opened unto you,' Mat. vii. 7. 'Be zealous, and repent' (that is the means to cure all former transgressions, 'repent'), 'and be zealous, and do *the former works*,' and 'To him that overcometh,' Rev. iii. 19, 21 (that is, he that is earnest, that will never leave off till he hath overcome), 'to him will I grant to sit with me on the throne; and to him that overcometh will I give to eat of the tree of life,' Rev. ii. 7. All the promises are to him that overcomes, to him that is zealous and earnest.

2. Then again, *The Spirit whereby a man is earnest is a victorious Spirit.* As Christians have the word and promise to build on, that leads them on, and encourageth them, so they are led by a mighty Spirit, that hath the force of wind and fire, that beats down all before it, that breaks through all oppositions and difficulties. Being led with a divine Spirit, what earthly thing can oppose that which is divine? It brings under and subdues all. Therefore 'the violent take it,' the Spirit of God seizing upon and possessing the heart, and carrying it with strength after these things.

3. And then only the violent take it, because *God hath set it at this rate.* 'He that heareth and doth,' 'he that perseveres to the end,' 'he that sells all for the pearl,' for the treasure in the field; there must be nothing retained; all must be parted with; we must be at any cost and charge and peril, and all little enough. It is offered to us upon these terms, of parting with all, of enduring anything, of breaking through all difficulties. Only such, and all such, shall obtain it by force.

4. And again, Only the violent, *because only they can prize it when they have it.* They only can prize grace and heaven. They know how they come by it. It cost them their pleasures and profits, it cost them labour, and danger, and loss of favour with men; and this pains, and cost, and loss, it endears the state of grace and glory to them; for God will never bring any man to heaven till he have raised his affections to that pitch, to value grace and glory above all things in the world. Therefore only those shall take it by violence; for only those shew that they set a right price on the best things. They weigh them 'in the balance of the sanctuary,' Dan. v. 27. They value things as God would have them valued.

Obj. But is not the kingdom of heaven and grace free? Therefore what needs violence to a thing that is free, and freely offered?

Ans. I answer, Because it is free, therefore it is violently taken. For, alas! if it were offered to us upon condition of our exact performing of the law, it might damp the spirits of men, as indeed usually such, if they be not better informed, they end their days in despair. But being freely offered, 'the publicans and harlots,' saith Christ, 'go into the kingdom of God before the proud Pharisees,' Mat. xxi. 31. Because it is free, it is free to sinners that feel the burden of their sins. 'Come unto me, all ye that are weary and heavy laden,' &c., Mat. xi. 28. 'Blessed are the poor in spirit, for theirs is the kingdom of heaven. Blessed are they that hunger and thirst after righteousness: they shall be satisfied,' Mat. v. 3–6. Thereupon he that hath a guilty conscience, he makes haste, and offers violence, when he hears of free pardon. What makes the condition of the devils so desperate? There is no hope of free pardon to them. What makes men so eagerly to embrace the gospel, notwithstanding their sins? Because it is freely offered. Thereupon it was that the Gentiles were so glad of it, that had been sinners and under Satan's kingdom before; and that makes miserable persons, that are humbled with afflictions and abasement in the world, glad of it—it being so great a thing, the kingdom of heaven, the favour of God, and freedom from misery, and so freely offered. It is so far from hindering violence because it is free, that therefore the humble afflicted souls that desire grace are the more eager after it. The proud Pharisees thought the kingdom of heaven belonged only to them; and therefore they despised Christ, and despised the gospel, because it was propounded to sinners, and to such mean persons that they thought were viler than themselves. But now when the meaner sort of people, and others that were abased with crosses in the world, saw what a kind of gospel it was, what great matters were offered, and that it was offered freely, they justified wisdom, Mat. xi. 19, and the counsel of God which others despised, and pressed for it with violence, Luke vii. 29, 30.

It is little comfort to hear of the excellency and necessity of these heavenly things, if there were not hope of them. Hope stirs up diligence and endeavour in the things of this world. What makes men adventure to the Indies, east and west? They hope for a voyage that shall enrich them all their life. Hope in doubtful things stirs up industry. What makes the poor husbandman diligent to plough and to sow? The hope that he shall have a harvest; yet this is under a providence that may guide it another way. But spiritual things are more certain. Therefore hope in spiritual things must needs stir up endeavour. We need not call them into question. And as it stirs up to diligence, so it stirs up in the use of the means; not to give over till we see our hopes accomplished. Then, in the third place, hope of success, that we shall not lose our labour, it enables and strengtheneth us to bear the tediousness of the time and the incumbrance of afflictions, and whatsoever is between us and the thing we expect. Though we have not that comfort from God that we would have, yet it makes us wait upon God.

Therefore when he saith, 'the violent take it by force,' it is to encourage us. The violent, eager, strong endeavours of a Christian in the ways of God, in the means of salvation, they are no successless endeavours.

He labours for that he knows he shall have; his violence is not in vain. He that is violent in good things hath a promise. He that wrestleth with God shall overcome, and he that overcometh shall have a crown. Here is a promise to build on. Therefore here is encouragement to be earnest and violent, 'he shall overcome,' he shall enter the castle at the last, if he continue striving, and give not over. Hence there is a difference to be observed between the endeavours of a Christian and of three sorts of other men.

(1.) First of all, If those only that offer violence to the kingdom of heaven, that set on it with encouragement, shall get it, and that by force, *what a great difference then is between them and those that in a contrary way offer violence to the kingdom of heaven;* that is, those that wrong Christ in his members, and hinder the means of salvation. What promise have they to speed? Surely they have no promise nor hope at all. Only their malice carries them amain in spite. Because the gospel reveals their hollowness and hypocrisy to all men, and forceth upon them a necessity to be other men than they list to be for the present, therefore they are eager in hating the gospel. There are threatenings enough against such as are violent against the gospel. They are violent in vain, for they 'kick against the pricks,' Acts ix. 5; they run themselves against a stone wall, and they shall dash themselves against it. Those that have ill will to Sion shall perish. There is one 'sits in heaven that laughs' all their attempts 'to scorn,' Ps. ii. 4. A Christian hath comfort in his endeavours. There is hope of good success, though there be inward and outward opposition. He shall prevail. Those that are enemies have nothing but discouragement. They shall be 'as grass on the house-top,' Ps. cxxix. 6, &c., that no man blesseth, but is cursed of every one. No man bestows a good word on them. It is a fruitless endeavour. They are under a curse.

(2.) Again, It shews us how *to judge of the courses of other men, that are violent in other courses, about the world.* A Christian he takes his kingdom at the last and enjoys it for ever; but those that are violent for the world, after pleasures, after baser things than themselves, alas! when they have it, they have but a shadow, and they become shadows in embracing it. Vanity embraceth vanity, and how soon are they stripped of all! If a man by violence scrape a great estate, he must leave it shortly. Here he found it, and here he must leave it, in spite of his heart, ere long; and 'all is but vanity' in the censure of him that knew all things the best of any man, even Solomon, that had gone through the variety of all things. And ofttimes they miss of that they labour for; 'they do not roast that they get in hunting,' Prov. xii. 27. They hunt after preferment and after riches, but ofttimes they do not enjoy them; and if they do, they get the curse of God with them, and ere long they are stripped of all. But here is that that may strengthen our endeavours. 'The kingdom of heaven suffereth violence, and the violent *take it*.' It is not an endeavour that is lost.

(3.) Then again, This shews that *the state of true Christians is different from the state of persons that are carried to good things, but not violently.* 'The violent take it.' He surpriseth the city at the last, he lays his siege, and will not remove till death. He will not give over till he have it. He will have it, or he will die in the business, and so at last he obtains his desire. The sluggish careless man he goes a little way. As Agrippa said to Paul, 'he was almost persuaded to be a Christian,' Acts xxvi. 28, so it is with such men. In some things they will be Christians, but there they are at a stand. They will go no farther. 'The sluggard desireth and wisheth, but his soul hath nothing,' Prov. xiii. 4. A sluggish, cold, lazy Christian he loseth all his pains. If a man be to go ten miles, and go but nine, and there sit down, he shall never come to his journey's end. If a man will give but seven or eight shillings for that which is worth ten, he shall go without it. Grace and glory are set at this price. There is required such strength of labour and endeavour and violence. Therefore without this, a man shall never attain it, unless he stretch himself to such a pitch. 'He shall never come to the end of his faith, to the salvation of his soul, to the high calling of God in Christ Jesus,' 1 Pet. i. 9. 'The sluggard wisheth and gets nothing.' The reason is, because he is a sluggard; because he will not strive; but the striver gets the fort, and hath all in it, and is a man made for ever.

'The sluggard thinks himself wiser than many men that can give a reason,' Ps. xxvi. 16. The sluggish discreet* Christian, I warrant you, he hath reasons for what he doth! It is not good to be too earnest! It will incur the disfavour of such a man or such a man! I shall be accounted so and so for my pains! But a wise man he seeth the excellency of the things, and he knows that his courses and his conscience will justify him at the last, and therefore he goes on, whatever comes of it.

God is not so weary of these precious things, these precious jewels of grace and glory, as to force them upon us. Is 'the kingdom of heaven' such a slight thing, that it should be obtruded to us whether we will or no? Shall we think to have it when our hearts tell us we esteem other things better? No. There are none ever come to heaven but their hearts are wrought to such an admiration of grace and glory, that they undervalue all things to it. Therefore there is no hope for any to obtain it, but he that takes it by violence. We see Moses esteemed the basest thing in the church better than the greatest excellencies in the world, that men are so violent after. He esteemed the very afflictions of God's people better than the treasures and pleasures of sin for a season, nay, than the pleasures of a court, Heb. xi. 25. When men shall esteem the base things of the world above all the treasures of heaven, above the state of Christianity, they have no hope of coming there. They may pretend God is merciful, and Christ died, &c. Ay, but whosoever he brings to salvation, he works such a sense of misery in them, and such an apprehension of grace, and of the means of grace, that there is an undervaluing of all other things. God will not bring them to heaven that shall not glorify him when they come there; and how shall they glorify him here or there when they value the world and these base things that they must leave behind them more than the things of heaven? This is the reason that few are saved, because they content themselves with easy, dull, and drowsy performances, and never consider with what proportion they are carried to things. When they had rather lose the advantage of that which will bring everlasting good to their souls, than lose the petty commodities of this world, and yet think themselves good Christians, what a delusion is this! It is the violent only that are successful, 'they take it by force.'

Obj. Ay, but what if the opposition grow more and more?

Ans. Then the grace of God and courage will grow and increase more and more. As Luther said well, 'The more violent the adversaries were, the more free and bold was he' (*a*). So the more the enemies rage, the more the Spirit of grace grows in God's people. It increaseth by opposition. As Noah's Ark, the higher the waters were, the nearer still it was carried to heaven. So we are nearer to God, and nearer to the 'kingdom of heaven,' the more opposition swells and rages. True courage grows with opposition. As the palm-tree riseth up against the burden that presseth it down, so the divine Spirit being a heavenly thing, and all opposition below of the devil and devilish-minded men being but earthly, what are they to the divine Spirit which sets us on and encourageth us? They cannot quell it, but the Spirit grows more and more in opposition. The apostles they ran all from Christ when he was to be crucified. They had but a little measure of the Spirit, but when the Holy Ghost was shed more plentifully on them, they began to stand courageously for the cause of Christ. When there was more opposition the Spirit grew more and more, till they sealed the truth with their blood. Therefore though opposition

* That is, '*over* prudent, cautious.'—G.

of enemies and their fury and rage grow, let us know whose cause we manage, and with what assurance of success. The violent at length 'shall take it by force.' Let us meditate upon this, that success is tied to violence. Therefore when you pray to God, if he seem to deny your request, offer violence, wrestle with him, let him not go without a blessing. When he seems to be an enemy, as sometimes he doth to try our strength, we must use an holy violence. When we are dull, and not fit to pray, nor fit for holy things, let us stir up the Spirit of God in us, and labour to get out of that estate; let us use violence, and violence will overcome at the last. A man that hath the Spirit of God gets the victory of whatsoever opposeth him. If there be snares offered from the world, he withstands them; if Satan come with his temptations, he resists him. He hath a promise for it: 'Resist the devil, and he will flee,' James iv. 7. Let us hold out and we shall get the victory, and overcome even God himself. How much more all other things! Therefore when either opposition without, or indisposition within, sets upon us in the course of religion and piety, let us think here, now is time and place for violence. I know, if I set myself about it, I shall have the victory and the crown. A Christian is alway in a hopeful state and condition, he hath somewhat to encourage him, he hath arguments to prevail over the state of opposition; he knows he shall win all at last if he go on, and that makes him courageous in what estate soever he is. Let us not be discouraged to hear of opposition. And let us be encouraged when we hear of good things, when we hear that the kingdom of heaven and grace is offered in the preaching of the gospel. 'Let us attend upon the posts of Wisdom's doors,' Prov. viii. 3, 4, and not give over till 'we come to peace of conscience and joy in the Holy Ghost,' Rom. xiv. 17. If we hear of comfort in the word of God against distress of conscience, let us never give over till we find it. If we hear that God is a God 'hearing prayer,' let us never leave knocking at heaven-gate, never leave wrestling, till our prayers be heard. When we hear what ill is to be avoided, and what good is offered, let us not cease till we avoid the one and obtain the other. 'The violent take it by force.'

The last point is the date of time from whence this kingdom of heaven suffereth violence.

'From the days of John Baptist until now.'

Quest. Was there not a kingdom of heaven that suffered violence before John Baptist's time? Did the kingdom of God begin then? Was Christ a king, and was heaven opened only then?

Ans. I answer, No. But now the things of God were more gloriously discovered. Therefore, John i. 51, 'henceforth you shall see heaven opened.' The kingdom of heaven was opened now by the preaching of the gospel more gloriously than before. Therefore the state of the gospel is called the 'kingdom of heaven,' partly in regard of the times before, and partly in regard of the times after.

The law *was full of servile bondage to ceremonies.* It was a heavy dark state. They were laden with a multitude of ceremonies, which were but cold things to the spirit of a man that desires peace. Though they were ceremonies of God's appointing, yet they were but outward empty things in comparison: 'weak and beggarly elements,' as the apostle saith, Gal. iv. 9. They were costly and painful and cold things, that had not the efficacy of spirit in them.

And secondly, Then it was *entailed to the Jews only.* Now, since Christ's time, it is enlarged; and being more large and free, this blessed estate is called 'a kingdom.' John Baptist now opening Christ clearly, and a better state than the church had yet enjoyed, when people saw an end of the ceremonies, and the beginning of the glorious liberty in Christ, this made them violently set on them.

Again, John Baptist *made way for Christ*, levelling the souls of men by his powerful preaching and his holy life. He taught them in what need they stood of Christ. He was the messenger sent before Christ for that end. He was as the morning star to the sun. He was powerful in his preaching, and holy in his life. He told every man his own. He told the Pharisees that they were a 'generation of vipers.' He shewed men their state by nature, and told them of a better state, that 'the kingdom of heaven was at hand,' Mat. iii. 2. And although he wrought no miracles, yet himself was a miracle. To teach such holy doctrine, and to live an austere holy life in those evil days, it was no less than a miracle. Therefore this violence to the kingdom of heaven, it hath the date from John Baptist's time; from his preaching, not from his birth. He being so excellent a preacher, no wonder there should be violence.

This shews the reason why the gospel in later times was embraced so greedily when Luther began to preach. Alas, people had been in a worse condition than Jewish in respect of ceremonies; and otherwise foolish idle men they will set God to school, they will have some fooleries alway that they will make as much of as of the worship of God; and so it had been in the times before Luther. In Saint Austin's time he was pestered with many vain ceremonies; and, good man, he yielded to the stream and custom in many things, though he could hardly endure the slavery of those things. Now when the times grew better, it is no wonder the world embraced the gospel with violence, as in Luther's time, when there was a freedom proclaimed from those beggarly rudiments and traditions. Antichrist had hampered the consciences of men with an intolerable mass of foolish, groundless ceremonies, making them equal with the word of God, as we see in the Council of Trent, (*b*) and this vexed the consciences of people like scorpions, as it is Rev. ix. 9. They oppressed the people with a multitude of weights and burdens, which when people could not assent unto, it stung their consciences. No wonder then if people thronged after Luther when he opened the doctrine of free justification by faith, that the consciences of men were not to be hampered with these things. He taught that God's people were only to have a few ceremonies for present order; but for the rest, to trouble men's consciences, and to make them of equal value with the word of God, he shewed it was an abominable doctrine, and wrote against it learnedly and sweetly. And therefore it is no marvel though the truths he taught were soon and cheerfully by multitudes embraced.

And the reason why now the gospel begins to be so little embraced and esteemed, is because, by reason of the long continuance of it, we are weary of this heavenly manna. As the people in Saint John Baptist's time, as eager as they were after John's preaching, yet it was but for a time that they rejoiced in his light. They grew weary of him. We never felt the burden of those Romish ceremonies, and therefore now grow weary of our liberty. Whereas in the beginning of Luther's time, because they were eased from many beggarly, and which is worse, tyrannical ceremonies of Rome, therefore with much joy and eagerness they embraced the truth when it came to be preached amongst them.

Therefore we are to praise God for the liberty of the church at this time, that we have the word of God to rule our consciences, and that other matters are not pressed on us but as matters of decency and order. Alas, if we were in bondage to those proud popish wretches, our consciences would be enthralled to a world of snares.

Last of all, 'From the days of the Baptist,' and so forward, 'the kingdom of heaven did suffer violence,' because from that time forward *the Spirit began to be more plentifully given.* Christ comes with his Spirit, which is soul of our soul, and the life of our life. The Spirit is like a 'mighty wind,' that moves the ship in the water. The ship is becalmed. It cannot move unless there be a wind. So the soul cannot move to that which is good without the Spirit. Now there is more abundance of the Spirit since the coming of Christ. Christ, who is the king of his church, the Lord of heaven and earth, he reserved the abundance of the Spirit till his own coming, especially till he entered into heaven. Then the Spirit came in abundance. 'It was poured upon all flesh,' Joel ii. 28. It was but, as it were, dropped before, but then it was 'poured out.' Then the Gentiles came in, and the apostles received the Spirit in abundance. Therefore no wonder that there was violence offered to the kingdom of heaven. Then hence we may observe,

That the more clearly Christ and the blessed mysteries of Christ are opened, the more effectual the Spirit is, and the more heavenly men are, and more eagerly disposed to spiritual things.

(1.) The reason and ground of it is in nature. *The affections follow the discovery of the excellency of things.* When first *the necessity of being in Christ is laid open ;* that there are but two kingdoms, the kingdom of Christ and the kingdom of the devil, and that a man must either enter into the kingdom of Christ, or be of the devil's kingdom still ;

(2.) And when, secondly, together with the necessity, *the excellency of Christ's kingdom is discovered*, that it is a state that will make us all kings; a state wherein we shall at length overcome all opposition of hell, sin, death, the wrath of God ; that whereas earthly kingdoms are opposed, and enthralled, and one dash against another, the kingdom of heaven is a state that subdues all that is against it by little and little. As Christ overcame death and the wrath of his Father, and now rules in heaven in his person, so all his members shall overcome all in time. When the excellency of this kingdom is laid open to the understandings of men, is it a wonder that their affections are set on fire? Will anything do it more than such a kingdom?

(3.) Then, in the third place, *when it is hopeful, too ; when, together with the necessity and excellency of it, there is assurance given us that we shall obtain it if we strive for it ;* when it is offered freely, even grace and glory, and we are entreated to receive grace : 'Come unto me, ye that are weary,' &c., Mat. xi. 28. Nay, we are threatened if we do not come, and we have example of the worst sort of people: of Zaccheus, and the poor woman out of whom the devils were cast ; of Peter, that denied Christ ; of Paul, that persecuted him ; such as had been wretched persons, that have come out of Satan's kingdom ; when these things are propounded, and understood, and apprehended, men that are in their wits, that are not besotted by the devil, men that are not in love with damnation, and hate their own souls, they will embrace them. When they see a state discovered in Christ wherein they are above angels, in some sort, above death and hell, that they triumph over all in Christ, that because it is as sure that they shall be crowned conquerors with Christ in heaven, as if they were there already; when it is propounded thus hopefully, who would not offer violence to this kingdom? When John Baptist laid it open so clearly to them, 'This is the Lamb of God, that takes away the sins of the world,' John i. 29, it made them offer violence to it.

And this is another reason why in the latter, the second spring of the gospel—for there was a winter in the time of popery, it being a kingdom of darkness, keeping people in ignorance—so many nations so suddenly embraced the truth. Luther was a man that was wondrously exercised and afflicted in conscience. This made him relish the doctrine of justification by grace in Christ, and thereupon to lay open the mysteries of Christ and the bondage of popery; and this being once a-foot, the people's minds being prepared out of the sense of their former bondage, whole kingdoms came in presently. As in the spring time, when there comes a fine sunshine day, the prisoners are let loose out of the earth after a cold winter, so after the winter of affliction and persecution, inward and outward, came the sunshine of the gospel, and made all come forth and flourish presently. Wheresoever Christ is taught powerfully and plainly, and the excellency and necessity of the state we have by him, and that men may partake of it, if they be not false to their own souls, there is always violence offered to these things, because where the riches of Christ are opened, the Spirit goes with it, and goes with violence, that it carries all before it.

Hence, again, we may see that popish spirits are witty* in opposing the unfolding of the gospel in the ministry, especially where there is conscience and skill to unfold Christ plainly. They know when Christ is opened, all their fopperies and inventions will grow base. The more Christ is unfolded, the more people will grow in hatred of antichrist. The more they see the light, the more they will hate darkness. For this cause they oppose the unfolding of the gospel to the understanding of the people; they would keep people in ignorance that they may make them doat upon them. It argueth a disposition dangerous, that shall never taste of the good things of God, to be in a bitter temper against the unfolding of the gospel of Christ. For we see here the discovery of it makes it wondrous effectual. John Baptist laying open Christ clearer than he was discovered before, 'the kingdom of heaven suffereth violence.'

Here we are instructed what way we should take if we would bring ourselves or others into a temper fit for heaven, to an earnest temper after holy things, not to begin with dead outward actions, but to begin, as becomes the condition of reasonable men, as God deals with man, befitting the nature of man; *begin with the understanding*. Let us meditate seriously of the truth of Christ's coming in the flesh, of the end of his coming, 'to dissolve the works of the devil,' 1 John iii. 8, to bring us out of the state of nature to a better condition. Meditate of the excellency of the state of grace, of the eternity and excellency of the state of glory. Let us warm our hearts with these things. When a man hath once these things and believes them, let him be cold and dull if he can. And so, if we would gain others to a fit disposition for heaven, let us labour to instruct them what their state by nature is; what kingdom they are born in; that they are liable to hell and damnation; that they are under the possession of the 'strong man,' the devil, if the stronger man bring them not out and dispossess him; and let them know withal the infinite love and mercy of God in Christ, offering a better state, giving the gospel and promising his Spirit with his truth; and if they be-

* That is, 'wise.'—G.

long to God, this will work upon them, or else nothing will. Other courses, to punish men in their purse, or imprison them, or the like, may subdue them to outward conformity, but if we would bring their souls to heaven, let us endeavour to enlighten their understandings to see the danger they are in, and to see the riches of grace and salvation that is proffered in Christ, and this will 'compel them to come in,' Luke xiv. 33. There will be no need of any other compulsion, no more than there can be need to bid a man escape away that sees wild beasts about him, or to bid a guilty person to flee to the city of refuge and take hold of the horns of the altar. Let John Baptist come before Christ to make way for him, and presently 'the kingdom of heaven suffers violence;' and after Christ's time, when the Spirit was more abundantly given, and the gospel more clearly opened, the world stooped to the gospel. The gospel at length overcame the proud sceptre of the Roman empire. They laid their crowns down before Christ's gospel. The cross of Christ got above the crown in the preaching of the gospel, it was so powerful. Thus, if we would have the number of heaven enlarged, let us desire that God's truth may be opened plainly and powerfully. John Baptist was a plain and powerful preacher; a man of holy life. They all reverenced John as a holy man. Thereupon his doctrine came to be so effectual. This is the way whereby God will do good to those he delights in. For others that are bitter atheists, whom God hath appointed to damnation, the gospel hardens them and makes them worse. The Pharisees were the worse by the preaching of Christ. When the gospel is preached, some are made worse by it, and malign, and persecute it as far as they dare. As the apostle saith, God is glorified in the damnation of such bitter opposers, Rom. iii. 8. We are not to look to gain all by preaching. Those that withstand it are sent by it with the more just damnation to hell, but those that do belong to him are gained this way.

Let us labour, therefore, for a clear manifestation of Christ. There is the treasure of all goodness in Christ, whatsoever is necessary to bring us to heaven. And the more he is discovered and applied, the more we are enriched with grace and comfort. Times of change may come; and if times of opposition and persecution come not, yet temptations will come, and the hour of death will come, when we shall have occasion to use all the strength and comfort we have; and the more dangerous the times are, the more sound and clear knowledge of Christ we should labour for, and that will breed this holy violence, that shall break thorough all oppositions whatsoever.

NOTES.

(*a*) P. 309.—'As Luther said well, "The more violent the adversaries were, the more free and bold was he."' An often-repeated saying of his 'Table-talk' and letters. Cf. note *uu*, Vol. III. page 533; also Vol. I. page 126.

(*b*) P. 311.—'As we see in the Council of Trent.' For history of this celebrated Council, see note-references in *jj*, Vol. III. page 532.

I take the present opportunity of correcting a mistake of Sibbes' in relation to this Council. See note *uuu*, Vol. III. page 536. He there makes Luther observe, that 'if they [the Papists] live and die peremptorily in all the points professed in the Tridentine Council, they cannot be saved.' Sibbes gives no authority; but it is plain that Luther could not adduce the *Tridentine* Council, as the following brief quotation from Bungener's History of the Council of Trent (by Scott, page 66) will shew: 'For the first time (it was now the 22d of February) the Council met to deliberate in good earnest. The legates appeared radiant with smiles. Why so? . . *Luther was dead.*'—G.

ANGELS' ACCLAMATIONS.

ANGELS' ACCLAMATIONS.

NOTE.

The 'Angels' Acclamations' forms the second of the four treatises which compose 'Light from Heaven' (4to, 1638). Its separate title-page is given below.* For general title-page, see Vol. IV. page 490. G.

* ANGELS
Acclamations:
OR,
THE NATIVITY
of CHRIST, celebrated by
the heavenly *Host.*

BY
The late learned, and reverend Divine
RICHARD SIBS,
Doctor in Divinity, Master of *Katherine Hall*
in *Cambridge*, and sometimes Preacher
at *Grayes-Inne.*

ISAI 9. 6.
To us a Child is borne, to us a Sonne is given.

1 PET. 1. 12.
Which things the Angels desire to looke into.

LONDON,
Printed by *E. P.* for *N. Bourne*, at the Royall
Exchange, and *Rapha Harford*, at the gilt Bible, in
Queenes head Alley, in Pater-noster-Row.
1638.

ANGELS' ACCLAMATIONS.

And suddenly there was with the angel a multitude of the heavenly host praising God, and saying, Glory to God in the highest, and on earth peace, good will towards men.—LUKE II. 13, 14.

THE words are few and pregnant, very precious, having much excellency in a little quantity. The heavens never opened but to great purpose. When God opens his mouth, it is for some special end; and when the angels appeared, it was upon some extraordinary occasion. This was the most glorious apparition that ever was, setting aside that it was at Christ's baptism, when the heavens opened, and the Father spake, and the Holy Ghost appeared in the likeness of a dove upon the head of Christ,' Mat. iii. 16, when all the Trinity appeared. But there never was such an apparition of angels as at this time; and there was great cause, for,

1. *There was never such a ground for it,* whether we regard the matter itself, the incarnation of Christ. There was never such a thing from the beginning of the world, nor never shall be in this world: for God to take man's nature on him; for heaven and earth to join together; for the Creator to become a creature.

2. Or whether *we regard the benefit that comes to us thereby.* Christ by this means brings God and man together since the fall. Christ is the accomplishment of all the prophecies, of all the promises. They were made in him and for him. Therefore he was the expectation of the Gentiles. Before he was born, he was revealed by degrees. First, generally, 'the seed of the woman,' &c., Gen. iii. 15. Then, more particularly, 'to Abraham and his seed,' and then to one tribe, 'Judah,' that he should come to him; then to one family, the house of David; and then, more particularly, 'a virgin shall conceive and bear a son,' Isa. vii. 14, and the place, 'Bethlehem,' Micah v. 2; till at last John Baptist pointed him out with the finger, 'Behold the Lamb of God, which taketh away the sins of the world,' John i. 29. Even as after midnight, the sun grows up by little and little, till his beams strike forth in the morning, and after it appears in glory, so it was with the 'Sun of righteousness;' as he came nearer, so he discovers himself more gloriously by degrees, till he was born indeed; and then you see here a multitude of angels celebrate his nativity.

Now, as before his birth he was revealed by degrees, so after his incarnation he was revealed to all sorts: to the old, in Simeon; to women, in Anna, a prophetess; to wise men and to silly shepherds; to all ranks of men; and to whomsoever the incarnation of Christ was revealed when he was born, they all entertained it with joy. The angels they sang and praised God; Simeon was even content then to die; and Zechariah, you see, beforehand breaks forth, 'Blessed be the Lord God of Israel,' &c., Luke i. 68; and the shepherds went away rejoicing. There is a special passage of divine providence in the carriage of this manifestation; for Christ was revealed to the wise men that were Gentiles by a star, because they were given to star-gazing. He was discovered to the shepherds by the apparition of angels. The scribes that were conversant in Scripture, they found it out by searching the Scriptures. God applies himself to every man's condition.

'And suddenly there was with the angel a multitude,' &c.

You see here, however, Christ lay in the cratch,* in the manger, yet notwithstanding there were some circumstances that shewed the greatness of his person, that he was no ordinary person. He lay in the cratch indeed, but the wise men came and adored him; and he appeared to the shepherds, poor men; yet notwithstanding, here is an host of angels that praise him. So likewise at his death he converted the good thief, and shadowed the sun itself, and then he gloriously rose again. So that there were some beams of his divine nature that broke forth in all his abasements. We see here an apparition of angels. In the words consider these things.

Here is, first of all, an apparition of heavenly angels.

And then their celebration of Christ's birth.

The apparition: 'And suddenly there was with the angel a multitude of the heavenly host.'

The celebration of it: 'praising God, and saying.'

The matter of the celebration and praising God,

'Glory to God in the highest,

'In earth peace,

'Good will towards men.'

I shall especially stand upon those words; but somewhat is to be touched concerning the apparition of these angels.

1. *The circumstances of their apparition.* They appear to poor shepherds.

God respects no callings.

He will confound the pride of men, that set so much by that that God so little respects; and to comfort men in all conditions.

2. Again, The angels appeared to them *in the midst of their business and callings;* and indeed God's people, as Moses and others, have had the sweetest intercourse with God in their affairs; and ofttimes it is the fittest way to hinder Satan's temptations, and to take him off, to be employed in business, rather than to struggle with temptations. We many times meet with comfort in our business, in our callings, that without † it, in speculation and otherwise, we should never have.

3. And then they appeared to them in the night.

God discovers himself in the night of affliction.

Our sweetest and strongest comforts are in our greatest miseries. God's

* That is, 'cradle.' Consult Haliwell, *sub voce.*—G.

† That is, 'outside of,' = apart from.—G.

children find light in darkness; nay, God brings light out of darkness itself. We see the circumstances then of this apparition.

He calls these angels 'a heavenly host,' in divers respects; especially in these:

(1.) An host *for number*. Here are a number set down. A multitude is distinct from an host; but in that they are an host, they are a multitude; as in Dan. vii. 10, 'Ten thousand times ten thousand angels attend upon God.' And so, Rev. v. 11, there are a world of angels about the church. In Heb. xii. 22, we are come to have communion with an 'innumerable company of angels.' He sets not down the number; and here appears 'a multitude of angels.' Worldly, sottish men that live here below, they think there is no other state of things than they see; they are only taken up with sense, and pleasures, and goodly shows of things. Alas! poor souls! There is another manner of state and frame of things, if they had spiritual eyes to see the glory of God, and of Christ our Saviour, and their attendants there—an host, a multitude of heavenly angels,

(2.) An host likewise implies *order;* or else it is a rout, not an host or army. 'God is the God of order, not of confusion,' 1 Cor. xiv. 33. If you would see disorder, go to hell. Surely disordered places and companies are rather hells than anything else; nay, in some respects worse; for there is a kind of order even among the devils themselves. They join together to destroy the church, and the members thereof. I note this by the way. Here was an host of angels; that is, they are an orderly company. What that order is, I confess with St Austin, is undetermined in Scripture; we must not rashly presume to look into these things (*a*).

(3.) Again, *Here is consent;* an host all joining together in praising God: 'Glory to God on high.' And sure it is a heaven upon earth, when a company of Christians, led with one Spirit, shall join in one work to praise God; to help one another in some spiritual way. When they meet together to hear the word, and to pray to God, all with one consent, their prayers meet in heaven. Christ commends union and consent. 'Where two or three are met together in my name, I will be in the midst of them,' Mat. xviii. 20; and 'whatsoever two or three shall ask in my name, if they agree' (if there be no jarring, nor schism, nor breach among them), 'I will grant it,' Mat. xviii. 19. Agreement in good is a notable resemblance of that glorious condition we shall enjoy in heaven. This multitude of angels they all agree with one consent.

(4.) An host of angels, it shews likewise their *employment*. An host is for defence or offence. That is the employment of angels here below especially, for the defence of the church, and for the offence of the enemies of the church. It is a great comfort to the church and children of God. The church is in the midst of devils here. We are all strangers in the way to heaven. We live in the midst of devils, and devils incarnate, devilish-minded men, that are led with the spirit of the devil. But here is our comfort, we have a multitude, an host of angels, whose office is to defend the church, and to offend the enemies of the church, as we see in Scripture.

(5.) Again, An host implies *strength*. We have a strong garrison and guard. We are kings in Christ, and we have need of a guard; and God hath appointed us a strong guard, a guard of angels. Angels severally are strong creatures. We see one of them destroyed all the first-born in Egypt; one of them destroyed the host of Sennacherib the Assyrian in one night. If one angel destroyed a whole host, consisting of many thousands, what can a multitude of heavenly angels do? Yet all are for the service of

Christ and of his church. These and such like observations we may gather hence, that they are said to be an host of angels.

Beloved, we have need of such comforts; and let it not seem slight unto us to hear of angels because we see them not. It is a thing forgotten of us too much. Why are we so cold, and dead, and dull, and distrustful in dangers? We forget our strength and comfort in this way. There is now at this time an earthly host against the church, men led with anti-christian spirits. Let us comfort ourselves, we have an heavenly host with us; as Elisha said to his servant, 'There are more with us than against us,' 2 Kings vi. 16. If God see it good, this outward host of heaven, the sun, moon, and stars, he can make them fight for his church, as in Sisera's case, Judges v. 20. But there is another host, that see the face of God; that is, that observe and wait on his will and command. We have an heavenly host within the heavens, that having a command from God, can come down quickly for the defence of the church, and for every particular Christian, not only one angel. That is but an opinion, that every one hath his angel; but even as God sees good, one or two, or more, a multitude, an host of angels.

God useth angels, not for any defect of power in himself to do things, that he must have such an host, but for the further demonstration of his goodness. He is so diffusive in goodness, he will have a multitude of creatures, that they may be a means to diffuse his goodness: angels to the church, and the church to others. It is for the spreading of his goodness, for he is all in all in himself. Let it take impression in us, that we have such glorious creatures for our service.

We see here this host of heavenly angels, they attend upon the Lord of hosts at his birth, for Christ is the creator of angels, the Lord of them; not only as God, but as Mediator. As God, he is the creator of angels; as Mediator, he is the head of angels, Col. i. 16. It was fit therefore that an host of angels should attend upon the Lord of angels; it was for the honour of Christ. God would let the world know—although they heeded it not, there was no such thought in Augustus's court at that time—that there was an excellent, glorious person born into the world. God himself took our nature: Christ, Immanuel. Though he were neglected of the world, and fain to lie in a manger, yet God took better notice of him than so. Heaven took notice of him when earth regarded him not. Therefore God, to shew that he had another manner of respect and regard to Christ than the world had, he sends a multitude, an host of heavenly angels, to celebrate the nativity of Christ.

There is much solemnity at the birth of princes; and God, that is King of kings and Lord of lords, he makes a solemnity likewise at the birth of his Son, the greatest solemnity that ever was, an host of heavenly angels. But these things I do but touch.

'And suddenly there was,' &c.

'Suddenly,' in an unperceivable time, yet in time; for there is no motion in a moment, no creature moves from place to place in a moment. God is everywhere. 'Suddenly:' it not only shews us,

1. *Somewhat exemplary from the quick despatch of the angels in their business*—we pray to God in the Lord's prayer, 'Thy will be done on earth as it is in heaven;' that is, willingly, 'suddenly,' cheerfully—

2. But also it serves *for comfort.* If we be in any sudden danger, God can despatch an angel, 'a multitude' of angels, to encamp about us 'suddenly.' Therefore, though the danger be present, and the devil present,

and devilish-minded men present to hurt us, God hath a multitude, an host of angels as present to defend us; nay, as himself is everywhere, so in the midst of his church he is present more than angels can be. He is not only among us, but he is in us by his Spirit, to comfort and strengthen us. Therefore let us stir up the Spirit of God in us, in all difficulties and dangers whatsoever, considering we have such grounds of comfort every way.

What is the use and end of this glorious apparition? In regard of the poor shepherds, to confirm their faith, and in them ours; for if one or two witnesses confirm a thing, what shall a multitude do? If one or two men confirm a truth, much more an host of heavenly angels. Therefore it is base infidelity to call this in question, that is confirmed by a multitude of angels. And to comfort them likewise in this apparition. We see by the way that for one Christian to confirm and comfort another, it is the work of an angel, an angelical work; for one man to discourage another, it is the work of a devil. When Christ was in his agony, the angels appeared to comfort him, Luke xxii. 43. We may take notice how willing and ready these glorious spirits were to attend upon our blessed Saviour Jesus Christ, in all the passages from his incarnation to his glory. We see they appeared here at his incarnation; they ministered unto him after his temptation; at his resurrection, then they were ready to attend him; and at his ascension, they were ready then; but oh the welcome when he entered into heaven! There was the glorious embracings, when all the host of heaven entertained him at his ascension. In the garden, as I said, they comforted him. Let us imitate them in this blessed work, if there be any in distress that need comfort and confirmation. We love examples of great, noted persons. Here you have an example above yourselves, the example of angels; who, to confirm and comfort the poor shepherds, appear in an host, 'a multitude of heavenly angels.' The angels, as they attend upon Christ, so for his sake they attend upon us too; for he is that Jacob's ladder. Jacob's ladder, you know, stood upon the earth, but it reached to heaven, and the angels went up and down upon the ladder; that is, it is Christ that knits heaven and earth together, God and man; and the angels by Christ, having communion and fellowship with us, as I noted out of the place, Heb. xii. 22, 'we are come to an innumerable company of angels;' so that they attend upon us for Christ's sake, whose members we are. They attend upon Christ mystical as well as Christ natural: 'For they are ministering spirits for the sakes of them that shall be saved,' Heb. i. 7. And therefore in our childhood and tender years they have the custody of us committed to them; as Christ saith, 'their angels behold the face of God;' and in our dangers they pitch their tents about us, and at our death they carry our souls to the place of happiness, as they carried Lazarus's soul into Abraham's bosom, and at the resurrection they shall gather our dead bodies together. So that as they never left our blessed Saviour from his birth to his ascension, so they always attend upon his members, his spouse. For his sake we have communion with the blessed angels. These things may be of some use. But it is not that I mainly intend. Thus much for the apparition.

2. Now *the celebration* is 'a multitude of the heavenly host praising God.'

The word signifies 'singing,'* as well as praise. It implies praise expressed in that manner; and indeed 'praising God,' it is the best expression of the affection of joy. The angels were joyful at the birth of Christ their Lord. Joy is no way better expressed than in 'praising God;' and it

* See any good Lexicon, under the word αἰνέω.—G.

is pity that such a sweet affection as joy should run in any other stream, if it were possible, than the 'praising of God.' God hath planted this affection of joy in the creature, and it is fit he should reap the fruit of his own garden. It is pity a clear stream should run into a puddle, it should rather run into a garden; and so sweet and excellent [an] affection as joy, it is pity it should be employed otherwise than 'in praising God' and doing good to men.

They express their joy in a suitable expression 'in praising God.' The sweetest affection in man should have the sweetest employment. The sweetest employment that joy can have is to be enlarged in love, 'to praise God,' and for God's sake to do good to others.

See here the pure nature of angels. They praise God for us. We have more good by the incarnation of Christ than they have; yet notwithstanding, such is their humility, that they come down with great delight from heaven, and praise and glorify God for the birth of Christ, who is not their, but our Redeemer. Some strength they have. There is no creature but hath some good by the incarnation of Christ; to the angels themselves, yet however they have some strength from Christ, in the increase of the number of the Church; yet he is not the Redeemer of angels. In some sort he is the head of angels, but he is our Redeemer. 'To *us* a child is born; to us a Son is given,' Isa. ix. 6. And yet see, their nature is so pure and so clear from envy and pride, that they even glorify God for the goodness shewed to us—meaner creatures than themselves; and they envy not us, though we be advanced, by the incarnation of Christ, to a higher place than they. For, beloved! the very angels have not such affinity to Christ in this as we. They are not the spouse of Christ. They make not up mystical Christ. The church doth. The church is the queen, as Christ is the king of all. It is married to Christ. Angels are not; and yet although they see us advanced in divers respects above them, yet they are so pure and free from envy, that they join in 'praising God' here in love to us.

Let us labour therefore for dispositions angelical; that is, such as may delight in the good of others, and the good of other meaner than ourselves.

And learn this also from them: shall they glorify God for our good especially? and shall we be dull and cold in praising God on our own behalf? Shall they come 'suddenly from heaven,' and cheerfully, and willingly, and 'to praise God' for his goodness to us, and shall we be frozen and cold in this duty, that is for our good more especially? I hasten to that that follows:

What is the matter of their celebration and gratulation?

'Glory to God in the highest,
'In earth peace,
'Good will towards men.'

There is some difference in the readings. Some copies have it, 'On earth peace to men of good will,' to men of God's good will; and so they would have it two branches, not three. If the word be rightly understood, it is no great matter (*b*).

1. First, The angels begin *with the main and chief end of all.* It is God's end; it was the angels' end, and it should be ours too, 'Glory to God on high.'

2. Then they wish *the chief good of all*, that whereby we are fitted for the main end, 'peace.' God cannot be glorified on earth unless there be peace wrought. For man else conceives God as an enemy. By this peace we are fitted to glorify God. If we find reconciliation with God through

Jesus Christ, then the sense of God's love in the work of reconciliation will inflame our hearts to glorify God. Therefore, next to the glory of God, they wish 'peace on earth.'

3. Then, thirdly, here is *the ground of all happiness* from whence this peace comes: from God's good will; from his good pleasure or free grace, 'to men of God's good will.' So if we go back again, the good will and pleasure of God is the cause and ground of peace in Christ; and peace in Christ puts us into a condition and stirs up to glorify God. So we see there is an order in these three.

To begin with the first:

'Glory to God in the highest.'

The angels, those blessed and holy spirits, they begin with that which is the end of all. It is God's end in all things, his own glory. He hath none above himself whose glory to aim at. And they wish 'glory to God in the highest heavens.'

Indeed, he is more glorified there than anywhere in the world. It is the place where his majesty most appears; and the truth is, we cannot perfectly glorify God till we be in heaven. There is pure glory given to God in heaven. There is no corruption there in those perfect souls. There is perfect glory given to God in heaven. Here upon earth God is not glorified at all by many. The whole life of many being nothing but a dishonouring of God, by abusing his ordinances, trampling upon his church and children, by slighting his word and sacraments, there is little honour given to God in the world, but only by a few, whom he intends to glorify for ever. And indeed, if we will glorify God here, we must raise our thoughts to heaven at that time; raise them above the world, to heaven, where we shall for ever glorify him; where we shall join with the blessed saints and angels, and sing, 'Holy, holy, holy, Lord God of hosts,' &c. In the mean time, let me add this by the way, that in some sort we may glorify God more on earth than in heaven. It may seem a paradox, but it is true. That is thus: here upon earth we glorify God in the midst of enemies; he hath no enemies in heaven, they are all of one spirit. Here upon earth we live not only among devils, but among men led with the spirit of the devil, where God is dishonoured; and if here we take God's side, and the truth, and gospel's side, and stand for God's cause, in some sort, we honour God here more than we are capable to do it in heaven, where there is no opposition. In this respect, let us be encouraged to glorify God, what we can here: for if we begin to glorify God here, it is a sign we are of the number that he intends to glorify with him for ever.

The verb is not set down here; whether it should be, Glory *is* given to God; or whether, by way of wishing, '*Let* glory be given to God; or by way of prediction or prophecy for the time to come, 'Glory *shall be* to God,' from hence to the end of the world. The verb being wanting, all have a truth. For, first, it cannot be a wish, unless it were a positive doctrinal truth, that all glory is due to God in the incarnation of Christ; and because all glory is due to him, thereupon comes the ground of wishing and of prayer, 'Let God be glorified.' Why? Because it is due. If it were not a positive doctrinal truth, there could be no foundation to raise a wish or a prayer: for what is a prayer, but the turning of a promise or truth into a prayer? And what is praise, but the turning of a truth into praise? So it is a doctrinal truth; first, that God is to be glorified especially in Christ; and in Christ, in this particular, in the incarnation of Christ. And it is a wish for the time to come, let him be glorified; and a prediction, God shall be glorified in the church. He shall alway have some to glorify him for Christ, and especially for his incarnation.

'Glory to God on high.'

Glory is excellency, greatness, and goodness, with the eminency of it, so as it may be discovered. There is a fundamental glory in things, that are not discovered at all times. God is always glorious, but, alas! few have eyes to see it. But here I take it for the excellency and eminency of the goodness and greatness of God discovered and taken notice of. In the former part of the chapter 'light' is called the 'glory of the Lord,' ver. 9. Light is a glorious creature. Nothing expresseth glory so much as light. It is a sweet creature, but it is a glorious creature. It carries its evidence in itself, it discovers all other things and itself too. So excellency and eminency will discover itself to those that have eyes to see it; and being manifested, and withal taken notice of, is glory.

In that the angels begin with the glory of God, I might speak of this doctrine, that

The glory of God, the setting forth of the excellencies and eminencies of the Lord, should be the end of our lives, the chief thing we should aim at.

The angels here begin with it, and we begin with it in the Lord's prayer, 'hallowed be thy name.' It should be our main employment. 'Of him and by him are all things, therefore to him be glory,' Rom. xi. 36. Therefore we should give God that which is his own; 'Thine is the glory,' as it is in the conclusion of the Lord's prayer. But this being a general point, I will pass it by and come to the particular, in which it will more comfortably appear, as this glory shines in Christ, in the incarnation of Christ, there is matter of glorifying God, both the* angels and men.

And here I do not take the incarnation of Christ abstractively from other things in Christ, but I take the incarnation of Christ as a foundation and prerequisite to all the other good we have by Christ; 'Glory to God on high, now Christ is born.' Why? Only that he is born? No. But by reason of this incarnation there is a union of the two natures, God and man. So that by the incarnation, now Christ is man, and holy man. The human nature in Christ is pure and holy, being sanctified by the Spirit and united to God. Now Christ being not only man, but pure man and God-man, God taking our nature to the unity of his person, hence it is that he comes to be qualified for all that he did, and suffered after. It was from hence that they had their worth. What was the reason that his being made a curse, and to die for us, should be of such worth? It came from a person that was God-man; nay, so near is the manhood to God, that what the manhood did God did, because the person was God; the second person taking the nature of man, and what he suffered in his human nature, God suffered according to man's nature. Hence comes that phrase of the communication of properties. Whatever was done or suffered in man's nature, God did as a mediator, God did it in that nature. Thereupon comes the price of it. Thus the incarnation is a prerequisite and foundation to all other benefits by Christ. Therefore take it conjoined, his incarnation, and his death, and resurrection, and ascension, and all.

Well then, *the incarnation of Christ, together with the benefits to us by it, that is, redemption, adoption, &c., it is that wherein God will shew his glory most of all.* That is the doctrinal truth. The glory and excellency of God doth most shine in his love and mercy in Christ. Every excellency of God hath its proper place or theatre where it is seen, as his power in the crea-

* Qu. 'by'?—Ed.

tion, his wisdom in his providence and ruling of the world, his justice in hell, his majesty in heaven; but his mercy and kindness, his bowels of tender mercy, do most of all appear in his church among his people. God shews the excellency of his goodness and mercy in the incarnation of Christ, and the benefits we have by it. Many attributes and excellencies of God shine in Christ, as,

His *truth*: 'All the promises of God are yea and amen in Christ,' 2 Cor. i. 20. There is an accomplishment of all the promises.

And then his *wisdom*, that he could reconcile justice and mercy, by joining two natures together. This plot was in heaven by God the Father, the Son, and the Holy Ghost, the Trinity, that God and man should be joined together. To join and knit two attributes seeming contrary, justice and mercy; to reconcile man by reconciling justice and mercy, and by such an excellent way that God should become man, Emmanuel, this was a great wisdom—to reconcile justice and mercy by such a person as should satisfy justice and give way to mercy, that is, by Christ. God will lose none of his attributes. His justice must be satisfied, that his mercy might be manifested. The wisdom of God found out that way. It is a plot the angels study in.

Likewise here is *justice*, justice fully satisfied in Christ. He became our surety who is God as well as man. If no creature can satisfy God, God can; when the second person took our nature, and was our surety, and died for us, he was the glory of his justice.

And of his *holiness*, that he would be no otherwise satisfied for sin. It was so foul a thing, that to shew his hatred of it he punished it in his own Son, when he became our surety. How holy and pure is God. That is, what a separation is there in the nature of God from sin, considering that he so punished it in his Son, our surety, that he made him cry out, 'My God, my God, why hast thou forsaken me?' Mark xv. 34. We cannot see the nature of God in anything in the world so much as in Christ. In Christ we see, as in a glass, his infinite sweet wisdom, his justice and holiness in hating and loathing of sin.

But the main of all is his mercy and goodness, which set him on work to contrive this great work of redemption by the incarnation and death of Christ. The infinite, rich, glorious, abundant mercy—that is the main thing wherein God is glorious now in Christ. Therefore everywhere you have these and the like titles put to his goodness and mercy. The bounty of God appeared, and the riches of his mercy, and the exceeding great height, and breadth, and depth of his love. There are no words large enough to set out the goodness and mercy of God in Jesus Christ. Therefore I will only speak of this attribute, because this bears the mastery among all the other attributes, though God be equally powerful and just; and yet he expresseth his mercy and grace most of all in Jesus Christ, towards poor wretched man. For after the fall man being miserable and sinful, what attribute can exalt itself, but mercy to misery, and grace to sinful man in pardoning his sin? Considering in what terms man stood, there was no other attribute could exalt itself but grace and mercy, to triumph over misery and sin. As it is in a city, those that are otherwise equal in honour, yet sometimes one bears rule above another; and he that is now magistrate and chief, take him at another time he is inferior to others; so since the fall the mercy of God bears office, and is chief governor and commander over all the attributes of God. For as I said, what moved God to set his wisdom on work to contrive such a thing as the salvation of mankind, to reconcile God and man in one person? His mercy moved him. What moved him to satisfy his justice? It was that an excellent way might be made, without prejudice to any other of his attributes, for his free grace and mercy; That is it that set all the other on work. That is the main triumphing attribute, considering man now standing in that exigence of mercy. Therefore 'glory to God in the highest heavens,' especially for his free grace and mercy in Christ.

Now that you may understand this sweet point, which is very comfortable, and indeed the grand comfort to a Christian, do but compare the glory of God, that is, the excellency and eminency of God's mercy, and goodness, and greatness of this work of redemption by Christ, with other things.

1. God is glorious *in the work of creation.* 'The heavens declare the glory of God,' and the earth manifests the glory of God. Every creature indeed hath a beam of the glory of God, especially those celestial bodies in the heavens, they praise God in their kinds, but with our mouths; they give us matter of praise. And if we have gracious hearts we take notice of it, and magnify him for his goodness. His goodness appears in the use of the creatures, and his greatness in the bulk of the creatures; his wisdom, in ordering and ranking of them. So that his mercy shines in all things in heaven and earth marvellously. Oh but, beloved, heaven and earth shall come to nothing ere long; and what is all this glory of the goodness and greatness of God to us, if we be sent to hell after this short life is ended? What comfort is it that we go on the earth, and enjoy the comforts that God gives us in this world, and then to perish for ever? Therefore the glory and goodness of God doth not so gloriously appear in the creation of the world.

2. Nay, the glory of God's love and mercy *shined not to us so, when we were in Adam;* not in Adam, for there God did good to a good man: he created him good, and shewed goodness to him. That was not so much wonder. But for God to shew mercy to an enemy, to a creature that was in opposition to him, that was in a state of rebellion against him, it is a greater wonder and more glory. It was a marvellous mercy for God to make man out of the earth; but here God was made man, he became man himself. There all was done with one word, 'Let us make man.' It was easily done. But in this, for Christ to become man for us, and to suffer many things, to be 'made a curse for us,' it was not so easy a matter. Therefore herein there is a great manifestation of the glory of God's goodness and mercy to us. For God hath set himself to be glorious in his mercy, and goodness, and grace, in Christ. He hath set himself to triumph over the greatest ill in man, which is sin, in the glorious work of redemption. So that you see here the greatest glory and mercy of God appears in our redemption by Jesus Christ, the foundation of which is his incarnation. In Exod. xxxiv. 6, God doth make an answer to Moses, who desired to see the glory of God, that he might have it manifested to him, not out of curiosity, but that he might love God the more, how doth God manifest his glory to him? 'Jehovah, strong, merciful, glorious, pardoning sin and iniquity.' When God would set himself to shew his glory in answering Moses's petition, he doth it in setting out his glorious mercy and grace, and loving-kindness, in pardoning sin and iniquity, to shew that he will now have his glory most appear in the sweet attribute of mercy and compassion in the forgiveness of sins, &c. In Titus ii. 12, 'The grace of God hath appeared, teaching us to deny ungodliness and worldly lusts,' &c. The grace of God hath appeared. Grace hath not a body to appear visibly; ay,

but Christ appeared; and when he appeared it was as if grace and love had been incarnate, and took a body. So that grace and mercy most of all shines in the incarnation of Christ.

I need not clear the point further, but only make a little use of it, and so end. Doth the grace, and love, and mercy of God, those sweet attributes, now appear and shew themselves in Jesus Christ? I beseech you, let us remember it—there is no point of divinity of more use and comfort —especially in the greatest plunges and extremities; for it answereth all objections, the greatest and strongest that can be made.

The sinner will object, My sins are great, of long continuance and standing; they are of a deep dye.

Look then upon God in Christ, and consider his end in the incarnation of Christ. It was that his mercy, and goodness, and grace should be exalted, and triumph over all man's unworthiness. The greater thy sin, the greater will be the glory of his mercy; and that is it God seeks for now, to be glorious in his mercy.

Again, Thy heart tells thee, that if there be any mercy shewed to such a wretch as thou art, it must be no ordinary mercy.

It is true. God's mercy is no ordinary thing. Of all attributes he will triumph in that. The glory of his mercy and goodness is that he seeks to have of men, by the incarnation and redemption wrought by Christ, above all things whatsoever.

Obj. Thou wouldst have infinite mercy.

Ans. Thou hast it in Christ.

Obj. Thy sins have abounded.

Ans. God's grace abounds much more.

Obj. Thy sins are mountains.

Ans. God's mercy is as the ocean, to cover those mountains.

Obj. But is it possible for God to forgive such a wretched sinner, that hath been a blasphemer, &c.?

Ans. It were not with men; but, saith God, 'My thoughts are not as your thoughts,' Isa. lv. 8. You are vindictive in your dispositions, and will not pardon; but my thoughts are as far above yours as the heavens are above the earth. Therefore bound not the infinite mercy of God, wherein he will triumph, with thy narrow thoughts, but let it have its scope, especially in plunges and assaults, and at such times as the best of us may be brought unto. In Hosea xi. 9, 'I am God, and not man,' implying that if he were man, we might have mean thoughts of him, confined thoughts; but 'I am God, and not man,' therefore comfort yourselves in this, consider how God sets himself to be glorious in his love and mercy to poor, miserable, wretched man in Jesus Christ.

You see the mercy of God in Christ, even in the sacrament. He doth not only give Christ to us—'*So* God loved the world, that he gave his only begotten Son,' John iii. 16, to be born and to die for us—but his mercy is a boundless mercy. We see he labours to strengthen our faith by these pledges, that we make use of this. What if God be merciful in Christ! and what if Christ be gracious, and there is nothing but grace and mercy! If there be not an application, if there be not an interest, what benefit have we by it? We must interest ourselves in this glorious person, interest ourselves in Christ, for it is founded upon Christ. All the glorious mercy of God is grounded upon satisfaction of justice; that is, in Christ. But this is nothing except we interest ourselves in Christ, and in the mercy of God; for our approbation is the ground of all comfort. God out of Christ is a 'fountain sealed.' He is a fountain of mercy, but he is sealed up. He is a 'consuming fire,' but in Christ he is a cheering, comforting fire. But this is nothing to us, unless we be in Christ. We must have interest in Christ. We must be 'bone of his bone, and flesh of his flesh.' He hath married our nature, that we might be married to him. We have no benefit by his incarnation else. Now all our comfort is by this union and communion with Christ, by marrying ourselves to Christ, by strengthening our faith in this union and communion, that so we may make use of the boundless mercy of God in Christ. Therefore how should we be encouraged to come to the sacrament, to enjoy this comfort!

You have heard, beloved, of the joy of the angels, of their manner of celebrating the birth of Christ; and if the angels should leave heaven, and come down upon earth, and take upon them bodies, how would they celebrate the incarnation of Christ!* You see here, 'Glory to God on high.' This would be the course wherein they would carry themselves to glorify God, answerable to their song. So should we do, if we will be like the blessed angels. We see how to celebrate the nativity of Christ. We need not go to fetch joy from hell to celebrate it. If the devil should be incarnate, and come to live among men, how would he celebrate the incarnation of Christ otherwise than in many places it is? If we do not love to have our portion with devils, surely we should not imitate those whose state and condition we are afraid of. The angels saw matter enough in the thing itself to make them sing, 'Glory to God on high, on earth peace, good will towards men.' What! Hath God been so rich in love to us in Christ, so wondrous in mercy, as to take our miserable nature, not at the best, but at the worst, and to take our condition upon him? Here is matter of joy; and shall we be beholden to the devil for joy, when we should rejoice for Christ? Will not the thing itself yield matter of rejoicing? Oh base dispositions, that we should not content ourselves with *homogeneal*, uniform joy to the thing itself. I desire repentance, and reformation of what hath been amiss. If there be any that have been guilty in this kind, that intend to come near God in these holy mysteries, let them know, that God will be honoured of all that come near him; let them take it to heart. As Tertullian said in his time, What! shall we celebrate that which is a public matter of joy to all the church, for a public shame, in a disgraceful way? (*c*)

I beseech you, consider of these things. 'Repent, for the kingdom of God is near,' saith the Baptist, Mat. iv. 17. What! shall we therefore give carnal liberty to all looseness, as if Christ came to bring Christians liberty to licentiousness? Shall we, instead of repenting, run further and further into guilt, and indispose ourselves to all goodness? Is that the reasoning of the Scriptures? No. 'Repent, for the kingdom of God is at hand.' Change your lives, for Christ and the fruits of the gospel are at hand. 'The grace of God hath appeared in Christ.' What! to teach us to live as we list, and to be more disordered than at other times? Oh no. 'To live soberly and justly,' Titus ii. 12, not to wrong any body, and holy and godly in this present world. This is the Scripture reasoning, and thus, if ever we look for comfort from God and Christ, we must reason too.

Let none think it too late to speak of these things now; but those that have not had the grace of God to keep them innocent, let them make use of the grace of God to repent; and as the phrase of some of the ancients is, repentance is a board to escape to the shore, after we have made ship-

* In margin here, 'These sermons were preached at the feast of Christ's nativity.' —G.

wreck, and done things amiss (*d*). Therefore, as I said, those that have not had the grace before to be innocent, let them make use of the grace of God, that now invites them to repentance, or not presume to come to these holy things. I speak it, not only to free mine own soul, but to free you from contracting further guilt; for do you think to make amends by coming to the sacrament, without repentance of what you have done before? 'What hast thou to do,' saith God, 'to take my name into thy mouth,' Ps. l. 16—to take my sacrament into thy mouth—'when thou hatest to be reformed?' God accounted his own service as the 'cutting off a dog's head,' when they came indisposed and unprepared, Isa. lxvi. 3. The sacrament is bane and poison to us, if we come without repentance. What saith the apostle? 'For this cause,'—because you come unreverently to the things of God—'some are sick, and some weak, and some sleep,' 1 Cor. xi. 30. God struck them with death for it. And it is a great cause why many are hardened in their sins, and go on still; because God executes these spiritual judgments for profaning these holy things, thinking to daub with God,* and to compliment with him in an easy performance.

I know those that belong to God are suffered sometimes to do things amiss, and to fall into errors and miscarriages, that they may know themselves better. And indeed, much of our spiritual wisdom is gotten by the sight of our own errors. We grow more stablished after, against the like temptations, for the time to come; and we can say by experience, It is good that I know the foolishness of my own heart, &c. But he that God hath no delight in, he swells and rages against any admonition, though it be in love to his soul. I hope there are none such here. Therefore, those that have made their peace with God, let them come to these holy mysteries with comfort, notwithstanding any thing before; for God hath prepared these things, not for angels, but for weak men, whose faith stands in need to be strengthened.

And let us not think that Christianity is a matter of compliment; that because we are baptized, and come to hear the word, and receive the sacrament, all is well. For we may do all this, and yet be greater sinners than Turks, or Jews, or pagans; for the most horrible sins are committed in the church. Where is the sin against the Holy Ghost committed? sins against light and against conscience, but where the conscience and understanding is most enlightened? There be the horrible, provoking sins, where there is more light and direction to live in another way. When the grace of God and the riches of Christ are opened, and yet men live in their sins, against conscience and the light of the gospel, so far is the outward performance from excusing in sickness and at the hour of death, that it aggravates our guilt and damnation when we make not a right use of the holy things of God.

That which I shall next stand upon, shall be to shew,

1. How we may know whether we glorify God for Christ or no;

2. And then the hindrances that keep us from glorifying God for this excellent good;

3. And the means how we may come to glorify God.

1. For the *first, of glorifying God in general*, I will not speak much. It would be large; and the point of glorifying God is most sweetly considered, as invested in such a benefit as this, when we think of it, not as an idea only, but think of it in Christ, for whom we have cause to glorify God, and for all the good we have by him.

(1.) First, then, we hold tune with the blessed angels in giving glory to

* Cf. Ezek. xxii. 28.—G.

God, *when we exalt God in our souls above all creatures and things in the world;* when we lift him up in his own place, and let him be in our souls, as he is in himself, in the most holy. God is glorious, especially in his mercy and goodness. Let him be so in our hearts, in these sweet attributes, above all our unworthiness and sin. For God hath not glory from us till we give him the highest place in our love and joy and delight, and all those affections that are set upon good, when they are set upon him as the chief good; then we give him his due place in our souls, we ascribe to him that divinity, and excellency, and eminency that is due to him. And this especially appears in competition and opposition of other things, when we will not offend God for any creature, when we can say as the psalmist, 'Whom have I in heaven but thee, and what is there in earth in comparison of thee?' Ps. lxxiii. 25. Therefore let us ask our own thoughts often what that is, that our affections of delight and joy and love, and all the sweetness and marrow of our souls, is spent on, and runs after. Is it the sweet love of God in Christ, the excellent state we have in Christ? It is an excellent sign. Surely the blessed saints in heaven, and those that are in earth that look for heaven, are thus disposed for the most part, especially when they set themselves in their devotions before God. Let us examine what is highest in our souls. 'The loving-kindness of the Lord is better than life itself,' saith the psalmist, Ps. lxiii. 3. Then we give God glory, when we set light by life itself, as holy Saint Paul could say. What! do you tell me of suffering at Jerusalem? 'I am not only ready' to do that, but to 'die for the name of Christ,' Acts xx. 24, and in Philip. i. 20, 'so God may be magnified by my life or death.' I am at a point; so if the question be whether we shall sacrifice this blood and life of ours, or dishonour God and wrong the gospel, or be any way prejudicial to the truth known, when we are ready to part with all, with father and mother, and houses and lands, and all for Christ, then with the angels we say, 'Glory be to God on high.' Therefore in a state of opposition, when we cannot enjoy both, let us leave the creature and cleave to God.

(2.) Then again, we give glory to God for Christ, when *we take all the favours we have from God in Christ*, when we see Christ in everything. 'All things are ours because we are Christ's,' 1 Cor. iii. 23. It is by Christ that we are heirs, that we have any comfortable interest. Therefore, when we accept all in Christ, and give God in Christ the glory of all, we practise this that the angels do here; we give glory to God.

(3.) Then again, we give glory to God *when we stir up others.* All the angels consent. There was no discord in this harmony of the angels. When we all join together and stir up one another, and labour to promote the knowledge of God in Christ all the ways we can—every one in our place and calling, magistrates and ministers, and every one in our families—labour that Christ may rule there, that God in Christ may be known. In Ps. ciii. 20, *seq.*, there the psalmist stirs up himself to glorify God, and he stirs up the angels, and here the angels stir up men, 'Glory to God on high,' &c. When there is a zeal of God's glory, and a disposition fit to glorify God, there will be a stirring up one of another—angels men, and men angels—and a wishing that God may have glory in heaven and earth. Therefore those that labour not in their places that the truth may be made known, that for base and worldly ends are opposers of the publishing of the gospel any way—as it is the fashion now, they will not appear openly, but cunningly undermine the gospel under pretences—they bear no tune with these blessed angels. For those that have dispositions like them will study how this blessed truth may be promoted and propagated, and spread even over the world. Therefore we should labour every one to spread the glorious gospel of Christ, especially those that are ministers, whose office it is to unfold and open the 'unsearchable riches of Christ.'

(4.) Again, We glorify God in Christ, *when we see such glory and mercy of Christ, as it doth transform us and change us*, and from an inward change we have alway a blessed disposition to glorify God, as I shewed out of 2 Cor. iii. 18.* This is the difference between the glass of the gospel and the glass of the law and of the creatures. In the law we see the beams of the justice of God, 'Cursed is every one that continueth not in all,' &c., Gal. iii. 10, and the beams of his power and goodness in the creature. But it doth not change and transform us to be good and gracious. But when we see the glory of God, of his goodness and infinite mercy, shining in the face of Jesus Christ—for we dare not look upon God immediately—it changeth the soul to be gracious like unto Christ. Therefore if we find that the knowledge of God in Christ hath changed our dispositions, it is a sign then we give glory to God indeed. For to glorify God is an action that cannot proceed but from a disposition of nature that is altered and changed. The instrument must be set in tune before it can yield this excellent music, to glorify God as the angels do; that is, all the powers of the soul must be set in order with grace by the Spirit of God. If the meditations and thoughts of the gospel have altered our dispositions to love God, and that that pleaseth God, to do good to men, to delight in goodness, it is a sign we are instruments in tune to glorify God, and that we have an apprehension of the love and mercy of God in Christ as we should. For it hath a transforming power to work this. 'The grace of God will teach us to deny ungodliness and wordly lusts, and to live holily,' Titus ii. 12. When the grace of God, that is, the free love of God in Christ, in the forgiving our sins and advancing us to heaven, hath this effect in our souls, it is a sign we have a true notion and apprehension of the excellency and eminency of God's grace. Otherwise, if we 'turn the grace of God into wantonness,' Jude 4, to make the benefits by Christ a pretence and covering for our wicked and loose lives, we know not what it is to glorify God; but though in words we say, 'Glory be to God,' yet in our lives we deny it, as the apostle saith, Titus i. 16. The hypocrites in Isa. lxvi. 5, they had good speeches in their mouths. Saith God, 'Hear the word of the Lord, ye that tremble at his word: your brethren that hated you, and cast you out for my name's sake, said, Let the Lord be glorified.' So you shall find those that are opposers and persecutors, and haters of sincerity, will sing '*Gloria Patri*,' 'God be glorified;' but what good will this do them if they have diabolical, Satanical dispositions, if they be like the devil in opposing the truth, and hating that that is good? The devils in the gospel could glorify God for their own ends: 'We know that thou art the Son of God,' Luke iv. 41. So devils incarnate can come to church and receive the sacraments, and seem to praise God. Oh, but there must be a change; for to glorify God is a work of the whole man, especially of the Spirit. 'All that is *within* me, praise his holy name,' Ps. ciii. 1. It came from the heart-root of a sanctified judgment, out of grounds why we do it. The wish of the angels here, 'Glory to God on high,' it came from a good ground, because they knew God is to be glorified in Christ. For judicious phrases are founded upon truths. So there must be a sanctified judgment to be the ground of it, and the affections must be in tune answerable to those

* Cf. 'Excellency of the Gospel above the Law,' Vol. IV. page 201, *seq.*—G.

truths. Then we are fit to glorify God. And all this is by the power of the gospel transforming us.

(5.) Again, We glorify God *when we take to heart anything that may hinder, or stop, or eclipse God's truth, and obscure it;* when it works zeal in us in our places, as far as we can; when it affects us deeply to see the cause of religion hindered any way. If there be any desire of glorifying God, there will be zeal. The heart will move with a kind of indignation when God is dishonoured, and his truth eclipsed with false doctrine or by ill practice. It cannot be otherwise. It is out of the nature of the thing itself. Therefore those that either are instruments of stopping or obscuring the truth, or causing it to be reproached by their wicked lives, or if they be not instruments, yet they do not take it to heart when they see God dishonoured, surely they can speak little comfort to themselves. They have neither angelical nor evangelical dispositions; for if they had the knowledge of the gospel it would work this in them.

(6.) Again, If we apprehend this glorious mystery of Christ in the gospel aright, *it will work in us a glorious joy;* for joy is a disposition especially that fits us to glorify God. Then we are fit to 'glorify God,' when our hearts are enlarged with joy; when we think of God in Christ; when we think of the day of judgment; when we think of heaven; when we think of hell with joy, as being subdued; and bless God for Christ; when we can think of all that is opposite as conquered in Christ. So that our joy is enlarged in the apprehension of our own blessed condition. It is a good sign we are in a disposition to 'glorify God.' But I will not enlarge myself further in this point.

2. This being so excellent a duty, to which we are stirred by the angels, 'Glory to God on high,' &c., what are the main hindrances of it, that we give not God more glory?

(1.) The main hindrances are, *a double veil of ignorance and unbelief,* that we do not see the glorious light of God shining in Jesus Christ; or else if we do not know it, we do not believe it; and thereupon, instead of that blessed disposition that should be in the soul, there comes an admiration of carnal excellencies, a delighting in base things.

This ignorance is partly from the darkness of our own hearts, being overcast sometimes, that such great things are too good to be true. Our hearts have a hell of unbelief in them.

And sometimes the policy of Satan, who casts dust in our eyes, and labours that we may not see the glory of God in the gospel: 2 Cor. iv. 4, 'The God of this world hath blinded their eyes,' &c. Ignorance arising from within or without is a great cause why we do not see the excellencies of God. Therefore no wonder if, where the gospel is not preached, that the devil hath a kind of reign, and God is not honoured at all, because the devil is the prince of darkness, and rules in darkness. That is one cause, ignorance.

(2.) So likewise *unbelief,* when we hear and see and know the notion of mercy and of Christ, and can dispute of these things, like men that talk of that they never tasted of. The devils know all these things better than any man; yet they do not 'glorify God,' because they do not believe that these things pertain to them. Men want a light suitable to the truth of the things themselves. A man may see them with a natural light, or with the light of education, or by books or the like; but not in a spiritual and proper light. He sees not spiritual, heavenly things, in a spiritual light. And that is the reason he believes them not. These two veils are the cause why we see not the light of God shining in the gospel, and why we do not glorify him. Light is a glorious creature. It was the first creature. It is not only glorious in itself, but it shews the glory of all other things too. If we had all the sights in the world presented to us, if there were no light to discover them, or no sight in our eyes, if either be wanting, all the glory of them would be lost. So it is in the gospel. Though there be wondrous admirable things there, if we want either light or sight; if the light shine round about us, 'and the god of this world have blinded our eyes,' and infidelity have blinded us, how can we 'glorify God,' wanting a heavenly, proper, peculiar, spiritual light, suitable to the things? For a natural man, by the light that he hath, cannot judge of them. These are the main hindrances, the veil of ignorance and unbelief.

(3.) And, on the contrary, there is another hindrance; that is, *too much light;* either want of light altogether, or too much light, when by the preaching of the word of God, awaking our conscience, and shewing our sins so enormous, so transcendent, so odious, that we forget mercy in Christ, and so dishonour Christ, to set the sins of the creature above the infinite mercy of the Creator; as those that doubt, and from doubting, proceed to despair of the mercy of God, seeing the vileness of their sins in the true colours of them, and seeing and feeling God's anger and wrath, together with their sins in the conscience; here is too much light one way, and not looking to the other light, this excellent, glorious, infinite light of God's mercy, shining in the gospel. They look not on God in 'the face of Christ.' Out of some stubbornness and pride they flatter themselves; they will not believe; they will not receive the consolations due to them, but dwell upon the consideration of their unworthiness and sins; and Satan holds them in that slavery and bondage. This is a great hindrance of glorifying of God, when we lift up our sins above the mercy of God in Jesus Christ. This is to take away God and Christ altogether; for if the mercy, and rich and bountiful goodness of God, wherein he will be infinitely glorious, were not greater than our sins, it were not the mercy and bounty of a God. God should not be glorious in it. But there are but few of these that miscarry; God usually shines upon them at the last. There are three ranks of men. Some are in the first profane, dead, loose Christans, that were never under the law, that never understood the corruption of nature, nor themselves. Some are brought from that to understand themselves a little too much, that are under the law, and feel the flashes of God's wrath. And some, in the third place, are brought from hence to be under grace. That is the only happy condition, to be under the grace of God in Christ. Some men never come to the second step. They never understand what sin is, and what the anger and wrath of God is. They will give their conscience no leisure to tell them what their condition is. There is hope of the second that they will come to the third rank; but for a company of profane persons, opposers of goodness, to talk of the mercy of God in Christ, they are not in the next step to it. A man must be sensible of his sins and of his misery before he can have grace. Therefore, for those that have too much light, though it be a great fault in some, and hinders God of much glory, and themselves of much comfort, out of this peevish stubbornness of theirs, yet there are not many of them, and, as I said, few of them miscarry.

Now, from these two veils that hinder the glory of God, there come other hindrances; for the soul of man will wonder and admire at somewhat. It will have somewhat in the eye of it. Hereupon, not seeing or not believing the mercy, and goodness, and love of God, and the excellent prerogatives of a Christian issuing from the goodness of God, and the fruits of it, they doat upon some worldly excellency; either they are proud of their parts, and so God is robbed of his honour, or on creatures meaner than themselves. For the base nature of man, since the fall, it doats upon earth, upon gold and silver, mean and base things, not to be compared to the excellency of man, or else upon some duties they perform, upon their own works, as if God should be beholden to them. For not knowing themselves well, and the infinite glory of God in Christ, that God must have all the glory, not only of happiness, but of grace that brings us to happiness, they glory in that they have done; as in popery, they think they merit much by their performance. In the night time a torch seems a goodly thing; and sometimes rotten wood will shine; but in the day time, when the sun appears, the very stars shine not; we care not for meaner lights. For what good do they then? So the soul, when it wants a sight of the greatest excellency, it doats upon rotten wood, upon every torch-light. Many vain things seem to be great. A man may see by the dispositions of many what they admire and stand upon most. Their carriages shews it well enough. It argues a corrupt and weak judgment. You see what are the main hindrances.

3. Now, the way to attain to this glorious duty, to glorify God. The next thing shall be to give some directions, because it is a most necessary duty. Is it not that we pray for in the Lord's prayer, 'Hallowed be thy name'? And what is the end that we were created and redeemed for, but that God may have some glory by us? Therefore, being a necessary absolute duty, let us hearken to some directions that may help us that way.

(1.) First, Therefore, if we would glorify God, *we must redeem some time to think of these things, and bestow the strength of our thoughts this way.* The soul being the most excellent thing in the world, it is fit it should be set on the excellentest duty. Man being in such an excellent condition, being heir of heaven, and having an understanding soul, it is fit the most excellent part of the most excellent creature should be set upon the most excellent object. Now, the most excellent part of the soul is the understanding. It kindles all the affections, and leads all the rest. Therefore let us take some time to meditate and think of these things. What we are by nature, and the misery we are exposed to by sin, that whatsoever we have more than hell is more than we deserve; and then withal, think what we are advanced to in Christ; what we are freed from,—that cursed condition; and what we shall be freed from,—the sting of death; and all that we fear for the time to come. Think of what we are freed from, and what we are advanced to, and by whom. By God becoming man: a mystery that might, nay, that doth ravish the very angels themselves; God-man, now in heaven, making good what he did on earth, by his intercession. And then the ground of all, the infinite love, and mercy, and bounty of God to poor distressed man. The thought of these things will inflame the heart. Now, they never work upon the heart thoroughly till they end in admiration; and indeed the Scripture sets it down in terms of admiration, '*So* God loved the world.' '*So*.' How? '*So*, as I cannot tell how, I cannot express it; and 'what love hath God shewed us, that we should be called the sons of God!' 1 John iii. 1. And then the fruits that we have by this incarnation of Christ, and by his death, they are admirable: 'peace that passeth understanding,' Philip. iv. 7, 'joy unspeakable and glorious,' 1 Pet. i. 8. So that the mystery is wonderful, and the dignity wonderful, and the fruits, the comfort, and peace, and joy, wonderful; everything is an object of admiration. Therefore when we think and meditate of these things, let us never end till our souls be wound up to admiration of the excellent love of God. We wonder at things that are new, and rare, and great. Is there anything more new and rare than that that never was the like, for God to become man? Is there anything more excellent than the benefits we have by Christ becoming man, to free us from so great misery, and to advance us to so great happiness? If anything be an object of admiration, surely it must be this. Therefore the apostle doth well to give all the dimensions to the love of God in Christ, 'height, and breadth, and depth, and length.' It is a love 'passing knowledge,' Eph. iii. 19.

Quest. What good will come by this?

Ans. When the soul is thus exercised, then it will be fit to 'glorify God.' When it is in this frame, it will think itself too good for any base service of sin. Eagles will not catch at flies. When the soul is lift up to consider God's love and mercy in Christ, will it be catching at every base thing in this world? No. It will not. The soul never sins, but when it loseth this frame, to have a judgment suitable to things. When our judgment and affections are lost of the best things, then comes in a judgment and affection to other things as better. So losing that frame the soul should be in, we fall to the creature, to commit spiritual fornication with that.

Let us labour to keep our souls in this temper, begin every day with this meditation, to think what we were, what we are now in Christ, what we shall be, and by what glorious means all this was wrought, that so the soul may be warmed with the love of God in Christ. This frame of spirit will not suffer the soul to sin, to stoop to base sinful lusts.

(2.) Now, to help this, in the next place, *beg of God the 'Spirit of revelation' to discover to us these things in their own proper light,* 'for they are spiritually discerned.' Now the Spirit knows the breast of God, what the love of God is to every one in particular, and he knows our hearts too. Therefore the apostle desires of God 'the Spirit of wisdom and revelation,' Eph. i. 17, to discover these things to us, not only that they are truths, but that they are truths to us. For unless we know these things belong to us in particular, we cannot glorify God as we should. They are in themselves glorious things: to hear of God's mercy in Christ; of God becoming man; to hear of kingdoms and crowns. Oh, but when there is a spirit of appropriation to make these our own, that God in Christ loves us—'who loved *me*, and gave himself for *me*,' Gal. ii. 20—then the soul cannot but break forth with the angels here, 'Glory to God on high.' Therefore beg the Spirit to reveal to us our part and portion, that he would shew his face to us, that he is to us a Father in Christ. Surely in hearing, meditation, and prayer, &c., we shall find a secret whispering and report from heaven, that God is our Saviour, and that our sins are forgiven, especially when we stand in most need of this comfort. Let us therefore beg of God to take away the veils of ignorance and unbelief, and openly to reveal his fatherly bowels and tender mercy to us in Christ; to discover to us in particular more and more our interest in the same by his Spirit, that only knows the secret of our hearts, and being above our hearts can settle our doubts. Only the Spirit can do it. For as God only works salvation, so the Spirit only can seal to our souls our salvation. This is one excellent way to help us to glorify God.

And add this as motive, as a plea, not to move God so much as to move and to satisfy our hearts, and to strengthen our faith, *that it is the end of our lives and the pitch of our desires to 'glorify God.'* Therefore we desire God to reveal himself so far to us, to be our Father in Christ, that we may glorify him. Surely it is a forcible plea. God will do that that is suitable to his end. 'He hath made all things for his own glory,' Prov. xvi. 4. Especially the work of redemption in Christ is for the glory of his rich mercy; and we desire the sense of his mercy and love for this end, that we may be fitter to glorify God. It is a prevailing argument, fetched from God's own end.

(3.) And let us labour daily more and more *to see the vanity of all things in the world.* Put the case we have honours and large possessions in the world, that we wanted nothing; if this were severed from God's love in Christ for life everlasting, what comfort could we have in this, especially at the hour of death? Let us see, therefore, the vanity and emptiness of all things else out of Christ, and the good we have by Christ, what all will be ere long. The daily thoughts of that will be a good means; for we must empty ourselves of that we are, that we may be filled with that we are not; and we must daily consider the emptiness of the creature wherewith we labour to support ourselves. For when men have no goodness in themselves, they will have an excellency in the creature. Therefore, when we see ourselves out of Christ, to be nothing but fuel for God's vengeance, and see that the creature can afford us nothing but vexation, these thoughts that these things are so, and out of experience, will make us draw near to God upon all occasions. It will make us glorify him and abase ourselves. What made Job abase himself and glorify God? When he drew near to God, and God drew near to him. 'I abhor myself,' Job xlii. 6; and so we see in Abraham, Gen. xviii. 27. Let us draw near to God upon all occasions, in the word and prayer, and in the sacraments, and this will make us see our own nothingness and God's greatness; for that is the way to honour him, to see his greatness, and a nothingness in the creature; that all things in him are so excellent, and out of him nothing, and worse than nothing.

Now we are to draw near to God in the sacrament; and the nearer to God, the more we honour him. Who honours God most? Surely Christ, because he is so near him, being God and man in one person; and next to him the blessed angels 'glorify God.' They are near him. Therefore, in Isa. vi. 2, they 'cover their faces,' it being impossible for the creature to comprehend the great majesty of God; and they cover their feet in modesty. The nearer we draw to God in the meditation and consideration of his excellency in the ordinances, the more humble and abased we shall be in ourselves; and the more we shall honour God, seeing his excellency, especially of his love. So next to the angels the saints: 'all thy works praise thee,' Ps. cxlv. 10; they give matter and occasion, but 'thy saints bless thee.' If it were not for a few saints on earth, though all the works of God are matter of praise, they could not praise God: 'thy saints bless thee.' And the nearer we come to God, the fitter we are for this. Now, there is a wondrous near-coming to God in the sacrament. If we come prepared, we come to have communion and strengthening in Christ. He is both the inviter and the feast itself. We come to be made one with him: 'bone of his bone, and flesh of his flesh.' Therefore, if we come prepared, this is the way to bring us to a disposition to glorify God. You see here the wondrous, infinite love of God in the sacrament, to stoop so low to his creature, to strengthen our faith by giving us these things. God had been good to us whether he had given us his oath and his seal or no, but he knows we are weak, and unbelieving, and doubting; therefore to help us he hath given us not only his promise, but his oath, and besides his oath he hath given us signs and seals. Here is wondrous mercy. Let us be encouraged to come in and admire the love of God, not only in giving his Son Christ for us, but in affording us other means to strengthen our faith. Let none be discouraged in the sight and sense of their own sins; but let them come in, and they shall glorify God the more. 'Where sin hath abounded' in their sense and feeling, there 'grace shall more abound.' And those that have been good, and have slipped any way, let them consider God's infinite love in Christ. It is not a cistern, but a spring. God's mercy in Christ, and the blood of Christ, is a 'fountain opened for Judah,' &c., Zech. xiii. 1; that is, it serves not for our first conversion only, but every day, upon every occasion, when we have made any breach with God, we may come and wash in that bath, Christ's blood. 'The blood of Christ purgeth,' 1 John i. 7. It is in the present tense. It runs continually in the vigour of it. There is a spring of corruption in us; there is a spring of mercy in God. There is a spring of Christ's blood, that hath a perfect efficacy to wash our souls. Therefore, if we have not yet been converted, and humbled, and cast down for our sins, let us now come in and give God the glory of his mercy; and if we have fallen again, consider there is a fountain opened for 'Judah and Jerusalem to wash in,' and let us come and renew our repentance and faith at this time.

'Peace on earth.'

The same holy affection in the angels that moved them to wish God to have his due of glory from the creature, it moves them to wish peace to men likewise; to shew this, by the way, that

There can be no true zeal of God's glory but with love to mankind.

They were not so ravished with the glory of God as to forget poor man on earth. Oh no! They have sweet, pure affections to man, a poorer creature than themselves. Therefore let them that are injurious and violent in their dispositions, and insolent in their carriage, never talk of glorifying God, when they despise and wrong men. There are some that overthrow all peace in the earth for their own glory, but he that seeks God's glory will procure peace what he can; for they go both together, as we see here, 'Glory to God in the highest, peace on earth.'

Now, their end of wishing peace upon earth, it is that men might thereby glorify God, that God being reconciled, and peace being stablished in men's consciences, they might glorify God. Hence observe this likewise, that

We cannot glorify God till we have some knowledge of our peace with him in Christ.

We must have the first act, to cast ourselves upon God's mercy in Christ, and adhere and cleave to that mercy; and then we shall feel so much comfort as shall make us glorify God, though we may question it in desertion sometimes. Here the angels, intending that God should have glory of all, they wish peace on earth, in the consciences of men especially.

The reason is, peace comes from righteousness. Christ is first the 'King of righteousness,' and then 'King of peace;' righteousness causeth peace. Now, unless the soul be assured of righteousness in Christ, it can have no peace. What saith the Virgin Mary? 'My soul doth magnify the Lord, and my spirit rejoiceth in God my Saviour.' She begins with magnifying the Lord. But what was the ground? She rejoiced in

God as a Saviour; therefore she magnified him. So in the Lord's Prayer we say 'Our Father,' which is a word of the covenant of grace, when the soul conceives of God as a gracious Father, reconciled in Christ. And then comes 'Hallowed be thy name,' insinuating that, till we know in some measure God to be our Father, we cannot with a gracious spirit say, 'hallowed be thy name.' For can we heartily wish for the manifestation of the glory of him that we think is our enemy, and him that we have no interest in his greatness and goodness? The heart of man will never do it, therefore God must first speak peace to the soul;—the angels knew that well enough;—and then we are fit to glorify God.

'Peace on earth.'

What is peace? It is the best thing that man can attain unto, to have peace with his Maker and Creator. Peace, in general, is a harmony and an agreement of different things. This peace here you may know what it is by the contrary, as the apostle saith, Eph. i. 10. The word there is very significant, *Anakephaliosis* (ἀνακεφαλαίωσις). There is a recapitulation or gathering all to a head in Christ. Out of Christ there is a division, a separation and a scattering, a breach, that is five-fold.

(1.) First, *There is a scattering and a division from God*, the fountain of good, with whom we had communion in our first creation, and his delight was in his creature. We lost that blessed communion, and our sins have separated between God and us, as the prophet saith.

(2.) Then there is *a separation between the good angels and us;* for they being good subjects, take part with their prince, and therefore join against rebels, as we are. Hence it is, that upon the sight of angels, the very hearts of good men have sometimes been stricken, considering that there is no very good terms between us and the angels, till we come to Christ again.

(3.) Then there is *a division and scattering between man and man.* No common Spirit of God will keep men together till they be in Christ, as it is said, God sent an evil spirit, 'a spirit of division,' between the men of Shechem, Judges ix. 23. So, since the fall, there is an ill spirit of division among men, till the gospel again bring peace; especially there is no sound peace between men in the state of nature and others that are God's children, nor with the ordinances of God. For men apprehend the ordinances of God as enemies. The word cuts and lanceth him. It is as the sentence of a judge to condemn him. Therefore he fears and trembles at the powerful opening of the word. The ordinance of God speaks no comfort to a carnal man. He is as Ahab. He never had a word of peace from the prophet. The word alway speaks ill to him. He is under the law, and it speaks nothing but terror and curses to him.

(4.) And then there is a division and separation *between a man and the creature*, which is ready to be in arms against any man that is in the state of nature, to take God's quarrel, as we see in the plagues of Egypt and other examples. If God do but give them leave, they presently make an end of sinful man; and they would glory in it too, to serve their Creator. It is part of their vanity to be subject to wicked men. They have no peace with the creature.

(5.) And they have no peace *with themselves*. They speak peace to themselves, but, alas! God speaks none to them. They make a covenant with death and hell, but death and hell make no covenant with them. So it is a forced, sleepy peace. It is a dead sleep. The peace they have, it is but a diversion to other things. They consider not themselves and the war they are in with God, with themselves, and with the creature; it is but a truce that they take up for a time. When God opens their conscience, there is a hell in their hearts and souls, that when it is loosed, makes them to suffer a hell upon earth. They enter into the pains of hell before their time. So there is 'no peace to the wicked' at all, Isa. lvii. 21. There is, since the fall, a separation between God and man, between angels and man, between man and the creatures, between man and himself.

Now, Christ at his coming, taking our nature upon him, brings all into one again. He brings God and man together again, by offering himself a sacrifice, by making full satisfaction to the justice of God; and sin, which is the cause of his displeasure, being taken away, God being gracious and merciful, his mercy runs amain on us. Sin only separates between God and us, and that Christ takes away. Therefore he is called by St Paul, 'Christ our peace,' Eph. ii. 14, and 'the Prince of peace,' Heb. vii. 2. He was qualified to be our peace. He was a friend to both parties, having married our nature of purpose, that he might in our nature bring God and us together, as it is 1 Peter iii. 18. His whole work was to 'bring us back again to God,' from whom we fell at the first.

Then if we be at peace with God, all other peace will follow; for good subjects will be at peace with rebels, when they are brought in subjection to their king, and all join in one obedience. Therefore the angels are brought to God again by Christ.

And so for men, there is a spirit of union between them. The same Spirit that knits us to God by faith, knits us one to another by love.

And we have peace with the creature, for when God, who is the Lord of hosts, is made peaceful to us, he makes all other things peaceable. The heathen could say, *Tranquillus Deus, tranquillat omnia* (*e*), when God is at peace, he makes all so.

So there is peace in our own hearts. We are assured by the Spirit of God that he is our Father. He seals it to our conscience by his Spirit, because the blood of Christ is set on by the Spirit of God, and not by our own, so that now God and we are brought to one, and angels and we, and all other things. Therefore now the angels say, 'Peace on earth,' when Christ was born.

Now, we will shew that this blessed peace, in all the branches of it, *is founded in Christ*. Christ is the cause and the foundation of it. For though these words were spoken at the incarnation of Christ, yet we refer them to the whole work of his mediatorship, in the state of his abasement and his state of exaltation. Our peace is wholly founded upon him. For he was born and became man, and became sin; that is, a sacrifice for sin for us; he became 'a curse for us,' to stablish a peace and to satisfy God's anger; and then he rose again, to shew that he had fully satisfied God's anger, and that peace was fully established. Therefore the Holy Ghost was sent after the resurrection, as a testimony that God was appeased; and now in heaven, he is ever there as a priest, to make intercession for us. So that Christ is our peace from his incarnation to his death, from thence to his resurrection, and ascension, and intercession; all peace with God, with angels, and with creatures is stablished in Christ.

Quest. And why in Christ?

Ans. Christ is every way fitted for it, for he is the mediator between God and man; therefore by office he is fit to make peace between God and man. He is Emmanuel, himself God and man in one nature;* therefore his office is to bring God and man together.

* Qu 'person'?—Ed.

(1.) It is fit it should be so *in regard of God*, who being a 'consuming fire,' will no peace with the creature without a mediator. It stands not with his majesty, neither can there ever be peace with us otherwise. Now Christ is a fit mediator, being a friend to God as the Son of God, and a friend to us, taking our nature upon him, to be a merciful Redeemer.

(2.) It was also fit, *in respect of us*, it should be so. Alas! 'who can dwell with everlasting burnings?' Isa. xxxiii. 14. Who can have communion with God, who is a 'consuming fire?' No. We cannot endure the sight of an angel. The Israelites could not endure the sight of Moses when he came from the mount, his face shone so; and can we endure the glorious presence of God, 'who dwelleth in light that none can attain unto'? 1 Tim. vi. 16. Therefore God derives all good to us in our flesh, that though we cannot see God directly in himself, yet in the flesh we can see God incarnate. We may see the sun in the water, though we cannot directly look on that creature without hazard. It was a comfort to the patriarchs, that they had Joseph their brother the second man in the kingdom. So it may be to every Christian, that now we have the second person in heaven, our brother in our nature. He is the steward of heaven and earth, to dispense all God's treasures to us. Will not he acknowledge us, that are 'bone of his bone, and flesh of his flesh,' when he took our nature for this end, to be a merciful Redeemer? It is most suitable to our condition, that Christ should be the foundation of our peace.

3. *If we look to Christ himself*, he being God's Son, and the Son of his love, for him to make us sons, and sons of God's love. Is it not most agreeable, that he that is the image of God, should again renew the image of God that we lost? Jacob's ladder knit heaven and earth together; so Christ knits heaven and earth, God and us, together. You know if a ladder lie upon the ground, it doth no good, or if it be kept above, it serves for nothing; so if Christ were only God, or only man, there could be no union wrought between God and man; but now, being both, he is a fit mediator between both. Christ is the foundation of our peace, in the gracious covenant that God hath made with us, in all his offices. For as a prophet, he proclaims peace. He preached before in the time of Noah. He published peace as the prophet of his church in himself, when he lived, and by his ministers when he left the world. And as a priest, he did work our reconciliation, offering himself a sacrifice. He made a peace between God and us, and is now in heaven, to make intercession between God and us. And as a king, he subdues the corruptions of our souls, he pulls down the pride of our thoughts, to bring the heart into subjection to him by his mighty power, which indeed requires an almighty power; also by his kingly office, he rules, and governs, and subdues all the enemies of his church, without and within. You see then, without further illustration, that Christ is the foundation of our peace, by his incarnation, death, resurrection, and ascension.

This should teach us, first, that whatsoever intercourse we have with God the Father, we should take Christ, take our Benjamin, our Beloved, with us. We must not offer sacrifice without the High Priest. Let us offer nothing to God without Christ. There is no intercourse between God and us, till we be reconciled in Christ, in whom we must offer all our sacrifices and endeavours. Therefore, let us not own an absolute God in our devotions: let us think of God 'reconciled' in Christ, and at peace with us, and a father in covenant in Christ; and then our persons, and prayers, and all, shall be accepted for the sacrifice of Christ, in whom he smells a sweet savour. As it is said concerning Noah, he offered a sacrifice to God, 'a sweet smelling sacrifice of rest,' Eph. v. 2. So doth God in Christ. He is the true mercy-seat in Christ, in looking to whom, God frees us from the curse of the law. Jerusalem was the glory of the world, and the temple was the glory of Jerusalem; but the mercy-seat was the glory of the temple, because that pointed to Christ, the Mercy-seat, in whom we have intercourse with God the Father.

We conceive not high enough of the majesty of God, when we go to him immediately. We must go to him in his Son, whom he hath sent, and anointed, and set forth, 'as the propitiation for our sins,' Rom. iii. 25, and 'him hath God the Father sealed,' John vi. 27. He cometh with authority. Therefore God will be reconciled in Christ. We may bind God himself, when we offer Christ. He is the foundation of reconciliation and peace, by God's appointment. He is 'the Prince of peace,' of his own anointing. Therefore we may go boldly to God, to the throne of grace in Christ.

And let us often seriously meditate of the sweet favour and reconciliation stablished now between God and us through Christ. It is the sweetest meditation.

First, To think in what ill terms we are with God by nature; and then think how near we are now to God in Christ, that we are at peace with him. Methinks the word is too short. There is more meant than is spoken. At peace with God in Christ: nay, now we are friends; nay, we are sons and heirs, fellow-heirs, fellow-kings with Christ; for God's favours are complete. As a God he stablisheth not a peace as men do, only to do them no harm that they are at peace with; but where he makes a peace, he confers all that is good: reconciliation, adoption, giving us the liberty of sons and friends, to go boldly to God as a Father in all our wants. Let us think more of this, and improve this blessed privilege every day.

'Peace upon earth.'

Quest. Why doth he say, 'peace on earth'?

Ans. Because peace was here wrought upon earth by Christ in the days of his flesh, when he offered himself 'a sacrifice of a sweet-smelling savour to his Father.'

Because here in earth we must be partakers of it. We ofttimes defer to make our peace with God from time to time, and think there will be peace made in another world. Oh, beloved, our peace must be made on earth. 'We must live godly, and righteously, and soberly in this present world,' Titus ii. 12. We must enter 'into the kingdom of heaven' here. Further entrance 'must be ministered here, by growing in grace daily more and more,' 2 Pet. iii. 18. If heaven be not entered into here, it shall never be entered afterwards; for the church is the seminary of the heavenly paradise. All that are taken to heaven, to be set there for ever, they are set in the church before they are planted, and grow up there a while, under the means of salvation. Therefore, labour to have this 'peace on earth,' or else we can never glorify God on earth; and if we glorify him not on earth, we shall never do it in heaven.

But to come to some trials, whether we have this peace made or no; whether we can say in spirit and truth, there is a peace established between God and us.

1. For a ground of this, that may lead us to further trial, know that Christ hath reconciled God and us together, not only by obtaining peace, by way of satisfaction, but by way of application also. *Whom he died for*

to obtain 'peace,' he gives a spirit of application to improve that peace, to improve 'Christ, the prince of peace,' *as their own.* For there is a mutual commerce between God and man, who is an understanding creature; and there is nothing that God doth for man, if we look to the general and head of benefits, but there is somewhat in man wrought by the Spirit to answer it again. God is reconciled to man in Christ. Man must be reconciled to God in Christ; in 2 Cor. v. 19, 'God was in Christ, reconciling the world.' When he was on the cross, God was there reconciled in Christ. Is that all? No. God by us entreats you to be reconciled to God. A strange condescending, that God should entreat us to be good to our own souls by his ministers. 'We entreat you to be reconciled,' 2 Cor. v. 20; that is, to accept of the reconciliation wrought by Christ, and to lay aside all weapons of rebellion, whereby you fought against God in the course of your vanity. We beseech you to be reconciled, and to 'repent, because the kingdom of God is at hand,' Mat. iii. 2. So that except there be reconciliation wrought by a spirit of application on man's part, it is not sufficient that God is reconciled in Christ, because God will alway have a reflex act from man. As he chooseth man, so man by grace chooseth him. As he loves and delights in man, so he will have man, by a spirit of sweetness, delight in him again above all the world. 'Whom have I in heaven but thee?' Ps. lxxiii. 25. So there is somewhat wrought by the Spirit to God again. Why should God be at good terms with us, but to enjoy the friendship of his poor creature? Unless, therefore, there be a gracious disposition wrought in the creature, to look back, to love and delight in God, as God doth in him, there is no actual reconciliation. There must be a forcible application by the Spirit. If God should not give a spirit of application, as well as Christ obtain heaven for us, those that are in the covenant of grace should not be stablished; but God by this means brings them so near, that he, loving them, loves them for ever, and they have an everlasting covenant and an everlasting union. The carnal heart of man is a poisonful thing, and hates God naturally. It wishes that there were no God to judge him. He may think well of God for the good things of this life, but when he thinks of God as a judge to cast him into hell, he wisheth with all his heart, Oh that there were no God! that I might have my full of the pleasures of sin. Now the soul when it is at peace with God, when God by his Spirit speaks to the soul, and saith, 'I am thy salvation,' Ps. xxxv. 3, 'Thy sins are forgiven thee,' Mat. ix. 2; and as Christ to the good thief on the cross, 'This day shalt thou be with me in paradise,' Luke xxiii. 43; when he whispers to the soul, 'Thou art mine, and I am thine,' Cant. ii. 16; then the soul becomes sweet and peaceable to God again, and studies to advance the glory of God's mercy by all means, and to advance the gospel of peace. It becomes friendly to God.

To come to some more familiar evidences, whether we be at peace with God, and whether we have the comfort of this peace, established by Christ, or no.

2. Those that are reconciled one to another *have common friends and common enemies.* If therefore there be 'peace' between God and us, it is so with us. We love all where we see any evidence of God's love. We love Christians as Christians. And whom God loves not, we love not; what God hates we hate in ourselves and others. We hate corruptions in ourselves and others, though we love their persons.

3. Another evidence of 'peace' made in Christ between God and us, *is a boldness of spirit and acquaintance with God.* 'Acquaint thyself with

God, and be at peace with him,' Job xxii. 21. A Christian being at 'peace' with God in Christ Jesus, he goes boldly to the throne of grace in all his necessities, as a poor child goes boldly to his father, and moves the bowels of his father by his petitions. When two kingdoms are at 'peace,' there is trading set up afresh again. So when God is at 'peace' with the soul, there is a heavenly intercourse and trading set up. There is no man that is at 'peace' with God, but he calls upon God in his person, in his family. He sets up the worship of God there. He labours to bring all to God that he can. He thinks it the most gainful trade in the world. In the want of grace and spiritual comfort he goes to the fountain of grace, and improves that blessed prerogative we have by peace in Christ. Those that have not the Spirit of God to improve it in communion and trading with God, it is a sign there is no peace. Strangeness shews that there is no peace. Alas, how strangely do many walk towards God, that from Sunday to Sunday scarce lift up their hearts to heaven for a blessing, but walk in the strength of their own mother-wit, and support themselves with the success of second causes, and bless themselves; they are strangers from the 'God of peace.' Let us take notice of this, and account it a great prerogative, that we may go to God with boldness, that it is not now as it was in paradise. There is no angel with a sword to shut us from heaven. But now there is an entrance to the throne of grace. We may go boldly in the name of Christ, to offer ourselves and all our endeavours.

4. A Christian that hath made his 'peace' with God, will never allow himself *in any sin against conscience,* because he knows sin is odious in itself, loathsome to God, and hurtful to his soul; therefore he will not be in league with any sinful, unjust course. What! to be in league with God, and to be at 'peace' with that that God hates more than the devil himself! He hates sin more than the devil, for he hates him for sin. Therefore a man that allows himself in known sins, there can be no peace between God and him, as he saith, 'Why do you talk of peace, as long as the witchcrafts and whoredoms of Jezebel remain?' 2 Kings ix. 22. A man that lives in sins against conscience, that is an open swearer, an unjust person, that cares not by what means he advanceth himself, what doth he talk of peace with God, when he is in league with God's enemy? Therefore, though such men,—out of 'the hardness of their hearts, which are harder than the nether millstone,' Job xli. 24, and God seals them up under a hard heart to damnation, except some terrible judgment awake them,—force a peace upon themselves, they ought to speak none, and they shall find it to their cost ere long. Therefore let us examine our own hearts how we stand affected to any sinful course. There may be infirmities and weaknesses hang upon the best that are besides* their purposes and resolutions, but for a man resolvedly to set himself in an ill way, how can he be at peace with God and with Satan at the same time? Let us take notice of these things, and not daub† with our own consciences.

5. Again, Where there is a true peace established, there is *a high esteem of the word of peace,* the gospel of reconciliation, as St Paul calls it, 2 Cor. v. 18, 'He hath committed to us the word of reconciliation.' Those that find this peace, there is stirred up by the Spirit in their breasts a high esteem of the ordinance of God, as being the word of their 'peace.' How come we to have peace between God and us? Is it not by opening the riches of God's love in Christ in the Scriptures? Therefore, saith the Scripture, 'blessed are the feet of them that bring glad tidings,' Isa. lii. 7.

* That is, 'beside.'—G. † Cf. Ezekiel xxii. 28.—

The meanest part of their body, their feet, are blessed. Therefore those that have despicable conceits of the ministry of the word, and place their happiness in depraving* the labour and pains of that office and calling, it is a sign that they have profane hearts; for whosoever hath had any grace wrought by the word of reconciliation and of peace, they will highly esteem it, and respect them for their office sake. It cannot be otherwise.

6. Lastly, Those that have found peace *are peaceable*. It is universally true God doth make an impression of the same disposition in us to others. We apprehending God in Christ to be peaceable to us, we are peaceable to others. Therefore, in Isa. xi. 6, *seq.*, the knowledge of God in Christ, it alters and changeth men's dispositions. It makes wolves and lions to be of a milder disposition and temper. Harsh, proud, sturdy dispositions, they never felt 'peace' and mercy themselves; therefore they are not ready to shew it to others. In the nature of the thing itself it is impossible for the soul to apprehend peace in the love of God, and not to have the disposition wrought upon to shew what it hath felt. Let us think of these and such like evidences daily, to keep our hearts from speaking false 'peace.' The greatest danger in the world, in this regard, is in the church; for people under the gospel speak false 'peace' to themselves. There is a spirit of delusion that carries them along *to* their death, and deceives them also *in* death; and so they are in hell before they be aware, and then too late. They see that they were never in good terms with God in all their life, because they looked on Christ making peace, without any consideration of the spirit of application.

There must be a sprinkling of the blood of Christ on our souls to make it our own: 'We are come to the blood of sprinkling,' Heb. xii. 24. It is not the blood of Christ that makes our peace only as blood; but as it is sprinkled by the hand of faith, that is as the hyssop that sprinkled the blood of the sacrifice upon the people. We must not think to have any good by the blood of Christ, when we want the blood of sprinkling, that is, this particular faith: 'Christ loved me, and hath chosen me,' Gal. ii. 20; and I choose him, and love him again; and so go with boldness to God as a Father. Unless there be this passage of the soul, between God and us, let us not talk of peace. For if we might have good by Christ, without a spirit of application, and if there were not a necessity of sprinkling the blood of Christ upon our souls by faith, all the world should be saved.

In the next place, to give a few directions to maintain this peace actually and continually every day.

1. To walk with God, and to keep our daily peace with God, *it requires a great deal of watchfulness over our thoughts*,—for he is a Spirit, *over our words and actions*. Watchfulness is the preserver of peace. Where there is a great distance between two that are at peace, it is not kept without acknowledgment of that distance, and without watchfulness. It is not here as it is in a peace that is between two kings that are co-ordinate with one another; but it is a peace between the King of heaven and rebels that are taken to be subjects; therefore we must walk in humble, low terms. 'Humble thyself, and walk with thy God,' 1 Pet. v. 6. We must watch over our carriage, that we do not 'grieve the Spirit of God;' for then, however the first peace established in conversion should be never taken away, yet God interdicts our comfort. We cannot daily enjoy our daily peace without watchfulness. But God suffers our knowledge, and our former illumination, to lash our conscience, and to be more miserable in our

* That is, 'undervaluing.'—G.

inward man, than a carnal man that never had sight of goodness. Oh the misery of a man that is fallen into ill terms with God, that had peace before! Of all men such a man hath most horror till he have made his peace again. Watchfulness will prevent this.

2. And because it is a difficult thing to maintain terms of peace with God, in regard of our indisposition, we fall into breaches with God daily; therefore *we should often renew our covenants and purposes every day.*

And if we have fallen into any sin, let us make use of our great peacemaker, Christ, who is in heaven to make peace between God and us. Let us desire God, for his sake, to be reconciled unto us, 'for God is, in Christ, reconciling us unto him,' 2 Cor. v. 19, still. The fruit of Christ's death remains still. Let us desire him to testify it unto us by his Holy Spirit.

3. And take that direction of the apostle, in Philip. iv. 6, when we find any trouble in the world, not to trouble ourselves over much. 'In nothing be careful,' &c. No. Shall we cast away all care? Cast your care upon God; let your requests be made known to God with thanksgiving; let your prayers be made to God; and let him have his tribute of thanksgiving for what you have received already. What then? 'The peace of God, that passeth all understanding, shall keep and preserve your hearts and minds in Christ Jesus,' Philip. iv. 7. Perhaps we shall not have what we pray for, when we have made our requests known to God. If we have not that we pray for presently, yet we shall have the 'peace of God, that passeth all understanding,' [which] shall 'keep our hearts and minds.' Therefore, when any thing troubles us, let us consider there is peace made between God and us, and put up our requests in the name of Christ, and we shall find that peace that passeth understanding.

4. Again, If we would maintain this peace, let us *be alway doing somewhat that is good and pleasing to God.* In the same chapter, Philip. iv. 8, 'Finally, brethren, whatsoever things are honest, whatsoever things are just, whatsoever things are pure,' &c., 'think of these things;' and what then? 'The God of peace shall be with you.' The peace of God and the God of peace shall be with you. There must be a thinking of whatsoever is good. The thoughts must be exercised that way, and there must be a practice of what we think of. This is one means to maintain this peace with God. The very heathen had this reward of God, I mean in this life, that when they did good to their country, and one to another, they had content of conscience, they had a peace suitable. For in this world there is a suitable pleasure of conscience and contentment upon everything that is good. God rewards it in this world. For as the heat followeth the fire alway—naturally it cannot be without heat—so the thinking and practising of that which is good, especially when it is joined with some opposition of corrupt nature, when the light of nature is above the corruption of nature. If a man be a pagan, he shall have this reward in this world, a kind of inward peace; for we see how comfortably they speak sometimes upon some notable performance for their country (*f*). Now, the God of peace will be with us much more when we have laid the foundation of our peace aright, in the mercy of God in Christ, besides what is reserved, heaven and happiness. In this world we shall find the peace of God in the doing that which is good.

As for those that live in the church, and are not yet in the state of grace, that have lived wicked lives, let them consider that yet the day of grace continues, as yet the sceptre of mercy is held forth in the ministry; there is a day of jubilee for them to return from their former captivity. Let them not abuse the patience of God, and think to do it afterward; for that is the way to harden the heart more and more. And this Scripture puts an effectual argument into the hearts of all that are in ill terms with God, that have not made their peace, or that have had peace and have broken it. Here is an effectual way of pleading with God. 'Glory to God on high,' &c. If the soul can say, I consider my folly and madness in running into sin; thou mightest justly damn me if thou wouldst; it is thy mercy I am not sent to hell. Oh, but thou shalt have the greater glory! If I find mercy therefore that I may say, 'Glory to God on high,' let me find peace on earth; speak peace by thy Spirit to my soul; say, 'I am thy salvation.' This was the end of thy sending of Christ, the end of creation, the end of providence, all to bring thee glory. Thou mightest have the glory of thy justice to damn me. Oh, but it will be the glory of thy mercy to save me; that as my sins have abounded, so thy glory shall more abound. O Lord, extend the bowels of thy mercy. Will not the Lord be jealous 'of his glory' when you allege it? Certainly he will. You see the angels here cry, 'Glory to God on high, peace on earth.' The way to bring 'peace' is to allege the glory of God's mercy in Christ. It is a prevailing way.

Now, to stir us up more and more to search the grounds of our peace, I beseech you, let us,

1. *Consider the fearful estate of a man that hath not made his peace with God.* However Christ have died, that will not serve the turn. But if Christ be food, if he be not eaten; if he be a garment, and not be put on; if Christ be a foundation, if we do not build on him, what benefit is it to us? Therefore those that have not been brought by the Spirit of God to communion with Christ, alas! they are under the wrath of God, however God doth use them; as princes do traitors in the Tower, he gives them the liberty of the prison, yet the sentence of death is not revoked. All the delights of a prisoner in the Tower doth not content him; he knows he is in ill terms with his prince. So, till we have made our peace with God, by hearty confession of our sins, by shaming of ourselves, by a particular faith, believing the forgiveness of our sins, and a resolution against all sin for the time to come, alas! we have not sued out our pardon; all our delights are but as those of a prisoner in the Tower. Therefore, ask thy soul, Hast thou sued out thy pardon? Is there reconciliation wrought between God and thee, and accounts made even? 'If we confess and forsake our sins, we shall find mercy,' 1 Kings viii. 35 and 1 John i. 9. It is the word of the God of heaven, who is truth itself. He hath pawned his fidelity and truth on it, to forgive us, if we confess. He is content to be thought unjust and unfaithful if he do not forgive, if we ingenuously, without all guile of spirit, lay open our sins, and take shame to ourselves.

2. If we do not make our peace with God, what a case are we in! God himself ere long will appear our enemy. *Christ, whom we think will save us, will be our judge*, and a terrible judge. The Lamb will be angry. 'Who shall cover us from the wrath of the Lamb?' Rev. ii. 12. We think of Christ as an innocent, meek lamb only, that will not be angry. The rebellious kings and potentates, that fight against Christ and his church, they think to trample on Christ and his gospel; but the time will come when they shall 'desire the mountains to cover them,' Rev. vi. 16; and 'if his wrath be kindled, who shall abide it?' Ps. ii. 12. He speaks there of Christ: 'Happy are they that trust in him.'

3. As for the Holy Ghost, how can they look for comfort from him?

They have grieved him, therefore he will grieve their conscience. The Holy Ghost, as he is the God of all comfort and consolation, so he is the ground of all terror to wicked men; when he hath knocked at their hearts, by the ministry of his word, to open and to let him in, but they would not.

4. *And the angels are ready executioners of God's vengeance* upon any occasion; and others, creatures, wait but for a command from God to execute his wrath upon sinners. The heavens are ready to rain upon them as in the flood, and the earth is ready to swallow them as it did Korah; the beasts that carry us, the creatures we use, wait for a command from God to destroy us; our meat to choke us, the air to infect us, the water to drown us. They are all ready to serve the Lord of hosts against his enemies; as he saith, Isa. i. 24, 'Ah, I will be avenged on mine ememies.' Indeed, here God shews his patience; and our long life, that we think a great favour, 'it is a treasuring up of wrath against the day of wrath,' Rom. ii. 5. And then, when God's wrath comes at the day of judgment, when God hath forsaken sinful men, when God the judge of all hath said, 'Depart, ye cursed,' Mat. xxv. 41, no creature shall minister them the least comfort. The sun shall shine upon them no more; the earth shall bear them no longer; as we see Dives (*g*), he had not a drop of water to comfort him in those flames, Luke xvi. 24. Therefore, if we be not at peace with the Lord of hosts, every creature is ready to be in arms against us.

5. *As for the devils*, they will be ready to be tormentors. They that are incentives to sin will be tormentors for sin afterwards.

6. *As for the church*, what comfort can a wicked man look for from the church, whom he hath despised, and whose ministry he hath rejected?

7. *And for the damned spirits*, they are all in that cursed condition with himself. Therefore, 'where shall the ungodly appear?' 1 Pet. iv. 18. Ere long whence shall he hope for comfort? Neither from God, nor angels, nor devils, nor wicked men, nor good men. None of them all will yield him a dram of comfort.

Let us not therefore delude ourselves, *but get into Christ*, get into the ark in time, that when any public calamity shall come, we may be safe in Christ. If we be at peace with God, by repentance of sins, and by faith in Christ, everything will minister thoughts of comfort to us. We cannot think of God, but as our Father; of Christ as our Redeemer and reconciler, that hath brought God and us together. The Holy Ghost takes upon him the term of a Comforter for such. Angels, they are ministering spirits. As for the church itself, God's people, they all have a common stock of prayers for us. Every one that saith, 'Our Father,' thinks of us; and all other things, they are at peace with us, as Job saith, 'The stones in the street,' Job v. 23; nay, the stone in a man's body, the terrible pangs that comes from that disease, they have a blessing upon them. In the greatest extremities, a soul that is at peace with God, however God do not deliver him from the trouble, yet he delivers and supports him in the trouble; and as the troubles increase, so his comforts increase; and the very troubles are peace with him. 'All work for the best to them that love God,' Rom. viii. 28. And in the greatest confusions and tumults of states, yet 'the righteous is afraid of no ill tidings,' Ps. cxii. 7, because his heart is fixed upon God's love in Christ. The wicked, when war and desolation, and signs of God's anger appear from heaven, they 'shake as the trees of the forest,' as a wicked Ahaz, Isa. vii. 2; as a Belshazzar, when there is but a fear of trouble. How did he know that the handwriting was against him? It was nothing but this naughty conscience. He knew not what it was till it was expounded. So when any troubles comes upon wicked men, their consciences upbraid them with their former life. Their knees knock together, and they grow pale as Belshazzar. Oh the misery of a man that hath not made his peace with God, in the evil day, and the comfort of a man that hath! There is the difference between godly and ungodly man. Consider them in calamities. The one is at peace with God, in the midst of all calamities and troubles; nay, as I said, even troubles themselves are peaceable to him.

Yea, when death comes, which is the upshot of all, the sting of it is taken away, and it is for our greatest good. He that hath made his peace with God, he can say, with old Simeon, 'Lord, now let thy servant depart in peace, for mine eyes have seen thy salvation,' Luke ii. 30. Mine eyes have seen Christ with the eye of faith. He is willing to yield his soul to God, because he is at peace with God. Their graves are their beds, and their souls rest with God. They die in peace, and commend their souls to God, 'as to a faithful Creator,' 1 Peter iv. 19, with a great deal of confidence: as Saint Paul saith, 'I have fought the good fight, I have kept the faith, I have run my race; henceforth is reserved for me a crown of righteousness; and not for me only, but for all those that love the blessed and glorious appearing of Christ.' Oh the comfort of a gracious soul in the hour of death, that hath made its peace with God, Job xviii. 14, when 'the king of fears,' death, shall look with a ghastly, terrible look upon men that have not made their peace. But to the other it is the end of misery, the inlet to eternal happiness. 'Blessed are those that die in the Lord,' in the peace of the Lord; 'they rest from their labours,' from the labour of sin, of callings, of afflictions, Rev. xiv. 13. There is no resting till then. Saint Paul himself was troubled with the remainders of sin, with afflictions and troubles of his calling; but blessed are they that die in the peace of God in Christ. They rest from their labours. And after death, what comfort are those in that have made their peace with God in Christ! Then their Saviour is to be their Judge. He that makes intercession for them in heaven will be their Judge; and will the head give sentence against the members, the husband against the wife and spouse? Oh no! Therefore the godly have comfortable and sweet thoughts of those blessed times, that astonisheth wicked men. They have a glorious expectation of the times to come. They cannot think of death and judgment, when their souls are in a good frame, without much comfort. 'Lift up your heads, for your redemption draws near,' Luke xxi. 28. Therefore let us not conceive slightly of this peace. It is not a freedom from petty ills, and an advancement to a little good; but it is a freedom from ills that are above nature; from the wrath of God, before which no creature can stand; no, not the angels themselves; from hell and damnation; the curse of God; from the kingdom of Satan. It is a freedom from that condition that all the powers of the world shall tremble at. How can they stand before the anger of God? And it is an advancement to the greatest good; a freedom from bondage; an advancement to sonship. Therefore let us have high thoughts of this peace; as the angels had, when they sang, 'Glory to God on high, on earth peace.'

'Good will towards men.'

Divers copies have it otherwise, 'On earth peace to men of good will.' Some have it, 'Good will towards men.' The sense is not much different.* Peace on earth, 'To men of God's good will, of God's good pleasure.' That God hath a pleasure to save, or 'good will towards men,' of God's good pleasure; 'Peace on earth,' to men of God's good will and pleasure; or God's good pleasure towards men.

'Good will towards men.'

This is the spring and root of all. The angels begin with 'Glory to God,' and then they come to 'peace among men,' because without peace and reconciliation with God the heart of man cannot be enlarged to glorify God. The angels would have men glorify God as well as themselves. Therefore they desire peace on earth, that God may be glorified in heaven. Now there is no peace but issues from grace. Grace is God's free good will and pleasure. Therefore the angels say, 'Good will towards men.'

The holy apostles, they could not have better teachers for their salutations in their epistles than to learn of the angels; as you have Saint Paul's prefaces, the same with this evangelical celebration and gratulation here to men, 'Grace, mercy, and peace,' so here, 'Peace on earth, good will towards men.' Only the apostles they begin, 'grace and peace;' and here the angels, 'peace and grace.' But the meaning of the angels and apostles is all one; for the angels, when they wish 'peace on earth,' they go to the spring of it, 'good will towards men.' The apostles, they begin with grace, the spring, and then go to peace after.

'Good will towards men.'

The words need not further to be explicated. There is no great difficulty in them. The points considerable are these.

1. God now hath a gracious good will towards men.
2. This good will is the foundation of all good.
3. And this is founded upon Christ.

The first of these I will but touch, because it doth but make way to the other.

1. *God shews now good pleasure towards men.*

The love that God bears towards man hath divers terms, from divers relations. As it is a propension in him to do good, so it is love. As it is his free, so it is his good, pleasure or grace. As it is to persons in misery, it is mercy. The fountain of all is love. But as the object is diversely considered, so the terms be divers. Good pleasure and grace imply freedom in the party loving, and mercy implies misery in the party loved.

Now this free good will and grace, it is towards men, towards mankind. He saith not, towards angels. It is more towards men, than even to good angels, in some sort. For now man is taken to be the spouse of Christ. Good angels are not so. Neither is it good will to evil angels; for their state is determined. There is no altering of their condition. Therefore God is called *Philanthropos*, not *Philangelos;* and the Scripture calls this *Philanthropia*, the love that God hath shewed to *men* in Christ.† Therefore we should have thoughts of God as gracious, loving our nature more than the angelical nature in some respects.

And learn this for imitation, to love mankind. God loved mankind; and surely there is none that is born of God, but he loves the nature of man, wheresoever he finds it. He will not stand altogether, whether it be good or bad, &c. But because we are now in the way, and our state is not determined, and because God loves the nature of man, therefore every

* Cf. note *a*.—G.

† That is, φιλανθρωπία.—G.

man that hath the Spirit of God loves mankind. He will labour to gain Turks, or Indians, &c., if he can, because he loves the very nature of man. But I pass from this point to the second.

2. This ἐυδοκια, '*good will of God' to restore lapsed man by the sending of his Son, is the ground of all good to man*, and hath no ground but itself. God's grace and love to the creature is altogether independent in regard of the creature. God fetcheth not reasons of his love from the creature, but from his own bowels. What can he foresee in 'persons that were dead'? nay, in persons that were in a contrary disposition to goodness? There is nothing but enmity in our nature to supernatural goodness. Can God foresee grounds of love in enmity?

As Moses tells the people of Israel in divers places, Deut. vii. 8, 'that it was not for any foresight of good in them,' they were the stubbornest people under heaven, therefore God, to shew his free love, he chose a stubborn people, and singled them out to be the object of his mercy. So God ofttimes takes the unlikeliest men in the world, and passeth by many, otherwise of sweet natures. So we see, even the means themselves, they are of God's free mercy and love.

We have whatsoever we have by virtue of the covenant; for what could we look for from God but in covenant, wherein he hath bound himself? Now, since the fall, this covenant is called the covenant of grace; that now, 'if we believe in Christ, we shall not perish, but have life and salvation,' John iii. 15. In all the parts of it, it is of God's free grace and good pleasure. What is the foundation of the covenant? Christ. Christ is of free grace. 'God so loved the world, that he *gave* his only Son,' verse 16. There is nothing freer than gift. Christ is a gift, the greatest gift. He came freely from God; he 'gave him to death for us all,' Rom. viii. 32.

And then whatsoever good thing we have in Christ, it comes freely too. He that gave Christ freely, shall he not 'with him give us all things too?' Rom. viii. 32.

Then the very grace to keep the covenant, repentance and faith, they are the gift of God. 'I will take away your stony heart, and give you new hearts, and cause you to walk in my statutes; I will circumcise your hearts,' Exek. xi. 19. So the grace to walk in the covenant of grace, it comes from God. God doth his part and ours too, to shew not only that the covenant of grace is a covenant of wondrous love, to give us grace here and glory hereafter, but that the foundation is of grace, and the performance on our part is of grace. Nay, it is of grace that he would enter into covenant at all. He humbled himself wondrously to vouchsafe to enter into covenant. It was humiliation on God's part, and exaltation to us. Therefore, as it is in Zechariah, we may cry, 'Grace, grace.' There is nothing but grace and free love in the whole carriage of our salvation.

If whatsoever good come to man be merely from God's good will, let us empty ourselves, and give him the glory of all. It is easily spoken and heard, but not so easily done. For man naturally is proud, and for flesh and blood to be brought to go out of itself and acknowledge nothing in itself, to give the glory of all goodness and happiness to God's free grace and goodness, it is hard to bring proud nature to do this. But we must beg grace of God to work our hearts to this more and more, to empty ourselves of ourselves, and to give God the glory of all. But,

I come to the last point, because I would end this text at this time.

3. *This free love and grace of God is only in Christ.*

Therefore the angels pronounce it now at the birth of Christ, 'good will to men.' All these agree very well: Christ's free grace, and faith. For what we have by grace, we have only by Christ; because he hath given satisfaction to God's justice, that so grace may be conveyed and derived unto us without prejudice to any other attribute in God; and then the embracing power and grace in us is faith. So these three agree. I say, whatsoever we have from God's free love now, we have it in Christ. The free love of God is grounded in Christ. We in ourselves, especially considered in the corrupt mass, cannot be the object of God's love. God cannot look upon us, but in him, the best beloved, first. Therefore all is in Christ in the carriage of it. We are elected in Christ, called in Christ, justified by Christ, sanctified by the Spirit of Christ, glorified in Christ. 'We are blessed with all spiritual blessings in heavenly things in Christ,' Eph. i. 3. 'This is my beloved Son; I am well pleased in him,' Mat. iii. 17. It is the same word there, εὐδόκησα, 'in whom I delight,' Isa. xlii. 1, out of which the Father takes his speech, 'This is the Son I delight in.' Now, all God's delight is first fixed in his Son and in us, because we must have communion with the Son. So the first object of God's free love is Christ, and then he looks upon us in him.

The Trinity have a wondrous complacency in looking upon mankind. Now in Christ God loves us, as redeemed by Christ; Christ loves us as elected by the Father, and given by the Father's choice to him to redeem. The Holy Ghost hath a special liking to us, as seeing the love of the Father in choosing us, and of the Son in redeeming us. And surely if we would see likewise those sweet interviews of God the Father, Son, and Holy Ghost, it should be our main delight too, to see how God hath chosen us and given us to Christ to save; how Christ hath redeemed us, from this very respect, that the Father hath chosen us and given us to him, as it is in John xvii. 6, 'Thine they were, thou gavest them me;' and how the Holy Ghost is a Spirit of communion—the 'communion of the Holy Ghost,' 2 Cor. xiii. 14—that hath communion with the Father and the Son, and issues and proceeds from them both; how he witnesseth this love to our souls, and applies it to us. The Holy Ghost applies all. The Father decreed and ordained all. The Son works and dispenseth all. The consideration of the point is wondrous comfortable.

Whatsoever good will the Father hath to us, it is as we are in Christ.

Quest. And why in Christ?

Ans. Because Christ is the first thing that God can love. He is 'the only begotten Son of God.' Whosoever is loved to glory in a spiritual order, is loved in the first beloved. Christ is loved of God as the character of his own image. The Son represents the Father. He is loved of God, as mediator by office. So God looks upon us in Christ as the 'Son of his love.' So he is called by Saint Paul, Col. i. 13.

Then if we consider ourselves, this must be so. Alas! we are not objects of God's love in ourselves, nor cannot be; but in some other that is loved first. For what are we? And what is the glory to which God loves us? To love such as we to such glory, and to free us from such misery due, it must be by another foundation than ourselves. Therefore God's good pleasure is founded upon his Son Christ. This is a clear point. The Scripture beats much upon it. He is our elder brother, and we must be conformed to him.

Use. To make some use of it.

First of all, then, we see here that all that are not in Christ lie open to the vengeance and wrath of God. His good will towards men is only in Christ.

Again, If all God's good will and pleasure be in Christ, as our high priest, without whom we can offer no sacrifice, as we know whatsoever was not offered by the high priest it was abominable, therefore we should look to God in Christ, love God in Christ, perform service to God in Christ, pray to God in Christ, give thanks to God in Christ, desire God in Christ to make all things acceptable for Christ's sake, because it is in Christ that God hath any good will and pleasure to us.

It is a point of marvellous comfort, that God's love and good pleasure is so well founded, as in Christ. He loves Christ eternally, and sweetly, and strongly. Is not God's love to us the same? Doth he not love us with the same love that he loves his Son? He loves his mystical body with one love, that is Christ, head and members: John xvii. 23, 'That the love thou bearest to me may be in them.' What a sweet comfort is this! God loves Christ and me with one love. He loves me strongly, and sweetly, and constantly, as he doth his own Son. His love to me is eternal, because the foundation of it is eternal. It is founded upon Christ. The love of a prince, if it be founded on a favourite he loves dearly, must needs be firm and strong. Now God's love to Christ is ardent, and strong, and sweet, as possibly can be conceived. Therefore it is so to us, his good will to us being founded on Christ.

Why should a believer fear that God will cast him away? He will as soon leave his love to his own Son, as to us, if we continue members of his Son. It is an undefeasible love. It is a point of wondrous comfort. 'What shall separate us,' saith the apostle, Rom. viii. 35, 'from the love of God founded in Christ? neither things present, nor things to come, nor life, nor death, nor anything.' Many things may sever the soul and body, but there is nothing in the world but sin, that shall sever either soul or body from the love of God in Christ, because both body and soul are members of Christ. Therefore let us treasure it up as a point wondrous comfortable.

To come to an use of trial, how shall we know whether God's good will be to us in Christ or no? How shall I know that he loves my person, that I am in the state of grace and love with him?

The Holy Ghost must ascertain this. For as the work of salvation was so great, that only God could satisfy God, so the doubts of man's heart, and the guilt of his conscience when it is upon him, and the fear of God's wrath upon just guilt, is such that God must assure him that God is reconciled to him. God the Son must reconcile God the Father, and God the Holy Ghost must seal and ascertain this to the soul. The soul will never be quiet, before it see and know in particular God reconciled in Christ. The Spirit that is God, that is above conscience, must seal it to the soul, being above conscience. He can set down and quiet our conscience. Now this Spirit that worketh this in us, and assures us of God's good pleasure, it alters and changeth our dispositions, that we shall have a good pleasure in God, for there is a mutual good pleasure. God hath a good pleasure in us as his, and we have a good pleasure in God wrought by the Spirit. The Spirit not only witnesseth, but worketh this sweet and gracious disposition to God. God delights in us, and we in God. God delights in the church above all things. The church is his wife and spouse, his body, his friends, his children, and those that have the Spirit of God delight in them too. Ps. xvi. 3, 'All my delight is in the excellent;' and Prov. viii. 31, 'My delight is in the sons of men,' saith Christ; which he shewed by taking the base nature of man upon him. So all that have the Spirit of Christ delight in the church and people of God: 'All my delight is in the saints on earth,' Hosea ii. God saith his delight is in his church. So all that have the Spirit of God, they delight in the people of God.

God delights in obedience more than sacrifice. God's people, that he delights in, they yield their bodies and souls a sacrifice to God: Rom. xii. 1, 'They will seek out what is well-pleasing and acceptable to God.' God accepts them in Christ, and he is acceptable to them in Christ Jesus, and they seek out what pleaseth him and is acceptable to him. As the sons of Isaac sought out what might please their old father, what he could relish, so God's children seek out what duties God relisheth best. Thanksgiving is a sacrifice 'with which God is well pleased.' Is it so? Then they will seek out that that may please him. God by his Spirit will work in them a disposition to please him in all things. Therefore the people of God are said to be a voluntary, free people, 'zealous of good works,' Titus ii. 14, being set at liberty. The Spirit infusing and conveying the love and good pleasure of God in Christ to them, it sets their wills at liberty, to devise to please God in all things. They have, as David prays, Ps. li. 12, 'a free Spirit.' As God, not out of any respect from us, but freely from his own bowels loved us, and gave Christ to us, and delighted in us, so the soul freely, without any base respects, loves God again. Those, therefore, that do duties for base aims, and forced, as fire out of a flint, not as water out of a spring, that duty comes not naturally and sweetly from them, God hath no pleasure in them, because they have none in God; but the good they do is extorted and drawn from them.

Let us try ourselves therefore. If we have tasted God's good will towards us, *we will have a good pleasure to him again.* Whatsoever is God's pleasure shall be our pleasure; what pleaseth him shall please us. If it please him to exercise us with crosses, and afflictions, and losses, what pleaseth God shall please me; for when he hath once loved me freely in Christ, every thing that comes from him tastes of that free love. If he correct me, it is out of free love and mercy. All the ways of God 'are mercy and truth.' His way of correction and sharp dealing, it is a way of love and free mercy. Therefore, if it please him, it shall please me; my will shall be his will.

Again, If we find the free love of God to us in Christ, *it will quicken us to all duties, and strengthen us in all conditions.* But these evidences shall suffice. Let us search our hearts how we stand affected to God, and to the best things. We delight in them, if God delight in us.

And if we do not find ourselves yet to be the people of God's delight, towards whom God hath thoughts of love, as the prophet speaks, Jer. xxix. 11, what shall we do?

Attend upon the means of salvation, the gospel of peace and reconciliation, and wait the good time, and do not stand disputing. This is that that hinders many, their disputing and cavilling, that perhaps God hath not a purpose to save me, and that the greatest part of mankind go the broad way, &c. Leave disputing, and fall to obeying. God hath a gracious purpose to save all that repent of their sins and believe in Christ. This is gospel. 'I will leave secret things.' 'They belong to God, revealed things belong to me,' Deut. xxix. 29. I will desire of God his Spirit, to repent of my sins, and to believe and cast myself in the arms of his mercy in Christ, and then let God do as he please. If I perish, I will perish in the arms of Christ. Let us labour to bring our hearts to wait in the use of the means, for God's good Spirit to enable me to see my state by nature, and to get out of it, by casting myself upon God's love in Christ.

And *object not the greatness of any sin to hinder the comfort of God's mercy.* It is a free mercy. The ground of it is from himself, and not from thee. It was free to Manassas, that had sinned, no man more. Being a king, and being the son of a good father, his sins spread further than ours can do, answerable to the greatness of his person. Being an infinite and free mercy, it extends to the greatest sinners. Let no man pretend any sin or unworthiness, if he seriously repent. If any sin or unworthiness could keep it back, it were something; but it is a free mercy and love from God's own bowels in Christ.

And consider how God *offers this in the gospel, and lays a command.* It is thy duty to have a good conceit of God in Christ. We ought not to suspect a man that is an honest man; and will God take it well at our hands to suspect him that he is so and so? He makes a show of his love and mercy in Christ, but perhaps he intends it not. Put it out of question by believing. If thou have grace to believe the mercy of God in Christ, thou makest thyself a member of Christ and an heir of heaven. Thou questionest whether thou be one that Christ died for or no? Believe in him, and obey him, and thou puttest that question out of the question. Thou doubtest whether God love thee or no? Cast thyself upon the love of God in Christ, and then it is out of question. Whosoever hath grace to cast himself upon the free love of God, he fulfils the covenant of grace. Stand not disputing and wrangling, but desire grace to obey; and then all questions concerning thy eternal estate are resolved; all is clear.

If these things will not move you, then let all men know, that live in a sinful condition, that they had better have lived in any part of the world than in these glorious times and places of light; for when they hear the love of God in Christ laid open to them, if they will come in and receive Christ, and cast themselves upon him, and be ruled by him, and they will not, it shall be easier for Sodom and Gomorrha, for Jews, and Turks, and pagans, and those that worship devils, than for us. For when God offers his free love and mercy in Christ if we will entertain it, and we will none of it, then justice alone shall not condemn us, but mercy shall condemn us; we will none of mercy. There is not the worst man but would have pardoning mercy. He is content to have God pardon his sin; but he will not take the whole mercy and love of God in Christ, curing, healing mercy. There are those that live in filthy courses, in profaneness, in swearing, &c. It is food to them to be malicious, to deprave the best things. Serpents feed on poison. They are content to have their sins pardoned, if God will let their filthy nature alone,—their poisonful, blasphemous disposition, that exalts itself against God,—and let them go on in their course. They will have one mercy but not another. But we shall never be saved without entire mercy, healing as well as pardoning. Whom God loves, he doth not only pardon their sins, but heals their nature, and makes it like unto Christ's, holy and pure.

Those that have not the Spirit in them, desiring, altering, and changing, and healing grace, as well as pardoning grace, they are hypocrites.

Let us remember this especially, because it is most useful; and most men are deceived in this. They think, Oh, God is merciful, and his love is free in Christ; and though I be unworthy, yet God will have mercy upon me. But hast thou a secret desire to partake of God's whole mercy and love, to make thee good, as well as to make thee his son, and entitle thee to heaven, to have thy nature altered, to see the deformity of sin and the beauty of grace? If thou hadst rather to have the image of God upon thee more than any favour in the world, that thou hadst rather be free from the bondage of sin than any other deliverance: if it be thus, thy state is good.

To hasten; considering God's free love opened now in Jesus Christ, I beseech you, let us study Christ, and labour to get into Christ daily more and more, that we may be members of Christ; and desire God, daily more and more, to reveal himself in Christ to us, that we may see his face in Christ, that we may know him in the sweet relations he hath put on him in the gospel.

To know God in general as a Creator and doing good, &c., the heathens did that by the light of nature; but we should labour to see him in the face of Christ; that is, to see him appeased and loving us, wishing us well. Concerning eternal glory, that must be by the light of the gospel, and by the Spirit. Therefore in hearing of the word, and reading and meditating, desire God above all to reveal by his Spirit his gracious face in Christ; that in Christ we may see him as a Father, as a husband, as a friend, in those sweet relations of love that he hath taken upon him. It should be our daily desire of God to manifest his love more to us in Christ Jesus than in any other fruits of his love; for there be common fruits, as to give us health, and friends, and liberty, and quiet government, which are great favours that we see denied to many nations. Oh, but the soul that is touched with the Spirit of God, and the sense of his own condition by nature, is thus disposed: Lord, I desire that thou wouldst shew the fruits of thy love to me; but I desire not so much those common fruits, that the reprobates may have as well as I. Oh shew me by thy Holy Spirit that thou hast a particular and peculiar love to me in Christ; and for this end give me grace to know the mystery of Christ more and more, and the mystery of my natural corruption, that knowledge that may drive me to make much of thy love and grace in Christ! Now, the Spirit that knows the deep things of God, the depth of God's love to any one in particular, and the depth of our hearts, if we beg the Spirit to reveal the good pleasure of God to us, in time God will shew unto our souls that he delights in us, and that he is our salvation. This shews that the soul is [in] an excellent temper, that it sets a right price and value on things, that it prizeth God's favour above all things. That is the nature of faith; for what is faith? Only to believe in general that Christ died, &c.? No. But to esteem God's love better than all the world; for God's love is entire in pardoning and curing too. By this the soul is raised up to esteem the love and mercy of God in pardoning and healing sin above life itself: Ps. lxiii. 3, 'Thy loving-kindness is better than life.'

To conclude all with this one motive, *the loving-kindness of God;* when we have it once, it is no barren, complimental kindness. It is a loving-kindness that reacheth from everlasting to everlasting, from God's love in choosing to his love in glorifying us. It is a love that reacheth to the filling of nature with all the happiness it is capable of. In this world, in all misery, one beam of God's loving-kindness will scatter all clouds whatsoever. What raised the spirit of Daniel in the lions' den? of the 'three young men' in the midst of the furnace? of St Paul in the dungeon? The beams of God's love in Christ brake into the prison, into the dungeon. A few beams of that will enlarge the heart more than any affliction in the world can cast it down. It is excellent that Moses saith, Deut. xxxiii. 16, 'The good pleasure of him that dwelt in the bush,' &c. You know that God appeared in the bush, when it was flaming. The flaming bush shewed the state of Israel, in the midst of the furnace of persecution; yet notwithstanding the bush was not consumed. Why? Because the good will of God was in the bush. So let us be in any persecution; put case we be like Moses's bush, all on fire; yet the fire shall not consume nor hurt us. Why? The good pleasure of him that dwelt in the bush is with us. In Isa. xliii. 2, 'I will be with thee in the fire, and in the water;' not to keep thee out, but I will be with thee in it. So that in the greatest persecutions that can be, in the fiery trial, as St Peter calls it, 'the good will of him that dwelt in the bush will be with us.' So that we shall not be consumed, though we be in the fire; 'afflicted, but not despair,' 2 Cor. iv. 8. Why? The good pleasure of God dwells in the bush, in the church. In the midst of afflictions and persecutions he is with us. Who can be miserable that hath the presence of God, the favour and good will of God? But this shall be sufficient for this time and text.

NOTES.

(*a*) P. 319.—'What that order is, I confess with St Austin, is undetermined in Scripture; we must not rashly presume to look into these things.' There are well-nigh innumerable allusions to the angels, scattered through the writings of this Father, all distinguished by that reverence and modesty of speculation, so characteristic of him in treating of the 'secret things' of God. Cf. *Indices* of Benedictine edition, *sub voce.*

(*b*) P. 322.—'There is some difference in the readings.' The Vulgate reads εὐδοκίας, its version being 'hominibus bonæ voluntatis.' The reading is found in some of the Fathers. The Syriac version renders 'good tidings to the sons of men.' Sibbes refers probably to both the Vulgate and Syriac. Dean Alford has a pungent note on the the popish adoption of εὐδοκίας.

(*c*) P. 328.—'As Tertullian said in his time: "What! shall we celebrate that which is a public matter of joy to all the church, for a public shame, in a disgraceful way"?' There are many such remonstrances and 'rebukes' in this Father. Cf. 'Apology,' c. xxxix.

(*d*) P. 329.—'As the phrase of some of the ancients is, repentance is a board to escape to the shore, after we have made shipwreck, and done things amiss.' The allusion is to Acts xxvii. 44, a very frequent accommodation with the Puritans.

(*e*) P. 339.—'The heathen could say, *Tranquillus Deus tranquillat omnia.*' We have not fallen in with this expression. Similar ones occur in Seneca, Cicero, and other heathen writers.

(*f*) P. 345.—'For we see how comfortably they speak sometimes upon some notable performance for their country.' Cicero, and Seneca, and later, the 'Thoughts' of the Emperor Marcus Aurelius Antoninus, which have been admirably rendered and interpreted by George Long, M.A. (1 vol. fc. 8vo, Bell and Daldy), furnish examples.

(*g*) P. 347.—'As we see Dives.' It is singular how the *un-named* 'rich man' of the parable has gone down to posterity as *Dives*, the Anglicised form of the Vulgate rendering of πλούσιος.

THE FRUITFUL LABOUR FOR ETERNAL FOOD.

THE FRUITFUL LABOUR FOR ETERNAL FOOD.

NOTE.

'The Fruitful Labour' appeared originally in 'The Beams of Divine Light (4to, 1639). Its separate title-page will be found below.* For general title-page see Vol. V. page 220. G.

*THE
FRVITFULL
LABOVR
FOR
Eternall Foode.
In two Sermons,
By the late Reverend and Learned
Divine RICHARD SIBS,
Doctor in Divinity, Master of Katherine Hall in
Cambridge, and sometimes Preacher at
Grayes-Inne.

ESAY. 55. 2.

Why doe you spend money for that which is not Bread? and your labour for that which satisfieth not? Hearken diligently unto mee, and eate yee that which is good, and let your soule delight it selfe in fatnesse.

JOHN 6. 55.

For my flesh is meate indeed, and my blood is drink indeed.

LONDON,
Printed by *G. M.* for *Nicholas Bourne* and *Rapha Harford*, 1639.

THE FRUITFUL LABOUR FOR ETERNAL FOOD.

Labour not for the meat that perisheth, but for the meat that endureth to everlasting life, which the Son of man shall give you: for him hath God the Father sealed.—John VI. 27.

Our blessed Saviour was mighty in word and deed. Witness what he did, what he taught, and both in this chapter.

What he did. He fed many with a few loaves. He came over the water without any help.

What he taught. Witness from this part of the chapter to the end.

The words are part of an answer of our blessed Saviour to his hypocritical followers, that followed him for the loaves, and not for any confirmation of their faith by his miracles. For upon occasion of those two miracles —mentioned in the former part of the chapter—they followed him; and perceiving that he was miracnlously come over the water, they began to ask him, 'Rabbi, how camest thou here? Our Saviour perceives that they meant to compliment with him. He sees with what hearts they came after him. Therefore, as most befitting the exigence of their state, because they were hypocrites, he answers, not to their question, but to their persons, 'Verily, verily, ye seek me, not because of the miracles, but because ye ate of the loaves, and were filled. Labour not for the meat that perisheth,' &c.

The verses together contain a conviction, and an injunction or direction.

A conviction, and that is serious and loving. *Serious*, 'Verily, verily, I say unto you, ye seek me, not because of the miracles, but because ye ate of the loaves,' &c. He convinceth them of their fault, of their hypocrisy, of their wicked and carnal aims in holy business. They come flattering of Christ: but as he was too holy to flatter, so he was too wise to be flattered. He deals therefore directly with them, thoroughly convinceth them of their hypocrisy and corrupt aims in following after him. We are all naturally prone to these carnal ends in holy actions. We must take heed with what minds, with what hearts, we come before God, whose eyes are brighter than the sun, who regards not so much what we do, as with what minds we do it.

As his conviction is serious, so it is loving; for with the *conviction or reproof follows the injunction or direction*, 'Labour not for the meat that perisheth.'

In the injunction there are two things:

First, He shews them what they should not follow. He takes them off from labouring after 'the meat that perisheth.'

And then, secondly, he instructs them in what they should follow, what they should seek after: 'but labour for the meat that endureth to everlasting life,' &c.

There are arguments in both. In the first, there is an argument dissuasive, and that is unfolded: 'Labour not for the meat that perisheth,' because it is meat that perisheth.

In the second, there are arguments persuasive, or enforcing to the duty, and they are three,

The necessity.

The excellency.

The possibillity of attaining.

The necessity. It is meat; and what so necessary as meat?

The excellency; and that is set forth, first, by the continuance. It is 'meat that endures.' Secondly, by the fruit or effect of it. It is 'meat that endures to everlasting life.' It is meat to life, and it is meat that tends to an everlasting, to a glorious life.

The possibility of attaining it. 'The Son of man shall give it you: for him hath the Father sealed.'

There are three things that must concur to make a thing attainable, and to be had:

A willingness in the giver.

Power and strength to give it.

And then authority with power.

Here are all these. *Here is will to bestow it.* He will give it. What freer than a gift? The Son of God became the Son of man upon purpose to give it. He will give it, and he will give it freely.

Here is *power and strength to give it;* for he is the Son of God as well as the Son of man.

And then here *is authority joined with that power*, for 'the Father hath sealed him.' The Father that created heaven and earth, that hath all power in his hands, that is King of kings and Lord of lords, 'he hath sealed him.' He hath given him full commission to be the Saviour of all that trust in him. Christ came not without authority from God the Father. He came out with God's broad seal as his commission.

So you see the arguments, both dissuasive, 'Labour not for the meat that perisheth,' and persuasive, 'but for the meat that endureth to everlasting life.' I shall but touch the former, and principally insist upon the latter branch."

To speak a little for the explication or the words. What is here meant by the 'meat that perisheth'?

We must enlarge the sense according to our Saviour's meaning. By 'the meat that perisheth,' he doth not intend only outward food, but all outward things whatsoever, they are the 'meat that perisheth.' All earthly and outward things are the food that the soul of a natural man feeds upon. The soul of a covetous man feeds upon his money, applauding himself that he is worth so much and so much. The ambitious man, chameleon-like, feeds upon the air, upon the airy applause of the people. The sensual man feeds upon base and sensual pleasures. In a word, all carnal men, natural men, are condemned to that sentence of the serpent, 'to eat dust,' to feed upon outward, earthly, perishing things. So that everything that is not grace and glory, or the means that lead to it, is a perishing thing.

Nay, to raise it a little higher, learning and knowledge, if it be only of perishing things, is food that perisheth; for as the frame of nature and the civil frame of the world must have an end and perish, so the knowledge of natural and civil things must needs be perishing also.

And to say no more, the very knowledge, the speculative and contemplative knowledge of religious things, if we have only the knowledge of the things in us, and are not turned into the things we know, is a perishing thing. The truths of God indeed are the food of the soul, but unless the goodness of those truths be the food of the will and affections, unless we are moulded and fashioned into the very form of those truths, unless we are framed to a love and liking of that which we know, that those truths be rooted and planted in us, it is 'food that perisheth.'

In a religious discourse, in preaching, all your ornaments, besides that which quickeneth and strengtheneth the soul to holy duties, is 'food that perisheth.' And your hearing, if it be only to hear witty sentences and turnings of speech, without regard to the truth itself, is 'food that perisheth.' Thus you see what a great latitude this food that perisheth hath in Christ's meaning.

Now our blessed Saviour takes them off from labouring for this by a strong argument. Would you have a greater argument? 'It is food that perisheth.' We do not regard the lustre of things, but their continuance. Why do we esteem of crystal more than glass? Because it continues. Flowers have a goodly gloss, but we regard them little, because they are fresh in the morning, and cast away at evening. And so it is with all excellencies, unless it be grace or glory. All flesh is grass, and the excellentest things of nature, wit, and honour, and learning, and all, though they be not as grass so common, yet they are as 'the flower of the grass; they are all fading and withering; but the word of God endureth for ever;' that is, the grace and comfort that we get by the blessed truths of God, 'that endures for ever,' and it makes us endure for ever. But all other things are food that perisheth, and we perish in the use of them. 'The world passeth away, and the concupiscence of it;' the world, the things lusted after perish; and in lusting after the world, the lust perisheth, and we perish too in the pursuit of them; nay, which is worse, the immoderate seeking after these things destroy us: we eternally perish. For by placing our affections on earthly things we turn earthly. Therefore in divinity we have our denomination from our affections. We are called good or ill, not from our knowledge, but from our affections. The devil knows good, but he is not good. It is loving, and joying, and delighting in good or ill that makes us good or ill. We have our form and being in religion from our affections.

Now by seeking after and placing our affections, that are ordained to close with better things—which shall make us happy in another world—by planting them on earthly things, we become like the things, earthly; by placing them on the world, we become the world, we become earthly. Therefore they are not only perishing in themselves, but we perish in the pursuit of them. It is a strong argument that is here used. All earthly things are 'food that perisheth.' For, alas! he that is rich to-day may be poor to-morrow. He may be as rich as Job in the morning, and as poor as Job at night. He may be in credit now with Haman, and be in discredit ere soon. He may be in health now, and sick ere long. We need not Scripture for this. Experience reads us this lecture enough; but we are so desperately set on earthly things, that neither faith nor experience, nor the strength of discourse, nor reason, is sufficient to take us off, till God by his Spirit convince us thoroughly of this. Therefore Moses prays that 'God would teach them to number their days,' Ps. xc. 12. So, though there is a sufficient argument in the discovery of these earthly things to be perishing things to enforce a dissuasion, yet we cannot loosen our affections to them, nor know the uncertainty of them till God teach us.

To make some use of this in a word, and so to go on to that which I more intend. If all things here below be grass, and as the flower of the grass, perishing and fading things, why then we should *take heed that we do not redeeem any perishing thing with the loss of that which doth not perish, with the loss of this soul of ours*, which is an eternal spiritual substance, breathed in by God in the creation, and redeemed by Christ; which is capable of immortality, capable of happiness, capable of the blessed impression of the image of God. 'What if one should gain the whole world,' saith Christ, that knows the price of a soul best, 'and should lose his own soul!' It is an argument sufficient even to a man that is led but with the strength of natural reason, not to labour for that which will perish, when he hath a soul that will not perish. To labour after that thing as his main chief good, that is of shorter continuance than himself, is extremity of folly. Therefore no carnal man, that seeks after these perishing things, can ever be a wise man, because he hath an end inferior to himself. He may be wise for particular ends, to be rich, to have great places, to get his pleasure. This is to be wise for particular ends. But he cannot be wise for the chief, and last, and best end, for his soul, for eternity. He cannot direct his course that way, that labours for the 'food that perisheth.'

And again, we should not pass* *to neglect any earthly thing, to gain advantage of our souls*, because they are perishing things. We should force ourselves to contentment in the loss of earthly things for the gain of spiritual. The loss of things perishing is an easy matter. We lose things that will perish whether we lose them or not. All earthly things perish either in our time or after us. We should not therefore be over-eager in getting of these earthly things. Let us leave things that perish to men that perish. You see therefore how strong a reason our Saviour Christ allegeth here, 'Labour not for the meat that perisheth, because it perisheth.'

And learn here from our blessed Saviour *a point of heavenly wisdom*. You see when he would take us off and dissuade us from the pursuit of earthly things, he takes an argument from the nature of them. They are perishing things; and therefore, when we look upon the outward lustre of earthly things, we should withal consider the perishing nature of them. When we are tempted to too much delight in the creature, we should present to ourselves the perishing and fading nature of outward things. When we are tempted to sin, either to commit or to leave that which is good for anything that is outward, we should consider, What do I now? I stain my soul, I crack my conscience, I contract guilt and grounds of terror for the time to come for that which is perishing. It is always good to have present to our souls and to our fancies the nature of earthly things, that they may be as present as the temptation that Satan from them urgeth and forceth upon the soul. It is good always to remember that they are perishing things, and that as they are perishing in themselves, so they will destroy us, cause us to perish in the pursuit of them. But my meaning is not to dwell long upon this.

* That is, = 'hesitate.'—G.

'Labour not for the meat that perisheth.'

What! Doth Christ mean that we should not labour at all for earthly things? Doth he read a lecture of ill husbandry, and unthriftiness, and negligence?

No. He doth as we do. When we would set a crooked thing straight, we bend it as much the contrary way. Our Saviour saw that they were desperately addicted to earthly things, that they followed him for their bellies, sought him for the loaves, therefore he bends the stick the contrary way: 'Labour not for the meat that perisheth;' that is, labour not for it in comparison of better things; labour not so inordinately, so immoderately, labour not so unseasonably. It is said of the Israelites that they brought Egypt into the wilderness, because they brought the love of the garlic and onions of Egypt with them, Num. xi. 5. We have many come to the church, to these holy exercises, to this holy place, but they bring the world with them. They come with carnal affections. Labour not so unseasonably. It should be our heavenly wisdom to lay aside importunate earthly thoughts of earthly things; to drive them away, as Abraham did the birds from the sacrifice, Gen. xv. 11. We should leave them as he did the beasts and his servants, at the bottom of the mount, when he went up to sacrifice unto God, Gen. xxii. 5. Thus, labour not; labour not immoderately; labour not inordinately; labour not unseasonably.

But how shall we know when our labour is immoderate, unseasonable, and inordinate after earthly things?

I answer, In a word, when they either hinder us from, or hinder us in, holy things; when they keep us from holy duties, as from the sanctifying of the Lord's day, or from any other service of God; or when they hinder us in them; when they fill us full of distractions; when they turn the soul from the business in hand, &c. Thus, when they do either hinder us from or hinder us in better things, we may know we offend against this dissuasion of Christ. 'Labour not for the meat that perisheth.'

But why doth our Saviour begin first with his dissuasion, 'Labour not for the meat that perisheth,' and then enjoin what they should seek after, but 'for the meat that endureth to everlasting life'?

Because he saw that their souls were corrupted, and desperately set upon the seeking after earthly things; and when the soul is invested to anything, there must first be a removal of that; as in ground, the thorns must first be rooted out before there be any sowing of seed; and in bodily distempers, there must first be a purging of the malignant humour before there be any cordials given. So Christ, he first takes them off from an immoderate and inordinate seeking after the world and earthly things, and then he directs them what they should do, what they should seek after: 'Seek the food that endures to everlasting life.'

Here is the prerogative of Christianity. A heathen man, out of the strength of moral discourse and outward experience, can teach the negative part, can tell you that all earthly things are vain and perishing. A stoic will declaim wittily and gravely from moral principles and daily experience upon these things; that these earthly things of themselves are all vain and fading, and that it is our conceit of them only that bewitcheth us to them: it is that only that renders them to us green and fresh. But now for the affirmative part, what we should seek after; here paganism is blind. That is only to be learned in the church of Christ. It is proper to Christianity to direct us here, as I shall discover better to you when I come to speak of the duty enjoined, which is that I especially aim at.

But before I come to enforce the act or duty which our Saviour here exhorts unto, I must unfold the object of that act: what is meant here by the 'meat that endures to everlasting life.'

The 'meat that endures to everlasting life' is our blessed Saviour Christ Jesus, as he is contained and wrapped up in the means of salvation, with all the blessed liberties, privileges, and prerogatives, graces, and comforts, that we have by him and in him. For our blessed Saviour never goes alone. He is never embraced naked; but with him goes his graces, comforts, prerogatives, and liberties. We have him not now as we shall see him 'face to face' hereafter in heaven; but he is to be considered as wrapped up in the word and sacraments. So is Christ the food that lasts to everlasting life. And in this latitude we must take it, or else we mistake and straiten the Holy Ghost.

But why is our blessed Saviour so considered, and the comforts, and prerogatives, and good things we have by him, termed food?

In divers respects. To instance in a few. But, first, you must know that as the soul hath a life as well as the body, so it hath a taste as well as the body; and as God, lest the body should pine away, hath planted in it an appetite, which is the body's longing after that which refresheth it—for if it were not for appetite, if it were not for hunger and thirst, who would care for meat and drink?—so God hath planted in the soul, lest it should pine away, a spiritual appetite, an earnest longing and desiring after that which is the most necessary good of the soul; for the soul hath that which the body hath, taste, and smell, &c., though in a more sublime and divine sense, but as really and truly, as we shall see afterwards. Now our blessed Saviour is this spiritual food of the soul. He is the bread of life that came down from heaven; he is the true manna; he is the true tree of life in paradise, in the church of God, the true paradise. He is the true shew-bread; he is the true Lamb of God.

He, considered with all the blessed prerogatives, and privileges, and comforts we have by him, is called meat or food for divers respects.

First, *Whatsoever sweetness, or comfort, or strength there is in meat, it is for the comfort, and strength, and good of the body;* so whatsoever is comfortable and cherishing in Christ, as indeed all comfort and cherishing is in him, it is for our good; to us he is given, for us he was born: 'To us a child is born, to us a Son is given,' Isa. ix. 6; all is for us, for us men, for us sinners. There is nothing in his natures, in his state and condition, both of abasement and exaltation, nothing in his offices, but it is all for our good. Consider him in his human nature, and join with his nature his abasement: that he was man, that he took upon him our nature, that he was abased in it, that he humbled himself to death, even to the death of the cross, to be a sacrifice for our sins; how doth the soul feed on this, on the wonderful love of God in giving Christ to be incarnate, and then to die for us! How doth the soul feed upon the death of Christ, because by that God's wrath is appeased, and he reconciled! 'Where the dead body is, there the eagles resort,' Mat. xxiv. 28. So doth the soul prey and feed upon the dead body of Christ. Christ crucified is the special food of the soul.

Consider him in his exaltation, in his glorious resurrection and ascension into heaven; how doth the soul feed upon that? Christ our surety has risen again. Therefore our debt is discharged, the justice of God is satisfied to the full. So for his ascension. When the soul is basely-minded on earthly things, it ascends to Christ, who is taken up to heaven for us.

So his sitting at the right hand of God. The soul feeds on that, because he sits there till he have triumphed over all his enemies, till he have trod them all under foot.

Consider him in his offices. In ignorance the soul feeds on him as a prophet to instruct it. In the sense of wrath and anger, the soul feeds on him as a priest to make peace and reconciliation. In want of righteousness, the soul feeds on his righteousness: 'he is our righteousness.' In the sense of corruption, the soul feeds on him as a king, that by his Spirit will ere long work out all corruption; that as he will tread down all our enemies without, so he will tread down all corruption within. He will never leave the soul till he have made it a glorious house, fit for himself.

So the prerogatives we have by him, the soul feeds on them, feeds on his redemption; that by his redemption we are freed from our enemies and all that hate us, and all that we feared; that we are set at liberty from the law, from sin, and from death; and notwithstanding all the debasements of this world, we are 'the sons of God and heirs of heaven.'

In a word, whatsoever is in Christ is for our good. He is all mine; his life is mine; his death is mine; his resurrection is mine; his ascension is mine; all is mine. He is expended and laid open for my good. That is the first.

Again, As in the bodily life *there is a stomach, a power to work out of the meat that which is for strength and nourishment*, so in the soul there is faith, the spiritual mouth and stomach of the soul, to work and draw out of Christ whatsoever is for the comfort and nourishment of it. As there is comfort in Christ, so the Spirit of God gives a man a hand, a mouth, as it were; gives a man faith to work out of Christ somewhat for comfort. What were food if there were not a stomach to digest it, to make it a man's own? So what were Christ if we had not faith to lay hold on him?

Again, thirdly, *As our life is nourished and maintained with that which is dead, with dead things*, so the chief dish that maintaineth and nourisheth the life of the soul, as I said before, is 'Christ crucified.' 'God forbid,' saith the apostle, 'that I should rejoice in anything but in Christ crucified.' When the soul of a poor sinner is pursued with accusations from Satan and his own conscience, when they take part with God against him, whither runs it? To the city of refuge. It runs to Christ, to Christ crucified. Thither the soul flies, being pursued with the guilt of sin; 'to the horns of the altar,' as Joab did when he was pursued, but with better success, for he was pulled from thence, 1 Kings ii. 28. But the soul that flies to Christ crucified, to the death of Christ, to Christ abased, to his satisfying the wrath of God by his death, and making of us friends with God, there it holds; there it lives; and there it will continue for ever. This keeps the soul alive.

And then again, *as in meat, before it can nourish us, there must be an union, an assimilation, a turning of it into us*, so Christ, except he be made one with us by faith, unless there be an union between him and us, he can never nourish and comfort us savingly.

Again, *As we oft eat, and after we have received food once, yet we eat again every day, because there is a decay of strength—and there are still new businesses, new occasions that require new strength—and therefore there is need of a continual repairing of our strength by food*, even so there is a perpetual exigence, a continual need that the soul hath to feed upon Christ, upon the promises of Christ, and the prerogatives by Christ, because every day we have fresh impediments, fresh assaults, and therefore we have need to fetch fresh supplies and refreshment from Christ, to have meat from Christ every day; to live on Christ not only at the first, but continually; that as our corruptions, and temptations, and infirmities return every day, so every day to feed on Christ for the repairing of our spiritual strength. Especially we are to make daily use of the death of Christ; for howsoever the death of Christ be transient in respect of the act of it, as one of the ancients saith (*a*), yet the fruit of it remains for our daily comfort and refreshment. His blood runs every day in the church afresh, like a fountain always poured out, for Judah and Jerusalem to wash in, Zech. xiii. 1. It always runs; that is, in regard of God's imputation, in regard of the fruit that comes to the soul; and therefore we should make daily use of it for the comfort and strength of our souls upon all occasions. 'We have an advocate with the Father, Jesus Christ the righteous: and he is the propitiation for our sins,' 1 John ii. 1. He is now an intercessor in heaven; he continually applies the fruit of his death now by his intercession in heaven.

Again, As, *after meat received and eaten, there is strength and comfort gotten for the affairs of this life*, so likewise after the soul hath digested and relished Christ, and the benefits and prerogatives that come by him, after we have made the heavenly truths of Christ our own, the soul is strengthened to holy duties. It is fit to do; it is fit to suffer; it is fit to resist temptations; it is fit to perform all the services of Christianity.

In these and divers other respects Christ is the blessed meat here mentioned; not himself alone, but considered with all the blessed good things which we have by him. For Christ, as I said before, is never alone. If we have him, we are sons in him; we are heirs in him; we are free in him; we are redeemed in him; we are kings in him; priests in him; prophets in him; we are all in him; we have with him all the good things that he hath; for as we have not them without him, so we have not him without them. Those that have the field, have the pearl in the field; and they that have the pearl in the field, have the field. They that have Christ, have Christ clothed with all his blessed prerogatives, and privileges, and comforts.

But wherein lieth the difference between this meat, this food of the soul, and other meat?

In these things. First of all, *Christ, as he is from heaven, so all the graces and comforts that we have by him are all from heaven*, and they carry us to heaven. All the other things are earthly.

Secondly, *All earthly food doth not give, but maintain life where it is; but Christ he is such a food as gives life.* He is as well life as food: 'I am the life,' John xi. 25.

Again, thirdly, *The nourishment we have from this outward food, we turn to ourselves; but Christ, this spiritual meat, turns us into himself*, transforms us into his own likeness; for Christ offered to us in the gospel being digested by faith, doth by his Spirit change us every way into his own likeness.

Lastly, *All other meats are consumed in the spending, and there will a time come when we shall not be able to relish any worldly thing; our mouth will be out of taste with these outward things.* But Christ, the food of the soul, is never consumed, but grows more and more; and when we can relish no other, we may relish this food that endures to everlasting life. It always satisfies the soul. All earthly things are as salt water, that increase the appetite, but satisfy not. Only Christ and grace, and the comforts we have by him, satisfy, and that everlastingly. They are as a spring that never dies.

As he himself in his own person endures to everlasting life, so all that we have by him is everlasting. Grace is everlasting. Grace ends in glory. Christ always satisfies, though not wholly here, because there must be a continual recourse to him; yet he will satisfy hereafter. 'Blessed are they that hunger and thirst after righteousness, for they shall be satisfied,' Mat. v. 6.

Thus you see what is meant by the 'food that endures to everlasting life,' and the reason of the resemblance and the difference that is between this and other meat.

Here are arguments enough then to enforce us to a labouring after this meat that endures to everlasting life, that is so agreeable to the best part of us, that is able to make us happy; to labour by faith to get them to be our own.

Now the labour required is especially to get a stomach to this meat. God requires nothing of us when we come to his delicacies but that we bring a good stomach with us. I will therefore speak a little of that, what we must do to get an appetite to this spiritual meat.

A good stomach, we know, is procured *by sharp things*. The paschal lamb was 'to be eaten with sour herbs,' Exod. xii. 8. If we would have an appetite after Christ, labour daily to consider what a cursed estate we are in without Christ. God hath left the law, as for other purposes, so for this, that we should feed upon the threatenings of it, that it should drive us to Christ. A legal faith is the way to evangelical. Labour therefore thoroughly to be convinced of the need thou standest in of Christ, and then I need not bid thee to labour for the food that endures to everlasting life. That will sharpen thy appetite after it. And beg of God illumination to see the ill that is in thee, and the ill that belongs to thee. God hath left infirmities and corruptions in us on purpose for this end, and likewise we have temptations without us. We carry not only a hell within us, which if God should not keep in would carry us to despair; but there is a hell without us, the temptations of Satan, the accusations of the law, the anger and wrath of God. Thus we should labour to be convinced of our wretched estate without Christ, the danger we are in if God should take us hence on a sudden. This will force every day a fresh appetite and stomach in the soul to feed on Christ.

Secondly, If we would sharpen our appetites to this food, *we must purge our stomachs*, which naturally surfeit of earthly things. Purge the soul by a consideration of the vanity of all other things that draw us from Christ. The reason why we have no better relish of Christ and heavenly things is, because we cleave in our affections so much to earthly things. We set up idols in our hearts instead of Christ, and we cleave in an adulterous and false affection unto them. Let us set before us arguments of the vanity of all things but Christ; and there can be no better argument than here is set down, 'they are all perishing things.' That which the soul neglects Christ, and heaven, and happiness for, and is so madly set upon, alas! they are all base in respect of the soul. The whole world is not worth a soul. They are all perishing things, of less continuance than the soul is. We should purge our souls by such considerations as these.

Then again, thirdly, *exercise getting a stomach*. Let us every day spend our spiritual strength in spiritual exercises, in resisting temptations, in withstanding the snares of Satan, in bearing those daily crosses that God lays upon us. Live as Christians should live, and the exercise of a Christian life will enforce us to go unto Christ to feed on him, to fetch from him spiritual strength. When in our daily exercise we shall see the continual need we have of pardon for daily sins, of comfort and strength against daily corruptions and infirmities, this will make us feed on Christ and on the promises made in him—not only on the promise of forgiveness, but on the promise of a supply of necessary grace, on that sweet promise, that 'he will not quench the smoking flax, nor break the bruised reed,' Mat. xii. 20—feed on him as a King to subdue our corruptions, &c. The daily exercise of a Christian life will force us unto Christ.

Again, To whet our appetite after Christ, *consider the necessity we have of spiritual strength and comfort.* When a man considers that he hath a journey to take, he will eat to enable him to his journey; as Elias was bid to rise up and eat, because he had a journey to go, 1 Kings xix. 7. We are all to take a journey as far as heaven, and we are to travel through the wilderness of this world; and we shall be daily assaulted, besides our inward corruptions, with divers temptations; and therefore we had need every day to fetch strength from Christ. And consider that sickness will come, and death will surprise us; and if we have not Christ, we are wretched creatures without him. And though we have applied Christ to ourselves, and made him our own, yet a time of desertion, a time of trial, will come. Thus the necessity of spiritual strength will force us to feed upon Christ.

Again, To get us a stomach to these things, *let us converse with those that are spiritual, with those that are heavenly-minded*, 'that have tasted of heavenly things,' Heb. vi. 4. When we see them delight in reading, delight in hearing; when we see them contemplate of heaven and heavenly things, on Christ and the benefits we have by Christ, on the blessed condition of a better life, and of the world to come; when we see these persons that are better than ourselves, that have less cause than we, take such pains for their souls, we will be ashamed of our own neglect; and it will be the discourse of a soul presently with itself, Surely there is some excellent strength and comfort in these things, some extraordinary sweetness and refreshment that these men find, that they so fall to them. It is a great advantage to converse with those that are spiritual.

And lastly, To put an edge to our dull appetites after this food, *consider we know not how soon this table that Christ hath spread, these dainties that wisdom hath provided for us in the ministry of the word, may be taken from us.* Therefore, let us fall to while we have them. We should do as those do, that, being at a feast, and have neglected feeding, at the latter end, when they see all ready to be taken away, fall to afresh. We know not how long we may enjoy these blessed opportunities. Therefore now with Joseph, let us lay up against a time of scarcity. There will a hard winter come. Therefore, let us imitate the wisdom of that poor creature the ant, to provide against winter, Prov. vi. 6. Now, while the jubilee is, let us take out a pardon. There is a time of spending to come; now let us 'get oil in our lamps,' Mat. xxv. 4. Now is the seed time; now are the waters stirred in the pool of Bethesda; now is the acceptable time of grace. We know not how long it shall continue. Therefore, now let us labour for the food 'that endureth to everlasting life.' I never knew any repent of the pains they had taken for their souls; but many that have lamented and bewailed the precious time they have spent, and that they have not been good husbands for their souls. It is one special point of heavenly wisdom to take advantage of our precious time, to fill it up with holy exercises. Let us often offer this consideration to our souls, Wherefore was I sent hither into this world? What is the end why I live here? Is it to scrape together perishing things, and so to perish with them? Or am I not rather sent hither to get out of the state of corruption wherein we all are by nature? to get into Christ, to make him mine own, to be turned into him, to feed on him, to get joy, and comfort, and strength from him? Is not this the end why I live here?

But to go on, and to make an use of trial, whether we have, as we should do, relished and tasted Christ, whether we have fed on this meat or no. How shall we know that?

I answer, We may easily know it. For, first of all, if we have relished Christ and the good things by him, *we disrelish all other things; we begin to have a baser esteem of all earthly things.* It is with the soul as it is with a balance. When Christ is high in the soul, other things are low; and when other things are high, Christ is low in the soul. Christ was high in Paul's soul; therefore he esteemed all as 'dung' in comparison of the excellent knowledge of Christ, Philip. iii. 8. The poor woman of Samaria, when she had heard Christ, and tasted the sweetness that was in him, down goes her water-pot, and she runs to the city and tells them, 'I have seen a man that hath told me all things; is not this the Messiah?' John iv. 29. Zaccheus, when he had tasted of grace, and had the pardon of his sins by Christ, 'half my goods I give to the poor,' &c., Luke xix. 8. When grace is planted in the soul, when the soul hath tasted once of better things, there will be a mean and base esteem of earthly things. The more the soul feeds on heavenly things, the less respect it hath to temporal things. The soul is a finite essence, and it cannot spend itself on all things. The more it runs into severals, the more shallow it is to others; as in a stream, when it is cut into many channels it runs weakly in the several, whereas it runs strongly in the main. So it is with the soul: when it is scattered, as the poor Israelites were about the land of Egypt to gather straw, to gather these perishing earthly things, it is weak to heavenly things; it hath little strength to those. But when the course of it is wholly bent to those, there are but weak or no desires running to these earthly things. When once the soul of a Christian hath had a true taste and relish of the things of heaven, it looks with a despising eye upon whatsoever is here below. When once it hath tasted of Christ, then especially it grows out of relish with poison; then away with popery! away with false doctrine! away with hypocrisy and formality in religion!

Again, secondly, We may know that we have tasted Christ, and fed on him, and on the good things that are by him, *when we are strengthened by our feeding; when we are strengthened to duties; strengthened against tentations* and against corruptions.* Thou sayest thou believest on Christ, and hast made him thine own; what comfort and strength feelest thou by Christ? Art thou able to encounter a tentation? Art thou able to resist a lust? Art thou able to perform holy services? If there be no strength in thee, but every tentation turns thee over, and thou yieldest to every base lust, where is Christ? Canst thou believe Christ to be thy King, and yet suffer thy lusts to bear sway in thee? Canst thou believe that Christ is a priest that died for thy sins, and yet cherishest and lovest sin? Canst thou believe that Christ is in heaven, and that thou art in heavenly places with Christ, and yet hast no mind of heavenly things, but art carried away with every earthly thing? No. Thou hast not yet tasted how good and gracious the Lord is; thou hast not relished the heavenly manna. The

* That is, 'temptations.'—G.

soul that feeds on Christ is strengthened from spiritual reasons, and supernatural grounds, and divine principles drawn from Christ, to duty, so that it is enabled even with a holy violence to do anything for Christ's sake; for the soul reasons thus: Christ gave himself to death for me; I will therefore, if need be, give myself to death for him. Christ thought nothing too dear for me, I will think nothing too dear for him. This pride, this vanity that I am tempted to, these were the spears that were the death of my Saviour. Thus the soul fetches reasons from the death of Christ to strengthen it against temptations, to strengthen it to duty; and so for the matter of comfort. After meat hath been received we are refreshed. If the soul be sweetly refreshed with the comforts that are to be had in Christ, and in the word of Christ, it is a sign we have tasted Christ. Those that have trembling and discouraging hearts and souls, that cannot rest nor receive comfort, it is a sign they have not rightly tasted Christ. 'Come unto me,' saith Christ, 'all ye that are weary and heavy laden, and ye shall find rest to your souls,' Mat. xi. 28. In Christ there is rest, out of Christ there is no rest. And so likewise those that have corruptions bearing sway in them. It is a sign they have not so much as touched Christ, for if they had but touched Christ, he would stop the issue of their corruptions. The poor woman in the gospel, as soon as she had touched Christ, her bloody issue was stayed; so, upon the least touch of Christ by faith, there will be an abating of corruption.

Thirdly, In the bodily life, we know after a good meal *the desire and appetite is satisfied*, so the soul that tastes of Christ, it hath sweet satisfaction and contentment. Oh the sweet satisfaction that a Christian soul hath above a heathen! A Christian, that hath Christ, need not go out of him for anything. It hath fulness and satisfaction in him in all estates, both in life and in death. Dost thou find Christ, and the privileges and prerogatives we have by him; dost thou find the word of Christ and the promises of the word fully and sufficiently satisfy thee? Then it argues that thou hast fed on Christ; for Christ being received by faith into the soul, gives it fulness and contentment.

Lastly, To name no more, as men, if they have the grace of God in their hearts, *will give thanks for their bodily food*, so it is an evidence that we have fed on Christ, when our hearts and tongues are enlarged to praise God for Christ, for the comforts, and contentment, and satisfaction that we find in him and in religion. Therefore St Paul begins his epistle to the Ephesians with 'Blessed be God the Father of our Lord Jesus Christ, who hath blessed us with all spiritual blessings in heavenly places in Christ,' Eph. i. 3. And St Peter, being led by the same blessed Spirit, his heart being full, his mouth is full of thanks: 'Blessed be God the Father of our Lord Jesus Christ, who hath begotten us again to an inheritance immortal, that fadeth not away, reserved for you in the heavens,' 1 Peter i. 4, for you that are reserved by faith to salvation. So, undoubtedly, the soul that tastes the sweet comforts of religion in Christ will be much in sweet enlargements of heart in thanksgiving. It cannot be otherwise. It is an universal reason. The more believing a soul is, the more thankful a soul is. Where there is no praise, there is no faith.

Thus you see how we may try whether we have tasted and relished, whether we have fed upon 'the food that endures to everlasting life' or no.

Taste is the most necessary sense of all, saith a wise searcher of the mysteries of nature: our life is maintained by taste (*b*). Every creature sees not, every creature hears not, but every creature hath taste. You may judge of yourselves by your taste and relish; and if once you have tasted and relished Christ, all the world cannot persuade you to fall from him. If all should say there were no sweetness in religion, that it were better to be a worldling, &c., you would defy* it; you would never believe it. There is no disputing against what a man tastes. If all men should say sugar were sharp, if I once tasted it I would say otherwise.

'Labour for the meat that endures to everlasting life.'

The arguments enforcing this act upon the object to labour for Christ are, that he is food, and food that endures; 'and food that endures to everlasting life.'

Let me from these arguments here in the text, for I will draw no other, enforce what I have said before. I have shewed you what this labour is, and rules how you may know whether you rightly labour for this food or no. Now to enforce this act, consider, first, the necessity of that our Saviour here enjoins us to; *it is food.*

It is a strange thing that persons should persuade themselves that they are Christians, and yet go from day to day without refreshing themselves with Christ, and with the meditation of the blessed estate they are in by him, both in respect of this world and that which is to come; without getting strength from Christ against tentations and against corruptions. Christ is food, and the promises and prerogatives we have by him are food. We should labour after it every day, feed on it every day. If a man should ask a man in his calling, Why do you take such pains, morning and evening, rising early and going to bed late? he would answer, It is to get bread; it is to get food to maintain my family. So should it be our answer to any that wonder why we take such pains for our souls, why we labour so after Christ. Oh, remember we take pains for life; to get and maintain life; and what is so necessary as life? And if life be so necessary, food which preserves it must be necessary. We see the patriarchs for food left their country; and the poor Egyptians sold themselves and their cattle, and all to get food to keep life. We famish eternally except we feed on Christ; except we have so much faith as makes us one with him; except by faith we digest him and get nourishment and strength from him. It will appear to be so when it is too late. Ere long nothing in the world will relish us; and then if we have not Christ and the things of another life to relish us, what will become of us? I beseech you, consider what opinion and judgment we shall have ere long of these earthly things, and of the better things of another world. At the hour of death, our judgments will be convinced that the things of heaven are the best things; and if it be true that they will be so then, why is it not true that they are so now? Labour to have the same judgment now.

With the necessity our blessed Saviour joineth the excellency of this food, 'It is food *that endures to everlasting life.*' Christ and the good things we have by him are of equal extent and of equal time with our souls. If we labour for earthly things, we labour after that which is of shorter continuance than our souls. We may outlive our happiness, and what a miserable state is that! But if we labour for the food that endures to everlasting life, our happiness is of the same continuance with our souls, and that is only true happiness.

If there were such a tree upon the earth now as there was in paradise, a tree of life, that whosoever should taste of the fruit of it should live,

* That is, in the literal sense, = disbelieve.—Ed.

though but on the earth here to enjoy his sensual pleasures, oh what would not men give for a little fruit of that tree, though it were to redeem a little time, and to lengthen out a fading, base life on earth, but much more to live for ever! Here is food 'that endures to everlasting life,' to such a life as is heavenly and glorious. Now, blessed be God that since we are cast out of the first paradise by sin, that now in our relapsed estate God is so merciful to us as to provide another manner of tree of life. That in paradise was but a typical tree. The true tree of life is Christ; and whosoever feeds on him shall not perish, but have everlasting life. Certainly if we believed this, it could not be, but it would wondrously set us on to labour after this meat, because it is not only food that tends to the preservation of life, but to life everlasting, to a life that endures as long as our souls.

And let us know that if we do not labour for this meat that brings to this life, look what degree of excellency we have had in the rank of the creatures, the same degree we shall have in misery; for as the angels in the degree of excellency were the most excellent creatures, but being fallen they are in the same degree of misery that they were in happiness, and are now the most accursed creatures of all others, so man, as he is a most excellent creature, if he feed on the food that endures to everlasting life; so if like Nebuchadnezzar he feed as a beast on earthly things, and forget his soul and affections, which are made to close and feed on Christ and better things, he shall have the same degree of misery that he hath in happiness, even next to the devils, the most wretched creature that can be. What if a man were clad as Aaron was in all his pontificality, in his priestly robes! What if he should feed deliciously every day as Dives! What and if he had the wisdom of Solomon, the strength of Samson! What and if he had all the kingdoms of the world! If he have not the 'food that endures to everlasting life,' he should be stripped of all these ere long. It is only Christ, and the good things that are to be had in him and by him, that continue everlastingly.

This should enforce us to labour after this food in the use of all good means. And before I leave the point, consider the reality, the truth of these heavenly things, of these things we have by Christ, 'the second Adam,' all things else are shadows. The food that nourisheth the body is not food in comparison of that. Earthly kingdoms are not kingdoms in respect of that; earthly sonship is not sonship to that; earthly riches they are nothing, they are vanity in comparison of that. Earthly inheritance is no inheritance in comparison of the inheritance we have by Christ. All other things are but titles of things. They are but empty things. There is a reality in Christ, a truth in the kingdom of grace. Alas! what is riches, what are pleasures, what are honours, what is sonship, what are all earthly things, in comparison of the soul, which is an immortal, a spiritual, an eternal substance? They are but shadows. Those things that are of equal extent and continuance with the soul; and not only of equal extent, but that raise the soul to have communion with God in heaven, with the Father, Son, and Holy Ghost; there is the reality, there is the truth, if we will have the truth of things. 'I am that bread,' saith Christ afterwards in this chapter, 'and my flesh is meat indeed, and my blood is drink indeed,' as if other meat and other drink refreshed not indeed, but were only shadows of things.

Labour therefore for this meat; and certainly, if so be the Spirit of God once convince your judgments that these things which I say are true, both for the necessity and excellency of this food, they will be effectual to stir you up to labour more after this food that endures to everlasting life. So much for that.

'Which the Son of man shall give you, for him hath God the Father sealed.'

To come now to the possibility of attaining this food, which is the third argument our blessed Saviour useth to enforce upon us this injunction, to 'labour for the food that endures to everlasting life.' Hope stirreth up endeavour, as we see in merchandizing. Though when we venture beyond the seas we commit all to wind and water, as they say, and it is doubtful what the issue may be, yet we hope, and that sets us on work. So the poor husbandman, but that he hopes to have a comfortable issue, to have a harvest, he would never set himself to work. Now here is hope; and hope on a better ground a great deal; for he that makes other things successful, he hath given Christ for this purpose; and Christ, you see here, he gives himself, 'which the Son of man shall give you.'

Here is all that we may ground and found our hope upon. Here is will, here is power, and here is authority to give it.

Here is will; Christ will give it. Why? Because he is the Son of man. What use is there of these words in this place? Why doth he not say, 'which the *Son of God* shall give you'?

Oh, the Son of God without the Son of man is indeed a fountain of good things, but he is a sealed fountain; alas! of no comfort. Our comfort is in Immanuel, God-man. All our comfort is to be brought back to God, from whom we fell in paradise, and we must be brought back again to God by God. But unless God had become man, man had never come back again to God. Therefore all the union and communion we have with God, it depends on this first union of Christ with our nature, that the Son of God became the Son of man, as St Austin saith (*c*); for now the next union, that we become the sons of God, it comes from this, that God became man. And therefore he saith here, 'the Son of man shall give it you.' You need not climb up to heaven to fetch this food that endures to everlasting life, for the Son of God is come down from heaven to earth to take the nature of man; and in that to die, in that to satisfy God's wrath, and so to become this blessed and everlasting food; the Son of man, 'the second Adam.' As by one man we all come to misery, so by the 'second Adam,' by man, we are restored to a blessed condition again. Therefore he saith here 'the Son of man,' because in the human nature all our salvation was wrought. Indeed, the worth and efficacy of our salvation comes from the divine nature; but it was wrought in man's nature, the divine nature could not work it alone. But I will not dwell on this.

'The Son of man shall give it you.' You need not fear it, God is become man on purpose to give it you. We may now boldly go to a mediator which is made bone of our bone and flesh of our flesh. We should have feared and trembled if he had only been God, but now all grace and comfort is hid in this nature of ours in Christ. If Christ had not took this poor, wretched nature of ours upon him, it had been a hateful nature to God. God hated the nature of man; but now, because the Son of God is become the Son of man, our nature is become lovely in the eyes of God; and not only lovely, but it is filled in him with all grace, and of his 'fulness we receive grace for grace,' John i. 16. He will give it therefore, because he is 'the Son of man.'

Here is will; ay, but what power and strength hath he to give it?

He is so the Son of man as that he is also the Son of God. Therefore we are said, Acts xx. 28, 'to be redeemed with the blood of God.' Christ by his eternal Spirit, by his Godhead, offered himself a sacrifice for sin. So that he can give it because he is God.

But what authority hath he?

He is 'sealed' to do it. That is the third; that is, he hath authority, for authority is here expressed by 'sealing.' Now, Christ is said to be 'sealed,' first, *because there is the impression of God upon him.* Even as the seal imprints in the wax the likeness of that which is in it, so God hath imprinted in Christ his own likeness. He is the image of God, for Christ as he is God is the character* of his Father; and his human nature is likewise as like God as nature can express. 'We saw,' saith the apostle, 'his glory, the glory as of the only begotten Son of God,' John i. 14. We saw a kind of divinity in him, as much as human nature could receive; the likeness of God sparkled in him; therefore he is said to be 'sealed.' But that is not all, nor the principal here meant.

Again, secondly, The use of a seal *is to appropriate and distinguish from other things;* so Christ is sealed, that is, God hath appropriated him to be his own Son, and to be a mediator of his own appointing, and hath distinguished him from all others by a blessed anointing and qualification of him above all. He is as Saul among the rest, higher than all; he is as Aaron, anointed with the oil of gladness, but above his fellows, and yet for his fellows. From him distils the blessed ointment of grace. It is poured on his head first, and descends from him down to all the skirts of his garment, to all his members. So here is in this sealing likeness, distinction, and appropriation.

But especially by sealing here is meant *authority:* for a thing sealed is not only to distinguish and appropriate to a man's use, but to authorise also. As a magistrate that hath the king's broad seal, he is authorised; so Christ he hath God's seal, God hath authorised him to be a mediator; and as he was foreordained before all worlds, as the apostle Peter saith, 'to be the head of them that should be saved, and to be their mediator,' 1 Pet. i. 9, *seq.*, so when the fulness of time was come, when he came in the flesh, he was authorised by the greatest testimony that ever was, by the blessed Trinity, God the Father, Son, and Holy Ghost, at his baptism. 'This is my beloved Son, hear him,' saith a voice from heaven, Mat. iii. 17. There was the Father, the Son in the voice, the Holy Ghost in the dove. There was the whole Trinity. So he was authorised from heaven.

And then he was authorised by his miracles. God gave him power to work those works which none could do but a Mediator. Therefore he saith, 'If you believe not me, yet believe me for my works' sake,' John x. 38.

He was authorised also by his resurrection, as the apostle saith, in Rom. i. 4: 'He mightily declared himself to be the Son of God by the resurrection from the dead.' The angels from heaven brought witness of him. He was witnessed by all kind of persons on earth, yea, by the devils themselves. So he is 'sealed' and authorised every way, by all kind of witnesses, to be a mediator.

This is set out in other phrases in the Scripture. In Ps. ii. 7, 'This my Son have I set upon my holy hill of Sion;' and Rom. iii., toward the latter end, ver. 25: 'Whom God hath set forth to be a propitiation.' God

* That is, χαρακτὴρ, the 'express image.'—Ed.

hath set him forth as the shewbread was set out under the law. And then again in another place, 'Whom he hath sent,' 1 John iv. 9, 10; and in 1 Cor. i. 30, 'He is made of God unto us wisdom,' &c. 'He is made of God;' that is, he is 'sealed,' appointed, authorised by God for that purpose.

So you see why Christ is said to be sealed, especially because he is authorised by God the Father, 'made,' 'sent,' 'set forth,' 'whom the Father hath sealed;' that is, the party offended by our sins, he hath sealed and authorised Christ to be a mediator.

If this be so, let us learn this use of it, to bless God the Father as well as Christ. 'Blessed be the Father of our Lord Jesus Christ;' and 'Blessed be Christ,' for him hath the Father 'sealed' by the Spirit. The blessed Trinity have all a hand in our salvation.

And then again consider, if we despise Christ, whom we despise. We despise the Father that hath 'sealed' him. It is a weighty matter. Read the second psalm, and you shall see there what it is to despise Christ, not to 'kiss the Son;' that is, when God hath anointed and sent forth a Saviour, and 'sealed him,' and authorised him by all the testimonies that can be, to be a mediator, not to receive him for our king, for our priest and prophet. It is a rebellion, not against Christ only, but against the Father who hath 'sealed' him.

And likewise it serveth wonderfully to strengthen our faith when we go to God for forgiveness of sins. Offer him his own broad seal, offer him Christ as a mediator authorised by himself. Lord, I am thus and thus a sinner, but notwithstanding, thou hast sent thy blessed Son and set him forth to be a Saviour for me, and him I offer to thee. Thou canst not deny or refuse thy own 'sealed' Mediator and Redeemer. If he had been a mediator of my own appointing and of my own sealing, it were another matter; but I offer thy own mediator, look on the death of him whom thou hast 'sealed' to be my intercessor. It is a wondrous prevailing argument with God. He cannot deny that which he hath devised himself, him whom he chose before all worlds for this great office.

But how shall I know whether he be 'sealed' for my good or no? Saith the soul that hears this, we hear much of an authorised Saviour, of an authorised mediator to be all-sufficient, but what is that to me?

Why? For whom is he 'sealed?' Is he 'sealed' for angels or for men? And amongst men is he 'sealed' for holy men or sinners? 'I come not to seek or to save whole men, or men that never were lost,' Mat. xviii. 11. No. He came to seek and to save men, but they are lost men, sick men; and it is a faithful saying, and worthy of all means to be embraced, 'that Christ came into the world to save sinners,' saith blessed Paul, 1 Tim. i. 15. Therefore he is 'sealed' to save thee if thou art a sinner, to save thee if thou wilt receive him; and thou art bound to receive him, under pain of the punishment of rebellion. Is it not rebellion not to receive a magistrate whom the prince has authorised under his broad seal? It is another manner of matter not to receive Christ. It is a greater sin than to sin against the law; for if a man sin against the law there is the gospel to help him, but if a man sin against the gospel there is not another gospel to him. Now to refuse Christ offered in the gospel is a sin against the gospel. Where then can there be hope of salvation? Salvation itself cannot save him that will not be saved, that refuses the remedy 'sealed' by God the Father, the party offended. Who can heal him that casts down the potion that is brought to heal him? that refuseth the physician that comes to cure him? I say he is 'sealed' to save thee if thou wilt be saved;

if thou wilt receive him; receive him not only to be thy Saviour, but to be thy king to rule thee, and thy prophet to teach and instruct thee, as we shall see afterwards.

But, to clear this a little better, we must know that there are three distinct sealings.

There is God's sealing of Christ, which I have unfolded to you.

And there is our sealing of God; that is, our sealing of God's truth.

And then again, there is God's sealing of us by his Spirit. And these follow one the other.

Why hath God sealed Christ, but that we hereupon should be stirred up to believe and to receive Christ, and so by consequence to seal, that God is true in sending such a blessed Mediator, as St John saith, 'He that believes in the Son hath set to his seal that God is true,' John iii. 33. God hath sealed him, that we, by receiving him, should seal God's truth.

Beloved, God comes to us for our testimonials, for our hands and seals. Oh how wondrously doth God condescend to weak man! He hath sealed Christ for the office of a mediator, and he offers him unto us, and he comes to us likewise that we would set to our seals too, that Christ is the Son of God. He counts it not sufficient that he hath sealed him himself, but he will have us seal too; and we seal him when we receive him. He that receives him hath set to his seal that God is true. He that doth not receive him, 'he makes God a liar,' saith St John, 1 John v. 10.

And what comes of this, when we receive Christ, and set to our seal that God in the promise of salvation by Christ is true? Then we having honoured him, he honours us by his Spirit, as the apostle saith, Eph. i. 13, 'In whom, after ye believed, ye were sealed.' So when we believe and set to our seal that God is true, God seals us by his Spirit; 'after ye believed you were sealed.'

But what is this seal of the Spirit whereby God seals us after we believe?

I answer, God seals us when he sets the stamp of his Spirit upon us; when the work and witness of his Spirit is wrought in us. For as in a seal the wax hath all in it, the whole likeness of the image that is in the seal, so the soul that is sealed by the Spirit hath the likeness of the Spirit of Christ stamped on it. God imprints in their spirits the likeness of his Son; that is to say, he makes them loving souls, humble souls, obedient as Christ was in all things, patient, meek, &c. You may see in the spirit of a believing man an expression of the spirit of Christ. So that if you would see Christ in his excellencies, look on the spirit of a true Christian. There you shall see a resemblance of Christ Jesus, not perfectly, but in some comfortable* measure. You shall see the very image of Christ. You shall see how full of love he is, how patient in crosses, how humble, how meek, how obedient to God in all things, both in a passive and active obedience. This is the stamp of the Spirit; when a man believes, God honours him by setting his image on him.

And yet this is not all. Besides this, we are sealed with the witness and comfort of the Spirit as well as with the work of the Spirit, the Spirit of God sweetly witnessing that we are the sons of God. And this sweet witness of the Spirit especially comes after we have honoured God by believing in temptation, when we are able to hold out and say as Job said, 'Though he kill me, yet will I trust in him,' Job xiii. 15. So when we can, after conflicts of doubting and despair, say, 'Though he kill me, yet will I trust in him,' I will set to my seal that he is true. Well, will you so? God, to

* Qu. 'conformable'?—Ed.

honour such a soul, seals him to the day of redemption; that is, he gives to the soul of such a one a sweet evidence and testimony that he is the Son of God.

And this seal of the Spirit is double: not only done by the witness and work of the Spirit inwardly, which I have shewed, but likewise the Spirit doth seal them outwardly, enabling them to make an outward confession of Christ and his truth; and therefore, in Rev. vii. 3, *seq.*, Christians are said to be 'sealed in the forehead,' that is, as they are marked and singled out in ill times, to be such as God hath set his special favour upon, so they are 'sealed' with a spirit of boldness, willingly and with forwardness to confess the truth of Christ in ill times.

Now, to apply it to our purpose, wouldst thou know whether thou be such a one, for the present, as for whom Christ is 'sealed' a mediator? Examine, first of all, whether thou hast put to thy seal that God is true, by receiving and believing Christ, and the promise of salvation through him. If thou hast done so, then thou wilt find another seal from God, even the work of the Spirit in sanctifying of thee, and conforming of thee to the image and likeness of Christ; and thou wilt find the witness and comfortable testimony of the Spirit, in telling thee that thou art the son of God; and withal thou wilt have a spirit of boldness, and readiness, and forwardness to confess Christ. Thou wilt not care for all that the world saith; but wilt, if need be, stand to the profession of religion to the death.

If thou canst find this in thyself, undoubtedly thou art not only such a one as Christ came to seal, but for the present thou mayest be assured that thou hast interest in this mediator, sealed by God for that purpose.

Thus you see that here is 'food that endures to everlasting life,' which is Christ and the benefits we have by him. You see that that blessed meat is attainable, because he is willing to give it; for he is become man for that purpose. He is able to give it, for he is God as well as man, and he hath authority to give it, for God the Father hath sealed him and fitted him for that office. If we receive him, he will seal us with his blessed Spirit; that is, the same Spirit that furnished Christ with grace, that sanctified him in the womb, will sanctify all those that are his members, will work a likeness and conformity in them to his blessed image; for the same Spirit that was in the natural Son is in all the adopted sons of God. And he will likewise give us the comfortable evidence and assurance that we are the sons of God, furnish us with boldness and resolution to profess Christ in all times.

Let me then, I beseech you, come again to re-enforce this exhortation. Take heed you refuse not Christ. Consider with what authority he comes. 'He is sealed.' It is no presumption therefore to receive him, though you be never such sinners, to receive him; I mean not only to be a priest to reconcile you to God, but to be a king to rule you, and a prophet to instruct you by his Spirit; to receive him on this manner is no presumption. To receive him indeed as a Saviour, but to neglect him as king, to refuse to come under his government, is great presumption; but to receive whole Christ is obedience and faith, and no presumption; nay, if you do not receive him you sin damnably, you commit the greatest sin that can be. He came to save all that will come under his blessed government, that will kiss the Son. 'Whosoever will, let him come and drink of the waters of life,' Rev. xxii. 17. All the good promised by Christ is promised upon our receiving of him, upon the obedience of our faith. There is nothing required but a will to embrace him, and to be under his government. There is no exception made of sins, or persons, or times. 'At what time soever a sinner repent,' 1 Kings viii. 30, *seq.*, whatsoever sinner, whatsoever time, or whatsoever the sins be, if he repents, Christ is ready to receive him.

If you pretend your unworthiness and want of excellencies, he takes away that objection. 'Come unto me, all that are weary and heavy laden,' Mat. xi. 28; 'Come, buy without money,' Isa. lv. 1; and here in the text, 'The Son of man shall give;' and what so free as gift?

If you pretend you have sinned since your calling, and that you have sinned against conscience and knowledge, and therefore now you have no further hope of Christ, remember that Paul, 2 Cor. v. 20, speaks to the Corinthians that were in the state of grace, 'I beseech you to be reconciled to God;' and in Jer. iii. 6, *seq.*, 'Return again, you backsliding Israel, and I will heal your backsliding;' and again, 'Will a man receive a wife that hath played the harlot, and broken the band of marriage? Yet return, O house of Israel, and I will receive you.' Therefore run not away from God. Though thou hast sinned after thou art in the state of grace, come again, I beseech you. Still Christ is to be received; the door of grace is always held open, and the golden sceptre continually held out as long as we live in this world.

But yet it is not good to neglect the time of grace. Receive Christ presently; defer not to come under his government; and receive him wholly, or else there is no receiving of him at all.

And to press this a little further; I beseech you, consider that if you leave not your sinful courses, and come under the blessed government of Christ, if you receive not this 'sealed' king, this 'sealed' priest and prophet, this 'sealed' mediator, whom God hath 'sealed' and sent unto you for salvation, there is not anything in the world that will one day more torment you than your refusal of him. Oh that we should ever live to hear of salvation so freely offered, and of a Saviour so authorised, yet notwithstanding that we should respect our sins more than our souls! and because we could not have him to be our Saviour except we came under his government and be ruled by him as a king, we refused him wholly altogether. Indeed, if we might have had salvation by him and the forgiveness of sins, and withal have remained under the rule and sway of our own lusts, and been led by them, we would have been contented to have had him; but rather than we would leave our blasphemous, our unclean, injurious, and covetous courses of life, we were content to let Christ go if he would. Oh that we should reject this 'sealed' Saviour! Oh that we should refuse salvation offered on such loving terms, when God was so loving as to seal and authorise his Son; when the Son was so loving as to give himself when he was 'sealed;' to refuse this and that for such base respects, will certainly one day, when the conscience is wakened, prove the greatest torment that can be!

See how the apostle notably enforceth this in the second of the Hebrews, ver. 3: 'If so be they did not escape that despised Moses' law, how shall we escape if we neglect so great salvation?' He doth not say, How shall we escape if we oppose Christ, if we rail on him, if we despise his image in his children, as many cursed wretches do? but, How shall we escape if we do but '*neglect* so great salvation,' so witnessed and authorised with all the signs, so offered and tendered with all the terms of love that may be?

And therefore, if there be any here that have lived in sinful courses, and have a purpose to break them off, that are weary of the government of their lusts, and of Satan that rules them by their lusts,—for all are under one government or other, either under the 'sealed' government of Christ, or under the base government of Satan that tends to damnation,—Oh leave it, and come under this governor 'sealed' by God the Father, authorised from heaven by the blessed Trinity, by miracles, and by all the arguments that can be; come under his blessed government and you shall do well. God the Father, the party offended with your sins, he hath 'sealed' him; and he cannot refuse a mediator of his own sealing.

And do not say your sins have been thus and thus; for consider what were these parties that he offers himself to here, that he saith to, 'Labour for the meat that endures to everlasting life.' Were they not cursed hypocrites, that followed him for the loaves, and yet he saith to them, 'Labour for the meat that endures,' &c. I am 'sealed' even for your salvation, if you will come out of your hypocrisy and be ruled by me. Therefore let none stand out from coming under the government of Christ, for he offers mercy, you see here, to the worst of men, even to cursed hypocrites.

And, to conclude with a word of comfort, if there be any poor distressed soul frighted in conscience with the sight of his sins and Satan's temptations, Oh let such consider the love of God in Christ. Satan pictures out God as a terrible judge; and so he is indeed to men that go on in their sins, 'a consuming fire.' But art thou weary of thy courses? art thou willing to come under a better covenant? Let not Satan abuse thee by setting God before thee as a terrible judge, and Christ as one that would not save thee. No. Come in, kiss the Son, 'for him hath the Father sealed,' 'sealed' for thee if thou be weary of thy sins. Enforce not upon thy soul any unwillingness to be in God. Wherefore doth God stoop so low, and labour by all these arguments here, as that Christ is the Son of man, and that he shall give it you, and that the Father hath sealed him for that end; wherefore is all this, but to shew his willingness to receive thee? Wherefore hath the Father 'sealed' Christ but in love to thee? Come in, therefore, and then, if you will seal to his truth, if you will believe and cast yourselves on God's gracious promise, even against doubting and distrust, you shall find God sealing you by his Spirit; you shall find his Spirit witnessing to your spirits that you are the 'sons of God.'

Here then you see is sure footing for poor doubting souls to fasten upon. God the Father, the party offended, hath 'sealed' his Son; hath authorised him to save thee, if thou repent and come in. What are all thy sins and unworthiness to Christ, God-man, 'sealed' and authorised by the Father, who is the party offended? If thou art willing to come in, bring all thy sins and oppose them to Christ, God-man, 'sealed' by the Father, and they will vanish as a cloud. But, as I said before, if thou wilt not come in and accept of this Saviour, if thou wilt not submit thyself to his government, thou sealest thy damnation.

Thus you see I have unfolded this blessed portion of Scripture. Christ Jesus, and all the prerogatives and benefits that come by him, is the food that endureth to everlasting life. You see the arguments our blessed Saviour useth to enforce us to labour after this food. It is 'food.' It is food that 'endures,' and it is food that 'endures to everlasting life;' and he 'will give it,' for 'him the Father hath sealed' and authorised so to do. He is both the gift and the giver; both the food and the inviter to the food; both the priest and the sacrifice. Labour therefore after this food.

There is an objection which I will briefly answer, and so end.

Labour after it. Why? Christ will give it; if he will give it, why must we labour after it? And if we must labour for it, how doth he give it? How can these two, gift and labour, stand together?

I answer, Very well; Christ will give himself, and forgiveness of sins, and life everlasting, and yet we must labour too. But we must know for what we must labour. We must not labour for any merit to the title unto heaven and happiness. Christ indeed gives that. But labour in the use of all good means to get knowledge and faith to receive this gift, to get the knowledge of Christ, what he is in his natures and offices, what he hath promised, what he hath done and what he hath suffered, what the intent of the gospel is; what the giver is; and what the authority is, that his Father hath given him. This requires labour. It is a labour to crack the shell, to understand the letter of the Scripture; to know what the gift and what the giver is. And it is likewise a labour to get faith to receive this gift; to get the soul emptied of all self-confidence; of all worth in itself and in the creature; for Christ must be received with a beggar's hand; and it will ask much labour to deny a man's self; for proud flesh will always have somewhat to trust to either in itself or in the creature.

So that these two may well stand together, labour and gift. We are taught to pray, 'Give us this day our daily bread.' God will give us our daily bread. We must not therefore stand still and do nothing; but though God will give it, yet he will give it in the use of means, in the use of our lawful callings. So here, God will give us this spiritual food; yet he will give it in labour. It is his ordinance; and whatsoever he gives, he gives not in idleness, but in obedience to his ordinance. He will have us to labour in the use of the means, in reading, hearing, receiving the sacrament, praying, meditating, and the like, to have a part in Christ this blessed gift. Nay, because he will give Christ, therefore labour. The one enforceth the other. The like reason Moses giveth the Israelites: 'Fight,' saith he, 'for the Lord hath given them into your hand,' Joshua x. 19. They might say, If our enemies be given into our hand, why should we fight? Yes; fight the rather, be encouraged to fight, because you shall be sure to conquer. So here, 'Labour for the meat that endures to everlasting life, for the Son of man will give it.' Therefore labour, because he will give it. In labouring we shall be sure to have it; do that which belongs to thee, and thou shalt be sure to have that which belongs to God; thou shalt find Christ, and heaven, and glory, and all in the use of the means. But he gives nothing without labour. There can be no good done in earthly things without labour; and do yon think to have heaven without labour? No. Spiritual things are against the stream. Heaven is up the hill. There must be labour, there must be striving against corruptions within, and against temptations without; and our labour it is a happy labour. It is not a barren labour; 'Our labour is not in vain in the Lord,' as the apostle saith, 1 Cor. xv. 58. We that labour for the food that endures to everlasting life, we labour for somewhat; but worldlings that beat their brains, and tire their spirits, and rack their consciences, and wear out their bodies, it is all for nothing; it is for that which is 'vanity and vexation of spirit,' Eccles. i. 14; for that which they must leave behind them. A true Christian, to encourage him to take all the pains that may be, he labours for something; it is a hopeful and not a barren labour. And, beloved, blessed are we that we can have this food for our labour; that since the fall we can recover by the 'second Adam' a better estate than we had by the first.

And our blessed Saviour, to the end he might distinguish true Christians from hypocrites, enjoins this duty of labouring so much the more; for we have many in the church that think to have Christ and his benefits without labour, as if heaven would drop into their mouths. They can say that God is merciful, and Christ died for us; but you shall in the mean time find them careless of reading, of hearing, of praying, of the communion of saints, &c., are idle in working out their salvation with fear and trembling, negligent in selling all that they have for the pearl, will part with nothing for Christ. I say, to distinguish these hypocrites from true Christians, therefore he saith, 'Labour,' to shew to us that only they that labour for Christ in the use of all good means; that labour for the true knowledge of him, and for faith to receive him; that sell all for him; that take pains to grow in grace and in union with Christ; that make him their best portion in the world, and delight in him: it is they only that have interest in Christ; only the painful* Christian is the true Christian.

Therefore, I beseech you, as you would have it discerned that you are not hypocrites in the church, be stirred up to use all sanctified means to know Christ, to believe in him, to know that you are in communion with him, that you belong unto him. Be not discouraged. You shall have rest ere long. 'There is a rest for the people of God,' as the apostle saith to the Hebrews, Heb. iv. 9. Indeed, so long as we are here below, there is labour joined with weariness; for we have great conflicts with corruptions and temptations, with enemies within and enemies without; but be of good comfort, we shall at last come to a rest, to a rest perpetual and everlasting. It is true, in heaven there shall be labour, for we shall be alway praising God; but it shall be labour without weariness, labour without conflict. There shall be no corruption within, nor no devil without. Satan could enter into paradise below, but he shall never enter into that heavenly paradise. Therefore be encouraged to labour for a while. Though it be tedious, because of corruptions and temptations, 'yet there is a rest for the people of God, an eternal rest.

* That is, 'painstaking.'—G.

(*a*) P. 366.—'Especially are we to make daily use of the death of Christ; for howsoever the death of Christ be transient in respect of the act of it, as one of the ancients saith; yet . . . .' The *thought* is common to Bernard and Augustine.

(*b*) P. 370.—'Taste is the most necessary sense of all, saith a wise searcher of the mysteries of nature; our life is maintained by taste.' Query, Bacon?

(*c*) P. 373.—'All . . . depends . . . as Saint Austin saith, for now . . .' This great fundamental doctrine of the Christian faith, is constantly dwelt upon throughout the works of Augustine. G.

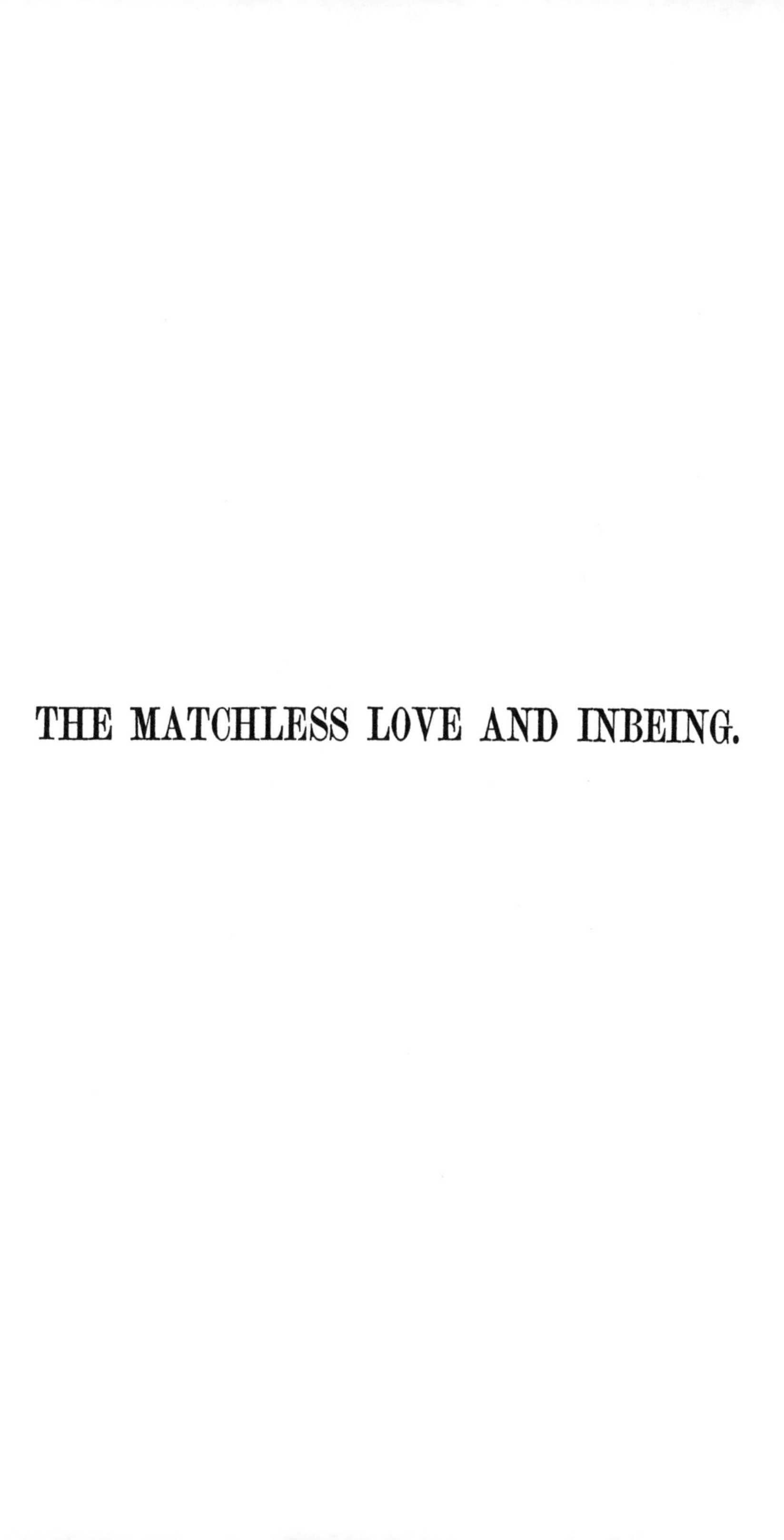

THE MATCHLESS LOVE AND INBEING.

THE MATCHLESS LOVE AND INBEING.

NOTE.

'The Matchless Love and Inbeing' appeared in the first edition of The Saint's Cordials, 1629. It will be observed from the full recapitulation in the commencement of the first of these sermons, that the two so designated formed part of a series, expository, in all probability, of the whole chapter. These not having been preserved, accounts perhaps for the withdrawal of 'The Matchless Love and In-Being' from the after editions, of 1637 and 1658, of the 'Cordials.' The title-page will be found below.*

G.

* THE

MATCHLES LOVE,

AND IN-BEING.

In two SERMONS.

Wherein is shewed,

That we may be Assured of Gods loue vnto vs:
Helpes for Weake Christians how to attaine vnto this loue:
Helps how to know that we haue it in vs:
That Christ is in all beleeuers:
How to know that Christ is in vs:
How in a seeming absence he is discouered to be in the Soule:
How to keepe Christ there, and how to recouer him being lost, &c.

[Woodcut here, as described in Vol. IV. page 60.]

VPRIGHTNES HATH BOLDNES.

EPHES. 3. 17, 18, 19.

That Christ may dwell in your hearts by Faith, that ye being rooted and grounded in loue, May be able to comprehend with all Saints, what is the bredth and length, and depth and height:

And to know the loue of Christ, which passeth knowledge, that ye might be filled with all the fulnesse of God.

LONDON,

Printed in the yeare 1629.

THE MATCHLESS LOVE AND INBEING.

SERMON I.

I have declared unto them thy name, and I will declare it; that the love wherewith thou hast loved me may be in them, and I in them.—JOHN XVII. 26.

THE dependence we have heard heretofore, when I entered upon the first part of this verse. Our Saviour intending to have committed his disciples to the love of his Father, that they might be the fitter objects of his love, he sets down here his own care for the present, and for the time to come; for it is hypocrisy in prayer when we pray for that that we endeavour not. For as he prays the Father to take them into his charge, so he sets down his own care about them: 'I have manifested thy name, and I will,' &c. The verse contains this blessed act of Christ.

1. What he hath done.
2. What he will do.
3. The end of it.

'I have declared thy name, and will declare it, that the love wherewith thou hast loved me may be in them, and I in them.' 'I have declared, and will declare.' This I unfolded at large the last day. Among many other things, this one I observed, that *we are in a perpetual proficiency in this life*. We never know so much, but we may know more, and we ought to know more. So that by consequence there is a perpetual necessity of Christ's prophetical office. 'I have declared, and I will declare,' &c. We see *the church in general grew to knowledge by degrees*, till Christ, the Sun of righteousness, came gloriously in the flesh; till John pointed at him with the finger, 'This is the Lamb of God,' &c., John i. 29. And as the whole body mystical, so every member; we grow to knowledge by degrees. 'I have declared,' &c. Christ doth fit his work to our exigents. We need further knowledge, and he is bountiful to promise a further declaration. 'I have, and I will.' *He is never weary of well-doing*. As his love is infinite, so his expression is unwearied that comes from his love. A ground of special comfort, as we shewed, to all Christians, especially to the labouring, weak Christians, that their beginnings are pledges of further degrees. For Christ, where he is Alpha, he will be Omega; and where he is the author, he will be the finisher of our faith; where he hath laid the first stone, he will set up the roof at length. 'He hath declared, and he will declare.'

He is not such an unwise builder as will leave his work.* He knows what he can do, and therefore we may enter upon all the means of saving knowledge, with this confidence, that we have a teacher that will carry us along from one degree of knowledge to another. And let us never despair for any insufficiency of parts. *It is no matter what the capacity or the incapacity of the scholar be, when there is such a teacher.* When God is the teacher, it is no matter how dull the learner is, for Christ doth not only bring doctrine, but he brings wit, grace, and ability to the inward man ; that is, not only a declaration, as man doth teach the outward man, but he unlocks and opens the heart, the ears of the inward man, as he opened Lydia's heart, &c., Acts xvi. 14. Let none distrust if they be conscionable* and careful in the use of good means. Many other things, I observed hence, which I will not be large in unfolding. 'I have declared to them thy name,' &c. ; that is, that whereby thou mightest be known. Now in the covenant of grace, God would be known by the sweet name of Father, by the attributes of mercy and love. That whereby he will be known is his name, his mercy in the covenant of grace in condescending to be our Father in Jesus Christ, together with the sweet attributes of love and mercy, from whence all spring. This is his name. Now he will not be known only to be the God of Abraham, Isaac, and Jacob ; the God that brought them out of the land of Egypt, or out of the North; but he will be known by the name of 'the Father of our Lord Jesus Christ,' and our Father ; to be the Father of mercy, and the God of all comfort. Thus we must labour to present God to us now in his right name. This name makes all other names sweet that he hath. For being once gracious and merciful, and a Father in covenant, his power is ours, his wisdom is ours, and all is ours. Then this name of God is set forth at large : 'Jehovah, Jehovah, merciful, forgiving iniquity,' &c., Exod. xxxiv. 7. 'I have declared thy name,' &c. But this I stood at large on.

What was the end of our blessed Saviour in this his gracious dealing ?

'That the love wherewith thou lovest me may be in them, and I in them.'

In unfolding of which words, I propounded these general heads, to omit other things. First, *That God doth love Christ, because he is the first object of his love, his own image ;* for he represents God's attributes, and whatsoever is good in him, every way exactly. He is the Jedidiah, the beloved of the Lord. He is the true Isaac, the true matter of joy. He is the first Son, the first beloved. This was the first thing we unfolded and made use of. The second was this, *That after Christ, God loves all that are Christ's with that love wherewith he loves Christ.* There is a former love, indeed, of God, to give us unto Christ ; but I speak of the carriage of our salvation, all which is in Christ. He loves Christ, and he loves us in Christ, and not otherwise. There is a love that moved him to give Christ, but this love must concur with the other attributes. It must be such love and mercy, and so apprehended, as must be without offering violence or wrong to other attributes. His justice and his holiness must not be wronged. And therefore though he bare love to those whom he knew before all worlds ; yet in the carriage of salvation he intended actually so to set his love upon them, as that it should be in one that should make satisfaction for them, being considered as sinners in themselves. And God would have, in our salvation, the glory, as of infinite love to man, so of infinite hatred of sin, and likewise of infinite wisdom, in reconciling these together. His infinite hatred to sin, how could he shew it more, than that rather than he would

* That is, 'conscientious.'—G.

not have it punished, his Son must become incarnate, to be a surety for sin and to take it away? How could he shew his infinite love more, than by giving such a gift as Christ, and his infinite wisdom, than to devise such a way as to bring these two together, justice and love, to reconcile them? So though God loved a certain company whom he foreknew to everlasting life, yet he intended, in the carriage of their salvation, to do it with the manifestation and glory of his attributes, that no attribute might be wronged nor complain, and that justice might fully be satisfied; but especially that his mercy and love might triumph. For what in God stirred up a fatherly heart? What stirred him up to reconcile justice and mercy, but love, that set on work all other attributes, his mercy, and love, and goodness? God loves us in Christ therefore, and only in Christ; because in Christ only his wrath is satisfied. Christ only is the mediator, the only treasury of the church to convey all to us. The adopted sons have their excellency, and all that they have, in the virtue of the natural Son. But this I have unfolded at large heretofore, and shewed the use of it last day; this was the second thing.

The third general thing out of the text is this, that *the love of God to us is in Christ, loving us in him, as electing us, and doing all good to us in him.* It is the ground of all other favours and graces whatsoever. And therefore he sets it here for all in all, 'I have declared, &c., that the love wherewith thou lovest me may be in them,' &c. What! doth he not say, that I might be merciful to them and pitiful, and that they may have other graces that love me? What needs all this? He sets down the spring of all, 'I have manifested thy name,' thy gracious name, that in the apprehension of that they may find my love. And so, when we feel the love of God and of Christ, know that all other graces flow from thence; for indeed all graces wrought in us issue from God's love to us first. Whence comes pity, and mercy, and love, but from God's shining in our hearts first by his love, that doth mould and frame the heart to all duties and graces whatsoever, and to the first grace to love God? For how can we love him unless we have an apprehension of his love first? You know iron, and stones, and things that are cold of nature, if they have any heat, we say it is the sun that hath heated them, or the fire that hath warmed them, because intrinsecally they have no heat. So when there is any goodness in the creature, any pity, mercy, or love to God, or to those that are his, it implies, that there hath been first the fire, the light of God's love to us. And therefore, saith Christ, 'I have manifested thy name to them, that thy love may be in them.' This love in them will be enough to set them on fire on all good things whatsoever. 'We love him, because he loves us first,' 1 John iv. 19. We know him, because he knows us first, Gal iv. 9, and we choose him, because he chooseth us first. We joy and delight in him, because he joys and delights in us first. All is a reflex from him, whatsoever of good comes from us. This was the third thing. We made thence use of it, and so brake off. To go on. The fourth thing which I propounded to speak of out of the words is this, *that this love of God to us may be known, and ought to be known of us.*

It may be known with an experimental and with an applicatory knowledge. The next was, that *the way to know God's love to us, is the manifesting of his name in the gospel:* that follows by the connection of them two together; and the last is, *Christ being in us,* which I cannot come to at this time. So then now, to clear this point, that *we may, and it is our duty to do it, to labour to know God's love to us.* We ought to labour that

God's love may be in us, and that we may know it, not generally that he loves us, but that his love is in us, that it is incorporate and invested into us, to have a taste and be sensible of it. For this is the end of Christ's prayer, 'That the love wherewith thou lovest me may be in them,' &c. And the next way to know it, which we shall speak of at this time among the rest, it is this, 'The manifesting of God's name by Christ.' For the first then.

Doct. 1. *That we may, and ought to know God's love to us in Christ.* That we ought to know it; what need I be large in the point? I will not, because it is so clear. For if it be, as I shewed the last day at large, the spring of all duties, of all other graces, which sets all on work, then surely we ought to labour for that which may make us good, and not only good, but comfortable. Now all our goodness, and comfort, it comes from this original, the knowledge of God's love to us, when that is in us, for we have no love to him until we know that we are beloved of him.

1. *We cannot be thankful to God till we know that he loves us in Christ.* I speak of his peculiar love as a child. Who can be thankful for that which he knows not? It overthrows all thankfulness and denies it. We ought to labour for the assurance of the love of God in Christ. For it is a duty to joy in the Lord as our portion. Now we must be certain of his love first. How else can we practise this duty of rejoicing in the Lord alway? What joy and cheerfulness can come without the love of God shining upon us and enlarging our hearts to joy? As the shining of the sun enlargeth the spirit of the poor creatures, the birds, in the spring time, to sing, so proportionably the apprehension of the sweet love of God in Christ enlargeth the spirit of a man, and makes him full of joy and thanksgiving. He breaks forth into joy, so that his whole life is matter of joy and thanksgiving.

2. Again, *In suffering any cross, any opposition, who will endure to lose his temporal goods, his life and liberty, to be restrained any way, that knows not God's love?* Who will abide anything for him that he loves not? What doth set us to suffer all things that may be for God? The apprehension that he loves us. What makes a man willing to end his life, and to yield up his soul to God? He knows he shall yield his soul to him as to a father that loves him, that will save his soul. Can a man be willing to leave his home here, when he knows not whether he shall have a better or no? Can a man commend his soul to one that he knows not to be his friend? No. Can he commend such a jewel to one that he knows not but to be an enemy? Can he say with Simeon, 'Lord, let thy servant depart in peace, for mine eyes have seen thy salvation'? Luke ii. 29. Doth not all joy and comfort come from the love of God in Christ? What should I enlarge the point? We can neither have grace, nor joy, nor suffer anything with thankfulness, nor end our days with joy and comfort, till we get assurance that we are in the covenant of grace, and that God's love is in us.

And therefore it is clear to anybody that knows anything in religion, or desires anything, that we ought to labour that God's love may be in us. I beseech you, therefore, make use of it to see the abominable doctrine of popery—I cannot speak too hardly of it—which teacheth that we ought to doubt of God's love. It cuts the sinews of endeavour. Who will endeavour after the attaining of the love of God, and this assurance, when this is laid in the way, that we ought not to do it? Are we not prone enough to distrust, but we must be taught it? Is not Satan malicious enough, but we must light a candle to him, and arm his malice with this doctrine, that we ought to doubt? He is the master of doubtings; for the works of darkness, and all the discomfort and sin that he brings on us is in darkness, in this particular darkness, that we know not whether we be the children of God or no. And therefore, say some, why should we leave our gain, our profit, and our present pleasures that we have? And what doth he aim at by the sins he tempts us to, but to shake our assurance of God's love? Well, they teach the doctrine of devils in divers things, amongst which this is one that strengthens the kingdom of Satan much, that people ought to doubt, and that there is no way or means to get assurance of God's love. This is to overthrow the intent of Christ's prayer. Wherefore doth he pray here, and what doth he promise in his prayer? That God would shew them his love, and that he may do it: 'I have declared thy love,' &c. So it is clear that we ought to answer Christ's aim. Why doth Christ declare his Father's name? And why are all the means of salvation, but that we may have God's love in us? Is it not our duty, then, to answer Christ's course, and his promise, and his love? Taking that, then, for a ground, that we ought to labour to have God's love to be in us, we will shew that we may attain to it, and come to know that God loves us. I will not be long in it, it is a clear point, which heretofore, upon another occasion, I have spoken of.

We may attain to it. Here is the way, as I shall shew in the next point, 'By the declaration of God's name.' For what is faith, which is the work of the gospel and grace of the new covenant, but the apprehension of the love of God in Christ? It is nothing else; and therefore we may attain to it in the covenant of grace. Faith is nothing but the act whereby we apprehend this effectual love of God to us in Christ. Therefore we that are Christians may attain to it, because we have the Spirit of God, which 'searcheth the deep things of God,' 1 Cor. iii. 10. Our spirit knows what is in us, and God's Spirit knows what is in God, and we have the Spirit of God to shew us the things of God, and all the benefits and fruits of his love, with the affection itself. The Spirit searcheth the deep things of God, as it is in 1 Cor. ii. 10. It is a point I have heretofore followed at large. A Christian in the covenant of grace, he knows that God loves him. There is no truth in the world so illustrious, so gloriously and apparently* true, as this. Would you have a better pledge of his love than Jesus Christ, the Son of his love, to be given for us, the dearest thing that God hath? He would not have us doubt of his love that hath given such an invaluable thing as his own Son to assure us of it, besides all that comes from this; for if he have given him once, he gives all things with him. He that hath given us his Son for our Redeemer and Saviour, he gives us heaven for our inheritance, and his Spirit for our conduct, guide, and sanctifier, Rom. viii. 32. He hath given angels for our attendants. He gives us peace, and joy, and all things. In Christ, we have all. But here, because it is a main point, I will enlarge myself a little, and speak as familiarly as I can to every conscience.

Quest. 1. How shall a sinner, that is not yet converted, be persuaded of God's love to him?

Quest. 2. And how shall we, in the time of temptation, deal with sinners in the state of grace? I speak of the ordinary course, how a Christian may be persuaded of it. For the first, which is, how those that are unconverted may be drawn to the sense of the love of God, to find that they have any

* That is, 'manifestly.'—G.

portion in it at all, that they may have it for the time to come, though they feel not yet any goodness in them.

Ans. 1. I answer, *We must draw them to a sense that they are not yet in the love of God, by those things, that their corruptions suggest to them to measure the love of God by.* As, for example, you have a company that think their case is good, because God hath given them outward blessings, and accompanies his blessings with patience and long-suffering; gives them parts and gifts, and preferments in the church; gives them place, great estimation, and such things. Hereupon they begin to reason, Certainly God is in love with me; though, if a man should search their lives and examine them, you shall find that there is no act, no evidence of God's special love to them at all. Such, therefore, must be convinced, that they must not measure God's love by these things; that that which is common to castaways cannot be a character and sign of God's love; but these things are common to castaways. Did Abraham give Ishmael, and the rest of his children, moveable things? but Isaac had the inheritance, Gen. xxv. 6, *seq.* Esau had his portion in the things of this life, but Jacob goes away with the blessing. The blessings of the left hand, castaways and reprobates may have in abundant measure. God fills their bellies with abundance of outward things, whose hearts he never fills with his love, as in Dives, Luke xvi. 25. Not to enlarge myself, look on such instances. What tend they to, but to shew that these outward things are no evidences of God's love? and for God's patience in enduring me in such a state as I am in, that is no argument. For God in his patience endures the vessels of wrath, who treasure up 'wrath against the day of wrath,' Rom. ii. 4, 5, God suffering them to prolong their days in judgment, that so he may pour the full vials of his wrath upon them. He suffers them, to lead them unto repentance; and they, not making a right use of it, God after justifies his vengeance and judgment the more, when he pours it upon them, so that plenty in outward things, accompanied with patience, is no true sign of God's love.

Like think of parts and gifts. Had not Judas excellent parts? Nay, the devil himself, who comes near him in the depth of understanding and policy? &c. Judas had a place in the church, he was an apostle. And for gifts, Ahithophel and Saul had gifts of government. All these are no evidences of the love of God to be in us as yet, or that he hath any interest in us. The way, therefore, to bring those that have not the love of God to love God, is to shew them their vain confidence, that they trust to a broken reed, and to that which in the time of sickness, the hour of death, and the day of judgment, will deceive them, seeing they trust unto a cracked title. Well, if the consciences of such as are not yet in the state of grace be once awaked, we may thus draw them to be within the compass of the love of God. Otherwise, when they see the vanities of other things, and likewise that there is sin in them, somewhat that lays them open to the wrath of God, then Satan will help their conscience, Satan and their conscience will tell them ofttimes all, and make them, reason, As for such a wretch as I, there is no hope; I had as good go on in a sinful course, and have somewhat in this world, as to want heaven and the comforts of this life too. And so Satan keeps them in darkness, because they think it is to no purpose to go about another course, and that it is impossible they should come to assurance. Such kind of conceits he hath.

But we must know, that in the covenant of grace now in the gospel, this is not put as a bar of God's love, that I am a sinner, that I have committed any degree of sin whatsoever. None are shut out but those that will be as they are. And therefore all objections are taken away in the promulgation of the gospel. Ay, but I am guilty, and Oh, I am laden with sin! 'Be of good comfort, thou art called, thou art the man. Come unto me all ye that are weary and heavy laden,' Mat. xi. 28. Oh that I might find mercy, says one. Why, 'Blessed are the hungry and thirsty; blessed are the poor in spirit; blessed are the mourners,' Mat. v. 3, 4; and 'Ho, every one that thirsteth, come,' Isa. lv. 1. There is hope for thee. He keeps open house for every one. He shuts out none but those that shut out themselves, that think these things are too good to be true, and therefore will enjoy their pleasures, and go on still and daub with their conscience. But if their hearts be awakened, if they will go to God and cast themselves upon his mercy, whosoever is weary, whosoever is athirst, whosoever is heavy laden, God is no accepter of persons, but at 'what time soever any sinner whatsoever repents of any sin whatsoever,' God will shew mercy, if he come in and accept of the proclamation of pardon, Ezek. xviii. 22. If he come in, and will not continue in his rebellion still, but cast himself upon his mercy, and resign, and yield himself to God and to Christ's government, to be ruled by him, as a subject should be, he shall find mercy. Let the devil, therefore, keep none in bondage, in the dungeon of ignorance and unbelief, for the end of the gospel is to bring in all such, if they will.

But to come more particularly to such as have true goodness in them, and yet the devil takes all advantages to hinder the apprehension of God's love to them in Christ.

Quest. 2. *How shall we in divers states and cases bring men to be persuaded of God's love in Christ, when conscience and Satan, together with some outward occurrents, urge them to unbelief and to stagger?*

For instance, a sinner that is converted and in the state of grace, he may ofttimes fall into some great sin; hereupon Satan, taking advantage of the sin, together with conscience, which always helps Satan in this case, speaks bitter things.

Ans. 1. Thus we must answer such as are drawn by Satan to sin, and after accused by Satan for sin, and to whom God is presented as a hateful God, &c., *that notwithstanding they should not be discouraged.* We have many examples in Scripture: 'If we sin, we have an advocate with the Father, Christ Jesus,' &c., 1 John ii. 1; and he is the propitiation for our sins. We ought not, therefore, to be discouraged from going to God, humbled as we ought to be. Here is place for humiliation, but there is no place for base discouragement, and calling God's love into question. A son under anger is a son; and therefore, though Satan presents to him an angry God for sin—for this temptation is then sharpened indeed, when it is made a weapon by Satan, by reason that God accompanies the sinner that is fallen into sin, with some judgment as a punishment—yet he ought to lay hold on the rich mercies of God in Christ. What should he else do? Shall he run away from God? No. A bastard, a slave, will do so; but he runs *to* God. Even as a child, when he hath offended his father, doth not run away from him; but, knowing that his father is merciful and loving, though he have offended him, and that he is now a son, though under his wrath, he goes and studies to appease his father, casts himself upon his favour and mercy, and will endure his correction gently. Thus ought we to do. Satan, when he hath gotten us to sin, he saith, Now you had as good run on still, for God follows you with judgments; you have offended

God, and there is no hope for you. So he keeps us without comfort, and God without service, by that means; whereby we run deeper and deeper into God's books. Oh come in betimes, and repent. It will be easier. Thy comfort will be stronger. God will be sooner pacified. Thy heart will not be so hardened. Do not call in question God's love to thee; for Satan tempts, and corrupts, and draws thee to sin, for that end, to call it in question. God may love thee, though he follow thee with shows of anger; for he may be angry, and yet love thee too, as we shall see afterwards.

Ans. 2. Again, Satan doth use as a weapon, to shake our sonship or adoption, and our estate in God's love, manifold temptations and crosses, and such like, to discourage us. He comes with 'If.' 'If thou wert in the love of God, and the love of God in thee, and did belong to thee any way, would God follow thee thus and thus, with these declarations of wrath and anger?'

I answer, A man may retort that upon Satan the tempter, and upon his own heart. The spirit retorts that upon the flesh: 'God corrects every son, and he is a bastard that hath not correction,' Heb. xii. 8. In this world, to thrive in a course of sin, when a man hath offended God, it is a sign of reprobation rather than otherwise. Every child God corrects; and for poverty, shame, and the like, we must not measure God's love by these, for God loves us as he loved Christ. Mark here Christ's prayer: 'That the love wherewith thou hast loved me may be in them.'

Quest. How was God's love in Christ? To fence him from poverty, from disgrace, from persecution, from the sense of God's wrath? No. But the first-begotten Son, the natural Son, he was persecuted as soon as he was born; he was disgraced, calumniated, slandered, and abused to the death. Nay, and he felt the wrath of God. 'My God, my God, why hast thou forsaken me?' Mat. xxvii. 46. We then may be in the love of God if we be no otherwise than the natural Son was, in whom the love of God was when he was at the worst. In the lowest degree of his abasement, God loved him then as much as at any other time, even when he was accompanied with the sense of the wrath of God. And therefore reject and beat back all temptations with this invincible argument, It is no otherwise with me than it was with his natural Son. Shall I desire to be loved any otherwise of God than Christ was loved? His love to Christ did not exempt him from slander, from disgrace, from abasement, from the sense of his wrath, when yet he was the Son of God always; and I, being in this case, shall I doubt of my adoption? Shall I dishonour God? Shall I add this sin to the rest of my sins?

Satan is wonderful prone to take these weapons, to sharpen them, as I said before, of sin, desertions, sometime of temptations and outward afflictions; and so he comes with his 'If,' 'If thou wert the Son of God, would he deal thus and thus with thee?' It was alway his course. We must therefore have present, to repel all such temptations, that God loves us as he loves his Son, that he chastiseth every son; and that God's love is not always and only manifested in exempting of us from these things. Let us measure God's love that he bears to us in Christ, by the best fruits of his love. What are those? An heart to seek him; to fear his name; love to his majesty; love to his children; delight in good things; hatred of that which is evil. None but his can esteem and value his love by these things. By these therefore, and the like peculiar marks and stamps of the Spirit that are in us, let us judge of his love, and not by any outward thing whatsoever; for all outward crosses whatsoever befell his own Son. And can we desire that he should love us otherwise than he loved him? We are predestinate to be conformable unto him, Rom. viii. 29, and why should we refuse to be conformable to him in abasement, with whom we hope to be conformable in glory? Let faith therefore plead against all the suggestions of Satan and accusations of conscience. By faith in the word of God persuade we ourselves that we are in the love of God. If we find any evidences of his love in our spirits, we shall come to them by and by. But, first, I will name one or two directions how we may come to have God's love in us, and how to know that his love is in us.

1. We may come to have his love in us, *if we be careful to preserve ourselves under the means of salvation, and if so we do present God to ourselves, as he is presented in our glorious gospel.* When we are convinced of sin first (I speak of such as are convinced thoroughly of a sinful state, such may come to the knowledge of God's love in Christ by the gospel, and by presenting God to their souls as he is presented in the gospel, to be the Father of mercy and the Father of Christ. The devil he puts other colours upon God: he presents him as a tyrant, as a judge, as a revenger, as one that hates him.

2. Again, Labour *to be such as God may love us.* God loves his own image. Wherefore doth he love Christ, but because he perfectly represents him? If we would come to have God's love in us, beg of him, that by his Spirit he would stamp his likeness in us; that as he is light, we may be light; as he is love, so we may have love; as he is pitiful, so we may have our hearts enlarged; as he is free in love, so we may be free in love; and that we may be holy, as he is holy; that as he hates sin, so we may hate it; that we may joy in him, affect what he doth affect, hate that which he hates; that so he may look upon us, as his own image, and delight in us, as the representation of his own likeness.

3. Again, We may come to have God's love, *by more and more sequestering ourselves and our affections from conformity with his enemies;* for this helps the other. If we would be like to God, and so come to have him delight and solace himself in us, we must withal labour to be unlike the world and wicked persons, that are yet in the state of corruption and danger of damnation. Let us labour not to conform ourselves to them, but to frame ourselves clean of another fashion; for you know, if we fashion ourselves to the world, the world is not of God, but it is God's enemy. How shall God delight in us, when we delight in courses that are sinful, wretched, and worldly? The world must perish, be condemned, as Paul saith, 'God afflicts us that we should not be condemned with the world,' 1 Cor. xi. 32. The world lies in mischief. Our especial care, therefore, must be, that we have no correspondency with it.

4. But especially, to come to that which I intend to make a distinct point, *by the Spirit, and Christ's manifesting of God himself in the gospel:* 'I have declared unto them thy name, and will declare it, that the love wherewith thou hast loved me may be in them.'

Exhortation. Beg of Christ, therefore, the spirit of revelation, as it is Eph. i. 17, that you may know what is the exceeding love of God in Christ; and see the height, and breadth, and depth of God's love in him. Beg of Christ to shew the Father to us. You know what that holy man said in the gospel, 'Shew us the Father, and it is sufficient,' John xiv. 8. So desire we no more but to see the Father once. We must go to Christ, that he would shew us the Father; and we must go to God the Father to discover his Son. For either or both discover the other. God draws us to

Christ. 'There is none come to me,' saith Christ, 'but the Father draws them.' And Christ opens and discovers the Father to us, and the Holy Ghost discovers them both; for as he proceeds from both, so he shews us the love of both. He shews us the love of the Father and the Son.

Labour, therefore, for the manifestation of Christ, that Christ would manifest his Father's love to us, and that God would manifest Christ by his Spirit: that the Father would give us his Spirit, and the Son would give us his Spirit, which is his love. For God's love is always with God's Spirit. This Spirit comes from him, and his love is always with his Spirit. The same Spirit that sanctifieth us, that witnesseth, is the Spirit of love. Now Christ doth manifest this. We must not only pray, but we must know how Christ manifests himself.

Christ doth manifest God's name to us, as I said before, which is his truth. He opens the understanding by his Spirit, and then he speaks to every man's particular soul by his Spirit. 'I am thy salvation;' he gives faith, &c., Luke xxiv. 45. All knowledge of God's love is from the knowledge of the gospel, together with his Spirit. For how can I know that God loves me, but by his own word and Spirit, by his own Son, Christ? I say, the Spirit and the word, which are divine, they persuade me of God's love. That must be above nature, above Satan, and above all opposition whatsoever, that convinces my heart of God's love in Christ. The arguments must be divine, taken out of God's truth; and those truths must be set on by the Spirit of God, which is above my spirit, and by Christ, God and man, who sends his Spirit. This will silence all objections whatsoever that the heart can make, as indeed our hearts are full of cavils against the love of God. God's Spirit will do it by Christ, together with the truth, the word and Spirit going together. And therefore, because I cannot enlarge myself, beg the Spirit of revelation; and because the Spirit and word go together, attend always upon the word, and think the promises are God's promises, and desire that Christ would set the promises upon our hearts, that we may know the things that belong to us in particular.

Use. Well, if this be so, that the declaring of God's favour and mercy is the way that his love may be in us, as it is, then what shall we think of those that are enemies to the declaration of the name of God, the preaching of the gospel, to the reading of Scripture? They are enemies of our comfort and of God's glory. For how shall I know that God loves me, but by declaring his name by the word, and by the Spirit? Christ by the Spirit and by the word declares his Father's name, and so I come to know the Father's love to me. How pitiful is the estate of those souls that live where there is no means, no word of God, no declaring of God's name? Can the love of God be in them? No; this manifesting of God's love, it is with the manifestation of the truths of the gospel. 'I have manifested thy name in the teaching of the word, that thy love may be in them.' Let us therefore be persuaded to attend upon the means of salvation, and upon the Spirit of God, together with the means. God will work together with the means of salvation, and persuade our hearts of his love to us in Christ, if we attend meekly upon them, at one time or other.

Obj. Oh, but I have attended long upon the means, and have prayed, and yet I cannot find the love of God to me.

Ans. 1. Wait, wait a while; all are not called at one hour. Josias was called when he was young, 2 Chron. xxxiv. 2; and so Timothy, 2 Tim.

iii. 15, and Joseph when they were young; Paul when he was old. Those that were converted at Peter's sermon were men of years, Acts ii. 38. Wait; the good hour will come. God perhaps will have thee under the law a little longer before thou come under grace. He will convince thee of thy cursed estate thou art in by nature, make thee see thyself more vile; and when he hath wrought and perfected the work of humiliation, then in time call thee. Leave not the porch of wisdom's house, leave not the manifestation of God's truth; for in time God will speak to thee, and will say to thy soul that he is thy salvation. To come to an evidence or two of this estate.

1. We may know that we have the love of God in us, among other things, *if we come by this love by the manifestation of God's name*, the manifestation of the truth of God, which is his name revealed in the gospel; if we have the love that we pretend we have of God in us, we can say it came by the declaration and manifestation of God's truth with his Spirit; from thence I came to know God's love to me.

2. I may know it likewise in that I *love God again freely*. He hath loved me, and therefore I love him. I will not offend him, if it were to save my life. I love his truth so, I value it as a pearl, above all things. I could sell all, I could part with all, rather than with that. Therefore God's love hath been heretofore certainly made known to me, in that I so love God and value his truth.

3. *Seasonable afflictions* (which the devil moves us to think evidences of God's hatred), *they are evidences of his love, if they be sanctified*, to make us jealous of our ways, and to see the depth of our corruptions the more, that we can never see sufficiently in this life. They are arguments of God's love. But especially this,

4. *If our love to God come from the word and Spirit, and from good things, that are manifested from thence.* When thou dost find God's love in thee in regard of some beginnings of faith, hope, love, hatred of evil, and that there is peace, and joy, and such like things in thee, which are peculiar, then comfort thyself in thy portion, whosoever thou art, whatsoever estate thou art in for outward things. St Paul, we see, for outward matters, what a kind of man he was. He reckons up his own afflictions and abasements; but how full of thankfulness was he, because he knew that God loved him in Christ, that God's love was in him! 2 Cor. xi. 26. Our Saviour, Christ, what did he care for all these outward things? He knew his Father loved him. Let us therefore labour to have our part and portion in this peculiar love of God, and to be assured that God's love is in us; and for other matters, let us leave them to God's wisdom, who knows what is good for us, and beg of God thus: Lord, I do not ask of thee riches, I ask not glory, I ask not preferment in the world, I ask none of these: I ask thy love, in which all is that is good. For the love of God it is a rich love, as that love that he bears to his Son. If he love me once, he loves me as he loves his Son. Now, he loves him freely, and richly, and unchangeably, and with an incomparable love. God's love both to him and us, it is an incomparable love. For what is the love of a father but a drop from his love? And what is the love of a mother? 'Can a mother forget her child? Yet if she could, I would not forget thee,' saith God, Isa. xlix. 15. So David, 'When my father and mother forsook me, God took me up,' Ps. xxvii. 10. Behold the incomparable love of God to us! And therefore if we have that, we have all that is good.

The love of God, though with afflictions, with crosses, with whatsoever in the world is contrary, yet it is the most desirable estate; for one glimpse of God's fatherly countenance in Christ, it will make us in such a case as we shall not care for any affliction whatsoever. Paul in the dungeon, God gave him a taste of his love, and what did he care for whipping? for the darksomeness, for the nastiness and noisomeness of the prison? Acts xvi. 25. He was, as it were, in paradise. God's love was in him. If God's love be in us, if we be with Daniel in the lions' den, the den shall be a kind of paradise. I say, where God is, there is paradise; yea, indeed, where God's love is, there is heaven itself. So we have God's love, it is no matter what we want; nay, it is no matter in what state of misery we are in this world.

If God have kindled love in us, there is no such sweet estate. If it come from God, it will make us digest anything. Love it will put such life in us, that we shall want or suffer anything quietly. When we feel the love of God in us, that he loves us to immortality, that he loves us to life everlasting, to an inheritance immortal and undefiled, that he loves us in things that accompany salvation, peculiar blessings, this will swallow up all discouragements whatsoever, it will make us be in heaven before our time. The sense of the love of God, when it is shed into our hearts, as it is Rom. v. 5, what will it do? It will make all tribulations, afflictions, crosses, and wants sweet unto us. 'The love of God,' saith he, 'is shed into our hearts by the Spirit.' When the Spirit of Christ Jesus is shed into our hearts, and witnesseth to us the love of God and of Christ, it makes us rejoice under hope, triumph in all tribulation, in all estates whatsoever, as he saith excellently, Rom. v. 3–5. But now to add one thing.

Quest. When doth Christ manifest his Father's love most to us by the Spirit?

Ans. I answer, *This is not at all times alike.* For it is with a Christian's soul as it is with the days of the year, or the seasons of the day. There is foul and fair, there is darkness and light, there is an intercourse, not always an even apprehension to us of God's love in Christ at all times. God sees reasons why it should not be so. Among many there are these,

1. *To sharpen our desires of heaven,* which is a constant, immutable, unchangeable estate.

2. And likewise *to make us watchful,* that when we have tasted of God's love we do not lose it.

3. *To make us observe how we lose it at first,* that so we may recover it again.

4. *To be a correction to us likewise for our boldness to sin, and keeping carnal company, &c.* Many ends God hath to withhold the taste and sense of his love to us, that we may fear him at one time as well as at another.

Quest. But when is it most of all?

Ans. God's love is in us most *when we stand most in need of it, in extremities.* When no creature can help us, when we stand most in need of the manifestation of God's love, we have it. When do parents shew their love most of all? Is it not in the extremities of their children? Then they [be]moan them, and pity them, whom before in the time of health they corrected sharply. But now they see the child is sick and distempered, now they shew all love to it. So when all comforts are taken away, then God's comforts come in place, and then especially; for then they are known to be God's, who doth all things as shall be most for his glory. Then it is most for his glory to help when none else can, and then it is most for the comfort of a poor distressed Christian; for then God comes, as it were, immediately, and doth help even to the ravishing of the soul. If a prince or a king, not sending any messenger, should come to a man immediately, in his own person, and should say to him, Fear not, you shall want nothing, you shall have the best encouragement I can, &c., Oh what a comfort would it be to any man! Yet what are all these to the sweet report of God's love in Jesus Christ? When nothing else can help us, then God's Spirit comes immediately to us, and tells us, Be of good comfort, heaven is yours, God is yours, Christ is yours: all is yours to work for your good. And he doth not only feed them with promises, but enlargeth the soul with present comfort.

Who would therefore be discouraged from enduring anything for God's name, being cast into extremity, when that is the time specially to feel God's love more than at other times? the sense and feeling whereof in Christ is the best estate in the world. There is no estate comparable to the sense of God's love. What makes heaven heaven, as it were, but the sense of his love? of his sweet fatherly face in Christ shining upon us in his Son, and persuading of us that we are his sons? Why, this divine comfort that comes from the favour of God, it is that that makes all nothing, commands all the creatures, rebukes all, Satan and all. The beams of such a rich and gracious God is above all discouragements; for they are human or diabolical; they go no higher; and if they be discouragements from the sense of the wrath of God, from divine desertion, when God shews himself an enemy, yet when he discovers himself a friend and a father in Christ, they all vanish, even as a cloud, as a mist, before the sun. What are all earthly discouragements to the sense of God's love in Christ? Thus we see how God's love is manifested to us by manifesting of God's name by Christ, and when especially, and to what end: 'That thy love may be in them,' saith Christ.

Use 1. Do but raise these thoughts in your meditations, *what a comprehensive thing this is that Christ aims at in his prayer, and in his endeavour;* 'I have declared thy name, and I will,' &c.

Is not this therefore a main thing that we should aim at, that Christ aims at? Must not this needs be an excellent state, to have the love of God in us? Let us therefore, to conclude all for this time, have it in our thoughts, and in our aims, that God's love may be in us. It is no matter who hates us, if God loves us; if God and his love be present with us, it is no matter what troubles be present. Though we be in the valley of the shadow of death, if God be with us, and the assurance of his love to our hearts, it is an heaven upon earth. Rejoice in your portion, whosoever you be, that find the love of God to you in regard of the best things.

We see it is the aim of Christ's prayer, and of his endeavour. It is the aim of the declaration of the gospel, that God's love may be in you; that when God, in regard of his Spirit, and grace, and comfort, is in you, you may have a rich portion. Would you have more than God himself, and his love? What if you want a beam? You have the sun itself, God's love. You want perhaps riches or friends; ay, but you have God's love, which is a wise love. If he saw it were for your good, you should not want them. If you want a stream, you have the spring itself. Rejoice therefore in this your portion; let it be an argument to comfort you, and an argument and motive of endeavour to us all, to labour to find this love of God in us; and to root and purge out of your souls all other things that cannot stand with the love of God. Desire God by his Spirit to subdue in us, and to work out of us mightily, by the strong operation of his blessed Spirit, whatsoever cannot stand with his love in Christ; that he would reign and rule in us by his blessed Spirit; that he would make us such, that he might, as it were, keep his court in us; that he would make our hearts, as it were, an heaven for himself to dwell in; that he would cast down all high and proud thoughts whatsoever; that his love may be in us.

Use 2. And *when we want any grace, pitiful hearts, love to men or God, we must take the method here laid down.* I know all this comes from the want of the feeling of God's love to me; for if God's love were rooted in my heart, if it were as hard as steel, it would make it flexible, pliable, pitiful, and tender to others, and I should love God again. My heart is cold and dead; what is the reason of it? I feel not God's love, and therefore it should edge our prayers thus: 'Lord, let me feel thy love in Christ; I cannot love holy duties without the manifestation of thy love; and therefore manifest thy love to my soul.' 'I give you a new commandment,' saith Christ, 'that ye love one another,' John xiii. 34.

Quest. Why, whence comes this commandment of love to the brethren in the gospel to be a new commandment?

Sol. Because the declaring of the name of God, of his mercy, and of his love in Christ, gives us new hearts; and where there is more manifestation of God's mercy, there is more love to others; and therefore, because there is a new enlargement of God's love in Christ, therefore it is a new commandment. The heart is set on fire now with the love of God, which is manifested in Christ, which was not declared before.

And therefore, if we would have new hearts for this new commandment, this love to God and to others, let us labour to have the declaration of the name of God; more of the mercy of God in Christ; more declaration by his word and Spirit; that so by his sanctified means, having his love in us, we may have new hearts, new love, and new affections to one another. This is the way, in the want of grace, to come to get the love of God in Christ; desire him that he would by his Spirit reveal himself, and reveal Christ to us; and that we may see the dimensions of his love, 'the height, and breadth, &c., of the love of Christ, which passeth knowledge,' Eph. iii. 19, and then all our grace and comfort will follow.

When we are in darkness we are glad to come into the light of the sun; so when we have any distemper in our souls, let us come to this light of God's love in Christ, and by oft meditation of God's word, see there how he presents himself to us a father in covenant; not only a friend, but a father, a gracious father; beg with all means, with reading, with hearing, with conference, with God's Spirit, to reveal his fatherly affection in Christ, and for other things they will be easy.

I speak this the rather, because men go plodding upon duties, and take not a right method. When we find any distemper and deadness of spirit, search what is the cause of it. If it be negligence, irreverence, or any such thing, let us repent, and do the first works. But let us always take this in: 'Lord, shew thyself, shew thy love; thy pardoning love first, and then thy curing love; thy forgiving love, and then thy giving love. I am in a sinful state, forgive that which is amiss, and give me that which I want; shew thy large love every way, both in giving and forgiving; heal me and cure me; let me feel this thy love in the sweetest peculiar fruits of it;' and then reformation will follow upon all, then our care will be continual, when we have the love of God so to walk as that we may abide in that love, and that love in us, that we do not displease him, nor give occasion of distaste.

Therefore there must be a great deal of reverence and love, much humility and watchfulness, if we would preserve ourselves in the love of God. For when one hath once tasted of his love, it is his desire alway to taste it, to taste how gracious the Lord is, Ps. xxxiv. 8. If we therefore would so do, let us watch narrowly, as he that would keep his acquaintance and love with a great person. For we must know the distance between the great God and us. There must be humility. Humble thyself, and walk with thy God, and 'make an end of your salvation with fear and trembling,' Philip. ii. 12. With a fear of jealousy, especially that we grieve not the Spirit, that 'seals us to the day of redemption,' Ephes. iv. 30. And therefore, if we have the Spirit witnessing this love, which is the cause of all comfort and all grace, grieve not the Spirit, quench not the Spirit. When the motions of it come, resist not the gracious Spirit with carnal delights; let the Spirit have a full work; let us lie open to the Spirit of God. God's love reigns in us then, when we will do nothing contrary to it.

Now the sweetest fruit of it in us is his Spirit. Let us not quench nor resist the Spirit, but cherish it by all duties, and by all holy means. One day led thus by a Christian, though with some conflict with corruption, in the taste and sense of God's love to him in Christ, is worth all contentment that this world can afford. And therefore David knew well enough what he wished, Ps. iv. 6, when he desires 'neither corn, nor wine, nor oil.' Let them, saith he, desire what they will, but, 'Lord, shew me the light of thy countenance,' and in it I shall have all that I desire to have; and without that I care neither for corn, nor wine, nor oil, nor any thing.

So let it be our prayer that God would shew his love and mercy, that he would shew his love to us in Christ, which is better than life itself. And then for other things, be at a point, be indifferent. We see the apostles' prayers in their epistles, all of them being led by the same Spirit. They pray for grace, and mercy, and peace. Why do they not pray for all other things? To shew if they had grace, and mercy, and the love of God, they have all. If we have not that, it is no matter what we have. But some other things there are to be unfolded, which must be referred till another time.

THE MATCHLESS LOVE AND INBEING.

SERMON II.

That the love wherewith thou hast loved me may be in them, and I in them.—JOHN XVII. 26.

I HAVE spoken at several times of this verse. We propounded formerly out of it these points to be handled:

First, That the love wherewith God loves his own Son is the love wherewith he loves those that be in him.

Secondly, That God loves his own Son best and first.

Thirdly, That the love of God is the cause of all good to us.

Fourthly, That this love of God may be known.

Fifthly, That one way and ground to know that God loves us with that love he loves his own Son, is the manifestation of God's name: the manifestation of God's truth in the gospel. By that we come to know that God loves us; for this is the coherence of the text, 'I have manifested thy name to them, that thy love may be in them.' So then, the scope, as we see hence, of the gospel, and the manifesting of it, is to lay open the riches of God's love to us, that we may know that God loves us in his beloved Son Christ Jesus. Indeed, so it is. For we have a throne of grace discovered to us in the gospel—God reconciled in Jesus Christ. All is love and mercy to those that are in Christ. 'I have manifested thy name, that thy love may be in them.' The more, therefore, God's name is manifested, God's truth and the covenant of grace, his love and mercy, his name whereby he is now known in the gospel, the more, I say, it is discovered and laid open, surely the more we know God's love, which is as a banner, Cant. ii. 4, 'displayed over us' in the gospel. The use of a banner, you know, was to draw swords under it. Now God's love in the gospel is displayed as a banner; and therefore it hath an attractive, drawing force, to bring us under the sweet government of God in the gospel, because there we are under God's love; and his love, where it is displayed, is like a banner. But this I shall have occasion to touch hereafter.

The point that I am now to take in hand is this: *That Christ doth manifest his Father's name, his love, his mercy, his goodness and truth, 'that God's love may be in them, and himself in them.'*

We see, then, that God's love and Christ do go together. Wheresoever his love is in the best things, there it is in Christ, and with Christ: 'That thy love may be in them, and I in them. 'This is eternal life, to know thee, and whom thou hast sent, Jesus Christ,' John xvii. 3. All comes from God's love to us, together with Christ and in Christ. Where Christ is not, there is not the love of God; and where the love of God is, there is Christ. The sweet combination of the Trinity is not only a pattern of love and agreement to us, that we should love one another, but a main ground of comfort likewise; for they join in love for our good. The Father loves us as he loves his Son, and with his Son. Where Christ is, there is his Father's love; and where his Father's love is, there is Christ. 'I am in the Father, and the Father in me,' John x. 38. All that the Father hath is mine, and all that I have is the Father's.

I say, it is not only a pattern of agreement, that we should labour to agree as the Trinity, which is an exact form of unity, but it is a ground of special comfort; they agree in our good and eternal salvation. The Father looks upon us as we are in his Son; as he hath given us to him to bring us to salvation by his merit and passion. Christ looks on us as we are in the Father's love. 'Thou gavest them me;' and we look on ourselves, first, in Christ, and then in God's love, when we see ourselves in Christ. So that there is this mutual interview, God loves us as we are in his Son: he is in the Father, and we in Christ. We see ourselves in Christ, know ourselves in him, and love ourselves in him, as having our being and living in him, and we are known by him, and his love is known by us, because they go both together. 'That thy love may be in them, and I in them.'

'And I in them.'

We are in Christ, as the branch in the vine, as the members in the head, knit to it in the body; and he is in us as the vine is in every particular branch; as the head is in the members by his influence, imparting unto them life, regiment,* and motion. 'In them;' that is, for the explication of the term, 'that I may be in them,' and dwell in them as in a temple, in a house; that I may infuse strength into them, as the vine into the branches; that I may impart spiritual life into them, as the head into the members. This is the end of my manifesting thy name, that I may be in them, that so thy love may be in them. I might hence observe—I will but touch it—that whosoever knows not Christ, nor hath a being in him, hath nothing to do with the Father, by combining of these two parts together, 'That thy love may be in them, and I in them.'

'I in them.'

Doct. The end of Christ's manifesting his Father's name is, that he may be in them, and that his Father's love may be in them. To unfold the connection a little.

Quest. How doth this hang together, 'I have manifested thy name to them, that I may be in them'?

As thus:

Sol. God's mercy and truth in the gospel, the covenant of grace, are all in Christ, and for Christ. This being discovered and manifested to the soul, the soul sees the love of God in the gospel. There it is opened and discovered. There is offered God's love and mercy in forgiving sins, and in giving all privileges in Christ, not only discovered, but offered to all believers that will receive Christ. Thus all the good in him being discovered and offered to the soul, hereupon it comes to lay hold upon Christ,

* That is, 'government.'—G.

and to embrace him, as offered of the Father, and presented unto it by the Spirit of God, given together with the gospel and the manifestation of it. The Spirit works faith and belief in the heart, which closeth with Christ thus offered; so Christ dwells in the heart by faith. Faith ascends to heaven, and lays hold on Christ; faith goes back to Christ crucified, and Christ dwells in the heart by faith, Eph. iii. 17. Upon the manifestation and discovery of the Spirit, it being given with manifestation, faith is wrought, by which Christ dwells in the heart. 'I have manifested thy name, that the love wherewith thou hast loved me may be in them,' &c. Now, for some observable points, observe this,

Doct. 2. *Christ is in all believers.*

His further dwelling and discovering himself to believers is the end of this manifestation of God's name in the gospel. Christ is in them, as the vine is in the branches; as the head is in the members, Christ is in them all.

Christ is in all believers.

Here is a notable bond of union between them, Christ by his Spirit is in them all, therefore they should all labour to be one. Christ is one in them all, not divided; his Spirit is the same spirit in them all. It were an excellent thing, if all the men in the world had the same thoughts, the same religion, the same aims, the same affection to good things, all as one man. How strongly would they then be carried against any opposition whatsoever! And how comfortable would they be in themselves, if all had one heart, one affection, one aim! This should be, and this is the end of Christ's prayer. It is the end of all, to bring us all to be one in ourselves, to be one in him and in the Father. Now here is one argument to enforce it, that all may agree in good things, in our aims, love, and affections. There is one Christ, there is one head of all the members. 'I in them.' We must take heed that we do not think this phrase to be a shallow phrase, as it is in common life. We say of two friends, there is one soul in two bodies, because the soul lives in the party loved; and so to make it nothing but a matter of affection.* No; 'I in them;' that is, I dwell in them, because I love them; so it would be, that we are in Christ because we love him; and so Christ and we make one soul in two bodies, as though it were nothing but an unity, a dwelling in regard of the affection he bears to us. No; I am in them, and I have manifested thy truth, that I may be further in them. It argues more than union in affection, as in marriage there is more than the union of love, there is the bond that interesteth the wife in all the goods of her husband. Christ is in us more than in love, for he is in us indeed.

Quest. Ay, but is he in us body and soul, and Godhead, and all? What need this, as the papists will have him in the sacrament?

Sol. No; but he is in us in regard of his human nature, because his Spirit is in us, and the same Spirit that sanctified that nature, the same Spirit sanctifieth us. So there is an union between us and his human nature, though it be in heaven. As I said, the last day, of the sun; the sun is in the house when the beams of the sun is there; so when we find the efficacy of Christ, that Christ dwells in us by his Spirit, though his human nature be not there, yet, notwithstanding, the power of the grace of Christ is there, because the same Spirit that sanctified his human nature sanctifies and comforts us, and doth all. It is a wonderful working and operative being when Christ is said to be in us. Even as the vine doth

* Cf. note *b*, Vol. II. p. 194.—G.

transfuse juice and life to the branch, whereupon it comes to be fruitful, so we must conceive deeply of this phrase, 'I in them.' To omit other things;

Quest. How shall we know that Christ is in us?

Sol. 1. This is one way, if Christ be born in us once. If he be in us by his Spirit, *he will work great matters in us, there will presently be tumults in the soul.* For Christ when he is in us, he comes not to friends, but he finds all in rebellion and in opposition; when he is in us therefore, presently there are stirs in the soul. Even as, as soon as ever he was born into the world, you know Herod was mightily troubled and all Jerusalem with him, Mat. ii. 3. Herod had little cause, but much troubled he was. He thought one was born that would have dispossessed him, and therefore he was jealous, much troubled, and labours to kill him if he could. So it is when Christ is born in the soul, there are tumults. Those lusts that bare sway before, those desires, down they go, they plead prescription, and are loath to yield. Natural desires, that have been from before, are loath to yield to Christ, a new comer. He is as a new conqueror that comes with new laws, fundamentally new. He overturns all the laws of lust and of the flesh. He comes in more strongly; and thereupon in conversion, wheresoever Christ is born, there is first a strife, the soul doth not presently yield to him. This is spoken of those that have not been converted from the beginning. There are some now in the bosom of the church, that have no violent conversion from a wicked estate to a good. But from a less degree to a greater, they grow more and more. They have the Spirit of Christ from the beginning. They are not much troubled with such inward oppositions.

2. Where Christ is, *he will drive out all that is contrary.* As when he entered into the temple, he drave out the money-changers, and whipped out those corrupt persons there, Mat. i. 12, so, as soon as ever he comes into the soul by his Spirit, out go those lusts, those desires that were there before, worldliness, profaneness, fury, and rage, wherewith the soul was transported before, that possessed the habitation that God should dwell in. When Christ comes in, he scourgeth out all. Where these therefore are in any force, there certainly Christ is not.

3. Again, *Where Christ is, he doth rule;* for he takes the keys of the house himself, and governs all in some measure. He gets into the heart, rules, and sets up a throne there. For I make account* if he go no deeper than the brain and tongue; that is, to give him no better entertainment than he had when he was born, to be put in a manger. No; where he is—I mean, where he is in the heart and affections—there he rules; and where he takes not his lodging in the affections and in the heart, in the joy, desire, and delight, he is not at all to any purpose. To have him in the brain to talk, and in the tongue to discourse, and to keep the heart for worldly lusts and such things, I account not this an inbeing of Christ to any purpose, to any comfort. Where Christ is comfortably, he takes his throne and lodging in the heart, he dwells in it by faith. By heart, I mean, especially, the will and affections. He draws the will to cleave to him, to choose him for the best good. And therefore where Christ dwells, there is an admiring of the excellencies, and of the good things that are in him, and contentment in him above all things in the world. For he dwells in the heart and affections, especially in the will. The will chooseth him to be an head and husband. It cleaves to him as the chief good. The affection of joy, it

* Qu. 'no account'?—Ed.

joys in him above all things. The affection of love and desire, of zeal in his cause, is strong against those that oppose him and his truth. Thus he takes up his seat and his throne in the heart wheresoever he is in truth.

4. And, therefore, this follows upon that too. Where Christ is in the heart by faith, and takes up the affections, *there is a base esteem of all the excellencies in this world whatsoever.* Moses did but see afar off the excellency that came by Christ, and he accounted all the pleasures of sin for a season to be nothing, Heb. xi. 27, and took upon him the rebuke of Christ rather. St Paul accounted all but dung and dross, Philip. iii. 8; all his former works, all his pharisaical excellency, and all things else he accounted as nothing, and of no value, having in his heart and soul an admiration of the all-sufficiency and excellency in Christ. Zaccheus, as soon as ever Christ came once into his house—but he was in his heart before he was in his house, or else he had never done it—he grew liberal: 'Half my goods,' saith he, 'I give unto the poor,' Luke xix. 8. He loved extortion and base courses before, but now down they go, he will be no base dealer, no oppressor any more. No; the half of his goods he gives to the poor, and he satisfies those whom he had wronged.

And so the disciples, howsoever they were busied before, when Christ once took up his lodging in their hearts, and opened their spirits by his Spirit, to see wherefore he came into the world 'to save sinners,' and opened their eyes to see the excellency that was in him, away goes all the trash that they were exercised in before, that they might follow Christ. Matthew follows him presently, Luke v. 27; and so the rest. It is impossible that the heart which entertains our blessed Saviour Jesus Christ into it, should have in over-much admiration any earthly excellency whatsoever. For it is the nature of the soul, upon the discovery of better things, to let the estimation of other things of less value to fall down presently. As we see in civil things, children, when they come to be men, they are ashamed of childish toys. So it is with a man that is converted: when Christ enters he so opens the understanding, and enlargeth the heart to see and admire better things, that presently it begins to care nothing for this world in comparison. Thus we see how we may know whether Christ hath taken his seat and lodging in us or no.

5. To go on a little further. If Christ be in us, *he doth frame us to himself.* He doth transform us to his own likeness, where he rules by the Spirit; for he is such a head as changeth his members, such an husband as changeth his spouse, 2 Cor. iii. 18. Moses could not change the complexion of his Ethiopian wife: she was black, and he left her black. But Christ renews and changeth his spouse. He is such a head as quickens his members; such a vine as puts life in the branches. And therefore you may know by this altering, changing, transforming power, whether he be in you or not. He alters and changeth us to his own likeness, that as he is set down in the gospel in his life, conversation, and disposition, so, if we have entertained him and he be in us, we should have the same disposition, the same mind, and the same will with him; for he will alter us to himself, that he may take the more delight in us. We shall judge of things as he judgeth of them, we shall judge meanly of outward things. There will be a delight to do our Father's will, as it was his meat and drink to do his Father's will, John iv. 34. We shall have a spirit of obedience, as he had, to look to our Father's glory, and to his commandment in all things. We shall have compassion and melting hearts to the misery of others, as he had bowels yearning to see sheep without a shepherd. We shall have humble

and meek hearts, as he had. 'Come, learn of me, for I am humble and meek,' Mat. xi. 29. For where he dwells, I say, and takes up his throne, he alters and changes the disposition in all things to be like his own. For when he comes to the soul, he takes up all the parts thereof, and keeps out all that may hinder his work. He takes up the eyes, the ears, the understanding, and the affections; and even as we shut up the doors and windows against all that is contrary to us, so the Spirit of Christ, where he is, shuts the door of the senses both to Satan and all his suggestions, and whatsoever else might hurt us.

6. Where he enters likewise, *he possesseth the whole inward and outward man to himself.* He changeth it like to himself; he rules the eyes, the ears, the hands; he renews all, that our delights are clean other than they were before. If there be such a power in his truth, that, like a scion engraffed, it doth change us into itself, certainly where Christ dwells, he hath as much power as his word. His word is like leaven, which alters the whole lump to be like itself. For the word engraffed makes the soul that believes it heavenly like itself, 1 Cor. v. 6. How is this? Because Christ comes with his word, leavens, alters, changeth, and turns the soul. Christ by his Spirit and word is said to do it, because the Spirit of Christ comes with the word, which doth all. Those therefore whose dispositions are contrary to Christ, Christ is not begotten in them. For certainly he doth alter and change and fit his temple for himself, and drives out and chaseth thence, as I said before, all that is contrary; and keeps the door of the senses, and possession against all. He useth every member as an instrument of the Spirit and weapon of defence.

7. Again, You may know who dwells within, *by what servants come out of the house, and who comes in.* Would you know who dwells in the soul? See what comes from within the house: filthy thoughts, blasphemous words, oaths, rotten discourse; eyes full of adultery, ears open to receive that which may taint the soul. Who dwells here? Christ? No; where nothing but filth comes out, the devil dwells there. These two are immediate opposites; there is no third; either Christ or the devil dwells in us. Now when nothing comes out of a man but scorning of goodness, and that which is rotten and offensive—if there be other things, they come from the brain, and not from the heart; they have no seat there—the devil is there; Christ and his messengers are not there. There come no good thoughts, no good desires, no good speeches; and is Christ there? Is Christ in the heart, that drinks in corruption at all the senses? that lets open all the senses to all that is naught,* to hear all kinds of things that may cherish corruption, that will be at these corrupting exercises, that will see all that may blow up the flesh? What is this within that is thus cherished? Is Christ fed with filthy discourse, with filthy spectacles? Doth Christ, in us, delight in these things? Oh no! Who dwells there, then, that is thus fed? Sure the spirit that is there fed is the devil. The devil dwells in our spirits, and in our corruptions, which are like the devil, in that proportion that he dwells in us, and stirs us up to feed him with these things, to the destruction of the soul. No, no, from the heart where Christ is proceed often prayer, sighs, and groans to God, and fruitful discourses to others; and all the senses and passages of the body are open for good things. He hath desires to see that which is good, which may edify. He desires to speak, and to have others to speak, that which may feed the soul. The lips of the wise feed many,' saith Solomon, Prov. x. 21. So where

* That is, 'naughty,' wicked.—G.

Christ is, Christ's Spirit is thus fed. Thus familiarly have I discovered to you how you may know whether Christ be in you or no.

Quest. What if he be not?

Sol. He must be, or else you are reprobates. So saith the apostle, 2 Cor. xiii. 5, 'Know you not that Christ is in you, except you be reprobates?' He means not eternal reprobates, but this, If Christ be not in you, the devil and corruption are. Anatomise a carnal man, and what is in him? In his brain, a company of wicked plots and devices of the world; in his heart, a deal of love of the world, and of money; in his memory, matter of revenge; in his conscience, that which will stare upon him at the day of death, and that which will damn him unless he repent. Examine yourselves, therefore. If Christ be not in you, you are reprobates; and he that hath not the Spirit of Christ, he is none of his. I beseech you, therefore, take a trial, and enlarge the point in your own meditations. Examine what spirit is in you. If we find the Spirit of Christ to be in us, as, indeed, he is in all his in some measure, what a comfortable state is this! He is the best guest that ever we could entertain in this world, for he doth that to the soul that the soul doth to the body. What doth the soul to the body? Whence hath the body the beauty that it hath? whence the vigour that it hath to work with? to move from place to place? whence hath it government to rule itself? whence all that is excellent, good and useful? From the guest that dwells in it, the soul—the reasonable, understanding soul. For as soon as the soul is out of the body, the body is an ugly, deformed thing, a dead creature, unfit for anything. It cannot stir itself, a loathsome thing; it cannot rule itself, a mere lump of earth. Now, as the soul is to the body, so is Christ to the soul, if he dwell there. For he gives beauty and loveliness unto it. He transforms it to his own likeness and image, that it may be the object of God's love; that he may love us, not only because we are in his Son, but because his Son's image is in us. We have not only beauty from Christ dwelling in us, but where he is he works and stirs us to all holy and heavenly duties.

8. Where the Spirit is, *there is often prayer*, as Christ often prayed; a perpetual endeavour of doing good, as his Spirit in him stirred him to go from place to place to do good. Where his Spirit is, there is holiness. If we consider what a sweet guest Christ is, where he is there is all beauty, work, comfort, strength, and all. And where he is, he is for ever. He never forsakes his lodging, he never forsakes his house and temple. He had two temples built with stone; one by Solomon, and another after the captivity. Both lie now in the rubbish, and are demolished for ever, and shall never be repaired again. But his spiritual temples he never leaves wholly; for whose souls he now dwells in, he will take them by that Spirit that dwells in them, and carry them to heaven, to be where he is. The divine Spirit, that dwells in our souls now, shall quicken our dead bodies, and make them like to his glorious body.

What an excellent honour and happiness is this, to entertain such an one as will rule, govern, and adorn our souls while we live, and carry them to himself and to his Father in heaven, and will quicken our bodies likewise! An everlasting inhabitant he is. If Christ be in us, therefore, we may comfort ourselves. But here must be an objection answered.

Obj. Christ doth seem oftentimes to be absent from the soul to which he was present before; he seems to leave his house and his temple sometimes.

Sol. I answer, He is said to leave that soul into which, shutting the door to his knocks, and resisting the sweet motions of his Holy Spirit, he never actually entered. But he never leaves that soul into which he is once entered to dwell. Indeed, sometimes he conveys himself into a corner of the soul; for when he does not entertain him and respect him as he should, and preserve the motions, comforts, and graces of his Spirit, but give way to the suggestions and temptations of the devil and ill company, &c., then he retires himself; but he is still in the soul. For even as God the Father, when he would have his own beloved Son Christ Jesus to be abased on the cross, withdrew not his divinity, but the sense and comforts thereof from Christ's human nature, that he might suffer for us on the cross, Matt. xxvii. 46—loving him still notwithstanding, so that the divinity did not forsake him, but only did rest and cease to support and comfort him at that time, that he might perform the work of satisfaction for our sins—so it is with us, though it be a different case, when God humbles us for our rashness, want of reverence, of careful walking before God, and preserving the sweet work of his Holy Spirit: then Christ hides himself only, takes not himself away.

Christ was God on the cross, but the comfort was withdrawn, that he might suffer. So the comfort of Christ's presence is withdrawn, that he may humble us for our former sins; that we might make more of this guest than we did before; that we may be stirred up to entertain him better, and might be more careful for the time to come, to cleave closer unto him. So much for the answer of that, that Christ is oftentimes in the soul, when he discovers not himself to be there; as he was near unto Mary, though her eyes being full of tears, she could not discern him, John xx. 15.

Quest. But how shall I know that he is there by any discovery at all, that he hath any being at all in the soul at such a time?

Sol. 1. Yes; a man may know he is there. There will be some pulses, some beating of the soul. Where Christ and the love of God is, they ever go together. Is there any love of God, any love to him? Again, Is there a longing after Christ's presence? Is there a grieving, when we feel not the comfort we had before? Oh this is a sign he hath been there. He hath left somewhat there by his Spirit. Though he be retired into a corner of the soul, yet he hath left somewhat behind him to work a desire of further communion and fellowship with him. As it is Cant. v. 5, when he left knocking at the door, when the spouse would not open, he left somewhat behind, the droppings of his fingers, that drew the love of the spouse to him. So that he never leaves us, no, not for to humble and abase us for our bold walking, but he leaves somewhat in the soul, some desires, some sense of his love, that they think their estate is not good till they have recovered their former estate. They linger after him, they are never pleased with earthly contentments in this temper of the soul. In desertion they are not themselves, they are not quiet, because they think Christ is lost. As Christ's mother, when she thought he was lost, was full of woe, Luke ii. 48, so a Christian soul, when it conceits that it hath lost Christ, it is never quiet till it have found him again.

Sol. 2. Again, Christ may be very near, and dwell in us sometimes, and we see him not: because we may so dwell upon corruption, and be so full [of] grief in affliction, that we forget Christ; as Mary, who, though Christ was near her, yet could not discern him, her eyes were so full of tears, John xx. 15; and as Hagar, who was so full of grief, that she could not see the fountain appear, Gen. xxi. 16. There may be, I say, in desertion of soul such grief for our other things, crosses, losses, fears, &c., that a man may forget Christ, till he recover himself by meditation, prayer, and conference with others that are more skilful than himself, that can tell what is in him by his pulses, discourse, and desires. Sometimes we must trust the judgment of others better than our own, to know what is in us. But I will not enlarge myself in this. Thus we may know that Christ is in us, which is a point of especial comfort.

Obj. But the soul thinks, Is the Spirit of Christ in us? Will such an Holy Spirit, as that we cannot conceive him in the height of his holiness and greatness, vouchsafe to dwell in such sinful spirits? We cannot conceive how the Spirit of Christ should dwell in us, that are so corrupt as we are.

Sol. Indeed, I must needs say, it is an argument of wonderful love, that infinite holiness should be joined with such corruption, that greatness will be in such narrow straits, that glory will be in such an obscure place and habitation as our souls. Here is a wondrous condescending; admirable mercy it must needs be. But let us not be discouraged; Christ by his Spirit is in us, notwithstanding our corruption, because he cannot be a whit corrupted by it. The Spirit is an active thing, it suffers nothing. The spirit is as fire, which endures nothing: it is always doing, always in action, it is an active element. So the Spirit of Christ in us, though it be in us, yet it joins not with our corruptions. As the sunbeams are pure still, though they shine upon impure and filthy places, so Christ's Spirit, it is a working, fiery thing. As fire consumes dross, so the Spirit, being like fire, though it be where corruption is, yet it is there, as an enemy to it, opposing, consuming, and wasting it by little and little.

Quest. But why doth he not do it all at once?

Sol. There are divers reasons: God will have us to have matter of abasement here, to make us desire to be with him. Yet in the mean time Christ will be so in the Church his spouse, cleansing and fitting her for himself, as that by his Spirit dwelling in her she shall daily oppose, and by little and little subdue and bring under all corruption whatsoever, till at last she have gotten a full and perfect conquest and triumph over all. All the imaginations, desires, and lusts, that exalt themselves against the Spirit of Christ, shall be brought down at last; the Spirit will subdue all. Stronger is the Spirit that is in us, than the spirit that is in the world, 1 John iv. 4, though it be in never so little a measure; and therefore by little and little will conquer all within us, without us, the devil and all at the last. Thus much to answer that doubt.

Use 1. That which further ariseth from hence, that Christ is in us, is not only matter of comfort, but likewise *it shews and directs us how to look on other Christians; to look upon them as the temples and houses where Christ dwells.* Why should we not reverence and respect Christians for the guest that is in them, the Spirit of Christ? If Christ vouchsafe to dwell in such a man, shall he not dwell in our love? Shall not one place contain us here, that heaven must contain ere long? We shall be all together in heaven, and shall we not be loving together here? Thus considering that Christ is in all his, how should we respect Christians, that are the habitation of Christ, the second heaven? For Christ hath but two heavens; the heaven where he is, and the heart of a believing Christian, where Christ is, and rules in a comfortable measure, and will rule more and more. How should we value such! Not as many cursed devilish spirits, that disgrace and oppose Christ in his members. That which they do to his image in his children, that they would to him himself, if they had him in their power.

Use 2. The last use shall be an use of direction, *how to keep Christ, and to preserve him, and the sense of his being in us with comfort,* seeing it is so comfortable an estate to have Christ in us, and that yet ofttimes we want the sweet comfort of his presence. In a word, mark here the dependence, 'I have manifested thy name. that thy love may be in them and I in them.' Christ is in us then, by manifesting of divine truth. He conveys himself into our hearts, by our understandings; he manifests his truth, the means of salvation, by his ordinance; he manifests divine truths to the understanding by his Spirit, which goes together with his word. From the understanding he goes to the heart, and there he dwells; for manifesting of divine truths, and Christ being in us, go together.

1. *Those that care not for the discovery and manifesting of Christ's truth in the gospel, let them never think to entertain Christ into their hearts,* for he will come with his word and with his own ordinance; his word and Spirit always go together. Therefore let this be one chief direction. If we will have Christ to be in us, to fill our hearts, and remain with us, let us attend upon the blessed means of salvation, and be where he is, and then he will be with us. He is in the church, and he is in every particular member; but especially where his ordinance is, there is he with the Spirit. God the Father, Son, and Holy Ghost are all there if we have Christ in us. And therefore oft attend upon the ordinances of God, and communion of saints, and then you shall find experience of Christ. Christ joined with the two disciples when they were talking of him, as they were going to Emmaus, Luke xxiv. 15; so let us oft stir up the grace of Christ in us by conferring of good things, and Christ will be with us, joining with good company, &c.

2. Again, Would we preserve Christ's presence in us? *Labour then that he may dwell largely in our hearts.* Now that which enlargeth the soul is humility. For it empties the soul, and makes it large. Pride swells the soul up, and drives out Christ. God gives grace to the humble; Christ dwells in the humble soul. You know he was born in an humble virgin's womb, and he is new born in the womb of an humble soul. Preserve therefore humble, base conceits of ourselves; that in us there is nothing that is good, nothing worthy to be respected, that so Christ may dwell largely in our hearts. Let us have no wit, no reason of our own, contrary to Christ. Let us have no wills, no desires contrary to his. Let us even give up the keys and the regiment* of our souls to him, and then he will dwell largely there. Humility keeps him there. If his word be our reason, his commandment our will, and his comfort our joy and delight, then he will dwell largely in us, for there is nothing in us to oppose him. But if we have several states of soul, distinct from his government, it is no wonder we banish him, when we will not live by faith in him, but by our wits, shifts, tricks, lusts, the examples of others, and by the spirit of the world. It is no wonder, I say, that we savour only of earthly things if we live thus. It is no wonder that Christ is not preserved in us if we be not ruled by his Spirit. It is no wonder that he departs from us when we set ourselves contrary to him, and have wills and reasons of our own repugnant and disagreeable to his, and ways to get wealth, and to raise ourselves contrary to his gospel and truth. Will Christ rule in such a soul? No. He subdues all. The Spirit of Christ is like a mighty wind, as it is compared by Christ to Nicodemus, John iii. 8, that beats all down before it. If we cherish contrary desires and contrary delights to Christ, it is no wonder if he delight not to dwell in such a soul.

* That is, 'government.'—G.

3. *Beg of Christ likewise that he would stay with us;* as they in the gospel, when he made as if he would have gone forward from them, Luke xxiv. 29, constrained him to stay, saying, 'Abide with us: for it is towards evening, and the day is far spent;' and he went in to tarry with them. So, lay we hold on Christ, by the means of salvation; stay him with us by prayer and importunity, especially when the night of death, and error, and superstition comes. Say, 'Lord, night is near, stay with us, depart not from us.' Lay an holy violence upon God, as Jacob did: 'Thou shall not go hence.' Lay hold on him by prayer, and do not leave him till we have drawn virtue and got some blessing from him; he must be kept by entreaty.

4. *And then desire him to perfume our souls for his dwelling*, as the church, Cant. iv. 16, 'Arise, O north wind; and blow, O south; that my beloved may come into his garden.' Desire Christ by his Spirit to blow upon us, that our beloved may come into his garden, that he may find somewhat there to solace himself withal—humility, love, pity, large and loving hearts, as himself had, to do all good. Desire him to plant those blessed spices of grace in our hearts, and that he would blow upon them by his Spirit, that they may prosper and thrive, that so he may come into his garden and solace himself. Let us still desire further and further communion with him; never be content. As the church, Cant. i. 1, 'Let him kiss me with the kisses of his mouth.' He hath been familiar, but I desire more still. So every Christian soul that hath once entertained Christ is never content till it be with Christ in heaven, but still desires a fuller measure of comfort, grace, strength, and assurance. And why doth the soul thus desire after him? 'Oh his love is better than wine,' Cant. i. 2. So saith the church, having had a sense and feeling of his love. 'Thy love is sweeter than wine,' and therefore 'let him kiss me with the kisses of his mouth.' Desire therefore a more nearer communion in his love; for it is sweeter than wine, being once tasted.

5. And having got enjoyment of communion with God, *shut the soul to other things.* The comfort of his presence is a heaven upon earth, sweeter than wine, and above all other things to be desired. Take we heed therefore that we grieve not his good Spirit, and force him to retire himself; that we quench not his sweet motions by anything contrary to him. Those that have guests which they respect will do nothing that may be offensive to them. So let us watch over our souls, that nothing come in that may grieve Christ, nor anything come forth to grieve his Spirit in us. Let us not thrust ourselves into such occasions and company as may do or speak such things as may grieve the Spirit of God in us. Let us neither grieve the Spirit in ourselves, by cherishing that which is evil in our own hearts, nor by thrusting ourselves into the company of those whom we know by experience will grieve the Spirit. A man cannot go into bad company, but he must either be grieved, or tainted, and corrupted. Who would redeem familiarity and favour with them? exchange comfort and sense of Christ's Spirit for the favour of such men as grieve the Spirit in us? No; a soul that walks in the strength of the comfort of Christ's dwelling in him must be watchful and jealous over himself, and preserve heavenly motions, cherish them, and make them strong, and banish all that is contrary.

Quest. But how shall I recover him again, if I have grieved the Spirit, and lost the sense of his being in me?

Sol. I will name but one means. *Observe how thou lost it, and recover him by the contrary.* If thou wilt renew the experience of his love, and his dwelling in thee comfortably, consider how didst thou lose him? Was it by negligence? by omission of duties? Didst thou not read when thou mightest, or hear when thou mightest? or gavest thou thy thoughts liberty to range? or didst thou not walk with God as thou shouldst? didst thou cast thyself into ill company, or cherish carnal desires? Take a contrary course then; converse with those that are good; stir up the grace of God in thee by meditation, and by renewing thy purposes and resolutions; hear as much as thou canst; speak to God as much as thou canst; maintain communion with saints, &c. As thou lost it, so endeavour the recovery by a contrary way, and then Christ will come again to the soul. We see, Cant. v. 3–6, that after Christ had stood knocking and calling to his spouse, 'Open to me, my sister, my love, my dove, my undefiled,' till his head was filled with dew, and his locks with the drops of the night, but found no entrance, he retired, and withdrew himself, because she would not rise and put on her coat. But afterward, when she endeavoured herself, and used contrary means to her former sluggishness, seeking him, and saying, 'What is become of my beloved?' &c., then Christ came again into his garden, returned to his spouse, and forgat the former unkindness.

We deal with such a Saviour, that though we lose the sense of his presence for a time, yet if we use contrary means, and knit ourselves to his ordinances, at last we shall refind his love to our souls. Nay, he is so loving, so indulgent, that he never upbraids us with our former sins; as we see in Peter, whom he upbraided not with his former denial. Who would not maintain love, respect, and communion with such a Saviour as this, especially considering what a sweet estate it is to have Christ with us at all times, and in all estates, and so to have the love of God, for both go together? And what are all discouragements where the love of God in Christ is? What are all the creatures to God's love, to Christ? Where the soul is persuaded that it is in covenant and peace with God through Christ, and when it knows that Christ's Spirit is in it, this is a comfort above all discouragements whatsoever. Discouragements are carnal, outward things; the comforts are the presence of divine things. The Spirit of Christ, whose presence drowns all things, it is precious above all creatures, strength, beauty, wit, &c., yea, and prevalent above all the afflictions and sufferings in the world.

All afflictions cannot hinder the life of reason, and can they hinder the life of grace? No. Paul saith excellently, the more 'our outward man decays,' the more we suffer in our outward man, 'the more the life of Christ is manifest in us,' 2 Cor. iv. 16. So far are we from being hurt by any outward sufferings in the world, or discouraged by them, that the life and presence of Christ in us is thereby made more glorious, Christ triumphs and rules the more, by how much the more outward opposition we have.

If God's love, and consequently Christ, be in us, what if all the creatures were against us? Is there not more in God and Christ, than in all the creatures? Made he not all things of nothing? What made the martyrs in the primitive church to sacrifice their blood so willingly and cheerfully? Because the love of God was manifested to them in Christ Jesus. His name was manifested and declared as a sweet ointment poured forth, which caused those virgins to follow him. The sense and apprehension of the love of God, manifested by the Spirit of Christ, begat in them such a love to God again, that was strong even to death. It engendered such an heat within, that made them endure all the heat and flame without; so that all the torments which the malice and wit of persecutors could devise, could not daunt their invincible spirit; but in all these things they were more than conquerors, through him that loved them. A sweet state it is.

I beseech you, therefore, every day examine whether Christ be in you, and in what measure he is in you; and labour to give him more room in your hearts. Will not the contrary daunt us? else we are reprobates, refuse creatures, and the devil is in us. But contrariwise, if he be in us, he will fit us to be with him. He comes to us, that we may come to be with him; for why doth he dwell in us? One main reason is, to fit us for heaven. Let us labour, then, that he may be in us, that he may fit us for himself, to dwell with him in heaven. Labour that none may rule us but his Spirit. In death, what a comfort will it be, that Christ is in us. The Spirit of Christ, that hath ruled me all my life, shall carry my soul to heaven, and shall raise my dead body. If Christ be in us, what need we fear judgment? Will the head condemn the members? Christ is in us while we live, and therefore joyfully we may expect judgment. Why? Our Redeemer, our Saviour, our Head, our Husband, will be our Judge. Therefore, of all estates in the world, get into Christ, and labour by all means to get Christ into us, by prayer, by getting grace, &c., that he may delight and solace himself in us. It is the best estate in the world.

Out of Christ, a man is as a branch cut from the vine, subject to the fire. Out of him, a man is as a member cut from the head, cut from the body, good for nothing, neither lively nor fruitful. Get into Christ: it is a state of all grace, for all grace is derived to us from him. It is a state of comfort in life and death, and for ever. He is the 'second Adam;' and as all our misery is derived and communicated by being born of the first, from whom sin and corruption is derived, and misery with sin, mortal diseases, and all other misery, so, as soon as the 'second Adam,' Christ, is got into us, his Spirit reigns to glory with us: he never leaves us till he have made us as himself. It should be our main endeavour in this world, therefore, to get out of the cursed estate we are in by nature, and to get into Christ, the 'second Adam,' and then we are safe. For there is more comfort in him than there was sin and misery in the first.

A HEAVENLY CONFERENCE.

A HEAVENLY CONFERENCE.

NOTE.

The 'Heavenly Conference between Christ and Mary' appeared originally in a small 18mo volume in 1654. A second edition in 4to appeared in 1656. The title-page of the latter will be found below.* It is usually appended to the Commentary upon 2 Corinthians Chap. IV., 4to, 1656. Cf. Note, Vol. IV. page 308. G.

*A HEAVENLY
CONFERENCE
BETWEEN
CHRIST
AND
MARY
AFTER HIS
RESURRECTION

WHEREIN,
The intimate familiarity, and near relation between
Christ and a Beleever is discovered.

By the Reverend RICHARD SIBBS, D.D.

LONDON,
Printed by *S. G.* for *John Rothwell*, and are to be sold at the
Fountain and *Bear* in *Cheapside*,
1656.

TO THE READER.

The scope and business of this epistle is not so much to commend the workman—whose name is a sweet savour in the church—as to give thee a short summary-view of the generals handled in this treatise. Though much might be said of this eminent saint, if either detraction had fastened her venomous nails in his precious name, or the testimony of the subscribers of this epistle might give the book a freer admission into thy hands. This only we shall crave leave to mind the reader of, that this bright star, who sometimes with his light refreshed the souls of God's people while he shone in the horizon of our church, set, as we may say, between the evening of many shadows and the morning of a bright hoped-for Reformation; which, though it be for the present overcast, yet being so agreeable to the mind of Jesus Christ, and ushered in with the groans and prayers of so many of his saints, we doubt not but will in God's own time break forth gloriously, to the dissipating of those clouds and fogs which at the present do eclipse and darken it.

Now, as it is the wisdom of God, in bringing about his own designs, to raise up fit and suitable instruments for the work of every generation, so it is also the gracious dispensation of God to put seasonable words into the mouths of those his servants, who by faith do fix their eyes on him for the guidance of his blessed Spirit; as every judicious reader may observe in the works of this reverend divine, who foreseeing, as it were, what a degeneracy of spirit professors in his time were falling apace into, that itch of questions and disputings, like a noxious humour, beginning then to break forth among professors,* like a skilful physician, applied himself to preserve the vitals and essentials of religion, that the souls of his hearers, being captivated with the inward beauty and glory of Christ, and being led into an experimental knowledge of heavenly truths, their spirits might not evaporate and discharge themselves in endless, gainless, soul-unedifying, and conscience-perplexing questions. For as it is in nature, a man that hath tasted the sweetness of honey will not easily be persuaded that honey is bitter, but he that hath only taken it up upon credit may soon be baffled out of it, because no act can go higher than its principles; and so it is in religion. For those good souls that have embraced the truths of Jesus Christ upon a supernatural principle, and experimented not only the truth, but the goodness of them in their own souls, they are the clinched Christians, the good hold-fast men, as Mr Fox styles some Christians in his

* In margin here, *Pruritus disputandi scabies ecclesiæ.*—Sir H. Wotton.—G.

days; they are the even and steady walkers. Whereas those that have only a 'form of godliness,' 2 Tim. iii. 5, a slight tincture—who have only out of novelty and curiosity, or pride and ambition, or other self ends, professed religion—will prove giddy and unconstant, 'like clouds carried about with every blast,' Eph. iv. 14, and while they promise themselves liberty, be a prey to the net of every fancy and opinion.

To the sound and practical Christian that is not squeesy-stomached,* will the truths in this treatise be grateful. Supposing therefore and desiring, if thou art not, thou mayest be such a one, here is offered to thy consideration a divine and heavenly discourse betwixt Christ and Mary, between a soul-burthened sinner and a burthen-removing Saviour.

That thou mayest here see how diligent Mary is to seek, how ready Christ is to be found. Mary hath her heart brimful of sorrow; Christ comes, as it were, 'leaping over the mountains,' Cant. ii. 8, with comfort and bowels of compassion. Mary was in a strong pang of affection, nay, her affections were wound so high that her expressions seem broken; and her actions might seem to savour of irregularity, were it not that the excellency of the object did warrant the height of her affection, and the compassion of Christ was large enough, not only to interpret for the best, but also to pardon and cover all her infirmities. The woman was better at her affections than expressions. 'They have taken away my Lord.' She speaks at random, names nobody, whether Jews, or disciples, or soldiers. But see the strength of her faith. She is not ashamed to call him 'Lord,' even in the lowest state of humiliation. Though Christ be reproached, persecuted, despised, rejected, dead, buried, yet he shall be Mary's Lord. Again, 'I know not where they have laid him.' She dreams of a bodily asportation† and resting of Christ somewhere, and speaks with indignation, as if she looked upon it as an indignity or incivility, nay, of cruelty—*Sævitum est in cadavera, sævitum est in ossa, sævitum est in cineres* (Cyprian)—of the Roman emperors' cruelty, to remove a dead body (*a*). What was done to Christ, Mary takes it as done to her; and, good heart, she thinks she hath so much right to him, that he should not be stirred without her knowledge. And 'I know not where,' &c.

Now while Mary is seeking Christ—who is never far absent from a seeking soul—he stands at her back. Christ is nearer to us many times than we think of. Sometimes a poor soul wants the sight of comfort more than matter of comfort, and is, like Hagar, weeping for water when the well is hard by. Seeking of Christ is the soul's duty; but Christ manifesting himself is the soul's comfort. Mary turned herself, and she saw Jesus. Gerson saith, the angels rose up at the presence of Christ, which Mary seeing, made her turn about.‡ But omitting that conjecture, the original word *στρέφεσθαι* is sometimes used for a turning of the face, but most frequently for a turning of the whole body. But to put it out of doubt here, it is said exegetically, *ἐστραφη ἐις τὰ ὀπίσω*, 'she turned herself back.' The same phrase the Septuagint§ use of Lot's wife looking back (*b*). Many times Christ hath his face towards us, when we have our backs upon him; and therefore if thou wouldst find Christ, turn thyself to him.

* That is, 'queezy,' 'squeamish,' = rising on the stomach.—G

† That is, 'a carrying away.' Cf. Richardson, *sub voce*.—G.

‡ In margin here, 'Ideo conversa est quia angeli assurrexerunt presentiæ Christi. —*Gerson*.

§ *Καὶ ἐπέβλεψεν ἡ γυνὴ αὐτοῦ εἰς τὰ ὀπίσω*; *i.e.*, se domum versus præter virum suum qui subsequebatur ipsam.—*Junius* in anal. in Gen.

Again, Here thou mayest see the true Joseph. He knows Mary when she knows not him, but takes him for the gardener. Christ is always beforehand with us in his grace. He loves us before we love him, and calls us before we call him. Mary travails with desires to find Christ, and Christ is full of yearnings towards her. Like Joseph, he could restrain no longer, and because the general manifestations of Christ wrought little, he calls her by her name, 'Mary;' and she being a sheep of Christ, 'knows his voice,' and answers him with a title of dignity, *Rabboni;* that is to say, 'My Master.'

We may see here that discoveries of grace are not fruitless. They stir up believers' reverence and obedience. 'Let us sin because grace abounds,' is the devil's application of Christ's doctrine, Rom. vi. 1.

These and several other particulars are with much brevity, spirituality, and perspicuity handled in this treatise, and with that liveliness that they shew they come from one whose own heart savoured what he taught to others. The largest part of this book is spent upon that sweet doctrine, viz., *a believer's interest in God as a Father, and the comforts that flow from that sweet relation.* The foundation of our relation to God is here handled, and how God is first a Father to Christ, and in him to us. What can be more comfortable in this earthly, interest-shaking, disjointing, confounding age, than to clear up our soul's interest in God? *Tolle meum, et tolle deum,* as he said (*c*). It were better for me there were no God, than that he should not be my God. This will be thy comfort, that when thou canst not say, My state, my liberty, my house, my land, my friend, my trade, thou mayest be able to say, 'My Father, my God.' If therefore thou savourest the things of God, this subject will be acceptable and grateful to thee; and if this treatise may be any ways instrumental for putting thee upon study how to get it, or upon practice how to improve it, or in case thy soul sits in darkness, how to endear and clear thy interest, the publishers shall have much of their aim, and thou wilt have no cause to repent thy cost in buying, or thy pains in reading. We shall add no more than this. Blessed is that man or woman that hath an interest in him who is the Father of Jesus Christ by eternal generation, and of all believers in Christ by adoption and regeneration; in which inheritance and portion, that thou mayest have a share, shall be the prayer of

Thy soul's and thy faith's servants in the work of the ministry for Jesus' sake,

SIMON ASH.*
JAMES NALTON.*
JOSEPH CHURCH.*

* For notices of these names, see Vol. IV. page 311.—G.

A HEAVENLY DISCOURSE BETWEEN CHRIST AND MARY, AFTER HIS RESURRECTION.

Jesus saith unto her, Mary. She turned herself, and said to him, Rabboni; that is to say, Master. And Jesus said to her, Touch me not; for I am not yet ascended to my Father: but go to my brethren, and say to them, I ascend to my Father, and your Father; to my God, and your God.—John XX. 16.

The same love of Christ that drew him from heaven to the womb of the virgin, from the womb of the virgin to the cross, and from the cross to the grave, the same love of Christ moved him to discover himself after he was risen from the grave to them that he knew did entirely and wonderfully love him. And therefore, before he would ascend to heaven, he did vouchsafe many apparitions* and discoveries of himself, partly to instruct them in the certainty of his resurrection, and partly, but especially, to comfort them: those that he knew did love him.

His first apparition of all was made to Mary, the woman out of whom he had cast seven devils, Luke viii. 2. She was much beholding to him, and therefore loved much, Luke vii. 47. No sex may discourage any sinner from Christ. She expresseth her love of Christ by her desire of finding him, by her seeking and weeping, notwithstanding all impediments, before she found him. As she wept, she stooped down and looked into the sepulchre, and there saw two angels in white: a colour of glory, purity, and joy, because it was a time of joy. They were one at the head, and the other at the feet. As in the law, when the mercy-seat was made, two cherubims were also framed, and placed one at the one end, and the other at the other end thereof, with their faces looking one towards another, Exod. xxv. 20. And when Christ was risen, there were two angels, one at the head, another at the feet, to shew that peace was to be expected in the true propitiatory, Jesus Christ.

One at the head, the other at the feet of the body of Jesus. And they sat there. It was a time of peace. Peace was made between heaven and earth, God and man; and here is a posture of peace, 'They sat quietly.' In Christ, angels and we are at one; God, and we, and all. There is a recapitulation and gathering of all things in heaven and earth, Col. i. 20.

* That is, 'appearances.'—G.

The angels, they attended on Christ in all the passages of his life and death till they brought him to heaven.* They brought news of his birth, comforted him in his agony; they were at his resurrection, and you see here they attend. At his ascension they accompany him. And as they did to the Head, so they will to the members. In our infancy, they take charge of our tender years; in our dangers, they pitch their tents about us; in our deaths, they carry our souls to Abraham's bosom, a place of happiness. At our resurrection, their office is to gather our bodies together. That service and attendance they afforded the Head they afford to the members; to mystical Christ as well as natural. Therefore let us comfort ourselves in the service they did to Christ.

Now, besides the apparition of the angels, here is the speech of the angels: 'Woman, why weepest thou?' They knew she had no cause of weeping, for Christ whom she sought was risen again.

She answereth, 'Because they have taken away my Lord, and I know not where they have laid him.' If it had been as she supposed, there had been cause enough of her weeping, if her Lord had been taken away; for when the Lord is taken away, what remaineth that is comfortable? And if the Lord be not taken away, it matters not what is taken away. For he is all in all. Carnal people, so they have their wealth, and friends, and comforts in the world, they care not what is taken away. But she is of another mind. 'They have taken away my Lord,' and what comfort can I have if my Lord be taken away?

But it was but the speech of an opinion; she did but think it. And there were two things might lead her, truth and probability, which is the foundation of opinion. *Probability:* he is not here, therefore he is taken away. *Truth:* Christ promised he would rise again, therefore he would take away himself. There was certain truth to ground faith, and weak probability to ground opinion. Yet such is the nature of weak persons in distress. If there be probability and certain truth, yet they will be sure to cleave to their probabilities. Oh, theirs be great sin! Ay, but there is greater mercy for faith to lay hold upon. So the presumptuous sinner saith, 'God is merciful.' Ay, but God hath excluded thee from heaven; thou art an adulterer, a swearer, a filthy person; thy opinion is grounded scarce upon probability. 'God is merciful,' but not to such sinners as live in sins against reconciliation as thou dost, 1 Cor. vi. 9. Therefore, when one hath but probability to ground opinion, and the other certain truth to ground faith, be so wise for our souls as to take the best and leave the other. If she had remembered his promise to raise himself out of the grave, she needed not to have doubted.

'They have taken away my Lord, and I know not where they have laid him.' '*They* have taken away.' She instanceth none. And when she had thus said, she turneth her back, and saw Jesus standing, and knew not that it was Jesus. The angels hold their peace when Christ speaks, and it is their place so to do.

But she knew not that it was Jesus in respect of her passion. Her senses were held partly by the power of God, and partly by a kind of passion that was a cloud between her and Jesus, that she knew him not at that time.

What doth Jesus say to her?

* In margin here, 'Ministry of angels towards Christ. Luke ii. 9, 10; Luke xxii. 43; John xii. 29; Acts i. 10; Heb. i. 14; Ps. xxxiv. 7; Luke xvi. 22; Mat. xxiv. 31.'—G.

'Woman, why weepest thou? whom seekest thou?' The first words that ever Christ spake after his resurrection to them he appeared to, is, 'Woman, why weepest thou?' It is a good question after Christ's resurrection. What cause of weeping when Christ is risen? Our sins are forgiven, because he, our head and surety, hath suffered death for us; and if Christ be risen again, why weep we? If we be broken-hearted, humbled sinners, that have interest in his death and resurrection, we have no cause to grieve. It is therefore a good question to them that believe, 'Why weepest thou? whom seekest thou?' They were questions, not for satisfaction to him—he knew it well enough—but to draw out her mind, and to draw out by confession what God had hid in her heart, that he might comfort her afterwards.

'But she, supposing him to be the gardener, said, Sir, if thou hast borne him hence, tell me,' &c.

She had a misconceit of Christ, as if he had been the gardener. Beloved, so it is with a sinner, especially in times of desolation of spirit and disconsolate condition. They present Christ to themselves as an enemy. She in passion thinks Christ the gardener. Do not many, when they be melancholy of body and troubled in mind, conceive of Christ as an austere judge, that will undoubtedly damn such wretches as they are, who present Christ to themselves in that fashion, that the Scripture doth not? Doth not he bid all that be weary and heavy laden come to him? Mat. xi. 28. And yet they, out of passion, will present Christ to be an austere judge, that will take them at their disadvantage, observe all their ways, and will surely damn them.

It is a great violence that passion and opinion offers to truth, and to saving truth, and the hardest matter in the world for a distressed conscience to apprehend God aright, and to apprehend Christ aright. Secure persons apprehend God under a false notion. They apprehend God as a God all of mercy, and Christ as if he were not a judge of the world; as if he observed them not, nor their sinful courses; and therefore they care not whether they serve him or no, Acts xvii. 31. And Satan presenteth Christ all of mercy, and Satan and their hearts meeting together, the mistake is dangerous. It is a great art of faith, and an excellent skill, to apprehend Christ suitable to our condition that we are in. When we be in any sin, then think him a judge; then think of Moses rather than of Christ; then think of Christ as one that will judge both quick and dead for their hard and wicked actions. But when we be humble and broken-hearted, and touched with sense of sin, present him as a sweet Saviour, inviting and alluring all to come to him: 'Come to me, all ye,' &c., Mat. xi. 28; present him as a gentle shepherd; present him in all the sweet relations he names himself by in the Scriptures, lest otherwise we do Christ dishonour, and ourselves wrong, Isa. xl. 11.

'If thou hast borne him hence, tell me where thou hast laid him, and I will take him away.'

She was a likely woman indeed to take Christ away; for a weak woman to take a heavy body away! But love thinks nothing impossible. Faith and love agree in this, nothing is impossible. 'Love is strong as death,' Cant. viii. 6. Neither love nor faith care for difficulties; they arm the soul to break through all.

'Tell me where thou hast laid him, and I will take him away.'

One would think the dead body might have frighted the woman, and the heavy body might have been above her strength. But she was in such an ecstasy of love and desire, and grief for want of desire, that she considered not well what she said.

They be words of passion; and, indeed, if you observe the story of Mary Magdalene, she was a woman of extremity in all conditions. Like Jonah, when he grieves, he grieves exceedingly; when he rejoices, his joy is wound to the highest pitch. So she was full of love when she loved, and full of grief when she grieved, and full of joy when she joyed. She had large affections. All were in the highest measure, and strained to the highest pin in her; and that made her say, 'If thou hast,' &c.

Jesus could not endure [to keep] her longer in this perplexed condition. He was too merciful; and therefore saith, 'Mary.' She turned to him, and saith, 'Rabboni,' which is to say, Master.

And Jesus said to her, 'Mary.'

The words are a sweet and loving intercourse between Christ and Mary. In a seasonable time, when she was in all her perplexity and depth of sorrow for loss of her Lord, Christ seasonably at length, as not being able to hold any longer, but must needs discover himself, saith to her, 'Mary.'

You see, first of all, Christ beginneth, and saith, 'Mary;' she answereth, in the second place, and saith, 'Rabboni;' and till Christ begins, no voice in the world can do any good. The angels they spake to her, but till Christ spake nothing could comfort her. Christ began, and till Christ began nothing would comfort Mary. Christ began himself, and used but one word. It is a word, and but one word. Nothing will comfort but the word of Christ. The word that comforted her when he spake, and it was but one word, and yet enough, there was such fulness of spirit and comfort in that one word. And she answereth with one word again.

You may ask why they spake but one word. Beloved, he was full of affection, and she was full of affection also, too full to express themselves in many words. As it is in grief, grief sometimes may be so great that scarce any words are able to express it: *ingentes dolores stupent;* and if any words, then broken words, which shew fulness of affection rather than any distinct sense. Christ was so full, and she so full, that a word discovers. And indeed there was so much sense, and so much love, so much contained in these little words 'Mary' and 'Rabboni,' that it is impossible to express them shorter; and her passion would not stay any longer discourse. It was by words, and by one word, 'Mary.' It was by a word which sheweth he took notice of her. Christ knows the names of the stars; he knows everything by name. He knows everything of a man, to the very hair. He knows their parts, and their very excrements of their parts. He knew her, and acknowledged her too: 'Mary.'

1. It is a word of knowledge, and familiar acquaintance, and acknowledgment.

2. It is a word of compassion; because he had held her long, and now could not longer. He pitieth the state she was in. He saw her ready to sink for grief and melt for sorrow, and therefore he said, 'Mary.'

3. As it is a word of compassion, so it is a word full of exceeding love.

4. And it is a word of peculiar appropriation, 'Mary,' whom I have so much respected heretofore. And a word of satisfaction on his part, out of his pity, and out of his love, and former familiarity and acquaintance. 'Mary,' I am the man that thou seekest; I know what all thy seekings tend to. Thou wantest him whom thou lovest; thou wantest me; I am he whom thou seekest.

She answered him again, 'Rabboni,' which is interpreted, Master. She returned him an answer again; she spake to him. He first began, then she follows. She found the virtue of his speech in her heart. There was an influence of it to her heart; and his love witnessing to her heart, raised her love to him again. So it was an answer of Christ's speech, and from the same affection: an answer of love, and an answer of exceeding large affection and satisfaction to her soul. O my 'Rabboni,' the soul of my soul, the life of my life, my joy, my rock, my all that can' be dear to me. 'Rabboni,' I have enough. As he desired to give her satisfaction, so she takes satisfaction in the word. And yet it was not full satisfaction; for after she clasps about him, and would not let him go. It was an affection that stirred up much desire more and more to have communion with him, so that he was fain to check her afterward: 'Touch me not, for I am not yet ascended to my Father.' She had not enough; as indeed a believing, affectionate soul hath never enough till it be in heaven.

And thus you see the sweet intercourse upon the apparition and first discovery of Christ to Mary. He spake to her, and she answered him again with the same affection. And it is a word of dependence, as it is fit, 'Rabboni, my Master.' It is not only a word of honour, not any superior, but a superior in way of teaching. There was submission of conscience to the 'Rabboni,' as the 'Rabboni,' labouring to sit in the consciences of people. It is a Syriac word, which signifieth in the original, 'multiplication of knowledge' in him that speaketh, and that laboureth to breed much knowledge in him that is spoken to; and therefore it is a word of great respect and dependence (*d*).

She might well call him 'Rabboni,' for he was 'Master of masters,' 'Rabboni of rabbonis,' the angel of the covenant, the great doctor of the church, the great 'Gamaliel,' at whose feet all must sit and be taught. So you see what sense and affections are in these little words. The fulness of heart that was in this couple cannot be expressed, were it possible to say all that could be said. And therefore we leave the hypothesis, and come to make application of it to ourselves.

Obs. 1. First, *We may learn here, that till Christ himself discovers himself, no teaching will serve the turn*. No. The teaching of angels will not serve the turn, till Christ himself by his Holy Spirit discovers himself. When Christ doth it, it is done. And therefore it should teach us so to attend upon the ministry as to look up to the great doctor that hath his chair in heaven, and teacheth the heart.* If he teach, it is no matter how dull the scholar is. He is able to make any scholar, if he instruct. I will not enlarge the point, because there be particular places wherein they will be enlarged.

Obs. 2. The second thing I will observe is this, *that Christ, when he teacheth, he doth it by words, not by crucifixes, not by sights*. We lost our salvation and all our happiness by the ear, and we must come to it by the ear again. Adam, by hearkening to Eve, and Eve to the serpent, lost all; and we must recover salvation therefore by the ear. As we have heard, so we shall see. We must first hear, and then see. Life cometh in at the ear as well as death. Faith, you know, is the quickening of a Christian, the spiritual life of a Christian. Now, faith comes by hearing; and therefore I beseech you in the bowels of Christ, set aside prejudice, and meekly attend God's ordinances. Do not consider who we are; we are but poor ministers, frail men as yourselves. But consider the Lord, that is pleased to convey life, and salvation, and grace, and whatsoever is fit to

* In margin here, '*Cathedram habet in cœlis qui corda docet.*'—G.

bring to heaven, this way. Therefore they that despise this way, set light by salvation; as the apostle saith, Acts xiii. 46, 'They judge themselves unworthy of the kingdom of heaven.' They can read at home, but is that the way God hath sanctified? Did not the manna stink when gathered on the Sabbath day? There is a curse upon all private industry and devotion when it is with neglect of public ordinances. She could have no comfort till Christ spake. Nay, the very sight of Christ could not comfort her. Let this, I pray you, be enough, that I may not enlarge the point any further. This is the way for comfort. We must hear him in his ministers here, if we will hear him comfortably speaking to us hereafter, 'Come, ye blessed of my Father,' &c., Mat. xxv. 34.

Obs. 3. It was but one word, 'Mary;' and is there so much force in one word? Yea, when it is uttered by Christ. One word coming from Christ, and set on the heart by the Spirit of Christ, hath a mighty efficacy. The word hath an efficacy in creating all things, *fiat, fuit.* Let it be done: it was done; 'Let there be light: there was light.' So let there be light in the understanding, and there it shall be presently. So in all Christ's cures, he said the word, and it was done. So in all spiritual cures, let him say the word, it is done. Nay, a very look of Christ, if the Spirit go along with it, is able to convert the soul. *Respexit Christus, flevit Petrus amarè:* Christ looked on Peter, he wept bitterly. What will his word do, when his look will do so much? It was but a word, and but one word: 'Say but the word,' saith he in the gospel, 'and my servant shall be healed,' Mat. viii. 8. This should make us desire that Christ would speak though but few words to the soul; that he would clothe the words of men mightily with his word and with his Spirit; and then they will be mighty in operation and works. One word, but it was a pregnant word. It was full of affection. She knew it well enough: 'Mary.' What! to call her so familiarly, so sweetly, by her accustomed name? It wrought on her bowels presently.

Obs. 4. But to go on. You see here again, *that Christ must begin to us before we can answer him.* He began to 'Mary,' and then she said 'Rabboni.' All the passages of salvation are done by way of covenant, by way of commerce and intercourse between God and man, but God begins first. In election, indeed, we choose him; but he chooseth us first. And he knoweth who are his, and we know him; but he knows us first. And in calling, we answer, Ay; but he calleth first, and we do but echo to his call. In justification, forgiveness of sins, we accept of justification, and submit to the righteousness of Christ, and God's purpose of saving man that way; but he giveth faith first, for faith is the gift of God. We glorify him here on earth, but it is from a result of God's glorifying us in heaven. Some earnests we have, but they are of God's giving. All we do is but reflection of his love first, or his knowledge first.

The Christian soul saith, 'Thou art my God;' ay, but he saith first, 'I am thy salvation,' Ps. xxxv. 3. As Austin saith, *Non frustra dicit anima, Deus salus tua:* when God saith, 'I am thy salvation,' it is easy for the soul to say, 'Thou art my God' (*e*). And this may teach us in our devotions, when we are to deal with God, when we are to bring to him any request, to desire him first to reveal himself to us, desire Christ to reveal himself by his Spirit to us. It is an error in the case of men's devotions. They think to bring something of their own strength, and to break in, as it were, upon God, without his discovery first. But Paul saith, Gal. iv. 9, 'We know God, or rather, are known of him.' We must desire that he would make known his heart to us first, and then we shall know him again; that he would speak to us by his Spirit, and then we shall answer to him again. That he would say to our souls, he 'is our salvation;' and then we may lay claim to him, 'he is our God.' Desire the 'Spirit of revelation,' to reveal his bowels and love to us in Christ by his Holy Spirit; for certainly, in every return of ours to Christ, God begins to us, all in all, though not sensibly. But we ought to pray, every day more and more, for a sensible revelation, that God would reveal his love to us in Christ. And we cannot but answer. If Christ saith, 'Mary,' Mary cannot but answer, 'Rabboni.'

Obj. But you will say then, It is not our fault, but Christ's fault, if he must begin. If God begins, we shall answer.

Ans. I answer briefly, that God doth always begin to us, and is beforehand with us in all dealings with ourselves. He giveth us many motions, and never withdraweth himself from us, but when he is despised and slighted first; therefore, let us take heed that we labour to answer Christ's call when he doth call. If we slight it, then in a judicious* course he ceaseth to speak further to us, if we slight his beginnings of revelations. There be many degrees and passages to faith and assurance. If we do not observe the beginning, how God begins to reveal himself to us by little and little, speaking to us by his Spirit in our hearts when he begins, then in a spiritual judgment sometimes he leaves us to ourselves. And therefore let us regard all the motions of the Spirit, and all the speeches of the Spirit of Christ, for he begins by little and little, else our consciences will say afterward, we are not saved, because we would not be saved. We would not yield to all the passages of salvation; but when he was beforehand with us, and offered many sweet motions, yet we loved our sins better than our souls, and so repelled all. Therefore, I beseech you, do not refuse the sweet messages from heaven, the gracious and sweet motions of the Spirit of Christ.† Make much of them. God hath begun to you, be sure to answer. Learn it of Mary. When Christ began, she set not her heart and infidelity against it, but she opened her heart, and said, 'Rabboni;' learn, therefore, the duty of spiritual obedience. When God speaks, 'Speak, Lord, for thy servant heareth,' 1 Sam. iii. 10. Do not shut your ears to the motions of God's blessed Spirit; do not harden your hearts against his voice, but open your hearts as she did: 'Rabboni.'

Our Saviour Christ here saith, 'Mary;' but when? After he had concealed himself from her a long time. It is not presently 'Mary,' nor 'Rabboni.' He had concealed himself a great while. Christ doth not usually open himself fully at first, though at first he doth in some degree; but he observeth degrees, as in the church in general. You see how that he discovers himself in his gracious promises by little and little; darkly at first, and at last the Sun of righteousness ariseth clearly. So the day-star ariseth in our hearts by degrees. It is a great while before Mary heareth the satisfying speech of Christ, 'Mary.'

Quest. But why doth Christ thus conceal himself in regard of his fuller manifestation?

It is partly to try and exercise our faith and other graces; and therefore God doth seem to withdraw himself in the sense of his love.

1. *To see whether we can live by faith*, or whether we be altogether addicted to sense, as the world is, who live altogether by sense, and not by faith.

* Qu. 'judicial'?—G. † In margin here, '*Alloquenti Christo fideles respondent.*'—G.

2. *He would have our patience tried to the utmost.* He would have 'patience have its perfect work,' James i. 4. She had much patience to endure all this. But her patience had not a perfect work till Christ spake.

3. *Christ will stir up and quicken zeal and fervency in his children;* and therefore he seemed to deny the woman of Canaan, Mat. xv. 21, *seq.*, and Mark vii. 27, 28; first, he giveth no answer but an harsh answer, 'A dog.' And she works upon it: 'Though I am a dog, yet dogs have crumbs.' All which denial was only to stir up zeal and earnestness. And therefore though Christ doth not manifest himself to us at first, yet it is to stir up zeal and affection to seek after him more earnestly. A notable passage there is of this, Cant. iii. 16. The soul sought Christ, and sought long, and sought in the use of all means; but at length she waited, and in waiting she found him.

4. *Christ doth this to set a better price upon his presence when he comes;* to make his presence highly valued when he doth discover himself. *Desiderata diu magis placent:* things long desired please more sweetly. And things, when wanted, are ingratiated to us, as warmth after cold, and meat after hunger; and so in every particular of this life. And therefore God, to set a greater price on his presence, and that he would be held more strongly when he doth reveal himself, he defers a long time. That is one reason why he did defer revealing himself to Mary, that she might have the more sweet contentment in him when he did reveal himself, as indeed she had. Long deferring of a thing doth but enlarge the soul. Want enlargeth the desire and capacity of the soul, so doth love. Now, when we want that we love, that emptieth the soul marvellously much; it mortifieth affection. When God keeps off a long time, and we see it is God only must do it, then the affection is taken off from earthly things, and the heart enlarged to God by love, and the want of the thing we love. And therefore we set a price on the thing, so that we are wonderfully pleasing to God. It is very beneficial to ourselves. What lost Mary by it? So shall we lose nothing. We have it at last more abundantly. We have it as a mighty favour. Mary taketh this as a new blessing altogether. When things are kept long from us, and God only must discover, when the heart is kept from second causes, the heart is enlarged. Certainly this comes from God, and God should have all the glory of it. God is wise; and therefore makes us to stay a long time for that we do desire.

We all of us are in Mary's case in a spiritual sense. Some times or other we miss Christ, I mean the sweet sense of Christ. Lay this down for a rule, that Christians ought to walk in sweet communion with God and Christ, and that it ought to be the life of a Christian to maintain the communion that Christ hath vouchsafed between us and himself. Then, certainly, we lose Christ wonderfully; and not against our minds, but willingly, by our own slighting of him, and by our own undervaluing of him, or by our negligence or presumption. Christ, though he be low, yet he is great, and he will have us to know his greatness. There must be communion with due respect. One way or other we deprive ourselves of the sense and sweetness of communion with Christ. What must we do, then? We must do as the woman did: turn over every stone; use all kind of means; leave not one till we find him; and when all means are used, wait still. Persevere in waiting, as Peter speaks. Believers, wait; hold out in waiting, for Christ in his time will come. He cannot hold long. As Joseph did suppress his love and affection for politic ends a great while, Gen. xlv. 3, but his pity towards his brethren was such that his bowels would not suffer him to conceal himself longer; his passion was above his policy: 'I am Joseph.' And so let us in the use of all things seek Christ and the sweet sense of his love, which is better than life itself. And, indeed, what is all without Christ? Christ is so full of compassion, he will not long suffer us to be prolonged, but will at length satisfy the hungry soul, Ps. lxiii. 5. How many promises have we to this end!

Take heed of such a temper of soul, as cares not whether we find Christ or no. Oh take heed of that! If we will seek him, seek him as Mary. She sought him early in the morning; she brake her sleep and sought him with tears. If anything be to be sought with tears, it is Christ and communion with him. She sought him instantly and constantly. She sought him so, that no impediment could hinder her, she was so full of grief and love.* She sought him with her whole heart, she waited in seeking. That is the way to find Christ. Seek him early, in our younger times, in the morning of our years. Oh that we could seek Christ as we seek our pleasures. We should find more pleasure in Christ than in all the pleasures of the world, if we could persuade our base hearts so much. Seek him above all other things. Awake with this resolution in our hearts, to find Christ, never to be quiet till we may say with some comfort, 'I am Christ's, and Christ is mine.' When we have him, we have all. Seek him with tears, at length we are sure to find him. He hath bound himself, that if we knock he will open; and if we seek we shall find: if we seek wisdom early with our whole hearts, entirely, sincerely. Seek Christ for Christ, and then we shall be sure to find him, as she did. Thus seek him in the word and sacraments, wherein he discovers himself familiarly. Seek him in the temple—'Christ was found in the temple,' Luke ii. 46—and then we shall be sure to find him both here and hereafter. Specially we shall find him in our hearts. You see how familiarly he comes to us in the word, speaks to us by a man like ourselves. And how familiarly by the sacrament, by common bread and common wine, sanctified to do great matters above nature, to strengthen faith. He cometh to us through our faces, into our souls in the sacrament. He cometh to us, through our ears in hearing the word, through our sight in seeing the bread broken. He comes by familiar things, and by a familiar manner of conveying, as if he should name every one, 'I come to thee, and give thee my body.' Think with ourselves, Now Christ cometh to me; when the minister reacheth the bread and comes to me, think of heavenly bread, and of the gift of Christ to me by means. And can he do it more familiarly? Is it not as if he would say, 'Mary'? And that is the excellency of the sacrament. It conveyeth Christ to all the saints, and to every one in particular, as if he named every one. And what an encouragement is this to answer again, to open our hearts to receive him, together with the elements! to embrace Christ, join with Christ, and then to keep him when we have him! Do not lose him. He will not be so dealt withal. Remember the covenant we have made to him. I beseech you, let these sweet considerations of Christ dwell in us, and work on every one of our hearts. If they do good on us here on earth, if we by faith lay hold on him, and have intercourse with him, what will it be in the day of judgment! How comfortable will it be to hear him say to every one in particular, 'Come thou, and thou, stand on my right hand, sit and judge the world with me?' 1 Cor. vi. 2. Doth he know our names now on earth, and giveth to every one particularly by

* In margin here, 'Mat. xxviii. 1, Mark xvi. 9, Luke xxiv. 1, John xx. 25.'—G.

himself, if we come worthily? and will not he know us then? Oh, that is far more worth than the world's good, to know us then and to call us by our names! Therefore, I beseech you, be acquainted with Christ. Have intercourse, all we can, with him in the word and sacraments, and never rest till we find this sweet result in the use of the means, 'that he is ours, and we are his.'

Take heed therefore in these times, desperately addicted to formality and popery. I say, take heed, we do depend not upon any outward thing, but look to Christ in all his ordinances, look to the Spirit. All God's children, the church of the first-born, they are θεοδίδακτος, such as are 'taught of God.' Who can take away the opposite disposition of man's nature to goodness, but God by his Spirit? Who can shine into the soul, and quicken the soul, but Christ by his Spirit? Who is above the heart and conscience, but Christ by his Spirit? Therefore take heed of formality; submit your hearts to the great prophet of the church, that Moses speaketh of, Deut. xviii. 18, who shall be the great teacher of the church; lift up our hearts to him, that he would teach our hearts, and remove the natural disposition that is in us; that he would 'take off the veil from our hearts,' and teach not only what to do, but teach the very doing of them. Teach us to hate what is ill, teach us to believe, and to resist all Satan's temptations. Who can teach but the great teacher, whose chair is in heaven? Therefore take heed of depending on formal things. Lift your hearts to God, that he would join his teaching with all other teachings. This cannot be too much stood upon. I beseech you, therefore, take it to heart.

Give me leave, therefore, to add a few things more. If Christ speaketh in general to Mary, she answereth in general; and when he speaks aloof to her, she answereth aloof to him, afar off, and never gave him a direct answer, till he gave a direct word to her. When he said, 'Mary,' she gave him a direct answer, 'Rabboni;' not before. I beseech you, therefore, let us not rest in general promises and the general graces, that be so much stood on by some, that God hath a like respect to all. Trust not to that. We must not enter into his secrets, but let us obey his precepts and commandments. And withal remember this, when we hear of a general mercy and commandment for all nations to believe, and that Christ came to save a world of sinners, alas! what is that to me, unless thou by thy Holy Spirit speakest to my soul, and sayest in particular, 'I am thy salvation,' and speakest familiarly to my soul? Generals are in some degrees comfortable. But if I find not particular interest by the witness of thy Holy Spirit to my soul, if thou sayest not to my soul, 'I am thine, and thou art mine,' all is to little purpose. Therefore in the desires of our souls in prayer, let us desire the Lord to reveal himself in particular. We trust too much in generals. God is merciful, and Christ came to redeem the world. They be truths, and good foundations for to found faith upon, but they will not do the deed, till by daily prayer we seek to the Lord, that he would in a particular manner reveal himself to us. This doth Paul pray for, Eph. i. 17, 'that God would vouchsafe to them the Spirit of revelation.' And this is the office of the Holy Spirit. His special office is, to reveal to every one in particular his estate and condition God-ward. The Holy Ghost knoweth the secrets in the breast of God, and in our own hearts.* Now the Holy Ghost can reveal the particular love that lieth in God's breast to our particular souls. And therefore we should desire God, that the Holy Spirit may be sent to seal to us our particular salvation, and never

* In margin here, '*Spiritus Dei, et Dei et hominis secreta cognoscit.*'—G.

be quiet till we be sealed in particular assurance, that we be they whom Christ came to save. This we ought to labour for. If we labour for it, we shall have it some time or other, for God loveth to be familiar with his children. He loveth not to be strange to them, if they seek his love, but to reveal himself first or last. And few seek it, but God revealeth himself by his Spirit to them before they die; if he doth not, they are sure of it in heaven. And therefore they that be against particulars, they are enemies to their own salvation. Mary regarded not, while Christ spake of generals, but when he came to particulars, then 'Rabboni,' and not before.

'Jesus saith unto her, Touch me not; I am not yet ascended to my Father,' &c.

This verse containeth Christ's prohibition, or Christ's commission or charge. His prohibition, 'Touch me not;' and his reason, 'for I am not yet ascended to my Father.'

His charge, 'Go to my brethren;' and then directeth what to say to them: 'I ascend to my Father, and your Father; to my God, and your God.'

The words be very natural, and need no breaking up to you. But I shall handle them, as they follow one another.

'Jesus said to her, Touch me not.'

'Touch me not.' Why? He would have Thomas not only touch, but to put his finger into his side; that is more than touching him, John xx. 27. But our Saviour's intent is to meet with a disposition in Mary something carnal, something low and mean, in regard of this glorious occasion, Christ being now risen and glorified, for his resurrection was the first degree of his glorification. And therefore, 'Touch me not.' She came with too much a carnal mind to touch him, when she said, Rabboni. It was not satisfaction enough for her to answer, 'Rabboni,' but she runneth to him, and claspeth him, and clingeth about him, as the affection of love did dictate to her. But saith he, 'Touch me not' in such a manner. This is not a fit manner for thee to touch me in, now I am risen again. In a word, she had thought to converse with Christ in as familiar a manner as before, when she poured ointment on his head. He was the same person, but the case is altered. That was in the days of his humiliation; now he was risen again, and it was the first degree of his glorification. There was another manner of converse due to him; and therefore, 'Touch me not.' Thou thinkest to touch me as thou didst before, but thou must not do it. She was too much addicted to his bodily presence.

1. *It is that that men will labour after, and have laboured for, even from the beginning of the world*, to be too much addicted to present things, and to sense. They will worship Christ, but they must have a picture before them. They will adore Christ, but they must bring his body down to a piece of bread; they must have a presence. And so instead of raising their hearts to God and Christ in a heavenly manner, they pull down God and Christ to them. This the pride and base earthliness of man will do. And therefore saith Christ, 'Touch me not' in that manner; it is not with me now as it was before. We must take heed of mean and base conceits of Christ. What saith Paul, 2 Cor v. 16? 'I know no man now, according to the flesh; no, not Christ himself, now he is risen.' Christ was of such a tribe, stature, had such gifts and qualities. What is that to me? Christ is now Lord of lords, and King of kings. He is glorious in heaven, and so I conceive of him: 'I know no man after the flesh; no, not Christ himself.' I forget what he was on earth, and think of him what he is now in heaven. Therefore to bring him down to our base con-

ceits, to sense, and the like, this is the humour of men that labour to cross the scope of the gospel. For why are men so addicted to outward things, outward compliments? It is pride, it is Satanical pride. They think that God is delighted with whatsoever their folly is delighted withal. Because amongst men there must be a deal a-doing, therefore they think God is well pleased with such things. God is a Spirit, and though outward things be necessary, yet all must not be turned outward, as in popery. We must not bring God down to our foolish conceits, as if he were delighted as we are, Joshua iv. 24.

2. *It is wonderful easy too.* All outward things, any naughty* men have them with their sins.† Let a man perform a little outward compliment, he may be what he will be, let him live as he will, and be possessed that outward things will serve the turn. He is safe; his conscience is daubed up, till God by sense of wrath awakeneth conscience; and then they shall find it another matter to deal with God than by compliment.

3. *There is also a great glory in outward things.* There is commendations, and men's observance of them, as in the Pharisees, and in popery. But the spiritual worship of Christ hath no observance to the eye of the world. It is between God and the soul. Men naturally love those things that be glorious. It is said of Ephraim, that he loved to tread out the corn, but not to plough, Hosea x. 11; that is, Ephraim will take that which is easy, but not that in God's worship which is hard. There be two things in God's service: an easy thing, which is outward compliment; an hard thing, which is to trust him, to deny ourselves, to rely upon him and live by faith.‡ And that Ephraim will not do. Ephraim will tread the corn, because the heifer may eat corn; but there be hard things in religion which he will not practise. He will not plough. 'Touch me not,' saith Christ. Thou hast not conceits spiritual enough to deal with me, now I am risen.

But what is the reason? 'Touch me not; *for* I am not yet ascended to my Father.' That seemeth to be a strong reason. But it seemeth to be a contrary reason. Touch me not now, when my body is present; but touch me when I am gone, and removed out of sight of all flesh. Touch me not now, when thou mayest touch me; and touch me when there is an impossibility of touching me. This is seemingly strange. But indeed there is no contrariety in it: 'Touch me not; *for* I am not yet ascended to the Father.'

There is a double meaning of the words. First of all, 'Touch me not; for I am not yet ascended,' &c. Thou needest not clasp and cling about me, as if I would stay no more with you below; 'I am not yet ascended to the Father.' There will be time enough afterwards. For the word 'touch,' in the original, doth not signify merely to touch, but clasp, associate, join, and solder with a thing (*f*).§ The Scripture speaking of the evil man, you shall not touch him; that is, not make him one with him. The devil shall not take him from Christ and make him one with himself. It is a strange word in the original: 'Thou claspest about me, thou dost more than touch me, thou clingest to me and wilt not leave me, as if I would go presently to the Father; but I am not yet ascended to the Father.' That is one part of the meaning.

* That is, 'wicked.'—G. † In margin here, '*Externa Deo placere nequeunt.*'—G.

‡ In margin here, '*Arduum et difficile est in fide vivere.*'—G.

§ In margin here, '*Non solum significat tangere, sed adhærere, conglutinari*, Isa. lii. 11, 2 Cor. vi. 17. *A tabernaculo impiorum hominum recedite*, Num. xvi. 27.'—G.

But there is a farther than that, 'I am not yet ascended to the Father; touch me not.' That is, it is another manner of touch that I look for—better for thee, and in some regard for me—to touch me by the hand of faith when I am ascended to the Father. Then touch me, and take thy full of touching me. But for the present I am not ascended; I have not done all; I have not manifested myself to my disciples in full. When I am ascended, all is done, and then there is place for touch. And that I take is meant here, I am not yet ascended to the Father. Thou thinkest I have done all that is to be done, but thou art deceived. I must ascend to the Father, and when I am there I expect to be touched after another manner, after a gracious, spiritual manner, which is by faith; as Augustine saith well, 'Send up thy faith to heaven, and then thou touchest Christ.'* As he said in the sacrament, '*Quid paras dentem et ventrem? Crede, et manducasti:* What dost thou prepare thy teeth and stomach for? Believe, and thou hast eaten' (*g*). So the best communion with Christ is to believe, till we come to heaven to have eternal communion with him. This touch will do thee little good, and it pleaseth me as little. When I am ascended to the Father, then touch me at the full. So you see what Christ meaneth.

The life of a Christian here, and the manner of the dispensation of Christ here, is by promise, and by his Spirit; that we should live by faith, and not by sense. The life of sight is reserved for another world, when we are fitted for it. She was not fit for a life of sense, but was to expect the Holy Ghost from heaven; to be filled with that, and then to be filled with faith and love; and then to have an holy communion with him in heaven. But 'I am not yet ascended.' Thus you see the meaning, 'Touch me not.'

There be two reasons of Christ's prohibition.

1. *Her respects were too carnal and ordinary*, considering he was in the state of glory. And then,

2. *For that there will be time enough.* Do not stand embracing of me, there is a greater work for thee to do. Christ preferred the great work of giving notice to his disciples of his resurrection, before the office of respect and service to himself. Go about a duty, that I more regard a great deal: 'Go, tell my brethren I ascend,' &c. So that every part of the text yields satisfaction to that prohibition.

'Go,' saith he, 'to my brethren.' I have another work for thee to do, 'Touch me not.' Thou clasps about me as if thou hadst nothing to do. There is another work to do that pleaseth me better, and more fit for thee: to comfort them that are in distress, my poor brethren and disciples. And therefore 'go to my brethren, and say unto them.' So that Christ prefers a work of charity to his poor disciples before a work of compliment to his own person. She clingeth about him; but 'this is not it I would have.' Those poor souls are mourning and disconsolate for me, as if I were clean taken away; go to them, and prevent their farther sorrow.

God hath a wonderful respect to others. It is strange that Christ should say, 'Go and be reconciled to thy brethren, and then offer thy sacrifice,' Mat. v. 24. As if he would have his own sacrifice neglected, rather than we should not be reconciled to others. And so a work of charity and love is preferred before an *officium* and compliment to himself. Let us shew our love to the first table in the second, our love to God by our love to man. Everything hath its measure and time. Away therefore with this over-much embracing and touching. Go thy way, thou hast another work

* In margin here, '*Mitte fidem in cœlum et tetigisti.*'—G.

to do: 'Go to my brethren.' And so you see, as I take it, the full meaning of the words.

Observe the circumstances. Who must go? Here is a commission and command. And to whom? To the disciples of Christ. And when doth Christ bid her go? When he was risen, and in the first estate of glory. What is the message? 'Tell my brethren I am ascending to my Father, and your Father; to my God, and your God.' It is worth your considering a little.

1. *Who is sent?* A woman. A woman to be the apostle of apostles, to be the teacher of the great teachers in the world. Mary Magdalene was sent to instruct the apostles in the great articles of Christ's resurrection and ascension to heaven. By a woman death came into the world, and by a woman life was preached to the apostles; because indeed she was more affectionate, and affection taketh all. And that makes that sex more addicted to religion, by the advantage of their affection; for religion is merely a matter of affection. Though it must have judgment shine before it, yet it is specially in the heart and affections. And she had shewed a great deal of affection. She stood out when the rest went away, John xix. 25. She was constant, and broke through all difficulties; and then God honoured her to be the first preacher of his resurrection.

God's course is to trust secrets in earthen vessels, that earthen vessels should carry heavenly treasure; and therefore stick not at the vessel, but look to the treasure, 2 Cor. iv. 7. A woman may teach the greatest apostle. Look not to the man, but to the message. Elias will not refuse the meat because the raven brought it, 1 Kings xvii. 4. And a condemned man will not refuse a pardon, because a mean man bringeth it. Take off pride in spiritual respects. When God honours any man to bring news of reconciliation, stoop to him, of what condition soever he be.

2. *To whom must she go?* 'Go, tell *my brethren*,' the apostles. Go to the apostles, that are disconsolate men, now orphans, deprived of their Master and Lord. Disconsolate men, and not in vain, so not without cause; for they had reason to be discomforted, not only for their want of Christ, but for their own ill carriage towards Christ. One of them denieth him, and the rest forsake him; and yet 'my brethren,' 'go tell *my* brethren.'

3. *When did he speak this?* After his resurrection, in the state of glory; in the beginning of it, and when he is ascending to heaven; and yet he owneth them as brethren, though such brethren as had dealt most unbrotherly with him.

But how came they to be his brethren? And how come we to be Christ's brother. Christ is the first-born of many brethren, Rom. viii. 29. He is the Son of God by nature; and all others now, by grace and adoption, Rom. viii. 17. Christ is the *primo-genitus* amongst many brethren; and in Christ we have one Father with Christ. We have one honour, and we shall be all kings and heirs of heaven, as he is. 'If sons, then heirs,' Gal. iv. 7; the apostle makes the coherence. Now we are all in Christ sons of God, heirs with him. To go to the condition of nature that he took, our nature; and therefore having our flesh, he is our brother, Heb. ii. 14. The very reprobate may say so. Yet that is a ground of comfort, that he is a man as we are. But that is not the main thing considerable. He is our brother in a spiritual respect, in regard of adoption. He is the first Son of God, and we in him sons. He is the first heir of God, and we in him are heirs. And therefore 'go to my brethren.'

Beloved, it is a point of marvellous comfort, that Christ was not ashamed to call them brethren, Ps. xxii. 22: 'I will declare thy name amongst thy brethren,' saith Christ. Our Saviour Christ alluded to that psalm in this passage; and so it is read, Heb. ii. 12, out of that psalm. Christ hath taken all relations, that are comfortable, upon him towards us. 'He is the everlasting Father, the Prince of peace,' Isa. ix. 6. He is 'a second Adam,' and therefore a father in that regard. The first Adam is the father of all that perish; the second Adam is the father of all that shall be saved. As he is our brother, so our husband. He could not be our husband, except he were our brother. He must take our nature, and be one with us, before we can be one with him. He is our friend. Before this time he called them friends, as you see in John: 'I will call you friends,' John xv. 15. But here is a sweeter term, 'brethren.' There is no relation that hath any comfort in it, but Christ hath taken it on him. He is our head, husband, friend, father, brother, and whatsoever can convey comfort to us.* And the truth of it is, he is these things more truly than any relation is made true on earth. For these relations of husband and wife, and brother and sister, and father and child, are but shadows of that everlasting relation that Christ hath taken upon him; the reality and truth itself is in Christ. We think there is no brother, but the brother in flesh; no father, but the father in flesh. Alas! these are but shadows, and quickly cease: 'the fashion of the world passeth away,' 1 Cor. vii. 31. Brother is another relation, whereof these are but shadows. These do but represent the best things that are in heaven. Christ is the father, brother, friend, and whatsoever is comfortable in heaven; therefore 'go tell my brethren.'

Obj. Ay, but saith the poor soul, I that have been so sinful, so unworthy a wretch, shall I have comfort in this, that Christ is my brother, and I am Christ's? I cannot do it.

Ans. 1. I profess thou canst not do it, 'flesh and blood must not teach it thee,' thou must be taught by the Spirit of Christ. But consider how the apostles used Christ. Thou canst not call Christ brother, because thou hast been a sinner, and hast carried thyself unkindly to Christ. And did not the disciples so? Did not they leave him, and one of them deny him, and that with oaths? Therefore, whatsoever our sins have been, deny not our relation to Christ. The poor prodigal said, 'I am not worthy to be called a son,' I am not worthy to be called a servant, Luke xv. 21.

He denied not that he was a son, but he was unworthy of it. And so I am unworthy to be a spouse and brother of Christ, yet do not our unfaithful hearts so much pleasure, as to deny our relation.

The apostles were so dignified, as to be called the 'pillars of the world,' Gal. ii. 9. But these left him, and yet for all that, in this time of their desertion of him, 'go tell my brethren.' Therefore be not discouraged. Go to Christ in our worst condition, in our greatest temptations, when our hearts misgive us most that we have used God most unkindly, and Satan plied us most with desperate temptations; yet own him for our brother, who owned his disciples when they dealt most unkindly with him.† I beseech you, count it a comfort unvaluable, which no tongue is able to express, that Christ after his resurrection should call 'brethren.' He might well call them brethren after his resurrection, because then all debts

* In margin here, '1 Cor. xi. 3; 1 Cor. xii. 27; Eph. v. 23; 1 John ii. 2, *seq.*; Rev. xxii. 3, *seq.*'—G.

† In margin here, '*Tentatio est ad Christum eundi opportunitas, ut nobis succurrat.*' —G.

were discharged by his death. He had paid their debts, and now the acquittance was due to them, because Christ as surety had paid all. Now I am risen, 'go and tell my brethren so.' If we can make use of the death and resurrection of Christ, and say, Christ hath died for my sins, and rose again for my justification; I will interest myself in his death, I will claim the virtue of his resurrection; then take the comfort of this. In popery, they had much comfort in those dark times, when a company of proud, carnal, beastly men ruled the roast according to their own lusts. These clergymen made a great pother with fraternity and brotherhood. And if they were of such a fraternity of Dominic or Francis, or merely in a friar's cowl, it was not only satisfactory, but meritorious, they could not do amiss. Away with these shadows. Here is the brotherhood that must comfort Christians, that Christ owned us for brethren after his resurrection. He paid dear for it, alas! Are we worth so much, that God should become man to die for us, to rise again for us, to justify us, and make us brethren? That infinite love, that God became man and died for us, and rose again to own us for his brethren, will satisfy all doubts. Shall we doubt anything of that love? When he out of his free love will own us as brethren, shall not we own him? I confess it is a marvellous thing, in times of temptation it is difficult to make use of it. Oh, but pray with the good apostle, 'Lord, increase our faith,' Luke xvii. 5; with the poor man in the gospel, 'I believe; Lord, help my unbelief,' Mark ix. 24. So when any temptation cometh for our unworthiness and our undeserving, then think Christ after his resurrection called his apostles 'brethren,' and he will be content to be my brother, if I will believe he died for me, and I will cast myself upon him; therefore away with all doubts.

There be many other observations out of the words.

(1.) *Will you have the first words in estate of glory, his first words after death?* 'Go and tell my brethren.' Think in a desperate extremity, think of the sweet message he sent by Mary Magdalene to his unworthy 'brethren,' that he died for, and [had] given his blood to make them his brethren. Think of his free love to you. It is not for your worthiness or unworthiness, but of his own free love, that he came from heaven to take your nature. It is his own free love that he came to die; and therefore conceive not of worthiness nor unworthiness, but consider the command of God to believe; and if we perish, perish there. Cast ourselves on our brother, that will own us in our worst condition. That is the grand use.

(2.) Again, If *God owns us in his glorious condition, shall we be ashamed of the doctrine of Christ, of the children of God, to own them?* What saith Christ? It is a terrible thunderbolt. 'He that is ashamed of me and of my word before men, I will be ashamed of him before my heavenly Father,' Mark viii. 38. Take heed of being ashamed to stand out a good cause, in matters of religion. Christ was not ashamed to call us brethren when we were at the worst, and he himself in a glorious condition; he was in glory, and the disciples drooping in consideration of their guilt, that they had forsaken him, and yet 'brethren' still. And shall not we own him, that owneth us in state of glory? How shall we look that he will own us hereafter, when he trusteth us with his cause and glory, and we betray all to pleasure such and such? Can we look Christ in the face with comfort, if we neglect his cause, his truth, and his church?

(3.) Again, Make this use of it, *Christ is our brother, and will not he take our parts?* Absalom was a disobedient son, yet Absalom would not let his sister Tamar be abused; he would be revenged of that. And will Christ suffer his sister, his spouse, his church to be abused long? Nay, will he leave his 'dove, his love, his undefiled one,' Cant. v. 2, where he hath placed all his joy and contentment, to the malice and fury of the enemy long? Certainly he will not. Certainly he will be avenged on his enemies. If nature, that he hath put into the wicked, sinful men, teach them to revenge indignities offered to their kindred, will Christ suffer his brethren, his sisters, to be abused? 'Saul, Saul, why persecutest thou me?' Acts ix. 4. Now he is in heaven, the church's case is his own. And therefore comfort ourselves with that sweet relation. Christ hath undertaken to be our brother in state of glory. What a comfort is it that we have a brother in heaven! What a comfort was it to the poor patriarchs, when they thought with themselves, we have a brother, Joseph, that is the second man in the kingdom! And so, what a great comfort is it for poor Christians to think, that the second in heaven, that sitteth at God's right hand, that is King of kings and Lord of lords, and that ruleth all, is our brother! Is not this a main comfort, yea, beyond all expression, if we could make use of it by faith answerable to our trouble? Therefore go to Joseph, that hath laid up comfort for us. He hath comfort enough for us, he hath treasures of comfort. Whatsoever is necessary for us, we may have in Christ our elder brother. And therefore 'go to my brethren.'

I beseech you, let us make a use of exhortation, to be stirred up, to labour by faith to be one with Christ; and then he will be our head, our husband, our brother, our friend, our all. Say what you can, Christ will be 'all in all' to all his. He hath enough in him: 'Of his fulness we shall receive, and grace for grace.' Oh labour to be one with Christ. Do not lose such a comfort as is offered. He offereth himself first to be our Saviour and Redeemer, and then our brother; never rest therefore till we have part in Christ. And then labour to make use of, in all temptations catch fast hold of, everything that is useful, as it is the nature of faith to do, like Benhadad's servants, who made use of that word 'brother.' He is my 'brother,' said the king of Israel, as common offices make kindred, 1 Kings xx. 33. He had but let pass the term of 'brother,' and they would not let it go, but catch at it: 'Thy brother Benhadad.' We see what wisdom flesh and blood can teach, to make an improvement of any comfort in the world, if by kindred, or office, or any relation in the world, they make use of them. And when we be in Christ, shall not we make use of them, when we be troubled with sense of sin, or in desperate conditions? When Christ calleth us brother, shall not we answer, 'I am thy brother'? Blessed be thy mercy and love, that descended so low as to make me thy brother! I beseech you, let us not lose the comforts we may have in the disciples' being called Christ's brethren, when they were in some sort enemies. But he knew their hearts were sound, and it was but their weakness; therefore let no weakness discourage thee. He will not 'quench the smoking flax, nor break the bruised reed,' Mat. xii. 20. Is thy heart right to Christ? art thou not a false hypocrite, a secret traitor to Christ, and to his cause and church? Then be of good comfort; thou mayest go to Christ as to thy brother. Though Peter denied him with his mouth, yet he confessed him with his heart. And therefore 'go tell my disciples,' *and Peter*—he hath most guilt, and therefore he hath most need of comfort. Be thy guilt never so great, if thou wilt come into covenant with God, here is mercy for thee, and therefore make this use of it. Never forget, in your worst condition that may be, since Christ will stoop so low to own you to be brethren, to make use of it, if your hearts be right towards him.

'Go to my brethren.' Now I come to the commission or charge given to her. 'Go to my brethren.' Who is the party charged? 'Mary.' And what is her charge? To go to the apostles under the sweet term of 'brethren.' When doth he call them so? After his resurrection; when he was in the state of glory. What is the message? It is very sweet, Go, say to them, 'I ascend to my Father, and your Father; to my God, and your God.' 'I ascend;' that is, I presently am to ascend, in a very short time I shall ascend. It was but forty days between Easter and Ascension, and all that time Christ appeared now and then. It is the nature of faith, where it is glorious, for to present future things as if present, especially when they be near. 'I ascend;' that is, I shall very shortly ascend, and it is all one as if I ascend presently. To whom do I ascend? 'I ascend to *my Father*.' To '*my* Father.' That is not comfort enough. Therefore 'to *your* Father too.' 'I ascend to God.' That is not comfort enough. Therefore 'to my God, and your God.' We shall unfold the words as we come at them.

First, Mary Magdalene, a woman, a sinner, is used in the great work of an apostle, to be an apostle to the apostles. I would there were that love in all men to teach what they know; and that humility in others, to be instructed in what they know not. It were a sweet conjunction if it were so. She was a mean person to instruct the great apostles. But, beloved, where there is a great deal of love, there they will teach what they know; and where there is humility, there they will be taught what they know not, though they be never so great. And God will humble the greatest to learn of the meanest sometimes. Therefore he sendeth Mary to the apostles.

I beseech you, in matters of salvation, stand not on terms. Let us take truth from Christ, let us see God and Christ in it, see our own comfort in it, not stand upon persons. Aquila and Priscilla teach the great men knowledge, Acts xviii. 2, *seq*. And so it is. Sometimes mean persons are honoured to be instruments of great comforts to persons greater than themselves. She is to go to the apostles under the name of brethren: 'Go tell my brethren.' And she must go to the apostles that were Christ's brethren, and owned to be so now, when he was in glory, when he was risen and exempt from all abasements of the cross and grave, where he was held captive three days under the dominion of sin, when he was freed from all enemies of salvation, and had triumphed over all. 'Go tell my brethren.' So you see there is a sweet affinity and nearness between Christ and his. Christ took our nature on him for this end: he became flesh of our flesh, and bone of our bone, that we spiritually might be flesh of his flesh and bone of his bone. It is no comfort at all; an inducing comfort it is, but no actual, present comfort, that Christ was incarnate for us; for all the world might have comfort in that, Turks, Jews, Pagans, that had the nature of man in them. And all have some comfort in it, as their nature is dignified; and that he took not on him the nature of angels, but the nature of man, his spouse, his church it is that hath the comfort of it. Therefore it is not sufficient that he be bone of our bone and flesh of our flesh; but we must be bone of his bone, and flesh of his flesh. We must be ingraffed and baptised into him by faith, and then the term holdeth, and never till then; so that there is a sweet nearness between Christ and his. 'Brother' is a most comfortable relation. It is a comfort that he took our nature upon him, that God would take 'dust and ashes,' earth, into the unity of his person. For God to become man is a great dignifying of man's nature. But to take not only our nature on him, but to take our person particularly near to him; thou and thou to be a member of Christ, there is the honour of it. It induceth us to come to Christ that hath loved our nature so much. But the other is an actual, present comfort, when we can say, 'I am my beloved's, and my beloved is mine.'

Our hearts are too narrow a great deal to embrace the whole comfort that this word affords unto us, that Christ should own us as his brother after his resurrection, for that sheweth a reconciliation. 'Brother' is a term of friendship, nay, more than a term of reconciliation, for a man may be reconciled to an enemy; but it is a term of amity, to shew that when we believe in Christ and are one with him, our sins are quitted; death is overcome; Satan's head is crushed when God is reconciled. What have they to do with us? They are only to serve our turns to bring us to heaven, and fit us for it. I beseech you, consider of the excellent freedom and dignity of a Christian; his freedom in that he is the brother of Christ; free from all, being owned by Christ after his resurrection, all being quit by his death who was our surety, else he should be in the grave to this day. And then think of our dignity, to be brother to him that is King of heaven, Lord of lords, ruler of the whole world; that hath all things subject to him. Oh that our hearts were enlarged to conceive the wonderful comfort that every Christian hath in this relation! 'Go tell my apostles,' under the sweet term of 'brethren.'

Who art thou, will Satan say, flesh and blood, a piece of earth, wretched sot; wilt thou claim kindred of Christ?

Ay, saith the Christian, believing soul, it is true. If it were my own worthiness it were another matter, but I will give him the lie. When he owned me for his brother after his resurrection, shall I deny the relation? Therefore never believe Satan's tempting words and sinful flesh; for Satan cometh to us in our own flesh, and maketh us think God and Christ to be such and such. Ay, but what saith Christ himself? Believe him and not Satan, that cometh to thee in thy own despairing, dark, doubting flesh. Believe the word of Christ, who calleth thee brother, if thou believest on him, and castest thyself upon him.

This sheweth the dignity of a Christian when he is once in Christ, the excellent, superexcellent, transcendent glory of a Christian. When they told our Saviour Christ that his mother and brethren were to speak with him, saith he, 'They that hear my word and do it, they are my brother, and sister, and my mother,' Luke viii. 21. This is the excellency of a Christian, that he is of so near a kin to Christ. When we believe Christ, it is all one as if we conceived Christ, as if we were brothers to Christ, as if we were of the nearest kindred to him. Nay, it is more; he preferreth mother before mother, brother before brother; mother in spirit before mother in the flesh, and brother in spirit before all other brothers. Therefore an excellent thing to be a Christian! When once a Christian giveth himself to Christ, and denieth his own doubting, despairing heart, which is the greatest enemy he hath, 1. Then what belongeth to him? Then God is his, and Christ is his; he must have an inheritance; he is fellow-heir without;* all are his. 2. What carrieth he in him? He carrieth in him the Spirit of the Father and the Son, and the graces of the Spirit, which make him lovely to God. 3. What cometh from him? Having the precious graces of the

* Qu. 'without doubt'?—Ed.

Holy Ghost in him, what can come from him as a Christian but grace and comfort to others? He is a tree of righteousness; and what can come from a good tree but good fruit? So far he is so.

So if you regard what belongeth to them, what is in them, the inheritance they shall have, or what cometh from a Christian, that is, brother of Christ, he is an excellent person, more excellent than his neighbour. There is no man in the world, never so great, but is a base person in comparison of a Christian. What will all be ere long? If a man be not in Christ, these things will add to our vexation. It will be a misery to have had happiness; the greater will be the misery when they must be parted withal. And therefore raise your hearts to consider of the excellent condition of a Christian when he is once the brother of Christ.

I confess it is an hidden dignity; as Paul saith, 'Our life is *hid* with Christ in God,' Col. iii. 3. We have a life, a glorious life, but it is hid. It is dark; sometimes under melancholy, sometimes under temptations, sometimes under the afflictions of the world and disgrace, and so it is an hidden excellency, but it is a true excellency. The world knoweth us not more than they know God and Christ. But it is no matter, God knoweth us by name. He knew Mary by name, as it is said in Isaiah, 'I have called thee by name,' xlv. 3. He is a shepherd, that knoweth his sheep by name, and is known of them. He knoweth thee, and thee, and thee, by name; yea, and the hairs of thy head are numbered; and therefore it matters not though thy dignities be hid with the world. Yet God knoweth them. He hath written all thy members in a book, and he hath a book of remembrance of thee. And therefore it is no matter though it be an hidden dignity. It is a true dignity to be a brother of Christ.

Let us oppose this to the disgrace of the world, and to all temptations of discouragement whatsoever. What are all discouragements to this? They fall all before this, that we are the sons of God and brethren of Christ. What can discourage a man that is thus apprehensive of this excellency upon good terms? I will enlarge the point no further, but leave it to your own meditations, and the Spirit of God work with it!

'Go to my brethren.' When doth he bid her go? Now after his resurrection, when he was to ascend to heaven. The first degree of his glory was his resurrection, after his lowest abasement in the grave. You see that honour doth not change Christ's disposition, as it doth amongst men. When they be advanced to great places, they will not look on their old friends and acquaintance; but Christ hath no such disposition, he owneth his poor disciples in their greatest abasements: 'Go tell my brethren.' Now when he was in a state of glory, ready to go to heaven, and he giveth them a more comfortable title now than ever before. In the gospel he called them 'servants,' and 'friends,' and 'apostles,' and 'disciples;' but now 'brethren,' a word of all sweetness, and nothing but sweetness. 'Go tell my brethren' presently; Christ would have no delay, for he saw they had present need. Christ's love is a quickening love, and the fruits of it are very speedy. There is more than angelical swiftness in Christ when there is need of him. God helpeth at need, in the most seasonable time, and he knoweth the time best of all. He did but rise in the morning, and the very same day, 'Go tell my brethren.' Ye have Cant. ii. 8, that Christ cometh 'leaping upon the mountains.' When he was to help his church, 'he leaped over the mountains;' as in the eighth verse, 'The voice of my beloved! behold, he cometh leaping upon the mountains, skipping upon the hills.' He cometh from heaven to earth, from earth to the grave; and now he is risen, he is all in haste, he maketh no stay, because his manner of despatch is, to help and comfort by the ministry of others. Go quickly; do not stand embracing of me, but 'go and tell my brethren.'

Obj. But why then do not we find comfort sooner, that are afflicted?

Ans. Beloved, where is the fault? Is it in Christ? You stand out at staves-end* with Christ; you will not embrace comforts when they be offered, or else you be not sufficiently humbled; for he is wise as he is swift, he knoweth which be the best times.

You see then that Christ, so soon as ever it is fit for him, he will come. If he should come sooner, he would come too soon; if afterward, it would be too late. He is the best discerner of times and seasons that can be, and therefore wait his leisure. If thou want comfort, humble soul, whosoever thou art, wait his leisure. Certainly he knoweth the best time, and when the time is come, he will come. 'He that will come shall come,' Heb. x. 37, there is no question of that.

Now as he sent her in all haste, preferring it before any compliment to his own person, so it is a constant love. As it is a quick love that God bears to his children, so it is a constant, invincible love. They had dealt most unbrotherly with him, for every one had forsaken him, and Peter had denied him; yet, 'Go tell my brethren.' One would think this water would have quenched this fire; this unkind and unbrotherly dealing would have quenched this love in Christ's breast. It is true, if it had been the mere love of man, it had been something; but it was the love of an infinite person, that took our nature out of love, and therefore it was a constant and invincible love. Nothing could conquer it, not the thoughts of their unkind dealings, no, not their denying and forsaking of him. But still, 'Go tell my brethren.' 'Love is strong as death,' Cant. viii. 6. Death could not hold Christ in the grave, but love held him on the cross. When he came to the work of our redemption, love then held him on earth; but when he was in the grave, it brake through all there. Indeed, it was stronger than death, in Christ.

Quest. Why is Christ's love so constant, so invincible, that nothing can alter it?

Resolution. The ground of it is, it is free love. He fetcheth the ground of his love from his own heart; not from our worthiness or unworthiness, but from his own freedom, and God's eternal purpose. God hath purposed to save so many, and those and no more he giveth to Christ to save. And God looketh on his own purpose, Christ's free love, and that is the ground of all. And therefore whom he loveth he loveth to the end, because he looked on us in his election. The Lord knoweth who are his; the foundation is so sure, if once we be God's we are ever God's.† For Christ looks on us in God's election. Therefore, if ever he sheweth his love to us, once his love and for ever his love. If anything in man could hinder it, it would have hindered it at our first conversion, when we were at worst, even enemies; if nothing could hinder it then, what can hinder it afterwards? as the apostle reasoneth strongly: Rom. v. 10, if we be reconciled by his death, much more will he save us by his life. 'If when we were enemies we were reconciled to God by the death of his Son, now much more, being reconciled, shall we be saved by his life.' If when we had no goodness, but opposition and rebellion in us, we were saved by his death,

* That is, = at a distance, or on ceremony.—G.

† In margin here, '*Fundamenta tamen stant inconcussa Syonis.*'—G.

Christ is much more able to save us now by his life, triumphing over death and being glorious in the heavens.

Obj. Oh but, saith the poor soul, I am a poor weak creature, and ready to fall away every day.

Ans. Ay but Christ's love is constant. 'Whom he loveth he loveth to the end.' What saith the apostle? Rom. viii. 38, 'Neither things present, nor things to come, shall be able to separate us from the love of Christ;' and therefore be strong in the Lord, and in the power of his might; do not trust to yourselves, nor trouble yourselves for things to come. If you be free from guilt of former sins, never question time to come. God is unchangeable in his nature, unchangeable in his love. He is 'Jehovah, I am,' always; not 'I was or will be,' but 'I am always.' If ever he loved thee, he will love thee for ever. You see the constancy of Christ's love, 'Go tell my brethren.' Now when they had most deeply offended him, they were renegadoes, having all left him; and then when he had most need of their comfort, being in greatest extremity; and yet 'Go tell my brethren.'

Beloved, let us not lose the comfort of the constancy and immutability of Christ's love. Let us conceive that all the sweet links of salvation are held on God's part strong, not on ours; the firmness is on God's part, not on ours. Election is firm on God's part, not on ours. We choose indeed as he chooseth us, but the firmness is of his choosing; so he calleth us, we answer, but the firmness is of his action. He justifieth; we are made righteous, but the firmness is of his imputation. Will he forgive sins to-day, and bring us into court and damn us to-morrow? No. The firmness is of his action. We are ready to run into new debts every day, but whom he justifieth he will glorify. The whole chain so holdeth, that all the creatures in heaven and earth cannot break a link of it. Whom he calleth he will justify and glorify. Therefore never doubt of continuance, for it holds firm on God's part, not thine. God embraceth us in the arms of his everlasting love, not that we embraced him first. When the child falleth not, it is from the mother's holding the child, and not from the child's holding the mother. So it is God's holding of us, knowing of us, embracing of us, and justifying of us that maketh the state firm, and not ours; for ours is but a reflection and result of his, which is unvariable. The sight of the sun varieth, but the sun in the firmament keepeth always his constant course. So God's love is as the sun, invariable, and for ever the same. I only touch it, as the foundation of wonderful comfort, which they undermine that hold the contrary.

The next point is, that Christ chose Mary to go tell his brethren, and under the sweet title of 'brethren,' to deliver this sweet message, 'I am going to my Father, and your Father; to my God, and your God.' He telleth them the sweetest words in the worst times.

This point differeth from the former thus. The former was, that Christ's love is constant, and always the same. But now Christ most sheweth his love when we are most cast down: in the worst times, if our casting down be with repentance. He never said 'brethren' before, but reserved the term of 'brethren' for the worst time of all. The sweetest discoveries of Christ are in the worst times of all to his children. Mothers will bring out any thing to their children, that is sweet and comfortable to them, in their sickness. Though they frowned on them before, yet the exigency of the child requires it. When there is need, any thing cometh out that may please the child. The poor disciples were not only in affliction, being the scorn of the world, the shepherd being smitten and the sheep scattered, but their inward grief was greater. They were inwardly confounded and ashamed to see Christ come to such an end. They were full of unbelief. Though Christ had told them he would rise again, they could not believe; and so what with fear, and what with doubt, and what with grief for their using of Christ so unkindly and leaving him, certainly they were in a perplexed and disconsolate condition; yet now, 'Go and tell my brethren.' We see, then, that after relapses, when we be in state of grace, to deal unkindly with Christ, must needs be matter of grief and shame; yet if we be humbled for it and cast down, even then Christ hath a sweet message for us by his Holy Spirit: 'Go, tell my brethren.' In the Canticles, the church, the spouse of Christ, had dealt unkindly with Christ, by losing him and forsaking him, chap. iii. 5. In the third chapter, she had lost him, and sought him on her bed, but found him not. She rose, and went to the watchmen, and then went through the city, but found him not. At length she found him whom her soul loved. Then Christ speaks most sweetly and comfortably to her in the beginning of the fourth chapter, but especially in the sixth chapter, after she had dealt most unkindly with Christ. He standeth at the door knocking and waiting, till his locks dropped with rain, in resemblance of a lover that standeth at the door, and is not suffered to come in. Afterwards he leaveth her for this unkindness, yet not so, but that there was some sweet relish left upon the door. God always leaveth something in his children to long after him; and at length, after much longing, Christ manifesteth himself sweetly to her, chap. vi. 4, and breaketh out, 'Thou art beautiful, O my love, as Tirzah, comely as Jerusalem, terrible as an army with banners; turn away thine eyes from me, for they have overcome me; thy hair is as a flock of goats,' &c., and so goeth on, 'My love, my dove, my undefiled one.' He could not satisfy himself in the commendations of his church, being, as it were, overcome with love. And this sheweth, that after we have dealt unkindly with Christ, and our consciences are ashamed and abashed with it, as it is fit they should, yet if we will wait a while, and be content, nor be desperate, nor yield to temptation, if we stay but a while, Christ will manifest himself to us, and shew that he valueth and prizeth the hidden graces we cannot see. He can see gold in ore. He can see hidden love, and hidden faith and grace, that we cannot see in temptations; and he will manifest all at length, and shew his love when we stand most in need of it. We see it in David, who was deeply humbled for his folly with Bathsheba, for there was not one, but many sins, as murder and adultery, &c.; yet being now humbled, God sent him and Bathsheba wise Solomon, to succeed him in his kingdom. He forgetteth all; and so you see our Saviour Christ forgetteth all their unkindness. He biddeth her not 'Go, tell my renegade disciples, that owned not me; they care not for me: I care not for them; I am above death and all, and now will use them as they did me.' Oh no. But 'Go, tell my brethren,' without mentioning any thing that they have done unkindly.

What is the reason? It is sufficient to a gracious soul that it is thus; it is the course of God. But there be reasons to give satisfaction.

Reason 1. First, *The love of Christ to a poor, disconsolate, afflicted soul is most seasonable.* When they have relapsed and dealt unkindly with Christ, then Christ not only forgiveth, but forgets all; nay, and calleth them under the term of 'brethren,' which is more than forgiving or forgetting. Oh now it is seasonable. For there is a wonderful dejection of spirit after unkind usage of Christ, in a soul that knows what Christ means. It is as a shower of rain after great drought. It falleth weighty upon the soul.

Reason 2. Secondly, *The freedom of Christ's love most appeareth then, when no desert of ours can move it.* For is not that love free, when we have dealt unkindly with him, and joined with the world and with the flesh, and dealt slipperily with him, that then he would speak kindly to us and make love to us? Lord, if I had had my due, what would have become of me? If he had sent them word according to their deserts, he might have said, 'Go, tell the apostate, base people that have dealt unworthily with me, whom I will send to hell.' Oh no. But 'tell my brethren.' His free love appeareth most at such times, when our souls are most dejected.

Reason 3. Thirdly, *Satan roareth then most, then he most of all sheweth his horns, when we are relapsed.* Oh, saith he, if thou hadst never found kindness, it had been something; but thou hast dealt unworthily that hast had so many favours, and dost thou so requite the Lord of glory? Now this love of Christ doth exceedingly confound Satan, and trouble his plots. He knoweth then that God leaveth men, and he joineth with a guilty conscience, and a guilty conscience maketh them to fear all they have deserved, Shall I look God in the face, and Christ in the face when I have used them thus? Shall I receive the sacrament and join with God's people? Now Satan doth join with guilt of conscience, and carrieth it further; and when God seeth them dejected and humbled for this, he speaketh more comfort to them than ever before.

There is none of us all, I can except none, but had need of this. Have we dealt so unkindly with Christ since our conversion? Have not we dealt proudly, and unkindly, and carelessly with him? And if we have the love of Christ in our breasts, it will shame and abash us. Now if we have joined with a temptation, Satan will say, Will you go to God, and to prayer, that have served God thus? Shall I yield to this temptation? If we can shame ourselves and say, Lord, I take all shame to myself, I have dealt most unworthily with thee, we shall hear a voice of comfort presently. And therefore whatsoever our conditions be, be invited to repentance, though thou hast fallen and fallen again. 'I have dealt unkindly.' Did not Peter so? and yet, 'Go, tell my disciples, and tell Peter.' The pope will have him head of the church. I am sure he was head in forsaking of Christ, and indeed Christ never* upbraided Peter with forsaking of him. Now only he biddeth him feed, feed, feed, that he might take more notice of it; but he was so kind that he never cast it into his teeth, John xxi. 15-17.

Obj. But saith the poor drooping soul, If I had never tasted of mercy it had been something.

Ans. But object not that, for though Peter's offence was great, yet his repentance was great; and though thy sins be great, yet if thy repentance and humiliation be answerable, thou shalt have most comfort of all. And therefore let no man be discouraged.

If we go on in sinful, desperate courses, as the fashion of the world is, speak what we can, if we speak out our lungs, many will not leave an oath, nor their profane base courses and filthy ways; ill they have been already, and ill they will be till they come to hell. Some such there be, but better we are to speak too. Whosoever thou art, that are weary of thy profane, base, godless courses, be humbled for them. When thou art humbled and broken-hearted, then think of Christ, as he offers himself; think of nothing but love, nothing but mercy. Satan will picture him thus and thus, but when thou beest humbled and broken-hearted, he is

* Misprinted 'ever.'—G.

readier to entertain thee than thou art to fly to him. And therefore at such times consider how Christ offereth himself to thee. He that died for his enemies, and seeks them that never sought him, that is found of them that sought him not, will he refuse them that seek him? If thou hast an heart humbled, and hast a desire of favour, will he refuse thee, that receiveth many in the world. Therefore do not despair. We as ambassadors beseech you, saith the apostle. Thou desirest God's favour and Christ's love. Thou desirest them, and Christ entreateth thee, and then thou art well met. Thou wouldst fain have pardon and mercy, so would Christ fain bestow it upon thee. Therefore join not to Satan. Take heed of temptations in such a case as this is. Take heed of refusing our own mercies. When God offers mercy in the bowels of his compassion, refuse it not. Christ is ready to shew great kindness in our greatest unkindness, if we be humbled for it.

But this belongeth to those that be broken-hearted, that can prize and value Christ. They that go on in presumptuous courses shall find Christ in another manner of majesty. They shall find him as a judge whom they despised as a brother; and they that will not come in and subject themselves to his mercy, they shall find his justice. If they will not come under this sceptre, they shall find his rod of iron to crush them to pieces. And therefore let no corrupt, careless person, that will go on, fortify their presumption from hence. It belongeth only to them to be humbled and abased with the sight of sin, and consideration of their unkindness and unworthy dealing with Christ. I know such as are most subject to discouragement, and Satan is most ready to close with them in strong temptations above all. Oh, but never let them despair, but consider what the apostle saith: 'While sin aboundeth, grace aboundeth much more,' Rom. v. 20. If there be height, depth, and breadth of sin in us, there is now more height, and depth, and breadth of mercy in Christ; yea, more than we can receive.

I have fallen from God, saith the soul. What if thou hast? but God is not fallen from thee. Peter denied Christ, but did Christ deny Peter? No. Christ hath not denied thee. What saith the Lord in Jeremiah? 'Will the husband take the wife when she hath been naught? no; yet return to me, O Israel,' Jer. iii. 1. But say, thou hast been false, and committed such and such sins; whatsoever they be, though adultery, yet return to me.

Quest. Oh, but is it possible God should do it?

Resol. Yea, it is possible with him: 'His thoughts are not as thy thoughts; his thoughts are as far above thine as heaven is above earth,' Isa. lv. 8.

Obj. Why, no man will do it.

Ans. Ay, but here is the mercy of a God, 'I am God, and not man;' therefore his comforts fail not. If he were so, he would not regard one that hath been so unkind; but he is God, and not man.

'Go to my brethren.' I come now to the matter of the commission. Tell them, 'I ascend to my Father, and your Father; to my God, and your God,' which is all included in 'brethren;' for if we be God's in Christ, then God is our Father. But we must not deal in few words with disconsolate souls, but come again and again with the same words. As how many times have you the comfort of the Messiah in Isaiah and the rest of the prophets, again and again? Our hearts are so prone to doubt of God's mercy, of Christ's love, especially after guilt, that all is little enough; and therefore our Saviour studieth to speak sweetly to the heart, 'Go, tell my brethren.' That which a carnal heart and curious* head would count tautology and superfluity of words, a gracious heart thinks to be scantiness. Oh, more of that still; I have not enough! This is the pride of men, that will have all things to satisfy the curious ear; but a gracious heart hath never enough. And therefore Christ addeth comfort to comfort: 'Go, tell my brethren, I ascend to my Father, and their Father; to my God, and their God.' The message itself is Christ's ascension. The place whither is to the Father, a common Father to him and them. Every word hath comfort.

'I ascend.'

I ascend to the Father, and to my Father and your Father too. Now I have quitted myself of death, and sin imputed to me as a surety, and I am going to heaven to make an end of all there: 'I ascend to God, to my God and to your God.' We have all one common Father, and one common God.

First, For his ascension. He did not yet ascend. Why then doth he speak for the present? 'I ascend;' that is, I am shortly so to do. And it was in his mind, it was certainly so to be; and therefore he speaks of it in present. It is the phrase of faith, to speak of things to come as if they were present. Faith makes them so to the soul, for it looketh on the word and all things as they are in that Word, who will make good whatsoever he saith. And therefore it is the evidence of things that are not yet, yet they be evident to a faithful soul. If we could learn this aright, to make things to come present, what kind of people should we be! Could we think of our resurrection and ascension and glory to come as present, they would be present to our faith; the things present, or sense, could not withdraw us. If we could set hell before us, could the pleasures of hell bewitch us? If the time to come were present, could anything in the world withdraw us? It could not be. And therefore it is an excellent skill of faith to set things to come before us as present.

He ascendeth. He implieth that he was risen. That was past, and therefore he nameth it not. All Christ's mind was on ascending. Those that are risen together with Christ, their mind is all on ascension, all on heaven. And this is one main reason, because where anything is imperfect, there the spirit resteth not till it attaineth to that perfection that it is destinated unto. When anything hath a proper element and place where it must rest, it resteth not till it be in its own proper place and element. The perfection of the soul is in heaven, to see Christ face to face, and God in Christ. Heaven is the element of a Christian. It is his proper region. He is never well till there; and there is his rest, his solace and contentment, and there all his desires are satiated to the utmost. Till we be in heaven, we be under desires; for we be under imperfections. All the while we are in imperfections we are in an uncomfortable estate; and while we be so, we are not as we should be. And therefore wheresoever any are partakers of Christ's resurrection, they mind the ascension as present. Where any grace is, there the thoughts are for heaven presently.

Let us take a scanting† of our dispositions from hence. There be many that think it good to be here always; they never think of ascending. If they could live here always, they would with all their hearts, but it is not so with a Christian. It is his desire to be where his happiness, his Saviour, his God and Father is, where his country and inheritance is,

* That is, 'over-curious.'—G.

† That is, 'proportion' = measure.—G.

and therefore he mindeth ascension and things to come. When anything is done, he thinks that what is done is not yet enough. As your great conquerors in the world, they forget what they have conquered, and remember what they have yet to do; so Christ, having got conquest over death, he thinks now of ascension, to conquer in the eyes of all; for it is not enough to conquer in the field, but he will conquer in the city; he will conquer to heaven, and make show of his conquest. I ascend to lead captivity captive, 'to make a show,' as it is expressed, Col. ii. 15. While anything is to do or receive, our souls should not be satisfied, but still stretched out to desire further and further still, more and more still, till we be there where our souls shall be filled to the uttermost; and there is no place of further desire, as heaven is the place to satiate, and fill all the corners of the soul.

Quest. But how shall we know whether we be risen with Christ or no?

Resol. Partly we may know it by our former courses. Christ when he was risen, all the clothes were laid together in the grave. He left them behind, and rose with an earthquake. There was a commotion; and after his resurrection he minded heaven. So if ye be risen with Christ, your former vile courses lie in the grave; your oaths are gone; profaneness and wickedness of life gone. Tell you me, you are risen, while you carry the bonds of your sins about you? You profane, wretched, swearing, ungodly persons, filthy speakers, that have an heart more filthy, vile in body and soul, can they have any part in Christ? Where is that that bound you before? You carry it about still. Therefore you be in the bonds of the devil; you be in the grave of sin; there is no rising. Resurrection is with commotion. There was an earthquake when Christ arose; and there is an heartquake when the soul riseth. Can the soul rise from sin without commotion? In the inward man there will* be division between flesh and spirit, without any ado at all? And therefore they that find nothing to do in their spirits, where is their rising again?

But that which is proper to the occasion in hand is the third. Where grace is begun, there will be an inward proceeding and ascending with Christ. How shall I know therefore whether I ascend?

1. *First, By minding things above.* The apostle telleth us directly, Col. iii. 1, 'Mind things above,' be heavenly-minded in some sort, live the life that Christ did, after his resurrection. All his discourse was, after his resurrection, of the kingdom of heaven, and his mind was on the place whither he was to go; and so a true Christian indeed, that is truly risen, his thoughts and discourse is, when he is himself, heavenly. Other things he useth as if he did not; as while we be in the world, we must deal with worldly things; but we must deal with them as that which is not our proper element, 1 Cor. vii. 37, 'They used the world, as if they used it not; and they married, as if they did not; for they knew the fashion of this world passeth away.' And therefore they that affect earthly glory, carnal affections and delights, they cannot think of these things with any comfort. They be moles which grovel in the earth. Some make a profession, and they ascend higher as kites do, but they look low; they make high professions, but their aims are low. The true eagles that ascend to Christ, as they ascend, so they look upward and upward still. They do not mind things below; they do not take a high pitch, and still continue earthly-minded; but they look high, as well as ascend high. Therefore let us not deceive ourselves.

* Qu. 'will there'?—ED.

2. Yet more particularly, those that ascend with Christ, they that are in heaven and they that are on earth *do the same things, though in different degrees and measure.* What do they in heaven? There they meddle not with defilements of the world; and so, though a Christian be on earth, he defileth himself not with the world, or ill company. He will converse with them, but not defile himself with them. They that be in heaven are praising God, and so be they much in praising of God here. They that be in heaven love to see the face of God, they joy in it. And they that be heavenly-minded here joy in the presence of God, in the word, the sacraments, and his children. If they be ascended in any degree and measure, this they will do. And then they will joy in communion with God all they can, as they do in heaven. You have some carnal dispositions that are never themselves but in carnal company like themselves. If ever we mean to be in heaven, we must joy in heaven on earth; that is, in them that be heavenly in their dispositions. If we cannot endure them here, how shall we ever live with them in heaven?

What was Christ to ascend for? What is the end of his ascension?

The end of his ascension was to take possession of heaven in his body, which had never been there before?

1. And he was to take possession of heaven in his body for his church; that is, his mystical body. So he ascended to heaven, carried his blessed body that he took in the virgin's womb with him.

2. And likewise he ascended to heaven, to take up heaven in behalf of his spouse, his church; as the husband takes up land in another country in behalf of his wife, therefore he did ascend.

3. And likewise he ascended to leave his Spirit, that he might send the Comforter. He taketh away himself, that was the great Comforter, while he was below. He was the bridegroom; and while the bridegroom was present, they had not such a measure of the Spirit. Christ's presence supplied all. But Christ ascended to heaven that his departure from them might not be prejudicial to them, but that they might have comfort through the God of comfort, the Spirit of comfort, the Holy Ghost: 'I will send the Comforter,' John xiv. 16, *seq.*

And though there was no loss by the ascension of Christ, they might fear by losing of Christ that all their comfort was gone. Ay, but Christ telleth them, 'I go to prepare a place for you.' He goeth to take up heaven for his church, and then to send his Spirit. What a blessed intercourse is there now, since Christ's ascension, between heaven and earth! Our body is in heaven, and the Spirit of God is here on earth. The flesh that he hath taken into heaven is a pledge that all our flesh and bodies shall be where he is ere long. In the mean time, we have the Spirit to comfort us, and never to leave us till we be brought to the place where Christ is. This is great comfort, and this is the main end why Christ ascended to the Father, that he might send the Comforter. And comfort might well come now in more abundance than before, because by the death of Christ all enemies were conquered, and by the resurrection of Christ it was discovered that God was appeased. The resurrection of Christ manifested to the world what was done by death; and now, all enemies being conquered, and God being appeased, what remains but the sweetest gift next to Christ, the Holy Ghost? And that is the reason why the Holy Ghost was more abundant after Christ's resurrection, because God was fully satisfied, and declared by the rising of Christ to be fully satisfied, and all enemies to be conquered.

4. One end likewise of his resurrection was 'to make a show of his conquest.' There is a double victory over the enemy. There is a victory in the field, and triumph together with it. And then there is triumphing *in civitate regia*, a triumphing in the kingly city. So Christ did conquer in his death, and shewed his conquest by resurrection; but he did not lead captivity captive and make show thereof till he ascended; and then he made open show of his victorious triumph *in civitate regia*.

5. One special end, likewise, why he would have this message sent, that he was to ascend, was that he might appear there in heaven for us, as Heb. ix. 11, *seq.*, 'He appears for ever in heaven for us, and maketh intercession for us.' When the high priest was to enter into the holy of holies, which was a type of heaven, he carried the names of the twelve tribes engraven in stone upon his breast. Christ, our true high priest, being entered into the holy of holies, carried the names of all his elect in his breast into heaven, and there appeareth before God for us. He carrieth us in his heart. Christ doth fulfil that which in John xvii. he prayeth for, appearing in heaven before his Father by virtue of his blood shed, and that blood that speaketh better things than the blood of Abel. It speaks mercy and pardon. The blood of Abel crieth for vengeance and justice; but the blood of Christ saith, Here is one that I shed my blood for. And when we pray to God, God accepts of our prayers; and by virtue of Christ's blood shed, there is mercy, and pardon, and favour procured, which is sprinkled by faith upon the soul; God manifesting to the soul by his Spirit, that Christ died in particular for such a soul, which soul praying to God in the name of Christ, that blood not only in heaven, but sprinkled upon the soul, speaketh peace there. The Spirit saith that to the soul, which Christ doth in heaven. Christ saith in heaven, I died for such a soul; the Spirit saith in the soul, Christ died for me; and the blood of Christ is sprinkled on every particular soul. As Christ in heaven appears and intercedeth for me, so the Spirit intercedeth in mine own guilty heart, that always speaks discomfort, till it be satisfied with particular assurance. Christ died for me, and God is mine, and Christ is mine. Thus particular faith sprinkleth the blood of Christ upon the soul. So that now my sins are not only pardoned in heaven, but in my soul. There is not only intercession in heaven, but in my soul. My soul goeth to God for pardon and for mercy, and rejoiceth in all the mercies it hath and hopeth to have. What is done in heaven, is done in a man's soul by the Spirit in some measure.

6. The last end is, that he might shew that our salvation is exactly wrought, that God is perfectly satisfied to the full, else he should never have risen, much less ascended to heaven. And therefore if we once believe in Christ for forgiveness of sins, and yet say, I doubt of salvation, it is all one as if you should go about to pluck Christ from heaven. The doubtful, distrustful heart, till it be subdued by a spirit of faith, saith, 'Who shall ascend to heaven, to tell me whether I shall go to heaven?' or 'Who shall enter into the deep, to tell me I am freed from hell?' I am afraid I shall be damned, saith the guilty heart, till the Spirit of God hath brought it under and persuaded it of God's love in Christ. Say not, 'Who shall ascend up to heaven? for that is to bring Christ down from heaven,' Rom. x. 7. And what an injurious thing is it to bring Christ down from heaven, to suffer on the cross! This is a great indignity, though we think not of it, to doubt of our salvation, and not cast ourselves on his mercy. For as verily as he is there, we shall be there. He is gone to take up a place

for us. He is there in our name, as the husband taketh a place for his spouse. And if we doubt whether we shall come there or no, we doubt whether he be there or no. And if we doubt of that, we doubt whether he hath wrought salvation or no, and so we bring him down to the cross again. Who shall descend to the deep? that is, to bring Christ from the dead again. Such is the danger of a distrustful heart. So that by Christ's ascending into heaven, we may know all is done and accomplished; all our enemies are subdued; God is appeased and fully satisfied, heaven is taken up in our room, and therefore labour for a large heart answerable to the large unchangeable grounds we have, for faith to pitch and bottom itself upon it. Therefore make this farther use of this ascension of Christ, and thereupon his intercession in heaven for us. He is there to plead our cause. He is there as our surety to appear for us, and not only so, but as a counsellor to plead for us; and not only so, but one of us, as if a brother should plead for a brother; and not only so, but a favourite there too. All favourites are not so excellent at counselling perhaps, but we have one that is favourite in heaven, and is excellent at pleading, that can non-suit all accusations laid against us by the devil. He is the Son of God, and he is one of us; he appeareth not as a stranger, for a stranger, as the counsellor is perhaps for his client, but he appears as our brother, Apoc. xii. 10. Let us think of the comforts of it. He appears for us to plead our cause, with acceptation of his person and cause. For he, before whom he pleadeth, God the Father, sent him to take our nature, die, and ascend into heaven for us, to sustain the persons of particular offenders. He must needs hear Christ, that sent him for that purpose. Where the judge appoints a counsel, it is a sign he favoureth the cause. Perhaps we cannot pray, are disconsolate, and vexed with Satan's temptations. The poor client hath a good cause, but cannot make a good cause of it. But if he get a skilful lawyer, that is favourable to him, and before a favourable judge, his comfort is, his advocate can make his cause good. If we would confess our sins, as that we must do, we must take shame to ourselves in all our distress and disconsolation of spirit; and we must lay open our estates to God, and complain; and then desire God to look upon us, and Christ to plead our cause for us and answer Satan; and when Satan is very malicious and subtile, as he is a very cunning enemy to allege all advantages against us, to make us despair, remember this, we have one in heaven that is more skilful than he 'that is the accuser of brethren,' Rev. xii. 10, that accuseth us to God and to our own souls, that accuseth every man to himself and maketh him an enemy to himself. But we have a pleader in heaven that will take our part against the accuser of our brethren, and quiet us at length in our consciences. Perhaps we may be troubled a while, to humble us; but remember that he is in heaven purposely to plead our cause.

It is a good plea to God, 'Lord, I know not what to say; my sins are more than the hairs of my head. Satan layeth hard to me. I cannot answer one of a thousand. I confess all my sins. Hear me, and hear thy Son for my sake. He is now at thy right hand, and pleadeth for me.' And desire Christ to plead for us. We have not only all the church to pray for us, 'Our Father;' but we have Christ himself to plead for us and make our cause good, if Christ saith, I shed my blood for this person, and [he] appears now by virtue of my redemption. And the condition of the covenant is, if we confess our sins, he is merciful to forgive. And if we sin, we have an advocate in heaven, to whom we must lay claim, 1 John ii. 1. The party hath confessed the debt; and therefore the bond must be cancelled. He hath performed the conditions on his part; and therefore make it good on thine own part. And being* the Spirit hath shamed thee for thy sins, what can the devil say? What saith Paul? 'It is God that justifieth; who shall condemn?' Rom. viii. 33. If God, the party offended, do justify, who shall condemn? It is Christ that died. That is not enough. 'That is risen again.' That is not enough. It is Christ that rose again, 'and sitteth at the right hand of God for us,' and maketh intercession for us. 'Who shall lay any thing to the charge of God's elect?' Let the devil accuse what he will, Christ is risen, to shew that he hath satisfied; and is now in heaven, there appearing for us. Oh that we had hearts large enough for these comforts! then should we never yield to base temptations.

It is against the pleasure of God that we should be disconsolate? Therefore we wrong our own souls, and sin against our own comfort, when we let the reins loose by inordinate and extreme sorrow. We lose that sweetness that we might enjoy, by giving way to discomfortable thoughts. Indeed, if a man examine his life from the beginning of his conversion to the end thereof, he may thank himself for all his trouble. The sin against the holy gospel is a kind of rebellion against God, though we think not so, when we will not be comforted, nor embrace grounds of comfort when we have them. The comforts of God ought not to be of small esteem to us. The sweet comforts, large, exceeding, eternal comforts of God, we ought to esteem of them as they be; and therefore our Saviour Christ sendeth to them speedily.

All Scripture is to this end, for consolation, even the Scripture that tendeth to instruction and direction, that so men may be in a state of comfort; for cordials are not good, but where there is purgation before. So all Scriptures that are purging, to tell us our faults, they be to bring us unto a comfortable condition. Other Scriptures, that tend to instruct our judgments and settle us in faith, what is the end of all, if we walk not comfortably towards God and strongly in our places? Therefore, when we look not to comfort and joy in all conditions, we abuse the intendments† of God.

But, I beseech you, make not a bad use of it; for if you know it to be so, if it worketh not graciously in you, and winneth you to respect God the more, and love him that is thus indulgent and gracious, but go on in offending conscience, and break peace off, then at length conscience will admit no comfort. Many that have excellent comforts have made havoc of their consciences, and will go on in spite of ministers, in spite of their consciences and God's Spirit joined with conscience. At length it is just with God to give them up to despair, wicked sinners that trample the blood of Christ under their feet. But for all other that strive against corruption, and would be better, it is a ground of marvellous comfort.

I shall come to the message itself. Tell them, 'I ascend.' He speaketh of that as present which was surely to be. So we should think of our future estate as if we were presently to go to heaven. Faith hath this force, to make things to come present. If we could keep it in us, and exercise it, could we live in any sin? But that it is distant, that is the cause of sinning. We put off things in a distance. If it be at the day of judgment, that is far off; and therefore they will not leave their present pleasure for that that shall not be, they know not when. But look on things in the word of a God that is Jehovah, that giveth a being to all, who

* That is, 'seeing,' or 'it being so that.'—G.

† That is, 'intentions.'—G.

hath spoken of things to come as if present, and then you will be of another mind. Faith is the privilege of a Christian, which maketh things afar off present. No wicked man but would leave his swearing and profaneness if he saw the joys of heaven and pains of hell; and it were no thanks to him. But to believe God on his word, that these things shall be, that is the commendations of a man, and the excellency of a Christian above another man. Another man doth all by sense; but the Christian will trust God on his word. 'I ascend,' saith Christ.

We must not think of the ascension of Christ as a severed thing from us, but if we would have the comfort of it, we must think of it as ourselves ascending with him. Think of Christ as a public person and surety for us, and then we shall have great comfort in that, that he saith, 'I ascend.' God prepared paradise before he made the creature. He would have him to come into a place of honour and pleasure. And so God, before ever we were born, provided a place and paradise for us in heaven, that we might end our days with greater comfort. We may be straitened here. Many a good Christian hath scarce where to lay his head; but Christ is gone to prepare a place for them in heaven. And this may comfort us in the consideration of all our sins; for sin past, and for corruption present, and sin that we may commit for time to come. For any thing that is past, if we confess our sins to God, he will forgive them. 'The blood of Christ cleanseth us from all sins,' 1 John i. 7, even from the present corruptions that attend on us. We have one that stands between God and us as a surety; and he will give us his Spirit to subdue our corruptions, and at length make us like himself, a glorious spouse, Eph. v. 27. If we were perfect men, we need not a mediator; and this may teach us comfort, rather because we are sinners, and daily subject to offend God. We have one to make our peace for time to come; if we sin, we have an advocate, 1 John ii. 1. When Christ taught us to pray, 'Forgive us our daily trespasses,' he supposed we should run daily into sins, Mat. vi. 12. We have an advocate in heaven every day to stand between God and us, to answer God, to undertake that at length we should cease to offend him; and for the present, we are such as he shed his precious blood for; and he appeareth for us by virtue of his death, which is a marvellous comfort. We think if we commit sin there is no hope. But what needs a mediator, but to make peace between the parties disagreeing? If all things were made up between God and us, what need of an intercessor? But God knoweth well enough we run into daily sins, by reason of a spring of corruption in us, which is never idle. And therefore we may daily go to God in the name of our advocate, and desire God for Christ's sake to pardon, and desire Christ to intercede for us. Let us therefore shame ourselves.

There is not a Christian but will be in himself apprehensive of being thrown into hell every day. There is a spring of corruption in him, and should God take a forfeiture of * his daily rebellions, his conscience tells him it were just. And therefore we must every day live upon this branch of his priestly office, his mediation. We must live by faith in this branch of Christ, and make use of it continually, for this will keep us from hell. And therefore if we sin every day, go to God in the name of Christ, and desire him to pardon us. This is to feed on Christ; and therefore we should more willingly come to the sacrament. When we be in heaven, we

* That is, 'from,' = should God regard his rebellion as a 'forfeiture,' &c.—G.

shall need a mediator no longer, for we shall be perfectly holy. We cannot think of these things too much. They be the life of religion and of comforts; and it may teach us to make a true use of Christ in all our conditions. Poor souls that are not acquainted with the gospel, they think God will cast them into hell for every sin, and they live as if they had not an high priest in heaven to appear for them.

The matter of the message is, Christ ascended to God, as a common Father and God to him and them. He doth not say, I ascend to *the* Father. That were no great comfort; for what were that to them? or to *my* Father only. Neither doth he say, 'I ascend to *our* Father,' for that is true in the order of it: for he is not in equal respect the God and Father of Christ, and the God and Father of us. And therefore he speaks of himself in the first place: 'I go to my God and your God.' For he is first and specially Christ's Father and Christ's God, and then ours; as we shall see in the particulars. We have a common Father and a common God with Christ. God the Father is Christ's Father by eternal generation, as he is God and man. We have therefore the nature of Christ as he is God and man.

There is this difference between God's being Christ's Father and the Father of any else.

First of all, God is Christ's Father from eternity. God had a being and was a Father from all eternity. There is no man of equal standing with his father. He is born after his father cometh to be a man. But Christ is of God from all eternity. His generation is eternal; and therefore there is a grand difference.

Then Christ is co-equal with the Father in glory and majesty every day. The son is not equal with the father, but Christ is with his Father.

Again, The son in other generations comes of the father, and is like the father, taken out of his substance, but of a different substance from the father. But Christ and the Father, both the persons are in one substance, in one essence. The essence of the Father differeth not from the essence of the Son. We must remember this, to give Christ the prerogative and pre-eminency, that God is his Father in another manner than ours. He is his Father by nature, ours by adoption. What he is by nature, we are by grace. Though Christ was intent upon his ascension, yet he forgetteth not this grand difference here, but mentioneth it: 'Go to my brethren.' We must not call him brother again. We may think of him as our brother; but 'My God and my Lord,' as Thomas saith, John xx. 28. If the greatest person should call us brother, yet it is most behoveful for the inferior to say, 'My God, my Lord;' to acknowledge Christ as a great person, and to make use of his love to strengthen our faith, not to diminish our respect to him in any way. It is his infinite mercy to term us brethren. But when we go to him we must have other terms.

Thus we see how to conceive of Christ after his resurrection. When he hath triumphed over all his enemies, and reconciled God by his death, then 'I go to my Father and your Father.' Then he is a common Father, by virtue of Christ's satisfaction to divine wrath and justice, and victory and triumphing over all his enemies. So we must not conceive of God as our Father, but in reference to Christ's victory over death. God is our Father by virtue of Christ's satisfaction to justice and conquest over all our enemies. 'The God of peace,' saith the holy apostle Paul in the epistle to the Hebrews, in the conclusion of that excellent epistle, 'that brought you from death to life through our Lord Jesus Christ,' John v. 24. How cometh he to be the God of peace to us, which brought us from death to life by our Lord Jesus? Why, the resurrection of Christ makes him the God of peace. Who raised him? He raised himself. But who together with himself? The Father raised him. And could the Father raise him if he were not reconciled? But now he is the 'God of peace;' for peace is made by the cross and blood of Christ, Col. iii. 15, the great peace-maker of heaven and earth; now we may conceive of God under the sweet relation of a Father.

Now this relation of a father teacheth us as what we may expect from God, so what we ought to return to God again, and how we ought to carry ourselves one towards another.

I. *What we may expect from God being a Father.*

(1.) *We may expect whatsoever a child may expect from a father.* God taketh not upon him empty names. He saith he will be a Father, not only called a Father, 'but I will be your Father, and you shall be my sons,' 2 Cor. vi. 18. All the fatherhood, and all the kindred in heaven and earth that is spiritual, the comfort of it cometh from God the Father, reconciled to us in Christ. The word in the original is so strong that we cannot express it in English. Fathers on earth are but poor fathers, and they be but beams of the fatherly affection that is in God. God will let us see by these beams of compassion that is in a father to a child, what real compassion he beareth to us. The true reality of fatherhood is in God. And therefore, when we hear of father, think of whatsoever lieth in the bowels of a father to a child; and that we may expect from God our Father, and infinite more. It is a great indulgence; as a father pitieth his child, so God will pity us, Mal. iii. 17. Will a father cast off his child? Indeed, he will cleanse the child. So God will take away our abominations, and purge us when we defile ourselves. It is because of an eternal relation he casteth us not off. We may expect from him indulgence; and it is an indulgence of indulgence. God needed no son when he made us sons. Yet he had his Son and angels to praise himself withal. Can we pity and pardon a child? and will not God pardon and pity us? Why should we conceive worse of him than of ourselves? Will we give pity to a father, and not pity to the Father of all bowels and compassion? And therefore think not that God will cast us off. God pardons us, and healeth our infirmities, and pitieth us as a father pitieth his own child, Ps. ciii. 13. It is a name under which no man must despair. What! Despair under the name of a father? Despair of mercy when we have a Father to go to? The poor prodigal, when he had spent his patrimony, his body, his good name, had lost all, and nothing left, yet he had a father, and 'I will go to him,' Luke xv. 18. And so, when we be at the last cast, and have spent all, we have a Father. Therefore go to him. What saith the church? Isa. lxiii. lxiv., 'Doubtless thou art our Father,' when the church was in a poor condition; 'Though our righteousness be as a menstruous cloth, and we be defiled, yet thou art our Father; we are the clay, thou art the potter,' &c. So that it is a name of his indulgence.

You have his disposition set down by the father of the prodigal. The son saith, he will *go* to the father; the father *runneth* to him and meeteth him when he is coming. God runneth to us, and is ready to meet us, when we begin to repent of sin, and are sensible of our faults. He is more ready to pardon, than we to ask pardon.

I touch only some principal things, that you may remember against the evil day and hour of temptation. He taketh not on him the relation of a

Father for nought, but will fill it up to the uttermost. It is no empty relation.

(2.) *It is a name likewise of comfort.* It is the speech of a natural man, 'A little punishment is enough from a father.' 'He knoweth whereof we are made, he remembers we are but dust,' Ps. ciii. 14, and Heb. xii. 6; he knoweth we are not iron or steel; he knoweth our making; and therefore he will deal gently with us when he doth correct us. It is as necessary as our daily bread to have gentle correction, to wean us from the world; yet he doth it gently. A little punishment will serve from a gracious father.

(3.) *It is a name likewise of provision,* that we may expect from God; that he will in all our exigences and necessities provide for us whatsoever shall be needful. What saith our Saviour Christ to the poor disciples doubting of want? 'It is your Father's good will to give you the kingdom.' What then? 'Fear not, little flock,' Luke xii. 32. He that will give you a kingdom, will not he give you daily bread, *viaticum,* provision for a journey? He that intendeth us heaven, certainly he will provide for us here. And therefore in the Lord's prayer, before all petitions, as a ground of all, he putteth in 'our Father'; and therefore, 'Give us our daily bread, our Father.' And therefore he will give us grace to sanctify his name, and do his will, and forgive us our sins. Expect all from our Father, which is the ground of all. Christ had much ado to persuade his disciples that they should not want necessaries; and therefore he makes whole sermons to strengthen their faith in this: 'Your heavenly Father knoweth what you stand in need of,' Mat. vi. 8. The son cannot ask, but the Father can interpret any sigh, any groan, and knoweth what we would have. And therefore being God's children, we may fetch provision from him in all conditions.

(4.) *And with provisions, protection likewise;* and therefore make this use of it. In the temptations of Satan, lie under the wing of our Father. We have a Father to go to; make use of him, make use of his protection, that God would shield us, that he would be a tower, as he is a tower, and 'the righteous man may fly to him,' Prov. xi. 8. Lie under his wings. He is a gracious Father, and he hath taken this sweet relation on him for this purpose, that we may have comfort in all conditions. You see then what we may expect from God, by this sweet relation he hath taken on him in Christ, to be our Father.

II. *This word, it is a word of relation.* It bindeth God to us and us to God. We are to honour him as our Father. This one word is sufficient to express our duty to a father, and that is a word of reverence; for it includeth a mixed affection of fear and love. And it is an affection of an inferior to a superior. He is great, therefore we ought to fear him. He is good, therefore we ought to love him. There is with him beams of majesty and bowels of compassion. As there is beams of majesty, we ought to fear him; as bowels of compassion, we ought to love him. So that fear and love mixed together is the affection we owe to God as our Father. If we tremble, and are afraid to go to him, we know not he is loving. If we go to him over-boldly and saucily, we forget that he is great. Therefore we must think of his greatness, that we forget not his goodness. We must so think of his goodness, that we forget not his greatness. Therefore go boldly to him, with reverence to the throne of Christ. In the word 'Father,' there is more saving power than in ten thousand. It toucheth his very bowels. When a child wanteth anything, and is in distress, let it but say, Father, or Mother, and the parents yearn upon him. If God be our Father, go to him boldly; but with reverence go with affiance* to his bowels. Oh, it is a persuasive word! What cannot we look from† that majesty that hath condescended to be called 'Father,' and to be a Father to us in all our necessities? Either we shall have what we want and lack, or else we shall have that which is better. He is a wise Father. He answereth not always according to our wills, but always according to our good. He seeth it is for our good that we are not presently comforted. The physician giveth a sharp potion. Oh, I cannot endure! And the chirurgeon lanceth. Oh, I cannot endure it! But the chirurgeon knoweth it is not healing time. Even so we would be presently taken off from under crosses; but God is a wise Father, and knoweth how long it is fit for us to continue under the cross.

Come to him boldly therefore, under the name of a father, that he may move his bowels, and surely will hear us. For in Ps. xxvii. 10, when all forsook me, 'My father and mother forsook me, but the Lord took me up.' Fathers in the flesh, and mothers, die, but the Lord taketh us up. He is an eternal Father, and therefore a ground of eternal boldness with God, and of everlasting comfort. He was our Father before we had a father in the world, and he will be our Father when we shall cease to be in the world, They be but instruments under God to bring us into the world. God is our true Father. Our other fathers are but under God, to give us a being, to fit us for heaven. He provideth the best inheritance and paternity for us in heaven. And therefore never be disconsolate, but remember, 'I go to my Father and your Father,' which is a word of eternal comfort. He was our Father from eternity in election; he will be our Father to eternity in glorification. 'Can a mother forget her child? yea, though she should, yet can I not forget thee, thou art written in the palm of my hand,' Isa. xlix. 15, 16. God hath us always in his eye. A mother cannot always think of her child. She sleepeth sometimes; but God is a Father that never sleepeth. 'The keeper of Israel neither slumbereth nor sleepeth,' Ps. cxxi. 4. And this is our comfort in all times and for eternity. And therefore we ought to carry ourselves to God reverently, and go boldly to him, and always make use of him.

And this we should learn likewise, to maintain a sweet frame between God and us. Shall God open such an advantage to us? Shall God be our Father, and bear the gracious eternal affection of a father? and shall not we, by prayer and faith, fetch from our Father all we stand in need of? As our Saviour saith, 'You that be earthly fathers, when your children ask such a thing, will you deny?' Mat. vii. 9, 10. And have we a Father so rich, so loving, and shall not we have intercourse with him in our daily necessities? What a trade is open to us, if we know what a comfort is laid up in the sweet relation of a father! 'Your Father knoweth what we stand in need of,' Mat. vi. 8, and he will give thee the spring of all graces, not only a broken heart, a spirit of life and vigour in his service, but go to God and he will give thee his Holy Spirit, which is the best thing next Christ that can be. And therefore be encouraged to make intercourse between thee and God, considering we have a brother in heaven, our nature is there, and our spirit is below. We have the best things in heaven, next Christ, on earth, and God hath our flesh in heaven by Christ; and therefore why should we not be much in prayer, and much in praises in all our necessities? Beloved, it is a comfort of that largeness that I cannot express

* That is, 'trust.'—G.

† Qu. 'look for him'?—Ed.

it. I rather leave it to your admiration, that you may see what use to make of this sweet relation of a father.

(1.) But we must know, that every one cannot say, 'my Father,' for there are a company of men in the world that may say, in some respects, 'our Father;' but in other respects they cannot. As our Saviour Christ saith peremptorily, John viii. 44, 'You are of your father the devil.' They bragged of God their Father, and they were of their 'father the devil.' Therefore, consider who is fit to take this name into their mouths, 'My Father.' Mark the disposition of the Scribes and Pharisees, and then you shall see who be fit to brag of God as their Father. They be very formal men, look to their outward devotion, who so devout as they? They studied it; but what were they for the inside? They were malicious men, they were Satanical men, men opposite to the power of religion, arrant hypocrites, painted sepulchres. It is no matter for compliment or formality. An hypocrite may have much of that in the eyes of the world, yet may be a child of the devil for all that, and a Pharisee for all that. Thou mayest be malicious against the truth, as the Pharisees sought Christ's blood. A man may be like Herod, seeking the blood of Christ in his members, persecuting Christ, as all cruel men do. They seek to devour Christ in his professors. What they can, they disparage and dishearten them. They are enemies to the power of religion and to the ordinances of God. They be the children of the devil, and therefore have no reason at all to brag that God is their Father. Indeed, an inward bitter disposition against the power of religion, though under any formality, is a character of a Satanical spirit, and such cannot say, 'Our Father.' If they do, it is an usurpation, for their true father is the devil.

(2.) *Who can say, Our Father?* Those that by the Spirit of the Father and the Son, by the Holy Ghost, are ingraffed into Christ by a spirit of adoption, and have the stamp of the Father upon them. The likeness of the Father and of Christ, whom God begets to his own likeness, that are, in a word, like Christ. Christ is the first Son, and in him, and for his sake, we are sons. He is the natural Son, and they may say 'Our Father' that labour to express the disposition of Christ, who is the first Son. See this disposition of Christ in the gospel, how marvellously patient he was under the hand of his Father, obedient to the death of his cross, humbled, full of love, full of goodness. 'He went about doing good,' Acts x. 38. Do we then walk as Christ did? Carry we the image of the 'second Adam'? Have we the patient, humble, meek disposition of Christ in our measure? Do we love Christ in his members, God in his image? Do we love the ordinances and the power of religion? This sheweth what we are. And is our conversation suitable to our inward disposition? Do we walk in light? Do we shew by our conversation whose children we are? Do our speeches give a character of the inward man? If this be in us, though in never so small a measure, with comfort we may say, 'Our Father.'

But may not another man, that is not in Christ, come to God under the sweet name of 'our Father?' Yea, he may come to him as his father by creation and providence, or sacramentally a father, or as brought into the church, and having God to create him and to provide for him. Lord, thou hast shewed thyself a gracious Father thus far, though I cannot from any inward persuasion say, 'My Father.' Thus far as I can I say, 'My Father.' Strive against our spiritual infidelity, believe God and cast ourselves on his gracious promises in Christ. God will meet us at the same time, and he will send us his Spirit to make us his sons. And therefore let no man that hath been a wicked liver be discouraged from going to God in the name of a father, in that wherein he is a father. Lord, thou hast created me and preserved me, and it is thy mercy I am not in hell. Yet thou offerest to be my Father in Christ—thou hast made gracious promises and invited me; and upon this, when the heart yieldeth to the gracious apprehensions of God as a Father, there is a spirit of faith wrought in the heart presently. Therefore think of the name of a father, and the very thoughts of it will bring the spirit of adoption.

Only it speaks no comfort to the bitter malicious satanical enemies of Christ, and the power of religion. They be children of the devil. But now poor souls, that groan under the burden of sin, let them think that God is a Father, and of the mercies of God, though they do not see they be interested in them. By the very contemplation of the mercies of God in Christ, and his inviting them to receive them, the Spirit of God will be wrought in the soul, whereby they may have confidence to come to God as a Father.

I desire you therefore to remember this. It is the first sermon of our Saviour Christ after his resurrection, and therefore forget not to think of God as a Father and Christ as a Brother. Indeed, whatsoever comfort is in any relation, God and Christ have taken it on them. A father is more comprehensive than any other title: Christ is Father, and Husband, and Spouse. And God is our Rock and Shield; and whatsoever is comfortable he hath taken on him, and in Christ we may command him to be so. And if we had ten thousand worlds, they could not be compared to the comforts that arise from hence, that we can call God, Father. It is more to us, if we could improve it in our spiritual trade for heaven, than if we had a thousand worlds, especially in days of affliction and in the hour of death. For it improveth whatsoever is in the bowels of God for poor distressed souls. When nothing else will comfort, this will comfort, if we can say to God, 'Father.' Though we cannot make a distinct prayer, yet if we can say 'Father,' God can pick matter out of our broken language. Now Christ is ascended up to heaven, he doth us more good than he did when he was upon the earth. The sun in the firmament yieldeth us heat and comfort; but if it were nearer it would do us hurt, or if further off it would not do us so much good. God hath placed it, being a common light of the world, high, to enlighten inferior bodies, and to convey influence by means into them. And so Christ, the Sun of righteousness, being ascended and advanced to heaven, doth more good than on earth. And therefore saith he, 'It is for your good that I ascend.' It is for our good that we have Christ in heaven, to appear there for us.

'I ascend to my Father, and to your Father.' 'Father' is here taken personally, not essentially; though it be true in that sense, 'to my Father,' as the first person of the Trinity especially. Christ may well say, 'I ascend to my Father' now; for he was risen again, and was mightily declared to be the Son of God by his resurrection from the dead. 'Thou art my Son; this day I have begotten thee;' that is, this day have I declared thee, Rom. i. 4, and Heb. i. 5. It is said of things, *fiunt, cum patefiunt*, they are done when they be open, and declared to be done. Christ was the Son of God when he rose again, because he was discovered by his glorious resurrection to be so indeed. And therefore Christ may well say after his resurrection, 'I go to my Father, and your Father.' Observe from hence, that God in Christ is our Father. We say, relations are *minimæ entitatis*,* they are little entities founded upon others, but they are *maximæ consequentiæ*, of great concernment.

I beseech you, before I leave the point, give me leave to go on a little further in this, to shew that wonderful mercy, that admirable goodness which the tongues and hearts of all the men in the world, and angels in heaven, are not able to express; that love of God which is contained in the relation he hath taken on him in Christ to be our Father.

(1.) *Consider who, and whom.* Who, the great God, that hath the Son to solace himself in. He did not adopt us because he wanted sons. He had sons of his own, and sons of his love to solace himself in. What need he have took traitors, rebels, enemies, to make them his sons? Oh it is a marvellous advancement of our nature, that God should in Christ become our 'Father.' It is said, Ps. cxiii. 6, 'God abaseth himself to behold things below;' and indeed so he doth, with reverence be it spoken to his great majesty: he abaseth himself in regard of things below, in regard of us worms of the earth, that be enemies, yea, devils by nature. For many, ye shall see the devil in them, in their lying and opposing of goodness. And God will always have some amongst men, to shew others what they would be, if God left them to themselves. God abaseth himself to behold things below. Not that it is a diminution of majesty to do it, but God in Christ hath stooped so low, that he could go no lower, and he is advanced as high in our nature as can be. How could God become a man, a curse, God in the second person with us, God in the first person to be so near to us as a Father, and God in the second person to make him a Father, to be so low as Christ was, which is to be as low as hell itself.

(2.) Consider to whom this message is sent. He is your Father, even a Father to you the disciples, now you are disconsolate. God owneth us for his children at the worst. He took our condition notwithstanding all our infirmities. When we be pronest by a work of the Spirit to condemn ourselves, then God is nearest to justify us. When the poor prodigal said, 'I am unworthy to be a son, make me an household servant,' you see how the father entertaineth him, Luke xv. 19. So the poor publican dareth not lift up his eyes, and yet went away justified, Luke xviii. 13. David, when he could not pray, but murmur and rebel, and said in his heart all men are liars, 'yet thou heardest the voice of my prayer,' Ps. cxvi. 11; even then, when he could not pray, but groan and sigh to God: 'I said, I am cast out of thy sight, yet thou regardest the voice of my prayers;' when he said, out of a murmuring spirit and rebelliousness of nature, I am cast out of thy sight—a speech that tended to desperation,—yet God heard the voice of his prayer. When Job said, 'I clothed myself in dust and ashes,' God said to him, 'I have accepted thee,' Job xlii. 6, 8. When we by the Spirit think ourselves unworthy to be accepted, or to look to heaven, or to tread upon the earth, then God looketh on us worthy in his Son; and never more worthy than when we acknowledge our own unworthiness. 'Go tell my disciples,' at this time when they had dealt so unworthily, 'I go to their Father.'

It is from his own bowels, and not any goodness in us, that he loveth us. He loveth the work of his own Spirit, his own nature, that that is of his own. Though the child hath many infirmities, yet the Father seeth the nature of the child, and therefore loveth it. God seeth his image of holiness in us in some poor measure, and he loveth his own in us. And he loveth our love to him, which is in some measure. Though the disciples

* Qu. '*entitates*'?—Ed.

had got into corners, after their unkind dealing with Christ, yet he knew they loved him. As where there is love, there will be a reflection of his love back again.

And then God knoweth if he should not shew mercy to sinners, he should have none to serve him on earth. And therefore saith the psalmist, Ps. cxxx. ver. 4, 'There is mercy with thee that thou mayest be feared;' that is, worshipped. If God were not merciful to sinners, where should he have any to worship him? And therefore God sheweth himself to be a Father, even to sinful creatures; even in their wickedness, he seeth his own nature in them. He seeth some love, some work of respect in them, and if he should not love them, he would have none to fear him.

Beloved, live upon this. I spake before of the love of Christ. Here is the love of God the Father, who is content to be a Father even in our sinful condition. If God be a Father to us, as to Christ, then let not our hearts be discouraged in afflictions, persecutions, temptations. God was a Father to Christ in his desertion. God leaveth us to ourselves sometimes, and we fear his love. Did not he leave his own Son upon the cross—'My God, my God, why hast thou forsaken me?' Mat. xxvii. 46—and yet he ceased not to be a Father.

For persecution of enemies: was not Christ's whole life filled up with persecution, and yet a Son? For temptations: thou art tempted, and thinkest thou art none of God's children. Satan did tempt our blessed Saviour, that he might be a merciful Saviour, and know how to succour thee in times of temptation. Therefore, be not discouraged. Say not, when thou art deserted, persecuted, afflicted, tempted, God is not thy Father; for by that reason thou mayest argue, God was none of Christ's Father. God was Christ's Father, notwithstanding his desertion for a time; and notwithstanding his afflictions in the world, his persecutions of all sorts of men, and notwithstanding his temptations, God was his Father still. This we must observe, 'father' is not a relation to-day, none to-morrow. It is an eternal relation. '*Dum percutis, pater es; dum castigas, pater es*,' saith Austin (*h*): 'While thou strikest us, thou art our Father; whilst thou correctest us, thou art our Father.' Parents are tender to their weakest and sick children; and God is most tender of all to them that be weak. 'Go, tell Peter.' And therefore, never be out of conceit of God or Christ. We cannot be in a condition wherein, on any sound grounds, we may run from God.

But if this be so, let us learn of God to be indulgent. If I were to speak to ministers, I should be large to advise them to preach the law and the gospel. The very law is preached in mercy. The Lord taketh a severe course, but it is to order us. All God's severity is reducible to mercy and Christ; all his afflictions, humiliations, and abasements, do they come from unfatherly affection? No; but to draw us home to him. And therefore, never be terrible to any, but with a bowel of compassion, but with a mind that they may see themselves, and see the comforts they have in Christ. We ought to be of his affection, the great Pastor and Bishop of the church. And so for ordinary Christians; they should be indulgent one to another. Some are always cutting in ulcers; always wounding and tearing themselves with ill usage and misconstruction; keeping themselves from growing up in a better life, by observing the infirmities of them that be better than themselves. Oh, but 'go, tell my brethren' that my Father owneth them for his children, which may be a use of marvellous comfort to us.

Shall a child be always prowling for itself? We think there is neither father nor mother to take care for it: your heavenly Father knoweth what you need. We ought to labour for contentment in all conditions; for God is our Father. And for others, if God be our Father, let us look to others that be our brethren; own them, and carry ourselves to them as brethren. Let the strong carry themselves lowly to the weak. It is a sign of greatest strength to be most indulgent. Many account it great commendations on their part to be censorious and to be severe. Ay, but that is the greatest part of their weakness, if they have any goodness in them. For who was more indulgent to the disciples than Christ, who saw their weakness? He bore with all their infirmities. Where we see any goodness, let us bear with many weaknesses. We ought to be peaceable men: *Beati sunt pacifici.** They that be appeased in their consciences, in sense of their own pardon, are ready to shew mercy to others. Busy, contentious, quarrelsome dispositions argue they never found comfort from God himself.

If God be a Father, and we are brethren, it is a levelling word; it bringeth mountains down and filleth up valleys. All are brethren, take them in what condition you will. If they be great in the world, brethren of high degree; yet 'brother' levelleth them. If they be of low degree, yet it filleth them up, and raiseth them to the height in this brotherhood. And therefore, 'Go, tell my brethren;' tell them all, for they be all equally brethren.

If I were to speak to persons of quality and great parts, as I am to speak to mean, let them be put in mind of their condition. Nothing should raise us up so high, as to forget the everlasting relation of brother. Infirmity should not so far prevail with us, as to forget that which the children of God have to eternity. And for other persons more eminent, if he be a king, let him not so mind that, as to forget all other. For all relations determine in death, and must be laid in the dust; all must stand on equal ground before God's bar, and they that have most to answer for, have the highest account of all, and therefore it is ground of humility to all. Let them that are in greatest eminency consider this. Paul, after conversion, could say, 'Henceforth, I know no man after the flesh,' 2 Cor. v. 16. There is a great deal of humanity in the world: compliment is very ordinary, which is the picture and outside of humanity; but Christian love, which is a degree above humanity, the apostle calleth it Φιλαδελφία, 'brotherly love,' that is the scorn of the world. They will own a brother in office; but owning them in the sweet bonds of brotherhood, as they are the sons of God, here is heaven; make much of them in that kind, that is a strange thing in the world. But we must know what it meaneth, before we come to heaven. We must respect a Christian, be he what he will be, under all his infirmities, if he hath a good spirit in him, which God the Father seeth and Christ seeth. We must bear love to all saints. Some will make much of an eminent man, that hath excellent parts, because there may be some countenance from such persons; but here is sincerity that beareth love to all saints. He wraps them up all in the general term, 'Go, tell Peter,' among the rest, that hath offended more than the rest.

If you will know whether you be true brethren or no, or sons of God or no, make a use of trial, by what is formerly delivered. I shall enlarge myself in that point, because all dependeth upon it. God is the Father of all by creation; he is the Father in a general covenant, of all that receive the sacrament and are baptized. But if they have no other relation to God but so, they may go to hell, as Judas and others did: there-

* That is, 'Blessed are the peace-makers.' Cf. Mat. v. 9.—G.

fore we must know whether we may claim this relation of Father on good grounds or no, else it is an usurpation.

1. Those that belong to God, *the Spirit of God witnesseth to them that they are sons.* They that are adopted have the Spirit of adoption in some degree. God sendeth his Spirit into their hearts, that assures them that they be God's children. And howsoever this is the first, yet God giveth some intimation by his Spirit, that they look to God in another familiar manner than before; and he looks on them in a fatherly manner. So there be some intimations, and insinuations, and hints, though the Spirit of adoption witnesseth not fully and gloriously to the soul always, because we are not fitted for it; but sometimes in great afflictions and desertions. Where the Spirit of God is, there is communion with God in the Spirit of adoption. And when the voice of the Spirit of adoption speaks not loudly, yet there is a work of the Spirit. There is something to us renewed by the Spirit; there is something of the new creature. When a Christian cannot hear God say to his soul, 'I am thy salvation,' yet a man may see a work of grace. There is a love to God, to the ordinances, to the people of God; a mourning, because he cannot mourn; a sighing, because he hath not an heart pliable. He is discordant with his condition when he is disconsolate. So that there is a work of the Spirit helpeth him in his worst condition.

Besides, there is a spirit of supplication in some measure. Though he cannot make set discourses to God, yet he can in a sweet manner lay open his sorrow and grief to God, and leave them in his bosom. They be broken words, perhaps, but God can pluck sense out of them. God knoweth the meaning of the sighing of his own Spirit, though broken speeches. So that where there is any tongue for God in a man, there is a spirit of prayer; there is not a strangeness of God to go altogether by, but the spirit hath a kind of acquaintance with God; and it goeth to God in a familiarity, and layeth forth grief, and putteth forth petitions, in another manner than the world doth.

Again, A Christian in the worst condition, God not only shineth on him through the cloud, but there is a spirit in him that sigheth to go through all thick clouds to God. There is a spirit of supplication and of love in some degree, for that is promised. 'The Spirit shall help our infirmities, when we know not how to pray,' Rom. viii. 26. The intercourse and communion with God is never broken off where there is any Spirit of adoption. Therefore Jonas and David, and the rest, though they could not pray, yet they sighed to God, and would not leave him. If they could embrace Christ, they would not leave him. If they could not embrace Christ, they would touch the hem of his garment. They will not yield to the stream altogether, but strive against it. And though they be carried away with the strength of the stream, and see no goodness in themselves, yet they that be with them shall see a spirit striving to another condition than they are in. Something of Christ's, something of God's Spirit there will be in them. And take them at the worst, they will appear better than the civil man, that thinks himself a glorious man, though he hath nothing but for show and fashion. Who would be in such a man's condition without some brokenness of heart, some sighs?

2. Likewise we may know it *by our sympathy and antipathy*—our sympathy with them that be good, and antipathy to that which is naught.* There is a love of that which is good. So things, good things, are connatural to a good man. There is a relish in good company and good

* That is, 'naughty,' = wicked.—G.

things. As there is sweetness in the best things, so there is something in the children of God that is answerable to the God whom they serve. He is never so out of taste but he findeth his chief comfort in this thing, and he is never himself so much as when he is conversant in these things, though in different measure : sometimes more, and sometimes less. There is an inward antipathy to God in a proud carnal man that hath not his heart subdued by grace ; there is a contrariety to the power of that grace which outwardly he professeth, and a sympathy with the world and the spirit of the world. Take a good Christian at the worst, he is better than another at the best. I beseech you, therefore, examine our dispositions ; how we stand affected to things of an higher nature than the things of the world ; to spiritual things, how we can relish spiritual things, God's ordinances, and anything that is holy. Surely if there be the life of God and Christ in us, there will be a kind of connaturalness and suitableness of taste to the sweetness that is in holy things.

To come to the next, mark the order here, 'Go to my Father, and your Father.' We are the sons of God at the second hand. God is the Father of Christ first, and then ours. He is his God first, then our God.

This is a weighty point for directing of our devotions, that we may know in what order to look on God. See God in Christ ; see all things in Christ first, and then in us. Look upon him as Father to Christ, and then to us. Look on him as a God to Christ first, and in Christ a God to us. Look on him as having elected us, but elect in Christ first. See ourselves justified, but see Christ justified first from our sins, and his justification declared by his resurrection. See our resurrection and ascension, and glorification in heaven, not directly, but in Christ our head, who is in heaven, and taketh up place for us. See God loving us, but look on it in Christ, who is *sedes amoris*.* The next thing to God is his Son, and he loveth none but in him. When we consider of any spiritual blessing, say with the apostle, 'Blessed be God, that hath filled us with all spiritual blessings in Christ,' Eph. i. 3. Otherwise we do not know ourselves nor God. Whatsoever is derived from God to us is through Christ. All promises are his first. They are made to him, and to our nature in him, and they are performed for his sake. He taketh them from God the Father, and they be performed for his sake. He is the true Aaron. We are but the skirts. The oil that is poured upon his head runneth down to his skirts. It runneth to the meanest Christian ; but the ointment of grace is first poured on his head. 'Of his grace we receive grace for grace, and of his fulness,' John i. 10. The first fulness is God himself ; the second receptacle of all is Christ, God-man ; the third are we ; we have it at the third hand. God emptieth himself into Christ, as mediator. In him are the fulness of all riches, the treasures of all wisdom and knowledge. We are completed in him, and in him we are full. His is not only a fulness of the vessel, as ours is, but a fulness of the fountain.

And it is for our comfort that it is so, that God's love is to Christ first. There is a firm foundation when God loveth us in his Son, and we are children in his natural Son, in whom we are adopted. Then our state is firm. Our first state in the first Adam was not firm, but now our nature is taken into the unity of the second person, it is firm. So that the love and care and fatherly disposition of God towards us, it is sweet to us, because it is tender to his Son. It is eternal to us, because it is eternal to him. He can as soon cease to love his Son, as cease to love us. For with

* That is, 'seat of love.'—G.

the same love he loveth all Christ mystical, head and members. There is not the least finger of Christ, the least despised member of Christ, but God looketh on him with that sweet eternal tenderness with which he looketh upon his Son, preserving the prerogative of the head. Oh, this is a sweet comfort, that now all the excellent privileges of a Christian are set on Christ and then on us; and therefore we should not lose them, for Christ will lose nothing. When the favour of a prince is founded on his son whom he always loveth, the affection is unalterable on the son, and therefore the case is good. So God's favour to us is founded on his love to his Son, and therefore unalterable and eternal. We should therefore look up to God in his Son; put up all our petitions to him in his Son; expect all from him in his Son. He is in heaven for us, to do that that belongeth to us. Expect all from God through Christ, and do all to God through Christ; love God in Christ, and Christ in God; ourselves in Christ, and ourselves in the love of God. Christ is in God, and God is in Christ. God and Christ are in us. There is a marvellous sweet relation and communion between God and us, and Christ and us. It is a sweet communion, and mysterious to us. How sweet is the communion between the soul and the body, the soul being so spiritual, and the body a piece of earth! But what is this to the mystery of mysteries, when God takes clay and dust into unity of his person; and all this is for this union. The great and glorious union of Christ to our natures is that he may take us into his mystical body, and so make us one with himself, and one with the Father. He took our natures that he might convey his fatherly goodness and love and Spirit to us. The sweet union of the two natures of Christ is to confirm union between the Father and us, and Christ and us. And we are never happy till we be assured that we are one with Christ, which is the issue of his excellent prayer, John xvii.

Our blessed Saviour fetcheth the comfort of our Father from this, that God is his Father first, and so to join both together; that God is our God, because he is his God first. It is a point very considerable, that whatsoever comfort we look for from God, and in God, we must see it in Christ first before we see it in ourselves, because we be but sons by adoption, and we have all we have from God through Christ. Whatsoever we see in Christ, think this will belong to us. And whatsoever we look should belong to us, see it first in him. As verily as he ascended, we shall ascend; as verily as he rose, we shall arise; as verily as he is at God's right hand, we shall be there too; for by faith we sit now in heavenly places with Christ; and 'we shall judge the world, and be for ever with the Lord,' 1 Cor. vi. 3. Whatsoever we see in Christ, interest ourselves in it. And therefore we must not conceive of Christ as a severe person, but conceive of ourselves in union and communion with Christ our head; and to conceive of Christ as our head and surety, and 'second Adam,' and as a quickening spirit, that communicateth all to us. And therefore when we are to deal with God, be sure to go through Christ; as we expect all from God through Christ, so give all to God through Christ again. Be sure to take Benjamin with us when we go; and come clothed with the garments of our elder brother, and do not doubt when we come with Christ, for else we dishonour Christ. Shall I come in the sweet name and mediation of my Saviour, that hath perfected salvation, and not be accepted of God, when God hath ordained him for that purpose? If we stagger, and doubt to receive anything at God's hand, we wrong not only God's bounty, but Christ the mediator. Carry this therefore all along with us.

Do all in him, and desire God to pardon all for his sake, and God will regard us.

Use. Let us therefore make use of it, and add this further, *that if so be God is first the Father of Christ before he is our Father, and first the God of Christ before he is our God, and that all our good is dependent upon what God is to Christ first, then doth not this follow from hence, that we should not only thank God for ourselves, but thank God for whatsoever he hath done to Christ; not only comfort ourselves in it, but let God have the glory of it?* And this the Spirit of God in the holy apostles Peter and Paul led them to. Eph. i. 3, 'Blessed be the God and Father of our Lord Jesus Christ.' What, and nothing but so? Nay, with a reduplication, 'Blessed be God the Father of our Lord Jesus Christ,' even because he is the Father of our Lord Jesus Christ; because out of his infinite depth of wisdom and goodness he hath found out a way to save us in Christ, to be a Father to him, and in him a Father to us. It is said of the Virgin Mary, 'All generations shall call her blessed,' Luke i. 48. Why? Because she was the mother of the person that was God; she was the mother of Christ in human nature, and of God, because we may not sever the persons. And shall we bless the Virgin Mary, as mother of God, and not God as Father of Christ? If she be the mother of Christ-man, then God is the Father of whole Christ; and therefore blessed be God, not only that he is our Father and our God, but that he might be thus with satisfaction to divine justice, he hath found out such a way to be the Father of Christ; and Christ, as man, is an object of God's love and predestination as well as we. We deserved nothing at God's hands, but he found out such a way by taking the nature of man into unity of his second person, and so became a Father of Christ and of us. And therefore bless God, who hath predestinated Christ to be the Lamb of God, that hath freed him from sin, and set him at his right hand, raised him from the dead; that hath carried him into heaven, and ordained him to be Judge of quick and dead. Are these things severed from us? No. They be favours that be ours in Christ; his first, then ours. And therefore whensoever we think of anything Christ hath of his glory in heaven, as he is king of heaven and earth, and hath all power committed to him, glorify God for it, and think of it, This is mine; he is mine husband, my head; he hath taken up that glory, and whatsoever is in heaven, and enjoyeth them, he hath taken it up for me, and therefore we should bless God for it. So the apostle Peter: 'Blessed be God the Father of our Lord Jesus Christ, that hath begot us again to an inheritance immortal, undefiled, that fadeth not away, reserved in the heavens,' 1 Peter i. 3. He hath begot us to a lively hope, 'through the resurrection of Christ from the dead.' So it is from the resurrection of Christ from the dead that Christ saith, 'God is my Father and your Father.' Since God's justice is satisfied by my resurrection; that is, declared to be satisfied; 'I ascend to my Father, and your Father; to my God, and your God.' I beseech you, let us not lose the comfort of these things, since our Saviour Christ intended them for comfort.

To come to the words. First, Christ saith, God was his God, and our God, because his God. In what sense is God Christ's God? As mediator, as man, both in regard of his person and in regard of his office, God is Christ's God every way. See Ps. xxii. 9, which is a psalm of Christ, David being but a type of him in it: 'Thou art my God from my mother's womb;' and so God is Christ's God in his particular person, from his mother's womb.

(1.) For, first, *God was Christ's God when by his Holy Spirit he sanctified him in his mother's womb, and brought him out into the world.* Let the foolish disputes of friars, and dreams, and dotages of dunsical times go. 'But thou art my God from my mother's womb.'

And (2.) *He is Christ's God, because he saved him from the massacre of the infants.* Our Saviour Christ makes that prayer in Psalm xxii., Mark xv. 34, on the cross, 'My God, my God, why hast thou forsaken me?'

(3.) *God was Christ's God in protecting of him in his young time,* and afterward in going along with him still to his death; and in death, 'My God, my God' still. He would own God to be his God still; when God had deserted him to his sense and feeling, yet 'My God' still. So God was Christ's God, as Christ was man. Take Christ as mediator, God is the God of Christ; for God the Father hath by his authority put on Christ whatsoever he hath. The Father hath sent him into the world; the Father 'sealed' him; the Father sent him out as a propitiation for our sins; the Father hath declared him and 'anointed' him; and all these terms of authority, whereby the Father hath shewed himself to be Christ's God, even in his office of mediatorship. So in regard of the care of his person from his mother's womb, and for ever; and in regard of his office as mediator he might well say, 'I go to my God.' In regard of the intimate familiarity and acquaintance maintained even on the cross, he might say, 'My God.'

But the comfort of it lieth in the second clause, that as God is the God of Christ, so he is our God, because he is the God of Christ.

What is it to be a God to any? In a word, to be a God is to be all-sufficient to any; to be sole sufficient, and to be self-sufficient.

To be a God is to be all-sufficient for every creature; to be all-sufficient when nothing else can be sufficient. And to be self-sufficient, to be sufficient of himself, and therefore to reduce all back again to himself. Now, God is a God of himself, for himself, and by himself. God is all-sufficient, self-sufficient, sole-sufficient; and whatsoever the creature hath, it hath it from him. There is, in a word, in God a sufficiency for all good and happiness, and an efficiency to apply that sufficiency for the good of the creature. And in particular to be a God to any, is to do for a creature that no creature in the world can do but God. To make it of nothing, to free it from misery that it is beset withal, when no other can free it, to recover it again. God is Jehovah, that hath a being of himself, giveth being to the creatures, that can make the creature of nothing, and being something, can make it nothing.

Now, if God be a God to any, he is not only to give being to us, in a certain rank of creatures, as we are advanced above other creatures, as to have a being, or a life of growing, or a life of sense, or to advance us to a life of creatures endowed with reason, whereby we are common in that fashion with angels, and understand God himself. Alas! this were a poor privilege if it went no further than to set us in that rank of creatures, though a great favour. But considering us in a lapsed estate, it is a poor favour to leave us here. And therefore God is said to be our God now in a state of grace, when he advanceth us to an higher being and life than all this, a life of grace here and of glory hereafter; when out of his sovereignty and power he reduceth all to help forward his main end, the salvation of his in particular. So God is a God in peculiar of some that he taketh out of base mankind. There is a world taken out of the world, as Austin useth to speak (*i*). And thus he is a God not to bestow a life of grace and supernatural being here, but a glorious condition hereafter in heaven; and to make all things serviceable to that, that we may say, 'All is ours, because we are Christ's, and Christ is God's,' 1 Cor. iii. 22, 23. So that whatsoever befalleth a Christian, is serviceable and conducible to the main and last end. And that is for God to be God indeed, to make us his in Christ Jesus, to give us a new creation and a new state, better than the first.

Now, what is the foundation of this, that God is our God in the covenant of grace? We say it is founded on Christ. God is Christ's God, and then our God; and that is the reason why Christ is called 'Immanuel,' which is as much as to say, as it is expounded, 'God with us.' Not only because when he took our nature on him, there was God and man in one person; but the meaning of the word is, Christ is Immanuel, 'God with us;' by being God in our nature, and satisfying divine justice in our nature, hath brought God the Father and us into a sweet covenant. So that God may be our God and our Father, notwithstanding his justice; because all is satisfied by Christ, who took our nature to die for us. Christ is Immanuel, because he hath made God and us one. So that God is our God, and not only so, but our Father in him. Thus you see how it cometh to pass that God is our Father by Christ, who came to bring us again to God, as his whole office was to bring a few that had been singled out of mankind to God again, from whom they fell; for we all had communion with God in Adam, but we lost it; and now must be brought again to God, which must be done by Christ, God and man.

Thus much for the foundation of the point, that God is Christ's God, and God in Christ is our God, to do all things for us, to bring us to an happy condition here and an everlasting happy condition in heaven.

We see here it is brought as a ground of comfort, and so indeed it is. And we may observe from hence, *that now by the resurrection of Jesus Christ, God is not only become a Father to us, but a God.* This is a ground of many comforts. 'Go, tell my disciples,' now I am risen again; and therefore justice is satisfied; and now they may have lively hope of a better condition hereafter. For God is my God, that hath raised me up, and who will raise up mine too. So that now we are copartners with Christ, sharers with him in the fatherhood of God, and God is God in common with Christ and us.

This may well be brought as a ground of comfort. If there were any comfort in the world of sweeter efficacy than this, our Saviour would have sent it to his disciples. Comfort being his main office and his main end, he would have the best comfort after his best resurrection. And he picks this from amongst them all, 'Go, tell them, I go to my Father, and their Father; to my God, and their God.' And therefore it is a pregnant comfort; and indeed no heart can conceive the comfort of it, that we have interest together with Christ in God, and with the Fatherhood of God. And both these the Scripture joineth together: 2 Cor. ii. 6, 'I will be your Father, and your God.'

To unfold the comforts more, God is said to be our God in covenant in Christ. He is the God of Christ, and therefore of us, because he hath made himself over to us. A thing is said to be another man's when the title is passed to another man. Now, God hath as it were passed over himself to his believing children and members of Christ. He hath made over himself to them to be their God; as he was the God of Abraham, Isaac, and Jacob, and all the patriarchs, prophets, and apostles, so he is of every good, believing Christian to the end of the world. God maketh himself over to be theirs; and, as the Scriptures' style is, he is their portion and their inheritance; a blessed portion, a blessed inheritance, more to us than if all the world were ours, than if heaven were ours, than if ten thousand worlds were ours, for he is our God that can create millions of worlds more than this if it were needful. *Habet omnia, qui habet habentem omnia:* he hath all things that hath him in covenant that hath all things. And therefore when the Scripture saith, 'I go to their God,' it implieth, I go to him that is all in all to them, that is larger than their hearts can be; for what heart can conceive the fulness of the comforts arising from hence, 'that God is our God'? Many know they need comfort of such a transcendent nature. The heart of man is so distrustful, so faithless, and the conscience is such a clamorous thing, and therefore he cannot think this is too much. I beseech you, therefore, do not lose the comfort of it, that in Christ God is our God; though we can say of nothing else, it is ours. Perhaps we cannot say, great houses are ours, or friends are ours, or inheritances ours. That is no matter. We can say, that is ours which is infinitely more than that. We can say, God is ours in Christ. Nay, being exhorted to say by the Spirit of faith, that God is ours in Christ, all things in the world are ours. As you have it in that place of Scripture, 'All things are yours.' Why? 'Because you are Christ's, and Christ is God's.' 'Whether things present, or things to come, Paul, Apollos, Cephas, life, death, all is yours; you are Christ's, and Christ is God's;' that is, all things must by a command from God conspire to make us happy: affliction, or Satan, or death, or trouble of conscience, or desertion, or everything to help us to heaven. The curse is taken away, and there is a blessing hid in everything that befalleth a Christian, to bring him to heaven. Therefore it is a comfort of infinite extent. All is yours, because God is yours.

You shall see the extent of the comforts further by retail, as it were. If God be ours, then all is ours too. What be they? The Scripture telleth you, and I should spend too much time in unfolding of them.

1. If God be ours, his wisdom must needs be ours, to find out ways to do us good; for his infinite wisdom hath found out a way in Christ, by satisfaction of his justice, to bring us to heaven. He can make us go beyond all the policy of our neighbours, for his wisdom is ours.

2. If we [are] in danger, his power is ours, to bring us out.

3. If we have sinned, his mercy is ours, to forgive us. He himself being ours, his mercy must needs be ours. The whole being ours, it followeth out of the strength of reason that the parts also must be ours.

4. In any want, his all-sufficiency is ours, to supply it or to turn it to good, and make it up in a better kind.

5. In a word, God being ours, whatsoever is in God, whatsoever God can do, whatsoever he hath, is ours, because himself is ours. And therefore, I beseech you, make this use of it, to get into Christ by faith; to be one with Christ, that so God may be our God. Get faith above all graces, the grace of union and the grace of communion; that being one with Christ, we are one with him. God being ours, all is ours; yea, the worst thing in the world is ours.

If God be not ours, it is no matter what else is ours. Alas! all things must be taken from us, we know not how soon, and we taken from all things else. What if we had a kingdom, as Saul had, if we be forsaken of God as he was? What if we had paradise? If we offend God, we shall be cast out. What if we had the dignity to be apostles? If with Judas we have not God, what will all come to? What if a man enjoy all the world? If out of Christ, it would yield him no comfort! As the emperor said, I have gone through all varieties of condition, *et nihil mihi profuit*, but it hath done me no good.* If we had all, what is it but 'vanity of vanities'? and not only so, but 'vexation'? Eccles. i. 2, ii. 17. Now, when we have God to be our God, he is able to fill the soul. He is larger than the soul, and he is able to quiet the soul; he is the rest of the soul, the soul is quiet; in him is the centre, as the place of quiet. If God be ours, then the soul resteth in it; for God filleth the soul, and quiets the soul, and hath always fresh comforts for the soul, infinite still to all eternity. There is nothing in the world but we do as it were *deflorare*, take away the flower of it by use, and it becometh stale. Though a man continue many thousand years in the world, yet he will be weary of all things in the world, because there is no freshness in them. It is finite, and the soul is larger than the comforts of the world. But in God is a spring of fresh comforts to everlasting. Consider the things that enable him to be our God, to fill the soul, and to be larger than the soul; to quiet and calm the soul in all the troubles of it; and then to have fresh springs of comforts. What a comfort is this, to have God for their God!

Let it therefore raise up our souls to labour after God, and never rest till we have some interest in this great portion, of God to be our God. When we can by faith go out of ourselves to Christ, and lay a right and just claim to God to be our God, this is a comfort which reacheth from everlasting to everlasting. It giveth us forgiveness of sins when we had lost ourselves; because we are in Christ, he hath forgiven us. In all extremities and troubles, when no creature can comfort us, it is his glory to shew himself a God. It reacheth to the resurrection of the body. God is Abraham's, and Isaac's, and Jacob's God when dead, because he was the God of whole Abraham, Isaac, and Jacob, and therefore of soul and body. And it reacheth from all favours of this world, so far as is for our good, to all eternity. Being our God, he will protect us from all extremities in this world; he will speak comfort to our souls, which nothing can do but God. When we be dead he will raise up our dust, because he is our whole God, the God of our souls and bodies, and we shall be for ever with the Lord. It is a comfort of wonderful extent.

Use. 1. Let us therefore make this use of it. *Labour to make him so to us;* for as he is to us, so God by his Spirit is our comforter, who being satisfied, giveth us his Spirit. We must make God our God, and then he will be a God to us. These be mutual wheresoever they be; wheresoever God is God to any, they by the Spirit obtained by Christ have grace to make him so to themselves. What is it for us to make God a God to us? It is this: to set up God a throne in our hearts; to give him a sovereignty over all things in the world, that we may say in truth of heart, God is our joy, God is our comfort, God is our rock, God is all in all to us. When we give him supremacy of affection above all the world, we esteem nothing above him; we value him above all esteem; his loving-kindness is better than life itself; for else we do not make him a God to us, and then it is no comfort to hear all the comforts spoken of before. For all to whom he is a God in the covenant of grace, and have hearts to make him so, the Spirit raiseth up their affections to make him a God to themselves. *Amor tuus, deus tuus*, as it is said of old, what we love most is our god. What we joy most in is our god, what we rely and trust in most is our god, as

* Cf. note *z*, Vol. III. p. 531.—G.

it was said of the 'wedge of gold,' Job xxxi. 24. And therefore if anything hath our affections more than God, or equal with God, that we make our god. It is a *quære* of the greatest concernment in the world to put to our hearts. What do I make my god? as David putteth the *quære* to himself: 'Now, Lord, what is my hope? is it not in thee?' And so put this *quære* to ourselves: Lord, what is my joy, what is my hope, what is my trust, what is my comfort? is it not in thee? If our hearts cannot make an answer to this in some sincerity, surely as yet we have not made God our God. Time may be that he may be so; but till by the Spirit of God we be brought to see an emptiness and vanity in the creature, and nothingness in all in comparison of God, that we can say, 'Whom have I in heaven but thee?' we have not comfort, because we do not make him ours by a spirit of mutuality. Where there is a covenant of grace there must be a mutual making of God our God, as he maketh himself to us.

Alas! we may be ashamed of it; the best do often forget themselves. Oh how do men value the favours of a man, and the promises of a man; the seal of a man for such and such a benefice; and how doth it grieve them to have the frowns of flesh and blood, the frowns of greatness! But when their consciences tell them they are under guilt of many sins, and God is not in good terms with them, how doth this affect them? And when their consciences cannot say they have promises sealed in Christ of the favours and mercies of God here and hereafter, alas! it is dead comfort: 'Εμοὶ τὸ παρὸν, Give me that which is present, and take you that which is to come, is the language of both. How few can say from sincerity of heart that they make good* to be their God? And therefore it is of greater concernment than we take it.

Use 2. As it is a ground and foundation of comfort, *so of all obedience to God*, as it is prefixed before the commandments, 'I am the Lord your God,' Exod. xx. 2, 'you shall have no other gods but me,' and do all in obedience to me from this ground. But much more now. Then he was the Lord God that brought them out of Egypt; but now God may prefix, 'I am your Lord God in Christ,' that have brought you from hell and damnation, that intend you heaven and happiness, and therefore do so and so. Since this is the spring of all obedience, we ought to labour to make it good, and often to examine ourselves, as before, what we make our god, and what we pitch our affections on. Alas! is our soul for anything but God? Hath not God made us for himself? and will our hearts rest in anything but God? Why then should we love vanity, and besot ourselves? When death comes, they may say, as Saul said, 'The Philistines are upon me, and God hath forsaken me,' 1 Sam. xiii. 12. Death is on me, trouble, sickness, vexation of conscience is on me, and God hath forsaken me; I have no God to go to. What a miserable estate is this! And therefore, I beseech you, let us labour to have interest in the covenant of grace, to make it good that God is our God in Jesus Christ.

Who giveth us a being to be Christians, to have a new nature, to have a good being, but God? Who maintaineth and preserveth that being but God? And who keepeth and preserveth us till we get into a glorious being in heaven but God, who is all-sufficient, self-sufficient, sole-sufficient, only sufficient? This God is our God now in Christ.

God is to us in a more special singular manner than to other creatures, because he hath raised us to be a more excellent being, not only as men, we being in the highest rank of creatures next the angels; and so he is a God

* Qu. 'god'?—Ed.

to us more than to inferior creatures that have a more circumscribed and narrow being. Man hath a large being, a reasonable soul, and is fitted by nature to have communion with God, who is wisdom itself, and with angels; but all this were little comfort unless we had higher degrees of being than this. If God be our God in Christ, we have a spiritual being, which is as much above the dignity and prerogative of our ordinary being as our being by nature is above the basest creature in the world. And so God setteth a style upon us suitable to the excellency of our spiritual being. There is nothing excellent in the world but we are termed by it now, to set out the advancement and excellency of the dignity we have from God in a special manner; to be 'sons,' 'jewels,' his 'portion,' his 'diadem,' to be whatsoever you can imagine that is glorious and excellent: an excellent condition, though spiritual and concealed from the world. God's children are concealed men, as you shall see afterward. They be hidden men. The world taketh no notice of them, because their excellency is seen with another eye than the world hath. 'The God of the world blindeth the eyes of worldlings,' 2 Cor. iv. 4. They cannot see into the excellency of God's children, no more than they know God himself and Christ himself. So you see what it is to be a God in nature and in grace; to be all in all unto us; to have our whole substance and dependence in him. 'In him we live, move, and have our being,' and well-being.

In this our excellency consisteth, that God is our God in Christ, who was God; and that he might bring God and us to good terms together; that he might make God our God. He was Immanuel, God with us, to make God with us in favour and love. The Godhead is nearest the human nature of Christ of any creature. It is nearer to Christ than to the angels; for God hath not taken the angels into hypostatical union, to be in the same person; but God in Christ is so near our nature, that there is an hypostatical union. They make one person, our nature being taken into the second person. By reason of this near union of the Godhead to our nature cometh that comfort and near union between God and our nature, whereby God hath sweet communion with us in Christ. God by his Spirit, though not hypostatically, yet graciously, is one with us, and hath communion with us now as his children. So that sweet intercourse between God and us now, is founded upon the nearness of the Godhead to our nature in Christ, in whom it is nearest of all, in whom it is advanced above the angelical nature. And therefore our blessed Saviour might well say, 'I go to my God, and your God;' to his God first, and then to our God.

Now we may say, God is our God; and upon good grounds, because God is Christ's God, and in him our God, which is a point of singular comfort; and therefore I will enlarge myself further in it.

Doct. For God to be our God, especially in having that in our hearts unfolded, in regard of our spirits and best being, is the most fundamental comfort that we have. For from this, that God is our God, cometh all that we have that is good in nature and grace. Whatsoever is comfortable cometh from this spring, that God in Christ is our God, our reconciled God; that God's nature and ours now are in good terms.

Beloved, what cannot we expect from God, that is now become our God! What he is, what he is able to do, what he hath, all is ours, considering himself is ours. If we have the field, we have the pearl in the field. And therefore the wise merchant in the gospel sold all for the field wherein the treasure was, Mat. xiii. 44. We have the field itself in having God, and we have all that God is or can do for us for our good, even as we have Christ, and all that Christ is, or hath done, and suffered, and enjoyeth; 'all is ours, because we are Christ's, and Christ is God's,' as the apostle saith. So that having God we have all, because we have him that possesseth all, the creator of all, and preserver of all, and disposer of all.

But to clear the objection a little: if God be ours, and all things else, how comes it that we want so many things?

Ans. I answer, It is our own fault for the most part. We want faith to make use of and improve this comfort. And then again, we want nothing that is for our good; want itself is for our good. And observe this, our God is so powerful a God, that he maketh the worst things we suffer a means to convey the greatest good oftentimes to us. If God be our God and Father in Christ, why have we sins? Why vexed with the devil? Why persecuted with men? Why frightened thus, and thus, and thus? All this is for our good. God is our God by these, and in the midst of these; and is never more our God than in the greatest extremity of all, for then we come nearest the fountain. There is a near and sweet communion between this God and us, when we take of the fountain. When the means are drawn away, the conduits of conveyance, and we have nothing to go to but God immediately, there is sweet communion and sweetest comfort in heaven; we shall have God in Christ, who will be all in all unto us. We shall need no magistracy, ministry, food, raiment, or defence against cold or injury; we shall be out of the reach of Satan and all enemies; God will be all in all immediately. The same God is all in all to us, either by means or immediately. When means fail, he conveyeth his sweetness and his power immediately, but ordinarily by means. And what sight doth in heaven, faith doth now in some proportion; for as sight in heaven seeth God in Christ all in all, and enjoyeth that happy vision, so faith seeth God to be all in all, and Christ to be all in all. Though in an inferior degree to sight and clearness of vision, yet for the capacity of this life we enjoy God now as they do in heaven. We have inward comforts when most deserted. God was never more near our blessed Saviour than on the cross, when he cried, 'My God, my God,' &c., for then he found invincible strength supporting him in the great undertaking under the wrath of his Father. And so God is never nearer than in extremity; in strength, though not in sense and feeling; and oftentimes in feeling itself. We never have sweeter comforts than in the want of all outward comforts whatsoever, when nothing else can comfort us but the presence of God. And we must know besides, that the state of a Christian in this world is an hidden condition; for it is to the eye of faith, not of sense; and therefore God is a God to his, though the world see it not. There is a secret, hidden influence, a secret passage between heaven and earth, that none seeth. Who observeth the influence of the sun, or the sweet influence of the stars upon the earth? Light we see, but there is a secret influence pierceth deeper than the light, to the very bowels of the earth, whence metals come. Where no light comes, there is an influence, though not discerned; and much more can there be influence of strength and power and hidden comfort, though there be no sight. Cannot God be our God in regard of strength, supporting and supplying, though there be no visible and sensible comfort, though we see it not ourselves? Certainly the soul is upheld by an invincible strength in the worst condition that can be. Therefore this is true, that God is our God in all conditions.

Use. Let us make use of this. To what use is riches and friends, if we do not use them? To what use is God and Christ, if we use them not? *Nostrorum* * *est, utamur nostro bono*. He is ours, let us use him for our special good on all occasions. Oh that we had faith answerable to our prerogative. It is a prerogative more than heaven and earth, that God is ours; and had we faith suitable, what kind of persons should we be in grace and comfort, and whatsoever is good? Therefore labour to make use of it. But more of this after we have spoken of some rules of trial, because whatsoever I may say this way may be misapplied. They be excellent comforts. But perhaps, saith the distressed soul, they belong not to me, to whom it doth belong. Perhaps it belongeth to me, saith another that is a stranger and a carnal man, to whom it doth not belong. Therefore our Saviour giveth some notes of distinctions, to know whether God be our God or no. Not to be much in the argument, yet to be plain in it.

(1.) *God is their God in this peculiar manner I speak; that is, in the covenant of grace, not otherwise;* and I speak not what God is by creation of man, for so the devil is God's, and every creature. But the question is, Whom God is a God to in the nearest bond of the covenant of grace? That is the only comfortable relation that can be; for if God be not our God in that, all other comforts will be nothing. It is better we be no creatures at all, than not creatures in the covenant of grace. It is therefore worthy the commending to you, especially considering our naughty hearts are prone to deceive us. Satan, and melancholy, and temptations do make some refuse the comfort, and some presumptuous persons to snatch at it when it doth not belong to them. Those to whom God is a God indeed, in a sweet relation of the covenant of grace to be their God, as to the patriarchs, prophets, and Christ and the apostles, he giveth his Holy Spirit to witness so much to them. Though the voice of the Spirit is not always heard in the best children of God, yet he giveth them the Holy Spirit, that though it doth not always witness, yet it always works something in them which may be an evidence that they are God's.

(2.) Now the spirit of adoption and sonship is known *by a spirit of supplication especially*. Whom God is a God to, he vouchsafeth a spirit of prayer, to go to him in all their necessities, which is an issue or branch of their faith. He giveth them faith to believe it, and prayer to make use of it; for God will not give this great privilege without hearts to make use of it, which is done by faith and prayer; and prayer is nothing but the frame of faith, Acts ix. 11. As soon as Paul was a good man, presently after his conversion, 'behold he prayeth.' The child crieth as soon as born, and the child of God is known by his praying; as soon as he is converted, an intercourse is opened between God and the soul, which a Christian soul will never neglect. If they are placed in the worst condition, they will pray to God, or at least sigh and groan, which is a prayer that God can make sense of.

Those that have any strong places of defence, in trouble they will be sure to fly to that; in times of war they will betake them to their castle and place of munition. And so they that be God's, in time of danger run presently to God; he is their rock, their refuge, and place of defence. [They] repair to him by faith and prayer. 'The name of the Lord is a tower of defence: the righteous in trouble fly thither, and they are safe,' Prov. xviii. 10. A man may know what his god is by his retiring in times

* Qu. '*nostrum*'?—Ed.

of extremity. Your carnal man, if he hath any place to retire to, it is to his friends, to his purse, to bring him out. He will go to that which his instinct will specially lead him to in times of trouble. As every creature, together with the nature of it, hath received an instinct from God to go to the place of refuge wherein it is safe—as the weakest creature hath strongest refuge — the conies, a poor weak creature, hide themselves most strongly, out of instinct they have of their own weakness—so God's child, being privy of his weakness, and need of support and strength, hath the strongest support that may be, and runneth to his God. Worldly men have many shifts, as the wily fox hath; but a Christian hath but one, but that is a great one: he goeth to his God in time of need. And therefore you may know who is in covenant with God in times of extremity, especially by a spirit of faith, a spirit of prayer.

In times of extremity, no man but a Christian can pray with any comfort, with any sweet familiarity, 'Abba, Father;' but they be like Pharaoh, 'Go, Moses, pray to your God,' Exod. ix. 28. He hath no such familiarity with God as to pray for himself. And so carnal men will say, 'Pray to your God.' And many, like devils, will have no communion with God in their prosperity, but their whole life is a provoking of God to enmity, by swearing, loose, debauched, irregular carriage, hateful even to moral men. Their hearts tell them they be even like Satan, 'What! dost thou come to torment us before our time?' Mat. viii. 29. What hast thou to do with me? What have they to do with God? They have scarce a Bible in their chambers; if one, it is for fashion's sake. And that they may not appear to be naught, they will hold conformity in public assemblies; but for private familiarity, they have nothing to do with it. The show of religion goeth under an opprobrious name, but if they would put off the show it were nothing, and not make ostentation of what they are not; but they have no communion with God in prayer. They will go for God's people, and own him for their God, when they have no trading with him so much as by prayer. Take heed we deceive not ourselves, I beseech you; salvation dependeth upon it.

(3.) We may further try *whether our claim of God to be our God be a good claim, on good grounds, by our siding, by our part-taking;* for those whom God is a God to in a peculiar manner will be sure to side with God. God hath two things in the world he prizes more than all the world; that is, his children and church, his cause and religion. They that be God's will be sure to side with the church, they will stand and fall with the church; and the cause of religion, they will live and die with it. But a carnal politician, that hath perhaps great parts of nature, he is 'Αλλὰ πρός ἄλλους, as the Grecian calleth him; they be for all turns; they can bring themselves to any figure, like water that will receive any figure (*j*). Take it, put it into a vessel that is square, it will be square; put it into a round vessel, it will be round. How can they own God for their God when they will not seek him, and they are yet to choose their God and religion? And because they will be sure to be safe in all times, they will own no religion in any time. And, beloved, is it possible any such should say with confidence, God is their God? Will he own them that will not own him, nor his church, nor his cause? You know Jehu crieth out, 'Who is on my side, who?' Cast her out. And so God, in doubtful times of danger, crieth out, 'Who is on my side, who?' Stand out; appear, if you be on my side; if you be on my side, own my cause; if you be not on my side, if you have no degree of goodness, it will appear. Christian wisdom is one thing, carnal policy is another thing. 'The wisdom of the flesh is enmity with God,' Rom. vii. 8. Many applaud, and think themselves for somebody in this kind; but this wisdom is enmity itself against God. When a man will be wise in a distinct kind of wisdom from God, when he will have a cause severed from God, and will not side with God, he must look that God will account him his enemy, and make him his; but especially in the hour of death and deep extremity, he shall not be able to look God in the face, to whom he hath been a traitor in the church and in the cause of religion. And therefore, as we will be able to own God for our God, especially in doubtful and dangerous times, side with the church, and side with religion. It was objected to that good Jehonadab, a good man, 'Have we anything to do with God's enemies?' Jer. xxxv. 6, *seq.* Now there be two sorts of enemies that we are especially to have nothing to do withal if we side with God: enemies within us, and enemies without us. Sin within us. We must take part against our sins; take God's part and the Spirit's part against corrupt motions and affections. Divinity must begin from within, else it is faction without. It is not religion, but faction, if the religion begin not in our hearts, and if we hate not sin in ourselves. Where there is true antipathy, the nearer anything is that is opposite to our nature, the more hateful it is. He that hateth a toad, hateth it in his bosom most of all. And he that hates sin as sin, hates it in his own heart most of all. And therefore they that will pretend religion, and be naught in their own particular, it cometh not from a true principle; for they that will side with God, side with God in their own hearts, and be good men in their own particulars. Therefore, I beseech you, try yourselves by this. Likewise, when men esteem God's enemy wheresoever they see it, and so far as their authority and power reacheth, they will take God's part in themselves against themselves, and in the world too. I will not enlarge the point, because it cometh in by way of trial, and I cannot but touch it as a trial. Thus you see how we may know whether we be God's or no, by owning his cause and siding with him. You have some expressions in Scripture to this purpose: Micah iv. 5, 'All people will walk every one in the name of his god, and we will walk in the name of the Lord our God for ever and ever.' Every man will walk and converse in the name of his god; they will own their god and take part with him; and we will walk in the name of our God for ever and ever, and own his cause at all times, and constantly, for ever and ever.

And likewise in Isa. xliv. 5, speaking of gracious times there, when men shall be bold for the Lord, as in all times some men will. 'One shall say, I am the Lord's, and another shall call himself by the name of Jacob, and another shall subscribe with his hand to the Lord, and term himself Israel.' God shall have his tongue, his hand, and all. He shall say, 'I am the Lord's,' he shall call himself 'by the name of God,' he shall subscribe to it, and own the cause.

(4.) Again, If we would know whether God be our God, *we must know whether we may lay just claim to our God as a peculiar God to us, or no, and that way in which God sheweth himself to be a God in peculiar respects to us.*

Quest. Now how doth God shew himself a God in a peculiar respect to his children?

Ans. He sheweth himself to have a peculiar respect to them,—

[1.] *By peculiar gifts, when he gives to them that which he giveth to none else.* Shall we imagine God to be our God by common gifts and common graces? No. For thou comest to hear the word; so Herod did. Thou receivest the sacrament; so did Judas, so did Simon Magus. Thou hearest the truth with some joy; so did the 'third ground,' Mat. xiii. 20. Thou hast excellent parts; so hath the devil himself.

But thou art in such a place of the church, teachest others; so did Judas. Are these evidences to try whether we be God's or no? What then is the peculiar gift and love-token that God bestows upon his favourites? They be the graces of his Spirit, especially in regard of God: an humble broken heart, and a believing heart, and a lowly heart, that goeth out of itself, that goeth unto God by faith, and towards man full of love, which argueth a great deal of self-denial, when a man can love others with denial of his own profit and ease. He that hath a humble, believing, lowly heart, hath more than all the world besides, for he hath God's peculiar gift. Many poor souls complain as if God had no regard to them, and yet in the mean time they have humble, broken hearts, which is more than if they had all the wealth and worth that the world hath, which have proud hearts, never broken. The return of these favours will be comfort in death and glory in heaven. What will the fruit of a believing heart be? He hath God and Christ. If he hath a lowly large heart to do good, he doth that which in the issue shall further his account at the day of judgment; and there is the love of God shewed in his special favour.

[2.] *So the love of God especially shall be a peculiar comfort that the world is ignorant of, especially in times of extremity.* Inward peace of conscience, inward joy, and inward comforts, these are signs of love that God bestoweth upon a man, when he will own him in the worst times, and speak peace to his soul when nothing in the world will speak peace. When the lions roar, [when] the great lions of the world roar in extremity, he hath inward peace and joy, and comforts of the Holy Ghost. That inward intercourse of God with the soul is a sign of God's peculiar love. When God speaketh peace to the soul, when he sheweth the light of his countenance, which David in Ps. iv. 7 prefers before all outward comforts whatsoever—God's revealing of himself, as the Scripture calleth it—when God revealeth himself to his to be theirs, with peace, and joy, and comfort accompanying it, this is peculiar.

[3.] Again, A peculiar favour and love-token of God *is to have seasonable and sanctifying correction.* To have corrections when they be seasonable; when we be in a way of straying, and God will bring us home by correction; and when we have sanctified correction, we find by experience that all is turned to our good. If I find anything turn me to my God, I know I am his; if my cross be seasonable and sanctified, he is my God, for he takes that course with me which he takes with his own people. These be singular signs of God's love, when he bestoweth the graces of his Spirit, his comforts, peace, and joy, though not largely, yet so much as shall sustain the soul. And then, when he seasonably meeteth us, and will not suffer us to thrive in an evil course. Oh it is a judgment of judgments to be hardened in sinful courses of life; how can it but end in desperation at length? And therefore it is a great favour to be chastised; it sheweth 'we are sons, and not bastards.' Thus we see how we may lay just claim to this, that God is our God in a peculiar manner.

(5.) To name but one more, to distinguish a spirit of presumption from a spirit of faith and truth, that God is our God, is this,

[1.] *If we have grace to answer his dealings towards us,* when we can echo to God's dealings. God hath chosen us, if we have grace to choose him for our God. We may know he hath called us effectually, when we answer God's call. When he biddeth us believe, he giveth an influence of power to be able to say, 'I believe; Lord, help my unbelief,' Mark ix. 24. We may know he loveth us, when we reflect love again, and love him. We may know he compasseth us, when we embrace him. We may know he delighteth in us, when we delight in him and his servants. Whence is the strength of this argument? From hence. All good things, whatsoever we do from God,* is by reflection. God shineth on us first; God owneth us for his first, and God must do so in order of causes. God being the spring of all goodness, he must begin. 'We love him because he loved us first,' 1 John iv. 19, else we could never love him. Therefore if we love him and truth, he loveth us. That is sure. 'What have I in heaven but thee, and in earth of comparison of thee?' Ps. lxxiii. 25. Surely he owneth us, because in order of causes we can have nothing but from him first.

[2.] And then again, *out of the nature of conscience; if we can go boldly to him as a reconciled God, notwithstanding guilt of conscience*, it is a sign he hath obtained peace of conscience, because it is the nature of conscience, if it hath not peace from God, not to dare to appear in God's presence. So then, when there is inward peace and love answering to God's love, choice answerable to God's choice, apprehending of him answerable to his apprehension, this reflection, and return, and rebounding back to God, is an invincible argument that God hath first shined upon that soul. God sometimes will let us see things in the effect, and hide them in the cause. Perhaps he will not persuade by his Spirit that he loveth us, hath chosen us, and that we are his; but he will work something in our hearts, because he will have us search our spirits, what good thing he hath wrought, what love, what choice of the best side are in any of these. Surely then God is theirs. Though there be not an open voice, yet they may know God hath loved this soul and spoken peace to that soul, because we can return nothing to God, but he must shine on us first.

Therefore, beloved, let us make use of this, and let us take heed of sacrilegious usurpations, that we do not usurp upon God's house or God in a peculiar respect. Indeed, we may come to God as his creatures—We are the workmanship of thy hands—and say the truth, though we be in a wicked course of life. But to say, 'Thou art my God in Christ,' 'I am thine, thou hast chosen me for thine,' when we have not chosen him for our God, nor loved him nor his cause, nor sided with him, nor have any stamp of him on the soul, have nothing but common favour, that castaways have as well as we, and the devils as well as we—for the devils go beyond all men in parts—and yet to usurp the prerogative of being God's in a peculiar manner, and to be bold with the holy things of God, as if we were of his family, this is a dangerous usurpation; take heed of it. And therefore they that live in courses of rebellion, and resolve not to mend, they take the holy things of God, as the psalmist speaks, Ps. l. 16, 17, in an holy indignation, 'What art thou, that takest my word in thy mouth, since thou hatest to be reformed?' Thou art an enemy to God and goodness, and wilt be so; thou art in a course of rebellion, and wilt be so. The devil's works you do and will do. Can we not take the word of the covenant into our mouths, and shall we take the seal of the covenant? Therefore resolve to amend, else have nothing to do with God; do not add one sin to another. 'It is the children's food, and not for dogs,' Mat. xv. 27; it belongeth to

* Qu. 'is from God'?—Ed.

them of the family. If thou be none of the family, what hast thou to do with them? If thou be of the family, whatsoever thy infirmities are, thou mayest come boldly, for the seals are to strengthen our weak faith. When the father is father of a child, the father will not cast away the child for breaking out with deformity or lameness. When God hath taken us into his family, infirmities cannot discard us. But I speak of them that in a wilful opposite course of sin shew they never had to do with God in familiar intercourse. God never gave them a spirit to alter their natures. Propriety,* and proportion, and suitableness of disposition go together: propriety joineth with suitableness; where God owneth any man, he makes them like himself by his word and Spirit, that their natures shall be even and agreeable to holy things, shall have a taste of holy things. And where there is not suitableness of holy things, there is no propriety. Will God own a man, and not make him suitable? Will God take his friend, and not give him a friendly nature? He will not, for he first fitteth our natures for communion with himself, else there can be no propriety. Let us not deceive ourselves, but if we find some beginnings of grace, and can say without arrogancy or usurpation, 'Doubtless thou art our Father, our God,' Isa. lxiii. 16; we be not worthy to be thine, but we be thine; if we find something that castaways cannot have, some grief of heart for sin, some faith, some little measure of love, some love of truth and inclination to the best things, then we may come boldly to increase our familiarity and communion with God. But otherwise it is dangerous to come to God. We approach 'a consuming fire,' Heb. xii. 29. 'Who shall dwell in everlasting burnings?' Isa. xxxiii. 14. Say they in Isaiah, And if God be not in covenant with us, Oh, he will be 'a consuming fire,' everlasting burnings, and we but stubble; and it will increase spiritual judgment in us, hardness of heart, and going on from sin to sin, till we be accursed for sin. Therefore it is a fearful thing to be given up to hardness of heart. They that do continue in sin, God giveth them up to hardness of heart, to be insensible of his dealings with him.

Use 3. If we can in any degree make it good that God is our God and we his people, then let us make use of it for our comfort in all times, *that we have a God to go to*. Though we have no friend in the world, yet we have him in whom all friends meet. If we have no comfort here, yet we have him in whom all comforts meet, for all concentre in him. He hath father and friends, and worth and grace, and peace and comfort in him; and all is in him. If we go to him, we shall find a confluence of everything that is good, suitable to any necessity of ours.

And therefore let us learn to single out of God whatsoever may help us to be in covenant with him. He having made himself over to be ours, let us learn this wisdom, to single out of God whatsoever is peculiar to our present condition; for considering he hath made himself a God to us, he is all-sufficient to every turn. Therefore out of his all-sufficiency, take out whatsoever is fit for any particular exigency. 'Lord, I am in a strait, and want wisdom.' Thou in Christ hast abundance of wisdom. Christ hath in him all treasures. I now want friends, I want counsel, I want help, I want strength. God hath a fulness of all this for his children. He hath it not only to content himself, and look on his own happiness, but for his friends that be in covenant with him, that be so near him that he will own him to be their God. If you ask, What is religion? it is to know God, to have all-sufficiency in him for any good, and then to make use of him

* That is, 'property or ownership.'—Ed.

by dependence on him for that good, and by advancing of him in giving him the due honour and thanks of it. And therefore we deserve not the names of religious persons, if we do not study what he is to his creatures in the covenant of grace. Then make use of it by a spirit of dependency, and always giving praise and thanks. This is our whole man, and what is all else? Nothing but trouble and vanity. Get our bonds sealed that he is our God, and then break with all the world beside. Come what can come, or what will come, we are sure to be safe. It is a comfort of wonderful large extent. The use of the sacrament is to seal that God is our God in particular, and that Christ is ours as verily as the bread and wine are ours. And let us desire the Lord to seal to every one of our souls, that are to have communion with him in particular, that he in Christ is ours: Christ with all his merits and fruits of them, forgiveness of sin and life everlasting, as verily as the outward man partakes of the outward seals; and then we shall come and go away with comfort, and be made partakers of that end and use of the sacrament for which our blessed Saviour instituted it.

Having spoken before of common favours, which devils and castaways may have as well as we, I shall enlarge myself a little in this, because it is a point of concernment. As in other sins we be like the devil, so in this sin a man is worse than the devil himself, if a man will be a common swearer, and opposer, and malicious against goodness, being only in love with some idle conceit of his own, which he will have God himself stoop to else he will not to heaven; he will not be saved but by his own foolery. A man that hath a bitter spirit against the power of grace, that is a common blasphemer, that carrieth a spite against religion, for him to say, 'God is his God,' the devil will as well say so. He will say of Paul and Silas, These are the people of God; but he will not say himself is, Acts xix. 15. For a man to live in sins against conscience, defend them, oppose all that opposeth his sins, and yet claim an interest while that disposition standeth in him, it is more than Satanical impudency, and it is extreme hardening of the heart against all goodness; for how many thousands in the church perish and sink to hell under this presumptuous conceit, 'I am God's, and God is mine,' when the title is false, and the evidence false. And therefore it is a point deserving thoroughly to be examined continually, what those evidences of graces be that we venture our souls and salvation upon. I will not stand much to press the point. But you see the necessity of it. Consider therefore, I beseech you, what I have said. If God be ours, there will be a separation. Where there is an owning of God for their God, there will be a separation from all that is not his, as well as a gathering to them that be his. The work of God's Spirit in his children is like fire, which hath two properties: to sever all heterogeneal and strange stuff, and dross, and the like, and gather all the homogeneal stuff of one nature. And so the works of the Spirit gathereth to the soul so much as is good, and refines that, and severeth that which is contrary. The Spirit of God, that telleth them that they be God's, it is a severing Spirit and a uniting Spirit. It severs contraries, and it uniteth things of the same nature. There is a joining to what is good, and a separating of what is evil.

I will add this farther, that wheresoever on good title we can say, 'I am God's,' there is a reflect act of the soul to say, 'God is mine.' God hath put a light of reason and friendship into man. Now friendship standeth in mutual office of duty and gift. Where this is not, there is no friendship, no reconciliation, no owning on good terms. The end why God saveth a company of men, and bringeth them to heaven; the body of

Christ, which we call the church; it is, that he may have eternal communion with them in the heavens, as he hath with the blessed angels; and in Christ a nearer communion than he hath with them. Now how can this communion be, unless we turn to God, unless we have something to answer God's love?

Again, Note, *God is ours, because Christ is ours.* The covenant is made first with Christ, and then with us. Whence we see a ground of particular application of that which we call particular faith; a ground of particular application by a Spirit of faith of God to us, and Christ to us; that God in Christ is my God and your God.

The ground of this is, as God offereth himself, we must apprehend him; but Christ offers God, and he knoweth how to offer him. He teacheth us how God is to be presented, and he presenteth him as our God and our Father; and therefore let us entertain him as ours. Thus you see a good ground of particular application of God the Father, and Christ to us in particular, in two respects; not only that every one in particular ought to have a particular faith, and not to think a general faith is enough, to believe as the church believeth, but to have a particular faith of the object; not only of the subject, but of the object; that that is his in particular, 'I go to my Father and your Father.'

God is the Father and the God of all the elect, and only the elect, and of every one of the elect, as we say, *in solidum*. That is said to be *in solidum*, when every one applieth the whole to himself, without diminution of any part. The sum is *in solidum* to every one that will make use of it, to enlighten every creature that shutteth not his eyes. As a common fountain is no man's in particular; for no man can say, This is my fountain, and yet every man can say, This is mine; so every saint can say of God, He is mine *in solidum*. Though he were alone, he may say, God is mine. If ten thousand have him, yet God is his God. God careth for all, as if there were but one, and for one, as if none but he. God offers himself, not only to his whole church, but to every one in particular, and therefore of every one he ought to be apprehended.

This is founded in all the great points and mysteries of religion. As for instance, what is the ground of all the petitions in the Lord's Prayer? 'Our Father.' What interest have we to all the petitions, and to every article of the creed? If there be not a particular application,—'I believe God the Father to be *my* God, Jesus Christ *my* Saviour, the Holy Ghost *my* sanctifier; remission of sins and life everlasting is mine,'—we do no more than the devils. Now every truth in Scripture is written for our comfort, and shall it be no more comfort to us than to the devils? Doth the Scripture intend us no more comfort than the devils? Yes. But the devil may say, for the church there is remission of sins, and a God and Saviour, but not for me; and that is his torment; he cannot come to particulars. So the sacraments are to seal a particular faith. As every one in particular taketh the bread and wine, so by a particular faith every one may say, Christ is mine; his death is mine; bloodshed mine; remission of sins and interest of Christ is mine. It doth not seal a general faith in the clouds, but a particular assurance, that it belongeth to every one. And so in the words of the catechise,* the ministerial questioning of sinners is intended, that every one that believeth should apply it, If thou believest, and if thou believest, thou shalt be saved; and thy sins shall be forgiven thee. So that if we regard prayer and faith, if we regard the sacraments,

* That is, the Church Catechism.—Ed.

or the use of the catechise, all enforce a particular faith. If we have not particular faith, we lose the virtue of all. So it is for the commandments. Put case, no man in particular, yet every one ought to ply in particular, that they ought to abstain from such a sin, and perform such a duty. If they do so, they shall be glorified; if not, they shall be punished. And there is the same reason in faith as in obedience. A man is condemned in law, though not named in law; because the general is set down here, and every man ought particularly to apply it; I ought not to have done so and so. So that it overturneth the end of all, if a man labour not for a particular faith. To go farther. Now if I disable this interest of particular faith of God's love, and Christ's love, I lose the comfort of weak faith where it is true. What condition were they in now, when Christ biddeth Mary go? Had not some of them denied Christ, and had they not all forsaken him? And yet notwithstanding, 'Go tell Peter,' and tell them all, 'I go to their Father and their God.' So that the interest that a soul hath in Christ, who hath true faith, though a weak faith joined with many infirmities, the interest he hath in Christ is not broke off, as you see by the example of the apostles. And therefore I beseech you, let us comfort ourselves in this, labouring for a particular faith, and then labour to maintain our interest, notwithstanding our infirmities and faults, notwithstanding our sins past. Let not Satan rob us of our claim, that God is our God and Father in Christ. Let us learn of Christ; we cannot have a better pattern. What doth Christ on the cross, when he had the sins of all the believing world upon him, and had there been ten thousand times more, it had been all one to so infinite a person, God-man; he had made full satisfaction to God's justice. But having so much upon him, did it take away his claim of God, as his God? It did not, but still he said, 'My God, my God.' Was it a claim that did him any good? Was it a useful claim? Yes. For it was made good by his resurrection and ascension; and therefore he might well say, 'I go to my God and your God.' I have overcome the wrath of God due for sin; and therefore when I, that had all the sins of the world upon me, acknowledged God to be my God, and underwent the burden of God's wrath, and satisfied for all sin, you may well say, '*My* God;' not only from the pattern of Christ, because he did so, but as a cause. I may say so now, because Christ said so then. For he hath fully satisfied his Father, who had laid that burden on him. You, therefore, that have particular burdens of your sins, and have not that other, but have a conscience troubling you, it is for good; because if you believe, that is taken away. But put case you had the guilt of your own sins, and many sins beside, what is that to this of Christ, who had the guilt of all sin? And therefore let no guile hinder you from a spirit of faith, to say, 'My Father, and my God.' Is Christ ascended to heaven, to be a mediator of intercession to appear before God? For whom? Is it not for sinners? What work is there in heaven for a mediator, if we were not daily sinners? Christ that hath satisfied for sin, biddeth us, after satisfaction, to think of God as a Father, and think of his ascension; even for this end to appear before God for us as our high priest, to make daily peace for us. His blood is of everlasting efficacy. And if Abel's blood cried for vengeance, the blood of Christ crieth for mercy, Heb. xii. 24. As the appearing of the blood of Abel spake for vengeance, so the very appearing of Christ speaks enough for mercy to the sinner.

It is a comfortable clause that in Hosea ii. 19, where God saith, 'He will marry them in everlasting mercy.' So that mercy is a part of the jointure of the church. God will marry them in mercy; in what mercy? In pardoning mercy; as the husband is to bear with the wife, the weaker vessel, not to put her away for infirmities. Shall we attribute mercy to men, and not to God? Can a friend bear the infirmities of a friend, and a husband of a wife? And cannot Christ bear the infirmities of his spouse? And therefore never think that our infirmities may hinder our claim. You see it did not here. But 'go to my Father, and your Father.' This comfort we shall be driven to make use of some time or other, and therefore make use of it now.

But you will say, This is not comfort for common sort of Christians. It is not, and I intend it not for them. It is children's bread, and it must not be cast to dogs. Therefore they that have not God for their God, and live in any sin, they can lay no claim to him, for they serve another god in their hearts. Their vile courses are instead of their god, and in their affections above their God, and therefore let them not think any promise belongeth to them in that course. Let them think of God as 'a consuming fire,' as 'everlasting burnings,' while they be such, and that their peace is as the peace that the soul hath when the strong man holdeth all in possession; when the conscience is speechless, and God hath given them up to hardness of heart, which is a desperate peace. This belongeth to them that are resolved not to live in any sin, that have given themselves up to God; and yet by reason of the remainder of corruption are driven to make use of that petition which Christ bids them to pray, 'Forgive us our daily sins.'

Use. Hence issueth this truth, *that a Christian may be assured of his salvation in this world.* For, first of all, grant that we ought particularly to apply, as God offers himself to us, and that no infirmities nor sins hinders this claim, then what followeth but a Christian, believing and repenting of his sins daily, may be assured that he is in a state of grace, because there be grounds of particular application. That, therefore, which seems to disable that interest, hinders not at all. And therefore labour to maintain that comfortable state of assurance by all means. The grounds of it is, particular application, notwithstanding of all sins and infirmities whatsoever, because Satan envieth it most, because it is a state wherein we honour God most.

I will not enter largely into the point, because I have spoken of it in other texts; but, forasmuch as concerneth this time, we must labour for that, without the which we cannot go through that which God calleth us to.

(1.) *There be many duties and dispositions that God requires which we cannot be in without assurance of salvation on good grounds.* What is that? God bids us be thankful in all things. How can I know that, unless I know God is mine and Christ is mine? Can I be thankful for that which I doubt of and think I ought to doubt of? Therefore it is such a state, without which I cannot perform other duty; and particularly the grand duty of thankfulness. And what a pitiful state is this, that a man should not be thankful for Christ, nor heaven, nor for the state of another world, that there should be such great matters, and yet they cannot thank God for them.

(2.) Again, *God enjoineth us to rejoice.* 'Rejoice, and again I say, rejoice,' Philip. iv. 4. Can a man rejoice that his name is written in heaven, and not know his name is written there? The disciples were very weak now; and yet, notwithstanding all their infirmities, they loved Christ; they cast themselves upon him, and had not chosen another Saviour. Therefore 'rejoice that your names are written in heaven,' Luke x. 20, and how can a man rejoice that knoweth it not to be so? By God's writing of the law in a man's heart, he may know his name is written in heaven. Can a man always rejoice if he hath not grounds why?

(3.) Again, *God requires cheerfulness.* 'God loveth a cheerful giver,' 2 Cor. ix. 7, and a cheerful doer. It is the disposition that is required in everything. 'Give me thy heart' in everything thou dost, Prov. xxiii. 26. Alas! how can I perform cheerful service to God, when I doubt whether he be my God and Father or no? Shall not I labour for a heart to yield cheerful obedience? Doth it not come deadly off? Surely it doth. We ought to comfort ourselves; and how can a man comfort himself in a condition full of uncertainties? No comforts are comfortable without this, that God is our God and our Father. Unless we know this, comforts themselves are not comfortable unto us. None of the comforts we have, the comforts of this life, are not comforts to us when the soul saith, Perhaps God feeds me to slaughter; and, perhaps, I have these mercies as my portion in this world; and how can he be comfortable when he apprehendeth not, that they issue from a spring of love? Alas! comforts themselves are uncomfortable. And therefore shall not I labour for that without which I cannot be comforted? especially it being a disposition for our good to be thankful, and cheerful, and joyful, and large-hearted.

(4.) God requires a disposition in us *that we should be full of encouragements, and strong in the Lord;* and that we should be courageous for his cause in withstanding his enemies and our enemies. How can there be courage in resisting our corruptions, Satan's temptations? How can there be courage in suffering persecution and crosses in the world, if there be not some particular interest we have in Christ and in God? It cannot be so. Unless we will deny obedience to all duty enjoyed,* we must have this assurance which enters into all, which is the spirit that quickeneth and enliveneth all. Therefore labour for it.

Use 2. Else *we shall take away the grounds that God enforceth good duties from in Scripture,* as he doth enforce duty from this ground, 'As elect, see ye put on bowels of compassion,' Col. iii. 12. I beseech you, 'by the mercies of God, offer yourselves a sacrifice to God,' Rom. xii. 1. Alas! I know not whether I shall have mercy or no. Why take away your ground and overthrow your principles? And therefore shall not we labour for that state of soul wherein we are fitted to be in that disposition, and to perform duty as God would have us? I therefore beseech you, labour for assurance of salvation.

That we may maintain it the better, see the grounds of it. It is not in our perfection, for then the poor disciples, where had they been? Alas! they had dealt unfaithfully with Christ. But the ground of firmness is on God's side, the certainty is on God's part, not ours. Tell them, 'I go to my Father, and my God; and their Father and their God.' Though we make breaches every day, yet God breaketh not, as Mal. iii. 6, 'Verily, I the Lord am not changeable; and therefore you are not consumed.' We change, ebb and flow, are to and fro, up and down every day, varying in our dispositions. Though there be some root and seed of grace in us always, yet there is a change in our dispositions every day; but it holdeth on God's part. And therefore Christ nameth not any qualification in them

* Qu. 'enjoined'?—Ed.

to build comfort on, but '*my* God and *your* God' will yet maintain the relation of a Father to you, that have not dealt as you should do; and maintaineth the relation of a God, notwithstanding your fall. So that we maintain not our assurance on any part in us, but on God's love. 'Whom he loveth, he loveth to the end,' John xiii. 1. Our God unchangeably loveth us, in whom there is not so much as a shadow of change. And therefore in the last of the Hebrews, it is called an 'everlasting covenant.' 'The God of peace that brought again from the dead our Lord Jesus, the great Shepherd of the sheep, through the blood of the everlasting covenant,' Heb. xiii. 20. By the blood of Christ there is an everlasting covenant. God will be our God to death, and in death, and for ever. For this relation being on God's part, extendeth itself from forgiveness of sins to life everlasting. It is always. The blood of Christ is the blood of an everlasting covenant. 'I will marry thee to me for ever,' Hosea ii. 19. It holdeth sure on God's part.

Let us labour to maintain this assurance of salvation from God's love.

Use 2. But for our comfort, *we must do our parts too, though it begin with God.* It beginneth on God's part. He loveth us first, and embraceth us first; and we must love again, and embrace again. We must desire of God grace to answer relation. Therefore I will prescribe some rules, how we may say, God is our God, with comfort. That we may have the comfort of it, by making good our interest in him, to make it good that we are sons, as well as to call him Father; that we are his people, as well as to call him our God; his spouse, as well as call him our husband. And because this cometh from God, join this with all our endeavours: Lord, thou must begin; I desire to shew myself as a spouse to thee; but thou must discover thyself to me. I desire to love thee, but discover thy love first; all I can do is but reflection. Thou must shine on me first. So desire God to reveal himself more and more in Christ Jesus; and then we cannot but carry ourselves to him as we should do in our relation.

This day we must perform the relation on our sides. There be two words that go to this heavenly bargain. The covenant consisteth of two parts. Now, desire God, by his grace, to enable us to do our part, for he doth both. And desire him, according to his promise, to teach us to love him, and 'to write his law in our hearts,' Jer. xxxi. 33, to do what is good; and circumcise our hearts, and give his Holy Spirit. We ask no more than he hath promised, and so go boldly to him. Lord, thou hast made a covenant with us; we cannot keep it without thee. Thou hast not only promised grace and gifts, but the grace to perform the covenant on our parts must come from thee. And this God will do. Therefore in the use of means, attend upon him; and looking to him, we shall have grace to do our parts, and then maintain this assurance, without which we cannot live as Christians should live.

That we may further maintain this relation, that God is our God, let us labour to get into Christ, for it is in him that God is our Father; and to grow up in Christ, to grow more and more, to grow up in faith and in all grace.

A gracious Christian never wanteth arguments of assurance of salvation. It is the dead-hearted Christian, the careless Christian. Therefore labour, as to be in Christ, so to grow up in the knowledge of Christ.

And so to know God in Christ, labour to see the face of God in Christ; for in him are all the beams of his love. As the beams of the sun in a glass are gathered, so the beams of all God's love meet in Christ. So lovely is God in Christ, whatsoever we have in Christ it is from God in Christ. And whatsoever we have from God, it is through Christ; therefore grow in the knowledge of Christ, in faith in Christ. To this end are the sacraments, that we might grow up in him, and be fed into Christ. And then we may make right use of it, as the ordinance that God hath sanctified for this end. And as God doth take us out and set a stamp upon us, so labour to make choice of God more and more, and choice of God in Christ; for there be the two objects of our faith and love. Choose God for our God, and esteem him above all, and renounce all other, and resign ourselves wholly to him; for all is ours when God is ours. He setteth us apart from other men—taking us out—and appropriateth us to himself, chooseth us for his jewels. I beseech you, labour daily to choose God to be your God. If we say, we are God's, let us make choice of him at the same time, and appropriate him with our choice. He is mine in particular. There is renunciation of all others. I have served other gods heretofore; the world, and the flesh, and the favour of man have been my god, but they shall be my god no more. If we choose him not, and appropriate him as ours, and renounce all other, and give ourselves to him, we cannot say he is 'our God.' This we should practise every day. In the solicitation of sin, or despair for sin, make use of this choice, and appropriation, and resignation. If we be tempted to any sin, Why, I am not mine own, I am God's. I have chosen him to be my God; I have appropriated myself to him; I have renounced all other; I have offered myself to him; therefore what have I to do with sin, with this temptation? I have taken the sacrament on it, that God is mine, and Christ is mine, with all his benefits. Therefore if there be any solicitation to sin, make this use of it; and so we shall grow in assurance of our interest in God, when we can make use of it on all occasions.

If when we be moved to any sin, by Satan, or our own flesh, which is a devil within us, this is contrary to my covenant, this is contrary to the renewing of the covenant, so often renewed in the sacrament, and therefore I will not commit it. It is contrary to the state I am advanced to, and contrary to my relation. God is my Father and my God, and therefore I must be his; and what have I to do with sin? What hath pride to do with a heart bequeathed to God? What hath lust and filthiness? What hath injustice, or anything else that is sinful, to do in a heart that hath dedicated and consecrated itself to God, who hath given up himself and all he can do, and to whom we have given up all we have? and shall we give our strength to sin and Satan, his enemies?

Thus we should grow in assurance, exercising the increase and knowledge of our interest. I beseech you, therefore, let us use these and the like things to make God our God. And if any temptation to sin be joined, as Satan cannot but solicit to sin, so he laboureth when we have sinned to tempt to despair for sin; for they be the two ways by which Satan prevails. Now, fetch comfort against both from hence, 'God is my God and my Father,' and Christ teacheth them to call him so; and therefore, notwithstanding sin, I may go to God and call him Father. The disciples, though their sin was great, yet on their humility they were to acknowledge God to be their Father and their God. And therefore answer Satan: I ought not to abuse, and break off, and deny my interest in God as my Father and my God for any sin, because the disciples did not so; and Christ hath taught how to make use of God, and to acknowledge him for my comfort. We cannot have a better guide than God; and therefore never think of God but as 'our God and our Father,' and labour to answer all Satan's temptations in that kind from hence.

Use 4. Again, This assurance, that God is our God in Christ, and our Father, *is wrought by the sealing of the Spirit, and sanctifying of us;* therefore take heed *we grieve not the Spirit of God.* God's Spirit moveth our hearts oftentimes in hearing the word, or reading, or praying; when we have any good motions, or when we entertain them; and therefore do not grieve the Spirit of God, whose office is 'to seal us to the day of redemption,' to assure us God is our God and our Father in Christ. Grieve him not, lest he grieve us, by racking and tormenting our consciences. That is the way to maintain our interest. Take heed of crossing the Spirit, especially by any sin against conscience. Conscience is God's deputy. Grieve not the Spirit. Grieve not conscience, for conscience is God's deputative. It is a little god within us. And therefore, if we will not alienate God from us, to whom we have given ourselves if we be true believers, do nothing against his deputy and agent, the Spirit that sanctifieth and sealeth us to the day of redemption.

This is the way to maintain assurance, that God is our God. For men may be led with a spirit of presumption, and say, God is my God. But if conscience telleth them, they live in sin against conscience and the motions of the Spirit, and suppress them, and kill them, as births that they would not have grow in their hearts; then they cannot say God is my God, but conscience telleth them they lie. And therefore, I beseech you, labour for an holy life. That faith that maketh this claim, that God is my Father and my God, is a purifying faith, 1 John iii. 3. It is a faith quickening the soul, a faith purifying, a faith cleansing. Faith is wonderfully operative, especially having these promises. What promises? 'I will be your God and your Father.' 'Having such promises, let us cleanse ourselves from all filthiness of flesh and spirit, and grow up in all holiness in the fear of the Lord.' And therefore labour for that faith that layeth hold upon this privilege, God is our Father and our God. Make it good by this, that it be a purifying faith, an operative faith, that worketh by love, that sheweth itself in our conversation. The more we labour and grow this way, the more we grow in assurance of salvation.

Beloved, favour cannot be maintained with great persons without much industry, and respect, and observance of distance. A man that will maintain the favour of great persons must be well read in their dispositions, must know how to please them, and yield them all observance and respect. And shall we think then to preserve respect with God without much industry and holiness? It cannot be. 'And therefore give all diligence,' not a little, 'to make your calling and election sure,' 2 Peter i. 10. It requireth all diligence, it is worth your pains. We live on this, that he is our God, and will be our God to death and in death, for ever and ever. That God is our God to everlasting, that he is of an equal extent with the soul, he liveth to fill it and make it happy, our souls being of an eternal subsistence. Therefore it standeth us upon 'to give all diligence to make our calling and election sure,' else it will not be maintained. Why do not Christians enjoy the comforts of this, that God is their God in Christ, more than they do? The reason is, they be negligent to maintain intercourse between God and them. We must know our distances, there must be reverent carriage to God, Ps. ii. 11. A loose Christian can never enjoy the comforts of God. He is so great, and we so mean, we ought to reverence him, we ought to 'love him with fear, and rejoice with trembling,'

Ps. ii. 11. Humble thyself to walk with thy God. Where there is a great deal of humility, it maintaineth friendship. We cannot walk with God as a friend, as Abraham is said to be God's friend. We must acknowledge ourselves to be 'dust and ashes,' know him in his greatness, and ourselves in our meanness, if he will maintain this to our hearts, that God is our God. If we be careful to maintain this, surely he that delighteth himself in the prosperity of his servants will delight to make himself more and more known to us, that we may be assured of our salvation.

All that hear me are such as have not yet made choice of God to be their God, or have made choice. Let me speak a word to both; for there be many that yet have their choice to make, that have other lords and other gods to rule over them. Let them consider what a fearful state it is not to be able to say, in regard of life everlasting, 'God is my God and my Father.' They can say they be God's creatures; but what a fearful condition is it not to be able to say, God is my Father. Will not these know whom he is not a God to in favour, he will be a God to in vengeance? He must be a friend or enemy. There is no third in God. God and the devil divide all mankind. They share all. If thou be not God's, and canst not say so on good titles, thou art the devil's. Yet God is daily pulling men out of the kingdom of the devil, by opening their eyes to see their miserable condition; yet all go under these two grand titles, God's and the devil's. If thou canst not say, God is thy God, then the devil is thy god; and what a fearful condition is it to be under the god of the world by a worldly, carnal disposition! And perhaps thou mayest die so, if thou be not careful to get out of it. If God be not our God, he is our enemy; and then creatures, angels, devils are against us, conscience against us, word against us. If he be for us, who is against us? If he be against us, who is for us? A terrible condition, and therefore get out of it, I beseech you.

But how shall I do? Is there mercy for such a wretch? Yea, he offereth himself to be thy God if thou wilt come in. Wherefore serveth our ministry, the word of grace, but to preach life to all repentant sinners. 'He that confesseth and forsaketh his sins shall have mercy.' And therefore God hath ordained ambassadors of peace to proclaim if you will come in. And he entreateth you to come in, and he chargeth and commandeth you. You be rebels, not only against him, but enemies to your own souls if you do not. And therefore I beseech you, if you be not yet come in. Add this more, you be sacrilegious persons if you be not Christians in earnest. Have not you given yourselves to God in baptism? And have not you in your lives given yourselves to lusts which you renounced at your baptism? Now you have alienated yourselves from God, to whom you were dedicated. Did not you engage yourselves to God in your baptism? And is not he willing to receive you? He thought of you when you could not think of yourselves. And therefore, as it bindeth you over to greater punishment if you will not come in, but continue sacrilegious persons from God to whom you have dedicated yourselves, so God preventeth* you with mercy.

He encourageth by the seal of election in baptism to make it good by faith, without which it will do no good, being but a seal to a blank. Therefore how many encouragements have you to come in? Take God's gracious offer. He giveth you time. Make your peace. It is nothing but wilful rebellion to stand out against God.

* That is, = 'God has come before with mercy, *e.g.*, baptism,' &c.—G.

For they that have given themselves to God, and now renewed their interest in him by the sacraments, let them conceive what a word of comfort they have in this, *that Christ is theirs and God is theirs.* What an ocean of comforts is it when all things leave you, as all things will; yet we have God, that will be a God for evermore. At the time of death, what comfort will it be to say, God is mine, Christ is mine. Life is mine no longer; world is mine no longer; friends forsake me, but I am interested in God, and have made covenant with God, who is a God for ever. The covenant I have made is an 'everlasting covenant.' It is of that largeness, the comfort is, that the angels themselves admire it,* the devils envy it, and it is a matter of glory and praise in heaven for ever. Therefore make much of such a privilege, that is the envy of devils, the admiration of angels, that is the joy of a Christian's heart here, and matter of glorifying God for ever, world without end. That God in Christ is become his God here and for ever, it is a ravishing consideration. It is larger than our hearts. Here be comforts larger than the capacity of our hearts. *Cor vestrum soli Deo patere debet:* our hearts ought all to lie open to divine things, for they have more in them than the heart can contain. If we will shut them, shut them to worldly things. Oh the comfort of a Christian that hath made his state sure: let him glory in the Lord.

There be three degrees of glory in all. Let him glory under hope of glory, glory in afflictions, and glory in God; that is, we glory in God to be our God. That in the sharing and dividing of all things God hath given himself to us; and what an offer is this, that when God divideth this world to the children of men, you shall have this and that, but you shall not have me. But to his children he hath given himself, and he hath nothing better to give, and indeed there is nothing else needs. For there is more in it than we can speak. But that when God divideth all things he should give such a share as himself, is not this a glory, that a poor creature should have God to be his, and all he hath to be his, to make use of it in life and in death? It is worth all the world; it is worth our endeavours 'to make our calling and election sure,' when we may have this comfort from it, 2 Peter i. 10.

* That is, 'wonder.'—G.

NOTES.

(*a*) P. 416.—'*Sævitum est in cadavera, sævitum est in ossa, sævitum est in cineres* (Cyprian)—of the Roman emperors' cruelty, to remove a dead body.' This Father has many eloquent passages on the reverence due to the 'body' of the believer, as formerly a 'temple' of the Holy Ghost; and the present is a reminiscence of one of them.

(*b*) P. 416.—'She turned herself back. The same phrase the Septuagint use of Lot's wife looking back.' Genesis xix. 26 in the LXX. is as follows:—Καὶ ἐπέβλεψεν ἡ γυνὴ αὐτοῦ εἰς τὰ ὀπίσω.

(*c*) P. 417.—'*Tolle meum, et tolle Deum*, as he said.' Qu. Bernard?

(*d*) P. 422.—'Rabboni. . . . It is a Syraic word.' See Robinson under Ῥαββι and Gesenius under רַב and רַבִּי By Syriac, Sibbes means Hebrew, a common use of the term by him and his contemporaries.

(*e*) P. 423.—'As Austin saith, *Non frustra dicit anima, Deus salus tua.*' Cf. Augustine, *De Arbitrio*, and *in loc.*

(*f*) P. 429.—'For the word "touch," in the original, doth not signify merely,' &c. The verb is ἅπτω, on which see Robinson, *sub voce;* and on the passage, for excellent remarks, consult Webster and Wilkinson.

(*g*) P. 430.—'As Augustine saith well, *Mitte fidem in cœlum et tetigisti.* As he said in the sacrament, *Quid paras dentem et ventrem? Crede et manducasti.*' For the first part of this reference see Com. or Hom. on Mat. ix. 21; for the latter, cf. Tract 26 in Joan; *e. g.*, 'Credere in Christum hoc est manducare vivum;' also in Joh. Evang. c. vi.

(*h*) P. 457.—'It is an eternal relation, *Dum percutis, pater es, dum castigas, pater es*, saith Austin.' One of the often-recurring apophthegms of the 'Confessions' and Theology of this Father.

(*i*) P. 463.—'"There is a world taken out of the world," as Austin saith.' Cf. remark under note *h*. It is the ground of his entire doctrine of Predestination.

(*j*) P. 471.—'As the Grecian calleth him; they be for all turns,' &c. See note *eeee*, Vol. III. p. 536.

G.

KING DAVID'S EPITAPH.

KING DAVID'S EPITAPH.

NOTE.

'King David's Epitaph' appeared originally in 'The Beams of Divine Light' (4to, 1639). The separate title-page is given below.* For general title-page, see Vol. V. page 220. G.

*KING
DAVID'S
EPITAPH:

OR,

An Epitome of the life and death
of King DAVID.

In three Sermons.

By
The late learned, and reverend Divine,
RICHARD SIBS.

Doctor in Divinitie, Master of Katherine-Hall
in *Cambridge;* and sometimes Preacher at *Grayes-Inne.*

Luke I. 74, 75.

That we being delivered from our enemies, might serve him in holinesse and righteousnesse before him, all the dayes of our lives.

2 Sam. 14. 14.

For we must needs die, and are as water spilt upon the ground.

LONDON,
Printed by *E. P.* for *Nicholas Bourne*
and *Rapha Harford.*

KING DAVID'S EPITAPH.

For David, after in his own generation he had served the counsel (or will) of God, he fell asleep, and was laid to his fathers, and saw corruption.—ACTS XIII. 36.

THE words are part of a sermon of blessed St Paul, wherein he proves out of the Old Testament, Ps. xvi. 10, that David prophesied of Christ, and not of himself. David saw corruption, but he of whom David spake 'saw no corruption,' therefore David was not the Messias. He shews that the things there spoken do no way agree to David, but to the Messias, who saw no corruption. 'For David, after he had served in his own generation, fell asleep, and saw corruption.' In general, observe this:

One of the best ways to understand the Scriptures is to compare the Old Testament and the New together.

1. *That which was spoken and foretold of Christ in the Old Testament, and fulfilled in the New, that must needs be true.* Christ is the true Messias. Why? It was foretold so of him in the Old Testament, and accomplished in the New. Therefore Christ is the true Messias, comparing the prophecy and the event together. For the Old and New Testament make up but this syllogism: he that should be so and so, as was prophesied, born of a virgin, that should come at such a time, in the latter end of Daniel's weeks, &c., he is the true Messias. But Christ was such a one; he was born of a virgin, came at such a time, he saw no corruption, for he rose the third day. Therefore Christ is the true Messias.

2. Again, *You see the Holy Ghost here could not mention David without terms of honour:* 'David, after he had served the will of God in his generation,' &c. Precious to God is both the life and death of his saints, Ps. cxvi. 15. The righteous shall be had in everlasting remembrance, Ps. cxii. 6. The name of Josias is as an ointment poured out. So indeed the names of holy men are as ointment poured out; they sweeten men when they are gone. David's body was buried among them; but David had a better tomb. He was buried in the best monument: in the hearts and remembrance of God's people, and in the remembrance of God. God wraps him up as a valiant man in his own colours. He mentions not David barely here, but his serving the will of God.

Let wicked men cast what aspersions they will upon the names of God's people, let them eclipse them and cloud them as they please, as their malice instigates them therein, the names and reputations of God's people are not in their keeping and power. For David shall have a good name, in spite of all the Doegs and Shimeis, when they are rotten, body and name together. We see here, many hundred years after, he is mentioned with titles of honour. It should encourage us, therefore, to serve God as we regard a good name.

Mark here *the language of the Holy Ghost, the language of Canaan.* When he speaks of a good man, he speaks of him in favoured terms. He doth not say that David, after he had been so long, or lived so long, or reigned and flourished so long, as we see in stories, such a man lived or reigned, &c., so long, and then died; yet this had been true; after he had lived and reigned so long, he died. But that is not the language of the Holy Ghost; but after he had 'served God' so long. The Scripture values men by that that God values them, and not as men do, by their life, and reign, and flourishing in the world, and their esteem with men, but as his carriage hath been to God. David 'served the will of God' in his generation.

And then, when he speaks of his death, 'he fell asleep;' he sweetens the harsh name of death with a sweet term the Scripture puts upon it. It is a comfortable thing to consider the very language of the Scripture; how savoury and heavenly it is, raising us up to comfortable and heavenly thoughts, even from the very manner of the phrase. Different, as I said, is the phrase of Scripture from other histories, that say, such a man lived and reigned so long, and then he died. And indeed a man may say of a wicked man, he was so long in the world; but if he did no good, a man can scarce say that he lived; for what is life without doing good but a mere being in the world? Or if his life be ill, we may say such a man troubled the world so many years, and then went to his own place, as it is said of Judas, Acts i. 25. But this is the epitaph of a holy man. He served God so long, and then he slept and had happiness of God: another manner of epitaph than other men have when they are gone. This I observe from the very language or phrase. 'David, when he had served the will, or counsel, of God,' as the word is (*a*).

3. Again, In the third place, observe this in general, *that God sets down David here only as he was a good man, and passeth by all his infirmities and breaches*, whereas, alas! David's life was woven with good and ill. There were some ill spots in that excellent garment; there were some ill parentheses made in that excellent speech; there was somewhat, by the infirmity of man, that was not so good. But doth God speak of that when he mentions David? Oh no. But David, after he had served God in his generation, &c. The Spirit of God in St Paul passeth by all that was amiss, and sets down that which is good, to shew us this comfortable point, *that God values those that are in Christ* (and have repented of their sins), *not by what they have been or have done at some time, but by what they are, and what they resolve to be.*

God values them by their better part; by that that is his in them, by that that is spiritual in them. He judgeth them by the tenor of their lives, and not by a particular flaw in their lives. This is God's infinite mercy; when he pardons, he pardons absolutely: he forgets as well as forgives. Therefore the phrase of Scripture runs, 'He will cast our sins behind his back, and cast them into the bottom of the sea, that they shall never rise up in remembrance,' Micah vii. 19. When we have once repented of our sins, they are to him as if they had never been done, they are as things forgotten. Peter, after his foul fall, he was not so much as upbraided by Christ in particular, 'Thou hast denied me,' &c.; only Christ comes sweetly over him with a question, 'Lovest thou me?' John xxi. 15. He tells him not, thou hast betrayed me thus and thus. No; he doth not so much as upbraid him with the mention of it. So curious* is God for troubling the peace of his people, that when they have soundly repented of their sins, they shall never hear of it to their confusion, nor at all, except it be to better them, and to perfect the work of humiliation.

Contrary to the fashion of the corrupt poisonful nature of man: if they have but one thing in all a man's life to hit him in the teeth with, he shall be sure to hear of it oft enough, and pass by whatsoever is good in him. God doth not so with his children; but though they have some breaches in their lives, he passeth by them, and takes notice of that which is good in them, as we see here the apostle doth, being directed by the Spirit of God.

But though God so sweetly pass by David's faults when he mentions him, and calls him a 'man after his own heart,' &c., yet there is one thing that God puts in as a scar upon David. 'He was a man after God's own heart in all things but in the matter of Uriah,' 1 Kings xv. 5 Why doth that come in Scripture? Surely God mentions that, because that was done with more deliberation and advice; it was done in cold blood. It was not infirmity, but presumption in that. Now the more will there is in any action of sin, the more heinous the sin is, the more the guilt is increased. There was more will in that, for it was not done in heat of passion, but deliberately, therefore it was a foul act. The Spirit of God takes notice both of the good and of the evil; as we see in the epistles, in Rev. ii., to the churches. He had found fault with them before, and indeed God discerns directly when we are to blame, 'yet this thou hast, that thou hatest the works of the Nicolaitans,' &c. If there be any good, God takes notice of it. David, after he had repented of that foul sin, and was sharply corrected for it, as indeed he was, David was a good man for all that, 'he served God in his generation.'

But to give you an item by the way: however God passed by the sin in David, and accounted him after his repentance a good man, yet he must be sharply corrected for it. Let no man therefore presume upon this that God will judge him by the tenor of his life, and therefore he will commit particular enormities. Oh no! It cost David dear; for besides his heart-smart in his own particular, God made his heart bleed. It cost him many a salt tear, besides that it was punished in his posterity. God raised up his own bowels to take arms against him; he made him wish a thousand times that he had not so offended God. It is ill trying conclusions with God. Though God afterwards pardon us, and turn all to good, yet it shall cost us dear first. Though God will bring us to heaven, yet if we will venture upon sins against conscience, and take liberty to offend God, he will take sharp courses with us. Yet it shall not prejudice our salvation. You see those sins of David, after he had repented and was corrected for them, they were forgotten, and David, in regard of the course of his life, 'served God.' His life was a service of God, notwithstanding some particular actions. These things may be useful to the best of us all. Therefore I observe them in general from God's manner of mentioning David here with honour, and passing by his infirmities. To come more particularly to the words.

* That is, 'careful or scrupulous.'—Ed.

'Then David, after he had served in his generation the will of God,' &c.

The words are a short epitome of the life and death of the blessed man David. First, I will speak of his life, and then of his death. In his life there are these two parts:

First, The time in which he lived; when this service was done, 'in his generation.'

And then the manner of his carriage in that time of his generation. It was a service of God, 'he served God.'

And this service of God is set down by the object of it, 'God.' By the rule of his worship, 'the will of God.' He served God, but how? As he had revealed his will to him, not at random. God will be served according to his own will. And then here is the act, 'he *served*.' So here is the proper object of worship, 'God,' in whom all our service is terminate. Whatsoever we do, it must rest in him. If we do good works to men, it must be for God's sake; we must serve God in it. Then here is the proper rule carrying us to that object, 'his will.' And then it must be a service; it must be done in obedience to God. 'David in his generation served the will, or counsel, of God,' as the word is (*b*). For his death, we shall speak of it after.

First, *For the time*: 'in his generation.' 'Generation,' in the Scripture, signifies a succession of men one after another, as you have it in Mat. i. 1, from such a one to such a one; so many generations, so many successions. You know in the Latin tongue, *seculum* is taken for an age or generation, the space of an hundred years, though Moses shut up the life of man in a shorter time. Succession of one man after another is a generation. Generation, sometimes in a general sense, is taken for all of one kind. The generation of Noah, and the generation of the righteous; that is, all of that kind, without restraining it to succession. But most commonly it is the consideration of men from succession of them, having the term from the way whereby we enter into the world, that is, by generation; therefore the succession of men from one to another is called generation.

Now, here generation implies both the times and the persons. The persons of men are a several generation, and the time wherein they live is a generation, and both are here included. 'David in his generation,' among the age of men, and in the time wherein he lived, 'served God.' The meaning of the place is clear. The points considerable here are,

First of all, That there is a generation, a succession of men one after another.

Secondly, That every man hath his particular generation. David had his generation, wherein he served the Lord.

Thirdly, That 'he served God in his generation;' that is, the whole time of his generation; yet with this limitation, he served God only in his generation while he was here, before he came to heaven. In heaven there is a kind of service, but it is not by way of work, but of reward. We must serve God in our generation here. If ever we look to reap hereafter, we must sow now. 'David served God *in* his generation.'

Obs. 1. First of all, *There is a generation, a succession of men.*

Particular men go off the stage, but the *species*, the kind, is eternal. Kinds of things continue for ever. Man dies not, but Paul, and Peter, and David die; there is a succession of particular men. It is with men as it is with the waves of the sea; one wave goes away, and another comes after. It is with men as it is with trees; for men are compared in Scripture to trees, trees of righteousness; and man, take him in his nature, is like a tree. The poet could say to that purpose (*c*). It is with men as with trees; some fall off in autumn, and others come in their place the next spring. So it is with men. They have their several generations. There is an autumn, a decay, and there is a spring of them. There is a succession of generations.

Use 1. To teach us this lesson, *that our time being short here*, every man hath his generation; one generation goeth away and another cometh, as the Scripture saith, Eccles. i. 4. We must be laid with our fathers, and others must stand up in our place. 'Rise up,' Joshua, 'for Moses my servant is dead, saith the Lord,' Josh. i. 2. One servant of God dies and another rises. There be many that must act their parts in this world. Therefore some must go off the stage, that others may come on. Therefore while we have time here, let us be sure to do good, before we be taken away, suddenly, we know not how soon, and there be no more generation. Here there will be a succession of generations, till we all meet in heaven, and then there will be no succession, there shall be no more death; but as the apostle saith, 'we shall be for ever with the Lord,' 1 Thes. iv. 17.

Use 2. And it should teach us likewise, considering that in regard of our being and natural condition in the world there are several successions, generation after generation, that now we are here, and presently after no more seen in the world, *to make sure an eternal generation; to be born anew of the immortal seed that never dies*, as St Peter saith, 1 Pet. i. 23, that tends to immortality. There is no death in that birth. A Christian, as he is a new creature, hath a generation to eternity; he never dies. In regard of our being here, there is generation after generation, successions of men; but when we are new born, though we cease to be here, we go to heaven. 'He that believes in me,' saith Christ, 'shall never die,' John xi. 26. 'Man that is born of a woman,' saith Job, 'hath but a short time to live,' and that short time 'is full of misery,' Job v. 7. But man that is born of the Spirit hath an eternal time to live, and that a happy life. All flesh is grass in regard of this life we lead, which is supported with meat and drink, and the comforts of this life: all flesh is grass, and the beauty of it as the flower of the grass; but the word of God endureth for ever; and as St John saith, 'he that doth the will of God endureth for ever,' vi. 27. The word of God endures for ever, because it makes us, having the Spirit of God, to endure for ever. The world passeth, and the lusts of it, but he that doth the will of God, that is new born by the word of God, and transformed to the obedience of God, he abides for ever. Would you abide for ever, and not pass from alteration to alteration—as wicked men, they alter and come to nothing, and worse than nothing? Then labour for this estate. This is the way to abide for ever. This life hath no date of days, no death.

Labour to plant ourselves in Christ by faith, that so in him we may have an eternal estate. 'Thou art our habitation from generation to generation,' Ps. xc. 1. It was a psalm that was made upon occasion of their falling away in the wilderness. They dropped away as leaves, and few of them came to Canaan. 'Well,' saith he, 'we fall away here, and wither as grass,' &c. 'But thou art our God from generation to generation;' that is, we have a perpetual subsistence in thee. A Christian when he is in God by being in Christ, hath a perpetual everlasting subsistence. As we are temples of God, so he is our temple. We dwell in him, 'thou art our habitation,' &c. Who would not labour to be in such an estate? for in this world there is nothing but a succession of generations.

Obs. 2. Secondly, *Every man hath a particular generation.* There is some emphasis in this. 'David in *his* generation.' For men drop not into the world at all adventure; but every man hath his own time appointed; when to come into the world and when to go out; some in one time, and some in another. Therefore the times wherein they live are foreknown of God. He hath set down when such a man shall be born, in such an age of the world. So long he shall live; such work he shall do; and when he hath done his work, he shall be taken away hence, and another shall come and stand up in his place. So every man hath his own generation designed, and appointed, and ordained by God himself from all eternity; not only his generation, but all the circumstances of it. The very place of his abode, the time, and season, and country where he shall live, all are set down.

Use 1. It is useful for this end *to observe in what times our lot is fallen, to what times God hath reserved us;* what generation and age we live in: to consider of the state of the times.

(1.) *Are they good? Bless God that hath reserved us to those times.* We pity some good men that lived in ill times; as our countrymen in Queen Mary's time, and other dark times. They were worthy men, and it was pity they lived not in better ages. Certainly they would have been excellent men then. Therefore we should bless God for reserving us to better times. What makes the times better? The discovery of salvation by Jesus Christ: the discovery of the means of happiness in another world. In what age there is a clearer discovery, where there is most Spirit working together with the outward means, that is a blessed age. The Spirit of God was not working so much in former times of darkness and popery. Then there were many that followed the beast to their eternal destruction, though God had mercy on many souls that followed him. As it is said in Scripture, 'they followed Absalom in the simplicity of their hearts, not knowing whither they went,' 2 Sam. xv. 11, so they followed popery in the simplicity of their hearts, not knowing the danger. God had mercy on them; yet certainly thousands of them were wrapped up in darkness. They were miserable times then. Those that know popery will say so. Those that read the story will say so. The world was wrapped in wars and miseries in those times.

It is true our times are not so good as they should be, and in many regards they are miserable times; and we must not murmur at this dispensation of God, if God hath so appointed that our lot shall be to live in hard and ill times. I say in some respects these are bad times; for the world, the older it grows, the worse it is. As it is in a sink, the farther it goes the more soil it gathers; so all the soil of former times are met in the sink of later times, and in that respect this generation is an ill generation.

(2.) *But if we consider what makes times good;* the manifestation of Christ's glorious gospel, that hath shined for a hundred years and more in our church; the discovery of the means of salvation so clearly; the abundance of the Spirit with the means, making men to apprehend the means; enlightening their understandings to make use of them, and working their hearts to obedience. Look in what age these are; they are happy times. Witness our Saviour, and he is the best judge: 'Happy are the eyes that see the things that ye see, and the ears that hear the things that you hear,' Mat. xiii. 17. Oh, in former times, if they had seen that that we see, and heard that that we hear, they would have accounted themselves happy. Oh, those that lived two hundred years ago, though they were good men, if they had lived to see that that we see, and to hear that that we hear, living in the glorious lustre and sunshine of the gospel, how would it have rejoiced them! Therefore, as we have cause to consider of the ills of the time and generation, that we be not swayed away with them, so we have cause on the other side to bless God, that hath reserved us to these times of knowledge. In regard of the ills we may say with St Austin, 'Lord, to what times are we reserved!' (*d*). But in regard of the good things we may say, Blessed be God, that hath reserved for us these things, that he hath cast our time thus; that we should be born in this generation; in the blessed time of the gospel; in this second spring of the gospel. We should bless God for it.

Use 2. Well, but that is not all. We are to be accountable to God for the time and means we enjoy here in our generation. *If we be not the better for it, we shall be so much the worse.* It had been better for us to have been born in times of popery and darkness, in places of ignorance, than livingi n the glorious times of the gospel, and in places where the light is discovered, and to be naught in the midst of such light. Those that are bad now are very bad. We see by experience, that of all men, the most outrageous wretched persons are those that are ill in good places; for God gives them up to more than an ordinary measure of profaneness. A man shall have better and more civil usage. He shall see better carriage in a pagan than in many Christians that are not good under the means. There be degrees of those that are naught. Some God gives up to a profane spirit in the midst of the means, a fearful brand. Those that are bad now in the glorious times of the gospel, their sins are presumptuous sins. They are not damned simply for sinning, so much as for sinning against the means, for sinning against such light, for sinning in these times. Those that lived in darkness they could do no better. What, to be swearers now! to be licentious, disordered persons now! to contemn holy things now! to be corrupt in our callings now! in this generation, when the light of the gospel hath so gloriously shined! What excuse can men have for their sins now? Certainly it shall aggravate their damnation, that they were children of darkness in the midst of light. Nothing will trouble their consciences so much as that they have offended against so many means, and so many helps as they had in the days they lived in. I beseech you, therefore, as we should bless God for reserving us for these times and places of knowledge and light, so let us take heed lest they be a means of aggravating our damnation afterward, that we shall wish that we had never been born in such times, but rather in times of darkness. It shall go better with our forefathers that lived in darker times, than with us, if we live in profane and ungodly courses.

Use 3. Now there is no generation so good, but there be gross sins in all times and generations, therefore *let every man be careful* (as to consider the good of the generation, to take good by it, so likewise) *to consider the sins of the times wherein he lives, that he be not tainted with the sins of that generation.* God's children have a counter-motion, a contrary motion to the motion of wicked persons in every generation; therefore in our generation let us do as David did in his generation, stand against the ills of the times, go against the stream in that which is ill. It is the commendation you see in the Old Testament. 'Noah was a good man in his generation,' Gen. vi. 9, and such and such were good men in their generations. 'David in his generation served God,' and yet the times were naught. 'Help, Lord,' saith he, 'for godly men perish from the earth,' Ps. xii. 1. The times were naught when he lived. There was Doeg, and Ahithophel, and Shimei, and other wicked men; yet David 'was a good man in his generation.' He was not carried with the stream of the times.

A godly man considers who are good and who are naught in his generation, and he walks to heaven with those that are good, though they be never so few. He goes in a contrary motion to others. He doth not conform to the world, Rom. xii. 2, 'he fashions not himself according to the world,' according to the wicked men in the generation he lives in; but he fashions himself to them that are of another world, that go a contrary way to the world.

Use 4. Every generation hath a genius both for manners and study; former times they were given to barbarism; now these times are more refined for outward respects. So for sins: *every age hath particular sins that reign;* superstition in former times, but now the clean contrary: profaneness, atheism, hardness of heart against the light, presumption, looseness, and the like. Now these being the sins of our times, we should go so much the stronger against the stream of profaneness and atheism. The devil discovers himself in divers shapes, in divers generations. Sometimes he prevails with ignorance, and then he is a spirit of darkness, sometimes he is a spirit of profaneness and looseness. Now consider by what sins the devil hath most advantage, and be sure to set ourselves against them.

Use 5. And let every one in his place *labour to make the generation we live in as good as we can.* Why doth God speak thus honourably of David? 'He served God in his generation.' That time was the better for him. We have all cause to bless God for such men, they are blessed men. Let every one of us in our generation carry ourselves so, that when we are gone, it may be said, Such a man did much good in his time and place, and hindered much ill. What a blessed thing is it when in our generation we hinder all the ill and do all the good we can, that others may say to our comfort and credit, The times and place was the better for such a man. Beloved, every one of us hath his generation. Some have a longer generation, some a shorter; some have a longer glass appointed to run out, some their glass is run out in a shorter time. Well, be it longer or shorter, let us be careful that we trifle not out our generation and time wherein we live unprofitably. That little part of time that God hath given us to work in, let us be sure to bestir ourselves in our generation, we know not how long or short our generation is.

Alas! if most men ask their own consciences, wherefore they live? what is the life of many, but an annoyance? They infect the air with their oaths, they are a burthen to the earth, they mis-spend the blessings of God; but what hath the times been the better for them? Their lives have been scandalous, wicked, and vicious. It should be our glory to shine in our times, 'as lights in the midst of a sinful generation,' Philip. ii. 15. I beseech you, therefore, let us take the counsel of holy St Paul: Gal. vi. 9, 'While we have time, let us do good.' While we have a part to act here upon the stage of this world, let us act our parts, do that wherefore we came into the world. We have not assurance from God that our generation shall hold thus long or thus long. Therefore whatsoever we have to do, let us do it presently; let us reform our wicked lives presently, 'before we go hence and be no more seen,' Ps. xxxix. 13. And for the good we have to do, do it presently, put it not off. No man is assured of his continuance here.

Obs. 3. In the next place, 'David served God *in his generation.*' He did not do it by starts and fits. He did not do this or that good act; but he served God in his whole generation. So must every man not only be content to do now and then a good action; for the veriest wicked man in the world may do good sometimes, and the best men may do ill sometimes; but in the whole course of our life, we must do good in our generation. Our course must be holy, the whole tenor of our lives, while we are in the world. All things have their time, but there is no time for sin; there is no time for vanity; no time for swearing; no time for sensuality and looseness.

Therefore let the whole course of our lives be spent in the service of God. What do we know but that that little time wherein we yield to the service of the devil may be the time when God will fetch us hence? And what will become of us then? Therefore resolve not a moment to serve sin. Our whole time is but short in respect of eternity. What is our generation to world without end? Therefore let us be content to serve God our whole generation.

'He served God *in his generation*,' that is, in his lifetime, while he was here. For God hath placed us in the world to do him some work. This is God's working place; he hath houses of work for us. Now our lot here is to do work, to be in some calling and course to work for God. We are not sent here into the world to play, or to live idly. Religion is no vocal profession. Every man must have some calling or other, and in his generation he must do good. For what will our account be afterwards else, when we shall give an account to God how we have spent our time in our generation, what good we did, what ill we hindered? It will be a fearful account when we have spent our time idly, perhaps scandalously and offensively, and sent others to hell by our example. We must serve God in our generation, in our life.

Thou that livest profanely day after day, when dost thou mean to serve God? At the hour of death? Did David serve God when he was to die only? No. 'He served God in his generation, and then fell asleep.' Alas, why do we put off? There is no sowing after this life. Then is the time of reaping. And why wilt thou defer the time of sowing till thou come to reap? It is a time to reap the comforts of religion at the hour of death. Shall we defer to serve God's will till we come to make our own will? And ofttimes it is forced what we do then. No. We must serve God all our time. 'David served God all his generation.' To do a few good works at our death only, it is a swinish doing good. The swine will do good when he is dead. Then there is profit of his flesh, though all his life he were noisome. Those men that put off thus, they are rather swine than men, beastly men. God seldom accepts the good they do then, and it is a forced good. If they were not to die then, no good at all would be done. That they do is because they can keep it no longer. It shews they have no grace nor faith at all, for if there had been faith to depend upon God they would have done good before. But they think, I may come to misery myself, and I know not what distasteful, base thoughts; therefore they will do no good in their lifetime. But we must serve God in our generation if we will be saved. These things are of some use, and we should not forget them. But I come to the service itself, which I shall a little more stand upon.

'David served the will of God.'

Here is considerable, as I told you, these three things.

The object whom he served, 'God.'

The rule by which he served him, 'his will.' And then

The service itself; for to know 'the will of God,' and not to serve him, it is to no purpose. All must go together. We must serve 'the will of God,' as we see here David did.

1. For the first, it is a known truth, *that God is the main object of all our service*. Indeed, we serve men; for in love, which is a very busy grace, we must serve one another in good works: but the love of God must set all on work, and all must be done in obedience to him. God is the object that must terminate all our service to men. Whatsoever duty we do, we must do it as to God. If we serve men, if we be Christians, it must be with reference to God, because he commands us, and that we may honour God. We can do no good to him, Ps. xvi. 2. What doth he care for our goods? But he hath substituted men in his place, he hath appointed such and such men in our generation to do good unto, and he accounts what we do to them for his sake, as done to him. God is the object of our service, God in Christ as our Father.

'God,' as God, without Christ a mediator, ought to be served for our very creation, if we were to go to hell when we had done, or should vanish to nothing with the beasts; for our very subordination and subjection to God as creatures implies service. He is the object of service, as being our maker, having given us a being, having given us reason to serve him. But now God considered as a Father in Christ in the covenant of grace, we ought to serve him in a higher regard; not as creatures the Creator only, and as servants their Lord, but as a gracious Father. So God the Father, Son, and Holy Ghost, and Christ, Mediator, God-man, are the objects of our service, the whole adequate, fit object. We must not go beyond them, for whatsoever else we do, it must be in reference to them. I will not dwell upon the point. It is a foundation to that I am to speak of.

The next thing is the rule of his service: 'He served *the will of God*.'

'The will of God.'

The word signifieth 'counsel,' and it is better translated 'counsel' than 'will,' because it is more emphatical. God's will is his counsel, not in regard of imperfection in counsel; for counsel implies somewhat imperfect, as deliberation and consultation. God sees all at once; he doth not deliberate, but in regard of that which is eminent in counsel; what is that? Wisdom. 'By counsel thou shalt be established,' Prov. xix. 18. So whatsoever is God's will, that is counsel. It is wise, it is weighed, it is as 'gold seven times tried,' Ps. xii. 6. Therefore we should stoop to whatsoever is God's will, either in his word or in events. His will is counsel. He is wise, he is not rash. A pattern to all those that would be like God, to do all by counsel and not by will. Those that are put to their will, if there be not answerable wisdom to guide it, to what mishief do they plunge themselves and others!

(1.) God must be served according *to his counsel or will*, as he hath discovered himself in his word; for service is nothing but an action done with an eye to the will of another. For if a man doth an action that one would have him do, if he do it not with respect to his command, it is no obedience nor service. He that hath not some care in the act, it is no obedience. As the civil law saith, *infringit obedientiam*, &c. (*e*), it breaks from the nature of obedience that hath no cause for it. He must know his reason; at the least there is the command of the superior must be a reason and ground for what he doth in all his obedience and service. Therefore there is a like necessity of the word of God as of his service, for what master will be served according to the will of his servant? Why doth the Scripture mislike will-worship, worship that is according to our own will? Because therein we make ourselves god; we serve ourselves, and not God. We must not serve God as we would be loath to be served ourselves. We would be loath to have a servant compliment with cap and knee, and then do as he list himself; and so for us to come and compliment with God, to hear his word as if we would be directed by him, to kneel and pray to him for fashion, and then all our life after to do as we list. It is a delusion to say we serve God, unless we serve him according to his *will*.

2. Therefore there must be a rule of our service, *and that rule is the written word of God*. There was a time when the word of God was not written, Heb. i. 1; and then God discovered his will by dreams and visions, and many other ways. But when the world was enlarged, and mankind spread further, traditions from hand to hand was not a fit means and way to deliver truths, because it was subject to corruption. God therefore would deliver his will, how he would be served, in writing; and God sanctified this course, and gave credit to it, by his own example, writing his own law with his own finger. The ten commandments were written by God himself. God was the first preacher and the first writer. He was the first preacher: he preached the gospel to Adam in paradise; and the first writer: the ten commandments being written by God himself. Now, we have the written word of God to be our rule, how God must be served, an exact and perfect rule. I will not speak by way of controversy. I hope we are grounded well enough, but by way of direction for a godly life. God's will is a sufficient rule.

What is requisite in a rule?

(1.) First, *A rule must be clear and open*, that it may be made use of by those that are to be regulated by it. Therefore we say, The secret will of God can be no rule, because it is secret. That which is a rule must be manifest and open. Therefore the revealed will of God, that every one may see, that is our rule. We may cross God's secret will and do well; and we may serve it and yet do ill. A father may pray for his child's life, and may cross the secret will of God, and yet doth well. God allows bowels in fathers. A wicked man may do according to God's secret will, and yet sin. Therefore that was not the rule of David's service, nor cannot be of ours. 'Secret things belong to God; but revealed things to us and our children,' saith blessed Moses, Deut. xxix. 29. The will of God, as it is discovered, must be the rule of our actions. A rule must be open, or else it is no rule.

(2.) Again, The rule by which we must lead our lives *it must be infallible:* not subject to error; for then it cannot be the rule of our service. The word of God is an infallible rule. It cannot deceive, because it is the word of God. Men wrote it, indeed, but it was God that dictated it. The finger writes, but the head dictates. Holy men wrote it according as they were guided by the Holy Ghost. The will of any man cannot be the rule of any man's service, further than it is agreeable to the first rule. Why? Because it is subject to error and mistake. That which must be the constant rule of a man's life, it must not be as popish traditions and the like. It must be infallible. Now, the word of God is so. It is infallible. A man may err, and be a man, and a good man too; but God cannot err, and be God. The word of God cannot be false and be the word of God. Therefore it is an infallible rule.

When this is applied to any creature, it is a grand lie, and the foundation of misery in that church. This is the first lie in the church of Rome, that the church, consisting of a company of men, cannot err. What a horrible absurdity is this, to make the will of man the rule, that the church cannot err, that popery cannot err! Though they err egregiously, they account rebellion service, and make traitors merit, &c.

But are our tenets subject to such gross things? No. We make the rule of obedience the infallible word of God, that cannot err. To attribute that of that which cannot err to that which can err, it is a horrible absurdity. But I will not enter into controversies.

(3.) Again, That which is a rule *must be perfect in commensuration, in measure*. It must be of equal extent to all things that are to be ruled. Now the things that are to be ruled is our whole carriage and conversation. Therefore that that is the rule for a man, it must rule his thoughts, his speeches, and actions. So the word of God, it rules the whole carriage of a man. There is a proportion between the rule and all things that are to be ruled by it. All things fall under the word of God to be directed and ruled by it. It gives direction to our thoughts, to our speeches, to our actions, in our callings. It gives direction to magistrates, to ministers, to masters, to servants, to all estates and conditions in life, in death. It is exceeding large, as David saith: 'All things come to an end, but thy commandments are exceeding large,' Ps. cxix. 96. It is a rule that extends to all things that are to be ruled whatsoever. No other rule but God's will doth so; for men's laws they have nothing to do with thoughts. Thought is free for them.

(4.) Again, A rule must be *authentical*. What is that? It must be credited for itself. It must have authority of and for itself, and not depend upon another, if it be the first rule. Indeed, there be subordinate rules. There is a rule ruled, and a rule ruling men's laws. The magistrates will it is a rule ruled by a higher rule; and, as long as it is so, it is a good rule. But there must be a rule ruling above all subordinate rules whatsoever. What is that? The word of God. It hath authority from itself, not borrowed of men. It is a rule that rules all, and is ruled of none other's rule but by this rule. This is a rule ruling the very rulers of the world. No man's will is a law further than it is squared by this law of laws.

(5.) It is an *inflexible rule*. It cannot be bent to men's purposes. Man would bring God's will to his will; but it is the measure that measures all, and is measured by none. For we must not judge the word, the word must judge us. You have some presumptuous persons that will judge and murmur at the word, but the word will be too good for them and judge them. He that judgeth the law, and gives sentence on the law, shews himself a fool; the law must judge him, much more the law of God. Therefore it is authentical.

These are the main properties of that that must be a rule to judge our lives by. Now the word of God is both known, and is not subject to error any kind of way, and it is equal to all things that may fall under it, and it is authentical, of credit for itself, let men say what they will. It must rule, and not be ruled. Therefore David, when he ordered his course of life by this will of God, he deserved this commendation, that 'in his generation he served the will of God.'

There be subordinate rules in their kind, as the law of nature, and the laws of men, direct in things of this life, to do them in that manner, according to the rule: a civil law for civil actions; men's laws for men's actions; but when we do anything holily, we must have direction from

God's law, and that must put the respect of service to God upon our actions. For howsoever we do things civilly by the civil law, and do things comely by the law of nature, nature teacheth us to carry ourselves in a decorum, to give every man his due; but it is not a service of God, except it be directed by the rule of God. A man cannot serve God without a higher rule than man can give.

But you will say, How shall we apply and make use of this rule in particular actions? The word is but short, but actions are infinite. The word of God directs me not to this or that action, and saith, You shall do this or that in particular, but gives general rules; how shall we come to carry ourselves in particular actions? Here is the skill, for a rule is not to hang up, a measure is not to be cast aside but to be applied. A rule is a thing in relation to a thing ruled, and a measure to things measured; and if we do not apply it, we lose the use of it. How shall we know how to serve the will of God in every particular action?

1. Besides the general word of God, we have some outward helps and some inward. *The outward helps are:*

(1.) First, The ministry. That is one main outward help. And what is the ministry for but to dig up the treasure, the mine of God; to lay open the will of God in particular; to branch out, and lay open, and anatomise the duties of such and such callings, by their ministerial gifts, which God hath given his servants in a competent measure to give particular directions? They have their callings for this end, 'to speak a word in season.' They have 'the tongue of the learned,' Isa. l. 4. God hath not set up this calling for nought. Therefore, as we go to the learned in the law, in doubts in that kind, so in particular doubts why do we not make use of those that study that way, if it be in such a case as perhaps we have no light in ourselves? It is one end of their calling, because perhaps our callings are such as that we cannot study particulars ourselves; therefore God hath sanctified that calling, that we might have the use of it. That is one.

(2.) Another outward help for particulars: *it is communion with good people,* those that are led with the Spirit of God; for we must know that God ofttimes lays up the practice of one man in the breast of another, because he would knit man to man. We are ofttimes at a loss, the best of us all, in particular directions what to do. Sometimes a meaner man, in some things, than ourselves, can give better directions in particular than ourselves. Shall we storm and swell at this? No. It is God's wisdom that one man should carry that which is for the special use of another, that we might take counsel and ask advice one of another. 'A wise man ordereth his doings by counsel,' saith the wise man, Prov. xii. 15; and ofttimes he that takes advice of himself hath a fool to his counsellor, and he beshrews himself that he would not take the benefit of another man's advice. Therefore, besides the public ministry, this is one help, our Christian friends and acquaintance, and they are reserved for such a time. 'A friend is made for adversity,' for ill times, in perplexed and doubtful cases. This is to make use and benefit of others.

(3.) Again, *The laws of men.* What are the laws, if they be good, but particular determinations of the will of God. We ought to have reverent conceits of the laws, for they do but bring God's generals to particulars, if they be good laws. If they have not their derivation from God's laws, they are naught;* but, if they back† that in anything, they are nothing

* That is, 'naughty,' = wicked.—G. † That is, 'support.'—G.

but a particular determining of the general rules in God's word, to give every man his due, &c. Therefore in many cases we may know what the will of God is, by the good laws of the kingdom which bind the conscience to obedience. There is no disobedience to men's laws, but where there is disobedience to God's laws first, which hath stablished men's laws.]

(4.) And then, in some particulars, when it doth not appear what we should do, *the example of good people, of the wisest and best in the rank and place where we live*, till we know the contrary. The best way is to rest in their judgment, to follow the advice of others, the direction of friends, or the laws and customs, and not to be refractory and opposite, except there be reason to the contrary. For man's spirit is a divine thing. It must alway be led with some reason, but with this reservation, a man may keep to others till it appear otherwise, till he see other light and direction to take this course. This is the disposition that should be in every peaceable man. These be some outward helps to know the will of God in particular actions.

2. *The inward helps to know what God's will in particular is*, together with the word of God unfolded.

(1.) *The Spirit of God*, which is as a voice behind us, saying, 'This is the way, walk in it,' Isa. xxx. 21. Wherefore serves the blessed Spirit but to be a counsellor? as Isa. ix. 7. Christ, he is the blessed counsellor. How comes he to be so? Not immediately by himself, but by his Spirit. All things he doth to his church is by his Spirit. He fills his church with his Spirit. Now the children of God, having this Spirit of counsel to advise them in particulars, they are 'led with the Spirit.' This is one inward help, and a main one. And surely, if we would give way to the blessed guidance of God's Spirit, and not grieve, and quench, and resist the Spirit, the Spirit of God would be ready to direct us upon all occasions. We should be guided in particular actions with a better Spirit than our own. And this Spirit we may have by prayer. God will give the Spirit to them that beg him, Luke xi. 13.

(2.) Then another inward help *is particular grace*, which God gives to his children. Particular prudence to speak words and to do actions in season, that everything may be beautiful in its time. There is sapience, wisdom, and prudence: 'I Wisdom dwell with prudence,' Prov. viii. 12. It is the wisdom of a man to understand his way, what to do in particular, or what not to do. It is prudence or discretion to discern of differences. Now that grace of God is in some measure given to all his children. He makes them wise to understand their own way. They are not so wise, perhaps, for other things. It is not their way. God lets some men go with a less measure of discretion to heaven than others; because he hath less work for them to do. But every man hath as much as will bring him to heaven. The less he hath himself, the more he shall have of others. Some men are excellent in gifts of wisdom. They can tell you generals out of the book of God excellent well. But come to directions in particular, and you shall have meaner men of better discretion than they. Either we have it ourselves, or else God will associate us, and by his providence cast us upon other acquaintance that have a greater measure of this grace that he will have us acquainted with. God gives every one of his a spirit to discern what to speak, how to advise, how to comfort, what to do. And the meanest Christian is more in this, for religious actions, than the greatest man in the world that hath not the Spirit of God; for he can tell in particular how to bear afflictions, and how to enjoy prosperity; because the Spirit directs him what to do.

(3.) Again, *God hath put into every man a conscience.* Wherefore serves conscience, but especially to direct in particulars. There is a faculty of the soul that we call a treasury, a preserving faculty, that is to lay up general rules out of the word of God, and directions out of good books, and from the counsel of other men. It is a faculty to treasure up rules. Therefore it hath the name of preserving. But there is a conscience under this. That being sanctified by the Spirit of God, and being directed in general by the word of God, it directs in particular. Conscience tells us, This in particular you ought to do; this you have done; in this particular you have done well, in this you have done ill. So conscience is put in us to check or direct us in particular. It is God's vicar in every man, together with the Spirit. Conscience, together with the Spirit, is a great help to know God's will in particulars. If men would not be too bold with conscience, conscience, together with God's Spirit, would be faithful to them. Conscience may say, as Reuben said to his brethren when they were in misery, 'Did not I tell you, do no hurt to the lad?' Gen. xlii. 21; deal not so hardly with Joseph as to cast him into the pit. So many men do many things amiss. Conscience may say, Did not I tell you this before? it was naught,* and yet you would needs do it. Yes, certainly; and when conscience is not hearkened unto as a director, it will scourge as a judge. It hath many offices, and it is good to keep this conscience in its office; to let conscience do its full duty, let conscience direct us to the full. Certainly, if we would hearken to this vicegerent in our hearts, this little god that God hath placed there in mercy to guide our lives in particular, it would be better with us than it is. We should end our days with more comfort, and give a better reckoning than we can.

(4.) Again, *Experience* may be added as another help. Experience is a great help in particulars, for indeed generals are raised out of experiments† in particular. Therefore] those that are wise politicians, statesmen, they are not so out of books altogether, but men of experience that can say, such a case hath been so at such a time. So that out of observation and particular experience they are able to say, upon the like case, it should be now at this time thus and thus. If therefore we would treasure up experience, it would be a good help to know what is to be done in particulars; to consider how it hath been in former time, and consider the experience of others. You see then what the rule of our service is, God's will; with these helps subordinate to it, how to direct ourselves in particular actions to serve the will of God. So much for that point.

'He served.'

Now I come *to the act of service.* God must be served according to his own will. We must search and try what is the good, and holy, and acceptable will of God, Rom. xii. 2. I have shewed how we may search in particular what the good and acceptable will of God is. Now when this is discovered, the next thing is to 'serve' God in the knowledge of his will; for all the blessings are annexed to service, and not to knowledge. 'If ye know this will.' Is there all? No. 'Happy are ye if ye *do* it,' John xiii. 17. If we know the rule and do it, we are happy. What if we do it not? 'He that knows his master's will, and doth it not, shall be beaten with many stripes,' Luke xii. 47. It will but aggravate our damnation, to know the rule, to have directions what to do, and not to do them. Then

* That is, 'naughty,' = wicked.—G. † That is, 'experiences.'—G.

the rule that we have hath another use. If we use it not for direction in what we do, it will be brought against us at the day of judgment, as a direction for God to damn us by: This you knew; this counsel you had; these motions of the Spirit you had; this, conscience told you; this, the ministry and your friends told you. Notwithstanding, you crossed and thwarted all. When it is not a direction for us to obedience, it will be a direction for God to give sentence. Therefore let us make conscience first to know the will of God, which is the rule of all our actions, by all the means we can, and then to give 'service to it.' David served the will of God. His life was not unfruitfully and wickedly spent; but 'he served' the counsel of God that had planted and placed him there in the world for that purpose. Why hath God planted us here in the paradise of the church? That we should not be barren trees, or bring forth ill fruit; but that we should 'serve' him, and be fruitful in our places.

This word 'service' is a harsh word, and such a thing as proud spirits could never digest. Why did the devils fall? They would be in a state independent, and not under others; they would have their own courses; and therefore the Scripture saith, 'They kept not their own standing,' Jude 6. God set them in one course, and they swelled and would not keep it. The particular is not set down in Scripture, but 'they kept not their own standing.' Neither the devil, who is a proud creature, nor men led with the spirit of the devil, can endure service. Every man would be a god to himself, to be guided by his own lewd will and lusts; and God knows, they are blind guides, and we shall know it to our cost if we have not a better guide. When the will of God is revealed, therefore, we must have a care to serve it.

Now, to 'serve,' implies two things especially: an action, and a reference of that action to the will of another. That is service, as I said before, to do a thing, and to do in obedience. For if a man do never so many things, if it be not in obedience to the will of another, it is no 'service.' He serves himself. So to 'serve' God is when we know the will of God, to do accordingly, and to do it because it is the will of God. Then it is service; or else it is a work indeed done, but no service or obedience.

All obedience is with looking to the will and pleasure of another, that hath authority to direct us; and then we 'serve' the revealed will of God, when the whole inward and outward man is fashioned and framed to that; when there is a measuring of both together, as when we obey the directions; when we tremble at the threatenings; when we imitate the examples of holy writ; when we are raised up with the comforts; when answerable to every divine truth there is an answerable disposition of soul; when there is a sweet harmony between God's truth and our inward and outward man. Rom. vi. 17, 'We must be cast into the mould of the word.' As a thing when it is moulded in another frame, it carries the print of the frame or mould, so we 'serve' the will and word of God when we are moulded answerable to that will.

Now, more particularly, this 'service' of the will of God, it is either immediate, inward 'service' of the will of God, or outward service.

(1.) *Inward service* is the obedience of the first commandment, when upon the knowledge of God we set him up in our souls, and cleave to him in our affections of trust, and joy, and love, and delight, to give him the supremacy of all these. Then we serve him with inward worship and service. And this indeed is to set the crown upon God's head, and to make him king and God in our hearts. He must have the prime of our inward service. When we love God above all, and fear him above all, and delight in him above all, and cleave to him when all things else fail us, this is the immediate 'service' of God in our hearts, when we give God his own in our hearts. Hence comes all other 'service' whatsoever, or else it is but the eye-service, that is not enlivened with the inward worship of God.

(2.) Now, besides this inward, there is a 'service' of God *that comes from this inward service, which is of the outward man;* that is, when we pray to God, and that requires our words, when we praise God in thanksgiving, when we come to hear the word and to receive the sacrament. And so all outward holy actions are the 'service' of God, and are drawn from the inward immediate worship of God that I spake of before.

(3.) Besides these (which come more immediately from a sanctified spirit), there is a service of God *that is the obedience of the second table,* when we do good to men with an eye to serve God, as we say. There is an elicit, proper service of God, and a commanded service of God, *cultus imperatus.* All duties to men are a 'service' of God, when we do them as commanded of God, as because I love God, therefore I honour my parents, and magistrates; and therefore I will not commit adultery: as Joseph, 'Shall I do this, and offend God'? Gen. xxxiv. 9. So the Scripture allegeth reasons out of the first table, when we are tempted to sins against the second table; and then the duties of the second table are a worship and 'service' of God, when they are commanded by the first. And this is the difference between a mere formal man and a Christian in his outward performances. A civil man is altogether for the second table, but he hath not his rise from the first. He gives every man his due, &c., but it is not in obedience to God, because God hath commanded him to do it; but because he sees it is a deformed thing to be unjust. Out of the light of nature he condemns the sin, but not out of religious respects. It is not a service of God all this while. Ay, but when it is from love to God, when that great command, 'Thou shalt love God above all,' sets him upon this, then all the duties he performs to man are a service of the will of God, for God commands them. Even the basest works are a service of God when they are done in obedience to God, as Saint Paul tells them in Col. iii. 22, and Eph. vi. 5, the poor servant 'serves the Lord Christ.' When a poor servant is at his work, employed in the business of man, poor, common things, yet he serves the Lord all the while. For God hath set them that calling, and he doth the second table in obedience to the first; and he serves men, those that are his governors, with an eye to the great Governor and Master that is above all, that will reward them for their poor service, however their master reward them, Eph. vi. 8. This is to serve the will of God then; to yield to him the immediate service of the soul, and the outward expressions of it; and to go through all other duties as they spring from the first. Then we are moulded, as I said before, answerable to the word of God.

To apply this to our blessed man David, and then to make use of it to ourselves.

Thus did David serve the will of God in his time; for you may see what he was. He is anatomised and laid open to our eyes in the Psalms. You may see his care of 'serving' God in his own writings. See how he cleaved to God in his affections in Ps. xviii. 30, *seq.*, how he loved God, and joyed in God, and in the word of God above all things in the world. He esteemed the light of 'God's countenance more than corn, or wine, or oil,' Ps. iv. 7. I give but a touch, to shew how this description is true of this blessed man, 'that he served the will of God.'

And for the expression of it in praise and prayer, he was 'a man after God's own heart;' especially in this, he was ready upon all occasions to bless and praise God. He kept his communion with God, as we see; though he were a king, yet his main care was to 'serve' God, as we see in Ps. i. 2, 'He meditated in the word of God day and night.' What time had he to rule his kingdom then? The meaning is, that all the spare time that he had it was to think of God; to look to the rule, the word of God, how to guide his life.

And for his outward calling. (There is a double calling wherein we 'serve' God as Christians, our general and our particular calling, wherein we are to deal with men.) What an excellent man was he! 'He served the will of God,' as a governor of a family. We see in Ps. ci. 2, how he carried himself in the midst of his house to all his servants. A liar should not abide in his house. You have a direction there how to guide your families. You see how he served the will of God as a governor. Yet there was a fault to him in that respect, he was too indulgent to Absalom and Adoniah. A man may be a good man, and yet be to blame in some particulars; but when his heart is right, God pardons the rest.

You see how he carried himself as a king. He was an excellent king, the delight of Israel. He carried himself every way as a king should do. He tempered mercy and judgment together: 'I will sing of mercy and judgment,' Ps. ci. 1. So he did in his whole carriage sweetly temper mercy and justice; he dispensed these two. And as a king must not only 'serve' God, so his care was to establish the worship of God, as you find in the story. David, when he saw all in peace and quiet, then he begins to take care for the ark, 2 Sam. vii. 2: 'I dwell in a house of cedar; but the ark of the Lord remains under curtains.' Therefore he took a course for that. So governors should do, when God hath settled them in their government quietly, to begin to think of God's house; for they rule not well, they 'serve not the will of God,' except, besides their own service, they call others to serve him. A magistrate must be the keeper of both tables himself, and cause others to do it; he must lay down his crown at the feet of Christ, as it is in Isaiah xlix. 7. Thus David was a nursing father to the church of God; he served God in his particular calling.

Now, to make use of another division, the will of God it is either in things to be done or to be suffered; and obedience answerable to that is either active or passive; as David 'served' God in doing, so he yielded obedience, and 'served the will of God' in his passive obedience; wherein he did deny himself exceedingly, as much as ever man did, next to Christ. You see how he denied himself in his carriage toward Saul, 1 Sam. xxiv.: in matter of revenge, how he overcame himself, because he knew that revenge was God's, and that God was his, and therefore would right him well enough. And in Shimei, 'God hath bid him rail.' He would not revenge. And other notable examples we have, how he submitted to God's will, as in 1 Sam. xxx. 6, when he was in extremity, he encouraged himself in the Lord his God. There he stayed himself in extremity; and in 2 Sam. xv. 25, there is a notable place how he submitted himself to God. 'The king said, Carry back the ark of God: if I have found favour in the eyes of God, he will bring me again; but if God say thus, I have no delight in him, behold here I am, let him do as seems good to him.' Here was a resignation of himself to the will of himself* in serving of him. So in Ps. xxxix. 1, 'I held my tongue, Lord, because thou didst it.' Thus you see how he 'served' the will of God, in the inward service of God, and in the outward to God and man; in both callings, as a good man, and a good governor, in his family; every way he 'served' the will of God.

Use. And wherefore is all this? Here is a pattern for us that we should serve the will of God: to serve the will of God immediately, to labour to bring our hearts to trust in him; to fear him above all; to delight in him above all; and to express it in our outward service of him, and in doing duties to men from inward respect to God; in conscience of our duty, to serve God when we serve men: to carry ourselves in our general calling, as Christians, and in our particular place, not only to be good men, but good in our callings; good students, good lawyers, &c. Let us shew our religion there, as David did. This is to serve the will of God. That is not religion that is left behind in the church: as Lactantius saith, that is no religion that we leave behind when we come to the church door (*f*). But that is religion when we learn our duty here, and carry it in our breasts to practise it every day in the week; when we shew it in our places. That is the service of God. Therefore let this holy man be an example to us. Wherefore are these particular things recorded of him in the Scriptures, but that we should transform ourselves to this blessed pattern.

The whole life of a Christian we see is a service of God. There is nothing that we do but it may be a 'service' of God. No. Not our particular recreations, if we use them as we should; as whettings to be fitter for our callings, and enjoy them as liberties, with thankfulness to God, that allows us these liberties to refresh ourselves. There is no passage of a man's life, but it may have the respect of a service of God. It is not the matter or stuff, but the stamp, that makes the coin; so it is not the work, but the stamp, that makes it 'a service,' when we do it with an eye to God. Let the king set a stamp but upon brass, upon a token, yet it will go for current if it have the king's authority and stamp upon it. Let it be but an action of our callings, suppose to give counsel in our studies or pleading of the law, &c., if it have God's stamp upon it; if there be prayer upon it to bless it, and it be done in obedience to God, and with justice; not against the rules of piety and charity, and as far as it may displease God, to baulk and avoid all temptations in our callings out of religious respects, it is a 'service' of God. Our whole life, not only in the church, but in our particular places, may be a 'service of God;' as it is said here, 'David served God.'

Oh, if we could think of this wheresoever we are, we would take no liberty to offend God in anything. We would not thrust religion into a corner, into a narrow room, and limit it to some days, and times, and actions, and places, and then take liberty to defraud and dissemble, to abuse ourselves this way and that way. Is this to serve God? To 'serve' God is to carry ourselves as the children of God wheresoever we are: so that our whole life is a service of God.

A Christian is no libertine, no man of freedom. He is a servant. Indeed, we have changed our master. We are set at liberty from the slavery of sin and Satan; but it is not that we should do nothing, to be Belials without yoke; but it is to serve God. We are taken from the service of Satan to be the Lord's freemen; and indeed it is to that end. We are

* Qu. 'God'?—Ed.

delivered that we might serve God, Luke i. 74. Therefore all the actions of our life should be a 'service' to God.

Quest. To make this a little clearer: How can this be, will some man think, that every common action should be a service of God?

Ans. I will make it clear by an instance. The beasts and other creatures and we have common actions, such as we do in common, as to eat, and to drink, and to move. The beast doth this, and man doth it. When a man doth them, they are reasonable actions, because they are guided with reason, and moderated by reason; but when the beast doth them, they are the actions of a beast, because he hath no better faculty to guide him. So common actions, they are not a service of God, as they come from common men, that have not grace and the Spirit of God in their hearts; they are mere buying and selling, and going about the actions of their callings, as the actions, of a beast are the actions of a beast. But let a Christian come to do them, he hath a higher life and a higher spirit that makes them spiritual actions that are common in themselves. He raiseth them to a higher order and rank. Therefore a Christian 'serveth God.' In all that he doth he hath an eye to God: that which another man doth with no eye to God, but merely in civil respects. We say of policy, it is an ancient observation, which is good and very fit. The knowledge of a commonwealth, it is a building knowledge, a commanding knowledge; for though a statesman doth not build, he doth not buy and sell and commerce; but he useth all other trades for the good of the state. It is a knowledge commanding all other inferior arts and trades, in a commonwealth, to the last end. They should all be serviceable to the commonwealth, and if they be not, away with them. So religion, and the knowledge of divine things, it is a commanding knowledge; it commands all other services in our callings, &c. It doth not teach a man what he shall do in particular in his calling; but it teacheth him how to direct that calling to 'serve God,' to be advantageous and helpful to his general calling; to further him to heaven, to make everything reductive to his last end, which he sets before him; that is, to honour and serve God in all things, to whom he desires to approve himself in life and death. He hath a principle, the Holy Ghost in him, and he labours to reduce everything to the main end. Oh that we were in this temper!

And as we must labour to imitate holy David in doing, so likewise in suffering. We must be careful that nothing of God's displease us, as we are careful, for ourselves, that nothing of ours displease God. In doing, we ought to be careful that nothing of ours displease God; in suffering, that nothing of God's dealing displease us; for there is rebellion in both, in passive obedience as well as active. There is rebellion when we murmur and will not be as God will have us, as if we were wiser than he, to appoint our own condition. Whereas we should resign ourselves, as David, 'Here I am; let the Lord do as it pleaseth him;' and as they said in the Acts, xxi. 14, 'The will of the Lord be done;' and as we pray in the Lord's prayer, 'Thy will be done,' insinuating not our own. We must be content to stoop in our sufferings obediently to God, because he is 'righteous in all his ways, and holy in all his works,' Ps. cxlv. 17, in all the courses he takes with us. We should be ready to justify God in all things.

Now, how did he 'serve God,' for the manner of his service? The manner of his service was as it should be, and so he was exemplary to us all in that. Amongst others, his service was,

1. First, *Universal*, to God and to men every way.

2. Secondly, *It was uniform.* He was good in all conditions, a good shepherd, a good king, he was good in his family, &c. So the service of the children and servants of God, it must be uniform in all estates, 'to know how to want, and how to abound,' &c.,

3. And then his service was *cheerful.* We see how oft he rouseth up himself in the Psalms: 'Awake; my harp and lute,' &c.,

4. And lastly, His service *was sincere.* It was to God. You may know his sincerity by this:

(1.) *He cared not for scoffings;* he practised duties that were scorned at. That is an evidence of sincerity, when in ill times the children of God stand to God and religion. When Michal mocked him, saith he, 'I will be yet more vile for God,' 2 Sam. vi. 22. When God may have glory, and religion defence, for men to stand for God in ill times, it is a sign of sincerity. An hypocrite will never do so. David did at all times, 'in his generation.'

(2.) And then it was a sign of sincerity, *that he would appeal to God.* 'Try me, Lord, if there be any way of wickedness in me,' Ps. cxxxix. 23. When a soul can go to God, and say, Lord, if there be any way of wickedness in me, any secret lurking corruption in me, that may endanger the state of my soul, that I know not of, discover it to me: that is a sign that a man is in league with no sin, but his service is sincere.

(3.) A man that is not sincere *hath no comfort.* So much sincerity, so much comfort. If a man do not things to God in sincerity, all is lost to God. A man may have commendations of the world, as the Pharisees had, which is nothing but a kind of curse: 'You have your reward,' Mat. vi. 2; that is, you have it here, and shall lose it hereafter. So much concerning the life of David, in those words, 'David in his generation served the counsel or will of God.' Now, to make a perfect discourse of it, we will speak something of his end.

'He fell asleep, and was gathered to his fathers, and saw corruption.'

'He fell asleep,' that is, he died; for sleep, in Scripture, it is a middle phrase, appliable to good and bad; for wicked men, in Scripture, are said to sleep, and good men are said to sleep. Only the difference is, as the persons are; for the sleep of wicked men it is like the sleep of a malefactor before his execution, that is ofttimes tripped in his sleep; or like the sleep of a man in sickness, or in a mad fit. His sleep doth but concoct the malignant humour, and after he wakes, he rageth three times more than he did before. So the sleep, the death of a carnal, wicked man, it is but a preparation to his execution; it is but the sleep of a distempered man that wakes with more horror, and terror, and rage, than ever before. Indeed, properly the death only of the godly is a sleep. But to observe something first briefly in general.

Obs. 1. *We see here is a time of dying as well as a time of living.*

There is a time to serve God in living, and there is a time to yield our souls to him, as well as a time to serve God in doing the actions and functions of this life.

Use 1. Which would teach us this, *not to fix our thoughts too much on life.* As there is a time for all things to the living, so there is a time to cease to live; and therefore to use the world with moderation, 'as though we used it not, knowing that the fashion of the world passeth away,' 1 Cor. vii. 31. It should teach us to serve God as well in living as in dying.

Use 2. And it should teach us *to do all the good we can while we have time.* David served God while he lived, and he served God in dying; because his death was in obedience. But, as I said before, after death properly there is no service of God, but a receiving of wages. Therefore let us serve God while we live, while we have time, because there is a time 'when night will come,' the night of sickness and of death, 'and then no man can work,' John ix. 4, if he would never so fain.

'He fell asleep.' Why did he not die before? He served God a great while; he did not die when he was first a good man.

Obs. 2. *God will have his children serve out their generation.*

(1.) *They must serve out their time.* As soon as ever we believe we have right to heaven, but God will have us bear the burden of the day awhile, *to bring others to heaven with us,* to go before others in the example of a godly life, to gain as many as we can.

(2.) *To try the truth of our graces before we come to heaven,* whether they be true or no, that they may be true, tried graces.

(3.) And he will have us *perfect* before we come to so holy a place. He will have us 'grow in grace,' as Ahasuerus his wives were to be perfumed and prepared before they came to him. It is a holy place that we hope for, a holy condition; therefore he will have us by little and little be fitted by the Spirit of God. Many such reasons there be why God in heavenly wisdom will have us go on here a time before we come to heaven, though as soon as we believe we are in the state of salvation; as Christ said to Zaccheus, '*This day* is salvation come to thine house,' Luke xix. 9.

Use. Therefore let us not repine that God will have us live. Indeed, as soon as a Christian hath faith, he hath life in patience and death in desire; for he is impatient to want his crown. Oh, but here is the time of service; and when he considers the eternity of the reward he shall have after, he will be glad to serve God, and he will be ashamed that he can do it no more. When he knows he shall have an 'eternal weight of glory,' 2 Cor. iv. 17, for a little service, then he will deny his lusts and pleasures to serve God in the place he lives in, whether he be magistrate or minister whatsoever, to undergo the burden of a little service.

Again, In that it is said here, '*then* he fell asleep,' not before, till he had served the counsel of God.

Obs. 3. *God hath allotted a man a time.*

He hath set him a glass that must be run, he hath given him a part to act, and he cannot be taken away till that be done. He can never fall asleep till he have served the counsel of God. As it is said in the gospel concerning our Saviour Christ, 'his hour was not yet come,' John vii. 30. They have laid wait for him, but his hour was not come. So there may be many snares laid for the children of God by Satan and his instruments, but till their hour be come, all the devils in hell, nor all the devil's instruments on earth, cannot shorten a man's life one minute of an hour; for he shall fall asleep when he hath served the counsel of God, when he hath done all that God will have him to do.

Use. Therefore it is ground of resolution, *let us go on in our places and callings, undauntedly and wisely too;* not to tempt God, to rush into dangers; but, I mean, without base fear and distrust; for we must serve God to-day and to-morrow, and then we shall be sanctified. We must serve God the appointed time that he will have us to live here; and then we shall 'fall asleep,' and not before. No creature hath power over the life of man to shorten his days.

Obs. 4. The next thing we will observe from the nature of sleep is, that

The death of the godly is a sleep, in respect of refreshing.

Sleep doth refresh and repair, and as it were recreate and make a man anew. Sleep and rest it is the blessed ordinance of God, it is an excellent thing to repair men; so after death nature shall be repaired better, we shall rise fresher; as it is Ps. xvii. 15, 'When I arise, I shall be satisfied with thine image.' We shall rise refreshed, better than we lay down. So that as we go to bed then, to sleep, to cut off all cares, so when we rest in death, all cares, and fears, and terrors, all annoyances, are cut off.

(1.) 'Blessed are the dead that die in the Lord: *they rest from their labours*,' Rev. xiv. 13; insinuating that there is no rest before. For to a man that knows that this world is a workhouse, and his life a service to God, he thinks of no rest till he be in his grave. So death it is a sleep in regard of that rest. We rest from the labour of sin, we rest from the wearisome labour of the body; from the labour of afflictions and oppressions, from the molestations of other men among whom we live. Every way this life is tedious, and death rest.

(2.) Again, It is in this respect a sleep; because a man goes to bed *with assured hope of rising again*, and therefore he goes quietly. Though it be a state of darkness for the time, all the senses are bound up, yet he knows that in God's ordinary providence he shall rise again. Therefore men not only quietly, but cheerfully, go to bed. So there is greater ground to know that we shall rise again out of our graves, than that we should rise out of our beds; for many men's beds have been their graves, in some sort; I mean, they have died in their beds. But for the resurrection, we have the word of Almighty God, that is a God of his word, that we shall rise again; and we have it in the pledge of our Saviour's resurrection. There is no doubt of that.

Therefore when we die, if we have faith, we should make no more of death than men do to go to bed; hoping undoubtedly of an assured and joyful resurrection. The want of faith in that kind makes us backward to this. You see in what respect death is said to be a 'sleep.' To speak only of those references and relations that are most pertinent between sleep and death.

(3.) David 'fell asleep,' and very willingly; for he had lived a painful life; he served God both as a private man, as a shepherd, and as a king; Eccles. v. 12, 'To a labouring man sleep is sweet;' so to a man that hath served God carefully in his calling, and kept a good conscience, death is very sweet. We see children that have been playing all day, they are loath to go to bed; but to a man that hath wrought all day, 'sleep is sweet,' as wise Solomon saith, 'to a labouring man.'

Use. Would we, then, have death as a sweet rest? Let us do as David did; that is, be painful,* and laborious in our particular place and in our general calling; let us be faithful in them to keep a good conscience, and set all in order as much as we can while we live; to leave no seeds of debate when we are gone. Some men die carelessly this way in disposing the good things that God hath given them. They lay a foundation of perpetual jarring afterward; and so their death is scarcely a 'sleep and rest.' They cannot but be disquieted when they think how they leave things, because they were not wise beforehand. David settled Solomon in his throne, and set all things right before he died; and that made him die, not only in rest but in honour; in 1 Chron. xxix. 28, 'David died in a good old age, full of riches and honour.'

* That is, 'pains-taking.'—G.

And let us labour to get assurance of a change for the better. David his flesh rested in hope, because he believed in Christ, that Christ's body should see no corruption, Ps. xvi. 10. So if we would have death sweet as a sleep, let us labour to get assurance by faith in Christ, and so our flesh may rest in hope, that as Christ raised his own flesh, so he will raise ours. Good Simeon, when he had seen Christ once, 'Lord, now let thy servant depart in peace,' &c., Luke ii. 29. So after we have gotten a sight of Christ to be our Christ, our Saviour and Redeemer, and have interest in him, 'Lord, now let thy servant depart in peace.' So much for the term seep.

It is added besides, that

'He was gathered to his fathers.'

'He was gathered to his fathers' both in regard of his body, and in regard of his soul; for his body went to the house of the dead, the grave, and his soul went to his fathers, to heaven. As I said before of sleep, so of this. It is a phrase of Scripture that must be understood as the persons are. When a man dies, his body goes to the place or house of all men, the house of darkness, the grave; but for his soul, that goes as the man is, to his fathers, to hell, if he be naught; to the souls of just and perfect men, as the apostle speaks, if he have lived a gracious and a good life; and so it must be understood here, because he speaks of a blessed man.

'He was put to his fathers.' He means not to his immediate fathers, but all believing men before him that were the children of Abraham. His soul went to them; his body to the first mother, the earth, out of which it was taken. So the general is nothing but this, that

Obs. 5. *When we die we are put to our fathers.*

Therefore this should moderate our fear of death, and our grief for the departure of others. Why? We are not lost when we die. The soul and body is taken asunder, it is taken in pieces, but both remain still. The body goes to the earth from whence it was taken, and the soul goes to God that gave it. And for our comfort, we go to those that we knew before, many of them; to our fathers, not to strangers. Especially in respect of our souls we go to our fathers, to our next forefathers and to our old fathers: to Abraham, Isaac, to Jacob, to David, to blessed Saint Paul and Peter, and all the blessed men that died in the faith. And when we are dead, we go to those that are more perfect than those that we leave behind us. This should moderate our grief. Oh, I leave my friends behind me, my father, and mother, and children! It is to go to better, to greater, and those that love thee better. Thou goest to greater, for they are in their pitch; they have attained their end, they are in heaven; and to better, they are refined from those corruptions that men here are subject unto, and then their love is perfect likewise. Therefore going to our fathers and not to strangers, to those that are better and greater, and love us more perfectly, why should we think much to die? They will be ready to entertain us. Oh the welcome that souls find in heaven! and at the day of the resurrection the sweet embracings, when all the blessed souls that have been from Adam to the last man shall meet together! Seeing therefore we go to our fathers, it should rather make us cheerful. Here, whom do we live with? Take them at the best, our friends. Men, subject to jealousies and weaknesses. Our jealousy makes us suspect them, and their weakness makes us think the meaner of them. So our love is not perfect, nor our graces are not perfect. Therefore we cannot have perfect love and contentment while we are here. But in heaven there shall be no jealousy, nor fear, nor imperfection, which is the ground of jealousy. We shall perfectly love them because they shall be perfectly good; and they shall perfectly love us because we shall be perfectly good; and one shall stand admiring the graces of God in another, and that will maintain a perpetuity of love. Therefore it is want of faith that makes us unwilling to yield our souls unto God at the point of death. It is a going to our fathers.

But then we must take heed what fathers we imitate here, Heb. xiii. 7. Take heed who are our patterns while we live; for if we do not imitate them here, we cannot live with them in heaven when we are dead. Therefore it is a very necessary item in Heb. xiii. 7, 'Look to them that rule over you, that speak the word; whose faith follow, considering the end of their labour.' Let us look before what kind of men those have been that we desire to live with in heaven, and mark the end of their conversation; for such as we delight in, and frame our carriage to here, such we shall live with hereafter. We must not think to live with Nero, and die with Paul; to live Epicures, and die Christians; to live dissembling and falsely in our places, and to die comfortably, and to go to the blessed souls at the hour of death, and at the resurrection. No. God will gather our souls with wicked men, if we fashion our carriage to wicked men. Such as we delight in, and live with, and set as patterns before us, with such we shall live for ever hereafter. 'He was gathered to his fathers.'

One sign of a man that shall be gathered to believing fathers, to his good forefathers, besides imitation, is this, to delight in the congregations of just men here. A man may know he shall go to the congregation of perfect souls in heaven, if he delight in the congregations of God's saints here; for surely he that hath a confidence to be in the proper heaven, heaven that is so blessed, he will have a care while he lives, as much as he can, to be and delight in the heaven upon earth. Now the chief heaven upon earth is the church of God. 'O how amiable is thy dwelling-place, O Lord,' Ps. lxxxiv. 1, where many souls meet together to join in speaking to God, and in hearing God speak to them. Those therefore that delight not in the congregations, that delight not in the service of God, what hope have they to be gathered to the congregation of the faithful when they are gone. So much for that, 'He was gathered to his fathers.'

'And he saw corruption.'

It is an Hebraism for 'he felt corruption,' 'he had experience of corruption.' All other senses are attributed to sight. That being the principal of all the senses, they have their term from it, because sight is the most excellent, the most capacious and quick sense. Therefore, I say, the actions of all the other senses are attributed to it, as we say, see how he speaks, and so here, 'he saw corruption,' that is, he had experience of it; because sight is a convincing sense. He could not properly see when he was dead: but the meaning is, he had experience of 'corruption.' The truth is this, in a word, that,

Obs. 6. *The best and greatest men in the world, when they are gone, they are subject to corruption.*

David was a king and a prophet, 'a man after God's own heart.' Yet this could not keep David's body from corruption.

Reason 1. The reason is, *we are but dead men here.* This is not the life that Christ hath purchased for us. We are going to death. Our natural life is but *cursus ad mortem*, a continual going to death. We are alive now, but, alas! our life is nothing but a continual dying; every day cuts off a part of our life. It is a statute that all must die.

Reason 2. And it *is our perfection to die*. We cannot otherwise see God and enjoy our crown. Death indeed is nothing but misery. But when we die we go to live. The best must 'see corruption.'

Use 1. Therefore this should be an argument *to support the soul;* when we think of the rottenness in the grave, and of that place, and time of horror, when we shall be no more here upon earth. It is no otherwise with us than it hath been with the best in the world. They all saw 'corruption' in their time.

Use 2. Again, considering we have but corruptible bodies here, bodies that must see corruption; *let us take care for the better part*. He is a madman, that having two houses, one free-hold, the other a rotten tenement, ready to fall about his ears, that shall take delight in that and neglect his own inheritance, which is a goodly thing. It is for want of wit; and it is as much want of grace, when we, having a double life, the life of grace, that ends in glory, the life of the soul, the life of God, as St Paul saith; and then the life of the body, which is communicated from the soul to the body, which is corruptible;—our bodies are but 'tabernacles of clay, whose foundation is in the dust,'—for us to take care of this vile body, as the apostle calls it, Philip. iii. 21, 'Who shall change our vile body, and make it like to his glorious body, according to his mighty power;' to take care of this vile body and to neglect our precious souls. It is the care of most (such is the carnal breeding of men, and they follow those that bred them in this brutishness, as if they had no souls; as if there were no life after this), their care is, 'what they shall eat, and what they shall drink, and put on,' Mat. vi. 25; what to commend themselves by in the outward man to the view of others; all their care is for their outward man. Alas! what is it but a corruptible vile body? It is but the case of the soul. They forget the jewel and look all to the casket, which is a base body, take it at the best while we are here.

Use 3. And take heed *we be not ensnared with the bodies of others*. This is the 'corruption' of men, to gaze in this kind. You see wise Solomon and others were much troubled with temptations in this kind. Consider that body that thou doatest on now, and which is made by the devil a snare to thee, what will it be ere long? So noisome that thou wilt not endure the presence of it. It is but a flower, and it is fading, fresh in the morning and dead at night. All flesh is but grass. It is a corruptible body. If thou wilt needs love, be acquainted with such as have excellent spirits that shall live eternally. Oh, there is an object of love indeed! That is the true love and acquaintance that is spiritual. Many things may be lovely in the outward person, but see that there be a heavenly spirit, that is mounting up, that savours of good things; a spirit that hath life begun in it, that shall be for ever happy in heaven. Unless there be this, there cannot be a fit ground for the love of any wise man.

To end all, you see here a short story of a good life and a blessed death. Let us make this blessed man of God exemplary to us in both. Let our whole life be nothing but a service of God, and let us consider the generation wherein we are to take and do all the good we can in our time. And then consider what death will be. When we come to die, it will be a sweet sleep to us, and our resurrection will be a refreshing. 'Our flesh shall rest in hope,' as David saith, 'we shall be gathered to our fathers;' we shall 'see corruption,' indeed. But mark what David saith, Ps. xvi. 9, 10,

'My flesh shall rest in hope, *because* thou wilt not suffer thy holy one to *see* corruption.' Then this is the upshot of all. Though we 'see corruption' when we are dead; yet, with the eye of faith, we see a rising again from 'corruption.' We see death but as a pot to refine us in. Even as it is with silver, when there is much corruption and heterogeneal matter mingled with it, the fire refines it, but it is not lost. So the grave refines the body, and fits it for a glorious resurrection. 'The flesh rests in hope' all the while, though the body see corruption. Because our head saw no corruption. If the head be above water, what if the body be down? Our head saw no corruption; that is, Christ, for he rose out of the grave before his body was putrified; for his body had a subsistence, and was gloriously united to the second person in Trinity; and, being united to the Lord of life, it saw no corruption. For that did not lie upon Christ as our Saviour to be corrupt, but to die, 'to be made a curse for us,' Gal. iii. 13, and then especially, I say, by reason of the near union of it to the God of life.

Well, then, what is David's argument of comfort? In Ps. xvi. 9, 10, 'My flesh shall rest in hope; because thou wilt not suffer thine holy one to see corruption.' Because Christ rose from the grave himself, the holy one of God, our flesh may rest in hope, though we see corruption. Because the same divine power that raised Christ our head out of the grave, that his body saw no corruption, will raise our bodies to be like his glorious body. Our blessed Saviour, that overcame death in his own person, by his power he will overcome death for all his mystical body, that is, his church. It shall be perfect in heaven, soul and body together, as he himself is glorious now in heaven. That we may say with David, notwithstanding our bodies see corruption, as his did, yet our flesh shall rest in hope, because God's holy one saw no corruption.

NOTES.

(*a*) P. 490.—'This I observe from the very language or phrase.' The phrase is, ὑπηρετήσας τῇ τοῦ Θεοῦ βουλῇ = having served the counsel of God, as Sibbes suggests. Cf. ver. 22.

(*b*) P. 492.—'"David in his generation served the will, or counsel, of God," as the word is.' See note *a* above.

(*c*) P. 493.—'Man, take him in his nature, is like a tree. The poet could say to that purpose.' This comparison is frequent in the Classics and in all languages. By *the* poet is probably intended Homer, and the reference to the famous passage Il. ζ 146—

Τυδείδη μεγάθυμε, τίη γενεὴν ἐρεείνεις;
Οἵη περ φύλλων γενεὴ, τοιήδε καὶ ἀνδρῶν·
Φύλλα τὰ μέν τ' ἄνεμος χαμάδις χέει, ἄλλα δέ θ' ὕλη
Τηλεθόωσα φύει, ἔαρος δ' ἐπιγίγνεται ὥρῃ·
Ὡς ἀνδρῶν γενεὴ, ἡ μὲν φύει, ἡ δ' ἀπολήγει.

Thus translated by Cowper:—

'Why asks Diomede of my descent?
For as the leaves, such is the race of men.
The wind shakes down the leaves, the budding grove
Soon teems with others, and in spring they grow.
So pass mankind. One generation meets
Its destined period, and a new succeeds.'

The Elizabethan poets furnish many splendid examples of the metaphor; *e.g.*, Ben Jonson, Massinger, and their compeers.

(*d*) P. 495.—'In regard of the ills, we may say with Saint Austin, "Lord, to what times are we reserved."' One of his lamentations during his passionate controversies with the Donatists, and when Hippo was besieged by the Vandals, during which calamity this illustrious father expired.

(*e*) P. 498.—'As the civil law saith, *infringit obedientiam*,' &c. Still a law-*maxim*.

(*f*) P. 507.—'As Lactantius saith, "that is no religion that we leave behind when we come to the church-door."' Cf. for the *thought*, his *De Falsa Religione* repeatedly. G.

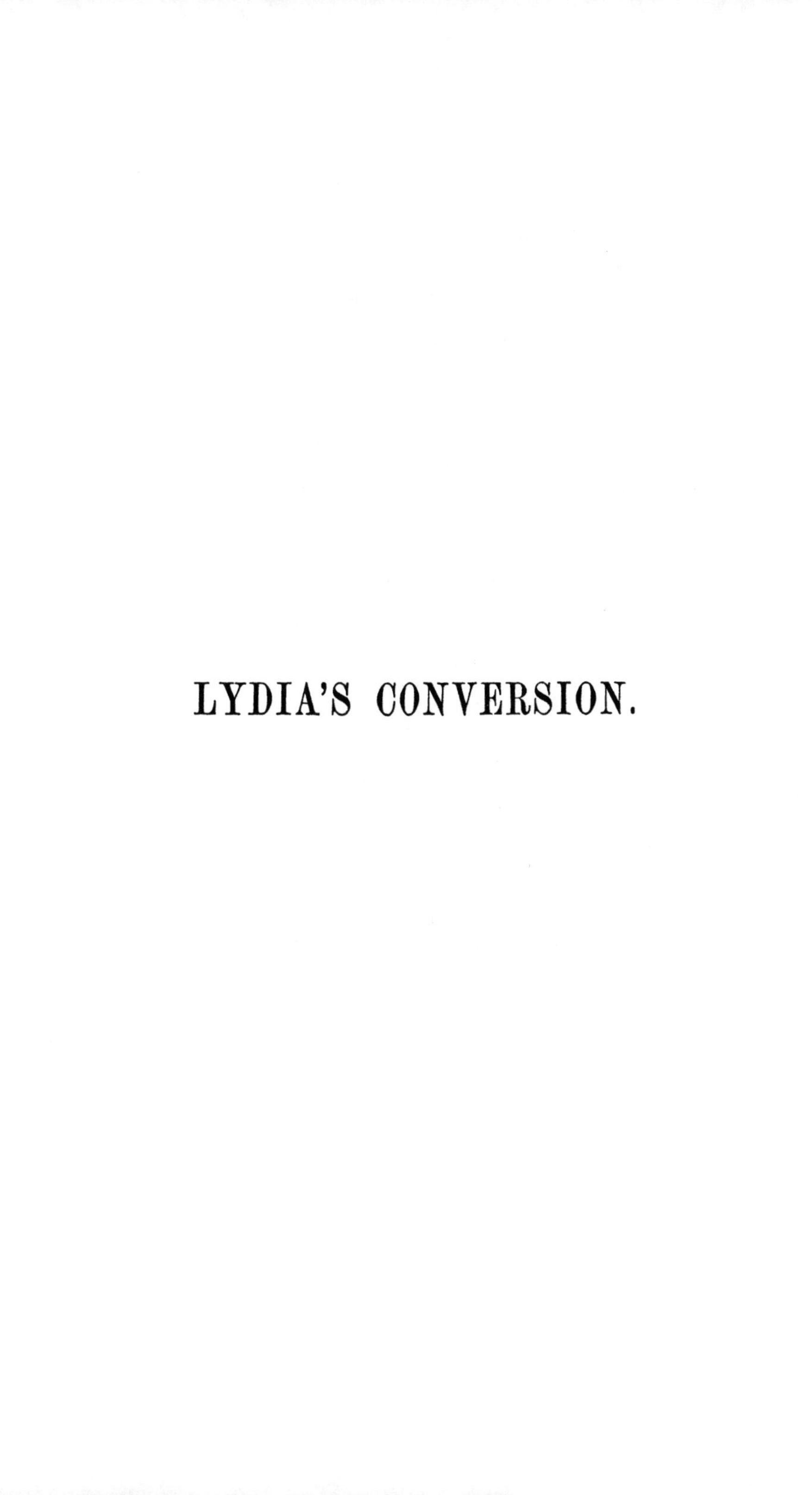

LYDIA'S CONVERSION.

LYDIA'S CONVERSION.

NOTE.

Lydia's Conversion' is the former of two short treatises published in a small volume (18mo) in 1638. The general title-page will be found below.* Prefixed is Marshall's miniature portrait of Sibbes. The 'Rescue from Death; or, Return of Praise,' will be found in its place in Vol. VII. This little volume is exceedingly uncommon. G.

* THE
RICHES
OF
MERCIE.
In two Treatises;
1. Lydia's *Conversion.*
2. *A Rescue from Death.*

By the late learned, and reverend
Divine, Richard Sibbs,
Doctor in Divinitie.

Published by the Authors owne
appointment, and subscribed
with his owne hand to prevent
imperfect Copies.

1 Sam. 2. 6.
The Lord killeth, and maketh alive;
hee bringeth downe to the Grave
and bringeth up.

London
Printed by I. D. for *Francis*
Eglesfeild, and are to be sold by
him at the signe of the Marigold in *Paul's* Church-
yard. 1638.

LYDIA'S CONVERSION.

And a certain woman, named Lydia, a seller of purple, of the city of Thyatira, that worshipped God, whose heart the Lord opened, that she attended to the things that were spoken of Paul. And when, &c.—Acts XVI. 14, 15.

The holy apostle, St Paul, a vessel of mercy, having found mercy himself of God, was a fit instrument to preach mercy to others.

Hereupon he was appointed to be a preacher to the Gentiles. Among the rest of the Gentiles, he was called to preach to them of Macedonia, and it was by a vision, as we see in the former part of the chapter. Verse 9: 'A man of Macedonia,' appeared to Paul by night, and said, 'Come to Macedonia and help us.' Indeed, the state of the people of Macedonia called for help; as now the state of many people doth. Though there be not such a vision as a man of Macedonia, yet their wretched estate, being under the kingdom of Satan, cries, 'Come and help us.' Though they do not cry with their mouths, yet their estate cries. The apostle upon this vision, takes his journey to come toward Macedonia; and he stayed there a good while; 'he abode certain days.'

Though God called him to Macedonia, yet God did not give him great encouragement for the present. This is the manner of God's carriage, not to discover at the present what he will do, but leads people on by gentle encouragements; and to humble them the more with little fruit at the first. He 'abode there certain days,' without any great fruit. Afterwards he goes out to Philippi, the chief city of Macedonia; and on the Sabbath day the people were gathered together, a company of women were resorted together, and there he preached to them. As indeed holy communion is never without a blessing. They met together on a good day, the Sabbath; and for a good end they were met together. Now Paul took the advantage of their meeting together on the Sabbath day. He cast his net, and he catcheth one with her family, namely, Lydia. The gospel was a sweet savour of salvation to her.

Hereupon there is a discourse of Lydia, a short story of Lydia, a story worthy to be thought of, which is in the words of my text.

'A certain woman named Lydia,' &c.

She is described, first, by her person and sex, 'a certain woman;' by her name, 'Lydia;' by her calling, 'a seller of purple;' by her city,

'Thyatira;' by her pious disposition, 'she worshipped God.' And then her conversion is set down by the cause of it: 'God opened her heart.' And what followed upon that opening of her heart: 'she attended to the things that were spoken by Paul;' and likewise, 'she was baptized with all her household. And then the sweet fruit that this conversion of her with all her household had, presently she shewed the love that she felt from God in converting her, to the blessed apostle and his company, 'She besought them, saying, If ye have judged me faithful to the Lord, come to my house,' &c., which words I shall unfold as I come to them.

'And a certain woman named Lydia, a seller of purple,' &c.

First, here is a description of her person, and sex, and name, and calling, and city, and disposition.

God takes notice of all the particulars of those that are his. He delights to speak of them. Those that have their names written in the book of life, he knows their names, and callings, and persons. They are jewels in his eyes. They are 'written on the palms of his hands,' Isa. xlix. 16. He takes more special notice of them than of the rest of the world. Therefore the apostle is very punctual in the description of all particulars.

For her person I will be very short. I will give but a note or two, and so come to that I mainly aim at, her conversion.

'A certain woman named Lydia.'

For her sex, she and the rest were women that were gathered together, as we see in the former verse. 'In Christ Jesus there is neither male nor female,' Gal. iii. 28. Sin came in by a woman; and the means of salvation was by a woman too. Here were a company of women gathered together.

For the most part women have sweet affections to religion, and therein they oft go beyond men.

Reason 1. The reason is, religion is especially seated in the affections; and they have sweet and strong affections.

Reason 2. Likewise they are subject to weakness, and God delights to shew his 'strength in weakness.'

Reason 3. And thirdly, Especially child-bearing women, bring others into this life with danger of their own; therefore they are forced to a nearer communion with God, because so many children as they bring forth, they are in peril of their lives. Therefore the apostle here mentions a company of women that were gathered together, and among the rest, a 'certain woman named Lydia.'

What! a woman to be the foundation of the church of Macedonia; a poor woman! and then a jailor afterward, a rugged, rough jailor! For these to be the foundation of so famous a church as Philippi, and other churches in Macedonia! Oh yes! The kingdom of heaven is as 'a grain of mustard seed,' Mat. xiii. 31, small in the beginning. It is so in regard of the church itself; and in regard of the grace that every particular member hath. It is little and weak beginnings. Christians are not as the angels were, perfect at the first. The church grows by little and little. Therefore we should not be discouraged when the plantation of the gospel hath poor success at the beginning, We see in the church of Macedonia there was little success at the first. A woman and a rough jailor; a jailor that both by calling, and disposition, and custom, was a man hard and hardened too. Yet these two were the foundation of a great church.

Was it not so strange ourselves? The church of later times, in the time of reformation, how began it? By a child and a woman; King Edward the sixth, and Queen Elizabeth of famous memory. Therefore as the prophet saith, 'Who art thou that despisest the day of little things?' Zech. iv. 10. Despise not little things. There is nothing less than grace at the first. But as Christ the stock of Jesse, rose from the dead, and rose up to heaven, and overspreads the world now; so every Christian riseth of mean beginnings; and so doth the church itself. 'A certain woman named Lydia.' She was the foundation of a famous church.

Then she is set down by her calling.

'A seller of purple.'

God allows callings.

The calling of Christianity is shewed in particular callings, which are sanctified by God to subdue the excess of corruptions. Men without callings are exceedingly vicious, as some gentlemen and beggars. In this I may rank them together. Those that have no callings, nor fit themselves for a calling, and that are out of a calling lawful.

Callings are lawful; and so this calling of commerce and trade, 'a seller of purple.' Though for the most part men gather a great deal of soil and corruption, by co-mixture of manners with those they deal with, yet there must be commerce, and this particular commerce of 'selling of purple.'

The body of man needs many callings. There is not a part of man's body, not one member, but it sets a particular calling on work. Therefore this life is a life of many necessities; and there must be callings and trading, and this particular trading, 'selling of purple.' It may seem superfluous, but it is not altogether; for garments are for three ends:

For necessity, ornament, distinction.

Now purple, however it be not for necessity, it is for ornament and distinction; for magistrates and the like, persons of great quality. However the pride of the times hath bred a confusion, that one will go as well as another; yet God that allows distinctions of callings and persons, allows distinction of habit and attire. Therefore selling of purple is lawful, and the wearing of rich attire. 'Kings' daughters' went in such, as it is said of David's daughters,

So there be not over-much delicacy; for delicacy in this in these times is fatal, as there be many in the city and in the countries that are given to over-much nicety and sumptuousness in this kind. It is a fore-runner of ruin.

Otherwise it is lawful, for those that may, to wear purple, as it is lawful to sell purple. So that, as he said to the great emperor (*a*), they do not consider the purple, so much as that the purple covers dust and base flesh, that must turn to dust and ashes and rottenness ere long; so that people be not lift up in that that is borrowed from the poor creature, from worms. It is a strange thing that men should be so sick in their fancy, as to think themselves the better for that they beg of the poor creature. So a man take heed of fancy and pride, it is lawful to use purple. 'She was a seller of purple.' So much for her calling.

'She worshipped God.'

She was perhaps a Jew, and looked for a Messiah. There were three sorts of people before Christ. The Jews, and those which we call proselytes, and religious persons fearing God. She might be one of tho three;

it is not certain what she was. Certainly she was one that feared God. She had some religion in her. Though yet she was not ripened in the true religion, she was a woman that 'feared God.'

From such kind of places as this, we have occasion to speak of works of preparation. St Paul was sent to her; she was a woman that feared God. To speak a little of works of preparation.

It is true God usually prepares those that he means to convert, as we plough before we sow. We do not sow among the thorns; and we dig deep to lay a foundation; we purge before cordials. It is usual in nature and in grace preparations; therefore preparations are necessary. There is such a distance between the nature and corruption of man and grace, that there must be a great deal of preparation, many degrees to rise by before a man come to that condition he should be in. Therefore preparations we allow, and the necessity of them.

But we allow this, that all preparations are from God. We cannot prepare ourselves, or deserve future things by our preparations; for the preparations themselves are of God.

And, thirdly, though we grant preparations, yet we grant no force of a meritorious cause in preparations to produce such an effect as conversion is. No. Only preparation is to remove the hindrances, and to fit the soul for conversion, that there may not be so great a distance between the soul and conversion as without preparation there would be.

Quest. But when is preparation sufficient?

Ans. When the soul is so far cast down as it sets a high price on Christ, and on grace, above all things in the world. It accounts grace the only pearl, and the gospel to be the kingdom of heaven. When a man sets a high price on grace more than all the world besides, then a man is sufficiently prepared.

Some poor souls think they are never prepared enough; but let them look to the end that God will have preparation for, that is, that a high price be set upon the best things, and value all things but grace meanly in their own rank. When a man is brought to that pitch that by the light of the Spirit he esteems all nothing but Christ, and that he must be had, and he must have saving grace, let him never talk whether he be prepared or no. This disposition shews that he is prepared enough, at least to bring him to conversion.

Now, God in preparation for the most part civiliseth people, and then Christianiseth them, as I may say; for the Spirit of God will not be effectual in a rude, wild, and barbarous soul; in men that are not men. Therefore they must be brought to civility; and not only to civility, but there must be a work of the law, to cast them down; and then they are brought to Christianity thereupon.

Therefore they take a good course that labour to break them from their natural rudeness and fierceness; as by nature every man is like 'a wild ass colt.' There cannot be more significant words, 'a colt, an ass colt, and wild,' Job xi. 12. Now, there is no sowing in the sand or on the water. There is no forcing of grace on a soul so far indisposed, that is, not brought to civility. Rude and barbarous souls therefore, God's manner is to bring them in the compass of civility, and then seeing what their estate is in the corruption of nature, to deject them, and then to bring them to Christianity, as we see here in Lydia.

For however there is no force of a meritorious cause in preparations to grace, to raise up the soul to grace; for, alas! that cannot be. It is not in it to produce such a blessed effect. Yet notwithstanding it brings a man to a less distance than other wild creatures that come not within the compass of the means. Therefore usually to those that use the talents of their understanding and will, that they have, well, God after discovers himself more and more.

Therefore let all be encouraged to grow more and more to courses of civility and religion, and wait the good time till God shine on them in mercy. For though those courses can never produce religion, yet it brings men to a proximity and nearness to God and Christ, more than those that stand further off. But I will not force this point further at this time. 'She was a woman that feared and worshipped God.' She was faithful in that light she had; 'and to him that hath shall be given,' Mat. xiii. 12.

'She worshipped God.'

Not in any sight of her own. She had the grace of God from the Spirit of God. All fear comes from the Spirit of God, initial fear and ripened fear; all fear is from God, But I will not conflict with adversaries at this time. You see the person, a woman; her calling, 'a seller of purple;' and her pious disposition, she was such a one 'as worshipped God,' 'and she heard Paul.'

The sweet providence of God brings those that belong to election under the compass of the means at one time or other. Let the devil, and the instruments of the devil, rage and oppose, and do what they can, those that belong to God, God will have a time to bring them within the compass of his calling, and effectually call them by his Spirit. As here Lydia, there was a sweet preventing* providence that she never thought of. God brought an apostle for the salvation of her soul. She heard Paul, and was converted. To come to the description of her conversion in the next words.

'Whose heart the Lord opened to attend to the things that were spoken of Paul.'

God opened her heart. To what purpose? 'To attend to the things spoken of Paul.'

'God, by the word preached,' opens the hearts to attend to the word. By the word we are fitted to the word. The Spirit and the word draw us to themselves; the Spirit and the word draw us to regard the word; by the word her heart was opened to attend to the word.

First, I will speak *of the opening her heart.* And then of her attending upon the word preached by Paul, 'God opened her heart.' She was a religious woman, yet her heart was shut before God opened it. She was religious in her kind, yet her heart must be further opened before she could be saved. There is no staying in preparations in this or that degree, as many abortives in our times that make many offers. They have the Spirit of bondage, and are cast down; but there they stick, and never come to proof. But those that will attain to salvation must not rest in religious dispositions, in good affections, and gracious offers. They must go on further and further, as we see here: 'God opened her heart.'

Observe then in the opening of the heart these things.

1. First, *The heart is naturally shut and closed up,* as indeed it is to spiritual things. It is open enough to the world, and to base contentments here; but it is shut to heaven and heavenly things. Naturally it is clean locked up.

* That is, 'going before,' = anticipating.—G.

Partly in its own nature, being corrupt and earthly; partly because Satan he besiegeth all the senses, and shuts up all. There is a spirit of deafness and blindness, and a spirit of darkness and deafness in people, before God hath brought them by the powerful work of the gospel from the kingdom of Satan, that possesseth every man naturally. Naturally therefore our hearts are not open, but locked and shut up. That is supposed here. So that except God be merciful to break the prison, as it were, whereby by unbelief and the wickedness of our nature we are shut up, there is no hope of salvation at all. God opens the heart.

2. The second thing is this, that as our hearts are shut and closed up naturally, *so God, and God alone, opens the heart*, by his Spirit in the use of the means. God opened Lydia's heart.

God hath many keys. He hath the key of heaven to command the rain to come down. He hath the key of the womb; the key of hell and the grave; and the key of the heart especially. 'He opens, and no man shuts; and shuts and no man opens,' Rev. iii. 7. He hath the key of the heart to open the understanding, the memory, the will, and affections. God, and God only, hath the key of the heart to open that. It is his prerogative. He made the heart, and he only hath to do with the heart. He can unmake it, and make it new again, as those that make locks can do. And if the heart be in ill temper, he can take it in pieces, and bring it to nothing as it were, as it must be before conversion; and he can make it a new heart again. It is God that opens the heart, and God only. All the angels in heaven cannot give one grace, not the least grace. Grace comes merely* from God. It is merely from God. All the creatures in the world cannot open the heart, but God only by his Holy Spirit. For nature cannot do above its sphere, as we say, above its own power. Natural things can do but natural things. For nature to raise itself up to believe heavenly things, it cannot be. Therefore as you see vapours go as high as the sun draws them up, and no higher, so the soul of man is lift up to heavenly things by the power of God's Spirit. God draws us and then we follow. God, I say, only openeth the heart.

(1.) Because there is not only want of strength in the soul to open itself, but likewise there *is enmity and poison in the heart to shut itself, and shut out all goodness*. A man hath no senses to spiritual things, no eyes, no ears, no taste, no life. Nay,

(2.) *There is an opposition to all.* 'A natural man perceiveth not the things of God, neither can he,' 1 Cor. ii. 14. He wants senses, and those senses he hath are set against goodness, as the apostle saith, 'he esteemeth them foolishness.' I need not be much in so easy an argument, that you are well enough acquainted with. Naturally the heart is shut, and God only must open it.

Use. This should teach us patience, when we can do little good with those that are under us by all our instructions and corrections, wait the due time. Grace is not of thy giving. The heart is not of thy opening, or of any man's opening. Therefore as it is 2 Tim. ii. 23, *seq.*, wait and bear 'with patience men of contrary minds,' waiting when God in due time gives them grace to repent. Grace is God's creature. It is none of our own. Therefore take heed that we be not short and angry spirited. If we cannot have all we would have of those that are under us, children or servants, let us wait God's time. He opens the heart in his time.

And if we find not grace wrought in our own hearts at the first, or second,

* That is, 'altogether.'—G.

or third sermon, let us do as he at the Pool of Bethesda, lie there till the angel stir the water, till God be effectual by his Spirit. God doth it, and he only doth it, only we must wait. He will do it in his good time. Be not over short-spirited. This we ought to observe out of these words, 'God opened the heart of Lydia.'

The heart is put for the whole soul. He opened her understanding to conceive; for all things begin with heavenly light of the understanding. All grace comes into the soul by the understanding.

There is no sanctifying grace in the affections but it comes by enlightening the understanding. We see the grounds of it in the understanding first. God opens the understanding, and then he opens the memory to retain. That the memory may be as the pot of manna to hold heavenly things, he opens and strengthens it with retention to keep them, and he opens the will to close with holy things, and the affections to joy and delight in them. So the heart is the whole inward man. He not only enlightens the understanding, but infuseth grace into the will and affections, into the whole inward man. We must take it in that extent, for else if God should only open the understanding, and not through the understanding flow into the will by the power of his Spirit, the will would alway rebel, as indeed it is a poisonful thing. There is nothing so malicious, next the devil, as the will of man. God will have one way, and it will have another. Therefore God doth not only open the understanding to conceive, but he opens the will to close with and to embrace that that is good; or else it will take arms against the understanding in that that is good, and never come to the work of grace. Therefore take it so. He opened the will and affections as well as the understanding, though whatsoever is in the will and affections comes through the understanding, as well as heat comes through light. God opened her heart, to what end?

'To attend to the things that were spoken of Paul.'

The word signifies to apply and set her mind to the things that Paul said, to join and fasten the mind to what Paul said (*b*).

First, You see then, here *is the opening of the heart before there is attending*. Before there can be any attending and applying of the mind, the mind must be sanctified and strengthened. The soul must be sanctified before it can attend.

The reason is, nothing can flow but from a suitable faculty, and ability to attend is a power and act of the soul. It must come from a sanctified power of the soul. The heart must first be opened, and then the heart attends. God saith, he will circumcise the heart, and then we shall love him. He sanctifies the heart, and then it loves him. God changeth and altereth the frame of the soul, and then holy actions come from it. First, grace begins with the abilities and powers of the soul. The heart is opened, and then come holy actions suitable. There is no proportion between holy actions and an unsanctified soul. The heart must first be opened, and then it attends.

'Whose heart the Lord opened that she attended,' &c.

You see then, in the next place, that God opening the heart of any Christian, it is to carry the attention to the word. God by grace carries the heart to the word. 'She attended to what Paul spake.' Where true grace is wrought, it carries not to speculation, or to practise this or that idle dream; but where the heart is open, grace carries to attend to the word, especially to the good word, the gospel of Christ. As grace is wrought by the word, so it carries the soul to the word.

Use. And therefore it may be a use of trial, to know whether we have our hearts wrought on by the grace of God or no; whether God by his Spirit have opened our hearts or no, if our hearts be carried to the blessed word of God to relish that. If they be, God hath opened our hearts to attend to the word. And there is no better evidence of a child of God, than that that is fetched from the affection that he carries to the word and blessed truth of God. Oh, he relisheth it as his appointed food. He cannot be without it. Take away that, and you take away his life. 'My sheep hear my voice,' John x. 3. You are none of mine, because you hear not my word. A delight in the blessed truth of God is an argument that God hath first opened the heart.

Therefore poor souls, when they want good evidence, when they doubt whether their estate be good or no, let them consider what relish they have of divine truths; whether it be co-natural to the word* or no; whether it be savoury or no; whether they could be without the means of salvation or no; and let them judge of themselves by their delight in God's truth. Her heart was opened 'to attend to the word.'

'She attended to the things which were spoken of Paul.'

Which were the blessed truths of salvation, the forgiveness of sins, the free mercy of God in Christ. The particulars are not set down, but it was the gospel, and she believed upon it. Therefore it must needs be the word of faith. We see here then that

The seed and ground of faith is the gospel.

Her heart was opened to attend to that that Paul spake, which was the gospel. And indeed so it is. The foundation of faith, the word of faith, is the gospel. Nothing can breed faith but the word of God; for how can we hope for heaven and happiness, but by the mind of God discovered? Can we look for anything but God must discover his mind to bestow it? And where have we the mind and bosom of God opened to us? Is it not from the Scriptures, the word of God, from the good word especially? It is called the 'word of grace,' and 'the word of the kingdom,' and 'of glory,' the 'word of life;' because by it all these blessed things are conveyed to us.

Now it is not the word simply here, but the word 'spoken by Paul;' that is, the word preached by an authorised minister is the usual means of faith. Her heart was opened to attend to what was spoken by Paul, an authorised minister. So the word preached is the ordinary, though not the sole foundation of faith. Therefore the apostle saith, that God by that converted the world, 'by the foolishness of preaching,' 1 Cor. i. 21. And in the ladder of heaven, in Rom. x. 14, *seq.*, 'How shall they call on him of whom they have not heard? . . . and how shall they preach except they be sent?' So there is no faith without teaching. The point is plain. You hear it oft. The word is the ground of faith; and the word especially as it is preached by a Paul, by a minister unfolding it.

Use. Therefore be stirred up, as ye favour the souls of God's people, to pray to God 'to send labourers into his harvest,' Mat. ix. 38; and to pray that the gospel, and the preaching of it, may have a free passage, that God would set up lights in all the dark corners of the kingdom, and everywhere to 'those that are in darkness, and in the shadow of death,' Ps. cvii. 10. And blessed are their endeavour that labour that the gospel may be preached in every part of the kingdom. For we see here it is the word unfolded, 'the unsearchable riches' of Christ spread open, the tapes-

* Qu. 'heart'?—Ed.

try laid open, that usually beget faith. The mine must be digged; people must see it familiarly laid open.

Therefore saith he here, Lydia's heart was opened, 'and she attended to the words spoken by Paul.'

Let this teach us to set a price upon the ordinance of God. Doth God set up an ordinance, and will he not give virtue and power to it? Yes. There is a majesty and a power in the word of God to pull people out of the kingdom of Satan, to the blessed light of God's kingdom. It was the word, and the word opened by the ministry of Paul.

But it was the word, and the word opened and attended to. She mixed it with her attention, and her heart closed with it. There are these three go together; the word, and the word preached, and then attending to the word preached. That was the ground of her faith; these three meeting together.

There are these four things must always be in the senses of our body. If we will see, there must be an object to see, we must see something; and a faculty to see, our eye; and then a light whereby we see; we cannot see in the dark. And then there must be an application of the eye to see the object by that light. So in spiritual things there is the blessed truth of God, the mercy of God in Jesus Christ. That we may see these things, we must have a light by which we may see them. And there must be a power to see, which is the sanctified, opened understanding. When the understanding is opened, then there is an application of the soul to attend to the word of God by the light of the word. So that there must be application and attention to the word. Before the word can do us good, it must be applied to the object, the taste to the thing tasted; and so in all the other senses.

Attention is a special thing. How many sermons are lost in this city, that are as seed drowned, that never come to fruit! I think there is no place in the world where there is so much preaching, and no place where there are so many sermons lost. Why? Because people want a retaining power and faculty to attend, and retain and keep what we hear. She '*attended* to the word preached.'

To give a little direction in this point of attending and applying the mind. Not to speak much, I will name two or three principal things that I think fit at this time.

1. If we should come, as we should, to the word preached: *Let us search our wants before we come, and all the occasions we shall have to encounter with; all temptations that we are like to encounter with, let us forecast by presenting to our souls.* I am weak in knowledge, and I want such graces. I am like to encounter with such temptations, I am too weak for it; I shall meet with such adversaries, I know not how to answer them; I am plunged in such businesses, I shall be lost in them without grace. Then the soul comes with a mind to be supplied; and then it will attend, and will pray for the preacher. Oh, Lord, direct him that he may speak fitly to me; somewhat for my understanding; somewhat for my affections; somewhat to help me against such and such a temptation. This is wanting; and therefore we profit no more by the word than we do.

2. Then when we come to hear the word, let us hear it *with all spiritual subjection, as that word that hath power to command the conscience.* This is the word of God. The minister of God speaks in the place of God to me. I must give an account of it. I will subject my conscience to it. It is spoken with evidence, and proved; I will stoop to it. Thus we should

come with subjection of soul and conscience to whatsoever is taught; and not come to judge and censure, or to delight in it as music, as if we came to a play, to hear some pretty sentences. But come to hear God, as to the ordinance of God, come as to that word that shall judge our souls at the latter day. That is the way to attend.

3. Then again, if we would attend when we have heard the word of God, *let us labour by all means to bring it near to us, that it may be an* 'engrafted word,' James i. 21; that the soul may be leavened by it, that it may be so engrafted in the understanding and affections, that we may think the better in the virtue of it, and love, and speak, and do the better, as a scion* savours of the plant it is put into. Let us labour that the word of God may be written in our souls, in the tables of our hearts, that the truth of God may be near us, as any temptation shall be near us, or any corruption near us. What is the reason we yield to corruptions and temptations? They are near and the word is far off. We never attended to the word to bring it near home. If the word were as near as corruptions and temptations, that it were engrafted and invested into the soul, we should have the word ready for every temptation. There should not be a temptation offered, nor a corruption arise, but we should subdue it and beat it down with the blessed truth of God accompanied with the Spirit. Let us labour to get it near us, that the reasons of the word and our reason, that the judgment of God and our judgment, that the will of God and our own will may be all one; and so to have it incorporated and naturalized into our hearts, that we may speak, and think, and do nothing but that which is divine; that is, to have the word written in our hearts, our attention should be to that end. Therefore, when we hear, we should do as nature doth with the meat we eat. It sucks out a strength suitable for every part. Every part hath a power to draw out nourishment, what is suitable to itself. So when we hear the word of God, we should be able to say, this is good for such and such an end; and never leave thinking of the word of God when we have heard it, till we have turned the word into our souls, till we have it fixed in our understandings, that we can say, now I know it; till we have subdued our hearts to it, and we be moulded and delivered up to it, that we can say, now I have it, now the word is mine. Let us never leave the truth we hear till we be brought to that. Alas! to what purpose is it to hear except we make it our own, as nature makes the meat our own that we eat. There is a second or third digestion that goes before digestion be perfectly made, and the meat turned into it. It is ruminating and meditating, and altering of that we hear, and working on it; that makes spiritual nourishment. Thus we should do to attend to purpose.

4. And that we may do it, *let us add some meditations to these practices.* Consider first of all whose word it is. It is the word of the great God, and the word of God for my good. It is the good word of God, and the word of God that brings me much good, eternal salvation, if I obey it. It is the word of God that brings eternal damnation, if I obey it not.

It is the word of the great King, a proclamation, a law whereby I shall be judged, and perhaps that word that I shall not hear another time. Perhaps the Spirit may work more now than at another time. Therefore I will be wise, and give way to the Spirit of God, and not beat it back. Perhaps I shall never have such a gale of the Spirit offered again. It may be the last sermon I shall hear while I live. We should have such meditations, we that speak, as if it were the last time we should speak; and you

* Spelled 'sience.'—G.

that hear, as if they should be the last things that ever you should hear. For how do we know but it may be so? It is another manner of matter to hear than we take it. 'Take heed how ye hear,' saith our blessed Saviour, Luke viii. 18. We hear nothing but it sets us forward in the way of grace to heaven, or forward to hell. We are helped by it to heaven, or else hardened by it further to hell. We had need to take heed how we hear. We must be judged by that we hear; and that that we hear now negligently and carelessly, God will make good at the day of judgment. We may shake off, as profane spirits do, the minister's exhortations; but will you shake off 'Depart, ye cursed,' at the latter day? Matt. xxv. 41. Will you shake off that sentence, 'You would not hear me, and I will not hear you'? Oh no. Therefore shake not that off now that will be made good then. If thou entertain the gospel now, God will make it good then; if thou receive mercy now, he will shew that thou art acquitted then before devils, and angels, and men. Let us regard this, and let it make us hear the word with attention, as this good woman here. God opened her heart, 'and she attended to the things that were spoken of Paul.'

Quest. But you will ask, How shall I know a man whose heart is opened, and attends better than another man doth?

Ans. 1. I will give two or three brief rules of discerning. He that by the Spirit of God attends to the good word of God to purpose with an opened understanding, he not only knows the words, and the shell in preaching the word of God, *but the things.* He knows not only what faith and repentance is in the words, but he hath a spiritual light to know what the things are, what repentance is, and faith, and love, and hope, and patience; he knows the things. And likewise he that hath attended to purpose, he can do the things. He not only knows what he should do, but by the grace of the Spirit, and attending upon the word of God, he knows how to do them. Grace teacheth him not only that he should deny himself and 'live soberly, and righteously, and godly,' Titus ii. 12, but it teacheth him how to live soberly, and righteously, and godly. Grace, when we attend upon the word as we should, teacheth us to do the things, not only that we should repent and pray, &c., but to do them. It opens the things, and gives ability to do them.

And in the next place, those that attend as they should do, *there is a spiritual echo in their souls to everything that is taught;* that is, when they are exhorted to believe, they answer, Lord, I will believe; Lord, I will hear, I will repent, and I will take heed of such sins by thy grace. When God saith, 'Seek my face,' 'Lord, thy face will I seek,' Ps. xxvii. 8. This is the answer of a good conscience, this echo. Where there is attention to the word of God by the Spirit, there is an echo to that the Spirit speaks. Lord, it is good, and it is good for me if I yield to this; if I do not, it is naught* for me to put off repentance till another day; I desire to yield now, and Oh that my heart were directed! If it be rebellious, and not yielding, there is a desire that the heart may be brought into subjection to every truth revealed, there is a gracious echo in them that attend to purpose.

3. Then again, those that do attend from a sanctifying grace, they see things by another light, by a spirit of their own, by a heavenly light, by a *species* in their own kind, spiritual things with a spiritual light. Many come and hear sermons, and can discourse, and wrangle, and maintain janglings of their own, and all this out of natural parts, and out of pride

* That is, 'naughty,' = wicked.—G.

of heart; but a gracious holy man sees spiritual things by a spiritual light in their own kind.

A man that is born in a dungeon, and never saw the light, when he hears discourse of the sun and stars, and earth, and flowers, and plants, he hath imaginations what they should be, but he fancies other things. So a man that never had spiritual eye-sight to see spiritual things in their kind, he fancies them to be this and that, but he sees them not by their own light. Many speak and talk of good things, but it is by the spirit of other men, out of books and hearing, and not by a spirit of their own. He that attends by grace, speaks out of a spirit of his own, and not out of other men's spirits. He sees spiritual things in their own colours. Thus we see how to discern spiritual attention.

4. And he that knows what this means, what it is to have his heart opened to attend, when he goes from hearing the word, *he judgeth of his profiting by it, not by what he can say by heart, but by how much the meeker he is, how much more patient, how much more able to bear the cross, to resist temptations, and to have communion with God.* So he values his attending upon the means and hearing the word by the growth of his grace, and the decay of his corruptions: 'she attended to the things that were spoken of Paul.'

'She was baptized, and her household.'

She had the means of salvation, and she had the seal likewise, which is baptism. We have all need of seals. We have need to have our faith strengthened. God knows it better than we ourselves. We think baptism and the communion small matters, but God knows how prone we are to stagger. He knows that all seals are little enough. Therefore it is said here, 'she was baptized, and all her household.' Baptism is a solemn thing; it is the seal of the covenant of grace. You are well enough acquainted, I imagine, with the thing; therefore I will not enter into the commonplace. It is needless. As the whole Trinity was at the baptism of Christ, so every infant that is baptised is the child of Christ. And it is a special thing that we should meditate of.

We slight our baptism, and think it needless. You see the holy woman here would be baptized presently; she would have the seal of the covenant. There are many that are not book-learned, that cannot read, at least they have no leisure to read. I would they would read their book in their baptism; and if they would consider what it ministers to them upon all occasions, they would be far better Christians than they are.

Think of thy baptism when thou goest to God, especially when he seems angry. It is the seal of the covenant. Bring the promise: Lord, it is the seal of thy covenant; thou hast prevented* me by thy grace; thou broughtest me into the covenant before I knew my right hand from my left. So when we go to church to offer our service to God, think, by baptism we were consecrated and dedicated to God. We not only receive grace from God, but we give ourselves to God. Therefore it is sacrilege for persons baptized to yield to temptations to sin. We are dedicated to God in baptism. When we are tempted to despair, let us think of our baptism. We are in the covenant of grace, and have received the seal of the covenant, baptism. The devil is an uncircumcised, damned, cursed spirit. He is out of the covenant. But I am in the covenant. Christ is

* That is, 'anticipated.'—G.

mine; the Holy Ghost is mine; and God is mine. Therefore let us stand against all the temptations of that uncircumcised, unbaptized, damned spirit. The thinking of our baptism thus will help us 'to resist the devil,' James iv. 7. He is a coward; if he be resisted, he will flee; and what will better resist him than the covenant of grace and the seal of it? When we are tempted to sin, let us think, What have I to do with sin? By baptism I have union with the death of Christ; he died to take away sin, and my end must be his. I must abolish sin in my nature. Shall I yield to that that in baptism I have sworn against? And then if we be tempted to despair for sin, let us call to mind the promises of grace and forgiveness of sins, and the seal of forgiveness of sins, which is baptism. For as water in baptism washeth the body, so the blood of Christ washeth the soul. Let us make that use of our baptism, in temptations, not to despair for sin. And in conversing among men, let us labour to maintain the unity of the Spirit 'in the bond of peace,' Eph. iv. 3, to live peaceably. Christians must not fall to jar. Why? 'There is one faith, and one baptism;' have we 'not all one Father,' ver. 5, one inheritance, one baptism, one religion? and shall we break one with another for trifles? They forget their baptism that are so in quarrels. Thus if we would think of it, it is such a book as would be ready at hand for all services.

And then for our children, those that God hath committed to us, let us make use of baptism. Do they die in their infancy? Make this use of it: I have assured hope that my child is gone to God. He was born in the covenant, and had the seal of the covenant, baptism; why should I doubt of the salvation of my child? If they live to years of discretion, then be of good comfort, he is God's child more than mine; I have dedicate him to God and to Christ, he was baptized in the name of Christ, Christ will care for him as well as for me. If I leave my children behind me, they are God's and Christ's children. They have received the seal of the covenant, baptism. Christ will provide for them. And he that provides heaven for them will provide all things in the way to heaven necessary. God hath said, 'I will be the God of thee and of thy children,' Ps. cxxxii. 12. They are in covenant. Thine they were, Lord. A man may commit his children to God on his deathbed: Thou gavest them me, and I commit them to thee again, as before I did by baptism. All this we have by thinking of our baptism. If we look no further, as profane spirits do not, than the water and the elements, we can have no comfort by these things; but we should consider God's blessed institution and ordinance to strengthen our faith. And to our children when they come to years, baptism is an obligation to believe; because they have received the seal beforehand, and it is a means to believe. 'She was baptized.'

'And her household.'

So good is God, where the governor of the family is good, he gives all the family good, because he makes conscience in governing and instructing them. God crowns their endeavours with success, that they shall be all good. As we see Abraham and his household, the jailor and his household, Zaccheus and his household. Oh, it is a blessed thing to be a good governor in a family. He brings a blessing upon his house, the church of God is in his house. There cannot be a more honourable title to any house than to say it is the church of God; that the governor of the family brings all in subjection to God; that as he will have all serve him, so he will have all serve God; that he will not have a servant but he shall be the servant of God, nor a child but he shall be the child of God; and he labours to make his wife the spouse of Christ. Thus it should be said of every Christian family, and then they are churches.

Alas! in many places now they are hells, because there is little regard had of instructing of them. Beloved, many poor souls have had occasion to bless God for ever that they have been grafted into such good families. And put case sometimes thou hast instructed them and taken pains, and there is no good done. When thou art dead, and twenty years after, it may come to their minds all those instructions when they are in worse families. Oh! in such a place, with such a master, I had such instructions, but I had no grace to take good by them, but now I call them to mind. So the seed that was sown long before may take effect then. This should encourage those that are governors of families to be good. 'Lydia was baptized, *and her household*.'

'And she besought them, saying, If you have judged me faithful to the Lord, come to my house, and abide there.'

Here is the fruit of Lydia's conversion. When she was converted and baptized, she entreated the apostles to come to her house and abide there; and she prevailed. She constrained them by a moral kind of violence; they suffered themselves to be overcome.

'If you have judged me faithful, &c., come to my house, and abide there.'

Here is her invitation, and the argument that she forceth it by. 'If you have judged me faithful to Christ, then come to my house.'

To speak a little of her argument, whereby she forced the blessed apostle and the rest to her house.

'If ye have judged me faithful.'

It is a most binding argument. If you judge me faithful, you must judge me a child of God, an heir of heaven, the spouse of Christ; you must judge me all these and the like. 'If you have judged me faithful, come to my house.' And if you judge me so, can you deny me this courtesy? It is a conjuring, wondrous forcible argument. 'If you have judged me faithful.'

It implies that St Paul and holy men would be more strange else; and so there should not be intimate familiarity—converse there may be, but not familiarity—with those that are not faithful. Indifferent carriage to all alike shews a rotten heart: those that make no difference between good Christians and formal hypocrites. No. But 'if you have judged me faithful, *come to my house*.' As if she had said, I know your spirits are such, that except you judge me faithful, you will not take this courtesy at my hands.

Again, she supposed, if Paul judged her faithful, he would not deny her that courtesy. Those that upon good grounds we judge faithful, we should be gentle to them and easy to be entreated. 'The wisdom that is from above is so,' James iii. 17. Grace sweetens the carriage and alters a man's disposition. Those that have felt pity from God are merciful to others. 'Therefore, if you have judged me faithful,' &c.

It was an argument of a great deal of sincerity to appeal to their knowledge and judgment. 'If you have judged me faithful.'

If she had not been sincere she would not have done so. But sincerity makes a man bold to appeal to God himself. 'Lord, thou knowest that I love thee,' saith St Peter, John xxi. 15; and 'If there be any iniquity in my heart,' saith David, Ps. lxvi. 18. They dare appeal to God and to God's people: 'If ye have judged me faithful.'

In this speech, likewise, she desires to have confirmation of her estate from the apostles. And indeed it is a great confirmation of weak Christians to have the judgment of strong Christians that they are good, 'If you have judged me faithful,' do me this courtesy. And would it not comfort her soul to have the judgment of so strong a man as Paul?

It is a great strengthening, not only to have the Spirit of God witness for us, but the Spirit of God in others. And sometimes in temptations, the judgment of others will do us more good than our own in a dark state. Therefore we should appeal to those that fear God to judge us faithful, though we be in a mist and in darkness sometimes, that we are not able to judge of our own condition.

And indeed, when we judge the people to be truly good and true-hearted to God, we owe them this duty: to think them good people, and to shew it, it is a debt. We wrong good persons when we take wrong conceits of them. Shall we not affect* and love them that God loves? It is as if she had said, God hath taken me into his family, and will admit me to heaven, and will not you come to my house? When Christ shall take men to be members of his body, shall not we take them into our company. It is a wrong to good people to be strange to them. Sometimes there may, by way of censure in some sin, be a little strangeness, but ordinary strangeness becomes not Christians. It becomes not that sweet bond, 'the communion of saints.' 'If you have judged me faithful.' That is the bond. Her invitation is,

'Come to my house, and abide there.'

You see many sweet graces presently after she believed. Here is a loving heart. Why did she desire them to come to her house? To express the love she did bear to them for their work's sake. She felt the love of Christ by their ministry; and now she desired to express the fruit of her love in maintaining them.

And not only so, but she desired to be edified by them. She was youngly planted, and she desired to be watered from them. She knew Paul would drop heavenly things, and give her that that might stablish her; therefore she desired that they would stay at her house, that she might have benefit by their heavenly discourse, and be built up and edified further and further.

So you see these two graces especially upon believing, a bountiful, loving heart. She entreated them not only to come to her house, but to abide there a good while, as they did. And here was her desire to be edified, and a boldness to appear to own Christ and his ministers in dangerous times. For in those times it was a dangerous thing to appear to be a Christian. They were worse hated than the Jews were. Though both were hated, yet Christians were above all. Therefore false Christians would be 'circumcised,' they would be Jews to avoid the cross, that they might not be accounted Christians.

You see in general true faith, that works love, and works by love. It works love in the heart, and by love it works all duties of hospitality and bounty by love. When it hath wrought that holy affection, it works by that holy affection. You see here it is never without fruit; presently faith brings forth fruit. As soon as she was baptised, she shews her love to the apostles, and their company, and her bounty and her boldness in the cause of Christ.

We say of a graft, it is grafted to purpose if it take and bring forth fruit;

* That is, 'choose.'—G.

so she being a new scion* graft into Christ, she took presently. As soon as she was baptised into Christ, here is the fruit of love, and bounty, and boldness in the cause of Christ. Zaccheus, as soon as ever he believed, 'Half my goods I give to the poor,' Luke xix. 8. So we see the jailor afterwards, presently upon believing he entertained the apostles with a feast, and washed their wounds.

Take heed of a barren, dead faith. It is a false faith. If thou believe indeed, faith will work love, and work by love, as it did in this blessed woman. Her faith knit her to Christ in heaven. Her love was as the branches of the tree. Her faith knit her to the root; but love as the branches reached to others; her branches reached fruit to the apostle and his company. So it is the nature of faith that knits us to Christ. The same spirit of love knits us to others, and reacheth forth fruit to all we converse with.

As we desire to have evidence of the soundness of our faith, let us see what spirit of love we have, especially love to these three things.

1. *Love to Christ*, to whom we are engrafted, and,

2. *Love to the ministers of Christ*. We cannot shew kindness to Christ. He is in heaven. But his ministers and his poor are upon the earth; when we can, buy ointment to pour on Christ's feet, his poor members, and his ministers.

3. And *love to the word of God*. They are the three issues of a gracious, believing heart, and where they are not there is no faith at all.

I beseech you, let us imitate this blessed woman. You see here the name of Lydia is precious in the church. The name of Lydia, as it is said of Josiah, it is a box of ointment poured out. The name of Lydia cannot be named in the church, but there is a sweet savour with it. As soon as she believed, the Holy Ghost, the Spirit of God blowing upon the garden of her heart, where the spice of grace was sowed, stirred up a sweet scent of faith, and of bounty, and liberality in the cause of Christ.

Let not this be in vain to us, but every one of us labour to be like Lydia. You see what loadstone drew Paul here to go unto her house; she had faith, and she expressed it in love.

Let us labour to have faith, and to express it in love to God, unto Christ, to his people, and word, and ordinances, that have his stamp on them; and let us boldly own the cause of Christ; let us not regard the censures of vain men that say thus and thus. Faith and love forget danger; it is bold. She forgot all the danger that she was in by countenancing Paul and such men.

Let us labour for faith and love, and we shall not say this and that. 'There is a lion in the way,' Prov. xxii. 13; but we shall go on boldly until we do receive the end of our faith and love, 'the salvation of our souls.'

* Spelled 'sience.'—G.

NOTES.

(*a*) P. 521.—'Purple.' Probably the reference is to Tertullian. Cf. footnote, page 89.

(*b*) P. 525.—'The word signifies to apply and set her mind,' &c. The word is προσέχω, on which cf. Dr Robinson's interesting article in his Lexicon, *sub voce*. Literally here = to apply the mind; but often in the Classics with the accessory idea of believing, giving credence. G.

THE BRIDE'S LONGING

FOR

HER BRIDEGROOM'S SECOND COMING.

THE BRIDE'S LONGING.

NOTE.

'The Bride's Longing for her Bridegroom's Second Coming' forms a small volume (18mo), published in 1638. Its title-page is given below.* Of Sir Thomas Crew, known by the venerable title of 'The poor man's lawyer,' nothing need be added to the splendid eulogium of Sibbes, which, as in the case of Milton's upon Bradshaw, has proved a more enduring monument than marble and brass. Prefixed to the volume is Marshall's miniature portrait of Sibbes. I have not traced a second copy of 'The Bride's Longing.' G.

* THE
BRIDES Longing
for her
BRIDE-GROOMES
second comming.
A
Sermon preached at the funerall
of the right Worshipfull, Sir
THOMAS CREVV, Knight,
Sergeant at Law to his
MAIESTIE.
By
The late learned and reverend Divine,
RICH. SIBS.
REV. 22. 17.
The Spirit and the Bride say, come, and let him that heareth, say, come.
LONDON:
Printed by *E. P.* for *G. Edwards*, at
the signe of the Angell in green
Arbour. 1638.

TO THE READER.

Loving Readers,—Lo, here the verifying of that ancient adage, *Quod differtur, non aufertur*, for long looked for comes at last. That which, before a solemn and sad assembly, was publicly preached and committed to the ears of some, is now printed and committed to the eyes of all that have a mind to read it; which thing hath with a long and longing desire been wished and waited for by sundry. This funeral sermon bespake your receiving and respecting of it in a double consideration, each of which, in my opinion, hath an important, rare, and singular ponderation. Behold, first, the man; secondly, the matter. The man by whom, and the man for whom it was made: the one, that worthy divine Dr Sibbes, who in his lifetime intended and approved it for the press, as it now comes forth; the other, that worshipful serjeant, Sir Thomas Crew; men of more than ordinary worth and goodness, whom to name is enough to those that knew them; for if I should enter into a particular discourse and discovery of their deserved worth, I fear I should more dishonour my undertakings, and wrong your expectation, than in any proportion answer the excellency of two such worthy themes. Secondly, for the matter, as the occasion and men's expectations were extraordinary, so shall you find his preparation. Read, and then judge. It sweetly and to the life sets forth the duty, desire, and disposition of the church and spouse of Christ echoing a faithful and prayerful Amen to all the truths of God, especially to the precious promises, and chiefly to that promise of promises, Christ's 'second coming;' which in cold blood undauntedly to desire, is an infallible mark of a true and thorough convert; which that we may do, we must make sure our espousal to Christ here, and get to be clad with the wedding garment of faith and repentance, teaching us to ponder and pray much, and then admirable shall be our confident standing before God, our rich hope, our quietness and heart's ease, our joy, as if we had one foot in heaven already. We shall be able with St Paul to cast down our gauntlet and bid defiance to devils, to men, to height, to depth, to things present and things to come. If all the hearts in the world were one heart, it could not comprehend those rich blessings wherewith true Christians are richly endowed, and those spiritual joys and comforts which shall rain upon them in sweet showers from heaven; rich they are in hand, but richer in hope; rich in possession, but richer in reversion. For what ravishing joy, what inexplicable sweetness shall then everlasting[ly] possess our souls, whenas we who have been a long time contracted to our Lord and husband, shall see that blessed time come, when we shall have that glorious marriage between him and us, really and royally solemnised, in the presence of God and his holy angels, and shall have the fruition of him and all his happiness, and enjoy such heavenly fellowship, familiarity, and acquaintance with him, transcendently above all the sweetest relations here below, I say, with him who is 'the Prince of peace,' 'the King of glory,' yea, the very glory of heaven and earth, 'the express image of his Father's person,' in whom 'those things which are invisible are seen,' 'the brightness of everlasting light,' the undefiled mirror of the majesty of God, and 'the desire of all nations.' Blessed are they which are called to the marriage supper of the Lamb, Rev. xix. 9. Whereunto, that you may be admitted as a welcome guest, you must both know and practise what in this treatise is contained.

To conclude, I am bold therefore, in the cause of God's honour and your salvation, to entreat you, as ever you would have interest in Christ's blood and blessedness, sufferings and satisfactions, as you mean to have any fellowship or communion in heaven with the blessed saints and angels, as you intend to have any part in that kingdom which the Lord Jesus hath purchased with his own blood, that you would up and be doing that which the wife of the Lamb is said to have done—Rev. xix. 7, 'Make yourselves ready;' which if you do, his speedy access shall bring to you speeding success; which that you may do, you shall not want his constant and instant prayers, who is

Your Christian and cordial well-wisher,

G. H.*

* These initials probably represent the Rev. George Hughes, B.D., of Plymouth, one of the 'Ejected' of 1662, and father-in-law of the illustrious John Howe.—G.

THE BRIDEGROOM'S PROMISES,

AND

THE BRIDE'S PRAYER.

He which testifieth these things saith, Surely I come quickly: Amen. Even so, come, Lord Jesus.—Rev. XXII. 20.

As the church of God, being the weakest and the most shiftless* part of mankind, is never without trouble in this world, so God would never have it to be without comfort. And therefore God reveals unto Christ in this book, and Christ unto the angel, and the angel unto John, 'things to come,' from the ascension of Christ unto his 'second coming;' that so, in all conditions of the church, the church might have recourse unto this book, to see what the issue of all would be. This is their comfort, that howsoever things may be carried in this world in a seeming confusion, in a cloud, and in a mystery, yet in conclusion all shall end well on the church's side. Their trouble shall end in peace, their abasement in glory, and their conflict in a crown. This we may see here verified. This revelation doth end in the description of the glorious condition of the church. In the two last chapters, as I take it, the evangelist Saint John sets down the glorious estate of the church of God, even in this world, yet so as it shall end and be consummate in perfect glory in the world to come. For the soul of a Christian, like Noah's dove, cannot rest in any glory here, till it return to the ark, till it come to the enjoyment of perfect glory, and have blissful communion with Christ for ever and ever in heaven. And therefore Christ doth terminate and end the sweetness of his promises in heaven, and at his last coming; and the church likewise stretcheth and raiseth up her desires to that. Howsoever, there shall be glorious times and things here, yet these are but as the first fruits to the whole harvest, and as a drop unto the ocean. Therefore, when you read of a glorious estate of the church to be here upon earth, your minds must have recourse to the upshot and consummation of all in heaven. Jerusalem which is from above must lead us to Jerusalem which is above.

Now, because that man's unbelieving heart is too prone to think that these things are too good to be true, and too great to be performed, seeing such an immeasurable disproportion between his own unworthiness and

* That is, 'without expedients.'—G.

the excellency of the things promised, hereupon the mercy of our blessed Saviour is such, that he confirms this his second glorious coming by all kind of witnesses that may be. Here is the angel, verse 6; Christ himself, verse 7; the spouse, and the Spirit in the spouse, verse 17; and Christ himself again in the words before the text, 'Behold, I come quickly.' Then you have the spouse's answer, 'Amen. Even so, come, Lord Jesus.' Beloved, faith is a supernatural thing. It hath no friend within us. It hath no help, no cause in the world, except God himself. Therefore, it hath need of all confirmation. God knows us and our needs better than we do ourselves, and you see he useth confirmation to help our unbelief. And besides the witnesses, the thing itself is repeated again and again, three or four times in this chapter: verses 7, 12, 20, 'Behold, I come quickly,' and 'Behold, I come quickly,' and, 'Surely I come quickly.' By every repetition, Christ seeks to gain upon our misgiving souls. 'Behold, I come.' Now because our spirit is exceeding short, and we are ready to cry out, as it is in the sixth of this book, 'How long, Lord, holy and true?' Rev. vi. 10. How long? Why, he answers, 'Behold, I come quickly.' You shall also find in the prophecies of the Old Testament, the same promises delivered and repeated again and again, because of our unbelief; which ariseth from an inward guilt, that cleaves to our consciences, because we are subject to failings, and are not so strict as we should be. But such are the yearning bowels of our blessed Saviour, that it grieves him to see his tender church afflicted and troubled in mind. Therefore he helps all that he can.

Note. Observe then, I beseech you, in the words, the sweet intercourse that is between Christ and his spouse. Christ promiseth again and again, 'Behold I come quickly;' and the church saith, 'Come;' 'Amen. Even so, come, Lord Jesus.' There is no intercourse in the world so sweet as is that between Christ and his church. But we will come unto the words themselves: 'Amen. Even so, come, Lord Jesus.'

In these words you have, first, the assent of the church; secondly, the consent—her assent to the truth; her consent to the goodness of the truth. 'Amen:' it is so. Nay, 'Amen:' it shall be so. Nay, 'Amen:' be it so; or, let it be so. There is a wishing included in it. All these are wrought by the Spirit. The Spirit convinceth us both of the truth and of the goodness of the truth. And besides that, in the next words, the same Spirit stirs up a desire and prayer: 'Even so, come, Lord Jesus.' Holy desires are turned into fervent prayers.

Note. 'Amen' is a short word, but marvellously pregnant, full of sense, full of spirit. It is a word that seals all the truths of God, that seals every particular promise of God. And it is never likely to arise in the soul, unless there be first an almighty power from heaven, to seize on the powers of the soul, to subdue them, and make it say, 'Amen.' There is such an inward rising of the heart, and an innate rebellion against the blessed truth of God, that unless God, by his strong arm, bring the heart down, it never will nor can say, 'Amen.'

Note. But now the heart will not be pent in or restrained. The Spirit is an enlarging thing; and therefore, besides 'Amen' (though 'Amen' includes that which follows), the spirit breaks forth and saith, 'Amen. Even so, come, Lord Jesus.'

A little of 'Amen.'

Christ is said, in the beginning of this book, to be 'Amen, the true and faithful witness,' Rev. iii. 14. And all the promises are said, in Christ

Jesus, 'to be yea and amen,' 2 Cor. i. 20; that is, they are made for his sake, and performed for his sake; they are made in him, and for him; and they are performed in him, and for him. And when 'Amen'—that is, Christ himself—shall say his 'Amen' to any thing, is it so much for us to give our 'Amen'?

The point I mean to raise out of this word 'Amen' is this:

Doct. 1. *That the hearts of the children of God are pliable to divine truths, to yield to the whole word of God, especially to the good word of God,* viz., *the promises; and of all promises, to the promise of promises, the second coming of Christ.*

They say 'Amen' to that, and that for these reasons:

Reason 1. Because *there is a suitableness of disposition, and a kind of connaturalness, between a sanctified heart and sanctified truths, between an holy heart and holy things;* insomuch, that if an holy truth, never heard of before, be heard by an holy heart, it will yield present assent; for his heart is subdued so, that he hath an 'Amen' for it presently.

Reason 2. *There is a sweet relish in all divine truths,* and suitable to the sweetness in them, there is a spiritual taste, which the Spirit of God puts into the soul of his children. Though there be never so much sweetness in things, if there be not a suitable taste, there is no relish in them. Therefore, the Spirit of God, in his children, works a taste of the sweetness that is in the word of God. And that is a main ground why they say 'Amen,' especially to comfortable truths.

Reason 3. Again, when the soul is once contracted unto God, *it hath no will of its own, but it yields up his will to God's will.* The spouse hath no will of her own, but her husband's will is her will. So if Christ say 'Amen, I come quickly,' the spouse of Christ saith 'Amen' too.

Reason 4. *God deals with his children, likewise, by way of a covenant and a contract.* And above all other covenants, the covenant of a contract is the sweetest covenant. Now, in it there must be a consent on our part; and therefore it is, that the Spirit always stirs up an 'Amen' on our parts too. When he saith 'Amen,' it shall be so, then the soul saith, 'Amen, Lord; let it be so.' As in civil marriage there is a contract, so here, in the spiritual; and seeing there is a contract, there is also an assent to the 'second coming' of Christ. The contracted spouse must needs say 'Amen' to the marriage day.

Reason 5. Lastly, the Spirit of God, in the hearts of his children, *stirs up in them this 'Amen,' as a seal of their effectual calling.* If you should ask me what effectual calling is, I answer, it is nothing else but the heart's echo and answer to God's speech. God calls, and we answer. This is by St Peter called, 'the answer of a good conscience,' 1 Pet. iii. 21. There must be in the soul the answer of a good conscience to all divine truths. Doest thou believe? I do believe. Doest thou repent? I do repent. 'Seek ye my face. Thy face, Lord, will I seek,' Ps. xxvii. 8. 'Return, ye backsliding children, and I will heal your backslidings. Behold, we come unto thee; for thou art the Lord our God,' Jer. iii. 22. Unless there be thus the answer of a good conscience, there is no effectual calling. Our calling is then effectual, when the Spirit stirs up in the heart an answer unto it. Therefore, you see there must needs be an 'Amen' wrought in the hearts of the children of God.

Use. Beloved, if this be so, I beseech you let us beg of God, if we find any stubbornness or renitency* in our souls to divine truths, the perform-

* That is, 'striving against.'—G.

ance of the covenant of grace, Lord, thou hast promised fleshy and sensible hearts, tender and yielding affections. Oh now grant them, and work them.

Note. For, beloved, this you must know, howsoever God deals with us by way of covenant, yet when he comes to perform the covenant, he works, in a manner, our part and his own too. In effect, he makes a testament, and not a covenant. In a testament we bequeath; we do not covenant and condition. So that, though God deals with his people by way of covenant, as if you repent, if you believe, if you obey, yet he gives, by way of testament, the grace that he bestows. Therefore, beg of God that, as he requires this condition, that we should assent and be pliable unto his word, so that he would make his covenant a testament and a will—I mean, that he would effectually work it, and make us to do it—this should be our desire of God. And so much the rather—

Motive 1. First, *Because God honours us by it, in having our consent.* Is not this a great honour to us, that he will not perform things without our consent? For indeed he will not accomplish the work of our everlasting salvation without it. But then, if we set our seals to God's seal, and we consent once, we even bind God himself. When he seals to us, and we to him, we bind God almighty, and by that power of faith, subdue hell and all our opposite enemies. When we seal to the truth of God, and cry 'Amen,' it is a word that fills heaven and earth. There is not a joyfuller word in the world, than when whole congregations can say and shout 'Amen.' When God says 'Amen' in heaven, if we presently can say 'Amen' to his truth upon earth, he will say 'Amen' to our salvation. Thus God honours us by it, when he comes for our consent.

Motive 2. *We honour God again, by our sealing to his truth.* Faith is that which seals to God's truth, and 'Amen' is the very voice of faith.

Use 2. It is a pitiful thing, but common in the world, that God should have no more credit with us. Poor distressed souls will say 'Amen' to the lies of their own hearts, and presumptuous persons will say 'Amen' to a liar, to a murderer, to an enemy, to Satan. But God hath so little credit with us, that if he command, we will not say 'Amen;' if he promise, we have no 'Amen' for him; if he threaten, we bless ourselves, saying, We shall do well enough: 'We shall have peace, though we walk after the imagination of our own hearts, adding drunkenness unto thirst,' Deut. xxix. 19. When the Spirit of God saith, 'He will stir up a fire in his anger, and his wrath shall burn unto the lowest hell,' Deut. xxxii. 22, against all such as go on in their sinful courses, yet they will flatter themselves. Well, beloved, we may shake off God's word in the ministry, as profane persons do; but when God comes in the execution of his threatenings, then his wrath shall burn to hell, and not be quenched. Who can avoid or abide that dreadful sentence, 'Go, ye cursed, into everlasting fire, prepared for the devil and his angels,' Mat. xxv. 41. God's words are not as wind. Indeed, they are such a wind as will blow down all impenitent sinners to hell. We must have a legal 'Amen' to the threatenings of God, as well as an evangelical 'Amen' to the sweet promises. St John here, by the Spirit of God, saith 'Amen' to the promises of the time to come; to wit, for the confusion of antichrist, for the conversion of the Jews, and for the glorious times to come, though he sees no evidence thereof for the present; and so must we to all divine truths.

But we have another kind and company of men that must be taxed, that have indeed an 'amen' and a seal, but it is to a blank. They are presumptuous persons, and such, which is worse, as will have God to say 'Amen' to their courses. They will be naught* and sinful, and then study and strive to bring God's word to stand bent to their bow; and so in their lying conceit make God say 'Amen' to their lusts. They account it not sufficient to have their will, but they will have God to be of their mind too, and they will always get some daubers that shall say, 'Go on and prosper.' An Ahab will always have his false prophets. What a wicked thing is this, that we should make an idol of God, and transform him into the likeness of Satan, his enemies, to make him like that which he hates most. We will continue in our sinful courses, and make as though we had the word of God for us; and, Oh we have the judgment of such and such, and thus bolster up ourselves by building upon such sandy foundations. When we should bring up our souls and resign them to God and his Spirit, we will bring God down to our bent, and make him to say this and that, agreeable to our carnal reason and corrupt affections.

But I must not enlarge myself in this. In a word, therefore, to conclude this point: As there is a sweet harmony in God's truth, so let there be a harmony in our hearts thereunto. God's truth always agrees with itself. Oh let our hearts agree with it. When we hear a threatening, a precept, or a promise, Oh let us say, 'Amen.' It is the sweetest harmony in the world when we can bring our hearts to close with God and his word, with his Spirit and truth, when we can be delivered 'into that form of doctrine which is delivered unto us,' Rom. vi. 17.

But now I go on. 'Even so, come, Lord Jesus.' We come from the assent unto the consent, yielding unto that which Christ said as true and good. We come unto the desire and prayer of the church: 'Even so, come, Lord Jesus.'

Note. 'Amen' is an Hebrew word, and it is still retained, to shew the consent of the Christian church with the Jewish, both with that which was before, and with that which shall be afterward.† And it is expressed and opened here, by a word following, 'yea,' or 'even so,' come, Lord Jesus. You see the church desires, and out of her desire prays, 'Come, Lord Jesus.'

Now, this desire of the church shews the gracious disposition of the church. These desires are the breathings and motions of the Spirit in the soul, tending to further union. Even as motion tends to rest, so desires tend to the uniting unto the thing desired. The church's desires here are the immediate issue of the soul, and therefore undissembled, and they shew the true character of a Christian soul. We may dissemble words and actions, but we cannot dissemble our desires and affections; we may paint fire, but we cannot paint heat. Therefore God judgeth us more by our desires and affections than by our words and actions.

Now you may know that our desires are holy and good, if so be that they be heavenly; for then it is a sign that they come down from heaven, even as a spring will arise and ascend as high as the spring-head whence it comes. If our desires rise to heaven, as the church's here do, then it is a sign they come down from heaven.

Our desires are as a stream, which I will shew you, by prosecuting that metaphor and allusion in sundry particulars.

1. *A good stream hath a good spring;* so must our desires. The spring of the church's desires here is love: she loves Christ, and therefore desires him to 'come quickly.'

2. A stream, you know, *carries all before it;* so our desires are an holy

* That is, 'naughty,' = wicked.—G. † Cf. Robinson's Lexicon, *sub voce*.—G.

stream issuing from a good spring and carrying all before them. They are efficacious, not a mere velleity,* as they say, a bare wishing and woulding.

3. A stream, *if it be stopped, will swell till it break down all opposition and carry all before it;* so let a good desire be stopped, and it will swell more and more, and grow bigger and bigger, till it makes way for itself.

4. A stream *is restless and incessant till it meet with the ocean and empty itself into the sea;* so, true and holy desires be restless and always in motion. They are not like a standing pool that rests, but they are in motion still, till they have emptied themselves into the boundless and bottomless ocean of endless pleasure.

5. As true streams that arise from a fountain *do wax bigger aud bigger the nearer they come to the ocean,* because other rivers join with them, and so they take advantage and augmentation by other streams that run into them, so, if our desires be true, *they are growing desires;* they increase bigger and bigger still till they come to heaven.

6. At length, *we see the streams empty themselves into the sea.* They are swallowed up there, where they have a more constant being than in themselves, namely, of the ocean, the true element and proper place of all waters; and so our desires, if they be holy, as they are restless and growing, so at last they empty themselves into Christ, and join with God and happiness for the time to come; for there is greater happiness for the souls of men, in God, in Christ, and in heaven, than there is in themselves, and there they are swallowed up.

7. Lastly, *We may try our desires by this.* Vapours in a low place do shew that there is a spring there. You know that the springs are there where there are most vapours constantly. So where there be breathings of the soul upward, as there is here of the church, surely there is a spring of love that yields these vapours, and whence these desires flow.

But I come more particularly unto this particular desire of the church, 'Come, Lord Jesus.' I shall make way by some propositions which I shall premise, before I come to the main thing which I shall stand upon at this time.

First, We must take it for granted;

Obs. 1. *That there will be a second glorious coming of Christ, that will be far more glorious than the former.*

The best times and things are to come for Christians every way. Every day they rise they are nearer to their happiness.

Again, We must know this;

Obs. 2. *That a Christian, if he hath true faith in the times to come, he will have answerable desires, and correspondent prayers.*

For, beloved, there is always an harmony between the heart and the brain, between the understanding and the will and affections. What we assent to as true, and consent to as good, that we shall both desire and pray for. Therefore, if you know there will be a glorious coming of Christ, and if you assent to it, that the best times are yet to come, surely there will be this prayer too. There is alway a sweet agreement and harmony between a sound convinced knowledge and gracious affections. Hence it is, that in Scripture what we do not wish and affect,† we are said not to know. We see not things in their proper light, when we know and affect them not; but we have received them only by tradition and from others. But when we see proper things with a proper light, spiritual things with a spiritual light, then there will be always prayers and desires accordingly.

* That is, 'wishing.'—G. † That is, 'choose,' 'love.'—G.

As the church here, after 'Amen, even so,' there is the desire. 'Come, Lord Jesus,' there is her prayer.

And therefore, we may know whether our knowledge be spiritual or not, by this, if the heart be subdued to yield unto it. Otherwise the heart will swell when it comes to petition, and to particular truths. What! Shall I yield to this? No. I have heard of this by the hearing of the ear, but I know not whether it be true or not; I have heard much talk of the Scriptures. But when the Scripture comes to cross a man in this or that particular lust, then if his knowledge be not spiritual, his heart will rise and swell against it, and begin to call into question and doubt; yea, and to think it folly and a base thing for a man to yield to it. I am sure of my pleasures, I am sure of my profits, but I am not sure whether this be true or no. And thus the heart of an atheist comes to stand out, because his knowledge is not spiritual. But if it be, then it carries an assent to it with it, and a desire drawn into a prayer.

Again, You must know this before we come unto the main point,

Obs. 3. *That a gracious heart turneth promises into desires and prayers.*

The promise was, 'I come quickly.' Here faith clasps about the promise, as a vine about the elm, and saith, 'Come, Lord Jesus.' Faith puts the promise into suit presently. Christ had no sooner said, 'I come quickly,' but the spirit of faith saith, 'Nay, come, Lord Jesus.' But then we must be sure that we have a promise out of the word of God. Faith hath no 'amen' for the word of a man, or for anything else but the word of God; and when it fastens upon that, as it doth here, you see it turns it into a holy desire and prayer, 'Come, Lord Jesus.' Beloved, we believe not the promise as we should do, else we would do so. We have rich, 'exceeding great and precious promises,' 2 Peter i. 4, but where is our rich, exceeding great and precious faith, to lay hold upon them, and to turn them presently into suits, desires, and prayers? Thus if we would do, we should bind God with his own word; he cannot deny himself, or falsify his truth.

Obs. 4. You see again, *that the more assured one is of anything, the more effectually it will make him to pray.*

An atheistical heart would say thus: Such a thing will be; Christ will come whether I pray or no; what need I pray then? Nay, therefore pray, because he will come. 'I come quickly;' therefore, 'Even so come, Lord Jesus.' Christ himself was fully assured that his Father would grant him all that he prayed for: 'I know that thou hearest me always,' saith he, John xi. 42; yet you see what an heavenly prayer he makes, John xvii. Nay, God bids him do it: 'Ask of me, and I will give thee the heathen for thine inheritance,' Ps. ii. 8, &c. Christ himself must ask before God will give him 'the uttermost parts of the earth for his possession.' So Ezek. xxxvi., where you have the covenant of grace itself, with many promises attending it; to all which it is added, ver. 37, 'Yet for all these things will I be inquired of by the house of Israel, saith the Lord.' Though he had made great promises to his church, yet he must be prayed to for the performance of them. He will have things received as fruits of our prayer, as well as of his promise and providence. We cannot be so thankful for things that come only as fruits of his providence, as when we look upon them as fruits of our prayers. David was a king of prayers; but Saul came by providence only, and by the people's importunity. Whether was the more blessed?

Oh then, my brethren, though we be never so much assured of things to come, yet let us join prayer thereto; for the assurance of the end will stir us up to the careful use of the means. None are so careful of the latter as they who are most assured of the former. Witness the church here.

The next thing I shall premise, as making way for that, that I mean more fully to speak of, is this :

Obs. 5. *That God's promises have gradual performances.*

They are made good by degrees. God goes by many steps to the performance of his great promises ; as here, the promise of Christ's 'second glorious coming' hath many degrees to the accomplishment thereof. So God promises 'a new heaven and a new earth,' Isa. lxvi. 22. That was one degree of the performance hereof, when the Jews came out of captivity. It had a second degree of performance when Christ came in the flesh. Then all things were new. There was a new priest, a new Sabbath, a new nation. So when the Gentiles were called, and came in, it had a third gradual performance. When the Jews shall be called, when there shall be 'a resurrection from the dead,' as it were, Rom. xi. 15, then all things shall be new. That was a fourth. And the last and full performance shall be, when all things shall be new indeed ; that is, when there shall be 'a new heaven and a new earth.' So this promise here, 'Come, Lord Jesus,' it hath a latitude and a breadth of performance ; 'Come, Lord,' into our hearts first, and set up thy kingdom and sceptre there ; subdue all therein unto thyself, throw down all lusts, thrust out Satan, take thine own interest in us.

And then 'come' into thy church, as you have it, Mark ix. 1. There is a powerful coming of Christ in the gospel; therein 'the kingdom of God comes with power.' Come thus in the ministry of thy word. When Christ was bodily ascending up into heaven, he came spiritually in his ordinances. And thus 'come' thou by thy Spirit.

And then 'come' to blast antichrist, and to consume 'that man of sin,' 2 Thes. ii. 3, and so make way for the other degree of thy coming. 'Come' in the fulness of the Gentiles, 'come' in the conversion of thy people of the Jews, that their riches may be an increase of our riches, that there may be golden times indeed, as surely then they will be.

And then, because there is a certain number of the elect of God, which must be accomplished and fulfilled; and Christ will delay his last coming till that be done ; therefore, 'come' and accomplish the number of thine elect, as you have it Rev. vi. 11, 'And white robes were given to every one of them ; and it was said unto them, that they should rest yet for a little season, until their fellow-servants also and their brethren, that should be killed as they were, should be fulfilled.' They must stay till the rest come in. As they that have invited a company of strangers to a feast, do stay till the last be come, so there will not be a glorious coming of Christ until all the elect be gathered into one body. And then shall be the coming of all comings, which is the glorious coming of Christ, to take us to himself, and to make us sit with him, 'to judge the world,' 1 Cor. vi. 2, as so many kings and judges of the world, and to be with him for ever. As the apostle saith, 'Then shall we be ever with the Lord,' 1 Thes. iv. 17, 18. And that is a comfort indeed. As he adds there, 'Wherefore comfort one another with these words.' And so you see the gradual performance thereof.

Now I come unto the last, and that which I mean most to stand upon, being a blessed truth, most suitable to this occasion.

Obs. 6. *That as it is the duty, so it is the disposition of a gracious heart, to desire the glorious coming of Christ Jesus ; and to desire all his other comings in way and order to this, as they make way for his last coming*

In the unfolding of this I shall shew you the grounds and reasons why the church doth so, and then make some trials whether we do so or no, and then give some few directions to help us therein.

Why doth the church desire so much this second and glorious coming of Christ?

Reason 1. *Because the church is in want till that time*, and the ground of all desire is want. We want our bodies, we want many of our friends, &c. But then there shall be a supply of all.

Reason 2. Because 'our life is hid with Christ in God,' and 'when Christ, who is our life, shall appear, then shall we also appear with him in glory,' Col. iii. 3, 4. Our glorious head is there already. When he shall be revealed, then our glory shall be revealed, for 'he shall come to be glorified in his saints, and to be admired in all those that do believe.'

Reason 3. *In regard of Christ himself:* Christ is in some sort imperfect till the latter day, till his 'second coming.' For the mystical body of Christ is his fulness. Christ is our fulness, and we are his fulness. Now Christ's fulness is made up, when all the members of his mystical body are gathered and united together; the head and the members make but one natural body. So Christ and the church are but one mystical: 1 Cor. xii. 12, 'As the body is one, and hath many members, and all the members of that one body being many, are one body, so also is Christ.' Hence it is that the saints are called 'the glory of Christ,' 2 Cor. viii. 23. Christ in this sense is not fully glorious therefore till that time. The church desires therefore that Christ may be glorious in himself, and glorious in them, that he may come to be 'glorious in his saints,' 2 Thes. i. 10.

Reason 4. Because, *where the treasure is, there will the heart be also*, Mat. vi. 21. Now where is the church's treasure but in Christ? Our spirits are supernatural, and carried to the best of spirits; and who is the best of spirits but Christ himself?

Reason 5. Because *the members are carried to union with the head*. The happiness of the soul is in union with the fountain of happiness, and the nearer the fountain of happiness the more happy. What is it that makes the blessed body of Christ more happy than all the angels and men, but because it is hypostatically united to the second person of the Trinity, and so to the fountain of the Godhead? The nearer to God the happier, the fuller of grace and glory, because he is the God of all grace and glory. Therefore the nearer to Christ the more happy. Now after the resurrection we shall be nearer both in soul and body. We may see this by the contrary. What is it that makes hell so horrible? Because there is an utter and eternal separation from the chiefest and choicest good, God himself. Here the wicked men of the world have the presence of God in the creatures. They taste the sweetness of God's goodness in them. But in hell they shall have none to all eternity. There shall be an utter separation between Christ and them. But now the joining to God, the fountain of all good in heaven, makes heaven to be heaven indeed. If Christ was not there, heaven would be no heaven. Therefore Paul saith, 'I desire to be dissolved and to be with Christ,' Philip. i. 23; and so the church here, 'Come, Lord Jesus.' Then we shall be near, not in soul only, but also in body and soul; and in both we shall be for ever joined to the fountain of all good. It is that which the church desires here; and in the Canticles, what is it that the church prays for in the beginning? 'Let him kiss me with the kisses of his lips,' &c., Cant. i. 2. There she desires the first coming of Christ. But you have it afterwards in the conclusion of the book: 'Make haste, my beloved, and be thou like to the young hart or roe upon the mountain of spices,' Cant. viii. 14. Such is the disposition of the church, that before Christ was come, good people were known by the desire of his coming. And therefore it was the description of holy men, that 'they waited for the consolation of Israel,' Luke ii. 25. O Lord, come quickly, come in the flesh! But now the first coming is past, they desire as much his 'second coming,' and therefore they are described in the epistle of St Paul to be such as 'love and long for the appearing of Christ; a crown of righteousness is laid up for all those that love his appearance,' 2 Tim. iv. 8. Therefore if we had the spirit of the church, we would echo to Christ when he saith, 'I come quickly,' and say, 'Make haste, my beloved,' &c., as the church saith in the latter end of the Canticles.

Reason 6. Beloved, do but compare the glory of that time with the glory which we have here, and that will shew another reason. I will shew it by way of comparison a little, why the church should be desirous of the 'second coming' of Christ.

If the good things that we have by grace here are such 'as eye hath not seen, or ear heard, neither have entered into the heart of man to consider of,' 1 Cor. ii. 9 (for the place is meant of grace especially, that is the natural and immediate meaning), how transcendently then unutterable and unconceivable are those things that are reserved against that time! If the 'first fruits' are so sweet, what is the full harvest! Rom. viii. 23. If the 'earnest' be so comfortable, what is the whole bargain! 2 Cor. v. 5; Eph. i. 14. If this 'joy be unspeakable and full of glory,' 1 Peter i. 8, and this 'peace pass all understanding,' Philip. iv. 7, what will the fulness of joy, peace, and pleasures which are at God's right hand for evermore,' Ps. xvi. 11, and which shall be then, do!

If the angels wonder at the wisdom of God, in the government of his church here, in the midst of confusion, how shall they be put into a new and greater wonderment, when they shall see Christ glorious in his saints!' 2 Thes. i. 10.

If when Christ was born in his abasement, they sang 'Glory to God on high, peace on earth, good will towards men,' Luke ii. 14, how joyful will those blessed spirits be, when Christ and all his members shall be joined in one body in heaven!

If Abraham rejoiced to foresee by the eye of faith the first coming of Christ in the flesh, how should we joy by faith to see the second coming of Christ! If John Baptist leaped in the womb for joy at the presence of Mary the mother of our Lord, how will our hearts dance when we shall see the Lord himself in the great glory and majesty of heaven! Luke i. 44.

If Peter was so ravished with a little drop and glimpse of heaven, when he saw the transfiguration of Christ in the mount, so that he even lost and forgat himself, and 'wist not what he said,' Mat. xvii. 4, how shall we be affected, think you, when we shall see Christ, not in his transfiguration, but in his glorification, for ever!

If old Simeon, when he saw Christ in his infancy, embraced him in his arms and said, 'Now, Lord, lettest thou thy servant depart in peace, according to thy word: for mine eyes have seen thy salvation,' Luke ii. 29, how shall we be transported with joy and admiration to see Christ, not in his swaddling clothes, nor in his infancy, but in heaven all glorious!

If the sight of Christ in his ordinances, in his word and sacraments, doth so affect a Christian's heart, as to transform him into the image of them,

2 Cor. iii. 18, what will it do to see Christ 'face to face,' without these glasses! 1 Cor. xiii. 12.

If the promises do so quicken us, as you have it in the Psalms, 'Thy word hath quickened me,' Ps. cxix. 25, *et alibi*, what will the full performance of them do!

If the communion of saints here be so sweet, even an heaven upon earth, 1 John i. 3, what will it be when all the blessed souls that have been from the beginning of the world unto the end shall be all together, and they altogether freed from all corruptions and infirmities! What a blessed sight will that be!

If so be that things prepared by men be so glorious as the temple of Solomon was, what is that glory which was prepared before the world was, and is in preparing still for the church!

If rest from labour be so sweet, what is 'the glorious liberty of the sons of God!' Rom. viii. 21. A little liberty from corruption, a little freedom and enlargement of spirit here, how sweet is that! When we are set at liberty to serve God, when we have the liberty of the spirit to go boldly to God and to the throne of grace, Heb. iv. 16, how pleasant is that! But oh the liberty of glory! that is true liberty indeed. Beloved, these things deserve and desire admiration,* rather than expression. Therefore I leave them to your wondering and admiring, rather than I will study long to express them. O ye blessed souls, stand still a little, and consider by the eye of faith these glorious things and times to come. You see then by this, the church hath great reason to say, 'Come, Lord Jesus.'

Reason 7. Besides, *do but consider the estate of the church here in this world;* even at the best, 'while we are present in the body, we are absent from the Lord,' 2 Cor. v. 6. But for the most part, the church is in this world as Daniel in the lions' den, as sheep in the midst of ravening wolves, as a ship in the midst of the waves, and as a lily among thorns. All the birds of prey do seize on the poor turtle dove of Christ, and they bear a special and implacable malice against God's church and children. Yea, oftentimes, those that profess religion in the form of it do let out the heart-blood of it indeed, and deny the power thereof. We see it hath been so ever since Christ's coming, and it will be so to the end of the world. Satan abuseth the great ordinances of God, and makes them serviceable to his own ends; so that there is nothing free from Satan's defilement, no, not the best ordinances of God. We see how boisterously and roughly the poor church of God is handled. Are there not oftentimes in the church within itself prejudices, surmises, jealousies one against another, that the company of one another is not so sweet and delightful? And 'woe to the world because of offences,' Mat. xviii. 7. Are there not scandals and offences in the church, that hinders the comfort of it, and many times do cause the falling out of those that are otherwise truly good? So that in regard of Christians themselves, there is not such a sweet complacency and delight one in another as there should be, and as there shall be then. Where there is a different sight and a different light, there will be different judgments and affections. Now all Christians in this life have both a different light and sight, one sees things clearer than another, and so their judgments differ a little, and therefore their affections too: those promises of the lion and the lamb dwelling together, Isa. xi. 6, shall not exactly be performed until this his 'second coming;' but there shall be something of the lion and of the wolf in the best Christians. But then it shall be fully satisfied. Then

* That is, 'wonder.'—G.

all wolfish and lionish dispositions shall be subdued; then there shall be no infirmity in others to displease us, nor any in us to give distaste to them; but then we shall have an eternal communion together. Therefore is there not, in regard of ourselves, good reasons for Christians to say, 'Amen. Even so, come, Lord Jesus'? Then, in regard of every one in his own particular, doth not every one find that true in himself that Paul saith of himself, that we carry about with us 'a body of sin and a body of death'? Our corruptions, that we carry about with us, are like a dead body tied unto a living body. Now, what an odious and loathsome thing is it for a man to carry about with him a dead body! Thus we do, and the more we grow in grace, the more noisome it will be to us; for the more we grow in grace, the more life we have, and therefore the more antipathy against sin. The more we grow in grace, the more light we have to discern the bad, and the more will our love to grace increase. Now the more light, and life, and love, the more shall we be annoyed carrying about with us this body of sin, and 'the thorn in the flesh,' 2 Cor. xii. 7. Some corruptions are as grievous to us as a thorn that rends the flesh. And this is the disposition of the best in this life. Therefore, in regard of the church and the enemies of it, in regard of ourselves and every particular Christian, in regard of their conflicting and afflicted condition, have we not cause to say, 'Amen; come, Lord Jesus'? Thus we see the grounds which the church hath to say so.

Let us now come to the second point, to try whether we can indeed express this desire that the Spirit of God makes. For it is only the Spirit in the spouse that saith, 'Come, Lord Jesus.' Let us see whether the Spirit says so in us.

We shall not say much. It may be known by that which hath been said in the beginning, and it is evident also besides. Therefore, in a word or two.

Trial 1. Let us try ourselves by this. *What benefit have we by the first coming of Christ, by his death, and the shedding of his blood?* Doth that pardon our sins? Are our consciences 'besprinkled by that from dead works to serve the ever-living God?' Heb. ix. 14. Are our hearts set at liberty to go to the throne of grace? Have we thus any benefit by his first coming? Then we cannot but with a long and longing expectation look for his second.

But, on the contrary, he that hath no good by the first, cannot truly desire nor comfortably expect the second coming of Christ: for why? The second coming is but to make good what is begun here. The first is to redeem our souls, the second is to glorify our bodies. If our souls be not redeemed, never look for the 'redemption of our bodies,' Rom. viii. 23. The first and second coming of Christ are of so near connection, that oftentimes they are comprised together, as the regeneration of our souls and the regeneration of our bodies, the adoption of our souls and the adoption of our bodies, the redemption of our souls and the redemption of our bodies; to shew that wheresoever there is the true redemption and adoption of the soul, there the redemption and adoption of the body will follow, and an expectation thereof also. Christ will be redemption to us when he hath been redemption to our souls first, in the assurance of the pardon of our sins. Look then to that first.

Trial 2. If we desire the second coming of Christ, *we will prepare for it.* If a man says, he desires to go to some great person, and yet never thinks of any preparation for it, it is but a pretended desire if he doth not put on his best clothes, and fit himself for it, as Joseph did for Pharaoh, Gen. xli. 14. So if a man hope for this coming of Christ, he will 'purify himself for it, even as he is pure,' 1 John iii. 3. He will not appear in his foul clothes, but will 'put off the old man, and put on the new,' Eph. iv. 22. He will fit himself as the bride for the coming of the bridegroom. Beloved, if the thoughts of Christ's second coming be not efficacious to work in the soul a great care to fit and prepare for it, it is but a false conceit and lying fancy, it is no holy desire.

Trial 3. Examine it by this, *whether your hearts be the kingdom of Christ, whether he rule in your hearts here?* Do we think to rule with him in heaven, in his kingdom, if we will not yield up our hearts to be his kingdom upon earth? No; he will come into our hearts before we shall come to him; he will come to rule in us here, before we shall ever think to come to rule with him in heaven. Therefore all they that stand out against the ordinances of God, and will live in sin against their knowledge and conscience, do they spend any thoughts or wishes on Christ's second coming? He will come indeed, but it will be a 'day of darkness and gloominess' unto them, Joel ii. 2. Such persons cannot say, 'Come, Lord Jesus, come quickly,' but 'Mountains come, and rocks come, come quickly: fall upon us, and hide us from the presence of him that sitteth upon the throne, and from the wrath of the Lamb,' Rev. vi. 16. Nothing will be more terrible to such than that day. Fire is the most comfortable thing, and the most terrible; and so God is most comfortable to his, and yet most terrible to such that do not prepare for his coming. 'Who amongst us,' saith the prophet, 'shall dwell with the devouring fire? Who amongst us shall dwell with everlasting burnings?' Isa. xxxiii. 14. Who shall appear before Christ? To them, then, that live in their sins, in this glorious light of the gospel, there is a most terrible threatening, even from the coming of Christ. 'If any man love not the Lord Jesus,' when he is discovered clearly in the gospel, 'let him be Anathema, Maran-atha,' 1 Cor. xvi. 22, which is a more terrible curse than any is in the law. As the greatest blessings are from the coming of Christ, so from the same is the more terrible threatening. There is not a more terrible curse in all the Scriptures again, as that is in the Corinthians. So that 'the Lord shall come in flaming fire, rendering vengeance to all them that know him not, and that obey not the gospel,' 2 Thes. i. 8. Therefore take heed of this.

Trial 4. Try it again *by holy exercises.* They that desire indeed the coming of Christ, they exercise themselves much in holiness: they exercise themselves in the beginning of heaven here upon earth, in reading and hearing the word, in the communion of saints, in praying and acquainting themselves with God, &c. In what else shall we be employed when we come to heaven? There shall be the perfection of these graces and exercises begun here upon earth. Many a profane wretch's heart swells when he comes to prayer or any divine exercise. He is proudly brought up, and his heart is not subdued to holy exercises here. Heaven will not brook* such, and such will not brook heaven. There is nothing but praising God continually. Now if you will not endure these holy exercises here, what should you do in heaven? Therefore let us not deceive our own souls, I beseech you. If we say this truly, 'Come, Lord Jesus,' undoubtedly it will have an influence into our lives, it will stir up all graces in the soul: as faith, to lay hold upon it; hope, to expect it; love, to embrace it; patience, to endure anything for it; heavenly-mindedness, to fit and pre-

* That is, 'endure.'—G.

pare for it; faithfulness in our callings, that we may make up our accounts before that time, &c. There is not a grace of the Spirit, but it is stirred up and quickened thereby. Therefore be not deceived. It is impossible that we should have dead, and dull, and cold hearts, and yet believe this, that there is such a glorious time to come. Undoubtedly it will inspire and cause strength and comfort in all our sufferings, and in all our doings, if our hearts do think with the spirit and thought of faith of this glorious appearing of Christ. Therefore we should shame ourselves. What! Can I hear of these things, and be no more affected with them than I am? Thus we should complain of the deadness and dulness of our hearts, and labour to work our hearts to an admiration of the excellencies that shall be revealed then.

But I go on, and come, in the last place, to some few directions how we should come to frame ourselves to this, to be able to utter this desire and prayer.

Direct. 1. *Labour to be reconciled to God.* Maintain and preserve thy peace and reconciliation with God, and then all things will be reconciled unto us, that are between us and the second coming of Christ. Nay, all shall be ours: death ours, devil ours, to help us to heaven. When we are at peace with God, all shall be at peace with us, John v. 23; Hos. ii. 18. And then we may have comfortable thoughts of that day; then we can think of death, and not be troubled; of hell and God's wrath, and not be disquieted. Therefore, above all, let us get the assurance of the grand point of justification, of being clothed with the righteousness of Christ. Let us be sure to be found in that, and appear in it, to understand that point well. St Paul was wonderful careful hereof. He desires to have it as a seal of the righteousness of faith, and 'to be found in him, not having his own righteousness,' &c., Phil. iii. 9, as if he were tender, to touch upon Christ's glory. If we be clothed with the garments of Christ's righteousness, we may go through the wrath of God; for that alone is wrath-proof. That will pacify God, and pacify the conscience too. It is a righteousness of God's own providing and accepting. Be sure that you understand it well; that you appear not in your own, but in his, and then may you think of that day with comfort.

Direct. 2. If we would think of the blessed times that are to come with comfort, then let us labour to grow in the new creature, to be more and more filled with the fulness of God, to strive to have more of Christ in us still. The more we have of Christ in us, the more shall we desire his coming to us. Let us desire and labour to have all the corners of the heart filled up with the Spirit of Christ, our understandings with knowledge, our affections with love and delight, and our wills with obedience. The Scripture calls it, 'being filled with all the fulness of God,' Eph. iii. 19. Now the more we enter into the kingdom of heaven, by growth in grace here, the fitter shall we be for it, and the more shall we desire it. The more suitableness there is between us and heaven, and the glorious condition to come, the more shall we long after it, and rejoice in the thoughts of it.

Direct. 3. *Be sure to do what you do quickly and thoroughly.* Satan is so wise that he knows his time is but short, and therefore lays about him with great wrath and fury, Rev. xii. 12. Oh let us be so wise as to know that our time is but short. God himself tells us that it is so. Our time is a little spot of time cut out between two eternities, before and after, 1 Cor. vii. 29. Then let us do our work quickly. We may be suddenly surprised before we be aware; and as the tree falleth, so it lies; as a man lives, so he dies; as death leaves us, so judgment, and the second coming of Christ, shall find us. We should therefore, as the apostle saith, 'work out our own salvation with fear and trembling,' Phil. ii. 12. Many men when they come to die are troubled about this; Oh, I have not done so; I should have done this and that, and have not; but I have done amiss, I have not thoroughly repented; something is not done that should have been; I have not made mine evidences sound, I have not 'made my calling and election sure,' 2 Peter i. 10. Oh my conscience is troubled, and my soul cannot find that peace in God, &c. Oh do you take warning by them, and now work out your salvation with fear and trembling; and that upon this ground, because the time is short and uncertain. Beloved, it is a great error in us. We think of reaping as soon as we begin to sow, nay, we begin to sow then when we should reap. Then we begin to think of God and goodness when we lie a-dying. That should be a time of reaping the comfort of all our former life, and to think of the time to come with joy. Oh what a comfortable thing would it be if we can with St Paul look backward and say, 'I have fought the good fight, I have finished my course, I have kept the faith,' &c., 2 Tim. iv. 7. He looks back with comfort, and therefore he looks forward with comfort too; 'From henceforth there is laid up for me a crown of righteousness, which the Lord, the righteous judge, shall give me at that day,' &c., verse 8. When a Christian man hath done the will of God, and looks backward and saith, I had a race to run, and I have run it; I had a faith to keep, and I have kept it; I had a fight to fight, and I have fought it; and then looks forward, and sees a crown of eternal glory before his eyes: what a comfort and ravishing joy will this afford! Whether he looks backward or forward, all is glorious. But if we be careless and negligent, and will not work out our salvation, then we cannot with Hezekiah look back with comfort, and say to God, 'Lord, remember how I have walked before thee in truth and uprightness of heart, and have done that which was right in thy sight,' Isa. xxxviii. 3. Neither can we with St Paul look forward with any comfort. Beloved, heaven is a pure place, and requires a great deal of purity in those that come thither; and Christ is holy and glorious. Therefore we must set no measure and pitch to any holiness in this life, but grow still more and more heavenly till we come to heaven. Therefore the apostle sets it down by way of wonderment in the last of St Peter: 'Seeing all these things shall be dissolved,' saith he, 2 Peter iii. 11. What saith he to that? He cannot tell what to say. Therefore he says nothing in particular, but in general: 'What manner of persons ought we to be in all holy conversation and godliness!' Some men will set a measure and stint to themselves, and if any go beyond their measure, then they are such and such, curious, nice, and precise, &c.* Why! What measure of holiness should be set to them that look for the second coming of Christ? 'What manner of persons ought we to be!' He cannot tell what to say in particular, and therefore leaveth it to admiration. We must not then set up our staff, and put any measure to any perfection here in this world; but still grow in grace and godliness, looking for and hasting unto the coming of the day of the Lord.

Direct. 4. *Let us take all advantages to help us in this desire and prayer for the second coming of Christ*, from all the crosses of this life, and from all the businesses of Satan. Satan was shut out of paradise, but he is still

* Cf. note *c*, Vol. II page 194.—G.

creeping into the paradise of the church. But in heaven he shall never come. He was once there, and was cast down from thence, never to come there again. But in the church he is always stirring. He is never so bound up but he hath some mischief to do. Now let the consideration of Satan and his instruments, that are always some way or other molesting of the church, and are as thorns in their sides, stir us up to desire the second coming of Christ. So from all particular losses and crosses let us help ourselves. If we have lost a friend, let us fill our hearts with comfort from the 'second coming' of Christ, and from the consideration of that, that then the time will come when all friends shall meet together. Do we leave anything in this world behind us? We shall meet with better there, better friends, a better place, better employment; all better. Therefore let us take advantage from everything to help forward that desire. In a word, I beseech you, because there be many things that might be spoken to this purpose, let it be your main care to fit yourselves for that time. It is a time of longing here, while we live. It is the time between the contract and the marriage. Let us labour to be fitted and prepared for that time.

Obj. But you shall have many a good soul cry out, Oh, I am not so desirous of the coming of Christ as I ought.

Ans. True. It may be so because of thy wants, because thou hast not prepared thyself, because thou art not spiritual, because thou art not mortified. This ariseth further, as from other causes, so from this. Thou art ignorant of the covenant of grace, that God is thy Father, and that he hath bound himself as a father to pardon the sins of his children. Therefore, if thy sins be but infirmities, that thou strivest against, thou mayest be comforted. Mark what the apostle saith, 'We ourselves, which have the first-fruits of the Spirit, even we ourselves do groan within ourselves, waiting for the adoption, even the redemption of our bodies,' Rom. viii. 23. If we labour against our corruptions, it should be so far from hindering our desire of Christ's coming, that we should desire it the rather, because we labour under them; for then we shall be fully rid of them. Labour to understand the covenant of grace more fully. Christ is a mediator and intercessor. For whom? For perfect men? No. But for them that unwillingly run into debt with God every day. Therefore we say in the Lord's prayer, 'Give us this day our daily bread, and forgive us our debts,' &c., Mat. vi. 11, 12. The ignorance of evangelical points makes us so cold, so dead and dull, as we are oftentimes.

Obj. But you will say, I desire to live still. Those that desire the 'second coming' of Christ, desire that he would come and fetch them out of the world when they have done their work. May not I do so?

Ans. Yes you may, but it must be with a reservation that you may bring to heaven as many as you can, that you may get further evidence of your salvation; and so in other respects you may desire to live, so it may be that God may honour himself by our lives. But simply, and as the thing is in itself, we ought to be of St Paul's mind, 'to desire to be dissolved, and to be with Christ,' which is far better, Philip. i. 23.

Therefore when the time of our dissolution comes, we are to be willing to resign up our souls unto God, not only patiently, but cheerfully. For why? The day of death is a day of jubilee, a day of coronation, a day of marriage, a day of harvest, a day of triumph. We are to be ashamed of the disproportion of our desires to earthly things and to heavenly. Is the labourer loath to think of a sabbath or a day of rest? Is a soldier loath to think of a day of victory and triumph? Is a contracted person loath to think of the day of marriage? or a king of the day of his coronation? They are all desirous of these things, and why should not we be of that time, when all these things shall indeed and really be performed? All those things are but shadows, and scarce that, of things to come, and yet how earnestly desirous are men of them? Have not we then just cause to take occasion to shame and blame ourselves, for the disproportion of our desires to earthly and heavenly things?

But now, when we have finished our work, when God hath been served by us in our generations—as it was said of David, 'that he served God in his own generation, by the will of God, and after that fell on sleep,' Acts xiii. 36—then God will take off our desire of living any longer, then he will make us even willing to die. As St Paul, in the last epistle that ever he made, when he had run his race and fought his fight, and finished his course, then nothing but a crown. 'Henceforth, there is laid up for me a crown of righteousness,' &c., 2 Tim. iv. 8. And in the same chapter afterward: 'The Lord shall deliver me from every evil work, and preserve me unto his heavenly kingdom,' ver. 18. So saith Christ, 'I have glorified thee on the earth: I have finished the work which thou gavest me to do. And now, O Father, glorify thou me with thine own self,' John xvii. 4, 5. So when the children of God have an item from the Spirit of God, that they have done all that God would have them for to do, then they will be most willing to go hence. In the mean time, they 'must run with patience the race that is set before them,' Heb. xii. 1; they must fight the fight that God hath pitched for them, and keep the faith; they must be willing to do all that God would have them, in an humble submission to his will. But when they have done all, then their hearts wlll be enlarged to desire the coming of Christ, that he would come and call them home.

So, then, this doubt is sufficiently answered. In a word, I will end with this.

When you find your hearts dull and cold, and inactive to good, then fetch fire from hence to inflame them: from the 'second coming' of Christ, from the love of God in Christ, from the love of his appearance. Oh, rouse up and quicken your hearts with such considerations. Do you conflict with any enemies, either without or within? Remember what the apostle saith: 'Fight the good fight of faith; lay hold on eternal life,' 1 Tim. vi. 12. What is the way to fight the good fight of faith? Why, lay hold on eternal life, and that will make a man fight indeed.

Are you in any disconsolate condition? If you be, see what the apostle Paul saith to the Thessalonians: 'Wherefore, comfort ye one another with these words,' 1 Thess. iv. 18. With what words? Why, 'We shall be ever with the Lord.' Oh these words will comfort indeed. Consider, when you have lost your friends, your estate, or anything, it shall be all fully made up there? Do you, as it were, make it up beforehand, with comforts of a higher nature? They be things that will comfort indeed.

And so, when you find yourselves dull in doing the work of the Lord, think upon the 'second coming' of Christ, and that he will not then come empty-handed, but 'he will bring his reward with him,' Rev. xxii. 12. Consider what St Paul said to Timothy: 'I charge thee, therefore, before God and the Lord Jesus Christ, who shall judge the quick and dead at his appearing, and his kingdom,' &c., 2 Tim. iv. 1. The holy apostle had no greater a conjuration to move Timothy to be diligent, and to quicken him in his ministry, than by the coming of our Lord Jesus. So let us stir up ourselves, and comfort ourselves hereby.

Beloved, the soul is never in such a tune, as when the thoughts of these glorious times have raised the affections to the highest pitch and peg. Then the soul is never uncomfortable; and so long as it is so affected, it cannot sin, for we lose our frame, we let down the soul in base desires, we let loose our thoughts from closing with Christ, and with the time to come, when we sin. When we let them loose, then they sink down to earthly things; and that is the cause of all sin and of all discomfort.

So long, then, as we keep our hearts in a blessed frame of faith, and in a love of the appearing of Christ, they are impregnable. Satan cannot come between us and our faith, but he labours to loosen our faith and love, and to distract us with the businesses of the world, that we shall have very seldom thoughts of these things. Alas, that we 'who are born again to an inheritance incorruptible and undefiled, and that fadeth not away, reserved in heaven for us,' 1 Pet. i. 4, should have so little and so light thoughts of our inheritance!

If a man were to go a journey by sea a year hence, he would be thinking every day upon his journey, what he should have to carry with him, and what will do him good when he comes there. We have all of us a long journey to go, from earth to heaven; and we should be thinking of it every day in the year.

But we have a company of men in the world, all whose happiness is in putting off all thoughts in that kind; in deferring the day of their death, and putting the evil day far away from them; not thinking upon them; that so they may drown themselves in pleasure and voluptuousness. Ah, what a pitiful case hath Satan and our own sinful dispositions brought us unto, that we should place our happiness, safety, and comfort in putting off the thoughts of death, in going on presumptuously in sin, and never thinking upon that great day! Alas, they cannot think of it but as Felix did, who, when he heard Paul dispute and reason of 'righteousness, and temperance, and judgment to come, trembled,' Acts xxiv. 25.

Why, let Felix tremble, and let the world tremble, but let every Christian that hath made his peace with God, rejoice. Even as poor birds do sing when the spring time is returned again—for it warms them, and puts life and spirit into them, and they entertain the light and heat of the sun with singing and melody—so let us, in our thoughts, entertain Christ's coming with joy and comfort, having made our peace, substantially and solidly, with God. Let us look up, and lift up our heads with joy, for our redemption draweth nigh, Luke xxi. 28.

Now I come to the particular occasion.

It is well known that the particular occasion of this meeting is, to celebrate and solemnise the funeral of that worthy man Sir Thomas Crew, one of the king's serjeants, in regard of whom I made choice of this text. If I wanted matter to speak of him, he had many natural excellent parts, which did commend him. I might speak of the quickness of his wit, of the firmness of his memory, of the readiness of his expressions, of the clearness and solidity of his judgment, able to penetrate into the depth of things, &c. And for his ability in his particular calling, I might say many things. He was a man very eminent in his calling: he was one of the oracles of the law in his time; one that had gathered very long and large experience, and wonderful great dexterity in that profession. And surely, beloved, these things are not to be neglected by us, though to God-ward they are not much regarded. For natural parts, the devil excels, and hath more than any man; but yet to men-ward, they are to be esteemed, for they vindicate men from the reproach and obloquy of the world. They will say, Such a man was a religious man, but he had no skill in his calling; a good man, but unlearned. Now then it takes away reproach and disgrace from religion, when it can be said, This was an excellent man in his profession, and withal, a very excellent good Christian. It is the guise and fashion of proud profaneness, to lay religion as low as they can. They will take away or diminish all parts from religious persons as near as they can, that religion itself may seem vile and contemptible. For if religion once should win credit, then their baseness would appear the more; and that their pride will not endure. Wherefore, if these things be to be regarded, in regard of men, we ought to thank God for it, when grace is graced with excellent parts. Therefore, God sometimes vouchsafeth to men that are truly religious, excellency of parts. Otherwise, grace is lovely in itself; but as a precious stone and pearl set in gold is more precious and glorious, so religion, set in the stem of nature and excellent parts, hath more lustre and beauty, and the larger improvement.

You have a company of profane wretches in the world, even in these glorious times of the gospel, that do glory only in their excellent parts, that will seek even to the devil himself, so they may out-brag others, and gain to themselves a reputation of wit; and some will vilely adventure upon sin against their conscience, thinking that they should lose all reputation of wit and parts, if they should become religious once. But you see that God oftentimes adorns religious men with excellent parts of nature. Religion indeed cuts off the froth, the exuberancy and redundancy of parts; but it increaseth the solidity of parts, and spiritualiseth them, and directs them to their right end, to the glory of God and good of mankind. Therefore, they may stand well enough together.

Now, in this worthy man there was a concentrating and joining together of the parts of nature and the parts of industry, and likewise of the parts of grace. And that which did steer his conversation, and rule all aright, was indeed the true fear of God, which caused him to set the stamp of religion on all his courses in his whole conversation.

For the Lord's day, it may a little be discerned by that. He had a wonderful care to keep it holy. He was as eminent as any in his profession for that. He would not intermeddle with the businesses of his calling on that day. He did not think it enough to hear the sermon and divine service, and then to go to the works of his calling. And in this he is to be commended. For whose good hath God appointed the Lord's day? Is it not for our own? Should not we grow base and earthly-minded, if one day in seven we should not be heavenly-minded, and think upon our everlasting condition in another world? Shall we think much then of that which God appoints for us?

But to return. Besides his care of the Lord's day, for he did not limit his religion to a day, he was careful in his family of having morning and evening prayers; yea, and private also, twice in a day at the least. And this, as it did bring strength to his soul, and put a beauty upon it, so it did also sanctify his labours and prosper his businesses, and bring them to a good issue. He lost nothing by it. And seeing it is almost impossible in these profane times but that such courses as these are should meet with envy and scorn from some, therefore he had learned with Moses 'to bear the reproach of Christ,' Heb. xi. 26. He did account nothing more glorious than the profession of religion. And truly religion is a glorious thing: it puts a glory and beauty upon the soul.

But there are many men in these days that will not own Christ in his cause. How will such look him in the face another day, when he hath said, 'Whosoever shall be ashamed of me, and of my words, in this adulterous and sinful generation, of him also shall the Son of man be ashamed, when he cometh in the glory of his Father, with his holy angels,' Mark viii. 38.

But this worthy man, I say, what he judiciously undertook he constantly went through withal. He would not be scorned or turned out of his course by any man. He was a child of wisdom, able to justify what he did against the spirit of gross and proud profaneness, and against an empty, formal, dead, cold profession. He had not only the word of God to back him, but his own excellencies, and the sweetness that he felt and found in his Christian course, to defend him. And this should all we labour for.

He was, moreover, a man exceedingly conscionable.* He had a very tender conscience, being willing in all doubtful things to be directed and resolved, which was an excellent thing. He knew, and so should all you, that the time would come ere long that a man would give a great deal to have a good conscience, and this was in him.

For his conversation in his family, he was very mild and gentle at all times; not as some, who being sweetened with a fee, are wonderful mild and calm to their clients, but are lions in their own houses. His carriage was not such.

For his conversation with other kind of men, it was sweet and loving, and very useful. He was full of goodness, and offices of love. He did not bear himself big upon his offices or place; but was, as David saith of himself, 'as a weaned child,' Ps. cxxxi. 2. Though his parts did raise him up, and advance him above the ordinary sort of men, yet his grace levelled him, that he made himself equal to the lower sort, and yet in such sort that he had wisdom to understand and know himself in his place, and so grace will teach a man to do.

He was a marvellous great encourager of honest, laborious, religious ministers, for their Master's sake, and for their work's sake, and he lost nothing by it. He had a prophet's reward, the prayers of all good men that were acquainted with him. And I hope that that commendation will not die with him, but that it will live in those that he lives in.†

For his disposition toward the poor, he was very merciful and compassionate. He was the poor man's lawyer; insomuch that the last cause that ever he pleaded was *sub formá pauperis*, for a poor man, and a minister; as it was publicly shewn to the greatest and most judicious magistrates in the kingdom. 'He was a foot to the lame, and eyes to the blind,' as Job saith he was, Job xxix. 15, and 'he made the widows to rejoice.' He was a helpful and fruitful man, 'a tree of righteousness,' full of good fruit. He made the times and places better where he lived. He was a great lover of his country, even in some degree to the prejudice of himself.

It pleased King James, of famous memory, to choose him with some other commissioners, to go into Ireland about public employment, which he performed with such care and conscience, that when he returned home again he was made the king's serjeant, and after that speaker in parliament, and the mouth of the Commons.

* That is, 'conscientious.'—G.

† Qu. 'leaves'?—Ed.

He was forty years a practitioner in his calling; in which time God blessed him with a great increase of his estate. God sometimes doth delight to make good his temporal promises to a religious, industrious, and faithful man, and that in the eyes of the world. Sometimes God carries things in a cloud and in a mystery. We cannot see how such and such men should go back in the world. This will appear to us another day, in the day of revelation. But because God would encourage religion, faithfulness, and industry, he makes good his temporal promises to such faithful men as he was. Such was his faithfulness, such was his dexterity and quickness in dispatching men's causes and business, that men were willing to put their causes and estates into his hands. Therefore it is no wonder, if in so long a time as forty years' practice, God blessed him with so great an estate.

Obj. But some may object his going to London of late times, when his infirmities grew upon him.

Ans. But this much I know, that the exigency and urgency of other men's occasions did importune, and in part draw him to it. And then again his staying at home was very tedious to him. It is death to an industrious man, that hath been in employment, to be idle, as it is death to an idle man to be employed. He was a man of an active spirit, and one that was not hindered by his journeys. Neither would it have holpen or eased him to have stayed at home. Therefore you must judge charitably of that.

But I come in a word to the time of his sickness, and so to the hour of his death.

For these later years he had two several severe churlish monitors that did put him in mind of his end, namely, the stone and the strangury. In these sore diseases he carried himself with wonderful great patience. None did ever hear any words fall from him that witnessed any impatience.

Toward his end, he considered that he was now for another and a better place. Therefore, when he was invited to dinner in the house of which he was, in Gray's Inn, saith he, 'I must dine in another place.'

When his sickness did seize upon him more sharply, though the pain thereof took away a great part of the powers of his soul, yet he did manifest a great deal of strength of faith by divers words that fell from him: 'As the hart brays after the rivers of water, so panteth my soul after thee, O God,' Ps. xlii. 1. And as the church doth here, 'Come, Lord Jesus, come quickly:' and, 'Lord, now lettest thou thy servant depart in peace, according to thy word.' He was displeased with them about him, that out of their love to him did recall him by cordials out of a swoon, and so protracted his life longer than he would have had it: 'You keep me too long from Christ,' saith he, 'God is merciful to me, and you are not,' with many the like. And when they heaved up his body, his spirit was so strong in him as if he desired to meet Christ before his time.

And thus, at length, this blessed man meekly yielded up his blessed soul into the hands of his blessed Saviour, that had so dearly bought it, sanctified it, and sealed it by his holy and blessed Spirit.

Beloved, I think there were but few men of later times, of whom we had more, and a more general loss, than of this worthy man. His servants lost a kind and loving master; his children lost a most tender and careful father; his friends, a true, cordial, and hearty friend; the professors of the law, a special ornament of it; the ministers especially, a sweet encourager; the poor clients, a loving patron; the richer sort, a grave, wise, and judicious counsellor; religion and justice, a great supporter; the country where he lived, a faithful magistrate. So that here is the loss of many.

But what hath he lost? He hath attained to that which he desired so earnestly, he hath joined himself to Christ and left behind him a monument of mortality, the sad remembrance and remainder of him, his dead body. He hath made an happy change, of earth for heaven; of the company of men for the company of perfect souls and angels in heaven; of troublesome employments here for glorious employments for ever. So that he is no loser.

He hath left behind him likewise another sweet memorial and remembrance of him, as sweet as the ointment of the apothecary, unto the church and people of God.

He lived, to end all, in the best times that have been in the church since the apostles' times all his days. He was born under the gospel and lived under the gospel. He began to favour the best things, even from his youth. And God lengthened his days very long for the good of us. Therefore God miraculously, almost, preserved his weak worn body. It was much that such a spirit should endure in such a body so long under such diseases. But, at length, being full of days, and full of honour with all good people, God having blessed him in his children (for his children's children inherit his blessing), in the comfort and assurance of an happy change, he yielded up his blessed soul, and triumphant spirit, into the hands of God, whom he had loved; whose cause he had owned here in the world, in the midst of this sinful generation, and whom he professed, even unto death; whose coming he desired so earnestly; where, and with whom, we now leave him.

And for you, beloved, that fully know, as the apostle Paul saith, 'his purpose, his manner of life, his faith, his long-suffering, his charity, patience,' &c., 2 Tim. iii. 10, I beseech you, let not his memory die with him; but let those virtues that were in him live in you, so long as you live. 'If there be anything praiseworthy, or of good report' (as indeed there was much in him), 'think on these things,' Phil. iv. 8. If there were any infirmities in him (as, I think, there were as few in him as in any man), love hath a mantle to cover them. He was a gracious man every way; one that adorned the doctrine and gospel of Christ in everything. Therefore, I beseech you, as the apostle saith, 'be followers of him, as he was of Christ.' We must one day give an account to God, not only for what sermons we have heard, but for the examples of those amongst whom we have lived; how we have profited by the lights that God hath set before us in the world, whether we have imitated their examples or no. We must give an account for all the good we might have received, not only by the means of salvation, but also by the precedents of worthy persons set before us.

I beseech you, in the bowels of the Lord Jesus, 'think on these things,' and 'the peace of God be with you!'

END OF VOL. VI.

THE WORKS OF
RICHARD SIBBES

THE WORKS OF
RICHARD SIBBES

VOLUME 7

Miscellaneous Sermons
& Indices

Edited by
Alexander B. Grosart

THE BANNER OF TRUTH TRUST

THE BANNER OF TRUTH TRUST

Head Office
3 Murrayfield Road
Edinburgh, EH12 6EL
UK

North America Office
610 Alexander Spring Road
Carlisle, PA 17015
USA

banneroftruth.org

The Complete Works of Richard Sibbes
first published in 7 volumes 1862-64
This reprint of volume 7 first published by
the Banner of Truth Trust 2001
Reprinted 2023

*

ISBN
Print: 978 0 85151 341 6

*

Printed in the USA by
Versa Press Inc.,
East Peoria, IL.

CONTENTS.

PREFATORY NOTE.

The present volume includes the whole of the 'single' Sermons not already given, and the whole of the remaining writings of Dr Sibbes; and now the Editor has to congratulate the subscribers to the Series, and himself, upon the completion of this first collective edition of the entire Works of this author.*

In so doing, he takes this opportunity of repeating the expression of his obligation to friends and correspondents for valuable suggestions and help kindly rendered from volume to volume. It is for others to judge how far, with such aid, he has succeeded in his arduous task; he only knows that, without that aid, he would not have succeeded so well.

In the Preface it was proposed to give, in a short essay, an 'analysis' and 'estimate' of Sibbes as a man and a writer, together with a view of his 'opinions' and 'character' as reflected in his books; likewise to try to shed a little light on his relations to others and theirs to him, and to guide the casual reader to the treasures of thought, wisdom, spiritual insight, tenderness, and consolation of this incomparable old worthy.† It will be found that all this has been forestalled in another shape—viz., in the somewhat minute 'analysis' of each important treatise contained in the 'contents' of the successive volumes, and in the 'notes,' elucidatory and illustrative, appended to the several dedications, epistles, and numerous allusions and quotations, in combination with the full *Indices* and *Glossary* in the present volume. All of these have much exceeded the original estimate, and *practically* fulfil the promise and enable each reader to do for himself what at best could only have been done imperfectly by another. The *Index of Topics* has received anxious attention, and, incorporating as it does the original tables drawn up by Sibbes and his original editors, will readily guide to what may be handled and sought. The most cursory use of it

* Cf. Preface, Vol I. page xiii. † *Ibid.* p. xv. ‡ Memoir, Vol. I. p. xix.

will reveal that the author gives forth no 'uncertain sound,' but definitely yet most catholically, scripturally yet most charitably, expresses his 'opinions,' which all bear the stamp of being *convictions.* He was a Puritan in 'doctrine,' but loyal to the Church of England with that touching loyalty shewn to the throne by illustrious contemporaries even when they despised its occupant. On almost every point of Theology the Works of Richard Sibbes will rarely be consulted 'in vain.' They are a casket of gems, and the lid needs but to be raised to flash forth wealth of spiritual thought.

In closing his onerous labours, the Editor would, in a few sentences, characterise the Works now collected and completed; and at once that epithet, which seems by universal consent to have been associated with the name of Richard Sibbes—'HEAVENLY'—recurs. It is the one distinctive adjective for him. For if there ever has been, since apostolic times, a 'heavenly' man, the meek 'Preacher' of Gray's Inn was he. Emphatically, 'he was a *good* man, and full of the Holy Ghost and of faith' (Acts xi. 24); and in accord with this, he is pre-eminently and peculiarly a 'son of consolation,' a 'comforter.' This, I should say, is the *merit* of these works. The minister of the gospel and the private reader will find abundant 'consolations' for bruised, tried, despondent, groping souls. Nor is this *characteristic* a small thing. It must be a growing conviction, with all who mark the 'signs of the times,' that the want of our age, in the church as in the world, is not more intellect or genius, learning or culture, but more reality of CHRISTIAN LIFE —more 'GOOD' rather than more 'great' men. Perhaps there never has been a period—speaking generally—of more intellect in intense activity, if not in mass, more learning and diffused culture, than the present; and certainly never was there an age of such thick-coming interrogation of all problems in all realms of thought and speculation. But these seem often lamentably disassociated from GOODNESS, from conscience, from spiritual integrity and truthfulness, and above all, from Christian LIFE.

For Sibbes, then, is not claimed the title of 'great'—so much abused, and indeed vulgarised—in the world's meaning. Weighed against contemporaries—Shakespeare, Bacon, Milton—he has no awful crown of genius. Placed beside other divines, Church and Puritan, he lacks the orient splendour of Jeremy Taylor, the massiveness of Barrow, the intensity of Baxter, the unexpected wit of Thomas Adams, the exhaustiveness of John Owen, the profundity of Thomas Goodwin; nor has he left behind him any great work such as that on the 'The Creed' by Pearson, or the 'Defensio' by Bull. In reading him, we never come upon recondite speculation, wide-reaching generalisation, sustained argument, burning eloquence, flashes of wit, aphoristic wisdom, not even, or but rarely, melody of words. But a 'soul of goodness' informs every fibre and filament of his thinking; nor is there a page without FOOD for the spiritually 'hungry.' He has few equals, and certainly no superior, for ingenuity in bringing 'comfort' to tried, weary ones, and in happy use of Scripture, his mere citation of a text being often like a shaft of light.* It should be noticed, that the very invariableness of Sibbes's excellence hides his richness and power, as the very commonness of the air makes us forget the wonder and the blessedness of it.

In a word, Richard Sibbes seems ever to come to us from his knees, ever brings with him a 'savour' of Christ, and beyond almost every contemporary approaches the office of the Holy Spirit, whose specific work is not to do '*great*' but '*good*' things, ever taking 'of the things of Christ and SHEWING THEM.' May THE MASTER own and use this edition of his long-departed servant's Works in these 'latter days.'

A. B. G.

* See 'Affliction' and 'Assurance' in General Index.

BALAAM'S WISH.

BALAAM'S WISH.

NOTE.

'Balaam's Wish' forms one of the sermons which compose 'Evangelical Sacrifices' (4to, 1640). [Cf. Vol. V. page 156.] Its separate title-page is given below.*

* BALAAMS
VVISH.

In one Funerall Sermon upon
NVMB. 23. 10.

BY
The late Learned and Reverend Divine,
RICH. SIBBS:
Doctor in Divinity, Mr of KATHERINE Hall
in *Cambridge*, and sometimes Preacher
to the Honourable Society of
GRAYES-INNE.

PRO. 13. 4.
The soule of the sluggard desireth, and hath nothing.

LONDON,
Printed by *E. Purslow*, for *N. Bourne*, at the Roy-
all Exchange, and *R. Harford* at the gilt
Bible in Queenes head Alley, in Pater-
Noster-Row. 1639.

BALAAM'S WISH.

Let me die the death of the righteous, and let my last end be like his!—NUMB. XXIII. 10.

THE false prophet Balaam goes about to curse, where God had blessed. But God reveals his wonders in his saints by delivering of them, and keeping them from dangers, when they never think of them. They never thought they had such an enemy as Balaam. The church of God is a glorious company, and the great God doth great things for it. So long as they keep close to him, their state is impregnable, as we may read here. Neither Balak nor Balaam, that was hired to curse them, could prevail, but the curse returns upon their own head.

These words I have read to you, they are Balaam's desire, Balaam's acclamation. Divers questions might be moved concerning Balaam, which I will not stand upon, but come directly to the words, wherein are considerable these things.

First, That the righteous men die, and have an end as well as others.

Secondly, That the state of the soul continues after death. It was in vain for him to desire 'to die the death of the righteous,' but in regard of the subsistence of the soul.

Thirdly, That the estate of righteous men in their end is a blessed estate, because here it was the desire of Balaam, 'Oh that I might die the death of the righteous!'

Fourthly, There is an excellent estate of God's people, and they desire that portion: 'Oh let me die the death of the righteous.' These are the four things I shall unfold, which discover the intendment of Balaam in these words.

For the first I will touch it briefly, and so go on.

Obs. 1. *The righteous die, and in the same manner outwardly as the wicked do.*

For Christ, in his first coming, came not to redeem our bodies from death, but our souls from damnation. His second coming shall be to redeem our bodies from corruption into a 'glorious liberty.' Therefore wise men die as well as fools. Those whose eyes and hands have been lift up to God in prayer, and whose feet have carried them to the holy place, as well as those whose eyes are full of adultery, and whose hands are full of blood, they die all alike, in manner alike. Ofttimes it is the same in the eye of the world. Death comes upon good and bad, but to the good for their greater glory; for the shell must be broken before they come to the pearl. Death it fits them for the blessed life after the body lying a while in the grave, the soul being in the hands of God. And death now it makes an end of sin, that brought in death; and it makes us conformable to the Son of God, our Elder Brother, that died for us. The point is pregnant, and full of gracious and serious meditations.

Use 1. It should enforce this excellent duty, that considering we have no long continuance here, therefore, while we are here, *to do that wherefore we come into the world.* As a factor, that is sent into a place to provide such goods beforehand, let us consider that here we are sent to get into a state of salvation, to get out of the state of nature into the state of grace, to furnish our souls with grace, to fit us for our dissolution to come. Let us not forget the main end of our living here. Considering we cannot be here long, let us do the work that God hath put into our hands quickly and faithfully, with all our might.

Use 2. And let it *enforce moderation to all earthly things.* 'The time is short, therefore let those that use the world be as if they used it not,' &c., 1 Cor. vii. 29. Those friends that have been joined together will part. Therefore let us use our bodies and souls so, that we may present them both comfortably to God. Let us beg of God to make a right use of this fading condition. But I hasten.

The second point is this, that,

Obs. 2. *The estate of the soul continues after death.*

For here he wisheth to die the death of the righteous, not for any excellency in death, but in regard of the subsistence and continuance of the soul after death.

Scripture and reason and nature enforceth this, that the soul hath a subsistence of itself, distinct from the life it communicates to the body. There is a double life, a life proper to the soul, and the life it communicates to the body. Now when the life it communicates to the body is gone to dissolution, itself hath a life in heaven. And indeed it is in a manner the whole man; for Abraham was Abraham when he was dead, when his soul was in heaven, and his body in the grave. It is the whole man.

Reas. 1. And it discovers, indeed, that it hath a distinct life and excellency in itself, by reason that *it thwarts the desires of the body when it is in the body.* Reason, if there be no grace in the soul, that crosseth the inclination of the body, grace much more.

Reas. 2. And we see ofttimes, *when the outward man is weak, as in sickness, &c., then the understanding, will, and affections, the inward man, is most sublime, and rapt unto heaven, and is most wise.* Take a man that hath been besotted all his lifetime, that hath been drunk with the pleasures of a carnal life, that hath been a covetous wretch, an earth-worm, that enjoys not heaven, but lives as his wealth and lusts carry him in slavery, yet at the hour of death, when he considers that he hath scraped together, and considers the way that his lusts have led him, and that all must leave him, now he begins to be wise, and speaks more discreetly. He can speak of the vanity of these things, and how little good they can do. Indeed many, nay, the most men, are not wise until that time. Therefore the soul of itself hath a distinct being, because, when the body is lowest, it is most refined and strong in its operations.

Reas. 3. Likewise it appears *by the projects that it hath of the time to come.* The soul, especially of men that are of more elevated and refined spirits, it projects for the time to come what shall become of the church and commonwealth, what shall become of posterity and of reputation and credit in the world. Certainly, unless there were a subsistence of itself, it would never look so much beforehand, and lay the grounds of the prosperity of the church and commonwealth for the time to come. I will not stand further on it, but rather make some use of it.

Use. Let us know which is our best part, namely, the soul, that hath a being after death, *that we do not employ it to base uses*, for which it was not made nor given us. Do we think that these souls of ours were made and given us to scrape wealth? to travel in our affections to base things worse than our souls? Are they not capable of supernatural and excellent things? Are they not capable of grace and glory, of communion with God, of the blessed stamp of the image of God? Let us use them, therefore, to the end that God gave them. And let us not deserve so ill of our souls as to betray them, to cast them in the dirt, to lay our crown in the dust. This is our excellency. What can keep our bodies from being a deformed, loathsome thing, if the soul be taken away? Yet so we abase this excellent part! Ofttimes we abase it to serve the base lusts of the body, which is condemned to rottenness. What is the life of most men but a purveying and prowling for the body? The lusts of the body set the wit and affections on work to prowl for itself. What a base thing is this! Were our souls given us for this end? And especially considering this, that our souls are immortal, that they shall never die, but be for ever. Let us not altogether spend this precious time that is given us to save our souls, and to get the image of God stamped upon them, I say let us not spend this precious time in things that will leave us when our souls shall live still; let us not carry the matter so, that our souls shall outlive our happiness. All worldlings and base creatures, they outlive their happiness. For where do they plant it? In the base things of this life. All their life long they are prowling for those things that they must leave when they die, whereas their souls shall not die, but everlastingly subsist.

What a misery is this, that these souls of ours shall have a being when the things wherein we placed our happiness, and abused our souls to gain them, they shall have an end! The souls of such men that seek the things of this life shall have a being in eternal misery. Indeed, so it is; for these souls of ours, the same degree they have in excellency if they be used as they should, if we do not abase them, the same degree they shall have in baseness and misery if we abuse them, and make them slaves to earthly things. For as the devils, the same degree they had of excellency when they were angels, the same degree they have in misery now they be devils. The more excellent the creature is when it keeps its excellency, the more vile it is when it degenerates. So these souls of ours that next to angels are the most excellent creatures of God, the more excellent it is if it get the image of God stamped upon it, and the new creature, and have the life of grace, the more cursed is the state of the soul if it subsist to everlasting misery.

It were happy if the souls of such creatures were mortal that labour for a happiness in this life. Oh that we would think of this! Most men in the bosom of the church, which is lamentable to think, they live as if they had no souls. They overturn the order that God hath set, and hath given us our bodies to serve our souls. They use all the strength and marrow of their wits, all the excellencies in their souls, for the base satisfaction of the lusts of the body. So much for that point.

The third is that,

Obs. 3. *There is a wide, broad difference between the death of the godly and of the wicked.*

The godly are happy in their death, for here we see it is a matter desirable. This caitiff, this wretched man Balaam, Oh, saith he, 'let me die the death of the righteous, and let my last end be like his.' It being the object of his desire, it is therefore certainly precious, 'the death of the righteous.' And indeed so it is; holy and gracious men, they are happy in their life. While they live they are the sons of God, the heirs of heaven; they are set at liberty, all things are theirs; they have access to the throne of grace; all things work for their good; they are the care of angels, the temples of the Holy Ghost. Glorious things are spoken of these glorious creatures even while they live.

But they are more happy in their death, and most happy and blessed after death.

In their death they are happy in their disposition, and happy in condition.

(1.) *Happy in their disposition.* What is the disposition of a holy and blessed man at his end? His disposition is by faith to give himself to God, by which faith he dies in obedience; he carries himself fruitfully and comfortably in his end. And ofttimes the nearer he is to happiness, the more he lays about him to be fruitful.

(2.) Besides his disposition, *he is happy in condition;* for death is a sweet close. God and he meet; grace and glory meet; he is in heaven, as it were, before his time. What is death to him? The end of all misery, of all sin of body and soul. It is the beginning of all true happiness in both. This I might shew at large, but I have spoken somewhat of this point out of another text.* They are happy in their death, for 'their death is precious in God's sight.' The angels are ready to do their attendance, to carry their souls to the place of happiness. They are happy in their death, because they are 'in the Lord.' When death severs soul and body, yet notwithstanding neither soul nor body are severed from Christ. 'They die in the Lord;' therefore still they are happy. Much might be said to this purpose, and to good purpose, but that the point is ordinary, and I hasten to press things that I think will a little more confirm it. They are blessed in death.

(3.) And blessed *after death especially;* for then we know they are in heaven, waiting for the resurrection of the body. There is a blessed change of all; for after death we have a better place, better company, better employment; all is for the better.

There are three degrees of life:

The life in the womb, this world, heaven.

The life in the womb is a kind of imprisonment; there the child lives for a time. The life in this world, it is a kind of enlargement; but, alas! it is as much inferior to the blessed and glorious life in heaven, as the life in the womb is narrower and straiter and more base than this life wherein we behold the blessed light and enjoy all the sweet comforts of this life. They are happy after death; then the image of God is perfect in the soul. All graces are perfected, all wants supplied, all corruptions wrought out, all enemies subdued, all promises accomplished, waiting their time for the resurrection of the body; and then body and soul shall sit as judges upon the wretches that have judged them on earth, and they shall be both to-

* See the Sermons on Phil. iii. 21. [Vol. V. pp. 143–152.]—G.

gether 'for ever with the Lord.' I might enlarge the point much. It is a comfortable meditation; and before I pass it, let us make some use of it.

If godly men be blessed and happy, not only before death, in the right and title they have to heaven, but in death, because then they are invested into possession of that that makes them every way happy,

Use 1. Therefore this may teach us *who are truly wise.* A wise man is he that hath a better end than another, and works to that end. A true Christian man, he hath a better end than any worldling. His end is to be safe in another world, and he works and carries his forces to that end. 'Let my last end be like his,' saith Balaam, insinuating that there was a better end in regard of condition and state than he had aimed at. A gracious man, his end is not to be happy here; his end is to enjoy everlasting communion with God in the heavens, and he frames all his courses in this world to accomplish that end, and he is never satisfied in the things that make to that end. A worldling he hath no such end. He hath a natural desire to be saved,—as we shall see afterwards,—but a man may know that is not his end, for he works not to it. He is not satisfied in prowling for this world; he is not weary of getting wealth; he is not satisfied with pleasure. So that his end is the things of this life. Therefore let him be never so wise, he is but a fool, for he hath not the true end, nor works to it. Wicked men are very fools in the manner of their reasoning; for they will grant that there is a happy estate of godly men in death, and after death better. If it be so, why do they not work and frame their lives to it? Herein they are fools, because they grant one thing and not another which must needs follow. They do believe there is such a happiness to God's children, and yet seek not after it.

Use 2. If there be such a blessed estate of God's children in death and after death, I beseech you *let us carry ourselves so as that we may be partakers of that happiness;* let us labour to be righteous men, labour to be in Christ, to have the righteousness of Christ to be ours, to be out of ourselves, in Christ; in Christ in life, in Christ in death, and at the day of judgment in Christ, 'not having our own righteousness,' as the apostle saith, 'but his righteousness,' Philip iii. 9, and then the righteousness of grace and of a good conscience will alway go with the other. For this makes a righteous man to be in Christ, and to have his righteousness, and to have his Spirit, and the beginnings of the new creature in us. Let us labour to be such as may live and die happily and blessedly, and be for ever happy. So much for that third point.

That which I intend mainly to dwell on is the last, and that is this, that *Even a wicked man, a wretched worldling, may see this; he may know this happiness of God's people in death, and for ever, and yet notwithstanding may continue a cursed wretch.*

Balaam here wishes, 'Oh that I might die the death of the righteous, and that my last end might be like his.' It was a strange speech of such a man as this was, that his soul should be rapt up in this manner; but indeed Balaam was scarce himself, he scarce understood what he said, no more than the beast that carried him.

But God will sometimes even stir up the hearts of wicked men to a sight and admiration of the excellent estate of God's children. Why? For diverse reasons. Among the rest for this, *that he may convince them the more of their own rebellion, when they see a more excellent estate than they are in, if they will not take the course to partake of it.* Therefore at the day of judgment it will justify the sentence of damnation upon such wretches, and they may pronounce self-condemnation upon themselves. Oh what a terror will it be when they shall think, I had a better estate discovered; I heard of it in the ministry of the word, and God's Spirit revealed an excellent estate, and I might have gotten it if I had improved the blessed means that God made me partaker of, and now I am shut out for ever and ever from communion in that estate. To convince wretched men, I say, and to justify the just sentence of damnation upon them, that their hearts may go with the sentence at the day of judgment, God thus enlightens them oftentimes, that they see better courses if they had grace to take them.

What a thing is this, that a wicked man should see such an estate and not take it! And what serves that knowledge for but to damn them the more! This is the estate of many men that live in the bosom of the church, and partake of the means of salvation, and yet live in sins against conscience. They get knowledge by the ministry, and by good books and acquaintance, and such like. They have a savour in the use of good things. Something they have, some little apprehension of the estate of a better life.

Again, for another end God reveals to them the excellent estate of his children sometimes, *to keep them in better order, to awe them, that they be not open enemies to the church, but may do good service;* for conceiting that there is such a happiness, and that perhaps they may partake of it, they will not carry themselves malignantly against those that are true professors.

There are several degrees of wicked men. Some are well-willers to good things, though they never come far enough. Some are open, malicious persecutors. Some again are better than so. They have a hatred to goodness, but they do not openly shew themselves; as hypocrites, &c. God reveals these good things to wicked men to keep them in awe. The net draws bad fish as well as good; so the net of the word, it draws wicked men, it keeps them from violence and open malice. Besides, even the majesty of the word, and the conviction of that excellent estate that belongs to God's children, it keeps them from open malice and persecution. This is another end that God aims at. What may we learn hence?

Use 1. Seeing this is so, it should teach us *that we refuse not all that ill men say; they may have good apprehensions, and give good counsel.* It had been good for Josiah to have followed the counsel of wicked Pharaoh, a heathen. God often enlightens men that otherwise are reprobates. Refuse not gold from a dirty hand; do not refuse directions from wicked men. Because they are so and so, refuse not a pardon from a man, a base creature. We ought not therefore to have such respect of persons as to refuse excellent things because the person is wicked. But that which I intend to press is this: If this be so, that wicked men may have illumination whereby they discover an excellency, and likewise may have desires raised up to wish and desire that excellency,

Use 2. It should stir us up *to go beyond wicked men.* Shall we not go so far as those go that shall never come to heaven? We see here Balaam pronounceth the end of the righteous to be happy. This should therefore stir us up to labour to be in a different estate from wicked men. Let us therefore consider a little wherein the difference of these desires is, the desires that a Balaam may have, and the desires of a sound Christian, wherein the desires of a wicked man are failing.

(1.) These desires, first of all, *they were but flashes:* for we never read that he had them long. They were mere flashes; as a sudden light, that rather blinds a man than shews him the way. So these enlightenings they are not constant. Wicked men ofttimes have sudden motions and flashes and desires. 'Oh that I might die the death of the righteous.' Oh that I were in such [a] man's estate. But it is but a sudden flash and lightning. They are like a torrent, a strong sudden stream, that comes suddenly and makes a noise, but it hath no spring to feed it. The desires of God's children they are fed with a spring, they are constant; they are streams, and not flashes.

(2.) Again, this desire of this wretched man, it was not *from an inward principle, an inward taste that he had of the good estate of God's children*, but from an objective delight and admiration of somewhat that was offered to his conceit by the Holy Ghost at this time. It was not from any inward taste or relish in himself that he speaks, but from somewhat outward, as a man that saw and heard excellent things, that ravished him with admiration, though he had not interest in them himself.

(3.) Again in the third place, this desire of the happiness of the estate of God's children, *it was not working and operative, but an uneffectual desire.* It had only a complacency and pleasing in the thing desired; but there was not a desire to work anything to that end. This wretch therefore would be at his journey's end, before he had set one step forward to the journey. It was a desire of the end without the means. It was not an operative effectual, but a weak transient desire. Where true desires are, they are not only constant, and proceed from an inward interest and taste of the thing desired, but they are effectual and operative. They set the soul and body, the whole man on work, partly to use the means to attain the thing desired, and partly to remove the impediments; for where desire is, there will be a removing of the impediments to the thing desired; as he that intends a journey, he will consider what may hinder him, and what may help him in it. He that sets not about these things, he never means it, for a man cannot come to his journey's end with wishing; we can attain nothing in this life with wishing. There is a working, I say, that tends to remove impediments so far as we may, and tending to use all means to effect and bring the thing to pass. We see, then, there is a main difference between the desires of this wretched man Balaam and the desires of the true church of God. To go on and follow the point a little further.

(4.) Where desires are in truth, the party that cherisheth those desires, *will be willing to have all help from others to have his desire accomplished.* If a man desire to demolish a place, if any will come and help him down with it, or if any man desire to weed his ground, he that will help him, he will thank him for his pains. Where there is a true desire, there is a willing closing with all that offer themselves, that the thing desired may be brought to pass. Where there is a desire of the happy estate of God's children, there will be a willing entertainment of any help. Let a man come to a man that desires grace and glory, and discover his especial sins that hinder him, you must weed out this, and you must pull down this, he will thankfully embrace all admonitions, because he truly desires the end; therefore he desires the means that tend to the end. He desires the removing of the hindrances; he will be thankful, therefore, for any help that he may have, and especially that of the ministry, that it may powerfully enter into his soul, and rip him up. Why? Because he desires to please God in all things, and he would not cherish a motion or desire contrary to the Spirit of God. Therefore the more corruption is presented and made odious to him, the more the 'inward man' is discovered, the more he blesseth God, and blesseth the blessed instruments; and of all means he is willing to attend upon such.

Where there is swelling and rising against the blessed means, either in private admonition or public teaching, let men pretend what they will, there is no true desire of grace and to be in the estate of God's people; for then they would not be contrary to the means. This wretched man Balaam, when the angel stood in his way, with his sword drawn, to stop his way, yet notwithstanding he goes on still. He was so carried with covetousness, and so blinded, that neither the miracle of the beast speaking, nor of the angel in his way, nor God in the way, could stop him. Alas! where was this desire then? No, no! The glory of earthly things dazzled the glory of the estate of God's people. Therefore we see he goes against all means that was used to stop him in his journey.

If a man desire to be good, and to leave his sins, he will not stand against the means.

Have we not many that stand against the ministry of God's ministers [who] are God's angels? They stand in the way, and tell people, if you live in this course you shall not inherit heaven; if you live in oppression and base lusts, unless you be changed, you shall all perish. They come to particular reproofs, and hold forth the sword of God's Spirit, yet men break through all and wreak their malice upon God's messengers. Is here a true desire when they are not willing to have the hindrances removed? when there is not respect of the means that should be used?

(5.) Again, true desires of grace, *they are growing desires.* Though they be little in the beginning, as springs are, yet as the springs grow, so do the waters that come from them. So these desires, they grow more and more still. They grow sometimes in God's children, that they will have no stop till they come to have their full desire, to have perfect union and communion with God in heaven. The desires of a blessed soul, they are never satisfied till it come to heaven. 'Let him kiss me with the kisses of his mouth,' saith the church,' Cant. i. 2. Oh, let me have nearer communion with Christ! It desires in the word and sacraments to come nearer and closer to God, and in death then, 'Come, Lord Jesus, come quickly,' Rev. xxii. 20. And when the soul is in heaven there is yet nearer union, a desire of the body's resurrection, that both may be for ever with the Lord. Till a Christian be perfect in body and soul, there is desire upon desire, till all desires be accomplished. They are growing desires, as St Peter saith: 'As new born babes desire the sincere milk of the word, that ye may grow thereby,' 1 Peter ii. 2. It is a desire that is never satisfied, because there is alway somewhat to be desired till we be perfectly happy.

(6.) And then they are desires *that will not be stilled.* A child, if it have not strong desires, it will be stilled with an apple; but if the desires be strong, nothing will still it but the dug. So God's children, if their desires be strong, it is no bauble they desire, nothing but grace and inward comfort will quiet the inward man. It is a desire that is growing and strong. It will not be stayed with anything in this world, but will break through all impediments; as a strong stream, it will never rest till it have communion with God. And therefore the desires that men think are good and earnest enough, that go on plodding in a constant course, and never labour to grow, they are no desires at all, no sanctified desires from a supernatural principle of grace. The desires of a Christian grow, and are never satisfied till he have perfect happiness.

The three worthies of David brake through the host, and got the water of Bethel for David: 'Oh that I had of the water of Bethel,' 2 Sam. xxiii. 15. So where there are strong desires they are like David's worthies, they carry the soul through all impediments, they grow stronger and stronger, and are never satisfied till they come to the water of life. Let us consider these things, whether we have this desire or no. If we have but sometimes flashes, inconstant, ineffectual desires, desires that grow not, that are soon satisfied, and are stilled with anything, alas! these desires the Spirit of God never kindled and bred in the heart; they are ordinary flashes, that shall serve for our deeper damnation. Therefore let us take heed, and not rest in a castaway's estate; let us not rest in Balaam's state, but labour that the desires of our souls may be as they should.

Desires, I confess, are the best character to know a Christian; for works may be hypocritical, desires are natural. Therefore we ought to consider our desires, what they are, whether true or no; for the first thing that issues from the soul are desires and thoughts. Thoughts stir up desires. This inward immediate stirring of the soul discovers the trnth of the soul better than outward things. Let us oft therefore examine our desires. And let me add this one thing to the other, let us examine our desires by this, besides the rest,

(7.) *Whether we desire holiness, and the restoration of the image of God, the new creature, and to have victory against our corruptions;* to be in a state that we may not sin against God, to have the Spirit, to be 'new born,' as well as we desire happiness, and exemption from misery. Balaam desired happiness, but he desired not the image of God upon his soul; for then he would not have been carried with a covetous devil against all means. No; his desire was after a glimpse of God's children's glory only.

A wicked man can never desire to be in heaven as he should be; for how should we desire to be in heaven? to be freed from sin, that we may praise God and love God; that there may be no combat between the flesh and the spirit. Can he wish this? No. His happiness is as a swine to wallow in the mire, and he desires to enjoy sensible delights. As for spiritual things, especially the image of God, and the vision of God, they are not fit objects for him, as far as it is a freedom from sin, but as he hath a conceit, oh they are goodly things to be seen, &c. So it corresponds with his disposition, but to be free from sin, and from the conflict of the flesh and spirit, and to be set at liberty to serve God alway, he cannot desire it so. Tell him of heaven, he loves it not. There is no gold, there is not that that he affects,* therefore he cares not for it, he cannot relish it, he is not changed. Therefore it is a notable character of a true Christian to desire heaven, to be freed from sin, to have communion with God in holiness. Other prerogatives will follow this.

Let us therefore consider what our desires are, how they are carried, for desires discover what the soul is. As a spring is discovered by the vapours that are about it, so is this hidden state of the soul discovered by the breaking out of desires. They are the breath and vapour of the soul. Let us consider what is set highest in our souls, what we desire most of all. Oh, a Christian soul that hath 'tasted of the loving-kindness of the Lord,' accounts it 'better than life itself,' Ps. lxiii. 3. It is not 'corn, and wine, and oil' he desires, 'but, Lord, shew me the light of thy countenance,' Ps. iv. 6. The desires of his heart are large to serve God, and to do good, more than for the things of the world. He desires earthly things, but as

* That is, 'loves,' 'chooses.'—G.

instruments for better things, and this is the desire of every sanctified soul in some measure.

Let us hence make a use of conviction of the folly of base men, that live in the church, and yet come not so far as Balaam, that come not so far as those that shall go to hell. They turn over all religion to a 'Lord, have mercy upon us,' and 'Christ died for us,' and 'we hope we have souls to God-ward,' as good as the best, and to a few short broken things. They turn religion to compendiums, to a narrow compass, and make the way to it wide and broad, and complain of preachers that they straiten the way to heaven.

This is the disposition of worldlings; whereas, alas! there must be a righteousness that must 'exceed the righteousness of the Scribes and Pharisees,' Mat. v. 20; there must be a righteousness from an inward principle; there must be a strong, constant desire of righteousness, more than of any thing in the world, before we can be assured of our interest and part with God's people. Let us take heed that we delude not ourselves this way.

But to come to an use of direction. How may we so carry ourselves, as we may have a spring of blessed desires, a spring of holy desires, that may comfort us, that we may have our interest and portion in the state of God's people?

That we may have these desires, *let us desire of God the spirit of revelation.* Desires follow discovery, for desires are the vent of the soul upon the discovery of some excellency it believes. Therefore let us beg of God the spirit of revelation, to discover the excellent estate of God's people. And because this is given in the use of means, let us present ourselves with all diligence under such means, as where we may have somewhat of the kingdom of God, that the riches of Christ being unfolded, our desires may be carried to such things; for there is never any discovery of holy and good and gracious things to a Christian soul, but there are new desires stirred up. Our souls are like a mill that grinds what is put into it; so the soul it works upon the things that are put into it. If it have good desires and good thoughts put into it, by good means used, and by prayer, it feeds upon them. Let us alway, therefore, be under some good means, that good thoughts may be ministered unto us, that may stir up gracious desires for the soul to work upon. Let us be in good company. 1 Sam. x. 12, 'Saul among the prophets,' we see he prophesied; and the heart is kindled and enflamed when we are among those that are better than ourselves, especially if their hearts be enlarged to speak of good things. But to come nearer.

2. That we may have holy and gracious and constant desires, *let us take notice and make trial continually of the state and frame of our souls, which way for the present they are carried, in what current our desires run.* If they run the right way, to heavenly things, it is well; if not, take notice what draws and diverts and turns the streams of our desires the false way. Let us think what the things be, and the condition of those things that draws our desires down, and make us earthly and worldly, whether the pleasures or profits or honours of this life. The way to have better desires is to wean ourselves from these things, by a constant holy meditation of the vanity of these things that the soul is carried after. Solomon, to wean his heart from these desires, from placing too much happiness in these things, he sets them before him and saith, 'they were vanity and vexation of spirit,' Eccles. i. 14. Let us set them before us as nothing, as they

will be ere long. 'Heaven and earth will pass away,' Mat. xxiv. 35; the world will pass away, and the concupiscence and lust of it. Let us consider the baseness, fickleness, and uncertainty of things that our souls are carried after, and this will be a means to wean them from them. And the soul being weaned from earthly things, it will run amain another way. Let us study, therefore, to mortify our base affections, and study it to purpose, to cut off the right hand and to pull out the right eye; spare nothing, that God may spare all. That God may have mercy upon us and spare us, let us spare nothing. These 'lusts they fight against our souls,' 1 Peter ii. 11.

And, as I said before, feed our souls; minister unto them better thoughts continually. Those that are governors of those that are young, season them while they be young with good things; for while the soul is not filled with the world, and while covetousness and ill lusts have not wrought themselves into the soul, good things and good desires are easily rooted and planted, and grow up in the soul. As letters graven in the body of a tree, they grow up with the tree, and the fruit of the tree grows up with the tree, and therefore the twigs break not with the greatness of the weight of it, because they grow up together. So plant good things in those that are young, inure them to know good things, to hate ill ways, plant in them blessed desires, and inure them to holy exercises and good duties, that good exercises may grow up with them, as the fruit with the tree. We see what a hard matter it is to convert an old man, to draw the desires of a carnal worldly man to heaven. When we speak of good things to him, his soul is full of the world. What is in his brain? The world. What is in his heart? The world. So he is dry, and exhausted of all good things, and that that is in him is eaten up with the world. It is a great improvidence in those that govern youth, that they labour not that their desires may be strong to the best things.

And let us all, both young and old, labour *for heavenly wisdom*, that when good things are ministered to us from without, or good motions stirred up by the Spirit of God, to close with them, and not to quench those motions and resist the Spirit, but to embrace those motions, and cherish them, till they come to resolutions, and purposes, and actions. If we have a motion stirring us up to repentance, let us ripen it till it come to perfect repentance, till we repent indeed, and have turned from all our evil ways, and turn to God with full purpose of heart, that it may be a motion to purpose. If it be a motion to faith, let us never leave cherishing of it by the promise till our hearts be 'rooted in faith.' If it be a motion to any other good thing, let us cherish and follow them to purpose, and embrace every motion, as an angel sent from heaven from God to a good end, to put us in mind, to invite us to good, and to drive us from ill.

And because desires are fickle and fading of themselves unless there be some art in helping of them, therefore let us add to these things a daily course of renewing of our covenant with God, that this day, as God shall enable me, I have a constant purpose against all sin, I will regard no iniquity in my heart, I will have respect to all good ways discovered. Renew our covenants and resolutions of old. Saith David, 'I have sworn and will perform it, that I will keep thy statutes,' Ps. cxix. 106. And as we determine and resolve, so make particular vows sometimes against particular hindrances, to abstain from such things.

Quest. What needs all this ado? saith the wicked atheist. Will not less serve the turn, but there must be these vows, and purposes, and resolutions?

Ans. No; God values us by our resolutions and purposes, and not by ineffectual glances and wishes. Will wishing help us take a journey, or to do anything in this world? And can we not do anything in this world with wishing, and can we for heaven? No; certainly there must be resolutions, and covenants, and purposes, &c. What is the difference between a Christian and another man? A Christian unlooseth his heart from base desires. Nothing shall tie him to the base world. But his conscience tells him that he is free from living in sins against conscience, and as for infirmities, he labours and resolves against them. Therefore he is fit to die and to resign his soul. Whensoever God shall take him, he is in a good way, in good purposes and resolutions. God values us according to our purposes and resolutions. David did not build the temple, Abraham did not offer Isaac, but they resolved upon it, and it was accounted as done. This is our comfort, that God takes the resolution for the deed; and the perfection of a Christian is, that God accepts of these resolutions when he determines on the best things, till he bring his heart in some measure to that estate.

Quest. What is the reason that many men at the hour of death will admit no comfort?

Ans. The reason is, their hearts were naught. They respected some iniquity in their hearts. They were in bad ways, and allowed some reigning sin; and till these be mortified, we can minister no comfort. It is only the resolved Christian that is a fit subject for comfort.

But to answer an ordinary let* or two that the devil casts in men's ways in these things.

Obj. But doth not God accept the will for the deed? Put the case I have a good will to do a thing; though I do it not, God accepts that.

Ans. I answer, God accepts the will for the deed, only where the impediments and hindrances are impossible to be removed; as, put the case a poor man would be liberal if he had it, God accepts the will for the deed, because he wants opportunity. But it never holds when a man can do it. God accepts not the will for the deed when a man hath a price in his hand to get wisdom, and yet is a barren plant and not a tree of righteousness. It is a sign of a naughty heart.

Obj. Oh, saith another, 'God quencheth not the smoking flax,' Mat. xii. 20, therefore, though I have weak desires, all shall be well.

Ans. It is true God doth not quench the smoking flax, but he doth not leave it smoking, but blows the spark, that in time it comes to a flame. Where there are beginnings of goodness embraced, it will grow from smoking flax to a flame. They are growing desires, as I said before. Therefore flatter not thyself that Christ will not quench the smoking flax. It is true, if there be a desire of growth, for then I must speak comfort to a poor Christian that cannot be so good as he would, but desires it, and complains, Oh 'that my ways were so direct, that I might keep thy statutes!' Ps. cxix. 5. With his desires, he complains that he cannot do it, and useth the means to grow. It is a good sign; God will not quench the smoking flax till he have brought corruption into subjection in us. Let every good soul comfort itself with this, if thou have these blessed desires, God meets with thee, for he desires thy salvation, and Christ desires thy reconciliation, and it is the desire of thy heart, and thou usest the means.

* That is, 'hindrance,' = objection.—G.

Thou wilt not live in sins against conscience. Be of good comfort. We that are the ministers of God, and I at this time, bring the news of pardon; Christ's desire and thine meet in one.

Let us enlarge these things in our own deep and serious meditation. Alas! for want of serious meditation in our hearts of such like truths as these, men perish and sink suddenly to hell. There is but a step between ordinary profane persons and hell, and yet they never think of renewing their covenants with God, and entering into the state of grace, but content themselves with that which comes short of thousands that are now in hell, that have had more wishes and desires. Men put all upon empty things, 'God is merciful,' &c. No; God will not be merciful to such as bless themselves in ill courses; his wrath shall smoke against such, as I said; for in thus reasoning, they make a covenant with hell and death as much as they can. They that do thus forget God and good courses, and God will forget them; they treasure up wrath, and God treasures up wrath against them. Let us take heed of Balaam's wishing, and labour to have such desires as may be accepted of God and comfortable to us.

THE UNPROSPEROUS BUILDER.

THE UNPROSPEROUS BUILDER.

NOTE.

'The Unprosperous Builder' is another of the sermons from 'Evangelical Sacrifices' (4to, 1640). Its separate title-page is given below.* G.

* THE
VNPROSPEROVS
BVILDER.

A Sermon preached upon the 5th of
November, in remembrance of Our
Deliverance from the Papists
Powder-Treason.

BY

The late Learned and Reverend Divine,
RICH. SIBBS:
Doctor in Divinity, Mr. of KATHERINE Hall
in *Cambridge*, and sometimes Preacher
to the Honourable Society of
GRAYES-INNE.

HAB. 2. 12.
Woe to him that buildeth a Towne with blood, and
establisheth a Citie by Iniquity.

LONDON,
Printed by *T. B.* for *N. Bourne*, at the Royall Exchange,
and *R. Harford*, at the guilt Bible in Queenes-head
Alley in Pater-noster-Row. 1639.

THE UNPROSPEROUS BUILDER.

Cursed be the man before the Lord that riseth up and builds this city Jericho: he shall lay the foundation of it in his first-born, and in his youngest son set up the gates thereof.—JOSHUA VI. 26.*

THE words are a terrible denunciation of a curse of the man of God Joshua; wherein you have the curse generally set down—'Cursed be the man before the Lord that riseth to build this city Jericho'—and then a specification in particular, wherein the curse stands. The two branches of the curse are these, 'He shall lay the foundation of it in his first-born, and in his youngest son set up the gates thereof.' It shall be with the raising† out of his posterity. So that the text is nothing else but a terrible denunciation, under a curse, of the destruction of the family of that person that should labour to build up Jericho again. I will not speak much of cursing or blessing, being not pertinent to my purpose, only to give a touch of it. As in blessing there are three things considerable, that come near one another,—there is a blessing, a prayer, and a prophecy: the prayer is for a blessing to come; the prophecy is of the certainty of it, that it shall be; the blessing is an efficacious application of the thing to the person; I mean those three, because the one gives light to the other,—so is it likewise in cursing: there is a prayer that God would pour forth his vengeance upon the enemies of the church, and a prophetical prediction that God will do it; and a cursing, when it comes from a qualified person, that is led by a better spirit than his own; for every one is not fit to cast these bolts. Cursing is an efficacious application of the curse to the person; when a man is, as it were, the declarative instrument whereby God works and brings the curse upon the person. So that we must account a curse to be a wondrous deep thing. The persons qualified for cursing or blessing, they are parents, either politic, as magistrates, or parents natural, to curse or bless their children, as we see in Noah,—'Cursed be Ham,' &c., Gen. ix. 25,—or else parents spiritual, whose office it is indeed especially to bless or curse. It is a greater matter than the world takes it for, a blessing or a curse, especially from a spiritual father. The apostles, that were spiritual fathers of the church, they began their epistles with blessings; and so the prophets and patriarchs.

Therefore we should regard the blessing that God gives by his ministers.

* Misprinted '10.'—G. † Qu. 'razing?'—ED.

Some are ready to run out before the blessing, as not esteeming either blessing or curse. Luther, a man of great parts and grace, saith of himself, 'That if a man of God should speak anything terrible to him, and denounce anything against him, he knew not how to bear it, it would be so terrible' (*a*). The Jesuits themselves, amongst the rest one De Lapide, he saith, 'The priest cannot sooner come into the pulpit, but if there be a nobleman there, down he falls, and all look for the blessing of the priest' (*b*). The devil is always in extremes, either to drive people to superstition, or else to profaneness and atheism; either to regard the blessing of those whom they should not regard, or not to regard any blessing at all; not to regard that good men should pray for them or their children. If the devil can bring men to hell by either extremes, he hath his will. As for the blessing of Rome, we expect it not; and for their curse, we need care no more for it than an armed man needs to care for a headless arrow or for a child's pop-gun.* But those men that come in the name of God, and are qualified with callings to pray and to bless, their prayers and blessings are highly to be esteemed; and so likewise their curses. I would it were more esteemed; it would be a means to convey God's blessing more than it is.

'Cursed be the man before the Lord.'

Take this caution by the way: though Joshua were a man of God, he was a mixed person; he was both a magistrate and, in some sort, a minister. As we say of kings, they are mixed persons, they are keepers of both tables: *custodes utriusque tabulæ*. There is more in the supreme magistrate than is common. Every one must not take upon him to curse upon every motion of the flesh; for here it is not, as one of the ancients saith well, 'the wrath of a man in commotion and fury, but the sentence of a man in a peaceable temper, who is the conveyer of God's curse' (*c*). It is passive here as well as active.

In the New Testament we are commanded to bless and not to curse. It is a common fault upon every distemper to fall a cursing; and ofttimes it lights, as an arrow shot upwards, upon the head of the curser. We are people of God's blessing, all true believers; and we should delight in blessing. Having felt the blessing of God ourselves upon our souls, we should be moved to blessing, both by way of gratitude to those that are our superiors and have done us good, that God would bless them, and by way of amity and friendship to those that are under us or about us, and by way of mercy to our very enemies. We should pray for and bless our very enemies themselves, as our blessed Saviour prayed for them that cursed him. This should be our ordinary disposition, we should be all for blessing. As for curses, we must take heed that we direct them not against any particular person; we have no such warrant, though the primitive church pronounced a curse against Julian, a notable enemy (*d*); and St Paul, he cursed Alexander the coppersmith, 2 Tim. iv. 14. But for us this time, the safest way is to pronounce all those curses in the Psalms and elsewhere in Scripture upon the implacable and incorrigible enemies of the church, the whole body of the malignant church, and so we should not err. I will not dwell longer upon this argument, only I thought good to remember you to regard the blessing of those that have the Spirit of God to bless, especially that have a calling to do it; and to take heed of cursing. But to come to the particulars.

'Cursed be the man before the Lord.'

* Misprinted 'pot.'—G.

That is, let him be cursed indeed. That that is done before the Lord is truly and solemnly done. This was a solemn curse, a heavy curse, and it did truly light upon him. And let him be cursed before the Lord, however the world bless him; as a man cannot do such a thing as to build a city, but the world will commend a man for doing such a thing, but it is no matter for the world's commendation, if a man set upon a cursed cause. So much for the phrase, 'Cursed be the man before the Lord;' that is, he is truly and solemnly cursed, and cursed before the Lord, though men bless him.

'That riseth and builds this city Jericho.'

That is the cause why he should be cursed, because he would build that city that God would have to be a perpetual monument of his justice. Why would not God have Jericho built again?

1. God would not have it built up, partly *because he would have it a perpetual remembrance of his goodness and merciful dealing with his people, passing over Jordan, and coming freshly into Canaan;* for we are all subject to forget. Therefore it is good to have days set apart for remembrance and somewhat to put us in mind, as they had many things in old time to help memory. If this city had been built again, the memory of it would have been forgotten; but lying all waste and desolate, the passengers by would ask the cause—as God speaks of his own people,—What is the reason that this city lies thus?—and then it would give them occasion of speaking of the mercy of God to his people. And likewise it would give occasion to speak of the justice of God against the idolatrous inhabitants, whose sins were grown ripe. God foretold in Genesis that the sins of the Amorites was not yet ripe; but now their sins were ripe, they were idolaters.

2. And likewise *it was dedicated to God as the first-fruits.* Being one of the chief mother cities of the land, it was dedicate and consecrated to God as a thing severed; it was to be for ever severed from common use. There are two ways of severing things from common use: one by way of destruction, as here the city of Jericho; another by way of dedication, as the gold of Jericho. God would have this city severed from common use, as a perpetual monument and remembrance of his mercy and justice.

3. And likewise he would have it never built up again, *for terror to the rest of the inhabitants*; for usually great conquerors set up some terrible example of justice to terrify others. Now, this being one of the first cities after their passing over Jordan, God would have the destruction of it to strike terror, together with this sentence of a curse, upon all that should build it again for ever.

4. And then that this terrible sentence might be a means *to draw others to come in to God's people to join with them, and submit, and prevent their destruction*, seeing how terribly God had dealt with Jericho. Many such reasons may be probably alleged; but the main reason of reasons, that must settle our consciences, *God would have it so.* Joshua he was but God's trumpet and God's instrument to denounce this curse, 'Cursed be the man before the Lord that shall build up this city Jericho.' We must rest in that. I will go over the words, and then make application afterwards to the occasion.

I come to the specification of the curse, wherein it stands: 'He shall lay the foundation thereof in his first-born.'

If any man will be so venturous to build it up again, as one Hiel did, in 1 Kings xvi. 34, if any man will be so audacious, he shall do it with the peril of the life of his first-begotten; and if he will not desist then, he shall finish the gates of it, he shall make an end of it, with the death of his younger son. It is God's custom to denounce a threatening of a curse before he execute it. It is a part of God's mercy and of his blessing, that he will curse only in the threatening; for therefore he curseth, that he might not execute it; and therefore he threateneth, that he might not smite; and when he smites, he smites that he might not destroy; and when he kills the body, it is that he might not destroy the soul; as 1 Cor. xi. 32, 'Therefore some of you are weak, and sick, and some sleep, that you might not be condemned with the world.' Thus God is merciful, even till it comes to the last upshot, that men by their rebellions provoke him. God's mercy strives with the sins of men. Mark here the degrees of it: first, God threatens the curse, 'Cursed be the man;' and then in the particulars, he begins with the eldest son. First, there is a threatening; and when the execution comes, he takes not all his sons away at once, but begins with the eldest; and if that will not do, he goes to the youngest.

This carriage of God, even in his threatenings, it should put us in mind of God's mercy, and likewise it should move us to meet God presently, before any peremptory decree be come forth, as we shall see afterward; for if we leave not sinning, God will never leave punishing. He might have desisted in the death of his first son; but if that will not be, God will strike him in his youngest son, and sweep away all between; for so we must understand it, that both elder, and younger, and all should die.

Now for the judgment itself.

'He shall lay the foundation thereof in his first-born.'

There is some proportion between the judgment and the sin. The sin was to raise up a building, a cursed city, contrary to God's will. The punishment is in pulling down a man's own building; for children, according to the Hebrew word, are the building, the pillars of the house (*e*); and since he would raise up a foundation and building contrary to God's mind, God would pull up his foundation. Cities are said to have life, and to grow, and to have their pitch, and then to die like men; and, indeed, they do: observing only a proportion of time, they are of longer continuance, but otherwise cities live and grow and die and have their period as men have.* Now he that would give life to a city, that God would have buried in its own ruins, God would have his sons die; he would have his sons as it were buried under the ruins of that city that he would build in spite of God, that would give life to that city that was cursed. Ofttimes we may read our very sins in our punishments, there is some proportion. But to go on to the particulars.

'He shall lay the foundation in his first-born.'

A heavy judgment, because the first-born, as you know he saith of Reuben, he was his strength; and he was king and priest in the family. The first-born had a double portion, he was redeemed with a greater price, as we see in Moses's law, than other sons. It was a heavy judgment to have his first-born smitten in this fashion, to be taken away.

If any ask why God was so severe, that he did not punish Hiel in himself, but take away his children, it may seem against reason.

But we must not dispute with God, for we must know that God hath the supreme power of life and death.

* Cf. Dr Vaughan's 'Ages of Great Cities,' wherein this truth is eloquently illustrated and enforced.—G.

Then we must know again that children are part of their parents; God punisheth the parents in their children, and it is a heavier punishment ofttimes in their esteem than in themselves, for they think to live and continue in their children. Now when they see their children took away it is worse than death. Men ofttimes live to see things worse than death, as those that see their children killed before them, as Zedekiah and Mauritius, the emperor, for indeed it is a death oft (*f*); a man dies in every child. This man he died in his eldest son, and he died in his youngest son; he died in regard of the apprehension of death. It was more sharp in apprehension than when he died himself. So it is a heavy judgment to be stricken in our children. God, when he will punish, he punisheth ofttimes in posterity; as we see it was the most terrible judgment of all upon Pharaoh, that in his first-born; God drew them all to let Israel go out, when 'he smote their first-born.' It is a heavy judgment for a man to be stricken in his first-born, either when they are dissolute, and debauched, and lawless, for God hath judgments for the soul as well as for the body, or else when they are taken out of the world.

But, thirdly, which is very likely another reason that moved God,—that we may justify God in all our sentence that we give of him,—he took them away, because they imitated their father in ill; and God hath a liberty to strike when he will, when there is cause; and whom he will, he will spare for so many generations.

Quest. You will say, Why doth he light on such a generation? and why not on such a place?

Ans. It is his liberty and prerogative, when all deserve it; and he lights upon one and not upon another. We must not quarrel with God, but leave him to his liberty. It is a part of his prerogative, 'Who art thou, O man, that disputest?' Rom. ix. 20. Why God, when all are equally sinners, strikes one and not another; why he executes judgments in one age and not in another; there may be reasons given of it; but it is a mystery that must not be disputed. But I cannot stand on these things.

'He shall lay the foundation thereof in his first-born, and in his youngest son set up the gates thereof.'

This terrible sentence we see executed in 1 Kings xvi. 34. In Ahab's time, there was one so venturous as to build Jericho again. There is an accent* to be set upon that, that it was in Ahab's time. Hiel would needs build Jericho again; and why should he build it? Hiel no doubt saw it a wondrous commodious place to found a city, being near to Jordan. And then he saw and considered that it was accounted a famous thing to be founder of a city. And then no doubt he thought that Ahab would not only permit him to do it, but [it] would gratify him: wicked Ahab, which had sold himself to work wickedness; that was an abominable idolater himself, and countenanced idolatry, and had set up the false worship of Baal. It was likely enough in his time that Jericho should be built; and therefore, no doubt but he did it partly to insinuate himself with Ahab. And to shew how little he cared for Joshua's or Jehovah's threatening, as usually such impudent persons that are grown up with greatness, that have sold themselves to be naught,† that have put off all humanity and modesty, they are fittest to carry wicked and desperate causes, being agreeable to them. So this wicked person was a fit man to do this, and he thought to please Ahab by it.

Man is a strange creature, especially in greatness of riches or place, &c.

* That is, 'emphasis'.—G. † That is, 'naughty' = wicked.—G.

A piece of earth that will be puffed up, if he have flatterers and sycophants about him, and a proud heart withal, he will forget, and dare the God of heaven, and trample under foot all threatenings and menaces whatsoever. As this wicked Hiel, rather than he will miss of his will, he will break through thick and thin, and redeem the fulfilling of his will with the loss of his own soul, and of his children, his first-born, and his last and all. *Mens mihi pro regno;* let a man be happy in his will, he cares not for all the world. If he may have his will, let all go upon heaps. This is the nature of man. One would think that this threatening might have scared a man that had loved himself, or his posterity. But nothing would keep him, he would venture upon it, as we see in that place, 1 Kings xvi. 34. Thus we have passed over the words.

To come to handle the words by way of analogy, how they may agree to other things by way of proportion, and in a spiritual mystical sense.

There are divers degrees of men that venture upon curses, and thereupon grow to be cursed themselves. Even as this man ventured upon the building of Jericho, so there be many that do the like in a proportionable kind. I shall name some few.

God did determine *that the Jewish ceremonies should determine and have an end and period.* Now, in St Paul's time, there were many that would put life into them, and join them with the gospel. St Paul tells them, 'Christ shall profit you nothing,' Gal. v. 2. Those are they that build Jericho again, that revive and put life into that that God hath determined should never revive again. When the Jewish ceremonies were honourably interred, and laid in their graves, these men would raise them out of their graves again, and so venture upon God's curse, and be excluded from Christ. These are one sort of men that raise Jericho again; and so afterwards in the church, there were those that would build up Jericho, that would still retain Jewish ceremonies, and heathenish in the church, and some at the first with no ill minds. But then afterwards, as Augustine complains, they so pestered the church with Jewish and heathenish ceremonies, that the Jews' condition was better than theirs, for these things should have been buried (*g*). Gerson, that had many good things in him, though he lived in ill times, 'Oh,' saith he, 'good Augustine, dost thou complain of those times? what wouldst thou have said if thou hadst lived now?' (*h*) What is popery but a mass of Jewish and heathenish ceremonies, besides some blasphemies that they have? I speak concerning what they differ from ours, which are decent and orderly. What a mass of ceremonies and fooleries have they, to mislead men that are taken away with fancies to distaste the truth of God, and to have respect to fancies, to outward pomp and gorgeous things, rather than the gospel? These men build up Jericho again, and bury the gospel as much as they can.

There are another sort of men that raise up Jericho, *that revive all the heresies that were damned to hell by the ancient Councils.* The heresy of Pelagius was damned to hell by the ancient councils. The African councils, divers of them, divers synods, wherein Augustine himself was a party, they condemned Pelagius's heresy.* Are there not men now abroad that will revive these heresies? And there must be expected nothing but a curse where this prevails; for they are opinions cursed by the church of God, that have been led by the Spirit of God heretofore; such opinions, I mean, as speak meanly of the grace of God, as if it were a weak thing, and advance the strength of free-will, and make an idol of that; and so, under

* Cf. Note *j*, Vol. II. page 194.—G.

the commendation, and setting up of nature, are enemies of grace. These are those that build up Jericho.

3. There are a company that build up Jericho likewise, *persons that will venture upon the curse of founders of colleges, &c.*, those that have left statutes, and testaments, and wills, established and sealed them with a curse, as it were, against the breakers of them; yet some make no more bones of breaking these, either statutes or wills, than Samson did of breaking his cords; as if they would venture upon the curse of former times, and persons that very likely were led by the Spirit of God, and could say amen to their curses, as if they were nothing like Hiel, that would venture upon the terrible curse of Joshua; come what would, he would break through all.

4. But the Jericho especially that a world of people go about to build again, *is popery*. How many have ye to build up the walls of Jericho again in this kind? But to make this a little clearer, because the occasion leads to this something, I will be the larger in it.

Quest. How came they to build these walls of Jericho? By what means came this religion that is so opposite to the religion of the Scripture; this religion, that was gathered by the Council of Trent into one sea, as it were, that whosoever drinks of it dies, as it is in the Revelation, xx. 14. How comes this religion? How crept it into the world?

Ans. I could be long to shew that it came by degrees. While the husbandmen slept, then the devil sowed his tares by heretics and such like. It grew by degrees. And then the world was scared and terrified with shows and fancies; as with the succession of Peter, that is a mere fancy; and then they were frighted with excommunications, the terrible sentence of the church. And then again it is a kingdom of darkness, popery is. By little and little they brought in ignorance, not only of the Scriptures, but of other things. They had their prayers in an unknown tongue, forbidding the Scriptures and the like. In the night they might do what they would, when they had put out the candle. When they had buried the knowledge of the word of God they might bring in any heresy; many ways they came in.

Now the preaching of the gospel is the means to pull down these walls of Jericho, it is the going about the walls of Jericho. By the preaching of Luther and others, the walls have fallen, though not utterly; yet notwithstanding, in the last hundred years there hath been a great ruin of popery.

Quest. What means have they now to build the walls again? How they bestir themselves! There is a new sect of Jesuits, that are the spirit of the devil for knowledge and industry. It is a strange project they have now to build up the walls of Jericho again; and three things they have in their project, and these are to set up the pope again, and a catholic king under him, as he is the catholic head of the church, and to set up the Council of Trent in the full vigour. These are the main projects they labour to set up, and so to build Jericho again this way; and what course do they take?

Ans. The devil hath a thousand wiles. I cannot reckon all the instruments of Satan. Who can tell all his wiles? They go about to build the walls of Jericho again among other ways.

By shutting out of all light by their terrible inquisition, a most cruel thing. By the tyranny of this inquisition, they shut out all light of God's truth in all places where popery is established.

Then again they have all Satan's arts to build up Jericho, by slanders and lies. They labour to estrange the hearts of people what they can against the truth of religion, and therefore they raise all the lies and slanders they can; nay, and they will not suffer so much as a Protestant writer to be named, but the name of such a one, say they, be blotted out. Then they have their *Index Purgatorius*,* to purge all that savour of truth that favour our cause. And then they have their dispensations. And, to cut off other things, for where should I end? indeed their policy is almost endless in this kind; they have the quintessence of their own wit and of Satan's to sharpen them in this kind.

They deal as the magicians of Egypt. When Moses came to do wonders, they imitated him in all the rest, except in one. So they strengthen themselves much in imitating the Protestants. We labour to build the walls of Jerusalem, they imitate us in building the walls of Jericho. We preach to shake off drowsiness, and they fall a preaching. We print, and they print. We publish books of devotion; they go beyond us. We set out books of martyrology (*i*), to shew the cruelty of them, and they have lost much by that. Hereupon they do so too, and aggravate things, and add their own lies. So by imitating our proceedings, wherein we have gained upon them, they, like the Egyptian magicians, do the like, and God hardens their hearts, as he did Pharaoh's, by the magicians.

Again, by labouring to make divisions between kings and their subjects, what they can in those places where their religion hath not obtained ground. That they may get a party they cherish division like the devil; they divide and rule.

It was Julian's policy to provide that no Christian should bear any office in the wars, to be captain, &c. So if the Jesuits and papists may have their will, no man that is opposite to them shall have any place. Those that shall have the place to manage offices, and such like, shall be those that incline to them. This they bring to pass if they can, and so for captains in the wars, &c. As Julian the apostate, he cared not for Judaism, but did what he did out of spite to the Christians; so in the most of their plots thus they work one way or other. I say there is no end of their plots, only it is good to know them; for so we may the better prevent them.

Quest. How shall the building up of Jericho be stopped, seeing they go about it so? And indeed they have built much of late years, and have raised up their walls very high, and labour what they can to stop the building of Jerusalem!

Ans. 1. The way to stop this Jericho, that it never go up again, *is the judicious knowledge of popery;* that it is a religion contrary to the blessed truth of God. God hath left us his testament, his will, wherein he hath bequeathed us all the good that we can challenge from him. Now this religion is contrary to our Father's will, and they know it well enough, and therefore they build their courses upon men's devices, and not upon divine truth. They know if people come to know the Testament, that they should lose, and therefore they labour to suppress knowledge, and extinguish it; we should labour to know the controversial truths between us and them, and to have the knowledge of the Scriptures; for knowledge is a notable means to strengthen us; there are none that know popery that will be deceived by it.

2. And then, together with the knowledge of their tenets, *to know their courses, and practices, and policy.* In 2 Tim. iii. 9, 'They shall prevail

* That is, 'Expurgatorius' = Index of Prohibited Books. Cf. Mendhan.—G.

no longer,' saith Saint Paul, 'for their madness shall be made manifest.' Why shall they not prevail any longer? Their madness shall be manifest. So that the manifesting of the madness of men is the cause why they shall prevail no longer. It were good to know all their undermining tricks, and all the policy of the Jesuits and papists, that lay their trains afar off, that they may be the less seen. As the spider gets into a corner, that she appear not, so themselves will not appear, but they draw women, and other licentious persons, and they have greater than them too. So they lay their trains afar off, that they may have their will. It is good to know their devilish practices, that so their diabolical madness may be manifest, that so they may prevail no longer; for undoubtedly, if their courses were laid open, there is no man that loves his own safety, and the safety of the kingdom, but would hate them.

3. Another way to stop the building of Jericho is *to have young ones instructed*. I would parents would have more care of catechising, and others in their places would have more care of grounding young ones in the grounds of religion. Popery labours to overthrow that. For the worshipping of images it is directly against the second commandment, and they are so guilty of it that they take it away in some of their books. The younger sort, that are the hope of the succeeding church, should be well grounded in religion. That that is right will discover that that is crooked. It would make them impregnable against all popish solicitations.

The neglect of this is the cause why many gentlemen, and of the nobility [apostatize]. The neglect of their education by those that should overlook them hath made them fit for Jesuits and priests to work on, having ripe wits otherwise. And all because of the atheism of those that have neglected their breeding, and filled their heads with other vanities; it hath been the ruin of many families in this kingdom. Therefore it is good to season younger years with the knowledge of the grounds of religion.

4. And in all the dark corners of the land *to set up lights that may shine;* for these owls fly in the dark. They cannot endure the light of the gospel by any means. They see the breath of God's mouth is too hot for them; and they must be consumed at length by that, by the preaching of the gospel. Not with the sword, but with the sword of Christ's mouth, Antichrist must especially be consumed. And they know this by experience. Therefore they labour underhand. They will not be seen in it, but ofttimes others are instruments more than they are aware, to stop the preaching of the gospel by all the policy they can.

5. Again, as I said before, popery is a kingdom of darkness, and nothing will undo it but light; therefore we should labour *to cherish all good learning*. It is a notable means to assist against popery. Julian knew that well enough. Therefore he would not suffer parents to send their children to school, but to be brought up in ignorance. And so papists would have a neglect of learning that might help this way.

6. And because they labour to reign in division, *let us labour to unite ourselves, and not break upon small matters, but to join together with one shoulder, as one man, against that malignant generation*, and mark those among us that are the causes of division; as the apostle saith, 'Mark them, they serve not Christ, but their own bellies,' Philip. iii. 19; they serve their own turns that reign in division. Let us labour as much as may be if we will join strongly against the enemies of God and his church, to unite our forces together, and not to entertain slight matters of breach one from another.

7. And with these let us join *our prayers to God, and our thanksgiving.* We are not thankful enough that God hath brought us out of the kingdom of darkness; not only out of the darkness of sin and Satan, but from the darkness of popery. We have not been thankful to God for that deliverance in Queen Elizabeth's time, out of the Egyptian darkness, and the deliverance in our late king's time, and deliverances in later times, we are not thankful enough. And we begin to shew it in not making much of religion, and growing in further and further obedience of religion. Is this our thankfulness to God? What, doth religion hurt us? Are we not beholden to God for our religion, and to religion for our peace and deliverance? Hath not God witnessed the truth of our religion from heaven by deliverances? Hath not God been with us strangely by the confusion of the plots of others. And how do we requite it? By growing to a lukewarm temper. A lukewarm temper is odious in the sight of God. 'I would thou wert hot or cold,' saith Christ, Rev. iii. 15. The best religion in the world is odious if it be cold. God will not endure us to join the ark and Dagon, Christ and Belial. Certainly, if we do, God will spue us all out. It will be the confusion of the church and state, and yet this is the thankfulness that we give to God for the gospel of peace, that we have been so much beholden to him for.

Therefore it is good to take occasions, as we have one ministered this day, to call to mind the former dealing of God to us, in the gunpowder treason and other deliverances, which we have had several occasions upon this day to speak of. And, to come nearer ourselves, let us stir up our hearts to thankfulness, which is the main end of this day, and among the rest for our gracious prince, that God hath delivered him as the three children in the fiery furnace (*j*). They were kept and preserved untouched of the fire; so God hath preserved him in the fiery furnace. The not being thankful for these things will be a means for God to lay us open to his and our enemies. Therefore let us make use of this day especially to stir us up to thankfulness. To go on.

8. For the building of the walls of Jericho what should I speak of popery and the like? *We should labour to overthrow that Jericho.* All of us have vowed in baptism to fight against the world, and the devil, and the main enemy of all that is within us, that is, our flesh. We could not be hurt by them. We betray ourselves, as Samson betrayed himself to Delilah. Those that are baptized, and especially that have renewed their vows by solemn fasting, and renewed their covenant in taking the communion, as there are none of us all but have vowed against our corruptions and sins in baptism, and have renewed their solemn vows in the communion and in public fasting. Well, when we go about to strengthen our corruptions, and the corruptions of the times in the places where we live, what do we go about? To build the walls of Jericho again. What do we go about, but to strengthen that that God hath cursed? There is nothing under heaven so cursed as this corruption of ours, that is the cause of all the curses of the creatures, of all the curses that ever were, or shall be, even to the last curse: 'Go, ye cursed, to eternal destruction,' Mat. xxv. 41. This pride, and sensuality, and secret atheism and infidelity that we cherish, and love more than our own souls, this is that that many go about to build, and oppose all the ways that are used to pull down Jericho, and hate nothing so heartily as the motions of God's Spirit, and the means that God's Spirit hath sanctified to pull down these walls of Jericho.

Must not this be a cursed endeavour, when we go about to build that

that we ourselves have vowed to pull down? when we go about to raise that that we have formerly destroyed by our own vows? As Saint Paul saith, Gal. ii. 18, 'If I again build the things I have destroyed, I make myself a transgressor.' Indeed, when we go about to build the things that we have vowed their destruction, we make ourselves transgressors.

Let us take notice of the wondrous poison and rebellion of the corruption of our hearts in this kind. Hath not the Lord threatened curse upon curse against many particular sins? 'Cursed is the man that calls evil good, and good evil,' Isa. v. 20. Have we not many that do so? In Deuteronomy there is curse upon curse to those that mislead others, xxvii. 16, *et alibi*. And in the New Testament there is curse upon curse; St Paul threateneth that such and such shall not enter into the kingdom of heaven, 1 Cor. vi. 9, 10. Yet, notwithstanding the curse, we go about to build Jericho again, to set up that that God hath pronounced a curse upon.

We cry out against popery, and well we may, when the Scripture directs curses against their particular opinions, as where it saith, 'If an angel from heaven shall teach other doctrine, let him be accursed,' Gal. i. 8. The Council of Trent hath cursed those that say traditions are not of equal authority with the Scriptures, and so they set curse against curse. We wonder at them that they are not afraid of the curse of God, nay, to counter-curse God as it were; when he curseth disobedience, to curse the practice of obedience to him. And then there is a curse to those that shall add or take away from the Scripture. St John seals the whole Scripture with a curse: 'Cursed is he that adds, or takes away,' &c., Rev. xxii. 18. Now they add to the Scripture that that is no scripture; and they take away what they list, as the second commandment and the cup in the sacrament. I say we wonder at them, that they will run upon the curses, that they will be stricken through with so many curses, more than Absalom with javelins, or Achan with stones: 'Cursed is he that worshippeth graven images,' Deut. xxvii. 15; besides particular things that are cursed in Scripture. We wonder at them that they are so desperately blind to run on. But are not we as ill? Are there not many curses in the Scripture, and denunciations of being excluded from the kingdom of God, against the courses that are taken by many men? And yet we venture on it. Will a negative religion bring any man to heaven, to say he is no papist, nor no schismatic? No. Certainly therefore profane persons that maintain corruptions, and abuses, and abominations, against the light of conscience, and nature, and Scriptures, they raise up Jericho again and they are under a curse.

Let me ask any one why Christ came?* The apostle saith, and they will be ready to say, 'To dissolve the cursed works of the devil,' 1 John iii. 8. It should seem by many, notwithstanding, especially at these times, that he came to establish the works of the devil; for what good we do in the ministry, in three quarters of a year, it is almost undone in one quarter. At the time when we pretend great honour to Christ, we live as if he came to build up the cursed wall of hell; to break loose all. Whereas he came to destroy the works of the devil: 'He came to redeem us out of the hands of our enemies, that we might serve him without fear, in holiness and righteousness, all the days of our life,' Luke i. 75. He came to redeem us from our vain conversation. Nay, many live as if he came to give liberty to all conversation. Is not this to raise Jericho? to raise a fort for Satan to enter into our souls and keep possession in us? to beat out God

* In margin here, 'Application concerning the feast of the nativity.'—G.

and his Spirit? to fight against our known salvation, when we rear up courses contrary to Christ's coming in the flesh, and to the end of Christ's dying for us, which was to free us from our vain conversation, and to redeem us from the world, that we should not be led as slaves to the customs of the world?

Therefore let us consider what we do, what our course of life is. If it be a proceeding, and edification, and building up ourselves more and more to heaven, a growing in knowledge and in holy obedience to the divine truths we know; if it be a pulling down of sin more and more, a going further and further out of the kingdom of darkness, and a setting ourselves at a gracious liberty to serve God; oh it is a happy thing if it be so! If our life be a taking part with Christ, and his Spirit, and his ministry, to grow in grace and piety, oh it is an excellent thing when we grow better the longer we live in the world, and this cursed Jericho, the corruption of nature, which, if we cherish, will be the cause of an eternal curse after, if it go down, and we ruin it more and more, and we suffer the word to beat down the forts of Satan, those strong imaginations, &c. But if our life be nothing else but a living answerable to our lusts; that as we are dead and cursed by nature, so we make ourselves twice dead, a hundred times dead by sin, and bring curse upon curse by our sinful conversation, we are then under God's broad seal cursed. We are all born accursed, till we get out of the state of nature; to free us from which Christ became a curse. If we get not out of this, but go on and feed our vanity and corruption, what will be the end of it but an eternal curse afterwards? Therefore let us consider what we do, when we maintain and cherish corruptions and abuses in ourselves and others. We build that that God hath cursed; we build that that we have vowed against ourselves.

And how will God take this at the hour of death? Thou that art a careless, drowsy hearer of the word of God, and a liver contrary to the word of God, how will God take this at thee, at the hour of death, when thy conscience will tell thee that thy life hath been a practice of sin, a strengthening of corruption? The 'old Adam' that thou hast cherished, it will stare and look on thee with so hideous a look that it will drive you to despair; for conscience will tell thee that thy life hath been a strengthening of pride, of vanity, of covetousness, and of other sins. Thy whole life hath been such; and now when thou shouldst look for comfort, then thy corruptions, which thou shouldst have subdued, they are grown to that pitch that they will bring thee to despair, without the extraordinary mercy of God to awaken thy heart by repentance. Why therefore should we strengthen that that is a curse and will make us cursed too? and will make the time to come terrible to us, the hour of death and the day of judgment? How shall men think to hold up their faces and heads at the day of judgment, whose lives have been nothing else but a yielding to their own corruption of nature, and the corruptions and vanities of the times and places they have lived in? that have never had the courage to plead for God; that have been fierce against God: 'Who ever was fierce against God, and prospered?' Job ix. 4. When men make their whole life fierce against God, against the admonitions of his word and Spirit, and their whole life is nothing but a practice of sin, how can they think of death and judgment without terror!

Now, it were wisdom for us to carry ourselves so in our lives and conversations, that the time to come may not be terrible, but comfortable to think of; that we may lift up our heads with joy when we think of death and judgment. But when we do nothing but build Jericho, when we raise up sin, that we should ruin more and more, what will the end of this be, but despair here and destruction in the world to come?

You may shake off the menaces and threatenings of the ministers, as Hiel shook off Joshua's. He was an austere, singular man, and it is a long time since Jericho was cast down, and God hath forgotten. Hath he so? He found that God had not forgotten; so there are many that think that words are but wind of men, opposite to such and such things. But, though our words may be shooken off now, and the word of God now in the preaching may be shook off, yet it will not when it comes to execution. When we propound the curse of God against sinful courses, you may shake off that curse; but when Christ from heaven shall come to judge the quick and the dead, and say, 'Go, ye cursed,' that were born cursed, that have lived cursed, that have maintained a cursed opposition to blessed courses, that have not built up your own salvation, but your corruptions, you that loved cursing, 'Go, ye cursed, to hell-fire, with the devil and his angels for ever,' Mat. xxv. 41. Will you shake off that? No, no! Howsoever our ministerial entreaties may be shaken off, yet when God shall come to judge the quick and the dead, that eternal threatening shall not be shaken off. Therefore, I beseech you, consider not so much what we say now, but what God will make good then. 'What we bind on earth,' out of the warrant of God's book, 'shall be bound in heaven,' Mat. xvi. 19, and God will say Amen to that we say agreeable to his word.

Think not light of that we speak, for God will make good every word. He is Jehovah, he will give being to every word. He is not only mercy but justice. We make an idol of him else. And we must fear him in his justice. 'He loves to dwell with such as are of a contrite spirit, that tremble at his word,' Isa. lvii. 15.

It is said of David, that when Uzzah was stricken, he trembled,' 2 Sam. vi. 6. Hiel, and such kind of persons, regard not the threatenings of God, but go on and treasure up wrath. It is a sign of a wicked man to hear the menaces and threatenings, and not to tremble. To end all with two places of scripture: Saith Moses, 'He that hears these things, and blesseth himself, my wrath shall smoke against him,' Deut. xxix. 20. God's wrath shall smoke and burn to hell against such a one as blesseth himself, that knows he is cursed under the seal of God, that doth ill, and yet he blesseth himself in doing ill. Therefore, take heed of that, add not that to the rest. God's wrath will smoke against such a one. And you know what St Paul saith: Rom. ii. 5, 'If thou go on and treasure up wrath,' thou buildest Jericho, that thou hast vowed the destruction of. Every time thou takest the communion, thou treasurest up wrath against the day of wrath. For there will be a day of the manifestation of the just wrath of God, and then these things will be laid to thy charge.

Let us every one labour to get out of the state of nature, to break off our wicked lives, and to get into Christ the blessed seed, and then we shall be blessed, we shall be made free, free from the curse of nature and of sin. Let us renew our covenants against all sin, and make conscience to be led by the Spirit of Christ, that we may gather sound evidence every day, that we are in Christ, and so out of the curse.

NOTES.

(*a*) P. 20.—'Luther, a man of great parts and grace, saith of himself, "That if,"' &c. The *sentiment* is found in his 'Table Talk,' on which cf. note *uu*, Vol. III. p. 533.

(*b*) P. 20.—'The Jesuits themselves, amongst the rest one De Lapide, he saith.' '*One* De Lapide' is somewhat contemptuous for a name so famous as Corneille de la Pierre, commonly called Cornelius à Lapide. His great 'Commentarii in Sacram Scripturam' (10 vols. folio) is an extraordinary chaos of wisdom and folly. The thing stated *ante* is a commonplace of popery.

(*c*) P. 20.—'As one of the ancients saith well, "the wrath of a man,"' &c. Probably Augustine, but I have failed to trace it.

(*d*) P. 20.—'The primitive church pronounced a curse against Julian.' It needeth not to annotate so familiar a fact in the early conflicts of Christianity; but perhaps it is as well to notice that 'curse' is not used technically. There was angry denunciation, yet scarcely excommunication *proper*.

(*e*) P. 22.—'Children, according to the Hebrew word, are the building, the pillars of the house.' The allusion here is not, as at first sight would seem, to 'first-born' in the text, but to the general word for children, viz., בָּנִים, and probably also to the Hebrew word for 'house,' בַּיִת (*quasi* בְּנֶת), both which words are derived from the verb בָּנָה, 'to build.' So we read the passage, 'Cursed be the man that riseth up and buildeth (בָּנָה) Jericho;' as if he said, 'that riseth up and maketh Jericho to have children and house. That man shall suffer for it, inasmuch as his *children* shall die, and his *house* be left desolate.'

(*f*) P. 23.—'As Zedekiah and Mauritius the emperor.' With respect to Zedekiah, cf. 2 Kings xxv. 7. 'Mauritius' is of course Mauricius Flavius Tiberius, one of the greatest of the emperors of Constantinople. Sibbes alludes to the well known fact, that his five sons were murdered in the church of St Antonomus, Chalcedon, while their father was compelled to look on.

(*g*) P. 24.—'As Augustine complains, they so pestered,' &c. Repeatedly in his *De Civitate Dei*, and in his Controversies.

(*h*) P. 24.—'Gerson . . . saith.' To distinguish this from other Gersons, it may be stated that Sibbes no doubt refers to John Gerson of Gerson [Charlier], whose writings are numerous. Died 1429.

(*i*) P. 26.—'We set out books of martyrology.' The great martyr-book is that of John Fox; but for others prior and subsequent to Sibbes, cf. Watt's Bib. Brit., *sub voce*. G.

(*j*) P. 28.—The reference is to the safe return of Prince Charles, afterwards Charles I., from the visit which he made in company with Buckingham into Spain, whence he returned on the 5th October 1623. His safe return is frequently referred to as a matter of thankfulness by the preachers of the period. There is already published in this Series a sermon preached on that occasion by Samuel Ward (Works, p. 134).

THE VANITY OF THE CREATURE.

THE VANITY OF THE CREATURE.

NOTE.

'The Vanity of the Creature' forms No. 18 of the Sermons in the Saint's Cordials of 1629. It is not contained in the editions of 1637, 1658. The separate title-page will be found below.* G.

* THE

VANITIE OF

THE CREATVRE.

In One SERMON.

WHEREIN IS SET FORTH,

The decaying condition of all naturall parts, and worldly comforts.

Together with the meanes how to attaine an estate supernaturall, to live with God in Christ.

Shewing who are the truly wise men in the world.

With sundry helps and directions to stirre up in Christians a longing desire after their best home, &c.

[The ornament here, described in Vol. IV. page 60. So in all the Sermons from the Saint's Cordials in this volume.—G.]

VPRIGHTNES HATH BOLDNES.

LONDON,

Printed in the yeare 1629.

THE VANITY OF THE CREATURE.

And Barzillai said to the king, How long have I to live, that I should go up with the king to Jerusalem? I am this day fourscore years old, &c.—2 SAMUEL XIX. 34–38.

I HAVE read, beloved, a large text. In the handling of it, we will do as the traveller doth that is belated; we will cast how we may post the next way to an end. The oration, you see, is very plain. We shall not need to spend much time in explicating the terms.

The words are part of a conference, you see; a passage between king David and Barzillai of Rogelim, in the county of Gilead. This Barzillai had been wondrous kind to David in the time of his distress. David being now restored from danger, remembers the kindness of his old friend, and, in way of requital, tenders him this offer, that in case he would go with him to the court of Jerusalem, he should be very welcome thither, and he should have such entertainment as the court would afford. This invitement* of the king foregoes† our text.

The old man Barzillai is now upon his answer in the words read, who doth,

1. First, *very modestly and mannerly put off the king's motion to him.*

2. *And then next he tenders and prefers a suit of his own.* For the king's motion, that he should turn courtier, Barzillai puts off very finely, as you may see in the text. He gives sundry reasons for his so doing.

1. The first is, *because that he was no fit man for the court.*

First, He was smitten in age, and therefore, in case he should go up, he could but only salute it; for, saith he, 'how many are the days of my years?' My years are brought to days; my days may quickly be numbered. I should die by that time I were warm there, and therefore what should I do at the court? Secondly, put the case he did draw breath there a while, that was all; for, saith he, 'Am I able now to discern between good and evil?' There is nothing that offers itself to my eye, to my ear, to my taste, to any of my senses, that will give me any great content, and therefore there is no great reason why I should be drawn thither. This is his first reason, from the unfitness of the thing.

* That is, 'invitation.'—G.

† That is, 'goes before,' = precedes, used as also 'fore-think,' and the like, by contemporaries.—G.

Second, Afterward he proceeds to other reasons in the text, that is first thus much: if he should live there, *it must be to do the king some service, at the least to yield him some contentment*. But so it was that he was under age's command, and was able for neither. He was neither fit for work nor fit for play. He found no great contentment in himself, and he could yield little to others, and therefore why should he be a burden to the king's court?

Third, The third reason is this, *that he had done what he had done for the king, but in duty*. It was his duty to do what he did, and it was but a little. All that he could do for the king was only to bring him a mile or two on his way; and why should the king trouble his thoughts about a recompence for this, saith he? Thus he puts off the king's motion; he craves leave that he may forbear the court, and be excused thence.

Fourth, This done, he comes in the next place, because he would give no offence, to tender a suit of his own, and that is double.

1. In regard of himself.

2. And then in regard of his son Chimham.

For himself he craves leave to go back again to his own dwelling; and here he doth finely set his petition by the king's motion.

1. He desires the king's leave, that he would give him leave to go home and die.

2. And next, that the king would be pleased so far to gratify him, that he may die in his own dwelling, where his habitation was.

Fain he would die as the hare doth in her own form, and as other creatures willingly do in their own nests. Then, in the next place, he adds another reason why he would be dismissed; because he would die where his father and his mother were buried. There he was bred, there he was born, there he drew his first breath, and there he would gladly resign himself again, and his breath, and be laid and gathered in mercy to his fathers. This is his suit for himself.

In the behalf of his son, he tenders him to the king's grace, as if he should say, Your motion is very gracious, far beyond my desert, and such as I should be very happy in the enjoying of, in case age did not hinder me. For proof whereof, I leave my son as a pledge and pawn.* This staff of my age, this stay of my comfort, I commend him to your grace; deal with him as shall seem best in your eyes. And thus Barzillai he hath commended his suit to the king.

Now this being thus delivered, it is further amplified and set forth from the effect that this wrought in the king.

1. First, King David he accepts of his excuse. He gives him to understand, if he will go, he shall be kindly welcome; if he stay behind, there is no offence shall be taken, but further, the king will be ready in any other kind to gratify him as occasion shall serve.

2. And next for his son, the king accepts of him, and promiseth to do for him that which should seem good in the eyes of his father.

These be the parts of this conference, and the effects of it; so that in sum you see here is a dialogue,

A conference between David and Barzillai.

We are now upon Barzillai's answer, which is set forth,

1. From the parts.

2. From the effects of it, as before we inferred.

Now from all these generals, sundry particular instructions might be

* That is, 'security.'—G.

raised. But I perceive the time hath prevented me; therefore we will briefly handle a point or two, and so for this time cease.

1. First of all, in the first place, we see that *Barzillai hath no mind to the court;* and he draws his argument and his reason from his state and from his age. 'How many,' saith the original, 'are the days of my years?' (*a*.) The motion* was very gracious on the king's part, and such as man's nature is ready enough to entertain. Naturally, we desire honour and preferment; at least an old man might take some contentment in the dainties and delicates of a court. Further than this, let a man be never so religious, in David's court a man might find much contentment, and might take much comfort and solace in the presence and company of such a prince. Notwithstanding all this, saith old Barzillai, my days are almost spent, my glass is almost run, and therefore what should I talk of a court? I will go home and die.

Doct. 1. In him we learn thus much, *how that no company, no comforts, no motions in the earth, should put off thoughts of death when death begins to creep upon us.* I say wheresoever we live, what offers soever are made us, whatsoever the motion be, for ease, for profit, for promotion, for any outward contentments, we must not lay down, we must not lay aside the thoughts of our mortality. No dream must put us out of these thoughts while we travel in this main roadway of all flesh. We must never be so busy in discourse, in contrivements,† as to forget our way, to forget which way we are going, but still our thoughts must be homewards; that as we deal with other journeys here upon earth; for these momentary homes that we have here, wheresoever we be, in company that we like wondrous well, where our entertainment is full of kindness, where our welcome is of the best, and all content is given; yet notwithstanding, thoughts eftsoons‡ will offer themselves of home, night will come, and it will grow late, I must home for all this, and leave all this company. So, my brethren, should it be concerning our long homes, which is that surest dwelling; wheresoever we be, howsoever for the present we be tempted or taken up, still, still our eye must be home; we must remember our latter end, remember whither we are going. This Barzillai teacheth us in his practice. A motion is made for the court. Tush! court me no courts, saith Barzillai; I am an aged man; I have one foot in the grave; let me go home and die. Here is an offer made him of comfort and contentment. No; I will go home and lie by my fathers. Death possesseth his thoughts; he minds nothing else now but dying. This Barzillai did, and thus the apostle would have us do in 1 Cor. vii. 29, 30. Our time, saith he, it is abbreviated. Now our time is nothing in comparison of that it was in the time of the patriarchs. A great part of our time is already run out, and there is but a little of it left behind. Our time being thus short, saith the apostle, 'Let him that is married, be as if he were not married; let him that weeps, be as if he wept not; let him that rejoiceth, be as if he did not rejoice; he that is in the world, as if he were not in the world.' Let us so carry ourselves, that we may be very indifferent towards all matters in this life. Let us so order the matter, that no occasion of grief, of sorrow, of comfort, of joy, of company, of one thing or another, public or private, may divert our thoughts, and turn them aside from thinking upon death. This is that which David and others press in sundry psalms.§ He calls upon rich and poor, upon high and low, one and another, in the 82d Psalm. He calls

* That is, 'proposal.'—G.
† That is, 'contrivances.'—G.
‡ That is, 'immediately.'—G.
§ In margin, 'Psalms xlix. and lxxxii.'—G.

upon judges and magistrates, though they be in place gods, yet in nature men, and must die as men. This is that which Solomon presseth too. But what needs particulars? We will not trouble you with particular instances of Scripture, much less with instances of other stories. Every man almost knows what some heathen princes have done this way. They had some to call upon them in their beds, some at their boards, to remember them that they were mortal, that they must die, to mind them of this in the midst of their greatest security, and in the midst of all their jollity (*b*). And indeed there is great reason why it should be thus, why it is good still to hold on the thoughts of our mortality and of our death, whatsoever occasion be offered.

1. It is needful for the preventing of evil.

2. And it is useful for the obtaining of good.

Reason 1. *These evils will be hereby prevented.* (1.) The constant thoughts of death and mortality *will tie us to our good behaviour*, that we shall not offer any injustice, any hard measure, to any man. Whereas let death be once out of the sight of the thoughts of a man, he grows wild, he grows unruly, he grows masterless. You see in the parable of the servant,* when he thought his master was gone afar off, that he would not come a great while, that his reckoning, his account would not be soon, it would not be sudden, he lays about him like a Nimrod, he smites and beats his fellow-servants, he makes no conscience of his dealing to his poor brethren. Whereas, on the other side, when Job presented to himself the thoughts of death and mortality, how that there was a Lord and a Judge that would call him to an account for all, he dares not lift up his hand, he dares not lift up his tongue, against any underling or inferior.†

(2.) Again, as this will prevent injustice towards men, so it will *prevent impenitency towards God.* The heart of man secures itself like the harlot, Prov. vii. 10, *et seq.* When she conceives her husband is gone afar off, and hath taken a great journey, she is secure. So the heart, the impenitent heart of man, when a man puts far from him the thoughts of death, and will not conceive that the Judge stands at the door, then he doth obstinate‡ himself in sinful courses, and doth what he can to stiffen himself against all the admonitions and rebukes of God's mouth.

(3.) Further, this is another evil that is prevented; the thoughts of mortality will *prevent dotage*, as it were, *about these worldly things.* The world will grow upon us and bewitch us, if we suffer the thoughts of death to fall once. If we do not see death stand at the end of all our earthly profits, of all our worldly pleasures and advantages, we shall be even almost mad after them, and we shall be too too glad of them when we have them, and too too much surfeit upon them; whereas, on the other side, the thoughts of this, that we must shortly leave them, and depart hence, this will cool our appetite to earthly things, it will make us have them as if we had them not, as you heard from the apostle.

(4.) Yea, these thoughts of our mortality in all estates and conditions, it is that which will *prevent the danger of death.* It will take away the sting of it, it will take away the terror of it. Death is a most terrible thing in its own nature you know, and the heathen could speak [so of] it. Death is most terrible, especially to him that doth not die in his thoughts daily. Whenas a man in his meditations doth daily present death to himself, and

* Mat. xxv. 15, *et seq.*—G. † Job xxxi. 13.—G.

‡ That is, 'hardens,' = grows stubborn.—G.

looks upon it, then death is like the prevented* basilisk, death hath lost the sting. It can do us no hurt; it proves like the brazen serpent looked upon. The beholding of that death puts an end to all other miseries, to all other maladies, to all other deaths whatsoever, so that there is much good gotten, at the least there is much evil prevented, in case we do constantly entertain in us thoughts of mortality and of death, as Barzillai did.

Reason 2. *Secondly,* As this thought of mortality is profitable for us in that respect, in preventing evil, so in a second regard proposed, that it doth even *help us to much goodness.* Thoughts of mortality, what will they do?

(1.) First, They will make a man painful† in his place, to dwell upon his own vocation, upon his own business; as Paul saith, 'Knowing the terror of the Lord, we exhort and admonish,' 2 Cor. v. 11. We being apostles, we do the duty of apostles. Upon this ground Barzillai, remembering his mortality, that he must shortly go hence, he betakes himself home, that death might find him in his own place.

(2.) Again, the thoughts of mortality, as they will make a man painful in his place, so they will make him *profitable consequently to men;* as apostle Peter speaks, 2 Peter i. 13, he stirs up himself to put the people of God in remembrance of those things they had learned, because he considered that 'shortly he was to lay down his tabernacle,' to make an end of his life.

(3.) And further, the thoughts of death and mortality, they will make a man *patient in the midst of all the hard measure that is offered to him;* in the midst of all preserves us, as the apostles speak, both James and Paul, that we shall be patient: 'Let your patience be known unto all men, because the Lord is at hand, because the time is short, because the Judge stands at the door,' &c., Philip. iv. 5, James v. 10. This is that which will make one quiet in all provocations; this is that will comfort him in all discouragements: I shall shortly be sent for, I shall be called from hence; then I shall be righted where I am wronged, I shall be cleared where I am accused, I shall have rest where I have trouble, all shall be well, and therefore why should I not be quiet?

(4.) Yea, this thought of mortality is that that will make one *prepare for death.* A man that resolves he must die, he goes about to set his house in order, to set his heart in order, to set all in order, and prepare now for that guest that is so near approaching.

So that whether we look to the evils that are prevented, or to the good things that are obtained and acquired, it will be a profitable course for every man to be of Barzillai's mind, to set aside all motions, and all solicitations, all other respects, and to take to himself thoughts of death and mortality. We will stand no longer in proving and clearing this plain point unto you, we will be as brief as we may in applying it, and that with all plainness.

Use 1. First, then, is this our duty? *Here we must shame and blame ourselves that we forget our home, and that we remember no better our latter end.* This is a matter of humbling to us, that we do not remember that which should be always in our thoughts. The end of a man's days should be at the end of all his thoughts. Still, as the goal is in the eye of the runner, as

* Alluding to the idea that if a man see a basilisk before it sees him, it cannot injure him, but dies.—Ed.

† That is, 'painstaking.'—G.

the white* is in the eye of the archer, so still a man's latter end should be in the eye of him whilst he is running his race and his course here in this world.

A man should be still bound for home, as it were, as you see all creatures be. Let a stone be removed from home, from the centre, let it be put out of its place, it will never be quiet till it be home again. Let a bird be far from the nest, and it grows towards night, she will home even upon the wings of the wind. Let every poor beast, and every creature, though the entertainment be but slender at home, yet if you let it slip loose it will home as fast as it can. Everything tends to its place; there is its safety, there is its rest, there it is preserved, there it is quiet. Now, sith it is so with every creature, why should it not be so with us? Why should not we be for our home? This, my brethren, is not our home, here is not our rest. That is our home where our chief friends be, where our Father God is, where our husband Christ is, where our chief kindred and acquaintance be, all the prophets, and apostles, and martyrs of God departed are, that is our home, and thither should we go.

Again, that is our home where our chief work, where our chief business lies. And where is chiefly a Christian's business but in heaven? His conversation must be there, his affection is there. He himself while he is on earth must be out of the earth, and raise himself from earth to heaven every day.

More than this, that is our home where our rest and peace is. Here we have no abiding city; there is our home, as our Saviour speaks, our mansion.† We have no abiding place till we come to heaven. While we are here, we are tossed to and fro from place to place; but when we are there, there we rest. We rest from our labours, we rest from sin, we rest from corruption, from all fears, from all tears, from all griefs, from all temptations; that is our home. Why do we not go home, then, my brethren? Why are we like a silly child, that when his father sends him forth, and bids him hie him home again, every flower that he meets with in the field, every sign he sees in the street, every companion that meets him in the way, stops him, and hinders him from repairing to his father? So it is with us for the most part; every trifle, every profit, every bauble, every matter of pleasure, every delight, is enough to divert and turn aside our thoughts from death, from home, from heaven, from our God, and we are taken up, and lose ourselves I know not where. This shews that either we conceive not heaven as our home, and earth as a pilgrimage and tabernacle, or else it shews we are too, too childish, like children in this behalf.

Use 2. But, secondly, here is another word of instruction for us, and that is thus much, *that every one of us now should labour after the example of this good man*, even to remember his latter end, to remember whither he is going, to remember his home.

Quest. What need this? will some say; how is it possible for a man to forget this point?

Ans. 1. Yes, my beloved, it is very possible. It is a very easy matter to speak of death, but it is an hard matter to think of it, and to think of it seriously, for a man to take it home to his own thoughts. It is a very difficult thing for a man to apprehend privations,‡ those things that are so far from eternity and being. It is the hardest thing in the world

* That is, 'mark' in the centre of the 'butt.'—G.
† John xiv. 2.—G.
‡ That is, 'negatives.'—G.

to do this in the greatest privation of all, in matter of death. A man is utterly unwilling, utterly unable. This argues he hath no mind to see death, nor no will to salute it.

Ans. 2. Besides, many men, upon many occasions, will labour to turn aside a man's thoughts this way. Hence it is, that though we say we are mortal, yet we scarce believe ourselves to be mortal; but we carry immortal hopes and immortal conceits in mortal breasts. Hence it comes to pass, that though we look into the graves of others, yet we little think that ourselves shall shortly be closed in the grave. Though we see others fall at our right hand and at our left, yet we hardly believe that those eyes of ours must shortly be closed up and stopped, and all our members must be forsaken, and left lifeless as a carcase. These things are far from our thoughts, and therefore it is needful for us to press this oft and oft upon our thoughts, namely, that we are mortal, and that we must away.

Obj. Why, will some man say, how can a man choose but think so, when he hath so many instances of mortality every day before his eyes? He sees rich and poor, young and old, one and another die, and therefore he cannot conceive but that he must die too.

Ans. But yet all this will not do, except a man be assisted by the divine Spirit. This Moses intimates, Ps. xc. 12. They fell in the wilderness by hundreds, nay, by thousands, and yet saith Moses, 'Lord teach us to number our days, &c., and give us wisdom to apply our hearts unto wisdom;' and to that sense and effect Moses prays. Moses, though he had instances enow of mortality, notwithstanding that he was an excellent man himself, and had to do with the best people that were then in the world, yet he sees reason to pray to God that God would teach them their mortality, and that God would make them wise, and that they might know how to number their days, and to remember their own estate. If Moses saw reason to put up this petition to God, certainly there is great need for us to do it. We had need pray Moses' prayer, and we had need to practise Moses' practice too.

(1.) First, *let us labour to take the sum of our life*, what it is in the gross, as he saith in that psalm, 'Our days are threescore years and ten, it may be one may come to fourscore;' he may arrive to such a number, or thereabouts; this is the life of man, Ps. xc. 10. And then,

(2.) Secondly, in the next place, *let us consider how much of this time is run out already*, how that the fourth part, or the third part, or the half of our days is already expired and run out. Let us do in this case as an apprentice doth reckon how many years he was bound for, how many he hath served already, and what is behind. Let us do as a traveller would do: So many miles I must go this day, so many are measured already, the remainder must be passed before night. So let us do in this apprenticeship, in this journey of death. Account what it is, how much of it is spent, how the time slides away in an insensible manner, [how] it steals away.

(3.) Nay, let us in the third place consider *how others fall on every hand before us*. Present this to thy own thoughts, and say, There dwelt such a gentleman the other day, now he is dead; there dwelt such a woman, such a neighbour of late, she is now departed; not long since there dwelt so many in that family, and there are few now left. Thus let us reckon, consider how death seizeth upon other men, and then reflect upon thyself. Who knows whose turn may be next?

(4.) Yea, let us in the last place consider, *how death steals on us too by* *degrees, how it takes possession of us.* It is with us as it is with an house. There falls down a window, and then comes down a piece of a wall, and then a door, &c.; so it is with a man, death seizeth upon his feet, and then upon his hands. Let us take notice how death steals on us, and say, Death is already in mine eye, I begin to be dim-sighted: death is already in mine ear, I begin to be thick of hearing; death is in my limbs and joints, they begin to be lazy, and stiff, and cold, I begin to feel the symptoms of death upon me already. Let us look oft upon ourselves to this purpose, take notice how nature begins to wither and decay. Let the whiteness of our hairs, the weakness of our joints, the wrinkles in our faces, be so many witnesses against us, as he speaks in that place in Job xvi. 8. Thus we must do, my brethren, to come to settle this in our thoughts, that we are mortal, and when we have once persuaded ourselves of this, then let us make preparation for death. Oh think of it by thyself alone, think what it is to die, think what is concluded* in that short word, think what is thy preparation to it, think what business is about it, think what treads on the heels of it when thou art gone. 'It is appointed to men to die once, and after that comes the judgment,' Heb. ix. 27. Consider, I say, by thyself, what it is to die, consider with other folk, with other people. Be ready to speak of it, as Barzillai doth, to mind thyself and others of mortality: and more than this, make preparation, set thy house in order, set thy heart in order.

Preparation to death. For thy house, for thy persons, goods, or children, look thou set them in order.

First, For thy persons, dispose of thy children as Barzillai doth here. Dispose of thy family, of thy kindred, place them in callings, dispose of them for thy habitation. As Isaac and Jehoshaphat, and others in Scripture, give them good instructions, leave them precepts that shall stick by them when thou art dead and gone.

Second, For thy goods, dispose of them; what is evil gotten restore, what is well gotten dispose to pious and merciful uses, to thy family, to those that may challenge right in thee. And it is good to set these things in order before such time as death cometh. Oh, my brethren, it is a miserable madness among the sons of men. They defer these weighty and important businesses to the last hour. When the powers of nature are shaken, when their wits and memories fail, when their speech and understanding leaves them, then, then they go about the most important business of all others. Do this in time; have thy will ready about thee, dispose of thy family, of thy estate, whilst thou art in memory and understanding.

Third, As thy house must be disposed of, *so much more thy heart must be disposed of.* 'Repent of thy sins, pluck out the sting of death, which is sin; 'the sting of death is sin.' Death cannot hurt where there is repentance of sin. Sin unrepented will bring a sting in the time of death. It will fill the heart with sorrow, and the soul with amazement, and the conscience with terror. Pull out the sting, and then thou shalt triumph over death, and over the grave, and say, 'O death, where is thy sting? O grave, where is thy victory?' 1 Cor. xv. 55. O hell, where is thy triumph? O Satan, where is thy malice and power? Nothing is able to do thee harm.

Fourth, In the next place, *labour to take possession of heaven now.* Make entrance into it while thou art here, by getting the life of Christ, and the life of faith in thee, by getting the saving graces of the Spirit in thee. If these things be in thee and be not unfruitful, then thou shalt have entrance,

* That is, 'shut up,' = included.—G.

as Peter speaks, 'into the inheritance and kingdom,' 2 Pet. i. 11. This then is somewhat, that we should have said more largely, if we had had more time and fitness to have spoken to the first point; and therefore we will but name to you some other particulars that we should have spoken to.

In the next place, you see his second reason why he would not be a courtier, is, that now his natural parts, his outward senses begin to fail, that he found his sight to decay, that he could not discern colours; his taste wasted, he could not distinguish between sweet and sour; his ears were not serviceable; now the mirth, and music, and melody of the court was nothing to him. Herein then we see in the next place how it fares with us.

Doct. 2. *That natural parts and powers will decay with age.* Age will decay and wear out our nature. All parts, and powers, and faculties whatsoever they be, time and age will wear out. The clothing both of the body and of the mind, age wears out the clothing of the body, and the garment of the mind, as it were. The mind and the soul is clothed with flesh. This body of ours, our flesh, is clothed with other raiment. Time wears out the one as well as the other. The heaven and the earth, which are more durable than man, yea, than a generation of men, as Solomon saith: Eccles. i. 4, 'Man dieth, a generation of men pass away, but the earth stands,' and much more the heavens continue; yet the heavens and the earth, they are as a garment, they wax old and are soon changed, as the Holy Ghost tells us, Isa. l. 9, much more the sons of men. Yea, the water by drops wastes the stones, nay, a rock of stones, nay, a mountain of stones, as it is in Job xiv. 19, and therefore it will consume in time flesh and blood. To stand to prove this is needless; I will give you some instances for the enlightening of the point, and so end.

1. First, Isaac, when he was an old man, when he waxed old, his sight was thick and dim, as in Gen. xxvii. 1. David in 2 Kings i., when he was stricken in age, when he was passed on in years, then saith the text, David's natural heat began to decay, and they were fain to apply means to help him; so Solomon in Eccles. xii. 1, a place known, tells us that evil days will come, and cloud will follow upon cloud, and then the keepers of the house, the hands, will wax feeble; the pillars of the house, the legs and thighs, will wax faint and weak; those that look out at the windows, the eyes, will be dark and duskish; then all the daughters of music, the ears, they will begin to wax thick too and heavy, and so of the rest, as we see there (*c*). We cannot stand on particulars.

Obj. If any man object, and say, How can this be, sith the soul of a man is no material thing, and it is the soul that sees, and the soul that hears, and not the body; and, therefore, why should the seeing, and hearing, and these senses decay?

Ans. The answer is very easy. The soul doth these things, but it useth the body as an instrument and organ, and so it must work according to the nature of the instrument. Let a man be never so good a horseman, and never so cunning in the way, he must travel as his horse will give him leave. So in this case, let the soul be never so active and full of life, it must perform its actions as the organ and instrument, the members of the body are disposed. Now the body is frail and mortal in a double regard.

First, In regard of the curse and sentence of God passed upon man, 'In the day that thou eatest thereof, thou shalt die the death,' Gen. iii. 8.

Secondly, In regard of the matter whereof man's body is compounded and made. If you make an house of weak and rotten timber, it will decay;

if you make a coat of that which is not very sound and durable, it will not last. Man's body is made of such matter, of such metal, of such timber, of such stuff, it will not hold out; therefore in time it wastes and rots in pieces.

Use 1. For the use of this, thus much in brief. Sith these bodies, the natural faculties and powers, will decay and wear out in time, *let us improve them while we have them;* let us make use of them, as we do of other instruments while they are fit for use. Memory will decay, therefore let us labour to treasure up good things in our memories, lay up things worthy to come into a treasury, and not bad things. That is Solomon's use that he makes: 'Remember thy Creator in the days of thy youth,' saith he, Eccles. xii. 1. Long before the evil days come, and before the decay of thy natural powers, employ thyself well, redeem the time. So say I to you; use memory whiles it lasteth, use wit whiles it lasteth, for the truth: 'Do nothing against the truth,' as Paul speaks of himself, 2 Cor. xiii. 8; so for thine eyes, let them be casements to let in fresh air, and not to let in corruption; use thy ears for wholesome instructions; use thy feet for good purposes, to follow the ways to the house of God; use thy hands, employ them in profitable business while you can work. This providence* men have for their outward estate, and for the body. When we are young we provide for age, we provide somewhat to keep us when we are old. Let us do somewhat for our spiritual estate. You that have young and fresh wits, fresh memories, and eyes, and ears, and hands, and feet, all the parts of your bodies and powers of your souls, ready to do service, improve your time, lay hold on the opportunity. Now is the time of reading, now is the time of learning, now is the time of gathering, now is the time of your harvest; provide for winter; there will evil days come, cloud will follow cloud, as Solomon speaks.

Use 2. Secondly, here is another point of instruction: since this is so, that the natural powers and faculties will fail, *let us therefore strive to get more than this which is natural.* Since this will away, let us provide some more durable substance. You know when an old suit fails, we think of getting a new suit of apparel; when the old lease is expired, we think where to get another habitation; we begin to take a new state, and a new lease. As we do thus in matters of this life, so we should do much more for matters of the soul. When we see the natural life will not hold out, and that it cannot continue long, oh, labour, labour, my brethren, for a better life, for another life, a life that is heavenly, a life that is supernatural; get the life of God in you, and then you shall never die. To this end, get the fountain of life, Christ, to be yours, receive him into your understandings by knowledge, into your hearts by love and affection; receive him, and clasp him, and take him to yourselves by faith, and he that believes in him shall never die; yea, though he die, he shall live; he shall live in death, and shall outlive death, as Christ tells us in that place of the Gospel, John xv. 26. And when you have this fountain of life, that Christ lives in you, that you live not your own life, that you live not the life of Adam, the life of nature,

First, *Labour to act to this life.* Life is made up of many actions, so is the life of God too.

Secondly, If we live the life of Christ, and act it when he puts life into us, we shall *labour to mortify the lusts of the flesh, and of the old man.* So much corruption, so much death; so far as sin lives, so far the man dies.

* That is, 'forethought,' = care.—G.

Thirdly, *Labour to exercise and to stir up those graces of the Spirit that Christ hath bestowed on us;* and so much as faith lives, and as patience lives, and as charity lives, and the graces of God's Spirit live in us, so much we live, and live that life that shall never be determined* and take end. That is another thing briefly.

Yet we add one thing more.

Use 3. In the third place, so this may serve *to shew who is the wisest man in the world,* who makes the wisest choice; for wisdom is most seen in comparative actions. When things are compared together, and a choice is made of things that excel each other, lay the comparison. Who is the wisest man? Some men are for outward things; no man is admired of them but for his natural parts. We look who hath the finest hand, who hath the finest eye, who hath the finest wit, and the best memory for natural regards. This man regards this man, and commends this. This man applauds a child, chooseth a wife, respects men for these things, and for these only. But now spiritual things, heavenly endowments, these things commend a man; they make the man in truth, they are the whole man, as in Eccles. xii. 13. You know that Christ saith, when he comes to determine the question between two sisters, 'Martha, Martha, Mary hath chosen the better part,' Luke x. 42. And why the better part? She hath chosen that which 'shall not be taken from her.' So he makes the best choice then, that prefers those things that are most durable, those things that will last, those things that death cannot kill, those things that sickness cannot make sick, those things that weakness cannot weaken, that no outward thing can deprive us of, those supernatural, spiritual, heavenly graces. A wise man prefers these before all natural parts whatsoever. That is the second thing.

Doct. 3. There is a third thing that we should have spoken to, and that is this, *that not only natural parts, but natural comforts and delights, wear away.*

So Barzillai tells us, he takes no comfort in that he sees, in that he tasted, in that he heard. All matter of delights in nature were taken from him. So that natural delights and comforts they wear out, that as it is said of Sarah, 'it was not with her after the former manner;' so we may say of all natural delights and comforts, in time it will be with the eye, it will be with the ear, it will be with the taste, that nature will be so, that it will not be with them after the manner of the eye, after the manner of the taste, after the manner of the ear; they shall be as if a man had no eyes, as if he had no taste, as if he had no hearing at all. This we might shew in many instances, but this shall suffice, because we would pass to the grounds; and the reason it is clear.

Reason 1. First, All natural objects from whence natural delights and contentments arise, they fail in time.

Reason 2. Secondly, The natural senses and means whereby men apprehend these, they wax dim, and slow, and heavy, and so they perform their actions and their functions with tediousness, because they do it not with alacrity, therefore it is not done with delight.

Reason 3. Further, again, because these very things in themselves in time will work a satiety of all natural delights, a man shall be filled with them, not only with the world, but with the lusts of the world. The desire of earthly things will vanish too, 1 John ii. 16, 17. So the eye is never satisfied with seeing, or the ear with hearing; these things cannot quiet the appetite, they cannot fill the mouth of the desire, these things cannot give con-

* That is, 'terminated'.—G,

tentment. All natural things are so short and finite, that in time they wear out, that a man shall be dulled and tired with them.

Use. The use we should make of this should have been thus much: first of all it serves to teach us this lesson, *that therefore we should not rest, we should not lean too much upon natural comforts and delights,* trust not to natural cheerfulness, to natural courage, as if these would bear us through all perils, and dangers, and fears, and as if these would carry us through all griefs and heart-breakings. No; nature is a little finite thing; it hath its latitude and its extent as a bow hath, which, drawn beyond the compass, breaks in pieces; or as an instrument, the string of an instrument, strain it to an higher pitch, it snaps asunder; so it is with nature too, draw it beyond the pitch, it breaks. You cannot lay much upon the back of nature, but it crusheth it, and breaks it, it falls asunder; and therefore rest not too much in natural parts, for wit and cheerfulness, all these shall fail in time.

Obj. Ay, but nature is propped up with art.

Ans. It may be so for a time, but that is patchery. It may be for a time. If natural delights fail, much more will artificial; if true fire cannot warm a man, and give him relief, painted fire cannot do it. But so it is that natural and artificial things fail in time. Let a man's eye be made of glass in spectacles, and that which is made of flesh as the natural eye, both the natural and artificial eyes, both turn to dust at length. Let a man have a leg, a crutch of wood, or a leg of flesh, as the natural leg, yet both come to dust and ashes in time. All natural and artificial things decay at the last.

Obj. Ay, but carnal delights will help a man.

Ans. Least of all: if wine will not comfort a man, poison will not. Now all carnal pleasures and delights are poison. Where shall we go then for comfort and delight? Yet above all the creatures, there be joys I confess to be had, that will drink up all tears, all sorrows; there be comforts to be had, that will carry a man over all discouragements and grievances; there be everlasting joys, unutterable comforts, inconceivable hopes, and peace of conscience, that will carry a man through sickness, and through pain, and through poverty and shame, through death and all, and will never give him over; a peace that will be with a man in his bed, that will run with him when he flies before the enemy; a peace that will follow him to his grave, and beyond the grave; a peace that will live with him when he dies, that will follow him to the throne and tribunal of Christ, and will set a crown of glory and grace upon him at the last. These joys and comforts be to be had. Oh make out for them, my brethren; seek the joys that are spiritual, seek the comforts of the Scriptures, rejoice in this, 'that your names are written in heaven,' Luke x. 20; rejoice in this, 'that God is your Father; rejoice that Christ dwells in you; rejoice that heaven is yours, that Christ is yours, that God is yours, that the promises and the covenant is yours; and these be the joys that no man can take from you, that nothing can take from you. These will make you rejoice in sorrow, these will make you live in death. As I said before, labour for these that may carry you over all troubles, and miseries, and terrors whatsoever. That is another point. There are divers others I was thinking to have said something to, for I intended no more but only to give you some general heads, some words of instruction in general out of this large text; but I know not how the time hath overslipped us in speaking this little that we have; and therefore we will go no further at this time.

NOTES.

(*a*) P. 37. '"How many," saith the Original, "are the days of my years?"' So commonly in the margin of our English Bible, 'How many days are the years of my life?' Cf. Ps. xc. 12.

(*b*) P. 38. 'The heathen had some to call upon them,' &c. Cf. Note *z*, Vol. II. p. 435.

(*c*) P. 43. 'Keepers of the house,' &c. It is interesting to compare this incidental exposition of a difficult figurative passage, with modern interpretations, *e. g.*, Wardlaw, Macdonald (of America), Moses Stuart, and Ginsburg. Sibbes differs somewhat. G.

DISCOURAGEMENT'S RECOVERY.

DISCOURAGEMENT'S RECOVERY.

NOTE.

'Discouragement's Recovery' forms No. 2 of the Sermons in the first edition of the Saint's Cordials (1629). It was withdrawn in the two subsequent editions. Valuable and suggestive in itself, this sermon has the additional interest of being from a verbally parallel text with that on which 'The Soul's Conflict' is based; and is thus, in all probability, its first form. The separate title-page is given below.* G.

* DISCOVRAGEMENTS
RECOVERIE.
WHEREIN THE SOVLE BY REFLEXI-
ON OF THE STRENGTH OF VNDERSTAN-
ding, quarrelling with it selfe, is at length reduced
and charged to doe that, which must and should be the
true vpshot of all Distempers.

VPRIGHTNES HATH BOLDNES.

PSAL. 31. 21, 22.

Blessed be the Lord, for he hath shewed me his maruellous kindnesse in a strong Citie.

I said in mine haste, I am cut off from before thine eyes, neuerthelesse thou heardest the voice of my supplications, when I cryed vnto thee.

LONDON,
Printed in the yeare 1629.

DISCOURAGEMENT'S RECOVERY.

Why art thou cast down, O my soul? and why art thou disquieted within me? hope in God; for I shall yet praise him, who is the health of my countenance, and my God.—Ps. XLIII. 5.

THIS psalm was penned by David, which shews the passions of his soul; for God's children know the estate of their own souls for the strengthening of their trust and bettering their obedience. Now this is the difference between psalms and other places of Scripture. Other scriptures speak mostly from God to us; but in the Psalms, this holy man doth speak mostly to God and his own soul; so that this psalm is *an expostulation of David with his own soul in a troubled estate*, when being banished from the house of God, he expostulates the matter with his soul: 'Why art thou cast down, O my soul? and why art thou disquieted within me?' The words contain,

1, David's perplexed estate; and, 2, His recovery out of it.

His perplexity is laid down in these words: 'Why art thou cast down, O my soul?' &c. His recovery out of it is first by questioning with himself: 'Why art thou cast down, O my soul?' and then by a charge laid upon his soul: 'Trust in God;' and this trust is amplified from the matter, for what his soul should trust in God: 'I shall yet praise him, and give him thanks;' that is, I shall be delivered, for which delivery my heart will be enlarged to give him thanks. Because this is my God, my salvation, and my help, there is the ground of my faith and trust.

1. For the first, which is his perplexity, *consider the way, how he comes to be thus perplexed.*

(1.) *He was in great troubles and afflictions.* So that it is seen, God suffers his children to fall into extremities, many and long and great afflictions and troubles, ere deliverance come. They are most sensible of spiritual crosses by reason of the life of grace that is in them; and therefore it is that these do cast them down more than all other things. The want of spiritual means makes them thirst more than any want else; yea, than the hart which brayeth after rivers of water, Ps. xlii. 1. Spiritual wants grieve much, spiritual thirst is strong, and the life of grace must be kept. Now to want the means which must do it, this toucheth him more than all the rest.

A soul that is lively in grace cannot endure to live under small means of salvation, much less to endure blasphemous reproaches. Therefore such persons who can content themselves with small or any means, with small comforts, without labouring and striving after more sweet and near communion with God, they have cause to fear their own estates. A child, so soon as it is born, if it be not still-born, cries and seeks for the breast, which puts it out of all question there is life in it, though never so weak. So the life of grace begun in us is known by our spiritual appetites and desire after the means of grace.

(2.) The second thing that troubled this holy man, was *the blasphemous words of wicked men.* Therefore if we would try our state to be good, see how we take to heart everything that is done against religion. Can a child be patient when he sees his father abused? When a man sees the gospel of God trodden down, for a man now to be quiet, that shews his heart is dead. It is better to rage than to be quiet in such a case; for that shews life, though with much distemper. God will set light by his salvation that sets light by his honour. The enemy said, 'Where is now thy God?' Ps. xlii. 10. This went to David's heart. What doth the enemy say now at this day? Where is now your God? your reformed religion? your Christ? where is your God? Well, they that are not affected with this are in an evil and in a dangerous state, let them judge of themselves what they will. God's children are sensible of such things; they are men, and not stones . flesh, and not iron. Therefore it is no wonder that they are so sensible of our times, and take them to heart as they do; forget their wounds, and mingle their passion with their afflictions, that so perplexeth their minds. Thus David was troubled, and over-troubled and grieved, and that too much, for he checks himself: 'Why art thou cast down, O my soul?' Indeed, by nature we have no bounds in our affections; if we joy, we joy too much; if we sorrow, we sorrow too much. Grace only doth qualify all our actions and affections, and where there is no grace there is either all joy or all sorrow. Nabal, when he did begin to joy, he joys over much, and when he did begin to sorrow, he exceeded in that, 1 Sam. xxv. 36, 37. A wicked man hath nothing to uphold him, and therefore he is over head and ears in all that he doth. The child of God is kept upright by that which is wrought in his heart, whereby his sorrow and joy is mixed together.

'Why art thou cast down, O my soul?' The point is this,

Obs. 1. *That it is a sin for a child of God to be too much discouraged and cast down in afflictions*, nay, I add more, *though the cause be good*, as it was here, to be banished and want means of comfort; in this case, to be too much cast down and disquieted, it argues a distempered heart.

Quest. But how shall we know when a man is cast down too much? for it is a sinful thing in a man not to be sensible of that which lies upon him.

Ans. The soul is cast down too much, to name this one for many, *when our mourning and sorrow brings us not to God, but drives us from God.* Grief, sorrow, and humility are good; but discouragement is evil. That which brings a man from delighting, from trusting in God, which hinders a man in his calling, either as he is a Christian, or in his particular calling, by this he may know he is in excess. As the children of Israel were in great trouble under Pharaoh, and heeded not therefore unto that which Moses spake unto them for anguish of spirit, Exod. vi. 9. The husband and wife must not live at odds, lest their prayers be interrupted, 1 Pet. iii. 7. No; though the cause be never so good, they must not be over much troubled; therefore, when Christians exceed in anything, they do it not as Christians, but as they are men overcome of their passions.

Quest. What is the ground why casting down and disquieting is a sin?

Ans. 1. *Because it doth turn to the reproach of religion and God himself,* as if there were not strength in the promises of God to uphold a soul in the time of trouble and disquietment.

2. *Because their so sinking under afflictions never yields any good fruit.* Yea, the devil himself, in such a case, will say, God neglecteth thee,—thus joining his temptations with thy corruptions,—then where art thou? And, therefore, I beseech you consider. What! Shall a father neglect his own children so much that they should be cast down, whenas he only* knoweth what they want, and hath in his own power to give all that is good?

3. *Because it hinders us both from and in holy duties.* For where the soul is cast down, either we do not perform holy duties at all, or otherwise they are done but weakly; for as the troubled eye cannot see well, so the troubled soul cannot do good, nor receive good. It is the quiet soul that both receiveth and doeth good as it ought to be done; for quietness is the stay of the soul, either to do or receive. Holy things are not accepted of God by the stuff of them, but by the willingness and cheerfulness in doing of them. Thus, when the soul is too much cast down, God accepts not so well of the actions, because they want life. Then it plainly appears to be a sin thus to be cast down. Therefore, holy David takes up his soul and chides himself downright: 'Why art thou cast down, O my soul? and why art thou so unquiet within me?' If this be so, that it is a sin to be too much cast down, what shall we say of those who disquiet themselves in and for a vain shadow? Ps. xxxix. 6. They trouble themselves so much about vain things that they are discouraged from doing good. The holy man doth in this case raise up his soul; for the Spirit of God saith, 'This is the way, walk in it; and this you should have done, but herein you fail, and here is your wants,' Isa. xxx. 21. Thus I thought good to enlarge this point.

Obs. 2. 'Why art thou cast down, O my soul?' The word in the original shews *it is the nature of sorrow to bring the soul downwards* (*a*). Sorrow and sin agree both in this, for as they come from below, so they bring the soul downwards to the earth. The devil, ever since he was cast down himself, labours to cast all down. His voice is, Down, down to the ground. He would have no man stay in going down in afflictions or desperation. The new creature created by the Spirit of God is clean contrary; for that is all upward. Where the hope is, there the soul loves to be in thought and meditation, and all that it doth or can do is to go upwards.

'Why art thou cast down, O my soul? and why art thou so disquieted?' Here are two words used, 'Why art thou *cast down?* why art thou so *disquieted?*'

Quest. What is meant by casting down? and why doth he find fault with himself for it?

Ans. Because it breeds disquieting. I say casting down, when it is not with humility, but discouragement, breeds disquieting; but when it is joined with humility, that raiseth the soul to see mercy, in which sort, if God doth cast us down to humble us, it is to raise us up with so much the sweeter consolation; for so much as the soul is cast down by God, so much it is raised up by God. But the soul that is cast down by Satan rests not in God, but is troubled, as Ps. xxxvii. 1, it is said, 'Fret not thyself,' &c.

* That is, 'he alone.'—G.

So a man may know when his soul murmurs, and his fretting is against God himself, or against the instrument of the sinful discouragement of his soul, being over much cast down. Here is no true humiliation, but abundance of corruption, which brings vexation and disquietments. But I hasten to that which I have further to deliver, 'Why art thou so cast down, O my soul?' He doth check himself because he was thus cast down and disquieted. Here, then, you see,

1, David's perplexity; and, 2, the particular branches thereof, casting down, and disquieting.

Quest. What was the reason why he was thus cast down?

Ans. The reason is in the words,—a reason from the contrary. He reproves his soul for being thus cast down; he doth check and command himself to wait and trust in God; he checks his soul; which shews he had no good reason why he was thus cast down. Wherefore should he ask this reason, but that there was no just cause, but sophistical reasoning, which bred this? As Jonah iv. 9, God demands, 'Dost thou well to be angry, Jonah?' As if he had said, There is no good cause. You may see, by this manner of asking, the cause was ignorance and false reasoning, false trust and want of trusting in God. There is no discouragement in any affliction or trouble whatsoever, but it is for the want of knowing the ground wherefore God doth it. First, sometimes for the exercise of our graces, as well as for our sins. Again, forgetfulness of God's dealing, as Heb. xii. 5, 'You have forgotten the consolation which speaks unto you,' &c. And sometimes we are troubled in affliction because we do not examine the cause rightly with our own souls. Many go to the highest step of the ladder, to their election, before they come to the fruits thereof, Rom. v. 1. I beseech you, let us be more wise. There be some people who do trouble themselves by seeking their comfort only in their sanctification, when it should be looked for in their justification; and some others who trouble themselves about the issue of things for time to come, when we are commanded not to care for to-morrow, Mat. vi. 34, and in the mean time neglect their duty in using lawful means, and trusting in God. Again, want of trusting in God; for when we trust not in God, then we have false trusts in the creature, or in something else. Then this follows: vanity will bring vexation of spirit.

Thus, when vanity goes before, there will come vexation after. Therefore when men do set upon doing any good, or suffering for good, by their own strength, and trust not in God for a constant supply, this moves God to take away his support, and then they fall most shamefully. Nay, when a man trusts in himself, and in his present grace, more than in God, he shall be sure to fall; for we must trust in God for time to come for fresh grace, and pray that God would renew his graces, to strengthen us in every trouble and affliction. The cause why God's children do so miscarry in times of trouble is, because they trouble themselves, and do not trust in God for a new supply of grace. We cannot perform new duties, and undergo new sufferings, with old graces. So now you have some causes why men are thus cast down and disquieted; false trust, or else not trusting in God, as if the prophet had said, 'Why art thou cast down, O my soul?' The reason is this, thou dost not trust in God as thou shouldst do; therefore it was our Saviour reproved Peter when he feared, saying, 'O thou of little faith,' Mat. xiv. 31. It was not the greatness of the waves, but the weakness of his faith, which made him faint. In truth, the cause of our trouble and disquieting is either for want of faith or want in faith, whereby we cannot rely upon God in our troubles and afflictions; for the soul being weak of itself, it hath need of something to rely upon, as a weak plant had need of a supporter. Now that which gives answerable strength is our relying upon God. When we omit this, then comes disquieting and troubles in our souls. And so I end the point of perplexity, and come to the charge that he lays upon his own soul, saying, Trust in God. His remedy is double.

1. First, A reflecting action upon his soul, 'Why art thou disquieted, O my soul?'

2. Secondly, A command laid upon his soul, 'Trust in God.'

Before I come to particulars, observe in general this point,

Doct. 3. *That God's children, in their greatest troubles, recover themselves.* For here was the trouble, and his disquietness for the trouble. He was in temptation, afflictions, and discouragements. Here was Satan tempting, and the corruptions boiling, and God withdrawing the sense of his love, leaving David for a while to himself; and yet, notwithstanding, at length he breaks through all, and expostulates the matter with himself. So God's children, when they are in troubles, though never so great, they can recover and comfort themselves. And in truth the holy Scripture shews this; for this trusting and relying on God in extremities is a difference betwixt the child of God and an hypocrite. A little cross will not try men's graces so as great ones. As in Saul, it brings him to great trouble, and then he goes to the witch, and then see what becomes of him, 1 Sam. xxviii. 7. But the child of God, in his greatest troubles, he having the Spirit of God to strengthen him, he rests upon God, as is shewed, Rom. viii. 26. In the greatest troubles, the Spirit doth help our infirmities; and in the lowest depth of trouble, there is the Spirit of comfort. Now this Spirit works faith, that enables us to send out strong prayers and cries, which cry loud in God's ear. The child of God can mourn, and cry, and chatter, striving against deadness, and against his infidelity, and strives for comfort as for life; so, when they are at the lowest, they can recover themselves. God's children, at the beginning of trouble, do labour to recover themselves presently: 'Why art thou disquieted within me?' He stops himself at the first. Jonah was to blame this way; he did feed and flatter himself, and would not stand to expostulate with his heart, Jonah iv. 9; but David doth not so here, but saith, 'Why art thou so cast down, O my soul? and why art thou so disquieted?' There is a contrary spirit in them who are not God's children; for they do feed upon mischief, wickedness, and dark conceits, according to which apprehensions they make their conclusions; but God's children, knowing their own estates, they reprove themselves, and say, 'Why art thou cast down, O my soul? why art thou so troubled?'

Doct. 4. Again, *see the excellent estate of the soul.* It is an atheistical conceit that the soul doth arise out of the temper of the body; for that cannot be, because we see the soul doth cross our nature, and cross itself; much more the body. How can this be, if it rise of the body, that it should cross itself, and the very inclinations to evil? For though the soul be ready to run to excess of melancholy and excess of joy, yet there is resistance in the soul, and striving against these things in some measure; for in every Christian there are three men.

(1.) First, The natural man, the good creature of God, having understanding, will, and affection.

(2.) There is nature under the 'spirit of bondage,' which we call 'the old man.'

(3.) There is the 'new man,' framed by the 'Spirit of God,' which doth strive against the corruption of his nature; for nature cannot but be troubled in afflictions. This we see in Adam in his innocency; yea, in Christ himself. Grace doth stay us in this state, then much more doth grace stop nature. In the excellent state of the soul, having the Spirit of God in him, whereby a man is raised up above himself, and humbles himself, this is the excellency of the spiritual nature of the soul, and especially the excellency of the Spirit in the soul. The soul can check the body, and the Spirit can check both soul and body. Well, this I speak but in a word; for I will not stand upon it, but only to shew the nature of the soul.

Quest. It may be asked, How shall we know in these things, when anything comes from the Spirit, and not from the natural soul? for here is nature, flesh, and the Spirit.

Ans. I answer, when there is [the] Spirit in a man, that doth cross the natural constitution of the body, and checks the constitution of his soul being in affliction and discouraged in it, that thereby a man recovers himself again.

Afflictions of the soul are the greatest and worst of all, yet in this estate his soul doth carry him upward; and therefore there must be something in him that is better and above nature, which enables him to check and reprove himself. Now, this must needs be an excellent thing. Why? Because this is the Spirit of God, which enables us to strive, as Job did: 'Though thou kill me, yet will I trust in thee,' Job xiii. 15. And our blessed Saviour in his depths of afflictions cries, 'My God, my God, why hast thou forsaken me?' Mat. xxvii. 46. The sense of his present state caused him to cry out as if God had forsaken him; yet herein the blessed Spirit doth raise him up, for he cries, 'My God.' Thus we see when there is a crossing of ourselves in that state which we are in, this is a sign that it comes from the Spirit of God, and not from nature: 'Why art thou so cast down, why art thou so disquieted within me, O my soul?'

Another thing that I observe is this,

Doct. 5. *That the prerogative of a Christian in these disquietings, and in all estates, is, he hath God and himself to speak unto, whereby he can remove solitariness.* Put him into a dungeon, yet he may speak unto God there, and speak unto himself.

This is an excellent state. He who hath laid up store of grace beforehand, he can reprove and cross himself, and in his depths cry out unto God. Therefore take a Christian in the worst estate of all others, yet he can improve his estate to the best before God, whereby, even then, he hath an happy communion with God. This is a comfort to a Christian, when he hath nothing to comfort himself withal; as David here had neither goods, nor comforts, nor prophets, nor the tabernacle with him, yet he had his good God to go unto, who was the only thing he had; and when he speaks comfortably unto him, then David speaks as comfortably unto his soul: 'Why art thou cast down, O my soul?'

Let all the tyrants in the world do their worst to a Christian, if God be with him, he is cheerful still. This is plentifully seen in David. He was vexed outwardly, punished, persecuted, and banished from God's house, yet he goes unto God; and though he were vexed in his soul in particular, yet he cries out, 'Why art thou so vexed within me, why art thou so unquiet?'

The point from hence is this,

Doct. 6. *The best way to establish the soul is to deal with our own souls, and to begin with them first, and proceed in a judicial manner*, as this holy prophet of the Lord did. When we are in any troubles and afflictions, do not go to the trouble, but go to the soul; for if the soul be not set in right frame, and quieted, we cannot endure anything. But if we can set and frame ourselves to God, all the tyrants in the world, and all the devils in hell, cannot hurt us. The devil comes to our Saviour, but he could do him no harm, because there was nothing within him for him to fasten upon, John xiv. 30. Therefore this is the way, if we be in trouble, let all other things go, and lay the foundation of our quiet in God, and deal with our own souls. And the way to do this is to cite our souls before ourselves, hereby to make ourselves offenders and judges, teachers and scholars, as the prophet doth here: 'Why art thou so unquiet, O my soul?' God hath erected a court in a man, that he may cite and condemn himself. God hath set up this court, and given us this liberty, to prevent another examination, and condemnation for ever in the world to come. Therefore, 1 Cor. xi. 31, it is said, 'If we will judge ourselves, we shall not be judged of the Lord.' The way to do this is to call our own souls to a reckoning. This is to be strongly endeavoured for many reasons, that I will not stand upon, but only name some one of them.

As, namely, *because it is an hard thing*. For there is an affection of nature, and an affection of rebellion, and strong motions, that keep the soul in such a thraldom that it cannot fully know itself; and for a man to know all things, and not to know himself, what a miserable thing is it! What! to look altogether abroad, and never to look at home, that is a misery of all miseries. Well, if ever we would be saved, we must do this. If we would begin with ourselves, we might put the devil and our tormenting conscience out of office; for the time will come when it will be objected, This and that have been our sins, and this is the state of your souls, will Satan say. Well, says the soul thus prepared, 'I know all this, I have accused myself before God for this, and I have made my peace with God.' But when we go on in sin, and leave all to God, then comes the devil and accuseth us, and our consciences take God's part; thus we go down to hell for ever. Therefore take warning of this betimes, and call thy soul to a reckoning. But I will not spend too much time to enforce this holy action. The way to bring our souls to this is, to furnish them with holy thoughts, to sanctify and season our judgments with holy touches, to know what is good, and to bring our souls to love and delight in it. But if we have not a judicature in us, we can never do this, for we must not go blindly about this work, but know what evil we have committed, and which is done against this law, and which against that commandment. Thus a Christian must and will examine himself. But an ignorant person goes and never lays up anything in his soul; and therefore though he hath power in his soul to do this, yet he doth it not, because he is an ignorant and blind man.

Use. Well, *let this serve to stir us up to be careful in this holy duty.*

Obj. But the hypocrite will say, Tush, this is hid, and the world sees it not; for me to take pains to work upon my soul, the world cannot see it; what profit comes by this course? But the child of God is most busy and carefully employed about that which carries with itself least applause with the world. This is always a sure sign of a good heart; for the best work of the new creature is within us, that the world cannot see. And therefore if ye will have sound assurance of salvation, then call often in question the state of your own souls, and labour to get this disposition, and inquire of your souls what is the reason. Do you well to be angry? What! thus angry? At this time, and upon this occasion? And, what! do you well to be merry thus now? If we could do this, what an excellent state of soul should we live in! It would clear religion of many scandals. For from whence comes all these scandalous actions we fall into, but because we do not check ourselves in evil things before they break out into our lives? The soul many times doth rise in rebellious motions, and troubles the Spirit of God in us; but what an honour is it to a Christion to be free from scandal in this life, and to suppress evil in the beginning! There is nothing that is evil but it is first in thought, then in affection, and then in action; therefore if we could think when we are tempted to any evil, this thing will be a scandal, it will be open in the mouths of wicked men, it will grieve the true-hearted servants of God, oh how glorious might the servants of God shine in these woeful, dark, and sinful days! Well, I beseech you, do but consider, and bring the practice and carriage of most men and women to this rule that I have laid down, and what a pitiful estate shall we find the most to be in, who would seem to be religious, whose lives declare this before men.

Do but ask a covetous man why he is so extremely carried away with the things of this world; he answers by and by, Oh, he hath a great charge, and the times are hard; and in the mean time he neglects wholly the making sure of his own salvation. Nay, come to God's children themselves, who do too much hunt after the things of this world, I say to them, and sometimes ye shall hear the same answer, But what, have not ye a Father to provide for you? and this your Father, hath he not all things at his own disposing—having promised, you shall want nothing that is good—even he who is an infinite, loving, and merciful Father? I beseech you, consider what can we want, if we have faith to rely upon God? And then consider how vile a thing covetousness is; what for an old man now to be worldly, when one foot is in the grave! So for a blasphemer to provoke the majesty of God, there is no reason to be given for it. For sin is an unreasonable thing, and it cannot endure this question, What reason is there for this and that? Therefore the Scripture calls all wicked and ungodly men unreasonable men and fools, because they cannot give a good reason for anything they do. And therefore when they are in hell they may well say, We fools thought this and said thus. I beseech you, consider what reason is there that a man should sell God's favour, and the assurance of his salvation, for a wicked action, and for his lust, and for a little honour; I say, consider what you shall get, and what you shall lose, even the hope of heaven, for the attaining at the best but of perishing things, and many times miss of them also.

These things considered, the Spirit of God doth well to call us to question with ourselves, to give a reason for that we do, and then to censure ourselves, as David in another place did: 'How foolish was I, like a beast,' Ps. lxxiii. 22.* And so, I beseech you, when you are tempted to any sin, then say, What a base thought is this! what base thing is this! is this according to my profession and religion? If we would but thus examine and question ourselves, accuse and condemn ourselves, oh how happy and blessed creatures might we be! And thus much for the first remedy.

* It is Asaph, not David, who says so.—G. See, however, the first sentence of the next sermon.—Ed.

Now come we to the second: 'Trust in God, wait on God.' Here is, 1, An action; 2, a fit object.

The action, trust; the object, God: 'wait on God,' for God is the only prop and rock whereon we may rest safe in time of danger. Waiting on God implies his meeting our souls, before we can have any comfort from him. Therefore all our care should be to bring God and our souls together. This trusting in God, and waiting for God, is an especial means to uphold us in our greatest troubles. This is the state of the new covenant; for we have fallen in Adam by our infidelity, and must now have faith to recover ourselves, which is the applying grace that doth help us up, and enable us to wait on God and his truth, for they are all one. As a man of credit and his word are all one, so is our trusting in God and his trust* and promises. But because I have spoken of this trusting in God out of another place of Scripture,† I will be brief in it; only I will now add something to help us on in this point, wherein our souls shall find so much comfort.

Doct. 7. 'Trust in God.' *This trusting in God is the way to quiet our souls, and to stay the same in every estate.* The reason is, because God hath sanctified this holy grace to this end. This is the grace of the new covenant, the grace of all graces, which stays the soul in all disquietings whatsoever.

The first thing that disquiets the soul is sin. Now God by his Spirit and word doth give us the pardon thereof. Therefore trust in God for this, and for life everlasting, and then trust in God in this life for whatsoever thou dost want. Know that the same love of God that brings thee to everlasting life will give thee daily bread. Therefore trust in God for provision, for protection, and for whatsoever thou dost want. For the first thing that a troubled soul doth look unto is for mercy, salvation, and comfort; and therefore in every troubled estate we have one thing or other still from God to comfort us. I say, if we be in trouble, there is answerable comfort given us of God. Are we sick? He is our health. Are we weak? He is our strength. Are we dead? He is our life. So that it is not possible that we should be in any state, though never so miserable, but there is something in God to comfort us. Therefore is God called in Scripture a rock, a castle, a shield. A rock to build upon, a castle wherein we may be safe, a shield to defend us in all times of danger, shewing that if such helps sometimes succour us, how much more can God. I beseech you, consider God is our 'exceeding great reward,' Gen. xv. 1. God is bread to strengthen us, and a Spirit of all comfort; and indeed there is but a beam in the creature, the strength is in God. And if all these were taken away, yet God is able to do much more, and to raise up the soul. What! can a castle or a shield keep a man safe in the time of danger? how much more can God! I beseech you, consider how safe was Noah when the ark was afloat, Gen. vii. 16. And why? Because God shut the door upon him and kept him there. Thus you see there is something in God for every malady, and something in the world for every trouble; then 'trust in God.' This is the way to quiet our souls. For as heavy bodies do rest when they come to the centre of the earth, so the soul, for joy, and for care, for trust, doth find rest in God when it comes to him and makes him her stay. The needle rests when it comes to the North Pole, and the ark rested when it came to the mount Ararat, Gen. viii. 4, so the soul rests safe when it comes to God, and till that time, it moves as the ark upon

* Qu. 'truth?'—Ed.

† See General Index under 'Trust,' and 'Soul's Conflict.'—G.

the waters. Therefore our blessed Saviour saith in Matthew, 'Come unto me, all ye that are weary and heavy laden, and you shall find rest in your souls,' Mat. xi. 28. This holy man would have rest, therefore he saith, 'O my soul, wait upon God.'

Quest. Well, in a word, how shall we know if we have this rest and trust in God or no?

Ans. By this which I have said; for if we trust in God, then we will be quiet, for faith hath a quieting power. Therefore, if thou canst stay thyself, and rest upon God for provision, for protection, for all that helps thee from grace to glory, thou art safe. Again, faith hath a comforting power. There is a distinction between alchymy gold and true gold; for that which is true will comfort the heart, but counterfeit faith, like alchymy gold, will not strengthen the heart. Therefore, if thou dost find thy faith strengthen thee, to cast thyself upon God and his mercy in Jesus Christ, then there is true faith. The garment of Christ, when it was but touched, there was virtue went out of it, so that the woman found strength therein to quench her bloody issue, Mat. ix. 21, xiv. 36; and dost not thou find strength from God to quench the bloody issue of sin in thy soul? Then hast thou cause to doubt of the truth of thy faith; for precious faith brings virtue from the root. As the tree doth draw strength from the earth to feed the body and the boughs, whereby it is fruitful, so faith brings virtue from Christ and his promises, which strengthens the soul.

I beseech you consider, if you have your soul strengthened by the promises of God, and the nature of God, it is a sign you have true faith. What a shame is it for Christians, when they have an infinite God for their God, who hath made abundant promises, and have a rich Saviour, and yet they live so unquiet and discontented, and sometimes for earthly trash, as if there were no Father for them in heaven, nor providence upon earth! Now, at this time, which are times of trouble abroad, wherein our faith should be exercised, how are the hearts of many cast down, as though God had cast away his care over his church! Consider, I pray you, doth an husband cast away his care over his wife in time of danger when she is wronged? No; but is the more inflamed to be revenged: much more will God arise to maintain his own cause, but we must wait the time, knowing 'they that believe make not haste,' as it is Isa. xxviii. 16.

Quest. But what is the matter for which we are to trust God? 'I shall yet praise him.'

Ans. His meaning is, though he be for the present in great afflictions, yet he shall be delivered. See the language of Canaan. The holy people of God, if they receive any deliverance, they give God the praise and glory, for this is all that God looks for; if thou art in any affliction, and God doth deliver thee, then to give him all the glory and the praise. So this holy man saith to his soul, 'God will deliver thee;' then saith the soul, 'I will praise him;' so he gives the delivered soul both matter and affection to praise his name. I beseech you, consider here when the soul hath nothing in itself to trust in, how it doth sustain itself by looking towards God. Christ himself, when he was in his extremities, looks upward to his Father in heaven, Mat. xxvi. 39, so this holy man comforts himself he shall be delivered. Thus he lays sound grounds in God, for there is no loose sands there. Therefore the ship of his soul rides safe. He trusts God for the present and for the time to come; as though he should say, Though I am now in great affliction, yet it shall be better with me, howsoever it be now.

Use. Let us raise this comfort to ourselves, *trust in God.* What if we should live here all the days of our life in this troubled estate that we are now in! 'Yet wait upon God, O my soul, for I shall yet praise him.' We live here in many troubles and afflictions, and we sit down by the rivers of Babel. Well! what if we die in this affliction? Yet I shall have glory with Christ. Thus, I beseech you, extend this comfort to the whole church of God; put the case the church be in trouble, what hath the church to do? 'To wait on God;' because it shall have delivery, and all the true church shall praise God upon their delivery. God will deliver his church, and in the mean time preserve and provide for it. It is as dear unto him as the apple of his eye, it is his jewel, his vine which himself hath planted; and therefore let us comfort ourselves with this. What though we are now cast down and in heaviness for the church of God abroad; yet God will redeem Israel from all his iniquities, much more out of all his troubles and afflictions, Ps. cxxx. 8. The church must be delivered, and Babel must fall. Nay, the Holy Ghost saith it is fallen, Rev. xviii. 2, to shew the certainty of it, for God will do it. The Red Sea and Jordan must return, and the church must sing praises for her delivery; and thus we do daily and continually wait upon God for the performance hereof.

Quest. What ground hath this holy man for this waiting?

Ans. He is my present help and my God, he is my salvation and my God. The word is 'salvations:' he hath more salvations than one (*b*). Therefore though we be troubled with poverty, shame, or any other affliction, yet God is salvations and helps. Consider this, if you are in trouble of conscience for sin, or Satan condemns you, then say that 'God is salvation;' if you are in trouble, God is deliverance; if you are persecuted by any wicked malicious enemies, God is a castle: as Ps. xviii. 2, 'The Lord is my rock, and my fortress, and my deliverer; my God, and my strength, in whom I will trust; my buckler, and the horn of my salvation, and my high tower.' 'Who is a rock, save our God? I will call upon the name of the Lord, so shall I be delivered from all mine enemies.' Thus you see how David after all his victories describes God to be his God, and his salvation both for body and soul, for the present and for the time to come, with means, without means, and against all means. What a comfort is this! He can command salvation, he can command the creature to save, and the devil himself to be a means to save us; and if there be no means for thee to see, yet he can create means to do it in an instant. Thus God is our help; and what a ground of comfort is this! Therefore I beseech you be not discouraged. Mourn we may like doves, but not roar like beasts in our afflictions; when we have humbled ourselves enough, then must we raise up our souls from our grief to another object. For a Christian must look to divers objects: look to the trouble with one eye, and to God with the other, and know him to be his salvation. Then, let the trouble be what it will be, if God be thy deliverer; it is no matter what the disease be, if God be thy physician. But many times we do betray ourselves into the hands of the devil for want of thinking of these things. 'He is my God.' There is another ground of his comfort. Give me leave a little to unfold this sweet point. Consider therein with me two things.

1. God is the God of his children. 2. He is so constantly.

This is the ground of all comforts, God is my God, and God is our God. First, because he doth choose us, and call us in his due time, and then makes a covenant with us to be our God, and then he knows us, loves us, and preserves us, and so he is our God; because they whom God doth choose, he knows them for his own, and stirs up answerable affections, that we may take God, and know God to be ours. For there must be an action on God's part in taking and choosing us, and an action of soul in us to choose God again. If God say to our souls, I will be thy God, then our souls should answer God, 'Thou art the strength of my salvation.' First, God doth love us, then know us, and then we reflect God's love upon God. Again, he knows us, and we know him again; he delights in us, and we delight in him. The Scriptures are full of speeches in this kind. There is a reciprocal natural passage between God and the soul; for in covenant there must be consent on both sides, and then we make him our God when we choose him before all creatures both in heaven and in earth. Then we have familiarity with him, love him, and trust in him in all our necessities.

Thus we see how God is said to be our God. First, God is ours by election, adoption, by sanctification and redemption. God is our God, by dwelling with us; and this propriety, '*My* God,' is the first of all; for when God saith, 'Thou art mine,' the soul saith, Thou art mine, and shalt be mine. This is an everlasting covenant of salvation: God doth endure world without end. Our salvation is according to the nature of God, from everlasting to everlasting, from election to glory. Thus God is the God of Abraham from everlasting to everlasting; he is the God of Abraham's body, now his soul is in heaven, and his body is in the dust, Mat. xxii. 32. Abraham hath a being in his love. And so we have an everlasting propriety therein, God takes us for ever, marries us for ever, Hos. ii. 19. Therefore we must trust in God, and wait upon God, for he is our God and our salvation.

Use 1. I beseech you, give me a little leave to press this; for certainly there is more comfort in this word '*My* God,' than in all the words of the world; for what is God to me if he be not my God, and so make me his? For this same propriety of comfort is more than all the comforts in the world. We account a little patch of ground, or corner of an house of our own, more than all the city and town where we live. This comforts a man, when he can say, This is mine. As a man that hath a wife, it may be, she is not of the best, or the richest, or the fairest, yet she comforts him more, and he takes more content in her, than in all the women in the world, because she is his wife; so if a man can say, 'O *my* God,' he needs not say any more, for it is more than if he could say, All the world is mine. If we have God we have all, and if we had a thousand worlds, all were nothing to this, if we cannot say 'God is my God.' Therefore, though the child of God may seem to be a poor man, yet he is the only rich man. Other men have the riches of this world, as a kind of usurpers, for they have not the highest right unto them. Worldly men are like unto bankrupts, who are taken to be rich men because they have a great deal of goods in their possession, but the true right belongs to others, and so they prove in the end to be worth nothing. I beseech you, consider what God's servants have said heretofore: 'God is my portion,' Lam. iii. 24. If God be our God, then he will supply all our wants, as it shall make for the best unto us. This is a great comfort to all Christians in what estate soever. God in dividing things, it may be, he hath given others honours, beauty, and riches, and parts of nature. Well! God falleth to thy lot. Let the worldlings, the lascivious and ambitious persons, make themselves merry with their portions in this life, yet let the Christian, in what estate soever, glory in his portion, for God is his, and all things else. Though there be many changes in thyself, why shouldst thou be discouraged or disquieted in any state whatsoever? God is thine to do thee good.

Use 2. Again, *Here is a ground of comfort against all losses whatsoever.* The world, and worldly men, may strip us of these earthly things, vex our bodies, and restrain our liberties, and take away outward things from us; but this is our comfort, they cannot take our God from us, for this is an everlasting portion, my God, my help, my all-sufficiency. In truth, friends, means, and life itself may be taken away, yet God will never fail nor forsake us. We are here to-day, and gone to-morrow, and life is the longest thing we have, for we may out-live our riches and honours. But what then? Ps. xc. 1, 2, it is said, 'Thou art an everlasting habitation, from everlasting to everlasting,' and we dwell in the fear of God. We had a being in thy love, O Lord, before ever we were born, and when we are dead, we are in thy love still. What a comfort is this to cause us to rest in our God, and that for ever! But as for the wicked, it is not so with them; their voice is, The 'Philistines are upon me, and God hath forsaken me,' 1 Sam. xxviii. 15. This is a fearful speech, and is, or shall be, the voice of every wicked man ere long. Now they ruffle it out,* and none so free from care and trouble as they; but where is their comfort when their consciences shall be awakened? Then their voice will be, Death and hell and all are upon me, and God hath forsaken me; what shall become of me and mine? But as for the children of God, let what will come upon them, yet God can command salvation, and he commands comfort to attend his people, for God is my God. I beseech you to enlarge these things in your own meditations, and do not disquiet yourselves, but believe in God for these things, and for your own happiness in heaven, and cast yourselves upon Christ for the pardon of sins in the first place; and then, 'trust in God,' and nothing in all the world that comes between you and heaven but God will remove it, and bring you safe thither; but, in this case, many doubts arise: 1. For perseverance.

Obj. I may fall away for time to come.

Ans. I answer, That God, that hath begun this good work in me, will finish it in his due time, Philip. i. 6.

Obj. Ay, but I am changeable.

Ans. It is true, but God is unchangeable; thou mayest be off and on, but God is not so, for the ground of his love is always alike. Therefore fear nothing for the present nor for the time to come.

Obj. Oh but I have a great charge, and these are hard and evil times.

Ans. God is thy God, and the God of thy seed, therefore labour to make this sure, that God is thy God, and in thus doing, thou providest for thyself and thy posterity; and when thou art dead and gone, then the living Father will be a God to thy posterity and children. Therefore I beseech you trust in God, wait upon him, and fear not the want of necessaries in this life. What foolish children are we, that think God will give us heaven when this life is gone, and yet we fear he will not give us such things as shall maintain this life, while we are here employed in his service! 'The heathen seek after all these things,' saith our Saviour, Mat. vi. 32; but 'it is your Father's pleasure to give you a kingdom,' Luke xii. 32.

Exhortation. Well, therefore, for provision and protection both in life and death, trust in God for all, and all shall be well with us; then wait upon God. I beseech you make one thing sure, that is, make God to be our God, by trusting in him, and walking worthy of him. And this one

* That is, are at 'the *height* of prosperity.' Cf. *Glossary, sub voce.*—G.

care will free you of all other cares. This one study is better than all other studies; for if we can make God our God, then we make all other things ours also. This requires more than ordinary of a Christian, to walk worthy of the Lord: 'Two cannot walk together if they be not agreed,' saith Solomon,* therefore this requires great mortification of soul, and much holiness, to walk with God. This world knows not what this is, to walk with God in the ways of heaven, where there is nothing but holiness. Therefore we must exercise our communion with God, by praying to him, and by hearing of him, and thinking upon his word and presence, and abstaining from all filthiness of the flesh and spirit. We have an holy God, therefore we must labour for a good measure of holiness, if we will maintain communion with God. This should enforce us thus to stand for God and his truth, because he is our God. It is strange to see how men do not walk this way. They will part with anything, or do anything for their lust, but yet they will not endure to part with anything for God, and for the comfort of their souls. Well! Christ stood for us unto the death, and gained us life, when it could not be had otherwise; and are we too good to stand for a good cause; nay, to die for the maintenance of God's cause? What! shall not we stand for God? Yes; for he is an 'hiding-place' to us; and if death come to us for this cause, he is life to us, and we have a being for ever in his love.

* It is Amos (iii. 3), not Solomon, who says this.—G.

NOTES.

(*a*) P. 53. 'The word in the original shews it is the nature of sorrow,' &c. More exactly the rendering is, 'Why wilt thou cast down,' &c., = dejection, self-rebuked.

(*b*) P. 61. 'Salvation.' See Note *j*, Vol. I. p. 294. G.

THE SAINT'S HAPPINESS.

THE SAINT'S HAPPINESS.

NOTE.

'The Saint's Happiness' forms one of the four 'Sermons' appended to 'The Saint's Comforts,' concerning which see Note, Vol. VI. page 160. Its title-page is given below.* Each of the four Sermons has separate pagination, but they do not appear to have been issued separately. G.

* THE
SAINTS
HAPPINESSE:

Shewing mans Happi-
nesse is in Communion
with God.

With the meanes, and trialls
of our Communion with God,
being the substance of
divers Sermons.

By that Faithfull and Reverend Divine, R. SIBBES, D.D.
and sometime Preacher to the Honorable Societie of
Grayes-Inne.

Printed at *London*, by *Tho. Cotes*, and are
to be sold by *Peter Cole.* 1637.

THE SAINT'S HAPPINESS.

But it is good for me to draw near to God.—Ps. LXXIII. 28.

THIS psalm is a psalm of Asaph, or of David, commended to Asaph, who was a seer and a singer. It represents one in a conflict afterward recovered, and in a triumphant conclusion. It begins abruptly, as if he had gained this truth: Say flesh and Satan what they can, yet this I am resolved of, I find God is yet good to Israel. Then he discovers what was the cause of this conflict. It was his weakness and doubt of God's promises in ver. 13, occasioned from the great prosperity that the wicked enjoyed, described from the 2d verse to the 13th. Then he sets down his recovery in the 17th verse. He went into the sanctuary, and saw what God meant to do with them at last. Then follows the accomplishment of the victory in the 23d verse. I am continually with thee. Thou hast holden me up. Thou wilt guide me now and bring me to glory. Therefore there is none in heaven but thee. Though nature may be surprised, yet God is my help; and for the wicked, they shall perish; nay, thou hast destroyed them. Therefore 'it is good for me to draw nigh to God.'

Now from that which hath been laid open we may observe,

Doct. First, *That God's dearest children are exercised with sharp conflicts in the faith of principles, yea, of God's providence.* This should comfort such as God suffers to cast forth mire and dirt of incredulity. It is the common case of God's dearest children, yea, of the prophets of God, David, Jeremiah, and Habakkuk, and therefore we ought not to be dejected too much; and the rather because,—which also we may note in the second place,—

Doct. [Second,] *God's children, though they be thus low, yet they shall recover*, and after recovery comes a triumph. They may begin to slip a little, but still God's hand is under them, and his goodness ever lower than they can fall; and this should teach us to discern of our estates aright, and to expect such conflicts, yet to know that still God's Spirit will not be wanting to check and repress such thoughts in the fittest time. Contrarily it is a principle to wicked men to doubt of God's providence, and therefore they suffer such temptations to rule in them.

In the next place observe,

Doct. [Third,] *The way for a Christian to recover his ground in time of temptation, is for him to enter into God's sanctuary*, and not to give liberty to his thoughts to range in, considering the present estate that he is in; but look to former experiences, in himself, in others; see the promises and apply them; it shall go well with the righteous, but woe to the wicked, it shall not go well with them. This is to go into the sanctuary; and happy man thou art, and in high favour, whom God admitteth so near to him. The world will tell thee of corn, and wine, and oil, and how great and glorious men are here; but the sanctuary will shew thee they are set in slippery places. Carnal reason will tell thee God hath left the earth; he sees not, he governs not, all are out of order. But the sanctuary will shew thee all things are beautiful in their time, Eccles. iii. 11. Mark the end of the righteous, Ps. xxxiii. 37. See Joseph, once a prisoner, after lord of Egypt; Lazarus, once contemned and despised, after in Abraham's bosom; Christ himself, once a rebuke and scorn of all on the cross, but now triumphing on 'the right hand of God, far above all principalities and power,' Eph. i. 21. All God's ways are mercy and truth, though we seem never so much forsaken for the present. Again, from David's observing the state of wicked men,—it is said, he saw the prosperity of wicked men,—we may gather,

Doct. [Fourth,] *Whether it be the eye of faith or the eye of sense, all serveth to bring us nearer to God.* God represents to the outward view of his children the example of his justice on others, to draw his children nearer home; and it is one main reason why God suffers variety of conditions in men, that his children may gain experience from seeing their behaviour and by conversing with them.

Last of all, from the connection of this text with the former words, observe,

Doct. [Fifth,] *That the course of the children of God is a course contrary to the stream of the world.* 'They withdraw away from thee, and shall perish,' saith the prophet, but 'it is good for me to draw near;' as if he had said, Let others take what course they will, it matters not much, I will look to myself, 'it is good for me to draw near to God;' and the reason is,

Reason 1. *Because they are guided by the Spirit of God*, which is contrary to the world, and the Spirit teacheth them to see, not after the opinions of the world that is their best friend, but God is my best friend, that will never forsake me. 'Many walk that are enemies to the cross of Christ, but our conversation is in heaven,' Philip. iii. 18. And then a Christian hath experience of the ways of God, and by it he is every day settled in them; by it he sees what the world works in others, and how God is opposite to them, and thereby he is made more zealous; as in winter time the body is more hot within than in summer. And those that are well grounded grow more strong by opposition; and however they may sometimes stagger, yet their motion is constant.

Use. If we will know our estates, *examine after what rule we lead our life, and what principles we follow.* If outward weights of the love of the world, self-love, or the like do move us, as clocks that go no longer than the weights hang on them, this shews that we are but actors of the life of a Christian, and that we are not naturally moved, that our nature is not changed, and that we are not made 'partakers of the divine nature,' 2 Peter i. 4; for then our motion would come from above: 'My life and flesh may fail, but thou, Lord, wilt never fail,' Ps. xl. 12. Therefore it is good for me to draw near to thee; which words proceeding from an experimental trial of David, of the goodness and happiness of this nearness to God, afford us this consideration,

Doct. [Sixth,] *That God's Spirit enableth his children by experience to justify wisdom.* He suffers his children to meet with oppositions, that they may see they stand by an almighty power above their own, and above the power of their enemies. *Nihil tam certum est, quam quod post dubium certum est*, and therefore those that have felt the bitterness of their sins know how bitter it is; and those that have been overcome in temptations know their nature is weak, and those that have felt the unconstancy of the world, and the vanity of it, know it is a bitter thing to be far from God, and therefore they resolve, Hosea ii. 7, 'I will go to my first husband; for then it was better with me than now;' and as the prodigal, 'There is meat enough in my father's house, why then do I perish here with hunger'? Luke xv. 17; and therefore, if we will ever think to stand out resolutely in our courses against trials, we must labour for experience, and diligently observe God's dealings. It is experience that breedeth patience and hope. Experience of a truth seals a truth with a *probatum est*. And without it, the best and strongest judgments will in time of trial be ready to be jostled out of the maintenance thereof, and great professors will be ashamed of their good courses.

But to come to the particulars. 'It is good;' that is, it puts in us a blessed quality and disposition. It makes a man to be like God himself; and, secondly, 'it is good,' that is, it is comfortable; for it is the happiness of the creature to be near the Creator; it is beneficial and helpful.

'To draw near.' How can a man but be near to God, seeing he filleth heaven and earth: 'Whither shall I go from thy presence?' Ps. cxxxix. 7. He is present always in power and providence in all places, but graciously present with some by his Spirit, supporting, comforting, strengthening the heart of a good man. As the soul is said to be *tota in toto*, in several parts by several faculties, so God, present he is to all, but in a diverse manner. Now we are said to be near to God in divers degrees: *first*, when our *understanding is enlightened; intellectus est veritatis sponsa;* and so the young man speaking discreetly in things concerning God, is said not to be far from the kingdom of God, Mark xii. 34. *Secondly, in minding;* when God is present to our minds, so as the soul is said to be present to that which it mindeth; contrarily it is said of the wicked, that 'God is not in all their thoughts,' Ps. x. 4. *Thirdly*, when the *will upon the discovery of the understanding comes to choose the better part, and is drawn from that choice to cleave to him*, as it was said of Jonathan's heart, 'it was knit to David,' 1 Sam. xviii. 1. *Fourthly*, when *our whole affections are carried to God*, loving him as the chief good. Love is the first-born affection. That breeds desire of communion with God. Thence comes joy in him, so as the soul pants after God, 'as the hart after the water springs,' Ps. xlii. 1. *Fifthly*, and especially, *when the soul is touched with the Spirit of God working faith*, stirring up dependence, confidence, and trust on God. Hence ariseth sweet communion. The soul is never at rest till it rests on him. Then it is afraid to break with him or to displease him. But it groweth zealous and resolute, and hot in love, stiff in good cases; resolute against his enemies. And yet this is not all, for God will have also the outward man, so as the whole man must present itself before God in word, in sacraments; speak of him and to him with reverence, and yet with strength of affection mounting up in prayer, as in a fiery chariot; hear him speak to us; consulting with his oracles; fetching comforts against distresses, directions against maladies. *Sixthly*, and especially, we draw near to him *when we praise him;* for this is the work of the souls departed, and of the angels in heaven, that are continually near unto him. And thus much for the opening of the words. The prophet here saith, 'It is good for me.' How came he to know this? Why, he had found it by experience, and by it he was thoroughly convinced of it; so

Doct. [Seventh,] *Spiritual conviction is the ground of practice;* for naturally the will followeth the guidance of the understanding; and when it is convicted* of the goodness of this or that thing, the will moveth toward it. Now there are four things that go to conviction: first, the understanding must be enlightened to see the truth of the thing, that there is such a thing, and that it is no fancy; secondly, we must know it to be good, as the gospel is called the good word of God; thirdly, that it is good for me; and lastly, upon comparing all these together, it is the best for me of all, though other things seem to be good in their kind. A wicked man may be convinced that heaven and grace are good things; but his corrupted affections persuade him it is better to live in pleasure and lust; and when death comes then he may repent, for God is merciful. But a good man preferreth drawing near to God above all, and therefore we should labour for this conviction of our spirits. For it is not enough to hear, read, discourse, pray, but we must get the Spirit to set to his seal to all upon our hearts; and this made Moses in sober balancing of things, choose rather to draw near to God and join with his afflicted brethren, than to be in honour in Pharaoh's court, to be the son of Pharaoh's daughter, or to enjoy the pleasures of sin, 'for he had respect to the reward,' Heb. xi. 25. He was convinced that there was more to be gotten with them than amongst the Egyptians. Thus Abraham came to forsake his country, and the disciples to forsake all and follow Christ. And undoubtedly the ground of all profaneness is from atheism that is within. Would the swearer trample upon the name of God, if he did believe and were convinced that he should not be guiltless? Would the filthy person come near strange flesh, if he were persuaded that God would judge? Would any wicked man change an eternal joy for a minute's pleasure, if he did believe the unrighteous should not inherit the kingdom of God? Nay, the best have a remainder of this corruption of atheism. David: 'So foolish was I, and a beast,' Ps. lxxiii. 22. From hence come all sin against knowledge and conscience in men, whereof David complains: 'Keep me, that presumptuous sins prevail not over me, or get not dominion over me,' Ps. xix. 13. And for remedy against this vile corruption, there is no way but the immediate help of the Holy Spirit; and therefore, John xvi. 9, it is said that the Spirit, when it comes, 'shall convince the world of sin;' that is, it shall so manifest sin to be in the whole world, because of the general unbelief, as they shall see no remedy but in Christ; and therefore we should beforehand search out the crafty allurements to sin, that we may be provided to give them an answer when they set upon us, lest we be suddenly overcome, and labour to see the excellency of the things that are freely given us of God, which amongst other titles are called a feast, 'a feast of fat things,' Isa. xxv. 6. Now if we will not feast with him, how do we ever think to suffer with him if he should call us thereto? 'It is good.' How is it good? Both in quality and condition; for while we are here in this world we are strangers, and in an estate of imperfection as it were. Paul saith, while he was present in the body he was absent from the Lord; and the more near perfection we are, the more near must we be to the ground of all perfection, and

* That is, 'convinced.'—G.

this is only in God. For, first, *he is goodness itself*. He hath the beauty of all, the strength of all, the goodness of all, originally in himself. He is the gathering together of all excellency and goodness. Secondly, he is *the universal good*. He is good to all. What all hath that is good, cometh from him. Of creatures, some have beauty, others riches, others have honours, but God hath all together. Thirdly, he is *the all-sufficient and satisfactory good*. The goodness of no creature can give full content; for the soul of man is capable of more than all created goodness together can satisfy. Only it is filled with God's likeness, and satisfied with communion with him. The best thing here to satisfy the soul, as Solomon witnesseth, is knowledge; and yet it contents not the heart of man: *sine Deo omnis copia est egestas*, [saith] Bernard.* God alone filleth every corner of the soul in him. We are swallowed up with 'joy unspeakable,' and 'peace that passeth understanding.' 'Eye cannot see it, ear cannot hear it, heart of man cannot conceive those things which even in this life are but beams of his brightness,' 1 Cor. ii. 9. Fourthly, God is a goodness *that is proportionable and fitting to our souls*, which is the best part in a man; and that which we draw near unto must communicate some loveliness, for that moves us to draw near to it. Now God is a Spirit fit to converse with our spirits; and he is love, and can answer the love and drawing near of our spirits with love and drawing near to us again. The things of this world cannot love us so as to give us content, or to help us in the day of wrath. Fifthly, *nothing can make us happy but drawing near to God*. If there were nothing in the world better than man, then man would be content with himself; but by nature it is evident man seeth a better happiness than is in himself, and therefore he seeketh for it out of himself. And as Solomon tried all things, and found no happiness but in the fear of God, so man cannot rest in any outward content till he comes to God as the Creator of all happiness, and the spring-head from whence the soul had its original; and therefore, 1 John i. 3, 'All the gospel is to this end, that we may have fellowship with the Father, and his Son Jesus Christ;' and 1 Pet. iii. 18, 'Christ's sufferings [were] to this end, that being dead in flesh, but quickened in the spirit, he might bring us again to God,' Eph. i. 10, and 22, 'That he might gather all into one head.' By sin we were scattered from God, from angels, and from our ourselves; but now by Christ we are made one, with one another, and with the holy angels, one with God our chief good.

For use hereof, it *should teach us to labour to attain to this estate of being spiritually convinced of the goodness of God*, that we may by experience say, 'It is good for me to draw near to God,' for God will not esteem of us according to our knowledge, but as our affections are, and therefore the wicked man he calls a worldling, because the world filleth him, let his knowledge be never so great. And the church in the Revelation is called heaven, because their affections and minds are that way, xxi. 1; and again, the more we are convinced of God's goodness, the better we are; for God's goodness, tasted and felt by the soul, doth ennoble it, as a pearl set in a gold ring maketh it the more rich and precious. But to come to the estate that is so commended to us, it is described to us by drawing near unto God, so as we may take this for a received ground, that

Doct. [Eighth,] *Man's happiness is in communion with God*. Before the fall of man, there was a familiar conversation with God; but by the sin of our first parents we lost this great happiness, and now we are strangers, and as contrary to God as light is contrary to darkness, and hell to heaven;

* A frequent sentiment in his Letters.—G.

he holy, we impure; he full of knowledge, we stark fools; and instead of delighting in him, we now tremble at his presence, and are afraid of such creatures as approach nigh to him, trembling at the presence of angels, nay, afraid of a holy man. 'What have I to do with thee, thou man of God? art thou come to call my sins to remembrance?' 1 Kings xvii. 18. And therefore we fly the company of good men, because their carriage and course of life do upbraid us; and hence it is that at the least apprehension of God's displeasure, wicked men do quake. The heathen emperor trembled at a thunder clap.* But God, in his infinite mercy and goodness, left us not, but entertaining a purpose to choose some to draw near unto him; and to this end he hath found out a way for man and him to meet, but no way for the angels; and the foundation of this union is in Christ, in whom he reconciled the world to himself; for he being God, became man, so to draw man back again unto God; and thus, like Jacob's ladder, one end of it is in heaven, the other on earth. The angels ascending and descending shew a sweet intercourse between God and man, now reconciled together, so as Christ is now 'a living way' for ever, being 'the way, the truth, and the life.' He is a way far more near and sure than we had in Adam; for in him God was in man, but now man subsisteth in God, so as our nature is now strengthened by him, who also hath enriched it and advanced it: and what he hath wrought in his own human nature, he by little and little will work in all his mystical members; so being once far off, we are now made near, and this he did principally by his death, for reconciliation is made by his blood, Col. i. 20; and thus, by the admirable mystery of his deep wisdom, he hath found a means to make the seeming opposite attributes of justice and mercy to kiss each other, so as we are saved, and yet his infinite justice hath full content. For how could his hatred of sin appear more gloriously than in punishing it upon his own only beloved Son? And therefore worthily he is called 'our peace;' for he is that great peacemaker offering himself up, and us in him, 'as a sweet-smelling sacrifice, acceptable to God,' Philip. iv. 8, being then thus brought near to God, to keep and maintain this nearness, so as nothing may separate us again. He hath put into us his own Spirit, so as we are one spirit with Christ; and by that Spirit he worketh in us and by us by that Spirit. We hear, read, pray, and as by the soul in us our bodies do live, breathe, and move, and the like, so he maketh his Spirit to move in us to a holy conversation and a heavenly life, being thus made 'partakers of the divine nature,' 2 Peter i. 4; and this sanctifies us to a holy communion with God; and therefore the apostle prays, 2 Cor. xiii. 14, 'The grace of our Lord Jesus Christ, the love of God the Father, and the communion of the Holy Ghost, be with them;' that is, for a fuller manifestation of the love of God in sending Christ, the grace of Christ in coming to us, and the communion of the Holy Spirit, because by it we are made to live a holy life, and to communicate with God; and thus the three persons in Trinity conspire together in reducing man back again to be more near to God.

Use 1. Now, for use of this, it should teach us *how to think on God*, not as all justice and power, hating sin and sinners, but as a Father, now laying aside terrible things that may scare us from drawing nigh to him, and as a God, stooping down to our human nature, to take both it and our miserable condition upon himself, and see our nature not only suffering with Christ, but rising, nay, now in heaven united to God; and this will feed the soul with inestimable comfort.

* This is told of Nero.—G.

Use 2. Secondly, Labour to be more near to him, *by the more full participation of his Spirit.* Those that have not Christ's Spirit are none of his. By it we in Christ have access to God; and therefore the more spiritual we are, the nearer access we have to the secrets of God. In our first estate, we are altogether flesh, and have no spirit; in our present estate of grace, we are partly flesh and partly spirit; in our third estate in heaven, we shall be all spiritual; yea, our bodies shall be spiritual, 1 Cor. xv. 44. It is sown natural, but it shall be raised spiritual, and shall be obedient to our souls in all things, and our souls wholly possessed and led by the Spirit of God, so as then God shall be all in all with us; and for means hereunto,

First, *Labour to be conversant in spiritual means*, as in hearing of the word, receiving of the sacraments. God annexeth his Spirit to his own ordinances; and thence it is that in the communion with God in the ordinances, men's apprehensions are so enlarged as they are many times spiritually sick, and do long after the blessed enjoying of God's presence in heaven. But take heed how we come, think what we have to do, and with whom. Come not without the garment of Christ; and it is no matter how beggarly we are, this food is not appointed for angels, but for men. And come with an humble heart, as Elizabeth. Who am I, that (not the mother of my Lord) God himself from heaven should come to me!' Luke i. 43.

Secondly, *Converse with those that draw near unto him.* God is present where two or three are assembled in his name, warming their hearts with love and affection, as it is said of the two disciples going to Emmaus, 'Did not our hearts burn within us while we walked in the way, and conferred of the sayings?' &c., Luke xxiv. 32. Oh, it is a notable sign of a spiritual heart to seek spiritual company; for when their hearts join together, they warm one another, and are hereby guarded from temptations; nay, the wicked themselves in God's company will be restrained. Saul, a wicked man, amongst the prophets will prophesy now, 1 Sam. x. 12. If by good company carnal men themselves do in a manner draw near to God, how acceptable ought this to be to us, and how powerful in us.

Thirdly, And especially, *be much in prayer;* for this is not only a main part of this duty of drawing near to God, but it is a great help thereunto. God is near to all that call upon him; for then are those most near to God when their understandings, affections, desires, trust, hope, faith, are busied about God; and therefore as Moses's face did shine with being in the presence of God, so those that are conversant in this duty of prayer have a lustre cast upon their souls, and their minds brought into a heavenly temper, and made fit for anything that is divine. I could wish that men would be more in public prayer, and that they would not forget private prayer, if ever they intend the comfort of their souls, not only hereafter, but even during this present life. For every day's necessities and dangers in the midst of many enemies, the devil, flesh, and world, ill company, and strong corruptions, should invite us to cast ourselves into the protection of an almighty Saviour. There is not a minute of time in all our life but we must either be near God or we are undone.

Fourthly, Observe *the first motions of sin in our hearts*, that may 'grieve the Spirit of God' in the least manner, and check them at the first. Give no slumber to thine eyes, then, nor the reins to thy desires: 'Thou, O man of God, fly the lusts of youth,' 2 Tim. ii. 22. The best things in us, if they come from nature in us, God abhors. Rebuke therefore the first motions, before they come to delight or action. God abhorreth one that gives liberty to his thoughts, more than one that falleth into a grievous sin now and then, through strength of temptation; and such shall find comfort sooner of the pardon of their sins, for they cannot but see their offences to be heinous, and so have ground of abasement in themselves; but the other, thinking of the smallness of their sins, or at least that God is not much offended with thoughts, do fill themselves with contemplative wickedness, and chase away the Spirit of God, that cannot endure an unclean heart. We must therefore keep ourselves pure and unspotted of this present world, 'for the pure in heart shall see God,' Mat. v. 8; and 'without holiness none shall ever see him,' Heb. xii. 14. The least sin in thought, if it be entertained, it eats out the strength of the soul, that it can receive no good from God, nor close with him, so as it performeth all duties deadly and hollowly: Ps. lxvi. 18, 'If I regard iniquity in my heart, the Lord will not hear my prayer;' and hence it is that so little good is wrought in the ordinances of God. Men bring their lusts along with them. They neither know the sweetness of the presence of God's Spirit, neither do they desire it. It is a true rule that every sin hath intrinsecally in it some punishment; but it is not the punishment that is the proper venom or poison of sin, but this, that it hinders the Spirit of God from us, and keeps us from him, and unfits us for life or for death. But this inward divorce from God's Spirit above all it is the most bitter stab that can befall any one that ever tasted of the sweetness of Christian profession. Now, for the better keeping of our thoughts, we should labour to watch against our outward senses, that by them thoughts be not darted into us. 'The eyes of the fool are in the corners of the world,' Prov. xvii. 24, saith the wise man; and therefore let men profess what they will, when they go to lewd company and filthy places, where corruptions are shot into them by all their senses, they neither can take delight to draw near to God, nor can God take any delight to draw near to them. Dinah, that will be straying abroad, comes home with shame; and that soul that either straggles after temptations, or suffereth temptations to enter into it uncontrolledly, both ways doth grieve God, and that good Spirit that should lead us to him. As for such as live in gross sins, as lying, blaspheming, swearing, drunkenness, adultery, or the like, let them never think of drawing near to God. They must first be civilised before they can appear to be religious; and they contrarily proclaim to the whole world that they say to God, 'Depart from us, for we will none of thy ways,' Job xxi. 14; so as God draws away from them, and they draw away from him.

Fifthly, *Be in God's walks and ordinances in a course of doing good*, in our Christian or civil calling, sanctified by prayer and a holy dependence upon God for strength, wisdom, and success. Go not out of those ways wherein he gives his angels charge of our persons and actions, and whatever we do. Labour to do it with perfection, as our Father in heaven is perfect.

Sixthly, *Observe God's dealings with the church*, both formerly and now in these days, and how he dealeth and hath formerly dealt with ourselves, that from experience of his faithfulness to us we may gather confidence to approach nigh him at any occasion. God's works and words do answer one another: 'Hath he said, and shall he not do it?' He is always good to Israel. Observe therefore how all things work together for thy particular drawing nigh unto him; for if all do work together for thy good, then it must be of necessity for thy drawing near to God, and drawing thee away from this present world; and observe how thy soul answereth the purpose of God, how thy affections are bent, and so how all comes out for thy benefit at last. See God in afflictions embittering ill courses in thee; in thy success in thy affairs, encouraging thee; and thus walk with God. But evermore think of him as of a Father in covenant with thee.

Seventhly, *Labour to maintain humility*, having evermore a sense of thy unworthiness, and wants, and continual dependence on God, and thus humble thyself to walk with him. Hence the saints in God's presence call themselves 'dust and ashes,' as Abraham, Gen. xviii. 27; 'and less than the least of God's mercies,' as Jacob, Gen. xxxii. 10. God is 'a consuming fire,' Heb. xii. 29, and will be sanctified in all that come nigh unto him. He will give grace to the humble, but beholdeth the proud afar off, as they look on others: James iv. 8, 'Draw near to the Lord, and he will draw near to you.' Humble yourselves under 'the mighty hand of God,' and he will lift you up. He that lifteth himself up, maketh himself a god; and God will endure no co-rivals. Contrarily, he dwelleth in the heart of the humble, Isa. lxvi. 2; and in the Psalms, 'An humble and a contrite heart, O God, thou wilt not despise.' But pride he abhorreth as an abomination of desolation.

Eighthly, *Labour for sincerity in all our actions.* Whatever we do to God or man, do it with a single eye, resolute to please God. Let men say what they will, 'a double-minded man is unstable in all his ways,' James i. 8; and what is a double-minded man, but one that hath one eye on God, another on a by-respect? If religion fail him, he will have favour of men, or wealth, yet would fain have both, for credit sake. Such are gross temporisers; and in time, of temporisers [it] will appear that their religion serves but for a cloak to their vile hypocrisy. This God loathes, and will 'spue them out,' Rev. iii. 16.

Ninthly, Observe *the first motions of God's Spirit;* and give diligent heed to them, for by these God knocks for entrance into the heart: Rev. iii. 20, 'Behold, I stand at the door and knock.' God is near when he knocks, when he putteth inclinations into the heart, and sharpeneth them with afflictions. If, then, we stop our ears, we may say 'the kingdom of God was near unto us;' but if he once ceaseth knocking, our mouths shall for ever be stopped; and for this reason it is that so many live daily under the means, and yet live in vile courses, as if God had determined their doom. They resisted the first motions, and close with their lusts, and so God pronounceth a curse: 'Make this people's heart fat,' Isa. vi. 10. On the contrary, those that will open to God while he continues knocking, God will come in and make an everlasting tabernacle in them, and sup with them, Rev. iii. 20.

Lastly, *Take up daily controversies that do arise in us, through the inconstancy of our deceivable hearts.* Repentance must be every day's work, renewing our covenant, especially every morning and evening; repair breaches by confession; and considering the crossness of our hearts, commit them to God by prayer: 'Knit my heart to thee, that I may fear thy name,' Ps. lxxxvi. 11.

A third use of this doctrine is of *instruction;* and, first, to teach us *that a Christian that thus draweth near to God is the wisest man.* He hath God's word, reason, and experience to justify his course. He is the wisest man that is wise for himself. The Christian feels it and knows it, and can justify himself, 2 Tim. i. 12. Paul suffered, and was not ashamed.

Why? 'I know,' saith he, 'whom I have believed.' Let men scorn, I pass* not for man's censure. They shall never scorn me out of my religion; and for them, the Scripture, that can best judge, calls those wicked men fools; for they refuse God, who is the chiefest good, and seek for content where none is to be found. Contrarily, if we do affect honour, or riches, or pleasure, God is so gracious as in religion he gives us abundance of these. In God is all fulness; in Christ are unsearchable riches; in God everlasting strength, 'and his favour is better than the life itself,' Ps. lxiii. 3. Ahithophel was wise, but it was to hang himself; Saul a mighty man, but to shed his own blood; Haman's honour ended in shame.

Secondly, Hence we may learn *how to justify zeal in religion*. If to be near God be good, then the nearer him the better; if religion be good, then the more the better; if holiness be good, then the more the better; it is best to excel in the best things. Who was the best man but Christ, and why? He was nearest the fountain. And who are next but the angels, and why? Because they are always in God's presence. And who next but those that are nearest to Christ. If we could get angelical holiness, were it not commendable? And therefore it should shame us to be backward, and cold, and to have so little zeal, as to be ashamed of goodness, as most are.

Thirdly, This should teach us *that a man must not break with God for any creature's sake whatever*. It is good to lose all for God. Why? Because we have riches in him, liberty in him, all in him. A man may be a king on earth, and yet a prisoner in himself; and if we lose anything, though it be our own life, for God, we shall save it. If we be swallowed up of outward misery, the Spirit of God, that 'searcheth the deep things of God,' 1 Cor. ii. 10, passes and repasses, and puts a relish into us of the 'unsearchable riches of Christ,' Eph. iii. 8. 'Taste and see how good God is,' Ps. xxxiv. 8. 'How excellent is thy lovingkindness, which thou hast laid up for them that fear thee,' Ps. xxxvi. 7. 'How precious are thy thoughts to me, O Lord,' Ps. xxxix. 17. 'Thou hast the words of everlasting life, whither then shall I go?' said Peter, when he felt but a spark of the divine power, John vi. 68.

A further use of this doctrine shall be an use of *trial, to know whether we draw near to God or not*.

First, therefore, where this is, there will be *a further desire of increase of communion with God*. The soul will not rest in measure, Exod. xxxiii. 11, *seq*. Moses had divers entertainments of God: he had seen him in 'the bush,' and in mount Sinai, and many other times; but not contented herewith, he would needs see God's face. And thus Abraham, he gathers upon God still more and more ground in his prayers: 'What if fifty, what if forty, what if twenty, what if ten righteous be found there?' saith he, Gen. xviii. 24, *seq*. And Jacob, how often was he blessed whom Isaac blessed, when he was to go into Paran! when he was there at his return; and yet when he comes to wrestle with the angel, 'I will not let thee go till thou bless me,' Gen. xxxii. 26. And the reason is, because as God is a fountain never to be drawn dry, so is man an emptiness never filled, but our desires increase still till we arrive in heaven; and therefore the more we work, and the more we pray, and the more good we do, the more do our desires increase in doing good.

Secondly, This will appear *in abasing or humbling ourselves*, as it was with Abraham. The more near God is, the more humbly he falls on his

* That is, 'pause,' = care for.—G.

face, and confesseth he is but 'dust and ashes.' The angels, in token of reverence, do cover their faces, 'being in the presence of God.' And it is an universal note, that all such as draw near to God, they are humble and reverent in holy duties; and therefore proud persons have no communion with God at all.

Thirdly, *The nearer we are to God, the more we admire heavenly things;* and count all others 'dross and dung,' as St Paul, Philip. iii. 8. When the sun riseth, the stars they vanish; and those that do not admire the joy, peace, and happiness of a Christian, are unacquainted with drawing near to God.

Fourthly, *When we have a sense and sight of sin, then we may truly be said to 'draw near,'* and to be near to God; for by his light are our eyes enlightened, and we are quickened by his heat and love; and hence we come to see little sins great sins, and are afraid of the beginnings of sin: 'Lord, purge me from my secret sins; create in me a new heart; oh let the thoughts of my heart be always acceptable in thy sight,' Ps. xix. 12. And those that make no scruple of worldly affairs on the Lord's day, of light, small oaths, as they call them, or of corrupt discourse, they neither are nor can draw near to God.

Fifthly, *The nearer we draw to God, the more is our rest.* 'Come unto me, all you that are weary and heavy laden, and you shall find rest unto your souls,' Mat. xi. 28. Ps. xvi. 4, 'The sorrows of those that worship another god shall be multiplied,' and therefore they may well maintain doubting. And therefore such, if they be in their right minds, never end their days comfortably.

Sixthly, *In all distresses, those that draw near to God will fly to him with confidence;* but a guilty conscience is afraid of God, as of a creditor that oweth him punishment, or that intendeth to cast him into perpetual prison. And as a child will in all his wrongs go and complain to his father, Rom. v. 2, *seq.*, so if we have the spirit of sons we have access to God, and peace with God, and can come boldly to the throne of grace, to find help in him at need.

Seventhly, *He that is near to God is neither afraid of God nor of any creature,* for God and he are in good terms. In the midst of thundering and lightning, Moses hath heart to go near, when the Israelites fly, and stand afar off: Ps. xxvii. 1, 'The Lord is the strength of my salvation, of whom shall I be afraid?' Ps. cxii. 7, 'He that feareth the Lord will not be afraid of evil tidings;' but, contrarily, on the wicked there are fears, and snares, and pits. They fear where no cause of fear is; and when God revealeth his terror, indeed then, Isa. xxxiii. 14, 'the sinners in Sion are afraid, and the hypocrites that make show of holiness are surprised with fearfulness; who amongst us shall dwell with devouring fire, and who amongst us shall dwell with everlasting burnings?'

Eighthly, *The nearer we are to God, the more in love we will be with spiritual exercises;* the more near to God, the more in love with all means to draw nigh to him; as of books, sermons, good company. My delight 'is in the excellent of the earth,' Ps. xvi. 3; 'Oh how I love thy law,' Ps. cxix. 97; 'How beautiful are thy dwelling-places, O Lord of hosts,' Ps. lxxxiv. 1.

Ninthly, He that is near God *is so warmed with love of him, so that he will stand against opposition,* and that out of experience—'He that delivered me out of the paw of the bear, will deliver me from the hands of this uncircumcised Philistine,' 1 Sam. xvii. 37,—and out of his experience he will be encouraged to use the ordinances of God. He will pray, because he hath found the sweetness of it; he will be in good company, because he finds it preserves him in a better temper for the service of God; he will hear the word spiritually and plainly laid open to him, because he hath found the power of it in renewing and quickening his affections and desires; and those that do not draw nigh to God, do either loathe, or at least are indifferent, to days, to companies, to exercises. All are alike to them; and they wonder at the niceness of Christians that take so much labour and pains, whenas a man may go to heaven at an easier rate by much; and, on the contrary, Christians do as much wonder at them, that they are so careless, whenas 'few are called;' and of those that are called, some 'hear the word, but receive it not.' Some receive, 'and in time of trial fall off,' Luke viii. 5, so as not the third part of hearers are saved. What then now remaineth but that we should be *encouraged unto this duty of drawing near unto God.* We see how Scripture, reason, and experience proves that it is a thing necessary and profitable; and those that are far from God shall perish, and those that go a-whoring from him he will destroy, as it is in the foregoing verse. Those that are either of a whorish judgment, or affections after lust or covetousness, or the like, God will curse, for all sin is but adultery, or defiling of the soul with the creature; and therefore labour for chaste judgments and affections; love him, and fear him above all, and this is the whole duty of man; and use other creatures in their own place, as creatures should be used. We know not what troubles and difficulties we shall meet with ere long, wherein neither friends nor all the world can do us any good; and then happy shall we be if, with a comfortable heart, we can go to God with David: Ps. xxii. 11, 'Be not far from me, for trouble is near, and there is none to help.' If God be then far off from us when trouble is near to us, we may go and cry to him; but his answer will be, Prov. i. 31, 'You shall eat the fruit of your own way; you have set at nought all my counsel, and would none of my reproof.' You would not draw nigh to me; you shall now call and seek to me, but now you shall not draw nigh to me, you shall not find me. What, then, can our friends do? What can the whole world then supply to us, when sickness comes as 'an armed man,' and death as a mighty giant, against whom is no resisting; but will we or nill we, away we must be gone? Then to have a God nigh us, to whom we may go as Peter did in the storm, 'O Master, save me, I perish,' Mark iv. 36; then to have a friend in heaven, who can for the present guide us by his counsel, and instruct us against Satan's wiles and our deceivable hearts, and be a safe guard to us in the fire and in the water, in the dungeon and when we are in the greatest depths of misery to outward sense; though in death, in the shadow of death, and in the valley of the shadow of death, yet can send us such cheerful remembrances of his love, as the cloud shall be scattered, the shadow taken away, and death, an enemy, shall be a friend; nay, a friendly meeting between God and the soul, so as the soul shall triumph in death, and shall delight to die, and desire it: 'Lord, now let thy servant depart in peace, for,' by the eye of faith, I have 'waited for thy salvation,' Luke ii. 29; I say, then will the sweetness of this estate of drawing near to God be manifested to us, and then shall we not repent of any labour or travail spent in our lifetime, in the attaining of such a condition.

DAVID'S CONCLUSION; OR, THE SAINT'S RESOLUTION.

DAVID'S CONCLUSION; OR, THE SAINT'S RESOLUTION.

NOTE.

'David's Conclusion' is one of the sermons of the 'Beams of Divine Light.' (4to, 1639. Cf. Vol. V. p. 220.) Its separate title-page is given below.*

DAVIDS
CONCLVSION:
OR,
THE SAINTS
RESOLVTION.

In one Sermon.

By the late learned, and reverend Divine,
RICHARD SIBBS.
Doctor in Divinitie, Master of Katherine-Hall
in *Cambridge;* and sometimes Preacher at *Grays-Inne.*

Ieremy 30. 21.
Who is this that ingageth his heart to approach unto me, saith the Lord?

James 4. 8.
Draw nigh to God, and he will draw nigh to you.

LONDON,
Printed by *E. P.* for *Nicholas Bourne*
and *Rapha Harford.*
1639.

DAVID'S CONCLUSION; OR, THE SAINT'S RESOLUTION.

But it is good for me to draw near to God.—Ps. LXXIII. 28.

This psalm is a psalm of Asaph, or a psalm of David, and committed to Asaph the singer, for Asaph was both a seer and a singer. Those psalms that David made were committed to Asaph, so it is thought to be a psalm of David. And if not of David, yet of Asaph, that likewise was a singer in the house of God (*a*).

The psalm represents to us a man in a spiritual conflict, by a discovery of the cause of it, and a recovery out of the conflict, with a triumphant conclusion afterwards.

1. He begins abruptly, as a man *newly come out of a conflict:* 'Truly God is good to Israel;' as if he had gained this truth in conflicting with his corruptions and Satan, who joins with corruption in opposing. Say the flesh what it can, say Satan what he can, say carnal men what they can, '*yet* God is good to Israel.'

2. After his conflict he sets down *the discovery*, first of his weakness, and then of his doubting of God's providence, and then the cause of it, the prosperity of the wicked, and God's contrary dealing with the godly. Then he discovers the danger he was come to, ver. 13, 'Verily I have cleansed my heart in vain, and washed my hands in innocency,' &c.

3. And then *the recovery*, in ver. 17: 'I went into the sanctuary, and there I understood the end of these men.' The recovery was by going into the sanctuary; not by looking upon the present condition, but upon God's intention, what should become of such men; and there he had satisfaction.

4. Then his *victory and triumph over all:* ver. 23, 'Nevertheless I am continually with thee.' It was a suggestion of the flesh that thou wast gone far from me, by reason of the condition of carnal men that flourish in the eye of the world. No: 'Thou art continually with me, and thou holdest me by my right hand.' Thou upholdest me, I should fall else. But what, would God do so for the time to come? 'He will guide me by his counsel,' while I live here and when I am dead. What will he do for me after? 'He will receive me to glory.' Whereupon saith he, 'Who have I in heaven but thee? and there is none in earth that I desire besides thee.' Therefore, though for the present 'my flesh fail,' yea, and 'my heart fail,'

yet God is the 'strength of my heart, and my portion for ever.' We see here his victory set down, and he gives a lustre to it, by God's contrary dealing with the wicked: 'For lo, they that are far from thee shall perish: thou hast destroyed all them that go a-whoring from thee.' Now, in the words of the text, you have his conclusion upon all this, 'Nevertheless it is good for me to draw near to God.'

This is the conclusion upon the former principles. This is, as it were, the judgment upon the former demurs. The sum of all comes to this: Let all things be weighed and laid together, I am sure this is true, 'it is good for me to draw near to God.' So he ends where he began, 'God is good to Israel.' Therefore, because God is so good to Israel, 'it is good to draw near to God.' So you see in what order the words come. They are the words of a man got out of a conflict, after he had entered into the sanctuary, and after he had considered the end of wicked men, at whose prosperity he was troubled and took scandal.

Before I come to the words, it is not amiss briefly to touch these points, to make way to that I am to deliver.

First of all, that,

1. *God's dearest children are exercised with sharp spiritual conflicts.*

God suffers their very faith in principles sometimes to be shaken. What is more clear than God's providence? Not the noonday. Yet God suffers sometimes his own children to be exercised with conflicts of this kind, to doubt of principles written in the book of God, as it were, with a sunbeam, that have a lustre in themselves. There is nothing more clear than that God hath a particular special providence over his; yet God's ways are so unsearchable and deep, that he doth spiritually exercise his children; he suffers them to be exercised, as you see here he comes out of a conflict; 'but it is good for me to draw near to God.' I will touch it. Therefore I will extend it only to God's people, that, if by reason of the remainders of corruption God suffer their rebellious hearts to cast mire and dirt, to cast in objections that are odious to the spiritual man, that part that is good, they may not be cast down too much and dejected. It is no otherwise with them than it hath been with God's dear children, as we see in Jeremiah, Habakkuk, and others. It is a clear truth. I only point at it that we might have it ready to comfort ourselves when such things rise in our souls. It is no otherwise with us than it hath been with other of God's dear children.

The second point is, that,

2. *God's children, when they are in this conflict, they recover themselves.*

God suffers them to be foiled, but then they recover themselves. First, there is a conflict, and then ofttimes the foil. A man is foiled by the worst part in him, and then after a while he recovers; and then, as in other conflicts, there is triumph and victory, as we see here his conflict and recovery.

For God's children go not far off from him, as it is in ver. 27, 'Lo, they that are far off from thee shall perish.' They may have their thoughts unsettled a little concerning God's providence, but they run not far off, they go not a-whoring, as carnal men do. They begin to slip, but God hath a blessed hand under them to recover them, that they do not fall away, that they fall not foully. They may slip and fall a little, to stand better and surer after, but they go not far off as wicked men do. They never slip so low but God's goodness is lower to hold them up. He hath one hand under them and another hand above them, embracing them, so that they cannot fall dangerously. This is the second; from this that we see here, he recovers out of this conflict.

Use. Which may serve *to discern our estate in grace.* If we belong to God, though such noisome imaginations rise, yet, notwithstanding, there is a contrary principle of grace always in God's children that checks them, at the least afterwards, if not presently. Such noisome thoughts as these rule and reign in carnal men, for they take scandal * at God's government, and they judge, indeed, that the ways of wicked men are happy. They have false principles, and they frame their course of life to such false principles and rules, from cherishing atheistical doubts of God's providence, and the like. It is far otherwise with God's children. There are conflicts in them, but there is a recovery; they check them presently; they have God's Spirit, and the seed of grace in them. That is never extinct.

3. *The way of recovery is to enter into God's sanctuary.* For we must not give liberty to ourselves to languish in such a course, to look to present things too much, but look into God's book, and there we shall find what is threatened to such and such ill courses, and what promises are made to good courses. And then apply God's truth to the example; see how God hath met with wicked men in their ruffe,† and advanced his children when they were at the lowest, when they were even at the brink of despair. Examples in this kind are pregnant and clear throughout the Scripture. The Lord saith, 'It shall go well with the righteous, and it shall [not] go well with the wicked,' Ps. xci. 8; 'Let him escape a thousand times. Doubtless there is a reward for the godly,' Ps. lviii. 11. Let us look in the book of God, upon the predictions, and see the verifying of those predictions in the examples that act the rules, and bring them to the view: let us see the truths in the examples. This entering into God's sanctuary it is the way to free us from dangerous scandals, and to overcome dangerous conflicts; for the conclusions of the sanctuary are clean contrary to sensible carnal reason. Carnal reason saith, Such a one is a happy man; sure he is in great favour; God loves him. Oh, but the sanctuary saith, It shall never go well with such a man. Carnal reason would say of Dives, Oh, a happy man; but the sanctuary saith, 'He had his good here,' and 'Lazarus had his ill here.' Carnal reason saith, Is there any providence that rules in the earth? Is there a God in heaven, that suffers these things to go so confusedly? Ay, but the word of God, the sanctuary, saith, there is a providence that rules all things sweetly, and that 'all things are beautiful in their time,' Eccles. iii. 11.

We must not look upon things in their confusion, but knit things. 'Mark the end, mark the end of the righteous man,' Ps. xxxvii. 37. Look upon Joseph in prison. Here is a horrible scandal! For where was God's providence to watch over a poor young man. But see him after, 'the second man in the kingdom.' Look on Lazarus at the rich man's door, and there is scandal; but see him after in Abraham's bosom. If we see Christ arraigned before Pilate, and crucified on the cross, here is a scandal, that innocency itself should be wronged. But stay awhile! See him at the right hand of God, 'ruling principalities and powers, subjecting all things under his feet,' Eph. i. 21.

Thus the sanctuary teacheth us to knit one thing to another, and not brokenly to look upon things present, according to the dreams of men's

* That is, 'make a stumbling-block of.'—G.

† Edward Philips, Sibbes's contemporary, uses the word 'ruffe' very much as here. See 'Godly Learned Sermons' (1605), p. 160. It seems = height of prosperity.—G.

devices ; but to look upon the catastrophe and winding up of the tragedy; not to look on the present conflict, but to go to the sanctuary, and see the end of all, see how God directs all things to a sweet end. 'All the ways of God to his children are mercy and truth,' Ps xcviii. 3, though they seem never so full of anger and displeasure. Thus you see God's children are in conflict ofttimes, and sometimes they are foiled in the conflict; yet by way of recovery they go into the sanctuary, and there they have spiritual eye-salve. They have another manner of judgment of things than 'flesh and blood hath.'

4. Again, we see, when he went into the sanctuary, *the very sight of faith makes him draw near to God.* Sometimes God represents heavenly truths to the eye of sense, in the examples of his justice. We see sometimes wicked men brought on the stage. God blesseth such a sight of faith, and such examples to bring his children nearer to him; as we see immediately before the text, 'thou wilt destroy all that go a-whoring from thee;' and then it follows, 'It is good for me to draw near to God.' So that the Spirit of God in us, and our spirits sanctified by the Spirit, takes advantage when we enter into the sanctuary, and see the diverse ends of good and bad, to draw us close to God.

Indeed, that is one reason why God suffers different conditions of men to be in the world, not so much to shew his justice to the wicked, as that his children, seeing of his justice and his mercy, and the manifestation and discovery of his providence in ordering his justice towards wicked men, it may make them cleave to his mercy more, and give a lustre to his mercy. 'It is good for me to cleave to the Lord.' I see what will become of all others.

5. The next that follows upon this, *that God's children, thus conflicting and going into the sanctuary, and seeing the end of all there, they go a contrary course to the world.* They swim against the stream. As we say of the stars and planets, they have a motion of their own, contrary to that rapt motion, whereby they are carried and whirled about in four-and-twenty hours from east to west. They have a creeping motion and period of their own, as the moon hath a motion of her own backward from west to east, that [she] makes every month; and the sun hath a several* motion from the rapt motion he is carried with that he goes about in a year. So God's children, they live and converse, and are carried with the same motion as the world is. They live among men, and converse as men do; but notwithstanding, they have a contrary motion of their own, which they are directed and carried to by the Spirit of God, as here the holy prophet saith, 'It is good for me to draw near to God.' As if he should say, For other men, be they great or small, be they of what condition they will, let them take what course they will, and let them see how they can justify their course, and take what benefit they can; let them reap as they sow; it do not matter much what course they take, I will look to myself; as for me, I am sure this is my best course, 'to draw near to God.'

So the sanctified spirit of a holy man, he looks not to the stream of the times, what be the currents, and opinions, and courses of rising to preferment, of getting riches, of attaining to an imaginary present happiness here; but he hath other thoughts, he hath another judgment of things, and therefore goes contrary to the world's course. Hear St Paul, Phil. ii. 21; saith he there, 'All men seek their own,—I cannot speak of it without weeping,—whose end is damnation, whose belly is their god, who mind

* That is, 'separate.'—G.

earthly things.' But what doth St Paul, when other men seek their own, and are carried after private ends? Oh, saith he, 'our conversation is in heaven, from whence we look for the Saviour, who shall change our vile bodies, and make them like his glorious body, according to his mighty power, whereby he is able to subdue all things to himself.' So you see the blessed apostle, led with the same Spirit as the man of God here, he considers not what men do, he fetcheth not the rules of his life from the example of the great ones of the world or from multitude. These are false, deceiving rules. But he fetcheth the rule of his life from the experimental goodness he had found by a contrary course to the world. Let the world take what course they will, 'it is good for me to draw near to God.'

6. I might add a little further, that *the course and corrupt principles of the world are so far from shaking a child of God, that they settle him.* They stir up his zeal the more. As we say, there is an *antiperistasis*, an increasing of contraries by contraries, as we see in winter the body is warmer by reason that the heat is kept in, and springs are warmer in winter because the heat is kept in; so the Spirit of God, in the hearts of his children, works and boils when it is environed with contraries. It gathers strength and breaks out with more zeal, as David, Ps. cxix. 126, when he saw men did not keep God's law. We see how he complains to God, 'It is time, Lord, for thee to work.' Indeed, it is the nature of opposition to increase the contrary. Those that have the Spirit and grace of God in truth, they gather strength by opposition.

Use. Therefore the use we are to make of it, is *to discern of ourselves of what spirit we are, what principles we lead our lives by;* whether by examples of greatness, or multitude, or such like, it is an argument we are led by the spirit of the world and not by the Spirit of God. God's children, as they are severed from the world in condition, they are men of another world, so they are severed from the world in disposition, in their course and conversation. Therefore, from these grounds their course is contrary to the world. 'But it is good for me;' 'but' is not in the original. It is, '*And* it is good for me;' but the other is aimed at. The sense is, '*But* it is good for me to draw near to God,' and so it is in the last translation (*b*). Thus you see what way we have made to the words. I do but touch these things, and it was necessary to say something of them, because the words are a triumphant conclusion upon the former premises.

7. And in the words, in general, observe this first of all, that *God by his Spirit enableth his children to justify wisdom by their own experience.*

To make it good by their own experience: 'It is good for me to draw near to God.' And this is one reason why God suffers them to be shaken, and then in conflict to recover, that after recovery they may justify the truth. *Nihil tam certum*, &c., nothing is so certain as that that is certain after doubting (*c*). Nothing is so fixed as that that is fixed after it hath been shaken, as the trees have the strongest roots, because they are most shaken with winds and tempests. Now God suffers the understanding, that is, the inward man, of the best men to be shaken, and after settles them, that so they may even from experience justify all truths; that they may say it is naught,* it is a bitter thing to sin. Satan hath abused me, and my own lust abused me, and enticed me away from God; but I see no such good thing in sin as nature persuaded me before. As travellers will tell men you live poorly here. In such a country you may do wondrous

* That is, 'naughty' = wicked.—G.

well. There you shall have plenty and respect. And when they come there, and are pinched with hunger, and disrespect, they come home with shame enough to themselves that they were so beguiled ; so it is with God's children. Sometimes he suffers them to be foiled, and lets them have the reins of their lusts awhile, to taste a little of the forbidden tree ; that after they may say with experience, it is a bitter thing to forsake God, it is better [to] go to my 'former husband,' as the church saith in Hosea, when God took her in hand a little, ii. 7. Sin will be bitter at the last. So the prodigal he was suffered to range till he was whipped awhile, and then he could confess it was better to be in his 'father's house.' God suffers his children to fall into some course of sin, that afterward, by experience, they may justify good things, and be able to say that God is good.

And the judgment of such is more firm, and doth more good than those that have been kept from sinking at all. God, in his wise providence, suffers this.

Use. We should labour, therefore, *to justify in our own experience all that is good.* What is the reason that men are ashamed of good courses so soon? It may be they are persuaded a little to pray, and to sanctify the Lord's day, to retire themselves from vanity and such like. Ay, but if their judgments be not settled out of the book of God, and if they have not some experience, they will not maintain this; therefore they are driven off. Now a Christian should be able to justify against all gainsayers whatsoever can be said, by his own experience. That to read the book of God, and to hear holy truths opened by men led with the Spirit of God, it is a good thing, I find God's Spirit sanctify me by it. To sanctify the Lord's-day, I find it good by experience. That where there is the communion of saints, holy conference, &c., I can justify it, if there were no Scripture for it: I find it by experience to be a blessed way to bring me to a heavenly temper, to fit me for heaven. So there is no good course, but God's children should be able, both by Scripture, and likewise by their own experience, to answer all gainsayers. When either their own hearts, or others, shall oppose it, he may be able to say with the holy man here, it is no matter what you say, 'it is good for me to draw near to God.' So much for the general. To come more particularly to the words.

'It is good for me to draw near to God.'

Here you have the justification of piety, of holy courses, which is set down by 'drawing near to God;' and the argument whereby it is justified, 'It is good.' This gloss put upon anything commends it to man; for naturally since the fall there is so much left in man, that he draws to that which is good; but, when he comes to particulars, there is the error, he seeks heaven in the way of hell, he seeks happiness in the way of misery, he seeks light in the way of darkness, and life in the way and path of death: his lusts so hurry him and carry him the contrary way. But yet there is left this general foundation of religion in all men; as the heathen could say, naturally all men from the principles of nature draw to that which is good. Here religious courses are justified and commended from that which hath the best, attractive, and most magnetical force. 'It is good to draw near to God.' 'Good' hath a drawing force; for the understanding, that shews and discovers; but the will is the chief guide in man, and answerable to the discovery of good or ill in the understanding, there is a prosecution or aversation* in the will, which is that part in the soul of man that cleaves to good discovered. To unfold the words a little.

* That is, 'turning from.'—G.

'*It is good*' to draw near to God, who is the chief good. It is good in quality, and good in condition and state. It is good in quality and disposition; for it is the good of conformity for the understanding creature to draw near to God the Creator, who hath fitted the whole inward man to draw near, to conform to him.

And then it is good in condition; for it is his happiness to do so. The goodness of the creature is in drawing near to God. The nearer anything is to the principle of such a thing, the better it is for it; the nearer to the sun, the more light; the nearer to the fire, the more heat: the nearer to that which is goodness itself, the more good; the nearer to happiness, the more happy; therefore it must needs be the happiness of condition to draw near to God. So you see what is meant, when he saith here, 'It is good.' It is a pleasing good, conformable to God's will; he commands it; and it is for my good likewise; it advanceth my condition to draw near to God.

'*To draw near.*' What is it to draw near to God? We shall see by what it is to go from God. God is everywhere. We are always near to God. 'Whither shall I go from thy presence? If I go to hell, thou art there,' &c., saith the psalmist, Ps. cxxxix. 8. God is everywhere indeed in regard of his presence, and power, and disposing providence; but then there is a gracious presence of God in the hearts of his children. And there is a strange presence of God to Christ, the *presence of union;* which makes the human nature of Christ the happiest creature that ever was, being joined by a hypostatical union to the second person. But we speak not of that nearness here. There is a gracious nearness when the Spirit of God, in the spirits of those that belong to God, sweetly enlargeth, and comforts, and supports, and strengtheneth them, working that in them that he works in the hearts of none else. For instance, the soul is in the whole man. It is diffused over all the members. It is in the foot, in the eye, in the heart, and in the brain. But how is it in all these? It is in the foot as it moves it. It is in the heart, as the principle of life. It is in the brain and understanding, using and exercising his reasoning, understanding power. So that, though all the soul be in the whole man, yet it is otherwise in the brain than in the rest. So, though God be everywhere, yet he is otherwise in his children than in others. He is in them graciously and comfortably, exercising his graces in them, and comforting them. He is not so with the rest of the world. You see how God is present everywhere, and how he is graciously present with his. So answerable we are said to be near to God. We are near him in what state soever we are, but then there is a gracious nearness when our whole soul is near to God, as thus: *when our understandings conceive aright of God;* as it is said of the young man in the Gospel, when he began to speak discreetly and judiciously, 'Thou art not far from the kingdom of God.' When men have a right conceit* of divine truths, they are not far from the kingdom of God, when there is clearness of judgment to conceive aright. Those that have corrupt principles are far off. If the understanding be corrupt, all the rest will go astray. There is the first nearness when the judgment is sanctified by the Spirit to conceive aright.

Then again, there is a nearness when we not only know things aright, but mind them; when the things are present to our minds; when God is in our thoughts. David saith of the wicked man, 'God is not in his thoughts.' When we mind and think of God and heavenly things, they are near to us, and we to them. For the soul is a spiritual essence. It

* That is, conception.—G.

goes everywhere, it goes to heaven, and is present with the things it minds. We are nearer to God and heavenly things when we mind them, and think on and feed our thoughts on them.

Again, we are near them *when our wills first make choice of the better part with Mary ;* when upon discovery of the understanding, the will chooseth deliberately. Upon consideration follows the determination and choosing of the will; and upon choice, cleaving, which is another act of the will. When it chooseth that which is spiritually best, every way best for grace and condition, then it cleaves to it. As it is said of Jonathan, 'His heart did cleave to David,' 1 Sam. xviii. 1. So the woman cleaves to her husband, as Saint Paul speaks, 1 Cor. vii. 10. When the will chooseth and cleaves to that which is good, then there is a drawing near.

And likewise, *when the affections are carried to God as their object,* then there is a drawing near to God; when our love embraceth God and heavenly things, for love is an affection of union. It makes the thing loved and he that loveth to be one. It is the primary, the first-born affection of the soul, from which all other affections are bred. When we love God, we desire still further and further communion with him. And where there is love, if we have not that we love, then the soul goes forth to God in desire of heavenly things. 'The heart pants after God, as the hart doth after the rivers of waters,' Ps. xlii. 1, and after holy things, wherein the Spirit of God is effectual. And when we have it in any measure, then the soul shews a sweet enlargement of joy and delight in God. Thus when we judge aright of and mind heavenly things, and make choice of them, and cleave to God with all our affections of love, and joy, and delight, when these are carried to God and heavenly things, then we draw near to him.

And especially when the 'inward man' *is touched with the Spirit of God.* Even as the iron that is touched with the loadstone, though it be heavy of itself, it will go up, so, when the inward man is touched by the Spirit of God with a spirit of faith, which is a grace by which we draw near to God with trust,—for it is confidence and trust that draws us near to God,—faith, it is wrought in the whole inward man, in the understanding, in the mind, in choosing and cleaving, but especially it is in the will; for faith is described to be a going to God, a coming to him, which is a promotion or going forth, which is an act of the will; so by faith and trust specially we draw near and cleave to God. Even as at the first we fell from God by distrusting of his word; saith the Devil, 'Ye shall not die at all,' Gen. iii. 4: we believed a liar more than God himself. Now we are recovered by a way contrary to that we fell; we must recover and draw near to God again by trusting and relying upon God. You see what is meant by the words, 'It is good for me to draw near to God.'

To come to observe some things from them, first this, that

Spiritual conviction of the judgment, it is the ground of practice.

It is good, and good *for me.* For we know in nature that the will follows the last design of the understanding. That which the understanding saith is to be done, here and now, all circumstances considered it is best, that the will chooseth and that a man doth, for the will rules and leads the outward man. Now where there is a heavenly conviction of the understanding of any particular thing, this at this time is good, all things considered; and weighed in the balance, on the one side and on the other, where this is, there comes in practice and drawing near to God alway. Conviction is when a man is set down, so that he cannot gainsay nor will not, but falls to practice presently; then a man is convinced of a thing.

That which is immediately before practice, and leads to practice, it is conviction. Now, there are these four things in conviction.

There is first truth. A man must know that such a thing is true. Then it must not only be a truth, but a good truth; as the gospel is said to be 'the good word of God,' Heb. vi. 5, and 'it is a true and a faithful saying,' 1 Tim. i. 15. It is a true saying, 'that Christ came to save sinners,' Matt. ix. 13; and it is a faithful, a good saying. If it be not good as well as true, truth doth not draw to practice as it is truth, but as it is good.

As it must be truth, and a good truth, so it must be good for me, as the holy man saith here, 'It is good for me,' &c. A thing may be good for another man. The devil knows what is good; and that makes him envy poor Christians so. Wicked men know that which is good when they sin against the Holy Ghost; but for them it is better to keep in the contrary. So that we must know it is a truth, and a good truth, and good for us in particular, that it is best for us to do so.

The fourth is this: Though it be true, and good, and good for us; yet before we can come to practice, *it must be a good that is comparative, better than other things that are presented, or else no action will follow.* A man must be able to say, This is better than that. A weak man that is led with passions and lusts, he ofttimes sees the truth of things, and sees they are good, and good for me, and wishes that he could take such a course; but such is the strength of his passions at this time, that it is better to do thus, it is better to yield to his lusts, and he trusts that God will be merciful, and he shall recover it afterwards. These four things, therefore, must be in conviction before we can take the best course; and these are all here in this holy man, for he saw it was a truth, a duty, and likewise that it was a good truth; for to be near to God, the fountain of good, it must needs be good. And then it was good for him to be so, nay, it was good, all things considered; for it is a conclusion, as it were, brought out of the fire, out of a conflict. Nay, say the flesh, and say all the world what it can to the contrary, 'It is good for me to draw near to God.' He brings it in as a triumphant conclusion. Put drawing near to God in one balance, and lay in that balance all the inconveniences that may follow drawing near to God,—the displeasure of great ones, the loss of any earthly advantage,—and lay in the other balance all the advantages that keep men from drawing near to God,—as if a man do not keep a good conscience, he may please this or that man, he may get riches, and advance himself, and better his estate,—consider all that be, yet notwithstanding, it is better to draw near to God, with all the disadvantages that follow that course, than to take the contrary. Thus you see the truth clear, that conviction is the way and foundation of practice.

Use. Therefore we should labour by all means to be convinced of the best things. It is not sufficient to have a general notion, and slightly to hear of good things. No; we must beg the Spirit of God that he would seal and set them upon our souls; and so strongly set and seal them there, that when other things are presented to the contrary, with all the advantages and colours and glosses that flesh and blood can set upon them, yet out of the strength of spiritual judgment we may be able to judge of the best things out of a spiritual conviction, and to say it is best to cleave to God. So said the blessed man of God Moses. There was in the one end of the balance the pleasures of sin, the honours of a court, there was all that earth could afford,—for if it be not to be had in a prince's court, where is it to be had? His place was more than ordinary; he was accounted the son of Pharaoh's daughter,—yet lay all that in the balance, and in the other part of the balance, to draw near to God's people, though the people of God were a base, forlorn, despised, afflicted people at that time, yet notwithstanding to draw near to the cause of religion, the disgraced cause of religion, 'to draw near to God' when he is disgraced in the world,—it is easy to draw near to God when there is no opposition,—but to draw near to God's part and side when it is disgraced in the world, Moses saw it the best end of the balance, put in the afflictions, and disgrace of God's people, or what you will. So it was with Abraham when he followed God as it were blindfold, and left all, his father's house and the contentments he had there. So it was with our Saviour's disciples. They left all to follow Christ; they were convinced of this, Surely we shall get more good by the company of Christ than by those things that we leave for him.

Let us labour therefore to be convinced of the excellency of spiritual things, and then spiritual practice will follow. And undoubtedly the reason of the profane conversation of the world, it comes from hidden atheism; that men make no better choice than they do, that they draw not near to God. Let them say what they will, it proceeds from hence. I prove it thus. When men are convinced of good things, they will do good, for conviction is the ground of practice; and when men do not take good courses, it is because they are not convinced of the best things. Therefore men that swear, and blaspheme, that are carnal, brute persons, at that time atheism rules in their hearts, that they believe not these things in the book of God to be true. Can the swearer believe that 'God will not hold him guiltless that takes his name in vain; that a curse shall follow the swearer,' Exod. xx. 7, and the whoremonger; 'that whoremongers and adulterers God will judge? Heb. xiii. 4, and so the covetous, and extortioners, they that raise themselves by ill means, 'shall not enter into the kingdom of heaven.' Can men believe this, and live in the practice of these sins? If they did believe these things indeed, as the word of God sets them down, if they did believe that sin were so bitter, and so foul a thing as the word of God makes it, certainly they would not; therefore it comes from a hidden atheism. Indeed, there is a bundle of atheism and infidelity in the heart of man, and we cannot bewail it too much. In the best there are some remainders of it: as this holy man, 'So foolish was I, and as a beast before thee,' Ps. lxxiii. 22, when he thought of his doubting of God's providence. Therefore considering that the cause of all ill practice is that we are not spiritually convinced of the contrary, that sin is a naughty and bitter thing, nor are we sufficiently convinced of the best things, let us labour more and more to be soundly convinced of these things.

Now, nothing will do this but the Holy Ghost, as ye have it John xvi. 7, *seq.*: 'Christ promiseth to send the Comforter, the Holy Ghost, and he shall convince the world of sin;' that is, he shall so set sin before the eyes of men's souls, that they shall know there is no salvation but in Christ. He shall convince them of unbelief, that horrible sin. They shall have it presented so to them, that they shall believe presently upon it. This the Holy Ghost must do.

But the Holy Ghost doth it in the use of means. Therefore it must be our wisdom to hear and pray and meditate much, that God would vouchsafe his Spirit to persuade us, to convince our understanding, to convince us of all our false reasonings against good things, that there may not a vile imagination rise in our hearts contrary to divine principles.

'It is good to draw near to God.' Therefore it is good to come to the sacrament, which is one way of drawing near to God. Let us be so convinced of it, that it is not only a necessary, but a comfortable and sweet duty to have communion with God; for will we suffer for Christ if we will not feast with him? What shall we say of those, therefore, that are so far from drawing near to God, when they have these opportunities, that they turn their backs? They clean thwart this blessed man here. He saith, 'It is good for me to draw near to God;' nay, say they, it is good for me to have nothing to do with God, nor Christ, no, not when he comes to allure me. Now, he is come near us indeed, that we might come near him. Because we were strangers to God, and could not draw near to him, simply considered, God became man, Emmanuel, God with us, that he might bring us to God. Christ is that Jacob's ladder that knits heaven and earth together. Christ, God and man, knits God and man together. This was the end of his incarnation and of his death, to make our peace, to bring those near that were strangers, nay, enemies before; and of our part and portion in the benefits of his death, we are assured in the sacrament. Therefore let us draw near to our comfort, with cheerfulness, for his goodness that we have these opportunities. Let us draw near to God to have our faith strengthened and our communion with him increased.

Only let us labour to come with clean hearts. 'God will be sanctified in all that come near him,' Lev. x. 3. Let us know that we have to deal with a holy God, and with holy things, and therefore cast aside a purpose of living in sin; let us not come with defiled hearts, for then, though the things be holy in themselves, they are defiled to us. Let us come with a resolution to renew our covenant, and come with rejoicing that God stoops so low to use these poor helps, that in themselves are weak, yet by his blessing they are able greatly to strengthen our faith.

NOTES.

(*a*) P. 81.—'This psalm is a psalm of David, or of Asaph.' Cf. Dr J. A. Alexander and Thrupp *in loco*. Modern criticism seems to have no doubt that Asaph was the author, not merely the 'singer,' of this psalm.

(*b*) P. 85.—"'But' is not in the original." Cf. above reference. Dr Alexander renders, 'And I,' &c. 'As for me—the approach of God to me (is) good.' The 'last translation' is our present authorised version. G.

(*c*) P. 85.—'*Nihil tam certum*,' &c. An apophthegm common to Philosophy, and met with in various forms; *e. g.* it is a common saying, 'He who never doubted, never believed.'

THE CHURCH'S BLACKNESS.

THE CHURCH'S BLACKNESS.

NOTE.

'The Church's Blackness' forms No. 17 of the sermons in The Saint's Cordials of 1629. It was withdrawn in the after-editions. Its separate title-page is given below.*

G.

* THE
CHVRCHES
BLACKNES.

In One Sermon.

SHEWING,

That the best of Gods Saints, whilest they are here, are in imperfect estate.
That though our estate be here unperfect, yet we must not be discouraged.
As also, that Christians have beauty as well as blacknesse.
And that there is a glory and excellency in the Saints of God, in the midst of all their deformities and debasements.

Prælucendo Pereo.

Vprightnes Hath Boldnes.

LONDON,
Printed in the yeare 1629.

THE CHURCH'S BLACKNESS.

I am black, but comely, O ye daughters of Jerusalem, as the tents of Kedar, and as the curtains of Solomon. Look not upon me, because I am black, because the sun hath looked upon me; my mother's children were angry with me; they made me the keeper of the vineyards: but mine own vineyard have I not kept.—CANT. I. 5, 6.

IN the former verses of this chapter, the church having shewed her fervent love and dear affection unto Christ, and longing for a nearer communion with him; having also confessed and professed her own weakness and inability to come towards him, for which cause she says, 'Draw me, we will run after thee;' in the words which I have read, and in the verse following, she comes to remove certain objections and impediments, which might either discredit her or discourage her daughters, which she doth by turning her speeches unto them, who are answered as though they had expressed their objection in direct words; for the Spirit knows how to meet with our secret thoughts, either present or to come. Now these daughters who here make the objection, are supposed to be such as have no sanctifying grace as yet in them, at least very little (as it appeareth by their contemning of the church, ver. 6, and disacquaintance with Christ, chap. v. 9), yet daughters of Jerusalem. Now the first objection the church hath to meet with, is by reason of such as live in the church, are bred and born there, partake of the ordinances, are in the church, though not all of it, and these the church hath to do withal. As for the daughters of Babylon, and those out of the church, they do not heed what she saith, nor understand in any measure her language, they are neither for her nor her love. Well, with these daughters she deals, and taking up their objection, first, she answers it, ver. 5; secondly, she enlarges her answer, ver. 6. The objection is, 'Thou art black;' and this is aggravated from a comparison; the manner with her affected love, thus: And is Christ indeed, as thou reportest him, the best lover, full of sweetness and holiness, a king? what an unwise woman art thou to entertain any hopes of marrying him, sith you have nothing, be poor, afflicted, filthy; in a word, black, yea, very black. This is the objection, which she answers nimbly two ways.

1. By yielding what was said: 'I am black;' that is, my estate here is imperfect, subject to sin, to affliction; not beautiful, therefore, in carnal eyes and judgments, but deformed.

2. By denying the argument, that therefore she must be despised of men, rejected of Christ as one that had nothing in her; nay, black folks may be handsome and desirable, and so saith she, I am to the eye contemptible, yet inwardly rich, desirable, and lovely, which she sheweth by two comparisons.

First, thus: It is with me as with the tents of Kedar. The Kedarenes dwelt in Arabia, they dwelt in tents covered with hair (as Solymus and Pliny speaks) (*a*), which tents were very coarse to look to, tanned, exposed to all weather, rough with the sun, and hard, and yet in those tents they had much treasure, they were full of wealth, in cattle, in spices, in gold, in precious stones. So is it with the church; though outwardly base, yet there are treasures within, and much glory, as further she shews, saying, she was like Solomon's curtains; his bed is after mentioned; and out of question all his doings were admirable.

This is her second comparison. You read what a glorious house he built, how long it was a-building. If the church therefore be like his curtains, she is very glorious, amiable, and rich. But how is she like them? Thus, as the curtains of Solomon's bed were most glorious, and yet did not lie open to every eye, it being for those especially favoured to be admitted into such a king's bedchamber, and inmost rooms, which be for the king and his spouse, so it is with the church; she is rich, though her riches be inward, and not discernible by every eye: as Ps. xlv. 13, 'The king's daughter is all glorious within; like Solomon's curtains and Kedar's tents.' As if she should say, 'I am black,' so are the tents of Kedar, and yet have treasures in them. And not to send you so far, ye daughters of Jerusalem, know that there is much treasure and glory in Solomon's palace, which every one sees not, and so in me. Thus she answers the objection, and next, ver. 6, she dwelleth upon it, and enlargeth it. But first of this. For the meaning thereof, you see what we conceive of it; we will not be prejudicial to any man's opinion (*b*). The very matter is, she contends that it is possible for her to be rich, glorious, and lovely inwardly, though not in show (because her outward blackness did expose her to censure in the eyes of most men), and this she proves by two instances, well known unto these daughters: 1, of the Arabians, who brought treasure yearly to Solomon, 2 Chron. ix. 14, which argued their riches, though they lived in sun-burnt tents; and 2, of Solomon, who was as rich within doors as without, though all saw it not. Thus you have the church's confession, and her defence; black outwardly, and inwardly for some corruption, as after this is objected. Thus much is yielded. Hence then learn we,

Point 1. The church of God and Christians, whilst they are here, *are in an unperfect state.* No Christian in this life attains to full happiness and brightness, but is attended on by those sins and sorrows that argue an unperfect estate. The church of God, and every converted Christian, must needs confess that they be black outwardly and inwardly. This we hear not only from her own mouth, in her first conversion, but after; for howsoever we conceive of these things in the first chapter and part of the second, to agree with the first age of a Christian especially, yet not only; for what is here said of her is ever true whilst here on earth, though the degree be somewhat varied. The Holy Ghost useth a fair comparison; he makes the church to be born in the night, and to travel towards the day; she is going towards perfection, as one that sets out before day; yea, she is gone so far that it draweth towards the dawning. There is a mixture of some light and darkness together, and so it will be till we come to heaven, both for sin and sorrow, for sins and defects in soul. So, 1 Peter ii. 20, the saints have faults in this life, and are buffeted for them; there must be addition of grace to grace, 2 Peter i. 5, so Eph. i. 18. The eye of our understanding is shut until it be opened; and we have wonderful things to look after beyond the power of our present condition; for outward estate, see Prov. iv. 18, the church's path is like the shining light, 'which shineth more and more unto the perfect day;' for both she is duskish between night and day, and so will be till that full morning come. So Ps. xlix., what is the whole tenor thereof, save only a large commentary of our frailties and imperfections whilst we live here? So we find by Paul's description of the church, Eph. iv. 12, she is a house not yet fully furnished, nor beautified, but exposed to storms, and imperfect; she is a body not yet grown, like the tabernacle, an imperfect thing. This we see, Rev. ii. 3. Every church there is noted for sins, or afflictions, or both. If we conceive these churches to be types, the proof is most pregnant; if not (for I am persuaded God hath done teaching his church by types; for, as Heb. i. 2, 'In these last and latter days he speaks unto us by his Son, whom he hath made heir of all things'), yet since no church was more famous than those, who yet had blemishes and frailties a-many, it warrants here, and strengthens the point we have in hand. Hence comes the church's confession here both of sin and sorrow. Hence Paul saith, 1 Cor. xiii. 9, speaking of the church's estate, 'We know in part, and prophesy in part. But when that which is perfect is come, then that which is in part shall be done away.' Hence 1 John i. 8, it is said, 'If we say we have no sin, we deceive ourselves, and the truth is not in us. The causes why God will have it so are,

Reasons. 1. First, In regard of outward infirmities, that we might be made conformable to his Son, Rom. viii. 17, and so reign with him, being first made suitable to the body. Christ was to be like us in all things, sin excepted, and to partake with us in flesh and blood, that he might destroy him that had the power of death; that is, the devil, Heb. ii. 14. And we are to partake of him and his afflictions, that so we may come to partake of the divine nature, and be all in a suit,* as servants of the same master.

2. Secondly, In respect of outward and inward infirmities, both because God's glory is seen in our infirmities, 2 Cor. xii. 7, his grace being sufficient to uphold us, and also in regard our weakness commends his strength, and our folly his wisdom.

3. Thirdly, Because he would draw us out of the earth, and have us hasten to accomplish the marriage and come away, therefore he sends us so many crosses, and so little rest in the flesh.

4. Again, Because God would have us humble, patient, and pitiful people, neither of which would be unless our state were imperfect; we would never know ourselves, our brethren, and God, unless it were so, that on both sides we saw the prints of our imperfections. The use is twofold.

Use 1. Is this so? Learn these lessons. First, *confess if we be of the church, so much.* No man is more ready to charge the church than she is to confess her infirmities. She never hideth them, she never justifieth them; she is black, she hath afflictions, she kept not her own vine, she wants knowledge, affection, discretion, love. She never denies it, but confesseth all freely from her heart; she hides not her sin, but tells what she

* That is, as elsewhere, 'wear the same dress.'—G.

is, what she hath done, that so she may give glory to the Lord God of Israel. And indeed, it maketh much for the honour of Christ, and commends his grace, that he, such a king, will set his heart and his eye upon such a deformed slut as the world deemeth her to be. It makes for the comfort of her poor children, and much stayeth them, when they shall hear the church in all ages, and in her Abraham, David, and Paul, saying, 'I am black,' I have affliction, corruption, as well as others. It makes for the silencing of all saucy daughters that will upbraid her; an ingenuous confession, stops their mouths, and puts them all to silence. It much quickens her to the use of the means, and maketh her cry, 'Shew me, O thou whom my soul loveth, where thou feedest.' And to seek her comfort in Christ Jesus. Oh it doth her good to receive the sentence of death, shame, poverty, damnation, in herself, that so she may be found in Christ, arrayed with the rich robes of his righteousness. Hence her plain-hearted openness in her confession. Let us do the like, and leave it to the harlot and whore of Babylon to say herself is a queen, she is glorious, she cannot err. But let us say with the church, we are black; yea, let us see it, let us speak it with sorrow, with shame, as the saints have done, and be so affected with our estate, that it may truly humble us, and cause us to say, 'It is the Lord's mercies that we are not consumed.' And let us so confess it in ourselves, that we pity others, and bear with them, though full of sins and miseries; so confess it, that we stir up others thereby to run, as Paul did, and use the ordinances with all diligence, to pray much, to read much, to hear, to confer, to advise, and be humble and sincere. A verbal confession of frailties, without humility, mercy, diligence, without the use of the means, is hypocrisy. If we will speak with the church, we must feel what we say, and so well understand ourselves and our estate, that we may gain humility, mercy, watchfulness by it.

Use. 2. In the second place, *thirst after heaven, nay, after the day of resurrection.* Well may it be called the day of refreshing, the day of marriage. Till then the church is parched with the sun, and not half tried, till then she is accompanied with sundry imperfections in her outside. The saints are subject to aches, shames; their bodies are vile, corruptible; though in the grave free from pain, yet not from dishonour. Imperfections within the soul there are many, conflicts, corruptions, temptations, fears, sorrows, &c. Imperfections also in company: she is not taken out of the world; she hath her dwelling in the tents of Kedar, meets with hypocrites, atheists, persecutions, devils. Imperfections for means; she seeth but in a glass, she beholds Christ but through a window; she is in prison, and speaks through it; and there are imperfections in services, repentance, faith, prayer; and imperfections in parts and members: some members be not called yet, and it grieves her; some being called are very sickly, weak, heady; the best on earth imperfect, those in heaven not perfected till we come also, Heb. xii. 23. Nay, Christ himself, as head of the body, not yet perfected in his members, and in his church, which is his fulness, as Paul speaks, Eph. i. 23. Oh then, sith nothing in the church attains its perfection till that day; sith Christ calleth, come away, that head and members may have the same glory together, sith the creatures here, and all saints cry, come; let us so well understand our estate here, and there, and the odds of both, that we may say also, come, fly, my beloved, and be like the roe, that so all the shadows may fly away; and therefore, not only pray and hasten ourselves, but others also, that so harvest may be ripe when we sow betimes.

Well, then, she yields herself to be black, but yet she is not discouraged; she will not be set down, she is comely for all her blackness, she will to Christ still, as the verse tells us. Hence learn,

Doct. 2. *Though our estate be here imperfect, yet we must not be discouraged.* God's children must so see their sins, and sorrow for them, as that though they be thereby sent to humiliation, yet they may retain hope of mercy. So the church does, Ps. xliv. 17, 'All this is come upon us, yet have we not forgotten thee, neither have we dealt falsely in thy covenant; our heart is not turned back,' &c. So Isa. lxiii. 17, though the church was hard-hearted, yet she goes to Christ to bemoan herself: 'Oh Lord, why hast thou made us to err from thy ways, and hardened our heart from thy fear? Return, O Lord,' &c.; yet she conceives hope. This was Samuel's counsel to the people, 'Fear not: ye have done all this wickedness: yet turn not aside from following the Lord, but serve the Lord with all your heart,' 1 Sam. xii. 20, 21. And David likewise to his soul, Ps. xlii. 11, 'Why art thou cast down, O my soul? and why art thou discouraged within me? yet trust in God.' So the like is Paul's practice, Rom. vii. 24, 'O wretched man that I am! who shall deliver me?' &c. Then he answers, 'I thank God, through Jesus Christ our Lord.' Thus you see the point is plain; now the reasons.

Reason 1. We have a great and mighty deliverer. He loves his children in the midst of all their deformities. Like a good father, he tenders us in our weaknesses of soul and body, and as a father pities his child the more for being sick, so here he calls her for all this, 'O thou fairest amongst women,' &c.

2. Secondly, He is able to help them in all estates; his grace is still sufficient, he hath present help. What needs the child be dismayed for pain, when the Father can remove it at his pleasure?

3. Thirdly, The saints of God in all ages have gone through imperfections; they have been sick, poor, doubtful, passionate, as well as we. God hath brought them to heaven, to happiness, through all storms. Though in their life they cried, 'we are black,' we are forsaken; and why should we fear to wade through those waters where all have escaped that went before us?

4. Fourthly, Uprightness may stand with imperfection, some gold may be amongst earth; as the church shews here, beauty and deformity may stand together, some light, some darkness. Now God bids the upright hope, rejoice, says he is blessed, Ps. xxiii. 6.

5. Lastly, Because the effects of discouragement are too bad, as fretting, Ps. xlii. 11; yea, this doth not only keep out praises, but causes neglect of all ordinances, drives from God, makes one fierce, envious, uncomfortable, impotent, &c.

Use 1. This is to humble ourselves for our weakness; for, alas! how soon are we swooning and discouraged. Every slight affliction, corruption, temptation, doth dismay and put us to silence. If storms fall, and winds blow, if flesh stir, and Satan be busy, our faith trembles, and hearts are shaken; we meditate, fear and suspect ourselves; we suspect God, and shun his presence, and say in our haste 'we are forgotten;' this is our death. Oh how unworthy Christ is this carriage! How unlike the church in this place. She is charged with faults, upbraided with baseness, yet she holds on, she prayeth still. To Christ she runs; no affliction, no temptation, no corruption shall keep her from him, because nothing can keep him from her, as Rom. viii. 38 is at length shewed. Where is our faith, strength, courage, patience? Where is the spirit of power, that we are so weak in every temptation? Verily, these faintings of spirit, these despairing questions, these violent fears, do argue much weakness. Let us be humbled for this; humbled, I say, but not discouraged; for even the church sometimes, sometimes Manoah, yea, a David, have thus failed.*

Use 2. Now learn to be courageous. Are afflictions upon thee? Be sensible of them, be humbled in them, but never shrink from thy hold of Christ or hope of mercy. Be of Paul's resolution; 'We are distressed,' saith he, 'but yet faint not.' See God at thy right hand, as David did, and therefore be not moved. See what is gained by affliction, 'the inward man grows.' See what is laid up for these light and short afflictions, 2 Cor. iv. 17, 'even a far more excellent and eternal weight of glory.' Art thou censured and scorned by men? Make use of it, but not to discouragement. Remember Christ was despised, counted a worm, judged wicked, and then say with the church, 'Rejoice not against me, O my enemy, though I fall I shall rise again: When I am in darkness, the Lord he will be a light unto me,' Micah vii. 8. Art thou assaulted by Satan? Cry with Paul, and bemoan thyself; but know therewith that God's 'grace is, and shall be sufficient for thee,' 2 Cor. xii. 9; that he hath overcome, and therefore resolve, with Job, to receive from God what he will put upon thee, yea, to die at his feet, Job xiii. 15. Art thou led captive with thy corruptions? Mourn with Paul, but say withal, 'It is not I, but sin in me; I thank God through Jesus Christ our Lord,' Romans vii. 17, 25. It is a most worthy service to give Christ the glory of his riches in poverty, of his power in weakness, grace in sin, life in death. Then we live by faith, then we shew forth the strength of the Spirit. To this purpose, first learn to know thyself, what thou art by nature, and all men else. The want of this knowledge breeds pride, discouragement, error in judgment, mistaking, misapplication of things. Secondly, know what Christ is, how lovely, how rich, how able, how true; how willing he is to help the distressed and miserable, never adding affliction unto affliction. Thirdly, see what he hath done for others, for thyself heretofore. Now lay graces by infirmities with the church here, and when the devil upbraids thee with thy maims, look on thy cures; when he sets before thee the tempestuous dark works of the first Adam, do thou oppose, and lay before thee the quiet fruit of righteousness and peace-making reconciliation and works of Christ, the second Adam, thy surety, who hath paid thy debts and satisfied divine justice to the full.

Further, in that the church here stands upon her comeliness, notwithstanding of all her deformities and infirmities, learn we,

Doct. 3. *There is a glory and excellence in the saints of God in the midst of all their deformities and debasements.* Though they be encompassed with many miseries, yet are they glorious even in this life. Indeed their glory is like Solomon's curtains, not obvious to every eye; like Kedar's tents, or a heap of wheat in the chaff, and outwardly base, but inwardly excellent. Their life is sanctified indeed, and they live the life of grace, hence they are termed glory, Isaiah iv. 5; hence, as Ps. lxviii. 13, after their misery, it is promised they should be as the wings of a dove, covered with silver, and her feathers with yellow gold; hence, Ps. xlv. 16, they are called princes in all lands, all glorious within, to be of excellent beauty; hence. Ps. cx. 3, their beauty is termed a holy beauty; yea, that which is said of the church of Smyrna, Rev. ii. 9, may be said of every church, 'She is poor,

* Cf. Judges xiii. and Ps. lxxi.—G.

but rich;' and that which Paul saith of the apostles may be said of all, they are poor and rich, base and honourable, dying and yet living, having nothing, and yet possessing all things, 2 Cor. iv. 8, *et seq*. And why?

Reason 1. Needs it must be so, for being converted, they obtain a new name, Rev. ii. 17; yea, they have this peculiar favour granted, as 1 John iii. 1, to be called the 'sons of God.' This is set down with a 'behold,' to admire the wonderful love of God and excellency of the saints, who are also called princes on earth, as Ps. xlv. 16.

2. Secondly, they have a new nature, being made partakers of the image of God, and so of the divine nature; as it is, 2 Pet. i. 4, 'having escaped that corruption which is in the world through lust.'

3. Thirdly, they have a new estate; Christ Jesus makes them free, as John viii. 35, and he makes them also rich, supplying all their wants with the riches of his glory: as Ps. iv. 3, the prophet says, 'But know that the Lord hath set apart him that is godly for himself,' &c.

4. Lastly, they have a new kindred and guide. God is their Father, they are members of Christ: 1 Cor. xii. 13, they are 'led by the Spirit of God.' God dwelleth in them, and the Spirit of glory rests upon them even in affliction, 1 Pet. iv. 14, and filleth them with glorious faith and precious graces.

[1.] *This first discovers a wonderful blindness in us*, who can see no such matter in the saints of God. Christians shine in the world as stars in a dark night, and as far excel all others as corn weeds, chaff; yea, as far as lilies and roses do thorns and briars; and yet we cannot see it, unless we have riches, titles, fashions, wit, beauty to grace them. We see no beauty in them, we do not regard nor reverence them, we neglect, nay, despise them. Oh hearts of flesh, oh carnal eyes, that can see nothing but outward gauds and toys! How do we stick in the outward mud of this world, that serve only the world! How do we judge by the outward appearance! How carnal to have the glorious faith of Christ in respect of persons! Jude 16. How blind are we who cannot see the sunshine, and no excellency in those whom all the glorious angels serve, whom the King of glory terms 'the fairest of women!' Brethren, what shall I say to you? If your eyes be so blinded that you cannot see the church like Solomon's curtains, cannot see beauty in a Christian's face, wisdom in his language, glory in his behaviour, even in affliction; when their happiness is revealed, it will be a proof against you that you have not that anointing of God which teaches you all things, that you are but natural. Ask yourselves, therefore, the question, what men do I most admire, reverence, and who is most glorious in my eye? And if the Christian be not, you have but fleshly eyes, hearts, and affections. Strive and labour reformation.

[2.] Secondly, *This is comfort to saints now and hereafter*. Now they be glorious, but yet they are but in the way going to glory; as Prov. iv. 18, 'The path of the just is as the shining light' that waxeth more and more unto the perfect day.' Yet 'their life is hid with God in Christ.' When Christ, 'which is their life, shall appear, then shall they likewise appear in glory,' Col. iii. 3. Now they are the sons of God; but it appeareth not in this world what they shall be; and if they be now such, whilst black, what when in heaven, when Christ is made glorious in them? If thus in their pilgrimage, what at home in their country? If thus, imperfect, what in perfection? If thus, in corruption, what when this corruption shall put on incorruption? And if thus, in mortality, what when mortality shall be swallowed up of life?

Thus we have heard the church's apology for her blackness. The next verse, which I cannot now speak of as I would, contains the remainder of her answer, wherein she proceeds to shew thus much, that the church and Christians, even at the worst, are not to be despised for infirmities. This she takes for granted, as formerly proved, and then goes on to shew the causes which wrought her blackness and misery.

1. First, outwardly; *The sun had parched her*, that is, many afflictions had overtaken her; and then, in her particular, her mother's sons had crossed her; false hypocrites, erroneous, proud professors, carrying the name of brethren, had vilified and taken all occasions to put base drudgery upon her.

2. The second cause was inward; *She kept not her own vineyard*, that is, she did not husband her own soul aright; she looked not to her own work and charge; which words contain not an extenuation of her blackness, but an amplification of the causes of it rather. Thus you see the church's mind: she thinks men should rather comfort and encourage her, than despise her for her many afflictions, seeing she doth so freely confess them; and those who are in misery ought to be comforted. Not to stand upon it: hence we learn,

Doct. 4. *We must not still be poring into the deformities of God's church and people*, like flies on galled places, or dogs upon garbage and raw flesh. For,

Reason 1. First, This is a practice which utterly crosseth God in his commandments, who chargeth us 'not to despise the day of small things,' Zech. iv. 10.

Reason 2. Secondly, This is quite against justice; for Christians have beauty as well as blackness, graces as well as corruptions.

Reason 3. Thirdly, This neither cometh from any good, nor worketh good. It ariseth from pride, ignorance, &c., and sheweth that a man neither knows his own estate, nor God's proceedings with his people, who brings them to honour through baseness, and confounds the glory of the world with base things.

Use 1. This condemneth those Christians who have their eyes still upon the blackness of the church, who are of three sorts:

First, papists, who deck a whore, and call her Christ's spouse, and in the mean time despise the church of Christ for blackness and outward deformities.

Secondly, against such who stumble as much at our inward deformities, as these at our outward debasements, at our discipline, preaching, ministry, sacraments, calling, ordinances, as though all were antichristian. Why will not such see white with black? good with bad? We confess that in our church, as in every church visible, there is corn and tares, fish, good and bad, sometimes children, sometimes bastards, only sons by the mothers' side: we never knew it otherwise in any church.

Thirdly, This is against such as like bats can see to fly in the dark only. The prosperity of Christians they cannot see, or graces, nor comforts, nor good works, to be provoked thereby to obedience; but if any one be crossed in his profession, they speak of it; if any fall into sin, they remember him; if any suffer shipwreck, if any live less comfortably, or die less cheerfully, oh then there is work enough: who would be a Christian? How doth it make men mopish and lumpish, and bring men out of their wits? And whence is all this; but from ignorance or great hypocrisy, or malice? In love there is no such offence, as John speaks, and therefore to these the church speaks, 'Look not upon me, because I am black, &c.

A word only of the causes of her affliction, and so I have done—which came by her mother's sons, such as live in the church. So that we see the church hath those who afflict her and persecute her even within herself. See for this point: Rebekah's sorrow and struggling within her, two nations, Gen. xxv. 22. Next, see how they use her, and why? They take her by violence, and force her to slavery, and exercise too much hardness over her; and the reason that she apprehends is, the neglects in her own business; lay these together: so we learn,

Doct. 5. *Then God's children pay for it, when they do not their own work, not keeping their own standing.* It is with them as soldiers and scholars, when they keep not their own places, and learn not their own lessons: they are met with on every side. And that,

Reason 1. First, because no man speeds well out of his own place, but Christians worst of all; as Prov. xxvii. 8, a thousand inconveniences befall to one's self, to his charge, when absent. God will be upon him, and leave him to himself, till he hath wound himself into woeful brakes.*

Reason 2. Secondly, Men will be upon his back, as Paul on Peter's, or else grow strange till he be humbled; but bad men they will curse him, all the hypocrites in the town will be at his heels.

Reason 3. Thirdly, The devil will be upon them, and having drawn them out of the way, will either still mislead them, or else cut their throats and steal all, or hold them, if possible he may, from returning unto God; as in the prodigal son.

Reason 4. Fourthly, Their own consciences will be upon them, and it is with them as with a child that plays truant, his heart throbs, he hath no peace: so a Christian, whether he prosper or not prospers, he hath no peace, he eats not, he sleeps not in peace. The uses briefly are two.

Use 1. Is this true? It first teacheth us to do as the church doth, *to examine ourselves when troubles come,* when the Lord sends officers to arrest us, sets dogs upon us to fetch us in. When we meet stirs and storms abroad, when wicked men bark and brawl, when they tyrannize and task, when good men look strangely on us, when God hides his face, and our consciences be not comfortable unto us, oh, then, let us ask ourselves the question, where am I? what have I done? wherein have I been negligent? This, this is that which God aimeth at. Therefore he makes our paths uncomfortable, to the end we should examine our vaunts; therefore he turneth loose wicked men, that we might inquire. This is that which will work us patience in all provocations, drive us to repentance, and bring us home; this will make one lay his face in the dust, and rather justify God, than charge him foolishly. Therefore let us not fret or chafe at men, their pride, malice, &c., but say, why doth living man fret? He suffers for sin: Lament. iii. 1, *et seq.*, say with the church here, 'I kept not mine own vine: and this hath hurt me.' And then howsoever God's people may sometimes smart for not keeping their vines, and performing their own duties; yet those crosses sting not, but comfort; they then ere long abound with joy, peace, increase of love and watchfulness, which are let in most an end by former negligences. God saw his people drowsy, worldly, secure, and therefore is constrained to send persecution, so that if evils be upon us, we have cause to say, 'I kept not mine own vine;' time was when I was idle all day in the vineyard, and did nothing, and yet I am too negligent.

* That is, 'thickets' = difficulties.—G.

Use 2. Secondly, Here see *what is the best way to prevent crosses.* All crosses be rods, as Christ speaks in the gospel, and scourges. Now if a child will do well, what father will whip him? If we will learn the lessons of our salvation, Christ, God will not scourge us; if we would follow the shepherd and not stray, what need dogs run at us? Why then, let us know the duties of our place and do them, and keep ourselves close to them, for all our safety, peace, comfort, lieth there. Our place is a ship on the seas. Now two ways we fail in our course. First, by out-running our callings. We grow too far over-busy, and indeed this is most incident to the church in her first beginning. She is then too nimble with others, and too busy; her zeal, as she thinks, carries her captive. Secondly, by running too slowly. This is incident to Christians of riper years. After a while they slack, cooling apace, and it is with us as with children, so eager to go to school at first, that there is no quiet, but after hardly* drawn. So it is with us. Amend, amend therefore these: turn neither to the right hand nor the left; for if thou doest, thou art like to smart for it. Then up and upon your callings as Christians, as masters, as servants, as magistrates, as husbands, as wives. Every one hath a vine to look to, look to your callings; and then whatsoever befall you, 'if you suffer not as evil doers, blessed are you,' 1 Peter iii. 14.

* That is, 'with difficulty.'—G.

NOTES.

(*a*) P. 96.—'They dwelt in tents, covered with hair (as Solymus and [as] Pliny speaks).' The tents of the Kedareens, a nomadic tribe of North Arabia (Gen. xxv. 13, Isa. xxi. 17), were and still are made of coarse cloth obtained from the shaggy hair of their black goats (Rosenmüller, Orient. iv. 939; Saalschütz, Archäologie der Hebräer, Erster Theil. p. 63). Cf. Guisburg among modern, and Robotham and Trapp among early, commentators *in loco*. For Sibbes's references to Pliny, see Natural History, lib. vi. c. 28; and for Solinus (not Solymus), c. 26; *i. e.*, Caius Julius Solinus, who has been called the 'ape of Pliny,' for the large use he makes of that writer's works. Among the many services to our early English literature by Arthur Golding, was a translation—racy and finely touched—of Solinus.

(*b*) P. 96.—'For the meaning, . . . we will not be prejudicial to any man's opinion.' Commentators named in above, note *a*, will shew the various 'opinions,'—the Puritans having much quaint fancy, and not less quaint lore. G.

MIRACLE OF MIRACLES.

MIRACLE OF MIRACLES.

NOTE.

'A Miracle of Miracles' originally appeared as a thin 4to, in 1638. The title-page is given below of the second edition (1656). It was appended to the Commentary upon 2 Corinthians chap. iv. See note Vol. IV., page 308. Cf. Memoir, Vol. I. pp. cxxv. for remarks of Fuller. G.

A
MIRACLE
OF
MIRACLES:
OR,
Christ in our Nature.

Wherein is contained
The Wonderfull Conception, Birth,
and Life of Christ, who in the fulnesse of
time became man to satisfie divine Justice
and to make reconciliation between
God and Man.

Preached to the honourable Society of
Grayes Inne, by that godly and faithfull Minister of Jesus Christ, *Richard Sibbes*, D.D.

Phil. 2. 5.

He made himselfe of no reputation, and took upon him the forme of a servant, and was made in the likenesse of men.

LONDON,
Printed by *W. H.* for *John Rothwell*, at the Sign
of the Beare and Fountaine in Cheapside, 1656.

MIRACLE OF MIRACLES.

(FIRST SERMON.)

The Lord himself shall give a sign; behold a virgin shall conceive, and bear a son, and shall call his name Immanuel.—ISAIAH VII. 14.

THE Jews at this time were in a distressed condition, by reason of the siege of two kings, Resin and Pekah : the one the king of Syria, the other the king of Israel. Whereupon the prophet labours to comfort them, and tells them that these two kings were but as two fire-brands, that should waste and consume themselves, and then go out. For confirmation thereof, because he saw the heart both of king and people astonished, he biddeth them 'ask a sign of things in heaven or earth.' No, saith king Ahaz, 'I will not tempt God ;' and making religion his pretence against religion, being a most wilful and wicked man, would not.

For he had framed an altar according to the altar which he had seen at Damascus, neglecting God's altar at Jerusalem as too plain and homely.

Man, unsubdued by the Spirit of God, admires the devices of men, and the fabric of his own brain.

And though this king was so fearful, that his heart, and the rest of their hearts, were 'as the leaves in the forest,' shaking, and trembling, and quaking at the presence of their enemies, and though he was surprised with fear and horror, seeing God his enemy, and himself God's enemy, and that God intended him no good, yet he would go on in his own superstitious course, having some secret confidence in league and affinity with other kings that were superstitious like himself. This, by the way.

We may learn by this wretched king, *that those that are least fearful before danger are most basely fearful in danger*. He that was so confident and wilful out of danger, in danger, his heart was 'as the leaves of the forest.' For a wicked man in danger hath no hope from God, and therefore is incapable of any intercourse with him. He will trust the devil and his instruments, led with a superstitious* spirit, rather than God: as this king had more confidence in the king of Syria, that was his enemy, and so shewed himself after, than in God. It is the nature of flesh and blood, being not sanctified by God, to trust in this means and that means, this carnal help and that carnal help, 'a reed of Egypt,' yea, the devil and lies, rather than to God himself.

The prophet, in an holy indignation for the refusing of a sign to confirm

* Cf. Acts xvii. 22.—G.

his faith that these kings should not do the church harm, breaketh forth thus: Know, O house of David, 'is it a small thing for you to weary men, but will you weary my God also?' God offers you a sign out of his love, and you dislike and contemn his blessed bounty. Therefore 'the Lord himself shall give you a sign.' What is that? 'A virgin shall conceive, and bear a son, and shall call his name Immanuel.'

From the inference, we may see *the conflict between the infinite goodness of God and the inflexible stubbornness of man;* God's goodness striving with man's badness. When they would have no sign, yet God will give them a sign. His goodness overcometh and out-wrestleth in the contention man's sinful strivings, his mercy prevails against man's malice.

To come to the text itself. 'Behold, a virgin shall conceive, and bear a son, and they shall call his name Immanuel.' It was not so much a sign for the present, as a promise of a miraculous benefit, which was to be presented almost eight hundred years after the prophet spake these words, even the incarnation of Christ, a miracle of miracles, a benefit of benefits, and the cause of all benefits. He fetcheth comfort against the present distress from a benefit to come. And to shew how this can be a ground of comfort at this time of distress, 'that a virgin shall conceive,' we must know that 'Christ was the Lamb slain from the beginning of the world,' Rev. xiii. 8. All the godly of the Jews knew it well enough, the Messiah being all their comfort. They knew that he was 'yesterday and to-day, and shall be the same for ever.' The church had in all times comfort from Christ. *Profuit antequam fuit:* he did good before he was exhibited in the world.

And thus the prophet applies the comfort to the house of David: 'A virgin shall conceive, and bear a son, and they shall call his name Immanuel, who shall be of the family of David.' And therefore the house of David shall not be extinct and dissolved. The reason is strong. You of the house of David are in fear that your kingdom and nation shall be destroyed; but know that the Messiah must come of a virgin, and of the house of David. And considering this mus certainly come to pass, why do ye fear, ye house of David?

Again, it hath force of a reason thus. The promise of our Messiah is the grand promise of all, and the cause of all promises; for all promises made to the church, are either promises of Christ himself, or promises in him and for his sake, because he takes all promises from God, and conveyeth them, and maketh them good to us. God maketh them, and performeth them in Christ and for Christ.

Now the reason stands thus, if God will give a Messiah, that shall be the 'son of a virgin,' and 'Emmanuel,' certainly he will give you deliverance. He that will do the greater will do the less. What is the deliverance you desire to the promised deliverance from hell and damnation, and to the benefit by the Messiah, which you profess to hope for and believe?

The apostle himself, Rom. ii. 8, reasons thus: 'God, that spared not his own Son, but gave him to death for us all, how shall not he with him give us all things?' If God will give Christ to be Emmanuel and incarnate, he will not stand upon any other inferior promises or mercies whatsoever.

Obj. But you will say, this promise was to come; and how could this confirm their faith for the present, that they should not be destroyed?

Ans. I answer, In regard of his taking our nature, he was 'to come,' yet Christ was always with his church before. They understood him in the 'manna;' he was the 'angel of the covenant.' They that were spiritually wise amongst the Jews, understood that he was the rock that went before them.

And again, it is usual in Scripture to give signs from things to come, as Isa. xxxvii. 30, 'The next year thou shalt eat that which groweth of itself,' &c., because where faith is, it maketh things 'to come' all one as if they were present.

And so we should make this use of the grand promises of Christ to comfort us against all petty matters and wants whatsoever. And to reason with the holy apostle, 'God spared not his only begotten Son, but gave him to death.' He hath given Christ, and will he not give things needful? Hath he given the greater, and will he stand with thee for the less? This is a blessed kind of reasoning. And so to reason from other grand things promised. God shall raise my body out of the dust and the grave, and cannot he raise my body out of sickness, and my state out of trouble? Cannot he raise the church out of misery? So saith St Paul, 2 Cor. i. 9, 'God that raised Christ, restored me again, that had received the sentence of death.' When we receive sentence of death in our persons, look to him that raised Christ from the dead, and to the grand promises to come. They before Christ comforted themselves in times of all distress by the grand promise of Christ 'to come.' But now the Messiah is come. And which may much more strengthen our faith, he hath suffered, and given his body to death for us; and therefore, why doubt we of God's good will in any petty matters whatsoever.

To come to the words more particularly, 'Behold, a virgin shall conceive, and bear a son,' &c.

You have diverse articles of our faith in these few words. As *Christ's conception* by the Holy Ghost, his being *born of the Virgin Mary*,' &c. You have here the *human nature* of Christ, 'A virgin shall conceive, and bear a son.' And the *divine nature* of Christ, his name shall be called Emmanuel, which signifieth also his office, 'God with us' by nature, and God with us by office, to set God and us at one. So you have divers points of divinity couched in the words, which I will only open suitable to the occasion.

'Behold.' This is the usual beacon set up, the usual harbinger to require our attendance* in all matters concerning Christ. And it hath a threefold force here. 'Behold,' as being a thing presented to the eye of faith. He mounteth over all the interim between the promise and the accomplishment, for faith knoweth no difference of times.

2. And then, it is to raise attention. 'Behold;' it is a matter of great concernment.

3. And not only attention, but likewise admiration.† 'Behold,' a strange and admirable thing. For what stranger thing is there than that a virgin should conceive, that a virgin should be a mother, and that God should become man.

We had need of strong grace to apprehend these strange things. And therefore God hath provided a grace suitable, above reason, and above nature, and that is faith. Reason mocketh at this. The devil knoweth it and envieth it. The angels know, and wonder at it. The soul itself, without a grace suitable to the admirableness of the thing, can never apprehend it. And therefore, well may it be said, 'Behold, a virgin shall conceive, and bear a son.'

'Behold, a virgin shall conceive, and bear.' And why a virgin? When God is to be born, it is fit for a virgin to be the mother. Christ was not

* That is, 'attention.'—G. † That is, 'wonder.'—G.

to come by the ordinary way of propagation. He was to come *from* Adam, but not *by* Adam; for he was to be sanctified by the Holy Ghost. Because he was indeed to be a sacrifice, and he must be without spot or sin himself, that was to offer himself for the sins of others. Therefore the foundation and ground of his nature must be pure and clean; and that is the foundation of all the purity of his life and conversation, and therefore a virgin.

This was typified in Aaron's rod, which budded though it had no root. No juice could come from a dry stick, yet by an almighty power the rod did bud. And so Moses's bush. It burned and did not consume. And that God that caused those things, caused a virgin to be a mother.

He enters into the womb of a virgin without any defilement at all, considering the Holy Ghost, from the Father and the Son, did purge and purify and sanctify that mass whereof the blessed body of our Saviour was made. The virgin afforded the matter, but the wise framer was the Holy Ghost. She was passive, the Holy Ghost was the agent.

Now, when did the virgin conceive? When upon the angel's coming to her and telling her 'that she was greatly beloved,' and that she should conceive; she assented, 'Be it so as the Lord hath spoken,' Luke i. 38. When she assented to the word, presently Christ was conceived; her faith and her womb conceived together. When her heart did conceive the truth of the promise, and yielded assent thereunto, her womb conceived at the same time also.

Obs. From hence learn something for ourselves: *It had been to little purpose though a virgin conceived Christ, unless Christ had been conceived likewise in her heart.* And there is no benefit by virtue of this conception to others, but to such as conceive Christ in their hearts also.

To which end our hearts must be in some measure made virgin hearts, pure hearts, hearts fit to receive Christ.

We must assent to promises of pardon and of life everlasting: 'Be it as the Lord saith.' A Christian is a Christian, and Christ liveth in his heart, at the time of the assenting to the promise. So that if you ask, When doth Christ first live in a Christian's heart? I answer, then, when the heart yieldeth a firm assent to the gracious promises made in Christ for the pardoning of sins and acceptation to the favour of God, and title and interest to life everlasting. For faith is the birth of the heart.

Christ was conceived in the womb of an humble and believing virgin. So that heart that will conceive Christ aright, must be a humble and believing heart: humble, to deny himself in all things; and believing, to go out of itself to the promises of God in Christ. When God by his Spirit hath brought our hearts to be humble and believing, to go out of themselves and believe in him, rest upon him and his promises, then Christ is conceived in our heart.

'Behold, a virgin shall conceive, *and bear* a son.' Here is the birth of Christ as well as the conception. Christ must not only be conceived in the womb, but also brought forth, because God must be manifested in the flesh; as St Paul saith, 'Great is the mystery of godliness, God manifested in the flesh,' 1 Tim. iii. 16. If he had only been conceived, and not brought forth, he had not been manifested. He was to do all things that befitted a Mediator.

And therefore he went along with us in all the passages of our lives. He was conceived as we are, remained in the womb so many months, born as we are born, brought into the light as we are; away therefore with idle, monkish devices and fond conceits, that affirm the contrary!

He was like to us in all things, 'sin excepted;' conceived, brought forth, hung upon the breast as we, an infant as we; hungry, and thirsty, and suffered as we.

And as he was in all things like to us, so in everything that was in him there was something extraordinary; as he was a man like to us, so he was an extraordinary man. He was conceived, but of a virgin, which is extraordinary. He was born as we are, but there his star appeared, and the wise men came to adore and worship him. He was poor as we are, but there were beams of his Godhead appeared. When he was poor, 'he could command a fish to furnish him,' Mat. xvii. 27. He died as we die, but he made the 'earth to quake, the veil of the temple to rend,' when he triumphed on the cross, Mat. xxvii. 51. All which declared he was more than an ordinary person.

And so we must all conceive Christ, and bear Christ in our words and actions. It must appear that Christ liveth in us; it must appear outwardly to man what we are inwardly to God. Our whole outward life must be nothing but a discovery of Christ living in us. 'I live, yet not I, but Christ liveth in me,' saith St Paul, Gal. ii. 20; which should appear by word, conversation, and action. Our lives should be nothing but an acting of Christ living in our souls.

This is not a mere analogical truth, but it floweth naturally. Whosoever are to have the benefit of his birth and conception, Christ sendeth into their heart the same Spirit that sanctified the mass whereof he was made, and so frameth a disposition suitable to himself. He sets his own stamp upon the heart. As the union of his human nature to the divine was the cause of all other graces of his human nature, so the Spirit of God, uniting us to Christ, is the cause of all grace in us. If we have not the Spirit of Christ, we are none of his.

'And shall call his name Emmanuel.' Many things might be observed concerning the ordinary reading of the words. Some read, '*She* shall call his name Emmanuel,' because he had no father; others, 'His name shall be called Emmanuel;' but they be doubtful, therefore I leave them (*a*).

But 'Jesus' was his name; therefore how can it be said, he shall be called 'Emmanuel'?

The meaning is, he shall be 'Emmanuel,' and shall be accounted and believed to be so; he shall be God with us indeed, and shall shew himself to be so; for in the Hebrew phrase, the meaning of a thing imports the being of the thing. The like phrase is in Isa. ix. 6, 'To us a child is born, to us a son is given; and his name shall be called Wonderful, Counsellor, the everlasting Father, the Prince of peace;' that is, 'He shall be believed to be so, and shall shew himself to be so, and shall be so indeed.' The like you have, because it is an answer to the cavil of the Jews, which object he was not called 'Emmanuel:' 'Judah shall be saved, Israel shall dwell safely; and this is his name, whereby he shall be called, The Lord our righteousness,' Jer. ii. 3. For indeed he is Jehovah our righteousness, and we have no righteousness to stand before God with but his. Divers other places of Scripture there be of the same nature; but these two are pregnant, and therefore I name them for all the rest.

Besides the conception and birth of Christ, you have here likewise the *divine nature* of Christ and the *offices* of Christ; for Emmanuel is a name both of nature and office.

It is a name of his nature, God and man; and of his office, which is to

* Qu. 'naming'?—ED.

reconcile God and man. We could not be 'with God,' but God must first be 'man with us.' We were once with God in Adam, before he fell; but there being a breach made, we cannot be recovered again till God be with us. He must take our natures, that he may reconcile our persons.

Now, Christ is 'Emmanuel;' first, in regard *of nature*, 'God with us,' or God in our nature. The pure nature of God, and the base nature of man, that were strangers ever since the fall, are knit together in Christ. What can be in a greater degree of strangeness, except the devil's, than men's unholiness and God's pure nature? Yet the nature of man and of God being so severed before, are met together in one Christ; so that in this one word 'Emmanuel' there is heaven and earth, God and man, infinite and finite; therefore we may well prefix 'behold.'

A true Saviour of the world must be 'God with man, whether we consider the greatness of the good we are to have by a Saviour, or the greatness of the evil we are to be freed from by a Saviour, both which do enforce that he must be Emmanuel, God with us.

I. (1.) First, The greatness of the good which we are to have, for he is to be God and man together, to satisfy the wrath of God, to undergo a punishment due to sin as our surety. He must give us title to heaven, and bring us thither, and who can do this but God?

(2.) Besides, secondly, he must know our hearts, our wants, our griefs, our infirmities; he must be everywhere to relieve us; and who can do this but God?

(3.) So, thirdly, in regard of evil, which we are to be freed from. He is to defend us in the midst of our enemies; and who is above the devil, and sin, and the wrath of God, and all the oppositions that stand between us and heaven, but God? So in regard of the good, in regard of the evil, and in regard of the preservation to an eternal good estate, and freedom from eternal evil, he must be 'Emmanuel, God with us.'

These grand principles are enough to satisfy in this point.

II. And, secondly, as he must be God, so there was a necessity of his being man. Man had sinned, and man must suffer for sin, and 'without blood there was no remission,' Heb. ix. 22; and then, that he might be 'a merciful and pitiful Saviour,' Heb. ii. 17, he must take that nature on him that he meaneth to save. There must be a suitableness and sympathy; suitableness, that the head and the members, the sanctified and the sanctifier, may be both of one nature; and a sympathy, that he might be touched with human infirmities.

III. Thirdly, This God and man must be one person; for if there were two persons, God one distinct person and man another, then there were two Christs, and so the actions of the one could not be attributed to the other.

As man died and shed his blood, it could not have been said that God died; but because there was but one person, God is truly said to die, though he died in man's nature, for he took man's nature into unity with his person; and whatsoever either nature did, the whole person is said to do; and therefore Christ is a Saviour according to both natures, as God and as man; for he was to suffer, and he was to overcome, and satisfy in suffering. He was not only to hear our prayers, but to answer them. Both natures had an ingredience* into all the work of mediation.

God died, and God suffered, and supported the manhood, that it might uphold the burden of the wrath of God, that it might not sink under it.

* That is, 'entrance.'—G.

And so in all his actions there was concurrence of divinity and humanity; the meaner works being done by the manhood, the greater works by the Godhead, so making one 'Emmanuel, God with us.'

For God must bring us to heaven by a way suitable to his holiness, and therefore by way of satisfaction; and that cannot be but by God equal with himself.

And that is the reason why the apostle joins together 'without Christ, without God,' Eph. iii. 12; that is, they that know not Christ God-man, to reconcile God and man, have nothing to do with God. For the pure nature of God, what hath it to do with the impure nature of man, without Emmanuel, without him that is God-man, to make satisfaction?

But now that Christ hath taken our nature, it is become pure in him, and beloved of God in him. And God in him is become lovely, because he is our nature; yea, in Christ, God is become a Father: 'I go to your Father, and my Father,' John xiv. 28. His nature is sweet to us in Christ; our nature is sweet to him in Christ; God loveth not our nature, but first in him in whom it is pure. And then he loveth our nature in us, because, by the Spirit of Christ, he will make our natures like to Christ's; and therefore we may conceive of God as Emmanuel, God well pleased with us, and we well pleased with him. Out of Christ we are angry with God, and he angry with us. We could wish there were no God, and choose rather to submit to the devil, to be led by his spirit to all profaneness and licentiousness. We have a rising against God and his image; and whatever comes from God, the proud, unmortified heart of man swelleth against it. But when the heart once believeth that Christ, Emmanuel, God with us, hath satisfied God's justice, now, God is taken by the believing heart to be a Father 'reconciled in Jesus Christ,' 2 Cor. v. 18. And we are taught to be his sons. And our nature is more and more purified and cleansed, and made like the pure nature of Christ; and so by little and little the terms between God and us are more sweet, till we get to heaven, where our nature shall be absolutely perfect and purged by the Holy Spirit. So that he is Emmanuel, God with us, to make God and us friends, which is two ways: first, *by satisfaction*, taking away the wrath of God; and then, secondly, *by the Spirit;* for God sendeth his Spirit into our hearts, to fit us for friendship and communion with him, when we have something of God in us.

From hence many things may be spoken, partly for instruction and comfort. I will name a few.

1. First of all, it is to be wondered at, and we cannot wonder enough, though we were angels, and had natures larger than they are, *at the marvellous mercies and love of God, that would stoop so low*, as that God in the second person should take our nature and become one with us. It is marvellous love that he would be one with us by such a means as his own Son, to make peace between him and us. It is a marvellous condescending and stooping in the Son to take our nature. When there be better creatures above us, that he would let pass all above us, and take our nature, that is dust, into unity of his person; that earth, flesh and blood, should be taken into one person with the Godhead, it is wonderful and marvellous.

He took not the nature of angels; so that we be above angels, by the incarnation of Christ. Because he took not the angels' nature, they are not the spouse of Christ, but every believing Christian is the spouse of Christ. He is married to Christ; he is the head, we the members. He is the husband, we the spouse; and therefore we may stand in admiration of the love of God, in taking our natures on him.

It requires hearts warmed by the Spirit of God to think of and admire these things answerable to their natures. The angels, when Christ was born, could not contain, but break out, 'Glory to God on high, on earth peace, good will towards men,' Luke ii. 13, 14, because there was then peace; peace between God and us, and by consequence with all the creatures, which do but take part with God and revenge his quarrel.

These things be matters of admiration; and we shall spend eternity in admiration thereof in another world, though here our narrow hearts can hardly conceive it. But what we cannot believe by understanding, as things above nature, let us labour to understand them by believing. Desire God we may believe them, and then we shall understand them to our comfort.

'Emmanuel, God with us.' If God be with us in our nature, then he is with us in his love; 'and if God be with us, who shall be against us?' Rom. viii. 31. For this Emmanuel hath taken our nature for ever; he hath taken it into heaven with him. God and we shall for ever be in good terms, because God in our nature is for ever in heaven, as an intercessor appearing for us. There is no fear of a breach now; for our Brother is in heaven, our Husband is in heaven, to preserve an everlasting union and amity between God and us. Now, we may insult* in an holy manner over all oppositions whatsoever. For if God be with us in our nature, and by consequence in favour, who shall be against us? and therefore with the apostle, 'let us triumph,' Rom. viii. 37, *seq.*

Let us make use of this Emmanuel in all troubles whatsoever, whether of the church or of our own persons. In troubles of the church; the church hath enemies, hell, and the world, and Satan's factors; but we have one, Emmanuel, God with us, and therefore we need not fear. You know whose ensign it is, whose motto, *Deus nobiscum* is better than *Sancta Maria*. *Sancta Maria* will down when *Deus nobiscum* shall stand (*b*).

I beseech you, therefore, let us comfort ourselves in regard of the church, as the prophet in the next chapter, verse 7, comforts the church in distress: 'He shall pass through Judah; he shall overflow and go over; he shall reach even to the neck: and the stretching out of his wings shall fill the breadth of thy land,† O Emmanuel.' It may seem a kind of complaint, 'The enemy stretcheth out their wings over thy land, O Emmanuel;' which may teach us in the person of the church to go to Emmanuel: Remember the enemies of thy church spread their wings over thy land and people; O Emmanuel, thou seest the malice of the enemy, the malice of antichrist and his supporters. He is the true Michael, that stands for his church. And then in the tenth verse, 'Take counsel together, and it shall come to nought; speak the word, and it shall not stand: for God is with us.' And as the church before Christ came in the flesh, much more may we, now he is come in the flesh, insult over all. Let all the enemies consult together, this king and that power, there is a counsel in heaven will disturb and dash all their counsels. Emmanuel in heaven laugheth them to scorn. And as Luther said, 'Shall we weep and cry when God laugheth?'‡ He seeth a company of idolatrous wretches, that conspire together to root out all protestants from the earth, if it lay in their power. They that are inspired with Jesuitical spirits, the incendiaries of the world,

* That is, 'triumph.'—G.
† In margin, 'church.'—G.
‡ Cf. Vol. I. page 126.—G.

have devoured all Israel and Christendom in their hopes; but the church, which is Emmanuel's land and freehold, sees it, and laughs them to scorn. God can dash all their treacherous counsels.

And so in all personal trouble whatsoever, 'Emmanuel, God with us,' is fitted to be a merciful Saviour. He was poor, that he might be with the poor. He took not on him an impassible nature, but he took our poverty, our miserable nature. He is poor with the poor, afflicted with the afflicted, persecuted with the persecuted. He is deserted with them that be deserted: 'My God, my God, why hast thou forsaken me?' He suffers with them that suffer; he hath gone through all the passages of our lives. In the beginning of it he was conceived and born; and he hath gone along with us, and is able to pity and succour us in our poverty, in prison, in bonds, in disgrace, in our conflict with God, in our terror of conscience, in all our temptations and assaults by Satan. He was tempted himself by Satan, for this purpose, that Emmanuel might in all these be merciful.

Let us not lose the comforts of this sweet name, in which you have couched so many comforts. In the hour of death, when we are to die, think of Emmanuel. When Jacob was to go into Egypt, saith God, 'Fear not, Jacob; go, I will go with thee, and bring thee back again,' Gen. xlvi. 3; and he did bring him back to be buried in Canaan. So fear not to die; fear not to go to the grave, Emmanuel hath been there. He will go into the grave; he will bring us out of the dust again; for 'Emmanuel' is 'God with us,' who is God over death, over sin, over the wrath of God, God over all, blessed for evermore; and hath triumphed over all. So that 'what shall separate us from the love of God in Christ Jesus?' Rom. viii. 35.

He is not only God with us in our nature, but he is God for us in heaven at all times. He is God in us by his Spirit. He is God amongst us in our meetings: 'Where two or three be gathered together in my name, I will be in the midst of them,' Mat. xviii. 20. He is God for us to defend us, for he is for us in earth, for us in heaven, and wheresoever we be, specially in good causes. And therefore enlarge our comforts as much as we can.

And shall not we then labour to be with him, as much as we can? All spirits that have any comfort by this Emmanuel, they are touched on by his Spirit, to have desires to be nearer and nearer to him.

How shall I know he is my Emmanuel, not only 'God with us,' but God with me? If by the same Spirit of his that sanctified his human nature, I have desires to be nearer and nearer to him, to be liker and liker to him; if I am on his side; if I be near him in my affections, desires, and understanding; if I side not against the church, nor join in opposition against the gospel; if I find inwardly a desire to be more and more with him, and like to him; if outwardly, in the place where I live, I side with him, and take part with his cause: it is a sign I have interest in him. And therefore let us labour to be more and more with Christ and with God in love and affections, in faith, in our whole inward man, because he is in us.

We must know this Emmanuel doth trust us with his cause, to speak a good word for him now and then, to speak a word for his church, and he takes it ill if we neglect him: 'Curse ye Meroz, because he came not out to help the Lord,' Judges v. 23. God trusteth us, to see if we will be on his side; and calls to us, as Jehu did, 'Who is on my side? who?'

2 Kings ix. 32. Now, if we have not a word for the church, not so much as a prayer for the church, how can we say, 'God with us,' when we are not used to speak to God by way of prayer, nor to man but by way of opposition and contestation? By this therefore examine the truth of our interest in Christ.

Those that intend to receive the communion must think, Now, I am to be near unto Christ, and to feast with him. Christ is with us in his word, in the sacrament. There is a near relation between the bread and the wine, and the body and blood of Christ. Now, the true child of God is glad of this most special presence of Christ. All true receivers come with joy to the sacrament. Oh, I shall have communion with Emmanuel, who left heaven, took my nature into a more near hypostatical union, the nearest union of all; and shall not I desire the nearest union with him again that can be possible? Oh, I am glad of the occasion, that I can hear his word, pray to him, receive the sacrament. Thus let us come with joy, that we may have communion with this Emmanuel, who hath such sweet communion with our nature, that our hearts may be as the Virgin's womb was to conceive Christ. I beseech you, enlarge these things in your meditations.

And because we know not how long we may live here, some of us be sick, and weak, and all of us may fall into danger we know not how soon, let it be our comfort that God is Emmanuel. He left heaven, and took our nature to bring us thither, where himself is. When times of dissolution come, consider, I am now going to him to heaven, that came down from thence to bring me to that eternal mansion of rest and glory. And shall not I desire an everlasting communion with him? God became man that he might make man like God, partaking of his divine nature, in grace here and glory hereafter. Shall not I go to him that suffered so much for me? Therefore saith St Paul, 'I desire to be dissolved, and to be with Christ,' Philip. i. 23; which is the effect of Christ's prayer, 'Father,' saith he, 'my will is, that where I am they may be also, John xvii. 24. And in this God heareth Christ, that all that believe in him shall be where Christ is, as he came down from heaven to be where we are. Lay up these things in your hearts, that so you may receive benefit by them.

NOTES.

(*a*) P. 110.—'Many things might be observed concerning the ordinary reading ol the words.' Cf. Dr Joseph Addison Alexander, Dr Henderson, and Maurer *in loco*, for the different readings and interpretations.

(*b*) P. 114.—'You know whose ensign it is, whose motto, *Deus nobiscum* is better than *Sancta Maria*.' Watchwords of the English and Spaniards respectively in the war of the Armada. G.

MIRACLE OF MIRACLES.

(THE SECOND SERMON.)

Behold, a virgin shall conceive, and bear a son, and shall call his name Immanuel.—ISAIAH VII. 14.

THE occasion of these words we have heard. The church was in great distress under two mighty kings, that threatened great matters; but indeed were but two smoking firebrands, that went out of themselves. Ahaz, being a wicked king (and wickedness being always full of fears, fearful *in* trouble, though not *before* trouble, for they that be least fearful of trouble be most fearful in trouble), and God intending comfort to the church, the prophet bids him ask a sign. Ahaz, out of guiltiness of conscience and stubbornness together, would ask none. God intended to strengthen his faith, and he would not make advantage of the offer; and therefore the prophet promiseth a sign, the grand sign, the sign of all signs, the miracle of all miracles, the incarnation of the Messiah.

Doct. By the way, I beseech you let me observe this: *It is atheistical profaneness to despise any help, that God in his wisdom thinketh necessary to prop and shore* our weak faith withal.* And therefore, when many out of confidence of their own graces and parts refuse the sacrament,—God knowing better than ourselves we need it,—unless it be at one time of the year, and refuse the other ordinance of preaching, which God hath sanctified, they seem to know themselves better than God, who out of knowledge of our weakness, hath set apart these means for the strengthening of our graces. And as Ahaz, refusing God's help, provoked God by it, so these must know they shall not escape without judgment, for it is a tempting of God, and proceedeth from a bad spirit of pride and stubbornness.

How this promise of the Messiah could be a sign to them to comfort them, we spake at large. We will now deliver something by way of addition and explication.

The house of David was afraid they should be extinct by these two great enemies of the church; but, saith he, 'A virgin of the house of David shall conceive a son,' and how then can the house of David be extinct? Secondly, heaven hath said it; earth cannot disanul it. God hath said it, and all the creatures in the world cannot annihilate it. It was the promise made to Adam, when he was fallen. It run along to Abraham, and afterwards to the patriarchs; so that it must needs be so.

* That is, 'support.'—G.

It was the custom of the men of God, led by the Spirit of God, in these times, in any distress, to have recourse to the promise of the Messiah, as for other ends, so for this, to raise themselves up by an argument drawn from the greater to the less. God will give the Messiah, God will become man. 'A virgin shall conceive a son;' and therefore he will give you less mercies.

I note this by the way for this end, to teach us a sanctified manner of reasoning. Was it a strong argument before Christ's coming, the Messiah shall come, and therefore we may expect inferior blessings? And shall not we make use of the same reason, now Christ is come in the flesh, and is triumphant in heaven? 'God having given Christ, will he not give all things necessary whatsoever?' Rom. viii. 32. Shall the reasonings before Christ's coming be of more force than these be, now Christ is come, and is in glory, appearing in heaven for us.

Beloved, it should be a shame to us, that we should not have the sanctified art of reasoning, to argue from the gift of Christ, to the giving of all things needful for us.

The ground of this reason is this, All other promises, whatsoever they are, are secondary to the grand fundamental promise of Christ. All promises issue from a covenant founded in God-man. Now covenants come from love; and love is founded in the first person, loved, and the foundation of all love. Therefore, if God giveth Christ the foundation of love, and out of love makes a covenant, and as branches of the covenant giveth many promises, then, having made good the main promise of all, Jesus Christ, will he not make good all the rest? And therefore we should have often in our hearts and thoughts, the accomplishment of all promises in Christ, and from thence make use of the expectation of all inferior promises; for they issue from that love of God in Christ, which is fully manifested already.

We have spoken of the preface, 'Behold,' which is a word usually prefixed before all the passages of Christ; his birth, his resurrection, his coming again. And great reason.

For what do we usually behold with earnestness? Rare things, new things, great things, especially if they be great to admiration, and that concern us nearly; useful things, especially if they be present. And is any thing rarer than that, 'A virgin shall conceive, and bear a son'? Then the incarnation of Christ. Never was the like in nature, never the like in heaven or earth, that God and man should be in one person. It is a rare thing, a new thing, it is great to wonderment; and therefore in the ninth chapter of this prophecy, 'His name shall be called Wonderful,' Isa. ix. 6, as in many other respects, so wonderful in his conception and birth.

And then all is for us. '*To us* a child is born, *to us* a Son is given,' in the same chapter. For us, and for us men, he came down from heaven. And then to the eye of faith all these things are present. Faith knoweth no difference of time.

Christ is present to the eye of faith now. We see him sacrificed in the sacrament and in the word. Faith knoweth no distance of place, as well as no distance of time. We see him in heaven, as St Stephen, sitting at the right hand of God for the good of his church, Acts vii. 56; and therefore 'behold.'

If ever any thing were, or shall be great, from the beginning of the world to eternity, this is great, this is wonderful. And if any thing in the world be fit for us; and if any thing dignifieth the soul, and raiseth the soul above itself, it is this wonderful object.

We, out of our weakness, wonder at poor petty things, as the disciples at the building of the temple, 'What stones are these?' Mat. xiii. 1. We wonder at the greatness of birth and place, but, alas! what is fit for the soul, being a large and capable thing, to stand in admiration of? Here is that that transcendeth admiration itself. 'Behold, a virgin shall conceive a son;' and therefore attend to the great matter in hand. This I thought good to add to what I formerly delivered in that particular.

'A virgin shall conceive a son,' &c.

You need not go farther than the text for wonders; for here are two great ones, a virgin a mother, and God man.

So in the words you have the *conception* and the *birth of Christ*, his human nature, his divine nature and his office, to reconcile God and us in one.

As he is God in our nature—he took our nature into communion of person—so his office is to bring God and man together; his two natures is to fit him for his office. God and man were as much distant terms as could be, unless between the devil and God. And therefore God-man in one person must perform the great office of bringing such as were in such opposite terms together.

Of his conception by the Virgin Mary we spake sufficiently, only we will add this for further explication. A further type of this was in the birth of Isaac. Isaac, you know, was born of a dead womb. Christ was conceived of a virgin, and in a manner far more improbable than the other. Isaac was the 'son of the promise,' Christ was 'the promised seed,' both in some sort miraculously born; for indeed it was a true wonder that Isaac should be born of a dead womb, and here that a virgin should conceive. Sarah had nothing to supply moisture and juice to the fruit; and so here was nothing of a man to further Christ's conception.

I will shew why there must be this kind of conception of Christ, which will help our faith exceedingly.

1. First, Christ must be *without all sin of necessity;* for else when he took our nature, stubble and fire had joined together. 'God is a consuming fire,' Heb. xii. 29;' and therefore the nature must be purified and sanctified by the Holy Ghost in the womb of the Virgin.

2. And then again, in the conception, there must be a *foundation of all obedience*, active and passive, and of all that was afterwards excellent in Christ. If there had been any blemish in the foundation, which was his conception, if he had not been pure, there had been defect in all that issued from him, his active obedience and passive obedience, for every thing savours of the principle from whence it cometh. And therefore it was God's great work in this strange conception, that sin might be stopped in the root and beginning; nature might be sanctified in the foundation of it. And so that he might pursue sin from the beginning to the end, both in his life, by living without sin, and also in his death, by making satisfaction for sin.

And therefore ground our faith on this, *that our salvation* is laid on one that is mighty, God-man, and on one that is pure and holy. And therefore in his obedience active, holy; and in his obedience passive, holy.

Again, He came to be a surety for us; and therefore he must pay our whole debt, he must pay the debt of obedience; he must pay the debt of punishment. Now obedience must come from a pure nature, and his death must extend to the satisfying of an infinite justice. And therefore he must be conceived of the Holy Ghost in the womb of a pure virgin.

And we must know that in this conception of Christ there were two or three things wherein there was a main difference between Christ and us.

(1.) Christ was in his human nature altogether *without sin*. We are sinful in our nature.

(2.) Again, Christ's human nature *had always subsistence in the divine*, and it was never out of the divine nature. As soon as his body and soul were united, it was the body and soul of God. Now our natures are not so.

(3.) And then *in manner of propagation*. His was extraordinary altogether. Adam was of the earth, neither of man, nor woman; Eve of man, without a woman; all other of Adam and Eve; Christ of a virgin, and without a man. But setting aside his subsistence in the second person, and extraordinary means of propagation, Christ and we are all one; he had a true human body and soul, and all things like ourselves, sin and the former differences excepted.

Why Christ must be man we have already heard. He became man to be suitable to us in our nature, and to sympathise in all our troubles.

And shall call his name Immanuel. 'He shall call his name Immanuel,' saith the New Testament, Mat. i. 23. That is, he shall be Immanuel indeed, and shall be known to be, and published to be so. Whatsoever hath a name is apparent.* Christ was before he took our flesh; but he was not called Emmanuel. It did not openly appear that he was God in our nature; he was not conceived in the womb of a virgin. They before Christ, knew that he should come, but when he was conceived and born, he was then called Emmanuel.

There were divers presences of Christ before he came. He was in the 'bush' as a sign of his presence. He was in the 'ark' as a sign of his presence. He was in the prophets and kings as a type of his presence. He took upon him the shape of a man as a representation of his presence, when he talked with Abraham and the patriarchs. But all this was not 'God with us,' in our nature. He took it on him for a time, and laid it aside again. But when he was Emmanuel, and was called and declared so to be, he took on him our nature, never to lay it aside again. He was born in our nature, brought forth in our nature, lived in our nature, died in our nature, was crucified in our nature, became a curse for us in our nature, buried in our nature, rose in our nature, is in heaven in our nature, and for ever will abide there in our nature.

All their faith before he came in the flesh was in confidence that he should take our flesh in the fulness of time. Now came the time when he was called Immanuel; and then the word became flesh and took our nature on him.

From hence, that God took our nature on him in the second person, come divers things considerable.

(1.) For, first, it appears *that he hath dignified and raised our nature above angels*, because he hath taken the seed of Abraham and not of the angels;—a wonderful advancement of our nature, for God to be with us, to marry such a poor nature as ours is; for the great God of heaven and earth to take dust into the unity of his person. If this may not have a 'behold' before it, I know not what may.

(2.) To join altogether. For the great God of heaven and earth, before whom the angels cover their faces, the mountains tremble, and the earth quakes, to take our flesh and dust into unity of his person, and for such

* That is, 'manifested' (?).—G.

ends, to save sinful man, and from such misery as eternal misery, from such great enemies, and then to advance him to such great happiness as we are advanced, to take Christ, Emmanuel, in the whole passage of his mediation, and there is ground of admiration indeed.

(3.) But consider it specially *in the raising and advancing of our natures to be one with God.* Shall God be God* with us in our nature in heaven, and shall we defile our natures that God hath so dignified? Shall we live like beasts, whom God hath raised above angels? Let swearers, beastly persons, and profane hypocrites, either alter their courses, or else say they believe not these truths. Shall a man believe God hath taken his nature into unity of his person, and hath raised it above all angels, and can he turn beast, yea, devil incarnate, in opposition of Christ and his cause? What a shame is this! Can this be where these things are believed? A Christian should have high thoughts of himself. What! shall I defile the nature that God hath taken into unity of his person?

(4.) And as he hath dignified, and raised, and advanced our nature so highly, so likewise *he hath infused and put all the riches of grace into our nature*; for all grace is in Christ that a finite nature can be capable of, for Christ is nearest the fountain. Now, the human nature being so near the fountain of all good, that is, God, it must needs be as rich as nature can possibly be capable of. And is not this for our good? Are not all his riches for our use?

And therefore seeing our nature is dignified by Emmanuel, and enriched exceedingly by his graces next to infinite—for our human nature is not turned to God as some are conceited; it is not deified, and so made infinite —yet as much as the creature can be capable of there is in Christ-man, and so shall we defile that nature?

(5.) And from hence, that our nature *is engrafted into the Godhead,* it followeth, that what was done in our nature was of wonderful extension, force, and dignity; because it was done when our nature was knit to the Godhead, and therefore it maketh up all objections. As,

How could the death of one man satisfy for the deaths of many millions?

Secondly, It was the death of Christ, whose human nature was engrafted into the second person of the Trinity. For, because they were but one person, whatsoever the human nature did or suffered, God did it. If they had been two persons, God had not died, God had not suffered, God had not redeemed his church.

And therefore the scripture runneth comfortably on this: 'God hath redeemed the church with his own blood,' 1 Peter i. 18. Hath God blood? No. But the nature that God took into unity of persons hath blood; and so being one person with God, God shed his blood. It is God that purchased a church with his blood. It is God that died. The Virgin Mary was mother of God, because she is the mother of that nature which was taken into unity with God.

Hereupon comes the dignity of whatsoever Christ did and suffered. Though he did it in our nature, yet the Godhead gave it its worth, and not only worth, but God put some activity, some vigour, and force into all that Christ did. It doth advance Christ Mediator according to both natures. And from hence ariseth communication of properties, as divines call it, which I will not now speak of. It is sufficient to see that whatsoever was done by Christ was done by God, he being Emmanuel, and therefore had

* Qu. 'one'?—Ed.

its worth and dignity to prevail with God. Hence cometh a forcible reason, that God must satisfy divine justice, because it was the action of a God-man. His great sufferings were the sufferings of the second person in our nature. And hereupon from satisfaction and merit comes reconciliation between God and us. God being satisfied by Christ, God and we are at terms of peace. Our peace is well founded if it be founded in God the Father, by God the Son taking our nature into unity of his person. These things must have influence into our comforts and into our lives and conversations, being the grand articles of faith. And therefore we ought to think often of them. We must fetch principles of comfort and holiness from hence, as from the greatest arguments that can be. Therefore I desire to be punctual* in them. God is Emmanuel, especially to make God and us one. Christ is our friend in taking our nature to make God and us friends again.

Quest. But how doth friendship between God and us arise from hence, that Christ is God in our nature? I will give two or three reasons of it.

(1.) First, It is good reason that God should be at peace with us, because *sin, the cause of division, is taken away.* It is sin that separateth between God and us, and if sin be taken away, God is mercy itself, and mercy will have a current. What stoppeth mercy but sin? Secondly, take away sin, it runneth amain. Christ therefore became Emmanuel, God with us, because 'He is the Lamb of God that taketh away the sins of the world.'

Before Adam had sinned there was sweet agreement and communion between Adam and God, but sin, that divided between God and the creature. Now Christ having made satisfaction for all our sins, there can be nothing but mercy.

(2.) Again, Christ is a fit person to knit God and us together, *because our nature is pure in Christ,* and therefore in Christ God loveth us. After satisfaction God looks on our nature in Christ, and seeth it pure in him. Christ is the glory of our nature. Now if our nature be pure in our head, which is the glory of our nature, God is reconciled to us, and loveth us in him that is pure, out of whom God cannot love us.

As Christ is pure, and our nature in him, so he will make us pure at length.

(3.) Thirdly, Christ being our head of influence, *conveyeth the same Spirit that is in him to all his members,* and by little and little by that Spirit purgeth his church, and maketh her fit for communion with himself, for he maketh us 'partakers of the divine nature,' 2 Peter i. 4. He took our frail human nature, that we might partake of his divine nature; that is, of his divine qualities, to be holy, pure, humble, and obedient as he was.

And thus Christ being a head, not only of eminence to rule and govern, but of influence to flow by his Spirit into all his members, is fit to be a reconciler, to bring God and us together, partly because our nature is in him, and partly because he doth communicate the same Spirit to us that is in himself, and by little and little maketh us holy like himself.

I hasten to the main use of all.

(4.) Then God the Father and we are in good terms, *for the second person is God in our nature for this end, to make God and us friends.* There is a notable place of Scripture which I note for the expression's sake, he speaking there of a 'day's-man:' 'There is no day's-man between us, that might lay his hand on us both,' Job ix. 33; that is, a middle person to lay his hand on the one and the other. Now Christ is the middle person, as the

* That is, 'exact,' 'accurate.'—G.

second person in the Trinity. And then he is God and man, and therefore he is fit to be mediator, to lay his hand on both sides, on man as man, on God as God. And Christ is a friend to both, to God as to God,* and to man as man, and therefore he is fit to be an umpire, to be a day's-man, to be a mediator. And he hath done it to purpose, making that good in heaven that he did on earth. And therefore labour to make a gracious use of all this. I know nothing in the world more useful, no point of divinity more pregnant, no greater spring of sanctifying duty, than that God and man were one, to make God and us one. He married our nature, that he might marry our persons.

Use 1. And if it be so that God and man are brought to terms of reconciliation on such a foundation as God-man, then ought *not we to improve this comfort?* Have we such a foundation of comfort, and shall not we make use of it? Shall we have wisdom in the things of this world, and not make use of the grand comforts that concern our souls?

Use 2. But how shall *we improve it?* In all our necessities and wants go to God. How? Through Christ, God-man, who is in heaven making intercession and appearing for us by virtue of his satisfaction made on earth, and therefore we may go boldly to the throne of grace to God, being reconciled by God. God hath God at his right hand, appearing for us, and shall we be afraid to go to the throne of grace? When we want strength, comforts, or anything, go to God, in the mediation of Emmanuel, and then God can deny nothing to us that we ask with the spirit of faith in the name of Christ.

I beseech you, therefore, let this be the main use, continually to improve the gracious privileges we have by Emmanuel. Our nature is now acceptable to God in Christ, because he hath purified it in himself, and God's nature is lovely to us, because he hath taken our nature. If God loved his own Son, he will love our nature as joined to his Son, and God's nature is lovely to us. He took our flesh upon him, and made himself bone of our bone. And shall not we like and affect that which was so graciously procured by Emmanuel.

Consider of it, and let it be ground of reverent and bold prayer, in all our wants to go to God in Emmanuel.

Use 3. Let us make use of it likewise in behalf of the church. The church is 'Emmanuel's land,' as ye have it in the next chapter: verse 8, 'The stretching out of his wings shall be the breadth of thy land, O Emmanuel.' The church of the Jews was Emmanuel's land, but then it was impaled within the pale of the Jews. But now the Gentiles are taken in. The church is scattered and spread abroad over the whole earth. And therefore go to God in behalf of the church. Thou tookest our nature into unity of thy person, that thou mightest be a gracious and a merciful head. And therefore look in mercy on thine own mystical body, the church. They, before Christ came in the flesh, who had the spirit of faith, knew the church of the Jews could not be extinct, because Emmanuel was to come of it.

And we may know the church shall never be destroyed till the second coming of Christ, because those things are not yet performed that God hath promised, and must be performed. And therefore we may go as boldly to Christ, and spread the cause of the church before him now, as they spread the cause of the Jews before him then; look upon thy land, look upon thy church, O Emmanuel.

* Qu. 'as God'?—Ed.

That there must be a church we must believe, and we cannot believe a *non ens*. We must have ground for our faith, and therefore never fear that heresy shall overspread the face of the church, 'Emmanuel's land' shall be preserved by some way or other, though not perhaps by the way we expect. God must have a church to the end of the world. The gospel must get ground. Antichrist must fall. God hath said it, and man cannot unsay it. And therefore in all estates of the church spread its cause before Emmanuel.

When Emmanuel came once, the church of the Jews wasted. Therefore, if you will have good arguments against the Jews, this is a good one to convince them, that Christ is come in the flesh. The church of the Jews was to continue till Emmanuel, but the church of the Jews hath ceased to continue, and is now no church. There is now no family of David, and therefore Emmanuel is come.

And for a further use, let us have thoughts of the second coming of Emmanuel, as they had thoughts of the first. Christ was called the consolation of Israel at his first coming, and in the New Testament it is everywhere expressed a sign of a gracious man to look for the appearing of Jesus Christ, and to love it. Now let us comfort ourselves that this Emmanuel will appear in our flesh ere long; let us wait for the 'consolation of Israel.' Emmanuel came down to us, to take our nature upon him, and to satisfy God's wrath, that he might take us to heaven with himself, and that we might be for ever with him in glory. And therefore let us, if we would make a true use of Emmanuel, desire to be with him. Christ delighted, before he came in the flesh, to be with the sons of men, and he is with us now by his Spirit, and so will be with his church to the end of the world; and shall not we be with him as much as we may? Indeed, he loved our nature so much, that he descended from the height of majesty to take our misery and business* upon him, and shall not we desire to be with him in glory?

There be divers evidences whether we have any ground of comfort in this Emmanuel or no. This shall be one.

(1.) We may know we have benefit by the first coming of Emmanuel, *if we have a serious desire of the second coming, if we have a desire to be with him;* if, as he came to us in love, we have desires to be with him in his ordinances as much as may be, and in humble resignation at the hour of death. How shall we be with him here? Be with him in thoughts, in meditation, in faith and prayer; meet with him wheresoever he is. He is in the congregation: 'Where two or three are gathered together in his name,' he is amongst them, Mat. xviii. 20. Be with them in all things where he vouchsafeth his gracious presence. It is the nature of love to desire perfect union, and therefore the Christian soul, touched with the Spirit of God, will desire 'to be dissolved and to be with Christ, as best of all,' Philip. i. 23; 'Come, Lord Jesus, come quickly,' Rev. xxii. 20; and therefore in the hour of death is willing to resign himself to God that he may go to Emmanuel, and enjoy his presence, that left the presence of his Father, to take our nature, and to be with us on earth.

(2.) But the main thing I desire you to observe, *is matter of comfort from this Emmanuel,* that now he having taken our nature upon him, that he might take our persons into unity of his mystical body, we might have comfort in all conditions. For he took our nature upon him, besides his other ends, that he might take our persons to make up mystical Christ.

* Qu. 'baseness'?—ED.

He married our nature to marry our persons. And therefore if he did it for this end, that we might be near him as our nature is near him, shall not we make it a ground of comfort, that our persons shall be near Christ as well as our natures?

As Christ hath two natures in one person, so many persons make up one mystical Christ, so that our persons are wonderfully near to Christ. The wife is not near* the husband, the members are not nearer the head, the building is not nearer the foundation, than Christ and his church are. And therefore comfort ourselves in this; Christ is Emmanuel, God with us in our nature. And will he suffer his church to want, that he hath taken so near to himself? Can the members want influence when the head hath it? Can the wife be poor when the husband is rich? Whatsoever Christ did to his own body, to his human nature taken into the unity of his person, that he will do in some proportion to his mystical body.

I will shew you some particulars. He sanctified his natural body by the Holy Ghost, and he will sanctify us by the same Spirit. For there is the same Spirit in head and members. He loveth his natural body, and so as never to lay it aside to eternity. And loveth his mystical body now in some sort more, for he gave his natural body to death for his mystical body. And therefore, as he will never lay aside his natural body, he will never lay aside his church, nor any member of his church. For with the same love that he loved his natural body he loveth now his mystical members. As he rose to glory in his natural body, and ascended to heaven, so he will raise his mystical body, that it shall ascend as he ascended. I beseech you, therefore, consider what a ground of comfort this is. God took our nature on him, besides the grand end of satisfaction, that he might make us like himself in glory, that he might draw us near to himself. And therefore now Christ being in heaven, having commission and authority over all things put into his hand; he 'having a name above all names in heaven and earth, that at the name of Jesus every knee should bow,' Philip. ii. 10, 11; that is, every subjection should be given; will he suffer any member of his body to suffer more than he thinks fit? No; seeing he is in heaven and glory, for his church's good. For all that he hath done and suffered is for the church and the church's use.

To conclude all, let us consider what we are. Let not a Christian be base-minded. Let him not be dastardly in any cause that is good, or God's. Let him be on God's side. Who is on his side? A Christian is an impregnable person. He is a person that can never be conquered. Emmanuel became man to make the church and every Christian to be one with him. Christ's nature is out of danger of all that is hurtful. The sun shall not shine, the wind shall not blow, to the church's hurt. For the church's head ruleth over all things, and hath all things in subjection. Angels in heaven, men on earth, devils in hell, all bow to Christ. And shall anything befall them that he loveth, unless for their greater good? Therefore though they may kill a Christian and imprison him, yet hurt him they cannot. 'If God be on our side, who can be against us?' Rom. viii. 30. But God is on our side, and on what grounds? God-man hath procured him to be our friend, he hath satisfied God, and therefore if we believe, we be one with Christ, and so one with God.

We have many against us. The devils are against us, the world is against us, to take away the favour of God, to hinder access to him in prayer, to stop the church's communion with God, and hinder the sweet

* Qu. 'nearer'?—Ed.

issue of all things that befall us as far as they can.'' But their malice is greater than their power. If God should let them loose, and give the chain into their own hand, though they seem to hurt, yet hurt they cannot in the issue. And shall not we make use of these things in times of distress? Wherefore serve they but to comfort us in all conflicts with Satan, and in all doubtings that arise from our sinful hearts? Answer with this, 'If God be with us, who can be against us?' If any be against us, name them; if not, be satisfied. And therefore come life, come death, Christ is our surety. He layeth up our dust, keepeth our acts* in the grave; and will Christ lose any member? 'Fear not, Jacob, to go down into Egypt, for I will bring thee back again.' So fear not to go down into the grave. The Spirit of God will watch over our dust, and bring us to heaven. Therefore fear nothing. God will be with us in life and death, yea, for ever; and we shall be for ever with the Lord, as the apostle saith in the Thessalonians, 1 Thes. iv. 17. And that issue of all that Emmanuel hath done, Christ was one in our nature, that he might bring God and us into favour, that we may be for ever with him in heaven, that we may be for ever with the Lord, which is the accomplishment of all the promises.

* Qu. 'bodies'?—Ed.

THE TOUCHSTONE OF REGENERATION.

THE TOUCHSTONE OF REGENERATION.

NOTE.

'The Touchstone of Regeration' forms No. 24 of 'The Saint's Cordials' of 1629, one of those displaced by others in the after-editions. Its separate title-page is given below.* G.

* THE
TOVCHSTONE
OF
REGENERATION.

In One SERMON.

WHEREIN THE VNDOVBTED
and true Signes of Regeneration are discovered, and the
Soule pointed to such a frame and temper of disposition,
which having attained, it may be comforted.

Prælucendo Pereo.

VPRIGHTNES HATH BOLDNES.

GALAT. 5. 22.

But the fruit of the Spirit is love, joy, peace, long-suffering, gentlenesse, goodnesse, faith.
Meeknesse, temperance, against such there is no law.

LONDON,
Printed in the yeare 1629.

THE TOUCHSTONE OF REGENERATION.

The wolf also shall dwell with the lamb, and the leopard shall lie down with the kid: and the calf, and the young lion, and the fatling together; and a little child shall lead them. The cow and the bear shall feed; their young ones shall lie down together: and the lion shall eat straw like the ox. And the sucking child shall play upon the hole of the asp, and the weaned child shall put his hand upon the cockatrice's den. They shall not hurt nor destroy in all my holy mountain, &c.—ISAIAH XI. 6–9.

I HAVE formerly, in divers sermons upon this scripture,* declared that it, by way of prophecy, foretelleth what shall be the fruits of Christ's kingdom under the gospel, shewing that miraculous change Christ should make upon men, shadowed out in this scripture under the similitude of beasts, as lions, wolves, bears, leopards, &c. The sum whereof is, that God will take from us that fierceness, malignity, and bitterness of nature in us, and bring us, in place thereof, to a loving, sweet, mild, and meek society together.

Many things already have been particularly handled out of this text; as,

1. First, from the condition and natural estate of men, wherein they may be called beasts, lions, serpents, &c.

2. And secondly, of that change Christ thereafter makes in us, which indeed is a miraculous change. This was the first thing handled.

First, That in every soul which shall come to heaven there must be a change.

Secondly, You have heard whereof the change must be; not of the substantial parts of a man's body, but of the corrupt qualities of the mind; or, if you will have it so, of the soul, and all the powers thereof.

Thirdly, I shewed upon whom this change was made—look verse 9; it is made upon the church of God in this world, which in my text is called God's holy mountain. So also, Heb. xii. 22, the church is called the mountain of God.

The fourth thing considered was, by whom this change was made; even by the spring-head of all. From the God of grace it cometh, and floweth to us by Jesus Christ our Lord, who was 'God manifested in the flesh.'

Fifthly, We inquired then by what means this change is wrought. This we shewed to be by the knowledge of the law, &c. And this is the reason

* These sermons have not been preserved; but cf. Vol. II. pp. 437–517.—G.

which is added why there shall be no hurt nor destroying in all this holy mountain, because the earth shall be full of the knowledge of the Lord as the waters cover the sea; meaning there shall then be an abundant knowledge, a deep knowledge, and a well-seasoned permanent knowledge, which shall keep every one within their limits, every one knowing his duty, so maintaining a mutual peace in all this holy mountain.

Next, now sixthly and lastly, for ending of this text, I am to speak of *the marks of this change;* or rather, I may call them, the effects of this change, the certain and infallible signs of the same. Yet look not that here I will undertake to handle a commonplace, and shew unto you all the signs of regeneration; only I will contain myself within this text, contented to shew you those which this scripture affordeth, which whosoever hath, may assure themselves of the rest. Wherein, ere we proceed further in particular, let us first make the general; that is, a taming, a subduing, a taking away of the fierceness and cruelty of our corrupt nature. This throughout the text is the main mark of the change; which will yet be more evident by the particulars.

What meaneth this, 'that the lion shall lie down with the calf, that the leopard shall lie down with the kid,' when they shall come from their own kind to another strange generation, as it were? What meaneth this, that they shall trust one another with their young ones? that the lion shall no more prey upon blood, as in times past, but eat straw with the ox? that the serpent shall let the little child play upon the hole of his den? and all these to be so tamed that a little child should lead them, take them, and rule them? What meaneth all this but this,

That it is an eminent and infallible mark of regeneration to have the violence and fierceness of our cruel nature taken away. This is a sure sign; for this look Rom. i. 29, how naturally the heart is filled with all maliciousness and sinful cruelty, which to be subdued and tamed is a special grace; so Gal. vi. 7–9, and Eph. iv. 17, *et seq.* There you may see the fruits of the old man to be idolatry, witchcraft, hatred, variance, wrath, strife, sedition, &c.; there you may also read of a change, of a renewing of the new man in love, joy, peace, long-suffering, gentleness, goodness, faith, meekness, temperance, against whom there is no law. There you may see what a great alteration this change maketh, and what the marks of corruption are.

But yet there it is worth the marking, that here in these places the Holy Ghost calleth for works of mercy, to perform duties to men, meekness, temperance, patience, &c., not mentioning duties directly due unto God. Why are these duties towards men so much urged, but to shew that our corruption is not so much manifested in the worship of God as in works of mercy to men? Therefore it is that all the prophets do so call for works of mercy, that Christ himself so inviteth thereunto, because men may deceive the world with a counterfeit show of outward justice to God, but in works of mercy there is no means to escape, Micah vi. 7. 'If the first-born, or ten thousand rivers of oil,' with a number of the like sacrifices, might please God, all would be given for the sin of the soul; but the Lord calleth for works of mercy, meekness, and to walk humbly with God.

Now the cause why men are so hardly brought to be merciful to others, and more easily to works of piety towards God's worship, I take to be, because, as it is John viii. 44, 'the devil is a liar and a murderer from the beginning.' Now his prime quality being to be a murderer, he worketh so in the children of disobedience, that, like unto him, they have a murderous disposition to shew no mercy, to relieve none, which sheweth that such are poisoned with the same sorts of poison wherewith he is infected. Thus you see there must be a general meekness in all who are heavenly wise, far from this murderous disposition. So James iii. 13, he saith, 'Who is a wise man, and endued with knowledge among you? let him shew out of a good conversation his works, with meekness of wisdom.' There he speaks of a devilish wisdom, which comes not from above, 'which is full of envying and strife; but the wisdom which is from above is first pure, then peaceable, gentle, and easy to be entreated, full of mercy and good fruits,' &c. Thus he shews by what coat-armour* a Christian must be known; how the sons of God must be discerned. This is the general mark: if that natural cruelty and bitterness bred in us be taken away, and meekness, gentleness, and the like, put in place thereof, this for the general is a sure sign that the change is made, regeneration is begun. Now I come to speak of these marks and infallible signs of regeneration contained in this text, which must be in some measure in the party regenerate. The first is,

1. *Harmlessness.*

Which, though it be a thing that runs along the body of my text, and is last named, yet here I bring it first, because it is partly implied in all; for in this, that it is said 'the little child shall play upon the hole of the asp,' and take no hurt, what doth this imply but a mild and harmless disposition, contrary to our natural fierceness and cruelty? It is written, Prov. iii. 27, 'Withhold not good from them to whom it is due, though it be in thy power to do it.' As I take it, by good in that place is meant works of mercy; that we must be so like God as may be in works of charity. He that refuseth works of mercy to those in need, he is a murderer. How can a man say he is renewed, unless in some sort he be like unto God in mercifulness? We see the wicked, it is a prime quality in them to do mischief; they delight in evil; it is meat and drink to them to do wickedly; they are still musing on some cursed deed or other. But it is a property of God's child to be harmless. Yet for further trial of this grace note we two signs of this sign.

First, *If we would not do evil, though we might do it unseen of any creature:* as, when a little child shall lay his hand on the cockatrice's den, the serpent might sting, and yet, unseen of any, pull in the head again. This, likewise, is a true sign of harmlessness—when, though a man may do some hurt unseen, yet he will not. Thus was not Herod; he abstained a-while from beheading of John Baptist, but it was more for fear of the people, than any other cause. Therefore, Christ, in another place, calleth him a fox, Luke xiii. 32, so far was he from this harmlessness we speak of. Thus we see the doctrine of Christ may be preached to a-many, but the power of the same extendeth but to a few.

Beloved, I would have all of us to consider this. We live, all of us, in the kingdom of Christ; but where is the man that, though he might do evil unseen, yet would not do it? We have a worthy pattern of this grace in Joseph, Gen. xxxix. 9, who, though he might have done evil unseen, yet would not, 'Oh,' saith he, 'how shall I do this evil, and sin against God?' and offend God. Oh, how many are there which withhold the passions of their tongues, and the violence of their hands, only because they are not able to work mischief! How many men now smooth the hands of God's people, and say as they say, only because they dare not,

* A heraldry term.—G.

and cannot do them mischief, who, if that opportunity served, would sting them! This will shew a change to be made, and we to be harmless, if, when opportunity of doing evil is offered, yet we can abstain.

A second sign of this sign is, *when, though a man hath provocation to do evil, yet he will abstain.* This is a sound trial. We see it is said, that the little child shall play upon the hole of the asp, and the weaned child shall lay his hand upon the cockatrice's den. Is not here provocation, and yet no hurt done? In this the Holy Ghost would give us a sure sign indeed. Many men are of a mild natural disposition, and so may, perhaps, forbear mischief when it is in their power. And so, many men, which are merely natural, may bear with religion for some by-respects. But, provoke them, and then you shall have them all of a fire, ready to fly in your face. What religion is there in this? For to do good for good, and evil for evil,—this, Christ says, even publicans may do: there is no thank in this; but if, when we are provoked, we can forbear to revenge, this is a blessed thing. If there be true love in our hearts, the apostle says, 1 Cor. xiii. 5, that it is not 'provoked.' And it is written, Isa. liii. 7, that Christ 'he was afflicted, oppressed, yet opened he not his mouth: he is brought as a lamb to the slaughter, and as a sheep before her shearers is dumb, so opened not he his mouth.' This he did, thus holy men have done, and this, if we would see life, we must do. Yet we see, though we should be like sheep, even they will now and then push at one another; but this is not with much violence; besides that, it doth not endure. The apostle wills us to forbear, forgive one another; so this strife hath an end. Therefore, if I cannot forgive in a small matter, but that either my tongue must fly out in words, or the heart be set on mischief, this is a woeful estate. If this be all our goodness, surely it is miserable goodness; here is no harmlessness: suspect thy estate. But the true goodness and blessed estate is to follow that counsel of our Saviour Christ, 'Bless them that curse and persecute you,' &c., Mat. v. 54. This, then, is harmlessness, when there is afforded unto us both secret occasion and provocation to do evil, and yet we abstain. So much for the first.

Now I pass to the second, which is

2. *Sociableness.*

Which is set out in the whole body of my text. But with whom is it that this society holdeth? Not of lions with lions, or wild beasts with wild beasts; and yet many of these cannot endure one another: for the rhinoceros and the unicorn, when they meet, they fight; so doth the wild horse and the bear; but if at length they agree, this sociableness of theirs is of wicked beasts one with another. But this is more, that the wolf and the lamb, the cow and the bear, the leopard and the kid, the calf and the young lion, shall lie down together, and that the little child shall play upon the hole of the asp. This implies, not only a simple society, as among wild beasts, but a sociableness, as it were, among those of another generation.*

To apply this unto ourselves: there be good bands of our sociableness one with another, both reason and speech; for, naturally, all of us have been lions, bears, and wolves, and unsociable haters of goodness in others. Now, then, this sociableness with those former servants of God, who have been called, this is a very sure mark of this change in us; so the apostle speaks, 1 John iv. 14, 'By this we know we are translated from death to life, because we love the brethren.' And so Christ, our master,

* That is, kind or species.—G.

speaketh, 'By this shall all men know that ye are my disciples, if ye love one another.' This nearness imports consanguinity. It is common, in the Scripture, to call the children of God brethren.

[1.] *No man can love a saint, as a saint, but a saint.* This is a sure sign of this sign. For this cause, the apostle to Philemon, he rejoiceth for his faith to God, and love to the brethren, ver. 5. And so again, ver. 7, it was his joy that the brethren were comforted. The reason hereof is, because, as there is a natural enmity among us by sin, to shew a difference, the children of God must rejoice in unity.

Further, a true trial of sociableness is, *when men will joy to sort themselves with those with whom formerly they have been most unsociable, and whose company they most loathed:* as, first, we see the wolf doth lie down with the lamb, which is a slow beast; secondly, the leopard with the kid; thirdly, the young lion and the calf, for these fat beasts are, for the most part, a prey to the lion; fourthly, the cow and the bear, for the cow is a prey to the bear; fifthly, the serpent is especially an enemy to mankind, as, Gen. iii. 15, God said, 'I will put enmity betwixt thy seed and that of the woman.' This, I confess, is chiefly meant of the devil, yet the extent thereof reacheth thus far unto us, who naturally loathe serpents, that so great shall this sociableness be, that even a little child shall play upon the hole of the asp, and receive no harm. Now, when all these are reconciled thus, where formerly was special envy, this is a true trial of sociableness. For further proof hereof, note an idolater when he is converted, none are so dear unto him as God's servants. The voluptuous man, having left his lust, loves none so well as Christ's people; the riotous man, having left his excess, loveth none so well as the sober; the atheistical, profane man delighteth, being changed, so much in none as the truest worshippers: so, we see, though before conversion men may roar like bears, as Isa. lix. 11, yet, being tamed, it is said, Jer. xxxi. 9, that then they shall come weeping, &c., and draw into sociableness with others formerly hated. When some men come to be of our religion, and yet keep such about them as are not sincere, this is no good sign. But, take this for a sure rule, that no man is truly turned unto God, but he that loveth the society he formerly hated.

[2.] A second sign of this sign is, *to love every brother, yea, though it were to lay down our life for a brother.* But how is this implied?—'The calf and the young lion shall lie down together.' If the young lion can endure not to raven on the calf, then it can endure any other of that kind. Beloved, it is a special grace to love all the brethren, without respect of persons. So the prophet David, Ps. cxix. 63, says, 'I am a companion of all those that fear thee.' Here is implied, not to love some one brother, but the brethren. I confess, for some special cause a man may rejoice and delight more in the company of some, than of others; as David, Ps. xvi. 2, 'But to the saints that are in the earth, and to the excellent, all my delight is in them.' So that, I say, for some special grace, or graces, one may love one better than another. Thus Christ loved John best, being called the beloved disciple, which was not for any special grace in John, but from a kind of sympathy in natures, which many times, from a hidden cause, produceth much love. But, if we have respect of persons, as it is, James ii. 3, we are to blame. If we respect a great rich man, with a little grace, more than a poor man with a great deal; or, if we respect not a poor man as a rich, with alike graces. We see, Acts viii. 14, *et seq.*, when Philip preached at Samaria, Simon Magus did cleave also to him; but it seems he did not stick so close to Philip for his graces, as it appeareth he did for somewhat in his person. Brethren, if partially we admire some for their persons, it is suspicious. It is dangerous too much to admire fleshly excellency, for those gifts of goodness in the same. If I do truly love goodness in rich apparel, why do I not also love it in rags? Beloved, if we love not thus, we love with the parrot, our love is not true; there ought ever to be the like love in kind, though not in measure.

Now I come to the third mark, which is,

3. *Constancy.*

How is this implied? By dwelling and lying together. You shall have beasts meet together, by chance, yet part asunder quickly again; but when they lie and dwell together in constant abode, this is a sure sign. You shall have many companions go with a man, for fashion's sake, to the church, and yet leave going ere it be long; you shall have some men sick, and then, like a serpent frozen in winter, which casts his skin, you shall have them cast their skin a little, that is, send for a preacher, or such a man, make confession of their sins, saying, Oh, if God will spare me, I will become a new man, I will never do as I have done, I will never any more haunt such company; but yet, when he is well, within a month after, where shall you find him? Not with the lambs, but with the bears, and wolves, and lions. Thus, when we can constantly hold on with an unmoved, constant affection, to the children of God, this is a sure sign.

But I hasten to the next. The fourth is,

4. *Inwardness.*

How is this implied? Their little ones shall lie down together. There is nothing so dear unto all creatures as their young ones, of which they are most jealous. There are no creatures which are not jealous and tender of their young ones, chiefly the bear, which is most of all tender, fighting sometimes, even to the death, in defence of her young ones. But this, that the little ones of the bear, and of the cow, shall lie together, this implies an inwardness together, such an inwardness as I think is meant, Acts iv. 32, where it is said, 'These dwelt together, and possessed all things in common use.' Yet not losing that title they had unto the same as their own; and, ver. 34, their charity is described, that 'no man lacked anything which another had, but in necessity all things were common.' This, their united charity to help others, was their little ones which did lie together. And this, also, must be our trial, if whatsoever is dear and near unto us, even our young little ones, if they be ready to lie down together with the necessities of others, this is inwardness. Think of this also, that this dwelling and lying together is a thing free, not any way constrained. This is a trial of our sociableness, not when we are tied together in a cage, but at liberty, and then we dwell together; for many keep company now together, both in dwelling and lying together, which would fly out if time served. We read in the book of Esther, that when the Jews had the better hand, many of their enemies joined with them, but not of love, but because they had the better hand of their enemies, Esther x. 3; and so, when the people of God came from Egypt, many of the people, because of their prosperity, did join with them; and now also, in the time of the gospel, I appeal to the consciences of many among us, whether they do not lie down with us for fear now. Let no man think amiss of me for that I thus speak, for now such join with us, who, if they had another day, would shew other strange tricks unto us; and, as it is, Jer. xviii 18, 'let us smite him with our tongues;' so many of these are ready to smite us with their tongues now, who seem to be inward with us. What would these do if the day were their own? Beloved, such men cannot be of God, who thus do malign the servants of God. You may couple beasts together in a chain, but, being loose, they run asunder again; so many now, like such beasts among us, are tied with chains for a while, but untie them once, and all is gone. Many of these, when once they are loose, keep company with bears and wolves.

But I hasten to the fifth, which is,

5. *Tractableness.*

How is this implied? A little child shall lead them and rule them. It is a true sign of grace when we become easy to be ruled and brought in compass. We read of lions to have been tamed to draw in chariots; this is tractableness. So when a poor servant of God hath nothing but his simplicity to bring us in, this is tractableness, when we can be content to be brought in even by men inferior to us, that are simple and of mean gifts. So when the husband can endure to be brought home by the wife, being wiser and of more knowledge than she; when the wife can be content to be brought home by the daughter or maid-servant, like Job, who despised not the counsel of his own servants, Job xxxi. 13; this is tractableness. To be brief, when men can be content to come to their old, ancient food.

6. *Simplicity,*

Which is the sixth and last sign of this change. This is a sure trial of regeneration. But how is this implied? That the lion shall eat straw like the ox. Beasts at the beginning were not thus cruel as since the fall of man, but did feed on grass, &c.; so the Holy Ghost doth imply, that when our state is come back to that it was at the beginning, as near as may be, that is to say, when the lost image of God is so restored in us that a man is come to his former food again, that as then, so now, he feeds on the contemplation of the wisdom of God, the justice of God, the mercy of God, the greatness and power of God, the abundant goodness and truth of God, &c., this is a sure sign of regeneration. Cain he was bloody, and fed upon blood; therefore, as it is John iv. 32, when a man is come thus far, that he hath meat which one seeth not, whereupon he feedeth, holy thoughts, holy meditations, &c., when he can suck the breasts of God's consolations, whereon his children feed, to draw virtue from the same unto himself, this is a sure sign that a man is most happy, and born again. In a word, as the apostle speaks, when thus striving for masteries, he becomes temperate in all things, 2 Tim. ii. 5, this is a sure mark and infallible. Now, I come to the uses, which are two:

1, For consolation; 2, for exhortation.

Use 1. The first thing is, for the place. But how shall this be brought in? What of the place? I say a trial by the place, where all shall be in: 'In my holy mountain.' It shall be therefore for trial of religion. Where the mountain is, there is the true religion, there is the church; look where you will, still it is in the mountain. Many now-a-days cry out and keep a stir to know where the true church is, and I affirm, it is in the mountain. So that in this I may say of the church, as sometime Elijah did speak of the true God, 1 Kings xviii. 24, 'Let him which answereth by fire be the true God;' so I say of the church and of true religion, Let that be the true religion that hath most fire in it, that which sheweth forth most piety and holiness. The papists they say they are the true church; but look on God's mountain, look which religion makes a man most mild, and tames his fierce nature, which takes away a man's dogged disposition, for a dog barks and then he bites, so the barking and biting of the Romish Church shews them not to be in the mountain; their church doth allow biting. Was there ever any doctrine like theirs, which teaches a man to murder his own king, to keep no faith, &c.? Was there ever any religion like theirs, that set poisoning afoot? which also set princes at variance? The last sacrament of theirs will never be forgotten, when that peace was proclaimed between both religions, then one would have thought all was well and ended, there were ten thousand massacred at one place called Labius, eighty slain with one sword, with many other of their cruelties; and the gunpowder treason, so odious and monstrous as the like hath not been heard (*a*). The like I may say of Garnet's part, who must not reveal this treason, because it was done in confession (*b*). Oh monstrous times, that confession should be so abused to barbarous, inhuman, matchless cruelty! If ever you take our religion to teach such things, though popery should prevail against us, as God forbid, we will claim no more right of the mountain. Never did, nor never will, our religion teach taking up of arms against our king, cruelty against superiors and others; but, by the contrary, our religion teacheth a man to suffer with and for Christ. It may be some cruel men may be among us, but we look what we profess, and teach that men with meekness must suffer; all this that I have said much concerneth us. If God will have no cruelty to be taught nor reign where he loveth, see what a thing it is to be thus cruel. If we be thus fierce and savage, let us not deceive ourselves, we are not yet come to the mountain of God; for, saith the prophet, 'They shall not hurt nor destroy in all my holy mountain.'

Use 2. Now I come to the second use, *for exhortation*. There is yet a little of the lion and the bear remaining in every one of us, which shews us to be not thoroughly renewed, yet I do not say that those who are angry are not regenerate; but I say, if this do rage and rule with us, all is not safe and well. A good tree sometimes may have some bare or crab stock on some side of the tree, that bears crabs, and yet the tree be good; but this must not be predominant. The apostle says, 'If there be divisions and dissensions among you, are you not carnal?' 1 Cor. iii. 3. I speak not of some little faults,—God help us! in all our natures there is much frailty,—but of such that rule in us. It is a wonder to see how uncharitable many men are to censure others for every little fault, when they themselves swallow down camels, I mean gross sins. Some man, for refusal of riotous excess, though he be full of excellent parts, yet say they, Such a one is a Puritan; and so again, if an honest man or woman fall by infirmity into some sin, Oh, say some, lo, now his hypocrisy discovers itself. Shall men be thus censured, as though perfection were on earth? This is far from covering thy brother's nakedness, this is far from St Paul's rule, 'to restore such a one with the spirit of meekness,' Gal. vi. 1. Beloved, God forbid that I should harden any man in sin; I speak these things only that since a little of the bear and the lion will still be in every one of us so long as we shall live in this world, let us learn to bear one another's infirmities, otherwise if thou chafe, censure, brawl, and chide still, I can give thee no comfort of thy state. Can such a one be regenerate? What! is the bear, and the lion, and the wolf come among us again? To conclude, as abroad, so look to thy conversation at home, among thy servants and friends; take heed thy authority deceive thee not, to think thou mayest set thy heart to raging and plotting envy and strife, to be angry and chafing still. If such raging be at home in thy house, I can give thee no comfort; as thou wouldest look for the evidences of thy lands, as certainly must thou look for this mildness, meekness, and this change in thyself. Mark this still, when a good man hath found out his sins, he is bound and doth lament for them; when he hath offended, he turneth the stream of his anger that way. So that, I say, if a man be thus bitter of his tongue, look what St James saith of such a one: 'That man's religion is in vain that cannot bridle his tongue,' James i. 26. 'Be not,' saith he, 'my brethren, many masters; for we have one Master,' &c., James iii. 1. If these contentions remain still among us, our stock yet bears crabs; we may suspect ourselves. But withal take with you this caution, let not men think it cruelty to execute the justice of God upon malefactors; but if magistrates do it cruelly, let them look to it, they shall dearly pay for it. The prophet David saith, Ps. ci. 1, 'I will sing of mercy and judgment,' &c. So for war, I call not that cruelty to fight God's battles; but if any man without a commission will take up the sword, he shall perish by the sword; so Christ saith unto Peter, Mat. xxvi. 52. This point is needful to be pressed still, because men cry Mercy, mercy; but, I say, judgment must be mingled; for as there may be a cruel justice, so there may be a cruel mercy, to suffer the lions to devour the sheep. We must, like God, temper them together, and make justice and mercy go hand in hand, that so the God of mercy may deal with us as we with others.

Thus you see what minds we must have if we look for an habitation in God's holy mountain. God, for his Christ's sake, grant unto us this tamedness and meekness, this thorough change of our cruel nature, that so we may come unto the assurance to be of that number for whom Christ died, seeing his Spirit hath wrought such an effectual, thorough change in us.

NOTES.

(*a*) P. 136.—'Ten thousand massacred at Labius,' &c. We have little doubt that there is a misprint here, and that the reading should be, 'there were ten thousand massacred; at one place in Calabria eighty slain with one sword.' The first reference we suppose to be to the massacre in Paris on St Bartholomew's Day, 1572. Davila estimates the number slain in that city on that day at ten thousand. The other reference we suppose to be to a massacre at Montalto, in Calabria, in 1560 when eighty-eight men had their throats cut by one executioner.

(*b*) P. 136.—'Garnet's part.' Cf. note *ooo*, Vol. III. page 535. G.

THE DISCREET PLOUGHMAN.

THE DISCREET PLOUGHMAN.

NOTE.

'The Discreet Ploughman' forms No. 26 of 'The Saint's Cordials' of 1629. It was withdrawn from the other two editions. The separate title-page is given below.*—G.

* THE

DISCREET

PLOVVMAN.

In One Sermon.

WHEREIN THE FRVITLES VA-
nity, and needlesse carking and vexing Cares of Gods
Children under the hand of God is reproved, and better Directions given them what to doe:

Informing them for the time to come, how to attaine a more
speedy and easie end of their Afflictions.

Prælucendo Pereo.

Vprightnes Hath Boldnes.

Iames 1. 4.

But let patience have her perfect worke, that ye may be perfect and intire, lacking nothing.

Iam. 4. 10.

Humble your selves in the sight of God, and he shall lift you up.

LONDON,
Printed in the yeare 1629.

THE DISCREET PLOUGHMAN.

Give ye ear, and hear my voice; hearken, and hear my speech. Doth the ploughman plough all day to sow? doth he open and break the clods of his ground? When he hath made plain the face thereof, doth he not cast abroad the fitches, and scatter the cummin, and cast in the principal wheat, and the appointed barley, and the rye, in their place? For his God doth instruct him to discretion, and doth teach him. For the fitches are not thrashed with a thrashing-instrument, neither is a cart-wheel turned about upon the cummin; but the fitches are beaten out with a staff, and the cummin with a rod. Bread-corn is bruised; because he will not ever be thrashing it, nor break it with the wheel of his cart, nor bruise it with his horsemen. This also cometh forth from the Lord of hosts, which is wonderful in counsel, and excellent in working.—Isa. XXVIII. 23–29.

The drift of these words is to comfort God's children in afflictions; and because in such smarting crosses, when one is sorrowful, weak, taken up and overpressed with grief, we are then unfit and incapable of instruction, the anguish of the suffering destroying our attention; he therefore says, doubling it four times, 'Give ye ear,' 'hear my voice,' hearken ye,' and 'hear my voice;' wherein he insinuates that the matter he is about to deliver requires attention. As though he should say, You can hearken to the world, to carnal reason, to the devil and his instruments, who lead you astray; but if you would have sound peace and comfort, you must hearken unto God's word, because it is his voice, one who loves you, tenders* your good, and does all things well.

Then he comes to the consolation, the sum whereof is, *that none loseth by God's afflictions, but rather they are gainers, and great gainers.* This he shews by two comparisons, both taken from a husbandman, who when he hath sowed will not harrow it always, but will give every ground sufficient labouring and manuring; who will sow seed, and every seed, and fit seed, in measure, time, and fit place. And then he shews, when God doth give this discretion to a husbandman, how much more doth he abound therein, who, John xv. 1, is called an husbandman; yea, he is the best husbandman who knows times and seasons, when to begin and when to make an end. This is the ground, as the wise husbandman's discretion teaches him how, when, and how much to plough his ground, and when and what seed

* That is, 'cares for.'—G.

to sow; so God is much more the greatest and wisest husbandman, who knows when and how much to afflict us; when to begin and when to make an end; when to sow, and how to make fruitful.

The second work of the husbandman is taken from the purging of his grain, where he shews the labourer will take and use fit instruments to cleanse it with. First, cummin, a cart-wheel is not turned about upon it; then, secondly, the fitches shall not be thrashed with a thrashing-instrument. Thirdly, then the third he shews as having most need, shall have the wheel to go over it; yet he shews the wheel shall not always go over it, nor break it so as to have any hurt by the pressure, for it shall lose nothing thereby but the chaff.

Now having declared thus much, then he shews, this discretion of wisdom in husbandry comes from the Lord of hosts, 'who is wonderful in counsel,' knowing with the height of deliberation and knowledge how to do all things. And then 'excellent in working,' to make all things frame to a good, sweet, seasonable, and happy end.

Before I come to the particulars, see in general he applies both comparisons to one and the same end, to evince* us of this great truth. As Pharaoh had his vision and dreams of the seven ears and seven lean kine doubled unto him, which two were but to confirm one thing that Pharaoh must be assured of; so here he deals in drawing us the right way to find comfort.

'Give ear, and hear my voice; hearken, and hear my speech,' &c.

Doct. 1. Hence observe, *the only way to quiet one's heart, and pacify one in all distresses, is to hearken what God says.* Therefore he goes over and over with it, 'give ear;' 'hearken,' and 'hear my voice,' for this shall quiet your souls, and bring you much quiet and peace of mind. In afflictions we toss, turmoil, and trouble ourselves more than we need. We cry out, Oh, none were ever so vexed and crossed as we are! and so say, Oh, I shall never get an end of this cross! this affliction will make an end of me! And then God comes to us to parley with us in this slumber, and hath much ado to wake us. He loves us best, and shews us this is our best way to find ease, to hear his voice.

Reasons. 1. First, Because God's word will work faith, which does purify the heart, overcome the world, and quenches the fiery darts of Satan.

2. Secondly, It will teach a man wisdom, whence and why it comes, and that struggling with God is in vain, and that in so doing we shall have the worse. The greatest hurt of our crosses comes from passion and distemper; for if we put no more in crosses than God puts in, all should be well; but we put in other things, our own impatience, false fears, fretting, and carnal reason, which makes this good purge of our heavenly Father's providing, be so bitter and heavy unto us. This we should by all means strive against, and make a good use of affliction, such as God would have and intends.

3. Thirdly, It will be a means to work patience in the heart. All the Scriptures are written to work patience in us; for God would have us submit, and our proud hearts can hardly be brought to stoop. This is the end of all.

4. Fourthly, If we hearken to God, this will make us go to God and pray, and prayer will bring comfort and ease to the heart ere long; but if we hearken to the flesh, the further we run this way, the more we plunge ourselves in misery. God, you know, bids us come to him, and says,

* That is, 'convince.'—G.

Wait a while, and all shall be well; he will come flying with deliverance when the hour is come. Thus, if a man do pray and wait, he shall be heart-whole quickly. What saith the apostle in this case? Phil. iv. 7, 'And the peace of God, which passes all understanding, shall keep your hearts and minds through Jesus Christ.' As though he should say, You think the cross causes this disquietness, carking and caring; but if you trust, wait, and pray, you shall have quietness and ease in the most boisterous afflictions.

Use. The use hereof is, *to take no more such unprofitabte courses for comfort and ease in afflictions, as we have done in running to broken cisterns that can hold no water.* It is usual with us, when afflictions are great, and pressing down, to complain, Oh, I have great crosses, never the like; they are beyond my strength; God is against me, and these and these afflict me. But the truth is, if we look to it, we may say, My folly, my pride, my foolishness, distrust, unbelief, and our great* hearts, these be the special causes that disquiets us. So that if we would have a quiet heart in trouble, and a happy end of it, we must hearken to God. He loves us as well in trouble as out of trouble, and there is a medicine in the word against all troubles whatsoever. Then he asks,

'Doth the ploughman plough all day to sow?' &c.

Doct. 2. Hence we see *all God's children must be ploughed.* All the elect are compared to God's husbandry, all who must be ploughed and humbled. To this the Lord exhorts them, Hos. x. 12, 'Sow to yourselves in righteousness, reap in mercy, break up your fallow ground,' &c. God hath no heath nor brakes in his church but are or shall be ploughed; they shall at one time or other have deep furrows made in them; they shall go whither they would not; all must be taken down.

Reason. And there is great reason for it; for naturally, all the elect of God be as subject to that would cross and keep down the seed as others. They have thorns and brambles growing, weeds of all sorts, which would quickly mar them if they were not soundly ploughed. Job for this purpose says that 'man new born is like an ass's colt; nay, like a wild ass's colt,' Job xi. 12. A tame ass might perhaps be ruled, but a wild ass's colt, this is worst of all. So is man following his own reason, led by his own affections, passions, desires, and actions. We would run riot, never be tamed unless the Lord did plough us and cause us break up our fallow ground. Even God's elect are foolish, worldly, covetous, full of envy, lusts, passions, mistakings, ignorance, and the like. God's ploughing helps all, tempers the ground better, digs out and keeps down the weeds, and makes the seed to grow, which otherwise would be cropped and destroyed. Thus, howsoever we may think of ourselves, and please ourselves in a thing of nought, no corn is more apt to have weeds amongst it than our hearts, unmastered, are unfit to bear or bring forth fruits of grace. We would think a husbandman foolish and mad that would sow corn amongst grass, where, having no root, it must rot, and not grow, the ground being unploughed. So we must hold this judgment in ourselves; for unless our hearts be tamed, no good seed will grow or take root there. To this effect our Saviour speaks: John xv. 2, 'Every branch in me that beareth not fruit he taketh away; and every branch that beareth fruit, he purgeth it, that it may bring forth more fruit.' If God be a husbandman, we shall be ploughed and pruned to make us be fruitful, lest we grow wild, and so be only fuel for condemnation.

* That is = 'proud.'—G.

The uses are,

Use 1. First, *not to envy those who are not thoroughly ploughed with afflictions*, for to admire the happiness of such, is no more than if a man should pass through a barren heath, and say this is good ground. I say no; if it were so, it should not lie unploughed. So we may fear of the state of many wicked men; unless they repent, they are not God's; were they of his husbandry they should be ploughed.

Use 2. Secondly, If we be of God's husbandry, and would be thought so indeed, then *think we not the fiery trial of our ploughing to be a strange new thing, that God should sometimes set so sore upon us and plough us to our cost.* If we would have an easier way, take the prophet's counsel, 'Plough up your fallow ground, and sow no more amongst thorns.' Oh, but some may say, I read and pray, and go to sermons. Ay, but you sow amongst thorns if thorns come up; look to this. The husbandman will plough indeed, but he will not sow amongst thorns. The church complains, Ps. cxxix. 3, 'The ploughers ploughed upon my back, and they made long their furrows.' Why did God suffer this? They were ploughed deep indeed, but had no hurt by it, but only ploughed them so as to be fit and good ground. Because in her ploughing she ploughed short, and left many balks and patches unploughed; therefore when we plough not ourselves as we should, it is a mercy of God to send us many ploughers. God will plough us rather than we should be overtaken with sins. God will find other means of afflictions to plough us. If, therefore, we plough ourselves soundly, crosses when they come will not do us so much hurt. If we ourselves be not guilty of neglect this way, afflictions when they come will be nothing so weighty, or of continuance. It follows:

The first comparison.

'Doth he open and break the clods of his ground, when he hath made plain the face thereof?' &c. The sum is, as if he should say, I appeal to your consciences, if you did see a husbandman ploughing and breaking the clods of his ground, casting out rubbish and the like, would you imagine he did spoil the ground, to break it up so always, and be still digging in it? Sure no. From our confession he would have it, that no husbandman knows so well how to plough, dig, and when to make an end of ploughing and afflicting as he doth, whose infinite knowledge and skill is beyond all others' knowledge, and therefore will make an end of ploughing his children in the best time. Whereby we learn thus much,

Doct. 3. *God will make a sweet and seasonable end of afflicting his children.* He doth correct us for our profit, that we may be partakers of his holiness: for, as it is, Ps. cxxv. 3, 'The rod of the wicked shall not rest upon the lot of the righteous, lest the righteous put forth his hand unto iniquity.' Miseries and afflictions never rest till they meet with wicked men; but on the righteous they come as a sojourner, which comes to tarry a while and so be gone; it shall not rest on them. And why so? Because, if God did not help us betimes, we would either murmur, or use some ill means to help ourselves. God will therefore make a good and seasonable end of the afflictions of his children.

Obj. Ay, but when will God will make an end of afflicting his servants? How shall it be known when he will make an end?

Ans. Why, as husbandmen, when the clods lie high, bring the harrow over the same, that the seed may spring through with the more ease; and when the weeds are ploughed and weeded out that would mar all, then he will make an end; and then affliction shall cease when the ground is made smooth and apt to bear and be fruitful in due season. Whence we may observe this much,

Doct. 4. *When the Lord hath made us plain, and hath fitted us with hearts to receive good seed, then is the time of rest.* If a man would plough in seed-time, we would think this a foolish, unwise action. God's ploughing is seasonable to cleanse and purge us, that we may have all fit helps to enable us for his service, as it is written, Isa. xxvii. 9, 'By this therefore shall the iniquity of Jacob be purged, and this is all the fruit to take away his sin,' &c.

Use. Therefore, if we would have a good and a speedy end of our crosses, fears, and afflictions, if we would have rest, and God to make an end of ploughing us, we must labour to be plain and even ground, to take down the pride of our hearts and wills; all high things, and everything which exalts itself, must be cast down and laid low. Many of God's children yet are weary, and suffering, and cry out, Oh when, when shall there be an end? In this case, I say, see in what fitness thy heart is brought to attend upon the word, look in what measure it is engrafted in thy heart. When we can hear the word with joy, and the stream of our endeavours is that way, then we are near an end of our affliction; when the ground is once made plain and fit, then the hour is come.

What remains then? When he hath made plain the face of the ground, he will sow seed, and the fittest seed, and do it in measure with wisdom. Whence observe:

Doct. 5. *When God hath humbled us by his word, then he will furnish and arm us with his word, and enable us with strength that way.* This is a difference betwixt his teaching of godly and wicked men: the one are the better, and mend by it; the other worse and worse; for the godly, with ploughing, he doth instruct and teach them, and make them pliable, it being contrary with the wicked. Many heaths, you know, do meet with streams and floods of water, and yet are nothing the better nor more fruitful; but God's arable, the saints, they are ploughed and instructed, as the psalmist speaks: 'Blessed is the man whom thou correctest, and teachest in thy law,' &c., Ps. xciv. 12. To have the one without the other is nothing, and does no good, but when correction and teaching go together, then one sees all the good of affliction, and why God sent it upon him. It is said in the Hebrews, that, 'he scourgeth every son whom he receiveth:' he corrects them, and convinces them of that evil by his word, of that sin which brought such and such a misery upon them, and makes them acknowledge God's justice in it. Conviction is this, when I bring evident reasons unanswerable, for to prove that which I would bring another to practise and believe. Now, we must acknowledge God's goodness unto us, that gives us not the one without the other, not correction only, but his word also to instruct and teach us. Hereby we know afflictions come from God's love, when they make us in love with the word, and cleave unto it. When we see a husbandman in a field ploughing, and one in a garden digging, we hope for good corn, fine herbs and flowers ere long; so we may say, Thus doth the Lord; now he is a-ploughing and digging of my heart: it is because he means to sow good seed, the seed of eternal life therein. Now, understand thou therefore by afflictions, when God is the husbandman, and afflictions the seed, there must come a good crop of it; God will make it multiply and increase abundantly to our comfort, whatsoever the difficulties be which may seem to hinder the growth of it. The reason hereof is added in the next place.

'For his God doth instruct him to discretion, and doth teach him.' Whence, in brief, learn we thus much:

Doct. 6. *Skill in husbandry is the gift of God, wisdom must come from him.* 'Every good gift, and every perfect gift,' says James, 'is from above, and cometh down from the Father of lights, with whom is no variableness, nor shadow of turning,' James i. 17. So, in other deep things, wherein we have ability to discourse of, know, and practise, let us give God the praise. Usually we are prone to sacrifice to our own nets, to magnify nature in our actions which we do wisely; but, know we, all is of God. If we did believe this, we would never be proud of our skill, and wit, and whatsoever gifts, but labour rather to use it to God's glory, and the good of others. Now comes

The second comparison.

'For the fitches are not threshed with a threshing instrument, neither is a cart wheel turned about upon the cummin,' &c. Hence see,

Doct. 7. *All God's grain needs threshing and ploughing; and as they need it, so they shall have it.* There is no husbandman but he sends his corn to the mill; wheat, or barley, and all sorts of grain must be purged and winnowed, ere it be useful and serviceable unto us. And whereas he speaks of divers grains, some more useful and excellent than others, this shews that some be of more excellent degree in the church than others. But the sum is, that all the best corn hath chaff, and all shall and must be purged, which shall ever be of use to God's service, and the good of others, as Zech. xiii. 9. All God's third must be purged and passed through the fire. As the best gold and silver hath dross in it, which must be purged and refined, so the best Christians must be melted, in a manner, and tried; but he shews they shall lose nothing by afflictions but the dross and chaff, which shall be purged out, during which trial as he brings them into the fire, so he will be with them in it, and bring them through it in safety. Again,

It is said, 'Bread corn is bruised, because he will not ever be threshing it.' This shews,

Doct. 8. *The best grain shall have the sorest trial, and hardest pressure.* So God proportions answerable crosses to our strength, and no further. The rest have not such manner of usage. The fitches are not threshed with a threshing instrument, but are beaten with a staff; neither is a cart wheel turned about upon the cummin, but beaten with a rod; but the wheat must have the wheel go on it. The meaning is an allusion unto that manner of the ancient Jews in treading their wheat, as appears by that precept, 'Thou shalt not muzzle the mouth of the ox or the ass that treadeth down thy corn,' Deut. xxv. 4, for then the oxen, drawing a wheel over the wheat, did so bruise it, but not break it. So the best Christians and patriarchs have been visited with sore and hard trials. Jacob, even after the blessing, how grievous crosses and afflictions endured he! how was he tossed and tumbled up and down! Alas, saith the prophet, speaking of a great calamity, 'it is a time of great trouble, there is none like it: it is like the time of Jacob's trouble; yet he shall be delivered,' Jer. xxx. 7. And Abraham, the friend of God, had many, and sore afflictions. The prophets also, you know how they had all their several crosses in life, many in life and death. Jeremiah complains of his persecutors, which were many. Holy David, a man of sorrows all his lifetime, how was he vexed with variety of crosses, one after another! What shall I say of Job, the mirror of patience, and his many sorrows? And the apostles, were they not the chiefest men next unto Christ? and yet all destinate to sore and great afflictions and trials, so that the nearer they were unto him, the greater were their afflictions.

Reason. And that because God thereby doth humble us and make us heavenly-minded, and keeps us low, for if God did not thus put water amongst our wine, and now and then give us vinegar and wormwood to drink, we would have been proud, and lifted up above measure: as we read of Paul, he was buffeted, and had a prick in the flesh to keep him under, 2 Cor. xii. 7. For, as the main posts and beams of a house are laid forth a long time ere they be used, endure many winds, storms, and tempests, lest, being unseasoned, they should warp, bear no weight, and shrink, marring the building, so God's warriors, the main posts of his spiritual building, if not seasoned with winds and tempests of afflictions, they would grow to ease and pomp, to abound in vanity. Therefore, that they may bear weight, and not warp or shrink, but hold out, Paul, a chosen vessel, what shall be told him? Why, this, 'I will tell him what he shall suffer for my name's sake,' saith our Lord, Acts ix. 16.

Use. The use hereof, briefly, is thus much, *to reform our judgments, to be comforted, not to be dismayed, nor condemn ourselves or others because of great afflictions.* The afflictions of wicked men make them more proud; but what afflictions bring out more prayers, and drive us nearer to God, these are happy afflictions. 'It is good for me,' saith David, 'that I have been afflicted, for thereby I have learned thy law,' Ps. cxix. 71. When we are come thus far, then we shall be no more bruised. He knows how to deliver his own out of temptation, and how to moderate the cross when they have been humbled, and make a speedy and a seasonable end, even of great crosses. As a wise husbandman knows when to stay the wheel of his cart, when the wheat is, and when it is not, enough bruised; as he is careful of the treading and bruising, so is he also of rest and ease, the work being done; much more so is the Lord careful of his spiritual husbandry, not to overdo, but to give his children sufficient ploughing, in measure, and not beyond measure. Oh, but some for all this cry out, Oh, I have been long afflicted, things are worse and worse, I see no hope of any end; the more I pray, all is one, no deliverance comes, I grow more impatient, not able to hold out. Sure, if this cross continue thus and thus, it will make an end of me. Oh the foolishness of flesh and blood! What is the matter? Knowest thou in whose hands thou art? Look about thee, unto the experience and confession of all the saints, and unto which of them canst thou turn thee, who have not been the better by their afflictions, and come forth as the gold, as Job assured himself he should before his delivery, Job xxiii. 10. Look upon them, and see what end the Lord made. This is as much as for thee to say, the Lord is an ill husbandman; he can, indeed, tread his corn, but he knows not when it is enough bruised, or he is careless of it, indifferent whether it be broken or spoiled, or what come of it. Oh take heed, know thou, that thy God, who gives the husbandmen all their discretion, much more doth he know the best time and fittest for thy deliverance. Which is now the next point to speak of.

'Bread corn is bruised, because he will not ever be threshing it, nor break it with the wheels of his cart, nor bruise it with his horsemen.' The point is this,

Doct. 9. *God almighty knows best, and he appoints what shall be the means, time, and measure of the trials of his children.* He knows what is the fittest instrument to purge his grain with. The husbandman, he knows the fittest instruments to purge his corn with: 'The fitches are beaten with a staff, and the cummin with a rod, the wheel going over the wheat;' much more God will have the fittest rod, to do all in love, and for our good. Thus he corrects all he loves. I note this so much the more, because, in a great cross we are ready to fly out, and say, Oh, if it had been any cross, any trouble but this, I could have borne it, but oh, this, this, I know not how to bear it. Why, what's the matter? Know, none was so good or fit for thee as this. Might the patient appoint the potion or plaster to be applied and taken, it is like he might perish, or the wound rot; he would endure no corrosive to eat out the proud* and dead flesh, nor anything to make him sick, and purge out his bad humours. So, if we might have what instrument or cross we list to appoint, our corruptions would never be mastered and cured. If a child should see his father use the wheel to bruise and fit the wheat for purging and winnowing, and should come and say, Father, why do you use this instrument? this were better; would not we judge such a one to be a foolish, rash child, and that a frivolous, idle question? Surely so is the case with us, when we cry out, Oh, were it any other instrument, or any other cross but this, I could bear it. No; thou deceivest thyself; we cannot, without him, bear the least, and supported by his strength, we shall be able to bear the greatest. Job had many and strong crosses, and many creatures against him,—the Sabeans, Chaldeans, wind, and fire from heaven,—yet he would not do them that credit, as to think or say, it was the Sabeans or Chaldeans that destroyed his substance, but this, 'The Lord giveth, and the Lord taketh, blessed be the name of the Lord,' Job i. 21.

Use. The use hereof is, Since the Lord himself appoints the instrument, time, measure, and ending of our afflictions, *therefore never fear, we shall not be overpressed or overborne by them,* as Isa. xxvii. 8, 'In measure he will contend with us, he stayeth his rough wind in the day of his east wind'; and Job xxxiv 23, it is said, 'He will not lay upon man more than right, that he should enter into judgment with God;' and the apostle says, 1 Peter i. 6, that 'these afflictions are but for a season (if need be), otherwise we should not be in heaviness through manifold temptations.' Therefore, always think and be persuaded of this, that his instrument is the best. Every one shall be beaten with the fittest rod, and not too long nor too much. He who is able to make a good and a holy use of a former affliction, having his ground made plain and fit for good seed, he shall have the cross mitigated or removed, with a comfortable issue of all his troubles.

But how shall all this be made good? What assurance may we have of this discreet and seasonable ploughing, in time, measure, and continuance, we having so many enemies without us, and corruptions within us? 'This also cometh forth from the Lord of hosts, which is wonderful in counsel, and excellent in working.' From hence we observe,

Doct. 10. *God, in the chastisements, trials, and afflictions of his elect, hath wonderful wisdom and power beyond our understanding.* He knows not only which is the best way to lead us to heaven, but also he is excellent in working, to bring his counsel to pass. See it in examples. As in Joseph, appointed to be the greatest save Pharaoh in all Egypt. First, he is sold for a slave. Secondly, accused falsely by his mistress; so cast into prison, that for a long time, as it is Ps. cv. 18, 'the iron entered in his feet, until the Lord's time was come.' What meant God thus to suffer an innocent man to be wronged and disgraced? He was 'wonderful in counsel' all

* That is, 'inflamed.'—G.

this while. One might think at first that counsel was darkened without knowledge; but, indeed, this affliction was the best means for him, as upon stairs, to climb up to his preferment. Besides all this, while in the prison, God so tamed him that he bare all patiently. He could not have come to this honour, nor borne it as became him, unless the Lord had first thus ploughed him. So David, after he was anointed king, in a state of honour, and all pomp and pleasure, how was he vexed and ploughed with many crosses? In all likelihood he lived a much better and quieter life when he was a shepherd. What means was this to raise him, to be so afflicted ere he came to it? He was humbled and acquainted with God by these trials, which drove him to prayer, to believe, trust, and wait upon God; and then, all these were helps to fit and enable him for his kingdom. So at Ziklag, his wives and all his goods were taken away; the flesh had a bout,* he wept till he could weep no more; yet then was God excellent in working; Saul was overthrown within a while; and the Amalekites, having much goods together, he asked counsel of God, being but four hundred men, and overtook, overthrew them, and had a great spoil, being able to send presents and rewards to all his men. So that which was at first a strange and uncouth thing, a most grievous cross, was turned into a very great blessing. So God was wonderful in counsel, to put all their store in his possession; secondly, he was excellent in working, his enemies had no heart to withstand him.

Use. The use is, therefore, *to be patient, because in all troubles and afflictions* 'he is wonderful in counsel;' and all his works are beautiful in time, which we shall see when both ends of the cross shall meet; and though we see not which way things shall be effected, yet he is infinite in wisdom. If we will but be quiet, stand still, and see his salvation, we shall see a wonderful issue, if we wait in patience.

Obj. Oh but, say some, they come, I know, from God; but I cannot bear this cross, I see no fruit of the working thereof upon me.

Ans. I say, Yet stay a while; as it is true his physic always works at length, so it is as true that he is not bound it shall work by and by at all times. Perhaps this is not good for thee; yet know, that as he is 'wonderful in counsel,' so he is also 'excellent in working.' We give counsel many times, and cannot make the party follow it; but God can, he hath power, and wisdom, and will abundantly; he who gives the purge, can cause it work to purpose; he who applies the plaster, can make it cure and heal, and in the best time; therefore we must be comforted in all our troubles with these considerations.

Lastly, to conclude, where he says, 'This also comes forth from the Lord of hosts,' thereby he shews,

Doct. 11. *That nothing can stay him from working, to hinder our comfort and deliverance in due time.* Why? Because 'he is Lord of hosts,' and all the creatures are his soldiers at command, and must do what he will, as, Isa. liv. 16, he most excellently shews, that no weapon without him shall prosper to hurt his people: 'For,' saith he, 'behold I have created the smith that bloweth the coals of the fire, and that bringeth forth an instrument for his work, and I have created the water† to destroy;' therefore he overrules all things to work for our good, so as we shall have a seasonable, happy, and blessed end to all our afflictions. Oh, if we could believe this, how happy were it for us!—that God is the Lord of hosts, that the devil is chained up, and all the creatures, from hurting us, till he

* That is, 'round' = turn.—G. † Qu. 'waster'?—Ed.

arm them with his power against us; that he is a fiery wall about us, and hath hedged us, and all that we have, about; that he loves us, pities us, delights not in chastising and afflicting us; that he doth it not willingly, but enforced, in a manner, for our good; and that all the while, as the prophet Isaiah speaks, 'he waits to have mercy upon us,' Isa. xxx. 18, having a certain appointed time for our deliverance. This, I say, being believed, would help to carry our heads above water, in all the tempestuous waves of our afflictions, so as to expect and hope for the accomplishment of this divine scripture: that, as the ploughman will not plough all the day to sow, &c., no more will our all-sufficient, only wise God; but will make a happy and comfortable end of his spiritual husbandry, in the best and fittest time, to the everlasting comfort and salvation of his children.

THE MATCHLESS MERCY.

THE MATCHLESS MERCY.

NOTE.

'Matchless Mercy' forms No. 22 of the original 'Saint's Cordials,' 1629. It was not included in the after-editions. Its separate title-page will be found below.*

G.

* THE
MATCHLES
MERCIE.

In One SERMON.

WHEREIN IS SHEWED
the Excellency and wonder of Divine Mercy in pardoning and subduing of sinne in us.

WITH THE REASONS WHICH
may induce the soule to beleeve and apprehend the same.

Prælucendo Pereo.

VPRIGHTNES HATH BOLDNES.

PSAL. 144. 9, 10.

The Lord is gracious and full of compassion, slow to anger, and of great mercy.
The Lord is good to all, and his tender mercies are over all his workes.

LONDON,
Printed in the yeare 1629.

THE MATCHLESS MERCY.

Who is a God like unto thee, that pardoneth iniquity, and passeth by transgression of the remnant of his heritage? he retaineth not his anger for ever, because he delighteth in mercy. He will turn again, he will have compassion upon us; he will subdue our iniquities: and thou wilt cast all their sins in the depth of the sea. Thou wilt perform the truth to Jacob, and the mercy to Abraham, which thou hast sworn unto our fathers from the days of old.—Micah VII. 18–20.

The drift and scope of this place is to shew God's infinite and constant mercies unto his children, who are tossed and tumbled in a world of miseries of this life, sometimes being altogether void of comfort and the sense of God's love; and this is two ways propounded:

1, In the benefits they receive; 2, in the reasons moving unto the same.

The benefits he promiseth are in number two:

1, Justification by the blood of Christ; 2, sanctification by his Spirit.

Now, this justification is set forth, for our better understanding, by divers arguments:

1. He shews what he will take away, viz.,

First, He says he will take away original sin, in these words, 'pardoneth iniquity.'

Secondly, He sheweth that he will take away our rebellion in these words, 'and passeth by transgression.' In sum, he sheweth that he will take away both the root and the fruits of sin.

2. He sheweth the fruits of this justification in this, what he will pass by.

'He passeth by the transgression of the remnant of his heritage.' The sum is, he will both forgive and forget. The original, in the time present, thus reads it, 'taking away,' arguing and shewing a continual act of God, even a continual act of mercy in him; implying, that as there is a continual spring of original corruption in us, which staineth all our best actions, making us continually liable to the wrath of God, so that in him there is a continual spring of mercy flowing from him, both to pardon and wash away this iniquity (*a*).

And now having shewed this benefit of justification, in the next place he cometh to describe the persons who shall obtain this great favour two ways:

1, They are but a remnant; 2, they are God's heritage.

Now, before he come unto the other benefit of sanctification, he answereth two objections:

Obj. First, Whereas some poor souls may object, What! how can this be? Is God such a God who pardoneth iniquity, and passeth by the same? I find my sins to lie heavy and sore upon me; they accuse me day and night, and they pursue me.

Ans. To this he answers, True it is God is forced to take notice of your sins, to let them accuse you, to curb and keep you in. If we will not take notice of our sins, then God must do tho same. Yet, saith he, for your comfort rejoice, he 'retaineth not his anger for ever;' be patient a while, and you shall see deliverance, it is for your good that you are thus afflicted.

Obj. Ay, but here, because the afflicted soul may again object, But I am not only troubled with outward crosses and afflictions, but also many inward tentations do assail me; I have committed sins of knowledge and presumption since my calling; I have trespassed against my enlightening, grieved the Spirit, I have forced God to depart from me; this seemeth hard, to be without the favour of God.

Ans. To this he answereth, It is true: God, to your thinking, seemeth to be gone from you. Ay, but despair not, stay your mind in peace a while; he hath but turned away his face for a little, he will turn again, he will have compassion upon you, &c. Though he correct and humble you for a while, yet you shall have a joyful issue of all. Now, having propounded this first mercy of our justification, he cometh to,

2. The second benefit, of sanctification, and it is amplified by two degrees:

1, In this life; 2, in the life to come.

For the first he says, 'He will subdue our iniquities;' that is, though at first we were sinful, ruled and overruled by our sins, yet now, when God cometh unto us thus in justification, working sanctification, he says he will subdue them; that is, by little and little he will master them, so that the force and power of them shall be taken away.

Secondly, He sheweth that all the sins of those whom he subdueth he will throw into the bottom of the sea. To understand which we must call to mind a history of former times, which is, that the Lord will deal with our sins as sometimes he did with the temporal enemies of his people. When Pharaoh and his army pursued them, the Lord did overthrow the chariots and horsemen of Egypt, and drowned them in the bottom of the sea; unto which the Spirit of God alludeth here, that he will, for assurance's sake, for ever drown all our sins; so that, as the Lord said to Moses, 'The Egyptians whom ye have now seen, ye shall not see any more,' Exod. xiv. 13; so here the Lord saith, that our sins, which vexed us, we shall never hereafter see any more, for he will drown all our sins from out of his sight; they shall never any more either vex us or grieve him, they shall be all cast into the bottom of the sea.

Now, the reasons moving God are taken from his nature:

1, From his mercy; 2, from his truth, aided with four reasons thereof.

For the first he saith, for mercy pleaseth him, or, 'he delighteth in mercy.'

For the second, of God's truth, because above all things we are full of infidelity, and hardly believe this, therefore he strengtheneth and confirmeth it with divers other reasons.

First, From antiquity. It is an ancient truth, even from the days of old, so that a thing of so ancient a truth must needs be believed.

Secondly, From the often repetition thereof: 'to Abraham, Isaac, and Jacob.' So that a truth that hath been so often repeated, must needs be true.

Thirdly, It is a truth confirmed by many witnesses, even a truth known of all our fathers; so that must needs be true which is confirmed by such a cloud of witnesses.

Fourthly, If all this will not serve, yet he says that 'God hath sworn it.' It is as true as God's truth; so that better it were that all the world should fail, than God should fail of his truth. And therefore, if we will needs keep and observe our oaths, much more must God. It stands him to defend his truth. Thus far of the opening and meaning of the words; now let us come to the instructions rising from hence.

And first, in that we see in the coherence of the text, he cometh in, as it were in a triumph, challenging all the powers in heaven and earth, angels and devils, with admiration, crying, 'Who is a God like unto thee,' &c., we learn that,

Doct. 1. *There is none so merciful as God.* So the Lord speaketh, Isa. xlix. 13, 'Can a woman forget her child, and not have compassion upon the son of her womb? Though they should forget, yet will not I forget thee,' &c. He sheweth here that all natural compassion is nothing to that great care God hath of us. So Ps. ciii. 13, 'As a father hath compassion on his children, so the Lord hath compassion on them that fear him.' So also we may see the same practised by examples. For at first when Adam had forfeited his estate, flying away out of God's presence, yet we see God cometh, and findeth him out, then forgives his sin, and lastly, comforts him in the promise of the blessed seed, Gen. iii. 15. And for the loss of a paradise upon earth, he bringeth him to a far more glorious and eternal paradise in heaven. So Saul, Acts ix. 3, *et seq.*, going unto Damascus in fury and rage to persecute the saints, we see Christ he comes unto him, finds him out, lovingly reasons the matter with him, and forgives him, sending him unto the means of his final conversion. Thus as of sins of nature, so of sins after regeneration, we may see the like. When David had sinned in adultery and murder, before he could half make confession of his sin, the Lord he meets him as it were half way, and pardoneth his sin, putteth it quite away from his sight, imputeth not the same unto him; so that we may justly cry out also with this prophet, 'Who is a God like unto thee?' &c. The reasons are divers.

Reason 1. First, Because mercy is God's nature. It is his name, even an attribute as infinite as himself. And he himself being infinite for measure, infinite in continuance, so his mercy must needs be as infinite as himself.

Reason 2. Secondly, Because all creatures in heaven and earth have their mercy by derivation from this mercy of God. In him it is his nature, in us derived, as a drop to the ocean, from him; so is all our mercy nothing else but a drop of his infinite mercy: so that he is merciful above all.

Reason 3. Thirdly, Because mercy in God is free, without any cause in us moving him to the same. In us mercy and love is still procured by something in the party we love. In God it is not so, for he loveth freely, without any moving cause in us: so that his mercy is over all his works.

Use. The use is, Is it so that mercy is God's nature, is an infinite essence, is free in him? Why then, in all distresses, let us come running freely unto him, and reaching out the hand of faith, let us confidently promise unto ourselves whatsoever mercies the best child hath ever found from the most kind and tender-hearted father and mother; for it is certain, if we come unto God, and have a good conceit of his mercy, and of the infinite immensible* depth, and length, and breadth, and height thereof, that we shall return from the throne of grace filled with a great measure of this mercy.

As the prodigal son, before he resolved to go unto his father, he had first a good conceit of him by a secret comparison and unequals,—'Oh,' saith he, 'how many hired servants are at my father's, and have bread enough, and I die for hunger! therefore, I will rise, and go to my father,' &c., Luke xv. 17,—even so we come unto God very often with small comfort. Why? Because we have not a high conceit of God's attributes; we judge of him like unto ourselves, and so we speed for the most part, departing as we came. And I pray you, if our children should lament, weep unto us, and bemoan themselves, would not we pity them? What pride then is this in us, to think better of ourselves than of God? If we be thus merciful, is not he much more merciful unto his children, since all our mercy is but a small drop of his infinite mercy? It was a good speech uttered by Benhadad, though a heathen man, who because of a flying report he had, that the kings of Israel were merciful, did humble himself in sackcloth, and found mercy; so, I say, if Ahab, a wicked man, upon this was merciful to Benhadad, though with his own destruction, how much more, do we think, doth God exceed in mercy? So many of us want comfort, because we will not go unto him for mercy; and therefore also do we want comfort even of our dearest friends, because God would have us run unto him, call earnestly for his mercy, be so much the more desirous thereof, and be acquainted with him.

Now, in the second place, where he beginneth to reckon up what this mercy is, first he sheweth that he pardoneth iniquity, which is remission of sins; where the doctrine is,

Doct. 2. *That it is the mercy of all mercies to have our sins forgiven, to have them covered, buried, and done quite away.* Now there be many reasons to prove this, that it is the mercy of mercies to have our sins forgiven.

Reason 1. First, Because other mercies reprobate men may have, as an abstinence from some sins; a show of sanctification, some outward gifts of the Spirit, &c., but this mercy none can have but the elect.

Reason 2. Secondly, Because this benefit is the chiefest fountain which flowed from Christ's blood: 'He hath loved us, and washed away our sins with his own blood.'

Reason 3. Thirdly, Because it bringeth unto us the happiest fruits and benefits here and hence; for, first, here; by this we are at peace with God, yea, in a more perfect peace than God had with Adam before his fall. Secondly, by this we have peace of conscience. When God favours us, then our conscience favours us, and all is at peace when once we are sprinkled with the blood of Christ. Thirdly, he hath peace with all the creatures, even in league with the beasts of the field, as Job speaketh: so also for the world to come.

Reason 4. Fourthly, This brings us to an everlasting peace in heaven, making us to be able that we may stand in the great day of his appearance without fear, as also now it is no small benefit, that God with forgiveness

* That is, 'unmeasurable.'—G.

of sins healeth the nature of his children, that sin and Satan shall never have their former dominion over them.

Use 1. Since, then, we see this is so great a benefit and mercy to have our sins forgiven, it must teach all of us earnestly to prize it, since such are so blessed who have their sins forgiven. The means is, to pray often and earnestly for the forgiveness of the same; to confess them often, and to appeal often to that payment which Christ hath already made for us; for if we come to confess our sins before God, we come but to get an acquittance of that debt which Christ hath formerly paid for us.

Use 2. Secondly, It is comfort unto such who have been sorry and grieved for their sins, who have got power against them, to be thankful for such deliverances, yea, to be thankful for all crosses in the mean time, for all such following crosses are but as wholesome medicines to cure our souls from our sins, that we may have our corruptions and the cry of sins removed. This is a great cause to rejoice, as Ps. ciii. 1, 'Praise the Lord, O my soul, and all that is within me praise his holy name; which forgiveth all thy sins,' &c.

Obj. But here the trembling soul may object. Oh, but I am sinful, and full of sins!

Ans. What then, if thou believe in Christ he hath paid all. Imagine two men did owe one of them a hundred thousand pounds, the other a small sum, having one surety for both, may not a man demand the hundred thousand of the party, as well as the little sum? Even so I say, it is all one to Christ thy surety, to pay thy great debts as well as thy small ones, if thou come unto him.

Obj. Ay, but here the trembling soul may object again, But I am a daily sinner, I sin again and again, how then shall I be sure to be still forgiven?

Ans. To this the Lord answereth, as it is in the original, in the present number, 'passing by iniquity,' arguing a constant, continual act in God of forgiving (*b*). He is more ready, saith he, to forgive than you to sin; as there is a continual spring of wickedness in you, so there is a greater spring of mercy in God. It is not, as many think, that God expects that after regeneration we should sin no more; no, he looks but that still we should be a-cleansing our bodies and souls, that we should still come unto him for new assurance. God he cleanseth us not like unto a cistern, which filleth* not again, but like unto a vessel that will fill* again, and so must still be emptied and filled, until it break by dissolution.

Use 3. It is for imitation. Is God thus merciful unto us, and ready to forgive? Why, then, we must labour to be like God, and merciful one to another.

Obj. Oh, but my enemy hath a spring of evils against me.

Ans. And I answer, But God hath a greater spring of mercy to forgive thee. Oh! but it is great! Oh! but God hath forgiven us much more. And yet further, as St Luke saith, It is a matter of great credit to forgive, Luke vi. 35, for thereby we are declared to be the children of our heavenly Father. It is also matter of comfort for us, for if we forgive, so shall we also be forgiven. If a poor man had a few shillings owing him, and he did owe the king many thousand pounds, were not he, think you, a mad man, that would not forgive the shillings to have the many thousand pounds forgiven him? Even so, we all owe many thousand pounds unto God; we must then forgive our shillings, that he may forgive our pounds.

* Qu. 'fouleth' and 'foul'?—Ed.

And thus we see how the poor, as well as the rich, may be merciful even to forgive wrongs, to love for hatred, and the like.

Having thus shewed you both what God doth forgive in the wonder of forgivenness of sins by a more wonderful mercy, and also how he doth forgive, none being like unto him, now he cometh to describe,

The persons who shall enjoy these great benefits; and first, he calleth them God's heritage; whence learn,

Doct. 3. *That God in a wonderful and special manner respecteth his heritage*, the proof whereof, I need not stand upon it, is evident enough, and known both by his working since the creation, and in our time of the gospel. I come to reasons thereof.

Reason 1. First, Because they are God's purchase; for, whereas the elect forfeited all their estates, he hath again purchased them by the blood of Christ. The rest of the world are none of his. If we then do make much of our purchases, much more will God do with his. This is the reason, because God hath paid a full and a valuable price for them all.

Reason 2. Secondly, Because of his providence, in that he keepeth a continual watch over them, as it is Isa. xxvii. 3; there the Lord saith, 'I the Lord do keep it, I will water it every moment; lest any hurt it, I will keep my vineyard night and day.' Again, he speaketh, John xv. 2, to same purpose, 'Every branch that beareth fruit, he purgeth it, that it may bring forth more fruit.'

Reason 3. Thirdly, Because he dwelleth amongst his church, and therefore he will have a special care of his own heritage, to do them all manner of kindnesses.

Use 1. The uses are, Since, therefore, the Lord is so ready, present, and willing to defend and prune his heritage, 1. We must labour to be fruitful unto him with some proportionable obedience, as Heb. vi. 7, 8. We see good ground will be fruitful and drink in the rain, and receiveth therefore a blessing from God; but that which bringeth forth thorns and briers is rejected, being nigh unto cursing and burning. It is no strange thing to see brambles and thistles in a heath, but to see such weeds in a watered garden of good ground were more than strange. So let us look to it, and be sure, that now, when God hath bestowed much cost upon us, he looketh for some answerable fruits.

Use 2. Secondly, It is matter of comfort unto us, that since God always dwelleth with his heritage, he therefore sees all our sorrows and cares; and because of this his abode, for this cause the church shall stand, because he loveth his dwelling-place; yea, though all the power of hell should be turned loose, yet they shall not hurt the church of God; yea, though their sin draw down judgments upon them, yet they shall not rest upon them for ever.

In the second place, we see the persons are described by calling them 'a remnant,' 'a little flock,' whence the point is,

Doct. 4. *That the people of God be but a remnant in regard of the wicked, even like the gleanings of the corn, a small company*, which is a cause they are so despised of the world. Whereof the uses are,

Use 1. First, We must not be discouraged though we see few go with us in the way to heaven. Many are ready to object and cavil against such, but few are ready to profess and suffer with them; yet, let all such who walk forward with the multitude, remember they are but a remnant which shall be saved.

Use 2. Secondly, Is it so, that this small remnant is so opposed and scoffed at? Why then, let us labour so much the more to love and make much one of another, and thus we shall be assured to do more good, than all the power of hell can procure hurt unto us. The devil he labours to sow sedition amongst us; but by love we shall overcome all. The church hath ever received more hurt by discord, than by open enemies.

Having thus described the parties on whom these great mercies shall be bestowed, now he proceedeth to prevent* an objection of some troubled souls, which might arise from the former doctrine.

Obj. You say that God is thus, and thus, and thus merciful, yet I feel him scourge me often and long together for my sins; I am sure he seems to be angry for the time.

Ans. To this he answereth, 'He retaineth not his anger for ever.' Whence the doctrine ariseth,

Doct. 5. *That the afflictions of God's children shall have a seasonable and a speedy end.* The Lord he knoweth best when it is good to begin, and when to make an end; so the Lord speaketh, Isa. liv. 7, 'For a small moment have I forsaken thee, but with great mercies will I gather thee; in a little wrath I hide my face from thee for a moment, but with everlasting kindness will I have mercy on thee, saith the Lord thy redeemer.' So saith the psalmist, 'Heaviness may come in the morning, but joy cometh in the evening,' Ps. xxx. 5. The reasons whereof be divers.

Reason 1. The first is taken out of Lam. iii. 33, 'Because the Lord doth not afflict willingly, nor grieve the children of men.' He doth it not to hurt us, but to mend us and make us come unto him, otherwise we would not come.

Reason 2. Secondly, Because we, having such a sure friend in the court of heaven, even Christ Jesus, to make intercession for us at the right hand of the Father, it is not possible but our afflictions should have a seasonable end; for if the church, having Esther, so sure a friend in the court of Ahasuerus, found by her so speedy and true deliverance, much more shall the church now, by the intercession of Christ, obtain deliverance from the court of heaven.

Reason 3. Thirdly, We shall have speedy and seasonable deliverance from afflictions, because by afflictions we gain instruction. This leadeth us to humiliation and confession of sins, and then the Lord having bound himself by promise and oath, it is not possible but we must have deliverance. He cannot choose but be merciful. Whereof the ground is, that, look how soon God hath his end, which is our unfeigned humiliation, confession, and amendment of life, instantly we have also our end, which is deliverance.

Reason 4. Fourthly, They shall have speedy and seasonable deliverance, because he correcteth them only for their profit; lest, therefore, they should faint and mourn under the burden, he will and hath promised to hasten help, as the psalmist speaketh: 'The rod of the wicked shall not always rest upon the just, lest the wicked oppress and triumph over him.' Excellently also to this purpose doth the Lord speak, Isa. lvii. 16, 'I will not contend for ever, neither will I always be wroth: for the spirit shall fail before me, and the souls which I have made.' So, certain it is, God will not beat his children unto death; he beateth not in revenge, but to bring home and amend us. The uses are,

Use 1. *Reproof to God's own dear servants*, who, in a sharp and quick cross, where they see no issue, they begin to murmur and repine, saying,

* That is, 'anticipate.'—G.

Oh! I shall never get out of this cross. But what, tell me, wouldst thou think of thy child, that, when thou art a-chastising him for some fault, would have such a conceit of thee, that thou wouldst beat him to death? Mightest not thou think him an unnatural child? Yet much more unnatural are we unto God, who is a great deal more loving; for if he once begin, we straight imagine that he will never make an end. But we ought not thus to repine, but rather quench his anger with repentant tears, and take away the fuel of sin which kindleth the sense of this wrath, and then the fire will cease. So let us take away the proud and dead flesh, and the plaster will quickly fall away.

Use 2. Secondly, We must hereby learn to imitate and be like unto God. If we will needs be now and then angry, let it be quickly gone; let us spend our anger upon our sins, and not let the sun go down upon our wrath.

But now here ariseth another objection, worse than the former, for the troubled soul might object, Oh! but I have driven God quite away by my innumerable sins; I have lost my feeling, angered my God, grieved the Spirit, and forced God to depart from me. This is a miserable estate; but yet the prophet, in the next verse, answereth, for the comfort of such, that he is not quite gone away, 'He will turn again,' saith he, 'and have compassion,' &c. Whence I gather,

Doct. 6. *Those who have once had any saving comfort, they shall have it again.* We see David, he quenched the Spirit, made a foul house, brought all things out of frame; he kept his union with God, but he lost his communion with Christ. The graces of the Spirit were seeming dead in him, yet this man had much comfort again, and did much good to the church, and died in peace and prosperity. So we see, Cant. iii. 1, the church at first quite lost Christ, in a manner; she had no feeling, yet she sought him up and down; nay, she went through all the means of salvation, yet found not Christ. It seems a strange thing, that sometimes one should use all holy means, and yet find no comfort or feeling; yet is it most true. But what then? She went a little further, and then she found him whom her soul loved. So let us always learn this much, that when we have used all the means to find feeling and comfort in vain, yet to go a little further, which is, to wait in patience for God's good time, and to hope above hope, &c., and then we see the issue—we shall find him whom our soul loveth; yea, then he will enable us to lay surer hold upon him than ever, and also keep him surer. So Peter, he fell for a while, yet we know Christ came again unto him, and made sure work, that he was the stronger for ever. The reasons are plain.

Reason 1. First, Because all God's saving graces be given for everlasting, therefore they shall never be finally taken away from his children, as those outward graces of the Spirit, which were in Saul, was.

Reason 2. Secondly, He will turn again and have compassion, though he turn away his face, because his heart is near unto us; like unto a mother, who in seeming anger turneth away her face from her child, yet she longeth until she turn again, even so the Lord when his face is turned from his children, he longeth until he turn again and have compassion, &c.

Reason 3. Thirdly, Because of all burdens the absence of God's favour is so intolerable, which absence Christ himself at that time could not endure, but cries out, 'My God, my God, why hast thou forsaken me?' Mat. xxvii. 46. And David, you know, he cries out, 'Thy loving kindness is better than life,' Ps. lxiii. 3. Therefore, I say, God being a most loving Father unto his children, and knowing how precious his favour is unto them, and how grievous his absence, that they cannot live without him, why then, as sure he is God, and goodness itself, no more can he be without them; he will turn again and have compassion, though not in our time, yet in a better time, even in such a time as he shall see fittest; therefore let us not be dismayed, but redouble our courage.

Use 1. The use hereof is, first, reproof unto such who say, that if their peace be once lost, oh! they shall never have it again, they shall never have comfort, favour, or feeling of God's love. But mark our error: we in this case judge God to be like unto a man, who will say, Oh! I will never again love this man, who hath deceived me. But let us remember that God did foresee all our errors and sins that ever we should commit, before we did commit the same. Now if these our sins, before our calling, which in the course of our life we were to commit, being all before God's face, could not hinder his love unto us, what folly is it to think that now, after our effectual calling, our sins which he foresaw can stay his mercies from us. This the apostle aimeth at, Rom. v. 10, 'For if, whilst we were enemies, we were reconciled unto God by the death of his son; much more, being reconciled, we shall be saved by his life.' So that most certain it is he will turn again and have compassion. For if a father should foresee such and such faults in his son, do you think he would punish his son for those faults which he foresaw would of necessity be in him? Certainly he would not. Though he seemed angry, yet he would love him still.

Use 2. Secondly, If we have lost our feeling, like the church, Cant. iii. 1, let us seek it again night by night, that is, constantly, diligently, and earnestly; as Isa. lxii. 7, let us give God no rest until he return; let us, with David, entreat him to 'restore unto us his Spirit again,' Ps. li. 12. Now, restoring argueth a former having, so he will return and have compassion, according to the multitude of his mercies.

Having thus at length propounded and spoken of the first benefit God promiseth, of justification, now he cometh unto the second, of

Santification, 1. In this life; 2. In the life to come.

First, then, *for this life*. After he hath spoken of justification, now he cometh to santification, as a necessary, inseparable fruit thereof; and sheweth, that whensoever God cometh to have mercy upon us, then he also subdueth our sins, and bringeth them in subjection. 'He will subdue,' saith he, 'our iniquities.' Whence learn that,

Doct 7. *Where God forgiveth sin, there he also subdueth sin*; as unto Paul, look how soon God was merciful unto him in effectual calling, so soon did he begin to subdue sin in him. So we see of Mary Magdalene, how penitent she was after forgivenness of sins; and so Peter, weeping bitterly after the same; so of Manasseh, that great sinner, who, when his sins were once pardoned, did leave off his sins;—they were subdued also.

Reason 1. The reasons are, first, Because the virtue of Christ's death can never be separated from the merit of the same. Now the merit of his death being the purchase of our free pardon by what he hath done for us imputed for forgiveness of sins, the virtue of his death, which is to kill and wound sin by degrees, to subdue and bring it under, to mortify the affections, can never be separated from the same.

Reason 2. Secondly, Because without this subduing of sin upon forgiveness, neither should we have comfort from him, nor he glory from us; for, so long as we groan under the burden and dominion of sin, we cannot rejoice in God heartily, we cannot serve him. Now, because God would have his servants to rejoice and serve him here fully, therefore upon acceptation of our persons, he will also loose our bands, and make us able to serve him.

Use 1. The use is, (1.) *reproof and terror* unto such who say they hope their sins are forgiven, when indeed they are not subdued; for it is certain that with forgiveness of sins God also healeth the nature in such, that the like be committed no more, at least there is a resolution, and a total, constant endeavour and striving, to leave all sin.

Use 2. Secondly, This serveth unto us for strong *consolation*, to see that this is not a death of sin here meant, but that it shall not assail so often, come so strong, act with such delight, and be so violent. No; the child of God in this life shall never have sin so subdued, as to find a death of it, only it shall be subdued. Therefore, this is a stronghold unto us, that if God have abated the force of sins in us, this is a sure sign of our justification.

Use 3. Thirdly, It is matter of *instruction* for us all, that whensoever we find our sins too strong for us, let us then fly out of ourselves unto him, who is stronger than all, and hath sworn to subdue them.

Obj. Some object, and say, Oh! I would come if I could but subdue this sin.

Ans. No, I say, because thou canst not overcome this or that sin, yet come. God, he bids thee come because thou art not able to subdue it, that he may come against it with his mighty power and subdue it; otherwise, if it were in our power to subdue our sins, we should be like unto so many gods. Now, I mean, we must go unto God in all his means, to prayer, to the word also, which is mighty to cast down holds, all strong mountains of sin. Again, we must go unto the sacraments, which, we must think, are as able to feed us to life, by eating and drinking of a little bread and wine, as the eating of a little unholy food was at first to bring upon us destruction. This is a stronghold to rest upon. Again, for subduing of our sins, let us bind them up in fetters and chains, let us bind one another by reproofs and holy admonitions. I deny not, for all this, God's children have, and may have, many vexing sins, but with humiliation let them be humbled for them. This is a death of sin, even this weakening and subduing of it.

Now followeth the second part of this santification, after this life, in these words, 'He will cast all our sins in the depth of the sea,' meaning that he will drown all our enemies, dealing with our spiritual enemies, as sometimes* he did with the temporal enemies of his church. Pharaoh and all his army he drowned in the bottom of the sea; so he says, at length he will drown and destroy all our spiritual enemies. After subduing of sins shall come drowning of them. Whence the doctrine is, that,

Doct. 8. *Those who have their sins subdued whilst they live, shall have them all drowned when they are dead.* We see, 1 Cor. xv. 26, it is said, 'The last enemy we have is death;' but this is only in regard of nature—to them it is a passage to heaven, for the others, unto hell. Rev. xiv. 13, the dead in the Lord are pronounced blessed, for then all their enemies are quite subdued. Here we labour under the burden of many crosses and afflictions, but then is deliverance; here we are troubled with many sins, but then cometh freedom from sin, then we labour no more, then all shall have an end. Wait but a little until then, and all shall appear most exceeding glorious; for then, for our comfort, all our sorrows and troubles, wherewith

* That is, = 'sometime.'—G.

we are now fined* in the furnace of affliction, shall be quite forgot, as though they had never been: former things shall be remembered no more.

Use 1. The use of all this is for us, since all our sins and sorrows shall then be subdued and forgot, to fight our battles cheerfully here, and look up unto heaven for help.

Use 2. Secondly, Again, that we should be exceedingly comforted in this, that our battle is so short, our victory so sure, and our reward so infinite and eternal; since after a little while all our sins and crosses shall be drowned, they shall be put as far from us as the east is from the west, as heaven is from hell: then, then our long tedious enemies shall all fly away.

Use 3. Thirdly, It is infinite consolation for us against the fear of death, that that death which parteth body and soul, shall also part us from all our sins, sorrows, and crosses for evermore. All those means we now do use, serve but to weaken sin, but death, this kills and vanquisheth it for evermore. So that the speech of Moses to the Israelites may as truly be said of our enemies, 'The Egyptians whom you have seen to-day, you shall never any more see,' Exodus xiv. 13. Even so, I say, though thou be vexed and troubled with many sins, crosses, and afflictions, yet stand still but a while, yet a little while, nay, a very little while, and all these crosses and sins which vex you, you shall never see any more: he will drown them all [in] the bottom of the sea.

I now come unto the reasons of these doctrines, which are in number two, wherein I must use brevity:

1, His mercy; 2, his truth.

I will only touch them, and so make an end. The first is, because he delighteth in mercy. If we will needs speedily and earnestly perform that wherein we do delight, much more will God. The point is, that,

Doct. 9. *That wherein God delighteth, it is impossible but it must needs come to pass.* Now he, delighting in mercy, therefore it is of necessity that he must needs pour upon us abundance of all his mercies; for he is the perfection of goodness, the perfection of love. Nothing can stay him from performing that wherein he delighteth, therefore all these excellent mercies must needs be bestowed upon his children.

The next reason, as I shewed in the opening, is taken from the truth of God, aided with many reasons: of antiquity, often repetition, many witnesses, and the oath of God confirming the same. So that the giving of these mercies, and certain assurance thereof, dependeth upon God's truth. Whence learn,

Doct. 10. *God is bound, in regard of his truth, to fulfil all his former mercies unto his children*; and therefore as certainly as God is true, as certainly all his benefits and mercies shall be given unto them.

Use 1. The use hereof is unto us, notwithstanding all these promises, to see our weakness, how in tentation† we are ready to rob God of his truth, neglecting the promises, because we find not present help. Behold how we deal with God! If a man promise us a thing again and again, we believe him; but if he swear and confirm the same with an oath, then we doubt no more; and yet when God he promiseth again and again unto us many precious promises, yea, and giveth us the earnest in hand, and sweareth unto us, yet, lo our wretchedness, we trust not with assured confidence in him; a mortal man would take it ill to be thus used at our hands. So every small tentation† maketh us to rob God of his truth, and to think that he will not be as good as his word.

* That is, 'refined' = purified.—G. † That is, 'temptation.'—G.

Use 2. Secondly, It must be matter of instruction for us all, that when we come unto God we must promise ourselves to have good speed, since God is most true of his promises, and we must labour by all means to remember and apply them, and so to turn them into prayers; thus reasoning the matter, What! I am in this and this necessity, God he hath promised to help; since he is true, it must needs be that he will have a care to fulfil his truth; for howsoever I should not be heard, yet God he should be the greatest loser, to lose his truth. O beloved, it is easy for us to speak, but in the evil day to put on our armour, to fly unto prayer, to hang upon God, to fight against tentations, to give unto God the praise of his attributes, that as he is true, loving, just, merciful, all-sufficiency, infinite, omnipotent, so to expect infinite love, infinite truth, infinite mercy from him,—this is no small matter, yea, it is true Christian fortitude, in tentation and affliction thus to reason the matter, to rely upon God, and as it were to bind his help near unto us with the chains of his loving promises. If a promise bind us, much more it bindeth God; for all our truth is but a small spark of that ocean of truth in him. And therefore to conclude all with this promise, worthy to be engraven in everlasting remembrance upon the palms of our hands, God he hath promised that all the afflictions of his children they shall work for the best, Rom. viii. 28. This is as true as God's truth, I shall one day see and confess so much if I wait in patience; why, therefore, I will wait. God is infinite in wisdom and power, to bring light out of darkness; so also he is true, and he will do it. Therefore because I believe 'I will not make haste;' I will walk in the perfect way until he shew deliverance. This must be our resolution, and then it shall be unto us according to our faith; which God, for his Christ's sake, grant unto us all!

NOTES.

(*a*) P. 153.—'The Original, in the time present, reads "taking away;"'
And again—

(*b*) P. 157.—'As it is in the Original, in the present number, "passing by iniquity."' The Hebrew is עֹבֵר עַל־פֶּשַׁע, = passing by transgression. So Dr Henderson, and all the early and recent Commentators. G.

THE SUN OF RIGHTEOUSNESS.

THE SUN OF RIGHTEOUSNESS.

NOTE.

The Sermon from Malachi iv. 2, 3 is appended to the Exposition of Philippians ii. 12–30. (See Vol. V. p. 2.) The pagination is continuous from Philippians and there is the simple heading,

A

SERMON

VPON MALACHIE. G.

THE SUN OF RIGHTEOUSNESS.

But unto you that fear my name shall the Sun of righteousness arise with healing in his wings; and ye shall go forth, and grow up as calves of the stall. And ye shall tread down the wicked; for they shall be as the dust in that day.—MALACHI IV. 2, 3.

In the former chapter we may read of a sort of wicked men, yet those not of the worst, that had in their corrupt observation noted that God did seem to approve of those that were notorious idolaters; therefore they contested with him, 'What profit is there,' say they, 'that we have kept his ordinances?' ver. 14 and 15. This God could not endure, and therefore, verse 8th and 13th, he reproves their boldness, telling them that they had robbed him, and had spoken stout and rebellious words against him, and from the laying open of their rebellious carriage, he proceeds to describe the carriage of some that were good, who spake often to one another; whence we may observe by the way, that *in the worst times some take God's part.* Some are notoriously wicked, carrying sin with a high hand, and some are more civil, yet irreligious, murmuring and complaining as if Christ were not king, and as if true religion were not to be cared for; and these are as hateful to God as the other. For this complaining proceeds either of anger, because things are not suitable to their humours, or from a murmuring at God's government, as if they were wiser to dispose of things than God; and there are likewise some that recover themselves from such misapprehensions of God's dealings, and justify God: 'Just art thou, O Lord, and righteous; and it is thy mercy we are not consumed,' Neh. ix. 33; and such look at those favours they have, though burdened with other calamities, and to these are these words spoken, 'But to you that fear my name,' &c.

In the former verse there is a terrible denunciation against the wicked, and therefore there is no ground that any should be offended at their prosperity. There is a day of vengeance, when they shall be burnt up, and there shall be left them neither root nor branch. This vengeance began to the Jews at the first coming of Christ, and was accomplished at the destruction of Jerusalem. They looked indeed for the Messiah, and the day of the Lord, but woe be to them, 'for it shall be a day of darkness,' Amos v. 8. The persons against whom this denunciation was threatened are said to be the proud men, such as sin against their own consciences, casting off God's rule and laws. When he bids them not to swear, they will; when he commands them to attend the means of salvation, they will not, they will live by their own law. So as pride is an ingredient in every sin, as humility is in every virtue; for humility gives God place above ourselves, and above our lusts. But to the present purpose; those words are a gracious promise made to those that fear. *In the worst times God hath a number that do fear him;* for else it would follow, there should be an act without an object, that we should believe a church where none is, and that there should be war without enemies, that there should be God without glory. For what glory hath God from such as rebel and shake off all rule? No; it is the saints that praise God: Ps. cxlv. 10, 'All thy works praise thee, and thy saints bless thee.' This should comfort us in that our posterity shall ever have some to stand for God in the worst times; nay, in the worst places, where Satan's throne is. In the next place we may observe, *that comfort belongs to such as are God's;* for here it is pronounced to those 'that fear.' The ground of which is in this, that Christ is given to them, and ministers should give 'such their portion,' and not grieve those that God grieves not; for such as do not thus are carnal in their disposition, and do steal the word from the people. But to proceed: good men are described here by this, that 'they fear the name of God;' that is, they fear lest by their infirmities there should be a divorce between God's outward favours and them, and fear lest they should offend so good a God, and so they fear his name; that is, fear him as he hath revealed himself in his word; for the devil will fear when God comes in his person. Therefore it is no thank for men to fear his presence; nay, those that fear God most when God declares his presence in his judgments, as when the wicked are smitten with horror and trembling, as Belshazzar was at the handwriting, they have the least true fear. And therefore to come to church at a set time with a composed carriage, and doing outward duties, is not enough to make a man such a one as fears God. Some solace themselves while they are in prosperity, Oh! they will repent when judgments come. The devil will do as much, he will tremble. Can there be any comfort in this fear? Can we think that a man who lives in all manner of notorious crimes till judgment overtake him, will heartily repent him of his faults, that he hath committed, out of love to God? No. It is the fear of wrath and judgment that terrifies him. If this be repentance, the damned in hell have it. How then shall this fear be discerned where it is? I answer, If we fear the name of God there will be *a jealousy over ourselves, and a special jealousy of our inward corruptions*, so as we fearing the traitor within us, will not give ear to everything, nor give our eyes liberty to look on temptations, but eat with fear, and converse with fear; for those that fear temptations are not secure, and fear not God.* Secondly, where this fear of [God] is, *it frees us from base fears.* We will fear no man when we are in a good cause. 'The man that feareth God shall not be afraid of evil tidings,' for his heart is fixed upon God, Ps. cxii. 7, and fears no creature further than as having a beam of God's glory. He fears not death itself, though the king of fears. God he fears as his king, father, husband, and master, and considers of him accordingly to stir up in him an awful reverence of so great a majesty. There is indeed a covenant between God and him, but so as it is with those that fear him.

'Shall the Sun of righteousness arise.' From the most glorious creature, 'the sun,' he expresseth the most glorious Creator, 'Christ Jesus,' taking

* That is, 'those that fear temptations and fear not God, are not secure.—G.

occasion to help our understandings in grace by natural things, and teaching us thereby to make a double use of the creatures, corporal and spiritual; out of the excellency of the creatures, raising up our minds to consider the excellency of the Creator, so as if these things have beauty and strength, and are comfortable; how much more he that endueth these things with these qualities. Thus, as the rivers lead to the sea, so these creatures should lead us to the glorious majesty of God. But the main observation is, *that Christ is the Sun of righteousness*, for as by nature there was no guile found in his lips, so is he habitually and actually righteous. He is wisdom, justification, sanctification, and redemption, 1 Cor. i. 30. He is compared to the sun, first, *because as all light was gathered into the body of the sun*, and from it derived* to us, so it pleased God that in him should the fulness of all excellency dwell, Col. i. 19; and therefore those that look for perfection out of Christ, do look for light without the sun. Secondly, *as there is but one sun*, so there is but one Sun of righteousness; and therefore what needeth two heads, or two husbands. One must needs be an adulterer. Christ doth all by his Spirit, which is his vicar. Other vicar needs not, though there were a thousand worlds more. Thirdly, *as the sun is above in the firmament*, so Christ is exalted up on high, to convey his graces and virtues to all his creatures here below; even as the sun conveys life, and quickens the earth, yea, all things thereon, though itself be but one. Fourthly, *as the sun works largely* in all things here below, so doth Christ. Fifthly, *as the sun is the fountain of light*, and the eye of the world, so Christ is the fountain of all spiritual light. 'I am the light of the world,' saith he of himself, John viii. 12. He was that light that enlightens the world, saith St John of him, John i. 9, and therefore Zacharias termeth him 'the day-spring from on high,' Luke i. 78. Sixthly, *as the sun directeth us whither to go, and which way*, so doth Christ teach us to go to heaven, and by what means; what duties to perform, what things to avoid, and what things to bear. Seventhly, *as the sun is pleasant*, Eccles. xi. 7, and darkness is terrible, so Christ is comfortable; for he makes all at peace where he comes, and sends his Spirit the Comforter. Now he is in heaven. Therefore as ignorance and error is expressed by darkness, so, contrarily, joy and honour and knowledge, which bringeth it, is expressed by light, Esther viii. 16; and Christ is our director, our supporter, and without him what are we? and what do we but glory in our shame? Eighthly, By the beams of the sun *is conveyed influence to make things grow*, and to distinguish between times and seasons. Thus Christ, by his power, makes all things cheerful, and therefore is called the 'quickening Spirit,' 1 Cor. xv. 45; for he quickens the dead and dark soul, which, till Christ shine on us, it is a dungeon of ignorance and unbelief; and as his Spirit blows on our spirits, so also it works a spring in growth of grace, or a summer in strength of zeal. Ninthly, *the sun works these effects not by coming down to us*, but by influence, and shall we, then, be so sottish as to imagine that Christ of necessity must come bodily in the sacrament to us, or that there is else no work of the Spirit by that ordinance. Can the sun be thus powerful in operation by nature, and shall not this Sun of righteousness be more powerful by the influence of his Spirit to comfort and quicken us, though he cometh not bodily down into a piece of bread? Tenthly, As the sun doth *work freely*, drawing up vapours to dissolve them into rain upon the earth, to cherish it when it is dry, so doth Christ. He freely came from heaven to us, and freely draws up our hearts to heaven, which cannot ascend thither but by

* That is, 'communicated.'—G.

his exhaling power. Christ is our loadstone, that draws these iron hard hearts of ours upward, causing us to contemn this base world, counting it 'dross and dung,' as the church is shadowed out in the Revelation treading the moon under our* feet. Eleventhly, *as the sun shines upon all, yet doth not heat all*, so Christ is offered to all. He shines on all where the gospel cometh, but all are not enlightened; and all that are enlightened do not burn in love to him; nay, some are more hardened by it, as it is the nature of the sun to harden some bodies. Twelfthly, and lastly, *as the sun quickens and puts life into dead creatures*, so shall Christ, by his power, quicken our dead bodies, and raise them up again when he shall come to judgment. And notwithstanding all these particulars, yet he is not everyway like it, for the sun shines upon all alike; but Christ doth not thus, for many are in eternal darkness, notwithstanding this light. He is mercy, yet many are in misery.

How, then, shall we know whether Christ be a sun to us or not?

I answer, *If we find that we feel the heat and comfort of a Christian*, it is a sign Christ hath effectually shined upon us. We know that a stone, being naturally cold, if it be hot, that either the sun hath shined on it, or it hath been near some fire. The papists ask us how we know faith to be faith. We may ask them how they know heat to be heat, or light to be light. Even so, by experience, do we find Christ his presence by enlightened hearts and holy affections. They, forsooth, will have the pope judge of these main things, and of the Scripture itself, and thus teach men to look for the sun by candle light.

Secondly, *He shall see his marvellous light*, and admire it, even as a man newly out of a dark prison, or a blind man restored to sight, how cheerful and joyous is he; or a cripple, when he is healed, oh how he skips and leaps; so a Christian he shews forth the joy of his own heart by telling how good God hath been to his soul. Carnal men wonder at fair buildings, precious jewels, and the like, but David crieth out, 'Lord, lift up the light of thy countenance upon me, and then I shall rejoice,' Ps. iv. 6.

Thirdly, If Christ have shined upon any effectually, *they will walk comely as children of the light;* and therefore if they live in a course of sin against conscience, the light will tell them their conscience belies them, if they think the light hath shined on them. And indeed it is a wonder how a man should be thus sottish to think he is a child of the light, and yet live in such sins as indeed a man should be ashamed to name; yea, such as the heathen did condemn. This shall be their condemnation, even because they sin against the light; 'light is come into the world, and yet they love darkness more than light, because their deeds are evil,' John iii. 19.

But how shall we carry ourselves, that Christ may shine on us?

For answer thereunto; we should ever be under sanctified means. All the light is gathered into the Scriptures. Attend we, in humility and obedience to God's commandment, on them, and let Christ alone for the profiting of us. It is he that gives us to will and to do according to his good pleasure. Use we the company of those that are good, for by conference God works strangely many times, as in the hearts of the two disciples that went to Emmaus, Luke xxiv. 13. Contrarily take we heed of filthy company. Christ will not shine on base houses, and company where all serves to fire temptations and strengthen our lusts.

Quest. But here may it be demanded what comfort was this to the Jews,

* Qu. 'her'?—G.

to whom this was spoken, whenas it was now near a hundred years after, before Christ came?

Ans. To which I answer, it was a comfort to them to be assured *that their seed and posterity should see this* 'Sun of righteousness.' Abraham rejoiced because the promise was made to him; the Jews rejoiced because of the conversion of the Gentiles which was to come; and where grace is, there will be joy for any good that ariseth to others that are led by the same Spirit, and one spiritual member is engaged in the good of another.

Secondly, *Christ was a son* before he was in the flesh.* He was 'a Lamb slain from the beginning of the world,' Rev. xiii. 8, in virtue and force, and also to the eye of faith, so as thereby those Jews saw this Sun of righteousness as present, and thus Abraham saw Christ's day and rejoiced; and thus is the second glorious coming of Christ present to every believer, and wraps up the soul in joy, as if it were in heaven; for faith regards no distance of time nor place, and therefore it sees Christ really present in the sacrament without the help of popish presence.

Now for use of this doctrine.

Use 1. Is Christ a Sun of righteousness? Then should *we pity their estate that are in darkness, and never had Christ to shine on them by his Spirit nor ordinances, as in many places of this kingdom.* It is a cruel bloody practice of those lay pastors, that for want of the ministry of the word do betray the souls of many poor people into the jaws of the devil.†

Use 2. Secondly, If Christ be the Sun of righteousness, we should, when we are cold and benumbed, *repair to him, and conceive of him as one having excellencies suitable to our wants.* Are we dark? He is light. Are we dull? He can heal us. Are we dying? He is life. And are we in discomfort? He is the fulness of love. He is therefore the Son,* that we should seek to him, and make him ours all in all; our Prophet, to direct us by his light; our Priest, to make atonement for us; our King, to help us overcome all our corruptions, and to make us more than conquerors.

'With healing in his wings.'

By wings are understood beams of the sun, for beams are spread from the lightsome body, as wings from the body; and thus Christ, though but one, can spread all his graces to all parts of the world; and by the beams are conveyed all that is in the sun, as light and power; and the like effects which grace works in us. Again, wings have a power to keep warm, and comfort the young ones; and therefore God is said to gather his children as a hen doth gather her chickens, Mat. xxiii. 37. In the beams there is a healing nature also. So as the meaning is evident, *that this Sun of righteousness shall be a healing sun.*

For naturally we are all sick and wounded. Some see and feel their diseases and pain, others do not; but those that do not are the most dangerously afflicted. We are all sick of a general spreading leprosy; and besides, we have every one of us our particular diseases. Some swell with pride, as men do with the dropsy; others that are covetous have ever a supposed hunger, crying ever 'Give, give;' some burn in wrath and anger, as men do in the hot ague; and as we are sick, so are we also wounded by terror of conscience, by Satan's temptations, and therefore have need of healing; and this is wrought by Christ, but after a wonderful manner, even from heaven he comes to invite us to come to him. 'Come to me, all ye that are weary,' Mat. xi. 28. Healing is ordinarily by natural medicines of drugs and the like; but Christ heals with a plaster of his own blood, even by

* Qu. 'Sun'?—Ed. † Cf. our Memoir of Sibbes, Vol. I. c. viii. p. lxxi.—G.

'his wounds and stripes are we healed,' Isa. liii. 5. He heals by his Spirit, enlightening our understandings, which by nature is dark, and soon led away to mistake light for darkness, and darkness for light. This he heals by his word breeding sound affections and judgments, whereby we esteem of things as they are, and accordingly do affect them. He heals our wounds of conscience that Satan makes by his darts and sharp temptations, whereby he would bear us in hand that we are reprobates, and that God is angry with us. Against these he strengthens our faith and trust in God, yea, though he kill us. These temptations, and many other, may gather together to cloud this Sun, but it will at length scatter them all. So as there is ever hope of comfort so long as we use good means. Indeed, amongst bodily diseases some there are that are called *opprobria medicorum*;* but in soul there is no disease but if it be felt it may be cured. The soul that hungers after comfort shall find it; for Christ is an universal healer, healing both bodies and souls of men, and healing them from all evil, both blindness and deafness of the heart; nay, the very dead heart he can restore to life. And this serves to reprove the carelessness of men. It is wonderful, if the head doth but ache, no cost nor labour is spared to redress it. The physician is sent for presently; but in the soul's sickness they are so far from sending for them as they hate them. Am not I your enemy because I tell you the truth? saith the apostle, Gal. iv. 16; and thus now-a-days none are greater enemies in the esteem of ordinary men than the minister that deals faithfully with them.

Again, this should teach us to take notice of our diseases in time, and go to the healing God, as he terms himself, Exod. xv. 26, and lay open our estates to him, and confess, as David did, Ps. xli. 4, 'Heal me, Lord, for I have sinned against thee.' And thus lay open our sores, as beggars use to do to move commiseration; for as there are beams of majesty in this Sun, so are there beams of mercy and bowels of compassion in him. And to this end we should claim his nature and truth in performance of his promises, and we should attend on the means; for there is a tree in the church of God, even 'the tree of life,' whose leaves are appointed 'to heal the nations,' Rev. xxii. 2, and this is the word of God. We should also take heed of despair. Though as yet Satan lulls us asleep, telling us that the sin we are tempted to is but a little one, and that God will dispense with it; that we may yet a while swear and commit adultery, and when we die we may repent. Believe him not, for when death approacheth he will alter his rhetoric. Oh! thou hast lived in sins against conscience a long while. Though thou hast been told of it often, thy sins are scandalous; thou hast resisted God, he will now resist thee; never hope for mercy, thou art mine. What comfort is there then for a poor miserable wretch, but to be well grounded in the knowledge of his Physician, and to be assured of his healing power that hath cured innumerable souls. We should furthermore take heed of ignorance; for many, when temptations come, have not the least knowledge of any healing power in Christ, and so they go on till death, and die like blocks. We should meditate of his commandments and promises; of his goodness and nature; of his encouragements given to us to come to him, 'Come to me, all ye that are weary,' Mat. xi. 38. We praise physicians that have peculiar sovereign medicines, that can work extraordinary cures. Now Christ he hath a medicine of his own able to cure any disease, though never so desperate, any person though never so sick; Mary Magdalene as well as Paul; Zaccheus as well

* That is, 'the shame of physicians' = incurable.—G.

as Manasseh; all come whole from him; and therefore when Satan would tempt us to despair, we should call to mind that we have a merciful God that 'forgives all our sins, and heals all our infirmities,' Ps. ciii. 3.

Quest. But it will be asked, Why then are we not healed? What means this that we are subject to these infirmities of ours?

Ans. I answer, Some of Christ's works are all at one time perfected, but some by degrees, by little and little. Christ heals the soul of guiltiness presently, but there remains the corruption and the dregs of this disease for heavenly purposes. And thus he heals by not healing, and leaves infirmities to cure enormities. He suffers us to be abased and humbled by our infirmities, lest we should be exalted above measure, as he dealt with Paul, 2 Cor. xii. 7, even as the body of a man is cured of an appoplex* by an ague, *est utile quibusdam ut cadant;* Peter did more profitably displease himself when he fell, than please himself when he presumed; and therefore we should retort Satan's accusations when he tempteth us to despair because of our sins, and reason thus, because we have infirmities, therefore we will pray the more earnestly, 'forgive us our trespasses;' because we are sick, we will go to Christ that took our nature not to cure the whole but the weak; for we may be sure Christ will not perfectly cure our weaknesses, because he will have us live by faith, every day going to the throne of grace, and depending on his promise for the forgiveness of our sins, assuring ourselves that the spirit, like David's house, shall grow stronger and stronger, and the house of Saul weaker and weaker, 2 Sam. iii. 1; and this flesh beginning once to fall, shall surely fall.

'And ye shall go forth, and grow up as calves of the stall.'

The most translations have it, 'you shall leap forth;' and the last translation is, 'you shall grow up.'† All is to one end, signifying a cheerful moving. The *terminus a quo* is sickness or bonds. Those that are sick are God's prisoners; but here it is taken for weakness of the spirit, and the promise is, that they should go forth in all good duties, and that they should walk with strength, so that Christ's benefits go together. Where there is forgiveness, there is also strength of grace promised; and where there is strength, there is promised increase thereof, even to fulness; for where Christ begins, he leaves not till his work be complete, in wisdom, righteousness, sanctification, and redemption; and therefore he comes both by water and blood also, for God is unchangeable; and that love that moves him to elect, moves him to justify, and sanctify, and glorify us; and all the promises do join these together, justification and sanctification: 'I will put my fear into their hearts, and they shall not depart away from me,' Jer. xxxii. 40. Where forgiveness of sin is, there is also power against sin, and strong resolutions to labour against it; and where there is justification, it will shew itself in works of sanctification. This will convict many to be no Christians that boast of the forgiveness of sins.

But where is this healing power of Christ seen? In their conversations. He that is cured can rise and walk,—as the cripple did,—in good duties of a holy life; for the spirit of adoption is the spirit of sanctification, and we are sick in the bed of sin if we come not out. In the next place we may observe, that in *every Christian there is a going out;* for so it is promised here, and this hath many degrees. There is *a going out of misery* in this life, for at this present the church was in great misery, and

* That is, 'apoplexy'.—G.

† That is, the Authorised Version of 1611.—G.

'a going out' was promised to them; for when a comfortable worldly estate is good for the church, it shall have it. Secondly, there is a going out *of the bonds of sin*, by little and little in this world; and because here we are in a warring estate, and our freedom here is but from the dominion of sin; there is another 'going out' at the last day, when we all shall go perfected out of the graves, body and soul being freed from sin; and then shall our joy be full. But in this world there is a going out to good duties, for true believers have hearts enlarged to 'go forth' in good duties. Their hearts are set at liberty, being freed from damnation, and free to walk in good courses; for where grace enables us to go, it enables us freely to go, so as *God's people are a free people*. In the building of the tabernacle and the temple, they did offer 'freely,' and David praised God for it, 1 Chron. xxix. 14, and Ezra likewise, Ezra ii. 4; and the reason is, because these have Christ's Spirit, which is a Spirit of liberty, 2 Cor. iii. 17; and it is a promise, Ps. cx. 3, that Christ's people shall be willing. God's people are all volunteers, doing holy duties freely; for they are freed from exaction and coaction. The Spirit that witnesseth the one worketh also the other, and setteth them at liberty. And as this is true, so it is also true that it is dearly bought. It cost Christ's blood, who redeemed us 'to serve him without fear,' Luke i. 74; and that we might be a holy people, zealous of all good works, Titus ii. 14; and therefore our lukewarm, cool carriage shews that we are not yet at liberty. And that is the reason we cannot spend an hour in good duties, but it is very irksome and tedious to us. It was otherwise with Zaccheus after his conversion; how free in charitable works! And with the jailor, how cheerful was he in feasting the apostle, whom a little before he had tormented! In the primitive church, how willingly did they endure persecutions, living together with one heart, one mind, and had all things common, Acts ii. 44. Thus is it in some measure in all Christians, when they are once heated by this Sun of righteousness. In the next place, God's people do not only go forth, but *grow up, and go on in a continued motion;* for it is promised that the soul shall grow strong in grace as well as the body in natural strength. And as nature doth enable the body, so doth grace enable the soul, giving ever a desire of liberty to grow up, and to grow in strength, thereby to overcome all weaknesses of the soul whatever, by those holy means appointed to that end. And this is necessary in regard of God, that he might have the more glory; for when we pray or do any good duty with strength, as when we can be resolute in the defence of a good cause, *God is honoured thereby*, and his truth honoured, and his wisdom justified. And it is likewise necessary *in regard of others*, that they may be won, and strengthened by our examples, they seeing that such things are possible to be done; and thus are they also won. When in our actions to one another we do them with all our might and cheerfulness, how grateful and lovely is it to them! And likewise *in regard of ourselves;* for the stronger we grow, the less burdensome will our profession be to us. For why are we so untoward and dead, that goodness comes from us as fire out of the flint, by force, but because we want this habit, that should grow upon us by practice? Therefore it is we are not grown yet; and therefore cannot pray privately, nor hear conscionably,* but with almost an insensible heart. And likewise this is necessary in regard *of oppositions*, which is such as must be gotten out of the fire, whatever good we labour for. We daily feel the strength of our own cor-

* That is, 'conscientiously.'—G.

ruptions of outward oppositions by indispositions of others and scandal of the times, and therefore we had need grow up.

Now, for means hereunto, we should first *purge and cleanse the soul of weakening matter.* Practise the duty of repentance daily; and though it be bitter, it is better to burn, to cut and lance here, than to die hereafter. It is better to renew our repentance daily, than to go on in security to desperation. And as it is in the body that is sick, the more it is nourished the greater is the strength that the humours do gather; or as it is in leaking ships, the longer we suffer the leak to open, the more danger the ship is in. The best of us daily gather ill humours, partly by reason of our own corruptions within us, partly by reason of the corruption in others with whom we converse; and these make us like sick men, either without stomachs, or with stomachs that can digest none but unwholesome meats; and these once purged out, makes us hunger after goodness, and stronger than before, and more intense in our love to Christ, as Peter was after his bitter tears.

In the next place, *we should come to good food.* When we have purged out the ill humours of our corruption, digest some comfortable truths, and that presently after we are humbled, lest Satan get advantages on us; therefore we should resort to the preaching of the word whiles we may. That study is accursed that takes up a man when he should be at God's ordinances; and the good that is gotten at home, when we may go to church on the Sabbath, is as the water of cursing, because it is gotten in contempt of God's ordinances.

And what though, as many poor Christians object, we forget immediately many times what we hear, yet for the present it will strengthen our souls to walk more strongly after it; as our meat doth when it is passed from us, yet the virtue thereof remaineth behind in us.

Thirdy, We should *use exercise of holy duties.* We see men that are given to daily labour, how strong they are to bear burdens, and what stomachs they have to their meat; and thus it is in those that are oft in prayer and meditation, how do they long after the word! and how sweet is it to them! and how do they treasure it up! Contrarily those that use no exercise, let them boast as they please, they are full, and care not for the word; and are graceless, however they may excel for civil* parts. If they come to church, or like of any of that breed,† it must be to their taste, or they will have none of it; gross meat their finer stomachs cannot digest. The preacher must be as a player upon a well-tuned instrument; and this sort of men are never good practitioners,‡ but commonly given to vanity.

But let us take heed we do not lightly esteem of God's ordinance, but in reverence use all means for the strengthening of our faith by the word, sacraments, and prayer. We have but a short time to work. Our wages are in heaven; and it should be a shame to us that we do no more work for so great a reward as we shall have. We should set no stay nor pitch in religion, but evermore pray and endeavour that God's kingdom may come, and that his will may be done on earth as it is in heaven. Be not dejected by the length of the way, nor the fierce serpents of this world. Take heed of returning into Egypt in our thoughts, but go on from grace to grace, and from one degree to another, till God shall call us to rest.

Quest. But doth a Christian perpetually grow?

* That is, 'moral and intellectual.'—G. ‡ That is, 'putters into practice.'—G

† Qu. 'bread'? and for 'like' = take?—G.

Ans. In answer, Not at all times in all parts. Trees we know, in winter time, grow in the root. Christians grow not always in all graces, but only in some one radical grace, as in faith, or humility, or the like. If there be any stop, it is to further his speediness afterwards, as we see in those that stumble in their course, and as water stopped, breaks out more outrageously. Thus was it in the slips of David and Peter. And God's children, after such times, are as a broken bone: after it is set, it grows stronger in that part than in any other.

Obj. But a man may say, I perceive not this growth.

Ans. To which I answer, We perceive not the corn grow, nor the shadow to move, yet in continuance of time we perceive the corn hath grown, and the shadow hath moved. So, though we perceive it not, yet every act of repentance and faith doth strengthen us. There may be many *turbida intervalla*, cloudy times in every Christian's life. David, a man after God's own heart, had many infirmities; and this may cloud a man's eyes that he may think he is going quite backward. But yet these should not hinder our faith in God's love; for God calls not every slip in a man's life to reckoning. Any traveller may set his foot awry and may go out of his way, yet at length he gets home; and God judges not of us by single acts, but by the tenor of our lives.

How then shall we know whether we are grown or not?

1. I answer, Our growth may be discerned by these signs: first, *if we can taste and relish the food of our souls, the word of God;* for it is with the soul herein as with the body. If our meat be not loathsome to us, our stomach is good, and it is a sign of health; so if we can hear the word of God with delight, and if it be not tedious to us, it is a sign of our Christian growth.

2. Another sign is, if we find ourselves *able to bear great burdens of the infirmities of our brethren;* and thus did Christ long bear the infirmities of his weak disciples that followed him; and the apostle, Gal. vi. 1, counts it the office of those that are strong, to restore such as are fallen with the Spirit of meekness.

3. A third sign of our growth is, if *we find ourselves able*, like Samson, *to break the green cords of pleasure and profits*, that they cannot bind us, and to run lightly away with a heavy load of afflictions, as Samson did with the city gates of Gaza, counting them light and momentary, as the apostle calls them, 2 Cor. iv. 17.

4. Lastly, our growth of grace is seen *in our performance of duties;* if they be strongly, readily, and cheerfully performed; an example whereof we have in the apostle, Phil. iv. 12, who could abound and suffer want, yea, could do all things through Christ that strengthened him: and this is in all Christians more or less, to content themselves in the will of God, and to run the race of God's commandments with a large and cheerful heart.

Ver. 3, 'And ye shall tread down the wicked, and they shall be as dust.

This is another promise made to the church, and in it to every member thereof, of victory over their enemies. God's children and the wicked are like scales, when the one is up, the other is down. Therefore, as this is a promise to the children of God, so is it a threatening to the wicked; for it is the happiness of the church 'to tread down the wicked,' which words must have a large interpretation; for the wicked generally seem to tread down the godly, and therefore we must know that these words were spoken to the Jews, and in them to all other Christians analogically; and it was fulfilled, first, when the good Jews saw the confusion of all the rebellious

Jews under Vespasian, when the temple and the city was destroyed, and they made a by-word unto the nations. Secondly, the words may have reference to the conversion of the Jews, whenas all the enemies of their glorious conversion shall be trodden down, as it is in Micah iv. 13, 'Arise, O Zion: thou shalt beat in pieces many people;' for undoubtedly there is a glorious conversion of the Jews to come, in what manner and at what time we hope ere long to know; for ever since this prophecy their estate and condition hath been very low and mean, and there must come a time of restoring. In the next place, these words may be intended as a promise to all God's church; for while they gloriously and powerfully profess the truth, they are the head and not the tail, ruling and not ruled, as appeareth by the Jews' example.

1. First, While they obeyed God, *they were a terror to the whole earth*, but once fallen from God, they were and remain a scorn to all people; and thus is it now where the white horse goes before, the red horse follows after, as it is in the Revelation, Rev. vi. 4. So long as the church keeps good terms with God, none so terrible as they, and their enemies knoweth this full well: 'Let us take him, God hath forsaken him, and he shall fall into our net,' Ps. lxxi. 11.

2. Secondly, The church treadeth down its enemies in regard *of true judgment and discerning of their estates;* for they do think and account of the wicked as a vile and abominable thing, and as of an object of pity; and this the wicked do know, and this makes them hate God's children.

3. Thirdly, The church of God tramples *on all things that rule wicked men*, as riches, honours, and the like; and therefore, in the Apocalypse, it is said to 'tread on the moon,' Rev. xii. 1; that is, putting all earthly, worldly things under it; and thus did Moses, Daniel, and Paul. All is dross and dung in comparison of Christ; and thus is the church and child of God a spiritual king.

4. Fourthly, The church and children of God tread down the wicked in regard *of their example, for by it and by the word* they subdue the spirits of the world, and bind kings in chains, bringing down their mighty strong corruptions and hard hearts to obedience, and if not, yet by making them inexcusable, we fasten a censure and a sentence of condemnation which hereafter is executed on them; and thus the saints in old time were said to condemn the world, and the white horse to go forth conquering; and there is no man but he must either yield or he is condemned already; and the arrows of God stick fast in him even here, and the liberty they seem to have is no other but as the liberty of the Tower.*

5. But lastly, this promise *is accomplished at the last day of judgment*, when we shall sit with Christ as kings, ruling with him, and as judges of the twelve tribes of Israel, judges of the world. We are here conquerors of the world, flesh, and devil; but then all things shall be put under our feet. And this should comfort us in our sufferings under wicked men; for at that time those that now triumph over us shall be trodden down as dust. And again, we should learn not to fret to see the prosperity of the wicked, Ps. xxxvii. 1. They are but flowers of a day's continuance. Who envies the estate or happiness of a base person that in a play acts the person of a king? This world is no other than a stage play. Let the wicked be in never so great a place, he must return to his rags; and the good man, though he acts the part of a beggar here for a while, he shall be a king

* That, is of 'the Tower of London,' within which State prisoners were confined. —G.

hereafter for ever, and in the mean time God considers of him as his dear son, and it is no matter how high or low he is in the subsidy* book.

If we see ill men therefore advanced, and scandalous men insult, let us enter into the sanctuary, and then we shall see their end to be cursing; and feed we ourselves with meditations, by faith seeing ourselves sitting in judgment on these wicked men. For God's truth and justice will not always suffer these men to ruffle,† for then the devil would be a better master than Christ. And for the present times, do we see that wicked men prevails and increases, take no scandal at it. We know we have as great promises as the Jews ever had; though by these trials God doth purge and quicken his church, it will not always be thus. The beast is going to destruction. They may serve for a while as scouring stuff to purge the church, or as horse-leeches to suck the corrupt blood of the church, and when this work is done, they shall be thrown on the dunghill. It will be thus ere long. 'Babylon is fallen;' and as Christ out of his deep and basest abasement under death did rise to the highest pitch of glory, so his enemy antichrist contrarily, when he is most high and lifted up, shall suddenly and irrecoverably come tumbling down, and at the judgment day shall be more despicable and confounded. He shall be cast into the lake of fire burning with brimstone, Rev. xix. 20. Amen!

* That is, 'the tax-book,' = how great or how small his income is.—G.

† See our Glossary, *sub voce*.—G.

DIVINE MEDITATIONS AND HOLY CONTEMPLATIONS.

DIVINE MEDITATIONS AND HOLY CONTEMPLATIONS.

NOTE.

The 'Divine Meditations and Holy Contemplations' appeared originally in a small volume (18mo.), published in 1638, having a finely-engraved title-page. A second edition was issued in 1651, and a third in 1658. The last is our text, and its title-page will be found below.* These 'Meditations' seem to have been taken from Sibbes's Commonplace book, or from his lips as they occurred in his Sermons, as many of them will be found scattered up and down his writings. G.

* DIVINE
MEDITATIONS
And
HOLY
CONTEMPLATIONS

BY

That Reverend Divine,
R. SIBBES D.D.
Master of *Catherine* Hall in *Cambridge*, and sometimes Preacher
of GRAYES INNE in
LONDON.

The third Edition Corrected.

LONDON,
Printed for *Simon Miller* at the Starre in
S[t] *Pauls* Church-yard, near the
West end. 1658.

TO THE CHRISTIAN READER.

Courteous Reader,—Thou hast here meditation upon meditation offered to thy consideration, as a help to thee when thou art privately alone.

As sweet spices yield small savour until they are beaten to powder, so the wonderful works of God are either not at all, or very slightly smelled in the nostrils of man, who is of a dull sense, unless they be rubbed and chafed in the mind, through a fervent affection, and singled out with a particular view; like them which tell money, who look not confusedly at the whole heap, but at the value of every parcel. So then a true Christian must endeavour himself to deliver, not in gross, but by retail, the millions of God's mercy to his soul; in secret thoughts, chewing the cud of every circumstance with continual contemplation. And as a thrifty gardener, which is loath to see one rose leaf to fall from the stalk without stilling;* so the Christian soul is unwilling to pass, or to stifle the 'beds of spices,' in the garden of Christ, without gathering some fruit, Cant. vi. 2, which contain a mystery and hidden virtue; and our 'camphire clusters' in the vineyards of Engedi,' Cant. i. 14, must be resolved into drops by the still of meditation, or else they may be noted for weeds in the herbal of men, which hath his full of all kinds. But some are slightly passed over, as the watery herbs of vanity, which grow on every wall of carnal men's hearts, and yield but a slight taste how good the Lord is, or should be to their souls. It therefore behoveth us, first, to mind the tokens of his mercy and love, and afterwards for the helping of our weak digestion, to champ and chew by an often revolution, every part and parcel thereof, before we let it down into our stomachs; that by that means it may effectually nourish every vein and living artery of our soul, and fill them full with the pure blood of Christ's body, the least drop whereof refresheth and cheereth the soul and body of him which is in a swoon through his sin, and maketh him apt to walk and talk as one who is now living in Christ.

By this sweet meditation the soul taketh the key where all her evidences lie, and peruses the bills and articles of covenant agreed and condescended unto between God and man. There she seeth the great grant and pardon of her sins, subscribed unto by God himself, and sealed with the blood of Christ.

There he beholdeth his unspeakable mercy to a prisoner condemned to

* That is, 'distilling.'—G.

die, without which at the last in a desperate case he is led and haled unto execution, by the cursed crew of hellish furies.

Here she learneth how the Holy Land is entailed, and retaileth by discourse the descent from Adam, unto Abraham and his son Isaac, and so forward unto all the seed of the faithful. By meditation the soul prieth into the soul, and with a reciprocal judgment examineth herself and every faculty thereof, what she hath, what she wanteth, where she dwelleth, where she removeth, and where she shall be.

By this she feeleth the pulses of God's Spirit beating in her; the suggestions of Satan; the corruptions of her own affections, who like a cruel step-dame mingleth poisons and pestilent things to murder the Spirit, to repel every good motion, and to be in the end the lamentable ruin of the whole man.

Here she standeth, as it were with Saul upon the mountains, beholding the combat between David and Goliah; between the Spirit and the uncircumcised raging of the flesh, the stratagems of Satan, the bootless attempts of the world.

Here appear her own infirmities, her relapses into sin, herself astonied by the buffets of Satan, her fort shrewdly* battered by carnal and fleshly lusts, her colours and profession darkened and dimmed through the smoke of affliction, her faith hidden because of such massacres and treasons; her hope banished with her mistrust; herself hovering ready to take flight from the sincerity of her profession.

Here she may discern, as from the top of a mast, an army coming, whose captain is the Spirit, guarded with all his graces; the bloody arms of Christ by him displayed, the trumpets' sound, Satan vanquished, the world conquered, the flesh subdued, the soul received,† profession bettered, and each thing restored to his former integrity.

The consideration hereof made Isaac go meditating in the evening, Gen. xxiv. 63.

This caused Hezekiah to 'mourn like a dove, and chatter like a pye' in his heart, in deep silence, Isa. xxxviii. 14.

This forced David to meditate in the morning, nay, all the day long, Ps. lxiii. 6, and cxix. 148th verse, as also by night in 'secret thoughts,' Ps. xvi. 7.

This caused Paul to give Timothy this lesson to meditate, 1 Tim. iv. 13, *seq.* And God himself commanded Joshua, when he was elected governor, that he should meditate upon the law of Moses both day and night, to the end he might perform the things written therein, Josh. i. 8.

And Moses addeth this clause, teaching the whole law from God himself, 'These words must remain in thy heart, thou must meditate upon them, both at home and abroad, when thou goest to bed, and when thou risest in the morning,' Deut. vi. 7.

This meditation is not a passion of melancholy, nor a fit of fiery love, nor covetous care, nor senseless dumps, but a serious act of the Spirit in

* That is, 'injuriously.'—G. † Qu. 'revived'?—G.

the inwards of the soul, whose object is spiritual, whose affection is a provoked appetite to practise holy things; a kindling in us of the love of God, a zeal towards his truth, a healing our benumbed hearts, according to that speech of the prophet, 'My heart did wax hot within me, and fire did kindle in my meditations,' Ps. xxxix. 3, the want whereof caused Adam to fall, yea, and all the earth, into utter desolation; for there is no man considereth deeply in his heart, Jer. xii. 16. If Cain had considered the curse of God, and his heavy hand against that grievous and crying sin, he would not have slain his own brother. If Pharaoh would have set his heart to ponder of the mighty hand of God by the plagues already past, he should have prevented those which followed, and have foreslowed* his haste in making pursuit, with the destruction of himself and his whole army.

If Nadab and Abihu had regarded the fire they put in their censers, they might have been safe from the fire of heaven.

To conclude, the want of meditation hath been the cause of so many fearful events, strange massacres, and tragical deaths, which have from time to time pursued the drowsy heart and careless mind; and in these our days is the butchery of all the mischiefs which have already chanced unto our countrymen; for whilst God's judgments are masked, and not presented to the view of the mind by the serious work of the same, though they are keen and sharp, it being sheathed, they seem dull, and of no edge unto us, which causeth us to prick up the feathers of pride and insolency, and to make no reckoning of the fearful and final reckoning which most assuredly must be made, will we, nill we, before God's tribunal. Hence it cometh to pass that our English gentlewomen do brave it with such outlandish manners, as though they could dash God out of countenance, or roist† it in heaven as they carve it here, so that thousands are carried to hell out of their sweet perfumed chambers, where they thought to have lived, and are snatched presently from their pleasant and odoriferous arbours, dainty dishes, and silken company, to take up their room in the dungeon and lake of hell, which burneth perpetually with fire and brimstone.

And for want of this, God's children go limping in their knowledge, and carry the fire of zeal in a flinty heart, which, unless it be hammered, will not yield a spark to warm and cheer their benumbed and frozen affections towards the worship and service of God, and the hearty embracing of his truth.

By this God's works of creation are slipped over, even 'from the cedar to the hyssop that groweth on the wall,' 1 Kings iv. 33.

The sun, the moon, the stars, shine without admiration; the sea and the earth, the fowls, fishes, beasts, and man himself, are all esteemed as common matters in nature. Thus God worketh those strange creatures without that glory performed which is due, and his children receive not that comfort by the secret meditation of God's creation as they might.

* That is, 'slackened beforehand.'—G.

† That is, 'roister.'—G.

Hence it proceedeth that they are often in their dumps, fearing as though they enjoyed not the light; whereas if they would meditate and judge aright of their estates, they might find they are the sons of God, and heirs of that rich kingdom most apparently * known and established in heaven, and shall suddenly † possess the same, even then most likely when their flesh thinketh it farthest off; as the heir being within a month of his age, maketh such a reckoning of his lands that no careful distress can trouble him. But this consideration being partly through Satan's, and partly through their own dulness and over-stupidness, they fare like men in a swoon, and as it were bereaved of the very life of the Spirit, staggering under the burden of affliction, stammering in their godly profession, and cleaving sometimes unto the world. Through this they carry Christ's promises like comforts in a box, or as the chirurgeon his salves in his bosom.

Meditation applieth, meditation healeth, meditation instructeth. If thou lovest wisdom and blessedness, meditate in the law of the Lord day and night, and so make use of these Meditations to quicken thee up to duty, and to sweeten thy heart in thy way to the heavenly Jerusalem. Farewell.—Thy friend,

EZEKIEL CULVERWELL.‡

* That is, 'manifestly.'—G.

† That is, 'quickly,' = 'soon.'—G.

‡ For notice of this profound thinker, see Dr Brown's reprint of 'The Light of Nature,' with Essay by Dr Cairns; and cf. our Bibliographical List of editions of Sibbes's Works at end of this volume, under 'Divine Meditations.'—G.

DIVINE MEDITATIONS.

---

1. That man hath made a good progress in religion that hath a high esteem of the ordinances of God; and though perhaps he find himself dead and dull, yet the best things have left such a taste and relish in his soul, that he cannot be long without them. This is a sign of a good temper.

2. A wife, when she marries a husband, gives up her will to him. So doth every Christian when he is married to Christ. He gives up his will and all that he hath to him, and saith, 'Lord, I have nothing but if thou callest for it thou shalt have it again.'

3. When we come to religion, we lose not our sweetness, but translate it. Perhaps before we fed upon profane authors, now we feed upon holy truths. A Christian never knows what comfort is in religion till he come to be downright; as Austin saith, 'Lord, I have wanted of thy sweetness over long; all my former life was nothing but husks.'*

4. God takes care of poor weak Christians that are struggling with temptations and corruptions. Christ carries them in his arms. All Christ's sheep are diseased, and therefore he will have a tender care of them, Isa. xl. 11.

5. Whatsoever is good for God's children, they shall have it; for all is theirs, to further them to heaven. Therefore if poverty be good, they shall have it; if disgrace be good, they shall have it; if crosses be good, they shall have them; if misery be good, they shall have it; for all is ours, to serve for our main good.

6. God's children have these outward things with God himself. They are as conduits to convey his favour to us; and the same love that moved God to give us heaven and happiness, the same love moves him to give us daily bread.

7. The whole life of a Christian should be nothing but praises and thanks to God. We should neither eat, nor drink, nor sleep, but eat to God, and sleep to God, and work to God, and talk to God; do all to his glory and praise.

8. Though God deliver not out of trouble, yet he delivers from the ill *in* trouble, from despair in trouble, by supporting the spirit. Nay, he delivers *by* trouble, for he sanctifies the trouble to cure the soul, and by less troubles he delivers from greater.

9. What are we but a model of God's favours? What do we see, or

* A frequent plaint of Augustine in the 'Confessions.'—G,

what do we taste, but matter of the mercies of God? The miseries of others should be matter of praise to us. The sins of others should make us praise God, and say, 'Lord, it might have been my case, it might have befallen me.'

10. God pities our weakness in all our troubles and afflictions. He will not stay too long, lest we out of weakness put our hands to some shifts.* He will not suffer the rod of the wicked to rest upon the lot of the righteous, Ps. cxxv. 3.

11. Is it not an unreasonable speech for a man at midnight to say it will never be day? And so it is an unreasonable thing for a man that is in trouble to say, 'O Lord, I shall never get out of this! it will always be thus with me.'

12. Do the wicked think to shame or fear good men? No; a spirit of grace and glory shall rest upon them. They shall not only have a spirit of grace rest upon them, but a spirit of glory, so that their countenances shall shine as Stephen's did when he was stoned, Acts vi. 15.

13. If God hides his face from us, what shall become of our souls. We are like the poor flower that opens and shuts with the sun. If God shines upon the heart of a man, it opens; but if he withdraws himself, we hang down our heads: 'Thou turnedst away thy face, and I was troubled,' Ps. xxx. 7.

14. When we have given up ourselves to God, let us comfort our souls that God is our God. When riches, and treasures, and men, and our lives fail, yet God is ours. We are now God's Davids, and God's Pauls, and God's Abrahams; we have an everlasting being in him.

15. A special cause of too much dejection is want of resolution in good things, when we halt in religion; for as halting is a deformed and troublesome gesture, so in religion, halting is always joined with trouble and disquiet.

16. God hath made the poorest man that is a governor of himself, and hath set judgment to rule against passion and conscience against sin; therefore reason should not be a slave to passion.

17. It is the peculiar wisdom of a Christian to pick arguments out of his worst condition, to make him thankful. And if he be thankful, he will be joyful; and so long as he is joyful he cannot be miserable.

18. God hath made himself ours, and therefore it is no presumption to challenge him to be our God. When once we have interest in God, he thinks nothing too good for us. He is not satisfied in giving us the blessings of this life, but he gives himself unto us.

19. As we receive all from God, so we should lay all at his feet, and say, 'I will not live in a course of sin that will not stand with the favour of my God;' for he will not lodge in the heart that hath a purpose to sin.

20. God's people have sweet intercourse with God in their callings. When we look for comfort, we shall find it either in hearing, reading, or praying, &c., or else in our callings.

21. We glorify God when we exalt him in our souls above all creatures in the world, when we give him the highest place in our love and in our joy, when all our affections are set upon him as the chiefest good. This is seen also by opposition, when we will not offend God for any creature, when we can ask our affections, 'Whom have I in heaven but thee?' Ps. lxxiii. 25.

* That is, 'expedients.'—G.

22. There is no true zeal to God's glory but it is joined with true love to men; therefore let men that are violent, injurious, and insolent, never talk of glorifying God so long as they despise poor men.

23. If we do not find ourselves the people of God's delight, let us attend upon the means of salvation, and wait God's good time, and stand not disputing, 'Perhaps God hath not a purpose to save me;' but fall to obedience, casting thyself into the arms of Christ, and say, If I perish, I will perish here.

24. The love of God in Christ is not barren kindness. It is a love that reaches from everlasting to everlasting; from love in choosing us, unto love in glorifying of us. In all the miseries of the world, one beam of this loving-kindness of the Lord will scatter all.

25. Our desires are holy if they be exercised about spiritual things. David desires not to be great, to be rich in the world, or to have power to be revenged upon his enemies, but that he may 'dwell in the house of the Lord, and enjoy his ordinances,' Ps. xxvii. 4.

26. Desires shew the frame of the soul more than anything; as where there is a spring, it discovers itself by vapours that arise; so the breathing of these desires shew that there is a spring of grace in the heart.

27. Desires spring from the will; and the will being as the whole man, it moves all other powers to do their duty, and to see for the accomplishing of that it desires. Those therefore that pretend they have good desires, and yet neglect all means, and live scandalously, this is but a sluggish desire.

28. An hypocrite will not pray always, but a child of God never gives over; because he sees an excellency, a necessity, and a possibility of obtaining that he desires. He hath a promise for it: 'The Lord will fulfil the desires of them that fear him,' Ps. cxlv. 19.

29. Prayer doth exercise all the graces of the Spirit. We cannot pray but our faith is exercised, our love, our patience; which makes us set a high price upon that we seek after, and to use it well.

30. God takes it unkindly if we weep too much, and over-grieve for loss of wife, child, or friend, or for any cross in the things of this life; for it is a sign we fetch not that comfort from him which we should and may do. Nay, though our weeping be for our sins, we must keep a moderation in that. We must with one eye look upon our sins, and with the other eye look upon God's mercy in Christ; and therefore if the best grief must be moderated, what must the other?

31. The religious affections of God's people are mixed; for they mingle their joy with weeping, and their weeping with joy, whereas a carnal heart is all simple. If he joy, he is mad; if he be sorrowful, unless it be restrained, it sinks him; but grace always tempers the joy and sorrow of a Christian, because he hath always something to joy in and something to grieve for.

32. We are members of two worlds. Now, whilst we live here, we must use this world; for how many things doth this poor life of ours need! We are passing away; and, in this passage of ours, we must have necessaries. But yet we must use the world as if we used it not; for there is a danger lest our affections cleave to the things of this life.

33. It is a poorness of spirit in a Christian to be over joyful, or over-grieved for things worse than ourselves. If a man hath any grace, all the world is inferior to him; and therefore what a poorness of spirit is it to be over joyful, or over-much grieved, when all things are fading and vanish

away. Let us therefore bear continually in our minds, that all things here below are subordinate.

34. A sincere heart that is burdened with sin, desires not heaven so much as the place where he shall be free from sin, and to have the image of God and Christ perfected in his soul; and therefore a sincere spirit comes to hear the word, not so much because an eloquent man preacheth, as to hear divine truths: because the evidence of [the] Spirit goes with it, to work those graces. You cannot still a child with anything but the breast; so you cannot still the desires of a Christian, but with divine truths, as, Isa. xxvi. 8, 'The desires of our souls is to thy name and to the remembrance of thee.'

35. There is a thousand things that may hinder good success in our affairs. What man can apply all things to a fit issue, and remove all things that may hinder? Who can observe persons, times, places, advantages, and disadvantages; and when we see these things there is naturally a passion, that it robs us of our knowledge: as, when a man sees any danger, there is such a fear or anger, that he is in a mist. So that, unless God give a particular success, there is none. As it is in the frame of a man's body; it stands upon many joints, [and] if any of these be out of frame it hinders all the rest.

36. If we will hold out, because the error is in want of deep apprehension of the miseries we are in by nature; let us labour therefore to have our hearts broken more and more. Upon this fault it was that the stony ground spoken of in the gospel wants rooting. Therefore it is Christian policy to suffer our souls to be humbled, as deep as possible may be, that there may be mould enough; otherwise there may be a great joy in divine truths, and they may be comfortable, but all will be sucked up like dew when persecution comes, if it be not rooted.

37. What is the reason that God's children sink not to hell when troubles are upon them? Because they have an inward presence strengthening them: for the Holy Ghost helps our infirmities, not only to pray, but to bear crosses, sweetening them with some glimpse of his gracious countenance. For what supports our faith in prayer, but inward strength from God.

38. In prosperity, or after some deliverance, it is the fittest time for praise; because then our spirits are raised up and cheered in the evidence of God's favour: for the greater the cross is from which we have been delivered, the more will the spirit be enlarged to praise God.

39. Whenever we receive any good to our souls, or to our bodies, whoever is the instrument, let us look to the principal; as in the gifts we receive, we look not to the bringer but to the sender.

40. Take heed of Satan's policy, 'That God hath forgotten me because I am in extremity;' nay, rather God will then shew mercy, for now is the special time of mercy, therefore beat back Satan with his own weapons.

41. Whatsoever God takes away from his children, he either supplies it with a great earthly favour, or else with strength to bear it. God gives charge to others to take a care of the fatherless and widow, and will he neglect them himself?

42. That is spiritual knowledge, which alters the taste and relish of the soul: for we must know there is a bitter antithesis in our nature, against all saving truths; there is a contrariety between our nature and that doctrine, which teacheth us, that we must 'deny ourselves,' Titus ii. 12, and be saved by another. Therefore the soul must first be brought to

relish, before it can digest: there must be first an holy harmony between our nature and truth.

43. If we walk aright in God's ways, let us have heaven daily in our eye, and the day of judgment, and times to come, and this will stern* the course of our lives, and breed love in the use of the means, and patience to undergo all conditions. Let us have our eye with Moses upon him that is invisible, Heb. xi. 27.

44. A man may know that he loves the world, if he be more careful to get than to use. For we are but stewards, and we should consider, I must be as careful in distributing as in getting: for when we are all in getting, and nothing in distributing, this man is a worldling; though he be moderate in getting, without wronging any man, yet the world hath gotten his heart, because he makes not that use of it he should.

45. It is a sottish conceit to think that we can fit ourselves for grace, as if a child in the womb could forward its natural birth. If God hath made us men, let us not make ourselves gods.

46. As natural life preserves itself by repelling that which is contrary to it, so, where the life of grace is, there is a principle of skill, of power, and strength to repel that which is contrary.

47. It is the nature of the soul, that when it sees a succession of better things, it makes the world seem cheap; when it sees another condition, not liable to change, then it hath a sanctified judgment to esteem of things as they are; and so it overcomes the world.

48. In the covenant of grace, God intends the glory of his grace above all. Now faith is fit for it, because it hath an uniting virtue to knit us to the mediator, and to lay hold of a thing out of itself; it empties the soul of all conceit of worth, or strength, or excellency in the creature: and so it gives all the glory to God and Christ.

49. What, we are afraid to speak before men, and to do for fear of danger, let us be afraid to think before God. Therefore we should stifle all ill conceits in the very conception, in their very rising: let them be used as rebels and traitors, smothered at the first.

50. The heart of man, till he be a believer, is in a wavering condition, it is never at quiet, and therefore it is the happiness of the creature to be satisfied, and to have rest: for perplexity makes a man miserable. If a man have but a little scruple in his conscience, he is like a ship in the sea, tossed with contrary winds, and cannot come to the haven.

51. The righteousness of works leaves the soul in perplexity. That righteousness which comes by any other means than by Christ, leaves the soul unsettled, because the law of God promiseth life only upon absolute and personal performance. Now the heart of man tells him, that this he hath not done, and such duties he hath omitted; and this breeds perplexity, because the heart hath not whereon to stay itself.

52. Glory follows afflictions, not as the day follows the night, but as the spring follows winter; for the winter prepares the earth for the spring: so doth afflictions sanctified prepare the soul for glory.

53. This life is not a life for the body, but for the soul; and therefore the soul should speak to the body, and say, 'Stay, body, for if thou movest me to fulfil thy desires now, thou wilt lose me and thyself hereafter.' But if the body be given up to Christ, then the soul will speak a good word for it in heaven; as if it should say, 'Lord, there is a body of mine in the

* That is, 'steer,' = place a helm at the stern.—G.

earth, that did fast for me, and pray with me:' it will speak for it as Pharaoh's butler to the king for Joseph, Gen. xli. 9.

54. Afflictions makes a divorce and separation between the soul and sin. It is not a small thing that will work sin out of the soul; it must be the spirit of burning, the fire of afflictions sanctified: heaven is for holiness, and all that is contrary to holiness afflictions works out, and so frames the soul to a further communion with God.

55. When the soul admires spiritual things, it is then a holy frame; and so long it will not stoop to any base comfort. We should therefore labour to keep our souls in an estate of holy admiration.

56. All those whom Christ saves by virtue of his merit and payment, to those he discovers their wretched condition, and instead thereof a better to be attained; he shews by whom we are redeemed, and from what, and unto what condition: the Spirit informing us thoroughly, that God enters into covenant with us.

57. Spiritual duties are as opposite to flesh and blood as fire to water; but, as anointing makes the members nimble, and strong, and cheerful, so, where the Spirit of God is in any man, it makes him nimble, and strong, and cheerful to good duties. But when we are drawn to them as a bear to the stake, for fear, or an inbred natural custom, this is not from the Spirit; for where the Spirit is, there duties are performed without force, fear, or hopes. A child needs no extrinsecal motion to make him please his father, because it is inbred and natural to him.

58. As the weights of a clock makes all the wheels to go, so artificial Christians are moved with things without them; for they want this inward principle to make them do good things freely. But where the Spirit of God is, it works a kind of natural freedom.

59. As the woman in the law, when she was forced by any man, if she cried out she was blameless, so if we unfeignedly cry unto Christ, and complain of our corruptions, that they are too strong for us, this will witness to our hearts that we are not hypocrites.

60. Good duties come from unsound Christians as fire out of the flint; but they flow from a child of God, as water out of a spring; yet because there is flesh in them as well as spirit, therefore every duty must be gotten out of the fire. And yet there is a liberty, because there is a principle in them that resists the flesh.

61. God's children are hindered in good duties by an inevitable weakness in nature, as after labour with drowsiness; therefore 'the spirit may be willing when the flesh is weak,' Mat. xxvi. 41. If we strive therefore against this deadness and dulness, Christ is ready to make excuse for us, if the heart be right, as he did for his disciples.

62. A child of God is the greatest freeman, and the best servant, even as Christ was the best servant, yet none so free; and the greater portion that any man hath of his Spirit, the freer disposition he hath to serve every one in love.

63. Sight is the most noblest sense. It is quick: it can see from earth to heaven in a moment. It is large: it can see the hemisphere of the heavens with one view. It is sure and certain: for in hearing we may be deceived. And, lastly, it is the most affecting sense. Even so is faith the quickest, the largest, the most certain, and most affecting. It is like an eagle in the clouds: at one view it sees Christ in heaven, and looks down into the world. It sees backward and forwards: it sees things past, present, and to come; and therefore it is, that faith is expressed by beholding.

64. A veil or covering had two uses amongst the Jews. One was subjection, and therefore the women were veiled; another was obscurity, and therefore was the veil on Moses's face. Both these are now taken away in Christ; for we serve God as 'sons,' and as a spouse her husband. We are still in subjection, but not servile; and now also with 'open face' we behold the glory of the Lord. We behold the things themselves; they are now clearly laid open; the veil is taken away.

65. Our happiness consists in our subordination and conformity to Christ; and therefore let us labour to carry ourselves, as he did to his Father, to his friends, to his enemies. In the days of his flesh he prayed whole nights to his Father. How holy and heavenly-minded was he, that took occasion from vines, and stones, and sheep, to be heavenly-minded. And when he rose from the dead, his talk was only of things concerning the kingdom of God. For his carriage to his friends, 'he would not quench the smoking flax, nor break the bruised reed,' Mat. xii. 20. He did not cast Peter in the teeth with his denial. He was of a winning and gaining disposition to all. For his carriage to his enemies, he did not call for fire from heaven to destroy them, but shed many tears for them that shed his blood. 'O Jerusalem,' &c., Mat. xxiii. 37; and upon the cross, 'Father, forgive them, for they know not what they do,' Luke xxiii. 34. So that if we will be minded like unto Christ, consider how he carried himself to his Father, to his friends, to his enemies, yea, to the devil himself. When he comes to us in wife, children, friends, &c., we must do as Christ did, bid 'Avoid, Satan;' and when we have to deal with those that have the spirit of the devil in them, we must not render reproach for reproach, but answer them, 'It is written.'

66. When we find any grace wrought in us, we should have a holy esteem of ourselves, as when we are tempted to sin. What! I that am an heir of heaven, a king, a conqueror, the son of God, a freeman, shall I stain myself? God hath put a crown upon my soul, and shall I cast my crown into the dirt? No; I will be more honourable. These are no proud thoughts, but befitting our estate.

67. Those that are besotted with the false lustre of the world, do want spiritual light. Christ himself, when he was here upon the earth, he lived a concealed life; only at certain times some beams broke out. So let it comfort us that our glory is hid in Christ. Now it is clouded with the malice of wicked men, and with our own infirmities. But let us comfort ourselves with this, that we are glorious in the eyes of God and his angels.

68. As men after a fit of sickness grow much, so God's children grow, especially after their falls, sometimes in humility, sometimes in patience. As we may observe in plants and herbs, they grow at the root in winter, in the leaf in summer, and in the seed in autumn; so Christians appear, sometimes humble, sometimes spiritual and joyful, and sometimes they grow in spiritual courage.

69. That which we drew from the 'first Adam' was the displeasing of God, but we draw from the 'second Adam' the favour of God. From the 'first Adam' we drew corruption, from the 'second Adam' we drew* grace: from the 'first Adam' we drew misery and death, and all the miseries that follow death. We draw from the 'second Adam' life and happiness. Whatsoever we had from the 'first Adam' we have it repaid more abundantly in the second.

70. Grace makes us glorious, because it puts glory upon the soul. It

* Qu. 'draw'?—Ed.

carries the soul above all earthly things: it tramples the world under her feet: it prevails against corruptions, that foil ordinary men. A man is not more above beasts than a Christian that hath grace is above other men.

71. It is an evidence that we are gracious men, if we can look upon the lives of others that are better than we, and love and esteem them glorious. A man may see grace in others with a malignant eye; for natural men are so vain-glorious, that when they see the lives of other men outshine theirs, instead of imitation they darken. What grace they will not imitate, they will defame. Therefore those that can see grace in others, and honour it in them, it is a sign they have grace themselves. Men can endure good in books, and to hear good of men that are dead, but they cannot endure good in the lives of others to be in their eyes, especially when they come to compare themselves with them. They love not to be out-shined.

72. As the sun goes its course, though we cannot see it go; and as plants and herbs grow, though we cannot perceive them: even so it follows not, that a Christian grows not, because he cannot see himself grow. But if they decay in their first love, or in some other grace, it is that some other grace may grow and increase, as their humility, their broken-heartedness. Sometimes they grow not in extension, that they may grow at the root. Upon a check, grace breaks out more; as we say after a hard winter, usually there follows a glorious spring.

73. God's children never hate corruption more than when they have been overcome by corruption. The best men living have some corruptions, which they see not till they break out by temptations. Now when corruptions are made known to us, it stirs up our hatred, and hatred stirs up endeavour, and endeavour revenge; so that God's children should not be discouraged for their falls.

74. When the truth of grace is wrought in a Christian, his desires go beyond his strength, and his prayers are answerable to his desires. Whereupon is it that young Christians oftentimes call their estate in question, because they cannot bring heaven upon earth, because they cannot be perfect; but God will have us depend upon him for increase of grace in a daily expectation.

75. Christ is our pattern, whom we must strive to imitate. It is necessary that our pattern should be exact, that so we might see our imperfections, and be humbled for them, and live by faith in our sanctification.

76. Consider Christ upon the cross as a public person, that when he was crucified, and when he died, he died for my sins, and this knowledge of Christ will be a crucifying knowledge. This will stir up my heart to use my corruptions, as my sins used Christ. As he hated my sin, so it will work the same disposition in me, to hate this body of death, and to use it as it used Christ, answerably. As we see this clearly, it will transform us.

77. With our contemplation let us join this kind of reasoning. God so hated pride, that he became humble to the death of the cross, to redeem me from it, and shall I be proud? And when we are stirred up to revenge, consider that Christ prayed for his enemies. When we are tempted to disobedience, think God in my nature was obedient to the death, and shall I stand upon terms? And when we grow hard-hearted, consider Christ became man, that he might shew bowels of his mercy. Let us reason thus when we are tempted to any sin, and it will be a means to transform us from our own cursed likeness into the likeness of Christ.

78. When we see God blasphemed, or the like, let us think, how would Christ stand affected if he were here? When he was here upon earth, how

zealous was he against profaneness, and shall I be so cold? When he saw the multitude wander as sheep without a shepherd, his bowels yearned; and shall we see so many poor souls live in darkness, and our bowels not yearn? Mat. ix. 36.

79. We must look upon Christ, not only for healing, but as a perfect pattern to imitate; for wherefore else did he live so long upon earth, but to shew us an example. And let us know that we shall be countable* for those good examples which we have from others. There is not an example of an humble, holy, and industrious life, but shall be laid to our charge; for God doth purposely let them shine in our eyes, that we might take example by them.

80. As the spirits in the arteries quickens the blood in the veins, so the Spirit of God goes along with the word, and makes it work. St Paul speaks to Lydia, but the Spirit speaks to her heart. As it was with Christ himself, so it is with his members. He was conceived by the Spirit, anointed by the Spirit, sealed by the Spirit. He was led into the wilderness by the Spirit. He offered up himself by the Spirit, and by the Spirit he was raised from the dead. Even so the members of Christ do answer unto Christ himself. All is by the Spirit: we are conceived by the Spirit. The same Spirit that sanctified him sanctifies us; but first we receive the Spirit by way of union, and then unction follows after. When we are knit to Christ by the Spirit, then it works the same in us as it did in him.

81. When a proud wit and supernatural truths meet together, such a man will have something of his own. Therefore in reading and studying of heavenly truths, especially the gospel, we must come to God for his Spirit, and not venture upon conceits of our own parts; for God will curse such proud attempts.

82. Many men think that the knowledge of divine truths will make them divine, whereas it is the Holy Ghost only that gives a taste and relish, for without the Spirit their hearts will rise when the word comes to them in particular, and tells them you must deny yourself, and venture your life for his truth.

83. When men understand the Scriptures, and yet are proud and malicious, we must not take scandal† at it, for their hearts were never subdued. They understand supernatural things by human reason, and not by divine light.

84. Those that measure lands are very exact in everything, but the poor man whose it is knows the use of the ground better, and delights in it more, because it is his own. So it is with those ministers that can exactly speak of heavenly truths, yet have no share in them; but the poor soul that hears them rejoiceth, and saith, These things are mine.

85. This life is a life of faith; for God will try the truth of our faith, that the world may see that God hath such servants as will depend upon his bare word. It were nothing to be a Christian if we should see all here. But God will have his children to live by faith, and take the promises upon his word.

86. The nature of hope is to expect that which faith believes. What could the joys of heaven avail us if it were not for our hope? It is the anchor of the soul, which being cast into heaven, it stills the soul in all troubles, combustions, and confusions that we daily meet withal.

87. It is too much curiosity to search into particulars, as what shall be the glory of the soul, and what shall be the glory of the body. Rather

* That is, 'accountable.'—G.

† That is, must not make it a 'stumbling-block.'—G.

study to make a gracious use of them, and in humility say, 'Lord, what is sinful man, that thou shouldst so advance him?' Ps. viii. 4. The consideration of this should make us abase ourselves, and in humility give thanks aforehand, as Peter did, 1 Peter i. 1. When he thought of an inheritance immortal and undefiled, and that fadeth not, he gives thanks, 'Blessed be God the Father of our Lord Jesus Christ, which, according to his abundant mercy, hath begotten us,' &c.

88. When we see men look big and swell with the things of this life, let us in a holy kind of state think of our happiness in heaven, and carry ourselves accordingly. If we see anything in this world, let us say to our souls, This is not that I look for; or when we hear of anything that is good, let us say, I can hear this, and therefore this is not that I look for; or when we understand anything here below, this is not the thing I look for: 'But for things that eye hath not seen, nor ear heard, nor that ever entered into the heart of man,' 1 Cor. ii. 9.

89. There are four things observable in the nature of love: first, an estimation of the party beloved; secondly, a desire to be joined to him; thirdly, a settled contentment; fourthly, a desire to please the party in all things. So there is first in every Christian an high estimation of God and of Christ. He makes choice of him above all things, and speaks largely in his commendations. Secondly, he desires to be united to him, and where this desire is, there is an intercourse. He will open his mind to him by prayer, and go to him in all his consultations for his counsel. Thirdly, he places contentment in him alone, because in his worst conditions he is at peace and quiet if he may have his countenance shine upon him. Fourthly, he seeks to please him, because he labours to be in such a condition that God may delight in him. His love stirs up his soul to remove all things distasteful. It seeks out, as David did: 'Is there never a one left of the house of Saul to whom I may do good for Jonathan's sake?' 2 Sam. ix. 1.

90. Infirmities in God's children preserves their grace. Therefore it is that in God's Scripture, where God honours the saints, their weaknesses are made known. Jacob wrestled with God and prevailed, but he halted, Gen. xxxii. 24; and Peter, 'Upon this rock will I build my church,' Mat. xvi. 18; yet, 'Get thee behind me, Satan,' Mat. xvi. 23. 'Paul was exalted above measure with revelations, but he had the messenger of Satan to buffet him,' 2 Cor. xii. 7.

91. It is the poisonful nature of man to quench a great deal of good for a little ill. But Christ cherishes a little grace, though there be a great deal of corruption, which yet is as offensive to him as smoke. Therefore we should labour to gain all we can by love and meekness.

92. Christians find their corruptions more offensive to them than when they were in the state of nature, and therefore it is that they think their estate is not good, but then corruption boils more, because it is restrained.

93. The more will, the more sin. When we venture upon sinful courses, upon deliberation, it exceedingly wastes our comfort. When we fall into sin against conscience, and abuse our Christian liberty, God fetches us again by some severe affliction. There shall be a cloud between God's face and us, and he will suspend his comforts for a long time. Therefore let no man venture upon sin, for God will take a course with him that shall be little to his ease.

94. The reason why mean Christians have more loving souls than men of greater parts, is because great men have corruptions answerable to their parts. Great gifts, great doubts. They are entangled with arguments,

and study to inform their brains, when others are heated with affection. A poor Christian cares not for cold disputes. Instead of that he loves; and that is the reason why a poor soul goes to heaven with more joy whilst others are entangled.

95. Many men are troubled with cold affections, and then they think to work love out of their own hearts, which are like a barren wilderness, but we must beg of God the Spirit of love. We must not bring love to God, but fetch love from him.

96. When we love things baser than ourselves it is like a sweet stream that runs into a sink. As our love therefore is the best thing we have, and none deserves it more than God, so let him have our love, yea, the strength of our love, that we may love him 'with all our souls, and with all our mind, and with all our strength,' Lev. xix. 18.

97. As the sun when it hath gotten to any height it scatters the clouds, so a Christian is then in his excellency when he can scatter doubts and fears, when in distress he can do as David did, comfort himself in the Lord his God.

98. Many men would be in Canaan as soon as they are out of Egypt, they would be at the highest pitch presently. But God will lead us through the wilderness of temptations and afflictions till we come to heaven. And it is a part of our Christian meekness to submit to God, and not to murmur, because we are not as we would be. But let us rather magnify the mercies of God that works in us any love of good things, and that he vouchsafes us any beginnings.

99. As noblemen's children have tutors to guide them, so God's children have the Spirit telling them, This you should do, and that you should not do. The Spirit not only changeth, but leads forward unto holiness. Wicked men have the Spirit knocking, and fain would enter, but they will not hear; but God's children have the Spirit dwelling in them.

100. A Christian is now in his nonage, and therefore not fit to have all that he hath a title to. But yet so much is allotted to him as will conduct him, and give him a passage to heaven. If therefore he be in want he hath contentment, and in suffering he hath patience, &c. All things are his, as well what he wants as what he hath.

101. The word of God is then in our hearts, when it rules in the soul, when it rules our thoughts, affections, and conversations, so that we dare not do anything contrary but we shall be checked. Who shall get out that which God's finger hath written in our hearts? No fire nor faggot, no temptation whatsoever.

102. We shall never be satisfied to our comfort, that the Scripture is the word of God, unless we know it from itself by its own light, and it shews itself abundantly to a believer in casting down the soul, and altering the mind and conversation. When the word is only in the brain, if there come a temptation stronger than our faith, then we despair. The word is far off from those that can only discourse and talk of it, when they see it only as a natural truth, when they look upon holy things, not in a divine, but in a human manner.

103. When the word dwells as a familiar in the heart, to direct, counsel, and comfort, then it is a sign it is there. The devil knows good and hates it, therefore knowledge alone is nothing. But when the promise doth alter the temper of the heart itself, then it is engrafted.

104. God excepts against none, if we do not except ourselves. Therefore thou, and thou, whosoever thou art, if thou beest a man or a woman,

and wilt come and take Christ upon his own terms, for thy Lord and husband, for better for worse, with persecutions, afflictions, crosses, &c. Take Christ thus, and take him for ever, and then thou shalt be saved.

105. When we believe divine truths by the Spirit, they work upon the heart and draw the affections after them. Therefore, if we spiritually believe the story of the gospel, we shall have our souls carried to love, and embrace it with joy and comfort,

106. We may be brought very low, but we shall not be confounded; yet we shall be brought as near confusion as may be, to shew us the vanity of the creature. In the judgment of the world we may be confounded, but a hand of mercy shall fetch us up again. Let the depth of misery and disconsolation be what it will be, we shall not be ashamed.

107. The reason why God's children do oftentimes with great perplexity doubt of their salvation, is because they have a principle of nature in them as well as of grace. Corruption will breed doubtings. As rotten wood breeds worms, and as vermin comes out of putrefaction, so doubtings and fears come from the remainder of corrruption.

108. For want of watchfulness God oftentimes gives us up to such a perplexed estate, that we shall not know that we are in grace, and though we may have a principle of grace in us, yet we shall not see it, but may go out of the world in darkness.

109. We ought not at any time to deny the truth, nor yet at all times to confess it. For good actions and graces are like princes that come forth attended with circumstances, and if circumstances in confession be wanting, the action is marred. It is true of actions as of words: 'A word spoken in season is like apples of gold with pictures of silver,' Prov. xxv. 11. Therefore discretion must be our guide, for speech is then only good when it is better than silence.

110. It is not lawful for any weak one to be present at the mass. Dinah ventured abroad, and came cracked home. It is just with God, that those that dally with these things should be caught, as many idle travellers are. It is pity but those should perish in danger that love danger.

111. He that will not now deny himself in a lust, in a lawless desire, will not deny himself in matter of life in time of trial. He that hath not learned the mortification of the flesh in time of peace will hardly be brought to it in time of trouble.

112. We must not only stand for the truth, but we must stand for it in a holy manner, and not swagger for it, as proud persons do. We must observe that in the first [Epistle] of Peter, iii. 15, to do it 'in meekness and fear.' We must not bring passion to God's cause, nor must our lives give our tongues the lie.

113. There is such a distance between corrupt nature and grace, that we must have a great deal of preparation; and though there be nothing in preparation to bring the soul to have grace, yet it brings the soul to a nearer distance than those that are wild* persons.

114. Nature cannot work above its own powers, as vapours cannot ascend higher than the sun draws them. Our hearts are naturally shut, and God doth open them by his Spirit in the use of the means. The children of Israel in the wilderness saw wonders upon wonders, and yet when they came to be proved they could not believe.

115. It is God's free love that hath cast us into these happy times of the gospel; and it is his further love that makes choice of some, and

* That is = 'in a state of nature.'—G.

refuses others. This should therefore teach us sound humility, considering that God must open or else we are eternally shut.

116. Seeing grace is not of our own getting, therefore this should teach us patience towards those that are under us, waiting if God at any time will give them repentance. Though God work not the first time, nor the second time, yet we must wait, as the man that lay at the pool of Bethesda for the moving of the water.

117. He that attends to the word of God, doth not only know the words, which are but the shell, but he knows the things. He hath spiritual light, to know what faith and repentance is. There is at that time a spiritual echo in the soul,—as Ps. xxvii. 8, 'When thou saidst, Seek ye my face; my heart answered, Thy face, Lord, will I seek,'—and therefore must men judge of their profiting by the word; not by their carrying of it in their memories, but by how much they are made able by it to bear a cross, and how they are made able to resist temptation, &c.

118. There should not be intimate familiarity but where we judge men faithful; and those whom upon good grounds we judge faithful, we must be gentle towards them, and easy to be entreated; and we wrong them if we shew ourselves strange unto them.

119. True faith works love, and then it works by love. When it hath wrought that holy affection, it works by it; as when the plant is engrafted and takes, it grows presently, and shews the growth in the fruits.

120. The word of God is ancienter than the Scripture; for the first word of the Scripture was the promise, 'The seed of the woman should break the head of the serpent,' Gen. iii. 15. The Scripture is but that *modus*, that manner of conveying the word of God. This Scripture is the rule whereby we must walk, and the judge also of all controversies of religion; and in spite of the Church of Rome, it will judge them. St Augustine hath an excellent discourse: 'When there is contention betwixt brethren, witnesses are brought; but in the end, the words, the will of the dead man is brought forth, and these words determine. Now, shall the words of a dead man be of force, and shall not the word of Christ determine? Therefore look to the Scripture' (*a*).

121. All idolaters shall be ashamed that worship images, that trust to 'broken cisterns.' Let those be ashamed that trust to their wits and policies. All those shall be ashamed that bear themselves big upon any earthly thing, for these crutches will be taken away, and then they fall. These false reports shall make them all ashamed.

122. The way to bring faith into the heart is, first, there must be a judicious,* convincing knowledge of the vanity of all things within us and without us that seems to yield any support to the soul, and then the soul is carried to lay hold on Christ; as David saith, 'I have seen an end of all perfection,' Ps. cxix. 96. Secondly, the soul must be convinced of an excellency in religion above all things in the world, or else it will not rest, for the heart of man would choose the best; and when it is persuaded that the gain in religion is above the world, then it yields. And, thirdly, a consideration of the firmness of the ground whereupon the promise is built. Put God to it, therefore, either to make his promise good, or to disappoint us; and he will be sure to make it good in our forgiveness of sin, proceeding in grace and strength, against temptations in time of trouble.

123. Man is naturally of a short† spirit; so that if he have not what he would, and when he would, he gives up, and shakes off all. There is not

* Qu. 'judicial'?—G.

† This is, 'hasty.'—G.

a greater difference between a child of God and one that wants faith, than to be hasty. Such men, though they may be civil, yet they are of this mind. They will labour to be sure of something here; they must have present pleasures and present profits. If God will save them in that way, so; if not, they will put it to a venture.

124. There be many things to hinder this grace of waiting. There is a great deal of tedious time, and many crosses we meet with; as the scorn and reproach of this world, and many other trials. God seems also to do nothing less than to perform his promise; but let us comfort ourselves with this, that he waits to do them good that wait on him.

125. We should labour to agree mutually in love, for that wherein any Christian differs from another is but in petty things. Grace knows no difference; the worms know no difference; the day of judgment knows no difference. In the worst things we are all alike base, and in the best things we are all alike happy. Only in this world God will have distinctions, for order's sake; but else there is no difference.

126. Christians are like to many men of great means, that know not how to make use of them. We live not like ourselves. Bring large faith, and we shall have large grace and comfort. We are scanted in our own bowels, therefore labour to have a large faith, answerable to our large riches. And though Christians be low enough in outward things, and oftentimes poorer than other men, yet they are rich; for Christ is rich unto them, in their crosses and abasements. That which they want in this world shall be made up in grace and glory hereafter.

127. We ought daily to imitate Christ in our places, to be good to all; as the apostle saith, 'Be abundant always in the works of the Lord,' 1 Cor. xv. 58. Let us labour to have large hearts, that we may do it seasonably, and abundantly, and unweariedly. The love of Christ will breed in us the same impression that was in him.

128. None come to God without Christ; none come to Christ without faith; none come to faith without the means; none enjoy the means but where God hath sent it. Therefore where there was no means of salvation before the coming of Christ, there was no visible intendment* of God ordinarily to save them.

129. Preventing mercy is the greatest. How many favours doth God prevent us with! We never asked for our being, nor for that tender love which our parents bore towards us in our tender years. We never asked for our baptism and engrafting into Christ. What a motive therefore is that to stir us up, that when we come to years, we may plead with the Lord, and say, 'Thou hadst a care of me before I had a being; and therefore much more wilt thou now have a care of me, whom thou hast reconciled unto thyself, and remember me in mercy for time to come.'

130. If God's mercy might be overcome with our sins, we should overcome it every day. It must be a rich mercy that must satisfy; and therefore the apostle never speaks of it without the extensions of love, 'the height and depth.' We want words, we want thoughts, to conceive of it. We should therefore labour to frame our souls to have rich and large conceits and apprehensions of so large mercy.

131. God is rich in mercy, not only to our souls, but in providing all we stand in need of. He keep us from ill, and so he is called a 'buckler;' he gives all good things, and so he is called a 'sun.' He keeps us in good estate, and advanceth us higher, so far as our nature shall be capable.

* That is, 'design,' or 'intention.'—G.

132. The sun shines on the moon and stars, and they shine upon the earth; so doth God shine in goodness upon us, that we might shine in our extensions of goodness unto others, especially unto them of the household of faith.

133. We are styled in Scripture to be good and righteous, because our understandings, our wills, and affections are our own; but so far as they are holy, they are the Holy Ghost's. We are the principal in our actions, as they are actions; but the Holy Ghost is principal of the holiness of the action. The gracious government of the new creature is from the Spirit. If the Holy Ghost take away his government, and do not guide and assist us in every holy action, we are at a stand, and can go no further.

134. Every man naturally is a god unto himself, not only in reflecting all upon himself, but in setting upon divine things in his own strength, as if he were principal in his own actions, coming to them in the strength of his own wit and in the strength of his own reason. This seed is in all men by nature, until God have turned a man out of himself, by the power of the Holy Ghost.

135. Those that care not for the word, they are strangers from the Spirit; and those that care not for the Spirit, never make right use of the word. The word is nothing without the Spirit; it is animated and quickened by the Spirit. The Spirit and the word are like the veins and arteries in the body, that give quickening and life to the whole body; and therefore where the word is most revealed, there is most Spirit; but where Christ is not opened in the gospel, there the Spirit is not at all visible.

136. When Christ comes into the soul by the Spirit, then he carries himself familiarly, discovering the secrets of God the Father, and shewing what love there is in God toward us. It teacheth us how to carry ourselves in all neglects, and when we are at a loss it opens a way for us; it resolves our doubts, it comforts us in our discouragements, and makes us go boldly to God in all our wants.

137. As we may know who dwells in a house by observing who goes in and them that come out, so we may know that the Spirit dwells in us by observing what sanctified speeches he sends forth, and what delight he hath wrought in us to things that are special, and what price we set upon them. Whereas a carnal man pulls down the price of spiritual things, because his soul cleaves to something that he joys in more; and this is the cause why he slights the directions and comforts of the word. But those in whom the Spirit dwells, they will consult with it, and not regard what flesh and blood saith, but will follow the directions of the word and Spirit.

138. A Christian will not do common things, but, first, he sanctifies them, and dedicates himself, his person, and his actions to God, and so he sees God in all things. Whereas a carnal man sees reason only in all that he doth; but a Christian sees God in crosses to humble him, and everything he makes spiritual. Yet because there is a double principle in him, there will be some stirring of the flesh in his actions, and sometimes the worser part will appear most. But here is the excellency of a Christian's estate, that the Spirit will work it out at last. It will never let his heart and conscience alone till it be wrought out by little and little.

139. The Spirit of God may be known to be in weak Christians. As the soul is known to be in the body by the pulses, even so the Spirit discovers itself in them by pulses, by groaning, sighing, complaining, that it is so with them, and that they are no better; so that they are out of love with themselves. This is a good sign that the Spirit is there in some measure.

140. Where the Spirit dwells largely in any man, there is boldness in God's cause, a contempt of the world: 'He can do all things through Christ that strengthens him,' Philip. iv. 13. His mind is content and settled. He can bear with the infirmities of others and not be offended, for it is the weak in spirit that are offended. He is ready in his desires to say, 'Come, Lord Jesus; come quickly,' Rev. xxii. 20. But where corruption bears sway there is, 'Oh stay a little, that I may recover my strength,' Ps. xxxix. 13; that is, stay a while that I may repent. For the soul is not fit to appear before God but where the Spirit dwells in grace and comfort.

141. When we are young carnal delights lead us, and when we are old covetousness drowns us; so that if our knowledge be not spiritual, we shall never hold out. And the reason why at the hour of death so many despair, is because they had knowledge without the Spirit.

142. God gives comforts in the exercise and practice of grace. We must not therefore snatch comforts before we be fit for them. When we perform precepts, then God performs comforts. If we will make it good indeed that we love God, we must keep his commandments. We must not keep one, but all. It must be universal obedience fetched from the heart root, and that out of love.

143. It is a true rule in divinity, that God never takes away any blessing from his people but he gives them a better. When Elijah was taken from Elisha into heaven, God doubled his Spirit upon Elisha. If God take away wife or children, he gives better things for them. The disciples parted with Christ's bodily presence, but he sent them the Holy Ghost.

144. God will be known of us in those things wherein it is our comfort to know him. In all our devotions, the whole counsel of heaven comforts us jointly. The second person prays to the Father, and he sends the third, and as they have several titles, so they all agree in their love and care to comfort.

145. In trouble, we are prone to forget all that we have heard and read that makes for our comfort. Now, what is the reason that a man comes to think of that which otherwise he should never have called to mind? The Holy Ghost brings it to his remembrance. He is a comforter, bringing to mind useful things at such times when we have most need of them.

146. Those that care not for the word of God, reject their comfort. All comfort must be drawn out of the Scriptures, which are the breasts of consolation. Many are bred up by education that they know the truth and are able to discourse of it, but they want the Spirit of truth; and that is the reason why all their knowledge vanisheth away in time of trial and temptation.

147. No man is a true divine but the child of God. He only knows holy things by a holy light and life. Other men, though they speak of these things, yet they know them not. Take the mysticallest points in religion, as justification, adoption, peace of conscience, joy in the Holy Ghost, the sweet benefit of communion of saints, the excellent estate of a Christian in extremity, to know what is to be done upon all occasions, inward sight and sorrow for sin, they know not what those things mean. For howsoever they may discourse of them, yet the things themselves are mysteries. Repentance is a mystery, joy in the Holy Ghost is a mystery. No natural man, though he be never so great a scholar, knows these things experimentally; but he knows them as physicians know physic, by their books, but not as a sick man by experience.

148. It is a great scandal to religion that men of great learning and parts

are wicked men. Hereupon the world comes to think that religion is nothing but an empty name; so that, without this inward anointing, they never see spiritual things experimentally; but though they know these things in the brain, yet secretly in their hearts they make a scorn of conversion and mortification; and though for his calling he may speak of these things excellently, and with admiration, yet in particular he hath no power of them in his heart.

149. It is good and comfortable to compare our condition with the condition of the men of the world; for howsoever they may excel in riches and learning, yet we have cause to bless God, as Christ saith in the 11th of St Matthew, ver. 25, 'I thank thee, O Father, Lord of heaven and earth, because thou hast hid these things from the wise and prudent, and hast revealed them unto babes.' It is good in all outward discouragements, when things go not well with us, thus to reason with ourselves. Wilt thou change thy estate with the men of the world? God hath advanced thee to a higher order. Let them have their greatness. Alas! they are miserable creatures, notwithstanding all that they do enjoy.

150. If we desire to have the Spirit, we must wait in doing good, as the apostles waited many days before the Comforter came. We must also empty our souls of self-love, and the love of the things of the world, and willingly entertain those crosses that bring our souls out of love with them. The children of Israel in the wilderness had no manna till they had spent their onions and garlic; so this world must be out of request with us before we can be spiritual. Let us therefore labour to see the excellency of spiritual things, and how cheap and poor all the glory of the world is to those. These things, thought and considered on, will make us more and more spiritual.

151. The Holy Ghost would not come till Christ, by his death, had reconciled his Father, and after that as an argument of full satisfaction had risen again, because the Holy Ghost is the best gift of God; and whatsoever grace or comfort was received before was by virtue of this; so that the sending of the Holy Ghost is the best fruit of God's reconciliation.

152. Let a particular judgment come upon any man, presently his conscience recalls back what sins have been committed by him; so that this waking of conscience shews that we are sinful creatures.

153. Every man by nature, though the wisest, till he be in Christ, is a slave to the devil, who abuses his wits and parts, and makes him work out his own damnation. This is not the condition of a few fools; but the greatest and wisest in the world. Satan leads them to honours and voluptuousness, as a sheep is led by a green bough. He goes with the stream of man's nature, and so is never discerned.

154. As a man that is called before a judgment-seat, being guilty of many crimes, yet the judge offers him his book, as meaning to save him by that means; but he cannot read. Now he is condemned, partly for his former faults, but especially because he cannot read, and cannot have the benefit of the law (*b*); so therefore a wicked man, not believing in Christ, because the remedy is prepared, and he takes no hold of it. In this sense, as some divines speak, no sin but infidelity condemns a man; for if a man could believe and repent, no sin should be prejudicial to his salvation. We had need, therefore, to look to our faith, when want of belief seals a man up under sin. A man is imprisoned in his conscience until he come to Christ, and his conscience is his jailor. His conscience, enlightened by the law, tells him that he is guilty of such and such sins, and hereupon keeps him to further judgment.

155. There is a miserable cosenage in sin. Naturally, men will deny sin, or else mince it, as Adam did, and as Saul, when Samuel came to convince him; 'I have,' saith he, 'done the commandment of the Lord;' and when he was driven from that, then 'he did but spare them for sacrifice;' but when nothing could satisfy, 'then, I pray thee, honour me before the people,' 1 Sam. xv. 30. Things that we cannot justify, yet we will excuse them, unless God come by his Spirit. We are ready to shift them off. But when the Spirit comes, and takes away all these fig-leaves, then it convinces him of his miserable condition, not only in general, but the Spirit, working together with the word, brings him to confess, 'I am the man.'

156. The affections of grief and sorrow follow upon the discovery of sin by the ministry of the word. Where the judgment is convinced, the affections are stirred up with hatred against that sin; and where this is not, there is no convincing. When a man cries for mercy as for life, this is an argument of sound condition. He that is truly convinced will be as glad of a pardon as a malefactor that stands at the bar condemned.

157. It is the policy of the devil to labour to make us slight the gracious work of conviction; for he knows that whatsoever is built upon a false foundation will come to nothing, and therefore he makes us slight the work of self-examining and searching of ourselves. But slight this, and slight all; for if thou beest slight in searching and examining thyself, thou wilt also be slight in thy repentance and obedience.

158. Naturally, men labour to put out all checks of conscience by sensuality. Men are loath to know themselves to be as they are. They are of the devil's mind, they would not be 'tormented before their time,' Mat. viii. 29. Such men, when they are alone, are afraid of themselves. As the elephant will not come near the waters because he hath an ill shape, he would not see himself, so men, by nature, will not come near the light, lest they should see their ill deformities. For nature is so foul, that when a man sees himself, unless he be set in a better condition, it will drive him to despair.

159. We ought to have especial high conceits of the lordship of Christ, as lord paramount over all our enemies, the fear of death, and wrath of God; yea, whatsoever is terrible indeed. He hath freed us from the fear of it.

160. No sin is so great, but the satisfaction of Christ and his mercy is greater. It is beyond comparison of father or mother. They are but beams and trains to lead us up to the mercy of God in Christ.

161. The greatest spite of a carnal man is, that he cannot go to heaven with his full swing; that he cannot enjoy his full liberty; and therefore he labours to suppress all the ordinances of God as much as he can.

162. The quintessence and the spirits of the things we ask in prayer are in God, as joy, and peace, and contentedness; for without this joy and peace, what are all the things in the world? and in the want of these outward things, if we have him we have all, because the spirits of all is in him.

163. Prayer is a venting of our desires to God, from the sense of our own wants, and he that is sensible of his own wants is empty. 'A poor man speaks supplications,' Prov. xviii. 23.

164. It is not so easy a matter to pray as men think, and that in regard of the unspirituatness of our nature, compared with the duty itself, which is to draw near to a holy God. We cannot endure to sever ourselves from our lusts. There is also a great rebellion in our hearts against anything

that is good. Satan also is a special enemy; for when we go to God by prayer, he knows we go to fetch help and strength against him, and therefore he opposeth all he can. But though many men do mumble over a few prayers, yet indeed no man can pray as he ought, but he that is within the covenant of grace.

165. A child of God may pray and not be heard, because at that time he may be a child of anger. If any sin lie unrepented of, we are not in a case fit to pray. Will a king regard the petition of a traitor that purposeth to go on in his rebellion? Therefore, when we come to God, we should renew our purposes of better pleasing him, and then remember the Scripture, and search all the promises as part of our best riches; and when we have them, we should challenge God with his promise, and this will make us strong and faithful in our prayers, when we know we never pray to him in vain.

166. When we pray, God oftentimes refuseth to give us comfort, because we are not in good terms with him; therefore we should still look back to our life past. Perhaps God sees thee running to this or that sin, and before he will hear thee, thou must renew thy repentance for that sin: for our nature is such, that it will knock at every door, and seek every corner before we will come to God; as the woman in the Gospel, she sold all before she came to Christ, Mat. ix. 20, *seq.* So that God will not hear before we forsake all helps, and all false dependence upon the creature; and then he gets the greatest glory, and we have the greatest sweetness to our souls. That water that comes from the fountain is the sweetest; and so divine comforts are the sweetest, when we see nothing in the creature, and he is the best discerner of the fittest time when to give us comfort.

167. When God means to bestow any blessing on his church or children, he will pour upon them the Spirit of prayer; and as all pray for every one, so every one prays for all. This is a great comfort to weak Christians; when they cannot pray, the prayers of others shall prevail for them.

168. A fool's eye is in every corner, and fools' afflictions are scattered. The only object of the soul is that 'one thing needful,' Luke x. 42, and this will fill all the corners of it. When a man hath sucked out the pleasure of worldly contentments, they are then but dead things; but grace is ever fresh, and always yields fresh and full satisfaction.

169. Desires are the spiritual pulse of the soul, always beating to and fro, and shewing the temper of it; they are therefore the characters of a Christian, and shew more truly what he is than his actions do.

170. In the ark there was manna, which was a type of our sacraments; and the Testament, which was a type of the word preached; and the rod of Aaron was a type of government. Wheresoever, therefore, there is spiritual manna, and the word preached, and the rod of Aaron in the government, there is a true church, though there be many personal corruptions.

171. The bitterest things in religion are sweet. There is a sweetness in reproofs; when God meets with our corruptions, and whispers to us that those and those things are dangerous, and that if we cherish them, they will bring us to hell. The word of God is sweet to a Christian, that hath his heart touched. Is not pardon sweet to a condemned man, and riches sweet to a poor man, and favour sweet to a man in disgrace, and liberty sweet to a man in captivity? So all that comes from God is sweet to a Christian, that hath his heart touched with the sense of sin.

172. It is not happiness to see, but sight with enjoyment, and interest. There are but two powers of the soul, understanding and will. When both

these have their perfection, that is happiness: when the understanding sees, and the will draws the affections. So there are these things concur to make up our everlasting happiness, the excellency of the thing, with the sight of it, and interest in it.

173. We see by experience that there is a succession of love. He that loves for beauty will despise when he sees a better; so it is in the soul, between heavenly and earthly things: when the soul sees more excellency, and more fruitfulness in heavenly things, then the love of earthly things falls down in his heart, as Saint Paul saith, Philip. iii. 7, 'I account all things dross and dung in comparison of Christ.'

174. In prayer we tempt God, if we ask that which we labour not for. Our endeavour must second our devotion; for to ask maintenance, and not put our hands to the work, it is as to knock at the door, and yet pull the door unto us that it open not. In this case, if we pray for grace and neglect the spring from whence it comes, how can it speed? It was a rule in the ancient time, 'Lay thy hand on the plough and then pray' (*c*). No man should pray without ploughing, nor plough without praying.

175. Wisdom is gotten by experience in variety of estates. He that is carried on in one condition, he hath no wisdom to judge of another's estate, or how to carry himself to a Christian in another condition; because he was never abased himself, he looks very big at him. And therefore, that we may carry ourselves as Christians, meekly, lovingly, and tenderly to others, God will have us go to heaven in variety, not in one uniform condition, in regard of outward things.

176. There is no condition but a Christian picks good matter out of it, as a good artsman sometimes will make a good piece of work of an ill piece of matter, to shew his skill. A gracious man is not dejected over-much with abasement, nor lifted up over-much with abundance, but he carries himself in an uniform manner, becoming a Christian, in all conditions; whereas those that have not been brought up in Christ's school, nor trained up in variety of conditions, they learn to do nothing. If they abound, they are proud; if they be cast down, they murmur and fret, and are dejected, as if there were no providence to rule the world.

177. There is a venom and a vanity in everything, without grace, wherewith we are tainted; but when grace comes, it takes out the sting of all ill, and then it finds a good in the worst.

178. Christianity is a busy trade. If we look up to God, what a world of things are required in a Christian, to carry himself as he should do: a spirit of faith, a spirit of love, a spirit of joy and delight in him above all. And if we look to men, there are duties for a Christian to his superiors, a spirit of subjection; to equals he must carry a spirit of love; and to inferiors a spirit of pity and bounty. If we look to Satan, we have a commandment to resist him, and to watch against the tempter. If we look to the world, it is full of snares. There must be a great deal of spiritual watchfulness, that we be not surprised. If we look to ourselves, there are required many duties to carry our vessels in honour, and to walk within the compass of the Holy Ghost; to preserve the peace of our consciences; to walk answerable to our worth, as being the sons of God and coheirs with Christ. He must dispense with himself in no sin; he must be a vessel prepared for every good work; he must baulk in no service that God calls him unto: and therefore the life of a Christian is a busy trade.

179. Sincerity is the perfection of Christians. Let not Satan therefore abuse us. We do all things, when we endeavour to do all things, and

purpose to do all things, and are grieved when we cannot do better, than* in some measure we do all things.

180. A Christian is able to do great matters, but it is in Christ that strengthens him. The understanding is ours, the affections are ours, the will is ours; but the sanctifying of these, and the carrying of these supernaturally, to do them spiritually, that is not ours, but it is Christ's.

181. We have not only the life of grace from Christ at the first, and then a spiritual power answerable to that again, whereby our powers are renewed, so as we are able to do something in our will, but we have the deed itself: the doing is from Christ, he strengtheneth us for the performance of all good.

182. God preserves his own work by his Spirit: first, he moves us to do, and then he preserves us in doing, and arms us against the impediments.

183. Though Christ be a head of influence that flows into every member, yet he is a voluntary head, according to his own good pleasure, and the exigents† of his members. Sometimes we have need of more grace, and then it flows into us from him accordingly. Sometimes we have need to know our own weakness, and then he leaves us to ourselves, that we may know that without him we cannot stand; and we may know the necessity of his guidance to heaven in the sense of our imperfections, that we may see our weakness and corruptions, that we had thought we had not had in us; as Moses, by God's permission, was tempted to murmur, a meek man, and David to cruelty, a mild man, that thought they had not had those corruptions in them.

184. God is forced to mortify sins by afflictions, because we mortify them not by the Spirit; and in the use of holy means God doth us favours from his own bowels, but corrections and judgments are always forced.

185. We may for the most part read the cause of any judgment in the judgment itself; as, if the judgment be shame, then the cause was pride; if the judgment be want, then our sin was in abundance: we did not learn to abound as we should when we had it.

186. As we say of those that make bold with their bodies, to use them hardly, to rush upon this thing and that thing; in their youth they may bear it out, but it will be owing them after; they shall find it in their bones when they are old: so a man may say of those that are venturous persons, that make no conscience of running into sin, these things will be owing to them another day; they shall hear of these in time of sickness, or in the hour of death; and therefore take heed of sinning upon vain hope, that thou shalt wear it out, for one time or other it will stick to thee.

187. When God visits with sickness, we should think our work is more in heaven with God than with men or physic. When David dealt directly and plainly with God, and confessed his sins, then God forgave him them, and healed his body too, Ps. xxxii. 5.

188. It were a thousand times better for many persons to be cast on the bed of sickness, and to be God's prisoners, than so scandalously and unfruitfully to use the health that they have.

189. It is an art wherein we should labour to be expert, to consider God's gracious dealing in the midst of his corrections; that in the midst of them we might have thankful and cheerful, and fruitful hearts, which we shall not have, unless we have some matter of thankfulness. Consider, therefore, doth God make me weak, he might have struck me with death;

* Qu. 'then'?—Ed.

† That is, 'exigencies.'—G.

or, if not taken away my mortal life, yet he might have given me up to a spiritual death, to an hard heart, to desperation.

190. In this latter age of the world, God doth not use the same dispensation. He doth not always outwardly visit for sin; for his government is now more inward. Therefore we should take the more heed, for he may give us up to blindness, to deadness, to security, which are the greatest judgments that can befall us.

191. We should labour to judge ourselves for those things that the world takes no notice of, for spiritual, for inward things; as for stirring of pride, of worldliness, of revenge, of security, unthankfulness, and such like unkindness towards God; barrenness in good duties, that the world cannot see. Let these humble our hearts; for when we make not conscience of spiritual sins, God gives us up to open breaches that stain and blemish our profession.

192. Many men put off the power of grace, and rest in common civil things, in outward performances; but when we regard not the manner, God regards not the matter of the things we do; and therefore oftentimes he punishes for the performance of good duties, as we see in 1 Cor. xi. 30, 31.

193. Our whole life under the gospel should be nothing but thankfulness and fruitfulness. Take heed, therefore, of turning the grace of God to wantonness. The state of the gospel requires 'that we should deny all ungodliness and worldly lusts, and live righteously and soberly and godly in the present world,' &c., Titus ii. 12. Therefore, when we find ourselves otherwise, we should think, Oh! this is not the life of a Christian under the gospel: the gospel requires a more fruitful, a more zealous carriage, more love to Christ, &c.

194. If any man be so uncivil, when a man shews him a spot on his garment, that he grows choleric, will we not judge him an unreasonable man? And so, when a man shall be told this will hinder your comfort another day, if men were not spiritually besotted, would they swell and be angry against such a man? Therefore take the benefit of the judgment of others among whom we live. This was David's disposition, when he was told of the danger, going to kill Nabal and his household. So we should bless God, and bless them that labour by their good counsel and advice, to hinder us from any sinful course, whatsoever it is.

195. Those that truss up the loins of their souls, and are careful of their ways, they are the only sound Christians. They are the only comfortable Christians, that can think of all conditions and of all estates comfortably.

196. It is an ill time to get grace when we should use grace; and therefore that we may have the less to do, when we shall have enough to struggle with sickness; and that we may have nothing else to do when we die, but to die, and comfortably to yield up our souls to God, let us be exact in our accounts every day.

197. God takes a safe course with his children, that they may not be condemned with the world. He makes the world to condemn them, that they may not love the world: he makes the world to hate them, that they may not love the world, but be crucified to the world. He makes the world to be crucified to them. Therefore they meet with crosses, and abuses, and wrongs in the world. Because he will not have them perish with the world, he sends them afflictions in the world, and by the world.

198. If God should not meet with us with seasonable correction, we

should shame religion, and shame Christ; and therefore God in mercy corrects us with fatherly correction.

199. In the governing of a Christian life we are carried naturally to second causes, whereas they are all but as rods in God's hands. Look, therefore, to the hand that smites; look to God in all. He chastiseth us, as David saith in the matter of Shimei, 2 Sam. xvi. 10; and as Job saith, 'It is the Lord that hath given, and the Lord that hath taken away,' Job i. 21.

200. We have oftentimes occasion to bless God more for crosses than for comforts. There is a blessing hidden in the worst things to God's children, as there is a cross in the best things to the wicked. There is a blessing in death, a blessing in sickness, a blessing in the hatred of our enemies, a blessing in all losses whatsoever; and therefore in our affections we should not only justify God, but glorify and magnify him for his mercy, that rather than we should be condemned with the world, he will take this course with us.

201. Though our salvation be sure, and that we shall not be condemned with the world, yet the knowledge of this doth not make us secure; for though God doth not damn us with the world, yet he will sharply correct us here. And by a careful, sober life we might obtain many blessings, and prevent many judgments, and make our pilgrimage more comfortable. Therefore it argues neither grace nor wit, that because God will save me, therefore I will take liberty. No; though God will save thee, yet he will [take] such a course with thee, thou shalt endure such sharpness for thy sin, that it shall be more bitter than the sweetest of it was pleasant.

202. Gracious persons in times of peace and quiet do often underprize themselves, and the graces of God in them, thinking that they want faith, patience, and love, who yet, when God calleth them out to the cross, shine forth in the eyes of others, in the example of a meek and quiet subjection.

203. God oftentimes maketh wicked men friends to his children without changing their disposition, by putting into their hearts some conceit for the time, which inclineth them to favour, as Nehemiah ii. 8. God put it into the king's heart to favour his people; so Gen. xxxiii. 4, Esau was not changed, only God for the time changed his affections to favour Jacob. So God puts into the hearts of many groundedly naught,* to favour the best persons.

204. Usually in what measure we in the times of our peace and liberty inordinately let loose our affections, in that measure are we cast down, or more deeply in discomfort. When our adulterous hearts cleave to things more than become chaste hearts, it makes the cross more sharp and extreme.

205. A man indeed is never overcome, let him be never so vexed in the world by any, till his conscience be cracked. If his conscience and his cause stand upright, he doth conquer, and is more than a conqueror.

206. Partial obedience is no obedience at all. To single out easy things that do not oppose our lusts, which are not against our reputation, therein some will do more than they need. But our obedience must be universal to all God's commandments, and that because he commands us.

207. In every evil work that we are tempted unto we need delivering grace, as to every good work assisting grace.

208. That Christian who is privy to his own soul, of good intentions to abstain from all ill, he may presume that God will assist him against all ill works for the time to come.

* That is, 'fundamentally wicked.'—G.

209. We should watch and labour daily to continue in prayer, strengthening and backing them with arguments from the word and promises, and marking how our prayers speed. When we shoot an arrow, we look to the fall of it; when we send a ship to sea, we look for the return of it; and when we sow seed, we look for a harvest; and so when we sow our prayers into God's bosom, shall we not look for an answer, and observe how we speed? It is a seed of atheism to pray, and not to look how we speed. But a sincere Christian will pray, and wait, and strengthen his heart with promises out of the word, and never leave till God do give him a gracious answer.

210. Take a Christian, and whatsoever he doth he doth it in fear. If he call God Father, it is in fear. He eats and drinks in fear, as St Jude speaks of them that eat 'without fear,' ver. 12. The true servant of God hath fear accompanying him in all his actions, in his speeches and recreations, in his meat and drink. But he that hath not this fear, how bold is he in wicked courses, and loose in all his carriages! But mark a true Christian, and you shall always see in him some expressions of an holy fear.

211. The relation of servant is of great consequence to put us in mind of our duty. If we will be God's servants, we must make it good by obedience, we must resolve to come under his government, and be at his command, or else he will say to us, as to them in the 10th of Judges, 'Go to the gods whom you have served,' x. 14. Therefore empty relations are nothing to purpose. If we profess ourselves God's servants, and [do] not shew it by our obedience, it is but an empty title. Therefore let us make our relations good, at least in our affections, that we may be able to say, 'I desire to fear thy name,' Ps. lxxxvi. 11.

212. In reading of the Scriptures, let us compare experiments* with rules: Neh. i. 8, 9, 'If you sin, you shall be scattered; and if you return again, I will be merciful.' We should practise this in our lives, to see how God hath made good his threatenings in our corrections, and his promises in our comforts.

213. Those that have had a sweet communion with God, when they have lost it, do count every day ten thousand till they have recovered it again; and when Christ leaves his spouse, he forsakes her not altogether, but leaves something on the heart that maketh her to long after him. He absents himself that he may enlarge the desires of the soul, and after the soul hath him again, it will not let him go. He comes for our good, and leaves us for our good. We should therefore judge rightly of our estates, and not think we are forsaken of God when we are in a desertion.

214. When men can find no comfort, yet when they set themselves to teach weaker Christians by way of reflection, they receive comfort themselves, so doth God reward the conscionable† performance of this duty of discourse, that those things we did not so sweetly understand before, by discourse we understand them better. This should teach us to be in love with holy conference, for besides the good we do to others we are much bettered ourselves.

215. We may use God's creatures, but not scrupulously, nor superstitiously, singling out one creature from another, nor yet may we use them as we list. There is a difference between right, and the use of right. The magistrate may restrain the use of our right, and so may our weak brother in case of scandal. So that all things be ours, yet in the use of them we must be sober, not eating nor drinking immoderately, nor using

* That is, 'experiences.'—G.

† That is, 'conscientious.'—G.

anything uncharitably, whereby others may take offence; for albeit we have a right to God's bounty, yet our right and use must be sanctified by the word and prayer.

216. Many men fall to questioning, Oh that I had assurance of my salvation! Oh that I were the child of God! Why, man, fall to obedience. Ay, but I cannot; for it is the Spirit that enables. But yet come to holy exercises, though we have not the Spirit; for many times in the midst of holy exercises God gives the Spirit; and therefore, attend upon the means until we have strength to obey. Wait upon God's ordinances till he stirs in thy soul. All that love your souls, attend upon the means, and have a care to sanctify the Lord's day: Rev. i. 10, 'John was ravished in the Spirit on the Lord's day.'

217. God takes nothing away from his children, but instead thereof, he gives them that which is better. Happy is that self-denial that is made up with joy in God. Happy is that poverty that is made up with grace and comfort. Therefore let us not fear anything that God shall call us unto in this world. It is hard to persuade flesh and blood hereunto; but those that find the experience of this as Christians, do find withal particular comforts flowing from the presence of Christ's Spirit. St Paul would not have wanted his whippings to have missed his comforts.

218. Christ doth chiefly manifest himself unto the Christian soul in times of affliction, because then the soul unites itself most to Christ; for the soul in time of prosperity scatters and loseth itself in the creature, but there is an uniting power in afflictions to make the soul gather itself to God.

219. Christ took upon him our nature, and in that nature suffered hunger, and was subject to all infirmities. Therefore, when we are put to pains in our callings, to troubles for a good conscience, or to any hardship in the world, we must labour for contentment, because we are hardly* made conformable unto Christ.

220. There is not any thing or any condition that befalls a Christian in this life but there is a general rule in the Scripture for it, and this rule is quickened by example, because it is a practical knowledge. God doth not only write his law in naked commandments, but he enlivens these with the practice of some one or other of his servants. Who can read David's Psalms but he shall read himself in them? He cannot be in any trouble but David is in the same, &c.

221. As children in the womb have eyes and ears, not for that place, but for a civil life afterwards among men, where they shall have use of all members, even so our life here is not for this world only, but for another. We have large capacities, large memories, large affections, large expectations. God doth not give us large capacities and large affections for this world, but for heaven and heavenly things.

222. Take a Christian that hath studied mortification, you shall see the life of Jesus in his sickness, in a great deal of patience and heavenly-mindedness, when his condition is above his power, his strength above his condition.

223. As men do cherish young plants at first, and do fence them about with hedges and other things to keep them from hurt, but when they are grown, they remove them, and then leave them to the wind and weather, so God, he besets his children first with props of inward comforts, but afterwards he exposes them to storms and winds, because they are better able to bear it. Therefore let no man think himself the better because he is free from troubles. It is because God sees him not fit to bear greater.

* That is, 'with difficulty.'—G.

224. When we read the Scriptures, we should read to take out something for ourselves; as when we read any promise, This is mine; when we read any prerogative, This is mine, it was written for me; as the apostle saith, 'Whatsoever was written aforetime was written for our learning,' &c., Rom. xv. 4.

225. As the Spirit is necessary to work faith at the first, so is it necessary also to every act of faith; for faith cannot act upon occasion but by the Spirit; and therefore we should not attempt to do or to suffer anything rashly, but beg the Spirit of God, and wait for the assistance, because according to the increase of our troubles must our faith be increased; for the life of a Christian is not only to have the Spirit work faith at first, but upon all occasions to raise up our former graces. For faith stirs up all other graces, and holds every grace to the word; and so long as faith continues, we keep all other graces in exercise.

226. There is no true Christian but hath a public spirit to seek the good of others, because as soon as he is a Christian, he labours for self-denial. He knows he must give up himself and all to God, so that his spirit is enlarged in measure unto God and to the church; and therefore the greater portion a man hath of the Spirit of Christ, the more he seeks the good of others.

227. If we would have hearts to praise God, we must labour to see everything we receive from God to be of grace, and abundance of grace answerable to the degrees of good. Whatsoever we have more than nature is abundant grace. Whatsoever we have as Christians, though poor and distressed in our passage to heaven, is abundant grace.

228. There are three main parts of our salvation: first, a true knowledge of our misery; and secondly, the knowledge of our deliverance; and then, to live a life answerable. The Holy Ghost can only work these. He only convinceth of sin; and where he truly convinceth of sin, there also of righteousness, and then of judgments.

229. That we may be convinced of sin, the Spirit must work a clear and commanding demonstration of our condition in nature. It takes away therefore all cavils, turnings, and windings; even as when we see the sun shine we know it is day. The Spirit not only convinceth in generals that we are all sinners, but in particulars, and that strongly, 'thou art the man.' This convincing is also universal, of sins of nature, of sins of life, sins of the understanding, of the will, and of the affections; of the misery of sin, of the danger of sin, of the folly and madness of sin, of sins against so many motives, so many favours. Proud nature arms itself with deftness,* strong translations,† strong mitigations. It is necessary therefore that the Holy Ghost should join with men's consciences to make them confess, 'I am the man.'

230. The convincing of the Spirit may be known from common conviction of conscience by this, that natural conviction is weak like a little spark, and convinceth only of breaches of the second table, and not of evangelical sins. Again, common conviction is against a man's will: it makes him not the better man, only he is tortured and tormented. But a man that is convinced by the Spirit, he joins with the Spirit against himself; he accuseth himself; he takes God's part against himself. He is willing to be laid open, that he may find the greater mercy.

231. It is not enough to know that there is a righteousness of Christ, but the Spirit must open the eyes of the soul to see, else we shall have a

* That is, 'dexterity.'—G.

† That is, 'transferences.' Cf. Gen. iii. 12, *seq.*—G.

natural knowledge of supernatural things. It is necessary to have a supernatural sight to see supernatural things, so as to change the soul; and therefore the Spirit only works faith to see Christ is mine. Further, only the Spirit can work the conscience to be quiet, because he is greater than the conscience, and can answer all inward objections and cavils of flesh and blood. Unless, therefore, the Holy Ghost apply what Christ hath done, the conscience will not be satisfied.

232. The best men in the estate of grace would be in darkness, and call their state into question, if the Holy Ghost did not convince them, and answer all cavils for them; and therefore we must not only be convinced at the first by the Spirit, but in our continued course of Christianity. This, therefore, should make us to come to God's ordinances with holy devotion. O Lord, vouchsafe the Spirit of revelation, and take the scales from mine eyes, that as these are truths, so they may be truths to me! Do thou sway my soul, that I may cast myself upon thy mercy in Christ!

233. Spiritual convincing is not total in this life, but always leaves in the heart some dregs of doubting, though the soul be safe for the main. As a ship that rides at anchor is tossed and troubled, but the anchor holds it, so it is with the soul that is convinced weakly: it is sure of the main, yet it is tossed with many doubts and fears, but the anchor is in heaven.

234. The Spirit of God doth so far convince every Christian of the righteousness of Christ, as preserves in him such a power of grace, as to cast himself upon the mercy of God. God will send his Spirit so far into the heart, as it shall not betray itself to despair. He will let such a beam into the soul, as all the powers of hell shall not quench.

235. When we neglect prayer, and set upon duties in our own strength, and in confidence of our own parts; if we belong to God we shall be sure to miscarry, though another man perhaps may prosper; and therefore we should be continually dependent upon God for his direction and for his blessing in whatsoever we go about.

236. As many women, because they will not endure the pain of childbirth, do kill their children in the womb, so many men, who will not be troubled with holy actions, do stifle holy motions. Therefore, let us take heed of murdering the motions of the Holy Spirit, but let us entertain them, that when they are kindled, they may turn to resolution, and resolution into practice.

237. This is a common rule, that we cannot converse with company that are not spiritual, but if they vex us not they will taint us, unless we be put upon them in our callings. We should therefore make special choice of our company, and walk in a continual watchfulness.

238. It is rebellion against God for a man to make away himself. The very heathens could say, that we must not go out of our station till we be called. (*d*). It is the voice of Satan, 'Cast thyself down.' But what saith St Paul to the jailor? 'Do thyself no harm, for we are all here,' Acts xvi. 28. We should so carry ourselves, that we may be content to stay here till God hath done that work he hath to do in us and by us; and then he will call us hence in the best time.

239. He is a valiant man that can command himself to be miserable; and he that cannot command himself to endure some bondage and disgrace in the world, it argues weakness. Christ could have come down from the cross, but he shewed his strength and power by enduring their reproaches and torments.

240. The reason why many Christians stagger, and are so full of doubts, is because they are idle, and labour not to grow in grace. There-

fore we should labour to grow in knowledge and mortification, for in that way we come to assurance.

241. Whatsoever good is in a natural man, is depraved* by a self-end. Self-love rules all his actions. He keeps within himself, and makes for himself: he is a god to himself: God is but his idol. This is true of all natural men in the world. They make themselves their last end; and where the end is depraved, the whole course is corrupted.

242. The sense of assured hope cannot be maintained without a great deal of pains, diligence, and watchfulness: 2 Pet. i. 10, 'Give all diligence to make your calling and election sure,' insinuating that it will not be had without it. It is the diligent and watchful Christian that hath this assurance; otherwise the Holy Ghost will suffer us to be in a damp,† and under a cloud, if we stir not up the graces of the Spirit. It is grace in the exercise, and love in the exercise, that is an earnest, and so faith and hope in the exercise is an earnest. If grace be asleep, you may have grace, and not know it. Therefore we should labour to put our graces into exercise.

243. Those that have assurance of their salvation have oftentimes troublesome distractions, because they do not always stand upon their guard. Sometimes they are lifted up to heaven, and sometimes cast down even to hell; yet always in the worst condition there is something left in the soul, that suggests to it that it is not utterly cast off.

244. He to whom this pilgrimage is over-sweet, loves not his country; yet the pleasures of this life are so suitable to our nature, that we should sit by them, but that God follows us with several crosses. Therefore let us take in good part any cross, because it is out of heavenly love that we are exercised, lest we should surfeit upon things here below.

245. In melancholy distempers, especially when there goes guilt of spirit with it, we can see nothing but darkness in wife, children, friends, estate, &c. Here is a pitiful darkness, when body, and soul, and conscience, and all are distempered, Now let a Christian see God in his nature and promises, and though he cannot live by sight in such a distemper, yet let him then live by faith.

246. Though God do personate an enemy, yet faith sees a fatherly nature in him. It apprehends some beams of comfort. Though there be no sense and feeling, yet the Spirit works a power in the heart, whereby the soul is able to clasp with God, and to allege his word and nature against himself.

247. The reason why the world seeth not the happy condition of God's children is, because their bodies are subject to the same infirmities with the worst of men; nor are they exempted from troubles. They are also subject to fall into gross sins, and therefore worldly men think, Are these the men that are happier than we? They see their crosses, but not their crowns; they see their infirmities, but not their graces; they see their miseries, but not their inward joy and peace of conscience.

248. To walk by faith is to be active in our walking, not to do as we list, but it is a stirring by rule. Since the fall, we have lost our hold of God, and we must be brought again to God by the same way we fell from him. We fell by infidelity, and we must be brought again by faith, and lead our lives upon such grounds as faith affords. We must walk by faith, looking upon God's promise, and God's call, and God's commandments, and not live by opinion, example, and reason.

249. In the exercise of our callings, when we think we shall do no good,

* That is, 'vitiated.'—G. † Qu. 'dump'?—G.

but all things seem contrary, yet faith saith, God hath set me here; I will cast in my net at thy commandment, Luke v. 5. Let us look upon God, and see what he commands, and then cast ourselves upon him.

250. A Christian hath sense and experience of God's love, together with his faith. It is not a naked faith without any relish, but that sense and experience we have here is given to strengthen faith for time to come; and therefore when we have any sweet feelings, we must not rest in them, but remember they are given to encourage us in our way, and to look for fulness in another world.

251. There is a double act of faith: first, the direct act, whereby I cast myself upon Christ, and there is a reflect act, whereby I know that I am in an estate of grace by the fruits of the Spirit. It is by the first act that we are saved. Feelings are oftentimes divided from the first act; for God may enable a man to cast himself upon Christ, and yet for some ends he shall not know it, because he will humble him. God gives the reflect act, which is assured hope, as a reward of exact walking, but we must trust to that closing act of faith as to that which saveth us. We ought to live by this direct act of faith till we come to heaven, but add this, that there is no man walks by faith that wants comfort.

252. God oftentimes defers to help his children until they be in extremity, till they be at their wits' end, because he will have them live by faith and not by sight; as good Jehoshaphat, 'We know not what to do, but our eyes are towards thee,' 2 Chron. xx. 12. So St Paul received the sentence of death in himself, that he might trust in the living God, 2 Cor. i. 9. This is the cause of divine desertions, why God leaves his children in desperate plunges, seeming to be an enemy to them, because he will have us live by faith; and when we live by it, then he rewards us.

253. Howsoever things are in sight, yet we should give God the honour to trust to his promises. Though his dealings towards us seem to be as to reprobates, yet let us believe his word. He cannot deny it. Say, 'Lord, remember thy promise to thy servant, wherein thou hast caused me to trust,' Ps. cxix. 49. Therefore wrestle with God, for thereby he doth convey secret strength to his children, that they may be able to overcome him.

254. The reason why many men at the hour of death are full of fears and doubtings, and their hearts are full of misgivings, is, because in their lifetime they have not been exercised in living by faith.

255. Confidence doth then arise from faith, when troubles make it the stronger. Therefore it is a true evidence, when confidence increaseth with opposition, great troubles breeding great confidence. Again, it is a sign a man's confidence is well bred, when a man can carry himself equal in all conditions, when he hath learned to want and to abound. He needs a strong brain that drinks much strong water. Now when a man hath an even spirit, to be content in all conditions, it argues a well-grounded confidence.

256. None can be truly confident but God's children. Other men's confidence is like a madman's strength. He may have the strength of two or three for a time, but it is a false strength; and it is when they are lifted up upon the wings of ambition and favour of men, but these men in the time of trial sink: 'The hope of the hypocrite shall perish,' Prov. xi. 7.

257. Wicked men depart out of this world like malefactors that are unwilling to go out of prison. But God's children, when they die, they die in obedience: 'Lord, now let thy servant depart in peace, according to thy word,' Luke ii. 29. To be in the body is a good condition, because

we live by faith; but it is better to be with the Lord, because then we shall live by sight.

258. An ambitious man is an underminer of others, and if any stand in his way, he will make way through blood, he will tread upon his friends to get to honour, so a soul that is graciously ambitious considers what stands in his way. He hates father and mother, nay, his own life; he pulls out his right eye, he cuts off his right hand, he offers violence to everything that stands betwixt him and his God.

259. We should study the Scriptures, that we may find what is acceptable to God and Christ. Now that which most pleaseth God is holiness. So doth grace and mercy. Therefore we should study to be holy, and gracious, and merciful. 'This is the will of God,' saith the apostle, 'even your sanctification, that is, to be holy as God is holy,' 1 Thes. iv. 3. Those that will be acceptable to God must be good in private, in their closet, because sincerity supposeth that God sees all. They must be humbled for the rising of sin, because these things are seen of Christ with grief and hatred.

260. If in our recreations or other lawful things we be so religious as we should, we will then have Christ in our eye, and see how this may further me in his service, or how this may hinder me; for the most glorious actions of religion are no service at all if not done in faith, and with respect to Christ.

261. Let no man be discouraged in the doing of good actions, though otherwise they may be bad men, having no interest in Christ; for so far as any outward action is outwardly good it shall be rewarded. The Scribes and Pharisees had the promise of men for their reward. The Romans were straight* in their civil government, and God so blessed them for it, that their commonwealth flourished for many hundred years. Let the people be what they will, if civil,† they shall have their reward suitable to that good they do. As for heaven and happiness in another world, they care not for it; yet every man shall have his 'penny,' Mat. xx. 13.

262. It is a great art in faith to apprehend Christ suitable to our present condition; as when we are fallen into sin, think of the terrors of the law, but when we are broken-hearted, then present him as a sweet Saviour, inviting all to come unto him; and thus neither shall Christ be dishonoured nor our souls wronged.

263. It is much to be desired that there were that love in all men to teach what they know, and that humility in others to be instructed in what they know not. God humbles great persons to learn of meaner; and it is our duty to embrace the truth whosoever brings it; and oftentimes mean persons are instruments of comfort to greater than themselves; as Aquila and Priscilla instructed Apollos, Acts xviii. 26.

264. He that seeks us before we sought him, will he refuse us when we seek after him? Let no man therefore despair or be discouraged. If there be in thee the height and depth, and length and breadth of sin, there is also much more the height and depth, and length and breadth of mercy in God. And though we have played the harlot with many lovers, yet return again: Jer. iii. 1, 'For his thoughts are not as ours,' and his mercies are the mercies of a reconciled God.

265. When we are under a cloud of temptations, let us take heed of opposing our comforts; for it wrongs Christ's intention, who would not have us at any time to be uncomfortable; and besides, whilst we are in such a condition, we are unfit to glorify God, for fear doth bind up the

* That is, 'exact,' 'strict.'—G. † That is, 'moral,' or 'equitable.'—G.

soul, and makes it in a palsy temper. We are not fit to do anything as we ought without some love and some joy; and though we be at present under a cloud, yet the sun is always the same. We may therefore for a time want the light of his gracious countenance, but never his sweet influence.

266. Most men if they could they would always live here, but whosoever is partaker of Christ's resurrection, his mind doth presently ascend; and here we are always enlarging our desires, because we are under a state of imperfection.

267. Many men that make a profession are like kites, which ascend high, but look low. But those that look high as they ascend high are risen with Christ. For a Christian being once in the estate of grace, he forgets what is behind, and looks upon ascending higher and higher, till he be in his place of happiness; and as at Christ's rising there was an earthquake, so such as are risen with him do find a commotion and division between the flesh and the spirit.

268. Christ hath an especial care of his children, when by reason of the guilt of sin they have most cause to be disconsolate; and therefore, where the heart of any man is upright towards God, it is not to be expressed what indulgence there is in him towards such a poor sinner; for though Peter had denied him, yet in Mark xvi. 7, 'Go tell his disciples, and tell Peter,' so that Christ took great care to secure him of his love, though he had most shamefully denied him.

269. God hath not in vain taken upon him the name of a Father, and he fills it up to the full. It is a name of indulgence, a name of hope, a name of provision, a name of protection. It argues the mitigation of punishment. A little is enough from a father. Therefore in all temptations it should teach us by prayer to fly under the wings of our heavenly Father, and to expect from him all that a father should do for his child, as provision, protection, indulgence, yea, and seasonable corrections also, which are as necessary for us as our daily bread; and when we die we may expect our inheritance, because he is our Father. But yet we must understand also, that the name of Father is a word of relation. Something also he expects from us. We must therefore reverence him as a Father, which consists in fear and love. He is a great God, and therefore we ought to fear him; he is also merciful, yea, hath bowels of mercy, and therefore we ought to love him. If we tremble at him, we know not that he is loving, and if we be over bold, we forget that he is a great God. Therefore we should go boldly to him with reverence and godly fear.

270. Those that are at peace in their own consciences will be peaceable towards others. A busy, contentious, querulous disposition argues it never felt peace from God; and though many men think it commendable to censure the infirmities of others, yet it argues their own weakness. For it is a sign of strength, where we see in men any good, to bear with their weaknesses. Who was more indulgent than Christ? He bore with the infirmities of his disciples from time to time. Therefore we should labour to carry ourselves lovingly towards them that are weak, and know that nothing should raise us so high in our esteem above others, so as to forget them to be brethren, inasmuch as those infirmities we see in them shall be buried with them.

271. Many men will make much of eminent persons, and men of excellent parts, but there may be a great deal of hypocrisy in that, and therefore the truth of our love is tried in this, if we bear a sincere affection to all the saints, Eph. vi. 18.

272. We must take heed of coming to God in our own persons or

worthiness, but in all things look at God in Christ. If we look at God as a Father, we must see him Christ's Father first. If we see ourselves acquitted from our sins, let us look at Christ risen first. If we think of glorification in heaven, let us see Christ glorified first, and when we consider of any spiritual blessing, consider of it in Christ first. All the promises are made to Christ. He takes them first from God the Father, and derives* them to us by his Spirit. The first fulness is in God, and then he empties himself into Christ. 'And of his fulness we all receive grace,' &c.

273. God is said to be our God, or to be a God unto us, whenas he applies for the good of his creature, that all-sufficiency that is in himself. God is our God by covenant, because he hath made over himself unto us. Every believing Christian hath the title passed over to him, so that God is his portion, and his inheritance. There is more comfort in this, that God is our God, than the heart of man can conceive. It is larger than his heart, and therefore though we cannot say, that riches, or honours, or friends, &c., are ours, yet if we be able to say by the Spirit of faith that God is ours, then we have all in him. His wisdom is ours to find out a way to do us good. If we be in danger, his power is ours to bring us out; if under the guilt of sin, his mercy is ours to forgive us; if any want, his all-sufficiency is ours to supply, or to make it good. If God be ours, then whatsoever God can do is ours, and whatsoever God hath is ours.

274. God is the God and Father of all the elect, and he is also a God and a Father unto every one of the elect. God is every saint's *solidum*. Even as the sun is wholly every man's, so is God. He cares for all as one, and for every one as if he had but one.

275. There is not only a mystery, but a depth in the mystery; as of election and reprobation, so of providence. There is no reason can be given why some of God's children are in quiet and others are vexed, why one should be poor and another rich. In Ps. xcvii. 2, 'clouds and darkness are round about him.' You cannot see him, he is hid in a cloud; ay, but righteousness and judgment are the foundation of his throne. Howsoever he wrap himself in a thick cloud, that none can see him, yet he is just and righteous. Therefore when anything befalls us, for which we can see no reason, yet we must reverence him and adore his counsels, and think him wiser than we.

276. When we are diligent in our calling, keeping a good conscience and labouring for a carriage answerable; when these three meet together, calling, and standing, and wise carriage: then whatsoever befalls us, we may with comfort say, 'The will of the Lord be done.' We are now in his way, and may then expect a guard of angels without, and a guard of his Spirit within.

277. All the contentions between the flesh and the spirit lies in this, whether God shall have his will or we ours. Now God's will is straight, but ours is crooked, and therefore if God will have us offer up our Isaac we must submit to him, and even drown ourselves in the will of God, and then the more we are emptied of ourselves, the freer we are by how much we are made subject to God. For in what measure we part with anything for him, we shall receive even in this world an hundredfold in joy and peace, &c.

278. Whatsoever outward good things we have, we should use them in a reverent manner, knowing that the liberty we have to enjoy them is purchased with the blood of Christ, as David, when he thirsted for the waters of Bethlehem, would not drink it, because it was the blood of his three worthies, 2 Sam. xxiii. 15, *seq*. So though we have a free use of the creatures, yet we must be careful to use them with moderation and reverence.

* That is, 'communicates.'—G.

279. There is nothing of God can please the world, because the best things are presented to the heart of a carnal man as foolishness. Man's nature above all things would avoid the imputation of folly, and rather than he will be counted a fool he will slander the ways of God to be* foolishness. Now the law of Christ constrains us, and makes us do many things for which the world doth think us out of our wits, and therefore we should labour to quit our hearts, and account of it a greater favour from God, when the Michals of this world scoff at us for our goodness, 2 Sam. vi. 22; for when they are offended at us God is delighted with us.

280. To discern of our estate in grace, let us chiefly look to our affections, for they are intrinsecal, and not subject to hypocrisy. Men of great parts know much, and so doth the devil, but he wants love. In fire all things may be painted but the heat. So all good actions may be done by an hypocrite, but there is a heat of love which he hath not. We should therefore chiefly examine the truth and sincerity of our affections.

281. We may apprehend the love of God, but we cannot comprehend it. All the fruits of his love passes our common understanding, and therefore we have the Holy Spirit given to us to take away the veil, and to make report of it to the soul; and then as soon as this love of Christ is apprehended, it constrains us to all holy duties, not as fire out of flint, but as water out of a spring. The love of a wife to her husband may begin from the supply of her necessities, but afterwards she may love him also for the sweetness of his person. So the soul doth first love Christ for salvation, but when she is brought to him, and finds that sweetness that is in him, then she loves him for himself.

282. It should be our continual care to manifest the sincerity of our hearts to God in our several places and callings, and this is done when we look at God in every action, and endeavour to yield our whole soul to the whole will of God, serving him in our spirits, and performing the works of our callings by his Spirit, according to his word, and unto his glory; and if we thus labour to approve ourselves to him, whatsoever be the issue, we shall be endued with a holy boldness, with inward peace and comfort, having carried ourselves as in the sight of God.

283. That a man may be fit to persuade others he must have love to their persons, a clear knowledge of the cause, and grace, that he may be able to speak in wisdom to their souls and consciences. As we are saved by love, so we are persuaded by the arguments of love, which is most agreeable to the nature of man, that is led by persuasion, not by compulsion. Men may be compelled to the use of the means, but not to faith. Many men labour only to unfold the Scriptures, for the increasing of their knowledge, that they may be able to discourse, whereas the special intent of the ministry is to work upon the heart and affections.

284. As we must approve ourselves to God and to our own consciences, so also to the consciences of others,—not to their humours and fancies,—that they may witness for us, that we love them and deal faithfully with them. We should labour to do all the good we can, especially to the souls of men that are redeemed with the blood of Christ. If we deserve well of them, they will give evidence for us; but if we walk scandalously, they will evidence that we by our ill courses and examples drew them to ill courses, and hardened them in evil. It should be our care therefore to approve ourselves to the consciences of men, that we may have them to witness for us, that such men of whom we have deserved well may be our crown at the last day.

* That is, = *as* foolishness.—G.

285. A man doth then keep a good conscience in relation to others, when he makes it appear that he can deny himself to do them good; when the consciences of other men shall think thus, Such a man regards my good more than his own; he seeks no advantage to himself; he lives so as that the world may see he is in good earnest; he speaks so as that he makes it good by his life. Now if our care be to walk thus, we shall approve ourselves to the consciences of men.

286. There are many that will give some way to divine truths, but they have a reservation of some sin. When Herodias is once touched, then John Baptist's head must off, Mat. xiv. 6. Such truths as come near makes them fret, because their conscience tells them they cannot yield obedience to all. The lust of some sins hath gotten such domination over their affections, that the conscience saith, I cannot do this; and then that hatred that should be turned upon the sin, is turned upon the word and the minister. Like unto some vermin, that when they are driven to a stand, they will fly in a man's face, so these men, when they see they must yield, they grow malicious, so that what they will not follow, that they will reproach; therefore it should be our care at all times to yield obedience, according to what we know.

287. There is a generation of churlish people, such as watch for offences, because they would go to hell with some reason. They will not see who are weak, and who are hypocrites, but they cast reproach upon all; and therefore oftentimes God in justice to them suffers good men to fall, that such men may take 'scandal' at them to their ruin.

288. A man may know that the word hath wrought upon his conscience, when he comes to it, that he may hear and learn and reform. A man that hath a heart without guile, is glad to hear the sharpest reproofs, because he knows that sin is his greatest enemy; but if we live in a course that we are loath should be touched, it is a sign our hearts are full of guile. Corrupt men they mould their teachers, and fashion them to their lusts; but a good and upright heart is willing that divine truths should have their full authority in the soul, giving way to our duty, though never so contrary to flesh and blood.

289. It is the duty of ministers to labour to prevent objections that may arise in the hearts of the people, so as to hinder the passage of their doctrine; and that truths may more readily come into the heart, we should labour to relish the person, for secret surmises are stones to stumble at; therefore both ministers and people should be careful to remove them.

290. A man ought not to commend himself, but in some special cases: first, because pride and envy in others will not endure it; secondly, it toucheth upon God's glory, and therefore we should take heed; thirdly, it deprives us of comfort, and hinders the apology* of others. The heathens could say, that the praising of a man's self is a burdensome hearing (*e*); let us take heed, therefore, that we snatch not our right out of God's hand. But now, on the contrary in some cases, we may praise and commend ourselves, as when we have a just calling to make an apology in way of defence, and for the conviction of them that unjustly speak evil of us; secondly, we may speak well of ourselves in way of example to others, as parents to their children; and this doth well become them, because it is not out of pride or vain glory, because the end is discovered to be out of love unto them.

291. It is the duty of those that are God's children, when they have just occasion, to take the defence of others upon them: and thus did the blind

* That is, 'defence.'—G.

man, John ix. 30; he defended Christ against the Pharisees; and Jonathan spoke to his father in the behalf of David, 2 Sam. xx. 30. Though he was the son of a rebellious woman, yet he knew that he ought* this unto the truth. God hath a cause in the world that must be owned, and therefore when the cause of religion is brought upon the stage, then God seems to say as Jehu did, 'Who is on my side, who?' 2 Kings ix. 32. God commends his cause and his children to us; and therefore 'Curse ye Meroz, saith the angel of the Lord, curse ye bitterly the inhabitants thereof, because they came not to the help of the Lord, to the help of the Lord against the mighty,' Judges v. 23. So a curse lies upon those that, when the truth suffers, have not a word to defend it.

292. Usually the defamers of others are proud, vainglorious persons. If a man will search for the spirit of the devil in men, let him look for it amongst vainglorious teachers, heretics, and superstitious persons. The ground of it is from the nearness of two contraries. There the opposition is the strongest, as fire and water when they are near make the strongest opposition; and who are so near God's children as vainglorious teachers that are of the same profession? Pilate, a heathen, shewed more favour to Christ than the Pharisees. And this use we should make of it, not to take scandal when we see one divine deprave† another, for it hath been so, and will be so to the end of the world.

293. All things out of God are but grass. When we joy in anything out of God, it is a childish joy, as if we joyed in flowers, that after we have drawn out the sweetness, we cast them away. All outward things are common to castaways as well as to us; and without grace they will prove snares; at the hour of death what comfort can we have in them, further than we have had humility and love to use them well. Therefore if we would have our hearts seasoned with true joy, let us labour to be faithful in our places, and endeavour according to the gifts we have to glorify God.

294. To glory in anything whatsoever, is idolatry, because the mind sets up a thing to glory in, which is not God; secondly, it is spiritual adultery to cleave to anything more than God; thirdly, it is false-witness-bearing to ascribe excellency where there is none. We have a prohibition, 'Let not the wise man glory in his wisdom, nor the strong man in his strength, nor the rich man in his riches,' Jer. ix. 23. God will not give his glory to another; and therefore when men will be meddling with glory, which belongs to God alone, he blasts them, and sets them aside, as broken vessels, and disdains to use them.

295. A Christian joys aright, when it proceeds from right principles, from judgment and conscience, not from fancy and imagination; when judgment and conscienoe will bear him out; when there is good terms between God and him: for our joy must spring from peace: Rom. v. 1, 'Being justified by faith, we have peace towards God.' The apostles begin their Epistles with mercy, grace, and peace: mercy in forgiveness; grace to renew our natures; and peace of conscience here. These are things to be gloried in. If we find our sins pardoned, our persons accepted, and our natures altered, then we may comfort ourselves in anything, in health, in wealth, in wife, in children, in anything, because all come from the favour of God. We may joy in afflictions, because there is a blessing in the worst things, to further our eternal happiness; and though we cannot joy in affliction itself, as being a contrary to our nature, yet we may joy in the issue. So that we may joy aright, when having interest in God, we

* That is, 'owed.'—G. † That is, 'undervalue.'—G.

glory in the testimony of a good conscience; when looking inward we find all at peace; when we can say upon good grounds, that God is mine, and therefore all is mine, both life and death and all things, so far as they may serve for good.

296. The hearts of men, yea, of good men, are apt to be taken up with outward things: when the weak disciples had cast out devils, they were ready to be proud; but Christ quickly spies it, and admonisheth them, 'not to rejoice that the devils were subject to them, but that their names were written in the book of life,' Luke x. 20. Therefore, when we find the least stirrings to glory in anything, we must check ourselves, and consider what grace we have to temper them; what love we have to turn these things to the common good; for whatsoever a man hath, if he have not withal humility and love to use it aright, it will turn to his bane.

297. It hath been an old imputation to lay distractedness upon men of the greatest wisdom and sobriety. John the Baptist was accused to have a devil, and Christ to be besides* himself, and the apostles to be full of new wine, and Paul to be mad; and the reason of this is, because as religion is a mystical and spiritual thing, so the tenets of it seem paradoxes to carnal men: as, first, that a Christian is the only freeman, and other men are slaves; that he is the only rich man, though never so mean in the world; that he is the only beautiful man, though outwardly never so deformed; that he is the only happy man in the midst of all his miseries. Now these things, though never so true in themselves, seem strange to natural men. And then again, when they see men earnest against sin, or making conscience of sin, they wonder at this commotion for trifles, as if we made tragedies of toys.† But these men go on in a course of their own, and make that the measure of all: those that are below them are profane, and those that are above them are indiscreet; by fancies and affections, they create excellencies, and then cry down spiritual things as folly; they have principles of their own, to love themselves, and to love others only for themselves, and to hold on the strongest side, and by no means to expose a man's self to danger. But now when men begin to be religious, they deny all their own aims, and that makes their course seem madness to the world, and therefore they labour to breed an ill conceit of them, as if they were madmen and fools.

298. God's children are neither madmen nor fools, as they are accounted. It is but a scandal cast upon them by the madmen of the world. They are the only wise men, if it be well considered; for, first, they make the highest end their aim, which is to be a child of God here, and a saint hereafter in heaven. Secondly, they aim to be found wise men at their death, and therefore are always making their accounts ready. Thirdly, they labour to live answerable to their rules. They observe the rule of the word, to be governed according to the same. Fourthly, they improve all advantages to advance their end; they labour to grow better by blessings and crosses, and to make a sanctified use of everything. Fifthly, they swim against the stream of the times, and though they eat, and drink, and sleep as others do, yet, like the stars, they have a secret course and carriage of their own, which the world cannot discern; and therefore a man must be changed, and set in a higher rank, before he can have a sanctified judgment of the ways of God.

299. Those that lay the imputation of folly and madness on God's children will be found to be fools and madmen themselves. Is not he a fool

* That is, 'beside.'—G. † That is, 'trifles.'—G.

that cannot make a right choice of things? and how do carnal men make their choice, when they embrace perishing things for the best? Secondly, a carnal man hath not parts to apprehend spiritual things aright. He cannot see things invisible. Thirdly, in his heart he accounts it a vain thing to serve the Lord. Fourthly, he judges his enemies to be his best friends, and his best friends to be his worst enemies. Fifthly, the principles of all his actions are rotten, because they are not directed to the right object; therefore all his affections are mad, as his joy, his love, his delight. His love is but lust, his anger vexation; for his confidence he calls God's love into question; but if a false suggestion comes from the devil, that he embraces, and therefore is he not now a madman? And this is the condition of all natural men in the world.

300. True freedom is when the heart is enlarged, and made subordinate to God in Christ. A man is then in a sweet frame of soul when his heart is made subject to God; for he, being larger than the soul, sets it at liberty. God will have us make his glory our aim, that he may bestow himself upon us.

301. When the love of Christ is manifested to me, and my love again to Christ is wrought by the Spirit, this causes an admiration to the soul, when it considers what wonderful love is in Christ; and the Spirit shall witness that this love of Christ is set upon me; from hence it begins to admire,* 'Lord, wherefore wilt thou shew thyself to us, and not to the world?' John xiv. 22. What is the reason thou lovest me, and not others? When the soul hath been with God in the mount, and when it is turned from earthly things, then it sees nothing but love and mercy, and this constrains us to do all things out of love to God and men.

302. When Joshua cursed the man that should build the walls of Jericho, he was not in commotion and fury, but in a peaceable temper, Joshua vi. 26. So that, when cursing comes from such a one, he is a declaratory instrument, and the conveyer of God's curse. Therefore every man must not take upon him to curse, for men oftentimes curse where they should bless, which is an arrow shot upright, that falls down upon his own head; but those that come in the name of the Lord, and are qualified for that purpose, their cursings or blessings are to be esteemed, for they are a means oftentimes to convey God's blessings or his cursings upon us.

303. It is over-curious to exact the first beginnings of grace, because it falls by degrees, like the dew, undiscernibly; and further, there is a great deal of wisdom as well as power in the working of grace. God offers no violence to the soul, but works sweetly yet strongly, and strongly yet sweetly. He goes so far with our nature, that we shall freely delight in grace. So that now he sees great reason why he should alter his course, God doth not overthrow nature. The stream is but changed, the man is the same.

304. When the soul desires the forgiveness of sin, and not grace to lead a new life, that desire is hypocritical; for a true Christian desires power against sin as well as pardon for it. If we have not sanctifying grace, we have not pardoning grace. Christ came as well by water to regenerate as by blood to justify. It should therefore be our continual care and endeavour to grow and increase in grace, because without it we shall never come to heaven. Without this endeavour our sacrifices are not accepted; without this we cannot withstand our enemies, or bear any cross; without it we cannot go on comfortably in our course; without this we cannot do anything acceptable and pleasing to God.

* That is, 'wonder.'—G.

305. God will be 'as the dew unto Israel, and he shall grow as the lily, and cast forth his roots as Lebanon,' Hos. xiv. 5. These are not words wastefully spent; for we have great need of such promises, especially in a distressed state, for then our spirits are apt to sink and our hearts to faint, and therefore we have need to have the same comforts often repeated. Profane hearts think, what need all this? but if ever thou beest touched in conscience for thy sins, thou wilt then be far from finding fault, when God useth all the secrets in the book of nature, and translates them, to assure us of his mercy and love.

306. God's children are strengthened by their falls. They learn to stand by their falls. Like tall cedars, the more they are blown, the deeper they are rooted. That which men think is the overthrow of God's children, doth but root them deeper; so that, after all outward storms and inward declinings, this is the issue, 'They take root downward, and bring forth fruit upwards.'

307. A Christian in his right temper is compared to the best of everything. If to a lily, the fairest; if to a cedar, the tallest; if to an olive-tree, the most fruitful: 'And his smell shall be as Lebanon.' We should therefore make use of all natural things, and apply them to spiritual. If we see a lily, think of God's promise and our duty; we shall grow as lilies. When we see a tall tree, think, I must grow higher in grace; and when we see a vine, think, I must grow in fruitfulness. When we go into our orchards or gardens, let the sight of these things raise our thoughts higher unto a consideration of what is required of us.

308. As it is the glory of the olive-tree to be fruitful, so it is the glory of a Christian to be fruitful in his place and calling; and the way to be fruitful, is to esteem fruitfulness a glory. It is a gracious sight to see a Christian answer his profession, and flourish in his own standing; to be fruitful, and shine in good works. When ability, and opportunity, and a heart answerable to all, meet for doing good, this is glorious.

309. When we go about any action or business, let us always ask our souls this question, Is this suitable to my calling, to my hopes? But if not, Why do I do it? I that am a king to rule over my lusts, doth this agree with my condition? This base act, this base company, shall such a man as I do this? When a man brings his heart to reason thus with himself, it will breed Ephraim's resolution, 'What have I any more to do with idols?' And in walking thus circumspectly, we shall find a heat of comfort accompanying every good action; and a sweet relish upon the conscience, with humility and thankfulness, acknowledging all the strength we have to be from the dew of his grace.

310. In times of calamity, God will have a care of his fruitful trees; as in chap. xx. of Deut., ver. 19, the Israelites were commanded that they should not destroy the trees that bare fruit. So though God's judgments come amongst us, yet God will have a special care of his children that be fruitful, but the judgments of God will light heavy upon barren trees. And howsoever God may endure barrenness in the want of means, yet he will not in the use of means. It were better for a bramble to be in the wilderness than in an orchard; nothing will bear us out but fruitfulness.

311. It may be observed that old men seem not to grow, nor to be so zealous as many young Christians; but the reason is, because there is in young Christians a greater strength of natural parts, and that shews itself, and makes a great expression. But aged men they grow in strength and stableness, and are more refined. Their knowledge is more clear, their

actions more pure, their zeal more refined, and not mingled with wild-fire; and therefore, though old Christians be not carried with a full stream, yet they are more stable and judicious, more heavenly-minded, more mortified. They grow in humility, out of a clearer sight of their own corruptions.

212. In true conversion the soul is changed to be of the same mind with Christ, that as he is affected, so the soul of such a one is affected; and as he loathes all ill, so upon this ground there must be a loathing of whatsoever is evil. But a carnal man is like a wolf driven from the sheep, that yet retains his wolfish nature; so these men that are driven from their sins only out of terror of conscience, they are affrighted with sin, but they do not hate it; therefore a loathing of evil is required as well as the leaving of it.

313. If we would make it evident that our conversion is sound, we must loathe and hate sin from the heart. Now, a man shall know his hatred of evil to be true, first, if it be universal; he that hates sin truly hates all sin. Secondly, where there is true hatred it is unappeasable; there is no appeasing of it but by abolishing the thing it hates. Thirdly, hatred is a more rooted affection than anger; anger may be appeased, but hatred is against the whole kind. Fourthly, if our hatred be true, it hates all ill in ourselves first, and then in others; he that hates a toad, hates it most in his own bosom. Many, like Judah, are severe in censuring of others, but are partial to themselves. Fifthly, he that hates sin truly, hates the greatest sin in the greatest measure; he hates it in a just proportion. Sixthly, our hatred is right if we can endure admonition and reproof for sin, and not be in rage with him that tells us of it; therefore those that swell against reproof hate not sin; only with this caution, it may be done with such indiscretion and self-love, that a man may hate the proud manner. Therefore in discovering our hatred of sin in others, we must consider our calling. It must be done in a sweet temper, with reserving due respect of those to whom we shew our dislike, that it may be done out of true zeal, and not out of wild-fire.

314. All love and associations that are not begun on good terms, will end in hatred. We should take heed whom we join in league and amity withal. Before we plant our affections, consider the persons what they are. If we see any signs of grace, then it is good; but if not, there will be a rent. Throughout our whole life this ought to be our rule. We should labour in all companies either to do good or receive good; and where we can neither do nor receive good, we should take heed of such acquaintance. Let men therefore consider and take heed how they stand in combination with wicked persons.

315. 'Whosoever will live godly in Christ Jesus, must suffer persecution,' 2 Tim. iii. 12. He must have his nature changed, and carry his hatred against all opposite courses; and therefore to frame a religion that hath no trouble with it, is to frame an idol. But neuters in religion are like unto bats, that men can scarce distinguish from mice, or flying fowl, because they have a resemblance of both. Take heed therefore of neutrality in religion. After the first heat many become lukewarm, and from that they fall into coldness; let us therefore look to our beginnings. Pure affection in religion must also be zealous.

316. Wise men will do nothing without great ends; and the more wise, the greater are their ends. Shall we attribute this to men, and not to the wisdom of God? Christ would never have appeared in our nature, and suffered death, but for some great end. Shall we think that this mystery

of God taking flesh upon him, was for a slight purpose? Now, the end of his coming was to save sinners, 1 Tim. i. 15; he came to bring us to God, 1 Peter iii. 18; but he that will save us must first bring us out of Satan's bondage, therefore Christ came to destroy the works of the devil, 1 John iii. 8. It must needs follow therefore that the salvation of our souls is of great consequence, seeing for this only end Christ took our nature upon him and suffered for us.

317. Christ came to destroy the works of the devil in us, but yet he makes us kings under him, to fight his battles; and as by his Spirit in us he destroys the works of the devil, so he doth it in the exercise of all the powers and parts of soul and body, and by exercising the graces of his Spirit in us. 'He hath made us kings and priests,' not that we should do nothing, but that we should fight, and in fighting overcome. The chiefest grace that God doth exercise in overcoming our corruptions is faith. We fell by infidelity and disobedience. Now, Christ comes and displants infidelity, and instead thereof he plants faith, which unites us to him; and then by a divine skill, it draws a particular strength from Christ, to fight his battles against corruption.

318. Temptations at first are like Elias's cloud, no bigger than a man's hand; but if we give way to them, they overspread the whole soul. Satan nestles himself when we dwell upon the thoughts of sin. We cannot withstand sudden risings, but by grace we may keep them that they do not abide there long. Let us therefore labour as much as we can to be in good company and good courses; for as the Holy Ghost works by these advantages, so we should wisely observe them.

319. It is hard to discern the working of Satan from our own corruptions, because for the most part he goes secretly along with them. He is like a pirate at sea; he sets upon us with our own colours; he comes as a friend; and therefore it is hard to discern, but it is partly seen by the eagerness of our lusts, when they are sudden, strong, and strange, so strange sometimes, that even nature itself abhors them. The Spirit of God leads sweetly, but the devil hurries a man like a tempest, that he will hear no reason; as we see in Ammon, for his sister Tamar. Again, when we shake off motions of God's Spirit, and mislike his government, and give way to passion, then the devil enters. Let a man be unadvisedly angry, and the devil will make him envious and seek revenge. When passions are let loose, they are chariots in which the devil rides. Some by nature are prone to distrust, and some to be too confident. Now, the devil he joins with them, and so draws them on further. He broods upon our corruptions; he lies as it were upon the souls of men, and there broods and hatches all sin whatsoever. All the devils in hell cannot force us to sin. He works by suggestions, stirring up humours and fancies; but he cannot work upon the will. We betray ourselves by yielding before he can do us any harm, yet he ripens sin.

320. There are some sins that let Satan loose upon us; as, first, pride; we see it in Paul, 2 Cor. xii. 7. Secondly, conceitedness and presumption; as we may see in Peter, Mat. xxvi. 33. Thirdly, security; which is always the forerunner of some great punishment or great sin, which also is a punishment, as we see in David. Fourthly, idleness; it is the hour of temptation, when a man is out of God's business. Fifthly, intemperance, either in looseness of diet or otherwise; therefore Christ commands us to be 'sober, and watch,' and look to sobriety in the use of the creatures. Sixthly, there is a more subtile intemperance of passion, for in what degree

we give way to wrath, and revenge, and covetousness, in that degree Satan hath advantage against us. Seventhly, when a man will not believe and submit to truths revealed, though but a natural truth; therefore God gave them up to vile affections, Rom. i. 26, because they would not cherish the light of nature, much more when we do not cherish the light of grace.

321. As Christ wrought our salvation in an estate of baseness, so in our way to glory we must be conformable to our Head, and pass through an estate of baseness. We are chosen to a portion of afflictions, as well as to grace and glory. God sees it needful also, because we cannot easily digest a flourishing condition. We are naturally given to affect* outward excellencies. When we are trusted with great matters, we are apt to forget God and our duty to others. This should therefore teach us to justify God when we are any ways abased in the world.

322. There are a world of poor, who yet are exceeding proud; but God sanctifies outward poverty unto his children, so as it makes way for poverty of spirit; that as they are poor, so they have a mean esteem of themselves. It makes them inwardly more humble and more tractable. Therefore when we are under any cross, observe how it works; see whether we join with God or no. When he afflicts us outwardly, whether inwardly we be more humble; when he humbles us and makes us poor, whether we be also poor in spirit; when God goes about to take us down, we should labour to take down ourselves.

323. Poverty of spirit should accompany us all our life long, to let us see that we have no righteousness of our own to sanctification; that all the grace we have is out of ourselves, even for the performance of every holy duty. For though we have grace, yet we cannot bring that grace into act without new grace; even as there is a fitness in trees to bear fruit, but without the influence of heaven they cannot. That which oftentimes makes us miscarry in the actions of our calling, is because we think we have strength and wisdom enough; and then what is begun in self-confidence, is ended in shame. We set upon duties in our own pride and strength of parts, and find success accordingly. Therefore it is a sign that God will bless our endeavours, when out of the sense of our own weakness we water our business with prayer and tears.

324. It is not sufficient for a Christian to have habitual grace. There is no vine can bring forth fruit without the influence of heaven, though it be rooted; so we cannot bring forth fruit unless God blow upon us. Our former strength will not serve when a new temptation comes. It is not enough to have grace, but we must use it. We must exercise our faith, love, patience, humility; and for this purpose God hath furnished us with the Spirit of all grace. Let us therefore remember, when we have any duty to do, to pray unto Christ to blow upon us with his Spirit.

325. God doth not so much look at our infirmities as at our uprightness and sincerity; and therefore when we are out of temptations, we should consider and examine what God hath wrought in us. And then though there be infirmities and failings, yet if our hearts be upright, God will pardon them; as we find that David and others were accounted upright, and yet had many imperfections.

326. Watching is an exercising of all the graces of the soul, and these are given to keep our souls awake. We have enemies about us that are not asleep, and our worst enemy is within us; and so much the worse,

* That is, 'love,' choose.—G.

because so near. We live also in a world full of temptations, and wicked men are full of malice. We are passing through our enemy's country, and therefore had need to have our wits about us. The devil also is at one end of every good action, and therefore we had need to keep all our graces in perpetual exercise. We should watch in fear of jealousy, taking heed of a spirit of drowsiness; labouring also to keep ourselves unspotted of the world.

327. It may be asked, how we shall know the Scripture to be the word of God? For answer, do but grant, first, that there is a God, it will follow then that he must be worshipped and served; and that this service must be discovered to us, that we may know what he doth require; and then let it be compared what the word of God can come near to be the same with this. Besides, God hath blessed the superstition of the Jews, who were very strict this way, to preserve it for us; and the heretics, since the primitive church, have so observed one another, that there can be no other to this word. But now we must further know, that we must have something in our souls suitable to the truths contained in it, before we can truly and savingly believe it to be the word of God, as that we find it to have a power in working upon our hearts and affections: Luke xxiv. 32, 'Did not our hearts burn within us, when he opened to us the scriptures?' Again, it hath a divine operation to warm and pacify the soul, and a power to make a Felix tremble. It hath a searching quality, to divide between the marrow and the bone. We do not therefore only believe the Scriptures to be the word of God because any man saith so, or because the church saith so; but also and principally because I find it by experience working the same effects in me that it speaks of itself. And therefore let us never rest, till, when we hear a promise, we may have something in us by the sanctifying Spirit that may be suitable to it; and so assuring of us that it is that word alone that informs us of the good pleasure of God to us, and our duty to him.

328. There is in God a fatherly anger. After conversion he retains that; and this fatherly anger is also turned away when in sincerity we humble ourselves. There is one saith well, 'A child of anger, and a child under anger' *(f)*. God's children are not children of wrath, but sometimes they are under wrath,—when they do not carry themselves as sons, when they venture on sins against conscience, &c. But if they humble themselves and reform, and fly to God for mercy, then they come into favour again, and recover the right of sons.

329. We may know that God loves us, when by his Spirit he speaks friendly to our souls, and we by prayer speak friendly to him again; when we have communion and familiarity with him. Whom God loves, to them he discovers his secrets, even such secrets as the soul never knew before. He reveals them to us when our hearts are wrought to an ingenuous confession of sin, and when we have no comfort but from heaven. Even as a father discovers his bowels most to his child when it is sick, so God reserves the discovery of his love, especially until such a time when we renounce all carnal confidence. Therefore if we can assure our souls that God loves us, let us then be at a point for anything that shall happen to us in this world, whether it be disgrace or contempt, or whatsoever, because we may fetch patience and contentedness from hence, that God's love supplies all wants whatsoever.

330. After a gracious pardon for sin, there are two things remaining in us, infirmities and weaknesses. Infirmities are corruptions stirred up,

which hinders us from good, and puts us forward to evil. But yet they are so far resisted and subdued, that they break not forth into action. Weakness is when we suffer an infirmity to break out for want of watchfulness; as if a man be subject to passion, when this is working disturbance in the mind, it is infirmity; but when, for want of watchfulness, it breaks forth into action, then it is weakness. And these diseases are suffered in us, to put us in mind of the bitter root of sin; for if we should not sometimes break forth into sin, we should think that our nature were cured. Who would have thought that Moses, so meek a man, could have so broken out into passion? We see it also in David, and Peter, and others; and this is to shew that the corruption of nature in them was not fully healed. But there is this difference between the slips and falls of God's children and of other men. When other men fall, it settles them in their dregs; but when God's children fall, they see their weaknesses, they see the bitter root of sin, and hate it the more, and are never at quiet till it be cast out by the strength of grace and repentance. Therefore let no man be too much cast down by his infirmities, so long as they are resisted, for from hence comes a fresh hatred of corruption; and God looks not upon any sin but sin ungrieved for, unresisted; otherwise God hath a holy end in suffering sin to be in us, to keep us from worse things.

331. There is none that out of sincerity do give themselves to holy conference but are gainers by it. Many men ask questions, and are inquisitive to know, but not that they might put in practice. This is but a proud desire to taste of the tree of knowledge; but the desire of true-affected Christians is to know that they might seek Christ. We gain oftentimes by discourse with those that are punies in religion. St Paul desires to meet with the Romans, though they were his converts, that he might be strengthened by their mutual faith, Rom. i. 12.

332. When once the Spirit doth fasten the wrath of God upon the conscience of one whom he means to save, then there follows these afflicting affections of grief and shame; and from hence comes a dislike and hate of sin; hence begins a divorce between the soul and the beloved sin; so that whereas there was before a sceptre of sin in the soul, now God begins to dispossess that strong man, and then follows a strong desire to be better, and a holy desperation, that if God in Christ be not merciful, then the soul saith, What shall become of me! and as the Spirit lets in some terrors, so he lets in also some hopes, as, 'What shall I do to be saved?' implying a resignation of the will to take any course, so he may be saved; and then all the world for one drop of mercy.

333. Christ never comes into any heart but where he is valued and esteemed; yet he delights not to hide himself from his poor creature. But when we are fit, when we truly judge ourselves unworthy of any favour, then he receives us. Here is comfort, therefore, for the worst of men; if they will come in, and submit to God's ordinances, they will be effectual to subdue our corruptions; and when once God hath taken up the heart of man for his temple, he will then bring into it all his treasures. There will be a mutual fellowship between God and the soul when we are once subdued.

334. God is so powerful an agent that he can overthrow all. He can overthrow the carnal principles of reason, which every natural man hath in the fort of his soul. He presents to men the condition they are in by nature, and lets in a taste of his vengeance. When God in his ordinances shews greater reasons for goodness than Satan can in his carnal courses, then all falls down. Those, therefore, that are not fully subdued, yet let

them come to the ordinances, for then they are within God's reach. When the word of God discovers the baseness, vileness, and danger of sin, then the soul stoops. Therefore let none despair; for though thy heart be stone, yet God can work powerfully. Nothing is difficult to infirmities; but it is a divine work to pull down a wicked sinner.

335. However we take pains in our callings, yet the ability and blessing comes from God. We pray for daily bread, and yet he gives it, though we labour for it. There is a gift of success, which, unless it be given us from above, we shall, with the disciples, 'catch nothing,' Luke v. 5.

336. Gifts are for grace, and grace for glory. Gifts are peculiar to some men, but grace is common to all Christians. Gifts are peculiar to many, and common to such as are not good. Gifts are joined with great sins, but grace hath love and humility to take down the soul. The devil hath lost little of his acuteness, but yet he remains mischievous. So many men have great parts, but they have also a devilish spirit. Grace comes from more special love, and yet men had rather be accounted devils than fools. Account them men of parts, and then count them what you will.

337. It is a hard matter to find out the least measure of grace and the greatest degree of formality; for as painting oftentimes exceeds the thing, so doth an hypocrite oftentimes make a greater show; but the least measure of saving grace is from desires. And these are known to be saving, if they proceed from a taste of the thing, and not merely from the object; and therefore we must distinguish between affections stirred up and the inward frame; for those that are suddenly stirred up do presently return. The waters in the bath* have a natural hotness, but water, when it is heated, will return to its former coldness.

338. Though we be sure of victory over our spiritual enemies, yet we must fight. The conquered kings must be fought withal. Christ, that fights for us, fights with us and in us, and crowns us when all is done. And the time will come, ere long, when we shall say of our enemies as Moses said of the Egyptians, 'Those enemies that we now see, we shall see them no more for ever,' Exod. xiv. 13; 'Be strong therefore in the Lord, and in the power of his might,' Eph. vi. 10.

* That is, 'hot-spring.'—G.

NOTES.

(*a*) P. 197.—'St Augustine hath an excellent discourse,' &c. A reminiscence rather than quotation of a frequent illustration from this Father. Cf. any Index of his works *sub vocibus*.

(*b*) P. 201.—'As a man that is called,' &c. See note *a*, Vol. V. p. 408.

(*c*) P. 204.—'It was a rule in the ancient time, "Lay thy hand,"' &c. As already noticed, this 'rule' is embodied in the *sentiment* 'Speed the plough.'

(*d*) P. 211.—'The very heathens could say, that we must not go out of our station till we be called.' A commonplace of Cicero and others of the ancients who have written striking things against suicide.

(*e*) P. 218.—'The heathens could say, that the praising of a man's self is a burdensome hearing.' This idea is found in Demosthenes' great speech 'De Coronâ.' [Reiske ed., p. 226, line 20; Bekker, § 4.]

(*f*) P. 226.—'There is one saith well, "A child of anger, and a child under anger."' Bernard and Augustine furnish the *thought*, and the distinction is common to all the Fathers. G.

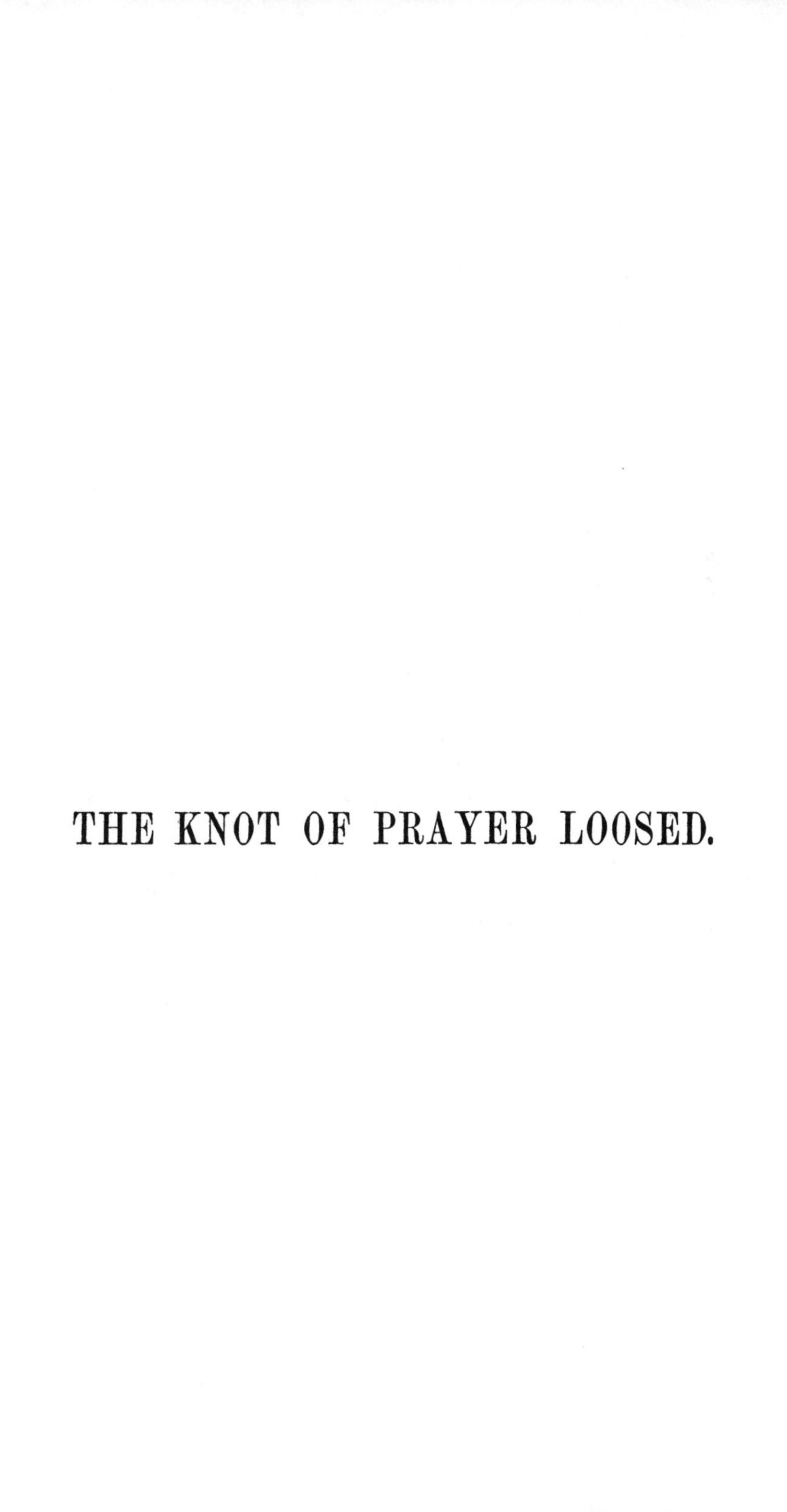

THE KNOT OF PRAYER LOOSED.

THE KNOT OF PRAYER LOOSED.

NOTE.

'The Knot of Prayer Loosed' forms No. 16 of 'The Saint's Cordials' of 1629. It was not inserted in the after-editions. Its separate title is given below.*

G.

* THE KNOT OF
PRAYER LOOSED.

In One Sermon.

Wherein is shewed,

The Conditions, Limitations, Qualities, Companions, and
Attendants of Prayer; The Causes of the Difficulties therein: How to
pray as we may be heard, nourishing and quick-
ning our Faith, &c.

Prælucendo Pereo.

Vprightnes Hath Boldnes.

Iames. 1. 5.

If any of you lacke wisedome, let him aske of God, who giveth to all men liberally, and upbraideth not, and it shall be given him.

LONDON,
Printed in the yeare 1629.

THE KNOT OF PRAYER LOOSED.

Ask, and it shall be given you; seek, and ye shall find; knock, and it shall be opened unto you: for every one that asketh, receiveth; and he that seeketh, findeth; and to him that knocketh, it shall be opened. Or what man is there of you, who, if his son ask bread, will give him a stone? or if he ask a fish, will give him a serpent? If ye then, being evil, know how to give good gifts unto your children, how much more shall your Father which is in heaven give good things to them that ask them?—MAT. VII. 7–10.

I HOPE it will not be offensive to any here present,—it may be profitable to some,—briefly to repeat what I have spoken in another place of this text.* The whole contains an exhortation to prayer, Christ's exhortation to Christ's hearers. The parts are two.

1. The exhortation strictly taken, pointing out the duty.
2. The motives and arguments enforcing the same. In brief,

The nail and the hammer.

The duty is laid down in these words, 'ask,' 'seek,' 'knock;' all of them whetting on our dulness; by which we may see, the pressing of these things in this manner imports diligence, that we should set on the same eagerly, yea, with an earnest desire of obtaining our suit, as we do with those we have occasion to speak with, whom by all means we importune for a despatch. Our Lord here would have us so to make haste, using all means and diligence for obtaining of our suit.

The motives are,

1. Ordinate, directly urging the duty.
2. Subordinate, standing as helps and supporters thereunto.

The motives ordinate are these: 'Ask, and receive;' 'seek, and find; knock, and it shall be opened unto you.' The argument is taken from a threefold promise, according to the threefold urging of the duty. In sum, the success they should have, that they shall speed.

The subordinate arguments follow the former, and they are of two sorts, simple or by comparison. The simple in these words, 'For every one that asketh receiveth, and he that seeketh findeth, and to him that knocketh it shall be opened.' And this simple argument is drawn, as it were, from the common experience of others, as if our Lord should have said, Since it is found by sure and certain experience, that every one that asketh

* The previous Sermons have not been preserved.—G.

receiveth, why should not ye also, if ye ask, think to speed as well as others?

Lastly, There is set down an argument of comparison, from the lesser to the greater, from fathers on earth, endowed with a little of that pity and mercy, the greater fountain and ocean whereof is in God; from which the inference is, that if earthly and evil parents will be ready to hear their children, and give good things unto them, how much more will our good and heavenly Father be ready to hear and grant our requests, that is, give good things to such as ask in faith? This is the sum.

From the exhortation note, the duty of prayer is a common task, so that every Christian, who would be in deed and not in name so called only, he must be a man of prayer. Then, in the next place, from the exhortation and reason laid together, note the potent means by which we shall be best enabled to receive from God what we would; and what we have need of is prayer. There might be, but needs not, many proofs of this, whereof there was delivered many uses then; the last and main whereof was, that we should learn to make more reckoning of our prayers than formerly we have done, that as we reckon our states in bonds and bills, and that we have beyond seas in stock, as well as that we have in possession by us; so we should reckon in our spiritual wealth, not only what we have and feel, but also that stock of prayer we have long since adventured to a far country, as merchants do of that they have adventured to East India: so much the rather, because these may fail in whole or in part, and so that stock may perish; but the adventure and return of this stock of prayer is most certain to increase more, which, if we do, we shall be sure of a more quick and speedy return. Hence we came to a knotty and great objection.

Obj. Whether all men in prayer have this assurance to be heard, seeing Christ's promise is so sure and firm?

Ans. There are indeed a great many Christians full of complaints and discouragements this way. Oh, say some, I have prayed thus and thus long, and am worse and worse; I have prayed and am not heard; better leave all, seeing I am not the better for it. I answer, Though our Lord do speak so confidently, yet God's charter must be interpreted to God's meaning, with such conditions and limitations as he hath revealed unto us out of his word, which, though not named here, yet must be understood. We are undone, every mother's son, if we lose any part of that charter Christ hath made, to think we can make no certain return of our prayers sent to our heavenly country; for it remains always sure, 'Ask, and ye shall receive; seek, and ye shall find; knock, and it shall be opened to you.' For the better answering of the objection, here comes two things to be considered,

1. Conditions on our part; 2. Limitations on God's part.

1. The first thing in the conditions on our part is concerning the party that must pray: he must be a free denizen in the state of faith and repentance. An outlawed man can put up no petitions with assurance to speed. St John saith, 'This is the confidence we have in him, that if we ask any thing according to his will, he heareth us,' 1 John v. 14. The will of God is, that he who prays be a man qualified; so all the promises of God are made, at least to such who hunger and thirst and desire to be in Christ. Faithless, godless, careless men are outlawed, as we see, Ps. l. 15, 16, the promise is, 'Call upon me in the day of trouble; I will deliver thee, and thou shalt glorify me;' and then presently he makes a stop. 'But unto

the wicked God saith, What hast thou to declare my statutes, or that thou shouldest take my covenant in thy mouth ? seeing thou hatest instruction, and castest my word behind thee.'

Obj. Here some may object, that even many heathens have been heard in their prayers who were not thus qualified.

Ans. To which I answer, It is not out of the privilege of this great charter here that such are heard; but out of his common goodness unto all, whereby he would draw even the most rebellious to admiration of his divine abundant mercies, yea, and even teach us, if such prevail thus, much more shall we, being within the covenant.

2. The second is, Our prayers must be made to God alone.

3. Thirdly, They must pass under the seal of the Mediator.

For though all Christians may claim a part in the charter, yet the title must be pleaded in the Mediator's name only; no Mediator to thee, no hearing.

4. Fourthly, Concerning the things prayed for, they must be lawful in kind also; not fore-excepted, nor under any general nor particular limitations forbidden. Not everything we desire is rightly asked, some of which may cross his nature and will; some things also are ill for us, by general and special decree forbidden, as exemption from afflictions and sufferings with him. If God hear us not in this, Christ forfeits not his word, but we our prayers.

5. Fifthly, That we have a right end in prayer; as James iv. 3, the apostle speaks, 'You ask, and receive not, because you ask amiss, that you may consume it upon your lusts.' If the end be naught, the prayer is confiscate.

6. Sixthly, The time; there be certain seasons and times wherein the Lord will be found; as Dan. ix. 2, when he knew the time of the captivity to be near expired, then he prays for the return of the people. If we wait and seek in season, we may obtain; but otherwise we may have a nap, and the door be knocked against our heads. Since then, 'there is a time that the Lord will be found,' as the prophet speaks, Isa. lv. 6, I would not have us omit our time, but now when there is a stirring of the Spirit, let us take the opportunity, lest we miss it when we shall have most need of it.

7. Seventhly, There is the manner, under which I comprehend the order of the things asked and desired. If we would speed in temporal things, we must first seek spiritual, saith our Saviour; 'But seek ye first the kingdom of heaven, and his righteousness, and all these things shall be added unto you,' Mat. vi. 33. If we miss of this, we may knock long ere we have entrance. To come to God and seek oil and wine, and the like things, and in the mean time to neglect the oil of grace, what a disorder is here. If in this case thou be crossed, it is not because he would put thee off without hearing, but because he would teach thee a better way to speed. For as when we eat our meat disorderly we want digestion, and for the most part buy experience at a dear rate, so many times God doth beat his dearest children, and put off their prayers for a long time, that he may teach them in due order what is first and principally to be desired; all these the party praying must carefully look unto for speeding in his suit.

Further, we have to observe in prayer,

1. The qualities. 2. The companions. 3. The attendants of prayer.

1. *The qualities of prayer.*

(1.) That it be the prayer *of faith;* not generally and confusedly of the Godhead only, but distinctly of the persons, and of the redemption purchased, and of the hearing of thy petitions, having interest in him, 'Believe and it shall be given thee.'

(2.) *Humility;* that a man go to God with a knowledge and a sense of his own insufficiency to succour himself. No man may come to God, but upon his knees. I speak not of the bowing of the knee, but of the heart; it is written, 'God will hear the desires of the humble,' Ps. ix. 12. In misery, affliction, sense of our necessity, and the like, we should assure ourselves to be heard.

(3.) *The heat and fervency of prayer.* Our God, which is a 'consuming fire,' Heb. xii. 29, doth not endure a cold prayer; the heart must be elevated, as Hannah, her heart spake unto the Lord, 1 Sam. i. 13; and Saint James saith, 'the effectual fervent prayer of a righteous man availeth much,' James v. 16. By the contrary, a cold prayer hath but a cold answer; that man is but a mocker of prayer, that would have God to hear him, when he hears not himself.

2. *The companions of prayer.*

(1.) First, *Charity* which extends itself toward all men, and a brotherly love toward the saints, joined with graciousness in ourselves; and it hath two things in it, giving and forgiving. He that would have mercy, must shew mercy; rich men may do the one, and all men may do the other, but the other is harder, to forgive. He that is able to give, and relieve others as their need shall require, and yet will not, let him not wonder if God deny his suit; and so he that will not forgive others, let him not look to be forgiven. 'Blessed is he,' saith the Scripture, 'that judgeth wisely of the poor, the Lord shall deliver him in the day of trouble,' Ps. xli. 1. If thou ask, and speed not, in this case marvel not; thou hast denied him in his own members asking of thee, and therefore it is just with him to deny thee.

(2.) The second is, *Thankfulness* for benefits and blessings received and enjoyed, with forgiveness of the old debts; thanksgiving ere we beg more mercies. For this cause we speed not in our suits; because we forget him, he forgets us.

3. *The attendants of prayer.*

(1.) First, *Perseverance,* called 'watching with prayer;' as we see our Lord teacheth us by the example of the importunate widow, and the unjust judge, thereby intimating for our comfort, how much more certainly, in the like case, we may assure ourselves to speed with him, who is the most just judge of the world, and goodness itself. So that he that will be sure to have this promise, 'Ask and ye shall have, seek and ye shall find,' made good unto him, he must make a trade of prayer, not for two or three times, and so have done, but he must still ask, and so obtain. As he desires constancy in holding out in our suits, so he would have us ask constantly without fainting; and as he will give conveniently in the best time, so he shews we shall still be set on work in begging, as his mercy shall be in giving.

(2.) The second is, *diligence in the means;* we tempt him, to ask for that we labour not for. As we pray, so our endeavours must second our devotion; for to ask maintenance, and not put our hands to the work, it is as to knock at the door, and yet to pull the door unto us that it open not. In this case, if we pray for grace, and neglect the spring from whence it comes, how can we then speed? It was a rule in the ancient time, 'Lay, thy hand on the plough, and then pray;' no man in old time might pray without ploughing, nor plough without praying (*a*).

(3.) The third is, *Expectation, waiting, perseverance in hope, until God hear us.* The reason is, because the Lord, who hath promised the thing, hath not limited the time. In this we may see what patience brings forth, as the prophet's experience is, Ps. xl. 1: 'I waited patiently for the Lord, and he inclined to me, and heard my cry;' and in another place he saith, 'It is good for man both to wait, and trust in the Lord,' ver. 4; so, Rev. iii. 10, he saith, 'because thou hast kept the word of my patience, I will also keep thee from the hour of temptation,' &c. This waiting doth interest us in him, when we are so earnest that we will not away till we speak with him; as, when a man knows a party he desires to speak with to be in such a house, and that he will come forth, he waits at the door, and will not away till he speak with him, so, if we were earnest, and had faith and assurance that God would come, we would stand still at the door till he came, and not be gone and faint upon every light occasion. All of us fail in this, that we wait not constantly at the door of grace till we obtain. Gross sins indeed, these cause a man to faint, that he dare not look God in the face but with much ado; but if we strive and labour to hold out, God accepts of the truth, though the measure be small, when we cannot do as we would. But if there be gross failings in this kind, that we fall into the old bias of our sins, and so leave knocking, or are quickly weary, we obtain not by and by, as though we might limit him the time. If, I say, in this case, like the raven sent out of the ark, our prayers return no more, and we faint and sink comfortless in desolation, anguish, and sorrow of mind, let us not blame our Saviour, whose promise is firm and inviolable without change. If we would learn to mend our prayers and wait, we should hear more from him. All these are limitations on our part.

Secondly, The limitations on God's part.

In general, we must be wary that our misunderstanding of providence make us not to fail: first, all such things are excepted, as God cannot give unto our prayers without crossing some part of his revealed will, or a secret government and providence of his, which we would not willingly cross, if we knew it, but rather submit ourselves unto the same, as Christ did in his agony, 'Nevertheless, not as I will, but as thou wilt,' Mat. xxvi. 39. I say then, God will so give, as may not cross himself in anything. There are some things God cannot grant, I speak with reverence, unless he forfeit his word. A man prays and says, 'Lord, forgive me my sins,' without a desire to leave them, or resolution of a new course of life, but goes on, swears and sins again; God cannot in this case hear such a one, because it is against his word to hear sinners, so long as with delight and without remorse they love the sin. The prophet saith, 'If I regard wickedness in my heart, the Lord will not hear me,' Ps. lxvi. 18. Therefore, seeing God cannot lie, repent, nor deny himself, such a one cannot be heard.

Again, an idle man in his calling, though he pray much and often to prosper therein, God, if he make his word good, will not grant his suit. As he hath said, 'the hand of the diligent maketh rich,' Prov. x. 4, so, on the contrary, he hath said in other places, 'that the sluggard shall be clothed with rags; that his soul shall desire, and have nothing; that because he will not plough in the cold, therefore he shall beg in harvest,' Prov. xx. 4, and thou, O sluggard, dost thou think then to obtain anything without pains-taking? So in another kind the Jews bade Christ to come down from the cross, and save himself, if he were the son of God; when in the mean time for the very same thing, because he was the Son of God, and had undertaken and promised to finish then the work of our redemption, he might not come down from the cross and save himself from that hour. And further, when a man blesseth himself in sin, as it is Deut. xxix. 19, saying in his heart, that 'he shall have peace, walking in the imagination of his heart; adding drunkenness to thirst,' &c., God hath passed his word, that he will not spare such a man, but his wrath shall smoke against him, and all the curses that are written in the book of God shall lie upon him. In this case, continuing and delighting in sin, God cannot hear such a prayer, unless he forget his word. Understand thou, man, God could never be held by such prayers that cross his will, and the manner of his government, yea, such against which he hath so often protested in his word.

Secondly, In the things asked, he understands that such should be good for us in lawfulness of circumstances, as,

1. The quality of the same good things. 2. The time. 3. The means. 4. The manner. 5. The measure.

I. For the first, ['*the quality*']. We know the main promise, made to the faithful, Rom. viii. 28, is, that 'all things work together for good unto them that love God.' Therefore, that which cannot be unto thee for good it is not intended, nor ever shall be given, if God do love thee. See also in my text, the last part of Christ's last argument is the same in effect: 'how much more shall your Father which is in heaven give good things to them that ask them?' The physician knows better than the patient what is good for him, so that I say, for this cause many things are profitably denied us, which could not conveniently without hurt be granted: as we see fathers will keep from their children knives, burning sticks, and all such sharp and dangerous things, not because they love them not, but because they love them so much, therefore they will keep from them all things hurtful.

II. Secondly, *For the time.* God gives us his bill, but he will pay at his pleasure. There is a time, but when, that is concealed; not that it is uncertain unto God, but it is hid from thee, as in Ps. lxxxvi. 7, 'He will hear,' but it is 'in the time of trouble;' yea, of great trouble and sorrow; betwixt the cup and the lip, as the proverb is. It was Abraham's experience: Gen. xxii. 14, 'In the mount of the Lord it shall be seen;' all things were there ready for a sacrifice, the wood was laid, the fire was ready, Isaac was bound, the hand and knife lifted up to kill and cut asunder the only son, and son of the promise; but at an instant came a stop unlooked for, which mercy being so great, it was then made unto us an instance for ever, that even in the most desperate cases we should not despair, but hope against hope, as he did. Now, why the Lord thus delays to help and hear us, there be divers reasons.

(1.) First, *That our faith and dependence on him might be the better tried*, which experience, though it be sore, yet we must be courageous, since the issue is joyful; though it be bitter, yet the victory obtained is great, as we may see in the woman of Canaan, a good suitor, having a good suit, yet how doth our Lord put her off a long time, that to others he might open the faith of this woman, and make her unto us a precedent for ever, Mat. vii. 6, *et seq.*

(2.) Secondly, Sometimes it is done *to humble men*, as Judges xx. In a good quarrel, having a good cause, we know what befell them. See what need we have of prayer to do all things aright. They consult with God what to do; they receive encouragement from him to go on, and yet are overthrown; the second time they weep, and mourn, and are beaten again. In such a case it seemeth strange to be overcome. Well, the third time they weep and fast, are humbled before God for their own sins, ere they seek revenge for other men's, then they prevail. Thus 'God resists the proud, and gives grace to the humble,' James iv. 6. Till we be nothing in our own eyes, he never comes with comfortable deliverance till we come to that pinch wherein we cry, Up, 'Lord, how long,' &c., as Paul saith of himself, 'We had the sentence of death in ourselves, that we might not trust in ourselves, but in God which quickeneth the dead,' 2 Cor. i. 9. The Lord brought him out of hope of life, that he might be humbled, and learn to know where only life, help, and comfort in all extremities is to be found.

(3.) Thirdly, *To quicken our appetite.* God puts us off the longer; we are unwise and think he doth it to put us off for ever; in which manner of working the Lord in a manner fisheth for us. The fisher, we know, doth draw back the hook when he finds the fish is like to bite, that the fish may follow. So God gives back from our suits sometimes, not to make us give over, but that we may press him so much the more. The experience hereof once found is very sweet, though smarting in the beginning, as we may see in the spouse: Cant. v. 2, 'She slept, and lost Christ by her sluggishness.' She made some idle excuses not to open unto him. Well, what came of it? When she would have opened to her best beloved her hands dropped myrrh; all her affection was not gone, for he had left so much with her as made her in love with him, but her beloved had withdrawn himself. Well, yet more. In search of him the watchmen 'beat her, wounded her, took away her veil.' Here she pays worthily for her sloth; she had all sweet words given her to open unto Christ: 'Open to me, my sister, my love, my dove, my undefiled;' but putting him off, as I have shewed, he departs and leaves her in the pursuit of him. And why goes he away? Partly to chastise her neglect of him, to whom she should have gone out, and opened with all cheerfulness and diligence; and partly it was to quicken on her desires, as we see it fell out, ver. 8, wherein she chargeth the daughters of Jerusalem, that if they find her beloved, to tell him that she was sick of love.

(4.) Fourthly, He delays and puts off our suits, *to enhance the price of those things he gives;* for what lightly comes, for the most part, as the proverb is, lightly goes; but what we come hardly by, that we highly prize, and have in estimation, as we see in the chief captain, Acts xxii. 28, when Paul had pleaded he was a Roman, he replied, 'With a great sum obtained I this freedom;' he bought it at a dear rate, and therefore he valued it highly. So if the things of God did not cost us sighs, tears, weepings, lamentations, watchings, strivings, earnest longings, and many prayers, we would think them easy, to be got at our pleasure, and so despise, contemn, or let them lightly pass as they came. God therefore, to enhance the price, doth keep them off till the bell ring, that we may know the rich value of these his commodities. All this is for the time.

III. The third circumstance is, *the means and way.* Here is all the strife. God would have it his way, and we would have it our way. Oh, saith Naaman, 2 Kings v. 11, 'Behold, I thought he would surely come out to me, and stand, and call upon the name of the Lord his God, and strike his hand over the place, and recover the leper.' But the Lord will not be tied to the means. When we see God, and fit means for effecting of such and such a thing, if then we grow secure therein, and think this is good, this is surely the way, and this will do it, herein we fail, because we see that alone, and do not principally and first of all see and seek unto God; and therefore in this case, because of our idolatrous conceit in lifting up the means beyond their places, God is forced many times to dash the means in pieces, and help us by some other way, of all others least expected, as we may see how God ordered the matter in Paul's shipwreck, Acts xxvii. 22. God did give unto him his own life, and the lives of all that were in the ship with him, but withal the ship must perish. A strange manner of deliverance! How should they then be saved, this being in all appearance the only means of safety? By the wreck of the ship God did perform his promise, some by swimming, the rest on boards, and some on broken pieces of the ship, all get on land; and even so, I say, we many times escape on boards, and broken pieces of a ship; I mean those means we least thought of, or least trusted unto, because we should not set up unto ourselves so many gods before us. Again, we may remember, Gen. xxxix., when Joseph was advanced into Potiphar's house, a great man and a prince of the state, then he might have thought he was likely now to rise, and that the accomplishments of his dreams were in fair way to speed; but this proved not the means. He becometh his enemy, and causeth him to be cast in a dungeon. Well, next a butler is made his friend by expounding of his dream; and now Joseph had good hope the butler would be a means of his enlargement, and no question he prayed also for good success, but God would not bless the same, because he will not have our means, and that we rest upon to speed. But at last God's means brings him out: Pharaoh dreams, is vexed, the butler then remembers; thus came his honour.

In France, the time was when their persecution was great, and their fears many; then they did trust on the king of Navarre, Oh what great matters he would do; but he failed them at their need. God indeed paid him home for disappointing the prayers and hopes of his people. Why did God suffer this? We may imagine this as a main cause, lest they should too much exalt the means, and say, the king of Navarre, the king of Navarre, the prince of Conde hath done this (*b*). God did cashier them, and set up another means of his praise. Judges vii., Gideon's army likewise is brought from thirty-two thousand to one thousand, and yet the Lord says they are too many, he will save Israel by three hundred only. Why? Lest Israel vaunt themselves against me, saying, 'My own hand hath saved me.' He knows how ready we are to attribute and sacrifice the fat of the offering unto man, and set up the means, forgetting him, the author and fountain of all the good things we enjoy; in all which and the like is verified, that which Saint Paul speaks, 1 Cor. i. 27, 'God hath chosen the foolish things of the world to confound the wise; and God hath chosen the weak things of the world to confound the mighty; and base things and naught, and things that are despised, hath God chosen, yea, and things which are not, to bring to nought things that are: that no flesh should glory in his presence; but all the praise be of him, and to him.'

These are the causes why God doth answer our prayers so often by those means we do not trust unto. If we send in a message at one door, what if we go about to another for an answer; let him appoint the means, and thy deliverance shall be so much the more speedy and comfortable. Many want comfort long for this cause, that they appoint unto themselves such and such means thereof. In afflictions, you shall have some say, Oh if I might speak with such and such a man I should be satisfied, he would ease my mind, when in the mean time, with this there is a sinful neglect of other men's ministry nearer, whose help we are bound to require. In this too much doating on the means, if we profit not, and our prayers remain unanswered, in this case, let us blame ourselves, who have prescribed him how to do his own work.

IV. The fourth circumstance is, *the limitation of the manner of granting.* We must distinguish of this,

(1.) *First, God will not be tied to the manner.* Sometimes when we ask, God doth give just the same we ask for, as 1 Sam. i. 11, Hannah prayed for a man-child unto the Lord, and she was heard, obtaining Samuel. If not so, yet then the Lord may answer us in value, though not in kind, giving us as good as we have desired. This is all one, if one pay us a sum in silver, do we ask him why it is not in gold? Moses, he desired to see the land of Canaan, God brought him not in thither, but yet he shews him it, Deut. xxxii, from the top of mount Nebo, whence he saw more of it by probability than he could have seen in any place of the land. He had his desire in value, though not in kind. So 2 Cor. xii. 7, alluding to Judges ii. 3, where it is said the Canaanites should be as thorns in their sides. A thorn in the flesh was sent to buffet St Paul, called the messenger of Satan, against which he prayed and prayed again (for nothing doth more grieve the child of God than to be humbled and buffeted with base temptations), but it was not removed. God's answer was, 'My grace is sufficient for thee, for my strength is made perfect in weakness.' Paul had it in value though not in kind. So many times our prayers are heard when we least think and perceive the same, and the good we desire done us, as it were, against our will. As apothecaries and surgeons use to deal with us, so many times God deals with men; when the plaster smarts, men cry to take it off, when in the mean time, by holding it on, the cure is done; and so it is with us, we cry out unto God to take away this pain, that he would pull away such a plaster, such a corrosive from us. Why? Oh, say they, that we may serve him better, and yield him more obedience, when indeed, with holding thee to it, and by binding, as it were, this cross fast upon thee, the very same thing God worketh in thee.

(2.) Again, in prayer, you shall have *many complaints of some.* Oh that I had more life! oh that I had more sense and feeling! oh that this lumpish heaviness were removed! when indeed the holding them off and delaying them in this suit is the highway to help them to their suit.

(3.) Finally, When God hears us not in any of the foresaid ways, yet in effect he shews *we have sometimes far better things than we desired*, as we see his promise is, Isaiah lx. 17, 'For brass I will bring gold, and for iron I will bring silver,' &c. Thus, many times when we pray for brass, iron, wood, and stones, we have gold, silver, brass, and iron in place of them; for when men labour in prayer, and have not the same things they have willed and asked for, God makes it up better another way. A man perhaps suffers poverty, loss, or wreck at sea, and is now driven nearer unto God by prayer, hath a more plentiful measure of the Spirit poured upon him, learns now to depend upon God, and know what true riches is: this man, if he could value grace, is a hundred times richer than before, having his eyes open to see afar off into things invisible. In this case, a man may come to complain, I have prayed thus and thus long, yet my prayers are not heard, yet this and this cross lies heavy upon me. But look if thou hast gotten patience, and canst see that God hath sent this upon thee; look if God have thereby driven thee off, and weaned thee from the world, and hath let in the oil of grace into thy heart, so as now thou art a new man, having thy conversation more in heaven than ever, remember in this, thy prayers are not lost, but double paid, and I hope there is no cause to complain when the payment is so good. Thus all God's promises, like rivers perpetuated, ending in the sea, do end in heaven, and to this tend all the comforts, promises, threatenings, and crosses to bring us thither. Unto all these I might also add this, that sometimes our prayers are not heard for others, when yet the reflex of that good we wish thee* comes upon ourselves, so that they are not lost; as we may see in the mission of the apostles, Mat. x. 13, they are willed in whatsoever house they come, to salute it, and if the house be worthy, that their peace be upon it. If there be a son of peace there, that peace be upon him, otherwise, our Lord saith, 'let your peace return to you.'

V. The last circumstance is, *the measure of proportion.* He hath set forth to no man any proportion of the things promised. To one he gives five talents, to another but one. Must every one have as much faith, hope, love, humility, honour, riches, and other qualities as others? Where then is that order which God hath appointed, to give the greatest and most eminent graces unto those he hath fitted for the greatest works and places. He gives thee not so much grace as another, because he hath not so much work for thee to do as for him unto others, or there is not so great trials and temptations appointed for thee to buckle with as is for such a one. It is a wonder to see how restless a great many are when they see others outstrip them in grace. They think nothing of that they have; unless they could pray as well as such a one and such a one, then all were well; but I say unto thee, content thyself if thou have any portion of grace, and be thankful for it. If God will open his hand in the use of the means, and give thee an increase, receive it joyfully; but fret not with thyself, or quarrel with him; if he keep thee of thy small measure, it shall serve thy turn to salvation as well as the greatest if he will give thee no more. Even as it was in the gathering of manna, Exod. xvi., he that gathered much had nothing over, and he that gathered little at the meeting† had no lack; so he that hath most grace, it shall bring him but to heaven, and thy small measure shall lead thee thither also. Say not, Oh I shall never come thither unless I have such and such a measure of grace, and can do as such and such a one. What if thy God will have thee contented with a little? His allowance shall suffice, the least measure shall bring us home. If in this case thou pray long and he hear thee not, blame thyself, striving thus to be thine own carver, not contented with allowance.

So there is a measure of the dispensation of things, as I touched before. He hears us going on in a course and trade of prayer, his grant includes a continual trading; as rain comes not all at once, but by degrees, that we might still have dependence for more, so God will give grace but by little and little, so as we shall still through the course of our life have cause to depend upon him and pray for increase. Thus, and many other ways, our Lord's promise is most sure. It stands always good. 'Ask, and you shall receive; seek, and ye shall find; knock, and it shall be opened unto you.' If the fault be not in ourselves, prayer shall bring down a blessing at one time or other, and we shall find the effect and fruit of it.

Now I come to the reasons, which are two: first, 'every one that asketh

* Qu. 'them'?—Ed. † Qu. 'meting?' that is, 'measuring.'—Ed.

receiveth;' as if he should say, for the Lord exempts no man that doth not disable himself. This promise, we must understand, is not a thing chained to some function, as most promises are, but this is as the Lord's common. All must and may pray, and are heard, always reserved the former exceptions.

The second is taken from fatherly compassion, so raising us up unto God, in and from whence these small streams we have flow, being much more abundantly merciful than any bowels of compassion which may be in us. !

But chiefly I would have you consider how here in this place our Lord doth press this matter again and again, assuring us we shall be heard in our prayer, of purpose, as it were, to hold up our heads above water, which in this our weary journey are so ready to sink. One would have thought this a very large charter, 'Ask, and ye shall receive; seek, and ye shall find; knock, and it shall be opened unto you;' and yet because he knew the difficulty of the same as well as the necessity, that it is a hard and a great task to pray in faith aright, and yet a thing absolutely needful, he follows it therefore, and presseth it home with several supporting arguments, which, God willing, we shall come to in their places.

First, we must consider *of the necessity of faith in prayer*. For he that comes to God must believe that he is a 'rewarder of them that diligently seek him,' Heb. xi. 6; and St James shews us, that he who asks must ask in faith, or else we speed not, James v. 15. Thus Jehoshaphat encourageth his fearful army to believe in God, but first he was encouraged himself. It was told him, and he told it them, that they should not need to fear; God was on their side, he would fight for them; and yet after this, Jehoshaphat shews how they must come by this deliverance: 'Believe in the Lord your God, so shall ye be established; believe his prophets, so shall ye prosper,' 2 Chron. xx. 20.

Brethren, it is true, the glory of God is put into our hands, as it were, to extend the same in obedience to every precept we are enjoined to observe; that so others, 'seeing our good works, may glorify our heavenly Father.' But most of all in believing we glorify him, and set forth his praises, because hereby we seal unto the truth of all the rest; where by the contrary, if we believe him not, it is the greatest dishonour and disgrace that may be; yea, John saith, 'Such a one hath made God a liar,' 1 John v. 10. Will you see an instance, how heinous this sin was in one of the best saints, in whom frailty no question for our comfort was suffered? Moses, Num. xx. 10–12, was bidden to speak to the rock, that water might come forth to that murmuring multitude; but in anger he smites twice on the same, uttering these words, 'Hear now, ye rebels, must *we* fetch ye water out of this rock,' as though if it came not, he was excused; and if it came, so, there it was. But for this, we know, he was not suffered to enter into the land of Canaan. We must trade in faith in all our actions, or we shall suffer loss in all; when by the contrary, if we go on in this, we shall have mercy unto mercy.

We read, Acts xiv. 9, that Paul, as he preached at Lystra, seeing an impotent cripple look on him stedfastly, in whom he saw faith to be healed, that by and by he made him stand up, and cured him; this was bred, no question, in him by the Spirit of God, but the special means thereof was his attending on the word preached. This attention, prizing, and valuing of the word, is a near way unto it; when by the contrary, the infidelity of men doth, as it were, bar up the way against themselves, that the power of the Spirit is not so lively in working amongst them: as we see Christ says of those he conversed amongst, that because of their unbelief, he could not do any great works amongst them; the infidelity of these, as it were, hindering him, bound his hands in a manner, they being uncapable thereof. Lo! what a necessity there is of faith in prayer, and how loathsome that stain of infidelity is! If our faith fall, all doth fall to the ground; if this abide, all goes well. Wherefore, as in war men take others' bonds and promises without further specialties, so do thou with thy God; take his bond, and go boldly unto him: believe his promise; there is a necessity thereof, it stands thee on thy life so to do.

Secondly, *for the difficulty of prayer with faith;* our Lord saw that there was no work more difficult to be done, and therefore he so presseth it with arguments.

The causes of the difficulty of prayer I take to be these:—

(1.) First, Because our profaneness and natural corruptions do most shew themselves in this action. Hence herein are those many and often complaints of our deadness, dulness, and hardness of heart in prayer, and of those world of things which violently, we know not whence, and suddenly thrust themselves into our minds. The devil helps also, and thrusts on, incensing* our corruptions.

(2.) Besides, this puts us down and out of heart from praying with assurance to be heard. The conscience of guiltiness gives stabs to our prayers. In this combat, the Egyptian or Israelite must die. If a man let loose himself to some gross sin, he shall be sure to find it in his prayer, sometimes to terrify him; sometimes to deaden his spirits, to weaken his faith; yea, at the best he shall be found not to pray with any life: as Mr Perkins tells us of a man who had stolen a sheep, who for all this, though he went on in his devotions, found no rest until he had confessed the same; till then the beast was ever in his way (*c*). Yea more, what checks and reproaches are then in the heart, sent close home by the accusing conscience! As, what! Wilt thou go unto God, and think to be heard; thou, so wretched and profane a creature; thou, that hast so often broken thy vows and promises; thou, that knowest so much of thy master's will, and doest so little; thou, that hast sinned against conscience and knowledge; that art so soiled and defiled with wallowing in the mire of sin?

Thus, though a man have prayed earnestly and often, it is not an easy matter to wash off the stain of sin, and quiet the conscience. As after a storm on the sea, though the tempest be gone, yet there is not by and by a calm, there will be a rolling and tossing of the waves up and down a long while after; so, to believe that God will hear our prayers, and that he hath done away all our sins out of his sight, it is not by and by done, there is a rolling and a stain of sin, that will toss up and down a long time after our prayers are done. Will you see the proof of this in one of the best saints, who was tossed thus for our comfort? The prophet David, after his great sin, and that he had confessed the same, 2 Sam. xii. 13, he had an absolution pronounced unto him by the prophet Nathan: 'The Lord also hath put away thy sin, thou shalt not die.' What could be more, and what now may hinder his joy? 'Blessed is he whose transgression is forgiven, and whose sin is covered,' Ps. xxxii. 1. But yet you see how the waves roll, and are troubled, though the storm be over; as Ps. li., how is he vexed! how earnestly doth he pray for mercy!—that 'his iniquities might be blotted out;' that his sin might 'be cleansed;' that he might 'hear

* That is, 'inflaming.'—G.

the voice of joy and gladness;' that 'the bones which he had broken might rejoice;' that God would not 'cast him from his presence, nor take his Spirit from him;' that he would 'restore unto him the joy of his salvation,' &c.

What was the cause of all this stir?

(1.) The filthiness of sin discovered, the Majesty offended, the punishment due, the scandal which came to others, to the dishonour of God by the party offending, together with the odious stain and filth which that sin left behind upon the soul, was such, that the greenness and yet smarting of the wound did not suffer him thoroughly to apprehend and fetch home the consolation. As we see, if a wound be raw, though suppling oil be brought unto it, and though it be applied with a light hand, which is commendable in that art, yet being touched, because of that rawness it smarts still; so the conscience being wounded, and the sore raw still, sin appearing like a monster in his colours, the punishment due apprehended, and the bitter belches thereof yet arising, though the comforts of God be like suppling oil applied by the hand of the skilful surgeon, to allay and cure the same, yet the comforts not being digested, nor able so soon to expel the former impressions, the Spirit being but raw in them, and the conscience of their own unworthiness being great, no comfort can fasten, but many fears remain in them for a long time.

(3.) Thirdly, Because there is a marvellous ignorance in us of the nature and dealing of God; not that we can be altogether ignorant of him, who is so glorious in all his creatures, filling heaven and earth with the majesty of his glory, yea, and is so good unto us; but as it is one thing to give rules of war, and another to practise the rules, so it is one thing to speak of God bravely, and another thing to practise those things we know and speak of. For when we have need to ask and beg of God those great and rich mercies to salvation, which should support and help us in all storms, diving into the use and depth of his attributes, in place thereof we draw unto ourselves a narrow scantling,* and false image of God, judging of him not as he is, but as we conceive him to be, like one of us. Which we see the Lord reproves, Isa. lv. 7: there God saith, 'Let the wicked forsake his way, and the unrighteous man his thoughts, and let him return unto the Lord, and he will have mercy on him; and to our God, for he will abundantly pardon.' And then it follows: 'For my thoughts are not your thoughts, neither are my ways your ways, saith the Lord. For as the heavens are higher than the earth, so are my ways higher than your ways, and my thoughts than your thoughts.' Is there sense in this? Dost thou ask what the sense is? As if he should say, alluding to thy senseless ignorant objections, What man could pass by these and these things! what father could pass by these offences in his child! how then shall I look for pardon of God? Unto this he answers, Measure not my working by scantling* the same after the proportion of any creature, or anything in his imagination, unless, I say, he have had his light from God, for my mercy outstrips all your conceits. Hence our prayers are weak and cold, because we make false images of God. But this point I shall meet with anon, therefore I let it pass.

(4.) Fourthly, Because we take a delay for a denial, and so are discouraged; that if we be not heard by and by, we throw down our armour and run away, or sit still astonished, so disabling ourselves.

(5.) Fifthly, The hardness and difficulty of the things we pray for hin-

* Cf. note *a*, Vol. I. page 117.—G.

ders our prayers; as John xi. 38, when Christ came to Lazarus's grave, and called to take away the stone, that he might raise him up, Martha cries out, 'Lord, by this time he stinketh, for he hath been dead four days.' This hinders our prayers, when we cry out it is too late, or the thing is so great, how can it be done? She was reproved, you know, and so must we be in this case. Another instance we have, 2 Kings vii., where, after Elisha had prophesied of that sudden plenty should be in the gate of Samaria after so great a famine, a lord, on whose hand the king leaned, answered the prophet, 'Behold, if the Lord would make windows in heaven, could this thing be?' He had an answer suiting his unbelief, and lived to see his infidelity punished, being trodden under foot by the people in the gate, as they went forth into the forsaken camp of the Assyrians. So, I say, these and the like things stand in our way, because they seem hard to be done. As in the East India adventures, a time was when men were quick and ready to buy other men's shares, because the returns were good; but when the business went in show backwards, many have been as busy in selling their parts again (*d*). So we seem rather to go back than forward in our prayers, because of the difficulty of the things we pray for. We are ready to leave all, and sell our adventure.

(6.) Lastly, The sixth impediment is Satan's opposition to our prayers, which he labours by all means to interrupt. For it stands him on it to bestir himself to quench our faith if he can, because it gives vigour, force, and life to prayer. It troubles not the devil the saying of a thousand *Paternosters* and *Ave Marias* without faith. If a man know not what he says, or cares not whether he pray or no, all is one to him, if there be no faith in prayer. Satan knows if faith lay not hold on God, God does not lay hold on us, and therefore his policy is to deal with us as Scanderbeg is reported to have used his enemies in fight, still to aim at the general (*e*); or rather like that stratagem of the king of Syria, 2 Chron, xviii. 30, neither to fight against great or small, but against the king of Israel; so Satan's special charge is to fight against faith and prayer, the special man; the which his subtile and cruel dealing towards us is much like unto that tyranny Pharaoh used toward the children of Israel in Egypt, Exod. iii. 18; he put them into extreme toiling servitude to make brick; so he commanded to slay the children; but when none of these succeeded to his mind, he then determined to kill all. So, many times before prayer, the devil puts men to make brick, by filling their hearts with many cares or temptations, or by their own sins, deadness, dulness, hardness of heart, or other things to be done, with a world of discouraging, and confused thoughts of God,—his mercy, justice, and the like; and all this to keep a man from prayer. But if the mercy of God help a man through these difficulties, that because of the command of God, that knowledge he hath of his will, and his own necessities, he will yet break through all, and go to prayer, notwithstanding all impediments; then, in the next place, he labours to make us kill the children in the birth; that is, whenas our weaknesses, and many wants and imperfections that way, should be as fuel to our prayers, and inducements to make us hold on, and in reverence contain ourselves, still begging and waiting at the throne of grace for what we want or desire, he turns the same into horrors, fears, and flying away from God. Yet if this will not serve the turn, but that our God doth allure and draw us unto his presence again, and that we resolve to pray, though with many tremblings, fears, and weaknesses, because we know not whither to fly from his presence; then, when our prayers are done, and we have striven as we are able, he persuades us to despair that our prayers are not heard, are nought, that our persons are abominable, that God loves us not, and that since Christ so turns us off still without comfort, we shall never, therefore, have any, &c.

The uses are,

Use 1. First, *Against the profaneness of such persons who make a mock of prayer.* But some may object there are none such. I wish there were not. But we know there are too many of this strain. I speak not of prayer established by law; none will, none dare meddle with that; it is dangerous. But for praying in houses, it is strange to see the profaneness in this kind. You shall have some say, Lo now these hypocrites; see what a stir they make; and he that doth keep some form of prayer in his own house constantly, though it may be but coldly done, yet he cannot escape, but is branded with the name of Puritan, when it may be, of all others, he least deserves it. But I will pass by this.

2. The second use is, *for reproof to such as think it an easy matter to pray.* Ask a beggar wandering through the country how he thinks to come to heaven, and he will answer, By my good prayers. So the dissolute and profane man, ask him how he thinks to come to heaven, he will say, By my good prayers. I confess, if you mean saying of a prayer, it is easy; but to pray aright, to pour out thy heart and soul before God, to believe he hears, and will come to help thee, to pray in faith, to rend thy heart before him, to lay hold of those things in him which are for thy humiliation and consolation, to wrestle with him, and strive for a blessing, to hope above hope, and, being delayed, to wait for him till he come, this is exceeding hard to be done. What then, profane man, hast thou not heard what is written? Zech. xii. 10, 'And I will pour upon the house of David, and upon the inhabitants of Jerusalem, the spirit of grace and supplication,' &c.; so, hast thou not read what is written? Ps. x. 17, 'Lord, thou hast heard the desire of the humble, thou wilt prepare their hearts,' &c. Hast thou not read what is written, Rom. viii. 16, 'Likewise the Spirit helpeth our infirmities; for we know not what we should pray for as we ought; but the Spirit itself maketh intercession for us, with groanings which cannot be uttered.' And dost thou, a lump of flesh, wallowing in thy sin, think to prevail by and bye in prayer? Those who are most forward thus in little esteeming and talking of prayer, many times are most to seek in sore and hard trials; as you shall have fencers, who make bravest flourishes when they play at blunt, are put most to their shifts when they come to the sharp (*f*); so, if such a one as I speak of fall into distress, he cannot draw out his sword, it rusts in the scabbard. It is a wonder to see grave and wise men to come so far short of this, that in the sorrows and discomforts of themselves or others, they cannot pray; a minister must be sent for to say somewhat unto them; they cannot themselves pray. I deny not but that God's dear children may be driven to this need upon divers occasions of sickness, sorrows, and temptations, to crave the help of others, that they may be humbled. Neither deny I but that book prayers may be good and profitable, and that there is a good and holy use of them, in which all our necessities may be included, if they be well and rightly penned; but yet for all this, it is a shame for men to be so ignorant that they cannot tell their mind to God in prayer, and plead for themselves and others in necessity, being more unfit to pray than David was to march in Saul's armour.

3. The third use is *for comfort.* To whom? To such as are good in

prayer, and yet are out of heart with their prayers. I would have such see how Jacob wrestled, wept, and prevailed with God in prayer. In some sort we must be contented to go away halting; there will be defects and imperfections in our best prayers, do what we can. 'That which is born of the flesh is flesh,' and will be so; and that which is born of the Spirit is spirit,' John iii. 6. You shall have those who are fullest of grace most complain, like rich men whining most when their bags are fullest, you shall have them complain, Lord, help me, I cannot pray; what shall I do? It is all to no purpose; better leave than go on in such a formal course. I am worse and worse. Surely, if I could pray aright, I should speed better. But I ask thee how? Dost thou not pray at all? Yes, will they say, I pray, but I pray not as I should, with faith, fervency, constancy, and feeling. I faint, and am discouraged in my journey. Hear me; thou seest a man go under a great burden, and perhaps so sinking under the same, that he must stoop and rest him often; and yet thou pitiest him, and thinkest for all this that he carrieth this burden, though he rest himself. So may it be with thee in prayer, seeing it is one of the hardest tasks of the world to pray with faith and feeling. If in this thou find stops and failings, be not discouraged; thou seest what a hard thing it is [to] go upright under so great a burden. Yet be not out of heart, though thou must sit down by the way; but know thy striving and endeavour shall bring thee through at the last. The bringing forth of a right prayer through so many oppositions, it is in a manner like the bringing forth of a child, in which there is much pain, anguish, and sorrow; so that we had rather do anything else; but when the child is born, then there is joy. Though with the remembrance of the throes of prayer thou art astonished, be comforted in this, the work is done, and thou hast made thy prayers known; the issue at one time or other shall be comfortable.

4. The fourth use is *for advice*. If the Lord have given us liberty at any time this way, that our hearts have been opened and enlarged, our faith strengthened, our eyes cleared, our consciences eased, so that our confessions have been large, bless God for this, and reckon it a most singular mercy. We fail all herein for want of thanksgiving. We can complain in wants, strivings, deadness, and senseless hardness. Oh my wants! Oh my ignorance! Oh my blockishness! Oh my hardness of heart! Oh my infidelity! But when our suit is granted, where is our thanksgiving? If thou bring forth a right prayer, let God have a sacrifice. It is a great matter.

5. A fifth use is, *for exhortation, to set on prayer as a work of great difficulty*. We must learn to whet and sharpen our tools first. As the prophet David out of meditations thus made prayers, thus must we prepare matter ere we pray. As the blood runs to the veins from the liver, made of the best and purest food concocted and digested; so we should prepare and digest fit matter, and not set on the same rashly and unpreparedly, as some think they may. Hear me: What will not men do in great important matters to compass them? So doth it much behove thee to consider what may humble thee, what may raise thee, what may encourage thee, and draw thee on before thy God, that thou mayest in thy distress make a right and proper use of the nature of God, and all these excellent things considerable in him. When we set on it slightly, it is no marvel though our return of consolation be of the same stamp. So in our general prayers we should have a fellow-feeling to set on edge our desires; but specially if we would be men of prayer. Christ would have set our faith on work

that this might fly to heaven, to fetch from thence whatsoever is good for us. Now in this case it is a marvellous cunning to dung our faith, as men dung the root of a tree to make it fruitful; though I confess somewhat else is to be done to the body, as the pruning and lopping of the branches, such as the increasing and scouring of our hope and love, with other graces, by the Spirit, which, as it hath an office in the branches, so doth it also descend into the root and help us there; so that the root of all prayer is the Spirit, but the root to thee is faith.

Now by what means should this be done, to dung our faith?

As in war they use a double help for their further security and strength.

1. The main;

2. The auxiliary helps;

So is it with our faith. The helps are divers.

(1.) First, *To labour to know and make clear our title to God, as a Father:* which is here implied: 'How much more shall your Father which is in heaven give good things to them that ask them?' To this, two main things belong: first, to consider the right how we come to this title? Only by faith in the Son of God: as it is John i. 12, 'But as many as received him, to them gave he power to become the sons of God, even to them that believe on his name.' Nothing can make them become the sons of God, but by faith in the Son of God. To clear this, it must be by the sign as well as by the cause. The apostle tells us, Gal. iv. 6, 'And because ye are sons, God hath sent forth the Spirit of his Son into your hearts, crying, Abba, Father.' Dost thou think thyself now in a blessed estate? Art thou one of the sons of God—for all his children are sons and daughters by adoption? Dost thou say thou art one of his sons and daughters? And dost thou say thou believest, being one with Christ, and so art justified by him? Take this also with thee; then he hath 'sent forth the Spirit of his Son into thy heart, to cleanse and sanctify thee: and hereby,' saith the apostle, 1 John iii. 24, 'we know that he abideth in us, by the Spirit which he hath given us.' If we make claim to justification, and omit sanctification: if no Spirit, we have no title of sons; for we know the same apostle saith, 'Whosoever is born of God, doth not commit sin, for his seed remaineth in him; neither can he sin, because he is born of God,' 1 John iii. 9.

(2.) Next, *To be careful to keep the evidences of our adoption always in repair:* I mean that we keep those graces which build us up hereunto, as fresh and flourishing as may be, that we read them fair in the time of trial. A man that in the country lays up his deeds and writings in the smoke, may find them so eaten and darkened, that when he should use them they cannot be read; so I doubt many of our evidences are smoky, and so blotted, that in our need we cannot read them. Our care hath not been to lay them up safe, and keep them in repair, by which it comes to pass that now we are to seek in those things which belong to our peace.

(3.) Lastly, as it is in Col. iii. 17, 'Whatsoever we do in word or in deed, we do all in the name of the Lord Jesus, giving thanks to God and the Father by him.' We do no honour to God, but through Christ; and so in the particular of our prayers we have the less joy, living in discouragements, not giving the beginning of all unto him, and the riches of his grace. When because we have nothing of our own to put in, whereupon we may build and rely, we go away heartless and discouraged, as though we should not be so bad, but somewhat should be in us to procure his mercy, never all this while having sufficiently seen our nakedness, that there is nothing in us, and that we must be covered altogether, and wholly in his presence, that no filthiness be discovered. We read, Exod. xxviii. 42, that the high priest going about his sacrifice must have on his linen breeches, from the loins even unto his thighs, that he might not bear iniquity, and die, discovering his nakedness. What! Such a high priest? so holy, so gloriously attired, so covered with rich robes? yet he shall die for all this if he want his linen breeches. I fear many of us come thus to God, not having soundly seen our own nakedness, and where only all our comfort is to be found. The apostle, 1 Cor. iii. 21, says, 'Therefore let no man glory in men: for all things are yours;' to wit, with the former limitations, to do us good. 'All things are yours; whether Paul, or Apollos, or Cephas, or the world, or life, or death, things present or things to come, all are yours:' but a man's title must be in Christ: for it follows, 'And you are Christ's, and Christ is God's.' So Rom. viii. 32, the apostle's argument is, 'He that spared not his own Son, but gave him up for us all, how shall he not with him freely give us all things?' If Christ be once given thee, Christ is more than heaven, and earth, and all; if he be given, God will deny thee nothing.

The auxiliary helps are as foreign soil to barren grounds, marl, lime, and the like, which make fruitful; and herein consider these things,

(1.) *The general graciousness of God to all his creatures.* This is a great help that he feeds the young ravens; yea, as it is Mat. vi. 26, that he feedeth all the fowls of the air. Whence from his general goodness the inference is, 'Wherefore, if God so clothe the grass of the field, which to-day is, and to-morrow is cast into the oven, shall he not much more clothe you, O ye of little faith?' The consideration of his graciousness unto all the sons of men, and especially to many evil men, when they have called upon him, of which God hath shewed us many instances that they have been heard, should make us not keep off, but hope to speed well; yea, and in this also to consider the graciousness of God in receiving great sinners unto mercy, which the prophet, admiring, thus speaks of: Micah vii. 18, 'Who is a God like unto thee, that pardoneth iniquity, and passeth by the transgressions of the remnant of his inheritance? he retaineth not his anger for ever, because he delighteth in mercy,' &c. I doubt many wrong themselves in this, because they erect before them a false image of God. If one should see a picture of God before him, as the papists do make him, like an old man with a cloak and a staff, and a great many about falling down before him, frowning on some, beating of others, kicking of others away, what an absurd thing would we think this (*g*)! What difference is there betwixt a false picture and a false image of God in thy heart? When thou canst not conceive of him but as terrible and incensed against thee, assure thyself, thou dost not prostrate thyself with right thoughts before him, if being a sinner thou thinkest he will smite thee down.

(2.) Secondly, *His all-sufficiency and omnipotency*, being in heaven above, and overruling all, who is excellent in knowledge, wonderful in working, all-sufficient to save, and powerful to put down the mighty from their seats, and to exalt the humble. He is beyond all fathers. They see but a little, they are not always present, they are not always able to help when they would, but he doth see thee at all times, is ever present, and able to help thee in all distresses; he is greater than all in breadth, in depth, in height, in length, in mercy, in power, as being in heaven above all; fathers are not so. These be two special helps.

(3.) Thirdly, *The promises, the faithfulness of God.* The precedents of them in former times to thyself, or others. As Ps. lxxvii. 5, David was in great and sore distress, yet, saith he, 'I have considered the days of old, the years of ancient times,' &c. And in another place the church pleads, 'Our fathers trusted in thee, and were delivered;' and so from thence raiseth a ground of confidence. Thus the prophet David he reasons the matter with Saul, when he was to go forth and fight with that great and terrible Philistine: 1 Sam. xvii. 34, 'Thy servant kept his father's sheep, and there came a lion and a bear, and took a lamb out of the flock; and I went out after him, and delivered it out of his mouth; and when he arose against me, I caught him by the beard, and smote him, and slew him. Thy servant slew both the lion and the bear; and this uncircumcised Philistine shall be as one of them.' The danger was now the same, wherefore having the like faith and protection, he looks for the like deliverance. So look what experience thou hast had of that which God hath done for thee, and make thy advantage thereof. Withal remember how even good men, where they have been bountiful, delight to give more and more still. Though it be not so always with men, yet it is so always with God; if once he have heard thee in mercy, he will hear thee always.

(4.) The last and principal one for this purpose, is that which lieth in the text, the first main reason which now fitly proffers itself, *the universality of the grant*, which is as a common, every commoner having interest therein, some more, and some less, yet all have interest less or more. As princes have masters of requests, who as grand officers have access unto them at all times, and are familiars, yet every man may deliver a petition to the king. Abraham we know was a holy man, and the friend of God; others there be inferior. Saint James wills those who are sick to send for the elders of the church, that they may pray over them, &c., James v. 14. Thus though all be not officers, yet all men have an universality of the grant: 'Every one that asketh, receiveth.'

Some may here object, What is that to me? I am not in the covenant. I answer, If thou be an outlaw, get thee in as soon as thou canst; but if thou art such an one that art not outlawed, then thou hast a title in the common, do as thou canst in carrying thyself as a commoner. Let us remember in the common cause we have need to be ready with our help, as we would be glad of help in the like case. In this let us ask ourselves, What have we done for others with our prayers? What for the church at home and abroad? It shall lie heavy upon us if we shall omit to help them now with our prayers at their need. In the city, when men have entered freemen, they use to pay scot and lot (*h*); so in Christianity, if we be entered as freemen, where is our scot and lot? Where are our prayers offered up for king, our country, for religion, against masses, the sins of the time, the judgments threatened, and the like?

Here some may object, and say, Alas! I am a poor servant, I cannot pray, let others pray that can; I am a poor ignorant man, with such like.

I answer, What if thou be! Thou art a citizen in Christianity; thou must pay scot and lot. How do men strive with their landlords for their commons? They will raise a mutiny, do anything, keep somewhat on it for possession's sake, rather than lose it, if it were but to keep one poor cow upon it. So, whatever thou be, maintain thy title in this common, do somewhat for it.

The last argument is taken from the lesser to the greater, from fathers on earth, declaring that if so much mercy, pity, affection, may be, and is in them to their children, how much more pity, love, mercy, and the like may we expect from our heavenly Father. I will go over but a few of these things, and so make an end, wherein I will not dispute all things, how fathers do and should do to their children, but limit myself within the compass of two examples only.

1. Of a good father to an ill son.

2. Of a good father to a good son.

1. That of 2 Sam. xviii. 33 shall be the first, where when Absalom had rebelled against his father, cast him out of the kingdom, abused his concubines, and was in pursuit of him for his life, yet when that battle was lost, wherein his son died, and the victory now on his side, how doth the king mourn, as though all had been lost! and though he was a magnanimous king, yet this made way to his passion, so that he went up and down weeping and crying, 'O Absalom, my son, my son Absalom, would God I had died for thee, O Absalom, my son!' Oh the love of a father to his son!

2. The second is that of Jacob, who when he had thought Joseph had been dead, it is said he rent his clothes, put on sackcloth, mourned for his death many days, which sorrow was so great, that when all his sons and daughters rose up to comfort him, he refused to be comforted, but said, 'I will go down into the grave unto my son mourning,' Gen. xxxvii. 35. So Gen. xliv. 30, when Benjamin was like to have been stayed prisoner by Joseph behind the rest, with what earnest affection doth Judah plead for his enlargement many ways! amongst which this was the chief, that Jacob's life was bound up in the life of his children.

Now, it is to considered, that though fathers be thus good, yet some may fail; but the thing is, they know how to be good, and are so ordinarily, unless it be when some, like monsters, prove unnatural in distemper of temptation, necessity, or some other sinister way. This dear affection the Lord excellently shews us, Isa. xlix. 15, 'Can a woman forget her sucking child, that she should not have compassion on the son of her womb? yea, they may forget, but I will never forget thee.' A father may prove unnatural to a son in a fit of temptation and distemperature, as Saul, who threw a javelin at his son Jonathan; sometimes necessity will cause unnaturalness, as 2 Kings vi. 28, in those women who consented to seethe their sons, one of them complaining to the king that she had done so, but the other would not. A miserable complaint, and most woeful misery, to hear of a woman who had buried her son in her own bowels. But this is rare and not usual. So a father may forget himself, and pass all affection in jealousy, as that Turk who made one strangle his own son out of a conceit he was too well beloved of his subjects. Thus with many the like occasions, parents may become churlish and unnatural to their children; but still this stands firm, they know at least how to be kind unto them. Our Lord would have us learn from hence, that he can do much more, and far surpasseth them all in whatsoever kindness can or may be in them.

See this last help to stay up our hands, to wit, that little picture of the great God in the dearness of affection which he hath placed in parents. If thou be a father or a mother, thou knowest it; but no man can know it but a father or a mother. Also, hast thou not seen what affection may be in a son to the father? As we read of the son of Crœsus, who, though he were dumb, yet when he saw the murderers to come in, who were ready to kill his father, violence of affection suddenly burst forth into these words, as the story shews, 'Oh, spare my father!' (*i*). If so much may be in a son unto thee, how much more may be in thy God for thee?

Now for all this, thou art afraid of thy imperfections, weaknesses, and manifold infirmities, that these shall stay good things from thee; and therefore thou criest out, Oh my prayers are lost, they are to no purpose! oh my sins, weaknesses, and infirmities, these stop the way to my prayers! What, man! Hast thou a son, and perhaps he marries without thy permission, or doth some other shrewd* turn, which grieves and vexeth thy spirit, and this child, perhaps, comes home wounded unto thee, with blood about his ears, and so falls down before thee, freely confessing his wandering and misdemeanours, and prays for thy favour and forgiveness; tell me, wouldst thou not embrace him, and cry out, 'Oh my son, my son!' all the rest should be forgotten and forgiven? What then, O man, thinkest thou of thy God, when thou sayest thou canst have no comfort in prayer? Thou beast, what wilt thou make of thy God? What! is he a God of cruelty, anger, and revenge only? No, no; in this case thou feignest unto thyself false and abominable conceits of God, and thence the returns of thy comforts are answerable unto thy wretched fancies. But if ever he hath turned thy heart unto him, and dealt graciously with thee, or hath allured thee unto him by his graciousness and kind dealing with others; or if thou findest in thyself how much thou canst pass by in thy child, though there be many great faults and omissions, make thy advantage of this, and go unto thy God; whatsoever thy case be, thou shalt find him more exceeding merciful, as the church doth, Micah vii. 9, and therefore she comes to triumph: ver. 18, 'Who is a God like unto thee, that pardoneth iniquity, and passeth by the transgressions of the remnant of his inheritance? he retaineth not his anger for ever, because he delighteth in mercy. He will turn again,' &c.

We are all much to blame in this, even those who have the greatest measures of grace, that we do not aright make use of the nature of God. Sometimes melancholy, temptation, and want of judgment are causes of our error, wherein our understanding, fancy, and other powers of the soul are disordered, until light come in to dispel these clouds. It is strange to think that when we were enemies to God, with our backs to him in our natural blindness, and in sin running from him, then to think he should receive us, and now to stab us with our faces towards him in the state of reconciliation.

To conclude, if it be such a hard thing to pray so as to obtain, if we have need of such and so many helps to lift and hold up our very hands, which are ready to fall down, the Lord teach us to know our faults, and tell us what is yet further to be done, that we may learn to wrestle with God, and prevail in prayer! If we have been faulty in times past, let us mend; and among other things, now when the ark is like to be in danger, let us not prove injurious unto God in forsaking his cause. Hear me; hath God brought the church in divers places now into such dangers, yea, and some great ones also, environed with fears and crosses, and shall we now prove so injurious to God as to retire from them (at least not to have the benefit of our help and prayers)? Was it accounted such a foul offence to cause Uriah to be left in danger in the foremost rank, and then command that the troops should retire; and shall we not now be much more faulty to leave them in this danger? Let us aid them, then, with our prayers, until God, who is wonderful in working, and excellent in power, bring light from this darkness. We know not what the issue may be; but in

* Cf. our Glossary, *sub voce*.—G.

the mean time, if we pray, this remaineth always sure, that 'if we ask, we shall receive.' Our Lord hath said it; it is so, it must be so.

NOTES.

(*a*) P. 235.—'It was a rule in the ancient time, "Lay thy hand on the plough," &c. See note *c* to '*Divine Meditations*,' page 229.

(*b*) P. 238.—'The king of Navarre . . . the prince of Conde.' It is only necessary here to notice that Sibbes evidently sees the 'finger of God' in the murder of Henry by Ravaillac. The apostasy of the great Huguenot points many 'a moral' to the Puritans. The services of Conde it were superfluous to annotate. He too was assassinated, by Montesquieu.

(*c*) P. 242.—'Mr Perkins tells us of a man,' &c. Cf. our Memoir of Sibbes, Vol. I. pages xxxviii., xxxix. See the 'Cases of Conscience' of this fervid and searching old Divine for the above and many other similar quaint illustrations.

(*d*) P. 244.—'As in the East India adventures.' India was the *El Dorado* of the age of Sibbes; and every year witnessed some scheme of romantic adventure and fabulous promise. Our *speculation* is not so modern a thing as many deem.

(*e*) P. 244.—'Deal with us as Scanderbeg is reported.' This is the celebrated warrior-king of Albania, renowned in song and story. There are various early English books, contemporary with Sibbes, about him. Cf. Watt *sub voce.*

(*f*) P. 245.—'Fencers make bravest flourishes when they play at blunt.' That is, in sport, or for practice, not in earnest. The weapons, or 'swords,' are then 'covered,' or 'blunted.' Hence the technical phraseology 'blunt,' being a pointless rapier or foil to fence with.

(*g*) P. 248.—'If one should see a picture of God before him.' Such 'pictures' are not at all uncommon; for it is a popular mistake that only God the Son, and, as the 'dove' or 'radiance,' God the Spirit, are represented. In Genoa there is at this day a painting very much corresponding with Sibbes's description. If I remember aright it is by Pietro Perugino.

(*h*) P. 249,—'Scot and lot.' These are the dues to the lord of the manor for ingress and egress.

(*i*) P. 250.—'The son of Crœsus.' . . . "Oh, spare my father." This touching and remarkable incident, which was the means of saving the life of Crœsus, took place at the siege of Sardis. The beautiful narrative of Herodotus has made it immortal.

G.

THE RICH PEARL.

THE RICH PEARL.

NOTE.

'The Rich Pearl' forms the second of the four 'Sermons' appended to 'The Saint's Comforts' (see Note, Vol. VI. page 160). Its separate title-page is given below.

G.

THE RICH
PEARLE.

In a Sermon upon the
Parable of a Merchant
man seeking good
pearles.

MATTH. 13. 45.

Shewing what that Pearle
is, how we may get it, how
we may know we have
it, how to improve
it, &c.

By that Faithfull and Re-
verend Divine, R. SIBBES,
D.D. and sometimes Preacher to
the Honorable Societie
of *Grayes-Inne.*

Printed at *London* by *Tho. Cotes* and
are to be sold by *Peter Cole.* 1637.

THE RICH PEARL.

And again, the kingdom of heaven is like unto a merchantman seeking goodly pearls, &c.—MAT. XIII. 45, 46.

ST PAUL expresseth in the Epistle to the Philippians what this parable typifies. There he teaches all is 'dung in comparison of Christ,' Philip. iii. 8. Here the Spirit teaches that all must be parted with to gain this pearl spoken of in this place; and as St Paul, so Christ, his thoughts were all heavenly. He came from heaven; and while he was on earth, his thoughts and speeches shewed whence he was. All his discourse is of heaven, sometime in plain doctrine, other whiles in parables; as in this chapter is manifested, comparing the kingdom of heaven to a sower, ver. 24; to a grain of mustard seed, ver. 31; to leaven, ver. 33; to an hidden treasure, ver. 44; and in these two verses to a merchant of pearls, beginning the verse with the word 'again,' to shew that he insisted upon the former matter. His love to mankind admits of no weariness in repetitions, and often inculcating the same things, thereby to work a strong impression in our minds, as knowing that they are above our understanding, and that we are indisposed to them naturally. And it should teach us *not to be weary of hearing the same things;* as also St Paul admonisheth us, in telling us it is safe for us: Philip. iii. 1, 'Though in itself it be tedious to the minister.'* And indeed it is the unhappiness of ministers to be often pressing the same thing; and yet they must not neglect it, seeing Christ stooped so low to take up this duty, for the benefit of our souls.

In the next place observe, *Christ teacheth by parables,* helping the soul by the body, the understanding by the sense; teaching us, out of objects of our sense, to raise up our souls to divine meditations, so as the soul is beholden to the body as well as the body to the soul, though not in so eminent a measure. But it may be questioned, Are not parables hard to be understood? I answer, It is true, if they be not unfolded they are hard; but if they be once manifested, they are of excellent use; and like the cloud, lightsome towards the Israelites, to give to them light, but towards the Egyptians a cloud of darkness. And carnal men are earthly in heavenly matters; and, on the contrary, those that are spiritually-minded are heavenly disposed in earthly matters. And it teacheth us our duty, viz., *to be of a holy disposition in the use of these outward things;* for the

* He says just the opposite, 'To me it is not grievous.'—ED.

creatures have a double use, one for the good of the body, another for the good of the soul, as Rom. i. 20, *seq.* The Godhead is so manifest in the creature, as it alone is sufficient to leave us without excuse; and therefore as we daily use them, so should our souls, by way of meditation, make them as a ladder to ascend on high. But for the parable itself, in it first we will expound the terms, and then pass to the observations. And, first, by the 'kingdom of heaven' is meant sometime the company of men that are under Christ's regiment,* that acknowledge him for their king; as we say it is not the walls that make the city, but the body of men united and governed by one law, custom, and privilege. But here it may be well taken for the blessed estate that doth belong to such, together with the means that bring them to this estate, and the prerogatives annexed to it, as peace, joy, grace, and the like; but most especially for the glorious estate of a Christian, begun here and perfected hereafter, for where this is supposed, it doth suppose the means and prerogatives also formerly spoken of. And therefore if we ever think to come to heaven, *it must be begun here in this kingdom of grace.* And hence it is that the word is sometimes called the 'kingdom of heaven;' for Christ will rule in those here by his Spirit that think to reign with him hereafter. And it should also comfort those that find in them the first-fruits of this kingdom, for they shall assuredly have the harvest at length. Fear not trials nor troubles; grace once begun, though as a grain 'of mustard seed,' will not leave growing till it ends in glory. And yet it must be supposed that our carriage here must be as if we were in heaven; our thoughts must suit with our estates. We are kings, our thoughts must be high; and take heed how we disesteem the gospel. If we neglect it, we neglect the kingdom of heaven; if we contemn it, we refuse also, and contemn grace, and so disclaim all title to heaven. It is further said that it is with this 'kingdom' as with a merchantman that seeks pearls. This merchant *is every Christian.* Our life is a continual merchandising of something, and taking other in exchange, *and taking such as are better than the things we part with,* else will our trade be soon at an end, and we never a whit the better. And therefore the Christian, like a good merchant, trades for pearls. A Christian life therefore is a life of trading, a venturing life; and therefore a life of danger, being ever as it were in danger of death, as the merchant is at sea, yet ever sure that his God will not forsake him, but assist and defend him off from the rocks of Satan's temptations, and accusations, and terror of conscience, and despair on the one side, and from the alluring waves of the world, that he falls not into that dangerous whirlpool on the other side.

His life is also *a life of labour,* labouring in his particular calling with faithfulness, having ever an eye on his other calling; and thus by an holy use of the things here below, his mind is ever climbing up the hill, to see the end of all his labour, and to aim at it in all his thoughts, words, and deeds. And as it is a life of labour, so it is not fruitless. It is† for pearls of honour, pleasure, or profit; but the Scripture counts these but dirt and thorns, although in our childish esteem we count them goodly jewels, being indeed but counterfeit glass. Yet there is a sort of higher spirit, that do indeed seek a pearl, having purposes to serve God; but they in seeking meet with counterfeits, with false teachers, that make glorious shows, yet indeed are but mountebanks, who shew and sell them much counterfeit pearl, and thereby seduce them from the right way. But such as God intends good unto, he informs them by his Spirit that this is not the right

* That is, 'government.'—G.

† Qu. 'is not'?—Ed.

orient pearl; and this they find by experience. It quiets not their hearts nor their consciences; it gives them no comfort. Briefly, it stands them in no stead; nay, it hinders them. And this makes them cast about anew for other treasure, as the woman of Samaria, a 'Messiah that will shew them all things,' John iv. 25; and at length they meet with this rich and precious pearl. And thus Augustine, a Manichee at the first, fell to doubting of his estate, and at length met with God indeed, which he formerly sought in vain.* To proceed: this merchant seeks, then finds, then sells all, to get the pearl that he thus found, wherein we will shew what this pearl is.

First, therefore, by this pearl is meant *Christ Jesus, with all his graces and prerogatives derived*† *to us, by the means of his ordinances.* Christ is the great pearl; all the rest are pearls, but no otherwise than as they lead us to Christ, the peerless pearl. Now, we know that pearls are bred in shell-fishes, of a celestial humour or dew; and like hereto was Christ, by heavenly influence formed in the womb of the Virgin. And as pearls, though formed in the water, yet originally are from the heavens, so the graces of God's Spirit are from heaven, though placed in earthly hearts. And again, as pearls, though here below, yet are like the heavens in clearness, so Christians by this gracious influence from this pearl Christ Jesus, though they live here on earth, are more like heaven than earth, wherein they are bred; and thus is Christ also. Though he took the flesh of man upon him, yet he hath the lustre of the Godhead, in whom all the attributes of God do plentifully shine. Again, a pearl is of great value and worth; and so Christ, one Christ of infinite value, and therefore became a ransom for many millions that were in bondage, so as all the whole church hath interest in him, and every particular Christian hath such a part in him, as if one only man had been in the world to have been saved by him, Christ must have died for him. He was given by God to purchase our redemption; and not only to purchase our deliverance, but also to make us acceptable, and to fill us with other things that are good in him. We have all that we stand in need of here and hereafter; all our grace and comfort ariseth from him. In him are the treasures of wisdom and counsel hid; 'and from his fulness we all receive grace for grace,' John i. 16. Furthermore, it is such a pearl as frees us from all ill; nay, it is powerful to turn all ill to the greatest good. It makes life out of death; it makes joy out of affliction; it makes the devil, our enemy, to be a means of hastening us to heaven. Lastly, this pearl makes us good. Like the philosopher's stone, it turns everything into gold. So this makes us God's jewels; and our High Priest doth now in heaven bear us in his breast, as the precious stones that were in Aaron's breastplate. It makes us kings and priests to God, and a spouse fitting for him our Husband. It adorneth us with all graces, it makes all ours, and entitles us to heaven, which we lost in our fall. Christ then is this pearl.

But now, in the second place, *let us see how we may come by this pearl.* We must therefore know that this pearl may be had; and we must have hope thereof, else there is no venturing for it; and therefore God, to prevent all excuse, he offers this pearl in his word. The pearl is sent from heaven to come to us. The ministry layeth open the riches of Christ, to make us long after him. He desires us to be good to our own souls, to receive the pearl thus offered. He entreats us to be reconciled to God,

* Cf. 'Confessions,' Introduction and throughout.—G.

† That is, 'communicated'.—G.

2 Cor. v. 20: 'Oh that my people would hear,' Deut. v. 29; 'O Jerusalem, how oft would I have gathered thee, as a hen gathereth her chickens!' Luke xiii. 31. What can we have more? We see it is no desperate matter, therefore it may be had. The ministry, though never so vile in account of men, yet hath made men rich: 2 Cor. vi. 10, 'Yet making many rich.'

In the next place, *what must we part with?* We see in this text the merchant parts with all, so must we give all that we have; and if we have nothing, then we must give ourselves, and God will give us ourselves again, but far better than we were when we gave ourselves to him. But what! may some say, doth God require we should forsake all indeed? I answer, not as the papists do, that vow wilful beggary,

1. But, in the first place, *we should part with the estimation of all.* We may keep them and use them, for God gave us these things to that end; but yet let us so use them as though we did not use them. Let them not have our chief affections, nor chief seats in our hearts.

2. Secondly, So we are to part with all things, *that we must have a heart prepared to part with all, if we cannot enjoy them, and this pearl too.* If the question be whether we had rather have this world than Christ, we must resolve to part with father, mother, lands, yea, with a man's own self, rather than with Christ. Without him honour shall be no honour, pleasure no pleasure. To us all things should be dung and dross in comparison of Christ; nay, 'the sufferings of this world are not worthy to be compared with that glory we shall have,' Rom. viii. 18. So as there is no proportion between them.

3. Thirdly, We must so part with these things as we must be ready *to sell all without constraint, to honour Christ in his poor members;* sell all for ointment for Christ's feet, part with anything that we may stand for Christ. Especially *we must part with all sins.* He that retains any one sin can never get this pearl; he that keeps in his heart but one beloved pleasure or profit of this life, let him read, pray, hear, profess never so much, the devil hath him sure by the leg or by the wing, and as sure as if the whole man were in his hands; for he will willingly suffer a man to go to, and use any good exercises, knowing they add to a man's damnation, so long as he retains a secret delight and liking to any lust, let it be never so small. And further, we must not part with sin only—for every sin hath some one good or other for its object, as covetousness of riches, ambition of honour, and such like; we must therefore 'sell all,' part with our affections, with all their branches and objects, if they will not stand with Christ; part with honour, riches, yea, our own lives, for they are far inferior to this precious pearl. Take heed of reservations of this one thing, this Zoar or that Rimmon, as Ananias and Sapphira. For who would not have Christ, if he might have pleasure, or profit, or honour with him? No, Christ will have all; and therefore this is the first lesson in Christ's school, deny ourselves, our reputation, the conceit of our own wisdom.

In the next place, let us see *what the gain of this trade will be.* We shall think ourselves no losers. We shall have Christ, and with him all things. What we give to him, he will return back, if they be fitting for us, and with them he will give us grace to use them, teaching us to want and to abound; and when we are come to give all for this pearl,—though indeed we have nothing here at all but only in our own esteem,—Christ will be worth all to us. Witness Moses, that chose to suffer affliction with the people of God before the pleasures of Pharaoh's court, Heb. xi. 25, *seq.*

And therefore Christ in this life promiseth a return of a hundred fold, which consisteth in abundance of comfort to our full satisfaction and content, which all the world cannot give, and that makes all things here to be 'vexation of spirit;' and therefore David, when he was a king, counted the testimonies of God better than gold, Ps. xix. 10; and St Paul counted these things here, notwithstanding his many privileges, to be 'dross, and dung, and loss in comparison of Christ,' Philip. iii. 8. *And it stands on God's honour not to make us losers* when we trade with him. If we part with riches, pleasures, and honours, life, world, we shall have better riches, better and more enduring pleasures and honours, eternal life, and 'a new heaven and a new earth, wherein dwelleth righteousness,' if we part with these for conscience' sake; whence we may learn *who are the true rich men*, even the Christian, that hath abiding riches, that will continue with him so long as his soul continueth, and such riches as make us good and acceptable in God's esteem, that in our extremities will stand us in stead, supporting and commending us to God, and in death doth not forsake us, but goes with us to heaven. But a worldling 'walks in a vain shadow, and disquiets himself in vain,' Ps. xxxix. 6, in heaping to himself riches and pleasures which he must part with, for he can carry nothing with him when he dies but a load of sins, which he commits in gathering this worldly pelf. All this gay clothing he must put off when he goes to his long home.

See, in the next place, *who is the right fool.* Is not he that in his judgment preferreth counters* before gold, and the baubles of this present life before that enduring substance in the heavens. We condemn Adam, Esau, and Judas for their foolish choice, when, alas! there is no worldling but is as ill as the worst of them, if not worse, if worse may be. Are there not many that sell Christ for less than thirty pieces? Are there not many that cast him away for nothing? What doth the common swearer and blasphemer but sell Christ, nay, cast away him, and all hope of happiness, for a mere presumptuous daring of God? And the best worldling sells Christ for a very thing of nought, a toy, a pleasure of sin, or a little profit. Such strongholds hath the king of this world in the hearts of the children thereof. But how shall we know when we have this pearl? *We should examine our hearts, what we could part with for Christ.* Many that make profession of Christ in this life shew that they affect† nothing but a bare title of profession; for their hearts tell them they never yet could find in their heart to deny pleasure or profit, no, not anything for Christ's sake; and yet are fully persuaded they must needs have this pearl. No, no! Christ is not to be had, neither is he to be kept upon such poor easy terms. Men 'cannot serve God and Mammon,' Mat. vi. 24.

Secondly, If we have this pearl, *we shall have a wonderful admiration at the excellency of the value thereof:* Ps. lxxxiv. 1, 'How beautiful are thy dwelling places;' Ps. cxix. 97, 'Oh how do I love thy law;' 1 Peter i. 8, 'Joy unspeakable;' and chap. ii. 9, 'Marvellous light.' What says the worldling? Oh, this or that marvellous rich man, goodly living, stately house, ancient family! Are these things for a Christian to wonder at, who entitles himself to glory in the highest heavens? No. Worldly respects fall down where heaven is advanced. When Paul is a convert, 'those things that were formerly gain to him, he counteth loss for Christ,' Philip. iii. 7.

Thirdly, Whosoever hath this pearl, it *works in him a wonderful joy above all worldly joy whatever,* 'above the joy of harvest,' Isa. ix. 3.

* Cf. Glossary, *sub voce.*—G. † That is, 'desire.'—G.

Zaccheus and the eunuch rejoiced; yea, in adversities this joy forsakes us not. It made St Paul sing in prison. But men will say, Who are more heavy and dejected than Christians? I answer, that God's Spirit appeareth not always in joy, but sometimes in mourning; for the want of the assistance of God's Spirit, which is an evidence of a taste and interest in the blessed estate of regeneration.

In the last place, if we have this pearl, *our affections and speeches will be busied evermore about it*, and our whole course of life will shew that we have it. In the next place, if we have this pearl, how shall we improve it to our most advantage? First, therefore, let us be as laborious in keeping it as Satan is laborious in striving to deprive us of it; and to that end we are to *watch over our especial and particular corruptions, and then most especially when the devil proffers us a good;* for we may be sure it is to deprive us of a better good. He gives an apple, but he looks to deprive us of a paradise. There was never man yet escaped from him a gainer; and therefore in such temptations, examine his offers by the light of sanctified reason, and we shall find ever he offers us loss. In the next place, let us look that *we preserve the vessels of our souls in purity*, that we may be fit for the pearl that must be set in gold. And in the next place, let us *make use of Christ and our interest in him.* If we be in bonds under sin, offer Christ to God. O Lord! Christ which thou gavest me is the righteousness which thou canst not but accept, seeing his righteousness is infinite, and thou hast made it mine. I am a beggar of myself, but thou hast made Christ all in all to me, to that end that thou mayest esteem of us all in all to thee. Oh how quiet and peaceable is that soul that is in this estate! 'How goodly are thy tents, O Jacob? who is like to thee, O Israel!' Num. xxiv. 5. Saved by the Lord, happy art thou! In less temptations, as afflictions, or death, that king of terrors, if that should seize on us, then consider, What do we lose? Nothing but that which we must one day leave of necessity. If we then have laboured formerly for this invaluable jewel, we are then most near it; our salvation then is most near even at that instant while we are labouring. Are we enjoying our treasure? shall not we be as desirous of the rich things that grace affordeth us as we are of the riches of this life? If the promises of such things do quicken us, how much more the things themselves. If we be troubled with losses, what lose we? Not our pearl, not grace, not our God, in whom is ever fulness of content. If he fills us with content, it is more than all this vain counterfeit world can afford us. What if we be robbed of pins, so long as we keep our jewels and hid treasure. Are we troubled with solicitations of Satan? are we subject to be drawn away of ill company? We should reject such things with scorn, and say, 'Avoid, Satan!' Your offers are loss to me; loss of peace, loss of comfort. The pleasures of sin are but for a season, godliness is profitable to all; nay, it is above all other riches. The time will come when nothing besides it will comfort us; nay, all other things will charge us with greater account, and load us with bitterness at the latter end. Let us therefore learn to be good husbands* for our souls. What is the glory of our nation? Is it not that we have mines of this invaluable riches, that we have ministers to draw out of this deep well, and to reveal this precious water of life to all, and that we may buy without money. Therefore let us take heed how we trifle away these privileges. The time will come when we shall want them, and then wisdom will laugh at us as if we have not been wise to lay up durable riches.

* That is, 'husbandmen.'—G.

SIN'S ANTIDOTE.

SIN'S ANTIDOTE.

NOTE.

'Sin's Antidote' forms No. 25 of the original edition of Saint's Cordials, 1629. It was not given in the other two editions. Its separate title-page will be found below.* G.

* SINNES
ANTIDOTE.

In One Sermon.

Wherein is shewed,

What sinne is.
The misery of it.
How it bindes over to condemnation.
How and in what sense it is said to be remitted.
How Iustice and Mercy joyne in this act of remission of sinnes.
That all the benefits of the new Covenant are given with remission of sins.
That it is possible to attaine unto the knowledge that our sins are remitted.
Lastly, how this knowledge is attained by the spirits threefold conviction.

Prælucendo Pereo.

Vprightnes Hath Boldnes.

1 Iohn 1. 9.

If we confesse our sinnes, hee is faithfull and just to forgive us our sinnes, and to cleanse us from all unrighteousnesse.

Rom. 3. 19.

For as by one mans disobedience many were made sinners, so by the obedience of one shall many be made righteous.

LONDON,
Printed in the yeare 1629.

SIN'S ANTIDOTE.

For this is my blood of the New Testament, which is shed for many, for the remission of sins.—MAT. XXVI. 28.

I HAVE already noted three things in the text.*

1. The name or title that is here given to the sacrament: it is called 'the blood of the new testament.' I have shewed the reason of it, and how all our good is made over to us by a new covenant which is sealed with the blood of Christ.

2. I have shewed also how this testament is confirmed, ratified, and established by the blood of Christ.

3. I have shewed the fruits and benefits by this covenant thus established, in the extent of it, which we spake of the last day, 'It is shed for many,' where I proved that many shall reap benefit by it; and not few, but many; and again, not all, but many; though many, not all.

Now it remains that we come to the main benefit itself, and that is, *the remission of sins*, which, that you may the better understand and make use of, I will first open the phrase clearly, what is meant by this same 'remission of sins.' Secondly, We will answer some doubts about the sense. Thirdly, We will gather the main conclusion, collect the main point intended, make application of it, and so conclude.

First, for the phrase that is here used, the great benefit that we have by the covenant, and by the blood of Christ, it is remission of sins: 'Shed for many for the remission of sins.' The word in the Greek, ἄφεσιν, 'remission,' properly signifieth the sending of a thing back again to the place from whence it was taken; so *remittere* is *retromittere*, to send a thing back again, as old Jacob in his prayer, 'The good Lord be merciful to you, my sons, and give you favour in the sight of the man, that he may send back again that my other son, and Benjamin also,' Gen. xliii. 14; there, to 'remit,' is to send them back again to the house from whence they came.†

So likewise Paul sent Onesimus back again to Philemon, in this sense, when he came away; that is the proper sense of the word, ver. 12. And if it should be taken properly, then to remit sin is to send it back again from

* The previous Sermon or Sermons have not been preserved.—G.

† Cf. Robinson *sub voce* in Greek, and Freund in Latin.—G.

whence it had its first being and beginning. Satan, the devil, tempted man, it is to send sin back from man to him, from whence it came first. But we need not tie the word so strictly. I say therefore the word is a metaphor, and so here only alludes to that same custom of releasing captives, or of releasing servants that were bound, in the year of jubilee, and the like; to release them from that yoke, bondage, and subjection to which they were tied: and so *remittere* is as much as *relaxare*, so it is used, to release and to free one from a yoke and bondage. Thus we have obtained remission of sins, when we are released from that bondage under which sin held us. That you may yet more clearly understand this, you must consider what opposition sin hath—

1. Against God.
2. Against his law.

1. *By discerning of these we shall know what it is to have sin remitted to a man*, howsoever these in the thing are but one and the same. There is no man transgresseth the law, but he sins against God, and there is no man that sins against God, but he transgresseth the law; yet, for doctrine's sake, and for your understandings, we will distinguish them, and shew you what that is that sin doth more directly against the majesty of God; and then what it doth against the law of God, and how it is said to be remitted in both these.

Every sin is an injury and wrong offered to God. Now, when God remits sin, he passeth by the wrong done to himself. In point of his honour and sovereignty, the creature is bound to his Creator, to give all his strength to his service. Now, when a man employs any of his strength, either of soul or body, in the service of anything against God, God is so far wronged, and therefore sometimes God takes this as a dishonour to himself, sometimes he accounts it as a rebellion against himself; so that in sin there is an enmity against God, and a dishonour to God. There is an enmity: so Rom. viii. 7, 'The wisdom of the flesh is enmity against God;' and he shews the reason why he calls it enmity against God, 'because it is not subject to the law of God, neither indeed can be;' that is, it doth not yield that orderly subjection to God which the creature should to the Creator, that subjection to the Lord that children should shew to their father; and therefore David, when he comes to confess his sins, Ps. li. 4, says, 'Against thee, against thee have I sinned, and done evil in thy sight.' He notes two things there in sin that aggravates it, and makes the sense more grievous, that it was before God, and done in his sight; and then, it was against God, 'Against thee have I sinned, and against thee have I done evil.' So that, when God doth remit sin, he doth as it were forgive that rebellion; he doth not account a man longer a rebel against himself; and though he have rebelled before, and have rebelled never so much, yet now he accounts him as a loyal subject, and now he recounts him a faithful servant, and an obedient child, because his rebellion is pardoned. That is the first thing.

Another thing in sin is, God is dishonoured. Why? 'If I be a father, where is my honour? if I be a master, where is my fear?' saith God in that same Mal. i. 6. He accounts obedience his honour, therefore disobedience is dishonourable to him. 'He that offers me praise, glorifies me,' saith he, 'and to him that orders his conversation aright, will I shew the salvation of the Lord,' Ps. l. 23. Now the ordering of a man's conversation, which is an actual and real praising of God, this is a glorifying of God; when a man orders his conversation amiss, when he disorders his conversation, and walks in a sinful course against the rule and against God, he dishonours God. Now, when God forgives sin, he doth put up all injuries done to his honour, and accounts him now as a man that had never dishonoured him at all. And that is the first thing.

2. Secondly, *Consider sin as it is a breach of the law*. So it is said of sin, 'It is a transgression of the law.' The law is the bond that binds all men; sin leaves a man in this bond. Now the law laps a twofold bond upon a man.

1. A bond of duty;

2. A bond of misery; if he shall neglect and fail in his duty.

(1.) The first is, *a bond of duty*, that is, a bond of obedience. Every man is bound by the law to obedience, to obey God according to that will which he hath manifested and revealed in his law. Now when a man fails, the bond is forfeited, he remains now under this bond, to expect all the danger that will follow upon the neglect of obedience; and therefore sin is called a debt: 'Forgive us our debts,' Mat. vi. 12. So that when God forgives a man's sins, he deals with him as a merciful creditor doth with his debtor, that though he were indebted to him, yet when he forgives him, he accounts it as if he were not in debt; and him, as if he had paid all, and there remains no more reckonings between them: so that God releases the bond now in respect of obedience, in the first sense, that is, in respect of that obedience, that should have been performed in time past; as it is, Rom. iii. 25, 'he is our reconciliation through faith in his blood, to declare the righteousness of God in the remission of the sins that are past;' that is, those sins that were committed before, they are now forgiven, and a man is acquitted even from that obedience that is due to the law for the time past. That is the first thing, that whereas he failed in the breach and transgression of the law, his disobedience is not imputed, it is not accounted, and he remains as if he had obeyed the law for the time past, though he had not obeyed it all.

(2.) But then, secondly, *there is something wherein a man is bound for the time to come;* that is, he is bound now to the curse of the law: 'Cursed is every one that continues not in all that is written in the law to do it,' Gal. iii. 10. Now when God remits sin, he frees a man from that curse; all that should have followed upon his neglect or failing in his obedience, 'He hath freed us from the curse of the law,' saith the apostle, 'inasmuch as he was made a curse for us,' Gal. iii. 13. So that, put all this together, and you now see what it is to have sin remitted. It is, for a man to be released and freed from all that guilt under which he was held, by which he was bound over to judgment for dishonour done to the majesty and glory of God; for rebellion against the sovereignty of God, for trangressing the law of God, and that curse under which he was bound; he is freed from all, so that God beholds a man now as one that had not at all dishonoured himself, or rebelled against him; God looks upon a man now, as a man that had not transgressed his law, or been under the curse and censure of the law in any point. So that you see there is a perfect and total forgiving and passing by of all sin, and a releasing of a man of the punishment of sin. When a man obtains this favour, to have his sins remitted him, this is that we call remission of sins. But now for the sense, there be two questions that must be answered.

Quest. 1. The first is, *Whether this remission of sins be all the benefit we have in this new covenant by the blood of Christ?* So it seems to be here, as if there were no other benefit but this: 'This is the blood of the new testament, shed for many, for the remission of sins.' There he names nothing but remission of sins.

Ans. 1. I answer, This is not all the benefit, though this include all the rest, and therefore it is only named. You shall find sometimes that this is left out: Jer. xxxi. 14, 'This shall be the covenant,' saith the Lord, 'that I will make with them; I will be their God, and I will put my fear in their hearts, and they shall not depart from me:' and there is no mention of remission of sins there. There sanctification is mentioned without justification; here again remission of sins is mentioned without the working of fear in their hearts; here is justification without sanctification, and so in that place of the Acts, x. 43.

Ans. 2. Secondly, We are said to be 'baptized for the washing away of sins.' There the washing away of sins is put for all the rest.

Sometimes again you shall have them both mentioned: and so in Jer. xxxi. 32, 'This shall be the covenant that I will make with thee, in those days,' saith God: 'I will be their God, and they shall be my people; I will forgive their iniquities, and give them a new heart, and I will take away their heart of stone, and give them an heart of flesh,' &c. Here is all put together now; sin remitted, and the new heart given, and all expressed and mentioned in the new covenant.

Quest. 2. *How comes it then that remission of sins is here put for the rest?*

Ans. 1. I answer, first, Because that this is the first mercy; and, secondly, This is the chiefest mercy, and the chiefest benefit in the new covenant, and therefore it is put for all the rest, by a figure usual in the Scriptures.

(1.) First, I say, it is that which God first doth, it is the first mercy which he shews. It is no hoping that he will bestow any gift on a man, until he receive him to favour. All those other gifts, those gifts of grace, they follow the gracious accepting of a man. First, God receives the person of a man, accepts him to favour, and then he bestows upon him all those gifts that are bequeathed by Christ in this testament. A king first receives a rebel to favour, forgives him his offence before he bestow any honour, any other privilege upon him. Now, because this is the first, therefore it is put for the rest, the rest follow it.

(2.) Then, secondly, because this is the chief, and so it includes all the rest under it; for, if this be once obtained, if this favour be once bestowed on a man, that God have forgiven him his sins, then he gives him everything else. So the apostle, Rom. v. 9, 10, saith he, 'If, when we were enemies, we were reconciled to God by the death of his Son; much more now, being reconciled, shall we be saved by his life.' If, when we were enemies, we were reconciled by the death of Christ, that is the first thing; and the greatest of all the great works of mercy was to remove and take away the impediments, the obstacles, the blocks that lay in the way. Sin, the conscience of sin, to purge the conscience from that, to forgive all that which laid a man open to the wrath of God, this is the greatest work; if this be done, it is an easy matter to obtain all the rest. And this may be noted the rather for the comfort of weak Christians, that doubt so much of strength of grace to subdue any corruption, for assistance and grace to persevere in an holy course. Hath God done the first work? Hath he forgiven thy sins? All the rest are less works than this; it is a less mercy, after sin is forgiven, to increase grace, to continue grace, to subdue corruption, and the rest; all will follow upon this, they are all included under this: therefore, I say, let a man make sure this to himself, first, that he hath forgiveness of sins, and then from thence let him raise arguments to strengthen his faith, and to encourage himself in asking another mercy at the hands of God; and so in any outward thing, in any outward want, distress, or difficulty, if God have done the greater, he hath forgiven thy sins. You know the apostle reasons from the giving of Christ, 'If he have given us his Son, with him he will give us all things,' Rom. viii. 32. Now the first and greatest gift, in the Son, it is this, to have our sins forgiven, and therefore he will certainly give all the rest with it; if a man can make good this one thing to his soul, all the rest will follow upon it. So much for the second question.

Quest. 3. Again, there is another, and that is this, *How can it be said here that this blood is shed for the forgiveness of sins?* It seems somewhat contradictory and opposite one to another; for, if sins be forgiven, How comes Christ to shed his blood for them? And if Christ shed his blood for them, How are they said to be forgiven?

Ans. 1. The shedding of Christ's blood supposeth merit. It was by the merit of his death that we obtained this mercy. Now where there is merit, what mercy is there in it? Forgiveness supposeth a free gift, a free grace; but where there was such a merit, as was procured by the blood of Christ, what free gift was in it? These two seem to fight one against another, and therefore we must reconcile them; for these two may well stand together, remission of sins, and yet the obtaining this by the blood of Christ. To this purpose you must consider in God,

Justice and mercy.

He is exactly just, and exactly merciful. He so shews mercy, as it must be done without injury to his justice. Justice must be fully satisfied, that mercy may be fully and comfortably manifested. Now there is the blood-shedding of Christ to satisfy justice, there is forgiveness of sins to declare mercy; for that is the common speech of people. Ask them how they hope to be saved? They will answer, They hope to be saved by the mercy of God. It is upon a mistake, for they do swallow up justice in mercy, as if God could not remain exactly just in shewing mercy; now tell them again, that God is as perfectly just as he is merciful. Ay, but they hope to find better than so, they hope they shall find mercy.

And therefore know, that there is no man that receives this mercy in the forgiveness of his sins till justice be satisfied even to the utmost. If the justice of God were not fully satisfied, I say, the infinite justice of God in the exact rigour, and in the perfect righteousness of it, if it had not been satisfied to the atmost, it had been impossible that any flesh should have been saved.

Ans. 2. And therefore, secondly, consider another thing, and that is, the comparison between Christ and us. Look upon Christ, and there is justice fully satisfied; look upon us, and there is mercy fully shewed. In us there is no merit, nothing but the guilt of sin; that if God would receive sinful men to favour, reckon, it must proceed from the tenderness of the bowels of his mercy, from the freeness of his love, by whom we have redemption through his blood, even the remission of our sins in his rich grace in the same, Eph. i. 7, 8; it is the tenderness of mercy, and the riches of grace, if he look on us, because there is nothing in us.

Now look upon Christ, who hath indeed satisfied the wrath of God to the utmost, and therefore he is declared to be a Saviour by the resurrection. If Christ should not have remained in the prison, as he was in the prison of the grave till he had paid the utmost farthing, God had not been just; he was indeed our surety, and there was no possibility of our being released from the debt, unless our surety had paid the utmost farthing. But now therefore, when Christ rose out of the grave, and was now released of the bonds of death, and was freed out of prison, into which he was cast as our surety, it is evident the debt is fully discharged, the creditor is fully satisfied, and now our peace is fully made, because Christ hath purchased us, and therefore in respect of Christ we are said to be bought: 'You are bought with a price, and therefore glorify God in your bodies and spirits.' And you are redeemed, saith the apostle; that is, you are bought, 'not with silver and gold, but with the precious blood of Jesus Christ,' 1 Peter i. 18. So that there was a price upon the blood of Christ, a value, a worth. Consider the person that shed that blood; it was one that had two natures: he was God, able to satisfy the wrath of an infinite, offended majesty, and therefore it is said that God purchased the church with his blood, Acts xx. 28; that is, because he that purchased the church with his blood was God as well as man. Now by this it comes to pass that his blood was meritorious, of an infinite value, worth, and price, and so he merited the favour of God. It was merited on Christ's part, but not on our part. Every way it is free to us. The gift of Christ is free, for that it comes from the free grace of God. 'To us a child is born, to us a son is given,' Isa. ix. 6. It is a gift, Christ was given, and then the application of Christ to us, the acceptation of us through Christ; this is a gift, and a gift of grace, as the apostle calls it in that same Rom. iv. 4. It is of free grace that God accepts us; he might have chosen others. We know that angels fell, and fell irrecoverably; Christ took not upon him the nature of angels, but he took upon him the seed of Abraham, and so he became a Saviour, not of angels, but of men, Heb. ii. 16. The angels that fell are fallen for ever, but Christ died that he might save men. So that every way it is free. It was free that God gave his Son to this abasement, it was free that God gave his Son for men, it was free that God should give men faith to lay hold upon his Son: 'Through faith you are saved by grace, and that not of yourselves, it is the gift of God,' Eph. ii. 8. So that remission of sins, though it be by the blood of Christ, it is an act of free mercy, an act of mercy whereto God is no way bound, but did it freely of his own love and mere motion, and of his own good pleasure. Thus you have the words opened. I have shewed you what remission is. I have shewed you also how these things stand together, the shedding of Christ's blood, and yet remission of sins by free grace.

Now let us come to the main point intended, and that is this, that

Doct. All the benefits that believers have by the new covenant, and so by the death of Christ, they are all of them given them in the remission of their sins. And therefore remission of sins is here put for the whole covenant, for all the privileges of the covenant, because all the rest are given in this and with it. Look what time God forgives a man's sins, at that time he gives him all other things, sanctification, and whatsoever else, as we see at large in Ezek. xxxvi. 26, the Lord speaks there of the intention of his goodness to his people: ver. 26, he shews what he will do, he will cleanse them from all their idols, and forgive all their sins, and then he will give them a new heart, he will cause them to walk in his ways; and then he comes with outward mercies too, as far as shall be good for them; he promiseth them deliverance from their enemies, and other good things, in the rest of the chapter, but all other things come in with remission of sins. A man that hath his sins forgiven, he hath the other things given with it. This point we are to prove and apply, it is a point of great weight, it is the very key of the gospel, which requires great attention in the hearer, and great care in the speaker; there is much in it, for the very not distinct and clear understanding of this causeth a world of doubts and scruples, and gives advantage to Satan for many temptations, as we shall shew when we come to open certain cases about this.

1. First, We must open the point, and make it appear to be a truth, *that all other privileges and benefits of the new covenant are given to believers in, and with the remission of their sins*, so that a man may conclude, he that hath his sins remitted and forgiven, he hath, and shall have all the rest of the promises of the new covenant; and therefore David, Ps. xxxii. 1, 2, saith, 'Blessed is the man whose iniquities are forgiven, blessed is the man to whom the Lord imputeth not sin.' The apostle, Rom. iv., expounding that text in the point of justification, he shews wherein the blessedness of a man consists; that is, in that he may appear before God without his sin, without his filth, without that that makes him abominable to God. And therefore such a man is truly blessed, for he hath with this all that can make him blessed. Look whatsoever a man would have to make up his blessedness, and to prove to his own soul that he is a blessed man, he hath all that here with remission of sins; you know, that other things, sanctification and the rest, are part of our blessedness, and therefore they must go along with this remission of sins. And so in another place of Scripture that speech of the apostle, Acts x. 43, is for us, 'To him give all the prophets witness, that through his name we have remission of sins.'

Now the prophets gave witness concerning Christ of many other things besides remission of sins. That we have in his name, that we have by him, but all other things come with this, and therefore he would have them chiefly to mark, that that which all the prophets would have the church to understand to be the great benefit they have by Christ, is the remission of sins. They all join in this, that this is the general benefit, as it were, the great gift of all, that supposeth and includeth all the rest in it, that 'whosoever believes in him shall have remission of sins;' 2 Cor. v. 19, 'God was in Christ, reconciling the world to himself, not imputing their sins.' God was in Christ, reconciling the world to himself, a marvellous great mercy! This consists in this, that their sins were not imputed. Ay, but there are many other things that a Christian would desire besides this; for what man that hath, in truth, his sins forgiven, that hath his faith working by love, by love to Christ, but he would desire also, that as his sins past might be pardoned, so he might walk before God in newness of life; and therefore that is that which David so much prayed for: 'Oh that my ways were so direct, that I might keep thy statutes,' Ps. cxix. 5. Now we have this into the bargain, we have this into the agreement, as it were, in with the rest, that our sins are not imputed. When this is granted we have this also with it, that they shall not condemn, as we see, Rom. viii. 1, 'There is no condemnation to them that are in Christ Jesus, which walk not after the flesh, but after the Spirit;' there is no condemnation to them. This is a great mercy, and this is one mercy that we have by Christ; but this is not all, for, saith he, 'they walk not after the flesh, but after the Spirit;' to shew that this walking after the Spirit, it is a thing that the Spirit of grace works in them, that is given to them by Christ; for 'the law of the Spirit of life which is in Christ hath freed me from the law of sin and of death.' So that now you see plainly there is something else given when sin is not imputed, and so a man is free from condemnation; all the rest comes in with it; that the law of the Spirit of life frees us from the law of sin and of death, and so by degrees perfects holiness and sanctification with it; and so in divers other places of Scripture I might allege for this purpose, but I intend not to dwell upon it. I will make it appear to you by some reasons, and so come to the uses. You see it is so, you shall see also it will be so, and it must be so when we have remission of sins, when this great mercy is bestowed on a man, that his sins are forgiven, all the rest are given with it.

Reasons. 1. The first reason is taken *from the nature of sin.* Consider that if sin be taken away once, that which hinders all our good is taken away, as Isa. lix. 1, 2, it is said, 'The hand of the Lord is not shortened, that it cannot help; nor his ear is not deaf, that he cannot hear: but your sins separate between you and your God, and hide his face and keep good things from you.' Good things are kept from us when God's face is hid from us. That which keeps good things from us, it is sin; saith the prophet, 'your sins separate between you and your God;' take away that now, take away sin that makes the separation, break down that partition wall, break down this distance between God and us, that keeps us from God, that we have not that access unto his presence, and keeps God from us, that there is not this free influence, as it were, of grace upon us. I say, take away that, and then a man is settled in all the other benefits, whatsoever comes by communion with God. Therefore this is the first thing, that remission of sins pulls down the wall, and brings a man into communion with God. Now by communion with God we have all good, we have all in him, all from him. There is no good denied to man when God hath received him to favour, and God never denies his favour to a man when he hath forgiven him his sins; for indeed that is the great act of his love, the great act of his favour and goodness, that he forgives sins to a man; that is the first thing.

2. Again, secondly, it will appear yet further, if you consider *the entireness of Christ, his perfectness.* How perfect a Saviour he is in every way! He is the head of the church, able to fill all his members, to fill the whole body, and therefore the church is called 'the fulness of Christ, that fills all in all, that fills all things,' Eph. i. 23. There would be some emptiness in a Christian if Christ should not fill the heart of man, fill the desires of the soul, if he should not also give something else with remission of sin. And therefore, 1 Cor. i. 30, saith the apostle, 'He is made to us of God the Father, wisdom, righteousness, sanctification, and redemption.' He is an entire perfect Saviour every way; he is made redemption to us; he is made, besides that, righteousness to us; besides that, he is made sanctification to us; besides that, he is made wisdom to us. Mark, if a man would have redemption, it is Christ; 'By him we have redemption, even forgiveness of sins,' saith the text. Now a man that hath redemption in Christ, that hath forgiveness of sins, he hath other things with it. He hath wisdom by Christ too, righteousness by Christ, and sanctification by Christ too. And so he hath everything, because he is an entire and perfect Saviour. And that is the second reason.

3. There is a third reason, and that is this, it is taken from *the chaining and tying of all the privileges of the new covenant together.* They are inseparably knit; they may be distinguished, but they are not divided; they are in the same subject. Where God gives one, he gives all; and there-

fore, Rom. viii. 30, it is said, 'Whom he predestinated, them also he called; and whom he called, them also he justified; and whom he justified, them also he glorified.' They go all together. If a man be a justified person, he is effectually called too; if he be effectually called, he was predestinated, and he shall be glorified. So that now there are many links in the chain, when all are joined together. If a man pull but one part of it, he takes all; they all follow, they are all chained together. The privileges of the new covenant they are coupled together. In the new covenant God doth not say, I will do this *or* thus, and so speak of them disjunctively; he will do one *or* another. I will give you a new heart, *or* I will forgive you your sins, *or* you shall be my people. He doth not do so; but the new covenant delivers them coupled so, that they are linked together; 'You shall be my people, *and* I will forgive you your sins, *and* I will give you a new heart,' &c., Ezek. xxxvi. 26. They are all joined together, and coupled together, and may not be divided asunder. If God give remission of sins, the rest goes with it, for they are coupled together in that grant, in the main grant; that is, in the covenant of grace itself. Thus then the point is opened and proved: I come to make some use of it. This is a point of great weight; the greatest work is to bring it home to the hearts of Christians.

The first use we will make of it shall be for instruction and exhortation, and we will come after to comfort, and to resolve certain cases, if time serve. The cases are many, and rise from mistake of the covenant.

Use 1. First, for exhortation and instruction, and that shall be to persuade every one, if they would make themselves happy in the enjoying of all things that are good, what course they should take for it. *Get this, their sins forgiven.* Let that be the first thing. If a man would make all comfort sure to himself, let him make this sure first to himself, that his sins are forgiven him. Therefore I beseech you consider this, and take it to heart, that we may persuade you to get the knowledge of the remission of your sins. We persuade you not to anything that is impossible or unnecessary. It is a thing that may be had, and it is a thing that is necessary you should have, if you will have any good. Make this first sure to thyself, that thy sin is pardoned.

I. I say, first, *it is possible.* It is that which the papists deny, and that which others question, and which natural reason is against; and therefore, because it is a point of faith, the Scripture is more large in it, and we must be more express in clearing of it, to make it appear to you that it is possible that a man may have the knowledge that his sins are forgiven him; that he may not only conclude that sins are forgiven to some, or, it may be, I may hope that my sins shall be forgiven to me; but he may conclude resolutely that my sins are forgiven me, and as truly and as certainly, and more certainly, than if an angel from heaven should tell a man so. A man would think when an angel shall come and tell Cornelius that his prayers and alms-deeds were accepted, there could be no certainer knowledge than that. When an angel shall come and tell Daniel that he was a man greatly beloved, there could not be more certainty of it by any means. All that Dives required was but that one might arise from the dead, that his brethren might certainly know the things in another world. But we will make it appear to you that there is a way to make it more certain to us than the voice of any that should rise from the dead, or the report of an angel. Men have been deluded by apparitions, and Satan may transform himself into an angel of light; but this way of making it known to a man's self that his sins are forgiven cannot deceive him, as we shall now shew to you. But that there is such a certainty,

(1.) First, Else how is it possible that the servants of God should have peace of conscience till a man may know that his sins are actually pardoned him? But to settle a man's conscience in quiet and in peace there must be an act in the court of heaven; and somewhat must be done in the court of conscience. Something Christ doth in heaven with God his Father, and something like that he doth in the heart of a man, he makes peace with God his Father for us. Now God is reconciled to a man; then again he doth by his Spirit give to a man the knowledge of this reconciliation with God by clear evidences out of the word, and then a man is at rest, then a man is at peace, and therefore a man may know it. Suppose a malefactor had a pardon granted in the court, as long as he knows not of it, he is full of trouble still, when it is brought home to his chamber, to his lodging, to the prison, or wheresoever he is, now he hath peace. The soul of a man is not at peace till the pardon be brought home to the consistory, to his chamber, to a man's own conscience. Now where there is one of these manifested evidently to him, that he may read it, and take notice of it, then he is at peace. Now it is possible for a man to have peace in this life: Rom. v. 1, 'Being justified by faith, we have peace with God, through Jesus Christ.' It was not only Paul's case that he had peace with God, but it was the case of the believing Romans, and therefore he joins the rest with himself, 'We being justified by faith, have peace with God.'

(2.) Again, it appears a man may know that his sins are pardoned by another thing, else how could a man pray for the pardon of sin? We are bound to pray for it; but what we ask we must ask in faith, and waver not, James i. 5, and whatsoever you ask, believe it shall be granted, and it shall be done to you, Mark xi. 24. A man must pray in faith; in praying for the particular thing, faith applies it to a man's self, applies it to his own soul, not in a wavering, suspensing, doubtful manner, but that upon knowledge: 'By his knowledge shall my righteous servant justify many.' There is a knowledge in faith; that is, such a knowledge as is grounded upon divine revelation, upon the truth of the word, whereupon faith looks, which, when a man knows and applies, now he hath peace; by this he knows that his sins are pardoned.

(3.) Again, to what use else is the sacrament, if it be not to make known to a man the forgiveness of sins? for that same giving to every particular man with the intent of it, to remember me, as Christ speaks, that which Christ did, as the end of it, that he died for sinners, and died for those particular sinners to whom he offereth himself, to whom he is given in the sacrament. All this is but to bring the knowledge and application of this forgiveness of sins to my own self.

(4.) Again, other of God's servants have known the forgiveness of their sins, that their sins have been forgiven, why may not we also? Doth the Spirit of God work diversely in the saints? did he work one way in David and another way in us? did he work one way in Paul and another way in us? It will appear otherwise: Ps. xxxii. 5, 'I said, I will confess against myself my sins,' saith David; 'and thou forgavest the iniquity of my sin.' David knew it was forgiven.

Ay, may some man say, David did it by some extraordinary revelation.

No, saith he; 'for this shall every one that is godly seek to thee,' &c. For this shall 'every man;' it is every man's case as well as mine, and they shall seek it the same way that I have done, that they may obtain the same mercy that I have found. And so the apostle Paul saith, I was a persecutor, and a blasphemer, and an oppressor, but I was received to mercy;' Paul knew he was received to mercy.

Ay, but Paul might know it by some extraordinary revelation.

Nay, saith the apostle for the comfort of those that shall believe hereafter to eternal life, 'God hath shewed on me all long-suffering and patience for the comfort of those that hereafter shall believe to eternal life.' This mercy manifested to Paul was for the comfort of others of God's servants that should afterward believe to eternal life. So it is not a thing impossible.

II. Again, secondly, when we persuade you to the knowledge of the forgiveness of your sins, we persuade you *to a thing that is as profitable as possible;* as it is possible to be had, so it is profitable, useful, and necessary for us. When a man will come and ask any mercy at God's hands, how shall he lay a foundation now of hope and faith, that he may speed with God in obtaining it, but in this first, that his sins are forgiven? And therefore it was even David's course, whensoever he came to beg any great mercy at the hands of God, he begins with this confession of sins, to beg pardon for sins. So, Dan. ix. 4, when he comes to beg a mercy for the whole church at the time in those times of sorrow, what course doth he take? First, he confesseth the sins of the church, he begs forgiveness of the sins of the church, as the great hindrances of mercy to the church. And therefore here is the thing, if a man would beg any good thing at the hands of God, begin here first, remove that which hinders. Till sin be done away, there will be hindrances of all our prayers. Every prayer is lost, whatsoever petition a man puts up, he shall never speed and obtain it till his sins be pardoned. Consider in the time of our Saviour Christ, whensoever he would bestow any special mercy upon men,—many came to him in several cases with several diseases,—the first speech of Christ is, 'Thy sins are forgiven;' when he healed their bodies and other particulars, or cast out devils, &c., it went along with this still, 'Thy sins are forgiven thee.' And therefore, of all things, it is most necessary that we may know how to speed in prayer, that we may know what right we have to come before God, and to make our requests known, that we know that our sins are forgiven and pardoned.

Quest. But how may I know that? Now I come to the main question, how a man may know that his sins are forgiven in particular.

Ans. I answer, *It is known by the testimony of the Spirit.* That which they stand so much upon, which is extraordinary revelation, it is not needful for this business; but yet a revelation from the Spirit is needful, and therefore it is called 'the Spirit of revelation,' Eph. i. 17; that is, the Spirit reveals to a man the things that are given him of God; and the apostle proves strongly that any believer may know the rich privileges of the new covenant, because any believer hath the Spirit; as, 1 Cor. ii. 9, &c., 'The things,' saith he, 'that eye hath not seen, that ear hath not heard, nor hath entered into the heart of man, are they that God hath laid up for those that love him.' What things are these? They are things that are laid up in heaven, though that be not denied; but the chief thing, the meaning there is, the great privileges that we have in the gospel, which God hath prepared for those that love him, and are laid up in the gospel; as in a rich treasury, there they lie; and therefore the promises are called 'precious promises,' because they contain these jewels and pearls, and these spiritual riches of a Christian in them. It is a rich cabinet that hath rich jewels in it, so they are precious promises that have such precious mercies in them. Thus these are such things as 'eye hath not seen, nor ear hath heard,' &c.

Obj. But some man will say, If no man ever saw them, if no man ever knew them, how shall we ever get the knowledge of them?

Ans. But, saith the apostle, 'God hath revealed them to us by the Spirit.' The eye of man, that is, the natural eye of man, can never see them, the natural heart of man can never conceive them, &c., yet, nevertheless, God hath revealed them to us by his Spirit; and so he goes on, ver. 14, 'The natural man knows not the things of God, but the spiritual man discerns all things.' Why so? Because the Spirit of God, who now causeth the light of the gospel to shine in his heart, reveals to him those things, that without that light can never be discovered or discerned by any man.

Quest. But now the great question is, How the Spirit of God reveals to a man that his sins are pardoned in particular? Every man will doubt of it.

'The same Spirit bears witness with our spirits, that we are the sons of God,' Rom. viii. 16. So there is a witness of the Spirit with the spirit of a man in the heart and conscience of a man, that he is accepted in the sight of God.

Quest. Oh, but now how doth the Spirit witness this? and what is the testimony that the Spirit gives of this, or by what way gives he it?

Ans. I answer, briefly, by alluding to that expression that you shall find John xvi. 7, 8: 'I will send,' saith Christ, 'the Holy Ghost. And when he is come he shall reprove the world; he shall convince the world of sin, of righteousness, and of judgment.' He shall convince the world, but of what shall he convince the world? 'Of sin, of righteousness, and of judgment. Of sin, because they have not believed in me: of righteousness, because I go to the Father: and of judgment, because the prince of this world is judged.' I say I allude to that, for there is such a work in this business that now we have in hand, as there is in that convincing the world concerning Christ; I say, there is such a work of the Spirit convincing a man 'of sin, of righteousness, and of judgment,' that he may reveal to him the pardon of his sins; there are certain works of the Spirit that we may express by these:

1. First, I say, *He convicts of sin*. The Spirit that testifies to a man that his sins are pardoned him, doth it first by convincing a man of his sins. Now, you know, there is more in conviction than bare discovery. It is a full and thorough discovery of the thing; and not only so, but an effectual discovery, such as works upon the soul; there is not only a light in the understanding, but some heat in the affection and in the will. Now, when the Spirit convinceth a man of sin, here is the first thing now whereby he knows that his sins are pardoned. You shall see this the better in the effects of it, and that is,

(1.) First, *It makes a man to see that there is no sweetness in sin;* it makes a man to find that sin is the greatest burden, the greatest misery, of this life. For that which makes a man delight in sin, is because it is presented to him in false shapes; but now when the Spirit of God comes to manifest sin, to discover sin in its own shape in the soul, and makes a man to look upon it in its own nature, as it is, then he finds it to be the most unprofitable burden that ever he bore in his life. Upon this comes that work upon the heart, which is that oppression of spirit, that a man comes laden and heavy burdened. You know this ever goes with forgiveness of sins: Mat. xi. 28, 'Come unto me, all ye that are laden and heavy burdened, and I will ease you.' That if a man would be eased of his sins he must be laden and heavy burdened first, that is, he must find a need of ease; and when he is laden and heavy burdened, that he may be assured he shall have ease if he come to Christ. That is the first effect.

(2.) Secondly, There is another thing that goes along with this, that sin being discovered thus to a man, *he comes to seek, above all things in the world, to be rid and to be eased of it;* as the apostle in that same 2 Cor. vii. 11 saith, 'Behold, what clearing of yourselves,' &c. He will get to be free from it rather than his life. Now, there is no clearing of a guilty person but by confession; for how shall a malefactor get to be cleared before the judge but by confessing his fault? If he sue for mercy, it may be he may obtain it; but if he stand out till it be proved against him, he will be cast. It fails with men many times, but it never fails with God; and therefore saith David, 'I said, I will confess against myself my sin, and thou forgavest the iniquity of my sin,' Ps. xxxii. 5, 6. So it is said, 'He that confesseth his sins, and forsakes them, shall find mercy,' Prov. xxviii. 13.

(3.) But, thirdly, *it is not a bare confession of sin, that may proceed from common knowledge and illumination; but there goes more in it, and that is, there is a loathing and a detesting of it.* By that the Lord describes the repentance of the people of Israel: Isa. xxx. 22, 'They shall defile the rich idols, and their apparel,' &c.; 'and shall cast them out, and shall say, Get you hence; they shall cast them out as a filthy thing, as a thing that they cannot endure to look on, and to have in their sight.' There is such a loathing of sin in the soul where God intends to forgive that sin.

(4.) Fourthly, There is yet a fourth thing in this conviction of sin, and that is this, *that all the care of a man is how he may free himself from the actual committing of sin,* how he may set himself in a right state again, how he may be right set; as Gal. vi. 1, 'If any be fallen by infirmity, you that are spiritual, set him in joint.' He is now like a man whose bones are out of joint, and he is in pain with it; therefore all his care is how he may be set in joint again, how he may be set into the estate that he was in before; for every time a man commits a sin, the soul is disordered by it, and a man is now much distempered. With that he is forward to commit other sins, he is backward to any good. And now the greatest care of a man is, when God hath thus fitted him by his conviction, by this work of the Spirit convincing him of sin, how to get his sin off, and how to get his soul rid of it; as Isa. i. 16, 18, 'Wash you, make you clean,' saith God; 'take away the evil of your works from before mine eyes; cease to do evil, and learn to do well; and then come and let us reason together: Though your sins were as crimson, they shall be as snow; though they be as scarlet, they shall be as wool.' He doth not mean that he would not at all forgive a man's sins till he have gotten such a victory over all his sins that he shall not at all commit any sin; but the meaning is thus, There should be in the soul such a contention, such a strife against sin, that it may appear that he endeavours nothing so much as to be rid of it. All his care is to be washed, to be made clean, and to have the evil of his works took from the eyes of God. Now, when a man sees the evil of sin, as it is contrary to God's holiness, and contrary to his word, and to his law, &c., seeing the evil of sin in himself, and the effects of it, he hates nothing so much, he strives against nothing so much, he desires not so much to be rid of anything as of sin; that is the first thing.

2. But then, secondly, *there is a conviction of righteousness:* 'He shall convince the world of righteousness;' that is, that a man now, when God hath forgiven him his sins, he is to look up to seek after righteousness. And this is certain, that God forgives no man his sins but by Christ, and through Christ, and for Christ; and he draws the eye of the soul, and the bent and the inclination of the heart, towards Christ; that now a man sets a price upon him, he prizeth him above all things: he prizeth him in his desire, till he may get assurance that he is his; and after he prizeth him in his estimation, walking in Christ, after he hath got assurance. There, I say, is the first thing then, he prizeth Christ before all things, he seeks nothing so much. You see the Lord works this disposition in the church in the Canticles, when the church had sinned by neglecting Christ; and now he withdrew himself from her, what doth she do? She comes and seeks him by the watchmen, and they smite her; she comes to those that kept the tower, and they mock her; she comes to the daughters of Jerusalem, and they slight her husband, him whom her soul loves; she goes on seeking still. This is the case of a Christian after relapse into sin, that he is not set again in his peace and comfort till he be made to prize Christ at an higher rate than before. So likewise he describes the church, Jer. l. 4, thus seeking after Christ: 'They shall go weeping as they go; and shall seek the Lord God, and shall ask the way to Zion, with their faces thitherwards.' They shall go; their end is to find out God, that God that was in covenant with them; to find out God, and they shall go weeping, and their faces towards Zion. This is the disposition of the soul of that man whose sins shall be forgiven him; he seeks nothing so much as Christ.

Again, he prizeth Christ at so high a rate, having forgiveness, that he will not part with him. The church saith, 'If she could get Christ, she would keep him in the chamber of her mother that brought her forth.' And when she hath him, what is her desire? 'Set me as a seal upon thy hand: for love is strong as death, and jealousy is cruel as the grave. Much water cannot quench love,' Cant. viii. 6, 7. She so loves Christ now, that she will never part with him again, but will continue with him for ever. So we see Mat. xiii. 44, 'The kingdom of heaven is like a treasure hid in a field; which when a man hath found, he hides it, and for joy of it he departeth, sells all, and buys it.' When a man hath found Christ, and the benefit of remission of sins by Christ, there is nothing that shall answer Christ in the esteem of his soul. Thus faith works by love, love to Christ; as we see the apostle Paul, Philip. iii. 8, he accounts 'all things as dung in comparison of Christ, that he might be found in him, not having his own righteousness, but the righteousness of Christ.' So then thus we see every way there is an high esteem of Christ, a seeking of him till he be found, and a keeping with him when a man hath gotten him, in prizing of Christ at a high rate, nothing in comparison of Christ; this now is because he is convinced that there is a righteousness to be had in Christ, and a righteousness that can be had nowhere else but in Christ, and such a righteousness as can make him perfectly righteous. It is the great thing that he desires above all the world, and that is the second thing. The Spirit doth this; as it draws, so it links a man to Christ.

3. There is a third thing, *the conviction of judgment;* such judgment as wherein 'the prince of this world is judged.' That a man falls now in condemning the motions of sin in his heart, and to condemn himself for the actions of sin before. That you may understand these things clearly,

(1.) First, I say, *a man condemns the actions of sin he hath committed he condemns them and himself for them.* This disposition is in all those whom Christ receives to forgiveness, whom he forgives these sins. 'Thou shalt judge thyself worthy to be cut off,' saith God, 'when I will be reconciled to thee,' Jer. xxxvi. 3. When God will be reconciled to his people, this is one thing, they shall judge themselves worthy to be cut off; and therefore, 1 Cor. xi. 31, 'if you would judge yourselves,' saith he, 'you should not be judged of the Lord.' So that this is that now which frees a man from the judgment of God; when he begins with his own heart, and judgeth himself for sin, he shall not be judged. It shall be judged once; and if a man will not judge himself, God will judge him; but if a man will judge himself, he shall not be judged of the Lord. Now, therefore, you have the conviction of judgment, when a man is now brought to judge himself, that is, to set himself against himself, as a judge sets himself against a malefactor: he arraigns him before him, he brings in evidence against him; he lays upon him the sentence of the law, he condemns him, and takes order that execution be performed upon him. Thus it is when a man sets himself to judge himself: he arraigns himself, he sets himself to a serious consideration before the tribunal of Jesus Christ, who is the judge of the quick and the dead, to consider how the matter stands between God and him, and he brings in evidence against himself, the testimony of his own conscience, the witness of the law; the books that shall be opened then are now opened to prevent that judgment. He looks upon the law, and it shews him what he should have done; he looks upon his conscience, and that shews him what he hath done; and, when he hath thus done, he comes to confess himself guilty; he proceeds now upon this conviction to condemn himself, and to acknowledge that all the curses in the law are due to him, and he wonders that God should bear with such a one as he to live upon the face of the earth thus long; he subscribes to the righteous judgment of God, if he should cast him into hell for his sins, for he judgeth himself worthy to be cut off; he extenuateth not any sin, he lessens not any sin that he hath committed; he desires nothing so much as to feel the weight of it in his heart, that he may indeed see the ugliness of sin more and more, and be brought to be more out of love with it; and thanks any man that will help him to aggravate his sins to himself, and to see the ugliness of them. When he hath done thus, he comes to execution, that is, he comes to that revenge upon himself; there is an indignation against sin, and a revenge upon himself too, because of sin; he judgeth himself unworthy of those liberties that he hath abused, and sometimes he ties and limits himself in those particulars, and denies himself of those things that by reason of his corruption he cannot tell how to use without sin; or otherwise he takes revenge upon himself for particular ills. I say, thus a man judgeth himself for his sins past. That is one thing.

(2.) But now secondly, *he judgeth the prince of this world, as well as himself;* that as he judgeth himself for his actions, so he judgeth all the motions of sin in his heart: that for the present, if any motion be rising from his own corruption, drawing him to a new act of evil, he judgeth and condemneth the sin in his heart, and this is the very original, and the root of that conflict in his soul, this work of the Spirit, a conviction of judgment, that now hath made a man as a judge against himself; and therefore now he sits as a judge doth, to prevent sin by all means; he sets himself against the motions of sin, which was the case of the apostle Paul: Rom. vii. 19, 'When I would do good, evil is present with me.' But what, doth he let this go on? No, he strives against it, that as the flesh lusteth against the spirit, so the spirit lusteth against the flesh; there is a seed, there is a work of grace striving to work out the corruption in his heart. This is in all the servants of God, in all those whom God bestows this mercy upon of the forgiveness of sins, to condemn the motions of sin, and therefore he sets against them. 'O wretched man! saith the apostle, 'who shall deliver me from this body of death?' He calls for help as it were against the body of death; he looks about to see if it be possible by any means to get it rooted out. When a man hath a thief gotten into his house, he calls for all his neighbours to help him, that he may take him there; so there is a thief got into the soul, for now sin is not in his heart as a lord, but as a thief, and therefore he calls for help, that seeing it is gotten in, he may get it out again. But this, I say, beloved, is in all the servants of God that shall have remission of sins, there is this conviction of judgment; that is, they are brought to this pass, that now they judge themselves and their sin, and condemn it in themselves. Now, upon this follows reformation and amendment of life, because they judge the prince of this world; they judge all the works of Satan, and all the motions of sin in their hearts; and therefore now they set themselves into a contrary way, to works of obedience, and amendment of life. So the promise is made that, 1 John i. 9, 'If you walk in the light, as he is in the light, the blood of Christ shall cleanse you from all your sins.' Thus you see now how a man may know and prove that his sins are forgiven. Put all this together, and let every man now examine his own heart; I know no man but would desire to partake of the comfort of this doctrine; and I told you already, there is great reason why every man should labour after it, to get the knowledge of this, that his sins are forgiven. We are yet but upon that point, how a man may know that his sins are forgiven. Now for this purpose, I say, consider what hath been said. It is a thing that is revealed to a man by the Spirit of God; the Spirit of God doth manifest in the word those grounds and texts upon which a man may gain this assurance to his soul. Now look on this threefold conviction of the Spirit, whereby it manifests this work, conviction of sin, conviction of righteousness, and conviction of judgment, for they all go together in that heart whose sins are forgiven. I say conviction of sin: first, it makes a man see the loathsomeness of his sin, the ugliness of it; it makes him account it a burden that he would fain be eased of it, and therefore he confesseth it; therefore he sets against it with all his might, and therefore he loathes and detests it. That is the first thing.

Now try yourselves by that, whether you yet apprehend your sins in that manner or no; not for a man to say generally, I am a sinner, &c., and to send forth some few sighs, slight and short, to no purpose, in a cursory and formal manner,—as the manner of many is,—but it is another manner of work. And therefore, I beseech you, consider seriously what is that inward secret work of the Spirit upon the heart; what effects it hath upon the affections of the soul, that is, upon the discovery of the filthiness of sin, to make a man weary of it, to loathe it, to hate it, to desire to be rid of it, to strive against it, to confess it, &c.

Whither hath this consideration sent thee? Hath it made thee to set a greater price upon Christ, and upon the gospel offering Christ unto thee; such a prizing of him as that thou lettest all go to seek him, that is, thou seekest Christ above all things; and if thou hast indeed gotten him, thou wilt not lose the comfort of him, but daily walk in him, that thy life is now a living in Christ. I beseech you, consider this, the walking of a man that hath received Christ, in the Scripture, is called a walking in Christ: 'As you have received Christ, so walk in him;' and the living of believers is said to be a living in Christ: 'Now I live, yet not I, but Christ liveth in me,' Gal. ii. 20; that is, in his whole life he lives to express the virtues of Christ; express Christ in thy life. I beseech you, consider this, that the affections are now set wholly on Christ, and that a man now gives himself to Christ, as a servant to his Lord, to be commanded and to be guided by him. So that nothing now sways in a man, nothing now carries him in his actions so as Christ shall, when he knows what is agreeable to the will of Christ, that shall most of all draw him to perform it. When he knows a thing is contrary to Christ, that shall make him set most of all against it.

Besides this, when he hath done this, there is a conviction of judgment; that now thou art the sharpest judger of thyself for thy sins past, and art the most watchful judger of the motions of sin present. This is thus in every one. I beseech you, take this home with you; consider of it now in the preparation to the sacrament that you are to receive; for the sacrament is a seal, as we shall shew you after, because it seals, as among other things, this, 'forgiveness of sins.' Now, that you may seal this comfort to yourselves, consider that the sacrament is a seal to none but to them that are sealed with the Spirit: 'In whom, after you believed, you were sealed with the Holy Spirit of promise,' Eph. i. 13. The Spirit, the inward seal, gives virtue to the sacrament, and to everything else that are seals of comfort, and nothing can seal comfort to a man, but the Spirit within, that makes everything effectual for that purpose; and therefore if the Spirit doth it, it doth it by this means; consider of this, therefore, seriously. There be in this divers cases that should be answered for the further opening of it, and for the settling of weak-hearted Christians in a settled estate, and somewhat for the casting off of presumptuous persons that are in the height of their pride, that we may give every one their portion; that the weakest may see against many particular temptations and doubts, that even his sins are forgiven; and that the other should see that they had but a false plea, a false claim all this while to the pardon of sins, when they cannot make it good by the testimony of the Spirit. But the work would be very large, and I have been already more large than I intended.

THE SUCCESS OF THE GOSPEL.*

Whereto then shall I liken the men of this generation? and what are they like?—LUKE VII. 31–35.

CHRIST in the former verses had commended St John's ministry, and in the verse next going afore he speaketh of the different success it found in the publicans, from that it found in the pharisees, who rejected the counsel of God. Now in the verses following he shews what success his own ministry had amongst them, and thus he doth by way of comparison or parable. And this he brings by way of asking a question, which implies admiration† and indignation, both shewing a deep passion, as it is in Isa.: 'What shall I do for my vineyard'? Isa. v. 4; and this shews in general, *that the refractory disposition of man is a matter of indignation and of admiration*, especially if we consider what it despiseth, and whom.

First, *They despise the word of God*, the saving word, the counsel and wisdom of God; nay, secondly, *they despise God clothed in flesh*, that was born and died for their sakes, and thereby offers salvation to them, and life everlasting; yet all this to the obdurate heart of man is as lightning that dazzleth the eyes and helps not the sight a whit; and therefore, Isa. vi. 10, the prophet is bidden 'to make the heart of the people fat.' Go tell this people, hearing they shall not understand, &c.; and therefore no marvel if God bears indignation against such. 'Whereto shall I liken the men of this generation,' Luke vii. 31; this generation of vipers, that are worse than any of the generations fore-passed, by how much they have had more means to be better.

Ver. 32. 'They are like unto children sitting in the market-place, and calling one to another, and saying, We have piped to you, and you have not danced; we have mourned to you, and ye have not wept.'

The comparison is to little children that, at marriages and times for

* 'The Success of the Gospel' forms the third of the four 'Sermons' appended to 'The Saints' Comforts' (See Vol. IV. page 160). The title-page is as follows:— 'The Svccesse of the Gospell. Shewing the diverse entertainements it hath in the World. In a Sermon Preached upon the 7. of Luke and 31. verse. By that Faithfull and Reverend Divine, R. Sibbes, D.D. and sometimes Preacher to the Honorable Societie of Grayes-Inne. Printed at London by Tho. Cotes and are to be Sold by Peter Cole. 1637.' It has distinct pagination, but does not appear to have been published by itself.

† That is, 'wonder.'—G.

feasting, piped and danced, and at funerals and times of mourning did mourn and use some fitting ceremony. Now there were some among them that were froward, and would neither be content with mourning nor piping, and playing, and to these Christ compares these great doctors, the scribes and pharisees; a froward generation, neither pleased with Saint John's austere course of life, nor with Christ's affability and meek carriage, and thus he crosseth their proud, froward disposition. For the custom itself, for that it is only related, and no whit censured, therefore I forbear to speak further thereof, but come to the reddition* of the comparison.

Ver. 33. 'For John Baptist came neither eating bread nor drinking wine; and ye say, he hath a devil.'

Ver. 34. The Son of man is come eating and drinking; and ye say, Behold a gluttonous man, and a wine-bibber, a friend of publicans and sinners!'

Where observe *God's gracious dealing with man.* He useth all kind of means, sendeth men of several natures, austere John, and meek Christ, and they use all means to convince the judgment, all methods to work upon the memories, all reasons to work upon the affections and wills. He turns himself into all shapes to gain wretched man unto him.

Secondly, Observe *the order God useth;* first, John, then Christ. John prepares the way, throwing down hills: 'O ye generation of vipers,' Mat. iii. 7. Oh, say they, this man is too harsh, I think he hath a devil. Then Christ comes with blessed: 'Blessed are the poor, blessed are you that weep,' &c., Mat. v. 3, *seq.* So he sent the law first, then the gospel; first he threatens, then promises.

Thirdly, Observe that the *manner of their teaching is double, by doctrine and life, and these agree,* wherein observe it is good that life and doctrine should suit; for John's life was austere and retired, his doctrine was also tending to beat down the proud conceits of man. Christ came to all, conversed with all meekly and lovingly; and the reason of God's making use of men of severe dispositions is, because of the different natures of men, whereof some can better relish one nature than another. Some love the hot and fiery nature, others delight in the meek spirit; and though there be diversity of gifts, yet they come from the same Spirit. Even as the diverse smells of flowers comes from the same influence, and the diverse sounds in the organs comes from the same breath, so doth the Spirit diffuse itself diversely, as it meets with diverse natures. Yet all tendeth to the perfecting of one work. We may hence therefore gather, that to converse fruitfully and lovingly is to be preferred before austerity, and commendable above it, because it is the conversation of Christ himself.

And the papists shall never be able to prove their foolish austere vows of a solitary life, &c., to be preferred before communication and society, unless they will prove John better than Christ. And again, this should teach us to moderate our censures of the diverse natures and carriage of men, as knowing that God in wisdom hath appointed it for excellent use, and that all agree in the building up of the spiritual temple of the church.

In the next place, observe that *where grace doth not overpower nature, no means will prevail* over the obdurate nature of man. Neither John nor Christ could work anything upon these Pharisees. Thus was it in the wilderness and Egypt. What admirable wonders did God work, yet how incredulous and stiff-necked were they! And the reason is, God gave not a heart, and in the conversion of a sinner *there must be another manner of*

* That is, 'rendering,' or application.—G.

grace than only offering and exhortation to accept of Christ; nay, the Spirit itself must do more than exhort, for it may lay open to us many motives, tell us of God's goodness, truth, and strength sealed to us; it may tell us of wrath and judgment, and on the other side of kingdoms, everlasting joys, perfection of happiness, yet all not work any remorse in the heart of man if the Spirit leaves him there. And the reason is, man is dead in sin by nature, and that 'strong man' having gotten the possession, cannot be cast out but by the 'stronger man,' which must quicken and give power, that may change every part of the soul, the understanding, will, and affections, else all means is to no purpose but for to make us unexcusable at the day of judgment. Hence therefore *we may see the shallowness of those that conceive of the word of God, as if it did only persuade the will.* No; it must alter the will and change it quite, else arguments are to no purpose; and in the second place, it teacheth us to *come to the ordinances with holy hearts*, begging God's power to soften our hard and stony hearts, and desiring him to join the powerful work of his Holy Spirit with the outward means, and that his word may be like to that word at the beginning, that no sooner commanded light, but 'there was light.'

And lastly, it teacheth us *to conceive of the word*, together with the goodness and power thereof, *with admiration and wonderment.*

In the next place, observe, from the calumniation of the scribes, *that rebellion and opposition against goodness is never without show of reason;* and men they will never go to hell, but they have reason for it. They will countenance rebellion by defaming and scandalisiug the people of God; and to that end they will be sure to take things with a strong hand. Austere John 'hath a devil;' sociable Christ 'is a wine-bibber.'

And the reason is, *the pride of man*, that will not be thought so foolish as to speak, or do anything without reason, and therefore when it is wanting they will feign one. In every calumniation they do so, and the calumniation and scandal here was the greater, because it was raised by the scribes and pharisees, the great doctors and the wise rabbis, whose word must carry such credit with it, as alone to condemn Christ: 'We would not have brought him to thee were he not worthy of death,' Mat. xxvi. 66; and whose life must be a rule to others: 'Doth any of the pharisees believe in him,' John vii. 48.

For use therefore of this doctrine, *let us account it no strange matter if we be traduced, disgraced, and scandalised*, for it was Christ's and John's lot. Great slanders must be maintained from great men, such as them that sit in Moses's chair, the pharisees and scribes. John's holiness should have procured reverence, and Christ's sociableness should have been rewarded with love; but it is the lot of them and all Christians: 'The disciple is not above his master,' Mat. x. 24. They may do well, but must look to hear ill. Wicked men when they learn to think well, they will learn to report well.

Let us grieve at their estate, and comfort ourselves in Christ, who will maintain our cause.

Thirdly, *Be innocent as doves*, and be ever doing good, that our lives may give them the lie, and stop others from giving credit to their malicious aspersions.

Fourthly, *Let us look that we approve ourselves to God*, who shall judge us. Stand or fall to him, and pass* not for the judgment of man, and of such as shall be judged themselves.

* Cf. Glossary, *sub voce.*—G.

Lastly, *Let us take heed we take not a thing in the wrong sense* and of vain prejudice. Men are witty* to lay stumbling-blocks in their own way to heaven. This preacher is too strict, that too mild; this too plain, that too poor. Like the children Christ speaks of here, nothing will please them: hence, in the last place, we may learn from the example of Christ, that it is not ill to speak ill of ill men, in case of apology and prevention of scandal; for Christ's example doth warrant it. But to proceed.

Ver. 35, 'But wisdom is justified of all her children.'

From the connection of these words with the former, by this word 'but,' we may observe, that *is is the lot of God's truth to have diverse entertainments in this world.* Some will be children of wisdom, and justify it; others, as the Pharisees, will scandalise it; and the reason is, *from the diversity of men's natures* in this world, wherein are contrary seeds† and contrary servants to contrary kingdoms. Some will flock after Christ; others will say, 'he deceiveth the people,' John vii. 12. Yet as there is 'a generation of vipers,' so there is a generation of children belonging to the kingdom, that swim against the stream, like the stars that have a retrograde motion to the residue. But for the meaning of the words, by 'wisdom' here is meant the doctrine of the gospel, not only as it is in books, but as it is in the ministry. And briefly the ways of God laid out in his ordinances, and taught by weak men, all this is understood in this word 'wisdom,' and this word 'justified,' that is approved and received 'of her children,' that is, of her followers, being such as wisdom begets to a new life. In these words let us consider, first, *that there is a doctrine which is wisdom;* and this teacheth what God intends to us, and we should return unto him. This reason will evince that God being so good unto man, he should have some thanks at his hands, and some acknowledgment of duty to him, by way of worship, which it is most fit God himself should institute; and the rule hereof, joined with practice, is that wisdom here meant, for there is diverse wisdoms: first, *as it is in God*, and so it is a depth unsearchable. 'Man knoweth not the price hereof,' Job xxviii. 13. Secondly, there is a wisdom *communicated to Christ*, who hath a twofold wisdom, infinite as God, and finite as man; and a wisdom as he is God and man joined together; and this is called wisdom of union. In the next place, there is a wisdom *of vision*, and this the saints and angels have in heaven, and we shall have hereafter; and there is a wisdom *of revelation*, which is revealed in the Scripture to us by the Spirit, and this is the wisdom meant in this place, as it is comprehended either in principles laid down in the gospel, or in conclusions inferred necessarily from them, or in our improvement of them, to the right and best end, which is God's glory and our salvation. This is wisdom; and called so here by way of emphasis, shewing it is the only excellent wisdom, which will further appear in these respects.

1. First, *It doth arise from a higher beginning than all other wisdom* whatever; for it comes from God's goodness and mercy.

2. Secondly, *The matter. It is a deep mystery.* Christ, God-man; his nature, offices, and benefits.

3. Thirdly, *It is more powerful* than all other wisdom; for it transforms us. It makes us wise, and changes us from wicked, and makes us good.

4. Fourthly, *It is better than the law*, which was a killing letter. This gives life.

5. Furthermore, this wisdom *is everlasting*, and it is ancientest: intended before the world was. It is also *inviolable*. God will change the course of

* That is, 'wise' = ingenious.—G. † Cf. Isa. lxv. 23, with i. 4.—G.

nature for his church's sake; and sooner will he break covenant with the day and night than this covenant, which shall be for ever, Ps. xix. 9.

6. The end of it is *to bring us home to God*, 1 John i. 3.

This wisdom hath the same *name with Christ*, who is the Wisdom of the Father. He gives his power to the word; and what reproach is done to it, he accounts it as done to himself.

Use 1. This serves, therefore, *to convince the atheists*, who cannot choose but acknowledge there is a God, that it is fit the creatures should depend upon him, and shew it by way of service; and that this service should be prescribed by God rather than by man. Let them know this is the wisdom and the word of God. No word like it in the convincing power it hath in purity and holiness; none so powerful to transform us from death to life, from nature unto grace.

Use 2. Secondly, it serves *to exhort us all to attend upon the commands of this wisdom*. Men are admired for their deep wisdom in policy, whereby they come to be great. This without grace is enmity to God; and the devil dwells in the heads of such as makes honours, ambition, or pleasures their sole aim. The wisdom of arts and sciences goes beyond that, yet comes far short of this; that being but temporary, and perishing with the things themselves, but this everlasting and eternal; and indeed policy and civil learning at the most do but civilize and make men morally wise; to which, if nothing else be adjoined, the life of such is but a smooth passage to hell.

Use 3. Lastly, this should teach us *to consider, magnify, and admire* at God's goodness*, that hath given such a wisdom to us as this, to be a lantern to light our way in this dark world, and to be as manna to feed us, that we faint not in the way, till we attain to everlasting life.

The second general thing is, that *there are children of wisdom, and that the world† it is fruitful and able to beget;* for it hath the Spirit of God accompanying it, which is fruitful. We see the sun and the rain beget herbs; trades makes men tradesmen, and arts artists; and shall we not think this wisdom should make men wise, and this trade make a man fitting for work? Yes, verily. No wisdom hath this begetting and operative spirit but this; for the law finds us dead, and leaves us dead. Again, this wisdom is the arm of God to salvation. By it 'we are begotten to be sons of God;' by it we are children 'made like to God,' holy, pure, heavenly, begotten to his image; and therefore as children we ought 'to obey the word' in performance of all duties; of prayer, hearing, reading. Furthermore, in that *we are scholars in Christ's school, which is wisdom itself*, we may be said to be 'sons of wisdom,' as those were called the sons of the prophets that were disciples to them. Now our teacher is a mighty teacher. It is no matter for the dulness of the scholar, this teacher can put wit and capacity where none was formerly, Ps. cxix. 12. Moreover, if this were not thus, then it would come to pass, that there should be a time when there would be no church; that Christ should be a king without subjects, and likewise a doctor without scholars.

1. From the doctrine we may observe, therefore, that those that follow the best rule, which is God's word, and intend the best end, which is their own salvation, *these are the most wise*, for they provide for the worst times, as the ant for winter; and with the wise steward they provide themselves of friends, and like Joseph they lay up for dear years. These are wise that procure shelter for themselves against all dangers, and are fruitful in doing good.

* That is, 'wonder.'—G. † Qu. 'word'?—Ed.

2. And, in the second place, let this *persuade us to attend upon wisdom*, be we who we will be, a publican, an extortioner, a persecuting Saul. This wisdom will 'of stones raise children up unto Abraham,' Mat. iii. 9.

3. In the next place, observe *the children of wisdom do justify it;* that is, they receive it, approve it, defend it, maintain it; for it is fitting that children should stand for their mother, and take to heart any wrong that is done to her; and therefore the child of wisdom privately believes it, and loves it; and openly, if the truth or any ordinance of God or holiness of life be spoken against, he will defend and maintain it, yea, to the death; for wisdom, though with the loss of all things, is rich enough. So Moses esteemed the rebukes of Christ more than the pleasures of a king's court, Heb. xi. 25.

Quest. But must we maintain it, so as to speak for it always, and in all companies?

Ans. I answer, No, but when we are called to it. Wisdom dwells with the prudent; and where it is, it will teach when to speak, and what, and in what manner. And the reasons of this observation are, first, it is fitting *that God's children should concur in judgment with God*, who justifies his wisdom in his children,' and admires his graces in them, 'O woman, great is thy faith,' Mat. xv. 38; as contrarily he doth admire the stubbornness of the heart of wicked men. Secondly, *wisdom in itself is justifiable;* for it justifies itself; for it carries a justifying spirit with it. It hath a power able to change. In all estates it justifies itself; in trouble and anguish it comforts. Yea, in death, when all other wisdom perisheth, this raiseth up. It is powerful above the power of nature. It pulls down the proud heart of man in prosperity.

Quest. But it may be said, if it be thus, what need is there that the children of wisdom should justify it?

Ans. I answer, in respect of itself, it needs not our help to justify it; but in regard of others, to draw them on to the loving and embracing thereof, and in respect of ourselves, to manifest the truth of grace in us.

The church also justifies it by proposing it, and declaring the goodness thereof by defending it and commending it. Yet is it not above the Scriptures, no more than we are above the truth of God, when we are said to 'seal it.' Children we are of the truth, and desire to be ruled by it, not to judge it, and all children agree herein to justify it, as it is said here, 'Wisdom is justified of all her children.' Though there be of divers countries, of divers nations and natures, yet all agree in commending and embracing this wisdom; and thereby are they known to be children of wisdom, for hereby *may we know what estate we are in, even by our carriage of ourselves towards wisdom.* How many, professing to be the children of wisdom, do notwithstanding condemn it. Diverse abroad, whom wisdom shall not judge, but they will judge wisdom, and are indeed the children of human tradition. And among ourselves, *are there not many that reject the ordinance of God?* Is not, say they, reading of good books at home as good as going to church? Do not such confess that the rivers of Damascus are as good as Jordan; whenas, if ever we come from this spiritual Egypt into the land of promise, we must go over this Jordan. We must come to heaven by the foolishness of preaching.

Again, are there not many, *because they see there is diversities of religions, they will be of none,* till it be decided which is the truth, and this is the way to die in no religion. These are bastards. They cannot be children of wisdom, for they know it not; as likewise they are such that justify ignorance, making it the mother of devotion (*a*). They profess they are the children of ignorance and error, and not of wisdom. Another sort there are that *in word justify wisdom*, saying it is the word of God, *but in their life and conversation do deny it.* Let such know, he that lives against the faith shall be damned, as well as he that believes against it. Good meat is commended more by eating and cheering than by talking. If such did truly believe the wisdom of God, it would purify them; and not to believe is madness; but to live so as if they believed not is desperate madness. The sinner denies God's presence, the covetous man denies God's providence, the despairing man denies God's mercy and Christ's merits, the sinner against conscience denies God's justice, else the terror of the Lord would move him. Yet if we see these things in us, and allow not of them, but condemn ourselves for them, God will be merciful and spare us.

This should encourage us, in the next place, *to proceed on in a resolute course of Christianity.* What though the wicked world laugh at us, and scorn us, God the Judge justifies us, his children justify us. As for other men, the Scripture calls them fools, for God hath given them over to a reprobate judgment in things that concern a godly life, and therefore if we be censured by such, let us account it our crown.

Moreover, this is a ground of exhortation, *to move us to this duty of justifying the ordinances and ways of God in life and conversation.* Justify Christ to be our Saviour by relying on him, and let the justified soul justify him to the world by repairing to him and depending on him. Justify God to be our Father, by repairing to him in all estates. Justify truth to be the best riches, by esteeming all other wisdoms dross and dung in comparison; and let us admire the goodness of wisdom, else wisdom will not lodge with us. Let it rule in our hearts, and it will abide with us; else it is a stranger, and will not tarry, In our days the voice of wisdom is heard. It uses all means. It hath sent men of all manner of conversations and gifts. Of all others, we are inexcusable if we entertain it not, and justify it not in our lives and conversations.

But it will be asked, How shall we justify wisdom?

I answer, *Let us strive first to empty ourselves and souls of corruption.* As a vessel full of bad liquor must be emptied before good can be put in, so we by nature are full of folly, and must empty ourselves before we can be enabled to justify wisdom; and in what proportion this folly is overruled in us, in the same proportion do we justify wisdom; for where wisdom is, it must dwell largely and purely; for itself is pure, and will endure no mixture. And therefore those that justify themselves in any ill course cannot justify wisdom; for when it once comes to cross him in his beloved course, let his words be never so good, his folly will discover itself. 'How can you believe, when you seek for glory one of another?' saith Christ, John v. 44.

Secondly, *Beg of God that he would take away the veil of our hearts, that we may know and love the best things in the best manner;* that he would open to us the wonders of his law.

Thirdly, *Labour that all our knowledge may be spiritual;* for if it be acquired out of books, and not written in our hearts, in time of temptation we shall never justify wisdom. This is evident out of the history of the martyrs. Many illiterate men stood out stiffly for the truth, and justified it with their blood, when many great clerks* gave over their profession; for when the Spirit teaches, it teaches to obey, to want, to abound, and to despise the

* That is, 'learned men.'—G.

glory of the world. Spiritual wisdom brings humility, other wisdom puffs men up with pride.

Fourthly, Therefore we should *pray for the Spirit of God*, that it would settle and seal truths into our hearts, and teach us to obey and practise the things it enjoins us.

Fifthly, We should also *condemn ourselves, and grow poor in spirit;* for what justifying is there like to that of those that, being abased by outward afflictions, are likewise inwardly humbled; so, condemning themselves, they justify God's wisdom; and therefore those that either trust to intercession of saints or their merits, in vain they think ever to come to the performance of this duty.

Sixthly, *Attend we on wisdom;* for what is more excellent than it, and without it all are fools. Wise they may be for the world to get riches, while their end is condemnation and perpetual beggary in hell. Many are wise to get high places here, and witty* to get a deep place in hell. They study for wisdom in the creatures, and when they die, their wisdom perisheth with them, and they want that true wisdom that should support them in death.

Seventhly, And *endeavour we to be rooted in it*, that we may be able to speak out of the power thereof in our souls, and to resist the temptations of Satan, with sound resolutions against them; and then when that day of revelation of all things shall come, Christ will own us, and justify us, when the children of this world shall tremble to hear that truth and wisdom condemn them perpetually, which here they hated and slandered.

Lastly, In all our wants and distresses, *so carry we ourselves that we may shew we have a Father to provide, a King to defend us in our desertions*, that we have a Priest in heaven to make our peace, and in all temptations that we have a Prophet that will direct us in the right way unto heaven, in spite of the malice of hell itself.

* That is, 'wise,' = ingenious.—G.

NOTE.

(*a*) P. 286.—'Ignorance . . . the mother of devotion.' This subsequently famous or infamous phrase was perhaps first used by Dr Cole in the great Disputation held at Westminster. Cole was an out-and-out defender of Popery. G.

MARY'S CHOICE.*

Now it came to pass, as they went, that he entered into a certain village: and a certain woman, named Martha, received him into her house, &c.—Luke X. 38–40.

This history is absolute of itself. Christ having despatched business elsewhere, went from place to place to do good, it being his whole aim and office. And now divine providence and holy love directs him to these two women, who formerly had entertained him in heart, and now in their house; yet did he feast them more liberally than they could him. And yet so studious they were in his entertainment, that they fall out in a manner about it. Mary she sat at Jesus's feet, knowing his custom, that his lips did ever drop down sweet-smelling myrrh in his gracious words, as it is Cant. v. 13; and therefore she forgat all other things. But to come to some observations.

First, From the coming of Christ to these women observe, *that where God hath begun grace, he will not discontinue, but will be perfecting of it till the day of the Lord;* directing by his providence continually for their good, and sending his servants the prophets to that end; for God's providence extendeth to the least things, even to the hairs of our head, and to sparrows, Mat. x. 29. The use is to teach us *to endeavour to be fruitful in communion one with another*, if we profess to be led by the same Spirit that Christ is guided with. The lips of the righteous are pleasant, and their tongues are refined silver. *Sometimes the sin of man makes instruction unseasonable*, and to swine it is pity to cast pearls, Mat. vii. 6. And many times *men are deluded with a vain despair of not profiting* by their speech, when no doubt if they did but trust on God in performing such duties, their exhortations or admonitions would take more effect than they

* 'Mary's Choice' forms the last of the four 'Sermons' appended to 'The Saint's Comforts' (see Vol. VI. page 160). Its title-page is as follows:—'Maries Choise. Wherein is laid down some directions how to choose the better part. Comforts for them that have chosen it. Signes whereby we may know we have chosen the better part. By that Faithfull and Reverend Divine, R. Sibbes, D.D. and sometimes Preacher to the Honorable Societie of Grayes-Inne. Printed at London by Tho. Cotes and are to be sold by Peter Cole. 1637.' It has distinct pagination, but does not appear to have been published separately. Henry Smith has a fine sermon from the same text and under the same title. Cf. 'Sermons,' 4to, 1675, pp. 149–157 of second division of the volume.—G.

look for, as oftentimes it falls out; for in man there is naturally a desire of good and profit. Sometimes *a spirit of dryness possesseth good men.* Christ had the fulness of the Spirit without measure, men have it according to their measure; and so through multitudes of occasions and businesses are overcome with a dryness, so as they can distil no grace as they should.

Against these *we should study and consider beforehand what occasions we are most like to meet with;* and study discourse fit for such occasions which we may best profit by. Study for sufficiency, that we may be like full clouds, or as paps that do pain themselves with fulness, till they be eased of their milk.

Secondly, And *lament over our deadness,* and beg spiritual influence, that may make us willing.

Thirdly, And *let all take Christ's example for a pattern,* to draw others to heaven, and to be ever busied in our calling.

Fourthly, And we should also imitate Mary; *be wise to draw from other men,* when they are not disposed to enlarge themselves. The wise man saith he is a fool that regards not the price in the hand of the wise. There is none but excels in one gift or other; and it is part of the honour due to such to take notice of them, and to make use of them; and it is unthankfulness to let such persons go without regard of those gifts. Many no doubt are dead, and their gifts with them, which had men been wise might have saved others much labour and increased knowledge much, if they had been displayed to others. Furthermore, it is said that Mary sat at Jesus's feet, implying her composed and settled demeanour, which helps to a quiet mind and attentive heart; 'but the eyes of a fool are in the corners of the world,' Prov. xvii. 24, which hinders attention. But Martha was troubled about serving. Mark as in this good woman, so in many of her sex, goodness troubled with passion. She chides with Mary. The grounds of it in her were either a mistaking of Christ's disposition, whom she thought looked for much entertainment; though she was therein much deceived, for that Christ came to feast them, not to feast with them. And for this she is gently rebuked of Christ, as if he would have told her that it concerned the glory of God more nearly to receive and take notice of his diffused mercies; and God requires it rather than performance of any outward duty of love to him. But for the words.

Verse 41, 'And Jesus answered, and said unto her, Martha, Martha.'

These and the ensuing words contain, first, a reproof of Martha; secondly, an instruction of her; thirdly, a justification of Mary, with the reason thereof. In the reproof of Martha, consider the compellation, wherein observe the ingemination,* 'Martha, Martha.' It implies *love* that Christ bare to her. He calls her gently by her own name. Christ saw in her good mixed with ill, and therefore is not over-sharp or bitter to her. It implies also *seriousness;* and therefore Christ doubles her name, even as Pharaoh's dreams. Two aiming at one end argueth the thing is sure; and as 'Lord, Lord' in prayer argues vehemency, so he reproved Martha for her inconsiderateness, and brought her thereby more seriously to ponder what she did. And *Christ's example should be a rule to us,* namely, in our reproofs, to imitate him who had all the parts of a good reprover.

And, *first,* we should be sure to reprove *out of love to the party,* else the proud nature of man will not endure it.

* That is, reduplication. Cf. Richardson *sub voce.*—G.

Secondly, It must be *done in wisdom;* first advise, then speak, else shame will return on us, and the other will be hardened.

Thirdly, It must be with *liberty of speech.* We must conceal nothing; and thus disposed was Christ. In him was the fountain of love and the treasures of wisdom; nay, he was wisdom itself, and he took liberty of speech. Though he was entertained, he doth not therefore sell his liberty; and though we say he that receives a benefit sells his liberty, but it was not so with Christ. Some there are if they give entertainment to a minister, they think they are bound to silence, and not to tell them of anything they see amiss in them; and therefore it was St Paul's wisdom not to take the offered kindness of the Corinthians, 2 Cor. xii. 14, *seq.*, lest he should be engaged to them. These things should be precedents to us, that we should be friends upon no other terms than to speak what is for their good; for some proud persons there are that think none friends but flatterers. Let us take heed of base engagements to such; for Balak will engage Balaam with gifts, if he can win him no other way to his humour. And it is reason that we should maintain this liberty of speech, for friends suffer disgrace for the folly of their friends. He that keeps company with adulterers shall be defamed, and therefore it is reason a man should have liberty of speech to reprove such.

'Thou art careful and troubled about many things.'

Not that Christ mislikes domestical business and hospitality; but by this Christ shews his pity of his* troublesome cares and distractions, which might have been passed over with far less burden to her, and hereby therefore he took occasion to heal her error in judgment, who thought Christ came to be feasted when he came to feast them; as also that he might free her from that hard opinion that she began to carry towards Mary her sister, whom she thought either negligent or proud in not helping her. It is therefore a ground to be supposed, that hospitality becomes both men and women. It is a part of that calling God commits to us, and it is commended to us from the example of Abraham, and the event of it, that he thereby entertained angels into his house, Heb. xiii. 2; and in this place it is implied under the words care and trouble, as if he had said, Thou dost trouble thyself too much, and more than there is need, giving us this lesson,

Doct. That in things that are lawful excess is easy in holy persons, for what more lawful than a calling? What more commendable than hospitality? Yet in this Martha is too much troubled.

The reason is, *because there is little or no fear of sin;* and where there is least fear there is most error; and security breeds neglect, and therefore it is the common plea, for excess in recreations and apparel, is it not lawful? Yes; who denies it? But is there not a mean? Nay, in their calling here may be excess, for there must be measure observed in them, and that is the reason no doubt.

And again, in *lawful things defect in any one circumstance makes the thing ill, though in itself never so good,* and therefore reformation of the state is good, but not by private persons. So here hospitality is good, but not when we should be hearing Christ speak. To a good action there is required not only that the nature of it be good, but that it be well done in every circumstance, for, failing many, one makes it vicious.

Use. And therefore *we should have a principal watch over our affections, and that in lawful things;* for good meanings do not always justify actions. Christ was crucified, and the martyrs burnt; and the actors in it thought they did

* Qu. 'her'?—Ed.

God good service, and shall this excuse? Peter had a good intent when he would have persuaded Christ from going to Jerusalem, yet received no better thanks than 'Get thee behind me, Satan,' Mat. xvi. 23. Therefore let us look in all our actions, how lawful soever they be, in the matter. It is not enough, but they must be lawfully done, according to the rule of the word of God, else it is sin to the doer, whate'er his intent be.

In the next place observe from the translation of the words, which is more exactly thus: 'Thou troublest thyself' (*a*), and true it is, that we *bring upon ourselves oftentimes more trouble than God lays on us*; and those that have lived any long time, if they advisedly consider of their labours past they shall find they may thank themselves for most of it; and in truth, without God's Spirit, we are self-tormentors, and our error is double in this kind; for either we *pull too great burdens on us, or they being laid on us, we make them too grievous to be borne by our careless laying them on us, or by our unhandsome and unseemly carriage under them*, as it is in ordinary burdens. Those that are skilful can carry a burden with a great deal less pain than another man can that wants skill, though it may be he be the stronger.

Secondly, And another reason hereof is *in our froward pettish natures*. An unmortified nature is like a sore, everything pierces to the quick, besides that it vexeth itself.

Thirdly, *And this is caused partly by too much passion in us, and partly by want of judgment, and ignorance or not remembering the end and issue of them*. Where these causes are, there cannot choose but be such effects. In the darkness everything scares us.

Use 1. Therefore *let us take heed of this infirmity and never excuse it*, saying, men need not care for me, I trouble none but myself; for thou sinnest against God, and thou art a sinner against the sixth commandment by self-murder in troubling thyself as well as by troubling others.

Use 2. Secondly, *Let us not be over much troubled at troubles*. Poor souls are much troubled this way. If they find but a little dulness of spirit, then they conclude they want grace, they are none of God's children.

Censure *not yourselves, nor vex not yourselves*. It made Jonah almost quarrel with God; and patient Job complain of his mother, of the day, of the night. Alas! what hurt did they him. And if we see others in this estate of censuring, vexing, or troubling themselves, *censure not them rashly*. The children of God are not always alike, nor always in tune; for a calm mind is a grace that God gives according to his good will and pleasure, and it ebbs and flows as he pleaseth. But to proceed; in the next place, observe *that the things of this life, meeting with a nature not mortified, are subject to trouble it*, and the reason is, they are inferior in themselves, empty and vain, giving no content, but bringing vexation, and are subject to mutability, and therefore not able to give the soul content, being of an higher nature, and more constant enduring, and therefore requires comforts and contents suitable, which these things, not able to afford, when they fail, as ever they do, the soul is vexed and offended.

For use thereof we should take notice of the nature of these things, and take heed of μερίμναις βιωτικαῖς, troubling ourselves about the things of this life. For it divides and weakens the soul; and the dividing of a river must weaken the force of the streams; and so Cyrus diverted the streams of Euphrates, and thereby took Babylon.* And the soul, when intent upon one thing, though then it be strong, yet being turned to many things, is

* Cf. note *a*, Vol. II. p. 248.—G.

much weakened, and the forces thereof scattered. And therefore we should meddle only with things that concern us, and so much with them as is fitting.

Ver. 42, 'But one thing is needful.' Christ doth not only reprove, but he doth instruct. He shews the disease and the remedy, to shew his love, and that his mind was not to gall or vex, but to heal and make peace. And this he doth by way of information, telling her these businesses are full of trouble, and not necessary, and therefore she was not to spend herself in them, but turn her to that one thing which is necessary, *which is to communicate with God in the use of all sanctified means of grace.* It is necessary to come out of our natural estate, and to be settled further into communion with God; and because holy means discovers our misery, opens a remedy, works grace in us to lay hold on Christ, therefore it is necessary also to attend on the means.

Quest. But it may be asked, What, are not meats and drinks, clothes and government in a commonwealth, are not these necessary? Wherefore serve callings? Nay, this whole life is a life of necessities, how then is there but one thing necessary?

Ans. I answer, It is true these things are necessary in their compass and sphere, for this present life, but this life itself is nothing without a better being, and we had better not be than be and not be translated hereafter to a better life, and therefore Christ applies himself to these means, as to that which conducteth us to that better life, which is only absolutely necessary.

Obj. But, it may be urged, is not Christ's righteousness, faith, God's Spirit, more than one; and yet are they not all necessary?

Ans. I answer, though they be diverse, yet they run all to one end. Even as many links make one chain, so all these tend to make a man one, that is a Christian; and therefore a wise soul considers them as one thing, and runs over them all at one view. He considers the word and the Spirit as that which, by working faith in him, brings him to Christ, who brings him to eternal glory; and therefore he doth not hear, to hear, but to be renewed inwardly, and so to have communion with Christ, and to attain to salvation; and therefore the word is called the kingdom of God, the word of reconciliation, of grace, of the kingdom, for by it we are conducted thither; and therefore, Acts xiii. 46, they that did neglect the gospel, which was the power of God to eternal life, are said to neglect eternal life. 'And therefore if we will ever profit by holy means,' consider them as chained to salvation; hear the word, and with it receive the Spirit, and with it faith, with it Christ, with him heaven and happiness. This is the one necessary thing, others are but accessary, and so we should esteem them. What is skill in reasoning, and not to be able to know the subtle sophistry of Satan? And to what purpose is skill in healing of sickness of the body, and to have a soul sick to the death? Tongues* are but the shell of knowledge; what good will deep skill in the law do us, if we be not able to make our title to salvation sure? What profit in ending controversies if we be not able to answer Satan's accusations and quarrels that he picks with us? And the reason is, all these are but for this life, short and uncertain. It would make the best of us ashamed, if we did but consider how little we live to God, or our own comfort, knowing many impertinent† things, and yet are ignorant of this our only main thing, and die before we live as we should. But, for the avoiding hereof, let us carefully observe these directions.

* That is, 'languages,' = learning.—G. † That is, 'things not pertinent.'—G.

And first, *Consider in everything what reference it hath to this one thing,* what reference it hath to grace and glory. So long as we neglect this, the devil cares not what we have, whither we go, in what company we are; all is one to him.

Secondly, *Carry ourselves respectively according to the necessity of the things that we are to be busied about,* whereof some are more, some less necessary, according as they have more or less good in them. Those that cannot stand with this main one thing, cut them off, for other things that are necessarily required for our well-being in this life, as our daily bread, our callings in these, and the like.

Thirdly, *Take heed of faithless cares, and beg wisdom to despatch business so as they prejudice not the main, and look still how they aim at the main end.* As travellers and warriors do unburden themselves of things less necessary, so let us take heed of entangling ourselves in the cares of this life, 2 Tim. ii. 4. The covetous man labours for riches, others for pleasures, that they may live sensually, wherein they never can come to the degree of that happiness that brutish creatures do, that have them without care and enjoy them without fear; but for a Christian this is the whole, 'to fear God and keep his commandments,' Eccles. xii. 13.

Fourthly, *In all business we should observe what the main end is, and labour to direct them to that main end.* In baptism, the one thing there, is the covenant; in funerals, the one thing is a work of charity, to commit the dead body to the ground. Yet in these and such like things, all the time is taken up in ceremonious preparations. In our buildings and dwellings we look for good air, good soil, good neighbours, but where is the main? Who inquireth what minister have we? What means of salvation? Tush! this enters not into their thoughts; and thus do they invert God's order. So, in bringing up of children, men look to teach them to read and to be fit for the course of life they intend they shall follow, and how to leave them enough to make them rich and great; but who desires and endeavours to have the image of God engraven in their hearts, and to provide an eternal inheritance for them.

Fifthly, *Every morning we should consider what is most necessary for the day.* Have we renewed our covenant with God and renewed our repentance? Have we armed ourselves by prayer against all occasions of temptations, and provided to avoid such as are likely to meet with us? Alas! how few trouble themselves this way. 'What shall we eat, drink, how shall we spend the time?' These things take up the minds of most; how to uphold a short troublesome life. And yet all their care cannot add one inch to their stature, or change the colour of a hair. 'But seek thou the kingdom of God and his righteousness,' this one thing, 'and all other shall be added,' Mat. vi. 33.

'And Mary hath chosen the better part,' and yet censured we see by Mary's example. *It is the lot of God's children sometimes to undergo the censures of those that are good,* for their forwardness; and thus did David's brethren censure David: 'We know the pride of thine heart; thou art come down to see the battle,' 1 Sam. xvii. 28. But let us be comforted, for as it often falls out that we suffer rebuke with Mary, so we shall have Christ to justify us as she had; and therefore,

Use. Let us resolve with Saint Paul not to pass for the censure of man, but remember that day when God will justify those that are his. Here we pass through a hidden eclipsed glory, but the time will come that we shall be approved; and it shall appear then what we are. Let us learn innocency, that though we undergo their censure yet we may not justly deserve it, and then whatever men do deem of us, we should be encouraged to bear it, in regard our witness is in heaven, in our own hearts, and in the hearts and spirits of good men.

But to proceed: Christ takes Mary's part, and justifies Mary's choice to be the best; in handling whereof we will lay down, in the first place, some grounds that I will go upon, as first that *there are diversity of parts, and diversity of ranks of good things;* and of these some concern this life, some concern the other life; and of either of these God gives to some more, to others less. Some have the goods of this life in plenty, others are endued with the gifts fitting them for a better life, and thus God sets forth his free rule over all creatures, and his free liberty to dispose them as he thinks best; and God exercises his children in the use of all sorts of things, and in discerning of things that differ.

A second ground is that there is a spirit of discretion planted in man, *to discern of the difference of things,* and this he is enabled to by the word especially, for man hath not this wisdom of himself.

Thirdly, *The best things in our minds must challenge the chiefest choice and first place in allowing them, then trying them, and lastly choosing them.* The good part here meant is *grace and glory.* This is that which Mary chose, to hear Christ speak for the strengthening of the graces in her, and that thereby she might assure her salvation to herself; and grace is good, because it makes us good. Outward things are snares, and makes us worse, but grace commends us to God. All other things are temporal, and death buries them, but grace and glory are in extent equal to our souls, extending to all eternity. Grace and the fruits thereof is our own; all other things are not ours. Grace brings us to the greatest good, and advanceth us to the true nobility of sons and heirs of God, and grace makes us truly wise. It makes us wise to salvation; it makes us truly rich with such riches as we cannot lose. Grace is so good, it makes ill things good, so as afflictions with the word and grace are better than all the pleasures in Pharaoh's court in Moses's esteem, Heb. xi. 25. Seeing it is thus, *let us be animated by this example of Mary;* and to that end, first, *beg the Spirit of revelation* to open our eyes to see the high prize of our calling, the happiness thereof; and to get a sense and taste of the pleasures thereof, that we may judge by our own experience. For the meanest Christian out of experience knows this to be the good part; and this it is which the apostle prays for, Philip i. 10, that the Philippians may approve the things that are excellent. The word signifies in all sense and feeling, to approve the things that are excellent, or do differ (*b*).

Secondly, Let us *endeavour to balance things, by laying and comparing them together.* For comparison gives lustre; and thus shall we see the difference and the excellency of some things above others, and the sooner be able to choose. Thus did David; and the effect thereof was this, 'I have seen an end of all created perfection, but thy commandments are exceeding broad or large,' Ps. cxix. 96.

Thirdly, *Labour for spiritual discretion to discern of particulars.* This is as it were the steward to all actions, teaching what to cut off, what to add. In all particular affairs of this life, what time and what place fitteth best, tells what company, what life, what way is the best. And when we have done this,

Fourthly, Proceed on *and make this choice.* If we do not choose it only, but stumble upon it, as it were, it is no thank to us. Though it be the fashion now-a-days; men read the word, and go to church; why? Not that they have, by balancing and the spirit of discretion, made choice of this as the best part, but they were bred up in it; and they went with company, and custom hath drawn them to it; they happen on good duties it may be against their wills; and this is the reason of those many apostates that fall off to embrace this present world, as Demas did, 2 Tim. iv. 10; for they not being grounded, must needs waver in temptation.

Fifthly, In the next place, when we have made this choice, *we must resolve with a deliberate resolution to stand by this choice.* It is not enough to make an offer, or to cheapen, as we say, but come with resolution to buy, to choose. So David, Ps. cxix. 30, 31, 'I have chosen the way of truth, and have stuck to thy statutes;' and ver. 57, 'I have said,' that is, set down with myself, 'that I would keep thy words:' for the will rules in our souls. If we be good, our will is good. There are many wicked men that understand and are persuaded what is best; but for want of this resolution and will they never make this determinate choice; and many rail at good men and persecute them. Let such know that God will not take men by chance. If they choose the worst part, they must look for to reap the fruit of their choice. Assuredly God will not bring any to heaven, but such as have chosen it here, as the best part before they die; and therefore it is no matter what the world think or speak. Let us take up that notable resolution of Joshua, 'I and my house will serve the Lord,' Josh. xxiv. 15.

If we go alone it is no shame; but to such as should accompany us, let them flout at us, and call us singular. If there be any way to heaven, the straightest,* and hardest, and least frequented is the right way. Let them take the delightful frequented broad way. Let us with Mary choose the better part. Though our choice be singular, it is Mary's choice. And take this as a sign that we are in the right way with Mary, if with her we still desire more and more growth in grace and knowledge, and never think that we know enough, that we are good enough, or faithful enough, and diligent enough in our ways.

Sixthly, In the next place, *come we often, and sit at Christ's feet,* as Mary here came to the ministry. 'He that heareth you heareth me,' saith Christ. Live under a powerful plain ministry.

Lastly, *Labour to draw on others* to this choice. By so much the more earnest endeavour, by how much the more we have been a means to draw them to ill heretofore, and this will seal up all the rest, it being a sure sign of our perfect and sincere choice.

'Which shall not be taken away from her.'

The best things are diversely commended unto us, and here that good part is commended by the continuance, that it shall be ours for ever. The means indeed shall end, for that time must come when Christ shall be all in all, but the fruit of them shall continue for ever in eternal glory; for hereby have we interest in the covenant, and the promises which are for ever assured to us, and the marriage between Christ and his church is an everlasting knot. We are an immortal seed. The image of God in our souls lasts for ever, and cannot be blotted out.

Secondly, *Our choosing this good part is an evidence God hath chosen us;* and once chosen, ever chosen. Our actions are but reflex. He chose us, loved us, knows us, and therefore we choose, love, and know him; and these being the gifts of God to us, are without repentance on his part. And who can take this part from us? God will not, for he is unchange-

* Qu. 'straitest'?—Ed.

able. Enemies cannot, for, as Christ said, 'My Father is greater than all,' John x. 29, and Christ is Lord of hell and death. 'What shall separate us? Not life nor death, principalities nor powers,' Eph. i. 21. Nothing can be able to separate. By grace are we kept to salvation, 'and by the power of God,' 1 Pet. i. 5; so as we shall not depart from him,' Jer. xxxii. 40. 'The peace of God preserves us,' Philip. iv. 7; and this *should comfort us and establish us.* We may lose wealth, friends, honours, health, by death. Those that have this 'good part' cannot lose it in all the changes that possibly can happen.

This also *may justify a Christian in his labours.* It is for the best part, that is everlasting, that which will accompany him in death. The wicked men of this world they labour and spend themselves in getting that which, as far as they know, the next hour they may be constrained to part with. They vex themselves with care in getting, with care in keeping, and with vexing grief in the parting from them.

In the next place, this should *content them that are poor and despised in this world.* If they have chosen this good part, they have that which will make them amiable in God's eyes; and this riches shall no man be able to take from them; and hereafter their enemies shall be ashamed, when they shall see these poor contemned ones to reign with Christ as princes a thousand years for evermore, and when they shall see those that were the rich men here to howl in perpetual misery. And therefore the consideration of this should *encourage us to set ourselves upon the best things,* and give no liberty to our consciences to rest till we have found that we have made this good choice; give our souls no rest till we have made an habitation for the God of Jacob in our hearts. In death we all look for comfort. Is it a time then to look for a choice? No. Men may shew a desire to repent, but few do it in earnest. They then send for ministers, but it is in fear. Few such ever die with comfort. However God in his mercy dispose of them, it must not be thus. If we look for comfort in death, we should now get oil in our lamps, now get the means of salvation; be at charges for it; spare no cost or labour. It will quit our cost, and we shall find it. Use prayers privately by ourselves with our families; care not for the jesting of men. He that shall judge the 'quick and the dead' will justify us in that day, and will give us that good part that shall never be taken from us. But how shall we know whether we have chosen this good part? I answer, we may gather divers signs from what hath been said; as first, our affections and esteem will testify what is of greatest esteem with us, and beareth the highest place in our hearts. That thing we have chosen; and therefore, if we love the means of grace principally, if we can say, with David, 'that we love God's testimonies above silver and gold,' Ps. xix. 10, and admire at the value of them, oh! how wonderful are thy commandments! how sweet! how do I love thy law! as if we count the feet beautiful of the messengers of peace, and the communion of saints sweet, this is a sign we have made this choice. Otherwise, if we count basely of the ministry, of the saints as of vile persons fit for scorn, whenas they are 'precious in God's eyes,' Ps. cxvi. 15, whatever we say, we are proud, empty, and vain persons. Peter was of another mind, John vi. 68; and let not men think, because Christ is in heaven, they go not from him when they turn from the word, for Christ saith, 'He that heareth you heareth me, and he that despiseth you despiseth me,' Luke x. 16. And because he would honour his ministers' and apostles' doctrine, he did accompany it with a more large portion of his Spirit working effectually than his own immediate ministry, as appeareth by the multitudes that his apostles did convert at one sermon. In the next place, *examine we ourselves if we be willing to part with anything for the means of salvation;* for if we love anything, and choose it, rather than we will part with that we will part with anything. If we love the pearl, we will sell all to gain it. Far from the humour of some, that will sell the pearl, sell the word, sell the care of the souls of men, to men of corrupt conversation for filthy lucre.

Thirdly, If we have made this choice, *we will have confidence to justify it against all depravers.** Michal's scorn cannot put David out of conceit with his dancing before the ark of God: 'I will be more vile than thus,' said he, 2 Sam. vi. 22. In vain we think to scorn usurers out [of] their trade. No. They find it is sweet. Their purse comforts them against all scorns. Thus it is with the child of God. Let men scorn, censure, rebuke, they comfort themselves; as Job, 'their witness is on high,' Job xvi. 19, and that makes them not pass for men's censure.

In the next place, if we *find that when all things fail us, we do retire ourselves to this as our stay, that our good part shall not be taken away*, nor ever will fail; and thus David, Ps. lxxiii. 26, 'My flesh and heart fail, but thou, Lord, art my portion for ever;' and make that use of it that David did: 'It is good for me to draw near to God.' As a man robbed of all his money, if his jewels be saved, he solaceth himself in them; and as Hezekiah, Isa. xxxviii. 3, if we can appeal to God in witness of our sincerity, 'Lord, remember how I have lived, how I have served thee in uprightness.' Then shall we find the comfort of this will never be taken away from us, else if we cannot thus appeal to God, we may call and cry to him but he will give us but a comfortless answer: 'Go to the gods which you have chosen,' Judges x. 14, let the world help you, let pleasures and riches deliver you; you would not choose me while I gave you all blessings of life and health, now, 'Go, ye cursed,' Mat. xxv. 41.

* That is, 'undervaluers.'—G.

NOTES.

(*a*) P. 294.—'Observe from the translation of the words, which is more exactly thus, "Thou troublest thyself."' The original is, Μάρθα, Μάρθα, *μεριμνᾷς καὶ τυρβάζῃ περὶ πολλά*, = 'art anxious and confused.'

(*b*) P. 297.—'The word signifies, in all sense and feeling, to approve the things that are excellent, or do differ.' The verb is *δοκιμάζω*, = to prove, test, assay. Cf. Bishop Ellicott *in loco*. G.

THE CHRISTIAN'S WATCH.*

Blessed are those servants, whom the Lord, when he cometh, shall find watching.—Luke XII. 37.

These words are part of a sermon that Christ made to his disciples concerning worldly cares, and concerning mercy to those that stand in need. Now in the last place he gives directions concerning watching: 'Blessed are those servants that shall be found watching when their master cometh.'

It was the custom of servants in those times to stand at night to watch for their master's coming.

Here Christ compares himself to a man that is lately married, solacing himself, and preparing a place for his spouse, and leaving a servant at home to wait for his return. Christ is gone into heaven to solace himself, and to prepare a place for us, and will come again to receive us into heaven. In the mean time we are to watch: 'Blessed are those servants that are found watching when their master cometh.'

In these words we are to consider, first, our relation, that we are 'servants.'

And then our condition, we are servants appointed 'to watch for our master's coming,' for our Lord is not yet come.

This life is a condition of waiting. We are always waiting for something, till we are taken up to Christ.

'Blessed are those servants that their lord shall find watching.' And then there is the relation and condition of them also, they wait for the return of their master. And their carriage is suitable, to wit, watching.

And then the encouragement, 'Blessed are those servants, that their Lord, when he cometh, shall find so doing.'

1. Concerning the relation *of servants*, in a word, some are so by office, as magistrates and ministers; but all are servants as Christians. It was the best flower in David's garland to be a servant to the Lord; and it is so for every one, be they never so great in dignity, to serve God; for to serve him is to run into the most noble service of all; for all God's servants shall be kings, nay, they are kings.

* 'The Christian's Watch' and 'Coming of Christ' were appended to the Exposition of Philippians, c. iii. (4to, 1639). [See note, Vol. V. page 2.] They are from different texts, but, as being on the same subject, could not be well separated. Neither has a separate title-page, only the heading as above.—G.

And then it is a rich and most beneficial service; for we serve a Lord that will reward to a cup of cold water. It is not such a service as Pharaoh's was, to gather stubble ourselves; but he will enable us to do, and where we fail he will pardon, and when we do anything he will reward, and when our enemies oppress us he will take our parts.

Observe here how the Scripture speaketh, when we are servants, but do not our duty, and when we do it. When David had committed that sin in numbering the people, he said to Nathan, 'Go tell David,' 2 Sam. xii. 1; but when he had an intent to build a temple to the glory of God, then he said, 'Go tell my servant David,' 2 Sam. vii. 5. When we are doing our duty towards God, then we are his 'servants,' but when we are about other service, God will not own us. Israel were the people of God when they were good, but when they committed idolatry, then, 'Go tell thy people,' saith God to Moses, 'that thou hast brought up out of the land of Egypt,' Deut. ix. 12. Let us therefore remember that we are God's servants, and if servants, then God will own us.

2. Now to go on: 'Blessed are those servants whom their Lord, when he cometh, shall find watching.'

We see here that there must be a constant waiting and watching for the coming of the Lord; whence we may learn *that it is the duty and office of every Christian constantly to watch and wait for the master's coming.*

Watching, you know, presupposes life; and hence first waking and then watching.

Sense springs from spiritual life, and then waking. All that have spiritual life are not all watchers, and all that wake do not watch. Waking is when the spirits return into the senses, and are in exercise. You know sleep binds up the senses; but when the spirits return the obstruction is dissolved.

And then there is waking when all the powers are in a readiness, and when there is a discessation* of vapours that stopped the senses before.

So, then, waking is the return of the spirits, either by some motion, as stirring up the body, or by some great shining light. So it is in the spiritual life. The vapours causeth sleep, but the Spirit of God, scattering a light, awakens us. By this light is meant either the light of his judgments, or the light of his mercies, or the light of divine truth; for by all these sometimes we are awakened.

There is first a waking condition, and then we watch. I intend to speak of watching. Now waking is a preparation to this.

'Watching' is when upon waking all the powers and graces are in exercise, preparing for good and avoiding of evil.

Now, for bodily watching, we have nothing to do with that here, because here it is spiritually meant; but yet taken so far as the body is an instrument of the soul in the action both of soul and body. As, when the body is surprised with any inordinate affection of the blessings of God, then the soul is unfit for watching; and therefore it is specially meant of spiritual watching.

In the primitive church, they had watchings bodily and spiritually; for, being under the tyranny of the heathen emperor, they had not liberty to serve God in the day. But afterwards they had their vigils, watching times, called vigils, preparations, which were before the word and sacraments, or when there was any great business in hand. And when superstition grew, they had their vigils too; but they made laws to bind the people to observe them three times in a night; but their prayers were in Latin. It was a per-

* That is = discession, *i.e.* going away, departure.—G.

verse imitation of David, that rose at midnight to praise God; that was when he was stirred up upon some extraordinary occasion, when there was some danger or some other occasion near, not that he did it ordinarily. But we are fallen into a contrary course than the ancient church was, to spend whole nights in prayers; for we have those that spend whole days in sleep. We cannot watch one hour with Christ; but we can spend whole nights in vanity.

Doct. That which I mean to stand upon at this time shall be this: *that the carriage of a Christian in this world is an estate of watching* till Christ come home.

I will shew this by some reasons why it should be so, and give some directions how we must be in a waking condition.

Reason 1. The first reason is this: *because we are in danger of sin, and in danger by sin.* This occasions watching, especially being ever in danger of sin; and besides many other sins, that sin of drowsiness, deadness, and heaviness of spirit; for every man by experience finds this spiritual drowsiness hanging upon him sometimes more than other. Therefore we ought to have the soul in a better condition.

And then we are in danger by sin, and that is more than I can express; for by drowsiness oftentimes we fall into sins whereby we offend God and the good angels, and give Satan advantage, and grieve the good Spirit of God, and put a sting into all other troubles. Yea, sin makes the blessings of God which we enjoy, no blessings, and hinders us from praising God as we ought for his blessings. So that thus we may see we are in danger *to* sin and *by* sin. Therefore we have need to keep a spiritual watch.

Reason 2. Again, consider *in what relation we are in this world, and what the life of a Christian is compared unto.* We are travellers through our enemies' country. This is Satan's place where he reigns, being 'god of this world;' therefore we had need to have our wits and senses about us.

And then again, the worst enemy is within us, our own hearts; which joins with Satan to betray us to the world, he being the god of this world.

Now carrying an enemy in our own bosom, therefore we need to watch, for that is the condition of travellers through their enemies' country. We also carry a jewel, a soul, a precious jewel in a brittle glass. If once the vessel break, all is lost.

Reason 3. And then again, *we run in a race.* Now those that run need have the goal in their eye, the price* of their high calling; they had need look upon that which may encourage them. And of all men runners need be watchful. We are all runners; therefore you see the necessity of a watch.

Reason 4. Again, our whole life is not only a race but *a warfare.* And of all conditions a warfare needs watching; for we have enemies to fight against that never sleeps. Satan our enemy never sleeps, 'but goes about like a roaring lion seeking whom he may devour,' 1 Peter v. 8. We sleep, but Satan sleeps not, nor those that are his instruments. The poor disciples slept, but Judas slept not. The traitors of the church sleep not, the poor disciples they fall asleep, and suffer Christ to manage his own cause. They have a time, and they will be sure to take it. We being therefore not only runners in a race, but born fighters, for every Christian is born so, therefore we must needs strive.

Now the strongest enemy is in our own bosom. Satan is said to depart from Christ for a time, but he never departs from us. We have an enemy,

* That is, 'prize.'—G.

that is, corruption, which hinders us from good, and taints that good we do. We carry corruption in us that seeks to betray us, and will give us no rest at all.

Reason 5. Again, not only thus, but we are all also *stewards*, and we have all of us 'talents,' of which we are to give an account. Now an estate of account ought to be a watchful estate.

We are all subject to give an exact account of that we have done in the flesh. Being therefore to give a strict account, we ought to be watchful.

Reason 6. Again, men *that are under observation* need be watchful. Now there is no Christian but is in perpetual observation, for there is in him a conscience. Though it be asleep for a time, yet that conscience will awake and stare him in the face. You know what is said in Genesis of Cain, 'Sin lieth at the door,' Gen. iv. 7. Conscience, like a sleepy dog, lieth at the door, and will fly in our face when we are going out of this world, and then it will be a heavy time. Thus we are in observation of conscience within us.

We are likewise in observation of Satan, that watches all whatsoever we speak or do.

And then God observes all that we do. All our sins are written with a 'pen of iron,' that they can never be gotten out of the soul without repentance.

If conscience fail, yet God will not fail. Therefore, being under observation, we had need be watchful.

I hope there is none that will deny this, but that they ought to watch.

Now, beloved, since our life is a vigil, a watching time, a warring time, and a race, we are therefore to stand in perpetual watch.

Let us now consider how we may be stirred up to watch. I will not speak all that may be said, but only give you a few things to shew you how we may keep the Lord's watch.

1. And that we may keep it the better, *let us labour to have waking considerations*, that we may preserve our souls, because consideration is a help to watchfulness. Know and believe that there is a God that watches, and an enemy that watches, and [that] conscience will do his office first or last; to know and believe also that there is a day of judgment wherein we must answer all that we have done.

2. Again, *consider the end wherefore we live here;* and let us also consider how suitable our actions are to that end, and whether they be for our good and the salvation of our souls.

3. And then to have a waking consideration *of the presence of God*, as Job had. 'Shall not God see if I do thus and thus?' Job xxxi. 4. And so Joseph, 'How shall I do this great wickedness and sin against God,' Gen. xxxix. 9. The eyes of the Lord goes through the world, seeing the good and bad. He hath an eye that never sleepeth. His eyes see into the dark thoughts of our hearts and sees our inward thoughts. All is naked to his eyes. Now the consideration of this may make us watch over our secret sins. What saith the heathen by the light of nature? What if thou hast nobody to accuse thee? Thou hast a conscience and a God that sees thee.* Think then when thou art in secret, that thou art in the presence of God, who is a judge. Consider of this, that we must all appear before the judgment-seat of Christ. St Paul was kept in a watching condition by the consideration of this: 'Knowing the terror of the Lord, we persuade men;' knowing also that it will be a terrible day, 2 Cor. v. 11. And

* Seneca.—G.

when Solomon would study an argument to startle young men, 'Go to, young man, take thy pleasure; but for all this, remember God will bring thee to judgment,' Eccles. xi. 9.

To this waking consideration add some further considerations.

4. *The fearful condition, to be found in an estate wherein we are not fit to die.*

A man is not in a good condition that is not fit to die. Add this also, that our life is short and uncertain. Now for us to live in an estate that we are not fit to die in is a fearful condition. Let us therefore take heed of promising mirth and jollity to ourselves to-morrow, for that may be the time of God's striking of thee. And that which he hath done to some may be done to thee. Ananias and Sapphira were stricken suddenly. The same may befall thee, and that resolution of thine in vain and sinful courses may be the time that God will take thee.

I might add many more; I only give you a taste of things. In a word,

5. *Labour for such an inward disposition as may dispose us to watchfulness.*

Now, there are two affections, when they are raised, will much help us, to wit, fear and love. See Jacob, when he was afraid of his brother Esau, he spent the night before in prayer and watching. Let us therefore labour to preserve the affection of fear, and in fear, the fear of reverence to offend so gracious a God. And let us watch over our hearts and lives, and labour for the fear of jealousy, because we have hearts subject to betray us. 'Blessed is the man that feareth always,' Prov. xxviii. 14; and 'make an end of your salvation with fear and trembling,' Philip. ii. 12. What fear? The fear of jealousy and reverence; for there is a great use of this fear.

Now if these will not prevail, then fear the day of judgment, and fear hell, if we will fear nothing else.

It is the atheism of these times to stand in awe of nothing; but he who hath a fear of reverence and jealousy is fit for all things. Besides, fear stirs up care, and care stirs up duty; for he that is afraid to offend will be careful to avoid offence and also to please.

So the affection of love; for as the soul is raised to the love of God and Christ, so it will be watchful.

This is a sweet affection, and keeps the soul watchful over anything that may displease the person whom we love.

And then it is full of invention, how he may give content to the person that is loved, and how to keep the soul in the presence of God. We never sin till the soul is drawn away from this, and we never have the soul in a better tune than when we are thus. We need therefore to wind up our affections every day. An instrument, though it be never so well in tune, let it but alone, it will be out; therefore it must be tuned every day. So we should deal with our souls, and when we find our affections to be down, wind them up with waking considerations; and let us do this daily, because they are ready to sink to present things, we are so nusselled* up in them. Those, therefore, that wish well to their souls, had need to wind them up, because they are for another world. And withal, labour to be wise and foresee; that is, to know ourselves both in good and evil, to know what we are naturally prone unto, and wherein we are subject to be overtaken, and then what hath done us good, and wherein we have been overcome. There is no creature will be taken in a snare if he see it. The dull ass, you cannot drive him through the fire. But man, since his fall, though he hath been catched, yet such is the pleasure of sin, that he will fall again thereinto, whereas he should be wiser than a dull beast.

* That is, 'nursed,' 'pampered.'—G.

Add hereunto, to have a soul fit for all advantages of doing good; let us labour for this, whereby we may know how to judge everything in its own worth, that so we may affect* it. Oh that hereby the soul may be raised up, otherwise it will fall. To know God in his greatness, Christ in his goodness, the world in its vanity, and sin in the danger thereof, will be means to stir up the soul to watchfulness. So long as the judgment is in a good frame, so long the soul will be fit for anything. And when we have advantages to anything, let us study how we may turn it to God's glory; and let us redeem those advantages, for this is one exercise of watching, to observe all advantages tending to the glory of God. It will grieve us one day, when we shall see at such a time we lost such an opportunity of doing good, and at such a time neglected such a duty; let us therefore labour to have such a disposition fit for all advantages, considering that this is our seed time. But, alas! how many advantages do we lose in not taking good and doing good!

And let us be wise to see what hinders us from doing good. As, too much business about the things of this world, as if we were born for them, whereas the Scripture limits our care for earthly things, telling us that we 'should use this world as though we used it not,' 1 Cor. vii. 31, but that we may enjoy these things here; but we must use them so as we may be wise unto salvation. Take heed 'of surfeiting, and drunkenness, and the cares of this world,' saith Christ, Luke xxi. 34. For when men are plunged in the cares of this world, they have their hearts eaten up, and thereby they lose many advantages of doing good and taking good. We should therefore labour to be in such a disposition that we may take heed of all hindrances. And we ought to do this, because our life is a warfare. We should therefore divide the day, and keep a daily watch.

First in the morning begin to awake with God before the world or the flesh thrust in, and bethink of all that may befall us that day, of all the dangers, of all the troubles; and we should likewise think with what armour we need to encounter with those accidents that may befall us. And then get provision, that whatsoever happens unto us, all may be for our good; and then let us consider how we stand prepared, and where we are like to be surprised strongly, there to prepare. And withal, before we set upon any good thing, let God have the first fruits of our time, and the first fruits of our hearts; let him have the first of the day by prayer, that when at any time we fall into any sin or affliction, we may not have cause to say, we have not commended ourselves unto God, and therefore this evil hath befallen us.

And this will be a comfort to us in all the actions of the day with this resolution. This is my comfort, I have commended myself and my prayers to God, and have set upon the day with this resolution, to do nothing that may offend God or a good conscience, and to regard no iniquity in my heart, but to pass the day under the shadow of the wings of the Almighty. We should labour to be in such a disposition as this; and afterwards in the day let us do nothing wherein we conceive God will not protect us; as in any evil way, for it is a fearful condition to be in any such, God not being in that place.

And then upon occasion be sure we carry a heavenly mind in earthly businesses, whereby we may serve God better, and fear him more; for there is nothing falls† in this life, but a gracious heart may draw out some-

* That is 'choose,' 'love' it.—G. † That is, 'befalls.'—G.

what of it to make his heart more religious. And to think with ourselves God hath set us in this place, and therefore we do this work.

Many other things may be given, but I name but some. So for recreations, in those whettings be watchful, especially above all things where we are ready to be surprised, as in prosperity. Therefore the Lord commands his people, take heed when thou art in the good land that floweth with milk and honey, that thou forget not the Lord thy God, Deut. iv. 9. Job knew this; therefore when his children were feasting, he offered sacrifice for them, lest they should dishonour God in their hearts, Job i. 5. It was a gracious heart in holy Job so to do. We should in like manner be watchful over ourselves, especially in that we are most prone to be overtaken in; and we should be watchful over ourselves when we are alone, for every man cannot use privacy well. Therefore our sequestration from company we should use in holy meditations. We should be watchful in that, because the devil is busy still. Oh when we are sequestered from others, our thoughts are a fit shop for the devil. Take heed, therefore, of privacy and idleness.

And so for company, by which we may either do good or receive good; for that is a great help to our watch—company—for one strengthens another, as stones in an arch. God hath sanctified the communion of those that are good for the strengthening of others. And therefore the Scripture saith, 'Stir up one another, and exhort one another,' Heb. iii. 13.

If we could account religion a serious thing, as it is, we would not hear these things as strange things, but we would think of them seriously, and practise them affectionately.

And so likewise, when we are to pass the occasions of the day, we should make use of that time we have spent, and go over all that we have done that day again. As God did when he created the world, he viewed all that he had done again. And let us not suffer our bodies to rest till our consciences are assured our sins are forgiven. Oh, it is dangerous to go to bed with a guilty conscience; for what do we know whether we shall see the world again or no? Let us therefore be sure to watch over this, and let us renew our resolution for the time to come. And if we find God's assistance and blessing upon our labours, then let us watch unto prayer, together with praising of our good God, observing all advantages of prayer and praises.

Now when we have observed in some measure that God hath been with us, then it is good to watch that God may have the honour by it.

3. Beloved, if this be so that we must take this course to watch continually, then mark what Christ saith, '*Blessed* is he that is found watching:' so that blessing goes along with watching. And by this blessedness, Christ encourageth us unto watchfulness. Those that keep their souls in a watching frame are blessed. Who saith this? Christ. He speaks and says, 'Blessed are those servants that he shall find watching when he cometh.' They shall be blessed in their life, and blessed at their death especially. Then we should give our souls to watching, because there is a meeting of all when he comes to us in death; for then we give ourselves to him.

Besides, look we to our former course of life, and to the glory that remains for us, and to Christ that is in heaven ready to receive us, and then to commit our souls to him; and to take heed of Satan's temptations, that we despair not thereby; and then to watch, for then Satan must have all or lose all, and so to end our days. Christ came to some in the first hour of the watch, to some the second, and to some the third hour of the watch; but happy is he that, when Christ shall come, he shall find watching. It is therefore good for young men to watch; but especially when men are in a declining age. It is good for them to watch for Christ's coming, because it cannot be long before he comes to them. Christ may come to the young and middle age, but those that are in the declining part, they should watch especially.

Beloved, Christ is come to us, and we every day go to him, for every day takes away part of our life. We should therefore every day fit ourselves for going to him by death. Our life should be nothing but a fitting ourselves for him; and what is good at the hour of death is good now. We have no security of our life. There is not the worst man but will then wish he had abstained from such and such courses. Do it now.

Beloved, I exhort you to nothing but that which is fit for us, namely, watchfulness; and what is watchfulness but a frame of soul fit to meet Christ. When our faith and hope, and our love about the object, and all the graces of the soul are fit, a man is as he should be.

It is the happiness of a man to be in an estate of well-doing; for what is the estate of heaven? Nothing but so; and to be watchful is the most excellent of all. Therefore as we ought to be watchful at that time, so now.

Now for preparation to the sacrament,* let us consider with whom we are to deal. We are to receive Christ; we are to feast with Christ. Natural wisdom teaches us, when we have to deal with great persons, to labour to have a suitable carriage, not only to speak that which is good, but to do it in all the circumstances exactly and comely. Let us so labour to come as we should do, by preparing our hearts, hungering and thirsting after this blessed means, and to come with hearts kindled with the love of God and Christ, because he gave himself for us; to come with hearts enlarged with thankfulness, and with holy resolutions for the time to come; and look better to our walking in the strength of that receiving. Now forty to one but Satan will set upon us: let us therefore especially watch afterwards; for when the devil knows we have gained any thing in the word and sacraments, by base thoughts, by base company and loose carriages, he seeks to overthrow us; let us therefore not only watch before, but after we have received, that we lose not the fruit. It is not the action that saves us, but the well-doing. 'Let a man therefore examine himself, and so let him eat,' 1 Cor. xi. 28: for as blessed is that servant whom his Master, when he cometh, shall find so doing, so blessed is that receiver whom the Lord shall find holy in preparation, holy in person, and holy in carriage.

* In margin here, 'This was preached before the sacrament, April 27. 1635.' Sibbes died on July 5. following.—G.

THE COMING OF CHRIST.

Behold, I come as a thief. Blessed is he that watcheth, and keepeth his garments close, lest he walk naked, and they see his shame.—Rev. XVI. 15.

We spake the last day concerning watching, out of the 12th of Luke and the 37th verse, 'Blessed are those servants whom their Master, when he shall come, shall find watching.' We will now go on in the argument a little, to add somewhat to that which hath been spoken, out of this 16th chapter of the Revelation, the 15th verse, being my present text.

'Behold, I come as a thief in the night. Blessed is he that watcheth, and keepeth his garments close, lest he walk naked, and be ashamed.'

After the sixth vial was poured out upon the enemies of the church, these words are brought in somewhat abruptly, out of Christ's care and love to his poor church in times of danger, 'Behold, I come as a thief in the night.'

You have in the words a prophetical premonition of watching and keeping our garments close, lest men walk naked, 'Behold, I come as a thief.' Beloved, Christ's coming is compared to the coming of a thief:

How comes a thief? He comes secretly and unexpectedly; secretly, lest he be discerned, and then with all advantages of surprisal, that he may not be taken himself while he is taking others. So Christ is said to come to judgment. He comes suddenly, and unexpectedly, and with a purpose to surprise. When people will take no warning, he watches the time of their destruction, so that here you have 'the goodness and the severity of God,' Rom. xi. 22; first, his goodness is shewed in that he will give warning in all dangers; but here is his severity also: when warning will not be taken, then he comes with judgment. The scripture runs thus, 'Prepare to meet thy God, O Israel,' Amos iv. 12; but when nothing will do, neither judgments nor mercies, then it is just with God to come with all advantage to our overthrow, as a thief in the night.

Comparisons usually are to be taken from that which is usually done, whether good or evil; for the goodness or badness of a thing is not regarded in comparisons.

The Spirit of God makes use of all things, ill things and good things. You see the diligence of the devil and the Jesuits, those old Jews and Pharisees that go about sea and land to make a proselyte. Why should not we be as diligent as they? A gracious heart will take good of them from their industry.

Christ here says 'he will come as a thief in the night,' and this his coming is by reason of our unfaithfulness. And his coming is sudden, unless to some of his children that he prepares by warning.

When he came into the world at his first coming, there were but a few 'waited for the consolation of Israel,' Luke ii. 25: the rest did not. So when he shall convert the Jews and judge the world 'Shall he find faith upon the earth?' Luke xviii. 8. When he comes to any man or nation in his judgments, doth he find faith? No; he finds them blessing themselves that to-morrow shall be as to-day. Beloved, let us take heed; for there be divers degrees of Christ's coming. He comes to a person, and comes to a nation. We here in this nation bless ourselves when all the world is in combustion and we are safe; as the three children in the fiery furnace. We bless ourselves, and cry, 'The temple of the Lord! Oh the temple of the Lord! but go to Shiloh, and see what the Lord hath done there,' Jer. vii. 12. Go to Bohemia, go to the Palatinate, and see what God hath done there. Oh, how should our hearts be awakened with the consideration of this, when we have such fair warning, and when the judgments of God are abroad.

But mark the prophecy spoken by Enoch, which was a thing to come—he was the seventh from Adam—'Behold, he comes in the clouds, with thousands of his saints,' Rev. i. 7. This prophecy was five thousand years ago, yet 'Behold, he cometh in the clouds.'

It is the nature of faith to answer all relations of God's dealings. That which God prophesies of, it is as sure as if it were past; so faith is affected with it. In matter of judgment, faith is affected with sorrow, and affected with a waking heart; in matter of joy, it is affected with delight. Alas! what is the difference of time between us and the last coming of all? what is this little distance? It is nothing. Therefore, 'Behold, I come as a thief in the night; blessed is he that watcheth, and keepeth his garments close.'

The Holy Ghost, the Spirit of Christ, here makes use of this his coming to stir us up to watch.

All that have spiritual life, labour to be waking Christians and then watching Christians. That which usually awakens is the noise of a trumpet, or some shining light. Now, living in the light of the gospel, and under the sound thereof, this should awaken us; if not this, the noise of the judgments round about us should. If ever we will be waking Christians, now is the time. And it is not enough that we be waking, but watchful Christians.

What is the difference between men, but that carnal men are sleepers, and spiritual men are waking? And what is the difference of Christians that are good, and that are not? The one is a watchful Christian, and the other not so. Wherein is one better than another? As the one is more careful to avoid sin than another. A weak Christian being watchful is better than a strong that is not so. See the difference between David and Joseph. Joseph was a servant tempted to folly, yet in the midst of his youth he avoided the temptation. David was a grown man, a holy man, a man of many experiences of God's mercies; yet you see with how small a temptation he was overtaken, because he was not watchful. So that thus Christians differ from themselves and others, as they are more or less watchful.

To come therefore to some directions how to carry ourselves, and among others remember this: we should have this waking and watchful consideration, that we have a soul immortal, and that we are for eternity; and whatever we do in the flesh, that shall be ever with us; and how that shortly we are going to the tribunal seat. In all these respects we should labour to be watchful at all times, because that time in which we take liberty to ourselves may be the time of our surprisal. We should therefore watch at all times, in prosperity and adversity. We should watch against all the sins of our persons, and the sins of the state we are in.

Moreover, we are not Christians indeed but when we are waking and watchful Christians, and we never live indeed but when we are watchful; neither can we give so good an account of our time.

Besides, if we use this course, we shall bring our souls to that awe as that they shall not dare to offend God, by reason they must come to be examined. And how will our souls be willing to be judged before Christ, when we are unwilling to set ourselves before ourselves? If we use this, it will bring a holy awe upon our souls, because they know they must come to examination for every sin.

But mark what follows: 'Blessed is he that watches and keeps his garments close, lest he walk naked.'

Watchfulness is for action; as 'Watch unto prayer,' Mat. xxvi. 41, and 'Watch unto thanksgiving,' 1 Peter iv. 7; as he saith here, 'Watch to the keeping of your garments close.' Now, this keeping of our garments close, is somewhat alluding to the ceremonial law; as if their garments were spotted, or as if they had touched some unclean body.

By garments here is meant, first, the keeping Christ close to the soul, and together with Christ all that is in him; for as a Christian is clothed with Christ, so also with his satisfaction, obedience, and righteousness, for Christ is given of God. Let us therefore keep our garments close; and not only so, but apply Christ for our sanctification. Put on the Spirit of Christ, and keep the soul in a holy frame. And keep not only the righteousness of Christ, but the holiness of Christ; and put on Christ, with the expression of his life in our life and conversation; as we are said to put on a man, when we express him in our life and conversation. And then keep Christ with his obedience, and keep him with his Spirit, with a holy desire to express him, keep all things close; and with Christ all the good we have by him, by using all means. Keep truth and our profession; keep the obedience of Christ and the graces of Christ; keep the Spirit of Christ and the truth of God, whereby all good is conveyed, and the profession of that truth keep unspotted. The danger is, 'lest you walk naked, and you be ashamed.'

You know sin and shame came in together. Adam was not ashamed of his nakedness till he saw it, and then he was loathsome to himself when his conscience was awakened; so it is sin that makes us ashamed. Therefore 'keep your garments close.' To come to that I mean to speak on, the words being clear,

1. First, Know *we have no garments of our own*. No man is born clothed; but God gives him wisdom to make use of all creatures for ornament for him, notwithstanding we are born naked.

Now, it is thus in spiritual things. We have no garments of our own since the fall; but before we had. We have none now but original corruption, that spreads over the soul. Besides that, men living unto years have another nature worse than the leprosy, custom. Here is all the clothing we have of ourselves; but for any spiritual good, we must fetch it from Christ. Since the fall we must have all our garments out of another wardrobe. That is here supposed that we have no garments of ourselves; and therefore 'Buy of me,' saith Christ, Rev. iii. 18.

2. Now, the second thing is this, we having none of ourselves, *therefore we must have garments;* and when we have them, we must keep them clean and close: 'Blessed is he that keeps his garments close.'

For the first, being born naked, there is a necessity for modesty to have garments to cover our shame. When God saw Adam naked, he would make him garments himself rather than he should be naked. There must be garments for defence; so in spiritual things there must be garments to defend us from the wrath of God, else we lie as naked to God's wrath as a man in a storm being naked lies open to the storm.

We must have garments of amity and friendship now. Being to entertain friendship with God, we must have something applied to us and wrought in us by the Spirit of God; for whatsoever is of Christ is amiable, because he is the only beloved.

Again, we must have garments for distinction. Now, garments do distinguish Christians at the day of judgment, for then God looks upon us to see what we have of his image; and if he find us in ourselves and not in Christ, then we are condemned with the world.

Garments that are coverings must be all over of equal extent. They cover the whole man. So head, hands, and heart, all must be sanctified as well as justified. So that those that look upon a Christian should see nothing in him but somewhat of Christ, his words, his callings, his thoughts. And as a man sees nothing of another man outwardly but his apparel, so the whole conversation of a Christian should be nothing but the expressing of Christ. He should speak by the Spirit of Christ, do all that he doth by the Spirit of Christ. We must labour to be 'wholly sanctified,' as the Scripture phrase is, 1 Thes. v. 23. There is an expression of this in the 2 Chron. xviii. 33: 'A certain man drew a bow, and smote the king of Israel between the joints of the harness.' There was some small place open, and that cost him his life. Let a man's profession be never so great, and let him have good expressions thereof, if there be any place for Satan's entrance, he will be sure to wound him in that place. So that by this you may see there must be an universal clothing.

And we must be clothed not only with garments, but armour, because we live in the midst of our enemies; by which we may perceive the necessity of the putting on of the one as well as the other.

Now, as we must have garments, and must keep them close, so also we must keep them from stains. The persons where these graces are, may be defiled, but the graces are pure. We should therefore labour to keep our actions unspotted. The reason why we should do so, among many other, is this, we live in a soiling age. The holy prophet could say, 'I am a man of polluted lips, and live among men of polluted lips,' Isa. vi. 5. We are defiled with corruption, and that soils all our actions; and therefore we ought, as much as in us lies, to keep our nature unspotted. We are polluted ourselves, and we live among men that are polluted. We live in an infected air, therefore we ought to keep our garment close, unspotted, and safe. Beloved, nothing will do us good but the application of things. All the virtue of things without us is conveyed unto us by application; therefore as the garments of a Christian are precious, so they must be applied. We must keep them close, and we must labour for the spirit of faith and of all graces. The truth must be engrafted into our spirits, that the word may be an engrafted word; for being from without us, we never have them to do us any good without the application. Therefore watchfulness is put before: 'Blessed is he that watcheth, and keepeth his garments close.'

The righteousness of Christ is an excellent garment, but it must be put on; and if we have Christ we have all. We will speak a little to shew you what is the reason men are tempted to despair, viz., because they keep not the garment of Christ clean, and close to their souls by the spirit of faith, for then the devil gets in between them and Christ. When garments are not close, the wind gets between them, or else perchance [they] fall off. So here we must labour to keep our garments close, and to renew our right in Christ every day, that we mày not fall away utterly; and that is the reason we so often take the sacrament to strengthen our faith, by which we are ready against all despair, and against all the temptations that Satan can administer; and so we have all necessary graces ready. We have our hope ready to set our souls quiet; our preparation to endure is ready; our meekness and our love is ready. 'Put on love,' saith the apostle, because it is the uppermost, the largest, and the richest garment; and set all other graces on work, as meekness, patience, &c., Col. iii. 14. We should therefore labour to have these graces ready, that is, by watching; for watchfulness is nothing but to have grace in readiness. And we have opportunity every day for one grace or other; but when we have them, we must keep them close by watching.

And so for truth, by which all comfort is conveyed unto us. When that is ready we are able to withstand temptations, but when that is to seek, mischief is ready to surprise us. Now if the word were engrafted in our hearts, then we should have some divine truths upon every occasion, and we should be ready against every sin, as Joseph was. We should therefore labour for this spiritual leaven, to season all other truths, that we may savour of them in all our thoughts and actions, and so shall our garments be close about us.

There is another thing intended in this Scripture. These are dangerous times, and there are spiritual cheaters abroad in the world. Therefore we should keep our profession close, and keep our truth and our judgments close, and get love into our affections; for we shall be set upon, and if we walk at large, then heretics and seducers will come between us and salvation, because our garments are not close. What a deal of loose profession have we! Were it not for authority that establisheth it, how many thousands have we would fall off? and all because they keep not their garments close. They fasten not truth to their souls. Their garments are loose about them, that so hereby the Jesuits have some points ready to fall upon by reason of unready Christians, for so they are taken. Therefore, 'Blessed is he that watcheth, and keepeth his garments close.'

So it is in the life and conversation; for in all men sin and corruption are ready, and where truth is not invested grace is not in the heart, but only in the brain. Some have some knowledge of things, but it is not ready, and hereupon they yield unto any temptation.

Now you have many halters in religion between God and Baal, between Christ and Belial. Our religion, beloved, must be our house. It is that with which we must cover our souls. We must build upon a rock, and our profession is our building, and the soul must not be so unsettled or loose, as not to know whether it should serve God or Baal.

If a man will have any good by religion he must cleave to religion. No loose profession shall ever come to heaven; for with the mouth we must confess, but we must believe with the heart to salvation. You have a company that think they may be saved in any religion, but the Scripture is directly for those that follow the best. Therefore we must take heed of unsettledness in religion.

And so in conversation men think they may be ambitious and unjust, and good Christians too. This loose profession never doth a man good; for we cannot join Christ and Mammon together. God will not be served with others. He will be served alone. He must be set up in our hearts and souls, and nothing with him. 'O Timothy, keep that which is committed to thee safe,' 1 Timothy vi. 20. Even so that truth that is committed to us, and that sacred depositance,* let us keep safe and close; for if we keep truth, truth will keep us: 'Because thou hast kept the word of my patience I will keep thee,' Rev. iii. 10. Oh but, saith some, if I keep truth I shall fall into this danger and that danger. No; but because thou kept the word of my patience, of all others thou shalt be safe. Therefore keep that as a jewel.

'Lest they walk naked, and men see their shame.' All shame arises from this, that we do not keep our garments close. So long as truth and Christ by truth have a place in the soul, so long we are safe. You see Adam could not be prevailed over till he wrung the truth from him. Then he stripped him of all God's image. When the children of Israel had cast their earrings into a calf, it is said the people were naked, Exod. xxxii. 25. So people when they keep not their garments close are naked. What make men loathsome to themselves? He hath in the eye of his soul his sin and his base courses. He hath not kept grace close in his heart, and that makes him naked. A man that hath grace in exercise he is a lovely object to himself, when he shall think with himself of his courses, how he hath abstained from such temptations, he is refreshed in the remembrance of them, as good Hezekiah said, 'Remember, Lord, how I walked before thee in truth of heart,' Isa. xxxviii. 2, *seq.*

A gracious man is lovely to himself, and sin makes him loathsome to his soul, and afraid of his own condition.

Now to give some directions how to keep our garments close.

1. First, Labour *for convincing knowledge*, because all grace comes into the soul by the light thereof. Grow therefore in grace and in the knowledge of our Lord Jesus Christ; and often propound queries to our judgments about the word and sacraments. Am I able to maintain this truth I have been brought up in? And do I find them true to my soul, &c.

There is scarce any point of religion but hath this savour in it. And who finds not this, that our nature is prone to the contrary? But when a man finds this, that he can justify things from experience, he resolves with himself, I know this, not because I have been taught it, but from experience I know it.

And so peace and joy that ariseth from judgment. I know I have found peace and joy in believing. When I was in a desertion, and when my conscience was awakened, I found this a comfortable point upon experience. By this means a man shall not easily fall from this truth. As for example, 'All things work together for the best to them that love God,' Rom. viii. 28. Few can by experience speak this, I have found God at such a time making this good unto me. But a Christian man can absolutely say this is true by experience. Wherefore we should beg of

* Cf. *Concio* in the present volume.—G.

God that he would engraft his truth into our soul; for this is the promise of grace, that he will teach our hearts, not our brains.

Christians are taught of God to love one another, therefore we should beg this of God. If that we will keep our garments close, we must labour every day more and more to grow in all grace, and then we shall have graces ready upon all advantages, and we must desire God to bless the words and sacraments for this end, and to use our profession as it should be, not to have an upper garment, to cover a naughty heart, but to labour more and more to put off the old man, and not to make religion a cloak and veil of hypocrisy; for besides all the sins we have, to make religion serve our turns, it makes our sin the greater.

When a man's religion shall be a cover to his sinful courses, that increases his sin, and makes his sins abominable.

'What hast thou to do to take my word into thy mouth, and hatest to be reformed?' Ps. l. 17. 'Take him, bind him hand and foot, and cast him into utter darkness,' Mat. xxii. 13.

It is a good phrase that is used in the sixth of the Romans: 'Let us be cast into the mould,' Rom. vi. 17 (*a*). We must fit ourselves for the word. That is the mould we must be cast into. If we hear any duty, say, 'Lord, fasten my soul to this duty, and when we are fastened to divine truths, then who shall come between truth and us, when truth is engrafted in us? But when it lies loose in the brain it may be removed, but when it hath gotten into the affections, who shall get Christ thereout.

A good conscience is a casket to keep divine truths in, and when we have gotten soul-saving truths, let us keep them by a good conscience.

Do nothing against the truth. Keep it in love. The affection of love must keep it.

If we have religion only in the brain, and not in love, we shall be stripped of all. Satan will rob us of any truth. Therefore it would be a great advantage for the putting on of Christ, if those that are young would labour to know all the points of religion betimes, that so they may get them rooted in the soul, that they may oversway our lusts, and strengthen the soul against temptations.

What is the reason many begin not to be religious till they be old? They have not divine truths engrafted into their hearts. They have a great advantage that are seasoned from the beginning; for that strengthens the soul against temptations. And if they fall into any sin they can recover themselves, because they have truth within them, and they are the readier to give way to any good counsel, because there is somewhat therein that will answer.

We must earnestly labour that the soul may be open to all divine truths, and then our hearts must close with them, so that thereby we may have comfort in all temptations, that when sickness, Satan, and the hour of death approaches, our knowledge fail us not, being rooted in our hearts.

And then we shall keep it in our affections, whereof love is the seat. In the Thessalonians, because they 'kept not the truth in the love of the truth,' they fell into gross errors, 2 Thes. ii. 10. Whatsoever, therefore, we know to be good, we should get it into our affections. Love all that is supernatural, keep all graces, and be in love with every one of them, as you have it, 2 Peter i. 5, *seq.* There is a furniture of graces, that if a man have one he must have another. We must keep all our graces, we must not lose one. Every part must be clothed. We must be clothed in our understanding with knowledge, and in our will with obedience, and in our affections with love. Our tongue must not only be clothed with good words, but we must labour that our hearts may be clothed also.

2. Those that will have good gardens will have flowers of every kind, *so a Christian must have graces of every kind.* When Ahab was killed there happened a weapon to strike through the joints of his harness, and killed him; to what purpose was it for him to have harness with loose joints? He should have had it complete. So we must have complete armour, and not any grace in part. We must not be right in opinion, and loose in action; not hot in affection, and weak in judgment. We must put on whole Christ for justification and sanctification, and we must add grace to grace; and when we have put on every grace we must keep them clean, and not defile our profession. Beloved, Christian religion is a pure religion. We must therefore keep our judgments pure, and we must take heed that we be not tainted with errors.

And as we judge, so we must affect and practise. If our judgments be naught, all is naught.

A Christian owes a due to truth; his understanding is a spouse to truth; he must not therefore cleave to this opinion and that opinion, but he must keep close all graces. In our place we must stand for the truth; and as Jacob's sons strove for the wells, so we should strive for the truth, and not incline to any schismatical or heretical opinion. What a poor thing were it for a man to drag an excellent garment through some sink-hole! Sure every man would say he were mad. Now, we have an excellent profession, and shall we suffer it to be stained? What is religion, but to keep ourselves unspotted of the world? We should therefore hate the garments spotted with the flesh, Jude 23. We should do with religion as we do with our clothes; he that is a neat man will not endure a spot upon his clothes. Beloved, shall we have such a garment, and care no more for it? Shall we care for our outward garments, and shall we endure spots in our profession and in our understanding?

We live in a leprous time, wherein men are spoiled in their affections, and are of a devilish disposition, hating God; whereas we ought to be of holy profession and conversation. A Christian should be glorious, for he hath a dignity above angels. Now, for a man that is a Christian to be failing in justice, what a shame it is! The very heathens abhorred this; and shall a Christian be no better than a pagan? Let us take heed of this our profession. And when we do anything, let us reason thus, Is this becoming my religion? and say thus to ourselves, I should walk worthy of Christ, and as it becometh the gospel; for what is the ornament of a Christian but the graces he hath? All the beauty we have is to be religious.

You know if a man be clothed we can see no deformity within him; so a Christian should be pure, that we may see no deformity in him, but all things that are pure; we should see Christ in his conversation. Indeed, we should all labour that the Spirit of Christ may speak and act; for every Christian hath the same Spirit that Christ hath to clothe his soul withal; therefore nothing should appear in him but Christ; the Spirit should so shine in him that all might appear glorious.

Shall that man look to have benefit by religion, who is a deceiver, a liar, a loose speaker? Is this to be clothed with the Spirit of Christ? Some men are of malicious minds, hating God and goodness; and yet they will take it as a great indignity to them if they should not have the title of Christians. But you see what they aim at; they know they should keep all their garments close, and that they should labour to fasten them upon their souls; that they may say of themselves as the church in the Canticles, 'My beloved is all fair,' v. 16; and as the mould gives the true impression of the print, so he may be all fair, not only having the righteousness of Christ, but may have some grace in all the parts of his soul.

We are clothed when we have the love of all grace and a desire to some of all grace; and when we complain that we are no better; and when we endeavour after all that is good, that wherein we fail we may comfort ourselves with this, that though our sanctification be imperfect, yet we are clothed with the perfect righteousness of Christ, which is the evangelical clothing.

This is a point of great consequence, that we have some evidences. We have put on Christ for our clothing, else there is no grace. Where there is faith to lay hold on the righteousness of Christ, there is likewise grace suitable; and as our souls desire both, so he gives both: he gives the righteousness of Christ and the Spirit of Christ. And then we may know we are clothed, if we have the righteousness of Christ.

And again, if we have a high esteem of that above all, as Paul had in the Philippians, iii. 8, 'I account all things dung and dross in comparison of Christ,' for all our righteousness is but as a 'polluted cloth,' Isa. xxx. 22.

A Christian hath put on Christ when he admires the righteousness of God-man; it is a righteousness of his own appointing and sending; what a high esteem therefore should we have of this!

And then we may know we are clothed when we love Christ, because our sins are forgiven. In the 7th of Luke, ver. 47, it is known that Mary* put on Christ, her love being such unto him because her sins were forgiven by him.

And then, when we have faith to believe this, that Christ is ours, and when we have boldness to go to God in our mediator's name, and can triumph over all our enemies, 'Who shall lay anything to the charge of God's people?' Rom. viii. 33. Out of the knowledge of this, that Christ died for me, and is now in heaven making intercession for me, I can triumph over all enemies. Alas! Satan will pick a thousand holes in our righteousness; but when we can look upon death and the day of judgment, and not be discouraged, it is a sign we are clothed. Let us therefore keep our garments close.

And let us make this use of our daily sins. Every day let us renew our right in Christ by repentance, saying thus, This day I have forfeited all, but now I will regain my right; there is a fountain open for sin and for uncleanness, Zech. xiii. 1.

The 'second Adam' takes away all sin; and therefore when we can make daily use of our justification, it is then a sign we live by faith. This is to feed upon Christ, when we feed upon his obedience.

The life of a Christian should be to live by faith. This use we should make of our daily infirmities, afflictions, and sins, to keep our garments close.

How doth Satan draw the souls of many to hell? When Christ is loose in their understanding, then the devil comes between them and their garments; and when conscience feels the weight of sin, and hath nothing to support it, then Satan robs them, because they want the spirit of faith.

They which walk in white here, shall walk in white in heaven; they which go on constantly here, they shall at the length walk in heaven with more white eternally with Christ.

* There is no good reason to believe that the 'woman which was a sinner' was Mary Magdalene.—Ed.

Now let us see our danger. If, on the contrary, we keep not our garments close, 'we shall be found naked.' Now, nakedness is a woeful condition; it is a curse. Therefore, when we are to appear before God, let us labour for the Spirit of Christ, that when Christ shall come to judge us, he may see his own stamp upon us.

And let us consider what a shame it will be unto us at that time if he shall find us naked.

What a shame is it to be a worldling! that when Christ is not upon our affections to turn Demases, as Demas followed Paul but afterwards embraced the world, 2 Tim. iv. 10; or, at the hour of death, what a shame is it that whereas many men went for religious men, but for want of keeping their garments close they then want comfort; and at the day of judgment shall be ashamed before God, angels, and men.

Let us therefore labour to make Christ ours, that then we may live clothed and die clothed; and then we shall be blessed: 'For blessed is he that hath Christ upon him here; he shall be blessed for ever hereafter.'

NOTE.

(*a*) P. 312.—'Let us be cast into the mould.' Sibbes's rendering of the τύπον of Paul is adopted by Webster and Wilkinson *in loco*, from whom I add this note: 'τύπον διδ. the scheme or mould of instruction to which ye were committed, ii. 20, 2 Tim. i. 13. The construction is by attraction for ὑπηκούσ. τῷ τυπῳ διδαχῆς εἰς ὃν παρεδόθητε. Cf. Acts xxi. 16. Their professed subjection to the gospel of Christ, their reception of the doctrine according to godliness was an acknowledgment of obedience to a new Master. They were put under a die or mould, from which they were to receive a new impression.' G.

THE GENERAL RESURRECTION.*

Jesus saith to her, Thy brother shall rise again. Martha saith unto him, I know that my brother shall rise again in the resurrection at the last day. —John XI. 23, 24.

Having formerly spoken of the communion of saints,† now we come to speak of the other two blessings and benefits which the Lord doth give and grant to the church in the life to come. The one whereof is, 'the raising of our bodies at the last day,' the other, 'life everlasting;' which be the blessings he hath reserved till the day of judgment, wherewith he closes up and makes an end of all, and yet not a final end with them, because they shall have no end, for the Lord will bestow eternal happiness on them; which day, though to some it shall prove a doleful day, yet it shall be joyful to the church of God, even a day that they have many a time looked for and desired.

In handling whereof, we are first to consider the order of God's distribution, who giveth us first the blessings and the benefits of this life, and then those of eternal life. Now that which is the order of God's distribution, must be the order in our intention.‡ We must labour to have communion with the saints here in this life, to have our sins pardoned, and then the Lord will raise up our bodies at the last day, and give us life everlasting; which, if we omit, we can have no hope to rise to everlasting life, but to perpetual shame and contempt. Therefore we must labour to entertain the communion of saints here. It is said, Rev. xx. 6, 'Blessed and holy is he that hath his part in the first resurrection, for on such the second death shall have no power.' Thus he is a blessed man that in this life rises out of his corruptions and sins, for on such a one 'the second death hath no power,' otherwise one must be held captive of the second death: for if one make a bargain, and giveth somewhat in hand, having

* 'The General Resurrection' forms No. 21 of the original edition of 'The Saint's Cordials' of 1629. It was not given in the after editions. Its separate title-page is as follows:—'The Generall Resvrrection.' In One Sermon. Declaring, The manner, time, and certainty of our Resurrection. In what estate our Bodies shall rise againe. Wherein the glory and excellency of the Saints shall consist after the Resurrection, shewed in sundry particulars. Together with the deplorable estate of the wicked in that day, &c. Prælucendo pereo. Vprightnes hath boldnes. London printed in the yeare 1629.'—G.

† See general Index, *sub voce*, also textual Index.—G.

‡ That is, = striving, intentness.—G.

received earnest, he looks for the bargain; even so the Lord hath made a bargain with us, to give us heaven and happiness, whereof, if he give us earnest in this life, the communion of saints, and the forgiveness of sins, then we may look to have our bodies raised to life everlasting: otherwise raised unto the second death.

Now in this great point of faith we are to consider divers particulars: the first whereof is,

Point 1. *That we believe, although we shall be laid into the grave, and dissolved into dust, yet one day we shall rise again by the power of Christ, and by virtue of his resurrection.* This is the proper faith of a Christian only; for heathens believe that they shall die and turn to dust. The Christian goes further, and believes to rise again; which is clear and manifest, both

1. By Scripture, and 2. by reason.

1. First we will prove it by Scripture, John v. 28, where Christ having spoken of that great work of raising up dead souls from the grave of sin to the life of grace, by his quickening and powerful word in the ministry; lest it should seem strange unto them, fetches a comparison from the resurrection of the body to life everlasting. 'Marvel not at this, for the hour is coming, in which all that are in the graves shall hear his voice, and shall come forth, they that have done good unto the resurrection of life; and they that have done evil unto the resurrection of condemnation.' So Dan. xii. 2, 'And many of them who sleep in the dust shall awake, some to everlasting life, and some to shame and perpetual contempt.' So 1 Cor. xv. 19, St Paul says, 'If in this life only we have hope in Christ, we are of all men the most miserable;' and then adds, ver. 21, a strong reason, 'For since by man came death, by man came also the resurrection from the dead. For as in Adam all die, so in Christ shall all be made alive. But every man in his own order,' &c. And Acts xvii. 31, he shews why all men are commanded to repent, everywhere: 'Because,' saith he, 'he hath appointed a day in which he will judge the world in righteousness by that man whom he hath ordained; whereof he hath given assurance unto all men, in that he hath raised him from the dead.' In another place he says, Acts xxiv. 15, making it the issue of his believing of all things in the law and prophets, 'And have hope towards God, which they themselves also allow, that there shall be a resurrection of the dead, both of the just and unjust.' Christ's threatenings to Chorazin and Bethsaida, Mat. xi. 22, shew that there shall be a day of judgment: so he threatens, Mat. xii. 36, 'But I say unto you, That every idle word that men shall speak, they shall give account thereof in the day of judgment.' And he proves the resurrection from an instance of Abraham, Isaac, and Jacob, he being their God, 'who is not a God of the dead, but the living,' Mat. xxii. 32, which also made the prophet Isaiah comfort the people: Isa. xxvi. 19—in that desperate estate of theirs, wherein they appeared as dead men without hope of recovery—from the similitude of the resurrection, 'Thy dead men shall live, together with my body shall they rise. Awake and sing, ye that dwell in the dust: for thy dew is as the dew of herbs, and the earth shall cast out the dead.' Many other strong proofs there are, both direct and by similitudes, besides the proof thereof in Christ, Enoch, Elias, and others. But I will pass them over, and end only with that one of St John's vision, Rev. xx. 12, 'And I saw the dead, both small and great, stand before God: and the books were opened; and another book was opened, which is the book of life: and the dead were judged out of those things which were written in the books, according to their works. And the sea gave up the

dead which were in it; and death and hell delivered up the dead which were in them: and they were judged every man according to their works.' And, therefore, seeing all things are come to pass which the Scripture hath foretold, and shall come; and seeing God is true, faithful, and almighty in power to do whatsoever he will: we may then also be sure of this, that God will raise again the dead at the last day.

Secondly, Thus much is proved by reasons of divers sorts, five in number.

1. From the power of God. 2. From the justice of God. 3. From the mercy of God. 4. From the end of Christ's coming. 5. From the resurrection of Christ.

(1.) [*Power of God.*] For the first Tertullian says well, 'It was a harder matter for God to make a man, being nothing, out of the dust of the earth, than now, being something, to raise him up and repair him again' (*a*). And he who spake the word, and made this great frame of heaven and earth, is able also, by his power, to raise up the dead at the resurrection; which made Christ, in that disputation with the Sadducees, Mat. xxii. 29, reprove their ignorance in this point: 'Ye do err, not knowing the Scriptures, nor the power of God.' Now of this, when we are once soundly convinced, then we can believe, and say with Job, 'I know thou canst do everything, that no thought can be withholden from thee; who is he that hideth counsel without knowledge?' &c., Job xlii. 3.

(2.) The second is drawn from his *justice;* for it is agreeable with his justice, that those who have been partakers in good and evil actions should participate in suitable rewards and punishments; but the bodies of men are partners in good and evil actions with the soul; therefore the Lord will raise up both, to reward and punish them, according as they have done good or evil. Tertullian saith, 'We must not think that God is slothful or unjust; 1, We may not think that God is unjust to reward the soul and destroy the body, or punish the one, and not the other; but he will raise up both, to reward both together, according to their sufferings and misdeeds. Again, we must not think him slothful, that he will not take pains to raise up dead bodies; no; he is indefatigable, not subject to any weariness. It is but for him to speak the word, think the thought, will it to be, and all shall be done,' (*b*). So, in regard of his justice, the body must rise also.

(3.) The third is drawn from the *mercy of God*, which is infinitely more in him than in us, extending itself in a large measure unto all. Now this mercy is in men, that, if they could raise all the dead bodies of their friends, they would do it. But the mercy of God being infinitely more than all our compassion can be, extends therefore itself to all the souls and bodies of men, to raise them up again, and perpetuate them; wherein, if the wicked had not forsaken their own mercy, they might have had joy and comfort with the rest. For this cause Christ tells us, Mat. xxii. 32, 'that he is the God of Abraham, Isaac, and Jacob,' not the God of the dead; for if it were so, then he should be only a God of one part of Abraham, and not of the other; but he is the God of both, therefore he will raise both soul and body at the last day, and the dead shall rise.

(4.) Fourthly, From *the end of Christ's coming*, as it is 1 John iii. 8, 'For this purpose appeared the Son of God, that he might loose* the works of the devil;' for the devil first brought in sin, and sin brought death. This was the great work the devil aimed at, to bring in sin and death; and

* The Greek word is λύω.—G.

therefore Christ coming to dissolve this great work, amongst the rest, which is not done unless there be a resurrection of the dead. Therefore the dead shall rise again.

(5.) The fifth is drawn *from the resurrection of Christ;* for Christ did not rise as a private person, like unto the widow's son, and as Lazarus did, but he rose as the public head of the church. St Paul says, 'that he was the first fruits of them that slept,' 1 Cor. xv. 20. So, in the rising of Christ, all the people of God rise, and that which went before in the head shall follow in the members, as Augustine speaks. And Cyril saith well, 'that Christ entered into heaven by the narrow passage of his sufferings and death; by his death and resurrection to make a wide passage for us unto heaven' (*c*). So in Christ's rising we rise. Here one may object, Oh, it was an easy matter for Christ to rise, because he was God. I answer, true; but as God-man, sustaining the burden and weight of all our sins, it was not so easy; for when we are laid in the grave, we have but the weight of our own sins to keep us down. Christ, he had the sins of all the elect people of God upon him, and therefore it was a harder matter for Christ to rise again than we suppose; and yet he broke through all, and rose again; therefore do not thou doubt but that he will at length raise thee again. So Christ's promise is, 'When I am lifted up, I will draw all men after me,' John xii. 32; only our care must be to have communion with Christ in our life and death; to live as he lived, die with him, lie in the grave with him, be as near in life, and lay our dead bodies as near his as may be, and then, when Christ, who is our life, shall appear, as it is in Col. iii. 1, 'then shall we likewise be raised up, and appear with him in glory.' Otherwise, we shall be raised, but unto all sorrow and misery in eternal torments, not as unto a head, but unto a terrible judge; where, when one hath lived a thousand years, they are as new to begin again; and so be tormented world without end. Now divers objections are made by atheistical persons against this main point of faith.

Obj. 1. The first is a common one, How is it possible, say they, that a body which hath lain rotting a thousand years in the grave should rise again, so turned into dust?

Ans. I answer, Though it be above reason, yet it is not against reason; for we see that the flies that be dead all the winter time, when the summer cometh, with the heat of the sun, they live again; so the corn rots in the ground, and revives again. Now if with the heat of the sun the one may be done, much more is the power of God able to raise up those who have lain in the grave a thousand years, to live again.

Obj. 2. Secondly, say they, It is impossible for men to rise again, because their dust is so mingled one with another, and with the dust of other creatures, as in a churchyard, where dust is mingled, one cannot well say This is the dust of my father, or This is the dust of my mother, things being so mixed; as, take a quantity of milk, and put into the sea, there both remain in substance, but so mingled, as that they cannot be parted one from another; and so, say they, it is with dead men, whose dust is so mingled together, as it is impossible to part them.

Ans. To this I answer, 1. In general, though it be an impossible work for man to do, yet it is not impossible for an Almighty God, unto whom all things are possible, it being an easy matter for him to give to every man his dust again, and sever it one from another, even as a man who hath a handful of divers seeds in his hand can easily distinguish and take one from another, putting each sort by itself again. We see that there be some men so cunning and skilful, that they can draw out of an herb or flower the four elements, fire, earth, air, and water. Now if so much cunning and skill may be in a man, how much more able is the Creator of men, who is only wise, of an all-seeing eye, to sunder every man's dust, and to bring them together again?

Obj. 3. Oh but, say they, what say you to this? When one man eats another, then that man's flesh becomes one with another man's flesh; in which case, if the one rise, the other cannot. To this I answer,

Ans. It is true indeed, one man eating another becomes a part of the other for the time; but yet he was a perfect man before he ate of the other, and the other a perfect man before he was eaten. Now it is a truth in divinity, that every man shall rise with his own flesh; but a man shall not rise with everything that was once a part of him. As, for instance, if a man have a tooth beaten out, and another come in the room of it, he shall not rise with both these; so likewise a man hath a piece of flesh stricken off with a sword, and new flesh comes in the room of it, he shall not rise with both, but with so much as shall make him a perfect man. Even so, though one man eats of another man's flesh, he shall not rise with that, but with so much as shall make him a perfect man; neither shall he who was eaten want anything of his perfection at the resurrection.

Obj. 4. Lastly, They bring one Scripture in show against us, and but one, which is this: 'That flesh and blood,' as the apostle speaks, 'cannot enter the kingdom of heaven,' 1 Cor xv. 50. To which I answer,

Ans. The meaning is figuratively spoken; that is, flesh, as it is corrupted and sinful, clothed with infirmities, and subject to mortality and death, so it shall not enter in. So this is expounded, Heb. ii. 14, 'Forasmuch, then, as the children were partakers of flesh and blood, he also himself likewise took part of the same, that through death he might destroy him that had the power of death, that is, the devil; and deliver them who, through the fear of death, were all their lifetime subject to bondage.' Therefore it is meant of flesh and blood in this transitory life, subject to infirmities; thus it shall not enter into heaven. And thus have we despatched the cavils of the atheists, against all which this point stands sure and firm, that the dead shall rise again.

Use 1. Seeing the dead shall rise again, therefore though we die as others do, and are dissolved into dust, *yet to be comforted, in regard that this is the worst our sins and the world can do unto us, to take from us a frail natural life,*—which, when they have done, it shall be restored unto us again in a far more excellent manner,—this, in all distresses and troubles, must comfort us, as it did Job, xix. 25, 26: 'I know that my Redeemer liveth, and that he shall stand at the latter day upon the earth; and though after my skin worms destroy this body, yet in my flesh shall I see God.' This also supported David, Ps. xvi. 9: 'Wherefore my heart is glad, and my tongue rejoices; and my flesh also resteth in hope: for thou wilt not leave my soul in the grave: neither wilt thou suffer thy Holy One to see corruption.' And so Christ himself says, Mat. xx. 19, unto his disciples: 'The Son of man shall be delivered unto the chief priests, and unto the scribes, and they shall condemn him to death, and deliver him to the Gentiles to scourge and to crucify: but the third day he shall rise again.' Now that which comforted Christ, Job, and David, must also comfort and support us in all crosses and troubles that befall us; for death, the seeming worst of things, shall prove advantage unto us. It was a comfort unto old Jacob that the Lord said unto him, 'Fear not, go down into Egypt; behold I will be with thee,' &c., Gen. xlvi. 3. So faith in death hears this comfortable voice of God, Fear not to go into the ground, to sleep in the grave a while; for behold I will go down with thee, keep thy ashes there, and raise thee up again; for death dealeth no otherwise with us, than David did by Saul when he was asleep: he took away his spear and his water-pot, which he restored unto him when he was awake. Even so death, he takes away our spear and our water-pot, our strength and a weak frail life, and when we awake again it is restored at the day of refreshing in a more excellent and more abundant manner.

Use 2. Secondly, Seeing the dead shall rise again, this must comfort us *in regard of our dead friends departed, that although death have sundered us for a time, yet we shall all meet together again.* So Martha here: 'I know that my brother shall rise in the resurrection of the just;' and, 1 Thes. iv. 14, the apostle saith, 'For if we believe that Jesus died and rose again, even so those who sleep in Jesus will God bring with him;' and then he adds, ver. 18, 'Wherefore comfort one another with these words.' Chrysostom says well, 'If a man take a long journey, his wife and children do not usually weep, because they expect his return ere long home again' (*d*). Even so it is, our friends who die in Christ, they are gone but a long journey, we must comfort ourselves that we shall meet again.

Use 3. Thirdly, Seeing the dead shall rise again, this must *make us careful therefore to spend our time well whilst we are here;* for if a man did not rise again, he might live as he list; but because we shall rise again with these bodies which have sinned, therefore we should be careful to pass our time here in holiness and righteousness, which is the use St Paul makes of it, Acts xxiv. 16, that because there shall be a resurrection both of the just and the unjust, 'herein,' saith he, 'I endeavour myself to have a clear conscience towards God, and towards man.' So should we in this case do. When Peter heard it was the Lord who was near him on the water, he girded his coat unto him, for he was naked. One would have thought that rather he should have put off his garment and have laid it aside; but Peter had this consideration, that when he came on the other side he should stand before his Master, and therefore he girded himself, that he might stand seemly and comely before him. Even so, seeing when we have passed the glassy sea of this world, we are to stand before God, therefore we are to have this consideration, that we gird ourselves and make everything ready, that we may come seemly and holily before God at the last day.

Point 2. The second main point is, *that we believe that we shall rise again at the last day with the same bodies.* So Job xix. 25, 'I know that my Redeemer liveth, and he shall stand [at] the last on the earth: and though after my skin worms destroy this body, yet in my flesh shall I see God: whom I shall see for myself, and mine eyes shall behold, and not another; though my reins be consumed within me.' And Ezek. xxxvii., there is shewed that life and sinews came into the same dry bones, and flesh grew upon them; which, though it be a parable, yet it enforceth that that which falleth being dead, shall rise again, because the strength of comfort therein set forth unto his people, is taken from the similitude of the resurrection. So Revel. xx. 12, John saith, 'And I saw the dead both great and small stand before God,' &c. Thus Tertullian says, that 'he will pray that the same body may rise again; for the resurrection is not of another body, but of the same that falleth: not a new creation, but a raising up' (*e*). St Jerome says, 'that it cannot stand with equity and right that one body should sin and another body be punished' (*f*). Neither will a just judge suffer a victorious person to die and another to have the crown of his deservings. Therefore the same body that sinned shall be punished, the same that hath gotten the victory shall be crowned, and that same body shall rise again. We see in Christ's resurrection, the same body that was wounded, the same body did rise again; he could, if he had pleased, in three days have cured his wounds, seeing that he could heal all sicknesses and diseases with a word, or a touch, but he let them alone to confirm his disciples, and to shew that he had the very same body which was crucified. Thus Thomas was bid, John xx. 27, to reach his finger and behold his hands, and reach his hand to put in his side, whereby appeared the same body and wounds remaining. Therefore, as in the head the same body which died rose again, so shall it be with all his members. Against this doctrine there be some objections.

Obj. 1. The first is out of 1 Cor. xv. 44, where it is said, 'that it is sown a natural body, but is raised a spiritual body,' so it is not the same body that riseth again. To this I answer,

Ans. That it is not spiritual in regard of substance, but in regard of the estate and condition which they shall be in; for a natural life is upheld by the use of meat, and drink, and sleep, physic, and rest, but then our bodies shall be upheld by the power of God, without the use of these means. Now our bodies are heavy, but then our souls shall be full of agility and nimbleness to move upwards or downwards at pleasure swiftly, so that it is a spiritual body, not in regard of substance, but in regard of quality and operation.

Obj. 2. Secondly, Say some, if the same bodies shall rise again, then they rise with a number of needless parts; for what shall a man need teeth, seeing they shall eat no meat? What shall they need a stomach, seeing there shall be no concoction or digestion? and what, shall a man need bowels, seeing there shall be no redundance to fill them?

Ans. Augustine shall answer for me: saith he, 'Concerning the teeth, they shall be needful and useful then, for we have a double use of them: they serve to eat with, and they are to further our speech, and therefore, though we shall have no need of teeth in regard of eating, yet we shall have need of them to speak with, for in heaven we shall praise God, and sing the song of Moses and of the Lamb. And as for the other parts of the body, they are, saith he, for sight and comeliness; for though there be no need of the stomach to concoct, nor of the bowels because there is no redundance, yet these shall be as ornaments to the body, to adorn and beautify it. For as there be some things not needful now save for ornament, as a man's beard and his breasts, which have no other use save this, even so, though we shall not need a stomach to concoct, nor bowels for redundance then, yet shall they be for an ornament to man'(*g*).

Obj. 3. Thirdly, It is objected, the same bodies do not rise, because they be heavy and ponderous; for how, say some, should heavy and weighty bodies stay above the clouds in the pure heaven, which is purer and thinner than the air? To this I answer,

Ans. (1.) That if a man may fill a great vessel of lead, and make it swim above the water, by drawing the air into it, why then may not God draw his Spirit into us, and fill us so with it, as to make our heavy bodies abide above the clouds, as well as a man to make a vessel of lead swim above water?

Ans. (2.) Again I answer, that everything abides in his own proper place at God's appointment. As, for example, the clouds are heavy and wet, and therefore would fall down to the ground, but that God hath appointed the air to be the proper place of them, where therefore they abide; so likewise the water would be above the land, but that God hath limited the proud waves to a confinement, where it must rest and advance no further. So, it being God's appointment which makes anything to remain where it doth, though contrary to the nature thereof; therefore, because heaven is the proper place of a glorified body, and earth of a mortal body, the same bodies shall remain here until the day of judgment, after which, being made glorified bodies, they shall remain for ever in heaven, the proper place of their assignment. The uses are,

1. First, That seeing we shall rise with the same bodies, therefore *we must be careful to keep them well, that they be pure and unspotted, without sin.* It is Paul's conclusion, 1 Cor. vi. 18, 'Fly fornication. Every sin that a man doth is without the body: but he who committeth fornication sinneth against the body.' So, because our bodies shall rise again, let us fly every sin and corruption, and keep our bodies unspotted, that so they may be presented before Christ holy and pure at that day. For what a shame will it be to stand before God in judgment, when we have wronged and grieved God by our sins; when our heavenly judge shall say unto us, Are not these the eyes wherewith you have let in lust and looked after vanity? are not these the tongues that ye have told so many lies with? are not these the mouths wherewith you have sworn and blasphemed my name? are not these the hands you have wrought wickedness with? are not these the feet which have carried you to sin, vanity, and disorder? And then how shall we be able to answer the Lord! Therefore let us be careful to live well, and keep our bodies unspotted, that we may have comfort at that day. We read, 2 Chron. xxxvi. 8, when Jehoiachim was dead, there was found the characters, marks, and prints of his sorcery; howsoever during his life he, being a king, bore it out, and kept it close; yet, being dead, there remained the prints of his abominations found on his body. So, howsoever sinners may hide and conceal their sins here, and deceive the world, yet when they be dead there shall be found the marks and prints of the foul sins that they have committed; therefore keep we our bodies pure and unspotted against that day.

2. Secondly, Seeing the same bodies shall rise again, therefore *we should depose and lay them down well at the day of death, to die in faith and repentance.* We see if a man put off his garment, and means to put it on again, he will not rend and tear it off his back, but pull it off gently, brush and lay it up safe, that so it may do him service again, and grace him before his friends. So, seeing our bodies are as a garment for our souls, when we put them off, let us labour to depose and lay them down well at the day of death, that they may do us credit at the day of judgment. We read, 2 Peter i. 14, saith he, 'I think it meet, so long as I am in this tabernacle, to stir you up, by putting you in mind; seeing I know that the time is at hand that I must lay down this my tabernacle, even as the Lord Jesus hath shewed me.' So Saint Paul, 2 Cor. v. 1: 'For we know, that if the earthly house of this tabernacle be dissolved, we have a building given us of God,' &c. Thus is he careful of a better building, in pulling down of the old. There is great difference between a soldier destroying of an house, and one that only dissolves it. He that destroys a house pulls down the timber and stones, and flings everything he cares not where, because he doth not purpose to use them again; but a man that dissolves a house, he will take it down piece by piece, laying up carefully every several parcel, because he intends to build with it again. Even so, because we know our

bodies shall rise again at the last day, we must not therefore destroy them, but labour to dispose of them, and lay them down well at the day of death.

3. Thirdly, Seeing the same bodies shall rise again, this should make us *live with fear, so to lay them down well at the day of death.* Here this great question may be answered: whether we may know one another at the day of judgment? But this needs be no question, seeing we shall rise again with the same bodies that we lay down here, therefore we shall know one another in heaven. The reasons are,

Reasons. 1. First, *Because our knowledge shall at that time be more perfect than ever Adam's was in the time of innocency,* in which state he did know his wife as soon as she was brought unto him, though he never saw her before; therefore much more we shall then know one another, seeing our knowledge, rising with the same bodies, shall be perfecter.

2. Again, *The disciples in the mount, at Christ's transfiguration, had but a glimpse or taste of the heavenly glory, and yet Peter knew Moses and Elias,* though they were dead many hundred years before. Wherefore, if he, having but a taste of heavenly glory, knew them, he being unglorified, much more we shall know one another, when we have fulness of glory.

3. *Because our happiness shall be greatly increased by the means of the mutual society one with another;* as, Mat. viii. 11, Christ says, 'But I say unto you, that many shall come from the east, and from the west, and shall sit down with Abraham, Isaac, and Jacob in the kingdom of God.' And therefore, seeing our happiness shall be greatly increased by mutual society, we are not to think that we shall go to a strange people, where we shall know nobody; but we shall go to all our godly friends and acquaintance, and to such as we know.

4. *We shall hear the indictment of the wicked at the day of judgment;* when, if we hear the same, we shall know the persons indicted of wicked men, such as oppressed the people of God, Cain, Pharaoh, Judas, Nero, and the like. And as we shall know the wicked, so we shall know the godly too, when they shall be rewarded. This, methinks, may be a motive to quicken us in our care to live holily and christianly, seeing we go not to a strange country, or people, but to our friends and acquaintance, and to such as we know.

The third general point is, the time when we shall rise.

Point 3. At the day of judgment, then, and never till then, as John xi. 23, Martha confesses, 'I know my brother shall rise again in the resurrection at the last day.' So, 1 Cor. xv. 51, Saint Paul says, 'We shall not all sleep, but we shall all be changed, in a moment, in the twinkling of an eye, at the last trumpet (for the trumpet shall blow), and the dead shall be raised up.' Of which there be four reasons.

Reasons. 1. First, *Because there might be a proportion betwixt Christ and his members;* for, when he died, he did not by and bye rise again, but he lay a while trampled and trodden under foot of death. So must we. Irenæus with this shuts up his book, saying, 'Even as our heavenly master did not fly to heaven by and bye, but did remain under death and in the grave for a time, even so all his servants must be contented to lie in the grave, and to be trampled under foot of death for a time before we go to heaven' (*h*).

2. Secondly, *Because the saints might meet the bodies of all the faithful which are gone before them together, they shall not rise to prevent one another in glory, but shall all go together;* as it is 1 Thes. iv. 14. This is an excellent comfort unto us who live in the last age of the world, that the saints

departed before us shall not rise to heavenly glory till we also be ready with them. Until this time they wait for our accomplishment in their graves; as 1 Sam. xvi. 11, when Samuel calleth all Jesse's sons before him, there being yet one of them wanting, said, Fetch him, we will not sit down till he be come, so all the people of God lie in their graves, and cannot rise till our time also be accomplished.

3. Thirdly, *For the further declaration of the power of Christ;* for it seems a greater matter that Christ should raise men who have been lying rotting in their graves a thousand years, than it is to raise men when they are newly dead. Therefore, when Christ was about to raise Lazarus from the death, Martha said to Jesus, 'My brother stinketh already, for he hath been dead these four days;' therefore she inferred, it was not so easy a matter to raise him then as at first, being new dead, and as it was to raise Jairus's daughter, and the widow's son. So Ezek. xxxvii. 3, when the Lord demanded this question of the prophet, 'Can these dead bones live? he answered, 'Lord, thou knowest;' as though he had said, It is not impossible to thee, but it is a hard matter to be done, or bring to pass.

4. Fourthly, *For the further confirmation of our faith;* for look how many there be of the dead bodies of the saints amongst us, so many pledges and pawns there are for our redemption; for although we might in ourselves doubt of our own bodies rising in regard of our sins, and of the badness of our lives, yet because there be so many bodies of the dead saints among us, we need not doubt but he will raise them up one day to glory. There are three bodies already ascended into heaven: Enoch before the law, Elias in the time of the law, and Christ in the time of the gospel; and for these three bodies he hath left many thousand of the dead saints' bodies remaining in the grave, to be pledges and pawns to us of our resurrection; to this purpose Saint Paul says, Heb. xi. 40, that God provided 'better things for us, that they without us should not be made perfect.' The uses are,

1. First, Seeing that the bodies of the saints do not rise till the day of judgment, therefore *we must be contented to be under affliction and trouble till God deliver us;* as the saints' bodies are trampled upon, and rest quietly till the day of deliverance.

2. Secondly, That seeing the bodies of the saints rise not till then, that *we should therefore desire and long for it, yea, and wait;* as it is said, Rom. viii. 21, both the creatures rational and irrational do groan and travail in pain towards that day of redemption, and glorious liberty of the sons of God. We see if a man have broken an arm, or put a leg out of joint, if one have promised him that he will come to set it in joint at such an hour, he will still be looking and longing for his coming; even so, seeing at the day of judgment the Lord will restore us again to our former integrity, we should long for that day, and be looking for it.

3. Thirdly, *This should moderate the delicate and too much pampering of our bodies,* which must ere long lie so trodden under and rotting in the grave, to be so careful about them, but to take care for our soul's good, and then both body and soul shall be raised up unto glory for ever.

Quest. Now here ariseth a question: Seeing our bodies must lie so many years and ages rotting in the grave, what may be our comfort to uphold and sustain us in the mean time?

Ans. 1. That God will be present with us, that he will not fail us nor forsake us, but will go to the grave with our dead bodies, watch over our ashes with the eye of his providence, to keep them, and raise up all again.

So that look how God encouraged Jacob, Gen. xlvi. 4, 'Fear not to go down into Egypt, for I will go with thee, and I will bring thee up again,' so God will go down into the grave with our dead bodies, watch over them, and bring them up again.

2. Secondly, That though our bodies lie rotting in the grave, yet that our souls shall be happy and blessed, which was Paul's comfort: 2 Cor. v. 1, 'For we know that if this earthly house of our tabernacle be dissolved, we have a building given us of God, not made with hands, but eternal in the heavens.' So Rev. vi. 11, the souls which lay under the altar, crying, 'How long, Lord'? were comforted with the long white robes given unto them; the present blessed estate of their souls.

3. Thirdly, This may comfort us, that although we lie in the grave a long time, yet that Christ hath sanctified and sweetened it unto us, by lying therein himself; so that the grave is now become a sweet bed to rest in peace in: as Isa. lvii. 2, he speaks of such, 'Peace shall be upon them, they shall rest in their beds, every one that walketh before me;' so that Christ hath now made this the plain way to heaven. Wherefore, as the children of Israel marched through the wilderness, where were fiery serpents, enemies, and many discouragements, overcoming all, because it was their way to Canaan, so the grave, being our way to heaven, let us overcome all doubts, and not fear to march that way unto it.

4. Fourthly, That although we lie a long time in the grave, that we have assured hope that we shall rise again; as David says, Ps. xvi. 9, 'Wherefore my heart is glad, and my tongue rejoiceth; my flesh also rests in hope: for thou wilt not leave my soul in the grave; neither wilt thou suffer thy Holy One to see corruption;' as it was true thus of Christ, so is it of all the members: when they are laid in the grave they are not gone and past hope. Though like Jonah, for the time swallowed up of a whale, the grave receive them, yet the Lord will in due time speak to the grave to cast them out again. Therefore it should teach us to live comfortably in this life, to encourage others; and when the time of our death cometh, then to depart in peace, seeing God will be with us, and our bodies shall rise again, heavenly glory in the mean time being appointed for our souls.

The fourth point is, the consideration by whose power we shall rise.

Point 4. That is, *by the power of Christ;* no power else can do it. It cannot be done by the power of nature; as Job xiv. 14, 'If a man die, shall he live again?' meaning, that if a man die he cannot rise of himself; so David says, Ps. xlix. 7, 'Yet a man can by no means redeem his brother, he cannot give his ransom to God.' So Ps. xlix. 15, 'But God shall deliver my soul from the grave; for he will receive me;' so all shall rise by the power of Christ, but with great difference: the godly with boldness, joy, and ravishment; the wicked with fear, shame, and astonishment.

The uses of which are,

Use 1. First, *To magnify and rely upon this mighty power of Christ*, by which we shall rise again out of the grave, and from the belly of rottenness.

2. Secondly, Therefore *to labour to feel the power of Christ here in this life to thy conversion and conscience quieting*, or else thou shalt feel the power of Christ to thy terror at the day of judgment.

3. Thirdly, Seeing all shall rise again at last, through the power of Christ, therefore *let us not doubt but that the Lord will raise us out of all troubles whatsoever in the best time*, as we see, Ezek. xxxvii. 3, the Lord there asks the prophet, 'Son of man, can these dead bones live'? then he bade him prophesy upon those bones, and bone ran to his bone, and the

flesh and sinews grew on them again, so that there stood up a great army. Now God applies this, ver, 11, 'Son of man,' saith he 'these bones are the whole house of Israel, which did lie in captivity and bondage;' wherefore God shewed the prophet that as he was able to raise these dead bones, so he was able to bring his people out of captivity and bondage again; therefore doubt not but thy God will raise thee out of thy troubles, whatsoever they be. So Ps. lxxxvi. 13, David confesseth, 'Great is thy mercy towards me, and thou hast delivered my soul out of the lowest grave.' This the saints have found, and this thou shalt find to thy comfort, therefore make a right use of the power of Christ.

The fifth point is, in what estate our bodies shall rise again.

Point 5. That is, *into an estate of glory*. Now our bodies are mortal and mutable, subject to a number of infirmities, hunger, cold, nakedness, sickness, and pains; now they are lumpish, dull, and heavy in the service of God, but at the resurrection then our bodies shall be made immortal, without subjection to any infirmities of nature, having strength to perform our own actions; in this goodly estate shall our bodies rise in.

If a physician should out of his art and skill give us such a potion that we should never hunger nor thirst after it, and to be freed also thereby from all griefs, pains, infirmities, and diseases, how would one strain to his utmost to buy such a potion? Yet such a potion the Lord hath freely provided for us at the last day, when he will give us such a cup to drink of as we shall never hunger, thirst, or feel any more pain, how should we therefore long and desire after the coming of Christ! We see what our Saviour says, Mat. xviii. 8, 'It were better for a man to enter heaven hurt and maimed, than otherwise to be cast into hell in never so great perfection of parts.' But thanks be to God, we may enter into heaven, and have all things in the state of perfection. Therefore how should this make us strive to be God's people, that we may attain unto this so excellent an estate?

But this question which St Paul propounds, 1 Cor. xv., in what estate our bodies shall rise at the last day, cannot be answered but with a distinction. The bodies of the godly rise in an estate of glory, the bodies of the wicked rise in an estate of shame and disgrace; so both rise, but in a different estate, as Gen. xl. 20, we read Pharaoh's two servants were both delivered out of prison, but in a diverse manner, the one to stand before the king, and give the cup into his hand, as formerly, the other to be executed and hanged. Even so it is with the godly and wicked at the last day, both of them shall be raised out of the grave, but the one to honour, to stand in the presence of God, the other to shame and perpetual contempt. So the bodies of the saints, though now weak, shall be glorious then; as Paul shews, 1 Cor. xv. 37, of corn, which, when it is sowed, it is but bare corn, but God giveth it a body at his pleasure; so, saith he, is the resurrection of the dead. Our bodies are sown in corruption, but raised in honour; it is sown in weakness, and is raised in power; it is sown a natural body, and is raised a spiritual body. So St Paul shews, 'Christ shall change our vile bodies, that it may be fashioned like unto his glorious body;' for look, in what estate Christ's body rose again, in the same estate shall all the bodies of the saints rise in; for the members must be conformable to the head; but Christ's body did rise in a far more glorious estate than ours are now. Therefore, when we look on our bodies, and see them weak, and poor, contemptible, crooked, and deformed, we should live well, and then comfort ourselves with this, that in the kingdom of God our bodies shall be made glorious and beautiful, and all deformities taken from them. One says well, that as the goldsmith melts his gold, and so frames a cup to serve the king, so the Lord only melts and refines us by death, to fit us to be vessels of glory hereafter. Therefore it is an excellent meditation to think often of the glory to come, to strengthen us against the terrors of death; as Job doth, chap. xix., when he was covered with griefs and sores; 'I am sure,' saith he, 'that my Redeemer lives, and he shall stand [at] the last on the earth; and though after my skin worms destroy this body, yet shall I see God with my flesh,' &c. So must we comfort ourselves in the like extremities. Now this glory shall not be from the redundance of the spirit only, but it shall be also in regard of the blessed and happy estate that the body shall be in at that time; which appears in

Six things, wherein the glory and excellency of the body shall consist after the resurrection.

1. First, *That all the parts of the body shall be then perfect and entire, and shall want nothing.* Howsoever now a man may be maimed and deformed, wanting a hand, eye, leg, arm, finger, or the like, yet all shall be supplied unto him then at that day; and that for two reasons.

(1.) First, Because all things then shall be reduced to their former estate; as Peter shews, Acts iii. 21, speaking of Christ, 'Whom,' saith he, 'the heavens must contain until the time cometh that all things shall be restored.' But in the beginning, man's body was made perfect and entire, wanting nothing either for beauty or comeliness; therefore to this estate it shall be restored again.

(2.) Secondly, Tertullian fetches it from another ground, Rev. xxi. 4, where it is said, 'There shall be no more death then.' 'Always,' saith he, 'in the greater is inferred the lesser. Now the lameness or deformedness of any member is the death of that member. Now if death be expelled from the whole man, so also must it be from every particular member; therefore the bodies of the saints shall rise again perfect and entire at the last day' (*i*).

Use 1. Therefore, *in any of the wants and imperfections of ourselves or our friends, we must labour to live a holy life,* draw them on also in goodness, and then be comforted. Whatsoever our imperfections are, God will help all at the last day.

Use 2. Again, seeing at the day of judgment all parts shall be perfected and restored, we should not now be afraid to give any of them for the name of Christ; for he that did restore the ear of Malchus, who was his enemy, much more will restore any part which his friends shall lose for his name's sake. Therefore we read, Heb. xi. 35, how those holy men there mentioned endured, and would not be delivered from those pains and torments which they endured of wicked men, that they might receive a better resurrection.

2. Secondly, *The glory of the body consists in this, that it shall be beautiful and lovely,* though now deformed and ill-favoured; being dead especially, which made Abraham desire to buy a place to bury his dead out of his sight, Gen. xxiii. 4; for these reasons:

Reason 1. First, look what estate Adam was in in the time of his innocency; in the same estate shall the bodies of the saints be at the resurrection. But in the beginning, the body of man was so beautiful, glorious, full of brightness and splendour which came from it, as all the beasts of the field came gazing, and stood looking on him; therefore the bodies of the saints shall be in the same state at the resurrection.

2. Secondly, Because all deformities, blackness, and ill-favouredness are punishments and penalties for sin; but when our sins shall cease, and our corruptions, then the penalty and punishment of them shall cease also. Oh how should this quicken up our care to repent us of our sins, to get faith in Christ, and to walk holily before him, that we may have our portion with the saints at last. Men cannot help deformedness, but God can. Both the temples were built, and defaced again, the last not so glorious as the first; but God will raise up all his, and make them more glorious than ever.

3. Thirdly, *The glory of the body shall then consist in this, that it shall be filled with brightness and splendour.* Now our bodies are dark and obscure, but then the bodies of the saints shall be like so many bright stars and shining lamps, when the wicked shall look dark and ugly to behold. We read, Dan. xii. 3, 'That they who be wise, shall shine as the brightness of the firmament; and they that turn many to righteousness, shall shine as the stars for ever and ever.' So Mat. xiii. 43, Christ enlargeth the same their shining, where he saith 'that the just shall then shine like the sun in the kingdom of their Father.' Therefore what glory they shall have is unconceivable of us. We see, when Moses had talked with God forty days, by the reflection of God's glory upon him, his face did so shine, that the children of Israel were not able to behold it; therefore how much more glorious shall the saints be to behold, when they shall stay, not forty days only with God, but for ever and ever? If in this case a spark was such, what shall the flame be? and what shall be the inward glory of the soul?

Use 1. The use hereof is, *that we should much and often solace ourselves with the meditation hereof,* abstracting our minds from this world; and, as Gen. xiii. 17, when the Lord had made a promise to Abraham of the land of Canaan, he bid him to arise and walk through the land in the length and breadth thereof, so seeing God hath promised us heaven, though we be not in actual possession, as we shall be, yet we should arise often, and walk through this land in the length and breadth thereof; that is, meditate and think of the surpassing glory and excellence of the place.

Use 2. Secondly, *Let us then be careful to live well, and spend our time in holiness and righteousness whilst we live here;* for how can we expect that God should honour us then, when we are not careful to honour him with our bodies now? It is a rule in art, that they who would finish their colours in brightness must lay light grounds; even so, if thou wouldst have Christ to finish up thy life in glory, never lay the sad grounds and black colours of sin and corruption, but repent of thy sins, purify thy heart by faith in Christ, wash thyself often in the blood of Christ, that so he may present thee pure and unspotted in that day.

4. Fourthly, *The body shall then be immutable and immortal.* Now our bodies are subject to many alterations and changes; as it is Job xiv. 2, 'Man shooteth forth as a flower, and is cut down: he vanisheth away as a shadow,' &c. Now our bodies are subject to hunger, and thirst, and many diseases, but then they shall be brought to such an estate of pre-eminency as they shall never hunger or thirst any more, nor have any alteration. So Rev. xvi. 7, it is said, 'They shall hunger no more, neither thirst any more, neither shall the sun light on them, neither any heat.' So Rev. xxii. 4, he shews God shall wipe away all tears from their eyes, and there shall be no more death, neither sorrow, neither crying, neither shall there be any more pain,' so they shall have rest. And as this is clear by the Scripture, so is it also by reason; for it is a ground in nature that all

things labour to attain to their last perfection, so to rest in it. We see in nature, if the shipman's needle be touched with a loadstone, it turns, and shakes, and never is at rest till it stand against the north pole, when, if it be hindered by anything, it stands trembling as discontented, resting when once it cometh there. So is it with the bodies of the saints that are touched with the loadstone, that is, who have touched Christ by faith; they be not in rest and quiet here, but subject to many sorrows and infirmities of nature, until they be brought to Christ, where they securely rest, and be immutable and unchangeable. Therefore, when we feel these diseases and decays of nature, let us take Peter's counsel, mentioned Acts iii. 19, 'Repent and turn to the Lord, that our sins may be put away, when the time of refreshing shall come out from the presence of the Lord.' It is a world to see what means men use to keep their bodies from putrefaction, to embalm them, keep them in lead with sweet spices, lay them in marble, yet none of these will serve, for all must stoop and yield to the grave and rottenness. But if we live a holy life, and get faith in the Lord Jesus, then at the last day the body shall be brought to such an estate as shall be immortal and immutable.

5. Fifthly, *They shall be spiritual bodies.* Now they are natural bodies, but then they shall be spiritual; as it is 1 Cor. xv. 44, 'It is sown a natural, and is raised a spiritual body.' Now, it shall not be a spiritual body in regard of substance, for it shall have breadth, and length, and thickness, parts and dimensions, as our bodies now have. So Christ told the disciples, Luke xxiv. 39, when entering the house, they supposed to have seen a spirit, but he says, 'Behold my hands and my feet, and handle me, for a spirit hath not flesh and bones.' Now, in two respects, our bodies are said then to be made spiritual.

(1.) First, Because then they shall be upheld and maintained by the Spirit. Now our bodies are upheld by meat and drink, sleep and physic; but then the Spirit of God shall quicken them, and they shall have no need of these helps. We know that Moses was forty days in the mount, where he was so filled with the glory of God, that he was neither thirsty nor hungry, nor desired to rest or sleep. Now if Moses was thus upheld with the glory of God in the estate of mortality,* without the use of meat and drink, much more shall the bodies of the saints be upheld in the state of glory, where God shall be all in all unto them (*j*).

(2.) Secondly, Because the body shall attend the spirit in all good duties, and shall be subject unto it; as Augustine speaks, 'It is not called a spiritual body, because, as some think, the substance of the body is turned into a spirit, but,' saith he, 'it is called a spiritual body, because it shall be subject to the spirit, and attend it' (*k*). The schoolmen, as Thomas Aquinas, confess thus much. It is a plain case that in glory the spirit shall not depend on the body, but the body shall be led by the spirit and attend it. For in the best there is now such reluctation betwixt the flesh and the spirit, as Gal. v. 17, that they being contrary to one another, we cannot do the things that we would; so Mat. xxvi. 40, when the disciples should have watched and prayed, Christ found them asleep; so Rom. vii. 22, 'For I delight in the law of God as touching my inward man: but I see another law in my members rebelling against the law of my mind, and leading me captive unto the law of sin which is in my members;' so Ezek. iii. 14, 'I went,' saith he, 'but it was in the bitterness of my spirit.' Thus the wrestling is great in us betwixt the flesh and the spirit, but one

* Qu. 'immortality'?—Ed.

day it is our comfort, the spirit shall have a final victory, and we shall be led by the spirit. When Rebecca had conceived, Gen. xxv. 22, she felt so great striving and struggling in her, that she was much perplexed, until she went to God, and had this answer, that two nations were in her, and that the elder should serve the younger. So must this be our comfort, that though now we be troubled with the flesh, which is the elder, yet that the time shall shortly come that the flesh shall submit, attend, and be subject to the younger, which is the spirit, last bred in us, in all things. If one bring a little spark of fire to a great heap of gunpowder, the fire will dissolve it and bring it to nothing; so, although there be a great heap of sin and corruption in us, yet if a man get but a little spark of the Spirit of God into us, it will dissolve our sins, and bring those purposes to nothing. Therefore now we must comfort ourselves with this, that though now our bodies be not ruled by the spirit, yet that one day they shall be subject unto it.

6. Sixthly, *In that it shall be a powerful body*; as 1 Cor. xv. 43. Now this power of the body appears in two things.

(1.) First, That it shall have power to perform the actions of the body without defatigation or weariness. Now we cannot do any action but in time we shall be weary of it, weary of going, sitting, standing; as it is said of Christ, John iv. 6, that being weary, he sat down upon the well; so Exod. xvii. 12, Moses's hands waxed weary in holding them up for Israel. So the best Christians are weary in the best duties, but at that day all duties shall be performed without any show of weariness, which should comfort us now amidst our imperfections, making us long for that day when we shall be enabled to serve God without ceasing.

(2.) Secondly, In that the body shall then move any way with ease, being able to walk in the air, on the water, even as now we can walk on the ground. Though now our bodies be heavy, yet then they shall have strength, as they shall be able to mount upwards, downwards, or forward or backward with as much ease as a man lifts up his hand; which should stir us up to live a holy life, that we may one day be partakers of these excellent privileges. Pliny reports of the little bees, that in a great wind or tempest, they fetch up little stones in their claws, to ballast themselves against the wind, that they be not carried away in it (*l*). So should we do in the time of temptation or trouble; ballast ourselves with the promises of God and hope of blessedness, that so we be not carried away with the wind of temptation and trouble. Thus far of the godly.

Now for the wicked, in what estate they shall rise in; it consists in two things.

1. First, *They shall rise in an estate of shame and disgrace.* 'And they shall go forth, and look upon the carcases of the men that have transgressed against me: for their worm shall not die, neither shall their fire be quenched; and they shall be an abhorring unto all flesh,' Isa. lxvi. 24. We see in sickness and pain, or a great fear, how our countenances alter and change; much more shall they then, in so great vexation and anguish of spirit.

2. Secondly, As the godly shall be free from hunger, cold, thirst, and all diseases and pains, so *the wicked shall be subject unto all these in much extremity for ever*, insomuch as if they should but, like the rich glutton, desire a drop of comfort to refresh them, they shall not have it. Wherefore seeing all the necessities and pains of nature, yea, and all the vengeance that the anger of an angry incensed God can inflict upon them, shall tor-

ment them for ever, let us now stir up ourselves to strive more than ever to shun this woeful miserable condition which the wicked shall then be in, and hearken unto the good counsel and advice of God's word, of the ministers, and of our godly friends to help us on in the good ways of God, which leads to heaven and happiness.

Thus I have done with the doctrine of the resurrection of the body; yet there remains some questions to be answered, which for mine own part I could be contented to pass over; because as David says, Ps. cxxxi. 1, 'I have not walked in great matters and hid from me.' And in the law, Exod. xix. 23, the priests as well as the people had their bounds set them, which they might not pass beyond. Yet, notwithstanding, because some are desirous to hear what further may be said, I will answer your desires, and make a further supply of them as far as the light of God's truth will lead me.

1. The first question is, Whether such as were born monsters and mis-shapen shall rise so at the last day?

Augustine answers, that they shall not rise monstrous deformed bodies at the last day, but corrected and amended in all parts. The reason he shews in another place is this, 'Because if a workman cast an ill favoured piece of work at first, he takes it and melts it again, until he make it an excellent piece; therefore much more God can and will melt these deformed bodies by death, and make them glorious, entire, and perfect' (*m*). Now to this judgment I assent thus far, that all the deformed bodies of the godly shall rise, melted by death, glorious and perfect in all parts; but that they who be wicked shall have the same deformities upon them at the day of judgment. My reason is, deformedness and mis-shapen-ness is a punishment of sin; but at the day of judgment the punishment of sin shall not be repealed unto the wicked, but shall be further increased. But the Schoolmen say, unto which I assent, that if a wicked man lose an eye or a hand for his offence, by the command of the magistrate, they shall be restored unto them at the day of judgment, to their further increase of torment. Lo, then the way to shun deformity, if thou be mis-shapen any way, live in the fear of God, believe in Christ, repent thee of thy sins, and then at that day all thy deformities shall be done away, and thy body made like unto Christ's glorious body for ever.

2. The second is, In what sex we shall rise, whether men shall rise men, and women women, or not?

I answer, They shall rise in the same sex; as Mat. xxii. 8, we see by the Sadducees' question propounded to Christ, of a woman who had seven husbands, whose wife she should be in the resurrection? Christ doth not say there shall be no women in the resurrection, but he says they shall not marry; so that the sexes shall not cease, but they shall be as the angels of God in heaven. And Saint Jerome upon that place affirms, that 'Christ gives us thereby to understand, where he says they shall not then marry, nor give in marriage, that both shall rise again in their proper sex, men shall rise men, and women shall rise women;' and the Greek text bears so much, though the Latin do not (*n*). So 1 Peter iii. 7, the apostle exhorts both men and women to live together as heirs of the grace of life. And Mat. xii. 42, there it is said that 'the queen of the south shall rise up in judgment against this generation, and shall condemn it,' &c.; so it is clear that both sexes shall rise again.

3. The third question is, In what age we shall rise, whether children shall rise children, and old men rise old men?

Augustine, unto whom the Schoolmen agree, answers, 'That all shall rise at the age of Christ, of thirty-three years of age' (*o*). But I dare not assent unto this opinion, because there is no warrant for it out of the Scriptures; for whatsoever is not of faith is sin; and that which hath not its warrant from the word cannot be of faith, which must be grounded on the Scripture. There is one place which seems to confirm the former opinion, that of Eph. iv. 13, 'Till we all meet together in the unity of the faith, and knowledge of the Son of God, into a perfect man, and into the age of the fulness of Christ.' Now by a consent of most of the fathers, they understand this place in another sense. Chrysostom saith, that in this place 'by the fulness of the age of Christ,' is meant not the full age of Christ, but the gifts and graces of Christ (*o*). So some others say to the same sense. St Jerome says, that 'by the age of Christ is not meant the grounds of the bodies of the godly, but the inward man, of the gifts and graces of the soul' (*o*). Again Tertullian differs from his judgment another way; saith he, 'Let Christians remember that our souls shall receive the same bodies from the which they departed; and therefore look in what stature and in what age they departed, in the same they shall rise again' (*p*). And in my judgment there be some reasons to prove the contrary.

1. First, That there is nothing in a child more than in a man to hinder him from the kingdom of God; for Christ saith, 'Suffer little children to come unto me, and forbid them not; for of such is the kingdom of God.' And I make no question, if in innocency Adam had had children, they should have been blessed; much more are they capable of blessedness in heaven.

2. Secondly, Children may perform the chiefest act of our work in heaven, namely, to praise God; as Ps. viii. 2, 'Out of the mouths of babes and sucklings thou hast ordained praise.'

3. Again, all those whom Christ raised, being upon earth, were raised in the same stature they were in when they died, as the maid, the widow's son, and Lazarus; and those who were raised at the resurrection of Christ, how shonld they else have been known of their friends if they had not risen the same they were? So that the imperfection of children is only in regard of labour and travail, not in regard of capacity to live a spiritual life.

Thus have I satisfied your desires in delivering my judgment in these weighty points, which I tie no man to believe further than the Spirit of God shall direct him. We must not be too curious in this great point, only stir up yourselves to the love and fear of God, to walk with him according to the prescription of his word, and then let it suffice us, we shall be raised up in a wonderful manner to everlasting glory and happiness, beyond all that we are able to think or speak; unto which, God of his mercy bring us all in due time. Amen.

NOTES.

(*a*) P. 318.—'Tertullian says well, "It was a harder matter for God to make a man, being nothing,"' &c. The present and after-references (*b*, *e*, *i*, *p*) combine, somewhat oddly, scattered reminiscences not only of this Father's great treatise *De Resurrectione Carnis*, but likewise of his *De Animâ*, and immortal 'Apology.' Cf. for the former c. xvii., for the next c. iv. and xxii., for the third c. xlviii.

Probably the present reference is to the last, which is eloquent and effective. Bp. Kaye's 'Tertullian,' c. iii. pp. 190–214, will reward consultation.

(*b*) P. 318.—'Again, Tertullian saith well, "We must not think,"' &c. Cf. note *a* above.

(*c*) P. 319.—'As Augustine speaks; and Cyril saith well, "that Christ entered,"' &c. As with Tertullian, Sibbes in his references brings together various scattered reminisences of Augustine. The *indices* to his *De Civitate Dei* furnish many references reflective of Sibbes's words. I suspect that Cyril is here a misreference for Basil, in whose Hexäemeron (Homil. viii.) the *thought* occurs, if I err not.

(*d*) P. 321.—'Chrysostom says well, "If a man take a long journey,"' &c. Consult as in note *o*.

(*e*) P. 321.—'Thus Tertullian saith, that "he will pray,"' &c. Cf. note *a*.

(*f*) P. 321.—'St Jerome says, "that it cannot stand with equity,"' &c. I find the *thoughts* under the following references in this Father's works (*Benedictine ed.*), iv. pp. 323, 325, 326. So much does Jerome enter into details in the statement of the doctrine of the resurrection of the body, that he intimates there will be no use of barbers in the resurrection state, the hair and nails having ceased to grow, as did those of the Israelites during their sojourn in the wilderness. This Father abounds in the most singular illustrations of Sibbes's oddest questions.

(*g*) P. 322.—'Augustine shall answer for me,' &c. Consult as in note *o*; but Jerome, as described in note *f*, is more curious.

(*h*) P. 324.—'Irenæus with this shuts up his book.' The 'book' referred to is his (fragmentary) *Adversus Hæreses*.

(*i*) P. 328.—'Tertullian fetcheth it from another ground,' &c. Cf. note *a*.

(*j*) P. 330.—'We know that Moses was forty days in the mount,' &c. Dr Adam Clarke, in his Commentary upon the place, furnishes us with a fine Rabbinical explanation. Relative, he says, to the 'forty days'' fast of Moses, there is a beautiful saying of the Talmudists: '"Is it possible that any man can fast forty days and forty nights?" To which Rabbi Meir answered, "When thou takest up thy abode in any particular city, thou must live according to its customs. Moses ascended to heaven, where they neither eat nor drink; therefore he became assimilated to them. We are accustomed to eat and drink; and when angels descend to us, they eat and drink also."' It was in very truth a 'heavenly,' not an 'earthly life,' in the case equally of Moses, Elijah, and the Lord.

(*k*) P. 330.—'Augustine speaks, "It is called a spiritual body,"' &c. Cf. as in note *o*; also various references under the text.

(*l*) P. 331.—'Pliny reports of the little bees.' This apocryphal statement is only one of many concerning bees and other creatures found in Pliny, and magnified in the early English translation by Philemon Holland.

(*m*) P. 332.—'Augustine answers, that they shall not rise,' &c. Cf. as in note *o*.

(*n*) P. 332.—'St Jerome upon that place (Mat. xxii. 8) affirms,' &c. Cf. note *f*.

(*o*) P. 333.—'Augustine answers,' &c. Cf. index-references of Augustine under Eph. iv. 13; also Chrysostom and Jerome. The point comes up repeatedly in these and in all the Fathers.

(*p*) P. 333.—'Again, Tertullian differs,' &c. Cf. note *a*. G.

SIBBES'S LAST TWO SERMONS; FROM CHRIST'S LAST SERMON.

HONORATISSIMO DOMINO,

DOMINO ROBERTO COMITI WARWICENSI,*

HAS MELLITISSIMI THEOLOGI RICHARDI SIBBS, S. THEOL. DOCTORIS,

(QUEM PERCHARUM HABUIT, CUJUSQUE CONCIONANTIS AUDITOR ERAT ASSIDUUS UNA CUM NOBILISSIMA FAMILIA),

CYGNEAS CONCIONES,

IN PIENTISSIMI AUTHORIS AFFECTUS, NECNON IPSORUM SINGULARIS OBSEQUII

μνημόσυνον.

D.D.D.

THOMAS GOODWIN.†
PHILIPPUS NYE.‡

* Robert Earl of Warwick, is a historic name in himself, and from his relations to the illustrious house of Sidney. See all the Peerage books.

† That is, Dr Thomas Goodwin, who discharged the office of editor to many of the Puritans besides Sibbes, *e.g.*, Burroughes, Thomas Hooker. Consult Dr Halley's 'Memoir,' prefixed to vol. ii. of works in this series.

‡ One of the most venerable worthies of Puritanism. Born in 1596, he died in 1672. See 'The Nonconformists' Memorial,' vol. i. 96–7. G.

LAST TWO SERMONS.

NOTE.

For the circumstances under which these 'Two Sermons' were delivered, consult our Memoir, c. xi. ult. Our text is taken from the 4th edition. Its title-page is given below.* Three editions preceded, as follows:—

(*a*) 1st, 1636. 4to. Pp. 69.
(*b*) 2d, 1636. 4to. Pp. 65. [The 'Prayer' first added to this ed.]
(*c*) 3d, 1637. 4to. Pp. 103.
(*d*) 4th, 1638. 18mo., as below.—G.

* Title-page—

TWO
SERMONS
Vpon the first words of
Christs last Sermon,
IOHN 14. 1.

Being also the *last* Sermons of

RICHARD SIBBS D.D.

Preached to the honourable society of Grayes Inne, *Iune* 21.
and 28. 1635.

Who the next Lords day following, dyed, and rested from all
his labours.

2 Sam. 23. 1. *These are the last words of
the sweet singer of Israel.*

The fourth Edition.

LONDON,
Printed by *Thomas Harper*, for *Lawrence Chapman*, and are to be sold at
his shop at Chancery lane end, in
Holborne, 1638.

THE AUTHOR'S PRAYER BEFORE HIS SERMON.

Gracious and holy Father! which hast sanctified this day for thy own service and worship, and for the furthering of us in the way of salvation; and hast made a most gracious promise, that when 'two or three be gathered together in thy name, thou wilt be there in the midst of them:'* vouchsafe, then, we beseech thee, the performance of this thy promise unto us, now gathered together in thy name, to pray unto thee, to hear and speak thy holy and blessed word, and so sanctify our hearts by thy Holy Spirit at this time, that we may perform these holy services as shall be most to thy glory and our own comfort. Unworthy we are in ourselves to appear in thy most holy presence, both by reason of the sins of our nature, and the sins of our lives, even since that time that we have had some knowledge of thy blessed truth; which holy truth we have not entertained nor professed as we should have done, but oftentimes against the light that thou hast kindled in our hearts by thy Word and Spirit, we have committed many sins; and, amongst the rest, we confess our sins against thy holy ordinance; our not preparing our hearts unto it, nor profiting by it as we should and might have done; giving thy Majesty hereby just cause to curse thy own holy ordinance unto us. But thou art a gracious and merciful Father unto us in Jesus Christ, in the abundance of thy love and mercy. In him we come unto thee, beseeching thee, for his sake, not to give us up to these inward and spiritual judgments; but vouchsafe us a true insight into our own estates, without deceiving of our own souls, and from thence, true humiliation. And then we beseech thee to speak peace unto us in thy Christ, and say to our souls by thy Holy Spirit, that thou art our salvation. And for clearer evidence that we are in thy favour, let us find the blessed work of thy Holy Spirit opening our understandings, clearing our judgments, kindling our affections, discovering our corruptions, framing us every way to be such as thou mayest take pleasure and delight in. And because thou hast ordained thy holy word 'to be a light unto our feet, and a guide and direction to all our ways and paths,'† and to be a powerful means to bring us more and more out of the thraldom of sin and Satan, to the blessed liberty of thy children, we beseech thee, therefore, to bless thy word to these and all other good ends and purposes for which thou hast ordained it. And grant, we beseech thee, that now at this time out of it we may learn thy holy will; and then labour to frame our lives thereafter, as may be most to thy glory and our own comfort, and that for Jesus Christ his sake, thine only Son, and our blessed Saviour. Amen.‡

* Matt. xviii. 20. † Ps. cxix. 105.

‡ This 'Prayer' appeared first in edition *b* of the 'Two Sermons.' It forms an item in Bishop Patrick's defence of 'printed' and 'read' prayers. See 'Continuation of the Friendly Debate' (Pt. ii., Works, vol. v. pp. 630–2). The authority on which Patrick rests in his statement that Sibbes used above single form of prayer does not bear him out. He refers to Geree (Vindiciæ Ecclesiæ Anglicanæ, 4to, 1644), but his words are, 'In prayer men many times limit themselves, as Doctor Sibbs *is said* to use one form of prayer before his sermons printed by Mr Goodwin and Mr Nye.' It is very improbable that Sibbes thus limited himself; and certainly neither Goodwin nor Nye make such an assertion.—G.

THE FIRST SERMON.

Let not your hearts be troubled: ye believe in God, believe also in me.—
JOHN XIV. 1.

HOLY men, as they be 'trees of righteousness,' Isa. lxi. 3, and desire to be fruitful at all times, so most especially towards their end; having but a short time to live in the world, they be willing to leave the world with a good savour. So it was with Jacob. So with Moses, as appears in his excellent Song made before his death. You may see it in King Solomon and David before their deaths. But especially in our Saviour. The nearer to heaven, the more heavenly-minded. When grace and glory are ready to join, the one to be swallowed up of the other, then grace is most glorious. All the passages of Christ are comfortable; but none more comfortable than those sermons of his, that were delivered a little before his death. Of all words that come from loving men to those they love, such are most remarkable as be spoken when they be ready to die; because then men are most serious, they being about the most serious business. Then they be wisest, and best able to judge; for the consideration of their end makes them wise. And therefore, saith God, 'O that my people were wise to consider their latter end!' Deut. xxxii. 29. And, 'teach me to number my days, that I may apply my heart to wisdom,' saith Moses, Ps. xc. 12. And indeed there is no wisdom to that; for it teacheth men to pass a right judgment upon all things in the world. They be no longer drunk with the prosperity of the world; they be no longer swayed with opinion, but they pass an estimation of things as they are.

Besides, love at that time is especially set on work. Therefore our blessed Saviour being now to offer himself a sacrifice on the cross, he sweetly delivereth these words before his departure, 'Let not your hearts be troubled.' Let us hear them therefore, as the dying words of our Saviour to his disciples, and in his disciples, to us all, as in the 17th of St John. 'I pray not for them only, but for all such as shall believe in me, through their word,' ver. 20. For his comforts concern us all, as his prayers did.

This chapter is sweetly mixed of comforts, counsels, and gracious promises; but especially it affords matter of comfort. Mark who it is that gives this comfort,—our blessed Saviour. And at what time,—when he was to sacrifice himself.

What admirable love, and care, and pity is in this merciful high Priest of ours, that should so think of comforting his disciples, as to forget himself, and his own approaching death! It is the nature of love so to do; and we should imitate our blessed Saviour in it. You see how he laboureth to strengthen them, especially towards his end. He knew they would then need it most, and therefore he endeavoureth by all means to strengthen them, both by counsel, as here; by the passover, and by a newly instituted sacrament, 1 Cor. xi. 23.

But what need we wonder at this in our blessed Saviour, who so regarded us, as he left heaven; took our nature; became man; put himself under the law; became sin?

The words contain *a dissuasion from over-much trouble,* and then *a direction to believe in God, and Christ.* Comforts must be founded on strong reasons. For we are reasonable and understanding creatures; and God works on us answerably to our principles. He stays our spirits by reasons stronger than the grievance. For what is comfort but that which establisheth and upholds the soul against that evil which is feared or felt, from a greater strength of reason which overmastereth the evil? If the grievance be but even with the comfort, then the consolation works not. But Christ's comforts are of an higher nature than any trouble can be. For he not only dissuades from trouble, but also persuades to confidence, 'Be of good comfort, I have overcome the world,' John xvi. 33.

The occasion of this comforting them, and of removing their discouragements, was this. In the former chapter, he had told them, that he should leave them, and that they should leave him; the best of them all, even Peter, should take offence at him, and deny him, and that all the rest should leave him. From whence they might gather, that the approaching trouble should be great, that should cause Peter to deny him, and them all to forsake him. And thence must needs arise great scandals. Our Saviour saw by the power of his Godhead into their hearts, and like enough, in their looks he saw a spirit of discouragement seizing on them, for his departure, and Peter's fall, their forsaking of him, and the persecutions that would follow. And therefore Christ discerning this dejection of their spirits, he raiseth them by this, 'Let not your hearts be troubled.' The heavenly Physician of our souls applieth then the remedy, when it is the fittest season.

There was some good in their trouble; something naturally, and something spiritually good. There was ground of natural trouble at the departure of such a friend, at the hearing of such persecutions. For we are flesh, not steel; and in that sense, Christ was troubled himself, to shew the truth of his manhood. Nay, trouble is the seasoning of all heavenly comforts, so as there were no comforts, if there were no trouble; and therefore this natural trouble was not disallowed by Christ. There was likewise something spiritually good, in this trouble. They loved their Master, who they saw was going away, and they knew it was a shameful thing for them to forsake him. There was love in them towards him all this while. Christ could discern gold in ore, some good in a great deal of ill; and therefore loved them again, and manifested it by comforting them, 'Let not your hearts be troubled.' They were right in this principle, that all comfort depends on the presence of Christ. And so the main ground of the sorrow was good. For as all heavenly light, and heat, and influence comes from the sun (it being all gathered into that body); so all heavenly comforts are gathered into Christ, and therefore must come to us from Christ's presence, bodily or spiritually. Their error was in tying all comfort to a bodily, a corporal presence; as if it were necessary for the sun to come down and abide upon the earth, to bestow its heat and influence. And therefore he tells them, that though he was to go away, yet he would send another comforter, the Holy Ghost.

And then they were overcome by an opinion that it would go worse with them when Christ was gone. Therefore Christ telleth them that it should be better for them; and indeed it was better. Christ did not take away his blessed presence for their disadvantage, but for their good. God never takes anything from his children, but he maketh it up in a better kind. If Christ takes away his bodily presence, he leaveth his spiritual presence, and more abundantly.

So that, though they were led with sensible things, and what they saw not they could hardly believe, yet Christ looks to what is good in them, and accepts it. He saw what was naught in them, with a purpose to purge it; what was naturally weak in them, to strengthen it; and therefore he counsels them, 'Let not your hearts be troubled.'

The thing that I will first observe out of the words is, *that the best Christians are subject to be troubled, to be pensive, and dejected more than should be.*

Indeed our Saviour Christ himself was troubled, but his trouble was like the shaking of clear water in a crystal glass. There was no mud in the bottom. But our trouble is of another kind, and apt to be inordinate.

We may carry this truth through the whole Scripture, and shew how Hannah was in bitterness of spirit, which exceeded so, that Eli, a good man, mistakes her, supposing that she was overcome with drink, 1 Sam. i. 13.

Hezekiah, a good king, was in such bitterness that, like a crane or swallow, he did chatter, Isa. xxxviii. 14. And David complained that his spirit was overwhelmed within him, Ps. lxxvii. 3; and Jonah cries out that he was 'in the belly of hell,' Jonah ii. 2.

And God will have it so, partly for conformity to our Head, and partly that we may be known to ourselves; that we may discern where our weakness lieth, and so be better instructed to seek to him in whom our strength lieth.

He suffers us, likewise, to be troubled for the preventing of spiritual sins, pride and security, and the like.

And partly in regard of others, that we may be pitiful. Christ was man for this end, that he might be a merciful High Priest; and we have much more need to know and feel the infirmities that are in ourselves, that we may be merciful to others; that we may not be harsh and censorious upon the troubles of others; from want of which consideration proceeded Eli's rashness in passing that censure upon Hannah.

But how shall we know that our hearts are more troubled than they should be? For I lay this for a ground: *That we may sin in being over much troubled at things for which it is a sin not to be troubled.* If they had not been at all affected with the absence of Christ, it had been a sin, and no less than stupidity; yet it was their sin to be over much troubled. In a word, therefore, for answer, a trouble is sinful when it hinders us *in* duty or *from* duty; when it hinders us in duties to God or to others; or from duty, that is, when the soul is disturbed by it, and, like an instrument out of tune, made fit for nothing, or like a limb out of joint, that moves not only uncomelily, but painfully, and becomes unfit for action. When we find this in our trouble, we may know it is not as it should be.

There be some affections especially, that are causes of over much trouble;

fear of evils to come, sorrow for evils that at present seize on us. Now, when these do hinder us from duty, or trouble us in duty, they be exorbitant and irregular.

Naturally, affections should be helps to duty, they being the winds that carry the soul on, and the spiritual wings of the soul. So that a man without affections is like the dead sea, that moves not at all. But then they must be regulated and ordered; they must be raised up and laid down at the command of a spiritual understanding. When they be raised up of themselves, by shallow and false conceits and opinions, they be irregular. When they be raised up by a right judgment of things, and laid down again when they ought to be, then they are right and orderly.

Now, besides the hurt that is in such affections themselves, Satan loves to fish in these troubled waters. The affections are never stirrred and raised up irregularly and exorbitantly but Satan joins with them. And therefore we have need to keep our affections of grief and fear within their due bounds. Satan is a curious observer of any excess in our passions; and in just correction, to speak the mildest of it, God lets loose Satan to join with that excess. And therefore the apostle saith wisely, 'Let not the sun go down upon your wrath, neither give place to the devil,' Eph. iv. 26, because as soon as ever we give way to any excess of affection, Satan fishes in these waters, and joins with that excess. He being a spirit of darkness, loves to dwell in the soul when it is in darkness. And therefore, when it is clouded by passion, as all passions beyond their due measure are as clouds that darken the soul, Satan, that works in darkness, then seizes on the soul presently.

That was Saul's case. He was envious at David, being of a proud and haughty spirit, that could not endure competition; and Satan took his time to work on him. And therefore it is said he was troubled with an evil spirit, 1 Sam. xvi. 23.

But trouble of spirit is too large an argument. I will not now stand upon it; only I will shew that we should not yield to excess of trouble any way. And the reasons are:—

First. We wrong our own selves when we give way to grief and sorrow, that is immoderate and inordinate. The soul is, as it were, put out of joint by it. We make actions difficult unto us. The wheels of the soul are thereby taken off. Joy and comfort are, as it were, oil to the soul. And therefore Nehemiah saith, 'the joy of the Lord is your strength,' chap. viii. 10. When, therefore, we give way to fear and grief, and such passions, it weakeneth the soul in action. And then again they are, as it were, a cloud betwixt God's love and us; and so the soul is hindered of much comfort and enlargement. Joy enlargeth the soul, but grief straiteneth it. Comfort raiseth up the soul, grief and sorrow weigh down the soul. A Christian should be of a straight, upright, and enlarged spirit. When, therefore, the spirit is straitened, when it is pressed down and dejected, a Christian is not in his right mind, in his due and proper frame.

Second. Besides, *if we regard God himself, we should take heed that the soul be not thus distempered;* for by over-much sorrow and grief, what a great deal of dishonour do we to God, in proceeding from a mistake of his goodness and providence! And with over-much fear and sorrow, there is always joined murmuring and discontent, and a spirit unsubdued to God, and his Spirit. There is a wronging, as of his care in providence, so of his graciousness in his promises. There is a grieving of his good Spirit; a questioning of his government, as if he did not dispose of things as he should; when we will have it one way, and God will have it another way. There is likewise a great deal of pride in dejections and discontent. The most discontented spirit in the world is the devil, and none prouder. It argues a great deal of pride and sullenness to be affectedly sad, and dejected; as if such worthy and excellent persons as we should be so afflicted: or there were greater cause for us to be dejected than raised up. Whereas if we balance our grounds of comfort, being Christians, as we should do, they would appear incomparably above the grounds of our discouragements. So it is a wrong to God, and his truth, and his gracious sweet government, to yield to a dejected sullen disposition.

It is likewise a wrong to others. For it maketh us unfit for any office of love to them, when we plod and pore so much upon our discontentments, and drink up our spirits, and eat up our hearts. It disables the soul, taking away not only the strength, but also the willingness of the soul; besides the scandal that it brings on religion, and the best ways; as if there were not enough in religion to comfort the soul.

But you will say, religion breeds a great deal of trouble and pensiveness. It is indeed the speech of the shallow people of the world, 'religion makes men sad.'

And it is true, that as our Saviour Christ here had made his disciples sad, by telling them that he would leave them; and that a great scandal would be taken at his cross, and shameful suffering; but yet withal, bids them not be troubled, and gives them grounds of comfort; so religion will make men sad; for it discovers truths, and sad truths. Aye, but the same religion will cheer them up again, yea, it casts them down, that it may raise them up. The sun in the morning raiseth clouds; but when it hath strength it scatters them. God intending solid and substantial comfort, doth first beget troubles, and discovers true grounds of trouble; he lets us see that all is not well. But still as religion brings any trouble, so it brings with it great remedies against these troubles; and that God that raiseth a soul to see just matter of grief, will by his Spirit shew its due and right portion, in comfort. Thus, to be sorrowful and sad, in some measure is from religion; but that which will prevent the excess and over-measure of it, is from religion likewise.

So that it is a scandal to religion to be overmuch dejected.

Third. Besides, though we should be troubled for sin, yet to be overmuch troubled for sin *is a dishonour to Christ, and to the love of God in Christ;* for it is as if we had not in him a sufficient remedy for that great malady. As, be it grief for the troubles of the church; as not to be troubled at the affliction of Joseph, is branded for a sin; so to be too much cast down, as if Christ had cast off the government from his shoulders, or had not the name of the church on his breast in heaven (as the high priest had the names of the twelve tribes in his breastplate); to be so cast down as to be taken off from prayer, and from the use of all good means to help the church, this is sinful. So also when grief for sin makes us forget the mercies of God in Christ; to forget the healing virtue of him our brazen serpent; to neglect to search our grounds of comforts, and to yield to Satan, to temptation. Overmuch sadness, even though it be for sin, or for the church, it is hurtful and scandalous.

Joshua was much cast down when he saw it went not well with Israel; but 'Get thee up, Joshua,' saith God, 'what dost thou lying here?' Up and do thy duty; consider what is amiss! There is an Achan in the camp. And so when things go not well, let not your thoughts be conversant about the matters of trouble, so much as about your duty. So we see it is incident to God's people to be overmuch troubled, and we see also the reasons why it should not be so, because it is injurious to God, to ourselves, and others every way.

And after all this, there is much reason in this, *that Christ hath forbidden it*, '*Let not* your hearts be troubled.'

Obj. But Christ could as well have cured it, being God, as easily as forbidden it.

Ans. It is true, but he cures it by forbidding it. With the words, there went forth a spirit of comfort into their hearts; an influence of grace accompanied his commands, for the word and Spirit go together. Christ deals with men by men. The Spirit of comfort is a spirit of truth; and therefore God comforts by truths. He gives us sanctified understandings and affections; and then works on them by sanctified truths.

And sometimes Christ cures it by real comforts; for comforts are either rational, which are fetched from grounds, which faith ministers; or real, from the presence of anything which comforts; as the sight of friends, or the accommodating of us in anything wherein we see the love of God conveyed. How many real comforts doth God bestow, when he fitteth us with conveniences in our way to heaven, so that we may read the love of God in them! God doth not only comfort us by his gracious promise, by his word and sacraments, administering heavenly comforts by them; but also by the conveying of himself and his love, by outward comforts that we enjoy in the world. Howsoever carnal men abuse them (making all things to work for the worst); yet that love, that intends heaven, sweetens all things in the passage to heaven, to his children; because they see the love of God in the least comfort.

Again, observe from this here, 'let not your *hearts* be troubled,' what is the seat of comfort, the heart. The seat of comfort is the seat of grief. There must be an application of comfort suitable to the grief, and the heart must be comforted.

And therefore in Isa. xl. 1, 2, 'Comfort ye, comfort ye my people, speak to the heart.' As the grief sinks and soaks to the root of the heart; so do Christ's comforts, like true cordials indeed, that go as deep as the grievance. If the grief goes to the heart, the comfort must go as deep. Now God, the Father of spirits, and the Holy Ghost, the Comforter, knows and searches our spirits. They know all the corners of the heart. They can banish fear and sorrow out of every cranny; and bring light, heat, and influence into every part of the soul. And therefore Christ saith, 'Let not your hearts be troubled.'

Now for the ways whereby we must labour to comfort our hearts (amongst many that I might speak of), I will name a few.

First of all, there must be a *due search into the heart, of the grounds of our trouble;* for oftentimes Christians are troubled, they cannot tell wherefore; as children that will complain they know not why. I speak not of hypocrites, that will complain of that which is not a true grief to them; like some birds that make greatest noise, when they be furthest from their nests. But of some poor Christians that are troubled, but distinctly know not the ground of it. But search the heart ingenuously and truly to the bottom of it, and see if there be not some Achan in the camp; some sin in the heart (for sin is like wind; when it gets into the veins, it will have vent, and a troublesome one; and so will sin, if it get into the soul). It is that indeed which causeth all trouble. And therefore search your hearts thoroughly;

what sin lieth there unrepented of, and for which you have not been humbled.

2. And when you have found out your sin, *give it vent by confession of it to God, and in some cases to others.*

3. And when we have done so, consider *what promises, and comforts, in that word of God are fitted to that condition.* For we can be in no condition but there are comforts for it, and promises fitted to yield comforts for every malady. And it will be the wisdom of a Christian to accommodate the remedy to the sore of his heart. And therefore we ought to be skilful and well seen in the word of God, that we may store up comforts beforehand. Our Saviour Christ tells them beforehand of the scandal of the cross, and of Peter's denial, that they might lay up strength and spiritual armour against the day of trial. Those comforts do not, for the most part, hold out in the day of adversity, which were not procured in the day of prosperity. *Non durant in adversis quæ non in pace quæsita.* It is not wisdom to be to learn religion when we should use it. And, therefore, let us be spiritual good husbands* for our souls, by storing up comforts out of the word of God; and then we shall have no more to do, than to remember the comforts that we did beforehand know.

And there be some promises of more general use, that are *catholica,* fitted for all sorts of grievances. And of these we must make use when we cannot think of particular ones, as the promises that concern forgiveness of sin. Think of God's mercy in pardoning sin with admiration; because sin will be presented us in such terrible colours, that if God be not presented in as gracious colours, we shall sink. And, therefore, set out Christ in his mercies, and all-sufficiency, when sin is aggravated to be in its heinousness, and out of measure, sinfulness; as the prophet Micah doth, 'Who is a God like our God, that pardoneth iniquity, transgression and sin?' vii. 18. Likewise, how many promises and comforts are there in that one promise, 'He will give his Spirit to them that ask him,' Luke xi. 13. And here our Saviour promiseth to send the Comforter. All graces and all comforts are included in the Spirit of grace and comfort. His Spirit is a Spirit of all grace; and, therefore, our Saviour thought that he promised enough when he said he would send them the Comforter. And so what a world of comfort is in that promise! 'All things shall work together for the best, to them that love God,' Rom. viii. 28. Yea, those things that are worst shall work together. Though they be hostile, and opposite one to another, yet they join issue in this, they be all for the good of God's people; as in a clock the wheels go several ways, but all join to make the clock strike. And so in the carriage and ordering of things, one passage crosses another, but in the issue we shall be able to say, 'all things work together for the best;' I found God turning all things for my good; and I could not have been without such a cross, such an affliction. And so for present assistance in your callings or straits, remember that promise made to Joshua, which is repeated in Hebrews xiii., 'I will not fail thee, nor forsake thee,' verse 5: a promise which is five times renewed in Scripture. And how much comfort is in that, that he will vouchsafe by his Spirit a gracious presence in all conditions whatsoever! And likewise that of David, Ps. xxiii. 4, 'Though I walk in the valley of the shadow of death, yet will I fear no ill, for thou art with me.' It was a terrible supposition made, that 'though he should walk in the valley of the shadow of death, yet he would fear no evil.' These promises

* That is, 'husbandmen.'—G.

well digested, will arm the soul with confidence, that it shall be able to put any case of trouble; as in the 27th Psalm, 1–3, David puts cases, 'The Lord is my strength, the Lord is the light of my countenance, of whom shall I be afraid? Though thousands shall rise against me, yet in this I will be confident.' If our hearts be established by the word of God, settled in the truth of such promises by the Spirit of God, we may set God and his truth against all troubles that can arise from Satan, and hell, and the instruments of Satan, or our own hearts. And, therefore, it is a great wrong to God, and his truth, if we know not our portion of comfort, and use it as occasion serves. More particulars I omit, leaving them to your own industry; the Scripture being full of them.

4. When we have these promises, *let us labour to understand them thoroughly;* to understand the grounds of our comfort in them, and to believe the truth of them, which are as true as God, who is truth itself. And then to love them, and digest them in our affections, and so make them our own, and then to walk in the strength and comfort of them.

5. Labour likewise to have them *fresh in memory.* It is a great defect of Christians, [that] they forget their consolation, as it is in the Hebrews, xii. 5. Though we know many things, yet we have the benefit of our comfort from no more than we remember.

6. But, above all, if we will keep our hearts from trouble, let us labour *to keep unspotted consciences.* Innocency and diligence are marvellous preservers of comfort. And, therefore, if the conscience be spotted and unclean, wash it in the blood of Christ, which is first purging, and then purifying. It first purgeth the soul, being set awork to search our sins, and confess them; which maketh us see our need of Christ, who died to satisfy divine justice. Then, God sprinkles our heart with his blood, which was shed for all penitent sinners; by which, when the heart is purged, the conscience will be soon satisfied also, by Christ's blood. And when it is purged and pacified, then keep it clean; for a foul soul is always a troubled soul; and though it may be quiet, yet it is sure to break out afterwards.

7. And because there can be no more comfort than there is care of duty, therefore, together with innocency, let us be careful *of all duties in all our several relations.* Let us consider in what relations we stand, and what duties we owe, and be careful to satisfy them all. Neglect of duty is a debt, and debts are troublesome. When the soul reflects upon the omission of a necessary duty; I owe such a duty to such a person; I should have done such a thing, in such a relation, but I have omitted it, it is a disquietment, and that upon good grounds; and if you have been negligent, there must be an actual renewing of the covenant, and a setting upon the duty, with fresh endeavours to make amends for former negligences; or else the soul shall have no comfort, nor will God suffer it to admit of comfort. And, therefore, 'work out your salvation with fear and trembling,' Philip. ii. 12. The reason that men do still tremble, and are troubled with this doubt and that fear, is, because their salvation is not wrought out; something is left undone, and their consciences tell them so.

8. But above all, that we may receive comfort, let us labour *for a spirit of faith.* Therefore here it is said, 'You believe in God, believe also in me.' Christ brings them to faith for comfort. And he sets down a double object of faith,—God, that is, the Father, Son, and Holy Ghost; and Christ, considered as Mediator; and Christ brings them to himself, 'Believe also in me,' John xiv. 1, because he would fence them against the future scandal of his suffering. As if he should say, You will hereafter, when you see me

so handled, and upon the cross, doubt and call in question whether I am God and the Messiah of the world or no. But if you believe in God, 'believe in me.' For howsoever, in love to you and mankind, I took man's nature on me, and am abased, yet, in my greatest abasement, remember this, that I am God. And surely there is nothing can stay the soul more, especially when it is deeply humbled, than to consider God in the second person incarnate, and abased and crucified, and made a curse and sin for us; to see the great God of heaven and earth, whose excellencies we cannot comprehend, to take our nature, and in our nature to suffer for us those things which he did endure. This will establish the soul indeed. Can the soul think that this was done for any small or to little purpose? Or can there be any grief or sin that should hinder comfort, or persuasion of the possibility of pardon, when the great God became man on purpose to die for sin? We may set this against all discouragements whatsoever. And therefore, 'believe in God, believe also in me.' Howsoever you see me abased, yet you may have comfort in my abasement, for it is for you. And therefore, saith Paul, 'I rejoice to know nothing but Jesus Christ, and him crucified,' 1 Cor. ii. 2. That which proud and atheistical heathens took scandal at, that he rejoiceth in, 'God forbid that I should glory in anything but in the cross of Christ,' Gal. vi. 14. Peace of conscience, joy in the Holy Ghost, reconciliation, and title to happiness, is all founded upon Christ crucified.

And then, again, you see he joins both together, 'Ye believe in God, believe also in me,' to shew the distinction of persons in the Trinity, God the Father, Son, and Holy Ghost. All our faith is resolved at length into one God, but yet withal into three persons in that divine nature, because, as there is God the Father offended, so there must be a God to satisfy that God, and there must be a God to reveal and apply that satisfaction. The soul is so full of doubtings, that nothing can set it down but that which is above the soul and above the devil. And therefore, for our salvation, and to give us comfort, there is a necessity of three persons in the Godhead. The Father is offended, God in the second person must satisfy offended justice, and God in the third person must reveal and apply that satisfaction for comfort. And therefore he names them distinctly, 'Ye believe in God,' &c. And because we cannot believe in God the Father but by believing in Christ, therefore he joins them together, 'Ye believe in God, ye believe also in me.' 'No man comes to the Father but by the Son,' John xiv. 6. God the Father dwells in the light that no mortal eye can approach unto; only he hath manifested himself in his Son, who is the engraven image of his person. God shines in the face of Christ, and as he comes down and makes himself known to us in his Son, so we must go up to him in his Son, as he saith afterwards, 'I am the way, the truth, and the life,' John xiv. 6. There is no going to the Father but by me. Nothing is more terrible than to conceive of God out of Christ, for so he is a 'consuming fire,' Heb xii. 29. Therefore think of God as ours in Christ. Carry Christ our elder brother with us, and desire God to look upon us in his Son.

Quest. Now, how doth faith in Christ ease the soul in trouble?

Ans. Many ways. I will name a few.

1. Faith in Christ *banisheth troubles, and bringeth in comfort,* because it is an emptying grace. It emptieth us of ourselves, and so makes us cleave to another, and thereby becomes a grace of union. It is such a grace as brings the soul and Christ together. Now, Christ being the fountain of comfort, God having treasured all comfort in him ('for the fulness of the

Godhead dwells in Christ,' Col. i. 19, and faith causeth Christ to dwell in us), brings the soul and Christ together, and so must needs make way for comfort. For it makes us one with the fountain of comfort, and by its repeated acts derives fresh comfort.

2. Again, faith *establisheth the heart*. Now, to establish the soul there must be a solid basis, as in building there must be a foundation, and a planting upon that foundation. Now here is a foundation, God and Christ; and there must be a grace to found and bottom the soul thereupon, and that is faith. And so the soul is established. The chain and connection of causes herein is this. God the Father in Christ, and by the Holy Ghost, conveys comforts, through the word laid hold upon by faith. It is not the word alone, for that is but as the veins and arteries that convey the blood and spirits. So the Spirit being conveyed by the promises, helpeth the soul to lay itself upon Christ by faith, which is a grace of union, by which union with him the soul is established.

3. And then, again, faith *stirreth up such graces as do comfort the soul*, as hope in all good things promised. And therefore in the next verse he adds, to comfort them, 'In my Father's house are many mansions,' and faith is the grace that apprehends the joys thereof; and hope expects that which faith believes, and that hope becomes an anchor to the soul, and stayeth the soul in all the waves and troubles of the world. And what is the ground of that hope but faith? Faith stirreth up hope, and hope pitcheth on the promise, especially of life everlasting. And thus faith becomes a quieting and a stilling grace, because it raiseth the soul, by representing and making real to it better things than the world can give or take, as it doth also at other times present heavier things than the world can threaten. Faith makes things present to the soul; and because it lays hold on divine things, greater than anything here below, therefore it overcomes the world, and all things in the world, yea, hell itself, because it lays hold on heaven and happiness, upon the power of God, and the mercy of God in Christ, and upon those rich promises. What is in the world, or in the rank of good things, but faith outbids it by setting heaven against it! and what evil is there but faith overcomes the fear of it by setting hell against it! I shall have such a good if I yield to such a lust. Aye, but what is that to heaven? saith faith. For faith being the hypostasis, the substance of things to come, makes them substantial and evident to the soul, as if they were already subsistent, being looked upon in the certainty of the word; and so it affects the soul deeply, and upholds it strongly, even as if the things themselves were present, and so it banisheth and dispels all discomforts. The 11th chapter to the Hebrews is a comment upon this truth in the example of Moses and many others. What greater object of fear might be presented to a man than the angry face and countenance of a terrible tyrant? Yet when by the eye of faith he saw him that was invisible, and then looked upon Pharaoh, what was Pharaoh to God? When Micaiah had seen God sitting on his throne, what was Ahab to him? And when the soul hath entered into the vail, and sees the glorious things of heaven and happiness, what are all things below? Faith sets the soul on a rock, above the reach of waves, upon the love of God in Christ. And therefore set the grace of faith on work, keep it on the wing, preserve it on exercise; and faith exercised will be able to comfort the most dejected soul in the world, and to raise it above all the troubles that can be imagined or befall us.

* Qu. 'in?'—G.

THE SECOND SERMON.

Let not your hearts be troubled : ye believe in God, believe also in me.—
JOHN XIV. 1.

THE words of dying men departing out of the world, as being the most serious and weighty, are most to be regarded. The children of God, the nearer they are to heaven, the more suitable they are to their heavenly condition. So was our Saviour Christ; and therefore he labours to furnish his disciples, and in them us, with good counsel to establish their hearts against the troubles and scandals to come. [This will appear] if you consider the time when he spake these words. It was when he himself was to be troubled more than ever was any creature. Yet he forgets himself and his future troubles, and thinks how to raise up and comfort them. He foresaw that Peter would deny him, that the rest would leave him; he foresaw that they would be dejected when he was gone. Yet 'let not your hearts be troubled.'

Oh, what a blessed and sweet Saviour have we, that thinks more of us than of himself, that he forgets his own troubles, and sufferings, and extremities, and thinks of the supporting and upholding of his disciples!

This came from the same love that drew him from heaven to earth, which moved him to take our nature, and in that nature to die for us. And what may we not expect from that sweet and large love? Out of the same bowels of pity and compassion was it (that they should not be overmuch dejected) that he saith, 'Let not your hearts be troubled.'

He knew his disciples were in the state of grace already, yet he foresaw they were such as would sin; nay, that Peter would deny him. Yet the foresight of Peter's and their unkindness did not take away his love, and pity, and compassion towards them. Yet, notwithstanding, he gives them sweet counsel; nay, after they had dealt unkindly with him, and denied and forsook him indeed, he took no advantage of their weakness. He knew they had a secret love to him, that they had in them a root of affection; and he was so far from taking advantage for it that presently after he saith, 'Tell my brethren that I ascend to my God and their God,' yea, and 'tell Peter so too,' John xx. 17, that hath dealt most unkindly of all with me. What a gracious and merciful Saviour have we, that foresees what ill we will do, and when we have done it, takes no advantage against us, but is careful to keep us from too much dejection, though he knew we would deal so unkindly by him! And, indeed, he did of purpose take our nature, that he might be a merciful High Priest.

Christians must distinguish betwixt *dejection* and *grief*. It had been a sin for them not to have grieved, as well as it was a sin for them to be over-much troubled. None are more sensible than a Christian. *Sentit dum vincit.* He feels troubles whiles he overcomes them.

Christ speaks to the heart, because the heart is the seat of trouble, 'Let not your *hearts* be troubled.'

Christ could speak to the ears and heart at once. His words were operative, and conveyed comfort with them. Together with his words, he let in his Holy Spirit, that comforted them. God's commands in the ministry of his word, suppose not that we have any ability to execute them, but together with his word there comes forth a power. As when Christ said, 'Lazarus, arise!' there went forth a power that caused Lazarus to arise; as in the creation he said, 'Let there be light;' for the word and the Spirit go together.

Having taken them off from trouble, he shews a way how to raise them, which is by faith, 'Ye believe in God, believe also in me.'

The object in believing is God, and Christ Mediator. We must have both to found our faith upon. We cannot believe in God, except we believe in Christ. For God must be satisfied by God, and by him that is God must that satisfaction be applied, the Spirit of God, by working faith in the heart, and for the raising of it up when it is dejected. All is supernatural in faith. The things we believe are above nature; the promises are above nature; the worker of it, the Holy Ghost, is above nature; and everything in faith is above nature. There must be a God in whom we believe; and a God through whom. If God had not satisfied God, the conscience would never have been satisfied; there would still have been misdoubtings. And yet if the Holy Ghost sets not down the heart, and convinceth it throughly of the all-sufficiency of that satisfaction, it would never believe neither. And, therefore, as 'ye believe in God, believe also in me,' for I am God too.

We may know that Christ is God, not only by that which Christ hath done, the miracles, which none could do but God, but also by what is done to him. And two things are done to him, which shew that he is God; that is, faith and prayer. We must believe only in God, and pray only to God. But Christ is the object of both these. Here he is set forth as the object of faith, and of prayer in that of Saint Stephen: 'Lord Jesus, receive my spirit,' Acts vii. 59. And, therefore, he is God; for that is done unto him, which is proper and peculiar only to God.

That which I shall now touch upon is this: We must remember what a strong foundation, what bottom, and basis, our faith hath. There is God the Father, Son, and Holy Ghost, and Christ the Mediator. That our faith may be supported, we have him to believe on who supports heaven and earth, as in Heb. i. 2, and Col. i. 16, 17. He created all things as well as the Father. He is honoured of all as well as the Father. He that supports the pillars of heaven and earth is able to support the pillars of thy soul.

But how doth faith in Christ ease the soul of trouble?

In a word, *as it carrieth the soul out of itself unto God in Christ, and unto Christ*, uniting and making us one with him, and so sets the soul above all trouble whatsoever. For, being one with Christ, we are already with him in heaven. And again, faith is a grace that *presents things to come, as pre-*

sent, and so establisheth the soul. It is the hypostasis of things, it gives subsistence to them in the promise, and it doth never leave to do it till the things subsist indeed. It is a grace that accompanieth the soul to heaven, looking upon things in the word of him that is truth itself, and so giving a kind of being to them, throughout all the way to heaven, till they have a being indeed. And then faith is out of office, yielding it up to sight, and the full enjoyment of all.

Quest. But did not the disciples believe already?

Ans. Yes, they did. But they had need to renew their faith, as occasions were renewed, and as troubles were to increase. 'Believe in me.' It is as he should have said: 'Now there is occasion for you to use your faith. I must be taken out of your sight. You must see me suffer. And you had need of an extraordinary measure of faith to see me in such abasement, and yet to believe that I am God.'

We must grow from faith to faith, that we may live by it continually; and we must increase with the increase of God, that as our difficulties do increase, our strength to go through them may increase also; as they prayed, 'Lord, increase our faith,' Luke xvii. 5.

I give some directions how we might not be troubled.

And first, we must labour to have our *part and portion in Christ*, else there is nothing belongs to us but trouble. There are two sorts of men in the church, some that usurp a peace and exemption from trouble, as if joy and comfort were their portion. Satan is wise enough not to trouble them, and they take an order with their consciences, that they shall not trouble them till needs must, till the hour of death, or some dismal accident. The only way for such is to be troubled, that their trouble may be a foundation of their comfort. For to such as live in their sins against conscience, apparently* so, that every man may see it, and yet are not troubled, they have no interest in comfort. Nothing but woe and misery belongs to them. Indeed, Christ came to save sinners, but it is broken-hearted sinners, penitent sinners, that are weary and heavy laden under the burden of sin. And, therefore, though they speak peace to themselves, yet we dare not speak any comfort to them from Christ. As Jehu said to Joram, 'What hast thou to do with peace, as long as the whoredoms of thy mother Jezebel are so many?' 2 Kings ix. 22. Dost thou talk of peace as long as thou art a swearer, a profane liver, a malicious person, against all that are truly good? What hast thou to do with peace?

Now, in the visible church, there is another sort that Satan laboureth to trouble. Since he cannot keep them in the state of nature, but they break from him—Christ pulling them out of Satan's kingdom by the power of his ordinances and Holy Spirit—he labours to trouble them in their peace all he can. Because they be, in the world, above the world, he envies their condition, that they should enjoy that paradise which he left, the comforts that he once had; and, therefore. he labours to disturb them in their comforts.

The estate of such is mixed here in this world. They have that in them, and without them, which will always be a cause and occasion of trouble. They have corruption in them not altogether subdued; and they have without them Satan taking advantage against them; and the world opposing them. These, although they have something in them that must be subdued, yet something also that must be cherished and strengthened. And therefore these are the persons to whom comfort properly belongs.

In heaven we shall have no need of being comforted, for there our peace

* That is, 'openly.'—G.

shall be to have no enemies at all. Our peace here is to have comfort in the midst of discomfort, and an heart enlarged in troubles.

He speaks this to them here who were believers already; ('Ye believe in God'), who he knew should not be troubled, ('Let not your hearts be troubled'). So that to the end we may be subjects capable of comfort, we must be such as by faith are one with Christ; and so reconciled to God. All motion ends in rest, and all the rest of the soul ends in God,—the centre of the soul. And therefore before the soul can settle itself, it must be brought to God, through Christ. That must be laid as a ground.

Now there is a threefold malady that troubleth us, and there must a threefold peace, and ground of comfort against them.

First, it is a trouble to the soul (when once it is awakened), that God and it should be in ill terms; when the soul looks upon God as angry, and displeased with it.

Secondly, Again, the soul is troubled, when it looks upon itself, and sees nothing but turmoils and seditions there.

Thirdly, when it looks upon the affairs of the world, and accidents here below, it is full of confusion for the present; and it is full of fears for time to come, that things will be worse and worse. Thus the soul, whilst it is in the world, is troubled about its peace with God, and with itself, and about this evil world.

Now before the soul can yield to any quiet, all these quarrels must be taken up.

First, a peace must be made betwixt God and us, by the great Peacemaker, who is also called 'our peace,' Eph. ii. 14; and when we be justified and acquitted from our sins by the blood of Christ, sprinkled on our souls by faith, that blood of Christ speaks peace to the soul in the pardon of sin; 'being justified by faith, we have peace with God, through Jesus Christ our Lord,' Rom. v. 1.

Then *secondly*, there must be another peace settled in some degree, and that is the *peace of government in the soul;* grace must be above corruption. They will be together in the soul whilst we are here, but sin must not have the dominion. This is such a peace, not as will admit of no conflict, but a peace wherein grace may get the better; and where grace gets the better, it will keep corruption under. And God gives his Spirit to whom he gives his Son; that as we be in good terms with God, so our natures may be like his; that we may love and delight in what he loves and delights in; and so may be as friends, enjoying acquaintance and communion together.

Aye, but *thirdly*, there is confusion in the world, and many accidents may fall out, that may disquiet us for time to come. Now before the soul can be at peace in that respect, *it must know that, being once in Christ, reconciled to God, and having the Spirit of God, it is under a gracious government and providence, that disposeth all things to good, and maketh everything peaceable. Tranquillus Deus tranquillat omnia* When God is at peace, all is at peace; yea, so far at peace, that they have a blessing in them. The curse and venom is taken out of them by Christ, who took the curse on himself, and satisfied the wrath of God; and now they be not only harmless, but medicinal, and helpful, so that they be all ours, and made in some sort serviceable to further our spiritual good.

When our husband hath all things committed unto him in heaven or earth, will he suffer anything to befall his dearly beloved spouse, that shall be disadvantageous, and prejudicial to the main? No, no; he will not suffer anything to befall her, which he will not rule, and order, and overrule for the good of the church; and so there comes to be that third peace.

And, for the time to come, a Christian knows, that whom 'Christ loves, he loves to the end,' John xiii. 1; and 'the good work begun shall be perfected to the day of the Lord,' Philip. i. 6. He knoweth he is in heaven already in his head. 'He that believes in Christ hath everlasting life,' John iii. 36, and is triumphing in glory in his head.

And, therefore, nothing can dismay a Christian that is truly in Christ. Grant the first, grant all. Stand upon good terms with Christ; be reconciled to God, and nothing can do thee hurt.

But when we at any time come to comfort such as have comfort for their portion, it sticks here. If I were a child of God indeed, or if I did believe, it were something. These be good comforts indeed, and certain, and true, for they be the word of God; but what is this to me? I find universally, that comfort sticks there, and therefore we must labour to remove that objection.

First of all, therefore, labour to have *a good judgment of main truths*: that these comforts are the comforts of the Holy Ghost, and that the word is the word of God. By a general knowledge of the truth of the promises, thou shalt be better able to apply them. If thou stick in the principles, so as not to know them, nor to believe them, there is no talking of the application of faith upon them. We must make that our own in particular, which we believe first in general. And therefore Christians must first be well seen in the Scriptures, and in the promises there, that they may know what belongs to them, and apply them to themselves.

Aye, but my faith is weak.

1. I answer, The office of faith is to knit to Christ, and the weakest faith will do that, as well as the strongest: and when we are once one with Christ, then our perfection is to be found in him. It is the office of faith to bring us to Christ; and then to look to him for all perfections and for thy title to heaven, and not to faith; and true faith is faith even in the least degree of it. As we say of the elements, every drop of water is water, and every spark of fire is fire. And, therefore, the argument will not hold, if we have not much faith, we have no faith; or if we have no feeling, we have no faith. There are many common errors which we must remove, that they may not hinder us in the application of Christ, by distinguishing between strong grace and true grace; and, above all, labour to know and understand the covenant of grace; the tenor of which requireth no set measures of grace; but 'if we believe, we shall not perish, but have everlasting life,' under so gracious and merciful a covenant are we.

2. But this is not sufficient to satisfy the soul. The very cleaving to Christ is indeed a sufficient ground of comfort, but yet to obtain actual comfort, *there must be a knowledge that we do cleave to Christ, and believe.* There may be adherence without evidence; and there must be an act of reflection to cause faith of evidence. It must appear to ourselves that we do believe before we can have comfort, though we may be true Christians, and go to heaven without it. Therefore, let us labour 'to make our calling and election sure,' 2 Pet. i. 10; that is, in ourselves, and in our own apprehension. Though it be never so sure in itself, and in God's breast, yet we must labour to make it sure in our own breasts; that sin may be pardoned in our own consciences; that all may be reconciled in our own hearts; that what is done in heaven may be done in our own hearts also being cleared to our own assurance. You see what advice the apostle gives 'Give all diligence.' It is not got without diligence, nor without 'all diligence, to make our calling and election sure,' that is, to make our election

sure by our calling, and to that end 'to add grace to grace,' 2 Pet. i. 5. It is the growing Christian that is the assured Christian. Whilst we are yet adding to every heap, 'we shall get more abundant entrance,' 2 Pet. i. 11, and further into the kingdom of Jesus Christ, as the apostle there speaks.

3. And when we have attained any evidence of true faith, labour to *keep that our evidence clear.* Let it not be spotted or defiled by any sinful acts. You have many a good evidence that is so blurred with negligences, and daily errors in speeches and conversation, that when they reflect upon themselves they conclude, Can such a wretch as I, that have so loose a tongue, that have no more watchfulness over my heart, have any faith at all? And thus God doth suspend their comforts so, that though they may be in a good estate for the main, yet they shall not know it; and all because they are not careful to keep their evidence, which we should preserve clear and bright, that it might be seen and read upon all occasions. And we should so keep them bright, that our consciences may witness with us, and that the Spirit and the word may join their witness with our consciences. The word saith, 'that he that loves the brethren is translated to life,' 1 John ii. 10, and he that hears the word, as the word, is Christ's sheep. Now, doth thy conscience tell thee, that though in weak measure, yet I do so? Then, here is the word, and thy conscience for thee. And doth the Spirit witness with thy conscience that it is so indeed? Then it is well. Thou keepest thy evidence to purpose.

4. And when we have done this, let us make conscience not *to yield to any base doubts, and fears, and objections of Satan, and our own hearts.* When we find any work of grace, deny not the work of God, lest we grieve the Spirit of God; as some melancholy Christians, that though every man may see the work of God in them, yet yield so slavishly to the misgivings of their hearts, and the temptations of Satan, that they conclude they have no faith, no love; though other Christians that can read their evidence better, see that they have these in them. What dishonour is this to God and his Spirit, when a dark humour shall prevail more than the word, the truth itself? This is a great bondage which Satan brings the soul into: that when there is evidence of faith in the fruits of it, yet men will believe a peevish humour, before the word and testimony of conscience, enlightened by the Spirit. Take heed of it as a great pride in the heart, when we yield more to a sturdy, dark, unsubdued humour, than to evidence itself.

Therefore in such cases hearken not to what fear says, or humour saith, or Satan saith, or what the world saith, but hearken what truth itself saith, and what conscience saith, when it is enlightened by the Spirit, as in good times when we are at the best. True Christians, though more remiss, shall have so much comfort as shall support them from falling into despair, yet not so much as shall strengthen them, and carry them into a vigorous life, fit for Christians.

5. When we have found any work of grace; and thereupon that our faith is true, *we ought to comfort ourselves, and to maintain our comfort by all means.* Every grace is but faith exercised. When our Saviour saith, 'Ye believe in God, believe also in me,' he might have said also in particular, Be patient, be contented, be comforted. But he names the root of all—Faith—wherein all graces are radically; which is therefore discerned in the fruits of it. So that if any grace be found, as love to the brethren, hope of life everlasting, or the like, there is faith. For the root and branches be together, though the root is not always discerned. And therefore when

we discover any true faith in the fruit of it, let us support and comfort ourselves with it.

For when a man is in Christ, and by Christ an heir of heaven, and a child of God, what in the world can befall him, that should deject overmuch, and cast him down? What loss, what cross, what want of friends? Hath he not all in God, and in Christ, and in the promise? Do not the promises weigh down all discouragements whatsoever? Surely they do. And therefore we must strive against dejection. For besides what I spake the last day, it is a dishonour to the profession of religion, which is in itself so glorious; a dishonour to God, and to Christ, that when we have such glorious prerogatives and privileges, which the angels themselves admire, yet every petty cross and loss that we meet withal in the world should cast us down. We should take heed exceedingly of this, and should labour every day to have a more and more clear sight of the promises that belong unto us, and to know the privileges of Christianity, and renew our faith in them continually, that they may be fresh to us in all temptations, and occasions whatsoever.

I beseech you, do but consider any one grand promise; which if it be rooted in the soul, how it is able to support the soul against all troubles whatsoever. As that, 'Fear not, little flock, for it is your Father's good pleasure to give you the kingdom,' Luke xii. 32. Or that other, 'If God spared not his Son for us, how will he not with him give us all things else?' Rom. viii. 32.

Labour to have these things fresh in memory, together with the privileges belonging to Christians. Think what it is to be a child of God, and an heir of heaven!

We must not look only to the blind and dark side of our condition. Christians have two sides, one to heaven-ward and God-ward; and that is full of glory, certain and immoveable. Another towards the world; and that is oftentimes full of abasement, full of disgrace, and dejection. That is moveable; sometimes better, sometimes worse, as God pleaseth to dispense his government in the church. Let us look to the grace, to the comforts that belong to that grace; to the promises; the best side; and not to be carried away with the darkness of the other.

It is a terrible sight to look upon sin, and misery, and hell, and judgment to come; but what are these to a Christian that is in Christ, that seeth them all subdued, and overcome to him? The afflictions of the world, and the crosses of the world, what are they to a soul, that is already in heaven by faith, and seeth them all overcome in his head Christ? 'Be of good comfort, I have overcome the world,' John xvi. 33. And therefore we must not be so malignant, as to look all upon one part of a Christian, and that the worser part, which is the object of sense. For shame, live not by sense! But if we be Christians, let us live by faith, look to the best part; look upwards and forwards to that which is eternal.

6. And withal labour to keep the graces of the Spirit *in continual exercise upon all occasions*. For grace exercised, brings certain comfort. It may be with a Christian in his feelings as with the worst man living; but he may thank his own negligence, his own dulness; his not stirring up of the graces of God in him. For therefore it is that he hangs the wing upon every petty cross, on every occasion. Labour to have an heart ready to exercise grace suitable to that occasion. For then grace will reflect sweetly, where there is sincerity and grace in exercise. Sincerity alone will not comfort a man, unless it grow up to fruitfulness; and fruitfulness which springs from the exercise of grace, hath

a sweet reflection upon the soul. 'Remember, Lord, how I walked before thee, in truth, and with a perfect heart,' saith Hezekiah, 2 Kings xx. 3. He stood then most in need of comfort; and this comforted him; this his reflection upon his former sincerity. So when a man can appeal unto God, as Peter did, 'Lord, thou knowest I love thee,' John xxi. 17. So much sincerity, so much boldness with God. And therefore let us keep grace in exercise, that we may be fruitful in our lives and conversations, and then we shall be always comfortable.

And to add a little, there is no grace in a Christian but, if it be exercised, there is a suitable comfort upon it even here in this world. There is a *præmium ante præmium*, a reward before a reward. Nay, the heathen men, Socrates and the best of them, so far as they exercised the natural goodness that was in them, their consciences reflected peace; so far as they were good, and did good, they had peace, much more peace than bad men had. God gave even them some rewards upon discharge of their duties. He will not be beholden to any man that exerciseth any degree of goodness that is in him. Much more therefore shall a child of God enjoy it, when he exerciseth his graces in any temptation. When he overcomes any unclean, earthly, vainglorious, vindictive, or any other base lust, he shall find peace of conscience suitable. And the more he grows in strength and resolution for the time to come, the more he groweth in inward peace. Righteousness and peace go together; not only the righteousness of Christ and our reconciliation before God, but also the righteousness of an holy life and peace in our own consciences.

The righteousness of Christ entitles to heaven; and the righteousness of an holy life sheweth my title unto comfort. As faith in Christ's righteousness brings peace, so sanctification also. Christ is first 'King of righteousness,' and then 'King of peace,' Heb. vii. 1. And therefore where there is no righteousness, there is no peace. But, on the contrary, as heat followeth the fire, and as the beams have an emanation from the sun, so doth comfort arise from grace, especially from grace exercised.

Therefore they that would have inward peace, let them labour to be gracious; and that not only in the inward frame of the heart, but in the exercise of grace upon all occasions. 'For they that walk according to this rule,' that is, of the new creature, 'peace be to them, and the whole Israel of God,' Gal. vi. 16. An exact and careful life will bring constant peace.

Therefore let us labour first for interest in Christ's righteousness, and then for the righteousness of an holy life; for a conscience to justify us, that we have no purpose to live in any sin; and a not accusing conscience will be a justifying conscience. What a blessed condition shall we be in, to be in Christ, and to know that we are so! O the heaven on earth of such a man as is in that condition! For which way soever he looks, he finds matter of comfort. If he looks backward, to the government of the Spirit that hath ruled him in the former part of his life, he may say with St Paul, 'I have fought a good fight, I have run the race that God hath set before me,' 2 Tim. iv. 7. And what a sweet reflection is this! He is not afraid to look back to his life past as other men. If he looks forward, he seeth a place prepared for him in heaven, and there he sees himself already in Christ. Henceforth 'there is laid up for me a crown of righteousness, which the righteous Judge shall give me at that day,' ver. 8; and all that love his appearing, saith he, there. When there comes ill tidings of the church abroad and at home, it doth not much dismay him. His heart is fixed; he believeth in God and in Christ, and that keeps him from being like a reed shaken with every wind. For reproaches and disgraces that he meets withal in the world, he wears them as his crown, if they be for religion and goodness' sake. For his witness is in heaven, and in his own conscience. And God in heaven, and his conscience within, do acquit him; and if he suffer for his deserts, yet in all afflictions God dealeth with him as a correcting Father. He knoweth he hath deserved them, but he looks on them as coming from a Father in covenant with him. And what can come from a father but what is sweet? He sees it moderated and sweetened, and in the issue tending to make him more holy. The sting is taken out, and a blessing is upon it, to make him better. And therefore what can make a Christian uncomfortable, when he hath the Spirit of Christ, and faith, the root of grace?

These comforts being warmed with meditation, will stick close to the heart. Comforts that are digested are they that work. Let them therefore not only enter into the brain and fleet* there, but let them sink into the heart, by often consideration of God's love in Christ, and the privileges of Christians here and in heaven, where our Head is, and where we shall be ere long. Warm the heart with these, and see if any petty thing can cast thee down!

* That is, 'flit.'—G.

THE SAINT'S PRIVILEGE.*

When he is come, he shall reprove the world of sin, righteousness, and judgment: of sin, because they believe not in me; of righteousness, because I go to my Father; of judgment, because the prince of this world is judged. Especially the 10th verse. *Of righteousness, because I go to my Father, and you shall see me no more.*—JOHN XVI. 8–10.

OUR blessed Saviour descending from heaven to earth for the redemption of man, after he had accomplished that great work, he ascended thither again. And knowing his disciples would take his departure very heavily, he labours to arm them against the assaults of all grief and sorrow that might otherwise oppress them; and that by many arguments. Among the rest, this is not the least, that when he is gone away he will 'send the Comforter unto them.' God never takes away anything from his children but he sends them a better. And this Comforter whom he promised to send shall bear them through in all their ministry, all function; and in effect he thus bespeaks them. You my disciples are to encounter with the world; be of good comfort, my Spirit shall go along with you, and 'he shall reprove the world of sin, righteousness, and judgment.' Of yourselves you are too weak, but the Spirit shall strengthen you, and make way into the hearts of those that shall be saved, by convincing them of 'sin, righteousness, and judgment.' So that be not discouraged; the Spirit shall breathe courage into you, and make way for your doctrine. 'When the Comforter is come, he shall reprove the world of sin, and of righteousness, and judgment: of sin, because they believe not in me; of righteousness, because I go to the Father; of judgment, because the prince of this world is judged.'

* 'The Saint's Privilege' appears to have been a favourite with the public. Besides more modern reprints, I possess the following editions:—(1.) 1638, 18mo. Its title-page is as follows:—'The Saints Priviledge or a Christians constant Advocate; Containing a short but most sweet direction for every true Christian to walke comfortably through this valley of teares. By the faithfull and Reverend Divine R. Sibs, D.D. and sometime Preacher to the Honourable Society of Grayes-Inn. London, Printed by G M for George Edwards dwelling in Green-Arbour at the signe of the Angell. 1638.' (2.) 1638, 4to. (3.) 1641, 4to. (4.) 1650. Appended to successive editions of 'The Returning Backslider. (Cf. Vol. II. page 250.) The *first* edition, which is our text, has Marshall's portrait of Sibbes prefixed, with the usual inscription.—G.

There are three main parts of salvation.

Knowledge of our misery, knowledge of our deliverance, and a life answerable. The Holy Ghost shall work all these. He shall convince the world of their own sin, of righteousness by a mediator, and of a reformation of life. So that the Holy Ghost shall go along with you in the carriage of the whole business of man's salvation. Where he begins, he makes an end. Where he convinces of sin, he convinces of righteousness, and then of a necessity of a reformation. He bears all afore him, and he doth it in a spiritual order.

1. First, He 'convinces the world of sin,' then 'of righteousness,' then 'of judgment;' because it were in vain to convince of the righteousness of Christ unless he hath before convinced of sin. For who cares for balm that is not wounded? Who cares for a pardon that is not condemned? Therefore he convinces of sin first. I have spoken heretofore of convincing of sin.

Here is a threefold convincing; of sin, of righteousness, and of judgment; and every one of these hath a reason added thereto. 'Of sin, because they believe not in me;' 'of righteousness, because I go to my Father;' 'of judgment, because the prince of this world is judged.'

The Holy Ghost begins with convincing of sin. What is this convincing? It is a clear and infallible demonstration of our condition. It brings a commanding light into the soul. It sets down the soul and takes away all cavils, all turnings and windings. To 'convince' is to make a man, as the psalmist's* phrase is, 'lay his hand upon his mouth.' Light is a convincing thing. Now we see the sun we see it is day. Though ten thousand men should say it is not day, we would not believe them, because the convincing hereof is undeniable, that he must be an unreasonable man that gainsays it.

So then, the Spirit of God brings a commanding light into the soul undeniable. Thou art thus and thus; here no shifting, no winding and turning will serve the turn when the Holy Ghost comes with this light. I do but plainly unfold this.

This conviction of the Holy Ghost is not in general only, that all men are sinners, but particular and strong. 'Thou art a sinner, and thou art in danger of damnation.' And it is universal, taking in sins of nature, sins of life, sins of the understanding, will, and affections; and it is not of sin only, but of the misery by sin, of the danger, folly, and madness of sin, and of the aggravations that greaten sin, as of stifling so many good motions, withstanding so many means, abusing so many mercies. The Holy Ghost convinces us thoroughly, that we can have nothing to reply. Because I have spoken of this before, I am short. Beloved, unless the Holy Ghost 'convince,' there will be no convincing. Our deceitful hearts have so many windings and turnings; proud nature arms itself with defences, as a hedgehog winds himself round and defends himself by his pricks. So you have many clothe themselves with strong words, ill translations upon others,† frivolous mitigations; the way of the multitude, as with a coat of mail to keep out this conviction, that did not the Holy Ghost strike in hard with their consciences, 'Thou art the man,' this work would never be done.

Quest. But you will ask me this question, How shall we know common conviction of conscience from this of the Spirit? For carnal men that go

* Qu. 'Job'?—Ed.

† That is, 'blaming others.' Cf. Genesis iii. 12, *seq.*—G.

to hell are 'convinced' by a common conviction. What is this saving conviction?

Ans. Difference 1. I answer, *common conviction by the light of nature is a weak conviction.* A little spark will shew a little light, but it will not enlighten a room. It must be the work of some greater light, as the sun. The Spirit is a strong light, stronger than natural conscience. Natural conscience, and common light, is of some breaches of the second table. Natural conscience never 'convinces' of corrupt nature, but the Spirit doth most of all, as you may see in David, Ps. li. 5, he resolves all into this, as if he should say, What should I tell you of my murder and adultery, 'in sin did my mother conceive me;' so a true Christian doth not look to the branches so much as to the root.

Difference 2. Then again, *a natural conscience, when it convinceth a man, it is against his will.* It makes him not the better man. He mends not upon it, but he is tortured and tormented. But a man that is 'convinced' by the Holy Ghost, he takes God's part against himself; he is willing to be laid open that he may find the greater mercy. So that there is a grand difference between common conviction of nature and the conviction of the Spirit. The conviction of the Spirit is the light of the Spirit, which is of a higher nature than that of natural conscience: 'I will send the Comforter,' when he comes he will greatly enlighten and overpower the soul.

Difference 3. Again, *the conviction of the Spirit sticks by a man*, it never leaves the soul. But that of an ordinary conscience it is but for a flash, and after they are worse than they were before.

I must cut off these things, because the time is always past upon these occasions before we begin.

Use 1. Come we therefore to make some *use.* The Spirit doth '*convince* of sin.' But how? By the ministry ordinarily, though not alone by the ministry. Therefore we must labour willingly to submit to the ministry 'convincing of sin.' Conscience will convince first or last. Is it not better to have a saving conviction now to purpose, than to have a bare desperate conviction in hell? Oh, beloved, all the admonitions we hear, if we regard them not now, we shall hereafter. Therefore labour to make good use of this 'sword of the Spirit' of God; and it is an argument of a good heart to wish, Oh that the ministry might meet with my corruption; that it may be discovered to me to the full. A true heart thinks sin the greatest enemy, and of all other miseries it desires to be freed from the thraldom thereof. For that defiles heaven and earth, and separates God from his creature. It is that that threw angels out of heaven, Adam out of paradise. What embitters blessings, and puts a sting into all afflictions but sin? If it were not for sin, we would take up any cross, and bear any affliction more quietly than we do.

Therefore as we desire to be saved, and to stand with comfort before God at the day of judgment, let us desire and endeavour to be thoroughly convinced of sin. Take heed of resisting the Spirit of God in the ministry. Why are many led captive of their lusts, but because they hate the ministry of the word? They look upon it as Ahab did upon Elias: 'Hast thou found me, O my enemy,' 1 Kings xxi. 20. They naturally are in love with their sins, and there is none so much hated as those that present themselves. A man, take him in his pure naturals, is a foolish creature; his heart rises against conviction. You see the pharisees, wise men, learned men, being convinced, they hated Christ to the death. Why? Because he did untomb them and discover the dead men's bones within, Mat. xxiii. 27.

So many now-a-days, that are convinced, hate any that by life or speech discover their sins unto them, if it were possible, and in their power, to the death. Thus the Holy Ghost convinces of sin. But before I leave this point, let me add this from the reason or ground of this conviction, 'Because they believe not in me.' That unbelief makes all other sins damnable. No sin is damnable if we could believe and repent. Therefore we are convinced of sin, because we do not believe; as we say of a man that is condemned, because he cannot read, therefore he is condemned. He should escape if he could read, being for no great fault.* So it is here. It is not believing in Christ and repenting makes all other sins deadly.

The differing of one man from another is their faith and repentance. Some there be whose sins are greater than others, yet by the Spirit of God and faith, they work them out every day. It is faith in the 'brazen serpent' that takes away the sting of the fiery serpents, Num. xxi. 9.

I have done with the conviction of sin. Let us now come to speak of the conviction of righteousness.

'Of righteousness, because I go to my Father, and you shall see me no more.' It is a fit time for the Holy Ghost to convince God's people of righteousness when they are convinced of sin before. Then they can relish Christ. Balm is balm indeed when the wound is discovered and felt. Oh then a pardon is welcome when the party is condemned. The reason of this conviction of righteousness is, 'because I go to my Father, and you shall see me no more.' The Holy Ghost, as he sets on sin upon the conscience, so he takes off sin by applying to the conscience the righteousness of Christ. This is his office, first, to convince the world of sin, and then to convince of righteousness, whereby we stand righteous before God.

And this righteousness here, is not our own inherent, but the righteousness of Christ a Mediator, God and man.

The Holy Ghost convinces of righteousness in this order of a fourfold gradation.

First, That there must be a righteousness, and a full righteousness.

The second is this, that there is no such righteousness in the creature.

Thirdly, That this is to be had in Christ the Mediator.

Fourthly, That this righteousness is our righteousness.

1. First, *There must be a righteousness;* for we have to deal with a God who is righteousness itself; and no unclean thing shall come into heaven, Rev. xxi. 7. Unless we have a righteousness, how shall we look God in the face, or how can we escape hell?

2. Now for the second, *that it is not in any creature, men or angels.* We have not a righteousness of our own; for there are divers things to be satisfied, God himself, and the law, and our own consciences, and the world. Perhaps we may have a righteousness to satisfy the world, because we live civilly.† Oh but that will not satisfy conscience. And then there must be a satisfaction to the law, which is a large thing that condemns our thoughts, desires, but God is the most perfect of all. Put case we have a righteousness of a good carriage among men; this will not satisfy God and the law; it will not satisfy conscience. Men they are our fellow-prisoners. Conscience will not be contented but with that which will content God, when conscience sees there is such a righteousness found out by the wisdom of God, that contents him, else conscience will be always in doubts and fears.

3. Thirdly, *This righteousness is to be had in Christ.* What is the right-

* The reference is to 'Benefit of Clergy.' Cf. note, Vol. V. page 408.—G.

† That is, 'morally.'—G.

eousness of Christ? The righteousness of Christ is that righteousness that is founded upon his obedience: active, fulfilling the law; and passive, discharging all our debts, satisfying God's justice. The meritoriousness of both of them is founded upon the purity of his nature. All his sufferings and doings had their excellency from the personal union of God and man; in reference to which union we may without blasphemy aver that God performed the law, God died for us.

4. Fourthly and lastly, *This righteousness is our righteousness.* The Spirit convinces that this belongs to all believers, for* it is better than Adam had. His righteousness was the righteousness of a man, this righteousness is the righteousness of a mediator; and it is such a righteousness, that when we are clothed with it, we may go through the justice of God. We may have access with boldness to the throne of grace, and say, 'Lord, I come in the righteousness of Christ, that hath appeased thy wrath and satisfied thy justice. This the Holy Ghost convinces of.

Quest. But you will ask me, How doth the Holy Ghost 'convince' me of the righteousness of Christ?

Ans. I answer, first, the Holy Ghost *presents to the soul the knowledge of this excellent righteousness, and then creates a hand of faith to embrace it, being proposed.* You that are humble and broken-hearted sinners, here is Christ for you. The Spirit of God doth not only reveal the excellency of Christ, but that this belongs to me, that Christ is given for me, and that 'revelation of the Spirit' doth sway the soul; when the Spirit doth not tell in general only that Christ is an excellent Saviour, but shall relate to a Christian soul, God gave Christ for thee. This sways the heart to rest upon Christ, whereupon the marriage is made up between the soul and Christ. The soul says, 'I am Christ's, and I give myself to Christ,' and to whatsoever accompanies Christ. And then as it is in marriage, the persons, by virtue of that relation, have interest into each other's substance and estate; so when this mystical marriage is made up between Christ and us, we have a right unto Christ by all rights, by titles of purchase and redemption. He hath purchased heaven for us, and us for heaven. All that Christ hath is ours; all his good is ours; our sins his, and his righteousness ours. So when the Holy Ghost convinces me of Christ's righteousness, and gives me faith to embrace it, then Christ is mine with all he hath. By this I have spoken, you may see how the Spirit convinces. Do but imagine what a blessed condition the soul is in when this match is made!

But you will ask me why is the sending of the Spirit necessary for the 'convincing of this righteousness'?

I answer, for divers reasons.

Reason 1. First, *Because it is above the conceit*† *of man* that there should be such a righteousness of God-man. Therefore it is discovered by the Spirit; and when it is discovered, the Spirit must open the eyes of the soul to see, else we shall have a natural knowledge of supernatural things; for a man, by a natural knowledge, may understand them, so as to be able to discourse of them; therefore, to change the soul, there must be a supernatural sight to see supernatural things. A devil incarnate may know all things, and yet want to see. Only the Holy Ghost gives inward sight, inward eyes, and works faith to see Christ as mine.

Reason 2. Again, the sending of the Holy Ghost is necessary for this conviction; *because he alone must set down the soul and make the conscience*

* Qu. 'and'?—G. † That is, 'conception.'—G.

quiet, who is greater than the conscience. Conscience will clamour, 'Thou art a sinner;' the Holy Ghost convinces, 'In Christ thou art righteous.' The Holy Ghost only knows what is in the heart of God the Father, and in the heart of every man. He only knows the intent of the Father to every Christian, and can answer all inward objections and cavils of flesh and blood raised up against the soul; therefore the convincing of the Holy Ghost is necessary. Howsoever Christ hath purchased our peace, yet the Holy Ghost must apply it; for the conscience is so full of clamours, that unless the Holy Ghost apply what Christ hath done, conscience will not be satisfied. God the Father hath appointed Christ, and Christ hath wrought it; but the third person must apply it to the soul, to assure us that this belongs to us. The application of all good things to the soul that Christ the Son hath wrought, is the proper office of the Third Person. In civil contracts here, there must not only be a purchase, but a seal. Though Christ hath wrought righteousness for us, the Spirit must seal it to every soul: 'This righteousness belongs to you;' 'Christ is yours, with all that is his.'

Reason 3. Again, it must needs be a work of the Spirit; *because flesh and blood is full of pride, and would fain have some righteousness of their own.* The Jews were of this temper; and it hath been the greatest question from the beginning of the world till this day, what is that righteousness whereby we must stand before God? But God's Spirit answers all objections. Beloved, the best of us, though in an estate of grace, if the Holy Ghost do not convince us, we shall be in darkness, and call all into question. Therefore we must not be convinced only at the first, but in a continued course of Christianity. Unless the Holy Ghost doth this, we shall fall into a dungeon of darkness; therefore the convincing of the Holy Ghost is necessary.

Beloved, this should make us take heed how we hear and how we read, even to beg this convincing of the Spirit in every ordinance: O Lord! vouchsafe 'the Spirit of revelation,' and take the scales off mine eyes, that as these are truths of themselves, so they may be truths to me; sway my soul, that I may cast myself upon thy mercy in Christ, &c.

Obj. I must answer some cases that many a poor soul is troubled withal: Alas! I am not 'convinced by the Spirit that Christ is my righteousness,' therefore what case am I in?

Ans. I answer, some are more strongly convinced, and some less. Let a man be careless of holy duties, and he is less convinced; but let him be constant therein, and he shall find the Holy Ghost convincing him more strongly that the righteousness of Christ is his. There are many presumptuous persons that 'turn the grace of God into wantonness,' Jude 4; who because through the enthusiasm of Satan, they never question their estate, but conceit themselves to be good men and in the estate of grace, think this to be the convincing of the Holy Ghost; whereas this is a general rule, spiritual convincing is not total, but always leaves in the heart some drugs* of doubting; as a ship that rides at anchor, though it may reel to and fro, yet is it safe for the main. So is it with the soul that is truly convinced. It is safe for the main, yet it is tumbled and tossed with many doubts and fears, but their anchor is in heaven.

Take this for a ground of comfort subscribed unto in the experience of all believers, that the Spirit of God so far convinces them of Christ's righteousness, as preserves in them such a power of grace as to cast them-

* Qu. 'dregs'?—G.

selves upon the mercy of God in Christ; and God will not quench that spark. Though there be little or no light, yet there will be heat. God will send his Spirit into the heart, so far as it shall not betray itself to despair, and let such a beam into the soul as all the power in hell shall not be able to keep out. But it is our own neglect that we are not more strongly convinced, so as to break through all. This is the privilege of a constant, careful Christian, to be strongly convinced of the righteousness of Christ.

Use. Thus we see how the Holy Ghost convinceth us of righteousness. Other things I must omit. If this be so, I beseech you, *let us not lose our privileges and prerogatives.* Doth God give grace, and give Christ with all his righteousness, and shall not we improve them? Let us use this righteousness in all temptations. Let us plead it to God himself, when he seems to be our enemy: Lord, thou hast ordained a righteousness, the righteousness of Christ, that hath given full satisfaction to thy justice, and he hath given me a title to heaven. Howsoever my soul be in darkness, yet, Lord, I come unto thee in the name of my Saviour, that thou wouldst persuade my soul of that righteousness. I would glorify thy name. Wherein wilt thou be glorified? In mercy or justice? Oh, in mercy above all. I cannot glorify thee in thy mercy, unless thou persuade me 'of the righteousness of Christ.' Can I love thee except thou love me first? Canst thou have any free and voluntary obedience from me, unless I be convinced that Christ is mine? Now, Lord, I beseech thee, let me be such as thou mayest take delight in. Beloved, since we have means of such a gift, let us never rest till we have it. If Satan set upon us, hold this out. If he tell thee thou art a sinner, tell him I have a greater righteousness than my own, even the righteousness of God-man; I have a righteousness above all my unrighteousness. Satan saith God is displeased with me: ay, but he is more pleased with me in Christ, than displeased with me in myself. Satan saith I have sinned against God; ay, but not against the remedy. Send Satan to Christ. Oh, but thou hast a corrupt nature that makes thee run into this sin and that sin; but there is a spring of mercy in God, and an over-running fountain of righteousness in Christ, an overflowing sea of the blood of Christ. Therefore let us labour to improve this righteousness of Christ to God and Satan against all temptations, yea, against our own consciences. I am thus and thus, yet God is thus and thus; all his attributes are conveyed to me in Christ. Let us exalt God and Christ, and set up Christ above our sins, above any thing in the world, as St Paul, who 'counted all things dung and dross for the excellent knowledge of Christ,' Philip. iii. 8.

Quest. You will ask me, How shall we know whether we be convinced of this righteousness or no?

Ans. I answer, We may know by the method Christ uses in convincing. First, he convinces of sin, and then of righteousness. For a man to catch at righteousness before he be convinced of sin, it is but an usurpation; for the Holy Ghost *first* convinces of *sin.*

Therefore you have many perish because they never were abased enough. Beloved, people are not lost enough and not miserable enough for Christ; and not broken enough for him; and therefore they go without him.

Quest. But how shall I know that the Holy Ghost hath convinced me enough of sin, so that I may without presumption apply the righteousness of Christ unto myself?

Ans. Only thus: if the Holy Ghost have discovered my sinful condition of nature and life, so as to work in me an hatred of sin, and to alter my bent another way, and so make Christ sweet unto me, then I am sufficiently convinced of sin.

This in answer to that question by the way. To return; in the next place, I may know I am convinced thoroughly of the righteousness of Christ *by the witness and work of the Spirit.* The Spirit brings light and faith. The work of the Spirit hath a light of its own; as I know I believe, when I believe. But sometimes we have not the reflect act of faith whereby to evidence our own graces to ourselves; but ever he that is convinced of the Spirit of God, his heart will be wrought to bear marvellous love to God. Upon this apprehension that God is mine, and Christ is mine, the soul is constrained to love; whereupon ensues an enlargement of heart, and a prevalency of comfort above all discomfort, for love casteth out fear. This one comfort that our sins are forgiven, and that we have a right and title to heaven, when the soul is convinced of this it is in a blessed condition. Then what is poverty and what is imprisonment? Not worthy to be reckoned in respect of the glory that shall be revealed.

Again, where the Holy Ghost convinces enough, *there is inward peace and great joy suitable to the righteousness.* As the righteousness is an excellent righteousness of God-man, so, that peace and joy that comes from it is unspeakable peace and joy. So that then the heart sees itself instated in peace and joy, as you have it, Rom. v. 1, 'Being justified by faith, we have peace towards God;' not only inward peace and joy, but a peace that will shew itself abroad; a glorious peace, a peace that will make us glory: ver. 3, 'We glory in tribulation.' A hard matter to glory in abasement. Not only so, but we glory in God. God is ours, and Christ's righteousness ours. When Christ hath satisfied God's wrath, then we may make our boast of God.

Again, where this conviction of righteousness is, *it answers all objections.* The doubting heart will object this and that, but the Spirit of God shews an all-sufficiency in Christ's obedience; and that sets the soul down quietly in all crosses, and calms it in all storms in some degree. Where the soul is convinced of the righteousness of Christ, there the conscience demands boldly: 'It is God that justifies, who shall condemn? It is Christ that is dead, and risen again, and sits at the right hand of God. Who shall lay any thing to the charge of God's elect?' Rom. viii. 33. So that a convinced conscience dares all creatures in heaven and earth. It works strongly and boldly. I shall not need to enlarge this. You know whether you are convinced.

Use. To end the point, I beseech you, *labour to live by this faith.* Here is an evidence if we can live by it. How is that? Every day to make use of the 'righteousness of Christ,' as every day we run into sin. Be sure we have our consciences sprinkled with the blood of Christ; that as we increase new guilt, so we may have a new pardon. Therefore every day labour to see God as reconciled, and Christ as our advocate with the Father. Christ is now in heaven. If we sin, make use of him. This should be the life of a Christian, to make use of Christ's righteousness. When you find nature polluted, go to God, and say, Lord, my nature, though foul in itself, yet is holy and pure in Christ. He took the weakness of the human nature unto him, that he might communicate the worth and efficacy of his divine nature unto me. And for my actions, I am a sinner; but Christ hath fully discharged all my debts, and is now in heaven. He hath performed all righteousness for me. Look not upon me as in myself, but look upon me in Christ. He and I are one. This should be every day's exercise, to see ourselves in Christ, and so see him and ourselves one. I should enlarge the point further, but I will speak a word of the reason.

What is the reason why the Comforter may and shall convince of righteousness? 'Because I go to the Father.' What strength is there in that reason? Why this: Christ took upon him to be onr surety; and he must acquit us of all our sins ere he can go to his Father. If one sin had been unsatisfied for, he could not have gone to his Father; but now he is gone to his Father, therefore all our sins are satisfied for. So that now the ascension of Christ is a sufficient pledge to me that my person is accepted, and my sins pardoned; because he is gone to his Father, to appear before the Father for us, which he could not have done had he not fulfilled all righteousness.

But wherefore did he go to the Father? Why, *to make application of what he had wrought.* If Christ should not have gone to the Father, he could not have sent the Holy Ghost to us. Therefore there is great use of this going to his Father. Satan pleads before God we are such and such. Ay, but saith Christ, I have shed my blood for them; and there he perfumes all our weak prayers. If we were not imperfect, what need we a Mediator in heaven? Therefore he is gone to heaven to disannul all Satan's accusations, and to provide a place for us. Die when we will, our place is ready.

Then again, he is gone to the Father *to clothe us with a sweet relation*, to make the Father our Father. For he saith, John xx. 17, 'I go to my Father and to your Father,' so that he is not ashamed to call us brethren. By virtue of this, we may go to God and call him Father; and when we die, we may without presumption say, 'Father, into thy hands I commend my spirit,' Luke xxiii. 46; for the Father loves us as he loved Christ, with one and the same love, though in a far different degree. What a comfort is this, that when we die, we go to our Father that is better than any earthly father. Therefore it should joy us when the time of our departure comes. We see old Jacob, when he saw the chariots come out of Egypt, how his heart leaped because he should go to see his son Joseph, Gen. xlv. 27, so when death is sent to transport us to Christ, to heaven, had we a strong faith we should be exceeding glad.

And let us learn here the art of faith from Christ. 'I go to the Father,' saith he. There was a great deal of time yet to pass, no less than forty days after his resurrection, before he went to the Father, yet he saith, 'I go to the Father,' to shew that faith presents things future as present, faith sees heaven as present, and the day of judgment as present, and doth affect the soul as if they were now existent. If we had a spirit of faith, it would thus present things far off as nigh at hand. Therefore when we meet with anything that may make our way to heaven seem long or troublesome, exercise your faith, and make your term present to your spirits. Though remote from sense, say, I go to the Father. What, though I go through blood and a shameful death, yea, perhaps a tormentful death, yet I go to the Father! When a man is once persuaded that God is his Father in Christ, it will make him walk to heaven before his time.

Use. Let us make use of this point of Christ's going to the Father. Beloved, there is not a point of religion but hath a wonderful spring of comfort; and it is want of faith that we do not draw more comfort from them. When, therefore, we part with our friends by death, think they are gone to their Father. If ye loved me, saith Christ, ye would rejoice because I said

'I go to the Father.' If we love our friends, we should rejoice when they die. Beloved, this should comfort us, Christ is gone to his Father! Oh, what welcome was there of Christ when he came into heaven. The same welcome will there be when we go to the Father. How joyful entertainment shall we have of the Father and the Son. Therefore death should not be troublesome to us; say, Christ's righteousness is mine; therefore I know I shall go to the Father. What care I, then, what kind of pains I go through. If a man be going to a desired place, howsoever the way be troublesome, the sweetness of the end will make him forget the discouragements of his passage. Perhaps we must wade to heaven through a sea of blood. It matters not. The end will recompense all. Though we lose our limbs by the way, it is better to limp to heaven than dance to hell.

April 10. 1638. *Imprimatur* THO. WYKES.

THE WITNESS OF SALVATION.*

For ye have not received the spirit of bondage again to fear ; but ye have received the Spirit of adoption, whereby we cry, Abba, Father. The Spirit itself beareth witness with our spirit, that we are the children of God.—Rom. VIII. 15, 16.

The apostle in this Epistle sets down a platform of Christian doctrine, whereupon all persons and Christian churches might safely build themselves ; shewing therein a sure way how those might come unto the Lord Jesus, who are to obtain salvation by him : which he delivereth in three heads.

1. First, Shewing *how God will convince the world of sin.*

2. He discovereth unto them *what that righteousness is, which without themselves is imputed unto them.*

3. He setteth forth *that righteousness inherent, created in us by sanctification of the Spirit, with the effects thereof and motions that help us thereunto.*

Answering that threefold work of the Spirit, John xvi. 8, where Christ promiseth that when the Comforter cometh, he shall reprove the world, 1. Of sin ; 2. Of righteousness ; 3. Of judgment.

First, He shews the comforter shall work a *conviction of sin,* leaving a man as vile, empty, and naked as may be. Not a bare confession of sin only, which a man may have and yet go to hell ; but such a conviction which stops a man's mouth that he hath not a word to speak, but sees a sink of sin and abomination in himself, such as the apostle had, Rom. vii. 18 : 'For I know that in me (that is, in my flesh) dwelleth no good thing,' &c. To attain unto this sight and measure of humiliation, there must be work of the Spirit.

* 'The Witness of Salvation' forms No. 12 of the original 'Saints' Cordial,' 1629. It was withdrawn in the after-editions. Its separate title-page is as follows :—'The Witnes of Salvation : or, God's Spirit Witnessing with ovr Spirits, that wee are the Children of God. In One Sermon. Wherein is shewed, What the spirit of Bondage is. Why God suffers his Children to be terrified therewith. The paralleling of the Witnesses in Heaven and Earth. What the witness of our spirit is. How to discerne of it. The order of the Witnesses. What the witnesse of Gods Spirit is : and, How to discerne the truth thereof. Prælucendo Pereo. Vprightnes Hath Boldnes. Iob 27. 5. God forbid that I should justifie you : till I dye I will not remove my integritie from mee. My righteousnesse I hold fast, and will not let it goe : my heart shall not reprove me as long as I live. London, Printed in the yeare 1629.'—G.

First, therefore, the apostle begins with the Gentiles in the first chapter, who failing grossly in the duties of the first table, God had given also over to err in the breach of all the duties of the second. Then the second chapter, and most part of the third, are spent on the Jews. They bragged of many excellent privileges they had above the Gentiles; as to have the law, circumcision; to be teachers of others; to have God amongst them; and therefore despised the Gentiles. The apostle reproves them, shewing, that in condemning the Gentiles they condemned themselves, they having a greater light of knowledge than they; which should have led them unto the true and sincere practice of what they were instructed in. Then he goes on, and shews naturally all to be out of the way, the 14th verse of the third chapter; and so concludes them to be under sin, 'that every mouth may be stopped, and all the world found guilty before God.' This is an end of the first part.

Now, this being done, in the latter end of the third chapter he goes on and proceeds to that second work of the Comforter, to convince the world *of righteousness*. But upon what ground? 'Because I go to my Father, and ye see me no more;' that is, he shall assure the conscience that there is now a righteousness of better things purchased for us; that Christ is wounded, condemned, and arraigned for us; that he was imprisoned, but now he is free, who was our surety; yea, and that he is not freed as one escaped, who hath broken prison and run away, for then he could not have stayed in heaven, no more than Adam in paradise after his fall: but now that Christ remains in heaven perfectly and for ever co-enthronized with his Father, this is a sure ground to us that the debt is paid, and everlasting peace and righteousness is brought in for our salvation.

This the apostle enlargeth, and shews this to be that righteousness only which Adam had, and which all we must trust unto, unto the sixth chapter. Then the apostle goes on unto the third point, and comes unto the convincing the world *of judgment and righteousness*, in the eighth chapter, which are two words signifying one thing; but because he had named righteousness before, which was that righteousness without a man, in Christ Jesus, in justification, he calls the third judgment, which is that integrity inherent, bred, and created in us, as we may see in that place of Isaiah xlii. 3. It is said of Christ, 'A bruised reed shall he not break, and the smoking flax shall he not quench, till he bring forth *judgment* unto victory.' He shews judgment there to be a beginning of righteousness in sanctification, even such a one as can never be extinguished. So Job xxvii. 2, the word is taken, where he expostulates the matter: 'As the Lord liveth, who hath taken away my judgment from me, all the while my breath is in me, and the Spirit of God in my nostrils, my lips shall not speak wickedness, nor my tongue deceit. God forbid that I should justify you: till I die I will not remove my integrity from me. My righteousness I hold fast, I will not let it go.' Here you see by judgment is meant integrity and that righteousness which is created and inherent in us, so that the ground of that place of Isaiah is, that God will never give over to advance and make effectual that weak righteousness and santification begun in us, until it shall prevail against and master all our sins and corruptions, making it in some a victorious sanctification. And the ground thereof is, 'For the prince of this world is judged;' he is like one manacled, whose strength and power is limited, so that now though he be strong, yet he is cast out by a stronger than he, that he cannot nor shall ever rule, as in times past. This strain of doctrine, the apostle holds in this epistle, shewing that, as that justification of righteousness by the blood of Christ is a thing without us, so sanctification is righteousness inherent and created in us, and is the ground of the witness of our spirit, as we shall hear in its own place. So that the blood of Christ doth two things unto us: 1. It covers our sins in justification; 2. And then in sanctification it heals our sins and sores; so that if there be any proud* flesh, it eats it out and then heals the wound. 'Therefore, saith he, not under the law, but under grace.' He that sees the law to be satisfied by another, and all to be under grace, he will not much stand on anything in himself for his justification, but fly unto grace, and be much in thankfulness; therefore we are commanded that sin have no dominion over us, 'for we are not under the law, but under grace.' Then he proceeds unto the particulars, and shews divers things, especially verse 12th of this eighth chapter, he drives unto the point of sanctification; as though he should say, You are freed from the law, as it is a judge of life and death, but yet the law must be your counsellor. You are debtors of thankfulness, seeing whence you are escaped, that ye may not live after the flesh. And then he proceeds to shew them how they should walk; that seeing they have received the Spirit, they should walk after the Spirit. Now that they had received that which should subdue and mortify the flesh and the lusts thereof, they should be no more as dead men, but quick and lively in operation, to live after the Spirit; otherwise they could not be the sons of God. And then he comes unto the words which I have now read, verse 15th, 'For ye have not received the spirit of bondage again to fear; but ye have received the Spirit of adoption, whereby we cry, Abba, Father.'

'For the Spirit itself beareth witness with our spirit that we are the sons of God.'

Here the apostle shews the ground of our union and communion with Christ, because having his Spirit, we are of necessity his; as St John speaks, 1 John iii. 24, 'And hereby we know that he abideth in us, by the Spirit which he hath given us.' What ties and makes one, things far asunder, but the same Spirit of life in both? So that Spirit which is in him, a full running-over fountain, dropping down and being also infused in us, unites us unto him; yea, that very Spirit communicated to me in some measure, which is in him in such fulness, that Spirit doth tie me as fast unto Christ as any joint ties member to member, and so makes Christ dwell in mine heart. As the apostle to this purpose speaks, Eph. ii. 21, 22, 'That thus by one Spirit we are built up and made the temple of God, and come to be the habitation of God by the Spirit.' So that now by this means we are inseparably knit and united unto him. For, I pray you, what is it that makes a member to be a member to another? Not the nearness of joining, or lying one to or upon another, but the same quickening spirit and life which is in both, and which causeth a like motion. For otherwise, if the same life were not in the member, it should be corrupt, dead, and of no use to the other; so that it is the same spirit and life which is in the things conjoined that unites. Yet to explain this more—as I have often in the like case spoken—imagine a man were as high as heaven, the same life and spirit being in all parts, what is that now that can cause his toe to stir, there being such a huge distance betwixt the head and it? Even that self-same life which is in the head being in it; no sooner doth the head will the toe to stir but it moves. So is it with us; that very Spirit which is in him being in us, and he in us, thereby we are united to him, grow in him, and live in him, rejoice in him, and so are kept and preserved to be glori-

* That is, 'inflamed.'—G.

fied with him. He is the 'second Adam,' from whom we received the influence of all good things, showering* down and distilling the graces of his Spirit upon all his members, that look, as it was said of Aaron, who was a type of the second Adam, and of that holy oil representing the graces of the Spirit, 'Which did not only run down his head and beard, but the skirts of his garments, and all his rich attire about,' Ps. cxxxiii. 2; so when I see the oil of the Spirit of grace not only rest upon the head, but also descend to his heel and run upon the members, making me now as one of them, in some sort another thing than I was or my natural state made me, by the same Spirit I know I am conveyed into Christ and united unto him. To this purpose is that which Christ so stands upon, John vi. 63, unto the Jews, where, speaking of the eating of his flesh, and that bread of life which came down from heaven, lest they should mistake him, he adds, 'It is the Spirit that quickeneth, the flesh profiteth nothing; the words that I speak unto you, they are spirit, and they are life.' So that we see it is the Spirit that gives a being unto the thing; and therefore the apostle also proceeds to shew, 'As many as are led by the Spirit of God, they are the sons of God,' Rom. viii. 13; 14; that look, as Christ is the true natural Son of God, so we as truly, by the conveyance of the same Spirit unto us, are his sons by adoption, and so heirs of God. This he begins to shew, ver. 15, that now being in this excellent estate, they were not only servants or friends—a most high prerogative—but they were 'the sons of God,' having 'the Spirit of adoption,' whereby they might boldly call God Father. In which verse he opposeth 'the spirit of bondage,' which doth make a man fear again, 'unto the Spirit of adoption,' which frees a man from fears, so as boldly to call God Father.

Now two things may be observed hence: first, *the order that the Spirit of God keeps*. Ere it comforts, it shakes and makes us fear. This the apostle speaks of, Heb. ii. 14, where he shews the end of Christ's coming was, that 'Because the children were partakers of flesh and blood, he also himself likewise took part with them; that through death he might destroy him that had the power of death, that is, the devil; and deliver them who through the fear of death were all their lifetime subject to bondage.' The first work then of the Comforter is to put a man in fear. Further, hence is shewed, that until this Spirit doth work this fear, a man doth not fear. The heart holds out. The obstinacy is so great, that if hell gates were open, a man will not yield till then that the Spirit worketh it. So St John speaks of the Comforter, that 'when he comes, he will convince or reprove the world of sin,' John xvi. 8; that is, he will convince and shew a man that he is but a bondman; and so he makes us to fear.

No man must think this strange, that God deals with men at first in this harsh manner, as it were to kill them, ere he make them alive; nor be discouraged, as if God had cast them off for ever as none of his; for this bondage and spirit of fear is a work of God's Spirit, and a preparative to the rest. But it is but a common work, and therefore, unless more follow it, it can afford us no comfort.

Obj. Why then doth God suffer his children to be terrified first with this fear?

Ans. I answer, that in two respects, this of all other is the best and wisest course to deal with us by the Holy Ghost, or else many would put it off, and never rightly come unto a sense of mercy. 1. In respect of God's glory; 2. In regard of our good.

* Misprinted 'shewing.'—G.

1. But now, let us see why is such a course good in respect *of God's glory.* Because, as in the creation, so in the work of redemption, God will have the praise of all his attributes. In the former, there appeared his infinite wisdom, goodness, power, justice, mercy, and the like, so would he in the greater work of redemption have all these appear in strength and brightness; for in so doing, we honour him. It is honour to acknowledge all these things to be in him in high perfection, whereby the contrary, it is his dishonour when we acknowledge not the excellency of his infinite attributes. Yea, I may safely say, the work of redemption was the greater; for therein appeared all the treasures of wisdom and knowledge, and in conveying it unto the church.

(1.) For his *wisdom.* There appeared infinite wisdom in so ordering the matter to find out such a means for the redemption of mankind, as no created understanding could possibly imagine or think of.

(2.) For his *mercy.* There could be no mercy comparable unto this, in not sparing his own Son, the Son of his love, to spare us, rather than we should perish, who had so grievously transgressed.

(3.) So there could not be so much *justice* seen in anything as in sparing us, not to spare his Son; in laying, as it were, his Son's head upon the block, and chopping it off, in renting and tearing that blessed body, even as the veil of the temple was rent—which was a type of him—so did he, as it were, tear him for us, and break him, when he 'made his soul an offering for sin.' This was the perfection of justice, and thus was he just, as the apostle speaks, 'that he might be a justifier of them who are of the faith of Jesus,' Rom. iii. 26. God would therefore in this great work have justice and mercy to meet and kiss each other. And that for two reasons: for the magnifying, 1. of his justice; 2. of his mercy.

1. *Justice.* For the former, the Spirit must first become a spirit of bondage and fear, for the magnifying of his justice, that God may have the glory thereof, as we see the prophet David, having sinned, was driven to this pinch: Ps. li. 4, 'Against thee, thee only have I sinned, and done this evil in thy sight, that thou mightst be justified when thou speakest, and be clear when thou judgest.' Thus he, an holy man, was brought to confess, to give God the glory of his justice. And so to this end, that a man might pass by, or through, the gates of hell into heaven, the Lord will have his justice extended and spread abroad to the full view; and therefore, for the present sight of mercy, he turns the law loose to have its course; and thus, as in the work of redemption, he would have the height of justice to appear. So neither, in the application thereof, would God suffer justice to be swallowed up of mercy. But even as that woman, 2 Kings iv. 1, who had nothing to pay, was threatened by the creditors to take away her two sons and put them in prison, so the law is let loose upon us, though we have nothing to pay, yet to threaten imprisonment and damnation; to affright and terrify us, to magnify the justice of God. This is the first cause.

Further, God hath set forth many terrible threatenings against sin and sinners. Shall all this be to no purpose? The wicked are insensible of them; must they therefore be in vain? Some people there be on whom they must work. 'Shall the lion roar, and no man be afraid?' Amos iii. 8. Since, then, those who should will not, some there are who must tremble, and those even his own dear children. This the prophet excellently sets forth, Isaiah lxvi. 2, where the Lord sheweth whom he will regard: 'But to this man will I look, even to him that is poor, and of a contrite spirit, and trembling at my words.' So that you see even some of his own must thus tremble and be humbled of necessity, and that it is not without just cause that God doth deal with his own children in this manner, though it be sharp in the experience. We must fear, tremble, and be humbled, and then we shall receive a spirit not to fear again.

That vain courage which some have to brag of, 'I fear not death,' this is not that meant here; for, alas! such braggers, out of ignorance of the thing, and desire to be out of misery in this life, may embrace death willingly, hoping it may put an end to their miseries. But this spirit not to fear again, is such a spirit that assures me of the forgiveness of all my sins, shewing me my freedom in Christ Jesus from hell and eternal condemnation, making me live an holy life, and from hence not to fear; and so seals us up unto the day of redemption, as we shall hear anon, when we come unto the witness of this Spirit. This is for the glory of his justice.

2. *Mercy*. Secondly, It is requisite that the Comforter should work a fear in men, for the glory *of his mercy*, which would never be so sweet, nor relish so well, nor be esteemed of us, if the awful terrors of justice had not formerly made us smart; as we may see in that parable, Mat. xviii. 23, whereunto our Saviour likens the kingdom of heaven, of that man who owed ten thousand talents unto the king his master. He shews he forgives him all. But what did he first? He requires the whole debt of him; and because he had nothing to pay, he commands him, his wife and children, and all that he had, to be sold, that payment might be made. First, he would have him pinch, thoroughly to know how much he was indebted; and in that case how high that favour was which he received in forgiving him all. Thus a king, for great faults, casts men into prison ere he pardon them, and then mercy is mercy indeed. So God deals with us. Many times he puts his children in fear, shews them how much they owe, how unable they are to pay, casts them into prison, and threatens condemnation in hell for ever. After which, when mercy comes to the soul, then it appears to be a wonderful mercy, yea, the acts of exceeding mercy. Why do so many find no savour in the gospel? Is it because there is no witness or matter of delight in it? No. It is because such have had no taste of the law and of the spirit of bondage; they have not smarted, nor found a sense of the bitterness of sins, nor of the just punishment due unto the same. Even as a king will suffer the law to pass on some grievous malefactor for high treason, and cause him to be brought to the place of execution, and lay his head on the block, ere he pardon, as we have had experience in this country. A man who otherwise would not cry, nor shed a tear for anything, despiseth death, and would not fear to meet an host of men, such a one now having at this instant a pardon brought from the king, it works wonderfully upon him, and will cause softness of heart and tears to come when nothing else could; whilst the wonder of this mercy is admired; which now appeareth so sweet and seasonable, that he is struck, and knows not what to say. So therefore, for this cause, God shews us first a spirit of fear and bondage, and prepares us to relish mercy; and then the Spirit of adoption, not to fear again.

And thus, by this order, the one is magnified and highly esteemed by the foregoing sense of the other.

If, therefore, this terror and fear be hard and troublesome unto us, yet if it be for God's glory, let us endure it. If he will give me over to a wounded, terrified conscience, to fears, tremblings, astonishments, yea, or to draw me to the fire itself, or to any other punishment, since it is for his glory, I must be contented. But what do I say? God gets nothing by us. All that we do is for ourselves. Our acknowledgment of him makes him no wiser, stronger, juster, nor better than he is, Job xxxv. 6, 7; but, in glorifying him, we do glorify ourselves, and so pass from glory to glory, until we be fully transformed into his image, 2 Cor. iii. 18. And herein consists our happiness in acknowledging of his wonderful attributes, that, by reflex of the knowledge of them, we may grow in them as much as may be for our good. He was as glorious, powerful, wise, just, happy, and good before the world was made as now. For if the case be put of glorifying him, the persons of the Trinity were only worthy of so great honour, not we, as we may read Prov. viii. 30. There Wisdom shews how it 'was with the Father before all time, and that they did mutually solace themselves in the contemplation of one another's glory.' Then, says Wisdom, 'was I by him, as one brought up with him, and I was daily his delight, rejoicing always before him;' and John xvii. 5, there we read the same in effect, where Christ prays, 'And now, O Father, glorify thou me, with thine own self, with the glory which I had with thee before the world was.' So that the beholding, magnifying, and admiring his glory as much as may be, labouring to be like him, is our glory. Thus much of the glory of God in beginning of his work in us by fear.

This second was, that this course is for our good, and that two ways,

1. In justification. 2. In sanctification.

1. *In justification.* For the first, we are such strangers unto God, that we will never come to him till we see no other remedy, being at the pit's brink, ready to starve, hopeless of all other helps. We are such wretched creatures, so hard frozen in the dregs of sin, delighting in our own ways, as we see in the parable of the prodigal son, Luke xv. 11, *seq.* He would never think of any return to his father till all other helps failed him, money, friends, acquaintance, all sort of food; nay, if he might have fed on husks with the swine, he would not have thought of returning any more to his father. This being denied him, then the text saith, 'He came to himself,' shewing us that whilst men run on in sinful courses they are madmen, out of themselves, even as we see those men in Bedlam. They are beaten, and kept under; comforts denied them till they come to themselves. Then what says he? 'I will go to my father, and confess that I have sinned,' &c. So it is with us, until the Lord humbles and brings us low in our own eyes, and shews us our misery and sinful poverty, and that in us is no good thing; that we be stripped of all helps in and without ourselves, and must perish for ever without we beg his mercy. We will not come unto him, as we see it was with that woman whom Christ healed of her bloody issue, Luke viii. 43, how long it was ere she came to Christ. She had been sick twelve years; she had spent all her substance on physicians, and nobody could help her. This extremity brought her. So that this is a means to bring us to Christ, to drive us on our knees, helpless, as low as may be,—to shew us where only help is to be found, and make us run into it.

Thus, therefore, when men have no mind to come unto Christ, he sends as it were fiery serpents to sting them, that they might look up unto the brazen serpent, or rather unto Christ Jesus, of whom it was a type, for help, Num. xxi. 8, John iii. 14. So unto others, being strangers unto him, he sends variety of great and strange afflictions, to make them come, that he may be acquainted with them. As Absalom set Joab's corn on fire because he would not come at him, being twice sent for, 2 Sam. xiv.

30, so God dealeth with us before our conversion many times; and with an iron whip he lasheth us home, turning loose the avenger of blood after us, and then we run and make haste unto this city of refuge for our life. Thus, I say, God doth shoot off his great ordnance against us, to make us run unto him. So John the Baptist in this manner came preaching of repentance, in attire, speech, diet, all strange; clothed with camel's hair, and with a girdle of skin about his loins, his meat locusts and wild honey; the place, in a wilderness; the speech, harsh and uncomfortable, thundering in voice, calling them generation of vipers, and telling them that now was the axe also laid to the root of the tree or under the wood, that every tree that brought not forth good fruit was hewn down and cast into the fire, Mark i. 6, *seq.*

As also we know in this manner, the Lord came unto Elias, 1 Kings xix. 11, *seq.* First, a great and strong wind rent the mountains, and brake in pieces the rocks before the Lord, but the Lord was not in the wind; and after them went an earthquake, but the Lord was not in the earthquake; and after the earthquake a fire, but the Lord was not in the fire. These were as a peal of great ordnance, shot off to prepare the way for him, to shew the King his coming. And after the fire a still small voice, and there the Lord was. So the Lord rends, tears, and shakes our consciences ofttimes to prepare the way for him, and then he comes unto us in that still and soft voice of consolation.

2. *For our sanctification.* It is good for us that the Comforter's first work is to work fear in us; for we are naturally so frozen in our dregs, that no fire in a manner will warm and thaw us. We wallow in our blood; we stick fast in the mire of sin up to the chin, that we cannot stir. So that this fear is sent unto us to put us from our corruptions, and to make us more holy. As we see a man having a gangrene beginning on his hand or foot, which may spread further and be his death, he is easily persuaded to cut off that, that it go no further. So doth God deal with us in this fear of bondage, that we may be clothed anew with his image, in holiness and righteousness.

Now, to effect this, the sharpest things are best. Such as are the law and threatenings of condemnation, the opening of hell, the racking of the conscience, and a sense of wrath present and to come. So hard-hearted we are by nature, being as children of the bond-woman, unto whom violence must do the work. Even as we see a man riding a wild and young horse to tame him, he will run him against a wall that this may make him afraid, ride him into deep and tough lands, or taking him up unto the top of some high rock, from whence bringing him to the bank thereof, he threatens to throw him down, and so makes him shake and quake for fear, whereby at last he is tamed. So deals the Lord by us. He gives us a sight of sin, and the punishment due thereunto, a sense of wrath; sets the conscience on fire; fills the heart with fears, horrors, and disquietness; opens hell thus unto the soul; brings one as it were unto the gates thereof, and threatens to throw him in; and all this to make us more lowly, or the more to hate sin. So that by this we see there must be strange mortifying and subduing of us by strong hand, to bring us unto Christ, for our sanctification.

Obj. Ere I proceed, give me leave to answer one objection of a troubled soul, which may arise from hence: Oh, may one say, 'what comfort, then, may I have of the first work of the Spirit in me, for as yet I have found none of these things? I have not been thus humbled, nor terrified, nor had such experience, as you speak of, in that state under the spirit of bondage.'

Ans. I answer, This, though it be the work of the Spirit, yet it is not the principal, sanctifying, and saving work of the Spirit. Yea, a child of the devil may come to have a greater measure of this than God's own dear children, whom for the most part he will not affright, torture, nor afflict in that terrible manner as he doth some of them; but the consequent of this is more to be accounted of than the measure, to see whither that measure I have, whatsoever it be, leads me. For if the measure were so absolutely necessary to salvation, then all God's children should have enough of it; for I make a difference still betwixt humiliation and humility, which is a grace of itself, and leads me along with comfort and life. Thus, therefore, I think of humiliation. If I have so much of it as may bring me to see my danger, and run unto the medicine and city of refuge for help, to hate sin for the time to come, and set myself constantly in the way and practice of holiness, it is sufficient. And so, I say, in the case of repentance. If a man could have a heart firmly set upon the sight of sin past, against all sin to come, the greater and firmer this were, the lesser measure of sorrow might suffice for sins past. As we see a wise father would never beat his child for faults past—he takes no delight in that but for prevention of what which is to come, for we see the child cries out in the time of correction, I will never do so more!—so God deals with us. Because our promises and resolutions are faint, and fail, and that without much mourning, humiliation, and stripes we attain not this hatred of sins past, and to have strength against them, therefore it is that the measure of our humiliation and sorrow must be proportionable to that work which is to be done, otherwise any measure of it were sufficient which fits us for the time to come.

I will add, there are indeed divers measures of it, according unto which the conscience is wounded. When there is a tough, melancholy humour, that the powers of the soul are distracted, good duties omitted, and the heart so much the more hardened; when upon this the Lord lets loose the bond of the conscience, oppressing the same with exceeding terrors and fears, this the Lord useth as a wedge to drive out a hard piece of wood to be cut. God then doth shew us, because we would not plough ourselves, we shall be ploughed: 'If ye would judge yourselves,' saith the apostle, 'you should not be judged,' 1 Cor. xi. 31. And therefore the church confesseth and complains, Ps. cxxix. 2, that 'the ploughers ploughed upon her back, and made deep furrows.' Why, how came this? 'She did not plough up her own fallow ground.' Wherefore the Lord sent her other ploughers, that ploughed her soundly indeed. Wherefore doth God thus deal? Because he is the great and most wise husbandman, who will not sow amongst thorns. Therefore when he is about to sow the seed of eternal life in the soul, which must take deep root and grow for ever, he will have that ground thoroughly ploughed.

The way, then, to avoid these things, so harsh and unpleasing to flesh and blood, is to take the rod betimes and beat ourselves. When we are slow, secure, and omit it, God doth the work; yet he makes a difference of good education in those who have kept themselves from the common pollutions and gross sins of the time. It pleaseth God that faith comes upon them, they know not how for the time. Grace drops in by little and little, now a little and then a little by degrees. Sin is more and more hated, and the heart inflamed with a desire of good things in a conscionable life. But in a measure, I say, such must have had, or have, or shall have, fears or terrors, so much as may keep them from sin, to go on constantly in the ways of holiness; or when they fly out of the way, they shall smart for it, and be whipped home again. Yet for the main they find themselves as it were in heaven, they know not how. But if a man have stuck deep and long in sin, he must look for a greater measure and more certain time of his effectual calling. There must be haling and pulling of such a man out of the fire with violence. That man must not look for peace and comfort with ease. God will thunder and lighten in this man's conscience in mount Sinai ere he speak peace unto him in mount Sion.

A second time also there is of a great measure of humiliation, which is, though a man be free of worldly pollutions and gross sins, when the Lord intends to shew the sense or feeling of his mercy to any in an extraordinary measure, or to fit them for some high service, then they shall be much humbled before, as we see Paul was, Acts ix. 8. God did thunder upon him, and beat him down in the highway, being stricken with blindness three days after.

And thus much shall suffice to have spoken of the 15th verse, touching 'the spirit of bondage' and the 'Spirit of adoption.' The apostle tells them, they may thank God the spirit of fear thus came, that hereafter they might partake of the Spirit of adoption to fear no more. He stirs them up, as it were, to be thankful, because now they had obtained a better state. Why, what estate? A very high one: ver. 16, 'The Spirit itself beareth witnesseth with our spirit, that we are the children of God.' The thing is then to know ourselves to be the children of God. There must be sound evidences. Here then are two set down, whose testimony cannot fail. I will touch them, by your patience, as briefly as I can, and so make an end.

1. The witness of our spirit. 2. The witness of God's Spirit with our spirit.

These be two evidences, not singly but conjoined, wherein you see there must be some work of our own spirit.

Obj. Our spirit is deceitful; how can our spirit work then in this manner to testify this?

Ans. I answer in this place, Our spirit is taken as an evidence of God from heaven; as it were a love-token given, and assuring me from good grounds that I have not misapplied the promises; that though God do write bitter things against me, yet I love him still, and cleave unto him; that for all this, I know that I hunger and thirst after righteousness; that I will not be beaten off, nor receive an ill report of my Lord and Saviour; that I rest, wait, serve, and trust in him still. In a word, the witness of our spirit I take to be a sanctified resolution upon deep sorrow and mature judgment both of God's mercies bestowed, and my obedience to the will of God; whence the soul gathers strength to wait and depend upon God, and serve him in all holiness, though for the present he hide his face and seem an enemy. When thus our valour and faith is tried, then comes the same Spirit, and seals with our spirit, that we are the children of God. When our seal is first put, then God seals with our spirit the same thing by his Spirit. To this effect, 1 John v. 8, we read of three witnesses there set down,

1. The Spirit; 2, the water; 3, the blood.

'And these three agree in one.' These three witness that we have everlasting life, and that our names are written in heaven. How do these three agree with these two witnesses? Very well, Saint John ranks them according to the order of their clearest evidence.

1. The Spirit; 2, then the water; 3, then the blood.

The apostle here ranks them according to their natural being: first, our spirit in justification; and sanctification is put next, and then God's Spirit. For the Spirit, of all other things, is the clearest evidence; and when this is bright and manifest, there needs no more. The thing is sealed. So the testimony of water is a clear evidence whereby is meant sanctification. This is put next unto the Spirit; for when the Spirit is silent, yet this may speak. For though I have many wants and imperfections in me, yet if my spirit can testify unto me that I have a desire to please God in all things, that I have resolved to set up his service as the pitch of all my utmost endeavours; that I with allowance will cherish no corruption, but have set myself against all: this water will thus comfort. It holds up a man from sinking, as we see in all the sore troubles of Job, chap. xxvii. 2–5, he still stood upon the integrity of his own spirit, and would not let that go though he were sore beaten of the Almighty, and slandered of his friends for a wicked person. But the water may be muddy, and the struggling of the flesh and spirit so strong, that we cannot well judge which is master. What then? In this case faith lays hold of the blood of justification, which though it be the darkest testimony, yet is it as sure as any of the other. Now in comparing these witnesses together in Saint John and in my text,

1. I rank the water and the blood with the testimony of our spirit. And,

2. The Spirit mentioned in St John and in my text to be all one.

Not as though we wrought them, but that we do believe them to be so. If a man ask, how I know that I am sanctified? the answer must be, I believe, I know it to be so. The work of working these things in me comes of God; but the work of discerning them is certain, how our affection stands in this case—comes of us. But yet to come nearer to the matter.

'The testimony of our spirit.'

I conceive to be, when a man hath taken a survey of those excellent things, belonging unto justification and sanctification; when according to the substantial truths which I know in the word belonging thereunto, I observe and follow as fast as I may what is there commanded; when I take the candle of the word, and with that bright burning lamp search what is to be done, and therewith lance my corruptions, *and so bring it home*, then is it mine. This is the ground-work of the witness of our spirit. As in the blood, with my spirit I must see what is needful to be done to be justified; what free promises of invitation belong thereunto. I must see how God justifies the sinner, what conditions on our part are required in justification, and my interest therein. I must see what footings and grounds of life give way, and hope for a graceless man to be saved, yea, even unto the worst person that may be. In this case a man must not look for anything in himself as a cause. Christ must not be had by exchange, but received as a free gift, which the apostle shews, Rom. iv. 16, 'Therefore it is of faith, that it might be by grace; to the end the promise might be sure to all the seed,' &c. I must therefore bring out* the receiving of Christ a bare hand; first, it must be of grace. God for this cause will make us let fall everything before we shall take hold of him. Though qualified with humiliation, I must let all fall; not trusting unto it, as to make me the worthier to receive Christ, as some think. When thus at first for my

* Qu. 'unto'?—Ed.

justification I receive Christ, I must let anything I have fall, to lay hold on him, that then he may find us thus in our shirts, as it were—in our blood—and in this sort God will take us, that all may be of mere grace.

Another thing is required, *that the promise may be sure.* If anything in us must be as a cause or help to our justification, a man should never be sure; therefore it is all of grace, that the promise may be sure. As though God should say, I care for nothing else, thou canst bring me in this case. Bring me my Son, and shew me him, and then all is well. And in this you see he doth not name hope or love, or any other grace, but faith. For the nature of faith is to let fall all things in laying hold of Christ. In justification faith is a sufferer only. But in sanctification it works and purgeth the whole man, and so witnesseth the certainty and truth of our justification, and so the assurance of salvation.

Hence, from the nature thereof in this work, 2 Pet. i. 1, the apostle writes unto them who had received the like precious faith. In this case, it was alike to all in virtue in this work, whatsoever the measure be. And I may liken it thus: Paul, we know, says, 'with these hands I got my living,' 1 Cor. iv. 12. Now, though strong hands may work more than weak, and so earn a great deal, yet a beggar who holds out his hands may receive more than some other can earn; so faith doth justify us by receiving, not working, as you may see, John i. 12, 'But as many as received him, to them gave he power to become the sons of God, even to them that believe in his name.' What then should we do to be saved? Why, receive him: that is, believe in him now. Come and take sure hold, as in the Revelation, 'and let him that is athirst come; and whosoever will, let him take of the water of life freely,' Rev. xxii. 17.

1. *Open house.* Now when I see that God keeps *open house,* come who will, without denying entertainment unto any, and when God's Spirit hath wrought the will in me, and I come and take God at his word, and believe in Christ, laying hold by degrees on the other promises of life, winding and wrapping myself in them as I am able, this is faith; but that persuasion, that I have, that I shall go to heaven, which many think to be faith, is not so, but rather a consequent thereof. The promise is made unto those who believe in Christ; for in him, saith the apostle, 'all the promises are yea and amen,' 2 Cor. i. 20. If a man weep much, and beg hard for the forgiveness of sins, he may weep and be without comfort unto the end of the world, unless he have received Christ, and applied his virtue home unto the trembling soul. A man must first receive Christ, and then he hath a warrant to interest himself in all the promises. So that now this being done, if such a man were asked, Hast thou a warrant to receive Christ? He will answer, Yes, I have a warrant. He keeps open house unto all who come, welcoming all, and I have a will to come. This is a good and sufficient warrant; if I have a will in me wrought for to come, and do come. And this is the first thing to be observed in the witness of our spirit.

2. *Invitation.* Now if a man do stagger, for all that the King keeps open house, so as he will not or doth not come, then in the second place comes *invitation.* Because we are slow to believe, therefore God invites us: Mat. xi. 28, 'Come unto me, all ye that labour and are heavy laden, and I will give you rest.' Many object, Oh, I am not worthy to come! But you see here is invitation to encourage me; yea, the sorer and heavier my load is, I should come so much the rather. So that if in this case the question should be asked of such a one, Friend, how came you hither?

What warrant had you to be so bold? Then he shews his ticket, as if he should say, Lord, thou gavest me a word of comfort, 'a warrant to come.' My load and burden indeed was very heavy, and my unworthiness great; but at thy invitation, in obedience to thy word, and faith in thy promise, I came hither. Now this invitation is directed to them who have no goodness yet wrought in them. When, then, my spirit warrants thus much unto me, that upon this word of promise and invitation, I have come in for relief and ease of my miseries unto Christ Jesus, the great physician, relying on him for cure, and lying, as it were, at his foot for mercy, this is the testimony of my spirit, that I do believe, and a ground for me to rest on, that now I am in the way of life, and justified by his grace.

3. *Entreaty.* Thirdly, Sometimes Christ meets with a slow and dull heart, lazy and careless, in a manner, what become of it; not knowing or weighing the dangerous estate it is in; making excuses. There Christ might justly leave us; for is it not too much that the King should invite us for our good, as he did those in the gospel, who, for refusing to come to his supper, were excluded from ever tasting thereof, and strangers were fetched in in their places? God might so deal with us; but you see, 2 Cor. v. 20, 'God sends an embassage to *entreat us*;' erects a new office, as it were, for our sakes. Says he, 'Now then we are ambassadors for Christ, as though God did beseech you by us: we pray you in Christ's stead, to be reconciled to God.' This may seem to be needless; we being weaker than he; ambassadors are sent to the stronger. The apostle reasons the matter: 'Are we stronger than he? Do we provoke the Lord to anger?' But here we see and may admire his infinite rich goodness, that he doth come to sue to us to be reconciled with him. We know it might be counted a kind of indignity for the king of Spain, so great a monarch, to sue unto the Hollanders for peace, who are so far inferior unto him. This dishonour God puts up at our hands, and says* unto us first, when rather it becomes us on our knees to beg for it. The effect of the embassage is, that we would be friends with him, and receive that which is so highly for our advancement. When, therefore, I see this quickness in my heart, so that, as St James speaks of the engrafted word to save our souls, I can bring it home, having some sweet relish and high estimation of it in my heart, that it begins to be the square and rule of my life, then I am safe. If this or any of these fasten upon the soul, and thereupon I yield and come in, it is enough to shew that I am a justified person, and from hence our spirit may witness, and that truly. This is a third thing in the witness of our spirit.

4. *Command.* Fourthly, If none of all this will do, then comes a further degree, *a command from the Highest*, You shall do it, as 1 John iii. 23, 'And this is his commandment, that we should believe on the name of his Son Jesus Christ, and love one another as he gave us commandment.' In the parliament of grace there is a law of faith, which binds one as strictly to believe as to keep any of the commandments. Saith the apostle, Rom. iii. 27, 'Where is boasting then? It is excluded. By what law? Of works? Nay, but by the law of faith.' So that if I will not believe on the Lord Jesus, who easeth me from the rigour of the law, and so is my righteousness, I shall perish for ever. What, may one object, *must* I needs believe? Yes, thou art as strictly bound to believe, as not to murder, not to be an idolater, not to steal. Nay, I will add more, that thy infidelity and contempt of that gracious offer, thy disobedience to the law of faith, is

* Qu. 'sues'?—Ed.

greater than thy disobedience to the law of works; when thou dost fling God's grace in his face again, and, as it were, trample under foot the blood of the covenant. See for this John xvi. 9. What is that great sin which Christ came to reprove? Even this infidelity, says he, 'because they believe not in me;' which in two respects is a great sin. First, because it sins against God's mercy; secondly, because it is a chain which links and binds all other sins together. Thus faith is sure, when it lies on the word, otherwise all other thoughts are but presumption, and will fail a man in the time of need. For what is faith, I pray you, but my assent to believe every word of God. He hath commanded me to believe, and to endeavour the practice.

5. *Threatenings.* Fifthly, If all this will not do, then comes *threatenings.* Then God swears, that such as refuse shall never enter into his rest. If the prince should sue unto a beggar's daughter for marriage, and she should refuse and contemn his offer, do you think he would be well pleased? So it is with us when the King of heaven's Son sends to us, will you be married to me? If we refuse, the Son doth take on wonderfully; and therefore, Ps. ii. 12, he says, 'Kiss the Son, lest he be angry, and ye perish in the way, when his wrath is kindled but a little. Blessed are all those that put their trust in him.' So Hebrews iii. 18: God swore because of infidelity those unbelieving Jews should never enter into his rest. All the rest of the threatenings in the law were not with an oath. There was some secret reservation of mercy upon the satisfaction of divine justice; but here there is no reservation. God hath sworn such shall never come to heaven. Look not for a third thing in God, as a mitigation of his oath. It cannot be. He hath sworn no unbeliever shall ever enter into his rest.

These five things are the grounds of faith even to the worst and unworthiest persons that may be, which, once wrought in the heart and the spirit, and the Spirit of God renewing our spirits, discerneth the same spirit. These are the witness of our spirit.

Now, our spirit having viewed all these things and the promises upon which they are grounded, thus it witnesses, as if one should demand of one, Are all these things presented to thy view true? Yes, will he say, true as the gospel. Then the next thing is, Are they good and profitable? Oh yes, saith he, all are very good and desirable. Then the upshot is, Are all good to thee? If then thou accept of this and warp and fold thyself in the promises, thou canst not wind thyself out of comfort and assurance to be in Christ Jesus; for, I pray you, what makes up a match but the consent of two agreeing. So the consent of two parties upon this embassage makes up the match between us and Christ, and unites and knits us unto him.

There are also, being now incorporate, other means to make us grow up in him, by which time discovers what manner of engrafting we have had in him. As we see four or five siens* may be engrafted in a stock and yet some of them not take root, but wither, so, many are by the word and sacraments admitted as retainers and believers of the promises who shrink and hold not out, because they never took root, but it only swimmed in the brain. Yet, howsoever, all that come to life must pass this way, if they look for sound comfort. Thus much shall suffice for the witness of our spirit in justification; but our spirit's testimony goes further, wherein I might shew you how in sanctification our spirit says, 'Lord, prove me, try me if there be evil in me, and lead me in the way for ever,' Ps. cxxxix.

* That is, 'scions,' = grafts.—G.

23. He loves the brethren, desires to fear God, as Nehemiah pleads, Neh. i. 11, 'Be attentive to the prayer of thy servant, and of thy servants, who desire to fear thy name,' &c. This is the warrant that I am partaker of that inward true washing, and not of that outward only of the hog, which being kept clean, and in clean company, will be clean till there be occasion of returning to wallow in the mire again. But when I find, though there were neither heaven to reward me nor hell to punish me, if opportunity were, yet my heart riseth against the sin because of him who hath forbidden it, this is a sure evidence, and testifies that I am the child of God. Thus much is for the first thing in bringing a man in to survey the promises concerning justification and sanctification, whereupon our spirit doth truly witness the assurance of our salvation.

Secondly, When I find Christ drawing and changing my nature, that upon the former reasonings and view, and laying hold of Christ, making me now have supernatural thoughts and delights,—for this a man may have,—then, certainly, my spirit may conclude that I am blessed; for, saith the Scripture, 'Blessed is the man whom thou choosest, and causest to come unto thee,' Ps. lxv. 4.

But some like drones do dream of this, I know not on what grounds; these men can have no comfort. But do I this waking with my whole soul? Doth my spirit testify it upon good grounds? Then I may rest upon it; it is as sure as may be. This is the testimony of our spirit. Yet, ere I come to the witness of God's Spirit with our spirit: there may be often an interposing trial betwixt; God may write bitter things against me, seem to cast me off, wound me for all this as with the wound of an enemy, and remove the sense of the light of his countenance from me. What then is to be done? What doth the witness of our spirit now? Why then I will trust in him, though he kill me, Job xiii. 15. Sure I am I have loved and esteemed the words of his mouth, more than mine appointed food, Job xxiii. 12; as Job speaks, 'I have laid hold of them to shew their power and believe them, I have desired to fear him and yield obedience to all his commandments.' If I must die, I will yet wait on him and die at his feet. Look here is the strength of faith. Christ had faith without feeling when he cried out, 'My God, my God, why hast thou forsaken me?' When sense is marvellous low, then faith is at the strongest. We must walk here by faith; we shall have sense and sight enough in another world. The apostle saith, 'We walk by faith, and not by sight, and by faith we stand;' as we may see a pattern in that woman of Canaan, Mat. xv. 22, *seq.* She was repulsed as a stranger, yet she went on; then she was called a dog. She might have been dashed and given over her suit; but see, this is the nature of faith, to pick comforts out of discomforts; to see out of a very small hole those things which raise and bring matter of consolation. She catcheth at that quickly, Am I a dog, Lord? Why yet it is well, 'The dogs eat the crumbs which fall from their master's table.' Thus faith was strong in her; and when this trial was past, then Christ says unto her, 'Woman, great is thy faith, have what thou wilt.'

I have done with the testimony of our spirit. And then from our believing God in generals and valorous resting upon him, taking him at his word, comes 'the testimony of God's Spirit, witnessing with our spirit, that we are the children of God.'

I say, this being done, and God letting us have trial what his strength is in us, he will not let us stand long in this uncomfortable state, but will come again and speak peace unto us; after two days gather us up, and the third day revive us, that we may live in his sight. As if he should say, What! hast thou believed me on my bare word? Hast thou honoured me so as to lay the blame and fault of all my trials on thyself for thy sins, and clear my justice in all things? Hast thou honoured me so as to magnify my mercy, to wait and hope in it for all this? Hast thou trusted me so as to remain faithful in all thy miseries? Then the Lord puts to the seal of his Spirit. As we may read Eph. i. 13, saith the apostle, 'In whom also ye trusted, after that you heard the word of truth, the gospel of your salvation: in whom also, after that ye believed, ye were sealed with the Holy Spirit of promise, which is the earnest of our inheritance,' &c.

Here is the difference betwixt faith and sense. Faith doth take hold of general promises, applies them, makes them her own, and lives and walks by them; and so squares his life by those rules in all things, as without sense she leads us on to heaven; but sense is another thing, when as Ps. xxxv. 3, there is a full report made unto the soul of its assured happiness. As in that place, 'Say unto my soul, I am thy salvation.' When a man hath thus been gathered home by glorifying him and believing his truth, then comes a special evidence unto the soul and says, 'I am thy salvation,' which, in effect, is that which Christ in another place speaks, 'He that loveth me shall be beloved of my Father, and I will love him, and manifest myself unto him,' John xiv. 21. And as it is Cant. i. 2, 'He will kiss us with the kisses of his mouth,' so as we shall be able to say, 'My well-beloved is mine, and I am his.' When God hath heard us cry a while until we be thoroughly humbled, then he takes us up in his arms and dandles us, making his Spirit after a sensible manner seal unto us the assurance of our salvation. So that a meditation of the word being past, a man having viewed his charter and his evidences, surveying heaven and the promises and privileges, with the glory to come, then the Spirit comes in and makes up a third guest; then comes joy unspeakable and glorious, and in such a measure that the soul is wonderfully pleased. It shall not continue always so, but at some times we shall have it; yet it endures so as that it shall never be taken quite away, as our Saviour's promise is, John xvi. 22: 'And you now therefore have sorrow; but I will see you again, and your heart shall rejoice, and your joy shall no man take from you.' This is the root of all consolation, that God will not forsake us for ever, but he will come at last and have compassion of us, according unto the multitude of his mercies.

Obj. Here some may object, What! doth the Spirit never seal but upon some such hard trials after the witness of our spirit?

Ans. I answer, The sealing of God's Spirit with our spirit is not always tied to sore, hard, and such foregoing trials immediately; for a man may be surveying heaven, or the glory to come, or praying earnestly in much humility, with a tender melting heart, applying the promises and wrestling with God; then at these or some such times God's seal many times may be, and is put to our seal: 'For as the wind bloweth where it listeth, and no man discerneth the coming thereof,' John iii. 8, so may the Spirit of God seal at divers times and upon divers occasions; yea, and why may it not seal in the time of some great suffering for the truth, as we read of the apostles, Acts v. 41, who went away from the council 'rejoicing that they were counted worthy to suffer any shame for his name'?

Lastly, *for trial;* we must now see how to distinguish this testimony of the true Spirit from the counterfeit illumination of the *Anabaptists* and some friars, who will now and then have some strange sudden joys, the devil, no question, transforming himself into an angel of light to deceive them. This trial is made, 1. By three things going before; 2. By three things following after.

First, *See that the ground-work be sure.* If a man be in the faith, and do believe the word; if, upon believing, meditation, opening unto the knock of Christ at first, not delaying him off, like the lazy spouse in the Canticles, if in this case the Spirit come and fill the heart with joy, then all is sure and well. It comes with promise, because then he hath promised to enter. If a man have a dull, dead, delaying ear to open unto Christ, or apply him upon good grounds, and therewith great fantastic joys, he may assure himself they are but idle speculations, not wrought in him by the right sanctification of the Spirit; but if this joy come upon the surveying of charters, evidences, &c., it is sure, we may build upon it.

Secondly, *A man must consider, if he hath as yet overcome strong passions and temptations, and passed through much hazard and peril,* having been buffeted with divers temptations, over which he hath obtained mastery. For this seal of God's Spirit with our spirit comes as a reward of service done; as we may see Rev. iii. 17, 'To him that overcometh will I give to eat of the hidden manna, and I will give him a white stone, and in the stone a new name written, which no man knoweth saving he that receiveth it;' whereby he means, in such a case he will give a secret love-token unto the soul, whereby it may rest assured of the unspeakable love of God and freedom from condemnation.

The Athenians had a custom, when malefactors were accused and arraigned, to have black and white stones by them, and so according to the sentence given, those acquitted had a white, those condemned had a black stone given them. Unto this the Holy Ghost here alludes, that this seal shall assure them of an absolute acquittance from condemnation, and so free them from the cause of fear. Again, he shews Christ will give a man a new name, that is, his absolution written in fair letters upon the white stone with a clear evidence; as if he should say, 'When Christ hath seen a man overcoming, and how he hath buckled with temptations, and yet holds out, pressing on for his crown unto the end of the race, he will come in then, and stroke him on the head, ease all his pains, fears, and sorrows with such a sweet refreshing as is unspeakable. When a man hath won it in sum, he shews he shall wear it.

Thirdly, *If the Spirit seal after meditation in the word,* it is right. The apostle saith, 'In whom, after ye believed, ye were sealed with the Holy Spirit of promise,' Eph. i. 13. Examine the root of your joys. The Spirit gives no comfort but by the word. If a man do meditate on the promises, and thereupon have a flame kindled, when he knows his interest in them, this is sure. A man may say, the word did stir it up. If it be God's comfort, assure thyself God would have his word to make way unto it. Those who find no sweetness in the word, what is the cause thereof? Because they chew not the cud to imprint it in their memories and hearts. If comfort comes whilst a man is meditating on the promises, and wedging them home upon the heart, it is of God, otherwise it is but counterfeit and false. These and divers others may be the forerunners to this seal. Now three things follow after, which the Spirit leaves behind it.

1. First, *Humility;* as in his knowledge, so in his sense, it makes a man more humble. There is naturally in all a certain pride which must be overcome; yea, of all sorts, spiritual pride is the most dangerous. Wherefore know the holiest are ever the humblest people. The apostle saith,

'What hast thou that thou hast not received? and if thou hast received it, why boastest thou?' &c., 1 Cor. iv. 7. By the contrary, the more near a man comes unto the glory of God, the more he sees him, and is truly acquainted with him, so much the more rottenness he finds in his bones; as we see in Job, what he says of himself in this case: Job xlii. 5, 'I have heard of thee by the hearing of the ear, but now my eye seeth thee.' His inference is—'wherefore I abhor myself, and repent in dust and ashes.' And the prophet Isaiah, he cries out, Isa. vi. 5, 'Woe is me, for I am undone, because I am a man of unclean lips, and I dwell in the midst of a people that is of unclean lips.' But wherefore is all this? saith he. 'For mine eyes have seen the Lord of hosts.' It is a certain thing, an humble soul is a sure and certain habitation for the Spirit of God. 'For thus saith the high and lofty One that inhabiteth eternity, whose name is the Lord of Hosts: I dwell in the high and lofty place, with him also that is of a contrite and humble spirit, to revive the spirit of the humble,' &c., Isa. lvii. 15. A proud spirit, therefore, but in vain brags of this seal of God's Spirit, which leaves a man humble, and the vilest of all others in his own sight; for then the brightest and best light hath shewed him more than ever his manifold and darkest corruptions, which abase him in his own eyes, seeing how far short he comes of what he should and ought to be.

2. A second thing which the Spirit leaves behind it, if it seal rightly, is, *a prevention of security to come.* In this case we must look for a new encounter. A false persuasion makes a man to fall into security; because Satan is then most malicious and busy, a man must stand faster than ever. The devil, he hates those most which are most endowed with God's image, whom, because he cannot reach, he persecutes his members. And therefore in this case, it must be with us as it was with Elias in his feast, 1 Kings xix. 8. After such an enlightening, a man must now think that he hath a great journey to go, and so walk on in the strength of that, long time. The devil, you see, watcheth a man at the best, then to overcome him, as we see in Adam and Eve. No sooner were they placed in that estate of innocency but he buckled with them. How much more a man having a sweeter taste of the Spirit and less strength now, may he look to be set upon? And therefore in these feasting days had need to be more in his watch and pray more; for we have more given unto us than Adam had. We have a new name give us, a secret love-token. Further, we see Christ saith, Rev. iii. 20, 'Behold, I stand at the door and knock: if any man will open unto me, I will come in and sup with him, and he with me.' Now, in such a case, if we be such parties who let our hearts fly open to let him in, we are safe; as if he should say, if you would be sure of reconciliation to be at peace with me, sup with me, and I will sup with you. For we know, if men formerly enemies be brought to keep company and eat together, we use to say, all is done and lapped up in the napkin; old reckonings are forgotten and taken away. Now they are certainly friends. But if, like the spouse in the Canticles, we let him stand knocking, and will not let him in, we may have great, many, and sound knocks ere we find him again, as we know it befell the church then, when she had lost her communion with him. Our Saviour, you see, knowing the devil's violence and subtilty in taking us unprovided, how often doth he command us to watch and pray, that we enter not into temptation. 'That I say unto you I say unto all men, Watch,' Mark xiii. 37. If we would therefore retain our comfort after such a sweet taste, or having lost it, recover the same, let us watch chiefly at that time, and prepare for a new assault. Then

again, in a loss, let us mark the knocks of the Spirit, when, as it is Isa. xxx. 21, 'A voice behind us says, Walk this way, and that way,' &c., and grieve him not by withstanding holy motions, and then we shall find him sealing our salvation, and witnessing with our spirit that we are the children of God. Men, you see, wait for the wind, and not the wind for them, else they may be long enough ere they reach home. So must we watch the knocks of Christ to let him in, that so his Spirit may seal us up to the day of redemption. Oh, how happy were it for us if thus we could do, and still watch and be ready for a new encounter! For let no man think to have more freedom from temptations than our blessed Saviour had, of whom it is written, Luke iv. 13, 'That when the devil had ended all his temptations against him, he departed from him *for a season*.'

The third thing the true Spirit leaves behind it is *love*. It makes a man the more enkindled with love to God. If a man do not love God more after such an enlightening, it is false and counterfeit. Saith the prophet David, 'I will love thee dearly, my Lord, my God, because thou hast heard my voice.' And the apostle saith, 2 Cor. v. 14, 'For the love of God constraineth us,' &c. And therefore, if we be obedient sons, we must shew it in loving and honouring our Father more and more; as Mal. i. 6, 'A son honoureth his father, and a servant his master; if I then be a father, where is mine honour?' Yea, then, this love will break forth unto others like fire, to warm and comfort them. 'Come unto me, all ye that fear the Lord, and I will tell you what he hath done for my soul,' &c., saith the prophet, Ps. lxvi. 16; so a holy soul in this case finds a fire like that of Elihu. It is like new wine in bottles that cannot hold. There is an holy rejoicing, an holy praising; holy flames sent towards others. Much love increased to them; admiration of such excellent surpassing things as remain in the life to come, if a taste be so much here.

I cannot go on further now. These, in brief, may serve us for a trial of the truth of God's Spirit witnessing with our spirit that we are the children of God, which now let us pray for, 'O Lord our God,' &c.

SAINT PAUL'S CHALLENGE.

What shall we then say to these things? If God be for us, who can be against us?—Rom. VIII. 31.

The words are a glorious conclusion and triumph of faith: the conclusion upon all the former particulars in the chapter, and the foundation of all the comforts that follow after, to the end of the chapter. They are as the centre of the chapter. All the beams of heavenly comfort in this divine chapter, they meet, as it were in one, in this short clause, 'What shall we say then to these things?' &c.

In the words, briefly, there is *first a question*, 'What shall we say to these things?'

And *then a triumph*, 'If God be with us, who can be against us?' It is a question answered with another question, 'What shall we say to these things?' He answers it with another question, 'If God be with us, who can be against us?'

'What shall we say to these things?'

To these things before mentioned. If we be in Christ, there is no condemnation to us; if we be led by the Spirit, if we be heirs of heaven and fellow-heirs with Christ, if we suffer with him, if we have the spirit of prayer to help our infirmities in the worst conditions, if all creatures groan with us, and if all work for our good, if God from all eternity hath written our names in heaven by election, and separated us from the rest of the world in vocation, and hath sanctified and justified us, and will after glorify us, 'what shall we say to these things?'

The heart of man is full of doubtings and misgiving, full of thoughts: 'According to the multitude of my thoughts, thy comforts refreshed my soul,' Ps. xciv. 19. A multitude of thoughts and a multitude of comforts. There is comfort after comfort, because there are thoughts after thoughts, and surmises after surmises. There is no waste comfort set down in this

* 'Saint Paul's Challenge' forms No. 8 of the Sermons entitled 'Beams of Divine Light' (4to, 1639). Its separate title-page is as follows:—'Saint Pauls Challenge. In one Sermon. By The late learned and reverend Divine, Rich. Sibbs: Doctor in Divinitie, M[r] of Katherine Hall in Cambridge, and sometimes Preacher at Grayes-Inne. Psal. 27. 3. Though an Host should encampe against me, my heart shall not fear; though warre should rise against me, In this will I be confident. London, Printed by E. P. for Nicholas Bourne, and Rapha Harford 1638.'—G.

chapter; and when he hath set down all, he comes and concludes in a triumphant manner, 'What shall we say to these things?' He propounds the *quære* to himself, he catechiseth his own heart and others. If these things be so, what can be said against them? Surely the unbelieving, doubting, dark, rebellious heart of man hath many things to say against divine truths; for though divine truths be lighter than the sun, and there is no greater evidence of anything in the world, yet they find no place in the unbelieving heart. Let God say what he will, the doubting heart is ready to gainsay it. But these truths are so pregnant and clear, that it is a wonder that anything should be said against them: 'What shall we say to these things?'

Again he means, what comfort can you have more? What can you desire more? What can be said more? What use will you make of all that hath been said? What will you suck out of it? If all this be true that hath been spoken before, that a Christian is so elevated above the common condition; if God love him from everlasting in election, and to everlasting in glorification; if in the middle time all shall work for the best, what comfort can the heart of man desire more? and what use can you make of this for courage and for comfort for the time to come? These things are implied in this question, 'what shall we say to these things?'

Use. It is good often to propound *quæres* and demands to our own hearts, when we read or hear divine truths; to ask our own hearts, You have heard these things, what say you to them? For whatsoever God saith in his word will do us no good till we speak to our own hearts, and be convinced of it, and say it is so. Therefore we should say to ourselves, Here are many comforts and duties pressed, but what sayest thou to it, my heart? Dost thou not stand out against comforts and advice? It is no matter what God saith, unless he overpower the unbelieving heart to say, 'What shall I say to these things?' Shall I not agree with God and his Spirit, and his comforts? Shall they be best in regard of an unbelieving heart? Oh no! Therefore let our care be to store them in the treasury of our memory, which should be like the pot of manna, to contain heavenly comforts. Let us treasure up all the truths we can, all will be little enough when we shall need comfort. But when we have them in our memory, let us ask ourselves, Are these things so or no? If they be so, believe them; if they be not so, then let us give liberty to ourselves, and away with hearing and reading, &c. If they be so, for shame let me yield to them.

Let us ask these questions with some fruit; let us deal thus with our own hearts, often call them to account whether we believe or no; for we have such a faculty and power, we can reflect upon ourselves. And we ought to desire of the Spirit of God to teach our hearts to reflect upon themselves, to examine whether we know, and if we know, whether we believe, and what use we make of these things, and why we should live thus? Doth this life and course of mine agree with these principles? The best of us all are tardy this way. Therefore let not that part without making some use of it. But I proceed to that I will more dwell on,

'If God be for us, who can be against us?'

Here is first a ground laid, and then a comfort built upon it. The ground that is laid is, 'If God be with us.' When he saith, 'If God be with us,' he doth not put the case, but lays it as a ground. 'If God be with us,' as indeed he is with all his in electing them, in calling them, in working all for their good, in glorifying them after, &c., 'If God be with us,' as he is, then this comfort is built upon this ground, 'who shall or can be against us?'

For the first, the ground that is laid is, that *God is with his children.*

Indeed, he is with the whole world. He is everywhere; but he is with his church and children in a more peculiar manner. The soul is spread in the whole body, but it is in the brain after another manner, as it understands and reasons. God is everywhere; but he is not everywhere comforting, and directing, and sanctifying, nor everywhere giving a sweet and blessed issue. So, besides the general respect, that I will not now stand on, God is 'with us' that are his in a more peculiar manner in all his sweet attributes: in his wisdom to direct us, with his power to assist and strengthen us, by his grace and love to comfort us; and he is with us in all our perplexities, to stay our souls. He is with us by his sweet and gracious mercy, to feed us with hidden manna, with secret comforts in the midst of discomforts. When there is no comfort else with us, then God is with us; and then he is with us in the issue of all that a godly man takes in hand in his name. He is with him in all crosses, to direct and turn them to his best good; 'All things work for the best to them that love God,' Rom. vi. 23. He is with them in all his sweet relations as a gracious Father in covenant, as a husband. He is with them in those sweet comparisons: as a hen, Mat. xxiii. 37; as an eagle, to carry them on his wings above all dangers, as he carried the Israelites in the wilderness, Deut. xxxii. 11. He is with them in all comfortable relations.

Therefore God, in the Scriptures, borrows names from everything that is comfortable. He is with them as a rock, to build on; as a shield, to defend them; in the time of heat and persecution, he is a shadow, to keep them from the heat; he is with them as a light. Christ is our life in death, our light in darkness, our righteousness in sinfulness and guilt, our holiness in impurity, our redemption in all our miseries. There is somewhat of God in every creature; therefore God takes names from his own creatures, because there is some strength or comfort in them. God gives himself variety of names, as there are variety of our distresses. Are we in misery? God is a rock, a shield, a tower of defence, a buckler; he is all that can be said for comfort. He is with us in his attributes and sweet relations, and all sweet terms that may support our faith, that whatsoever we see comfortable in the creature, we may rise more comfortably to God, and say, God is my rock and shield, and my light and defence.

And then God is with us in every condition and in every place whatsoever. He is not only a God of the mountains and not of the valleys, or a God of the valleys and not of the mountains, as those foolish people thought, 1 Kings xx. 28, but he is in all places, and at all times with his. If they be in prison, he goes with them: Acts xvi. 22, *seq.*, he made the prison a kind of paradise, a heaven. If they be banished into other countries, he goes with them; 'I will go with thee, O Jacob, into Egypt, and bring thee back again,' Gen. xlviii. 21. If they be in death, he is with us to death and in death: 'In the valley of the shadow of death, thou art with me,' Ps. xxiii. 4. At all times whatsoever, and in all conditions, God is with us.

In all our affairs whatsoever God is with us. 'Fear not,' Joshua; 'fear not,' Moses. What was the ground of their comfort? 'I will be with thee.' He was with St Paul in all conditions, therefore he bids him 'fear not,' Acts xxvii. 24. So our blessed Saviour, the head of all, in Acts x. 38, in the speech of Peter to Cornelius, he did all things well, 'for God was with him.' You see how God is with his children.

What is the ground that the great, and holy, and pure God, blessed for ever, should be with such sinful and wretched creatures as we are? that he should not only be with us, and about us, and compass us as a shield, but be in us?

The ground of all is his free love in Christ. Christ was God with us first. God, that he might be with us, ordained that Christ should be God with us; 'Emmanuel,' that he should take our nature into unity of person with himself. Christ being God with us, that he might satisfy the just wrath of God for our sins, and so reconcile God and us together, he hath made God and us friends. So that this, that God is with us, it is grounded upon an excellent and sound bottom; upon the incarnation of our blessed Saviour, that for this very end, that God might be with us, was God with us; that is, he was God and man, to bring God and man together; he was God and man in one, to bring God and man, that were at contrary terms, to terms of reconciliation; to recollect and bring us back again to God, from whence we fell. So the reason why God the Father, Son, and Holy Ghost are with us, it is because Christ, the second person, God and man, is with us, or else there could be no such sweet terms as these are. You see how it is founded. Christ took our nature, and advanced and enriched it. Now he having taken our nature and our persons to be one with him, how near are Christ and we together! There is one common Spirit in him and us, one common Father, 'I go to my Father and your Father, to my God and your God,' John xx. 17. There is one common kingdom and inheritance. We are fellow-heirs with him. Oh, how near is Christ to us! Our souls are not so near our bodies as Christ is to us, and God in Christ. So you see this, that God is with us. It is founded upon an excellent, wonderful, comfortable mystery. This I suppose is clear; therefore I come to that I intend further to enlarge; that is, the comfort built upon this ground, 'If God be with us, who shall be against us?'

One would think this a strange question; for a Christian no sooner comes to be one with Christ, and so to be reconciled to God, but he hath against him all the powers of hell; and then he hath the whole world against him presently, Satan's kingdom; and then he hath an enemy that is worst of all, that stirs up strife and rebellion and contention even in his own heart, his own flesh. So that we may say, who is not against a Christian? If God be with us, all else but God will side against us. There are two grand sides in the world, to which all belong. There is God's side, and those that are his; and there is another side, that is, Satan's, and those that are his; two kingdoms, two seeds, two contrary dispositions, that pursue one another, till all the one be in hell, Satan and all his seed together, the devil and all that fight under his banner, that are led with his malignant, poisonful spirit. Though it may be they cannot do more hurt, or do not out of politic respects, though they have poisonful hearts, yet these never leave contending till they be in hell; and the other never leave till they be in heaven together. Christ makes it his prayer, 'My will is, that where I am, they may be also,' John xvii. 24, and his will must be performed; so that he need not ask the question, 'If God be with us, who shall be against us?' There will be enow against us.

It is true. But in what sense are they against us, and how far are they against us?

They are thus far against us in their wit,* in their plots and policies; in their wills they would devour all if they could. They are against us in

* That is, 'wisdom.'—G.

their endeavours. They do what they can against the church and people of God. They are against us in their prevailing likewise. Their endeavours are not idle, but prevail very far over God's people, even to insolency: 'Where is now their God?' Ps. xlii. 10, as it is oft in the Psalms, and to the dejection of God's people; 'The Lord hath forsaken me; the Lord hath forgotten me,' Ps. xxxi. 12. God's people are brought very low, to the pit's brink; the pit almost shuts her mouth upon them. So you see they are against them many ways. God gives a great length to their tether.

And many reasons God hath to let them prevail, both to draw out their malice the more, and then to shew his people their corruptions the more, and then to exercise their graces in waiting, and for the just confusion of their enemies at the latter end, and for the sweet comfort of his children at the end—when God sees the fittest time to meet with the enemies—that they might have sweet experience of God's seasonable care, however God put off a long time for some respects. So you see they may prevail a long time. Yet who can be against us in this sense, that is, to prevail altogether? Who shall be against us, so far as to have their will in the issue? They prevail a great way. What do they intend? Not to prevail over the person of God's church and people, but the cause, which, in spite of Satan and his instruments, and all, must stand invincibe to the end of the world. They intend likewise to prevail over the courage of God's people. That they cannot neither; for Saint Paul saith after, in this chapter, 'In all these things we are more than conquerors,' Rom. viii. 37; that is, abundant conquerors, a strange high term. But in some sense we are more than conquerors; for if we consider what weak persons God's children are, what strong enemies they have, and what weak means they prevail with in the sight of the world, to flesh and blood, that such persons should prevail over such enemies, by such weak means as they do, in this respect, they are more than conquerors. So he may say, 'Who can be against us?' that is, to have their wills, to overthrow the cause of Christ, and the courage of God's children; they may prevail in this or that particular, but at the last all their plots and counsels shall prove abortive, and bring forth a lie. All is but to magnify God's power the more in letting them go so far, and then to dash all their moulds and plots. God's children, they have the devil and all his company, the world and the flesh [against them]. But there is God the Father, Son, and Holy Ghost for them, the blessed Trinity, that are able to blow away the other three, and all the strength and support they have whatsoever.

'Who shall be against us?'

It is not a question of doubting, or inquisition to learn anything, but it is a question of triumph. He doth, as it were, cast a bank, and bid defiance to all enemies whatsoever. 'Who shall be against us?' Let them stand out, Satan and the world, and all Satan's supports; let them do their worst. There is a strange confidence which is seated in the hearts of God's children, that they dare thus dare hell and earth, and all infernal powers; they set God so high in their hearts, that they dare say with a spirit of confidence, 'Who shall be against us?' The meaning is not, who shall be against us, to take away our lives or liberties, &c. As the speech is, they may kill us, but they cannot hurt us. The worst they can do is to send us to heaven, and make us partakers of that we desire most. First, we desire that God will be with us here; and, secondly, that we may be with God in heaven. They make God's children partakers of their desires by killing of them. Let tyrants and all persons that have a malignant disposition to the church of God, and armed with power, let them do their worst, the cause must stand impregnable. Christ will have a church and kingdom in the world, and their spirits will be impregnable against them. They may kill them, but they cannot hurt them; they may kill them, but they cannot kill their courage. As we see in the martyrs, there was the Spirit of God in them above all the dealings of the persecutors; there was a fire of God's Spirit in them above all outward fire whatsoever. You see it must be taken for granted, that the church of God and every particular Christian hath many enemies against them, as it is Ps. cxxix. 1, 'From my youth up,' saith the church, 'they have fought against me, but they have not prevailed.' From my youth up; from Abel to the last saint that shall be in the world, there will be alway some against God's people, yet their comfort is that none shall be against them to prevail, either over the Spirit of God in them, or over the cause that they manage.

Use. First of all you see then, that the state of a Christian in this world is an impregnable state, and a glorious condition. Here is glory upon glory, from this clause to the end of the chapter: 'If God be with us, who shall be against us? If God gave his Son for us, shall he not with him give us all things else?' There is another glorious speech, 'Who shall lay anything to the charge of God's people?' Another glorious triumphant speech, another glorious speech, 'Who shall separate us from the love of God founded in Christ?' He loves Christ first, and us in Christ as members; and as he loves them* eternally, so he loves us eternally too. Therefore you see every way the state of a Christian is a glorious condition. 'Who can be against us?' You see the state of God's people. It is an impregnable and glorious condition. Then by this means those that are strange paradoxes to flesh and blood, yet they agree in a Christian. He is never alone. When he is alone, God is with him; the Father, Son, and Holy Ghost are with him, angels are with him. God is not only with him, but his guard is with him; and God's Spirit is with him, and in him victoriously both in grace and comfort. Christ saith to his disciples, when they thought to leave him alone; saith he, you cannot leave me alone, 'my Father is with me,' John viii. 16; and St Paul towards his latter end, that had deserved so well of the Christian world: 'All forsook me,' saith he, 'but the Lord forsook me not, but delivered me out of the mouth of the lion,' 2 Tim. iv. 17. So a Christian is not alone; he is not left to the mercy of his enemies, but God is with him, and who shall be against him to prevail over him?

Again, though a Christian be a worm, a person trampled upon, for so the church is the most afflicted part of mankind, yet 'fear not thou, worm Jacob,' Isa. xli. 14. The world accounts them as worms, and they account themselves so. They are trodden on as worms. They are worms upon earth, yet they have a glorious head in heaven, and a glorious guard about them. Strange things agree in a Christian. Therefore let us not stumble, though we see not these things presently. The life of a Christian is a mystery.

Again, hence we see that a Christian profession, to be a sound Christian, to have true faith in Christ, to be one with Christ, and to be taken out of the state of nature, this condition and the happiness of it, it hath the strongest foundation of any life in the world. Christianity is founded upon the strongest and the greatest reasons that can be. Faith stands with

* Qu. 'him'?—Ed.

the greatest reason that a thing can do. Why? The comfort of a Christian is that he hath no enemy that shall prevail over him, and what is the ground of that? God is with him; God the Father, Son, and Holy Ghost. Faith is that that lays hold upon that presence, and promise, and covenant of God. And is not faith well bottomed? A Christian that carries himself valiantly and courageously, is not his course grounded on sound reason? Is not God with him? God the Father is his Father, God the Son is his Redeemer, God the Holy Ghost is his Comforter. There is no other men that have strong reason for their course, for that choice that they make of their religion and of their ways. They prove but fools in the conclusion. Only the sound Christian that by the Spirit of God hath his eyes opened to see the cursed estate he is in by nature, and what it is to be in Christ, and by a Spirit of faith is made one with Christ, he is the truly wise man in his faith and affiance, that the world mocks at, that he hath no common supports in the world, which he cares not for if God be on his side. He cares not what man can do against him, as it is Ps. cxviii. 6. You see on what ground it is founded. God is with him, and none can be against him.

Let us labour to lay up these principles. We work according as our principles are. Principles are the foundation of all conclusions that arise from them. As our grounds are, so are we in our faith, and working, and grace, and comfort every way. If we have rotten principles, if the grounds of our comfort be rotten, our course will be rotten and uncomfortable in the conclusion. Let us build upon the rock, to be well bottomed and founded, that our principles and grounds be strong, and that they be so to us; for what if God be with his, if he be not so to us? Let us labour to lay up sound grounds. Grounds have influence into the whole course of our lives. This one text hath influence into all the parts of our lives, in doing, in suffering, in all conditions. I know not a more pregnant, fruitful principle in the Scripture than this, 'If God be with us, who can be against us?' It is like a pearl, little in quantity, few in words, but strong in sense, large in the fruit that issues from it. Therefore as we may carry pearls or precious things wheresoever we go, because there is a great deal of worth in them, and they be small in quantity, so we may carry this principle with us, let us be sure to lay it up and make use of it. There be these two, that there is a God, and that God is with his children, and so with his children that he will subvert and overthrow all their enemies, and all their plots and endeavours, a principle of wonderful comfort.

If this principle be well laid, it is a ground of a Christian's courage in all conditions whatsoever. It is no matter how many enemies he hath; for as Cyprian saith, *Non potest seculum, &c.*: the world cannot hurt him that in the world hath God for his protector. For the devil, he is crushed already. Though he keep ado, and stir up storms, he perisheth in the waves, as he saith. He hurts himself more than anybody else; he increaseth his own torment, and so do all his children. The flesh likewise it bustles against the Spirit, but it loseth; and the Spirit gains upon every foil. Why? Here is the principle, 'God is with us.' There is no power can resist God, for then God should withstand himself. The power that the creature hath, it is but a borrowed power; and if by a borrowed power it should withstand God's purpose, God must be against himself, his kingdom must be divided, which is a contradiction. Therefore this is the ground of the courage of a Christian in all conditions. What is the reason that the Scripture hath this phrase so often, 'Fear not, I am with thee,' as to Paul, and Joshua, and the rest? Because it is the ground of all courage. We see weaker creatures than man: a dog in the sight of his master, he will fight courageously, because he hath a superior nature by him, that he thinks will back him. And shall not a Christian, when he hath laid up this principle, that God is with him, God incarnate, God in his nature, when he is a member of God as it were, of that person that is God, shall he not be courageous when he hath him to look upon him, and to back him?

And if God be with us, he is not so with us as to neglect us. He is so with us as he hath interest in the cause we have, and in our persons. He is with us as one with us, nay, as in us by his Spirit, and whosoever toucheth us toucheth the apple of his eye: 'Saul, Saul, why persecutest thou me?' Here is ground of courage in whatsoever may befall us, to stand it out in all conditions whatsoever. Nothing can sever Christ and a Christian; this body will never be beheaded; Christ will never be separated from his body; he will not lose the poorest member he hath. You see it is the duty of a Christian to be courageous and undaunted in the cause of God; and from this ground, because God is with him, and 'who can be against him?' Let all the world be against God, and against the cause that a Christian professeth, they do but kick against the pricks. They dash against a rock; as the waves that break themselves, they do not hurt the rock a whit. They do but cast stones upward, that fall upon their heads again. Therefore it is a desperate cause that malicious spirits manage, who have more parts than grace, and arm themselves and their wits to hurt the people and church of God, and slander his cause, and do all the hurt they can.

It is a ground likewise of encouragement in our callings. When God calls us to anything in our places that is good, he will be with us. Therefore in our places and standing, let us do that that belongs to us; let us not fear that we shall want that which is necessary, or miscarry any way. When Moses pretended he could not speak, 'Who gives a mouth?' saith God to him, Exod. iv. 11. Therefore let us take courage, not only in suffering and opposition, but in our places and standings. God will be with us; he gives his angels charge to keep us in our ways, Ps. xci. 11. We have a guard over us.

Here is a ground likewise of all contentment in any condition in the world. What can be sufficient to him that God cannot suffice? God, all-sufficient, is with thee; thou canst want nothing that is for thy good. Thou mayest want this and that, but it is for thy good that thou wantest it: 'Those that fear God shall want nothing that is good,' Ps. xxxiv. 11. It is a ground of all contentment, God is with them, to fill their souls to utmost. He is made for the soul, and the soul for him; for our end is to have communion with God in Jesus Christ here, and everlastingly in heaven. God is fitted for us, and we for him. Here is fresh comfort for the soul alway: he can fill up every corner of the soul, he is larger than our souls. Therefore let us be content; in what condition soever we are in, God is with us. Therefore 'let the peace of God, which passeth all understanding, guard our hearts,' Philip. iv. 7; even from this very ground and conclusion, 'God is with us, who can be against us?' Let Moses be cast into a basket of bulrushes, if God be with him, he shall not be drowned. Let Daniel be cast into the den, if God be with him, God will come between the lions' teeth and him. Let the three blessed men be cast into the fiery furnace, a fourth shall be with them, and keep them from the hurt of the flame. Let God be with Noah, he shall swim upon the waters; and the greater the waters, the more safe he, and the nearer to heaven. Let God be with us, and we may be content with any condition whatsoever.

Again, let us not be over-much discouraged with our infirmities and corruptions: 'If God be with us, who can be against us?' Our corruptions are against us, and they are worse to me than the devil and all enemies, saith a poor Christian. Indeed they are, for the devil hath no advantage against us but by our corruptions; but if thou account thy corruptions thine enemies, they are God's enemies and Christ's enemies as well as thine. He will be with thee, and thy corruptions shall more and more be wasted; for the flesh shall fall before the Spirit. This Dagon shall fall before this blessed ark, 1 Sam. v. 3. Stronger is he that is in us than he that is in the world, 1 John iv. 4. The Spirit of God is stronger in us than corruption in us, or the world without us; it ministers stronger grounds of comfort than all other can do of discomfort. If you be under the Spirit and under grace, 'sin shall not have dominion over you,' Rom. vi. 14. It may be in you, but it shall not have dominion, because ye are under the covenant of grace. Therefore though corruption be in us, for our exercise and humiliation, yet it shall not be against us, to abridge us of comfort. They serve to drive us nearer to God. Let none be discouraged, 'Christ came to destroy the works of the devil,' 1 John iii. 8; therefore he came to destroy sin in us, which is the work of the devil. He came to take away not only the guilt, but the very being of sin, as he will at last; for if God and Christ be with us, who shall be against us?

Obj. But it may be objected by some, But I find not God with me.

Ans. It is true, sometimes God hides himself: 'Thou art a God that hidest thyself,' Is. xlv. 15. He seems as a stranger in his own church; to be 'as a wayfaring man,' as the prophet saith, Jer. xiv. 8. He takes no notice of his church and their afflictions; he seems not to take them to heart, nor to pity his church. Oh, but this is but for a time, and for trial: 'Can a mother forget her child?' Isa. xlix. 15. Put case she should, yet will not I forget thee. God hides himself but a while, to try the graces of his children, and to give way to the enemies; to let his children to see their corruptions, and his wise dispensation. And these desertions we must be acquainted with. God seems to be away from his children, yet he is with them, and supports them with invisible strength. He seems to be with wicked men in prospering them in the world, that they have all at their will in outward things, yet he is far from them. He withdraws himself in spiritual things; they have no grace, no sound inward comfort. And he seems opposite to his children; he leaves them outwardly in regard of assistance and friends, but they have an invisible inward presence of the Spirit to support and strengthen them; therefore measure not desertions, God's being or not being with us, by outward respects; for so he is with the enemies of the church ofttimes, and not with his children. But he is with his in the sweetest manner, supporting of them when they are in darkness, and see no light of God's countenance; yet they have so much light, though they think they see it not, as makes them trust in God: 'Let him that is in darkness, and sees no light, trust in the name of God,' Isa. l. 10. Therefore, as I said, it is a principle pregnant for comfort and use. If God be with us, he is with us in life and death; for whom he loves he loves everlastingly, from everlasting to everlasting.

Quest. If this be so, what shall we do to God again? What is the best evidence to know that God is with us?

Ans. There is a relation between God and his. He is so with them, as that they are with him likewise in all passages. Doth he choose them? They in time choose him: 'Whom have I in heaven but thee? and there is none in earth that I desire in comparison of thee,' Ps. lxxiii. 25. Doth he call them? they answer. Doth he justify and free them from their sins? they make that answer of faith that Peter speaks of, 'I do believe; Lord, help my unbelief,' Mark ix. 24. They have faith to lay hold upon the forgiveness. And likewise, if God be with them, they can delight in God's presence. Can God delight to be present with them that have not grace to delight in him? God's children maintain their communion with him in all the sanctified means they can; they are afraid to break with God. Therefore those that, to please and give content to others, and for base ends will displease their God, it is a heavy sign that God as yet hath not shewed himself in his gracious mercy in Christ Jesus to them.

If God be with us, we will be of his side; and his enemies shall be our enemies, and his friends our friends. He that claims this, that God is with him, he will say, I will be with God and for God. God hath two things in the world that we must have a care of, his church and his cause. Take them out of the world, the world is but a hell upon earth; a company of miscreants, profane, godless, impudent, poisonful creatures. Take away the cause of God, religion, and the people that are begotten by religion, and what is the rest of mankind? The world would not stand, but be all upon heaps, for a company of sinful wretches that will have their wills; but it is for the church and people of God that the world stands. Now he that hath God with him, and he is in terms with God, that they are friends, as Abraham was the friend of God, he will side with God and religion. God's cause shall be his cause, and God's people his people. He will cleave to God's side as the safest. If he may have never so much preferment in the world, he will not join with antichrist. He will not betray the cause of religion if he might have a world for it. Why? Because he knows if God be with him, who can be against him? God hath given us understanding and grace to maintain friendship with him, to have common friends and common enemies: therefore, if we stand not for God, let us never talk of God's presence with us. He will be present to confound us, to overthrow us, and pursue us to hell; but not graciously present without we labour to maintain the cause of religion as far as we may. 'God is with us, if we be with him,' 2 Chron. xv. 2. If we be with God to take his part, he will be with us to protect and defend us, to guide and comfort us, and to give issue to all our affairs. Not that our being with him is the prime cause of his being with us, but it is an evidence to know whether he be with us, as we make profession, when as far as our callings will suffer, we be with him and maintain his cause.

Again, If we would know whether we be with God, and he with us, ask conscience whether it be with thee; for conscience is God's vicar. Is conscience with thee? Dost thou not sin against conscience? What conscience saith, God saith; and what it forbids, God forbids, especially when it is enlightened by the word. Doth conscience speak peace to thee from the word? Then thou art with God, and God is with thee. Especially in the great point of justification, doth conscience speak peace to thee in the blood of Christ? Is thy heart sprinkled with it, that it is not as the blood of Abel, that cries for vengeance? Hast thou a spirit of faith, to believe that Christ shed his blood for thee in particular? Then thou art with God, and he with thee, because God hath sprinkled the blood of Christ upon thy heart.

Quest. What course shall we take to keep God comfortably with us?

Ans. Look thou be in covenant with him, and not only at large in covenant; but look that continually upon all occasions thou renew thy covenant. For sometimes God's children may be in covenant, they may be his children; yet because they renew not their covenant, especially after some breaches, God is not with them so comfortably as he would, to free them from their enemies, as we see in the case of the Benjamites, Judges xx. 35. God's people sometimes may have the worst, though they be in covenant, because they have committed some sin, and have not renewed their peace and covenant with God. Therefore, if we would make a comfortable use of this truth, that God is with us, and would find him so in our affairs and business, let us renew our covenant upon all occasions, and our purpose to please God.

And then look *to the cause we take in hand, and to our carriage in that cause.* If our persons be good, be in covenant, and the cause good, and our conscience good, and our carriage suitable, then God will be with us. Let us make use of these principles, that we may be in love with the comfortable secure condition of a Christian. There is no state so glorious, so comfortable, so secure, and free from danger. If we were in heaven, and should look down below upon all snares and dangers, what would we care for them? Now if he be with us, and we with him, 'God is our habitation,' 'we dwell in the secret of the Almighty, he is our high tower, the way of wisdom is on high, to escape the snares below,' Ps. xci. 9. Therefore let us raise our souls as high as heaven and God is; and set ourselves where our hopes are, where our God is, and we have set ourselves in our tower; that we have set God in our hearts, and set ourselves in him; then we may overlook the devil, and men, and death, and danger, and all. As a man that stands upon the top of a rock, that is higher than all the waves, he overlooks them, and sees them break themselves upon the rock, so when we see God with us, and ourselves with him, by a Spirit of comfort we can overlook all with a holy defiance, as the apostle saith here, 'Who can be against us?' 'What can separate us?' Oh, the excellent state of a Christian when he is assured of his condition! Who would not labour for assurance that yields this abundant comfort in all conditions?

A word of the occasion* for which I made choice of this portion of Scripture. Here is a double fitness to the occasion, both at home and abroad, 'If God be with us, who can be against us!'

God was at home in '88.† He was with us in the powder treason: he was with us in the great sickness to preserve us,‡ and to give us our lives for a prey. He hath been with us; and we ought not to forget this, but upon occasion of this great deliverance, to call all former deliverances to mind, national and personal; to consider how often God hath given us our lives, and how oft he hath preserved us from death; and to take occasion to bless God for all at once, and so to make some special use of these meetings.

Then if we look abroad, God hath been with us in that he hath been his church,§ for they and we make but one body. That member that hath not a sympathy with the body, it is but a dead member. Therefore if we

* In margin here, 'Novemb. 5,' 'The Gunpowder Plot.'—G.

† That is, 1588, the Armada year.—G.

‡ That is, 'The Plague.'—G.

§ Qu. 'with his church'?—Ed.

we be not affected with the presence of God with the armies abroad, we are dead members. We may say, in regard of these outward deliverances, 'God hath been with us, and none hath been against us.' If God had not been with us in the powder-plot, where had we been? Our lives would have been made a prey. That that would have been done, would have been more than the blowing up of the parliament. They would have blown up the kingdom with the king, and religion with religious persons, and the state with statesmen. It would have brought a confusion of all, and would have moulded all after an idolatrous antichristian fashion. It would have overthrown the state, and persons, and all. The issues would have been worse than the present thing. And, therefore, if God had not been with us, as he was graciously with us, what would have become of us? as it is in Ps. cxxiv. 1. If God had not been with us, they had made us a prey, and overwhelmed and devoured us all; there had been no hope.

Have not we cause to bless God and be thankful? Therefore let us labour to do it for ourselves and our neighbours. How shall we shew our thankfulness to God? Not in outward manifestations only, which is laudable, and a good demonstration of the affections of people. But alas! what is that? We must shew our thankfulness in loving that religion that God hath so witnessed for, and defended so miraculously. Labour to love the truth, to entertain it in the love of it, and to bring our hearts to a more perfect hatred of popery; for if we wax cold and indifferent, or oppose God's cause, and undermine it, do we think that God would suffer this long? Would he not spue us out of his mouth?—with reverence I speak it. Though he have defended us again and again, he will be gone with his truth and religion. It came not alone, nor it will not go alone. If religion go, our peace and prosperity, and the flourishing of our state, all will go. It is our ark. If that go away, our happiness goes away. Let us make much of religion. That is the way to be thankful.

Again, Let us shew our thankfulness by giving and doing some good to the poor, by refreshing their bowels, that they may have occasion to bless God.

And for the time to come let us trust in God; that God will be with us if we be with him, and to stick to him. Who then shall be against us? Let the devil, and Rome, and hell, be all against us, if God be with us. Bellarmine goes about to prove Luther a false prophet (*a*). Luther, as he was a courageous man, and had a great and mighty spirit of faith and prayer, so his expressions were suitable to his spirit. What saith he? The cause that I defend is Christ's and God's cause, and all the world shall not stand against it. It shall prevail. If there be a counsel in earth, there is a counsel in heaven that will disappoint all. God laughs in heaven at his enemies, and shall we weep?* And things are in a good way if we can go on and help the cause of God with our prayers and faith that God will go on; and with our cheerfulness and joy that God may delight to go on with his own cause. We may encourage ourselves, though perhaps we shall not see the issue of these things, yet posterity shall see it.

* Cf. Vol. I. page 126.—G.

NOTE.

(*a*) P. 397.—'Bellarmine goes about to prove Luther,' &c. Any of the numerous treatises of the great Jesuit will furnish examples of his 'railing' against the greater Reformer. See specially his *Disputationes*.—G.

THE DEAD MAN.*

And you hath he quickened, who were dead in trespasses and sins.—
EPH. II. 1.

THE matter of this excellent epistle is partly doctrinal and partly exhortatory, as it was St Paul's course in all his epistles to lay the foundation of practice in doctrine. The heart must be moved, but the brain must be instructed first. There is a sympathy between those two parts; as in nature, so in grace. The doctrinal part of the epistle sets out the riches of Christ—chiefly in the first chapter—in regard of the spring of them, God's eternal election. Then in this chapter, by way of comparison, by comparing the state of grace to the state of nature: 'You hath he quickened, who were dead in trespasses and sins.'

The dependence of this verse, I take it to be from the 19th verse of the first chapter. The apostle there prays that the Ephesians might have 'the eye of their understandings opened and enlightened,' that they might know, among other things, what the exceeding great power of God is towards us that believe: 'According to the working of his mighty power that he wrought in Christ, when he raised him from the dead,' that they might have experience of that mighty power that raised Christ from the dead. Now, here in this chapter he saith, 'They were raised together with Christ, and set together with him in heavenly places.' His reason is in this manner: those that are raised up and quickened with Christ to sit in heavenly places with him, have experience of a mighty power; but you are raised up and quickened with Christ to sit in heavenly places with him; therefore you have experience of a mighty power that raised Christ, for those that are raised and quickened with Christ have experience of that power that Christ had when he was raised up.

The second thing that he intends especially in this chapter is, to shew that, *being raised with Christ, they are brought nearer to God, both Jews and*

* 'The Dead Man' forms another of the Sermons in the 'Beams of Divine Light' (4to, 1639), being No. 3 therein. Its title-page is as follows:—'The Dead-Man, or, The State of Every Man by Nature. In one Sermon. By the late Reverend and Learned Divine Richard Sibs, Doctor in Divinity, Master of Katherine Hall in Cambridge, and sometimes Preacher at Grayes Inne. John v. 25. Verily, verily I say unto you, the houre is comming and now is when the dead shall heare the voice of the Sonne of God, and they that heare shall live. London, Printed by G. M. for Nicholas Bourne and Rapha Harford. MDCXXXIX.'—G.

Gentiles, that of themselves were far off. Now, he shews that they 'were raised and quickened with Christ, and brought near to God in Christ,' that they might magnify the free grace of God in Christ—all is by grace —and thereupon to be stirred up to a suitable, comfortable, and gracious life. To come to the words, 'And you hath he quickened,' &c. They are an application of the former comfortable truths to them, 'you hath he quickened,' &c. These words, 'hath he quickened,' are not in the original in this place. They are after in verse 5, 'When we were dead in sins, he quickened us;' but they are put in in the translation, because they must be understood to make the full sense.

In the words consider these things:

First of all, here the apostle puts them in mind *of their former condition.*

And then he sets down *in particular what it was:* 'they were dead in trespasses and sins.'

Then he tells them *wherein they were dead,* what was the cause of their death, and the element wherein they were dead: 'in trespasses and sins.'

Lastly, *Not in one trespass and in one sin,* but 'in trespasses and sins.'

And then to speak a little of 'quickening,' to take it out of the 5th verse: 'You hath he quickened.' There is the benefit with the condition. That which I aim at is especially to shew our estate by nature, and how we are raised out of that. I shall touch the points briefly as I have propounded them.

1. St Paul here first minds them of their former condition—'You were dead in trespasses and sins,'—for contraries give lustre one to another; and it magnifies grace marvellously to consider the opposite condition. He that never knew the 'height, and breadth, and depth' of his natural corruption, will never be able to conceive 'the height, and breadth, and depth' of God's infinite love in Jesus Christ. St Paul had deep thoughts of both as ever man had; therefore he could never enter into the argument of abasing man and extolling the love of God in Christ, that he could satisfy himself, but his spirit carries him from one thing to another, till he set it out to the full. And every one of us should be skilful in this double mystery, the mystery of the corruption of nature, that is unsearchable. There is corruption in the heart that none knows but God only; and we must plough with his heifer, that carries a light into the hidden parts of the soul, and discovers corruption. There is a mystery of that as well as of the gospel, of our deliverance out of that cursed estate from the guilt and thraldom of it. I do but touch it only, to shew the scope of the apostle.

Now, besides the consideration of it for this end—to magnify the grace of God, and to understand what our former estate was the better—there are many other ends; as to stir up our thankfulness, when we consider from what we are delivered, to glorify God the more. There is no soul so enlarged to glorify God as that soul that hath large thoughts of its estate by nature; and that estate by nature made worse by custom, our second ill nature and bondage voluntary. Considering God's mercy in delivering and freeing us from all sins and trespasses, this will make us thankful indeed. And it is a spring of love to God. When we consider what great sins we have forgiven us, it will make us humble all the days of our lives and pitiful to others. But this may be handled fitter from another portion of Scripture. To come therefore to the words:

'Who were dead in trespasses and sins.'

Their condition is, 'they were dead.' The specification of their death, 'in sins and trespasses,' and not in one, but in 'sins and trespasses.' Here I might digress and tell you a discourse of life and death at large: every man knows by experience what they are. In a word, death is a privation of life. What is life? and whence ariseth it? Not to speak of the life of God,—God is life and Christ is life,—but of life in us, it ariseth from the soul. First there is a soul, and then a life from the union with that soul; and then there is a secret-kindled motion and operation outward wheresoever life is. Life in man, I say, springs from the soul. The soul hath a double life, a life in itself, and a life it communicates to the body. The life in itself it liveth when it is out of the body,—it hath an essential life of its own,—but the life of the body is derived from its union with the soul; and from that union comes lively motion and operation. The spiritual life of the soul is by the Spirit of Christ, when our soul hath union with the quickening Spirit of Christ, and by Christ's Spirit is joined to Christ, and by Christ to God, who is life itself, and the first fountain of all life: then we have a spiritual life. The Spirit is the soul of our souls; and this spiritual soul, this Spirit in us, is not idle. Wherever life is there is motion and operation inward and outward, suitable and proportionable to the fountain of life, the Spirit of God himself.

So on the contrary it is with death. What is death? Death is nothing else but a separation from the cause of life, from that from whence life springs. The body having a communicated life from the soul, when the soul is departed it must needs be dead. Now death, take it in a spiritual sense, it is either the death of law, our sentence,—as we say of a man when he is condemned, he is a dead man,—or death in regard of disposition; and then the execution of that death of sentence in bodily death and in eternal death afterward. Now naturally we are dead in all these senses.

1. First, *By the sin of Adam*, in whose loins we were, we were all damned. There was a sentence of death upon all Adam's rotten race; as we say, *damnati antequam nati*, we were damned before we were born, as soon as we had a being in our mother's womb, by reason of our communion with Adam in that first sin.

And then there is corruption of nature as a punishment of that first sin, that is a death, as we shall see afterward, a death of all the powers: we cannot act and move according to that life that we had at the first; we cannot think; we cannot will; we cannot affect*; we cannot do anything [that] savours of spiritual life.

2. Hereupon comes *a death of sentence upon us*, being damned both in Adam's loins and in original sin, and likewise adding actual sins of our own. If we had no actual sin it were enough for the sentence of death to pass upon us, but this aggravates the sentence.

3. We are *dead in law* as well as in disposition. This death in law is called guilt, a binding over to eternal death. It breeds horror and terrors in the soul for the present, which are the flashes of hell-fire, and expectation of worse, even of the 'second death,' for the time to come, which is an eternal separation from God for ever—an eternal lying under the wrath and curse of God in body and soul, after they are united at the resurrection,—because we would sin eternally if we did live eternally here. And, no satisfaction being made for man after death, there must be an eternal sentence and punishment upon him. A terrible condition! If we were

* That is, 'choose,' love.—G.

not afraid of the first death, we should be afraid of the second death that follows. 'We are all dead in trespasses and sins.'

Now what is the reason of it why we are dead?

First of all, The ground of it is: by sin we are separated from the fountain of life; therefore we are all dead.

Secondly, By sin we lost that first original righteousness which was comproduced with Adam's soul. When Adam's soul was infused, it was clothed with all graces, with original righteousness. The stamp of God was on his soul. It was co-natural to that estate and condition to have that excellent gracious disposition that he had. Now, because we all lost that primitive image and glory of our souls, we are dead.

We are dead likewise, not only in regard of the time past, but for the time to come. No man by nature hath fellowship with the second Adam till he be grafted into him by faith, which is a mere* supernatural thing. In these regards every man naturally is dead.

Nay, sin itself, it is not only a cause of death,—of temporal death as it is a curse, and so of eternal death; of that bitter sentence and adjudging of us too, both that we feel in terrors of conscience and expect after,—but sin itself is an intrinsecal death. Why? Because it is nothing but a separation of the soul from the chief good, which is God, and a cleaving to some creature; for there is no sin but it carries the soul to the changeable creature in delight and affection to its pride and vanity, one thing or other. Sin is a turning from God to the creature, and that very turning of the soul is death: every sinful soul is dead. In these and the like considerations you may conceive we are all dead.

'And you hath he quickened who were dead,' &c.

Let us consider a little what a condition this is, to be 'dead in trespasses and sins.' Not to speak of the danger of the death of sentence, when a man by the state of nature lies under the wrath of God, that hangs over his head and is ready to crush him every moment, but to speak of that death that seizeth upon our dispositions, we are dead by nature. And what doth death work upon the body?

1. *Unactiveness, stiffness;* so when the Spirit of God is severed from the soul it is cold, and unactive, and stiff. Therefore those that find no life to that that is good, no, nor no power nor strength, it is a sign that they have not yet felt the power of the quickening Spirit; when they hear coldly and receive the sacrament coldly, as if it were a dead piece of work and business; when they do anything that is spiritually good coldly and forced, not from an inward principle of love to God, that might heat and warm their hearts, but they go about it as a thing that must be done, and think to satisfy God with an outward dead action.

2. Again, death makes the body *unlovely*. Abraham would buy a piece of ground that he might bury his dead out of his sight; he could not endure the sight of his own beloved wife when she was dead. Death takes away the beauty and the honour that God hath put upon the body, so that it is not honourable to those that behold it after death. The image of God stamped upon the soul of man by the Spirit, it is the glory of a man; after sin it is an unlovely soul. 'We are all deprived of the glory of God,' as St Paul saith, Rom. iii. 23.

3. And not only so, but there is a *loathsomeness* contrary to that honour that was in it before. Though all art and skill be used that may be to set out a dead body,—with flowers, or whatsoever you will,—to please the

* That is, 'altogether.'—G.

fancy of the living, yet it is but a dead body, and the stench will be above all other sweet smells. So let any natural man be as witty, and as learned, and as great, and as rich as you will, or as he can be set out with all these ornaments and flowers, yet he is but a carrion, a loathsome creature to God, if his soul be separate from God and inwardly cleave to the creature. If he have not a new heart, he is abominable and loathsome to God, and to all that have the Spirit of God. A dead soul is abominable to all God's senses. The scripture thus familiarly condescends unto us; he will not behold him. 'He looks upon the proud afar off,' Isa. ii. 12. And he smells no favour* from their performances, 'The very sacrifice of the wicked is abominable,' Isa. i. 13. He looks upon them as we do upon a dunghill, as a loathsome thing: 'The prayers of the wicked are an abomination to God,' Prov. xxviii. 9; he turns away his face from them, he cannot endure them. And for his ears, 'He will not hear the prayers of the wicked.' And for feeling, he is wearied with their sins, 'as a cart is with sheaves,' Amos ii. 13. Nay, he is wearied with their very good actions, as it is Isa. i. 8, *seq.* Whatsoever wicked men perform, it is abominable to God; he cannot behold them; he cannot endure them; he is burdened with their sins; and those also that have the Spirit of God in them, as far as they see the foulness of their sins, they loathe them.

But herein a wicked man agrees with a dead body: a dead body is not loathsome to itself. So take a carnal man, he pranks up himself; he thinks himself a jolly man; especially when he is set out in his flowers,—those things that he begs of the creatures,—he sees not his loathsomeness; he thinks himself a brave man in the world, in the place he lives in; and he hath base conceits of others, of God, and all things of God. Dead men are not loathsome to themselves, because they want senses. As in a prison, the noisome savour is not offensive to them, because they are all acquainted with it; it hath seized upon and possessed their senses. So wicked men they smell no ill savour and scent, one from another, because they are all dead persons. One dead man is not loathsome to another; as a company of prisoners they are not offended with the noisomeness of one another.

4. Again, *we sever dead persons from the rest.* So, indeed, a dead soul, as he is severed from God, so, *de jure*, he should be severed from the company of others. There should be a separation; and as soon as the life of grace is begun, there will be a separation between the living and the dead. 'Let the dead follow the dead, and bury the dead,' saith our Saviour in the gospel, Mat. viii. 22.

5. Where bodily death is it deprives *of all senses.* There is no use of any, either of the eye or tongue, &c. It makes them speechless. So he that is spiritually a dead man, he can speak nothing that is savoury and good of spiritual things. If he doth, he is out of his element. If he speak of good things, he speaks with the spirit of another man. If he speak of the writings of other men, it is with the spirit of the writer. He cannot speak to God in praise, or to others in experience of the work of grace, because he hath a dead soul. Put him to his own arguments, to talk of vanity, to swear, or to talk of the times, you shall have him in his theme; but to talk of God and divine things, unless it be to swear by them and to scorn good things, he cannot. He is speechless there; it is not his theme. And as he is speechless, so he hath no *spiritual eyes to see God in his works.* There is nothing that we see with our bodily eyes, but our souls should

* Qu. 'savour'?—Ed.

have an eye to see somewhat of God in it; his mercy and goodness and power, &c. And so he hath *no relish to taste of God* in his creatures and mercies. When a man tastes of the creatures, he should have a spiritual taste of God and of the mercy in him. Oh how sweet is God! A wicked man hath no taste of God. And he cannot hear what the Spirit saith in the word. He hears the voice of man, but not of the Spirit when the trumpet of the word sounds never so loud in his ears. These things ought not to be over much pressed. Much curiosity must not be used in them, but because the Holy Ghost raiseth the proportion from these things, something must be said of them.

6. As there is no sense *nor moving to outward things*, so no outward thing can move a dead body. Offer him colours to the eye, food to the taste, or anything to the feeling, nothing moves him. So a dead soul, as it cannot move to good, so it is moved with nothing. That that affects a child of God, and makes him tremble and quake, it affects not a carnal man at all.

7. And as in bodily death, the longer it is dead, *the more noisome and offensive it is* every day more than other, so sin it makes the soul more loathsome and noisome daily, till they have filled up the measure of their sins, till the earth can bear them no longer. We say of a dead body it is heavy; so dead souls, I am sure, they are heavy, heavy to God, and to Christ that died for sin, and heavy in themselves. They sink to earthly things in their affections, and thereby they sink lower and lower to hell, and never leave sinking till they be there. As the life of grace is like the sun when it riseth, it grows still till it come to full perfection, till it come to the life of glory, so, on the contrary, this death is a death that is more and more increased in the loathsomeness and noisomeness of it every way; so that the longer a carnal man lives, the more guilt he contracts. 'A child of a hundred years old,' Isaiah lxv. 20, as the prophet saith, the longer he lives, the more vengeance is stored for him; 'he treasures vengeance up against the day of vengeance,' Rom. ii. 5, and it is a curse for a man in his natural estate to live long, for he grows more and more abominable every way. These things help to understand the Scripture, and therefore so far we may well think of them.

If this be so, I beseech you *let us learn to know what we are by nature*, not to make ourselves in our own conceits better than indeed we are. We judge of ourselves as we are to civil things. A man that hath natural parts, that can discourse and understand the mysteries of law and of the state, we value men by these. Alas! poor soul, thou mayest be dead for all this. What are all these abilities for? Are they not for the spiritual life? What is this to the life of grace? They only blow thee up with pride, and set thee further off, and make thee incapable of grace. If thou talk of learning, the devil is a better scholar than any man. He knows matters of state and other things better than thou dost, and yet he is a devil for all that. Therefore never stand upon these things. But there is a company that are more to blame than these. One would think that these have something to be proud of, that they might set themselves against God and goodness; but there is a generation that have little in them, that yet think themselves the only men in loose licentious life, despising all, caring for none, and think it the only life to live as they list, to go where they list, in what companies they list, to have bounds of their own. These think themselves the only men, when indeed they are nobody; they are dead, loathsome creatures. It is the mercy of God that the ground doth not sink under them; and yet they carry themselves as if they only were alive.

Again, if we be all dead by nature, and there ought to be a separation of the living from the dead, *let us take heed in our amity and society, that we converse not with natural men too much, that have not spiritual goodness in them;* that we converse not with them with delight and complacency. It is a tyrannical thing to knit dead and living bodies together, and he was accounted a tyrant that did so. Surely, in choosing our society, conjugal or friendly, any intimate society, to join living and dead souls together, we are tyrants to our own souls. We wrong our souls to join with dead persons; who would converse with dead corses and corpses?* The very creatures startle at the sight of a dead body; nature startles at that that is dead. If we had the life of grace, further than the necessity of civil conversation, and the hope of bettering them forceth it upon us, we would have no society with those that we see are in the state of nature. What issues from them but stench? eyes full of adultery; nothing that is pleasing can come from them; nothing can come from all their senses but rottenness and stench. What comfort can a man that loves his own soul, and hath any desire to be saved, have by intimate converse with such persons? Let them have never so good parts, they hurt more one way than they do good another. You see we are all dead by nature, and what this death is.

Obj. But you will say there is a difference between natural death and spiritual death; for in natural bodily death there is no moving, but in this spiritual death of the soul men have senses and motion, &c.

Ans. It is true thus far they differ; though a man be spiritually dead, yet notwithstanding he hath feet to carry him to the house of God; he hath ears to hear the word of God; he hath abilities of nature upon which grace is founded. God works grace upon nature. Now a man living in the church of God, that is a grace when a man hath grace to live within the compass of the means. He can, by common grace, without any inward change of nature, come and hear the word of God; and when he is there, he may yield an ear to listen, and he hath common discourse and understanding to know what is said, and upon what ground. He can offer himself to the work of the Spirit; he can come to the pool, though he be not thrust in this day or that day, when God stirs the waters. This, by common grace, any man living in the church may do.

Therefore, though we be all dead, even the best of us, by nature, yet let us use the parts of nature that we have, that God hath given us, to offer ourselves to the gracious and blessed means wherein the Spirit of God may work. Let us come to hear the word of God: John v. 25, 'The time is come, and now is, that the dead shall hear the voice of God,' where the voice of God is in the ministry, 'and so they shall live.' As in the latter day the noise of the trumpet shall raise the dead bodies, so the trumpet of the word of God, sounding in the ears of men, together with the Spirit, shall raise the dead souls out of the grave of sin. Therefore I beseech you, as you would be raised up out of this death, hear the noise of God's trumpet. Come within the compass of the means. As God is the God of life, and Christ calls himself the life, and the Spirit the Spirit of life, so the word 'is the word of life,' because, together with the word, God conveys spiritual life. The word of God in the ordinance is an operative, working word. As it was in the creation, God said, 'Let there be light, and there was light,' so in the ministry it exhorts and stirs up to duty; and there is

* Spelled 'courses' and 'corps,' an apparent pleonasm.—G.

a clothing of the ministerial word with an almighty power. It is a working word; as when Christ spake to Lazarus when he stank in his grave, he said, 'Lazarus, come forth,' it was an operative working word. There went an almighty power to raise Lazarus. Therefore, though we find ourselves dead, and have no work of grace, yet let us present ourselves more and more to the ordinance of God. God will be mighty in his own ordinance. The blessed time may come; let us wait when the waters are stirred, and take heed that we despise not the counsel of God, which is to bring man to spiritual life this way.

And object not, I am dead and rotten in sin many years; I am an old man.

You know many were raised in the Gospel; some that had been dead few days. Lazarus was rotten, and stank. It shews us that though a man be dead and rotten in sin, yet he may be raised first or last. The blessed time may come, therefore wait. Never pretend long custom and long living in sin. All things are in obedience to God. Though they have a resistance in themselves, yet God can take away that resistance, and bring all to obey him. All things in the world, though they be never so opposite to God's grace, they are in obedience to his command. Therefore though there be nothing but actual present resistance in the soul to that that is good, and a slavery to the bondage of sin, yet attend meekly upon the ordinance. God can make of lions lambs; he can take away that actual resistance. As Christ, when he was raised, the stone that lay upon the grave was removed, so when God will quicken a man, he will remove the stone of long custom that is upon him. Though he have been dead so many years, yet God can roll away the stone, and bid him rise up. Therefore let none despair. God is more merciful to save those that belong to him, than Satan can be malicious to hinder any way.

The best of us all, though we be not wholly dead, yet there are some relics of spiritual death hanging upon us, there be corruptions which in themselves are noisome. Therefore let all attend upon the means, that the Spirit of God by little and little may work out the remainders of death, the remainders of death in our understandings, and of rebellion in our wills and affections. For there be usually three degrees of persons in the church of God. Some open rotten persons, that are as graves, open sepulchres, that their stink comes forth, and they are profane ones. There are some that have a form of godliness that are merely ghosts; that act things outwardly, but they have not a spirit of their own. They have an evil spirit and yet do good works. They walk up and down, and do things with no spirit of their own. The second are more tolerable than the first in human society; because the other stink and smell to common society: common swearers and profane persons, that stink to any except it be to themselves. But the godly have this death in part. The life of sentence is perfect, the life of justification; but spiritual life in us is by little and little wrought in the means. The Spirit of life joins with the word of life, and quickens us daily more and more. A word of these words,

'And you hath he quickened.'

Suitable to the occasion.* This being our estate, let us know how much we are beholding to God 'who hath quickened us.' God quickens us with Christ and in Christ. It is a comfortable consideration, in that God hath quickened Christ and raised him from the grave, it shews that his Father's wrath is pacified, or else he would not have quickened him. He gave him

* In margin here, 'Easter-day.'—G.

to death, and quickened him again; therefore we may know that he hath paid the price for us. And he quickens us with Christ and in Christ. Whatsoever we have that is good, it is in Christ first: 'That Christ in all things might have the pre-eminence,' Col. i. 18. Christ first rose and ascended and sits in heaven, and then we rise, and ascend, 'and sit in heavenly places with Christ.'* Therefore, as St Peter saith well in 1 Peter i. 20, 'God hath raised Christ, that our faith might be in God.' If Christ had not been raised up, our faith and hope could not have been in God that he would raise us up. We are quickened and raised in Christ. All is in Christ first, and then in us. The ground of this is, that Christ was a public person in all that he did in his death; therefore we are crucified and buried with him; in his resurrection and ascension, therefore, we are quickened with him, 'and sit in heavenly places with him.' He is the 'second Adam.' And if the first Adam could convey death to so many thousands so many thousand years after, and if the world should continue millions of years he would convey death to all, shall not Christ, the second Adam, convey life to all that are in him? So think of all things, both comfortable and uncomfortable, in Christ first. When we think of sin, think of it in him our surety; and when we think of freedom from death and damnation, think of his death. When we think of our resurrection, think of his when he rose again. In his resurrection, the acquittance from our sins was sealed. Thereby we know that the debt is paid, because he rose again. Let us see an acquittance of all in the resurrection. And if we think of the glory that God hath reserved for us, think of it in Christ. See Christ glorious first, and we in him. See Christ at the right hand of God, and we in him. Carry Christ along with us in our contemplations. We are quickened with Christ. Christ takes away all the deaths I spake of before. Christ by his resurrection took away the death of sentence. He rose again for our justification, 'so that now there is no condemnation to them that are in Christ,' Rom. viii. 1. So again in regard of that deadly disposition that is in us, Christ quickens us in regard of that, by infusing grace by his Spirit, for Christ is an universal principle of all life. Now Christ, by his death pacifying his Father, obtained the Spirit, and by that Spirit, which he infuseth as a principle of life, he more and more quickens our nature, and makes it better and better, till it be perfect in heaven. As Adam was a principle of death, and the more we live in the state of nature, the worse we are, till we come to hell, so when we are in Christ, the Spirit sanctifies us more and more, till he have brought us to perfection. And as we are quickened from the death of sentence and of disposition, so we are quickened in regard of that hope of glory that we have. For now in Christ we are in heaven already; and though there come bodily death between, yet notwithstanding, that is but a fitting us for glory. The body is but fitted and moulded in the grave for glory. This very consideration will quicken a man in death: my head is in heaven above water, therefore the body shall not be long under water. And faith makes that that is to come present, and affects the soul comfortably. Christ is in heaven already, and I am there in Christ; and I shall be there as verily as he is there. I am there *de jure*, and *de facto* I shall be there. In these considerations, Christ quickens us. Therefore, saith St Peter, 'Blessed be God the Father of our Lord Jesus Christ, who hath begotten us again through the resurrection of Christ from the dead to a lively hope of an inheritance immortal,' &c. We are begotten again to this

* In margin here, 'See the Sermons upon Rom. viii. 2.' Cf. Vol. V. pp. 225-247.—G.

inheritance by the resurrection of Christ, who is risen again to quicken himself and all his. The consideration of this should affect us as it did St Peter, 'to bless God.'

Now all this quickening power ariseth from our union with Christ. We must have a being in Christ before we can have comfort by death with him or by rising with him. Our union with Christ springs from faith. Faith is cherished by the sacrament. The word and sacrament beget faith. Faith unites us to Christ. Union with Christ makes us partake of his death and the benefits of it, and of his resurrection and ascension to glory. Therefore the more we attend upon this ordinance of the word, and the seal of the word, the sacrament, the more our faith is increased; for God invites us to communion and fellowship with Christ, and all his benefits and favours; and the more we find faith assured of Christ, the more union and fellowship we have with Christ; and the more we feel that, the more Christ is a quickening Spirit, quickening us with the life of grace here, and the hope of glory afterward. Therefore let us comfortably attend upon the ordinance of God sanctified for this purpose, to strengthen this our union with Christ.

THE DANGER OF BACKSLIDING.*

For Demas hath forsaken me, and embraced this present world.—2 Tim. IV. 10†

Blessed St Paul, being now an old man, and ready to sacrifice his dearest blood for the sealing of that truth which he had carefully taught, sets down in this chapter what diverse entertainment he found both from God and man in the preaching of the gospel. As for men, he found they dealt most unfaithfully with him, when he stood most in need of comfort from them. Demas, a man of great note, in the end forsook him. Alexander the coppersmith,—thus it pleaseth God to try his dearest ones with base oppositions of worthless persons,—did him most mischief. Weaker Christians forsook him, &c. But mark the wisdom of God's Spirit in the blessed apostle in regard of his different carriage towards these persons. Demas, because his fault was greater, by reason of the eminency of his profession, him he brands to all posterity, for looking back to Sodom and to the world, after he had put his hand to the plough. Alexander's opposing, because it sprung from extremity of malice towards the profession of godliness, him he curseth: 'The Lord reward him according to his works.' Weaker Christians who failed him from want of some measure of

* 'The Danger of Backsliding' forms No. 10 of 'The Saint's Cordials,' 2d edit., 1637. It had previously appeared in the 1629 edition, under the title of 'Experience Triumphing; or the Saint's Safety,' from 2 Timothy iv. 17, 18. Probably the change of title was owing to other sermons having been published in the interval, under the title 'The Saint's Safety,' for which see Vol. I. pp. 293–334. There was no separate title-page for the 'Danger of Backsliding' in the 2d edition, but that of the first is as follows:—'Experience Trivmphing, or, The Saints Safetie. In One Sermon. Wherein is shewed, how the Comfort of Former Experiences of Gods Goodness and Mercy, doe and ought support and stay the soule for the expectation and assurance of Deliuerances and helpe for time to come, &c. Prælucendo Pereo. Vprightnes Hath Boldnes. Psal. 63, 6, 7. When I remember thee vpon my bed, and meditate on thee in the night watches: Because thou hast beene my help, therefore in the shadow of thy wings will I reioyce. London, Printed in the yeare 1629.' It may be proper to state that the present Sermon, from the second edition, is much shorter than in the first, the explanation being that Sibbes had elsewhere, *e.g.*, in 'The Saint's Safety' *supra*, used the omitted portions, and so had wished it to appear in its abbreviated form thereafter; another incidental confirmation of my supposition that the text of the Saint's Cordials of 1637 had received his sanction.—G.

† Misprinted 1 Timothy in second and third editions.—G.

spirit and courage, retaining still a hidden love to the cause of Christ, their names he conceals, with prayer that God would not lay their sin to their charge. But whilst Paul lived in this cold comfort on earth, see what large encouragement had he from heaven! Though all forsook me, yet, says he, 'God did not forsake me, but stood by me, and I was delivered out of the mouth of the lion,' ver. 17.

Obs. In the words we have, 1. This remarkable observation, *that it is the lot of God's dearest children to be oftentimes forsaken of those that have been most near unto them.* Thus it was with Christ himself. His disciples fled and left him, Mat. xxvi. 56. David complaineth that his friends forsook him, Ps. cxix. 87, and xxvii. 10. And Elias mourneth because he was 'left alone, and they sought his life also,' 1 Kings xix. 10.

Reason 1. And God suffers his dearest children to be thus forsaken, that they may be made conformable to their head Christ Jesus, who was left alone of his beloved disciples, and had none to comfort him.

Reason 2. Again, God suffers this to draw them to the fountain, that they might fly to Christ, in whom all true comfort lies, and see whether he is not better than ten sons, as Eli spake to Hannah, 1 Sam. i. 8. The Lord oft embitters other comforts to men that Christ may be sweet to them. Our hearts naturally hang loose from God, and are soon ready to join with the creature. Therefore we should soar much aloft in our meditations, and see the excellencies of Christ, and adhere to him. This will soon take off the soul from resting upon other props. When David began to say, 'My hill is strong,' then presently 'his soul was troubled,' Ps. xxx. 6, *seq.* Out of God there is nothing fit for the soul to stay itself upon; for all outward things are beneath the worth of the soul, and draw it lower than itself. Earthly things, such as are riches, honours, friends, &c., are not given us for stays to rest upon, but for comforts in our way to heaven. Whatever comfort is in the creature the soul will spend quickly, and look still for more; whereas the comfort that we have in God, 'is undefiled, and fadeth not away,' 1 Peter i. 4.

God hath therefore planted the grace of faith in us, that our souls thereby might be carried to himself, and not rely upon vain things, which only are so far good as we do not trust in them. Who would trust to that for comfort, which by very trusting proves uncomfortable to him? If we trust in friends, or estate, more than God, we make them idols.

There is still left in man's nature a desire of pleasure, profit, and whatever the creature presents as good; but the desire of gracious comforts, and heavenly delights is altogether lost, the soul being wholly infected with a contrary taste. Man hath a nature capable of excellency, and desirous of it, and the Spirit of God in and by the word discovers where true excellency is to be had; but corrupt nature leaving God, seeketh it elsewhere in carnal friendship and the like, and so crosseth its own desires, till the Spirit of God discovers where these things are to be had, and so nature is brought to its right frame again, by turning the stream into its right current. Grace and sinful nature have the same general object of comfort, only sinful nature seeks it in broken cisterns, and grace in the fountain. The beginning of our true happiness is from the discovery of true and false objects; so as the soul may clearly see what is best and safest, and then stedfastly rely upon it. For the soul is as that which it relies upon; if on vanity, itself becomes vain; if upon God and Christ, it becomes a spiritual and heavenly soul. It is no small privilege then which the Lord vouchsafeth some, by knocking off their fingers, and crossing their greedy appetites after earthly comforts, that he may refresh them with pleasures of a higher nature. Alas! what is the delight that we have in friends, or children, and the like, to the joy of God's presence, and the pleasures at his right hand for evermore?

Obs. But to bring the text a little closer to ourselves, the thing that I would have you chiefly to observe is this, *that those that have gone far in religion may yet notwithstanding fall away, and become apostates.*

Reason 1. The reason is, 1. *Because they rest on their own strength, and there is no support in man to uphold himself.* Without Christ we can do nothing. We see how weak the apostles themselves were, till they were endued with strength from above. Peter was blasted with the speech of a damsel. Therefore in all our encounters and fear of falling, we should lift up our hearts to Christ, who hath Spirit enough for us all, and say with good Jehoshaphat, 'Lord, we know not what to do, but our eyes are towards thee,' 2 Chron. xx. 12. The battle we fight is thine, and the strength whereby we fight must be thine. If thou goest not out with us, we are sure to be foiled. Satan knows that nothing can prevail against Christ, or those that rely upon his power; therefore his study is, how to keep us in ourselves and in the creature; but we must carry this always in our minds, that that which is begun in self-confidence will end in shame.

Reason 2. *Because Satan, that grand apostate, is fallen from the truth himself, and he labours to draw others to fall back with him;* for being a cursed spirit, cast and tumbled down himself from heaven, where he is never to come again, he is full of malice, and labours all that he can to ruin and destroy others, that they may be in the same cursed condition with himself. By his envy and subtlety we were driven out of paradise at the first, and ever since he envies us the paradise of a good conscience. He cannot endure that a creature of meaner rank than himself should enjoy such happiness.

Use. I beseech you, therefore, let us learn that exhortation of the apostle, 'Let him that standeth, take heed lest he fall,' A watchful Christian stands, when careless spirits have many a fall. It is no easy matter to keep our ground. We see tall cedars oftentimes to shake and fall. How many are like buds in a frosty morning, nipped suddenly. We have no more truth of grace than we hold out to the end.

Quest. But how shall we persevere in goodness?

Ans. 1. *Labour for true grace.* What is sincere, is constant. That is true grace which the Spirit of God doth work in us, and is not built on false grounds, as to have respect to this or that man, or by-ends of our own.

Now, that we may have true grace, let us labour to be throughly convinced of sin, after which conviction of our evil ways, grace will follow. To which end we should pray earnestly for the Spirit, which will 'convince us of all sin,' John xvi. 9, and work this grace of constancy, and all other graces in us. For where the Spirit is, there is a savour and relish in all the ways of God. How sweet is the goodness of God in our redemption, justification, and preservation, to a spiritual heart! If there be a relish in the meat, and not in the man, all is nothing.

Ans. 2. Again, if we would hold out, *get a strong resolution against all oppositions*, for, know this, scandals will come, difficulties will arise, but firm resolution will carry us through all. Those that go forth to walk for pleasure, if a storm comes, they return in again presently; whereas he that is to go a journey, though he meets with never so many storms and tempests, yet he will go through all, because he hath so resolved beforehand. Things are either good or evil, as a man willeth them. The bent of the soul to God makes a man good.

Ans. 3. That thou mayest persevere to the end, *labour, as for the obedience of faith, to believe the truth, so for the obedience of practice.* Labour to know the truth, and to practise what thou knowest, that so thou mayest be built on the rock Christ Jesus. If thou fall, it is thy own fault for building on the sand. Therefore, often put this question to thy soul, Is this truth that I hold? would I die for it? If so, then hold it fast, otherwise suspect there is unsoundness.

Ans. 4. Above all things, *get the love of God in thy heart.* This will constrain us to obedience. If we look altogether upon our discouragements, alas! we shall soon flag and fall away. But if we eye our encouragements, it is impossible we should desert Christ, or his truth. Who would not hold out, having such a captain, and such a cause as we fight for. Where the truth is received in the love of it, there is constancy.

Ans. 5. *Strive to grow daily in a denial of thyself.* None can come to heaven, but he must first strip himself of himself. He must not own his own wit, will, or affections; he must be emptied of himself wholly. He must deny himself in all his aims after the world, in the pleasure, profit, or preferment of it. He must not respect anything if he will follow Christ. A respective religion is never a sound religion. A true Christian hath a single eye; he serves God for himself. A man that hath worldly aims hath a double eye as well as a double heart; such a one cannot but waver. Bring therefore single eyes, hearts, and aims to receive the word. It is the great fault of many; they bring false hearts with them to the ordinances of God. It is said of Israel that he brought Egypt into the wilderness, Num. xi. 18. So it is with most men, they think to have religion and their lusts together; but whatsoever doth begin in hypocrisy will end in apostasy. And know this, that he that hath religion needs not go out for aims or good company. He hath acquaintance with God and Christ, and he hath an eternal inheritance to aim at. There be encouragements enough in religion itself. We need not go out and look abroad for more. I speak this the rather, because false aims and ends is the ready means to undo men, when we have respect to such a man or such a thing in our practice of holiness. Joash was a good king all the while Jehoiada lived. This respect kept him in awe. The eye of a great person keeps some men in, and causeth them oft to blaze forth in a greater show, than many others less outwardly apparent, but more inwardly sincere.

Ans. 6. *Labour, therefore, to have divine truths engrafted in thee;* not to have them loose, for then they will never grow, but get them engrafted in thy heart, that so they may spring forth in thy life, as that which is set in a stock turns the stock into the same nature with it. We should embrace truths inwardly. And indeed God's children will have truths as belonging to themselves. As a wife receiving a letter from her husband, saith, This is sent to me, it belongs to me, so we should say in every truth, this was penned for me, and directed to my soul in particular.

Ans. 7. Lastly, That thou mayest grow deeper in religion, *grow deeper and deeper in humiliation.* Then a man is humble when he accounteth sin his greatest evil and grace his chiefest good. Such a one will hold out in time of trial; and if temptations come on the right hand, of profit or preferment, Oh, saith he, Christ is better to me! And if sin comes on the left hand, to draw him aside, Oh, saith he, this is the vilest thing in the world; it is the worst of all evils, I may not yield to it.

Obs. But to go on, from Demas his forsaking of Paul, and embracing of the present world, we learn, *that the love of Christ and the world cannot lodge together in one heart.*

Reason 1. The reason is, 1, *They are two masters, ruling by contrary laws.* Christ was resolved to suffer, but the world saith, 'Spare thyself,' Mat. xvi. 22. How can these agree? I deny not but a man may be truly religious, and abound with all outward blessings; but the *love* of the world, and love of religion, cannot harbour in one breast. When the love of the world entered into Judas, it is said the devil entered into him, John xiii. 2. Now, Christ and Satan are contrary one to the other. Where religion is, it carries the soul upwards to heaven and heavenly things; but where the love of the world is, it brings the soul downward to the earth and things below.

Use. This discovereth the gross hypocrisy of such men as labour to bring God and the world together, which cannot be. Where the world hath got possession in the heart, it makes us false to God and false to man. It makes us unfaithful in our callings, and false to religion itself. Labour therefore to have the world in its own place, under thy feet; for if we love the world, we shall break with religion, with our friend, with the church, and with God himself. We see how it hindered the man in the Gospel from blessedness. When once Christ told him he must 'sell all that he had, and give to the poor,' he went away sorrowful, 'for he had great possessions,' Mat. xix. 22. Oh how do these things steal the good word out of our hearts, as the birds did the seed that was on the 'highway side,' Mat. xiii. 4. It even chokes the word, as the tares did the corn when it was sprung up, Mat. xiii. 26. Where this worldly love is, there can be no true profession of Christ, let men delude themselves never so much.

Quest. But how shall I know I love the world?

Ans. That will be seen by observing the bent of our heart, how it is swayed towards God and his service, and how towards things below. When two masters are parted, their servants will be known whom they serve, by following their own master. Blessed be God, in these times we enjoy both religion and the world together; but if times of suffering should approach, then it would be known whose servants we are. Consider therefore beforehand what thou wouldst do. If trouble and persecution should arise, wouldst thou stand up for Christ, and set light by liberty, riches, credit, all in comparison of him?

Yet we must know it is not the world simply that draws our heart from God and goodness, but the love of the world. Worldly things are good in themselves, and given to sweeten our passage to heaven. They sweeten the profession of religion, therefore bring not a false report upon the world. It is thy falseness that makes it hurtful, in loving it so much. Use it as a servant all thy days, and not as a master, and thou mayest have comfort therein. It is not the world properly that hurts us, but our setting our hearts upon it; whenas God should be in our thoughts, our spirits are even drunk with the cares below. Thorns will not prick of themselves, but when they are grasped in a man's hand they prick deep. So this world and the things thereof are all good, and were all made of God for the benefit of his creature, did not our immoderate affection make them hurtful, which indeed embitters every sweet unto us. This is the root of all evil. When once a man's heart is set upon the world, how doth he set light by God, and the peace of his conscience, to attain his ends! How doth he break with God, his truth, religion, and all, to satisfy a lust! And indeed as we fasten our love, so we are either good or bad. We are not as we know, but as we love. If we set our love on earthly things, we ourselves become base and earthly; but if we love heavenly things, our conversations will be spiritual and divine. Our affections are those things which declare what we are. If we do not love religion, it is no matter what we know or talk of it.

He that loves the world, brings it into the church with him. It is chief in his thoughts, and therefore he carries it about with him in his heart wherever he goes. As it is said of Israel, they carried Egypt into the wilderness, so these bring the world to the ordinances of God, they come to the hearing of the word like drones, leaving their stings behind them.

Paul saith not here 'Demas did forsake him' for fear of persecution, but 'for the love of the world.' Faults are in their aggravation as they are in deliberation. Peter denied his Master, but it was not with deliberation, whereas Demas did it in his cold blood. He loved the world, he set up the creature in his heart higher than the Creator.

Use. Labour therefore to know the world, that thou mayest detest it. In religion, the more we know the more we will love; but all the worldly things, the more we know the less we will affect them; as a picture afar off, it will shew well, but come near it and it is not so. Let us see, then, what the world is. Alas! it is but the 'present world,' which will vanish away suddenly. Poor Demas thought a bird in the hand was worth two in the bush, and therefore he would brave it out a while; but, alas! what is become of him now? A worldling oftentimes, in seeking these things, loseth himself and the world too; but a Christian never loseth that which he seeks after, God and Christ, and the things of a better life. The more we know the vanities of the world and the excellencies of grace, the more we will love the one and hate the other.

Labour, then, for faith, that you may overcome the world. It was an excellent speech of Christ when he sent forth his disciples, 'Did you lack anything?' and they said, 'Nothing at all,' Luke xxii. 35. Labour therefore for faith to rely on the promise; for provision, protection, and all things needful. If God be our shepherd, we are sure to lack nothing.

And cherish a waking heart; lay hold of eternal life. The way to get this is not to be drunk of the world, but to be wise, redeeming your time; and balance these earthly things with heavenly. See what these fading comforts are to eternity. All the things we see here are temporal, but the things which are not seen, they are eternal, 2 Cor. iv. 18. Therefore we should let our affections run the right way, and have Abraham's eyes to see afar off, and feed our meditations with the things which we shall have hereafter, as Moses did.

I beseech you, let us prize the favour of God above all that the earth affords. What though we endure hardness here! Did Christ leave heaven to suffer for us, and shall not we suffer some straits for him? Faith can see a greater good in Christ than in the creature. This is that that will set out the vanity of the world and the excellency of heaven, the certainty of the one and the perishing condition of the other. It will make things to come as present with us, and find out a sufficiency in the worst estate.

FAITH TRIUMPHANT.*

These all died in faith, not having received the promises, but having seen them afar off, they were persuaded of them, and embraced them, and confessed that they were strangers and pilgrims on earth.—HEB. XI. 13.

THIS chapter is a little book of martyrs. It discovers the life and death of the holy patriarchs, and by what means God's children are brought into possession of that that they have an interest and right unto upon earth. It is by faith. By faith we do and suffer all that we do and suffer, all that God hath ordained us to go through, till he have brought us and invested us to heaven, which is prepared for us.

In the former part of the chapter there is an induction, the instances of particular blessed patriarchs; and after he had named diverse particulars, he sums them up in this general, 'All these died in faith.'

In this verse there is,

First, The general set down, '*All* these died in faith.'

And then the particular unfolding of this. 'They received not the promises, having seen them afar off, and were persuaded of them, and embraced them, and confessed they were strangers and pilgrims on earth.' He sets down their faith particularly, hereby setting down what might hinder it and yet did not hinder it, 'the not receiving of the promises.' 'They received not the promises, and yet they believed the promises;' that is, the things promised. They were afar off, and yet they saw them.

'They saw them.' That is the first degree.

'They were persuaded of them.' That is the second.

'They embraced them.' That is the third.

'They confessed they were pilgrims and strangers.' That is the fourth.

'All these died in faith.'

There is one faith from the beginning of the world. As there is one Christ, one salvation, so there is one uniform faith for the saving of our souls. We hope to be saved by Jesus Christ as they were. I do but touch that.

* 'Faith Triumphant' forms 'five' of the Sermons of 'Evangelical Sacrifices' (4to, 1640). Its separate title-page is as follows:—'Faith Trivmphant. In five Sermons, on Heb. 11. 13. By the late Learned and Reverend Divine, Rich. Sibbs. Doctor in Divinity, Mr. of Katherine Hall in Cambridge, and sometimes Preacher to the Honourable Society of Grayes-Inne. Luke 7. 50. And hee said to the woman, thy faith hath saved thee, goe in peace. London, Printed by T. B. for N. Bourne, at the Royall Exchange, and R. Harford, at the guilt Bible in Queenes-head Alley in Pater-noster-Row. 1639.'

Then again, here is implied *a continuance and perseverance in faith.* 'All these *died* in faith;' that is, they lived in faith and by faith till they died, and then they died in faith. Faith first makes a Christian, and then after, he lives by faith. It quickens the life of grace, and then he leads his life by that faith. He continues in it till he come to death, which is the period of all, and then he dies by that faith. But of perseverance to the end and the helps to it, I spake at large upon another occasion, therefore I omit it.* 'All these died in faith.' Faith carried them along all their lifetime till death itself. Now that faith that helped them through all the difficulties of this life, that faith by which they lived, in that faith they died.

'*They died* in faith.'

In the faith of the Messiah, in faith of Canaan, in faith of heaven. For the patriarchs, they had not Canaan till many hundred years after. It was a type of heaven. They had not Christ till some thousands of years after. So they died in faith of Christ, of Canaan, and of heaven. The benefits by Christ is the upshot of all this. 'They died in faith.' He doth not say how otherwise they died, because it is not material whether they died rich or poor, great or mean. God takes no great notice of that, nor a Christian takes no great notice of it. 'They died in faith.' Whether they died a violent or a peaceable death it is no matter; they died blessed, in that they died in faith. 'They died in faith,' which in other phrase is, 'to die in the Lord,' 'to sleep in the Lord;' because whosoever dies in faith, dies in Christ. Faith lifts them up to Christ, and they sleep in Christ. It is a happy thing to die in Christ. Now those that die in faith, they die in Christ. 'Blessed are those that die in the Lord, they rest from their labours,' saith the apostle, Rev. xiv. 13.

'All these died in faith.'

They continued in faith to death, and then they ended their days in faith. When death closed up the eyes of their bodies, then with the eye of faith they looked upon Christ, upon God in Christ reconciled to them. The point is clear, that

Doct. The grace of faith, it is such a grace that it carries a Christian through all the passages of this life.

It enableth him to hold out to the end, to suffer those things that he is to suffer, and in the end by it he dies. And when all things else leave him in death, when riches leave him, when friends leave him, when honour and great places leave him, when his life and senses leave him, when all leave him, yet faith will never leave him till it have put him in full possession of heaven, and then it ceaseth when it hath done the work it hath to do, which is to bring us to heaven. Then it is swallowed up in vision and sight, and hope into fruition, and enjoying of the thing hoped for. It is a blessed grace, that stands by us, and goes along with us, and comforts us in all the passages of this life, and even in death itself, in those dark passages. It never forsakes us till it have put us in possession of heaven.

'All these died in faith.'

Quest. What is it to die in faith?

Ans. To die in faith, as I said, is to die in the Lord by faith; and it looks to the time past, present, to come.

1. *To the time past.* To die in faith is to die in assurance of the forgiveness of sins, when by faith and repentance we have pulled out the sting of sins past. For faith looks upon Christ, and Christ hath taken the sting

* The perseverance of the saints will be found frequently discussed by Sibbes throughout his works. For references see the Index.—G.

of death in his own, and death ever since hath been stingless and harmless to his members. He hath disarmed it. Death had nothing to do to kill Christ. Now seizing upon him, who should not have died, who was our surety, death hath lost his sting. So that to die in faith is to die in assurance of forgiveness of sins past by Christ.

2. *For the present.* In the present instant of death, to die in faith is to see God reconciled to us in Christ, and with the eye of Stephen, to see Christ ready to receive our souls, Acts vii. 59, to see Christ sitting at the right hand of God, to break through all that is between, to see ourselves sitting 'at the right hand of God, in heavenly places with Jesus Christ,' Eph. i. 20. This is to die in faith; to see ourselves there with our head, where we shall be ere long. Faith makes things to come present. To die in faith is to die in assurance of that blessed salvation presently, even at that instant of time, at the parting of soul and body, that Christ will receive our souls, that are redeemed with his precious blood, that cost him so dear. He will not suffer the price of his blood to miscarry. Faith apprehends that Christ will go down with us to the grave. As God said to Jacob, 'Fear not to go down into Egypt; I will go with thee,' Gen. xlvi. 3, so God would not have us fear to go down into the grave, those dark cells and dungeons; God will go down with us. 'Our flesh shall rest in hope,' Ps. xvi. 9, because Christ, our surety, was raised out of the grave, and sits in heaven in glory and majesty. Therefore 'our flesh rests in hope;' as it is, Ps. xvi. 10, 'Thou wilt not suffer thy Holy One to see corruption.' Therefore our flesh rests in hope till the resurrection; because God did not suffer his Holy One to see corruption. This is to die in faith.

3. And *for the time to come.* To die in faith is by faith to overcome all the horror of death. Death is a terrible thing; and of all the passages wherein we have occasion to use faith, it is most exercised in death. It requires more to die in faith than to live in faith; for then the soul it looks to the horror of the grave, it sees nothing there but dust and rottenness. It looks to the pangs of death, sense and nature doth. And likewise the soul, so far as it hath nothing but nature in it, it looks to the dissolution of two friends, the body and the soul, who have been long coupled together, and their parting is bitter. And then it looks to the parting with friends here, with whom they have lived lovingly and sweetly. In death, nature sees an end of all employment in this world, of all the comforts of this life, &c., and therefore it is a terrible thing. Now to die in faith is to die in conquering all these, with a spirit above all these. What doth faith in the hour of death? It overcomes all these, and all such like.

For when the soul by faith considers the horror of the grave as the chambers of death, faith considers they be but resting places for the body, that it sleeps there awhile till the day of the resurrection, and then they meet again. And it considers that the flesh rests there in hope of a glorious resurrection; and faith sees a time of restoring, as St Peter saith, 'There shall be a day of restoring of all things,' Acts iii. 21. There is a day of refreshing and restoring to come, when those eyes wherewith we now look up to heaven, and those feet that carry us about our callings, and about the exercises of religion, and those hands that have been lift up to God, that body that hath been the vessel of the soul, shall be restored, though it be turned to dust and rottenness. Faith seeth the faithfulness of God, that God in Christ hath taken these bodies of ours in trust. 'I know whom I have believed, and he is able to keep that I have committed to him,' 2 Tim. i. 12. I have committed to him my soul, my body, my whole salvation. I know he is able to keep that I have committed to him. 'And I know that my Redeemer liveth,' saith Job. It was his comfort in all extremity, that he should see him with his very same eyes.

And then for the pangs of death, which nature trembles and quakes at, faith considers of them as the pangs of child-birth. Every birth is with pangs. Now, what is death but the birth to immortality, the birth of glory? We die to be born to glory and happiness. All our lifetime we are in the womb of the church, and here we are bringing forth glory. Now death, I say, it is the birth-day of glory, and a birth is with pain. Faith sees it is a birth-day. It sees that presently upon it there shall be joy. As with a woman after she hath brought 'a man-child into the world,' John xvi. 21, so it comforts itself against the pangs of death. Again, faith sees them short, and sees the glory after to be eternal. It is a little dark passage to an eternal glorious light.*

Then for the dissolution and parting of two friends, soul and body, faith sees that it is but for a while, and then that that parting is a bringing in a better joining; for it brings the soul immediately to her beloved, our Saviour Christ Jesus; and faith sees that it is not long till body and soul shall be re-united again for ever, 'and they shall be for ever with the Lord,' .

And then for friends. Faith sees, indeed, that we shall part with many sweet friends; but faith saith we shall have better friends. We go to God, we go to the souls of perfect men, we go to [an] innumerable company of angels, Heb. xii. 22, we go to better company a great deal.

And for all the employments we have here, that we have below, faith sees that there will be exercise in heaven. We shall praise God with angels and all the blessed and glorious company of heaven. So consider what you will that is bitter and terrible in death, faith conquers it. It sees an end of it, and opposeth to it better things; because, notwithstanding death cuts off many comforts, yet it brings better. It is a blessed change; it is a change for the better every way. Faith sees that there is a better place, better company, better employment, better liberty,—all better. And, which is more, to die in faith is to die in assurance that all is ours, as the apostle saith, 1 Cor. iii. 16. Even death is ours. Paul is yours, Christ is yours, death is yours. This is our comfort when our days shall be closed up with death. Faith believes that death is ours, that is, it is for our good; for, as I said, it brings us to our wished haven; it brings an end to all misery, an end to our sins, an end to our pain, an end to our vexations, an end to our discomforts, and to all scandals here below; an end to all the temptations of Satan. 'The Lord will wipe all tears from our eyes then,' Rev. vii. 17. And it is the beginning of happiness that shall never end. So, indeed, faith sees that the day of death is better than the day of birth. When we come into misery, it is not so good as when we go out of misery, and enter into happiness. This is to die in faith. For the time past to see the forgiveness of all our sins, to see the sting pulled out; and for the present to look to Christ, ready to receive our souls, and to see him present with us to comfort us, to strengthen us against the pangs of death; and for the time to come, by faith to overlook the grave, to overlook death and all, and to see all conquered in Christ; to see ourselves in heaven already with Christ. And thus a Christian being upheld with this grace, he ends his days in faith.

* Cf. note *c*, Vol. I. p. 350.—G.

Use. This should stir us up, if this be so, *to get this grace of faith; above all graces, to get assurance that we are in Christ Jesus*, that so we may live with comfort, and end our days with comfort, and live for ever happy in the Lord. It is only faith, and nothing else, that will master this king of fears,—this giant that subdues all the kings of the earth to him. This monster death he outfaceth all (*a*). Nothing can outface him but faith in Christ, and that will master him. As for your glorious speeches of pagans, and moral, civil men, they are but flourishes, vain, empty flourishes. Their hearts give them the lie. Death is a terrible thing when it is armed with our sins, and when it is the messenger of God's wrath, and citeth us before God. It is the end of happiness and the beginning of torment. When we look upon it in the glass of the law and in the glass of nature, it is the end of all comforts. It is a curse brought in by sin. It is a terrible thing. Nothing can conquer and master it but faith in Christ. Oh, let us labour, therefore, to get it while we live, and to exercise it while we live, that we may live every day by faith.

It is not any faith that we can die by. It must be a faith that we have exercised and tried before. It is a tried, a proved faith, that we must end our days by. For, alas! when death comes, if we have not learned to live by faith before, how can we end our days in faith? He that, while he lives, will not trust God with his children, that will not trust God with his soul; he that will not trust God with his estate, but will use ill means, and put his hand to ill courses to gain by; he that will not trust God for his inheritance, that will not 'cast his bread upon the waters,' Eccles. xi. 1, and trust God to see it again; he that will not do this while he lives, how shall he trust God for body and soul and all, in death? He cannot do it. It must be a faith that is daily exercised and tried, whereby we must commit our souls to God when we die, that we may die in that faith; that we may be able to say, All the days of my life I had experience of God's goodness; I depended upon him, and I have found him true in all his promises. I committed myself and my ways to him, and I found him good and gracious in blessing me. I found him giving me a good issue; and now I am strengthened thereby to trust God, that hath been so true to me all my lifetime. I will trust him now with my soul that he will never fail me.

Let us all labour for this faith; for though it cannot be said of us that we die rich, or that we die great in the world, perhaps we may die a violent death, as there be divers diseases that lead the body into distempers. It is no matter how we die distempered, and in any estate, so it may be said of us we die in a blessed faith.

Obj. But it may be objected that all God's children die not in faith, because some die raging and distempered, and in such fits.

Ans. But we must know that they die in faith notwithstanding all that, for then they are not themselves. The covenant between God and them was made before: they have given up themselves to God, and committed their souls to God before; for a Christian gives up himself every day. He commits himself, soul and body, continually to God, as a blessed sacrifice of a free-will offering; so he learns to die daily, daily labours to live in the estate he would die in. He ought to do thus; and many Christians do thus. Therefore, notwithstanding these distempers, the covenant between God and the soul remains still, and he dies in faith. It is said here, they 'all died in faith.' He saith not they all died in feeling. A man may die in faith, and yet not die in feeling; and sometimes the strongest faith is with the least feeling of God's love. Feeling may be reserved sometimes for heaven. Yet notwithstanding, we must not take it so as if there were no feeling where there is faith; for there was never faith yet but upon the touch of faith, the soul drew some strength and some inward feeling. Though it be not discerned of the soul in regard of the immoderate desire of the soul to have more, yet there is alway so much feeling, and strength, and comfort, that supports the soul from despair, take the child of God at the worst. Therefore when I speak of feeling, I speak of a glorious demonstration that God sometimes takes away from his children. They died in faith, though not alway in feeling of it; they died in faith, though not alway by a fair death or in a comely manner outwardly, to the applause of the world. It is no matter for that; they all died in faith, and that is sufficient.

It is the desire of God's children that they may die in faith and die in Christ, as they have lived in faith and lived in Christ. Faith is a blessed grace. By it we live, by it we stand, by it we conquer and resist, by it we endure, by it we die, by it we do all those worthy matters we do, in spite of the devil and his kingdom. This is that excellent grace of faith by which we live and by which we die.

'These all died in faith.'

For they lived as they died, and died as they lived. It is a usual general rule, as men live, so they die. He that lives by faith, dies by faith. He that lives profanely, dies profanely. If we suffer the devil to lead us and abuse us all the time of our life, we must think God in just judgment will give us up, that he shall delude us and abuse us at the hour of death. Carnal confidence disposeth men to think they shall step out of their filthy blasphemous course of life, out of their sinful cursed condition, to leap to heaven presently. It is no such matter. Alas! * heaven it must be entered into on earth. There must be a fitting and preparing time on earth for heaven. We must look to die as we live. There is but one example of a man that died by faith that did not live by faith; that is, the good thief; and yet that little time of life we see how fruitful it was. But the rule is, all that will die in faith must live in faith; and usually men are affected and disposed, and their speeches and carriage are on their death-bed as they were when they lived, God in just judgment giving them up to that course.

Many wish that they may live in popery, and enjoy the liberty of that carnal religion, but they would not die by that religion. They live by that religion, and die by ours. When they have had the sweetness and liberty that is given them there to sin, and then open all in confession and be clean, and then sin again; and such easy courses they have that betrays thousands of souls to damnation. Now this is their course: when conscience is awakened, they fly to salvation by Christ, if they understand any thing at all, or else they die desperate, if they look to be saved by that religion as they live by it. If we look to die by faith, we must live by it.

'These all died in faith, not having received the promises.'

For God promised them Canaan, and they died many hundred years before. Their posterity came into Canaan. He promised them Christ, and they died long before Christ came. He promised them heaven, and they entered not into heaven till death. So they received not the promises, that is, they received not the things promised; for else they received the promise, but not that that was promised. They received not the type, Canaan, nor the things typified,—Christ and heaven. This is

* Another example of Sibbes's peculiar use of 'alas.'—G.

added as a commendation of their faith, that though they received not the things that they looked for, yet notwithstanding they had such a strong faith, that they continued to live by faith and died in faith. The promises here are taken for the blessed things promised.

This should teach us this lesson, that God's promises are not empty shells; they are real things. And then, whatsoever God promiseth it is not barely propounded to the soul, but in a promise. It is wrapped up in a promise. He gives us not empty promises nor naked things; but he gives us promises of things which we must exercise our faith in, in depending upon him for the performance of them till we be put in possession. For here all the blessings they looked for is wrapped up in the name promises. 'They received not the promises.' The meaning is, they received not Canaan; they received not Christ in the flesh, nor life everlasting. Now the believing soul, it looks upon all the good things that it looks for from God, not nakedly, but as they are involved and wrapped and lapped* up in promises. It must have a word for it; it looks to God's word. For the soul looks not now immediately, as it shall do in heaven. It looks not to God and to Christ directly; but it looks to Christ, and heaven, and happiness, as it is in a promise. It dares not expect any thing of God but by a promise. Alas! the guilty soul, how dares it look God in the face but by a promise, except he have engaged himself by promise? And he hath engaged himself by promise that he will do it. He hath pawned his faithfulness that he will do it. And then the soul looks to the promise; and in that it looks to Christ and grace, and heaven and happiness, and all good things.

A presumptuous idle person, that knows not what God is, that he is a 'consuming fire,' he rusheth into God's presence. Faith dares not go to God, but first it pleads his word to him; it pleads his promise to him; it looks on God by a promise. The very phrase enforceth this upon us that we should make great account of the promises, because we have all good wrapped in them. The promises are the swaddling clouts.† Christ and heaven is wrapped in them. And when we have a promise, let us think we are rich indeed; for God will perform his promise. From the promise then the soul goes to the nature of God. Then he thinks of his justice: his justice ties him to perform it. It thinks of his mercy and truth, 'faithful is he that hath promised,' Heb. x. 23. Then it thinks of that great name Jehovah, that gives being to the world, gives being to all things, nay, and that will turn all things that are now to nothing; as when they were nothing he gave them being at the first. That Jehovah hath made these promises of life everlasting, of necessary grace to bring us thither. He hath made a promise of perseverance and of comfort under the cross and affliction; a promise of provision and the like. That great God Jehovah, that gave being to all, is faithful: he hath bound himself; he hath laid his faithfulness to pawn, that he will make all good that is here promised. The soul, after it sees the promise, it riseth up and looks to God. 'They received not the promises,' that is, the things promised. So much I desire to observe from the phrase.

'They received not the promises.'

He speaks in the plural number, though he mean but one main promise, that is, the Messiah, for all other were types of him. Believers are called 'children of the promise,' Gal. iv. 28. Here they are called promises, for the repeating of them. The promise of the same thing it was made oft:

* That is, 'covered up,' *e.g.* lap, a covering.—G. † That is, 'clothes.'—G.

there was no new promise. The promise of the same thing it was seven* times repeated and renewed to Abraham presently one after another. So they are called promises, to shew that the promise can never be too much thought on, though it be the same promise of life everlasting; the same promise of grace and of comfort; the same promise of the resurrection, &c. All the promises of good things to come we cannot think of too oft, nor receive the sacrament, the seal of the promise, too oft. God knows what we are. He will have us oft receive the sacrament, and oft hear the same things. We see the prophet Isaiah and the rest, how oft they inculcate the same promises of comfort to the people in captivity, concerning their deliverance out of it. They repeat it again and again. The same reason should enforce the soul to have recourse to the promises again and again; when there is any doubt or darkness ariseth, to comfort the soul with the promise again and again. Satan puts clouds and darkness before the soul every day. There is a repeating of sin, of infirmities and darkness every day. We should every day repeat the promises still, though it be the same promise, and the seal of them. This I observe from the number.

'They received not the promises.'

There is a distinction of the words *Evangelion* and *Epangelia* in the Greek.† They have a different signification. *Epangelia* is of the time of the promises that were before Christ, and they were all in expectation of the promise, of the promised Messiah. The time of that dispensation was *Epangelia; Evangelion*, that was the time of the gospel, when the promise was brought into performance, when our salvation was wrought by Christ in his first coming. So they lived under the promise, but they lived not under the things promised. They had *Epangelia*, the promise made to them; but they had not *Evangelion*, that is, the dispensation of time wherein Christ lived; which were indeed glorious times, when Christ came in the flesh. They received not those, yet notwithstanding they died in faith, to shame us, that have so many means and helps, and yet notwithstanding are so earthly-minded, and so stagger and doubt in matters of salvation, and have our faith to seek; when all these blessed worthies, the patriarchs, died in the faith that they lived in, and yet 'they received not the promises,' no, not the type of the promises. They received not Canaan, which was an earthly type of heavenly Canaan, which was promised them. They came not to reap that till long after, when they came out of Egypt; as for Abraham, Isaac, and Jacob, they lived in the land of promise as strangers.

'They received not the promises.'

They were comforted notwithstanding, that their posterity should receive them. Canaan was a type of Christ and of heaven. I observe this by the way that,

Obs. God doth not reveal all things at all times.

God doth leave diverse things to be revealed in diverse ages of the church. God doth not reveal everything in every time, to comfort all ages of the church. We see not everything in our times; we must be content.

There is to come the conversion of the Jews. Many good souls desire that. There is to come the confusion of antichrist, and many good things that God will bring to pass in another age. Our posterity they shall see it. Let it comfort us. By faith we see the promises. Though we do not receive the things promised, we have the promise in the Scriptures.

* Qu. 'several'?—Ed. † That is, εὐαγγέλιον. ἐπαγγελία.—G.

Let us comfort ourselves in that, that the benefit is reserved to our posterity. Every age hath several privileges: that that one age hath not, another hath. These grand patriarchs saw not what their posterity saw. Their posterity saw not what those that lived in the time of Christ saw. Those in Christ's time saw not the discovery of antichrist which we see. Our posterity shall see the confusion of antichrist, which, it may be, we shall not see.

Again, this should help us against the common infirmity that Christians are subject unto. We should be thankful for some things, though we have not all that we would have. These 'received not the promises.' They had the promise, they had the word, though they had not the things promised; and that comforted them. Though they had not the thing, no, not so much as the type of the thing, not Canaan,—these blessed patriarchs, Abraham, Isaac, and Jacob,—yet they were thankful and cheerful, and died in faith.

It is a common infirmity which our nature is too prone to. If the church be not in all things as we would, we will not hear, we care for nothing. Like curst children, if they have not all they would have, they care for nothing. These all, they had the promises, they had not the things promised; but did they take pet upon this? Oh no! 'they embraced the promises,' and looked for the things promised in due time, though they had them not themselves. So it is with particular Christians. Other Christians they see go comfortably in their Christian course, and they have nothing,—no grace, no faith, no love, no goodness. Because they have not all they would have, therefore they have nothing. What an ill affection is this! We should be thankful for that we have, that we can deny ourselves; and we should be content to wait for that we have not. This is the disposition of a Christian that is in a right temper; and that is it which holds many from comforts, that they do not thankfully acknowledge that they have. Our covetousness and greediness of that that we have not, and yet would have it, makes us that we do not see that we have already. We all look forward, we would have more and more, and are not thankful for the present grace. The patriarchs were not so. They wanted many things that they desired heartily to have, and yet they comforted themselves, and died in faith. Though 'they did not receive the promises,'

'They saw them afar off.'

'They saw them afar off, and were persuaded of them and embraced them,' &c. This is the order of God's Spirit; first to open the eye to see, and by sight to persuade, and upon persuasion to stir up the heart and affections to embrace; for good things are brought into the soul through the understanding, by the spiritual sight of the understanding, and from that into the will and affections by embracing the things we know. This is God's course daily. Therefore he saith they first saw them, and then were persuaded of them, and then embraced them.

'They see them afar off.'

Indeed, they saw them afar off. They were not fulfilled till many years and generations after, yet they see them.

By what eye?

By the eye of faith. Faith makes things present, though in themselves they be far off. It is the nature of faith to make things that are absent to be present to the believing soul; and it affects the soul somewhat as if it were present. We know things work not upon the soul but as present; a danger that is many years to come, it affects not the soul unless it be apprehended as present; nothing affects the soul but as present. Now there are two ways of things being present. One is, when the things themselves be present; that is, when we shall be in heaven and enjoy Christ and all the joys of heaven, then the things are present themselves. And then there is a presence of faith. When faith apprehends the things promised to us as present, faith makes the things present in some sort, not in all respects, for then faith were all one with vision and possession, but in regard of certainty they are present, and in regard of sound comfort. Therefore God gives other graces, between faith and possession, to strengthen and enable faith that it do not sink in the work. Between faith and the full possession of the good things we believe, we have patience and hope, and many other sweet graces; but all dispose the soul comfortably to wait for the accomplishment of the things believed. Now, though the presence of faith affect not so much as the presence of sight, yet it doth affect. What is the reason that a holy man is so much affected with heavenly things? He feels no more* joy many times than a wicked man. It is the nature of faith that so represents them to him, and sets before his eyes the excellency of the things that he sees them as present.

Faith hath her eye, faith hath her senses, faith hath feet of her own, whereby she goes to Christ; faith hath arms of her own to grasp and to clasp Christ. Faith hath ears of her own to hear the word of God and believe it. Faith hath eyes of her own; and what kind of eyes? To see things afar off; to see things invisible; to see things within the veil; to see things that are upward, things that sense and reason can never reach unto. Reason sees more than sense; but faith sees more than reason. Faith sees the resurrection of the body; faith sees the glory in heaven, that all the eyes in the world cannot see. Faith correcteth the error of reason; reason corrects the error of sense. 'They saw him afar off,' with the blessed eye of faith. Faith hath an eye that sees afar off; it sees things remote both in time and place.

1. It sees things far off in place. Faith sees things in heaven; it sees Christ there; it sees our place provided for us there; it sees God reconciled there; by it we see ourselves there, because we shall be there ere long. Faith sees all this; it breaks through and looks through all; it hath most piercing beams, the eye of faith. And it works in an instant; it goes to heaven in a moment and sees Christ.

And for distance of time, the eye of faith it sees things past and things to come. It sees things past. It sees the creation of the world; it sees the redemption of us by Jesus Christ; it sees our sins there punished in Christ our surety; it sees us crucified with Christ Jesus; it sees all discharged by him. Faith sees this in the sacrament: when we take the bread, faith hath recourse presently to the breaking of the body of Christ and the shedding of the blood of Christ. Then Christ is crucified to us and dies to us. When we believe Christ was crucified for us and died for us, faith makes it present.

And so for the time to come, faith hath an eye that looks afar off. It sees the resurrection of the body and life everlasting. Faith sees the general judgment. It sees eternal happiness in heaven; it sees things afar off. It is the evidence of things not seen.

What is the reason of it?

It makes things not otherwise seen be seen, and presently seen; it gives

* Qu. 'feels more'?—Ed.

a being to things. It is a strange power that faith hath. Faith is the eye of the sanctified soul; it is the light of the soul.

In the dark, though things have a colour and a lustre in them, yet till light come to make them clear, they are all as if they were not, they are not seen; but when the light discovers them, then those things that were impossible to be seen and had in them colour and lustre, they come to be actually seen. So it is with faith; there is the happiness of a Christian; there is glory and grace. Reason, it seeth not this. Here is a night of all these things, if there be not light in the eye of faith. Now, when there comes the promise of God as a light discovering them, and the eye of faith to see all this, then here is an evidence of the things, a clear sight of them, which without faith are as excellent things in the night, that no eye can see. Faith is a further light, a light beyond all, a supernatural heavenly light and sight. It sees beyond all other eyes, beyond the eye of the body, or beyond the other eye of the soul, which is reason.

Now this work of faith is called sight; among other respects for this, that sight is the most capacious and comprehending sense. It apprehends its object quickly; and sight it works upon the affections. So faith hath a quick eye-sight; it pierceth through the dark things of the world; it pierceth through contraries. God's children, though they see their estate ofttimes contrary to the promise, as if God did not regard them, yet they break through that. You know God's manner of working is in contrary estates. When we die, faith sees life; when we most apprehend our sins, faith sees the forgiveness of sins; when we are in the greatest mystery, faith hath so quick a sight that it sees happiness and glory through all. It sees afar off, notwithstanding the interposing of anything contrary by flesh and blood.

Faith is sometimes called taste, and by the name of other senses; but especially by the name of sight. As in sight there is both the light outward and a light in the eye, and the application of the light in the eye to the object, so in faith there is a light in the things revealed, a promise and discovery of it by the light of the gospel, and an inward light in the soul answerable to the inward light in the eye. For a dead eye sees nothing, and a quick living eye sees nothing without the light of the air. So there is a double revelation, by the word and by the Spirit. The Spirit works an eye of faith in the soul, and then it discovers to it the things of God.

'They saw them afar off.'

God created a new eye in the soul, a new sight which they had not by nature; for even as the natural eye cannot see things that are invisible, so the natural man cannot see the things of God, which are seen not by a natural, but by a supernatural eye. 'Eye hath not seen, nor ear heard, nor hath entered into the heart of man to conceive, what God hath prepared for his children,' 1 Cor. ii. 10, 11. The eye therefore that must see things afar off, it must be a supernatural eye; and the light that must discover them must be the light of God's truth. For reason cannot see the resurrection of the body, and the life to come, and such glorious things as the word of God reveals to us.

Quest. If you ask why this sight of faith is so necessary, this supernatural sight;—

Ans. I answer, nothing can be done in religion without the supernatural eye of the soul, nothing at all; for a man may see heavenly things with a natural eye and be never a whit the better. A man may see the joys of heaven; he may hear much of heaven and happiness and forgiveness, and think, Oh, these are good things; but yet notwithstanding he doth not see these things with a supernatural eye; he doth not see these things to be holy and gracious, and to be fit for him; he wisheth them with conditions, but not with the altering of his disposition. As a man may see an earthly thing with a heavenly eye, because he sees God in it, and there is somewhat of God in it to lead him to see him, so a man may see heavenly things with a carnal eye, as Balaam wished 'to die the death of the righteous,' Num. xxiii. 10. A carnal man may be ravished with heavenly things; but he must look upon them as things suitable, or else all is to no purpose.

Quest. How doth faith see this? How comes faith to have this strength?

Ans. Because faith sees things in the power of God. It sees things in the truth of God. He is Jehovah; he gives being to things. Therefore, as God Almighty gives being to things in their time, when they are not, so faith in his promises sees that these things will be.—It sees things in the truth of God, in the promise of God. There it hath these eyes to see afar off. Itself is wrought by the mighty power of God in the soul, for it is a mighty power for the soul to neglect the things it sees, to neglect riches, and honours, and pleasures, and to stand admiring of things that it sees not. For a man to rule his course of life upon reasons which the world sees not, because there is a happiness to come and a God that he believes in, &c., it is a mighty power that plants such a grace in the heart. Faith is wrought by the mighty power of God. As itself is wrought by the power of God, so it lays hold upon the power of God, that the promises shall be performed. In all the promises it sees and lays hold on the mighty power and truth of God, and therefore it hath such an eye.

Use. Our duty then is to labour to have our faith clear, to have this eye of faith, to have a strong faith, a strong sight.

Quest. When is the sight of faith strong?

Ans. When it is as the faith of these patriarchs was.

There are three things that makes a strong sight, that makes us conceive that the sight of faith is a strong sight.

1. *When the things are far off that we see*, then if the eye see them, it is a strong sight. A weak eye cannot see afar off.

2. Secondly, *When there are clouds between, though the things be near.* Yet when there are clouds between, to break and pierce through them, there must be a strong sight.

3. Then, thirdly, *when there is but a little light.* When there are many obstacles in the midst, and to break through all by a little light to see things remote, here is a strong eye; and this was the sight of these blessed men. They had a strong eye.

1. For the things they looked on *were remote, afar off.* Divers thousands of years, they saw Christ by faith. The soul mounted up on the wing of faith. It flew over many thousands of years in a moment, and saw Christ the Messiah, and saw heaven itself typified in Canaan.* So swift is the eye of faith, it mounts over all in a moment. As the eye of the body in a moment can look to the visible heavens, so a strong faith it sees Christ in heaven.

2. And then between them and that they looked to *what difficulties were there!* Blessed Abraham, who was a type of Christ, how many difficulties had he, besides other of the patriarchs! We see God commanded him to slay his son, a command one would think against reason, against affection, against hope. It was faith against faith, as it were. It was against reason

* 'Saw,' misprinted twice 'see.'—G.

in the eye of flesh. Now in this case to strive against all these difficulties, what a-many clouds must Abraham break through here, against sense and against affection. He must hope against hope ; he must have faith against faith, he must deny affection, he must go and take his only begotten son Isaac, and he must be the executioner and butcher himself, and slay him for a sacrifice. Here must be a strong faith in the power of God, that must see God raising Isaac from the dead, as he did after a sort ; for when he was bound for a sacrifice ready to be slain, he caused a ram to be taken in the thicket, and to be offered, and Isaac escaped. It was a strong faith to break through all these. Indeed, blessed Abraham saw more excellency and power in the work of God than in his beloved Isaac. So faith that is strong, it sees more comfort, and joy, and matter of benefit and blessing to the soul in the promises and in the word of God than in Isaac ; that is, than in the dearest thing in our own account that we have, that the faithful soul had rather part with all than with God. It will not part with his promises for all that is in the earth, not for the dearest thing in this world ; Isaac shall go rather.

3. Then for their light to go by, *it was but little.* What a little light had they ! Promises. They saw things in types and glasses, a few promises. And what was that they sought ? A heritage far off. We, on the contrary, have all set nearer hand that may help us ; but we have a weaker faith. One would think it should greatly help us to lead our lives till we come to heaven ; for that that we believe is nearer, heaven is nearer. How little a time is between us and the day of judgment ! How little a time between us and the glory that is to be revealed ! For the clouds that we have between they are none in comparing our light with theirs. How many promises have we discovered beforehand ! We have Christ come in the flesh and risen again ; we have the Gentiles called, and all these things. We have light upon light. We have larger promises, and a larger unfolding of divine truths. The canon is enlarged, the Bible is enlarged more than it was then. There are many books added, and the New Testament. Now how doth it come to pass that we see not so well as they, nor so strongly as they ? I answer, the reason is this,—their light was less, but their sight was stronger. We have more light and less sight. We have things nearer, but our sight is weaker ; the more shame for us. A strong eye may see afar off by a little light, when a weak eye cannot see so far by a greater light. The eye of their soul, the eye of faith was stronger and more lightsome. The Spirit of God was stronger in Abraham, but his light of revelation was lesser, he had fewer promises ; for he desired to see Christ's day, and saw it not.

So it is with Christians sometimes ; when there is a great strength of faith, yet it may be there is not so much light. A weak Christian may have more light, but he hath a weaker eye, and he in that respect sees better than a stronger. To a stronger, God doth not discover to him so much outwardly sometimes, suitable to his inward. God's dispensations are diverse in this kind.

Now to help our sight to heaven, this sight of faith, that we may every day ascend with the eye of our souls with this blessed sight.

1. *Let us take heed of the god of this world, Satan*, that he do not with the dust of the world dim our sight. What is the reason that many cannot see the glorious things of God ? 'The god of this world,' saith the apostle, 'hath blinded their eyes.' He casts dust in their eyes. They are covetous, they are blind in their affections, they have dark souls. The

soul when it is led by affections and lusts, when the affections will not suffer it to see, it covers the eyes of it. And then the outward things of the world, they are cast into the eyes. We must take heed of these inward and outward lets; take heed of Satan, that he do not with outward objects bewitch us. For as it is in prospective glasses, you know such glasses, some are of that nature they represent to a man things that are afar off as if they were near; so faith it is a kind of prospective glass, it presents to the soul by reason of this supernatural light, things that are far off as if they were near. Now, as God hath his prospective glasses to see afar off, so the devil hath prospective glasses that when things are near he makes them seem afar off,—as such glasses there are too. When death, and danger, and damnation are near; when a man carries the sentence of damnation in his bosom, when he carries a stained, defiled conscience, the devil with his prospective glass makes him see death and destruction as afar off. I may live so many years and enjoy my pleasure and my will. Now this is but a false glass, the devil abuseth them; for your life is but a death, and when we begin to live we begin to die. Why should we account therefore of the time to come? Death and life go in equal pace one with another. Every day we live, so much is taken from our life, and then the cutting off of all is uncertain. Let us take heed that Satan blind us not.

2. And withal *desire God to open our eyes every day*, to take the scales from the eye of our souls, that we may see the promises, that we may see Christ, that we may see God shining on us in Christ; that he would take away the veil from the things by exposition, that he would open the truth to us by his ministers, and that he would take away the veil from our hearts, that our hearts may join with the things; that when by ministerial means the things are clear, that there may not be a veil of infidelity on our hearts, but that our hearts may sweetly join with them. Let us beg daily that God would take away the things that hinder, inward and outward, that we may see the things afar off; that we may not be, as Peter saith, mop-eyed (*b*), that we cannot see afar off; but that we may set heaven before our eyes, and the judgment and the happiness to come, that we may see, and view, and eye those things by faith, and that we may square our lives answerable.

3. Then, again, to help our sight of Christ and happiness, *let us get a fresh sight of our corruption and sin every day;* let us every day look on that terrifying object of our corruption of nature, hang it in the eye of our souls as an odious object, to humble us. Let us see every day what a corrupt heart we carry about us; see how odious these things are to God, how it offends him; see how it exposes us to the wrath of God, if he should take us in the midst of our sins and corruptions. Let us have these things fresh in our eyes every day, and that will clear our sight. Men are loath to look in the book of their consciences, because they are loath to be disturbed from their pleasures.

Let us see what need we stand in of Christ. The view of our corruptions will make us glad to see a better object. It will make us turn our eyes to Christ, to the promises, and all things that we have by Christ; we shall be glad to look to him. What is the reason we have no more delight to see the glorious things afar off? We see not the dimensions of our corruptions, for then we would be glad to see all the dimensions of God's love in Christ; the height, and breadth, and depth and all. So much for that.

'They saw them afar off.'

'They were persuaded of them.'

It was such a sight of the things as was with convincing, with persuasion. And indeed this follows well upon sight, for sight of all other senses persuades best. Hearing is not so persuasive as sight (*c*). Supernatural sight brings forth supernatural persuasion. Sight is a convincing sense, even outward sight. So inward sight it is a convincing thing; it persuades and sets down the soul that a thing is so, when a man sees it. All the men in the world cannot persuadē the weakest man in the world when it is day or night, when the sun shines or it is dark, that it is not so. When he sees it, he will believe his own eyes more than all the world besides. And as it is in sensible things we believe our own eyes, so much more in spiritual things we believe our eyes. When there is a spiritual light of revelation in the word discovering such things, and also to spiritual light a spiritual eye, when the Spirit puts an eye into the soul to see supernatural things that reason cannot attain to, then there is persuasion. Though all the world should persuade the soul that such a thing were not so, it would say it is so, it will believe its own eyes. If all the world should persuade a Christian that there is no such excellency in religion, that his ways are not good, that he is but foolish, &c., he knows the contrary, and will not be scorned out of his religion, and driven out of it by any contrary persuasion of men whom he pities—though perhaps they are otherwise beyond him—in the state of nature, for sight it is a convincing thing.

Especially when there is some taste with sight, for taste together with sight convinceth of the goodness of things; as we see in those that lead their life by tasting and feeling. The creatures maintain their life by tasting some proportionable food fit for them; so a Christian, when once he hath tasted of spiritual things, the proper food of his soul, when he hath seen and tasted of them, he will never be driven out of his religion and his course by any means; when he hath seen and tasted, he is thoroughly persuaded. A man must not dispute against taste. When he hath tasted a thing to be so, talk to him otherwise, he saith, I have tasted, and feel, and see it to be so; and therefore we see that after sight comes persuasion.

Now, this persuasion is a supernatural persuasion, and it is general and particular.

A general persuasion of the things, of the general truths, and a particular personal persuasion of our interest in them. When we are persuaded that the truths are so, generally, that are revealed in the word of God, and when we are persuaded, by the help of the Spirit, that we have a particular interest in them, a portion in them; and both are here meant. 'They saw them afar off, and were persuaded of them;' they were convinced both of the truth and goodness of them, and of the truth and goodness to them in particular.

Now, persuasion is a settled kind of knowledge. Persuasion comes divers ways. There be divers degrees tending to persuasion.

1. First, The poorest degree of the apprehension of things *is conjecture*, a guessing that such a thing may be so or otherwise, but I guess it rather to be so.

2. Beyond conjecture there is *opinion*, when a man thinks it is so, upon more reasons swaying him one way; and yet in opinion there is fear on the contrary, that it may be otherwise.

3. And the third degree beyond opinion *is certain knowledge;* when a

man is not only conceited* that the thing is so, his opinion is so upon some reasons inducing him, but he knows it by arguments and reasons. That is science and knowledge when the mind is persuaded by arguments. But that is not so much here meant, the persuasion by argument.

4. There is another degree then of knowledge, which is *by the authority of the speaker*, a persuasion from thence. When I know not the thing by the light of the thing so much, because I see the reason of the thing, but because I know such a one saith it, that is the persuasion of faith; when one is persuaded of a thing not so much out of his own knowledge, out of the principles of the thing, setting out the causes of the thing, as out of the credit of the person that speaks. Now, this persuasion riseth out of faith in the authority of the person. When I believe a thing for the authority of the speaker, it ariseth from the knowledge of him that speaks, that he is able, and that he is true, and that he is honest, and good; that he will not deceive because he is good, and he will not be deceived because he is wise. We conceive that he is wise, and holy, and able withal; one that we trust. If together with this knowledge and persuasion from the authority, and truth, and goodness, and wisdom of the speaker, there be joined sense and experience, we see it proved; and when there is experience, there is reason why we should believe that he saith, because we have found the thing to be so. So when there is both the authority of the speaker and some inward sense—some sight, and taste, and feeling, and experience of the thing spoken—here comes that settled persuasion, for he is undoubtedly true that hath spoken it, and I have found in some degree the thing true that he hath spoken. Now, both are here meant in some degrees, 'they saw the things afar off,' both by the authority of the promise, as likewise by their own sight, and some taste they had.

For God reserves not all for heaven. God gives his children some taste and feeling, some little joy and comfort, the 'first-fruits of the Spirit' here, Rom. viii. 23. So they were persuaded from the authority of the speaker, and some sense and feeling of the thing in some measure.

Now, this persuasion hath its degrees.

There is a *full persuasion*.

And there *is a persuasion that is not so full*, that is growing to further persuasion still.

And this persuasion hath degrees, both in the general persuasion of the truths themselves, and in their particular interest; for all Christians are not alike persuaded of divine truths themselves, nor all Christians are not alike persuaded of their particular interest in those truths. There be degrees in both respects.

1. *For the things themselves*, we may grow stronger and stronger persuaded; even as the light and our eye grows clearer the stronger is our sight, so our persuasion while we are here may grow stronger and stronger. It was strong in Abraham; yet not so uniformly strong, but that it was weaker some times than others, as we see in the story.

2. And so for *particular persuasion*. The Spirit of God may give assurance that may be shaken; ay, but he recovers himself presently. The tenor of a Christian's life is usually a state of sight and persuasion, when he is himself and when he remembers his own principles.

To come particularly, you see here that

Spiritual persuasion is necessary.

Both of the things in general, and of our interest in them.

* That is, 'conceives'—G.

Quest. It may be asked, whether there may be a persuasion of the truth in general, without a persuasion of our own particular interest in them?

Ans. I answer, No; not a sound, undoubted, spiritual persuasion. There is a double conviction, a conviction when a man cannot tell what to say against it; but spiritual conviction is when a man is convinced of the truth and goodness of the thing, and this always draws the other with it, first or last. A man may be convinced that he cannot tell what to say against the truth, but that is not properly persuasion. A man is persuaded by divine truth that all the promises are true in the gospel, and it draws with it a particular light; he sees, and is persuaded, of his own interest in it, first or last. For a strong persuasion of divine truth, of God's word, when I know it is God's word, it works in my flesh, it changeth me, it lifts me up, it casts me down, &c. So that a Christian knows that the word of God is the word of God by a spiritual persuasion, wrought by the efficacy of the word, from an intrinsecal principle in the word itself.

But sometimes it falls out that a Christian may be convinced of the truth of the word in general that it is God's word, and that the promises of salvation are true, and yet notwithstanding he may not feel the particular persuasion of the forgiveness of his sins, and of his acceptation to life everlasting, and his interest in Christ. These two are sometimes separable in regard of feeling. A Christian hath alway a persuasion of the truth of God, of the things, but he hath not alway a like persuasion of his own interest in them.

Quest. How do you prove that these are severed sometimes?

Ans. Thus: there is the birth and infancy of a Christian. When a Christian is in his birth, he is not persuaded of his own good estate, as he is after when he is grown. Then he knows his estate. A soul that is in the state of grace, that hungers and thirsts after good things, at that time it may be it is not acquainted that it shall be satisfied; it is not acquainted of its own interest, but stretcheth itself forward for entire satisfaction, and it shall be satisfied; that is, the soul that hungers and thirsts after the persuasion of God's love in Christ, and the forgiveness of sins, and life everlasting, there is never soul that thus hungers and thirsts, but God satisfies it at length; for the most part in this world, or else certainly in the world to come for ever. But alway where there is this persuasion supernatural, that the word of God is true indeed, that there is salvation to all true believers, when it is wrought by the Spirit, there is either a persuasion of our interest, or somewhat tending to persuasion, some hungering and thirsting, some desire that God accepts for the deed, to shew that such a man is in the state of grace.

I speak this the rather, because some are deceived in their own estates. They do not conceive aright of themselves. They think they are not in the state of grace, when they find not that particular, strong, assured persuasion.

I answer, they may be in the state of grace notwithstanding. A Christian knows not his own estate alway, at all times. It is one grace to be in a good estate, and another to have the knowledge of it. They be different gifts of God, and God suspends the knowledge of a man's being in a good estate for several ends.

1. Sometimes, among the rest for this one, *to humble us*, to keep us from security, to make us careful and diligent; to make us know that he hath the keeping of our feeling and persuasion in his own hands. As he hath the keeping of all our grace, so he hath the keeping of the knowledge

that we have grace, and of our comfortable walking, that we may know we have everything from him, both grace and the feeling of grace; and if we take liberty to ourselves, he will take liberty to keep our feeling at that time, to make us humble, and to make us seek reconciliation again. It is one part of God's dispensation with his children to hinder their persuasion of their particular interest sometimes.

Sometimes the children of God may be in such a condition, as that they may think for a time in their judgment, that they be in a contrary estate; they are mispersuaded of themselves not to be God's children, as it were. God may suffer this, that they shall not only have a weak, staggering persuasion, but a persuasion to the contrary, though it be a false persuasion.

Quest. But how shall they know that they are God's children at that time? They say they are so shaken, and at a stand, they are so conceited* that they are none of God's; that God hath left them, and forsaken them.

Ans. You may know it by this, that at the same time they are *conscionable*† of all heavenly duties, at the same they neglect no means of salvation; at the same time they complain against their own corrupt course of life that hath given God occasion to leave them thus to themselves; at the same time they strive against this, and labour to be persuaded of God's truths in general. And though the devil sometimes shake that persuasion, that God's truth is not God's truth, and make them question whether it be the word of God or no, and whether there be such a thing as life everlasting,—the devil shakes us in principles sometimes,—but yet a Christian in such temptations, though he be shaken in his principles by the force of wickedness, yet he attends upon the means, and goes on more conscionably, he doth not give back, but labours for satisfaction and further settling still, and is ashamed of himself that he should have such beastly thoughts, as the psalmist saith, 'so foolish was I and ignorant, and as a beast before thee,' Ps. lxxiii. 22, when he began to stagger in the principle of the providence of God. So sometimes a Christian is brought to stagger in principles, in the main general persuasion of the word of God; but he likes not himself, he accounts himself as a beast, and labours for satisfaction still in sanctified means, and never gives over, though he have not particular persuasion, he gives not over holy duties, but goes on in spiritual duties; he labours to obey God in all things; he is conscionable to God in fear and trembling, in the least thing. A man may say to such a soul, it shall find peace at the length; for God's ways are unsearchable. God hath cause and reason why he keeps such a soul under for a time, and withholds some sense and persuasion; but usually God's comforts come more abundantly to such a soul, he reserves it for the time of affliction or the hour of death.

The truth is, it is a constant rule, that though it may be thus with some in some cases, yet ordinarily God's children may be persuaded of their particular condition; yea, and they ought to labour after this persuasion and assurance, that their souls may be filled with marrow and fatness, and that they may joy in God, and have boldness to come before God in prayer, that they may be fruitful in all holy duties; that they may be strong to suffer afflictions, and to resist temptations. Therefore though God sometimes, in his wise dispensation, suffer them to be hindered, yet notwithstanding, this [is] a thing that is both attainable, and that they ought to labour for, and never give their hearts rest till they attain to it.

* That is, 'they so conceive.'—Ed.

† That is, 'conscientious.'—G.

I say we ought to labour for it; for the soul is never in such a frame as it ought to be but when it hath gotten some assurance of God's love. But I must add this, we must labour that this persuasion be supernatural, by the Spirit of God, both of the truths in general, of the promises in general, and of our interest in particular in them. We must labour that it be by the Spirit to our spirits; that the Spirit may seal them to our spirits. For it is not sufficient to know the word of God to be the word of God, and the promises to be the promises, because we have been brought up in them, and can say them by heart, and it were a shame for us to conceive the contrary. That is not sufficient, for that will deceive us. We must labour (as I said of knowledge, that we may be supernaturally convinced, so also that is from that knowledge), that it may be spiritual, or else it will deceive us.

Quest. How do we prove that?

Ans. To make it a little clearer, because it is a point of some consequence, even as I shewed of what consequence the sight of faith is, so I may say of this persuasion. We must labour therefore to know how we come by this persuasion, and whether it be such as we can hold out in; whether it be such by which we can stand out in the time of temptation. If there be nothing but that argument of breeding, and of general light, of discourse, that we see one thing how it follows from another, I say it will deceive us, because constant obedience will never follow upon such a persuasion; nor constant holding out to death, nor constancy in death, if the conscience be once awakened; neither will we be fruitful in our lives and conversations. To make this clear.

1. If the soul be not persuaded by the Spirit of God, together with the Spirit of the Scripture; for the same Spirit that is in the Scripture must be in our spirit, working our natures suitable to the Scriptures to be holy; if we do not, by that Spirit by which the Scripture was indited, know those truths, *we shall never be obedient to them, not constantly.* For what is the reason that men when they are told, God doth forbid you to take his name in vain; God forbids you to seek after earthly things; God forbids you by the Scriptures to defile your vessels; he forbids you to seek these things below; he forbids you these courses?* Now a man that hath knowledge that is not supernatural, that hath it not by the Spirit, he hears these things with a kind of scorn, and despiseth them as niceties; he never makes scruple of these things, because he knows they are forbidden or commanded of God, because he hears so. But he hath not known by the Spirit of God that penned the Scriptures, that these indeed are God's divine truths. The Spirit hath not sealed these truths to his soul, this is God's word. He hath not felt it in converting his soul, in mortifying his corruptions, in raising him being cast down, in working wonders in his conscience, in bringing all into a spiritual subjection. When he hath not felt the word work thus, for all his general knowledge by education, and breeding, and reading, he may be a disobedient wretch, and live and die a rebel, and bitter opposite against the power of grace, because he hath not knowledge of the word of God, and of particular truths by the Spirit of God, it is no persuasion of the Spirit.

And this is that that men wonder at, that know not the mystery of these things, to see great scholars, men of great knowledge, perhaps divines, that are preachers to others, to see such an one vicious, to see him carnally disposed as others. When a man seeth this he thinks, What, do you talk

* The sentence is left thus unfinished.—G.

of the word of God? If there were such a thing, men that know these things must needs lead their lives after the rule. It is no wonder. The devil hath knowledge enough, but he is no divine at all, because he hath it from his nature, being a spirit. So a man may be a devil incarnate, he may have knowledge of these things, and yet no true divine. But he that is taught by the Spirit of God the things in the word of God, the Spirit works a taste in them. Historical truths are known by their own light. There is no such need of the Spirit to discover them; but the promises, and threatenings, and such things are known by the Spirit. A man feels the power of the word of God. Then a man is convinced. Otherwise if the Spirit do not reveal these things, a man will never obey, but be rebellious.

2. And as there will be no obedience, *so there will be no holding out in time of peril and temptation*. The persuasion that a carnal man hath, that is not a sanctified persuasion, it will not hold out in the hour of death, in the time of temptation, in strong temptation, either on the right hand by preferments and favours, or on the left hand by threatenings and persecutions. It is but a seeming persuasion. When anything comes that is stronger than it, it will not hold. When there is afflictions and persecutions in the church, we see many excellent learned men hold not out in their profession. Why? They were drawn to the profession of religion by dependence on such kind of men, or they only followed religion as they saw reason for it, or they have been so bred in it, &c. Now reason may be brought against reason. When men have no other motives than these; when persecution comes that they must lose their preferments or their friends, or their life, they fall away altogether, because that persuasion that they seemed to have before, it was no spiritual persuasion wrought from intrinsecal grounds of divine truth, that hath a majesty and a spiritualness in itself, but it was merely wrought out of foreign grounds. Now we see a meaner man that hath his knowledge wrought by the Spirit of God, the same Spirit it seals that knowledge to him with the word of God that indited the Scripture, and acted the holy men of God that wrote the Scriptures. As his portion is incomparably great, so he is persuaded of his interest in those good things. The same Spirit that convinceth him of the truth, and of the certainty of the things, it convinceth him likewise of his part in them, and this supernatural persuasion, together with his interest in those good things persuaded of, sets down the soul so as it will not move. He holds out in persecution, because he hath felt the work of divine truth in his soul. He hath found the Spirit of God casting him down, and raising him up to comfort, therefore he holds out in his persuasion in all trials, and never apostatiseth from that estate and condition.

3. And so *for unfruitfulness in conversation*. Notwithstanding all those motives we have in the word of God, a man that is not convinced spiritually of those excellent things, he goes on deadly, as if there were no motives, because the Spirit of God hath not sealed them to his spirit. He hath not given him an apprehension of the divine encouragements wrapped up in the promises in the Scripture; and when death and danger come, for the most part such men are desperate, notwithstanding all their learning and knowledge literal that they have; for it will not hold water. All knowledge that is not wrought by the Spirit of God sealing divine truth to the soul, with some evidence of the power of it, it will not hold out in the trial.

Especially when Satan with his fiery darts comes with strong temptations, for the soul never felt the working power of the word. It feels then the temptation, it apprehends the poisonful fiery temptation, but it hath not so inwardly digested the truths of the Spirit, and therefore is surprised with horror and despair. There is not wrought in the heart an experimental feeling of knowledge, and therefore the heart cannot beat back the temptation.

When the devil shall come and tell men, You have been thus and thus, and they have not felt the truth of that they seemed to believe, conscience tells them, It is true I have heard and read such and such things; I never believed them; they never sunk deeply into my heart. When temptation shall be nearer the soul than the truth shall be, when temptation presseth sore, they are swallowed up of despair. Therefore let us labour that our general knowledge from the word, and our particular knowledge and persuasion, that it may be spiritual.

Quest. Now how doth the Spirit work this particular persuasion?

Ans. I answer, the Spirit of God works it in the soul together with the word: the Spirit and the word go together. All the men in the world cannot persuade the soul without the Spirit of God join. Paul preached, but God opened Lydia's heart, Acts xvi. 40, *seq.* We have it not of ourselves. It must come from without, from God's Spirit opening our eyes, and persuading and convincing our hearts: 'God persuades Japhet to dwell in the tents of Shem,' Gen. ix. 27. No creature can do it. It is passive. It is said here 'they were persuaded.' That persuasion that is sound, that carries a man to heaven, by which he dies in faith, it must be from the Spirit of God. All the words of the ministry, and all reasons, nothing will do it but God. God must persuade the soul.

Quest. Now what doth the Spirit here?

Ans. The Spirit enlightens the understanding, which I spake of before. It opens the understanding in persuasion. It doth propound arguments and motives from the excellency of the things promised, and the privileges of religion, and the good things we have by Christ, &c.; and, together with propounding these excellent encouragements and motives, the Spirit strongly works upon the disposition, upon the will, and affections. It works upon the soul, and so doth persuade and convince.

And thereupon comes embracing, which I shall have occasion to speak of afterward. The soul being persuaded, embraceth.

Now this persuasion is not only by propounding of arguments by the word and Spirit, but likewise a working upon the will; from whence there follows an inclination of the will, and an embracing of the things we are persuaded of.

For let all the arguments in the world be brought to a man to persuade him that God will be merciful to him in Christ, tell him of the free offer, 'Whosoever will, let him come in,' Rev. xxii. 17; all that will: a large offer; let him join to that offer of mercy the inviting, 'Come unto me, all ye that *are weary and heavy laden,*' Mat. xi. 28, and I will ease you; a sweet inviting; join with the invitation a command, 'It is his command that we should believe in his Son Jesus,' Acts xvii. 30; let him strengthen that command with the threatening, 'He that believes not is damned already,' John iii. 18; let a man remove all objections that the soul can make of its unworthiness, 'Come unto me, all ye that are weary and heavy laden, and I will ease you,' though you groan under the burden of your sin; let a man object again, I have nothing worthy in myself; why, come and buy, though you have no money; let him strengthen all these proposals with examples of the mercy of God to Manasseh, to Peter, to Paul, a persecutor, to Mary Magdalene, and the like; let all these arguments be wondrous effectually propounded, the soul will not yield, unless God's Spirit join with these arguments, and all in that kind, and convince the soul of our particular interest in these things, and persuade the will to embrace these things offered.

That, God hath reserved in his own power to bring our hearts and the promises together, to bring our hearts and divine truths together. Let there be never so much set before us in the ministry, he hath reserved this prerogative and authority, that our hearts and the truth should close together to embrace them in hearing. All things depend upon the Spirit; when we do not regard the Spirit in hearing and reading, &c., let all the things the Scripture hath be propounded, and set on with all the excellency and eloquence that may be, God hath reserved it to himself, by his Spirit, to give faith to persuade our souls that these belong to us, and to incline and draw the will.

I have shewed you, then, the kinds of persuasion, general and particular, and how it is wrought by the Spirit; that unless this persuasion be wrought by the Spirit, we shall never hold out in it. Though we have all the arguments in the world, we shall be disobedient. Disobedience comes when things are not discovered by the Spirit, and apostasy when the persuasion is not wrought by the Spirit, and desperation when the knowledge is not spiritual.

Now the manner is by removing contraries, and moving the heart, and drawing it. With the word of man, God enters into the very will and affections; for, as he made the soul, and framed it, so he knows how to work upon it, and to draw it sweetly by reasons, but yet strongly, that it may be carried to the things revealed. God at the same time works strongly by carrying the soul, and sweetly with reasons. For God first comes into the soul by divine light, by reasons, and then he sinks into the soul by his Spirit, to draw the soul to these reasons. Without this, we never yield to those reasons, but stand out in rebellion.

1. God persuades the soul *sweetly of the truth*, by shewing a man the goodness of it, and the suitableness to our condition, and the reasons of it, how they agree to our nature. He doth not force the soul, but doth it with reasons and arguments sweetly.

2. And he doth it *strongly*, that the soul, when it is persuaded, would not for all the world be of another mind. It is so strong, that the persuasion and the promises are stronger than the temptations of Satan and the corruptions of the flesh, or than the scandals of the world; that nothing can separate us from Christ, nothing can drive us from our faith and hope. The persuasion is set so strongly upon the soul, because it is a divine persuasion.

It is a strong work to persuade the soul.

For the Spirit of God, when it brings a light into the soul, it brings a great many graces with it. When it shines upon the soul, and discovers better things, it brings other graces to persuade, and to embrace the things it discovers.

As it is an infinite mercy and goodness of God to discover to our souls such excellent things as we may be persuaded of, as of our estate to be such as indeed it is above our comprehension in this world—'Neither eye hath seen, nor ear heard, nor hath entered into the heart of man, the things that God hath prepared for them that love him,' Isaiah lxiv. 4,—so likewise it is God's infinite work of power to frame the soul to be persuaded of this. It is as much power to work the soul to this persuasion, as it is mercy to discover them in a manner. There is such inward rebellion and distrust in the soul calling these truths into question, as if these things were too good to be true. Considering our own unworthiness and vileness, and the excellency of these things, laying these together, the unbelieving heart of man is prone to unbelief above all other sins. He can hardly conceive that there are such things for God's children, except the heart be mightily wrought on; unless, together with persuasion, there be some work in the soul whence it may gather by the work of the Spirit that they are those to whom such good things belong, because the Spirit of God hath singled them out, and set his seal and stamp on them, above other men, by some evidences of grace.

It is another manner of work than the world takes it to be; for, as I said before, together with the Scripture, there must a Spirit of persuasion go. There is a secret messenger goes with the outward speech both of the preacher and of the Scripture, or else all the arguments will not be to purpose; they will be of no efficacy.

As the Israelites they had arguments and motives enow to persuade them of God's love and care to them, yet notwithstanding God gave them not a heart, Deut. xxix. 4. In Christ's time what miracles did they see! Yet their hearts were hardened, because God, together with his shining in the outward means, did not subdue the rebellion of their wills and affections; and therefore the more they saw, the more they were hardened, the Scribes and Pharisees, and some of their desperate followers.

Use. Well, then, considering that the Spirit doth this great work, *let us labour that our knowledge may be spiritual;* that our persuasion of divine truth in general, and our part and portion in divine truth, that it may be spiritual. For, as St Paul divinely and excellently sets it down, 1 Cor. ii. 10, 11, that 'as no man knows the things that are in man, but the spirit that is in man: so no man knows the things of God's word,' divine truths, nor his part and portion and interest in them, but by the Spirit of God. If we bring the engine of our own wit and parts to God's truth, to sermons and books, we may never be the better, if we come not with a spiritual intention,* with reverent and humble hearts, and implore the teaching of the Spirit, that together with the revelation of the word there may be a removing of the veil by the Spirit; that with the outward teaching there may be the inward teaching of the Spirit; that with the sound opening the ear there may be the opening of the heart; that he that hath the key of David may open, and incline, and persuade the heart; that he may 'persuade Japhet,' as the Scripture phrase is.

It is sacrilegious presumption to come to holy places, and to set upon holy duties, to hear or read the word of God, without lifting up our hearts to God for his Holy Spirit. We cannot plough without his heifer. Can we know the mind of God without the Spirit of God? What arrogancy is this to think I shall be saved; and the Spirit never tells us with the word so: but it is only a presumptuous conceit. This is a sacrilegious usurpation upon God's glory. The Spirit of God knows what things are in God towards us, and reveals to our spirits God's inward love to us. 'The Spirit teacheth us to know the things that are given us of God.' We only know the good that God means us by his own Spirit; and therefore let us labour every day more and more to be spiritual and heavenly-minded.

And, above all things, to make it the pitch of our desires, as it is Luke xi. 13, to pray for the Spirit, 'he will give his Holy Spirit to them that

* That is, 'intentness.'—G.

beg it.' It is the best and the chief gift of all; for this makes our knowledge heavenly, our persuasion heavenly, and sound and constant in life and death. And this Spirit carries the whole soul with it: this Spirit makes us like the word of God. Because it is spiritual, it makes us so; and we love it in our inward man, and consent to it, and joy in it. Whereas naturally there is inward rebellion in the greatest scholar in the world against the word of God. The heart riseth against divine truths. They are as opposite as fire and water, as heaven and hell. The proud heart of man slights the promises of mercy, as nothing to petty things of the world. It slights the comforts of the word to carnal comforts, and the commandments of God in respect of the commandments of men. The proud man looks scornfully upon the things of conscience and of the Spirit; only the Spirit of God brings the proud heart of man to be subject to the word of God. Nothing that is not spiritual will hold out. Whatsoever is not spiritual, Christ will not own at the day of judgment. If the Spirit seal us and set a stamp upon us, Christ will look on his own stamp of the Spirit; where the first fruits are not, the harvest will not follow. The Spirit is an 'earnest.' Where the 'earnest' is not, the bargain will not follow. I beseech you, let us labour for the Spirit in the use of all means: let us attend upon the word, 'which is the ministry of the Spirit,' and we shall find that the Spirit will alter and change us, and shew us our interest in the promises, and the goodness of them. The more we attend upon the means, the more we shall see it; and the more we pray, the more we shall have the Spirit; and the more we obey God, the more we shall have the Spirit of God. God gives his Spirit to 'them that obey him.'

Use. And this should *teach us when we come to hear or to read the word of God,* Lord, open mine eyes! Lord, persuade my soul! Lord, bow the neck of my soul! of my inward man, that iron sinew. Lord, take away my hard heart, and give me a heart of flesh, teach my heart. Thou must persuade and incline me; incline my heart, Lord!

We want religious carriage in this. We come presumptuously upon confidence of our wit, to hear sermons, and to read the word; and so we come away worse than we went. Why? We do not pray to God to persuade us.

'They were persuaded of them.'

Mark here, first, he opens the eyes, and so he persuades. God persuades the inward man with enlightening. He shews a reason. The devil, and antichrist his vicar, they persuade by darkness, by maintaining a kingdom of darkness. The devil allures: he shews no reason; he keeps the soul in darkness and blindness. Antichrist persuades men to their religion. How? By fleshly allurements; not instructing them and opening their eyes, enlightening their understandings; but God opens their eyes to see, and then teaches and persuades. The devil's instruments they persuade, and so they teach and draw away. They persuade with carnal objects and the like, to draw and bewitch the affections, and so the judgment is dark still; but where there is true dealing there is no fear of the light.

Therefore, those that are enemies to the means of salvation, that fear God's people should know too much, they take a course contrary to God. For God enlightens, and then persuades; and knowledge enlighteneth: so that knowledge is necessary. All divine persuasion of faith hath the name of knowledge. They were persuaded by the Spirit of God of the truth of God, having their eyes opened.

It is an evidence we are not persuaded. We come to church, and attend upon the means. We go on in a course of sin: we are not divinely persuaded. God hath not persuaded our hearts. He hath not enlightened us; for if the covetous man were persuaded, 'that neither covetous, nor extortioners, should enter into the kingdom of heaven,' 1 Cor. vi. 10, would he not leave that course? Light and persuasion alway rule the action: for we work as we see and are persuaded in every thing.

The very beasts do as they see, and as sense leads them. An ass bears burdens. You know nature hath framed and made him for it; but can you drive the silly creature into the fire? He knows that will consume him. So that men they are brutish: they will not be persuaded by the Spirit of God. They run into courses that, if they had light in their souls, and if they were persuaded whither it tends, they would never run into hell fire. If there were a pit open before a man's eyes, would he plunge himself into that pit that were before his eyes? A man that lives in sins against conscience, he runs into a pit. There are no manner of liars, of whoremongers, of covetous persons, of such wretches as take the name of God in vain, that shall escape unpunished. Men lead a life in a course wherein they see a pit before them, and yet they run on. Are they persuaded? No, no! Certainly they are not persuaded.

And so for the means of salvation. Men that care not for hearing the word, are they persuaded it is the word of God to salvation? They are not persuaded. We may know the truth of our persuasion by the power it hath to rule our lives and conversations. What is the reason that a simple man, a weak man, he lives Christianly, and dies in the faith he lived by, whenas a great man, in conceit in knowledge, he lives wickedly, and dies worse? Because the one hath not this knowledge of the Spirit. The Spirit of God never opened his eyes: the Spirit of God never persuaded him. He hath it in books, and by education and the like. There are none that ever hold out but those that have the Spirit of God to be their teacher and persuader. We must see things in their own proper light. The Spirit of God hath to deal with the heart. God hath only power of that. He must deal with the heart. We must not trust therefore to education, or to outward things. If a man should ask the reason of men, Why do you leave these courses? why do you do this good? A Christian doth not say, I was brought up to this, or I cannot do otherwise; but I do it from a principle of the 'new creature.' Let us desire God, that we may do things from reasons of Scripture, from reasons of pleasing God; that we may do them from a holy sanctified affection; that we may be persuaded by the Spirit, and then it will hold out. 'They were persuaded of them,

'And embraced them.'

They embraced the promises, the good things promised: Christ's coming in the flesh, and Canaan, the type of heaven, and heaven itself. Though they had not these things, yet they embraced what they had, they embraced the promises. That is the nature of faith. If it have not that it looks for, as it hath not till it come to heaven, yet it makes much of that it hath; it embraceth the promises, and in the promises the thing itself promised.

Now these things follow one another in a most natural order; for sight brings persuasion, sight and conviction brings strong persuasion, and persuasion breeds embracing. For we embrace that in our affections that we are persuaded of to be good. According to the strength of conviction and persuasion is the strength of the affections. Those things that we have a weak persuasion of we have a weak affection to. Those things that we are fully persuaded of, and are great withal, the affections cannot but stretch forth themselves to embrace them. When the understanding was enlightened to see the truth, and to be persuaded of the truth of the promises, then the will and affections, they join and embrace those things. The will makes choice of them, and cleaves to them, the affection of desire extends itself to them, the affection of love embraceth them, the affection of joy delights in them. Spiritual conviction always draws affection. For God hath framed the soul so, that upon discovery of a good out of itself, it doth stretch out itself to embrace that object, the good thing presented. It cannot be otherwise.

We see the eye, it cannot but delight in beautiful objects, so the understanding of itself, it delights in true things, and the will in things that are good, that are delightfully good, or spiritually and conveniently good to the person. It cannot but be so.

The author of nature, God, doth not overthrow nature, but preserves it in its own work. Therefore where he gives a light to discover and persuade, both of the truth in general and of our particular interest in those things, he gives grace likewise to the will and affections, to that part of the soul that is carried to good things to embrace them. And upon discovery of evil, in that part of the soul that is affected to evil, there is an aversion and loathing of things that are inconvenient and hurtful. It must needs be so in the light of reason.

We may know whether the Spirit of God have wrought anything in us by our embracing of good things; for, as I said, God hath made our souls thus, when the soul is convinced of the truth and goodness of a thing, and is persuaded, the affections will always follow that that is shewed to be the best. Now when the Spirit of God discovers to the soul the excellencies of religion to be above all other excellencies whatsoever, 'that the favour of God is better than life itself,' Ps. lxiii. 3, and discovers to the soul the vanity of all other things, then comes the soul to embrace them. For the soul cannot but embrace that which the understanding being convinced designs to be best, and best for me; in comparison of all other things, this is now at this time, all things considered, best for me to do. Hereupon comes embracing always. The affections follow spiritual persuasion.

There be two main branches of faith: one is spiritual conviction and persuasion that things are so good, and that they belong to us; another branch of faith is to go out, and close, and meet with the things. Upon discovery of the excellency of the things, the heart opens itself to let in those things.

It is in grace as it is in nature: the heart is open upwards, and pointed downward. So the heart and soul of a man opens to heavenward. When those things are discovered by the soul to be best, the Spirit opens and closeth with those things.

A man may know what he is in religion by his affections, by his affection of love; for the affection of love will open to the things that are discovered to be best, whereof he is persuaded. And his affection of joy; he will delight in those things. And his affection of grief; his heart will be shut to things that are contrary; and his affection of zeal in the pursuit of the means, and in opposing that that is an enemy to that good. It is alway so. The heart embraceth what we are persuaded of.

God hath made the affections of the soul for supernatural things, he hath made our understanding to conceive of the heavenly light, and those prerogatives and privileges, and he hath made our affections to embrace those heavenly things. And then a man is in his right subordination, in his right state under God; he is framed as he should be. He is in a right frame of soul, when his soul is convinced of the excellency of the best things, and when his affections of joy and love and delight, of zeal and trust, and all are set on those things. For then a man is raised above the condition of an ordinary man. Such a man is come to his perfection. He is come out of that cursed estate that naturally all are in. For now the soul is set upon things that make it better than itself. For the soul is as the things are it is carried to. When the soul is persuaded of heavenly things and of its interest in them, and is carried to them by the sway and weight of the affections of love, and joy, and delight,—which is called here embracing,—then the things embraced transform the soul to be like them, as they be heavenly, and glorious, and excellent. There is nothing in the world to be named with them. All else is dung and dross. Then a man comes to be holy, and heavenly, and spiritual. He is raised in a condition far above others, above all other men, though he be never so mean in the world. When his soul is enlightened, and answerable to the light, there is heat; when there is light in the understanding, and heat in the affections accordingly to embrace, then the soul is in a right temper, a man is a holy and happy man. Therefore no wonder if upon persuasion and sight they embraced those things.

Let us try the truth of our estate by our affections, by our embracing of good things, by opening our hearts to the best things, by our joy and delight in them. Is there a holy wonderment at them? 'Oh how I love thy law!' Ps. cxix. 97; and 'one day in thy courts is better than ten thousand elsewhere,' Ps. lxxxiv. 10; and 'Oh the depth of his mercies!' Rom. xi. 33; and 'one thing have I desired of the Lord; that I may dwell in the house of the Lord all the days of my life,' Ps. xxvii. 4. When the soul stands in admiration of God and good things, when it is ready to welcome Christ and heavenly things and the state of religion: now away all former vanities! away all lusts of youth! away all confidence in beauty, and strength, and riches! All these are but dung to the soul. The soul hath seen better things. There is a discovery of better things; and now the respect of all other things falls down in the soul when there is a discovery of better things.

The soul cannot do otherwise when it is convinced supernaturally. The same Spirit that discovers better things opens the soul to follow them. It is so with every soul that hath the true work and stamp of the Spirit in it. It is set upon heavenly things. It saith with St Paul, 'I account all dung and dross in comparison of the excellent knowledge of Christ,' Philip. iii. 8. There is an attractive, a drawing, magnetical power in heavenly things when they are propounded to the soul by the Spirit, to draw the affections, and to make us spiritual like themselves.

Let us therefore labour more and more to have our affections wrought upon. As we are in our affections, we are in religion.* It is impossible that a Christian should be spiritually convinced that there are such excellent things belong to religion, and that he hath his part and portion in them, and not be transformed to a spiritual state and frame of soul, to love and delight in holy things, and to despise that which is contrary.

And when he is in such a state, what is all the world to him? What cares he for riches, or pleasures, or honours, when the soul sees incomparable better things? 'Whom have I in heaven but thee? and what do I desire on earth in comparison of thee? saith David, Ps. lxxiii. 25, when

* Cf. Edwards's Treatise of 'The Religious Affections,' which is only a splendid expansion of this sentiment, as developed in the sequel.—G.

he had a little meditated of the vanity of earthly things, and saw the goodness of God to his children. 'It is good for me to draw near unto God,' Ps. lxxiii. 28. It is a speech of conviction. The soul is convinced that it is good and best to draw near to God in holy means, and in holy duties to keep close to him, and then it cries out, 'Whom have I in heaven but thee?'

Therefore let us never rest in such a knowledge of holy things as doth not convince us of the goodness of them, and of our interest in them, so far as may draw and work upon our affections to embrace those things.

When we find our hearts and affections wrought on, that holy things, as they are excellent in themselves, so they have an answerable place in our hearts, that as they are holy, and high, and best, so they have a high place in our hearts, then a man is in the estate of a Christian, or else a man may very well doubt of his estate, when he can hear of heaven, and happiness, and of the excellency of the children of God, that they are heirs of heaven, &c., and his heart be not affected with these things. He may well question himself, Do I believe those things? Here are rich and precious promises, but where is my precious faith to close with and to embrace these things? Do I believe them? If I do, how is it that I am no more affected with them? And so let us stand in the meditation of the excellencies of religion so long till our hearts be affected and warmed with them. This will follow affections, a desire to think oft of them; as David joins both together: 'Oh, how do I love thy law! it is my meditation continually.' That that a man loves he oft thinks of. That stirs up love, and love makes him oft consider of it; and when it is thus with a man, he is in such a condition as these holy patriarchs, fit to live and die by his faith. 'They saw them, and were persuaded of them, and embraced them.'

Therefore, I say, we may know whether we have this spiritual light, whether we have true faith or no, if we have these embracings. If we be so persuaded of them that we embrace them with delight, and desire, and love, and joy; if we make choice of them, and esteem them highly, and cleave constantly to that which is revealed to us: then it is a divine light and persuasion, because we embrace them.

Certainly there is nothing in religion divine, unless the affections be carried with it. True faith carries the whole soul, to whole Christ, out of a man's whole self. It carries the understanding to see, and the will to choose and to cleave; it carries the affections to joy and delight and love; it carries all. Therefore, those that when holy things are discovered they have not a high esteem of them; that they prize them not above earthly things; that they cleave not to them with a disesteem of other things; that they joy not in them as their best portion; that they do not embrace them: there is no true faith at all, for where there is true faith there is this embracing.

God hath made the soul, as I said, for these heavenly things; and when the soul and they close together, there is a sweet embracing. Then the soul is raised above itself; the soul is quieted, and stilled, and satisfied. There is nothing in the world else will better the soul but the embracing of these things; nothing else will beautify and adorn the soul in God's sight. Our souls are made for them, our desires are made to embrace them, our love and our joy to delight in them, our wills to cleave to them and make choice of them above other things.

We abuse our souls. They are not made to close and grasp with the world; they are not made for those things that are baser than ourselves. We abase our souls. A covetous man makes himself worse than he is;

therefore he is called the world,* because he hath nothing in him better than the world. If we embrace Christ and the promises of salvation, the things of another life, the embracing of these raiseth the soul to be excellent like the things, and it doth quiet and rest the soul. For nothing will rest but in its own element. As the heavy bodies rest not but in the centre, in the middle point of the earth, and light bodies rest coming to their place above, so the soul it rests in God and in Christ. Faith resting in the power of God quiets the soul, carrying it to the thing it is made for. As these holy men, in all the turmoils and troubles of the world, in all confusions, the souls of these blessed men rested in Christ.

We may say of all earthly things, as Micah hath this sentence of them, Micah ii. 10, 'Go ye hence, here is not your rest.' So we may say to the soul concerning riches, and honours, and friends, 'Here is not your rest.' You were not made to embrace and to cleave to these things. Our rest is in Christ and in the good things we have by him. These good men embraced him with their whole soul.

This shews that many men have not faith; they know not what it means. Where there is true faith, there is alway love, and joy, and delight in the things believed. It carries the soul with it. In what measure we apprehend the goodness of a thing, in that measure our love is to it. In what measure we apprehend the greatness and fitness of a thing, in that measure our affections are carried to it. The understanding reports it to the affections of love and liking, and they are naturally carried to that which the soul makes report of to be useful. The understanding makes them follow it. Therefore it is a sign our understandings are not persuaded, our eyes are not opened, when we love not good persons and good things, when we cleave not to them above all things. Those that do not embrace and cleave in their will and affections to good things, let them say what they will, they do not believe. If there were but a light conjecture in men, if there were but a guessing that there were such a happiness and that there were such horrible torments for sinners that live in sin, they would live otherwise than they do. Therefore deadness in the affections discovers atheism in the judgment and heart; it shews there is unbelief. For how is it possible that a man should not be carried in his affections to a good that he is persuaded of. And how is it possible he should not loathe ill and destructive things? If he were persuaded that hell were such as it is, and that these courses lead to hell and destruction, and estrange him from the favour of God, 'whose loving-kindness is better than life itself,' Ps. lxiii. 3, if men were persuaded of these things in any strength, their souls would not be affected as they are.

Therefore if we would know whether nature be corrupted or no, we may do it by this. You have some men that are conceited, especially when they are in their ruff† and have all things plenty. Divines talk much of the corruption of nature and such things. They think all is well. Oh, but do but lay these things together, the excellency of the things promised and the terror of the things threatened, and our indisposition to these things in regard of persuasion, that we live as if we did not think these things to be true. What a disposition of soul is that that calls divine truths into question! To believe the lies of our own hearts and the temptations of the devil, and the world that lies in mischief, before the resolved truth of God itself, that is sealed with the oath of God. And yet the heart of man is naturally carried to believe these things more than God himself. Witness

* Cf. 1 Cor. ii. 12, xi. 32, *et alibi* (?).—G. † That is, = in state, grandeur.—G.

the lives of men who have dead, carnal, base affections in regard of heavenly things, they shew that they are not persuaded of them, notwithstanding all the sweet arguments and persuasions that the Scripture hath. They do not profess that they call them in question, yet they live as if they made no doubt that they are all false. It is a folly not to believe those things that are sealed by so many evidences as divine things are; but it is more desperate folly to live as if we did not believe them at all.

If these things were digested, they would make us out of love with our own natural estate, and to labour for a spirit of faith to persuade our souls, both that those things are so indeed that God hath revealed, and to get assured persuasion of our part and interest in them. Indeed, a dead faith is no faith at all. It is the effect of the whole Epistle of St James, that it is no faith that is dead; it doth not work upon the heart and affections, nor the life and conversation. A dead faith is no faith at all.

Let us shame ourselves therefore: Lord, do I profess I see things above nature? that I see Christ in heaven and see myself there? and do I profess that I am persuaded that the word of God is true, and am I no more affected? Where is my love? Where is my joy? Where is my comfort? Doth my heart run after other things, that profess myself to be persuaded of better things? Let us never rest, but be angry and wroth with our hearts and affections, for they are made for these promises. Our precious faith is made to embrace precious promises, and to carry the whole soul to them.

And let us help this with complaining of ourselves and with prayer. Lord, thou hast discovered excellent things in thy word, and hast persuaded me. Lord, open my heart; the heart is thy throne; the heart, and will, and affections thou dealest with especially. Lord, incline my heart, enlarge my heart. The Lord hath promised in the new covenant to teach our bowels to love; Lord, teach my heart to love thee. Thou hast opened my understanding to conceive holy things, or else I had never been able to understand thee and thy truth. Teach my bowels also to love; teach them to cleave to the things; take off my love, my joy, and delight from earthly things, and plant them where they should be; enlarge them the right way; fill my heart with thyself, as thou hast made it for thyself. This should be our desire.

Quest. What be the affections whereby the soul embraceth these good things it is persuaded of?

Ans. The soul embraceth these things in the affections of faith and hope in the first place; for faith is an empty grace in itself; it is carried to somewhat out of itself that it embraceth and layeth hold on; and hope is with faith alway. Together with the work of faith and hope there is a sanctified affection of the embracing soul; there is a love of the things promised, which is embracing, and a love of the means, and likewise joy and delight in them expressed by thankfulness. As you see the patriarchs in the story of Genesis, when God discovered holy things to them afresh, that he would give them the land of Canaan and the Messiah to come, and all that happiness, there was thankfulness, presently they built altars to God; and which alway accompanies thankfulness, humility. As Abraham, Gen. xvii. 3, down he falls when God made him such a large promise; he falls down on his face, as if he were unworthy of such a thing. So this disposition alway accompanies a soul that embraceth. Together with faith and hope, that leads the affections after them, there is love, expressed in a constant obedience and care of duty to God many ways, as it is an affection that will not be concealed. And joy and delight, with thankfulness and humility, considering the excellency of the things and our unworthiness; that we cannot but have this disposition alway, thankfulness and humility. And likewise contentment to end our days, a disposition that follows embracing in faith; for, where embracing of faith and love is in an imperfect estate, there will be joy when that comes that makes way to full embracing; that is, in heaven itself, as Simeon rejoiced when he embraced Christ in his arms. What did the old man, think we, when he came to heaven, when Christ and he met there? And Abraham rejoiced to see Christ's day with the eye of faith; and likewise embraced it with faith, and that wrought joy. What did Abraham then when he came to heaven, when he saw all ended there? I say, death, that makes way to full enjoining* and embracing, in this very respect it is not only patiently entertained of God's children, but comfortably, as letting them in to the good things that they esteem above all the world besides; to the possession of Christ; to heaven and happiness. Let us consider of these things.

To come to direct us a little about this embracing in faith, and hope, and love, and joy, and the whole soul, when the soul as it were goes out to the things we are persuaded of.

Quest. How shall this be wrought upon the soul?

Ans. This embracing we see it follows upon persuasion, and persuasion follows seeing: 'They saw them far off, and were persuaded of them, and thereupon they embraced them.'

1. Therefore *let us labour for a clear understanding of divine things.* That which the eye sees, the heart grieves for in ill, and that that the eye sees the heart embraceth in good. And in what measure our eyesight of heavenly things is clearer, and our persuasion stronger, in that measure our embracing is lovely and full of joy and delight. Therefore let us labour to grow in knowledge, in supernatural spiritual knowledge, and that our persuasion may be stronger every day more and more; for answerable to that our affections will grow, and will be carried to the things discovered.

And there is nothing more effectual to commend knowledge to us than this, that it is a means to work a holy and heavenly disposition and temper in us, especially if it be spiritual. And let us meditate upon what we seem to know and are persuaded of; let us dwell upon things still, to work them upon the will and affections; let us dwell upon them till our hearts be warmed well with the things known, and that we profess ourselves to be persuaded of.

And join with it an inquiry upon the soul, Are these things so? Do I know these things? and am I persuaded of these things that they are so? How is my disposition answerable then? am I so affected as I should be? Is my love so hot, and my joy so working, and spiritly,† and quick as it should, or no? And hereupon take occasion to stir up ourselves, and to check our own souls: Alas! that I should have such things discovered, and that I should see such things, in such a strong persuasion in the book of God, and profess myself to be persuaded of these things, and yet be so dead at all times.

And if we find our affections anything working, that we are disposed to embrace these things, then we cannot but be in an excellent temper, and bless God that vouchsafed, together with the excellency of the things themselves, to shew us our portion by his Holy Spirit, to enlighten our understandings, and to persuade us. Let us bless God for this, for it is a work above nature.

* Qu. 'enjoying'?—G. † Qu. 'sprightly'?—G.

And withal, because the soul cannot close with and embrace these things but it must let loose other things (for, you know, in embracing there must be a letting go of those things that were formerly within the grip), if we would grip these things in our affection and will, *we must have them only; we must not think to grasp the world and them together*, the things here below and them together; as we shall see after in that point, 'they accounted themselves strangers' to earthly things. Therefore this is one way to come to this embracing, to come to the sight of the vanity and insufficiency of all things in comparison of Christ, and the happiness we have by Christ. To see in matter of judgment the insufficiency of works and merit, and such like, in the matter of justification, the insufficiency of all such trash as the popish religion abuseth the world withal. And so in matter of conversation, to see the insufficiency, and emptiness, and vanity, yea, the vexation of all things besides these good things here offered. The good things that God's Spirit offers to the eye of our souls, that he offers to our wills and affections, what are all to these? And effectually think so, think what should draw a man's affections after it. Beauty or strength! Consider what will become of these ere long.

And then withal consider the excellency of the estate of the body and soul in heaven, if we carry ourselves as we should do, and preserve ourselves in our spiritual condition. Let us lay these things together, and then we shall see how infinitely the one is beyond the other. If it be for honour and favour of the world, consider the vanity of them and how short a time we may enjoy them, and the things themselves are subject to alteration. And withal consider the constant excellency of the favour of God in Christ Jesus, which will comfort us in life, in death, and for ever. And so for riches and possessions in this world, consider how soon all here must be left, and how the soul is larger than all these things, if we had a thousand times more abundance than we have; and that our souls that are more large and more excellent, they are not made for these things, but for better; and what use we shall have of better things when these fail, the soul being immortal and eternal. This will make us let go earthly things in our affections, and hold them in their place, in a secondary place, as things serviceable in the way to heaven, and not to grasp them in our affections, for then they pierce the soul to death and damnation.

And if we would be affected as we should be to good things, *let us keep our affections tender*, and keep them clear from the guilt of any sin that may work fears and doubts, for together with sin goes fears and doubts. They are bred in sin naturally; therefore if we would maintain this embracing, oh let us keep our souls! As we keep our understandings clear, so keep our affections tender by all means, and keep our consciences unspotted, that so our affections of joy, and delight, and love, may be ready pressed to good things, even to the best things.

Another way is in particular *to meditate of the love of Christ, the love of God in Christ, and of his embracing of us;* for we must know that our embracing is upon persuasion of God's embracing of us. We embrace not the promises of Christ as a man embraceth a dead post, that cannot return embraces to him again. This embracing of Christ and heaven, it is a mutual embracing; and it is a second, reflexive embracing. We embrace God and Christ, because we find God in Christ embracing our souls first in the arms of his love; therefore we embrace him again in the arms of our affections, because we find Christ embracing us in the arms of his affections.

Therefore let us attend upon the means, upon private reading of the word and upon the ministry; for what are the ministers but to contract Christ and the soul together? They are 'friends of the Bridegroom,' to discover Christ's love to us, and his loveliness,—his loveliness in himself, his riches in himself, and his love to us, to allure us again to Christ. The ministry is for this end especially, to draw Christ and the soul together. And what is the Scripture in the intent and scope of it, but to discover to us the excellency of Christ, and the good things we have by him, his love and good intention to our souls? Now, hearing these things in the ministry, they are effectual, together with the Spirit, to draw our affections back again to him; and, naturally, we cannot but love those that love us. Now, when we are persuaded of God's love to us in Christ, and Christ's love to us (God having made our souls for love to himself, and friendship with himself, and the nearest and sweetest conjugal friendship, now therefore) the more his love is discovered to us, the more we shall love him.

Therefore *let us be constant in attending upon good means.* We shall alway hear something that will either strengthen our faith in the promises of God, or shew us our duty to God again. We shall have something discovered whereby the Spirit will be effectual to help this embracing. Let us go to reading and hearing with this scope and intention. Now, I come to hear, I come to have my soul wrought on, I come to hear some message from heaven, to hear some good thing to draw my mind from the world and worldly things; and upon hearing our duty to God, to walk lowly in thankfulness for those good things that we have, and that we hope for in another world. It is no wonder that men lose their affections that are careless in the use of means; and if they lose them, will they not lose all? The best man living, if he be careless in using the means of salvation, and give himself to the world altogether or to his calling,—things not in themselves unlawful,—his affections will be dead, he shall lose them; for God hath ordained that our affections should be quickened by heavenly means, and God knoweth better than we ourselves, that hath sanctified these means to this purpose. In attending upon the means, we shall hear a discovery of good things, and hear comforts, and have our light strengthened by new discovery of new Scripture, or by old Scriptures lively applied; something to increase the life of our persuasion, at every sermon and reading good books, and by every good company. And that which increaseth knowledge and persuasion, makes our affection and embracing stronger.

I beseech you, let us take these courses, or else all is to no purpose. The main thing in religion is the will and affections, and when the will and affections are wrought on, the work is done in the matter of grace. And there is no other way to know whether the former work of the understanding and persuasion be effectual and to purpose or no, but this; to know whether the will choose and cleave to good things, and whether our affections joy and delight in them. There is the trial of the main work. The work indeed is especially in the judgment, when it hears soundly and supernaturally of the ills that are to be avoided, and of the good things that are to be embraced, but where is the trial of the judgment, but when it carries the whole soul with it, when it carries the stern of the soul with it? Now that which is immediate to our souls is our affection of joy and delight, and the like. Therefore let us take to heart these things, and never think we are anything in religion till our hearts and affections be wrought upon; till our knowledge be such as may sway that whole inward man.

Again, *consider the excellency of those good things that we have discovered to us in the gospel*, that are the object of our embracing, together with the necessity of them, that without them we are wretched creatures, there is no hope for us. Let us every day consider what ground of hope we have, though the things be not yet possessed, whether the things be true that we hope for, whether they be confirmed to be true or no, and how we rest on them. For let things be never so excellent and necessary, unless the soul conceive of them as things attainable, as things belonging to us, all is to no purpose, this effect of embracing will not be wrought in the soul. Therefore consider more and more *the hopefulness of them*. That may help this embracing.

A Christian, when he believes and hopes for that happiness that shall be revealed to him, the things promised, what a world of grounds of hope hath he for it? He hath the word of God for an 'inheritance immortal and undefiled,' 1 Peter i. 4; he hath the will of Christ: 'Father, I will that where I am, they may be,' John xvii. 24. His prayer to his Father is his will, and his will must be performed; for he lives for ever to make good his own legacy to his church. And he is now in heaven, preparing that happiness for us that we so embrace with faith. And he hath left us here his Spirit to be a pledge that he will come again. He hath left his Spirit, and hath taken our flesh to heaven, to strengthen our hope, that this shall follow. Our flesh is in heaven in him already, and his Spirit is in earth in us; as a mutual *depositum* in trust between him and us; and all to strengthen the hope of that happiness that is reserved.

Besides *the seal of the sacrament*, the end of which is to cherish hopefulness of Christ, and of all the good we have by him, his oath is added to his promise, that all things might be immutable and unchangeable of the forgiveness of sins and life everlasting, &c. Now especially when we find our hearts to sink downward, and not to have that life as they should have, by meditating on these things, of their excellency and necessity, and to conceive in Scripture the grounds of hope of them, it will quicken us.

Add likewise, for our own interest, what work of the Spirit we have, and then what singular promises we have, that where God hath begun he will make an end. For why is the work of the Spirit called an earnest, but that God will make good the bargain? Consider what work of the Spirit we have; for whatsoever is spiritual is eternal in a man. What joy is spiritual, what love is spiritual, what knowledge is spiritual, it shall be made up in perfection, it shall never be taken away.

See then how the Spirit seals us by the work of it, and what earnest we have, in peace of conscience and the work of it. This will cherish hope; for that is part of this embracing, to embrace them with faith and hope.

And this should be a daily course, to work upon the affections, to estrange them from all things, and from the meditation of all things, else. And as I said before, to consider the love of God to us, and to love him again. And consider likewise the hopefulness of good things, that nothing in the world is so made good to us as the things of a better life; the things of grace and glory. And God hath borrowed from all assurance amongst men, terms to shew the assurance of the good things we have in hope and faith. The pledge of the Spirit, the earnest of the Spirit, the seal of the Spirit, the witness of the Spirit.* What terms are there used among men that may confirm anything, that you have not used to strengthen this super-

* Cf. Eph. i. 14; Rev. viii. 2; 1 John v. 9.—G.

natural assurance of these supernatural good things? God herein succours our weakness, knowing how prone we are to call these things into question. And consider especially our own unworthiness, our vileness and baseness, that we deserve none of this. When conscience is once awaked to know aright our own unworthiness, then we shall find it a difficult thing to believe these things. Therefore it is a work worthy of our daily endeavour, to search the Scriptures, which applies itself to our capacity, and confers all the help in the world to increase our grounds of hope of the best things, and then our disposition is as it should be.

And let us deeply consider of the necessity of heavenly things, and the foulness of sin, and the danger of our natural condition, and this will make us embrace better things. He that sees himself in danger of drowning will embrace that that may stay him. He that sees himself in danger to be pulled away from that that upholds him from sinking, he will clasp about it fast. Let us consider what a-many things we have in this world to pull us away from God and good things, and to loose our grip, that we may not lay such hold of them. The devil envies our embracing of these things, and there are many things to loose our affections from them. Consider the danger, and withal the necessity of these good things, that if they be lost, we do not only lose them, but we lose them with the loss of our souls, with eternal damnation in the world to come. We do not simply lose them, but we plunge ourselves into the contrary. Let us consider of this, and it will make us clasp fast, and keep our hold by all means possible. In that measure that we apprehend the danger, in that measure we shall embrace these excellent things.

Case. Now to answer a doubt and a case or two by the way. How happens it, then, that God's children sometime, when their judgment is convinced, yet their affections are not so quick, they are something flat in their affections? As God's people complain sometimes, Alas! that I should believe such a happiness as heaven is, and such glory, and yet find my affections no more stirred! Is it possible that I should be the child of God, and believe these things, and find myself no more affected?

Sol. Indeed, this troubles the peace of God's children sometimes; and good reason: for we see here, *after sight comes persuasion, then embracing.* The will and affections cannot but entertain that good they are persuaded of, and so there is great ground for the objection.

But there may be some mistake in this; for sometimes the judgment may be convinced, and yet the affections not be so quick, because there may be a diversion at the same time. There may perhaps be some present cross that may befall thee, or some present thing lawfully loved, that takes up the affections at that time. As, for example, the presence of father, mother, wife, or children, or of other friends, may take up the affections for the time. Now the affections running that way at that time, perhaps not sinfully neither, they are not so enlarged to heavenly things. God knows our capacity, and what our affections can do.

Then again, *there may be some present grief upon them,* that God, to humble a man, may take up his affections, so that at that time he shall not be so affected with good things, though ordinarily he comfort himself with the best things; and so he doth afterward, when he hath given his grief and his present affections some liberty. There is a love of intention* and of valuing: a man may be deceived that way. A man values his child more than a stranger that he entertains, yet for the present he may give a

* Cf. Glossary, *sub voce.*—G.

stranger better looks and better entertainment. Though he set more value on his child, or his dear friend that he hath secured himself of, yet he will not shew such countenance to them as to a stranger on the sudden.

So it is here. God's children their constant joy is in the best things, and they are judiciously carried to the best things; but on the sudden there may be an entertaining of some other thing, and perhaps not unlawful neither. Perhaps it may be sinful, to humble God's children; but that is but on the sudden. His course is to carry his affections above all earthly things.

Again, in another case, *God's children are deceived this way sometimes:* for they think they have no affections when they have affections. How is that seen? In case of opposition. Let God, and Christ, and heavenly things be opposed, and you shall see then that they have affections. Those that, for want of stirring up the grace of God in them, or for want of good means, or by indisposition of body, seemed to be dull in their affections, let religion be disgraced or opposed any way, and you shall find then their affections deep in their hearts to heavenly things; but they appeared not before, because there was no opposition. These, and such like thoughts, we may have to content the soul that is disquieted this way. But the rule is certain, that a man's affections are as his persuasion is, and his persuasion as his light is. As he hath a heavenly light, discovering heavenly things, so is his persuasion of a better estate than the world can yield; and, answerable to his persuasion, his soul is raised up to delight in the best things. This is his course. If it fall out to be otherwise, there be reasons for it, which we must discreetly judge of, and not trouble the peace of a good conscience. To go on.

'They confessed they were strangers and pilgrims on earth.'

These words contain what they were in regard of earthly things; their disposition and carriage to all things besides the promises, to the things below. They were strangers and pilgrims in regard of their condition below. It sets down how they apprehended themselves to be, and how they discovered themselves to the world to be.

They were in regard of heaven indeed, heirs of happiness, heirs of a kingdom; in regard of the world and earthly things they were 'strangers and pilgrims.' And as they were, so they made themselves to be no better than they were. They confessed it. They were not ashamed of it. They apprehended themselves to be as they were, and they carried themselves answerable. Their life and course spake as much as their tongues. They confessed both in word and in deed that they were 'strangers and pilgrims.'

Now in the words I say you have their disposition and their profession, their condition and their confession; their disposition and carriage, and state and condition; 'they were strangers and pilgrims.'

The discovery of it, 'they confessed' they were so. And this confession is double.

Their confession was either verbal, as Jacob confessed when he came before Pharaoh: 'Few and evil have the days of the life of my pilgrimage been,' saith old Jacob, Gen. xlvii. 9.

Or it was a real confession, discovered by their carriage that they were strangers: their course spake louder than their words.

Those that in the whole course of their life shew a weaned affection to earthly things, though they talk not gloriously, as some idle persons do in a bravery, 'we are but strangers here, and we must be gone,' &c. Though, I say, they do not speak thus, as some do that never think so, yet, notwithstanding, their carriage bewrays it; their course, and company, and conversation shews that indeed they 'confess themselves pilgrims and strangers.'

Now the order of the words is this, 'strangers and pilgrims.' There is little difference between these two. 'Strangers' shews our absence from home, that we are abroad in another country, that we are in another place.

And 'pilgrims' shews our carriage to our country, our going home: a pilgrim or traveller is he that is going homeward. They confessed themselves that they were not at home, but they were going toward that that was their home, toward heaven, to that city 'whose builder and maker was God himself,' Heb. xi. 10. We are 'strangers,' to shew what we are here on earth. In regard of heaven we are strangers on earth, and not mere strangers that rest, and do nothing, but such strangers as are passing home toward their country; 'we are strangers *and* pilgrims' on earth. The one implies our absence, the other implies our moving to the place of our abode.

The points considerable are, first, this, *that God's children upon earth here are strangers and pilgrims;* They are not at home, but are travelling toward their country.

The second is this, that

They profess themselves to be so. They know they are so, and they confess that they are so. They are not ashamed of it.

For the first,

Doct. It is the disposition of him that hath truly interest in better things (though but in faith and hope) *to be a stranger and a pilgrim in regard of all things here below.*

And this follows the other; for where the eyes of the understanding are opened, and a man is persuaded, there is an embracing of better things as our proper good things; there is a considering of all other things as things that do not belong to us; in a manner we are strangers. When faith apprehends Christ and heaven and happiness to be our own, and our country to be above, faith apprehending and grasping these things, and embracing them, at the same time it is to be supposed, and necessarily follows, that we are strangers.

It follows out of the necessity of the thing itself; for, upon the very consideration that a man is an heir of heaven, that he hath another country and condition, out of the necessity of the thing itself, though there were no other reason for it, the affections of the soul will be closed up, as it were, to other things, and he will consider of other things in an inferior condition as they are.

For the things, though they be good in their kind and order, both the things above and the things below, yet there being such a difference in these good things and the things here below, the contentments here on earth being so meanly good, and so short in continuance, and so weak in their satisfaction of the soul, that they cannot be possessed, together with the blessed assurance of better things, but with the affections of strangers and pilgrims, this follows, I say, from the nature of the thing, that in whose eyes heavenly things are great, in his eyes earthly things are mean. They are accounted as they are, secondary, mean things of the way, to help him forward home.

If a man were on the top of a great mountain, he would see the things below to be very little, and the things above would appear greater to him; so when the soul is raised up to see great things, though they be afar off, as these did with the eye of faith, at the same time, his soul looking to things below must needs apprehend them to be little in quantity, as indeed they are.

If a man were in body lift up to heaven, and should look upon the earth, what were the earth but a poor silly point, the whole earth itself, much more a man's own possession; so when the soul is lifted up to heaven by faith,—which sets a man in heaven before his time,—when it looks from thence to the earth and earthly things, it must of necessity consider them, as they are, to be poor mean things. Therefore this follows, that being persuaded of the promises, that is, of the good things promised in religion in the word of God, to earthly things they were 'strangers and pilgrims.'

He that is from home, and hath another home which he is not at, he is a stranger; but Christians have another home.

1. For, first, *they are bred from heaven, they are born from heaven, they are born in Jerusalem that is from above; they are born in the church by the seed of the word and Spirit.* Now as they are from heaven, so their bent is to heaven again; for everything naturally riseth as high as it springeth. As we say of water, it mounts as high as the head of it is, so our affections mount as high as the spring of them is. Now a Christian being born from heaven, he tends to that in his affections, that is his country. It is his country, because his Father is there in his glory, and his Saviour is there, and a great part of his kindred are there; the souls of perfect men, and the glorious angels in a most glorious manner,—though they be in their attendance upon the earth,—there is his country, his city, his house, there is his happiness, his home. I shall not need, therefore, to prove that the godly are strangers. If heaven be his country, earth must needs be the place of his pilgrimage; there is no question but that follows.

It is said here 'they were pilgrims and strangers upon earth.' 'Upon earth;' because, wherever a Christian is, if it be upon any place upon earth, he is a stranger and a pilgrim. If he be in his own house, he is upon earth, and therefore he is a stranger in his own house; if he be in his own possession, he is upon earth, and therefore he is a stranger in his own possession. As David confessed, though he were a king, 'I am a stranger and a pilgrim here, as all my fathers were,' 1 Chron. xxix. 15. A king in his kingdom is upon God's earth, and therefore he is a stranger in his own kingdom here. As Austin saith very well, '*Quisque domus suæ*,' &c., every man is a stranger in his own house.* We are strangers here on earth, therefore. It is not any condition on earth that exempts a child of God from being a stranger, when the greatest kings in the world have confessed that they were strangers and pilgrims; so that all Christians, of what condition soever they are, from the highest to the meanest, they are all strangers upon earth. It is a clear point.

And it must needs be so, for the head of Christians was a stranger. His love made him a stranger; for he left his Father's bosom. His love drew him from heaven to earth, and here he conversed as a stranger. He dwelt in his body here as a tabernacle, which he laid aside for a while, to work the work of our redemption, and then after to dwell in it for ever. He was the prime stranger of all strangers. He that makes us all strangers here, and citizens of heaven, he was a stranger on earth. He was not indeed a stranger, for he was Lord of heaven and earth, yet in regard of his state of exaltation that was to come after, in regard of dispensation, he was here as a servant: he lived here as a stranger. And indeed he was as strangely

* Sibbes's previous sentences are a paraphrase of Augustine *in loco*.—G.

used; 'for he came among his own, and his own knew him not,' as it is in John i. 10. He was not known among his own countrymen the Jews; 'he was a stranger on earth.'

He conversed with us here, and was among us as a stranger. You see how his speech and carriage and conversation on earth it was as a stranger's. He was talking alway of his Father's house and of the kingdom of heaven. When he speaks of the estate of the church, which is the only company of people here in whom God rules by his Spirit, yet because they are ordained for the kingdom of heaven, he calls them strangers here, and terms them by that that they are ordained to. All his mind was of the kingdom of heaven. We see after he was risen, the matter of his discourse, as the gospel tells, it was of the kingdom of heaven. He talked of things that belonged to the kingdom of God; all his speeches were that way, and his comparisons were fetched that way. 'The kingdom of heaven is like' to such a thing and such a thing. And all his work was to draw men from the earth. As it was his grand work to redeem men from the earth, that is, from hell, and from their cursed condition, so the matter of his teaching was answerable to his work, to draw men to heaven. All the pains that he took before and after his death, till he was taken into heaven, it tended that way.

He came from heaven to earth to woo us to be a spouse to himself. He came from heaven into a strange country, to take us for his spouse, to take our nature, and in our nature to win us, to die for us. He carried himself as a stranger every way; he regarded not earthly things. Now answerable to our head Christ, must all Christians be in their affections and dispositions. We must be conformable to him; we must be strangers as he was.

All that look to die in the faith of Christ, and to be happy for ever, they must witness their believing and loving of better things by an answerable carriage to all things here below; they must have the affection of strangers and travellers. Faith doth enforce this. It is the nature of the soul, from a principle and ground of nature, that when the soul is carried up one way, it is shut another; when it cleaves unto, and embraceth better things, when it is open to heaven, the point of the soul is shut to the earth; and we look upon these things as strangers and pilgrims, only for necessary use.

These holy men the patriarchs were strangers.

1. Strangers *in their own esteem*. As Abraham and Jacob, they confess they were sojourners; and David, though he were a king, yet he saith 'he was a stranger, as all his fathers were.' So all the patriarchs they professed themselves to be strangers and sojourners; and they did it not in word only, but in deed. They shewed it by dwelling in tabernacles and tents; poor things, fit for strangers. Heaven was their house. Tabernacles are moveable, weak things, that have no foundation; so they knew their life was like a tabernacle here. And their manner of life shewed what they looked for; they carried themselves as those that hoped and looked for better things. They were strangers in their dispositions; they affected things above, and cared no more for these things than for necessary use, to help them to serve God in their places; and those that are strangers in their dispositions, they desire to be at home.

2. Again, they were strangers *in God's esteem*. God termed them so; and so it is with all that believe in Christ. When we once believe, and are new creatures, new born to a better inheritance, presently at the same time we are strangers here.

3. Strangers likewise *in the esteem of the world.* The world used them as strangers, strangely. When a man leaveth the world and cleaveth to God, presently the world setteth on him by reproaches, and all they can. Because they think he will disgrace them by his change, therefore they labour to make him as black as they may that way: they use all strangely that break from them. God will have it so. Because he will have his children not to love the world, therefore he will have the world hate them. So they are strangers in that respect: they think it strange that they do not as they did formerly; that they do not as they do. Wicked men think it strange that they 'run not with them into the same excess of riot,' 1 Pet. iv. 4: so they are strangers in the esteem of wicked men.

4. So they are strangers *in regard of their place.* Heaven is their hope. They are 'begotten to an inheritance immortal, undefiled,' &c., 1 Pet. i. 4; they live in a place where they are strangers; they are every way strangers.

Obj. But you will say, Wicked men are strangers, and pilgrims too?

Ans. I answer, They are indeed so, for in regard of the shortness of their lives, and the uncertainty of the things they enjoy,—for they outlive all their happiness here,—they are snatched hence before they be aware, therefore they are but travellers here; but they go from ill to worse. Yet in regard of their affections they are no strangers, but account themselves at home from a spirit of infidelity, and pride, and earthliness. Therefore they are called men of the earth, and those that 'dwell on the earth,' in the Revelation, Rev. iii. 10, because they look no further than the earth; and here they root and fix their affections upon this earth. They do not fix their hearts and affections upon the things above; they look not after them; they care not for them; they value them not, nor esteem them. Therefore, answerable to their thoughts, and bent of their soul and mind, is their discourse, their speech and carriage; and thereupon they are called 'men of the earth,' and called 'the world,' because they love nothing but the world; they are as it were changed into the things they love; they are earth, as the prophet saith, 'O earth, earth,' &c., Jer. xxii. 29; and they are the world, because their affection of love joins them to these earthly things. The church in the Revelation is called heaven; but the beast is said 'to rise out of the earth,' Rev. xiii. 11; for that which bred the carnal religion of popery, it was nothing but earth and earthly respects. Therefore, however they are strangers here, that they cannot be here long, and they have souls that are of an everlasting continuance; yet because their affections and the bent of their souls are all here, they account themselves at home here, and here they plant themselves and their posterity; therefore, though in some sense they be strangers, yet not in that sense that the children of God are.

Every Christian is born from above, and born to things above, and he is a stranger here. All his course, from his new birth till he come to the possession of his inheritance in heaven, it is nothing but a travelling. He never sits down, but is alway in his motion and passage. Every good work is a step of his way: he is in motion still; he takes degrees from better to better, from grace to grace, from knowledge to knowledge, till he come to his home.

Let us make a trial of ourselves, how our affections stand to these things, whether our hearts be weaned from earthly things. Undoubtedly, if we have embraced Christ, we shall use the world as though we used it not. We shall be transformed into the image of Christ; and he used the things of this world as a stranger, only to comfort him in the way. We shall have the same mind that he had. We shall carry ourselvers as strangers, as those that hope for a country in heaven. Therefore I will name some particulars, to shew the condition and carriage of a stranger.

1. First of all, a stranger *is travelling to another country*—to join both in one; for the one follows the other. He that is a stranger, that apprehends what he is, and apprehends that he hath a country to go to, he travels toward it.

2. A stranger that is travelling homeward, he *is content with his present condition*, for he knows he shall have better at home. In Jer. xlv. 4, God, by Jeremiah, speaks to Baruch, a good man: 'I will destroy all these things; and dost thou seek great things for thyself?' If a Christian did consider, I am going to heaven, to God, what do I seeking great things here, which God will destroy? What will become of heaven and earth, and all things here ere long? And if the time be long ere heaven and earth be destroyed, yet what will become of me ere long? I shall be turned to earth, and shall I seek great things here upon earth? Shall I not be content with my portion? Certainly a stranger is content with his present portion. He that is a traveller, when he comes to his inn, if perhaps things be not so clean, if his usage be not so good, he thinks it is but a night and away: it is no great matter. This is not the main. He will not be over much discontent, and quarrel at any unkind usage in the way, for he knows he shall have better usage when he comes home. Therefore, as he will be content with little, be it what it will be, he knows it is not the main.

3. So he will be *patient* if he meet with unkind usage: he will not stand quarrelling by the way, and so hinder himself in his journey; he will be patient in the injuries and wrongs in this life. If a prince be misused in another country, he is contented, and thinks with himself, I have a country where I shall be more respected; and therefore he bears it the more willingly. So a Christian is a king, he is an heir; and being a stranger, he shall meet with dogs in this world; as, who do dogs bark at, but at strangers? Now being strangers we must look for dogged usage. It is no wonder that dogs bark at strangers; it is their kind. They consider it is the disposition of wicked men to do so; they do but their kind. Would a man have dogs not to bark? And would we have wicked men that have evil tongues not to scorn that they know not? To do otherwise is to forget their kind. A Christian knows they do but their kind. He pities them; and he doth not stop his journey and his course for it. He will not be scorned out of his religion by a company of profane spirits; he will not be laughed out of his course; he knows what he doth better than they. They are mad and fools; he knows it, and they shall know it themselves ere long. He knows that he is in a serious judicious course that he can approve, and they cannot theirs; therefore he will not be scorned out of his course.

Thus faith in Christ makes him that is a stranger here, content and patient. He whose soul hath embraced Christ is contented with anything: anything is sufficient to his soul that is filled with better things. Nothing will content a covetous earthly man, a man of earth. Such men think themselves at home; they make a league with hell and death. The men of the world they think they shall live here alway; but a Christian that embraceth a better life with Christ in happiness to come, he knows he shall not be here long. He is here but as a stranger, and shall shortly be at home; and therefore he is contented with anything.

4. Likewise the knowledge of this that we are strangers and pilgrims, it will make a man not only content and patient, *but thankful, for any kindness he finds in this world*; that God sweetens his absence from heaven and his pilgrimage on earth [some]what; that God should love me so, not only to give me heaven, but to give me contentments on the earth to sweeten my way to heaven: what a mercy is this! He is thankful for any contentment; he is thankful to the world, to those that do anything for him, that afford him any courtesy here that may help him in his pilgrimage, and make it less troublesome and cumbersome to him.

All the saints in former time were wondrous thankful for that they had; for what can a traveller look for but discourtesies and hard usage? And if he find anything better he will be thankful: certainly it is more than I looked for, saith he. When a man is bent toward heaven, he cannot but look for hard usage from the world. We see when Christ did but look toward Jerusalem, the Samaritans had enough; they began to malign him. Why? 'His face was toward Jerusalem,' Luke ix. 53. So when base worldlings see that a man will to heaven, and leave their company and courses, they cannot digest this. A man with an ill conscience, when he sees another oppose that course that he resolved to stick to, he sees he confutes his course, he sees his face is toward heaven, and therefore labours to disgrace him. As the wench said to Peter, 'Thou speakest as one of Galilee; thy speech bewrays thee,' Mat. xxvi. 73; so when a man is going toward heaven, every base person, the veriest rascal of all, hath pride enough to scorn religion. So we see they make not much of the world, nor the world of them; therefore they are contented and thankful if they find better; for what can a stranger look for but strange usage in a strange place?

And therefore we see in Scripture how thankful they were, even for refreshings, for meat and drink. Our Saviour Christ was known by 'breaking of bread.' He used to be thankful. 'In all things give thanks,' Eph. v. 20. They saw the favour and love of God in a crumb of bread, and in a drop of refreshing in any kind. Oh, here is a blessed God, that hath given us these comforts in the way. The saints of God are wondrous thankful for the comforts of their pilgrimage, the comforts of this life.

And this should make us more thankful, because all men's pilgrimages are not alike; for do we not see the life of some more cumbersome? Some live in a great deal of want; some live in a great deal of opposition more than others do; others go in a smoother way to heaven. God sees his children's weakness; he sees they have not strength; and if in pity he keeps them that they shall not encounter with opposition, but lead them a better way than others, it is special matter of thankfulness to God and men too.

5. He that is a stranger, *he is glad of any good company*. Oh, if he meet with a man of his own country, he is a man alone for him; so it is with a Christian that walks in the way to heaven with him, he is comforted much in it.

6. A stranger, *he hath his prime intention* home to his country*, and what he doth in the way, it is in virtue of his prime intention, though he doth not, in every particular action that he doth, think of it. A traveller when he rides on the way he doth not think of home in every step. Ay, but he doth that that he doth in virtue of his prime intention when he first set out, and calls to remembrance ofttimes as he goes home; he thinks of his journeys. And by the way,

* Cf. Glossary, *sub voce*.—G.

I observe this note of some weak Christians that think they are not heavenly-minded, except they do nothing but think of heaven and heavenly things. That is but a weak and silly conceit. It should be our thought in the morning. Our thoughts should open with that. It should be the key to open the morning, the thought of this course what will become of us ere long in heaven. But then all that we do should be in virtue and strength of that prime intention to please God, and to go to heaven. Though we think not alway of the present business, yet it is good as much as may be to quicken our endeavour.

7. And hence it is that there is another property of a stranger that is going to a place, *perhaps he may step out of the way, yet notwithstanding, by virtue of his first intention, he gathers himself homeward again.* If he take other matters in hand, he gathers home still, though he go out of his way, in he comes; he considers, this is not my way. So a child of God, sometimes he diverts and turns aside, yet notwithstanding he considers, doth this way lead to Godward, to heavenward? Be these actions Christian actions? Are they the way to heaven? If he see they be not, though he have stepped awry, he comes in again, and is gathering homeward. Though he may perhaps forget himself a little—a traveller—yet his bent is homewards. So a Christian man, though perhaps in some particular he may forget himself, yet he is alway gathering home; his bent is home, and his course is godly. Take a Christian, perhaps he may step awry, but his course is godly, and he labours to recover himself; and if a traveller stay at any time by the way, he makes amends afterwards by making more haste. So doth a Christian, if we consider him with his affections loose to good things; yet he recovers himself again, and sets upon religious actions and courses with more violence of spirit, and recovers his former loss again.

8. A traveller and stranger he *provides beforehand for all encumbrances.* He knows though he meet not with troubles, yet he may, therefore he will be sure to go with weapons, and he will go with that that may sustain him by the way. Religion teacheth a man to gather out of the word of God comforts beforehand, and munition beforehand, to carry with him. Put the case he never use them; he may have cause to use them, and then if he have them not, what will become of him? He lies open to adversaries by the way. Therefore there is a spirit in a Christian, an instinct that stirs him up; he will be reading the word of God, and good books, and hearing the word. This I may have use of at such a time; this I will lay up for such an occasion. Put the case that such an occasion come not, he loseth nothing. He seasoneth his soul in the mean time, and prepares it for worse things if worse come.

Woe to those that have not laid up strength and comfort against evil times beforehand. If a man go to sea, and be not provided beforehand; if he take a journey, and be not provided beforehand, then when a storm comes, what a case is he in! It pleaseth God to teach us by these resemblances heavenly things. Therefore because they are fit means to convey holier things unto us, it is good to take this help that God affords us, considering that he shews us by these shadows better things. When we travel, and are going on in our journey towards heaven, it is good to consider higher things, it is a good meditation. Therefore to go on a little further.

9. A traveller and stranger *is inquisitive of the way,* whether he be in the way or out of the way. He asks not at random. That doth not content him, whether he go west, or north, or south, or east; it doth not content

him to ask where lies my country, eastward? &c. No; but he will ask the particular towns, and particular turnings and windings, how he may avoid going out of his way, and which is the right way, and he will ask upon every occasion, because he knows if he go but a little out of his way it will be a long time ere he shall recover it, and he will be ashamed to come back again; and the more he goes out of the way, the more trouble it is to come back again. So it is with a Christian, he doth not only desire to know in general, but he desires to have daily direction, what shall I do in such a case of conscience, and in such a case? How shall I overcome such a temptation if I meet with it? And so he is willing to have daily direction how to walk with God day by day, that he go not out of his way in anything.

For even as every step that a man takes is a part of his journey, so every action of a man's life it is a part of his journey to heaven, and therefore he is willing to have direction for every step, that he may walk step upon step upon good ground. Therefore he goes upon good grounds of a good conscience, in the duties of Christianity. He will have sound conviction what is good, and what is true in religion; what religion is true that he may venture his soul upon, and what use he may make of his particular calling; what he may do with a safe conscience, and what not; and what he may not do that he will not meddle with, and what is clear to his conscience that he will do. So every step he takes, though it be in his particular calling, it helps him forward. As St Paul saith, in the Epistle to the Colossians, of servants, that they serve God in serving their master, so a poor servant in his drudgery may serve God. So in our ordinary professions we are in the way to heaven, if they be sanctified by prayer beforehand, and do it in conscience and obedience to God, that hath set us in this way.

There are two callings, our general and particular calling, and we shew religion, that is our general calling, in our particular calling, as we are placed in this or that calling; and what we do in either of these callings is the way to heaven. Now the care of a Christian is, that he be well advised what to do, and on what ground.

10. And even as a traveller considers of things by the way as they make to his end, *to further his journey or hinder his journey*, he looks to heaven as his country that he hopes for, and therefore he doth not tangle himself with any more than may help him home. If they hinder him once, away they go; if they may help him, he takes them. A Christian in his travel in the way to heaven considers of things that may fall out by the way, as they may help and further him to heaven. If I find that things, though they be indifferent in themselves, if they trouble me in my way to heaven (it may be they are not so to another, but they are to me), though another can do it, yet I must consider whether I can do it, and find myself enlarged to heaven as at other times. If not, away with it. It is not indifferent to me, because it hinders my journey to heaven. A wise traveller will venture upon things and courses as they serve or hinder the main, though they be things perhaps that he cannot over-well spare, yet if they trouble him in his journey, off they go, that he may be more expedite and right in his way.

I wonder at the boldness of many that profess themselves religious, and yet dare venture upon anything. Undoubtedly, if they did search their own hearts, they could not but say that such courses do dead and dull them, and make them forget religion; that such company is not safe to keep. I find myself the worse by it, why should I venture upon anything that may stop and hinder, or cool and dead me in my way to heaven?

If a man be wise, he will consider of things as they help or hinder him to that.

As for sins whereof we are convicted, it is the apostle's counsel, Heb. xii. 1—he puts it out of all question—'We must cast off all that burden, that presseth down,' &c. A traveller will not have a burden upon him. The sin that hangs so fast on we must labour to mortify, to kill our lusts and corruptions more and more, and never leave till we have cast them off. These things are undeniable. I spake before of things in themselves indifferent, and to other men indifferent, if they have a larger measure of wisdom; but for corruptions and sins, they fight against the soul, they fasten us to the world, therefore above all things we must cast off them; as St Peter saith excellently, in 1 Peter ii. 11, 'I beseech you, brethren, as pilgrims and strangers, abstain from fleshly lusts, which fight against your souls:' insinuating that pilgrims and strangers should altogether abstain from lusts, from the cherishing of carnal lusts, for these fight against the soul, they fight against the comforts of the soul, against the graces of the soul, and against the eternal well-being of the soul. The more a man cherisheth base lusts, the more it damps his comfort and grace, and weakens his assurance of life everlasting. They fight against all good in the soul; therefore let us abstain 'from fleshly lusts, that fight against the soul.' That is clear; all confess that. But the other that I spake of before, carefulness of things indifferent, if we find them not so to us, till we get more mastery of ourselves, we must even be careful of our liberties, and not give ourselves those liberties that others do, if we find they hinder us in particular. Yet with a secret concealing of it, not to entangle the consciences of other men, who perhaps may use those things with less hindrance than we do: a wise Christian will be wary in that kind. If he find the things of the world to hinder him, he will not have his heart eaten up with the world, nor eaten out with lawful things. Being therefore to prepare for a better life, and to do God's business, he will only take the things of this life as they may make for a better life, and be a furtherance of him to his home. He winds home by all means, he useth all advantages to come nearer to God, and whatsoever hinders him he labours to avoid.

11. Again, he that accounts himself a stranger here, *he doth not value himself by outward things*. Faith teacheth a man, when he is an heir of heaven, not to value himself by earthly things. He thinks himself a stranger in his own house, as David did, though he were a king, as I said. Every Christian is a stranger at home. He values not himself by his honours, nor dignity, nor by the things that he hath here; nor he doth not disvalue himself by poverty or disgrace. He knows he is a stranger; he is going home; therefore he values himself by that he hath at home. Christians are kings and heirs; they esteem not or disesteem of themselves by what they have here below; they account them as things in the way, that God gives them, if they be good, to sweeten their pilgrimage; if they be ill, to sharpen their journey. It is necessary that God should give them these things, good things to sweeten their journey; and if they loiter in their way to heaven, then that they should have crosses to drive them homeward.

In all confusions in the world, faith teacheth a man to stand as a man upon a rock immoveable, because he is a stranger. If anything fall out in the city or place where a stranger is, he carries his own jewels and things about him, and so goes away, his goods are not of that place; so in all confusions of the world, a Christian hath good things of another world. The good things he carries with him are not subject to losses or crosses, they are not subject to the misusing of the world. When all things shall be on fire, a Christian hath his treasure laid up in heaven, in a place where no earthly creature hath power of it. It is not subject to any ill, and that makes him in all estates contented and patient. Let heaven and earth go together. A Christian when he hath embraced better things, a Christian thinks himself a stranger that is going home; therefore in all his life he carries himself as a stranger. To go on a little further.

12. A traveller in his way *must of necessity have refreshings by the way, or else he will fail;* therefore sometimes he sings, and sometimes useth other refreshings. Now, what saith David? 'Thy statutes have been my song in the house of my pilgrimage,' Ps. cxix. 54; that is, when I want other comforts, they are my song, my joy, and delight. A traveller must needs have comforts that may revive him in his fainting; he must have some pleasant walks for meditation. Let us therefore, when we grow weary, refresh ourselves in walking, in holy meditation. Take a turn there, to think of the vanity of all earthly things, and how soon they come to an end; and of the excellency and eternity of our glorious condition and estate when we come home, and then think of the helps and comforts by the way, and such like. The art of divine meditation is an art for this end, that since we are all travellers, that we are from home, and that we are going home, we may walk in wisdom. Let us learn that art, to feed and strengthen our souls with such meditations as may clear them by the way, to set some time apart when we grow dull and indisposed in religion. Then let us think how to cherish and refresh our souls with those excellencies, that are indeed above our comprehension; our hearts cannot conceive of it. It is set out in the word of God to our conceit, but as it is we cannot conceive here what is reserved for us when we shall come home. Therefore let us do as travellers, often think of home, and what is at home for us; and that will make us when we are in the way, and any comfort would draw us out of our way, to think, Oh, these are good comforts, but this is not my home. I have better at home than this, and this will stay me from home. Therefore the cross is necessary for travellers, that they may know they are not at home, that they may embitter his comforts. This consideration, that he is not at home, and that this is not his country, as it will keep a Christian from temptations, so it will draw him on to constancy in his love and in going on; for a traveller sits not down to stay there. He thinks, Here I am, and home I must go, and I shall not come home by sitting here.

So the oft thinking of home, it will both sweeten our troubles, and likewise the comforts that we meet with in this world. It will make us that we shall not be ensnared with them; because, though they be comfortable things, yet, alas! what are these? These indeed are fit to make a man forget home, to forget heaven, as a man that sees goodly things, goodly houses. These things, saith he, are they that make a man unwilling to go out of the world (*d*). But he that is assured of a country, and knows that he hath a better home than all these earthly things, that are shadows and vanity, he thinks these are very goodly things; but what are these to that that is reserved? And if I sit down by these, if a traveller sit down by delights, and gaze upon things by the way, when shall he come home? Let us think oft of home; there be many uses to think and meditate of that blessed day; this among the rest, that it draws us on forward and forward still, that we shall not sit quiet, but go on still, and not rest till we come home.

And the nearer we are home, the more busy and the more cheerful we should be; as a traveller, when he comes near home he is more cheerful, when he hath home in his eye; when he sees the smoke of his country, he rejoiceth. As these patriarchs, they saw the promises afar off. As men when they see the tops of steeples and houses, they think, Now we have them continually in our eye, we see something of home; and the nearer they come the more they see, and the nearer they come still the more they see. So the longer a Christian lives, the nearer and nearer he comes home. If he understand himself, and have any assurance in any degree, it makes him more joyful towards his end.

Thus it was with God's people. When they were nearer their end, then they sung sweetly the swan's song, and then they were enlarged in their spirits; as Jacob, when he was dying we see what a will he made, what legacies to his children. And Joseph, when he was dying, and Moses the man of God; the song of Moses, and David, the 'sweet singer of Israel.' The last words of David, what sweet words they were! And St Paul, when he was to go out of the world, 'I have fought the good fight, I have finished my course, I have kept the faith: henceforth is laid up for me the crown of righteousness,' &c., 2 Tim. iv. 7. And our blessed Saviour, toward his end, we see how heavenly he was in his prayer. And good Simeon, 'Lord, now let thy servant depart in peace,' &c., Luke ii. 29. When he had grasped Christ once, he was loath to live any longer. So it should be with Christians as it is with travellers: the nearer they are home, the more and more comfortable they should be still.

It is a shame for old men to fear when they come near their end, when they are near the haven, then to fear. It is as if a man in a storm should fear the haven; or a man that travels and sees a city, to be afraid of his own house; whereas he should rejoice and think he is nearer his happiness than other men, as Saint Paul tells the Romans, 'Your salvation is nearer now than when you first believed,' xiii. 11. So we should think our salvation and happiness in heaven is nearer now than when we first believed; and therefore the less time we have to travel here with incumbrances in the way to heaven, the more joyful we should be. The nearer we are to death, the nearer to our preferment, the nearer to our country and our home. These are the advised thoughts of a Christian; and when other thoughts come into a man, when he is stricken in years, surely they are not in him as a Christian, but as he is weak and wants faith and assurance of salvation. Oh let us therefore labour to get assurance of another, a better country; for what made these holy men confess themselves strangers and pilgrims here? 'They saw the promises afar off, and were persuaded of them and embraced them;' and in that measure they were assured of a better condition, 'they carried themselves as strangers and pilgrims here.'

To wind up all in a word, you see here their disposition. I beseech you, make this text your pattern to be moulded into. You see how these blessed men long ago lived in faith when their light was less than ours is; and they died in faith, and will welcome us when we shall come to heaven. We shall go to Abraham, Isaac, and Jacob, and the rest of the patriarchs and holy men. It will be a blessed time when all the blessed men that have gone before shall welcome us to heaven. If we look to be happy as they are, we must live as they did, and die as they did. Though we cannot so strongly as they did see that with the eye of faith that no eye else can see, yet let us desire God to persuade us of these truths more strongly than the devil of* our own lusts shall persuade us to the contrary; let us desire God to set on his truths so strongly that all other things may not hinder us, that we may embrace them with our best affections of love, of desire, of contentment; that we may witness all this by our demeanour to earthly things; by our base esteem of them, and carry ourselves as pilgrims and strangers on earth. If we do thus live in faith and die in faith, we shall live with Abraham, Isaac, and Jacob in the kingdom of heaven eternally.

* Qu. 'or'?—Ed.

NOTE.

(*a*) P. 418.—'Death . . . this king of fears.' Cf. note *e*, Vol. IV. page 38. I would supplement this note with a fuller quotation from Aristotle, to whose blank despair, when he treats of death, Sibbes alludes repeatedly: Eth. Nic. iii. 5, 4, *φοβερώτατον δ' ὁ θανατος. πέρας γὰρ, καὶ οὐδὲν ἔτι τῷ τεθνεῶτι δοκεῖ οὔτ 'αγαθὸν οὔτε κακὸν εἶναι.*

(*b*) P. 427.—'As Peter saith, mop-eyed.' Cf. 2 Peter i. 9. Mop-eyed means short-sighted, and very well translates τυφλός, = natural state of *blindness*, and worse—closing the eyes to the light as follows: μύωψ = contracting the eyelids as one who cannot see clearly = short-sighted.

(*c*) P. 428.—The author seems to have had in his mind the well-known lines of Horace—

'Segnius irritant animos demissa per aurem,
Quam quæ sunt oculis subjecta fidelibus.'

(*d*) P. 459.—'These things, saith he, are they that make a man unwilling to go out of the world.' This remark anticipates by more than a century a similar one ascribed to Dr Samuel Johnson, to Edmund Burke, and to John Foster the essayist, 'These are what make a death-bed terrible.' It seems to be one of those memorable things that have got inwrought into our language. G.

THE RUIN OF MYSTICAL JERICHO.*

By faith the walls of Jericho fell down, after they had been compassed about seven days.—Heb. XI. 30.

This verse suits somewhat to the occasion :† therefore I have made choice of it at this time. This chapter contains the triumph of faith in the hearts and souls of those in whom this blessed grace is planted; so that the excellency and office of all graces are attributed to it. There is a stirring up of all other graces whatsoever in faith. All the worthies that are spoken of before, they did that they did, and 'obtained a good report by faith.' The Spirit of God goes on here, and shews a glorious effect of this blessed grace, in the falling down of the walls of Jericho. This short verse is taken out of the story of the conquest of Jericho, mentioned in Josh. vi., in the latter end of the chapter, where you have the whole story set down at large. I need not rehearse it; and withal you have there a curse set down, that whosoever should go about again to build the walls of Jericho, he should lay the foundation in his first-born, and in his youngest son he should set up the gates. He that would raise up such a cursed building again, he should do it with the overthrow of his own building, of his own family; as the Scripture calls a man's house a building.‡ He should lay the foundation in his eldest son, and build the gates at the death of his youngest son.

And a little to acquaint you with the fulness of the word, before I come to the story, you have an audacious cursed attempt to build the walls of Jericho again, in 1 Kings xvi. toward the latter end, ver. 34, in a wicked king's time, in Ahab's time. There was one so adventurous, one Hiel, that he would build Jericho. He laid the foundation in Abiram, his first-born,

* 'The Ruin of Mystical Jericho' is another of the Sermons included in 'Evangelical Sacrifices' (4to. 1640). Its separate title-page is as follows :—'The Rvine of Mystical Iericho. A Sermon preached upon the 5th of November, in remembrance of Our Deliverance from the Papists Powder-Treason. By the late Learned and Reverend Divine, Rich. Sibbs. Doctor in Divinity, Mr. of Katherine Hall in Cambridge, and sometimes Preacher to the Honourable Society of Grayes-Inne.—Iosh. 6. 10. And it came to passe when the people heard the sound of the Trumpet, and the people shouted with a great shout, that the Wall fell downe flat, &c. London, Printed by T. B. for N. Bourne, at the Royall Exchange, and R. Harford, at the guilt Bible in Queenes-head Alley in Pater-noster-Row. 1639.'—G.

† In margin, 'Novemb. 5.'—G.

‡ בן, a *son*; from בנה, to build.—Ed.

and set up the gates in his youngest son Segub, according to the word of the Lord spoken by Joshua the son of Nun. You see whence this story is fetched. 'By faith the walls of Jericho fell down, after they had been compassed about seven days.' They were compassed about seven days, and the ark in the midst; and the seventh day they went seven times about, and then the walls fell down, as you have it in the story. But to come to the words; and to hasten to that I specially mean to touch at this time.

First of all, observe here, that Jericho had mighty walls, as you see in the story. It had walls, and trusted in these walls; or else they would have come out and have made conditions of peace with Israel. But as they had walls, so they were confident in them; as you see the spies, in Num. xiii. 28, they tell what walled cities they had, and that terrified them.

And next you see here, that God overthrows their walls; and by what means? By poor and base means, by trumpets of rams' horns. They had silver trumpets, but they used not them, but meaner instruments, rams' horns. Those were the means; and the time that they used them, seven days together; and then that by faith, using these means, they overthrew the walls of Jericho, they fell down. From hence, by analogy and proportion, we may see,

First of all, that carnal men they build up walls, and put their trust in them.

The second is, that God confounds these courses.

The third is, that God doth it by weak and silly means, believed by faith.

The last point is, that faith in the use of these means overcomes all. 'By faith the walls of Jericho fell down, after they had been compassed about seven days.' And then we shall come to other things that concern us, and apply it to the time.

Doct. 1. *Natural men, since the fall, they must have somewhat to trust to.*

Since man lost his first prop and confidence, and communion with God, he turns to the creature. There is always some confidence in some creature; and men leave God in what measure they trust that. When Cain was banished his father's house, then he falls to building of cities; he must have some contentment. And those that were escaped the flood, within a hundred years after the flood, they must build a tower of Babel, that should reach to heaven, to get themselves a name, wanting better courses. Every one will have some castle and wall of Jericho to trust to. Riches are the rich man's stronghold, as Solomon saith, Prov. xi. 16. Ahithophel trusted to a shrewd head and policy, that proved his ruin afterwards. The Jews had outward sanctity to trust to, opposing it to the righteousness of Christ; the righteousness of faith, Rom. x. 6. They would set a-foot a dead righteousness that could not stand; and therefore they were shut from the righteousness of God in Christ. Man will have a holiness, a wisdom, a strength, and power of himself, in the things below here, as I might shew at large, both in examples and otherwise. Naturally we find it in ourselves. If we be sick, we trust to the physician and other means. If we be in danger, we flee to the arm of flesh, to some mighty man; we trust in some great friend, if we have any. If we be in danger of invasion, or such like, we trust our walls and defences; and till strong temptations come, we trust in our own strength, till Satan pick so many holes in it, that we cannot stay there, and that conscience upbraids us. Always a man hath somewhat to trust to, till he be brought to desperate conditions; and rather than he will have nothing to trust to, he will trust to the broken reed of Egypt; he will trust to that that will deceive him and hurt him, as the reed of Egypt did the Jews; rather than they would trust God, and the word brought by the prophets, they would trust Asshur, and Egypt, 2 Kings xviii. 21.

Now the Spirit of God in the Scriptures takes notice of this proneness to false confidence. 'Trust not in uncertain riches. If riches increase, set not your hearts on them,' 1 Timothy vi. 17. And man, when he sets his heart upon false confidence, the issues are more dangerous; he will come against God; he doth not only set up these holds that he hath in rebellion against God, but he proclaims, as it were, defiance to God, and his word, and his ordinances, till afterwards God destroy all his false confidence, and bring him to shame.

In 2 Cor. x. 4 there is a notable place to shew what holds there are in the heart of man, that oppose against God and his truth in his word; holds that Satan keeps in man, and man, joining with Satan the enemy, holds against God and his truth: 'The weapons of our warfare,' saith he, 'are not carnal, but mighty through God to cast down strongholds.' The holds are within us, and we are so far from preparing ourselves to grace, and to entertain grace when it is offered, that naturally we set up holds against God and grace. There must be strong power to overturn all, to lead them into captivity to the obedience of Christ: 'To cast down the imaginations, and every high thing, every high thought that exalts itself against the knowledge of God, and to bring in captivity every thought,' 2 Cor. x. 5. So there are three mighty things in every natural man.

(1.) *This false reasoning and sophistry.* There is no man will go to hell without reason. Take the debauchedest wretch that lives, he is mad with some reason, and he will be damned with some reason. 'God is merciful,' 'Christ is come,' and 'others are as bad as I,' and 'I hope in time to repent;' this vile reasoning must be turned out of a man before he can be saved.

(2.) Then *there are proud thoughts.* What, shall I yield to such a one as he? I am better than he; I understand these things as well as he. As that proud cardinal in Germany said, 'I confess these things that Luther finds fault with are naught; but shall I yield to a base monk?' (*a*) So men think, shall I yield to a minister? The proud rebellious heart of man is lift up in proud thoughts against God.

(3.) And then there be *forecasts.* If I do thus, this danger will come of it; I shall provoke such an enemy; I shall lose such a friend; I shall endanger myself. Now, when the truth of God comes, down goes all these sophistries and high thoughts, and all these forecasts; they all lie flat when the Spirit of God comes in the power of the word. But naturally every man hath these; he builds up some castle against God; he builds up the walls of Jericho, and trusts in them too. 'Thy wisdom hath caused thee to rebel,' saith God to the king of Babylon, Isa. xlvii. 10. 'Let not the wise man trust in his wisdom,' Jer. ix. 23, insinuating that wise men are subject to trust in their wisdom, and the rich man in his riches, and the strong man in his strength; therefore God commands that they should not do so. 'Thy wisdom hath made thee to rebel.'

Use. Let us take notice of this, and make this use of trial of it, that if, by the power of God's Spirit, we can use all outward means and not trust in them; that we can trust in God, and not to our strength, then we have somewhat in us above nature; for naturally every man, before he be in communion and covenant with God, he hath some earthly false support or other to trust on; either within him, some policy and wisdom, or without him, some friends or riches, some bulwark or other; and this sets him against God and against the means of salvation, till God come in effectual calling and overturn all. But this doth but make way to other things, therefore I only touch it.

The second thing is this, that,

Obs. 2. *God first or last overturns all vain confidence in the creature.*

The walls of Jericho, down they must; and whatsoever exalts itself against God, either it shall end in conversion or confusion, because the time must come that God must have all the glory. 'Was there ever any man fierce against God, and prospered?' Job ix. 4. 'The rage of man turns to the glory of God,' saith the psalmist, Ps. lxxvi. 10. 'There is neither wisdom nor policy, counsel nor strength, or any earthly thing against the Lord,' as the wise man saith, Prov. xxi. 30. 'God will confound all; he scattered the proud in the imagination of their own hearts,' as the blessed virgin saith, Luke i. 51. And when they had built Babel, to get them a name, they found confusion. There is a notable place in Isa. l. 11: 'Behold, all ye that kindle a fire, that compass yourselves about with sparks: walk,' saith God, 'in the light of your fire, and in the sparks that ye have kindled. This ye shall have at my hand; ye shall lie down in sorrow.' Men that will walk in the light of their own fire, that will have a wisdom of their own, distinct, nay, contrary ofttimes to God's;— Well! go on, walk in the light of your own fire that ye have kindled; but take this withal with you, 'You shall have this at my hands,' saith God, 'ye shall lie down in sorrow.' What became of Haman's plots? What became of Ahithophel's policy? They all turned upon their own heads. Although men build up castles to secure themselves in their earthly defences and munition, yet God overturns all.

Use. Therefore let us make that use that Jeremiah doth, Jer. ix. 23: 'Therefore let not the wise man trust in his wisdom, or the strong man in his strength, or the rich man in his riches.' Let a man joy in none of these; but if he will joy, let him joy in this, that he knows the Lord, that he is in covenant with God. That for the second, briefly.

The third is this, that,

Obs. 3. *God doth this by base and weak means.*

He confounds great and mighty enterprizes and mighty persons, and useth but base and despised means; as here, the walls of Jericho fell down with the noise of rams' horns. This I might carry along through all the stories in the Scripture, from the creation to this present time, to shew how God doth great things by despised means; sometimes by no means at all, sometimes clean contrary to all means. When our Saviour Christ gave sight to the blind, he put clay upon his eyes, that, one would think, were fitter to put them out. We see in the story of the Israelites what an ox-goad did, and what Samson did with the jaw-bone of an ass. We see by what a trick the Midianites were put to flight by Gideon.* In all the stories we see, when God would do great matters, he doth it by base means. When he would confound the pride of Pharaoh, he will do it by frogs and lice, and such base creatures, that were fittest in God's wisdom to overthrow the pride of that wretched king. God, as he overturns the pride of men, so for the most part he doth it by weak and despised means.

Reason. And the reason is clear, *that he may have all the glory.* Some-

* Cf. (1) John ix. 6, (2) Judges iii. 31, (3) Judges xv. 16, (4) Judges vii. 16.—G.

times the means he useth have no influence at all to effect the thing, but are only joined with the thing; as here, what influence could poor trumpets of rams' horns have to cast down walls? They could have none; but only it was a thing joined before the walls fell down; they were things that must be used to try their obedience; and that they might know that it was not by chance that they fell down, but by God's power; and for other reasons. But if there be any influence from the cause to the effect, it is supposed it cannot produce the effect of itself, therefore, I say, God doth this that he may have all the glory; for that is his end, and it ought to be our end. We see here, though they had silver trumpets, yet they must by God's appointment use these base means, trumpets of rams' horns.

Now, they were to use them seven days together, and therefore on a Sabbath day; but it was no breach of the day, because God can dispense with his own law. In case of charity, good works may be done on the Sabbath, and in case of duty likewise, as the priests kill the sacrifice on the Sabbath. So here was sufficient warrant for them; God gave them a command; God, that made the law, can dispense with his own law in things that touch not upon his nature, as his truth and purity, &c., doth. In things that touch his nature, he should deny himself if he should dispense. God cannot lie, because truth is natural to him. God cannot do anything that is unfit for his nature; but for things that are out of him, he is Lord of days; he is Lord of goods and life; he hath a right to dispense here, as we see in the taking away the Egyptian's jewels and the like; they were outward things. But for those things that are intrinsecal in God, he cannot command that which is contrary to his truth and nature. Other things belong to his sovereignty. But that by the way.

They were to compass the walls seven days. If they had made an end before the seventh day, the walls had never fallen down. Howsoever, there was no power in their going about to effect that, yet God would not work the effect till he was waited on in all the seven days; the means appointed by God must be used, and so long as God will have them used, there must be a depending and waiting upon God all the time.

Quest. To give a little further light to that I touched before, you will ask why God useth means and doth not work immediately? why he did not cast down these walls by his own will and pleasure?

Ans. Besides that I said before, God useth second causes, not for defect of power, but for demonstration of his goodness; and for the trial of our obedience, and the like. Therefore, being Lord of hosts, he hath multiplicity of ranks of creatures which he useth to effect those things that he could do himself if it pleased him. Therefore let such questions cease; it pleased God so to do.

The last point is this—

Obs. 4. *It was by faith in the use of means that the walls of Jericho fell down.*

If they had not depended upon God in their going about seven days, the walls had stood still. It was by faith they did it; and it was a great faith that, using such a ridiculous stratagem as this, to go about the walls with rams' horns, they should think the walls would fall. It might shake their faith, and likewise expose them to the scorn of those of Jericho within, therefore it was a great faith in them. Not that all had faith, for certainly divers of them were unbelieving persons; but Joshua their captain, and some others of them, had faith, and all of them had hope of the best. It was faith that believed this in this unlikelihood of second causes, for there is the strength of faith; when second causes are weak, then faith is strong.

Abraham's faith was the stronger by reason there was more indisposition in the second causes, in Sarah's womb to conceive a child; for her womb was dead; in the course of nature she could not conceive. Therefore it is said by Saint Paul, Rom. iv. 20, 'He being strong in faith, gave glory to God:' strong faith gives glory to God. So here was a strong faith, because the means were weak, or none at all; for these means had nothing in themselves to work such a glorious effect as this, that the falling of the walls should follow. It was but a means adjoined. That it should be done by such a poor thing as this, it was the strength of faith. But was it the strength of faith in itself? Could faith do this?

Oh no; but that which that faith lays hold on doth, that faith is said to do. God honours the grace of faith by terming that to be done by it that he doth himself; for it was the power of God, the goodness of God to them, and the justice of God against the sins of these people, that overturned the walls of Jericho. Faith, it was but an empty hand to lay hold upon this power. It was the grace, whereby they went out of themselves, and denied themselves, and gave glory to God, in accomplishing the truth of his word, and his wisdom, and power, and justice. So God did it. But it is said to be done by faith, because, as I said, God honours faith thus much. What strength God and Christ hath, when faith lays hold on them, faith hath that strength, because it builds upon them. Faith sets a man upon God and Christ, and upon the truth of God. Hereupon it comes to be so victorious and conquering a grace as it is, because it carries us to that that doth all. By faith they did this.

But here were other graces likewise that sprang from faith, that helped them also. There was a great deal of patience to go about after that silly fashion with rams' horns seven days together. Here was patience, and perseverance, and hope. But, as I said before, because faith doth enliven all other graces, it gives life to all, and stirs up all, therefore that is named. In the whole chapter the exercise of other graces is attributed to faith, because they draw strength from that to quicken them all, and to stir them all to their several offices. Strengthen faith, and strengthen all other graces whatsoever. Thus you see we have briefly gone over these four main things.

Now, let us by way of proportion raise them higher, and make use of them to other things. To give a little touch. The walls of Jericho represent to us many things.

1. *The kingdom of Satan in general, the power of the devil in himself and in his instruments*, who hinders what he can, our coming out of Egypt to Canaan. He labours to come between us and heaven; to hinder us all he can by all means. He hath walls of many kinds; the strength of tyrants, the subtilty of heretics. What a world of ado was there to bring Israel out of Egypt! God was put to it, as it were, to work so many miracles to bring that poor despised people out of Egypt, to bring them through the Red Sea. When they were in the wilderness, what ado was there to bring them thence! what opposition! And then when they came to Jordan, what miracles were wrought! The division of the waters by the ark coming through; and then the first, the frontier town, that was, as it were, the key to let in all and to stop all, Jericho, the first town for the entrance into Canaan. There was opposition made when they would have entered into Canaan. It is no easy thing to come out of Egypt and to enter into Canaan. It is a mighty work to bring a poor Christian out of the kingdom of Satan, to bring him out of spiritual Egypt through the wilderness of

this life; to bring him through Jordan, those waves of death; to put him into heaven, to bring him at length to his own country, to Canaan; because there is spiritual wickedness stands in the way, both in regard of Satan himself, and in regard of the instruments he useth.

But Christ came 'to destroy the works of the devil,' as it is said 1 John iii. 8; and he himself overcame Satan and triumphed over him, as it is Col. ii. 15. He led him in triumph. He triumphed over Satan himself, and he will triumph over Satan in all his members. As he overcame Satan in himself, so he will overcome in us all: 'For stronger is he that is in us than he that is in the world,' 1 John iv. 4. The Spirit of God, as he is in us, is stronger than Satan. Not only Christ our glorious captain overcame him and is now in heaven, but the Spirit of God in us weak creatures, with faith laying hold upon the word of God, is stronger than he that is in the world; he is stronger than the devil and all that are against us.

2. But besides Satan, *there is in us much opposition that must be subdued before we come to Canaan.* As we saw before in 2 Cor. x. 5, those reasonings and sophistries, proud high thoughts, all must be brought down, because Satan doth join with these; and if it were not for enemies within us, Satan could not prevail over us. As it was Delilah that betrayed Samson, or else the Philistines could not have hurt him, so it is with our own corruptions. There be these walls within us. These betray us to Satan. He could not hurt us but that we betray ourselves.

Now, by little and little all these walls shall fall; not all at once, as the walls of Jericho did, but they shall moulder in pieces by little and little. God by degrees will perfect the work of mortification and sanctification till he make us like his Son Christ, like our husband and head, that we may be fit for so glorious a head.

3. But to come to the particular occasion. Besides other enemies that are between us and heaven, Satan is powerful, and effectual, and strong *in the kingdom of antichrist.* And by all means, that church which is opposite to Christ hath studied to build up walls, to build up Jericho, and to stop the church of Christ, to hinder it what they could. Now, what walls have they built up? As Pharaoh said, 'Let us deal wisely,' Exod. i. 10. How wittily have they gone to work to overthrow the church of God in all times, and to set up themselves and their own kingdom. It were a large discourse; it would take up the whole time to shew their policy and the plots they have had. To give an instance in a few.

How strongly have they built up walls in their own conceit when they had got the whole world almost into subjection to them! Before Luther's time, all the world followed them. They had used the matter so, that kings themselves had betrayed their very crowns to them, they had betrayed their kingdoms, they were rather vassals to them than kings. They had gotten the temporal sword into their hands as well as the spiritual. And they had raised up to themselves a bloody inquisition to suppress all light of truth as soon as ever it sparkled out. All beams of truth were stopped with their bloody inquisition. They thought they had fenced themselves safe enough. Then again, they had disabled all the kings and princes of Christendom. And then because the pope would engage princes to him to strengthen the walls higher, and to make them stronger, the young sons of princes, he would make them cardinals. And then he would arrogate to himself a power absolute to dispense in case of marriage, and oaths, and such like. And besides, what plots have they had for the counterfeiting of authors, for falsifying of authors, purging out true authors, that they might have none give witness against them! What tricks have they to keep people in ignorance, because it is a kingdom of darkness! The Bible they must have, God hath preserved that; but they would have it in an unknown tongue. And what other devices to abuse the people withal. How have they fenced themselves, by applying themselves to humour all sorts of people! For even as the devil enlargeth his kingdom by applying himself to the cursed sinful disposition of men, so doth the pope here upon earth apply himself to the sinful disposition of all sorts of men. There are no kind of men but they have a bait in popery. For loose libertines, there are stews. For others that are of a more reserved and severe disposition, there are monasteries. For superstitious persons, there they have a world of ridiculous ceremonies, devised to themselves of their own brain, and never used in the primitive church. For those that are covetous, they have the riches of the world in their own hands, they have had at least before more than they now have. For proud, ambitious persons, they have honours of all sorts. For the people, they have many carnal liberties for them. And for all the senses of the body, they have something to delight them, to draw people from the power of religion to carnal outward worship. So they have studied and whetted their wits all the ways that might be, to apply themselves to the dispositions of all sorts of men whatsoever, that so they might strengthen the walls of Jericho. I might be large; I give you but a taste.

Well, but what hath God done? God hath infatuate and overthrown their walls, and by weak means. Luther, a poor monk, with a trumpet of rams' horns, with his preaching and with his writing, you see how he shook the walls of Rome, how much they have lost within the last hundred years. The last age, the last century of years, they have lost a great part of this western part of the world, that they had in slavery before; and how? By weak means, as you heard, by the preaching of the gospel, by learning, and knowledge. It is no wonder that the devil hates knowledge and learning. As Luther saith well, 'He hates the quills of geese, because they are instruments to write against them' (*b*). He hath a kingdom of darkness, and hell, and the pope is a king of darkness. Now when the light of knowledge, the light of the word of God, the ordinance of God, when preaching came, these poor trumpets did shake the Church of Rome. As we see in England, the walls of Jericho fell down. By what means? By a child, in a manner, King Edward the Sixth, and after by a woman;* and if the word of God had gone on in like proportion in other places, popery had been lower than it is.

So we see then, that as high as they built, and as much as they fortified, though they be not wholly cast down, yet they are shaken, and that by weak means. Now the way to effect this, that these walls may fall down more and more, it must be by the spiritual means that God will use. We must use the means that God hath appointed us, poor contemptible means, trumpets of rams' horns, the preaching of the word, the discovery of the truth; and by this means we shall more and more gain upon them. And undoubtedly, let them but give free liberty to the preaching of the word in other countries, and we shall see them shortly as heretical, as they term it, even as London and England is. Such a power there is in God's ordinance, the Spirit of God accompanying it, that it carries all before it, it lays all flat, it beats all strongholds down before it.

What shall we do then?

* Elizabeth.—G.

By faith use the means that God hath appointed. The weapons appointed and sanctified by God, they are strong through God to beat down all strongholds. And take heed especially that we do not build up the walls of Jericho again, nor suffer them to build them. You know Joshua pronounceth a curse upon all that should build the walls of Jericho. He should lay the first stone in the death of his eldest son, and the last at the death of his younger; and so, as we have it in the story of Hiel, it was made good. I beseech you, therefore, let every one of us in our place labour to ruinate these walls of Jericho, and take heed how we build them again, or suffer any to build them again.

Quest. What way have we to prevent their building, that the walls of Jericho be not built again? They go about it what they can. We see what course they take. They have all the art of hell to help them, lies and equivocations. How many kings and great ones have they at this day to support and help them, to keep them from falling! They do all that they can to keep life now. How shall we prevent this, that they build not up the walls of this spiritual Jericho again?

Ans. 1. First of all, *every one labour to do what they can in their callings. Magistrates* to execute the laws of the kingdom, which, as those say that are well acquainted with them, are very beneficial to the church of God. Therefore the magistrates in their place should do what appertains to them.

2. *And so for ministers.* The spiritual means whereby such heresies must be confounded, *it is by the breath of the mouth of Christ;* as it is 2 Thes. ii. 8, 'He shall consume him with the breath of his mouth.' For things are dissolved contrary to that way that they were raised at the first, and contrary to that way they were maintained. Popery, as it was raised, so it is maintained, by darkness, and blindness, and ignorance of the word of God and of divine truth. The way to hinder it, therefore, from being built again, is to lay open divine truths, and to plant the ministry. Every one must labour for this, to be faithful in their place and standing. St Paul saith, 2 Tim. iii. 9, 'They shall prevail no longer, because their madness shall be manifest.' How doth that follow? The very manifestation of error hinders the prevailing of it. That is the way to hinder popery from prevailing, to manifest it by preaching, and writing, and such good means. For the demonstration of errors to be so is a refuting of them; for who would willingly be deceived? Therefore the laying open of the madness of popery, and the folly of their devices, it hinders their prevailing. No man willingly would have his soul led into error. Therefore let us lay their errors open in the ministry, and the grounds of them; the danger of popery, how pernicious it is. When this is discovered in the ministry, men, as they love their own souls, will take heed. That is the way therefore to keep the walls of Jericho from being built, to set an able ministry everywhere, and to countenance them, and those that are God's captains to fight his battles against them.

It is a world of hurt that comes to the church by impropriations, especially in the north parts, as we hear too much by reports. In great and mighty parishes to set up poor and weak men, and others wholly to receive the revenues; and that is the reason of the swarm of dangerous papists in those parts. Oh, that these things had been looked to in time! The walls of Jericho had not been built again in those parts so much as they are. This is one main way, the planting of an able ministry; for this painted harlot, she cannot endure the breath of the ministry. It discovers all her painting; it lays her naked and open; she knows it well enough.*

3. Then again, *take heed of the spreading of infections.* Men should be careful this way. They build up their religion thus, that else would fall down more and more. We are so confident in our cause, that we suffer men to read any popish treatises. They on the other side watch all things, so that there cannot a spark of our light break into them, what by their Inquisition, and other courses that they take. Confidence in our cause hath made us careless and secure in this kind. Therefore care this way is one means to help it.

4. And then *encouragement of good learning.* Popery fell with the beginning of good learning. Religion and good learning came in together. If I were in some place I should speak more of this; for, as I said before, it is a dark religion, not only in regard of the religion itself, but it grows and thrives with ignorance and barbarism, and not understanding of arts and tongues. They have helped very much towards the overthrow of these walls of Jericho. 'Every one should contend for the faith once given,' as St Jude admonisheth, ver. 3. Every one, the poorest man, may contend with his prayers. He that saith, 'Thy kingdom come,' what doth he pray for? If he pray in faith, he desires that God would pull down all opposite kingdoms to the kingdom of his Son Christ; that the kingdom of Christ may come, more and more in the hearts of his people; that he may reign everywhere more freely and largely than he doth. Every one may help forward the kingdom of Christ; he may help forward Jerusalem, and pull down Jericho; every one that hath a fervent devotion of prayer.

5. *And by a holy life;* for when men are vicious and carnal, they occasion God,—for not loving and embracing the truth,—to give them up to popish errors and such like. Many ways there be to stop the building up of Jericho.

6. But this is one especial, which this day occasions; that is, *thankfulness to God, a thankful remembrance, how God hath fought for us;* how God hath by little and little ruinated the walls of this Jericho, and hath helped us to build the walls of our Jerusalem. A thankful remembrance is a notable means to hinder the growth of popery; for when we remember their attempts, how God hath cursed and crossed them, it will make us love our religion that God hath witnessed to by so many deliverances, and it will make us hate theirs the more. Therefore it was a worthy work of that reverend bishop, that set out in a treatise all the deliverances that have been from popish conspiracies, from the beginning of Queen Elizabeth's time to this present. It was a worthy work, beseeming that grave and reverend person (*c*). 'Prayer gets blessings, but thankfulness keeps them.' So thankfulness to God for that which is past, for so many deliverances, is a means to preserve God's love and care of us still; that he will be our buckler, and castle, and hold, and all defence; thankfulness will do this.

We are over-prone to look upon civil grievances,—which are to be regarded and helped in season,—but naturally our nature is subject to complain more than to be thankful. We are so sensible of ill as to pray for remedy; but then let us alway be thankful to God for the good we have had these many years together, and the good that still, blessed be God, we enjoy. What cause have we to be thankful, that we are as the 'three young men' in the furnace! All Europe hath been in combustion, and we have been untouched and safe in the midst of the furnace under a quiet government.

* Cf. Memoir, Vol. I. p. 60, *seq.*—G.

What cause have we to bless God, for continuing the liberties of the gospel, whereby the soul is built up in saving knowledge, and ignorance banished! It was a fault in Rehoboam's time, in the beginning of his reign, it was a fault in these men, they could complain of the government of Solomon; and certainly there were many grievances in Solomon's: he was a great builder, and it was not without some cause they complained. Yet notwithstanding Solomon's time was a blessed time, and they had great cause to bless God for the government of Solomon. Now it is very likely in the story that they forgat it, and only lighted upon some grievance. I beseech you, let us in these times stir up our hearts to be thankful; as upon other occasions, so upon occasion of this day we are to bless God for this glorious deliverance, which we have spoken of so oft, again and again; and therefore we need not be much in the particular setting out the facinorous* and prodigious fact, that gives the day occasion to be remembered, as it hath oft done before. Let that remembrance, I say, stir us up to thankfulness, to shew our thankfulness, and love to that truth that God hath defended. 'Hath God been a wilderness to us?' Jer. ii. 31, as the prophet complains. Hath religion done us any harm? Why should we grow cold and lukewarm? Why should we decay in our first-love? Why should we be so unfruitful, when God hath given us so many encouragements to be thankful and fruitful, as he hath done? I beseech you, let us consider with ourselves, if we be not more thankful upon these occasions for these deliverances, and work our hearts to love religion, and to hate popery more, it will be just with God that they shall be thorns in our sides more than they have been, and pricks in our eyes; that we shall see what a dangerous faction they are, and what case we are in. For those that are drunk with the cup of this harlot, it takes away their wits from them. Those that worship images and stocks, they are stocks themselves. Though the danger be great to themselves, yet they labour to make others worse than themselves. There is no trusting to them. We should more fear them than foreign enemies. Both reasons of state, and reasons of religion, and reasons of our own safety, all should be forcible to have a special regard to prevent the growth of popery.

For ourselves, that hear of the destruction of this Jericho, we have heard what Jericho was before it was destroyed. For aught we know, God may destroy Jerusalem, as well as Jericho, and by a worse people than themselves, as the prophet saith, Ezek. xvii. 14, by 'a base people.' It is no matter, though others be worse than ourselves. God, when he plagues his people, will do it by worse than themselves, and cast the rod into the fire when he hath done; 'Asshur, the rod of my wrath,' Isa. x. 5. Therefore let us look to ourselves, that we be thankful to God. It will be no plea that we have been safe thus long, thus many years; for these people of Jericho, God let them alone four hundred years, as it is in Gen. xv. 16, They were threatened, but 'the sins of the Amorites were not yet full.' Jericho was a part of that country; but when their sins were full, then they were destroyed. God had patience four hundred years to the sins of the Amorites, to this people; and at last judgment came upon them fearfully. So howsoever God hath been forbearing and long-suffering towards us, yet let us look about us; oh, destruction may be near. It is not sufficient to think that God will destroy antichrist, that the walls of Jericho shall down. He may do that, and yet he may destroy us. There may be danger towards us too; and it is no comfort to them neither that

* That is, 'wicked to excess.'—G.

God will punish us; for that easeth not their overthrow neither, 'for if he do so to the green tree, what will he do to the dry?' Luke xxiii. 31. If his children be whipped with scorpions, what will he do to rebels? 'If the children of God scarcely be saved, where shall the sinner and ungodly appear?' 1 Pet. iv. 18. If the children taste of the wrath of God, then the enemies shall taste of the dregs of his wrath. It is no comfort for them, for their doom is set down, 'Babylon is fallen,' Rev. xiv. 8. It will not be so much comfort to us that God will destroy them, as it will be to look to ourselves in time before a peremptory decree come forth, to make our peace with God. The king of Sodom and others were delivered by Abraham, but afterwards we see how fearfully they perished. Pharaoh was let alone for a time, yet after he was destroyed in the sea. Jerusalem had warning after warning, yet afterwards it was destroyed. So, though we have had deliverance upon deliverance, yet if we make not more of religion, and grow more in detestation of that religion, that God would have us set ourselves against, it will be just with God to punish us, and to lay us open to them that we have sinfully favoured.

Use. We see what great matters faith will do in the use of means, though they be poor, weak, base means. Therefore let us set upon popish religion, in our places and callings, in a spirit of faith, in the use of means; and let us never think we are too weak; and now they are mighty and strong. It was said to Luther, when he began to write against the pope, Oh, poor monk, get thee into thy cell, and say, Lord have mercy upon thee! dost thou think to overcome the whole world with thy writing? (*d*). So the walls of Jericho may seem so mighty, the opposite power that we are to set against, as if we should lose our labour to set against it; but whatsoever is opposite to Christ, we have a promise it shall be overthrown. Let us in a spirit of faith set upon them in the use of means, and God will make it good, as in former times.

And for all other things that stand between us and heaven, all the walls of Jericho, all opposition, let us set upon them with a spirit of faith in the use of means; for he that hath overcome us,* as I said, will by little and little overcome in us. These corruptions of ours shall fall before the Spirit of God by little and little. And as Haman's wife could tell him, 'If thou begin to fall before that people, thou shalt certainly fall,' Esther vi. 13; so if the work of grace be begun in us, that corruptions begin to fall, undoubtedly and certainly they shall fall. They cannot stand before the Spirit; for grace is in growing, and corruption is in decaying, continually in a Christian.

Quest. Why doth not God all at once subdue these walls of Jericho in us, but by little and little?

Ans. 1. *God will exercise our faith and patience.* We are warriors here in this world. Our life is a warfare, and he will exercise grace in us; he will have us combat with enemies; these inward enemies among the rest.

2. Again, *He will let us see what he hath done for us.* If we were not exercised with enemies, we should not be thankful sufficient for victory over the devil. When we have been vexed with the devil's temptations, then blessed be God and Christ, that at last these troubles are ceased. How much are we beholden to Christ, that hath freed us from the danger of these! We are only annoyed with the trouble. This will make us thankful when we have smarted.

3. *This keeps us likewise from soul-devouring sins.* Less infirmities in us

* Qu. 'for us'?—Ed.

keep us from pride and security. God hath many ends; but to cut off other things, because the point is large, I only give a taste.

Let this comfort us, that the walls of Jericho, that is to say, whatsoever opposeth us in our coming out of the state of nature, and our entrance into the state of heaven, whatsoever opposition is between, shall fall. Therefore let us strengthen our faith in the use of means.

Quest. How shall we strengthen our faith this way?

Ans. Faith is strengthened *by the knowledge of the attributes of him, whom we lay hold upon, whose power doth all.* The more we know him, the more we shall trust him. Let us labour to know God in covenant to be our Father, and to know Christ as he is, in his nature and offices, what he is to us: to know his wisdom, and power, and truth, that there may be a bottom for faith to build on. The more we grow in spiritual knowledge the more we shall grow in faith; and the more we grow in faith, the more we shall grow in other graces, whereby we overcome all our enemies that set against us.

Again, *Let us make use of all former experience to strengthen faith.* Hath God begun the work? Do the walls of Jericho begin to fall? 'He that hath begun a good work will finish it to the day of the Lord,' Philip. i. 6. Let us take in trust the time to come, by experience of God's truth for the time past; for the work of the Spirit is a continued work. The Spirit of God, in subduing our corruptions, he would not have begun if he had meant to have left off and interrupted the work. The Spirit suffers us to fall sometimes, but it is to teach us to stand better afterward. He turns our very falls and slips to our good. Let us strengthen faith, therefore, from former experience, as David did. We have overcome the bear and the lion; therefore let us set on the Philistine, 1 Sam. xvii. 37. And as Joshua set his foot on the necks of the ten kings, and said, 'Thus shall the Lord thy God destroy all thine enemies,' Joshua x. 24, *seq.*, so hath the Spirit of God set his foot as it were upon some corruptions. Thus shall God deal with all corruptions and temptations at length, and never leave the blessed government of us till he have subdued all. Let us rise from one experiment* to another, to strengthen faith. God is alike in all truths. You know in Judges v. 31, saith the holy woman Deborah, 'So let all thine enemies perish.' The heart of that blessed woman was, as it were, enlarged prophetically. When one falls, they shall all fall, there is like reason. See how gloriously Hannah in her song enlargeth her faith, by God's power and goodness, because she had experience in herself. So experience in ourselves or others will enlarge our faith to look for greater matters still from our gracious, powerful God. Thus we ought to labour to strengthen our faith.

And the third thing to help faith in all spiritual oppositions that we meet with, is *daily exercise in using it, to make it brighter continually every day, by working with it upon our enemies.* And in the estate of grace to live by it, both for this present life, to depend upon God for all things, and likewise for necessary grace; as the disciples when they were enjoined a hard duty, 'Lord, increase our faith,' say they, Luke xvii. 5, they go to exercise their faith upon it. If that be increased, all is increased. And so in our callings, exercise it by depending upon God for strength and success. Saith Peter to Christ, 'Lord, at thy word I will cast out the net,' Luke v. 5, though it were very unlikely it should do any good. They had fished all day, and catched nothing, but yet he would wait, and go on still:

* That is, 'experience.'—G.

'At thy word I will cast out the net.' He did it, and the net brake with the multitude of fish. Let us exercise our faith in daily obedience to God, depend upon him in the use of means.

And learn this, to wait in the exercise of our faith; as they that went about the walls of Jericho, they did it seven days. Put case they had done it six, and no more, the walls had stood still. He that hath ten miles to go, and goes but nine, he shall never come to his journey's end. When God hath set down such a time, so long thou shalt wait, and use the means, and depend upon me by faith, in the use of the means; if we be short-spirited, and lengthen and strengthen not our faith in the use of the means, we shall never attain our desire, therefore let us labour to wait. Here is the difference between Christians and others. There is no man but he would be happy if so be it were not for this waiting. If a wicked man should see hell open, would he commit sin if he should see it present? If he should see heaven open, and Christ coming with his reward with him, he would be godly. There is not the vilest wretch in the world but he would be so if these things were present. But because it is only discovered in the word of God, and faith must believe, and wait for the reward, and faith must wait all the time of our life, here is the trial. So that a Christian differs nothing from a worldly man, but in a spirit of faith and waiting, and continuance of that faith in the mean time before a man come to enjoy and receive what he looks for. Faith gives God the glory of all his attributes. The glory of his truth; he hath spoken, and therefore he will make it good. The glory of his wisdom; that he hath found out such a course for us to walk in. The glory of his mercy; that he hath made such promises to such wretches. So all other attributes faith gives glory to. Therefore God glorifies faith, and the special act of faith is waiting: 'If I tarry long, wait thou,' Hab. ii. 3. And we have need of patience. Faith stirs up patience to help and assist it, as we see here, these waited seven days. Remember therefore to exercise faith in continual dependence upon God. Take heed of being short-spirited. Though God defer the rewarding of the righteous, and the punishment of the wicked, yet hold out still. He that hath promised will come in time, and make good that that he hath said in due time. Give God the glory of appointing the fittest time. He is the best discerner of opportunities: 'Our times are in his hand,' Ps. xxxi. 15, all kind of times; therefore let us depend upon him for that; only labour to have a strong spirit of faith, that we may wait his good leisure.

And to help us, do but consider what if we wait a few years, what is that to eternity? I might enlarge the point.

What great matters faith will do both in heaven and earth every way. We see here faith shakes the very earth. God he is the Lord of heaven and earth. The earth is the Lord's. Because these walls were built upon God's earth, we see here one puff of God blows them all down; and faith laying hold upon this casts them down. Though faith doth it not immediately, yet God doth it, because he is laid hold on by faith.

Let us labour therefore to have faith above all other graces. It is the mother grace. It is the grace that is the spring of all graces. If we would have patience, and hope, and love, and perseverance, and constancy together, let us labour to have faith strengthened; and to feed our faith the more, let us look to the word of God, make it familiar to us. The Spirit goes together with the word to strengthen and increase our faith, and that being strengthened, all is strengthened whatsoever.

Now the way to try whether we have this faith or no, not to speak largely of the point, but as the text leads me, is, if we humbly attend upon the means that God hath appointed, though they seem base to carnal reason. As how do we know that these Israelites had faith when they went about the walls of Jericho? Because they have humbled themselves to use the base means that God had appointed, though they were very unlikely. Naaman, out of the pride of his heart, saith he, what are the waters of Jordan? Have not we waters that can do as much? But if the servants had not been wiser than the master, he had gone home a leper as he came, 2 Kings v. 11, *seq.* So when men hear the word preached, they think, Cannot we read good books at home? And for the sacrament, it is a poor ordinance. What is there but wine and bread, and such like? Take heed of a proud heart. God will have weaker means to try us whether we will humble ourselves to his wisdom or no. Where there is true faith it will be careful to use all good means, or else it is a tempting of God, and not a trusting of him, when we do not use the means that he hath sanctified.

And where there is faith, as there will be a careful use of all means, so there will be a care in the use of means, not to depend upon the means, but to trust in God. There will be a joining of both together. Faith doth not take away the use of means, nay, he that is most certain of the end should strive to be most careful of all means used to that end. There ought no man to be more diligent in using the means, than he that is most certain of the end; because he is encouraged to use the means, knowing that he shall not beat the air, that he shall not lose his labour; so if we by faith lay hold upon God for the destruction of antichrist, and that God would subdue our corruptions, and that they shall fall before the Spirit by little and little; if by faith we lay hold upon this, that God will perfect the good work he hath begun in the use of good means: this will stir us up to use all means with cheerfulness and constancy. There are none that are more careful of the means than those that are most sure of the issue. Those that are careless of the means, let them pretend what they will, they are presumptuous persons, they have no faith; for that will stir us up to use the means, and in the use of means to depend upon God. So careful is faith to use the means, as if without them God would do nothing, and yet in the means it is so careful to depend upon God, as if the means could not do anything without God. Thus faith walks between the means and the great God.

Let us go on constantly in living the life of faith, and using all the blessed means that God hath sanctified. God hath sanctified the preaching of the word to beat down all these spiritual walls. Let us go on all our lifetime; and at length the last trump shall sound, another trumpet shall sound, and then not only the walls of Jericho, but the walls of heaven and earth shall fall down, and then we shall enter into that heavenly Canaan, both body and soul. In the mean time, let us exercise faith, and to quicken our faith the more, let us have those blessed times in the eye of our soul, let us see them as present. It is the nature of faith to apprehend things to come as present. Let us see heaven and earth on fire, see Christ coming to judgment. Let us see all the walls down, the graves open, whatsoever opposeth and stands between us and glory, see all gone. Let us see ourselves at the right hand of Christ, and triumphing in heaven. For the Scripture speaks of that that is to come, as if it were past. 'We sit in heavenly places with Christ,' Eph. ii. 6, and we are saved by faith, and we are glorified. Thus the spirit of faith speaks of the glorious times to come, when all enemies shall be trodden under foot. Satan and all enemies whatsoever shall go to their place. The opposite church shall be no longer. When the last trump shall blow we shall all stand together at the right hand of Christ, and be for ever glorious with him.

NOTES.

(*a*) P. 464.—'As that proud cardinal in Germany said, "I confess,"' &c. This saying is imputed to the Cardinal Cajetan, but whether a good authority we do not know.

(*b*) P. 469.—'As Luther saith well, "He hates the quills of geese,"' &c. One of his 'Table Talk' sayings. Cf. note *uu*, Vol. III. page 533.

(*c*) P. 471.—'It was a worthy work, beseeming that grave and reverend person.' The following is no doubt the work referred to by Sibbes:—'A Thankfull Remembrance of God's Mercy, in an historical collection of the great and mercifull deliverances of the Church and State of England since the Gospel began here to flourish from the beginning of Queen Elizabeth.' 1627. 4to. The author was George Carleton, Bishop of Chichester.

(*d*) P. 473.—'It was said to Luther when he began'. A taunt often met with in the contemporary controversies, and one which, at times, flung a shadow of doubt over the great Reformer himself, as witnessed in his 'Table Talk.' G.

THE DEMAND OF A GOOD CONSCIENCE.*

The like figure whereunto even baptism doth also now save us (not the putting away the filth of the flesh, but the answer of a good conscience toward God) by the resurrection of Jesus Christ.—1 PET. III. 21.

THE dependence of these words upon the former is this. The blessed apostle had spoken before of those that were before the flood, and of Noah's saving in the ark, whereupon he mentions baptism: 'The like figure whereunto is baptism, which also saveth us.' 'Christ was yesterday, to-day, and the same for ever,' Heb. xiii. 8. He was the same unto them before his incarnation, and the same unto them that lived in his time, and to us that shall be for ever. All were saved by Christ, and all had several sacrifices that were types of Christ. As there were two cities of the world from the beginning of the world figured out in Cain and Abel, the beginners of both, so God hath carried himself differently to the citizens of both. He always had a care to save his Noahs in the midst of destruction; he had an ark alway for his Noahs. 'God knoweth how to deliver his,' saith the apostle Peter, 2 Pet. ii. 9. It is a work that he hath practised a long time, since the beginning of the world; and for the other that are not his, that are of Cain's posterity, God carries himself in a contrary way to them; he destroys them. But to come to the words, 'The like figure whereunto even baptism doth now save us,' &c. The saving of Noah in the ark was a correspondent answerable type to baptism; for as baptism figures Christ, so did the saving of Noah in the ark. They are correspondent in many things.

1. As all that were *without the ark perished*, so all that are without Christ, that are not engrafted into Christ by faith, whereof baptism was a seal, they perish.

2. And as the same water in the flood *preserved Noah in the ark, and destroyed all the old world*, so the same blood and death of Christ, and his sufferings, it kills all our spiritual enemies. They are all drowned in the

* 'The Demand of a Good Conscience' forms one of the 'Sermons' which compose 'Evangelical Sacrifices' (4to, 1640). Its separate title-page is as follows:—'The Demand of a Good Conscience. In one Sermon, upon 1 Pet. 3. 21. By The late learned and Reverend Divine, Rich. Sibbs: Doctor in Divinity, Master of Katherine Hall in Cambridge, and sometimes Preacher to the Honourable Society of Grayes-Inne. 2 Cor. 1. 12. For our reioycing is this, the testimony of our Conscience, &c. London, Printed by E. Purslow, for N. Bourne, at the Royall Exchange, and R. Harford, at the gilt Bible in Queenes head Alley, in Pater-Noster-Row. 1640

Red Sea of Christ's blood, but [it] preserves his children. There were three main waters and deluges, which did all typify out Christ: the flood, that drowned the old world; the passing through the Red Sea; and the waters of Jordan. In all these God's people were saved, and the enemies of God's church destroyed, whereunto Micah the prophet alludes when he saith, 'He shall drown our sins in the bottom of the sea,' chap. vii. 19. He alludes to Pharaoh and his host drowned in the bottom of the sea. They sunk as lead; so all our sins, which are our enemies, if we be in Christ, they sink as lead.

3. As Noah, when he went to make the ark and to get into it, *was mocked of the wretched world*, so all that labour to get into Christ and to be saved, they are derided.

Yet notwithstanding, Noah was thought a wise man when the flood came; so when destruction comes, then they are wise that get into the ark, that get into Christ before. Many such resemblances there be. I name but a few, because I go on.

'The like figure whereunto baptism also saveth us,' &c.

Here, first of all, in a word, is a description of the means of salvation, how we are saved: 'baptism saveth us.'

Then there is a prevention of an objection, 'not the putting away of the filth of the flesh,' the outward part of baptism.

Then he sets down how baptism saves us, but 'the answer of a good conscience.'

And then the ground of it, 'by the resurrection of Jesus Christ.'

The former I pass over, that I may come to that which I specially intend. I come, therefore, to the prevention* of the objection, which I will not speak much of, but somewhat, because it is a useful point. When he said that baptism saves us, he saith, not that baptism which is a putting away 'the filth of the flesh;' insinuating this, that baptism hath two parts. There is a double baptism: the outward, which is the washing of the body; the inward, which is the washing of the soul; the outward doth not save without the inward. Therefore he prevents them, lest they should think that all are saved by Christ that are baptized, that have their bodies washed outwardly with water. The apostle knew this, that people are naturally prone to give too much to outward things. The devil in people is in extremes; he labours to bring people to extremes, to make the sacraments idols or idle, to make the outward sacrament a mere idol, to give all to that, or to make them idle signs. The devil hath what he would in both. The apostle knew the disease of the times, especially in his time, they attributed too much to outward things. St Paul, writing to the Galatians, he is fain twice to repeat it, 'Neither circumcision availeth anything, or uncircumcision, but a new creature,' Gal. v. 6. You stand too much on outward things. That that God requires especially is the 'new creature.'

So in the Old Testament, when God prescribed both outward and inward worship, they attributed too much to the outward, and let the inward alone. As in Ps. l. 16, God complains how they served him; therefore, saith he, 'What hast thou to do to take my covenant into thy mouth, and hatest to be reformed?' And so in Isa. i. 13, and Isa. lxvi. 3, we see God's peremptory dealing with them: 'I will none of your new moons, I abhor your offerings.' And in Isa. lxvi. 3, 'It was as the cutting off of a dog's neck, the offering of sacrifice;' and yet they were sacrifices appointed by God himself. What was the reason of this? They

* That is, 'anticipation.'—G.

played the hypocrites with God, and gave him only the shell; they brought him outward performances, they attributed too much to that, and left the spiritual part that God most esteems. So our Saviour Christ to the Pharisees, we see how he takes them up: 'Say not with yourselves, We have Abraham to our father,' Mat. iii. 9. They boasted too much of their outward privileges. You see through the current of the Scriptures, those especially that belong not to God, they are apt to attribute too much to outward things. It were well if they would join the inward too, which they neglect. There are two parts of God's service, outward and inward, that is harsh to flesh and blood. As in baptism there are two parts, outward and inward washing; and in hearing the word, is the outward man and inward soul, when it bows to hear what God saith; so in the Lord's Supper, there is outward receiving of bread and wine, and inward making of a covenant with God. Now people give too much to the outward, and think that God is beholding to them for it; but now for the inward, because they are conscious of their lust, they care not for that.

But more particularly, the reason is in corrupt nature.

First, Because the outward part *is easy and glorious to the eye of the world.* Every one can see the sacrament administered, every one can see when one comes and attends, and hears the word of God. They are easy and glorious in the eye of the world.

Second, And then again, people rest in them, because somewhat is done by it *to daub conscience*, that would clamour if they should do nothing, if they were direct atheists. Therefore, say they, we will hear the word, and perform outward things, and being loath to search into the bottom of their conscience, rest in outward things, and satisfy conscience by it. These and the like reasons there are.

Use. Let us take notice of it, *and take heed of the corruption of nature in it;* let us know that God regards not the outward without the inward, nay, he abhors it. He abhors his own worship that he hath appointed himself, if the inward be not there, much more devices and ceremonies of men's own devising. Popery is but an outside of religion. They labour to put off God with the work done. They have an opinion fit to corrupt nature; that is, that the sacrament administered confers grace, without any disposing of the party. One of the chief of them, a great scholar, he will have the water itself to be elevated above its own nature to confer grace, as if grace had any communion with a dead element (*a*). And thus they speak, to make people doat too much upon outward things. I will not stand to confute this opinion. This very text sheweth that the outward part of baptism, without the inward, is nothing; not the washing of the body, but 'the answer of a good conscience,' saith St Peter.

Let us labour, therefore, in all our services of God, to bring especially the spiritual part. The prophet Hosea finds fault with Ephraim: 'They loved to tread out the corn, but not to wear the yoke,' Hosea x. 11. Now the ox that wears no yoke, it is no trouble to tread out the corn; they fed upon the corn as they trod it. 'Thou shalt not muzzle the mouth of the ox that treadeth out the corn,' Deut. xxv. 4. So Christians are like Ephraim. They are content to take the easy part of religion, but to take the yoke, that which is hard, that they love not. Now we must labour to bear the yoke of religion. What the heart doth is done in religion; what the heart doth not, is not done; and there is a kind of divinity, a divine power in all the parts of God's worship that is requisite besides the bringing of the outward man. As in hearing there is required a divine power to make a man hear as he ought to do, to bow the neck of the inward man of the soul. And so to receive the sacrament, more is required than the outward man. There is a form and power in all the parts of religion. Let us not rest in the form, but labour for the power. There is a power in hearing of the word to transform us into the obedience of it, and a power in the sacrament to renew our covenants with God for a new life, and to cast ourselves altogether upon God's mercy in Jesus Christ—besides the outward elements—to have further communion with Christ.

We see what kind of persons those were in 2 Tim. iii. 5, that practised 'a form of religion, without the power.' He names a catalogue of sins there: 'they were lovers of pleasures more than lovers of God.' Yet these people will have a form of religion notwithstanding, but they deny the power of it. But I hasten to that that I will more dwell on.

Use 2. The ministers likewise are *to learn their duty hence, to observe the dispositions of people, and what bars they lay to their own salvation.* If we see them superstitious, that they swell in outward performances, and so are deluded by Satan in an ill state, and feed themselves with husks, then we are to take away such objections as much as we can, as St Peter here, when he had said that baptism answers to the flood. Both shew the deliverance of God's people by the blood of Christ. Ay, saith he, not the outward baptism, the washing of the body, but 'the answer of a good conscience.'

So Christ takes away a secret objection. Say not with yourselves, 'We have Abraham to our father,' Mat. iii 9. And to feed people in their ill humours, this is not the way, but to labour to make them spiritual, for God is a Spirit, and he loves that part of his worship that is spiritual and inward. We shall have no man damned in the church if there were not an inward spiritual part of God's worship, for the worst men of all will be busiest in outward performances, and glory most in it of any other. It is a delusion that brings thousands to hell; and that made me a little dwell upon it. But I go on. 'Not the washing away the filth of the body,'

'But the answer of a good conscience.'

Upon the preventing of an objection and removing their false confidence, he positively sets down what that is that doth save in baptism. Saith he, it is 'the answer of a good conscience.' The scope of the words should have moved the holy apostle to have said thus, 'not the putting off the filth of the body, but the putting off the filth of the soul.' But instead of that he sets down the act of the soul, which is an 'answer of a good conscience to God,' by the resurrection of Jesus Christ.

Where, first of all, you must know this for a ground. Indeed, it is a hard place of Scripture. I will only take that that I think fittest, and raise what observations I think fit for you, that out of that you must know for a ground that—

There is a covenant of grace.

Since God and man brake in the creation, there is a covenant which we call a 'covenant of grace.' God hath stooped so low, he hath condescended to enter into terms of covenant with us. Now, the foundation of this covenant is, that God will be our God, and give us grace and glory, and all good in Christ, the mediator of the new covenant. Christ is the foundation of the covenant, the mediator of the covenant, a friend to both: to God as God, to man as man, God and man in himself and by office; such is his office, as to procure love and agreement between God and man. He being the foundation of the covenant, there must be agreement in him. Now Christ is the foundation of the covenant, by satisfying God's justice, else God and we could never have come to good terms, nor conscience could ever have been satisfied; for God must be satisfied before conscience be satisfied. Conscience else would think God is angry, and he hath not received full satisfaction; and conscience will never be satisfied but with that that God is satisfied with. God is satisfied with the death of the mediator; so conscience being sprinkled with the blood of Christ, applying the death of Christ, conscience is satisfied too. Now, what doth shew that the death of the Mediator is a sufficient sacrifice and satisfaction? The resurrection of Christ; for Christ our surety should have lain in the grave to this day, if our sins had not been fully satisfied for.

Christ is the foundation of the covenant of grace, by his humiliation and by his exaltation, whereof the resurrection was the first degree. Now, in this as in other covenants, there is the party promising, making the covenant, and the parties that answer in the covenant. God promises life everlasting, forgiveness of sins, through the death of Christ, the mediator. We answer by faith, that we rely upon God's mercy in Christ; this is the answer of conscience. Now, this sound answer of conscience, it doth save us, because it doth lay hold on Christ that doth save us. Christ properly saveth us, by his death and passion. An argument of the sufficiency of his salvation was his resurrection. He is now in heaven triumphing; but because there is somewhat in us that must lay hold of this salvation, it is attributed to that that is the instrument of salvation, that is, to the answer of a good conscience. Now, this answer of a good conscience doth afford us this observation, that

There must be something in us before we can make use of what good is in God or Christ.

In a covenant, both parties must agree. There must be somewhat wrought in us that must answer, or else we cannot claim any good by the promises in Christ, or by any good that Christ hath wrought: that is the answer of a good conscience. Or else Christ should save all, if there were not the answer of a good conscience required, that only God's elect children have. But to shew the reasons of this, that there must on our part be this answer.

Reason 1. The reason is partly from the nature of the covenant. There must be consent on both sides, or else the covenant cannot hold; there are indentures drawn up between God and us. God promiseth all good, if we believe and rest on Christ; we again rest upon Christ, and so have interest in all that is good. There is a mutual engagement then in the covenant. God engageth himself to us, and we engage ourselves to God in Christ; and where this mutual engagement is, there the covenant is perfect; as here, there is 'the answer of a good conscience.' That is the first reason, then, from the nature of the covenant, there must be this answer.

Reason 2. The second reason, that there must be somewhat in us, is because *when two agree, there must be a like disposition.* Now, there must be a sanctifying of our nature, from whence this blessed answer comes, before that God and we can agree. There must be a correspondency of disposition. Of necessity this must be, for we enter into terms of friendship with God in the covenant of grace. Now, friends must have the same mind; there must be an answering. Now, this answer is especially faith, when we believe, and from faith, sanctified obedience. That is called the restipulation or engagement of a good conscience to God.

When the promise is made, we engage ourselves to believe, and to live as Christians.

Use. Now from this, that there must be an answer in us, an engagement on our part, I beseech you, let us in general therefore know that we must *search our own hearts for the evidence of our good estate in religion.* Let us not so much search what Christ hath done, but search our own hearts how we have engaged ourselves to God in Christ, that we believe and witness our believing, that we lead a life answerable to our faith, renounce all but Christ. This mutual engagement is in the form in baptism, that was used by the apostles and by the ancient church; for we know that in the ancient church that they that were baptized, they were questioned, Do you believe? I do believe. Do you renounce the flesh, and the world, and devil? I do renounce them. These two questions were made. Now, when they answered this question from a good conscience, truly, faithfully, and sincerely, then they had right in all the good things by Christ. Something alway therefore in the church was required on our part. Not that we answer by our own strength, for it is the covenant *of grace.* Why is it a covenant of grace? Not only because the things promised are promised of grace, but because our part is of grace likewise. We believe of grace, and live holily of grace; every good thought is from grace; it is by grace that we are that we are. All is of grace in the new covenant, merely of grace. God requires not any answering by our strength, for then he should require light of darkness and life of death. There is nothing good in us. He requires obedience, that he may work it when he requires it. For his commands in the covenant of grace, they are operative and working. When he commands us to believe and obey, he gives us grace to believe and obey. It is ourselves that answer, but not from ourselves, but from grace. Yet notwithstanding let us make this use of it, let us search ourselves, though it be not from ourselves, that we answer God's promise by faith and his command by obedience; yet we must have this obedience, though from him, before we can challenge anything at God's hands. It is arrogant presumption to hope for heaven and salvation before we have grace to answer all God's promises and commands, by a good conscience.

To come more particularly to the words, some will have it, 'the questioning,' 'the demand' of a good conscience, but that follows the other; for when we answer truly the interrogatories in baptism, when we believe and renounce, then we may from a good conscience demand of God all the good in Christ. We may call upon him, and pray unto him, Hath not Christ died, and made peace between thee and us? And may we not triumph against all enemies when there is the answer of good conscience? If Satan lay anything to our charge, Christ died, and rose, and sits at the right hand of God: 'Who shall lay anything to the charge of God's people?' Rom. viii. 33. We may, with a heart sprinkled with the blood of Christ now ascended into heaven, answer all objections, and triumph against all enemies. We may go boldly to God, and demand the performance of his promises.

Hence comes all the spirit of boldness in prayer from the answer of a good conscience, for that draws all other after it. Now, to come more particularly to the words, 'the answer of a good conscience.' It would take up all the time to speak of conscience in general, and it were not to much purpose. I will take it as it serves my purpose at this time. A good conscience, in this place, is a conscience peaceable and gracious.

Peace and purity make up a good conscience. To make this clearer, there be three degrees of a good conscience, though the last be here meant especially. There is, first, a good conscience that is troubled, a troubled good conscience; and then a pacified good conscience, and then a gracious good conscience.

1. *A troubled good conscience* is when the Spirit by conviction opens to us what we are in ourselves. He opens our sins, and the danger and foulness of our sins, whereupon our conscience is terrified and affrighted. Therefore this good conscience, whereby we are convinced of our estate by nature, in itself it is a good conscience, and tends to good; for it tends to drive us to Christ. There is a good conscience therefore that hath terror with it.

2. The second degree of a good conscience is that that comes from the other; when we are convinced of sin, and of the misery that comes by sin, then that good conscience *speaks peace to us*. When God shines upon the conscience by his Spirit, from whence there is peace, that is a peaceable good conscience, for God takes this course. After he hath terrified conscience by his Spirit and word, then he offers in the gospel; and not only offers, but commands, us to believe. He offers all good in Christ, and commands us; and not only so, but invites us: 'Come unto me, all ye that are weary,' &c., Mat. xi. 28. Nay, he beseecheth us: 'We beseech you to be reconciled,' 2 Cor. v. 20. He takes all courses. Now, his Spirit going with these entreaties, he persuades the soul that he is our gracious Father in Christ Jesus. Christ hath suffered such great things; and he is God and man, he is willing and able to save us. Considering he is anointed of God for this purpose, hereupon conscience is satisfied, and doth willingly yield to these gracious promises. It yields to this command of believing, to these sweet invitings. This is a peaceable good conscience.

3. Hereupon comes, in the third place, *a gracious good conscience*, which is a conscience, after we have believed, that resolves to please God in all things; as the apostle saith, Heb. xiii. 18, 'We have a good conscience, studying to please God in all things.' We have a good conscience toward God and toward men. When the conscience is appeased and quieted, then it is fit to serve God, as an instrument that is in tune. An instrument out of tune yields nothing but harsh music; so when the soul and conscience is distempered, and not set at peace, it is not gracious. So now you see the order: there is a troubled good conscience, and a peaceable good conscience, and then a gracious heart; for while conscience is not at peace by the blood and resurrection of Jesus Christ, by considering him, and by application of him, there is no grace nor service of God with that heart; but the heart shuns God, it hates God, and murmurs against God. Men think, why should they do good deeds when they believe not? When they cast not themselves upon Christ, and when conscience is not sprinkled with the blood of Christ, they are able to do nothing out of the love of God; and 'whatsoever is not of faith and love, it is sin,' Rom. xiv. 23. The heart cannot but be afraid of God, and wish there were no God, and murmur and repine till it be pacified. That is the reason why the apostles, in the latter part of their epistles, they press conscience of good duties when they had taught Christians before and stablished them in Christ, because all duties issue from faith; if they come not thence, they are nothing. If there be first faith in Christ, then there will be a good conscience in our lives and conversations.

And from the gracious conscience comes the increase of a peaceable conscience. There must be peace before we can graciously renew our covenants to please God; but when we have both these, faith in Christ and a resolution to please God in all things, there comes an increase of peace; for then there is an argument to satisfy conscience, when first of all conscience goes to Christ, to the foundation. I have answered God's command; I have believed, and cast myself upon Christ; I have answered God's promise. He hath promised, if I do so, he will give me Christ with all his benefits; I have yielded the obedience of faith. Hereupon comes some comforts; here is the foundation of this obedience. But then when conscience likewise from this resolves to please God in all things, in the duties to God and man, hereupon comes another increase of peace, when I look to the life of grace in my own heart. For a working, careful Christian hath a double ground of comfort: one, in the command to believe, and in the promise, whether he hath evidences of grace or no; but when he hath power by the Spirit to lead a godly life, and to keep a good conscience in all things, then he hath comfort from the evidence of grace in his own heart, from whence an increase of peace comes. You see what a good conscience is here in this place: 'the answer of a good conscience.' I will not speak largely of it. To come a little further to the point.

Quest. How know we that a man hath a good conscience, a peaceable good conscience, when it is troubled? For here is the difficulty, a conscience is never so peaceable and gracious but there is a principle of rebellion in us, the flesh, that casts in doubtings, and stirs up objections, as indeed our flesh is full of objections against God's divine truth. There be seeds of infidelity to every promise, and of rebellion to every command in the word. How shall a man know that he hath a peaceable good conscience in the midst of this rebellion?

Ans. 1. Let him look *if the conscience answer God in the midst of opposition and rebellion.* My flesh and blood saith thus, My sins are great, and Satan lays it hard to my charge; yet notwithstanding, because God hath promised and commanded, I cast myself upon God. Let us ask our own hearts and consciences what they say to God, what is the answer to God. We see what Job saith: 'Though he kill me, yet I will trust in him,' Job xiii. 15; flesh and blood would have shewed its part in Job, as if God had neither respected nor loved him; yet when Job recovered himself, 'Though he kill me, I will trust in him.' So a man may know, though conscience be somewhat troubled; yet it is a gracious peaceable conscience if peace get the upper hand, and grace subdue corruption, when the conscience, so far as it is enlarged by God's Spirit, can check itself. 'Why art thou disquieted, O my soul?' Ps. xlii. 5. Why art thou troubled? Trust in God. Trust in God reconciled now in Christ. When conscience can lay a charge upon itself, and check itself thus, it is a sign that conscience hath made this gracious answer.

2. Again, one may know, though conscience be troubled somewhat, yet it is a gracious peaceable conscience *when it always allows of the truth of God in the inward man.* Whatsoever the flesh say, the word is good, the commandment is good, the promise is good; as St Paul saith, 'I allow the law of God in my inward man,' Rom. vii. 22. By this a man may know, though his peace be somewhat troubled, that yet, notwithstanding, there is the answer of a good conscience.

3. Again, *when a man can break out of trouble, and such an estate* as the

devil weakens our faith by; for he useth the troubles of the church, and our own troubles, to shake our faith, as if God did not regard us: now when conscience can rise out of this, as in Ps. lxxiii. 1, 'Yet God is good to Israel; yet, my soul, keep silence to the Lord.' Though things seem to go contrary to a man, as if God were not reconciled, as if he had not part in Christ, 'yet, my soul, keep silence, and God is good to Israel.' This conflict shews that there is a gracious part in the soul, and that conscience is a gracious conscience. It is said here, it is 'the answer of a good conscience towards God.'

For conscience, indeed, hath reference to God, and that will answer another question; for conscience, as it performs holy duties, as it is a gracious conscience, it looks to God.

Quest. Whether may a man know, or how shall he know, that he doth things of conscience? whether he be in the state of grace, and doth things graciously?

Ans. He may; for why is conscience set in man but to tell him what he doth, with what mind he doth it, in what state he is? This is a power of the soul which conscience shews. A man may know what estate he is in, and whether he perform things graciously or no.

Quest. Now how shall a man know whether he doth things of conscience or no?

(1.) First, *Whatsoever the answer of conscience is, it is towards God.* If a man do things from reasons of religion, if a man be charitable to his neighbour, if he be just and good, if it be from reasons of religion, because God commands him, this is a good conscience. A good conscience respects God and his command. What we do for company or for custom is not from a good conscience. A good conscience doth things from God, with reasons from God, because he commands it. It is God's deputy in our hearts.

(2.) Again, what we do from a good conscience we do *from the inward man*, from an inward principle, from the inward judgment, because we think it is so, and from an inward affection. When we have not a right judgment of what we do, and do it not out of love, and from the inward man, we do it not out of a good conscience. What is done out of conscience is done from the inner man. Therefore in all our performances let us examine ourselves, not what we do, but upon what ground we do it, in conscience to God, to obey him in all things. I cannot dwell upon these things.

The answer of a good conscience, that saves us, together with baptism; when there is the answer of a good conscience, then baptism seals salvation. To come more near to the answer of a good conscience in baptism.

Obj. You will object, If the answer of a good conscience in baptism do all, and not the outward washing of the body, why are children baptized then; they cannot make the answer of a good conscience?

Ans. I answer, The place must be understood of those of years of discretion. For infants that die in their infancy we have a double ground of comfort concerning them. First, they are within the covenant. Have they not received the seal of the covenant, which is baptism? And however they actually answer not the covenant of grace by actual believing, yet they have the seed of believing, the Spirit of God in them, and God doth comprehend them by his mercy, being not able to comprehend him. Nay, we that are at years of discretion are saved by God's comprehending and embracing us. We are comprehended of him, as the child is of the nurse or of the mother. The child holds the nurse, and the nurse the child. The child is more safe from falling by the nurse and the mother's holding of it, than by its holding of them. Those that are at years must clasp and grasp about Christ, but Christ holds and comprehends them; much more doth God comprehend those that are children, that are not able to comprehend him. For those that live to years of discretion, their baptism is an engagement and obligation to them to believe, because they have undertaken, by those that answered for them, to believe when they come to years; and if, when they come to years, they answer not the covenant of grace and the answer of a good conscience, if they do not believe, and renounce Satan, all is frustrate. Their baptism doth them no good, if they make not good their covenant by believing and renouncing. It is spoken, therefore, of those that are of years of discretion. We leave infants to the mercy of God. Those, therefore, that are at years of discretion must have grace to answer the covenant of grace by believing and renouncing. To come, therefore, to ourselves.

We that will answer to the covenant made in baptism must perform it, especially that that we then covenanted. What was that? We answered that we would believe. Dost thou believe? I believe every article of the faith. And do you renounce the devil and all his works? I do. Therefore, unless now we believe in Christ, and renounce the devil, we renounce our baptism. It doth us no good. There are divers kinds of people that overthrow their own baptism.

Those that live in sins against conscience, they do renounce their baptism in some sort, those that feed their corruptions; for in baptism we are consecrated in soul and body to God, we are given up to him, 'we are not our own,' 1 Cor. vi. 20; his name is called on us; we are called Christians. Therefore our eyes are not our own, our hands are not our own, our thoughts and affections are not our own. There must be a renouncing and a denial of all sin, as far as it is contrary to Christ's spirit. Those, therefore, that labour to feed their corruptions, what do they else so far but renounce their baptism, and under the livery of Christ serve the enemy of Christ, the devil, that they should renounce? Those that feed their eyes with seeing of vanity, and their ears with filthy discourse; those that suffer their feet to carry them to places where they infect their souls; those that, instead of renouncing their corruptions, feed them, and their hearts tell them they cherish those corruptions they should renounce by baptism: what shall we think of these? And yet they think to be saved by Christ; 'God is merciful,' and 'Christ died,' when they live in a continual renouncing of baptism.

For a use therefore of exhortation, if so be that this be the effectual baptism, the chief thing that we ought to stand on, this answer of a good conscience, then I beseech you let us all labour for this echo, for this answer: when God saith, 'Seek ye my face,' to answer, 'Thy face, Lord, will I seek,' Ps. xxvii. 8; when he saith, 'I will be your God,' to answer, 'We will be thy people.' When he saith in the ministry, 'Believe,' to answer, 'Lord, I believe, help my unbelief,' Mark ix. 24. Let us labour to echo: this holy echo is the answer in the covenant of grace.

This answer of our faith is set down in Scripture alway when it speaks of the estate of those that are in the covenant of grace. It is mentioned on our part that we take God for our God, and Christ for our Christ: 'My beloved is mine, and I am my beloved's,' Cant. ii. 16, and vi. 3. There is a mutual owning of both sides. Therefore, if we would answer the covenant of grace, let us work our hearts to answer. When we hear in the ministry, and in the covenant of grace, answer, Lord, I desire to believe this; and when there is anything commanded, let our hearts answer, and desire God to bow our inward man to obedience, that we may be pliable. Let us labour to have that free spirit that holy David prays for, Ps. li. 12. That was stopped by reason of his sin; for when we renew sins against conscience, we stop the mouth of our prayers, that we cannot go to God; we stop the mouth of conscience, that we cannot go boldly to God; therefore he had then lost that freedom of spirit. Let us labour to be pliable to the Spirit, ready to answer God in all that we are exhorted to, and to yield the obedience of faith to all the promises. That is the state of those that are in the covenant of grace; there is the answer of a good conscience. Therefore let us resolve to take this course, if we would attain the answer of a good conscience.

First of all, labour *that our consciences may be convinced of the ill that is in us*, that we may have a good troubled conscience: first, that we may know thoroughly what our estate by nature is; and then labour, in the second place, *to have peace*, and then raise and renew our purpose to serve God in all things; and to try the truth of this, let us put interrogatories to ourselves; let us ask ourselves, Do I believe? do I not daub with my heart? do I obey? do I willingly cast myself into the mould of God's word, and willingly obey all that I hear? do I not deceive myself? Let us propound these interrogatories: 'God is greater than our conscience,' 1 John iii. 20. If we answer God with reservations, I will answer God in this, and not in this,—I will yield to religion as far as it may stand with my own lusts and advantage;—this is not the answer of a good conscience. What is done to God must be done all; what is done zealously and religiously, hath respect to all God's commandments and promises, to one thing as well as another. If our hearts tell us there are reservations from false grounds, here is not 'the answer of a good conscience.' Therefore let us search ourselves, and propound questions to ourselves, whether we believe and obey or no, and from what ground we do it.

And let us make use of our baptism upon all occasions, as thus,

1. *Satan hath two ways of tempting. One is, he tempts to sin, and then he tempts for sin*, to accuse our consciences to make a breach between God and us, that we dare not look upon God. When he tempts us, or our corruptions move us, or the world by allurements would draw us to any sin, let us think of our baptism, and the answer we have made there, and make use of it. Is this agreeable to the promise I made? Surely I have renounced this. Shall I overthrow my own promise? I make conscience to make good my promise to men, and shall I break with God? I have promised to God to renounce the flesh, the world, and the devil; to renounce all these corruptions. Let us have these thoughts when we are solicited to sin, when proud nature would have us set up the banner of pride. I have renounced these proud affections; I shall overthrow my baptism if I yield. And so for the enlarging of our estates, or for getting up to honour to please men's humours, to break the peace of my conscience. These things we have renounced, the world and the vanities of it in our baptism.

The life of many is nothing but a breach of their vow and covenant in baptism. How will they look at the hour of death, and the day of judgment, that God should keep his promise with them to give them life everlasting, when they never had grace to keep touch* with him, notwithstand-

* Qu. 'troth'?—Ed.

ing their engagements in baptism and their so often repeating it at the communion, and their renewing of their vows when they have been sick? How can we look for performance on God's part, when we have not had grace to perform our part, but our whole life hath been a satisfying of our base lusts! Let us make that use in temptations to sin; let us fetch arguments against sin from our baptism, from the answer that we made then; for we must make good now that that was made then, or else it is in vain.

2. Again, *when we are solicited by Satan to be discouraged*, let us consider that we are baptized 'in the name of the Father, and of the Son, and of the Holy Ghost;' and consider that the promise is made whensoever we repent, without any exception of time, nay, though we have broke with God,—for Satan will use that as a chief weapon, 'Thou hast fallen, thou hast fallen,'—yet as it is Jeremiah iii. 1, *seq.* Though a man will not take his wife after a breach, yet God transcends us; he is God, and not man. Therefore, after breaches, if we yet answer his command and his promise,—for the command of believing is upon us while we live,—if we believe, and 'confess our sins, we shall have mercy,' if we come and cast ourselves upon Christ. Therefore, after relapses, let not Satan abuse them to make us despair. Baptism is a seal of our faith, and faith is enjoined us all the days of our life. All this time of life is a time of grace, and we are commanded to repent and believe. Let not Satan therefore discourage us after sin; let us go to our baptism. It is a seal to us of faith and repentance whensoever we believe and repent.

3. When we are solicited *to distrust in God for the things of this life any way*, as if God cared not for us, let us consider that we have answered, that 'we believe in God the Father Almighty;' therefore he is our Father, he knows what is good for us, and he loves us. He is an almighty God. It is an article of our faith that we have answered to: let us make it good upon all temptations in that kind. Doth not God care for us? He had an ark for Noah in the worst times, when the flood overwhelmed the whole world. So if there be the answer of a good conscience, he will have an ark for his Noahs, to save, and protect, and defend us; he is a Father Almighty. Let us know the grounds of our religion, the articles of our faith, the grounds and foundation of our faith. Let us consider the good things promised there, and consider withal that we have all engaged ourselves to believe those things, and to make use of our faith upon all occasions. Those that cannot read, if they have no other, let them look on these two books, the book of their baptism and the book of conscience. They would be sufficient to instruct them. Some people pretend ignorance. Consider what thou art baptized to: the grounds of religion; consider there what thou hast renounced; consider in particular whether this thing that thou art moved to be God's or the devil's command, and answer Satan and thy lusts by not answering of them; give them their answer, and tell them a good conscience must answer God's command and promise. But they must have their answer by denial, by this answer of a good conscience. Those that cannot read, and are not learned, let them make use of the learning of their baptism. There is a world of instruction and comfort, a treasury of it in baptism. I dare be bold to say, if any Christian, when he is tempted to any sin, to despair or discouragement, if he consider what a solemn promise he hath made to God in baptism, it would be a means to strengthen his faith, and to arm him against all temptations. There is no man sins, but there is a breach with God first in wronging the

promise he hath engaged himself to in baptism. We all that are here have been baptized, let us learn to make more conscience of this blessed sacrament than we have done, and let us labour to have the answer of a good conscience at all times.

What a comfort is it when our hearts and consciences makes a gracious answer to God in believing and obeying, and in renouncing all God's and our enemies! What a comfort is such a conscience! It will uphold us in sickness, in death, and at the day of judgment, in all ill times in this life. A conscience that hath answered God by believing his promises, and hath renewed the covenant to obey God in all things, what a wondrous peace hath it! Let the devil object what he can; let our unbelieving hearts object what they can, yet notwithstanding, if it be a renewed sanctified conscience, it can out of the privity of its own act say, I have believed; I have cast myself upon God's mercy in Christ; I have renounced these motions, and suggestions, and courses, and though I be overcome with temptations, yet I heartily hate them. What a comfort is this!

Conscience, it is either the greatest friend or the greatest enemy in the world. It is the chiefest friend when it is privy to itself of this resolute answer, that it hath obeyed God in all things. Then conscience is our friend, it speaks to God for us at all times. Then again at the hour of death, what a comfort it is that we have this answer of a good conscience, especially at the day of judgment, when we can look God in the face. A sincere heart, a conscience that hath laboured to obey the gospel, and to keep covenant with God, it can look God in the face. For what in the covenant of grace goes for perfect obedience, but sincerity and truth? God requires that. When the heart can say with Hezekiah, 'Lord, thou knowest that I have walked perfectly before thee,' Isa. xxxviii. 3; Lord, I have believed, and laboured to express it in my life and conversation, though with much weakness, yet in truth; this sincerity will make us look God in the face, in the hour of death, and at the day of judgment, and in all troubles in this life.

A Christian that hath the answer of a good conscience, he hath Christ to be his ark in all deluges (*b*). Christ saves us not only from hell and damnation, but in all the miseries of this life. If anything come upon us for the breach of God's covenant,—as God threateneth, Lev. xxvi. 21, *seq.* 'to send war and famine,' &c., for the breach of his covenant,—what a comfort is it then for such as have kept the covenant! For then God hath an ark for such in ill times; for every deliverance in evil times, it comes from the same ground as the deliverance from hell doth. Why doth God deliver me from hell and damnation? Because he loves me in Christ, and that moves him to deliver me in evil times, if I keep a good conscience; and that love that gives me heaven, gives me the comforts of this life. If I labour to have this answer the apostle speaks of, what a comfort is this in the worst times?

Those that live in rebellion, and make no conscience of their vows and covenants to God, that they have made and repeated ofttimes, and renewed in taking of the Lord's supper, but go on still in their sins, alas! what comfort can such as these have! How can they look for an answer from God of any promise that he hath made, when their lives are rebellious. Their conscience tells them that their lives do not witness for God in keeping covenant with him, but they rebel against him. Their hearts tell them they cannot look to heaven for comfort. They carry a hell in their bosom, a guilty conscience; they do not labour to be purged by the blood of Christ, nor labour for the Spirit of God to sanctify them, in renewing them to holy obedience to God. Those that have their conscience thus stained, especially that purpose to live in sin, they can look for nothing but vengeance from God. It is not known now who are the wisest people. In the times of trouble, and at the hour of death, at such times it will be known that they are the wisest people that have made conscience of keeping their covenant with God, of renewing their covenant with God, first, in all things that would serve him better, and then when they have renewed their covenant with God, as we have cause now indeed, if ever, to renew them, when we are warned by public dangers; or when we have cause to take occasion to renew our covenants that we made with God in baptism, to bind our consciences to closer obedience; and those that have renewed their covenant, and have grace to keep it, those are wise people. We see in the current of Scripture, in dangerous times there was still renewing of their covenants with God. And those that God delights in, he puts his Spirit into them, that they shall be able, by the help of his Spirit, to keep their covenant in some comfortable measure; and those God will choose and mark out in the worst times.

NOTES.

(*a*) P. 480.—'One of the chief of them, a great scholar, he will have the water itself to be elevated,' &c. Query, Bellarmine? It is, however, a commonplace of the Baptismal controversy.

(*b*) P. 490.—'He hath Christ to be his ark in all deluges.' This recalls the title of one of Brooks's most searching and valuable books, viz., his 'Ark for all God's Noahs in a Gloomy Stormy Day,' 1662. G.

A GLIMPSE OF GLORY.*

According to his divine power, who hath given unto us all things that pertain to life and godliness, through the knowledge of him who hath called us unto glory and virtue.—2 PETER I. 3.

YOU have often heard in these two verses, how the apostle lays down the groundwork of that his prayer, which he had made in the second verse, wherein he wishes the multiplication of grace and peace unto them, 'through the knowledge of God, and our Lord Jesus Christ.' And further, in these verses he makes manifest, that we have a grant and gift given us of all things pertaining to life and godliness, by that same way by which he had formerly wished unto them the multiplication of grace and peace, 'through the knowledge of him who hath called us unto glory and virtue,' which in the fourth verse he clears, and shews that by the virtue of God's calling on his part, and our acknowledgment on our part, he hath given unto us those precious promises by which we may be, and are, made partakers of the divine nature, of which a sure sign and evidence is, that such 'do fly the corruption which is in the world through lust.'

Something does yet remain of the third verse untouched, and then, God assisting us, we shall come unto the fourth.† In the third verse, the sum whereof you have heard, we have considered,

1. A gift: 'he hath given us.'
2. The fountain from whence: 'his divine power.'
3. The kind of gift: 'things pertaining to life and godliness.'
4. The extent thereof: 'all things.'
5. The means of conveyance by which this great gift is made ours: 'by the knowledge of him who hath called us to glory and virtue.'

Knowledge, then, is the means by which we make claim to, and make use of, this great charter, grant, and gift of God. Not by every divine

* 'A Glimpse of Glory' forms No. 20 of the original 'Saints' Cordials,' 1629. It was withdrawn in the after-editions. Its separate title-page is as follows:—'A Glimpse of Glorie. In One Sermon. Wherein is shewed, The excellency and necessity of a particular calling. What our calling to glory is. Divers particulars to ravish the soule in admiration of it. &c. Prælucendo Pereo. Vprightnes Hath Boldnes. 1 Cor. 2. 9. But as it is written, Eye hath not seene, nor eare heard, neither have entred into the heart of man the things which God hath prepared for them that love him. London, Printed in the yeare 1629.'—G.

† The other sermons have not been preserved.—G.

knowledge of God, nor by a general knowledge of every branch of divinity, but by the knowledge of him only who 'calleth us to glory and virtue.' Then, I say, the immediate or mediate calling of God and Christ is considerable, or both if you will. This is that we must take knowledge of, if we mean to make claim either to piety in this world, or life in that to come. If once we come to have, and be assured of this calling, then therewith all things also pertaining to life and godliness are given us. And the reasons thereof are,

1. Such is the efficacy of this calling; 'not of men, but of God.'
2. Such is the fidelity of him who calleth us.
3. Such is the continual supply he will make of all things to us.

If he hath called us, he will supply us with all things, with piety here, and crown us hereafter in glory.

Thus far we went. Now let us go on. Something yet remains to be handled of the conveyance, where he saith, 'He hath called us. This word *us* hath his proper weight, and must not slightly be passed over. For although we have already spoken of calling in general, and the necessity thereof, yet now it is also fit to consider thereof in particular for our proper interest therein; for, as it is not sufficient to have a general knowledge of God in his power, justice, mercy, goodness, or other his attributes, or of Christ in his person and function, but I must know how he is merciful and good unto me, how he justifies and conveys life to me,—for unless we know God in Christ in particular, the general will not serve,—to know only that there is a covenant, a gospel, and life therein, that there is a Mediator, thou mayest know all this and more, and yet it be unprofitable to thee; so it will not suffice us to know there is a calling to glory and virtue, but in particular we must know him calling us to glory and virtue; for if we cannot say, He hath called *us*, we have small reason to rejoice, or be content of our estate. I enlarged this the last day by the similitude of a rich inventory and a will; a man may have a rich inventory, and read of many brave things and moveables therein, and know them also, but unless from the gift of the testator he may make claim to somewhat given him by name in the will, he is a poor man, for all his rich inventory. So is it of calling; a man may have a general calling, but he must have it by name: 'Who hath called *us* to glory and virtue.'

The point then is,

Doct. 1. *That whereby a Christian may have title, interest, and comfort, in life and glory.* It is not a knowledge of calling in general, but of that particular calling of ourselves to glory and virtue. This doth interest us in the promises of God. See Acts ii. 39, where, after they had been pricked with his sermon, he says, to comfort them, and invite all to hope and seek, 'For the promise is made to you and to your children;' and then he adds the condition, 'Even to as many as the Lord our God shall call.' No calling, no promise. Nay, further, without this there is no encouragement to holiness. 1 Tim. vi. 12, there Paul wills Timothy 'to fight the good fight of faith, to lay hold upon eternal life;' but on what ground is this? 'Whereunto thou art also called.' This is the reason why he is encouraged to lay hold; God had sanctified, and made a change in him, therefore he had good reason to lay hold of eternal life. So I would have every one of you know, that it is a command of God that every man should make 'his calling and election sure,' 2 Peter i. 10, as is shewed in the tenth verse of this chapter, where my text is. And for this, that we may be stirred up unto it, see both reason and example.

The reason is, because by this knowledge of our calling we draw home to our election. See for this Rom. viii. 30: 'Whom he called, them also he justified; and whom he justified, them also he glorified,' and so elected and predestinated.

By our calling, therefore, which is by an eternal purpose and grace of God in time, changing and renewing us unto holiness of life, we come to know the eternal decree of God, which otherwise were presumption to search, and may not be looked unto. For, as a prince's secret mind is made known by edicts and proclamations, which before we durst not search into, neither could know, so when God's secret counsel to execution is manifested, by changing our hearts, by calling us from the world to an holy calling, in a sanctified life: this, then, is no presumption, but duty in us, by our calling, to judge of our election, and so of our calling to glory and virtue.

If you look for an example of this, see that of St Paul, Gal. ii. 20, where that Paul gives a proof of his hope of life and calling, says, 'Nevertheless I live; yet not I, but Christ liveth in me: and the life which I now live in the flesh, I live by the faith of the Son of God, who loved me, and gave himself for me.' What doth Paul mean here? Doth he mean to engross unto him only, and make a monopoly of Christ? No; but he invests and puts himself into the common inheritance of the saints, because Christ loved him, and had given himself for him, because Christ dwelt in him, and that he had attained to lead a holy life. This was the ground of his assurance to eternal life, and of his calling to glory and virtue.

Obj. But some may object, and say, What speak you of St Paul? This was peculiar unto him, he was a chosen vessel, others cannot attain the like; chiefly the papists, they object most against this, who would have no assurance of calling but by special revelation. But the apostle, 1 John iv. 16, saith far otherwise. There he saith not, *we hope*, for he knew so weak a word could not express so great a matter and such assurance as he was about to declare unto them, but 'we *have known* and *believe* the love wherewith God hath loved us.' To know God's calling, and not our interest therein, it is a punishment, rather than any comfort unto us; as Christ speaketh of the Jews, Mat. viii. 11, 'For I say unto you, That many shall come from the east and west, and shall sit down with Abraham, and Isaac, and Jacob in the kingdom of heaven. But the children of the kingdom shall be cast out into utter darkness.' It is a small comfort to the children of the kingdom to know much, and yet to be thrust into utter darkness; but we must labour to know and believe this love of God to us, as the apostle did. Not that I exclude hope from faith, for though there be a distinction between them, yet there can be no separation; faith hath ever hope with it: a strong faith, a strong hope; a weak faith, a weak hope; a staggering faith, a staggering hope; a pale faith, a pale hope; but this we must do, make it our own, know it, believe it, apprehend it for our own. Many may know Christ in a sort, but not apprehend him. What is my knowledge, but so much the more misery to me, if I apprehend not Christ? For this I must crave leave to tell you a tale which shall make this I say good. There was not long ago a revolting wretch, one Francis Spira, beyond seas, who in the midst of his torments and despair, being told of the mediation of Christ's justification, the virtue of his blood, and merits of the same, burst out in this strange unexpected speech, 'I know all this, and more than any of you, and yet I cannot lay hold thereof to me' (*a*).

Then further, let us by the way add one point more, which formerly in part I touched.

Doct. 2. *That this knowledge of our particular calling is one of the strongest motives unto all goodness*, against that opinion of the papists, that say this doctrine opens a door to all licentiousness. Nay, it is so far from opening a door to all licentiousness, that like that angel of paradise, which with a flaming sword was set to keep the tree of life, he shuts all such liberty and licentiousness out of doors. So we see the apostles in their opinions still urge holiness and sanctification from this ground of the assurance of calling and election. Gal. v. 13, the apostle wills them 'not to use their liberty as an occasion to the flesh;' but on what grounds presseth he this? 'Ye have been called unto liberty.' Eph. iv. 2, he desires them 'to forbear one another in lowliness and meekness, endeavouring to keep the unity of the Spirit in the bond of peace.' But on what ground? 'That ye walk worthy of the vocation wherewith you are called.' Col. iii. 12, he exhorts them 'to put on bowels of mercies, kindness, humbleness of mind, meekness, and long-suffering, forbearing and forgiving one another.' But on what ground? 'As the elect of God, holy and beloved.' I might mention many places to this purpose; take this one more: 1 Thes. v. 9, after he hath exhorted them unto 'watchfulness and sobriety, to be sober, putting on the breastplate of faith and love, and for an helmet, the hope of salvation.' What is his ground? 'For God hath not appointed us to wrath, but to obtain salvation through our Lord Jesus Christ.' He that hath no assurance of this calling can have little comfort in performing of holy duties. A fearful, doubting soul lives in much vexation. Now I come to the uses, which are three.

1, Confutation; 2, trial; 3, instruction.

Use 1. The first is *against all such as oppugn this doctrine*, chiefly the papists, who are for that, that a man should not inquire after the assurance of his salvation. Such kind of men, I pray you what do they but do as much as in them lieth to overthrow and pluck up the root of faith, and of all obedience unto God? Oh, what should water my heart, and make it melt in obedience unto my God, but the assurance and knowledge of the virtue of this most precious blood of my Redeemer, applied to my sick soul, in the full and free remission of all my sins, and appeasing the justice of God? What should bow and break my rebellious hard heart and soften it, but the apprehension of that dear love of my Saviour, who hath loved me before I loved him, and now hath blotted out that hand-writing that was against me? What should enable my weak knees, hold up my weary hands, strengthen my fainting and feebled spirit in constant obedience against so many crosses and afflictions, temptations and impediments, which would stop up my way, but the hope of this precious calling unto glory and virtue? Down, then, with this false opinion and perverse doctrine, which overthroweth all the comfort of godliness, faith, and obedience to God.

Use 2. The second is, *that every man then must try his title, what calling he hath*. The trumpet of God is come and sounded loud in our ears; I mean, as it is Titus ii. 11, 'The grace of God, that bringeth salvation unto all men, hath appeared, teaching us to deny all ungodliness and worldly lusts,' &c. Not that it bringeth salvation unto all men, but unto all nations, to some of every sort. Now inquire whether this grace be come home unto thy heart, what power thou hast against thy corruptions, what sanctification and calling thou hast.

Exception. There is no man, I hope, that from hence needs to gather any matter of despair or discomfort, for that which hath not been it may be. God may have a time for thee; for who knows, but even whilst now that we are speaking of calling, the Lord may call thee, and touch thy heart with a sense of his love. I say to thee, be not discouraged, for there may be a time for thee. But I say unto such who think they are called, Art thou called? Hast thou had comfort of thy calling? Deceive not thyself; look from whence thou art called; if he have called thee, as it is 1 Peter ii. 9, out of darkness, he hath called thee to light, yea, out of darkness into his marvellous light. Hast thou seen a rare light in the gospel? Hast thou seen what palpable darkness thou hast been in? Hath he enlightened thee now from darkness into holiness, that now thou delightest thyself to do the works of God? If thus thou be called, then hath he called thee 'to a fellowship in his Son.' Shew me what conformity hast thou with him? Believest thou in him? at least, dost thou receive him offered unto thee? If thou receive him offered to thee, then cheer up thy heart, thou art called; so saith John i. 12, 'But as many as received him, to them gave he power to become the sons of God,' &c. What apprehension and feeling of this there wants, if thou hast received Christ, yet power is given thee to be the son of God, thou mayest have it.

Further, I say unto such, what peace hast thou obtained through him? Having him, thou hast peace; 'he is our peace.' Look what thou once wast, look now, what remission of sins, what dominion thou hast over them, what peace of conscience thou hast obtained! His blood hath a purging and a cleansing virtue to wash us from all sin, in delight, love, and approbation, as Heb. ix. 13, the apostle sheweth, 'that if the blood of bulls and goats, and the ashes of an heifer, sprinkling the unclean, sanctified them, as to the purifying of the flesh, how much more shall the blood of Christ, who through the eternal Spirit offered himself without spot to God, purge your consciences from dead works, to serve the living God!' Hast thou then peace, and a clean conscience with God and man? Hath he made it clean? Hast thou seen thy sin and thy impiety? and hath he cleansed thee from it by means of life? Hast thou in thy body been dead, and then art thou alive, and quickened from the dead? Hast thou found thyself to be alive? If thus thou be called, thou art also certainly justified. There is a calling and an election begun, that shall lead thee to life and glory. Be of good cheer then: thou mayest rejoice in peace; thou art certainly called to glory and virtue.

Yet to go on; he says, 'called us.' This was necessary to be stood upon in particular, that a man might not be deceived of his estate. For as there are some who presume on false and no titles, having no right, so there are some who have good title to glory, yet dare not make claim to the same, nor have any comfort thereof: as, on the contrary, we see some will boast of faith, and yet not know what it meaneth; but a liking of godliness in others, a seeming show of it in themselves, haunting of good company, for some respects, and the like, makes a shew of faith; when those others who cannot see their calling and election, nor their title, are indeed more happy. For whence is their discomfort? Not because they want a title, but because they see it not, for either affliction and crosses hath so slurred and dimmed the print, that they cannot for the present read it; or by temptations, Satan hath cast a blot upon their evidence, that they know it not; or their eyes are so full of tears, and their mind carried, that they cannot duly consider thereof, though indeed their title be good still. Even as a print of a seal, though the print be dimmed, and not apparent, yet is a good sufficient evidence in law, though it be not so fairly stamped, and the seal so evident, as that of other seals: so I say unto thee, be not discouraged though thy seal be smooth, and little; yet look if any measure of faith be in thee in truth, or any light of God have shined in thine heart, though there remain faith and doubting still in thee. This dims the print, but mars not quite the evidence; as though the legs and knees be not so strong as others, yet thou wilt not deny, but having weak legs and knees, thou hast such members as well as others, and art able to go; thou hast them in truth, though not in such strength as well as they; so I say, thy weak and dim evidence may be true as the strongest. When we desire for more, wish for more, endeavour for more, and are not content of that we have, in this case, the evidence is but blotted, we want not the title.

Use 3. The third is *for instruction.* If this be so, let not then any man dare to confound the external calling of men with the internal calling of God. You shall at some times see some men at a word of God falling suddenly upon them, struck as with a clap of thunder, and go away bleeding, as one struck on a galled wound; this affects much for the present, but continueth not.

So again, the calling of God by the ministry, breeds in some a certain amazement, when the majesty and glory of the word, overcoming our senses, doth for the present ravish us with a marvellous conceit of the excellency thereof; as those in the Gospel, who having heard of the excellency of the kingdom of God, do thereupon send out this confession, 'Blessed are they that eat bread in the kingdom of heaven,' and yet in neither of these a true calling. A man, if he have no more, may have small comfort in either, save by the one he may be convicted, and by the other condemned. The market, indeed, by the preaching of the gospel, is set open, the banquet is provided, and the guests invited to it, but where is thy warrant to come? where is thy invitation? where is thy wedding garment? what answer canst thou make unto the Lord of the feast? where are the fruits of thy faith? where is thy sanctity? where is the sense of thy poverty and wretched misery? where is thy hunger and thirst, and desire of Christ? Look to this well.

Again, we must not think that the particular calling of men, either to magistracy or ministry, is this calling to glory and virtue; the first whereof, is to

1. Execution; 2. Action.

For if an outward calling to the ministry be sufficient, then Judas, who had such a calling to assist Christ in his ministry, and had, with the other, power to cast out devils, had this calling, Luke ix. 1. But he was not thus called; he knew it not, for if he had known it, he had been saved and lived.

Further, how precious this calling should be unto us, we may see, Luke x. 20, whereupon the seventy disciples returned rejoicing, that the spirits were subject unto them. Christ reproves them, saying, 'Notwithstanding, in this rejoice not, that the spirits are subject unto you; but rather rejoice, because your names are written in heaven.'

Here is only cause of true joy. We know this was a great and excellent work, to subdue spirits and devils, to relieve poor souls, and in this to shew forth his exceeding power, who had sent them; and yet all is nothing to this calling. Christ he wills them to look to their election, and rejoice therein, as though all other joys were in vain, until a man might rejoice in this.

Let not, therefore, a man rejoice in any outward calling only; nay, not in this, that he is called to be a minister in the church of God, without this particular calling.

By this then be sure to take thy warrant of rejoicing, fetch it out of this calling, that God hath called thee to glory and virtue, which is the next thing to consider of; our calling to glory and virtue; I mean, a consideration of these things whereunto we are called, glory and virtue.

1. *Glory*. Glory is the end of all. The glory of God is the furthest reach and end of all things, and virtue is the way leading unto glory. Glory, the extent of glory, is set before virtue, the means and way thereunto: why unto virtue, and not by virtue, I have shewed already, I will not now insist. The liberty of the Scripture is manifold in the like. Glory; what is glory? Glory with men is nothing else but an estate in the world, that draws amazement and admiration after it; this it is, not that which we look after. Of such a kind of glory we read, Gen. xlv. 13, of Joseph, whereof he speaks to his brethren, 'And you shall tell my father of all my glory in Egypt.' This was a glory, and a glory, I confess, not to be despised, when God gives it as a favour and pledge of future glory, as it was unto him.

Further, we read of another glory, which was put from Moses upon Joshua, Num. xxvii. 20, where God said to Moses, that he shall bring Joshua before the priest, and shall put some of his glory upon him, and his Spirit, that he might be honourable before the people: this was the glory of endowments, but it is not that glory we inquire after. We read of another glory, Prov. xxii. 4, the reward of humility, and the fear of the Lord, is riches, glory, and life; neither is this that glory we inquire for, ours is of a higher strain. This glory then we speak of, is the reward of goodness, and is ever attended with virtue. For as shame and sin still go together, so do glory and virtue, even by the testimony of the consciences of all good and ill men. The glory then we speak of is an eternal glory.

'Called to glory and virtue.'

It is not meant, when he says 'called to glory,' that a Christian is only called unto that, and unto nothing else by the way, but by the way he is called unto virtue, and by occasion unto afflictions. When God will give physic, humble, purge, and fit us by the way, then accidentally come afflictions and crosses, that if there be anything in us which hinders and makes us unfit for glory, these afflictions and crosses scour us, and purge away.

But God's end of calling us is unto glory; as 1 Thes. ii. 12, there they are exhorted to 'walk worthy of God, who hath called you unto his kingdom and glory.' Rom. ix. 23, the children of God are called the 'vessels of mercy, which he had afore prepared to glory.' This glory is only of his mercy, from whence glory floweth unto us; mercy is the ground thereof. What shall I say of glory? See what is written, Rev. xix. 9, when a voice came to him and willed* Write, what doth he write? 'Blessed are they which are called unto the marriage supper of the Lamb.' There was a glorious feast, full of glory; and then it followeth, 'These are the true sayings of God,' for to comfort and assure the faithful, of the excellency and truth of this happiness, and to stir them up to a pursuit thereof. Why thus blessed? Because by this marriage supper is meant that great,

* Qu. 'called'?—Ed.

general wedding feast in heaven after the resurrection, where the King of glory and the angels are, where the Lamb's wife, as it is in the former verse, and all shall meet, at which all the creatures in their greatest glory, heaven and earth and all, shall put on new habits; for as a vesture shall they all be changed, Heb. i. 12; 2 Peter iii. 7, they shall be renewed. Here shall be glory, and surpassing glory, as it is written, 1 Cor. i. 9, then to be 'called unto fellowship with Christ;' yet more, as Rom. viii. 17, to be heirs; nay, yet a step more, to be co-heirs with him together in glory. Men cannot reward their servants thus, but it is the only excellency of our great Master,* that he can make all his servants heirs, and all his sons kings. Thus as it is upon this strong tower, whereupon now we stand, and rejoice in the hope of the glory of God; as it is called the glory of God, so, 2 Thes. ii. 14, we are stirred up to thankfulness for the same, as being called by the gospel to the obtaining of the glory of the Lord Jesus Christ; and, 1 Peter v. 4, it is there called a crown of glory that fadeth not away.

And, finally, what use and advantage the faithful make of this glory against all the crosses, afflictions, storms, and tempests of this life, the apostle sheweth; 2 Cor. iv. 17, saith he, 'For our light affliction, which is but for a moment, worketh for us a far more excellent and eternal weight of glory.' The more affliction, the more glory. Our thoughts cannot bear nor reach to that exceeding depth of the apostle's conceit of glory.

But perhaps like unto some great glory of a prince, it may continue but for a day, though but a day in this great glory were a wonderful thing, and passing all the glory of this world. No, saith the apostle, it shall be eternal. What more? It shall be a load, a weight, an exceeding weight, of glory. Oh how the apostle grows full, and lifts himself higher and higher, striving to express a thing unexpressible! Why doth he thus, but to move our hearts, and ravish us also in exceeding admiration of the greatness of this glory?

What can be said more? If yet you desire to hear more of glory, consider we, if you will,

1, The place, where; 2, the company, with whom; 3, the title, what; 4, the time, how long.

1. First, *For the place.* It is heaven, the proper seat and mansion of all glory, where Christ is. So Christ speaketh in that prayer of his: John xvii. 24, 'Father, I will that they also whom thou hast given me be with me where I am, that they may behold my glory.' This needs not much proof. So also 1 Thes. iv. 17, 'Then we which are alive and remain shall be caught up together with them in the clouds, to meet the Lord in the air: and so shall we ever be with the Lord.' Oh if the outside, skirts, and suburbs of the palace (the stars and planets, chiefly those two great lights, the sun and moon) of this great King be so glorious, that with our eyes we cannot look upon the splendour of the same, what brightness of glory is in the chamber of presence, innermost court, and *sanctum sanctorum* itself! And if now, in the state of corruption, where sin hath abated such a deal of their glory, these creatures are yet so glorious, what shall they be when they shall be changed and renewed in that state of incorruption? And if they then be glorious, how much more shall the glory of the Creator! Yea, when all the creatures shall put on their new habits, gloriously arrayed for this marriage feast; when the

* That is, the 'excellency' of Christ alone.—G.

general kinds of all creatures shall be changed, renewed, and delivered from the estate of corruption and vanity unto the glorious liberty of the sons of God; for that they shall be delivered it is clear, Rom. viii. 21. So the apostle Peter speaks of a new heaven and a new earth, 2 Peter iii. 13; not new in substance or quality, but renewed and purged. I say, when the glory of all these creatures shall meet, renewed in exceeding glory, what a deal of glory shall be there, both in heaven and earth! And if the servants at that day shall be glorious, judge you what shall be the glory of the bride and bridegroom.

2. The second thing *is the company, with whom.* No chaff shall be there mingled with the wheat, no darnel shall be amongst the corn, no unclean thing shall enter therein or be amongst them, Rev. xxi. 27, but there we shall be with innumerable millions of God's holy angels; and not so only, but with Jesus Christ the Mediator of the new covenant, and God the judge of all, &c.; as the apostle shews, Heb. xii. 22. To which he sheweth we are now already come in this life, and entered with them; but then is the full time, that we shall find the full comfort and perfection thereof in that meeting.

And therefore the Queen of the South's spirit did fail her when she had seen all Solomon's magnificency, his wisdom, the glory of his house, his meat, table, the attendance of his ministers, their apparel, &c., pronouncing those men and servants to be happy which might stand continually before him to hear his wisdom, 2 Chron. ix. 7. Blessed Lord, how great shall our felicity be to be continually with our God, who is the fountain of all wisdom, and to behold his face continually in so wonderful a light!

3. Thirdly, *The title, what.* Not of creatures, or of servants, not so only, but of sons and heirs, and co-heirs with Christ. This, one would think, were sufficient; and yet the Scripture gives us others to the like effect, as that we shall be kings and priests unto God. What can be more? But what shall be our condition then in this so excellent an estate? Oh, who can tell? Surely I cannot. But as those spies who went to view the land of Canaan, by some of the grapes and fruits which they brought, did judge of the fertility of the land, so, I say, if by the word of God those first-fruits of the Spirit, the love of God shed abroad in our hearts, those beginnings of grace, the divers working and operation of the same Spirit, those feelings and joys of the faithful raised thereby, peace of conscience, and all that which shines in the glory of the gospel, we may think of the same. If by these grapes, these fruits of our celestial Canaan, we may judge of our condition then, I will speak my mind to you. This we know for certain, that the image of God shall then be perfectly renewed in us, so to know and feel no more labour, no more pensiveness of heart, no more sin, sorrow, nor temptations, which shall all then cease, and then again to be holy as God is holy, I mean not in that habit of holiness he is holy, but in that manner. And so here we shall have a happiness beyond that estate of Adam's innocency; for at the best all he received was but a possibility to stand if he would, but we shall receive an impossibility ever to fall again.

So again, for our bodies, they shall have no manner of disturbance or subjection to corruption; then they shall know nothing but glory, glory within and glory without, all glorious. So the apostle Paul, 1 Cor. xv. 42, sets down the same of the body in four heads:

(1.) Says he, the body is sown in corruption, but raised in incorruption. Then no more mortality, nor tribulation, nor any sense of sorrow. Some interpreters have thought good to express this by the word impassible, signifying an impossibility of feeling any more hunger, cold, thirst, sorrow, and the like; in brief, not capable of suffering any more; for at first, sin brought in corruption, but then all sin being abolished, corruption, and all things thereunto belonging, must needs cease.

(2.) He says it is sown in dishonour, and is raised in glory. Thus we see how loathsome a dead body is generally to all, yea, even that of our dearest friends; we cannot then endure to see it. Some may say this is but passion for friends which causes this. I grant, but yet generally there is an hatred naturally in all to look upon a dead body. Ay, but then it shall be a glorious body, a bright, shining body, as Mat. xiii. 43, 'Then shall the righteous shine forth as the sun in the kingdom of their Father.'

We see here how things of great splendour do affect and move us, as the heat and light of the sun, and the glory of the heavens, the moon and stars, and the like. Consider, then, how glorious thou shalt be, to shine as the sun in the firmament, yea, as the sun when he riseth in his might.

(3.) So again, these bodies, though lame, dismembered, disfigured, abortive, or what you will of the like kind, shall rise again without all deformities, caused either through want and defect of nature, or time; and therefore the apostle, though he say, 'it is sown in weakness,' yet he adds, 'it is raised in power,' strong with the qualities and necessities thereunto.

(4.) So also, lastly, the apostle unto the power addeth agility, nimbleness, spiritualness. It is sown 'a natural body, it is raised a spiritual body;' subtile as it were, like a spirit, not unable by lumpish heaviness to move upwards, but being uncapable of anything pressing downwards; a glorious body, not clogged with mortality; and the soul, no more imprisoned, then is swift, nimble, and spiritual. Not that I say it shall not then keep the bodily dimensions, to be a body truly, for it shall do so still, but by reason of alteration of qualities, swiftness and agility, so it shall be a spiritual body. And if the glory of the body shall be such, what think you shall be that exceeding glory of the soul?

A taste hereof we have set forth, 1 John iii. 2: 'For we know that, when he shall appear, we shall be like him; for we shall see him as he is.' What can be more? And, Phil. iii. 20, the apostle says, 'But our conversation is in heaven; from whence also we look for the Saviour, the Lord Jesus Christ, who shall change our vile body, that it may be fashioned like unto his glorious body.' May some say, This is soon said; how shall this be done? He answers, By that mighty power whereby he is able to subdue all things unto himself. If he hath power over all things, then hath he power to bring to pass this also.

4. Now we want but *the time, how long.* What can be said of eternity? Think what we can, this is ever beyond the reach of all our thoughts, only I may say thereof as it is Ps. lxxxiv. 10. If the prophet David did make so great account of one day, in the sanctuary upon earth, 'that he had rather be one day in God's court, as a door-keeper, than be a thousand otherwhere, or dwell in the tents of wickedness,' what shall it be to be not one day in the court of heaven; for even but one day were a great happiness to be there; but to be there for ever, out of all time! For then, the angel in the Revelation, 'Time shall cease, and be no more,' Rev. x. 6. What is time, but the measure of motion, which, once ceasing, time shall cease also, and we shall have eternal rest. As no minute of time shall ever be that shall give any release to the torments of the damned, so shall there never again be any time which shall give the least intermission to the

joys of the elect. Oh, where are our hearts? How should they be lift up to hear of these things; what should we leave undone that may be done, once at last, to have life eternal? Now I come to

The uses. 1. If this, then, as is proved, be the only calling that we are called unto, unto glory and virtue, *let us labour to acknowledge the excellency of the calling of God, and set a due price upon the same.* Why stagger we herein? We are full of false fears, and discouragements, because we hear that 'all that will live godly in this world shall suffer persecution,' 2 Tim. iii. 12; therefore we give back, and are shamefully dismayed; and yet what lose we by this suffering? for, saith the apostle, 'If we suffer with him, we shall reign with him,' 2 Tim. ii. 12. Is not, then, the reigning beyond the suffering? Oh but if it were to suffer only, it were somewhat! But herein we must war and fight. Oh but it is for a kingdom; would we be crowned and not fight? and in fight would we have no enemies? Ay, but we may be overcome in the fight. No, but we are sure to overcome. Who would not then fight? God, when he calls us to conquer, then he conquers for us, and he conquers in us; and, as it is Rom. viii. 37, 'We are more than conquerors in him.'

No man, we know, how base soever, even the greatest coward that may be, but he would fight, if he were sure to overcome. What cowards then are we. Every one of us would be reputed stout and valiant; where, then, is our valour, whenas every barking of a dog, as I may so call them, or every touch of a fly, makes us deny our master? Oh, the shame of our profession; what is this temporising but to draw to lukewarmness, and so to denial, that we are ashamed in this or that company for these and these causes of our profession! Well, remember, if we deny him, he will deny us; if we be ashamed of him, he will be ashamed of us, Mat. x. 33. In this case, what shall, what can we answer him at that great day?

But if nothing in the excellency of this great calling will encourage us to war thus, yet let glory do it. 'Called to glory,' as it is Heb. xii. 2. Set glory before thy eyes, this or nothing will make thee go on. Look at Christ Jesus, 'who, for the joy that was set before him, endured the cross, and despised the shame, and is now set down at the right hand of God.' This will encourage thee to go on; and if thou so run that thou mayest obtain, so shalt thou in time be.

This is that which formerly hath been taught us out of the former chapter, Heb. xi. 10. Of all those famous champions, what made them hold out so in all their troubles and crosses but this, that they look at 'a better city, which hath foundations, whose builder and maker is God?' Here, therefore, stir up your fainting spirits to despise these base things you so delight in here, and look at glory; and to stir you up a little thereunto, give me leave to tell you a story which may help you to see what base delights we rejoice so in.

It is written of Cæsar that, travelling in his journey through a certain city, as he passed along, he saw the women for the most playing with monkeys and parrots, at which sight, thinking it strange, he said, What, have they no children to play with? So, I say, it is a base thing for us to be so toying* with these worldly delights, as though we had no better things to look to, when we are carried away with fair buildings, rich household stuff, riches, high birth, and the like; what are all these but monkeys and parrots unto this glory?

I confess, in themselves they are good things, but when these put Christ

* That is, 'trifling'—G.

out of doors, and take up your heart so as we think most of them, then all is not well. Nay, even in the church, how are our hearts carried away from better things? When we see one with a better fashioned gown than we, one with a better plume, oh our hearts run on this all the sermon time, never resting until we have the like. If it be thus with us still, O God, where is our calling to glory and virtue? Where is that kingdom we aspire after, when we hunt so eagerly after these things, in themselves so vain, got with so much ado, kept with so many fears, and parted with [with] such a deal of sorrow, and thus forget that calling of him who calleth us to glory and virtue?

It were good, methinks, that every man, when he is a-going to these idle sports, should thus reason with himself: O my soul, whither now art thou a-going? to see such a show, to see such a fair house, to see this mask and yonder play, and this and that company? If these seem to delight thee, yet what are they compared to glory? Are they not all vanity? Why art thou so eager in vain things. Oh why are we told here of a calling unto glory and virtue, but to stir and lift our hearts unto the search of such a calling which we are called unto, and in regard thereof to set a low price on all the things of this earth? There are many of you, I know, that dare not in your hearts say against that which I now speak, and yet you labour not for the same. Well, I wish you deceive not yourselves. Never think that you have learned anything, until your hearts be warned* and affected at these things. Oh worldly-minded men, and so taken up with the things of this life, with the base trudgery of this world!

2. The next is, to *value the children of God highly for the graces of God in them*, so judging of them. Not that I take upon me, as some have foolishly done, to judge and know certainly such a one to go to heaven or not. I determine not of such, only I mean that such in whom we see God's graces shine in a holy life, we must judge that such are called. And to what are they called? To glory, and eternal glory. You see how much ado we make here of great heirs, though we shall never be the better for them. How we do prize, embrace, dandle them in our arms, who at age never thank us again. If we delight so in these great heirs, why prize we not the heirs of heaven? why delight we not in God's children, who are greater heirs? Perhaps they are in their minority and nonage, yet are they heirs of heaven, kings and priests of God. But perhaps they are wronged and abused by some in this world, yet are they great heirs still. How darest thou despise or abuse any of these little ones? Sayest thou that thou art called to glory and virtue? Hast thou any portion in Christ, and despisest such? If thou wert called to glory, thou wouldst highly esteem of such.

3. The last is *for consolation*, a man that hath this calling unto glory, Oh how marvellously may such an one be joyful in all tribulations, sorrows, and crosses. Oh but, says one, I am in poverty, what shall I do? Stay a while, and glory will come, and thou shalt be rich as the best. Oh, may some other say, but I am tormented with sorrow and sickness, yea, am so loathsome, as doth make me stink in my own sight, and be a burden to myself and others,—a thing which may befall even God's dear children. Oh but think then even this loathsome vile body is appointed unto glory, and glory will come ere it be long. And so in my children and friends, in whose death, as a heathen said, we die often (*b*); yet I will rest in this, in that God hath taken them into perpetual rest, in that they are laid up in

* Qu. 'warmed'?—Ed.

the bosom of my Saviour, and are heirs of glory. I will think them all most safe. Oh but grisly death comes; what of all this? This shall cheer me most of all. There may well be a little struggling, but I shall overcome: this shall be to me the door of life and rest. Then will I think and expect the bright morning shall come, and look for a glorious wakening. So of all Satan's temptations, how many, mighty, or great soever they be, though they vex me sore for a time, yet I shall get double strength by them, having once overcome, for he who most wrestles thus hath most strength at last. All they shall make me but so much the stronger to contend for this glory; yea, all the sufferings of this life shall not be able to rob me of the same; for strong is my Redeemer to confirm me unto the end. What shall I say more? If we were not novices, and unacquainted in this our calling to glory, we could not be so distempered at our own crosses and losses, and those of others. What will not the hope of glory go through? Lord, so work upon our hearts, that we may know what the excellence of this our calling is to glory, that so we contend for the same.

NOTES.

(*a*) P. 494.—'One Francis Spira.' See note, Vol. III. page 533, note *qq*.

(*b*) P. 503.—'So in my children and friends, in whose death, as a heathen said, we die often.' Seneca, in his *Epistolæ;* but it is a commonplace of the Classics.

G.

THE PATTERN OF PURITY.*

And every one that hath this hope in him purifieth himself, even as he is pure.
—1 John III. 3.

I shall not need to stand on any curious division of these words: if you please shortly for your memory's sake to observe these three things:

1. The workman. 2. The work. 3. The pattern to be imitated.

1. *The workman* is 'every one that hath hope in him,' every one that looks to be like the Lord Jesus in the kingdom of glory, he is the man must set about this task. 2. Secondly, *The work* is a work to be wrought by himself; he is a part of the Lord's husbandry, and he must take pains as it were to plough his own ground, to weed his own corn, he must purify himself; this is the work. 3. Thirdly, *The pattern by which he must be directed* is the pattern of the Lord Jesus his purity. Put him for a pattern and instance; look unto him that is the author and finisher of our faith; as you have seen him do, so do you; as he is pure, so labour you to express in your lives the virtue of him who hath redeemed you. These be the three particulars.

Not to stand on curiosity, but to fall to the work in hand, *the work is purity*, 'to purify ourselves;' that howsoever this is a task which is now laughed out of countenance,—purity is become a nickname, those that will be thus are counted the scorn of the world, a reproach to men,—yet it is a point so absolutely needful unto salvation, that if thou despise it thou despisest thyself. If thou hast a hope to be saved, thou must do this; so that if a man do not purify himself, and take pains this way and overgo the scorns of the world, and cannot get the mastery, but will be kept out of heaven for a laugh of the world, he is worthy to go to his place, he is worthy of damnation.

But for *the workman* that God puts this task on, it is 'every one that hath this hope.' What hope is that, you see in the verse before. Now we are the sons of God; it doth not yet appear what we shall be: but we

* 'The Pattern of Purity' forms No. 18 of the original edition of the Saint's Cordials. 1629. It was withdrawn in the other two editions. Its separate title-page is as follows:—'The Patterne of Pvritie: Wherein is shewed, What Purity of heart is. The necessitie and excellency thereof. The meanes how to purifie our selves. With divers other particulars concerning the same. Prælucendo Pereo. Vprightnes Hath Boldnes. London, Printed in the yeare 1629.'

know that when he appears, we shall be like him as he is, that is, they they that look to be like to the Lord Jesus in glory, they must be conformable in grace. Wilt thou be glorious as he is in heaven, thou must have the image of his grace on earth; so that if we will be glorious, we must be pure.

Thou must not continue with a common heart, as foul hands are called common hands in the Scripture, we must wash ourselves, make ourselves clean. Now from hence I observed in another place this doctrine,

Doct. 1. *That a man that is careless of purifying himself, that man must have no hope.*

A harsh point, to bring a thing to desperate issue, but what shall we do? Shall we encourage men to that hope, that they shall carry with them to hell? May we say, thou mayest hope to be like Christ in glory, when thou dost not labour to be like him in purity in this world? We should betray souls. And do you know, this is the beginning of salvation.

When a man hath run hitherto in a naughty course, and now comes to be resolved in his conscience, that if he continue thus and thus, and alter not his course, he shall perish, I say the revolving of his conscience that way is the beginning of his conversion. When a man sees no hope, if he do not alter and turn, this will make him good or nothing,—I proved it from many places of Scripture,—so that, 'he that purifies not himself hath no true hope.' The point I then chiefly insisted upon was, to take away all the objections that the devil, and flesh and blood, could make to keep a man from purifying himself with a false hope, that surely men may come to heaven notwithstanding this hard task; I put to you the infiniteness of God's mercy, the mediation of Jesus Christ, the intercession of all saints, all the prayers thou canst make, all thy cries to God in extremity, all thou canst say, I proved they should not help thee one whit. No; the more infinite God's mercy is, the heavier his wrath shall burn against thee, that dost not prepare thyself to receive that mercy; thou hast counted the blood of the covenant an unclean thing. He hath washed us with his blood, but thou wilt not be washed; thou rejectest that blood, delighting in uncleanness, that it had been better for thee Christ had never been incarnate, he is so far from helping thee that he shall pronounce sentence of damnation against thee, 'Go, thou cursed, I know thee not.' If all the saints in the world should lift up their hands to God for thee, all will do no good as long as a man resolves to continue in iniquity: 'If I regard iniquity in my heart, the Lord will not hear my prayer.' If thou continuest in the course of the world, and wilt not take pains to cleanse thy heart, there is no hope of thy salvation; so that this is harsh, but I say it is true, it is a thing not possible to be altered. Heaven and earth shall pass, before the truth of this I have delivered shall pass. That man that taketh not pains to purify himself, that man must have no hope to be saved.

Obj. But if a man object, How doth this stand true, as soon as men have this hope they purify themselves?

Ans. I answer, Where the Scripture speaks of hope it is a divine hope, a work of grace that shall never disappoint a man; for hope is upheld and sustained by faith, as Hebrews xi. 1. For what is faith? 'It is the substance of things hoped for.' It is that that sustains and bears up the thing hoped for; so that hope is a pillar that is grounded on faith. Nothing is hoped for but what is first believed, on grounds taken from the word of God. As in faith, there is a dead faith, and a lively faith; now it is not every faith that saveth, but only that faith that is lively, and shews itself by good works; as James saith, 'What profiteth it, my brethren, if a man say he hath faith, and not works? can that faith save him? No', James ii. 14. Therefore the Scripture speaks of a lively hope, as well as of a lively faith: 'Blessed be the Lord, that hath regenerated us to a lively hope,' 1 Peter i. 3.

So that here is the difference between this hope and the other: the one hath for his foundation faith, laying hold firmly on the mercies of God—it is as sure every whit; Christian hope, that divine grace, is a thing as certain and infallible as faith is; for all that is hoped is picked from faith, faith is the ground of the thing hoped for; so that if faith cannot be shaken, hope cannot, which is settled upon and sustained by it.

Now, on the other side, an impure man that walks on in iniquity, what sustains his hope? Faith in God's promises? No; see God's book if there be any promise made to such a one: 'The mercies of God are from everlasting to everlasting towards them that fear him,' Ps. ciii. 17. And in the second commandment, 'The Lord will shew mercy to thousands of them that love him,' Exod. xxxiv. 7. There be promises that way, but where is the least promise, the least syllable in all God's book, that if thou continuest not in his fear he will shew thee mercy? Nay, if a man say, I shall be delivered, notwithstanding I do thus and thus, the Lord will not shew mercy to that man. Deut. xxix. 29, he says, 'Thou that thinkest thou hast a promise of God's mercy, and hast no word to put thee in hope, but to put thee out of hope, know the godly's hope is a work of God's Spirit in their heart, it is sustained by a promise;' faith in the promise makes it God's word, and cannot fail; but the hope of a wicked man is not upheld by faith in the promises, but by a foolish, a presumptuous conceit that he fancies in his own brain.

Indeed, beloved, it is a mad conceit that he hath, that he may do thus and thus; a strong presumption clean contrary to all that God hath set down in his word. It is as impossible as that God should be forsworn, as in the song of Zacharias: Luke i. 70, *et seq.*, 'The oath that he swore unto our fathers, that we being delivered out of the hands of our enemies, we might serve him without fear, in holiness and righteousness before him, all the days of our life.'

It is an old oath, God sware that if thou be delivered out of the hands of thine enemies, if thou be freed and rescued from everlasting damnation, God hath taken an oath that thou shalt serve him. Now for a man that will not serve him in holiness and righteousness, and yet persuade himself that he shall be delivered from his enemy, what hope is this?

But you will say, 'If hope be so certain, what difference is there between faith and hope, if one be as sure as the other.' Many will grant, we may hope for salvation, but doubt whether they may believe it, they think there be many things come between this and that. But I say, it is a foolish distinction in respect of the point of certainty, for the certainty must of force be the same, for nothing is hoped for but it is first believed.

'Faith is the substance of things hoped for,' giving the strength and sustentation to it. Therefore, Heb. vi. 19, it is called 'the hope which we have, as an anchor of the soul, both sure and stedfast, and which entereth into that which is within the veil,' that for certainty and infallibility giveth as great firmness as the anchor doth to a ship, that keeps it from wavering; and the reason is, hope is not like the anchor cast downward, but upwards, entering into that within the veil, is pitched on Jesus Christ, the rock of our salvation. Therefore, if we go by sea while we are in the sea of this world, this is it that bears us up against all surges and billows.

But to the point propounded, that I may not forget to shew what is the difference between faith and hope, if one be as sure as the other. I answer, The difference it is not in certainty, but in another respect, that is thus: *faith is a thing that hath neither time nor place, but makes anything present.* It puts a man as it were in real possession of eternal life; when he believes he hath it, he is in heaven already, but now hope carries us in expectation of it. There is a difference between them, we must stay in the mean time; for now 'it doth not appear what we shall be.' Now are we the sons of God, and faith apprehends that certainly, being an heir, I shall have a kingdom in heaven, faith puts me in real and actual possession of that great inheritance. But stay a while, you are not there yet, 'it doth not appear what we shall be;' then comes hope and qualifies that. Oh that I should be here born to so great estate, and yet be scorned and despised in the world, and kept so long from it; here comes hope and quiets it. It is a patient expectation of that which is firmly believed by faith, that is the difference between hope and faith. Read Rom. viii. 24; there the apostle points to that difference, 'Hope that is seen is not hope: for what a man sees, why doth he yet hope for it? But if we hope for that we see not, then do we with patience wait for it.' As faith, so hope is of things unseen, hope is certain it shall enjoy the thing unseen. Where is the difference then? Faith puts me as it were in real possession of it, the other makes me patiently to expect the full performance of it. If we hope, we do certainly expect. This distinguisheth these two virtues so near. And then this patience is a thing described by hope: 1 Thes. i. 3, 'Remembering without reasoning* your work of faith, and labour of love, and patience of hope in our Lord Jesus Christ, in the sight of God and our Father.' So that this patience, this expectation, this waiting, as it were, of God's leisure, is the thing that stays the stomach in the mean time, and that that doth distinguish this divine hope from faith. It is not the certainty, for they are equally certain, but the one brings always with it a settlement of the heart, with a patient expectation of the full fruition of the thing hoped for.

Then what follows? Nothing is so certain as the accomplishment of God's promise. He that builds his hope on faith in God's promises, nothing is so sure as he shall attain his desire. On the other side, he that builds his hope on the presumptuous conceit of his own brain, there is nothing so certain as that man's hope shall be vain, as Rom. v. 23, 'We,' saith he, 'have peace with God;' and not only so, 'we glory in tribulations: knowing that tribulation worketh patience; and patience, experience; and experience, hope: and hope maketh not ashamed.' What is the meaning of that?

Beloved, it is as much as if he had said, there is a difference between divine and human hope. The one hope is, when I repose confidence in the promise of a man, and when I look for the thing hoped for, the man breaks, so that my hope cannot be firmer than that I grounded on. It breaks, I am ashamed and confounded, that I did repose my hope and confidence that way; for this, see Job vi. 15, in the winter time, there comes land floods: 'My brethren,' saith he, 'have dealt deceitful as a brook, and as the stream of brooks they pass away; which are black by reason of the ice, and wherein the snow is hid: what time they wax warm, they vanish away: when it is hot, they are consumed out of

* Qu. 'ceasing'?—Ed.

their place. The paths of their ways are turned aside; they go to nothing, and perish. The troops of Tema looked, the companies of Sheba waited for them. They were confounded, because they hoped; they came thither, and were ashamed.' In the winter time, when waters abound and there is no need of waters, there will be a mighty stream, but in summer being parched with heat, he turns himself thither, and there is no water to be found, he is ashamed; when a man's hope is disappointed, it makes him ashamed.

Then here is the difference between the hope of God's child, that purifieth himself, and of an impure person; when the time comes he shall have need of hope, his hope is gone, as this hope will, that he shall be saved, though he purify not himself. The devil may continue it as long as he continues, but come to death, there is the difference, he is ashamed and disappointed. You see, Prov. x. 18, which is cited there, 'The hope of the righteous shall be gladness, but the expectation of the wicked shall perish;' that is, thou mayest hope for salvation, as well as God's children, but what is the difference? 'The hope of the righteous shall be gladness, but the expectation of the wicked shall perish.' Again, chap. xi. 7, 'When the wicked dies, his expectation shall perish, and the hope of unjust men perisheth.' So they have a hope, but a hope that shall perish as well as themselves, that shall be quite gone at the time of their death. Therefore, Job xxvii. 8, saith he, 'What is the hope of the hypocrite, though he hath gained, when God taketh away his soul?' Give me that hope that I shall have the comfort of when God takes away my soul. Now, while thou art in this world, thou hast a hope as strong as God's child, and thou wilt not be beaten from it, but when the Lord takes away thy soul what wilt thou get by it? It shall stick upon the world without end; it shall vex and gnaw thy soul, that thou shouldst stick to a hope that deceived thee.

So you see what a case a man is in that takes no pains to purify. We can speak no more to a man's discomfort than to tell him thou canst have no hope. It is said of the Gentiles, before they knew Christ, 'they were strangers from the commonwealth of Israel, being without hope in the world,' Eph. ii. 12; and that is thy case. Let not the devil feed thee with a false hope, and say thou shalt be like Christ in glory, though thou art not like Christ in purity in this world. It is false, it cannot be; thou art in the case of a very Turk, notwithstanding thou hearest much of the Lord Jesus; thou hast received baptism, yet as yet there is no hope for thee unless thou repent. I beseech you, as you tender your own salvation, yield to the truth of God's word. Let not Satan lead you on, and train you to destruction, to think that things may be otherwise than this preacher speaks, as the oracles of God. If we say that a man that purifies not himself cannot have hope, this is confirmed in heaven; whosoever hath this vain hope shall be ashamed. Therefore every one that hath this divine hope, that looks to be saved, to be like Christ in glory, he must without delay purify himself. So much for the workman.

Now, to come to the work. Then, what is the work? 'To purify himself.' 'Every one that hath this hope,' &c.

Doct. 2. *Whosoever hopes to be saved, must set himself upon this work, to purify himself.* But here is as great a difficulty as the other. Doth it lie in the power of a man to purify himself? That is the work of God; and that David knew well enough, as in the 51st Ps., ver. 10, 'Create in me a clean heart, O God, and renew a right spirit within me;' and we know it is the great purchase of Christ; they are purified that are purchased by him.

You must not make one truth of God to destroy another; therefore, for the clearing of it, consider what the apostle writes to them: Philip. ii. 12, 'Work out your salvation with fear and trembling. For it is God that worketh in you, both to will and to do of his good pleasure.' Mark how one depends on another, and then you shall see these things may stand very well together: 'work out your own salvation with fear and trembling.' We must go about the work; but why so? 'For it is God that worketh in you both to will and to do of his good pleasure.'

The meaning is, God doth not work things in us or with us, as we do with a spade or a shovel; that is, that we shall be mere patients only, but he works with us suitably to the reasonable soul he hath bestowed upon us. He hath given us understanding and will, so, though the Lord be the first mover and worker, and that we are not able to do anything, yet notwithstanding, as soon as God's grace hath seized on us, presently it puts us on doing; what God worketh in thee, thou must work thyself.

Therefore know, that when God finds a man at the first, when he is without grace, he is not able to stir, nor to do anything; talk of purifying himself, you may as well talk to a dead man. When God first visits with grace, we are not able to work, to do anything, why, we are stark dead; as it is said, 'And you that were dead in trespasses and sins hath he quickened,' Eph. ii. 1, so that God comes first, and finds a man stark dead. He may work natural works, civil works, moral works, but to do works he shall find in heaven, to lay a foundation for the time to come, he is able to do nothing of that; for things of heaven, he is utterly dead in sins and trespasses. Therefore, John v. 25, it is said, 'The hour is coming, and now is, that the dead shall hear the voice of the Son of God: and as many as hear his voice shall live;' that is, the force of God's quickening Spirit, the voice of Jesus Christ coming to a dead man, the powerful word of God, seconded with the lively Spirit of Jesus Christ, this finding a dead man conveys life into him, that presently he begins to hear and see. Though first there be an influence of life coming to us from Christ Jesus, yet presently, as soon as life is infused, wherein we are mere patients, presently, I say, as soon as the life of grace is come, we hear, and do, and work, though God works the first act of a man's conversion, 'Behold, I stand at the door and knock,' saith God; 'if any man opens, I will come in;' as soon as grace is infused, let me come in, Christ is there, and thou wert not aware of him.

But as soon as a stock of grace is given, presently, thy will must work, and thou must say, Lord, come in; he knocks as soon as thou hast grace, he enables thee to give a will, that thou mayest open. Though principally God, yet there is a concurrence between God and thee; and this is grace, when thy will is made active and able to do things, that now the things done by God's grace are attributed to men. Ezek. xviii. 31, God says, 'Cast away from you all your transgressions, and make you a new heart and a new spirit: for why will ye die, O house of Israel?' make you a new heart. So in 2 Cor. vii. 1, saith God, 'Having therefore these promises, let us cleanse ourselves from all filthiness of the flesh and spirit, perfecting holiness in the fear of God.' So that here is grace indeed, when thy will is enabled to open to Christ, to repent, to believe, to pray to Christ thyself. This is a thing needful to be stood on, because many will be very willing to hear that on God's part; Oh, if God will send grace, that they may not be put to take pains, then all is well, they like that well. But if thou hast hope, thou must work thyself, not as if thou didst it of thyself, no, God hath given thee ability, he hath given thee life, he would have thee go about thy business, he gives a stock whereby thy will is freed to do so much as God will accept; thou shalt have power to do that which God will accept of as well as the best service. I alway remember that place, Rev. iii. 8, 'I know thy works: behold, I have set before thee an open door, and no man can shut it: for thou hast a little strength, and hast kept my word, and hast not denied my name.' Mark, oh, if I had so much grace as others, I would purify myself; nay, but hast thou any strength, a little grace? Be not a dastard, a coward, but resolve in the work God hath called thee to and then thou wilt do'it.

'Thou hast kept my word,' a little strength and a good heart will do it. Thou idle servant, that which thou countest little is a talent, it is a gift fit for the great King of heaven and earth, it will carry thee far, if thou hast not a deceitful heart; if thou hast an upright heart, God giveth thee strength, that thou mayest purify thyself, as he is pure. But wherefore serves grace?

If the Lord have given grace, he will not have thee idle, but this grace frees the will, that thou must go about the work with success. Therefore, I beseech you, that ye be not deluded by this, so making one truth oppose another. When the Son visits with grace, thou art free; wherefore comes the Son? To make thee free. Thou hast thy will bound up, thou couldest not affect* the ways of God; the Son of God hath freed this will, and now requires that thou shouldst use it, to purify thyself as he is pure; so for that point it is clear.

Now for this, that a man should purify himself, what need I bring many arguments; if the first will not do it, nothing will do it; if thou doest not, thou art lost, there is no hope.

1. This must be done; and then, 2. It may be done.

Therefore God gives his Spirit and grace, that though the work comes originally from him, 'For except the Lord build the house, they labour in vain that build it,' Ps. cxxvii. 1, yet if a man say, I will do nothing except the Lord build the house, let him build it if he will have it built. No; the Lord will have it built, but thou must be a workman. 'The foundation of God standeth sure. The Lord knoweth who are his. And let every one that nameth the name of Christ depart from iniquity,' 2 Tim. ii. 19. The foundation of God standeth sure; the Lord knoweth who shall believe in him. There is a privy seal put to this, 'the Lord knoweth who are his;' but there is never a seal, but this purging that is for letters patent that be open; this is not a close rule, but thou mayest view and read it thyself; 'and let every one that nameth the name of Christ depart from iniquity.' There is the broad seal, whereby I may know that I am one of the number, that I shall appear in glory when Christ appears. Therefore if a man purge himself from these, he shall be a vessel to honour, sanctified and meet for the Master's use, and prepared for every good work.

Mark how a man works actively and passively. He is 'prepared and sanctified for the master's use,' but is he a mere patient? No; he must purge himself from these things. So there must be an active and passive working. When the Lord hath done the first work, the Lord looks thou shouldst put thine hand to, and be doing; but I say, there is no hope if I do not take pains, and therefore I must of necessity purify myself. All the matter is now, seeing it cannot be avoided, it must be done, and is facible.

* That is, 'choose.'—G.

How may it be done?

Resolve on the thing, that it must be done, and then I will give directions how to do it. The examples of the world are like a stream that carries a man clean out of the way of purity; but seeing there is no way but that I must, through good report and bad report, what must I do then?

1. *Remember we come to do service to a Father;* that is, for encouragement. God did of his own free accord, not for any goodness in us, cast his love on us; he hath adopted thee for his son; he puts thee about his work; he will spare thee, as a man spareth his own son. This is thy case, thou art not like a mercenary servant, that is only to earn his wages; thou hast it by inheritance, because thou art a son, and the Lord looketh for filial, and no servile service of thee. If a servant doth not his work, the master puts him off, and takes a better; but God doth not stand with thee on the strict observance of the law, as if he were to reckon with thee for wages, the Lord requires that thou do thy best, and the Lord will spare thee. Go truly and painfully* about thy work with the strength God hath given thee; the Lord will spare thee, and will not turn thee off, and take another, but will deal with thee as with his son; he takes it in good part when thou doest thy best: that is for thy encouragement. The keeping of God's word, as he will accept, may be done with a little strength: then how shall I do?

(1.) First, *Go to the fountain; let the cock run.* What is the fountain of all cleanness? The blood of Christ; as Rev. i. 5, 'Unto him that loved us, and washed us from our sins in his blood.' There is the first thing, begin with faith. It is the blood of Jesus Christ that must wash me from sin. Thou must not go like a moral man, to labour by multitude of acts to get a new habit; but thou must work from another principle: all this cleansing must come from the blood of Jesus Christ. And how may I apply this? By faith. So thou must go every morning, and present thy soul before the Lord, and look on him crucified, and say, Lord, thou didst shed thy blood to cleanse my soul from the spots of sin; have faith, rinse† thy soul, as it were, in the blood of this immaculate Lamb; apply the blood of Jesus Christ not only for justification to free thee from the guilt of sin, but let faith work, as it may be applied for sanctification, to wash away the spots and pollutions of sin. This is certainly the most effectual means that can be imagined. Go to the well-head; look to that main and principal beginning, like a Christian, and not like a moral man; that though thou art polluted and defiled, yet the blood of the Lord Jesus will purge thee from all sin, spot as well as guilt, as we see written, Heb. ix. 13, 14; 'For if the blood of bulls and goats, and the ashes of an heifer sprinkling the unclean, sanctifieth to the purifying of the flesh; how much more shall the blood of Christ, who through the eternal Spirit offered himself without spot to God, purge your consciences from dead works to serve the living God.' Mark that. You talk of a purgatory: there is the purgatory. That true purgatory is the fountain that is laid open for the house of Judah to wash in: serving not only for expiation of thy sin, that it shall not be laid to thy charge, but it serves to purge thy conscience from dead works to serve the living God. It is as effectual for sanctification, being applied by faith, as it is for justification.

Therefore, as I may speak with reverence, make thy breakfast, as I may say, every morning, of the flesh and blood of Jesus Christ, and this will give thee more life, more ability, and strength, the multiplying and con-

* That is, 'painstakingly.'—G.

† Spelled 'rence.'—G

tinual repetition every day of the act of faith, laying hold on Christ's body broken, his blood shed. It is a most effectual means; try it, and you shall find the experience of it.

(2.) No means in the world so effectual than, when a man would go to Christ, *to look to his ordinances*. What are they? His word and his sacraments. Come like a Christian, and not like a moral man. Go to the fountain for justification and sanctification where it may be had, thou shalt find then greater effects than ordinary. Then for the word, it is an effectual means whereby we may purify ourselves: we may read Eph. v. 26, 'Even as Christ loved his church, and gave himself for it, that he might sanctify and cleanse it, with the washing of water by the word.' The blood of Jesus Christ washeth thee, there is the main washing; but notwithstanding, there be certain conduits and pipes, whereby the virtue of this is conveyed. Christ doth sanctify and purify thee, by washing, by water, by the word; so that when a man comes with faith in his word, in his promises, this is a special means. Note one place more: John xv. 2, 'Every branch in me that beareth not fruit, he taketh away, and every branch that beareth fruit, he purgeth it, that it may bring forth more fruit.' 'Now you are clean through the word that I have spoken unto you:' nothing is more plain; the word of God taken with faith is a special ordinance, whereby thou mayest come to purify thy heart. But how is that? How may I apply the word thus?

1. First, *Consider the word of God is a word of power.* When thou comest to the ministry of the word, remember that God hath made them able ministers of the Spirit, not only of the letter. Christ is with them to the end of the world. They are not only such as do prescribe barely this and that, and give no strength. No; we are ministers sealed: the Lord accompanies the external ministry of the word with the internal power of his Spirit, that when thou comest to church, thou comest only for the ordinance sake; the Lord hath pleased to make that a door of grace effectual, and he shall not only barely command, but he shall be a minister of the Spirit, shall enable me to do the things God requires. Oh, if a man come as to a market of grace, and say, Lord, thou, thou hast commanded me to come, and to expect from their mouth the donation of the Spirit, thou hast touched their tongue with the fire of thy blessed Spirit, to shew that that shall be a means to convey grace. Now if a man could come thus, the word would go far, and be very effectual, whereas we come now to hear rather a lecture of moral philosophy than for God's Spirit.

2. Again, *The promises in the word of God, when thou dost apprehend them spiritually, they are a wonderful means to purge.* Many think that they should apprehend only the promises of justification. Nay, faith extends; wheresoever God hath a tongue in his word, there faith hath an ear to hear, and a hand to lay hold on. The oath that he swore to our forefathers, that we should serve him in holiness and righteousness before him all the days of our life: there is a word God hath sworn, that I shall serve the Lord Jesus; and beloved, if this be a word of truth, and if my faith can apprehend and apply it, notwithstanding many difficulties, though there be oppositions of men and angels, I am yet to wrestle with principalities and powers. But look to the Lord, the Lord hath sworn thou shalt serve him, all thine enemies shall not hinder. Where is thy faith now? Bring faith to this promise, this oath of God: and what will it make a man do? It will make us go out against all oppositions, though we have walls of brass and chariots of iron against us. But hath God said they shall go out?

Lay hold on that; believe that as firmly as thou wilt believe the promise of justification. So the word of God will be made a wonderful effectual means; only let us come, like believers, like true Christians, and the Lord will do wonders, above all we can imagine and think, if we can come in the right way. Well, that is the word.

3. But the Lord hath appointed his *sacraments*. It is a strange thing that the first sacrament of regeneration there should be so little use made of it. It is a popish error, and cannot be yet weeded out of men's hearts. They think, what is in baptism? It washeth away what is there for the present, but it serves for no other matter to purify afterward; a gross and popish error. You must know it hath virtue and effect, that must be made useful for cleansing thyself even at this hour: as Rom. vi. 1–4, 'What shall we say then? Shall we continue in sin, that grace may abound? God forbid. How shall we that are dead to sin, live any longer therein? Know you not that as many of us as were baptized into Jesus Christ were baptized unto his death? Therefore we are buried with him in baptism into death; that like as Christ was raised up from the dead by the glory of the Father, even so we should also walk in newness of life.' Mark how the apostle fetches his ground and foundation from baptism, not as past, but as having present operation and force. If thou hast faith to overcome thy corruptions now, the force and effect of baptism is in thee; it hath a regard for the time to come, as well as for the time past; therefore say, Lord, thou hast appointed thy blessed sacraments, to be a seal for the confirmation of thy promises which thou hast made, that I should be washed; Lord, I present thy word, thy own seal; I beseech thee, make it good to my soul. So that if a man look to his baptism, and present it to the Lord, I say, it will be a more effectual means of cleansing thee, than if thou look back, and apply it only for thy present state at the time of baptism; and so of the Lord's Supper. But I cannot go to particulars, these be the main things.

First, Remember to whom thou goest, to a Father; then go to Jesus Christ, then to his word and promises, then make use of his seals and his blessed sacraments, sue God of his word and deed, challenge them, and when thou art thus prepared,

3. *Then go and read a lecture to thyself of watchfulness.* What it is to watch, that implies when a man is in great danger to be surprised, that all is untrusty within him, and false abroad; then reason, I had need of a strong watch of every side; I have a false nature, and this flesh of mine is ready to betray me into the hands of the world and of the devil; therefore there must be a marvellous strong guard. I must not suffer my affections to rove, that is the way to bring in the devil, even seven devils, whereas if I keep a watch all will be well. James i. 14, it is said, when a man is tempted, he is tempted of his own lust, but is he not sometimes with the world and the devil? No; all the temptations of the world and devil will do no hurt. Look to that within; there is a concupiscence; the world and devil cannot tempt thee but by working on thine own lusts; therefore look to thyself within, that there be no parley, no intercourse between them. Make a covenant with thine eyes, with thy tongue: perhaps thou wilt go to a place where there is nothing but filthiness; is this watchfulness? Dost thou know the corruption of thine own nature? 'Be not deceived, evil words corrupt good manners;' put what gloss thou wilt upon them, evil words shew an evil heart, and evil words and an evil heart, hid before in the cinders, now make a great flame. Therefore seeing this corruption will

not be wholly weeded out, yet it must be kept under, that the forces without may not join with them within.

Oh, much ado we have to keep ourselves from being surprised within. Then suppose the devil comes not as to Eve, but to Adam, for Adam's temptation was more dangerous than Eve's. If the devil comes in his own colours, then it is nothing, every one will flee from him; but he comes as to Adam, by the woman, perhaps by a friend, by a great man. Let us know when there is any temptation, any motion this way, this is a way to let in these and these enemies: as 2 Kings vi. 32, 'Elisha sat in his house, and the elders sat with him, and the king sent a man before him; he said to the elders, see how this son of a murderer hath sent to take away my head, look when the messenger comes, shut the door, and hold him fast at the door: Is not the sound of his master's feet behind him?' Mark, let this be thy case: within, thou hast a false heart; there is danger without; one comes and entices thee to do this and that; what shalt thou do? Shalt thou entertain and listen to, and suffer this treacherous motion to enter into thy soul? Let not thy lust lay hold on it within, then care not for a thousand devils, for ten thousand worlds, for 'the feet of his master follows, his master' the devil will be there presently, on the first motion.

A man that hath this resolution to suppress sin at the first motion, as soon as it is born,—resolving, I will shut the door, there is the feet of the devil behind, that will murder my soul,—shall find comfort. And then again, a man that is resolved not to live in any known sin (perhaps there be some sins of infirmity that will stick to a man's soul), but there be sins that waste the soul, uncleanness, swearing, extortion, and especially such sins as we are subject unto by our calling, and the course we follow, utterly unlawful and unwarrantable, and known by the word of God to be so. As if a man make a trade of living on usury, this is a sin goes with me all the days of my life; it is with me waking and sleeping, a main sin that compasseth me round. If thou mean to purge thyself, thou must not live in any one known sin, for that wastes grace. When a man multiplies sin, he increaseth the stock of original corruption. There is nothing more sure than that we say, that original corruption is equal in all. It is true naturally. Every man's face answereth to his neighbour's, as face to face in water; none better than the other; but though there be an equality that way, I may add weight myself. Two men are weighed, they are just alike heavy; but if one of them contract his spirits, he oversways* the other; if he add his will to his natural poise, he is heavier than the other. So, notwithstanding, the wickedness of sin is perhaps as much in one as another; yet when I use my will, and multiply and repeat, that is a sign that custom of sin hardens the heart, and makes the stain and spot grow deeper, that now thou canst not wash it out. Therefore be sure, if thou wilt go to heaven, that thou do not continue one hour in any known sin, for the more thou dost, the more thou strengthenest thyself in sin.

I should now go to the third point, the pattern to which we should conform ourselves. The glass we should imitate is our Saviour Jesus Christ, as he is pure. It is not meant thou shouldst ever hope to be as pure in quantity. *As* is not a note of quantity, but of quality, it shews a likeness. 'Thy will be done in earth, *as* it is in heaven;' that is, as by the angels in heaven, cheerfully, readily, and willingly, though not in the same quantity; so that the life of our Saviour Jesus Christ, and the word of God, must be

* That is, = 'outweighs.'—G.

our pattern. But you will say, How am I able to attain to this? I answer, the law of God prescribes to us a perfect form of obedience, though it be not possible for me to fulfil it, and so the life of our Saviour Christ, we are not able to express the virtues in him, and his purity; yet there cannot be a better pattern than the law, and the life of our Saviour Christ.

A man that would have his child to write a fair hand, he will not give him an ill copy to write by, but as fair as may be, though there be no possibility the child should write so well as it. So we cannot possibly attain to that purity in Christ, yet the copy must be fair. Scholars, if they will have an elegant style, they set the best orators before them. Thus, though the law of God be perfect, though such a thing as a man is not able to fulfil, yet it is a fit pattern; the copy must be fair, that I may mend my hand by it.

And thus, if we go on following our pattern, as the scholar's hand, by practice, mends every day, though it never come near the copy, so shall we grow in grace; for, as the prophet speaks, 'then shall we know if we go on in knowing,' Hos. vi. 3. A Christian must mend his pace every day, as he learns his Master's will, so to be transformed into the image thereof, that the virtues of God may shine forth in him, that his 'path may be brighter and brighter unto the perfect day,' Prov. iv. 18, and towards that measure of the age of the fulness of Christ Jesus. But I cannot now press the point further, because of the time.

THE BEAST'S DOMINION OVER EARTHLY KINGS.*

For God hath put into their hearts to fulfil his will, and to agree to give up their kingdoms to the beast, until the word of God shall be fulfilled.—Rev. XVII. 17.

The occasion of this day's solemnity hath been long and well known, and we have often in this place spoken of it; and it were a thing not unseasonable for the day to set out in its lively colours that facinorous† act, which will scarcely be credible to posterity. It exceeds my conceit to set it out in the right colours. I have therefore taken a text tending that way, and serving for our present purpose.

It pleaseth our blessed Saviour, out of his love to his church, not only to give directions what to do and what not to do, what to believe and what not to believe, but to foretell likewise all future calamities, that so the church might be fore-armed, and might not be surprised with terror upon the sight of some sudden or strange accident, as especially the flourishing estate of Antichrist. He therefore foretells all, both the beginning, the growth, the strength, the proceeding, and at last the destruction of that man of sin.

The church in this world is always under some prophecy, it is always under somewhat that is unfulfilled; for until we come to heaven, there is not an accomplishment of all prophecies.

This Book is a setting down of prophecies of future events to the end of the world.

* 'The Beast's Dominion' is one of the three gunpowder-plot anniversary sermons contained in 'Evangelical Sacrifices' (4to, 1640). Its separate title-page is as follows:—'The Beasts Dominion over Earthly Kings. A Sermon preached upon the 5th of November, in remembrance of Our Deliverance from the Papists Powder-Treason. By the late Learned and Reverend Divine, Rich. Sibbs. Doctor in Divinity, Mr. of Katherine Hall in Cambridge, and sometimes Preacher to the Honourable Society of Grayes-Inne. Revel. 16. 14. For they are the Spirits of Devils working Miracles, which goe forth to the Kings of the earth. London, Printed by T. B. for N. Bourne, at the Royall Exchange, and R. Harford, at the Bible in Queenes-head Alley in Pater-noster-Row. 1639.' As explaining and qualifying the unmeasured language of the present and kindred sermons, it may be permitted me to refer to my Memoir of Dr Sibbes, Vol. I. p. lxiii.—G.

† That is, 'wicked to excess.'—G.

This chapter sets out in lively colours the state of the pontificality, the state of Rome, under the bishop of Rome, the pope, and not the state of Rome under the heathen emperors. It sets down likewise the judgment of God in this life upon this beast, and upon the whore that sits upon the beast.

The description is large in the former part of the chapter. It would take up a great deal of time to unfold that; but because I have divers other things to speak of, I will pass that by.

The judgment of God upon the beast and whore, is set down partly in the verse before the text: 'The ten horns which thou sawest upon the beast shall hate the whore, and make her desolate and naked, and shall eat her flesh, and burn her with fire. For God hath put into their hearts to fulfil his will, and to agree to give up their kingdoms to the beast,' &c.

Here the judgment is set down, what it is and by whom it shall be: by the ten horns, that is, the ten kings. And, secondly, what they shall do; and that is set down in order.

First, These ten horns, these ten kings, western kings, 'they shall hate the whore.'

Hatred is the beginning of all actions that are offensive; for it is the strongest and stiffest affection of ill, as love is the strongest of good affections. 'They shall hate the whore;' it is not only anger, but hatred.

'They shall make her desolate and naked:' that is the second degree. They shall leave her; they shall strip this strumpet of her ornaments and strength, whereby she set out herself.

'They shall eat her flesh:' that is the third. That is, what they have given her before to enrich her withal, that which made her in such well liking, that which commended her, that which is her living, the riches of the pope's clergy, gotten, most of it, by ill means, they shall take from her.

But that is not all, but there is a higher degree than all this: 'they shall burn the whore with fire.'

So that in the foregoing verse you see is set down what the judgment is, and who shall be the executioners of this judgment.

But why must all this come to pass? He riseth to the highest cause: 'God hath put into their hearts to fulfil his will, and to agree with one consent to give their kingdoms to the beast.' God afterwards put into their minds to hate the beast.

So that in this verse is the severity and the mercy of God, his justice and his goodness. His severity in putting into the hearts of these kings to agree with one consent to give up their kingdoms to the beast. A great judgment so to besot them. But here is a limitation of that severity at last, till the time come, until the word of God shall be fulfilled; that is, until they shall cease to be thus deluded by the bishop of Rome, and then they shall begin to hate the whore as much as ever they were deluded by her, 'and shall eat her flesh, and consume her with fire.'

For the explication of these words, they being somewhat hard, I will spend a little time to unfold them. And, first, I must shew who is this beast.

'For God hath put into their hearts to fulfil his will, and to agree to give up their kingdoms to the beast.'

The beast is mentioned in three places in the Revelation: in the ninth chapter there is mention of the beast coming out of the bottomless pit; and in the thirteenth, of the beast that rose out of the sea; and here in this seventeenth, of a scarlet-coloured beast, 'having seven heads and ten horns.'

The beast, in a word, is the state of Rome, sometime under the heathenish emperors, sometime under the pontificality. The question is, Whether the beast here spoken of be the state of Rome under the Roman persecuting emperors before Christianity prevailed much, or the state of Rome under the usurpation of the bishop of Rome?

I answer, undoubtedly it is here meant of the state of Rome as it is upheld, the whore; the beast, that beast; for it is meant here of one that seduced by lying miracles, of one that should come in a mystery, of one that should deal with fornication and such courses.

Now heathenish Rome, it overcame men by violence and by force, and not by whorish insinuations, by drawing them on to idolatry. It is said in the fifth verse that upon her forehead was a name written, 'Mystery, Babylon the Great, Mother of Harlots.' Babylon in a mystery, and this mystery is a great word too with them. The mystery of the mass; in everything there is a mystery; all their ceremonies are mysteries. This word 'mystery' therefore, in the forehead of the whore, sheweth what beast it is that is here meant.

It is observed by divers writers, that in the frontlet of the pope's diadem there is written this name, 'Mysterium,' as in Julius the Second's time; but afterwards, when they smelled that he was construed thereby to be the very whore, they razed out that, and put in Julius Secundus, &c.*

'And she sits upon many waters.' 'She sits.' Mark, the Spirit of God will not suffer us to err. What is the regiment† of the pope called? 'Sitting.' Such a pope sat so long; the whore sits in the very phrase. And what is the seat called? The see of Rome, the see of antichrist. Divers other particular things there are to shew that he means Rome, that is, the state of Rome under the bishop of Rome, to be the beast here spoken of.

Especially considering the connection of this chapter with that following, where is set down the final destruction of this beast. Now we know that heathenish Rome ended long ago; therefore that beast which is here meant must needs be that which follows in the next chapter, and therefore it must needs be Rome as it is under the bishop, the pope of Rome.

It is said in the thirteenth chapter that this beast made the former beast to speak, did enliven and quicken the former beast. So indeed this beast, Rome considered under the pope, which succeeds that beast, Rome as it was under the Roman emperors, quickens the former beast; for now all is as glorious as ever it was in heathenish Rome. For after that the Goths and Vandals had possessed Rome, the pope put some life into the empire of Rome, and did himself become emperor. For indeed the emperor of Germany, though he be entitled King of Rome, yet that is but a mere titular thing; the eagle is deplumed of her feathers, of her authority; it is only the title he bears. And if any emperor come to Rome, the pope will make him swear fealty; and he must not long stay in Rome, he cannot endure that.

And it is well said in the Revelation that this beast is the image of the former beast, for the pope is altogether like the emperors almost in everything. For the emperors were crowned, the pope for failing hath three crowns; the emperors had their scarlet, this is a purple-coloured whore in scarlet. They spake the Latin tongue, and forced all nations almost to

* Cf. note *d*, Vol. V. p. 539.—G.

† That is, 'government.'—G.

speak Latin, as a monument of their slavery; so all in the popish church is in Latin, their prayers in Latin, all in Latin, even for the simple and sottish people to use. Ancient heathen Rome had their grave senators, the pope hath his cardinals. The heathen emperors, as Domitian and others, would be adored as gods; so likewise is the pope of Rome adored. And mark the slight, he hath a crucifix upon his feet, and kings must kiss that; and so with adoring of the cross they adore his person, as they did Heliodorus, that heathen emperor (*a*). Thus in everything almost they agree with ancient Rome, and in many other things I might run over their likeness to the former beast.

Now this beast, to describe him a little better, that we might know what these kings did, when they gave up their kingdoms and thrones to the beast, it is said in the thirteenth chapter that the dragon gave power to the beast. The dragon is the devil; and as he wrought effectually in the former beast in heathen Rome, to make war with the saints, so is this beast, pontifical Rome, stirred up, and acted by the devil, the dragon, to persecute the church. So that this beast hath the power and the spirit of the dragon, the devil himself.

And that you may discern that I do them no wrong, consider how the dragon and this beast, which is moved, and led, and acted by the spirit of the dragon, agree in their courses. I will name two or three to you.

The dragon's course is to make us distrust God. You know how in paradise he taught our first parents to distrust the word of God: 'Ye shall be as gods, knowing good and evil,' Gen. iii. 5. So the force of popery is to dishonour and to discredit God's truth, to put out the people's eyes, to lead them blindfold, to make the Scripture a matter of error and heresy, and bid the people take heed of it; as if God meant to deceive them, to go beyond them in giving them his word; as though it were not a word of salvation. As the dragon himself said to Christ, 'If thou wilt fall down and worship me, all these will I give thee,' Mat. iv. 9, so the pope takes upon him the dragon's power. These that will be good sons of their church, these and these preferments will he give them, when he hath as much right to them as the devil had to those.

The devil fell from heaven at the preaching of the word, at the preaching of the gospel. The apostles, when they returned from preaching, told our Saviour that they saw Satan fall down like lightning (*b*). So antichrist falls by the preaching of the gospel, by the breath of the Lord's mouth. He is not able to stand before it no more than Dagon before the ark. The word preached is as fire to consume him. So he is like the dragon in that.

In disposition he is like the dragon. The devil is a liar and a murderer from the beginning, the father of lies. So likewise the pope is a liar; all popery is nothing but lies. Therefore, 2 Thes. ii. 11, it is said, 'they are given over to believe lies.' Popery is a grand lie. It is a lie in the primacy;* for it came in by forgery and intrusion. It is a lie in purgatory, which is a mere conceit. It is a lie in their miracles, which they have devised to maintain their false worship with. It is a lie in their works of supererogation, that they can fulfil more than the Law requireth. So that all popery, consider it distinctly from our religion, because they have that which we have, and some patches of their own, consider it by itself, it is a mere lie.

Besides that, they maintain the doctrine of equivocation, which is a lie, a justifier of lies, which is worst of all.

* That is, in the pope as claiming to be successor of Peter.—G.

And to murder: this present day and occasion tells us that murders come from them. Their doctrine maintains it; and they make orations in commendations of traitors, as Sixtus Quintus did in praise of him that killed Henry the Third, king of France, and the bloody massacre of France is pictured up in the pope's court (*c*). As the devil is a liar and a murderer, so is this son of the devil, who is led by the spirit of the dragon; in disposition they are alike.

In course of life they are alike. The dragon is said to draw the third part of the stars of heaven down to the earth; that is, to draw men which were as the stars of heaven, to make them deny their religion. So this dragon, this pope, the instrument and vassal of Satan, he draws the third part of the stars from heaven, and he draws men from the love of the truth by preferment and honour. Men that are learned, men that are otherwise of excellent parts, he draws them from heaven to earth; that is, he draws them from the knowledge of the truth and goodness to earth, and lower than earth too if they do not repent, even to hell itself, from whence he came. Thus I might go on to shew that this beast is Rome under the pontificality, and not Rome under the heathen emperors; likewise that this beast is acted, led, and guided by the spirit of the dragon, by reason of the resemblance which it holds parallel with him in these and other things. So much for explication of this beast.

But why is the state of Rome called the beast?

Daniel first knew the great empires: the one of Babylon, called a lion; the Persian monarchy, a bear; the Grecian, a leopard; but here in this chapter is a strange beast, that hath all the cruelty and fierceness of all those monarchies, called therefore a beast for her fierceness and cruelty.

God's church, they are sheep and lambs. Christ himself the Lamb of God; the opposite church of antichrist, a beast, a cruel beast. If you go to plants, God's church are lilies; the opposite kingdom are thorns. If you go to fowls, God's church are doves, turtles, mild and gentle; the opposite church are eagles and birds of prey.

But I say they are called beasts for their cruelty. The state of Rome under those heathenish emperors was a beast; and in those ten persecutions the emperors are rightly called beasts. So likewise Rome papal is a beast. Our religion, true religion entertained, makes of beasts men; the true knowledge of Christ alters their natures, turns lions into lambs, as the prophet saith, Isa. xi. 6. But the popish religion, it makes of men beasts, makes them worse than themselves. For these gunpowder traitors, many of them, as they were by birth gentlemen, so their dispositions were gentle and mild, divers of them, not of the worst dispositions, only that bloody religion made them worse than their nature was. So I say papal Rome is a beast, and popish religion makes men beasts.

Well, I will not enlarge myself in the uses of this point, because I shall speak of it afterward, if the time will give me leave, only this, have nothing to do with this beast, keep out of her paws, keep out of her claws. A lion, or a cruel beast, may seem to be calm for a while, but a lion will, as we say, shew a lion's trick once a year. Meddle not, therefore, with this beast. It is a beast. So much for that, what the beast is, the state of Rome under the bishop of Rome.

'For God hath put into their hearts to fulfil his will, and to agree to give up their kingdoms to the beast.'

Whose? The angel sets down in the verse before, 'the ten horns, the ten kings, the ten western kings.' Whether it be a certain number for an uncertain, or whether it be a certain number, I will not dispute of now, but take it so as it cannot be disputed against, a certain number for an uncertain. A number of the western kings gave up their kingdoms for a while to the beast, until the word of God should be fulfilled.

But mark the phrase, 'God put it into their hearts to give up their kingdoms to the beast.' Will God put it into their hearts to give up their kingdoms to the beast? Why, then, the pope of Rome need not pretend Constantine's donation,* that he three hundred years after Christ gave unto them many territories about Rome; but they may depend upon a higher donation, 'God put it into the hearts of the kings to give up their kingdoms to the beasts.' Here is a higher title than the donation of Constantine.

But we must know that this is not meant, as if God gave him a right by putting into the hearts of the kings to give up their kingdoms to the beast, but God seeing these ten horns, these ten kings to be in a sinful estate, who deserved to be left of him, and to be given up to further illusion, and by withdrawing his grace to give them up to the occasions of sin, so this seducing beast and whore, he put into their hearts to give up their kingdoms to the beast.

But this must be a little cleared. Is God the author of sin? 'God put it into their hearts.' He did not only rule the events, 'but he put it into their hearts,' &c.

I answer, the phrases of the Scripture are well enough known in this kind. 'God gave them up to a reprobate sense,' Rom. i. 21. The falling of the people from Rehoboam, it is said, 'it was of the Lord;' and God bade Shimei rail. Divers such phrases there are in the Scripture. How must these be understood? Thus: not that God doth allow or command any thing that is evil, much less that he doth infuse any evil into men, so that when it is said he put these things into their hearts, here is neither an outward command nor an inward infusion. What is it, then? Here is a finding of them in an evil and sinful estate, and God useth that evil, and mischief, and wickedness that he finds to his own end and purpose; he infuseth no malice or evil, but finding of it, he useth it to his own particular end and purpose, and makes way and vent for it upon particular occasions. These ten kings, he infuseth no love of superstition into them, but finding them evil, and not as they should be, subjects of his kingdom, and misliking his sweet government, it was just with God to give them up to be slaves to the beast, and by consequence to the devil himself, that spake and wrought by the beast. So I say God took away the impediments, and opened a way to their evil disposition. He used their evil disposition to this or that particular thing, even as a workman that finds an ill piece of timber, he makes not the timber ill, but when he finds it ill, he useth it to his own good purpose; and as a man, it is Luther's comparison (*d*), as a man that moves a horse that is lame, he doth not put lameness into the horse, but useth him to his own purpose being lame, so God, finding these men evil in the general, he directs this ill into particular courses, to work itself this way and not that, in this particular action, not in that. For God, although he be not the author of evil, yet he is the orderer of it; and he determines and directs it both to the object and also to that end which he pleaseth,

In a word, consider sin in three distinct times: before the commission, in it, and upon the performance. *Before*, God doth not command it, nor infuse it, but disallow and forbid it. *In* the sin, he permits it to be done.

* That is, 'gift.'—G.

How? By subtracting of his grace in not working, then by offering occasions that are good in themselves, and thirdly, by tradition, by giving men up to Satan; as here the beast is given up to Satan, and the kings are given up to the beast. So that God gives men up by subtraction of his grace, and by tradition; and then he doth uphold them in the committing of sin, upholds the powers. And when it is done, applies them to this particular, and not to that particular. In the doing of it, he limits it, he sets the bounds of it, both for the time of it, as also for the measure of it, as here in the text, 'Thus long shall the ten kings give up their crowns to the beast, and thus far shall they go, until the time come that the word of God shall be fulfilled.' So he limits sin in the committing of it, both for the measure and also for the time. 'The rod of the wicked shall not rest upon the back of the righteous,' Ps. cxxv. 3.

Thus you see the meaning of the words, 'God will put into their hearts;' that is, by withdrawing of his grace, which they deserved by their sinful courses; and offering to them this man of sin, this beast, which shall come with such efficacies of error, so that his grace being withdrawn, and they given up to the devil, to Satan and the beast, they shall without doubt be deluded and seduced, but with this limitation, until the time come that the word of God shall be fulfilled.

I might be large in this point, but it is not so suitable to the occasion, only somewhat must be said for the unfolding of the text. So much, therefore, for that.

'God put into their hearts to fulfil his will, and to agree to give up their kingdoms to the beast.'

They agree all unto it; and therefore it was not a thing done by force. Rome and the heathen emperors did compel men, did overcome men by force of arms. These agree. It was a voluntary and a free act in them. Necessary it was in regard of God's judgment, but it was free and voluntary in regard of themselves; for with one consent they gave up their kingdoms to the beast.

Thus having unfolded the meaning, we come to observe some truths and conclusions that do arise out of the words. I will not mention all, or the most that might be observed, but only some special.

'God put into their hearts to give up their kingdoms to the beast.'

Here, first of all, from this ariseth, *God's special providence in ill.* In the greatest evil that can be, there is his special providence apparent: 'God put into their hearts to give up their kingdoms to the beast.' Observe here many acts of his providence, the withdrawing of his grace, the giving them up to Satan, and to ill occasions; the presenting them with good occasions, which, meeting with an ill disposition, makes them worse; for good occasions meeting with an ill disposition makes it worse, makes it rage the more, as the stopping of a torrent makes it rage and swell the more; as also the limitation of all this, 'until his word shall be fulfilled.' Thus in this work, heaven, and earth, and hell meet in one action. Thus it was in that great action of the crucifying of our blessed Saviour. There is the action of God in giving his Son to be a sweet sacrifice, and the action of Judas, and the devil in him, betraying of Christ, and the action of the soldiers in crucifying him. Saint Augustine, in the unfolding of this point, of the providence of God in evil, observes how many may concur in one action, God without blame, man without excuse (*e*). God without blame; he finds men ill, and leaves men deserving to be left; he takes away his grace, and as a judge gives men up to Satan. Man without excuse, because man works willingly: 'They with one consent gave up their kingdoms to the beast.' That is the first.

The second is this, *that the will of man may be swayed by divine governance, and yet notwithstanding work most willingly and freely.*

Here God puts into their hearts to do this, and yet they willingly and with one consent gave their crowns to the beast.

God first hath his providence in ill, and then that providence is such that it doth not rob man of his liberty, because God finding man in an ill course, he forceth him not to this or that particular ill, but directs him only: 'The hearts of kings are in the hand of the Lord, as the rivers of waters,' Prov. xxi. 1. A man when he findeth a river of water, he doth not make the stream, but only makes way that it may run this or that way, as it pleaseth him. So God finding the hearts of kings, or the hearts of any, as the rivers of water, he opens vent that they should run this and not that way; that they should be given to this, and not to that. Here is the action of God, and yet the free liberty of man.

But how could this be free, when they could not avoid it?

I answer, They were not privy to God's directing; they worked not in conscience* of God's moving, but they followed their own lusts and will. Between God's work and man's will there is always sin. God never works immediately in man's will; for man's will is free, but man's sinful free will is the next cause in sin. Although God put it into their hearts, yet he found them sinfully disposed.

And then, the judgment is not bound or tied. The hearts of these kings told them that they might give their crowns or not give them to the beast. Their judgment saw they had reason to do it, though their judgment were corrupt. So a sinner sees reason to do this or that, and although it be corrupt reason, yet it moves him at that time. His judgment is not bound up, but God lets his judgment be free, though he take away his heavenly light, and so he judges perversely. That is the second.

The third is, *that it is a terrible judgment of God to be given up to a man's own will, to leave a man to his own consents.*

It is here spoken by way of judgment, that 'God put it into their hearts to give up their kingdoms to the beast.' And indeed so it is a terrible judgment.

There are some objections to be taken away for the clearing of this weighty point.

How is it a judgment or a punishment when it is voluntary? 'They willingly gave up their kingdoms.'

I answer, The more voluntary and free a man is in sin, the more and greater the judgment is; and as when sin is more restrained, either inwardly by the Spirit, and by the conscience, or outwardly by the laws and terror, the more mercifully God deals with men. So the more free the current of the disposition runs in ill ways, the more wretched a man is.

Yea, but will the heart of some atheistical person presently say, What punishment is it, as long as I have liberty in evil, and meet with no hindrance in my courses, and feel no harm, but rather the contrary, as many that get their riches by ill means, and those great papists, those great usurpers, we see what estates they get to themselves?

I answer, Spiritual judgments are so much the greater, by how much they are less sensible, because if they be not sensible to us here, they will be the more sensible to us hereafter. And those that have their will most

* That is, 'consciousness.'—Ed.

here, shall suffer most against their will hereafter. It is the greatest judgment in this world for a man to have his will in sinful courses. He that shall make an idol of his will, especially a man that is in great place of honour, that shall make all ways serve for the accomplishment of his will when he hath it, he is the most miserablest man in the world; for he that hath his will most in courses unjustifiable, shall suffer most against his will when he cometh to a reckoning. Such men therefore are the more miserable, because such taking themselves to be absolute persons, and their ways the best ways, though they have many determents from their base courses, yet they will hear no counsel, and therefore the harder to be reclaimed. It doth not therefore take away from their punishment, but rather aggravate it.

I beseech you, let me press this a little, that these judgments are great judgments, although we do not feel them, when with a free consent we give ourselves unto ill. It is a heavy judgment when God leaves us to our own lusts, and takes away the guidance of his Spirit. We had better that God should give us up to the devil for a while to be tormented; we had better be in hell, if a man might come out at a certain time, than to be given up all our life-time to do with our own consent and will, that which is liking to our own will and lust, because by yielding to our own will we yield to the devil that rules in a man's affections and will. For a man's affections, when they are carried to evil, they are the chariots of Satan. When the devil sees excessive sinful affections, as excessive sinful joy and delight in sinful pleasures, he being about us, is always carried in these affections, and carries us also strongly in the ways that lead unto eternal perdition.

We judge, when a man suffers some outward punishment, as casting into prison or the loss of his sight, oh, he is in a fearful case; but what is the case of a man blinded by Satan and his own lusts? a man that is a slave to his own base affections, and by consequent to the devil, which rules in his affections, and so consequently to damnation? a man that lies under the wrath of God, that hath no heart to repent? If a man had spiritual eyes to consider the case of that man, he would never pity so much the case of those men that suffer outward losses, as he would pity those which he sees to live, and oftentimes to die, in evil courses of life.

This should therefore be an use of direction to us, that seeing we hear that God rules the hearts of men; that he takes away his Spirit, and leaves men to occasions, we should pray to God to rule our hearts himself. Lord, take thou the rule of our hearts, to govern them thyself. It was a good prayer of the ancient church: 'O God, from whom all holy desires and all good counsels do proceed,' &c. *(f)*. Indeed, it is he from whom all good counsels do proceed. These ten horns, they were ten kings. No doubt but as they were men of great place, so of great parts; but without God's Spirit, without his light, the greatest and the wisest man is but mad. He is as a man out of his wits, puzzled in darkness, and knows not which way to go. When God gives men over to their own lusts, to their blind affections, they lead men to judgment, and they must needs fall into the pit.

Let us desire God to put into our hearts holy desires, holy purposes, for from him all holy desires come. Let us desire him not only to govern our estate, and to preserve our bodies from danger, but, Lord, keep thou our hearts. We cannot keep our hearts of ourselves. Do thou bend our understandings, bow our affections and our wills, that they may run in the right way.

And to stir us up to this the more, we must know, that that evil which we do not, we are beholding to God for, as much as for the good we do. Why do not men, having an ill disposition and corrupt nature, do ill? Because God offers not occasions of ill. If God should offer occasions, they would commit the evil as well as others. It is God that puts into men's hearts to hate that evil. If God should take away his Spirit, men would not hate evil when occasions are offered, as these men did not when the occasion was offered: 'They gave up their kingdoms and thrones to the beast.' So that we are beholding to God for all the ill that we do not; either it is his not offering occasions, or else his giving us strength in the occasions. This we forget. We are apt to say, This wicked man hath done this; this good man is fallen into this; this man hath done that. But where is our devotion at this time? We should rather say, Lord, it was thee, for causes thou best knowest; for if thou hadst left me, especially when occasions were presented and offered, and there was a correspondent corruption in my heart to close with the occasion, I had fallen into the like sin. It was thy keeping, and not my goodness.

One thing more; the beast is expressed before in chap. xiii. to be led by the devil. So that howsoever the devil, who by St Paul is called the god of this world, and the pope the subordinate vicar to the devil, and so by consequence he is the devil, for the devil, the dragon rules him. Howsoever, I say there be the devil, the god of this world, and the pope in this world, the vicar of that dragon; yet there is but one monarch, one that rules all, both devil and pope, and all the wicked limbs of both to his own ends. It was God that put it into the hearts of these kings to give up their kingdoms to the beast. It is he alone that is absolute, that gives up the liberty of the chain, both to men and devils: thus far they shall go, and no further. It is a good saying of the schools, That there is no ill so ill, as there is good that is good: there is not any ill so strong as God is good, but every ill must come under the government of God. The devil himself, nor the vile heart of man, cannot go out of his rule, yet may run out of his commandments. But then it runs into his justice. He may go against the revealed will of God, but then he runs into his secret will. There is no ill ill in that degree that God is good; but every ill is in somewhat, and from somewhat, and for somewhat, that is good, as it is over-ruled by God. The crucifying of Christ, which was the worst action that ever was, yet it tended to the greatest good, viz., the salvation of mankind. So this giving to the beast of these ten thrones by these ten kings, it was a sin and a punishment of their sin; but it was for a good end, as we shall see afterward, if the time will give leave.

This should teach us absolute dependence and subjection to this great God. They need fear no creatures that fear God. They need fear no devil, nor Turk, nor pope, nor all the limbs of them; for God is the absolute monarch of the world. He can do what he will; and if God be on our side, who can be against us? It is said he is a wise politician that can make his own ends out of his enemies' designs. The great governor of heaven and earth can do so. He can put a hook into the nostrils of the leviathans of this world, and can draw them and rule them as he pleaseth. They may do many things, but it shall be all to accomplish his ends and purposes. They shall do his will. God put it into the hearts of these kings to fulfil his will; he put it into their hearts to agree to give up their kingdoms to the beast, and so they did submit themselves to antichrist for a great while.

In the next place, it is expressed how this came: 'They *gave* their kingdoms to the beast.' We are to see how far faulty these kings were, and how far faulty the pope, the beast, was, to whom they gave their kingdoms. For it may be objected that these men they did but obey God, for he put it into their hearts; and for the pope, they offered their kingdoms to him, and who would not receive offered gold? But here is a deal of devilish deceit. For, first, God gave them over to themselves, and they gave themselves and their kingdoms to the beast. What then was sinful in them? This, to give their kingdoms to the beast.

This, they betrayed their kingdoms. Here is a wrong to God, a wrong to themselves, and a wrong to their subjects. A wrong to God, whose vicegerents they were. Did he give them their kingdoms to give them to his enemy, to give them to the beast, and by consequence to the devil? Doth God raise up men to rule that they should enthral themselves and their kingdoms to the beast, to give them to God's enemies? No; kings reign by him. The pope saith, By me. Is their constitution of men? No, kings reign by God; they derive their authority from him: 'It is he that hath power over kings,' Dan. ii. 21. They reign not if he will, and they may rule if he will, by his will permitting, else no man can reign. 'By me kings reign.' If, then, they reign by him, it is a treason against God to betray the kingdoms that he hath given them into the hands of his enemies. It is a wrong to Christ. Whereas they should kiss the Son by kisses of subjection; as princes use to do in the eastern countries, to fall down and kiss their sovereigns' toes, they do in this the clean contrary.

Here is a wrong to themselves. They betray their own authority; that when God hath made them kings to rule they will be slaves; and it is a great sin for a man not to maintain his standing, as it is well observed by his Majesty, who, if ever prince did, doth vindicate himself, and challenge his regal authority: and it shall continue, and make him live even to the world's end (*g*). It is the greatest sin for a man to betray himself. Every man is to maintain that place and standing that God hath set him in. These ten horns they wronged themselves and their place; God made them kings over their people, and they become slaves to an antichristian priest.

It was a great wrong to their subjects. Kingdoms, we know, follow their kings; and if Jeroboam make Israel to sin, all Israel will quickly sin. Diseases come from the head; if the head be naught,* there will be a disease in the body ere long. A greater stone being tumbled down from a hill, it carries lesser stones along with it: so great kings, when they fall themselves, they draw their kingdoms after them (*h*). Therefore the phrase of the Scripture is, 'God put into their hearts to give,' not only themselves, but their kingdoms, to the beast. For commonly the idol of the people is their king, and, being led by sense and not by faith, they fear him more than they fear God; and their own restraint more than they fear hell; and so they come to this damned religion by depending upon him. Therefore it is a wrong to the people, knowing they are so slavish by nature and wanting faith, are fearing, terror-led by the present command of their king. Thus it was a wrong in these kings every way.

But the pope, the beast, what was to blame in him? He did but take that which was offered him. 'They gave their kingdoms to the beast.'

I answer, Indeed, he took that which was offered him, but he abused these kings, he abused the Christian world. He had no title to these kingdoms, but was a fraudulent possessor of them, because he came to them by a slight.† He raised himself to the popedom by the ruins of the

* That is, 'naughty,' = diseased.—G. † That is, 'sleight, = craft.—G.

empire; for, upon the divisions of the empire, the emperor having enemies in the east, he was fain to rest in Constantinople, and thereupon Rome being much neglected, at last was overrun by the Goths and Vandals; and the pope, taking occasion of the absence of the emperor, set up himself, thus raising himself by the ruins of the empire; and then, he being established, set up Pepin, father of Charles the Great, and put down Childerick; who, being a weak prince, he deposed, and set the other up, that he might gratify him so. So he collogued* with princes.†

And then again, he won‡ respect and authority from the horns by diabolical and vile courses. For, first, he abused their understandings, keeping them from the Scriptures, and then he abused their affections, and drew them this way and that way with toys.§ They gave him great matters, and he gave them indulgences and pardons, and consecrated grains, (*i*) and such like things.

Then again, he would oft force them to yield by excommunications, and many false titles of Peter's successor and Peter's chair; so, by the terror and dread of excommunication he awed them.

Again, he wrought by subtilty, joining with one prince against another, setting one against another; and, if he joined with any party, he had such a slight that he would be sure to make him a slave to the papacy, one way or other, or else he would excommunicate him; and then, before they should be absolved, they must either pay a great sum of money, or else they must go such a voyage, or set such men or such on such an enterprise.

And then again, he gave dispensations to sell souls; and so men might do what they would, they should have pardon, otherwise they should have excommunication.

And then again, he had preferments for the sons of the horns; cardinals' places for their second sons, that they should be great princes; he had high places for them.

Then again, he laid his foundation on false grounds. He would be universal bishop; and the church could not err; and all of them must fetch and determine of their matters from him; and appeal must be made to none but to him; and in certain cases none could satisfy the conscience but him. So that he greatly raised his authority by these false and cozening means; and all that yielded to him were a deluded company of people, that were deluded by the false and subtile courses he took. And therefore, although they gave their kingdoms to him, yet he possessed them by a fraudulent title; the means he used were diabolical.

'They gave their kingdoms to the beast, till the word of God should be fulfilled.'

Well! we see here the judgment of God upon the Christian world. It was not only a judgment upon these kings, as they were kings, but God punished the people's sin in the slavery of these kings to the beast.

See here the judgment of God upon kings and princes for not esteeming, as they should do, the glorious gospel of Christ; for they, both princes and people, had it, but they esteemed it not, but delighted in untruths; therefore God gave them up to believe lies.

We are not, therefore, over much to pity our ancestors. Though they deserve pity, yet we excuse them overmuch this way; for certainly God is just in his judgment, who, seeing them delight in lies more than in his

* That is, 'entered into league,' = plotted.—G.
† These are the commonplaces of history now.—G.
‡ Printed 'wan.'—G. § That is, 'trifles.'—G.

truth, took away his grace, and gave them up to this beast, that they should give up their authority, both prince and people, to him. And because they would not be ruled by God's will, thinking themselves wiser than he, he appointed them to be ruled by one that should be ruled by the devil; for the devil was in the pope, and who would serve the devil if he knew it? But because they would not yield unto Christ's sweet government, therefore he gave them over to a government fit for them, even to be governed by the beast.

I beseech you take notice of this point. When we entertain not the glorious gospel of Christ, the good word of God, that word that declares salvation unto us, and which is an instrument to work grace in us, to fit us for heaven; that word that is the seed and the food of our new birth, the evidence of our inheritance; that good word which is the greatest jewel under heaven; when we do not value that, it is the greatest error that can be, and it is just with God to give us up to this and to that error, if not unto popery, yet unto some one error that the devil is in, and contrary to the Spirit of God. Do ye think, if a master should see his servant take ill courses, and would not do according to his appointment and admonition, that he would not leave him to take his own course, and so let him do his own will, that thereby he might see his folly in not being ruled by him? So it is just with God, when he sees that we do not make much of his gospel, of his soul-saving gospel, that we will not have that alone, but traditions with it, and that, besides Christ, we must have other mediators, as if Christ were not rich enough, it is just with God to give both prince and people up to the beast. Let us, therefore, make much of the gospel. What moved God to give up the eastern empire, those glorious churches in Saint John's time, unto the Turk? Nothing but this: they did not value the gospel. What moved God to give up those western kings to Romish antichrist,—for those two, the Turk and pope, are twins; they had their beginning at once, about seven hundred years after Christ,—what moved this, but only, when God had dealt graciously with them at the first, and gave them his truth to save their souls, which is the most comfortablest thing in the world to have God discover what he means to do with us, and what he would have us to do, when he discovered his will to them, and saw them leave his will, saw them leave gold, and take dross, prefer the traditions and wisdom of men before the wisdom of God, it was just with him to give them up to believe lies.

'They gave their kingdoms to the beast' (mark the limitation here 'until') 'until the word of God should be fulfilled.'

I see I cannot make an end of the text. A little further, and so I will conclude.

Here is an 'until;' here is a stop. The devil and the beast had their time to seduce the kings, and the kings had their time to be seduced, and to give up their kingdoms, but God hath his time, Christ hath his time. Christ gives his enemies time, and then takes time himself, 'until the time that the word of God shall be fulfilled.'

We see here, then, a mixture of mercy with justice; that after God had given them up justly, not only the eastern empire, but also the western kings to the pope, yet notwithstanding here is an 'until.' God limits ill not only for the measure of it, but also for the time of it. God at length turns the stream of things; so that these kings that were thus abused and baffled by this man of sin, this beast, at last they grow wise, by the instinct of God, and hate the beast as much as ever they loved her.

So, then, this is the point, that the same God that by divine providence gave way to these kings to abuse the doctrine of the gospel, and that gave way to these people, that were unthankful, to yield themselves in such slavery to the pope, yet notwithstanding, in mercy, God at the last put into the hearts of these kings to withdraw their necks from this yoke, and to put their necks under Christ's yoke.

This 'until' hath had a beginning many years ago, for we know, to omit other kings of other countries, King Henry the Eighth, of famous memory, take him without those things we cannot upbraid,* now he was a man of great and excellent parts, as he was of great vices. He was an excellent instrument of Christ to unhorse the pope, to shake off his government, to hate the whore, and to eat her flesh; that is, to overthrow the monasteries, those cages of unclean birds, and those Peter pence, those exactions; for indeed the pope made England his ass to bear his burdens. It would move any man's patience to see how pitifully the popes of Rome have abused this island, so that we may now truly say, as Christ saith, 'If the Son make you free, you are free indeed,' John viii. 36. Christ hath made us free, the gospel hath made us free, and ever since the coming of the gospel we have flourished. King Henry shook off the yoke first, and after him King Edward, and after him Elizabeth of blessed memory, and now our gracious king. So that this 'until' it begun long since to hate the beast, and to eat her flesh. One thing there is yet undone, 'to burn her with fire.' If they hate the beast, and eat her flesh, this will come too, to burn her with fire; even the ten kings that were subject to her before shall do that.

We see wickedness shall not thrive always. It shall not always be night, but the sun shall arise at the last. Impostures shall not always abuse the world. Their madness shall be made manifest at length, as Paul saith, 2 Tim. iv. 18. This is our comfort, that there is an 'until,' a time prefixed of God to discover and to lay open all impostures; and now the time is come that most of this should be fulfilled. Some of these words of God are fulfilled. The beast is hated; and now the beast is known to be the beast, to be cruel. Witness the blood of saints, the murder of kings, those horrible acts that are allowed from Rome. The beast, I say, is now discovered and hated.

The affections that are due to the beast is hatred. If ever we hated anything, we may hate the state of Rome. It is a beast, and the object of hatred, and ever was; and if ever, I say, we hated anything that was deservable of our hatred, it is that. Why? Do we not hate a harlot? Do we not hate an old strumpet, an old painted strumpet? Do we not hate her that is a bawd? There was never bawd, there was never whore, that did the thousandth part of that harm that this bawd, this beast, this whore of Rome hath done, drawing so many thousand souls to hell.

Of all the judgments that ever were since the beginning of the Christian world that God hath visited the pride and wickedness of men with, there was none so grievous as to suffer this man of sin to rule in the church. The spiritual judgment of the papacy it is the greatest judgment of God that was ever inflicted upon any.

We hate them that misuse us under the pretence of love, that cheat and cozen us, and we delight in their punishment. There was never cheater, never cozener like this. And surely so God hath fulfilled his word, that

* That is, 'exaggerate.' We have here an excellent example, awanting in Richardson, *sub voce*, of the use of this word in this (now obsolete) sense.—G.

she is hated even in our children, that know but the grounds of religion, to whom Christ hath shined by the evidences of his truth, that have the Spirit of God in them. They hate those impostures, those abuses of Christian religion, with which this beast hath deluded the Christian world, which shews that they have a contrary spirit to the Spirit of God. And indeed so they have; for, besides their own base government, they maintain the corruptions of men, feeding the pride and vanity of men's natures with outward, formal, empty things; so that the very weak ones, even children, now they hate the whore, hate her impostures, hate her cruelty, hate her lying, and all.

I see the time is past: I can go no further, but will draw to an end, only a little to stir us up. Shall God then reveal and discover this painted strumpet, this bawd, and shall we labour to conceal her ill? shall we daub, shall we make her better than she is? Shall we hinder God's purpose? God's word is, that she shall be revealed; the princes shall hate her, and consume her with fire. Let every one of our purposes help God's purpose, and providence, and decree in this point. That this shall be, it is God's purpose; and whosoever stops it, certainly they bring the judgment of God upon them. Those that would rear up Jericho again, we know what befell them; and they that rear up Rome, that begins now to be discovered, they bring the judgment of God upon them. God will perform this as well as he performed the other. As he put it into the hearts of these kings to betray their kingdoms to the beast, so he will put it into their hearts to hate the whore.

Now that we may hate her, let every one labour in his place: ministers in their place to lay open their impostures, their cozenings, and all their filthiness, whereby they deceive the people; magistrates in their place to countenance the ministers, to see the laws executed as they may. These that through ignorance are seduced, that are not Jesuited, for there is no hope of them; but others, their persons many times in the policy of state may have favour, but not their religion.

Let us all take heed that we grow in knowledge: let us labour to make more of the gospel of Christ. The more Christ appears in glory, the more antichrist will appear in shame. Let us labour by prayer, and not give God over by prayer, to plant the love of the truth in our hearts, to entertain the truth with love, to value it according to the respect it deserves at our hands, and let us labour to be moulded into that truth, to obey it; else, though we have it, yet if we do not love it, if we be not transformed into it, though our wits and parts be never so great, we may be seduced to error. God gave over these kings, men of great place and of great parts,—because they did not love the truth,—to believe lies.

My purpose was to have shewed the danger, if we do not further God's purpose in discovering this wicked antichrist: a state wherein the devil, the dragon, is effectual, and this book wondrously sets down the danger. It is another manner of danger now to relapse, and to apostatize, after the appearing of the glorious gospel of Christ, than it was a hundred years ago under darkness; and we know it to be so. Of all the judgments in this world it is the greatest for God to give up a man to decay in his love to the truth, to affect* this cursed religion, that the sentence of God hath passed upon, and it must be fulfilled, 'That they shall hate the whore, and burn her with fire, that she shall be left desolate and naked.'

But you may object. Alas! how is that likely to be, when we see now

* That is, 'love,' 'choose.'—G.

what strength the beast hath gotten, and how he ruffleth in the world at this time; how he triumpheth and trampleth the poor church under his feet?

Well, it is but a living before death. Undoubtedly Babylon is fallen, it is 'fallen,' saith John in his time, Rev. xiv. 8; that is, it is as sure to fall as if it had fallen already. The word of God hath said so. The power of man cannot hinder it. He hath put it into the heads and hearts of the kings to betray their kingdoms; he shall also put it into their hearts and heads to hate and burn the whore with fire at the last. It must be so. The angel said it was done, as if it were done already. It is as sure as if it were done. Therefore let us never take scandal at the flourishing state of the enemies of the church abroad; let us never dislike our religion for that. Babylon is fallen. The time will come when it shall be done. Heaven hath concluded it, and earth cannot hinder it; no, nor hell neither: God hath said it, and shall not he do it? It is the word of him that is Lord of his word; because he is Lord of hosts, and Lord of the creatures. It is the word of him that is Lord of lords, that is Lord of heaven and earth, Lord of all things. He hath said that Babylon is fallen; and therefore it must be so, he being Governor and Lord of all things, and of his word too, that can make all things prove serviceable to his purpose. Let us comfort ourselves, therefore, as if it were present, and not take offence at the state of the beast, and the whore's flourishing, but present him to yourselves as he is set out in the text. See him growing, see him rising, see him decaying, and at last see him cast into the bottomless pit, to burn in the lake of fire for ever. It is, you see, the word of God from heaven, that he is fallen, and cast into the earth as a millstone, and shall never rise again. He shall never quicken* again. Heathen Rome was quickened by papal Rome: the pope quickened the former beast; but there shall never be beast after this Rome, and therefore he is said in this chapter, 'to go into destruction;' that is, he, and his state, and all without repentance, shall so go into destruction, that there shall never be other beast.

And that that shall help this destruction forward, shall be the course that themselves take. God as he hath decreed their destruction, so he hath appointed that their own plots, which they have devised for their own maintenance, shall turn to their confusion. Do you not think that the ruin of the pope will be by the Jesuits, who are grown, by their pressing themselves, and by their pragmatical meddling into princes' affairs, by their drawing and assuming all business to themselves, and by their striving and bringing all to their profession, to such hatred of the world, that even these means, which they themselves take, will be the means of the overthrow and downfall of popery? As the counsel of Ahithophel was the means to infatuate him, so their own courses will cause their own overthrow.

In the powder treason, they thought they had been made for ever, but God turned their wickedness upon their own heads. And now in these later times we may see that God takes his cause into his own hands; and you know who spake it by observation, Haman's wife, 'If thou begin to fall, thou shalt not prevail, but shalt surely fall before him,' Esther vi. 13. So if God take the matter into his own hands, as he hath done already, let them fear. For they shall surely fall and not prevail, until he hath wrought his work in Sion; until he hath thoroughly purged his church, they shall prevail. There is a little time allotted them, but it is nothing. Let us see by the eye of faith what this book saith of them, that they shall be

* That is, 'live,' = 'be made alive.'—G.

destroyed; and let us look on the courses they themselves take which will cause their destruction. Was there ever anything that weakened popery so much as this desperate attempt that we now celebrate this day? Indeed, if we go to an ignorant papist, and tell him what doctrine they teach, and what upholds their doctrine, tell him of the powder treason, ask him concerning the traitors, he will mince the matter, Oh, they were unfortunate gentlemen, &c. But how did Sixtus Quintus mince the matter when they had success in the massacre in France; when many thousands of people were slain against the law, slain under pretence of being married and bidden to a marriage? (*j*) He was so far from disallowing the act, as that he caused it to be pictured in his palace. So if these had achieved this, they had not been unfortunate gentlemen; they had been made, they had been sainted, as some of them are, St Garnet! St Devil!* If the devil himself will help them, and further popery, he shall be sainted; and if they be never so base, yet for their rebellion and destruction of kings, they shall be sainted by them. Will not this provoke men to hate the beast and the whore, to make her desolate and naked, and to eat her flesh, and to burn her with fire?

Well, the time is past, I cannot finish the text as I thought to have done. To speak to the particular occasion I need not, it is yet fresh. And what should we speak of the gunpowder treason? The Jesuits and priests, having the devil for their midwife, they are big of such like plots; hell, Rome, and Satan, and the Jesuits, those frogs of the bottomless pit, they are full of devising such attempts. But I rather thought to speak against popery, against the beast and her religion at this time, than rhetorically to amplify that act of theirs, when indeed we are ready to have a new one continually, for they are always plotting and devising, I mean those Jesuits. Our comfort is to look to the Scripture, to look here what shall be the end of these frogs and of the beast. Ere long they shall be cast into the burning lake. Let us bless God that we live under this government, of so gracious a prince, that hath more weakened the pope by his learned writings, that ever any prince did.† So much for this time.

* Cf. note *ooo*, Vol. II. page 535.—G. † Cf. note *g*, page 534.—G.

NOTES.

(*a*) P. 520.—'Kings must kiss that . . . as they did Heliodorus.' Query, the private secretary of the Emperor Hadrian, and himself subsequently prefect of Egypt? Sibbes's name of 'emperor' would make it seem so: but the trait would better suit the haughty Heliodorus, author of the famous romance at the end of which he has proudly told that he was of the family of priests of the Syrian god of the sun (Τῶν ἀφ' Ἡλίου γένος).

(*b*) P. 520.—'The apostles, when they returned from preaching.' This is a singular slip on the part of Sibbes. It was Jesus who thus 'saw' Satan 'fall,' whatever the mysterious words may mean. The apostles told how the 'devils' had been subject to them. Probably this was running in Sibbes's mind at the time. Cf. Luke x. 18, *et seq.*

(*c*) P. 521.—'As Sixtus Quintus,' &c. The murderer of Henry III. (on August 1st 1589) was Jacques Clement, a Dominican friar. In Henry III. the House of Valois became extinct. By the 'bloody massacre' is no doubt intended that of St Bartholomew. The papal approbation, if we may not say exultation, on both occasions is a commonplace of history.

(*d*) P. 522.—'And as a man, it is Luther's comparison, that moves a horse.' The 'comparison is common to various of the early Fathers, *e. g.* Augustine and Basil, also Lombard, as well as Luther. Dr John Boys has worked it in very well, with much additional lore, in shewing how the Spirit is said to lead in temptation. Cf. Works, p. 234 (1629).

(*e*) P. 523.—'St Augustine, in the unfolding of this point, of the providence of God in evil.' See the reference to Boys in previous note (*d*). The reconciliation often recurs in Augustine.

(*f*) P. 525.—'It was a good prayer of the ancient church, Oh God, from whom all holy desires and all good counsels do proceed,' &c. One of the *memorabilia* of the *Book of Common Prayer.*

(*g*) P. 527.—'His majesty, who, if ever prince did, doth vindicate himself.' Sibbes seems, from this and other tributes, to have held a high opinion of James I. (VI. of Scotland). Let this be placed against more modern depreciations.

(*h*) P. 527.—'Kings . . . they draw their kingdoms after them.' Probably the author was thinking of Horace's line—

'Quicquid delirant reges, plectuntur Achivi.'

(*i*) P. 528.—'Consecrated grains.' Query, the 'wafer' of the host?

(*j*) P. 533 —'Sixtus Quintus.' Tillemont has pronounced this pope 'the most extraordinary man of his time (1585).' Sibbes would seem to refer to the great massacre on the '*Festival*' of St Bartholomew, Aug. 24. 1572; but the then reigning pope was Gregory XIII. Cf. note *c supra.* G.

THE CHURCH'S ECHO.*

And the Spirit and the bride say, Come.—REV. XXII. 17.

THIS book of the Revelation is an history of the state of the church, from the first coming of Christ to his second coming.

These two last chapters set down the glorious condition of the church, in the latter end of the world, and as it shall be in the consummation of all things, when the present state of things shall determine* in the 'second coming' of Christ. For howsoever, no doubt but there is set down the glorious condition of the church in this world in part, yet the desire of the church rests not in any condition here, therefore it is carried to the consummation and perfection of all. There shall be a kind of new world at the conversion of the Jews; but when the church is under that blessed condition, yet it is under desires still of farther perfection, till an end be made of all things. Therefore this saying here, 'Come,' hath reference to the future state of the church. All the desires of the church are restless till the consummation of all things in the latter coming of Christ. It carries all before it in a desire; 'come, Lord,' therefore to call the Jews; 'come, Lord,' to confound antichrist, which must be before that. For the Jews will never come in till the scandal† of idolatry be removed, and when all this is fulfilled, then 'come, Lord,' to make an end of this sinful world.

As it is with a river, it carries all before it, till it discharge itself into the ocean, where it is swallowed up, so it is with the desires of a Christian. They carry all in the mean time, between heaven and them, in a stream, and never rest till they be swallowed in heaven itself, and the 'second coming' of Christ to finish all things; and then is the period of all happiness, and the accomplishment of all promises, 'when Christ shall come to be glorious in his saints,' 2 Thes. i. 10.

* 'The Church's Echo' forms one of the sermons included in the 'Beams of Divine Light' (4to, 1639). Its separate title-page is as follows:—'The Chvrches Eccho. In one Sermon. By The late learned and reverend Divine, Rich. Sibbs: Doctor in Divinitie, Mr of Katherine Hall in Cambridge, and sometimes Preacher at Grayes-Inne. Isay 64. 1. Oh that thou wouldst rent the heavens and come downe, that the Mountaines might flow downe at thy presence. London, Printed by E. P. for Nicholas Bourne, and Rapha Harford, 1638.' G.

* That is, 'end.'—G.

† That is, 'stumbling-block.'—G.

The words they are, as it were an echo, an answer back again of the bride, the spouse of Christ, unto his promise of his coming, which he makes twice in this chapter, in ver. 7, 'Behold, I come quickly;' and in ver. 12, 'Behold, I come quickly;' and he comes not empty-handed, 'My rewards is with me.' Now the church here echoes back again: Christ saith, 'I come,' and the Spirit and the bride say, 'Come.' The words contain the most heavenly desire that can be, of the most excellent personage in this world, the queen, the bride of Christ; and it is a desire to the most excellent person absolutely, Christ himself, a desire of his coming; and it is stirred up by the most excellent Spirit, the Holy Spirit of God. For the meaning of the words is this, 'The Spirit and the bride say, Come,' not as distinct and severed, but the bride by the Spirit saith, 'Come,' the Holy Ghost in the bride, as it is Rom. viii. 26, 'We know not what to pray, but the Spirit makes intercession.' How is that? The Spirit makes intercession, by making us make intercession; for what Christ doth, the Spirit causeth us to do, for there is one Spirit in Christ and us. So the bride, by the motion of the holy and blessed Spirit, says, 'Come.' The order of our discourse upon these words shall be this,

First, to speak *of the person wishing, and her condition*, the bride.

And then of *the desire of this excellent personage*, the bride.

And then of *the moving cause that stirs up the bride to desire the coming of Christ.*

First, *For the person*, the bride.

The church is sometime compared to a woman for weakness; sometimes to a wife, for faithfulness to her husband Christ; sometimes to a bride, because she is contracted to Christ in this world; sometimes to a mother for her fruitfulness; sometimes to a virgin for her chastity; here to a bride, because this life is but the time of contract, but the consummation of the marriage shall be in heaven. Now this contract [is] between the church and Christ, and between every particular soul and Christ; for both are the bride of Christ. Even as it is the same soul that is in the little finger and in all the whole body, the same soul enlivens both, so it is the same Spirit in the bride in general, and in every particular Christian, therefore the bride is both every particular Christian's and the whole church's. Now the contract that is made between the soul, and between the church and Christ, it is by the Spirit of God, which knits the soul to Christ, and Christ to the soul; and for this end, that Christ might be a husband, and contract this bride to himself in our nature, he married our nature that he might marry our persons.

There is a threefold degree of union:

An union of nature, grace, glory.

The union *of nature* was, when Christ took *our nature* upon him. The union *of grace* is, when we take his nature, when we partake of the divine nature. The union *of glory* is when we shall all be in heaven. The first is for the second, and the second for the third. Christ became bone of our bone in nature, that we might be 'bone of his bone' with him in grace; and so perfectly one with him in glory. We see the bride, that is the person. Here I might take occasion to speak of the sweet comfort that issues from this, that the second person in the Trinity should dignify us so much, as to take us to unity with and contract us to himself. But I will not speak much of this point, having spoken more at large of it out of the Canticles.*

* Cf. 'Bowels Opened,' Vol. II. *in loc.*—G.

If marriage be honourable, what is this marriage and contract which is indeed the pattern of all other? Others are but shadows to this.

Use 1. Hence comes *the sweet security and peace of the church, from this contract between Christ and it;* for all our debts are discharged by this. He took upon him our sins. And then the church hath interest in him and all his in this contract and marriage which is to be consummate; all that he is and hath is the church's. 'All is yours, because you are Christ's,' 1 Cor. iii. 21, *seq*. What a large comfort is this, if we had hearts to consider of it and to improve it! His grace serves for the church: 'of his fulness we receive grace for grace.' John i. 16. So we may say of all the privileges that Christ hath, they are first in him and then in the church. The church shines in his beams. And as it is matter of wondrous comfort, so it is likewise matter of more special comfort, in case of infirmities. The church is a woman, therefore the weaker vessel. Now God, that bids us 'bear with the woman, as the weaker vessel,' 1 Peter iii. 7, to honour her with the honour of gentle usage,—for that honour is meant,—he that teacheth man his duty, will he not perform it himself, to bear with his church, as the weaker vessel? Especially when it is the condition of the marriage, Hosea ii. 19, 'I will marry thee to me in mercy.' We may claim mercy as a part of our dowry by Christ, pardoning mercy, forbearing, pitying mercy. We make not use of this comfort when we are discouraged.

Use 2. But this teacheth us likewise how *to carry ourselves to Christ as we should do, chastely*. To take heed how we judge of things, we must keep our judgments chaste. A Christian hath not liberty to riot in his opinion, to run at random, to see what carnal reason saith. No; he must think what Christ thinks, and submit his judgment to him. And he must have no will of his own; he must give it up to his contracted husband, Christ, and be content to be ruled by him in all things; he must forget his father's house and his former condition, and not to make this marriage, as carnal professors do, a cover for their adulterous unfaithfulness. What is the course of many Christians? They make the profession of religion a cover for their ill dealing, for their unfaithful courses. What a shame is this! It is abominable. What makes the faults of wives worse than the fault of single persons? Because they are contrary to covenants, besides many other inconveniences, the confusion of offspring and the like. But this is one grand difference, to make the exaggeration of the fault, it is contrary to former covenant. Those that are swearers and filthy persons, that disgrace religion, and yet notwithstanding cover themselves under pretence that they are contracted to Christ, they are baptized and come to the sacrament, &c., such wretched persons shall know ere long what it is to dally with religion. What is the aggravation of the faults of such persons? They deal as filthy adulteresses do, they make religion a cover for their wretched courses. God is merciful, Christ died, we are Christians, we are baptized, &c. This is an obligation to a stricter life. It gives men no liberty, but is a stricter bond to a holy life, the renewing of the new covenant again and again. Therefore there is no comfort for any such wretched persons, that countenance themselves under the profession of religion. It adds a greater degree to their offence. O ye adulterers and adulteresses, saith St James, 'know ye not that the love of the world is enmity with God'? James iv. 4. When we let our hearts loose to vain things, and yet pretend that we are contracted to Christ, we are adulterers and adulteresses.

I beseech you therefore, in the name of Christ, for it is our office that are ministers, to bring Christ and his spouse together, we are *Paranymphi,** friends of the bridegroom, as it is in the New Testament. Let me entreat you in good earnest, those that have not seriously given up their names to Christ, to be contracted to him, to join with him in good earnest, and to resign all to him in your inward man, in your judgments, and wills, and affections, and then you shall find it the most comfortable condition in this world. Indeed, all is nothing to the comfort of this condition, to be in deed and not in outward profession only, in covenant with Christ, to be contracted to him. If not, if you will take liberty under the profession of religion, to live loosely, to be swearers and filthy persons, to use your tongues as you list,† as if you had made no promise to Christ, as indeed we all have, what will be the confusion of your souls ere long! Oh that we dallied with religion! that we were entreated to be as we should be by all sweet bonds! and yet we preferred our own lusts and base affections. This will be the aggravation of hell and damnation itself; this entreaty of Christ, and the excellent prerogatives and privileges that we have in Christ. And in the mean time we stand more upon our own base courses, and will not leave anything to give up ourselves to Christ. But I mean not to dwell on this point. This is the person, 'the bride.' She is called 'the bride,' and not the wife, because she is only contracted here on earth; and she is called 'the bride,' in opposition to the whore of Babylon in this book, that is, the filthy adulteress, the false church. The true church of Christ is a bride and a virgin; in heaven she shall be a wife. The false church is a whore. She defiles herself with idolatry and abominations. So partly for distinction from itself in heaven, where it shall be a wife, and partly in opposition to the false church, she is here called a bride.

To come, in the next place, *to the desire of the church.* How should the church know she is a bride? This is one way, the desire of the marriage. Where there is a true contract, there is a desire of the marriage, of the consummation of it, a desire of the coming of Christ. In this there are two things considerable.

First, *that Christ will come.*

And then the church hath a desire of this coming. That Christ will come, I need spend no time to prove it, for it is an article of faith, 'He shall come to judge the quick and the dead.' And he will come to make an end of what he hath begun here. He came to redeem our souls. He must, and he will come to redeem our bodies from corruption. He came to be judged and to die for us. He must come to be judge of the quick and dead. He came to contract us, he will come again to marry us and to take us where he is. He loved us so, that he came from heaven to earth where we are, to take our nature, that he might be a fit husband, but he will come to take us to himself. We shall enter 'into his chamber, to the palace of the great King,' Ps. xlv. 15. He will come, there is no question of that.

The uneven carriage of things in this world to the eyes of men evinceth so much. You see how it is here with mighty persons that shake off Christ's yoke, how they bear sway, how Satan plays freaks‡ in opposing Christ; he rules in the children of pride. This must not alway be so. There must and will be a time when Christ will 'be glorious in his saints.' Now the life of Christ in the saints is a 'hidden' life; there must be a day of revelation. And even as it was in Christ's first coming, there was all kind of arguments and witnesses to prove that he should come in the flesh, a choir

* That is, from παρανυμφιος = brideman.—G.

† That is, 'choose.'—G. ‡ Misprinted 'reaks.'—G.

of angels from heaven to witness it; and on earth, the wise men among the Gentiles; and among the Jews, old Simeon. There was men and women, all kind of witnesses. So in his 'second coming,' there is all kind of witnesses. In this chapter here is Christ, and the angel, and John, and the Spirit, and the spouse, the church in general and every particular soul. Their desire of his coming shews that he will come; for the desires stirred up in the heart by the Holy Ghost, they will not be in vain. The desires of his coming shew that he will come; for spiritual desires must have their accomplishment. There will be a coming of Christ, there is no question of that.

And the church here desires it. It is the disposition of the church to be carried in her desires to it; wherein we will shew the ground of this desire, and then the use that we are to make of it.

The grounds why the church desires the coming of Christ are manifold.

1. First of all, look but to the present condition of things in this world, the state of things, *the scandals that are in the church.* There will be a desire in the church that all scandals and offences may be removed, as it is in the gospel, 'Christ will come and take away all that offend.'

2. Look again to the state of the church here, it is but *a persecuted, afflicted estate*, nay, those that should countenance the poor church, how roughly is the poor church used ofttimes of those! Those that should encourage the church, their rugged and rough usage stirs up this desire in the church, when those that should be most encouragement are ofttimes the greatest discouragement.

3. Then again the church hath *antichrist to oppose it, and false brethren in it*, false persons that hang in their affections to the world. And however they make a show, yet their minds are carried to pomp and to a false religion, because they are besotted with a proud carnal disposition, which they prefer before the simplicity of the gospel; vain persons in the bosom of the church, that know not what the glory of the church is.

4. Then again, if we regard even *the weakness of the church itself*, it breeds a desire of Christ's coming; for, alas! there is but a weak sight in men; and variety of sight where there is weakness, breeds variety of judgment; and where there is variety of judgment, there will be jealousies even among good persons; and these are irksome to the Spirit of God in any that love the sweet peace and concord of Christians, that are contracted to Christ. This will not be avoided in this world. Only those that are wise and strongest in grace, they will be the greatest peace-makers, and bear with the weak in this kind.

5. Then again, while we are in this world, there is not the best thing *but Satan will put his foot and claw in*, except grace overpower him. The magistracy and ministry, alas! how are they many times profaned and abused by Satan and corrupt-hearted men, that know not how to manage them graciously and fruitfully? The magistracy that is for good, it is turned ofttimes for grievance, as if all the world were made for them, and they to do nothing but to have others idolise them. And then for the ministry, those that should be teachers of others, many times discourage those that they should cherish; and as the prophet complains in this time of the false prophets, they discourage those that they should encourage, and strengthen the bands of the wicked, and grieve those that God doth not grieve by their false carriage, taking contrary ways to God's Spirit. They grieve those that they should cherish and comfort, and strengthen the hearts of those that they should take down, by flattery and false applications. This will

be to the end of the world, notwithstanding the excellent ordinance of God, by which God works his own good ends. While the world stands there will be a taint upon God's ordinance till Christ come, and then all that grieve and offend shall be taken away. There shall be no sun nor moon then, for the Lamb will do all. There shall be no magistracy nor ministry then, 'God will be all in all,' 1 Cor. xv. 28.

And so for all conditions. There is no condition nor nothing that is good in the world, but Satan labours to bring a vanity upon it, and the corrupt heart of man is prone to yield to him; this will be to the end of the world. Therefore we should not be over much offended, to see things carried otherwise than we would have them. Why should we wish for that condition that will never be in this world? Wish we may, but we must wish it in its own time. It will be hereafter. Let us labour that it may be so then, and bear with all here as patiently as we can.

6. Again, take the best Christians of all, in themselves, in their own particulars. Alas! *what a conflicting life hath a Christian with his own heart!* Sometimes, in general, he can see truths very clear, but, in a particular, some passion or other, of anger or revenge, &c., it clouds his judgment, that he cannot see what is to be done, what is best. The reason is, the imperfection of the work of mortification, hinders him in his passages and business, that he cannot clearly decide of what is best at this time. St Paul complains of this, that he '*could not do the good that he would, and that he did the ill that he would not*,' Rom. vii. 21. There are none but they carry some of these dregs with them in this world, that hinders them in their designs and determinations. Only those that have the power of God's Spirit in a greater portion than the rest, they get more victory over these things, and can more clearly see anything than others. Yet notwithstanding, all have some impediment this way, even the best.

7. *The necessities of this life enforce a great deal of trouble;* the supplying the necessities of nature and of the condition that God hath set us in, which all shall have an end then.

8. Then again, *the relation between Christ and this contracted spouse, and every faithful soul*, enforceth a desire of his coming. It is the time of the church's contract; she is a bride now, she is contracted. Now all the time between the contract and the marriage, it is a time of longing and desire; therefore the church cannot but desire the second coming of Christ. It is the nature of imperfection, where there is truth in imperfection, to desire perfection. You see the little seed that is sown in the ground, it breaks through the thick clods, because it is not in its perfection till it be in the ear. Nature hath given it an instinct to break out. So where the seed of grace is, it will break out and shoot forward to desire still and still, till it comes to perfection. Grace being an imperfect state here, it puts forward in desiring that perfection that it cannot attain in this world, but in the world to come. Therefore the Spirit and the spouse say, 'Come.'

9. And then, *from the nature of the affection of love itself, where it is planted.* It is an affection of perfect union. Contract will not serve, but marriage must come after. Love will not satisfy itself in imperfect union, but it cries, 'Come, come,' still. It is carried in a restless desire till it come to perfection. Therefore put the case the Jews were called and converted, and antichrist subdued, hath the church an accomplishment of the period of her desires, to say no more, 'Come?' Oh no! Yet Christ is not come as he will. There is not a perfect consummation of all; until

that of time itself, there will be a desire of the bride and spouse to say, 'Come.' Thus we see what grounds there are of this desire.

Quest. But is this only true of the church militant here below? Doth not the church in heaven say, 'Come,' too?

Ans. Yes, the church in heaven saith, 'Come,' too. The church in heaven and earth are but one family. They are, as it were, but one parliament. There is the higher house in heaven, and the lower on earth, and both say 'Come.' What is the reason that the church in heaven saith, 'Come?' Because the church in heaven have bodies that be rotting in earth; which bodies helped them to serve God on earth, fasted with them and prayed with them, and endured pains and toil with them. The soul accounts itself imperfect till it be joined to its old companion the body again. Therefore it desires, 'Come, Lord,' that my body may be united to me again; that so we may both perfectly praise thee in heaven.

Then again, they have not all their company; all the saints are not gathered; and they will not be merry indeed till they all meet in heaven. Therefore that all may meet, even the church in heaven hath a desire, 'Come, Lord.' So both heaven and earth agree in this, they meet in this desire.

Use 1. This may be a ground of trial, *whether we be truly the bride of Christ or no.* The ground of the trial may be gathered hence. Whither is the bent of our desire carried? Is our condition so here, as that we desire to be as we are still? Then all is naught with us. The church, we see, saith 'Come.' Nothing will content her in this world. So those hearts that are wrought upon by the Spirit of God, nothing here will content them, but still they say, 'Come.' The disposition in carnal persons is clean contrary. They say, as it is in Job, 'Depart from us, we will none of thy ways,' Job xxi. 14; they are of the mind of the devil in the Gospel, 'Why dost thou come to torment us before our time? Mat. viii. 29. Do not come. If it were in the power of most men in the church, whether Christ should come to judge the world or no, do you think they would give their voice that way, that Christ should come? They would never do it: for they know how unfit a condition they are in for the second coming of Christ. If thieves and malefactors might have liberty to choose whether there should be assizes or no, surely they would never have any. So it is with the men of the world, that live in sinful, wretched courses; that abuse their tongues and their bodies; are they of the disposition of the bride, to say, 'Come'? Oh no! They know they have not done their duty. Therefore let us enter deeply into our own souls, and try whether cordially we can yield this desire of our hearts to say, 'Come'?

(1). Therefore, to spend a little time in further search, if we can truly say 'Come,' *we will desire Christ to come into our souls now*, to rule our souls now, to come and make way for himself in our hearts. Is it possible for the soul to desire to go to Christ, that will not suffer him to come to it? If Christ rule not in us, we shall never reign with Christ: if Christ's kingdom come not to us, we shall never enter into Christ's kingdom. Therefore the soul that hath this desire truly, to say, 'Come,' it will give Christ entrance into it and let him 'come' by his ordinances. 'Come,' Lord, by thy word! come by thy Spirit into my heart! close with my heart! drive out whatsoever is there that will not give thee liberty to reign as thou wilt! These desires will be in a true heart. It will not cherish wilfully those desires that are contrary to this.

Shall we think that that Christian that saith these words in good earnest will put Christ away in his ordinances, and not care for to hear his word, nor care to meet Christ here in earth, and yet pretend a desire to meet him in heaven? Where is Christ here? Is he not in his congregations and assemblies of his saints? Those, therefore, that despise the ordinances of God, and yet pretend that they desire that Christ should come, do they not profane the Lord's prayer when they say, 'Hallowed be thy name,' 'Thy kingdom come'? They patter* it over; they do not mean it in good earnest. When they despise the ministry and the ministers, and whatsoever is Christ's, despise the motions of his Spirit, and will not suffer him to rule in their hearts, but are ruled by rules of policy and reason and flesh, can they say, 'Come'? No! They do abominably profane the Lord's prayer. What kind of service is that, when their desires are quite clean contrary? It is a protestation contrary to their faith, and therefore it is a nullity. They profess in their prayers that they would have Christ to come, and yet their course of life is contrary; they would not have him come.

(2.) Again, those that truly desire Christ should come, *they will be subordinate helpers under Christ, to promote those things that tend to his coming.* Before Christ comes, antichrist must be abolished and consumed; the Jews must be converted, and the number of the elect must be consummate and finished. Therefore what shall we say, when those that pretend to desire the coming of Christ shall countenance heresies that must have an end first? And those that are against wholesome laws to be made in that kind, those that countenance idolatry and false worship, stablishing what Christ must abolish before he come, can they say, 'Come,' in good earnest? Their course is contrary to what they pray. Therefore in deed and in good earnest we pray, 'Thy kingdom come,' and say with our souls as the church here, 'Come,' when we set ourselves to abolish heresy and false worship of God, that is adulterous, and promote the true service of God; when we labour in our places that the number of the elect may be consummate; when we labour that our children may be God's children, and our servants may be God's servants, and every one in our places labour that the kingdom of Christ may be enlarged—if we put not to our helping hand to that we pray for, it is a contradiction. Those, therefore, that live scandalous lives, in scandalous courses and speeches, and hinder the conversion of people's souls, and labour to draw them to wicked, hellish courses, when they post to hell themselves, and labour to draw others into cursed society with themselves, they cannot truly say, as the church here, 'Come.' Let us take it to heart, that we do not mock and dally with religion. It is a greater matter than we take it for. It is impossible but a Christian that saith his prayers in earnest, should be thus affected, unless we make a mockery of religion.

(3.) Again, if we can indeed say 'Come,' *there will be a fitting for this coming*, a preparing ourselves for it, for our going to Christ. Is it not so in civil things? And doth not grace work that that nature doth, in a higher degree? If we desire that a great person should come to us, will there not be a fitting of our houses, of our apparel, and entertainment suitable to the worth of the person? or else a man may say, Surely you look for nobody this day; there is nothing fitted and prepared. So if we pretend we desire Christ to 'come,' and yet notwithstanding we are careless of getting knowledge and of purging our souls, of growing in grace, careless of being such as Christ may delight to come unto, this carelessness of fitting and preparing

* The allusion is to the *pater noster* of popery.—G.

ourselves shews that we do but in hypocrisy speak the words when we have no such thing in our hearts. Those that desire the kingdom of Christ, and the happy condition of Christians in another world, they desire the way of it here, that is, by fitting and preparing themselves for that estate; and indeed it will work those effects as it is Tit. ii. 12, and other places. What is the motive there to live a holy and righteous and sober life? 'Looking and waiting for the glorious appearing of our Lord and Saviour Jesus Christ.' There he inserts a holy life between the two comings of Christ, shewing that the believing the end of both, will work this effect in the change of our lives, 'to be sober to ourselves, and just to others, and holy to God.' 'The grace of God hath appeared,' that is, in the first coming of Christ, 'teaching us to deny all ungodliness and worldly lusts,' &c., and then looking forward still for the second coming of Christ, ver. 13. So that he believes that the grace of God hath appeared in saving our souls by the death of Christ in his first coming; and he that believes that he will come to be glorious after in his second coming, certainly he will live justly and soberly and righteously in this present world; he will fit himself for that estate that he professeth to desire. Let us try ourselves by these evidences in some measure, and not think our state good till we can say from our hearts, 'Come.'

But are Christians always in this state of soul that they can say, 'Come'?

Ans. I answer, they are alway in some degree fitting themselves for Christ; but, notwithstanding, they are not alway so exact and watchful, that they could wish that he should come at this time. Take the comparison from a wife, a spouse: she heartily desires the coming home of her husband; yet perhaps sometimes things may not be in so good order as to wish that he were here now; nay, I have not yet prepared. This is the state of careless Christians, that have soundness of grace, and yet are careless. They desire the coming of Christ, and they love the glory of the life to come, and endeavour weakly for it; yet they are so careless; some corruption hangs on them, that they have not so mortified and subdued as they should do; they are not yet so fitted as they should be. Therefore God often rouseth such by afflictions and other courses in this world, to wean them more from the love of the world, and to prepare us, because we are slothful and careless to prepare ourselves. So I say that sometimes the best Christians may be more indisposed than at others, by reason of security growing on our souls, so weak are we and beset with temptations. Therefore let none be over much discouraged with that, but let us strive as the church here, to be in such an estate as we may alway say, 'Come.'

Well, upon trial, if we find ourselves not so disposed as we should, how shall we carry ourselves that we may say, 'Come'?

Use 1. Let us labour *to purge ourselves by mortification more and more.* 'He that hath this hope purgeth himself,' 1 John iii. 3. And let us endure God's purging of us, and justify God's purging of us by afflictions, and think that God hath this aim. Certainly this is to make me more heavenly-minded, to raise my affections up. I will therefore bear the anger of God; I have deserved it, and he hath holy ends in it to make me partaker of his righteousness. Let us purge ourselves by grace, and endure the course that God takes to purge us by daily crosses, for God aims by it to wean us more and more from the world.

Use 2. And let us *labour daily more and more to unloose our hearts from the things below.* Those that would remove a tree, they loosen it from the root of it: so our affections are rooted to earthly things, therefore we should labour to loose them daily more and more, by the consideration of the uncertainty and vanity of all things. They are not that that will stick to us and give us content, when we shall stand in most need of them. Here we must leave the things of the world, as we find them here, we must part with them. Therefore we should labour to unloose our hearts, and to plant, and set, and pitch them where they may be safe, and swallowed up in better things.

Use 3. And to this end often meditate of the excellency that shall be in the second coming of Christ. Oh the glorious time then! See the means how the church comes to be stirred up here to say, 'Come.' Christ saith before, that he was 'the root of David,' the 'bright morning star.' He sets out himself gloriously, and the gloriousness of that time. Then the church, hearing what the excellency of that state will be then, and the excellency of Christ, the Church hath desires suitable to those manifestations. Therefore let us meditate of the state of the church what it will be, and of the excellency and glory of Christ when he shall come to be glorious in his saints, what a happy condition it will be! And to feed our meditations, let us be oft in hearing and reading of these things. If we hope for anything to come in this world, as if a young heir that shall have great possessions, the more he grows towards years, the more he thinks, I shall have this manor and that, he thinks of the possessions he hath; so a Christian, the nearer he grows to heaven, the more he thinks upon and talks and is willing to hear of that condition that he shall have. The more we are in meditation, and, to help meditation, the more we are in thinking, and speaking, and conferring of these things, what will befall us ere long, if we be God's, the more our affections will be raised up, as we see in the spouse here; upon the manifestation of the excellency of Christ comes this desire after the coming of Christ. This is one reason of the deadness of our hearts. We do not awaken them with such holy thoughts as we should, and we are not under those means as we might ofttimes. There cannot be anything more sweet and powerful to draw up our souls than meditation in this kind.

Use. 4. Again, that we may be able to say 'Come,' let us *labour to be more and more spiritual*, that the Holy Spirit may rule our spirits; and then the Spirit is always for 'Come.' Nature saith not Come, because it is above nature; I mean nature not corrupt saith not 'Come.' It is a hidden secret to nature. Nature saith, Stay still. It hath no desire to it. The flesh is contrary altogether. But the Spirit in the spouse saith, 'Come.' The Spirit doth all. As the soul doth all in the body,—it acts it, and leads it, and comforts it, and gives beauty to it,—so the Spirit first knits Christ and us together. There is the same Spirit in Christ the head and in the church, there is one common Spirit in head and members. And when it hath done so, it acts, and leads, and sanctifies, and purifies the church. It acquaints the church with the good things that God hath given her, acquaints her with the deep meaning of God, the love of God in Christ. It acquaints God with our desires. He knows our meaning in our prayers, and we know his meaning. It acquaints us with the state we shall have after, and assures us of it. It is the 'earnest' of the inheritance. The Spirit and the graces of it are not only the earnest but a part of that inheritance, a part of heaven where our bodies shall be spiritual; not that they shall turn to be spirits, but they shall be ruled wholly by the Spirit, as the soul rules the body.

As it is in a river, it is impossible that the stream should run higher than the spring-head from whence it comes, so it is impossible that our desires should rise higher than the spring from whence they come. The desires of nature cannot go higher than nature. The desires of the flesh are fleshly, but spiritual desires, as they spring from heaven, they have a noble original and head, so they carry to heaven again. Therefore, as the Spirit comes from God the Father and the Son, so it carries us back again to the Father and the Son; as it comes from heaven, so it carries to heaven back again. That is one way to know whether our desires be spiritual or no. Our desire of death and of the coming of Christ, if it be from wearisomeness of life, and from afflictions in the world, so nature may desire. I were better be dead than to be thus, as Jonas wished death, and the children of Israel, and Elias in a passion, Oh that I were dead, &c. But if those desires spring from the Spirit, then they come from heaven, from the consideration of the excellency of the state we shall have there, that it shall be better with us, and that death is but a dark passage to a glorious condition. We may know our desires are spiritual from the rise of them, if they come from spiritual and holy and heavenly considerations. The Spirit doth all in the spouse that is holy and spiritual.

Therefore let us give entertainment to the Spirit of God, and be where we may have further and further communion with the Spirit in spiritual ordinances. The preaching of God's holy word, though it be meanly esteemed by the world, it is the ministry of the Spirit. In the hearing of it the Spirit is given. If we would have the Spirit, let us attend upon the ministry of the Spirit. And let us study Christ, and make him all in all. Saint Paul questions with the Galatians; saith he, 'I would know of you, how came ye by the Spirit? by hearing of Christ's gospel or of the law preached?' No; it was by the gospel, Gal. iii. 2. So that not only the ministry in general, but the evangelical ministry that unfolds Christ, and the infinite love of God in Christ, the excellent condition we have in this world and look for in the world to come; the Spirit is effectual with these thoughts to make us holy and heavenly. The law beats down, but the gospel, especially these evangelical truths, make us spiritual. Therefore we should be willing to hear spiritual points. There are a company of men that love to hear curious * and nice points, and if a minister be quaint, and satirical, and unfold points suitable to their apprehension, they can digest this; but come to speak of things about nature, of Christ, and the benefits by him, they are spiritual, they are remote and transcendent about their nature, that they cannot relish them. But he that hath the Spirit of Christ, of all points, there are none to those that unfold Christ and the benefits by him, the glory that we hope for by him in another world.

And let us not grieve the Spirit, but give way to his motions. The Spirit is now among us in his ordinance, knocking at our hearts, and desiring entertainment. Let us give way, and not quench the good motions that he stirs up; and the Spirit shall be given more and more to us: 'The Holy Ghost is given to them that obey him,' Acts v. 32. And let us beg the Spirit. God 'will give his Holy Spirit to those that ask him,' Luke xi. 13. As if he should say, the Spirit is the best thing God can give. You that are evil can give 'good things to your children;' but your heavenly Father hath one good thing instead of all; he will give his Spirit. Therefore, when we find our hearts dead, and dull, and earthly, and base-minded, think thus, Alas, I am a lump of flesh now. Where is the Spirit of God? Certainly if I had the Spirit in me, I could not be as I am. If we love our

* That is '*over*-curious.'—G.

souls, we will take this course; we trifle with religion else. God doth all by the Spirit. The Spirit is Christ's vicar. Here is no need of a ministerial head between the spouse and Christ, the Spirit and the spouse are so near together. There is such a conjunction between Christ and his church, that where the Spirit is, he stirs up desires of his coming. Only let us attend upon the means and ordinances that he hath left in his church, and let us consider we are are not for this life; we are not to live here alway. The child in the womb is not for that life, and when it is in the world, it is not for this life. There is a third life that we are for. An imperfect state rests not till it come to perfection. Our best is behind. Let those that are naught* fear the second coming of Christ. Let Herod, and Judas, and the beast of Rome fear, that shall be cast into the burning lake. Let Felix tremble, the corrupt judge, and all that live in corrupt courses. But we that profess ourselves to be Christians, and hope for better things in another world, let us labour to banish base fears: and to this end let us labour to be spiritual, and not to be led by the flesh. Whosoever is Christ's, hath the Spirit of Christ, or else he is none of his, as it is sweetly, and largely, and heavenly proved, Rom. viii. 14, *seq.* We have nothing to do with Christ, unless we have his Spirit, to stir up motions and desires of better things than this world can afford.

* That is 'naughty,' = wicked.—G.

ANTIDOTUM CONTRA NAUFRAGIUM FIDEI ET BONÆ CONSCIENTIÆ.*

[DEDICATION.]

VIRO INSIGNI,

TUM PIETATE TUM ERUDITIONE PRÆCLARO, REVERENDISSIMO

Do. Do. JOAN. ARROWSMITH,† D.D., S., STÆ.

ET INDIVIDUÆ TRINITATIS COLLEGII APUD CANTABRIGIENSES PRÆFECTO,

HANC CONCIONEM AD CLERUM.

L. M. Q. D. D.

N. W. G.‡

* This 'Concio' is the only specimen of Sibbes's Latinity extant. It was published in a tiny volume in 1657, which is excessively rare. Its title-page is as follows:—'Antidotum Contra Naufragium Fidei & Bonæ Conscientiæ. Concio Latine Habita Ad Academicos Cantabrig. in Ecclesia S. Mariæ 9 die Octobris, 1627. Authore Rich: Sibbs, S. S. Th. D.D. & Aulæ Catharinæ Præside. Londini, Excudebat J. G. pro Nath: Webb & Guliel: Grantham apud signum nigri Ursi in Cœmeterio Paulino. 1657.' If the Latinity, with mosaic of Greek, be somewhat rude, this 'Concio' is yet a piece of vigorous high-toned Protestantism, much needed in these days of lukewarmness.

† It were superfluous to annotate a name so eminent as that of Dr John Arrowsmith. He died in 1659. Cf. Brook's Lives of the Puritans, vol. iii. pp. 315–318, and every history of Puritanism.

‡ These initials probably represent the publishers Nathaniel Webb and William Grantham, the W being used for the surname of the former and the Christian name of the latter. G.

ANTIDOTUM CONTRA NAUFRAGIUM FIDEI ET BONÆ CONSCIENTIÆ.

Custodi præclarum depositum per Spiritum Sanctum habitantem in nobis.—
2 TIM. I. 14.

SANCTAM animam Deo jam brevi redditurus Paulus, et cœlo proximus, Timotheum filium instruit in iis quæ et ipsi et ecclesiæ usui essent. Cum autem salva doctrina salva sint omnia, urget curam ὑποτυπώσεως sacrorum verborum, quam ut fortius premat, repetita hortatione, sed aliis verbis utitur, 'custodi depositum,' &c. Scriptura cum τὸ αὐτὸ λέγει οὐ ταυτολογεῖ, quasi dixisset, tu, mi Timothee, mihi (ad cælestis vitæ præmia evocato) superstes futurus es, hoc unum in votis est, ut depositam a Christo doctrinam custodias; prævideo tempestates, sed ne succumbas, præsto erit Spiritus in subsidiis.

In his verbis tria spectanda,

1. Commendatum.
2. Mandatum.
3. Argumenta vim addentia.

Ex parte objecti depositum est, ex parte adjuncti præclarum, ex parte subjecti, juvabit Spiritus: Depositum est, ut jure debeas; præclarum est, ut libenter velis; juvabit Spiritus, ut facile possis.

Quid ergo reliquum est (mi Timothee) nisi ut custodias præclarum depositum, per Spiritum sanctum habitantem in nobis?

Primo vobis considerandum est quid sit depositum, et qui sint depositarii.

Quadruplex depositum Timotheis omnibus committitur.

1. Populus Dei ipsius sanguine redemptus.
2. Munus docendi.
3. Dona ad docendum idonea; qui dedit homines dedit dona hominibus.
4. Ipsa doctrina salutis, pabulum vitæ, quam cum Tertulliano hic præcipue intelligimus depositum.

Bellarminus per depositum intellexit traditiones non scriptas (*a*); sed facessat illa sententia, siquid enim Paulus tradidit, a Christo prius accepit, 1 Cor. xv. 3. At papales traditiones spuriæ sunt, incerto patre natæ. Recte Hieronimus contra Helvidium, 'Credimus quia legimus, non quia non legimus' (*b*). Audiat apostolum væ ipsis angelis fulminantem, siquid præter tradiderint, Gal. i. 8. Nobis ergo depositum sit sacra doctrina, quæ aut matrix omnis doctrinæ ipsa scriptura, aut articuli fidei ex scripturis deducti, aut corpus doctrinæ articulis fidei consonum, ex scripturis concinnatum; quales sunt confessiones fidei ecclesiarum.

Antequam ostendam quinam sunt depositarii, quatuor hæc fundamenti loco præmittenda.

1. Esse aliquod depositum; hæc enim connexa sunt, Deus, homo, reli-

gio, revelatio, unde fundetur religio. Deus enim ex suo præscripto coli vult, non nostro.

2. Esse hoc depositum unum, licet articuli sunt multi, corpus tamen unum; extra fidem est quicquid extra unam fidem. *Hillar.*

3. Esse scriptum hoc depositum. Traditio enim non tutus est tradendi modus: licet natura Dei innotescat aliquatenus ex creaturis, ex scripto tamen debet constare de voluntate.

4. Esse aliquem cœtum qui custos sit hujus depositi, quem ecclesiam vocamus, quam vix melius definieris, quam quod sit custos præclari hujus depositi per Spiritum sanctum habitantem in ea.

Ambigitur inter nos et pontificios, quinam sint meliores fidei depositarii. Nos eos reos agimus coram toto mundo multipliciter violati depositi; multa addiderunt, ut nova sacramenta, novos articulos fidei, novam formam juramenti annexam concilio Tridentino: multa detraxerunt, poculum e cœna, &c., multum transmutarunt, sacramenta in sacrificia, præcepta in consilia, regimen ecclesiæ in visibilem monarchiam. In multis depravarunt doctrinam fidei, pœnitentiæ, clavium; quid non, excepta doctrina de Trinitate, ab istis Harpiis fœdatum? Quod ad sacrum codicem spectat, dandum est eos aliquatenus custodire; custodiunt, sed in versione varie corrupta; in sensu violento, quem vi inferunt, non auferunt. At verba vagina tantum sunt, sensus est gladius; custodiunt, sed in lingua plebi ignota, cum scriptura sit publici juris. E re sua esse norunt populum non nimis sapere: Sit veritatis cursus liber, et liceat populo credere quantum ei persuaderi potest ex literis fidei, et brevi videbimus ipsam Hispaniam et Italiam æque orthodoxam atque est ipsa Anglia. Custodiunt, sed aliis non sibi; non suo, sed latentis apud eos ecclesiæ bono. Custodiunt ut fures, quod non suum. Custodiunt sibi, sed in crucem; consumit enim eos Christus non tam ore gladii, quam hoc gladio oris sui. Custodiunt, sed adjungunt alios custodes ne noceat, ut traditiones et Apocrypha. Alias sibi metuunt ab hoc deposito ut rebus suis inimico. Magno redemptum vellent nullum esse depositum; quando hoc consequi non possunt, conantur omnibus modis delumbare scripturas. Sed κριτήρια sanæ doctrinæ nonnihil perpendamus, ut hinc judicium fiat penes quos sit depositum.

1. Quæ a Deo est doctrina fontem malorum ostendit, mysterium latentis vitiositatis recludit; peccatum enim impedit sui ipsius cognitionem. Quam dilute de hoc sentiunt papistæ, satis notum est. Sana hujus articuli doctrina peculiaris ecclesiæ, sensus piis in ecclesia.

2. Doctrina a Deo inspirata conscientiam pacat, vim habet quietativam (ut alia taceam), in agone luctantis conscientiæ; a doctrina justitiæ Christi nobis imputatæ quanta menti serenitas! Hanc justitiam ut supra angelicam, utpote Christi Θεανθρώπου ipsi infenso Deo opponimus. Hac freta fides paterna Dei viscera introspicit, et ut lyncei ei sunt oculi, cernit post nubila solem. Pura doctrina est instar maris vitrei prælucidi, in quo benignam faciem Dei in Jesu Christo cernimus. Aurum verum dignoscitur a chymico, quod verum confortat cor, Ps. xix. 10. At pontificii pavidis conscientiis inextricabilibus casibus cruces erigunt. Locustæ illæ cruciant animos non satis edoctos ex verbo.

3. Vera doctrina congrua est naturæ ipsius Dei, qui spiritus est, et in spiritu coli vult. At papistica quid aliud quam farrago ineptiarum? Indignissime de Deo sentiunt, quem his crepundiis se posse demereri putant. Vera religio conjungitur cum vera sapientia.

4. Quæ desuper est sapientia casta est, pacifica, &c. [Jac. iii. 17.] Id est, tales præstat homines qualis ipsa est, non parricidas et æquivocos

impostores, quales papæ pleni vel ex parricidalibus doctrinæ principiis, etiam reclamante genio, seipsis facti deteriores. Qui quintessentiam papisticæ doctrinæ hauserunt, ut nec Deo fidem, sic nec principi fidelitatem servant. Christi cognitio mutat non homines in leones, sed leones in homines.

5. Ex antipathia inter sapientiam carnis et mundi, et cælestem veritatem, liquet quæ sit vera religio. Ejusmodi est qualis inter medicinam et peccantes humores. Hæc est indoles cælestis doctrinæ, ut nunquam emergat non fremente Sathana et suis, quia vagis animi cupiditatibus frænum injicit; unde quo quisque impurior est, eo infensius odit veritatem. Veritas odio est (ut Lactantius) ob insitam austeritatem (*c*). At pontificii religionem excogitarunt naturæ gratam, rebus suis aptam, hominibus dementandis idoneam. Norunt apud ambitiosos honorem, apud avaros lucrum, apud dissolutos libertatem, apud superstitiosos cerimoniarum larvam valere. Hinc tot allicia, et auctoramenta apud eos, quibus sibi devinctos reddunt homines, ut non mirum sit, si de numero glorientur.

6. Ex consanguinitate cum apostolicis ecclesiis et doctrina constat quæ sit fides semel tradita; hic illud valet, '*prior tempore, potior jure*.' Sed veritati non præscribitur a doctrina nudiustertius inventa, de mendacio præjudicanda est quæ sapit adversus semel traditam. At si Romam in Roma quærimus, frustra erimus; 'quomodo fidelis civitas facta est meretrix!' [Isaiah i. 21.]

Consensus universalis omnium ecclesiarum, etiam ipsius papanæ, qua aliquid sani retinet. Quæ enim unquam ecclesia non agnovit positiva nostræ ecclesiæ dogmata? Docemus scripturam esse regulam fidei, esse legendam, fide nos justificari, Christum esse mediatorem, Deum esse invocandum. Annon ipsi patres, annon ipsi pontificii? Solum illos male habet innocens illa exclusiva sola, a qua tamen, aut eandem vim habente, non abhorrent literæ sacræ, non patres, non ipsi in agone mortis, utpote tutissimo asylo. Litem intendunt nobis non tam de iis quæ credimus, quam de iis quæ non credimus; unde scoptice religionem nostram negativam vocant. Sed probe novimus esse quasdam additiones perimentes; æque subjacet maledicto qui addiderit, ac qui subtraxerit. Nos metuimus nobis a fulmine apostolico; metuimus nobis ab interminatione qua obsignatur canon (*d*); metuimus nobis a sacrilegii reatu, si gloriam Deo debitam demus alteri. Non aliter Deus adoratur quam si solus; non aliter in Christum creditur, quam si in solum, mors ergo in olla religionis Romanæ; sanguineum hoc et tabidum mare, unde quicunque bibit moritur.

Quæritur quænam doctrina sit magis catholica? Vel ipsis judicibus, nonne illa quam ipsi communiter nobiscum tenent? At nos rejicimus eorum assumenta, ut et purior ecclesia. Hinc apparet quam puerilis sit ille *κόκκυσμος*,—'Ubi vestra ecclesia ante Lutherum? Vix octogenaria est' (*e*). Respondemus, ecclesiam ante Lutheri tempora esse congeriem heterogeneam, in qua defæcatior pars idem depositum custodivit nobiscum, quoad fundamentalia; placita enim scholæ non sunt dogmata fidei, neque unaquæque veritas theologica est de fide; quoad primaria fidei dogmata nobiscum senserunt: religio quædam habet æternitatis, quædam temporis, ut ritus qui variant. Doctrina semel tradita æterna est, et æterna est ecclesia in illa æterna veritate.

A deposito commendato accedo jam ad officium demandatum custodiendi. Hic supponenda sunt tria,

1. Ecclesiam non esse dominam, judicem, vel authorem fidei, sed custodem tantum. Ecclesia *οὐκ ἀυθεντεῖ ἀνδρὸς*, Dei est deponere, ecclesiæ tantum proponere.

2. Arduam esse depositi custodiam, quam tantopere premit apostolus.

3. Non eandem omnino rationem esse hujus depositi, et aliorum: Hoc enim ita depositum est, ut sit talentum, et Thesaurus, cujus ususfructus noster est, licet dominium sit Christi, et nostro bono apud nos deponitur.

Hic positis, nosse oportet custodiendum esse hoc depositum ex voluntate deponentis, qui deposuit hoc, 1. ad cognoscendum; 2. deinde ornandum; 3. augendum; 4. defendendum; 5. communicandum; 6. propagandum.

Primum ergo cognoscendum, quia sapienter nobis credendum est, et rationale obsequium postulat Deus: ut interventu lucis transfunditur calor cælestis, sic mediante luce accenduntur omnes sancti habitus, et dilatationem intellectus sequitur dilatatio voluntatis. Est et quædam obedientia intellectus, nec permittenda est lascivientibus ingeniis licentia quidvis sentiendi; sunt et opinionum monstra: intellectus sponsa est veritatis; et est quædam castitas judicii. Et hic major cura adhibenda est, quia ubi non bene creditur non bene vivitur; vitium primæ concoctionis non corrigitur in secunda. Debile fundamentum fallit opus. Hinc diabolus, princeps tenebrarum, tenebras primo offundit intellectui, ut cum lucem eripuerit ducat quo velit. Ad parandam hanc cognitionem deglutiendus sacer est codex, et in succum et sanguinem convertendus, ut nobis familiaris sit et in numerato, et arma inde ad manum parata. Ad hujus intellectum multæ a theologis traduntur regulæ, partim ad speculationem, partim ad interiorem sensum spectantes. Quod ad theoriam, loca pauciora intelligenda per plura, obscuriora per liquida; verbi causa, si de perseverantia quæratur, quorsum attinet vexare locos dubios, cum dicat Johannes, 1 Ep. iii. 9. 'Qui natus est a Deo non peccat, nec potest,' &c., multa sunt ejusmodi loca adeo clari ut solis radio scripta videantur. Si quid dubii occurrat, non tam videndum quid in transitu dicat scriptura, quam quid ubi destinato et disertis verbis aliquid profert. Deinde phrasis et dicendi modus observandus est. Instemus in sacramentario negotio, quod multos torsit, unde symbolum pacis factum est Μῆλον Ἔριδος. Quidam licet aversentur portentiloquia transubstantiationis, consubstantiationis, volunt tamen Christum adesse in pane, tantum nescire se quo modo. At verba (ut recte Philippus) (*f*) non sunt propter panem, sed propter hominem. Signatum dicitur de signo majoris certiorationis causa, ut non ficte accedentes in possessionem quasi corporis Christi immittat. Ut alia mittam, averruncandæ sunt cupiditates, quæ nubem obducunt intellectui, unde res non *καθ' ὑπόστασιν* sed *κατ' ἔμφασιν* videntur. Surdus venter nil audit, cæca ambitio nihil videt in spiritualibus, superbo oculo veritas non videtur; ubi ventris negotium non agitur, aut honori non velificantur, papistæ satis recte sapiunt. Respectus ad terrena, et pruritus ad propria in causa est cur draconis cauda tot stellæ detractæ sunt e cœlo ecclesiæ. Caveamus etiam ne divinam veritatem nostro modulo circumscribamus, ut non aliter verum esse judicemus, quam si nos assequamur; quasi noster intellectus mensura esset judiciorum divinorum. Sunt quædam inaccessa, ad quæ exclamat apostolus, *ὦ βάθος*! [Rom. xi. 33.] Sed quibusdam D. Paulo acutioribus hæc vadosa et pervia sunt. Cur hunc non illum eligit Deus, in causa est, quia præviderat hunc non illum crediturum; quasi præviderit aliquid Deus quod non decreverat dare, qui author totius entis et in natura et in gratia. Hinc tot quasi de cœlo tacta, et syderata ingenia, quæ in arcam audacius quam fælicius introspicere gestiunt. Est quædam lux quæ fulguris instar terret, et occæcat, non dirigit et illustrat. Sed optimum ad Scripturam intelligendam compendium est pietas. Ergo et sensu opus est ad intelligendum depositum. Aliter intelligit ægrotus quid sit morbus, aliter medicus ex scriptis. Aliter novit transmarinas regiones qui αὐτόπτης vidit, quam qui in tabulis tantum geographicis. Sentitur res cujus virtus cognoscitur; vita spiritualis ut et naturalis gustu ducitur. Non patitur promissa evangelica sibi eripi qui dulcedinem eorum degustavit: ut Petrus cum vim verborum Christi in intimis præcordiis sensisset, statim clamat, 'Domine quo abirem? tu verba vitæ æternæ habes,' Joh. vi. 68. Ad sensum necessaria crux est tentatio; mysterium enim crucis sine cruce non intelligitur; voluptatibus ebrii, stupidi sunt, nec gustum ullum veri boni habent, quia, ut loquitur Augustinus, deest iis spirituale palatum. Horum judicium nullum est præjudicium in rebus a sensu remotis. Ad sensum etiam conducit particularis fiducia, cujus est promissa, ἰδιοποιεῖσθαι ut peculium et patrimonium nostrum.

Multa etiam intelliguntur in ipsis exercitiis pietatis; quid sit amare et credere, soli amantes et credentes intelligunt. Hinc illud apostoli ad Timotheum, 'Exerce te ad pietatem,' 1 Ep. iv. 7. Sed hic ante omnia necessarium est subsidium a Spiritu sancto, qui velum tollat a cordibus; alias res divinas tantum intelligimus humano modo, et non in sua propria luce. Nihil homini impuro cum sacrosancto hoc deposito, nisi mentem purgaverit Spiritus. Sincerum est nisi vas, quodcunque infundis acescit. Ubi Spiritus non domat insitam contumaciam, veritas sæpe in rabiem agit homines.

2. Nec tantum intelligendum proponitur hoc depositum, sed et ornandum; non enim hic est ut in mathematicis principiis, quorum finis est nuda speculatio; ornabimus autem si toti totum hoc depositum, et solum custodiamus. Nam Deo in totum hominem jus est. Anima debet esse instar arcæ in qua positæ sunt tabulæ Testamenti, et unaquæque facultas instar arculæ; memoria sit instar urnæ in qua custoditur manna, sit Thesaurus hujus Thesauri: hinc eat in voluntatem, affectus, et in totum hominem. Theologia præcipue versatur circa voluntatem et affectus dirigendos, unde boni vel mali dicimur, non a cognitione. Retinendum ergo depositum est in medio cordis ut in propria sua sede. Sit σύμφυτος λόγος, intimis affectibus insitus, ut surculus vertens nos in suam naturam; ut omnia dicta, facta, cogitata sapiant depositam veritatem. Sit in deliciis ad admirationem usque. Sapientis est alias res non admirari, at hic solius sapientis est mirari (*g*). Vas et theca hujus pretiosi depositi est bona conscientia, honestum cor, cui fixum, et in proposito cordis est tradere se in typum verbi fingendum et formandum. Dedignatur hæc sacra veritas sui copiam facere nisi illis qui se totos illi in obsequium tradiderint: ea lege custoditur, si regnet, et a consiliis nobis sit in omnibus. Datur enim non ad ostentationem scientiæ, sed ad regulam vitæ. Sic ornabimus depositum. Vomicæ sunt et dehonestamenta religionis qui sub forma ejus vim abnegant, quorum culpa fit ut religio male audiat. Perinde Sathanæ sive male vivat quis, sive male credat; profanus vivit contra fidem, hæreticus credit contra fidem; uterque damnandus. Excusatius peccant qui nunquam de evangelio audiverunt: nos tanto deteriores quanto meliores esse debebamus; et deterior conditio spretæ, quam non agnitæ veritatis.

Ut a totis, sic totum servandum est, quia totum utile, et est ea parte ἀλληλουχία: ita apta omnia in theologia et connexa sunt, ut quemadmodum in arcuatis fornicibus si vel unus laxetur lapis, tota ruit compages: sic in fide integritas totius pendet ab integritate partium. Hinc illud, fides non eligit objectum, sed fertur in omne revelatum. Ut totum sic et solum servandum est in negotio fidei. Nil ultra scire est omnia scire, et ut Tertullianus, cum credimus, hoc credimus, nihil esse quod ultra credamus (*h*).

3. Deinde requiritur ad custodiam depositi, ut proficiamus in fide; pro-

ficiat fides, non mutetur, ut Vincentius Lyrinensis. Prodigiosum est si plura sint membra, non si explicentur et crescant; idem senex qui et puer; illustrare licet depositum, non alia pro aliis subjicere, et nove, non nova. Angustiora sunt vasa nostra quam ut capiant plenitudinem illius depositi, unde locus est perpetuo profectui; et paulatim superandæ difficultates, donec adolescamus in virum perfectum. Alia ratio theologiæ in idea, alia in subjecto, hic semper imperfecta: unde Bernardus, 'Si dixeris, *Sufficit*, peristi.' Tepidi sunt qui dicunt, Nolumus majoribus nostris esse meliores.

4. Defendendum est hoc depositum, partim a calumnia, partim a sophisticis argutiis; et primo vindicandum a calumniis est, quia hypocritæ causam Dei deformant, et devenustant mendaciis, ne aliter sine causa sensîsse videantur. Nil tam veretur veritas quam ne ignota damnetur; vindiciæ ergo hic necessariæ. Contra eos etiam qui rationibus oppugnant defendendum, contendendum est pro fide semel data, nec dicendum tantum de veritate, sed pro veritate; utendum sinistra æque ac dextra: multis melior dextra quam sinistra, melius oppugnant aliena, quam defendunt sua: est et præclarum certamen æque ac præclarum depositum. Isaaci servi contendunt de puteis, multo magis nobis de vitæ fonte etiam ad sanguinem resistendum. Noluit David bibere de aqua Bethleemitica quam cum periculo vitæ heroes attulerant, quia sanguis illorum fuit; magni ergo æstimandus sanguis coram domino est pro domino effusus. Veritas hæc ipse est sanguis martyrum (*i*): sed et hic cavendum est ne adversarios suis ipsorum telis petamus, non eget tali defensione causa Christi; depositum hoc armamentarium est, ex se suppeditat tela. Sint adversariis piæ fraudes, pia convitia, ἐξουθενισμοὶ, veros authores castrent, depravent, falsos supponant, certissimo indicio deploratæ causæ. Non veretur Sixtus Senensis laudare superstitiosum illud silicernium, Pium Quintum, quod indicibus expurgatoriis locum dederit. Possevino (*j*) etiam hac in re plus oris est, minus mentis; nos ut causa, sic et agendi modo vincamus, et vicimus sane. Illi enim solis Sathanæ artibus instructi nos adoriuntur, nec aliis nutabundus papismus fulcitur tibicinibus. Sed veritas non eget vanitate ad sui subsidium.

Quod ad fratres nonnihil dissentientes attinet, optandum est, ut coalefieremus, ut junctis viribus hostes oppugnaremus. Inter regia Jacobi regis κατορθώματα et hoc censendum, quod præcipitem contentionis rotam Synodo sufflaminare conatus est (*k*). Cui (licet ab aliis indictæ) momentum addidit tanti regis authoritas. Cui pacis consilio si successus non responderit, in causa est quorundam intemperies, quibus nihil gratum nisi quod suum; quibus cordi est ut sint ungues in ulcere. Inter beatam illam animam Philippum et Calvinum pia et ecclesiæ utilis intercessit concordia, licet in nonnullis dissenserint. Inter Dei servos (ut ait Ambrosius) collatio sit, non contentio; contentionibus enim impeditur invocatio, distrahuntur affectus et studia, aluntur suspiciones, quibus alter alteri redditur inutilis; et quod sanguineis lachrymis deplorandum esset, multi non mali alienantur ab ecclesiis nostris, suæque impietati hoc pretexunt ἄθεοι; et in his paroxysmis omnia plerunque augentur in majus; et certe altercationibus raro quæritur veritas, sæpe amittitur, semper periclitatur. Et fere aliquid vitii adjunctum habet etiam justa defensio; humani enim aliquid patiuntur sæpe viri optimi. Non est tamen redimenda pax veritatis jactura, quæ nobis omnibus charitatibus pretiosior esse debet; nec ea lege indulgenda est errantibus quam petunt tolerantia, ut liceat iis spargere sua dogmata, nobis interim silentibus. Intrepide hic explicanda sententia est, error enim cui non resistitur approbatur.

Interim hoc concedendum est paci ecclesiæ, ut sine felle feramus privatim dissentientes, paratos cedere meliora docentibus, dum sibi tantum sapiunt. Si qui autem sint dolosi operarii, qui prætextu nescio cujus moderationis veritatem actis cuniculis subruere conantur, et miscellam quandam religionem ex adulterio veritatis conflare moliuntur, his quantum in nobis est nullus locus est dandus. Deformem hanc claudicationem ferre non potest Deus, ut qui non vult homines de alieno, multo minus de divino esse liberales. Malefida semper fuit religionum ferruminatio, et prævia publicis calamitatibus. Periculose ergo suadetur inter nos et pontificios unio, non obstante tanto hiatu; castam Christi sponsam decet casta concordia.

Facit et hoc ad defensionem depositi, ut veritas muniatur adversus scandala; commodis ergo verbis explicanda veritas, et a crudis maleque sonantibus sententiis abstinendum, quantum sine veritatis præjudicio fieri potest. Non est enim deserenda veritas propter scandala. Odium faciunt quidam causæ bonæ verbo non bono, *irresistibilis;* vox etiam physicæ actionis quibusdam cætera orthodoxis, ut horridius quidem sonans, non satis placet. Sed modo constet de re ipsa, in verbis difficiles esse non decet, et hæc explicatione molliuntur. Nec patiendum ut contemptim loquantur homines de iis quorum opera usus est Deus in restituendo deposito. Apud Deum sit in benedictione, apud nos in honore nomen eorum. Sunt qui fidem nostram sannis adversariorum exposuerunt, dum mittunt εἰς κόρακας homines rectius se sentientes. Hinc pontificii, En quos correctores antiquitatis, quos reformatores habuit Ecclesia Anglicana! Quorum nominibus parco; interim in nullius verba ita jurandum, ut singula præstemus quæ dixerint. Novimus enim magnis luminaribus suas esse eclipses, ne cuiquam nimis addicti essemus. In primæva ecclesia προσωποληψία induxit προσωπολατρέιαν, illa mortuorum ἁγιολατρίαν, hæc εἰδωλολατρίαν; ut nullus terminus falso est. Cautio ergo hic adhibenda est et candor; cautio, ne nimio vini amore fæces bibamus; candor, ut cuique suus constet honos.

5. Insuper et hoc depositum communicandum est; talentum enim est quod tum custoditur cum aliorum usui impenditur. Custodimus etiam cum non custodimus. Non producimur in hanc scenam ut simus κῶφα πρόσωπα, ut speculationibus indulgeamus; ut condi simus tantum, non promi, ut conchæ, non canales: maledictus qui abscondit frumentum; et fælices nos quorum opera uti dignatur Deus in vinea sua, quod non simus rejicula turba, fracta, et inutilia instrumenta, sed quorum industriam in alto loco posuerit Deus. Fatendum quidem est nonnihil diminutum a majestate theologiæ præpopera quorundam praxi, sed hoc faciat ad excitandam aliorum industriam. Tacerent forsitan graculi si canerent cygni. Cuique suum σιτομέτριον distribuendum est. Thesis ad hypothesin aptanda. Non tantum ad ministrum spectat ὀρθοποδεῖν, sed et ὀρθοτομεῖν. Nostrum est explicare divitias Christi, ut quanta habeat sponsa Christi in Christo, quantum fulgeat mariti sui radiis intelligat.

6. Propagandum etiam est. Hinc illud ad Timotheum suum, 2 Ep. ii. 2. 'Quæ audisti a me commenda fidelibus hominibus, qui idonei erunt et alios docere.' Vos qui præestis studiis adolescentum, et bene natis ingeniis dominamini, instillate in dicata Christo pectora hujus amorem depositi; magnas familias pessundabit neglecta prima institutio. Indocti enim tibiarum similes nihil sonant nisi ab aliis inflati; et videndum ne qui formant aliorum studia imbuant eos odio optimorum et hominum et rerum. Male tincta enim ingenia ut nigræ lanarum nullum alium colorem imbibunt. Juventus est purissima pars ecclesiæ, et primitiæ spiritus sunt suaviores et

fervidiores. Hinc est quod his præcipue insidietur Sathan, ut sibi in posterum reddat obnoxios. Foveamus ergo adolescentum studia, ne quod apes capere oportet fuci intercipiant. Nemini fraudi aut damno sit pietati fuisse addictiorem ; quid enim aliud hoc est quam Christum infantem in juvenum cordibus, Herodis instar, occidere? Hisce omnibus adminicula sunt matricum linguarum, artiumque scientia ; una cum sacra doctrina sacræ etiam linguæ restitutæ sunt ; frangenda enim nux ei qui nucleum edere vult. Nec ulla ars est quæ non ancillarem operam præstat huic dominæ, nec elegantem respuit theologia literaturam ; Spiritus sanctus mundus est, aversatur sordes, etiam has literarum et sermonis. Cum Christus venit in mundum politior literatura in suo solstitio erat ; florebant tum ingeniorum apices. At cum antichristus erat in sua auge et zenith, barbaries regnabat in scholis, qua e solio suo deturbata, religionis, literarum, linguarumque simul erat παλιγγενεσία. Spissa errorum caligine discussa, suus et literis redditus nitor. Et sane logicis rhetoricisque lacertis vibrata theologica tela fortius feriunt, altius penetrant ; multum refert quo brachio hasta torqueatur. Nec neglectim habenda philosophia ; si enim ad illius appellemus tribunal, stare non possunt nupera illa dogmata de media scientia, et de prævisa fide, quæ tollunt dependentiam causarum inferiorum a prima, quæ intimius agit in iis quam ipsæ. Unde Jesuitæ non aliter sua probare possunt dogmata, quam si novam cudant philosophiam. Sed artium encomia suis prælectoribus relinquo. Imprimis autem utile erit cognoscere quodnam fuerit in singulis ætatibus hujus depositi fatum, quinam adversarii, a quibus intercessum, quomodo a prima veritate deflexum sit ; quam sinuosi hæresium anfractus. Magdeburgensium hic elaboravit industria, magnum quid hic præstitit ecclesiasticorum annalium consarcinator, in quo major industriæ laus quam fidei, fidei quam judicii. Huic mos est (ut observat Wintonensis) (*l*) ut si quid non sit ad stomachum, vel eradat ex historiis, vel arrodat in historia, alias non malus si non omnia torsisset ad statuminandam Romanam monarchiam (*m*). Ad historiam redeo ; in qua, ut observat Rhenanus (*n*), plurimum sibi indulsit antiquitas, dum formam vitæ delineare cupiebat. Non diu mansit ecclesia virgo ; sed attentarunt Christi sponsæ pudicitiam hæretici, qui ex pastoribus facti lupi. Alia et alia ecclesiæ facies, prout major vel minor cura hujus depositi, et suus cuique seculo genius ; hoc autem omnibus commune, quod neglectis fontibus cumularunt ridiculas ceremonias, de quo conquestus Augustinus, aiens, tolerabiliorem fuisse Judæorum conditionem : si tuo tempore sic dolebas (O bone Augustine) quid nostra tempestate dixisses? inquit Gerson. Auream illam apostolorum ætatem excepit argentea, illam secuta est ferrea. Nonum et decimum seculum fere exhaustum bonis literis et viris. Decimum seculum produxit nobis scholasticos, pugnaces homines, qui rixatricem induxerunt theologiam, et seposito hoc deposito Lombardi racemationes substituerunt (*o*) (*p*). Fuerunt hi (ut tempora tunc erant) docti et ingeniosi homines, sed depositum miscuerunt argutiis philosophicis, et quæstionum minutiis rerum fregerunt pondera. Nimia sublimitas infesta veritati est, ut virtuti. Aranearum telis quid subtilius, quid inutilius? Non desunt tamen ex illis qui Augustinum sequuntur, qui satis recte sapiunt, inter reliquos Georgius Ariminensis (*q*), magnus gratiæ patronus. Quia nobis negotium est cum papistis, quibus patriarchæ scholastici, qui nomen theologi tueri vult, non debet esse omnino hospes in schola ; sed male primo ablegant studiosos ad scholasticos, cum longe plus sit spiritus theologici et apostolici in patribus vel ultimæ antiquitatis. Hoc in illis laudibile est, quod missis laciniosis et inerticibus declamationibus, stringunt res. Utile erit ὑποτυπώσει aliqua sanorum verborum, tanquam saburra librare et solidare judicium, priusquam solvamus in oceanum authorum; alias misere fluctuabimus.

Tandem ecclesiæ suæ misertus Deus excitavit heroas qui religionem reformarunt, non formarunt; idem speculum detersum pulvere quod et ante, sed nitidius. Postquam autem a papatu secessimus, quidam e nostris damnatas ab ecclesia veteri opiniones recoxerunt, quibus si Augustinum præferamus, non habent quod ægre ferant. Scripsit historiam Pelagianam post Latium (*r*) Vossius (*s*), sed partibus addictior, alias vir doctus et modestus, nimis multa haurit a Jesuitis, aliisque non optimis fidei authoribus: singulæ (*t*) hæreses suas habent historias, quas non inconsultum esset contexere. Harum indago difficilis, quia dum dormierunt agricolæ, sparsa sunt zizania; et verecunda, ut vitiorum, sic errorum initia; ut liquet si singulorum errorum census habeatur. Cuneis in hoc non dissimiles, qui tenues primo lignis impacti locum faciunt crassioribus, donec paulatim fissum dissiliat lignum. Error errori viam struit; sed ut et errorum natales ignoti fuerint, satis tamen est ut si cum fide semel data non consentiunt, pro damnatis habeantur. E re etiam erit observare quodnam in pravis dogmatibus, πρῶτον ψεῦδος unde alia fluunt. Ut ecclesiam, *i. e.* papam non posse errare; quod non solum error, sed errandi principium, unde jus cuivis errori. Hoc intuitu vitium non erit vitium, proditio non proditio. Audite Bellarminum; 'Si papa erraret prohibendo virtutes, præcipiendo vitia, teneretur ecclesia credere vitia esse bona, virtutes esse malas,' &c (*u*). Quid est contra Deum, contra naturam, contra veritatem bellum gerere, si hoc non est? Quasi veritas non in rebus ipsis sed in opinione sita esset. At αἰσχρὸν αἰσχρὸν κἂν δοκῇ κἂν μὴ δοκῇ, hoc est terminos a Deo positos mutare, qui æternum divorcium posuit inter lucem et tenebras, bonum et malum. Sic aiunt; concupiscentiam Adamo fuisse naturalem, tantum fræno originalis justitiæ cohabitam. Hinc post baptismum non tam habere rationem culpæ quam pœnæ. Quorsum hoc, nisi ut inferant, non obstante concupiscentia legem posse impleri, operibus nos justificari, mereri, supererogare (*v*)? Unde indulgentiæ, purgatorium, et quid non.

His positis, ostendamus jam paucis, quo affectu et conatu custodiendum sit hoc depositum.

1. Sancte habenda est hæc sacrosancta fides: arca minus reverenter excepta multas clades intulit; sunt qui in hoc deposito ludos sibi faciunt.

2. Sincere. Aurum accepimus, aurum reddamus, non superstruendæ stipulæ aut fænum; nec scenæ serviendum. Infernum suum circumferunt, qui depositum hoc ad aliorum libidinem inflectunt. Non miscendo nostros affectus cum sacro hoc deposito; quod fecisse quibusdam morituris tormento fuit. Augustinus suo tempore questus est, vix quæri Jesum, propter Jesum; quæ utinam querela nostro tempore locum non haberet.

3. Constanter etiam adhærescendum; parum est verbis et calumniis peti, ne vita quidem contra hoc depositum chara est; omnia patiamur ne quid patiatur depositum; quo amisso ut alia omnia possideremus, tamen miseri sumus. Apostatarum princeps Sathanas conatur omnes eadem ruina involvere; non desinit (inquit Cyprianus) perditos perdere.

Cum ebullit aliqua novitas, statim apparet paleæ levitas, et frumenti gravitas; nam levia et desultoria ingenia cito transferuntur, et semper sunt ancipites temporum palpatores. Vespertiliones in fide, qui nunc in avibus nunc in muribus habentur.

4. Studiose et solicite; nam id nunc verum est quod olim questus Hilarius, ingeniosam rem esse nunc esse Christianum; sola innocentia non satis tuti sumus (*w*). Ne ergo securis nobis elabi, aut invitis eripi depositum

catiamur. Omnia sunt latronibus infesta, et invasori Sathanæ fere una pura ut Thesauro hoc nos spoliet; non prævaluit ejus malitia, quo minus elucesceret sacra veritas; at si effecerit ut non custodiamus, hoc ei satis erit. Cavendum hic et a vivis et a mortuis impostoribus, vix hic cavet etiam qui cavet. Ait Plinius, scorpium caudam subinde ad lapides acuere ne desit occasioni; sic adversarii nostri intenti sunt omnibus occasionibus; an nos stertemus? An acrius illi ad perniciem, quam nos ad salutem? Judas (ut dicitur) non dormit.

1. Restat jam ut ad argumenta moventia accedam; primo depositum est. In depositario requiritur ut fidelis sit. Mutua est obligatio depositi inter Deum et nos; ille penes nos depositam suam veritatem voluit; nos item nosmetipsos, salutem nostram, et coronam apud eum deponimus? At qua fiducia pendebimus ab ejus fide, si nos proditores depositi fuerimus? Si depositum hoc nostra culpa detritum, mutilatum fuerit, actio malæ fidei in nos competet. Apud homines turpe est eos fallere qui nisi nobis credidissent non fallerentur.

2. Secundo, præclarum hoc est depositum, eminenter bonum. Ita a Deo facti sumus, ut præclaris moveamur: τὸ καλὸν καλεῖ, evocat ad sui amorem vi quadam magnetica. Bonum est unde nos ipsi boni; unde maxima nobis et offeruntur, et exhibentur bona; unde communio nobis intercedit cum summo bono. Hinc Deum alloquimur, et suis promissis luctamur cum eo. Hinc Sathanam in fugam damus; ortu, forma, materia divinum est, usu salutiferum, effectis mirandum. Hinc enim visus cœcis, vita mortuis, ab inferis erutos in cœlo ponit: sanctitate authorem refert, mysterio profundum, majestate gloriosum, unde nos transmutamur a gloria in gloriam; duratione æternum, unde nos æterni sumus, et æterna nobis bona legantur. Absque hoc deposito esset quam atra nox (*x*) incumberet animis nostris? Quanta opinionum divortia, et confusio? Quam inermes essemus in medio cingentium hostium? Hic ipsius Dei non os tantum apertum audimus, sed mentem etiam nudatam cernimus. His qui non movetur ignorat τὸ τοῦ καλοῦ καλόν. Vilis ei salus cui depositum hoc vile. Quomodo evademus (inquit apostolus) si neglexerimus tantam salutem? Hoc depositum est in quo prærogativam sibi vendicat ecclesia. Non sic omni nationi.

Habita semper est hæc academia custos depositi. Beda et Alcuinus nostrates erant, Augustini doctrinam amplexi; pluris apud nos sit majorum nostrorum authoritas quam nescio quorum turbatorum vicinarum ecclesiarum. Hoc ad decus gloriosum, ad conscientiam pium, ad fructum utile, ad eventum tutum fuerit, si hanc nobis gloriam constantem esse velimus. Depositum hoc verum palladium est, quo in tuto nos tuti; unica averruncandorum imminentium malorum ratio, custodia depositi. Circumspiciamus regiones circumjacentes, Eamus ad Siloh, ut loquitur propheta, videbimus abominationem desolationis ibi erectam ubi pura Christi doctrina sonabat [Jerem. vii. 12]. Gloria eorum discessit ab iis; caveamus ergo ab iis qui doctrinæ formam mutatam vellent. Servat servata fides. Quia custodisti verbum meum, custodiam te, inquit Christus [Joann. xvii. 6]. Non longum vitæ curriculum nobis concessit Deus, quanti erit si morituri cum apostolo dicere possimus, 'Fidem servavimus, bonum certamen certavimus' [2 Ep. Tim. iv. 12]. Alia scripta magna pollicentur, sed plus in titulo quam in pyxide; cedit medecina morbo, relinquunt stimulum omnis mali peccatum. Ac docet hoc nostrum depositum exarmata esse omnia mala, et nobis in bonum servire; hinc ergo doceamus, hinc discamus: Felices nos quos ad hæc tempora servavit

Deus! Quidam iniquissimi rerum æstimatores contemnunt lucem nunc divinitus accensam, digni quorum ingrata superbia conspuantur. Inhæreamus huic deposito, tum minor sensus præsentium malorum, dum a sacris cogitationibus nos avelli non patimur, terrena omnia ut infra nos posita cernimus; calamitates adversus pectus hoc deposito munitum nihil possunt.

At non est nostrarum virium in tanta mentium caligine, tanta infirmitate, tanta mole impedimentorum, tanto Sathanæ furore et malitia, et ministrorum ejus versutia ac numero, custodire depositum. Certe non est, et expedit hoc scire quod non sit, ut nobis diffisi toti aliunde pendeamus. Addit ergo *per Spiritum sanctum* quo uncti omnia scimus, omnia possumus, omnia vincimus; omnia Spiritui prona cedunt. Quæ ut liquidius constent, sciendum est, omnia a divina natura proficisci mediantibus personis, et inter personas, a Patre, in Filio, per Spiritum sanctum, qui ut substantialis amor et vigor ab utroque procedit. Hic Spiritus est vinculum unionis, deinde communionis inter nos et Christum, in quo, ut primo amabili fundatur Dei in nos amor; unde Spiritus primo in Christo requiescit, tum in nobis, ut unguentum in caput Aaronis effusum usque ad oram vestium ejus descendit: præsentia autem hæc spiritus in Christo non est hypostatica, sed mystica, ipsius personâ Spiritûs, licet non personalis; eodemque modo in Christo est ac in nobis, servata capitis prærogativa. Sed quomodo Spiritus in Christo et nobis? Respondeo, mysterium hoc magnum est; hic valet illud Durandi, motum sentimus, modum nescimus, præsentiam credimus; habitat ergo in nobis Spiritus; pulsat quidem corda aliorum, sed non habitat in iis. De Spiritu Christi solum vivit corpus Christi, inquit Augustinus (*y*). Nec nudus venit in nos, sed omnium gratiarum satellitio stipatus, unde gratiarum nomen a Spiritu, cujus fructus sunt. Quoad inferiora quædam dona Spiritus sanctus est in multis, sed qua sanctificans, in solo corpore mystico, cujus solius est servator; ut anima est in toto corpore, sed prout ratiocinatur, in arce capitis sedem fibi figit. Non diversatur ut abiturus, sed habitat; nec unquam destituit nos, ne in sepulchro quidem cineres nostros, donec deduxerit (ut angelus ille in deserto) ad cælestem Canaan. Non est corpus Christi quod non erit cum eo in æternum. Hinc recte Irenæus, Templum Dei non participare salutem quomodo non maxima blasphemia est? Nec circa nos, aut cum nobis habitat, sed in nobis, præsentia operosissima et efficacissima, sed (ut loquuntur) modificata, et attemperata ad modum nostrum. Et per modum voluntarii agentis, nec agentis tantum, sed et regentis, vincentis, et tandem triumphantis, cum erit omnia in omnibus, et ipsum corpus reddatur spirituale. Stupenda dignatio! Spiritum sacrosanctum velle inter medias sordes et inimicitias sedem suam figere, ubi delicietur, κειμήλια sua reponat, secreta revelet.

Ut in nobis, et solis, sic in singulis habitat. Unde Paulus (non habitantem in me sed) in nobis. Quia Spiritus est commune vinculum inter nos et caput, et omnia membra. Ut idem spiritus qui est in organis pneumaticís, est et in singulis fistulis, sed modulus est varius; sic idem Spiritus non pari modo dilatat se in omnibus, sed fortis in Paulo, fervidus in Petro, sublimis in Johanne, sanctus in Davide, sed idem in omnibus, pro mensura donationis Christi.

Cæterum triplex hic notanda συζυγία. 1. Inter Spiritum et depositum; 2. Inter Spiritum et nos custodientes; 3. Inter mandatum et vires subministratas.

1. Inter Spiritum et depositum. Verbum est vehiculum Spiritus, Spiritus anima verbi. Spiritus inspirat verbum, et ab eodem Spiritu custoditur. Talis inter venas et arterias est συζυγία; spiritus in arteriis fovet sanguinem

in venis, sanguis in venis alit spiritum in arteriis. Hinc respondetur ad illa quæsita, quænam est formalis ratio credendi verbum esse verbum Dei? Respondemus, authoritatem divinam in verbo se Spiritui in nobis ingerentem. Sed unde judicium fit de hoc Spiritu? Si a verbo ad verbum nos ducat. Spiritus enim officium est ducere nos in omnem veritatem. Hinc dicitur Spiritus veritatis quam obsignat in cordibus nostris; non credendum ergo est spiritui qui abducit a deposito ad humana commenta (*z*).

2. Συζυγία inter nos et Spiritum. Nos custodimus, sed per Spiritum qui agit primo in nobis, tunc per nos; nos credimus, sed Spiritus aperit cor; nos audimus, sed Spiritus aperit aures; nos loquimur, sed Spiritus aperit os; facimus, sed facit Spiritus ut faciamus; agimus, sed acti; sequimur, sed tracti; movemus, sed moti, ut orbes inferiores moventur a primo motore.

Nec offert Spiritus sanctus gratiam si velimus, sed inspirat ut velimus. Ipsa potestas, ipsa voluntas, ipsa actio custodiendi est a Spiritu, qui movet et applicat ad agendum, sustentat in agendo, removet impedimenta, et promovet ad eum gradum ad quem visum est ei nos perducere. Recte Augustinus, A nobis custodimur, sed non de nobis; liberi sumus, sed in quantum liberati; domini sumus actionum nostrarum, sed sub domino; non tam ἀυτεξόυσιοι quam ὑπεξόυσιοι; subordinatio hic, non coordinatio. Nec ulla libertatis hic læsio, quia ut fortiter in nobis agit Spiritus, sic suaviter, salvo nostro agendi modo. Prævium enim semper est mentis judicium. Non ergo laborandum tantum est nobis, sed et orandum; non innitendum (*aa*) tantum, sed et Spiritui innitendum, fustra enim (ut pulchre Bernardus) nititur qui non innititur.

3. Συζυγία inter mandatum evangelicum et vires simul administratas. Custodi, sed per Spiritum; Spiritus indit vires, jubet, sed juvat; operativa enim sunt verba, ut in creatione *fiat et fuit*. Sed hoc in fœderatis tantum; nec aliis tamen mandando illuditur, quia vellicat eorum conscientias; elicit contumaciam, ut quodammodo convicti sint, licet non victi. Vocat eos Deus, et provocat ulterius quam ipsi vellent. Quomodo alias resisterent Spiritui sancto nisi ei reniterentur ad altiora ducenti? Sed potuit Deus tollere hanc contumaciam; recte, volenti enim hominem salvum facere, nullum humanum resistit arbitrium, ut Augustinus. Cur ergo non tollit? Tu quis homo? Salva maneat summo regi sua prærogativa. Non ergo sequitur ratio a mandato ad vires nostras, sed ad vires a Spiritu sancto suppeditatas. Agit Deus nobiscum per modum collationis, loquitur ad modum nostrum, sed agit ad modum suum; humanitus loquitur, sed divinitus operatur, et dum vocat omnes, per Spiritum evocat suos. Ne ergo quæramus subsidium desidiæ ab infirmitate nostra, quia dabit Spiritum sanctum petentibus. Rogandus, flagitandus ergo Deus, ut Spiritus sui luce nos dirigat, virtute fulciat, solatio erigat, robore sustentet. Apostolis, cum pericula ingravescerent, crevit animus, sufficiente illis invictum adversus omnia robur Spiritu sancto, ut flores pluvia decidui flaccescunt, donec solis radiis erigantur; idem nos patimur si Spiritus non affulgeat. Ut Sampson rasa cæsarie nihil aliis validior, sic nos, nisi Spiritus moneat, moveat, removeat impedimenta, et ad summum gradum paulatim promoveat. Spiritus hic petentibus promittitur, obedientibus datur, a non resistentibus et extinguentibus custoditur. Agite ergo; quid resistamus? quid causemur? vela pandamus huic Spiritu. Aperiamus portas nostras huic regi; animorum nostrorum ædes vacivas faciamus huic hospiti. Et O felices nos tali hospite! ut rationalis hic spiritus statuit nos in creaturarum ordine supra animalia quæ in ventrem prona finxit Deus; sic Spiritus hic sanctus nos supra vulgarem hominum censum elevat. Christi spiritu imbutus sublimius

quiddam est quam reliqui homines. Omnia infra se videt, utpote quæ nihil juris habeant in spiritum. Quicquid ab orbe condito heroicum, et supra modum humanum, id totum ab hoc Spiritu. Christiani hoc munimentum habentes in pectore, adversus omnia mala intrepidi steterunt.

Ut omnia contrahamus; depositum hoc præclarum a Christo nobis relictum, ab apostolis traditum, a patribus per omnium seculorum memoriam propagatum, a majoribus nostris de manu in manum transmissum, sanguine tot martyrum obsignatum, principum authoritate firmatum, legibus munitum, divinitus defensum, omni modo commendatissimum, tueamur ipsi, ut et preciosissimum thesaurum posteris relinquamus. Debemus hoc (academici) Christo, debemus ecclesiæ Christi sponsæ, debemus matri academiæ, debemus hoc piæ juventuti indies hic succrescenti. Quorsum academia, quorsum tot indulta privilegia, et præclare fundata collegia, nisi ut hic felicia alantur ingenia in spem ecclesiæ? Nisi ut iis studeamus in terris quorum fructus nos manet in cœlo? Hoc ergo unum agamus, in hoc simus nos, qui sacræ huic militiæ nomina dedimus; ut pectora nostra hoc deposito locupletemus ipsi, et deinde stillemus ut ros super sitibundas populi mentes. Πάρεργα nobis ne sint ἔργα, summæ enim infelicitatis est (ut bene philosophus) singula speculari. Cæteris suus locus et ordo sit, sed suus. Formicas dicunt eandem terere semitam, sic et nos. Sæpe obversetur nobis depositi hujus dignitas, mandati gravitas, et ad promovendum omnem pium conatum paratæ, Spiritus sancti suppetiæ, qui cum Spiritus veritatis sit, veritatis assertores non destituet. Dicamus cum Nazianzeno, τὰ ἐμαυτοῦ καὶ τὸν ἐμαυτὸν δίδωμι τῷ πνεύματι, μόνον ἀγέτω καὶ κινείτω, &c. (*bb*). Divinum, inquit, sum instrumentum, a divino musico pulsandum; videamurque nobis sæpe audire Sanctum Paulum hæc verba auribus nostris ingerentem, 'Custodite præclarum depositum per Spiritum sanctum habitantem in nobis.'

NOTES.

(*a*) P. 548.—Bellarminus. Cf. Opera, 'Traditiones,' in Indic. (*b*) P. 548.—Hieronimus, *i. e.* St Jerome. The reference is to his 'Contra Helvidium de B. Mariæ Virginitate,' &c. (*c*) P. 550.—Lactantius. Cf. his 'De Mortibus Persecutorum.' (*d*) P. 550.—Apocalypse xxii. 19. (*e*) P. 550.—'Ubi vestra', &c. Cf. note *sss*, Vol. III. page 536. (*f*) P. 551.—Philippus, *i. e.* as onward, Philip Melancthon. (*g*) P. 552.—'Nil admirari,' &c. The allusion is no doubt to the Nil admirari, &c., of Horace, for which see note *h*, Vol. II. p. 518. (*h*) P. 553.—Tertullianus. Cf. 'Apologia,' under *fides*. (*i*) P. 553.—'Sanguis martyrum.' Cf. note *m*, Vol. III. p. 530. (*j*) P. 553.—Qu. Possevinus? *i. e.* Antonius Possevinus, a learned Jesuit and theological writer. Died 1611. (*k*) P. 553.—Synod, *i. e.* of Dort. (*l*) P. 555.—Winton, *i. e.* Bishop Andrewes. (*m*) P. 555.—History, *i. e.* Baronius. (*n*) P. 555.—Rhenanus. Misprinted Rhevanus. (*o*) P. 555.—'Substituerunt.' Misprinted 'substituerint.' (*p*) P. 555.—Lombard That is, the great 'Master of the Sentences.' (*q*) P. 556.—Georgius Ariminensis. That is, George Amira, a famous Maronite. (*r*) P. 556.—Latius, *i. e.*, Joh. Latius, author of 'Comm de Pelagianis et Semipelagianis.' 1617. (*s*) P. 556.—Vossius, *i. e.* probably the famous scholar and critic, who must not be confounded with the Socinian, if not atheistic, canon of Windsor, Isaac, his son. (*t*) P. 556.—'Singulæ.' Misprinted 'singulas.' (*u*) P. 556.—Bellarminus. Cf. note *g*, Vol. I. p. 313. (*v*) P. 556.—'Supererogare.' Misprinted 'superogare.' (*w*) P. 557.—Hilarius. Cf. note *l*, Vol. IV. p. 305. (*x*) P. 557.—'Nox quæ.' The 'quæ' dropped out. (*y*) P. 558.—Augustinus. Cf. note *hhhh*, Vol. III. p. 537. (*z*) P. 559.—'Veritatem.' Some lines here have been 'broken up' in the original edition. They are restored conjecturally. (*aa*) P. 559.—'Non innitendum.' Query, Non intendum? (*bb*) P. 560.—Nazianzen. Cf. note *g*, Vol. V. p. 455.

SIBBES AND GATAKER.*

To the Right Worshipful Mr ROBERT OFFLEY, Master of the Company of Haberdashers, and the Right Worshipful Sir JOHN GARRET, Knight, Mr Alderman HAMMERSLY, Mr Alderman WHITMORE, Mr Alderman RANTON, and other worthy Fathers and Brethren of the said Company, all prosperity in this world, and happiness in the world to come.

RIGHT WORSHIPFUL,

Albeit the expressions of a gracious heart by lively voice breed deeper impressions (God attending his own ordinance of preaching with a more special blessing), yet writing hath in this respect a prerogative, that holy truths thus conveyed to the world spread further, and continue longer. Those, therefore, deserve well of the church that this way impart those things to public and future use, by which God wrought on the hearts of the hearers for the present. In which respect, this funeral sermon, preached out of love and honour of the graces of God in a poor yet well esteemed Christian (Master Winter), may gain acceptance, as being not only for matter sound, for handling clear, but for the times seasonable. For what were necessary in these times, wherein many are ashamed of the downright profession of that religion by which they hoped to be saved, than to press constant faithfulness in known truths, unto which all promises are entailed? Particular points have been much and long urged amongst us; it is very needful that constant cleaving to all those blessed truths likewise be enforced. And from what stronger encouragement can this be, than from a crown of life here promised to the crown of all graces, *Perseverance?* Since the fall, one dangerous disease of the soul is, unsettledness in good purposes, especially where either discouragements or allure-

* The above 'Epistle Dedicatory' by Sibbes, which has hitherto escaped all notice, is prefixed to a 'Funeral Sermon,' the title-page of which is as follows:—'Christian Constancy crowned by Christ: a Funerall Sermon on Apocalyps 2: 10. Preached at the buriall of Mr William Winter Citizen of London. Together with the Testimony then given unto him. By Thomas Gataker, B of D. and Pastor of Rotherhyth. Veritas Filia Temporis. London Printed by Anne Griffin for Edward Brewster, and are to be sold at the signe of the Bible, at Fleet-bridge. 1637.' This characteristic 'Epistle' forms another contribution to chap. ix. of our Memoir. G.

ments are offered. But what will not a soul break through, that hath in the eye of it a crown, held out to all that hold out to the end, by him who hath both obtained it for us, and keepeth it for us, and us for it? There is a mutual passage of trust between God and us, for thus graciously he condescendeth to us. We trust him with the salvation of our souls, he trusteth us with his truth, which, if by grace we be enabled to keep, it will keep us, and raise up our hearts to an expectation of all good from our faithful and good God, even at that time when our souls gasp for comfort, at the hour of death. And at the day of judgment the sentence will pass, not according to greatness of parts and place, but according to faithfulness, Well done, not learned, wise, rich, but faithful servant, &c. This sermon, entreating of things thus useful, is presented by me, as entreated by the widow of the late deceased (Master Winter), and some others whom I respect, and to you as chief of that company whereof he was a poor member; and this by willing consent of the author, my reverend and ancient friend, of whom I am not willing to take this occasion to speak: his long, faithful, learned labours in the church have made him sufficiently known. He gave her full power of the copy for her use; which, in her behalf, and at her desire, I offer unto your worships as a testimony of her respect; as likewise, if there be a blessing in your hands in the behalf of the orphans of such as have been of your company, I was not unwilling to take this advantage of presenting her estate to your merciful considerations, considering she traineth up a son at the university, for the future service of the church. It is a special blessing of God, where he hath given power and a willing mind to do good, to offer likewise the opportunity of fit objects, that bounty be not misplaced, which here undoubtedly you shall have, and the blessing of the fatherless and widow shall come upon you. The Lord lead you on in a course of faithfulness, to which we are here encouraged, that in the end you may receive the crown of life which is here promised.

Yours in all Christian service,

R. Sibbs.

Gray's Inn, *Jan.* 2. 1623.

*** Gatakor has received the highest praise of, earlier, Salmasius, Aenius, Morhof, Baillet, Witsius, and, later, of Hallam and Dr Wordsworth. He died 1654. His works, 'Opera Critica,' were collected by Witsius into 2 vols. folio, 1698; his 'Sermons,' &c., occupy a noble folio, 1637. The 'sermon' to which Sibbes's epistle was prefixed, is contained in it. The 'son' of 'Master Winter,' referred to, afterwards became minister of West Acre, Norfolk; several fugitive sermons were published by him. G.

INDEXES, &c.

I.—BIBLIOGRAPHICAL LIST OF THE WORKS OF RICHARD SIBBES, D.D.

NOTE.

Agreeably to my promise in Preface, there is herewith appended a chronological catalogue of the several books and tracts of Dr Sibbes, with references to the places in the respective volumes of our edition in which they will be found. To save mere repetition, these references are intended also to guide therein, to the exact title-pages and accounts of different editions of every volume and single sermon. I have departed from my intention to record more modern reprints of the few treatises that have been reprinted, as, with the exception of Pickering's two volumes, these are of no bibliographical interest or value. G.

I. *Latin Verses in University Collections.*—1. On death of Dr William Whitaker, 1595. See Memoir, vol. I. p. lxxxii. 2. On birth of James, Duke of York, 1633. See Memoir, vol. I. p. lxxxiii.

II. *The Saint's Cordials.* Folio (large). 1st edition. There is no date in the general title-page; but the separate sermons all bear the date of 1629. Besides title, pp. 453. 2d edition—Folio (small), general title-page, titles, texts, and doctrines of the sermons, pp. 8 (unpaged), and pp. 395. 3d edition—Folio (small), general title-page, titles, texts, and doctrines of the sermons, pp. 8 (unpaged), and pp. 395.

*** The third is the handsomest book, and contains the same sermons with the 2d edition. For the full title-pages of the three editions, see vol. iv. p. 60.

The following are the contents of the 1st edition. At end of each 'sermon' in this list is given its place in the original, and in our edition:—1. The Art of Contentment, title, and pp. 2–17, vol. v. p. 176. 2. Discouragement's Recovery, title, and pp. 21–32, vol. vii. p. 50. 3, 4. Judgment's Reason, title, and pp. 35–50, 51–62, vol. iv. p. 76. 5. Experience Triumphing; or the Saint's Safety: also called 'The Danger of Backsliding' (as *infra*), title, and pp. 65–85, vol. vii. p. 408. 6, 7. The Matchless Love and In-being, title, and pp. 89–101, 103–113, vol. vi. p. 384. 8–11. Josiah's Self-Reformation, title, and pp. 117–129, 131–141, 143–157, 159–171, vol. vi. p. 28. 12. The Witness of Salvation, title, and pp. 175–191, vol. vii. p. 367. 13. The Pattern of Purity, title, and pp. 195–204, vol. vii. p. 505. 14, 15. Spiritual Mourning, title, and pp. 207–217, 219–231, vol. vi. p. 266. 16. The Knot of Prayer Unloosed, title, and pp. 235–253, vol. vii. p. 230. 17. The Church's Blackness, title, and pp. 259–267, vol. vii. p. 94. 18. The Vanity of the Creature, title, and pp. 271–281, vol. vii. p. 34. 19. The Right Receiving, title, and pp. 285–297, vol. iv. p. 60. 20. A Glimpse of Glory, title, and pp. 301-311, vol. vii. p. 492. 21. The General Resurrection, title, and pp. 315-330, vol. vii. p. 316. 22. The Matchless Mercy, title, and pp. 333-343, vol. vii. p. 152. 23. The Poor Doubting Christian Drawn to Christ. (By Thomas Hooker of New England, and therefore necessarily excluded.) 24. The Touchstone of Regeneration, title, and pp. 369-376. vol. vii. p. 128. 25. Sin's Antidote, title, and pp. 379-393, vol. vii. p. 262. 26. The Discreet Ploughman, title, and pp. 397-405, vol. vii. p. 140. 27, 28. The Life of Faith, title, and pp. 409-421, 423-432 (misprinted, 418), vol. v. p. 358. 29. Salvation Applied, title, and pp. 423-453, vol. v. p. 386. The 2d edition of Saint's Cordials does not contain No. 2, nor 12 to 26 of the 1st edition, these having probably been withdrawn to make room for others that were included in it; and these sermons preferably as being imperfectly reported, and, moreover, consisting, in nearly every case, of single sermons of a series not preserved. Of the omitted sermons, the whole, except Nos. 13, 17, and 23 (Hooker's), are ascribed to Sibbes in that valuable and authoritative compilation by Osborne and Crowe, 'The Catalogue of our English Writers of the Old and New Testament, either in whole or in part: whether Commentators, Elucidators, Annotators, Expositors, at large or in single Sermons.' Our references are to 'The second impression, corrected and enlarged, 1668,' 12mo. Nos. 13 and 17 seem to have been overlooked; they authenticate themselves, being full of Sibbes's recurring phrases and words. Nos. 3 and 4 of the 1st edition are in the 2d entitled 'The Art of Self-judging.' No. 5 of the 1st edition, from 2 Timothy iv. 17, 18 (misprinted 1 Timothy, in 2d and 3d editions), has its title changed to 'The Danger of Backsliding,' evidently because of the other sermons entitled, 'The Saint's Safety.' Nos. 6 and 7 in the 1st edition, are called 'The Saints' Assurance' in the 2d; and so No. 11, 'The Saints' Refreshing,' instead of 'The Peace-gathering Privilege' in the 1st. The following nine sermons, contained in the 2d and 3d editions, were not in the 1st. As before, I append to each the reference to our edition—1. Christ's Sufferings for Man's Sin, vol. i. p. 352. 2, 3. The Saint's Safety in Evil Times, vol. i. p. 296. 4 Christ is Best, vol. i. p. 336. 5, 6. The Church's Visitation, and The Ungodly's Misery, vol. i. p. 372, and p. 385. 7. Difficulty of Salvation, vol. i. p. 395. 8, 9. The Saint's Hiding-place, vol. i. p. 401. Nos. 1 to 4, and 5 to 9 respectively, had previously been published. For the former, see under IV; for the latter, under V.

*** Of Nos. 8 to 10 I have in my library beautifully written *manuscript* 'Notes,' which are much more vivid and directly personal than the published editions, evidencing that they had been taken down from Sibbes's lips, and carefully re-copied. The volume is a handsome quarto, in contemporary morocco binding, gilt edged, richly tooled and gilded, and with the letters L. P. stamped in gold on both sides. The opening paragraph of the first sermon, 'The Tender Heart,' from our MS., may be compared with the printed copy (vol. vi. p. 29): 'You have heard lately, how in the former two verses the prophetesse Huldah (vpon Josiah's message vnto her fearinge Judgment to come) had denovnced a fearfull threatning against Jerusalem and the inhabitants thereof, from whence we noted divers Lessons: as, first, what weake meanes God vses to doe greate matters when it pleases him; a silly weake woman is stirred vp to counsaile and comfort a great religious king; and then her wisdome, how she backs her message, and puts the glorie where it is due, "Thus saith the Lord." Then in the manner of the denvntiation, "Beholde," we observed this word to be a forerunner of some strange thinge: and so it was yt the Lord should punish soe severely his owne beloved people: vpon wch we put you in minde of God's long-sufferinge and patience, wch the longer it be abused, vpon soe manie warnings, at length produceth soe much the more judgment upon the contemners. From hence we obserued, that whatsoeuer the instruments of affliction be, yet the Lord directs all, and in the end makes it appeare that no privilege can procure any safetie to a people if they goe on in a sinfull course of life, and doe not make their peace with God.' There follows fully other two pages, and then, with slight verbal changes, come in the opening words, as printed. So throughout.

III. *The Bruised Reed and Smoking Flax.* 1st edition, 1630, 18mo. Title; dedication, pp. 17 (unpaged); to the Christian reader, pp. 20 (unpaged); table of the contents, pp. 9 (unpaged), and pp. 347. For title-page and other editions, see vol. i., page 34.

IV. *The Saint's Safety in Evil Times.* For title-page, &c., see vol. i. p. 296. For the separate sermons *above*, after contents of the Saint's Cordials. Title, 1st sermon, 'The Saint's Safety,' pp. 1-75, and 79-173; 'Christ is Best,' pp. 177-239; 'Christ's Sufferings for Man's Sin,' pp. 243-302.

V. *The Church's Visitation.* For title-page, &c., see vol. i. p. 372. For the separate sermons, as in IV. The edition of IV in 1634, which was a mere re-issue of that of 1633, with a new title-page, has V. appended. Title, pp. 240; table, pp. 20 (unpaged). This table includes IV. The sermons of V. are Nos. 5, 6, 7, 8, and 9 of Saint's Cordials, 2d and 3d editions.

VI. *The Soul's Conflict.* 1st edition, 1635, 12mo. Title; dedication, p. 1; to the Christian reader, pp. 21; treatise, pp. 728; table, pp. 18. For title-page and other editions, see vol. i. p. 120. Cf. also note *g*, pp. 290-294 in refutation of Bp. Patrick.

VII. *Two Sermons upon the First Words of Christ's Last Sermon.* 1st edition, 1636, 4to. Title, and pp. 69. For title-page and other editions see vol. vii. p. 336.

VIII. *The Spiritual Man's Aim.* 1st edition, 1637, 18mo. Title, and pp. 1-92; table, pp. 6; 'licence,' p. 1 (unpaged); portrait by Marshall. For title-page, and other editions, see vol. iv. p. 40.

IX. *A Fountain Sealed.* 1st edition, 1637, 18mo. Title, dedication, pp. 7; the contents, pp. 11 and pp. 252; errors to be corrected, and a page before the treatise. For title-page and other editions, see vol. v. p. 410.

X. *The Christian's Portion* (or the Charter of a Christian). 1st edition, 1639, 18mo. Title and pp. 67; 'licence,' p. 1. For title-page, &c., see vol iv. p. 2.

XI. *Divine Meditations and Holy Contemplations.* 1st edition, 18mo. Fine engraved title-page; title; to the Christian reader, pp. 20 (unpaged), and pp 274. For title-page and other editions, see vol. vii. p. 180.

XII. *Light from Heaven Discovering the Fountain Opened, &c.* 4to. Title; dedication, pp. 5; to the reader, pp. 5; contents, pp. 4 (all unpaged). 'The Fountain Opened,' and 'Angels' Acclamations' are separately paged 1-297, and 'The Church's Riches by Christ's Poverty,' and 'The Rich Poverty, or the Poor Man's Riches,' 1-157; table for both at close, pp. 13 (unpaged). The following are the contents, with references:—1. The Fountain Opened, vol. v. p 458. 2. Angels' Acclamations, vol. vi. p. 316. 3. The Church's Riches by Christ's Poverty, vol. iv. p. 490. 4. The Rich Poverty, or the Poor Man's Riches, vol. vi. p. 230. For general title-page, see vol. iv. p. 490.

XIII. *The Riches of Mercy,* in two Treatises: 1. Lydia's Conversion; 2. A Rescue from Death, with a Return of Praise. 18mo, 1638. Title and pp. 108 and table (unpaged) pp. 15 and pp. 146. 'Licence,' and portrait. For title-page, &c., see vol. vi. p. 518. It may be stated here that 'The Rescue from Death' is erroneously assigned in the note to Lydia's Conversion to vol. vii., whereas both are in vol. vi. See p. 135.

XIV. *Yea and Amen; or, Precious Promises and Privileges.* 18mo, 1638. Pp. 429, *i. e.* 1-215 and 217-429. For title-page, &c., see vol. iv. p. 114 for 'Yea and Amen,' and vol. v. p. 250 for 'The Privileges of the Faithful.'

XV. *The Saint's Privilege; or, A Christian's Constant Advocate.* 18mo, 1638. Title; table, pp. 6; licence, pp. 47. For title-page and editions see vol. vii. p. 357.

XVI. *The Bride's Longing for her Bridegroom's Second Coming.* 1638, 18mo. Title; to the reader (unpaged), pp. 12; the contents, pp. 7 (unpaged) and pp. 138; licence. For title-page see vol. vi. p. 536.

XVII. *Two Sermons Preached by that Faithful and Reverend Divine, Richard Sibbes, D.D.* 18mo, 1638. Title and licence; dedication; and pp. 83. For title-page of the former, 'The Spouse, her Earnest Desire after Christ,' see vol. ii. p. 198; for the latter, 'The Power of Christ's Resurrection,' vol. v. p. 196.

XVIII. *A Glance of Heaven; or, A Precious Taste of a Glorious Feast.* 1638, 18mo. Engraved frontispiece by Marshall; title; to the Christian reader, pp. 7 (unpaged); table, pp. 12 (unpaged). Sermons i.-iii. pp. 211, and then iv. pp. 59. For title-page see vol. iv. p. 152. The secondary head-line title is, 'Hidden Secrets Revealed by the Gospel.'

XIX. *The Saint's Comforts.* 1638, 12mo. Title; contents of the sermons upon Ps cxxx. and pp. 113. For title-page, &c., see vol. vi. p. 160.

The following sermons belong to this volume—1. The Saint's Happiness, vol. vii. p. 66. 2 The Rich Pearl, vol. vii. p. 254. 3. The Success of the Gospel, vol. vii. p. 280. 4. Mary's Choice, vol. vii. p. 288.

XX. *A Miracle of Miracles; or, Christ in our Nature.* 1638, 4to. Title and pp. 25 and 27; licence. For title-page, &c., see vol. vii. p. 106.

XXI. *The Christian's End.* 1639, 4to. Title and pp. 111. Fine portrait. For title-page see vol. v. p. 288.

XXII. *Christ's Exaltation purchased by Humiliation.* 1639, 18mo. Title; contents (unpaged), pp. 6 and pp. 196. For title-page see vol. v. p. 324.

XXIII. *The Returning Backslider.* 1st edition, 1639, 4to. Portrait; title; to the reader (unpaged), pp. 4; sum of the treatise (unpaged), pp 7 and pp. 482. For title-page, &c., and other editions see vol. ii. p. 250.

XXIV. *Beams of Divine Light.* 1639, 4to. Title; dedication, pp. 5 (unpaged); to the reader (unpaged), pp. 3 and pp. 330 and 232; table (unpaged), pp. 14. For general title-page see vol. v. p. 220.

The following are the separate sermons—1. A Description of Christ, vol. i. p. 144. 2. God's Inquisition, vol. vi. p. 206. 3. The Dead Man, vol. vii. p. 398. 4. The Fruitful Labour, vol. vi. p. 358. 5. Violence Victorious, vol. vi. p. 294. 6. The Church's Complaint and Confidence, vol. vi. p. 182. 7. The Spiritual Jubilee, vol. v. p. 220. 8. St Paul's Challenge, vol. vii. p. 386. 9. The Church's Echo, vol. vii. p. 535. 10. David's Conclusion; or, The Saint's Resolution, vol. vii. p. 80. 11. King David's Epitaph, vol. vi. p. 488.

XXV. *The Excellency of the Gospel above the Law.* 1639, 12mo. Title; contents (unpaged), pp. 17 and pp. 650. For title-page see vol. iv. p. 302.

XXVI. *A Breathing after God.* 1639, 18mo. Title; to the Christian reader (unpaged), pp. 9; license, contents, pp. 8; portrait. For title-page see vol. ii. p. 210. A friend suggests that the initials 'To the reader' more probable represent Henry Jessey.

XXVII. *An Exposition of the Third Chapter of the Epistle of St Paul to the Philippians.* Two sermons of Christian Watchfulness; an exposition of part of the second chapter of the Epistle to the Philippians; a sermon upon Malachi. 1639, 4to. Title; dedication; to the reader, pp. 8 (unpaged); directions to the reader; a table, pp. 12; Exposition of Philip. iii. pp. 1–256; table, 2 pages; works of Sibbes; Christians' Watch and Coming of Christ, pp. 1–146; The Christian Work, pp. 47–173; on Malachi, pp. 174–204. The Exposition of Philippians was issued separately. For general title-page see vol. v. p. 2.

The following are the several portions, with references:—1. Philippians chap. iii., vol. v. p. 56. 2. Christian's Watch, vol. vii. p. 298. 3. The Coming of Christ, vol. vii. p. 306. 4. The Christian Work, vol. v. p. 6. 5. Of the Providence of God, vol. v. p. 35. Nos. 4 and 5 make the exposition of 'part of Philippians chap. ii.' In the 'note' to title-page of XXVII. I promise a notice of Cole, one of Sibbes's publishers. I found it in Edwards's Gangræna (2d part, pp. 50, 51, edit. 1646), in an account of an interview in the shop of 'Mr Smith, Cornhill,' whereby it appears he was at one with Edwards as to 'Liberty of Conscience and Tolerations,' which were as 'the unpardonable sin' to the hot-headed and wrong-headed Presbyterian. He says—'In December 1644, coming into Mr Smith's shop in Cornhill, near the Exchange, where some persons were, there was some discourse about liberty of conscience; whereupon I spoke against it, and Mr Cole, bookseller, confessed he was against a general liberty of conscience by what he saw and knew,' &c. &c. There is another glimpse of Cole in an address of 'The Stationer to the Reader'—said stationer being one 'Dr Newman'—prefixed to Burroughs' 'Gospel Remission' (4to, 1668). Among other things extraneous, this occurs: 'Knowing that Mr Peter Cole (who formerly printed many of the author's works) had long laid wait and endeavoured to get this copy out of the hands of those that published the author's books, offering a great reward for the same, but could not obtain it,' &c &c. Pity that these old booksellers and publishers have no memorial. It is a literary mine all unwrought. Surely it will tempt some worthy antiquary some day. The Coles, and Simmonses, and Parkhursts, and Calverts to whom we owe many a stately folio and precious quarto, and equally priceless lesser volumes, deserve to have their names and labours revived. Cole's heraldic shield is proudly displayed in his book catalogues, *e.g.*, prefixed to Thomas Hooker's volumes. The date is 1316.

XXVIII. *Bowels Opened.* Sermons on 'Canticles.' 1st edition, 1639, 4to. For title-page and editions see vol. ii. p. 2.

XXIX. *The Spiritual Favourite at the Throne of Grace.* 1640, 18mo. Pp. 101. For title-page, &c., see vol. vi. p. 92.

XXX. *Evangelical Sacrifices in Nineteen Sermons.* 1640, 4to. General title; dedication, pp. 5; to the reader, pp 4 (unpaged), and pp. 318 and 218; table, pp. 8.

The following are the several sermons, with references:—1. The Beast's Dominion over Earthly Kings, vol. vii. p. 517. 2. The Ruin of Mystical Jericho, vol. vii. p. 462. 3. The Unprosperous Builder, vol. vii. p. 18. 4, 5. The Successful Seeker, 2 Sermons, vol. vi. p. 110. 6–10. Faith Triumphant, vol. vii. p. 414. 11, 12. The Hidden Life, vol. vi. p. 204. 13. The Redemption of Bodies, vol. v. p. 156 14. Balaam's Wish, vol vii. p. 2. 15, 16. The Faithful Covenanter, vol. vi. p. 2. 17. The Demand of a Good Conscience, vol. vii. p. 478. 18, 19. The Sword of the Wicked, vol. i. p. 104. For general title-page see vol. v. p. 156.

XXXI. *A Consolatory Letter to an Afflicted Conscience.* 1641, 4to. See Memoir, vol. I. pp. cxiv–cxvi.

XXXII. *The Glorious Feast of the Gospel.* 1650, 4to. Title; to the reader, pp. 8 (unpaged); table, pp. 6 (unpaged), and pp. 156, alphabetical table, pp. 5. For title-page see vol. ii. p. 438. In the prefatory 'note' I refer to mistakes in pagination in this tractate; but as this is shared by it with numerous others of the early editions, it is not deemed needful to specify them.

XXXIII. *A Heavenly Conference between Christ and Mary.* 18mo, 1654. For title-page, &c., see vol. vi. p. 414.

XXXIV. *A Learned Commentary or Exposition upon the First Chapter of the 2d Epistle of St Paul to the Corinthians.* 1655, folio. Title; to the reader, pp. 3 (unpaged), and pp. 1–581; alphabetical table, pp. 18 (unpaged); fine portrait in style of Hollar. For title-page, &c., see vol. iii. p. 2.

XXXV. *A Learned Commentary or Exposition upon the Fourth Chapter of the 2d Epistle of St Paul to the Corinthians.* 1656, 4to. Title; to the reader, pp. 5 (unpaged); errata and pp. 273, &c. For the title-page, vol. iv. p. 308. For the other pieces mentioned in title-page see VIII. XX. and XXXIII.

XXXVI. *Antidotum contra Naufragium Fidei,* &c. 1657, 18mo. For title-page, &c., see vol. vii. p. 547.

XXXVII. For 'Epistles' Dedicatory and Prefatory by Sibbes to the books of others, see chap. ix. of our Memoir, pp. lxxxiii–cx and vol. vii. p. 462.

II.—GLOSSARY.

NOTE.

This Glossary is given in fulfilment of our promise in Preface (Vol. I. page xiv). It may be stated that, *as a rule*, we have not given separate references to the different grammatical forms of the words, *i. e.*, noun, adjective, verb, &c., are placed under a *single* form. There will be found in these references not a few excellent early examples of now classic words, and also some in the transitional state, half-English only at the time. In nearly every case the references guide to explanations *in the places*.—G.

Abased, ii. 135.*
Abroach, iii. 336, 514.
Absolutely, iv. 328.
Abstractively, ii. 230—v. 283.
Acception, iii. 17, 382.
Acquisite, iii. 526.

III.—NAMES QUOTED AND REFERRED TO.

IV.—GENERAL INDEX.

NOTE.

The principle acted upon in the construction of this General Index was to select *thoughts* rather than mere *words*. An effort has been made to include all the former. The 'Tables' given in the original and early editions are *substantially* incorporated, but frequently under more definite and concise headings. Where, as in '*Christ*,' the references would have been so numerous as to confuse, as many as possible have been distributed under other topics. G.

V.—TEXTS.

NOTE.

In this Index will be found the whole of those texts which are discussed fully in Treatise or Sermon, and likewise such incidental citations and explanations of others, as have called for notice in the *Notes*. The references to the latter have a * prefixed. It was very soon discovered that more than this was inexpedient. There are thousands of other texts quoted by Sibbes, and more or less fully elucidated, illustrated, or applied; but it had demanded a goodly volume to enumerate them alone. Consequently, but with some reluctance, these were left to be traced by the *Index of Subjects*. G.

CONCLUDING NOTE: ERRATA AND EMENDATIONS.

In so large a work it is to be expected that a few *errata* will occur. It is believed that they are neither numerous nor important. The following include such as have been noticed, along with a few emendations :—

Vol. I. p. cxxv., footnote ‡. Besides B. R. and S. C., Sibbes's 'Divine Meditations' (1638) was also in Leighton's Library. It is bound up with the B. R., and in common with the others, bears numerous markings and pencillings, shewing Sibbes to have been a favourite with the saintly Archbishop. I may also state that, in the recently issued 'Fourth Series' of the 'Collections of the Massachusetts Historical Society' (Boston, 1863), which consists of 'Letters,' hitherto unpublished, of nearly all the eminent Puritans, from the Winthrop MSS., a letter from Humfrey has this postscript: 'I have sent you those new books that are lately come out . . . and now Dr Sibs' "Bruised Reed" (p. 4). His books were well read by the Fathers of New England.'

Vol. I. p. 171, line 26 from top, insert 'here,' and read, 'This is that which here put,' &c.

Vol. I., Note *f*, p. 290. I gladly withdraw the long current charge against Sterne, in the light of Fitzgerald's new 'Life' (2 vols. 1864). One is always glad to have any stain removed from a great name: and though much in Sterne remains to be deplored, it must now be admitted that the creator of 'Uncle Toby' was not the poor wretch which tradition has made him, and Thackeray sanctioned.

Vol. II., p. 3, 'family papers at Kimbolton.' The following is the work referred to, now *published*: 'Court and Society from Elizabeth to Anne. By the Duke of Manchester,' 2 vols. 8vo, 1864. Scarcely a name of note contemporary with Sibbes but has light cast upon it in this work. It may be worth while mentioning, that in the only reference to Sibbes, his name is mis-read 'Gybbes.' The connection and mention of his successor Potter, at Gray's Inn, shews that he was intended. Cf. 'Letter of Leicester to Mandeville,' Vol. i. cxxi, p. 364.

Vol. II., Note *s*, p. 195, 'lilies.' As 'white' was the royal colour among the Hebrews, perhaps our Lord's comparison of Solomon's robes is, after all, to the 'royal lily,' or crown imperial, common in Judea still, and which is 'white.' Herod arrayed our Lord in *ἐσθῆτα λαμπρὰν*, as King of the Jews; and *λαμπρὰν* seems to express the idea of 'white,' and shining like the light (Luke xxiii. 11). On the other hand, the imperial colour among the Romans was 'purple,' aud thus Pilate's soldiers put upon our Saviour *ἱμάτιον πορφυροῦν*, a 'purple robe' (John xix.)

Vol. II., Note *u*, p. 195, 'If God is mine.' I have since learned that the author of this hymn, as of others, is Beddome, an eminent 'Baptist' minister, whose 'Sermons' received the praise of Robert Hall.

Vol. II., Note *o*, p. 434, Beelzebub. More properly read 'Beelzebul.'

Vol. II., Note *c*, p. 517, '*Manna.*' There are two etymologies of the word: מָן הוּא, = 'What's this?' and מן, = a portion, *i. e.*, man-ha; or manna from a supposed old form, מַנָּה. The former, as in our Note, seems preferable.

Vol. III., Note *h*, p. 47. Sibbes's reference will be found in St Chrysostom, a little onward. I had stopped short too soon.

Vol. III., p. 529. What Irenæus relates is that St John refused to go into the public baths when he heard the heretic Cerinthus was there. This he had from the martyr Polycarp, St John's own scholar and disciple.

Vol. IV., Note *e*, p. 78, 'Death, ... Aristotle.' The fuller expression of '*the* philosopher's' blank despair concerning death, is found in his *Eth. Nic.*, iii., 6. 6, as follows :—*φοβερώτατον δ' ὁ θάνατος· πέρας γὰρ, καὶ οὐδὲν ἔτι τῷ τεθνεῶτι δοκεῖ οὔτ' ἀγαθὸν οὔτε κακὸν εἶναι.*.

Vol. IV., Notes *d*, p. 58, and Note *k*, p. 305, 'Sic transit Gloria Mundi.' I add the following earlier notice: 'In Rom. Pontificum inauguratione interea dum de more sacellum D. Gregorii declaratus prætergreditur, ipsum præit ceremoniarum magister gestans arundines seu cannas duas, quarum alteri sursum apposita est candela ardens, quam alteri cannæ, cui superpositæ stuppæ sunt, adhibet, incenditque dicens: PATER SANCTE, *sic* TRANSIT GLORIA MUNDI. Quod et ipsum tertio iterat. Unde Paradinus sumpsit symbolum quod inter heroica sua possuit: NIL SOLIDUM. Hoc olim non ignorarunt Romani. Nam si alicui ex ipsorum ducibus vel Imperatoribus ob res feliciter gestas, et hostibus devictis, triumphus a Senatu decretus esset, et is in curru triumphali maxima pompa urbem ingrederetur, eodem curru carnifex minister publicus vehebatur, [Zonaras lib. ii.] qui pone coronam auream gemmis distinctam sustinens, eum admonebat, ut respiceret, id est, ut reliquum vitæ spacium provideret, nec eo honore elatus superbiret. Appensa quoque erat currui nola et flagellum: quæ innuebant eum in tantas calamitates incidere posse ut et flagris cæderetur, et capite damnaretur. Nam qui ob facinus supremo supplicio afficiebantur nolas gestare solebant, ne quis inter eundum contactu illorum piaculo se obstringeret.'—Philippi Camerarii *Meditationes Historicæ*, 1644, p. 76.

Vol. IV., Note *b*, p. 200, 'Take all from me,' Augustine. Cf. Cowper, close of 'The Task.'

Vol. IV., Note *k*, p. 486, Augustine. Cf. also De Civitate Dei, xxii. 5.

Vol. IV., Note *kk*, p. 488, 'Vespertiliones.' There is a curious parallelism to this quoted from St Bernard, Serm. II. in Corn. A Lapide, *On the Minor Prophets*, p. 3, 'in terrenis lynces, in cælestibus talpæ.'

Vol. V., Note *ee*, p. 34, 'Harmless.' For 'without harm,' read, as with Sibbes, p. 23, 'without horn;' and the Greek word is not ἀμεμπτος, but ακέραιος.

Vol. V., foot-note, p. 163, for Cowper read Watts.

Vol. V., foot-note, p. 183, I add, that *a la mort* means 'going to die,' *i.e.*, so they fancy, or 'like dead men.'

Vol. V., Note *b*, p. 247, 'Law.' Perhaps Sibbes's reference may be to Cæsar's classic saying on proceeding to cross the Rubicon. According to Suetonius Cæsar 30) he quoted the lines of Euripides (Phœnisse, 534–5):

"If I must be unjust, 'tis best to be so
Playing for empire; just in all things else."

Vol. V., *Lady Brooke*, p. 411. In the 'Memoir' contained in Parkhurst's funeral sermon for this illustrious and venerable 'lady,' will be found a very interesting notice of Sibbes's visits to her, and of their mutual regard.

Vol. V., Note *b*, p. 539, 'Common and profane;' read rather κοινός. 'The reason' seems to be that holiness or religious purity, as well as everything belonging to religion, was connected by the ancients (especially the Hebrews) with the notion of something *set apart* or *separate;* and whatsoever was not thus set apart, or was outside the sacred enclosure, was *common* and *profane*, whether used in good or bad sense.

Vol. V., p. 153, 'Ferus.' I rather take to be Dr Joh. Wild (Latinised Ferus), a celebrated Franciscan preacher and expositor at Mentz at the time of the Reformation. The only other name of the kind known, is that of the celebrated Spanish Dominican, S. Vincent Ferrar, who died in 1419.

Vol. V., p. 256, Credo quia impossibile est, is the famous paradox of Tertullian.

Vol. V., p. 435. Does 'civil men' mean men of the world, 'natural men,' as our translators call them, and not 'moral men'?

Vol. V., p. 353. In the remark of Calvin with regard to whether our Lord merited personally, &c., the marks of quotation are wrongly placed. It ought to be: Saith he, 'Whether He did or no, it is curious to search, it is,' &c.

⁂ I have mislaid my reference to Sibbes's quotation of 'likeness' being the ground of 'communion.' The reader chancing upon it will be glad to have it confirmed with the noble passage in Plato: Theætetus, 176, A, πειρᾶσθαι χρὴ ἐνθένδε ἐκεῖσε φεύγειν ὅ τι τάχιστα φυγὴ δὲ ὁμοίωσις θεῷ κατὰ· τὸ δυνατόν. ὁμοίωσις δὲ δίκαιον καὶ ὅσιον μετὰ φρονήσεως γενέσθαι.

A. B. G.

END OF VOL. VII.